Berlitz®

Polish

Standard Dictionary

Polish–English • English–Polish

Berlitz Publishing

New York · Munich · Singapore

Original edition edited by the Langenscheidt editorial staff.

Project management: Rafał Sarna

Lexicographical work: Klaudyna Hildebrandt, Brian Kelly, Prof. Dr. Tadeusz Piotrowski, Mirosław Rusek, Bogusław Solecki, Karolina Stefaniak

Book in cover photo: © Punchstock/Medioimages

Berlitz Publishing
193 Morris Avenue
Springfield, NJ 07081
USA

Printed in Germany
ISBN 978-981-268-521-6

1 2 3 4 5 13 12 11 10 09

Contents

Spis treści

Preface

The present Polish-English and English-Polish dictionary has been compiled by a team of experienced authors in accordance with the current standards in lexicography. While working on the dictionary, the authors aimed at making it up-to-date, clear and useful to the reader.

The present dictionary is extremely comprehensive: it consists of approximately 120 000 references. While selecting them, the authors were guided by their frequency in contemporary Polish and English. The reader will find the newest Polish words, such as **czat**, **oszołom** or **wypasiony**, as well as the most modern English expressions, e.g. **chill out**, **flextime** and **scoop**. The authors have included both British and American English, and the two varieties are systematically distinguished. Apart from the general vocabulary and everyday language, the dictionary contains modern terminology used in the most rapidly developing fields, such as new media, business, economy and medicine.

The present dictionary has been written according to the current standards in lexicography. Blue headwords give it clarity and facilitate finding the desired information. As far as explanations are concerned, not only primary meanings are covered but also those less frequent and idiomatic ones. Differences between individual equivalents are described by means of special labels as well as glosses in the form of synonyms and collocators occurring with a given meaning. In many cases the dictionary presents typical usage examples, collocations and fixed phrases. There is a lot of information on grammar and style, providing the reader with guidance on how to use an equivalent in the correct way. The English-Polish part of the dictionary includes pronunciation and division of the English headwords.

The dictionary is supplemented by short Polish and English grammars as well as a list of English irregular verbs. Geographical names and the most important abbreviations have been incorporated into the main part of the dictionary as separate entries.

The content and structure of the dictionary make it suitable for users at different levels of language ability. It is a good basis for expanding vocabulary and a reliable aid in everyday communication both in Polish and in English.

Prof Tadeusz Piotrowski

Przedmowa

Prezentowany słownik polsko-angielski, angielsko-polski został opracowany przez zespół doświadczonych autorów zgodnie z aktualnymi standardami leksykografii. Pracując nad słownikiem, twórcy postawili sobie za cel jego aktualność, przejrzystość oraz przydatność dla użytkownika.

Słownik jest bardzo obszerny: zawiera w obu częściach około 120 000 haseł i zwrotów. Przy ich wyborze autorzy kierowali się częstotliwością ich występowania we współczesnym języku polskim i angielskim. W słowniku znajdziemy także najnowsze wyrazy, tak polskie: **czat**, **oszołom** czy **wypasiony**, jak też angielskie: **chill out**, **flextime** lub **scoop**. Uwzględniono i konsekwentnie rozróżniono dwa podstawowe warianty angielszczyzny: brytyjską i amerykańską. Oprócz słownictwa ogólnego i języka potocznego, Czytelnik znajdzie aktualne terminy z najszybciej rozwijających się dziedzin, takich jak nowe media, biznes, ekonomia oraz medycyna.

Słownik został opracowany zgodnie z obecnymi standardami leksykografii. Niebieskie wyrazy hasłowe zapewniają przejrzystość i umożliwiają szybką orientację w słowniku. W opisie znaczeń uwzględniono nie tylko te podstawowe, lecz także mniej częste i idiomatyczne. Różnice pomiędzy poszczególnymi ekwiwalentami są opisane za pomocą kwalifikatorów oraz glos w formie synonimów lub kolokacji używanych z danym znaczeniem. W wielu przypadkach słownik podaje typowe przykłady, inne kolokacje lub zwroty frazeologiczne. Liczne informacje gramatyczne i stylistyczne umożliwiają prawidłowe użycie ekwiwalentu. Po stronie angielsko-polskiej podano wymowę angielskich wyrazów hasłowych oraz zaznaczono ich miejsca podziału.

Słownik uzupełniają krótkie gramatyki: polska i angielska, oraz wykaz angielskich czasowników nieregularnych. Nazwy geograficzne oraz najważniejsze skróty zostały uwzględnione w częściach hasłowych.
Słownik ze względu na zawartość i budowę przeznaczony jest dla użytkowników na różnych poziomach zaawansowania. Stanowi dobrą podstawę do poszerzania słownictwa oraz niezawodną pomoc w codziennej komunikacji w języku polskim i angielskim.

prof. dr hab. Tadeusz Piotrowski

Guide to Using the Dictionary

Wskazówki dla użytkownika

All headwords are entered in strict **alphabetical order**. Derivatives are nested in one entry. The list of headwords includes irregular word forms with a cross-reference to their base forms.

Headwords appear in **bold type**. The first headword in an entry is additionally printed in ***blue***.

gwint ... **gwintować** ... **gwintownik**
jet ... **jet-'black** ... **'jet en•gine**

Other variants of the given headword, examples, expansions of abbreviations, and prepositions used in syntactic structures are given in ***bold italic type***.

cat•a•logue ['kætəlɒg] *Br,* ***cat•a•log*** *Am*
murować ⟨***wy-***⟩ (*-ruję*)
emulsja *f* (*-ji; -je*) emulsion; ***~ do opalania*** suntan lotion
ID [aɪ'diː] *abbr* (=***identification, identity***) dowód *m* tożsamości
change [tʃeɪndʒ] **I** *v/t* **1.** zmieniać ⟨-nić⟩ (***for*** na *A*)

Inflected forms, special labels and explanatory notes concerning the headword or its meaning are given in *fair italics*.

numer *m* (*-ru; -ry*) **1.** number **2.** (*ubrania, butów*) size **3.** (*czasopisma*) issue, numer
mat•ey ['meɪtɪ] *adj Br infml:* ***be ~ with*** bratać się z *I*, kumplować się z *I*

Wszystkie wyrazy hasłowe podane są **w porządku alfabetycznym**. Wyrazy pokrewne zostały zgromadzone w jednym gnieździe. Na liście haseł umieszczono także nieregularne formy fleksyjne wraz z ich odesłaniem do formy podstawowej.

Pogrubionym drukiem oznaczono wyrazy hasłowe. Pierwsze wyrazy hasłowe w gnieździe wyróżniono dodatkowo ***kolorem niebieskim***.

gwint ... **gwintować** ... **gwintownik**
jet ... **jet-'black** ... **'jet en•gine**

Pogrubioną kursywą zaznaczane są warianty haseł, przykłady, rozwinięcia skrótów oraz przyimki w schematach składniowych.

cat•a•logue ['kætəlɒg] *Br,* ***cat•a•log*** *Am*
murować ⟨***wy-***⟩ (*-ruję*)
emulsja *f* (*-ji; -je*) emulsion; ***~ do opalania*** suntan lotion
ID [aɪ'diː] *abbr* (=***identification, identity***) dowód *m* tożsamości
change [tʃeɪndʒ] **I** *v/t* **1.** zmieniać ⟨-nić⟩ (***for*** na *A*)

Jasną kursywą podawane są formy fleksyjne, kwalifikatory oraz dodatkowe uwagi odnoszące się do wyrazu hasłowego lub jego odpowiednika.

numer *m* (*-ru; -ry*) **1.** number **2.** (*ubrania, butów*) size **3.** (*czasopisma*) issue, numer
mat•ey ['meɪtɪ] *adj Br infml:* ***be ~ with*** bratać się z *I*, kumplować się z *I*

In collocations and examples the headword or the part of it that appears to the left of the vertical bar (|) is replaced with the **swung dash**. If the spelling of the first letter of the given word changes (form the upper case to the lower case and vice versa), the **swung dash with a circle** (~̊) is used.

dziurk|a *f* (*-ki; -ki*) (small) hole; ***~a od klucza*** keyhole; ***mieć czegoś po ~i w nosie*** be sick of s.th.
pole [pəʊl] *s* biegun *m*; ***the North ~̊*** Biegun Północny

English headwords are followed by their British **pronunciation** given in square brackets [ ]. For this purpose the International Phonetic Alphabet (IPA) has been applied. Explanation of the rules of Polish and English pronunciation and a list of phonetic symbols used are given on pp. 18–23.

na•tive ['neɪtɪv]
pag•i•na•tion [pædʒɪ'neɪʃn]

In the case of English **compounds,** instead of their pronunciation, there is an apostrophe preceding the stressed syllable.

rac•ing ['reɪsɪŋ]
'rac•ing bi•cy•cle
'rac•ing car

Bold dots in English headwords indicate the way the word can be divided.

ad•ven•ture
talk•a•tive

Tylda (~) zastępuje we frazach i przykładach wyraz hasłowy lub jego część znajdującą się po lewej stronie pionowej kreski (|). Jeżeli zmienia się pisownia pierwszej litery wyrazu (z dużej na małą lub na odwrót), używa się **tyldy z kółeczkiem** (~̊).

dziurk|a *f* (*-ki; -ki*) (small) hole; ***~a od klucza*** keyhole; ***mieć czegoś po ~i w nosie*** be sick of s.th.
pole [pəʊl] *s* biegun *m*; ***the North ~̊*** Biegun Północny

Po angielskich wyrazach hasłowych podano w nawiasach kwadratowych [ ] ich **wymowę** w wersji brytyjskiej. W tym celu zastosowano międzynarodową transkrypcję fonetyczną IPA. Na stronach 18–23 omówiono podstawowe zasady wymowy języka polskiego i angielskiego oraz zestawiono stosowane znaki fonetyczne.

na•tive ['neɪtɪv]
pag•i•na•tion [pædʒɪ'neɪʃn]

W przypadku angielskich **wyrazów złożonych** zamiast wymowy zamieszczono małą kreseczkę ('), która poprzedza sylabę akcentowaną.

rac•ing ['reɪsɪŋ]
'rac•ing bi•cy•cle
'rac•ing car

Grube kropki w angielskich wyrazach hasłowych wskazują na dopuszczalne miejsca podziału.

ad•ven•ture
talk•a•tive

Homonyms are given as separate entries and marked with successive Arabic numerals in superscript ($^{1\ 2\ 3\ ...}$).

piec^1 *m (-ca; -ce)*
piec^2 ⟨**u-**⟩ *(piekę)*
check^1 [tʃek] *v/t* **1.** sprawdzać
check^2 [~] *s (wzór)* krata

Roman numerals (**I II ...**) indicate successive lexical classes (e.g. noun, adjective, adverb) in which the given headword can appear. The classes are presented in the order set in the grammar, and each Roman numeral is followed by a label standing for the relevant part of speech.

kościelny I *adj...* **II** *m (-nego; -ni)* ...
tease [tiːz] **I** *v/i* ... **II** *v/t* ... **III** *s* ...

Arabic numerals (**1. 2. ...**) indicate successive meanings of the given headword (within one lexical class).

nabijać ⟨**-bić**⟩ *(-jam)* **1.** *broń:* load **2.** *fajkę:* fill **3.** *butlę:* fill up
hire [haɪə] **I** *v/t* **1.** wynajmować ⟨-jąć⟩; ***a ~d killer*** wynajęty zabójca **2.** wypożyczać ⟨-czyć⟩ **3.** zatrudniać ⟨-nić⟩ **II** *s* wynajem *m*, wypożyczanie *n*

Letters of the alphabet (**a) b) ...**) introduce successive meanings of a given collocation.

nie do podważenia **a)** *argument:* impregnable, irrefutable **b)** *dowód:* ironclad
at s.o.'s instigation **a)** z czyjejś inicjatywy **b)** za czyjąś namową

Homonimy podano w osobnych hasłach i oznaczono kolejnymi cyframi arabskimi w indeksie górnym ($^{1\ 2\ 3\ ...}$).

piec^1 *m (-ca; -ce)*
piec^2 ⟨**u-**⟩ *(piekę)*
check^1 [tʃek] *v/t* **1.** sprawdzać
check^2 [~] *s (wzór)* krata

Za pomocą **cyfr rzymskich** (**I II ...**) wyróżniono kolejne kategorie gramatyczne (np. rzeczownik, przymiotnik, przysłówek), w których występuje dany wyraz hasłowy. Kategorie te zostały podane w ustalonej w gramatyce kolejności, a po liczbie rzymskiej podano skrót oznaczający odpowiednią część mowy.

kościelny I *adj...* **II** *m (-nego; -ni)* ...
tease [tiːz] **I** *v/i* ... **II** *v/t* ... **III** *s* ...

Za pomocą **cyfr arabskich** (**1. 2. ...**) wyróżniono kolejne znaczenia danego wyrazu hasłowego (w ramach jednej kategorii gramatycznej).

nabijać ⟨**-bić**⟩ *(-jam)* **1.** *broń:* load **2.** *fajkę:* fill **3.** *butlę:* fill up
hire [haɪə] **I** *v/t* **1.** wynajmować ⟨-jąć⟩; ***a ~d killer*** wynajęty zabójca **2.** wypożyczać ⟨-czyć⟩ **3.** zatrudniać ⟨-nić⟩ **II** *s* wynajem *m*, wypożyczanie *n*

Za pomocą **liter alfabetu** (**a) b) ...**) podano kolejne znaczenia danej frazy.

nie do podważenia **a)** *argument:* impregnable, irrefutable **b)** *dowód:* ironclad
at s.o.'s instigation **a)** z czyjejś inicjatywy **b)** za czyjąś namową

Differences in meaning are explained by: field and register labels (see p. 24), preceding synonyms or other explanatory notes, given in round brackets, attributes, objects or nouns being defined.

Różnice znaczeniowe objaśniane są za pomocą: kwalifikatorów dziedzinowych i stylistycznych (patrz s. 24), poprzedzających synonimów lub innych wskazówek objaśniających podanych w nawiasach okrągłych, poprzedzających przydawek, dopełnień lub określanych rzeczowników.

lotka *f* (*-ki*; *-ki*) **1.** *SPORT* shuttlecock **2.** *ptaka:* flight feather **3.** *TECH* aileron
old•ie ['ouldɪ] *s infml* **1.** (*person*) staruszek *m* **2.** (*song*) przebój *m* sprzed lat
poszukiwani|e *n* (*-nia*; *-nia*) **1.** *pracy:* search, hunt **2.** *złota:* digging; **3.** *prawdy, szczęścia:* quest

lotka *f* (*-ki*; *-ki*) **1.** *SPORT* shuttlecock **2.** *ptaka:* flight feather **3.** *TECH* aileron
old•ie ['ouldɪ] *s infml* **1.** (*person*) staruszek *m* **2.** (*song*) przebój *m* sprzed lat
poszukiwani|e *n* (*-nia*; *-nia*) **1.** *pracy:* search, hunt **2.** *złota:* digging; **3.** *prawdy, szczęścia:* quest

Grammar

Verbs

As a rule Polish imperfect verbs appear as headwords. Imperfect verbs that have the perfect aspect are followed by angle brackets 〈〉 in which a prefix or a suffix that is used to form the perfect aspect of the verb is given.
Verbs that have only the imperfect aspect are marked *v/im*.
Perfect verbs are labelled *v/p*.
Verbs that are used in both aspects are marked *v im/p*.
The infinitive form is followed by the ending of the first person singular given in round brackets.

logować się 〈**za-**〉 (*-guję*)
mrugać 〈**-gnąć**〉 (*-gam*)
bać się *v/im* (*boję*)
dopilnować *v/p* (*-nuję*)
importować *v im/p* (*-tuję*) import

Most perfect verbs are cross-referred to their imperfect forms.

dorosnąć *v/p* → ***dorastać***

Regular forms of English verbs, formed with *-ed*, are not included. Appropriate irregular forms are given in round brackets. Polish imperfect verbs appear as their equivalents. A prefix or a suffix that is used to form the perfect aspect of the verb is given in angle brackets.

get [get] (*get; got/Am gotten*) *v/t* **1.** dostawać 〈-tać〉 **2.** kupować 〈-pić〉
steal [stiːl] (*stole; stolen*) *v/t* kraść 〈u-〉

Wskazówki gramatyczne

Czasowniki

Jako wyrazy hasłowe występują z reguły polskie czasowniki niedokonane. Przy czasownikach niedokonanych posiadających wariant dokonany podano w nawiasach trójkątnych 〈〉 przedrostek lub przyrostek, za pomocą którego tworzy się formę dokonaną.
Czasowniki mające wyłącznie aspekt niedokonany oznaczone są skrótem *v/im*.
Czasowniki dokonane oznaczono skrótem *v/p*.
Czasowniki dwuaspektowe są wyróżnione za pomocą skrótu *v im/p*.
Po formie bezokolicznika w nawiasach okrągłych podawana jest końcówka pierwszej osoby liczby pojedynczej.

logować się 〈**za-**〉 (*-guję*)
mrugać 〈**-gnąć**〉 (*-gam*)
bać się *v/im* (*boję*)
dopilnować *v/p* (*-nuję*)
importować *v im/p* (*-tuję*) import

Większość czasowników dokonanych odsyłana jest do ich wariantu niedokonanego.

dorosnąć *v/p* → ***dorastać***

Regularne formy czasowników angielskich, tworzone za pomocą końcówki *-ed* nie są w słowniku uwzględniane. Podano natomiast w nawiasach okrągłych odpowiednie formy nieregularne. Jako odpowiedniki polskie występują czasowniki niedokonane. W nawiasy trójkątne ujęto przedrostek lub przyrostek, za pomocą którego tworzy się formę dokonaną.

get [get] (*get; got/Am gotten*) *v/t* **1.** dostawać 〈-tać〉 **2.** kupować 〈-pić〉
steal [stiːl] (*stole; stolen*) *v/t* kraść 〈u-〉

Many English verbs are followed by *phrasal verbs* they form.

pay ... **pay back** ... **pay in** ... **pay off** **pay out** ... **pay up**

The list of headwords includes irregular *Past Simple* and *Past Participle* forms that are cross-referred to their infinitive forms.

grew [gruː] *Past Simple* → **grow**
sawn [sɔːn] *Past Participle* → **saw²**

Nouns

Polish noun headwords are always labelled with the abbreviation of their gender (*m, f, n*). The endings of genitive singular and nominative plural are given in round brackets. Words having only plural forms are marked *pl*.

dołek *m* (*-łka*; *-łki*)
ewolucja *f* (*-ji*; *-je*)
gimnazjum *n* (*indecl*; *-ja*)
igrzyska *pl* (*igrzysk*)

English noun headwords are marked *s*. Irregular plural forms follow the label *pl*.

Polish equivalents are accompanied by the abbreviation of their gender.

child [tʃaɪld] *pl children* [ˈtʃɪldrən] *s* dziecko *n*
stew [stjuː] COOK **I** *s* **1.** mięso *n* duszone z jarzynami **2.** gulasz *m* **3.** potrawka *f*

Po wielu czasownikach angielskich zestawiono tworzone przez nie czasowniki frazowe (*Phrasal vebs*).

pay ... **pay back** ... **pay in** ... **pay off** **pay out** ... **pay up**

Na liście haseł zamieszczono nieregularne formy *Past Simple* i *Past Participle*, wraz z odesłaniem do formy podstawowej czasownika.

grew [gruː] *Past Simple* → **grow**
sawn [sɔːn] *Past Participle* → **saw²**

Rzeczowniki

Polskie hasła rzeczownikowe opatrzone są zawsze skrótem rodzaju gramatycznego (*m*, *f*, *n*). W nawiasach okrągłych podano końcówki dopełniacza liczby pojedynczej oraz mianownika liczny mnogiej.
Wyrazy występujące tylko w liczbie mnogiej mają oznaczenie *pl*.

dołek *m* (*-łka*; *-łki*)
ewolucja *f* (*-ji*; *-je*)
gimnazjum *n* (*indecl*; *-ja*)
igrzyska *pl* (*igrzysk*)

Angielskie hasła rzeczownikowe opatrzone są skrótem *s*. Nieregularne formy liczby mnogiej podane są po symbolu *pl*.
Przy ekwiwalentach polskich zamieszczono odpowiedni skrót rodzaju gramatycznego.

child [tʃaɪld] *pl children* [ˈtʃɪldrən] *s* dziecko *n*
stew [stjuː] COOK **I** *s* **1.** mięso *n* duszone z jarzynami **2.** gulasz *m* **3.** potrawka *f*

Adjectives

Adjectives are marked *adj*. Polish adjective headwords are listed in the positive degree of the nominative singular. Irregular comparative and superlative forms of Polish and English adjectives are given in round brackets. These forms are, moreover, included as separate entries.

mocny *adj* strong
bad [bæd] (*worse; worst*) *adj* zły
lepszy *adj comp* → ***dobry*** better

Numerals

Cardinal numerals are labelled *num*. Ordinals are treated as adjectives and marked *adj*.

szesnasty *adj* the sixteenth
szesnaście *num* sixteen
four•teen [fɔː'tiːn] *num* czternaście
four•teenth [fɔː'tiːnθ] *adj* czternasty

Syntax

In the case of differences between Polish and English, appropriate syntactic structures are presented; they show how to use the given word in the correct way. To this end relevant prepositions and pronouns, as well as case labels (e.g. *A* = accusative) and other abbreviations (e.g. ***s.th.*** = something) are provided.

kryć się **1.** (*chować się*) hide (***za*** *I* behind); **~ *z czymś*** conceal s.th.
poblíż|e: ***w ~u*** *G* nearby, close to
fright [fraɪt] *s* **1.** strach *m;* ***give s.o. a ~*** przestraszyć kogoś
hel•lo [hə'ləʊ] **I** *interj* cześć!, halo! **II** *s* ***say ~*** przywitać się (***to*** z *I*)

Przymiotniki

Przymiotniki są oznaczane skrótem *adj*. Polskie hasła przymiotnikowe występują w mianowniku liczby pojedynczej stopnia równego. Nieregularne formy stopnia wyższego i najwyższego przymiotników polskich i angielskich podawane są w nawiasach okrągłych. Ponadto formy te zostały ujęte na liście haseł.

mocny *adj* strong
bad [bæd] (*worse; worst*) *adj* zły
lepszy *adj comp* → ***dobry*** better

Liczebniki

Liczebniki główne zostały opatrzone skrótem *num*. Liczebniki porządkowe zostały potraktowane jak przymiotniki i oznaczone skrótem *adj*.

szesnasty *adj* the sixteenth
szesnaście *num* sixteen
four•teen [fɔː'tiːn] *num* czternaście
four•teenth [fɔː'tiːnθ] *adj* czternasty

Informacje składniowe

W przypadku różnic pomiędzy językiem polskim i angielskim w słowniku podawane są odpowiednie schematy składniowe, pozwalające prawidłowo użyć danego słowa. W tym celu wymieniane są odpowiednie przyimki, zaimki oraz używane są symbole przypadka (np. *A* = biernik) i inne skróty (np. ***s.th.*** = something).

kryć się **1.** (*chować się*) hide (***za*** *I* behind); **~ *z czymś*** conceal s.th.
poblíż|e: ***w ~u*** *G* nearby, close to
fright [fraɪt] *s* **1.** strach *m;* ***give s.o. a ~*** przestraszyć kogoś
hel•lo [hə'ləʊ] **I** *interj* cześć!, halo! **II** *s* ***say ~*** przywitać się (***to*** z *I*)

Special Labels

Field labels (e.g. *INF*, *REL*) indicate the area of knowledge in which the given headword or expression is used.

piasta *f* (*-ty; -ty*) *TECH* hub
ma•ple 'syr•up *s COOK* syrop *m* klonowy

Register labels indicate the register the given headword or expression comes from. If its Polish or English equivalent belongs to the same register, the label is not repeated.

rzygać ⟨***-gnąć***, ***wy-***⟩ (*-gam*) *infml* puke (up)
en•treat [ɪn'triːt] *v/t form* błagać, usilnie prosić

British and American variety of English are distinguished from each other with *Br* and *Am* respectively. These abbreviations are also used to label the British and American equivalents of Polish headwords and expressions.

au•thor•i•sa•tion [ɔːθəraɪ'zeɪʃn] *Br*, ***au•thor•i•za•tion*** *Am*
mieszkanie *n* (*-nia*; *-nia*) *Br* flat, *Am* apartment

Kwalifikatory

Kwalifikatory dziedzinowe (np. *INF*, *REL*) wskazują dziedzinę wiedzy, w której używana się danego wyrazu hasłowego lub frazy.

piasta *f* (*-ty; -ty*) *TECH* hub
ma•ple 'syr•up *s COOK* syrop *m* klonowy

Kwalifikatory stylistyczne wskazują na styl języka, z którego pochodzi wyraz hasłowy lub fraza. Jeśli jego odpowiednik polski lub angielski należy do tej samej płaszczyzny stylistycznej, kwalifikator nie jest powtarzany.

rzygać ⟨***-gnąć***, ***wy-***⟩ (*-gam*) *infml* puke (up)
en•treat [ɪn'triːt] *v/t form* błagać, usilnie prosić

Brytyjską i amerykańską odmianę języka angielskiego rozróżniono za pomocą skrótów *Br* i *Am*. Oznaczeń tych używa się także przy podawaniu brytyjskich i amerykańskich odpowiedników polskich wyrazów hasłowych i fraz.

au•thor•i•sa•tion [ɔːθəraɪ'zeɪʃn] *Br*, ***au•thor•i•za•tion*** *Am*
mieszkanie *n* (*-nia*; *-nia*) *Br* flat, *Am* apartment

Notes on Polish Pronunciation

Polish vowels

letter	sound	pronunciation	example
a	a	similar to English *a* in luck	mama
ą	ɔ̃	similar to English *ow*, in know	mąż
e	ɛ	between English *a* in man and *e* in men	chleb
ę	ɛ̃	similar to English *en* in ten	męski
i	i	as English *i* in he	mina
	ĭ	as English *y* in year	talia
o	ɔ	as English *o* in boy	okno
ó	u	as English *oo* in moon, but shorter	ósmy
u	u	as English *u* in put	suma
y	i	between English *i* in sit and *e* in set	syn

Pronunciation of nasalised vowels

1. When used at the end of a word the vowels **ą, ę** lose their nasality
ę → /e/, ą → /o/, e.g.:
daję → /*daje*/, *gazetę* → /*gazete*/, *są* → /*so*/, *dają* → /*dajo*/
2. Pronunciation of nasalised vowels **ą, ę** before consonants
before **p, b** – **ą, ę → /om/, /em/**, e.g.:
skąpy → /*skompy*/, *kąpie* → /*kompie*/, *trąba* → /*tromba*/
następny → /*nastempny*/, *tępy* → /*tempy*/, *zęby* → /*zemby*/
before **t, d, c, dz, cz** – **ą, ę → /on/, /en/**, e.g.:
piąty → /*pionty*/, *kąty* → /*konty*/, *gorąco* → /*goronco*/
piętro → /*pientro*/, *chętnie* → /*chentnie*/, *więc* → /*wienc*/
before **ć, dź** – **ą, ę → /oń/, /eń/**, e.g.:
płynąć → /*płynońć*/, *bądź* → /*bońć*/, *mąci* → /*mońci*/
pięć → /*pieńć*/, *zdjęcie* → /*zdjeńcie*/, *wszędzie* → /*fszeńdzie*/
before **k, g** – **ą, ę → /oŋ/, /eŋ/**, e.g.:
rąk → /*roŋk*/, *strąk* → /*stroŋk*/, *drągiem* → /*droŋgiem*/
ręka → /*ręŋka*/, *węgiel* → /*weŋgiel*/, *tęgi* → /*teŋgi*/
before **l, l, ł** – **ą, ę → /o/, /e/**, e.g.:
zaczął → /*zaczoł*/, *zaczęli* → /*zaczeli*/
before **w, w, f, f, s, ś, z, ź, ż (rz), ch (h), ch, h** – **ą, ę** do not lose their nasality, e.g.:
wąs → /vąs/, kęs → /kęs/

Polish consonants

letter	sound	pronunciation	example
c	ts	as English *ts* in its	cały
ch	x	as English *h* in hand	chyba
cz	tʃ	as English *tch* in itch	czas

ć (ci)	tç	as softly *tch*	bić, ciocia
dz	dz	as in English red zone	chodzę, dzwon
dź (dzi)	ðž	as softly *dz*	dźwig, działo
dż, drz	dʒ	as English *j* in just	dżem, drzwi
h	x	as English *h* in hand	herbata
ł	w	as English *w* in wet	stół, miło
ń (ni)	ɳ	as English *ni* in onion	koń, koniec
r	r	as English *r* in red	rak
rz	ʃ	as English *s* in ship	krzak
	ʒ	as English *s* in pleasure	rzeka
s	s	as English *s* in yes	sala
sz	ʃ	as English *sh* in show	szal
ś (si)	ç	as softly *s*	świt, siwy
w	v	as English *v* in voice	woda
z	z	as English *z* in zebra	zadanie
ź (zi)	ž	as softly *z*	późno, zimno
ż	ʒ	as English *s* in pleasure	żaba

Pronunciation of consonants

Most voiced consonants have voiceless equivalents, e.g. **b – p**, **w – f**, **d – t**, **z – s**, **dz – c**, **ż – sz**, **dż – cz**, **ź – ś**, **dź – ć**, **g – k**.
Voiced consonants become voiceless in the following contexts:
–at the end of a word, e.g.: *klub* → */klup/*, *bagaż* → */bagasz/*
–before voiceless consonants, e.g.: *babka* → */bapka/*, *brzydki* → */brzytki/*, *wszyscy* → */fszyscy/*
The consonant **ł** is not pronounced when situated between 2 consonants, e.g. *jabłko* → */japko/*.
on, **om**, **en**, **em** are pronounced **ą**, **ę**, before the following consonants: **f, w, s, z, t, d, dz, n, ł,** *e.g.: sens* → */sęs/*, *konsul* → */kąsul/*, *komfort* → */kąfort/*.

Stress in Polish

Stress in Polish is regular and usually falls on the penultimate syllable, e.g.: *gotowanie, przemówienie, robotnik, klasówka.* Stressed syllables are pronounced longer than unstressed syllables.
Exceptions:
a) The third syllable from the end is stressed in the first and second person plural, e.g: *czytaliśmy, zwiedzaliście*, as well as in all singular forms and third person plural of the conditional, e.g.: *zrobiłabym, widzieliby.*
b) The third syllable from the end is stressed in nouns ending in *-yka, -ika*, e.g.: *matematyka, turystyka, polemika.*
c) The fourth syllable from the end is stressed in the first and second person plural of the conditional, e.g.: *zrobilibyśmy, widzielibyście.*

Zestawienie symboli fonetycznych w języku angielskim

Samogłoski i dwugłoski

znak fonetyczny	zbliżony polski odpowiednik	przykłady
iː	*i*	see, read
ɪ	*y*	in, chips
e	*e*	bed, head
ɜː	*e (długie)*	first, nurse
ə	*a (zanikowe)*	about, butter
æ	*a*	bad, cat
ʌ	*a (krótkie)*	much, love
ɑː	*a (długie)*	father, start
uː	*u (długie)*	too, two
ʊ	*u (krótkie)*	good, put
ɔː	*o (długie)*	door, law
ɒ	*o (krótkie)*	shop, lot
aɪ	*ay (łączne)*	ride, try
eɪ	*ey (łączne)*	day, face
ɔɪ	*oy (łączne)*	boy, choice
ɪə	*ya (łączne)*	here, beer
eə	*ea (łączne)*	hair, pear
ʊə	*ua (łączne)*	poor tour
aʊ	*au (łączne)*	now, mouth
əʊ	*ou (łączne)*	home, no

Spółgłoski

znak fonetyczny	zbliżony polski odpowiednik	przykłady
p	*p*	pen, happen
b	*b (rozdźwięcznione)*	body, job
t	*t*	toy, better
d	*d (rozdźwięcznione)*	odd, day
k	*k*	key, school
g	*g (rozdźwięcznione)*	ghost, go
f	*f*	coffee, physics
v	*w*	heavy, very
θ	*f (wymawiane międzyzębowo)*	think, path
ð	*z (wymawiane międzyzębowo)*	this, other
s	*s lub z (po dźwięcznej spółgłosce)*	sister, glass, dogs
z	*z (rozdźwięcznione)*	zero
ʃ	*sz*	shop, fish
ʒ	*ż (rozdźwięcznione)*	pleasure, television
tʃ	*cz*	church, much
dʒ	*dż (rozdźwięcznione)*	age, just
h	*h (wymawiane wydechowo)*	hot, whole
m	*m*	more, hammer
n	*n*	nice, sun
ŋ	*n (jak np. w bank)*	thing, long
l	*l*	light, feel
r	*r (bryt. ang. wymawiane tylko przed samogłoskami)*	right, hurry
j	*j*	yes, use
w	*ł*	one, when

The Polish Alphabet

	Pronunciation
a	[a]
ą	[ɔ̃]
b	[bɛ]
c	[tsɛ]
ć	[tɕɛ]
d	[dɛ]
e	[ɛ]
ę	[ɛ̃]
f	[ɛf]
g	[gɛ]
h	[xa]
i	[i]
j	[jɔt]
k	[ka]
l	[ɛl]
ł	[ɛw]
m	[ɛm]
n	[ɛn]
ń	[ɛɲ]
o	[ɔ]
ó	[ɔ krɛskovanɛ]

	Pronunciation
p	[pɛ]
r	[ɛr]
s	[ɛs]
ś	[ɛɕ]
t	[tɛ]
u	[u]
w	[vu]
x	[iks]
y	[i grɛk]
z	[zɛt]
ź	[zɛt]
ż	[ʒet]

Compound letters

ch	[xa]
cz	[tʃɛ]
dz	[dzɛ]
dź	[dzɛ]
dż	[dʒɛ]
rz	[ɛrzɛt]
sz	[ɛʃ]

Alfabet angielski

	wymowa		wymowa
a	[eɪ]	**n**	[en]
b	[biː]	**o**	[əʊ]
c	[siː]	**p**	[piː]
d	[diː]	**q**	[kjuː]
e	[iː]	**r**	[ɑː]
f	[ef]	**s**	[es]
g	[dʒiː]	**t**	[tiː]
h	[eɪtʃ]	**u**	[juː]
i	[ai]	**v**	[viː]
j	[dʒeɪ]	**w**	['dʌbljuː]
k	[keɪ]	**x**	[eks]
l	[el]	**y**	[waɪ]
m	[em]	**z**	[zed]

Abbreviations
Skróty

także	*a.*	also
biernik	*A*	accusative
skrót	*abbr*	abbreviation
przymiotnik	*adj*	adjective
administracja	*ADM*	administration
przysłówek	*adv*	adverb
rolnictwo	*AGR*	agriculture
amerykański	*Am*	American
anatomia	*ANAT*	anatomy
architektura	*ARCHIT*	architecture
przedimek	*art*	article
sztuka	*ART*	arts
astronomia	*ASTR*	astronomy
motoryzacja	*AUTO*	motoring
biologia	*BIOL*	biology
brytyjski	*Br*	British
budownictwo	*BUILD*	building
stopień wyższy	*comp*	comparative
handel	*COMM*	commerce
spójnik	*conj*	conjunction
kulinarny	*COOK*	cooking
celownik	*D*	dative
zdrobniały	*dim*	diminutive
ekonomia	*ECON*	economy
rodzaj żeński	*f*	feminine
w znaczeniu przenośnym	*fig*	figurative
kino, film	*FILM*	cinema
finanse	*FIN*	finance
oficjalny	*form*	formal
dopełniacz	*G*	genitive
geografia	*GEOGR*	geography
geologia	*GEOL*	geology
gramatyka	*GRAM*	grammar
historia	*HIST*	history
żartobliwy	*hum*	humorous
narzędnik	*I*	instrumental
nieodmienny	*indecl*	indeclinable
informatyka	*INF*	computers
potoczny	*infml*	informal
wykrzyknik	*interj*	interjection

ironiczny	*iron*	ironic
nieregularny	*irreg*	irregular
prawo	*IUR*	law
miejscownik	*L*	locative
literacki	*lit*	literary
rodzaj męski	*m*	masculine
matematyka	*MATH*	mathematics
górnictwo	*MIN*	mining
muzyka	*MUS*	music
mianownik	*N*	nominative
rodzaj nijaki	*n*	neuter
bez liczby mnogiej	*no pl*	no plural
liczebnik	*num*	numeral
imiesłów	*part*	participle
partykuła	*particle*	particle
filozofia	*PHIL*	philosophy
fotografia	*PHOT*	photography
fizyka	*PHYS*	physics
liczba mnoga	*pl*	plural
polityka	*POLIT*	politics
zaimek dzierżawczy	*poss*	possessive pronoun
przyimek	*prep*	preposition
zaimek	*pron*	pronoun
psychologia	*PSYCH*	psychology
chroniony znak towarowy	®	registered trademark
radiofonia	*RADIO*	radio
religia	*REL*	religion
rzeczownik	*s*	noun
liczba pojedyncza	*sing*	singular
sport	*SPORT*	sport(s)
stopień najwyższy	*superl*	superlative
technika	*TECH*	technical
telekomunikacja	*TEL*	telecommunications
teatralny	*THEAT*	theatre
czasownik	*v*	verb
czasownik posiłkowy	*v aux*	auxiliary verb
czasownik dwuaspektowy	*v im/p*	perfective and imperfective verb
czasownik nieprzechodni	*v/i*	intransitive verb
czasownik niedokonany	*v/im*	imperfective verb
czasownik dokonany	*v/p*	perfective verb
czasownik przechodni	*v/t*	transitive verb
wulgarny	*vulg*	vulgar, obscene
zobacz	→	see, refer

Polish – English

A

a I *conj* and; ***dwa, ~ nie jeden*** two, not one; ***~ co więcej*** and what is more **II** *particle* and; ***~ nie mówiłem?*** I told you so!; ***~ to niespodzianka!*** what a surprise! **III** *interj* ***~!*** ah!; ***~ psik!*** achoo!, *Br* atishoo!

abażur *m* (*-ru*/*-ra*; *-ry*) lampshade

abdykacja *f* (*-ji*; *-je*) abdication; **abdykować** *v im*/*p* (*-kuję*) abdicate

abecadło *n* (*-ła*; *-ła*) **1.** alphabet, ABC **2.** (*podstawy*) the ABC

abiturient *m* (*-ta*; *-nci*), **~ka** *f* (*-ki*; *-ki*) *Br* A-level student

abonament *m* (*-tu*; *-ty*) **1.** (*subskrypcja*) subscription **2.** (*opłata*) ***~ radiowo-telewizyjny*** the TV and radio licence fee; ***~ telefoniczny*** line rental

abonent *m* (*-ta*; *-nci*), **~ka** *f* (*-ki*; *-ki*) **1.** (*subskrybent*) subscriber; ***~ telefoniczny*** telephone customer **2.** *radiowy*, *telewizyjny*: licence payer

abonować ⟨**za-**⟩ (*-nuję*) subscribe (*A* to)

aborcj|a *f* (*-ji*; *-je*) abortion; ***dokonać ~i*** perform an abortion

absencja *f* (*-ji*; *-je*) absence

absolutn|y *adj* **1.** absolute; ***masz ~ą rację*** you are absolutely right; ***słuch ~y*** perfect pitch; ***zero ~e*** PHYS absolute zero **2.** *cisza*, *spokój*: total

absolutorium *n* (*indecl*; *-ria*): ***udzielić zarządowi ~*** accept the financial report of the board

absolutyzm *m* (*-mu*; *no pl*) absolutism

absolwent *m* (*-ta*; *-nci*), **~ka** *f* (*-ki*; *-ki*) graduate

absorb|ować ⟨**za-**⟩ (*-buję*) absorb; ***~ować czyjąś uwagę*** hold s.o.'s attention; ***~ują go studia*** he is absorbed in his studies; **absorpcja** *f* (*-ji*; *no pl*) absorption

abstrah|ować *v*/*im* (*-huję*) abstract away (***od*** *G* from); ***~ując od*** *G* apart from

abstrakcj|a *f* (*-ji*; *no pl*) abstraction; ***to czysta ~a!*** it is totally divorced from reality!; ***żyć w świecie ~i*** live in an unreal world; **abstrakcyjn|y** *adj* abstract; ***sztuka ~a*** abstract art

abstynencja *f* (*-ji*; *no pl*) abstinence

abstynent *m* (*-ta*; *-nci*), **~ka** *f* (*-ki*; *-ki*) *Br* teetotaller, *Am* teetotaler

absurd *m* (*-du*; *-dy*) nonsense; ***doprowadzić coś do ~u*** take s.th. to absurd levels; ***teatr ~u*** theatre of the absurd; **absurdalny** *adj* nonsensical

absynt *m* (*-tu*; *-ty*) absinthe

aby I *conj* (in order) to; ***powiedz jej, ~ tu przyszła*** tell her to come here; ***~ go nie obudzić*** (so as) not to wake him up **II** *particle* ***~śmy mogli*** so that we can

aceton *m* (*-nu*; *no pl*) CHEM acetone

acetylen *m* (*-nu*; *no pl*) CHEM acetylene

ach *interj* oh, ah

Achilles: ***pięta ~a*** Achilles' heel

aczkolwiek *conj* although, *form* albeit

Adam: ***w stroju ~a*** in the nude, naked; ***jabłko ~a*** ANAT Adam's apple

adamaszek *m* (*-szku*; *-szki*) damask

adaptacja *f* (*-ji*; *-je*) **1.** adaptation; ***~ filmowa*** *Br* film adaptation, *Am* movie adaptation; ***~ sceniczna*** stage adaptation **2.** *budynku*: conversion; ***~ na biura*** conversion into offices, office conversion

adapter *m* (*-ra*/*-ru*; *-ry*) record player

adaptować ⟨**za-**⟩ (*-tuję*) **1.** *dzieło*: adapt **2.** *budynek*: convert (***na*** *A* to); ***adaptować się*** adapt

adekwatny *adj* **1.** appropriate **2.** (*trafny*) accurate

adept *m* (*-ta*; *-pci*), **~ka** *f* (*-ki*; *-ki*) student; ***~ nauk humanistycznych*** arts student

adidasy *pl* (*-sów*) *Br* trainers, *Am* sneakers

adiunkt *m* (*-ta*; *-kci*) *Br* reader, *Am* assistant professor

adiustować *v*/*im* (*-tuję*) edit

adiutant *m* (*-ta*; *-nci*) aide-de-camp

administracj|a *f* (*-ji*; *-je*) **1.** administration, management **2.** (*organy władzy państwowej*) ***~a państwowa*** the Civil Service; ***pracownik ~i państwowej*** civil servant; **administracyjny** *adj* administrative, managing; ***pracownik ~*** administration worker, administration officer; ***podział* ~** administrative division

administrator *m* (*-ra*; *-rzy*), **~ka** *f* (*-ki*; *-ki*) **1.** administrator, manager; **~ *budynku*** building manager **2.** INF administrator

administrować *v/im* (*-ruję*) administer, manage

admirał *m* **1.** (*-ła*; *-łowie*) admiral **2.** (*-ła*; *-ły*) (*motyl*) ***rusałka* ~** red admiral

adnotacja *f* (*-ji*; *-je*) annotation, note

adopcj|a *f* (*-ji*; *-je*) adoption; ***oddać do* ~i** give up for adoption

adoptować ⟨**za-**⟩ (*-tuję*) adopt; **adoptowany** *adj* adopted

adorator *m* (*-ra*; *-rzy*), **~ka** *f* (*-ki*; *-ki*) admirer

adorować *v/im* (*-ruję*) adore, admire

adrenalina *f* (*-ny*; *no pl*) adrenaline

adres *m* (*-su*; *-sy*) address; **~ *domowy*** home address; **~ *zwrotny*** return address; ***wysłać list na czyjś* ~** send a letter to s.o.'s address; ***powiedzieć coś pod czyimś* ~em** address s.th. to s.o.

adresat *m* (*-ta*; *-saci*), **~ka** *f* (*-ki*; *-ki*) **1.** *listu*, *przesyłki*: addressee **2.** *książki*, *filmu*: audience

adresować ⟨**za-**⟩ (*-suję*) address (**do** *G* to)

Adriatycki *adj*: ***Morze* ~e** the Adriatic Sea; **Adriatyk** *m* (*-ku*) the Adriatic

adwent *m* (*-tu*; *-ty*) Advent; ***pierwsza niedziela* ~u** Advent Sunday

adwentysta *m* (*-ty*; *-tyści*), **-tka** *f* (*-ki*; *-ki*) Adventist

adwokack|i *adj*: ***zespół* ~i** legal team; ***kancelaria* ~a** law firm; **adwokat** *m* (*-ta*; *-kaci*), **~ka** *f* (*-ki*; *-ki*) lawyer, *Br* barrister, *Am* attorney

aerobik *m* (*-ku*; *no pl*) aerobics

aerodynamiczny *adj* aerodynamic

aeroklub *m* (*-bu*; *-by*) flying club

aerozol *m* (*-lu*; *-le*) aerosol; ***dezodorant w* ~u** aerosol deodorant

afek|t *m* (*-tu*; *no pl*) JUR the heat of passion; ***działać w* ~cie** act in the heat of passion; ***zbrodnia w* ~cie** crime of passion; **afektacja** *f* (*-ji*; *no pl*) affectation; **afektowany** *adj* affected

afer|a *f* (*-ry*; *-ry*) **1.** scandal; **~*a szpiegowska*** spying scandal **2.** (*awantura*) *infml* rumpus; ***zrobić* ~ę** kick up a rumpus

aferzysta *m* (*-ty*; *-rzyści*), **-tka** *f* (*-ki*; *-ki*) swindler, wheeler-dealer

Afganistan *m* (*-nu*) Afghanistan

Afgańczyk *m* (*-ka*; *-czycy*), **-ganka** *f* (*-ki*; *-ki*) Afghan

afgański *adj* Afghan; ***chart* ~** Afghan hound

afirmacja *f* (*-ji*; *no pl*): **~ *życia*** affirmation of life; **afirmować** *v/im* (*-muję*) affirm

afisz *m* (*-sza*; *-sze*) poster, bill; ***wejść na* ~** THEAT open; ***zejść z* ~a** THEAT close; ***nie schodzić z* ~a** THEAT run; **afiszować się** *v/im* (*-szuję*) parade, flaunt (**z** *I*)

aforystyczny *adj* aphoristic; **aforyzm** *m* (*-mu*; *-my*) aphorism

afront *m* (*-tu*; *-ty*) affront, insult; ***zrobić* ~** affront, insult

Afryka *f* (*-ki*) Africa

Afrykanin *m* (*-na*; *-kanie*), **-kanka** *f* (*-ki*; *-ki*) African

afrykański *adj* African

agat *m* (*-tu*; *-ty*) agate

agawa *f* (*-wy*; *-wy*) agave

agencja *f* (*-ji*; *-je*) **1.** agency; **~ *reklamowa*** advertising agency; **~ *towarzyska*** escort agency; **~ *turystyczna*** travel agency **2.** (*oddział*) branch

agencyjn|y *adj* agency; ***wiadomości* ~e** agency news

agenda *f* (*-dy*; *-dy*) **1.** branch **2.** (*terminarz*) timetable, schedule

agent *m* (*-ta*; *-nci*), **~ka** *f* (*-ki*; *-ki*) agent; **~ *wywiadu*** agent, spy; **~ *handlowy*** representative; **~ *ubezpieczeniowy*** insurance agent; **agentura** *f* (*-ry*; *-ry*) **1.** branch **2.** (*szpiegowska*) spy ring

agitacja *f* (*-ji*; *no pl*) campaigning, canvassing; **~ *przedwyborcza*** canvassing (for votes); **agitacyjn|y** *adj*: ***akcja* ~a** campaign

agitator *m* (*-ra*; *-rzy*), **~ka** *f* (*-ki*; *-ki*) campaigner, canvasser; **agitować** *v/im* (*-tuję*) campaign (**za** *I* for; **przeciw** *D* against), to canvass (**za** *I* for)

aglomeracja *f* (*-ji*; *-je*) agglomeration; **~ *miejska*** urban agglomeration

agonalny *adj*: ***być w stanie* ~m** be dying

agoni|a *f* (*-nii*; *no pl*): ***być w ~i*** be dying
agrafka *f* (*-ki*; *-ki*) safety pin
agrarny *adj* agrarian
agregat *m* (*-tu*; *-ty*) *TECH* unit; ***~ chłodniczy*** freezing unit; ***~ prądotwórczy*** electrical power generator
agresj|a *f* (*-ji*; *-je*) **1.** aggression **2.** (*napaść*) ***~a zbrojna*** armed aggression; ***dokonać ~i*** commit aggression
agresor *m* (*-ra*; *-rzy*) aggressor
agrest *m* (*-tu*; *-ty*) gooseberry
agresywność *f* (*-ści*; *no pl*) aggression; **agresywny** *adj* aggressive
agronom *m* (*-ma*; *-mowie*) agronomist; **agronomia** *f* (*-mii*; *no pl*) agronomy
agroturystyka *f* (*-ki*; *no pl*) rural tourism
aha *interj* **1.** (*zrozumienie*) aha, yeah; ***~, już rozumiem*** oh, now I see **2.** (*przypomnienie*) oh
AIDS *abbr m indecl* AIDS; ***chory na ~*** AIDS sufferer, AIDS victim; ***być chorym na ~*** suffer from AIDS; ***test na ~*** HIV test
ajencj|a *f* (*-ji*; *-je*) **1.** (*dzierżawa*) lease; ***dać w ~ę*** lease (out); ***wziąć w ~ę*** lease **2.** (*oddział*) branch
ajent *m* (*-ta*; *-nci*), **~ka** *f* (*-ki*; *-ki*) **1.** (*dzierżawca*) lessee **2.** (*agent*) representative, agent
ajerkoniak *m* (*-ku*; *-ki*) advocaat
AK *abbr f indecl* (= **Armia Krajowa**) *HIST* (*Poland's underground resistance organization in WWII*) Home Army
akacja *f* (*-ji*; *-je*) **1.** black locust **2.** (*tropikalna*) acacia; **akacjowy** *adj* **1.** black locust **2.** (*dotyczący akacji tropikalnej*) acacia
akademia *f* (*-mii*; *-mie*) **1.** academy; ***~ medyczna*** medical college; ***≈ Muzyczna*** the Academy of Music; ***~ rolnicza*** the college of agriculture; ***≈ Sztuk Pięknych*** the Academy of Fine Arts; ***≈ Wychowania Fizycznego*** the College of Physical Education **2.** (*uroczystość*) commemoration (***ku czci*** *G* of)
akademick|i *adj* academic; ***dom ~i*** *Br* hall of residence, *Am* dormitory; ***młodzież ~a*** students; ***rok ~i*** academic year; ***kwadrans ~i*** *15-minute grace period for lecturers at the beginning of classes*
akademik[1] *m* (*-ka*; *-ki*) (*internat*) *Br* hall, *Am* dorm
akademik[2] *m* (*-ka*; *-cy*), **-miczka** *f* (*-ki*; *-ki*) **1.** (*naukowiec*) academic **2.** (*członek akademii*) academician
akant *m* (*-tu*; *-ty*) *BIOL ARCHIT* acanthus
akapit *m* (*-tu*; *-ty*) paragraph
akcent *m* (*-tu*; *-ty*) **1.** accent; ***mówić z obcym ~em*** speak with a foreign accent; ***kłaść ~*** put an emphasis (***na*** *A* on) **2.** (*w językoznawstwie*) stress; **akcentować** ⟨**za-**⟩ (*-tuję*) **1.** stress **2.** *szczegóły*: emphasize
akcept *m* (*-tu*; *-ty*) *ECON* acceptance; **akceptacja** (*-ji*; *no pl*) **1.** acceptance **2.** (*aprobata*) approval; **akceptować** ⟨**za-**⟩ (*-tuję*) **1.** accept **2.** (*aprobować*) approve
akces *m* (*-su*; *no pl*): ***zgłosić ~*** **a)** *do organizacji*: apply to join (***do*** *G*) **b)** *do konkursu*: enter (***do*** *G*)
akcesoria *pl* (*-riów*) accessories; ***~ samochodowe*** car accessories
akcj|a *f* (*-ji*; *-je*) **1.** action; ***~a protestacyjna*** protest; ***film ~i*** *Br* action film, *Am* action movie; **2.** (*operacja*) operation; ***~a ratunkowa*** rescue operation; ***~a zbrojna*** military operation **3.** (*kampania*) campaign; ***~a wyborcza*** election campaign **4.** *ECON* share **5.** *SPORT* attack
akcjonariusz *m* (*-sza*; *-sze*), **~ka** *f* (*-ki*; *-ki*) shareholder
akcydensow|y *adj*: ***druki ~e*** jobwork *sing*
akcyjn|y *adj*: ***spółka ~a*** joint-stock company; ***kapitał ~y*** share capital
akcyza *f* (*-zy*; *-zy*) *ECON* excise
aklamacj|a *f* (*-ji*; *no pl*): ***przez ~ę*** **a)** (*jednogłośnie*) unanimously **b)** (*bez potrzeby głosowania*) by acclamation
aklimatyzacja *f* (*-ji*; *no pl*) acclimatization; ***aklimatyzować się*** ⟨**za-**⟩ (*-zuję*) acclimatize
akompaniamen|t *m* (*-tu*; *no pl*) accompaniment; ***przy ~cie*** to the accompaniment (*G* of); **akompaniator** *m* (*-ra*; *-rzy*) accompanist; **akompaniować** *v/im* (*-niuję*) accompany
akord *m* (*-du*; *-dy*) **1.** *MUS* chord **2.** *ECON* piecework; ***pracować na ~*** do piecework
akordeon *m* (*-nu*; *-ny*) accordion

akordow|y *adj* piecework; ***praca ~a*** piecework; ***robotnik ~y*** pieceworker
akredytacja *f* (*-ji*; *-je*) accreditation; **akredytować** *v im/p* (*-tuję*) accredit
akrobacje *pl* (*-ji*) acrobatics; ***~ lotnicze*** aerobatics; **akrobata** *m* (*-ty*; *-baci*), **-tka** *f* (*-ki*; *-ki*) acrobat; ***~ na trapezie*** trapeze artist; **akrobatyczn|y** *adj* acrobatic; ***gimnastyka ~a*** acrobatic gymnastics
aksamit *m* (*-tu*; *-ty*) velvet; **aksamitka** (*-ki*; *-ki*) **1.** (*wstążka*) velvet ribbon **2.** (*roślina*) marigold; **aksamitny** *adj* **1.** velvet **2.** *skóra*: velvety
aksjomat *m* (*-tu*; *-ty*) axiom
akt *m* (*-tu*; *-ty*) **1.** act; ***~ płciowy*** sexual act; ***~ przemocy*** act of violence; ***~ rozpaczy*** act of despair; ***~ wiary*** act of faith **2.** ART nude **3.** (*dokument*) certificate; ***~ chrztu*** baptism certificate; ***~ kupna*** bill of sales; ***~ oskarżenia*** indictment; ***~ notarialny*** notarial deed; ***~ ślubu*** wedding certificate; ***~ urodzenia*** birth certificate; ***~ zgonu*** death certificate **4.** (*uroczystość*) ceremony; ***~ otwarcia*** opening ceremony **5.** THEAT act; ***w trzech ~ach*** in three acts
akta *pl* (*akt*) files, records; ***~ osobowe*** personal records; ***~ sądowe*** court records
aktor *m* (*-ra*; *-rzy*) actor; **aktorka** *f* (*-ki*; *-ki*) actress; **aktorsk|i** *adj* **1.** acting; ***szkoła ~a*** drama school **2.** *fig* theatrical; **aktorstwo** *n* (*-wa*; *no pl*) acting
aktówka *f* (*-ki*; *-ki*) briefcase
aktualizować ⟨**z-**⟩ (*-zuję*) update; **aktualnie** *adv* currently, at present; **aktualność** *f* (*-ści*; *no pl*) topicality; ***tracić ~*** become out of date; ***zachowywać ~*** remain up to date; ***aktualności*** **a)** (*wiadomości*) news **b)** (*problemy*) current issues; **aktualny** *adj* **1.** current **2.** (*na czasie*) up-to-date **3.** (*ważny*) valid
aktywa *pl* (*-wów*) ECON assets
aktywista *m* (*-ty*; *-wiści*), **-tka** *f* (*-ki*; *-ki*) activist
aktywizować ⟨**z-**⟩ (*-zuję*) mobilize, energize
aktywność *f* (*-ści*; *no pl*) activity; ***wykazywać ~*** be active; **aktywny** *adj* active
akumulacja *f* (*-ji*; *no pl*) accumulation; ***~ ciepła*** heat accumulation; **akumulator** *m* (*-ra*; *-ry*) AUTO battery; **akumulować** ⟨**z-**⟩ (*-luję*) accumulate
akupunktura *f* (*-ry*; *no pl*) acupuncture
akurat *adv* **1.** (*dokładnie*) exactly **2.** (*właśnie*) just; ***~ gdy wychodziłem*** just as I was leaving; ***~!*** *infml* oh, come on!, you must be joking!
akustyczny *adj* acoustic; **akustyka** *f* (*-ki*; *no pl*) acoustics
akuszerka *f* (*-ki*; *-ki*) midwife
akwaforta *f* (*-ty*; *no pl*) etching
akwamaryna *f* (*-ny*; *no pl*) aquamarine
akwarela *f* (*-li*; *-le*) *Br* watercolour, *Am* watercolor
akwariow|y *adj* aquarium; ***rybki ~e*** aquarium fish; ***rośliny ~e*** aquarium plants
akwarium *n* (*indecl*; *-ria*) fish tank, aquarium
akwedukt *m*(*-tu*; *-ty*) aqueduct
akwizycja *f* (*-ji*; *no pl*) direct selling, door-to-door selling; **akwizytor** *m* (*-ra*; *-rzy*) door-to-door salesman; **akwizytorka** *f* (*-ki*; *-ki*) door-to-door saleswoman
AL *abbr f indecl* (= **Armia Ludowa**) HIST (*Poland's underground army organization in WWII*) People's Army
alabaster *m* (*-tru*; *-try*) alabaster; **alabastrowy** *adj* alabaster
alarm *m* (*-mu*; *-my*) **1.** alarm; ***bić na ~*** raise the alarm; ***~ przeciwwłamaniowy*** burgler alarm; ***~ przeciwpożarowy*** fire alarm; ***~ samochodowy*** car alarm **2.** (*gotowość*) alert ***~ pożarowy*** fire alert; **alarmować** ⟨**za-**⟩ (*-muję*) alarm; **alarmow|y** *adj* alarm; ***sygnał ~y*** alarm; ***stan ~y*** state of alert; ***urządzenie ~e*** warning device; **alarmujący** *adj* alarming
Alaska *f* (*-ki*) Alaska
Albania (*-nii*) Albania; **Albańczyk** *m* (*-ka*; *-czycy*), **-banka** *f* (*-ki*; *-ki*) Albanian; **albańsk|i** *adj* Albanian; ***mówić po ~u*** speak Albanian
albatros *m* (*-sa*; *-sy*) albatross
albinos *m* (*-sa*; *-sy/-si*) albino
albo *conj* or; ***~..., ~*** either... or; ***~ też*** or
albowiem *conj lit* because, for
album *m* (*-mu*; *-my*) album; ***~ fotograficzny*** photo album
alchemia *f* (*-mii*; *no pl*) alchemy

ale **I** *conj* but **II** *particle* **~ *chce mi się pić!*** I'm so thirsty!; **~ *piękny widok!*** what a beautiful view!; **~ *pogoda!*** what weather!; **~ *smaczne!*** absolutely delicious **III** *n indecl* ***żadnych ~!*** no buts!
alegoria *f* (*-rii*; *-rie*) allegory; **alegoryczny** *adj* allegorical
aleja *f* (*alei*; *-je*) avenue
alergia *f* (*-gii*; *-gie*) allergy (**na** *A* to); **~ *na kurz*** allergy to dust; **alergiczny** *adj* allergic
alergik *m*(*-ka*; *-gicy*), **-giczka** *f* (*-ki*; *-ki*): ***być ~iem*** be allergic, have an allergy
alert *m* (*-tu*; *-ty*) alert
alež *particle* but; **~ *skąd!*** of course not!; **~ *tak!*** yes, of course!
alfabet *m* (*-tu*; *-ty*) alphabet; **~ *Braille'a*** Braille; **~ *Morse'a*** Morse code; ***według ~u*** alphabetically
alfabetyczny *adj* alphabetical
alfons *m* (*-sa*; *-si*/*-sy*) *infml* pimp
alga *f* (*-gi*; *-gi*) alga; ***algi*** algae
algebra *f* (*-ry*; *no pl*) algebra; **algebraiczny** *adj* algebraic
Algieria *f* (*-rii*) Algeria
Algierczyk *m* (*-ka*; *-czycy*), **-rka** *f* (*-ki*; *-ki*) Algerian; **algierski** *adj* Algerian
aliancki *adj* allied; **aliant** *m* (*-ta*; *-nci*), **~ka** *f* (*-ki*; *-ki*) ally; ***alianci*** *HIST* the Allies
alibi *n indecl* alibi
alienacja *f* (*-ji*; *no pl*) alienation
alimenty *pl* (*-tów*) *Br* maintenance *sing*, *Am* alimony *sing*; **alimentacyjny** *adj*: ***obowiązek ~*** obligation of maintenance
alkaliczny *adj* alcaline
alkohol *m* (*-lu*; *-le*) alcohol; ***poziom ~u we krwi*** level of alcohol in the blood; ***uzależniony od ~u*** addicted to alcohol; ***zawierać 10% ~u*** contain 10% alcohol; ***alkohole*** (*napoje*) alcoholic beverages
alkoholik *m* (*-ka*; *-licy*), **-liczka** *f* (*-ki*; *-ki*) alkoholic; **alkoholizm** *m* (*-mu*; *no pl*) alcoholism; **alkoholowy** *adj* alcoholic
alkomat *m* (*-tu*; *-ty*) breathalyser, *Am* Breathalyzer®
alleluja *n indecl* hallelujah; ***Wesołego ~!*** Happy Easter!
aloes *m* (*-su*; *-sy*) aloe
alpejsk|i *adj* Alpine; ***fiołek ~i*** cyclamen; ***kombinacja ~a*** Alpine combined
alpinista *m* (*-ty*; *-niści*), **-tka** *f* (*-ki*; *-ki*) mountaineer, climber; **alpinizm** *m* (*-mu*; *no pl*) mountaineering, climbing
Alpy *pl* (*Alp*) the Alps
alt *m* (*-tu*; *-ty*) alto
altana *f* (*-ny*; *-ny*), **altanka** *f* (*-ki*; *-ki*) **1.** (*na działce*) summer house **2.** (*w parku*) *Br* arbour, *Am* arbor
alternator *m* (*-ra*; *-ry*) *AUTO* alternator
alternatywa *f* (*-wy*; *-wy*) alternative; **alternatywny** *adj* alternative
altówka *f* (*-ki*; *-ki*) viola
altruista *m* (*-ty*; *-ruiści*), **-tka** *f* (*-ki*; *-ki*) altruist; **altruistyczny** altruistic; **altruizm** *m* (*-mu*; *no pl*) altruism
altysta *m* (*-ty*; *-tyści*), **-tka** *f* (*-ki*; *-ki*) violist
aluminiow|y *adj* *Br* aluminium, *Am* aluminum; ***folia ~a*** tinfoil; **aluminium** *n indecl* *Br* aluminium, *Am* aluminum
aluzj|a *f* (*-ji*; *-je*) **1.** hint, allusion; ***robić ~e*** allude (**do** *G* to) **2.** (*literacka*) allusion
aluzyjnie *adv*: ***wspomnieć ~ o*** *L* hint at
Alzacja *f* (*-ji*) Alsace
alzacki *adj* Alsatian; ***owczarek ~*** Alsatian
ałun *m* (*-nu*; *-ny*) alum
amalgamat *m* (*-tu*; *-ty*) amalgam; ***plomba z ~u*** amalgam filling
amant *m* (*-ta*; *-nci*) **1.** (*wielbiciel*) admirer **2.** (*kochanek*) lover; **~ *filmowy*** screen lover
amarantowy *adj* amaranth, purplish red
amarylis *m* (*-su*; *-sy*) amaryllis, belladonna lily
amator *m* (*-ra*; *-torzy*), **~ka** *f* (*-ki*; *-ki*) **1.** amateur; ***fotograf ~*** amateur photographer **2.** (*miłośnik*) lover; **~ *win*** wine lover **3.** (*reflektujący*) **~ *na kupno czegoś*** s.o. interested in buying s.th.
amatorsk|i *adj* **1.** (*nieprofesjonalny*) amateur; ***teatr ~i*** amateur theatre **2.** (*niefachowy*) amateurish; ***po ~u*** amateurishly; **amatorsko** *adv* **1.** (*nieprofesjonalnie*) ***zajmować się ~ fotografią*** be an amateur photographer

2. (*niefachowo*) amateurishly; **amatorszczyzna** *f* (*-ny*; *no pl*) amateurishness
Amazonka[1] *f* (*-ki*) (*rzeka*) the Amazon
Amazonka[2] *f* (*-ki*; *-ki*) (*wojowniczka*) Amazon
amazonka *f* (*-ki*; *-ki*) horsewoman
ambaras *m* (*-su*; *no pl*) *dated* embarrassment; ***narobić ~u*** cause trouble
ambasada *f* (*-dy*; *-dy*) embassy; **ambasador** *m* (*-ra*; *-rzy*) ambassador; ***~ Francji w Polsce*** the French ambassador to Poland
ambicj|a *f* (*-ji*; *-je*) **1.** (*pragnienie*) ambition; ***~e artystyczne*** artistic ambitions; ***ktoś ma ~e coś zrobić*** s.o.'s ambition is to do s.th.; ***kogoś żżera ~a*** s.o. is consumed by ambition; ***nie mieć ~i*** lack ambition; ***zaspokoić swoje ~e*** fulfil one's ambitions **2.** (*duma*) pride; ***zranić czyjąś ~ę*** hurt s.o.'s pride
ambitny *adj* ambitious
ambona *f* (*-ny*; *-ny*) (*w kościele*) pulpit
ambulans *m* (*-su*; *-se*) ambulance
ambulatorium *n* (*indecl*; *-ria*) (*przy szpitalu*) out-patient department; **ambulatoryjn|y** *adj* out-patient; ***leczenie ~e*** out-patient treatment
ameba *f* (*-by*; *-by*) *Br* amoeba, *Am* ameba
amen *n indecl* amen; ***pewny jak ~ w pacierzu*** (as) certain as death and taxes; ***na ~*** for good
Ameryka *f* (*-ki*; *-ki*) America; ***~ Południowa*** South America; ***~ Północna*** North America; ***~ Środkowa*** Central America
Amerykan|in *m* (*-na*; *-kanie*), **~ka** *f* (*-ki*; *-ki*) American; ***jest ~ką*** she is American
amerykanka *f* (*-ki*; *-ki*) (*fotel*) chair bed
amerykański *adj* American
ametyst *m* (*-tu*; *-ty*) amethyst
amfibia *f* (*-bii*; *-bie*) **1.** *BIOL* amphibian **2.** *TECH* amphibious vehicle
amfiteatr *m* (*-ru*; *-ry*) *Br* amphitheatre, *Am* amphitheater
amfora *f* (*-ry*; *-ry*) amphora
aminokwas *m* (*-su*; *-sy*) amino acid
amnesti|a *f* (*-tii*; *-tie*) amnesty; ***powszechna ~a*** general amnesty; ***udzielić komuś ~i*** grant s.o. an amnesty
amnezja *f* (*-ji*; *no pl*) amnesia
amok *m* (*-ku*; *no pl*) amok, frenzy; ***być w ~u*** run amok; ***wpaść w ~*** go into a frenzy
amoniak *m* (*-ku*; *no pl*) ammonia
amoralny *adj* amoral
amorek *m* (*-rka*; *-rki*) *ART* putto
amortyzacja *f* (*-ji*; *no pl*) **1.** *TECH* shock absorption **2.** *obiektów*, *urządzeń*: depreciation **3.** *kredytu*: amortization; **amortyzator** *m* (*-ra*; *-ry*) shock absorber
amortyzować ⟨**z-**⟩ (*-zuję*) **1.** *wstrząsy*: absorb **2.** *upadek*: cushion **3.** *obiekty*, *urządzenia*: depreciate; ***amortyzować się*** pay for itself
amory *pl* (*-rów*) *infml* **1.** (*flirt*) flirtation *sing* **2.** (*romans*) love affair *sing*
amperomierz *m* (*-rza*; *-rze*) ammeter
ampułka *f* (*-ki*; *-ki*) ampoule
amputacja *f* (*-ji*; *-je*) amputation; **amputować** *v im/p* (*-tuję*) amputate
Amsterdam *m* (*-mu*) Amsterdam
amulet *m* (*-tu*; *-ty*) amulet
amunicja *f* (*-ji*; *no pl*) ammunition; ***ostra ~*** live ammunition; ***ślepa ~*** blank ammunition
anaboliczn|y *adj* anabolic; ***środki ~e*** anabolic steroids
anachroniczny *adj* anachronistic, outdated
analfabet|a *m* (*-ty*; *-beci*), **~ka** *f* (*-ki*; *-ki*) illiterate; ***są ~ami*** they're illiterate; **analfabetyzm** *m* (*-mu*; *no pl*) illiteracy
analityk *m* (*-ka*; *-tycy*), **-tyczka** *f* (*-ki*; *-ki*) analyst
analiz|a *f* (*-zy*; *-zy*) analysis; ***~a krwi*** blood analysis; ***~a matematyczna*** mathematical analysis; ***~a rynku*** market analysis; ***poddać coś ~ie*** subject s.th. to analysis; ***przeprowadzić ~ę*** conduct an analysis; **analizować** ⟨**z-**⟩ (*-zuję*) *Br* analyse, *Am* analyze
analny *adj* anal
analogia *f* (*-gii*; *-gie*) analogy; **analogiczny** *adj* analogous
ananas *m* (*-sa*; *-sy*) **1.** (*owoc*, *roślina*) pineapple **2.** *infml* (*urwis*) urchin; **ananasowy** *adj* pineapple
anarchia *f* (*-chii*; *no pl*) anarchy; **anarchiczny** *adj* anarchic; **anarchista** *m* (*-ty*; *-chiści*), **-tka** *f* (*-ki*; *-ki*) anarchist; **anarchistyczny** *adj* anarchist

anatomia *f* (*-mii*; *no pl*) anatomy; **anatomiczny** *adj* anatomical
Andora *f* (*-ry*) Andorra
androny: ***pleść ~*** spout nonsense
andrzejki *pl* (*-jek*) **1.** (*dzień*) *the eve of St Andrew's day* **2.** (*zabawa*) *party held on the eve of St Andrew's day*
Andy *pl* (*-dów*) the Andes
anegdota *f* (*-ty*; *-ty*) anecdote; **anegdotyczny** *adj* anecdotal
aneks *m* (*-su*; *-sy*) *Br* annexe, *Am* annex (**do** *G* to); ***~ kuchenny*** kitchen area; **aneksj|a** *f* (*-ji*; *-je*) annexation; ***dokonać ~i*** annexe; **anektować** ⟨**za-**⟩ (*-tuję*) annex
anemia *f* (*-mii*; *no pl*) *Br* anaemia, *Am* anemia; **anemiczny** *adj Br* anaemic, *Am* anemic
anestezjolog *m* (*-ga*; *-lodzy*) *Br* anaesthetist, *Am* anesthetist
angażować ⟨**za-**⟩ (*-żuję*) **1.** (*zatrudniać*) employ, hire **2.** (*zajmować*) involve **3.** *środki finansowe*: apopropriate (**w** *A* for) **4.** *mięśnie*: work; ***angażować się*** **1.** (*przyjąć pracę*) take a job **2.** (*udzielać się*) get involved (**w** *A* in); ***~ się uczuciowo*** get involved emotionally
Angielka *f* (*-ki*; *-ki*) Englishwoman; ***jest Angielką*** she is English
angielsk|i I *adj* English; ***~a flegma*** British phlegm; ***jak to powiedzieć po ~u?*** how do you say it in English?; ***język ~i*** English; ***mówić po ~u*** speak English; ***po ~u*** in English; ***ziele ~ie*** allspice, pimento **II** *m* (*-kiego*; *no pl*) English; ***lekcja ~iego*** English lesson
angielszczyzna *f* (*-ny*; *no pl*) English
angina *f* (*-ny*; *no pl*) acute tonsillitis, *infml* sore throat
Anglia *f* (*-lii*) England
anglicyzm *m* (*-mu*; *-my*) anglicism
Anglik *m* (*-ka*; *-licy*) Englishman; ***oni są ~ami*** they are English
anglikanin *m* (*-na*; *-kanie*), **-kanka** *f* (*-ki*; *-ki*) Anglican; **anglikański** *adj* Anglican; ***Kościół ~*** the Church of England
anglistyk|a *f* (*-ki*; *no pl*) English studies; ***studiować ~ę*** study English
anglojęzyczny *adj* **1.** *osoba*, *kraj*: English-speaking **2.** *literatura*: English; **anglosaski** *adj* Anglo-Saxon
angora *f* (*-ry*; *no pl*) angora
ani I *conj* or; ***~..., ~*** neither..., nor!; ***~ mnie to ziębi, ~ grzeje*** I don't care about it; ***nie kradł, ~ nie kłamał*** he did not steal or lie **II** *particle* not (even); ***~ myślę*** no way!; ***~ razu*** not even once; ***~ jeden*** none; ***~ trochę*** at all; ***~ śladu*** no trace; ***~ słowa!*** not a word!; ***~ mi się śni!*** like hell I will! *infml*; ***~ grosza*** *Br* not a penny; ***~ mru-mru!*** hush!
anielsk|i *adj* **1.** *skrzydła*: angel **2.** *uśmiech*: angelic **3.** ***~a cierpliwość*** the patience of a saint **4.** ***włosy ~ie*** tinsel
animacja *f* (*-ji*; *-je*) animation; **animowany** *adj* animated; ***film ~*** (animated) cartoon
animusz *m* (*-szu*; *no pl*) spirit; ***nie tracić ~u*** not lose one's spirit; ***dodać ~u*** give s.o. heart
anioł *m* (*-ła*; *-łowie*/*-ły*) angel; ***≈ Pański*** Ave Maria; ***~ stróż*** guardian angel
ankieta *f* (*-ty*; *-ty*) **1.** (*formularz*) questionnaire; ***~ personalna*** personal questionnaire **2.** (*sondaż*) poll
ankietować *v*/*im* (*-tuję*) poll; **ankietowany** *m* (*-nego*; *-ni*), **-na** *f* (*-nej*; *-ne*) respondent
ano *particle* well; ***~ tak*** yes, *infml* yeah; – ***„Zgadzasz się?"*** – ***„≈ tak."*** 'Do you agree?' 'Yes I do.'
anoda *f* (*-dy*; *-dy*) anode
anomali|a *f* (*-lii*; *-lie*) anomaly; ***~e atmosferyczne*** weather anomalies
anonim[1] *m* (*-ma*; *-mowie*) **1.** (*osoba*) anonymous person **2.** (*autor*) anonymous author
anonim[2] *m* (*-mu*; *-my*) (*list*) anonymous letter; **anonimowo** *adv* anonymously; **anonimowy** *adj* anonymous
anons *m* (*-su*; *-se*/*-sy*) **1.** (*ogłoszenie*) advertisement, ad **2.** (*zawiadomienie*) announcement, notice; ***dać ~*** put an ad (**do** *G* in); ***zamieścić ~*** place an advertisement (**w** *L* in)
anoreksja *f* (*-ji*; *no pl*) anorexia
antagonista *m* (*-ty*; *-niści*), **-tka** *f* (*-ki*; *-ki*) antagonist; **antagonizm** *m* (*-mu*; *-my*) antagonism; ***~ rasowy*** racial antagonism; **antagonistyczny** *adj* antagonistic
antarktyczny *adj* Antarctic
Antarktyda *f* (*-dy*) Antarctica

antenla *f* (*-ny*; *-ny*) antenna, aerial; ***~a satelitarna*** satellite dish; ***na ~ie*** *RADIO* on (the) air
antenat *m* (*-ta*; *-naci*) forefather
antenowy *adj* antenna; **czas ~** airtime
antidotum *n* (*indecl*; *-ta*) antidote (**na** *A* to)
antologia *f* (*-gii*; *-gie*) anthology
antrakt *m* (*-tu*; *-ty*) *THEAT* intermission
antresola *f* (*-li*; *-le*) mezzanine
antropolog *m* (*-ga*; *-lodzy*/*-gowie*) anthropologist; **antropologia** *f* (*-gii*; *no pl*) anthropology; **antropologiczny** *adj* anthropological
antrykot *m* (*-tu*; *-ty*) *COOK* entrecôte
antyaborcyjnly *adj* anti-abortion; ***ustawa ~a*** anti-abortion law
antyalkoholowly *adj* **1.** *kampania*: anti-alcohol **2.** *terapia*: (alcohol) detoxification, *infml* detox **3.** ***poradnia ~a*** *Br* alcohol advice centre
antybiotyk *m* (*-ku*; *-ki*) antibiotic
antychryst *m* (*-ta*; *-ty*) **1.** *RELIG* the Antichrist **2.** *infml* heathen
antycypować *v*/*im* (*-puję*) anticipate
antyczny *adj* **1.** *świat*, *epoka*: ancient **2.** *meble*: antique
antydatować *v*/*im* (*-tuję*) backdate
antydepresyjny *adj* antidepressant; ***środek ~*** antidepressant
antydopingowly *adj*: ***kontrola ~a*** drug test
antyfaszystowski *adj* anti-fascist
antyfeministyczny *adj* anti-feminist
antygen *m* (*-nu*; *-ny*) antigen
antyk *m* (*-ku*; *-ki*) **1.** (*okres*) antiquity **2.** (*mebel*) antique; ***sklep z ~ami*** antique shop
antykapitalistyczny *adj* anti-capitalist
antyklerykalny *adj* anticlerical
antykomunistyczny *adj* anti-communist
antykoncepcja *f* (*-ji*; *no pl*) contraception; **antykoncepcyjnly** *adj* contraceptive; ***środek ~y*** contraceptive; ***pigułka ~a*** contraceptive pill, the pill
antykorozyjny *adj* anti-corrosive
antykwariat *m* (*-tu*; *-ty*) **1.** (*z książkami*) second-hand bookshop **2.** (*z antykami*) antique shop; **antykwariusz** *m* (*-sza*; *-sze*) **1.** (*księgarz*) second-hand bookseller **2.** (*sprzedawca antyków*) antique dealer; **antykwaryczny** *adj* (*związany z antykami*) antique; ***handel ~*** antique dealing
antylopa *f* (*-py*; *-py*) antelope
antynarkotyczny *adj* anti-drug
antynuklearny *adj* anti-nuclear
antypaństwowy *adj* anti-national
antypatia *f* (*-tii*; *-tie*) antipathy
antypatyczny *adj* unpleasant, unsympathetic
antypiracki *adj* anti-piracy
antypolski *adj* anti-Polish
antysemicki *adj* anti-Semitic; **antysemita** *m* (*-ty*; *-mici*), **-tka** *f* (*-ki*; *-ki*), anti-Semite; **antysemityzm** *m* (*-mu*; *no pl*) anti-Semitism
antyseptyczny *adj* antiseptic
antyspołeczny *adj* antisocial
antytalent *m* (*-tu*; *-ty*) **1.** (*brak zdolności*) **mieć ~** have no talent (**do** *G* for) **2.** (*osoba*) untalented person; ***być ~em językowym*** have no talent for languages
antyterrorystycznly *adj* anti-terrorist; ***brygada ~a*** anti-terrorist squad; ***akcja ~a*** anti-terrorist action
antywirusowy *adj* *INF* antivirus; ***program ~*** antivirus (program)
antywłamaniowy *adj* antiburglar
antywojenny *adj* anti-war
anulować *v im*/*p* (*-luję*) **1.** cancel **2.** *wyrok*: remit; **anulowanie** *n* (*-nia*; *no pl*) cancellation
anyż *m* (*-żu*; *-że*) **1.** (*przyprawa*) aniseed **2.** (*roślina*) anise; **anyżowy** *adj* aniseed; **anyżówka** *f* (*-ki*; *-ki*) anisette
aorta *f* (*-ty*; *-ty*) aorta
aparat *m* (*-tu*; *-ty*) **1.** (*urządzenie*) ***~ fotograficzny*** camera; ***~ telefoniczny*** telephone; ***~ rentgenowski*** X-ray machine; ***~ słuchowy*** hearing aid; ***~ tlenowy*** breathing apparatus **2.** (*system*, *układ*) apparatus; ***~ państwowy*** the state apparatus; **aparatura** *f* (*-ry*; *-ry*) apparatus
apartament *m* (*-tu*; *-ty*) suite
apaszka *f* (*-ki*; *-ki*) neck kerchief
apatila *f* (*-tii*; *no pl*) apathy; ***popaść w ~ę*** fall into apathy
apatyczny *adj* apathetic
apel *m* (*-lu*; *-le*) **1.** appeal; ***zwrócić się z ~em*** make an appeal (**do** *G* to) **2.** (*w szkole*) assembly **3.** (*w wojsku*) roll call

apelacj|a *f* (*-ji*; *-je*) **1.** *JUR* appeal; **wnieść ~ę** *Br* lodge an appeal, *Am* file an appeal **2.** *wina*: appellation

apelacyjny *adj JUR* appeal; **sąd ~** court of appeal, appelate court; **apelować** ⟨**za-**⟩ (*-luję*) appeal (**o** *A* for)

Apeniny *pl* (*-nów*) the Apennines; **apeniński** *adj*: **Półwysep ≈** the Italian Peninsula

apetyczny *adj* appetizing; **apetyt** *m* (*-tu*; *-ty*) appetite (**na** *A* for); **odebrać komuś ~** spoil s.o.'s appetite; **pobudzić czyjś ~** *fig* whet s.o.'s appetite; **stracić ~** lose one's appetite; **mieć na coś ~** feel like (eating) s.th.

aplauz *m* (*-zu*; *-zy*) applause; **przyjąć z ~em** applaud; **spotkać się z ~em** be met with applause

aplikacja *f* (*-ji*; *-je*) **1.** *INF* application **2.** *JUR* apprenticeship, *Br* training contract **3.** (*naszyty wzór*) appliqué; **aplikant** *m* (*-ta*; *-nci*), **~ka** *f* (*-ki*; *-ki*) *JUR* **1.** (*adwokacki*) trainee solicitor **2.** (*sądowy*) trainee judge

aplikować ⟨**za-**⟩ (*-kuję*) *lek*, *zastrzyk*: administer; **za~ komuś lek** administer medicine to s.o.

apodyktyczny *adj* domineering, *infml* bossy

apogeum *n* (*indecl*; *-gea*) apogee; **osiągnąć ~** reach its apogee

apokaliptyczny *adj* apocalyptic

apolityczny *adj* apolitical

apopleksja *f* (*-ji*; *no pl*) apoplexy; **apoplektyczny** *adj* apoplectic; **atak ~** apoplectic fit

aport *interj*: **~!** fetch!; **aportować** ⟨**za-**⟩ (*-tuję*) fetch

apostolsk|i *adj* apostolic; **Dzieje ≈ie** the Acts of the Apostles; **Stolica ≈a** the Holy See; **apostoł** *m* (*-ła*; *-łowie*) apostle

aprobata *f* (*-ty*; *no pl*) approval; **aprobować** ⟨**za-**⟩ (*-buję*) approve (*A* of)

apteczka *f* (*-ki*; *-ki*) **1.** (*pierwszej pomocy*) first-aid kit **2.** (*szafka*) medicine cupboard

apteka *f* (*-ki*; *-ki*) pharmacy, *Br* chemist's, *Am* drugstore; **aptekarsk|i** *adj*: **waga ~a** pharmaceutical scales; **aptekarz** *m* (*-rza*; *-rze*), **-rka** *f* (*-ki*; *-ki*) pharmacist, *Br* chemist, *Am* druggist

Arab *m* (*-ba*; *-bowie*), **~ka** *f* (*-ki*; *-ki*) (*osoba*) Arab

arab *m* (*-ba*; *-by*) (*koń*) Arab

Arabia Saudyjska *f* (*-bii Saudyjskiej*) Saudi Arabia

arabsk|i I *adj* **1.** Arab; **Półwysep ≈i** the Arabian Peninsula; **Zjednoczone Emiraty ≈ie** United Arab Emirates **2.** *język*, *literatura*, *cyfra*: Arabic; **po ~u** in Arabic **3.** *koń*, *pustynia*: Arabian; **guma ~a** gum arabic **II** *m* (*-kiego*; *no pl*) (*język*) Arabic; **mówić po ~u** speak Arabic

arachidow|y *adj*: **orzeszki ~e** peanuts

aranżacja *f* (*-ji*; *-je*) *MUS* arrangement; **aranżować** ⟨**za-**⟩ (*-żuję*) *MUS* arrange

arbiter *m* (*-tra*; *-trzy*) **1.** *JUR* arbitrator **2.** (*autorytet*) arbiter; **~ dobrego smaku** arbiter of taste **3.** (*w piłce nożnej*, *koszykówce*) referee **4.** (*w tenisie*) umpire

arbitraż *m* (*-żu*; *-że*) arbitration

arbitrażowy *adj*: **sąd ~** court of arbitration

arbuz *m* (*-za*; *-zy*) watermelon

archaiczny *adj* archaic

archanioł *m* (*-ła*; *-łowie*/*-ły*) archangel

archeolog *m* (*-ga*; *-lodzy*/*-gowie*) *Br* archaeologist, *Am* archeologist

archeologia *f* (*-gii*; *no pl*) *Br* archaeology, *Am* archeology; **archeologiczny** *adj Br* archaeological, *Am* archeological

archidiecezja *f*(*-ji*; *-je*) archdiocese

archipelag *m* (*-gu*; *-gi*) archipelago

architekt *m* (*-ta*; *-kci*), **~ka** *f* (*-ki*; *-ki*) architect; **~ wnętrz** interior designer; **architektoniczny** *adj* architectural; **architektura** *f* (*-ry*; *no pl*) architecture; **~ wnętrz** interior design

archiwaln|y *adj* archival; **film ~y** archive film; **nagrania ~e** archive records

archiwista *m* (*-ty*; *-wiści*) archivist; **archiwum** *n* (*indecl*; *-wa*) archive

arcybiskup *m* (*-pa*; *-pi*) archbishop

arcydzieło *n* (*-ła*; *-ła*) masterpiece

arcykapłan *m* (*-na*; *-ni*) high priest

arcyksiążę *m* (*-sięcia*; *-żęta*) archduke

arcymistrz *m* (*-rza*; *-rzowie*) grand master

areał *m* (*-łu*; *-ły*) acreage

aren|a *f* (*-ny*; *-ny*) arena; **na ~ie międzynarodowej** in the international arena

aresz|t *m* (*-tu*; *-ty*) **1.** (*aresztowanie*) arrest; **~t domowy** house arrest; **~t tymczasowy** custody; **w ~cie** under arrest; **w ~cie śledczym** in custody **2.** (*pomieszczenie*) lockup
aresztowa|ć ⟨**za-**⟩ (*-tuję*) arrest; **jest pani ~na** you're under arrest; **aresztowani|e** *n* (*-nia*; *-nia*) arrest; **nakaz ~a** arrest warrant; **aresztowany** *m* (*-nego*; *-ni*), **-na** *f* (*-nej*; *-ne*) arrestee
Argentyna *f* (*-ny*) Argentina
Argentyńczyk *m* (*-ka*; *-czycy*), **-tynka** *f* (*-ki*; *-ki*) Argentinian
argentyński *adj* Argentinian
argument *m* (*-tu*; *-ty*) argument (**za** *I* for; **przeciw** *D* against); **argumentować** *v/im* (*-tuję*) argue (**za** *I* for; **przeciw** *D* against)
aria *f* (*-rii*; *-rie*) aria
arianin *m* (*-na*; *-rianie*) Arian; **ariański** *adj* Arian
arka *f* (*-ki*; *no pl*) the ark; **Ꞩ Noego** Noah's Ark; **Ꞩ Przymierza** the Ark of Covenant
arkad|a *f* (*-dy*; *-dy*) arch; **~y** arcade
arkan *m* (*-nu*; *-ny*) lasso
arkana, **arkany** *pl* (*-nów*) secrets
arktyczny *adj* Arctic
arkusz *m* (*-sza*; *-sze*) sheet; **~ papieru** a sheet of paper; **~ kalkulacyjny** spreadsheet
arlekin *m* (*-na*; *-ny*/*-ni*) harlequin
armata *f* (*-ty*; *-ty*) canon; **armatni** *adj* cannon; **kula ~a** cannonball; **mięso ~e** cannon fodder
armator *m* (*-ra*; *-rzy*) **1.** (*właściciel*) ship owner **2.** (*zarządca*) ship operator
armatura *f* (*-ry*; *-ry*) fittings
Armenia *f* (*-nii*) Armenia
armeński *adj* Armenian
armi|a *f* (*-mii*; *-mie*) army; **w ~i** in the army; **wstąpić do ~i** join the army
arogancja *f* (*-ji*; *no pl*) arrogance; **arogancki** *adj* arrogant
aromat *m* (*-tu*; *-ty*) **1.** (*zapach*) aroma **2.** (*dodatek*) *Br* flavouring, *Am* flavoring
aromaterapia *f* (*-pii*; *no pl*) aromatherapy
aromatyczny *adj* aromatic, fragrant; **aromatyzowany** *adj Br* flavoured, *Am* flavored
aronia *f* (*-nii*; *-nie*) black chokeberry
arras *m* (*-su*; *-sy*) tapestry
arsenał *m* (*-łu*; *-ły*) arsenal
arszenik *m* (*-ku*; *no pl*) arsenic
art. *abbr* (= **artykuł**) article
arteria *f* (*-rii*; *-rie*) artery
arterioskleroza *f* (*-zy*; *no pl*) MED arteriosclerosis
artezyjsk|i *adj* artesian; **studnia ~a** artesian well
artretyczny *adj* arthritic; **artretyzm** *m* (*-mu*; *no pl*) arthritis
artykuł *m* (*-łu*; *-ły*) article; **~ wstępny** editorial; **~y gospodarstwa domowego** household goods; **~y luksusowe** luxury goods; **~y pierwszej potrzeby** basic necessities; **~y spożywcze** groceries; **artykułować** ⟨**wy-**⟩ (*-łuję*) articulate
artyleria *f* (*-rii*; *no pl*) artillery; **~ przeciwlotnicza** anti-aircraft artillery; **artyleryjski** *adj* artillery
artysta *m* (*-ty*; *-ści*), **-tka** *f* (*-ki*; *-ki*) artist; **~ malarz** painter; **~ cyrkowy** circus performer
artystyczn|y *adj* artistic; **działalność ~a** artistic activity; **rzemiosło ~e** craft; **szkoła ~a** art school
artyzm *m* (*-mu*; *no pl*) artistry
aryjski *adj* Aryan
arystokracja *f* (*-ji*; *no pl*) aristocracy; **arystokrata** *m* (*-ty*; *-raci*), **-tka** *f* (*-ki*; *-ki*) aristocrat; **arystokratyczny** *adj* aristocratic
arytmetyczn|y *adj* arithmetic; **średnia ~a** arithmetic mean; **arytmetyka** *f* (*-ki*; *no pl*) arithmetic
as *m* (*-sa*; *-sy*) ace; **~ karo** the ace of diamonds
asceta *m* (*-ty*; *-ceci*) ascetic; **ascetyczny** *adj* ascetic; **asceza** *f* (*-zy*; *no pl*) asceticism
asekuracja *f* (*-ji*; *no pl*) **1.** (*zabezpieczenie*) safety measures **2.** (*przy wspinaczce*) belay **3.** (*na siłowni*) spotting; **asekuracyjny** *adj* **1.** *towarzystwo*: insurance **2.** *liny*, *haki*: belay
asekurancki *adj* over-cautious; **asekurant** *m* (*-ta*; *-nci*): **być ~em** be over-cautious
asekurować *v/im* (*-ruję*) **1.** protect **2.** (*przy wspinaczce*) belay **3.** (*na siłowni*) spot; **asekurować się** play safe; **~ się przed** *I* protect oneself from
aseptyczny *adj* aseptic

asfalt *m* (*-tu*; *no pl*) tarmac; **asfaltować** ⟨**wy-**⟩ (*-tuję*) tarmac; **asfaltow|y** *adj* tarmac; ***droga ~a*** tarmac road
askorbinowy *adj*: ***kwas ~*** ascorbic acid
asocjacja *f* (*-ji*; *-je*) *lit* association
asortyment *m* (*-tu*; *-ty*) range, assortment
ASP *abbr f indecl* (= ***Akademia Sztuk Pięknych***) the Academy of Fine Arts
aspekt *m* (*-ty*; *-ty*) aspect
aspiracje *pl* (*-ji*) aspirations; ***~ literackie*** literary aspirations, ***mieć wysokie ~*** have high aspirations, aim high; **aspirant** *m* (*-ta*; *-nci*), **-tka** *f* (*-ki*; *-ki*) candidate
aspirować *v/im* (*-ruję*) aspire (**do** *G* to)
aspiryna *f* (*-ny*; *no pl*) aspirin
aspołeczny *adj* anti-social
aster *m* (*-tra*; *-try*) aster
asteroida *f* (*-dy*; *-dy*) asteroid
astma *f* (*-my*; *no pl*) asthma; **astmatyk** *m* (*-ka*; *-tycy*), **-tyczka** *f* (*-ki*; *-ki*) asthmatic; **astmatyczny** *adj* asthmatic
astraln|y *adj* astral; ***ciało ~e*** astral body
astrofizyka *f* (*-ki*; *no pl*) astrophysics
astrologia *f* (*-gii*; *no pl*) astrology
astronauta *m* (*-ty*; *-nauci*), **-tka** *f* (*-ki*; *-ki*) astronaut
astronautyka *f* (*-ki*; *no pl*) astronautics
astronomia *f* (*-mii*; *no pl*) astronomy; **astronomiczny** *adj* astronomical
astygmatyzm *m* (*-mu*; *no pl*) astigmatism
asygnata *f* (*-ty*; *-ty*) FIN cash voucher; **asygnować** ⟨**wy-**⟩ (*-nuję*) **1.** *sumę*: allocate (***na*** *A* for) **2.** *czek*: sign
asymilacja *f* (*-ji*; *no pl*) assimilation
asymilować ⟨**z-**⟩ (*-luję*) assimilate; ***asymilować się*** assimilate (**z** *I* into)
asy|sta *f* (*-ty*; *-ty*) company; ***w czyjejś ~ście*** in the company of s.o.; **asystent** *m* (*-ta*; *-nci*), **-tka** *f* (*-ki*; *-ki*) **1.** assistant **2.** (*na uczelni*) *Br* lecturer, *Am* instructor
asystować *v/im* (*-tuję*) **1.** (*pomagać*) assist **2.** (*towarzyszyć*) accompany
Asyż *m* (*-żu*) Assisi
atak *m* (*-ku*; *-ki*) **1.** attack; ***~ serca*** heart attack; ***~ lotniczy*** air raid **2.** *epilepsji*, *kaszlu*: fit; ***~ śmiechu*** a fit of laughter; ***~ płaczu*** crying fit **3.** SPORT *Br* attack, *Am* offense; ***ona gra w ~u*** she's a forward
atakować ⟨**za-**⟩ (*-kuję*) attack
ateista *m* (*-ty*; *-teiści*), **-tka** *f* (*-ki*; *-ki*) atheist; **ateistyczny** *adj* atheistic
ateizm *m* (*-mu*; *no pl*) atheism
atelier *n indecl* studio; ***~ filmowe*** film studio
Ateny *pl* (*Aten*) Athens
atest *m* (*-tu*; *-ty*) (quality) certificate; **atestować** *v im/p* (*-tuję*) *produkt*: certify
atlantycki *adj* Atlantic; ***Ocean 2*** the Atlantic Ocean
Atlantyk *m* (*-ku*) the Atlantic
atlas *m* (*-su*; *-sy*) atlas; ***~ samochodowy*** road atlas
atleta *m* (*-ty*; *-leci*) strongman; **atletka** *f* (*-ki*; *-ki*) strongwoman; **atletyczn|y** *adj*: ***~a budowa ciała*** strong build; **atletyka** *f* (*-ki*; *no pl*) athletics; ***lekka ~*** *Br* athletics, *Am* track and field
atłas *m* (*-su*; *-sy*) satin; **atłasowy** *adj* satin
atmosfera *f* (*-ry*; *-ry*) atmosphere; **atmosferyczn|y** *adj* atmospheric; ***ciśnienie ~e*** atmospheric pressure; ***warunki ~e*** atmospheric conditions; ***zimny front ~y*** cold front; ***zjawiska ~e*** atmospheric phenomena
atol *m* (*-lu*; *-le*) atoll
atom *m* (*-mu*; *-my*) atom; **atomow|y** *adj* **1.** nuclear; ***bomba ~a*** nuclear bomb; ***energia ~a*** nuclear power **2.** *liczba*, *masa*: atomic; ***jądro ~e*** nucleus
atrakcja *f* (*-ji*; *-je*) attraction; ***~ turystyczna*** tourist attraction; **atrakcyjność** *f* (*-ści*; *no pl*) attractiveness; **atrakcyjny** *adj* attractive
atrament *m* (*-tu*; *-ty*) ink; ***~ sympatyczny*** invisible ink; **atramentow|y** *adj* ink; ***drukarka ~a*** ink-jet printer
atrapa *f* (*-py*; *-py*) **1.** imitation **2.** TECH radiator cover
atropina *f* (*-ny*; *no pl*) atropine
atrybut *m* (*-tu*; *-ty*) **1.** (*cecha*) mark; ***~ męskości*** mark of masculinity **2.** (*symbol*) symbol; ***~ władzy*** symbol of power **3.** INF attribute
atut *m* (*-tu*; *-ty*) **1.** (*zaleta*) advantage; ***elokwencja jest jej ~em*** eloquence is her trump card; ***znajomość komputera będzie ~em*** computer literacy would be an asset **2.** (*w kartach*) trump; ***mieć wszystkie ~y w ręku***

hold all the trump cards; **atutowy** *adj* trump
audiencja *f* (*-ji*; *-je*) audience
audiowizualny *adj* audio-visual, AV
audycja *f* (*-ji*; *-je*) broadcast; **~ *dla dzieci*** *Br* children's programme, *Am* children's program
audytorium *n* (*indecl*; *-ria*) **1.** (*słuchacze*) audience **2.** (*sala*) lectur theatre, *Am* auditorium
Augiasz: ***stajnia ~a*** Augean stable
aukcj|a *f* (*-ji*; *-je*) auction; ***na ~i*** at auction
aula *f* (*-li*; *-le*) hall
aura (*-ry*; *no pl*) *lit* **1.** (*pogoda*) weather **2.** (*nastrój*) aura; ***otaczała go ~ smutku*** he had an aura of sadness about him
aureola *f* (*-li*; *-le*) halo
auspicj|e *pl*: ***pod ~ami*** under the auspices (*G* of)
Australia *f* (*-lii*) Australia
Australijczyk *m* (*-ka*; *-czycy*), **-jka** *f* (*-ki*; *-ki*) Australian; ***jest ~iem*** he's Australian; **australijski** *adj* Australian
Austria *f* (*-rii*) Austria; **austriacki** *adj* Austrian
Austriak *m* (*-ka*; *-riacy*), **-riaczka** *f* (*-ki*; *-ki*), Austrian; ***są ~ami*** they're Austrian
aut *m* (*-tu*; *-ty*) out; ***rzut z ~u*** throw-in; ***wybić piłkę na ~*** knock the ball out of play; ***wyjść na ~*** go out of play
autentyczny *adj* **1.** *obraz*, *podpis*: authentic **2.** *historia*, *fakt*: true **3.** *wydarzenie*, *postać*: real **4.** *zainteresowanie*, *talent*: genuine; **autentyczność** *f* (*-ści*; *no pl*) authenticity; **autentyk** *m* (*-ku*; *-ki*) original
auto *n* (*-ta*; *-ta*) car
autoalarm *m* (*-mu*; *-my*) car alarm
autobiografia *f* (*-fii*; *-fie*) autobiography; **autobiograficzny** *adj* autobiographical
autobus *m* (*-su*; *-sy*) bus; ***~em*** by bus
autocasco *n indecl* car damage and loss insurance
autochton *m* (*-na*; *-ni*), **~ka** *f* (*-ki*; *-ki*) native
autograf *m* (*-fu*; *-fy*) autograph
autoironia *f* (*-nii*; *no pl*) self-irony
autokar *m* (*-ru*; *-ry*) bus, *Br* coach
automat *m* (*-tu*; *-ty*) **1.** (*ogólnie*) automatic machine; ***~ telefoniczny*** payphone **2.** (*broń*) automatic gun **3.** (*do sprzedaży*) vending machine, slot machine; ***~ z papierosami*** cigarette vending machine **4.** (*do rzutek*) dart machine;
automatyczn|y *adj* automatic; ***~a sekretarka*** answering machine; ***~y ołówek*** mechanical pencil; ***pralka ~a*** automatic washing machine
automatyzacja *f* (*-ji*; *no pl*) automation; **automatyzować** ⟨**z-**⟩ (*-zuję*) automate
automyjnia *f* (*-nii*; *-nie*) car wash
autonaprawa *f* (*-wy*; *-wy*) car service
autonomia *f* (*-mii*; *no pl*) autonomy; **autonomiczny** *adj* autonomous
autopoprawka *f* (*-ki*; *-ki*) *amendment to a parliamentary bill made by the bill's author*
autoportret *m* (*-tu*; *-ty*) self-portrait
autopsj|a *f* (*-ji*; *-je*) autopsy; ***znać coś z ~i*** know s.th. from experience
autor *m* (*-ra*; *-rzy*), **~ka** *f* (*-ki*; *-ki*) author
autorski *adj*: ***prawo ~e*** copyright; ***egzemplarz ~*** author's copy; **autorstwo** *n* (*-wa*; *no pl*) authorship
autoreklama *f* (*-my*; *no pl*) self-advertising
autorytatywny *adj* **1.** *rządy*: authoritatian **2.** *ton*, *opinia*: authoritative
autoryzowany *adj* authorized
autorytet *m* (*-tu*; *-ty*) **1.** (*szacunek*) respect; ***cieszyć się ~em*** enjoy respect **2.** (*osoba*) authority (***w dziedzinie*** *G* on)
autoserwis *m* (*-su*; *-sy*) car service
autostop *m* (*-pu*; *no pl*) hitch-hiking; ***jechać ~em*** hitch-hike
autostopowicz *m* (*-cza*; *-cze*), **~ka** *f* (*-ki*; *-ki*) hitch-hiker
autostrada *f* (*-dy*; *-dy*) *Br* motorway, *Am* freeway
autow|y *adj*: ***linia ~a*** touchline; ***piłka ~a*** out-of-bounds ball
autystyczny *adj* autistic; **autyzm** *m* (*-mu*; *no pl*) autism
awangar|da *f* (*-dy*; *no pl*) **1.** ART avant-garde **2.** (*oddział żołnierzy*) vangard; ***w ~dzie*** *fig* in the vangard (*G* of)
awans *m* (*-su*; *-se*/*-sy*) promotion; ***~em*** in advance; ***~ społeczny*** social advancement; ***dostać ~*** be promoted;

awansować *v im/p* (*-suję*) **1.** (*dać awans*) promote **2.** (*otrzymać awans*) be promoted

awantura *f* (*-ry*; *-ry*) row, fight; **awanturnica** *f* (*-cy*; *-ce*) rowdy; **awanturnictwo** *n* (*-wa*; *no pl*) rowdiness

awanturniczy *adj* (*kłótliwy*) rowdy; **awanturnik** *m* (*-ka*; *-nicy*) rowdy; **awanturować się** *v/im* (*-ruję*) quarrel, fight (**o** *A* over)

awaria *f* (*-rii*; *-rie*) **1.** failure; **~ *linii telefonicznej*** telephone line failure; **~ *silnika*** engine failure **2.** *pojazdu*, *maszyny*: breakdown; **awaryjn|y** *adj*: ***hamulec ~y*** emergency brake; ***wyjście ~e*** emergency exit

awersja *f* (*-ji*; *no pl*) *lit* aversion

AWF *abbr m* (*AWF-u*; *no pl*) (=***Akademia Wychowania Fizycznego***) the College of Physical Education

awista: ***rachunek ~*** *Br* current account, *Am* checking account

awitaminoza *f* (*-zy*; *no pl*) vitamin deficiency

awizo *n* (*-za*; *-za*) advice (note)

awizować ⟨**za-**⟩ (*-zuję*) (*informować*) notify (*A* of)

awokado *n indecl* avocado

azalia *f* (*-lii*; *-lie*) azalea

azbest *m* (*-tu*; *no pl*) asbestos; **azbestowy** *adj* asbestos

Azer *m* (*-ra*; *-rzy*), **~ka** *f* (*-ki*; *-ki*) Azerbaijani, Azeri

Azerbejdżan *m* (*-nu*) Azarbaijan

azerbejdżański *adj* Azerbaijani

Azja *f* (*-ji*) Asia; ***~ Mniejsza*** Asia Minor

Azjata *m* (*-ty*; *-jaci*), **-tka** *f* (*-ki*; *-ki*) Asian; **azjatycki** *adj* Asian

azot *m* (*-tu*; *no pl*) nitrogen; **azotowy** *adj* nitric; ***kwas ~*** nitric acid; ***nawóz ~*** nitrogen fertilizer

azyl *m* (*-lu*; *-le*) **1.** (*polityczny*) asylum; ***otrzymać ~*** be granted asylum; ***prawo ~u*** the right of asylum; ***ubiegać się o ~*** seek asylum **2.** (*miejsce*) safe haven

azylant *m* (*-ta*; *-nci*), **~ka** *f* (*-ki*; *-ki*) refugee

aż I *conj* until, till; ***~ tu nagle*** when all of a sudden; ***czekała, ~ przestanie padać*** she waited for the rain to stop; ***prosił ją, ~ się zgodziła*** he kept on asking till she agreed **II** *particle* ***~ 15 lat*** as many as 15 years; ***~ 100 złotych*** as much as 100 zlotys; ***~ nadto dobrze*** only too well; ***~ strach pomyśleć*** one shudders to think; ***~ tak źle*** so bad; ***~ tyle*** so much; ***impreza trwała ~ do 3 rano*** the party didn't stop till 3 a.m.; ***doszli ~ do rzeki*** they went as far as the river; ***mieć ~ 200 lat*** be as old as 200 years; ***to nie jest ~ takie trudne*** it is not that difficult; ***wody było ~ po kolana*** the water reached as high as the knees; ***wystawa była czynna ~ do wczoraj*** the exhibition only closed yesterday

ażeby → ***aby***

ażurowy *adj* openwork

B

b. *abbr* **1.** (=***były***) ex- **2.** (=***bardzo***) v.

baba *f* (*-by*; *-by*) **1.** (*kobieta*) *infml* woman; ***głupia ~*** stupid woman; ***≈ Jaga*** Baba Yaga; ***latać za ~mi*** chase skirts **2.** (*stara kobieta*) *infml* old woman **3.** (*handlarka*) *infml* street vendor **4.** (*ciasto*) traditional cake **5.** (*mężczyzna*) *infml* sissy

babeczka *f* (*-ki*; *-ki*) (*ciastko*) cup cake

babcia *f* (-ci; -cie) **1.** grandmother, *infml* grandma **2.** (*staruszka*) old woman; ***~ klozetowa*** toilet cleaning lady

babi *adj*: ***~e lato*** **a)** (*pajęczyna*) gossamer **b)** (*pora*) Indian summer

babiarz *m* (*-rza*; *-rze*) *infml* skirt chaser; **babieć** ⟨**z-**⟩ (*-bieję*) *infml* **1.** (*o kobiecie*) grow old **2.** (*o mężczyźnie*) become effeminate

Babilon *m* (*-nu*) Babylon

babiloński *adj* Babylonian

babka *f* (*-ki*; *-ki*) **1.** (*babcia*) grandmother, *infml* grandma **2.** (*staruszka*) old woman **3.** (*młoda kobieta*) *infml* girl **4.** (*ciasto*) traditional cake; ***~ z piasku*** mud pie **5.** (*roślina*) plantain

babochłop *m* (*-pa*; *-py*) *infml* butch

babrać ⟨**za-**, **u-**⟩ (*-brzę*/*-ram*) *infml* **1.** (*brudzić*) dirty **2.** (*smarować*)

B

smear; **babrać się** **1.** (*brudzić się*) get dirty **2.** (*robić powoli*) dawdle
babranina *f* (*-ny*; *no pl*) drudgery
babski *adj* women's; **~e gadanie** women's talk
babsko *n* (*-ka*; *-ka*), **babsztyl** *m* (*-la*; *-le*) *infml* hag, old bag
babunia *f* (*-ni*; *-nie*), **babusia** *f* (*-si*; *-sie*) *dim* grandma, *Br* gran
baby-sitter *m* (*-ra*; *-rzy*), **baby-sitter** *f* *indecl* babysitter
baca *m* (*-cy*; *-cowie*) *head shepherd in the Tatra mountains*
bach *interj* bang
bachor *m* (*-ra*; *-ry*) *infml* brat
backup *m* (*-pu*; *-py*) INF back-up
bacówka *f* (*-ki*; *-ki*) mountain hut
bacznoś|ć *f* (*-ści*; *no pl*): **~ć!** attention!: **stać na ~ć** stand to attention; **mieć się na ~ci** be on one's guard (**przed** *I* against); **baczn|y** *adj* **1.** (*osoba*) attentive **2.** (*uwaga*) close; **mieć ~e oko na** *A* keep a watchful eye on
bacz|yć: **nie ~ąc na** *A* undaunted by
bać się *v/im* (*boję*) **1.** (*odczuwać strach*) be scared (*G* of); **~ czegoś jak ognia** be scared to death of s.th.; **~ o własną skórę** be afraid of one's life; **~ własnego cienia** be scared of one's shadow; **bój się Boga!** good God! **2.** (*martwić się*) be worried (**o** *A* about) **3.** (*nie śmieć*) **~ się coś zrobić** be afraid to do s.th.
badacz *m* (*-cza*; *-cze*), **~ka** *f* (*-ki*; *-ki*) **1.** (*naukowiec*) researcher; **~ przyrody** naturalist **2.** (*odkrywca*) explorer
badać ⟨**z-**, **prze-**⟩ (*-dam*) **1.** examine **2.** *rynek*, *problem*: research; **~ naukowo** research **3.** *sprawę*: investigate **4.** *puls*: take **5.** *krew*: test **6.** *literaturę*: study; **badać się** have a check-up
badani|e *n* (*-nia*; *-nia*) **1.** examination; **~e opinii publicznej** opinion poll; **~e rynku** market research **2.** (*lekarskie*) check-up, examination; **~e krwi** blood test; **~e wzroku** eye test **3.** **~a naukowe** research
badany *m* (*-nego*; *-ni*), **-na** *f* (*-nej*; *-ne*) **1.** (*ankietowany*) respondent **2.** (*poddany testom*) subject
badawczo *adv*: **spojrzeć na kogoś ~** give s.o. a searching look; **badawcz|y** *adj* **1.** (*dotyczący badań*) research; **prace ~e** research; **wyprawa ~a** research expedition; **zespół ~y** research team **2.** (*przenikliwy*) searching, scrutinizing; **~e spojrzenie** searching look
badminton *m* (*-na*; *no pl*) badminton; **grać w ~a** play badminton
badyle *pl* (*-li*) **1.** (*łodygi*) stalks **2.** (*rośliny*) plants
badziewie *n* (*-wia*; *-wia*) *infml* trash
bagatela *f* (*-li*; *-le*) trifle; **w cenie, ~, 2500 zł** at a trifling PLN 2500; **bagatelizować** ⟨**z-**⟩ (*-zuję*) **1.** (*lekceważyć*) make light of; **~ niebezpieczeństwo** disregard the danger **2.** (*umniejszać*) belittle **3.** (*nie doceniać*) underrate
bagaż *m* (*-żu*; *-że*) *Br* luggage, *Am* baggage; **~ podręczny** *Br* hand luggage, *Am* hand baggage; **odbiór ~u** *Br* baggage reclaim, *Am* baggage claim; **przechowalnia ~u** *Br* left-luggage office, *Am* baggage room; **bagażnik** *m* (*-ka*; *-ki*) **1.** (*w samochodzie*) *Br* boot, *Am* trunk; **~ na dachu** roof rack **2.** (*rowerowy*) carrier; **bagażowy** **I** *adj* *Br* luggage, *Am* baggage; **wagon ~** *Br* luggage van, *Am* baggage car **II** *m* (*-wego*; *-wi*) porter
bagienny *adj* **1.** *teren*: marshy, swampy **2.** *roślinność*: marsh, swamp
bagietka *f* (*-ki*; *-ki*) baguette
bagnet *m* (*-tu*; *-ty*) bayonet
bagnisty *adj* *teren*: marshy, swampy
bagno *n* (*-na*; *-na*) **1.** marsh, swamp **2.** *fig* morass
Bahama: **wyspy ~** the Bahama Islands, the Bahamas
bajać *v/im* (*-jam*) tell stories
bajarz *m* (*-rza*; *-rze*), **-rka** *f* (*-ki*; *-ki*) story teller
bajda *f* (*-dy*; *-dy*) balderdash; **bajdurzyć** *v/im* (*-rzę*) *infml* talk balderdash, tell stories
bajeczka *f* (*-ki*; *-ki*) fairy tale; **bajeczny** *adj* fabulous
bajer (*-ru*; *-ry*) *infml* **1.** (*dodatek*): **bez ~ów** with no frills, plain; **ze wszystkimi ~ami** with all bells and whistles **2.** (*kłamstwo*) fib; **wcisnąć ~** fib; **bajerancki** *adj* *infml* cool; **bajerant** *m* (*-ta*; *-nci*) *infml* fibber; **bajerować** ⟨**z-**⟩ (*-ruję*) *infml* **1.** (*okłamywać*) fib **2.** (*nabierać*) trick
bajk|a *f* (*-ki*; *-ki*) **1.** (*baśń*) fairy tale; **~a na dobranoc** bedtime story **2.** (*zwierzęca*) fable; **~i Ezopa** Aesop's Fa-

bles; **bajkopisarz** *m* (*-rza*; *-rze*) **1.** (*autor baśni*) fairy-tale writer **2.** (*autor bajek zwierzęcych*) fabulist; **bajkowy** *adj* fairy-tale

Bajkał (*-łu*) Lake Baikal

bajoński *adj*: ***~e sumy*** colossal amounts

bajoro *n* (*-ra*; *-ra*) **1.** (*staw*) pool **2.** (*kałuża*) puddle

bajt *m* (*-ta*/*-tu*; *-ty*) INF byte

bajzel *m*(*-zlu*; *-zle*) *infml* mess

bak *m* (*-ku*; *-ki*) (*na paliwo*) fuel tank

baki *pl* (*-ków*) (*włosy*) sideburns

bakalie *pl* (*-lii*) *mixture of dried fruits and nuts*; **bakaliow|y** *adj*: ***lody ~e*** ice cream with dried fruits and nuts

bakcyl *m* (*-la*; *-le*) *dated* bug; ***połknąć ~a*** *fig* get the bug

bakier: ***na ~*** (*na ukos*) aslant; ***być na ~ z I*** **a)** (*nie zgadzać się*) be at odds with **b)** (*nie umieć*) be no good at; ***być na ~ z prawem*** (*o osobie*) be a lawbreaker

bakłażan *m* (*-na*; *-ny*) *Br* aubergine, *Am* eggplant

bakteri|a *f* (*-rii*; *-rie*) bacterium; ***~e chorobotwórcze*** pathogenic bacteria; **bakteriobójczo** *adv*: ***działać ~*** have antiseptic properties; **bakteriobójczy** *adj* antiseptic; ***środek ~*** antiseptic; **bakteriologiczny** *adj* bacteriological

bakteryjn|y *adj* bacterial; ***flora ~a*** bacterial flora; ***kolonia ~a*** bacterial colony

bal[1] *m* (*-la*; *-le*) (*kłoda*) log

bal[2] *m* (*-lu*; *-le*) (*zabawa*) ball; ***~ przebierańców*** fancy-dress party

balanga *f* (*-gi*; *-gi*) *infml* party, bash

balans *m* (*-su*; *no pl*) (*balansowanie*) balance; **balansować** *v/im* (*-suję*) balance; ***~ na krawędzi przepaści*** be on the verge of collapse

balas *m* (*-sa*; *-sy*) baluster

balast *m* (*-tu*; *no pl*) **1.** ballast **2.** *fig* a ball and chain; ***uważać coś za zbędny ~*** consider s.th. unnecessary

baldachim *m* (*-mu*; *-my*) canopy; ***łóżko z ~em*** four-poster

balet *m* (*-tu*; *-ty*) ballet; **baletki** *pl* (*-tek*) ballet shoes; **baletnica** *f* (*-cy*; *-ce*) ballerina, ballet dancer; **baletowy** *adj* ballet

balia *f* (*-lii*; *-lii*) tub

balistyczny *adj* ballistic; ***pocisk ~*** ballistic missile

balkon *m* (*-nu*; *-ny*) balcony; **balkono|wy** *adj* balcony; ***drzwi ~e*** French window, *Am* French door; ***wnęka ~a*** loggia

ballada *f* (*-dy*; *-dy*) ballad

balon *m* (*-nu*; *-ny*) balloon; ***zrobić kogoś w ~a*** *infml* take s.o. for a ride;

balonik *m* (*-ka*; *-ki*) **1.** (*zabawka*) balloon **2.** (*policyjny*) *Br* breathalyser, *Am* Breathalyzer®

balować (*-luję*) **1.** *v/im* (*tańczyć*) dance **2.** ⟨**za-**⟩ (*imprezować*) party; **balow|y** *adj* ball; ***sala ~a*** ballroom

balsa *f* (*-sy*; *no pl*) balsa

balsam *m* (*-mu*; *-my*) **1.** balm; ***~ do ciała*** body lotion; **balsamować** ⟨**za-**⟩ (*-muję*) embalm

balustrada *f* (*-dy*; *-dy*) balustrade

bałagan *m* (*-nu*; *-ny*) mess; ***narobić ~u*** make a mess; **bałaganiarstwo** *n* (*-wa*; *no pl*) messiness, untidiness; **bałaganiarz** *m* (*-rza*; *-rze*) slob *infml*; **bałaganić** ⟨**na-**⟩ (*-nię*) make a mess

bałałajka *f* (*-ki*; *-ki*) balalaika

bałamucić ⟨**z-**⟩ (*-mucę*) **1.** (*flirtować*) flirt (*A* with) **2.** (*wprowadzać w błąd*) mislead

bałamutny *adj* (*mylący*) misleading

Bałkany *pl* (*-nów*) the Balkans

bałkański *adj* Balkan; ***Półwysep ~*** the Balkan Peninsula

bałtycki *adj* Baltic; ***Morze ~e*** the Baltic Sea

Bałtyk *m* (*-ku*) the Baltic

bałwan *m* (*-na*; *-ny*) **1.** (*śniegowy*) snowman; ***lepić ~a*** make a snowman **2.** REL idol

bałwochwalca *m* (*-cy*; *-cy*) idolater; **bałwochwalczy** *adj* idolatrous

bambosz *m* (*-sza*; *-sze*) carpet slipper

bambus *m* (-su/-sa; -y) bamboo; **bambusowy** *adj* bamboo

banalność *f* (*-ści*; *no pl*) banality; **banalny** *adj* banal; **banał** *m* (*-łu*; *-ły*) banality

banan *m* (*-na*; *-ny*) banana; **bananowy** *adj* banana

banda *f* (*-dy*) **1.** (*grupa*) gang **2.** (*na lodowisku*) boards **3.** (*w bilardzie*) cushion

bandaż *m* (*-ża*; *-że*) bandage; ***~ elastyczny*** elastic bandage; **bandażo-**

B

wać ⟨*za-*⟩ (*-żuję*) bandage
bander|a *f* (*-ry*; *-ry*) flag, ensign; ***pod polską ~ą*** under the Polish flag
banderola *f* (*-li*; *-le*) (*akcyzowa*) excise sticker
bandycki *adj* criminal; ***~ napad*** criminal assault; **bandyta** *m* (*-ty*; *-dyci*) criminal, thug; **bandytyzm** *m* (*-mu*; *no pl*) violent crime, thuggery
bandzior *m* (*-ra*; *-ry*) thug
bani|a *f* (*-ni*; *-nie*) (*kulisty przedmiot*) ball; ***szklana ~a*** glass ball; ***być do ~*** *infml* be no good; ***na ~*** *infml Br* tanked up, *Am* tanked; **baniak** *m* (*-ka*; *-ki*) (*zbiornik*) tank
banialuki *pl* (*-luk*) balderdash *sing*; ***opowiadać ~*** talk balderdash
baniasty *adj klosz, naczynie*: ball-shaped
bank *m* (*-ku*; *-ki*) bank; ***~ danych*** databank; ***~ emisyjny*** the bank of issue; ***~ spermy*** sperm bank; ***na ~*** *infml* for sure; ***rozbić ~*** *fig* break the bank
bankier *m* (*-ra*; *-rzy*) banker
bankiet *m* (*-tu*; *-ty*) banquet (***na cześć*** *G* in honour of)
banknot *m* (*-tu*; *-ty*) *Br* note, banknote, *Am* bill
bankomat *m* (*-tu*; *-ty*) ATM, *Br* cash machine
bankowość (*-ści*; *no pl*) banking
bankructwo *n* (*-wa*; *-wa*) bankruptcy; **bankrutować** ⟨*z-*⟩ (*-tuję*) go bankrupt
bańk|a *f* (*-ki*; *-ki*) **1.** (*pęcherzyk*) bubble; ***~i mydlane*** soap bubbles **2.** (*pojemnik*) can; ***~a na mleko*** milk can **3.** (*lecznicza*) cupping glass; ***stawiać komuś ~i*** cup s.o.
baon *m* (*-nu*; *-ny*) battalion
baptysta *m* (*-ty*; *-ptyści*), **-tka** *f* (*-ki*; *-ki*) Baptist; **baptystyczny** *adj* Baptist
bar[1] *m* (*-ru*; *-ry*) **1.** (*gastronomiczny*) cafe; ***~ przekąskowy*** snack bar; ***~ samoobsługowy*** cafeteria; ***~ szybkiej obsługi*** fast-food restaurant, *infml* fast-food joint **2.** (*kontuar*) bar; ***siedzieć przy ~ze*** sit at the bar
bar[2] *m* (*-ru*; *no pl*) *CHEM* barium
bara-bara *indecl infml* fooling, *dated* hanky-panky
barak *m* (*-ku*; *-ki*) **1.** *small building used for temporary offices, warehouses or accommodation* **2.** (*mobilny*) Portakabin® **3.** (*w obozie*) barracks; **barakowóz** *m* (*-wozu*; *-wozy*) caravan
baran *m* (*-na*; *-ny*) **1.** (*zwierzę*) ram; ***jak stado ~ów*** like sheep; ***liczyć ~y*** count sheep; ***wziąć kogoś na ~a*** give s.o. a piggyback ride **2.** *infml* (*osoba*) fool **3.** ***≈*** *ASTR* Aries; ***być spod znaku ≈a*** be an Aries
baranek *m* (*-nka*; *-nki*) lamb; ***≈ Boży*** the Lamb of God; ***łagodny jak ~*** (as) gentle as a lamb
barani *adj* **1.** (*z futra*) sheepskin; ***kożuch ~*** sheepskin coat; ***skóra ~a*** sheepskin **2.** (*z mięsa*): mutton; ***mięso ~e*** mutton **3.** ***patrzeć ~m wzrokiem na*** *A infml* look dumbly at
baranieć ⟨*z-*⟩ (*-nieję*) be stupified, be struck stupid
baranina *f* (*-ny*; *no pl*) mutton
baraszkować ⟨*po-*⟩ (*-kuję*) frolic
barbakan *m* (*-nu*; *-ny*) *ARCHIT* barbican
barbarzyńca *m* (*-cy*; *-cy*) barbarian; **barbarzyński** *adj* barbaric; **barbarzyństwo** *n* (*-wa*; *no pl*) barbarism
Barbórka *f* (*-ki*; *-ki*) *St Barbara's Day* (Miners' Day)
barczysty *adj* broad-shouldered
bardziej *adv* more; ***coraz ~*** more and more; ***im ~,... tym ~*** the more..., the more; ***jeszcze ~*** even more; ***tym ~, że*** the more so because, especially as
bardzo *adv* **1.** (*przed przymiotnikami, przysłówkami*) very; ***~ dobry*** (*stopień*) A; ***nie ~*** not really; ***tak ~*** so much; ***za ~*** too much **2.** (*z czasownikami*) very much; ***~ mi się podobasz*** I like you very much; ***~ proszę*** (*prośba*) please; ***~ dziękuję*** thank you very much; ***proszę ~*** (*odpowiedź na podziękowanie*) not at all; ***~ przepraszam*** I'm so sorry
barek *m* (*-rku*; *-rki*) (*mebel*) drinks cabinet
bariera *f* (*-ry*; *-ry*) barrier; ***~ dźwięku*** sound barrier; ***~ ochronna*** (*przy drodze*) safety barrier; ***~ psychologiczna*** psychological barrier; ***~ językowa*** the language barrier; ***~ celna*** tariff barrier
bark *m* (*-ku*; *-ki*) *ANAT* shoulder; ***wziąć coś na swoje ~i*** take s.th. on one's shoulders; ***zrzucić coś na czyjeś ~i*** burden s.o. with s.th.
barka *f* (*-ki*; *-ki*) barge
barkowy *adj ANAT* shoulder; ***pas ~*** shoulder girdle; ***staw ~*** shoulder joint

barłóg *m* (*-łogu*; *-łogi*) **1.** (*łóżko*) messy bedding **2.** (*ze szmat*) bed of rags **3.** (*niedźwiedzi*) den
barman *m* (*-na*; *-ni*) barman, *Am* bartender; **barmanka** *f* (*-ki*; *-ki*) barmaid, *Am* bartender
barok *m* (*-ku*; *no pl*) baroque, Baroque; **barokowy** *adj* baroque, Baroque
barometr *m* barometer
baron *m* (*-na*; *-nowie*) baron; **baronowa** *f* (*-wej*; *-we*) baroness
barow|y *adj krzesło*, *urządzenie*: bar; ***danie ~e*** café meal; ***stołek ~y*** bar stool
barszcz *m* (*-czu*; *-cze*) borsch, beetroot soup; ***~ czerwony*** red borsch, red beetroot soup; ***~ biały*** white borsch; ***tani jak ~*** dirt cheap
barw|a *f* (*-wy*; *-wy*) *Br* colour, *Am* color; ***~a dźwięku*** timbre; ***~y narodowe*** *Br* national colours, *Am* national colors; ***~y ochronne*** camouflage
barwić ⟨**za-**⟩ (*-wię*) dye; ***~ na niebiesko*** dye blue; ***barwić się***: ***~ na czerwono*** become red
barwnik *m* (*-ka*; *-ki*) dye
barwny *adj* **1.** (*wielobarwny*) *Br* colourful, *Am* colorful **2.** (*nie czarno-biały*) *Br* coloured, *Am* colored
bary *pl* (*-rów*) (*ramiona*) shoulders; ***wziąć się za ~ z*** *I* grapple with
barykada *f* (*-dy*; *-dy*) barricade; **barykadować** ⟨**za-**⟩ (*-duję*) barricade
baryłka *f* (*-ki*; *-ki*) barrel
baryton *m* (*-nu*/*-na*; *-ny*) (*głos*, *śpiewak*) baritone
bas *m* (*-su*/*-sa*; *-sy*) (*instrument*, *głos*, *śpiewak*) bass
baseballówka *f* (*-ki*; *-ki*) baseball cap
basen *m* (*-nu*; *-ny*) **1.** (*pływacki*) pool, swimming pool; ***~ odkryty*** outdoor swimming pool; ***~ kryty*** indoor swimming pool **2.** GEOL basin **3.** (*zlewisko*) drainage basin **4.** (*naczynie*) bedpan; ***~ portowy*** *Br* harbour basin, *Am* harbor basin
basetla *f* (*-li*; *-le*) *bass fiddle used in Polish folk music*
Bask *m* (*-ka*; *-kowie*), **~ijka** *f* (*-ki*; *-ki*) Basque
baskijsk|i *adj* Basque; ***po ~u*** in Basque; ***mówić po ~u*** speak Basque
Baskonia *f* (*-nii*; *no pl*) the Basque Country
basowy *adj* bass; ***klucz ~*** bass clef
bastard *m*(*-da*; *-dzi*) bastard
basza *m* (*-szy*; *-szowie*) pasha
baszta *f* (*-ty*; *-ty*) (castle) tower
baśniowy *adj* fairy-tale; **baś|ń** *f* (*-śni*; *-śnie*) fairy tale; ***~nie Andersena*** Andersen's Fairy Tales; ***~nie ludowe*** folk tales
bat *m* (*-ta*; *-ty*) whip; ***jak z ~a strzelił*** in a flash; ***~y*** **a)** (*chłosta*) whipping **b)** *infml* beating; ***dostać ~y*** take a beating
batali|a *f* (*-lii*; *-lie*) (*bitwa*) battle; ***toczyć ~ę*** *fig* battle (**o** *A* for); **batalista** *m* (*-ty*; *-liści*) (*malarz*) battle scene painter
bateri|a *f* (*-rii*; *-rie*) **1.** (*elektryczna*) battery; ***~a do latarki*** torch battery; ***na ~e*** battery-powered **2.** (*łazienkowa*) *Br* mixer tap, *Am* mixer faucet; ***~a dział*** battery of guns
bateryjka *f* (*-ki*; *-ki*) *dim* (small) battery
baton *m* (*-na*; *-ny*) chocolate bar
batut|a *f* (*-ty*; *-ty*) baton; ***pod czyjąś ~ą*** conducted by
batyst *m* (*-tu*; *-ty*) batiste; **batystowy** *adj* batiste
Bawarczyk *m* (*-ka*; *-czycy*) Bavarian; **Bawaria** *f* (*-rii*) Bavaria; **Bawarka** *f* (*-ki*; *-ki*) Bavarian
bawarka *f* (*-ki*; *-ki*) (weak) tea with milk
bawarski *adj* Bavarian
bawełn|a *f* (*-ny*; *no pl*) cotton; ***nie owijać w ~ę*** *fig* not beat around the bush; **bawełniany** *adj* cotton
bawi|ć ⟨**za-**⟩ (*-wię*) **I** *v/t* (*rozweselać*) amuse; ***to mnie nie ~*** I don't think it's funny **II** *v/i lit* (*przebywać*) stay; ***~ć u kogoś z wizytą*** (*w domu*) stay at s.o.'s house; ***bawić się*** **1.** (*grać*) play (*I* with); ***~ć się lalkami*** play with dolls; ***~ć się czyimś kosztem*** have fun at s.o.'s expense; ***~ć się w berka*** play tag; ***~ć się w kotka i myszkę*** *fig* play cat and mouse **2.** (*spędzać czas*) ***dobrze się ~ć*** have fun
bawidamek *m* (*-mka*; *-mki*) ladies' man
bawoli *adj* buffalo; **bawół** *m* (*-wołu*; *-woły*) buffalo
baza *f* (*-zy*; *-zy*) base; ***~ danych*** database; ***~ noclegowa*** accommodation
bazaltowy *adj* basalt

B

bazar *m* (*-ru*; *-ry*) **1.** market **2.** (*na Bliskim Wschodzie*) bazaar
bazgrać ⟨**na-**⟩ (*-rzę*) scrawl; **~ *jak kura pazurem*** write in a spidery scrawl
bazgranina *f* (*-ny*; *-ny*) scrawl
bazgrolić ⟨**na-**⟩ (*-lę*) *infml* scrawl
bazgroły *pl* (*-łów*) *infml* scrawl *sing*
bazia *f* (*-zi*; *-zie*) catkin
bazować *v/im* (*-zuję*) **1.** (*być opartym*) be based (***na*** *L* on) **2.** (*polegać*) rely (***na*** *L* on)
Bazylea *f* (*-lei*) Basel
bazylia *f* (*-lii*; *-lie*) basil
bazylika *f* (*-ki*; *-ki*) basilica
bazyliszek *m* (*-szka*; *-szki*) basilisk; **bazyliszkow|y** *adj*: ***~e spojrzenie*** basilisk stare
bażant *m* (*-ta*; *-ty*) pheasant
bąbel *m* (*-bla*; *-ble*) **1.** (*bańka*) bubble **2.** (*na skórze*) blister; **bąbelek** *m* (*-lka*; *-lki*) *dim* (small) bubble; ***~ powietrza*** air bubble
bączek *m* (*-czka*; *-czki*) (*zabawka*) top
bądź I *conj* or; **~... ~** either... or **II** *particle* ***~ co ~*** after all; ***co ~*** anything; ***gdzie ~*** anywhere; ***kto ~*** anybody; ***który ~*** any one **III** *v* → ***być***
bąk *m* (*-ka*; *-ki*) **1.** (*trzmiel*) bumblebee **2.** (*bydlęcy*) horse fly **3.** (*zabawka*) (spinning) top **4.** (*dziecko*) tot **5.** ***puścić ~a*** *infml* break wind; ***zbijać ~i*** *infml* laze around
bąkać ⟨**-knąć**⟩ (*-kam*) mumble; ***~ pod nosem*** mumble
bdb. *abbr* (= ***bardzo dobry***) (*ocena*) A
be: ***ani ~, ani me*** not a single word
beatyfikacja *f* (*-ji*; *-je*) beatification; **beatyfikować** *v im/p* (*-kuję*) beatify
bebechy *pl* (*-chów*) *infml* guts
bebeszyć ⟨**wy-**⟩ (*-szę*) (*patroszyć*) *infml* gut
becik *m* (*-ka*; *-ki*) baby wrap
beczeć ⟨**za-**⟩ (*-czę*) **1.** (*o owcy, kozie*) bleat **2.** (*o osobie*) *infml* blubber; **beczenie** *n* (*-nia*; *no pl*) *owcy, kozy*: bleating
beczk|a *f* (*-ki*; *-ki*) **1.** (*pojemnik*) barrel; ***~a na wino*** wine barrel; ***piwo z ~i*** *Br* beer on draught, *Am* beer on draft; ***~a prochu*** *fig* time bomb; ***gruby jak ~a*** (as) fat as a pig; ***zacząć z innej ~i*** *fig* change the subject; ***zjeść z kimś ~ę soli*** *fig* know s.o. inside out **2.** (*w akrobacji powietrznej*) roll; ***kręcić ~i*** do rolls
beczkować ⟨**za-**⟩ (*-kuję*) barrel
beczkowóz *m* (*-wozu*; *-wozy*) water tanker
beczkow|y *adj*: ***piwo ~e*** *Br* draught beer, *Am* draft beer
beczułka *f* (*-ki*; *-ki*) keg
bedeker *m* (*-ra*; *-ry*) travel guide
bedłka *f* (*-ki*; *-ki*) agaricus
bednarz *m* (*-rza*; *-rze*) cooper
befsztyk *m* (*-ka*/*-ku*; *-ki*) steak; ***~ tatarski*** steak tartare
bejca *f* (*-cy*; *-ce*) stain; **bejcować** ⟨**za-**⟩ (*-cuję*) stain
bek *m* (*-ku*; *-ki*) **1.** *kozy, owcy*: bleating **2.** *osoby*: *infml* blubber
bekać ⟨**-knąć**⟩ (*-kam*) *infml* burp, belch
bekas *m* (*-sa*; *-sy*) snipe
bekhend *m* (*-du*; *-dy*) SPORT backhand
beknąć *v/p* → ***beczeć***, ***bekać***
bekon *m* (*-nu*; *-ny*) bacon
beksa *f/m* (*-sy*; *-sy*) *infml* crybaby
bela *f* (*-li*; *-le*) bale; ***pijany jak ~*** blind drunk, *infml* blotto
beletrystyka *f* (*-ki*; *no pl*) fiction; **beletrystyczn|y** *adj* fictional; ***książka ~a*** work of fiction
belfer *m* (*-fra*; *-frowie*/*-frzy*) *infml* teacher, pedagogue
Belg *m* (*-ga*; *-gowie*) Belgian; ***jest ~iem*** he's Belgian; **Belgia** *f* (*-gii*) Belgium; **Belgijk|a** *f* (*-ki*; *-ki*) Belgian; ***jest ~ą*** she's Belgian; **belgijski** *adj* Belgian
belka *f* (*-ki*; *-ki*) **1.** TECH beam **2.** (*naszywka*) *infml* stripe
bełkot *m* (*-tu*; *-ty*) gibberish; **bełkotać** ⟨**wy-**⟩ (*-kocę*) **1.** (*mówić niewyraźnie*) mumble **2.** (*mówić niejasno*) talk gibberish
bełt *m* (*-ta*; *-ty*) **1.** (*wino*) *infml* cheap wine, *Br* plonk **2.** (*plusk*) splash
bełtać ⟨**z-**⟩ (*-tam*) stir
bemol *m* (*-la*; *-le*) MUS flat
benedyktyn *m* (*-na*; *-ni*) Benedictine; **benedyktyńsk|i** *adj* Benedictine; ***~a cierpliwość*** the patience of Job
beniaminek *m* (*-nka*; *-nki*/*-nkowie*) SPORT newly promoted team
benzen *m* (*-nu*; *no pl*) CHEM benzene
benzoesowy *adj* CHEM benzoic; ***kwas ~*** benzoic acid
benzyna *f* (*-ny*; *no pl*) **1.** (*napędowa*) *Br* petrol, *Am* gasoline, *infml* gas **2.** (*do

czyszczenia) *Br* white spirit, *Am* mineral spirit; **benzynow|y** *adj Br* petrol, *Am* gasoline; ***stacja ~a*** *Br* petrol station, *Am* gas station
berbeć *m* (*-cia*; *-cie*) tot
berberys *m* (*-su*; *-sy*) berberis, barberry
ber|ek *m* (*-rka*; *no pl*) (*zabawa*) tag; ***bawić się w ~ka*** play tag
beret *m* (*-tu*; *-ty*) beret
Berlin *m* (*-na*) Berlin
berlińczyk *m* (*-ka*; *-czycy*), **-linianka** *f* (*-ki*; *-ki*) Berliner; **berliński** *adj* Berlin; ***mur ~*** *HIST* the Berlin Wall
berło *n* (*-ła*; *-ła*) *Br* sceptre, *Am* scepter
bermudy *pl* (*-dów*) (*spodenki*) Bermuda shorts, Bermudas
bernardyn *m* **1.** (*-na*; *-ni*) (*zakonnik*) bernardine **2.** (*-na*; *-ny*) (*pies*) St Bernard
Berno *n* (*-na*) Bern
beryl *m* **1.** (*-lu*; *-le*) (*kamień*) beryl **2.** (*-lu*; *no pl*) *CHEM* beryllium
bessa *f* (*-sy*; *-sy*) *ECON* slump
bestia *f* (*-tii*; *-tie*) beast; **bestialski** *adj* bestial; **bestialsko** *adv* bestially; ***~ zamordowany*** cruelly killed; **bestialstwo** *n* (*-wa*; *-wa*) bestiality
bestseller *m* (*-ru*; *-ry*) best-seller
besztać ⟨**z-**⟩ (*-tam*) scold, rebuke
Betlejem *n indecl* Bethlehem
beton *m* (*-nu*; *-ny*) **1.** *TECH* concrete **2.** (*ludzie*) the old guard; **betoniarka** *f* (*-ki*; *-ki*) cement mixer; **betonować** ⟨**za-**⟩ (*-nuję*) concrete; **betonowy** *adj* concrete
bety *pl* (*-tów*) *infml* **1.** (*posłanie*) messy bedding *sing* **2.** (*rzeczy*) stuff *sing*
bez[1] *m* (*bzu*; *bzy*) lilac; ***czarny ~*** elder
bez[2] *prep* (*G*) without; ***~ dwóch zdań*** without doubt; ***~ granic*** without borders, without frontiers; ***~ krzty zdrowego rozsądku*** (***ambicji***) with no common sense (ambition) whatsoever; ***~ liku*** *form* aplenty, *infml* galore; ***~ ładu i składu*** chaotically; ***~ mała*** virtually; ***~ paniki!*** don't panic!; ***~ potrzeby*** unnecessarily; ***~ pożegnania*** without saying goodbye; ***~ pytania*** without asking for permission; ***~ szwu*** seamless; ***~ tchu*** out of breath; ***~ ustanku*** incessantly; ***~ wad*** defectless, spotless; ***mówić*** (***pisać***) ***~ ładu i składu*** ramble; ***powiedzieć coś ~ ogródek*** say s.th. straight
beza *f* (*-zy*; *-zy*) *COOK* meringue
bezalkoholowy *adj* non-alcoholic; ***napój ~*** soft drink
bezapelacyjnie *adv* **1.** *zwyciężyć*: outright **2.** *rozstrzygnąć*: irrevocably
bezapelacyjny *adj* **1.** *zwycięstwo*: absolute **2.** *wyrok*: final **3.** *decyzja*: irrevocable
bezawaryjny *adj* failure-free
bezbarwny *adj* **1.** (*bez koloru*) *Br* colourless, *Am* colorless **2.** (*nijaki*) bland
bezbłędny *adj* **1.** *odpowiedź*, *rozwiązanie*: correct **2.** *działanie*: faultless **3.** *rozumowanie*: flawless
bezbolesny *adj* painless
bezbożnik *m* (*-ka*; *-nicy*) heathen; **bezbożny** *adj* godless
bezbramkowy *adj remis*: goalless
bezbronność *f* (*-ści*; *no pl*) defencelessness
bezbronny *adj* defenceless
bezbrzeżny *adj* **1.** *pustynia*, *miłość*: boundless **2.** *oddanie*: utter
bezcelowość *f* (*-ści*; *no pl*) pointlessness; **bezcelowy** *adj* pointless
bezcen *indecl*: ***za ~*** for a song, *infml* dirt cheap; **bezcenny** *adj* **1.** *kolekcja*, *klejnot*: priceless **2.** *pomoc*, *informacja*: invaluable
bezceremonialny *adj* unceremonious
bezchmurny *adj* cloudless
bezcłowy *adj* duty-free
bezczelność *f* (*-ści*; *no pl*) insolence, impudence, *infml* cheek; **bezczelny** *adj* insolent, impudent, *infml* cheeky
bezcześcić ⟨**z-**⟩ (*-czeszczę*) desecrate
bezczynność *f* (*-ści*; *no pl*) **1.** inactivity **2.** *rządu*, *administracji*: inaction **3.** *osoby*: idleness; ***słodka ~*** sweet idleness; **bezczynny** *adj* **1.** *urządzenie*, *rząd*: inactive **2.** *osoba*: idle
bezdenny *adj* bottomless
bezdeszczowy *adj* dry
bezdomny **I** *adj* **1.** *osoba*: homeless **2.** *pies*: stray, homeless **II** *m* (*-nego*; *-ni*), **-na** *f* (*-nej*; *-ne*) homeless person; ***bezdomni*** homeless people, the homeless
bezdroża *pl* (*-ży*) wilderness *sing*
bezdrzewny *adj* treeless
bezduszny *adj* callous, unfeeling

B

bezdyskusyjny *adj* **1.** *kwestia, dowód*: indisputable **2.** *odmowa*: flat
bezdzietność *f* (*-ści; no pl*) childlessness; **bezdzietny** *adj* childless
bezdźwięczny *adj* **1.** *ruch*: soundless **2.** *głoska*: voiceless
beze *prep*: **~ mnie** without me
bezeceństwo *n* (*-wa; -wa*) wickedness; **bezecny** *adj* wicked
bezglutenowy *adj* gluten-free
bezgotówkowy *adj* cashless
bezgraniczny *adj* **1.** *stepy, rozpacz*: boundless **2.** *zaufanie*: absolute
bezgwiezdny *adj* starless
bezimienny *adj* **1.** nameless **2.** (*anonimowy*) anonymous
bezinteresowny *adj* selfless
bezkarnie *adj* with impunity; ***coś uszło komuś ~*** s.o. went away with s.th.
bezklasowy *adj* classless
bezkofeinowy *adj* caffeine-free, decaffeinated
bezkolizyjn|y *adj* collision-free; ***skrzyżowanie ~e*** *Br* flyover, *Am* overpass
bezkompromisowy *adj* uncompromising
bezkonfliktowy *adj* peaceable
bezkonkurencyjny *adj* **1.** *Br* unrivalled, *Am* unrivaled **2.** *cena, oferta*: unbeatable
bezkres *m* (*-su; -sy*) *lit* infinity; **bezkresny** *adj lit* boundless
bezkręgowce *pl* (*-ców*) invertebrates
bezkrwawy *adj* bloodless
bezkrytyczny *adj* uncritical
bezksiężycowy *adj* moonless
bezkształtny *adj* shapeless
bezlitosny *adj* merciless; **bezlitośnie** *adv* mercilessly
bezludn|y *adj* **1.** (*niezamieszkały*) uninhabited; ***~a wyspa*** desert island **2.** (*wyludniony*) deserted
bezludzie *n* (*-dzia; no pl*) wilderness
bezład *m* (*-du; no pl*) disorder; **bezładny** *adj* **1.** *działania, ruchy*: chaotic **2.** *mowa, myśli*: confused
bezmiar *m* (*-ru; no pl*) *lit przestrzeni, oceanu*: vastness; ***~ szczęścia*** (***cierpień***) boundless love (suffering); **bezmierny** *adj lit* boundless
bezmięsny *adj* meatless, vegetarian
bezmyślny *adj* thoughtless, mindless
beznadzieja *f* (*-dziei; no pl*) **1.** (*brak nadziei*) hopelessness **2.** (*beznadziejna rzecz*) *infml* ***to ~!*** it's hopeless!; ***beznadziejny*** *adj* hopeless
beznamiętny *adj* **1.** *wyraz twarzy, głos*: impassive **2.** *obserwator*: dispassionate
beznogi *adj* **1.** (*bez nogi*) one-legged **2.** (*bez nóg*) legless
bezobjawowy *adj* asymptomatic, symptomless
bezoki *adj* eyeless
bezokolicznik *m* (*-ka; -ki*) infinitive
bezołowiowy *adj benzyna*: unleaded
bezosobowy *adj* impersonal
bezowocny *adj* fruitless, futile
bezpański *adj pies*: stray
bezpaństwowy *adj* stateless
bezpartyjny *adj* non-party, independent
bezpestkowy *adj* seedless
bezpieczeństw|o *n* (*-wa; no pl*) **1.** safety; ***~o i higiena pracy*** occupational health and safety; ***hamulec ~a*** emergency brake; ***kaftan ~a*** straitjacket; ***pas ~a*** safety belt; ***wyjście ~a*** emergency exit **2.** (*ochrona*) security; ***Rada ~a*** the Security Council; ***siły ~a*** security force
bezpiecznik *m* (*-ka; -ki*) **1.** (*elektryczny*) fuse **2.** (*w broni*) safety catch, safety lock
bezpieczn|y *adj* **1.** safe; ***~y seks*** safe sex **2.** (*chroniony*) secure, safe
bezplanowy *adj* planless
bezpłatny *adj* **1.** free; ***~ bilet*** free ticket **2.** *urlop*: unpaid
bezpłciowy *adj* **1.** BIOL asexual **2.** (*nijaki*) *infml* bland
bezpłodność *f* (*-ści; no pl*) infertility, sterility; **bezpłodny** *adj* sterile, infertile
bezpodstawny *adj* groundless, baseless
bezpośredni *adj* **1.** direct **2.** *sąsiedztwo*: immediate **3.** *transmisja*: live; **bezpośrednio** *adv* **1.** directly; ***~ po*** immediately after **2.** *transmitować*: live
bezpotomny *adj* heirless
bezpowrotny *adj* irretrievable
bezprawie *n* (*-wia; no pl*) lawlessness; **bezprawny** *adj* unlawful, illegal
bezprecedensowy *adj* unprecedented

bezpretensjonalny *adj* **1.** *osoba*, *styl*: unpretentious **2.** *strój*: plain **3.** *zachowanie*: natural
bezproblemowy *adj życie*: trouble-free
bezprocentowy *adj* interest-free
bezprzedmiotowy *adj spór*: groundless
bezprzewodowy *adj* cordless
bezprzykładny *adj* unparalleled
bezradność *f* (*-ści*; *no pl*) helplessness; **bezradny** *adj* helpless
bezrękawnik *m* (*-ka*; *-ki*) **1.** (*kamizelka*) *Br* waistcoat, *Am* vest **2.** (*sukienka*) *Br* pinafore, *Am* jumper
bezręki *adj* **1.** (*bez ręki*) one-armed **2.** (*bez rąk*) armless
bezrobocie *n* (*-cia*; *no pl*) unemployment; ***wysokie ~*** high unemployment
bezrobotn|y **I** *adj* unemployed **II** *m* (*-nego*; *-ni*), **-na** *f* (*-nej*; *-ne*) unemployed person; ***zasiłek dla ~ych*** unemployment benefit; ***~i*** the unemployed
bezrozumny *adj* irrational, mindless
bezruch *m* (*-chu*; *no pl*) stillness; ***stać w ~u*** stand still
bezsenność *f* (*-ści*; *no pl*) insomnia; **bezsenny** *adj* sleepless
bezsens *m* (*-su*; *-sy*) **1.** nonsense **2.** *życia*: meaninglessness; **bezsensowny** *adj* absurd
bezsilny *adj* helpless (***wobec*** *G* against)
bezskutecznie *adv* unsuccessfully, ineffectively; **bezskuteczny** *adj* unsuccessful, ineffective
bezsolny *adj* salt-free
bezsporny *adj* indisputable, undeniable
bezsprzeczny *adj* indisputable
bezstronny *adj* impartial, unbiased
bezszelestnie *adv* silently; **bezszelestny** *adj* silent
bezśnieżny *adj* snowless
bezterminowo *adv* indefinitely, for an indefinite period; **bezterminowy** *adj* **1.** *umowa*: for an indefinite period **2.** *kredyt*: with no fixed repayment date **3.** *wyrok*: indefinite
beztłuszczowy *adj* fat-free
beztreściowy *adj* vacuous
beztroska *f* (*-ki*; *no pl*) **1.** (*brak trosk*) light-heartedness, nonchalance **2.** (*lekkomyślność*) carelessness; **beztroski** *adj* **1.** (*niemający trosk*) carefree, light-hearted **2.** (*lekkomyślny*) careless; **beztrosko** *adv* **1.** (*bez trosk*) light-heartedly **2.** (*lekkomyślnie*) carelessly
bezustannie *adv* incessantly; **bezustanny** *adj* incessant
bezusterkowy *adj praca*: failure-free
bezużyteczność *f* (*-ści*; *no pl*) uselessness; **bezużyteczny** *adj* useless
bezwartościowy *adj* worthless
bezwarunkowo *adv* **1.** unconditionally **2.** (*koniecznie*) absolutely; **bezwarunkowy** *adj* unconditional; ***odruch ~*** unconditioned reflex
bezwiedny *adj* involuntary
bezwietrzny *adj* windless
bezwizowy *adj* visa-free
bezwład *m* (*-du*; *no pl*) **1.** (*bierność*) inertia **2.** (*paraliż*) paralysis; **bezwładność** *f* (*-ści*; *no pl*) *PHYS* inertia; **bezwładny** *adj* **1.** *PHYS* inert **2.** (*sparaliżowany*) *Br* paralysed, *Am* paralyzed
bezwolny *adj* **1.** (*bierny*) passive **2.** (*uległy*) submissive, yielding
bezwonny *adj Br* odourless, *Am* odorless
bezwstyd *m* (*-du*; *no pl*) shamelessness; **bezwstydnica** *f* (*-cy*; *-ce*) *dated* hussy; **bezwstydnik** *m* (*-ka*; *-nicy*) shameless person; **bezwstydny** *adj* shameless
bezwyjątkowy *adj* with no exceptions
bezwyznaniowy *adj* **1.** unreligious **2.** *szkoła*: secular
bezwzględność *f* (*-ści*; *no pl*) (*okrucieństwo*) ruthlessness; **bezwzględn|y** *adj* **1.** (*okrutny*) ruthless **2.** (*absolutny*) absolute; ***~a większość*** absolute majority
bezzałogowy *adj* unmanned
bezzasadnie *adv* groundlessly; **bezzasadny** *adj* groundless
bezzębny *adj* toothless
bezzwłocznie *adv* promptly; **bezzwłoczny** *adj* prompt
bezzwrotny *adj butelka*, *pożyczka*: non-returnable
beż *m* (*-żu*; *-że*) beige; **beżowy** *adj* beige
bęb|en *m* (*-bna*; *-bny*) drum; ***grać na ~nach*** play the drums; **bęben|ek** *m* (*-nka*; *-nki*) *dim* **1.** *MUS* (small) drum **2.** *ANAT* eardrum; ***~ki mi pękają*** *fig* the noise is hurting my ears **3.** (*rewolweru*) cylinder; **bębenkow|y** *adj*: ***bło-***

B

na ~a tympanic membrane; **bębnić** *v im/p* (*-nię*) **1.** drum; **~ *palcami o*** *A* drum one's fingers on **2.** (*o deszczu*) patter (**o** *A* against); **bębnowy** *adj hamulec*, *skaner*: drum

bęc *interj* bang

bęcwał *m* (*-ła*; *-ły*) *infml* oaf

będą, ***będę***, ***będzie*** → ***być***

bękart *m* (*-ta*; *-ty*) bastard

bhp, ***BHP*** *abbr n indecl* (= ***bezpieczeństwo i higiena pracy***) occupational health and safety

biada *interj* woe, betide

biadolić *v/im* (*-lę*) moan (***nad*** *I* about)

białaczka *f* (*-ki*; *no pl*) *Br* leukaemia, *Am* leukemia

białko *n* (*-ka*; *-ka*) **1.** BIOL protein **2.** (*jajka*, *oka*) white; **białkowy** *adj* BIOL proteinaceous

biało *adv* white; ***pomalować coś na ~*** paint s.th. white; ***ubrany na ~*** dressed in white; **biało-czerwony** *adj* red and white

białodrzew *m* (*-wu*; *-wy*) white poplar

Białorusin *m* (*-na*; *-ni*), **~ka** *f* (*-ki*; *-ki*) Byelorussian; **białoruski** *adj* Byelorussian; **Białoruś** *f* (*-rusi*) Byelorussia

białość *f* (*-ści*; *no pl*) white

biał|y I *adj* white; ***~a kawa*** coffee with milk, *Br* white coffee; ***~e pieczywo*** white bread; ***~y jak ściana*** (as) white as a sheet; ***~e wino*** white wine; ***~y ser*** cottage cheese; ***do ~ego rana*** till dawn; ***doprowadzić kogoś do ~ej gorączki*** make s.o.'s blood boil; ***w ~y dzień*** in broad daylight **II** *m* (*-ego*; *biali*), **~a** *f* (*-łej*; *-łe*) white person; ***biali*** white people, the white

biathlon *m* (*-nu*; *no pl*) biathlon

bibelot *m* (*-tu*; *-ty*) knick-knack

bibka *f* (*-ki*; *-ki*) *infml* bash, *Br* do

Biblia *f* (*-lii*; *-lie*) Bible; **biblijny** *adj* biblical

biblioteczka *f* (*-ki*; *-ki*) **1.** (*kolekcja książek*) library **2.** (*mebel*) bookcase; **biblioteczny** *adj* library

biblioteka *f* (*-ki*; *-ki*) library; ***~ publiczna*** public library; **bibliotekarski** *adj etat*, *kadra*: library

bibliotekarz *m* (*-rza*; *-rze*), **-rka** *f* (*-ki*; *-ki*) librarian

bibuła *f* (*-ły*; *-ły*) **1.** (*papier*) blotting paper; ***~ filtracyjna*** filter paper **2.** (*wydawnictwa*) *infml* underground publications; **bibułka** *f* (*-ki*; *-ki*) tissue paper; ***~ papierosowa*** cigarette paper

bicie *n* (*-cia*; *-cia*) **1.** (*uderzanie*) beating; ***~ serca*** heartbeat; ***z ~m serca*** with a pounding heart **2.** *dzwonu*: ringing **3.** *zegara*: chimes **4.** (*w szachach*) capture **5.** (*ubój*) slaughter

bicz *m* (*-cza*; *-cze*) whip; ***~ boży*** scourge (of God); ***~ wodny*** jet shower; ***jak z ~a strzelił*** in a flash; **biczować** ⟨**u-**⟩ (*-czuję*) whip

bić ⟨**z-**, **po-**⟩ (*biję*) **I** *v/t* **1.** (*uderzać*) beat (*I* with; **po** *L* on); ***~ kogoś po twarzy*** hit s.o. in the face **2.** *rywala*: beat **3.** *rekord*: break **4.** (*zabijać*) slaughter **5.** *monety*: mint **II** *v/i* **1.** (*o sercu*) beat **2.** (*o zegarze*) chime **3.** (*o dzwonie*) ring **4.** (*o źródle*) gush; ***~ brawo*** applaud; ***~ na alarm*** raise the alarm; ***~ na głowę kogoś*** be head and shoulders above s.o.; ***bije od niej siła i pewność siebie*** she emanates power and self-confidence; ***to bije w oczy*** it's plain to see; ***z jego twarzy biła radość*** his face radiated joy; ***bić się*** (*walczyć*) fight; ***~ się w piersi*** beat one's chest; ***~ się z myślami*** have a hard time deciding

bidet *m* (*-tu*; *-ty*) bidet

bidon *m* (*-nu*; *-ny*) water bottle

biec, ***biegnąć*** (*biegnę*) ⟨**po-**⟩ **1.** run (**po** *A* for); ***~ kłusem*** trot **2.** (*o czasie*) pass

bied|a *f* (*-dy*; *-dy*) **1.** (*nędza*) poverty; ***~a z nędzą*** grinding poverty; ***klepać ~ę*** be badly off; ***cierpieć ~ę*** *lit* suffer poverty **2.** (*kłopot*) trouble; ***cała ~a w tym, że*** the trouble is that; ***pół ~y*** it's not so bad; ***ujdzie od ~y*** it's not so bad

biedactwo *n* (*-wa*; *-wa*) poor thing; **biedaczka** *f* (*-ki*; *-ki*) **1.** (*dziewczyna*) poor girl **2.** (*kobieta*) poor woman; **biedaczysko** *n/m* (*-ka*; *-ka*) poor thing; **bieda|k** *m* (*-ka*; *-dacy*/*-ki*) **1.** (*nędzarz*) poor man; ***on jest ~kiem*** he is poor; ***~cy*** the poor **2.** (*nieszczęśnik*) poor guy

biednieć ⟨**z-**⟩ (*-nieję*) **1.** (*stawać się biednym*) get poor **2.** (*stawać się biedniejszym*) get poorer

biedn|y I *adj* poor **II** *m* (*-nego*; *-ni*), **~a**

(*-nej*; *-ne*) poor person; ***pomagać ~ym*** help the poor

biedota *f* (*-ty*; *no pl*) (*biedni*) the poor; **biedować** *v/im* (*-duję*) live in poverty

biedronka *f* (*-ki*; *-ki*) *Br* ladybird, *Am* ladybug

biedzić się ⟨**na-**⟩ (*-dzę*) take a lot of trouble (***nad*** *I* over)

bieg *m* (*-gu*; *-gi*) **1.** (*czynność*) run; ***~iem*** (*szybko*) quickly; ***przyśpieszyć ~u*** (*o pociągu*) speed up; ***w ~u*** **a)** (*biegnąc*) at a run, running **b)** (*w pośpiechu*) in a hurry **c)** (*w ostatniej chwili*) on the run **2.** SPORT race; ***~ krótki*** sprint; ***~ maratoński*** marathon race; ***~ przełajowy*** cross-country race; ***~ przez płotki*** hurdles; ***~ sztafetowy*** relay; ***~ z przeszkodami*** obstacle race; ***~ zjazdowy*** downhill race; ***~i*** running **3.** AUTO gear; ***~ jałowy*** neutral gear; ***na ~u*** in gear ***wsteczny ~*** reverse (gear); ***zmienić ~*** *Br* change gear, *Am* shift gear **4.** (*tok*, *nurt*) course; ***dolny*** (***górny***) ***~ rzeki*** the lower (upper) course of the river; ***z ~iem rzeki*** downstream; ***z ~iem czasu*** in time

biegacz *m* (*-cza*; *-cze*), ***~ka*** *f* (*-ki*; *-ki*) runner

biegać ⟨**po-**⟩ (*-gam*) **1.** run **2.** (*dla zdrowia*) jog; ***~ po sklepach*** shop around; **bieganina** *f* (*-ny*; *no pl*) hustle (and bustle)

biegle *adv* *mówić*: fluently; ***mówić ~ po francusku*** be fluent in French

biegłość *f* (*-ści*; *no pl*) **1.** proficiency (***w*** *L* in) **2.** (*w mowie*) fluency; **biegł|y I** *adj* **1.** proficient (***w*** *L* in) **2.** (*w mowie*) fluent; ***z ~ą znajomością angielskiego*** fluent in English **II** *m* (*-łego*; *-gli*), ***-ła*** *f* (*-łej*; *-łe*) (*sądowy*) court-appointed expert

biegnąć → ***biec***

biegowy *adj* **1.** *trasa*, *konkurencja*: running **2.** *narty*: cross-country

biegun *m* (*-na*; *-ny*) PHYS GEOGR pole; ***~ północny*** the North Pole; ***fotel na ~ach*** rocking chair; ***koń na ~ach*** rocking horse

biegunka *f* (*-ki*; *-ki*) *Br* diarrhoea, *Am* diarrhea

biegunowo *adv* diametrically; ***~ różne*** diametrically opposed

biel *f* (*-li*; *-le*) white; ***~ cynkowa*** zinc white; ***w ~i*** in white

biele|ć (*-leję*) **1.** ⟨**z-**⟩ (*stawać się białym*) whiten, turn white **2.** *v/im* (*jaśnieć*) ***na zboczach ~ją płaty śniegu*** there are white patches of snow on the slopes; **bielić** ⟨**po-**⟩ (*-lę*) **1.** *mur*: whitewash **2.** *płótno*: bleach

bielik *m* (*-ka*; *-ki*): ***orzeł ~*** white-tailed eagle

bielinek *m* (*-nka*; *-nki*): ***~ kapustnik*** large white (butterfly)

bielizna *f* (*-ny*; *no pl*) **1.** (*odzież*) underwear; ***~ damska*** lingerie **2.** (*pościelowa*) bed linen

bieliźniarka *f* (*-ki*; *-ki*) (*mebel*) linen cabinet

bielmo *n* (*-ma*; *-ma*) leucoma; ***mieć ~ na oczach*** *fig* be blind; ***zdjąć komuś ~ z oczu*** open s.o.'s eyes

bielony *adj* **1.** *papier*: bleached **2.** *mur*: whitewashed; **bielszy** *adj comp* → ***biały*** whiter

bieluń *m* (*-nia*; *-nie*) datura, thorn apple

bielutki *adj dim* white

bierka *f* (*-ki*; *-ki*) (*w szachach*) piece; ***bierki*** (*gra*) pick-a-stick

biernik *m* (*-ka*; *-ki*) GRAM accusative

bierność *f* (*-ści*; *no pl*) passivity, passiveness; **biern|y** *adj* passive; ***strona ~a*** GRAM the passive (voice)

bierz, ***bierzesz*** → ***brać***[2]

bierzmować *v im/p* (*-muję*) confirm; **bierzmowanie** *n* (*-nia*; *no pl*) confirmation

bies *m* (*-sa*; *-sy*) devil, demon

biesiada *f* (*-dy*; *-dy*) feast

Bieszczady *pl* (*-czad*/*-dów*) the Bieszczady Mountains

bież. *abbr* (= ***bieżący***) → ***bieżący***

bieżąco *adv*: ***być na ~ z*** *I* be up to date with; ***regulować płatności na ~*** not be in arrears with one's payments; **bieżąc|y** *adj* **1.** *rachunek*, *sprawy*: current **2.** *rok*, *kwartał*: this, current **3.** *woda*: running; ***~y numer*** (*gazety*) current issue; ***metr ~y*** *Br* metre, *Am* meter

bieżnia *f* (*-ni*; *-nie*) SPORT (running) track

bieżnik *m* (*-ka*; *-ki*) *opony*: tread; **bieżnikować** *v/im* (*-kuję*) retread

bigamia *f* (*-mii*; *no pl*) bigamy; **biga-**

B

mista *m* (*-ty*; *-miści*) bigamist
bigos *m* (*-su*; *-sy*) (*Polish dish of sauerkraut, meat, sausage and mushrooms*) bigos; ***narobić ~u*** *fig* make a mess
bigot *m*(*-ta*; *-goci*), **~ka** *f* (*-ki*; *-ki*) religious bigot; **bigoteryjny** *adj* bigoted
bijak *m* (*-ka*; *-ki*) SPORT bat
bijatyka *f* (*-ki*; *-ki*) fight, brawl; ***~ na pięści*** fist fight
bikini *n indecl* bikini
bil *m* (*-la*; *-le*) (billiard) cue
bila *f* (*-li*; *-le*) (billiard) ball
bilans *m* (*-su*; *-se*) **1.** ECON balance sheet; ***~ handlowy*** balance of trade; ***roczny ~ księgowy*** annual accounts; ***~ płatniczy*** balance of payments; ***~ ujemny*** negative balance **2.** *fig* final outcome; **bilansować** ⟨**z-**⟩ (*-suję*) **1.** ECON balance **2.** (*podsumowywać*) sum up
bilard *m* (*-du*; *no pl*) billiards; **bilardowy** *adj* billiard
bilet *m* (*-tu*; *-ty*) ticket; ***~ kolejowy*** train ticket; ***~ lotniczy*** air ticket; ***~ powrotny*** *Br* return (ticket), *Am* round-trip ticket; ***~ ulgowy*** discount ticket; ***~ wizytowy*** visiting card; ***~ w jedną stronę*** one-way ticket; ***~ wstępu*** admission ticket
bileter *m* (*-ra*; *-rzy*), **~ka** *f* (*-ki*; *-ki*) **1.** (*w kinie*) box office attendant **2.** (*na dworcu*) ticket office attendant; **biletow|y** *adj* ticket; ***kasa ~a*** **a)** (*w kinie, teatrze*) box office **b)** (*na dworcu*) ticket office
bilion *m* (*-nu*; *-ny*) trillion
billboard *m* (*-du*; *-dy*) billboard, *Br* hoarding
billing *m* (*-gu*; *-gi*) TEL itemized bill
bilon *m* (*-nu*; *no pl*) coins *pl*, *infml* (loose) change
bimba|ć *v/im* (*-bam*) *infml*: ***ktoś ~ sobie na*** *A* s.o. doesn't care about
bimber *m* (*-bru*; *no pl*) bootleg, *Am* moonshine
binarny *adj* binary; ***system ~*** binary system
bio- (*w złożeniach*) bio-
biochemia *f* (*-mii*; *no pl*) biochemistry
biodegradacj|a *f* (*-ji*; *no pl*) biodegradation; ***ulegający ~i*** biodegradable
biodr|o *n* (*-ra*; *-ra*) hip; ***obcisły w ~ach*** tight around the hips; ***wąski w ~ach*** (*o osobie*) narrow-hipped; **biodrow|y** *adj* hip; ***kość ~a*** hip bone; ***przepaska ~a*** loincloth
biodrówki *pl* (*-wek*) *Br* hipsters, *Am* hiphuggers
biografia *f* (*-fii*; *-fie*) biography; **biogram** *m* (*-mu*; *-my*) biographical note
biolog *m* (*-ga*; *-lodzy*/*-gowie*) biologist; **biologia** *f* (*-gii*; *no pl*) biology; **biologiczn|y** *adj* biological; ***broń ~a*** biological weapons
biometeorologiczny *adj* biometeorological
bioprąd *m* (*-du*; *-dy*) bioelectric current
biorca *m* (*-cy*; *-cy*) recipient
biotechnologia (*-gii*; *no pl*) *f* biotechnology
biorą, ***biorąc***, ***biorę*** → **brać**[2]
biret *m* (*-tu*; *-ty*) **1.** *księdza:* biretta **2.** *profesora*: cap
bis *m* (*-su*; *-sy*) (*występ*) encore; ***na ~*** as an encore
biseksualny *adj* bisexual
biskup *m* (*-pa*; *-pi*) bishop; **biskupi** *adj* **1.** *konsekracja*, *pałac*: bishop's **2.** *synod*: bishops'; **biskupstwo** *n* (*-wa*; *-wa*) bishopric
bisować ⟨**za-**⟩ (*-suję*) give an encore
bistro *n* (*-ra*; *-ra*) bistro
biszkopt *m* (*-tu*; *-ty*) **1.** (*ciasto*) sponge cake **2.** (*herbatnik*) biscuit; **biszkoptow|y** *adj*: ***ciasto ~e*** sponge cake
bit *m* (*-tu*; *-ty*) INF bit
bitewny *adj* battle
bitk|a *f* (*-ki*; *-ki*) *infml*: ***skory do ~i*** brawling
bitki *pl* (*-tek*) COOK cutlets
bitny *adj* valiant
bitw|a *f* (*-wy*; *-wy*) battle; ***pole ~y*** battlefield
bitumiczny *adj* bituminous
bit|y *adj* **1.** (*ubity*): ***~a droga*** compacted dirt road; ***~a śmietana*** whipped cream **2.** *godzina*, *kilometr*: full; ***być nie w ciemię ~ym*** be no fool
biuletyn *m* (*-nu*; *-ny*) bulletin, newsletter
biurko *n* (*-ka*; *-ka*) desk
biuro *n* (*-ra*; *-ra*) office; ***~ podróży*** travel agency; ***~ pośrednictwa pracy*** unemployment office; ***~ prasowe*** press office

biurokracja *f* (*-ji*; *no pl*) bureaucracy, red tape; **biurokrata** *m* (*-ty*; *-raci*) bureaucrat; **biurokratyczny** *adj* bureaucratic; **biurowiec** *m* (*-wca*; *-wce*) office building; **biurowy** *adj* office

biust *m* (*-tu*; *-ty*) **1.** (*kobiecy*) breasts **2.** (*rozmiar*, *popiersie*) bust; **biustonosz** *m* (*-sza*; *-sze*) bra

biwak *m* (*-ku*; *-ki*) camp; **biwakować** *v/im* (*-kuję*) camp

bizantyjski *adj* Byzantine

bizmut *m* (*-tu*; *no pl*) CHEM bismuth

biznes *m* (*-su*; *-sy*) business; ***otworzyć ~*** set up a business; **biznesmen** *m* (*-na*; *-ni*) businessman; **biznesmenka** *f* (*-ki*; *-ki*) businesswoman; **biznespartner** *m* (*-ra*; *-rzy*) business partner; **biznesplan** *m* (*-nu*; *-ny*) business plan; **biznesowy** *adj* business

biżuteria *f* (*-rii*; *no pl*) *Br* jewellery, *Am* jewelery; ***sztuczna ~*** *Br* costume jewellery, *Am* costume jewelery

blach|a *f* (*-chy*; *-chy*) **1.** (*materiał*) sheet metal; ***~a falista*** corrugated metal **2.** (*arkusz*) metal sheet **3.** (*do pieczenia*) baking tray; ***wykuć coś na ~ę*** *infml* learn s.th. by rote; **blacharski** *adj*: ***warsztat ~*** AUTO *Br* (vehicle) body repair workshop, *Am* (auto) body shop; **blacharz** *m* (*-rza*; *-rze*) AUTO *Br* (vehicle) body repairer, *Am* (auto) body repairer

bladł, ***bladła***, ***bladło*** → ***blednąć***

blado *adv* **1.** palely; ***wyglądać ~*** look pale **2.** *świecić*: dimly **3.** *uśmiechać się*: feebly; **bladoniebieski** *adj* pale blue; **bladość** *f* (*-ści*; *no pl*) paleness

blad|y *adj* **1.** pale; ***~y jak śmierć*** (***ściana***) (as) pale as death (a sheet); ***~ym świtem*** at the crack of dawn; ***~a twarz*** *fig* paleface; ***~y ze strachu*** (***złości***) pale with fear (anger) **2.** *światło*: dim **3.** *uśmiech*: feeble **4.** (*nieciekawy*) bland

bladziej *comp* → ***blado***

blaga *f* (*-gi*; *-gi*) fabrication; **blagier** *m* (*-ra*; *-rzy*), **~ka** *f* (*-ki*; *-ki*) liar; **blagować** *v/im* (*-guję*) lie

blaknąć ⟨**wy-**, **z-**⟩ (*-nę*) fade

blankiet *m* (*-tu*; *-ty*) form

blanszować *v/im* (*-szuję*) COOK blanch

blask *m* (*-ku*; *-ki*) **1.** *świateł*, *słońca*, *chwały*: blaze **2.** *klejnotów*: glitter; ***~i i cienie*** the good and bad sides; ***przy ~u księżyca*** by moonlight; ***przy ~u świec*** by candlelight

blaszan|y *adj* metal; ***instrumenty ~e*** brass instruments

blaszka *f* (*-ki*; *-ki*) **1.** (*metalowa*) metal plate **2.** *grzyba*: gill, lamella **3.** *liścia*: blade, lamina

blat *m* (*-tu*; *-ty*) top; ***~ stołu*** table top

blednąć ⟨**z-**⟩ (*-nę*) **1.** (*o człowieku*) turn pale **2.** (*o kolorach*) fade **3.** (*o zmartwieniach*) fade away

bledszy *comp* → ***blady***

blef *m* (*-fu*; *no pl*) bluff; **blefować** *v/im* (*-fuję*) bluff

blekot *m* (*-tu*; *-ty*) fool's parsley

blenda *f* (*-dy*; *-dy*) **1.** ARCHIT blank window **2.** (*minerał*) blende

blezer *m* (*-ra*; *-ry*) blazer

blichtr *m* (*-ru*; *no pl*) glitter, glitz

blis|ki *adj* **1.** close, near; ***~ki ideału*** almost perfect; ***~ki płaczu*** close to tears; ***w ~kiej przyszłości*** in the near future; ***są sobie bardzo ~cy*** they are very close **2.** *przyjaźń*, *krewny*, *współpraca*: close **3.** *sąsiad*: next-door **4.** ***≈ki Wschód*** the Middle East; ***nasi ~cy*** (*rodzina*, *przyjaciele*) our nearest and dearest

blisk|o **I** *adv* **1.** close, near; ***strzelić z ~a*** fire from close range; ***zobaczyć kogoś z ~a*** see s.o. up close **2.** *współpracować*: closely **3.** *spokrewniony*: closely **4.** (*prawie*) nearly **II.** *prep* (*G*) close to, near

bliskość *f* (*-ści*; *no pl*) **1.** (*w przestrzeni*) nearness, closeness **2.** (*zażyłość*) intimacy, closeness

bliskowschodni *adj* Middle Eastern

bliskoznaczny *adj* synonymous

blizn|a *f* (*-ny*; *-ny*) scar; ***~a po operacji*** surgical scar; ***~y po ospie*** pockmarks

bliźni *m* (*-niego*; *-ni*) *lit Br* neighbour, *Am* neighbor

bliźniaczka *f* (*-ki*; *-ki*) twin sister; **bliźniaczo** *adv*: ***~ podobny*** identical; **bliźniacz|y** *adj* (*identyczny*) twin, identical; ***~e podobieństwo*** exact likeness

bliźniak *m* **1.** (*-ka*; *-ki*/*-niacy*) (*brat*) twin **2.** (*-ka*; *-ki*) (*dom*) *Am* duplex; ***połowa ~a*** semi-detached house

Bliźnięta *pl* (*-niąt*) ASTR Gemini

bliżej *adv comp* → ***blisko*** **1.** closer; ***~ nieznany*** little known **2.** *poznać*:

better; **bliższy** *adj comp* → **bliski** closer; ***potrzebujemy ~ch danych*** we need more data

bloczek *m* (*-czka*; *-czki*) *TECH* pulley

blok *m* (*-ku*; *-ki*) **1.** block; ***~ programowy*** programming block; ***~ startowy*** *SPORT* starting block **2.** (*mieszkalny*) *Br* block of flats, *Am* apartament building **3.** *POLIT* bloc **4.** (*zeszyt*) ***~ rysunkowy*** sketch pad

blokada *f* (*-dy*; *-dy*) **1.** *policyjna*, *ekonomiczna*: blockade; ***~ drogowa*** road block **2.** *kierownicy*: lock; **blokować** ⟨**za-**⟩ (*-kuję*) **1.** block; ***~ komuś drogę*** block s.o.'s way **2.** *urządzenie*: lock

blokowisko *n* (*-ka*; *-ka*) *Br* tower block estate, *Am* apartment building complex

blond *adj włosy*: blonde, fair; **blondyn** *m* (*-na*; *-ni*) blond; ***jest ~em*** he's blonde; **blondynk|a** *f* (*-ki*; *-ki*) blonde; ***jest ~ą*** she's blonde

bluszcz *m* (*-czu*; *-cze*) ivy

bluza *f* (*-zy*; *-zy*) **1.** (*sportowa*) sweatshirt; ***~ dresowa*** tracksuit top **2.** ***~ dżinsowa*** denim jacket **3.** (*część munduru*) tunic; **bluzka** *f* (*-ki*; *-ki*) blouse

bluzgać ⟨**-gnąć**⟩ (*-gam*) **1.** (*tryskać*) gush **2.** ⟨**na-**⟩ (*przeklinać*) curse

bluźnić *v/im* (*-nię*) blaspheme

bluźnierca *m* (*-cy*; *-cy*) blasphemer; **bluźnierczy** *adj* blasphemous; **bluźnierstwo** *n* (*-wa*; *-wa*) blasphemy

bł. *abbr* (= **błogosławiony**) blessed

błagać *v/im* (*-gam*) beg, plead (**o** *A* for); **błagalny** *adj spojrzenie*, *modlitwa*: pleading; **błaganie** *n* (*-nia*; *-nia*) *o pomoc*: plea

błahostka *f* (*-ki*; *-ki*) trifle; **błahy** *adj* trivial

bławatek *m* (*-tka*; *-tki*) bluebottle, cornflower

błaz|en *m* (*-zna*; *-zny*) **1.** clown; ***robić z siebie ~na*** make a fool of oneself **2.** (*dworski*) jester; **błazeński** *adj* clownish; ***strój ~*** jester's outfit; **błazeństwo** *n* (*-wa*; *-wa*) fooling; **błaznować** *v/im* (*-nuję*) clown (around)

błaźnić się ⟨**z-**⟩ (*-nię*) make a fool of oneself

błąd *m* (*błędu*; *błędy*) error, mistake; ***~ drukarski*** printing error; ***~ ortograficzny*** spelling mistake; ***~ w rozumowaniu*** fallacy; ***być w błędzie*** be wrong; ***popełnić ~*** make a mistake; ***wprowadzić w ~*** mislead; ***wyprowadzić kogoś z błędu*** put s.o. right

błądzi|ć (*-dzę*) ⟨**za-**⟩ **1.** (*włóczyć się*) wander **2.** (*szukać drogi*) walk round in circles **3.** (*mylić się*) be wrong; ***~ł wzrokiem*** his eyes kept straying

błąkać się ⟨**za-**⟩ (*-kam*) roam; ***~ po mieście*** wander around (the) town

błędnie *adv* wrongly, incorrectly; **błędn|y** *adj* **1.** wrong, incorrect **2.** *wzrok*: hazy, confused; ***~e koło*** vicious circle; ***~y ognik*** will-o'-the-wisp; ***~y rycerz*** knight-errant

błędy *pl* → **błąd**

błękit *m* (*-tu*; *-ty*) blue; **błękitnooki** *adj* blue-eyed; **błękitn|y** *adj* **1.** sky-blue **2.** *niebo*: blue; ***~a krew*** *fig* blue blood; ***~e hełmy*** (UN) blue helmets

błocić ⟨**za-**⟩ (*-cę*) muddy, soil with mud

błogi *adj* blissful; **błogo** *adv* blissfully; ***czuć się ~*** feel so good

błogosławić ⟨**po-**⟩ (*-wię*) bless; **błogosławieństwo** *n* (*-wa*; *-wa*) blessing; **błogosławiony I** *adj* blessed; ***w ~m stanie*** pregnant **II** *m* (*-nego*; *-wieni*), **-na** *f* (*-nej*; *-ne*) *REL* blessed person; **błogosławieni** the blessed

błogostan *m* (*-nu*; *no pl*) blissful serenity; **błogość** *f* (*-ści*; *no pl*) bliss, blissful serenity

błona *f* (*-ny*; *-ny*) *BIOL* membrane; ***~ dziewicza*** hymen; ***~ fotograficzna*** film; ***~ pławna*** web; ***~ śluzowa*** mucous membrane

błonica *f* (*-cy*; *no pl*) *MED* diphtheria

błonie *n* (*-nia*; *-nia*) common

błonka *f* (*-ki*; *-ki*) *dim* → **błona**

błonnik *m* (*-ka*; *no pl*) *Br* fibre, *Am* fiber

błotnik *m* (*-ka*; *-ki*) **1.** *samochodowy*: *Br* wing, *Am* fender **2.** *rowerowy*: *Br* mudguard, *Am* fender; **błotnisty** *adj* muddy; **błotn|y** *adj* **1.** *ptactwo*: marsh **2.** *kąpiel*: mud; ***lawina ~a*** mudslide

błot|o *n* (*-ta*; *-ta*) mud; ***obrzucać kogoś ~em*** *fig* sling mud at s.o.; ***wyrzucać pieniądze w ~o*** *fig* throw money down the drain; ***~a*** swamps

błysk *m* (*-ku*; *-ki*) (*błyśnięcie*) flash; ***~ pioruna*** a flash of lightning; ***wypo-***

lerować na ~ shine; **błyskać** ⟨***-snąć***⟩ (*-kam*) **1.** flash **2.** (*wyróżniać się*) shine; ***błyskać się***: ***błyska się*** it's lightning

błyskawica *f* (*-cy*; *-ce*) lightning; ***jak ~*** (as) fast as lightning; **błyskawicznie** *adv* **1.** (*szybko*) in a flash **2.** (*natychmiast*) instantly; **błyskawiczn|y** *adj* instant; ***zamek ~y*** zipper, *Br* zip; ***zupa ~a*** instant soup

błyskotka *f* (*-ki*; *-ki*) trinket; **błyskotliwość** *f* (*-ści*; *no pl*) brilliance; **błyskotliwy** *adj* **1.** *osoba*, *umysł*: brilliant **2.** *umysł*: sharp

błyskow|y *adj*: ***lampa ~a*** *PHOT* flash; **błysnąć** *v/p* → ***błyskać***

błyszczący *adj* **1.** shiny **2.** *papier*: glossy; **błyszczeć** ⟨**za-**⟩ (*-czę*) **1.** shine **2.** (*o gwiazdach*) twinkle **3.** (*o oczach*) sparkle, shine; ***błyszczeć się*** **1.** shine **2.** (*o gwiazdach*) twinkle **3.** (*o oczach*) sparkle, shine; **błyszczyk** *m* (*-ku*; *-ki*) (*do ust*) lipgloss

błyśnięcie *n* (*-cia*; *-cia*) → ***błysk***

bm. *abbr* (=***bieżącego miesiąca***) of this month

bo I *conj* because; ***nie ruszaj się, ~ skoczę*** don't move, or I'll jump **II** *particle* ***~ ja wiem?*** how should I know?

boa[1] *m indecl* (*wąż*) boa; ***~ dusiciel*** boa constrictor

boa[2] *n indecl* (*szal*) boa; ***~ z piór*** feather boa

boazeria *f* (*-rii*; *-rie*) *Br* panelling, *Am* paneling

bobas *m* (*-sa*; *-sy*) baby, tot

bobkow|y *adj* bay; ***liście ~e*** bay leaves

bobslej *m* (*-ja*; *-je*) *Br* bobsleigh, *Am* bobsled; **bobslejowy** *adj Br* bobsleigh, *Am* bobsled; ***tor ~*** bobsleigh track

bochen *m* (*-chna*; *-chny*), **bochenek** *m* (*-nka*; *-nki*) loaf; ***~ chleba*** a loaf of bread

bocian *m* (*-na*; *-ny*) stork; **bociani** *adj* stork's; ***gniazdo ~e*** (*na statku*) crow's-nest

bocz|ek *m* (*-czku*; *-czki*) *COOK* bacon; ***jajecznica na ~ku*** scrambled eggs with bacon

bocznica *f* (*-cy*; *-ce*) siding; **boczn|y** *adj* side; ***~a ulica*** side street; ***nawa ~a*** *ARCHIT* aisle; ***wiatr ~y*** crosswind

boczyć się *v/im* (*-czę*) be in a sulk (***na*** *A* with)

boćwina *f* (*-ny*; *no pl*) → ***botwina***

bodaj, ***bodajże*** *particle* **1.** (*prawdopodobnie*) probably **2.** (*przynajmniej*) at least **3.** (*chyba*) perhaps

Bodeński *adj*: ***Jezioro ~e*** Lake Constance

bodziec *m* (*-dźca*; *-dźce*) **1.** stimulus **2.** (*zachęta*) incentive

bodziszek *m*(*-szka*; *-szki*) cranesbill

bogacić ⟨**wz-**⟩ (*-cę*) make rich; *fig* enrich; ***bogacić się*** get rich; **bogactw|o** *n* (*-wa*; *-wa*) **1.** (*zamożność*) wealth **2.** (*różnorodność*) richness; ***~o dźwięków*** a rich array of sounds; ***~a*** riches; ***~a naturalne*** natural resources

bogacz *m* (*-cza*; *-cze*), ***~ka*** *f* (*-ki*; *-ki*) rich person; ***być ~em*** be rich; ***~e*** the rich

bogatka *f* (*-ki*; *-ki*): ***sikorka ~*** great tit

bogato *adv* **1.** (*obficie*) richly; ***~ wyposażony*** well-equipped **2.** (*drogo*) expensively; ***~ wyjść za mąż***, ***~ się ożenić*** marry money; ***boga|ty*** *adj* **1.** rich; ***~ci*** the rich **2.** *doświadczenie*: wide **3.** *twórczość*: extensive

bogini *f* (*-ni*; *-nie*) goddess

boginka *f* (*-ki*; *-ki*) nymph

bogobojny *adj* god-fearing

Bogurodzica *f* (*-cy*; *no pl*) (*old Polish religious hymn*) Mother of God

bohater *m* (*-ra*; *-rowie*/*-rzy*) **1.** hero; ***~ narodowy*** national hero **2.** *książki*, *filmu*: main character, *form* protagonist; **bohaterka** *f* (*-ki*; *-ki*) **1.** heroine **2.** *książki*, *filmu*: main character, *form* protagonist; **bohaterski** *adj* heroic; **bohaterstwo** *n* (*-wa*; *no pl*) heroism

bohomaz *m* (*-zu*/*-za*; *-zy*) daub

boi się → ***bać się***

boisko *n* (*-ka*; *-ka*) (playing) field, ground; ***~ do piłki nożnej*** football field; ***~ do siatkówki*** volleyball court

boja *f* (*boi*; *-je*) buoy

bojaźliwość *f* (*-ści*; *no pl*) fearfulness; **bojaźliwy** *adj* fearful

bojaźń *f* (*-źni*; *no pl*) *lit* fear

bojer *m* (*-ra*; *-ry*) ice boat

boję, ***boję się*** → ***bać się***

bojkot *m* (*-tu*; *-ty*) boycott; **bojkotować** ⟨**z-**⟩ (*-tuję*) boycott

B

bojownik *m* (*-ka*; *-nicy*), **-niczka** *f* (*-ki*; *-ki*) fighter; **~ o wolność** freedom fighter

bojowo *adv* **1.** combatively; **być nastawionym ~** have a combative attitude **2.** *wykorzystać*: in combat; **bojow|y** *adj* **1.** *oddziały*, *sprzęt*: combat **2.** *organizacja*: paramilitary **3.** *działacz*, *zawodnik*: combative; **chrzest ~y** baptism of fire; **głowica ~a** warhead; **okrzyk ~y** war cry

bojówka *f* (*-ki*; *-ki*) raiding party

bok *m* (*-ku*; *-ki*) side; **leżeć na ~u** lie on one's side; **na ~!** stand aside!; **odłożyć coś na ~** put s.th. aside; **odwrócić się na drugi ~** turn over; **po ~ach** at either side; **podparty pod ~i** with arms akimbo; **popatrzeć** (**przesunąć**) **się w ~** look (move) sideways; **przesunąć się na ~** move aside; **u czyjegoś ~u** at s.o.'s side; **pod ~iem** at hand; **robić ~ami** be in financial straits; **to mi wychodzi ~iem** I'm fed up with it; **trzymać się z ~u** stay away; **wziąć kogoś na ~** take s.o. aside; **z ~u na ~** from side to side; **zrywać ~i ze śmiechu** split one's sides; **żarty na ~** joking aside

bokobrody *pl* (*-dów*) sideburns

boks[1] *m* (*-su*; *-sy*) **1.** (*w biurze*, *szatni*) cubicle **2.** (*w stajni*) box (stall)

boks[2] *m* (*-su*; *no pl*) boxing

bokser *m* **1.** (*-ra*; *-rzy*) SPORT boxer **2.** (*-ra*; *-ry*) (*pies*) boxer

bokserski *adj* boxing; **boksować** *v/im* (*-suję*) box; **boksować się** box

bolący *adj* aching; **bolączka** *f* (*-ki*; *-ki*) problem, *Br* bugbear

bolec *m* (*-lca*; *-lce*) **1.** pin **2.** (*gwintowany*) bolt

bol|eć[1] ⟨**za-**⟩: **to ~i** it hurts; **~ą kogoś plecy** s.o.'s back hurts; **~i kogoś gardło** s.o. has a sore throat; **~i kogoś głowa** (**ząb**) s.o. has a headache (toothache); **niech cię o to głowa nie ~i** *fig* don't worry about it; **oczy ~ą patrzeć na to** *fig* it's an eyesore

bole|ć[2] *v/im* (*-leję*) deplore (**nad** *I*); **~ję, że** I regret that

bolesny *adj* painful; **boleś|ć** *f* (*-ści*; *-ści*) anguish; **jęk ~ci** anguished groan; **~ci** acute pains; **od siedmiu ~ci** rotten, lousy; **w ~ciach** in agony

bolimuszka *f* (*-ki*; *-ki*) stable fly

Boliwia *f* (*-wii*) Bolivia; **Boliwijczyk** *m* (*-ka*; *-czycy*), **-jka** *f* (*-ki*; *-ki*) Bolivian; **boliwijski** *adj* Bolivian;

bolszewik *m* (*-ka*; *-wicy*) Bolshevik

bom *m* (*-mu*; *-my*) (*na statku*) boom

bomba *f* (*-by*; *-by*) **1.** (*pocisk*) bomb; **~ atomowa** nuclear bomb; **~ zegarowa** time bomb; **~ pułapka** booby trap **2.** (*sensacja*) *infml* sensation; **bombardować** ⟨**z-**⟩ (*-duję*) **1.** (*zrzucać bomby*) bomb **2.** *pytaniami*: bombard (*I* with); **bombardowanie** *n* (*-nia*; *-nia*) bombardment

bombastyczny *adj* bombastic

bombka *f* (*-ki*; *-ki*) glass ball, bauble

bombonierka *f* (*-ki*; *-ki*) chocolate box

bombowiec *m* (*-wca*; *-wce*) bomber; **bombowo** *adv infml* fantastically; **wyglądać ~** *Br* look smashing, *Am* look awesame; **bombowy** *adj* **1.** bomb; **atak ~** bomb attack; **nalot ~** air raid **2.** (*fantastyczny*) *infml Br* smashing, *Am* awesame

bon *m* (*-nu*; *-ny*) voucher

bonifikata *f* (*-ty*; *-ty*) **1.** ECON reduction **2.** SPORT bonus

BOR *abbr m* (*BOR-u*; *no pl*) (= **Biuro Ochrony Rządu**) Bureau for Protection of the Government

bor *m* (*-ru*; *no pl*) CHEM boron

boraks *m* (*-su*; *no pl*) borax

bordo *n indecl* maroon, dark brownish red; **bordowy** *adj* maroon, dark brownish-red

borny *adj*: **kwas ~** boric acid

borować ⟨**wy-**⟩ (*-ruję*) drill, bore

borowik *m* (*-ka*; *-ki*) boletus, cep

borowina *f* (*-ny*; *-ny*) (*torf*) (therapeutic) peat; **borowinow|y** *adj*: **kąpiel ~a** (therapeutic) peat bath

borówka *f* (*-ki*; *-ki*) blueberry; **~ amerykańska** highbush blueberry; **~ czarna** bilberry

borsuczy *adj nora*, *skóra*: badger; **borsuk** *m* (*-ka*; *-ki*) badger

borykać się *v/im* (*-kam*) struggle (**z** *I* with)

bosak[1]: **na ~a** barefoot

bosak[2] *m* (*-ka*; *-ki*) **1.** (*pożarniczy*) fire hook **2.** (*żeglarski*) boat hook

Bosfor *m* (*-ru*) Bosporus, Bosphorus

bosk|i *adj* divine; **łaska ~a** the grace of God; **na miłość ~ą!** for heaven's

sake!; ***Matka** ≈**a*** the Virgin Mary; ***rany ~ie!*** my God!; **bosko** *adv* divinely
bosman *m* (*-na*; *-ni*) boatswain, bosun
boso *adv* barefoot; **bosonogi** *adj* barefoot; **bosy** *adj* **1.** *człowiek*: barefooted **2.** *stopa*: bare
Bośnia *f* (*-ni*) Bosnia; ***~ i Hercegowina*** Bosnia and Herzegovina; **bośniacki** *adj* Bosnian; **Bośniak** *m* (*-ka*; *-niacy*), **-niaczka** *f* (*-ki*; *-ki*) Bosnian
botaniczny *adj* botanical; **botanik** *m* (*-ka*; *-nicy*), **-niczka** *f* (*-ki*; *-ki*) botanist; **botanika** *f* (*-ki*; *no pl*) botany
botki *pl* (*-ków*) boots
botwina *f* (*-ny*; *no pl*), **botwinka** *f* (*-ki*; *no pl*) **1.** (*liście*) young beetroot leaves **2.** (*zupa*) *soup made with young beetroot leaves*
bowiem *conj lit* for, because
boy *m* (*boya*; *boye*) (*w hotelu*) bellboy, pageboy
Bozia *f* (*-zi*; *no pl*) *infml* God
bożek *m* (*-żka*; *-żki*) god, idol, *fig* idol
bożonarodzeniowy *adj* Christmas
boż|y *adj* God's, divine; ***z ~ej łaski*** *iron* mediocre; ***~a krówka*** *Br* ladybird, *Am* ladybug; ***≈e Ciało*** Corpus Christi; ***≈e Narodzenie*** Christmas; ***Królestwo ≈e*** the Kingdom of God; ***Syn ≈y*** the Son of God; ***palec ~y*** the finger of God; ***po ~emu*** (*uczciwie*) honestly
bożyszcze *n* (*-cza*; *-cza*) idol
bób *m* (*bobu; no pl*) broad beans; ***dać komuś bobu*** teach s.o. a lesson
bóbr *m* (*bobra*; *bobry*) beaver; ***płakać jak ~*** cry one's eyes out
Bóg *m* (*Boga*; *no pl*) God; ***~ Ojciec*** God the Father; ***~ zapłać!*** God bless you!; (***między***) ***Bogiem a prawdą*** in truth, to tell the truth; ***Bogu ducha winien*** (as) innocent as a lamb; ***broń Boże!*** God forbid!; ***dzięki Bogu*** thank God; ***jak Boga kocham!*** cross my heart!; ***o Boże!*** My God!; ***Pan ~*** God, the Lord; ***szczęść Boże!*** God bless!
bóg *m* (*boga*; *bogowie*) god; ***~ miłości*** (***wojny***) god of love (war); ***bogowie mitologii greckiej*** the gods of Greek mythology
bój *m* (*boju*; *boje*) fight; ***plac boju*** battlefield; ***toczyć boje o*** fight for; ***w boju*** in combat, in action
bójka *f* (*-ki*; *-ki*) fight; ***~ na pięści*** fist fight
ból *m* (*-lu*; *-le*) pain; ***~ brzucha*** stomach ache; ***~e porodowe*** *Br* labour pains, *Am* labor pains; ***~ gardła*** sore throat; ***~ głowy*** headache; ***~ ucha*** earache; ***~ zęba*** toothache; ***z ~em serca*** with a heavy heart
bór *m* (*boru*; *bory*) *lit* forest
bóstwo *n* (*-wa*; *-wa*) deity; ***wyglądać jak ~*** look divine; ***zrobić się na ~*** *infml* doll oneself up
bóść ⟨***u-, bodnąć***⟩ (*bodę*) (*rogami*) butt
bóżnica *f* (*-cy*; *-ce*) synagogue
bp *abbr* (= **biskup**) bp., bishop
br. *abbr* (= **bieżącego roku**) this year
bracia *pl* → **brat**
braciszek *m* (*-szka*; *-szkowie*) **1.** *dim* little brother **2.** (*zakonny*) brother, friar; **bractwo** *n* (*-wa*; *-wa*) **1.** *strzeleckie*: fraternity **2.** *HIST* guild
brać[1] *f* (*braci*; *no pl*) *lit*: ***~ studencka*** students
brać[2] ⟨**wziąć**⟩ (*biorę*) **I** *v/t* **1.** take; ***~ coś do ręki*** take hold of s.th., take s.th. in one's hand; ***~ coś pod uwagę*** take s.th. into account; ***~ kogoś do niewoli*** take s.o. prisoner; ***~ kogoś do wojska*** *Br* conscript s.o. into the army, *Am* draft s.o. into the army; ***~ kogoś na ręce*** pick s.o. up; ***~ na serio*** take seriously; ***~ rozwód*** get divorced; ***~ ślub*** get married; ***~ udział w*** *L* take part in; ***~ winę na siebie*** take the blame; ***~ w ramiona*** embrace; ***~ ze sobą*** take **2.** *kąpiel*, *prysznic*: *Br* have, *Am* take **3.** (*pomylić*) mistake (**za** *A* for) **II** *v/i* (*o rybie*) bite; **brać się 1.** (*pochodzić*) come from; ***skąd się to bierze?*** where does that come from? **2.** (*chwytać*) ***~ się za ręce*** hold each other's hands **3.** (*zabierać się*) ***~ się do pracy*** get down to work; ***wziąć się w garść*** pull oneself together; ***~ się za coś*** start doing s.th.
brajl *m* (*-la*; *no pl*) Braille
brak[1] *m* (*-ku*; *-ki*) **1.** lack; ***~ apetytu*** lack of appetite; ***~ doświadczenia*** lack of experience, inexperience; ***~ odpowiedzialności*** irresponsibility; ***z ~u*** for lack (*G* of); ***cierpieć na ~*** be short (*G* of); ***mieć ~i w wykształceniu*** be poorly educated **2.** (*wada*) defect

B

brak[2] *v/irreg*: **~ *komuś pieniędzy*** **a)** (*ktoś ma za mało*) s.o. is short of money **b)** (*ktoś nie ma wcale*) s.o. has no money; ***~ mi ciebie*** I miss you; ***~ mi słów*** words fail me; ***~ mu odwagi*** he lacks courage; ***nie ~ mu odwagi*** he is not short of courage

braknąć *v/p* → ***brakować***

brakoróbstwo *n* (*-wa*; *no pl*) defective production

brak|ować ⟨**-knąć**⟩: ***~uje czegoś*** s.th. is lacking; ***~uje mi ciebie*** I miss you; ***komuś ~uje czegoś*** s.o. lacks s.th.; ***komuś ~uje pieniędzy*** s.o. is short of money; ***nie ~uje jej odwagi*** she doesn't lack courage; ***niewiele ~owało*** it was a close call; ***tego tylko ~owało*** *iron* that's just what we needed

brama *f* (*-my*; *-my*) gate; ***~ wjazdowa*** entrance gate; **bram|ka** *f* (*-ki*; *-ki*) **1.** (*wejście*) gate **2.** SPORT goal; ***stać na ~ce*** play in goal; ***strzał do ~ki*** shot at the goal; ***strzelić ~kę*** score a goal; **bramkarz** (*-rza*; *-rze*) SPORT goalkeeper, *infml* goalie; **bramkowy** *adj* SPORT goal

brandenbursk|i *adj* Brandenburg; ***Brama ~a*** the Brandenburg Gate

bransoletka *f* (*-ki*; *-ki*) bracelet

branża *f* (*-ży*; *-że*) industry; **branżowy** *adj* industry; ***sklep ~*** specialist shop

brat *m* (*-ta*; *bracia*) **1.** brother; ***~ bliźniak*** twin brother; ***~ cioteczny*** cousin; ***~ przyrodni*** half-brother **2.** (*zakonny*) brother, friar; ***być za pan ~*** be on friendly terms (**z** *I* with)

bratanek *m* (*-nka*; *-nkowie*) nephew; **bratanica** *f* (*-cy*; *-ce*) niece

bratek *m* (*-tka*; *-tki*) pansy

braterski *adj* brotherly; **braterstwo** *n* (*-wa*; *no pl*) brotherhood in arms

bratni *adj* brotherly; ***podać komuś ~ą dłoń*** give s.o. a helping hand; ***~a dusza*** soul mate, *lit* kindred spirit

bratobójca *m* (*-cy*; *-cy*) fratricide; **bratobójczy** *adj* fratricidal; **bratobójstwo** *n* (*-wa*; *-wa*) fratricide

bratowa *f* (*-wej*; *-we*) sister-in-law

brawo *n* (*-wa*; *-wa*) applause; ***bić ~*** applaud; ***~!*** bravo!

brawura *f* (*-ry*; *no pl*) bravado

brawurowy *adj* **1.** (*śmiały*) daring **2.** (*ryzykancki*) foolhardy; **brawurowo** *adv* with bravado

Brazylia *f* (*-lii*) Brazil; **Brazylijczyk** *m* (*-ka*; *-czycy*), **-jka** *f* (*-ki*; *-ki*) Brazilian **brazylijski** *adj* Brazilian

brąz *m* (*-zu*; *-zy*) **1.** (*kolor*) brown; ***opalony na ~*** brown **2.** (*metal*, *medal*) bronze; ***epoka ~u*** the bronze age; **brązowy** *adj* **1.** *kolor*: brown **2.** (*z brązu*) bronze; ***~ medal*** bronze medal

brednie *pl* (*-ni*) *Br* rubbish *sing*, *Am* hogwash *sing*; **bredzić** *v/im* (*-dzę*) **1.** (*w gorączce*) speak deliriously **2.** (*mówić głupstwa*) rave, spout nonsense

breja *f* (*brei*; *no pl*) **1.** pulp **2.** (*śnieg*, *błoto*) slush

breloczek *m* (*-czka*; *-czki*) **1.** pendant **2.** (*przy kluczach*) (key) fob

Brema *f* (*-my*) Bremen

Bretania *f* (*-nii*) Brittany

brew *f* (*brwi*; *brwi*) eyebrow

brewerie *pl* (*-rii*) commotion *sing*; ***wyczyniać ~*** run riot, *infml* cause a rumpus

brewiarz *m* (*-rza*; *-rze*) breviary

brezent *m* (*-tu*; *-ty*) tarpaulin

briefing *m* (*-gu*; *-gi*) (press) briefing

brnąć ⟨**prze-**⟩ (*-nę*) wade (**przez** *A* through); ***~ w śniegu*** trudge through the snow; ***~ w długi*** sink into debt

broczyć *v/im* (*-czę*): ***~ krwią*** bleed

brod|a *f* (*-dy*; *-dy*) **1.** ANAT chin **2.** (*zarost*) beard; ***zapuścić ~ę*** grow a beard; **brodaty** *adj* bearded

brodawka *f* (*-ki*; *-ki*) (*na skórze*) wart; ***~ sutkowa*** nipple

brodzić *v/im* (*-dzę*) wade (**w** *L* through); **brodzik** *m* (*-ka*; *-ki*) *Br* paddling pool, *Am* wading pool

broić ⟨**na-**, **z-**⟩ (*broję*) *infml* make mischief; ***co zbroiłeś?*** what've you been up to?

brokat *m* (*-tu*; *-ty*) **1.** (*drobinki*) glitter **2.** (*tkanina*) brocade; **brokatowy** *adj* **1.** *puder*: glitter **2.** *suknia*: brocade

brokuły *pl* (*-łów*) COOK broccoli *sing*

brom *m* (*-mu*; *no pl*) CHEM bromine

brona *f* (*-ny*; *-ny*) harrow

bronchit *m* (*-tu*; *-ty*) bronchitis

bronić ⟨**o-**⟩ (*-nię*) **1.** defend; ***~ dostępu do*** *G* bar the way to; ***~ tytułu*** SPORT defend one's title; ***broń Boże!*** God forbid! **2.** (*strzec*) protect (**przed** *I* from);

bronić się defend oneself (***przed*** *I* against)
bronować ⟨**za-**⟩ (*-nuję*) harrow
broń[1] → ***bronić***
broń[2] *f* (*-ni; no pl*) **1.** (*narzędzie*) weapon; ***nosić ~*** carry arms **2.** (*zbiorowo*) arms *pl*, weapons *pl*; ***~ atomowa*** nuclear weapons; ***~ palna*** firearms; ***~ masowego rażenia*** weapons of mass destruction, WMD; ***chwycić za ~*** take up arms; ***złożyć ~*** lay down one's arms
broszka *f* (*-ki; -ki*) brooch
broszura *f* (*-ry; -ry*) brochure; ***~ polityczna*** political pamphlet; ***~ reklamowa*** advertising brochure
browar *m* (*-ru; -ry*) brewery; **browarniczy** *adj przemysł*: brewing
bród *m* (*brodu; brody*) ford; ***przejść rzeką w ~*** ford a river; ***czegoś jest w ~*** there's plenty of s.th.
bródka *f* (*-ki; -ki*) (*zarost*) beard; ***kozia ~*** goatee
brr *interj* **1.** (*zimno*) brr **2.** (*wstręt*) yuck! *infml*
brud *m* (*-du; -dy*) dirt; ***~y*** (*ubranie*) dirty clothes; **brudas** *m* (*-sa; -sy*) slob
bruderszaft *n* (*-tu; -ty*) *ceremony celebrating the passage to first-name basis*
brudno *adv*: ***tu jest ~*** the place is dirty; ***pisać coś na ~*** make a rough draft of s.th.; **brudnopis** *m* (*-su; -sy*) **1.** (*tekst*) rough draft **2.** (*brulion*) rough book; **brudny** *adj* dirty
brudzić ⟨**po-**, **za-**, **u-**, **wy-**⟩ (*-dzę*) dirty, soil; ***brudzić się*** get dirty
Brugia *f* (*-gii*) Brugges
bruk *m* (*-ku; -ki*) cobblestone paving; ***wyrzucić kogoś na ~*** *fig* throw s.o. out onto the street; ***znaleźć się na ~u*** *fig* be out on the street, be down and out
brukać ⟨**z-**⟩ (*-kam*) *lit honor, dobre imię*: sully
brukiew *f* (*-kwi; -kwie*) *Br* swede, *Am* rutabaga
brukować ⟨**wy-**⟩ (*-kuję*) cobble, pave with cobblestones
brukowiec *m* (*-wca; -wce*) (*pismo*) tabloid; **brukow|y** *adj*: ***pismo ~e*** tabloid; ***prasa ~a*** the gutter press
Bruksela *f* (*-li*) Brussels
brukselka *f* (*-ki; -ki*) Brussel(s) sprout; **brukselski** *adj* Brussels
brulion *m* (*-nu; -ny*) **1.** (*zeszyt*) notebook **2.** (*brudnopis*) rough book
brunatny *adj* dark brown; ***niedźwiedź ~*** brown bear; ***węgiel ~*** lignite
brunet *m* (*-ta; -neci*) dark-haired man; ***on jest ~em*** he has dark hair; **brunetka** *f* (*-ki; -ki*) brunette
brusznica *f* (*-cy; -ce*): ***borówka ~*** cowberry
brutal *m* (*-la; -le*) brute; **brutalność** *f* (*-ści; no pl*) brutality; **brutaln|y** *adj* brutal; ***~a siła*** brute force
brutto *adj* gross; ***ciężar ~*** gross weight; ***zysk ~*** gross profit
bruzda *f* (*-dy; -dy*) *w ziemi, na twarzy*: furrow
bruździć *v/im* (*-rużdżę*): ***~ komuś*** hinder s.o., put a spoke in s.o.'s wheel
brwi *pl* → ***brew***
brwiowy *adj*: ***łuk ~*** superciliary ridge; ***rozbić komuś łuk ~*** split s.o.'s brow open
bryczesy *pl* (*-sów*) riding breeches; jodhpurs
bryczka *f* (*-ki; -ki*) britzka, (horse-drawn) carriage
brydż *m* (*-dża; no pl*) bridge
brygada *f* (*-dy; -dy*) **1.** brigade; ***~ antyterrorystyczna*** antiterrorist unit **2.** (*ekipa*) team
brygadzista *m* (*-ty; -dziści*) foreman; **brygadzistka** *f* (*-ki; -ki*) forewoman
bryk *m* (*-ka; -ki*) crib, revision book
brykać ⟨**-knąć**⟩ (*-kam*) (*o dziecku, zwierzęciu*) frisk
brykiet *m* (*-tu; -ty*) briquette
brylant *m* (*-tu; -ty*) diamond; **brylantowy** *adj* diamond
brylantyna *f* (*-ny; -ny*) brilliantine
bryła *f* (*-ły; -ły*) **1.** *węgla, gliny*: lump; ***~ lodu*** block of ice; ***~ ziemi*** clod **2.** MATH solid
bryłka *f* (*-ki; -ki*) *dim* → ***bryła 1***
bryłowaty *adj ziemia*: lumpy
bryndza *f* (*-dzy; no pl*) ewe's milk cheese
brystol *m* (*-lu; -le*) Bristol board
brytan *m* (*-na; -ny*) mastiff
brytfanna *f* (*-ny; -ny*) roasting pan
Brytyjczyk *m* (*-ka; -czycy*) British person, *infml* Briton; ***jest ~iem*** he is British; ***Brytyjczycy*** the British; **Brytyjka** *f* (*-ki; -ki*) Britishwoman; **brytyjski** *adj* British; ***Wyspy ≈e*** the British Isles

B

bryza *f* (*-zy*; *-zy*) sea breeze
bryzg *m* (*-gu*; *-gi*) splash; **bryzgać** ⟨**-znąć**⟩ (*-gam*) splash
brzana *f* (*-ny*; *-ny*) barbel
brzask *m* (*-ku*; *-ki*) daybreak; ***o ~u*** at daybreak
brzdąc *m* (*-ca*; *-ce*) *infml* tot
brzdąkać *v/im* (*-kam*) *na gitarze*: strum
brzdęk *m* (*-ku*; *no pl*) **1.** *strun*: twang **2.** *szkła*, *monet*: clink **3.** *metalu*: clank
brzeg *m* (*-gu*; *-gi*) **1.** (*krawędź*) edge; *naczynia*: rim; ***wypełniony po ~i*** **a)** *sala*: filled to capacity **b)** *naczynie*: filled to the brim; ***pierwszy z ~u*** **a)** *rzecz*: any **b)** *osoba*: anyone **2.** *jeziora*, *morza*: shore; ***na ~u*** on the shore, ashore **3.** *rzeki*: bank; ***rzeka wystąpiła z ~ów*** the river burst its banks; **brzegow|y** *adj*: ***linia ~a*** shoreline
brzemienny *adj lit* pregnant; ***być ~m w skutki*** have serious consequences
brzemię *n* (*-mienia*; *-miona*) *lit* burden
brzeszczot *m* (*-tu*; *-ty*) blade
brzezina *f* (*-ny*; *-ny*) (*las*, *drewno*) birch wood
brzeżek *m* (*-żka*; *-żki*) *dim* (*krawędź*) edge
brzęczeć ⟨**za-**⟩ (*-czę*) **1.** (*o owadzie*, *dzwonku*) buzz **2.** (*o szkle*) clink **3.** (*o metalu*) clank **4.** (*o strunach*) twang; **brzęczenie** *n* (*-nia*; *no pl*) **1.** *owada*, *dzwonka*: buzz(ing) **2.** *strun*: twang(ing); **brzęczyk** *m* (*-ka*; *-ki*) buzzer
brzęk *m* (*-ku*; *-ki*) **1.** *strun*: twang **2.** *szkła*, *monet*: clink **3.** *tłuczonego szkła*: crash **4.** *metalu*: clank
brzmi|eć ⟨**za-**⟩ (*-mię*) sound; ***~eć dobrze*** sound good; ***piosenka ~ała w oddali*** a song could be heard in the distance; ***rozkaz ~ał*** the order was; ***tekst ~ał następująco*** it read as follows; **brzmienie** *n* (*-nia*; *-nia*) **1.** MUS sound **2.** *tekstu*: wording
brzoskwinia *f* (*-ni*; *-nie*) peach; **brzoskwiniowy** *adj* peach
brzoza *f* (*-zy*; *-zy*) birch; **brzozowy** *adj* birch
brzuch *m* (*-cha*; *-chy*) belly; ***ból ~a*** stomach ache, *infml* bellyache; ***leżeć do góry ~em*** laze about; ***mięśnie ~a*** abdominal muscles; ***na ~u*** on one's belly; ***taniec ~a*** belly dance; ***wiercić dziurę w ~u*** badger, pester
brzuchaty *adj osoba*: pot-bellied
brzuchomówca *m* (*-cy*; *-cy*) ventriloquist
brzuszek *m* (*-szka*; *-szki*) belly, *infml* tummy; **brzuszny** *adj* abdominal; ***dur ~*** typhoid fever
brzydactwo *n* (*-wa*; *-wa*) ugly thing; **brzydal** *m* (*-la*; *-le*) ugly man; ***jest ~em*** he's ugly
brzydki *adj* **1.** ugly **2.** *pogoda*: bad; ***~e słowa*** bad language; **brzydko** *adv* **1.** *wyglądać*: ugly **2.** *postąpić*, *zachować się*: badly; ***~ się wyrażać*** use bad language
brzydnąć ⟨**o-**, **z-**⟩ (*-nę*) get ugly; ***zbrzydło mi to*** I'm sick of it
brzydota *f* (*-ty*; *no pl*) ugliness; **brzydul|a** *f* (*-li*; *-le*) ugly girl; ***jest ~ą*** she's ugly
brzydzić się *v/im* (*-dzę*): ***~ czymś*** feel disgust for s.th., find s.th. disgusting
brzydziej *comp* → ***brzydko***
brzytwa *f* (*-wy*; *-wy*) razor
bubek *m* (*-bka*; *-bki*) *infml* whippersnapper
bubel *m* (*-bla*; *-ble*) dud, trash
buc *m* (*-ca*; *-ce*) *infml* big head
bucha|ć ⟨**-chnąć**⟩ (*-cham*) *ogniem*, *dymem*: belch (out); ***~ć żarem*** glow with heat; ***dym ~ł z kominów*** chimneys belched smoke
buchalteria *f* (*-rii*; *no pl*) accountancy
buchnąć *v/p* → ***buchać***
bucik *m* (*-ka*; *-ki*) *dim* (small) shoe; **bucior** *m* (*-ra*; *-ry*) boot, *infml* clodhopper
buczeć ⟨**za-**⟩ (*-czę*) **1.** (*o owadzie*, *urządzeniu*) hum **2.** (*o urządzeniu*, *syrenie*) drone **3.** (*o dziecku*) *infml* blubber
buczyna *f* (*-ny*; *no pl*) (*las*, *drewno*) beech wood
buda *f* (*-dy*; *-dy*) **1.** shed; ***~ na narzędzia*** tool-shed **2.** (*dla psa*) kennel, *Am* doghouse **3.** (*na targu*) booth, stall **4.** *kabrioletu*: hood **5.** (*szkoła*) *infml* school
Budapeszt *m* (*-tu*) Budapest
buddyjski *adj* buddhist; **buddysta** *m* (*-ty*; *-dyści*) buddhist; **buddyzm** *m* (*-mu*; *no pl*) buddhism
budka *f* (*-ki*; *-ki*) **1.** box; ***~ telefoniczna*** telephone booth, *Br* phone box;

~ ***wartownicza*** sentry-box; ~ ***dla ptaków*** nest-box, nesting box **2.** (*mała buda*) (small) shed **3.** (*kiosk*) ~ ***z gazetami*** news stand **4.** (*na targu*) booth, stall

budow|a *f* (*-wy*; *-wy*) **1.** (*budowanie*) construction; ***plac ~y*** construction site; ***w ~ie*** under construction **2.** (*struktura*) structure **3.** (*konstrukcja*) construction **4.** (*plac budowy*) construction site **5.** *ciała*: build

budować ⟨**z-**, **wy-**⟩ (*-duję*) **1.** build **2.** (*konstruować*) construct; ***budować się***: ***coś się buduje*** s.th. is being built; ***ktoś się buduje*** s.o. is having a house built

budowla *f* (*-li*; *-le*) **1.** structure **2.** (*budynek*) building, structure

budowlan|y *adj* building, construction; ***przedsiębiorca ~y*** builder, building contractor; ***branża ~a*** the construction industry

budownictwo *n* (*-wa*; *no pl*) **1.** (*branża*) the construction industry; ~ ***mieszkaniowe*** residential construction **2.** (*budowanie*) building; **budowniczy** *m* (*-czego*; *-czowie*) builder

budujący *adj przykład*, *opowieść*: edifying; **budulec** *m* (*-lca*; *-lce*) building material

budynek *m* (*-nku*; *-nki*) building; ~ ***mieszkalny*** residential building

budyń *m* (*-dyniu*; *-dynie*) *thick milk pudding with potato flour and vanilla, chocolate or fruit flavouring*

budzenie *n* (*-nia*; *no pl*) **1.** waking up **2.** (*usługa*) alarm call; **budzenie się** *n* (*-nia*; *no pl*) waking up

budzi|ć (*-dzę*) **1.** ⟨**o-**, **prze-**⟩ wake (up) **2.** ⟨**wz-**⟩ *sympatię*, *litość*, *zainteresowanie*: arouse; ***~ć obawy*** arouse concern **3.** ⟨**wz-**⟩ *wątpliwości*: raise; ***~ć w kimś podziw*** (***niesmak***) fill s.o. with admiration (disgust); ***coś ~ czyjś zachwyt*** s.th. delights s.o.; ***budzić się*** wake up; **budzik** *m* (*-ka*; *-ki*) alarm clock

budżet *m* (*-tu*; *-ty*) budget; ***projekt ~u*** draft budget; ***przekroczyć ~*** go over budget; **budżetowy** *adj* budget

bufe|t *m* (*-tu*; *-ty*) **1.** café **2.** (*na dworcu*) buffet **3.** (*kontuar*) bar, counter; ***przy ~cie*** at the bar **4.** (*stół*) buffet table; ***zimny ~t*** cold buffet

bufiasty *adj rękaw*: puff(ed)

bufon *m* (*-na*; *-ni*) *infml* big-head

bufor *m* (*-ra*; *-ry*) buffer

buhaj *m* (*-ja*; *-je*) *bull kept for breeding*

bujać (*-jam*) **1.** ⟨**po-**⟩ (*kołysać*) rock **2.** ⟨**na-**⟩ *infml* (*kłamać*) fib; ***przestań ~*** stop telling fibs; ~ ***w obłokach*** *infml* daydream; ***bujać się*** **1.** (*kołysać się*) rock **2.** (*huśtać się*) swing **3.** (*kochać się*) *infml* ~ ***w*** *L* have a crash on

bujd|a *f* (*-dy*; *-dy*) *infml* fib, story; ***opowiadać ~y*** tell stories

bujn|y *adj* **1.** *roślinność*, *włosy*: luxuriant, lush; ***~a roślinność*** lush vegetation **2.** *wyobraźnia*: vivid **3.** *życie*: eventful

buk *m* (*-ku*; *-ki*) beech

Bukareszt *m* (*-tu*) Bucharest

bukiet *m* (*-tu*; *-ty*) **1.** *kwiatów*: bunch; (*uroczysty*) bouquet; ~ ***ślubny*** wedding bouquet **2.** (*wina*) bouquet

bukmacher *m* (*-ra*; *-rzy*) bookmaker

bukować ⟨**za-**⟩ (*-kuję*) book

bukowy *adj* beech

buksować ⟨**za-**⟩ (*-suję*) (*o kole*) spin

bukszpan *m* (*-nu*; *-ny*) box

bulaj *m* (*-ja*/*-ju*; *-je*) porthole

buldog *m* (*-ga*; *-gi*) bulldog

buldożer *m* (*-ra*; *-ry*) bulldozer

bulgotać ⟨**za-**⟩ (*-goczę*/*-gocę*) **1.** gurgle, bubble **2.** (*w garnku*, *czajniku*) bubble

bulić ⟨**wy-**, **za-**⟩ (*-lę*) *infml* shell out *infml*

bulimia *f* (*-mii*; *no pl*) MED bulimia (nervosa); **bulimiczka** *f* (*-ki*; *-ki*) bulimic, bulimia sufferer

bulion *m* (*-nu*; *-ny*) consommé, stock; ~ ***w kostkach*** stock cubes

bulwa *f* (*-wy*; *-wy*) **1.** *roślin kwiatowych*, *cebuli*: bulb **2.** *ziemniaka*: tuber

bulwar *m* (*-ru*; *-ry*) boulevard; **bulwarowy** *adj prasa*: tabloid

bulwersować ⟨**z-**⟩ (*-suję*) shock, scandalize

bulwiasty *adj nos*, *narośl*: bulbous

buława *f* (*-wy*; *-wy*) mace: ~ ***marszałkowska*** marshal's baton

bułeczka *f* (*-ki*; *-ki*) *dim* → ***bułka***

Bułgar *m* (*-ra*; *-rzy*) Bulgarian; ***jest ~em*** he is Bulgarian; **Bułgaria** *f* (*-rii*) Bulgaria; **Bułgarka** *f* (*-ki*; *-ki*) Bulgarian

B

bułgarsk|i *adj* Bulgarian; ***mówić po ~u*** speak Bulgarian; ***po ~u*** in Bulgarian
bułka *f* (*-ki*; *-ki*) (bread) roll; ***~ paryska*** French loaf; ***~ tarta*** breadcrumbs; ***słodka ~*** bun
bumelanctwo *n* (*-wa*; *no pl*) *infml* loafing (around); **bumelować** *v/im* (*-luję*) *infml* loaf (around)
bumerang *m* (*-gu*; *-gi*) boomerang
bunkier *m* (*-kra*; *-kry*) bunker
bunt *m* (*-tu*; *-ty*) **1.** rebellion **2.** (*na statku*) mutiny **3.** (*protest*) protest
buntować ⟨**z-**⟩ (*-tuję*): ***~ kogoś przeciw*** *D* turn s.o. against; ***~ kogoś, żeby coś zrobił*** incite s.o. to do s.th.; ***buntować się*** rebel (**przeciw** *D* against); **buntowniczy** *adj* rebellious; **buntownik** *m* (*-ka*; *-nicy*) **1.** rebel **2.** (*na statku*) mutineer
buńczuczny *adj* **1.** (*wyzywający*) provocative **2.** (*pełen werwy*) dashing
bur|a *f* (*-ry*; *-ry*) *infml* dressing-down; ***dostać ~ę*** get a dressing-down
buraczany *adj* beetroot; **buraczki** *pl* (*-ków*) COOK beetroot salad *sing*
buraczkowy *adj* **1.** beetroot **2.** (*kolor*) maroon; **burak** *m* (*-ka*; *-ki*) **1.** (*ćwikłowy*) *Br* beetroot, *Am* beet **2.** (*pastewny*) beet **3.** (*cukrowy*) sugar beet
bur|czeć ⟨**-rknąć**⟩ (*-czę*) **1.** ***~czy mi w brzuchu*** my stomach is rumbling **2.** (*zrzędzić*) grumble
burda *f* (*-dy*; *-dy*) **1.** (*bójka*) brawl **2.** (*kłótnia*) row
burdel *m* (*-lu*; *-le*) **1.** (*dom publiczny*) brothel **2.** (*bałagan*) mess
burgund *m* (*-da*; *-dy*) burgundy
burkliwy *adj* gruff
burknąć *v/p* (*-nę*) grunt
burmistrz *m* (*-rza*; *-rzowie*) mayor
bursa *f* (*-sy*; *-sy*) *Br* hall of residence; *Am* dormitory
bursztyn *m* (*-nu*; *-ny*) amber; **bursztynowy** *adj* amber
burt|a *f* (*-ty*; *-ty*) side; ***człowiek za ~ą!*** man overboard!; ***lewa ~a*** port, larboard; ***prawa ~a*** starboard; ***wyrzucić coś za ~ę*** throw s.th. overboard
bury *adj* dun
burz|a *f* (*-rzy*; *-rze*) storm; ***cisza przed ~ą*** the calm before the storm; ***~a piaskowa*** sandstorm; ***~a śnieżna*** snowstorm; ***~a mózgów*** brainstorming; ***~a w szklance wody*** *Br* a storm in a teacup, *Am* a tempest in a teapot; ***~a z piorunami*** thunderstorm
burzliwość *f* (*-ści*; *no pl*) **1.** *dyskusji*: heat **2.** *życia*, *czasów*: turbulence; **burzliwy** *adj* **1.** *dyskusja*: heated **2.** *oklaski*: thunderous **3.** *życie*, *czasy*: turbulent
burzow|y *adj* *pogoda*, *dzień*: stormy; ***chmura ~a*** storm cloud; ***kanał ~y*** storm drain
burzyć ⟨**z-**⟩ (*-rzę*) **1.** *dom*, *mur*: knock down, demolish **2.** (*niszczyć*) destroy **3.** *włosy*: ruffle **4.** *spokój*: disturb; ***burzyć się*** **1.** (*o włosach*) ruffle **2.** (*buntować się*) rebel (**przeciw** *D* against) **3.** (*denerwować się*) seethe
burżuazyjny *adj* bourgeois
burżuj *m* (*-ja*; *-je*) *iron* capitalist
busola *f* (*-li*; *-le*) compass
busz *m* (*-szu*; *no pl*) (the) bush; **buszować** *v/im* (*-szuję*) (*po szufladach*, *szafkach*) rummage (**po** *L* through) **2.** (*po lesie*) scour; ***~ po Internecie*** surf the Internet; ***~ po sklepach*** shop around
but *m* (*-ta*; *-ty*) **1.** shoe **2.** (*z cholewką*) boot; ***głupi jak ~*** *Br* (as) daft as a brush
buta *f* (*-ty*; *no pl*) haughtiness
butelczyna *f* (*-ny*; *-ny*) bottle; **buteleczka** *f* (*-ki*; *-ki*) *dim* (small) bottle
butelk|a *f* (*-ki*; *-ki*) bottle; ***~a wina*** bottle of wine; ***nabić w ~ę*** *infml* take s.o. for a ride; **butelkowy** *adj* **1.** *piwo*, *mleko*: bottled **2.** (*kolor*) bottle green
butik *m* (*-ku*; *-ki*) boutique
butla *f* (*-li*; *-le*) **1.** (large) bottle **2.** (*z gazem*) cylinder, bottle; ***~ tlenowa*** oxygen cylinder
butny *adj* haughty
butonierka *f* (*-ki*; *-ki*) (lapel) buttonhole
butwieć ⟨**z-**⟩ (*-wieję*) rot, decay
buzi|a *f* (*-zi*; *-zie*) **1.** (*usta*) mouth; ***dać komuś ~*** give s.o. a kiss **2.** (*twarz*) face
buziak *m* (*-ka*; *-ki*) (*całus*) kiss
buzować *v/im* (*-zuję*) blaze
by **I** *conj* to; ***powiedziała mu, ~ został*** she told him to stay **II** *particle* (*w trybie warunkowym*) ***poszedłby, gdyby mógł*** he would go if he could
byci|e *n* (*-cia*; *no pl*) being; ***~e szczęśliwym*** being happy; ***sposób ~a*** manner
byczek *m* (*-czka*; *-czki*) bull calf; **by-**

C

cz|y *adj* **1.** bull's; **~a skóra** bullhide **2.** *farma*, *kark*: bull; **byczyć się** *v/im* (*-czę*) *infml* laze around

być *v/im* (*jestem*) be; **będę pamiętać** I will remember; **~ może** maybe; **~ za** *I* (*popierać*) *Br* be in favour of, *Am* be in favor of; **~ z kimś na ty** be on the first-name basis with s.o.; **było ich trzech** there were three of them; **było mi smutno** I was sad; **było późno** it was late; **co będzie, jeśli ona nie przyjdzie?** what if she doesn't come?; **co jest na obiad?** what's for dinner?; **co ci jest?** what's wrong with you?; **czy jest? a)** is there? **b)** (*w sklepie*) do you have?; **czy jest Bóg?** is there a God?; **jestem samochodem** I've come by car; **jestem z Europy** I'm from Europe, I come from Europe; **jesteśmy po śniadaniu** we've (already) had breakfast; **jest mi głupio** I feel stupid; **jest mi zimno** I'm cold; **jest moim chłopakiem** he is my boyfriend; **(jest) już po wszystkim** it's all over; **jest zima** it is winter; **nie może ~!** it can't be!; **tak jest!** yes sir!; **to jest ze szkła** it's made of glass; → **nie ma**

bydlę *n* (*-lęcia*; *-lęta*) beast; **bydlęcy** *adj* **1.** *wagon*, *choroba*: cattle **2.** *życie*: beastly

bydło *n* (*-ła*; *no pl*) cattle

byk *m* (*-ka*; *-ki*) **1.** (*zwierzę*) bull **2.** (*błąd*) *infml* (spelling) mistake; **silny jak ~** (as) strong as an ox; **stoi jak ~** it's in front of your eyes; **wziąć ~a za rogi** take the bull by its horns **3.** **~** *ASTR* Taurus

byle I *adv* any; **~ co a)** (*jakakolwiek rzecz*) (just) anything **b)** (*tandeta*) trash; **~ gdzie** (just) anywhere; **~ jak** (just) anyhow; **~ jaki a)** (*jakikolwiek*) any **b)** (*kiepski*) trashy; **~ kto** (just) anybody; **nie ~ jaki wyczyn** no mean feat **II** *conj* (*aby*) (in order) to

byli → **być**

bylina *f* (*-ny*; *-ny*) perennial

był, **była**, **było** → **być**

były, **była** *adj* ex-, former; **~ mąż** ex-husband; **~ Związek Radziecki** the former Soviet Union

bynajmniej *particle lit*: **~ nie** by no means; **~!** not in the least!

by-pass *m* (*-su*; *-sy*) bypass; **operacja wszczepienia ~u** bypass (operation)

bystrość *f* (*-ści*; *no pl*) **1.** *umysłu*: brightness, *form* acuity **2.** *wzroku*: sharpness, *form* acuity **3.** *nurtu*: swiftness, rapidity; **bystry** *adj* **1.** *osoba*: bright, sharp-witted **2.** *wzrok*: acute, sharp **3.** *nurt*: swift, rapid

byt *m* (*-tu*; *-ty*) **1.** (*egzystencja*) existence **2.** *PHIL* being; **racja ~u** raison d'être; **walka o ~** struggle for survival; **bytność** *f* (*-ści*; *no pl*) stay; **bytow|y** *adj* existential; **warunki ~e** living conditions

bywa|ć *v/im* (*-wam*) **1.** (*na koncertach*, *na zebraniach*) go (**na** *L* to) **2.** (*z wizytą*) visit (**u** *G*) **3.** (*zdarzać się*) happen; **~, że** (sometimes) it happens that; **~ł zazdrosny** he was sometimes jealous

bywalczyni *f* (*-ni*; *-nie*) **1.** frequent visitor **2.** (*stała klientka*) regular, *form* patron

bywalec *m* (*-lca*; *-lcy*) **1.** frequent visitor **2.** (*stały klient*) regular, *form* patron; **bywały** *adj* **1.** (*doświadczony*) frequent visitor **2.** (*światowy*) worldly

b.z. *abbr* (= **bez zmian**) no change

bzdet *m* (*-tu*; *-ty*) *infml* nonsense, *Br* rubbish

bzdur|a *f* (*-ry*; *-ry*) nonsense, *Br* rubbish; **pleść ~y** talk nonsense; **bzdurny** *adj* nonsensical

bzik *m* (*-ka*; *no pl*) *infml*: **dostać ~a** go nuts; **mieć ~a** be nuts (**na punkcie** *G* about)

bzów, **bzu** → **bez**[1]

bzyczeć ⟨**bzyknąć**⟩ (*-czę*) hum, buzz

C

cackać się *v/im* (*-kam*): **~ z kimś** (**czymś**) handle s.o. (s.th.) in kid gloves; **cacko** *n* (*-ka*; *-ka*) gem

cacy *adj infml* lovely

cal *m* (*-la*; *-le*) inch; **dżentelmen w każdym ~u** every inch a gentleman

C

cali *pl* → **cały**
calówka *f* (*-ki*; *-ki*) *folding rule marked in inches and centimetres*
całka *f* (*-ki*; *-ki*) *MATH* integral; **całkiem** *adv* **1.** (*zupełnie*) entirely, completely; **~ sam** all alone **2.** (*dość*) quite, *infml* pretty; **~ nieźle** not (so) bad
całkowicie *adv* totally, completely; **~ popieram** I totally agree; **~ umeblowany** fully furnished
całkowit|y *adj* **1.** total, complete; **~e zaćmienie Słońca** total solar eclipse; **mieć ~ą rację** be entirely right **2.** *suma*: total
całkowy *adj*: **rachunek ~** integral calculus
cało *adv*: **wyjść ~** (*z wypadku*) escape unhurt
całodobowy *adj* 24-hour; **całodniowy**, **całodzienny** *adj* **1.** *wycieczka, wyjazd*: all-day, *Am* daylong **2.** *praca*: full day's **3.** *bilet*, *wyżywienie*: daily
całokształt *m* (*-tu*; *no pl*) the whole; **~ sytuacji** the whole situation; **nagroda za ~ twórczości** lifetime achievement award
całonocny *adj* all-night; **całoroczny** *adj* **1.** *przerwa*: yearlong **2.** *zysk*: yearly
całostronicowy *adj* full-page
całościowy *adj* **1.** *opracowanie*, *ujęcie*: comprehensive **2.** *obraz*, *charakter*: overall
całoś|ć *f* (*-ści*; *no pl*) whole; **iść na ~ć** *infml* go the whole hog; **przeczytać artykuł w ~ci** read the whole article; **w ~ci poświęcony** devoted entirely to
całotygodniowy *adj* **1.** *wizyta*, *przerwa*: week-long **2.** *utarg*: weekly
całować ⟨**po-**, **u-**⟩ (*-łuję*) kiss; **~ kogoś w usta** kiss s.o.'s lips; **całować się** kiss
całun *m* (*-nu*; *-ny*) shroud
całus *m* (*-sa*; *-sy*) kiss; **posłać komuś ~a** blow s.o. a kiss
cał|y *adj* **1.** whole; **~y czas** all the time; **~y dzień** all day (long); **na ~y głos** at the top of one's voice; **na ~y regulator** at full volume; **na ~ym świecie** all over the world; **z ~ej siły** with all one's strength; **~e szczęście, że** fortunately **2.** (*nieuszkodzony*) intact **3.** (*zdrów*) unhurt; **~y i zdrowy** safe and sound **4.** (*jedyny*) only; **to ~y mój majątek** that's all I have

camping → **kemping**
cap *m* (*-pa*; *-py*) *infml* dork
capnąć *v/p* (*-nę*) *infml* **1.** (*chwycić*) grab **2.** (*aresztować*) nab *infml*
capstrzyk *m* (*-ku*; *-ki*) tattoo
car (*-ra*; *-rowie*) tsar, czar; **caryca** *f* (*-cy*; *-ce*) tsarina, czarina; **carski** *adj* tsarist, czarist
cążki *pl* (*-ków*/*-żek*) pincers; **~ do paznokci** nail clippers
CD *n indecl* CD, compact disc
CD-ROM *m* (*-ROM-u*; *-ROM-y*) (*pamięć*) CD-ROM
cdn. *abbr* (= **ciąg dalszy nastąpi**) cont., contd
ceb|er *m*: **leje jak z ~ra** it's raining cats and dogs
cebula *f* (*-li*; *-le*) onion; **cebulka** *f* (*-ki*; *-ki*) **1.** *dim* (small) onion **2.** *rośliny*: bulb **3.** *włosa*: root; **cebulowaty** *adj* bulbous; **cebulkowy** *adj rośliny*: bulbous **cebulow|y** *adj* onion; **zupa ~a** onion soup
cech *m* (*-chu*; *-chy*) guild
cecha *f* (*-chy*; *-chy*) feature; **~ charakteru** character trait; **~ charakterystyczna** characteristic (feature)
cechować *v/im* (*-chuję*) be characteristic of; **cechować się**: **~ się czymś** be characterized by s.th., be marked by s.th.
cedować ⟨**s-**⟩ (*-duję*) cede (**na** *G* to)
cedr *m* (*-ru*; *-ry*) cedar; **cedrowy** *adj* cedar
ceduła *f* (*-ły*; *-ły*) *FIN* official quotation list
cedzak *m* (*-ka*; *-ki*) colander
cedzić (*-dzę*) **1.** ⟨**prze-**⟩ *kartofle*: strain **2.** *napój*: sip; **~ słowa** ⟨**wy-**⟩ drawl
cegielnia *f* (*-ni*; *-nie*) brickyard; **cegiełka** *f* (*-ki*; *-ki*) *fig* contribution
ceglany *adj* brick; **ceglasty** *adj* (*kolor*) brick-red; **cegła** *f* (*-ły*; *-ły*) **1.** brick **2.** (*gruba książka*) *infml* tome
Cejlon *m* (*-nu*) Ceylon; **cejlońsk|i** *adj* Ceylonese; **herbata ~a** Ceylon tea
cekaem *m* (*-mu*; *-my*) heavy machine gun
cekin *m* (*-na*/*-nu*; *-ny*) sequin
cel *m* (*-lu*; *-le*) **1.** (*obiekt starań*) aim, goal; **bez ~u** aimlessly; **~ sam w sobie** a goal in itself; **~ uświęca środki** the end justifies the means; **mijać się z ~em** be pointless **2.** (*przeznaczenie*)

purpose; ***do ~ów dydaktycznych*** for educational purposes; ***mieć na ~u*** aim at; ***na ~e dobroczynne*** for charity; ***w ~u zrobienia czegoś*** in order to do s.th.; ***w tym ~u*** for this purpose **3.** (*tarcza*, *obiekt*) target; ***do ~u*** at the target **4.** (*miejsce przeznaczenia*) destination; ***~ podróży*** destination

cela *f* (*-li*; *-le*) cell; ***~ więzienna*** prison cell; ***~ śmierci*** death cell

celebrować *v/im* (*-ruję*) **1.** *mszę*: celebrate **2.** *czynność*: make a ritual of

celiakia *f* (*-ki*; *no pl*) MED *Br* coeliac disease, *Am* celiac disease

celiba|t *m* (*-tu*; *no pl*) celibacy; ***żyć w ~cie*** be celibate

celnik *m* (*-ka*; *-nicy*), **-niczka** *f* (*-ki*; *-ki*) customs officer

celność *f* (*-ści*; *no pl*) **1.** *strzału*: accuracy **2.** *uwagi*: aptness

celny[1] *adj* **1.** *strzał*: accurate **2.** *uwaga*: apt

celn|y[2] *adj* (*dotyczący cła*) customs; ***opłata ~a*** (customs) duty; ***urząd ~y*** customs office; ***odprawa ~a*** customs clearance

celofan *m* (*-nu*; *no pl*) cellophane

celować[1] ⟨**wy-**⟩ (*-luję*) (*mierzyć*) take aim (**do** *G* at)

celować[2] *v/im* (*-luję*) (*wyróżniać się*) excel (**w** *L* in/at); **celownik** *m* (*-ka*; *-ki*) **1.** (*w broni*) sight(s); ***~ lunetowy*** telescopic sight **2.** GRAM dative **3.** PHOT viewfinder; **celowo** *adv* **1.** (*umyślnie*) on purpose, intentionally **2.** (*w jakimś celu*) purposefully; **celowość** *f* (*-ści*; *no pl*) purposefulness; **celowy** *adj* **1.** (*umyślny*) intentional, deliberate **2.** (*przemyślany*) purposeful

Celt *m* (*-ta*; *-towie*) Celt; **celtycki** *adj* Celtic

celujący *adj* excellent

celuloza *f* (*-zy*; *no pl*) cellulose

cement *m* (*-tu*; *-ty*) cement; **cementować** ⟨**za-**, **s-**⟩ (*-tuję*) cement; **cementownia** *f* (*-ni*; *-nie*) cement works; **cementowy** *adj* cement

cen|a *f* (*-ny*; *-ny*) price; ***~a kupna*** purchase price; ***po ~ie obniżonej*** at a reduced price; ***za ~ę*** *G* at the price of; ***za pół ~y*** (at) half-price; ***za wszelką ~ę*** at all costs

cenić *v/im* (*-nię*) value; ***wysoko sobie ~*** highly value; ***cenić się*** value oneself

ceniony *adj* valued; ***wysoko ~*** highly valued, highly regarded

cennik *m* (*-ka*; *-ki*) price list; **cenny** *adj* precious, valuable

cenowy *adj* price

centrala *f* (*-li*; *-le*) **1.** *instytucji*: head office **2.** TEL (telephone) exchange **3.** (*w firmie*, *hotelu*) TEL switchboard; **centralizacja** *f* (*-ji*; *no pl*) centralization; **centraln|y** *adj* central; ***~e ogrzewanie*** central heating

centrum *n* (*indecl*; *-ra*) *Br* centre, *Am* center; ***~ handlowe*** shopping centre; ***~ obliczeniowe*** computational centre

centymetr *m* (*-ra*; *-ry*) **1.** (*jednostka*) *Br* centimetre, *Am* centimeter **2.** (*taśma*) tape measure

cenzura *f* (*-ry*; *no pl*) censorship; **cenzurka** *f* (*-ki*; *-ki*) school certificate; **cenzurować** ⟨**o-**⟩ (*-ruję*) censor

cep *m* (*-pa*; *-py*) **1.** (*narzędzie*) flail **2.** (*osoba*) *infml* dork

cera[1] *f* (*-ry*; *no pl*) (*skóra*) complexion

cera[2] *f* (*-ry*; *-ry*) (*w pończosze*) darn

ceramiczny *adj* ceramic; **ceramika** *f* (*-ki*; *no pl*) **1.** ceramics; ***~ szlachetna*** fine ceramics **2.** (*z gliny*) pottery

cerata *f* (*-ty*; *-ty*) oilcloth

ceregiel|e *pl* (*-li*) *infml*: ***bez ~i*** **a)** (*bez ceremonii*) without ceremony **b)** (*bez problemów*) with no hassle; ***robić ~e*** make a fuss

ceremonia *f* (*-nii*; *-nie*) ceremony; **ceremonialny** *adj* **1.** ceremonial **2.** (*formalny*) *form* ceremonious

cerkiew *f* (*-kwi*; *-kwie*) (Orthodox) church; **cerkiewn|y** *adj* (Orthodox) church; ***muzyka ~a*** Orthodox church music

cerować ⟨**za-**⟩ (*-ruję*) *pończochę*: darn

certolić się *v/im* (*-lę*) *infml*: ***~ z kimś*** (***czymś***) handle s.o. (s.th.) in kid gloves

certyfikat *m* (*-tu*; *-ty*) certificate; ***~ pochodzenia*** certificate of origin

cesarski *adj* imperial; ***~e cięcie*** *Br* Caesarean section, *Am* Cesarean section; **cesarstwo** *n* (*-wa*; *-wa*) empire

cesarz *m* (*-rza*; *-rze*) emperor; **cesarzowa** *f* (*-wej*; *-we*) empress

cesja *f* (*-ji*; *-je*) **1.** JUR assignment **2.** POLIT cession

C

cetnar *m* (*-ra*; *-ry*) hundredweight
cewka *f* (*-ki*; *-ki*) **1.** TECH coil; **~ *zapłonowa*** ignition coil **2.** ANAT duct; **~ *moczowa*** urethra
cewnik *m* (*-ka*; *-ki*) catheter
cez *m* (*-zu*; *no pl*) *Br* caesium, *Am* cesium
cezar *m* (*-ra*; *-rowie*) Caesar
cęgi *pl* (*-gów*) pincers
cętk|a *f* (*-ki*; *-ki*) spot; ***w ~i*** spotted; **cętkowany** *adj* spotted
chaber *m* (*-bra*; *-bry*) bluebottle, cornflower; **chabrowy** *adj* sapphire
chadecja *f* (*-ji*; *no pl*) Christian democrats *pl*; **chadecki** *adj* Christian democrat; **chadek** *m* (*-ka*; *-decy*) Christian democrat
chadzać *v/im* (*-dzam*) **1.** (*udawać się*) go (from time to time) **2.** (*nosić*) wear (**w** *L*)
chała *f* (*-ły*; *-ły*) *infml* trash
chałat *m* (*-tu*; *-ty*) Jewish gaberdine
chałka *f* (*-ki*; *-ki*) plaited bread, challah
chałtura *f* (*-ry*; *-ry*) *infml* **1.** (*dodatkowa praca*) extra job **2.** (*sztuka, książka*) potboiler
chałup|a *f* (*-py*; *-py*) **1.** (*na wsi*) cottage, hut **2.** (*mieszkanie*) *infml* place; ***w ~ie*** at one's place
chałupnictwo *n* (*-wa*; *no pl*) cottage industry
chałupnik *m* (*-ka*; *-nicy*), **-niczka** *f* (*-ki*; *-ki*) homeworker
chałwa *f* (*-wy*; *-wy*) halva(h)
cham *m* (*-ma*; *-my*); **~ka** *f* (*-ki*; *-ki*) cad, boor; **chamski** *adj* boorish, caddish; **chamstwo** *n* (*-wa*; *no pl*) *Br* boorish behaviour, *Am* boorish behavior
chan *m* (*-na*; *-nowie*) HIST khan
chandr|a *f* (*-ry*; *no pl*) the blues; ***mieć ~ę*** be down in the dumps *infml*
chaos *m* (*-su*; *no pl*) chaos; **chaotyczny** *adj* chaotic
charakter *m* (*-ru*; *-ry*) charakter; ***być człowiekiem bez ~u*** have a weak character; ***~ pisma*** handwriting; ***czarny ~*** villain; ***w ~ze gościa*** as a guest; ***z ~em*** of character; **charakterystyczn|y** *adj* characteristic (***dla*** *G* of); ***cecha ~a*** characteristic; **charakterystyka** *f* (*-ki*; *-ki*) **1.** (*opis*) profile **2.** TECH characteristic; **charakteryzacja** *f* (*-ji*; *-je*) THEAT make-up; **charakteryzator** *m* (*-ra*; *-rzy*), **~ka** *f* (*-ki*; *-ki*) make-up artist
charakteryz|ować (*-zuję*) **1.** ⟨**s-**⟩ (*opisywać*) characterize, describe **2.** *v/im* (*cechować*) ***coś ~uje kogoś*** (***coś***) s.o. (s.th.) is characterized by s.th. **3.** ⟨**u-**⟩ THEAT *twarz*: put make-up on; ***charakteryzować się*** be characterized (*I* by)
charczeć (*-czę*) **1.** ⟨**za-**⟩ (*rzęzić*) wheeze **2.** ⟨**wy-**⟩ (*mówić*) speak in a hoarse voice
charkot *m* (*-tu*; *-ty*) wheeze
chart *m* (*-ta*; *-ty*) greyhound; ***~ afgański*** Afghan hound; ***~ perski*** saluki; ***~ rosyjski*** borzoi, Russian wolfhound
charytatywn|y *adj działalność*: charity; ***instytucja ~a*** charity; ***na cele ~e*** for charity
charyzma *f* (*-my*; *no pl*) charisma; **charyzmatyczny** *adj* charismatic
chaszcze *pl* (*-czy*/*-czów*) thicket *sing*
cha|ta *f* (*-ty*; *-ty*) **1.** (*na wsi*) cottage, hut **2.** (*mieszkanie*) *infml* place; ***w ~cie*** at one's place
chc|ieć *v/im* (*-cę*) **1.** (*pragnąć*) want; ***~ieć coś zrobić*** want to do s.th.; ***~ę, żebyś przyszła*** I want you to come; ***~iałbym*** I'd like; ***~iałbym coś zrobić*** I'd like to do s.th.; ***czy ~iałbyś zostać?*** would you like to stay?; ***jak ~esz*** as you wish **2.** (*mieć ochotę*) feel like; ***~e mi się płakać*** I feel like crying; ***~e mi się jeść*** (***pić***) I'm hungry (thirsty) **3.** (*z rzeczownikami nieżywotnymi*) ***zamek nie ~iał się otworzyć*** the lock wouldn't open
chciwie *adv* greedily; **chciwiec** *m* (*-wca*; *-wcy*) greedy person; **chciwość** *f* (*-ści*; *no pl*) greed; **chciwy** *adj* greedy (***na*** *A* for); ***~ na pieniądze*** greedy for money, money-greedy
chełbia *f* (*-bi*; *-bie*) moon jellyfish
chełpić się *v/im* (*-pię*) brag (*I* about); **chełpliwość** *f* (*-ści*, *no pl*) boastfulness; **chełpliwy** *adj* boastful
chemia *f* (*-mii*; *no pl*) chemistry; ***~ nieorganiczna*** inorganic chemistry; **chemiczka** *f* (*-ki*; *-ki*) chemist; **chemiczn|y** *adj* chemical; ***pralnia ~a*** dry cleaner's; **chemik** *m* (*-ka*; *-micy*) chemist; **chemikalia** *pl* (*-liów*) chemicals; **chemioterapia** *f* (*-pii*; *no pl*) chemotherapy

cherlak *m* (*-ka*; *-lacy*) weakling; **cherlawy** *adj* sickly
cherubinek *m* (*-nka*; *-nki*) cherub
chę|ć *f* (*chęci*; *chęci*) **1.** (*pragnienie*) desire; ***mieć ~ć coś zrobić*** feel like doing s.th.; ***z ~cią*** with pleasure **2.** (*wola*) will; ***~ć do życia*** (***pracy***) a will to live (work) **3.** (*zamiar*) intention; ***mieć dobre ~ci*** mean well; ***pomimo najszczerszych ~ci*** despite best intentions
chętk|a *f* (*-ki*; *-ki*) *infml* hankering, *Br* fancy; ***mieć ~ę na*** *A* **a)** have a hankering for **b)** (*na kogoś*) *Br* fancy; **chętnie** *adv* willingly; ***~!*** with pleasure!; **chętny** *adj* willing; ***~ do pomocy*** (***nauki***) willing to help (study)
chichot *m* (*-tu*; *-ty*) giggle; **chichotać** ⟨**za-**⟩ (*-choczę*) giggle (**z** *G* at)
Chile *n indecl* Chile
chili *n indecl Br* chilli, *Am* chili
chilijski *adj* Chilean
chimer|a *f* (*-ry*; *-ry*) (*potwór*, *fantazja*) chimera; ***~y*** (*kaprysy*) whims; **chimeryczny** *adj* capricious, fickle
chinina *f* (*-ny*; *no pl*) quinine
Chink|a *f* (*-ki*; *-ki*) Chinese woman; ***jest ~ą*** she is Chinese; **Chiny** *pl* (*Chin*) China *sing*; **Chińczyk** *m* (*-ka*; *-czycy*) Chinese; ***są ~ami*** they are Chinese; **chińsk|i** *adj* Chinese; ***po ~u*** in Chinese; ***mówić po ~u*** speak Chinese
chińszczyzna *f* (*-ny*; *no pl*) **1.** (*język*) Chinese; ***to dla mnie ~*** *fig* it's all Greek to me **2.** COOK Chinese food
chip *m* (*-pa*; *-py*) chip, microchip
chipsy, **czipsy** *pl* (*-sów*) *Br* crisps, *Am* chips
chiromancja *f* (*-ji*; *no pl*) palmistry
chirurg *m* (*-ga*; *-rdzy*/*-gowie*) surgeon; **chirurgia** *f* (*-gii*; *no pl*) surgery; ***~ plastyczna*** plastic surgery; ***~ urazowa*** wound surgery
chirurgiczny *adj* surgical; ***zabieg ~*** operation, surgery
chlać *v/im* (*-lam*/*-leję*) *infml* booze *infml*
chlapa *f* (*-py*; *-py*) *infml* rainy weather; **chlapać** ⟨**na-**, **-pnąć**⟩ (*-pię*) splash; ***chlapać się*** splash around
chlastać ⟨**-snąć**⟩ (*-tam*/*-szczę*) (*uderzać*) smack; ***chlastać się*** (*ciąć*) slash oneself
chleb *m* (*-ba*; *-by*) bread; ***~ z masłem*** bread and butter; ***o ~ie i wodzie*** on bread and water; ***zarabiać na ~*** earn a living; **chlebak** *m* (*-ka*; *-ki*) haversack
chlebodawca *m* (*-cy*; *-cy*), **-czyni** *f* (*-ni*; *-nie*) employer
chlebow|y *adj piec*, *ciasto*: bread; ***drzewo ~e*** breadfruit
chlew *m* (*-wu*; *-wy*) pigsty; **chlewn|y** *adj*: ***trzoda ~a*** swine, pigs
chlipać ⟨**-pnąć**⟩ (*-pię*) sob
chlor *m* (*-ru*; *no pl*) CHEM chlorine; **chlorek** *m* (*-rku*; *-rki*) chloride; ***~ sodu*** sodium chloride; **chlorofil** *m* (*-lu*; *no pl*) chlorophyll; **chloroform** *m* (*-mu*; *no pl*) chloroform; **chlorować** *v/im* (*-ruję*) chlorinate; **chlorowodór** *m* (*-ru*; *no pl*) hydrogen chloride
chlub|a *f* (*-by*; *no pl*) pride; ***być ~ą*** be the pride (*G* of); ***przynosić komuś ~ę*** do s.o. credit; **chlubić się** *v/im* (*-bię*) take pride (*I* in); **chlubn|y** *adj czyn*, *wyjątek*: glorious; ***dawać ~e świadectwo*** do credit to
chlupać ⟨**-pnąć**⟩ (*-pię*) **1.** (*o wodzie*) splash **2.** (*o błocie*) squelch; ***chlupać się*** splash around
chlustać ⟨**-snąć**⟩ (*-tam*) **1.** (*wylewać*) splash **2.** (*tryskać*) spurt, gush **3.** (*o brzeg*) splash
chłam *m* (*-mu*; *no pl*) *infml* trash
chłeptać ⟨**wy-**⟩ (*-pczę*/*-pcę*) lap
chłodek *m* (*-dku*; *-dki*) the cool; **chłodnawo** *adv*: ***jest ~*** it's fairly cold; **chłodnawy** *adj* fairly cold, coolish; **chłodnia** *f* (*-ni*; *-nie*) **1.** (*pomieszczenie*) refrigerated room **2.** (*pojazd*) refrigerated truck; **chłodnica** *f* (*-cy*; *-ce*) AUTO radiator; **chłodniczy** *adj* **1.** *technika*, *urządzenia*: refrigeration **2.** *pomieszczenie*, *pojazd*: refrigerated
chłodnik *m* (*-ka*; *-ki*) *fruit or beetroot soup served cold*
chłodno *adv* **1.** ***jest ~*** it's rather cold **2.** *odezwać się*, *przywitać*: coolly; **chłodny** *adj* cool
chłodząc|y *adj* cooling; ***napoje ~e*** cold drinks
chłodziarka *f* (*-ki*; *-ki*) refrigerator; **chłodzić** ⟨**o-**⟩ (*-dzę*) **1.** (*ochładzać*) cool, chill **2.** (*zamrażać*) freeze **3.** (*o lodówce*) refrigerate; ***chłodzić się*** **1.** (*o napoju*) be chilling **2.** (*o czło-*

C

wieku) cool oneself down; **chłodzony** *adj*: **~ wodą** water-cooled

chłonąć ⟨**w-**⟩ (*-nę*) **1.** absorb **2.** *słowa*, *widoki*: drink in; **chłonność** *f* (*-ści*; *no pl*) absorption capacity; **chłonny** *adj* **1.** *materiał*: absorbent **2.** *umysł*: receptive **3. węzeł ~** ANAT lymph gland

chłop *m* **1.** (*-pa*; *-pi*) (*rolnik*) peasant **2.** (*-pa*; *-py*) (*mężczyzna*) *infml* man, *Br infml* chap; **chłopak** *m* (*-ka*; *-ki*/*-pacy*) **1.** boy **2.** (*sympatia*) boyfriend; **chłopczyca** *f* (*-cy*; *-ce*) tomboy; **chłopczyk** *m* (*-ka*; *-ki*) *dim* (little) boy

chłopiec *m* (*-pca*; *-pcy*) **1.** boy **2.** (*sympatia*) boyfriend; **~ *na posyłki*** office boy; **~ *okrętowy*** ship-boy

chłopięcy *adj* **1.** *odzież*, *zabawy*, *chór*: boys' **2.** *figura*, *wdzięk*: boyish; ***wiek*** **~** boyhood

chłopka *f* (*-ki*; *-ki*) peasant woman; **chłopski** *adj* peasant; **~ *rozum*** common sense; **chłopstwo** *n* (*-wa*; *no pl*) peasantry

chłost|a *f* (*-ty*; *-ty*) whipping; ***kara ~y*** whipping; **chłostać** ⟨**wy-**⟩ (*-szczę*) whip

chłód *m* (*-łodu*; *-łody*) **1.** (slight) cold **2.** (*oziębłość*) coldness

chłystek *m* (*-tka*; *-tki*) whippersnapper *infml*

chmara *f* (*-ry*; *-ry*) **1.** *owadów*, *ptaków*: swarm **2.** *ludzi*, *dzieci*: horde

chmiel *m* (*-lu*; *no pl*) hop

chmura *f* (*-ry*; *-ry*) cloud; **~ *deszczowa*** rain cloud; **chmurka** *f* (*-ki*; *-ki*) *dim* (small) cloud; **chmurny** *adj* **1.** *niebo*, *dzień*: overcast **2.** *osoba*: sulky **3.** *wzrok*: gloomy

chmurzyć ⟨**na-**⟩ (*-rzę*): **~ *czoło*** frown; ***chmurzyć się*** ⟨**za-**, **na-**⟩ **1.** (*o niebie*) become cloudy **2.** (*o osobie*) frown

chochla *f* (*-li*; *-le*) ladle

chochlik *m* (*-ka*; *-ki*) imp; **~ *drukarski*** misprint

chociaż **I** *conj* although, though **II** *particle* (*przynajmniej*) at least; **chociażby**, ***choćby*** **I** *conj* even if **II** *particle* (*przynajmniej*) at least

chodak *m* (*-ka*; *-ki*) clog

chodnik *m* (*-ka*; *-ki*) **1.** (*na ulicy*) *Br* pavement, *Am* sidewalk **2.** (*dywanik*) runner **3.** GÓRN gallery

chody *pl* (*-dów*): ***mieć ~*** have connections, have friends in high places; → ***chód***

chodząc|y *adj*: ***~a dobroć*** the embodiment of goodness; ***~a encyklopedia*** know-all

chodzi|ć *v/im* (*-dzę*) **1.** (*pieszo*) walk; ***~ć na ryby*** (***grzyby***) go fishing (mushrooming); ***~ć na palcach*** tiptoe; ***~ć na spacer*** go for a walk; ***~ć na zakupy*** do the shopping; ***~ć o lasce*** walk with a stick; ***~ć po mieście*** walk around town; ***~ć za kimś*** follow s.o.; ***chodźmy!*** let's go!; ***chodź tu!*** come here! **2.** (*bywać*, *uczęszczać*) go; ***~ć do szkoły*** (***pracy***) go to school (work) **3.** (*nosić*) wear (**w** *L*) **4.** (*spotykać się*) go out (**z** *I* with), *Am* date (**z** *I*) **5.** *infml* (*funkcjonować*) work **6.** *infml* (*być włączonym*) be working; ***~ mi o*** *A* I mean, I'm talking about; ***~ o to, że*** the thing is (that); ***jeżeli o mnie ~*** as far as I'm concerned; ***o co ~?*** what's the matter?, what's the problem?; ***o co ci ~?*** what are you talking about?

choink|a *f* (*-ki*; *-ki*) **1.** (*w lesie*) spruce **2.** (*świąteczna*) Christmas tree; ***dostać coś pod ~ę*** get s.th. for Christmas

choinkowy *adj* **1.** *ozdoby*: Christmas tree **2.** *zagajnik*: spruce

choler|a *f* (*-ry*; *no pl*) **1.** (*choroba*) cholera **2.** (*przekleństwo*) *infml* ***~a!*** damn!; ***~y można od tego dostać!*** it's driving me crazy!; ***idź do ~y*** go to hell!; ***jak ~a*** like hell; ***po ~ę?*** what the hell for?

cholern|y *adj infml* **1.** damn, *Br* bloody; ***miał ~e szczęście*** he was damn lucky **2.** *bałagan*: terrible

cholerstwo *n* (*-wa*; *-wa*) *infml* beast, bugger

choleryczny *adj* **1.** *osoba*: hot-tempered; ***mieć ~ temperament*** be hot-tempered **2.** *cmentarz*: cholera; **choleryk** *m* (*-ka*; *-rycy*) hot-tempered person; ***być ~iem*** be hot-tempered

cholesterol *m* (*-lu*; *no pl*) cholesterol

cholew|a *f* (*-wy*; *-wy*) (boot) upper; ***buty z ~ami*** boots; **cholewka** *f* (*-ki*; *-ki*) (shoe) upper

chomąto *n* (*-ta*; *-ta*) (horse) collar

chomik *m* (*-ka*; *-ki*) hamster; **chomikować** ⟨**za-**⟩ (*-kuję*) hoard
chorągiew *f* (*-gwi*; *-gwie*) **1.** (*flaga*) flag **2.** (*w harcerstwie*) area; **chorągiewka** *f* (*-ki*; *-ki*) (small) flag; **chorąży** *m* (*-żego*; *-żowie*) warrant officer
choreograficzny *adj* choreographic
chorob|a *f* (*-by*; *-by*) **1.** (*schorzenie*) illness, disease **2.** (*stan*) illness; **~a Heinego-Medina** polio; **~a morska** seasickness; **~a popromienna** radiation sickness; **~a serca** heart disease; **~a szalonych krów** mad cow disease, BSE; **~a umysłowa** mental illness; **~a zakaźna** infectious illness, contagious disease; **~a zawodowa** occupational disease; **z powodu ~y** due to illness
chorobliwy *adj* morbid; **chorobotwórczy** *adj* pathogenic; **chorobow|y** *adj* **1.** *objawy*: disease **2.** *zmiany*: pathological **3.** *ubezpieczenie*: medical; **karta ~a** medical record; **zasiłek ~y** *Br* sickness benefit; **chorobow|e** *n* (*-wego*; *no pl*) *infml Br* sickness benefit; **na ~ym** on sick leave
chorować ⟨**za-**⟩ (*-ruję*) be ill; **~ na serce** have a heart problem; **~ na grypę** have the flu
chorowitość *f* (*-ści*; *no pl*) sickliness
chorowity *adj* sickly
Chorwacja *f* (*-ji*) Croatia; **chorwack|i** *adj* Croatian; **mówić po ~u** speak Croatian; **po ~u** in Croatian
Chorwat *m* (*-ta*; *-waci*), **~ka** *f* (*-ki*; *-ki*) Croat; **są ~ami** they are Croatian
chory **I** *adj* **1.** *osoba*, *zwierzę*: ill, sick; **być ~m na AIDS (grypę)** have AIDS (the flu); **być ~m na serce** have a heart problem; **~ umysłowo** mentally ill **2.** *noga*, *serce*, *ząb*: bad **3.** *roślina*, *gospodarka*: sick **4.** *infml* (*szalony*) mental **II** *m* (*-rego*; *-rzy*), **-ra** *f* (*-rej*; *-re*) **1.** (*chora osoba*) sick person **2.** (*pacjent*) patient
chować (*-wam*) **1.** ⟨**s-**⟩ (*ukrywać*) hide **2.** ⟨**s-**⟩ (*wkładać*) put; **~ ręce do kieszeni** put one's hands in one's pockets **3.** ⟨**s-**⟩ (*trzymać*) keep **4.** ⟨**po-**⟩ (*do grobu*) bury **5.** ⟨**wy-**⟩ (*wychowywać*) bring up; **~ urazę** hold a grudge; **chować się 1.** ⟨**s-**⟩ (*ukrywać się*) hide **2.** ⟨**wy-**⟩ (*rosnąć*) grow up
chowan|y **I** *m* (*-nego*; *no pl*): **bawić się w ~ego** play hide and seek **II** *adj podwozie*: retractable
chód *m* (*chodu*; *chody*) **1.** walk, gait **2. ~ sportowy** SPORT race walking **3. na chodzie** *infml* in (good) working order; → **chody**
chór *m* (*-ru*; *-ry*) **1.** (*zespół*) choir; **~em** in chorus **2.** (*utwór*) chorus; **chóralny** *adj muzyka*: choral; **chórek** *m* (*-rku*; *-rki*) *infml* backing singers
chórzysta *m* (*-ty*; *-rzyści*), **-tka** *f* (*-ki*; *-ki*) choir member, choir singer
chów *m* (*chowu*; *no pl*) breeding
chrabąszcz *m* (*-cza*; *-cze*) cockchafer
chrapać ⟨**-pnąć**⟩ (*-pię*) snore; **chrapanie** *n* (*-nia*; *no pl*) snoring
chrapk|a *f*: **mieć ~ę na** *A* **a)** have a hankering for, itch for **b)** (*na kogoś*) *Br* fancy
chrapliwy *adj* hoarse
chrapy *pl* (*chrap*/*-pów*) nostrils
ChRL *abbr f indecl* (= **Chińska Republika Ludowa**) PRC, People's Republic of China
chrobot *m* (*-tu*; *-ty*) **1.** grating **2.** *myszy*: scratching; **chrobotać** ⟨**za-**⟩ (*-boczę*/*-bocę*) **1.** grate **2.** (*o myszy*) scratch
chrom *m* (*-mu*; *no pl*) CHEM chrome
chromosom *m* (*-mu*; *-my*) chromosome
chromować *v*/*im* (*-muję*): **~ coś** chrome s.th., plate s.th. with chrome; **chromowany** *adj* chrome-plated
chroniczny *adj* chronic
chronić ⟨**o-**, **u-**⟩ (*-nię*) protect; (**przed** *I* from); **chronić się 1.** ⟨**s-**⟩ (*kryć się*) take cover **2.** ⟨**u-**⟩ (*zabezpieczać się*) protect oneself (**przed** *I* from) **3.** (*unikać*) avoid (**przed** *I*)
chroniony *adj* protected
chronologiczny *adj* chronological
chropawy, **chropowaty** *adj* rough
chropowatość *f* (*-ści*; *no pl*) roughness
chrupać ⟨**s-**⟩ (*-pię*) crunch (*A* on); **chrupiący** *adj* crunchy
chrupki **I** *adj* crunchy; **pieczywo ~e** crispbread **II** *pl* (*-pek*) crisps
chrust *m* (*-tu*; *no pl*) brushwood
chryja *f* (*-ryi*; *-je*) *infml* fracas, *infml* rhubarb
chrypk|a *f* (*-ki*; *-ki*) hoarse throat; **mieć ~ę** be hoarse; **chrypliwy** *adj* hoarse, raspy; **chrypnąć** ⟨**o-**⟩ (*-nę*) get hoarse

C

chrystianizacja *f* (*-ji*; *no pl*) Christianization
Chrystus *m* (*-sa*; *no pl*) Christ
chryzantema *f* (*-my*; *-my*) chrysanthemum
chrzan *m* (*-nu*; *no pl*) horseradish; ***do ~u*** *infml* no good; **chrzanić** ⟨**s-**⟩ (*-nię*) *infml* **1.** (*psuć*) mess up **2.** (*mówić głupstwa*) talk nonsense; ***chrzanić się*** (*psuć się*): ***radio się chrzani*** something's wrong with the radio
chrząkać ⟨**-knąć**⟩ (*-kam*) **1.** (*o osobie*) clear one's throat **2.** (*o świni*) grunt; **chrząkanie** *n* (*-nia*; *no pl*) **1.** (*o osobie*) clearing one's throat **2.** (*o świni*) grunting
chrząstka *f* (*-ki*; *-ki*) **1.** COOK gristle **2.** ANAT cartilage
chrząszcz *m* (*-cza*; *-cze*) beetle
chrzciciel: ***Jan*** ~ REL John the Baptist
chrzcić ⟨**o-**⟩ (*chrzczę*) **1.** (*udzielać chrztu*) baptize **2.** (*nadawać imię*) christen
chrzcielnica *f* (*-cy*; *-ce*) (baptismal) font
chrzciny *pl* (*chrzcin*) christening party
chrzest *m* (*chrztu*; *chrzty*) baptism
chrzestn|y *adj*: ***matka ~a*** godmother; ***ojciec ~y*** godfather; ***rodzice ~i*** godparents; ***syn ~y*** godson
chrześcijanin *m* (*-na*; *-janie*), **-nka** *f* (*-ki*; *-ki*) Christian
chrześcijański *adj* Christian; **chrześcijaństwo** *n* (*-wa*; *no pl*) Christianity
chrześniaczka *f* (*-ki*; *-ki*) goddaughter, **chrześniak** *m* (*-ka*; *-niacy*) godson
chrzęst *m* (*-tu*; *-ty*) *żwiru*, *śniegu*: crunch; **chrzęścić** *v/im* (*chrzęszczę*) (*o żwirze*, *śniegu*) crunch
chuch *m* (*-chu*; *no pl*) *infml* **1.** (*oddech*) breath; ***nieświeży ~*** bad breath **2.** (*chuchnięcie*) puff (of breath)
chuchać ⟨**-chnąć**⟩ (*-cham*) **1.** blow (a puff of breath) **2.** (*rozpieszczać*) dote (***na*** *A* on)
chuchro *n* (*-ra*; *-ra*) weakling
chuć *f lit* (*chuci*; *chucie*) lust
chuderlawy *adj* scraggy, frail; **chudnąć** ⟨**s-**⟩ (*-nę*) lose weight; ***schudła 3 kilo*** she lost 3 kilos; **chudość** *f* (*-ści*; *no pl*) thinness
chudy *adj* **1.** thin; ***~ jak patyk*** (as) thin as a rake **2.** *mięso*: lean **3.** *mleko*, *ser*: low-fat; **chudzielec** *m* (*-lca*; *-lcy*/*-lce*) bag of bones
chuj *m* (*-ja*; *-je*) *vulg* prick, cock
chuligan *m* (*-na*; *-ni*) hooligan
chuligaństwo *n* (*-wa*; *no pl*) hooliganism
chusta *f* (*-ty*; *-ty*) scarf; **chusteczka** *f* (*-ki*; *-ki*) handkerchief, *infml* hanky: ***~ do nosa*** handkerchief; ***~ higieniczna*** (facial) tissue; **chustka** *f* (*-ki*; *-ki*) kerchief
chwalebny *adj* **1.** (*godny pochwały*) praiseworthy, *form* commendable **2.** *zamiary*, *śmierć*: *Br* honourable, *Am* honorable; **chwalić** ⟨**po-**⟩ (*-lę*) praise; ***~ sobie*** *A* be satisfied with; ***chwalić się*** boast (*I* about/of); **chwalipięta** *f*/*m* (*-ty*; *-ty*) *infml* boaster
chwała *f* (*-ły*; *no pl*) glory; ***~ Bogu*** thank God
chwast *m* (*-tu*; *-ty*) weed
chwiać ⟨**za-**⟩ (*chwieję*) shake; ***chwiać się*** **1.** (*o osobie*) stagger **2.** (*o krześle*) wobble **3.** (*o płomieniu*) flicker
chwiejność *f* (*-ści*; *no pl*) **1.** *uczuć*, *nastrojów*: instability **2.** *poglądów*: changeability; ***~ chodu*** stagger; **chwiejny** *adj* **1.** *nastroje*: unstable **2.** *poglądy*: changeable **3.** *płomień*: flickering; ***~ chód*** stagger; ***iść ~m krokiem*** stagger
chwil|a *f* (*-li*; *-le*) moment; ***~a wytchnienia*** (a moment of) respite; ***co ~a*** all the time; ***do ~i obecnej*** until now; ***lada ~a*** any moment; ***na ~ę*** for a moment; ***od tej ~i*** from now on; ***po ~i*** after a moment; ***przed ~ą*** a moment ago; ***przez ~ę*** for a moment; ***w tej ~i*** at the moment; ***w tej ~i!*** this minute!; ***za ~ę*** in a minute; ***z ~ą, gdy*** the moment (that); ***w jednej ~i*** **a)** (*szybko*) in no time **b)** (*nagle*) all of a sudden; ***~e*** (*czas*) time; ***~ami*** sometimes
chwileczk|a *f* (*-ki*; *-ki*), **chwilk|a** *f* (*-ki*; *-ki*) moment; ***~ę!*** just a minute!
chwilowo *adv* **1.** (*tymczasowo*) temporarily **2.** (*obecnie*) at the moment **3.** (*przez chwilę*) for a moment; **chwilowy** *adj* **1.** (*krótkotrwały*) momentary **2.** (*tymczasowy*) temporary
chwycić *v/p* → ***chwytać***
chwyt *m* (*-tu*; *-ty*) **1.** hold, grip **2.** (*sztuczka*) trick

chwy|tać ⟨**chwycić**, **s-**⟩ (*-tam*) **I** *v/t* **1.** (*brać*) take hold of; **~tać powietrze** gasp for air; **~tać za pióro** *fig* put pen to paper; **~tać za serce** *fig* touch the heart; **mróz ~cił** it's freezing **2.** ⟨**s-**⟩ (*mocno*) grasp **3.** ⟨**s-**⟩ (*gwałtownie*) grab **4.** ⟨**s-**⟩ (*w locie*) catch **5.** ⟨**s-**⟩ *przestępcę*: capture **6.** ⟨**u-**⟩ *sens*: grasp **7.** ⟨**u-**⟩ *chwilę*: seize **II** *v/i* (*o pomyśle*) catch on; **chwytać się**: **~** *G* take hold of, grab; **~tać się na czymś** catch oneself doing s.th.; **~tać się za głowę** put one's head in one's hands

chwytliwy *adj melodia*, *slogan*: catchy; **chwytny** *adj ogon*: prehensile

chyba I *particle* probably; **~ masz rację** you're probably right; **~ zapomniał** he may have forgotten **II** *conj* **~ że** unless; **~ tak** (**nie**) I (don't) think so

chybcik: **na ~a** sloppily

chybi|ać ⟨**-bić**⟩ (*-biam*) miss; **ani ~** for sure, without fail; **~ać celu** miss the target; **na ~ł trafił** at random; **chybiony** *adj* **1.** *decyzja*, *posunięcie*: wrong **2.** **~ strzał** miss **3.** *próba*: unsuccessful **4.** *zarzut*: unfounded

chybotać ⟨**za-**⟩ (*-boczę*) **I** *v/t* **1.** *stołem*: wobble **2.** *łodzią*: rock **II** *v/i* (*o płomieniu*) flicker; **chybotać się 1.** (*o krześle*) wobble **2.** (*o łodzi*) rock; **~ się na boki** rock from side to side

chybotliwy *adj* **1.** *drabina*, *krzesło*: wobbly **2.** *płomień*: flickering

chylić ⟨**po-**, **s-**⟩ (*-lę*): **~ czoła przed** *I* bow before; **chylić się** bend over; **~ się ku upadkowi** be in decline, be falling into decline

chyłkiem *adv* stealthily, sneakily; **wymknąć się ~ z pokoju** sneak out of a room

chytrość *f* (*-ści*; *no pl*) **1.** (*przebiegłość*) cunning **2.** (*chciwość*) greed

chytrus *m* (*-sa*; *-sy*/*-si*) (*skąpiec*) scrooge, *infml* cheapskate

chytry *adj* **1.** (*przebiegły*, *pomysłowy*) cunning; **~ jak lis** (as) sly as a fox **2.** (*skąpy*) mean

chyży *adj lit* swift

ci I *pron* **1.** these; **~ chłopcy** these boys; → **ten 2.** you; **powiem ~** I'll tell you; → **ty II** *particle* **to ~ historia!** what a story!; **masz ~ los!** oh dear!

ciachać ⟨**-chnąć**⟩ (*-cham*) *infml* cut, chop; **ciachać się** cut oneself

ciałk|o *n* (*-ka*; *-ka*) **1.** (*ciało*) body **2.** *BIOL* corpuscle; **białe** (**czerwone**) **~a krwi** white (red) blood cells

ciał|o *n* (*-ła*; *-ła*) **1.** body; **Boże 2o** Corpus Christi; **~o niebieskie** *ASTR* heavenly body; **~o obce** foreign body; **~o pedagogiczne** teaching staff; **część ~a** body part; **na całym ciele** all over (the body); **angażować się duszą i ~em w** *A* commit oneself body and soul to **2.** (*tkanka*) flesh; **na gołe ~o** on one's bare flesh **3.** *PHYS* substance; **~o stałe** solid

ciamajda *f*/*m* (*-dy*; *-dy*) *infml* clodhopper

ciamkać *v/im* (*-kam*) **1.** (*mlaskać*) smack one's lips **2.** (*głośno jeść*) munch

ciapa *f*/*m* (*-py*; *-py*) (clumsy) oaf; **ciapowaty** *adj infml* clumsy, bumbling

ciarki *pl* (*-rek*) shivers, creeps; **przeszły mnie od tego ~** it gave me the creeps

ciasno *adv stłoczeni*, *spleceni*: tightly; **mieć w domu ~** live in cramped conditions; **jest mi w tej sukience ~** this dress is too tight; **ciasnota** *f* (*-ty*; *no pl*) lack of space; **~ umysłu** narrow-mindedness; **ciasny** *adj* **1.** *buty*, *spodnie*: tight **2.** *mieszkanie*: cramped, small **3.** *przejście*: narrow; **mieć ~ umysł** be narrow-minded

ciastkarnia *f* (*-ni*; *-nie*) cake shop

ciastko *n* (*-ka*; *-ka*) cake

ciasto *n* (*-ta*; *-ta*) **1.** (*słodki wypiek*) cake; **~ francuskie** puff pastry **2.** (*nadziewane*) pastry **3.** (*masa*) dough **4.** (*na naleśniki*) batter

ciaśniej *comp* → **ciasno**

ciaśniejszy *comp* → **ciasny**

ciąć ⟨**po-**⟩ (*tnę*) **I** *v/t* cut; **~ powietrze** cut through the air **II** *v/i* **1.** (*o deszczu*) lash down **2.** (*o komarach*) bite **3.** (*o osach*) sting

ciąg *m* (*-gu*; *-gi*) **1.** *liczb*, *zdarzeń*: sequence **2.** *budynków*, *sklepów*: row **3.** *opowiadania*: course **4.** *silnika*: thrust **5.** *gęsi*: string; **~ dalszy** continuation; **~ dalszy nastąpi** to be continued; **~ myśli** a train of thought; **~ powietrza** *Br* draught, *Am* draft; **w ~u** *G* (*podczas*) during; **w ~u dnia** by day; **w ~u dwóch dni** in two days; **w dalszym ~u** still

ciągać *v/im* (*-gam*) drag; **~ kogoś po**

C

sądach drag s.o. through the courts
ciągle *adv* **1.** (*nadal*) still; **oni ~ żyją** they're still alive; **2.** (*nieustannie*) continuously **3.** *powtarzać się*: constantly; **~ narzekać** keep on complaining
ciągliwy *adj metal*: ductile, malleable
ciągłość *f* (*-ści*; *no pl*) continuity; **ciągły** *adj* continuous; **w ~m ruchu** (**strachu**) in constant motion (fear)
ciągnąć ⟨**po-**⟩ (*-nę*) **I** *v/t* **1.** pull; **~ kogoś za włosy** (**rękę**) pull s.o.'s hair (hand); **~ losy** draw lots; **~ korzyści z** *G* derive profit from **2.** (*wlec*) drag **3.** (*pociągać*) **coś kogoś ciągnie** s.o. is attracted to s.th. **II** *v/i* (*kontynuować*) **~** (**dalej**) go on, continue; **tu ciągnie** *Br* there's a draught here, *Am* there's a draft here; **ciągnąć się** **1.** (*trwać długo*) drag (on) **2.** (*o polach*, *lesie*) stretch
ciągnienie *n* (*-nia*; *-nia*) (*loterii*) draw, *Am* drawing
ciągnik *m* (*-ka*; *-ki*) tractor
ciąż|a *f* (*-ży*; *-ży*) pregnancy; **przerwać ~ę** abort a pregnancy; **w ~y** pregnant; **zaawansowana ~a** late pregnancy; **zajść w ~ę** get pregnant
ciążenie *n* (*-nia*; *no pl*) gravity, gravitation; **ciążowy** *adj* **1.** *test*: pregnancy **2.** *sukienka*, *spodnie*: maternity
ciążyć ⟨**za-**⟩ (*-żę*) **~ komuś a)** (*psychicznie*) be a burden to s.o. **b)** (*fizycznie*) weigh s.o. down; **ciąży na kimś obowiązek zrobienia czegoś** s.o. is obliged to do s.th.
cichaczem, **cichcem** *adv* stealthily; **wymknąć się ~** sneak out
cichnąć ⟨**u-**⟩ (*-nę*) **1.** (*o głosach*, *gwarze*) die away **2.** (*o wietrze*) die down, abate **3.** (*o burzy*) subside, abate
cicho *adv* quietly; **bądź ~!** be quiet!; **~!** quiet!; **jest ~** it's quiet
cichobieżny *adj silnik*, *wentylator*: quiet-running, silent; **cichutko** *adj dim* quietly; **cich|y** *adj* **1.** quiet; **po ~u** quietly **2.** *głos*, *szept*: low, quiet **3.** *morze*: calm **4.** *wielbiciel*: secret
ciebie *pron* you; **u ~** (**w domu**) at your place; → **ty**
cie|c *v/im* (*ciekne*) **1.** (*kapać*) drip **2.** (*strumieniem*) trickle; **łzy mi ~kły po policzkach** tears were running down my cheeks **3.** (*przeciekać*) leak
ciecz *f* (*-czy*; *-cze*) fluid
cieczk|a *f* (*-ki*; *-ki*): **mieć ~ę** *Br* be on heat, *Am* be in heat
cieć *m* (*ciecia*; *ciecie*) *Br* caretaker, *Am* janitor
ciekawi|ć ⟨**za-**⟩ (*-wię*) interest; **~ mnie, co myślisz** I wonder what you think; **ciekawie** *adv* **1.** (*interesująco*) interestingly **2.** (*z ciekawością*) curiously; **ciekawostka** *f* (*-ki*; *-ki*) **1.** (*informacja*) interesting fact **2.** (*rzecz*) curiosity
ciekawoś|ć *f* (*-ści*; *no pl*) curiosity; **z ~ci** out of curiosity
ciekawski *adj infml* nosy, prying
ciekawy *adj* **1.** (*interesujący*) interesting; **~ jestem, czy** I wonder if **2.** (*zainteresowany*) curious
ciekły *adj* liquid
cieknąć *v/im* (*-nę*) → **ciec**
cielak *m* (*-ka*; *-ki*) calf
cielesny *adj* **1.** *potrzeby*, *nietykalność*: physical **2.** *kara*: corporal
cielę *n* (*-lęcia*; *-lęta*) calf; **cielęcina** *f* (*-ny*; *no pl*) veal; **cielęc|y** *adj kotlet*: veal; **~a skóra** calfskin; **~e mięso** veal
cielić się ⟨**o-**⟩ (*-lę*) calve
cielisty *adj Br* flesh-coloured, *Am* flesh-colored
cielna *adj krowa*: pregnant, with calf
ciem → **ćma**
ciemiączko *n* (*-ka*; *-ka*) *ANAT* fontanelle
ciemieniowy *adj ANAT* parietal
ciemię *n* (*-mienia*; *-miona*) *ANAT* the crown (of the head), vertex; **być nie w ~ bitym** be no fool
ciemięga *f/m* (*-gi*; *-gi*) *infml* clumsy oaf
ciemiężca *m* (*-cy*; *-cy*), **ciemiężyciel** *m* (*-la*; *-le*) oppressor; **ciemiężyć** ⟨**u-**⟩ (*-żę*) oppress
ciemku: **po ~** in the dark
ciemnia *f* (*-ni*; *-nie*) darkroom
ciemniak *m* (*-ka*; *-ki*/*-niacy*) *infml* dimwit
ciemnieć ⟨**po-**, **ś-**⟩ (*-nieję*) darken
ciemno *adv* dark; **~ choć oko wykol** pitch-dark; **jest ~** it's dark; **pomalowany na ~** painted dark; **randka w ~** blind date; **robi się ~** it's getting dark; **w ~** *Br* on spec; **zrobiło mu się ~ przed oczami** all went dark for him
ciemnoblond *adj* dark blond; **ciemnoczerwony** *adj* dark red; **ciemnoskóry** *adj* (*czarny*) black

ciemność *f* (*-ści*; *-ści*) darkness
ciemnota *f* (*-ty*; *no pl*) ignorance
ciemnowłosy *adj* dark-haired
ciemny *adj* **1.** dark **2.** *chleb*: brown **3.** (*podejrzany*) shady **4.** (*głupi*) *infml* dumb; **~ jak tabaka w rogu** (as) daft as a brush
cieniej *comp* → **cienko**
cieniować ⟨**wy-**⟩ (*-niuję*) **1.** *rysunek*: shade **2.** *włosy*: layer; **cieniowanie** *n* (*-nia*; *no pl*) **1.** *rysunku*: shading **2.** *włosów*: layering
cienisty *adj* shady
cieniutki *adj dim* very thin; **cienki** *adj* **1.** thin **2.** *głos*: high-pitched **3.** (*kiepski*) *infml* lame
cienko *adj* thinly; **~ prząść** (*być biednym*) live from hand to mouth
cienkopis (*-su*; *-sy*) fine-tip felt pen
cienkość *f* (*-ści*; *no pl*) thinness
cie|ń *m* (*cienia*; *cienie*) **1.** *osoby*, *przedmiotu*: shadow **2.** (*miejsce*) shade; **w ~niu** in the shade; **bez ~nia wątpliwości** beyond a shadow of a doubt; **~nie pod oczami** shadows under one's eyes; **~ń do powiek** eyeshadow; **~ń nadziei** a glimmer of hope
cieńszy *comp* → **cienki**
cieplarnia *f* (*-ni*; *-nie*) greenhouse; **cieplarniany** *adj* **1.** greenhouse; **efekt ~** greenhouse effect **2.** *warunki*: *Br* favourable, *Am* favorable
cieplej *adv comp* → **ciepło²** warmer; **cieplejszy** *adj comp* → **ciepły** warmer
cieplny *adj energia*, *izolacja*: thermal
cieplut(eń)ki *adj dim* very warm
ciepławy *adj* warmish
ciepło¹ *n* (*-ła*; *no pl*) **1.** warmth **2.** PHYS heat
ciepło² *adv* **1.** (*o temperaturze*) warm; **jest ~** it's warm; **jest mi ~** I'm warm; **robi się ~** it's getting warm **2.** *przywitać*, *ubierać się*: warmly; **trzymaj się ~!** take care!
ciepłokrwisty *adj* warm-blooded
ciepłota *f* (*-ty*; *no pl*): **~ ciała** body temperature
ciepłownia *f* (*-ni*; *-nie*) heating plant
ciepł|y *adj* **1.** warm **2.** *słowa*: friendly; **~e kraje** warm climes; **~e kluchy** *infml* loser
ciernik *m* (*-ka*; *-ki*) three-spined stickleback
cierniow|y *adj*: **korona ~a** a crown of thorns; **ciernisty** adj thorny
cierń *m* (*-nia*; *-nie*) thorn; **ciernie** (*krzewy*) thorn bushes
cierpiący *adj* suffering (**na** *A* from); **~ na chorobę morską** seasick; **nie ~ zwłoki** urgent
cierpieć ⟨**u-**⟩ (*-pię*) **I** *v/t* **1.** suffer; **~ głód** starve **2.** (*znosić*) **nie ~** detest, hate **II** *v/i* **1.** suffer (**na** *A* from); **~ z powodu** *G* suffer because of **2.** (*doznawać szkody*) suffer
cierpienie *n* (*-nia*; *-nia*) suffering
cierpki *adj* **1.** tart **2.** *zapach*: acrid **3.** *humor*: bitter
cierpliwoś|ć *f* (*-ści*; *no pl*) patience; **nie mieć ~ci do** *G* have no patience with; **musisz uzbroić się w ~ć** be prepared for a long wait; **cierpliwy** *adj* patient
cierpn|ąć ⟨**ś-**⟩ (*-nę*) (*drętwieć*) go numb; **na myśl o tym ~ie mi skóra** it gives me the creeps
cieszyć ⟨**u-**⟩ (*-szę*): **coś kogoś cieszy** s.o. is glad about s.th., s.o. is happy with s.th.; **bardzo mnie to cieszy** I'm very glad about it; **cieszy mnie, że** I'm glad that; **cieszyć się 1.** (*być zadowolonym*) be glad (**z** *G* about), be happy (**z** *G* with) **2.** *zdrowiem*, *życiem*: enjoy **3.** *szacunkiem*: command; **~ się powodzeniem** be successful
cieśla *m* (*-li*; *-le*) carpenter
cieśnina *f* (*-ny*; *-ny*) strait
cietrzew *m* (*-wia*; *-wie*) black grouse
cię *pron* you; **kocham ~** I love you; → **ty**
cięci|e *n* (*-cia*; *-cia*) cut; **~a budżetowe** budget cuts
cięciwa *f* (*-wy*; *-wy*) **1.** (*łuku*) bowstring **2.** MATH chord
cięgi *pl* (*-gów*) thrashing *sing*; **dostać ~** get a thrashing
cięty *adj* **1.** *kwiaty*, *rana*: cut **2.** *uwaga*: cutting **3.** *język*: biting **4.** (*zawzięty*) **być ~m na** *A* pick on
ciężar *m* (*-ru*; *-ry*) **1.** weight; **podnoszenie ~ów** SPORT weightlifting; **~ odpowiedzialności spoczywa na** *L* the weight of responsibility falls on **2.** *fig* burden; **stać się ~em dla** *G* become a burden to
ciężarek *m* (*-rka*; *-rki*) weight; **ciężarna I** *adj* pregnant **II** *f* (*-nej*; *-ne*) preg-

C

nant woman; **ciężarowy** *adj transport*: heavy; **samochód ~** *Br* lorry, *Am* truck
ciężarówka *f* (*-ki*; *-ki*) *Br* lorry, *Am* truck
ciężej *comp* → **ciężko**
ciężk|i *adj* **1.** heavy; **~ie pieniądze** *fig* big money, loads of money; **waga ~a** SPORT heavyweight **2.** *praca*, *czasy*, *życie*: hard; **~ie roboty** *Br* hard labour, *Am* hard labor **3.** *choroba*: serious
ciężko *adv* **1.** heavily **2.** *pracować*: hard; **żyło się ~** life was hard **3.** *chory*, *ranny*: seriously
ciężkostrawny *adj posiłek:* heavy
ciężkoś|ć *f* (*-ści*; *no pl*) heaviness; **siła ~ci** PHYS gravity; **środek ~ci** PHYS *Br* centre of gravity, *Am* center of gravity
ciocia *f* (*-ci*; *-cie*) aunt
cios *m* (*-su*; *-sy*) (*uderzenie*) blow; **~ poniżej pasa** low blow; **~y** (*kły*) tusks
ciosać (*-sam*) **1.** ⟨**o-**⟩ *skałę*, *drewno*: hew **2.** ⟨**wy-**⟩ *figury*: carve
ciota *f* (*-ty*; *-ty*) *infml* queer, *Am* fag
cioteczn|y *adj*: **~a babka** great-aunt; **~a siostra** cousin; **~y brat** cousin
ciotka *f* (*-ki*; *-ki*) aunt
cipa *f* (*-py*; *-py*) *vulg* cunt, pussy
cipka *f* (*-ki*; *-ki*) *vulg* pussy
cis[1] *m* (*-su*; *-sy*) (*drzewo*) yew
cis[2] *n indecl* MUS C sharp; **fuga ~-moll** fugue in C sharp minor
ciskać ⟨**-snąć**⟩ (*-kam*) (*rzucać*) fling
cisnąć *v/p* (*-nę*) **1.** (*o bucie*) pinch **2.** (*naciskać*) push
cisz|a *f* (*-szy*; *no pl*) silence; **~a morska** calm sea; **~a przed burzą** the calm before the storm; **proszę o ~ę!** quiet please!; **ciszej** *comp* → **cicho**
ciśnienie *n* (*-nia*; *-nia*) pressure; **~ powietrza** (**krwi**) air (blood) pressure; **ciśnieniomierz** *m* (*-rza*; *-rze*) pressure gauge
ciuchcia *f* (*-ci*; *-cie*) *infml* choo-choo
ciuchland *m* (*-du*; *-dy*) *infml* second-hand clothes shop
ciuchy *pl* (*-chów*) *infml* clothes, *infml* duds
ciuciubabka *f* (*-ki*; *no pl*) *Br* blind man's buff, *Am* blind man's bluff
ciułać ⟨**u-**⟩ (*-łam*) hoard money
ciupa *f* (*-py*; *-py*) (*więzienie*) *infml* the clink
ciupaga *f* (*-gi*; *-gi*) *Polish highlanders' climbing stick*
ciurkiem *adv*: **płynąć ~** trickle
ciut *adv infml* a bit
cizia *f* (*-zi*; *-zie*) *infml* chick
ckliwy *adj* soppy, slushy
clić ⟨**o-**⟩ (*clę*) impose duty (*A* on)
cł|o *n* (*cła*; *cła*) (customs) duty; **wolny od ~a** duty-free
cmentarny *adj* cemetery; **cmentarz** *m* (*-rza*; *-rze*) **1.** cemetery, graveyard **2.** (*przy kościele*) churchyard
cmentarzysko *n* (*-ka*; *-ka*) prehistoric burial site; **~ starych samochodów** graveyard for cars
cmokać ⟨**-knąć**⟩ (*-kam*) **1.** smack one's lips **2.** (*całować*) peck
cnot|a *f* (*-ty*; *-ty*) **1.** virtue **2.** (*dziewictwo*) virginity; **pas ~y** HIST chastity belt; **cnotliwy** *adj dated lit* **1.** virtuous **2.** (*czysty*) chaste
co I *pron* **1.** what; **~ innego** something else; **~ mu jest?** what's the matter with him?; **~ słychać?** how are things?; **~ to jest?** what's this?; **~ do** as for; **czego chcesz?** what do you want?; **nie wiem, ~ robić** I don't know what to do **2.** (*który*) which; **ci, ~ wyszli** those who left **II** *prep* **1. ~ drugi dzień** every second day; **~ tydzień** every week; **~ wieczór** every night **2.** (*wykrzyknik*) **~ za niespodzianka!** what a surprise! **III** *particle* **a ~ dopiero** not to mention; **~ bądź** anything; **~ było robić** nothing doing; **~ jest grane?** *infml* what's going on?; **~ nieco a)** (*trochę*) a little **b)** (*coś*) something; **~ najmniej** at least; **~ najwyżej** at most; **~ niemiara** in abundance, galore; **~ prawda** as a matter of fact; **~ się tyczy** as for; **~ takiego?** what (did you say)?; **i ~ z tego?** so what?; **jeszcze czego!** oh, come on! **IV** *conj* **~ gorsza** worse still; **~ się stało, to się nie odstanie** what's done cannot be undone; **~ więcej** what's more; **czym starszy, tym przystojniejszy** the older he gets, the better he looks
c.o. *abbr* (= **centralne ogrzewanie**) central heating
codziennie *adv* every day, daily; **codzienność** *f* (*-ści*; *no pl*) everyday life; **codzienny** *adj* **1.** everyday **2.** *gazeta*, *wiadomości*: daily

cofać ⟨**-fnąć**⟩ (*-fam*) **1.** *rękę, obietnicę*: take back; withdraw **2.** *auto, decyzję*: reverse **3.** *zegar*: put back **4.** *zlecenie*: cancel; ***cofać się*** **1.** (*usunąć się*) move back **2.** (*o aucie*) reverse **3.** (*wracać*) go back; ***~ się myślą do*** *G* cast one's mind back to **4.** (*o wojsku*) pull back; ***nie ~ się przed niczym*** *fig* stop at nothing

cofanie *n* (*-nia*; *no pl*) *samochodu*: reversing; ***cofanie się*** (*o wojsku*) pulling back; **cofnięcie** *n* (*-cia*; *no pl*) withdrawal

cogodzinny *adj* hourly

cokolwiek **I** *pron* anything; ***~ robił, myślał o niej*** whatever he was doing, he was thinking about her **II** *adv* a little

cokół *m* (*-kołu*; *-koły*) pedestal

comber *m* (*-bra*; *-bry*) COOK saddle; ***~ barani*** saddle of mutton

comiesięczny *adj* monthly

conocny *adj* nightly

coraz: ***~ bardziej*** more and more, *form* ever more; ***~ lepiej*** better and better ***~ więcej*** more and more; ***robi się ~ cieplej*** it's getting warmer and warmer

coroczny *adj* annual, yearly

coś *pron* **1.** something; ***~ mocniejszego*** (*alkohol*) *infml* (the) hard stuff; ***~ w rodzaju*** something like **2.** (*w pytaniach*) anything; ***czy mogę dostać ~ do picia?*** can I get something to drink?; **cośkolwiek** → ***cokolwiek***

cotygodniowy *adj* weekly

córeczka *f* (*-ki*; *-ki*) *dim* (little) daughter; **córka** *f* (*-ki*; *-ki*) daughter

cóż **I** *pron* (*co*) what(ever); ***~ to za pytanie?*** what kind of question is that?; → **co** **II** *particle* **1.** well; ***~, nie mogę ci pomóc*** well, I can't help you **2.** (*dlaczego*) why; ***cóżeś taki zły?*** why are you so angry?

cuchnąć *v/im* (*-nę*) stink (*G* of)

cucić ⟨**do-**, **o-**⟩ (*-cę*): ***~ kogoś*** try to bring s.o. round; ***o~ kogoś*** bring s.o. round

cud *m* (*-du*; *-da*) **1.** REL miracle **2.** (*niezwykłe zjawisko*) wonder, marvel; ***~a natury*** (***techniki***) the marvels of nature (technology); ***~em*** by a miracle; ***czynić ~a*** work wonders; ***jakim ~em?*** how on earth?; ***siedem ~ów świata*** the Seven Wonders of the World; ***to ~, że*** it's a miracle that; ***uratować się ~em*** miraculously survive

cudaczny *adj* weird; **cudak** *m* (*-ka*; *-dacy*/*-ki*) freak; **cudny** *adj* wonderful

cudo *n* (*-da*; *-da*) beauty; **cudotwórca** *m* (*-cy*; *-cy*) wonder-maker; **cudownie** *adv* **1.** wonderfully **2.** (*cudem*) by a miracle

cudown|y *adj* **1.** (*wspaniały*) *Br* marvellous, *Am* marvelous; ***~e dziecko*** (child) prodigy **2.** (*nadprzyrodzony*) miraculous; ***~y lek*** wonder drug

cudzołożyć *v/im* (*-żę*) *dated* commit adultery; **cudzołóstwo** *n* (*-wa*; *-wa*) *lit* adultery

cudzoziemiec *m* (*-mca*; *-mcy*), **-mka** *f* (*-ki*; *-ki*) foreigner

cudzoziemsk|i *adj* foreign; ***legia ~a*** the Foreign Legion

cudzy *adj* somebody else's

cudzysł|ów *m* (*-łowu*; *-łowy*) quotation marks *pl*; ***w ~owie*** in quotation marks

cugle *pl* (*-li*) reins

cukier *m* (*-kru*; *-kry*) sugar; ***~ w kostkach*** sugar cubes; ***~ puder*** *Br* caster sugar, *Am* powdered sugar

cukierek *m* (*-rka*; *-rki*) sweet, *Am* candy

cukiernia *f* (*-ni*; *-nie*) confectioner's; **cukiernica** *f* (*-cy*; *-ce*) sugar bowl; **cukiernik** *m* (*-ka*; *-nicy*) confectioner

cukinia *f* (*-nii*; *-nie*) *Br* courgette, *Am* zucchini

cukrownia *f* (*-ni*; *-nie*) sugar factory; **cukrow|y** *adj* sugar; ***burak ~y*** sugar beet; ***trzcina ~a*** sugar cane

cukrzyca *f* (*-cy*; *no pl*) diabetes

cukrzyć ⟨**po-**⟩ (*-rzę*) sugar; **cukrzyk** *m* (*-ka*; *-rzycy*) diabetic

cuma *f* (*-my*; *-my*) mooring rope; ***cumy*** moorings; **cumować** ⟨**za-**⟩ (*-muję*) **I** *v/t* moor **II** *v/i* be moored

cwał *m* (*-łu*; *no pl*) gallop; ***~em*** at a gallop; **cwałować** ⟨**po-**⟩ (*-łuję*) gallop

cwaniactwo *n* (*-wa*; *no pl*) *infml* slyness, low cunning; **cwaniak** *m* (*-ka*; *-niacy*/*-ki*) *infml* (sly) fox

cwany *adj* sly, wily

cyborg *m* (*-ga*; *-gi*) cyborg

cybuch *m* (*-cha*; *-chy*) (pipe) stem

cycek *m* (*-cka*; *-cki*) *infml* **1.** *zwierzęcia*: teat **2.** *kobiety*: tit *vulg*, boob *infml*

cyferblat *m* (*-tu*; *-ty*) dial, face

cyfra *f* (*-ry*; *-ry*) **1.** digit, figure **2.** *arabska*, *rzymska*: numeral; **cyfrowy** *adj TECH* digital

Cygan *m* (*-na*; *-nie*), **~ka** *f* (*-ki*; *-ki*) Gypsy

cyganeria *f* (*-rii*; *no pl*) bohemians *pl;* **cyganić** ⟨**o-**⟩ (*-nię*) cheat

cygańsk|i I *adj* **1.** Gypsy **2.** (*artystyczny*) bohemian **II** *m* (*-kiego*; *no pl*) (*język*) Gypsy, Romany; ***mówić po ~u*** speak Romany

cygarniczka *f* (*-ki*; *-ki*) cigarette holder; **cygaro** *n* (*-ra*; *-ra*) cigar

cyjanek *m* (*-nku*; *-nki*) cyanide; ***~ potasu*** potassium cyanide

cykać ⟨**-knąć**⟩ (*-kam*) **1.** (*o zegarze*) tick **2.** (*o koniku polnym*) chirp

cykada *f* (*-dy*; *-dy*) cicada

cykl *m* (*-lu*; *-le*) **1.** cycle; ***~ miesięczny*** menstrual cycle **2.** (*seria*) series

cyklamen *m* (*-nu*; *-ny*) cyclamen

cykliczny *adj* **1.** cyclic(al) **2.** *audycja*, *program*: serial

cykliniarka *f* (*-ki*; *-ki*) floor grinder; **cyklinować** ⟨**wy-**⟩ (*-nuję*) *podłogę*: grind

cyklon *m* (*-nu*; *-ny*) **1.** (*wir*) cyclone **2.** *CHEM* Zyklon

cyknąć *v/p* → ***cykać***

cykor *m* (*-ra*; *-ry*) *infml* **1.** (*tchórz*) scaredy-cat **2.** (*strach*) ***mieć ~a*** be scared, have cold feet

cykoria *f* (*-rii*; *-rie*) **1.** (*sałatowa*) *Br* endive, *Am* chicory **2.** (*korzeniowa*) *Br* chicory, *Am* endive

cykuta *f* (*-ty*; *-ty*) hemlock

cylinder *m* (*-dra*; *-dry*) **1.** *TECH* cylinder **2.** (*kapelusz*) top hat; **cylindrowy** *adj*: ***cztero~*** 4-cylinder; **cylindryczny** *adj* cylindrical

cymbał *m* (*-ła*; *-ły*) *infml* dork; **cymbały** *pl* (*-łów*) *MUS* dulcimer *sing*; **cymbałki** *pl* (*-ków*) *MUS* glockenspiel *sing*

cyna *f* (*-ny*; *no pl*) **1.** tin **2.** (*do lutowania*) solder

cynaderki *pl* (*-rek*) *COOK* kidney stew *sing*

cynamon *m* (*-nu*; *no pl*) cinnamon; **cynamonowy** *adj* cinnamon

cynfolia *f* (*-lii*; *no pl*) tinfoil

cyngiel *m* (*-gla*; *-gle*) trigger

cyniczny *adj* cynical; **cynik** *m* (*-ka*; *-nicy*) cynic; **cynizm** *m* (*-mu*; *no pl*) cynicism

cynk *m* (*-ku*; *no pl*) *CHEM* zinc; **cynkować** ⟨**o-**⟩ (*-kuję*) galvanize; **cynkowy** *adj* zinc

cynober *m* (*-bru*; *no pl*) (*kolor*) vermilion

cynować ⟨**o-**⟩ (*-nuję*) tin

cypel *m* (*-pla*; *-ple*) headland

Cypr *m* (*-ru*) Cyprus; **Cypryjczyk** *m* (*-ka*; *-czycy*) Cypriot; **cypryjski** *adj* Cypriot

cyprys *m* (*-su*; *-sy*) cypress

cyranka *f* (*-ki*; *-ki*) garganey

cyrk *m* (*-ku*; *-ki*) **1.** circus **2.** *infml* farce

cyrkiel *m* (*-kla*; *-kle*) (a pair of) compasses

cyrkon *m* (*-nu*; *-ny*) **1.** *CHEM* zirconium **2.** (*minerał*) zircon

cyrkowiec *m* (*-wca*; *-wcy*), **cyrkówka** *f* (*-ki*; *-ki*) circus performer; **cyrkowy** *adj* circus; ***namiot ~*** (the) big top

cyrkulacja *f* (*-ji*; *-je*) circulation; **cyrkulować** *v/im* (*-luję*) circulate

cyrograf *m* (*-fu*; *-fy*): ***podpisać ~*** sign a pact with the devil

cyrylica *f* (*-cy*; *no pl*) the Cyrillic alphabet

cysta *f* (*-ty*; *-ty*) cyst

cysterna *f* (*-ny*; *-ny*) (*pojazd*) tanker, tank truck

cysters *m* (*-sa*; *-si*) Cistercian

cyt *interj* hush!

cytadela *f* (*-li*; *-le*) citadel

cytat *m* (*-tu*; *-ty*) quotation, citation

cytologia *f* (*-gii*; *no pl*) cytology; **cytologiczny** *adj* cytological

cytować ⟨**za-**⟩ (*-tuję*) quote, cite

cytrusow|y *adj* citrus; ***owoce ~e*** citrus fruit

cytryna *f* (*-ny*; *-ny*) lemon; **cytrynek** *m* (*-nka*; *-nki*) brimstone (butterfly); **cytrynowy** *adj* lemon; **cytrynówka** *f* (*-ki*; *-ki*) lemon vodka

cywil *m* (*-la*; *-le*) civilian; ***w ~u*** *infml* **a)** (*o ubraniu*) in civvies **b)** (*o życiu*) in civvy life *infml*, *Br infml* in Civvy Street

cywilistyka *f* (*-ki*; *no pl*) (the) civil law

cywilizacja *f* (*-ji*; *-je*) civilization; **cywilizacyjn|y** *adj* civilization; ***choroby ~e*** the diseases of civilization

cywilizowany *adj* civilized

cywiln|y *adj* **1.** civil; ***obrona ~a*** *Br* civil defence, *Am* civil defense; ***odwaga ~a*** civil courage; ***prawo ~e*** (the) civil law; ***stan ~y*** marital status; ***ślub ~y*** civil marriage; ***urząd stanu ~ego*** *Br* register office, *Br infml* registry office; ***wziąć ślub ~y*** get married in a civil ceremony **2.** *ubranie*: plain; ***policjant w ~ym ubraniu*** plain-clothes policeman

cz. *abbr* (= **część**) p.

czad *m* (*-du*; *no pl*) carbon monoxide; ***więcej ~u*** *infml* pump up the volume

czador *m* (*-ru*/*-ra*; *-ry*) chador

czaić się ⟨**za-**⟩ (*czaję*) (*o osobie, niebezpieczeństwie*) lurk; ***~ na*** *A* **a)** (*czekać*) lie in wait for **b)** (*skradać się*) stalk

czajka *f* (*-ki*; *-ki*) (northern) lapwing

czajnik *m* (*-ka*; *-ki*) kettle

czambuł: ***w ~*** across the board

czap|a *f* (*-py*; *-py*) (*czapka*) hat; ***dać komuś w ~ę*** *infml* clock s.o. (one)

czapka *f* (*-ki*; *-ki*) **1.** (*wełniana*) hat **2.** (*z daszkiem, płaska*) cap; ***~ niewidka*** invisible cap

czapla *f* (*-li*; *-le*) heron

czar *m* (*-ru*; *-ry*) (*wdzięk*) charm; ***rzucić ~ na*** *A* cast a spell on; ***~y*** magic

czara *f* (*-ry*; *-ry*) (drinking) bowl

czarniusieńki *adj dim* pitch-black

czarno *adv* black; ***pomalować coś na ~*** paint s.th. black; ***pracować na ~*** work illegally, get paid under the table; ***ubrany na ~*** dressed in black

Czarnogóra *f* (*-ry*) Montenegro

czarnoksiężnik *m* (*-ka*; *-nicy*) sorcerer

czarnomorski *adj* Black Sea

czarnooki *adj* black-eyed; **czarnorynkowy** *adj* black market; **czarnoskór|y** *adj* black; ***~zy*** blacks; **czarnowłosy** *adj* black-haired

czarnoziem *m* (*-mu*; *-my*) chernozem, black earth

czarnuch *m* (*-cha*; *-chy*) *infml* nigger

czarn|y *adj* **1.** black; ***~a dziura*** *ASTR* black hole; ***~a jagoda*** bilberry; ***~a ospa*** black pox, black smallpox; ***~a porzeczka*** blackcurrant; ***~a robota*** donkeywork; ***~a rozpacz*** black despair; ***~a skrzynka*** *TECH* black box; ***~y charakter*** villain, black guy; ***~y rynek*** black market; ***odłożyć coś na ~ą godzinę*** save s.th. for a rainy day **2.** *myśli*: dark

czarodziej *m* (*-ja*; *-je*), **~ka** *f* (*-ki*; *-ki*) wizard; **czarodziejski** *adj* magic, **czarodziejstwo** *n* (*-wa*; *no pl*) wizardry

czarować (*-ruję*) **I** *v/im* do magic **II** ⟨**o-**⟩ *v/t* (*olśnić*) charm

czarownica *f* (*-cy*; *-ce*) witch; **czarownik** *m* (*-ka*; *-nicy*) **1.** sorcerer **2.** (*szaman*) witch doctor; **czarowny** *adj* enchanting

czart *m* (*-ta*; *-ty*) *lit* fiend

czarter *m* (*-ru*; *-ry*) charter; **czarterować** ⟨**wy-**⟩ (*-ruję*) charter; **czarterowy** *adj* charter

czarujący *adj* charming

czas *m* (*-su*; *-sy*) **1.** time; ***co jakiś ~*** at times; (***najwyższy***) ***~ coś zrobić*** (it's) high time to do s.th.; ***~ gry*** playing time; ***~ miejscowy*** local time; ***~ pracy*** working time; ***mieć ~ na*** *A* have time for; ***mieć mało ~u*** have little time; ***na ~*** in time; ***na ~ie*** up to date; ***nie ma ~u na*** there's no time for; ***od ~u*** (***jak***) since; ***od ~u do ~u*** from time to time; ***od tego ~u*** ever since; ***po ~ie*** too late; ***przed ~em*** ahead of time; ***przez jakiś ~*** for some time; ***szkoda ~u*** it's a waste of time; ***we właściwym ~ie*** in due time; ***w ~ie*** *G* during; ***w ~ie, gdy*** while; ***w krótkim ~ie*** in a short time; ***wolny ~*** free time, leisure; ***w późniejszym ~ie*** later; ***za moich ~ów*** in my days; ***z ~em*** in time **2.** *GRAM* tense; ***~ przeszły*** past tense; ***~ przyszły*** future tense; ***~ teraźniejszy*** present tense; **czasami**, **czasem** **1.** sometimes **2.** (*przypadkiem*) by any chance

czasochłonny *adj* time-consuming

czasopismo *n* (*-ma*; *-ma*) **1.** magazine **2.** (*naukowe*) journal, periodical

czasownik *m* (*-ka*; *-ki*) *GRAM* verb

czasowo *adv* temporarily; **czasowy** *adj* temporary

czasza *f* (*-szy*; *czasz*) **1.** *anteny*: dish **2.** *spadochronu*: canopy; **czaszka** *f* (*-ki*; *-ki*) skull; ***trupia ~*** death's head

czat *m* (*-tu*; *-ty*) *INF* chat; ***być na czacie*** chat on the net; ***stać na ~ach*** be on the lookout; **czatować** *v/im* (*-tuję*) **1.** ***~ na*** *A* lie in wait for **2.** *INF* chat

cząsteczka *f* (*-ki*; *-ki*) **1.** *CHEM* molecule **2.** *PHYS* particle; **cząstka** *f* (*-ki*; *-ki*) **1.** (*mała część*) (small) part **2.** *PHYS* particle **3.** *pomarańczy*: segment; **cząstkowy** *adj* partial

C

czci → ***cześć***
czciciel *m* (*-la*; *-le*), **~ka** *f* (*-ki*; *-ki*) worshipper
czcić⟨**u-**⟩ (*-czę*) **1.** REL worship **2.** (*świętować*) celebrate; **~ *pamięć*** commemorate; **czcigodny** *adj* venerable
czcionka *f* (*-ki*; *-ki*) **1.** type **2.** TECH INF font
czczą, **czczę** → **czcić**
czczo *adv*: ***na ~*** on an empty stomach; **czczy** *adj lit* **1.** *słowa*, *obietnice*: empty **2.** *gadanina*: idle
Czech *m* (*-cha*; *Czesi*) Czech
Czechosłowacja *f* (*-ji*) Czechoslovakia
Czechy *pl* (*Czech*) **1.** (*państwo*) the Czech Republic **2.** HIST Bohemia
czego *pron* what; → ***co***; **czegokolwiek** → **co**(***kolwiek***)
czegoś → ***coś***
czek *m* (*-ku*; *-ki*) *Br* cheque, *Am* check; ***~iem*** by cheque; ***~ na 250 zł*** a cheque for PLN 250
czeka|ć ⟨**po-**, **za-**⟩ (*-kam*) **I** *v/i* wait (***na*** *A* for); ***~ć na swoją kolej*** wait one's turn; ***~j no!*** *infml* (just) you wait! **II** *v/t* await; ***~ go przykra niespodzianka*** he's in for a surprise
czekan *m* (*-na*; *-ny*) SPORT *Br* ice axe, *Am* ice-ax
czekolada *f* (*-dy*; *-dy*) chocolate; **czekoladka** *f* (*-ki*; *-ki*) chocolate; **czekoladowy** *adj* **1.** chocolate **2.** (*o kolorze*) chocolate (brown)
czekow|y *adj Br* cheque, *Am* check; ***książeczka ~a*** *Br* chequebook, *Am* checkbook
czeladniczy *adj* *świadectwo*: apprenticeship; **czeladnik** *m* (*-ka*; *-nicy*) apprentice
czele → **czoło**
czelność: ***mieć ~ coś zrobić*** have the audacity to do s.th.
czeluść *f* (*-ści*; *-ście*) abyss
czemu *pron* (*dlaczego*) why; → ***co***; **czemukolwiek** → ***cokolwiek***; **czemuś** → ***coś***
czep|ek *m* (*-pka*; *-pki*) cap; ***~ek kąpielowy*** swimming cap; ***w ~ku urodzony*** born with a silver spoon in one's mouth
czepiać się *v/im* (*-piam*) **1.** (*chwytać*) clutch at **2.** (*lgnąć*) cling to **3.** (*krytykować*) *infml* ***~ czegoś*** be fussy about s.th.; ***~ kogoś*** pick on s.o.
czereda *f* (*-dy*; *-dy*) pack
czeremcha *f* (*-chy*; *-chy*) bird cherry
czerep *m* (*-pu*; *-py*) (*czaszka*) skull
czereśnia *f* (*-ni*; *-nie*) cherry
czerniak *m* (*-ka*; *-ki*) MED melanoma
czernica *f* (*-cy*; *-ce*) bilberry
czernić *v/im* (*-nię*) blacken; **czernieć** ⟨**s-**⟩ (*-nieję*) turn black, blacken; **czer|ń** *f* (*-rni*; *no pl*) black; ***w ~ni*** in black
czerpać *v/im* (*-pię*) **1.** draw **2.** *wiedzę*, *przyjemność*: derive; ***~ korzyści z*** *G* profit from; **czerpak** *m* (*-ka*; *-ki*) (*naczynie*) dipper
czerpany *adj*: ***papier ~*** wove paper
czerstwieć ⟨**s-**⟩ (*-wieję*) (*o pieczywie*) go stale; **czerstwy** *adj* **1.** *pieczywo*: stale **2.** *staruszek*: hale and hearty
czerw *m* (*-wia*; *-wie*) (*larwa*) maggot
czerwcowy *adj* June; **czerwiec** *m* (*-wca*; *-wce*) June
czerwienić się ⟨**za-**⟩ (*-nię*) **1.** (*stawać się czerwonym*) redden **2.** (*być czerwonym*) be red **3.** (*rumienić się*) blush (**z** *G* with), redden; **czerwienieć** ⟨**po-**⟩ (*-nieję*) → **czerwienić się**
czerwień *f* (*-ni*; *no pl*) **1.** red **2.** (*w kartach*) hearts
czerwonawy *adj* reddish
czerwonka *f* (*-ki*; *no pl*) MED dysentery
czerwono *adv* red; ***pomalowy na ~*** painted red; ***ubrany na ~*** dressed in red; **czerwonoskóry** *m* (*-rego*; *-rzy*) (American) Indian; **czerwonoś|ć** *f* (*-ści*; *no pl*) redness; ***rozgrzany do ~ci*** red-hot
czerwon|y **I** *adj* red; ***~a kartka*** red card; ***~e wino*** red wine; ***~y jak burak*** (as) red as a beetroot; ***~y Krzyż*** the Red Cross **II** *m* (*-ego*; *-ni*), **-na** *f* (*-nej*; *-ne*) red
czesać ⟨**u-**⟩ (*-szę*) comb; ***czesać się*** comb one's hair; ***gdzie się czeszesz?*** where do you have your hair done?; ***~ się krótko*** (***w kok***) wear one's hair short (in a bun)
czesankowy *adj* *wełna*: combed
czesk|i *adj* Czech; ***mówić po ~u*** speak Czech; ***po ~u*** in Czech
czesne *n* (*-nego*; *no pl*) tuition (fees)
Czeszka *f* (*-ki*; *-ki*) Czech
cześć *f* (*czci*; *no pl*) **1.** (*szacunek*) reverence; ***na ~*** *G* in honour of **2.** REL worship; ***oddawać ~*** worship **3.** ***~!***

a) (*na powitanie*) hi, hello! **b)** (*na pożegnanie*) see you!, bye!

często *adv* often

częstochowski *adj*: ***rymy ~e*** doggerel verse

częstokroć *adv lit* oftentimes

częstotliwość *f* (*-ści*; *-ści*) frequency; ***mała*** (***duża***) **~** low (high) frequency

częstować ⟨**po-**⟩ (*-tuję*): **~** ***kogoś czymś*** offer s.o. s.th.; ***częst|ować się*** help oneself; ***~ujcie się!*** help yourself!

częsty *adj* frequent, common

częściej *adv* more often, more frequently

częściowo *adv* partly, partially; **częściowy** *adj* partial

częś|ć *f* (*-ści*; *-ści*) part; ***~ć mowy*** part of speech; ***~ć składowa*** component; ***~ć zapasowa*** spare part; ***lwia ~ć*** lion's share; ***po ~ci*** partly, partially; ***większa ~ć*** (*większość*) majority

czipsy → ***chipsy***

czkać ⟨**-knąć**⟩ (*-kam*) hiccup

czkawka *f* (*-ki*; *-ki*) (the) hiccups

człapać *v/im* (*-pię*) trudge

człek **I** *m* (*-ka*; *no pl*) man **II** *pron* one

człekokształtn|y *adj*: ***małpy ~e*** (anthropoid) apes

człon *m* (*-nu*; *-ny*) **1.** *nazwiska*: part **2.** *zdania*: clause **3.** *rakiety*: module

człon|ek[1] *m* (*-nka*; *-nki*) **1.** (*penis*) penis **2. *~ki*** *lit* (*kończyny*) limbs

członek[2] *m* (*-nka*; *-nkowie*), **-nkini** *f* (*-ni*; *-nie*) (*osoba*) member; **~ *partii*** party member; **~ *załogi*** crew member, crewman; **członkostwo** *n* (*-wa*; *no pl*) membership; **członkowski** *adj* **1.** *legitymacja*, *opłata*: membership **2.** *kraje*: member

człowieczeństwo *n* (*-wa*; *no pl*) humanity

człowiek **I** *m* (*-ka*; *ludzie*) human being, man; **~ *interesu*** businessman; ***~u!*** man!; ***młody ~*** young man **II** *pron* one, you; → ***ludzie***

czmychać ⟨**-chnąć**⟩ (*-cham*) make off

czochrać ⟨**roz-**⟩ (*-ram*) *włosy*: tousle, rumple

czołg *m* (*-gu*; *-gi*) tank; **czołgista** *m* (*-ty*; *-giści*) tank crewman, tankman; **czołgowy** *adj* tank

czołgać się *v/im* (*-gam*) **1.** crawl (low) **2.** *fig* grovel (***przed*** *I* before)

czoł|o *n* (*-ła*; *-ła*) **1.** forehead; ***stawić ~a*** face **2.** (*przód*) front; ***na czele*** (*z przodu*) in front of; ***stać na czele czegoś*** head s.th., be in charge of s.th.

czołobitny *adj* servile

czołow|y *adj* **1.** (*zderzenie*) head-on **2.** (*wybitny*) leading **3.** (*przedni*) frontal; ***zatoki ~e*** ANAT frontal sinuses

czołów|ka *f* (*-ki*; *-ki*) **1.** *filmu*: opening credits **2.** (*czołowa grupa*) ***~ka graczy*** top players; ***~ka polityków*** leading politicians; ***Szwecja jest w światowej ~ce eksporterów*** Sweden is one of the world's leading exporters; ***w ~ce rankingu*** at the top of a ranking **3.** (*w gazecie*) ***trafić na ~ki gazet*** make the headlines

czop *m* (*-pa*/*-pu*; *-py*) plug; **~ *woskowinowy*** impacted cerumen; **czopek** *m* (*-pka*; *-pki*) suppository

czosnek *m* (*-nku*; *no pl*) garlic; **czosnkowy** *adj* garlic

czółenka *pl* (*-nek*) (*buty*) *Br* court shoes, *Am* pumps

czółno *n* (*-na*; *-na*) canoe, boat

czterdziest|ka *f* (*-ki*; *-ki*) forty; ***być po ~ce*** be in one's forties; **czterdziestoletni** *adj osoba*, *budynek*: forty-year-old; **czterdzieści** *num* forty

czterech, **czterej** *num* four

czternastka *f* (*-ki*; *-ki*) fourteen; **czternastolatek** *m* (*-tka*; *-tki*) fourteen-year-old boy; **czternastolatka** *f* (*-ki*; *-ki*) fourteen-year-old girl; **czternast|y** *adj* fourteenth; **o** (***godzinie***) ***~ej*** at 2 (o'clock) p.m.; **czternaście** *num* fourteen

cztero- (*w złożeniach*) four-; **czterokrotny** *adj zwycięzca*: four-time; **czterolatek** *m* (*-tka*; *-tki*) four-year-old boy; **czterolatka** *f* (*-ki*; *-ki*) four-year-old girl; **czteroletni** *adj osoba*, *samochód*: four-year-old; **czteroosobowy** *adj* **1.** *samochód*: four-seat **2.** *pokój*: four-bed; **czterosuwowy** *adj* four-stroke; **czterotomowy** *adj* four-volume

cztery *num* four; ***rozmowa w ~ oczy*** tête-à-tête; **czterysta** num four hundred

czub *m* (*-ba*; *-by*) (*u ptaka*) crest; ***mieć mocno w ~ie*** *infml* be wasted; **czubaty** *adj łyżka*, *talerz*: heaped

C

czub|ek *m* (*-bka*; *-bki*) **1.** tip; ***~ek palca*** fingertip; ***~ek góry lodowej*** the tip of the iceberg; ***na ~ku języka*** on the tip of one's tongue **2.** *drzewa*, *głowy*: top **3.** (*wariat*) *infml* nut

czucie *n* (*-cia*; *no pl*) feeling

czu|ć ⟨**po-**⟩ (*czuję*) **1.** feel; ***~ć sympatię wobec*** *G* have a liking for, like; ***~ć, że*** feel that **2.** *zapach*: smell; ***~ję spaleniznę*** I can smell something burning; ***~ć pismo nosem*** smell a rat; ***czuć się*** feel; ***~ć się dobrze*** (***źle***) feel well (unwell); ***jak się ~jesz?*** how are you feeling?, how are you?; ***~ć się jak ryba w wodzie*** be in one's element; ***~ć się jak u siebie w domu*** feel at home; ***czy ~jesz się na siłach to zrobić?*** do you feel up to the job?

czujka *f* (*-ki*; *-ki*) TECH detector; ***~ pożarowa*** fire detector; **czujnik** *m* (*-ka*; *-ki*) TECH sensor; **czujność** *f* (*-ści*; *no pl*) watchfulness, alertness; **czujny** *adj* **1.** (*uważny*) watchful, alert **2.** (*wrażliwy*) sensitive **3.** *sen*: light

czule *adv* affectionately, tenderly; **czulić się** *v/im* (*-lę*) (*pieścić*) cuddle

czułki *pl* (*-ków*) feelers

czułostkowy *adj* sentimental; **czułość** *f* (*-ści*; *-ści*) **1.** affection, tenderness **2.** *przyrządu*: sensitivity **3.** *filmu*: speed

czuły *adj* **1.** affectionate, tender **2.** *przyrząd*: sensitive; ***~ na światło*** sensitive to light; ***mieć ~ słuch*** have acute hearing

czupiradło *n* (*-ła*; *-ła*) *infml* fright, scarecrow

czupryna *f* (*-ny*; *-ny*) mop

czupurny *adj* provocative, combative

czuwać *v/im* (*-wam*) **1.** (*być czujnym*) be alert **2.** (*o straży*) keep watch **3.** (*pilnować*) watch (***nad*** *I* over)

czwartek *m* (*-tku*; *-tki*) Thursday; ***tłusty ~*** *the last Thursday before Lent*, Fat Thursday; ***Wielki ~*** Holy Thursday; **czwartkowy** *adj* Thursday

czwart|y *adj* fourth; ***jedna ~a*** one fourth; ***o*** (***godzinie***) ***~ej*** at four (o'clock); ***po ~e*** fourthly

czworaczki *pl* (*-ków*) quadruples; **czworak|i**: ***na ~ach*** on all fours

czworo *num* four; ***byliśmy we ~*** there were four of us; ***złożony we ~*** folded in four; **czworobok** *m* (*-ku*; *-ki*) quadrilateral; **czworokąt** *m* (*-ta*; *-ty*) quadrangle; **czworonożny** *adj* four-footed, quadrupedal

czwórk|a *f* (*-ki*; *-ki*) **1.** four; ***byliśmy we ~ę*** there were four of us; ***~ami*** in fours **2.** (*stopień szkolny*) B

czy **I** *particle* **1.** (*w pytaniach*) ***~ to prawda?*** is it true?; ***~ znasz ją?*** do you know her?; ***~ kiedykolwiek tam byłeś?*** have you ever been there?; ***~ umiesz pływać?*** can you swim? **2.** (*w zdaniach podrzędnych*) if, whether; ***nie wiem, ~ to prawda*** I don't know if it's true **II** *conj* or; ***tak ~ inaczej*** one way or another

czyhać *v/im* (*-ham*) **1.** lie in wait (***na*** *A* for) **2.** (*o niebezpieczeństwie*) lurk

czyj, **czyja**, **czyje** *pron* whose; **czyjkolwiek** *pron* anyone's, anybody's; **czyjś** *pron* someone's, somebody's

czyli *conj* **1.** that is **2.** (*inaczej*) or

czym *pron* what; ***o ~ jest ten film?*** what is this film about?; ***~ to zrobiłeś?*** what did you do it with?; → ***co***; **czymkolwiek** → ***cokolwiek***; **czymś** → ***coś***

czyn *m* (*-nu*; *-ny*) act, deed; ***~ przestępczy*** criminal offence; ***człowiek ~u*** the man of action; ***wprowadzić coś w ~*** put s.th. into action

czyni|ć (*-nię*) **1.** ⟨**u-**⟩ do; ***~ć postępy*** make progress; ***~ć zadość*** *prawu*, *prośbie*: comply with; ***okazja ~ złodzieja*** opportunity makes the thief **2.** ⟨**po-**⟩ *ustępstwa*: make

czynieni|e: ***mieć do ~a z*** *I* deal with, have to do with

czynnie *adv* actively; **czynnik** *m* (*-ka*; *-ki*) factor; **czynnoś|ć** *f* (*-ści*; *-ści*) action; activity; ***codzienne ~ci*** daily routine; ***zawieszony w ~ciach*** suspended from one's duties

czynn|y *adj* **1.** active; ***~a napaść*** assault and battery; ***strona ~a*** GRAM the active (voice) **2.** *sklep*: open

czynsz *m* (*-szu*; *-sze*) rent

czyrak *m* (*-ka*; *-ki*) boil

czysta *f* (*-tej*; *-te*) (*wódka*) (straight) vodka; → ***czysty***

czystka *f* (*-ki*; *-ki*) purge; ***~ etniczna*** ethnic cleansing

czysto *adv* **1.** clean; ***w pokoju jest ~*** the room is clean; ***przepisać coś na ~*** make a fair copy of s.th.; ***wyjść na ~***

break even **2.** (*wyłącznie*) purely **3.** *wymawiać*: clearly **4.** *śpiewać*: in tune
czystość *f* (*-ści*; *no pl*) **1.** *pokoju, ubrania*: cleanliness **2.** *substancji*: purity **3.** (*przejrzystość*) clarity **4.** *lit* (*płciowa*) chastity
czyst|y *adj* **1.** *pokój, ubranie*: clean; ***~ej krwi*** thoroughbred **2.** *niebo, sumienie*: clear **3.** *substancja*: pure **4.** (*przejrzysty*) clear **5.** *zysk*: net **6.** *śpiew*: in tune **7.** *wódka*: straight, pure
czyszczący *adj*: ***środek ~*** cleaner
czyszczenie *n* (*-nia*; *-nia*) cleaning
czyścić ⟨**wy-**⟩ (*czyszczę*) clean; ***~ szczotką*** brush
czyściec *m* (*-śćca*; *no pl*) purgatory
czyściej *comp* → **czysto**; **czyściejszy** *comp* → **czysty**
czyściutki *adj dim* clean, spick and span
czytać ⟨**prze-**⟩ (*-tam*) read; ***~ między wierszami*** *fig* read between the lines
czytadło *n* (*-ła*; *-ła*) light reading; **czytanie** *n* (*-nia*; *-nia*) reading
czytanka *f* (*-ki*; *-ki*) text (in a reader)
czytelnia *f* (*-ni*; *-nie*) reading room
czytelnik *m* (*-ka*; *-nicy*), **-niczka** *f* (*-ki*; *-ki*) reader; **czytelnicz|y** *adj*: ***karta ~a*** library card; **czytelny** *adj* **1.** *napis*: legible **2.** (*jasny*) clear
czytnik *m* (*-ka*; *-ki*) reader
czytywać *v/im* (*-tuję*) (sometimes) read
czyż → **czy**
czyżyk *m* (*-ka*; *-ki*) siskin

Ć

ćma *f* (*ćmy*; *ćmy*) moth
ćmić *v/im* (*ćmię*) *fajkę*: puff (*A* on)
ćpać *v/im* (*ćpam*) *infml* do drugs
ćpun *m* (*-na*; *-ny*), **~ka** *f* (*-ki*; *-ki*) *infml* junkie
ćw. *abbr* (= **ćwiczenie**) ex.
ćwiartka *f* (*-ki*; *-ki*) quarter; **ćwiartować** ⟨**po-**⟩ (*-tuję*) quarter
ćwiczebny *adj lot, skok*: training; **ćwiczeni|e** (*n -nia; -nia*): **~e gimnastyczne** exercise; **~a a)** *uniwersyteckie*: classes **b)** *wojskowe*: exercises **2.** (*czynność*) practice
ćwiczyć ⟨**wy-**⟩ (*-czę*) **I** *v/t* **1.** *Br* practice, *Am* practise **2.** *umysł*: exercise **II** *v/i* **1.** *Br* practice, *Am* practise **2.** (*gimnastykować się*) exercise; ***ćwiczyć się*** *Br* practice, *Am* practise (***w*** *L*)
ćwiek *m* (*-ka*; *-ki*) **1.** (*gwóźdź*) hobnail **2.** (*dekoracyjny*) stud; ***zabić ~a*** stump
ćwierć *f* (*-rci*; *-rci*) quarter
ćwierćfinałow|y *adj*: ***mecz ~y*** quarter-final; ***rozgrywki ~e*** quarter-finals; **ćwierćnuta** *f* (*-ty*; *-ty*) MUS *Am* quarter note, *Br* crotchet; **ćwierćwiecz|e** *n* (*-cza*; *-cza*) quarter of a century; ***w pierwszym ~u*** in the first quarter of the century
ćwierkać ⟨**-knąć**⟩ (*-kam*) chirp
ćwikła *f* (*-ły*; *no pl*) COOK *beetroot and horseradish salad*; **ćwikłowy** *adj*: ***burak ~*** *Br* beetroot, *Am* beet
ćwok *m* (*-ka*; *-ki*) *infml* dork, blockhead

D

da → ***dać***
dach *m* (*-chu*; *-chy*) roof; ***bez ~u nad głową*** without shelter; ***mieć ~ nad głową*** have a roof over one's head; **dachować** *v/im* (*-chuję*) (*o samochodzie*) roll over; **dachowy** *adj konstrukcja*: roof; **dachówka** *f* (*-ki*; *-ki*) (roof) tile
dacza *f* (*-czy*; *-cze*) dacha
da|ć *v/p* (*dam*) give; ***~jmy na to*** say; ***nie ~ne mu było tam wrócić*** he was not destined to return there; ***dać się***: ***długo, jak się tylko ~*** as long as possible; ***ile się ~*** as much as possible; ***kraść co się ~*** steal what one can; ***nie ~j się!*** don't give up!; ***szukać oszczędności gdzie się ~*** try to make savings wherever possible

D

daktyl *m* (*-la*; *-le*) **1.** (*owoc*) date **2.** (*w wierszu*) dactyl; **daktylowiec** *m* (*-wca*; *-wce*) date palm

dal *f* (*-li*; *-le*) distance; ***skok w ~*** long jump; ***w ~i*** in the distance; ***z ~a*** from afar; ***z ~a od*** *G* far (away) from

dalece *adv* **1.** *lit* (*z przymiotnikami*) very **2.** (*z czasownikami*) much, far

dalej *adv comp* → ***daleko*** **1.** (*w przestrzeni*) farther **2.** (*w czasie*) further; ***~!*** go ahead!; ***i tak ~*** and so on; ***mówić ~*** go on

dalek|i *adj* **1.** far (**od** *G* from); ***z ~a*** from afar **2.** *kraj*: faraway; ***~i Wschód*** the Far East **3.** *przyszłość*, *krewni*: distant **4** *podobieństwo*: remote

daleko *adv* far; ***~ idący*** *zmiany*, *skutki*: far-reaching; ***~ lepiej*** far better; ***~ więcej*** far more; ***do tego jeszcze ~*** far from it; ***jak ~?*** how far?

dalekobieżny *adj pociąg*: long-distance; **dalekopis** *m* (*-su*; *-sy*) *Br* teleprinter, *Am* teletypewriter; **dalekosiężny** *adj* **1.** *cele*, *plany*: long-term **2.** *zmiany*, *skutki*: far-reaching

dalekowidz *m* (*-dza*; *-dze*) ***być ~em*** *Br* be long-sighted, *Am* be far-sighted; **dalekowzroczność** *f* (*-ści*; *no pl*) **1.** *Br* long-sightedness, *Am* far-sightedness **2.** *fig* far-sightedness; **dalekowzroczny** *adj* **1.** *Br* long-sighted, *Am* far-sighted **2.** *fig* far-sighted

dalia *f* (*-lii*; *-lie*) dahlia

dalmatyńczyk *m* (*-ka*; *-ki*) (*pies*) dalmatian; **dalmatyński** *adj* Dalmatian

dalmierz *m* (*-rza*; *-rze*) rangefinder

dalsz|y *adj comp* → ***daleki*** **1.** further; ***ciąg ~y nastąpi*** to be continued; ***~y ciąg*** continuation; ***~y rozwój*** further development **2.** *odległość*: farther; ***na ~ą metę*** in the long run; ***na ~ym planie*** in the background **3.** *dopełnienie*: indirect

dam → ***dać***

dama *f* (*-my*; *-my*) **1.** lady **2.** (*w kartach*) queen

damasceńsk|i *adj* Damascene; ***stal ~a*** Damascus steel

Damaszek *m* (*-szku*) Damascus

damka *f* (*-ki*; *-ki*) **1.** (*w warcabach*) king **2.** (*rower*) women's bike; **damsk|i** *adj* women's; ***fryzjer ~i*** hairdresser; ***krawiec ~i*** dressmaker; ***toaleta ~a*** *Br* the ladies, *Am* the ladies' room

dan|e *pl* (*-nych*) data; ***baza ~ych*** database; ***~e osobowe*** personal details, personal data; ***ochrona ~ych osobowych*** personal data protection; ***przetwarzanie ~ych*** data processing

Dania *f* (*-nii*) Denmark

danie *n* (*-nia*; *-nia*) **1.** (*potrawa*) dish **2.** (*część posiłku*) course; ***drugie ~*** main course

daniel *m* (*-la*; *-le*) fallow deer

danina *f* (*-ny*; *-ny*) tribute

dansing *m* (*-gu*; *-gi*) dance

dan|y *adj* **1.** (*określony*) given; ***w ~ej chwili*** at a given moment **2.** (*ten*) this; ***w ~ym przypadku*** in this case

dar *m* (*-ru*; *-ry*) gift; ***dać coś komuś w ~ze*** present s.o. with s.th.; ***mieć ~ wymowy*** be articulate; ***w ~ze*** as a gift

daremnie *adv* in vain; **daremność** *f* (*-ści*; *no pl*) futility; **daremny** *adj* futile

darł, ***darłam***, ***darłem*** → ***drzeć***

darmo *adv*: (**za**) **~** (*bezpłatnie*) (for) free; ***na ~*** in vain; ***za pół ~*** for a song; **darmoch|a** (*-chy*; *no pl*) *infml*: ***za ~ę*** (for) free; **darmowy** *adj* free; **darmozjad** *m* (*-da*; *-dy*) *infml* sponger

darnina *f* (*-ny*; *-ny*), **darń** *f* (*-rni*; *-rnie*) turf

darować ⟨**po-**⟩ (*-ruję*) **1.** (*dać*) give (***komuś coś*** s.o. s.th.) **2.** (*ofiarować*) present (***komuś coś*** s.o. with) **3.** (*wybaczyć*) forgive; ***~ komuś winę*** REL absolve s.o. **4.** (*oszczędzić*) ***~ komuś życie*** spare s.o.; ***~ sobie*** spare oneself: ***~ komuś karę*** pardon s.o.; **darowizn|a** *f* (*-ny*; *-ny*) donation; ***akt ~y*** deed of gift

darzyć ⟨**ob-**⟩ (*-rzę*): ***~ sympatią*** like; ***~ szacunkiem*** have respect for; ***~ zaufaniem*** have confidence in, trust

dasz → ***dać***

dasz|ek *m* (*-szka*/*-szku*; *-szki*) **1.** awning **2.** (*czapki*) *Br* peak, *Am* visor; ***czapka z ~kiem*** *Br* peaked cap, *Am* visor cap **3.** (*znak graficzny*) circumflex

dat|a *f* (*-ty*; *-ty*) date; ***być człowiekiem starej ~y*** be old-fashioned; ***~a ważności*** expiry date

datek *m* (*-tku*; *-tki*) contribution, donation

datować *v/im* (*-tuję*) date; ***datować się***: ***~ się od*** date from; **datownik** *m* (*-ka*; *-ki*) date stamp

dawać ⟨**dać**⟩ (*daję*) **1.** give **2.** *ogłoszenie*: put, place **3.** *zysk*: yield, generate **4.** (*pozwolić*) let; **~ komuś coś zrobić** let s.o. do s.th.; **daj mi spokój** leave me alone; **~ cień** provide shade; **~ coś do naprawy** have s.th. repaired; **~ dowód męstwa** prove one's courage; **~ komuś popalić** *infml* give s.o. a hard time; **~ komuś znać** let s.o. know; **~ słowo** give one's word; **~ sobie spokój z** give up; **~ sobie radę** manage (**z** *I* to do); **~ wyraz** (*wyrazić*) express; **~ za wygraną** give up; **~ o sobie znać** make one's presence felt; **dawać się**: **czegoś nie da się uniknąć** s.th. cannot be avoided, you can't avoid s.th.; **dać się słyszeć** can be heard; **~ się komuś we znaki** give s.o. a hard time; **tego zamka nie da się otworzyć** the lock won't open; **to da się zrobić** it can be done

dawca *m* (*-cy*; *-cy*), **-czyni** *f* (*-ni*; *-nie*) donor; **~ krwi** blood donor

dawka *f* (*-ki*; *-ki*) dose; **dawkować** *v/im* (*-kuję*) dose, dosage; **dawkowanie** *n* (*-nia*; *no pl*) dosage

dawniej *adv comp* → **dawno** before; **~ był tu sklep** there used to be a shop here; **jak ~** as before; **Myanmar, ~ Birma** Myanmar, formerly Burma; **dawno** *adv* long ago; **~ jej nie widziałem** I haven't seen her for a long time; **~ temu** a long time ago; **jak ~?** how long ago?

dawn|y *adj* **1.** (*stary*) old **2.** (*były*) former; **od ~a** for a long time; **w ~ych czasach** in the past; **z dawien ~a** from time immemorial; **z ~ych lat** from the old days

dawstwo *n* (*-wa*; *no pl*) donating; **~ krwi** blood donating

dąb *m* (*dębu*; *dęby*) oak; **stawać dęba a)** (*o włosach*) stand on end **b)** (*o koniu*) rear; **dąbrowa** *f* (*-wy*; *-rów*) oak wood

dąć ⟨**za-**⟩ (*dmę*) blow; **~ w trąbkę** blow a trumpet

dąsać się ⟨**na-**⟩ (*-sam*) sulk (**na** *A* about/with); **dąsy** *pl* (*-sów*) sulk *sing*

dążenie *n* (*-nia*; *-nia*) **1.** pursuit (**do** *G* of), quest (**do** *G* for); **~ do doskonałości** the pursuit of perfection; **~ do władzy** the quest for power **2.** (*ambicja*) aspiration; **dążność** *f* (*-ści*; *-ści*) **1.** pursuit (**do** *G* of) **2.** (*ambicja*) aspiration

dążyć *v/im* (*-żę*) **1.** *do celu*, *szczęścia*: pursue (**do** *G*) **2.** *do władzy*, *doskonałości*: strive (**do** *G* for)

dba|ć ⟨**za-**⟩ (*dbam*) **1.** (*troszczyć się*) take care (**o** *A* of); **~ć o linię** watch one's weight **2.** (*zważać*) care; **nie ~ć o** *A* not care about; **nie ~m o to** I don't care (about it)

dbałość *f* (*-ści*; *no pl*) **1.** (*troska*) care (o *A* for) **2.** (*uwaga*) attention; **~ o szczegóły** attention to detail; **dbały** *adj* **1.** (*troskliwy*) caring **2.** (*zwracający uwagę*) attentive (**o** *A* to)

dealer *m* (*-ra*; *-rzy*) dealer; **~ narkotyków** drug dealer

debata *f* (*-ty*; *-ty*) debate (**nad** *I* on); **debatować** *v/im* (*-tuję*) debate (**nad** *I* on)

debel *m* (*-bla*; *-ble*) SPORT doubles *pl*

debet *m* (*-tu*; *no pl*) **1.** (*w księgowości*) debit **2.** (*na koncie*) overdraft; **debetow|y** *adj* debit; **karta ~a** debit card

debil *m* (*-la*; *-le*), **~ka** *f* (*-ki*; *-ki*) *infml* moron; **debilizm** *m* (*-mu*; *no pl*) moronism, moronity; **debilny** *adj infml* moronic

debiut *m* (*-tu*; *-ty*) debut; **debiutować** ⟨**za-**⟩ (*-tuję*) make one's debut; **debiutant** *m* (*-ta*; *-nci*), **~ka** *f* (*-ki*; *-ki*) debutant

decentralizacja *f* (*-ji*; *-je*) decentralization; **decentralizować** ⟨**z-**⟩ (*-tuję*) decentralize

dech *m* (*tchu*; *no pl*) breath; **bez tchu** out of breath; **nabrać tchu** draw breath; **biec co tchu** run as fast as one's legs will carry one; **jednym tchem** *przeczytać*: at one sitting; **zapierać komuś ~ w piersiach** take s.o.'s breath away; **zatrzymać się, by nabrać tchu** stop for breath; **z zapartym tchem** with bated breath

dech|a *f* (*-chy*; *-chy*) plank, board; **gaz do ~y!** *infml* step on it!; **w ~ę** *infml* fab, swell; **na wsi zabitej dechami ~ami** out in the sticks

decy- (*w złożeniach*) deci-

decydent *m* (*-ta*; *-nci*) decision-maker; **decydować** ⟨**z-**, **za-**⟩ (*-duję*) **1.** (*podejmować decyzję*) decide; take a decision (**o** *L* on); **~ o czyimś losie** decide s.o.'s fate; **~, że** decide that

D

2. (*podejmować decyzje*) make decisions **3.** (*przesądzać*) determine (**o** *L*); **decydować się 1.** make up one's mind, decide (**na** *A* on); **~ się coś zrobić** decide to do s.th. **2.** (*o losach*) be decided

D

decydujący *adj* decisive; **decyzj|a** *f* (*-ji*; *-je*) decision (**o** *L* about); **podjąć ~ę** take a decision

dedykacja *f* (*-ji*; *-je*) dedication; **dedykować** ⟨**za-**⟩ (*-kuję*): **~ coś komuś** dedicate s.th to s.o.

defekt *m* (*-tu*; *-ty*) **1.** fault, defect; **~ wymowy** speech defect; **z ~em** faulty, defective **2.** (*ułomność*) handicap

defensyw|a *f* (*-wy*; *-wy*) *Br* defence, *Am* defense; **w ~ie a)** *być*: on the defensive **b)** *grać*: *Br* in defence, *Am* on defense; **defensywny** *adj* defensive

defetyzm *m* (*-mu*; *no pl*) defeatism

deficyt *m* (*-tu*; *-ty*) **1.** ECON deficit; **~ budżetowy** budget deficit **2.** (*niedobór*) shortage; **deficytowość** *f* (*-ści*; *no pl*) unprofitability

deficytowy *adj* **1.** *przedsiębiorstwo*: loss-making **2.** *budżet*: deficit **3.** *towar*: in short supply

defilada *f* (*-dy*; *-dy*) (military) parade; **defilować** ⟨**prze-**⟩ (*-luję*) parade

definicja *f* (*-ji*; *-je*) definition; **definiować** ⟨**z-**⟩ (*-niuję*) define; **definitywny** *adj* definitive, final

deflacja *f* (*-ji*; *no pl*) deflation

deformować ⟨**z-**⟩ (*-muję*) deform; **deformować się** become deformed

defraudacja *f* (*-ji*; *-je*) embezzlement; **defraudant** *m* (*-ta*; *-nci*) embezzler; **defraudować** ⟨**z-**⟩ (*-duję*) embezzle

degeneracja *f* (*-ji*; *no pl*) degeneration; **degenerat** (*-ta*; *-raci*) degenerate; **degenerować się** ⟨**z-**⟩ (*-ruję*) degenerate

degradacja *f* (*-ji*; *no pl*) degradation; **~ środowiska** environmental degradation; **degradować** ⟨**z-**⟩ (*-duję*) degrade

degustacja *f* (*-ji*; *-je*) tasting; **~ wina** wine tasting

deka *n indecl* decagram, 10 grams

dekada *f* (*-dy*; *-dy*) decade

dekadencki *adj* decadent

dekagram *m* (*-mu*; *-my*) decagram, 10 grams

dekalog *m* (*-gu*; *-gi*) **1.** REL the Decalogue **2.** *fig* code

dekapitalizacja *f* (*-ji*; *no pl*) decapitalization

dekarz *m* (*-rza*; *-rze*) roofer

dekiel *m* (*-kla*; *-kle*) (*pokrywka*) lid

deklamacja *f* (*-ji*; *-je*) recitation; **deklamator** *m* (*-ra*; *-rzy*) reciter; **deklamować** ⟨**za-**, **wy-**⟩ (*-muję*) recite

deklaracj|a *f* (*-ji*; *-je*) **1.** declaration; **~a celna** customs declaration; **~a podatkowa** tax declaration; **≈a Praw Człowieka** the Declaration of Human Rights; **złożyć ~ę** make a declaration **2.** (*zobowiązanie*) pledge

deklarować ⟨**za-**⟩ (*-ruję*) **1.** (*ogłaszać*) declare; **~ poparcie** declare one's support **2.** (*przyrzekać*) pledge; **~ pomoc** pledge one's support; **deklarować się** *Br* declare (**po stronie** *G* for)

deklinacja *f* (*-ji*; *-je*) GRAM declension

dekoder *m* (*-ra*; *-ry*) decoder; **dekodowanie** *n* (*-nia*; *-nia*) decoding

dekolt *m* (*-tu*; *-ty*) (*w sukience*) neckline; **głęboki ~** low neckline; **sukienka z ~em** low-cut dress; **dekoltować się** ⟨**wy-**⟩ (*-tuję*) wear low-cut dresses

dekomunizacja *f* (*-ji*; *no pl*) decommunization

dekoniunktura *f* (*-ry*; *no pl*) recession, (economic) crisis

dekonspirować ⟨**z-**⟩ (*-ruję*) unmask; **dekonspirować się** reveal one's identity

dekoracj|a *f* (*-ji*; *-je*) **1.** decoration; **~a orderem** decoration, conferment of an order **2.** FILM THEAT set; **zmiana ~i** set change

dekoracyjn|y *adj* decorative; **rośliny ~e** decorative plants; **dekorator** *m* (*-ra*; *-rzy*), **~ka** *f* (*-ki*; *-ki*) designer; **~ teatralny** theatre set designer

dekorować ⟨**u-**⟩ (*-ruję*) decorate

dekować się ⟨**za-**⟩ (*-kuję*) *infml* dodge the draft; **dekownik** *m* (*-ka*; *-nicy*) *infml Br* scrimshanker, *Am* draft-dodger

dekret *m* (*-tu*; *-ty*) decree; **wydać ~** issue a decree

delegacja *f* (*-ji*; *-je*) **1.** delegation **2.** (*wyjazd służbowy*) business trip **3.** (*zaświadczenie*) (travel) expense report

delegalizacja *f* (*-ji*; *no pl*) delegalization; **delegalizować** ⟨**z-**⟩ (*-zuję*) ban, delegalize
delegat *m* (*-ta*; *-gaci*), **~ka** *f* (*-ki*; *-ki*) delegate; **delegatura** *f* (*-ry*; *-ry*) **1.** branch **2.** *rządu*: office
delegować ⟨**wy-**⟩ (*-guję*) delegate
delektować się *v/im* (*-tuję*) *Br* savour, *Am* savor
delfin *m* (*-na*; *-ny*) **1.** dolphin **2.** SPORT butterfly
delicje *pl* (*-ji*) **1.** (*przysmaki*) delicacies **2.** (*ciastka*) jaffa cakes
delikatesy *pl* (*-sów*) **1.** (*przysmaki*) delicacies **2.** (*sklep*) delicatessen
delikatność *f* (*-ści*; *no pl*) **1.** delicacy; **~ w postępowaniu** sensitivity, delicacy **2.** *światła*: softness **3.** *towaru*: fragility **4.** *sugestii*: gentleness **5.** *mięsa*: tenderness
delikatny *adj* **1.** delicate **2.** *światło*: soft **3.** *towar*: fragile, delicate **4.** *sugestia*: gentle **5.** *mięso*: tender, delicate; **~ wietrzyk** light breeze
delikwent *m* (*-ta*; *-nci*), **~ka** *f* (*-ki*; *-ki*) poor guy
delta *f* (*-ty*; *-ty*) GEOGR delta
demagogiczny *adj* demagogic
demarkacyjn|y *adj*: **linia ~a** demarcation line
demaskować ⟨**z-**⟩ (*-kuję*) expose; **demaskować się** reveal oneself
dementować ⟨**z-**⟩ (*-tuję*) deny
demilitaryzacja *f* (*-ji*; *no pl*) demilitarization
demobil: **jeep z ~u** army surplus jeep
demobilizować ⟨**z-**⟩ (*-zuję*) **1.** *żołnierzy*: demobilize **2.** *pracowników*: demotivate
demograficzny *adj* demographic; **wyż** (**niż**) **~** (*okres*) baby boom (bust)
demokracja *f* (*-ji*; *-je*) democracy; **demokrata** *m* (*-ty*; *-raci*), **-tka** *f* (*-ki*; *-ki*) democrat; **demokratyczny** *adj* democratic; **demokratyzacja** *f* (*-ji*; *no pl*) democratization
demolować ⟨**z-**⟩ (*-luję*) vandalize, *infml* trash
demoludy *pl* (*-dów*) *infml* the Eastern bloc *sing*
demon *m* (*-na*; *-ny*) demon; **demoniczny** *adj* demonic
demonstracja *f* (*-ji*; *-je*) demonstration; **~ siły** a demonstration of power; **demonstracyjny** *adj* ostentatious; **demonstrant** *m* (*-ta*; *-nci*), **~ka** *f* (*-ki*; *-ki*) demonstrator; **demonstrować** ⟨**za-**⟩ (*-ruję*) demonstrate
demontaż *m* (*-żu*; *-że*) disassembly, dismantling; **demontować** ⟨**z-**⟩ (*-tuję*) dismantle
demoralizacja *f* (*-ji*; *no pl*) corruption; **demoralizować** ⟨**z-**⟩ (*-zuję*) corrupt; **demoralizować się** become corrupt; **demoralizujący** *adj* corrupting
den → **dno**
denacjonalizacja *f* (*-ji*; *no pl*) denationalization
denat *m* (*-ta*; *-naci*), **~ka** *f* (*-ki*; *-ki*) the deceased
denaturat *m* (*-tu*; *no pl*) methylated spirit(s)
denazyfikacja *f* (*-ji*; *no pl*) denazification
denerw|ować ⟨**z-**⟩ (*-wuję*) **1.** (*irytować*) annoy; **on mnie ~uje** he gets on my nerves **2.** (*niepokoić*) **~ować kogoś** make s.o. nervous; **denerwować się** **1.** (*złościć się*) be angry **2.** (*być zirytowanym*) be annoyed **3.** (*niepokoić się*) be nervous, be anxious
denerwująco *adv* annoyingly; **działać na kogoś ~** annoy s.o.; **denerwujący** *adj* annoying
denko *n* (*-ka*; *-ka*) **1.** (*wieczko*) lid **2.** *kapelusza*: crown **3.** (*dolna część*) bottom
denny *adj* **1.** *flora*, *fauna*: bottom-dwelling, benthic **2.** (*bezwartościowy*) *infml* crummy
denominacja *f* (*-ji*; *-je*) redenomination
dentysta *m* (*-ty*; *-ntyści*), **-tka** *f* (*-ki*; *-ki*) dentist; **dentystyczny** *adj* **1.** *gabinet*, *fotel*: dentist's **2.** *sprzęt*, *nić*: dental; **technik ~** dental technician; **dentystyka** *f* (*-ki*; *no pl*) dentistry
denuncjator *m* (*-ra*; *-rzy*), **~ka** *f* (*-ki*; *-ki*) informer; **denuncjować** ⟨**za-**⟩ (*-juję*) denounce
departament *m* (*-tu*; *-ty*) department; **≈ Stanu** the State Department
depesza *f* (*-szy*; *-sze*) **1.** (*telegram*) telegram, cable **2.** (*prasowa*) dispatch
depilacja *f* (*-ji*; *no pl*) depilation; **depilator** *m* (*-ra*; *-ry*) hair remover; **depilować** ⟨**wy-**⟩ (*-luję*): **~ nogi** (**ciało**) remove hair from one's legs (body)

D

deponować ⟨**z-**⟩ (*-nuję*) *pieniądze, kosztowności*: deposit
deportacja *f* (*-ji*; *-je*) deportation; **deportować** *v/im* (*-tuję*) deport
depozyt *m* (*-tu*; *-ty*) deposit; **~ bankowy** bank deposit; **oddać do ~u** deposit
deprawacja *f* (*-ji*; *no pl*) depravation; **deprawować** ⟨**z-**⟩ (*-wuję*) deprave
deprecjacja *f* (*-ji*; *no pl*) depreciation; **~ waluty** currency depreciation
depresj|a *f* (*-ji*; *-je*) depression; **popaść w ~ę** fall into depression
deprymować ⟨**z-**⟩ (*-muję*) dishearten; **deprymujący** *adj* disheartening
deptać ⟨**po-**⟩ (*-pczę*/*-pcę*) **1.** tread (**po** *L* on); **~ komuś po piętach** be at s.o.'s heels; **nie ~ trawników!** keep off the grass! **2.** *fig* trample (*A*); **deptak** *m* (*-ka*; *-ki*) **1.** (*w mieście*) pedestrian precinct **2.** (*nad morzem*) promenade
deputat *m* (*-tu*; *-ty*) perk
deputowany *m* (*-nego*; *-ni*), **-na** *f* (*-nej*; *-ne*) deputy
deratyzacja *f* (*-ji*; *no pl*) rodent extermination
derby *pl* (*-bów*) derby *sing*
dereń *m* (*-renia*; *-renie*) (*krzew*) dogwood
deresz *m* (*-sza*; *-sze*) (*koń*) roan
derka *f* (*-ki*; *-ki*) horse-cloth
dermatolog *m* (*-ga*; *-lodzy*) dermatologist; **dermatologia** *f* (*-gii*; *no pl*) dermatology
desant *m* (*-tu*; *-ty*) **1.** (*operacja*) landing; **~ powietrzny** air landing **2.** (*oddziały*) landing troops; **desantowiec** *m* (*-wca*; *-wce*) (*statek*) landing-craft; **desantow|y** *adj* landing; **operacja ~a** landing operation
deseczka *f* (*-ki*; *-ki*) *dim* (small) board
deseń *m* (*-seniu*/*-senia*; *-senie*) pattern, design
deser *m* (*-ru*; *-ry*) dessert; **na ~** for dessert; **deserow|y** *adj* dessert; **łyżeczka ~a** dessert spoon
desk|a *f* (*-ki*; *-ki*) **1.** (*cienka*) board; **~a do prasowania** ironing board; **~a surfingowa** surfboard; **od ~i do ~i** *fig* from cover to cover; **ostatnia ~a ratunku** *fig* the last resort **2.** (*gruba*) plank **3. ~i a)** (*narty*) skis **b)** *THEAT* the stage
deskorolka *f* (*-ki*; *-ki*) skateboard
deskowanie *n* (*-nia*; *-nia*) boarding
desperacki *adj* desperate; **desperat** *m* (*-ta*; *-raci*) desperado
despotyczny *adj* **1.** *rządy, władca*: despotic **2.** *ojciec, mąż*: domineering, tyrannical
destrukcyjny, **destruktywny** *adj* destructive
destylacja *f* (*-ji*; *-je*) *CHEM* distillation; **destylować** ⟨**prze-**⟩ (*-luję*) distil
desygnować *v im/p* (*-nuję*) appoint (**na** *A* as)
deszcz *m* (*-czu*; *-cze*) rain; **~ drobny** light rain; **~ ulewny** heavy rain; **kwaśny ~** acid rain; **pada ~** it's raining; **rosnąć jak grzyby po ~u** mushroom; **w ~u** in the rain; **złapał nas ~** we got caught in the rain; **z ~u pod rynnę** out of the frying pan and into the fire
deszczomierz *m* (*-rza*; *-rze*) rain gauge; **deszczownia** *f* (*-ni*; *-nie*) (*rozpylająca wodę*) sprinkler; **deszczowo** *adv*: **było ~** (*o dniu*) it was a rainy day; **deszczow|y** *adj* rainy; **pora ~a** rainy season; **deszczówka** *f* (*-ki*; *no pl*) rainwater
deszczułka *f* (*-ki*; *-ki*) (small) board
deszczyk *m* (*-ku*; *-ki*) light rain
detal *m* (*-lu*; *-le*) **1.** (*szczegół*) detail; **opisywać coś z ~ami** describe s.th. in detail **2.** *ECON* retail; **cena w ~u** retail price
detalicznie *adv*: **sprzedawać ~** sell retail; **detaliczn|y** *adj* retail; **cena ~a** retail price; **handel ~y** retail (trade)
detektor *m* (*-ra*; *-ry*) detector; **~ gazu** gas detector
detektyw *m* (*-wa*; *-wi*) detective; **detektywistyczny** *adj* detective; **sprzęt ~** detective equipment
detergent *m* (*-tu*; *-ty*) detergent
determinacja *f* (*-ji*; *no pl*) determination; **determinować** ⟨**z-**⟩ (*-nuję*) determine
detonacja *f* (*-ji*; *no pl*) detonation; **detonator** *m* (*-ra*; *-ry*) detonator; **detonować** ⟨**z-**⟩ (*-nuję*) detonate
detronizować ⟨**z-**⟩ (*-zuję*) dethrone
dewaluacja *f* (*-ji*; *-je*) devaluation
dewastacja *f* (*-ji*; *-je*) **1.** *własności publicznej*: vandalization **2.** *środowiska*: devastation; **dewastować** ⟨**z-**⟩ (*-tuję*) **1.** *własność publiczną*: vandalize **2.** *środowisko*: devastate

deweloper *f* (*-ra*; *-rzy*) (property) developer
dewiacja *f* (*-ji*; *-je*) deviation
dewiza *f* (*-zy*; *-zy*) motto; **dewizowy** *adj konto, dochód*: foreign currency; **dewiz|y** *pl* (*dewiz*) foreign currency *sing*; ***kursy ~*** foreign currency exchange rates
dewocja *f* (*-ji*; *no pl*) (religious) bigotry
dewocjonalia *pl* (*-liów*) devotional articles
dewotka *f* (*-ki*; *-ki*) (religious) bigot
dezaktualizować się ⟨**z-**⟩ (*-zuję*) become outdated
dezaprobat|a *f* (*-ty*; *no pl*) disapproval; ***z ~ą*** with disapproval
dezercja *f* (*-ji*; *-je*) desertion; **dezerter** *m* (*-ra*; *-rzy*) deserter; **dezerterować** ⟨**z-**⟩ (*-ruję*) desert
dezinformacja *f* (*-ji*; *no pl*) **1.** misinformation **2.** (*świadoma*) disinformation; **dezinformować** *v/im* (*-muję*) **1.** misinform **2.** (*świadomie*) disinform
dezodorant *m* (*-tu*; *-ty*) deodorant; ***~ w sprayu*** spray deodorant; ***~ w sztyfcie*** stick deodorant
dezorganizacja *f* (*-ji*, *no pl*) disorganization; **dezorganizować** ⟨**z-**⟩ (*-zuję*) *życie, pracę*: upset
dezorientować ⟨**z-**⟩ (*-tuję*) confuse
dezynfekcja *f* (*-ji*; *no pl*) disinfection; **dezynfekcyjny** *adj komora*: disinfection; ***środek ~*** disinfectant; **dezynfekować** ⟨**z-**⟩ (*-kuję*) disinfect
dezynsekcja *f* (*-ji*; *no pl*) insect control
dębieć ⟨**z-**⟩ (*-bieję*) be dumbfounded
dębina *f* (*-ny*; *-ny*) oak wood; **dębow|y** *adj* oak; ***aleja ~a*** avenue of oaks; ***las ~y*** oak wood; ***dęby*** *pl* → ***dąb***
dętka *f* (*-ki*; *-ki*) **1.** (*w kole*) (inner) tube **2.** (*w piłce*) bladder
dęty *adj orkiestra, instrument*: wind
diabelnie *adv* **1.** (*jak diabeł*) devilishly **2.** *nudny*: excruciatingly **3.** *inteligentny*: fiendishly **4.** *gorąco, zimno*: hellishly; ***~ szybki*** fast like hell; **diabeln|y** *adj* **1.** (*diabelski*) devilish **2.** *upał, mróz*: hellish; ***mieć ~e szczęście*** have the luck of the devil; **diabelski** *adj* devilish; ***~ młyn*** Ferris wheel; **diabelsko** *adv* → ***diabelnie***
diab|eł *m* (*-bła*; *-bły*) devil; ***bolało jak ~li*** it hurt like hell; ***co*** (***kto***) ***do ~ła?*** what (who) the hell?; ***co nagle, to po ~le*** haste makes waste; ***~eł tkwi w szczegółach*** the devil is in the detail; ***~li wiedzą*** the devil only knows; ***do ~ła!*** *infml* hell!, damn!; ***do ~ła i trochę*** *infml* hell of a lot; ***gdzie ~eł mówi dobranoc*** in the middle of nowhere; ***idź do ~ła!*** go to hell!; ***jeden ~eł!*** (it's) no bloody difference! *infml*; ***nie taki ~eł straszny, jak go malują*** the devil is not as black as he is painted, s.th. is not as black as it is painted; ***pieniądze ~li wzięli*** the money has gone down the drain; ***po kiego ~ła?*** what the hell for?; ***zimno jak ~li*** (it's) cold as hell
diabełek *m* (*-łka*; *-łki*) **1.** (*chochlik*) imp **2.** (*dziecko*) little devil; **diablica** *f* (*-cy*; *-ce*) she-devil; **diaboliczny** *adj* diabolical
diagnoz|a *f* (*-zy*; *-zy*) diagnosis; ***postawić ~ę*** make a diagnosis; **diagnozować** ⟨**z-**⟩ (*-zuję*) diagnose
diagonalny *adj* diagonal
diagram *m* (*-mu*; *-my*) diagram
diakon *m* (*-na*; *-ni*) deacon
diakrytyczn|y *adj*: ***znaki ~e*** diacritics
dialekt *m* (*-tu*; *-ty*) dialect; **dialektyczny** *adj* dialectical
dializa *f* (*-zy*; *-zy*) dialysis; **dializacyjny** *adj* dialysis; ***płyn ~*** dialysis fluid, dialysate
dialog *m* (*-gu*; *-gi*) dialogue, *Am* dialog
diament *m* (*-tu*; *-ty*) diamond; **diamentow|y** *adj* diamond; ***~e gody*** diamond wedding
didżej *m* (*-ja*; *-je*) DJ
diecezja *f* (*-ji*; *-je*) diocese; **diecezjalny** *adj* diocesan
diesel *m* (*-sla*; *-sle*) diesel; **dieslowski** *adj* diesel
die|ta *f* (*-ty*; *-ty*) **1.** diet; ***być na ~cie*** be on a diet, diet; ***ścisła ~ta*** strict diet **2.** (*w podróży*) travel allowance **3.** ***~ty poselskie*** MP's salary
dietetyczn|y *adj* diet; ***kuchnia ~a*** diet cooking; **dietetyczka** *f* (*-ki*; *-ki*) dietician; **dietetyk** *m* (*-ka*; *-tycy*) dietician
dinozaur *m* (*-ra*; *-ry*) dinosaur
dioda *f* (*-dy*; *-dy*) diode
disc jockey *m* (*-keya*; *-keye*) disc jockey
disco *n indecl* disco; ***muzyka ~*** disco music

D

dla *prep* (*G*) for; **~ *jaj*** *infml* for laughs; **~ *zrobienia czegoś*** to do s.th.; ***film ~ dorosłych*** *Br* adult film, *Am* adult movie; ***miły ~ kogoś*** nice to s.o.; ***przejście ~ pieszych*** *Br* pedestrian crossing, *Am* crosswalk; ***przyjazny ~ środowiska*** environmentally friendly; ***zatrzymać się ~ nabrania tchu*** stop for breath

dlaczego *pron* why; **~ *nie?*** why not?

dlatego *pron* so; **~, *że*** because

dł. *abbr* (= **długość**) l.

dławić (*-wię*) **1.** *v/im* choke **2.** ⟨**z-**⟩ *bunty*: stifle; **dławić się** ⟨**u-**⟩ choke

dławiec *m* (*-wca*; *no pl*) diphtheria

dławik *m* (*-ka*; *-ki*) (*cewka*) choke

dłoniasty *adj liście*: palmate

dło|ń *f* (*dłoni*; *dłonie*) **1.** (*wewnętrzna część ręki*) palm; ***jasne jak na ~ni*** clear as day **2.** (*ręka*) hand; ***podać komuś pomocną ~ń*** *fig* give s.o. a helping hand; ***uścisnąć sobie ~nie*** shake hands

dłubać ⟨**po-**⟩ (*-bię*) **1. *~ w nosie*** (***zębach***) pick one's nose (teeth) **2.** *figurki*: carve **3.** (*majstrować*) *infml* tinker (**przy** *L* with)

dług *m* (*-gu*; *-gi*) debt; **~ *publiczny*** *ECON* national debt; ***mieć ~i*** be in debt; ***mieć ~ wdzięczności wobec*** *G* owe a debt of gratitude to; ***wpaść w ~i*** get into debt

długawy *adj* longish

długi *adj* long; **~ *do kolan*** knee-long; **~ *do kostek*** ankle-long; **~ *na 15 metrów*** 15 metres long; ***jak dzień ~*** all day long; ***upaść jak ~*** fall flat on the ground

długo *adv* long; ***jak ~?*** how long?; ***tak ~ (,) jak*** as long as

długodystansowiec *m* (*-wca*; *-wcy*) long-distance runner; **długodystansowy** *adj* long-distance

długofalowo *adv planować*: long term; **długofalowy** *adj planowanie*, *cel*: long-term

długogrając|y *adj*: ***płyta ~a*** long-playing record, LP

długoletni *adj* long-standing; **długometrażowy** *adj*: ***film ~*** feature film; **długonogi** *adj* **1.** long-legged **2.** *kobieta*: leggy *infml*

długopis *m* (*-su*; *-sy*) (ball-point) pen

długoś|ć *f* (*-ści*; *-ści*) length; ***~ć fali*** *PHYS* wavelength; ***~ć geograficzna*** longitude; ***mieć dwa metry ~ci*** be two metres long

długoterminowy *adj* long-term

długotrwały *adj* **1.** *związek*, *skutek*: long-lasting **2.** *choroba*, *stres*, *oklaski*: prolonged **3.** *pamięć*: long-term

długowieczność *f* (*-ści*; *no pl*) longevity; **długowieczny** *adj* **1.** long-lived **2.** *baterie*: long-life

długowłosy *adj* long-haired

dłut|o *n* (*-ta*; *-ta*) chisel; ***~a Michała Anioła*** by Michelangelo

dłużej *adv comp* → **długo** longer

dłużnik *m* (*-ka*; *-nicy*), **-niczka** *f* (*-ki*; *-ki*) debtor

dłużny *adj* **1. *być ~m*** owe (***komuś coś*** s.o. s.th./s.th. to s.o.) **2. *skrypt ~*** *FIN* debt certificate, IOU

dłuższ|y *adj comp* → **długi** longer; ***od ~ego czasu*** for a long while; ***na ~ą metę*** in the long run; ***na ~y czas*** for a long while

dłużyć się *v/im* (*-żę*) drag (on); ***czas się dłużył*** time dragged on; **dłużyzna** *f* (*-ny*; *-ny*) (*w filmie*) longueur

dmą, **dmę** → **dąć**

dmuchać ⟨**-chnąć**⟩ (*-cham*) blow; ***nie dam sobie w kaszę ~*** I won't let myself be led by the nose, I won't play the game by their rules; **dmuchawa** *f* (*-wy*; *-wy*) blower

dmuchawiec *m* (*-wca*; *-wce*) blowball

dmuchnąć *v/p* (*-cham*) (*ukraść*) *infml* pinch; → **dmuchać**

dn. *abbr* (= **dnia**) (*data*) on; ***dn. 21 marca 2004*** *Br* on 24 March 2004, *Am* on March 21, 2004

dna[1] *f* (*dny*; *no pl*) *MED* arthritis

dna[2], **dnem** → **dno**

dni, **dnie** → **dzień**

dnie|ć: ***~je*** the day is dawning

dniówk|a *f* (*-ki*; *-ki*) **1.** (*płaca*) daily wage; ***pracować na ~ę*** be paid on a daily basis **2.** (*dzień pracy*) working day

dniu → **dzień**

dn|o *n* (*dna*; *dna*) **1.** bottom; ***do ~a!*** bottoms up!; ***do góry ~em*** bottom up; ***drugie ~o*** *fig* hidden meaning; ***odbić się od ~a*** *fig* bottom out; ***pójść na ~o*** go down; ***stoczyć się na ~o*** *fig* hit rock bottom; ***wypić do ~a*** drink up **2.** *morza*, *rzeki*: bed, bottom **3.** *do-*

liny, *jaskini*, *oceanu*: floor **4.** (*coś bezwartościowego*) ***to ~o*** *infml* it sucks

do *prep* (*G*) **1.** to **2.** (*w kierunku*) to; ***~ szkoły*** to school; ***iść ~ domu*** go home **3.** (*nie dłużej niż*) until, till; ***czekał ~ piątku*** he waited until Friday; ***od... ~*** from... to; ***będzie gotowe ~ poniedziałku*** it will be ready by Monday **4.** (*nie dalej niż*) to; ***od... ~*** from... to **5.** (*do wnętrza*) into; ***~ pudełka*** into a box; ***wejść ~ pokoju*** enter a room **6.** (*nie więcej niż*) up to; ***~ dwóch godzin*** up to two hours **7.** (*o przeznaczeniu*) for; ***coś ~ jedzenia*** something to eat; ***klucz ~ drzwi*** door key; ***list ~ ciebie*** a letter for you; ***szczoteczka ~ zębów*** tooth brush; ***dwa razy ~ roku*** two times a year; ***~ roboty!*** (let's) get to work!; ***~ widzenia!*** good-bye!; ***~ zobaczenia!*** see you!; ***wpół ~ drugiej*** half past one

dob|a *f* (*-by*; *-by*) **1.** day (and night), 24 hours; ***czynny całą ~ę*** open round the clock; ***w ciągu ostatniej ~y*** in the last 24 hours **2.** (*epoka*) age

doberman *m* (*-na*; *-ny*) Dobermann (pinscher)

dobić *v/p* → ***dobijać***

dobiec *v/p*: ***~ do mety*** reach the finish line; → ***dobiegać***

dobieg *m* (*-gu*; *no pl*) SPORT finish

dobie|gać ⟨**-biec**⟩ (*-gam*) **1.** (*o dźwięku*, *głosie*) come **2.** (*zbliżać się*) ***~gać czterdziestki*** be pushing forty *infml*; ***~gać końca*** come to an end; ***~ga północ*** it's almost midnight; ***już ~gała do autobusu, gdy zamknęły się drzwi*** she almost made it to the bus when the door closed

dobierać ⟨**-brać**⟩ (*-ram*) **1.** (*wybierać*) select, choose; ***starannie ~ słowa*** carefully choose one's words **2.** (*dopasowywać*) match (**do** *G* to); **dobierać się 1.** (*dostawać się*) get (**do** *G* at) **2.** (*seksualnie*) *infml* make a pass (**do** *G* at) **3.** (*łączyć się*) ***~ się parami*** form pairs

dobi|jać ⟨**-bić**⟩ (*-jam*) **I.** *v/t* **1.** *człowieka*, *zwierzę*: kill off **2.** (*psychicznie*) ***ta pogoda mnie ~ja*** the weather is killing me; ***ta wiadomość go ~ła*** he was devastated by the news; ***~jać targu*** strike a deal **II.** *v/i* (*przyłączać się*) join (**do** *G*); ***~jać do brzegu*** reach the shore; ***~jać się*** bang at the door

dobitk|a *f* (*-ki*; *-ki*) SPORT second shot; ***na ~ę*** to top it all

dobitny *adj* **1.** (*wyraźny*) emphatic **2.** (*dosadny*) blunt

doborowy *adj* **1.** *towarzystwo*: select, elite **2.** *oddziały*: crack, elite; ***~ strzelec*** crack shot

dobosz *m* (*-sza*; *-sze*) (army) drummer

dobowy *adj opóźnienie*: 24-hour; → ***doba***

dobór *m* (*-boru*; *no pl*) selection; ***~ naturalny*** BIOL natural selection

dobra *pl* (*dóbr*) **1.** (*majątek*) property *sing* **2.** (*towary*) goods; ***~ konsupcyjne*** consumer goods

dobrać się *v/p* (*-biorę*) (*dopasować się*): ***świetnie się dobrali*** they are a great match; → ***dobierać się***

dobranoc *n indecl*: ***~!*** good night!; ***przeczytać komuś bajkę na ~*** read s.o. a bedtime story; **dobranocka** *f* (*-ki*; *-ki*) *infml bedtime TV cartoon*

dobrany *adj* **1.** well-matched **2.** (*z przysłówkami*) matched; ***dobrze ~*** well-matched; ***źle ~*** badly matched

dobre: ***na ~*** for good; → ***dobry***

dobrnąć *v/p* (*-nę*) manage to reach (**do** *G*); ***~ do końca książki*** manage to get to the end of a book

dobr|o *n* (*-ra*; *-ra*) good; ***~o społeczne*** the public good; ***dla ~a firmy*** for the good of the company; ***dla ~a dzieci*** for the sake of (the) children; ***dla twojego ~a*** for your own good; ***zapisać 100 złotych na ~o rachunku*** credit 100 zlotys to an account

dobrobyt *m* (*-tu*; *no pl*) prosperity

dobroczynność *f* (*-ści*; *no pl*) charity; **dobroczynn|y** *adj* **1.** *akcja*, *impreza*: charity; ***działalność ~a*** charity; ***na cele ~e*** for charity **2.** *wpływ*, *sen*: beneficial

dobroczyńca *m* (*-cy*; *-cy*) benefactor

dobroć *f* (*-roci*; *no pl*) goodness

dobroduszność (*-ści*; *no pl*) good nature, kind heart; **dobroduszny** *adj* good-natured, kind-hearted

dobrodziejstwo *n* (*-wa*; *-wa*) (*korzyść*) benefit, blessing

dobrosąsiedzki *adj Br* neighbourly, *Am* neighborly

D

D

dobrotliwość *f* (*-ści*; *no pl*) good heart; **dobrotliwy** *adj* kind-hearted

dobrowolny *adj* voluntary

dobr|y *adj* good (**na** *A* for, **do** *G* for; **w** *L* at); ***brać coś za ~ą monetę*** *fig* take s.th at face value; ***być ~ej myśli*** hope for the best; ***dzień ~y!*** **a)** (*rano*) good morning! **b)** (*po południu*) good afternoon!; ***~a!*** *infml* all right!; ***~a wola*** goodwill; ***~y wieczór!*** good evening!; ***działać w ~ej wierze*** act in good faith; ***~e sobie!*** it's ridiculous!; ***na ~ą sprawę*** actually; ***na ~e i na złe*** for better or (for) worse; ***wszystkiego ~ego!*** all the best!; ***wszystko ~e, co się dobrze kończy*** all's well that ends well; → ***dobre***

dobrze *adv* **1.** well; ***~ ubrany*** well-dressed; ***~ wychowany*** well mannered; ***~ znany*** well-known; ***komuś się ~ powodzi*** s.o. is well off; ***życzyć komuś ~*** wish s.o. well **2.** *wyglądać, czuć się, smakować*: good; ***~!*** good!; ***ona ~ się uczy*** she is a good student; ***~ ci tak!*** it serves you right!; ***~ postąpić*** do the right thing; ***~ widziany*** welcome; ***mieć się ~*** be all right; ***równie ~ mógłbyś powiedzieć, że*** you might as well say that; ***to ~ robi na*** *A* it's good for

dobudowywać ⟨**-dować**⟩ (*-dowuję*) *skrzydło, oficynę*: add, build

dobudówka *f* (*-ki*; *-ki*) *Br* extension, *Am* addition

dobudzić *v/p* (*-dzę*) wake up

dobyć *v/p* → ***dobywać***

dobytek *m* (*-tku*; *no pl*) **1.** property **2.** (*ruchomy*) belongings *pl*

dobywać ⟨**-być**⟩ (*-wam*) *lit miecza, szabli*: draw

docelowy *adj* **1.** *grupa, klienci*: target **2.** *stacja, lotnisko*: destination; ***port ~*** port of destination

doceniać ⟨**-nić**⟩ (*-niam*) appreciate; ***nie ~*** underestimate, underrate

docent *m* (*-ta*; *-nci*) *Br* reader, *Am* associate professor

dochodowość *f* (*-ści*; *no pl*) profitability; **dochodowy** *adj* profitable; ***podatek ~*** income tax

dochodzenie *n* (*-nia*; *-nia*) investigation, enquiry; ***~ sądowe*** prosecution

dochodzić ⟨**dojść**⟩ (*-dzę*) **1.** (*do miejsca, celu*) get (**do** *G* to), reach (**do** *G*) **2.** (*o liście, przesyłce*) arrive **3.** (*o zapachu*) come **4.** (*o dźwięku, głosie*) be heard; ***z dołu dochodziły głosy*** voices could be heard from downstairs; ***doszły nas słuchy, że*** we've heard rumours that **5.** (*o drodze*) lead (**do** *G* to) **6.** *praw*: claim **7.** (*osiągać*) reach (**do** *G*); ***~ do formy*** get into shape; ***~ do perfekcji*** achieve perfection; ***~ do zdrowia*** recover; ***doszło do wypadku*** there was an accident; ***~ do siebie*** (*odzyskiwać przytomność*) come around; ***~ prawdy*** seek the truth; ***dochodzi ósma*** it's almost eight; ***nie dali mi dojść do słowa*** *Br* I couldn't get a word in edgeways, *Am* I couldn't get a word in edgewise; ***spotkanie nie doszło do skutku*** there was no meeting, the meeting was cancelled

dochowywać ⟨**-chować**⟩ (*-chowuję*): ***~ tajemnicy*** keep a secret; ***~ wierności*** remain faithful; **dochowywać się** (*zachować się*) survive

dochód *m* (*-chodu*; *-chody*) income; ***czysty ~*** net profit; ***~ ze sprzedaży biletów*** revenue from ticket sales; ***dochody*** income

dociąć *v/p* → ***docinać***

dociągać ⟨**-gnąć**⟩ (*-gam*) pull (**do** *G* to) *pas, śrubę*: tighten

dociekać ⟨**-ciec**⟩ (*-kam*) **1.** investigate (*G*), enquire (*G* into); ***~ przyczyn*** investigate the causes **2.** *prawdy, znaczenia*: seek

dociekanie *n* (*-nia*; *-nia*) investigation, enquiry; **dociekliwy** *adj* enquiring; ***~ umysł*** enquiring mind

docierać ⟨**dotrzeć**⟩ (*-ram*) **I** *v/i* **1.** *do miejsca, celu*: get (**do** *G* to), reach (**do** *G*) **2.** (*o liście*) arrive **3.** (*o głosie*) ***do pokoju docierały ich głosy*** their voices could be heard in the room **II** *v/t samochód*: run in

docinać ⟨**-ciąć**⟩ (*-nam*) cut to size; ***~ coś do czegoś*** cut s.th. to fit s.th.; **docinek** *m* (*-nka*; *-nki*) jibe, cutting remark

dociskać ⟨**-snąć**⟩ (*-kam*) *wieko, śrubę*: tighten; ***~ śrubę*** *fig* tighten up; ***dociskać się***: ***dosisnąć się gdzieś*** push one's way somewhere

do cna *adv* completely; ***dom spłonął ~*** the house burnt to the ground; ***zepsuty ~*** corrupt to the bone

docucić *v/p* → ***cucić***
doczekać *v/p* (*-kam*) **1.** (*dotrwać*) wait (*G* till) **2.** (*dożyć*) live (*G* to); **~ starości** live to an old age; **doczekać się**: ***nie mogę się ~*** I can't wait (*G* for)
doczepiać 〈**-pić**〉 (*-piam*) attach, couple (**do** *G* to)
doczesny *adj* **1.** *życie, świat*: earthly **2.** *dobra*: worldly
doczołgać się *v/p* (*-gam*) crawl (**do** *G* to)
doczytywać 〈**-tać**〉 (*-tuję*) read (**do** *G* to); ***~ do końca*** read to the end
dodać *v/p* → ***dodawać***
dodat|ek *m* (*-tku*; *-tki*) **1.** addition; ***na ~ek, w ~ku*** in addition **2.** (*do żywności, benzyny*) additive; ***z ~kiem*** *G* with **2.** (*do pensji*) allowance; ***~ek mieszkaniowy*** *Br* housing benefit; ***~ek rodzinny*** *Br* child benefit **3.** (*do pisma*) supplement; ***~ek nadzwyczajny*** special **4.** ***~ki*** (*do ubioru*) accessories
dodatkowo *adv* **1.** (*w dodatku*) in addition, additionally **2.** *zapłacić, zarobić*: extra; **dodatkow|y** *adj* additional; ***~y personel*** extra staff; ***informacje ~e*** additional information, supplementary information; ***opłata ~a*** extra charge, surchage
dodatni *adj* positive
dodawać 〈**-dać**〉 (*-daję*) add (**do** *G* to); ***~ gazu*** *infml* step on it; ***~ komuś otuchy*** boost s.o.'s morale
dodawani|e *n* (*-nia*; *no pl*) *MATH* addition; ***znak ~a*** plus sign
dodruk *m* (*-ku*; *-ki*) reprint, reimpression
dodzwonić się *v/p* (*-nię*) get through (**do** *G* to); ***nie mogłem się do niej dodzwonić*** I tried calling her but there was no answer
dofinansowywać 〈**-sować**〉 (*-sowuję*) *ECON* (financially) support
dog *m* (*-ga*; *-gi*) Great Dane
dogadywać się 〈**-dać**〉 (*-duję*) **1.** (*mówiąc w obcym języku*) understand each other **2.** (*zostać zrozumianym*) make oneself understood **3.** (*po negocjacjach*) come to an arrangement (**z** *I* with)
dogadzać 〈**-godzić**〉 (*-dzam*) please; ***~ czyimś zachciankom*** pander to s.o.'s every whim; ***~ sobie*** indulge oneself; ***nie można dogodzić wszystkim*** you can't please everyone
doganiać 〈**-gonić**〉 (*-niam*) **1.** (*zrównywać się*) catch up (**z** *I* with) **2.** (*łapać*) catch
dogasać 〈**-snąć**〉 (*-sam*) (*o płomieniu*) dye down
doglądać *v/im* (*-dam*) (*opiekować się*) tend to
dogłębny *adj wiedza, analiza*: in-depth
dogmat *m* (*-tu*; *-ty*) dogma; **dogmatyk** *m* (*-ka*; *-tycy*) dogmatist
dogodność *f* (*-ści*; *no pl*) *lokalizacji, połączenia*: convenience; **dogodny** *adj* **1.** convenient; ***w ~m dla kogoś terminie*** at s.o.'s convenience **2.** *warunki*: good, *Br* favourable, *Am* favorable **3.** *okazja*: good
dogodzić *v/p* → ***dogadzać***
dogonić *v/p* → ***doganiać***
dogorywać *v/im* (*-wam*) be dying in agony
dogrywać 〈**-rać**〉 (*-wam*) **1.** *grę, partię*: finish **2.** (*nagrać*) record **3.** (*grać*) ***~ coś do końca*** play s.th. to the end **4.** (*ustalać*) *infml* agree (the details of); **dogrywka** *f* (*-ki*; *-ki*) *SPORT* *Br* extra time, *Am* overtime
dogryzać 〈**-ryźć**〉 (*-zam*) jibe (*D* at)
dogrzewać 〈**-rzać**〉 (*-wam*) heat; ***~ (jeszcze) wody*** heat more water
doić 〈**wy-**〉 (*doję*) milk
doigrać się *v/p* (*-ram*): ***doigrał się*** he got what was coming to him
dojadać 〈**-jeść**〉 (*-dam*) **1.** *posiłek*: finish **2.** *ciastko, surówkę*: finish up; ***nie ~*** *Br* live on the breadline
dojarka *f* (*-ki*; *-ki*) **1.** *TECH* milking machine **2.** (*osoba*) milkmaid
dojazd *m* (*-du*; *-dy*) **1.** (*podróż*) travel; ***~ do pracy*** commute (to work) **2.** (*droga*) access; **dojazdow|y** *adj*: ***droga ~a*** access road
dojechać *v/p* → ***dojeżdżać***
dojeść *v/p* → ***dojadać***
dojeżdżać 〈**-jechać**〉 (*-dżam*) **1.** (*docierać*) get (**do** *G* to); ***~ do domu*** get home, arrive home **2.** (*zbliżać się*) approach **3.** (*regularnie*) travel; ***~ do pracy*** commute
dojmujący *adj lit* **1.** *ból*: acute **2.** *zimno*: bitter **3.** *wrażenie*: profound
dojny *adj krowa*: milk

D

dojrzałoś|ć *f* (*-ści*; *no pl*) **1.** maturity; ***~ć płciowa*** sexual maturity **2.** *owocu*: ripeness; ***egzamin ~ci*** final exams; ***świadectwo ~ci*** *Br* GCSE, *Am* high school diploma; **dojrzały** *adj* **1.** mature; ***wiek ~*** maturity **2.** *owoc*: ripe

dojrzeć *v/p* (*-rzę*) (*ujrzeć*) see; **dojrzewać** ⟨**-rzeć**⟩ (*-wam*) **1.** mature; ***ktoś dojrzał do zrobienia czegoś*** *fig* s.o. is mature enough to do s.th. **2.** (*o owocach*) ripen

dojrzewani|e *n* (*-nia*; *no pl*); ***~e płciowe*** puberty; ***okres ~a*** adolescence; ***problemy wieku ~a*** adolescent problems

dojści|e *n* (*-cia*; *-cia*) **1.** (*droga*) way **2.** (*dostęp*) access **3.** (*piechotą*) walk; ***~e do porozumienia*** reaching an agreement; ***~e do władzy*** rise to power; ***mieć ~a*** *infml* have connections

dojść *v/p* → **dochodzić**

dok *m* (*-ku*; *-ki*) dock; ***w ~u*** in dock

dokańczać ⟨**-kończyć**⟩ (*-czam*) finish

dokazywać *v/im* (*-zuję*) frolic

dokąd *pron* where; ***~ bądź*** anywhere; ***nie mieć ~ pójść*** have nowhere to go; ***powiedz mi, ~ idziemy*** tell me where we are going; **dokądkolwiek** *pron* anywhere; ***~ szedł, zabierał ją za sobą*** he took her wherever he went

doker *m* (*-ra*; *-rzy*) docker

dokładać ⟨**dołożyć**⟩ (*-dam*) (*dodawać*) add; ***dołożył nam brakującą sumę pieniędzy*** he gave us the rest of the money we needed; ***~ komuś ryżu*** give s.o. more rice; ***~ starań, by coś zrobić*** make every effort to do s.th.; ***musiała dołożyć do tego interesu*** she lost on the deal; ***~ komuś*** *infml* give s.o. a bashing; ***dokładać się*** contribute (**do** *G* to)

dokładk|a *f* (*-ki*; *-ki*) second helping, *infml* seconds *pl*; ***na ~ę*** (*w dodatku*) on top of that

dokładnie *adv* **1.** exactly; ***w tym ~ momencie*** at that exact moment **2.** *zmierzyć*: accurately, precisely **3.** *skontrolować*: closely **4.** (*szczegółowo*) in detail

dokładność *f* (*-ści*; *no pl*) accuracy, precision; ***z dokładnością do 0,1 mm*** with 0.1 mm precision; **dokładny** *adj* **1.** *osoba*, *pomiar*: accurate, precise **2.** *kopia*: exact **3.** *kontrola*: close **4.** (*szczegółowy*) detailed

dokoła **I** *adv* around **II** *prep* (*G*) around; ***rozglądać się ~*** (***siebie***) look around

dokonać *v/p* → **dokonywać**

dokonanie *n* (*-nia*; *-nia*) achievement, accomplishment; **dokonany** *adj czasownik*: perfective; ***postawić kogoś przed faktem ~m*** present s.o. with a fait accompli

dokonywać ⟨**-nać**⟩ (*-nuję*) **1.** *wyboru*, *transakcji*, *odkrycia*: make **2.** *zbrodni*: commit **3.** *bohaterskiego czynu*: perform; ***~ korekty błędu*** rectify a mistake; ***~ włamania do mieszkania*** *Br* burgle a flat, *Am* burglarize an apartment; ***dokonywać się*** take place

dokończenie *n* (*-nia*; *-nia*) **1.** (*ostatnia część*) final part; ***~ w następnym numerze*** to be continued in the next issue **2.** *pracy*, *budowy*: completion

dokończyć *v/p* → **dokańczać**

dokopywać ⟨**-pać**⟩ (*-puję*) *infml* beat; ***dokopywać się*** dig down (**do** *G* to)

dokręcać ⟨**-cić**⟩ (*-cam*) **1.** *śrubę*: tighten **2.** *kran*: turn off

dokształcać się ⟨**-cić**⟩ (*-cam*) **1.** (*samodzielnie*) broaden one's knowledge **2.** (*w szkole*) further one's education

doktor *m* (*-ra*; *-rzy*/*-rowie*) **1.** doctor **2.** (*nauk humanistycznych*) PhD, Doctor of Philosophy; ***~ honoris causa*** honorary doctor; ***~ medycyny*** MD, Doctor of Medicine; **doktorat** *m* (*-tu*; *-ty*) doctorate, doctor's degree; ***robić ~*** study for one's doctorate

doktorsk|i *adj* doctoral; ***praca ~a*** *Br* doctoral thesis, *Am* doctoral dissertation; **doktoryzować się** *v/im* (*-zuję*) take a doctorate (**z** *G* in)

doktryna *f* (*-ny*; *-ny*) doctrine; **doktrynerski** *adj* doctrinaire

dokuczać ⟨**-czyć**⟩ (*-czam*) **1.** (*złośliwie*) ***~ komuś z powodu czegoś*** to tease s.o. about s.th. **2.** (*o dolegliwościach*) trouble; ***komuś dokucza ból*** s.o. is in pain; ***komuś dokucza głód*** s.o. feels pangs of hunger, s.o. is hungry

dokuczliwy *adj* **1.** *osoba*, *kaszel*, *komary*: troublesome **2.** *ból*: nagging **3.** *mróz*, *wiatr*: biting **4.** *upał*: oppressive

dokuczyć *v/p* → **dokuczać**

dokument *m* (*-tu*; *-ty*) document; **~ tożsamości** proof of identity, ID; **dokumenty** (*stwierdzające tożsamość*) ID, papers

dokumentacja *f* (*-ji*; *-je*) documentation; **dokumentalista** *m* (*-ty*; *-liści*) **1.** (*w biurze*) documentalist **2.** (*filmowiec*) documentary maker

dokumentalny *adj* documentary; **film ~** documentary; **dokumentować** ⟨**u-**⟩ (*-tuję*) document

dokupywać ⟨**-pić**⟩ (*-puję*) buy more

dol. *abbr* (= **dolar**) dollar

dol|a *f* (*-li*; *no pl*) (*los*) lot; **~e i niedole** ups and downs

dolać *v/p* → **dolewać**

dolar *m* (*-ra*; *-ry*) dollar

dol|atywać ⟨**-lecieć**⟩ (*-tuję*) **1.** (*o pasażerze*) reach one's destination; **~ecieć na Alaskę** reach Alaska **2.** (*o zapachu*, *odgłosie*) come

dolega|ć *v/im*: **co ci ~?** what's the matter?; **nic jej nie ~** she's all right

dolegliwoś|ć *f* (*-ści*; *-ści*) **1.** ailment **2.** (*poważna*) condition; **cierpieć na ~ci sercowe** have a heart condition; **dolegliwy** *adj ból*: acute

dolepiać ⟨**-pić**⟩ (*-piam*) (*przyklejać*) stick (**do** *G* to)

dolewać ⟨**-lać**⟩ (*-wam*) pour more (**do** *G* into); **~ komuś zupy** give s.o. more soup

doliczać ⟨**-czyć**⟩ (*-czam*) **1.** (*włączać*) include (**do** *G* in); **~ odsetki** add interest **2.** (*liczyć*) count; **doliczyć się**: **nie mogła się doliczyć kilku łyżek** she was a few spoons short

dolina *f* (*-ny*; *-ny*) valley; **~ rzeki** river valley

doln|y *adj* **1.** (*niżej położony*) lower; **~a warga** lower lip; **~a Odra** the lower Oder; **~y Śląsk** Lower Silesia **2.** (*najniższy*) bottom; **~a szuflada** bottom drawer

dolutowywać ⟨**-tować**⟩ (*-towuję*) solder (**do** *G* to/onto)

doładowywać ⟨**-dować**⟩ (*-dowuję*) **1.** (*załadowywać*) load more **2.** *baterię*: recharge

dołączać ⟨**-czyć**⟩ (*-czam*) **1.** (*przyłączać się*) join (**do** *G*) **2.** *pismo*, *zdjęcie*: enclose (**do** *G* with); **dołączać się** (*o osobach*) join (**do** *G*)

doł|ek *m* (*-łka*; *-łki*) **1.** hole; **być w ~ku** *fig* be down in the dumps **2.** (*w policzku*, *brodzie*) dimple; **dołem** *adv* (*pod*) underneath

dołożyć *v/p* → **dokładać**

doły *pl* (*-łów*): **~ społeczne** lower classes; → **dół**

dom *m* (*-mu*; *-my*) house; **w ~u** at home; **iść do ~u** go home; **~ akademicki** *Br* hall of residence, *Am* dormitory; **~ dziecka** children's home; **~ handlowy**, **~ towarowy** department store; **~ kultury** *Br* community centre, *Am* community center; **~ mieszkalny** residential house; **~ poprawczy** *Br* borstal, *Am* reformatory; **~ publiczny** brothel; **~ starców** old people's home; **~ wariatów** *infml* madhouse; **czuć się jak u siebie w ~u** feel at home; **u kogoś w ~u** at s.o.'s house; **ona zajmuje się ~em** she is a housewife; **pan ~u** host; **pani ~u** hostess; **z ~u** (*o kobiecie*) née

domaciczny *adj* intrauterine; **~ środek antykoncepcyjny** intrauterine device, IUD

domaga|ć się *v/im* (*-gam*) **1.** (*żądać*) demand **2.** (*potrzebować*) be in need (*G* of); **jego żołądek ~ł się jedzenia** he felt the pangs of hunger

domalowywać ⟨**-lować**⟩ (*-lowuję*) paint in

domator *m* (*-ra*; *-rzy*), **~ka** *f* (*-ki*; *-ki*) homebody

domek *m* (*-mku*; *-mki*) (small) house; **~ dla ptaków** birdhouse; **~ jednorodzinny** single-family house; **~ kempingowy** camping bungalow; **~ letniskowy** holiday home; **~ z kart** house of cards

domiar *m*: **na ~ złego** to make matters worse, *infml* to top it all

domieszać *v/p* (*-szam*) mix (**do** *G* into); **domieszk|a** *f* (*-ki*; *-ki*) **1.** addition; **z ~ą czegoś** with s.th.; **koń z ~ą krwi arabskiej** horse with some Arab blood **2.** (*do paliwa*) additive **3.** *ironii*: tinge

domięśniowy *adj* intramuscular

Dominikana *f* (*-ny*) the Dominican Republic

D

dominikanin *m* (*-na*; *-kanie*) Dominican; **dominikański** *adj* Dominican
domino *n* (*-na*; *-na*) domino
domin|ować ⟨**z-**⟩ (*-nuję*) dominate (**nad** *I*); ***katedra ~uje nad miastem*** the cathedral dominates the city; **dominujący** *adj* dominant
domknąć *v/p* → ***domykać***
domniemany *adj* alleged
domofon *m* (*-nu*; *-ny*) *Br* Entryphone®, intercom
domokrążca *m* (*-cy*; *-cy*) *Br* pedlar, *Am* peddler; **domokrążny** *adj*: ***~ handel*** door-to-door selling
domorosły *adj* **1.** (*o samouku*) self-taught **2.** (*dyletancki*) unprofessional, dilettante
domostwo *n* (*-wa*; *-wa*) homestead; **domownik** *m* (*-ka*; *-nicy*) household member
domow|y *adj* **1.** *telefon*, *adres*: home **2.** *zwierzę*, *obowiązki*: domestic **3.** *jedzenie*: home-made; ***areszt ~y*** house arrest; ***~ej produkcji*** home-made; ***gospodarstwo ~e*** household; ***gospodyni ~a*** housewife; ***porządki ~e*** house cleaning; ***pomoc ~a*** domestic help; ***prace ~e*** housework; ***wojna ~a*** civil war; ***zadanie ~e*** homework
domyć *v/p* (*-mywam*): ***~ coś*** wash s.th. clean
domyka|ć ⟨**-knąć**⟩ (*-kam*) shut (tight); ***domykać się*** shut well; ***okno się nie ~*** the window won't shut
domysł *m* (*-łu*; *-ły*) guess, speculation; ***snuć ~y*** speculate (***na temat*** *G* about/on)
domyślać się *v/im* (*-lam*) (*podejrzewać*) suspect
domyślić się *v/p* (*-lę*) (*zgadnąć*) guess; **domyślność** *f* (*-ści*; *no pl*) shrewdness; **domyślny** *adj* **1.** *osoba*: shrewd **2.** *INF* default
donica *f* (*-cy*; *-ce*) (*na kwiaty*) (large) flowerpot; **doniczka** *f* (*-ki*; *-ki*) flowerpot; **doniczkow|y** *adj*: ***kwiaty ~e*** *infml* plants
doniesienie *n* (*-nia*; *-nia*) **1.** (*wiadomość*) news **2.** (*donos*) denunciation
donieść *v/p* → ***donosić***
donikąd *adv* nowhere; ***coś prowadzi ~*** s.th. leads nowhere
doniosłość *f* (*-ści*; *no pl*) momentousness, great importance; **doniosły** *adj* momentous
donos *m* (*-su*; *-sy*) denunciation, *infml* tip-off; ***złożyć na kogoś ~*** denounce s.o.; inform against s.o.
donosiciel *m* (*-la*; *-le*), **~ka** *f* (*-ki*; *-ki*) informer
donosić ⟨**-nieść**⟩ (*-szę*) **1.** (*składać donos*) denounce (**na** *A*), inform (**na** *A* against) **2.** (*informować*) inform (**o** *L* about) **3.** (*przynosić*) bring, carry **4.** (*przynosić więcej*) bring more; ***~ płód***, ***~ ciążę*** carry the baby to term
donośny *adj* loud
dookoła → ***dokoła***
dopad|ać ⟨**-paść**⟩ (*-dam*) **1.** (*chwytać*) catch, get **2.** (*dobiegać*) run up (**do** *G* to); ***~ła kogoś burza*** s.o. got caught in the storm; ***~ła kogoś chandra*** s.o. is down in the dumps *infml*; ***~ła go grypa*** he went down with the flu
dopalać ⟨**-lić**⟩ (*-lam*) *papierosa*: finish; ***dopalać się*** burn down
dopasowany *adj* **1.** (*kolorystycznie*, *wzorniczo*) matching (**do** *G*) **2.** (*rozmiarem*) well-fitting; ***~ do ciała*** close-fitting; ***~ do potrzeb klienta*** tailored to customer needs
dopasowywać ⟨**-sować**⟩ (*-sowuję*) **1.** *elementy*: fit (**do** *G* to/into) **2.** *kolorystycznie*, *wzorniczo*: match (**do** *G* with); ***dopasowywać się*** *do warunków*: adapt (**do** *G* to)
dopaść *v/p* → ***dopadać***
dopatrywać się ⟨**-rzyć**⟩ (*-ruję*) **1.** (*dostrzegać*) see **2.** (*znajdować*) find
dopełniacz *m* (*-cza*; *-cze*) *GRAM* genitive
dopełni|ać ⟨**-nić**⟩ (*-niam*) **1.** *obowiązku*: meet **2.** *formalności*: complete **3.** (*uzupełniać*) supplement (*I* with); ***to ~ło miary*** this was too much
dopełnienie *n* (*-nia*; *-nia*) **1.** *GRAM* object; ***~ bliższe*** (***dalsze***) direct (indirect) object **2.** (*dodatek*) addition (*G* to)
dopędzać ⟨**-dzić**⟩ (*-dzam*) catch up (*A* with)
dopi|ąć *v/p* (*-pnę*) (*osiągnąć*) achieve; ***~ąć celu*** reach one's goal; ***~ąć swego*** get what one wants; ***~ęty na ostatni guzik*** set, *infml* ready to roll
dopić *v/p* → ***dopijać***
dopie|kać ⟨**-piec**⟩ (*-kam*): ***~c komuś***

give s.o. a hard time; **~c komuś do żywego** cut s.o. to the quick *infml*

dopieprzać ⟨**-rzyć**⟩ (*-rzam*) (*bić*) *infml* bash

dopiero *particle* **1.** only, not until; ***przyjechałem ~ wczoraj*** I only arrived yesterday; ***wypuszczono nas ~ we wtorek*** we were not released until Tuesday **2.** (*przed chwilą*) (only) just; ***~ co*** (only) just; ***~ skończyła*** she's only just finished **3.** (*tylko*) only; ***a co ~*** let alone; ***a to ~!*** never!, *dated* well, I never!

dopieszczać ⟨**-pieścić**⟩ (*-czam*) (*wykańczać*) add the finishing touches to, polish

dopijać ⟨**-pić**⟩ (*-pijam*) finish

dopilnować *v/p* (*-nuję*): ***~ czegoś*** see to s.th.; ***~, żeby ktoś coś zrobił*** see to it that s.o. does s.th., make sure that s.o. does s.th.

dopinać ⟨**-piąć**⟩ (*-nam*) → ***dopiąć***

doping *m* (*-gu*; *no pl*) **1.** (*publiczności*) cheering **2.** (*farmakologiczny*) doping **3.** (*zachęta*) *fig* encouragement; **dopingować** ⟨**z-**⟩ (*-uję*) **1.** SPORT cheer on **2.** (*motywować*) motivate, give a boost; **dopingow|y** *adj*: ***kontrola ~a*** drug test; ***środek ~y*** performance-enhancing drug *infml*, dope; **dopingujący** *adj*: ***środek ~*** performance-enhancing drug, *infml* dope

dopisek *m* (*-sku*; *-ski*) **1.** note **2.** (*postscriptum*) postscript

dopis|ywać ⟨**-sać**⟩ (*-suję*) **I** *v/t* (*dodawać*) add **II** *v/i* (*o pogodzie*) be good; ***pogoda nie ~ała*** the weather was bad; ***szczęście komuś (nie) ~uje*** s.o. is lucky (out of luck); ***zdrowie komuś ~uje*** s.o. enjoys good health

dopłac|ać ⟨**-cić**⟩ (*-cam*) pay extra; ***~ić 20 dolarów*** pay an extra 20 dollars; **dopłata** *f* (*-ty*; *-ty*) **1.** surcharge, extra charge **2.** (*za nadbagaż*) excess fare **3.** (*do listu*) excess postage

dopłynąć *v/p* (*-nę*) **1.** (*o statku*) arrive (**do** *G* at); ***~ do brzegu*** reach the shore **2.** (*o osobie*, *rybie*) swim up (**do** *G* to) **3.** (*o wodzie*, *prądzie*) reach (**do** *G*); → ***dopływać***

dopływ *m* (*-wu*; *-wy*) **1.** *rzeki*: tributary **2.** *prądu*, *informacji*: supply

dopływać ⟨**-łynąć**⟩ (*-wam*) (*zbliżać się*) approach (**do** *G*); → ***dopłynąć***; **dopływowy** *adj* *rura*: supply

dopomagać ⟨**-móc**⟩ (*-gam*) *lit* help (*I* with)

dopominać się ⟨**-mnieć**⟩ (*-nam*) **1.** demand (**o** *A*) **2.** *o prawa*: claim (**o** *A*) **3.** (*odczuwać brak*) be crying out (*G* for)

dopomóc *v/p* → ***dopomagać***

dopowiadać ⟨**-wiedzieć**⟩ (*-dam*) add; ***nie ~ do końca*** not finish

dopowiedzenie *n* (*-nia*; *-nia*) (*uzupełnienie*) supplement

dopowiedzieć *v/p* → ***dopowiadać***

dopóki *conj* **1.** (*póki*) as long as; ***dopóty pracował, ~ mógł*** he worked as long as he could **2.** (*aż*) until

dopracowywać ⟨**-cować**⟩ (*-cowuję*) polish (up)

dopraszać się ⟨**-rosić**⟩ (*-szam*) (*wciąż prosić*) keep asking (**o** *A* for); ***nie mógł się ich doprosić o pieniądze*** he kept asking for money but they wouldn't give him any

doprawdy *adv*: ***~?*** really?

doprawiać ⟨**-wić**⟩ (*-wiam*) season (*D* with)

doprosić się *v/p* → ***dopraszać się***

doprowadzać ⟨**-dzić**⟩ (*-dzam*) **I** *v/t* **1.** (*zabierać*) take (**do** *G* to) **2.** (*wskazując drogę*) lead (**do** *G* to) **3.** *krew*: carry **4.** *prąd*, *gaz*: supply; ***~ łącze internetowe*** provide Internet access; ***~ do porządku*** tidy up; ***~ do skutku*** *plan*, *zamiar*: carry out; ***~ kogoś do wściekłości*** drive s.o. mad; ***~ kogoś do rozpaczy*** (***ruiny***) bring s.o. to despair (ruin) **II** *v/i* **5.** ***~ do*** *G* result in; ***doprowadzać się***: ***~ się do porządku*** spruce (oneself) up

dopust *m* (*-tu*, *no pl*): ***~ boży*** **a)** act of God **b)** (*nieszczęście*) scourge of God

dopuszcz|ać ⟨**-puścić**⟩ (*-czam*) **I** *v/t* **1.** (*zezwalać*) let; ***~ać kogoś do egzaminu*** admit s.o. to an examination; ***~ać kogoś do głosu*** let s.o. speak; ***~ać kogoś do kogoś*** let s.o. near s.o **2.** *możliwość*: allow for; ***nie ~am takiej możliwości*** it's impossible **II** *v/t* ***~ać do czegoś*** let s.th. happen; ***nie ~ę, by to zrobił*** I won't let him do it; ***dopuszczać się*** *przestępstwa*: commit

dopuszczalny *adj* **1.** acceptable **2.** *prędkość*: maximum (permissible)

D

dopuścić *v/p* → **dopuszczać**
dopytywać się ⟨**-tać**⟩ (*-tuję*) ask, *form* enquire (**o** *A* about)
dorabiać ⟨**-robić**⟩ (*-biam*) **1.** (*wykonywać*) make (another); **~ klucz** have a key cut **2.** (*zarabiać*) **~** (**sobie**) make extra money; **dorabiać się** (*wzbogacać się*) grow rich (**na** *D* on); **~ się majątku** make a fortune **3.** *pozycji*: attain
doradca *m* (*-cy*; *-cy*), **-czyni** *f* (*-ni*; *-nie*) adviser; **~ prawny** (**inwestycyjny**) legal (investment) adviser; **doradczy** *adj* advisory
doradzać ⟨**-dzić**⟩ (*-dzam*) advise; **doradztwo** *n* (*-wa*; *no pl*) consulting, advice
dorastać ⟨**-rosnąć**⟩ (*-tam*) **1.** (*rosnąć*) grow **2.** (*osiągać dorosłość*) grow up **3.** (*osiągać*) reach (**do** *G*); **nie ~ do** *G* not match up to; **nie ~ komuś do pięt** be no match for
dorastający *adj młodzież*: adolescent
doraźnie *adv* **1.** (*na razie*) temporarily, for the time being **2.** *pomóc*: immediately **3.** *karać*: summarily; **doraźn|y** *adj* **1.** *środek*: temporary **2.** *cel*, *korzyści*: immediate **3.** *sąd*: summary; **pomoc ~a** emergency aid
doręczać ⟨**-czyć**⟩ (*-czam*) *list*: deliver; **doręczenie** *n* (*-nia*; *-nia*) delivery; **doręczyciel** *m* (*-la*; *-le*) **1.** deliverer **2.** (*listonosz*) *Br* postman, *Am* mailman
dorobek *m* (*-bku*; *no pl*) **1.** (*majątek*) possessions **2.** *artystyczny*, *naukowy*: output, work; **~ kulturalny** cultural achievements
dorobić *v/p* → **dorabiać**
dorobkiewicz *m* (*-cza*; *-cze*) nouveau riche
doroczny *adj* annual
dorodny *adj owoc*: ripe and healthy
dorosły I *adj* **1.** *osoba*: adult, grown-up; **być ~m** be of age **2.** *zwierzę*: adult **II** *m* (*-łego*; *-rośli*), **-ła** *f* (*-łej*; *-łe*) adult
dorosnąć *v/p* → **dorastać**
dorośle *adv zachowywać się*, *wyglądać*: mature; **dorośleć** ⟨**wy-**⟩ (*-leję*) grow up
dorożka *f* (*-ki*; *-ki*) (horse-drawn) cab
dorówn|ywać ⟨**-nać**⟩ (*-nuję*): **~ywać komuś w** *L* be s.o.'s equal in; **nie ~ywać komuś** (**czemuś**) not match up to s.o. (s.th.); **nie ~ywać komuś urodą** be no match for s.o.'s looks; **nikt im nie ~uje** they have no match
dorsz *m* (*-sza*; *-sze*) cod
dorwać się *v/p* (*-wę*) get hold (**do** *G* of); **~ do władzy** grab power
dorysowywać ⟨**-sować**⟩ (*-sowuję*): **~ coś** add s.th. (to a drawing)
dorywczo *adv*: **pracować ~** *Br* do casual jobs; **dorywczy** *adj praca*: *Br* casual
dorzecze *n* (*-cza*; *-cza*) basin; **~ Amazonki** the Amazon basin
dorzucać ⟨**-cić**⟩ (*-cam*) **1.** throw as far as (**do** *G*) **2.** (*dokładać*) throw (more) (**do** *G* into) **3.** (*dopowiadać*) add
dosadnie *adv* **1.** bluntly **2.** *przeklinać*: crudely; **dosadny** *adj* **1.** blunt **2.** *słowo*: crude
dosalać ⟨**-solić**⟩ (*-lam*) add more salt (*A* to)
dosiadać ⟨**-siąść**⟩ (*-dam*) *konia*, *motocykla*: mount; **dosiadać się 1. ~ się do czyjegoś stolika** join s.o. at the table; **czy mogę się dosiąść?** can I join you? **2.** (*siadać obok*) **~ się do kogoś** sit next to s.o.
dosiąść *v/p* → **dosiadać**
dosiedzieć *v/p* (*-dzę*): **~ do końca filmu** sit through to the end of a film
do siego: **~ roku!** Happy NewYear!
dosięgać ⟨**-gnąć**⟩ (*-gam*) reach (**do** *G*)
doskakiwać ⟨**-skoczyć**⟩ (*-kuję*) **1.** jump (**do** *G*) **2.** (*w dal*) jump as long as (**do** *G*) **3.** (*wzwyż*) jump as high as (**do** *G*)
doskonale *adv* **1.** perfectly **2.** *wyglądać*: perfect; **~!** perfect!; **doskonalenie** (**się**) *n* (*-nia*; *no pl*) improvement; **~ zawodowe** professional training
doskonalić ⟨**u-**⟩ (*-lę*) improve; **doskonalić się**: **~ się zawodowo** develop professionally, gain new skills
doskonałość *f* (*-ści*; *no pl*) perfection; **doskonał|y** *adj* perfect, excellent; **zbrodnia ~a** perfect crime
doskwiera|ć *v/im* (*-ram*): **komuś coś ~** s.o. is troubled by s.th.; **komuś ~ głód** s.o. feels hunger pangs
dosłać *v/p* → **dosyłać**
dosłownie *adv* literally; **dosłowny** *adj* literal; **w ~m znaczeniu tego słowa** in the literal sense of the word
dosłysz|eć *v/p* (*-szę*): **nie ~eć** have trouble hearing; **przepraszam, nie ~ałam** I'm sorry, I didn't catch that

dosolić *v/p* → **dosalać**
dospać *v/p* → **dosypiać**
dostać (się) *v/p* → **dostawać (się)**
dostarcz|ać ⟨**-czyć**⟩ (*-czam*) **1.** *towar, przesyłkę*: deliver **2.** *dowody*: provide; ***coś ~a komuś przyjemności*** s.o. takes pleasure in s.th.
dostatecznie *adv* **1.** (*wystarczająco*) sufficiently **2.** (*zadowalająco*) satisfactorily; **dostateczny** *adj* **1.** (*wystarczający*) sufficient **2.** (*zadowalający*) satisfactory **3.** (*ocena*) D
dostat|ek *m* (*-tku*; *-tki*) **1.** (*bogactwo*) wealth; ***żyć w ~ku*** be well-off **2.** (*obfitość*) plenty; ***mieć czegoś pod ~kiem*** have plenty of s.th.; **dostatni** *adj* wealthy; ***prowadzić ~e życie*** be well-off
dostaw|a *f* (*-wy*; *-wy*) delivery; ***termin ~y*** delivery date; ***przy ~ie*** on delivery
dostawać ⟨**-tać**⟩ (*-taję*) **1.** get; ***~ lanie*** get a beating; ***~ świra*** *infml* go nuts; ***~ w łapę*** *infml* be bribed; ***~ wypieków*** flush; ***~ za swoje*** get what one deserves **2.** *zastrzyk*: have **3.** *grypy*: catch **4.** *kaszlu*: develop **5.** (*dosięgać*) get (**do** *G* at) **6.** (*zostać pobitym*) be beaten **7.** (*zostać postrzelonym*) get shot; **dostawać się 1.** get (**do** *G* to/into) **2.** *do szkoły*: be admitted (**do** *G* to); ***~ się na studia*** get into university; ***dostało się komuś*** s.o. got a roasting *infml*; ***~ się do niewoli*** be taken prisoner; ***~ się w czyjeś ręce*** fall into s.o.'s hands
dostawca *m* (*-cy*; *-cy*) *ECON* supplier; ***~ Internetu*** Internet provider; **dostawczy** *adj*: ***samochód ~*** delivery van
dostawiać ⟨**-wić**⟩ (*-wiam*) **1.** *krzesło*: pull in an extra **2.** *stół*: add an extra **3.** ***~ prawą stopę do lewej*** bring the right foot to the left
dostąpić *v/p* (*-pię*) *lit zaszczytu, łaski*: be granted
dostęp *m* (*-pu*; *no pl*) access; ***~ do Internetu*** Internet access; **dostępny** *adj* **1.** *towar*: available; ***łatwo ~*** easily available; ***ogólnie ~*** freely available; ***trudno ~*** hard to get **2.** *miejsce, sposób*: accessible
dostojeństwo *n* (*-wa*; *-wa*) dignity; **dostojnik** *m* (*-ka*; *-nicy*) dignitary; **dostojny** *adj* **1.** *gość, dama*: distinguished **2.** *mina*: dignified
dostosowanie *n* (*-nia*; *-nia*) *BIOL* adaptation; **dostosowawczy** *adj* adaptative
dostosowywać ⟨**-sować**⟩ (*-sowuję*) (*regulować*) adjust (**do** *G* to); ***~ coś do potrzeb klientów*** tailor s.th. to customers' needs; **dostosowywać się 1.** adapt (**do** *G* to) **2.** (*przestrzegać*) conform (**do** *G* to)
dostrajać ⟨**-roić**⟩ (*-jam*) **1.** *instrument*: tune **2.** *radio*: tune (in); ***dostrajać się*** tune in (**do** *G* to)
dostrzegać ⟨**-rzec**⟩ (*-gam*) **1.** (*widzieć*) see **2.** (*zauważać*) notice; ***nie ~*** overlook
dostrzegalny *adj* noticeable: ***ledwo ~, ledwie ~*** hardly noticeable
dosuwać ⟨**-sunąć**⟩ (*-wam*) **1.** *do stołu*: pull (**do** *G* to) **2.** *do ściany*: push (**do** *G* to)
dosychać ⟨**-schnąć**⟩ (*-cham*) dry up
dosyć *adv* **1.** (*wystarczająco*) enough; *~* (***tego***)*!* that's enough (of that)! **2.** *dobry, miły*: fairly, quite, *infml* pretty **3.** *biedny, brzydki*: rather; ***mam tego ~ a)*** I'm fed up with this **b)** (*wyraża zniecierpliwienie*) I've had enough; ***nie ~ na tym*** that's not all; ***nie ~, że jest śliczny, to jeszcze uroczy*** not only is he pretty but also charming; ***od ~ dawna*** for quite a while
dosyłać ⟨**-słać**⟩ (*-łam*) send more
dosypać *v/p* → **dosypywać**
dosypiać ⟨**-spać**⟩ (*-piam*) sleep (**do** *G* until); ***nie ~*** not sleep enough
dosypywać ⟨**-pać**⟩ (*-puję*) add (**do** *G* to)
doszczętnie *adv* utterly, totally; ***~ spalony*** burnt to a crisp; **doszczętny** *adj zniszczenie, wytępienie*: utter, total
doszkalać ⟨**-kolić**⟩ (*-lam*) provide additional training (*A* for)
doszlifowywać ⟨**-fować**⟩ (*-fowuję*) (*kończyć szlifowanie*) polish up
dosztukowywać ⟨**-kować**⟩ (*-kowuję*) (*doszywać*) sew on, add (**do** *G* to)
doszukać się *v/p* (*-kam*) find; **doszukiwać się** *v/im* (*-kuję*) (*szukać*) look for
dościgać ⟨**-gnąć**⟩ (*-gam*) **1.** (*doganiać*) catch up (*A* with) **2.** (*łapać*) catch
dość → **dosyć**
dośpiewywać ⟨**-piewać**⟩ (*-piewuję*) (*kończyć śpiewanie*) finish singing; ***~ sobie*** *fig* guess

D

dośrodkowanie *n* (*-nia*; *-nia*) SPORT cross; **dośrodkowy** *adj* centripetal; **dośrodkowywać** ⟨**-kować**⟩ (*-kowuję*) SPORT cross (the ball)

doświadcz|ać ⟨**-czyć**⟩ (*-czam*) **1.** experience **2.** (*poddawać próbie*) try; ***~ać czegoś na własnej skórze*** experience s.th. oneself; ***los ciężko kogoś ~ył*** s.o.'s life was filled with trials and tribulations

doświadczalny *adj* experimental; ***królik ~*** *fig* guinea pig

doświadczeni|e *n* (*-nia*; *-nia*) **1.** *życiowe, zawodowe*: experience; ***brak ~a*** inexperience; ***mieć ~e w*** *L* be experienced in; ***nie mieć ~a w*** *L* be inexperienced in; ***z ~a*** from experience **2.** (*eksperyment*) experiment (***na*** *L* on)

doświadczony *adj* **1.** *osoba*: experienced **2.** *ucho, oko*: trained; **doświadczyć** *v/p* → ***doświadczać***

dot. *abbr* (= ***dotyczy***) re

dotacja *f* (*-ji*; *-je*) subsidy

dotarcie *n* (*-cia*; *no pl*) **1.** (*przyjazd*) arrival **2.** *do klienta*: reaching (***do*** *A*) **3.** *samochodu*: running in; **dotarty** *adj samochód*: run-in

dotąd *pron* **1.** (*tak daleko*) this far, that far; ***stąd ~*** from here to there **2.** (*tak wysoko*) that high **3.** (*do teraz*) so far, until now

dotkliwy *adj* **1.** *chłód, porażka*: severe **2.** *ból, kłucie*: acute **3.** *straty*: heavy

dotknąć *v/p* (*-nę*) **1.** touch **2.** (*doświadczyć*) affect; → ***dotykać***

dotknięcie *n* (*-cia*; *-cia*) **1.** touch **2.** *pędzla*: stroke; **dotknięty** *adj* **1.** (*urażony*) offended **2.** *chorobą*: afflicted (*I* with)

dotleniać się ⟨**-nić**⟩ (*-niam*) get some fresh air

dotować *v/im* (*-tuję*) subsidize

dotrwa|ć *v/p* (*-wam*) **1.** (*przetrwać*) survive (***do*** *G* to) **2.** (*wytrzymać*): ***nie ~łem do końca filmu*** I didn't get to the end of the film

dotrzeć *v/p* → ***docierać***

dotrzymywać ⟨**-mać**⟩ (*-muję*): ***~ komuś kroku*** keep up with s.o.; ***~ komuś towarzystwa*** keep s.o. company; ***~ obietnicy*** (***słowa***) keep one's promise (word); ***~ terminu*** meet the deadline; ***~ umowy*** (***warunków umowy***) comply with an agreement (the terms of an agreement)

dotychczas *adv* so far; **dotychczaso|wy** *adj* **1.** (*trwający dotychczas*) so far; ***jego ~e życie*** his life so far; ***jej ~a praca*** the work she's done so far **2.** (*obecny*) present

dotyczący *adj* **1.** concerning, related to **2.** (*mający zastosowanie*) applying (*G* to)

dotyczy|ć *v/im* (*-czę*) **1.** concern; ***to mnie nie ~*** it has nothing to do with me; ***wszystko, co ~*** *G* all related to **2.** (*mieć zastosowanie*) apply (*G* to)

dotyk *m* (*-ku*; *no pl*) touch; ***miękki*** (***szorstki***) ***w ~u*** soft (rough) to the touch; ***zmysł ~u*** the sense of touch

dotykać ⟨**-tknąć**⟩ (*-kam*) **1.** touch **2.** (*badać dotykiem*) feel **3.** (*urażać*) offend **4.** (*o nieszczęściu, chorobie*) afflict; ***dotknęło go nieszczęście*** a misfortune befell him *lit* **5.** (*dosięgać*) reach **6.** (*wspominać*) touch (*G* on); ***dotykać się*** touch

dotykalny *adj* tangible; **dotykowy** *adj wrażenia, wrażliwość*: tactile

douczać ⟨**-czyć**⟩ (*-czam*) *Br* coach; **douczać się** (*kształcić się*) further one's education

doustny *adj* oral

dowalać ⟨**-lić**⟩ (*-lam*) (*uderzać*) *infml* bash

dowartościowywać ⟨**-ciować**⟩ (*-ciowuję*): ***~ kogoś*** increase s.o.'s self-appreciation; ***dowartościowywać się*** increase one's self-appreciation

dowcip *m* (*-pu*; *-py*) **1.** (*kawał*) joke; ***zrobić komuś głupi ~*** play a stupid trick on s.o. **2.** (*cecha*) wit **3.** (*humor*) *Br* humour, *Am* humor

dowcipkować *v/im* (*-kuję*) joke, *infml* crack jokes; **dowcipniś** *m* (*-nisia*; *-nisie*) joker; **dowcipny** *adj* witty

dowiadywać się ⟨**-wiedzieć**⟩ (*-duję*) **1.** learn (***o*** *L* about) **2.** (*dopytywać się*) enquire (***o*** *A* about)

dowierzać *v/im* (*-rzam*): ***nie ~*** mistrust; ***nie ~ własnym oczom*** (***uszom***) not believe one's eyes (ears)

dowieść *v/p* → ***dowodzić***

dowieźć *v/p* → ***dowozić***

dowlekać ⟨**-wlec**⟩ (*-kam*) drag; **dowlekać się** drag oneself, crawl

dowodow|y *adj* evidential; ***materiał ~y*** the evidence, evidential material; ***postępowanie ~e*** evidentiary proceedings
dowodzeni|e *n (-nia; no pl)* **1.** *(dowództwo)* command; ***objąć ~*** take command (*G* of) **2.** *(rozumowanie)* reasoning; ***~ twierdzeń*** MATH theorem proving
dowodzić ⟨**-wieść**⟩ *(-dzę)* **1.** *(sprawować dowództwo)* be in command (*G* of) **2.** *(udowadniać)* prove
dowolność *f (-ści; no pl)* freedom
dowolny *adj* **1.** *(jakikolwiek)* any **2.** *(swobodny)* free; ***program ~*** *(w łyżwiarstwie)* free skate; ***taniec ~*** free dance
dowozić ⟨**-wieźć**⟩ *(-wożę)* **1.** *osoby*: take, drive (**do** *G* to) **2.** *towar*: deliver
dowód *m (-wodu; -wody)* **1.** proof; ***na ~ czegoś*** to prove s.th.; ***w ~ wdzięczności*** (***uznania***) as a token of gratitude (appreciation) **2.** JUR (piece of) evidence; ***~ rzeczowy*** **a)** (piece of) material evidence **b)** *(w sądzie)* exhibit **3.** *(pokwitowanie)* receipt; ***~ nadania*** receipt of postage; ***~ zakupu*** proof of purchase **4.** *(dokument)* ***~ osobisty*** ID (card); ***~ tożsamości*** proof of identity
dowódca *m (-cy; -cy)* commander; ***~ plutonu*** platoon commander; ***naczelny ~*** commander-in-chief
dowództw|o *n (-wa; -wa)* **1.** *(dowodzenie)* command; ***naczelne ~o*** command-in-chief; ***objąć ~o*** take command; ***pod ~em*** *G* under the command of **2.** *(sztab)* headquarters
dowóz *m (-wozu; -wozy)* delivery
doz|a *f (-zy; -zy)* dose; ***z dużą ~ą prawdopodobieństwa*** in all probability
dozbrajać ⟨**-roić**⟩ *(-jam)* arm better
dozgonny *adj* **1.** *wdzięczność*: undying **2.** *przyjaźń*: lifelong
doznani|e *n (-nia; -nia)* **1.** experience **2.** *(zmysłowe)* sensation; ***przyjemne ~a*** pleasant sensations, pleasure
doznawać ⟨**-nać**⟩ *(-naję)* **1.** experience **2.** *zawodu, straty, szoku*: suffer **3.** *kontuzji, obrażeń*: sustain **4.** *życzliwości*: meet with
dozorca *m (-cy; -cy)*, **-czyni** *f (-ni; -nie)* *Br* caretaker, *Am* janitor; **dozorować** *v/im (-ruję)* supervise
dozować *v/im (-zuję)* administer (in doses)
dozór *m (-zoru; no pl)* **1.** supervision **2.** *(opieka)* care
dozwolony *adj* permitted; ***film ~ od lat osiemnastu*** X-rated film
dożyć *v/p* → ***dożywać***
dożylny *adj* intravenous
dożynki *pl (-nek)* harvest festival *sing*
dożywać ⟨**-żyć**⟩ *(-wam)*: ***~ stu lat*** live to be a hundred; ***~ późnego wieku*** reach old age; ***~ do rana*** last the night; ***ja już tego nie dożyję*** I won't live long enough to see it happen
dożywiać ⟨**-wić**⟩ *(-wiam)* provide extra food (*A* to)
dożywoci|e *n (-cia; -cia)* **1.** *(wyrok)* life sentence **2.** *(okres więzienia)* life imprisonment; ***zostać skazanym na ~*** be sentenced to life (in prison); **dożywotni** *adj renta, tytuł*: life; ***~e więzienie*** life imprisonment; ***skazana na ~e więzienie*** sentenced for life; **dożywotnio** *adv* for life
dób → ***doba***
dóbr → ***dobro***
dół *m (dołu; doły)* **1.** *(otwór)* hole **2.** *(grób)* pit **3.** *(dolna część)* bottom; ***od góry do dołu*** from top to bottom; ***na dole*** **a)** at the bottom **b)** *(na niższym piętrze)* downstairs; ***na ~*** **a)** down **b)** *(na niższe piętro)* downstairs; ***u dołu*** at the bottom; ***w ~*** down; ***w ~ rzeki*** downstream; ***z dołu*** **a)** from below **b)** *(z niższego piętra)* from downstairs **c)** *płatny*: in arrears
dr *abbr* (= **doktor**) dr
drab *m (-ba; -by)* *(oprych)* thug
drabina *f (-ny; -ny)* ladder; ***~ składana*** stepladder; ***~ społeczna*** the social ladder; **drabinka** *f (-ki; -ki)* ladder; ***~ sznurowa*** rope ladder
dragi *pl (-gów)* *(narkotyki)* *infml* dope *sing*
drajwer *m (-ra; -ry)* INF driver
draka *m (-ki; -ki)* *infml* fracas
drakoński *adj* draconian
dramat *m (-tu; -ty)* **1.** *(rodzaj literacki)* drama **2.** *(nieszczęście)* tragedy; ***robić z czegoś ~*** make a drama out of s.th.
dramatopisarz *m (-rza; -rze)*, **-rka** *f (-ki; -ki)* playwright
dramaturgia *f (-gii; no pl)* drama; **dra-**

D

maturgiczn|y *adj* dramatic; **twórczość ~a** drama(s); **dramatyczn|y** *adj* **1.** *aktor*, *utwór*: dramatic; **twórczość ~a** drama(s) **2.** *sytuacja*: tragic; **dramatyzować** *v/im* (*-zuję*) dramatize

D

drań *m* (*drania*; *dranie*) bastard *infml*; **draństwo** *n* (*-wa*; *no pl*) (*świństwo*) dirty trick

drapacz *m* (*-cza*; *-cze*): **~ chmur** skyscraper

drap|ać ⟨**-pnąć**⟩ (*-pię*) **1.** ⟨**po-**⟩ scratch (**w** *A*); **kogoś ~ie w gardle** s.o. has an itchy throat **2.** (*o ubraniu*) itch **3.** (*o dymie*) sting; **drapać się** scratch; **~ać się w głowę** (**plecy**) scratch one's head (back); **~ać się pod górę** *infml* clamber up

drapak *m* (*-ka*; *-ki*) (*dla kotów*) scratching post; **dać ~a** *infml* make a bolt for it; **drapanie** *n* (*-nia*; *no pl*) (*dźwięk*) scratching

draperia *f* (*-rii*; *-rie*) drapery

drapieżnik *m* (*-ka*; *-ki*) predator; **drapieżność** *f* (*-ści*; *no pl*) predation; **drapieżn|y** *adj* predatory; **ptaki ~e** birds of prey

drapnąć *v/p* → **drapać**

drapować ⟨**u-**⟩ (*-puję*) drape

drasnąć *v/p* (*-nę*) graze

drastyczny *adj* **1.** *scena*, *opis*: shocking **2.** *środki*, *metoda*: drastic

draśnięcie *n* (*-cia*; *-cia*) graze

drażetka *f* (*-ki*; *-ki*) **1.** (*pigułka*) sugar-coated tablet **2.** (*cukierek*) dragee

drażliwość *f* (*-ści*; *no pl*) *osoby*: touchiness (**na punkcie** *G* about); **drażliwy** *adj* **1.** *osoba*: touchy, sensitive (**na punkcie** *G* about) **2.** *kwestia*, *temat*: sensitive

drażniąco *adv* irritatingly; **działać ~** irritate

drażnić ⟨**roz-**⟩ (*-nię*) **1.** irritate **2.** (*dokuczać*) tease

drą → **drzeć**

drąg *m* (*-ga*; *-gi*) pole; **drągal** *m* (*-la*; *-le*) *infml* beanpole

drążek *m* (*-żka*; *-żki*) **1. ~ sterowy** control stick; **~ biegów** *AUTO* gear lever **2.** *SPORT* horizontal bar

drążyć ⟨**wy-**⟩ (*-żę*) **1.** *tunel*: drive **2.** *owoce*: core **3.** *temat*: dwell (*A* to)

drelich *m* (*-chu*; *-chy*) **1.** (*materiał*) drill **2.** (*ubranie*) overalls

dren *m* (*-nu*; *-ny*) drain; **drenaż** *m* (*-żu*; *-że*) drainage; **~ mózgów** brain drain; **drenować** *v/im* (*-nuję*) drain

dreptać ⟨**po-**⟩ (*-pczę*/*-pcę*) **1.** mince (along) **2.** (*o małym dziecku*) toddle; **~ w miejscu** *fig* make no progress

dres *m* (*-su*; *-sy*) tracksuit; **bluza od ~u** tracksuit top; **dresiarz** *m* (*-rza*; *-rze*) *Br infml* yob

dreszcz *m* (*-czu*; *-cze*) shiver; **~e** shivers; **mieć ~e** be shivering, have the shivers; **przyprawiać kogoś o ~e** make s.o. shiver

dreszczowiec *m* (*-wca*; *-wce*) *Br* horror film, *Am* horror movie

dreszczyk *m* (*-ku*; *-ki*) **1.** (*dreszcz*) shiver **2.** (*podniecenie*) thrill; **opowieść z ~iem** thriller; **~ podniecenia** thrill

drewniak *m* (*-ka*; *-ki*) clog; **drewniany** *adj* wooden; **instrumenty ~e** *MUS* woodwind instruments

drewnieć ⟨**z-**⟩ (*-nieję*) **1.** lignify **2.** (*twardnieć*) harden

drewno *n* (*-na*; *no pl*) **1.** wood; **~ na opał** firewood **2.** *BUILD Br* timber, *Am* lumber **3.** (*kawałek*) piece of wood

drę → **drzeć**

dręczący *adj wątpliwości*, *ból*: nagging; **dręczyciel** *m* (*-la*; *-le*) tormentor; **~ zwierząt** animal abuser

dręcz|yć *v/im* (*-czę*) (*znęcać się*) maltreat; **kogoś ~ą wątpliwości** (**kontuzje**) s.o. is troubled by doubts (injuries); **kogoś ~y bezsenność** (**sumienie**) s.o. suffers sleeplessness (remorse); **dręczyć się** (*samego siebie*) agonize (*I* over)

drętwieć ⟨**z-**⟩ (*-wieję*) go numb; **~ z zimna** (**strachu**) go numb with cold (fear)

drętwo *adv*: **na przyjęciu było ~** the party was a drag *infml*; **drętwy** *adj* **1.** (*zdrętwiały*) numb **2.** (*nudny*) dull

drg|ać ⟨**-gnąć**⟩ (*-gam*) **1.** (*o strunie*, *powietrzu*) vibrate **2.** (*o powiece*) twitch; **ani nie ~nąć** stand still, not budge

drgania *pl* (*-gań*) **1.** *PHYS* vibration *sing* **2.** (*elektryczne*) oscillation *sing*; **drgaw|ki** *pl* (*-wek*) convulsions; **dostać ~ek** go into convulsions

drgnąć *v/p* → **drgać**

drink *m* (*-ka*; *-ki*) drink

drobiarstwo *n* (*-wa*; *no pl*) poultry farming

drobiazg *m* (*-gu*; *-gi*) **1.** (*rzecz*) small thing **2.** (*detal*) minor detail **3.** (*błahostka*) trifle; **~!** (*reakcja na podziękowanie*) sure!, no problem!

drobiazgowo *adj opisywać*, *omawiać*: in detail; **drobiazgowość** *f* (*-ści*; *no pl*) meticulousness; **drobiazgowy** *adj* **1.** *osoba*: meticulous **2.** *opis*, *badanie*: detailed **3.** *kontrola*: close

drobić *v/im* (*-bię*) (*stawiać kroki*) trip, mince

drobina *f* (*-ny*; *-ny*) particle

drobiowy *adj* poultry

drobne *pl* (*-nych*), **drobniaki** *pl* (*-ków*) *infml* (*pieniądze*) (small) change *sing*; ***rozmienić na ~*** change; **drobnica** *f* (*-cy*; *no pl*) *COMM* general cargo; **drobniut(eń)ki** *adj dim* → ***drobny***

drobno *adv* **1.** *pokrojony*, *zmielony*: finely **2.** *zadrukowany*: densely

drobnomieszczański *adj* petit-bourgeois; **drobnomieszczaństwo** *n* (*-wa*; *no pl*) the petit bourgeoisie

drobnostka *f* (*-ki*; *-ki*) → ***drobiazg***

drobnoustrój *m* (*-roju*; *-roje*) microorganism

drobnoziarnisty *adj* fine-grained

drobn|y *adj* **1.** small; ***~a przedsiębiorczość*** small business; ***~ym drukiem*** in small print **2.** *deszcz*, *pył*: fine **3.** *szczegół*, *problem*: minor **4.** *blondynka*, *figura*: petite **5.** *mężczyzna*: slight **6.** *przestępca*: petty **7.** *przemysł*: small-scale; ***pisać ~ym maczkiem*** have small handwriting

droczyć się *v/im* (*-czę*) tease (**z** *I*)

droga[1] *adj* → ***drogi***[2]

drog|a[2] *f* (*-gi*; *-gi*) **1.** road; ***~a boczna*** side road; ***~a główna*** main road; ***~a gruntowa*** dirt track; ***~a startowa*** runway; ***~a wylotowa*** exit road **2.** (*trasa*, *kierunek*) way; ***2a Krzyżowa*** *REL* the Stations of the Cross; ***~a okrężna*** detour; ***~a wolna!*** **a)** the way is clear! **b)** *fig* do what you will!; ***~ą elektroniczną*** by e-mail; ***~ą lotniczą*** (***morską***) by air (sea); ***po drodze*** on the way; ***pytać o ~ę*** ask the way; ***sprowadzić kogoś na złą ~ę*** lead s.o. astray; ***w pół ~i pomiędzy*** *I* halfway between; ***zejść komuś z ~i*** get out of s.o.'s way **3.** (*podróż*) journey; ***w drodze powrotnej*** on the way back; ***wyruszyć w ~ę*** set off; ***przez całą ~ę*** all the way; ***szczęśliwej ~i!*** have a good trip! **4.** (*odległość*) distance; ***2a Mleczna*** *ASTR* the Milky Way; ***choroby przenoszone ~ą płciową*** sexually transmitted diseases, STD; ***swoją ~ą*** *fig* by the way; ***w drodze wyjątku*** by way of exception **5.** ***~i oddechowe*** (***moczowe***) the respiratory (urinary) tract

drogeria *f* (*-rii*; *-rie*) *Br* chemist's, *Am* drugstore

drogi *adj* **1.** (*kosztowny*) expensive; ***~e kamienie*** precious stones **2.** (*kochany*) dear; ***mój ~*** my dear

drogo *adv*: ***coś kosztuje ~*** s.th. is expensive; ***~ zapłacić za*** *A fig* pay dearly for; **drogocenny** *adj* precious

drogowiec *m* (*-wca*; *-wcy*) road worker; **drogownictwo** *n* (*-wa*; *no pl*) road building and maintenance

drogowskaz *m* (*-zu*; *-zy*) signpost; **drogow|y** *adj* road; ***kodeks ~y*** *Br* the Highway Code; ***kontrola ~a*** vehicle check; ***opłata ~a*** (*za przejazd*) toll; ***policja ~a*** traffic police; ***roboty ~e*** *Br* roadworks; ***wypadek ~y*** road accident; ***znaki ~e*** road signs

drogówka *f* (*-ki*; *no pl*) *infml* traffic police, *Br infml* black rats *pl*

drops *m* (*-sa*; *-sy*) drop; ***~y owocowe*** fruit drops

drozd *m* (*-da*; *-dy*) thrush

drożdże *pl* (*-dży*) yeast *sing*; **drożdżow|y** *adj* yeast; ***ciasto ~e*** yeast cake; **drożdżówka** *f* (*-ki*; *-ki*) bun

drożeć ⟨**po-**, **z-**⟩ (*-żeję*) become more expensive, go up (in price); **drożej** *comp* → ***drogo***; **droższy** *comp* → ***drogi***; **drożyzna** *f* (*-ny*; *no pl*) high prices *pl*, *infml* highway robbery

drób *m* (*drobiu*; *no pl*) poultry

dróg → ***droga***[2]

dróżka *f* (*-ki*; *-ki*) (narrow) path; **dróżnik** *m* (*-ka*; *-nicy*) level-crossing keeper, gatekeeper

druciak *m* (*-ka*; *-ki*) *infml* scourer; **druciany** *adj* wire; **drucik** *m* (*-ka*; *-ki*) **1.** wire **2.** (*w żarówce*) filament

drucz|ek *m* (*-czka*; *-czki*) (*blankiet*) form; ***drobnym ~kiem*** in small print

drug|i *adj* **1.** (the) second; ***~i kwietnia*** the second of April, April the second; ***~a klasa*** **a)** second class **b)** (*w szkole*) *Br* second form, *Am* second

D

grade; ***numer ~i*** number two; ***~ie śniadanie*** (*kanapki*) *Br* packed lunch, *Am* bag lunch; ***~ie danie*** the main course; ***co ~i*** every other, every second; ***do ~iej potęgi*** *MATH* to the power of two; ***~ie co do wielkości miasto*** the second-largest city; ***~i gatunek*** grade B; ***obywatele ~iej kategorii*** second-class citizens; ***po ~ie*** second, secondly; ***towary ~iego gatunku*** seconds; ***zająć ~ie miejsce*** come second; ***z ~iej ręki*** second-hand **2.** (*inny*) another; ***jeden po ~im*** one by one, one after another **3.** (*jeden z dwóch*) the other; ***na ~im końcu świata*** at the other end of the world; ***na ~im planie*** in the background; ***po ~iej stronie*** on the other side; ***z ~iej strony*** *fig* on the other hand; ***~ie tyle*** **a)** (*z rzeczownikami niepoliczalnymi*) twice as much **b)** (*z rzeczownikami policzalnymi*) twice as many **4.** ***jest*** (***godzina***) ***~a*** it's two (o'clock); ***wpół do ~iej*** half past one, *Br infml* half one

drugoklasista *m* (*-ty*; *-lasiści*) *Br* year-two pupil, *Am* second-grader

drugoplanow|y *adj* **1.** *szczegół fotografii*, *motyw obrazu*: background **2.** *sprawa*: minor, of secondary importance; ***rola ~a*** *FILM* supporting role; ***postacie ~e*** *FILM* supporting characters

drugorzędny *adj* **1.** (*pomniejszy*) minor **2.** (*niższej kategorii*) second-rate

druh *m* (*-ha*; *-howie*) **1.** (*towarzysz*) companion **2.** (*harcerz*) (boy) scout; **druhna** *f* (*-ny*; *-ny*) **1.** (*na ślubie*) bridesmaid **2.** (*harcerka*) *Br* girl guide, *Am* girl scout

druk *m* (*-ku*; *-ki*) **1.** (*drukowanie*) printing; ***ukazać się ~iem*** appear in print; ***jakość ~u*** print quality; ***pójść do ~u*** go to press **2.** (*blankiet*) form **3.** (*czcionka*) type; ***tłustym ~iem*** in bold type; ***drobnym ~iem*** in small print **4.** (*deseń*) print; **5.** ***~i*** (*wydawnictwa*) printed matter *sing*; ***~i reklamowe*** printed advertising (material)

drukarka *f* (*-ki*; *-ki*) printer; ***~ atramentowa*** (***laserowa***) ink-jet (laser) printer; **drukarnia** *f* (*-ni*; *-nie*) printing-house, printer's; **drukarski** *adj* (*maszyna*, *papier*) printing; ***błąd ~***, ***chochlik ~*** misprint; ***skład ~*** typesetting, composition

drukarstwo *n* (*-wa*; *no pl*) the printing industry; **drukarz** *m* (*-rza*; *-rze*) printer; **drukować** ⟨**wy-**⟩ (*-kuję*) print

drukowan|y *adj* printed; ***litery ~e*** block letters; ***pisać ~ymi literami*** print

drut *m* (*-tu*; *-ty*) **1.** wire; ***~ kolczasty*** barbed wire; ***prosty jak ~*** *infml* simplicity itself; ***ciągnąć ~a*** *vulg* blow **2.** (*do robótek*) (knitting) needle; ***robić na ~ach*** knit

druzgotać ⟨**z-**⟩ (*-goczę*/*-gocę*) crush

drużba *m* (*-by*; *-bowie*) (*na ślubie*) best man

drużyna *f* (*-ny*; *-ny*) team; ***~ harcerska*** scout troop

drużynowo *adv* *SPORT* in the team event, in the teams; **drużynowy** **I** *adj* team **II** *m* (*-wego*; *-wi*), **-wa** *f* (*-wej*; *-we*) scout leader, *Br* scouter

drwa *pl* (*drew*) firewood *sing*

drwal *m* (*-la*; *-le*) woodcutter, *Am* lumberjack

drwiąco *adv* mockingly; ***uśmiechnąć się ~*** smile mockingly, sneer; **drwiący** *adj* mocking; ***~ uśmiech*** mocking smile, sneer

drwić ⟨**za-**⟩ (*-wię*) **1.** mock (**z** *G*) **2.** *z niebezpieczeństwa*: laugh (**z** *G* at); **drwina** *f* (*-ny*; *-ny*) mockery, derision

dryblas *m* (*-sa*; *-sy*) *infml* beanpole

dryblować ⟨**prze-**⟩ (*-luję*) dribble

dryf *m* (*-fu*; *no pl*) drift; **dryfować** *v/im* (*-fuję*) drift

dryg *m* (*-gu*; *no pl*) *infml*: ***mieć ~ do*** *G* have a knack for

dryl *m* (*-lu*; *no pl*) drill

drylować ⟨**wy-**⟩ (*-luję*) *owoce*: stone

drzazg|a *f* (*-gi*; *-gi*) splinter; ***rozbić coś w ~i*** break s.th. into pieces, shatter

drzeć ⟨**po-**, **wy-**⟩ (*drę*) **1.** tear; ***~ na kawałki*** tear up; ***~ coś na strzępy*** rip s.th. to shreds; ***~ mordę*** *infml* yell; ***drą za sobą koty*** they are at loggerheads, they fight like cat and dog **2.** *buty*, *ubranie*: wear out; **drzeć się** **1.** tear **2.** (*o butach*, *ubraniu*) wear out **3.** (*krzyczeć*) *infml* yell

drzem|ać *v/im* (*-mię*) doze; ***~ią w nim wielkie możliwości*** *fig* he has a great potential

drzemk|a *f* (*-ki*; *-ki*) nap; ***~a poobiednia*** after-dinner nap; ***uciąć sobie ~ę*** have a nap; ***zapaść w ~ę*** doze off
drzewce *n* (*-ca*; *-ca*) **1.** *dzidy*, *strzały*: shaft **2.** *sztandaru*: pole
drzewko *n* (*-ka*; *-ka*) *dim* (small) tree
drzewny *adj* **1.** *pień*, *kora*: tree **2.** *przemysł*: *Br* timber, *Am* lumber **3.** *pulpa*, *wełna*: wood; ***węgiel ~*** charcoal
drzewo *n* (*-wa*; *-wa*) **1.** tree; ***~ iglaste*** coniferous tree, conifer; ***~ genealogiczne*** family tree; ***~ liściaste*** deciduous tree; ***~ owocowe*** fruit tree **2.** (*drewno*) wood **3.** (*budulec*) *Br* timber, *Am* lumber
drzeworyt *m* (*-tu*; *-ty*) **1.** (*odbitka*) woodcut **2.** (*technika*) wood engraving
drzewostan *m* (*-nu*; *-ny*) tree stock
drzwi *pl* (*drzwi*) door *sing*; ***~ami*** through the door; ***~ wejściowe*** entrance door; ***stać w ~ach*** stand in the doorway; ***~ na balkon*** **a)** balcony door **b)** (*podwójne*) French window, *Am* French door; ***~ obrotowe*** revolving door; ***~ rozsuwane*** sliding door; ***~ stoją otworem przed*** *I* the door is opened to; ***~ szafy*** wardrobe door; ***pokazać komuś ~*** show s.o. the door; ***przy ~ach zamkniętych*** *proces*: in camera; ***wyrzucić kogoś za ~*** throw s.o. out; ***wyważać otwarte ~*** reinvent the wheel; ***za ~!*** get out!
drzwiczki *pl* (*-czek*) (small) door *sing*; **drzwiowy** *adj* door; ***samochód 4-~*** 4-door car
drżący *adj* trembling
drż|eć ⟨**za-**⟩ (*-żę*) **1.** shake, tremble (**z** *G* with); ***~eć z zimna*** shiver (with cold); ***~ę na samą myśl o tym*** I shudder to think **2.** (*bać się*) fear (**o** *A* for); **drżenie** *n* (*-nia*; *no pl*) shaking, trembling
ds. *abbr* (= ***do spraw***) for; ***zespół ~ kontroli jakości*** quality control team; ***dyrektor ~ eksportu*** export director
dst. *abbr* (= ***dostateczny***) (*ocena*) D
dubbing *m* (*-gu*; *no pl*) dubbing; **dubbingować** *v/im* (*-guję*) dub; **dubbingowany** *adj film*: dubbed
dubeltówka *f* (*-ki*; *-ki*) *Br* double-barrelled gun, *Am* double-barreled gun
dubler *m* (*-ra*; *-rzy*), **~ka** *f* (*-ki*; *-ki*) **1.** *FILM* (body) double **2.** *THEAT* understudy
dublować ⟨**z-**⟩ (*-luję*) **1.** (*powtarzać*) duplicate **2.** *SPORT* lap **3.** *FILM* double (*A* for) **4.** *THEAT* understudy
duch *m* (*-cha*; *-chy*) **1.** spirit; ***~ czasu*** the spirit of the age, Zeitgeist; ***iść z ~em czasu*** move with the times; ***ani żywego ~a*** not a living soul; ***2 Święty*** the Holy Spirit, the Holy Ghost; ***być z kimś ~em*** be with s.o. in spirit; ***~ walki*** fighting spirit, morale; ***podnieść kogoś na ~u*** lift s.o.'s spirits, boost s.o.'s morale; ***upaść na ~u*** lose heart; ***w głębi ~a*** deep down; ***wyzionąć ~a*** give up the ghost; ***niespokojny ~*** restless soul **2.** (*zjawa*) ghost
duchota *f* (*-ty*; *no pl*) stuffiness
duchowieństwo *n* (*-wa*; *no pl*) (the) clergy
duchown|y **I** *adj* **1.** *stan*, *osoba*: clerical; ***osoba ~a*** **a)** (*mężczyzna*) clergyman **b)** (*kobieta*) clergywoman **2.** *władza*: religious; ***seminarium ~e*** seminary **II** *m* (*-nego*; *-ni*) **a)** (*mężczyzna*) clergyman **b)** (*kobieta*) clergywoman
duchowo *adv* spiritually; **duchowy** *adj* spiritual
dud|ek *m* (*-ka*; *-ki*) (*ptak*) hoopoe; ***wystrychnąć kogoś na ~ka*** make a fool of s.o.
dudnić *v/im* (*-nię*) **1.** rumble **2.** (*o deszczu*) drum
dudy *pl* (*dud*) bagpipes, pipes; **dudziarz** *m* (*-rza*; *-rze*) piper
duet *m* (*-tu*; *-ty*) **1.** (*zespół*, *para*) duo **2.** (*utwór*) duet
dukać ⟨**wy-**⟩ (*-kam*) (*jąkać się*) stammer
dukat *m* (*-ta*; *-ty*) ducat
dukt *m* (*-tu*; *-ty*) (*w lesie*) ride, track
dulka *f* (*-ki*; *-ki*) *Br* rowlock, *Am* oarlock
dum|a *f* (*-my*; *no pl*) pride (**z** *G* in); ***napawać ~ą*** fill with pride; ***urazić czyjąć ~ę*** hurt s.o.'s pride
dumać *v/im* (*-mam*) muse (**o** *L* on/over)
dumny *adj* proud (**z** *G* of); ***~ jak paw*** (as) proud as a peacock
dumping *m* (*-gu*; *no pl*) dumping; **dumpingowy** *adj* dumping
Dunaj *m* (*-ju*) the Danube
Dunk|a *f* (*-ki*; *-ki*) Dane; ***ona jest ~ą*** she is Danish

D

Dunkierka *f* (*-ki*) Dunkirk
Duńczyk *m* (*-ka*; *-czycy*) Dane; ***on jest ~iem*** he is Danish; **duński** *adj* Danish; ***mówić po ~u*** speak Danish; ***po ~u*** in Danish
dup|a *f* (*-py*; *-py*) *vulg* **1.** *Br vulg* arse, *Am infml* ass; ***do ~y*** crap; ***mieć coś w ~ie*** not give a shit about s.th.; ***dawać ~y*** (*oddawać się*) fuck **2.** (*kobieta*) *Br vulg* piece of arse, *Am infml* piece of ass
duperele *pl* (*-li*) *infml* rubbish *sing*
dur[1] *m* (*-ru*; *no pl*): ***~ brzuszny*** *MED* typhoid fever; ***~ plamisty*** *MED* spotted fever
dur[2] *n/m indecl MUS* major; ***A-~*** A major
dur|eń *m* (*-rnia*; *-rnie*) fool; ***zrobić ~nia z*** *G* make a fool of
durny *adj infml* dumb
durowy *adj MUS* major
durszlak *m* (*-ka*; *-ki*) colander
durzyć się ⟨**za-**⟩ (*-rzę*) be infatuated (**w** *L* with)
dusiciel *m* (*-la*; *-le*) (*osoba*) strangler; ***boa ~*** boa constrictor
dusić (*-szę*) **1.** ⟨**u-**, **za-**⟩ (*zabijać*) choke, strangle **2.** *v/im (o dymie)* suffocate **3.** ⟨**u-**⟩ *COOK* simmer; ***~ pod przykryciem*** stew **4.** ⟨**z-**⟩ *łzy, złość*: choke back **5.** ⟨**z-**⟩ *śmiech*: suppress, stifle **6.** *v/im* (*ściskać*) squeeze; ***dusić się*** **1.** (*umierać*) suffocate, choke (*I* on) **2.** (*nie móc oddychać*) ***duszę się tutaj*** I fell stifled here **3.** *COOK* simmer **4.** (*być przytłoczonym*) feel suffocated **5.** (*o astmatyku*) feel breathless
dusigrosz *m* (*-sza*; *-sze*) *infml* pennypincher
dusz|a *f* (*-szy*; *-sze*) soul; ***bratnia ~a*** kindred spirit; ***~a towarzystwa*** the life (and soul) of the party; ***czego ~a zapragnie*** anything you want; ***ile ~a zapragnie*** to one's heart's content; ***w głębi ~y*** deep down; ***z całej ~y*** with all one's heart; ***ani żywej ~y*** not a living soul; ***oczyma ~y*** in one's mind's eye; ***mieć ~ę na ramieniu*** have one's heart in one's mouth
duszący *adj zapach*, *dym*: suffocating, stifling
duszek *m* (*-szka*; *-szki*) elf
duszkiem *adv* in one gulp
dusznica *f* (*-cy*; *no pl*): ***~ bolesna*** *MED* angina pectoris; **duszność|ć** *f* (*-ści*; *-ści*) **1.** breathlessness; ***mieć atak ~ci*** feel breathless **2.** (*w powietrzu*) sultriness
duszno *adv*: ***jest ~*** **a)** it's stifling **b)** (*w pomieszczeniu*) it's stuffy; **duszny** *adj* **1.** *dzień*, *powietrze*: sultry **2.** *zapach*, *atmosfera*: stifling, suffocating **3.** *pomieszczenie*: stuffy
duszpasterski *adj* priestly; **duszpasterz** *m* (*-rza*; *-rze*) priest
dużo *adv* **1.** a lot (*G* of), *form* a great deal (*G* of); ***za ~ ludzi*** too many people; ***za ~ cukru*** too much sugar; ***~ więcej*** (***mniej***) much more (less); ***dość ~*** quite a lot (*G* of) **2.** (*z rzeczownikami niepoliczalnymi w pytaniach i przeczeniach*) much **3.** (*z rzeczownikami policzalnymi w pytaniach i przeczeniach*) many
duż|y *adj* **1.** big, large; ***w ~ej mierze*** to a large extent; ***~y palec*** **a)** (*u ręki*) thumb **b)** (*u nogi*) toe; ***jest ~e zachmurzenie*** it's very cloudy; ***~e pieniądze*** big money; ***mieć ~e zdolności*** be very talented **2.** *mróz*: hard **3.** *litery*: capital; ***pisany ~ą literą*** spelled with a capital letter **4.** *inteligencja*, *gorączka*: high
dw|a *num* two; ***~a razy*** twice; ***co ~a dni*** (***tygodnie***) every two days (weeks); ***~a kroki stąd*** close by, around the corner; ***w ~óch słowach*** in a word; ***bez ~óch zdań*** no doubt about it; **dwadzieścia** *num* twenty; **dwaj** *num* two; **dwanaście** *num* twelve
dwie *num* two; **dwieście** *num* two hundred
dwoić się *v/im* (*dwoję*): ***~ i troić, żeby*** be going all out to; ***~ komuś w oczach*** s.o. is seeing double
dwoisty *adj* dual; **dwojaczki** *pl* (*-ków*) twins; **dwojaki** *adj* twofold; **dwojako** *adv* in two ways
dwoj|e *num* two; ***jedno z ~ga*** one or the other; ***na ~e***, ***we ~e*** (*na pół*) in two; ***romantyczny wieczór we ~e*** a romantic evening for two; ***na ~e babka wróżyła*** it could go one way or the other
dwom → ***dwa***
dworcowy *adj poczekalnia*, *bufet*: station

dworek *m* (*-rku*; *-rki*) (small) country house; **dworski** *adj* **1.** *życie*, *błazen*: court **2.** *maniery*, *tańce*: courtly; **dwory, dworze → dwór**

dworzanin *m* (*-na*; *-rzanie*) courtier

dworzec *m* (*-rca*; *-rce*) station; **~ kolejowy** railway station, train station

dwóch *num* two; **dwóchsetlecie** *n* (*-cia*; *-cia*) **1.** (*jubileusz*) bicentenary **2.** (*okres*) two hundred years

dwójk|a *f* (*-ki*; *-ki*) **1.** two; **~ami** in pairs; **we ~ę** (*razem*) together **2.** (*ocena*) D **3.** (*łódź*) double

dwójnasób: **w ~** twofold

dwóm → dwa

dwór *m* (*dworu*; *dwory*) **1.** (*królewski*) court **2.** (*ziemiański*) manor **3. wyjść na ~** go out, go outside; **na dworze** outside

dwu *num* two; **dwu-** (*w złożeniach*) two-; **dwuaktówka** *f* (*-ki*; *-ki*) THEAT two-act play; **dwubarwny** *adj* *Br* two-coloured, *Am* two-colored; **dwubój** *m* (*-boju*; *-boje*) biathlon

dwucyfrowy *adj* two-digit; **dwucylindrowy** *adj* two-cylinder; **dwuczęściowy** *adj* **1.** two-part **2.** *kostium*, *suknia*: two-piece

dwuczłonowy *adj* **1.** *nazwisko*: two-part **2.** *konstrukcja*: two-piece; **dwudaniowy** *adj* two-course; **dwudniowy** *adj* **1.** *wyjazd*, *termin*: two-day **2.** *noworodek*: two-day-old; **dwudrzwiowy** *adj* *szafa*, *samochód*: two-door

dwudziest|ka *f* (*-ki*; *-ki*) twenty; **po ~ce** in one's (early) twenties

dwudziesto- (*w złożeniach*) twenty-; **dwudziestoczterogodzinny** *adj* twenty-four-hour, 24-hour; **dwudziestokilkuletni** *adj* **1.** *osoba*: over twenty, *infml* twenty-something **2.** *okres*: over twenty years long

dwudziestolatek *m* (*-tka*; *-tki*) twenty-year-old man; **dwudziestolatka** *f* (*-ki*; *-ki*) twenty-year-old woman; **dwudziestolecie** *n* (*-cia*; *-cia*) **1.** (*jubileusz*) twentieth anniversary **2.** (*okres*) twenty years; **~ międzywojenne** the interwar period

dwudziestoletni *adj* **1.** *okres*: twenty-year **2.** *osoba*: twenty-year-old; **dwudziestowieczny** *adj* twentieth-century

dwudziestozłotówka *f* (*-ki*; *-ki*) (*banknot*) *Br* twenty-zloty note, *Am* twenty-zloty bill

dwudziest|y *adj* twentieth; **~y pierwszy** twenty-first; **lata ~e** the twenties; **o** (**godzinie**) **~ej** at 8 p.m.

dwuetapowy *adj* *proces*, *zabieg*: two step, two-stage

dwugarbny *adj* *wielbłąd*: Bactrian, two-humped; **dwugłoska** *f* (*-ki*; *-ki*) diphthong; **dwugodzinny** *adj* two-hour

dwuizbowy *adj* *parlament*: bicameral

dwujęzyczność *f* (*-ści*; *no pl*) bilingualism; **dwujęzyczny** *adj* bilingual

dwukierunkowy *adj* two-way; **dwukołowy** *adj* two-wheeled; **dwukondygnacyjny** *adj* *Br* two-storey, *Am* two-story; **dwukropek** *m* (*-pka*; *-pki*) colon

dwukrotnie *adv* **1.** twice; **~ większy** twice bigger; **~ wzrosnąć** (*podwoić się*) increase twofold, double; **~ szybciej niż** twice as fast as; **dwukrotny** *adj* **1.** *zwycięzca*: two-time **2.** *wzrost*: double

dwulatek *m* (*-tka*; *-tki*), **-tka** *f* (*-ki*; *-ki*) two-year-old

dwuletni *adj* **1.** two-year **2.** *dziecko*: two-year-old; **roślina ~a** biennial (plant); **dwulicowość** *f* (*-ści*; *no pl*) two-facedness, hypocrisy; **dwulicowy** *adj* two-faced; **dwumasztowy** *adj* two-masted; **dwumian** *m* (*-nu*; *-ny*) MATH binomial

dwumiejscowy *adj*: **samolot ~** two-seater; **dwumiesięcznik** *m* (*-ka*; *-ki*) bimonthly; **dwumiesięczny** *adj* **1.** *okres*, *wakacje*: two-month **2.** *dziecko*: two-month-old

dwunastka *f* (*-ki*; *-ki*) twelve; **dwunastnica** *f* (*-cy*; *-ce*) ANAT duodenum

dwunasto- (*w złożeniach*) twelve-; **dwunastogodzinny** *adj* twelve-hour; **dwunastoletni** *adj* **1.** *okres*: twelve-year **2.** *dziecko*: twelve-year-old

dwunastu *num* twelve

dwunast|y *adj* twelfth: **o** (**godzinie**) **~ej** at 12 (o'clock); **~a w nocy** 12 (o'clock) at night

dwunożny *adj* *zwierzę*, *robot*: two-legged, bipedal; **dwuodcinkowy** *adj* *serial*: two-part

dwuosobowy *adj* **1.** *pokój*, *łóżko*: double **2.** *zespół*: two-person **3.** *kajuta*:

D

D

two-berth; **dwupasmow|y** *adj*: ***droga ~a*** **a)** dual two-lane road **b)** (*przedzielona pasmem zieleni*) *Br* dual carriageway, *Am* divided highway
dwupłatowiec *m* (*-wca*; *-wce*) biplane
dwupłciowy *adj* bisexual; **dwupokojowy** *adj* two-room; **dwupoziomowy** *adj* **1.** *skrzyżowanie*: two-level **2.** *pokój*, *mieszkanie*: split-level
dwurzędowy *adj* *marynarka*: double-breasted; **dwusetny** *adj* two-hundredth
dwusilnikowy *adj* *samolot*: twin-engined; **dwuskrzydłowy** *adj* *drzwi*: double; **dwustopniowy** *adj* **1.** two-stage **2.** *wybory*: two-round
dwustronny *adj* **1.** *umowa*, *rozmowy*: bilateral **2.** *druk*: two-sided **3.** *materiał*: reversible; **dwustuletni** *adj* **1.** *dom*, *drzewo*: two-hundred-year-old **2.** *historia*: two-hundred-year
dwusuwowy *adj* AUTO two-stroke; **dwusylabowy** *adj* two-syllable; **dwuszereg** *m* (*-gu*; *-gi*): ***w ~u*** in a two-deep line; **dwutlenek** *m* (*-nku*; *-nki*) CHEM dioxide; ***~ węgla*** carbon dioxide
dwutomowy *adj* two-volume
dwutygodnik *m* (*-ka*; *-ki*) biweekly; **dwutygodniowy** *adj* **1.** *okres*: two-week **2.** *dziecko*: two-month-old; **dwutysięczny** *adj* two-thousandth; ***rok ~*** (the year) two thousand
dwuwarstwowy *adj* **1.** *materiał*, *papier*: two-ply **2.** *struktura*: two-tier, two-layer
dwuwiersz *m* (*-sza*; *-sze*) couplet
dwuwymiarowy *adj* two-dimensional
dwuzłotówka *f* (*-ki*; *-ki*) (*moneta*) two-zloty coin
dwuzmianowy *adj* two-shift
dwuznaczność *f* (*-ści*; *no pl*) ambiguity; **dwuznaczny** *adj* **1.** ambiguous **2.** *uśmiech*, *żart*: suggestive
dybać *v/im* (*-bię*): ***~ na czyjeś życie*** seek s.o.'s life
dyby *pl* (*-bów*) the stocks; ***zakuty w ~*** locked in the stocks
dycha *f* (*-chy*; *-chy*) *infml* tenner *Br*
dychawica *f* (*-cy*; *no pl*) MED asthma
dydaktyczny *adj* **1.** educational **2.** *pomoce*, *ośrodek*: teaching **3.** *poemat*: didactic
dyferencjał *m* (*-łu*; *-ły*) differential (gear)
dyfteryt *m* (*-tu*; *no pl*) diphtheria
dyftong *m* (*-gu*; *-gi*) diphthong
dyfuzja *f* (*-ji*; *no pl*) PHYS diffusion
dygać ⟨**-gnąć**⟩ (*-gam*) curtsy (**przed** *I* to)
dygnitarz *m* (*-rza*; *-rze*) dignitary
dygotać ⟨**za-**⟩ (*-goczę*/*-gocę*) tremble, quiver (**z** *G* with); ***~ z zimna*** shiver (with cold)
dygresja *f* (*-ji*; *-je*) digression; ***poczynić ~*** digress
dykcja *f* (*-ji*; *no pl*) diction
dykta *f* (*-ty*; *no pl*) plywood
dyktafon *m* (*-nu*; *-ny*) Dictaphone®
dyktando *n* (*-da*; *-da*) (*ćwiczenie*) dictation; ***robić wszystko pod czyjeś ~*** do what one is told by s.o.
dyktator *m* (*-ra*; *-rzy*) dictator; ***~ mody*** top (fashion) designer; **dyktatura** *f* (*-ry*; *-ry*) dictatorship
dyktować ⟨**po-**⟩ (*-tuję*) dictate
dyl: ***dać ~a*** *infml* make a bolt for it
dylemat *n* (*-tu*; *-ty*) dilemma; ***mieć ~*** be in a dilemma
dyletancki *adj* unprofessional
dyletant *m* (*-ta*; *-nci*), **~ka** *f* (*-ki*; *-ki*) dilettante
dyliżans *m* (*-su*; *-se*) stagecoach
dym *m* (*-mu*; *-my*) smoke; ***~ z papierosa*** cigarette smoke; ***pójść z ~em*** go up in smoke; ***nie ma ~u bez ognia*** there is no smoke without fire; ***puścić coś z ~em*** burn s.th., reduce s.th. to ashes
dymić ⟨**za-**⟩ (*-mię*) smoke; ***dymić się*** smoke
dymisj|a *f* (*-ji*; *-je*) **1.** (*rezygnacja*) resignation; ***podać się do ~i*** resign **2.** (*zwolnienie*) dismissal; **dymisjonować** ⟨**z-**⟩ (*-nuję*) dismiss
dymka *f* (*-ki*; *-ki*): ***cebula ~*** spring onion
dymnik *m* (*-ka*; *-ki*) (*okno*) skylight; **dymn|y** *adj* *sygnał*: smoke, ***świeca ~a*** smoke bomb; ***zasłona ~a*** smokescreen
dynamiczny *adj* dynamic; **dynamika** *f* (*-ki*; *no pl*) dynamics
dynamit *m* (*-tu*; *no pl*) dynamite
dynamo *n indecl*/*n* (*-ma*; *-ma*) dynamo
dynastia *f* (*-tii*; *-tie*) dynasty
dyndać ⟨**za-**⟩ (*-dam*) dangle
dynia *f* (*-ni*; *-nie*) pumpkin
dyplom *m* (*-mu*; *-my*) **1.** (*ukończenia*

uczelni) diploma; ***mieć ~ wyższej uczelni*** have a university degree **2.** (*ukończenia szkoły, kursu*) certificate; ***~ uznania*** letter of recognition
dyplomacja *f* (*-ji; no pl*) diplomacy
dyplomata *m* (*-ty; -maci*), **-tka** *f* (*-ki; -ki*) diplomat; **dyplomatyczny** *adj* diplomatic
dyplomowany *adj* **1.** qualified **2.** *pielęgniarka*: registered; **dyplomow|y** *adj*: ***praca ~a*** **a)** *magisterska, doktorska*: thesis **b)** (*zawodowa*) final project
dyr. *abbr* (= **dyrektor**) director
dyrdymały *pl* (*-łów/-mał*) *infml* balderdash *sing*
dyrekcja *f* (*-ji; -je*) management; ***pod ~ą*** *G* (*o orkiestrze*) conducted by; **dyrektor** *m* (*-ra; -rzy/-rowie*) **1.** *firmy*: director, manager **2.** *szkoły*: headmaster, principal
dyrektywa *f* (*-wy; -wy*) directive
dyrygent *m* (*-ta; -nci*) conductor; **dyrygować** *v/im* (*-guję*) **1.** *orkiestrą*: conduct **2.** ***~ kimś*** *fig* boss s.o. around
dyscyplina *f* (*-ny; -ny*) discipline; ***~ sportowa*** sport; **dyscyplinarn|y** *adj* disciplinary; ***zwolnienie ~e*** disciplinary dismissal, disciplinary discharge
dysertacja *f* (*-ji; -je*) dissertation
dysfunkcja *f* (*-ji; -je*) malfunction
dysharmonia *f* (*-nii; no pl*) disharmony
dyshonor (*-ru; no pl*) *Br* dishonour, *Am* dishonor
dysk *m* (*-ku; -ki*) **1.** disc, *Am* disk **2.** INF disk; ***~ twardy*** hard disk **3.** SPORT discus; ***rzut ~iem*** discus-throwing
dyskietka *f* (*-ki; -ki*) floppy disk, *infml* floppy
dyskobol *m* (*-la; -le*), **~ka** *f* (*-ki; -ki*) discus-thrower
dyskomfort *m* (*-tu; no pl*) discomfort
dyskonto *n* (*-ta; no pl*) discount
dyskoteka *f* (*-ki; -ki*) disco; **dyskotekow|y** *adj* disco; ***muzyka ~a*** disco music
dyskrecj|a *f* (*-ji; no pl*) discretion; ***prosić kogoś o ~ę*** ask s.o. to be discreet, ask s.o. to keep the matter confidential
dyskredytować ⟨**z-**⟩ (*-tuję*) discredit
dyskretny *adj* **1.** *osoba*: discreet **2.** *makijaż*: light **3.** *światło, muzyka*: soft
dyskryminacja *f* (*-ji; no pl*) discrimination; **dyskryminować** *v/im* (*-nuję*) discriminate
dyskusj|a *f* (*-ji; -je*) discussion; ***poddać coś pod ~ę*** raise s.th. for discussion; ***to nie podlega ~i*** there's no doubt about it, it's indisputable; **dyskusyjny** *adj* **1.** *forum*: discussion **2.** *pogląd*: controversial **3.** *klub*: debating
dyskutant *m* (*-ta; -nci*), **~ka** *f* (*-ki; -ki*) debater
dyskut|ować *v/im* (*-tuję*) discuss (**o** *L*/**nad** *I*); ***nie ~uj!*** don't argue!
dyskwalifikacja *f* (*-ji; -je*) disqualification; **dyskwalifikować** ⟨**z-**⟩ (*-kuję*) *zawodnika, kandydata*: disqualify
dysleksja *f* (*-ji; no pl*) dislexia; **dyslektyk** *m* (*-ka; -tycy*) dislexic
dysonans *m* (*-su; -se*) dissonance
dyspensa *f* (*-sy; no pl*) dispensation (**od** *G* from)
dysponować ⟨**za-**⟩ (*-nuję*) *form czasem, gotówką*: have
dyspozycj|a *f* (*-ji; -je*) *form* **1.** (*polecenie*) instruction **2.** (*skłonność*) disposition (**do** *G* towards); ***mieć coś do ~i*** have s.th. at one's disposal; ***być do czyjejś ~i*** be at s.o.'s disposal
dyspozycyjność *f* (*-ści; no pl*) *pracownika*: ability to work flexible hours, flexiblility; **dyspozycyjny** *adj pracownik*: able to work flexible hours, flexible
dyspozytor *m* (*-ra; -rzy*) *ruchu*: manager
dysproporcja *f* (*-ji; -je*) disproportion
dysputa *f* (*-ty; -ty*) *form* dispute
dystans *m* (*-su; -se/-sy*) distance; ***zachować ~*** keep one's distance; ***trzymać kogoś na ~*** keep s.o. at arm's length; ***z ~em*** with reserve
dystansować ⟨**z-**⟩ (*-suję*) outdistance; ***dystansować się*** distance oneself (**od** *G* from)
dystrybucja *f* (*-ji; no pl*) distribution
dystrybutor *m* **1.** (*-ra; -rzy*) ECON distributor **2.** (*-ra; -ry*) ***~ napojów*** drink dispenser; ***~ paliwa*** *Br* petrol pump, *Am* gas pump
dystyngowany *adj* distinguished, dignified; **dystynkcja** *f* (*-ji; no pl*) refinement, distinguished manner
dystynkcje *pl* (*-ji*) (*wojskowe*) insignia
dysydent *m* (*-ta; -nci*), **~ka** *f* (*-ki; -ki*) dissident

D

D

dysza *f* (*-szy*; *-sze*) nozzle
dyszeć *v/im* (*-szę*) pant; ***ciężko ~*** pant heavily; ***ledwo ~*** be all-in *Br infml*, be beat *infml*
dyszel *m* (*-szla*; *-szle*) *przyczepy*: towbar, drawbar
dywagacje *pl* (*-ji*) *form* divagations, digressions
dywan *m* (*-nu*; *-ny*) carpet
dywanow|y *adj*: ***wykładzina ~a*** fitted carpet
dywersja *f* (*-ji*; *no pl*) sabotage
dywidenda *f* (*-dy*; *-dy*) dividend
dywizja *f* (*-ji*; *-je*) division; **dywizjon** *m* (*-nu*; *-ny*) squadron
dyżur *m* (*-ru*; *-ry*) **1.** duty hours; ***mieć ~*** **a)** be on duty **b)** (*o aptece*) be open all night **2.** *lekarza*: *Br* surgery hours *pl*, *Am* office hours *pl*; ***nocny ~*** night duty; ***ostry ~*** *Br* accident and emergency, *Am* emergency
dyżurny **I** *adj* ***lekarz*** (***oficer***) ***~*** duty doctor (officer) **II** *m* (*-nego*; *-ni*), **-na** *f* (*-nej*; *-ne*) **1.** person on duty; ***~ ruchu*** dispatcher **2.** (*uczeń*) monitor
dyżurować *v/im* (*-ruję*) **1.** be on duty **2.** (*o aptece*) be open all night
dzban *m* (*-na*; *-ny*) jug; **dzbanek** *m* (*-nka*; *-nki*) (small) jug; ***~ do herbaty*** teapot; ***~ do mleka*** milk jug; ***~ do kawy*** coffee pot
dziać się *v/im* (*dzieję*) happen, go on; ***co się tu dzieje?*** what's going on here?; ***co się z tobą dzieje?*** what's the matter with you?; ***niech się dzieje, co chce!*** come what may!
dziad *m* (*-da*; *-dy*) **1.** (*żebrak*) beggar **2.** (*starzec*) old man **3.** (*przodek*) forefather; ***z ~a pradziada*** for generations
dziadek *m* (*-dka*; *-dkowie*) **1.** (*krewny*) grandfather, *dim* grandad **2.** (*staruszek*) old man **3.** ***~ do orzechów*** nutcracker
dziadkowie *pl* (*-ków*) (*rodzice rodziców*) grandparents
dziadostwo *n* (*-wa*; *no pl*) (*tandeta*) trash
dziadowski *adj* (*nędzny*) shabby, trashy; ***być rozpuszczonym jak ~ bicz*** be a spoiled brat
dziadówka *f* (*-ki*; *-ki*) (*żebraczka*) beggarwoman; **dziadyga** *m* (*-gi*; *-gi*) old geezer; **dziadzieć** ⟨**z-**⟩ (*-dzieję*) *infml* **1.** (*stawać się biednym*) come down in the world, *infml* go to the dogs **2.** (*starzeć się*) grow old
dziadziuś *m* (*-dziusia*; *-dziusiowie*) *dim* grandpa
dział *m* (*-łu*; *-ły*) **1.** (*dziedzina*) branch; **2.** *firmy*: department, section; ***~ kadr*** personnel department, HR department **3.** *czasopisma*, *biblioteki*: section **4.** ***~ wodny*** watershed
działacz *m* (*-cza*; *-cze*), **~ka** *f* (*-ki*; *-ki*) activist; ***~ partyjny*** party activist; ***~ podziemia*** resistance fighter; ***być ~em społecznym*** be involved in social work
działać ⟨**za-**⟩ (*-łam*) **1.** (*funkcjonować*, *pracować*) work **2.** (*czynić*, *postępować*) act; ***~ cuda*** work wonders; ***~ na własną rękę*** act on one's own **3.** (*o firmie*) operate **4.** (*oddziaływać*) ***~ komuś na nerwy*** get on s.o.'s nerves; ***~ usypiająco*** induce sleep **5.** ***~ wstecz*** JUR apply retrospectively, be retroactive
działalność *f* (*-ści*; *no pl*) activity; ***~ gospodarcza*** business activity; ***prowadzić ~ gospodarczą*** run a business
działani|e *n* (*-nia*; *-nia*) **1.** (*czynność*) action **2.** (*funkcjonowanie*) operation **3.** (*postępowanie*) activities **4.** MATH operation **5.** (*oddziaływanie*) effects *pl*; ***~e uboczne*** side effect **6.** (*walka*) ***~a wojenne*** military operations
działka *f* (*-ki*; *-ki*) **1.** (*grunt*) plot; ***~ budowlana*** building plot **2.** (*ogródek*) garden plot, *Br* allotment **3.** *infml narkotyku*: hit **4.** (*część*) *infml* share
działkowicz *m* (*-cza*; *-cze*) allotment gardener; **działkowy** *adj*: ***ogródek ~*** garden plot, *Br* allotment
działo *n* (*-ła*; *-ła*) cannon
działo się → ***dziać się***
działow|y *adj*: ***ścianka ~a*** partition wall
dzianina *f* (*-ny*; *-ny*) **1.** (*tkanina*) knitted fabric **2.** (*ubranie*) knitwear
dziarski *adj* bouncy; ***~ staruszek*** sprightly old man
dziąs|ło *n* (*-ła*; *-ła*) gum; ***zapalenie ~eł*** gingivitis
dzicz *f* (*-czy*; *no pl*) **1.** (*teren*) wilderness **2.** (*tłum*) mob; **dziczeć** ⟨**z-**⟩

(-*czeję*) **1.** go wild **2.** (*o roślinie*) grow wild **3.** (*o człowieku*) *fig* coarsen, become brutalized

dziczyzna *f* (-*ny*; *no pl*) venison

dzida *f* (-*dy*; -*dy*) spear

dzidzia *f* (-*dzi*; -*dzie*) baby; **dzidziuś** *m* (-*dziusia*; -*dziusie*) baby

dzieci *pl* → **dziecko**

dzieciak *m* (-*ka*; -*ki*) *infml* kid; ***nieznośny* ~** brat; **dzieciarnia** *f* (-*ni*; *no pl*) kids *pl*

dzieciątko *n* (-*ka*; -*ka*) baby; ***~ Jezus*** the baby Jesus

dziecięcy *adj* **1.** *ubranie*, *literatura*: children's; ***~ głos*** (***śmiech***) **a)** child's voice (laughter) **b)** (*jak u dziecka*) childlike voice (laughter); ***wiek ~*** childhood **2.** (*niemowlęcy*) baby

dziecinada *f* (-*dy*; *no pl*) *Br* childish behaviour, *Am* childish behavior

dziecinnie *adv* childishly; ***to ~ proste*** it's child's play; **dziecinn|y** *adj* childish; ***pokój ~y*** nursery; ***wózek ~y*** **a)** (*głęboki*) *Br* pram, *Am* baby carriage **b)** (*spacerowy*) *Br* pushchair, *Am* stroller; ***~a igraszka*** *fig* child's play

dzieciństwo *n* (-*wa*; *no pl*) childhood

dzieciobójstwo *n* (-*wa*; -*wa*) infanticide

dzieciuch *m* (-*cha*; -*chy*) *infml* kid

dzieck|o *n* (-*ka*; -*ci*) **1.** child; ***dom ~a*** children's home; ***cudowne ~o*** child prodigy; ***od ~a*** since childhood; ***ktoś jest ~iem szczęścia*** s.o. was born under a lucky star; ***wylać ~o z kąpielą*** *fig* throw the baby out with the bath water **2.** (*małe*) baby; ***~o z probówki*** test-tube baby

dziedzic *m* (-*ca*; -*ce*) **1.** (*sukcesor*) heir, successor **2.** (*właściciel majątku*) squire; **dziedzictwo** *n* (-*wa*; -*wa*) *kulturowe*: heritage; **dziedziczka** *f* (-*ki*; -*ki*) (*sukcesorka*) heiress

dziedziczność *f* (-*ści*; *no pl*) **1.** *BIOL* heredity **2.** *tronu*: hereditary succession; **dziedziczny** *adj* **1.** *cecha*, *władca*: hereditary **2.** (*otrzymany w spadku*) inherited

dziedziczyć ⟨**o-**⟩ (-*czę*) inherit (**po** *L* from)

dziedzin|a *f* (-*ny*; -*ny*) **1.** field; ***nagroda Nobla z ~y*** *G* the Nobel prize for; ***specjaliści z ~y marketingu*** marketing specialists **2.** *działalności*: area

dziedziniec *m* (-*dzińca*; -*dzińce*) courtyard

dzieg|ieć *m* (-*gciu*; *no pl*) wood tar; ***łyżka ~ciu w beczce miodu*** a fly in the ointment

dziej|e *pl* (-*jów*) (*historia*) history *sing*; ***od zarania ~ów*** from the dawn of history; ***~e Apostolskie*** *REL* the Acts of Apostles; ***wspominać stare ~e*** to remember the old days; → ***dziać się***

dziejowy *adj* **1.** *misja*: historic **2.** *sprawiedliwość*: historical

dziekan *m* (-*na*; -*ni*) dean; **dziekanat** *m* (-*tu*; -*ty*) (*na uczelni*) dean's office

dziekański *adj*: ***urlop ~*** (university) leave of absence; ***dzień ~*** university holiday

dzieleni|e *n* (-*nia*; *no pl*) **1.** dividing **2.** *MATH* division; ***znak ~a*** division sign

dzielić ⟨**po-**⟩ (-*lę*) **1.** divide (**na** *A* into); ***~ włos na czworo*** *fig* split hairs **2.** (*rozdzielać*) distribute (**między** *A* between/among) **3.** *MATH* divide (**przez** *A* by) **4.** (*mieć wspólne*) share (**z** *I* with); **dzielić się 1.** (*składać się*) be divided (**na** *A* into) **2.** (*dawać*, *komunikować*) share; ***~ się doświadczeniami*** share experiences; ***~ się opłatkiem*** share the wafer **3.** *MATH* be divisible (**przez** *A* by)

dzielna *f* (-*nej*; -*ne*) *MATH* dividend

dzielnica *f* (-*cy*; -*ce*) **1.** *miasta*: district, quarter; ***~ mieszkaniowa*** residential district; ***~ podmiejska*** suburban district **2.** *HIST* province; **dzielnicowy I** *adj* district **II** *m* (-*wego*; -*wi*) *Br* beat officer

dzielnik *m* (-*ka*; -*ki*) *MATH* divisor

dzielność *f* (-*ści*; *no pl*) bravery; **dzielny** *adj* brave

dzieł|o *n* (-*ła*; -*ła*) work; ***~o sztuki*** work of art; ***przystąpić do ~a*** set to work; ***być ~em przypadku*** be a coincidence; ***umowa o ~o*** contract for a specific task

dziennie *adv* daily; ***dwie godziny ~*** two hours a day

dziennik *m* (-*ka*; -*ki*) **1.** (*gazeta*) daily **2.** (*program*) the news **3.** (*szkolny*) register **4.** (*pamiętnik*) diary, journal; ***~ podróży*** travel journal; ***~ okrętowy*** log; ***~ urzędowy*** official journal

D

D

dziennikarka *f* (*-ki*; *-ki*) (female) journalist

dziennikarsk|i *adj* journalistic; ***kaczka ~a*** canard; **dziennikarstwo** *n* (*-wa*; *no pl*) journalism; **dziennikarz** *m* (*-rza*; *-rze*) journalist

dzienn|y *adj* **1.** *płaca*, *utarg*: daily; ***porządek ~y*** agenda; ***być na porządku ~ym*** *fig* be an everyday occurence; ***światło ~e*** daylight; ***wyjść na światło ~e*** see the light of day **2.** *studia*: full-time **3.** *zajęcia*: day **4.** *temperatury*: daytime **5.** *zwierzę*: diurnal

dzień *m* (*dnia*; *dni*) **1.** day; ***~ wolny*** day off; ***~ świąteczny*** holiday; ***~ tygodnia***, ***~ powszedni*** weekday; ***~ roboczy*** *Br* working day, *Am* workday; ***cały ~*** all day (long); ***~ dobry!*** **a)** (*rano*) good morning! **b)** (*po południu*) good afternoon!; ***w ciągu dnia*** during the day; ***co*** (***drugi***) ***~*** every (other) day; ***na drugi ~*** the next day; ***za dnia*** by day; ***z dnia na ~*** **a)** (*nagle*) overnight **b)** (*stopniowo*) day by day **c)** *żyć*: from day to day; ***do dziś dnia*** to this day; ***w biały ~*** in broad daylight; ***lada ~*** any day (now) **2.** (*data*) date; ***dnia siódmego lipca*** on the 7th of July; ***~ urodzin*** birthday

dziergać ⟨**wy-**⟩ (*-gam*) *szalik*, *sweter*: knit

dzierżaw|a *f* (*-wy*; *-wy*) lease; ***oddać w ~ę*** lease (out); ***wziąć w ~ę*** lease; **dzierżawca** *m* (*-cy*; *-cy*) lessee, leaseholder

dzierżawczy *adj*: ***zaimek ~*** GRAM possessive pronoun; **dzierżawić** ⟨**wy-**⟩ (*-wię*) lease

dzierżyć *v/im* (*-żę*) *lit*: ***~ władzę*** wield power

dziesiątk|a *f* (*-ki*; *-ki*) ten; ***trafić w ~ę*** hit the bullseye; ***~i czegoś*** dozens of s.th.; **dziesiątkować** ⟨**z-**⟩ (*-kuję*) decimate; **dziesiąt|y** *adj* tenth; ***jedna ~a*** one tenth; ***dwa i pięć ~ych*** two point five; ***o ~ej*** (***godzinie***) at ten (o'clock)

dziesięcio- (*w złożeniach*) ten-; **dziesięcioboista** *m* (*-ty*; *-boiści*) decathlete; **dziesięciodniowy** *adj* **1.** *dziecko*: ten-day-old **2.** *okres*, *urlop*: ten-day; **dziesięciokrotny** *adj* tenfold; **dziesięciolecie** *n* (*-cia*; *-cia*) **1.** (*okres*) decade **2.** (*rocznica*) tenth anniversary; **dziesięcioletni** *adj* **1.** *dziecko*, *samochód*: ten-year-old **2.** *okres*: ten-year **3.** *doświadczenie*: ten years'

dziesięciomiesięczny *adj* **1.** *dziecko*: ten-month-old **2.** *okres*: ten-month; **dziesięciominutowy** *adj* *przerwa*: ten-minute; **dziesięcioro** *num* ten; **dziesięciozłotówka** *f* (*-ki*; *-ki*) (*banknot*) *Br* ten-zloty note, *Am* ten-zloty bill

dziesięć, **dziesięciu** *num* ten; **dziesiętny** *adj* decimal

dziewanna *f* (*-ny*; *-ny*) mullein

dziewczęta *pl* (*-cząt*) girls; **dziewczęcy** *adj* **1.** *bluzka*: girl's **2.** *wygląd*, *uśmiech*: girlish

dziewczyna *f* (*-ny*; *-ny*) **1.** girl **2.** (*sympatia*) girlfriend; **dziewczynka** *f* (*-ki*; *-ki*) (little) girl

dziewiarski *adj* knitting

dziewiątka *f* (*-ki*; *-ki*) nine; **dziewiąt|y** *adj* ninth; ***o (godzinie) ~ej*** at nine (o'clock)

dziewica *f* (*-cy*; *-ce*) virgin; **dziewictwo** *n* (*-wa*; *no pl*) virginity

dziewicz|y *adj* virgin; ***błona ~a*** ANAT hymen; ***~y rejs*** maiden voyage; ***Wyspy ~e*** Virgin Islands

dziewięcio- (*w złożeniach*) nine-; **dziewięciokrotny** *adj* ninefold; **dziewięcioletni** *adj* **1.** *dziecko*, *samochód*: nine-year-old **2.** *okres*: nine-year **3.** *doświadczenie*: nine years'; **dziesięcioro** *num* nine

dziewięć, **dziewięciu** *num* nine; **dziewięćdziesiąt** *num* ninety; **dziewięćset** *num* nine hundred; **dziewiętnasto-** (*w złożeniach*) nineteen-; **dziewiętnastoletni** *adj* **1.** *chłopak*: nine-year-old **2.** *przerwa*, *okres*: nine-year; **dziewiętnast|y** *adj* nineteenth; ***o (godzinie) ~ej*** at seven (o'clock) p.m.; **dziewiętnaście** *num* nineteen

dzieworództwo *n* (*-wa*; *no pl*) BIOL parthenogenesis

dzięcioł *m* (*-ła*; *-ły*) woodpecker

dziękczynny *adj* **1.** *modlitwa*, *ofiara*: thanksgiving **2.** *list*: thank-you

dzięki **I** *prep* thanks (*D* to); ***~ Bogu!*** thank God! **II** *interj* ***~!*** thanks!; ***wielkie ~*** thank you very much; **dziękować** ⟨**po-**⟩ (*-kuję*) thank (***za*** *A* for)

dzik *m* (*-ka*; *-ki*) (wild) boar

dzik|i **I** *adj* **1.** wild; ***~ie wino*** Virginia creeper **2.** *plemiona*, *ludy*: savage

3. *wysypisko*: illegal; **~i lokator** squatter **4.** (*nietowarzyski*) antisocial **5.** *strajk*: wildcat **II** *m* (*-kiego*; *dzicy*) savage

dzikus *m* (*-sa*; *-sy*), **~ka** *f* (*-ki*; *-ki*) savage

dziobać ⟨**-bnąć**⟩ (*-bię*) **1.** peck (**w** *A* at) **2.** *widelcem*, *palcem*: prod

dziobak *m* (*-ka*; *-ki*) (duck-billed) platypus

dziobaty *adj* pockmarked

dziób *m* (*dzioba*; *dzioby*) **1.** beak; **zamknij ~!** *infml* shut your face! **2.** *kaczki*, *gołębia*: bill **3.** *statku*; bow **4.** *samolotu*: nose

dzisiaj, **dziś** *adv* **1.** today; **~ rano** this morning; **~ wieczorem** tonight, this evening; **~ w nocy** tonight; **którego ~ mamy?** what date is it today?; **od ~** from now on; **pogoda na ~** today's weather **2.** (*obecnie*) nowadays

dzisiejsz|y *adj* **1.** today's; **dzień ~y** today **2.** (*współczesny*) present-day; **~a młodzież** today's young people, the youth of today

dziś → **dzisiaj**

dziupla *f* (*-li*; *-le*) hollow (in a tree)

dziur|a *f* (*-ry*; *-ry*) **1.** hole; **szukanie ~y w całym** *fig* nitpicking; **wiercić ~ę w brzuchu** *fig* keep pestering **2.** (*w zębie*) cavity **3.** (*w dętce*) puncture

dziurawić ⟨**prze-**⟩ (*-wię*) make a hole (*A* in) perforate; **dziurawiec** *m* (*-wca*; *-wce*) (*roślina*) St John's wort

dziuraw|y *adj* **1.** (*z dziurą*) with a hole in it **2.** (*z dziurami*) with holes in it **3.** *dach*: leaky; **mieć ~e ręce** *infml* have butterfingers

dziurk|a *f* (*-ki*; *-ki*) (small) hole; **~a od klucza** keyhole; **mieć czegoś po ~i w nosie** be sick of s.th.

dziurkacz *m* (*-cza*; *-cze*) (hole) punch; **dziurkować** ⟨**prze-**⟩ (*-kuję*) punch

dziw *m* (*-wu*; *-wy*) *lit* wonder; **nie ~, że** no wonder

dziwactwo *n* (*-wa*; *-wa*) (*cecha*) eccentricity, freakishness

dziwaczeć ⟨**z-**⟩ (*-czeję*) become eccentric, get freaky; **dziwaczka** *f* (*-ki*; *-ki*) eccentric, *infml* oddball; **dziwaczny** *adj* odd, bizarre; **dziwak** *m* (*-ka*; *-wacy*/*-ki*) eccentric, *infml* oddball

dziwić ⟨**z-**⟩ (*-wię*) surprise; **dziwić się** be surprised

dziwka *f* (*-ki*; *-ki*) *vulg* tart *infml*, *Am infml* hooker

dziwn|y *adj* strange; **~a rzecz** a strange thing; **nic ~ego, że** no wonder; **~ym trafem** by a strange coincidence

dziwo: **o ~** surprisingly (enough)

dziwoląg *m* (*-ga*; *-gi*) **1.** (*osoba*) freak **2.** (*rzecz*) oddity, curiosity

dzwon *m* (*-nu*; *-ny*) **1.** bell; **bić w ~y** ring the bells **2.** **~y** (*spodnie*) flares

dzwoneczek *m* (*-czka*; *-czki*) *dim* (little) bell

dzwonek *m* (*-nka*; *-nki*) **1.** bell; **~ do drzwi** doorbell; **ostatni ~** *fig* the last chance **2.** (*roślina*) bellflower **3.** (*w kartach*) diamond

dzwoni|ć ⟨**za-**⟩ (*-nię*) **1.** ring; **~ć do drzwi** ring at the door; **~ mi w uchu** I have a ringing in my ear **2.** (*telefonować*) call, ring (up) (**do** *G*); **czy mogę zadzwonić?** can I make a phone call?

dzwonko *n* (*-ka*; *-ka*) *śledzia*: slice

dzwonnica *f* (*-cy*; *-ce*) belfry; **dzwonnik** *m* (*-ka*; *-nicy*) bell-ringer

dźgać ⟨**-gnąć**⟩ (*-gam*) prod (*I* with), jab (*I* with)

dźwięcz|eć *v/im* (*-czę*): **jej słowa wciąż ~ały w jego uszach** her words still rang in his ears; **dźwięczny** *adj* **1.** *głos*: resonant **2.** *śmiech*: ringing **3.** *głoska*: voiced

dźwięk *m* (*-ku*; *-ki*) sound; **~ C** C note; **barwa ~u** tone, timbre

dźwiękonaśladowczy *adj* onomatopoeic; **dźwiękoszczelny** *adj* soundproof

dźwiękow|y *adj* sound; **ścieżka ~a** soundtrack

dźwig *m* (*-gu*; *-gi*) **1.** crane; **operator ~u** crane operator **2.** (*winda*) *Br* lift, *Am* elevator

dźwigać ⟨**-gnąć**⟩ (*-gam*) **1.** (*podnosić*) lift; **~ z gruzów** *fig* rebuild from ruins **2.** (*nosić*) carry; **dźwigać się 1.** (*wstawać*) stand up **2.** (*podnosić się*) lift oneself up

dźwigar *m* (*-ra*/*-ru*; *-ry*) BUILD girder

dźwignia *f* (*-ni*; *-nie*) TECH lever; **~ zmiany biegów** *Br* gear lever, *Am* gear shift

dżdżownica *f* (*-cy*; *-ce*) earthworm

dżdżysty *adj* rainy

dżem *m* (*-mu*; *-my*) jam

D

dżentelmen *m* (*-na*; *-ni*) gentleman; **dżentelmeńsk|i** *adj* gentlemanly; ***~a umowa*** gentleman's agreement
dżersej *m* (*-ju*; *-je*) jersey
dżet *m* (*-tu*; *-ty*) jet
dżinsow|y *adj* denim; ***spodnie ~e*** jeans; **dżinsy** *pl* (*-sów*) jeans
dżip, ***jeep*** *m* (*-pa*; *-py*) jeep
dżoint, ***joint*** *m* (*-tu*; *-ty*) joint
dżokej *m* (*-ja*; *-je*), **~ka** *f* (*-ki*; *-ki*) jockey
dżul *m* (*-la*; *-le*) joule
dżuma *f* (*-my*; *no pl*) (bubonic) plague
dżungla *f* (*-li*; *-le*) jungle; ***~ przepisów*** red tape, jungle of regulations

E

E

e *interj* **1.** (*negatywne emocje*) oh! **2.** (*zwracanie uwagi*) hey!
EBOiR, ***EBOR*** *abbr* (*EBOiR-u; no pl*) (= ***Europejski Bank Odbudowy i Rozwoju***) EBRD, the European Bank for Reconstruction and Development
ebonit *m* (*-tu*; *no pl*) ebonite, vulcanite
ech! *interj* **1.** oh! **2.** (*lekceważenie*) huh!
ech|o *n* (*echa*; *echa*) **1.** echo; ***rozbrzmiewać ~em*** echo **2.** *fig* echo, reaction; ***odbić się szerokim ~em w mediach*** have wide media coverage; ***pozostać bez ~a*** go unnoticed
echolokacja *f* (*-ji*; *no pl*) echolocation; **echosonda** *f* (*-dy*; *-dy*) echosounder
ecu *n indecl* ecu, ECU
Eden *m* (*-nu*) Eden
edukacja *f* (*-ji*; *no pl*) education; **edukacyjny** *adj* educational; ***system ~*** education system
edycja *f* (*-ji*; *-je*) edition
edykt *m* (*-tu*; *-ty*) edict
Edyp: ***kompleks ~a*** Oedipus complex
edytor *m* (*-ra*; *-rzy*) editor; ***~ tekstu*** word processor; **edytorski** *adj* editorial
efekciarstwo *n* (*-wa*; *no pl*) showiness
efek|t *m* (*-tu*; *-ty*) effect; ***w ~cie*** in effect; ***przynieść pożądane ~ty*** have the desired effects; **efektowny** *adj* **1.** impressive **2.** *widowisko*: spectacular
efektywność *f* (*-ści*; *no pl*) **1.** effectiveness **2.** (*wydajność*) efficiency; **efektywny** *adj* **1.** effective **2.** *osoba*: efficient
efemeryczny *adj lit* ephemeral, short-lived
egalitarny *adj* egalitarian
Egejski: ***Morze ~e*** the Aegean Sea
egid|a: ***pod ~ą*** under the aegis (*G* of)
Egipcjanin *m* (*-na*; *-janie*), **-janka** *f* (*-ki*; *-ki*) Egyptian; **egipski** *adj* Egyptian; ***panowały ~e ciemności*** it was pitch dark; **Egipt** *m* (*-tu*) Egypt
ego *n indecl* ego
egocentryczny *adj lit* egocentric, self-centered
egoista *m* (*-ty*; *-goiści*), **-tka** *f* (*-ki*; *-ki*) egoist; **egoistyczny** *adj* egoistic, selfish
egoizm *m* (*-mu*; *no pl*) egoism, selfishness
egz. *abbr* (= **egzemplarz**) **1.** (*egzemplarz*) copy **2.** (*egzemplarze*) copies
egzaltowany *adj* (over)emotional
egzamin *m* (*-nu*; *-ny*) exam, *form* examination; ***~ z matematyki*** maths exam; ***~ na prawo jazdy*** driving test; ***~ wstępny*** entrance examination; ***~ dojrzałości*** final exams
egzaminacyjn|y *adj* exam, *form* examination; ***sesja ~a*** end-of-semester examinations; **egzaminator** *m* (*-ra*; *-rzy*) examiner
egzaminować ⟨**prze-**⟩ (*-nuję*) examine
egzekucja *f* (*-ji*; *-je*) **1.** *skazańca*, *testamentu*: execution **2.** *opłat*, *podatku*: enforcement; **egzekucyjny** *adj* **1.** *sala*: execution **2.** *postępowanie*: enforcement; ***pluton ~*** firing squad; ***tytuł ~*** writ of execution
egzekutor *m* (*-ra*; *-rzy*) **1.** (*komornik*) bailiff **2.** *testamentu*: executor
egzekwować ⟨**wy-**⟩ (*-wuję*) *długi*, *prawo*: enforce
egzema *f* (*-my*; *no pl*) MED eczema
egzemplarz *m* (*-rza*; *-rze*) **1.** *pisma*, *książki*, *płyty*: copy; ***w dwóch ~ach*** in duplicate **2.** *produktu*: unit **3.** (*okaz*) specimen
egzorcyzmy *pl* (*-mów*) exorcisms
egzotyczny *adj* exotic

egzystencj|a *f* (*-ji*; *-je*) existence; ***warunki ~i*** living conditions
egzystencjalizm *m* (*-mu*; *no pl*) existentialism; **egzystencjalny** *adj* existential; ***lęk ~*** existential fear
egzystować *v/im* (*-tuję*) *lit* exist
ej! *interj* hey!
ejże! *interj* hey!
EKG *abbr n indecl* (= **elektrokardiogram**) ECG, *Am* EKG
ekierka *f* (*-ki*; *-ki*) *Br* set square, *Am* triangle
ekipa *f* (*-py*; *-py*) team; ***~ telewizyjna*** TV crew; ***~ rządowa*** government team
ekler *m* (*-ra*; *-ry*) **1.** COOK eclair **2.** (*zamek*) zipper
ekologia *f* (*-gii*; *no pl*) ecology; **ekologiczny** *adj* **1.** ecological **2.** (*bezpieczny dla środowiska*) environmentally-friendly **3.** *żywność*, *gospodarstwo*: organic **4.** *katastrofa*: environmental
ekonomia *f* (*-mii*; *no pl*) **1.** (*nauka*) economics **2.** (*gospodarka*, *oszczędność*) economy; **ekonomiczny** *adj* **1.** (*gospodarczy*) economic **2.** (*oszczędny*) economical
ekonomika *f* (*-ki*; *no pl*) (*nauka*) economics
ekonomista *m* (*-ty*; *-miści*), **-tka** *f* (*-ki*; *-ki*) economist
ekosystem *m* (*-mu*; *-my*) ecosystem
ekoturystyka *f* (*-ki*; *no pl*) ecotourism
ekran *m* (*-nu*; *-ny*) screen; ***szeroki ~*** wide screen; ***wejść na ~y*** be released, open; **ekranizacja** *f* (*-ji*; *-je*) **1.** (*wersja filmowa*) film version **2.** (*filmowanie*) filming
ekranizować ⟨**z-**⟩ (*-zuję*): ***~ coś*** adapt s.th. for the screen
eks- (*w złożeniach*) ex-
ekscelencja *f/m* (*-ji*; *-je*) excellency
ekscentryczny *adj* eccentric; **ekscentryk** *m* (*-ka*; *-rycy*) eccentric
ekscesy *pl* (*-sów*) incidents, disturbances
ekscytacja *f* (*-ji*; *no pl*) excitement; **ekscytujący** *adj* exciting
ekshibicjonista *m* (*-ty*; *-niści*) exhibitionist, *infml* flasher; **ekshibicjonizm** *m* (*-mu*; *no pl*) exhibitionism
ekshumacja *f* (*-ji*; *-je*) exhumation
ekskluzywny *adj* exclusive
ekskomunikować *v im/p* (*-kuję*) excommunicate
eksmisj|a *f* (*-ji*; *-je*) eviction; ***nakaz ~i*** eviction notice; **eksmitować** ⟨**wy-**⟩ (*-tuję*) evict
ekspansja *f* (*-ji*; *no pl*) expansion
ekspatriacja *f* (*-ji*; *no pl*) *form* expatriation
ekspedient *m* (*-ta*; *-nci*), **~ka** *f* (*-ki*; *-ki*) *Br* shop assistant, *Am* sales clerk
ekspediować ⟨**wy-**⟩ (*-diuję*) *form* dispatch; **ekspedycja** *f* (*-ji*; *-je*) **1.** (*wyprawa*) expedition **2.** (*wysyłanie*) dispatch; **ekspedycyjny** *adj* **1.** *namiot*: expedition **2.** *korpus*: expeditionary **3.** *biuro*: dispatch
ekspert *m* (*-ta*; *-rci*) expert; ***~ w dziedzinie*** *G* expert in; **ekspertyza** *f* (*-zy*; *-zy*) (expert) examination, expertise; ***~ sądowa*** forensic examination
eksperyment *m* (*-tu*; *-ty*) experiment (***na*** *L* on); **eksperymentalny** *adj* experimental; **eksperymentować** *v/im* (*-tuję*) experiment (***na*** *L* on)
eksploatacj|a *f* (*-ji*; *no pl*) *form* **1.** (*używanie*) use **2.** (*wydobywanie*) exploitation; ***rabunkowa ~a*** overexploitation, uncontrolled exploitation; ***w ~i*** in operation; ***oddać coś do ~i*** put s.th. into operation; **eksploatować** ⟨**wy-**⟩ (*-tuję*) **1.** (*używać*) use **2.** (*wydobywać*) mine **3.** *robotnika*: exploit
eksplodować *v im/p* (*-duję*) explode; **eksplozja** *f* (*-ji*; *-je*) explosion
eksponat *m* (*-tu*; *-ty*) exhibit; **eksponować** ⟨**wy-**⟩ (*-nuję*) **1.** (*prezentować*) display, put on display **2.** (*podkreślać*) highlight
eksport *m* (*-tu*; *no pl*) export; ***na ~*** for export; **eksporter** *m* (*-ra*; *-rzy*) exporter; **eksportować** ⟨**wy-**⟩ (*-tuję*) export; **eksportow|y** *adj* export; ***towary ~e*** exports
ekspozycja *f* (*-ji*; *-je*) **1.** (*wystawa*) exhibition **2.** PHOT exposure
ekspozytura *f* (*-ry*; *-ry*) **1.** (*oddział*) branch (office) **2.** (*agencja*) agency
ekspres *m* (*-su*; *-sy*) **1.** (*pociąg*) express (train) **2.** (*przesyłka*) special delivery **3.** (*do kawy*) coffee maker; ***kawa z ~u*** espresso; **ekspresow|y** *adj* **1.** *pociąg*, *autobus*: express **2.** *list*: special delivery; ***herbata ~a*** tea bags
ekspresja *f* (*-ji*; *no pl*) expression; **eks-**

E

presjonizm *m* (*-mu*; *no pl*) expressionism
ekstaza *f* (*-zy*; *no pl*) extasy
eksterminacja *f* (*-ji*; *no pl*) extermination
eksterytorialny *adj* extraterritorial
ekstra *adv* **1.** (*dodatkowo*) extra **2.** (*super*) *infml* super

E

ekstradycja *f* (*-ji*; *-je*) extradition
ekstraklasa *f* (*-sy*; *-sy*) *SPORT* premiership, Premier League
ekstrakt *m* (*-tu*; *-ty*) extract
ekstrawagancki *adj* extravagant
ekstremalny *adj* extreme
ekstremista *m* (*-ty*; *-miści*), **-tka** *f* (*-ki*; *-ki*) extremist
ekstremistyczny *adj* extremist; **ekstremum** *n* (*indecl*; *-rema*) *form* extreme
ekumeniczny *adj* ecumenical
ekwipunek *m* (*-nku*; *no pl*) equipment, gear
ekwiwalent *m* (*-tu*; *-ty*) equivalent
elastyczność *f* (*-ści*; *no pl*) flexibility; **elastyczny** *adj* **1.** flexible **2.** *bandaż*, *rajstopy*: elastic
elegancja *f* (*-ji*; *no pl*) elegance; **elegancki** *adj* elegant; **elegancko** *adv* **1.** elegantly **2.** *wyglądać*: elegant
elegijny *adj* elegiac
elekcyjny *adj* elective
elektor *m* (*-ra*; *-rzy*) elector; **elektorat** *m* (*-tu*; *no pl*) electorate
elektro- (*w złożeniach*) elektro-; **elektrociepłownia** *f* (*-ni*; *-nie*) combined heating and power plant; **elektroda** *f* (*-dy*; *-dy*) electrode; **elektrokardiogram** *m* (*-mu*; *-my*) electrocardiogram; **elektroliza** *f* (*-zy*; *-zy*) electrolysis
elektromagnes *m* (*-su*; *-sy*) electromagnet; **elektromechanik** *m* (*-ka*; *-nicy*) electrical engineer; **elektroniczny** *adj* **1.** electronic **2.** *zegarek*: digital; **elektronowy** *adj* *PHYS* electron; **elektrotechnika** *f* (*-ki*; *no pl*) electrical engineering
elektrownia *f* (*-ni*; *-nie*) power plant, *Br* power station; **~ *wodna*** (***atomowa***) hydroelectric (nuclear) power plant
elektrowstrząs *m* (*-su*; *-sy*) electroshock; **elektrowóz** *m* (*-wozu*; *-wozy*) electric locomotive
elektryczność *f* (*-ści*; *no pl*) electricity
elektryczn|y *adj* **1.** electric; ***sieć ~a*** power (supply) network **2.** *awaria*: electrical; **elektryfikacja** *f* (*-ji*; *no pl*) electrification
elektryk *m* (*-ka*; *-rycy*) electrician; ***inżynier ~*** electrical engineer; **elektryzować** ⟨**na-**⟩ (*-zuję*) electrify
element *m* (*-tu*; *-ty*) element
elementarz *m* (*-rza*; *-rze*) (reading) primer
elewacja *f* (*-ji*; *-je*) *budynku*: elevation
elewator *m* (*-ra*; *-ry*) (grain) elevator
eliminacj|a *f* (*-ji*; *no pl*) **1.** elimination **2. *~e*** qualifying (rounds); ***eliminacyjn|y*** *adj* *mecz*, *turniej*: qualifying; ***biegi ~e*** the heats
eliminować ⟨**wy-**⟩ (*-nuję*) eliminate
elipsa *f* (*-sy*; *-sy*) **1.** *MATH* ellipse **2.** (*opuszczenie*) ellipsis
elita *f* (*-ty*; *-ty*) elite; **elitarny** *adj* elite
elokwencja *f* (*-ji*; *no pl*) eloquence; **elokwentny** *adj* eloquent
e-mail *m* (*-la*; *-le*) e-mail; ***~em*** by e-mail
emalia *f* (*-lii*; *-lie*) **1.** (*szkliwo*) enamel **2.** (*farba*) enamel (paint); **emaliowy** *adj* enamel
emancypacja *f* (*-ji*; *no pl*) emancipation; ***~ kobiet*** the emancipation of women
eman|ować *v/im* (*-nuję*) *form* emanate; ***~uje z niej spokój***, ***~uje spokojem*** she emanates calm
emblemat *m* (*-tu*; *-ty*) emblem
embrion *m* (*-na*/*-nu*; *-ny*) embryo; **embrionalny** *adj* embryonic
ementaler *m* (*-ra*; *-ry*) Emmental (cheese)
emeryt (*-ta*; *-ryci*), **~ka** *f* (*-ki*; *-ki*) (old-age) pensioner, senior citizen; **emerytalny** *adj* **1.** *wiek*, *świadczenia*: retirement **2.** *fundusz*: pension
emerytowany *adj* retired; **emerytur|a** *f* (*-ry*; *-ry*) **1.** (*świadczenie*) pension **2.** (*okres*) retirement; ***być na ~ze*** be retired; ***przejść na ~ę*** retire; ***wcześniejsza ~a*** early retirement
emfatyczny *adj* *form* emphatic
emigracj|a *f* (*-ji*; *-je*) emigration; ***być na ~i*** be an expatriate; ***~a zarobkowa*** economic emigration; **emigracyjny** *adj* **1.** emigration **2.** *literatura*: émigré; ***rząd ~*** government-in-exile
emigrant *m* (*-ta*; *-nci*), **~ka** *f* (*-ki*; *-ki*)

1. emigrant 2. (*z przyczyn politycznych*) émigré
emigrować ⟨**wy-**⟩ (*-ruję*) **1.** emigrate **2.** (*z przyczyn politycznych*) go into exile
eminencja *f/m* (*-ji*; *-je*) eminence; ***szara ~*** eminence grise
emisja *f* (*-ji*; *-je*) **1.** *gazów, promieni*: emission **2.** *akcji, znaczków*: issue **3.** *RADIO TEL* broadcast; ***~ na żywo*** live broadcast
emitować ⟨**wy-**⟩ (*-tuję*) **1.** *gazy, promienie*: emit **2.** *akcje, znaczki*: issue **3.** *RADIO TEL* broadcast; ***~ na żywo*** broadcast live
emocja *f* (*-ji*; *-je*) emotion
emocjonalny *adj* emotional; **emocjonować się** *v/im* (*-nuję*) be excited (*I* about); **emocjonujący** *adj* exciting
empatia *f* (*-tii*; *no pl*) *lit* empathy
empiria *f* (*-rii*; *no pl*) *lit* experience; **empiryczny** *adj* empirical
emulsja *f* (*-ji*; *-je*) emulsion; ***~ do opalania*** suntan lotion
encefalografia *f* (*-fii*; *no pl*) encephalography; **encefalogram** *m* (*-mu*; *-my*) encephalogram
encyklika *f* (*-ki*; *-ki*) encyclical
encyklopedia *f* (*-dii*; *-die*) encyclopedia, *Br* encyclopaedia; **encyklopedyczny** *adj* encyclopedic, *Br* encyclopaedic
endokrynologia *f* (*-gii*; *no pl*) endocrinology
energetyczny *adj* **1.** *surowce, kryzys, napój*: energy **2.** *przemysł, linie*: power; **energetyka** *f* (*-ki*; *no pl*) (*dział gospodarki*) power industry
energi|a *f* (*-gii*; *no pl*) energy; ***~a elektryczna*** electric energy, power; ***bez ~i*** (*o człowieku*) without energy, listless; **energiczny** *adj* energetic
energochłonny *adj* energy-consuming; **energooszczędny** *adj* energy-saving
enigmatyczny *adj* enigmatic
enklawa *f* (*-wy*; *-wy*) *lit* enclave
entuzjastyczny *adj* enthusiastic; **entuzjazm** *m* (*-mu*; *no pl*) enthusiasm; **entuzjazmować się** ⟨***roz-***⟩ (*-muję*) enthuse (*I* about)
enzym *m* (*-mu*; *-my*) enzyme
epatować *v/im* (*-tuję*) (*szokować*) *form* shock (*I* with)
epicentrum *n* (*indecl*; *-ra*) *Br* epicentre, *Am* epicenter
epicki *adj* epic
epidemia *f* (*-mii*; *-mie*) epidemic; **epidemiczny** *adj* epidemic
epigon *m* (*-na*; *-ni*) epigone
epigram *m* (*-mu*; *-my*) epigram
epika *f* (*-ki*; *no pl*) epic, epic literature
epilepsja *f* (*-ji*; *no pl*) epilepsy; **epileptyczny** *adj* epileptic
epileptyk *m* (*-ka*; *-tycy*), **-tyczka** *f* (*-ki*; *-ki*) epileptic
episkopat *m* (*-tu*; *-ty*) episcopate
epitafium *n* (*indecl*; *-fia*) epitaph; **epitet** *m* (*-tu*; *-ty*) **1.** (*określenie rzeczownika*) epithet **2. ~y** (*wyzwiska*) invectives; ***obrzucić kogoś ~ami*** hurl abuse at s.o.
epizod *m* (*-du*; *-dy*) **1.** episode **2.** (*rola*) minor role; **epizodyczny** *adj* **1.** episodic **2.** *rola*: minor
epoka *f* (*-ki*; *-ki*) epoch; ***~ kamienia*** (***żelaza***) the Stone (Iron) Age; ***~ lodowcowa*** the Ice Age; **epokowy** *adj* epoch-making, momentous
epopeja *f* (*-pei*; *-je*) epic
er|a *f* (*ery*; *ery*) **1.** age, era; ***przed naszą ~ą*** *Br* BC, *Am* B.C.; ***naszej ~y*** *Br* AD, *Am* A.D.; ***~a nowożytna*** modern history **2.** *GEOL* era
erekcja *f* (*-ji*; *-je*) *prącia, sutka*: erection
erka *f* (*-ki*; *-ki*) (*karetka*) (emergency) ambulance
erogenny *adj* erogenous; **erotoman** *m* (*-na*; *-ni*) sex maniac, erotomaniac
erotyka *f* (*-ki*; *no pl*) **1.** (*erotyzm*) eroticism **2.** (*w księgarni*) erotica; **erotyczny** *adj* erotic; **film ~** erotic film, *infml* blue movie; **erotyzm** *m* (*-mu*; *no pl*) erotism
erozja *f* (*-ji*; *-je*) erosion; **erozyjny** *adj procesy*: erosion, erosional
errata *f* (*-ty*; *-ty*) errata
erudycja *f* (*-ji*; *no pl*) erudition
erupcja *f* (*-ji*; *-je*) **1.** *GEOL* eruption **2.** *emocji, agresji*: outburst
erytrocyt *m* (*-tu*; *-ty*) erythrocyte
esbek *m* (*-ka*; *-becy*) *HIST* secret police officer
eseista *m* (*-ty*; *eseiści*) essayist; **esej** *m* (*-ju*; *-je*) essay
esencja *f* (*-ji*; *-je*) essence; ***~ herbaciana*** strong tea brew

E

esesman *m* (*-na*; *-ni*) SS man, member of the SS
eska *f* (*-ki*; *-ki*) (*rozmiar*) *infml* (size)
eskadra *f* (*-ry*; *-ry*) **1.** squadron **2.** (*w lotnictwie*) flight
eskalacja *f* (*-ji*; *no pl*) escalation
eskapada *f* (*-dy*; *-dy*) (*wyprawa*) foray
E
Eskimos *m* (*-sa*; *-si*) Eskimo, Innuit; **Eskimoska** *f* (*-ki*; *-ki*) Eskimo woman, Innuit woman; **eskimoski** *adj* Eskimo, Innuit
eskort|a *f* (*-ty*; *-ty*) escort; ***pod ~ą policji*** under police escort; **eskortować** *v/im* (*-tuję*) escort
esowaty *adj* S-shaped
esperanto *n indecl* Esperanto
estakada *f* (*-dy*; *-dy*) (*wiadukt*) *Br* flyover, *Am* overpass
esteta *m* (*-ty*; *esteci*), **-tka** *f* (*-ki*; *-ki*) *Br* aesthete, *Am* esthete; **estetyczny** *adj* **1.** *Br* aesthetic, *Am* esthetic **2.** (*gustowny*) tasteful **3.** (*ładny*) easy on the eye *infml*
Estonia *f* (*-nii*) Estonia; **Estończyk** *m* (*-ka*; *-czycy*), **-tonka** *f* (*-ki*; *-ki*) Estonian; **estoński** *adj* Estonian
estrad|a *f* (*-dy*; *-dy*) **1.** (*podwyższenie*) platform **2.** (*przemysł rozrywkowy*) show business; ***gwiazdy ~y*** show-business stars; **estradowy** *adj występ*: stage; ***artysta ~*** (stage) entertainer
estragon *m* (*-nu*; *no pl*) tarragon
estrogen *m* (*-nu*; *-ny*) *Br* oestrogen, *Am* estrogen
estym|a *f* (*-my*; *no pl*) *form* esteem; ***cieszyć się*** (***wielką***) ***~ą*** be held in (high) esteem
esy *pl*: ***~-floresy*** curlicues, flourishes
e tam! *interj* oh, come on!
etap *m* (*-pu*; *-py*) **1.** stage; ***~ami*** in stages **2.** *wyścigu*, *podróży*: leg, stage; ***na tym ~ie*** at this stage; **etapowy** *adj*: ***konkurs 2-~*** 2-stage competition
etat *m* (*-tu*; *-ty*) (*posada*) position; ***pełny ~*** full-time job; ***na pełny ~*** (***pół ~u***) full-time (part-time); ***wolny ~*** vacancy; **etatowy** *adj* full-time; ***pracownik ~*** full-time employee, FTE
etażerka *f* (*-ki*; *-ki*) display cabinet
eter *m* (*-ru*; *no pl*) **1.** ether **2.** ***na falach ~u*** over the airwaves; ***cisza w ~ze*** dead air; **eteryczny** *adj* **1.** ethereal **2.** *olejek*: aromatic

Etiopia *f* (*-pii*) Ethiopia; **etiopski** *adj* Ethiopian
etiuda *f* (*-dy*; *-dy*) **1.** MUS étude, *Br* study **2.** (*ćwiczenie*) exercise
etniczny *adj* ethnic
etnografia *f* (*-fii*; *no pl*) ethnography
etola *f* (*-li*; *-le*) fur stole
etyczny *adj* ethical; **etyka** *f* (*-ki*; *no pl*) ethics
etykieta *f* (*-ty*; *-ty*) **1.** (*na towarze*) label **2.** (*reguły zachowania*) etiquette; **etykietk|a** *f* (*-ki*; *-ki*) label; ***przyczepić komuś ~ę*** *G fig* label s.o. as
etylina *f* (*-ny*; *no pl*) *Br* high-octane petrol, *Am* high-octane gas
etymologiczny *adj* etymological
eucharystia *f* (*-tii*; *no pl*) the Eucharist
eufemistyczny *adj* euphemistic; **euforia** *f* (*-rii*; *no pl*) euphoria
eukaliptus *m* (*-sa*; *-sy*) eucalyptus; **eukaliptusowy** *adj olejek*: eucalyptus
eunuch *m* (*-cha*; *-chowie*/*-chy*) eunuch
euroczek *m* (*-ku*; *-ki*) Eurocheque
Europa *f* (*-py*) Europe; **Europejczyk** *m* (*-ka*; *-czycy*), **-jka** *f* (*-ki*; *-ki*) European; **europejski** *adj* European; **europejskość** *f* (*-ści*; *no pl*) European character
eutanazja *f* (*-ji*; *no pl*) euthanasia
ewakuacja *f* (*-ji*; *-je*) evacuation; **ewakuacyjny** *adj* **1.** *plan*: evacuation **2.** *wyjście*: emergency
ewakuować *v im/p* (*-kuuję*) evacuate
Ewangelia *f* (*-lii*; *-lie*) Gospel; ***~ według św. Jana*** the Gospel according to St John, St John's Gospel
ewangelicki *adj* evangelical; **ewangelik** *m* (*-ka*; *-licy*), **-liczka** *f* (*-ki*; *-ki*) Evangelical
ewenement *m* (*-tu*; *-ty*) (*osobliwy wypadek*) unusual thing
ewentualnie *adv* **1.** (*w razie potrzeby*) if needed **2.** (*albo*) or; **ewentualność** *f* (*-ści*; *-ści*) possibility, *form* eventuality; ***przygotowany na każdą ~*** prepared for every eventuality; **ewentualny** *adj* possible
EWG *abbr f/n indecl* (= ***Europejska Wspólnota Gospodarcza***) EEC, European Economic Community
ewidencja *f* (*-ji*; *-je*) record, records *pl*, files *pl*; ***~ ludności*** census
ewidencjonować ⟨**z-**⟩ (*-nuję*) record,

file; **ewidencyjny** *adj* **1.** record **2.** *stan*: recorded
ewidentny *adj* evident
ewolucj|a *f* (*-ji*; *-je*) (*proces*) evolution; ***teoria ~i*** the theory of evolution; **ewolucje** *pl* (*-ji*) **1.** (*gimnastyczne*) acrobatics **2.** (*samolotowe*) aerobatics;
ewolucyjnie *adv* **1.** evolutionarily **2.** *rozwijać się*: by evolution; **ewolucyjny** *adj* evolutionary; **ewolucjonista** *m* (*-ty*; *-niści*), **-tka** *f* (*-ki*; *-ki*) evolutionist
exposé *n indecl* (first) policy speech
ezoteryczny *adj* esoteric

F

fabrycznie *adv*: ***~ nowy*** brand new; ***~zapakowany*** in the original packaging; **fabryczn|y** *adj* **1.** *robotnik*: factory **2.** *dzielnica*: industrial; ***hala ~a*** (work)shop; **fabryka** *f* (*-ki*; *-ki*) factory; **fabrykować** ⟨**s-**⟩ (*-kuję*) (*fałszować*) fabricate
fabularny *adj*: ***film ~*** feature film
fabuła *f* (*-ły*; *no pl*) *filmu*, *powieści*: plot
facet *m* (*-ta*; *-ceci*) *infml* guy, man; **facetka** *f* (*-ki*; *-ki*) *infml* woman
fach *m* (*-chu*; *-chy*) trade; ***kolega po ~u*** fellow professional; colleague in the field; ***znać swój ~*** know one's stuff
fachowiec *m* (*-wca*; *-wcy*) **1.** (*ekspert*) expert **2.** (*profesjonalista*) professional; **fachowo** *adj* professionally; **fachowość** *f* (*-ści*; *no pl*) professionalism; **fachowy** *adj* professional
fagot *m* (*-tu*; *-ty*) bassoon
fajans *m* (*-su*; *no pl*) faience, faence; **fajansowy** *adj* faience, faence
fajerka *f* (*-ki*; *-ki*) stove lid
fajerwerki *pl* (*-ków*) fireworks
fajka *f* (*-ki*; *-ki*) **1.** pipe; ***~ pokoju*** peace pipe **2.** (*papieros*) *infml* fag *Br* **3.** (*znak*) tick
fajnie *adv infml* **1.** great **2.** *ubrany*, *urządzony*: nicely; **fajny** *adj infml* great; **fajowy** *adj infml* grand, *Am* swell
fajtłapa *m*/*f* (*-py*; *-py*) *infml* **1.** (*niezdara*) clumsy oaf **2.** (*osoba niezaradna*) loser
faks *m* (*-su*; *-sy*) fax
fak|t *m* (*-tu*; *-ty*) fact; ***po ~cie*** (*zbyt późno*) too late; ***postawić kogoś przed ~tem dokonanym*** present s.o. with a fait accompli; ***oparty na ~tach*** based on fact
faktur|a *f* (*-ry*; *-ry*) **1.** ECON invoice ***wystawić ~ę*** issue an invoice **2.** *materiału*, *kompozycji*: texture
faktyczny *adj* **1.** actual; ***stan ~*** facts, actual state (of affairs) **2.** *kontrola*: effective
fakultatywny *adj* **1.** optional **2.** (*nadprogramowy*) extra-curricular
fakultet *m* (*-tu*; *-ty*) **1.** (*wydział*) faculty **2.** (*przedmiot*) optional subject
fal|a *f* (*-li*; *-le*) **1.** wave; ***~e dźwiękowe*** sound waves; ***~e morskie*** sea waves; ***~e radiowe*** radio waves; ***na ~ach eteru*** over the airwaves; ***~e krótkie*** (***UKF***) RADIO short-wave (VHF) band; ***~a protestów*** a wave of protest(s); ***~a przestępstw*** crime wave; ***~ami*** in waves
falbana *f* (*-ny*; *-ny*), **falbanka** *f* (*-ki*; *-ki*) frill
falisty *adj* **1.** *włosy*: wavy **2.** *blacha*: corrugated; ***~ teren*** rolling hills, rolling countryside
falochron *m* (*-nu*; *-ny*) breakwater
falować *v*/*im* (*-luję*) **1.** wave **2.** (*o morzu*, *terenie*) roll; **falowanie** *n* (*-nia*; *no pl*) **1.** waving **2.** *morza*: swell
falset *m* (*-tu*; *-ty*) falsetto; ***~em*** *infml* in a shrill voice
falstart *m* (*-tu*; *-ty*) false start
falsyfikat *m* (*-tu*; *-ty*) forgery
fałd *m* (*-du*; *-dy*), **fałda** *f* (*-dy*; *-dy*) fold; ***spódnica w ~y*** pleated skirt
fałdować się ⟨**po-**, **s-**⟩ (*-duję*) **1.** crinkle **2.** (*o sukience*) ruck up
fałdzisty *adj suknia*: full pleated
fałsz *m* (*-szu*; *-sze*) **1.** (*nieprawda*, *obłuda*) untruth, falsehood; ***prawda czy ~?*** true or false? **2.** (*fałszywa nuta*) wrong note; **fałszerka** *f* (*-ki*; *-ki*) (female) forger; **fałszerstwo** *n* (*-wa*; *-wa*) forgery; **fałszerz** *m* (*-rza*; *-rze*) forger; ***~ pieniędzy*** counterfeiter

F

fałszować ⟨**s-**⟩ (*-szuję*) **I** *v/t* **1.** *obraz*, *podpis*: forge **2.** *pieniądze*: counterfeit **3.** *dane*: falsify **II** *v/i* **1.** (*śpiewać*) sing out of tune **2.** (*grać*) play out of tune

fałszywiec *m* (*-wca*; *-wcy*) *infml* deceiver, hypocrite

fałszywość *f* (*-ści*; *no pl*) (*nieprawda*, *obłuda*) falsehood, untruth; **fałszywy** *adj* **1.** false **2.** *pieniądze*: countereit, fake **3.** *obraz*: forged **4.** *osoba:* deceitful, two-faced **5.** *nuta*: off-key

fama *f* (*-my*; *no pl*) **1.** (*wiadomość*) news *sing*; ***rozeszła się ~, że*** the word spread that **2.** (*pogłoska*) *Br* rumour, *Am* rumor

familijny *adj* family

fan *m* (*-na*; *-ni*), **~ka** *f* (*-ki*; *-ki*) fan

fanaberie *pl* (*-rii*) whims

fanatyczny *adj* fanatical; **fanatyk** *m* (*-ka*; *-tycy*), **-tyczka** *f* (*-ki*; *-ki*) fanatic; **fanatyzm** *m* (*-mu*; *no pl*) fanatism

fanfara *f* (*-ry*; *-ry*) fanfare

fanfaronada *f* (*-dy*; *no pl*) buffoonery

fant *m* (*-tu*; *-ty*) **1.** (*w grze*) forfeit **2.** (*na loterii*) prize

fantasta *m* (*-ty*; *-taści*), **-tka** *f* (*-ki*; *-ki*) (*marzyciel*) dreamer; ***pisarz ~*** science-fiction writer

fantastyczny *adj* fantastic

fantazj|a *f* (*-ji*; *no pl*) **1.** (*wyobraźnia*) imagination, fantasy; ***puścić wodze ~i*** give rein to one's imagination; ***wytwór czyjejś ~i*** a figment of one's imagination; ***robić coś z ~ą*** do s.th. with flair **2.** (*zmyślenie*) fantasy **3.** (*fikcja*) fiction **4.** MUS fantasia; **fantazjować** *v/im* (*-juję*) fantasize (***o*** *L* about); **fantazyjny** *adj strój*, *deseń*: fancy

fantow|y *adj*: ***loteria ~a*** prize lottery

faraon *m* (*-na*; *-nowie*/*-ni*) pharaoh

farb|a *f* (*-by*; *-by*) **1.** paint; ***~a drukarska*** printing ink; ***puścić ~ę*** *infml* spill the beans **2.** (*do włosów*) dye **3.** ***~y*** (*pudełko*) paint set *sing*

farbiarnia *f* (*-ni*; *-nie*) dye-house; **farbiarz** *m* (*-rza*; *-rze*) dyer

farbki *pl* (*-bek*) (*pudełko*) paint box *sing*

farbować (*-buję*) **I** *v/t* ⟨**u-**, **za-**, **prze-**⟩ *włosy*: dye **II** *v/i* (*w praniu*) run

farfocel *m* (*-cla*; *-cle*) *infml Br* piece of fluff, *Am* piece of lint

farma *f* (*-my*; *-my*) farm

farmaceutyczny *adj* pharmaceutical; **farmacja** *f* (*-ji*; *no pl*) pharmacy; **farmakologia** *f* (*-gii*; *no pl*) pharmacology; **farmakologiczny** *adj* pharmacological

farmazony *pl* (*-nów*) *lit* balderdash *sing*, nonsense *sing*

farmerki *pl* (*-rek*) *Br* dungarees *sing*, *Am* (bib) overalls

farsa *f* (*-sy*; *-sy*) farce

farsz *m* (*-szu*; *-sze*) stuffing

fart *m* (*-ta*/*-tu*; *no pl*) *infml* (a stroke of) luck: ***mieć ~*** be lucky

fartuch *m* (*-cha*; *-chy*) **1.** *kucharki*, *kelnera*: apron **2.** *lekarza*: gown **3.** (*roboczy*) *Br* overall; **fartuszek** *m* (*-szka*; *-szki*) *dim kucharki*, *kelnera*: apron

faryzeusz *m* (*-sza*; *-sze*) Pharisee

fasada *f* (*-dy*; *-dy*) facade

fascynować ⟨**za-**⟩ (*-nuję*) fascinate; ***fascynować się*** be fascinated (*I* by); **fascynujący** *adj* fascinating

fasola *f* (*-li*; *-le*) **1.** (*roślina*) bean **2.** (*ziarna*) beans *pl*; **fasolka** *f* (*-ki*; *-ki*) (*szparagowa*) *Br* French beans *pl*, *Am* string beans *pl*; **fasolowy** *adj zupa*: bean

fason *m* (*-nu*; *-ny*) (*krój*) cut; ***z ~em*** *fig* with aplomb

fastryga *f* (*-gi*; *-gi*) (*ścieg*) tack; **fastrygować** ⟨**s-**⟩ (*-guję*) tack, baste

faszerować ⟨***na-***⟩ (*-ruję*) stuff (*I* with); **faszerowany** *adj* stuffed

faszystowski *adj* fascist; **faszyzm** *m* (*-mu*; *no pl*) fascism

fatalistyczny *adj* fatalistic

fatalnie *adv* **1.** terribly **2.** *czuć się*, *wyglądać*: terrible, appalling; **fatalny** *adj* **1.** *pogoda*, *nastrój*: appalling **2.** *skutki*, *błąd*: disastrous

fatyg|a *f* (*-gi*; *no pl*) trouble; ***szkoda ~i*** it's not worth the trouble; **fatygować** ⟨**po-**⟩ (*-guję*) trouble; ***fatygować się*** take the trouble; ***proszę się nie ~*** please don't trouble yourself

faul *m* (*-lu*/*-la*; *-le*) SPORT foul

faworki *pl* (*-ków*) **1.** COOK angel wings

faworyt *m* (*-ta*; *-ryci*), **~ka** *f* (*-ki*; *-ki*) *Br* favourite, *Am* favorite; **faworyzować** *v/im* (*-zuję*) *Br* favour, *Am* favor

faza *f* (*-zy*; *-zy*) phase

fe! *interj* yuck!

febra *f* (*-ry*; *no pl*): ***żółta ~*** yellow fever

federacja *f* (*-ji*; *-je*) federation; **federalny** *adj* federal
fekalia *pl* (*-liów*) *Br* faeces, *Am* feces
feldmarszałek *m* (*-łka*; *-łkowie*) field marshal
feler *m* (*-ru*; *-ry*) *infml* **1.** (*defekt*) defect **2.** (*wada*, *minus*) drawback
felga *f* (*-gi*; *-gi*) (wheel) rim
felieton *m* (*-nu*; *-ny*) column
feministka *f* (*-ki*; *-ki*) feminist; **feministyczny** *adj* feminist
Fenicja *f* (*-ji*) Phoenicia; **Fenicjanin** *m* (*-na*; *-janie*), **-janka** *f* (*-ki*; *-ki*) Phoenician; **fenicki** *adj* Phoenician
fenig *m* (*-ga*; *-gi*) pfennig
Feniks *m* (*-sa*; *no pl*) phoenix
fenol *m* (*-lu*; *-le*) phenol, carbolic acid
fenomen *m* (*-nu*; *-ny*) phenomenon
fenomenalny *adj* phenomenal
feralny *adj* unlucky
ferie *pl* (*-rii*) holiday *sing*; **~ świąteczne a)** (*wielkanocne*) Easter break **b)** (*bożonarodzeniowe*) Christmas break
ferma *f* (*-my*; *-my*) (specialized) farm
ferment *m* (*-tu*; *-ty*) *polityczny*, *kulturalny*: ferment; **fermentacja** *f* (*-ji*; *-je*) fermentation; **fermentować** ⟨**s-**⟩ (*-tuję*) ferment
ferować *v/im* (*-ruję*) *form*: **~ wyroki** judge
ferwor *m* (*-ru*; *no pl*) *Br* fervour, *Am* fervor; ***w ~ze walki*** in the heat of the battle
festiwal *m* (*-lu*; *-le*) festival
festyn *m* (*-nu*; *-ny*) *Br* fête, *Am* carnival
fetor *m* (*-ru*; *-ry*) stench
fetować *v/im* (*-tuję*) celebrate
fetysz *m* (*-sza*; *-sze*) fetish; **fetyszysta** *m* (*-ty*; *-szyści*) fetishist
feudalizm *m* (*-mu*; *no pl*) feudalism; **feudalny** *adj* feudal
fifka *f* (*-ki*; *-ki*) cigarette holder
figa *f* (*-gi*; *-gi*) **1.** (*owoc*) fig **2.** (*nic*) *infml* nothing; ***~ z makiem!*** forget it!; ***figi*** *pl* (*fig*) panties
fig|iel *m* (*-gla*; *-gle*) prank; ***spłatać komuś ~la*** play a prank on s.o.
figlarny *adj* playful; **figlarz** *m* (*-rza*; *-rze*) joker, prankster; **figlować** *v/im* (*-luję*) play pranks
figowiec *m* (*-wca*; *-wce*) fig tree; **figowy** *adj* fig; ***listek ~*** fig leaf
figura *f* (*-ry*; *-ry*) **1.** figure; ***~ stylistyczna*** figure of speech **2.** (*w szachach*) piece **3.** (*w kartach*) face card, *Br* court card; **figurować** *v/im* (*-ruję*) (*w spisie*) appear; **figurow|y** *adj* figure; ***jazda ~a na lodzie*** figure skating
figurówki *pl* (*-wek*) *infml* figure skates
fikać ⟨**-knąć**⟩ (*-kam*) **1.** (*podskakiwać*) frolic **2.** (*prowokować*) *infml* be spoiling for a fight; ***~ koziołki*** do somersaults
fikcja *f* (*-ji*; *-je*) fiction; **fikcyjny** *adj* **1.** fictitious **2.** *bohater*, *świat*: fictional **3.** (*zmyślony*) imaginary; ***żyć w ~m świecie*** live in an imaginary world
fiksacja *f* (*-ji*; *-je*) *infml* fixation; **fiksować** ⟨**s-**⟩ (*-suję*) *infml* go nuts
fikus *m* (*-sa*; *-sy*) rubber plant
fikuśny *adj* **1.** (*śmieszny*) funny **2.** (*wymyślny*) fanciful
filantrop *m* (*-pa*; *-pi*) philanthropist; **filantropijny** *adj* philanthropic; **filantropka** *f* (*-ki*; *-ki*) (woman) philanthropist
filar *m* (*-ru*/*-ra*; *-ry*) **1.** ARCHIT pillar, pier **2.** *fig* pillar, backbone; ***ona jest ~em zespołu*** she is the backbone of the team
filatelista *m* (*-ty*; *-liści*), **-tka** *f* (*-ki*; *-ki*) philatelist; **filatelistyka** *f* (*-ki*; *no pl*) philately
filcować się ⟨**s-**⟩ (*-cuję*) felt; **filcowy** *adj* felt
filet *m* (*-tu*; *-ty*) fillet
filharmonia *f* (*-nii*; *-nie*) **1.** (*sala*) philharmonic hall **2.** (*organizacja*) philharmonic (society); **filharmoniczn|y** *adj*: ***orkiestra ~a*** philharmonic (orchestra)
filia *f* (*-lii*; *-lie*) **1.** (*oddział*) branch **2.** (*agencja*) agency
filigranowy *adj* **1.** *przedmiot*, *osoba*: dainty **2.** *dziewczyna*: petite
Filipiny *pl* (*-pin*) the Philippines
filiżanka *f* (*-ki*; *-ki*) cup; ***~ do herbaty*** (***kawy***) teacup (coffee cup); ***~ herbaty*** (***kawy***) a cup of tea (coffee)
film *m* (*-mu*; *-my*) **1.** FILM *Br* film, *Am* movie; ***~ dokumentalny*** documentary; ***~ rysunkowy*** cartoon; ***~ mi się urwał*** *infml* I had a blackout **2.** PHOT film; **filmoteka** *f* (*-ki*; *-ki*) *Br* film library, *Am* movie library

F

filmować ⟨**s-**⟩ (*-muję*) film, shoot; **filmowiec** *m* (*-wca*; *-wcy*) *Br* film-maker, *Am* movie-maker; **filmowy** *adj Br* film, *Am* movie

filologi|a *f* (*-gii*; *-gie*) philology, language and literature; ***~a klasyczna*** Classics; ***student ~i polskiej*** student of Polish; ***studiować ~ę angielską*** read English, study English; ***dyplom ~i angielskiej*** a degree in English; **filologiczny** *adj* philological

F

filozof *m* (*-fa*; *-fowie*) philosopher; **filozofia** *f* (*-fii*; *-fie*) philosophy; ***to żadna ~*** it is not rocket science; **filozoficzny** *adj* philosophical; **filozofować** *v/im* (*-fuję*) philosophize; ***nie filozofuj!*** don't get philosophical!

filtr *m* (*-ru*/*-ra*; *-ry*) filter; ***~ do kawy*** coffee filter; ***papierosy z ~em*** filter cigarettes; **filtrować** ⟨**prze-**⟩ (*-ruję*) filter

filuterny *adj* playful

Fin *m* (*-na*; *-nowie*), **~ka** (*-ki*; *-ki*) Finn; ***on jest ~em*** he is Finnish

finalista *m* (*-ty*; *-liści*), **-tka** *f* (*-ki*; *-ki*) finalist; **finalizować** ⟨**s-**⟩ (*-zuję*) *transakcję*: complete

finał *m* (*-łu*; *-ły*) **1.** (*zakończenie*) end, conclusion **2.** *SPORT* final **3.** *MUS* finale; **finałowy** *adj* final; ***mecz ~*** final

finans|e *pl* (*-sów*) **1.** finance *sing*; ***Ministerstwo ≈ów*** the Ministry of Finance **2.** (*środki*) finances; **finansować** ⟨**s-**⟩ (*-suję*) fund, finance

finansowo *adv* financially; **finansow|y** *adj* financial; ***kłopoty ~e*** financial problems

finezja *f* (*-ji*; *no pl*) finesse; **finezyjny** *adj* subtle, refined

fingować ⟨**s-**⟩ (*-guję*) *atak*, *swoją śmierć*: fake

finisz *m* (*-szu*; *-sze*) *SPORT* finish; **finiszować** *v/im* (*-szuję*) (*o biegaczu*) sprint for the line, spurt

Finlandia *f* (*-dii*) Finland

fiński *adj* Finnish; ***nóż ~*** bowie knife, sheath knife

fiolet *m* (*-tu*; *-ty*) **1.** (*kolor*) purple **2.** (*do dezynfekcji*) gentian violet, crystal violet; **fioletowy** *adj* purple

fioł *infml*: ***mieć ~a*** be nuts (***na punkcie*** *G* about)

fiołek *m* (*-łka*; *-łki*) violet; ***~ alpejski*** cyclamen; **fiołkowy** *adj* violet

firanka *f* (*-ki*; *-ki*) (net) curtain

firma *f* (*-my*; *-my*) **1.** company, business **2.** (*nazwa*) business name; **firmow|y** *adj* **1.** *konto*: business, company **2.** *samochód*: company **3.** (*markowy*) brand; ***znak ~y*** trademark; ***danie ~e*** (house) specialty, *Br* (house) speciality

fisharmonia *f* (*-nii*; *-nie*) harmonium

fiskaln|y *adj* fiscal; ***kasa ~a*** cash register

fistaszki *pl* (*-ków*) peanuts

fiszbin *m* (*-nu*; *-ny*) whalebone

fiszka *f* (*-ki*; *-ki*) index card

fiut *m* (*-ta*; *-ty*) (*penis*) *vulg* dick

fizjologia *f* (*-gii*; *no pl*) physiology; **fizjologiczny** *adj* physiological

fizjonomia *f* (*-mii*; *-mie*) physiognomy

fizyczn|y *adj* **1.** physical; ***wychowanie ~e*** physical education, PE **2.** *praca*: physical, manual **3.** *pracownik*: manual, blue-collar

fizyk *m* (*-ka*; *-zycy*) physicist; **fizyka** *f* (*-ki*; *no pl*) physics; **fizykoterapia** *f* (*-pii*; *no pl*) physiotherapy

flacha *f* (*-chy*; *-chy*) *infml* bottle

flaczeć ⟨**s-**⟩ (*-czeję*) get flabby

flaczki *pl* (*-ków*) *COOK* tripe soup *sing*

flaga *f* (*-gi*; *-gi*) flag; **flagowy** *adj*: ***okręt ~*** flagship

flaki *pl* (*-ków*) **1.** guts **2.** *COOK* tripe soup *sing*; ***nudne jak ~ z olejem*** (as) dull as watching paint dry, (as) dull as ditch-water

flakon *m* (*-nu*; *-ny*) **1.** (*wazon*) vase **2.** (*buteleczka*) bottle; **flakonik** *m* (*-ka*; *-ki*) *dim* **1.** (*wazon*) (small) vase **2.** (*buteleczka*) (small) bottle

flamandzki *adj* Flemish

flamaster *m* (*-tra*; *-try*) marker, felt-tip pen

flaming *m* (*-ga*; *-gi*) flamingo

flanca *f* (*-cy*; *-ce*) seedling; **flancować** *v/im* (*-cuję*) plant (out) seedlings

Flandria *f* (*-rii*) Flanders *pl*

flanelowy *adj* flannel

flanka *f* (*-ki*; *-ki*) flank

flaszka *f* (*-ki*; *-ki*) bottle

flądra *f* (*-ry*; *-ry*) flounder

flecista *m* (*-ty*; *-ciści*), **-tka** *f* (*-ki*; *-ki*) *Br* flautist, *Am* flutist

flegma *f* (*-my*; *no pl*) phlegm; **flegmatyczny** *adj* phlegmatic

flejtuch *m* (*-cha*; *-chy*) *infml* slob

flek *m* (*-ka*/*-ku*; *-ki*) tap
fleksja *f* (*-ji*; *no pl*) **1.** *GRAM* flexion
flesz *m* (*-sza*; *-sze*) *PHOT* flash(gun); ***robić zdjęcia z ~em*** take flash photos
flet *m* (*-tu*; *-ty*) (*poprzeczny*) flute; ***~ prosty*** recorder, English flute
flirciarz *m* (*-rza*; *-rze*) flirt; **flirt** *m* (*-tu*; *-ty*) flirt; **flirtować** *v/im* (*-tuję*) flirt
flisak *m* (*-ka*; *-sacy*) raftsman
floks *m* (*-sa*; *-sy*) phlox
flora *f* (*-ry*; *no pl*) flora
florecista *m* (*-ty*; *-ciści*), **-tka** *f* (*-ki*; *-ki*) foilist
Florencja *f* (*-ji*) Florence
floret *m* (*-tu*; *-ty*) foil
flota *f* (*-ty*; *-ty*) **1.** fleet **2.** (*marynarka*) navy; ***~ wojenna*** navy; **flotylla** *f* (*-li*; *-le*) (*w marynarce wojennej*) flotilla
fluid *m* (*-du*; *-dy*) **1.** fluid **2.** (*kosmetyk*) foundation ***dobre ~y*** good vibes
fluktuacja *f* (*-ji*; *-je*) fluctuation; ***~ kadr*** staff turnover
fluor *m* (*-ru*; *no pl*) *CHEM* fluorine; ***pasta z ~em*** fluoride toothpaste
fluorescencja *f* (*-ji*; *-je*) fluorescence
fobia *f* (*-bii*; *-bie*) phobia
fochy *pl* (*-chów*) **1.** (*dąsy*) sulk *sing* **2.** (*kaprysy*) whims; ***stroić ~*** be fussy
foka *f* (*-ki*; *-ki*) seal
foksterier *m* (*-ra*; *-ry*) fox terrier
fokstrot *m* (*-ta*; *-ty*) foxtrot
folder *m* (*-ra*/*-ru*; *-ry*) **1.** brochure **2.** *INF* directory
folia *f* (*-lii*; *-lie*) **1.** (*plastikowa*) plastic film, *infml* plastic; ***~ spożywcza*** *Br* cling film, *Am* plastic wrap **2.** (*metalowa*) foil; **foliowy** *adj* **1.** (*plastikowy*) plastic **2.** ***kwas ~*** folic acid
folklor *m* (*-ru*; *no pl*) folklore
folwark *m* (*-ku*; *-ki*) *HIST* (estate) farm
fon *m* (*-nu*; *-ny*) *PHYS* phone; **fonetyczny** *adj* phonetic; **fonetyka** *f* (*-ki*; *no pl*) phonetics; **fono-** (*w złożeniach*) phono-
fonoteka *f* (*-ki*; *-ki*) music library
fontanna *f* (*-ny*; *-ny*) fountain
foremka *f* (*-ki*; *-ki*) *dim* **1.** *Br* (small) mould, *Am* (small) mold **2.** (*do pieczenia ciasta*) *Br* cake tin, *Am* cake pan **3.** (*zabawka*) sand form; **foremny** *adj kształt*, *wielokąt*: regular
form|a *f* (*-my*; *-my*) **1.** form; ***przybrać ~ę*** take the form (*G* of) **2.** (*sprawność*) shape; ***w dobrej ~ie*** in good shape; ***nie w ~ie*** out of shape **3.** (*do pieczenia*) *Br* baking tin, *Am* baking pan **4.** *odlewnicza*: *Br* mould, *Am* mold **5.** ***~y towarzyskie*** (social) manners
formacja *f* (*-ji*; *-je*) **1.** *GEOL BIOL* formation **2.** (*oddział*) unit **3.** (*ugrupowanie*) group
formalina *f* (*-ny*; *no pl*) formalin
formalistyczny *adj* **1.** formal **2.** *PHIL ART* formalistic; **formalność** *f* (*-ści*; *-ści*) formality; ***czysta ~*** a mere formality; **formalny** *adj* formal
format *m* (*-tu*; *-ty*) **1.** format **2.** *fig Br* calibre, *Am* caliber; ***człowiek wielkiego ~u*** man of high calibre; **formatować** ⟨**s-**⟩ (*-tuję*) *INF* format
formować (*-muję*) **1.** ⟨**u-**, **s-**⟩ (*tworzyć*) form **2.** ⟨**u-**⟩ (*kształtować*) shape, form
formularz *m* (*-rza*; *-rze*) form
formuła *f* (*-ły*; *-ły*), **formułka** *f* (*-ki*; *-ki*) formula; ***~ grzecznościowa*** courtesy, polite phrase; **formułować** ⟨**s-**⟩ (*-łuję*) formulate
fornir *m* (*-ru*; *-ry*) veneer
fors|a *f* (*-sy*; *no pl*) *infml* dough, money; ***przy ~ie*** in the money; ***gruba ~a*** big money; ***mieć ~y jak lodu*** have money to burn; **forsiasty** *adj infml* loaded
forsować (*-suję*) **1.** ⟨**s-**⟩ *przeszkodę*: overcome **2.** ⟨**s-**⟩ *rzekę*: cross **3.** ⟨**prze-**⟩ *projekt*: push through; **forsować się** exert too much effort, overstrain; **forsowny** *adj* arduous
forsycja *f* (*-ji*; *-je*) forsythia
forteca *f* (*-cy*; *-ce*) fortress
fortel *m* (*-lu*; *-le*) stratagem
fortepian *m* (*-nu*; *-ny*) (grand) piano; ***na ~*** for piano; **fortepianowy** *adj* piano
fortun|a *f* (*-ny*; *no pl*) fortune; ***zbić ~ę na L*** make a fortune on
fortyfikacja *f* (*-ji*; *-je*) fortification
fory *pl* (*-rów*) **1.** (*względy*) ***mieć ~ u G*** *Br* be in favour with, *Am* be in favor with **2.** ***dać komuś ~*** *SPORT* **a)** (*w szachach*) give odds to s.o. **b)** (*w biegu*) give s.o. a headstart
fosa *f* (*-sy*; *-sy*) moat
fosfor *m* (*-ru*; *no pl*) *CHEM* phosphorus; **fosforyzujący** *adj* phosphorescent, luminous

F

F

fotel *m* (*-la*; *-le*) **1.** (*w mieszkaniu*) armchair; **~ *bujany*** rocking chair **2.** (*w pojeździe*, *w kinie*) seat; **~ *ministra*** *fig* ministerial office; **~ *dentystyczny*** dentist's chair
fotka *f* (*-ki*; *-ki*) *infml* snap, snapshot *infml*; **~*i z wakacji*** *Br* holiday snaps, *Am* vacation snaps
fotoamator *m* (*-ra*; *-rzy*) amateur photographer
fotogeniczny *adj* photogenic
fotograf *m* (*-fa*; *-fowie*) photographer; **fotografia** *f* (*-fii*; *-fie*) **1.** (*sztuka*) photography **2.** (*zdjęcie*) photo, photography; **fotograficzny** *adj* photographic; ***aparat*** **~** camera; **fotografować** ⟨**s-**⟩ (*-fuję*) photograph
fotokomórka *f* (*-ki*; *-ki*) photocell; **fotokopia** *f* (*-pii*; *-pie*) photocopy; **fotokopiarka** *f* (*-ki*; *-ki*) photocopier; **fotomodelka** *f* (*-ki*; *-ki*) photographic model; **fotomontaż** *m* (*-żu*; *-że*) photomontage, trick photograph; **fotoreportaż** *m* (*-żu*; *-że*) photo essay
fotoreporter *m* (*-ra*; *-rzy*), **~ka** *f* (*-ki*; *-ki*) (press) photographer
fotos *m* (*-su*; *-sy*) *FILM* still
fotoskład *m* (*-du*; *no pl*) photosetting; **fotosynteza** *f* (*-zy*; *no pl*) *BIOL* photosynthesis
fracht *m* (*-tu*; *-ty*) freight; **frachtowiec** *m* (*-wca*; *-wce*) cargo ship
fragment *m* (*-tu*; *-ty*) fragment; **fragmentaryczny** *adj* fragmentary
frajd|a *f* (*-dy*; *no pl*) *infml* fun; ***mieć*** **~*ę*** have fun; ***wielka*** **~*a*** great fun
frajer *m* (*-ra*; *-rzy*), **~ka** *f* (*-ki*; *-ki*) *infml* sucker; ***za*** **~** for free
frak *m* (*-ka*; *-ki*) tailcoat
frakcja *f* (*-ji*; *-je*) faction; **frakcyjny** *adj* **1.** *destylacja*: fractional **2.** *walki*: factional
framuga *f* (*-gi*; *-gi*) frame; **~ *drzwiowa*** (***okienna***) door (window) frame
franciszkanin *m* (*-na*; *-kanie*) Franciscan; **franciszkański** *adj* Franciscan
Francja *f* (*-ji*) France
francusk|i *adj* French; ***mówić po*** **~*u*** speak French; ***ciasto*** **~*ie*** puff pastry; ***klucz*** **~*i*** monkey wrench; ***miłość*** **~*a*** oral sex; ***śpiewać po*** **~*u*** sing in French; **Francuz** *m* (*-za*; *-zi*) Frenchman; ***oni są*** **~*ami*** they are French; ***Francuzi*** the French; **Francuzk|a** *f* (*-ki*; *-ki*) Frenchwoman; ***jest*** **~*ą*** she is French
frank *m* (*-ka*; *-ki*) franc
frant: ***z głupia*** **~** out of the blue
frapujący *adj* intriguing
fraszka *f* (*-ki*; *-ki*) **1.** (*błahostka*) trifle **2.** (*wiersz*) epigram
frazeologia *f* (*-gii*; *no pl*) phraseology
frazes *m* (*-su*; *-sy*) (*oklepany zwrot*) cliché; **~*y*** (*slogany*) empty talk *sing*
fregata *f* (*-ty*; *-ty*) frigate
frekwencja *f* (*-ji*; *no pl*) **1.** (*uczęszczanie*) attendance; ***duża*** (***mała***) **~** high (low) attendance **2.** (*wyborcza*) turnout
freon *m* (*-nu*; *no pl*) *CHEM* freon
fresk *m* (*-ku*; *-ki*) fresco
fretka *f* (*-ki*; *-ki*) ferret
frez *m* (*-zu*; *-zy*) (milling) cutter; **frezarka** *f* (*-ki*; *-ki*) milling machine
frezja (*-ji*; *-je*) freesia
frędzle *pl* (*-li*) **1.** (*w rzędzie*) fringe *sing* **2.** (*w pęku*) tassel *sing*
fron|t *m* (*-tu*; *-ty*) front; ***na*** **~*cie*** at the front; **frontowy** *adj* **1.** *drzwi*, *elewacja*: front **2.** *żołnierze*: front-line
froterka *f* (*-ki*; *-ki*) floor polisher; **froterować** ⟨**wy-**⟩ (*-ruję*) polish
frotté *n indecl* terry; ***ręcznik*** **~** terry towel
frunąć *v/p* (*-nę*) fly
frustrować ⟨**s-**⟩ (*-ruję*) frustrate; ***frustrować się*** get frustrated
fruwać *v/im* (*-wam*) fly
frycowe *n* (*-wego*; *no pl*) *infml*: ***zapłacić*** **~** learn the hard way
frykasy *pl* (*-sów*) delicacies
frytki *pl* (*-tek*) *Br* (potato) chips, *Am* (French) fries; **frytkownica** *f* (*-cy*; *-ce*) deep-fat fryer
frywolny *adj hum*, *piosenka*: risqué, blue
fryz *m* (*-zu*; *-zy*) **1.** *ARCHIT* frieze **2.** (*fryzura*) *infml* hairdo
Fryzja *f* (*-ji*) Friesland
fryzjer *m* (*-ra*; *-rzy*), **~ka** *f* (*-ki*; *-ki*) hairdresser; **~ *męski*** barber; ***u*** **~*a*** at the hairdresser's; **fryzjerski** *adj nożyczki*: hair, hairdresser; ***zakład*** **~** hairdresser's shop, hairdresser's salon
fryzura *f* (*-ry*; *-ry*) hairstyle, haircut
fuch|a *m* (*-chy*; *-chy*) *infml* **1.** odd job; ***brać*** **~*y*** moonlight **2.** (*wykonywana regularnie*) sideline, job on the side

fuga *f* (*-gi*; *-gi*) **1.** *MUS* fugue **2.** (*zaprawa*) grout
fujara *f/m* (*-ry*; *-ry*) *infml* clumsy oaf, butterfingers *pl*; **fujarka** *f* (*-ki*; *-ki*) pipe
fukać ⟨**-knąć**⟩ (*-kam*) (*o człowieku*) snap (**na** *A* at)
fuks *m* (*-sa*; *no pl*) *infml* fluke; **~em** by a fluke; **fuksiarz** *m* (*-rza*; *-rze*) *infml* lucky devil
fuksja *f* (*-ji*; *-je*) fuchsia
ful I *m* (*-la*; *-le*) (*w pokerze*) full house **II** *adv infml* **~ czegoś** lots of s.th.; ***na ~ grać***: at full blast
fundament *m* (*-tu*; *-ty*) foundation; **fundamentalista** *m* (*-ty*; *-liści*) fundamentalist; **fundamentalizm** *m* (*-mu*; *no pl*) fundamentalism; **fundamentalistyczny** *adj* fundamentalist
fundator *m* (*-ra*; *-rzy*), **~ka** *f* (*-ki*; *-ki*) founder
fundnąć *v/p* (*-nę*) *infml*: ***~ komuś coś*** buy s.o. s.th., treat s.o. to s.th.
fundować (*-duję*) **1.** ⟨**u-**⟩ (*zakładać*) found **2.** ⟨**za-**⟩ (*kupować*) ***~ komuś coś*** buy s.o. s.th., treat s.o. to s.th.; ***ja funduję*** my treat; **fundusz** *m* (*-szu*; *-sze*) fund
funkcj|a *f* (*-ji*; *-je*) **1.** function **2.** (*stanowisko*) position; ***pełnić ~ę dyrektora*** be director (*G* of); ***pełnić ~ę przewodniczącego spotkania*** chair a meeting; **funkcjonalny** *adj* functional; **funkcjonariusz** *m* (*-sza*; *-sze*): ***~ policji*** police officer
funkcjonować ⟨**za-**⟩ (*-nuję*) function; **funkcyjny** *adj klawisz*: function; ***dodatek ~*** post-related allowance
funt *m* (*-ta*; *-ty*) pound; **50 ~ów** 50 pounds, *Br infml* 50 quid
fura *f* (*-ry*; *-ry*) **1.** (*wóz konny*) (horse) wagon **2.** (*samochód*) *infml* car, *infml* wheels **3.** **~ czegoś** *infml* loads of s.th.
furczeć ⟨**-rknąć**⟩ (*-czę*) **1.** (*o fladze, żaglu*) flap **2.** (*o maszynie*) whirr
furgonetka *f* (*-ki*; *-ki*) van
furi|a *f* (*-rii*; *no pl*) fury; ***wpaść w ~ę*** fly into a fury
furiat *m* (*-ta*; *-riaci*), **~ka** *f* (*-ki*; *-ki*) maniac, raving lunatic
furkotać *v/im* (*-koczę*/*-kocę*) **1.** (*o fladze, żaglu*) flap **2.** (*o maszynie*) whirr
furman *m* (*-na*; *-ni*) (horse wagon) driver; **furmanka** *f* (*-ki*; *-ki*) horse wagon
furtk|a *f* (*-ki*; *-ki*) gate; ***zostawić sobie ~ę*** leave oneself a way out
fusy *pl* (*-sów*): ***~ po kawie*** coffee dregs; ***~ po herbacie*** tea leaves
fuszerka *f* (*-ki*; *no pl*) botch-up
futbolowy *adj Br* football, *Am* soccer
futerał *m* (*-łu*; *-ły*) case; ***~ na okulary*** glasses case
futerkowy *adj zwierzę, zabawka*: furry
futro *n* (*-ra*; *-ra*) **1.** (*sierść*) fur **2.** (*okrycie*) fur coat
futryna *f* (*-ny*; *-ny*) frame; ***~ drzwiowa*** (***okienna***) door (window) frame
futrzan|y *adj* fur; ***~a kurtka*** fur jacket; **futrzarski** *adj sklep, przemysł*: fur
futurystyczny *adj* futuristic
fuzja[1] *f* (*-ji*; *-je*) *ECON* merger
fuzja[2] *f* (*-ji*; *-je*) (*strzelba*) shotgun

G

g. *abbr* (= **godzina**) o'clock; ***w niedzielę o g. 15:00*** on Sunday at 3 p.m.
gabardyna *f* (*-ny*; *-ny*) gaberdine
gabaryty *pl* (*-tów*) dimensions
gabinet *m* (*-tu*; *-ty*) **1.** (*do pracy*) office; ***~ lekarski*** consulting room, *Br* doctor's surgery, *Am* doctor's office; ***~ kosmetyczny*** *Br* beauty salon, *Am* beauty shop **2.** (*w domu*) study **3.** *POLIT* cabinet; **gabinetowy** *adj POLIT* cabinet
gablotka *f* (*-ki*; *-ki*) showcase
gacek *m* (*-cka*; *-cki*): ***~ wielkouch*** brown long-eared bat
gach *m* (*-cha*; *-chy*) *infml* lover
gacie *pl* (*-ci*) *infml* **1.** (*majtki*) underpants, *Br* pants **2.** (*spodnie*) *Br* trousers, *Am* pants
gad *m* (*-da*; *-dy*) **1.** reptile **2.** (*człowiek*) *infml* rat
gada|ć *v/im* (*-dam*) talk; ***~ć od rzeczy*** talk nonsense; ***~ła jak najęta*** she wouldn't stop talking
gadani|e *n* (*-nia*; *no pl*) talk; **czcze ~e**

empty talk; ***bez ~a*** (*niewątpliwie*) no doubt; ***bez ~a!*** don't argue!; **gadanina** *f* (*-ny*; *no pl*) *infml*: **czcza ~** empty talk; **gadatliwy** *adj* talkative

gadk|a *f* (*-ki*; *-ki*) *infml* gab; ***~a szmatka*** chit-chat; ***mieć ~ę*** have the gift of the gab

gadu-gadu: ***my tu ~, a*** here we are chit-chatting and

gadulstwo *n* (*-wa*; *no pl*) talkativeness; **gaduła** *m*/*f* (*-ły*; *-ły*) *infml* chatterbox; ***straszny z niego ~*** he never stops talking

G

gadzina *f* (*-ny*; *-ny*) *fig* reptile, rat

gaf|a *f* (*-fy*; *-fy*) gaffe, faux pas; ***popełnić ~ę*** make a gaffe

gagatek *m* (*-tka*; *-tki*) *infml* scamp

gaj *m* (*-ju*; *-je*) grove

gajowy *m* (*-wego*; *-wi*) forester; **gajówka** *f* (*-ki*; *-ki*) forester's house

gal|a *f* (*-li*; *-le*) **1.** (*uroczystość*) gala **2.** (*strój*) ***w pełnej ~i*** in full dress

galaktyka *f* (*-ki*; *-ki*) galaxy

galanteria *f* (*-rii*; *no pl*) **1.** (*dodatki*) accessories; ***~ skórzana*** leather accessories **2.** (*grzeczność*) courtesy

galare|ta *f* (*-ty*; *-ty*) jelly; ***nóżki*** (***wieprzowe***) ***w ~cie*** (pig) trotters in aspic; **galaretka** *f* (*-ki*; *-ki*) jelly; ***~ owocowa*** fruit jelly

galera *f* (*-ry*; *-ry*) galley

galeria *f* (*-rii*; *-rie*) **1.** gallery; ***~ sztuki*** art gallery **2.** (*pasaż handlowy*) *Br* (shopping) arcade, *Am* shopping mall

galernik *m* (*-ka*; *-nicy*) HIST galley slave

galimatias *m* (*-su*; *no pl*) shambles

galon[1] *m* (*-nu*; *-ny*) (*jednostka*) gallon

galon[2] *m* (*-nu*; *-ny*) (*taśma*) braid

galop *m* (*-pu*; *no pl*) canter, (easy) gallop; ***~em*** at a canter; **galopować** ⟨***po-***⟩ (*-puję*) (*o koniu*) canter

galopujący *adj inflacja*: galloping

galowy *adj koncert*: gala; ***ubiór ~*** full dress

galwanizacja *f* (*-ji*; *no pl*) galvanization; **galwanizować** *v*/*im* (*-zuję*) galvanize

galwanometr *m* (*-ru*; *-ry*) galvanometer

gałązka *f* (*-ki*; *-ki*) **1.** twig **2.** (*z liśćmi*) sprig; **gałąź** *f* (*-łęzi*; *-łęzie*) branch

gałgan *m* (*-na*; *-ny*) **1.** (*szmata*) rag **2.** (*urwis*) *infml* urchin **3.** ***~y*** (*łachmany*) rags

gałka *f* (*-ki*; *-ki*) **1.** (*pokrętło*) knob; ***~ drzwiowa*** doorknob; ***~ oczna*** ANAT eyeball; ***~ muszkatołowa*** nutmeg **2.** *lodów*: scoop

gały *pl* (*gał*) *infml*: ***wlepiać ~ w*** *A* gawk at; ***wytrzeszczać ~*** goggle

gama *f* (*-my*; *-my*) **1.** MUS scale **2.** *towarów*, *kolorów*: range, array

gamoń *m* (*-monia*; *-monie*) *infml* dumbo

Gandawa *f* (*-wy*) Ghent

ganek *m* (*-nku*; *-nki*) porch

gang *m* (*-gu*; *-gi*) gang; ***~ samochodowy*** gang of car thieves

gangrena *f* (*-ny*; *no pl*) gangrene

gangster *m* (*-ra*; *-rzy*) gangster; **gangsterski** *adj film*: gangster

ganiać *v*/*im* (*-niam*) **1.** (*biegać*) run **2.** (*próbować złapać lub zdobyć*) chase (***za*** *I*)

ganić ⟨***z-***⟩ (*-nię*) scold, rebuke (***za*** *A* for)

gap *m* (*-pia*; *-pie*): ***tłum ~iów*** crowd of onlookers

gap|a *f* (*-py*; *-py*) gawk; ***jechać na ~ę*** fare-dodge, *infml* steal a ride; ***pasażer na ~ę*** fare dodger

gapić się ⟨***za-***⟩ (*-pię*) *infml* stare, *infml* gawk; (***na*** *A* at); ***~ z otwartymi ustami na*** *A* gape at; ***zagapił się*** **a)** (*nie uważał*) he wasn't paying attention **b)** (*stracił poczucie czasu*) he forgot time; **gapiostwo** *m* (*-wa*; *no pl*) **1.** (*nieuwaga*) inattentiveness **2.** (*roztargnienie*) absent-mindedness; **gapiowaty** *adj* gawky

gar *m* (*-ra*; *-ry*) *infml* (big) infml; ***myć ~y*** do the dishes; ***stać przy ~ach*** do the cooking

garaż *m* (*-żu*; *-że*) garage

garb *m* (*-bu*; *-by*) hump; ***mieć ~*** have a humped back

garbarnia *f* (*-ni*; *-nie*) tannery; **garbarz** *m* (*-rza*; *-rze*) tanner

garbaty *adj* **1.** *osoba*: humpbacked **2.** *grzbiet*: humped; **garbić się** ⟨***z-***⟩ (*-bię*) stoop

garbować ⟨***wy-***⟩ (*-buję*) (*wyprawiać skórę*) tan

garbus *m* **1.** (*-sa*; *-si*/*-sy*) (*osoba*) hunchback **2.** (*-sa*; *-sy*) (*auto*) Beetle; **garbuska** *f* (*-ki*; *-ki*) hunchback

garderoba *f* (*-by*; *-by*) **1.** (*ubiory*) wardrobe **2.** THEAT dressing room

gardło *n* (*-ła*; *-ła*) *ANAT* throat; ***wąskie ~*** *fig* bottleneck; ***boli kogoś ~*** s.o. has a sore throat; ***na całe ~*** at the top of one's voice

gardłowy *adj* **1.** *głos*: guttural **2.** *ANAT* pharyngeal

gardzić ⟨**po-**, **wz-**⟩ (*-dzę*) **1.** despise **2.** (*odtrącać*) scorn

gardziel *f* (*-li*; *-le*) **1.** throat **2.** *wulkanu*: mouth

garmażeryjn|y *adj*: ***wyroby ~e*** delicatessen

garnąć się *v/im* (*-nę*) (*lgnąć*) be attracted (***do*** *G* to); ***~ do nauki*** (***pracy***) be eager to learn (work)

garncarstwo *n* (*-wa*; *no pl*) pottery; **garncarz** *m* (*-rza*; *-rze*) potter

garn|ek *m* (*-nka*; *-nki*) infml; ***nie mieć co do ~ka włożyć*** live from hand to mouth

garnirować *v/im* (*-ruję*) garnish

garnitur *m* (*-ru*; *-ry*) suit

garnizon *m* (*-nu*; *-ny*) garrison

garnusz|ek *m* (*-szka*; *-szki*) (*kubek*) (small) mug; ***być na czyimś ~ku*** live off s.o.

garsoniera *f* (*-ry*; *-ry*) studio

garsonka *f* (*-ki*; *-ki*) (skirt) suit

garstka *f* (*-ki*; *-ki*) (*ilość*) handful (*G* of); **garś|ć** *f* (*-ści*; *-ście*) **1.** (*ilość*) handful (*G* of) **2.** (*dłoń*) hand; ***trzymać coś w ~ci*** hold s.th. in one's hand; ***wziąć się w ~ć*** *fig* pull oneself together; ***mieć kogoś w ~ci*** *fig* have s.o. in one's grip; ***czerpać pełnymi ~ciami z*** *G fig* draw heavily on

gasić (*-szę*) **1.** ⟨**z-**⟩ *ogień*, *papierosa*: put out **2.** ⟨**z-**⟩ *światło*, *silnik*: turn off **3.** ⟨**u-**⟩ *pragnienie*: quench **4.** ⟨**z-**⟩ *zapał*: dampen; **gasnąć** ⟨**z-**⟩ (*-nę*) **1.** (*o ogniu*, *świetle*) go out **2.** (*o silniku*, *samochodzie*) stall **3.** (*o entuzjazmie*) wane

gastronomia *f* (*-mii*; *no pl*) **1.** (*usługi*) catering (services) **2.** (*sztuka kulinarna*) gastronomy; **gastronomiczny** *adj usługi*: catering

gaśnica *f* (*-cy*; *-ce*) (fire) extinguisher

gat. *abbr* (=**gatunek**) grade

gatun|ek *m* (*-nku*; *-nki*) **1.** *towaru*, *materiału*: grade; ***pierwszy*** (***drugi***) ***~ek*** grade A (B) **2.** (*typ*) type **3.** (*jakość*) quality; ***najwyższego ~ku*** top quality; ***towary drugiego ~ku*** seconds **3.** *BIOL* species *sing* **4.** *literacki*, *filmowy*: genre

gatunkow|y *adj* **1.** *BIOL* species; ***skład ~y*** species composition **2.** *towar*: quality; ***wino ~e*** quality wine **3.** *cechy utworu*: genre; ***ciężar ~y*** *fig* significance

gawęda *f* (*-dy*; *-dy*) (*opowieść*) story, tale

gawędzić ⟨**po-**⟩ (*-dzę*) chat

gawiedź *f* (*-dzi*; *no pl*) *dated* (the) rabble

gaworzyć *v/im* (*-rzę*) (*o dziecku*) babble

gawron *m* (*-na*; *-ny*) rook

gaz *m* (*-zu*; *-zy*) **1.** *PHYS* gas; ***~ ziemny*** natural gas; ***~ łzawiący*** tear gas **2.** (*pedał*) *Br* accelerator, *Am* gas pedal; ***na pełnym ~ie*** at full speed; ***~ do dechy!*** *infml* step on it!; ***na ~ie*** *infml* tanked (up) **3.** (*paliwo samochodowe*) (road fuel) gas

gaza *f* (*-zy*; *-zy*) gauze; ***~ opatrunkowa*** gauze dressing

gazda *m* (*-dy*; *-dowie*) highland farmer (in the Tatra Mountains)

gazeciarz *m* (*-rza*; *-rze*) paper boy; **gazeta** *f* (*-ty*; *-ty*) (news)paper; **gazetka** *f* (*-ki*; *-ki*) (*pismo*) (news)paper; ***~ ścienna*** board newsletter; **gazetowy** *adj*: ***papier ~*** newsprint

gazik[1] *m* (*-ka*; *-ki*) (*samochód*) jeep

gazik[2] *m* (*-ka*; *-ki*) (*opatrunek*) gauze pad

gazociąg *m* (*-gu*; *-gi*) gas pipeline; **gazomierz** *m* (*-rza*; *-rze*) gas meter

gazować ⟨**po-**, **przy-**⟩ (*-zuję*) **1.** *ludzi*: gas **2.** (*pędzić*) *infml* speed; **gazowany** *adj* **1.** *woda*: sparkling, carbonated **2.** *napoje*: carbonated, *Br* fizzy; **gazownia** *f* (*-ni*; *-nie*) gas works; **gazowy** *adj ogrzewanie*, *komora*: gas; ***w stanie ~m*** in gaseous form

gazy *pl* (*-zów*) (*wiatry*) *Br* wind *sing*, *Am* gas *sing*

gaźnik *m* (*-ka*; *-ki*) *Br* carburettor, *Am* carburetor

gaża *f* (*-ży*; *-że*) *aktora*: fee

gąbczasty *adj* spongy; **gąbka** *f* (*-ki*; *-ki*) sponge

gąsienica *f* (*-cy*; *-ce*) **1.** *BIOL* caterpillar **2.** *TECH* track; **gąsienicowy** *adj pojazd*: tracked

gąsior *m* (*-ra*; *-ry*) **1.** (*samiec gęsi*) gander **2.** (*butla*) demijohn

G

gąska *f* (*-ki*; *-ki*) **1.** (*gęś*) gosling **2.** (*dziewczyna*) silly girl **3.** (*grzyb*) tricholoma

gąszcz *m* (*-czu*; *-cze*) **1.** thicket; ***~ włosów*** thick mop of hair **2.** *przepisów, statystyk*: maze, thicket

gbur *m* (*-ra*; *-ry*) churl, boor; **gburowaty** *adj* churlish, boorish

gdakać ⟨***-knąć***⟩ (*gdaczę*) (*o kurze*) cackle

gderać *v/im* (*-ram*) grumble

gdy *conj* when; ***~ tylko*** as soon as; ***podczas ~*** while

G

gdybanie *n* (*-nia*; *no pl*) speculating, theorising

gdyby I *conj* if **II** *particle* if only; ***~m tylko miała więcej czasu!*** if only I had more time!; ***jak ~ nigdy nic*** as if nothing had happened

gdyż *conj* because, since

gdzie I *adv* where; ***~ indziej*** somewhere else; ***~ okiem sięgnąć*** as far as the eye can see **II** *particle* ***~ tam!*** nothing of the kind!

gdziekolwiek *adv* **1.** (*obojętnie gdzie*) anywhere **2.** (*wszędzie, gdzie*) wherever; **gdzieniegdzie** *adv* here and there

gdzieś I *adv* **1.** somewhere; ***mam to ~*** *infml* I don't give a damn about it **2.** (*w pytaniach*) anywhere; ***czy widziałeś ją ~?*** have you seen her anywhere? **II** *particle* (*około*) around; **gdzież** *adv* where

gehenn|a *f* (*-ny*; *no pl*) ordeal, hell; ***przechodzić ~ę*** go through hell

gej *m* (*-ja*; *-je*) gay; ***być ~em*** be gay; **gejowski** *adj* gay

gejzer *m* (*-ra*; *-ry*) geyser

gem *m* (*-ma*; *-my*) (*w tenisie*) game

gen *m* (*-nu*; *-ny*) gene

gencjana *f* (*-ny*; *-ny*) gentian

genealogiczn|y *adj* genealogical; ***drzewo ~e*** family tree

generacja *f* (*-ji*; *-je*) generation

generalicja *f* (*-ji*; *no pl*) generalization

generalizować *v/im* (*-zuję*) generalize

generaln|y *adj* **1.** general; ***próba ~a*** dress rehearsal; ***~e porządki*** big clean-up, spring cleaning; ***sekretarz ~y*** Secretary General; ***dyrektor ~y*** director-general **2.** *sztab*: chief

generał *m* (*-ła*; *-łowie*) general

generator *m* (*-ra*; *-ry*) TECH generator; ***~ drgań*** oscillator

genetyczny *adj* genetic; **genetyk** *m* (*-ka*; *-tycy*) geneticist; **genetyka** *f* (*-ki*; *no pl*) genetics

geneza *f* (*-zy*; *no pl*) origin

genialn|y *adj* brilliant; ***~e dzieło*** work of genius; ***~y człowiek*** (***pisarz***) man (writer) of genius

genitalia *pl* (*-liów*) genitals

geniusz *m* (*-sza*; *-sze*) genius

genom *m* (*-mu*; *-my*) genome; **genotyp** *m* (*-pu*; *-py*) genotype

geodeta *m* (*-ty*; *-deci*) **1.** surveyor **2.** (*naukowiec*) geodesist; **geodezja** *f* (*-ji*; *no pl*) **1.** surveying **2.** (*nauka*) geodesy; **geodezyjny** *adj sprzęt*: surveying

geograf *m* (*-fa*; *-fowie*) **1.** geographer **2.** (*nauczyciel*) geography teacher; **geografia** *f* (*-fii*; *no pl*) geography; **geograficzn|y** *adj* geographical; ***szerokość ~a*** latitude; ***długość ~a*** longitude

geolog *m* (*-ga*; *-lodzy*) geologist; **geologia** *f* (*-gii*; *no pl*) geology; **geologiczny** *adj* geological

geometria *f* (*-rii*; *no pl*) geometry; **geometryczny** *adj* geometric

georginia *f* (*-nii*; *-nie*) dahlia; **gepard** *m* (*-da*; *-dy*) cheetah; **geranium** *n indecl* geranium; **gerbera** *f* (*-ry*; *-ry*) gerbera

germanista *m* (*-ty*; *-niści*), **-tka** *f* (*-ki*; *-ki*) **1.** (*nauczyciel*) German teacher; teacher of German **2.** (*absolwent*) German graduate, graduate in German **3.** (*filolog*) Germanist

germanistyka *f* (*-ki*; *no pl*) German studies *pl*

germanizować ⟨**z-**⟩ (*-zuję*) Germanize; **germański** *adj* Germanic, Teutonic

gest *m* (*-tu*; *-ty*) gesture; ***zrobić ~*** make a gesture; ***mieć*** (***szeroki***) ***~*** *fig* be generous, be open-handed; ***przywołać ~em*** beckon

gestapo *n indecl* Gestapo; **gestapowiec** *m* (*-wca*; *-wcy*) Gestapo officer

gesti|a: ***w ~i*** *G* under the jurisdiction of, in the hands of

gestykulacja *f* (*-ji*; *no pl*) gesticulation; **gestykulować** *v/im* (*-luje*) gesticulate

getry *pl* (*-rów*) gaiters

getto *n* (*-ta*; *-ta*) ghetto

gęb|a *f* (*-by*; *-by*) *infml* **1.** (*usta*) trap; ***zamknij ~ę!*** shut your trap!; ***być mocnym w ~ie*** have the gift of the gab; ***mieć niewyparzoną ~ę*** have a big mouth; ***zapomiałeś języka w ~ie?*** have you lost you tongue?; ***pełną ~ą*** *fig* in the full sense of the word **2.** (*twarz*) mug; ***dać komuś w ~ę*** whack s.o. in the face

gębow|y *adj*: ***jama ~a*** oral cavity

gęgać ⟨**za-**⟩ (*-gam*) (*o gęsi*) honk; **gęsi** *adj jaja, pióra*: goose; ***~a skórka*** *Br* goose pimples, *Am* goose bumps; ***~ego*** in single file; ***~e pióro*** (*do pisania*) quill

gęstnieć ⟨**z-**⟩ (*-nieję*) **1.** thicken **2.** (*tężeć*) coagulate: **gęsto** *adv* thickly, densely; ***~ zaludniony*** densely populated; ***~ się tłumaczyć*** to have some explaining to do; **gęstość** *f* (*-ści*; *no pl*) density; ***~ zaludnienia*** population density

gęstwina *f* (*-ny*; *-ny*) thicket; **gęst|y** *adj* **1.** thick, dense; ***~e włosy*** thick hair **2.** *sieć, siatka*: fine

gęś *f* (*gęsi*; *gęsi*) goose; ***głupia ~*** *fig* dumb woman

giąć ⟨**wy-**⟩ (*gnę*) bend; ***giąć się*** bend

gibki *adj ruchy, kibić*: lithe

gicz *f* (*-czy*; *-cze*) *cielęca*: *Br* knuckle, *Am* shank

giełda *f* (*-dy*; *-dy*) FIN exchange; ***~ papierów wartościowych*** stock exchange; ***~ antyków*** antique market, antique fair; ***~ samochodowa*** (used) car mart; **giełdowy** *adj transakcja, notowanie*: stock exchange; ***makler ~*** stockbroker

gierki *pl* (*-rek*) *infml* little games

giermek *m* (*-mka*; *-mkowie*) HIST squire

giez *m* (*gza*; *gzy*) warble fly

giętki *adj* **1.** flexible **2.** *ciało*: supple, flexible **3.** *umysł*: nimble; **giętkość** *f* (*-ści*; *no pl*) **1.** flexibility **2.** *umysłu*: nimbleness

gigant *m* (*-ta*; *-nci*/*-ty*) **1.** giant **2.** (*w mitologii*) titan; ***slalom ~*** giant slalom; **gigantyczny** *adj* gigantic

gil *m* (*-la*; *-le*) **1.** (*ptak*) bullfinch **2.** (*z nosa*) *infml* snot

gildia *f* (*-dii*; *-die*) HIST guild

gilotyna *f* (*-ny*; *-ny*) **1.** HIST guillotine **2.** TECH guillotine, cutter

gimnastyczka *f* (*-ki*; *-ki*) SPORT (female) gymnast; **gimnastyczn|y** *adj sprzęt*: gymnastic; ***sala ~a*** gym, *form* gymnasium; (***szkolny***) ***kostium ~y*** (school) sports kit

gimnastyk *m* (*-ka*; *-tycy*) SPORT gymnast; **gimnastyka** *f* (*-ki*; *no pl*) **1.** SPORT gymnastics **2.** (*ćwiczenia*) exercise; ***~ poranna*** morning exercise; **gimnastykować się** *v/im* (*-kuję*) **1.** exercise **2.** (*starać się*) bend over backwards (***żeby coś zrobić*** to do s.th.)

gimnazjalista *m* (*-ty*; *-liści*), **-tka** *f* (*-ki*; *-ki*) middle school student

gimnazjalny *adj* middle school; **gimnazjum** *n* (*indecl*; *-ja*) middle school

ginący *adj gatunek*: dying

gin|ąć ⟨**z-**⟩ (*-nę*) **1.** (*gubić się*) go missing, be lost; ***zginęły mu klucze*** he (has) lost his keys **2.** (*umrzeć*) die **3.** (*niknąć*) disappear; ***droga ~ie w oddali*** the road vanishes into the distance **4.** (*o tradycji*) die, vanish

ginekolog *m* (*-ga*; *-lodzy*) *Br* gynaecologist, *Am* gynecologist; **ginekologiczny** *adj Br* gynaecological, *Am* gynecological

gips *m* (*-su*; *-sy*) **1.** (*materiał, opatrunek*) plaster; ***w ~ie*** in plaster **2.** (*minerał*) gypsum; **gipsować** ⟨**za-**⟩ (*-suję*) plaster; **gipsowy** *adj* plaster

girlanda *f* (*-dy*; *-dy*) festoon

giry *pl* (*gir*) (*nogi*) *infml* stumps

gitara *f* (*-ry*; *-ry*) guitar; **gitarowy** *adj* guitar

gitarzysta *m* (*-ty*; *-rzyści*), **-tka** *f* (*-ki*; *-ki*) guitarist, guitar player

gladiator *m* (*-ra*; *-rzy*) gladiator

glanc *infml*: ***wypucować na ~*** shine; **glancować** ⟨**wy-**⟩ (*-cuję*) shine

glazura *f* (*-ry*; *no pl*) **1.** (*płytki*) (wall) tiles **2.** (*powłoka*) glaze; **glazurować** ⟨**po-**⟩ (*-ruję*) *naczynia*: glaze

gleba *f* (*-by*; *-by*) soil; **glebogryzarka** *f* (*-ki*; *-ki*) cultivator

glejt *m* (*-tu*; *-ty*) HIST safe conduct (pass)

ględzenie *n* (*-nia*; *no pl*) *infml* **1.** (*gadanie*) yakking, blathering **2.** (*marudzenie*) griping; **ględzić** *v/im* (*-dzę*) *infml* **1.** (*gadać*) yak, blather **2.** (*marudzić*) gripe

gliceryna *f* (*-ny*; *no pl*) *Br* glycerine, *Am* glycerin

G

glin *m* (*-nu*; *no pl*) CHEM *Br* aluminium, *Am* aluminum
glina *f* (*-ny*; *glin*) **1.** clay **2.** (*policjant*) *infml* cop
glinianka *f* (*-ki*; *-ki*) (*chata*) mud hut; **glinian|y** *adj dzbanek*, *figurka*: clay, earthenware; ***naczynia ~e*** pottery, earthenware
gliniarz *m* (*-rza*; *-rze*) (*policjant*) cop
gliniasty *adj* **1.** *ziemia*: clayey **2.** *chleb*: doughy
glinka *f* (*-ki*; *-ki*) clay; ***~ kaolinowa*** china clay

G

glista *f* (*-ty*; *-ty*) **1.** (*pasożyt*) roundworm **2.** (*dżdżownica*) (earth)worm
glob *m* (*-bu*; *-by*) (the) globe; **globalny** *adj* global; **globus** *m* (*-sa*; *-sy*) globe
glon *m* (*-nu*; *-ny*) alga; ***~y*** algae
gloria *f* (*-rii*; *no pl*) glory; **gloryfikować** *v/im* (*-kuję*) glorify
glosa *f* (*-sy*; *-sy*) *lit* gloss
glukoza *f* (*-zy*; *no pl*) glucose
gluten *m* (*-nu*; *no pl*) gluten
gł. *abbr* (= **główny**) main
gładki *adj* smooth; **gładko** *adv* smoothly; ***~ ogolony*** clean-shaven
gładkość *f* (*-ści*; *no pl*) smoothness
gładzić ⟨**po-**, **wy-**⟩ (*-dzę*) **1.** (*głaskać*) stroke; ***~ kogoś po karku*** stroke s.o.'s neck **2.** (*wyrównywać*) smooth; **gładziutki** *adj tkanina*, *skóra*: silk-smooth
głaskać ⟨**po-**⟩ (*-szczę*/*-kam*) stroke; **głaskać się**: ***~ się po brzuchu*** stroke one's belly; ***dają się ~*** you can stroke them
głaz *m* (*-zu*; *-zy*) boulder; ***~ narzutowy*** erratic (boulder); ***milczeć jak ~*** be as silent as the grave; ***zimny jak ~*** (as) cold as stone
głąb[1] *m* (*-ba*; *-by*) **1.** *kapusty*: stalk **2.** (*głupiec*) *infml* dork, wuss
głąb[2] *f* (*głębi*; *głębie*): ***w ~*** *skierować*, *biec*: inward; ***w ~*** *G* (deep) into; ***w ~ kraju*** inland; ***ekspedycja w ~ Australii*** expedition into the interior of Australia
głębi|a *f* (*-bi*; *-bie*) **1.** *oceanu*: the depths **2.** *myśli*, *utworu*: depth; ***~a ostrości*** PHOT depth of field; ***w ~*** *fotografii*: in the (distant) background; ***z ~ domu*** from inside the house; ***w ~ serca*** deep down, at heart; ***z ~ serca*** from the bottom of one's heart; ***wzruszony do ~*** deeply moved
głębinowy *adj* deep-sea
głęboki *adj* **1.** deep; ***~ na dwa metry*** *Br* two metres deep, *Am* two meters deep; ***~ talerz*** soup plate; ***~ dekolt*** low neckline, décolletage; ***pogrążony w ~m śnie*** fast asleep **2.** *ukłon*: low, deep **3.** *analiza*: in-depth, deep **4.** *wyrazy współczucia*: deepest; **głęboko** *adv* **1.** (*w głąb*) deep **2.** *fig* deeply; ***~ kogoś urazić*** cut s.o. to the quick; **głębokoś|ć** *f* (*-ści*; *-ści*) depth; ***mieć dwa metry ~ci*** *Br* be two metres deep, *Am* be two meters deep; ***na ~ci 20 metrów*** *Br* at the depth of 20 metres, *Am* at the depth of 20 meters; ***~ć zanurzenia*** *Br* draught, *Am* draft
głębszy *m* (*-szego*; *-sze*) (*kieliszek*) *infml* shot
głodnieć ⟨**z-**⟩ (*-nieję*) get hungry
głodny *adj* hungry; **głodomór** *m* (*-mora*; *-mory*) big eater
głodować *v/im* (*-duję*) starve; **głodow|y** *adj* **1.** *strajk*: hunger **2.** *porcja*: starvation; ***śmierć ~a*** (death from) starvation; ***umrzeć śmiercią ~ą*** starve to death
głodówka *f* (*-ki*; *-ki*) **1.** (*strajk*) hunger strike **2.** (*dieta*) starvation diet
głodzić ⟨**za-**⟩ (*-dzę*) starve; **głodzić się** starve oneself
głos *m* (*-su*; *-sy*) **1.** voice; ***na ~*** aloud, out loud; ***na cały ~*** at the top of one's voice; ***prosić o ~*** ask to speak; ***zabrać ~*** speak, take the floor; ***stracić ~*** lose one's voice **2.** *zwierzęcia*: voice, cry **3.** (*dźwięk*) sound **4.** (*w głosowaniu*) vote; ***oddać ~*** vote, cast a vote; ***50% ~ów*** 50% of the vote; ***~ wstrzymujący się*** abstention
głosiciel *m* (*-la*; *-le*), ***~ka*** *f* (*-ki*; *-ki*) advocate; **głosić** *v/im* (*-szę*) advocate
głoska *f* (*-ki*; *-ki*) sound (of speech)
głosować ⟨**za-**⟩ (*-suję*) vote (***nad*** *I* on, ***za*** *I*/***na*** *A* for; ***przeciwko*** *D* against); **głosowani|e** *n* (*-nia*; *-nia*) vote; ***w ~u tajnym*** by secret ballot; ***w ~u powszechnym*** in a general election; **głosow|y** *adj ćwiczenia*: vocal; ***struny ~e*** vocal cords; ***poczta ~a*** voice mail
głośnik *m* (*-ka*; *-ki*) (loud)speaker; **głośno** *adv* **1.** loudly; ***mówić ~ o*** *L*

fig speak out about; ***zrobiło się o kimś*** (***czymś***) ~ s.o. (s.th.) came to fame **2.** (*na głos*) aloud, out loud; **głośność** *f* (*-ści*; *no pl*) **1.** loudness **2.** TECH volume; **głośny** *adj* **1.** loud **2.** (*sławny*) famous **3.** (*hałaśliwy*) noisy

głow|a *f* (*-wy*; *-wy*) head; ***~a państwa*** (***rodziny***) head of state (a family); ***ból ~y*** headache; ***bez ~y*** headless; ***na ~ę*** (*na osobę*) each, a head; ***PKB na ~ę*** GDP per capita; ***uderzyć komuś do ~y*** go (straight) to s.o.'s head; ***przyszło mi do ~y, że*** it occured to me that; ***mieć ~ę na karku*** have one's head screwed on (the right way); ***tracić ~ę*** lose one's head; ***tracić ~ę dla*** *G* fall head over heels for; ***nie tracić ~y*** keep one's head; ***włos ci z ~y nie spadnie*** you won't get hurt; ***stawiać coś na ~ie*** turn s.th. on its head; ***~a do góry!*** chin up!; ***od stóp do głów*** from head to toe; ***upaść na ~ę*** *fig* be off one's head, be out of one's mind; ***mam inne rzeczy na ~ie*** I have other things on my mind

głowica *f* (*-cy*; *-ce*) **1.** TECH head; ***~ bojowa*** warhead **2.** ARCHIT capital

głowić się *v/im* (*-wię*) puzzle (***nad*** *I* over); ***~, jak coś zrobić*** try to puzzle out how to do s.th.

głownia *f* (*-ni*; *-nie*) *szabli*: blade

głód *m* (*głodu*; *no pl*) **1.** hunger; ***~ wiedzy*** hunger for knowledge; ***~ narkotykowy*** **a)** (*zaburzenia*) withdrawal symptoms **b)** (*pragnienie*) craving **2.** (*klęska głodu*) famine; ***śmierć z głodu*** (death from) starvation; ***umrzeć z głodu*** starve to death

głóg *m* (*głogu*; *głogi*) (*roślina*) hawthorn; ***nalewka z głogu*** hawthorn extract

główka *f* (*-ki*; *-ki*) **1.** head; ***~ szpilki*** pinhead; ***~ maku*** poppy-head; ***~ czosnku*** head of garlic **2.** SPORT header

główkować ⟨**po-**⟩ (*-kuję*) **1.** SPORT head the ball **2.** (*myśleć*) think; ***~, jak coś zrobić*** try to figure out how to do s.th.

głównie *adv* mainly, primarily; **głównodowodzący** *m* (*-cego*; *-cy*) commander-in-chief; **główn|y** *adj* **1.** main; ***nawa ~a*** nave **2.** *księgowy*: chief **3.** *liczebnik*: cardinal

głuchnąć ⟨**o-**⟩ (*-nę*) go deaf

głucho *adv*: ***zamknięty na ~*** locked up tight; ***dudnić ~, bębnić ~*** thud; ***zrobiło się o kimś ~*** s.o. (has) disappeared from the public eye; **głuchoniemy** *adj* deaf-and-dumb; **głuchoniemi** *pl* (*-mych*) the deaf and dumb; **głuchota** *f* (*-ty*; *no pl*) deafness

głuch|y **I** *adj* **1.** deaf (***na*** *A* to); ***~y jak pień*** (as) deaf as a post **2.** *dźwięk*: dull, muffled; ***~e uderzenie*** thud **3.** *cisza, milczenie*: dead **II** *m* (*-chego*; *głusi*) deaf person; → ***głusi***

głupawy *adj* silly; **głupek** *m* (*-pka*; *-pki*) *infml* idiot

głupi *adj* **1.** stupid; ***udawać ~ego*** play stupid, play dumb; ***~ jak but*** (as) daft as a brush **2.** (*niezręczny*) awkward; **głupiec** *m* (*-pca*; *-pcy*) fool; **głupieć** ⟨**z-**⟩ (*-pieję*) **1.** grow stupid **2.** (*tracić głowę*) lose one's head

głupio *adv* stupidly; ***jest mi ~*** I feel stupid; **głupiutki** *adj* silly

głupkowaty *adj* foolish; **głupol** *m* (*-la*; *-le*) *infml* dumbo; **głupot|a** *f* (*-ty*; *no pl*) (*bezmyślność*) stupidity; ***~y*** nonsense *sing*; **głupstwo** *n* (*-wa*; *-wa*) **1.** stupidity; ***palnąć ~*** say a stupid thing; ***zrobić ~*** do a stupid thing **2.** (*błahostka*) little thing; ***byle ~*** any little thing; **głuptas** *m* (*-sa*; *-sy*) silly

głusi *pl* (*głuchych*) deaf people, the deaf

głusza *f* (*-szy*; *-sze*) (*odludzie*) wilderness

głuszec (*-szca*; *-szce*) capercaillie; **głuszy|ć** (*-szę*) **1.** ⟨**za-**⟩ *chwasty*: choke **2.** ⟨**wy-**⟩ *dźwięki*: muffle; ***wrzawa ~ła jej słowa*** her words were lost in the din

gm. *abbr* (= **gmina**) commune

gmach *m* (*-chu*; *-chy*) edifice; ***~ szkolny*** (***opery***) school (opera) building

gmatwać ⟨**za-**⟩ (*-wam*) *sprawę*: confuse; ***gmatwać się*** get complicated; ***~ się w zeznaniach*** give conflicting testimony

gmatwanina *f* (*-ny*; *-ny*) tangle

gmerać *v/im* (*-ram*) *infml* dig (***w*** *I* around in)

gmina *f* (*-ny*; *-ny*) **1.** ADM commune, municipality **2.** REL community; **gminny** *adj* **1.** ADM communal, municipal **2.** REL community

G

gnać ⟨**po-**⟩ (*gnam*) (*o osobie*) rush
gnat *m* (*-ty*; *-ty*) *infml* **1.** (*kość*) bone **2.** (*broń*) gun
gnębić ⟨**z-**⟩ (*-bię*) **1.** (*o władcy*) oppress **2.** (*o samotności*, *myślach*) haunt, trouble; ***co go ~?*** what's bothering him? **3.** (*o nauczycielu*) pick on
gniady *adj koń*: bay
gniazdko *n* (*-ka*; *-ka*) **1.** (*gniazdo*) nest **2.** ***~ elektryczne*** *Br* socket, *Am* outlet
gniazdo *n* (*-da*; *-da*) nest; ***~ wtykowe*** *Br* socket, *Am* outlet; **gniazdować** *v/im* (*-duję*) nest
gnicie *n* (*-cia*; *no pl*) decay, rot; **gnić** ⟨**z-**⟩ (*gniję*) rot, decay; ***~ w więzieniu*** rot in prison
gnida *f* (*-dy*; *-dy*) **1.** nit **2.** (*osoba*) *infml* louse
gnieść ⟨**z-**⟩ (*gniotę*) **1.** (*miąć*) crumple, crease **2.** (*ściskać*) squeeze **3.** (*o butach*) pinch **4.** *ciasto*: knead; ***gnieść się*** **1.** (*o materiale*) crease **2.** (*o pasażerach*) be crammed (together)
gniew *m* (*-wu*; *no pl*) anger; ***unieść się ~em*** flare up; **gniewać** ⟨**roz-**⟩ (*-wam*) anger; ***gniewać się*** be angry (***na*** *A* with, ***o*** *A* about)
gniewny *adj* angry
gniewosz *m* (*-sza*; *-sze*) smooth snake
gnieździć się *v/im* (*gnieżdżę*) **1.** nest **2.** (*tłoczyć się*) live cheek by jowl, live on top of each other
gnilny *adj proces*: decomposition
gnoić ⟨**z-**⟩ (*gnoję*): ***~ kogoś*** *infml* kick s.o. in the teeth
gnojek *m* (*-jka*; *-jki*) *infml* bastard, *Am* asshole; **gnojowica** *f* (*-cy*; *-ce*) manure pit; **gnojówka** *f* (*-ki*; *-ki*) liquid manure
gnój *m* **1.** (*gnoju*; *no pl*) manure, muck **2.** (*gnoja*; *gnoje*) (*osoba*) *infml* bastard
gnuśnieć ⟨**z-**⟩ (*-nieję*) **1.** (*tracić energię*) lose energy **2.** (*być bezczynnym*) be idle; **gnuśny** *adj* slothful, idle
go *pron* **1.** (*o osobie*) him **2.** (*o przedmiocie*, *zwierzęciu*) it; → ***on***
godło *n* (*-ła*; *-ła*) emblem; ***~ państwowe*** national emblem
godnie *adv* **1.** (*należycie*) properly, duly **2.** (*z godnością*) with dignity; **godność** *f* (*-ści*; *-ści*) **1.** dignity; ***jak pana ~?*** what's your name? **2.** (*funkcja*) *lit* post
godny *adj* **1.** (*zasługujący na*) deserving (*A*), worthy (*G* of); ***~ zaufania*** trustworthy; ***~ podziwu*** admirable; ***~ polecenia*** recommended; ***~ uwagi*** noteworthy, worthy of note; ***być ~m szacunku*** deserve respect; ***~ pochwały*** praiseworthy; ***~ pozazdroszczenia*** enviable; ***~ pogardy*** contemptible; ***pożałowania ~*** *skutki*, *wygląd*: miserable, pathetic; ***nic godnego uwagi*** nothing of interest **2.** *mistrza*, *ojca*: worthy (*G* of)
godowy *adj sezon*, *okres*: mating
gody *pl* (*-dów*) mating season *sing*; ***złote ~*** *Br* golden wedding, *Am* golden anniversary
godz. *abbr* (= **godzina**) h; ***o ~ szóstej*** at six (o'clock)
godzić (*-dzę*) **I** *v/t* **1.** ⟨**po-**⟩ (*pojednać*) reconcile **2.** ⟨**po-**⟩ (*łączyć*) combine **3.** ⟨**u-**⟩ (*trafić*) hit; ***kula ugodziła go w ramię*** the bullet hit him in the arm **II** *v/i* (*zagrażać*) jeopardize, threaten; ***godzić się*** **1.** (*wyrażać zgodę*) agree (***na*** *A* to) **2.** (*jednać się*) become reconciled, make up **3.** (*oswajać się*) come to terms (***z*** *I* with)
godzin|a *f* (*-ny*; *-ny*) hour; ***jest ~a druga*** it's two o'clock; ***o ~ie drugiej*** at two o'clock; ***która ~a?*** what time is it?; ***o której ~ie?*** what time?; ***~y otwarcia*** (***urzędowania***) opening (office) hours; ***~y przyjęć*** *Br* surgery hours, *Am* office hours; ***~a przyjazdu*** (***odjazdu***) arrival (departure) time; ***~y nadliczbowe*** overtime; ***~a policyjna*** curfew; ***w ~ach szczytu*** at rush hour; ***za ~ę*** in an hour, an hour from now; ***na ~ę*** per hour; ***o umówionej ~ie*** at the appointed time; ***~ami*** for hours
godzinka *f* (*-ki*; *-ki*) *dim* hour; **godzinki** *pl* (*-nek*) REL canonical hours; **godzinny** *adj* an hour's; **24-~** 24-hour; **godzinow|y** *adj stawka*: hourly; ***wskazówka ~a*** hour hand
godziwy *adj zarobki*: fair
gofr *m* (*-ra*; *-ry*) waffle; **gofrownica** *f* (*-cy*; *-ce*) waffle iron
gogle *pl* (*-li*) goggles
goguś *m* (*-gusia*; *-gusie*) fop
goić ⟨**za-**⟩ (*goję*) heal; ***goić się*** heal
gol *m* (*-la*; *-le*) goal; ***strzelić ~a*** score a goal
golarka *f* (*-ki*; *-ki*) razor

golas *m* (*-sa*; *-sy*) *infml* naked person; ***na ~a*** *infml* naked
golec *m* (*-lca*; *-lce*) (*biedak*) *infml* beggar
goleni|e *n* (*-nia*; *no pl*) shaving, shave; ***maszynka do ~a*** razor; ***elektryczna maszynka do ~a*** shaver, electric razor; ***krem do ~a*** shaving cream; ***płyn po ~u*** aftershave (lotion)
goleniow|y *adj*: ***kość ~a*** shinbone; **goleń** *f* (*-leni*; *-lenie*) shin
golf[1] *m* (*-fa*; *no pl*) SPORT golf
golf[2] *m* (*-fa*/*-fu*; *-fy*) **1.** (*z wywiniętym kołnierzem*) *Br* polo neck, *Am* turtleneck **2.** (*z obcisłym kołnierzem*) *Br* turtleneck, *Am* mock turtle; **golfow|y** *adj* SPORT golf; ***pole ~e*** golf course
golić (się) ⟨**o-**⟩ (*-lę*) shave
golnąć *v/p* (*-nę*) *infml*: ***~ sobie jednego*** have a quick one
golonka *f* (*-ki*; *-ki*) COOK pork knuckle, *Am* pork hocks *pl*
golutki *adj* (*nagi*) stark naked
gołąb *m* (*-łębia*; *-łębie*) pigeon; ***~ pocztowy*** carrier pigeon; ***~ pokoju*** dove of peace; **gołąbek** *m* (*-bka*; *-bki*) **1.** *dim* pigeon; ***~ pokoju*** dove of peace **2.** (*grzyb*) russula; ***gołąbki*** *pl* (*-ków*) COOK stuffed cabbage rolls
gołębi *adj jajo*: pigeon, pigeon's; ***mieć ~e serce*** be soft-hearted
gołębiarz *m* (*-rza*; *-rze*) pigeon keeper; **gołębica** *f* (*-cy*; *-ce*) dove; **gołębnik** *m* (*-ka*; *-ki*) dovecot(e)
goło *adv* (*nago*) naked
gołoledź *f* (*-dzi*; *no pl*) **1.** glaze ice, glazed frost, *Am* glaze **2.** (*na jezdni*) black ice
gołosłowny *adj zarzut*: groundless; ***aby nie być ~m, podam przykład*** the following example will illustrate my point
goł|y *adj* **1.** bare; ***pod ~ym niebem*** in the open air; ***~ymi rękoma*** with one's bare hands; ***z ~ymi rękami*** emptyhanded; ***~ym okiem*** with the naked eye; ***z ~ą głową*** bare-headed; ***z ~ymi nogami*** bare-legged; ***~y jak święty turecki*** (as) poor as a church mouse **2.** *ciało*: naked **3.** (*bez pieniędzy*) broke
gonada *f* (*-dy*; *-dy*) gonad
gondola *f* (*-li*; *-le*) gondola
gonić ⟨**do-**⟩ (*-nię*) chase; ***~ resztkami sił*** be at the end of one's tether
goniec *m* **1.** (*gońca*; *gońcy*) messenger, errand runner **2.** (*gońca*; *gońce*) (*w szachach*) bishop
gonitwa *f* (*-wy*; *-wy*) **1.** SPORT race **2.** (*gonienie*) chase (**za** *I* for), pursuit (**za** *I* of); ***~ za pieniądzem*** pursuit of money; ***~ myśli*** racing thoughts
gonokoki *pl* (*-ków*) gonococci
gont *m* (*-tu*/*-ta*; *-ty*) shingle
gończy *adj*: ***list ~*** wanted poster; ***pies ~*** hound
GOPR *abbr m* (*GOPR-ru*; *no pl*) (= **Górskie Ochotnicze Pogotowie Ratunkowe**) mountain rescue service
gorąco I *adv* **1.** hot; ***jest ~*** it's hot; ***jest mi ~*** I'm hot; ***robi się ~*** it's getting hot; ***na ~*** COOK (served) hot **2.** *witać*, *przyjmować*: warmly **II** *n* (*-ca*; *no pl*) heat
gorąc|y *adj* **1.** hot; ***~y okres*** hectic time; ***mamy ~y okres*** things are (really) busy, it is all go; ***w ~ej wodzie kąpany*** hot-headed; ***złapać kogoś na ~ym uczynku*** catch s.o. red-handed **2.** *powitanie*: warm, hearty **3.** *prośba*: urgent, big **4.** *uczucie*: passionate **5.** *patriota*: ardent
gorączk|a *f* (*-ki*; *no pl*) fever; ***mieć wysoką ~ę*** have a high fever; ***~a złota*** gold rush; **gorączkować** *v/im* (*-kuję*) have a temperature; ***gorączkować się*** get excited, get worked up; **gorączkowy** *adj przygotowania*, *pośpiech*: feverish, frantic
gorczyca *f* (*-cy*; *-ce*) mustard
gordyjski *adj*: ***przeciąć węzeł ~*** cut the Gordian knot
gorliwość *f* (*-ści*; *no pl*) eagerness; ***~ religijna*** religious zeal, *Br* religious fervour, *Am* religious fervor; **gorliwy** *adj* **1.** *uczeń*, *pracownik*, keen, eager **2.** *zwolennik*, *wyznawca*: fervent, ardent **3.** *służbista*: officious
gors *m* (*-su*; *-sy*) **1.** (*biust*) bosom, bust **2.** (*dekolt*) neckline; **gorset** *m* (*-tu*; *-ty*) **1.** (*pod suknią*) corset, girdle **2.** (*pas ortopedyczny*) (body) brace
gorszący *adj* **1.** demoralizing, scandalous **2.** (*oburzający*) outrageous **3.** *dowcip*: obscene
gorsz|y *adj comp* → **zły** worse; ***co ~a*** what's worse; ***zmiana na ~e*** change

for the worse; ***nie ma nic ~ego niż*** there is nothing worse than
gorszyć ⟨**z-**⟩ (*-szę*) **1.** demoralize **2.** (*oburzać*) scandalize; ***gorszyć się*** be scandalized
gorycz *f* (*-czy; no pl*) bitterness; **goryczka** *f* (*-ki; -ki*) **1.** BIOL gentian **2.** (*smak*) slight bitterness
goryl *m* (*-la; -le*) **1.** gorilla **2.** (*ochroniarz*) *infml* bodyguard
gorzałka *f* (*-ki; -ki*) vodka
gorzeć *v/im* (*-rzeję*) (*palić się*) *lit* be ablaze

G

gorzej *adv comp* → ***źle*** worse
gorzelnia *f* (*-ni; -nie*) distillery
gorzkawy *adj* slightly bitter, bitterish; **gorzki** *adj* **1.** bitter **2.** (*niesłodzony*) unsweetened, without sugar; ***~e żale*** REL Lenten Lamentations; **gorzknieć** ⟨**z-**⟩ (*-nieję*) **1.** (*o osobie*) become embittered **2.** (*o jedzeniu*) turn bitter; **gorzko** *adv* **1.** bitterly **2.** *smakować*: bitter
gospod|a *f* (*-dy; -dy*) inn; ***właściciel ~y*** innkeeper
gospodarcz|y *adj* **1.** economic **2.** *narzędzia, budynki*: farm; ***prace ~e*** maintenance and cleaning
gospodarka *f* (*-ki; -ki*) **1.** economy; ***~ rynkowa*** market economy; ***~ rolna*** agriculture, farming **2.** (*gospodarowanie*) management; ***zła ~*** mismanagement
gospodarność (*-ści; no pl*) **1.** good management skills *pl* **2.** (*oszczędność*) frugality, thrift; **gospodarny** *adj* **1.** ***być ~m*** have good management skills **2.** (*oszczędny*) frugal, thrifty; **gospodarować** *v/im* (*-ruję*) **I** *v/t funduszem*: manage; ***umiejętnie ~*** be a good manager **II** *v/i* farm (***na*** *L*)
gospodarski *adj* **1.** *zwierzęta, prace*: farm **2.** *córka*: farmer's; **gospodarstw|o** *n* (*-wa; -wa*): ***~ rolne*** farm; ***~ domowe*** household; ***artykuły ~a domowego*** household items
gospodarz *m* (*-rza; -rze*) **1.** (*pan domu, organizator*) host **2.** (*rolnik*) farmer **3.** *kamienicy, mieszkania*: landlord **4.** (*właściciel gospody*) innkeeper; **gospodyni** *f* (*-ni; -nie*) **1.** (*pani domu*) hostess; ***~ domowa*** houswife **2.** (*żona rolnika*) farmer's wife **3.** (*rolnik*) (woman) farmer **4.** *kamienicy, mieszkania*: landlady **5.** (*właścicielka gospody*) innkeeper; **gosposia** *f* (*-si; -sie*) housekeeper
gości|ć (*goszczę*) **I** *v/t* ⟨**u-**⟩ **1.** (*na przyjęciu*) entertain **2.** (*dawać nocleg*) ***~liśmy ich*** they stayed with us **3.** (*w programie*) ***~liśmy kogoś*** s.o. was our guest **II** *v/i* ⟨**za-**⟩ **1.** (*przebywać*) stay (***u*** *G* with) **2.** (*w programie*) guest (***w*** *L* on) **3.** (*odwiedzić*) visit (***u*** *G*)
gościec *m* (*-śćca; no pl*) MED rheumatism
gościn|a *f* (*-ny; no pl*) **1.** (*pobyt*) ***być w ~ie u*** *G* stay with; ***zaprosić kogoś w ~ę*** invite s.o. to stay; ***przyjechać w ~ę*** come to stay with **2.** (*krótka wizyta*) ***być w ~ie u kogoś*** pay s.o. a visit; ***podziękować za ~ę*** thank s.o. for his hospitality
gościniec *m* (*-ińca; -ińce*) *dated* (countryside) highway; **gościnność** *f* (*-ści; no pl*) hospitality; **gościnny** *adj* **1.** *osoba*: hospitable **2.** *występ, pokój*: guest
gość *m* (*-ścia; -ście*) **1.** guest; ***~ hotelowy*** hotel guest; ***stały ~*** regular, patron **2.** (*odwiedzający*) visitor **3.** (*facet*) *infml* guy, *Br* bloke
gotować ⟨**u-**⟩ (*-tuję*) **1.** cook; ***~ na parze*** steam **2.** *wodę, ziemniaki*: boil; ***gotować się*** **1.** cook **2.** (*o wodzie, ziemniakach*) boil **3.** (*przygotowywać się*) *lit* make ready (***do*** *G* for)
gotowanie *n* (*-nia; no pl*) cooking; **gotowan|y** *adj* boiled
gotowość *f* (*-ści; no pl*) readiness (***do*** *G*); ***~ bojowa*** combat readiness
gotowy *adj* **1.** ready (***na*** *A*/***do*** *G* for); ***~ do drogi*** ready to go, ***~ do użycia*** ready-to-use, ready-made; ***~ na wszystko*** ready for anything **2.** *wyrób*: finished
gotów → ***gotowy***
gotówk|a *f* (*-ki; no pl*) cash; ***~ą*** (in) cash; ***płatne ~ą*** payable in cash; **gotówkowy** *adj* cash
gotycki *adj* Gothic; **gotyk** *m* (*-ku; no pl*) Gothic, the Gothic style
goździk *m* (*-ka; -ki*) **1.** (*kwiat*) carnation **2.** COOK clove
gór|a *f* (*-ry; -ry*) **1.** (*wzniesienie*) mountain; ***~a lodowa*** iceberg; ***iść pod ~ę*** go uphill; ***schodzić z ~y*** go downhill **2.** ***~y*** mountains; ***jechać w ~y*** go to

the mountains **3.** (*o kierunku*) ***w ~ę***, ***do ~y*** up; ***z ~y*** down; ***w ~ę rzeki*** up the river; ***do ~y nogami*** *fig* upside down; ***ręce do ~y!*** hands up! **4.** (*sterta*) pile, heap **5.** (*część*) upper part, top; ***~a sukni*** bodice; ***u ~y*** at the top; ***od ~y do dołu*** from top to bottom; ***~a domu*** (the) upstairs; ***mieszkać na ~ze*** live upstairs, ***wchodzić na ~ę*** go upstairs; ***schodzić z ~y*** go downstairs; ***płacić z ~y*** pay in advance; ***z ~ą*** (*ponad*) over; ***~a*** (*najwięcej*) at most; ***brać ~ę*** *fig* prevail, have the upper hand

góral *m* (*-la*; *-le*), **~ka** *f* (*-ki*; *-ki*) highlander

górk|a *f* (*-ki*; *-ki*) hill, hillock; ***pod ~ę*** uphill; ***z ~i*** downhill

górnictwo *n* (*-wa*; *no pl*) mining; **górniczy** *adj* **1.** *sprzęt*, *przemysł*: mining **2.** *czapka*: miner's; **górnik** *m* (*-ka*; *-nicy*) miner

górnolotny *adj* high-flown

górn|y *adj* **1.** upper **2.** *szuflada*, *półka*: top; ***~a kreda*** GEOL Upper Cretaceous; ***~y Śląsk*** Upper Silesia

górować *v/im* (*-ruję*) **1.** (*być wyższym*) tower (***nad*** *I* over) **2.** (*wyróżniać się*) ***~ nad kimś inteligencją*** surpass s.o. in intelligence, be more intelligent than s.o.; **górsk|i** *adj pasmo*, *rower*: mountain; ***ratownictwo ~e*** mountain rescue service

górzysty *adj* mountainous

gówniarz *m* (*-rza*; *-rze*) *infml* squirt

gówno *n* (*-na*; *-na*) *vulg* shit *infml*; ***~ mnie to obchodzi!*** I don't give a shit (about it)!; ***~!*** shit!

gr. *abbr* (= **grosz**) grosz

gr|a *f* (*gry*; *gry*) **1.** (*zabawa*, *dyscyplina*) game; ***~a w piłkę nożną*** *Br* football, *Am* soccer; ***~a w szachy*** (game of) chess; ***~a w chowanego*** game of hide and seek; ***~a pojedyncza*** (***podwójna***) (*w tenisie*) singles (doubles) **2.** (*granie*) playing; ***~a na fortepianie*** piano playing; ***~a na skrzypcach*** violin playing; ***~a aktorska*** acting; ***~a na giełdzie*** playing the stock market, speculating on the stock market **3.** *kolorów*, *świateł*: play; ***~a słów*** wordplay; ***nie wchodzić w ~ę*** be out of the question; ***to ~a nie warta świeczki*** the game is not worth the candle

grab *m* (*-ba*/*-bu*; *-by*) hornbeam

graba *f* (*-by*; *-by*) *infml* paw, mitt

grabarz *m* (*-rza*; *-rze*) gravedigger

grabi|ć ⟨**za-**, **o-**⟩ (*-bię*) **1.** *liście*, *ziemię*: rake (up) **2.** (*rabować*) rob **3.** (*łupić*) plunder; **grabie** *pl* (*-bi*) (*narzędzie*) rake *sing*

grabieć ⟨**z-**⟩ (*-bieję*) go numb; ***~ z zimna*** go numb with cold

grabież *f* (*-ży*; *-że*) *lit* plunder; **grabieżca** *m* (*-cy*; *-cy*) *lit* plunderer

grabowy *adj* hornbeam

graca *f* (*-cy*;*-ce*) draw hoe

gracj|a *f* (*-ji*; *no pl*) grace; ***z ~ą*** with grace

gracz *m* (*-cza*; *-cze*) player

grać ⟨**za-**⟩ (*gram*) **1.** play; ***~ w tenisa*** play tennis; ***~ na gitarze*** play the guitar; ***~ komuś na nerwach*** get on s.o.'s nerves; ***~ na zwłokę*** play for time; ***~ na giełdzie*** play the stock market, speculate on the stock market; ***to nie gra roli*** it doesn't matter; ***~ w otwarte karty*** lay one's cards on the table; ***wszystko gra*** everything's all right; ***coś tu nie gra*** something's wrong here; ***co jest grane?*** *infml* what's going on? **2.** ***gdzie grają tę komedię?*** where is that comedy showing? **3.** (*o aktorze*) act; ***~ rolę*** play a role; ***grała w „Mężu fryzjerki"*** she was in 'The Hairdresser's Husband'

grad *m* (*-du*; *no pl*) hail; ***~ pocisków*** hail of bullets; ***pada ~*** it is hailing; **gradobicie** *n* (*-cia*; *-cia*) hailstorm

graficiarz *m* (*-rza*; *-rze*) graffiti artist

graficzny *adj* **1.** graphic; ***układ ~ tekstu*** text layout **2.** *karta*: graphics; **grafik** *m* **1.** (*-ka*; *-ficy*) (*artysta*) graphic designer; ***~ komputerowy*** computer graphics designer **2.** (*-ka*; *-ki*) (*wykres*) chart; **grafika** *f* (*-ki*; *-ki*) **1.** graphic design; ***~ komputerowa*** computer graphics **2.** (*sztuka*) graphic arts *pl* **3.** (*dzieło*) print

grafit *m* (*-tu*; *-ty*) **1.** (*minerał*) graphite **2.** (*wkład*) lead

grafologia *f* (*-gii*; *no pl*) graphology; **grafologiczny** *adj* graphological

grafoman *m* (*-na*; *-ni*), **~ka** *f* (*-ki*; *-ki*) (talentless) hack *infml*

graham *m* (*-ma*; *-my*) wholemeal bread; **grahamka** *f* (*-ki*; *-ki*) wholemeal roll

G

grajek *m* (*-jka*; *-jkowie*) (amateur) musician; **~ *uliczny*** busker, street musician

gram *m* (*-ma*; *-my*) gram, *Br* gramme

gramatyczny *adj* grammatical; ***rodzaj ~*** grammatical gender; **gramatyka** *f* (*-ki*; *no pl*) grammar

gramofon *m* (*-nu*; *-ny*) record player, gramophone; **gramofonowy** *adj płyta*: gramophone

gramolić się ⟨**w-**⟩ (*-lę*) *infml* climb (***do*** *G* into; ***na*** *A* up on)

G

granat[1] *m* (*-tu*; *-ty*) **1.** (*kolor*) navy blue **2.** (*owoc*) pomegranate **3.** (*minerał*) garnet

granat[2] *m* (*-tu*; *-ty*) grenade: **~ *ręczny*** hand grenade; **granatnik** *m* (*-ka*; *-ki*): **~ *przeciwpancerny*** bazooka

granatowy *adj* navy blue

graniastosłup *m* (*-pa*; *-py*) prism

granic|a *f* (*-cy*; *-ce*) **1.** boundary; ***w ~ach miasta*** *Br* within (the) city boundaries, *Am* within (the) city limits; ***w ~ach rozsądku*** within reasonable bounds; ***miłość bez ~*** boundless love **2.** (*między państwami*) border; ***za ~ą, za ~ę*** abroad **3.** (*między pojęciami*) borderline **4.** TECH limit; ***górna ~a*** upper limit; **graniczn|y** *adj kontrola*, *przejście*: border; ***wartość ~a*** boundary value, limit; **graniczyć** *v/im* (*-czę*) **1.** border (***z*** *I*) **2.** *fig* border, verge (***z*** *I* on)

granit *m* (*-tu*; *-ty*) granite; **granitowy** *adj* granite

grant *m* (*-tu*; *-ty*) grant

granulowany *adj* granulated

grań *f* (*grani*; *granie*) ridge

grasica *f* (*-cy*; *-ce*) ANAT thymus (gland)

grasować *v/im* (*-suję*) **1.** (*o zwierzęciu*) prowl **2.** (*o chorobie*) be rampant **3.** (*o bandytach*, *złodziejach*) operate

grat *m* (*-ta*; *-ty*) **1.** piece of junk; ***~y*** junk **2.** (*samochód*) heap, *Br infml* banger

gratis *adv* free (of charge); **gratisowy** *adj* free (of charge)

gratka *f* (*-ki*; *-ki*): ***trafiła mu się ~*** fortune smiled on him, he was lucky

gratulacje *pl* (*-ji*) congratulations; ***moje ~e!*** congratulations!; ***składać komuś ~*** congratulate s.o. (***z okazji*** *G* on); **gratulować** ⟨**po-**⟩ (*-luję*) congratulate (***z okazji*** *G* on)

gratyfikacja *f* (*-ji*; *-je*) **1.** (*nagroda*) reward **2.** (*dodatek*) bonus

grawerować ⟨**wy-**⟩ (*-ruję*) engrave; **grawerunek** *m* (*-nku*; *-nki*) engraving

grawitacja *f* (*-ji*; *no pl*) gravity, gravitation; **grawitować** *v/im* (*-tuję*) gravitate (***ku*** *D* to/toward)

grążel *m* (*-la*; *-le*) water lily

grdyka *f* (*-ki*; *-ki*) Adam's apple

Grecja *f* (*-ji*) Greece

grecki *adj* Greek; ***mówić po ~u*** speak Greek; **greckokatolicki** *adj* Greek Catholic, Uniate; **Greczynk|a** *f* (*-ki*; *-ki*) Greek woman; ***ona jest ~ą*** she is Greek; **Gre|k** *m* (*-ka*; *Grecy*) Greek; ***on jest ~kiem*** he is Greek; ***~cy*** the Greek, Greek people; ***udawać ~ka*** play stupid, play dumb; **greka** *f* (*-ki*; *no pl*) Greek

gregoriański *adj* Gregorian

grejpfrut, ***grapefruit*** *m* (*-ta*; *-ty*) grapefruit; **grejpfrutowy** *adj* grapefruit

gremialnie *adv* all together; **gremialny** *adj* mass; **gremium** *n* (*indecl*; *-mia*) **1.** *ekspertów*: panel, body **2.** (*ciało*) body **3.** (*zgromadzenie*) assembly **4.** (*komisja*) committee **5.** (*rada*) board

grenadier *m* (*-ra*; *-rzy*) grenadier

Grenlandia *f* (*-dii*) Greenland; **grenlandzki** *adj* Greenland

grill *m* (*-la*; *-le*) barbecue; **grillować** *v/im* (*-luję*) barbecue

grobla *f* (*-li*; *-le*) causeway

grobowiec *m* (*-wca*; *-wce*) tomb; **grobowy** *adj* **1.** *pomnik*: tomb **2.** *nastrój*: grim **3.** *cisza*: dead

groch *m* (*-chu*; *no pl*) **1.** (*roślina*) pea, pea-plant **2.** COOK peas *pl*; ***~ z kapustą*** *fig* complete mess, *Br* hotchpotch, *Am* hodgepodge; **grochowy** *adj* pea; **grochówka** *f* (*-ki*; *-ki*) pea soup

grochy *pl* (*-chów*) (*deseń*) polka dots; ***sukienka w ~*** polka-dot dress

grodzić ⟨**o-**⟩ (*-dzę*) fence (in)

grodzki *adj sąd*: magistrate's

grom *m* (*-mu*; *-my*) thunder; ***jak ~ z jasnego nieba*** like a bolt from the blue; ***czegoś jest od ~a*** *infml* there are loads of s.th.

gromada *f* (*-dy*; *-dy*) **1.** (*grupa*) group **2.** BIOL class; **gromadka** *f* (*-ki*; *-ki*) (small) group; **gromadnie** *adv* **1.** *żyć*: in groups **2.** *przybywać*: in large numbers; **gromadny** *adj*: ***pro-***

wadzić ~ tryb życia (*o zwierzętach*) live in groups

gromadzić ⟨**z-**, **na-**⟩ (*-dzę*) **1.** gather; ***~ zapasy*** *G* stock up on; ***~ zbiory*** build up a collection **2.** *fundusze*, *wojska*: raise **3.** *oszczędności*: make; ***gromadzić się*** **1.** (*o osobach*) gather **2.** (*o zanieczyszczeniach*) accumulate

gromić ⟨**roz-**⟩ (*-mię*) *przeciwnika*: trounce

gromki *adj* **1.** *śmiech*: booming **2.** *oklaski*: thunderous

gromnica *f* (*-cy*; *-ce*) blessed candle

gronkowiec *m* (*-wca*; *-wce*) staphylococcus

gron|o *n* (*-na*; *-na*) **1.** (*grupa*) circle; ***~o nauczycielskie*** teaching staff; ***w ~ie rodzinnym*** with one's family; ***~o znajomych*** circle of friends **2.** (*winogrona*) bunch of grapes

gronostaj *m* (*-ja*; *-je*) (*zwierzę*) stoat; **gronostaje** *pl* (*-jów*/*-tai*) (*futro*) ermines

gronowy *adj* grape

gros *indecl* (*większość*) a majority (*G* of), most

grosz *m* (*-sza*; *-sze*) grosz; ***nie mieć ani ~a*** have no money at all, be penniless; ***nie być wartym złamanego ~a*** not be worth a penny; ***nie mieć za ~ rozumu*** have no common sense whatsoever; ***co do ~a*** down to the last penny; ***za ~e*** dirt cheap; ***kosztować ~e*** be dirt cheap

groszek *m* (*-szku*; *-szki*) **1.** COOK (sweet) peas *pl* **2.** (*roślina*) lathyrus; ***~ pachnący*** sweet pea

groszki *pl* (*-ków*) (*deseń*) spots; ***w ~*** spotted; ***w czerwone ~*** with red spots

groszkowy *adj kolor*: light green

groszow|y *adj*: ***~a sprawa*** (*drobna kwota*) minor amount

grot *m* (*-tu*; *-ty*) **1.** ***~ strzały*** arrowhead; ***~ dzidy*** spearhead **2.** (*żagiel*) mainsail

grota *f* (*-ty*; *-ty*) grotto

groteskowy *adj* grotesque

grotołaz *m* (*-za*; *-zi*/*-zy*) *Br* caver, potholer, *Am* spelunker

groz|a *f* (*-zy*; *no pl*) horror; ***zdjęty ~ą*** horror-stricken; ***wzbudzać w kimś ~ę*** fill s.o. with horror; ***wzbudzający ~ę*** terrible, dreadful; ***filmy ~y*** *Br* horror films, *Am* horror movies

grozić ⟨**za-**⟩ (*grożę*) threaten (*I* with); ***ktoś grozi, że coś zrobi*** s.o. threatens to do s.th.; ***coś grozi śmiercią*** s.th. may result in death; ***~ zawaleniem*** be in danger of collapse; ***za coś grozi kara więzienia*** s.th. carries a penalty of imprisonment; ***komuś grozi kara więzienia*** s.o. is liable to imprisonment

groźb|a *f* (*-by*; *-by*) **1.** threat ***pod ~ą czegoś*** under threat of; ***pod ~ą użycia siły*** under threat of violence **2.** *pożaru*, *zawalenia*: risk; ***~a pożaru*** risk of fire

groźny *adj* **1.** dangerous **2.** *spojrzenie*, *głos*: menacing, threatening

grób *m* (*grobu*; *groby*) grave; ***milczeć jak ~*** be silent as the grave; ***≈ Nieznanego Żołnierza*** the Tomb of the Unknown Soldier; ***zza grobu*** *fig* from beyond the grave; ***wpędzić kogoś do grobu*** *fig* be the death of s.o., send s.o. to an early grave

gród *m* (*grodu*; *grody*) **1.** (*osada*) fortified settlement **2.** (*miasto*) *lit* town **3.** (*zamek*) castle

grubas *m* (*-sa*; *-sy*) fat man, *infml* fatty, fatso; **grubasek** *m* (*-ska*; *-ski*) (*dziecko*) chubby child; **grubaska** *f* (*-ki*; *-ki*) fat woman, *infml* fatty, fatso

grubiański *adj* boorish, burly

grubieć ⟨**z-**⟩ (*-bieję*) **1.** thicken **2.** (*o osobie*) grow fat **3.** (*o głosie*) deepen

grubo *adv* **1.** *smarować*: thickly **2.** *ubierać się*: warmly **3.** *wyglądać* fat **4.** *mielić*: coarsely **5.** *przesadzić*: greatly, grossly; ***~ się mylić*** be greatly mistaken

gruboskórny *adj* uncouth; **gruboś|ć** *f* (*-ści*; *no pl*) thickness; ***mieć 10 cm ~ci*** be 10 cm thick; **gruboziarnisty** *adj piach*, *sól*: coarse

grub|y *adj* **1.** thick; ***~e pieniądze*** big money; ***jelito ~e*** large intestine; ***z ~sza*** roughly; ***przedstawić w ~szych zarysach*** outline; ***~a ryba*** *fig* big shot **2.** *człowiek*: fat **3.** *głos*: low **4.** *rysy*: coarse **5.** *błąd*: gross, grave **6.** *żwir*, *piach*: coarse

gruchać *v/im* (*-cham*) coo

gruchnąć *v/p* (*-nę*) *infml* **1.** crash **2.** (*o wieści*) break (out)

gruchot *m* **1.** (*-ta*; *-ty*) (*samochód*) *infml Br* banger, *Am* jalopy **2.** (*-tu*;

G

no pl) (*dźwięk*) crash; **gruchotać** ⟨**po-, z-**⟩ (*-choczę*|*-chocę*) **I** *v/i* rattle **II** *v/t kości*: crush

gruczoł *m* (*-łu*; *-ły*) gland; **gruczołowy** *adj* gland

grud|a *f* (*-dy*; *-dy*) lump; ***~a ziemi*** clod (of earth); ***coś idzie jak po ~zie*** *fig* s.th. is an uphill struggle

grudka *f* (*-ki*; *-ki*) (small) lump; **grudkowaty** *adj* lumpy

grudniowy *adj* December

grudzień *m* (*-dnia*; *-dnie*) December

grun|t *m* (*-tu*; *-ty*) **1.** (*teren*) land; ***~ty orne*** arable land **2.** (*gleba*) soil **3.** (*substancja*) primer **4.** (*powłoka*) priming; ***~t to*** the most important thing is; ***z ~tu*** basically; ***w ~cie rzeczy*** in fact; ***stać na twardym ~cie*** *fig* be on firm ground

gruntować ⟨**za-**⟩ (*-tuję*) prime; **gruntowny** *adj* **1.** thorough **2.** *zmiany*: radical, sweeping; **gruntow|y** *adj* **1.** *pomidory*: outdoor **2.** *woda*: ground **3.** *podatek*: land **4.** *droga*: earth; ***farba ~a*** primer

grupa *f* (*-py*; *-py*) group; ***~ krwi*** blood group, blood type; **grupka** *f* (*-ki*; *-ki*) (small) group; **grupować** ⟨**z-**⟩ (*-puję*) group; ***grupować się*** group; **grupowo** *adv* **1.** (*w grupach*) in groups **2.** (*w grupie*) in a group; **grupowy** *adj* group

grusza *f* (*-szy*; *-sze*) pear tree

gruszk|a *f* (*-ki*; *-ki*) **1.** pear; ***obiecywać ~i na wierzbie*** *fig* promise the moon; ***~a do lewatywy*** enema syringe **2.** SPORT punching bag; **gruszkowaty** *adj* pear-shaped; ***~ kształt*** pear shape; **gruszkowy** *adj* pear

gruz *m* (*-zu*; *-zy*) rubble; → ***gruzy***

gruzełkowaty *adj narośl*: lumpy

Gruzin *m* (*-na*; *-ni*), **~ka** *f* (*-ki*; *-ki*) Georgian; **gruzińsk|i** *adj* Georgian; ***mówić po ~u*** speak Georgian

Gruzja *f* (*-ji*) Georgia

gruzowisko *n* (*-ka*; *-ka*) heap of rubble

gruz|y *pl* (*-zów*) **1.** (*szczątki*) rubble; ***legnąć w ~ach*** **a)** (*o budynkach*) be reduced to rubble **b)** (*o planach*) come to nothing **2.** (*ruiny*) ruins

gruźlic|a *f* (*-cy*; *no pl*) tuberculosis, TB; ***szczepionka przeciw ~y*** TB vaccine; **gruźlik** *m* (*-ka*; *-licy*), **-liczka** *f* (*-ki*; *-ki*) tuberculosis patient

gryczan|y *adj* buckwheat; ***kasza ~a*** whole buckwheat (kernels), kasha

gryf[1] *m* (*-fu*; *-fy*) **1.** (*gitary*) fretboard **2.** (*skrzypiec*) stringboard

gryf[2] *m* (*-fa*; *-fy*) (*w mitologii*) griffin

gryka *f* (*-ki*; *no pl*) buckwheat

grymas *m* (*-su*; *-sy*) grimace; **grymasić** *v/im* (*-szę*) **1.** (*wybrzydzać*) be fussy; ***~ przy jedzeniu*** be a fussy eater **2.** (*narzekać*) whine; **grymasy** *pl* (*-sów*) **1.** (*narzekanie*) whining *sing* **2.** (*kaprysy*) whims; **grymaśny** *adj* **1.** (*wybrzydzający*) fussy **2.** (*narzekający*) whiny

grynszpan *m* (*-nu*; *no pl*) verdigris

gryp|a *f* (*-py*; *no pl*) flu, *form* influenza; ***mieć ~ę*** have the flu; ***epidemia ~y*** flu epidemic; **grypowy** *adj sezon*, *infekcja*: flu, *form* influenza

gryps *m* (*-su*; *-sy*) secret letter

grysik *m* (*-ku*; *no pl*) (*kaszka manna*) semolina

grywać *v/im* (*-wam*) play (from time to time)

gryzak *m* (*-ka*; *-ki*) teether, teething ring; **gryzący** *adj* **1.** (*zębami*) biting **2.** *zapach*, *dym*: pungent, acrid; ***~ w oczy*** eye-stinging **3.** *sweter*: scratchy **4.** *ironia*: biting, pungent

gryzipiórek *m* (*-rka*; *-rki*) *Br* pen-pusher, *Am* pencil-pusher

gryzmolić ⟨**na-**⟩ (*-lę*) scribble, scrawl; **gryzmoły** *pl* (*-łów*) **1.** (*pismo*) scribble *sing*, scrawl *sing* **2.** (*rysunki*) scribbles, scrawls

gryzoń *m* (*-zonia*; *-zonie*) rodent

gry|źć ⟨**u-, po-**⟩ (*gryzę*) **I** *v/t* **1.** bite; ***co cię ~zie?*** *fig* what's eating you?; ***kogoś ~zie sumienie*** s.o. has pangs of conscience **2.** (*żuć*) chew; ***~źć kość*** chew on a bone **II** *v/i* **1.** bite **2.** (*o dymie*) sting; ***~źć w oczy*** sting in the eyes **3.** (*o wełnie*, *swetrze*) scratch; ***gryźć się*** **1.** (*dręczyć się*) fret (*I* about) **2.** (*o psach*) fight **3.** (*kłócić się*) fight **4.** (*o kolorach*) clash

grzać ⟨**o-, za-**⟩ (*grzeję*) **I** *v/t* **1.** *wodę*: heat (up) **2.** *ręce*: warm **II** *v/i* **1.** (*o grzejniku*) be hot **2.** (*o słońcu*) shine; ***grzać się*** **1.** (*o wodzie*) heat (up) **2.** *przy piecu*: warm up; ***~ się w słońcu*** bask in the sun

grzałka *f* (*-ki*; *-ki*) immersion heater

grzaniec *m* (*grzańca*; *grzańce*) mulled wine

grzanka *f* (*-ki*; *-ki*) (piece of) toast
grządka *f* (*-ki*; *-ki*) bed; **~ *kwiatowa*** flower bed
grząski *adj* **1.** *teren*: boggy **2.** *błoto*: sticky
grzbiet *m* (*-tu*; *-ty*) **1.** back **2.** *książki*: spine **3.** *góry*: ridge
grzebać ⟨**po-**⟩ (*-bię*) **I** *v/t zmarłego*: bury **II** *v/i* **1.** *w torebce*, *szufladzie*: dig (**w** *L* through), go (**w** *L* through) **2.** (*kopać*) dig (**w** *L* in) **3.** *w przeszłości*: dig (**w** *L* into); ***grzebać się*** (*guzdrać się*) dawdle (**z** *I* with)
grzebień *m* (*-bienia*; *-bienie*) **1.** (*do włosów*) comb **2.** *koguta*: crest; **grzebyk** *m* (*-ka*; *-ki*) *dim* little comb
grzech *m* (*-chu*; *-chy*) sin; ***popełnić ~*** sin; **~ *pierworodny*** original sin; ***~y młodości*** youthful mistakes
grzechotać *v/im* (*-choczę*/*-chocę*) rattle; **grzechotka** *f* (*-ki*; *-ki*) rattle; **grzechotnik** *m* (*-ka*; *-ki*) rattlesnake
grzecznościowy *adj* polite
grzecznoś|ć *f* (*-ści*; *-ści*) **1.** (*uprzejme zachowanie*) politeness; ***z ~ci*** out of politeness **2.** (*przysługa*) *Br* favour, *Am* favor; ***wyświadczyć komuś ~ć*** do s.o. a favour **3.** (*uprzejme słowa*) courtesy; ***wymienić ~ci*** exchange courtesies; **grzeczny** *adj* **1.** polite **2.** *dziecko*: good, well-behaved
grzejnik *m* (*-ka*; *-ki*) **1.** heater **2.** (*kaloryfer*) radiator
grzesznik *m* (*-ka*; *-nicy*), **-nica** *f* (*-cy*; *-ce*) sinner; **grzeszny** *adj* sinful
grzeszyć ⟨**z-**⟩ (*-szę*) sin; ***nie ~ urodą*** not be blessed with good looks; ***nie ~ rozumem*** be lacking in wisdom
grzewczy *adj* heating
grzęda *f* (*-dy*; *-dy*) perch, roost
grzęzawisko *n* (*-ka*; *-ka*) quagmire, bog; **grzęznąć** ⟨**u-**⟩ (*-nę*) sink (**w** *L* into); ***ugrzęznąć w czymś*** get stuck in sth
grzmieć *v/im* (*-mię*) **1.** (*o człowieku*) thunder **2.** (*o armatach*, *głosie*) boom; ***grzmi i pada*** it's thundering and raining
grzmocić ⟨**-motnąć**⟩ (*-cę*) bash (repeatedly); **grzmot** *m* (*-tu*; *-ty*) *pioruna*: thunder; **grzmotnąć** *v/p* **I** *v/t* **1.** bang (**o** *A* against) **2.** (*rzucić*) slam (**o** *A* against) **3.** *kogoś*: bash **II** *v/i* ***~ o ziemię*** crash to the ground
grzyb *m* (*-ba*; *-by*) **1.** (*w lesie*) mushroom; **~ *trujący*** poisonous mushroom, toadstool; ***iść na ~y*** go mushrooming **2.** BIOL fungus **3.** (*pleśń*) *Br* mould, *Am* mold; **grzybiarz** *m* (*-rza*; *-rze*) mushroom picker
grzybica *f* (*-cy*; *-ce*) fungal infection, mycosis
grzybień *m* (*-bienia*; *-bienie*) water lily
grzybnia *f* (*-ni*; *-nie*) (fungal) mycelium, mushroom spawn; **grzybobójczy** *adj*: ***środek ~*** fungicide; **grzybobranie** *n* (*-nia*; *-nia*) mushroom picking; **grzybowy** *adj* mushroom
grzywa *f* (*-wy*; *-wy*) mane; **grzywacz** *m* (*-cza*; *-cze*) (*gołąb*) ring dove, wood pigeon; **grzywka** *f* (*-ki*; *-ki*) *Br* fringe, *Am* bangs
grzywn|a *f* (*-ny*; *-ny*) fine; ***nałożyć ~ę na*** fine
gubernator *m* (*-ra*; *-rzy*/*-rowie*) governor
gubić ⟨**z-**⟩ (*-bię*) **1.** lose; **~ *wątek*** **a)** (*mówiąc*) lose one's thread **b)** (*słuchając*, *czytając*) lose the thread; **~ *pogoń*** lose one's pursuers **2.** (*doprowadzać do zguby*) ***to go zgubiło*** that was his undoing; ***gubić się*** get lost; **~ *się w domysłach*** be lost in conjecture
gula *f* (*-li*; *-le*) *infml* lump
gulasz *m* (*-szu*; *-sze*) goulash
gułag *m* (*-gu*; *-gi*) gulag
gum|a *f* (*-my*; *-my*) **1.** rubber; ***~a do żucia*** chewing gum; ***~a arabska*** gum arabic **2.** (*do majtek*) elastic **3.** (*opona*) *Br* tyre, *Am* tire; ***złapać ~ę*** *Br* have a puncture, *Am* have a flat (tire)
gumiak *m* (*-ka*; *-ki*) rubber boot
gumk|a *f* (*-ki*; *-ki*) **1.** (*do majtek*) piece of elastic; ***szorty na ~ę*** *Br* shorts with an elastic waist **2.** (*do wycierania*) eraser, *Br* rubber **3.** (*do pakowania*) *Br* elastic band, *Am* rubber band
gumować *v/im* (*-muję*) rubberize; **gumowiec** *m* (*-wca*; *-wce*) rubber boot; **gumowy** *adj* rubber
gupik *m* (*-ka*; *-ki*) guppy
guru *m indecl* guru
GUS *abbr m* (*GUS-u*; *no pl*) (= ***Główny Urząd Statystyczny***) Central Statistical Office
gusła *pl* (*-seł*) *lit* witchcraft *sing*
gust *m* (*-tu*; *-ty*/*-ta*) taste; ***sprawa ~u*** a matter of taste; ***w złym guście*** in

G

bad taste; ***nie w moim guście*** not to my taste; ***on nie jest w moim guście*** he is not my type; ***coś w tym guście*** something of that kind; ***na mój ~*** to my taste

gustować *f v/im* (*-tuję*) have a liking (**w** *L* for), like; **gustowny** *adj* tasteful

guwernantka *f* (*-ki*; *-ki*) governess

guz *m* (*-za*; *-zy*) **1.** (*stłuczenie*) bump; ***nabić sobie ~a*** get a bump; ***szukać ~a*** look for trouble **2.** MED *Br* tumour, *Am* tumor

guzdrać się *v/im* (*-ram*/*-rzę*) dawdle

guzek *m* (*-zka*; *-zki*) **1.** (*stłuczenie*) (small) bump **2.** *Br* (small) tumour, *Am* (small) tumor

guzik *m* (*-ka*; *-ki*) button; ***~ mnie to obchodzi*** I don't give a hoot (about it)

gwałciciel *m* (*-la*; *-le*) rapist; **gwałcić** ⟨**po-**, **z-**⟩ (*-cę*) **1.** *kobietę*: rape **2.** *prawo*: violate

gwałt *m* (*-tu*; *-ty*) **1.** (*na kobiecie*) rape **2.** (*przemoc*) violence; ***~em*** by force; ***na ~*** rapidly

gwałtowność *f* (*-ści*; *no pl*) **1.** *reakcji*, *ataku*: violence, vehemence **2.** *zmian*: suddenness **3.** *osoby*: impetuosity **4.** *burzy*: violence, fury; **gwałtowny** *adj* **1.** *reakcja*, *zamieszki*: violent **2.** *zmiana*: sudden **3.** *osoba*: impetuous **4.** *potrzeba*: urgent **5.** *burza*: violent, heavy **6.** *ulewa*: torrential **7.** *śmierć*: instant

gwar *m* (*-ru*; *no pl*) buzz; ***~ rozmów*** babble of voices

gwara *f* (*-ry*; *-ry*) (*dialekt*) dialect

gwarancj|a *f* (*-ji*; *-je*) **1.** guarantee **2.** COMM warranty, guarantee; ***posiadać 3-letnią ~ę*** come with a 3-year warranty; ***być jeszcze na ~i*** be still under warranty; **gwarancyjny** *adj* *karta*: warranty, guarantee; **gwarant** *m* (*-ta*; *-nci*) guarantor; **gwarantować** ⟨**za-**⟩ (*-tuję*) guarantee

gwardia *f* (*-dii*; *-die*) (the) guards; ***~ honorowa*** *Br* guard of honour, *Am* guard of honor; ***≈ Narodowa*** the National Guard; ***stara ~*** (*koledzy*) friends from the old days, *infml* the old gang

gwardzista *m* (*-ty*; *-dziści*) guardsman

gwarny *adj* bustling, noisy

gwarowy *adj* dialect(al)

gwarzyć *v/im* (*-rzę*) chat

gwasz *m* (*-szu*; *-sze*) gouache

gwiazd|a *f* (*-dy*; *-dy*) star; ***~a filmowa*** *Br* film star, *Am* movie star; ***niebo usiane ~ami*** the star-studded sky; ***urodzony pod szczęśliwą ~ą*** born under a lucky star; ***~a spadająca*** shooting star; ***zobaczyć wszystkie ~y*** *fig* see stars (before one's eyes)

gwiazdk|a *f* (*-ki*; *-ki*) **1.** (*na niebie*) little star **2.** (*znak*) asterisk **3.** (*Boże Narodzenie*) Christmas; ***prezent na ~ę*** Christmas gift; **gwiazdkowy** *adj* Christmas

gwiazdor *m* (*-ra*; *-rzy*) **1.** star; ***~ filmowy*** *Br* film star, *Am* movie star **2.** (*Święty Mikołaj*) Santa Claus, St. Nicholas; **gwiazdozbiór** *m* (*-bioru*; *-biory*) constellation

gwiaździsty *adj* **1.** *niebo*, *noc*: starry **2.** *przedmiot*: star-shaped **3.** *kształt*: star **4.** *sklepienie*: star, stellar **5.** (*promienisty*) radial; **gwiaździście** *adv*: ***rozchodzić się ~*** radiate

gwiezdny *adj* star

gwint *m* (*-tu*; *-ty*) (screw) thread; ***jasny ~!*** *infml* holy cow!; **gwintować** ⟨**na-**⟩ (*-tuję*) thread; **gwintownik** *m* (*-ka*; *-ki*) tap

gwizd *m* (*-du*; *-dy*) whistle; **gwizdać** ⟨**-dnąć**⟩ (*gwiżdżę*) **1.** whistle **2.** (*o publiczności*) boo

gwizd|ek *m* (*-dka*; *-dki*) whistle; ***na pół ~ka*** half-heartedly; **gwizdnąć** *v/p* (*-nę*) **1.** give a whistle **2.** (*ukraść*) pinch; → **gwizdać**

gwoździk *m* (*-ka*; *-ki*) (*gwóźdź*) (small) nail

gwóźdź *m* (*gwoździa*; *gwoździe*) nail; ***~ programu*** *fig* highlight; ***być gwoździem do trumny*** *fig* be a nail in s.o.'s coffin

gzy *pl* → **giez**

gzyms *m* (*-su*; *-sy*) **1.** ARCHIT cornice **2.** *skalny*: ledge

G

H

habilitacja *f* (*-ji*; *-je*) postdoctoral degree
habit *m* (*-tu*; *-ty*) habit, frock
haczyk *m* (*-ka*; *-ki*) **1.** hook; **~ *na ryby*** (fish-)hook; ***połknąć ~*** swallow the hook, take the hook **2.** (*szczegół*) catch; **haczykowaty** *adj* hooked
hafciarka *f* (*-ki*; *-ki*) embroideress; **hafciarstwo** *n* (*-wa*; *no pl*) embroidery
haft *m* (*-tu*; *-ty*) embroidery; **haftka** *f* (*-ki*; *-ki*) hook and ear; **haftować** ⟨**wy-**⟩ (*-tuję*) **I** *v/t* embroider **II** *v/i* (*wymiotować*) *infml* puke, *Am* barf
Haga *f* (*-gi*) the Hague
hak *m* (*-ka*; *-ki*) hook; **~ *holowniczy*** tow hook; ***z ~iem*** *infml* plus
haker *m* (*-ra*; *-rzy*) hacker
hala[1] *f* (*-li*; *-le*) (*sala*) hall; **~ *fabryczna*** workshop; **~ *odlotów*** departure lounge, departure hall; **~ *przylotów*** arrivals hall
hala[2] *f* (*-li*; *-le*) (*łąka*) mountain meadow
halibut *m* (*-ta*; *-ty*) halibut
halka *f* (*-ki*; *-ki*) slip
halny *adj*: ***wiatr ~*** *foehn wind in the Tatra Mountains*
halo[1] *interj* **1.** (*przez telefon*) hello **2.** (*przywołanie*) hey
halo[2] *n indecl* halo; ***wielkie ~!*** *infml* big deal!
halogenowy *adj* halogen
halowy *adj* SPORT indoor
halucynacja *f* (*-ji*; *-je*) hallucination; **halucynogenny** *adj* hallucinogenic
hałas *m* (*-su*; *-sy*) noise; ***narobić ~u*** *fig* make a fuss
hałastra *m* (*-ry*; *no pl*) rabble
hałasować *v/im* (*-suję*) make noise
hałaśliwie *adv* noisily; **hałaśliwy** *adj* noisy
hałda *f* (*-dy*; *-dy*) (slag) heap, mound
hamak *m* (*-ku*; *-ki*) hammock
hamować (*-muję*) **I** *v/i* **1.** ⟨**za-**⟩ brake, slow down; ***ostro ~*** brake sharply **II** *v/t* **1.** ⟨**po-**⟩ *wzruszenie*, *gniew*: control **2.** ⟨**po-**⟩ *łzy*: hold back **3.** ⟨**za-**⟩ *rozwój*: hinder, inhibit **4.** ⟨**przy-**⟩ (*spowalniać*) slow down; ***hamować się*** control oneself
hamujący *adj czynnik*, *wpływ*: inhibiting, inhibitory
hamulcowy *adj* brake; **hamulec** *m* (*-lca*; *-lce*) **1.** brake; **~ *bezpieczeństwa*** emergency brake **2.** (*zahamowanie*) inhibition
handel *m* (*-dlu*; *no pl*) trade, commerce; **~ *zagraniczny*** foreign trade; **~ *krajowy*** domestic trade; **~ *wymienny*** barter; ***prowadzić ~*** trade
handlarz *m* (*-rza*; *-rze*), **-rka** *f* (*-ki*; *-ki*) vendor; **~ *uliczny*** street vendor; ***narkotyków*** drug dealer; **~ *dziełami sztuki*** art dealer
handlować *v/im* (*-luję*) **1.** trade (*I* in), deal (*I* in) **2.** *narkotykami*: deal (*I* in), traffic; **handlowiec** *m* (*-wca*; *-wcy*) **1.** trader **2.** (*w dziale sprzedaży*) salesperson, salesman; **handlow|y** *adj* **1.** *korespondencja*, *szkoła*: business **2.** *centrum*, *dzielnica*: shopping, retail **3.** *przedstawiciel*: sales **4.** *spółka*: commercial; ***izba ~a*** chamber of commerce
handryczyć się *v/im* (*-czę*) bicker, squabble
hangar *m* (*-ru*; *-ry*) hangar
haniebny *adj* disgraceful, ignominious
hantle *pl* (*-li*) dumbbells
hańba *f* (*-by*; *no pl*) *Br* dishonour, *Am* dishonor; **hańbić** ⟨**z-**⟩ (*-bię*) *Br* dishonour, *Am* dishonor
haracz *m* (*-czu*; *-cze*) **1.** extortion (fee) **2.** HIST tribute
haratać ⟨**po-**⟩ (*-tam*) **1.** (*drapać*) scratch **2.** (*kaleczyć*) cut
harce: ***wyczyniać ~*** romp around
harcerz *m* (*-rza*; *-rze*), **-rka** *f* (*-ki*; *-ki*) scout; **harcerski** *adj* scout; **harcerstwo** *n* (*-wa*; *no pl*) scouting (movement)
hardość *f* (*-ści*; *no pl*) haughtiness, pride
hardware *m indecl* INF hardware
hardy *adj* haughty
harem *m* (*-mu*; *-my*) harem
harfa *f* (*-fy*; *-fy*) harp; **harfiarz** *m* (*-rza*; *-rze*), **-rka** *f* (*-ki*; *-ki*) harpist
harmider *m* (*-ru*/*-dru*; *no pl*) din
harmonia *f* (*-nii*; *-nie*) **1.** harmony **2.** (*instrument*) melodeon; **harmonijka** *f* (*-ki*; *-ki*) MUS mouth organ, harmonica; **harmonijny** *adj* harmonious

harmonizować ⟨**z-**⟩ (*-zuję*) harmonize (**z** *I* with)
harmonogram *m* (*-mu*; *-my*) schedule
harować *v/im* (*-ruję*) *infml* slave (away); **~ jak dziki osioł** sweat blood, *Br infml* work one's arse off, *Am infml* work one's ass off
harówka *f* (*-ki*; *-ki*) *infml* sweat and toil
harpun *m* (*-na*; *-ny*) harpoon
hart *m* (*-tu*; *no pl*): **~ ducha** fortitude, (a) stout heart
hartować ⟨**za-**⟩ (*-tuję*) TECH temper; **hartować się** raise one's resistance to cold
hasać *v/im* (*-sam*) frolic (around)
hasło *n* (*-ła*; *-ła*) **1.** password **2.** (*dewiza*) motto **3.** (*sygnał*) signal **4.** (*slogan*) slogan **5.** (*wyraz w słowniku*) headword **6.** (*artykuł w słowniku*) entry
haszysz *m* (*-szu*; *no pl*) hashish
haubica *f* (*-cy*; *-ce*) howitzer
haust *m* (*-tu*; *-ty*) (*łyk*) gulp; **jednym ~em** in one gulp; **zaczerpnąć ~ powietrza** take in a lungful of air
Hawaje *pl* (*-jów*) Hawaii *sing*; **hawajski** *adj* Hawaiian
hazard *m* (*-du*; *no pl*) (*gry hazardowe*) gambling; **uprawiać ~** gamble; **hazardow|y** *adj* gambling; **gra ~a** gambling game
hazardzista *m* (*-ty*; *-dziści*) gambler
heban *m* (*-nu*; *no pl*) ebony
hebel *m* (*-bla*; *-ble*) plane; **heblować** ⟨**wy-**⟩ (*-luję*) plane
hebrajsk|i *adj* Hebrew; **mówić po ~u** speak Hebrew
hec|a *f* (*-cy*; *-ce*) *infml*: **dla ~y** for fun, for a laugh
hegemonia *f* (*-nii*; *no pl*) hegemony
Heinego-Medina: **choroba ~** polio
hejnał *m* (*-łu*; *-ły*) trumpet call
hektar *m* (*-ra*; *-ry*) hectare
hel *m* (*-lu*; *no pl*) CHEM helium
helikopter *m* (*-ra*; *-ry*) helicopter
hełm *m* (*-mu*; *-my*) helmet; **~ ochronny** hard hat; **hełmofon** *m* (*-nu*; *-ny*) **1.** (*czołgisty*) tank helmet **2.** (*pilota*) flight helmet
hemofilia *f* (*-lii*; *no pl*) *Br* haemophilia, *Am* hemophilia
hemoroidy *pl* (*-dów*) piles, *Br* haemorrhoids, *Am* hemorrhoids
hen *adv*: **~ daleko** far away
henna *f* (*-ny*; *no pl*) henna
heraldyka *f* (*-ki*; *no pl*) heraldry
herb *m* (*-bu*; *-by*) **1.** coat of arms, arms **2.** (*państwowy*) emblem
herbaciany *adj* tea; **herbaciarnia** *f* (*-ni*; *-nie*) tea shop, tea room; **herbata** *f* (*-ty*; *-ty*) tea; **~ ekspresowa** tea bags *pl*; **herbatnik** *m* (*-ka*; *-ki*) *Br* biscuit, *Am* cookie
herbowy *adj* heraldic, armorial
herc *m* (*-ca*; *-ce*) hertz
heretycki *adj* heretical; **heretyk** *m* (*-ka*; *-tycy*) heretic; **herezja** *f* (*-ji*; *-je*) heresy
hermafrodyta *m* (*-ty*; *-dyci*) hermaphrodite
hermetyczny *adj* **1.** *pojemnik*: airtight **2.** *świat*: hermetic, closed **3.** *język*: impenetrable, recondite
heroiczny *adj* heroic; **heroina** *f* (*-ny*; *no pl*) **1.** (*narkotyk*) heroin **2.** (*bohaterka*) *lit* heroine; **heroinowy** *adj* heroin
herszt *m* (*-ta*; *-szci*/*-ty*) ringleader
heteroseksualny *adj* heterosexual
hetman *m* **1.** (*-na*; *-ni*) HIST hetman; **≈ Wielki Koronny** Grand Royal Hetman **2.** (*-na*; *-ny*) (*w szachach*) queen
hiacynt *m* (*-tu*/*-ta*; *-ty*) hyacinth
hibernacj|a *f* (*-ji*; *no pl*) **1.** (*u zwierząt*) hibernation; **w stanie ~i** in hibernation **2.** (*człowieka*) cryonic suspension
hiena *f* (*-ny*; *-ny*) hyena; **~ cmentarna** graverobber
hieroglif *m* (*-fu*; *-fy*) hieroglyph(ic)
higiena *f* (*-ny*; *no pl*) hygiene; **~ jamy ustnej** dental hygiene
higieniczn|y *adj* hygienic; **podpaska ~a** *Br* sanitary towel, *Am* sanitary napkin; **chusteczka ~a** tissue
higroskopijny *adj* hygroscopic
Hindus *m* (*-sa*; *-si*), **~ka** *f* (*-ki*; *-ki*) (*mieszkaniec Indii*) Indian
hiper- (*w złożeniach*) hyper-
hiperbola *f* (*-li*; *-le*) **1.** MATH hyperbola **2.** (*w utworze literackim*) hyperbole
hipika *f* (*-ki*; *no pl*) riding, horse riding
hipis *m* (*-sa*; *-si*), **~ka** *f* (*-ki*; *-ki*) hippie, hippy; **hipisowski** *adj* hippie, hippy
hipnotyzer *m* (*-ra*; *-rzy*), **~ka** *f* (*-ki*; *-ki*) hypnotist
hipnotyzować ⟨**za-**⟩ (*-zuję*) hypnotize; **hipnoz|a** *f* (*-zy*; *no pl*) hypnosis; **poddać ~ie** hypnotize

hipochondryk *m* (*-ka*; *-rycy*), **-ryczka** *f* (*-ki*; *-ki*) hypochondriac

hipodrom *m* (*-mu*; *-my*) racecourse, racetrack

hipokryta *m* (*-ty*; *-ryci*) hypocrite

hipopotam *m* (*-ma*; *-my*) hippopotamus, *infml* hippo

hipoteczny *adj* mortgage; **hipotek|a** *f* (*-ki*; *-ki*) mortgage; ***pożyczka pod ~ę*** mortgage loan

hipotetyczny *adj* hypothetical; **hipoteza** *f* (*-zy*; *-zy*) hypothesis

histeri|a *f* (*-rii*; *no pl*) hysteria; ***zbiorowa ~a*** mass hysteria; ***wpaść w ~ę*** get hysterical, *infml* have hysterics; **histeryczny** *adj* hysterical

histori|a *f* (*-rii*; *-rie*) **1.** (*dzieje*, *nauka*) history; ***~a choroby*** case history; ***przejść do ~i*** make history, go down in history (**jako** *N* as) **2.** (*wydarzenie*) story; ***opowiadać niestworzone ~e*** tell stories

historyjka *f* (*-ki*; *-ki*) story; ***~ obrazkowa*** comic strip; **historyk** *m* (*-ka*; *-rycy*) historian; **historyczny** *adj* **1.** historical **2.** (*ważny*) historic

Hiszpan *m* (*-na*; *-nie*) Spaniard; ***jest ~em*** he is Spanish; **Hiszpania** *f* (*-nii*) Spain; **Hiszpanie** *pl* (*-nów*) the Spanish; **Hiszpank|a** *f* (*-ki*; *-ki*) Spanish woman; ***jest ~ą*** she is Spanish; **hiszpańsk|i** *adj* Spanish; ***mówić po ~u*** speak Spanish

hit *m* (*-tu*; *-ty*) hit

hitlerow|iec *m* (*-wca*; *-wcy*) Nazi; ***~cy*** the Nazis; **hitlerowski** *adj* Nazi

hobbista *m* (*-ty*; *-biści*), **-tka** *f* (*-ki*; *-ki*) hobbyist

hobby *n indecl* hobby

hochsztapler *m* (*-ra*; *-rzy*), **~ka** *f* (*-ki*; *-ki*) con artist

hodować ⟨**wy-**⟩ (*-duję*) **1.** *zwierzęta*, *rośliny*: breed **2.** *brodę*: grow

hodowca *m* (*-cy*; *-cy*) **1.** *zwierząt*: breeder **2.** *roślin*: grower

hodowla *f* (*-li*; *-le*) **1.** breeding; ***~ jedwabników*** sericulture **2.** *bakterii*, *komórek*: culture **3.** (*miejsce*) breeding farm; **hodowlan|y** *adj farma*, *metody*: breeding; ***rasa ~a*** breed

hojnie *adv* generously; **hojność** *f* (*-ści*; *no pl*) generosity; **hojny** *adj* generous

hokeista *m* (*-ty*; *-keiści*) hockey player; **hokej** *m* (*-ja*; *no pl*): ***~ na lodzie*** ice hockey; ***~ na trawie*** field hockey

hol[1] *m* (*-lu*; *-le*) **1.** (*pomieszczenie*) (main) hall **2.** (*w teatrze*) foyer **3.** (*w hotelu*) lobby

hol[2] *m* (*-lu*; *-le*) (*lina*) tow rope; ***na ~u*** on tow

Holandia *f* (*-dii*) the Netherlands *pl*, Holland

Holend|er *m* (*-dra*; *-drzy*) Dutchman; ***on jest ~rem*** he is Dutch

holender *inter*: ***~!*** blast!

Holenderk|a *f* (*-ki*; *-ki*) Dutchwoman; ***ona jest ~ą*** she is Dutch; **holendersk|i** *adj* Dutch; ***mówić po ~u*** speak Dutch

holować *v/im* (*-luję*) tow; **holowniczy** *adj lina*, *hak*: tow; **holownik** *m* (*-ka*; *-ki*) tugboat

hołd *m* (*-du*; *-dy*) **1.** (*wyrazy czci*) tribute, homage; ***złożyć ~*** pay tribute (*D* to), pay homage (*D* to); ***w ~zie*** *Br* in honour (*D* of), *Am* in honor (*D* of) **2.** HIST homage; ***złożyć ~*** pay homage (*D* to); **hołdować** *v/im* (*-duję*) *lit zasadzie*, *prawdzie*: hold to

hołota *f* (*-ty*; *no pl*) riff-raff, *Am infml* trash

hołubić *v/im* (*-bię*) *lit* cherish

homar *m* (*-ra*; *-ry*) lobster

homeopatia *f* (*-tii*; *no pl*) homeopathy; **homeopatyczny** *adj* homeopathic

homogeniczny *adj* homogenous

homogenizowany *adj* homogenized; ***serek ~*** cream cheese

homonim *m* (*-mu*; *-my*) homonym

homoseksualista *m* (*-ty*; *-liści*) homosexual, gay; **homoseksualny** *adj* homosexual, gay

honor *m* (*-ru*; *no pl*) *Br* honour, *Am* honor; ***słowo ~u*** *Br* word of honour, *Am* word of honor; ***~y*** *Br* honours, *Am* honors; ***oddać ~y*** (*o żołnierzach*) salute

honorarium *n* (*indecl*; *-ria*) fee

honorować *v/im* (*-ruję*) **1.** *prawa*, *umowy*: *Br* honour, *Am* honor **2.** *kartę kredytową*: accept; **honorowo** *adv*: ***postąpić ~*** *Br* behave honourably, *Am* behave honorably; **honorowy** *adj* **1.** *osoba*: *Br* honourable, *Am* honorable **2.** *członek*, *urząd*: honorary **3.** *dawca krwi*: volunteer

hop *interj*: ***~!*** jump!; ***nie mów ~, póki nie przeskoczysz*** don't count your chickens before they are hatched

horda *f* (*-dy*; *-dy*) horde
hormon *m* (*-nu*; *-ny*) hormone; **hormonalny** *adj kuracja*, *równowaga*: hormone, hormonal
horoskop *m* (*-pu*; *-py*) horoscope
horrendalny *adj* **1.** *cena*: horrendous, exorbitant **2.** *bzdura*: utter
horror *m* (*-ru*; *-ry*) **1.** (*film*) *Br* horror film, *Am* horror movie **2.** (*książka*) horror book **3.** (*sytuacja*) horror
horyzon|t *m* (*-tu*; *-ty*) **1.** horizon; ***na ~cie*** on the horizon **2.** ***~ty*** (*perspektywy*) prospects; ***poszerzać czyjeś ~ty*** broaden s.o.'s horizons; ***mieć ciasne ~ty*** be narrow-minded
H
hossa *f* (*-sy*; *-sy*) (*na giełdzie*) bull market
hostessa *f* (*-sy*; *-sy*) hostess
hostia *f* (*-tii*; *-tie*) REL the Host
hot dog *m* (*-ga*; *-gi*) hot dog
hotel *m* (*-lu*; *-le*) hotel ***mieszkać w ~u*** stay at a hotel; ***~ robotniczy*** workers' hostel; **hotelarstwo** *n* (*-wa*; *no pl*) **1.** hotel business **2.** (*branża*) the hotel industry; ***~ i gastronomia*** the hospitality industry; **hotelowy** *adj* hotel
hoży *adj* **1.** blooming, robust **2.** *dziewczyna*: buxom
hrabia *m* (*-biego*; *-biowie*) **1.** count **2.** (*w Anglii*) earl; **hrabina** *f* (*-ny*; *-ny*) countess; **hrabiowski** *adj* count's; ***tytuł ~*** countship, the title of count
hrabstwo *m* (*-wa*; *-wa*) *Br* shire, *Am* county
huba *f* (*-by*; *-by*) bracket fungus
hucz|eć *v/im* (*-czę*) **1.** (*o morzu*) roar **2.** (*o działach*) roar, boom **3.** (*buczeć*) drone **4.** (*o wodospadzie*) crash **5.** (*o wietrze*) howl; ***~y mi w głowie*** my head is ringing; ***~eć od plotek*** be buzzing with gossip; **huczn|y** *adj* **1.** *uczta*, *obchody*: lavish **2.** *oklaski*: roaring; ***~a zabawa*** revelry
hufiec *m* (*-fca*; *-fce*) (*w harcerstwie*) district
huk *m* (*-ku*; *-ki*) **1.** (*przy wybuchu*, *upadku*) bang; ***z ~iem*** with a bang **2.** *silnika*, *fal*: roar **3.** *pioruna*: crack, rumble **4.** *wodospadu*: crash
hukać ⟨***-knąć***⟩ (*-kam*) (*o sowie*) toot; **huknąć** *v/t* **1.** (*uderzyć*) *infml* bang, *infml* whack; ***~ głową*** (***kolanem***) ***o*** bang one's head (knee) on **2.** (*zganić*) snap (***na*** *L* at); ***huknąć się***: ***~ się w głowę*** bang one's head
hulać *v/im* (*-lam*) **1.** (*bawić się*) revel, carouse **2.** (*o wietrze*) howl
hulajnoga *f* (*-gi*; *-gi*) scooter
hulanka *f* (*-ki*; *-ki*) revelry; **hulaszczy** *adj* riotous, rakish; ***prowadzić ~ tryb życia*** lead a riotous life
hultaj *m* (*-ja*; *-je*) rogue, rascal
humanistyczn|y *adj* humanistic; ***nauki ~e*** arts, the humanities
humanitarny *adj* **1.** *organizacje*, *pomoc*: humanitarian **2.** *traktowanie*, *zabijanie*: humane
humanizm *m* (*-mu*; *no pl*) humanism
humor *m* (*-ru*; *no pl*) **1.** *Br* humour, *Am* humor; ***mieć poczucie ~u*** have a good sense of humour **2.** (*nastrój*) mood; ***w dobrym*** (***złym***) ***~ze*** in a good (bad) mood; ***~y*** *pl* (*-rów*) **a)** (*dąsy*) sulk *sing*, moodiness *sing* **b)** (*kaprysy*) whims; ***miewać ~y*** be moody; **humoreska** *f* (*-ki*; *-ki*) humorous sketch
humorystyczny *adj* humorous
humorzasty *adj* moody
hura *interj* hurrah; ***hip, hip, ~!*** hip, hip, hurrah!; ***robić coś na ~*** *fig* rush headlong into s.th.; ***kupić coś na ~*** buy s.th. on impulse
huragan *m* (*-nu*; *-ny*) hurricane; **huraganowy** *adj wiatry*: hurricane
hurmem *adv infml* all together; ***wchodzić ~ do*** crowd in
hurt *m* (*-tu*; *no pl*) wholesale; ***~em*** **a)** *kupować*: wholesale **b)** *infml* all at once
hurtownia *f* (*-ni*; *-nie*) **1.** (*magazyn*) warehouse **2.** (*przedsiębiorstwo*) wholesaler; **hurtownik** *m* (*-ka*; *-nicy*) wholesaler; **hurtowo** *adv kupować*: wholesale; **hurtowy** *adj* wholesale
hurysa *f* (*-sy*; *-sy*) houri
husaria *f* (*-rii*; *no pl*) (Polish) hussars *pl*; **husarz** *m* (*-rza*; *-rze*) (Polish) hussar
husycki *adj* Hussite
huśtać ⟨***po-***⟩ (*-tam*) **1.** swing **2.** *łódką*: rock; ***huśtać się*** **1.** swing **2.** *na falach*: rock
huśtawka *f* (*-ki*; *-ki*) **1.** (*pionowa*) swing **2.** (*pozioma*) see-saw; ***~ nastrojów*** mood swings
huta *f* (*-ty*; *-ty*) foundry, mill; ***~ stali*** steelworks; ***~ szkła*** glassworks; **hutnictwo** *n* (*-wa*; *no pl*) **1.** metallurgy **2.** (*stali*) the steel industry

hutniczy *adj przemysł*: metallurgic, smelting; ***piec ~*** furnace; **hutnik** *m* (*-ka*; *-nicy*) **1.** foundry worker **2.** (*w hucie stali*) steelworker

hybryda *f* (*-dy*; *-dy*) hybrid

hydrauliczn|y *adj* **1.** *hamulec*, *pompa*: hydraulic **2.** *roboty*: plumbing; ***instalacja ~a*** plumbing; **hydraulik** *m* (*-ka*; *-licy*) plumber

hydro- (*w złożeniach*) hydro-; **hydroelektrownia** *f* (*-ni*; *-nie*) hydroelectric power plant; **hydroenergia** *f* (*-gii*; *no pl*) water power; **hydrofor** *m* (*-ru*; *-ry*) booster pump; **hydroplan** *m* (*-nu*; *-ny*) *Br* seaplane, *Am* hydroplane; **hydroterapia** *f* (*-pii*; *no pl*) hydrotherapy

hymn *m* (*-nu*; *-ny*) hymn; ***~ państwowy*** national anthem

I

i I *conj* and; ***~ zdrowy, ~ bezpieczny*** both healthy and safe; ***~ tak*** (*tak czy owak*) anyway **II** *particle* ***~ już!*** and that's that!; ***~ tak*** (*w ten sposób*) in this way

iberystyka *f* (*-ki*; *no pl*) Iberian studies *pl*

ich I *pron* them; ***nie było ~*** they were not there; → ***oni***, ***one*** **II** *poss* **1.** (*przed rzeczownikiem*) their **2.** (*bez rzeczownika*) theirs

ichtiologia *f* (*-gii*; *no pl*) ichthyology

idą → ***iść***

ide|a *f* (*idei*; *idee*) **1.** (*cel*) cause; ***służyć ~i*** serve a cause; ***walczyć w imię ~i*** fight for a cause **2.** (*pomysł*, *pojęcie*) idea, concept

idealista *m* (*-ty*; *-liści*), **-tka** *f* (*-ki*; *-ki*) idealist; **idealistyczny** *adj* idealistic

idealizować ⟨**wy-**⟩ (*-zuję*) idealize

idealny *adj* ideal; **ideał** *m* (*-łu*; *-ły*) ideal; ***~ kobiety*** (***męża***) the ideal woman (husband); ***dążyć do ~u*** strive for perfection

identyczny *adj* identical

identyfikacyjny *adj numer*, *kod*: identification; ***numer ~*** identification number, ID; **identyfikator** *m* (*-ra*; *-ry*) **1.** (*plakietka*) ID badge **2.** *użytkownika*: ID, identification

identyfikować ⟨**z-**⟩ (*-kuję*) identify; ***identyfikować się*** **a)** *z bohaterem*: identify (**z** *I* with) **b)** (*popierać*) identify oneself (**z** *I* with)

ideolog *m* (*-ga*; *-lodzy*) ideologist; **ideologia** *f* (*-gii*; *no pl*) ideology; **ideologiczny** *adj* ideological

ideowy *adj* ideological; ***schemat ~*** schematic diagram

idę → ***iść***

idiocieć ⟨**z-**⟩ (*-cieję*) *infml* go stupid, *Br* go daft, *Am* go goofy

idiom *m* (*-mu*; *-my*) idiom

idiot|a *m* (*-ty*; *idioci*), **-tka** *f* (*-ki*; *-ki*) idiot; ***słodka ~ka*** bimbo

idiotyczny *adj* idiotic; **idiotyzm** *m* (*-mu*; *-my*) idiocy

idol *m* (*-la*; *-le*) idol

idylla *f* (*-li*; *-le*) idyll; **idylliczny** *adj* idyllic

idziemy → ***iść***

idź → ***iść***

igiełka *f* (*-ki*; *-ki*) *dim* (small) needle

iglasto-liściasty *adj las*: mixed

iglast|y *adj* coniferous; ***drzewo ~e*** conifer

iglica *f* (*-cy*; *-ce*) **1.** ARCHIT spire **2.** (*w broni palnej*) firing pin **3.** GEOL pinnacle

igliwie *n* (*-wia*; *no pl*) (conifer) needles

igł|a *f* (*-ły*; *-ły*) needle; ***~a do szycia*** sewing needle; ***~a gramofonowa*** phonograph needle, stylus; ***~a do strzykawki*** hypodermic needle; ***jak spod ~y*** brand new

ignorować ⟨**z-**⟩ (*-ruję*) ignore

igrać *v/im* (*-ram*) play (**z** *I* with); ***~ z ogniem*** play with fire

igraszk|a *f* (*-ki*; *-ki*) (*zabawa*) game; ***być*** (***dziecinną***) ***~ą*** be child's play

igrzyska *pl* (*igrzysk*): ***~ olimpijskie*** the Olympic Games, the Olympics; ***~ zimowe*** the Winter Olympics

ikona *f* (*-ny*; *-ny*) icon

ikr|a *f* (*-ry*; *no pl*) **1.** (*w wodzie*) spawn; ***składać ~ę*** spawn **2.** (*w rybie*) (hard) roe; ***facet z ~ą*** *fig* guy with (plenty of) guts

ilast|y *adj*: ***gleba ~a*** loam

ile *pron* **1.** (*z rzeczownikami niepoliczalnymi*) how much; ***~ wina?*** how much wine?; ~ ***to kosztuje?*** how much is it?; ***tyle pieniędzy, ~ potrzebujesz*** as much money as you want; ***można jeść, ~ dusza zapragnie*** you can eat as much as you want **2.** (*z rzeczownikami policzalnymi*) how many; ~ ***kieliszków?*** how many glasses?; ~ ***masz lat?*** how old are you?; ***tyle samochodów, ~*** as many cars as **3.** (*mnóstwo*) ~ ***ludzi!*** what a lot of people!; ~ ***pieniędzy!*** what a lot of money!; ***o ~ wiem*** (***pamiętam***) as far as I know (remember); ~ ***sił w nogach*** as fast as possible; ~ ***wlezie*** *infml* as much as possible, as much as one can; ***nie tyle ważna jest cena, ~ jakość*** the price is not as important as quality; ***o ~*** (*jeśli*) if, provided that; ***o ~ nie*** unless, if not

I

ilekroć *pron* whenever; **ileś** *pron* a certain number of; **ileż** *pron* **1.** (*z rzeczownikami niepoliczalnymi*) how much **2.** (*z rzeczownikami policzalnymi*) how many

iloczyn *m* (*-nu*; *-ny*) product

iloma → ***ile***

iloraz *m* (*-zu*; *-zy*) quotient; ~ ***inteligencji*** IQ, intelligence quotient

ilościowy *adj* quantitative; **ilość** *f* (*-ści*; *-ści*) **1.** (*z rzeczownikami niepoliczalnymi*) amount, quantity; ~ ***i jakość*** quantity and quality **2.** (*z rzeczownikami policzalnymi*) number

ilu → ***ile***

iluminacja *f* (*-ji*; *-je*) illumination; **iluminować** *v/im* (*-nuję*) illuminate

ilustracja *f* (*-ji*; *-je*) illustration

ilustrować ⟨**z-**⟩ (*-ruję*) illustrate; **ilustrowany** *adj* illustrated

iluzj|a *f* (*-ji*; *-je*) illusion; ***ulegać ~i, że*** be deluded that

iluzjonista *m* (*-ty*; *-niści*), **-tka** *f* (*-ki*; *-ki*) illusionist; **iluzoryczny** *adj* illusory

ił *m* (*iłu*; *iły*) clay

im **I** *pron* them; ***powiedz ~*** tell them; ***daj ~ to*** give it to them; → ***on***, ***ona*** **II** *adv* the; ~ ***prędzej, tym lepiej*** the quicker the better

im. *abbr* **1.** (= ***imię***) (first) name **2.** (= ***imienia***) ***szkoła im. Stefana Batorego*** Stefan Batory School

imać się *v/im* (*imam*) *zajęć*: take

imadło *n* (*-ła*; *-ła*) *Br* vice, *Am* vise

imaginacja *f* (*-ji*; *no pl*) imagination

imbecyl *m* (*-la*; *-le*) imbecile

imbir *m* (*-ru*; *no pl*) ginger; **imbirow|y** *adj* ginger; ***piwo ~e*** ginger beer

imbryk *m* (*-ka*; *-ki*) teapot

imieniny *pl* (*imienin*) name day *sing*; **imieninowy** *adj* name-day; **imiennie** *adv wymienić*: by name; **imiennik** *m* (*-ka*; *-nicy*) namesake; **imienny** *adj* **1.** *zaproszenie*: personal **2.** *akcje*: registered

imiesłów *m* (*-łowu*; *-łowy*) participle; ~ ***czynny*** present participle; ~ ***bierny*** past participle; ~ ***uprzedni*** perfect participle

imię *n* (*imienia*; *imiona*) **1.** (first) name; ***jak masz na ~?*** what's your name?; ***mam na ~ Ania*** my name is Ania; ***drugie ~*** middle name; ***ona mówi mi po imieniu*** she calls me by my first name; ***w czyimś imieniu*** on behalf of s.o.; ***w ~*** *G* in the name of **2.** (*nazwa*) name; ***szkoła imienia Stefana Batorego*** Stefan Batory School; ***dobre ~*** *fig* good name, reputation; ***nazywać rzeczy po imieniu*** *fig* call a spade a spade

imigracja *f* (*-ji*; *-je*) immigration; **imigracyjny** *adj* immigration; **imigrant** *m* (*-ta*; *-nci*), **~ka** *f* (*-ki*; *-ki*) immigrant

imigrować *v im/p* (*-ruję*) immigrate

imiona *pl* → ***imię***

imitacja *f* (*-ji*; *-je*) imitation; ~ ***skóry*** imitation leather; **imitować** *v/im* (*-tuję*) imitate

immatrykulacja *f* (*-ji*; *-je*) **1.** matriculation **2.** (*uroczystość*) matriculation ceremony; **immatrykulować** *v im/p* (*-luję*) matriculate

immunitet *m* (*-tu*; *-ty*) immunity; ~ ***poselski*** parliamentary immunity

immunologiczny *adj system*: immune

impas *m* (*-su*; *-sy*) deadlock, impasse; ***znaleźć się w ~ie*** reach a deadlock; ***przełamać ~*** break a deadlock

imperialistyczny *adj* imperialistic; **imperializm** *m* (*-mu*; *no pl*) imperialism

imperium *n* (*indecl*; *-ria*) empire; ~ ***rzymskie*** the Roman Empire

impertynencja *f* (*-ji*; *-je*) *lit* impertinence; **impertynencki** *adj lit* impertinent; **impertynent** *m* (*-ta*; *-nci*), **~ka** *f* (*-ki*; *-ki*) *lit* impertinent person

impet *m* (*-tu*; *no pl*) (*pęd*) momentum; ***nabierać ~u*** gain momentum; ***tracić***

~ lose momentum; **z ~em** impetuously

implant *m* (*-tu*; *-ty*) implant

imponować ⟨**za-**⟩ (*-nuję*) impress (**komuś** *I* s.o. with); ***zaimponowało jej to, że*** it impressed her that; **imponujący** *adj* **1.** impressive **2.** (*ogromny*) imposing

import *m* (*-tu*; *no pl*) import; ***towary z ~u*** imports, imported goods; **importować** *v im/p* (*-tuję*) import; **importowy** *adj* **1.** *licencja*, *cło*: import **2.** *towary*: imported

impotencj|a *f* (*-ji*; *no pl*) impotence; ***cierpieć na ~ę*** be impotent; ***cierpieć na ~ę twórczą*** (*o pisarzu*) have writer's block

impregnacja *f* (*-ji*; *no pl*) **1.** *tkanin*: proofing **2.** (*na działanie wody*) waterproofing **3.** (*na działanie ognia*) fireproofing **4.** *drewna*: impregnation; **impregnować** ⟨**za-**⟩ (*-nuję*) **1.** *tkaninę*: proof **2.** (*na działanie wody*) waterproof **3.** (*na działanie ognia*) fireproof **4.** *drewno*: impregnate; **impregnowany** *adj* **1.** (*nieprzemakalny*) waterproof **2.** (*niepalny*) fireproof

impresariat *m* (*-tu*; *-ty*) entertainment agency

impresja *f* (*-ji*; *-je*) impression; **impresjonizm** *m* (*-mu*; *no pl*) Impressionism

imprez|a *f* (*-zy*; *-zy*) **1.** (*wydarzenie*) event; ***~a sportowa*** sporting event **2.** (*przyjęcie*) party, *Br infml* do; ***robić ~ę*** *infml* throw a party; **imprezować** *v/im* (*-zuję*) *infml* party

improwizacja *f* (*-ji*; *-je*) improvisation, *infml* improv; **improwizować** ⟨**za-**⟩ (*-zuję*) improvise

impuls *m* (*-su*; *-sy*) impulse; ***pod wpływem ~u*** on impulse; **impulsywny** *adj* impulsive

inaczej *adv* **1.** (*w inny sposób*) differently; ***~ niż się spodziewałam*** not as I expected; ***tak czy ~*** one way or another; ***~ mówiąc*** in other words **2.** (*w przeciwnym razie*) otherwise **3.** (*innymi słowy*) or

inauguracja *f* (*-ji*; *-je*) opening, inauguration; **inauguracyjny** *adj* inaugural, opening; **inaugurować** ⟨**za-**⟩ (*-ruję*) open, inaugurate

incydent *m* (*-tu*; *-ty*) incident

indagować *v/im* (*-guję*) *form* question (**o** *A* on)

indeks *m* (*-su*; *-sy*) **1.** index; ***~ rzeczowy*** subject index; **2.** ***~ górny*** superscript; ***~ dolny*** subscript **3.** (*studenta*) (student's) record book

indeksacja *f* (*-ji*; *no pl*) indexation

Indianin *m* (*-na*; *-dianie*), **-nka** *f* (*-ki*; *-ki*) Native American, (American) Indian; **indiański** *adj* Native American, (American) Indian

Indie *pl* (*-dii*) India *sing*

indoeuropejski *adj* Indo-European

Indonezja *f* (*-ji*) Indonesia

indonezyjski *adj* Indonesian

indor *m* (*-ra*; *-ry*) turkeycock

indukcja *f* (*-ji*; *no pl*) induction; **indukcyjny** *adj* inductive

indyczka *f* (*-ki*; *-ki*) turkey hen; **indyczy** *adj* turkey

indygo *n indecl* indigo

indyjsk|i *adj* Indian; ***Ocean ~*** the Indian Ocean; ***curry po ~u*** Indian curry

indyk *m* (*-ka*; *-ki*) turkey

indywidualista *m* (*-ty*; *-liści*), **-tka** *f* (*-ki*; *-ki*) individualist

indywidualność *f* (*-ści*; *no pl*) **1.** individuality **2.** (*osoba*) personality; **indywidualny** *adj* **1.** individual **2.** *wrażenie*: personal

indywiduum *n* (*indecl*; *-dua*) individual

indziej: ***gdzie ~*** somewhere else; ***kiedy ~*** some other time; ***niedostępny nigdzie ~*** not available anywhere else

inercja *f* (*-ji*; *no pl*) inertia

infantylny *adj* infantile

infekcja *f* (*-ji*; *-je*) infection; **infekcyjny** *adj* infectious; **infekować** ⟨**za-**⟩ (*-kuję*) infect

infiltracja *f* (*-ji*; *no pl*) infiltration

inflacja *f* (*-ji*; *no pl*) inflation

informacj|a *f* (*-ji*; *-je*) **1.** (*wiadomość*) (piece of) information (**o** *L* about/on); ***~e z ostatniej chwili*** the latest news **2.** (*dane*) information; ***~a genetyczna*** genetic information **3.** (*biuro*) information office; ***centrum ~i turystycznej*** *Br* tourist information centre, *Am* tourist information center; ***~a telefoniczna*** *Br* directory enquiries, *Am* directory assistance, *Am* information; **informacyjny** *adj* information

informator *m* **1.** (*-ra*; *-ry*) (*książka*) guide, directory; ***~ wydawniczy*** pub-

I

lications directory **2.** (*-ra*; *-rzy*) (*osoba*) informant

informatyk *m* (*-ka*; *-tycy*), **-tyczka** *f* (*-ki*; *-ki*) **1.** computer scientist **2.** (*w firmie*) IT specialist **3.** (*nauczyciel*) computer (science) teacher

informować ⟨**po-**⟩ (*-muję*) inform (**o** *L* of/about)

ingerencja *f* (*-ji*; *no pl*) interference (**w** *L* in); **ingerować** ⟨**za-**⟩ (*-ruję*) interfere (**w** *L* in)

inhalator *m* (*-ra*; *-ry*) inhaler; **inhalować** *v/im* (*-luję*) inhale

inicjacja *f* (*-ji*; *-je*) initiation; **inicjator** *m* (*-ra*; *-rzy*), **-rka** *f* (*-ki*; *-ki*) initiator

inicjatyw|a *f* (*-wy*; *-wy*) **1.** (*plan*, *samodzielność*) initiative; ***z własnej ~y*** on one's own initiative; ***wykazywać ~ę*** use one's initiative **2.** (*propozycja*) proposal **3.** (*pomysł*) idea; ***forum powstało z jego ~y*** the forum was created (based) on his idea, it was his idea to create the forum

I

inicjować ⟨**za-**⟩ (*-juję*) initiate; ***~ działalność*** (*o firmie*) start operations

iniekcja *f* (*-ji*; *-je*) injection

inkasent *m* (*-ta*; *-nci*) meter reader; **inkaso** *n* (*-sa*; *no pl*) collection; **inkasować** ⟨**za-**⟩ (*-suję*) collect

inklinacja *f* (*-ji*; *-je*) *form* inclination (**do** *G* to)

Inkowie *pl* (*-ków*) the Incas

inkrustacja *f* (*-ji*; *je*) incrustation, encrustation; **inkrustowany** *adj* inlaid; ***~ złotem*** gold-inlaid, inlaid with gold

inkubacyjny *adj*: ***okres ~*** incubation period

inkubator *m* (*-ra*; *-ry*) incubator

inkwizycja *f* (*-ji*; *no pl*) REL inquisition; ***Święta ~*** the Holy Inquisition; **inkwizycyjny** *adj* inquisitional

inną ***inne***, ***inni*** → ***inny***

innojęzyczny *adj odpowiedniki*, *wersje*: foreign-language

inność *f* (*-ści*; *no pl*) different nature, being different; ***zaakceptować czyjąś ~*** accept that s.o. is different

innowacja *f* (*-ji*; *-je*) *form* innovation

innowierca *m* (*-cy*; *-cy*) infidel

inn|y I *pron* **1.** (*różny*) different; ***jest ~a niż wszystkie*** she is different from everyone else; ***być ~ego zdania na temat*** have a different view on **2.** (*nie ten*) ***~e rzeczy*** other things; ***w ~ym mieście*** in another town; ***co ~ego*** something else; ***kto ~y*** someone else; ***~ym razem*** some other time; ***nikt ~y*** no one else, nobody else; ***między ~ymi*** (*o rzeczach*, *zjawiskach*) among other things; ***~ymi słowy*** in other words **II** *m* (*-nego*; *-ni*) **3.** another person; ***~a*** another woman; ***~i*** others

inscenizacja *f* (*-ji*; *-je*) staging, production; **inscenizować** ⟨**za-**⟩ (*-zuję*) stage

insektobójczy *adj* insecticidal; ***środek ~*** insecticide; **insekty** *pl* (*-tów*) insects

inseminacja *f* (*-ji*; *-je*) artificial insemination

inskrypcja *f* (*-ji*; *-je*) inscription

inspekcj|a *f* (*-ji*; *-je*) **1.** (*kontrola*) inspection; ***przeprowadzać ~ę*** inspect **2.** (*organizacja*) inspectorate, regulator; ***Państwowa ~a Pracy*** the National Labour Inspectorate; **inspektor** *m* (*-ra*; *-rzy*) inspector; ***~ szkolny*** school inspector; **inspektorat** *m* (*-tu*; *-ty*) inspectorate

inspekt *m* (*-tu*; *-ty*) (cold) frame, hotbed

inspiracj|a *f* (*-ji*; *-je*) inspiration; ***z czyjejś ~i*** at s.o.'s suggestion; **inspirować** ⟨**za-**⟩ (*-ruję*) inspire; **inspirujący** *adj* inspiring

instalacja *f* (*-ji*; *-je*) **1.** (*czynność*) installation **2.** (*zespół urządzeń*) system; ***~ wodno-kanalizacyjna*** water supply and drainage; ***~ wodociągowa*** plumbing; ***~ elektryczna*** wiring; **instalator** *m* (*-ra*; *-rzy*) **1.** (*osoba*) installer, fitter **2.** INF installation wizard; **instalować** ⟨**za-**⟩ (*-luję*) install

instancj|a *f* (*-ji*; *-je*): ***sąd pierwszej ~i*** court of first instance; ***sąd wyższej ~i*** higher level court; ***sąd najwyższej ~i*** the supreme court; ***najwyższa ~a*** the highest (level of) authority

instrukcja *f* (*-ji*; *-je*) **1.** (*polecenie*) instruction **2.** (*przepisy*) instructions *pl*; ***~ obsługi*** manual; ***~ przeciwpożarowa*** fire safety instructions

instruktaż *m* (*-żu*; *no pl*) training; **instruktażowy** *adj film*, *kurs*: instructional

instruktor *m* (*-ra*; *-rzy*) instructor; ***~ jazdy*** driving instructor; ***~ pilotażu*** flight instructor

instrument *m* (*-tu*; *-ty*) instrument; **~y strunowe** stringed instruments; **instrumentalnie** *adv*: **traktować kogoś ~** treat s.o. like an object; **instrumentalny** *adj* instrumental
instrumentariusz *m* (*-sza*; *-sze*), **~ka** *f* (*-ki*; *-ki*) surgeon's assistant
instruować ⟨**po-**⟩ (*-ruuję*) instruct
instynkt *m* (*-tu*; *-ty*) instinct; **~ samozachowawczy** self-preservation instinct, survival instinct; **instynktowny** *adj* instinctive
instytucja *f* (*-ji*; *-je*) institution; **~ małżeństwa** the institution of marriage; **instytucjonalny** *adj* **1.** institutional **2.** *klient*: business
instytut *m* (*-tu*; *-ty*) institute; **~ badawczy** research institute
insulina *f* (*-ny*; *no pl*) insulin
insygnia *pl* (*-niów*): **~ królewskie** royal insignia
insynuacja *f* (*-ji*; *-je*) false allegation; **insynuować** *v*/*im* (*-nuuję*) (falsely) allege
integracja *f* (*-ji*; *no pl*) integration; **integralny** *adj* integral
integrować ⟨**z-**⟩ (*-ruję*) integrate
intelektualista *m* (*-ty*; *-liści*), **-tka** *f* (*-ki*; *-ki*) intellectual; **intelektualny** *adj* intellectual
inteligencja *f* (*-ji*; *no pl*) **1.** (*cecha*) intelligence **2.** (*warstwa społeczna*) (the) intelligentsia; **inteligencki** *adj*: **w środowisku ~m** among the intelligentsia; **inteligentny** *adj* intelligent
intencj|a *f* (*-ji*; *-je*) intention; **mieć dobre ~e** mean well, have good intentions; **na ~ę** *G* for
intencyjny *adj*: **list ~** letter of intent
intendent *m* (*-ta*; *-nci*) **1.** (*w wojsku*) commissary **2.** (*stołówki*) steward
intensyfikować ⟨**z-**⟩ (*-kuję*) intensify
intensywność *f* (*-ści*; *no pl*) intensity; **intensywn|y** *adj* **1.** intensive; **oddział ~ej opieki** intensive care ward, intensive care unit **2.** *kolor, światło*: intense
interaktywny *adj* interactive; **interdyscyplinarny** *adj* interdisciplinary
interes *m* (*-su*; *-sy*) **1.** (*sprawa*) business; **nie twój ~** none of your business; **mam do niego ~** I'd like to have a word with him **2.** (*korzyść*) interest; **w czyimś ~ie** in s.o.'s (best) interest; **zrobić ~ na** make money on **3.** (*transakcja*) deal; **ubić ~** cut a deal; **złoty ~** *fig* a gold mine **4.** (*firma*) business; **człowiek ~u** businessman; → **interesy**
interesant *m* (*-ta*; *-nci*), **-tka** *f* (*-ki*; *-ki*) client
interes|ować ⟨**za-**⟩ (*-suję*) interest; **~uje ją sport** she is interested in sport; **interesować się** be interested (*I* in); **interesowny** *adj* self-interested, mercenary
interesujący *adj* interesting; **interesy** *pl* (*-sów*) business *sing*; → **interes**
interna *f* (*-ny*; *no pl*) (*dział medycyny*) *infml* internal medicine
internat *m* (*-tu*; *-ty*) dormitory; **szkoła z ~em** boarding school
internauta *m* (*-ty*; *-nauci*) Internet user, web user
Internet *m* (*-tu*; *no pl*) the Internet
internista *m* (*-ty*; *-niści*), **-tka** *f* (*-ki*; *-ki*) specialist in internal medicine, *Am* internist
internować *v im*/*p* (*-nuję*) intern
interpretacja *f* (*-ji*; *-je*) interpretation; **interpretator** *m* (*-ra*; *-rzy*), **~ka** *f* (*-ki*; *-ki*) interpreter
interpretować ⟨**z-**⟩ (*-tuję*) interpret
interpunkcja *f* (*-ji*; *no pl*) punctuation; **interpunkcyjny** *adj* punctuation; **błąd ~** punctuation error
interwencja *f* (*-ji*; *-je*) intervention; **interwencyjny** *adj* *program*: intervention; **telefon ~** hotline; **interweniować** *v im*/*p* (*-niuję*) intervene
intonacja *f* (*-ji*; *no pl*) intonation; **intonować** ⟨**za-**⟩ (*-nuję*) **1.** (*śpiewać*) intone **2.** (*zaczynać śpiew*) start singing, launch into
intratny *adj* lucrative
introligator *m* (*-ra*; *-rzy*) bookbinder; **introligatornia** *f* (*-ni*; *-nie*) bookbindery
intruz *m* (*-za*; *-zi*) intruder
intryga *f* (*-gi*; *-gi*) intrigue; **intrygancki** *adj* intrigant; **intrygant** *m* (*-ta*; *-nci*), **~ka** *f* (*-ki*; *-ki*) schemer, plotter
intrygować ⟨**za-**⟩ (*-guję*) intrigue; **intrygujący** *adj* intriguing
intuicja *f* (*-ji*; *no pl*) intuition
intymność *f* (*-ści*; *no pl*) intimacy; **intymny** *adj* intimate
inwalida *m* (*-dy*; *-dzi*), **-dka** *f* (*-ki*; *-ki*) disabled person; **~ wojenny** disabled

I

war veteran; **inwalidzi** *pl* (*-dów*) the disabled

inwalidzki *adj renta, zasiłek*: disability; **wózek ~** wheelchair; **inwalidztwo** *n* (*-wa*; *no pl*) disability

inwazja *f* (*-ji*; *-je*) invasion

inwencja *f* (*-ji*; *no pl*) (*pomysłowość*) inventiveness; **~ twórcza** creativity

inwentaryzacja *f* (*-ji*; *-je*) (*towarów*) *Br* stocktaking, *Am* inventory; **inwentarz** *m* (*-rza*; *-rze*) **1.** inventory (list) **2.** *zabytków*: schedule **3.** **żywy ~** livestock; **drobny ~** small livestock

inwestor *m* (*-ra*; *-rzy*) investor

inwestować ⟨**za-**⟩ (*-tuję*) invest

inwestycja *f* (*-ji*; *-je*) **1.** investment **2.** (*projekt*) development project **3.** (*obiekt*) development; **inwestycyjn|y** *adj* **1.** investment; **nakłady ~e** capital expenditure **2.** *projekt*: development

inwigilacja *f* (*-ji*; *-je*) surveillance

inż. *abbr* (=**inżynier**) M.Eng.; **dr ~** D.Eng.

inżynier *m* (*-ra*; *-rowie*) **1.** engineer; **~ budowlany** construction engineer; **~ elektryk** electrical engineer **2.** (*tytuł*) M.Eng.

inżynieria *f* (*-rii*; *no pl*) engineering: **~ genetyczna** genetic engineering; **~ lądowa** civil engineering

iracki *adj* Iraqi; **Irak** *m* (*-ku*) Iraq

Iran *m* (*-nu*) Iran; **irański** *adj* Iranian

ircha *f* (*-chy*; *no pl*) chamois, *Br* chamois leather

Irlandczycy *pl* (*-czyków*) the Irish; **Irlandczyk** *m* (*-ka*; *-czycy*) Irishman; **jest ~iem** he is Irish; **Irlandia** *f* (*-dii*) Ireland; **Irlandka** *f* (*-ki*; *-ki*) Irishwoman; **irlandzki** *adj* Irish

ironi|a *f* (*-nii*; *no pl*) irony; **~a losu** irony of fate; **jak na ~ę** ironically; **ironiczny** *adj* ironic

irygacja *f* (*-ji*; *no pl*) irrigation; **irygacyjny** *adj* irrigation

irys *m* (*-sa*; *-sy*) **1.** (*roślina*) iris **2.** (*cukierek*) toffee

irytacja *f* (*-ji*; *no pl*) irritation; **irytować** ⟨**po-**, **z-**⟩ (*-tuję*) irritate; **irytować się** get irritated

iskać *v/im* (*-kam*) (*o zwierzętach*) groom; **iskać się** **1.** (*o ptaku*) preen itself **2.** (*o zwierzęciu*) groom itself

iskierka *f* (*-ki*; *-ki*) *dim* spark; **~ nadziei** a flicker of hope

iskra *f* (*-ry*; *-ry*) spark; **iskrzyć** *v/im* (*-rzę*) spark; **iskrzyć się** **1.** sparkle **2.** (*o urządzeniu*) spark

islamski *adj* Islamic

Islandczyk *m* (*-ka*; *-czycy*) Icelander; **Islandia** *f* (*-dii*) Iceland; **Islandka** *f* (*-ki*; *-ki*) Icelander; **islandzki** *adj* Icelandish

istnie|ć *v/im* (*-nieję*) **1.** exist; **firma ~je od 1902 roku** the company was established in 1902; **czy ~je życie na Marsie?** is there life on Mars?; **takie pojazdy nie ~ją** no such vehicles exist **2.** (*o nadziei, możliwości, zależności*) be; **~je zależność między** there is a relationship between; **istnienie** *n* (*-nia*; *-nia*) (*życie*) existence

istn|y *adj szaleństwo*: real; **~e cudo** a real beauty

istota *f* (*-ty*; *-ty*) **1.** (*stworzenie*) creature; **~ żywa** living creature; **~ ludzka** human being **2.** (*sedno*) *lit* essence, crux; **~ rzeczy** the crux of the matter **3.** (*natura*) *lit* nature, character; **w istocie** in fact **4.** (*znaczenie*) meaning

istotnie **I** *adv* **1.** (*znacznie*) significantly **2.** (*naprawdę*) really **II** *particle* (*rzeczywiście*) indeed; **~, spotkaliśmy się** indeed, we met; **istotny** *adj* **1.** (*ważny*) important, significant **2.** (*znaczny*) significant

iść ⟨**pójść**⟩ (*idę*) **1.** go (**do** *G* to); **~ do domu** go home; **~ pieszo** walk, go on foot; **~ za kimś** follow s.o.; **~ spać** go to bed; **~ na zakupy** go shopping; **~ na koncert** go to a concert; **~ do lekarza** go to the doctor; **~ na ryby** go fishing; **~ na studia** go to university; **~ sobie** go away, leave; **~ dalej** go on; **~ w górę** go up; **~ w dół** go down; **~ na dno** (*o statku*) go down; **jak idzie?** how is it going?; **~ na coś** (*zgadzać się*) go with s.th.; **co za tym idzie** as a result, consequently; **~ na całość** go the whole hog; **~ na ustępstwa** make concessions; **~ na marne** be wasted; **nasze wysiłki nie poszły na marne** our efforts were rewarded; **~ w parze z I** *fig* go together with, go hand in hand with; **~ jak woda** *fig* sell like hot cakes **2.** (*o wiośnie, burzy*) come;

idzie wiosna spring is coming; → **chodzić**, **przychodzić**, **pójść**

itd. *abbr* (= ***i tak dalej***) etc.

itp. *abbr* (= ***i tym podobne***) etc.

izba *f* (*-by*; *-by*) **1.** (*pomieszczenie*) room; ***~ przyjęć*** admission room **2.** (*w parlamencie*) house, chamber; ***~ wyższa*** (***niższa***) upper (lower) chamber; ***≗ Gmin*** the House of Commons **3.** (*urząd*) office; ***≗ Handlowa*** Chamber of Commerce

izolacja *f* (*-ji*; *-je*) **1.** isolation **2.** TECH insulation; **izolacyjny** *adj warstwa*: insulating, insulation; **izolat|ka** *f* (*-ki*; *-ki*) **1.** (*w szpitalu*) isolation ward **2.** (*w więzieniu*) **w ~ce** in solitary confinement; **izolator** *m* (*-ra*; *-ry*) **1.** (*materiał izolujący*) insulator **2.** PHYS nonconductor

izolować (*-luję*) **1.** ⟨**od-**⟩ isolate **2.** ⟨**za-**⟩ TECH insulate; ***izolować się*** isolate oneself

Izrael *m* (*-la*) Israel; **Izraelczyk** *m* (*-ka*; *-czycy*), **-lka** *f* (*-ki*; *-ki*) Israeli; **izraelski** *adj* Israeli

iż *conj lit* that; → ***że***

J

j. *abbr* (= ***język***) language; ***j. angielski*** Eng., English

ja I *pron* I; ***to nie byłam ~*** it wasn't me **II** *n indecl* **1.** (*własna osoba*) self **2.** (*ego*) ego

jabłecznik *m* (*-ka*; *-ki*) **1.** (*ciasto*) apple cake, apple pie **2.** (*wino*) cider

jabłko *n* (*-ka*; *-ka*) apple; ***zbić na kwaśne ~*** beat to a pulp; ***niedaleko pada ~ od jabłoni*** like father, like son; the apple doesn't fall far from the apple tree

jabłonka *f* (*-ki*; *-ki*) *dim* (small) apple tree; **jabło|ń** *f* (*-łoni*; *-łonie*) apple tree; ***kwiat ~ni*** apple blossom; **jabłuszko** *n* (*-ka*; *-ka*) *dim* (small) apple

jacht *m* (*-tu*; *-ty*) yacht; **jachting** *m* (*-gu*; *no pl*) yachting

jacy → ***jaki***

jad *m* (*-du*; *-dy*) venom, poison; ***~ kiełbasiany*** botulin; ***zatrucie ~em kiełbasianym*** botulism

jadaczk|a *f* (*-ki*; *-ki*) *infml* gob; ***kłapać ~ą*** yap

jadać *v/im* (*-dam*) **1.** eat **2.** *śniadanie*, *obiad*: have; **jadalnia** *f* (*-ni*; *-nie*) **1.** (*w domu*) dining room **2.** (*sala*) dining hall; **jadalny** *adj* edible; ***pokój ~*** dining room

jadą, ***jadę*** → ***jechać***

jadł, ***jadła*** → ***jeść***

jadłodajnia *f* (*-ni*; *-nie*) eating place, *infml* eatery; **jadłospis** *m* (*-su*; *-sy*) menu; **jadłowstręt** *m* (*-tu*; *no pl*) sitophobia; ***~ psychiczny*** anorexia

jadowitość *f* (*-ści*; *no pl*) **1.** *węża*: venomousness **2.** *człowieka*: venom; **jadowity** *adj* **1.** *wąż*, *atak*: venomous **2.** *słowa*: biting; **jadow|y** *adj*: ***gruczoły ~e*** venom glands

jaglan|y *adj*: ***kasza ~a*** (whole) millet, (whole) millet groats

jagniątko *n* (*-ka*; *-ka*) *dim* (little) lamb; **jagnię** *n* (*-nięcia*; *-nięta*) lamb; **jagnięc|y** *adj* lamb; ***mięso ~e*** lamb; ***skóra ~a*** lambskin

jagoda *f* (*-dy*; *-gód*) **1.** berry; ***wilcza ~*** deadly nightshade **2.** (*czarna jagoda*) bilberry; **jagodowy** *adj* (*z czarnych jagód*) bilberry

jagodzianka *f* (*-ki*; *-ki*) bun with berries, *Am* bilberry muffin

jagódka *f* (*-ki*; *-ki*) *dim* **1.** (small) berry **2.** (small) bilberry

jaguar *m* (*-ra*; *-ry*) jaguar

jaja *pl* (*jaj*) (*jądra*) *infml* balls; ***to facet z ~mi*** he's got balls; ***robić sobie ~*** **a)** (*wygłupiać się*) fool around **b)** (*żartować*) be kidding; ***robić sobie ~ z G*** take the piss of; ***ale ~!*** *fig* what a pisser, *Br* oh, bugger!

jajcarski *adj infml* wacky; **jajcarz** *m* (*-rza*; *-rze*) *infml* joker, prankster

jajczarsk|i *adj*: ***przemysł ~o-drobiarski*** the egg and poultry industry

jajeczkowanie *n* (*-nia*; *-nia*) ovulation

jajecznica *f* (*-cy*; *-ce*) scrambled eggs

jajk|o *n* (*-ka*; *-ka*) egg; ***~o na twardo*** hard-boiled egg; ***~o na miękko*** soft-boiled egg; ***~o sadzone*** fried egg; ***~a w proszku*** dried egg; ***obchodzić***

się z kimś jak z ~iem treat s.o. with kid gloves

jajnik *m* (*-ka*; *-ki*) ovary

jajo *n* (*-ja*; *-ja*) egg; **jajogłowy** *m* (*-wego*; *-wi*) egghead

jajorodny *adj* oviparous; **jajowaty** *adj* **1.** egg-shaped **2.** *kształt*: egg(-like); ***mieć ~ kształt*** be egg-shaped; **jajow|y** *adj*: ***komórka ~a*** egg cell, egg

jak I *pron* **1.** (*w pytaniach*) how; ***~ długo?*** how long?; ***~ się masz?*** how are you?; ***~ leci?*** how's it going?; ***~ to wygląda?*** what does it look like?; ***~ mu tam*** what-d'you-call-him **2.** (*w zdaniach zależnych*) how; ***powiedz mi, ~ to zrobić*** tell me how to do it; ***nie wiem, ~ on wygląda*** I don't know what he looks like; ***zrobiłem, ~ kazałaś*** I did as you told me; ***~ gdyby*** as if; ***~ gdyby nigdy nic*** as if nothing had happened; ***w miarę ~*** as **3.** (*ekspresywnie*) how; ***~ szybko!*** how fast! **4.** (*w rozwinięciu wyrażenia*) ***~ zawsze*** as always **II** *conj* **1.** (*w porównaniach*) like; ***lekki ~ piórko*** as light as a feather; ***~ na*** for **2.** (*we wtrąceniach, dopowiedzeniach*) as; ***takie ~*** such as **3.** (*kiedy*) when; ***~ go zobaczysz, daj mi znać*** when you see him, let me know; ***~ tylko*** as soon as **4.** (*jeśli*) if; ***~ nie*** if not; ***~ nie przestaniesz, zacznę krzyczeć*** if you don't stop, I'll scream **5.** (*łączy zdania równorzędne*) ***~ i, ~ też*** and, as well as **III** *particle* ***~ najwięcej*** as much as possible; ***~ najlepszy*** the best possible; ***~ najbardziej!*** of course!; ***nic innego ~*** nothing less than; ***~ na owe czasy*** at that time; ***~ to?*** how come?; ***~ sobie chcesz*** as you like; ***~ przychodzi co do czego*** when it comes to the crunch

jakby I *conj* **1.** (*w porównaniach*) as if **2.** (*gdyby*) if **II** *particle* (***tak***) ***~*** sort of

jaki *pron* **1.** (*w pytaniach*) what?; ***w ~ sposób?*** how?; ***po ~emu oni mówią?*** what language are they speaking?; ***~m cudem*** how on earth?; ***~m prawem?*** by what right? **2.** (*w wykrzyknieniach*) ***~ piękny wieczór!*** what a beautiful night!; ***~ słodki!*** how sweet (it is)!; ***~ bądź fragment*** any fragment; ***byle ~ a)*** (*jakikolwiek*) any **b)** (*kiepski*) shoddy, trashy

jakikolwiek *pron* any; **jaki|ś** *pron* **1.** some; ***~eś dziecko*** a child; ***przez ~ś czas*** for some time; ***~ś taki*** somewhat, sort of **2.** (*około*) about **3.** (*przed przymiotnikiem*) somewhat, sort of

jakkolwiek *pron* **1.** (*bez względu na to jak*) however, no matter how **2.** (*byle jak*) anyhow **3.** (*chociaż*) although

jako I *prep* as; ***~ tako*** *infml* so-so **II** *conj* ***~ że*** because, since; **jakoby I** *particle* allegedly **II** *conj* ***nieprawdą jest, ~ było to niemożliwe*** the opinion that it is impossible is not true; **jakoś** *pron* somehow; ***~ś to będzie!*** it'll work out somehow!

jakościowo *adv* qualitatively; ***lepszy ~*** better in quality; **jakościowy** *adj* **1.** qualitative **2.** *certyfikat*: quality

jakoś|ć *f* (*-ści*; *no pl*) quality; ***produkt wysokiej ~ci*** high-quality product

jakże *adv lit* how; ***a ~!*** of course!, *infml* you bet!; ***~ się cieszę!*** I'm so happy!, how glad I am!

jałmużna *f* (*-ny*; *no pl*) alms

jałowcowy *adj* juniper; **jałowiec** *m* (*-wca*; *-wce*) juniper

jałowość *f* (*-ści*; *no pl*) **1.** *opatrunku* sterility **2.** *dyskusji*: pointlessness **3.** *ziemi*: barrenness; **jałowy** *adj* **1.** *opatrunek*: sterile **2.** *dyskusja*: pointless, arid **3.** *ziemia*: barren **4.** *bieg*: neutral

jałówka *f* (*-ki*; *-ki*) heifer

jama *f* (*-my*; *-my*) **1.** (*w ziemi*) pit; ***lisia ~*** fox hole **2.** (*jaskinia*) cave **3.** ANAT cavity

jamb *m* (*-bu*; *-by*) iamb

jamnik *m* (*-ka*; *-ki*) dachshund

jamochłon *m* (*-na*; *-ny*) coelenterate

jankes *m* (*-sa*; *-si*) **1.** *infml* Yank **2.** HIST Yankee

jantar *m* (*-ru*; *-ry*) *lit* amber

japa *f* (*-py*; *-py*) *infml* kisser, trap

Japonia *f* (*-nii*) Japan

Japonka *f* (*-ki*; *-ki*) Japanese woman

japonki *pl* (*-nek*) flip-flops, *Am* thongs

Japończycy *pl* (*-czyków*) the Japanese, Japanese people; **Japończyk** *m* (*-ka*; *-czycy*) Japanese person; ***jest ~iem*** he is Japanese; **japońsk|i** *adj* Japanese; ***mówić po ~u*** speak Japanese

jar *m* (*-ru*; *-ry*) gorge, ravine

jard *m* (*-du*/*-da*; *-dy*) yard
jarmarczny *adj* **1.** *dzień*, *kram*: market **2.** *ozdoby*: tacky; **jarmark** *m* (*-ku*; *-ki*) market
jarmuż *m* (*-żu*; *-że*) (curly) kale
jarosz *m* (*-sza*; *-sze*) vegetarian
jarski *adj* vegetarian
jary *adj jęczmień*: spring; ***stary, ale ~*** still going strong, hale and hearty
jarząb *m* (*-rzębu*; *-rzęby*): ***~ pospolity*** rowan, mountain ash; ***~ mączny*** whitebeam
jarzeniowy *adj lampa*: fluorescent; **jarzeniówka** *f* (*-ki*; *-ki*) *infml* strip light
jarzębiak *m* (*-ku*; *-ki*) rowan vodka; **jarzębina** *f* (*-ny*; *-ny*) **1.** (*drzewo*) rowan (tree) **2.** (*owoce*) rowanberries
jarzm|o *m* (*-ma*; *-ma*) yoke; ***w ~ie*** *G fig* under the yoke of
jarzyć się ⟨**roz-**⟩ (*-rzę*) glow
jarzyna *f* (*-ny*; *-ny*) vegetable; **jarzynowy** *adj* vegetable
jasełka *pl* (*-łek*) nativity play *sing*
jasiek *m* (*jaśka*; *jaśki*) (*poduszka*) small pillow
jaskier *m* (*-kra*; *-kry*) buttercup
jaskinia *f* (*-ni*; *-nie*) cave; **jaskiniowiec** *m* (*-wca*; *-wcy*) caveman; **jaskiniowy** *adj* cave; ***człowiek ~*** caveman
jaskółcz|y *adj*: ***~y ogon*** dovetail joint; ***~e ziele*** greater celandine; ***~e gniazdo*** swallow's nest; ***zupa z ~ych gniazd*** bird's-nest soup; **jaskółka** *f* (*-ki*; *-ki*) (*ptak*) swallow; ***pierwsza ~*** *fig* harbinger; ***jedna ~ nie czyni wiosny*** one swallow does not make a summer
jaskra *f* (*-ry*; *no pl*) MED glaucoma
jaskrawo- (*w złożeniach*) bright
jaskrawoczerwony *adj* bright red
jaskrawy *adj* **1.** *kolor*, *światło*: bright **2.** (*rażący oczy*) glaring **3.** *przykład*: glaring
jasno- (*w złożeniach*) light
jasno *adv* **1.** *świecić*: brightly **2.** *tłumaczyć*, *określać*: clearly; ***czy mówię ~?*** do I make myself clear? **3.** (*nie ciemno*) light; ***robiło się ~*** it was getting light; **jasnoblond** *adj* light blonde; **jasność** *f* (*-ści*; *no pl*) **1.** (*światło*) brightness **2.** *wypowiedzi*: clarity
jasnowidz *m* (*-dza*; *-dze*) clairvoyant
jasnowłosy *adj* fair-haired
jasn|y *adj* **1.** *światło*: bright; ***~e jak słońce*** (as) clear as day **2.** *kolor*: light; ***piwo ~e*** lager **3.** *włosy*: fair **4.** (*zrozumiały*, *oczywisty*) clear; ***~e!*** sure!, of course!; ***~e, że wiem*** of course I know; ***cholera ~a!*** *infml* damn it!
jastrząb *m* (*-rzębia*; *-rzębie*) hawk
jaszczur *m* (*-ra*; *-ry*) **1.** (*wymarły gad*) saurian; **jaszczurka** *f* (*-ki*; *-ki*) lizard
jaśmin *m* (*-nu*; *-ny*) jasmine
jaśnieć *v/im* (*-nieję*) **1.** (*o słońcu*) shine **2.** (*o włosach*) get lighter **3.** (*o kolorze*) fade
jaśniej *comp* → ***jasno***
jaśniejszy *comp* → ***jasny***
jatka *f* (*-ki*; *-ki*) (*rzeź*) slaughter, carnage
jaw: ***wyjść na ~*** **a)** come to light **b)** (*o kłamstwie*) be revealed; ***wydobyć na ~*** bring to light
Jawa *f* (*-wy*) Java
jaw|a *f* (*-wy*; *no pl*) **1.** (*niespanie*) waking; ***życie na ~ie*** waking life; ***śnić na ~ie*** daydream **2.** (*rzeczywistość*) reality
jawić się *v im*/*p* (*-wię*) appear (***jako*** to be)
jawnie *adv* openly; **jawn|y** *adj* **1.** *głosowanie*: open **2.** *pogarda*, *niechęć*: open, manifest **3.** *sprzeczność*: apparent; ***spółka ~a*** registered partnership
jawor *m* (*-ru*; *-ry*) sycamore
jaz *m* (*-zu*; *-zy*) weir
jazd|a *f* (*-dy*; *-dy*) **1.** (*prowadzenie samochodu*) driving; ***prawo ~y*** *Br* driving licence, *Am* driver's license; ***nauka ~y*** (*lekcje*) driving lessons; ***podczas ~y*** while driving; ***rozkład ~y*** *Br* timetable, *Am* schedule **2.** (*na rowerze*) (bicycle) riding, cycling; ***~a konna*** horse riding; ***~a na nartach*** skiing; ***~a na łyżwach*** skating; ***~a figurowa na lodzie*** figure skating; ***~a stąd!*** *infml* get out (of here)!
jazgarz *m* (*-rza*; *-rze*) ruffe
jazgot *m* (*-tu*; *no pl*) **1.** (*wrzawa*) din, racket **2.** (*gadanie*) *infml* yapping **3.** *maszyn*: rattle; **jazgotać** *v/im* (*-goczę*/*-gocę*) **1.** (*o osobie*) *infml* yap **2.** (*o maszynie*) rattle; **jazgotliwy** *adj osoba*: vociferous
jazz *m* (*-zu*; *no pl*) jazz; **jazzman** *m* (*-na*; *-ni*) jazzman; **jazzowy** *adj* jazz
jaź|ń *f* (*-źni*; *-źnie*) ego; ***rozdwojenie ~ni*** split personality

ją *pron* her; → ***ona***
jądro *n* (*-ra*; *-ra*) **1.** ~ ***komórkowe*** *BIOL* cell nucleus; ~ ***atomowe*** *PHYS* atomic nucleus **2.** *ziemi*: core **3.** *ANAT* testicle **4.** *problemu*: heart **5.** *orzecha*: kernel; **jądrow|y** *adj* nuclear; ***energia*** **~a** nuclear energy; ***elektrownia*** **~a** nuclear power station
jąkać ⟨**wy-**⟩ (*-kam*) *infml* stammer (out), stutter (out); ***jąkać się*** *v/im* stammer, stutter
jąkała *m/f* (*-ły*; *-ły*) *infml* stammerer, stutterer; **jąkanie się** *n* (*-nia*; *no pl*) stammer, stutter
jątrzyć *v/im* (*-rzę*) (*podburzać*) provoke
je[1] *pron* them; → ***one***, ***ono***
je[2] → ***jeść***
jechać ⟨**po-**⟩ (*jadę*) **1.** go (**do** *G* to); ~ ***do domu*** go home; ~ ***rowerem*** ride a bicycle, cycle; ~ ***samochodem*** go by car; ~ ***na nartach*** ski; ~ ***na łyżwach*** skate; ~ ***konno*** ride (a horse); ~ ***koleją*** go by train **2.** (*prowadzić samochód*) drive **3.** (*śmierdzieć*) *infml*: ***jechało od niego piwem*** his breath reeked of beer
jeden *num* one; ~ ***raz*** once, one time; ***jeszcze*** ~ one more; ~ ***jedyny*** just one; ~ ***jedyny raz*** one single time; ~ ***drugiego*** each other; ***uczą się*** ~ ***od drugiego*** they learn from each other; ***dni mijają*** ~ ***po drugim*** days pass one after another; ***dwa samoloty wystartowały*** ~ ***po drugim*** two planes took off one after the other; ~ ***przy drugim*** close to each other; ***sam*** ~ all alone; ***jednego dnia*** one day; ~ ***do zera*** *Br* one nil; ***ani*** ~ not a single one; ***nie widziałem ani jednego motyla*** I haven't seen a single butterfly; ***co to za*** **~?** who is he?; ***pójść na jednego*** go for a quick one; → ***jedna***, ***jedno***
jedenastka *f* (*-ki*; *-ki*) **1.** eleven **2.** (*zespół*) team **3.** (*rzut karny*) penalty
jedenastodniowy *adj* **1.** *dziecko*: eleven-day-old **2.** *urlop*: eleven-day; **jedenastolatek** *m* (*-tka*; *-tkowie*) **1.** (*dziecko*) eleven-year-old child **2.** (*chłopiec*) eleven-year-old boy; **jedenastolatka** *f* (*-ki*; *-ki*) eleven-year-old girl; **jedenastoletni** *adj* **1.** *dziecko*, *samochód*: eleven-year-old **2.** *okres*: eleven-year; **jedenastomiesięczny** *adj* *dziecko*: eleven-month-old **2.** *okres*: eleven-month; **jedenastu** *num* eleven
jedenast|y *adj* eleventh; ***godzina*** **~a** eleven o'clock; ***o*** **~*ej rano*** (***wieczorem***) at 11 a.m. (p.m.); **jedenaście** *num* eleven
jedlina *f* (*-ny*; *-ny*) **1.** (*dekoracja*) fir twigs *pl* **2.** (*drewno*) fir (wood)
jedna *f* (*-nej*; *no pl*) one; ~ ***druga*** (one) half; ~ ***trzecia*** one third; ***z jednej strony..., z drugiej strony*** on the one hand..., on the other hand; → ***jeden***
jednać ⟨**z-**⟩ (*-nam*): ~ ***sobie*** **a)** *szacunek*: earn **b)** *zwolenników*: win over; ~ ***sobie czyjąś sympatię*** win s.o. over; ***jednać się*** ⟨**po-**⟩ become reconciled
jednak *particle* but; ***a*** ~ but, and yet
jednakowo *adv* **1.** *dobry*, *korzystny*: equally **2.** *traktować*: equally **3.** *ubrany*: identically **4.** *wyglądać*: identical; **jednakowy** *adj* identical; ***w*** **~*m stopniu*** to the same extent
jednakże *particle lit* but
jedni *pl* (*-nych*) some; → ***jeden***
jedno *n* (*-nego*; *no pl*) one; ***wszystko*** ~ it doesn't matter; ***komuś jest wszystko*** ~ it is all the same to s.o.; ***jednym słowem*** in a word; (***to***) ***na*** ~ ***wychodzi*** same difference, it amounts to the same thing; → ***jeden***
jednoaktówka *f* (*-ki*; *-ki*) one-act play; **jednobarwny** *adj* *Br* one-colour, *Am* one-color; **jednobrzmiący** *adj* identical; ***w dwóch*** **~*ch egzemplarzach*** in two counterparts; **jednocyfrowy** *adj* one-digit; **jednoczesny** *adj* simultaneous; **jednocześnie** *adv* at the same time, simultaneously
jednoczyć ⟨**z-**⟩ (*-czę*) *ludzi*: unite; ***jednoczyć się*** unite
jednodaniowy *adj* one-course; **jednodniowy** *adj* **1.** *wycieczka*, *wyjazd*: one-day **2.** *niemowlę*: one-day-old
jednogłośnie *adv* unanimously
jednogodzinny *adj* *spotkanie*: one-hour; **jednoizbowy** *adj* *parlament*: unicameral
jednojajowy *adj* *bliźnięta*: identical, monozygotic; **jednojęzyczny** *adj* monolingual; **jednokierunkowy** *adj* *ulica*, *ruch*: one-way
jednokolorowy *adj* *Br* one-colour, *Am* one-color; **jednokomórkowy** *adj* unicellular, single-cell

jednokrotn|y *adj* **1.** single; ***CD ~ego zapisu*** write-once CD **2.** *uczestnik*: one-time

jednolitość *f* (*-ści*; *no pl*) uniformity, homogeneity; **jednolity** *adj* **1.** uniform, homogeneous **2.** *konsystencja*: smooth

jednomandatowy *adj*: ***okręg ~*** single-member constituancy

jednomiesięczny *adj* **1.** *okres*, *urlop*: one-month **2.** *dziecko*: one-month-old; **jednominutowy** *adj przerwa*, *spóźnienie*: one-minute

jednomyślnie *adv* unanimously; **jednomyślny** *adj* unanimous

jednonogi *adj* one-legged; **jednooki** *adj* one-eyed

jednoosobowy *adj* **1.** *pokój*, *kajak*: single **2.** *spółka*: one-person; **jednopartyjny** *adj* one-party; **jednopłatowiec** *m* (*-wca*; *-wce*) monoplane

jednopokojowy *adj* one-room

jednorazowo *adv* once; **jednorazow|y** *adj* **1.** *strzykawka*, *opakowanie*: disposable; ***~ego użytku*** disposable **2.** *bilet*: single; **jednorazówka** *f* (*-ki*; *-ki*) **1.** *strzykawka*: disposable syringe **2.** *igła*: disposable needle

jednoręki *adj* one-handed; ***~ bandyta*** one-armed bandit

jednoroczn|y *adj*: ***roślina ~a*** annual (plant); **jednorodny** *adj* homogeneous, uniform; **jednorodzinny** *adj dom*: single-family

jednorożec *m* (*-żca*; *-żce*) unicorn

jednorzędowy *adj marynarka*: single-breasted; **jednoskrzydłowy** *adj drzwi*: single

jednospadowy *adj*: ***dach ~*** pent-roof, shed roof; **jednostajny** *adj* (*monotonny*) monotonous

jednostka *f* (*-ki*; *-ki*) **1.** unit; ***~ miary*** unit of measure; ***~ wojskowa*** military unit; ***~ pływająca*** vessel; ***~ systematyczna*** BIOL taxonomic group **2.** (*osoba*) individual

jednostkowo *adv rozpatrywać*: individually; **jednostkowy** *adj* **1.** *zdarzenie*, *przypadek*: isolated **2.** *cena*: unit **3.** *doświadczenie*: individual

jednostopniowy *adj proces*, *wzmacniacz*: single-stage; **jednostronicowy** *adj pismo*: one-page; **jednostronny** *adj* **1.** *ruch*: one-way **2.** *druk*: single-sided **3.** *rozwój*: one-sided; **jednosylabowy** *adj* monosyllabic

jedność *f* (*-ści*; *no pl*) (*jednolitość*, *spójność*) unity

jednośladowy *adj* two-wheeled; **jednotomowy** *adj* single-volume; **jednotorowy** *adj kolej*: single-track

jednowymiarowy *adj* one-dimensional; **jednozłotowy** *adj* one-zloty; **jednozmianowy** *adj praca*: single-shift; **jednoznaczny** *adj* **1.** unambiguous, unequivocal **2.** *wyrazy*: synonymous

jedwab *m* (*-biu*; *-bie*) silk; **jedwabisty** *adj* silky; **jedwabnictwo** *n* (*-wa*; *no pl*) (*hodowla*) sericulture; **jedwabniczy** *adj*: ***przemysł ~*** the silk industry

jedwabnik *m* (*-ka*; *-ki*) silkworm; **jedwabny** *adj* silk

jedynaczka *f* (*-ki*; *-ki*) only child, only girl; **jedynak** *m* (*-ka*; *-nacy*) only child, only boy

jedynie *adv* only; **jedyn|ka** *f* (*-ki*; *-ki*) **1.** (*liczba*) one **2.** (*mieszkanie*, *autobus*) number one; ***mieszkać pod ~ką*** live at number one **3.** (*ocena*) fail, F **4.** AUTO first (gear); ***na ~ce*** in first **5.** (*kajak*) single kayak

jedyny *adj* **1.** only; ***~ w swoim rodzaju*** unique, one of a kind **2.** (*ukochany*) dearest

jedz, ***jedzą*** → ***jeść***

jedzenie *n* (*-nia*; *no pl*) food

jedzie, ***jedziecie***, ***jedziesz***, ***jedź*** → ***jechać***

jego *poss* **1.** (*w odniesieniu do osób*) his; ***~ świątobliwość*** His Holiness; ***~ wysokość*** His Highness; → ***on*** **2.** (*w odniesieniu do rzeczy*, *zwierząt*) its; → ***ono***

jegomość *m* (*-ścia*; *-ście*) *lit* gentleman

jej **I** *poss* **1.** (*w odniesieniu do osób*) her; ***to jest mój samochód, a to jest ~*** this is my car, and that is hers; → ***ona*** **2.** (*w odniesieniu do rzeczy*, *zwierząt*) its; → ***ona*** **II** *pron* her; ***powiedziałem ~*** I told her; → ***ona***

jeleni *adj*: ***rogi ~e*** (red) deer antlers

jeleń *m* (*-lenia*; *-lenie*) **1.** (red) deer **2.** (*frajer*) *infml* sucker

jelito *n* (*-ta*; *-ta*) intestine; ***~ grube*** large intestine; ***~ cienkie*** small intestine; ***~ proste*** rectum; ***~ ślepe*** *Br* caecum, *Am* cecum; **jelitowy** *adj* intestinal

jelonek *m* (*-nka*; *-nki*) **1.** (*młody jeleń*) fawn **2.** (*chrząszcz*) stag beetle
jełczeć ⟨**z-**⟩ (*-czeję*) go rancid
jełop *m* (*-pa*; *-py*) *infml* dork
jem → ***jeść***
jemioła *m* (*-ły*; *-ły*) mistletoe
jemu *pron* **1.** (*w odniesieniu do osoby*) him; → ***on*** **2.** (*w odniesieniu do rzeczy, zwierząt*) it; → ***ono***
jeniec *m* (*jeńca*; *jeńcy*) prisoner; ***~ wojenny*** prisoner-of-war, POW; **jeniecki** *adj* prisoner-of-war, POW; ***obóz ~*** prisoner-of-war camp, POW camp
jenot *m* (*-ta*; *-ty*) racoon dog
Jerozolima *f* (*-my*) Jerusalem
jesienny *adj* autumn, *Am* fall; **jesie|ń** *f* (*-sieni*; *-sienie*) autumn, *Am* fall; ***~nią*** in autumn, *Am* in (the) fall
jesion *m* (*-nu*; *-ny*) ash
jesionka *f* (*-ki*; *-ki*) light overcoat
jesionowy *adj* ash
jesiotr *m* (*-ra*; *-ry*) sturgeon
jest → ***być***
jesz → ***jeść***
jeszcze *particle* **1.** (*wciąż*) still **2.** (*z przeczeniem*) yet; ***~ nie*** not yet; ***~ nie przyszła*** she hasn't come yet **3.** (*ze stopniem wyższym*) even; ***~ lepszy*** even better **4.** (*ponadto*) ***coś ~?*** anything else?; ***co ~?*** what else?; ***~ raz*** once more; ***~ czego!*** no way!
jeść ⟨**z-**⟩ (*jem*) eat; ***~ śniadanie*** have breakfast; ***co jadłaś na kolację?*** what did you have for supper?; ***zjedliśmy kurczaka z ryżem*** we had chicken and rice; ***chce mi się ~*** I'm hungry; ***~ nożem i widelcem*** eat with a knife and fork; ***dać komuś ~*** feed s.o.; ***~ komuś z ręki*** *fig* eat out of s.o.'s hand
jeśli *conj* if; ***~ nie*** if not, unless; ***~ chodzi o coś*** as for s.th., as far as s.th. is concerned; ***a co ~ przegramy?*** and what if we lose?
jezdni|a *f* (*-ni*; *-nie*) road(way); ***przejść przez ~ę*** cross the road
jezior|o *n* (*-ra*; *-ra*) lake; ***nad ~em*** at the lakeside
jezuicki *adj* Jesuit; **jezuita** *m* (*-ty*; *-zuici*) Jesuit
jeździć *v/im* (*jeżdżę*) **1.** go (**do** *G* to); ***~ do domu*** go home; ***~ rowerem*** ride a bicycle, cycle; ***~ samochodem*** go by car; ***~ na nartach*** ski; ***~ na łyżwach*** skate; ***~ konno*** ride (a horse); ***~ koleją*** go by train **2.** (*prowadzić samochód*) drive **3.** (*podróżować*) travel; ***~ po świecie*** travel around the world
jeździec *m* (*-źdźca*; *-źdźcy*) rider; **jeździecki** *adj* riding; **jeździectwo** *n* (*-wa*; *no pl*) riding, *Br* horse riding, *Am* horseback riding
jeż *m* (*-ża*; *-że*) hedgehog; ***fryzura na ~a*** crew cut; ***ostrzyc się na ~a*** have a crew cut
jeżeli *conj* if; → ***jeśli***
jeżowiec *m* (*-wca*; *-wce*) sea urchin
jeżozwierz *m* (*-rza*; *-rze*) porcupine
jeżyć ⟨**na-**, **z-**⟩ (*-żę*): ***kot zjeżył sierść*** the cat bristled; ***być najeżonym trudnościami*** be fraught with difficulties; ***jeżyć się*** bristle
jeżyna *f* (*-ny*; *-ny*) blackberry
jęczeć ⟨**jęknąć**⟩ (*-czę*) **1.** moan, groan; ***~ z bólu*** moan in pain **2.** (*narzekać*) whine
jęczmienn|y *adj* barley; ***kasza ~a*** pearl barley; **jęczmień** *m* (*-mienia*; *-mienie*) **1.** (*roślina*) barley **2.** (*na powiece*) sty(e)
jędrny *adj* *owoc*, *skóra*, *pośladki*: firm
jędza *f* (*-dzy*; *-dze*) witch, hag; ***stara ~*** old hag; **jędzowaty** *adj* cantankerous
jęk *m* (*-ku*; *-ki*) moan, groan; ***~i*** moaning *sing*, groaning *sing*; **jękliwy** *adj* **1.** moaning **2.** (*żałosny*) plaintive; **jęknąć** *v/p* (*-nę*) moan, groan
jęzor *m* (*-ra*; *-ry*) tongue; ***~ lodowca*** glacier tongue
języczek *m* (*-czka*; *-czki*) **1.** *dim* tongue **2.** *ANAT* uvula **3.** (*u wagi*) pointer
język *m* (*-ka*; *-ki*) **1.** tongue; ***wystawić ~*** stick one's tongue out; ***mleć ~iem*** *infml* yap; ***mam to na końcu ~a*** it's on the tip of my tongue; ***ugryźć się w ~*** *fig* bite one's tongue; ***mieć długi ~*** *fig* have a loose tongue; ***mieć wspólny ~*** *fig* speak the same language; ***~i ognia*** tongues of fire **2.** (*mowa*) language; ***~ angielski*** English, the English language; ***~ ojczysty*** mother tongue; ***kaleczyć ~ polski*** (***angielski***) speak (in) broken Polish (English); ***zasięgnąć ~a*** enquire, *Am* inquire
językow|y *adj* **1.** *szkoła*, *kurs*: language; ***zdolności ~e*** a gift for languages; ***umiejętności ~e*** language skills **2.** *normy*: linguistic **3.** *mięśnie*:

J

tongue; **językoznawstwo** *n* (*-wa; no pl*) linguistics
jidysz *m indecl* Yiddish
jod *m* (*-du; no pl*) CHEM iodine
jodełk|a *f* (*-ki; -ki*): ***w ~ę*** herringbone
jodła *f* (*-ły; -ły*) fir; **jodłować** *v/im* (*-łuję*) yodel; **jodłowy** *adj* fir
jodowan|y *adj sól*: iodized
jodyn|a *f* (*-ny; no pl*) (tincture of) iodine
joga *f* (*-gi; no pl*) Joga
jogging *m* (*-gu; no pl*) jogging
jogurt *m* (*-tu; -ty*) yog(h)urt
jon *m* (*-nu; -ny*) ion; **jonizacja** *f* (*-ji; no pl*) ionization; **jonizować** ⟨**z-**⟩ (*-zuję*) ionize
Jońsk|i *adj*: ***Morze ~e*** the Ionian Sea
joński *adj* Ionic
Jordania *f* (*nii*) Jordan; **jordański** *adj* Jordanian
jot|a: ***co do ~y*** *wypełnić polecenie, spełnić się*: to the letter
Jowisz *m* (*-sza*) ASTR Jupiter
joystick *m* (*-ka; -ki*) joystick
jubilat *m* (*-ta; -laci*), **~ka** *f* (*-ki; -ki*) *person celebrating a birthday or anniversary*
jubiler *m* (*-ra; -rzy*), **~ka** *f* (*-ki; -ki*) jeweller, *Am* jeweler; ***u ~a*** *Br* at the jeweller's, *Am* at the jeweler's; **jubilerski** *adj* jeweller's, *Am* jeweler's; ***wyroby ~e*** jewellery, *Am* jewelery; **jubilerstwo** *n* (*-wa; no pl*) **1.** *Br* jewellery making, *Am* jewelery making **2.** (*usługi*) **złotnictwo i ~** *Br* goldsmiths and jewellers, *Am* goldsmiths and jewelers
jubileusz *m* (*-szu; -sze*) jubilee, anniversary; **jubileuszowy** *adj* jubilee, anniversary
juczn|y *adj* pack; ***zwierzę ~e*** pack animal, beast of burden
judaizm *m* (*-mu; no pl*) Judaism
Judasz *m* (*-sza; -sze*) **1.** Judas **2.** *~* (*w drzwiach*) peephole
judo *n indecl* judo; **judoka** *m* (*-ki; -docy*), **-doczka** *f* (*-ki; -ki*) judoka, judo player
judzić *v/im* (*-dzę*) stir up, incite
Jugosławia *f* (*-wii*) Jugoslavia; **Jugosłowianin** *m* (*-na; -wianie*) **-wianka** *f* (*-ki; -ka*) Yugoslav, Yugoslavian
juhas *m* (*-sa; -si*) *shepherd in the Tatra Mountains*
junior *m* (*-ra; -rzy*), **~ka** *f* (*-ki; -ki*) junior; ***zawody ~ów*** junior competition
jurajski *adj* Jurassic
jurny *adj* virile
juror *m* (*-ra; -rzy*), **~ka** *f* (*-ki; -ki*) juror
jurta *f* (*-ty; -ty*) yurt
jurysdykcja *f* (*-ji; no pl*) jurisdiction
justować ⟨**wy-**⟩ (*-tuję*) INF justify
juta *f* (*-ty; -ty*) jute
Jutlandia *f* (*-dii*) Jutland
jutowy *adj* jute
jutr|o I *adv* tomorrow; ***~o wieczorem*** tommorow night **II** *n* (*-ra; no pl*) tomorrow; ***do ~a!*** see you tomorrow!; **jutrzejszy** *adj* tomorrow's; ***dzień ~*** tomorrow
jutrzenka *f* (*-ki; -ki*) (*świt*) daybreak, dawn
juwenalia *pl* (*-liów*) *annual student festival with street events and parades*
już *adv* **1.** (*w zdaniach twierdzących*) already; ***~ skończyłem*** I've already finished; ***~ nie*** no longer; ***~ nigdy*** never again; ***~ w roku 1960*** as far back as 1960; ***powinnaś ~ iść*** you'd better go now; ***~ po wszystkim*** it's all over; ***~ miała wyjść, gdy*** she was about to leave when **2.** (*w pytaniach*) yet; ***czy ~ to słyszałaś?*** have you heard it yet?; ***i ~!*** and that's that!
jw. *abbr* (= ***jak wyżej***) ditto, as above

K

k. *abbr* (= ***koło***) near
kabaczek *m* (*-czka; -czki*) *Br* marrow, *Am* (marrow) squash
kabał|a *f* (*-ły; -ły*) REL Kabbalah; ***wpakować się w ~ę*** get into a (fine) mess
kabanos *m* (*-sa; -sy*) kabanos (sausage)
kabaret *m* (*-tu; -ty*) cabaret; **kabaretowy** *adj* cabaret; **kabaretki** *pl* (*-tek*) fishnet stockings
kabel *m* (*-bla; -ble*) cabel
kabina *f* (*-ny; -ny*) **1.** *kierowcy*: cab **2.** *prysznicowa*: cubicle **3.** (*przymierzalnia*) (fitting) room **4.** (*pilota, na statku*) cabin **5.** *telefoniczna*: booth

kablować *v/im* (*-luję*) (*donosić*) *infml* snitch; **kablow|y** *adj*: ***telewizja ~a*** cable television, cable TV
kabłąk *m* (*-ka*; *-ki*) bow; ***zgięty w ~*** with one's back arched
kabotyn *m* (*-na*; *-ni*) poseur, poser
kabriolet *m* (*-tu*; *-ty*) convertible
kabura *f* (*-ry*; *-ry*) holster
kabz|a: ***nabić sobie ~ę*** *infml* line one's pockets
kac *m* (*-ca*; *-ce*) *infml* hangover; ***mieć ~a*** have a hangover
kaczan *m* (*-na*; *-ny*) **1.** (*głąb kapusty*) stump **2.** (*kolba kukurydzy*) cob
kaczątko *n* (*-ka*; *-ka*) duckling
kaczeniec *m* (*-czeńca*; *-czeńce*) marsh marigold, *Br* kingcup
kaczk|a *f* (*-ki*; *-ki*) duck; ***~a dziennikarska*** *fig* canard; ***puszczać ~i*** play ducks and drakes; **kaczor** *m* (*-ra*; *-ry*) drake; **kaczy** *adj* duck; ***~ chód*** waddle

K

kadencja *f* (*-ji*; *-je*) **1.** term **2.** MUS cadence
kadłub *m* (*-ba*; *-by*) **1.** *statku*: hull **2.** *samolotu*: fuselage **3.** (*tułów*) trunk
kadr *m* (*-ru*; *-ry*) frame
kadra *f* (*-ry*; *-ry*) **1.** (*pracownicy*) personnel, staff **2.** (*zespół*) team; ***~ kierownicza*** management (team) **3.** (*wojskowi*) cadre
kadrowicz *m* (*-cza*; *-cze*) SPORT national team member; **kadrowy** *adj zmiany*, *polityka*: staff, personnel
kadry *pl* (*kadr*) personnel *sing*, human resources
kadzić *v/im* (*-dzę*) **1.** incense **2.** (*chwalić*) *infml* butter up; **kadzidło** *n* (*-ła*; *-ła*) incense
kadź *f* (*-dzi*; *-dzie*) vat
kafar *m* (*-ra*; *-ry*) piledriver
kafejka *f* (*-ki*; *-ki*) cafe, café
kafel *m* (*-fla*; *-fle*) tile
kafeteria *f* (*-rii*; *-rie*) cafeteria
kaflowy *adj*: ***piec ~*** tiled stove
kaftan *m* (*-na*; *-ny*) (*ubranie*) smock; ***~ bezpieczeństwa*** straitjacket; **kaftanik** *m* (*-ka*; *-ki*) baby jacket
kaganek *m* (*-nka*; *-nki*) oil-lamp
kaganiec *m* (*-gańca*; *-gańce*) muzzle
Kair *m* (*-ru*) Cairo
kajak *m* (*-ka*; *-ki*) kayak, *Br* canoe; **kajakarstwo** *n* (*-wa*; *no pl*) kayaking, *Br* canoeing; **kajakarz** *m* (*-rza*; *-rze*) kayaker, *Br* canoeist; **kajakowy** *adj*: ***spływ ~*** kayaking trip
kajdanki *pl* (*-nek*/*-ków*) handcuffs; ***założyć ~*** handcuff; **kajdany** *pl* (*-nów*/*-dan*) irons
kajtek *m* (*-tka*; *-tki*) *infml* kid
kajuta *f* (*-ty*; *-ty*) cabin
kajzerka *f* (*-ki*; *-ki*) Kaiser roll
kakao *n indecl* cocoa; **kakaowiec** *m* (*-wca*; *-wce*) cacao (cocoa) tree; **kakaowy** *adj* cocoa
kaktus *m* (*-sa*; *-sy*) cactus
kalać ⟨**po-**⟩ (*-lam*) *lit honor*, *dobre imię*: sully
kalafior *m* (*-ra*; *-ry*) cauliflower; **kalafiorowy** *adj* cauliflower
kalambur *m* (*-ru*; *-ry*) pun
kalarepa *f* (*-py*; *-py*) kohlrabi
kalcyt *m* (*-tu*; *-ty*) calcite
kalectwo *n* (*-wa*; *-wa*) disability
kaleczyć ⟨**s-**⟩ (*-czę*) cut; ***kaleczyć się*** cut oneself; ***~ się w rękę*** cut one's hand
kalejdoskop *m* (*-pu*; *-py*) kaleidoscope
kaleka *m*/*f* (*-ki*; *-ki*) cripple; ***~ życiowy*** failure; **kaleki** *adj osoba*: crippled
kalendarz *m* (*-rza*; *-rze*) calendar; **kalendarzowy** *adj* calendar; **kalendarzyk** *m* (*-ka*; *-ki*) *Br* diary, *Am* datebook; ***~ małżeński*** the rhythm method
kalenica *f* (*-cy*; *-ce*) (roof) ridge
kalesony *pl* (*-nów*) drawers, *infml* long johns
kaletnictwo *n* (*-wa*; *no pl*) leatherworking; **kaletnik** *m* (*-ka*; *-nicy*) leatherworker
kalib|er *m* (*-bru*; *-bry*) *Br* calibre, *Am* caliber; ***dużego ~ru*** large-calibre; ***wielkiego ~ru*** (*o człowieku*) of great distinction, distinguished
kaligrafia *f* (*-fii*; *no pl*) calligraphy; **kaligrafować** ⟨**wy-**⟩ (*-fuję*) calligraph
kalina *f* (*-ny*; *-ny*) (*koralowa*) guelder rose
kalka *f* (*-ki*; *-ki*) **1.** (*techniczna*) tracing paper **2.** (*maszynowa*) carbon paper **3.** (*językowa*) calque, loan translation; **kalkomania** *f* (*-nii*; *-nie*) *Br* transfer, *Am* decal; **kalkować** ⟨**prze-**⟩ (*-kuję*) **1.** copy **2.** (*za pomocą kalki technicznej*) trace
kalkulacja *f* (*-ji*; *-je*) calculation; **kalkulacyjny** *adj* calculation; ***arkusz ~***

spreadsheet; **kalkulator** *m* (*-ra*; *-ry*) calculator

kalkulować ⟨**s-**⟩ (*-luję*) calculate; ***kalkulować się*** *infml* be worthwhile

kaloria *f* (*-rii*; *-rie*) calorie; **kaloryczność** *f* (*-ści*; *no pl*) calorific value; **kaloryczny** *adj* calorific

kaloryfer *m* (*-ra*; *-ry*) radiator

kalosz *m* (*-sza*; *-sze*) *Br* wellington, *Am* rubber boot

kalwinizm *m* (*-mu*; *no pl*) Calvinism; **kalwiński** *adj* Calvinist

kał *m* (*-łu*; *no pl*) excrement, *Br* faeces *pl*, *Am* feces *pl*

kałamarnica *f* (*-cy*; *-ce*) squid

kałamarz *m* (*-rza*; *-rze*) ink bottle, inkwell

kałuża *f* (*-ży*; *-że*) puddle, pool; ***~ krwi*** pool of blood

Kambodża *f* (*-dży*) Cambodia

kambr *m* (*-ru*; *no pl*) GEOL the Cambrian

kamea *f* (*-mei*; *-mee*) camellia

kameleon *m* (*-na*; *-ny*) chameleon

kamera *f* (*-ry*; *-ry*) (film) camera; ***~ wideo*** video camera, camcorder

kameralny *adj* **1.** *muzyka*, *orkiestra*: chamber **2.** *nastrój*, *grono*: intimate **3.** *teatr*: studio

kamerdyner *m* (*-ra*; *-rzy*) butler

kamerton *m* (*-nu*; *-ny*) tuning fork

kamerzysta *m* (*-ty*; *-ryści*) cameraman; **kamerzystka** *f* (*-ki*; *-ki*) camerawoman

kamfora *f* (*-ry*; *no pl*) camphor; ***zniknąć jak ~*** *fig* vanish into thin air; **kamforowy** *adj*: ***olejek ~*** camphor oil

kamica *f* (*-cy*; *no pl*): ***~ nerkowa*** MED nephrolithiasis; ***~ żółciowa*** MED cholelithiasis

kamieniarstwo *n* (*-wa*; *no pl*) masonry; **kamieniarz** *m* (*-rza*; *-rze*) (stone) mason

kamienica *f* (*-cy*; *-ce*) tenement (building); **kamienicznik** *m* (*-ka*; *-nicy*) tenement owner

kamienieć ⟨**s-**⟩ (*-nieję*) **1.** (*twardnieć*) fossilize **2.** (*nieruchomieć*) petrify

kamieniołom *m* (*-mu*; *-my*) quarry

kamienisty *adj plaża*, *droga*: stony

kamienn|y *adj* **1.** stone; ***~a posadzka*** stone floor; ***~e serce*** heart of stone; ***epoka ~a*** the Stone Age; ***zachowywać ~y spokój*** keep a cool head **2.** *cisza*: stony **3.** *węgiel*: hard

kamienować ⟨**u-**⟩ (*-nuję*) stone (to death)

kamień *m* (*-mienia*; *-mienie*) **1.** stone; ***~ szlachetny*** precious stone; ***~ węgielny*** cornerstone; ***~ nazębny***, ***~ kotłowy*** scale; ***~ żółciowy*** gallstone; ***~ milowy*** milestone; ***~ spadł mi z serca*** it was a weight of my mind; ***przepaść jak ~ w wodę*** disappear into thin air; ***być kamieniem u szyi*** be a millstone around s.o.'s neck, *infml* be a drag **2.** (*w zapalniczce*) flint

kamikadze *m indecl* kamikaze

kamionka *f* (*-ki*; *-ki*) **1.** (*naczynia*) stoneware **2.** (*glina*) stoneware clay; **kamionkowy** *adj* stoneware

kamizelka *f* (*-ki*; *-ki*) *Br* waistcoat, *Am* vest; ***~ ratunkowa*** life jacket; ***~ kuloodporna*** bullet-proof vest

kampania *f* (*-nii*; *-nie*) campaign; ***prowadzić kampanię*** campaign (***na rzecz*** *G* for; ***przeciwko*** *D* against)

kamuflaż *m* (*-żu*; *-że*) camouflage; **kamuflować** ⟨**za-**⟩ (*-luję*) camouflage; ***kamuflować się*** camouflage (oneself)

kamyczek *m* (*-czka*; *-czki*) **1.** (little) stone **2.** (*otoczak*) pebble; **kamyk** *m* (*-ka*; *-ki*) **1.** stone **2.** (*otoczak*) pebble

Kanadyjczyk *m* (*-ka*; *-czycy*), **-jka** *f* (*-ki*; *-ki*) Canadian; ***jest ~iem*** he is (a) Canadian; **kanadyjka** *f* (*-ki*; *-ki*) (*łódź*) open canoe, Canadian; **kanadyjski** *adj* Canadian

kanalia *f* (*-lii*; *-lie*) scoundrel

kanalik *m* (*-ka*; *-ki*): ***~i łzowe*** tear ducts

kanalizacja *f* (*-ji*; *no pl*) drainage (and sewage) system; **kanalizacyjny** *adj sieć*, *rura*: drainage, sewage

kanalizować ⟨**s-**⟩ (*-zuję*) **1.** to install a sewage system **2.** *fig* channel

kanał *m* (*-łu*; *-ły*) **1.** (*droga wodna*) canal; ***≈ Sueski*** the Suez Canal **2.** (*rów*) channel, canal; ***~ irygacyjny*** irrigation channel, irrigation canal **3.** *telewizyjny*: channel **4.** (*przewód*) duct; ***~ wentylacyjny*** ventilation duct **5.** ***~ ściekowy*** BUILD sewer **6.** (*cieśnina morska*) channel; ***≈ La Manche*** the English Channel **7.** ***~ remontowy*** AUTO inspection pit **8.** (*dla orkiestry*) (orchestra) pit; **kanałowy** *adj leczenie*: root-canal

K

kanapa *f* (*-py*; *-py*) sofa, couch
kanapka *f* (*-ki*; *-ki*) **1.** (*z dwóch kromek*) sandwich **2.** (*z jednej kromki*) canapé
kanar *m* (*-ra*; *-ry*) *infml* ticket inspector; **kanarek** *m* (*-rka*; *-rki*) canary; **kanarkowy** *adj* canary-yellow; ***kolor ~*** canary yellow
Kanaryjski *adj*: ***Wyspy ~e*** the Canary Islands
kancelaria *f* (*-rii*; *-rie*) office; ***~ adwokacka*** legal office; ***~ prezydenta*** president's office; **kancelaryjny** *adj praca*: office; ***papier ~*** A3
kanciarz *m* (*-rza*; *-rze*) *infml* trickster, swindler
kanciasty *adj* **1.** angular **2.** *ruchy*: awkward, stiff
kanclerz *m* (*-rza*; *-rze*) chancellor
kandelabr *m* (*-ru*/*-ra*; *-ry*) candelabra
kandydat *m* (*-ta*; *-daci*), **~ka** *f* (*-ki*; *-ki*) candidate (**na** *A*/**do** *G* for); ***~ do tytułu*** contender for a title; ***~ do pracy*** job applicant; ***~ na studia*** university applicant; ***~ na prezydenta*** presidential candidate
kandydatur|a *f* (*-ry*; *-ry*) candidacy; ***wysunąć czyjąś ~ę na prezydenta*** nominate s.o. for presidency; **kandydować** *v/im* (*-duję*) be a candidate (**na** *A* for); ***~ na prezydenta*** run for presidency
kandyzowany *adj owoce*: candied
kangur *m* (*-ra*; *-ry*) kangaroo
kania *f* (*-ni*; *-nie*) **1.** (*grzyb*) parasol mushroom **2.** (*ptak*) kite
kanibal *m* (*-la*; *-le*) cannibal; **kanibalizm** *m* (*-mu*; *no pl*) cannibalism
kanister *m* (*-tra*; *-try*) (*na benzynę*) jerrycan, petrol can
kanka *f* (*-ki*; *-ki*) (small) milk can
kanon *m* (*-nu*; *-ny*) canon
kanonada *f* (*-dy*; *-dy*) cannonade
kanoniczn|y *adj* canonical; ***prawo ~e*** REL canon law
kanonier *m* (*-ra*; *-rzy*) gunner; **kanonierka** *f* (*-ki*; *-ki*) gunboat
kanonik *m* (*-ka*; *-nicy*) canon
kanonizować *v im*/*p* (*-zuję*) canonize
kant *m* (*-tu*; *-ty*) **1.** edge **2.** *spodni*: crease **3.** (*oszustwo*) *infml* con, trick
kantor[1] *m* (*-ru*; *-ry*): ***~ wymiany walut*** (foreign) exchange office; bureau de change
kantor[2] *m* (*-ra*; *-rzy*) (*śpiewak*) cantor
kantować ⟨**o-**⟩ (*-tuję*) *infml* cheat, trick
kantyna *f* (*-ny*; *-ny*) canteen
kanw|a *f* (*-wy*; *-wy*) (*tło*) foundation; ***powstać na ~ie*** *G* be based on
kapa *f* (*-py*; *-py*) **1.** (*na łóżko*) bedspread **2.** REL cope
kapać ⟨**-pnąć**⟩ (*-pię*) drip
kapary *pl* (*-rów*) capers
kapcanieć ⟨**s-**⟩ (*-nieję*) *infml* go downhill, *Br* lose vigour, *Am* lose vigor
kapeć *m* (*-pcia*; *-pcie*) slipper
kapela *f* (*-li*; *-le*) **1.** folk group **2.** (*zespół młodzieżowy*) *infml* band
kapelan *m* (*-na*; *-ni*) chaplain
kapelmistrz *m* (*-rza*; *-rze*/*-rzowie*) bandmaster
kapelusik *m* (*-ka*; *-ki*) *dim* (small) hat; **kapelusz** *m* (*-sza*; *-sze*) **1.** hat **2.** *grzyba*: cap; **kapelusznik** *m* (*-ka*; *-nicy*) hatter
kapilarny *adj naczynie*: capillary
kapiszon *m* (*-na*; *-ny*) (*do pistoletu zabawki*) cap
kapitalik *m* (*-ku*; *-ki*) (*czcionka*) small capital
kapitalista *m* (*-ty*; *-liści*), **-tka** *f* (*-ki*; *-ki*) capitalist; **kapitalistyczny** *adj* capitalist
kapitalny *adj* capital; ***remont ~*** **a)** *maszyny*: complete overhaul **b)** BUILD complete renovation
kapitał *m* (*-łu*; *-ły*) capital; ***~ początkowy*** initial capital, start-up capital; ***~ podstawowy***, ***~ zakładowy*** share capital; ***~ własny*** equity; **kapitałow|y** *adj* capital; ***inwestycje ~e*** capital investment
kapitan *m* (*-na*; *-nowie*) captain; **kapitanat** *m* (*-tu*; *-ty*) (*kierownictwo portu*) port authority; **kapitański** *adj* captain; ***mostek ~*** (the) bridge
kapitel *m* (*-lu*; *-le*) capital
kapitulacja *f* (*-ji*; *-je*) capitulation, surrender; ***bezwarunkowa ~*** unconditional surrender
kapitularz *m* (*-rza*; *-rze*) (*w klasztorze*) chapter room
kapitulować ⟨**s-**⟩ (*-luję*) **1.** capitulate (**przed** *I* to) **2.** *fig* give up
kapituła *f* (*-ły*; *-ły*) REL chapter
kaplica *f* (*-cy*; *-ce*) chapel; **kapliczka** *f* (*-ki*; *-ki*): ***~ przydrożna*** roadside shrine

kapłan *m* (*-na*; *-ni*) priest; **kapłanka** *f* (*-ki*; *-ki*) priestess; **kapłański** *adj* priestly; ***święcenia ~e*** ordination; ***otrzymać święcenia ~e*** be ordained

kapnąć *v/p* (*-nę*) drip; ***kapnąć się*** *infml* get (it), *Br* twig

kapok *m* (*-ka*; *-ki*) life jacket, *Am* life vest

kapota *f* (*-ty*; *-ty*) *infml* coat

kapotaż *m* (*-żu*; *-że*) *samolotu*: nose-over

kapować (*-puję*) *infml* **1.** ⟨**za-**⟩ (*donosić w szkole*) snitch **2.** ⟨**za-**⟩ (*donosić policji*) squeal, *Br* grass **3.** ⟨**s-**, **za-**⟩ (*rozumieć*) *infml* get (it); ***kapuję*** I get it

kapral *m* (*-la*; *-le*) corporal

kaprys *m* (*-su*; *-sy*) **1.** whim **2.** MUS capriccio; **kaprysić** *v/im* (*-szę*) **1.** (*grymasić*) be fussy **2.** (*dąsać się*) sulk; **kapryśny** *adj* **1.** capricious **2.** (*wybredny*) fussy **3.** (*humorzasty*) moody **4.** *pogoda*: unpredictable, capricious

kapsel *m* (*-sla*; *-sle*) (crown) cap

kapsuła *f* (*-ły*; *-ły*), ***kapsułka*** *f* (*-ki*; *-ki*) capsule

Kapsztad *m* (*-du*) Cape Town

kaptować ⟨**s-**⟩ (*-tuję*) win over

kaptur *m* (*-ra*; *-ry*) hood; ***bluza z ~em*** hooded jacket; **kapturek** *m* (*-rka*; *-rki*) *dim* hood; ***~ dopochwowy*** diaphragm, *Br* cap; ***Czerwony* ≈** Little Red Riding Hood

kapucyn *m* (*-na*; *-ni*) Capuchin (Friar)

kapusta *f* (*-ty*; *-ty*) cabbage; ***~ włoska*** kale; ***kiszona ~*** sauerkraut

kapuś *m* (*-pusia*; *-pusie*) *infml* **1.** squealer, *Br* grass **2.** (*w szkole*) snitch

kapuściany *adj* cabbage; ***głąb ~*** *fig* dimwit; **kapuśniaczek** *m* (*-czku*; *no pl*) (*deszcz*) drizzle; **kapuśniak** *m* (*-ku*; *-ki*) **1.** (*zupa*) cabbage soup **2.** (*deszcz*) drizzle

kar|a *f* (*-ry*; *-ry*) **1.** punishment (**za** *A* for); ***za ~ę*** as a punishment **2.** (*za wykroczenie, przestępstwo*) penalty; ***~a grzywny*** fine; ***~a pozbawienia wolności***, ***~a więzienia*** imprisonment, prison sentence; ***~a śmierci*** capital punishment, death penalty; ***podlegać ~ze więzienia*** be punishable with imprisonment; ***skazać kogoś na ~ę więzienia*** give s.o. a prison sentence

karabela *f* (*-li*; *-le*) karabela sabre

karabin *m* (*-nu*; *-ny*) rifle; ***~ maszynowy*** machine gun; **karabinek** *m* (*-nka*; *-nki*) **1.** (*karabin*) carbine **2.** (*haczyk*) snap-hook; **karabinowy** *adj* **1.** rifle **2.** (*dotyczący karabinu maszynowego*) machine-gun

karać ⟨**u-**⟩ (*-ram*) punish (**za** *A* for); ***~ grzywną*** fine

karafka *f* (*-ki*; *-ki*) decanter

karaibski *adj* Caribbean; ***Wyspy* ≈*e*** the Caribbean Islands

karakuły *pl* (*-łów*) (*futro*) Persian lamb *sing*

karalność *f* (*-ści*; *no pl*) punishability; ***zapytanie o ~*** request for a criminal record; **karalny** *adj* punishable; ***czyn ~*** punishable offence

karaluch *m* (*-cha*; *-chy*) cockroach

karambol *m* (*-lu*; *-le*) **1.** (*wypadek*) pile-up, multiple crash **2.** (*gra*) carom billiards

karany *adj* with a criminal record; ***był ~*** he has a criminal record

karaś *m* (*-rasia*; *-rasie*) crucian (carp)

karawan *m* (*-nu*; *-ny*) hearse

karawana *f* (*-ny*; *-ny*) caravan

karb *m* (*-bu*; *-by*): ***kłaść coś na ~*** *G* put s.th. down to; ***trzymać kogoś w ~ach*** keep s.o. under control; ***wziąć kogoś w ~y*** bring s.o. under control

karbid *m* (*-du*; *no pl*) carbide; **karbidówka** *f* (*-ki*; *-ki*) carbide lamp

karbon *m* (*-nu*; *no pl*) GEOL the Carboniferous

karbować *v/im* (*-buję*) **1.** *blachę*: corrugate **2.** *włosy*: wave; **karbowany** *adj* **1.** *blacha*: corrugated **2.** *włosy*: wavy

karcąco *adv spojrzeć*: reproachfully

karciany *adj* card; **karciarz** *m* (*-rza*; *-rze*) (avid) card player

karcić ⟨**s-**⟩ (*-rcę*) scold, rebuke

karczek *m* (*-czku*; *-czki*) **1.** neck **2.** *sukienki*, *koszuli*: yoke

karczemn|y *adj*: ***~a awantura*** mighty row; **karczma** *f* (*-my*; *-my*) inn; **karczmarz** *m* (*-rza*; *-rze*) innkeeper

karczoch *m* (*-cha*; *-chy*) (globe) artichoke

karczować ⟨**wy-**⟩ (*-czuję*) *las*: clear

kardiochirurg *m* (*-ga*; *-rdzy*) cardiac surgeon, heart surgeon; **kardiochirurgia** *f* (*-gii*; *no pl*) cardiac surgery, heart surgery

kardiogram *m* (*-mu*; *-my*) cardiogram; **kardiolog** *m* (*-ga*; *-lodzy*) cardiologist; **kardiostymulator** *m* (*-ra*; *-ry*) pacemaker

kardynalny *adj* cardinal; **~ błąd** cardinal error

kardynał *m* (*-ła*; *-łowie*) cardinal

karencja *f* (*-ji*; *no pl*) **1.** grace **2.** (*w spłacie kredytu*) grace period **3.** (*w ubezpieczeniach*) waiting period

kareta *f* (*-ty*; *-ty*) **1.** *HIST* coach **2.** (*w pokerze*) four of a kind; **karetka** *f* (*-ki*; *-ki*) **1.** ***~ pogotowia*** ambulance **2.** *TECH* carriage

kariatyda *f* (*-dy*; *-dy*) *ARCHIT* caryatid

karier|a *f* (*-ry*; *-ry*) **1.** (*przebieg pracy*) career **2.** (*sukces*) successful career; ***zrobić ~ę jako*** *N* be successful as; **karierowicz** *m* (*-cza*; *-cze*), **~ka** *f* (*-ki*; *-ki*) careerist

karimata *f* (*-ty*; *-ty*) (foam) sleeping mat

kark *m* (*-ku*; *-ki*) nape (of the neck), neck; ***skręcić ~*** break one's neck; ***mieć głowę na ~u*** have one's head screwed on (the right way); ***pędzić na złamanie ~u*** rush headlong; ***mieć czterdziestkę na ~u*** be in one's forties; **karkołomny** *adj* **1.** *akrobacje*: daredevil **2.** *tempo*: breakneck

karkówka *f* (*-ki*; *-ki*) *COOK* neck

karlica *f* (*-cy*; *-ce*) (female) dwarf, (female) midget

karłowacieć ⟨**s-**⟩ (*-cieję*) become dwarfed; **karłowaty** *adj* dwarf

karły *pl* → ***karzeł***

karma[1] *f* (*-my*; *no pl*) (*pasza*) (animal) fodder

karma[2] *f* (*-my*; *-my*) *REL* karma

karmazyn *m* **1.** (*-nu*; *no pl*) (*kolor*) scarlet, crimson **2.** (*-na*; *-ny*) (*ryba*) Norway haddock; **karmazynowy** *adj* scarlet, crimson

karmel *m* (*-lu*; *no pl*) caramel; **karmelek** *m* (*-lka*; *-lki*) caramel

karmelicki *adj* Carmelite; **karmelita** *m* (*-ty*; *-lici*), **~nka** *f* (*-ki*; *-ki*) Carmelite

karmelkowy *adj* caramel

karmiący *adj matka*: breastfeeding

karmić ⟨**na-**⟩ (*-mię*) feed; ***~ piersią*** breastfeed; **karmienie** *n* (*-nia*; *-nia*) feeding; ***~ piersią*** breastfeeding

karmin *m* (*-nu*; *no pl*) carmine; **karminowy** *adj* carmine

karmnik *m* (*-ka*; *-ki*) **1.** (*deseczka*) bird table (feeder) **2.** (*skrzynka*) feeding box

karnacja *f* (*-ji*; *no pl*) complexion

karnawał *m* (*-łu*; *-ły*) carnival; **karnawałowy** *adj* carnival

karnet *m* (*-tu*; *-ty*) season ticket, pass

karniak *m* (*-ka*; *-ki*) *infml* **1.** *SPORT* penalty **2.** (*wódka*) penalty drink (*given to latecomers to the party*)

karnie *adv* in a disciplined way

karnisz *m* (*-sza*; *-sze*) curtain track, curtain pole

karność *f* (*-ści*; *no pl*) discipline

karny I *adj* **1.** *odpowiedzialność*, *prawo*, *kodeks*: criminal **2.** *obóz*: penal **3.** *SPORT* penalty; ***rzut ~*** penalty (shot) **4.** (*posłuszny*) disciplined **II** *m* (*-nego*; *-ne*) *SPORT* penalty

karo *n* (*-ra*; *-ra*) **1.** (*kolor w kartach*) diamonds *pl*; ***as ~*** ace of diamonds **2.** (*karta*) diamond **3.** (*dekolt*) square-cut neckline

karoca *f* (*-cy*; *-ce*) coach

karoseria *f* (*-rii*; *-rie*) body(work)

karoten *m* (*-nu*; *no pl*) carotene

karp *m* (*-pia*; *-pie*) carp

kart|a *f* (*-ty*; *-ty*) **1.** card; ***~a kredytowa*** credit card; ***~a telefoniczna*** phone card; ***~a pocztowa*** postcard; ***~a tytułowa*** title page; ***~a wstępu*** admission ticket; ***~a członkowska*** membership card; ***~a rejestracyjna*** *AUTO* (vehicle) registration certificate; ***~a informacyjna*** reference card; ***Ꞩa ONZ*** the UN Charter; ***grać w ~y*** play cards; ***grać w otwarte ~y*** *fig* lay one's cards on the table; ***postawić wszystko na jedną ~ę*** go for broke *infml* **2.** (*menu*) menu; ***z ~y*** à la carte

Kartagina *f* (*-ny*) Carthage

karteczka *f* (*-ki*; *-ki*) *dim* slip of paper

kartel *m* (*-lu*; *-le*) cartel

kartka *f* (*-ki*; *-ki*) **1.** ***~ (papieru)*** sheet (of paper); ***~ pocztowa*** postcard; ***~ urodzinowa*** birthday card; ***~ z życzeniami*** greetings card; ***~ kalendarza*** calendar page; ***~ żywnościowa*** (food) ration card; ***żółta ~*** *SPORT* yellow card; ***czerwona ~*** *SPORT* red card; ***otrzymać czerwoną kartkę*** be redcarded **2.** (*w książce*) leaf; ***przeczytać kilka kartek*** read a few pages

kartkować ⟨**prze-**⟩ (*-kuję*) leaf through

kartof|el *m* (*-fla*; *-fle*) potato; ***~le w mundurkach*** jacket potatoes; ***~le tłuczone*** mashed potatoes
kartoflanka *f* (*-ki*; *-ki*) potato soup; **kartoflan|y** *adj* potato; ***placki ~e*** potato pancakes
kartograf *m* (*-fa*; *-fowie*) cartographer; **kartografia** *f* (*-fii*; *no pl*) cartography; **kartograficzny** *adj* cartographic
karton *m* (*-nu*; *-ny*) **1.** (*pudło*) cardboard box **2.** (*pudełko*) carton; ***~ mleka*** carton of milk; ***~ papierosów*** carton of cigarettes **3.** (*papier*) cardboard **4.** (*do rysowania*) Bristol paper; **kartonowy** *adj pudło*: cardboard
kartoteka *f* (*-ki*; *-ki*) **1.** files **2.** (*indeks*) *Br* card index, *Am* card catalog
karuzela *f* (*-li*; *-le*) merry-go-round, *Br* roundabout, *Am* carousel
kary *adj koń*: black
karygodny *adj* reprehensible
karykatura *f* (*-ry*; *-ry*) caricature; **karykaturować** ⟨**s-**⟩ (*-ruję*) caricature; **karykaturzysta** *m* (*-ty*; *-ryści*), **-tka** *f* (*-ki*; *-ki*) caricaturist
karzeł *m* (*-rła*; *-rły*) **1.** dwarf, midget **2.** (*istota baśniowa*) dwarf, gnome
kasa *f* (*-sy*; *-sy*) **1.** (*w sklepie*) *Br* cash desk **2.** (*w hipermarkecie*) checkout **3.** (*urządzenie*) cash register, *Br* till **4.** ***~ biletowa*** **a)** (*na dworcu*) ticket office **b)** (*w kinie, teatrze*) box office **c)** (*okienko*) ticket window, ticket desk **5.** (*skrzynka*) cash box; ***~ pancerna*** safe **6.** *infml* cash; ***nie mieć kasy*** be short of cash; ***robić kasę*** make big money **7.** (*fundusz*) ***~ chorych*** health fund
kasacja *f* (*-ji*; *-je*) **1.** JUR annulment, appeal **2.** (*wycofanie z użytku*) scrapping
kaseta *f* (*-ty*; *-ty*) **1.** (*z taśmą*) cassette; ***~ wideo*** video cassette **2.** (*z tonerem, filmem*) cartridge; **kasetka** *f* (*-ki*; *-ki*) **1.** box **2.** (*na kosztowności*) *Br* jewellery box, *Am* jewelery box; **kaseton** *m* (*-nu*; *-ny*) ARCHIT coffer; **kasetowy** *adj*: ***magnetofon ~*** cassette recorder
kasiarz *m* (*-rza*; *-rze*) *infml* safe cracker, safe breaker
kasjer *m* (*-ra*; *-rzy*), **~ka** *f* (*-ki*; *-ki*) **1.** cashier **2.** (*w banku*) teller
kask *m* (*-ku*; *-ki*) **1.** helmet **2.** *motocyklisty*: crash helmet **3.** (*na budowie*) hard hat
kaskada *f* (*-dy*; *-dy*) cascade
kaskader *m* (*-ra*; *-rzy*) stuntman; **kaskaderka** *f* (*-ki*; *-ki*) stuntwoman
kasłać ⟨**kaszlnąć**⟩ (*-łam*) cough
kasować ⟨**s-**⟩ (*-suję*) **1.** *bilet*: punch **2.** *plik, dane*: delete **3.** *nagranie*: erase **4.** *wyrok*: annul, rescind **5.** *infml samochód*: crash
kasownik *m* (*-ka*; *-ki*) **1.** (*w autobusie, tramwaju*) ticket puncher **2.** MUS natural
kasowy *adj wpływy, okienko*: cash; ***~ film*** box-office success
Kaspijski *adj*: ***Morze ~e*** the Caspian Sea
kasta *f* (*-ty*; *-ty*) caste
kastaniety *pl* (*-tów*) castanets
kastet *m* (*-tu*; *-ty*) knuckle-duster, *Am* brass knuckles
kastowy *adj* caste; ***system ~*** caste system
kastracja *f* (*-ji*; *no pl*) castration; **kastrować** ⟨**wy-**⟩ (*-ruję*) castrate
kasyno *n* (*-na*; *-na*) **1.** casino **2.** (*dla wojskowych*) mess
kasza *f* (*-szy*; *-sze*) groats, kasha; ***~ gryczana*** buckwheat kernels, kasha; ***~ manna*** semolina; ***~ perłowa*** pearl barley; ***~ jaglana*** millet groats
kaszak *m* (*-ka*; *-ki*) sebaceous cyst
kaszalot *m* (*-ta*; *-ty*) BIOL sperm whale
kaszanka *f* (*-ki*; *-ki*) *Br* blood pudding, *Am* blood sausage
kasz|el *m* (*-szlu*; *no pl*) cough; ***atak ~lu*** coughing fit
kaszka *f* (*-ki*; *no pl*): ***~ manna*** semolina; ***~ z mlekiem*** *fig* pushover
kaszlać, kaszleć ⟨**-lnąć**⟩ (*-lę*) cough; **kaszlnięcie** *n* (*-cia*; *-cia*) cough
kaszmirowy *adj* cashmere
kasztan *m* (*-na*; *-ny*) **1.** chestnut **2.** (*niejadalny*) horse chestnut; **kasztanow|y** *adj* **1.** chestnut; ***aleja ~a*** avenue of chestnut trees **2.** *włosy*: auburn, chestnut
kasztelan *m* (*-na*; *-ni*/*-nowie*) castellan
kat *m* (*-ta*; *kaci*) **1.** executioner **2.** (*wieszający przestępców*) hangman
kataklizm *m* (*-mu*; *-my*) cataclysm
katakumby *pl* (*-kumb*) catacombs
katalizator *m* (*-ra*; *-ry*) **1.** CHEM cata-

K

lyst; ~ **przemian** *fig* catalyst for change **2.** *AUTO* catalytic converter
katalog *m* (*-gu*; *-gi*) catalogue, *Am* catalog; ~ **rzeczowy** *Br* subject catalogue, *Am* subject catalog; **katalogować** ⟨**s-**⟩ (*-guję*) catalogue
katana *f* (*-ny*; *-ny*) **1.** (*miecz*) katana **2.** (*kurtka*) jacket
katapulta *f* (*-ty*; *-ty*) **1.** catapult **2.** *pilota*: ejector seat; ***katapultować się*** *v im/p* (*-tuję*) eject
katar *m* (*-ru*; *-ry*) runny nose, cold; ~ ***sienny*** hay fever; ***ktoś ma*** ~ s.o.'s nose is running, s.o. has a cold
katarakta *f* (*-ty*; *-ty*) (*zaćma*) cataract
katarynka *f* (*-ki*; *-ki*) barrel organ; ***gadać jak*** ~ *infml* yap on and on
kataster *m* (*-tru*; *-try*) cadastre
katastrofa *f* (*-fy*; *-fy*) **1.** disaster, catastrophe; ~ ***ekologiczna*** environmental disaster **2.** (*wypadek*) crash; ~ ***lotnicza*** plane crash; **katastrofalny** *adj* disastrous
katecheta *m* (*-ty*; *-checi*), **-tka** *f* (*-ki*; *-ki*) religion teacher, catechist; **katecheza** *f* (*-zy*; *-zy*) catechism; **katechizm** *m* (*-mu*; *-my*) catechism
katedra *f* (*-ry*; *-ry*) **1.** *REL* cathedral **2.** (*wydział*) faculty **3.** (*stanowisko*) chair **4.** (*pulpit*) lectern **5.** (*stół*) (lecturer's) desk; **katedralny** *adj* cathedral
kategori|a *f* (*-rii*; *-rie*) category; ***pierwszej*** ~***i*** first-rate; **kategoryczny** *adj* categorical
katharsis *n indecl* catharsis
kation *m* (*-nu*; *-ny*) cation
katiusza *f* (*-szy*; *-sze*) Katyusha (rocket launcher), *infml* Stalin organ
katoda *f* (*-dy*; *-dy*) cathode
katolicki *adj* Catholic; **katolicyzm** *m* (*-mu*; *no pl*) Catholicism; **katolik** *m* (*-ka*; *-licy*), **-liczka** *f* (*-ki*; *-ki*) Catholic
katorga *f* (*-gi*; *no pl*) *Br* forced labour, *Am* forced labor; *fig* ordeal
katować ⟨**s-**⟩ (*-tuję*) **1.** (*torturować*) torture **2.** (*bić*) (brutally) beat
katusze *pl* (*-szy*) *lit* agony *sing*; ***przeżywać*** ~ be in agony
kaucj|a *f* (*-ji*; *-je*) **1.** deposit **2.** *JUR* bail; ***zwolniony za*** ~***ą*** released on bail
kauczuk *m* (*-ku*; *no pl*) india rubber, natural rubber; **kauczukowy** *adj* india rubber, natural rubber
kaukaski *adj* Caucasian
Kaukaz *m* (*-zu*) Caucasus
kawa *f* (*-wy*; *-wy*) coffee; ~ ***naturalna*** real coffee; ~ ***rozpuszczalna*** instant coffee; ~ ***bezkofeinowa*** decaffeinated coffee; ~ ***mrożona*** iced coffee; ~ ***zbożowa*** cereal coffee
kawalarz *m* (*-rza*; *-rze*) *infml* joker
kawaler *m* (*-ra*; *-rzy*/*-rowie*) **1.** (*nieżonaty*) bachelor; ***jest*** ~***em*** he's single **2.** (*młodzieniec*) *dated* youth **3.** *orderu*: holder
kawaleria *f* (*-rii*; *no pl*) cavalry
kawalerka *f* (*-ki*; *-ki*) studio, *Br* studio flat, *Am* studio apartment; **kawalerski** *adj* bachelor; ***wieczór*** ~ stag party
kawaleryjski *adj* cavalry; **kawalerzysta** *m* (*-ty*; *-rzyści*) cavalryman
kawał *m* (*-łu*; *-ły*) **1.** (*część*) (large) piece, chunk; ~ ***drogi*** a long way; ~ ***chłopa*** big guy; ~ ***drania*** *infml* bastard **2.** (*dowcip*) joke **3.** (*psikus*) trick, joke; ***zrobić komuś*** ~ play a trick on s.o.; ***dla*** ~***u*** for fun; **kawałeczek** *m* (*-czka*; *-czki*) *dim* (little) bit, (small) piece
kawał|ek *m* (*-łka*; *-łki*) **1.** piece, bit; ***na*** ~***ki*** (in)to pieces; ***w jednym*** ~***ku*** in one piece **2.** (*utwór*) *infml* piece
kawałkować ⟨**po-**⟩ (*-kuję*) divide into pieces
kawiarenka *f* (*-ki*; *-ki*) (small) café, (small) coffee shop; **kawiarnia** *f* (*-ni*; *-nie*) café, coffee shop; ~ ***na świeżym powietrzu*** *Br* pavement café, *Am* sidewalk café; **kawiarniany** *adj* café
kawior *m* (*-ru*; *no pl*) caviar(e)
kawka *f* (*-ki*; *-ki*) **1.** (*ptak*) jackdaw **2.** (*kawa*) *dim* coffee
kawowy *adj* **1.** coffee **2.** *kolor*: coffee-(brown)
kazać *v im/p* (*każę*) tell; ~ ***komuś coś zrobić*** tell s.o. to do s.th.; ~ ***komuś na siebie czekać*** keep s.o. waiting; ***rób, co ci każę!*** do what I tell you!; ***kazał sobie za to zapłacić*** he wanted to be paid for it; ***jak zwyczaj każe*** according to tradition, as customary
kazalnica *f* (*-cy*; *-ce*) pulpit; **kazanie** *n* (*-nia*; *-nia*) **1.** sermon; ***wygłosić*** ~ ***o*** *L* preach about, preach a sermon on **2.** *fig* lecture
kazeina *f* (*-ny*; *no pl*) *BIOL* casein
kazirodczy *adj* incestuous; **kazirodztwo** *n* (*-wa*; *no pl*) incest

K

kaznodzieja *m* (*-dziei*; *-je*) preacher
kaźń *f* (*-źni*; *no pl*) *lit* **1.** (*męka*) suffering **2.** (*stracenie*) execution
każdorazowo *adv* every time; **każdorazowy** *adj* every, each
każd|y *pron* **1.** every; ***~ego roku*** every year, each year; ***za ~ym razem*** every time, each time; ***w ~ej chwili*** any time; ***o ~ej porze*** any time, always; ***w ~ym razie*** in any case; ***na ~ym kroku*** at every turn **2.** (*z danej grupy*) each **3.** (*osoba*) anyone
kącik *m* (*-ka*; *-ki*) **1.** *dim* corner **2.** (*rubryka*) column
kądziel: ***po ~i*** on the distaff side
kąkol *m* (*-la*; *-le*) corncockle
kąpać ⟨**wy-**⟩ (*-pię*) *Br* bathe, *Am* bath; ***kąpać się*** **1.** (*w basenie*, *jeziorze*) (have a) swim **2.** (*w wannie*) *Br* have a bath, *Am* take a bath
kąpiel *f* (*-li*; *-le*) **1.** (*w wannie*) bath; ***~ lecznicza*** therapeutic bath; ***zażyć ~i słonecznej*** go sunbathing **2.** (*w basenie*, *jeziorze*) swim
kąpielisko *n* (*-ka*; *-ka*) **1.** (*plaża*) swimming beach, (outdoor) swimming area **2.** (*basen*) swimming pool **3.** (*miejscowość*) seaside resort; **kąpielowy** *adj* swimming; ***kostium ~*** swimsuit, swimming costume; **kąpielówki** *pl* (*-wek*) (swimming) trunks
kąsać ⟨***ukąsić***⟩ (*-sam*) bite; **kąsek** *m* (*-ska*; *-ski*) morsel; ***smaczny ~*** tasty morsel
kąśliwy *adj* **1.** *dowcip*: biting **2.** *uwaga*: cutting
kąt *m* (*-ta*; *-ty*) **1.** (*róg*) corner; ***chodzić z ~a w ~*** walk back and forth; ***własny ~*** one's own place; ***zapadły ~*** the back of beyond **2.** MATH angle; ***pod ~em prostym*** at right angles, at a right angle; ***pod ~em 30 stopni*** at an angle of 30 degrees; ***pod ostrym ~em*** at an acute angle; ***pod ~em*** *G* (*pod względem*) in terms of; ***~ widzenia*** point of view; ***obserwować kogoś ~em oka*** watch s.o. out of the corner of one's eye
kątomierz *m* (*-rza*; *-rze*) protractor; **kątownik** *m* (*-ka*; *-ki*) **1.** (*element*) angle **2.** (*przyrząd*) square; **kątowy** *adj miara*: angular
k.c. *abbr* (= **kodeks cywilny**) the civil code, *Br* the civil procedure rules

kciuk *m* (*-ka*; *-ki*) thumb; ***trzymać ~i*** keep one's fingers crossed
kebab *m* (*-bu*; *-by*) kebab, *Am* shish kebab
keczup *m* (*-pu*; *no pl*) ketchup
kefir *m* (*-ru*; *-ry*) kefir
keks *m* (*-su*; *-sy*) fruit cake
kelner *m* (*-ra*; *-rzy*) waiter; **kelnerka** *f* (*-ki*; *-ki*) waitress
kemping *m* (*-gu*; *-gi*) *Br* campsite, *Am* campground; **kempingow|y** *adj* camping; ***pole ~e*** *Br* camping site, *Am* campground; ***przyczepa ~a*** caravan; ***domek ~y*** camping bungalow
keratyna *f* (*-ny*; *no pl*) keratin
keyboard *m* (*-du*; *-dy*) keyboard
kędzierzawy *adj włosy*: curly
kędzior *m* (*-ra*; *-ry*) curl
kępa *f* (*-py*; *-py*) **1.** *drzew*, *krzewów*: clump, copse **2.** *trawy*: tuft; **kępka** *f* (*-ki*; *-ki*) *trawy*, *włosów*: tuft
kęs *m* (*-sa*; *-sy*) bite
ki: ***po ~ego diabła?*** why the hell? *infml*
kibel *m* (*-bla*; *-ble*) *infml Br* the loo, *Am* the john
kibic *m* (*-ca*; *-ce*) *sportowy*: (sports) fan; ***~ piłki nożnej*** *Br* football fan, *Am* soccer fan; **kibic|ować** *v/im* (*-cuję*) **1.** (*dopingować*) cheer on **2.** (*być kibicem*, *być za*) support; ***której drużynie ~ujesz?*** which team do you support?
kibić *f* (*-bici*; *-bicie*) *lit* waist
kiblować *v/im* (*-luję*) *infml* repeat a year (at school)
kicać ⟨**-cnąć**⟩ (*-cam*) hop
kichać ⟨**-chnąć**⟩ (*-cham*) sneeze; ***kicham na*** *A infml* I don't care a fig about; **kichnięcie** *n* (*-cia*; *-cia*) sneeze
kicia *f* (*-ci*; *-cie*) pussy (cat)
kicnąć *v/p* → **kicać**
kicz *m* (*-czu*; *no pl*) kitsch, trash; **kiczowaty** *adj* kitschy, trashy
kić *m* (*kicia*; *kicie*) *infml Br* the clink, *Am* the can; ***pójść do kicia*** *Br* be put in the clink, *Am* be put in the can
kidnaper *m* (*-ra*; *-rzy*) kidnapper; **kidnaping** *m* (*-gu*; *no pl*) kidnapping
kiecka *f* (*-ki*; *-ki*) *infml* **1.** (*spódnica*) skirt; ***latać za ~mi*** chase skirts **2.** (*sukienka*) dress
kiedy **I** *pron* when; ***~ indziej*** some other time; ***~ bądź*** any time; ***od ~ ?*** since when?; ***rzadko ~*** only occasion-

ally, very rarely **II** *conj* **1.** when, as; **~ tylko zechcesz** when(ever) you want **2.** (*podczas gdy*) while, when; **kiedykolwiek** *pron* **1.** (*kiedyś*) ever; **czy byłeś ~ w Anglii?** have you ever been to England? **2.** (*obojętnie kiedy*) whenever; **kiedyś** *pron* **1.** (*w przeszłości*) once; **czy byłeś ~ w Polsce?** have you ever been to Poland?; **~ była piękna** she used to be beautiful **2.** (*w przyszłości*) some day; **kiedyż** *pron lit* when

kielich *m* (*-cha*; *-chy*) **1.** (*do wina*) goblet; **~ mszalny** chalice **2.** BIOL calyx **3.** (*korona kwiatu*) corolla; **4.** (*porcja alkoholu*) *infml* **iść na ~a** go for a drink

kieliszek *m* (*-szka*; *-szki*) glass; **~ do wina** wine glass; **~ wina** glass of wine; **~ do wódki** shot glass; **~ wódki** glass of vodka; **~ do jaj** egg cup; **lubić zaglądać do kieliszka** *fig* like the hard stuff

K

kielnia *f* (*-ni*; *-nie*) trowel

kieł *m* (*kła*; *kły*) **1.** canine (tooth), eyetooth **2.** *psa*, *wilka*: fang **3.** *słonia*, *dzika*: tusk

kiełb *m* (*-ba*; *-bie*) gudgeon

kiełbasa *f* (*-sy*; *-sy*) sausage; **kiełbasiany** *adj wyroby*: sausage; **jad ~** botulin; **zatrucie jadem ~m** botulism; **kiełbaska** *f* (*-ki*; *-ki*) (small) sausage

kiełbasić się ⟨**po-**⟩ (*-szę*) *infml* get confused; **wszystko się komuś pokiełbasiło** s.o. has it all mixed-up

kieł|ek *m* (*-łka*; *-łki*) sprout; **~ki pszenicy** sprouted wheat; **kiełkować** ⟨**wy-**⟩ (*-kuję*) sprout

kiełznać ⟨**o-**⟩ (*-nam*) **1.** *konia*: bridle **2.** *fig* tame

kiep *m* (*-pa*; *-py*) *dated* clod; **kiepski** *adj* poor; **kiepsko** *adv* poorly; **~ z kimś** s.o. is in a bad way

kier *m* (*-ra*; *-ry*) **1.** (*kolor w kartach*) hearts *pl*; **as ~** ace of hearts **2.** (*karta*) heart

kierat *m* (*-tu*; *-ty*) **1.** treadmill **2.** *fig* treadmill, *infml* grind; **~ codziennych obowiązków** the daily grind

kiermasz *m* (*-szu*; *-sze*) fair, sale; **~ książki** book fair

kierować (*-ruję*) **1.** ⟨**po-**⟩ direct (**do** *G* to); **~ ruchem** direct the traffic; **~ swoje słowa do** *G* address, speak to; **~ wzrok na** *A* look at; **~ swoje kroki do** *G* head for, go to; **kieruje kimś ambicja** (**ciekawość**) s.o. is driven by ambition (curiosity) **2.** ⟨**po-**⟩ *zespołem*, *wydziałem*: head **3.** ⟨**po-**⟩ *firmą*: run **4.** ⟨**po-**⟩ *pracą*: be in charge of **5.** ⟨**po-**⟩ *pojazdem*: drive **6.** ⟨**s-**⟩ *broń*: aim **7.** ⟨**s-**⟩ *pacjenta*: send **8.** ⟨**s-**⟩ *klienta*: refer; **kierować się 1.** ⟨**s-**⟩ (*udawać się*) head (**do** *G* for/to), go (**do** *G* to) **2.** ⟨**po-**⟩ (*postępować*) **~ się zdrowym rozsądkiem** (**emocjami**) be guided by common sense (emotions)

kierowca *m* (*-cy*; *-cy*) driver; **~ autobusu** bus driver; **~ taksówki** taxi driver; **kierownica** *f* (*-cy*; *-ce*) **1.** *samochodu*: steering wheel **2.** *roweru*: handlebars *pl*

kierownictw|o *n* (*-wa*; *no pl*) **1.** *firmy*, *szkoły*: management; **~o budowy** site management **2.** *partii*: leadership; **pod ~em** *G* **a)** headed by **b)** (*o orkiestrze*) conducted by; **kierowniczka** *f* (*-ki*; *-ki*) (woman) manager; **~ wydziału** department head; **~ szkoły** *Br* head (teacher), *Am* principal

kierowniczy *adj* **1.** *stanowisko*, *kadra*: managerial **2. układ ~** TECH steering; **kierownik** *m* (*-ka*; *-nicy*) manager; **~ wydziału** department head; **~ szkoły** *Br* head (teacher), *Am* principal

kierowy *adj* of hearts

kierun|ek *m* (*-nku*; *-nki*) **1.** direction; **w ~ku** *G* towards; **w ~ku zachodnim** to the west; **w przeciwnym ~ku** in the opposite direction; **pod czyimś ~kiem** under s.o.'s guidance; **~ek działania** course of action **2.** (*tendencja*) trend **3.** (*wydział*) (university) department; **kierunkowskaz** *m* (*-zu*; *-zy*) *Br* indicator, *Am* turn signal, *infml* blinker; **kierunkowy** *adj* **1.** *antena*: directional **2. numer ~** TEL *Br* dialling code, *Am* area code

kies|a *f* (*-sy*; *-sy*) *dated* (money) pouch; **z państwowej ~y** from the public purse; **nabijać sobie ~ę** line one's own pockets

kiesze|ń *f* (*-szeni*; *-szenie*) **1.** pocket; **~ń wewnętrzna** inside pocket; **włożyć coś do ~ni** put s.th. in one's pocket; **z własnej ~ni** out of one's own pocket; **znać coś jak własną ~ń** know s.th. like the back of one's hand; **to nie na**

moją ~ń I can't afford it; ***na każdą ~ń*** to suit every pocket; ***mieć węża w ~ni*** be tight-fisted, be stingy **2.** (*w komputerze*) drive **3.** *magnetofonu*: cassette compartment

kieszonka *f* (*-ki*; *-ki*) *dim* (small) pocket

kieszonkowe *n* (*-wego*; *no pl*) pocket money; **kieszonkowiec** *m* (*-wca*; *-wcy*) pickpocket; **kieszonkowy** *adj słownik*, *lusterko*: pocket; ***złodziej ~*** pickpocket

kij *m* (*-ja*; *-je*) **1.** stick; ***~ do szczotki*** broomstick; ***włożyć ~ w mrowisko*** *fig* cause a stir, stir up a hornet's nest; ***każdy ~ ma dwa końce*** it's a mixed blessing, it's a double-edged sword **2.** (*do golfa*) (golf) club **3.** (*bilardowy*) cue

kijanka *f* (*-ki*; *-ki*) (*larwa*) tadpole

kijek *m* (*-jka*; *-jki*) *dim* stick; ***~ narciarski*** ski pole, ski stick

Kijów *m* (*-jowa*) Kiev

kikut *m* (*-ta*; *-ty*) stump

kil *m* (*-lu*; *-le*) keel

kilim *m* (*-mu*; *-my*) kilim

kilka *pron* a few, several; ***~ razy*** a few times, several times; **kilkadziesiąt** *pron* a few dozen; ***~ tysięcy*** tens of thousands; **kilkakrotnie** *adv* a few times, on several occasions; **kilkakrotny** *adj* **1.** *próba*: repeated **2.** *mistrz*, *wzrost*: multiple; **kilkanaście** *pron* a dozen or more; **kilkaset** *pron* a few hundred, several hundred

kilkudniowy *adj* **1.** *okres*, *pobyt*: few days' **2.** *dziecko*: of a few days; **kilkugodzinny** *adj spotkanie*, *pobyt*: few hours'; **kilkuletni** *adj* **1.** *dziecko*: small, of a few years **2.** *samochód*: few years'; **kilkumiesięczny** *adj* **1.** *pobyt*, *wyjazd*: few months', of several months **2.** *dziecko*: little, of a few months; **kilkuminutowy** *adj przerwa*, *spotkanie*: few minutes'

kilkunasto- → ***kilkanaście***

kilkunastodniowy *adj wyjazd*, *pobyt*: of several days, lasting more than ten days; **kilkunastoletni** *adj* **1.** *dziecko*: teenage **2.** *pobyt*, *okres*: of over ten years; **kilkunastotysięczny** *adj* **1.** *suma*: of more than ten thousand **2.** *miasto*: of more than ten thousand inhabitants

kilkuosobowy *adj* **1.** *zespół*: of a few people **2.** *pokój*: for a few people; **kilkupiętrowy** *adj Br* several-storey, *Am* several-story; **kilkuset** → ***kilkaset***; **kilkusetletni** *adj* **1.** *tradycja*, *dąb*: centuries-old, ancient **2.** *panowanie*, *okres*: centuries-long; **kilkustopniowy** *adj* **1.** *proces*, *eliminacje*: multistage **2.** *ocieplenie*: by several degrees; **kilkutomowy** *adj* in several volumes; **kilkutysięczny** *adj* **1.** *suma*: of a few thousands, four-digit **2.** *tłum*: of a few thousands

kilof *m* (*-fa*/*-fu*; *-fy*) pickaxe, pick

kilogram *m* (*-ma*; *-my*) kilogram, kilo; ***na ~y*** by the kilogram; **kilometr** *m* (*-ra*; *-ry*) *Br* kilometre, *Am* kilometer; ***50 ~ów na godzinę*** 50 kilometres per hour

kilowat *m* (*-ta*; *-ty*) kilowatt; **kilowolt** *m* (*-ta*; *-ty*) kilovolt

kilowy *adj paczka*: one-kilo

kilwater *m* (*-ru*; *-ry*) wake

kiła *f* (*-ły*; *no pl*) MED syphilis

kim *pron* who, whom; ***~ ona jest?*** **a)** who is she? **b)** (*z zawodu*) what does she do?; ***o ~ mówisz?*** who are you talking about?; ***z ~*** with whom; → ***kto***, ***któż***

kimać ⟨***prze-***⟩ (*-mam*) *infml* doss, *Br* kip; ***iść ~*** go hit the sack

kimono *n* (*-na*; *-na*) kimono; ***uderzyć w ~*** *infml* hit the sack

kimże *lit* → ***kim***

kinematografia *f* (*-fii*; *no pl*) **1.** (*sztuka*, *technika*) cinematography, film-making, *Am* movie-making **2.** (*przemysł*) film industry, *Am* movie industry

kineskop *m* (*-pu*; *-py*) picture tube, cathode ray tube

kinkiet *m* (*-tu*; *-ty*) wall light, wall lamp

kin|o *n* (*-na*; *-na*) **1.** (*budynek*) *Br* cinema, *Am* movie theater; ***iść do ~a*** *Br* go to the cinema, *Am* go to the movies **2.** (*sztuka*) cinema, film **3.** (*przemysł filmowy*) film industry, *Am* the movies; **kinoman** *m* (*-na*; *-ni*), **~ka** *f* (*-ki*; *-ki*) *Br* film-goer, *Am* moviegoer

kinowy *adj* **1.** *sala*: *Br* cinema, *Am* theater **2.** *wersja*: wide-screen

kiosk *m* (*-ku*; *-ki*) **1.** kiosk **2.** (*z gazetami*) *Br* newsagent's, *Am* newsdealer's **3.** (*na okręcie podwodnym*) conning tower; **kioskarz** *m* (*-rza*; *-rze*), **-rka** *f* (*-ki*; *-ki*) *Br* newsagent, *Am* newsdealer

kipiący *adj woda*, *mleko*: boiling; **kipieć** *v/im* (*-pię*) (*o wodzie*, *mleku*) boil; **~ ze złości** boil with anger; **kipiel** *f* (*-li*; *-le*) **1.** (*fale*) surf **2.** (*wir*) whirlpool

kirkut *m* (*-tu*; *-ty*) Jewish cemetery

kisić ⟨**u-**⟩ (*-szę*) pickle (in brine); **~ kapustę** make sauerkraut; **kisić się** (*o ogórkach*) pickle

kisiel *m* (*-lu*; *-le*) *jelly-type dessert*; **dziesiąta woda po ~u** very distant relative

kisnąć ⟨**s-**⟩ (*-nę*) **1.** (*o mleku*) turn sour **2.** (*fermentować*) ferment

kiszk|a *f* (*-ki*; *-ki*) *infml* gut; **ślepa ~a** appendix; **~i mi marsza grają** *fig* I'm starving; **kiszkowaty** *adj* long and narrow

kiszonka *f* (*-ki*; *-ki*) silage

kiszon|y *adj*: **~a kapusta** sauerkraut; **~e ogórki** cucumbers in brine, brined cucumbers

kiść *f* (*-ści*; *-ście*) bunch; **~ winogron** bunch of grapes

kit *m* (*-tu*; *-ty*) putty; **~ pszczeli** bee glue, propolis; **do ~u** *infml* no good

kit|a *f* (*-ty*; *-ty*) (*ozdoba*) plume; **lisia ~a** fox's brush; **odwalić ~ę** *infml* kick the bucket

kitel *m* (*-tla*; *-tle*) coat, *Br* overall

kitować ⟨**za-**⟩ (*-tuję*) **1.** putty **2.** *infml* (*kłamać*) fib

kiwać (*-wam*) **1.** ⟨**-wnąć**⟩ (*przywoływać*) beckon (**na** *A* to) **2.** ⟨**wy-**⟩ (*oszukiwać*) *infml* trick **3.** ⟨**po-**, **-wnąć**⟩ (*potwierdzać*) **~ głową** nod one's head; **kiwać się 1.** wobble **2.** *SPORT* dribble

kiwi *n indecl* kiwi

kiwnąć *v/p* (*-nę*): **nie ~ palcem w bucie** not lift a finger; → **kiwać**

k.k. *abbr* (= **kodeks karny**) the criminal code

kl. *abbr* (= **klasa**) class

klacz *f* (*-czy*; *-cze*) mare

klajster *m* (*-tru*; *-try*) paste, starch glue; **klajstrować** ⟨**za-**⟩ (*-ruję*) paste

klakson *m* (*-nu*; *-ny*) horn; **nacisnąć na ~** blow one's horn

klamerka *f* (*-ki*; *-ki*) **1.** *dim* buckle **2.** (*do bielizny*) peg

klamka *f* (*-ki*; *-ki*) handle; **~ zapadła** there is no turning back

klamra *f* (*-ry*; *-ry*) **1.** (*przy ubraniu*) buckle **2.** (*nawias*) brace **3.** *TECH* clamp

klap|a *f* (*-py*; *-py*) **1.** (*pokrywa*) lid, top **2.** (*wyłóg*) lapel **3.** (*z tyłu samochodu*) tailgate, tailboard **4.** (*fiasko*) *infml* flop; **zrobić ~ę** flop, be a flop; **~a bezpieczeństwa** safety valve

klapek *m* (*-pka*; *-pki*) flip-flop; **klapk|a** *f* (*-ki*; *-ki*) **1.** flap **2.** (*na oczach*) *Br* blinker, *Am* blinder; **mieć ~i na oczach** *fig* be narrow-minded; **klapnąć** *v/p* (*-nę*) flop down

klaps *m* (*-sa*; *-sy*) slap, smack; **dać ~a** slap, smack

klarnecista *m* (*-ty*; *-ciści*), **-tka** *f* (*-ki*; *-ki*) clarinet player; **klarnet** *m* (*-tu*; *-ty*) clarinet

klarować ⟨**wy-**⟩ (*-ruję*) **1.** *wino*, *sok*: clear, purify **2.** (*wyjaśniać*) clarify; **klarować się 1.** (*o winie*) clear **2.** (*o sytuacji*) become clear; **klarowny** *adj* clear

klas|a *f* (*-sy*; *-sy*) **1.** class; **bilet drugiej ~y** second-class ticket; **~a robotnicza** the working class; **~a średnia** the middle class; **pierwszej ~y** *infml* first-rate **2.** (*grupa uczniów*) class, *Am* grade **3.** (*sala*) classroom **4.** (*gra*) hopscotch *sing*; **grać w ~y** play hopscotch

klaser *m* (*-ra*; *-ry*) stamp album

klaskać ⟨**-snąć**⟩ (*-szczę*/*-kam*) clap (one's hands)

klasow|y *adj* class; **praca ~a** test; **klasówka** *f* (*-ki*; *-ki*) test

klasycyzm *m* (*-mu*; *no pl*) classicism; **klasyczny** *adj* **1.** *muzyka*, *filologia*: classical **2.** *przykład*: classic; **styl ~** *SPORT* breaststroke

klasyfikować ⟨**za-**⟩ (*-kuję*) classify; **klasyfikować się** be classified

klasyk *m* (*-ka*; *-sycy*) **1.** (*autor*) classic author; **~ science fiction** classic science fiction writer **2.** (*utwór*) classic; **klasyka** *f* (*-ki*; *no pl*) classics *sing*

klasztor *m* (*-ru*; *-ry*) **1.** (*męski*) monastery **2.** (*żeński*) convent; **klasztorny** *adj* **1.** (*dotyczący klasztoru męskiego*) monastic **2.** (*dotyczący klasztoru żeńskiego*) convent

klaśnięcie *n* (*-cia*; *-cia*) clap

K

klatka *f* (*-ki*; *-ki*) **1.** (*dla zwierząt*) cage; **~ *piersiowa*** chest; **~ *schodowa*** staircase, stairwell **2.** *filmowa*: frame
klaustrofobia *f* (*-bii*; *no pl*) claustrophobia
klauzula *f* (*-li*; *-le*) clause
klawesyn *m* (*-nu*; *-ny*) *MUS* harpsichord
klawiatura *f* (*-ry*; *-ry*) keyboard
klawisz *m* (*-sza*; *-sze*) key; **klawiszowy** *adj instrument*: keyboard; ***skrót ~*** *INF* shortcut key combination
klawy *adj infml* swell
kląć ⟨**za-**⟩ (*klnę*) curse, swear; **~ *na*** *A* swear at; **~ *jak szewc*** swear like a trooper; **~ *na czym świat stoi*** swear like mad; ***kląć się*** swear; **~ *się na Boga*** swear by God
klątw|a *f* (*-wy*; *-wy*) curse; ***rzucić ~ę na*** *A* put a curse on
klecha *f* (*-chy*; *-chy*) *infml* holy Joe
klecić ⟨**s-**⟩ (*-cę*) knock together
kleić ⟨**s-**⟩ (*kleję*) glue (together); ***kleić się*** *v/im* (*o rękach*) be sticky; ***kleją mi się oczy*** my eyelids are drooping
kleik *m* (*-ku*; *-ki*) **1.** cereal; **~ *ryżowy*** rice cereal **2.** (*kleisty wywar*) pap; **~ *kukurydziany*** mush; **kleisty** *adj* sticky, glutinous
klej *m* (*-ju*; *-je*) glue, adhesive; **klejąc|y** *adj*: ***taśma ~a*** *Br* Sellotape®, *Br infml* sticky tape, *Am* Scotch tape
klejnot *m* (*-tu*; *-ty*) jewel, gem
klekot *m* (*-tu*; *no pl*) clatter; **klekotać** *v/im* (*-kocę*/*-koczę*) **1.** clatter **2.** (*o bocianie*) clatter its bill
kleks *m* (*-sa*; *-sy*) blot
klepać ⟨**-pnąć**⟩ (*-pię*) pat; **~ *kogoś po ramieniu*** pat s.o.'s shoulder; **~ *biedę*** *Br* live on the breadline; ***klepać się***: **~ *się po brzuchu*** pat one's stomach
klepisko *n* (*-ka*; *-ka*) earth floor
klepk|a *f* (*-ki*; *-ki*) **1.** (*podłogowa*) floor board **2.** (*w beczce*) stave ***brak mu piątej ~i*** he has a screw loose
klepnąć *v/p* → ***klepać***
klepsydra *f* (*-ry*; *-ry*) **1.** (*do pomiaru czasu*) hourglass **2.** (*nekrolog*) death notice
kleptomania *f* (*-nii*; *no pl*) kleptomania
kler *m* (*-ru*; *no pl*) clergy; **kleryk** *m* (*-ka*; *-rycy*) seminarian, seminarist; **klerykalny** *adj* clerical
kleszcz *m* (*-cza*; *-cze*) (*owad*) tick
kleszcze *pl* (*-czy*/*-czów*) **1.** (*cęgi*) pincers **2.** *ANAT* claws **3.** (*porodowe*) forceps; **kleszczowy** *adj*: ***poród ~*** forceps delivery
klęczeć *v/im* (*-czę*) kneel; **klęczk|i** *pl* (*-czek*): ***na ~ach*** on one's knees; **klęcznik** *m* (*-ka*; *-ki*) kneeler
klękać ⟨**-nąć**⟩ (*-kam*) kneel
klęli, ***klęłam*** → ***kląć***
klęsk|a *f* (*-ki*; *-ki*) **1.** (*przegrana*) defeat; ***ponieść ~ę*** be defeated, suffer defeat **2.** (*katastrofa*) disaster; ***~a żywiołowa*** natural disaster; ***~a głodu*** famine
klient *m* (*-ta*; *-nci*), **~ka** *f* (*-ki*; *-ki*) **1.** customer; ***stały ~*** regular customer **2.** *prawnika*, *firmy*: customer, client; **klientela** *f* (*-li*; *no pl*) customers *pl*, clientele
klif *m* (*-fu*; *-fy*) cliff
klika *f* (*-ki*; *-ki*) clique, cronies *pl*
klikać *v/im* (*-kam*) click
klimakterium *n indecl* menopause
klimat *m* (*-tu*; *-ty*) **1.** climate **2.** (*atmosfera*) *infml* atmosphere; **klimatyczny** *adj* climatic, climate **klimatyzacja** *f* (*-ji*; *no pl*) air-conditioning; **klimatyzator** *m* (*-ra*; *-ry*) air-conditioner; **klimatyzować** *v/im* (*-zuję*) air-condition
klin *m* (*-na*; *-ny*) **1.** wedge; ***zabić komuś ~a*** put s.o. on the spot **2.** (*kawałek materiału*) gusset
klincz *m* (*-cza*; *-cze*) clinch
klinga *f* (*-gi*; *-gi*) blade
kliniczn|y *adj* clinical; ***śmierć ~a*** clinical death; **klinika** *f* (*-ki*; *-ki*) clinic
klinkier *m* (*-ru*; *no pl*) clinker
klinować się ⟨**za-**⟩ (*-nuję*) **1.** (*utykać*) get stuck **2.** (*zacinać się*) jam (up)
klinow|y *adj*: ***pismo ~e*** cuneiform (writing); ***pasek ~y*** V-belt
klip *m* (*-pu*; *-py*) video
klips *m* (*-sa*; *-sy*) earclip
klisza *f* (*-szy*; *-sze*) **1.** *PHOT* film **2.** (*w poligrafii*) plate
klitka *f* (*-ki*; *-ki*) *infml* cramped room
kloc *m* (; *-ce*) block; **kloc|ek** *m* (*-cka*; *-cki*) **1.** block **2.** (*zabawka*) (building) block; ***~ki lego*** Lego® blocks **3.** ***~ek hamulcowy*** *TECH* brake pad
klomb *m* (*-bu*; *-by*) flower bed
klon[1] *m* (*-nu*; *-ny*) (*drzewo*) mapl (tree)
klon[2] *m* (*-nu*; *-ny*) *BIOL* clone
klonować ⟨**s-**⟩ (*-nuję*) clone; **klonowanie** *n* (*-nia*; *no pl*) cloning

K

klonowy *adj* maple; ***syrop ~*** maple syrup, *Am* maple sirup
klops *m* (*-sa*; *-sy*) meat loaf; ***no to ~!*** *infml* that's done it!; **klopsik** *m* (*-ka*; *-ki*) meat ball
klosz *m* (*-sza*; *-sze*) **1.** *lampy*: (lamp)-shade; ***trzymać kogoś pod ~em*** *fig* keep s.o. wrapped in cotton wool **2.** (*krój*) flare; ***spódnica w ~*** flared skirt; **kloszowy** *adj spódnica*, *spodnie*: flared
klown *m* (*-na*; *-ni*/*-ny*) clown
klozet *m* (*-tu*; *-ty*) lavatory; **klozetow|y** *adj* lavatorial; ***muszla ~a*** toilet bowl; ***babcia ~a*** toilet attendant
klub *m* (*-bu*; *-by*) club; ***~ sportowy*** sports club; **klubowy** *adj* club; ***fotel ~*** lounge chair
klucz *m* (*-cza*; *-cze*) **1.** key; ***zamknąć na ~*** lock; ***pod ~em*** under lock and key **2.** MUS clef **3.** *ptaków*: 'V' formation **4.** (*narzędzie*) *Br* spanner, *Am* wrench; ***~ nastawny*** *Br* adjustable spanner, *Am* monkey wrench; **kluczowy** *adj fig* key, crucial (***dla*** *G* to)

K

kluczyć *v/im* (*-czę*) **1.** weave one's way **2.** (*o drodze*) wander (along) **3.** (*w rozmowie*) hedge
kluczyk *m* (*-ka*; *-ki*) (small) key; ***~i do samochodu*** car keys
kluć się ⟨**wy-**⟩ (*kluję*) (*o pisklętach*) hatch
klusk|a *f* (*-ki*; *-ki*) dumpling; ***mieć ~i w gębie*** mumble
kła → ***kieł***
kłaczek *m* (*-czka*; *-czki*) *dim* wisp
kładka *f* (*-ki*; *-ki*) footbridge
kładziesz → ***kłaść***
kłak *m* (*-ka*; *-ki*) tuft; ***niewart funta ~ów*** not worth a look; ***kłaki*** (*włosy*) messy hair, straggly hair
kłam *m* (*-mu*; *no pl*): ***zadać ~*** *lit* belie, give the lie to
kłamać ⟨**s-**⟩ (*-mię*) lie; ***~ w żywe oczy*** lie through one's teeth; **kłamca** *m* (*-cy*; *-cy*) lier
kłamczuch *m* (*-cha*; *-chy*), ***~a*** *f* (*-chy*; *-chy*) *infml* (little) lier; **kłamliwy** *adj* **1.** *osoba*: untruthful **2.** *plotka*: untrue; **kłamstewko** *n* (*-ka*; *-ka*) white lie; **kłamstwo** *n* (*-wa*; *-wa*) lie
kłaniać się ⟨**ukłonić**⟩ (*-niam*) **1.** (*pochylać się*) bow **2.** (*pozdrawiać*) greet
kłapać ⟨**-pnąć**⟩ (*-pię*): ***~ zębami*** snap
kłapouchy *adj osioł*: lop-eared
kłaść ⟨**położyć**⟩ (*kładę*) **1.** put; ***~ rękę na*** *L* put one's hand on; ***~ kogoś spać*** put s.o. to bed; ***~ czemuś kres*** put an end to s.th.; ***~ nacisk na*** *A* place emphasis on, emphasize **2.** *płytki*, *dywan*: lay; ***kłaść się*** **1.** (*na łóżku*, *na podłodze*) lie down **2.** (*iść spać*) go to bed; ***nie ~ się spać*** stay up
kłąb *m* (*kłębu*; *kłęby*) **1.** *dymu*, *kurzu*: cloud **2.** *zwierzęcia*: withers; ***wysokość w kłębie*** height at (the) withers
kłącze *n* (*-cza*; *-cza*) rhizome
kłębek *m* (*-bka*; *-bki*) **1.** *wełny*: ball; ***~ nerwów*** *fig* a bundle of nerves; ***zwinąć się w ~*** curl oneself up into a ball **2.** *waty*: wad; **kłębiast|y** *adj*: ***chmura ~a*** cumulus; **kłębić się** *v/im* (*-bię*) **1.** (*o chmurach*) billow **2.** (*o myślach*) swirl around; **kłębowisko** *n* (*-ka*; *-ka*) **1.** *węży*: tangle **2.** *dymu*, *myśli*: whirl
kłod|a *f* (*-dy*; *-dy*) log; ***spać jak ~a*** sleep like a log; ***rzucać komuś ~y pod nogi*** put stumbling blocks in s.o.'s way
kłopot *m* (*-tu*; *-ty*) problem, trouble; ***mieć ~*** have a problem; ***mieć ~ z*** *I* have trouble with, have difficulty with; ***w czym ~?*** what's the problem?; ***być w kłopocie*** have trouble; ***wpaść w ~y*** get into trouble; ***sprawić komuś ~*** give s.o. trouble, inconvenience s.o.; ***nie rób sobie ~u*** don't bother; ***mieć ~y ze zdrowiem*** have health problems; ***~y pieniężne*** financial troubles
kłopotać się *v/im* (*-poczę*/*-pocę*) worry (***o*** *A* about); ***nie kłopocz się!*** don't bother!; **kłopotliwy** *adj* **1.** *sytuacja*: embarrassing **2.** *pytanie*: awkward
kłos *m* (*-sa*; *-sy*) ear; ***~ pszenicy*** ear of wheat; **kłosie** *n* (*-sia*; *no pl*) *zboża*: ears *pl*
kłócić się *v/im* (*-cę*) **1.** quarrel (***o*** *A* about/over), argue (***o*** *A* about/over) **2.** (*o kolorach*) clash
kłódk|a *f* (*-ki*; *-ki*) padlock; ***zamknięty na ~ę*** padlocked
kłótliwy *adj* quarrelsome; **kłótnia** *f* (*-ni*; *-nie*) quarrel, argument
kłucie *n* (*-cia*; *no pl*) (*ból*) stabbing pain; ***~ w boku*** (*kolka*) stitch in one's side; **kłu|ć** ⟨**u-**⟩ (*kłuję*) prick; ***~ło go w boku*** (*miał kolkę*) he had a stitch in his side; **kłujący** *adj* **1.** prickly **2.** *ból*: stabbing, piercing

kłus *m* (*-su*; *no pl*) trot; **~em** in a trot; **kłusak** *m* (*-ka*; *-ki*) trotter
kłusować[1] *v/im* (*-suję*) (*o koniu*) trot
kłusować[2] *v/im* (*-suję*) (*o kłusowniku*) poach; **kłusownictwo** *n* (*-wa*; *no pl*) poaching; **kłusownik** *m* (*-ka*; *-nicy*) poacher
kłuty *adj rana*: stab
kły *pl* → ***kieł***
kłykieć *m* (*-kcia*; *-kcie*) knuckle
KM *abbr* (= **koń mechaniczny**) hp
kminek *m* (*-nku*; *no pl*) caraway
kmiotek *m* (*-tka*; *-tki*) *infml* redneck
knajpa *f* (*-py*; *-py*) *infml* joint
knebel *m* (*-bla*; *-ble*) gag; **kneblować** ⟨**za-**⟩ (*-luję*) gag
knedle *pl* (*-li*) (plum) dumplings
knieja *f* (*kniei*; *-je*) forest
knocić ⟨**s-**⟩ (*-cę*) botch, mess up
knot *m* (*-ta*; *-ty*) **1.** (*w świecy*) wick **2.** *infml* trash
knowania *pl* (*-wań*) intrigues
knuć ⟨**u-**⟩ (*knuję*) plot; **~ *zemstę*** plot revenge
knur *m* (*-ra*; *-ry*) boar
knykieć *m* (*-kcia*; *-kcie*) knuckle
koalicja *f* (*-ji*; *-je*) coalition; **koalicyjny** *adj* coalition; ***rząd ~*** coalition government
kobalt *m* (*-tu*; *no pl*) CHEM cobalt; **kobaltowy** *adj* cobalt
kobiałka *f* (*-ki*; *-ki*) basket
kobieciarz *m* (*-rza*; *-rze*) womanizer; **kobieco** *adv wyglądać*: feminine; **kobiecość** *f* (*-ści*; *no pl*) femininity; **kobiecy** *adj* **1.** *czasopismo*, *choroby*: women's **2.** *intuicja*, *urok*: feminine, woman's **3.** *figura*, *cechy*: feminine, womanly **4.** *zachowanie*: feminine **5.** *narządy*: female
kobier|zec *m* (*-rca*; *-rce*): ***stanąć na ślubnym ~cu*** *fig* get married, *infml* tie the knot
kobieta *f* (*-ty*; *-ty*) woman; **~ *pilot*** woman pilot
kobuz *m* (*-za*; *-zy*) (Euroasian) hobby
kobyła *f* (*-ły*; *-ły*) mare
koc *m* (*-ca*; *-ce*) blanket
kocanka *f* (*-ki*; *-ki*) helichrysum
kocha|ć *v/im* (*-cham*) love; ***~m cię*** I love you; ***kochać się*** **1.** be in love (***w*** *I* with) **2.** (*fizycznie*) make love
kochanek *m* (*-nka*; *-nkowie*) lover; **kochanie**: **~!** darling!, honey!, *Am infml* baby!; **kochanka** *f* (*-ki*; *-ki*) lover, mistress; **kochany I** *adj* dear **II** *m* (*-nego*; *-ni*), **-na** *f* (*-nej*; *-ne*) darling; ***mój ~*** my darling
kocher *m* (*-ra*; *-ry*) camping cooker, camping stove
kochliwy *adj* amorous
koci *adj* **1.** feline, cat's; ***~e łby*** *fig* cobblestones; ***~a muzyka*** caterwauling (music); ***żyć z kimś na ~ą łapę*** *infml* shack up with s.o. **2.** *karma*: cat; **kociak** *m* (*-ka*; *-ki*) **1.** (*kot*) kitten **2.** *infml* (*dziewczyna*) chick
kocica *f* (*-cy*; *-ce*) she-cat; **kocić się** ⟨**o-**⟩ (*-cę*) (*o kotce*) have kittens; **kocię** *n* (*-cięcia*; *-cięta*) kitten
kocioł *m* (*kotła*; *kotły*) **1.** (*kuchenny*) cauldron; ***przyganiał ~ garnkowi*** the pot calling the kettle black **2.** *parowy*: boiler; **kociołek** *m* (*-łka*; *-łki*) kettle
kocmołuch *m* (*-cha*; *-chy*) *infml* slut
kocur *m* (*-ra*; *-ry*) tomcat
kocyk *m* (*-ka*; *-ki*) *dim* (small) blanket
koczkodan *m* (*-na*; *-ny*) guenon (monkey)
koczować *v/im* (*-czuję*) lead a nomadic life; **koczowniczy** *adj* nomadic; ***prowadzić ~ tryb życia*** lead a nomadic life; **koczownik** *m* (*-ka*; *-nicy*) nomad
kod *m* (*-du*; *-dy*) code; **~ *pocztowy*** *Br* postcode, *Am* Zip code
kodeks *m* (*-su*; *-sy*) code; **~ *karny*** the criminal code; **~ *postępowania cywilnego*** the civil code; **~ *drogowy*** *Br* the Highway Code, *Am* the Rules of the Road
kodować ⟨**za-**⟩ (*-duję*) (en)code
kodyfikować ⟨**s-**⟩ (*-kuję*) codify
koedukacyjny *adj* co-educational, *infml* co-ed
koegzystencja *f* (*-ji*; *no pl*) coexistence
kofeina *f* (*-ny*; *no pl*) caffeine
kogel-mogel *m* (*kogla-mogla*; *kogle-mogle*) *yolk mixed with sugar to a cream*
kognitywny *adj* cognitive
kogo *pron* who, whom; **~ *spotkałaś?*** who(m) did you meet?; ***od ~ to dostałeś?*** who did you get it from?; **~ *nie ma?*** who is absent?; → ***kto***, ***któż***
kogoż *pron lit* who
koguci *adj* cock; **~ *grzebień*** cockscomb; ***waga ~a*** SPORT bantamweight; **kogucik** *m* (*-ka*; *-ki*) *dim* cockerel;

kogut *m* (*-ta*; *-ty*) **1.** *Br* cock, *Am* rooster **2.** (*włosy*) standing-up hair
koić ⟨**u-**⟩ (*koję*) **1.** *ból*: soothe **2.** *cierpienia*: ease **3.** *nerwy*: calm
koja *f* (*koi*; *-je*) berth, bunk
kojarzyć ⟨**s-**⟩ (*-rzę*) **1.** (*w myślach*) associate **2.** *małżeństwa*: arrange; ***kojarzyć się*** associate (**z** *I* with); ***to się kojarzy z*** *I* it brings to mind; ***to mi się kojarzy z*** *I* it makes me think of
kojący *adj* soothing
kojec *m* (*-jca*; *-jce*) **1.** (*dla dziecka*) playpen **2.** (*klatka*) coop
kok *m* (*-ka*; *-ki*) bun; ***włosy upięte w ~*** hair pulled up in a bun
kok|a *f* (*-ki*; *no pl*) **1.** (*narkotyk*) *infml* coke, crack; ***brać ~ę*** do coke *infml* **2.** (*roślina*) coca plant
kokain|a *f* (*-ny*; *no pl*) cocaine; ***zażywać ~ę*** take cocaine
kokard|a *f* (*-dy*; *-dy*) bow; ***związany na ~ę*** tied in a bow

K

kokieteria *f* (*-rii*; *no pl*) flirtatiousness, *lit* coquetry; **kokieteryjny** *adj* flirtatious, *lit* coquettish; **kokietka** *f* (*-ki*; *-ki*) flirt, *lit* coquette; **kokietować** *v/im* (*-tuję*) flirt (*A* with)
koklusz *m* (*-szu*; *no pl*) *MED* whooping cough
kokos *m* (*-sa*/*-su*; *-sy*) coconut; ***robić ~y*** *infml* be coining money; **kokosowy** *adj* coconut
kokoszka *f* (*-ki*; *-ki*) hen
kokota *f* (*-ty*; *-ty*) cocotte
koks *m* (*-su*; *no pl*) **1.** coke **2.** *SPORT* dope
koksownia *f* (*-ni*; *-nie*) coking plant; **koksowniczy** *adj* coking
koktajl *m* (*-lu*; *-le*) cocktail; ***~ mleczny*** milkshake, shake
kol. *abbr* (= **kolega**) colleague
kolaboracja *f* (*-ji*; *no pl*) collaboration; **kolaborant** *m* (*-ta*; *-nci*), **~ka** *f* (*-ki*; *-ki*) collaborator
kolacj|a *f* (*-ji*; *-je*) **1.** supper; ***jeść ~ę*** have supper **2.** (*wczesna i obfita*) dinner
kolanko *n* (*-ka*; *-ka*) **1.** *dim* knee **2.** *TECH* elbow **3.** *BIOL* joint
kolan|o *n* (*-na*; *-na*) knee; ***po ~a w*** *L* knee-deep in; ***sukienka do ~*** knee-length dress; ***buty do ~*** knee-high boots; ***siedzieć komuś na ~ach*** sit on s.o.'s lap; ***posadzić kogoś na ~ach*** sit s.o. on one's lap; ***~a się pod kimś uginają*** s.o. goes weak at the knees; ***łysy jak ~o*** (as) bald as a coot; **kolanowy** *adj* knee
kolarski *adj wyścig*, *spodenki*: cycling, cycle; **kolarstwo** *n* (*-wa*; *no pl*) cycling; **kolarz** *m* (*-rza*; *-rze*) cyclist
kolaż *m* (*-żu*; *-że*) collage
kolba *f* (*-by*; *-by*) **1.** (*część broni*) butt **2.** *BIOL* cob; ***~ kukurydzy*** cob, *Br* corn cob **3.** (*naczynie*) flask **4.** (*lutownica*) soldering iron
kolczatka *f* (*-ki*; *-ki*) (*zwierzę*) echidna, spiny anteater; **kolczasty** *adj* prickly, spiny; ***drut ~*** barbed wire; **kolczuga** *f* (*-gi*; *-gi*) (chain) mail; **kolczyk** *m* (*-ka*; *-ki*) (*w uchu*) earing; ***~ w nosie*** nose ring
kolebka *f* (*-ki*; *-ki*) cradle
kolec *m* (*-lca*; *-lce*) **1.** *róży*: thorn **2.** *kaktusa*: prickle **3.** *jeża*, *jeżozwierza*: spine **4.** (*z metalu*, *drewna*) spike **5.** ***kolce*** *SPORT* spikes
kole|ga *m* (*-gi*; *-ledzy*) **1.** friend; ***~ga ze szkoły*** school friend; ***~ga ze studiów*** fellow student; ***~dzy ze studiów*** other students **2.** (*z klasy*) classmate **3.** (*z biura*) colleague **4.** (*z fabryki*) fellow worker
kolegialny *adj* (*grupowy*) collective
kolegiata *f* (*-ty*; *-ty*) collegiate church
kolegować się *v/im* (*-guję*) be friends (**z** *I* with)
koleina *f* (*-ny*; *-ny*) rut
kole|j *f* (*-lei*; *-je*) **1.** (*środek komunikacji*) *Br* railway, *Am* railroad; ***~j linowa*** cable railway ***jeździć ~ją*** travel by train, travel by rail; ***pracować na ~i*** be a railway worker **2.** (*kolejność*) turn; ***czekać na swoją ~j*** wait one's turn; ***normalna ~j rzeczy*** ordinary course of events; ***~j na ciebie*** it's your turn; ***po ~i*** in the right order; ***nie po ~i*** out of order; ***z ~i*** in turn; (***zmienne***) ***~e życia*** (changing) fortunes
kolejarz *m* (*-rza*; *-rze*) *Br* railwayman, *Am* railroader
kolej|ka *f* (*-ki*; *-ki*) **1.** (*rząd ludzi*) line, *Br* queue; ***w ~ce*** in a line; ***stać w ~ce po*** *A* stand in line for, *Br* queue for **2.** (*środek komunikacji*) (commuter) train; ***~ka podmiejska*** local train; ***~ka podziemna*** underground train; ***~ka linowa*** cable car, funicular; ***~ka gór-***

ska (*w wesołym miasteczku*) roller coaster **3.** (*zabawka*) train set **4.** (*porcja trunku*) round (of drinks); ***stawiać ~kę*** buy a round of drinks
kolejnictwo *n* (*-wa*; *no pl*) *Br* railway industry, *Am* railroad industry
kolejno *adv* in turn; **kolejnoś|ć** *f* (*-ści*; *no pl*) order, sequence; ***w ~ci alfabetycznej*** in alphabetical order; ***poza ~cią*** out of turn; **kolejny** *adj* **1.** (*następny*) next **2.** (*jeszcze jeden*) another
kolejowy *adj* **1.** *stacja*, *bilet*, *katastrofa*: train **2.** *linia*, *transport*: *Br* railway, *Am* railroad; ***dworzec ~*** train station, *Br* railway station
kolekcja *f* (*-ji*; *-je*) collection; **kolekcjoner** *m* (*-ra*; *-rzy*), **~ka** *f* (*-ki*; *-ki*) collector; **kolekcjonować** *v/im* (*-nuję*) collect
kolektura *f* (*-ry*; *-ry*) lottery outlet, lottery booth
kolektyw *m* (*-wu*; *-wy*) collective; **kolektywny** *adj* collective
kolender *m* (*-dru*/*-dra*; *no pl*), **kolendra** *f* (*-ry*; *no pl*) coriander
koleś *m* (*-lesia*; *-lesie*) *infml* **1.** (*kumpel*) *Br* mate, *Am* bud **2.** (*facet*) guy, *Am* dude
koleżank|a *f* (*-ki*; *-ki*) **1.** (female) friend; ***~a ze szkoły*** school friend; ***~a ze studiów*** fellow student; ***~i ze studiów*** other students **2.** (*z klasy*) classmate **3.** (*z biura*) colleague **4.** (*z fabryki*) fellow worker; **koleżeński** *adj* friendly, helpful; **koleżeństwo** *n* (*-wa*; *no pl*) friendship
koleżka *m* (*-ki*; *-kowie*) *Br* mate, *Am* buddy
kolęda *f* (*-dy*; *-dy*) **1.** (*pieśń*) (Christmas) carol **2.** (*śpiewanie kolęd*) carol singing; **kolędnik** *m* (*-ka*; *-nicy*) carol singer, caroler; **kolędować** *v/im* (*-duję*) sing carols
kolia *f* (*-lii*; *-lie*) necklace
koliber *m* (*-bra*; *-bry*) humming bird
kolidować *v/im* (*-duję*) **1.** (*o terminach*, *godzinach*) clash **2.** (*być niezgodnym*) conflict; ***~ z prawem*** conflict with the law
koligacja *f* (*-ji*; *-je*) kinship, family connection
kolisty *adj* circular
koliście *adv* in a circle
kolizj|a *f* (*-ji*; *-je*) **1.** (*zderzenie*) collision **2.** (*konflikt*, *sprzeczność*) conflict, clash; ***być w ~i z prawem*** be in conflict with the law; ***wejść w ~ę z prawem*** come into conflict with the law
kolk|a *f* (*-ki*; *-ki*) **1.** (*u niemowląt*) colic **2.** (*ból w boku*) stitch; ***mieć ~ę*** have a stitch
kolokwium *n* (*indecl*; *-wia*) (*na uczelni*) test
Kolonia *f* (*-nii*) Cologne
kolonia *f* (*-nii*; *-nie*) colony; ***~ letnia*** summer camp; ***~ karna*** penal colony; **kolonializm** *m* (*-mu*; *no pl*) colonialism; **kolonijny** *adj* **1.** colony **2.** (*dotyczący kolonii letniej*) summer camp; **kolonista** *m* (*-ty*; *-niści*), **-tka** *f* (*-ki*; *-ki*) **1.** (*osadnik*) colonist **2.** (*dziecko*) camper; **kolonizować** ⟨**s-**⟩ (*-zuję*) colonize
koloński|i *adj*: ***woda ~a*** (eau de) cologne
kolor *m* (*-ru*; *-ry*) **1.** *Br* colour, *Am* color; ***jaki ~ ma jej bluzka?*** *Br* what colour is her blouse?; ***~ czerwony*** *Br* (the colour) red; ***w ~ze niebieskim*** blue; ***pod ~*** *G Br* to match the colour of **2.** (*w kartach*) suit; **kolorować** ⟨**po-**⟩ (*-ruję*) **1.** *obrazki*: *Br* colour in, *Am* color in **2.** (*farbować*) *Br* colour, *Am* color; **kolorowo** *adj* **1.** *Br* colourfully, *Am* colorfully; ***żyć ~*** *Br* lead a colourful life **2.** *wyglądać*: *Br* colourful, *Am* colorful; **kolorowy** *adj* **1.** (*wielobarwny*) *Br* colourful, *Am* colorful **2.** *telewizja*, *film*: *Br* colour, *Am* color **3.** *papier*, *szkło*, *ludność*: *Br* coloured, *Am* colored
kolory *pl* (*-rów*) **1.** *Br* colours, *Am* colors **2.** (*rumieńce*, *koloryt*) *Br* colour *sing*, *Am* color *sing*; **koloryt** *m* (*-tu*; *no pl*) **1.** *obrazu*: tone **2.** *lokalny*: *Br* colour, *Am* color
koloryzować *v/im* (*-zuję*) **1.** (*przesadzać*) exaggerate **2.** (*upiększać*) embellish
kolos *m* (*-sa*; *-sy*) colossus; **kolosalny** *adj* colossal
kolportaż *m* (*-żu*; *no pl*) distribution; **kolporter** *m* (*-ra*; *-rzy*), **~ka** *f* (*-ki*; *-ki*) distributor; **kolportować** *v/im* (*-tuję*) *pisma*, *reklamy*: distribute
Kolumbia *f* (*-bii*) Columbia

kolumna *f* (*-ny*; *-ny*) **1.** column **2.** (*głośnik*) (loud)speaker

kolumnada *f* (*-dy*; *-dy*) colonnade; **kolumnowy** *adj sala*: columned; ***szyk ~*** column (formation)

kołatać ⟨**za-**⟩ (*-łaczę*/*-łacę*/*-tam*) **1.** (*do drzwi*) knock (**do** *G* at/on) **2.** (*o sercu*) pound; ***kołatać się*** *v/im* (*o myśli*) keep popping, keep ringing; **kołatka** *f* (*-ki*; *-ki*) (*przy drzwiach*) knocker

kołchoz *m* (*-zu*; *-zy*) kolkhoz

kołczan *m* (*-nu*; *-ny*) quiver

kołdra *f* (*-ry*; *-ry*) (continental) quilt, *Br* duvet

kołduny *pl* (*-nów*) *meat dumplings served in broth*

koł|ek *m* (*-łka*; *-łki*) **1.** (*wieszak*, *palik*) peg **2.** (*rozporowy*) wall plug, *Br* Rawlplug® **3.** (*do łączenia elementów*) dowel **4.** ***język komuś stanął ~kiem*** s.o. got tongue-tied

K

kołem *adv* in a circle; ***otoczyć ~*** circle, surround; ***historia ~ się toczy*** history repeats itself

kołnierz *m* (*-rza*; *-rze*) **1.** collar; ***nie wylewać za ~*** *fig* like the hard stuff **2.** TECH flange, collar; **kołnierzyk** *m* (*-ka*; *-ki*) collar

koł|o[1] *n* (*-ła*; *-ła*) **1.** circle; **w ~o a)** (*dookoła*) around **b)** (*ciągle*) over and over (again); ***~o przyjaciół*** circle of friends; ***~a polityczne*** political circles; ***~o ratunkowe*** life belt; ***~o polarne*** the Polar Circle; ***~o podbiegunowe*** **a)** (*północne*) the Arctic Circle **b)** (*południowe*) the Antarctic Circle; ***błędne ~o*** vicious circle; ***piąte ~o u wozu*** fifth circle; ***kwadratura ~a*** squaring the circle; ***w ~o Macieju*** over and over (again) **2.** *pojazdu*: wheel; ***przednie ~o*** front wheel; ***tylne ~o*** rear wheel; ***~o zapasowe*** *Br* spare tyre, *Am* spare tire; ***~o fortuny*** wheel of fortune **3.** TECH wheel; ***~o zębate*** cog(wheel); ***~o pasowe***, ***~o transmisyjne*** pulley; ***młyńskie ~o*** mill wheel; ***~o garncarskie*** potter's wheel **4.** (*zrzeszenie*) association

koło[2] *prep* (*G*) **1.** near, by; ***siedzieć ~*** *G* sit next to; ***przejść ~*** *G* walk by **2.** (*około*) about, around; ***~ drugiej*** about two o'clock; ***~ północy*** around midnight

kołonotatnik *m* (*-ka*; *-ki*) spiral notebook

kołowacieć ⟨**s-**⟩ (*-cieję*) *infml* stiffen; **kołowacizna** *f* (*-ny*; *no pl*) **1.** (*choroba*) gid, staggers *pl* **2.** *fig* dizziness, tailspin

kołować *v/im* (*-łuję*) **1.** (*o samolocie*) taxi **2.** (*zataczać kręgi*) circle

kołowrotek *m* (*-tka*; *-tki*) **1.** (*przy wędce*) *Br* reel, *Am* spool **2.** (*do przędzenia*) spinning wheel **3.** (*przy studni*) well-wheel, winch; **kołowrót** *m* (*-rotu*; *-roty*) **1.** (*urządzenie*) winch, windlass **2.** (*krzyżak*) turnstile **3.** *fig* whirl; **kołowy** *adj* **1.** *przekrój*: circular **2.** *pojazd*: wheeled; ***ruch ~*** road traffic

kołpak *m* (*-ka*; *-ki*) TECH hubcap

kołtun *m* (*-na*; *-ny*) **1.** (*osoba*) philistine, ignoramus **2.** (*włosy*) matted hair; **kołtuneria** *f* (*-rii*; *no pl*) narrow-mindedness

kołtuński *adj* narrow-minded

kołysać ⟨**za-**⟩ (*-szę*) **1.** swing; ***~ nogami*** swing one's legs **2.** *łodzią, dziecko*: rock; ***~ kogoś do snu*** lull s.o. to sleep **2.** *biodrami*: sway; ***kołysać się*** **1.** swing, rock **2.** (*o gałęziach*) sway **3.** (*o łodzi*) roll; **kołysanka** *f* (*-ki*; *-ki*) lullaby; **kołysk|a** *f* (*-ki*; *-ki*) cradle; ***od ~i*** from the cradle

koma[1] *f* (*-my*; *no pl*) (*śpiączka*) coma

koma[2] *f indecl* (*przecinek*) *lit* point

komando *n* (*-da*; *-da*) commando (unit)

komandor *m* (*-ra*; *-rzy*) (*w marynarce*) commodore; **komandorski** *adj*: ***krzyż ~*** commanders' cross

komandos *m* (*-sa*; *-si*) **1.** commando **2.** (*żołnierz jednostki powietrznodesantowej*) paratrooper

komandytow|y *adj*: ***spółka ~a*** limited partnership

komar *m* (*-ra*; *-ry*) mosquito

komasacja *f* (*-ji*; *no pl*) *gruntów*: consolidation

kombajn *m* (*-nu*; *-ny*) (*w rolnictwie*) combine, *Br* combine harvester

kombatant *m* (*-ta*; *-nci*) veteran

kombi *n indecl*: (***samochód***) *~ Br* estate car, *Am* saloon car

kombinacj|a *f* (*-ji*; *-je*) **1.** combination; ***~e*** wheelings and dealings, underhand dealings **2.** SPORT combined event; **~a norweska** Nordic combined; **~a alpejska** Alpine combined

kombinat *m* (*-tu*; *-ty*) (industrial) conglomerate

kombinator *m* (*-ra*; *-rzy*), **~ka** *f* (*-ki*; *-ki*) **1.** wheeler-dealer **2.** (*spryciarz*) sly old fox

kombinerki *pl* (*-rek*) (pair of) pliers

kombinezon *m* (*-nu*; *-ny*) **1.** *Br* overalls *pl*, *Am* coveralls *pl*; **~ narciarski** ski suit; **~ astronauty** spacesuit

kombin|ować ⟨**s-**, **wy-**⟩ (*-nuję*) **I** *v/i* (*zastanawiać się*) ***~ować, jak coś zrobić*** try to figure out how to do s.th. **II** *v/t*; (*knuć*) be up to something; ***oni na pewno coś ~ują*** they must be up to something

komedia *f* (*-dii*; *-die*) **1.** comedy **2.** *fig* farce; **komediancki** *adj* theatrical, histrionic; **komediant** *m* (*-ta*; *-nci*), **~ka** *f* (*-ki*; *-ki*) *dated* player, actor

komediopisarz *m* (*-rza*; *-rze*), **-rka** *f* (*-ki*; *-ki*) comedy writer; **komediowy** *adj* **1.** *serial*: comedy **2.** *element*, *aktor*, *talent*: comic

komend|a *f* (*-dy*; *-dy*) **1.** command; ***objąć ~ę nad*** *I* take command of; ***jak na ~ę*** all at once, as if by command **2.** (*siedziba dowództwa*) headquarters *sing*; ***~a policji*** police headquarters; **komendant** *m* (*-ta*; *-nci*) **1.** (*w wojsku*) commandant, commanding officer **2.** (*w policji*, *straży pożarnej*) chief; ***~ policji*** police chief, *Br* chief constable

komenderować *v/im* (*-ruję*): ***~ kimś*** push s.o. around

komentarz *m* (*-rza*; *-rze*) **1.** (*uwaga*) comment (***na temat*** *G* on/about); ***bez ~a*** no comment **2.** (*objaśnienia*) commentary **3.** *SPORT* (running) commentary

komentator *m* (*-ra*; *-rzy*), **~ka** *f* (*-ki*; *-ki*) commentator; **komentować** ⟨**s-**⟩ (*-tuję*) comment (*A* on)

komercjalizacja *f* (*-ji*; *no pl*) commercialization; **komercyjny** *adj* commercial

kometa *f* (*-ty*; *-ty*) comet

kometka *f* (*-ki*; *-ki*) badminton

komfortowo *adv* *żyć*: in comfort; ***~ wyposażone auto*** luxury car; **komfortowy** *adj* **1.** *samochód*: luxury **2.** *warunki*, *sytuacja*: comfortable; ***w ~ch warunkach*** in comfort

komiczność *f* (*-ści*; *no pl*) *Br* humour, *Am* humor; **komiczny** *adj* (*zabawny*) comical, funny

komik *m* (*-ka*; *-micy*) comedian

komiks *m* (*-su*; *-sy*) **1.** comic **2.** (*krótka historyjka*) comic strip

komin *m* (*-na*; *-ny*) **1.** chimney **2.** (*statku*, *lokomotywy*) smokestack, *Br* funnel; **kominek** *m* (*-nka*; *-nki*) fireplace

kominiarka *f* (*-ki*; *-ki*) (*czapka*) balaclava; **kominiarz** *m* (*-rza*; *-rze*) chimney sweep

komis *m* (*-su*; *-sy*) **1.** (*pośrednictwo*) consignment (sale) **2.** (*sklep*) second-hand shop, *Am* consignment store

komisariat *m* (*-tu*; *-ty*): ***~ policji*** police station; **komisaryczny** *adj*: ***zarząd ~*** **a)** (*zarządzanie*) receivership **b)** (*grupa osób*) (team) of receivers; **komisarz** *m* (*-rza*; *-rze*) **1.** *policji*: commissioner **2.** *ludowy*: commissar

komisja *f* (*-ji*; *-je*) **1.** committee, commission; ***~ badawcza*** committee of inquiry, commission of inquiry; ***~ do spraw nauki*** (***budżetowa***) science (budget) committee; ***≈ Europejska*** European Commission **2.** *egzaminacyjna*, *lekarska*: board

komisyjny *adj* **1.** *egzamin*: before a board (of examiners) **2.** *oględziny*: done by a committee

komitet *m* (*-tu*; *-ty*) committee; ***~ rodzicielski*** parents' association

komityw|a *f* (*-wy*; *no pl*): ***żyć w ~ie z*** *I* be on good terms with

komiwojażer *m* (*-ra*; *-rowie*) *Br* travelling salesman, *Am* traveling salesman

komizm *m* (*-mu*; *no pl*) *Br* humour, *Am* humor

komnata *f* (*-ty*; *-ty*) chamber

komoda *f* (*-dy*; *-dy*) *Br* chest of drawers, *Am* bureau

komora *f* (*-ry*; *-ry*) **1.** *TECH* chamber; ***~ gazowa*** gas chamber; ***~ celna*** customs house **2.** *serca*: ventricle

komorne *n* (*-nego*; *no pl*) rent

komornik *m* (*-ka*; *-nicy*) *Br* bailiff, *Am* law enforcement officer

komórk|a *f* (*-ki*; *-ki*) **1.** *BIOL* cell; ***~a jajowa*** egg (cell); ***szare ~i*** *fig Br* grey matter, *Am* gray matter **2.** (*telefon*) *infml Br* mobile, *Am* cellphone

K

3. (*pomieszczenie*) cubbyhole, small room; **komórkowy** *adj* cellular; ***telefon ~*** *Br* mobile phone, *Am* cellular phone

kompakt *m* (*-tu*; *-ty*) **1.** (*płyta*) CD **2.** (*odtwarzacz*) CD player **3.** (*samochód*) compact car, *Am* compact; **kompaktow|y** *adj*: ***płyta ~a*** compact disc; ***odtwarzacz ~y*** CD player

kompan *m* (*-na*; *-ni*) *Br* mate, *Am* buddy

kompania *f* (*-nii*; *-nie*) company; ***~ honorowa*** *Br* guard of honour, *Am* guard of honor

kompas *m* (*-su*; *-sy*) compass

kompatybilny *adj form* compatible (***z*** *I* with)

kompensacja *f* (*-ji*; *no pl*) *form* **1.** compensation **2.** (*wzajemnych zobowiązań*) netting

kompensata *f* (*-ty*; *no pl*) compensation

K

kompensować 〈**s-**〉 (*-suję*) *form* **1.** compensate (*A* for) **2.** FIN offset **3.** *wzajemne zobowiązania*: net

kompetencj|e *pl* (*-ji*) *form* (*uprawnienia*) (area of) competence *sing*, (area of) authority *sing*; ***być w zakresie czyichś ~i*** be within s.o.'s competence; ***to przekracza moje ~e*** it is not my responsibility; ***przekroczyć swoje ~e*** overstep one's authority

kompetentny *adj* competent; ***~ do zrobienia czegoś*** authorized to do s.th., competent to do s.th.

kompleks *m* (*-su*; *-sy*) **1.** (*zespół*) complex; ***~ budynków*** complex of buildings **2.** PSYCH complex (***na punkcie*** *G* about), hang-up (***na punkcie*** *G* about); ***~ niższości*** inferiority complex; ***~ Edypa*** Oedipus complex; ***bez ~ów*** *osoba*: self-assured, uninhibited

kompleksowo *adv* comprehensively; **kompleksowy** *adj* comprehensive

komplemenciarz *m* (*-rza*; *-rze*) flatterer; **komplement** *m* (*-tu*; *-ty*) compliment; ***prawić komuś ~y*** pay s.o. compliments, compliment s.o.

komplementarny *adj* complementary

komplet *m* (*-tu*; *-ty*) **1.** *narzędzi*, *naczyń*, *bielizny*: set; ***~ do kawy*** coffee set **2.** *mebli*: suite, set; ***~ wypoczynkowy*** living-room suite, three-piece suite **3.** *pracowników*, *uczniów*: full complement; ***na sali był ~ widzów*** the auditorium was filled to capacity; ***mieć ~ pasażerów*** be fully booked; ***jesteśmy w komplecie*** we're all here

kompletny *adj* complete; ***z ~m wyposażeniem*** fully equipped; **kompletować** 〈**s-**〉 (*-tuję*) **1.** *kolekcję*, *zestaw*: complete **2.** *drużynę*, *zespół*: assemble

komplikacj|a *f* (*-ji*; *-je*) complication; ***nastąpiły u niej ~e*** MED she developed complications

komplikować 〈**s-**〉 (*-kuję*) complicate; ***komplikować się*** become complicated

komponent *m* (*-tu*; *-ty*) component; **komponować** 〈**s-**〉 (*-nuję*) compose

kompot *m* (*-tu*; *-ty*) **1.** (*napój*) compote; ***wpaść jak śliwka w ~*** *fig* get into trouble **2.** (*narkotyk*) Polish heroin

kompozycja *f* (*-ji*; *-je*) **1.** composition **2.** *kwiatowa*: arrangement; **kompozytor** *m* (*-ra*; *-rzy*), **~ka** *f* (*-ki*; *-ki*) composer

kompres *m* (*-su*; *-sy*) compress

kompresja *f* (*-ji*; *-je*) compression

kompromis *m* (*-su*; *-sy*) compromise; ***dojść do ~u*** reach a compromise; ***pójść na ~ w kwestii*** *G* compromise on

kompromitacj|a *f* (*-ji*; *-je*) disgrace (*G* to), embarrassment (*G* to); ***z obawy przed ~ą*** for fear of compromising oneself

kompromitować 〈**s-**〉 (*-tuję*) **1.** disgrace, embarrass **2.** (*demaskować*) compromise; ***kompromitować się*** compromise oneself; **kompromitujący** *adj* embarrassing, compromising

komputer *m* (*-ra*; *-ry*) computer; ***~ osobisty*** PC, personal computer; **komputerowy** *adj* computer; **komputerowiec** *m* (*-wca*; *-wcy*) computer expert, *infml* computer buff

komputeryzować 〈**s-**〉 (*-zuję*) computerize

komu *pron* who, whom; → ***kto***

komuch *m* (*-cha*; *-chy*) *infml* Commie

komun|a *f* (*-ny*; *-ny*) **1.** (*komunizm*) communism, communist regime; ***za ~y*** in communist times **2.** (*wspólnota*) commune

komunalny *adj mieszkanie*, *grunty*: *Br* council, municipal
komunał *m* (*-łu*; *-ły*) platitude, cliché
komuni|a *f* (*-nii*; *-nie*) REL communion, Communion; ***przyjąć ~ę*** take communion; ***przystąpić do pierwszej ~i*** make one's First Communion
komunikacja *f* (*-ji*; *no pl*) **1.** (*porozumiewanie się*) communication **2.** (*łączność*) communications *pl* **3.** (*transport*) *Br* transport, *Am* transportation; ***~ miejska*** public transport; ***~ lotnicza*** air transport; **komunikacyjny** *adj* **1.** (*dotyczący transportu*) *Br* transport, *Am* transportation; ***węzeł ~*** transport hub **2.** (*dotyczący łączności*) communications
komunikat *m* (*-tu*; *-ty*) **1.** announcement; ***podać ~*** make an announcement **2.** *prasowy*: release, report **3.** *pogodowy*: report; **komunikatywny** *adj* **1.** *osoba*, *funkcja*: communicative **2.** *język*: accessible, easily understood
komunikować 〈**za-**〉 (*-kuję*) announce, communicate; ***komunikować się*** *v/im* communicate, be in contact
komunista *m* (*-ty*; *-niści*), **-tka** *f* (*-ki*; *-ki*) communist; **komunistyczny** *adj* communist
komunizm *m* (*-mu*; *no pl*) communism
komża *f* (*-ży*; *-że*) surplice
konać 〈**s-**〉 (*-nam*) be dying; ***~ ze śmiechu*** almost die laughing
konający *m* (*-cego*; *-cy*), **-ca** *f* (*-cej*; *-ce*) dying person
konar *m* (*-ra*/*-ru*; *-ry*) bough, limb
koncentracj|a *f* (*-ji*; *no pl*) concentration; ***zdolność ~i*** powers of concentration
koncentracyjny *adj obóz*: concentration
koncentrat *m* (*-tu*; *-ty*) concentrate; ***~ pomidorowy*** tomato paste, tomato concentrate
koncentrować 〈**s-**〉 (*-ruję*) concentrate; ***~ uwagę*** concentrate, focus (**na** *L* on); ***koncentrować się*** **1.** concentrate (**na** *L* on) **2.** (*ogniskować się*) *Br* centre, *Am* center (***wokół*** *G* around), be concentrated (***wokół*** *G* around)
koncepcja *f* (*-ji*; *-je*) idea, conception; **koncept** *m* (*-tu*; *-ty*) idea, *lit* conceit
koncern *m* (*-nu*; *-ny*) concern
koncert *m* (*-tu*; *-ty*) **1.** concert **2.** (*utwór*) concerto (**na** *A* for); ***~ skrzypcowy*** violin concerto; ***~ życzeń*** listeners' choice, *Br* request programme **3.** *fig* virtuoso display (*G* of); **koncertować** *v/im* (*-tuję*) give concerts; **koncertow|y** *adj* **1.** concert; ***sala ~a*** concert hall **2.** *fig* virtuoso, brilliant
koncesja *f* (*-ji*; *-je*) **1.** *Br* licence, *Am* license; ***~ na sprzedaż alkoholu*** licence to sell alcohol **2.** (*ustępstwo*) concession; **koncesjonować** *v/im* (*-nuję*) license; **koncesjonowany** *adj* licensed
koncha *f* (*-chy*; *-chy*) **1.** (*muszla*, *sklepienie*) conch **2.** ANAT concha
kondensować 〈**s-**〉 (*-suję*) condense
kondolencje *pl* (*-ji*) condolences; ***składać komuś ~*** offer one's condolences to s.o.; **kondolencyjny** *adj*: ***list ~*** letter of condolence
kondukt *m* (*-tu*; *-ty*): ***~ żałobny*** funeral procession, cortege
konduktor *m* (*-ra*; *-rzy*) conductor; **konduktorka** *f* (*-ki*; *-ki*) conductress
kondycj|a *f* (*-ji*; *no pl*) **1.** fitness; ***być w dobrej ~i*** be fit, be in good shape; ***nie być w ~i*** be out of shape **2.** *finansowa*: standing; **kondycyjny** *adj trening*, *ćwiczenia*: fitness
kondygnacja *f* (*-ji*; *-je*) *Br* storey, *Am* story
koneksje *pl* (*-ji*) connections
koneser *m* (*-ra*; *-rzy*) connoisseur
konewka *f* (*-ki*; *-ki*) watering can
konfederacja *f* (*-ji*; *-je*) **1.** confederation **2.** POLIT confederacy
konfekcja *f* (*-ji*; *no pl*) (ready-to-wear) clothing
konferansjer *m* (*-ra*; *-rzy*) master of ceremonies, MC, *Br* compère; **konferansjerka** *f* (*-ki*; *no pl*) (*zajęcie*) emceeing
konferencja *f* (*-ji*; *-je*) conference
konfesjonał *m* (*-łu*; *-ły*) confessional
konfident *m* (*-ta*; *-nci*), **~ka** *f* (*-ki*; *-ki*) informer
konfigurować 〈**s-**〉 (*-ruję*) configure
konfirmacja *f* (*-ji*; *-je*) confirmation
konfiskata *f* (*-ty*; *-ty*) confiscation; **konfiskować** 〈**s-**〉 (*-kuję*) confiscate
konfitury *pl* (*-tur*) conserve *sing*

K

konflikt *m* (*-tu*; *-ty*) conflict; ***wejść w ~ z I*** come into conflict with; ***~ pokoleń*** the generation gap; ***~ serologiczny*** *MED* rhesus incompatibility; **konfliktowy** *adj* **1.** *osoba*: confrontational **2.** *sytuacja*: conflict

konformizm *m* (*-mu*; *no pl*) conformism

konfrontacja *f* (*-ji*; *-je*) **1.** (*konflikt*) confrontation **2.** (*porównanie*) comparison, contrast; **konfrontować** ⟨**s-**⟩ (*-tuję*) compare, contrast (**z** *I* with)

kongres *m* (*-su*; *-sy*) congress

koniak *m* (*-ku*; *-ki*) brandy

koniczyna *f* (*-ny*; *-ny*) clover; ***czterolistna ~*** four-leaf clover

koniec *m* (*końca*; *końce*) **1.** end; ***~ tygodnia*** the end of the week; ***pod ~ roku*** at the end of the year; ***~ świata*** the end of the world; ***na końcu*** at the end (*G* of); ***w końcu*** (*wreszcie*) finally, eventually; ***do*** (***samego***) ***końca*** to the (very) end; ***do końca świata*** till the end of time; ***dobiec końca*** come to an end; ***bez końca*** endlessly, on end; ***od początku do końca*** from beginning to end; ***od końca*** from the end; ***i na tym ~*** and that's it; ***na dzisiaj ~!*** that's all for today!; ***nie idę i ~!*** I'm not going and that's final!; ***nie do końca rozumiem*** I don't quite understand; ***z nami ~!*** (*do chłopaka*, *dziewczyny*) we are finished!; ***na szarym końcu*** at the very end **2.** *języka*, *palca*: tip **3.** *igły*: point, end

koniecznie *adv* absolutely, really; ***nie~*** not necessarily; ***ten film trzeba ~ zobaczyć*** the film is an absolute must; **koniecznoś|ć** *f* (*-ści*; *no pl*) necessity (*G* of), need (*G* for); ***z ~ci*** out of necessity; **konieczn|y** *adj* necessary; ***obrona ~a*** self-defense

konik *m* (*-ka*; *-ki*) **1.** *dim* (small) horse; ***~ polny*** grasshopper; ***~ morski*** sea horse **2.** (*zabawka*) toy horse **3.** (*hobby*) hobby **4.** (*w szachach*) knight **5.** (*sprzedający bilety*) *infml Br* tout, *Am* scalper

koniugacja *f* (*-ji*; *-je*) *GRAM* conjugation

koniunktura *f* (*-ry*; *no pl*) **1.** (*sytuacja*) situation **2.** ***dobra ~*** *ECON* boom; ***zła ~*** *ECON* slump

koniuszek *m* (*-szka*; *-szki*) tip

konkluzja *f* (*-ji*; *-je*) conclusion

konkretny *adj* **1.** (*określony*) specific **2.** (*dokładny*) precise, exact **3.** *dowód*, *propozycja*: concrete **4.** *osoba*: businesslike, matter-of-fact

konkret *m* (*-tu*; *-ty*) (*informacja*) concrete information; ***przejść do ~ów*** get down to business, *infml* get down to the nitty-gritty; **konkretyzować** ⟨**s-**⟩ (*-zuję*) specify

konkubent *m* (*-ta*; *-nci*) cohabiting partner, common-law husband; **konkubina** *f* (*-ny*; *-ny*) cohabiting partner, common-law wife; **konkubina|t** *m* (*-tu*; *no pl*) cohabitation, common-law marriage; ***żyć w ~cie*** cohabit (**z** *I* for)

konkurencja *f* (*-ji*; *-je*) **1.** *ECON* competition **2.** *SPORT* event

konkurencyjność *f* (*-ści*; *no pl*) competitiveness, competitive edge; **konkurencyjny** *adj* **1.** *cena*: competitive **2.** *firma*, *sklep*: rival

konkurent *m* (*-ta*; *-nci*), **~ka** *f* (*-ki*; *-ki*) competitor, rival

konkurować *v/im* (*-ruję*) compete (**o** *A* for)

konkurs *m* (*-su*; *-sy*) competition, contest; ***~ piękności*** *Br* beauty contest, *Am* beauty pageant; ***~ radiowy*** radio quiz show; ***poza ~em*** (*o filmie*) outside the competition; **konkursow|y** *adj* competition; ***prace ~e*** entries for a competition

konno *adv*: ***jechać ~*** ride (on) horseback

konn|y *adj* **1.** *przejażdżka*: horseback **2.** *wóz*: horse-drawn; ***jazda ~a*** riding, *Br* horse riding, *Am* horseback riding; ***wyścigi ~e*** horse racing

konopie *pl* (*-pi*) hemp *sing*

konował *m* (*-ła*; *-ły*) *infml* quack

konsekwencja *f* (*-ji*; *-je*) **1.** consistency **2.** (*skutek*) consequence **3.** (*wytrwałość*) determination; **konsekwentny** *adj* **1.** consistent **2.** (*wytrwały*) determined

konserw|a *f* (*-wy*; *-wy*) **1.** canned food, *Br* tinned food; ***~a rybna*** canned fish **2.** (*opakowanie*) can, *Br* tin; ***otwieracz do ~*** can-opener; *Br* tin-opener

konserwacja *f* (*-ji*; *no pl*) **1.** *TECH* maintenance **2.** *zabytków*: conservation, preservation **3.** *żywności*: preservation; **konserwacyjny** *adj* **1.** *TECH*

K

maintenance **2.** (*dotyczący zabytków*) conservation, preservation
konserwant *m* (*-tu*; *-ty*) preservative
konserwator *m* (*-ra*; *-rzy*) **1.** TECH maintenance technician, maintenance person **2.** *zabytków*: conservator, restorer
konserwatorium *n* (*indecl*; *-ria*) *Br* conservatoire, *Am* conservatory
konserwatysta *m* (*-ty*; *-tyści*), **-tka** *f* (*-ki*; *-ki*) conservative
konserwatywny *adj* conservative
konserwować ⟨**za-**⟩ (*-rwuję*) **1.** TECH maintain **2.** *zabytki*: conserve, protect **3.** *żywność*: preserve; **konserwowy** *adj* **1.** *żywność*, *szynka*: canned, *Br* tinned **2.** *ogórki*: pickled; **konserwujący** *adj*: ***środek ~*** preservative
konsolidacja *f* (*-ji*; *-je*) consolidation
konsorcjum *n* (*indecl*; *-ja*) consortium
konspekt *m* (*-tu*; *-ty*) synopsis, summary
konspiracja *f* (*-ji*; *no pl*) **1.** (*organizacja*) the underground **2.** (*działalność*) underground activities *pl*; **konspiracyjny** *adj organizacja*, *działalność*: underground; ***działacz ~*** member of the underground; **konspirować** *v/im* (*-ruję*) conspire
konstatować ⟨**s-**⟩ (*-tuję*) *form* **1.** observe **2.** *fakt*: state
konstelacja *f* (*-ji*; *-je*) constellation
konsternacj|a *f* (*-ji*; *no pl*) consternation, dismay; ***wprawić w ~ę*** dismay
konstrukcja *f* (*-ji*; *-je*) **1.** (*struktura*) structure **2.** (*budowanie*) construction, building; **konstrukcyjny** *adj* **1.** *element*: structural **2.** *materiał*: construction
konstruktor *m* (*-ra*; *-rzy*), **~ka** *f* (*-ki*; *-ki*) **1.** design engineer, designer **2.** (*wykonawca*) constructor
konstruktywny *adj* constructive; **konstruować** ⟨**s-**⟩ (*-ruuję*) **1.** (*projektować*) design **2.** (*budować*) construct
konstytucja *f* (*-ji*; *-je*) constitution; **konstytucyjny** *adj* constitutional; **konstytuować** ⟨**u-**⟩ (*-tuuję*) constitute, form; ***konstytuować się*** be constituted, be formed
konsul *m* (*-la*; *-lowie*) consul; **konsularny** *adj* consular; **konsulat** *m* (*-tu*; *-ty*) consulate
konsultacja *f* (*-ji*; *-je*) consultation; **konsultacyjny** *adj*: ***punkt ~*** **a)** *Br* information centre, *Am* information center **b)** (*dla osób uzależnionych*, *studentów*) *Br* counselling service, *Am* counseling service
konsultant *m* (*-ta*; *-nci*) consultant; **konsulting** *m* (*-gu*; *no pl*) consulting services *pl*, consultancy
konsultować ⟨**s-**⟩ (*-tuję*) consult (**coś z** *I* s.o. about); ***konsultować się*** consult (**z** *I* with; ***w sprawie*** *G* about)
konsumencki *adj* consumer; **konsument** *m* (*-ta*; *-nci*), **~ka** *f* (*-ki*; *-ki*) **1.** consumer; ***ochrona praw ~a*** consumer protection **2.** (*klient*) customer
konsumować ⟨**s-**⟩ (*-muję*) **1.** consume **2.** *małżeństwo*: consummate; **konsumpcja** *f* (*-ji*; *no pl*) consumption; **konsumpcyjn|y** *adj* consumer; ***artykuły ~e*** consumer goods
konsylium *n* (*indecl*; *-lia*) (*lekarskie*) case conference
konsystencja *f* (*-ji*; *no pl*) consistency
konszachty *pl* (*-tów*) shady connections; ***mieć ~*** **z** *I* have shady connections with, *infml* be in cahoots with
kontak|t *m* (*-tu*; *-ty*) **1.** contact; ***być w ~cie*** **z** *I* be in touch with, be in contact with **2.** (*gniazdko*) socket; ***włączyć do ~tu*** plug in; ***wtyczka do ~tu*** plug **3.** (*wyłącznik*) switch
kontaktować ⟨**s-**⟩ (*-tuję*) **1.** ***~ kogoś z kimś*** put s.o. in contact with s.o. **2.** (*o wtyczce*, *kablu*) ***coś nie kontaktuje*** there is a loose connection in s.th. **3.** (*być osowiałym*): ***nie ~*** *infml* be spaced out, *Am* be spacey; ***kontaktować się*** **1.** (*być w kontakcie*) be in touch, be in contact (**z** *I* with) **2.** (*nawiązywać kontakt*) get in touch (**z** *I* with)
kontaktow|y *adj* **1.** contact; ***szkła ~e*** contact lenses **2.** *osoba*: outgoing
kontekst *m* (*-tu*; *-ty*) context; ***wyrwany z ~u*** (taken) out of context
kontener *m* (*-ra*; *-ry*) container; **kontenerowiec** *m* (*-wca*; *-wce*) container ship
kontestacja *f* (*-ji*; *no pl*) **1.** (*kwestionowanie*) challenging **2.** (*protest*) protest (*G* against) **3.** *polityczna*, *religijna*: dissent

K

kon|to *n* (*-ta*; *-ta*) account; ***wpłacić na ~to*** pay into an account; ***ma wiele sukcesów na swoim ~cie*** *fig* he has many successes to his credit
kontra[1] *f* (*-ry*; *-ry*) **1.** (*kontratak*) counterattack **2.** (*w boksie*) counter **3.** (*w brydżu*) double
kontra[2] *prep* (*N*/*D*) versus; ***argumenty pro i ~*** arguments for and against
kontrabanda *f* (*-dy*; *no pl*) contraband
kontrabas *m* (*-su*; *-sy*) double bass
kontrahent *m* (*-ta*; *-nci*), **~ka** *f* (*-ki*; *-ki*) **1.** (*partner*) (business) partner **2.** (*klient*) customer **3.** (*wykonawca, dostawca*) contractor
kontrakt *m* (*-tu*; *-ty*) contract; **kontraktowy** *adj* **1.** *pracownik*: contract **2.** *warunki*, *zobowiązanie*: contractual
kontrargument *m* (*-tu*; *-ty*) counter-argument
kontrast *m* (*-tu*; *-ty*) contrast; **kontrastować** ⟨**s-**⟩ (*-tuję*) contrast; **kontrastowy** *adj kolory*, *charaktery*: contrasting
kontrasygnować *v/im* (*-nuję*) countersign
kontratak *m* (*-ku*; *-ki*) counterattack
kontrkandydat *m* (*-ta*; *-daci*), **~ka** *f* (*-ki*; *-ki*) rival, rival candidate
kontrofensywa *f* (*-wy*; *-wy*) counteroffensive
kontrol|a *f* (*-li*; *-le*) **1.** (*sprawdzenie*) check, inspection; ***~a antydopingowa*** *Br* drugs test, *Am* drug test; ***~a biletów*** ticket inspection; ***~a paszportowa*** passport control **2.** (*nadzór*) control; ***~a urodzeń*** birth control; ***~a lotów*** air traffic control; ***przejąć ~ę nad** I* take control of **3.** (*zespół*) inspection team, inspectors *pl*
kontroler *m* (*-ra*; *-rzy*), **~ka** *f* (*-ki*; *-ki*) inspector, controller; ***~ biletów*** ticket inspector; ***~ ruchu lotniczego*** air traffic controller
kontrolka *f* (*-ki*; *-ki*) (*dioda*) control LED
kontroln|y *adj* **1.** *jazda*: test **2.** *wieża*: control; ***badanie ~e*** check-up; ***praca ~a*** test; ***lista ~a*** checklist; ***pakiet ~y*** controlling interest; ***urządzenie ~e*** **a)** (*sterujące*) control device **b)** (*monitorujące*) monitoring device; **kontrolować** (*-luję*) ⟨**s-**⟩ **1.** (*sprawdzać*) check, inspect **2.** (*kierować, panować nad*) control
kontrować ⟨**s-**⟩ (*-ruję*) **1.** SPORT counter **2.** (*w brydżu*) double
kontrowersyjny *adj* controversial
kontrrewolucja *f* (*-ji*; *-je*) counter-revolution; **kontruderzenie** *n* (*-nia*; *-nia*) counter-attack; **kontrwywiad** *m* (*-du*; *-dy*) counter-intelligence
kontuar *m* (*-ru*; *-ry*) **1.** (*w sklepie*) counter **2.** (*w barze*) bar
kontur *m* (*-ru*; *-ry*) outline, contour; **konturówka** *f* (*-ki*; *-ki*) lip liner
kontuzja *f* (*-ji*; *-je*) injury
kontynent *m* (*-tu*; *-ty*) continent; **kontynentalny** *adj* continental
kontyngent *m* (*-tu*; *-ty*) **1.** (*wojskowy*) contingent **2.** ECON (import) quota
kontynuacja *f* (*-ji*; *-je*) continuation; **kontynuować** *v/im* (*-nuuję*) continue
konwalia *f* (*-lii*; *-lie*) lily of the valley
konwenanse *pl* (*-sów*) social conventions, proprieties
konwencja *f* (*-ji*; *-je*) convention; **konwencjonalny** *adj* conventional
konwersacja *f* (*-ji*; *-je*) conversation; **konwersacyjny** *adj* conversational
konwersja *f* (*-ji*; *no pl*) conversion
konwój *m* (*-woju*; *-woje*) convoy
konwulsje *pl* (*-ji*) convulsions; **konwulsyjny** *adj* convulsive
koń *m* (*konia*; *konie*) **1.** horse; ***jechać na koniu*** ride a horse; ***~ na biegunach*** rocking horse; ***~ pełnej krwi*** thoroughbred; ***~ mechaniczny*** horsepower; ***stary ~*** *fig* full-grown man; ***zrobić kogoś w konia*** take s.o. for a ride; ***znać się jak łyse konie*** know each other inside out; ***darowanemu koniowi w zęby się nie zagląda*** don't look a gift horse in the mouth **2.** (*w szachach*) knight **3.** SPORT (vaulting) horse
końcowy *adj* **1.** final; ***przystanek ~*** final stop, terminus **2.** *produkt*: end **3.** *linia*: boundary
końcówka *f* (*-ki*; *-ki*) **1.** end **2.** *filmu*, *wyrazu*: ending **3.** SPORT finish **4.** *wiertła*: tip **5.** (*pozostałość*) remainder
kończyć ⟨**s-**⟩ (*-czę*) **1.** finish; ***~ 20 lat*** turn 20 **2.** *z piciem*, *paleniem*: be through (**z** *I* with) **3.** *w więzieniu*: end (**w** *L* in); **kończyć się** **1.** end

2. (*wyczerpać się*) run out; ***kończą nam się pieniądze*** we're running out of money
kończyna *f* (*-ny*; *-ny*) limb
końsk|i *adj grzywa*, *głowa*: horse's; ***~i ogon*** (*fryzura*) ponytail; ***mieć ~ie zdrowie*** be as fit as a fiddle; ***~a dawka*** *fig* megadose
kooperacja *f* (*-ji*; *no pl*) cooperation; **kooperować** *v/im* (*-ruję*) cooperate
koordynować ⟨**s-**⟩ (*-nuję*) coordinate
kop *m* (*-pa*; *-py*) *infml* kick, boot
kopa *f* (*-py*; *-py*): ***~ siana*** haystack; ***kopę lat!*** long time no see!, it's been ages!
kopać ⟨**-pnąć**, **wy-**⟩ (*-pię*) **1.** (*w ziemi*) dig **2.** (*nogą*) kick; ***prąd go kopnął*** *infml* he got a shock **3.** *ziemniaki*: lift
kopalina *f* (*-ny*; *-ny*) fossil
kopalnia *f* (*-ni*; *-nie*) mine; ***~ węgla*** coal mine, pit; ***~ odkrywkowa*** *Br* opencast mine, *Am* strip mine; ***~ wiedzy*** mine of knowledge; **kopalniany** *adj szyb*: mine; **kopalny** *adj gady*: fossil
koparka *f* (*-ki*; *-ki*) excavator, digger
kopcić ⟨**na-**, **za-**⟩ (*-cę*) smoke
Kopciuszek *m* (*-szka*; *no pl*) Cinderella
Kopenhaga *f* (*-gi*) Copenhagen
koper *m* (*-pru*; *-pry*) dill; ***~ włoski*** (sweet) fennel; **koperkowy** *adj* dill
koperta *f* (*-ty*; *-ty*) **1.** envelope **2.** *płyty*: sleeve, *Am* jacket
kopia[1] *f* (*-pii*; *-pie*) (*odtworzenie*, *odbitka*) copy; ***~ kserograficzna*** photocopy
kopia[2] *f* (*-pii*; *-pie*) (*broń*) lance
kopiarka *f* (*-ki*; *-ki*) (photo)copier
kopiasty *adj* heaped
kopiec *m* (*-pca*; *-pce*) **1.** mound; ***~ mrowiska*** anthill; ***~ mogilny*** burial mound **2.** *ziemniaków*: clamp
kopiować ⟨**s-**⟩ (*-piuję*) copy
kopnąć *v/p* → ***kopać***; **kopniak** *m* (*-ka*; *-ki*) kick; **kopnięty** *adj infml* nuts
koptyjski *adj* Coptic
kopulacja *f* (*-ji*; *-je*) copulation; **kopulować** *v/im* (*-luję*) copulate
kopuła *f* (*-ły*; *-ły*) dome
kopytka *pl* (*-tek*) potato dumplings
kopytny *adj zwierzęta*: hoofed
kopyto *n* (*-ta*; *-ta*) **1.** hoof; ***na jedno ~*** *fig* pretty much the same, done in the same style **2.** (*szewskie*) last
kora *f* (*-ry*; *-ry*) **1.** bark **2.** ANAT cortex; ***~ mózgowa*** cerebral cortex **3.** (*tkanina*) seersucker
koral *m* (*-la*; *-le*) **1.** coral **2.** (*paciorek*) bead **3.** ***~e*** (string of) beads; **koralik** *m* (*-ka*; *-ki*) bead
koralowiec *m* (*-wca*; *-wce*) coral; **koralow|y** *adj* coral; ***rafa ~a*** coral reef
korba *f* (*-by*; *-by*) crank; **korbowy** *adj* crank; ***wał ~*** crankshaft
korci|ć *v/im* (*-cę*): ***kogoś ~, żeby coś zrobić*** s.o. is itching to do s.th.
kordon *m* (*-nu*; *-ny*) cordon; ***otoczyć ~em*** cordon off; ***~ graniczny*** border posts
Korea *f* (*-rei*) Korea; ***~ Północna*** North Korea; ***~ Południowa*** South Korea
Koreańczyk *m* (*-ka*; *-czycy*), **-reanka** *f* (*-ki*; *-ki*) Korean; **koreańsk|i** *adj* Korean; ***mówić po ~u*** speak Korean; ***napisany po ~u*** written in Korean
korek *m* (*-rka*; *-rki*) **1.** *butelki*: stopper, cork; ***wyciągnąć z czegoś ~*** uncork s.th. **2.** (*do wanny*): plug **3.** (*zator*): ***~ uliczny*** traffic jam **4.** (*bezpiecznik*) fuse; ***wysiadły korki*** the fuses blew **5.** (*masa korkowa*) cork **6.** ***korki*** (*lekcje*) *infml* private lessons
korekt|a *f* (*-ty*; *-ty*) **1.** *tekstu*: proofreading; ***robić ~ę*** proofread **2.** (*poprawka*) correction; **korektor** *m* (*-ra*; *-ry*) **1.** (*-ra*; *-rzy*) (*osoba*) proofreader **2.** (*mazak*) correction pen, *Br* Tipp-Ex®, *Am* whiteout **3.** (*w płynie*) correction fluid, *Br* Tipp-Ex®, *Am* whiteout **4.** (*krem*) cover cream **5.** INF spell-checker **6.** MUS equalizer
korepetycje *pl* (*-ji*) private lessons, *form* private tuition *sing*
korespondencj|a *f* (*-ji*; *no pl*) **1.** correspondence; ***utrzymywać ~ę*** keep up correspondence, be in correspondence **2.** (*artykuł*) report; **korespondencyjnie** *adv Br* by post, *Am* by mail; **korespondencyjny** *adj* **1.** *adres*: mailing **2.** *kurs*: correspondence
korespondent *m* (*-ta*; *-nci*), **~ka** *f* (*-ki*; *-ki*) correspondent
korespondować *v/im* (*-duję*) correspond (**z** *I* with)
korkociąg *m* (*-gu*; *-gi*) **1.** corkscrew **2.** (*w akrobacji lotniczej*) spin; **korkować** ⟨**za-**⟩ (*-kuję*) **1.** *butelkę*: cork **2.** *ulicę*: block; **korkowy** *adj* cork

K

kornet *m* (*-tu*; *-ty*) cornet
kornik *m* (*-ka*; *-ki*) woodworm
korniszon *m* (*-na*; *-ny*) *Br* gherkin, *Am* pickle
korodować ⟨**s-**⟩ (*-duję*) corrode
korona *f* (*-ny*; *-ny*) crown; **koronacja** *f* (*-ji*; *-je*) coronation
koronka *f* (*-ki*; *-ki*) **1.** (*tkanina*) lace **2.** (*na ząb*) crown; **koronkow|y** *adj bielizna, kołnierzyk*: lace; ***~a robota*** *fig* superb (piece of) work
koronny *adj* crown, royal; ***zeznawać jako świadek ~*** *Br* turn Queen's evidence, *Br* turn King's evidence, *Am* turn State's evidence
koronować ⟨**u-**⟩ (*-nuję*) crown (**na** *A*); ***koronować się*** be crowned
korowody *pl* (*-dów*) (*zamieszanie*) fuss *sing*, hussle *sing*, hussles
korowód *m* (*-wodu*; *-wody*) procession parade
korporacja *f* (*-ji*; *-je*) corporation
korpulentny *adj lit* corpulent, fleshy
korpus *m* (*-su*; *-sy*) **1.** ANAT trunk **2.** *dyplomatyczny*: corps **3.** (*w wojsku*) corps *sing* **4.** TECH body **5.** (*zbiór tekstów*) corpus
korrida *f* (*-dy*; *-dy*) bullfight(ing), corrida
korsarz *m* (*-rza*; *-rze*) buccaneer, corsair
Korsyka *f* (*-ki*) Corsica; **korsykański** *adj* Corsican
kort *m* (*-tu*; *-ty*) SPORT court; ***~ tenisowy*** tennis court; ***~ ziemny*** clay court; ***~ trawiasty*** grass court
korumpować ⟨**s-**⟩ (*-puję*) corrupt
korupcja *f* (*-ji*; *no pl*) corruption; **korupcyjn|y** *adj* corruption; ***afera ~a*** corruption scandal
korygować ⟨**s-**⟩ (*-guję*) *form* correct
koryncki *adj* Corinthian
korytarz *m* (*-rza*; *-rze*) **1.** corridor; ***na ~u*** in the corridor, *Am* in the hallway **2.** (*w kopalni*) gallery
koryto *n* (*-ta*; *-ta*) **1.** (*naczynie*) trough **2.** (*łożysko*) channel; ***~ rzeki*** river channel
korzenić się ⟨**za-**⟩ (*-nię*) root; **korzeniowy** *adj* root
korzenn|y *adj* spicy, spice; ***przyprawy ~e*** spices; **korze|ń** *m* (*-rzenia*; *-rzenie*) root; ***zapuścić ~nie*** **a)** (*o roślinie*) take roots **b)** (*o osobie*) put down roots; ***wyrwać z ~niami*** uproot; ***~nie*** **a)** (*przyprawy*) spices **b)** (*pochodzenie*) roots
korzon|ek *m* (*-nka*; *-nki*) *dim* (small) root; ***~ki włosów*** hair roots; ***~ki nerwowe*** nerve roots
korzyć się ⟨**u-**⟩ (*-rzę*) *lit* humble oneself
korzystać ⟨**s-**⟩ (*-tam*) **1.** (*używać*) use (**z** *G*); ***~ z czyichś usług*** make use of s.o.'s services **2.** (*odnosić korzyść*) benefit (**z** *G* from) **3.** (*zyskiwać*) profit (**z** *G* from) **4.** (*wykorzystywać*) make use (**z** *G* of), use (**z** *G*); ***~ z czyichś doświadczeń*** draw on s.o.'s experience; ***~ z okazji*** to seize an opportunity; ***~ z prawa*** to exercise a right
korzystny *adj* **1.** *rozwiązanie, warunki pogodowe, wrażenie*: *Br* favourable, *Am* favorable **2.** *oferta*: advantageous; ***~ dla*** *G* beneficial to, advantageous to; ***~ dla zdrowia*** beneficial to health; ***wzajemnie ~*** mutually beneficial
korzyś|ć *f* (*-ści*; *-ści*) **1.** (*pożytek*) benefit; ***na czyjąś ~ć*** to s.o.'s advantage; ***decyzja na czyjąś ~ć*** *Br* decision in s.o.'s favour, *Am* decision in s.o.'s favor; ***czerpać ~ci z*** *G* benefit from; ***zmienić się na ~ć*** change for the better **2.** (*zysk*) profit; ***przynosić ~ci*** be profitable
kos *m* (*-sa*; *-sy*) blackbird
kosa *f* (*-sy*; *-sy*) scythe; **kosiarka** *f* (*-ki*; *-ki*) mower; ***~ do trawy*** lawnmower; **kosić** ⟨**s-**⟩ (*-szę*) **1.** (*kosiarką*) mow **2.** (*kosą*) scythe
kosmaty *adj* **1.** *futro, włosy*: shaggy **2.** *osoba*: hairy
kosmetyczka *f* (*-ki*; *-ki*) **1.** (*kobieta*) beautician **2.** (*na kosmetyki*) make-up bag, vanity bag **3.** (*na mydło, szczoteczkę*) toilet bag; **kosmetyczn|y** *adj* cosmetic; ***gabinet ~y*** beauty salon; ***mleczko ~e*** cleansing milk
kosmetyk *m* (*-ku*; *-ki*) cosmetic; ***~i do włosów*** hair-care products; **kosmetyka** *f* (*-ki*; *no pl*) **1.** beauty care **2.** (*upiększanie*) *fig* cosmetic work
kosmiczn|y *adj* **1.** cosmic; ***przestrzeń ~a*** outer space **2.** *lot, stacja, prom*: space; ***statek ~y*** spaceship
kosmita *m* (*-ty*; *-mici*) alien

K

kosmonauta *m* (*-ty*; *-nauci*) astronaut; **kosmos** *m* (*-su*; *no pl*) **1.** (*przestrzeń kosmiczna*) (outer) space **2.** (*wszechświat*) the cosmos, the universe
kosmyk *m* (*-ka*; *-ki*) wisp
kosodrzewina *f* (*-ny*; *-ny*) (dwarf) mountain pine
Kostaryka *f* (*-ki*) Costa Rica
kostium *m* (*-mu*; *-my*) **1.** (*specjalny strój*) costume; ***~ kąpielowy*** swimsuit, *Br* swimming costume; ***~ gimnastyczny*** *Br* sports kit **2.** (*damskie ubranie*) suit; **kostiumowy** *adj*: ***film ~*** costume drama; ***bal ~*** fancy dress party
kost|ka *f* (*-ki*; *-ki*) **1.** *lodu*, *cukru*: cube; ***cukier w ~kach*** sugar cubes; ***~ka bulionowa*** stock cube; ***kroić w ~kę*** dice **2.** *mydła*: bar **3.** *masła*: block **4.** (*u nogi*) ankle (bone); ***woda do ~ek*** ankle-deep water; ***sukienka do ~ek*** ankle-length dress **5.** (*u ręki*) wrist bone **6.** *zdr* (*mała kość*) (small) bone **7.** (*do gry*) dice **8.** *gitarowa*: pick
kostnica *f* (*-cy*; *-ce*) morgue, mortuary
kostnieć ⟨**s-**⟩ (*-nieję*) ossify; ***~ z zimna*** go numb with cold
kostn|y *adj* bone; ***mączka ~a*** bonemeal
kostucha *f* (*-chy*; *-chy*) the Grim Reaper
kostyczny *adj lit* **1.** *uwaga*: caustic **2.** *osoba*: acerbic, sarcastic
kosz *m* (*-sza*; *-sze*) basket; ***~ na śmieci*** *Br* rubbish bin, *Am* garbage can; ***grać w ~a*** *infml* play basketball, *Am* shoot hoops; ***rzucić ~a*** *infml* score; ***dostać ~a*** *fig* be turned down
koszary *pl* (*-szar*) barracks
koszerny *adj* kosher
koszmar *m* (*-ru*; *-ry*) nightmare; ***~ wojny*** the horror of war; **koszmarny** *adj* nightmarish, terrible; ***~ sen*** nightmare
koszt *m* (*-tu*; *-ty*) cost; ***~y utrzymania*** the cost of living; ***~ przesyłki*** shipment costs; ***~em czegoś*** at the cost of s.th.; ***czyimś ~em*** at s.o.'s expense; ***bawić się czyimś ~em*** have fun at s.o.'s expense; ***tanim ~em*** at a low cost, cheaply
kosztorys *m* (*-su*; *-sy*) (cost) estimate
kosztować (*-tuję*) **I** *v/i v/im* cost; ***ile to kosztuje?*** how much is it?, how much does it cost?; ***~ drogo***, ***~ wiele*** cost a lot **II** *v/t* ⟨**s-**, **za-**⟩ (*próbować*) taste
kosztowności *pl* (*-ści*) valuables; **kosztowny** *adj* expensive, costly
koszula *f* (*-li*; *-le*) shirt; ***~ nocna*** *Br* nightdress, *Am* nightgown; **koszulka** *f* (*-ki*; *-ki*) **1.** (*z krótkim rękawem*) T-shirt **2.** (*bielizna*) *Br* vest, *Am* undershirt; ***~ bez rękawów*** *Br* singlet **3.** (*na dokumenty*) sleeve
koszyk *m* (*-ka*; *-ki*) (small) basket
koszykarz *m* (*-rza*; *-rze*), **-rka** *f* (*-ki*; *-ki*) *SPORT* basketball player; **koszykówka** *f* (*-ki*; *no pl*) basketball
kościany *adj* bone; **kościec** *m* (*-śćca*; *-śćce*) skeleton
kościelny **I** *adj* church **II** *m* (*-nego*; *-ni*) sexton
kościotrup *m* (*-pa*; *-py*) skeleton
kościół *m* (*-cioła*; *-cioły*) church; ***chodzić do kościoła*** go to church; ***≈ rzymskokatolicki*** Roman Catholic Church; ***≈ ewangelicki*** Evangelical Church
kościsty *adj* **1.** bony **2.** *osoba*: skinny, bony
koś|ć *f* (*-ści*; *-ści*) **1.** bone; ***~ć ogonowa*** coccyx, tailbone; ***~ć słoniowa*** ivory; ***~ć niezgody*** bone of contention; ***przy ~ci*** plump; ***skóra i ~ci*** skin and bone; ***zmarznąć na ~ć*** be frozen to the bone; ***do szpiku ~ci*** to the bone; ***dać komuś w ~ć*** give s.o. a hard time; ***rozejść się po ~ciach*** die a natural death **2.** (*układ scalony*) chip **3.** (*do gry*) dice; ***grać w ~ci*** play dice
koślaw|y *adj* **1.** *litery*: crooked **2.** *styl*: clumsy; ***~e nogi*** **a)** (*iksowate*) knock knees **b)** (*pałąkowate*) bow legs
kot *m* (*-ta*; *-ty*) **1.** cat; ***tyle co ~ napłakał*** next to nothing; ***biegać jak ~ z pęcherzem*** run around like a headless chicken **2.** (*kurz*) *infml* ball of dust **3.** (*w wojsku*) *infml* rookie
kotara *f* (*-ry*; *-ry*) curtain
kot|ek *m* (*-tka*; *-tki*) **1.** *dim* pussycat; ***grać w ~ka i myszkę z I*** *fig* play cat and mouse with **2.** (*młody kot*) kitten **3.** (*zdrobnienie*) ***~ku!*** honey! **4.** ***~ki*** (*bazie*) catkins
koteria *f* (*-rii*; *-rie*) coterie, clique
kotka *f* (*-ki*; *-ki*) (female) cat, she-cat
kotlet *m* (*-ta*; *-ty*) chop, cutlet; ***~ schabowy*** pork chop; ***~ mielony*** *Br* rissole, *Am* meat patty
kotlina *f* (*-ny*; *-ny*) basin

K

kotłować się *v/im* (*-łuję*) **1.** (*o cieczy*) churn, seethe **2.** (*o myślach*) swirl around

kotłownia *f* (*-ni*; *-nie*) **1.** (*pomieszczenie*) boiler room **2.** (*budynek*) boiler house; **kotły** *pl* → **kocioł**

kotna *adj kotka*: in kitten, pregnant

koturn *m* (*-nu*/*-na*; *-ny*) **1.** (*but damski*) platform (shoe) **2.** *THEAT* cothurnus, buskin

kotwic|a *f* (*-cy*; *-ce*) anchor; ***rzucić ~ę*** drop anchor

kotwiczyć ⟨**za-**⟩ (*-czę*) anchor

kotylion *m* (*-na*; *-ny*) (*taniec*) cotillion

kowadł|o *n* (*-ła*; *-ła*) anvil; ***między młotem a ~em*** *fig* between the devil and the deep blue sea

kowal *m* (*-la*; *-le*) (black)smith; **kowalski** *adj młot*: (black)smith's; **kowalstwo** *n* (*-wa*; *no pl*) smithery

kowbojski *adj* cowboy

K

koz|a *f* (*-zy*; *-zy*) **1.** goat; ***raz ~ie śmierć!*** you can only die once! **2.** (*z nosa*) *infml Br* bogey, *Am* booger

Kozak *m* (*-ka*; *-zacy*) Cossack

kozak *m* (*-ka*; *-ki*) **1.** (*but*) (high) boot **2.** (*grzyb*) birch bolete

kozer|a *lit*: ***nie bez ~y*** not without reason

kozetka *f* (*-ki*; *-ki*) couch

kozi *adj mleko*, *ser*: goat's; ***~a bródka*** goatee; **kozica** *f* (*-cy*; *-ce*) chamois

kozioł *m* (*-zła*; *-zły*) **1.** (*samiec kozy*) goat; ***~ ofiarny*** *fig* scapegoat **2.** (*samiec sarny*) buck **3.** *SPORT* buck, (vaulting) horse **4.** (*odbicie*) bounce; ***fiknąć kozła*** do a somersault

koziołkować ⟨**prze-**⟩ (*-kuję*) turn somersaults, somersault

kozioroż|ec *m* (*-żca*; *-żce*) **1.** (*zwierzę*) ibex **2.** *ASTR* Capricorn; ***zwrotnik ~ca*** the Tropic of Capricorn

kozłek *m* (*-łka*; *-łki*) valerian

kozłować *v/im* (*-łuję*) *piłkę*: bounce

koźlątko *n* (*-ka*; *-ka*) *dim* kid; **koźlę** *n* (*-lęcia*; *-lęta*) kid; **koźlęc|y** *adj*: ***~a skóra*** kid(skin); ***z ~ej skóry*** kid

kożuch *m* (*-cha*; *-chy*) **1.** (*futro z owczej skóry*) sheepskin coat **2.** (*na mleku*) skin; **kożuszek** *m* (*-szka*; *-szki*) *dim* sheepskin jacket

kół → ***koło***[1]

kółk|o *n* (*-ka*; *-ka*) **1.** (small) wheel; ***~o zębate*** cog(wheel); ***w ~o*** **a)** (*dookoła*) around **b)** (*ciągle*) over and over (again); ***siedzieć za ~iem*** *infml* be behind the wheel; ***usiąść za ~iem*** *infml* take the wheel; ***cztery ~a*** *infml* wheels **2.** (*kształt*) circle; ***~o i krzyżyk*** *Br* noughts and crosses, *Am* tic-tac-toe, tick-tack-toe **3.** *olimpijskie*: ring **4.** (*w szkole*) club **5.** (*zrzeszenie*) association

kózka *f* (*-ki*; *-ki*) *dim* (little) goat

kpiarski *adj* mocking; **kpiarz** *m* (*-rza*; *-rze*) mocker; **kpiąco** *adv* mockingly; **kpić** ⟨**wy-**, **za-**⟩ (*kpię*) **1.** (*drwić*) mock (**z** *G*) **2.** (*śmiać się*) laugh (**z** *G*); **kpin|a** *f* (*-ny*; *-ny*) mockery; ***robić sobie z kogoś ~y*** mock s.o.

kra *f* (*kry*; *kry*) (ice) floe

krab *m* (*-ba*; *-by*) crab

krach *m* (*-chu*; *-chy*) **1.** crash; ***~ na giełdzie*** stock market crash **2.** (*niepowodzenie*) fiasco

kraciasty *adj Br* chequered, *Am* checkered

kradzież *f* (*-ży*; *-że*) theft; ***~ samochodu*** car theft; ***~ w sklepie*** shoplifting; ***~ z włamaniem*** burglary; **kradziony** *adj* stolen

kraina *f* (*-ny*; *-ny*) **1.** *lit* land; ***~ baśni*** fairyland; ***~ cieni*** the land of the dead **2.** (*region*) region

kraj *m* (*-ju*; *-je*) country; ***wyjechać z ~u*** leave the country; ***~ rodzinny*** motherland; ***~ związkowy*** Land; ***wiadomości z ~u*** domestic news

krajać ⟨**po-**⟩ (*-ję*) cut; ***~ w kostkę*** dice; **krajalnica** *f* (*-cy*; *-cy*) (food) slicer

krajan *m* (*-na*; *-nie*), **~ka** *f* (*-ki*; *-ki*) compatriot

krajobraz *m* (*-zu*; *-zy*) landscape

krajowy *adj* **1.** domestic **2.** *rozgrywki*: national; **krajoznawczy** *adj wycieczka*: sightseeing, local; **krajoznawstwo** *n* (*-wa*; *no pl*) local touring

kra|kać ⟨**za-**⟩ (*kraczę*) caw; ***nie ~cz!*** *fig* look on the bright side!

Kraków *m* (*-kowa*) Cracow

kraksa *f* (*-sy*; *-sy*) crash, *Am* wreck

kram *m* (*-mu*; *-my*) **1.** stall, stand **2.** (*bałagan*) *infml* mess

kran *m* (*-nu*; *-ny*) *Br* tap, *Am* faucet; ***woda z ~u*** tap water

kra|niec *m* (*krańca*; *krańce*) **1.** (*koniec*) end; ***na ~ńcu świata*** at the end of the world **2.** (*krawędź*) edge

kranówka *f* (*-ki*; *no pl*) *infml* tap water
krańcowy *adj* **1.** (*skrajny*) extreme **2.** *element*, *część*: outermost
krasnal *m* (*-la*; *-le*), **krasnoludek** *m* (*-dka*; *-dki*) **1.** dwarf **2.** (*w ogrodzie*) gnome
krasomówca *m* (*-cy*; *-cy*) *lit* orator; **krasomówczy** *adj lit* oratorical, rhetorical
kraść ⟨**s-**, **u-**⟩ (*kradnę*) steal
krat|a *f* (*-ty*; *-ty*) **1.** grating **2.** (*pręty*) bars *pl* **3.** (*osłona*) grille **4.** (*deseń*) check; ***koszula w ~ę*** check shirt; ***szkocka ~a*** tartan
kratk|a *f* (*-ki*; *-ki*) **1.** (*deseń*) check; ***koszula w ~ę*** check shirt; ***pogoda w ~ę*** *Br* patchy weather, *Am* spotty weather **2.** (*kwadrat*) square; ***zeszyt w ~ę*** graph-paper notebook, notebook with graph paper pages **3.** (*konstrukcja*) grating, grate **4.** (*osłona*) (small) grille **5.** (*pręty*) bars *pl*; ***za ~ami*** *infml* behind the bars
kratkowany *adj zeszyt*, *papier*: squared; **kratownica** *f* (*-cy*; *-ce*) TECH truss
kraul *m* (*-la*; *no pl*) SPORT crawl; ***pływać ~em*** do the crawl
krawat *m* (*-ta*/*-tu*; *-ty*) tie, *Am* necktie
krawcowa *f* (*-wej*; *-we*) dressmaker
krawęd|ź *f* (*-dzi*; *-dzie*) **1.** edge **2.** (*granica*) verge, brink; ***na ~zi*** *G* on the verge of
krawężnik *m* (*-ka*; *-ki*) *Br* kerb, *Am* curb
krawiec *m* (*-wca*; *-wcy*) (*męski*) tailor; (*damski*) dressmaker; **krawiecki** *adj przybory*: sewing; **krawiectwo** *n* (*-wa*; *no pl*) *męskie*: tailoring; *damskie*: dressmaking
krąg *m* (*kręgu*; *kręgi*) **1.** circle; ***~ światła*** circle of light; ***~ znajomych*** circle of friends; ***w ~*** (all) around; ***w kręgu znajomych*** among friends **2.** (*zakres*) range; ***~ zainteresowań*** range of interests; **krągł|y** *adj* **1.** round, full **2.** *kształty*: rounded; ***czyjeś ~e kształty*** s.o.'s curvacious lines
krążek *m* (*-żka*; *-żki*) **1.** *cebuli*: ring **2.** *cytryny*, *kiełbasy*: slice **3.** (*płyta*) *infml* disc **4.** SPORT puck; ***~ linowy*** TECH pulley; ***~ dopochwowy*** diaphragm
krążeni|e *n* (*-nia*; *no pl*) circulation; ***układ ~a*** the cardiovascular system
krążownik *m* (*-ka*; *-ki*) cruiser; **krążyć** ⟨**o-**⟩ (*-żę*) **1.** (*o krwi*, *powietrzu*, *plotce*) circulate; ***krążą plotki, że*** *Br* it is rumoured that, *Am* it is rumored that **2.** (*o planecie*, *księżycu*) revolve (***dokoła*** *G* around); orbit (***dokoła*** *G*) **3.** (*o ptaku*, *muchach*) circle (***dokoła*** *G* around) **4.** (*być podawanym*) be passed around **5.** (*o osobie*) wander (around), walk around
kreacja *f* (*-ji*; *-je*) **1.** (*strój*) creation, outfit; ***~ wieczorowa*** evening gown **2.** (*tworzenie*) *lit* creation **3.** (*rola*) role; **kreator** *m* (*-ra*; *-rzy*), **~ka** *f* (*-ki*; *-ki*) creator; ***~ mody*** fashion designer
kreatura *f* (*-ry*; *-ry*) scoundrel
kreatywny *adj* creative
krech|a *f* (*-chy*; *-chy*) (thick) line; ***mieć ~ę*** *infml* be in the doghouse (***u*** *G* with)
kreci *adj* mole; ***~ kopiec*** molehill; ***~a robota*** *infml* double-dealing
kreda *f* (*-dy*; *-dy*) **1.** chalk; ***biały jak ~*** (as) white as a sheet **2.** (*okres geologiczny*) the Cretaceous (period)
kredens *m* (*-su*; *-sy*) cupboard, *Br* dresser
kredka *f* (*-ki*; *-ki*) *Br* coloured pencil, *Am* colored pencil; ***~ woskowa*** crayon; ***~ do oczu*** eyeliner; ***~ do brwi*** (eye)brow pencil; ***~ do ust*** lipstick
kredowy *adj* **1.** *papier*: art **2.** *okres*, *osady*: Cretaceous
kredyt *m* (*-tu*; *-ty*) loan; ***na ~*** on credit; ***wziąć ~*** take out a loan; **kredytobiorca** *m* (*-cy*; *-cy*) borrower; **kredytodawca** *m* (*-cy*; *-cy*) lender
kredytować ⟨**s-**⟩ (*-tuję*) *inwestycję*: give credit for; **kredytowy** *adj* credit
krem *m* (*-mu*; *-my*) cream; ***~ do golenia*** shaving cream; ***~ do opalania*** suntan cream; ***~ do rąk*** hand cream; ***~ nawilżający*** moisturizer; ***~ na dzień*** day cream; ***~ na noc*** night cream
kremacj|a *f* (*-ji*; *-je*) cremation; ***poddać ~i*** cremate; **krematorium** *n* (*indecl*; *-ria*) crematorium
kremować[1] ⟨**s-**⟩ (*-muję*) cremate
kremować[2] ⟨**na-**, **po-**⟩ (*-muję*) apply cream (*A* on); **kremowy** *adj* cream
kreować ⟨**wy-**⟩ (*kreuję*) *lit* **1.** (*tworzyć*) create **2.** *rolę*: play
krepa *f* (*-py*; *-py*) crêpe

kres *m* (*-su*; *-sy*) end; ***położyć czemuś ~*** put an end to s.th.; ***~y*** borderland(s); ***≈y wschodnie*** the Eastern borderlands

kreska *f* (*-ki*; *-ki*) **1.** (*linia*) line **2.** (*łącznik*) hyphen **3.** (*nad literą*) accent **4.** (*w alfabecie Morse'a*) dash; **kreskowan|y** *adj*: ***o ~e*** the letter ó

kreskowy *adj*: ***kod ~*** barcode; **kreskówka** *f* (*-ki*; *-ki*) (animated) cartoon

kreślarz *m* (*-rza*; *-rze*) *Br* draughtsman, *Am* draftsman; **kreślarka** *f* (*-ki*; *-ki*) *Br* draughtswoman, *Am* draftswoman; **kreślarsk|i** *adj* drawing; ***kalka ~a*** tracing paper

kreślić (*-lę*) **1.** ⟨**wy-**⟩ (*rysować*) draw **2.** ⟨**prze-**⟩ (*przekreślać*) cross out **3.** ⟨**na-**⟩ *plan*: outline

kret *m* (*-ta*; *-ty*) mole

Kreta *f* (*-ty*) Crete

kretes: ***przegrać z ~em*** suffer a total defeat

K

kretowisko *n* (*-ka*; *-ka*) molehill

kretyn *m* (*-na*; *-ni*) *infml* idiot, moron

krew *f* (*krwi*; *no pl*) blood; ***grupa krwi*** blood group; ***badanie krwi*** blood test; ***komuś leci ~*** s.o. is bleeding; ***ktoś ma coś we krwi*** s.th. runs in s.o.'s blood; ***zachować zimną ~*** stay cool, keep a cool head; ***z krwi i kości*** of flesh and blood, full-blooded; ***mrożący ~ w żyłach*** blood-curdling; ***morderstwo z zimną krwią*** cold-blooded murder; ***bez rozlewu krwi*** without bloodshed; ***~ mnie zalewa, gdy*** it makes my blood boil when; ***iść jak ~ z nosa*** *infml* be a tough slog, be an uphill struggle; ***wejść komuś w ~*** become s.o.'s second nature; ***do ostatniej kropli krwi*** to the last breath; ***koń czystej krwi arabskiej*** pure-bred Arab

krewetka *f* (*-ki*; *-ki*) shrimp, prawn

krewki *adj* hot-blooded

krewna *f* (*-nej*; *-ne*), **-ny** *m* (*-nego*; *-ni*) relative

kręcić (*-cę*) **I** *v/t* **1.** ⟨**po-**⟩ (*obracać*) turn **2.** ⟨**za-**⟩ *włosy*: curl **3.** ⟨**na-**⟩ *film*: shoot **II** *v/i* (*oszukiwać*) *infml* cheat, fib; ***~ głową*** shake one's head; ***~ nosem*** *fig* be fussy, pick and choose; ***kręcić się*** **1.** (*obracać się*) turn (round) **2.** (*wirować*) spin; ***komuś kręci się w głowie*** s.o. feels dizzy, s.o.'s head is spinning **3.** (*o planecie, życiu*) revolve (***wokół*** *G* round) **4.** (*o włosach*) curl **5.** (*wiercić się*) fidget **6.** (*przebywać*) *infml* hang around (***koło*** *G*); ***interes się kręci*** business is doing well

kręcony *adj* **1.** *włosy*: curly **2.** *schody*: winding

kręg *m* (*-gu*; *-gi*) ANAT vertebra; ***~i szyjne*** cervical vertebrae; **kręgarstwo** *n* (*-wa*; *no pl*) chiropractic

kręg|iel *m* (*-gla*; *-gle*) (bowling) pin; ***grać w ~le*** play bowling, go bowling; **kręgielnia** *f* (*-ni*; *-nie*) bowling alley

kręgosłup *m* (*-pa*; *-py*) spine, backbone; **kręgowiec** *m* (*-wca*; *-wce*) vertebrate; **kręgowy** *adj* spinal; ***rdzeń ~*** spinal cord

krępować ⟨**s-**⟩ (*-puję*) **1.** (*wiązać*) tie (up) **2.** *fig* make feel uncomfortable; ***krępować się*** feel uncomfortable; ***nie krępuj się*** don't be shy

krępujący *adj* embarrassing

krępy *adj* stocky

krętactw|o *n* (*-wa*; *-wa*) deviousness; ***~a*** double-dealing, *infml* monkey business

krętacz *m* (*-cza*; *-cze*), **~ka** *f* (*-ki*; *-ki*) double-dealer, cheat

kręty *adj* winding

krnąbrność *f* (*-ści*; *no pl*) waywardness, *Br* wilfulness, *Am* willfulness; **krnąbrny** *adj* wayward, *Br* wilful, *Am* willful

krochmal *m* (*-lu*; *no pl*) starch; **krochmalić** ⟨**wy-**⟩ (*-lę*) starch

krocie *pl* (*-ci*) *lit* fortune *sing*; ***zarobić ~ na*** *L* make a fortune on

krocze *f* (*-cza*; *-cza*) **1.** crotch **2.** ANAT perineum; **kroczek** *m* (*-czka*; *-czki*) (small) step; **kroczyć** *v/im* (*-czę*) **1.** walk **2.** (*dużymi krokami*) stride **3.** (*maszerować*) march

kroić ⟨**po-**⟩ (*kroję*) **1.** cut; ***~ na kawałki*** cut into pieces **2.** (*na plasterki*) slice

krok *m* (*-ku*; *-ki*) **1.** step; ***stawiać ~i*** take steps; ***~ za ~iem*** step by step; ***co ~, na każdym ~u*** at every turn; ***to dwa ~i stąd*** it's just around the corner **2.** (*tempo*) pace; ***szybkim ~iem*** at a quick pace; ***dotrzymywać komuś ~u*** keep up with s.o. **3.** (*odgłos*) footstep **4.** (*krocze*) crotch; ***w ~u*** in the crotch

krokiet[1] *m* (*-ta*; *-ty*) COOK pancake roll
krokiet[2] *m* (*-ta*; *no pl*) SPORT croquet
krokodyl *m* (*-la*; *-le*) crocodile; **krokodyl|i** *adj* crocodile('s); ***wylewać ~e łzy*** shed crocodile tears
krokowy *adj*: ***gruczoł ~*** prostate gland
kromka *f* (*-ki*; *-ki*) slice
kronika *f* (*-ki*; *-ki*) **1.** chronicle; ***~ filmowa*** newsreel **2.** (*w gazecie*) column; **kronikarz** *m* (*-rza*; *-rze*) chronicler
kropelka *f* (*-ki*; *-ki*) droplet
kropi|ć ⟨**po-**⟩ (*-pię*) **1.** sprinkle **2.** ~ (*o deszczu*) *Br* it's spitting, *Am* it's sprinkling
kropidło *n* (*-ła*; *-ła*) aspergillum
krop|ka *f* (*-ki*; *-ki*) **1.** dot; ***być ~ka w ~kę jak*** *N* be the spitting image of; ***być w ~ce*** be in a fix; ***z ~ką*** (*nuta*): dotted **2.** (*znak interpunkcyjny*) full stop, *Am* period **3.** (*na tkaninie*) spot, polka dot; ***w ~ki*** dotted **4.** (*po cyfrze*) point; **kropkowany** *adj linia*: dotted
kropl|a *f* (*-li*; *-le*) drop; ***~a deszczu*** raindrop; ***~a w morzu*** *fig* a drop in the ocean; ***~a potu*** bead of sweat; ***~a drąży skałę*** little by little does the trick; ***~e do oczu*** eye drops; ***~e do nosa*** nose drops; ***są podobni jak dwie ~e wody*** they look like two peas in a pod
kroplówka *f* (*-ki*; *-ki*) drip
kropnąć *v/p* (*-nę*) (*zabić*) *infml* gun down, bump off
krosno *n* (*-na*; *-na*) loom
krosta *f* (*-ty*; *-ty*) pimple, *Br* spot
krowa *f* (*-wy*; *-wy*) cow; ***choroba szalonych krów*** mad cow disease; **krowi** *adj* **1.** *mleko*: cow's **2.** *ser*, *łajno*: cow; ***~ placek*** *Br* cowpat
krócej *comp* → **krótko**; **króciutki** *adj* tiny, very short
krój *m* (*kroju*; *kroje*) cut; ***~ czcionki*** typeface
król *m* (*-la*; *-lowie*) king; ***~ strzelców*** top scorer; ***Święto Trzech ~i*** Epiphany
królestwo *n* (*-wa*; *-wa*) kingdom
królewicz *m* (*-cza*; *-cze*) prince; king's son; **królewna** *f* (*-ny*; *-ny*) princess; king's daughter; ***~ Śnieżka*** Snow White; ***Śpiąca ~*** Sleeping Beauty
królewsk|i *adj* royal; ***przyjąć kogoś po ~u*** give s.o. a royal welcome
króliczy *adj futro*, *nora*: rabbit; **królik** *m* (*-ka*; *-ki*) rabbit; ***~ doświadczalny*** guinea pig
królowa *f* (*-wej*; *-we*) queen; ***~ pszczół*** queen bee
królować *v/im* (*-luję*) **1.** reign **2.** *fig* reign supreme
krótki *adj* short; ***z ~mi rękawami*** short-sleeved; ***~e spodenki*** shorts
krótko *adv* **1.** *trwać*, *zostać*: (for) a short time; ***spotkanie trwało ~*** the meeting was short **2.** *opisać*, *przedstawić*: briefly **3.** *obciąć*: short; ***~ mówiąc*** in short, to cut a long story short
krótkodystansowy *adj*: ***bieg ~*** sprint
krótkofalarstwo *n* (*-wa*; *no pl*) amateur radio, *infml* ham radio; **krótkofalówka** *f* (*-ki*; *-ki*) **1.** short-wave radio **2.** (*przenośna*) walkie-talkie
krótkometrażowy *adj*: ***film ~*** short (subject); **krótkość** *f* (*-ści*; *no pl*) shortness; **krótkoterminowy** *adj* short-term; **krótkotrwały** *adj* short-lived
krótkowidz *m* (*-dza*; *-dze*) *Br* short-sighted person, *Am* near-sighted person; ***być ~em*** be short-sighted
krótkowłosy *adj* short-haired
krótkowzroczność *f* (*-ści*; *no pl*) *Br* short-sightedness, *Am* near-sightedness; **krótkowzroczny** *adj Br* short-sighted, *Am* near-sighted
krótszy *adj comp* → **krótki** shorter (**od** *G* than)
krówka *f* (*-ki*; *-ki*) **1.** *dim* (little) cow **2.** (*cukierek*) cream fudge
krtań *f* (*-ni*; *-nie*) larynx
krucho *adv*: ***~ u kogoś z czasem*** (***pieniędzmi***) s.o. is pressed for time (money); ***z kimś jest ~*** **a)** (*jest chory*) s.o. is in a bad way **b)** (*ma kłopoty*) s.o. is in a tight spot, s.o. is in trouble
kruchta *f* (*-ty*; *-ty*) vestibule, porch
kruch|y *adj* **1.** *skała*, *lód*: brittle **2.** *pieczywo*: crisp **3.** *chleb*: crumbly; ***~e ciasto*** short-crust pastry **4.** *mięso*: tender **5.** (*delikatny*) fragile
krucjata *f* (*-ty*; *-ty*) crusade
krucyfiks *m* (*-su*; *-sy*) crucifix
kruczek *m* (*-czka*; *-czki*) **1.** (*pułapka*) catch **2.** (*wybieg*) trick **3.** (*w przepisach*) loophole

K

kruczoczarny *adj* raven-black; **kruk** *m* (*-ka*; *-ki*) raven

krupy *pl* (*krup*) **1.** (*kasza*) (barley) groats **2.** (*śnieg*) snow grains; **krupnik** *m* (*-ka*; *-ki*) **1.** (*zupa*) barley soup **2.** (*gorący napój*) hot mead

kruszec *m* (*-szcu*; *-szce*) ore

kruszeć ⟨**s-**⟩ (*-szeję*) **1.** crumble **2.** (*o mięsie*) become tender

kruszonka *f* (*-ki*; *-ki*) crumble topping

kruszyć (*-szę*) **1.** ⟨**po-**⟩ crumble **2.** ⟨**s-**⟩ *skałę*: crush **3.** ⟨**s-**⟩ *lód*: break **4.** ⟨**na-**⟩ (*śmiecić*) drop crumbs; ***kruszyć się*** crumble

kruszyna *f* (*-ny*; *-ny*) (*okruch*) crumb **2.** (*dziecko*) mite, moppet

kruszywo *n* (*-wa*; *-wa*) aggregate

krużganek *m* (*-nka*; *-nki*) (*w klasztorze*) cloister

krwawiący *adj* bleeding; **krwawić** ⟨**za-**⟩ (*-wię*) bleed

krwawnik *m* (*-ka*; *-ki*) (*roślina*) yarrow

krwawoczerwony *adj* blood-red; **krwawy** *adj* **1.** bloody **2.** *łuna*, *kolor*: blood-red

krwiak *m* (*-ka*; *-ki*) *Br* haematoma, *Am* hematoma; **krwink|a** *f* (*-ki*; *-ki*) blood cell; ***białe*** (***czerwone***) ***~i*** white (red) blood cells

krwiobieg *m* (*-gu*; *-gi*) **1.** (*krążąca krew*) bloodstream; ***dostać się do ~u*** pass into the bloodstream **2.** (*krążenie*) blood circulation **3.** (*układ krwionośny*) circulatory system; **krwiodawca** *m* (*-cy*; *-cy*), **-czyni** *f* (*-ni*; *-nie*) blood donor; **krwiodawstwo** *n* (*-wa*; *no pl*) blood donation

krwionośn|y *adj*: ***naczynia ~e*** blood vessels; ***układ ~y*** **a)** ANAT cardiovascular system **b)** (*krążąca krew*) bloodstream; **krwiożerczy** *adj* blood-thirsty

krwist|y *adj* **1.** *wysięk*: bloody **2.** *befsztyk*: rare; ***~a czerwień*** blood red

krwotok *m* (*-ku*; *-ki*) *Br* haemorrhage, *Am* hemorrhage; ***~ z nosa*** nosebleed

kryć (*kryję*) **1.** ⟨**po-**⟩ (*pokrywać*) cover **2.** ⟨**u-**⟩ hide, conceal **3.** *v/im* (*zawierać*) hide **4.** ⟨**po-**⟩ SPORT BIOL cover **5.** *v/im* (*przed odpowiedzialnością*) *infml* cover for; ***kryć się*** (*chować się*) hide (***za*** *I* behind); ***~ się z czymś*** conceal s.th.; ***coś się za tym kryje*** there's more behind it than meets the eye

kryjówka *f* (*-ki*; *-ki*) hiding place

Krym *m* (*-mu*) Crimea

kryminalista *m* (*-ty*; *-liści*), **-tka** *f* (*-ki*; *-ki*) criminal; **kryminalny** *adj* **1.** criminal **2.** *film*: detective

kryminał *m* (*-łu*; *-ły*) **1.** (*powieść*) detective novel, *infml* whodunit **2.** (*film*) *Br* detective film, *Am* detective movie **3.** (*więzienie*) the slammer

krypta *f* (*-ty*; *-ty*) crypt, vault

kryptonim *m* (*-mu*; *-my*) code name

krystaliczny *adj* **1.** crystalline **2.** *woda*, *powietrze*: crystal clear; **krystalizować się** ⟨**s-**⟩ (*-zuję*) crystallize

kryształ *m* (*-łu*; *-ły*) crystal; ***czysty jak ~*** crystal-clear; ***~ górski*** rock crystal; ***cukier ~*** granulated sugar; **kryształowo** *adv*: ***~ przezroczysty*** crystal-clear; **kryształowy** *adj* **1.** crystal **2.** *powietrze*: crystal-clear **3.** *charakter*: impeccable

kryterium *n* (*indecl*; *-ria*) criterium; ***kryteria*** criteria;

kryty *adj* **1.** *kort*, *basen*: indoor **2.** ***~ dachówką*** tiled; ***~ strzechą*** thatched

krytyczny *adj* critical; ***stan ~*** critical condition; **krytyk** *m* (*-ka*; *-tycy*) critic; **krytyk|a** *f* (*-ki*; *-ki*) **1.** criticism; ***zostać entuzjastycznie przyjętym przez ~ę*** win critical acclaim **2.** (*krytycy*) critics *pl*

krytykanctwo *n* (*-wa*; *no pl*) fault-finding; **krytykować** ⟨**s-**⟩ (*-kuję*) criticize (***za*** *A* for)

kryza *f* (*-zy*; *-zy*) ruff

kryzys *m* (*-su*; *-sy*) crisis; ***~ gospodarczy*** economic crisis; ***~ rządowy*** cabinet crisis; **kryzysowy** *adj* **1.** *sytuacja*: crisis **2.** *zespół*: emergency response

krzaczasty *adj* bushy; **krzak** *m* (*-ka*; *-ki*) bush, shrub

krzątać się ⟨**za-**⟩ (*-tam*) bustle (around); **krzątanina** *f* (*-ny*; *no pl*) (hustle and) bustle

krzem *m* (*-mu*; *no pl*) CHEM silicon

krzemień *m* (*-mienia*; *-mienie*) flint

krzemionka *f* (*-ki*; *no pl*) silica

krzepa *f* (*-py*; *no pl*) brawn; **krzepiący** *adj słowa*: uplifting, reassuring

krzepić ⟨**po-**⟩ (*-pię*) (*o słowach*) uplift, reassure; ***krzepić się*** *lit* fortify oneself (*I* with)

K

krzepki *adj osoba*: robust
krzepliwość *f* (*-ści*; *no pl*) coagulability; **krzepnąć** ⟨**s-**⟩ (*-nę*) **1.** (*o krwi*) coagulate **2.** (*o wosku*) solidify **3.** (*o galarecie*) set
krzesać ⟨**wy-**⟩ (*-szę*) *ogień*: strike
krzesełkowy *adj*: ***wyciąg ~*** chairlift
krzesło *n* (*-ła*; *-ła*) chair; ***~ składane*** folding chair
krzew *m* (*-wu*; *-wy*) bush, shrub
krzewić *v/im* (*-wię*) *lit* **1.** promote **2.** *oświatę*: spread
krztusić się ⟨**za-**⟩ (*-szę*) **1.** choke (*I* on) **2.** (*o silniku*) cough, sputter
krztusiec *m* (*-tuśca*; *no pl*) *MED* whooping cough
krztyn|a *m* (*-ny*; *-ny*) a bit, an ounce; ***~ę*** a bit
krzyczący *adj niesprawiedliwość*: glaring
krzyczeć ⟨**krzyknąć**⟩ (*-czę*) **1.** (*wołać*) shout (**do** *G* to) **2.** (*pod wpływem emocji*) scream, shout (**na** *A* at); ***~ z bólu*** scream in pain **3.** ⟨**na-**⟩ (*strofować*) yell (**na** *A* at) **4.** (*o ptaku*) cry, scream
krzyk *m* (*-ku*; *-ki*) **1.** (*wołanie*) shout(ing); ***to ostatni ~ mody*** *infml* it's all the rage now; ***i po ~u*** it's all over **2.** (*pod wpływem emocji*) scream(ing), shout(ing) **3.** (*protest*) outcry, hue and cry, *infml* fuss; ***podnieść ~*** *infml* kick up a fuss **4.** *ptaka*: cry, scream
krzykliwy *adj* **1.** *osoba*: loud, noisy **2.** *kolor*: gaudy, garish **3.** *głos*: shrill
krzyknąć *v/p* → ***krzyczeć***
krzywa *f* (*-wej*; *-we*) *MATH* curve; → ***krzywy***
krzywd|a *f* (*-dy*; *-dy*) harm; ***wyrządzić komuś ~ę*** do s.o. harm, hurt s.o.; ***zrobić sobie ~ę*** hurt oneself; ***nie stanie ci się ~a*** you won't get hurt; ***~a społeczna*** social injustice; ***naprawić ~ę wyrządzoną komuś*** make amends to s.o.
krzywdzić ⟨**s-**⟩ (*-dzę*) **1.** (*być niesprawiedliwym*) be unfair to, wrong **2.** (*fizycznie*) harm, hurt
krzywica *f* (*-cy*; *no pl*) *MED* rickets *sing*
krzywić ⟨**s-**⟩ (*-wię*) bend; ***~ usta*** wince; ***~ usta z bólu*** wince in pain; ***krzywić się*** **1.** bend, be bent **2.** (*robić grymas*) wince; ***~ się z bólu*** wince in pain **3.** (*okazywać niechęć*) wince (**na** *A* at)
krzywizna *f* (*-ny*; *-ny*) curvature
krzywo *adv* **1.** crookedly, askew **2.** *uśmiechnąć się*: wrily; ***patrzeć ~ na*** *A* frown on; **krzywoprzysięstwo** *n* (*-wa*; *no pl*) perjury
krzyw|y *adj* **1.** crooked; ***~y zgryz*** bad bite; ***mieć ~e nogi*** **a)** (*iksowate*) be knock-kneed **b)** (*pałąkowate*) be bow-legged; ***patrzeć ~ym okiem na*** *A* frown on, *lit* look askance at **2.** *powierzchnia*: uneven **3.** *uśmiech*: wry
krzyż *m* (*-ża*; *-że*) **1.** cross; ***Czerwony ~*** the Red Cross; ***parę osób*** (***domów***) ***na ~*** only a handful of people (houses) **2.** (*część kręgosłupa*) *infml* lower back; ***bóle w ~u*** backache
Krzyżak *m* (*-ka*; *-żacy*) Teutonic Knight
krzyżak *m* (*-ka*; *-ki*) **1.** (*pająk*) garden spider **2.** (*część stołu*) treble **3.** (*stojak*) stand **4.** *TECH* cross
krzyżować (*-żuję*) **1.** ⟨**s-**⟩ cross; ***~ nogi*** cross one's legs **2.** ⟨**s-**⟩ *zwierzęta*: cross(-breed) **3.** ⟨**po-**⟩ *plany*: thwart, ruin **4.** ⟨**u-**⟩ *człowieka*: crucify; ***krzyżować się*** cross
krzyżow|y *adj* **1.** (*w kształcie krzyża*) cross-shaped; ***wyprawa ~a*** crusade; ***ogień ~y*** crossfire; ***wziąć w ~y ogień pytań*** cross-examine; ***Droga ~a*** the Way of the Cross **2.** *ANAT* sacral; ***kość ~a*** (the) sacrum
krzyżówka *f* (*-ki*; *-ki*) **1.** (*w gazecie*) crossword **2.** (*połączenie*) cross **3.** *BIOL* cross(-breed) **4.** (*skrzyżowanie*) *infml* crossroads *sing*; **krzyżyk** *m* (*-ka*; *-ki*) **1.** (small) cross **2.** (*znak*) cross, X; ***zaznaczyć właściwą odpowiedź ~iem*** put a cross by the right answer
ks. *abbr* (= **ksiądz**) Rev.
ksenofobia *f* (*-bii*; *no pl*) xenophobia
ksero *n indecl* **1.** (*odbitka*) (photo)copy, Xerox® copy; ***zrobić ~*** (photo)copy, xerox **2.** (*urządzenie*) (photo)copier, Xerox® machine **3.** (*sklep*) copy shop; **kserokopia** *f* (*-pii*; *-pie*) photocopy; **kserokopiarka** *f* (*-ki*; *-ki*) photocopier
kserować ⟨**s-**⟩ (*-ruję*) (photo)copy, xerox
ksiądz *m* (*księdza*; *księża*) **1.** priest **2.** (*przed imieniem*) the Reverend, Father

K

książeczka *f* (*-ki*; *-ki*) **1.** *dim* (small) book **2.** (*dokument*) book; **~ oszczędnościowa** savings book; **~ zdrowia** health record
książę *m* (*księcia*; *-żęta*) **1.** (*syn króla*) prince **2.** (*tytuł*) duke; **książęcy** *adj* prince's, duke's; **tytuł ~** title of duke
książk|a *f* (*-ki*; *-ki*) book; **~i dla dzieci** children's books; **~a kucharska** cookbook, *Br* cookery book; **~a w twardej (miękkiej) okładce** hardback (paperback); **~a telefoniczna** phone book, telephone directory
książkowy *adj* **1.** *wydanie*, *wiedza*: book **2.** *styl*, *wyrażenie*, *bohater*: literary; **mól ~** bookworm
księg|a *f* (*-gi*; *-gi*) book; **~a pamiątkowa** visitors' book; **~a wieczysta** land and mortgage register; **prowadzić ~i** FIN keep the accounts
księgarnia *f* (*-ni*; *-nie*) *Br* bookshop, *Am* bookstore; **~ wysyłkowa** mail order bookshop; **księgarski** *adj* **1.** *rynek*, *targi*: book **2.** *katalog*, *serwis*: bookseller's **3.** *półki*: *Br* bookshop, *Am* bookstore
księgarstwo *n* (*-wa*; *no pl*) bookselling; **księgarz** *m* (*-rza*; *-rze*) bookseller
księgować ⟨**za-**⟩ (*-guję*) record (in the accounts); **księgowość** *f* (*-ści*; *no pl*) bookkeeping, accounting
księgowy I *adj wartość*: book **II** *m* (*-wego*; *-wi*), **-wa** *f* (*-wej*; *-we*) accountant; **główny ~** chief accountant
księgozbiór *m* (*-bioru*; *-biory*) book collection
księstwo *n* (*-wa*; *-wa*) duchy; **księżna** *f* (*-nej*; *-ne*) duchess; **księżniczka** *f* (*-ki*; *-ki*) princess
księżyc *m* (*-ca*; *-ce*) moon; **~** the Moon; **~ w pełni** full moon; **przy świetle ~a** by moonlight; **lot na ~** flight to the Moon; **księżycowy** *adj* **1.** *krajobraz*, *kalendarz*, *orbita*: lunar **2.** *noc*: moonlit
ksylofon *m* (*-nu*; *-ny*) xylophone
ksywa *f* (*-wy*; *-wy*) *infml* **1.** *przestępcza*: alias **2.** *infml* nickname
kształcenie *n* (*-nia*; *no pl*) education, training
kształc|ić ⟨**wy-**⟩ (*-cę*) (*uczyć*) educate, train; **podróże ~ą** travel broadens the mind; **kształcić się** (*uczyć się*) study
kształ|t *m* (*-tu*; *-ty*) shape; **w ~cie** *G* in the shape of, in the form of; **w ~cie serca** heart-shaped; **w ~cie kuli** spherical; **coś na ~t** *G* something like; **przybrać realne ~ty** become reality; **kobiece ~ty** feminine curves
kształtny *adj* shapely, well-formed; **kształtować** ⟨**u-**⟩ (*-tuję*) shape; **kształtować się** develop; **dochody netto powinny ~ na poziomie 5-6 mln zł** net income should be between PLN 5 million and PLN 6 million
kto *pron* **1.** who; **~ tam?** who's that?, who's there?; **kim jest ten chłopak?** who's that boy?; **kim są z zawodu?** what's their job?; **o kim mówisz?** who are you talking about?; **od kogo to dostałeś?** who did you get it from?; **mało ~** hardly anyone **2.** (*każdy*) whoever
ktokolwiek *pron* **1.** (*każdy kto*) whoever **2.** (*byle kto*) anybody, anyone; **ktoś** *pron* **1.** somebody, someone; **~ inny** somebody else, someone else **2.** (*w pytaniach*) anybody, anyone
którędy *pron* which way
któr|y *pron* **1.** (*w pytaniach*) which; **~a godzina?** what's the time?, what time is it; **o ~ej godzinie?** what time?; **~ego dziś mamy?** what's the date today?; **~y z nich?** which one of them? **2.** (*w zdaniach zależnych*) which, that; (*osobowy*) who, whom; (*dzierżawczy*) whose; **dom, w ~ym** the house in which; **ludzie, ~ym** people who; **dzieci, dla ~ych** children for whom **3.** (*ktokolwiek*) any; **mało ~y** hardly any
którykolwiek *pron* **1.** whichever, any (one); **~ z** *G* **a)** any of **b)** (*z dwóch*) either of **2.** (*niezależnie który*) whoever; **któr|yś** *pron* some; **~yś z nich** one of them; **~egoś dnia** one day
któż *pron* who; → **kto**
ku *prep* (*D*) to, towards; **~ górze** up(wards); **~ dołowi** down(wards); **zbliżać się ~ końcowi** be drawing to an end; **~ czci** in memory of; **~ czyjemuś zdziwieniu** to s.o.'s surprise
Kuba *f* (*-by*) Cuba; **Kubańczyk** *m* (*-ka*; *-czycy*), **-banka** *f* (*-ki*; *-ki*) Cuban
kubański *adj* Cuban
kub|ek *m* (*-bka*; *-bki*) **1.** mug **2.** *plastikowy*: cup; **~ki smakowe** ANAT taste buds

kubeł *m* (*-bła*; *-bły*) (*wiadro*) bucket; **~ na śmieci** *Br* rubbish bin, *Am* garbage can

kubistyczny *adj* cubist; **kubizm** *m* (*-mu*; *no pl*) cubism

kucać ⟨**-cnąć**⟩ (*-cam*) squat (down)

kucharsk|i *adj umiejętności*: cooking; **książka ~a** cookbook; **kucharz** *m* (*-rza*; *-rze*), **-rka** *f* (*-ki*; *-ki*) cook

kuchenka *f* (*-ki*; *-ki*) **1.** (*pomieszczenie*) kitchenette **2.** (*urządzenie*) cooker; **~ turystyczna** camping stove; **kuchenny** *adj* kitchen

kuchmistrz *m* (*-rza*; *-rze*) (*szef*) chef

kuchni|a *f* (*-ni*; *-nie*) **1.** (*pomieszczenie*) kitchen; **od ~** *fig* from the inside **2.** (*gotowanie*) cooking **3.** *polska*, *włoska*: cuisine **4.** *gazowa*, *elektryczna*: cooker **5.** *węglowa*: stove

kucki: **siedzieć w ~** squat on one's haunches; **kucnąć** *v/p* → **kucać**

kucyk *m* (*-ka*; *-ki*) **1.** (*koń*) pony **2.** (*uczesanie*) pigtail

kuć ⟨**wy-**⟩ (*kuję*) **I** *v/t* **1.** *metal*: forge **2.** (*uczyć się*) *infml Br* swot up on **II** *v/i* **1.** *w kamieniu*: carve (**w** *L* in) **2.** (*uczyć się*) *infml Br* swot, *Am* cram

kudłaty *adj* **1.** *futro*, *zwierzę*: shaggy **2.** *człowiek*: hairy; **kudły** *pl* (*-łów*) shaggy hair *sing*

kufel *m* (*-fla*; *-fle*) mug

kufer *m* (*-fra*; *-fry*) **1.** (*skrzynia*) chest **2.** (*na bagaż*) trunk **3.** (*bagażnik*) *Br* boot, *Am* trunk

kuglarz *m* (*-rza*; *-rze*) juggler

kujon *m* (*-na*; *-ny*) *infml Br* swot, *Am* grind

kukać ⟨**kuknąć**⟩ (*-kam*) cuckoo

kukiełka *f* (*-ki*; *-ki*) (stick) puppet; **kukiełkowy** *adj* puppet; **kukła** *f* (*-ły*; *-ły*) dummy

kuksaniec *m* (*-sańca*; *-sańce*) **1.** poke **2.** (*łokciem*) nudge

kuku *interj*: **a ~!** peekaboo!

kukułczy *adj* cuckoo; **kukułka** *f* (*-ki*; *-ki*) cuckoo

kukurydza *f* (*-dzy*; *-dze*) **1.** (*roślina*) *Br* maize, *Am* corn **2.** (*warzywo*) *Br* sweetcorn, *Am* corn; **prażona ~** popcorn; **kukurydzian|y** *adj*: **płatki ~e** cornflakes; **mąka ~a** *Br* cornflour, *Am* cornstarch

kukuryku *interj* cock-a-doodle-doo

kul|a *f* (*-li*; *-le*) **1.** ball; **~a śnieżna** snowball; **~a ziemska** the globe; **~a u nogi** *fig* ball and chain **2.** (*bryła*) sphere **3.** (*pocisk*) bullet **4.** SPORT shot; **pchnięcie ~ą** the shot-put **5.** (*inwalidzka*) crutch; **chodzić o ~ach** walk on crutches

kulawo *adv iść*, *działać*: poorly; **kulawy** *adj* **1.** *osoba*, *rymy*: lame **2.** *mebel*: wobbly

kuleczka *f* (*-ki*; *-ki*) (small) ball, pellet

kuleć *v/im* (*-leję*) **1.** limp **2.** (*o gospodarce*) be ailing

kulfon *m* (*-na*; *-ny*) *infml* (*nos*) beak, *Br* conk; **~y** (*pismo*) scrawl; **stawiać ~y** scrawl

kulić ⟨**s-**⟩ (*-lę*): **~ ramiona** hunch one's shoulders; **kulić się 1.** (*z zimna*) huddle up **2.** (*ze strachu*) cower **3.** (*w łóżku*) curl up

kulig *m* (*-gu*; *-gi*) sleigh ride

kulinarny *adj* culinary

kulis|y *pl* (*-sów*) **1.** (*przejścia dla aktorów*) the wings **2.** (*zaplecze*) backstage *sing*; **za ~ami** *fig* behind the scenes

kulisty *adj* spherical, ball-shaped

kulka *f* (*-ki*; *-ki*) **1.** (small) ball **2.** TECH ball **3.** (*pocisk*) bullet, *Am infml* slug; **kulkowy** *adj łożysko*: ball

kulminacyjny *adj* culminating, climactic; **punkt ~** climax

kuloodporny *adj* bulletproof

kulszow|y *adj* MED sciatic; **rwa ~a** sciatica

kult *m* (*-tu*; *-ty*) cult, worship; **~ jednostki** personality cult; **~ świętych** the worship of saints; **miejsce ~u** place of worship; **kultowy** *adj* cult

kultur|a *f* (*-ry*; *-ry*) **1.** culture; **dom ~y** community centre; **~a osobista** good manners; **o dużej ~ze osobistej** well-mannered **2.** *fizyczna*: fitness; **kulturalny** *adj* **1.** cultural **2.** *osoba*: cultured, well-mannered

kulturowy *adj* cultural; **kulturoznawstwo** *n* (*-wa*; *no pl*) cultural studies *pl*, study of culture

kulturystyka *f* (*-ki*; *no pl*) bodybuilding

kultywować *v/im* (*-tywuję*) cultivate

kuluar|y *pl* (*-rów*) corridors; **rozmowy w ~ach** *fig* behind-the-scenes talks

kułak: **śmiać się z kogoś w ~** laugh in s.o.'s face

K

kuma|ć ⟨**s-**⟩ (*-mam*) *infml* get (it); **~sz?** are you with me?
kumać się ⟨**s-**⟩ (*-mam*) *infml Br* be pals, *Am* pal around (**z** *I* with)
kumkać ⟨**za-**⟩ (*-kam*) (*o żabie*) croak
kumpel *m* (*-pla*; *-ple*), **~ka** *f* (*-ki*; *-ki*) *Br* mate, *Am* buddy; **kumpela** *f* (*-li*; *-le*) *infml* (girl)friend
kumplować się *v/im* (*-luję*) *infml* be friends, *Br* be pals, *Am* pal around (**z** *I* with)
kumulacja *f* (*-ji*; *no pl*) accumulation
kuna *f* (*-ny*; *-ny*) marten
kundel *m* (*-dla*; *-dle*) mongrel
kunszt *m* (*-tu*; *no pl*) artistry; **kunsztowny** *adj* **1.** artful **2.** (*misterny*) ornate, intricate
kup|a *f* (*-py*; *-py*) **1.** (*stos*) heap, pile; ***zebrać coś do ~y*** put s.th. together; ***nie trzymać się ~y*** *fig* **a)** not hold together **b)** (*o teorii*, *planie*) not hold water **2.** (*dużo*) *infml* lots of, piles of; ***~a śmiechu*** a good laugh **3.** (*kał*) *infml Br* poo, *Am* poop, *infml* turd; ***zrobić ~ę*** have a poo; ***zrobić ~ę w majtki*** mess one's pants
kuper *m* (*-pra*; *-pry*) rump
kupić *v/p od* **kupować**
kupiec *m* (*-pca*; *-pcy*) **1.** HIST merchant **2.** (*handlowiec*) trader **3.** (*nabywca*) buyer; **kupiecki** *adj* **1.** *szlak*: trade **2.** *rodzina*, *statek*: merchant **3.** *izba*: commercial, of commerce
kupka *f* (*-ki*; *-ki*) **1.** *dim* (small) heap, (small) pile **2.** (*kał*) *Br* poo, *Am* poop
kupno *n* (*-na*; *no pl*) purchase; **kupny** *adj zasłony*: ready-made; *ciasto*: shop
kupon *m* (*-nu*; *-ny*) coupon; ***~ toto-lotka*** lottery ticket
kupować ⟨**-pić**⟩ (*-puję*) buy (**za** *A* for); ***~ za gotówkę*** buy with cash; ***~ kota w worku*** buy a pig in a poke
kupujący *m* (*-cego*; *-cy*), **-ca** *f* (*-cej*; *-ce*) buyer
kura *f* (*-ry*; *-ry*) hen; ***~ domowa*** *infml* housefrau; ***pisać jak ~ pazurem*** scribble; ***wyglądać jak zmokła ~*** look like a drowned rat
kuracj|a *f* (*-ji*; *-je*) treatment, therapy; ***przechodzić ~ę*** receive treatment, be in therapy; ***~a odwykowa*** withdrawal treatment
kuracjusz *m* (*-sza*; *-sze*), **~ka** *f* (*-ki*; *-ki*) visitor, patient
kuratel|a *f* (*-li*; *-le*) **1.** JUR custody; ***sprawować ~ę nad*** *I* have custody of **2.** *fig* (close) supervision
kurator *m* (*-ra*; *-rzy*), **~ka** *f* (*-ki*; *-ki*) *wystawy*: curator; ***~ sądowy*** probation officer; ***~ oświaty*** *Br* chief education officer, *Am* superintendent of schools; **kuratorium** *n* (*indecl*; *-ria*) education authority, *Am* board of education
kurcz *m* (*-czu*; *-cze*) cramp; ***chwycił mnie ~*** *Br* I've got cramp, *Am* I have a cramp
kurczak *m* (*-ka*; *-ki*) chicken; **kurczątko** *n* (*-ka*; *-ka*) chick
kurczę I *n* (*-częcia*; *-częta*) chicken **II** *interj Br* gosh, *Am* shoot
kurczowo *adv* tightly; **kurczowy** *adj* tight
kurczyć ⟨**s-**⟩ (*-czę*) *nogi*: tuck (up); ***kurczyć się*** **1.** shrink **2.** (*o mięśniach*) contract
kurde *interj infml Br* gosh, *Am* shoot
kurdupel *m* (*-pla*; *-ple*) *infml Br* shortarse, *Am* short-ass
kurdyjski *adj* Kurdish
kurek *m* (*-rka*; *-rki*) **1.** (*kran*) *Br* tap, *Am* faucet **2.** (*w beczce*) spigot
kurewski *adj vulg* fucking
kurhan *m* (*-nu*; *-ny*) burial mound
kuria *f* (*-rii*; *-rie*): ***~ diecezjalna*** diocese offices; ***~ rzymska*** the Roman Curia
kurier *m* (*-ra*; *-rzy*), **~ka** *f* (*-ki*; *-ki*) courier, messenger; **kurierski** *adj* courier
kuriozalny *adj infml* ridiculous
kurka *f* (*-ki*; *-ki*) (*grzyb*) chanterelle
kurnik *m* (*-ka*; *-ki*) hen house
kuropatwa *f* (*-wy*; *-wy*) partridge
kurować ⟨**wy-**⟩ (*-ruję*) treat; ***kurować się*** undergo treatment
kurs *m* (*-su*; *-sy*) **1.** (*szkolenie*) course; ***~ na prawo jazdy*** driving course; ***~ językowy*** (foreign) language course **2.** FIN rate; ***~ wymiany*** exchange rate; ***~ akcji*** share price; ***~ otwarcia*** (***zamknięcia***) opening (closing) price **3.** (*kierunek*) course **4.** *autobusu*: run **5.** *taksówki*: trip **5.** (*obieg*) circulation
kursant *m* (*-ta*; *-nci*), **~ka** *f* (*-ki*; *-ki*) student, (course) participant
kursor *m* (*-ra*; *-ry*) cursor; **kursować** *v/im* (*-suję*) **1.** (*o pociągu*, *autobusie*) run **2.** (*o statku*) sail, travel

kursyw|a *f* (*-wy*; *no pl*) italics; **~ą** in italics
kurtka *f* (*-ki*; *-ki*) jacket
kurtuazyjny *adj wizyta*: courtesy
kurtyna *f* (*-ny*; *-ny*) curtain
kurwa *f* (*-wy*; *-wy*) *vulg* **1.** (*prostytutka*) whore **2.** (*obraźliwie o kobiecie*) slut, *Br* slag; **~ (mać)!** fuck!, shit!
kurz *m* (*-rzu*; *-rze*) dust
kurzajka *f* (*-ki*; *-ki*) wart
kurz|y *adj jaja*, *ferma*: chicken; ***~a ślepota*** night blindness; ***~e łapki*** crow's feet; ***~y móżdżek*** birdbrain
kurzyć ⟨**na-**⟩ (*-rzę*) **1.** *fajkę*: puff (on) **2.** (*o samochodzie*) raise (clouds of) dust; **kurzyć się** ⟨**za-**⟩ (*pokrywać się kurzem*) get dusty; ***wiał, aż się kurzyło*** he was running for his life
kusiciel *m* (*-la*; *-le*) tempter; **kusicielka** *f* (*-ki*; *-ki*) temptress; **kusicielsko** *adv* **1.** seductively **2.** (*wyglądać*) seductive
kus|ić ⟨**s-**⟩ (*-szę*) **1.** (*namawiać*) tempt; ***~i kogoś, żeby coś zrobić*** s.o. is tempted to do s.th.; ***~ić los*** *fig* tempt fate **2.** (*przyciągać*) lure, tempt (*I* with); ***~zą go młode dziewczęta*** he is drawn to young girls
kustosz *m* (*-sza*; *-sze*) *muzeum*: curator
kusy *adj spódniczka*: short
kusza *f* (*-szy*; *-sze*) crossbow
kuszący *adj* **1.** tempting **2.** (*uwodzicielski*) seductive
kuszetka *f* (*-ki*; *-ki*) couchette
kuśnierz *m* (*-rza*; *-rze*) furrier
kuśtykać ⟨**do-**⟩ (*-kam*) limp
kutas *m* (*-sa*; *-sy*) *vulg* dick
kuter *m* (*-tra*; *-try*): ***~ rybacki*** fishing cutter; ***~ torpedowy*** motor torpedo boat, MTB
kutwa *f* (*-wy*; *-wy*) *infml* Scrooge
kuty *adj* **1.** *żelazo*: wrought **2.** *brama*: wrought-iron; ***być ~m na cztery nogi*** be a sly devil
Kuwejt *m* (*-tu*) Kuwait
kuzyn *m* (*-na*; *-ni*), **~ka** *f* (*-ki*; *-ki*) cousin
kuźnia *f* (*-ni*; *-nie*) forge, smithy
kwadra *f* (*-ry*; *-ry*) ASTR quarter
kwadrans *m* (*-sa*; *-se*) quarter (of an hour); ***za ~ druga*** *Br* a quarter to two, *Am* a quarter of two; ***~ akademicki*** *the right of students to miss a class if the lecturer is more than 15 minutes late*
kwadrat *m* (*-tu*; *-ty*) square; ***podnosić do ~u*** square; ***do ~u*** MATH squared; ***idiota do ~u*** *infml* utter idiot; **kwadratura** *f* (*-ry*; *-ry*): ***~ koła*** *fig* squaring the circle; **kwadratowy** *adj* square
kwakać ⟨**-knąć**⟩ (*kwaczę*) quack
kwalifikacj|a *f* (*-ji*; *-je*) classification; ***mieć odpowiednie ~e*** be suitably qualified; **kwalifikacyjn|y** *adj* qualifying; ***rozmowa ~a*** interview; **kwalifikować** ⟨**za-**⟩ (*-kuję*) (*klasyfikować*) classify; ***kwalifikować się*** *do finału*, *do dotacji*: qualify (**do** *G* for)
kwapić się ⟨**po-**⟩ (*-pię*): ***nie ~ do nauki*** be not too keen on studying; ***nie ~ z odpowiedzią*** be in no hurry to answer a question
kwarantann|a *f* (*-ny*; *-ny*) quarantine; ***przechodzić ~ę*** be in quarantine
kwarc *m* (*-cu*; *-ce*) quartz; **kwarcówka** *f* (*-ki*; *-ki*) quartz lamp, sunlamp
kwartalnik *m* (*-ka*; *-ki*) quarterly; **kwartalny** *adj* quarterly
kwartał *m* (*-łu*; *-ły*) **1.** (*okres*) quarter (of a year) **2.** (*domy*) block
kwartet *m* (*-tu*; *-ty*) quartet
kwas *m* (*-su*; *-sy*) **1.** acid **2.** (*smak*) sour tang **3.** **~y** *fig* bad feelings, grudges; **kwasek** *m* (*-sku*; *no pl*) acid; ***~ cytrynowy*** citric acid
kwasić → ***kisić***
kwaskow(at)y *adj* slightly sour, sourish
kwasowy *adj* acid
kwaszony → ***kiszony***
kwaśnieć ⟨**s-**⟩ (*-nieję*) turn sour; **kwaśnawy** *adj* slightly sour, sourish
kwaśn|y *adj* **1.** sour; ***zbić kogoś na ~e jabłko*** beat s.o. black and blue, beat s.o. to a pulp **2.** *mleko*: soured **3.** *deszcz*, *odczyn*: acid
kwater|a *f* (*-ry*; *-ry*) **1.** (*mieszkanie*) lodgings *pl*; ***~y prywatne*** private rooms **2.** (*dla wojska*) billet, quarters *sing*; ***~a główna*** headquarters; **kwaterunkowy** *adj* **1.** *mieszkanie*: council **2.** *urząd*: housing
kwesta *f* (*-ty*; *-ty*) collection
kwesti|a *f* (*-tii*; *-tie*) **1.** (*problem*) issue, question; ***być ~ą*** *G* be a question of **2.** *aktora*: line; **kwestionariusz** *m* (*-sza*; *-sze*) **1.** (*ankieta*) questionnaire

K

2. (*formularz*) form; **kwestionować** ⟨**za-**⟩ (*-nuję*) question
kwestować *adj* (*-tuję*) collect (money)
kwękać *v/im* (*-kam*) *infml* whine, moan
kwiaciarka *f* (*-ki*; *-ki*) florist; **kwiaciarnia** *f* (*-ni*; *-nie*) (the) florist's, flower shop
kwiat *m* (*-tu*; *-ty*) **1.** flower; ***w ~y*** flowered, flowery **2.** (*roślina*) plant; ***~ doniczkowy*** pot plant **3.** *fig* flower, cream; ***w kwiecie wieku*** in the prime of life
kwiatek *m* (*-tka*; *-tki*) (small) flower; **kwiatostan** *m* (*-nu*; *-ny*) inflorescence; **kwiatowy** *adj* **1.** flower **2.** *wzór*: floral
kwiczeć ⟨**za-**⟩ (*-czę*) squeal
kwiecień *m* (*kwietnia*; *kwietnie*) April
kwiecisty *adj styl*, *sukienka*: flowery
kwietnik *m* (*-ka*; *-ki*) **1.** (*klomb*) flower bed **2.** (*mebel*) flower stand
kwietniowy *adj* April
kwik *m* (*-ku*; *-ki*) squeal
kwilić ⟨**za-**⟩ (*-lę*) whimper
kwintal *m* (*-la*; *-le*) quintal
kwintet *m* (*-tu*; *-ty*) quintet
kwit *m* (*-tu*; *-ty*) receipt, ticket; ***~ bagażowy*** *Br* luggage ticket, *Am* baggage check
kwita *infml*: ***być ~*** be quits, be square (**z** *I* with)
kwit|ek *m* (*-tka*; *-tki*) receipt, ticket; ***odprawić kogoś z ~kiem*** send s.o. away empty-handed
kwitnący *adj roślina*: flowering, blooming; **kwitnąć** ⟨**za-**⟩ (*-nę*) **1.** (*o roślinie*) flower, be in bloom **2.** (*o handlu*, *życiu kulturalnym*) flourish **3.** (*o interesie*) thrive **4.** (*o życiu nocnym*) be buzzing
kwitować (*-tuję*) **1.** ⟨**po-**⟩ (*potwierdzać*) sign for; ***~ odbiór*** confirm receipt (*G* of) **2.** ⟨**s-**⟩ (*odpowiadać*) respond, greet (*I* with); ***~ śmiechem*** laugh off, dismiss with laughter; ***~ wzruszeniem ramion*** shrug off
kwiz *m* (*-zu*; *-zy*) quiz
kwoka *f* (*-ki*; *-ki*) mother hen
kwota *f* (*-ty*; *-ty*) (*suma*) amount

L

L

labirynt *m* (*-tu*; *-ty*) **1.** labyrinth **2.** (*w ogrodzie*) maze **2.** *fig* maze, labyrinth
laborant *m* (*-ta*; *-nci*), **~ka** *f* (*-ki*; *-ki*) laboratory technician, *infml* lab technician
laboratorium *n* (*indecl*; *-ria*) laboratory, *infml* lab; **laboratoryjny** *adj* laboratory, *infml* lab
lać ⟨**w-**, **z-**⟩ (*leję*) **I** *v/t* **1.** *ciecz*: pour; ***~ wodę*** *fig Br* beat about the bush, *Am* beat around the bush, *Br infml* waffle (on) **2.** (*bić*) *infml* beat, give a thrashing **II** *v/t* **1.** (*o deszczu*) pour (down); ***leje*** (***deszcz***) it's pouring (with rain) **2.** *infml* piss; ***lać się*** **1.** (*o cieczy*) flow, pour; ***pot lał się z nas strumieniami*** sweat was pouring off us **2.** (*z kranu*) run
lada[1] *f* (*-dy*; *-dy*) counter; ***~ chłodnicza*** refrigerated (display) counter
lada[2] *particle*: ***~ dzień*** any day (now); ***to była nie ~ sztuka*** it was no mean feat
lafirynda *f* (*-dy*; *-dy*) *infml* floozy
laicki *adj* (*świecki*) secular, lay; **laicyzacja** *f* (*-ji*; *no pl*) secularization; **laik** *m* (*-ka*; *laicy*) layman
lak *m* (*-ku*; *-ki*) sealing wax
lakier *m* (*-ru*; *-ry*) **1.** varnish, laquer; ***~ do paznokci*** nail polish, *Br* nail varnish; ***~ do włosów*** hairspray **2.** *samochodowy*: paint; **lakierki** *pl* (*-ków*) patent leather shoes
lakiernia *f* (*-ni*; *-nie*) paint shop; **lakierować** ⟨**po-**⟩ (*-ruję*) **1.** varnish **2.** *samochód*, *paznokcie*: paint
lakmusowy *adj*: ***papierek ~*** litmus paper
lakoniczny *adj* laconic
lakować ⟨**za-**⟩ (*-kuję*) seal (with wax)
lalka *f* (*-ki*; *-ki*) **1.** doll **2.** THEAT puppet; **laluś** *m* (*-lusia*; *-lusie*) pretty boy
lama[1] *f* (*-my*; *-my*) BIOL llama
lama[2] *m* (*-my*; *-mowie*) REL lama
lamentować *v/im* (*-tuję*) lament (***nad*** *I*)
laminat *m* (*-tu*; *-ty*) laminate; **laminować** ⟨**za-**⟩ (*-nuję*) laminate
lamówka *f* (*-ki*; *-ki*) trimming

lampa *f* (*-py*; *-py*) lamp; ~ ***stojąca*** *Br* standard lamp, *Am* floor lamp; ~ ***jarzeniowa*** fluorescent tube; ~ ***błyskowa*** flash(light); ~ ***kineskopowa*** cathode ray tube

lampart *m* (*-ta*; *-ty*) leopard

lampion *m* (*-nu*; *-ny*) lantern

lampka *f* (*-ki*; *-ki*) **1.** (small) lamp; ~***nocna*** bedside lamp; ~ ***nagrobkowa*** memorial candle **2.** (*kieliszek*) glass **3.** *kontrolna*: light

lamus *lit*: ***odejść do ~a*** go out of use, go out of date

landrynka *f* (*-ki*; *-ki*) *Br* boiled sweet, *Am* hard candy; **landrynkowy** *adj* **1.** (*w kolorze landrynek*) *Br* candy-coloured, *Am* candy-colored **2.** (*przesłodzony*) saccharine

lanie *n* (*-nia*; *-nia*) beating, *infml* hiding; ***sprawić komuś porządne*** ~ give s.o. a good beating, *infml* give s.o. a good hiding; ~ ***wody*** *fig Br* beating about the bush, *Am* beating around the bush; **lan|y** *adj*: ***~e kluski*** egg noodles; ***~y poniedziałek*** Easter Monday, Wet Monday

lansować ⟨**wy-**⟩ (*-suję*) promote

lapidarny *adj* concise, succint

lapis-lazuli *m indecl* lapis lazuli

Laponia *f* (*-nii*) Lapland; **lapoński** *adj* Lappish

laptop *m* (*-pa*; *-py*) laptop

larwa *f* (*-wy*; *-wy*) larva; ***larwy*** larvae

laryngolog *m* (*-ga*; *-lodzy*) throat specialist, ENT specialist

las *m* (*-su*; *-sy*) forest, woods *pl*; ~ ***liściasty*** (***iglasty***) deciduous (coniferous) forest; ***nie wywołuj wilka z ~u*** let sleeping dogs lie; ***być z czymś*** (***jeszcze***) ***w lesie*** *fig* not be ready with s.th.; **lasek** *m* (*-sku*; *-ski*) (small) wood

laser *m* (*-ra*; *-ry*) laser; **laserowy** *adj* laser

laska *f* (*-ki*; *-ki*) **1.** (*do podpierania*) (walking) stick, cane; ***chodzić o lasce*** walk with a stick **2.** *cynamonu*, *dynamitu*: stick **3.** *wanilii*: pod **4.** (*dziewczyna*) *infml* chick **5.** *marszałkowska*: staff

laskowy *adj*: ***orzech*** ~ hazelnut

lastryko *n* (*-ka*; *no pl*)/*indecl* terrazzo

lata *pl* (*lat*) years; ~ ***sześćdziesiąte*** the sixties; ***ile masz lat?*** how old are you?; ***od lat***, ***przez*** ~ for years; ***za dwa*** ~ in two years, in two years' time; ***sto lat!*** many happy returns!; ***przed laty*** years ago; ***mieć*** (***już***) ***swoje*** ~ (*o osobie*) be no spring chicken; ***latami*** for years; → ***rok***

latać *v/im* (*-tam*) **1.** fly **2.** (*biegać*) *infml* run; ~ ***po sklepach*** shop, run around shops; ~ ***za spódniczkami*** chase women; ~ ***z wywieszonym jęzorem*** *fig* run around like a chicken with its head cut off

latanina *f* (*-ny*; *-ny*) *infml* running around

latarka *f* (*-ki*; *-ki*) *Br* torch, *Am* flashlight; ~ ***kieszonkowa*** penlight; **latarnia** *f* (*-ni*; *-nie*): ~ ***uliczna*** street lamp; ~ ***morska*** lighthouse; ***chińska*** ~ Chinese lantern

latawiec *m* (*-wca*; *-wce*) kite

lat|o *n* (*-ta*; *-ta*) summer; ***~em***, ***w lecie*** in (the) summer; ***babie ~o*** **a)** (*pajęczyna*) gossamer **b)** (*pora*) Indian summer

latorośl *f* (*-li*; *-le*): ***winna*** ~ vine, grapevine

latynoamerykański, ***latynoski*** *adj* Latin American

laufer *m* (*-fra*; *-fry*) (*w szachach*) bishop

laur *m* (*-ru*; *-ry*) (*nagroda*) laurels *pl*; ***spocząć na ~ach*** rest on one's laurels

laureat *m* (*-ta*; *-reaci*), **~ka** *f* (*-ki*; *-ki*) winner; ~ ***Nagrody Nobla*** Nobel prize-winner

laurk|a *f* (*-ki*; *-ki*) **1.** (self-made) greetings card **2.** *fig* puff; ***wystawić komuś ~ę*** sing s.o.'s praises

laurowy *adj*: ***listek*** ~ bay leaf; ***wieniec*** ~ laurel wreath, laurels

lawa *f* (*-wy*; *no pl*) lava

lawenda *f* (*-dy*; *no pl*) lavender; **lawendowy** *adj* lavender

lawina *f* (*-ny*; *-ny*) avalanche; **lawinowy** *adj* **1.** *zagrożenie*: avalanche **2.** *wzrost*: dramatic **3.** *efekt*: snowball

lawirant *m* (*-ta*; *-nci*), **~ka** *f* (*-ki*; *-ki*) trimmer, *infml* smooth operator; **lawirować** *v/im* (*-ruję*) *Br* manoeuvre, *Am* maneuver

ląd *m* (*-du*; *-dy*) land; ~ ***stały*** mainland; ***wyjść na*** ~ go ashore, come ashore

lądować ⟨**wy-**⟩ (*-duję*) land; **lądowanie** *n* (*-nia*; *-nia*) landing; ***przymusowe*** ~

L

forced landing; **lądowisko** *n* (*-ka*; *-ka*) airstrip; **lądow|y** *adj* land; ***drogą ~ą*** overland

lebioda *f* (*-dy*; *-dy*) fat hen

lec, ***legnąć*** *v/p* (*legnę*) *lit* **1.** (*położyć się*) lie down **2.** (*w walce*) fall; ***~ u podstaw*** lie at the root of, underlie; ***~ w gruzach*** **a)** (*o mieście*) be reduced to rubble **b)** (*o planach*) go up in smoke, be ruined

lecieć ⟨**po-**⟩ (*-cę*) **1.** fly **2.** (*o wodzie, krwi*) flow, run; ***kupowała wszystko jak leci*** she bought whatever was available (on sale) **3.** (*spadać*) fall **4.** (*biec*) run, rush **5.** (*o czasie*) pass; ***jak leci?*** how's it going?, how are things? **6.** (*o filmie w kinach*) be showing, be on **7.** (*o piosence*) be playing **8.** (*pożądać*) *infml* be after (**na** *A*)

leciutki *adj* **1.** (very) light **2.** *dotknięcie*: (very) light, (very) gentle

leciwy *adj lit* aged

lecz *conj* but; ***nie tylko…, ~ także*** not only…(,) but also

L

leczenie *n* (*-nia*; *no pl*) treatment; therapy; **lecznica** *f* (*-cy*; *-ce*) clinic; ***~ dla zwierząt*** animal clinic

lecznictwo *n* (*-wa*; *no pl*) health care; **leczniczo** *adv* therapeutically; **leczniczy** *adj* **1.** *dawka*, *działanie*: therapeutic **2.** *źródła*, *właściwości*: healing; ***środek ~*** medication

leczyć ⟨**wy-**⟩ (*-czę*) **1.** (*kurować*) treat **2.** (*przywracać zdrowie*) cure; ***leczyć się*** be treated, undergo treatment; ***~ się samemu czymś*** heal oneself with s.th.

ledwie, ***ledwo*** **I** *particle* **1.** (*prawie nie*) barely, hardly; ***~ wyczuwalny*** hardly noticeable; ***~ żywy*** *infml* dead-beat; ***~ mogła mówić*** she could hardly talk; ***~ zdążyłem na pociąg*** I (only) just made it in time to catch the train **2.** (*tylko*) only; ***znamy się ~ miesiąc*** we've only known each other for a month **3.** (*dopiero co*) **~** (**co**) only just **II** *conj* barely, hardly; ***~ zasnęła, zadzwonił telefon*** she had barely fallen asleep when the phone rang

legalizacja *f* (*-ji*; *no pl*) **1.** legalization **2.** (*stwierdzenie zgodności*) approval, authorization; **legalizować** ⟨**za-**⟩ (*-zuję*) **1.** legalize **2.** (*stwierdzać zgodność*) approve, authorize

legalny *adj* legal

legenda *f* (*-dy*; *-dy*) legend; **legendarny** *adj* legendary

legia *f* (*-gii*; *-gie*) legion; ***≈ Cudzoziemska*** the Foreign Legion; **legionista** *m* (*-ty*; *-niści*) **1.** (*żołnierz*) legionary **2.** (*w Legii Cudzoziemskiej*) legionnaire

legitymacja *f* (*-ji*; *-je*) (identity) card, ID card; ***~ członkowska*** membership card

legitymować ⟨**wy-**⟩ (*-muję*) check s.o.'s ID; ***legitymować się*** **1.** (*pokazać dokument*) show one's ID **2.** (*posiadać w dorobku*) have (to one's name)

legowisko *n* (*-ka*; *-ka*) **1.** (*dzikiego zwierzęcia*) lair **2.** (*dla psa*) (dog) bed

lej *m* (*-ja*; *-je*) crater; ***~ po bombie*** bomb crater

lejce *pl* (*-ców*) reins

lejek *m* (*-jka*; *-jki*) funnel; **lejkowaty** *adj* **1.** funnel-shaped **2.** *kształt*: funnel-like

lek *m* (*-ku*; *-ki*) **1.** drug, medicine; ***~ przeciwbólowy*** painkiller; ***~ uspokajający*** tranquilizer; ***~ na raka*** cure for cancer **2.** *fig* remedy, cure

lek. med. *abbr* (= ***lekarz medycyny***) Dr, MD

lekarka *f* (*-ki*; *-ki*) (woman) doctor; **lekarski** *adj porada*: medical; ***gabinet ~*** surgery, doctor's office; ***zwolnienie ~e*** sick note; ***na zwolnieniu ~m*** on sick leave

lekarstwo *n* (*-wa*; *-wa*) **1.** drug, medicine; ***jak na ~*** hardly at all, next to nothing **2.** *fig* remedy, cure

lekarz *m* (*-rza*; *-rze*) doctor; ***iść do ~a*** see a doctor, go to the doctor; ***~ rodzinny*** general practitioner, GP; family doctor; ***~ specjalista*** specialist, *Br* consultant; ***~ weterynarii*** *Br* veterinary surgeon, *Am* veterinarian

lekceważący *adj* **1.** *stosunek*, *ton*: dismissive, irreverent **2.** *uwaga*: slighting **3.** *uśmiech*: disparaging; **lekceważenie** *n* (*-nia*; *no pl*) **1.** (*bagatelizowanie*) disregard (*G* for/of); ***~ swoich obowiązków*** neglecting one's duties **2.** (*brak szacunku*) disrespect (*G* for); **lekceważyć** ⟨**z-**⟩ (*-żę*) **1.** (*bagate-*

lizować) disregard; **~ swoje obowiązki** neglect one's duties **2.** (*okazywać brak szacunku*) show disrespect (*G* for/to) **3.** (*ignorować*) ignore; **~ przepisy** flout the rules

lekcj|a *f* (*-ji*; *-je*) **1.** lesson; **~a gry w tenisa** tennis lesson; **~a języka angielskiego** English lesson; **po ~ach** after school; **prowadzić ~ę** teach a lesson, give a lesson; **odrabiać ~e** do one's homework **2.** (*godzina*) period

lekcyjn|y *adj*: **godzina ~a** (class) period; **sala ~a** classroom

lekk|i *adj* **1.** light; **~i jak piórko** (as) light as a feather **~a atletyka** *Br* athletics, *Am* track and field; **kobieta ~ich obyczajów** woman of easy virtue **2.** (*niewielki*, *nieznaczny*) slight **3.** (*niewyraźny*) faint **4.** *śmierć*: painless

lekkoatleta *m* (*-ty*; *-leci*), **-tka** *f* (*-ki*; *-ki*) *Br* athlete, *Am* track and field athlete; **lekkoatletyka** *f* (*-ki*; *no pl*) *Br* athletics, *Am* track and field; **lekkoatletyczny** *adj Br* athletic, *Am* track and field

lekkomyślność *f* (*-ści*; *no pl*) recklessness; **lekkomyślny** *adj* reckless

lekkość *f* (*-ści*; *no pl*) lightness

lekkostrawny *adj* light

lekomania *f* (*-nii*; *no pl*) pill addiction, *infml* pill-popping

leksykalny *adj* lexical; **leksykografia** *f* (*-fii*; *no pl*) lexicography

leksykon *m* (*-nu*; *-ny*) lexicon

lektor *m* (*-ra*; *-rzy*) **1.** (*na uczelni*) foreign language teacher **2.** RADIO TEL announcer; **głos ~a** (*w filmie*) voice-over; **lektur|a** *f* (*-ry*; *-ry*) **1.** (*czytanie*) reading **2.** (*książka*) set book; **spis ~** reading list; **~y obowiązkowe** required reading

lemoniada *f* (*-dy*; *-dy*) lemonade

len *m* (*lnu*; *lny*) **1.** (*roślina*) flax **2.** (*tkanina*) linen

lenić się *v/im* (*-nię*) **1.** (*być leniwym*) be lazy **2.** (*ociągać się*) dawdle; **lenistwo** *n* (*-wa*; *no pl*) **1.** (*cecha*) laziness **2.** (*stan*) idleness

leniuch *m* (*-cha*; *-chy*) *infml* lazybones *sing*; **leniuchować** *v/im* (*-chuję*) *infml* laze around, lounge around

leniwiec *m* (*-wca*; *-wce*) (*zwierzę*) sloth

leniwy *adj* **1.** *uczeń*, *pracownik*: lazy **2.** *spacer*, *rozmowa*: leisurely

lennik *m* (*-ka*; *-nicy*) liege(man); **lenno** *n* (*-na*; *-na*) (*ziemia*) fief(dom), fee

leń *m* (*lenia*; *lenie*) lazy person, idler, *infml* lazybones *sing*; **być leniem** be lazy

lep *m* (*-pu*; *-py*): **~ na muchy** flypaper

lepić ⟨**u-**⟩ (*-pię*) *bałwana*, *figurki z gliny*: make; **lepić się** ⟨**z-**⟩ be sticky; **~ od brudu** be grimy

lepiej *adv comp* → **dobrze** better; **tym ~** all the better; **~ już idź** you'd better go now

lepki *adj* **1.** sticky **2.** PHYS viscous

lepsz|y *adj comp* → **dobry** better; **zmienić się na ~e** change for the better; **pierwszy ~y** the first one to come along, just any

lesbijka *f* (*-ki*; *-ki*) lesbian

lessowy *adj gleby*: loess

leszcz *m* (*-cza*; *-cze*) bream

leszczyna *f* (*-ny*; *-ny*) hazel

leśnictwo *n* (*-wa*; *-wa*) **1.** (*dziedzina*) forestry **2.** (*obszar*) forest district; **leśniczówka** *f* (*-ki*; *-ki*) forester's lodge

leśniczy *m* (*-czego*; *-czowie*) forester; **leśnik** *m* (*-ka*; *-nicy*) forester; **inżynier ~** forestry engineer; **leśny** *adj* **1.** forest **2** *obszar*: wooded

letarg *m* (*-gu*; *no pl*) lethargy; **zapaść w ~** fall into lethargy

letni *adj* **1.** summer; **czas ~** *Br* summer time, *Am* daylight saving time **2.** (*ciepławy*) lukewarm, tepid

letnik *m* (*-ka*; *-nicy*) *Br* holidaymaker, *Am* vacationer; **letnio** *adv ubrany*: lightly

letnisko *n* (*-ka*; *-ka*) summer resort; **letniskow|y** *adj sezon*: summer holiday; **miejscowość ~a** summer resort

leukocyt *m* (*-tu*; *-ty*) leukocyte, white blood cell

lew *m* (*lwa*; *lwy*) **1.** lion; **~ morski** sea lion **2.** ASTR Leo

lew|a[1] *f* (*-wej*; *-we*) (*strona*) the left; **po ~ej** on the left, to the left; → **lewy**

lew|a[2] *f* (*-wy*; *-wy*) (*w kartach*) trick

lewacki *adj* extreme leftist

lewarek *m* (*-rka*; *-rki*) jack

lewatywa *f* (*-wy*; *-wy*) enema

lewic|a *f* (*-cy*; *no pl*) POLIT the left; **działacz ~y** left-wing activist; **partie ~y** left-wing parties; **lewicowiec** *m*

L

(*-wca*; *-wcy*) leftist; **lewicowy** *adj* **1.** leftist **2.** *działacz*: left-wing
lewkonia *f* (*-nii*; *-nie*) stock
lewo *adv*: ***patrzeć* (*skręcić*) *w ~*** look (turn) left; ***na ~ od*** to the left of; ***drzwi na ~*** the door on the left; ***na ~*** (*nielegalnie*) *infml* on the side, illegally; ***kupić coś na ~*** buy s.th. under the counter; → ***lewy***
lewobrzeżny *adj* left-bank; **leworęczny** *adj* left-handed
lewostronny *adj* left-side; ***w Australii obowiązuje ruch ~*** in Australia they drive on the left
lew|y *adj* **1.** left; ***po ~ej stronie*** on the left side; ***po ~ej stronie od*** *G* to the left of **2.** (*fałszywy*) *infml* fake, *infml* phoney; → ***lewa***, ***lewo***
leźć ⟨**po-**⟩ (*lezę*) *infml* **1.** (*wlec się*) shamble, drag oneself **2.** (*wdrapywać się*) climb
leżak *m* (*-ka*; *-ki*) deckchair; **leżanka** *f* (*-ki*; *-ki*) couch; **leżakować** *v/im* (*-kuję*) **1.** (*o winie*) mature **2.** (*odpoczywać*) rest
leżąco *adv*: ***na ~*** lying (down); ***czytać na ~*** read lying down
leżąc|y *adj* lying; ***miejsce ~e*** berth
leżeć *v/im* (*-żę*) **1.** lie; ***~ w szpitalu*** be in hospital; ***~ do góry brzuchem*** *infml* lie around; ***~ w gruzach*** lie in ruins; ***~ nad rzeką*** lie on a river; ***~ u podstaw*** *G* lie at the root of, underlie **2.** (*znajdować się*) lie, be; ***na podłodze leżał but*** there was a shoe (lying) on the floor **3.** (*o sukni*, *spodniach*) fit
lędźwie *pl* (*-wi*) loins
lęg *m* (*-gu*; *-gi*) (*wylęganie się*) hatching; **lęgnąć się** ⟨**wy-**⟩ (*-nę*) (*z jaja*) hatch; **lęgowisko** *n* (*-ka*; *-ka*) breeding ground
lęgowy *adj okres*, *miejsce*: breeding
lęk *m* (*-ku*; *-ki*) fear, anxiety; ***~ wysokości*** fear of hights; **lękać się** *v/im* (*-kam*) *lit* fear (**o** *A* for); **lękliwy** *adj osoba*: timid
lgnąć ⟨**przy-**⟩ (*-nę*) **1.** (*przylegać*) cling (**do** *G* to) **2.** (*garnąć się*) flock around (**do** *G*)
liana *f* (*-ny*; *-ny*) liana
libacja *f* (*-ji*; *-je*) drinking bout
Liban *m* (*-nu*) Lebanon; **Libańczyk** *m* (*-ka*; *-czycy*), **~banka** *f* (*-ki*; *-ki*) Lebanese; **libański** *adj* Lebanese
liberalizować ⟨**z-**⟩ (*-zuję*) liberalize; **liberalny** *adj* liberal; **liberał** *m* (*-ła*; *-łowie*) liberal
liberia *f* (*-rii*; *-rie*) livery
Libia *f* (*-bii*) Libya; **Libijczyk** *m* (*-ka*; *-czycy*), **~bijka** *f* (*-ki*; *-ki*) Libyan; **libijski** *adj* Libyan
licealista *m* (*-ty*; *-liści*), **-tka** *f* (*-ki*; *-ki*) *Br* secondary school student, *Am* (senior) high school student
licencj|a *f* (*-ji*; *-je*) *Br* licence, *Am* license; ***na czyjejś ~i*** under licence from s.o.
liceum *n* (*indecl*; *-cea*) *Br* secondary school, *Am* (senior) high school
lich|o *n* (*-cha*; *-cha*) evil spirit, fiend; ***do ~a!*** hell!, damn!; ***~o nie śpi*** you never know what might happen; ***~o wie*** devil only knows; ***do ~a i trochę*** a hell of a lot; ***gdzie* (*kto*) *u ~a?*** where (who) the hell?
lichtarz *m* (*-rza*; *-rze*) candlestick
lichwa *f* (*-wy*; *no pl*) usury; **lichwiarz** *m* (*-rza*; *-rze*) usurer
licować *v/im* (*-cuję*): ***nie ~ z*** *I lit* be out of keeping with, be unbecoming of
licytacj|a *f* (*-ji*; *-je*) **1.** auction; ***na ~i*** at auction **2.** (*w grach*) bidding; **licytator** *m* (*-ra*; *-rzy*) auctioneer; **licytować** ⟨**z-**⟩ (*-tuję*) **1.** (*sprzedawać*) auction **2.** (*oferować*) bid **3.** (*w kartach*) bid; ***licytować się***: ***licytowali się czymś*** they tried to outdo each other in doing s.th.
liczba *f* (*-by*; *-by*) number; ***~ pojedyncza*** the singular; ***~ mnoga*** the plural
liczbowo *adv* (*w liczbach*) in numbers; **liczbow|y** *adj dane*, *wartość*: numerical; ***gra ~a*** lottery
liczebnie *adv*: ***przeważać ~ nad kimś*** outnumber s.o.; **liczebnik** *m* (*-ka*; *-ki*) numeral; **liczebn|y** *adj*: ***stan ~y*** strength; ***mieć nad kimś przewagę ~ą*** outnumber s.o.
licznik *m* (*-ka*; *-ki*) **1.** *gazu*, *wody*: meter **2.** ***~ prędkości*** AUTO speedometer; ***~ kilometrów*** AUTO odometer, *infml* clock **3.** *Geigera*: counter **4.** MATH numerator; **liczny** *adj* numerous
liczyć ⟨**po-**⟩ (*-czę*) **I** *v/t* **1.** count; ***~ w pamięci*** count in one's head **2.** *cenę*, *wielkość*: calculate; ***~ coś na kalkulatorze*** work s.th. out on a calculator **3.** (*mieć*) have; ***~ sobie pięćdziesiąt***

lat be fifty years old **4.** (*kazać zapłacić*) charge **II** *v/i* count (***na*** *A* for); ***liczyć się*** **1.** (*mieć znaczenie*) count, matter **2.** (*brać pod uwagę*) take into account; ***~ się ze słowami*** watch one's mouth; ***~ się z każdym groszem*** count every penny; ***nie ~ się z*** *I* ignore, pay no attention to; ***nie ~ się z czyimś zdaniem*** disregard s.o.'s opinion

liczydło *n* (*-ła*; *-ła*) abacus

lider *m* (*-ra*; *-rzy*) leader

liga *f* (*-gi*; *-gi*) **1.** league **2.** *SPORT* league, division

lignina *f* (*-ny*; *no pl*) cellulose wadding

ligowy *adj* league

likier *m* (*-ru*; *-ry*) liqueur, *Am* cordial

likwidacja *f* (*-ji*; *-je*) **1.** (*usunięcie*) elimination **2.** *firmy*, *spółki*: liquidation, winding-up **3.** *sklepu*, *zakładu*: closing down; **likwidować** ⟨**z-**⟩ (*-duję*) **1.** (*usuwać*) eliminate **2.** *firmę*, *spółkę*: liquidate, wind up **3.** *sklep*, *zakład*: close down

lila *adj* lilac

lilia *f* (*-lii*; *-lie*) lily; **liliowy** *adj* lilac

limfatyczny *adj* **1.** *układ*: lymphatic **2.** *gruczoł*, *węzeł*: lymph

limit *m* (*-tu*; *-ty*) limit; **limitować** *v/im* (*-tuję*) limit

limuzyna *f* (*-ny*; *-ny*) limousine

lin *m* (*-na*; *-ny*) tench

lin|a *f* (*-ny*; *-ny*) rope; ***stalowa ~a*** steel cable; ***chodzić po ~ie*** walk the tightrope

linczować ⟨**z-**⟩ (*-czuję*) lynch

lingwistyka *f* (*-ki*; *no pl*) linguistics *sing*

lini|a *f* (*-nii*; *-nie*) **1.** line; ***~e papilarne*** skin lines, *ANAT* dermatoglyphics; ***odciski ~i papilarnych*** fingerprints; ***dbać o ~ę*** watch one's waistline **2.** *autobusowa*: route

linieć ⟨**wy-**⟩ (*-nieję*) *Br* moult, *Am* molt

linijka *f* (*-ki*; *-ki*) **1.** (*wiersz*) line **2.** (*przyrząd*) ruler; **liniowo** *adv* linearly, in a linear fashion; **liniowy** *adj* **1.** *MATH* linear **2.** *podatek*: flat-rate **3.** ***sędzia ~*** linesman

linka *f* (*-ki*; *-ki*) cord, rope

linoleum *n indecl* linoleum, *Br infml* lino

linoskoczek *m* (*-czka*; *-czkowie*) tightrope walker

linow|y *adj drabinka*: rope; ***kolejka ~a*** cable car, cableway

lipa *f* (*-py*; *-py*) **1.** *BIOL* lime **2.** (*bujda*) *infml* rubbish, *Am* baloney **3.** (*tandeta*) *infml* junk, *Am* schlock

lipcowy *adj* July; **lipiec** *m* (*-pca*; *-pce*) July

lipny *adj* (*tandetny*) *infml* shoddy

lipowy *adj* **1.** lime **2.** *aleja*: of lime trees

liryczny *adj* **1.** (*dotyczący liryki*) lyric **2.** (*nastrojowy*) lyrical; **liryka** *f* (*-ki*; *no pl*) lyric (poetry)

lis *m* (*-sa*; *-sy*) fox; ***szczwany ~*** wily old fox; ***~y*** (*futro*) fox; **lisi** *adj* fox; ***~ ogon*** fox's tail, brush; **lisica** *f* (*-cy*; *-ce*) vixen

list *m* (*-tu*; *-ty*) letter; ***~ polecony*** registered letter; ***~ lotniczy*** airmail letter; ***~em priorytetowym*** by priority mail; ***~ gończy*** arrest warrant; ***~ przewozowy*** waybill; ***~y uwierzytelniające*** credentials, letters of credence

lista *f* (*-ty*; *-ty*) list; ***~ płac*** payroll; ***~ przebojów*** the charts; ***~ obecności*** (*w szkole*) register

listek *m* (*-tka*; *-tki*) **1.** (*liść*) (small) leaf **2.** (*arkusik*) (small) sheet, paper

listonosz *m* (*-sza*; *-sze*) *Br* postman, *Am* mailman; **listonoszka** *f* (*-ki*; *-ki*) *Br* postwoman

listopad *m* (*-da*; *-dy*) November; **listopadowy** *adj* November

listowie *n* (*-wia*; *no pl*) foliage

listowny *adj* by post, by mail; **listowy** *adj papier*: letter

listwa *f* (*-wy*; *-wy*) **1.** strip of wood; ***~ podłogowa*** *Br* skirting (board), *Am* baseboard **2.** *tkaniny*, *obrazu*: border

liszaj *m* (*-ja*; *-je*) **1.** lichen **2.** (*rumieniowaty*) lupus

liściasty *adj BIOL* deciduous, broad-leaved

liś|ć *m* (*-ścia*; *-ście*) leaf; ***~ć dębu*** oak leaf; ***jesienne ~cie*** autumn leaves

litania *f* (*-nii*; *-nie*) litany

liter|a *f* (*-ry*; *-ry*) letter; ***dużymi ~ami***, ***wielkimi ~ami*** in capitals, in block letters; ***pisać coś wielką ~ą*** capitalize s.th.; ***cztery ~y*** *infml* behind, backside

literacki *adj* literary; ***pismo ~e*** literary journal

literat *m* (*-ta*; *-raci*) author, writer

L

literatka *f* (*-ki*; *-ki*) **1.** (*autorka*) (woman) author, (woman) writer **2.** (*szklaneczka*) shot glass
literatura *f* (*-ry*; *-ry*) literature; **~ *piękna*** poetry and fiction, belles-lettres; **~ *fachowa*** specialist literature; **~ *faktu*** non-fiction
literaturoznawstwo *n* (*-wa*; *no pl*) literary studies *pl*, study of literature; ***studiować* ~** study literature
literować ⟨**prze-**⟩ (*-ruję*) spell
litewsk|i *adj* Lithuanian; ***mówić po ~u*** speak Lithuanian
litościwy *adj* **1.** *osoba*: merciful **2.** *spojrzenie*: compassionate; **litoś|ć** *f* (*-ści*; *no pl*) **1.** (*żal*) pity; ***z ~ci*** out of pity **2.** (*łaska*) mercy; ***bez ~ci*** without mercy, mercilessly
litować się ⟨**z-**⟩ (*-tuję*) **1.** (*odczuwać żal*) pity (***nad*** *I*) **2.** (*okazywać łaskę*) have mercy (***nad*** *I* on)
litr *m* (*-ra*; *-ry*) *Br* litre, *Am* liter; **litraż** *m* (*-żu*; *no pl*) capacity (in litres); **litrowy** *adj Br* litre, *Am* liter
liturgia *f* (*-gii*; *-gie*) liturgy
Litwa *f* (*-wy*) Lithuania; **Litwin** *m* (*-na*; *-ni*), **-ka** *f* (*-ki*; *-ki*) Lithuanian
lity *adj drewno*: solid
lizać ⟨**-znąć**⟩ (*liżę*) lick; ***lizać się*** (*całować się*) *infml* smooch, *Br* snog; **lizak** *m* (*-ka*; *-ki*) lollipop
Lizbona *f* (*-ny*) Lisbon
lizus *m* (*-sa*; *-sy*) toady, bootlicker, *Br* creep
lm. *abbr* (= ***liczba mnoga***) pl.
lnian|y *adj* **1.** *tkanina*, *obrus*: linen **2.** *olej*: linseed; ***siemię ~e*** linseed
LO *abbr n indecl* (= ***Liceum Ogólnokształcące***) *Br* secondary school, *Am* (senior) high school
Loara *f* (*-ry*) the Loire
loch *m* (*-chu*; *-chy*) dungeon
locha *f* (*-chy*; *-chy*) sow
loczek *m* (*-czka*; *-czki*) *dim* curl
lodołamacz *m* (*-cza*; *-cze*) ice-breaker; **lodowacieć** ⟨**z-**⟩ (*-cieję*) freeze; **lodowaty** *adj* **1.** *ręce*, *woda*: ice-cold **2.** *wiatr*, *spojrzenie*: icy
lodowcowy *adj* glacial; **lodowiec** *m* (*-wca*; *-wce*) glacier; **lodowisko** *n* (*-ka*; *-ka*) ice rink
lodow|y *adj tor*, *epoka*: ice; ***góra ~a*** iceberg; **lodówka** *f* (*-ki*; *-ki*) refrigerator, *infml* fridge; **~ *turystyczna*** cool box;
lody *pl* (*-dów*) ice cream; **~ *na patyku*** ice cream on a stick
lodziarnia *f* (*-ni*; *-nie*) *Br* ice-cream parlour, *Am* ice-cream parlor; **lodziarz** *m* (*-rza*; *-rze*), **-rka** *f* (*-ki*; *-ki*) ice-cream vendor
lodżia *f* (*-dżii*; *-dżie*), **loggia** *f* (*-gii*; *-gie*) **1.** (*balkon*) (recessed) balcony **2.** (*część budynku*) loggia
logarytm *m* (*-mu*; *-my*) logarithm
logiczny *adj* logical; **logika** *f* (*-ki*; *no pl*) logic; **logistyczny** *adj* logistical; **logistyka** *f* (*-ki*; *no pl*) logistics *sing*
logo *n indecl* logo
logopeda *m* (*-dy*; *-dzi*) speech therapist
logować się ⟨**za-**⟩ (*-guję*) log in, log on; **~ *do systemu*** log into the system
lojalność *f* (*-ści*; *no pl*) loyalty; **lojalny** *adj* loyal
lok *m* (*-ka*; *-ki*) curl
lokaj *m* (*-ja*; *-je*) **1.** (*służący*) footman **2.** *fig* lackey
lokal *m* (*-lu*; *-le*) **1.** (*mieszkanie*) *Br* flat, *Am* apartment; **~ *mieszkalny*** dwelling unit **2.** (*pomieszczenie*) **~ *biurowy*** office; **~ *gospodarczy*** commercial space, commercial premises; **~ *wyborczy*** *Br* polling station, *Am* polling place **3.** (*restauracja*) restaurant; **~ *nocny*** night club
lokalizować ⟨**z-**⟩ (*-zuję*) locate; **lokalny** *adj* local
lokata *f* (*-ty*; *-ty*) **1.** (*w banku*) deposit **2.** (*inwestycja*) **~ *kapitału*** investment **3.** SPORT place
lokator *m* (*-ra*; *-rzy*), **~ka** *f* (*-ki*; *-ki*) occupant; ***dziki* ~** squatter
lokomocj|a *f* (*-ji*; *no pl*): ***środki ~i*** *Br* means of transport, *Am* means of transportation; **lokomotywa** *f* (*-wy*; *-wy*) engine, locomotive
lokować ⟨**u-**⟩ (*-kuję*) **1.** (*umieszczać*) place **2.** (*w banku*) deposit **3.** (*lokalizować*) locate **4.** *wczasowiczów*: accommodate
lokówka *f* (*-ki*; *-ki*) curling tongs *pl*
lombard *m* (*-du*; *-dy*) pawnshop
Londyn *m* (*-nu*) London
lont *m* (*-tu*; *-ty*) fuse
lornetka *f* (*-ki*; *-ki*) binoculars *pl*; **~ *teatralna*** opera glasses
los *m* (*-su*; *-sy*) **1.** (*przeznaczenie*) fate **2.** (*koleje życia*) fate, lot; ***przeciwnoś-***

ci ~u adversities; ***zmienne koleje ~u*** changing fortunes; ***masz ci ~!*** o dear!, just my luck! **3.** (*na loterii*) ticket; ***pusty ~*** losing ticket; ***ciągnąć ~y*** draw lots
losować ⟨**wy-**⟩ (*-suję*) **1.** (*ciągnąć losy*) draw **2.** *partnera*: draw for **3.** (*wygrywać*) win; **losowani|e** *n* (*-nia*; *-nia*) draw; ***drogą ~a*** by draw
losow|y *adj kolejność*: random; ***gra ~a*** game of chance; ***zdarzenie ~e*** **a)** random event **b)** (*w ubezpieczeniach*) chance event, accident
lot *m* (*-tu*; *-ty*) flight; ***widok z ~u ptaka*** bird's-eye view; ***w ~*** at once
loteri|a *f* (*-rii*; *-rie*) lottery; ***wygrać na ~i*** win a lottery
lotka *f* (*-ki*; *-ki*) **1.** SPORT shuttlecock **2.** *ptaka*: flight feather **3.** TECH aileron
lotnia *f* (*-ni*; *-nie*) hang-glider; **lotniarstwo** *n* (*-wa*; *no pl*) hang-gliding; **lotniarz** *m* (*-rza*; *-rze*) hang-glider
lotnictwo *n* (*-wa*; *no pl*) **1.** (*dziedzina*) aviation **2.** (*siły zbrojne*) air force; **lotnicz|y** *adj* **1.** *transport*, *katastrofa*: air **2.** *przemysł*, *paliwo*: aviation; ***linie ~e*** airlines; ***port ~y*** airport; ***drogą ~ą*** by air; ***poczta ~a*** airmail; ***pocztą ~ą*** by airmail; ***alarm ~y*** air-raid warning
lotnik *m* (*-ka*; *-nicy*) airman; **lotnisko** *n* (*-ka*; *-ka*) **1.** (*port lotniczy*) airport **2.** (*lądowisko*) airfield; **lotniskowiec** *m* (*-wca*; *-wce*) aircraft carrier; **lotniskowy** *adj* airport
lotn|y *adj* **1.** (*gazowy*) gaseous **2.** (*szybko parujący*) volatile **3.** *umysł*: agile; ***~e piaski*** quicksand
Lozanna *f* (*-ny*) Lausanne
loża *f* (*-ży*; *-że*) **1.** THEAT box **2.** *masońska*: lodge
lód *m* (*lodu*; *lody*) **1.** ice; ***rzeka skuta lodem*** ice-bound river; ***mieć forsy jak lodu*** *infml* be rolling in money; ***zostać na lodzie*** *fig* be left in the lurch, be left out in the cold; → **lody**
lp. *abbr* (= ***liczba pojedyncza***) sing.
lśniący *adj* **1.** *włosy*: shiny **2.** *tafla wody*: glistening; ***~ czystością*** spick and span; **lśnić** *v/im* (*-nię*) **1.** (*o włosach*) shine **2.** (*o tafli wody*) glisten
lub *conj* or; ***~ też*** or (else)
luba *f* (*-bej*; *-be*) *hum* beloved
lubczyk *m* (*-ka*; *-ki*) lovage
lubiany *adj* **1.** well-liked **2.** (*o nauczycielu*, *aktorze*) popular (***przez*** *A* with); **lubić** *v/im* (*-bię*) like; ***~ czytać książki*** like reading books, like to read books
lubieżnik *m* (*-ka*; *-nicy*) lecher; **lubieżny** *adj starzec*, *spojrzenie*: lecherous
lubować się *v/im* (*-buję*) *lit* revel (***w*** *L* in)
luby *m* (*-bego*; *-bi*) *hum* beloved
lud *m* (*-du*; *-dy*) people; ***wywodzić się z ~u*** be of low origin; **ludek** *m* (*-dka*; *-dki*) (*figurka*) man, figure; **ludność** *f* (*-ści*; *no pl*) population; **ludny** *adj* populous
ludobójca *m* (*-cy*; *-cy*) perpetrator of genocide, mass murderer; **ludobójstwo** *n* (*-wa*; *no pl*) genocide
ludowy *adj* **1.** *muzyka*, *strój*: folk **2.** *demokracja*: people's **3.** *partia*: peasant
ludożerca *m* (*-cy*; *-cy*) cannibal; **ludożerstwo** *n* (*-wa*; *no pl*) cannibalism
ludzi|e *pl* (*-dzi*) people; ***przy ~ach*** in public; **ludzik** *m* (*-ka*; *-ki*) (*figurka*) man, figure
ludzk|i *adj* **1.** (*dotyczący człowieka*) human; ***istota ~a*** human being; ***rodzaj ~i*** mankind; ***to przechodzi ~ie pojęcie*** this is incredible **2.** (*humanitarny*) humane **3.** (*dobry*) kind; ***po ~u*** **a)** (*życzliwie*) kindly **b)** (*przyzwoicie*) decently
ludzkość *f* (*-ści*; *no pl*) humankind
lufa *f* (*-fy*; *-fy*) **1.** (*część broni*) barrel **2.** (*kieliszek wódki*) *infml* shot
lufcik *m* (*-ka*; *-ki*) window vent
luft: ***do ~u*** *infml* no good
luk *m* (*-ku*; *-ki*) **1.** (*otwór*) hatch(way) **2.** (*ładownia*) hold
luka *f* (*-ki*; *-ki*) **1.** gap **2.** *prawna*: loophole
lukier *m* (*-kru*; *-kry*) *Br* icing, *Am* frosting
lukratywny *adj* lucrative; **lukrecja** *f* (*-ji*; *-je*) *Br* liquorice, *Am* licorice; **lukrować** ⟨**po-**⟩ (*-ruję*) *Br* ice, *Am* frost
Luksemburg *m* (*-ga*) Luxembourg
luksus *m* (*-su*; *no pl*) luxury; **luksusowy** *adj* luxury
lulać ⟨**u-**⟩ (*-lam*): ***~ kogoś do snu*** lull s.o. to sleep
lumbago *n indecl* lumbago
lump *m* (*-pa*; *-py*) *infml* bum

L

lunapark *m* (*-ku*; *-ki*) *Br* funfair, *Am* carnival
lunatyk *m* (*-ka*; *-tycy*), **-tyczka** *f* (*-ki*; *-ki*) sleep walker
luną|ć *v/p*: ***~ł deszcz*** it started pouring down
luneta *f* (*-ty*; *-ty*) telescope
lupa *f* (*-py*; *-py*) magnifying glass
lura *f* (*-ry*; *-ry*) *infml* wish-wash; **lurowaty** *adj infml kawa*, *zupa*: watery, wishy-washy
lusterko *n* (*-ka*; *-ka*) (small) mirror; ***~ boczne*** *AUTO* wing mirror; ***~ wsteczne*** *AUTO* rear-view mirror
lustracja *f* (*-ji*; *-je*) **1.** (*kontrola*) inspection **2.** *POLIT* vetting; **lustracyjny** *adj POLIT* vetting
lustro *n* (*-ra*; *-ra*) **1.** mirror **2.** (*powierzchnia*) surface; **lustrować** ⟨**z-**⟩ (*-ruję*) **1.** (*kontrolować*) inspect **2.** *POLIT* vet
lustrzanka *f* (*-ki*; *-ki*) *PHOT* reflex camera; ***~ jednoobiektywowa*** SLR, single-lens reflex camera; **lustrzan|y** *adj* **1.** mirror; ***~e odbicie*** reflection, mirror image **2.** (*lśniący*) shining
lut *m* (*-tu*; *-ty*) solder
luterański *adj* Lutheran
lutnia *f* (*-ni*; *-nie*) lute; **lutnik** *m* (*-ka*; *-nicy*) violin maker
lutować ⟨**z-**⟩ (*-tuję*) solder; **lutownica** *f* (*-cy*; *-ce*) soldering iron
lutowy *adj* February; **luty** *m* (*-tego*; *-te*) February
luz *m* (*-zu*; *-zy*) **1.** (*wolne miejsce*) room **2.** (*wolny czas*) free time **3.** (*swoboda zachowania*) *infml* ease; ***gość na ~ie*** laid-back guy, easy-going guy **4.** *TECH* clearance, play; ***~ kierownicy*** steering play; → ***luzem***
luzak *m* (*-ka*; *-zacy*) *infml* laid-back guy; ***być ~iem*** be laid-back, be easy-going
luzem *adv* (*bez opakowania*) loose
luzować ⟨**po-**⟩ (*-zuję*) *nakrętkę*, *linę*: loosen
luźny *adj* **1.** *ubranie*, *kartki*: loose **2.** *znajomość*, *uwaga*: casual **3.** (*wolny*) free
lwi *adj grzywa*, *skóra*: lion's; ***~a część*** the lion's share; **lwica** *f* (*-cy*; *-ce*) lioness
Lwów *m* (*Lwowa*) Lviv, Lvov, Lwów
lwy *pl* → ***lew***
lżejszy *comp* → ***lekki***
lżyć ⟨**ze-**⟩ (*-żę*) *lit* revile, abuse

Ł

Ł

łabędzi *adj* swan's; ***~ śpiew*** *fig* swansong; **łabędź** *m* (*-dzia*; *-dzie*) swan
łacha *f* (*-chy*; *-chy*) **1.** (*odnoga rzeki*) dead arm **2.** (*mielizna*) sandbank
łachmany *pl* (*-nów*), **łachy** *pl* (*-chów*) *infml* rags
łaciaty *adj* spotted
łacina *f* (*-ny*; *no pl*) **1.** Latin **2.** (*przekleństwa*) *infml* bad language; **łaciński** *adj* Latin
ład *m* (*-du*; *no pl*) order; ***doprowadzić coś do ~u*** put s.th. in order; ***dojść z kimś do ~u*** come to terms with s.o.; ***bez ~u i składu*** chaotically; ***mówić bez ~u i składu*** ramble, speak incoherently
ładnieć ⟨**wy-**⟩ (*-nieję*) get prettier
ładn|y *adj* **1.** *osoba*, *twarz*: pretty **2.** *piosenka*, *obrazek*: lovely, pretty **3.** *fryzura*, *nogi*, *gest*: nice **4.** *pogoda*: good, fine; ***~ych parę lat*** quite a few years; ***~a historia!*** that's nice!
ładować ⟨**wy-**⟩ (*-duję*) **1.** *towar*: load **2.** *baterię*: (re)charge; ***ładować się*** (*pchać się*) push one's way, barge in
ładownia *f* (*-ni*; *-nie*) hold; **ładowność** *f* (*-ści*; *no pl*) (load) capacity, (carrying) capacity; **ładowny** *adj bagażnik*, *plecak*: spacious, roomy
ładunek *m* (*-nku*; *-nki*) **1.** (*samochodowy*) load **2.** (*okrętowy*, *samolotowy*) cargo **3.** *PHYS* charge; ***~ wybuchowy*** **a)** (explosive) charge **b)** (*bomba*) bomb
łagodnieć ⟨**z-**⟩ (*-nieję*) **1.** (*o osobie*, *głosie*) soften **2.** (*o bólu*) ease **3.** (*o wietrze*) ease off; **łagodność** *f* (*-ści*; *no pl*) (*charakteru*) gentleness
łagodny *adj* **1.** *osoba*, *klimat*: gentle **2.** *smak*, *mydło*, *zima*: mild **3.** *światło*: soft **4.** *wyrok*: lenient **5.** *nowotwór*: benign

łagodząco *adv*: ***działać ~*** have a soothing effect; **łagodzący** *adj* **1.** *krem*: soothing **2.** *okoliczności*: extenuating, mitigating
łagodzi|ć (*-dzę*) **1.** ⟨**z-**, **za-**⟩ *ból*: ease, soothe **2.** ⟨**z-**, **za-**⟩ *cierpienie*, *stres*: relieve **3.** ⟨**za-**⟩ *napięcie*: ease, relax **4.** ⟨**za-**⟩ *konflikt*: reduce, *form* mitigate; ***muzyka ~ obyczaje*** music soothes the savage beast
łajać ⟨**z-**⟩ (*-jam*) scold, rebuke
łajba *f* (*-by*; *-by*) *infml* (*łódź*) boat
łajdactwo *n* (*-wa*; *-wa*) wickedness; **łajdaczyć się** *v/im* (*-czę*) **1.** lead a debauched life **2.** (*o kobiecie*) whore around; **łajdak** *m* (*-ka*; *-dacy*/*-ki*) scoundrel
łajno *n* (*-na*; *-na*) *krowie*, *końskie*: dung
łaknąć *v/im* (*-nę*) *lit miłości*, *deszczu*: long for; ***~ wiedzy*** be eager to learn; **łaknieni|e** *n* (*-nia*; *no pl*) appetite; ***brak ~a*** loss of appetite
łakocie *pl* (*-ci*) *Br* sweets, *Am* candy *sing*, *dated* sweetmeats; **łakomczuch** *m* (*-cha*; *-chy*) glutton, big eater
łakomić się ⟨**po-**⟩ (*-mię*) covet, crave (**na** *A*); **łakomstwo** *n* (*-twa*; *no pl*) **1.** greed **2.** (*grzech*) gluttony
łakomy *adj* **1.** *osoba*: greedy (**na** *A* for); ***~ na pieniądze*** money-greedy **2.** *kąsek*: tasty
łam *m* (*-mu*; *-my*) (*strona gazety*) column; ***na ~ach gazet*** in the papers
łamać (*-mię*) **1.** ⟨**z-**, **po-**⟩ break; ***z~ rękę*** break one's arm; ***~ sobie głowę nad*** *I* puzzle over, rack one's brains over; ***~ sobie język*** twist one's tongue; ***łamie mnie w kościach*** my bones are aching **2.** ⟨**z-**⟩ *przepisy*: violate, break **3.** ⟨**z-**⟩ *opór*: break, crush; ***łamać się*** **1.** break; ***nie łam się!*** *infml* cheer up!, don't let it get you down!; ***~ się z kimś opłatkiem*** *share the Christmas wafer with s.o. and exchange wishes* **2.** (*o głosie*) falter
łamaga *f* (*-gi*; *-gi*) *infml* clumsy oaf, *Am* klutz
łamany *adj angielszczyzna*: broken
łamigłówka *f* (*-ki*; *-ki*) **1.** puzzle, brainteaser **2.** *fig* puzzle, conundrum
łamistrajk *m* (*-ka*; *-ki*) strike-breaker, *infml* scab
łamliwy *adj* brittle
łan *m* (*-nu*; *-ny*) cornfield
łania *f* (*-ni*; *-nie*) doe
łańcuch *m* (*-cha*; *-chy*) chain; ***na ~u*** on a chain; ***~ górski*** mountain range; **łańcuchow|y** *adj reakcja*, *pies*: chain; ***piła ~a*** chainsaw; **łańcuszek** *m* (*-szka*; *-szki*) chain
łap|a *f* (*-py*; *-py*) **1.** (*zwierzęcia*) paw **2.** (*ręka*) *infml* paw, *infml* mitt; ***~y przy sobie!*** hands off!, ***dać komuś w ~ę*** bribe s.o., *Br infml* give s.o. a backhander
łapać ⟨**z-**⟩ (*-pię*) **1.** catch (**za** *A*); ***~ kogoś na czymś*** catch s.o. doing s.th.; ***z trudem ~ oddech*** be gasping for breath; ***~ kogoś za słowa*** pick holes in s.o.'s words **2.** *za rękę*: take hold (**za** *A* of); grab (**za** *A*) **3.** *taksówkę*: get **4.** *okazję*: grab, seize **5.** *stację*: pick up **6.** (*kontaktować się*) *infml* get hold (**za** *A* of) **7.** (*rozumieć*) *infml* get (it) **8.** **złapał go kurcz** *Br* he had cramp, *Am* he had a cramp; ***łapać się***: ***~ się na czymś*** catch oneself doing s.th.; ***~ się za głowę*** (***brzuch***) clutch one's head (belly)
łapanka *f* (*-ki*; *-ki*) round-up
łapczywy *adj* greedy
łapka *f* (*-ki*; *-ki*) **1.** (*łapa*) (little) paw **2.** (*ręka*) *infml* (little) hand; ***~ na muchy*** fly swatter; ***~ na myszy*** mouse trap; ***kurze łapki*** *fig* crow's feet
łapownictwo *n* (*-wa*; *no pl*) bribery; **łapówka** *f* (*-ki*; *-ki*) bribe
łapserdak *m* (*-ka*; *-ki*) ragamuffin
łapu-capu *infml*: **na ~** **a)** (*w pośpiechu*) in a rush **b)** (*byle jak*) sloppily, any old how
łasica *f* (*-cy*; *-ce*) weasel
łasić się *v/im* (*-szę*) (*przymilać się*) fawn (**do** *G* on)
łask|a *f* (*-ki*; *-ki*) **1.** (*względy*) *Br* favour, *Am* favor; ***być zdanym na czyjąś ~ę*** be at s.o.'s mercy; ***zrobić coś z ~i*** do s.th. with bad grace; ***niech pan z ~i swojej*** could you please; ***bez ~i!*** *infml* OK, forget it!; ***co ~a*** it's up to you **2.** JUR pardon, reprieve; ***prawo ~i*** *Br* prerogative of mercy, *Am* clemency power **3.** REL grace
łaskawy *adj* **1.** *król*, *życie*: kind; ***~ Panie!*** Dear Sir! **2.** *los*, *rok*: *Br* favourable, *Am* favorable **3.** *Bóg*: graceful, benevolent

Ł

łaskotać 〈**po-**〉 (*-koczę*) tickle
łaskot|ki *pl* (*-tek*): ***mieć ~ki*** be ticklish; ***nie lubić ~ek*** not like to be tickled
łasy *adj* greedy (**na** *A* for); ***być ~m na słodycze*** have a sweet tooth; ***~ na pieniądze*** money-greedy
łaszki *pl* (*-ków*) *infml* gear *sing*
łata *f* (*-ty*; *-ty*) (*na ubraniu*, *sierści*) patch; **łatać** 〈**za-**〉 (*-tam*) *ubranie*: patch
łatwizn|a *f* (*-ny*; *no pl*) *infml* cinch, piece of cake; ***iść na ~ę*** *infml* take the easy way (out)
łatwo *adv* easily; ***~ coś zrozumieć*** s.th. is easy to understand; ***~ powiedzieć*** it's easy to say; ***coś ~ poszło*** s.th. was easy; ***przychodzić komuś ~*** come easy to s.o.; ***nie miała ~*** she did not have it easy
łatwopalny *adj* flammable
łatwoś|ć *f* (*-ści*; *no pl*) ease; ***z ~cią*** easily, with ease; ***~ć wysławiania się*** eloquence
łatwowierny *adj* gullible, credulous
łatw|y *adj* easy; ***~y w obsłudze*** easy to use, user-friendly; ***lektura ~a i przyjemna*** light reading
ław|a *f* (*-wy*; *-wy*) **1.** bench; ***na ~ie oskarżonych*** in the dock; ***~a przysięgłych*** the jury **2.** (*stół*) coffee table; **ławą** *adv* all together, en masse
ławica *f* (*-cy*; *-ce*) *ryb*: school, shoal; ***~ piasku*** shoal
ławka *f* (*-ki*; *-ki*) **1.** bench; ***~ w parku*** park bench; ***~ rezerwowych*** substitutes' bench **2.** (*w szkole*) desk **3.** (*w kościele*) pew
ławnik *m* (*-ka*; *-nicy*) juror
łazęga *f*/*m* (*-gi*; *-gi*) *infml* tramp
łazić *v*/*im* (*łażę*) *infml* **1.** go, *infml* traipse **2.** (*wspinać się*) climb; ***~ po drzewach*** climb trees
łazienka *f* (*-ki*; *-ki*) bathroom; **łazienkowy** *adj* bathroom
łazik *m* (*-ka*; *-ki*) (*samochód*) jeep
łaźnia *f* (*-ni*; *-nie*) bath
łącze *n* (*-cza*; *-cza*) connection, line; **łączniczka** *f* (*-ki*; *-ki*) (female) liaison; **łącznie** *adv* (*w sumie*) in total; ***~ z*** *I* including; ***pisać coś ~*** write s.th. as one word
łącznik *m* **1.** (*-ka*; *-nicy*) (*osoba*) liaison **2.** (*-ka*; *-ki*) (*znak*) hyphen **3.** (*-ka*; *-ki*) TECH connector **4.** (*-ka*; *-ki*) MUS tie; **łączność** *f* (*-ści*; *no pl*) **1.** (*kontakt*) contact; ***~ radiowa*** radio contact **2.** (*komunikacja*) communication; **łączn|y** *adj* **1.** *tkanka*: connective **2.** *wartość*, *nakład*: total; ***pisownia ~a*** one-word spelling; ***~a suma*** total (sum)
łączyć 〈**po-**〉 (*-czę*) **1.** (*w całość*) join; ***~ ze sobą*** join (together) **2.** (*zapewniać komunikację*) connect **3.** TEL connect, put through **4.** (*jednoczyć*) unite **5.** (*godzić*) combine; ***~ przyjemne z pożytecznym*** combine business and pleasure; ***~ w sobie*** combine; ***łączę pozdrowienia*** best regards; **łączyć się 1.** (*w całość*) be joined, join **2.** (*mieć związek*, *połączenie*) be connected **3.** (*jednoczyć się*) unite **4.** CHEM combine **5.** TEL connect, get through **6.** RADIO go over (**z** *I* to)
łąka *f* (*-ki*; *-ki*) meadow
łeb *m* (*łba*; *łby*) **1.** head **2.** *infml* nut ***na ~, na szyję*** headlong; ***patrzeć spode łba*** scowl; ***~ w ~*** neck in neck **3.** (*umysł*) *infml* brains
łeb|ek *m* (*-bka*; *-bki*) head; ***~ek szpilki*** pinhead; ***od ~ka***, ***na ~ka*** *infml* a head, per head; ***robić po ~kach*** *infml* scamp, do cursorily
łechtaczka *f* (*-ki*; *-ki*) clitoris, *infml* clit
łechtać 〈**po-**〉 (*-chczę*/*-chcę*) tickle; ***mile ~*** *fig* flatter
łepek → ***łebek***
łezk|a *f* (*-ki*; *-ki*) *dim* tear; ***z ~ą w oku*** *fig* tearfully
łęg *m* (*-gu*; *-gi*) **1.** (*łąka*) marshy meadow **2.** (*las*) riverine forest
łgać *v*/*im* (*łżę*) *lit* lie; **łgarstwo** *n* (*-wa*; *-wa*) *lit* lie; **łgarz** *m* (*-rza*; *-rze*) *lit* lier
łkać 〈**za-**〉 (*łkam*) *lit* sob
łobuz *m* (*-za*; *-zy*) **1.** (*urwis*) urchin **2.** (*chuligan*) hoodlum, lout; **łobuzerski** *adj* *uśmiech*: roguish
łobuzeria *f* (*-rii*; *no pl*) (*łobuzy*) hoodlums *pl*, louts *pl*; **łobuzerstwo** *n* (*-wa*, *no pl*) **1.** roguery **2.** (*chuligaństwo*) hooliganism
łobuziak *m* (*-ka*; *-ki*) (little) rascal; **łobuzować** *v*/*im* (*-zuję*) make mischief
łodyga *f* (*-gi*; *-gi*) stalk, stem
łoić 〈**z-**〉 (*łoję*) *infml*: ***~ komuś skórę*** tan s.o.'s hide
łojotok *m* (*-ku*; *no pl*) *Br* seborrhoea, *Am* seborrhea

łojow|y *adj*: **gruczoły ~e** sebaceous glands
łok|ieć *m* (*-kcia*; *-kcie*) elbow; **trącić ~ciem** nudge; **rozpychać się ~ciami** elbow one's way, jostle
łom *m* (*-mu*; *-my*) crowbar
łomot *m* (*-tu*; *-ty*) **1.** (*huk*) bang **2.** (*głuchy odgłos*) thump, thud **3.** *kół*: rumble **4.** *serca*: pounding; **łomotać** ⟨**za-**⟩ (*-moczę*/*-mocę*) **1.** (*do drzwi*) bang **2.** (*głucho*) thump, thud **3.** (*o kołach*) rumble **4.** (*o sercu*) pound
łon|o *n* (*-na*; *-na*) **1.** (*macica*) womb **2.** (*kolana*) *lit* lap **3.** (*piersi*) *lit* bosom; **na ~ie natury** out in nature; **łonowy** *adj włosy*, *kość*: pubic; **wzgórek ~** mons pubis
łopata *f* (*-ty*; *-ty*) **1.** shovel **2.** (*szpadel*) spade **3.** (*część śmigła*) blade; **łopatka** *f* (*-ki*; *-ki*) **1.** ANAT shoulder blade **2.** (*zabawka*) (toy) spade **3.** COOK shoulder **4.** TECH blade
łopian *m* (*-nu*; *-ny*) burdock
łopot *m* (*-tu*; *no pl*) flap, flutter; **łopotać** ⟨**za-**⟩ (*-poczę*/*-pocę*) flap, flutter; **~ skrzydłami** flap its wings
łoskot *m* (*-tu*; *-ty*) **1.** (*huk*) bang **2.** *fal*, *grzmotu*: crash **3.** *kół*, *pociągu*: rumble
łososiowy *adj* (*o kolorze*) salmon pink; **łosoś** *m* (*-sosia*; *-sosie*) salmon
łoś *m* (*łosia*; *łosie*) elk
łotewsk|i *adj* Latvian; **mówić po ~u** speak Latvian
łotr *m* (*-ra*; *-ry*/*-rzy*) villain
Łotwa *f* (*-wy*) Latvia; **Łotysz** *m* (*-sza*; *-sze*), **~ka** *f* (*-ki*; *-ki*) Latvian
łowca *m* (*-cy*; *-cy*) hunter; **~ głów** headhunter
łowić ⟨**z-**⟩ (*-wię*) catch; **~ ryby** fish
łowiecki *adj sezon*, *klub*: hunting; **łowiectwo** *n* (*-wa*; *no pl*) hunting
łowisko *n* (*-ka*; *-ka*) **1.** (*rybackie*) fishing ground, fishery **2.** (*myśliwskie*) hunting ground; **łown|y** *adj*: **zwierzyna ~a** game; **łowy** *pl* (*-wów*) hunt
łoza *f* (*-zy*; *-zy*) *Br* grey sallow, *Am* gray sallow
łoż|e *n* (*-ża*; *-ża*) *lit* bed; **~e małżeńskie** double bed; **na ~u śmierci** on one's deathbed; **z nieprawego ~a** illegitimate
łożyć *v/im* (*-żę*) (*finansować*) fund (**na** *A*); **~ na czyjeś utrzymanie** provide for s.o.; **~ na czyjąś edukację** pay for s.o.'s education
łożysko *n* (*-ka*; *-ka*) **1.** ANAT placenta **2.** TECH bearing; **~ kulkowe** ball bearing **3.** (*rzeki*) (river) bed
łódka *f* (*-ki*; *-ki*) (small) boat
łódź *f* (*łodzi*; *łodzie*) boat; **~ motorowa** motor boat; **~ rybacka** fishing boat; **~ podwodna** submarine; **~ ratunkowa** lifeboat; **~ żaglowa** *Br* sailing boat, *Am* sailboat
łój *m* (*łoju*; *no pl*) **1.** (*wydzielina*) sebum **2.** COOK suet
łóżeczko *n* (*-ka*; *-ka*) **1.** *dim* (small) bed **2.** (*ze szczebelkami*) *Br* cot, *Am* crib; **łóżk|o** *n* (*-ka*; *-ka*) bed; **~o piętrowe** bunk beds; **iść do ~a** go to bed; **łóżkow|y** *adj*: **sprawy ~e** *infml* sex (life)
łubin *m* (*-nu*; *-ny*) *Br* lupin, *Am* lupine
łucznictwo *n* (*-wa*; *no pl*) SPORT archery; **łucznik** *m* (*-ka*; *-nicy*), **-niczka** *f* (*-ki*; *-ki*) archer
łudząco *adv*: **jest ~ podobny do matki** he is the spitting image of his mother
łudzić *v/im* (*-dzę*) tantalize; **łudzić się** delude oneself; **~ się nadzieją, że** hope against hope that; **nie łudź się!** don't fool yourself!
ług *m* (*-gu*; *no pl*) lye
łuk *m* (*-ku*; *-ki*) **1.** (*broń*) bow **2.** (*zakrzywienie*) curve **3.** (*kształt*) arc; **~ tęczy** the arc of a rainbow; **~ elektryczny** electric arc **4.** ARCHIT ANAT arch; **łukowaty** *adj* **1.** (*wygięty*) curved **2.** *okno*, *drzwi*: arched; **łukow|y** *adj sklepienie*: arched; **miara ~a kąta** radian
łuna *f* (*-ny*; *-ny*) glow
łup *m* (*-pu*; *-py*) loot; **~y wojenne** the spoils of war; **paść ~em złodziei** be stolen
łup|ać ⟨**-pnąć** ⟩ (*-pię*) *orzechy*: crack; **kogoś ~ie w kościach** s.o.'s bones are aching
łupek *m* (*-pka*; *-pki*) slate
łupić ⟨**z-**⟩ (*-pię*) plunder, loot
łupież *f* (*-żu*; *no pl*) dandruff
łupieżca *m* (*-cy*; *-cy*) *lit* plunderer
łupina *f* (*-ny*; *-ny*) **1.** (*twarda*) shell; **~ orzecha** nutshell **2.** (*miękka*) peel
łupnąć *v/p* (*-nę*) *infml* whack, wallop; → **łupać**
łuska *f* (*-ki*; *-ki*) **1.** (*ryby*) scale **2.** (*naboju*) shell **3.** BIOL husk; **łuskać** *v/im* (*-kam*) shell

Ł

łuszczyca *f* (*-cy*; *no pl*) MED psoriasis; **łuszczyć się** ⟨**z-**⟩ (*-czę*) peel (off), flake (off)
łut: **~ *szczęścia*** a bit of luck
łydka *f* (*-ki*; *-ki*) calf
łyk *m* (*-ku*/*-ka*; *-ki*) swallow, gulp; ***pociągnąć ~*** *G* take a gulp of; **łykać** ⟨**-knąć**⟩ (*-kam*) swallow
łyko *n* (*-ka*; *no pl*) bast; **łykowaty** *adj mięso*: stringy
łypać ⟨**-pnąć**⟩ (*-pię*) glance
łysawy *adj* balding; **łysieć** ⟨**wy-**⟩ (*-sieję*) go bald; **łysiejący** *adj* balding; **łysienie** *n* (*-nia*; *no pl*) hair loss; **łysina** *f* (*-ny*; *-ny*) **1.** (*ubytek*) bald spot **2.** (*głowa*) bald head
łyso *adv*: ***ogolony na ~*** with a shaved head; ***ogolić się na ~*** shave one's head
łys|y I *adj* bald; ***~y jak kolano*** (as) bald as a coot; ***~a pała*** *infml* bald coot **II** *m* (*-sego*; *-si*) baldman
łyżeczka *f* (*-ki*; *-ki*) teaspoon; **łyżka** *f* (*-ki*; *-ki*) **1.** spoon; ***~ wazowa*** (soup) ladle; ***~ do butów*** shoehorn **2.** (*miara*) spoonful
łyżwa *f* (*-wy*; *-wy*) (ice-)skate; ***jeździć na ~ch*** skate; **łyżwiarstwo** *n* (*-wa*; *no pl*) (ice) skating; **łyżwiarz** *m* (*-rza*; *-rze*), **~rka** *f* (*-ki*; *-ki*) skater
łyżworolk|i *pl* (*-lek*) in-line skates, *Br* Rollerblades, *Am* Roller Blades; ***jeździć na ~ach*** Rollerblade
łza *f* (*łzy*; *łzy*) tear; ***śmiech przez łzy*** laughter through tears; ***na otarcie łez*** as a consolation
łzawiący *adj gaz*: tear; **łzawić** *v/im* (*-wię*) water
łzaw|y *adj*: ***~y film***, ***~a opowieść*** tear jerker; **łzowy** *adj* tear

M

m *abbr* (=***metr***) m
m. *abbr* (=***mieszkania***) *Br* flat, *Am* apt.; ***ul. Cicha 15 m. 3*** *Br* flat 3, 15 Cicha St, *Am* 15 Cicha St., apt. 3
ma[1] → ***mieć***
ma[2] *pron lit* my; → ***mój***
macać ⟨**wy-**⟩ (*-cam*) **1.** feel **2.** (*lubieżnie*) grope
Macedonia *f* (*-nii*) Macedonia; **Macedończyk** *m* (*-ka*; *-czycy*), **-donka** *f* (*-ki*; *-ki*) Macedonian; **macedoński** *adj* Macedonian
machać ⟨**po-**, **-chnąć**⟩ (*-cham*) **1.** (*do kogoś*) wave; ***~ ręką*** wave one's hand; ***~ komuś na pożegnanie*** wave goodbye to s.o., wave s.o. goodbye **2.** *szablą*, *kijem*: brandish; ***~ nogami*** swing one's legs; ***~ ogonem*** wag its tail; ***~ skrzydłami*** flap its wings
machina *f* (*-ny*; *-ny*) **1.** (big) machine; ***~ oblężnicza*** siege engine **2.** *państwa*: machinery; **machinacje** *pl* (*-ji*) machinations, scheming *sing*
machinalny *adj* automatic, involuntary
machlojki *pl* (*-jek*) *infml* cons, monkey business *sing*
machnąć *v/p* (*-nę*): ***~ ręką na coś*** *fig* give s.th. up; → ***machać***
macica *f* (*-cy*; *-ce*) ANAT womb, uterus; ***~ perłowa*** mother-of-pearl
macie → ***mieć***
maciejka *f* (*-ki*; *-ki*) night-scented stock
macierz *f* (*-rzy*; *-rze*) **1.** MATH matrix **2.** *lit* ***wrócić do ~y*** (*do Polski*) return to Poland, be reincorporated into Poland
macierzanka *f* (*-ki*; *-ki*) thyme
macierzyński *adj instynkt*, *uczucia*: maternal; ***urlop ~*** maternity leave; **macierzyństwo** *n* (*-wa*; *no pl*) motherhood
macierzysty *adj* **1.** *firma*: parent **2.** *komórka*: stem **3.** *port*: home
maciora *f* (*-ry*; *-ry*) sow
macka *f* (*-ki*; *-ki*) tentacle
macocha *f* (*-chy*; *-chy*) stepmother
macosz|y *adj*: ***traktować kogoś po ~emu*** treat s.o. badly
maczać *v/im* (*-czam*) dip (***w*** *L* in); ***~ palce w*** *L fig* have a hand in
maczuga *f* (*-gi*; *-gi*) club
mać: ***kurwa ~!*** *vulg* fuck!
Madryt *m* (*-tu*) Madrid
mafia *f* (*-fii*; *-fie*) mafia; ***~ sycylijska*** the Mafia; **mafijny** *adj* mafia
mag *m* (*-ga*; *-gowie*) magus; ***~owie*** magi

M

magazyn *m* (*-nu*; *-ny*) **1.** (*budynek*) warehouse, storehouse **2.** (*pomieszczenie*) storeroom **3.** (*czasopismo, audycja*) magazine; **magazynek** *m* (*-nka*; *-nki*) **1.** (*pojemnik na naboje*) clip **2.** (*pomieszczenie*) (small) storeroom; **magazynier** *m* (*-ra*; *-rzy*) warehouse worker, warehouseman

magazynować ⟨**z-**⟩ (*-nuję*) store; **magazynow|y** *adj zapasy, urządzenia*: warehouse; ***powierzchnia ~a*** storage space

magia *f* (*-gii*; *no pl*) magic; **magiczny** *adj* **1.** *zaklęcie, sztuczka*: magic **2.** *wpływ, właściwości*: magical

magiel *m* (*-gla*; *-gle*) (*maszyna*) mangle

magik *m* (*-ka*; *-gicy*) magician, conjurer

magister *m* (*-tra*; *-trzy*/*-trowie*) **1.** master's degree holder **2.** (*nauk humanistycznych*) master of arts, MA, M.A. **3.** (*nauk przyrodniczych i ścisłych*) master of science, MSc, M.Sc.; **magisterski** *adj tytuł, praca*: master's; ***studia ~e*** MA courses

magistrala *f* (*-li*; *-le*) **1.** (*kolejowa*) main line **2.** INF bus

maglować ⟨**wy-**⟩ (*-luję*) **1.** *odzież*: mangle, press **2.** (*na egzaminie*) *infml* grill

magnat *m* (*-ta*; *-naci*) magnate; **magnateria** *f* (*-rii*; *no pl*) magnates *pl*, high nobility

magnes *m* (*-su*; *-sy*) magnet

magnetofon *m* (*-nu*; *-ny*): ***~ kasetowy*** **a)** cassette recorder **b)** (*część systemu*) cassette deck; **magnetofonowy** *adj taśma, kaseta*: audio

magnetowid *m* (*-du*; *-dy*) video recorder; **magnetyczny** *adj* magnetic

magnez *m* (*-zu*; *no pl*) CHEM magnesium

magnolia *f* (*-lii*; *-lie*) magnolia

mahometanin *m* (*-na*; *-tanie*), **-tanka** *f* (*-ki*; *-ki*) Muslim; **mahometański** *adj* Muslim

mahoniowy *adj* mahogany

maj *m* (*-ja*; *-je*) May; ***1 ~a*** May Day

majaczenie *n* (*-nia*; *-nia*) delirium, (feverish) ravings *pl*; **majaczyć** *v/im* (*-czę*) **1.** (*bredzić*) be delirious, rave **2.** (*być widocznym*) appear dimly, loom

majaki *pl* (*-ków*) (*senne*) nightmares

mają → ***mieć***

majątek *m* (*-tku*; *-tki*) **1.** (*własność*) property **2.** (*firmy*) assets *pl* **3.** (*dobra ziemskie*) estate **4.** (*fortuna*) fortune; **majątkowy** *adj* **1.** *prawo, straty*: property **2.** *status*: material, financial

majdan *m* (*-nu*; *no pl*) *infml* caboodle

majeranek *m* (*-nku*; *-nki*) marjoram

majesta|t *m* (*-tu*; *no pl*) *lit* majesty; ***obraza ~tu*** lese-majesty; ***w ~cie prawa*** in the name of the law; **majestatyczny** *adj lit* majestic

majętny *adj lit* wealthy, affluent

majolikowy *adj* majolica

majonez *m* (*-zu*; *-zy*) mayonnaise

major *m* (*-ra*; *-rzy*/*-rowie*) major

Majorka *f* (*-ki*) Majorca

majowy *adj* May; **majówka** *f* (*-ki*; *-ki*) picnic

majster *m* (*-tra*; *-trowie*) **1.** (*rzemieślnik*) master-craftsman **2.** (*budowlany*) foreman; ***~-klepka*** *hum* handyman

majsterkować *v/im* (*-kuję*) do DIY (jobs); **majsterkowicz** *m* (*-cza*; *-cze*) DIY enthusiast, *infml* DIY'er

majstrować (*-ruję*) *infml* **1.** tinker (***przy*** *L* with) **2.** ⟨**z-**⟩ (*budować*) to make

majteczki *pl* (*-czek*) panties, *Br* (little) pants; **majtki** *pl* (*-tek*) **1.** (*damskie*) panties, *Br* knickers, *Am* underpants **2.** (*męskie*) underpants

mak *m* (*-ku*; *-ki*) **1.** (*roślina, kwiat*) poppy **2.** (*nasiona*) poppy seeds *pl*; ***bułka z ~iem*** poppy-seed roll; ***w drobny ~*** to pieces, to smithereens

makabryczny *adj* gruesome, macabre

makaron *m* (*-nu*; *-ny*) **1.** (*ogólnie*) pasta **2.** (*spaghetti*) spaghetti **3.** (*w zupie*) noodles **4.** (*rurki*) macaroni **5.** (*nitki*) vermicelli

makaroniarz *m* (*-rza*; *-rze*) *infml* wop

makata *f* (*-ty*; *-ty*) tapestry, kilim

makieta *f* (*-ty*; *-ty*) model, mock-up

makijaż *m* (*-żu*; *-że*) make-up

makler *m* (*-ra*; *-rzy*) (stock)broker

makolągwa *f* (*-wy*; *-wy*) (common) linnet

makowiec *m* (*-wca*; *-wce*) poppy-seed cake; **makowy** *adj ciasto, olej*: poppy-seed

makówka *f* (*-ki*; *-ki*) poppy-head

makrela *f* (*-li*; *-le*) mackerel

makro **I** *adj* macro **II** *n* (*-ra*; *-ra*) INF macro

M

makroekonomia *f* (*-mii*; *no pl*) macroeconomics

maksi *adj sukienka*, *rozmiar*: maxi; **maksimum I** *n* (*indecl*; *-sima*) maximum; ***ustawić temperaturę na ~*** set the temperature to maximum **II** *adv* at the most, maximum

maksyma *f* (*-my*; *-my*) maxim

maksymalny *adj* maximum, maximal

makulatur|a *f* (*-ry*; *no pl*) waste paper; ***papier z ~y*** recycled paper

malachit *m* (*-tu*; *-ty*) **1.** (*minerał*) malachite **2.** (*kolor*) emerald green; **malachitowy** *adj* **1.** (*z malachitu*) malachite **2.** (*kolor*) emerald green

Malaje *pl* (*-jów*) Malaya; **malajski** *adj* Malay

malaria *f* (*-rii*; *no pl*) malaria

malarka *f* (*-ki*; *-ki*) (woman) painter; **malarski** *adj* **1.** *technika*, *pędzel*: painting **2.** *pracownia*: painter's **3.** *opis*: picturesque; **malarstwo** *n* (*-wa*; *no pl*) painting

malarz *m* (*-rza*; *-rze*) painter; ***~ pokojowy*** house painter, decorator

malec *m* (*-lca*; *-lcy*) little kid, *Br infml* nipper; **maleć** ⟨**z-**⟩ (*-leję*) **1.** (*o liczbie*, *produkcji*, *wpływie*) decrease, decline **2.** (*o poparciu*) fall **3.** (*o gorączce*) drop, go down **4.** (*o bólu*, *mrozie*) ease **5.** (*o oddalającym się obiekcie*) get smaller **6.** (*kurczyć się*) shrink

M

maleńki *adj dim* tiny; **maleństwo** *n* (*-wa*; *-wa*) **1.** (*dziecko*) (tiny) little baby **2.** (*rzecz*) (tiny) little thing

malign|a *f* (*-ny*; *no pl*) raving delirium; ***bredzić w ~ie*** rave in delirium

malina *f* (*-ny*; *-ny*) raspberry; **malinka** *f* (*-ki*; *-ki*) *fig* love bite, *Am infml* hickey; **malinowy** *adj* raspberry; ***w kolorze ~m*** *Br* raspberry-coloured, *Am* raspberry-colored

malkontent *m* (*-ta*; *-nci*) malcontent, grumbler

malować (*-luję*) **1.** ⟨**na-**⟩ paint **2.** ⟨**po-**⟩ *mieszkanie*: paint, redecorate; ***~ coś na niebiesko*** paint s.th. blue; ***~ usta*** paint one's lips; ***malować się*** ⟨**u-**⟩ (*nakładać makijaż*) make (oneself) up; ***przyszłość maluje się w jasnych*** (***ciemnych***) ***barwach*** the future is bright (bleak)

malowanki *pl* (*-nek*) (*książeczka*) *Br* colouring book *sing*, *Am* coloring book *sing*; **malowidło** *n* (*-ła*; *-ła*) painting; **malowniczy** *adj* picturesque, scenic

Malta *f* (*-y*) Malta; **Maltańczyk** *m* (*-ka*; *-czycy*), **-tanka** *f* (*-ki*; *-ki*) Maltese; **maltański** *adj* Maltese

maltretować ⟨**z-**⟩ (*-tuję*) **1.** (*znęcać się*) ill-treat, abuse **2.** (*bić*) batter

maluch *m* (*-cha*; *-chy*) **1.** (*dziecko*) tot, *Br infml* nipper **2.** (*samochód*) Fiat 126p; **malutki** *adj dim* tiny

malwa *f* (*-wy*; *-wy*) **1.** (*ślaz*) mallow **2.** (*prawoślaz wysoki*) hollyhock

malwersacja *f* (*-ji*; *-je*) embezzlement

mało *adv* **1.** *robić*, *pracować*: not much, little; ***~ mówić*** not speak much, speak little **2.** *wody*, *piasku*: little **3.** *ludzi*, *jabłek*: few **4.** *ważny*: not very, ***~ znany*** little-known; ***~ prawdopodobny*** not very likely, (rather) unlikely; ***~ brakowało, by przegrała*** she almost lost; ***o ~ nie zginął*** he almost died; ***~ kiedy*** hardly ever; ***~ kto to wie*** few people know that; ***~ tego*** and that's not all

małolat *m* (*-ta*; *-ty*), **~a** *f* (*-ty*; *-ty*) *infml* kid

małoletni *adj* minor; ***~ przestępca*** juvenile delinquent

małolitrażowy *adj*: ***samochód ~*** small car, *Br infml* runabout

małomiasteczkowy *adj* parochial, smalltown; **małomówny** *adj* taciturn, silent; ***człowiek ~*** man of few words; **małoobrazkowy** *adj aparat*: 35mm

Małopolska *f* (*-ki*) Little Poland

małorolny *adj*: ***chłop ~*** small farmer, *Am* smallholder; **małostkowy** *adj osoba*: petty; **małowartościowy** *adj* of little value, inferior

małpa *f* (*-py*; *-py*) **1.** monkey **2.** (*człekokształtna*) ape; **małpi** *adj* **1.** *futro*: monkey's **2.** *zręczność*: of a monkey; ***dostać ~ego rozumu*** *infml* go ape; **małpować** ⟨**z-**⟩ (*-puję*) ape

mał|y I *adj* **1.** small, little; ***~y palec*** little finger, *infml* pinkie; ***~ymi literami*** in lower case; ***od ~ego*** since childhood; ***o ~y włos nie zapomniałem*** I almost forgot; ***~a czarna*** *fig* (small) coffee **2.** *prędkość*: slow **II** *m* (*-łego*; *mali*), **-ła** *f* (*-łej*; *-łe*) **1.** (*dziecko*) kid, little one **2.** (*zwierzę*) young **3.** ***~e*** (the) young

małż *m* (*-ża*; *-że*) **1.** bivalve **2.** (*jadalny*) clam, mussel

małżeński *adj* **1.** *miłość*, *obowiązek*: marital **2.** *para*: married **3.** *łoże*: conjugal; ***związek ~*** matrimony; **małżeństwo** *n* (*-wa*; *-wa*) **1.** marriage **2.** (*para małżeńska*) married couple

małżonek *m* (*-nka*; *-nkowie*), **-nka** *f* (*-ki*; *-ki*) spouse; ***małżonkowie*** married couple

małżowina *f* (*-ny*; *-ny*) (*uszna*) auricle

mam → ***mieć***

mama *f* (*-my*; *-my*) *Br* mum, *Am* mom

mam|er: ***siedzieć w ~rze*** *infml* be in the slammer; ***pójść do ~ra*** be sent to the slammer

mamić ⟨**z-**⟩ (*-mię*) **1.** (*kusić*) tempt **2.** (*oszukiwać*) beguile, lure

maminsynek *m* (*-nka*; *-nki*|*-nkowie*) *Br* mummy's boy, *Am* mommy's boy; **mamka** *f* (*-ki*; *-ki*) wet nurse

mamlać, ***mamleć*** *v*/*im* (*-lę*) (*żuć*) chew

mammografia *f* (*-fii*; *no pl*) mammography

mamrotać ⟨**wy-**⟩ (*-roczę*|*-rocę*) mumble

mamuci *adj* mammoth

mamusia *f* (*-si*; *-sie*) *Br* mummy, *Am* mommy

mamut *m* (*-ta*; *-ty*) mammoth

manatki *pl* (*-ków*) (*rzeczy*) *infml* stuff *sing*, *Br infml* clobber *sing*

mandarynka *f* (*-ki*; *-ki*) tangerine, mandarin

mandat *m* (*-tu*; *-ty*) **1.** (*kara*) ticket, fine **2.** (*w parlamencie*) seat **3.** (*pełnomocnictwo*) mandate

mandolina *f* (*-ny*; *ny*) mandolin

manekin *m* (*-na*; *-ny*) dummy

manele *pl* (*-li*) *infml* stuff *sing*

manewr *m* (*-ru*; *-ry*) *Br* manoeuvre, *Am* maneuver; ***~y*** *Br* manoeuvre, *Am* maneuver; **manewrować** *v*/*im* (*-ruję*) *Br* manoeuvre, *Am* maneuver

mangan *m* (*-nu*; *no pl*) manganese

mania *f* (*-nii*; *-nie*) mania; ***~ wielkości*** delusions of grandeur; ***~ prześladowcza*** persecution complex

maniak *m* (*-ka*; *-niacy*), **-niaczka** *f* (*-ki*; *-ki*) maniac; ***~ komputerowy*** computer freak, computer nerd; ***maniakalny*** *adj* **1.** PSYCH *infml* manic **2.** (*obsesyjny*) obsessive

manicure *m* (*-re'u*; *no pl*) manicure

manier|a *f* (*-ry*; *-ry*) **1.** mannerism **2.** (*sposób*) manner **3.** ***~y*** manners; ***mieć dobre ~y*** be well-mannered

manierka *f* (*-ki*; *-ki*) canteen, water bottle

manifest *m* (*-tu*; *-ty*) manifesto; **manifestacja** *f* (*-ji*; *-je*) **1.** *uczuć*: manifestation **2.** *uliczna*: demonstration; **manifestacyjny** *adj sposób, zachowanie*: ostentatious

manifestant *m* (*-ta*; *-nci*), **~ka** *f* (*-ki*; *-ki*) demonstrator; **manifestować** ⟨**za-**⟩ (*-tuję*) demonstrate

manikiurzystka *f* (*-ki*; *-ki*) manicurist

manipulacja *f* (*-ji*; *-je*) manipulation; **manipulować** *v*/*im* (*-luję*) manipulate; ***~ przy*** *I infml* fiddle with

mankament *m* (*-tu*; *-ty*) **1.** (*minus*) drawback **2.** (*wada*) flaw

mankiet *m* (*-tu*; *-ty*) cuff

manko *n* (*-ka*; *-ka*) cash shortage

manna *f* (*-ny*; *no pl*) (*kaszka*) semolina; ***~ z nieba*** manna from heaven

manowce *pl* (*-ców*) wilderness *sing*; ***zejść na ~*** *fig* go astray; ***sprowadzić kogoś na ~*** *fig* lead s.o. astray

mansarda *f* (*-dy*; *-dy*) mansard

manto *n* (*-ta*; *no pl*) *infml*: ***spuścić komuś ~*** give s.o. a hiding

manualny *adj* manual

manuskrypt *m* (*-tu*; *-ty*) manuscript

mańkut *m* (*-ta*; *-kuci*|*-ty*) left hander

mapa *f* (*-py*; *-py*) map; ***~ samochodowa*** road map

mara *f* (*-ry*; *-ry*): ***~ nocna*** nightmare

maraton *m* (*-nu*; *-ny*) marathon; **maratończyk** *m* (*-ka*; *-czycy*) marathon runner; **maratoński** *adj* marathon

marazm *m* (*-mu*; *no pl*) *lit* lethargy; ***na rynku panuje ~*** the market is in the doldrums

marcepan *m* (*-nu*|*-na*; *-ny*) marzipan

marchew *f* (*-chwi*; *-chwie*), ***marchewka*** *f* (*-ki*; *-ki*) carrot

marcowy *adj* March

marek: ***nocny ~*** night owl

margaryna *f* (*-ny*; *-ny*) margarine

margerytka *f* (*-ki*; *-ki*) ox-eye daisy

marginalny *adj* marginal

margines *m* (*-su*; *-sy*) (*kartki*) margin; ***zapisany na ~ie*** written in the margin; ***~ społeczny*** underclass, *infml* riff-raff; **marginesowy** *adj* marginal

M

marihuana *adj* (*-ny*; *no pl*) marijuana, cannabis
marionetka *f* (*-ki*; *-ki*) marionette, puppet
mark|a *f* (*-ki*; *-ki*) **1.** COMM brand **2.** (*samochodu*) make **3.** (*reputacja*) reputation; ***mieć dobrą ~ę*** have a good reputation **4.** (*jakość*) ***dobrej ~i*** good-quality, of good quality
marker *m* (*-ra*; *-ry*) marker, *Br* marker pen
marketingowy *adj* marketing
markiza *f* (*-zy*; *-zy*) **1.** (*daszek*) awning **2.** (*parasol*) sunshade
markotnieć ⟨**z-**⟩ (*-nieję*) become sad, become gloomy; **markotny** *adj* sad, glum
markować *v/im* (*-kuję*) **1.** (*udawać*) feign **2.** SPORT feint
markowy *adj* **1.** branded, brand name **2.** (*wysokiej jakości*) (good-)quality
marksistowski *adj* Marxist
marmolada *f* (*-dy*; *-dy*) (fruit) preserve
marmur *m* (*-ru*; *-ry*) marble; **marmurowy** *adj* marble
marnieć ⟨**z-**⟩ (*-nieję*) **1.** (*o osobie*) waste away **2.** (*o roślinie*) wilt
marność *f* (*-ści*; *-ści*) *lit* (*życia*) vanity
marnotrawca *m* (*-cy*; *-cy*) waster, *lit* squanderer; ***~ czasu*** time waster; **marnotrawić** ⟨**z-**⟩ (*-wię*) waste, *lit* squander; **marnotrawny** *adj*: ***syn ~*** prodigal son
marnotrawstwo *n* (*-wa*; *no pl*) waste, wastefulness
marnować ⟨**z-**⟩ (*-nuję*) **1.** *czas*, *pieniądze*: waste **2.** *okazję*: miss; ***marnować się*** be wasted
marn|y *adj* **1.** *produkt*, *pracownik*, *zdrowie*: poor **2.** *los*: miserable; ***pójść na ~e*** go to waste; ***pracować za ~e grosze*** *infml* work for peanuts; ***komuś spotkał ~y koniec*** s.o. came to a sorry end
Mars *m* (*-sa*) ASTR Mars; **Marsjanin** *m* (*-na*; *-janie*) Martian
marskość *f* (*-ści*; *no pl*): ***~ wątroby*** MED cirrhosis
marsz *m* (*-szu*/*-sza*; *-sze*) march; ***z ~u*** straight away; ***odpowiedzieć z ~u*** answer off the cuff, answer offhand; ***naprzód ~!*** forward march!; ***~ do łóżka!*** off to bed (with you)!
marszałek *m* (*-łka*; *-łkowie*) **1.** (*w wojsku*) marshal **2.** POLIT (the) Speaker
marszczyć (*-czę*) **1.** ⟨**z-**⟩ wrinkle; ***~ nos*** wrinkle one's nose; ***~ czoło*** wrinkle one's forehead, furrow one's brow **2.** *sukienkę*: gather; ***marszczyć się*** **1.** (*o materiale*) crease **2.** (*o skórze*) become wrinkled
marszruta *f* (*-ty*; *-ty*) itinerary
martwica *f* (*-cy*; *no pl*) *tkanek*: necrosis
martwić ⟨**z-**⟩ (*-wię*) worry; ***martwić się*** worry (**o** *A* about)
martwieć ⟨**z-**⟩ (*-wieję*) (*o kończynach*) go numb
martwota *f* (*-ty*; *no pl*) lifelessness
martw|y **I** *adj* dead; ***~y wzrok*** lifeless look, blank stare; ***~a natura*** still life; ***~y sezon*** off season; ***utknąć w ~ym punkcie*** come to a standstill **II** *m* (*-wego*; *-wi*) dead person
martyrologia *f* (*-gii*; *-gie*) *lit* martyrdom
maruda *m*/*f* (*-dy*; *-dy*) *infml* grumbler, *infml* whiner; **maruder** *m* (*-ra*; *-rzy*) **1.** (*żołnierz*) marauder **2.** (*spóźnialski*) straggler; **marudny** *adj* grumpy
marudzić *v/im* (*-rudzę*) grumble, whine
marycha *f* (*-chy*; *no pl*) *infml* grass, *infml* pot
marynarka *f* (*-ki*; *-ki*) **1.** (*ubranie*) jacket **2.** (*flota*) (the) navy; ***~ handlowa*** merchant navy
marynarski *adj* **1.** *mundur*, *czapka*: sailor's, sailor **2.** *służba*, *stopień*: naval; **marynarz** *m* (*-rza*; *-rze*) sailor
marynata *f* (*-ty*; *-ty*) **1.** (*z warzyw*, *owoców*) pickle **2.** (*do mięs*, *ryb*) marinade; **marynować** ⟨**za-**⟩ (*-nuję*) **1.** (*w occie*) pickle **2.** (*przed gotowaniem*) marinate
marzec *m* (*-rca*; *-rce*) March
marzenie *n* (*-nia*; *-nia*) dream; ***coś jest ~m ściętej głowy*** s.th. is a pipedream; ***~ ściętej głowy!*** dream on!
marznąć ⟨**z-**⟩ (*-nę*) freeze
marzyciel *m* (*-la*; *-le*), **~ka** *f* (*-ki*; *-ki*) dreamer; **marzycielski** *adj* *spojrzenie*: dreamy; **marzycielstwo** *n* (*-wa*; *no pl*) dreaminess
marzyć *v/im* (*-rzę*) dream (**o** *L* of/about); ***marzyć się***: ***komuś coś się marzy*** s.o. dreams of s.th.
marża *f* (*-ży*; *-że*) COMM margin

M

mas|a *f* (*-sy*; *-sy*) **1.** mass; **~a ciała** body weight; **ciemna ~a** *infml* numbskull; **~y** (*ludzie*) the masses **2.** (*mnóstwo*) lots (*G* of), loads (*G* of) **3.** (*uziemienie*) *Br* earth, *Am* ground **4.** (*nadzienie*) filling
masakra *f* (*-ry*; *-ry*) massacre; **masakrować** ⟨**z-**⟩ (*-ruję*) massacre
masarnia *f* (*-ni*; *-nie*) (*sklep*) the butcher's; **masarski** *adj*: **wyroby ~e** meat products; **masarz** *m* (*-rza*; *-rze*) butcher
masaż *m* (*-żu*; *-że*) massage; **masażysta** *m* (*-ty*; *-żyści*) masseur; **masażystka** *f* (*-ki*; *-ki*) masseuse
maseczka *f* (*-ki*; *-ki*) mask
maselniczka *f* (*-ki*; *-ki*) butter dish
mask|a *f* (*-ki*; *-ki*) **1.** mask; **~a przeciwgazowa** gas mask; **~a pośmiertna** death mask; **pod ~ą obojętności** behind a mask of indifference **2.** (*samochodu*) *Br* bonnet, *Am* hood
maskarada *f* (*-dy*; *-dy*) masquerade
maskotka *f* (*-ki*; *-ki*) mascot
maskować ⟨**za-**⟩ (*-kuję*) **1.** *obiekt wojskowy*: camouflage **2.** *ból, strach*: mask
maskowy *adj bal*: masked
masł|o *n* (*-ła*; *no pl*) butter; **iść jak po maśle** go like clockwork, *infml* go swimmingly; **~o maślane** tautology; **bułka z ~em** *fig* a piece of cake
masochista *m* (*-ty*; *-chiści*), **-tka** *f* (*-ki*; *-ki*) masochist; **masochistyczny** *adj* masochistic
masoneria *f* (*-rii*; *no pl*) Freemasonry
masować ⟨**wy-**⟩ (*-suję*) massage; **~ komuś stopy** give s.o. a foot massage
masowo *adv* in large numbers; **produkować ~** mass-produce; **masow|y** *adj produkcja*, *turystyka*, *groby*: mass; **środki ~ego przekazu** the mass media
mass media *pl* (*-diów*) the mass media
masturbacja *f* (*-ji*; *no pl*) masturbation; **masturbować się** *v/im* (*-buję*) masturbate
masyw *m* (*-wu*; *-wy*) GEOGR massif; **~ górski** mountain range; **masywny** *adj* massive
masz → **mieć**
maszerować *v/im* (*-ruję*) march
maszkara *f* (*-ry*; *-ry*) **1.** (*straszydło*) monster, bogeyman **2.** (*maszkaron*) mascaron
maszt *m* (*-tu*; *-ty*) mast
maszyna *f* (*-ny*; *-ny*) machine; **~ do pisania** typewriter; **~ do szycia** sewing machine
maszynista *m* (*-ty*; *-niści*) (*kolejowy*) train driver
maszynka *f* (*-ki*; *-ki*) **1.** machine; **~ do golenia** razor; **elektryczna ~ do golenia** shaver, electric razor; **~ do mięsa** *Br* mincer, *Am* meat grinder **2.** (*kuchenka*) *Br* portable cooker, *Am* portable stove
maszynopis *m* (*-su*; *-sy*) typescript; **maszynowo** *adv* by machine; **maszynowy** *adj* **1.** machine; **karabin ~** machine gun **2.** *papier*: typing
maś|ć *f* (*-ści*; *-ści*) **1.** (*do smarowania*) ointment **2.** *konia*: *Br* (coat) colour, *Am* (coat) color; **wszelkiej ~ci** *fig* of all descriptions
maślak *m* (*-ka*; *-ki*) slippery jack
maślanka *f* (*-ki*; *-ki*) buttermilk
mat[1] *m* (*-ta*; *-ty*) (*w szachach*) checkmate; **dać ~a** checkmate
mat[2] *m* (*-tu*; *no pl*) (*brak połysku*) *Br* matt (finish), *Am* mat (finish)
mata *f* (*-ty*; *-ty*) mat
matactwo *n* (*-wa*; *-wa*) swindle
matczyny *adj* motherly
matematyczka *f* (*-ki*; *-ki*) (*nauczycielka*) *Br* (female) maths teacher, *Am* (female) math teacher; **matematyczny** *adj* mathematical, *Br infml* maths, *Am infml* math
matematyk *m* (*-ka*; *-tycy*) **1.** (*nauczyciel*) *Br* maths teacher, *Am* math teacher **2.** (*naukowiec*) mathematician; **matematyka** *f* (*-ki*; *no pl*) mathematics, *Br infml* maths, *Am infml* math
materac *m* (*-ca*; *-ce*) mattress
materi|a *f* (*-rii*; *no pl*) **1.** (*substancja*) matter; **przemiana ~i** metabolism **2.** (*przedmiot*) subject; **materialistyczny** *adj* materialistic; **materialny** *adj* **1.** *świat*: material, physical **2.** *sytuacja*: financial
materiał *m* (*-łu*; *-ły*) **1.** material; **~ wybuchowy** explosive; **~ dowodowy** evidence; **powtórzyć ~** revise (material) **2.** (*tkanina*) material, fabric **3. ~y** (*wyposażenie*) supplies; **~y biurowe** office supplies
matka *f* (*-ki*; *-ki*) mother; **~ chrzestna** godmother; **~ natura** Mother Nature;

spółka **~** parent company; **~ *Boska***; the Mother of God
matkować *v/im* (*-kuję*) mother
matma *f* (*-my*; *no pl*) *Br* maths, *Am* math
matni|a *f* (*-ni*; *-nie*): ***w ~*** trapped
matoł *m* (*-ła*; *-ły*) *infml* moron
matowieć ⟨**z-**⟩ (*-wieję*) **1.** (*o farbie*) dull **2.** (*o metalu*, *lustrze*) tarnish
matowy *adj Br* matt, *Am* mat
matriarchalny *adj* matriarchal
matryca *f* (*-cy*; *-ce*) TECH matrix, die
matrymonialn|y *adj plany*: marriage; ***biuro ~e*** marriage bureau; ***ogłoszenia ~e*** singles ads
matura *f* (*-ry*; *-ry*) **1.** (*egzaminy*) school-leaving examinations *pl*, *Br* A-levels *pl* **2.** (*świadectwo*) school-leaving certificate, *Br* A-level certificate, *Am* high-school diploma; **maturaln|y** *adj*: ***egzamin ~y*** school-leaving examinations, *Br* A-levels; ***świadectwo ~e*** school leaving certificate, *Br* A-level certificate, *Am* high-school diploma
maturzysta *m* (*-ty*; *-rzyści*), **-tka** *f* (*-ki*; -ki) **1.** (*zdający egzamin*) *Br* (secondary) school leaver, A-level student, *Am* diploma candidate **2.** (*absolwent*) *Br* (secondary) school graduate, *Am* high school graduate
mawia|ć *v/im* (*-wiam*) say; ***zawsze ~ł, że*** he always used to say (that)
mazać (*mażę*) **1.** ⟨**u-**⟩ (*smarować*) smear (*I* with) **2.** ⟨**u-**⟩ *farbą*, *błotem*: daub **3.** ⟨**na-**⟩ (*bazgrać*) scribble; **mazać się** (*płakać*) *infml* snivel; **mazak** *m* (*-ka*; *-ki*) felt tip
mazgaić się *v/im* (*-gaję*) snivel; **mazgaj** *m* (*-ja*; *-je*) *infml* crybaby
mazisty *adj* **1.** sticky **2.** (*obrzydliwie*) slimy
Mazowsze *n* (*-sza*) Masovia
Mazur *m* (*-ra*; *-rzy*) Mazurian
mazur *m* (*-ra*; *-ry*) MUS mazur, mazurka
mazurek *m* (*-rka*; *-rki*) **1.** MUS mazurka **2.** COOK (traditional) Easter cake
Mazurski *adj*: ***Pojezierze ~e*** the Masurian Lakeland
Mazury *pl* (*-zur*) Masuria
maź *f* (*mazi*; *mazie*) **1.** sludge, *infml* gunk **2.** (*smar*) grease
mąciciel *m* (*-la*; *-le*) troublemaker
mącić ⟨**z-**, **za-**⟩ (*-cę*) **1.** *wodę*: cloud **2.** *spokój*, *ciszę*: disturb; ***~ komuś w głowie*** confuse s.o.
mączka *f* (*-ki*; *-ki*) (*proszek*) meal; ***~ rybna*** fishmeal; ***~ kostna*** bonemeal: ***~ ziemniaczana*** potato flour
mączny *adj produkty*: flour
mądrala *m/f* (*-li*; *-le*) *infml* know-it-all, *Am* wise guy; **mądrość** *f* (*-ści*; *no pl*) wisdom
mądry *adj* **1.** wise **2.** *pies*: clever; **mądrzeć** ⟨**z-**⟩ (*-rzeję*) grow wiser
mądrzyć się *v/im* (*-rzę*) *infml* play the wise guy
mąka *f* (*-ki*; *-ki*) (potato) starch
mątwa *f* (*-wy*; *-wy*) squid
mąż *m* (*męża*; *mężowie*) husband; ***~ stanu*** statesman; ***jak jeden ~*** unanimously; ***wyjść za ~*** get married; ***wyjść za ~ za kogoś*** marry s.o.
mdleć ⟨**ze-**⟩ (*-leję*) faint, pass out
mdli|ć ⟨**ze-**⟩: ***~ mnie*** I feel sick
mdłości *pl* (*-ści*) nausea; ***czuć ~*** feel nauseous; **mdły** *adj zapach*: nauseous, nauseating
me *poss lit* my; → ***mój***
mebel *m* (*-bla*; *-ble*) piece of furniture; ***meble*** furniture; **meblościanka** *f* (*-ki*; *-ki*) wall unit; **meblować** ⟨**u-**⟩ (*-luję*) furnish; ***meblować się*** furnish one's home; **meblowóz** *m* (*-wozu*; *-wozy*) *Br* removal van, *Am* moving van; **meblowy** *adj sklep*: furniture
mecenas *m* (*-sa*; *-si*) **1.** (*patron*) patron **2.** (*prawnik*) lawyer; **mecenat** *m* (*-tu*; *-ty*) patronage
mech *m* (*mchu*; *mchy*) moss; **mechacić się** ⟨**z-**⟩ (*-cę*) pill
mechaniczn|y *adj* **1.** *urządzenie*: mechanical **2.** *napęd*, *pojazd*: motor; ***koń ~y***, ***konie ~e*** horsepower; **mechanik** *m* (*-ka*; *-nicy*) mechanic; ***~ samochodowy*** car mechanic; **mechanika** *f* (*-ki*; *no pl*) mechanics
mechanizm *m* (*-mu*; *-my*) mechanism; ***~ obronny*** defence mechanism; ***~ zegarowy*** clockwork; ***~ różnicowy*** differential gear; **mechanizować** ⟨**z-**⟩ (*-zuję*) automate
mechaty *adj tkanina*: fluffy
mecz *m* (*-czu*; *-cze*) match, game; ***~ tenisowy*** tennis match, game of tennis
meczeć *v/im* (*-czę*) (*o kozie*) bleat
meczet *m* (*-tu*; *-ty*) mosque

medal *m* (*-lu*; *-le*) medal; ***na ~*** *infml* top notch; ***druga strona ~u*** the other side of the coin; ***medalik*** *m* (*-ka*; *-ki*) medallion
medalista *m* (*-ty*; *-liści*), **-tka** *f* (*-ki*; *-ki*) *Br* medallist, *Am* medalist
media *pl* (*-diów*) the media
mediacj|a *f* (*-ji*; *-je*) mediation; ***~e pokojowe*** peace talks; **mediator** *m* (*-ra*; *-rzy*) mediator
Mediolan *m* (*-nu*) Milan
meduza *f* (*-zy*; *-zy*) jellyfish
medycyna *f* (*-ny*; *no pl*) medicine; **medyczny** *adj* medical; **medyk** *m* (*-ka*; *-dycy*), **-dyczka** *f* (*-ki*; *-ki*) *infml* medic
medytacja *f* (*-ji*; *-je*) meditation; **medytować** *v/im* (*-tuję*) meditate
mega- (*w złożeniach*) mega-
megabajt *m* (*-ta*; *-ty*) *INF* megabyte
megafon *m* (*-nu*; *-ny*) megaphone
megaloman *m* (*-na*; *-ni*) megalomaniac; **megalomania** *f* (*-nii*; *no pl*) megalomania
mego *poss lit* my; → ***mój***; **mej** *poss lit* my; → ***mój***
Meksyk *m* (*-ku*) Mexico
meksykański *adj* Mexican
melancholia *f* (*-lii*; *no pl*) melancholy; **melancholijny** *adj* melancholy
melanż *m* (*-żu*; *-że*) mélange, mixture
melasa *f* (*-sy*; *no pl*) *Br* treacle, *Am* molasses
meldować ⟨**za-**⟩ (*-duję*) **1.** (*informować*) report (*D* to) **2.** *lokatora*: register; ***meldować się*** **1.** (*o żołnierzu*) report **2.** (*w hotelu*) check in
meldunek *m* (*-nku*; *-nki*) **1.** (*doniesienie*) report **2.** (*prawo pobytu*) residence; **meldunkow|y** *adj* registration; ***biuro ~e*** residents' registration office
melina *f* (*-ny*; *-ny*) *infml* **1.** (*złodziejska*) hideout **2.** (*z alkoholem*) shebeen, *Am* speakeasy **3.** (*spelunka*) dive
melioracja *f* (*-ji*; *no pl*) land improvement
melisa *f* (*-sy*; *-sy*) lemon balm
melodia *f* (*-dii*; *-die*) tune, melody
melodramatyczny *adj* melodramatic
melodyjność *f* (*-ści*; *no pl*) melodiousness; **melodyjny** *adj* melodious; **meloman** *m* (*-na*; *-ni*), **~ka** *f* (*-ki*; *-ki*) music lover
melon *m* (*-na*; *-ny*) melon
membrana *f* (*-ny*; *-ny*) membrane
memoriał *m* (*-łu*; *-ły*) **1.** *SPORT* memorial contest **2.** (*dokument*) memorandum
MEN *abbr m* (*MEN-u*; *no pl*) (= ***Ministerstwo Edukacji Narodowej***) Ministry of Education
menadżer *m* (*-ra*; *-rowie*) manager; **menadżerski** *adj* managerial, management
menel *m* (*-la*; *-le*) *infml* bum
mennica *f* (*-cy*; *-ce*) mint
menstruacja *f* (*-ji*; *-je*) menstruation; **menstruacyjn|y** *adj* menstrual; ***bóle ~e*** period pains
mentalność *f* (*-ści*; *no pl*) mentality; **mentalny** *adj* mental
mentolowy *adj* menthol
mentor *m* (*-ra*; *-rzy*) mentor; **mentorski** *adj ton*: condescending
menu *n indecl* menu
menzurka *f* (*-ki*; *-ki*) graduated cylinder
merdać *v/im* (*-dam*): ***~ ogonem*** wag its tail
meritum *n indecl*: ***~ sprawy*** *lit* the crux of the matter, the heart of the matter
merynos *m* (*-sa*; *-sy*) merino
merytoryczny *adj* **1.** *kwestie*: content-related **2.** *błąd*: factual
Mesjasz *m* (*-sza*; *no pl*) Messiah
meszek *m* (*-szku*; *no pl*) down
met|a *f* (*-ty*; *-ty*) **1.** *Br* finishing line, *Am* finish line; ***na dłuższą*** (***krótką***) ***~ę*** in the long (short) run **2.** (*z alkoholem*) *infml* shebeen, *Am* speakeasy
metabolizm *m* (*-mu*; *no pl*) metabolism; **metafizyczny** *adj* metaphysical; **metafora** *f* (*-ry*; *-ry*) metaphor
metal *m* (*-lu*; *-le*) **1.** metal **2.** *MUS infml* metal; **metaliczny** *adj* metallic; **metalik** *adj* (*kolor*) metallic paint
metaloplastyka *f* (*-ki*; *no pl*) (decorative) metalwork; **metalowiec** *m* (*-wca*; *-wcy*) metal worker; **metalowy** *adj* metal; **metalurgia** *f* (*-gii*; *no pl*) metallurgy
metan *m* (*-nu*; *no pl*) methane
meteor *m* (*-ru*; *-ry*) meteor
meteorolog *m* (*-ga*; *-lodzy*/*-gowie*) meteorologist; **meteorologia** *f* (*-gii*; *no pl*) meteorology; **meteorologiczny** *adj* **1.** *stacja*: meteorological **2.** *prognoza*, *warunki*: weather
meteoryt *m* (*-tu*; *-ty*) meteorite

metka *f* (*-ki*; *-ki*) **1.** (*przyszywana*, *przyklejana*) label **2.** (*doczepiana*) tag
metoda *f* (*-dy*; *-dy*) method; **metodologiczny** *adj* methodological; **metodyczny** *adj* methodical
metr *m* (*-ra*; *-ry*) *Br* metre, *Am* meter; **~ kwadratowy** *Br* square metre, *Am* square meter; **~ sześcienny** *Br* cubic metre, *Am* cubic meter
metraż *m* (*-żu*; *-że*) (*powierzchnia*) (metric) area; **krótki ~** short subject; **długi ~** feature film
metr|o *n* (*-ra*; *no pl*) metro, *Br* underground, the Underground, *Am* subway; **~em** by metro, *Br* by underground, *Am* by subway
metropolia (*-lii*; *-lie*) metropolis
metrowy *adj Br* one-metre (long), *Am* one-meter (long)
metryczny *adj system*: metric
metryka *f* (*-ki*; *-ki*) **1.** *urodzenia*, *chrztu*: certificate **2.** (*psa*) pedigree
metylowy *adj* methyl
mewa *f* (*-wy*; *-wy*) seagull, gull
męczarnia *f* (*-ni*; *-nie*) torment; **męczący** *adj* tiring, tiresome
męczennik *m* (*-ka*; *-nicy*), **-nica** *f* (*-cy*; *-ce*) martyr
męczeński *adj śmierć*: martyr's
męczy|ć (*-czę*) **1.** ⟨**z-**⟩ (*powodować zmęczenie*) tire; **bardzo kogoś zmęczyć** tire s.o. out **2.** (*zadawać ból*) torment **3.** (*naprzykrzać się*) pester (*I* with); **kogoś ~ kaszel** s.o. has a bad cough; **męczyć się 1.** (*odczuwać zmęczenie*) tire, get tired (*D* with) **2.** (*odczuwać ból*) suffer **3.** (*wysilać się*) sweat (**nad** *I* over)
męczydusza *m/f* (*-szy*; *-sze*) *infml* nuisance, *infml* drag
mędrkować *v/im* (*-kuję*) *Br* be a smart alec, *Am* be a smart aleck
mędrzec *m* (*-rca*; *-rcy*) sage, wise man
męka *f* (*-ki*; *-ki*) torment, agony; **męki** agony
męsk|i *adj* **1.** *moda*, *obuwie*, *chór*: men's **2.** *wygląd*: manly **3.** *imię*, *narządy płciowe*, *osobnik*: male **4.** *rodzaj*, *rysy*, *głos*: masculine; **fryzjer ~i** barber; **po ~u** like a man
męskoosobowy *adj rodzaj*: masculine-personal, virile
męskość *f* (*-ści*; *no pl*) **1.** manhood **2.** (*uroda*) masculinity

M

męstwo *n* (*-wa*; *no pl*) *Br* valour, *Am* valor
mętlik *m* (*-ku*; *no pl*) confusion; **mieć ~ w głowie** be confused
mętnieć ⟨**z-**⟩ (*-nieję*) cloud
mętny *adj* **1.** *woda*: cloudy **2.** *zarys*, *wyjaśnienia*: vague
męty *pl* (*-tów*) dregs; **~ społeczne** the dregs of society, scum, riff-raff
mężatk|a *f* (*-ki*; *-ki*) married woman; **ona jest ~ą** she is married
mężczyzna *m* (*-ny*; *-czyźni*) man
mężnieć ⟨**z-**⟩ (*-nieję*) grow into a man; **mężny** *adj* brave, valiant
mgiełka *f* (*-ki*; *-ki*) *dim* haze, mist
mglisty *adj* **1.** *dzień*: foggy **2.** *zarys*: blurry **3.** *obietnice*, *pojęcie*: vague **4.** *wspomnienia*: misty, vague
mgł|a *f* (*-ły*; *-ły*) mist; (*gęsta*) fog; **zajść ~ą** mist up, fog up; **pamiętać jak przez ~ę** remember vaguely; **mgławica** *f* (*-cy*; *-ce*) nebula
mgnieni|e *n* (*-nia*; *-nia*): **~e oka** instant, brief moment; **w ~u oka** in a flash, in the twinkling of an eye
mgr *abbr* (= **magister**) **1.** (*nauk humanistycznych*) MA, M.A. **2.** (*nauk przyrodniczych i ścisłych*) MSc, M.Sc.
mi *pron* me; → **mnie**
miał *m* (*-łu*; *-ły*) (*kamienny*) dust; **~ węglowy** fine coal
miałki *adj węgiel*, *żwir*: fine
miano *n* (*-na*; *-na*) *lit* name; **mianować** *v im/p* (*-nuję*) appoint
mianowicie *conj* that is; **a ~** namely, that is
mianownik *m* (*-ka*; *-ki*) **1.** GRAM nominative **2.** MATH denominator; **wspólny ~** *fig* common denominator
miar|a *f* (*-ry*; *-ry*) **1.** measure; **~a długości** measure of length; **szyty na ~ę** custom-made, made-to-measure; **w ~ę** (*dość*) fairly, rather; **w ~ę jak** as; **w ~ę możliwości** to the best of one's abilities; **wielkiej ~y** *fig* of great stature; **w pewnej mierze** to a certain extent; **w dużej mierze** to a large extent; **ze wszech ~** *lit* by all means; **żadną ~ą** by no means **2.** (*taśma*) measuring tape **3.** (*rozmiar*) measurement
miarka *f* (*-ki*; *-ki*) measure; **~ się przebrała** this is too much

miarodajny *adj* **1.** *źródła*: reliable **2.** *opinia*: authoritative
miarowy *adj* **1.** *krok*: steady **2.** *oddech*: even, regular
miasteczko *n* (*-ka*; *-ka*) (small) town; **~ *studenckie*** campus; ***wesołe* ~** amusement park, *Br* funfair
miast|o *n* (*-ta*; *-ta*) **1.** town; ***~o rodzinne*** home town; ***iść do ~a*** go to town, go downtown **2.** (*duże*) city
miauczeć ⟨**za-**⟩ (*-czę*) meow, *Br* miaow
miazg|a *f* (*-gi*; *no pl*) pulp; ***~a zębowa*** dental pulp; ***zetrzeć na ~ę*** pulp, crush to a pulp; ***zetrzeć kogoś na ~ę*** *fig* make mincement of s.o., wipe the floor with s.o.
miażdżący *adj fig porażka*: crushing
miażdżyca *f* (*-cy*; *no pl*) arteriosclerosis; **miażdżycowy** *adj* arteriosclerotic; **miażdżyć** ⟨**z-**⟩ (*-dżę*) crush
miąć ⟨**po-**, **wy-**, **z-**⟩ (*mnę*) **1.** *ubranie*: crease **2.** *papier*: crumple; ***miąć się*** (*o ubraniu*) crease
miąższ *m* (*-szu*; *no pl*) *owocu*: flesh
miech *m* (*-cha*; *-chy*) bellows *pl*
miecz *m* (*-cza*; *-cze*) **1.** sword **2.** (*część łodzi*) *Br* centreboard, *Am* centerboard; **mieczyk** *m* (*-ka*; *-ki*) **1.** (*ryba*) swordfish **2.** (*kwiat*) gladiolus, sword lily
mieć *v/im* (*mam*) **1.** have; ***jak masz na imię?*** what's your name?; ***mam na imię Magda*** my name's Magda; ***czy mam przyjść?*** should I come?; **~ *coś komuś za złe*** hold s.th. against s.o.; **~ *coś na sobie*** be wearing s.th., have s.th. on; **~ *miejsce*** (*zdarzyć się*) take place; **~ *ochotę coś zrobić*** feel like doing s.th.; **~ *rację*** be right; ***ktoś miał coś zrobić*** s.o. was supposed to do s.th.; ***miano coś zrobić*** s.th. was to be done; ***nie ma jak*** there is nothing like; ***masz!*** here!; ***mam cię!*** I've got you! **2.** (*liczyć sobie*) be; ***ile masz lat?*** how old are you?; ***on ma 30 lat*** he's thirty; **~ *180 cm*** (***wzrostu***) be 180 cm tall; **~ *10 metrów*** be ten metres long; **~ *2 kilo*** weigh 2 kilo **3.** ***ma*** COMM credit; ***mieć się***: ***jak się masz?*** how are you?; **~ *się dobrze*** be fine, be doing well; **~ *się za kogoś*** consider oneself s.o.
miednica *f* (*-cy*; *-ce*) **1.** (*naczynie*) bowl, basin **2.** ANAT pelvis
miedza *f* (*-dzy*; *-dze*) balk, *Br* baulk
miedziany *adj* copper; **miedzioryt** *m* (*-tu*; *-ty*) copperplate; **miedź** *f* (*-dzi*; *no pl*) copper
miejscami *adv* in places, here and there, in parts
miejsc|e *n* (*-ca*; *-ca*) **1.** place; ***~e pracy*** workplace; ***~e zamieszkania*** address, place of residence; ***~e urodzenia*** birthplace; ***~e spotkania*** meeting place; ***~e przeznaczenia*** destination; ***~e wypadku*** scene of the accident; ***~e siedzące*** seat; ***czułe ~e*** soft spot; ***kłaść coś na swoim ~u*** put s.th. back; ***mieć ~e*** (*wydarzyć się*) take place; ***na ~a, gotowi, start!*** ready! steady! go!; ***na twoim ~u*** if I were you; ***ustąpić czemuś ~a*** give way to s.th.; ***w innym ~u*** in some other place; ***zająć pierwsze ~e*** be first, come in first; ***zginąć na ~u*** die on the spot; ***z ~a*** right away; ***nie na ~u*** inappropriate, out of place; ***w którym ~u?*** where? **2.** (*wolna przestrzeń*) space, room **3.** (*w hotelu*) vacancy; ***wolnych ~ brak*** no vacancies
miejscownik *m* (*-ka*; *-ki*) GRAM locative
miejscowość *f* (*-ści*; *-ści*) place; **~ *wypoczynkowa*** resort
miejscowy **I** *adj* local **II** *m* (*-wego*; *-wi*) local; **miejscówka** *f* (*-ki*; *-ki*) seat reservation
miejski *adj* **1.** *komunikacja*, *tereny*, *życie*: urban **2.** *zarząd*, *rada*: municipal **3.** *ratusz*: town
mielą, ***miele***(**sz**), ***mielę*** → ***mleć***
mieliście → ***mieć***; **mieliśmy** → ***mieć***
mieli|zna *f* (*-ny*; *-ny*) sandbank; ***osiąść na ~źnie*** run aground
mielon|y *adj* ground; ***mięso ~e*** minced meat; ***kotlet ~y*** (minced meat) patty, hamburger
mienić się *v/im* (*-nię*) (*skrzyć się*) shimmer
mienie *n* (*-nia*; *no pl*) *form* possessions *pl*, property; **~ *państwowe*** public property; **~ *prywatne*** private property
mierniczy **I** *adj* measuring **II** *m* (*-czego*; *-czowie*) surveyor
miernik *m* (*-ka*; *-ki*) **1.** TECH gauge **2.** (*miara*) measure **3.** *fig* measure, yardstick
miernota *f/m* (*-ty*; *-ty*) mediocrity; **mierność** *f* (*-ści*; *no pl*) mediocrity;

M

mierny I *adj* mediocre **II** *m* (*-nego*; *-ne*) (*ocena*) D

mierzeja *f* (*-rzei*; *-je*) sandbar

mierzi|ć ⟨**z-**⟩ (*-rzę*): ***coś kogoś ~*** s.o. is sickened by s.th., s.o. hates s.th.

mierzn|ąć ⟨**ob-**⟩ (*-nę*) *lit*: ***coś komuś ~ie*** s.o. is fed up with s.th.

mierzwić ⟨**z-**⟩ (*-wię*) ruffle

mierzyć (*-rzę*) **1.** ⟨**z-**⟩ measure; ***~ komuś temperaturę*** take s.o.'s temperature; ***~ wzrokiem*** eye **2.** ⟨**z-**⟩ *suknię, buty*: try on **3.** ⟨**wy-**⟩ (*celować*) aim (***w*** *A* at); ***wysoko ~*** aim high, be a high flyer; ***mierzyć się*** **1.** (*mierzyć swój wzrost*) take one's height **2.** (*dorównywać*) match; ***nie móc się mierzyć z*** *I* be no match for **3.** *z przeciwnościami*: cope (***z*** *I* with)

miesiąc *m* (*-ca*; *-ce*) month; ***raz na ~*** once a month; ***za ~*** in a month; ***~ami*** for months; ***miodowy ~*** honeymoon; ***być w szóstym ~u*** be six months pregnant

miesiączk|a *f* (*-ki*; *-ki*) period; ***mieć ~ę*** have a period; **miesiączkować** *v/im* (*-kuję*) menstruate

miesięcznik *m* (*-ka*; *-ki*) monthly; **miesięczny** *adj* **1.** *czynsz, bilet*: monthly **2.** *niemowlę*: one-month-old

mieszać (*-szam*) **1.** ⟨**wy-**, **za-**, **po-**, **z-**⟩ *łyżką*: stir **2.** ⟨**wy-**, **po-**, **z-**⟩ (*łączyć*) mix (***z*** *I* with), blend **3.** ⟨**po-**⟩ (*mylić*) confuse, mix up **4.** ⟨**w-**⟩ (*wplątywać*) involve (***w*** *A* in), mix up (***w*** *A* in); ***~ kogoś z błotem*** *fig* sling mud at s.o.; ***~ komuś w głowie*** confuse s.o.; ***mieszać się*** **1.** (*łączyć się*) mix **2.** (*mylić się*) mix up; ***wszystko mi się pomieszało*** I'm all mixed up **3.** (*wtrącać się*) interfere (***do*** *G* with), meddle (***do*** *G* with) **4.** (*wplątywać się*) get mixed up (***w*** *A* in) **5.** (*być speszonym*) be confused

mieszaniec *m* **1.** (*-szańca*; *-szańce*) BIOL cross-breed **2.** (*-szańca*; *-szańcy*) (*człowiek*) *infml* half-caste

mieszanina *f* (*-ny*; *-ny*) mixture; **mieszanka** *f* (*-ki*; *-ki*) **1.** blend **2.** TECH mixture; **mieszany** *adj* mixed

mieszczański *adj* bourgeois; **mieszczaństwo** *n* (*-wa*; *no pl*) the bourgeoisie

mieszczuch *m* (*-cha*; *-chy*) townie *infml*

mieszkać (*-kam*) **1.** live; ***~ przez ścianę*** live next door **2.** (*w hotelu*) be staying

mieszkalny *adj* **1.** *budynek*: residential **2.** *warunki*: living

mieszkanie *n* (*-nia*; *-nia*) *Br* flat, *Am* apartment

mieszka|niec (*-kańca*; *-kańcy*), **-nka** *f* (*-ki*; *-ki*) **1.** *domu*: occupant **2.** *miasta, wsi*: inhabitant; ***~ńcy miast*** (***wsi***) city (country) dwellers **2.** *kraju*: resident, inhabitant

mieszkaniow|y *adj* **1.** *dzielnica, osiedle*: housing, residential **2.** *kredyt*: home; ***budownictwo ~e*** housing industry

mieści|ć ⟨**z-**⟩ (*mieszczę*) **1.** (*o naczyniu*) hold **2.** (*o sali*) house **3.** (*zawierać*) contain; ***mieścić się*** **1.** (*znajdować się*) be located; ***to nie ~ się w głowie!*** it's hard to believe, the mind boggles **2.** (*mieć odpowiednie rozmiary*) fit (***w*** *L* into)

mieścina *f* (*-ny*; *-ny*) (small) town, (provincial) town

miewać *v/im* (*-wam*) have (from time to time); ***miewać się***: ***jak się pan***(***i***) ***miewa?*** how are you doing?

mięciutki *adj* very soft

mięczak *m* (*-ka*; *-ki*) **1.** (*zwierzę*) mollusc **2.** (*osoba*) *infml* wimp

międlić ⟨**z-**⟩ (*-lę*) (*gnieść*) squeeze

między *prep* (*I*/*A*) **1.** between; ***~ nami mówiąc*** between you and me **2.** (*w otoczeniu*) among; ***~ innymi*** **a)** (*o rzeczach*) among other things, including **a)** (*o osobach*) among others, including

międzykontynentalny *adj* intercontinental; **międzylądowanie** *n* (*-nia*; *-nia*) stopover; **międzyludzki** *adj* interpersonal; **międzynarodowy** *adj* international

Międzynarodówka *f* (*-ki*; *no pl*) (*pieśń*) the Internationale; **międzynarodówka** *f* (*-ki*; *-ki*) (*organizacja*) International; **międzypaństwowy** *adj* *stosunki*: international; ***mecz ~*** *Br* international; **międzypokoleniowy** *adj* *konflikt*: generational

międzysemestraln|y *adj*: ***przerwa ~a*** vacation

międzyszkoln|y *adj*: ***wymiana ~a*** *Br* student exchange programme, *Am* student exchange program

M

międzywojenn|y *adj* interwar; ***lata ~e*** the interwar period
miękk|i *adj* **1.** soft; ***jajko na ~o*** soft-boiled egg; ***książka w ~iej oprawie*** paperback **2.** *warzywa, mięso*: tender
miękkość *f* (*-ści*; *no pl*) **1.** softness **2.** *warzyw, mięsa*: tenderness; **mięknąć** ⟨**z-**⟩ (*-nę*) soften; ***gotować coś, aż zmięknie*** cook s.th. until tender
mięsak *m* (*-ka*; *-ki*) MED myoma; **mięsień** *m* (*mięśnia*; *mięśnie*) muscle; ***mięśnie brzucha*** stomach muscles
mięsisty *adj* fleshy; **mięsny** *adj* meat; ***sklep ~*** the butcher's (shop); **mięso** *n* (*-sa*; *-sa*) meat; ***~ armatnie*** *fig* cannon fodder
mięsożerny *adj* carnivorous
mięśniowy *adj* **1.** *tkanka*: muscle **2.** *bóle*: muscular
mięta *f* (*-ty*; *-ty*) **1.** mint; ***~ pieprzowa*** peppermint **2.** (*herbata*) (pepper-) mint tea
miętosić ⟨**z-**⟩ (*-szę*) crumple
miętowy *adj* **1.** *smak, lody*: mint; ***cukierek ~*** mint **2.** *olejek*: peppermint
miętus *m* (*-sa*; *-sy*) **1.** (*cukierek*) *infml* mint **2.** (*ryba*) burbot
mig: ***na ~i*** **a)** (*za pomocą gestów*) by gesture **b)** (*w języku migowym*) in sign language; ***porozumiewać się na ~i*** sign; ***w ~*** in a flash
migacz *m* (*-cza*; *-cze*) *Br* indicator, *Am* turn signal, *infml* blinker
migać ⟨**-gnąć**⟩ (*-gam*) **1.** (*o światełku, ekranie*) flicker **2.** (*o kierunkowskazie*) blink **3.** (*o błyskawicy*) flash **4.** (*przemykać*) flash **5.** (*porozumiewać się w języku migowym*) sign; **migać się** *infml* shirk (**od** *G*)
migawka *f* (*-ki*; *-ki*) **1.** (*urządzenie*) shutter **2.** (*zdjęcie*) (snap)shot; **migawkowy** *adj fig* snapshot, brief
migdalić się *v/im* (*-lę*) *infml* smooch, *Br* snog
migdał *m* (*-łu*; *-ły*) almond; **migdał|ek** *m* (*-łka*; *-łki*) ANAT tonsil; ***wycięcie ~ków*** tonsillectomy; **migdałowiec** *m* (*-wca*; *-wce*) almond tree; **migdałowy** *adj* almond
migiem *adv* in a flash, in no time
mignąć *v/p od* ***migać***
migotać ⟨**za-**⟩ (*-goczę*/*-gocę*) **1.** (*o płomieniu, świecy*) flicker **2.** (*o gwiazdach*) twinkle **3.** (*o rzece*) glimmer; **migotanie** *n* (*-nia*; *no pl*): ***~ komór serca*** atrial fibrillation; **migotliwy** *adj płomień, obraz*: flickering
migowy *adj*: ***język ~*** sign language
migracja *f* (*-ji*; *-je*) migration; **migracyjny** *adj* migratory
migrena *f* (*-ny*; *-ny*) migraine
migrować *v/im* (*-ruję*) migrate
mijać ⟨**minąć**⟩ (*-jam*) **I** *v/im* **1.** (*o terminie*) pass **2.** (*o czasie*) pass, go by **3.** (*o bólu*) pass, ease off; ***ich miłość minęła*** their love is gone **II** *v/t idąc, jadąc*: pass; ***kara*** (***nagroda***) ***kogoś nie minie*** s.o. will not go unpunished (unrewarded); ***mijać się*** **1.** (*o pojazdach, przechodniach*) pass each other **2.** (*nie spotkać się*) miss (**z** *I*) **3.** (*o listach*) cross (in the mail); ***coś mija się z celem*** s.th. is pointless; ***~ się z powołaniem*** miss one's vocation; ***ktoś minął się z prawdą*** s.o. departed from the truth
mijanka *f* (*-ki*; *-ki*) **1.** (*dla samochodów*) passing place **2.** (*dla pociągów*) siding
mika *f* (*-ki*, *no pl*) mica
Mikołaj *m* (*-ja*; *-je*): ***Święty ~*** Santa (Claus); ***prezent na ~a*** gift from Santa Claus; **mikołajki** *pl* (*-jek*) St Nicholas' Day *sing*; **mikołajkowy** *adj* St Nicholas' Day
mikro *adj* micro
mikrobus *m* (*-su*; *-sy*) minibus; **mikroby** *pl* (*-bów*) microbes; **mikroelementy** *pl* (*-tów*) microelements
mikrofalow|y *adj*: ***kuchenka ~a*** microwave (oven)
mikrofaza *f* (*-zy*; *no pl*) *Br* microfibre, *Am* microfiber; **mikrofilm** *m* (*-mu*; *-my*) microfilm; **mikrofon** *m* (*-nu*; *-ny*) microphone, *infml* mike; ***mówić do ~u*** speak into a microphone
mikroskop *m* (*-pu*; *-py*) microscope; **mikroskopijny** *adj* microscopic; **mikroskopowy** *adj* microscopic
mikser *m* (*-ra*; *-ry*) **1.** (*do mieszania*) mixer **2.** (*do rozdrabniania*) blender **3.** MUS mixer; **mikserski** *adj* mixing
miksować ⟨**z-**⟩ (*-suję*) **1.** mix **2.** (*rozdrabniać*) blend; **mikst** *m* (*-ta*; *-ty*) SPORT mixed doubles *pl*; **mikstura** *f* (*-ry*; *-ry*) **1.** mixtura **2.** *magiczna*: potion

M

mila *f* (*-li*; *-le*) mile; **~ *morska*** nautical mile

milczący *adj* **1.** silent **2.** *zgoda*: tacit; **milczeć** *v/im* (*-czę*) be silent; ***milcz!*** be quiet!; **~ *jak głaz*** be (as) silent as the grave; **milczek** *m* (*-czka*; *-czki*) man of few words; **milczenie** *n* (*-nia*; *no pl*) silence

mile *adv*: **~*widziany*** welcome; **~*zaskoczony*** pleasantly surprised; **~ *spędzić czas*** have a nice time; **~ *coś wspominać*** have fond memories of s.th.; **~ *przyjąć*** receive warmly

miliard *m* (*-da*; *-dy*) billion; **miliardowy** *adj* **1.** billionth **2.** *koszty*, *straty*: running into billions

milicja *f* (*-ji*; *-je*) police; **milicjant** *m* (*-ta*; *-nci*) policeman; **milicyjny** *adj* police

miligram *m* (*-ma*; *-my*) milligram; **milimetr** *m* (*-ra*; *-ry*) *Br* millimetre, *Am* millimeter

milioner *m* (*-ra*; *-rzy*), **~ka** *f* (*-ki*; *-ki*) millionaire

milionowy *adj* **1.** millionth **2.** *koszty*, *straty*: running into millions

militarny *adj* military; **militarystyczny** *adj* militarist(ic)

milknąć ⟨**za-**⟩ (*-nę*) **1.** (*przestawać mówić*) fall silent **2.** (*cichnąć*) die away

M

milowy *adj* one-mile; ***kamień* ~** *fig* milestone; ***zrobić* ~ *krok naprzód*** take a major step forward

milusińscy *pl* (*-skich*) *infml* little ones

milutki *adj dim* lovely

miłek *m* (*-łka*; *-łki*) pheasant's eye

miło *adv* **1.** nicely, pleasantly; **~ *mi panią poznać*** nice to meet you; ***to* ~ *z pana strony*** that's very kind of you; ***było* ~** we had a nice time; **~ *coś wspominać*** have fond memories of s.th. **2.** *przyjąć*, *przywitać*: warmly

miłosierdzie *n* (*-dzia*; *no pl*) mercy; **miłosierny** *adj* merciful

miłosny *adj* **1.** *wiersz*, *list*: love **2.** *spojrzenia*, *westchnienia*: amorous; **miłostka** *f* (*-ki*; *-ki*) (love) affair, romance

miłość *f* (*-ści*; *no pl*) love; **~ *bliźniego*** *Br* love of one's neighbour, *Am* love of one's neighbor; **~ *własna*** self-love, amour propre, ego; ***uprawiać* ~ *z*** *I* make love to; ***wyznał jej* ~** he said he loved her; ***na* ~ *boską!*** for God's sake!

miłośnik *m* (*-ka*; *-nicy*), **-niczka** *f* (*-ki*; *-ki*) lover; **~ *sztuki*** art lover

miłować *v/im* (*-łuję*) *lit pokój*, *prawdę*: love

mił|y *adj* **1.** nice; ***bądź tak* ~*y i*** be so kind and; ***z* ~*ą chęcią*** with pleasure **2.** *nastrój*, *widok*: pleasant **3.** *słowa*: kind **4.** (*drogi*) dear

mim *m* (*-ma*; *-mowie*) mime; **mimiczn|y** *adj* facial; ***zmarszczki* ~*e*** laughter lines, worry lines; **mimika** *f* (*-ki*; *no pl*) **1.** facial expression **2.** *THEAT* mime

mimo *prep* (*G*) despite, in spite of; **~ *to***, **~ *wszystko*** still, yet; **~ *woli*** involuntarily; **~ *że*** even though, despite the fact that

mimochodem *adv* in passing

mimowolny *adj* **1.** *ruch*: involuntary **2.** *sprawca*: unwitting, unwilling

mimoza *f* (*-zy*; *-zy*) mimosa; ***wrażliwy jak* ~** sensitive as a flower

m.in. *abbr* (= ***między innymi***) **1.** (*o rzeczach*) among other things, including **2.** (*o osobach*) among others, including

min|a[1] *f* (*-ny*; *-ny*) (*wyraz twarzy*) face; ***stroić* ~*y*** pull faces; ***robić dobrą* ~*ę do złej gry*** put on a brave front, grin and bear it; **~*a mu zrzedła*** his face fell

mina[2] *f* (*-ny*; *-ny*) (*ładunek wybuchowy*) mine; **~ *lądowa*** landmine

minąć *v/p* → ***mijać***

mineraln|y *adj* mineral; ***sole* ~*e*** mineral salts; **minerał** *m* (*-łu*; *-ły*) mineral

mini I *adj* ***spódniczka* ~** miniskirt **II** *n/f indecl infml* mini

minia *f* (*-nii*; *no pl*) red lead, minium

miniatur|a *f* (*-ry*; *-ry*) miniature; **~*a samolotu*** miniature airplane; ***w* ~*ze*** in miniature; **miniaturowy** *adj* miniature

minimalistyczny *adj* **1.** (*w sztuce*) minimalist **2.** *potrzeby*: minimal; **minimalny** *adj* minimum, minimal

minimum I *n* (*indecl*; *-nima*) minimum; ***koszty należy ograniczyć do* ~** costs should be kept to a minimum; **~ *socjalne*** subsistence wage **II** *adv* (*co najmniej*) at least

miniony *adj* past

minispódniczka *f* (*-ki*; *-ki*) miniskirt

minister *m* (*-tra*; *-trowie*) *Br* minister, *Am* secretary; **~ *edukacji*** the Minister of Education, *Am* the Secretary of Education; **~ *spraw wewnętrznych*** the Minister of the Interior, *Br* the Home Secretary; **~ *spraw zagranicznych*** the Foreign Minister, *Br* the Foreign Secretary, *Am* the Secretary of State; **~ *obrony narodowej*** *Br* the Defence Secretary, *Am* the Secretary of Defense; ***rada ministrów*** the Cabinet; **ministerialny** *adj* ministerial, departmental

ministerstwo *n* (*-wa*; *-wa*) ministry, department; **~ *spraw zagranicznych*** the Foreign Ministry, *Br* the Home Office, *Am* the State Department; **~ *obrony*** *Br* the Ministry of Defence, *Am* the Department of Defense

ministrant *m* (*-ta*; *-nci*) altar boy

minorowy *adj* **1.** *skala*: minor **2.** *nastrój*: gloomy, *Br* sombre, *Am* somber

minować ⟨**za-**⟩ (*-nuję*) mine; **minow|y** *adj*: ***pole ~e*** minefield

mintaj *m* (*-ja*; *-je*) walleye pollock

minus *m* (*-sa*; *-sy*) minus; ***piątka z ~em*** (*w szkole*) A minus; ***nosić ~y*** *infml Br* be short-sighted, *Am* be nearsighted; **minusowy** *adj* **1.** negative **2.** *temperatury*: sub-zero

minut|a *f* (*-ty*; *-ty*) minute; ***za ~ę*** in a minute; ***jest za ~ę trzecia*** it's one minute to three; ***~a ciszy*** minute's silence; **minutka** *f* (*-ki*; *-ki*) *dim* minute; **minutowy** *adj* **1.** *opóźnienie*: one-minute **2.** *wskazówka*: minute

miodowy *adj kolor*: honey; **~ *miesiąc*** honeymoon

miot *m* (*-tu*; *-ty*) BIOL litter

miotacz *m* (*-cza*; *-cze*) **~ka** *f* (*-ki*; *-ki*): **~ *kulą*** shot-putter; **~ *dyskiem*** discus-thrower; **~ *ognia*** flame-thrower

miotać *v/im* (*-tam*) (*rzucać*) throw; **~ *kulą*** put the shot; **~ *obelgami na*** *A* hurl abuse at; ***miotać się*** thrash around, flail around

miotany *adj*: **~ *gniewem*** wild with anger; **~ *nienawiścią*** seething with hatred; **~ *sprzecznymi uczuciami*** torn between conflicting emotions; **~ *zazdrością*** blinded by jealousy

miotła *f* (*-ły*; *-ły*) broom

miód *m* (*miodu*; *miody*) honey; **~ *pitny*** mead

mirabelka *f* (*-ki*; *-ki*) mirabelle

miraż *m* (*-żu*; *-że*) mirage

mirt *m* (*-tu*; *-ty*) myrtle

misa *f* (*-sy*; *-sy*) (*naczynie*) (large) bowl; **miseczka** *f* (*-ki*; *-ki*) **1.** (small) bowl **2.** *biustonosza*: cup

misiek *m* (*miśka*; *miśki*) *infml* **1.** (*niedźwiedź*) bear **2.** (*zabawka*) teddy (bear), *Br infml* teddy **3.** (*futro*) fake fur

misja *f* (*-ji*; *-je*) mission

misjonarz *m* (*-rza*; *-rze*), **-rka** *f* (*-ki*; *-ki*) missionary

miska *f* (*-ki*; *-ki*) (*naczynie*) bowl, basin; **~ *klozetowa*** toilet bowl

misterny *adj* **1.** *wzór*, *haft*: intricate, elaborate **2.** *plan*: elaborate

mistrz *m* (*-rza*; *-rzowie*) **1.** master; **~ *murarski*** master bricklayer **2.** SPORT champion; **~ *świata*** world champion

mistrzostw|o *n* (*-wa*; *-wa*) **1.** (*biegłość*) mastery **2.** SPORT championship; ***~a świata*** World Championships; ***~a świata w piłce nożnej*** World Cup; ***zdobyć ~o świata*** become a world champion

mistrzowsk|i *adj* **1.** *gra*, *pokaz*: masterly, brilliant; ***po ~u*** in masterly fashion, brilliantly **2.** *egzamin*, *dyplom*: master craftsman's; ***tytuł ~i*** SPORT championship (title)

mistrzyni *f* (*-ni*; *-nie*) **1.** master, mistress **2.** SPORT champion; **~ *świata*** world champion

mistyczny *adj* mystical, mystic

mistyfikacja *f* (*-ji*; *-je*) deception, hoax

mistyk *m* (*-ka*; *-tycy*), **-tyczka** *f* (*-ki*; *-ki*) mystic; **mistyka** *f* (*-ki*; *no pl*) mysticism

misyjny *adj* missionary

miś *m* (*misia*; *misie*) **1.** (*niedźwiedź*) bear **2.** (*niedźwiadek*) (bear) cub **3.** (*zabawka*) teddy bear, *Br infml* teddy **4.** (*futro*) fake fur **5.** ***misiu!*** (*pieszczotliwie*) honey!

mit *m* (*-tu*; *-ty*) myth; **mitologia** *f* (*-gii*; *-gie*) mythology; **mitologiczny** *adj* mythological; **mitoman** *m* (*-na*; *-ni*), **~ka** *f* (*-ki*; *-ki*) mythomaniac; **mityczny** *adj* mythical

mizdrzyć się *v/im* (*-drzę*) **1.** (*kokietować*) flirt (**do** *G* with) **2.** (*przymilać się*) fawn (**do** *G* on), coax (**do** *G*)

mizeria *f* (*-rii*; *-rie*) cucumber salad

mizernieć ⟨**z-**⟩ (*-nieję*) waste away; **mizerny** *adj* **1.** *osoba*, *twarz*: haggard **2.** *kwota*, *zarobki*: paltry

M

mknąć *v/im* (*-nę*) **1.** (*o samochodzie*) tear along (**po** *L*) **2.** (*o chmurach*) scud **3.** (*o czasie*) fly fast; **~ jak strzała** go like the wind

mlaskać ⟨**-snąć**⟩ (*-kam*/*-szczę*) make smacking sounds

mlecz *m* (*-czu*/*-cza*; *-cze*) **1.** (*mlecz polny*) sowthistle **2.** (*mniszek lekarski*) dandelion

mleczarnia *f* (*-ni*; *-nie*) dairy; **mleczarski** *adj wyrób*: dairy; **mleczarstwo** *n* (*-wa*; *no pl*) dairy industry; **mleczarz** *m* (*-rza*; *-rze*) **1.** (*pracownik mleczarni*) dairyman **2.** (*roznoszący mleko*) milkman

mleczko *n* (*-ka*; *-ka*) *dim* milk; **~ kosmetyczne** cleansing milk; **ptasie ~** chocolate marshmallow

mlecznobiały *adj* milky white, milky

mleczn|y *adj* **1.** *produkt*, *czekolada*, *krowa*: milk; **bar ~y** milk bar **2.** *światło*: milky; **Droga ~a** Milky Way **3.** *żarówka*: pearl **4.** *gruczoły*: mammary **5.** *zęby*: baby, *Br* milk

mleć ⟨**ze-**⟩ (*mielę*) **1.** *kawę*: grind **2.** *zboże*: mill **3.** *mięso*: mince; **~ jęzorem** *infml* yap

mleko *n* (*-ka*; *no pl*) milk; **pełne ~** whole milk, *Br* full-cream milk; **chude ~** skimmed milk; **~ w proszku** powdered milk; **zsiadłe ~**, **kwaśne ~** curds, sour milk; **krowie ~** cow's milk; **~ matki** mother's milk; **wyssać coś z mlekiem matki** be weaned on s.th.

M

mln *abbr* (= **milion**) m, million

młocka *f* (*-ki*; *no pl*) thrashing

młockarnia *f* (*-ni*; *-nie*) thrashing machine

młode *n* (*-dego*; *-de*) (*zwierzę*) young; → **młody**

młodnieć ⟨**od-**⟩ (*-nieję*) **1.** (*stawać się młodszym*) get younger **2.** (*czuć się młodszym*) feel younger

młodo *adv* young

młodociany **I** *adj* juvenile **II** *m* (*-nego*; *-ni*), **-na** *f* (*-nej*; *-ne*) juvenile

młodoś|ć *f* (*-ści*; *no pl*) youth; **być nie pierwszej ~ci** **a)** (*o osobie*) be past one's prime **b)** (*o rzeczy*) have seen better days

młodsz|y *adj comp* → **młody** **1.** younger; **ona jest trzy lata ~a ode mnie** she is three years my junior **2.** (*rangą*) junior, lower

młod|y *adj* **1.** young; **pan ~y** (bride-)groom; **panna ~a** bride; (**państwo**) **~zi** newly-weds; **~zi** (*młodzież*) (the) young; **za ~u** in one's youth **2.** *wino*, *ziemniaki*: new **3.** *wygląd*: youthful

młodzieniec *m* (*-dzieńca*; *-dzieńcy*) *lit* youth

młodzieńczy *adj* youthful

młodzież *f* (*-ży*; *no pl*) young people, (the) youth; **~ szkolna** school children; **~ akademicka** university students; **młodzieżowy** *adj* **1.** youth **2.** *muzyka*: young people's, teenage

młodzik *m* (*-ka*; *-ki*) SPORT cadet, sub-junior

młodziutki *adj* very young

młokos *m* (*-sa*; *-sy*) whelp

młot *m* (*-ta*; *-ty*) hammer; **~ pneumatyczny** pneumatic drill, *Am* jackhammer; **ryba ~** hammer fish; **rzut ~em** the hammer; **między ~em a kowadłem** *fig* between the devil and the deep blue sea

młotek *m* (*-tka*; *-tki*) hammer

młócić ⟨**o-**, **wy-**⟩ (*-cę*) **1.** *zboże*: thresh **2.** *osobę*: give a thrashing

młyn *m* (*-na*; *-ny*) mill; **diabelski ~** Ferris wheel; **być wodą na czyjś ~** *Br* be all grist to s.o.'s mill, *Am* be all grist for s.o.'s mill; **mieliśmy straszny ~** *infml* we were run off our feet; **młynarz** *m* (*-rza*; *-rze*) miller; **młynek** *m* (*-nka*; *-nki*) grinder; **~ do kawy** coffee grinder; **~ do pieprzu** pepper mill

młyński *adj* mill; **kamień ~** millstone

mną *pron* me; **ze ~** with me; → **ja**

mniam: **~**, **~** yum-yum

mnich *m* (*-cha*; *mnisi*) monk

mnie *pron* me; **o ~** about me; **ode ~** from me; **u ~** (**w domu**) at my place; **nie ma ~ w domu** I'm not at home, I'm out; → **ja**

mniej *adv comp* → **mało** **1.** (*z niepoliczalnymi*) less; **~ więcej** more or less **2.** (*z policzalnymi*) fewer, less; **nie ~ niż pięć** no fewer than five

mniejsza: **~ o to**, **~ z tym** never mind, it doesn't matter

mniejszość *f* (*-ści*; *-ści*) minority; **mniejszościowy** *adj* minority; **mniejszy** *adj comp* → **mały** smaller (**od** *G* than)

mniemać *v/im* (*-mam*) *form* **1.** (*sądzić*) believe, think **2.** (*przypuszczać*) pre-

sume; **mniemani|e** *n* (*-nia*; *-nia*) opinion, belief; ***mieć wysokie ~e o*** *L* think highly of; ***w czyimś ~u*** in s.o.'s opinion
mnisi *adj habit*: monk's; → ***mnich***
mniszek *m* (*-szka*; *-szki*) (*roślina*) dandelion
mnog|i *adj ciąża*: multiple; ***liczba ~a*** *GRAM* the plural; **mnogość** *f* (*-ści*; *no pl*) multitude
mnożenie *n* (*-nia*; *-nia*) *MATH* multiplication; **mnożna** *f* (*-nej*; *-ne*) *MATH* multiplicand; **mnożnik** *m* (*-ka*; *-ki*) *MATH* multiplier
mnożyć ⟨**po-**⟩ (*-żę*) **1.** *MATH* multiply (**przez** *A* by) **2.** *kapitał*: increase; ***mnożyć się*** multiply
mnóstwo *n* (*-wa*; *no pl*) plenty (*G* of), a lot (*G* of)
mobilizacja *f* (*-ji*; *-je*) mobilization; **mobilizować** ⟨**z-**⟩ (*-zuję*) **1.** *wojsko*: mobilize **2.** (*do działania*) stimulate (**do** *G* to do s.th.), mobilize; ***mobilizować się***: ***~ się do czegoś*** bring oneself to do s.th.
mobilizujący *adj* stimulating (**do** *G* to); **mobilność** *f* (*-ści*; *no pl*) mobility; **mobilny** *adj* mobile
moc *f* (*-cy*; *-ce*) **1.** (*siła*) strength; ***nie leżeć w czyjejś ~y*** not be in one's power; ***robić wszystko co w czyjejś ~y*** do everything in one's power; ***z całej ~y*** with all one's might **2.** *wiatru*: force **3.** *magiczna*, *obliczeniowa*: power **4.** *alkoholu*: strength, proof **5.** *PHYS* power **6.** *żarówki*: wattage **7.** *produkcyjna*, *przerobowa*: capacity **8.** ***~ prawna*** *JUR* legal force, legal validity; ***mieć ~ prawną*** be in force; ***pozostawać w ~y*** remain in force
mocarstwo *n* (*-wa*; *-wa*) superpower
mocniejsz|y *adj comp* → ***mocny***: ***coś ~ego*** a (strong) drink
mocno *adv* **1.** *uderzyć*: hard **2.** *trzymać*: tight **3.** *pragnąć*: strongly, very much **4.** *zawiązać*: tightly **5.** *przesadzony*: wildly; ***~ spać*** be fast asleep; ***~ stąpać po ziemi*** be down-to-earth; ***była ~ umalowana*** she had a lot of make-up on
mocn|y *adj* **1.** strong; ***~a strona*** *fig* strength; ***on ma ~ą głowę*** he can hold his drink **2.** *sen*: deep, sound **3.** *słowa*: harsh, strong

mocodawca *m* (*-cy*; *-cy*) *JUR* principal
mocować ⟨**za-**⟩ (*-cuję*) **1.** fix (**do** *G* to); ***~ coś na ścianie*** mount s.th. on a wall **2.** (*w imadle*) clamp, secure; ***mocować się*** wrestle (**z** *I* with)
mocz *m* (*-czu*; *no pl*) urine; ***oddawać ~*** pass urine
moczary *pl* (*-rów*) swamps, *lit* morass *sing*
mocznik *m* (*-ka*; *no pl*) urea
moczopędny *adj* diuretic; **moczowód** *m* (*-wodu*; *-wody*) ureter; **moczow|y** *adj* **1.** urinary; ***pęcherz ~y*** (urinary) bladder; ***cewka ~a*** urethra; ***drogi ~e*** urinary tract **2.** *kwas*: uric
moczyć ⟨**z-**⟩ (*-czę*) **1.** wet **2.** *bieliznę*: soak; ***moczyć się*** **1.** (*o bieliźnie*) soak **2.** (*oddawać mocz*) wet oneself
moczymorda *m* (*-dy*; *-dy*) *infml* boozer
mod|a *f* (*-dy*; *-dy*) fashion; ***w ~zie*** in fashion, fashionable; ***coś wyszło z ~y*** s.th. has gone out of fashion
model[1] *m* (*-lu*; *-le*) (*wzór, kopia*) model
model[2] *m* (*-la*; *-le*) **1.** *ART* model **2.** (*w modzie*) (male) model, fashion model
modelarstwo *n* (*-wa*; *no pl*) *Br* modelling, *Am* modeling; **modelka** *f* (*-ki*; *-ki*) model; **modelować** ⟨**wy-**⟩ (*-luję*) **1.** model **2.** *włosy*: style; **modelowy** *adj* model
modem *m* (*-mu*; *-my*) *INF* modem
modernistyczny *adj* modernist; **modernizm** *m* (*-mu*; *no pl*) modernism
modernizować ⟨**z-**⟩ (*-zuję*) modernize
modlić się ⟨**po-**⟩ (*-lę*) pray (**o** *A* for)
modliszka *f* (*-ki*; *-ki*) **1.** (*owad*) praying mantis **2.** (*kobieta*) man-eater
modlitewnik *m* (*-ka*; *-ki*) prayer book; **modlitwa** *f* (*-wy*; *-wy*) prayer
modł|a: ***na ~ę*** *G* after the fashion of
modły *pl* (*-łów*) *lit* prayers; ***zanosić ~*** say prayers
modny *adj* **1.** fashionable **2.** *słowo*, *zawód*: popular
modry *adj* (cornflower) blue
modrzew *m* (*-wia*; *-wie*) larch
modulacja *f* (*-ji*; *-je*) modulation; **modulować** *v/im* (*-luję*) modulate
moduł *m* (*-łu*; *-ły*) module
modyfikować ⟨**z-**⟩ (*-kuję*) modify
mogą, ***mogę*** → **móc**
mogiła *f* (*-ły*; *-ły*) grave; ***wspólna ~*** mass grave

mogli, ***mogłam***, ***mogłem*** → ***móc***
moher *m* (*-ru*; *no pl*) mohair; **moherowy** *adj* mohair
moi, ***moja***, ***moje*** → ***mój***
Mojżesz *m* (*-sza*; *no pl*) Moses
mokasyn *m* (*-na*; *-ny*) moccasin
moknąć ⟨**z-**⟩ (*-nę*) get wet
mokradła *pl* (*-deł*) marshes, swamps
mokrawy *adj* wettish; **mokro** *adv* wet; ***jest ~*** it's wet; ***dziecko miało ~*** the baby was wet; **mokr|y** *adj* wet; ***~a robota*** *infml* hit
molekularny *adj* molecular
molestować *v/im* (*-tuję*) **1.** (*dręczyć*) pester, nag **2.** (*seksualnie*) harass, molest
molo *n* (*-la*; *-la*) pier
moloch *m* (*-cha*; *-chy*) monster, behemoth
Mołdawia *f* (*-wii*) Moldova
momencik *m* (*-ku*; *-ki*) *dim* moment, *infml* sec; ***~!*** just a moment!, just a sec!
moment *m* (*-tu*; *-ty*) moment; ***~ bezwładności*** *PHYS* moment of inertia; ***~y*** (*w filmie*) *infml* hot moments, sex scenes
momentalnie *adv* instantly; **momentalny** *adj* instant, immediate
MON *abbr n* (*MON-u*; *no pl*) (= ***Ministerstwo Obrony Narodowej***) the Ministry of Defence
Monachium *n indecl* Munich
monarcha *m* (*-chy*; *-chowie*) monarch; **monarchia** *f* (*-chii*; *-chie*) monarchy; **monarchiczny** *adj* monarchic; **monarchini** *f* (*-ni*; *-nie*) monarch
monet|a *f* (*-ty*; *-ty*) coin; ***na ~y*** coin-operated; ***wziąć coś za dobrą ~ę*** *fig* take s.th. at face value; **monetarny** *adj jednostka*, *system*: monetary
Mongolia *f* (*-lii*) Mongolia; **mongolizm** *m* (*-mu*; *no pl*) mongolism
mongolski *adj* Mongolian
monit *m* (*-tu*; *-ty*) reminder
monitor *m* (*-ra*; *-ry*) **1.** monitor **2.** *INF* monitor, display unit **3.** (*pismo*) gazette, official journal
monitoring *m* (*-gu*; *-gi*) monitoring; **monitorować** *v/im* (*-ruję*) monitor
mono *adj* mono, monophonic
monogamia *f* (*-mii*; *no pl*) monogamy; **monografia** *f* (*-fii*; *-fie*) monograph; **monogram** *m* (*-mu*; *-my*) monogram; **monolog** *m* (*-gu*; *-gi*) monologue, *Am* monolog
monopol *m* (*-lu*; *-le*) **1.** *ECON* monopoly; ***mieć ~ na*** *A* have a monopoly on **2.** (*sklep*) *infml Br* off-licence, *Am* liquor store; **monopolowy** *adj* **1.** *ECON* monopolistic **2.** *wyroby*: alcoholic; ***sklep ~*** *Br* off-licence, *Am* liquor store
monoteizm *m* (*-mu*; *no pl*) monotheism; **monotematyczny** *adj*: ***ktoś jest ~*** s.o. has a one-track mind
monotonia *f* (*-nii*; *no pl*) monotony; **monotonny** *adj* monotonous
monstrancja *f* (*-ji*; *-je*) monstrance
monstrualny *adj* monstrous
montaż *m* (*-żu*; *-że*) **1.** (*złożenie z elementów*) assembly **2.** (*instalacja na miejscu*) installation, fitting **3.** *rusztowań*, *konstrukcji*: erection **4.** *filmu*, *programu*: editing **5.** *ART* montage; **montażowy** *adj schemat*, *plan*; assembly
montażysta *m* (*-ty*; *-żyści*), **-tka** *f* (*-ki*; *-ki*) **1.** (*filmu*) editor **2.** (*robotnik*) assembler
monter *m* (*-ra*; *-rzy*) fitter
montować ⟨**z-**, **za-**⟩ (*-tuję*) **1.** (*składać z elementów*) assemble **2.** (*instalować na miejscu*) instal(l), fit **3.** *film*, *program*: edit; **montownia** *f* (*-nii*; *-nie*) assembly shop
monumentalny *adj* monumental
mops: ***nudzić się jak ~*** be bored stiff, be bored to death
morale *n indecl* morale
moralizator *m* (*-ra*; *-rzy*), **~ka** *f* (*-ki*; *-ki*) moralizer
moralizować *v/im* (*-zuję*) moralize
moralność *f* (*-ści*; *no pl*) morality, morals *pl*; **moralny** *adj* moral; **morał** *m* (*-łu*; *-ły*) moral; ***prawić ~y*** preach (*D* at), moralize
mord *m* (*-du*; *-dy*) **1.** murder **2.** (*masowy*) slaughter
mord|a *f* (*-dy*; *-dy*) **1.** (*zwierzęcia*) muzzle **2.** (*człowieka*) *infml* mug; ***dać komuś w ~ę*** punch s.o. in the face
morderca *m* (*-cy*; *-cy*) murderer; **morderczy** *adj instynkty*, *skłonności*: murderous; **morderczyni** *f* (*-ni*; *-nie*) murderess; **morderstwo** *n* (*-wa*; *-wa*) murder; ***~ na tle rabunkowym*** murder and robbery; ***~ na***

M

tle seksualnym sex murder

mordęga *f* (*-gi*; *no pl*) *infml* drudgery

mordobicie *n* (*-cia*; *-cia*) *infml* brawl, *Br infml* punch-up

mordować ⟨**za-**⟩ (*-duję*) murder; ***mordować się*** **1.** (*nawzajem*) kill each other **2.** (*męczyć się*) plug away (**z** *I* with)

mordownia *f* (*-ni*; *-nie*) *infml* dive

morela *f* (*-li*; *-le*) apricot; **morelowy** *adj* apricot

morena *f* (*-ny*; *-ny*) moraine

morfem *m* (*-mu*; *-my*) morpheme

morfina *f* (*-ny*; *no pl*) morphine

morfologia *f* (*-gii*; *no pl*) BIOL GEOL morphology

moro *adj* camouflage, *infml* camo

mors *m* (*-sa*; *-sy*) walrus

morsk|i *adj* **1.** *woda*, *sól*: sea **2.** *zwierzęta*, *żegluga*: marine **3.** *mila*: nautical **4.** *baza*, *bitwa*: marine; ***choroba ~a*** seasickness; ***zachorować na chorobę ~ą*** get seasick; ***drogą ~ą*** by sea; ***kolor ~i*** sea green; ***latarnia ~a*** lighthouse; ***port ~i*** seaport; ***świnka ~a*** guinea pig; ***wilk ~i*** sea dog

morszczuk *m* (*-ka*; *-ki*) (European) hake

morszczyn *m* (*-nu*; *-ny*) fucus

morświn *m* (*-na*; *-ny*) *Br* (harbour) porpoise, *Am* (harbor) porpoise

morwa *f* (*-wy*; *-wy*) mulberry

morz|e *n* (*-rza*; *-rza*) sea; ***domek nad ~em*** cottage by the sea; ***jechać nad ~e*** go to the seaside; ***na ~u*** at sea; ***wakacje nad ~em*** holidays at the seaside; ***z widokiem na ~e*** with sea view

morzy|ć (*-rzę*): **1.** ⟨**za-**⟩ ***~ć głodem*** starve **2.** ⟨**z-**⟩ ***kogoś ~ sen*** s.o. feels drowsy

mosiądz *m* (*-dzu*; *no pl*) brass; **mosiężny** *adj* brass

moskit *m* (*-ta*; *-ty*) sandfly; **moskitiera** *f* (*-ry*; *-ry*) mosquito net

Moskwa *f* (*-wy*) Moscow

most *m* (*-tu*; *-ty*) bridge; ***~ zwodzony*** drawbridge; ***~ wiszący*** suspension bridge; ***~ powietrzny*** airlift

mostek *m* (*-tka*; *-tki*) **1.** (small) bridge; ***~ kapitański*** bridge **2.** (*w gimnastyce*, *stomatologii*) bridge **3.** ANAT breastbone, sternum **4.** COOK brisket

moszcz *m* (*-czu*; *no pl*) must, stum

moszna *f* (*-ny*; *-ny*) scrotum

mościć ⟨**wy-**⟩ (*moszczę*) pad; ***~ sobie posłanie*** make one's bed; ***mościć się*** ⟨**u-**⟩ snuggle (down)

motać ⟨**na-**⟩ (*-tam*) **1.** *wełnę*, *nici*: wind **2.** (*plątać*) tangle; **motek** *m* (*-tka*; *-tki*) hank, skein

motel *m* (*-lu*; *-le*) motel

motłoch *m* (*-chu*; *no pl*) the rabble

motocykl *m* (*-la*; *-le*) motorcycle; **motocyklista** *m* (*-ty*; *-liści*), **-tka** *f* (*-ki*; *-ki*) motorcyclist, *infml* biker; **motocyklowy** *adj* motorcycle

motor *m* (*-ru*; *-ry*) **1.** (*motocykl*) *infml* bike **2.** (*silnik*) engine, motor; **motorniczy** *m* (*-czego*; *-czowie*) *Br* tram driver, *Am* streetcar driver

motorower *m* (*-ru*; *-ry*) moped

motorowodn|y *adj*: ***sporty ~e*** motorboating, powerboating; **motorowy** *adj* motor; **motorówka** *f* (*-ki*; *-ki*) motorboat; **motorynka** *f* (*-ki*; *-ki*) (small) moped

motoryzacj|a *f* (*-ji*; *no pl*): ***rozwój ~i*** motorization; ***fani ~i*** car fans; ***pismo dla miłośników ~i*** car magazine; ***o ~i*** about cars; **motoryzacyjny** *adj* **1.** *magazyn*: car **2.** *sklep*: auto **3.** *przemysł*: automobile

motyka *f* (*-ki*; *-ki*) hoe

motyl *m* (*-la*; *-le*) butterfly; **motylek** (*-lka*; *-lki*) *dim* **1.** (small) butterfly **2.** SPORT butterfly **3.** TECH wing nut; **motyli** *adj* **1.** *skrzydła*: butterfly **2.** *lot*: of a butterfly

motyw *m* (*-wu*; *-wy*) **1.** ART LIT motif; ***powracający ~*** recurring theme; ***na ~ach*** based on **2.** (*powód*) motive; ***~ zbrodni*** motive for a crime

motywacja *f* (*-ji*; *-je*) motivation; **motywacyjn|y** *adj czynnik*: motivating; ***list ~y*** (letter of) application; ***premia ~a*** incentive

motywować (*-tywuję*) **1.** ⟨**u-**⟩ (*uzasadniać*) justify (*I* with) **2.** ⟨**z-**⟩ (*zachęcać*) motivate (**do** *G* to do s.th.)

mow|a *f* (*-wy*; *-wy*) **1.** speech; ***~a zależna*** reported speech; ***wygłosić ~ę*** give a speech; ***biegła znajomość języka angielskiego w ~ie i piśmie*** fluent written and spoken English; ***odebrało mu ~ę*** he was speechless, he was dumbstruck; ***nie ma ~y!*** it's out of the question! **2.** (*język*) lan-

M

guage; **~a ciała** body language
mozaika *f* (*-ki*; *-ki*) mosaic
mozolić się ⟨**na-**⟩ (*-lę*) toil (away) (**nad** *I* at/over); **mozolny** *adj* arduous
moździerz *m* (*-rza*; *-rze*) mortar
może *particle* maybe, perhaps; **~ pójdziemy na spacer?** how about going for a walk?, we could go for a walk; → **móc**
możecie, **możemy**, **możesz** → **móc**
możliwie *adv* possibly; **~ szybko**, **~ jak najszybciej** as soon as possible; **możliwoś|ć** *f* (*-ści*; *-ści*) **1.** possibility; **w miarę ~ci** if possible **2.** (*szansa*) opportunity, chance; **~ci** (*zdolności*) abilities; **~ci rozwoju** potential for development
możliw|y *adj* **1.** possible; **~y do zrobienia** feasible; **~e, że** it's likely that, it's possible that **2.** (*niezły*) *infml* passable, not bad
można *v/irreg*: **~ tam posłuchać dobrej muzyki** you can listen to good music there; **~ by** we could, why don't we?; **o ile ~, jeśli ~** if possible; **jak ~ zostać stylistką?** how can one become a stylist?; **~ wytrzymać** *infml* not too bad, it's OK; **~ tam parkować** parking is allowed there, **tu nie ~ palić** smoking is not allowed here; **czy ~ otworzyć okno?** do you mind if I open the window?; **jak ~ najszybciej** as quick as possible; **nie ~ tak mówić!** you mustn't say things like that!
możnoś|ć *f* (*-ści*; *no pl*) *lit* possibility; **w miarę ~ci** as far as possible
możnowładztwo *n* (*-wa*; *no pl*) high nobility, the magnates *pl*
możny *adj* wealthy and powerful
móc *v/im* (*mogę*) **1.** be able, can; **~ coś zrobić** be able to do s.th.; **nie mogę tego zrobić** I can't do it; **czy możesz to zrobić?** can you do it?; **być może** maybe, perhaps; **robię, co mogę** I'm doing my best; **nie może być!** it can't be!, it's impossible!; **dziękuję, już nie mogę** no thanks, I'm full; **mógł zapomnieć** he may have forgotten **2.** (*pozwolenie*) be allowed, can **3.** (*prawo*) may, can; **ktoś może coś zrobić** s.o. may do s.th., s.o. can do s.th.
mój *poss* **1.** (*przed rzeczownikiem*) my; **~ przyjaciel** my friend; **z mojej strony** for my part **2.** (*bez rzeczownika*) mine; **ta książka jest moja** this book is mine; **mój przyjaciel** a friend of mine
mól *m* (*mola*; *mole*) moth; **~ książkowy** *fig* bookworm
mówca *m* (*-cy*; *-cy*), **-czyni** *f* (*-ni*; *-nie*) speaker
mówi|ć ⟨**powiedzieć**⟩ (*-wię*) **I** *v/i* **1.** speak (**o** *L* about/of); **~ć po polsku** speak Polish; **~ć do siebie** talk to oneself; **halo, ~ Aga** hello, Aga speaking; **coś ~ samo za siebie** s.th. speaks for itself; **nie ma o czym ~ć** forget it; **~ć serio** be serious, speak seriously; **~ć przez nos** speak through one's nose, speak nasally **2.** (*rozmawiać*) talk **II** *v/t* **1.** say (**coś** *D* s.th. to), tell (**komuś** *A*, s.o. s.th.); **~ć bzdury**, **~ć od rzeczy** talk nonsense; **~ć do rzeczy** talk sense; **nic mi to nie ~** it tells me nothing, it doesn't ring a bell (with me); **~ą, że** it is said (that), they say (that); **a nie ~łem?** I told you so; **~ąc między nami** between you and me **2.** *prawdę, kłamstwa*: tell
mównica *f* (*-cy*; *-ce*) rostrum, lectern
mózg *m* (*-gu*; *-gi*) ANAT brain; **mózgownica** *f* (*-cy*; *-ce*) *infml* skull; **mózgow|y** *adj* ANAT cerebral; **kora ~a** cerebral cortex; **opony ~e** meninges; **zapalenie opon ~ych** meningitis
móżdżek *m* (*-dżka*/*-dżku*; *-dżki*) **1.** ANAT cerebellum; **mieć ptasi ~** *fig* be a birdbrain **2.** COOK brains *pl*
mroczny *adj* **1.** *zaułek*, *myśli*: dark **2.** *nastrój*, *obraz*: gloomy; **mrok** *m* (*-ku*; *-ki*) darkness; **zapadał ~** darkness was falling
mrowić się *v/im* (*-wię*) swarm; **mrowie** *n* (*-wia*; *no pl*) **1.** myriad, multitude **2.** *ludzi*: swarms *pl*
mrowienie *n* (*-nia*; *no pl*) tingling
mrowisko *n* (*-ka*; *-ka*) anthill; **wsadzić kij w ~** *fig* stir up a hornet's nest
mrozić ⟨**z-**, **za-**⟩ (*mrożę*) **1.** freeze; **~ krew w żyłach** make one's blood curdle **2.** (*chłodzić*) chill; **mrozić się** chill
mrozoodporny *adj* frost resistant
mroźno *adv*: **jest ~** it's freezing; **mroźny** *adj* **1.** frosty **2.** *powietrze*: icy
mrożonki *pl* (*-nek*) frozen foods; **~ warzywne** frozen vegetables; **mrożon|y** *adj* frozen; **~a kawa** iced coffee

M

mrówczy *adj praca*: painstaking; **mrówk|a** *f (-ki; -ki)* ant; **~i** *(mrowienie)* pins and needles
mrówkojad *m (-da; -dy)* anteater
mrówkowiec *m (-wca; -wce) infml* high-rise
mróz *m (mrozu; mrozy)* frost; ***jest 15 stopni mrozu*** it's 15 degrees below zero, it's minus 15 degrees; ***był trzaskający ~*** it was biting cold
mruczeć ⟨***mruknąć***⟩ *(-czę)* **1.** murmur; ***~ coś pod nosem*** mutter s.th. under one's breath **2.** *(o kocie)* purr
mrug|ać ⟨***-gnąć***⟩ *(-gam)* **1.** blink (one's eyes) **2.** *(okiem)* wink (one's eye) (**do** *G* at); ***nie ~nąć okiem*** *(nie okazać emocji) Br* not bat an eyelid, *Am* not bat an eye **3.** *(o gwiazdach, światłach)* twinkle, flicker
mrugnięcie *n (-cia; -cia)* **1.** *(jednym okiem)* wink **2.** *(oczami)* blink
mruk *m (-ka; -ki)* gruff person; **mrukliwy** *adj osoba*: gruff
mruknąć *v/p* → ***mruczeć***
mrużyć ⟨**z-**⟩ *(-żę)*: ***~ oczy*** squint (one's eyes), narrow one's eyes
mrzonka *f (-ki; -ki)* mirage, pipedream
MSW *abbr n indecl* (= ***Ministerstwo Spraw Wewnętrznych***) the Ministry of the Interior
MSZ *abbr m (MSZ-etu; no pl)* (= ***Ministerstwo Spraw Zagranicznych***) Foreign Ministry
msz|a *f (-szy; -sze)* **1.** REL Mass, service; ***iść na ~ę*** go to Mass; ***odprawiać ~ę*** celebrate Mass; ***służyć do ~y*** serve at Mass **2.** MUS mass; **mszaln|y** *adj* Mass; ***wino ~e*** altar wine; **mszał** *m (-łu; -ły)* missal
mszyca *f (-cy; -ce)* aphid
mściciel *m (-la; -le)*, **~ka** *f (-ki; -ki)* avenger
mścić ⟨**po-**⟩ *(mszczę)* avenge; ***mścić się*** ⟨**ze-**⟩ take (one's) revenge, avenge oneself (**za** *A* for)
mściwość *f (-ści; no pl)* vindictiveness; **mściwy** *adj* vindictive
mu *pron* him; → ***on***
much|a *f (-chy; -chy)* **1.** *(owad)* fly; ***padać jak ~y*** die like flies; ***on nawet ~y by nie skrzywdził*** he wouldn't hurt a fly; (**że**) ***~a nie siada*** *infml* top notch, absolutely great **2.** *(ozdoba)* bow tie
muchołapka *f (-ki; -ki)* flypaper; **muchomor** *m (-ra; -ry)* toadstool; ***~ czerwony*** fly agaric; ***~ sromotnikowy*** death cap
muczeć ⟨**za-**⟩ *(-czę) (o krowie)* moo
mudżahedin *m (-na; -ni)* mujahedin
mufka *f (-ki; -ki)* muff
muflon *m (-na; -ny)* mouflon
Mulat *m (-ta; -laci)*, **~ka** *f (-ki; -ki)* person of mixed race, mulatto
mulina *f (-ny; -ny)* (embroidery) floss
mulisty *adj* muddy
multi- *(w złożeniach)* multi-
multimedia *pl (-diów)* multimedia; **multipleks** *m (-su; -sy)* multiplex, *Br* multiscreen cinema, *Am* multiscreen movie theater; **multiwitamina** *f (-ny; -ny)* multivitamin
multum *pron* multitude (*G* of)
muł[1] *m (-łu; -ły) (substancja)* mud, sludge
muł[2] *m (-ła; -ły) (zwierzę)* mule
mumia *f (-mii; -mie)* mummy; **mumifikować** ⟨**z-**⟩ *(-kuję)* mummify
mundial *m (-lu; -le)* the World Cup
mundur *m (-ru; -ry)* uniform; **mundur|ek** *m (-rka; -rki) (szkolny)* (school) uniform; ***ziemniaki w ~kach*** jacket potatoes; **mundurowy** *adj* **1.** *policjant*: uniformed **2.** *bluza*: uniform
mur *m (-ru; -ry)* wall; ***~ pruski*** half-timbering; ***~ Berliński*** the Berlin Wall; ***na ~-beton*** *infml* for sure; ***być przypartym do ~u*** have one's back to the wall; ***walić głową w ~*** bang one's head against a brick wall; ***stanąć ~em za kimś*** give s.o. one's full support; ***w ~ach miasta*** within the city walls
murarsk|i *adj pomocnik*: bricklayer's; ***prace ~ie*** bricklaying; ***zaprawa ~a*** mortar; **murarstwo** *n (-wa; no pl)* bricklaying
murarz *m (-rza; -rze)* bricklayer
murawa *f (-wy; -wy)* **1.** *(gęsta trawa)* turf **2.** *(boisko)* field
murek *m (-rka/-rku; -rki)* **1.** (low) wall **2.** *(na krawędzi mostu, dachu)* parapet
murena *f (-ny; -ny)* morey (eel)
murować ⟨**wy-**⟩ *(-ruję)* **1.** lay bricks **2.** *dom, mur*: build; **murowany** *adj* **1.** *(z cegły)* brick **2** *(z kamienia)* stone **3.** *wygrana*: sure, sure-fire
murszeć ⟨**z-**⟩ *(-szeję)* rot

M

Murzyn *m* (*-na*; *-ni*) black (man); ***on jest ~em*** he is black
Murzynek *m* (*-nka*; *-nki*) black child; **murzynek** *m* (*-nka*; *-nki*) (*ciasto*) chocolate cake; **Murzynk|a** *f* (*-ki*; *-ki*) black (woman); ***jest ~ą*** she is black; **murzyński** *adj* black
mus[1] *m* (*-su*; *-sy*) (*substancja*) mousse
mus[2] *m* (*-su*; *no pl*) (*konieczność*) necessity; ***z ~u*** out of necessity
mus|ieć *v/im* (*-szę*) **1.** must; ***~zę to mieć*** I must have it; ***nie ~iałeś tego robić*** you needn't have done it **2.** (*być zmuszonym*) have to; ***czy ~zę?*** do I have to? **3.** (*prawdopodobieństwo*) ***on ~i być teraz w domu*** he must be at home now; ***~iała wyjść*** she must have gone out
muskać ⟨***-snąć***⟩ (*-kam*) **1.** brush **2.** (*o kuli*) graze
muskularny *adj* muscular; **muskuł** *m* (*-łu*; *-ły*) muscle
musli *n indecl* muesli
musnąć *v/p* → ***muskać***
musować *v/im* (*-suję*) fizz; **musujący** *adj* **1.** *wino*: sparkling **2.** *tabletka*: effervescent
muszelka *f* (*-ki*; *-ki*) (small) shell
musz|ka *f* (*-ki*; *-ki*) **1.** (*owad*) (small) fly; ***~ka owocowa*** fruit fly **2.** (*w broni*) front sight, bead; ***na ~ce*** in one's sights **3.** (*krawat*) bow tie
muszkatołow|y *adj*: ***gałka ~a*** nutmeg
muszla *f* (*-li*; *-le*) shell; ***~ klozetowa*** toilet bowl; ***~ koncertowa*** band shell
musztarda *f* (*-dy*; *-dy*) mustard; ***~ po obiedzie*** *fig* it's too late in the day; **musztardowy** *adj* mustard; **musztardówka** *f* (*-ki*; *-ki*) *infml* mustard jar
musztra *f* (*-ry*; *-ry*) (military) drill; **musztrować** *v/im* (*-ruję*) drill
musz|y *adj*: ***waga ~a*** SPORT flyweight
muślin *m* (*-nu*; *-ny*) muslin
mutacj|a *f* (*-ji*; *-je*) mutation; ***~a głosu*** voice breaking; ***ktoś przechodzi ~ę*** s.o.'s voice breaks; **mutować** *v/im* (*-tuję*) mutate
muza *f* (*-zy*; *-zy*) muse
muzealny *adj* museum; **muzeum** *n* (*indecl*; *-zea*) museum
muzułmanin *m* (*-na*; *-manie*), **-nka** *f* (*-ki*; *-ki*) Muslim; **muzułmański** *adj* Muslim
muzyczn|y *adj* **1.** musical **2.** *sklep*, *branża*: music; ***szkoła ~a*** school of music, music school
muzyk *m* (*-ka*; *-zycy*) musician; **muzyka** *f* (*-ki*; *no pl*) **1.** music; ***~ poważna*** classical music; ***~ rozrywkowa*** popular music; ***~ do filmu*** score **2.** (*ścieżka dźwiękowa*) soundtrack
muzykalny *adj* musical; **muzykant** *m* (*-ta*; *-nci*) **1.** musician **2.** (*uliczny*) street musician, busker
muzykologia *f* (*-gii*; *no pl*) musicology; **muzykować** *v/im* (*-kuję*) (*grać*) play music
my *pron* we; ***o nas*** about us; ***z nami*** with us; ***bez nas*** without us
myć ⟨***u-***, ***wy-***⟩ (*myję*) **1.** wash; ***~ naczynia*** do the dishes, *Br* wash up **2.** *zęby*: brush **3.** *okna*, *podłogę*: clean; ***myć się*** wash
mydelniczka *f* (*-ki*; *-ki*) **1.** (*podstawka*) soap dish **2.** (*pudełko*) soapbox; **mydlany** *adj bańka*, *opera*: soap
mydlić ⟨***na-***⟩ (*-lę*) soap; ***~ komuś oczy*** *infml* pull the wool over s.o.'s eyes; ***mydlić się*** **1.** (*o osobie*) soap **2.** (*o mydle*) lather
mydliny *pl* (*-lin*) (soap)suds; **mydło** *n* (*-ła*; *-ła*) soap; ***~ w płynie*** liquid soap
myjnia *f* (*-ni*; *-nie*): ***~ samochodowa*** car wash
mylić ⟨***po-***⟩ (*-lę*) confuse, mix up (***z*** *I* with); ***~ kogoś z*** *I* mistake s.o. for; ***o ile mnie pamięć nie myli*** if memory serves me right; ***~ ślady*** lay a false trail; ***pozory mylą*** appearances are deceptive; ***czy oczy mnie nie mylą?*** am I seeing right?; ***mylić się*** **1.** (*popełniać błąd*) make a mistake, err; ***o ile się nie mylę*** I may be wrong but (I think); ***często myli mi się*** I often confuse, I often mix up **2.** (*popełniać błędy*) make mistakes **3.** (*być w błędzie*) be wrong
mylnie *adv* wrongly, erroneously; ***~ poinformować*** misinform; ***~ zrozumieć*** misunderstand; **mylny** *adj* **1.** wrong, erroneous **2.** *ślad*, *przesłanki*: false
mysi *adj ogon*, *nora*: mouse; ***~ kolor*** *Br* mouse grey, *Am* mouse gray
mysikrólik *m* (*-ka*; *-ki*) goldcrest
mysz *f* (*-szy*; *-szy*) mouse; ***~y*** mice; ***siedzieć jak ~ pod miotłą*** be (as) quiet as a mouse

M

myszk|a *f* (*-ki*; *-ki*) **1.** (little) mouse **2.** *INF* mouse **3.** (*na ciele*) mole **4.** ***trącić ~ą*** be behind the times, be old hat; **myszkować** *v/im* (*-kuję*) poke around

myszołów *m* (*-łowa*; *-łowy*) buzzard

myśl *f* (*-li*; *-li*) **1.** thought; ***mieć na ~i*** mean; ***w ~ach*** in one's mind; ***przyjść komuś na ~*** occur to s.o.; ***pogrążony w ~ach*** deep in thought; ***być dobrej ~i*** be optimistic; ***być ~ami z*** *I* be in spirit with; ***złote ~i*** words of wisdom; ***to jest ~!*** that's a thought!, that's an idea! **2.** (*pomysł*) idea

myślący *adj* **1.** thinking **2.** (*inteligentny*) intelligent

myśl|eć ⟨**po-**⟩ (*-lę*) think (**o** *L* about/of); ***~eć o niebieskich migdałach*** *fig* daydream; ***~ę, że tak*** I think so; ***~ę, że nie*** I don't think so, ***tak ~isz?*** you think so?; ***niewiele ~ąc*** without much thought

myśleni|e *n* (*-nia*; *no pl*) thinking; ***dawać komuś do ~a*** make s.o. think; ***dawać do ~a*** be food for thought

myśliciel *m* (*-la*; *-le*) thinker

myślistwo *n* (*-wa*; *no pl*) hunting; **myśliwiec** *m* (*-wca*; *-wce*) (*samolot*) fighter; **myśliwski** *adj* hunting; **myśliwy** *m* (*-wego*; *-wi*) hunter

myślnik *m* (*-ka*; *-ki*) dash

myślowy *adj* mental

mżawka *f* (*-ki*; *-ki*) drizzle; **mżyć** *v/im* (*mżę*) drizzle; **mżysty** *adj* drizzly

N

n. *abbr* (= **nad**) (*położony nad rzeką*) on

na *prep* (*I*/*A*) **1.** on; ***~ podłodze*** on the floor; ***~ urlopie*** on holiday, on leave **2.** in; ***~ obrazku*** in the picture; ***~ ulicy*** in the street, on the street; ***~ korytarzu*** in the corridor; ***~ wsi*** in the country; ***~ Węgrzech*** in Hungary; ***~ drzewie*** in a tree; ***~ północy*** in the north; ***~ słońcu*** in the sun **3.** at; ***~ stacji*** at the station; ***~ uniwersytecie*** at university; ***~ dole strony*** at the bottom of the page **4.** for; ***~ 2 dni*** for 2 days; ***~ co?*** what for?; ***~ śniadanie*** for breakfast **5.** to; ***iść ~ zebranie*** go to a meeting; ***~ zachód od*** *G* to the west of **6.** ***~ zewnątrz*** outside; ***stojak ~ CD*** CD rack: ***grać ~ gitarze*** play the guitar; ***być chorym ~ grypę*** have the flu, *Br* have flu: ***jechać ~ rowerze*** ride a bicycle; ***jeździć ~ nartach*** ski; ***~ leżąco*** lying; ***~ wznak*** on one's back; ***sto mil ~ godzinę*** one hundred miles per hour

nabawić się *v/p* (*-wię*) **1.** *choroby*: catch, contract **2.** (*bawić się*) have fun

nabazgrać *v/p* → ***bazgrać***

nabazgrolić *v/p* → ***bazgrolić***

nabiał *m* (*-łu*; *no pl*) eggs and dairy products *pl*

nabić *v/p* (*-biję*): ***~ sobie guza*** bump one's head; → ***nabijać***

nabieg|ać ⟨**-biec**⟩ (*-gam*): ***łzy ~ły mu do oczu*** tears welled up in his eyes; ***krew ~ła jej do twarzy*** her face flushed with blood; ***nabiegać się*** *v/p* (*szukając, załatwiając sprawy*) run around

nabierać ⟨**-brać**⟩ (*-ram*) **1.** (*ręką*) take **2.** *wody ze studni*: draw **3.** *zwyczaju*: develop **4.** *szybkości*: pick up, gain **5.** *wartości*, *znaczenia*; grow in **6.** *pewności siebie*: gain in **7.** (*żartować*) pull s.o.'s leg **8.** (*oszukiwać*) take in, con; ***~ ochoty na*** *A* feel like doing s.th.; ***~ powietrza*** take a breath; ***~ sił*** grow in strength; ***~ rumieńców*** *Br* get one's colour back, *Am* get one's color back; ***~ ciała*** put on weight

nabijać ⟨**-bić**⟩ (*-jam*) **1.** *broń*: load **2.** *fajkę*: fill **3.** *butlę*: fill up; ***~ kogoś w butelkę*** *infml* take s.o. in, take s.o. for a ride; → ***nabić***; ***nabijać się*** make fun (**z** *G* of)

nabity *adj* **1.** *broń*: loaded **2.** *sala*: crammed (full), packed (full) **3.** *ciało*: compact; → ***nabijać***

nabluzgać *v/p* → ***bluzgać***

nabłonek *m* (*-nka*; *-nki*) *ANAT* epithelium

nabożeństwo *n* (*-wa*; *-wa*) **1.** *REL* service **2.** (*uroczysta powaga*) *lit* reverence

N

nabożn|y *adj*: **~a cześć** reverence; **~e milczenie** solemn silence
nabój *m* (*-boju*; *-boje*) cartridge; **~ z tuszem** ink cartridge; **ślepy ~** blank cartridge
nabór *m* (*-boru*; *-bory*) recruitment
nabrać *v/p*: **dać się ~** be taken in (**na** *A* by); → **nabierać**
nabroić *v/p* → **broić**
nabrudzić *v/p* → **brudzić**
nabrzeże *n* (*-ża*; *-ża*) (*w porcie*) wharf; **nabrzeżny** *adj* **1.** *ptactwo*: coastal, shoreline **2.** *osada*: coastal, waterfront
nabrzmiały *adj* **1.** swollen **2.** *fig* urgent; **nabrzmienie** *n* (*-nia*; *-nia*) MED swelling; **nabrzmiewać** ⟨**-mieć**⟩ (*-wam*) swell
nabujać *v/p* → **bujać**
naburmuszony *adj infml* sulky; **naburmuszyć się** *v/p* (*-szę*) go into a sulk
nabytek *m* (*-tku*; *-tki*) purchase, acquisition; **nabywać** ⟨**-być**⟩ (*-wam*) **1.** (*kupować*) *form* purchase, acquire **2.** *doświadczenia*, *umiejętności*: gain; **~ wprawy** *Br* become skilful, *Am* become skillful
nabywca *m* (*-cy*; *-cy*) purchaser
nabywcz|y *adj* **siła ~a** purchasing power
nacechowany *adj* **1.** marked (*I* by) **2.** *emocjonalnie*: charged
nachalny *adj* **1.** *osoba*: *infml* pushy, *form* importunate **2.** *reklama*: aggressive; **nachalność** *f* (*-ści*; *no pl*) **1.** *osoby*: *infml* pushiness, *form* importunateness **2.** *reklamy*: aggressiveness
nachlapać *v/p* → **chlapać**
nachodzić ⟨**najść**⟩ (*-dzę*) **1.** (*przychodzić*) intrude (*A* on) **2.** (*przychodzić wielokrotnie*) pester **3.** (*nakładać się*) **~ na siebie** overlap; **nachodzić się**: **nachodziłem się** I'm tired of walking
nachylać ⟨**-lić**⟩ (*-lam*) bend; **nachylać się** lean (foreward), bend (foreward); **nachylenie** *n* (*-nia*; *no pl*) slope; **nachylony** *adj* **1.** *dach*: sloping **2.** *osoba*: bent
naciąć *v/p* → **nacinać**
naciąg *m* (*-gu*; *no pl*) **1.** (*stopień naprężenia*) tension **2.** (*tenisowy*) string **3** MUS string set
naciągacz *m* (*-cza*; *-cze*) *infml* con artist
naciąg|ać ⟨**-gnąć**⟩ (*-gam*) **I** *v/t* **1.** *linę*: tighten, pull tight **2.** *płótno*, *fakty*: stretch **3.** *łuk*: draw **4.** *kołdrę*: pull **5.** *pończochy*, *rękawiczki*: pull on **6.** *mięsień*: strain, pull **7.** *dowody*: strain **8.** (*wyłudzać*) *infml* scrounge (**od** *G* off); **~nął mnie na pożyczkę** he wheedled me into lending him some money **II** *v/i* (*o herbacie*) infuse, draw
naciągany *adj argument*, *porównanie*: far-fetched
naciek *m* (*-ku*; *-ki*) **1.** *żywicy*: (dried) drip **2.** GEOL dripstone
nacierać ⟨**natrzeć**⟩ (*-ram*) **I** *v/t* (*wcierać*) rub; **~ coś kremem** rub cream into s.th. **II** *v/i* (*atakować*) charge (**na** *A* at); **nacierać się**: **~ się czymś** rub s.th. into one's skin
nacierpieć się *v/p* (*-pię*) suffer a great deal
nacieszyć się *v/p* (*-szę*) enjoy (to the full); **ktoś nie może się czymś nacieszyć** s.o. cannot get enough of s.th.
nacięcie *n* (*-cia*; *-cia*) **1.** cut **2.** (*rowek*) notch
nacinać ⟨**-ciąć**⟩ (*-nam*) **1.** incise, make an incision **2.** (*robić rowek*) notch, cut a notch; **nacinać się** *infml* get conned, be tricked
nacisk *m* (*-ku*; *-ki*) **1.** pressure; **wywierać ~** exert pressure **2.** (*akcent*) emphasis; **kłaść ~ na** *A* stress, emphasize
naciskać ⟨**-snąć**⟩ (*-kam*) **1.** *przycisk*, *pedał*: press, push **2.** *klamkę*: press, push down **3.** *spust*: pull; **~ na** *A fig* put pressure on, press; **~ gaz do dechy** *infml* step on it
nacja *f* (*-ji*; *-je*) nation; **nacjonalista** *m* (*-ty*; *-liści*) nationalist; **nacjonalistyczny** *adj* nationalist
nacjonalizować ⟨**z-**⟩ (*-zuję*) nationalize
na czele → **czoło**
naczelne *pl* (*-nych*) BIOL primates
naczelnik *m* (*-ka*; *-nicy*) **1.** *wydziału*: head; **~ poczty** postmaster **2.** *więzienia*: governor **3.** *powstania*: commander **4.** *plemienia*: chief
naczelny *adj* **1.** chief; **redaktor ~** editor-in-chief **2.** *dyrektor*: general, *Br* managing

N

naczyni|e *n* (*-nia*; *-nia*) **1.** vessel; **~a kuchenne** kitchenware; **~a szklane** glassware; **myć ~a** wash the dishes, *infml* do the dishes **2.** *laboratoryjne*: container **3.** ANAT vessel; **~a krwionośne** blood vessels
naczynko *n* (*-ka*; *-ka*) ANAT vessel
naczytać się *v/p* (*-tam*) read (plenty of)
nać *f* (*naci*; *no pl*) top (leaves); **~ pietruszki** parsley leaves
naćpany *adj infml* stoned
nad *prep* (*I*/*A*) **1.** (*ponad*) over, above; **~ łóżkiem** over the bed; **~ poziomem morza** above sea level **2.** (*w pobliżu*) **~ morzem** at the seaside; **jechać ~ morze** go to the seaside; **~ brzegiem morza** on the seashore; **~ rzeką** by the river; **~ ranem** at daybreak; **~ Wisłą** on the Vistula **3.** (*na temat*) **pracować ~** *I* work on; **myśleć ~** *I* think about **4.** (*zależność*) over; **kontrola ~** *I* control of, control over; **opieka ~** *I* care of
nadać *v/p* → **nadawać**
nadajnik *m* (*-ka*; *-ki*) transmitter
nadal *adv* still
nadanie *n* (*-nia*; *no pl*) *tytułu*: conferment; **~ obywatelstwa** naturalization
nadaremnie *adv* in vain
nadarzać się ⟨**-rzyć**⟩ (*-rzam*) (*o okazji*) arise
nadawać ⟨**-dać**⟩ (*-daję*) **I** *v/t* **1.** *list*, *przesyłkę*: mail, send **2.** *imię*, *wygląd*: give **3.** *tytuł*: confer **4.** RADIO broadcast **5.** *prawo*: grant, bestow; **~ obywatelstwo** naturalize **II** *v/i* (*mówić*) *infml* yap; **nadawać się** be suitable (**do** *G*/**na** *A* for); **nadający się** suitable
nadawca *m* (*-cy*; *-cy*), **-czyni** *f* (*-ni*; *-nie*) sender; **nadawczy** *adj stacja*: transmitter
nadąć *v/p* → **nadymać**
nadąsany *adj* sulky; **nadąsać się** *v/p* go into a sulk
nadążać ⟨**-żyć**⟩ (*-żam*) **1.** (*dotrzymywać kroku*) **nie ~ za** *I* not keep up with; **nie ~ z pracą** fall behind with one's work **2.** (*rozumieć*) follow
nadbagaż *m* (*-żu*; *-że*) excess baggage
nadbałtycki *adj kraje*: Baltic
nadbiegać ⟨**-biec**⟩ (*-gam*) run up, come running
nadbrzeże *n* (*-ża*; *-ża*) **1.** waterside; **~ rzeki** riverside; **~ jeziora** lakeside **2.** (*morskie*) (sea)shore **3.** (*portowe*) quay; **nadbrzeżny** *adj* waterside
nadbudowa *f* (*-wy*; *-wy*) **1.** (*część budynku*) *Br* (upper) extension, *Am* addition **2.** PHIL superstructure; **nadbudowywać** ⟨**-dować**⟩ (*-dowuję*) *piętro*: add; **nadbudówka** *f* (*-ki*; *-ki*) **1.** (*część budynku*) *Br* (upper) extension, *Am* addition **2.** (*na statku*) superstructure
nadchodzący *adj miesiąc*, *rok*: coming; **nadchodzić** ⟨**-dejść**⟩ (*-dzę*) come
nadciągać ⟨**-gnąć**⟩ (*-gam*) **1.** come **2.** (*o chmurach*, *burzy*) come up
nadciśnienie *n* (*-nia*; *no pl*) **1.** MED hypertension **2.** PHYS overpressure
nadczłowiek *m* (*-ka*; *-dludzie*) overman, superman
nadczynność *f* (*-ści*; *no pl*) hyperfunction; **~ tarczycy** hyperthyroidism
naddarty *adj* slightly torn
naddatek *m* (*-tku*; *-tki*) extra, surplus
nade: **~ wszystko a)** (*przede wszystkim*) above all **b)** (*bardziej niż cokolwiek innego*) more than anything else; → **nad**
nadejście *n* (*-ścia*; *no pl*) (the) coming, arrival; **nadejść** *v/p* → **nadchodzić**
nadepnąć *v/p* (*-nę*) step, tread (**na** *A* on); **~ komuś na odcisk** *fig Br* tread on s.o.'s toes, *Am* step on s.o.'s toes
nader *adv lit* most
naderwać *v/p* → **nadrywać**; **naderwany** *adj* (partly) torn
nadesłać *v/p* → **nadsyłać**
nadęty *adj infml* **1.** *bufon*, *styl*: pompous **2.** (*nadąsany*) sulky
nadfioletowy *adj* ultraviolet
nadganiać ⟨**-gonić**⟩ (*-niam*) *fig* catch up (*A* with)
nadgarstek *m* (*-tka*; *-tki*) wrist
nadgnić *v/p* (*-niję*) start to rot; **nadgniły** *adj* rotting
nadgodziny *pl* (*-dzin*) overtime *sing*
nadgonić *v/p* → **nadganiać**
nadgorliwość *f* (*-ści*; *no pl*) overzealousness, overeagerness; **nadgorliwy** *adj* overzealous, overeager
nadgraniczny *adj* border
nadgryzać ⟨**-gryźć**⟩ (*-zam*) **1.** (*wgryzać się*) bite into **2.** (*odgryzając część*) bite a piece off

nadjeżdżać ⟨**-jechać**⟩ (*-dżam*) **1.** (*zbliżać się*) come, approach **2.** (*przybywać*) arrive
nadkładać ⟨**-dłożyć**⟩ (*-dam*): **~ drogi** take the long way round
nadkrawać ⟨**-kroić**⟩ (*-wam*) cut into
nadkwasota *f* (*-ty*; *no pl*) hyperacidity
nadlatywać ⟨**-lecieć**⟩ (*-tuję*) **1.** come flying **2.** (*zbliżać się*) approach
nadleśnictwo *n* (*-wa*; *-wa*) forestry office; **nadleśniczy** *m* (*-czego*; *-czowie*) forest manager
nadliczbow|y *adj* extra, surplus; ***godziny ~e*** overtime
nadludzki *adj* superhuman
nadłamany *adj* partly broken
nadłamywać ⟨**-mać**⟩ (*-muję*) **1.** (*łamać częściowo*) break partly **2.** (*odłamywać kawałek*) break off a bit of
nadłożyć *v/p* → ***nadkładać***
nadmanganian *m* (*-nu*, *no pl*): **~ *potasu*** potassium permanganate
nadmia|r *m* (*-ru*; *no pl*) excess; ***w ~rze*** in excess; ***~r informacji*** information overload
nadmieniać ⟨**-nić**⟩ (*-niam*) mention
nadmiernie *adv* excessively; **nadmierny** *adj* excessive
nadmorski *adj* **1.** *plaża*, *ośrodek*: seaside **2.** *roślinność*, *ptactwo*: coastal; **~ *port*** seaport
nadmuchiwać ⟨**-chać**⟩ (*-chuję*) blow up, inflate; **nadmuchiwany** *adj* inflatable; **~ *materac*** air mattress
nadnaturalny *adj* supernatural
nadnercze *n* (*-cza*; *-cza*) adrenal gland
nadobowiązkowy *adj* **1.** *przedmiot*: optional, elective **2.** *zajęcia*: extracurricular **3.** *lektura*: optional
nadopiekuńczy *adj* overprotective
nadpalać ⟨**-lić**⟩ (*-lam*) partially burn
nadpijać ⟨**-pić**⟩ (*-jam*) *wina*: take a sip of
nadpleśniały *adj Br* (slightly) mouldy, *Am* (slightly) moldy
nadpłacać ⟨**-cić**⟩ (*-cam*) pay in excess, overpay; **nadpłata** *f* (*-ty*; *-ty*) excess payment, overpayment
nadpływać ⟨**-łynąć**⟩ (*-wam*) **1.** (*zbliżać się*) approach **2.** (*o kaczkach*) swim over
nadpobudliwy *adj* **1.** (*ruchowo*) hyperactive **2.** (*nadwrażliwy*) hypersensitive
nadprodukcja *f* (*-ji*; *no pl*) overproduction, overrun
nadprogramowy *adj* **1.** extra **2.** *zajęcia*: extracurricular
nadprzyrodzony *adj* supernatural
nadpsuty *adj owoce*: rotting, (a bit) off
nadrabiać ⟨**-robić**⟩ (*-biam*) *stracony czas*: make up for; ***~ zaległości w pracy*** clear a backlog; ***~ zaległości w nauce*** (***szkolnej***) catch up with one's (school) work; ***~ braki w umiejętnościach*** compensate for one's poor skills, compensate for one's lack of skills; ***~ drogi*** take a roundabout route; ***~ miną*** put on a brave face
nadruk *m* (*-ku*; *-ki*) print
nadrywać ⟨**-derwać**⟩ (*-wam*) **1.** tear slightly **2.** *ścięgno*: rupture; ***nadrywać się*** tear slightly
nadrzewny *adj zwierzęta*: tree-dwelling
nadrzędny *adj* **1.** *zasada*: overriding **2.** *władza*: superior **3.** *zdanie*: main
nadskakiwać *v/im* (*-skakuję*) fawn (*D* over)
nadspodziewany *adj* unexpected
nadstawiać ⟨**-wić**⟩ (*-wiam*): ***~ karku*** *fig* risk one's neck; ***~ uszu*** prick (up) one's ears; ***~ policzek do pocałowania*** turn one's cheek to be kissed
nadstawka *f* (*-ki*; *-ki*) (*mebel*) top section
nadsyłać ⟨**-desłać**⟩ (*-łam*) send
nadszarpnąć *v/p* (*-nę*) **1.** *oszczędności*: deplete, eat into **2.** *reputację*: tarnish, damage **3.** *nerwy*: tax **4.** *zdrowie*: damage, undermine; **nadszarpnięt|y** *adj nerwy*: frayed; ***ktoś ma ~e zdrowie*** s.o.'s health has deteriorated
nadtłuczony *adj* chipped
nadto *adv lit* (*ponadto*) furthermore; ***aż ~*** more than enough
nadużyci|e *n* (*-cia*; *-cia*) **1.** abuse; ***~a prawa*** abuse of law; ***~e podatkowe*** tax evasion **2.** (*przestępstwo finansowe*) misappropriation (of funds)
nadużywać ⟨**-żyć**⟩ (*-wam*) abuse
nadwag|a *f* (*-gi*; *no pl*) excess weight; ***mieć ~ę*** be overweight
nadwątlić *v/p* (*-lę*) *zdrowie*: undermine
nadwerężać ⟨**-żyć**⟩ (*-żam*) strain; ***~ swoje siły*** overtax one's strength; ***nadwerężać się*** overtax oneself

N

nadwodny *adj* **1.** *roślinność*: waterside **2.** *część*: above-water
nadworny *adj* court
nadwozie *n* (*-zia*; *-zia*) body(work)
nadwrażliwość *n* (*-ści*; *no pl*) hypersensitivity; **nadwrażliwy** *adj* hypersensitive
nadwyżka *f* (*-ki*; *-ki*) surplus
nadymać ⟨**-dąć**⟩ (*-mam*): **~ policzki** puff (out) one's cheeks; **nadymać się 1.** (*o żaglu*) swell (out) **2.** (*dąsać się*) go into a sulk
nadymić *v/p*: **~ w pokoju** fill a room with smoke
nadziać *v/p* → **nadziewać**; **nadziać się 1.** impale oneself (**na** *A* on) **2.** (*na osobę*) *fig* bump (**na** *A* into)
nadziany *adj infml* loaded
nadzie|ja *f* (*-dziei*; *-je*) hope; **mieć ~ję** hope; **pokładać ~je w** *L* pin one's hopes on; **pełen ~i** hopeful; **z ~ją, że** in the hope that; **przy ~i** *dated* with child
nadziemny *adj* **1.** *pędy*, *parking*: above-ground **2.** *linia wysokiego napięcia*: overhead **3.** *kolej*: elevated, overhead
nadzienie *n* (*-nia*; *-nia*) **1.** (*ciasta*, *czekoladki*) filling **2.** (*potrawy*, *mięsa*) stuffing
nadziewać ⟨**-dziać**⟩ (*-wam*) **1.** impale (**na** *A* on), skewer (**na** *A* on) **2.** *potrawę*, *mięso*: stuff; **nadziewany** *adj* **1.** *ciasto*, *czekoladki*: filled, with a filling **2.** *warzywa*, *mięso*: stuffed
nadzorca *m* (*-cy*; *-cy*), **-czyni** *f* (*-ni*; *-nie*) supervisor; **~ niewolników** slave overseer; **nadzorcz|y** *adj* supervisory; **rada ~a** supervisory board; **nadzorować** *v/im* (*-ruję*) supervise, oversee
nadzór *m* (*-zoru*; *no pl*) supervision, control
nadzwyczaj *adv* unusually, extremely; **nadzwyczajny** *adj* **1.** remarkable, extraordinary **2.** *dodatek*, *posiedzenie*: special; **profesor ~** *Br* reader, *Am* associate professor
nadżerka *f* (*-ki*; *-ki*) erosion
naelektryzować *v/p* → **elektryzować**
nafaszerować *v/p* → **faszerować**
nafta *f* (*-ty*; *no pl*) *Br* paraffin (oil), *Am* kerosene
naftalina *f* (*-ny*; *no pl*) naphthalene; **~ w kulkach** mothballs *pl*
naftow|y *adj* **1.** oil; **ropa ~a** petroleum, (crude) oil **2.** *produkty*: petroleum **3.** *lampa*: oil, *Am* kerosene
nagabywać ⟨**-bnąć**⟩ (*-buję*) **1.** (*zaczepiać*) accost **2.** (*prosić ciągle*) pester (**o** *A* about)
nagadać *v/p* (*-dam*) *infml* **1.** (*naopowiadać*) tell; **~ mnóstwo bzdur** come up with a lot of nonsense **2.** (*obmówić*) backbite (**na** *A*); **nagadać się** talk a lot
nagan|a *f* (*-ny*; *-ny*) reprimand; **otrzymać ~ę** be reprimanded; **udzielić ~y** reprimand
naganiać ⟨**-gonić**⟩ (*-niam*) drive
naganny *adj* reprehensible
nagarniać ⟨**-nąć**⟩ (*-niam*) **1.** gather **2.** (*na kupę*) heap, gather into a pile
nagi *adj* **1.** *osoba*: naked **2.** *ściana*, *skała*: bare **3.** *model*: nude
nagiąć *v/p* → **naginać**
nagietek *m* (*-tka*; *-tki*) marigold
nagimnastykować się *v/p* (*-kuję*) *infml* bend over backwards; struggle (**z** *I* with)
naginać ⟨**-giąć**⟩ (*-nam*) bend (**do** *G* to); **naginać się** (*do czyjejś woli*) bend (**do** *G* to)
naglący *adj* urgent, pressing
nagle *adv* suddenly
nagli|ć: **czas ~** time is short
nagłaśniać ⟨**-łośnić**⟩ (*-niam*) **1.** (*w mediach*) publicize **2.** *pomieszczenie*: provide sound for; **nagłośnienie** *n* (*-nia*; *no pl*) (*dźwięk*) sound; **nagłośnieniow|y** *adj*: **aparatura ~a** sound system, PA system
nagłowić się *v/p* (*-wię*) rack one's brains
nagłów|ek *m* (*-wka*; *-wki*) **1.** heading; **~ki gazet** (newspaper) headlines **2.** *listu*: letterhead
nagły *adj* **1.** sudden, unexpected **2.** *wydatek*: unforeseen **3.** (*pilny*) urgent; **w ~ch wypadkach** in urgent cases, in (case of) emergency
nagminny *adj* common, widespread
nagniotek *m* (*-tka*; *-tki*) corn
nag|o *adv* **1.** (*bez ubrania*) naked; **rozebrać się do ~a** strip naked **2.** (*pusto*) bare
nagolennik *m* (*-ka*; *-ki*) **1.** SPORT shin guard **2.** HIST greave
nagonić *v/p* → **naganiać**

nagonka *f* (*-ki*; *-ki*) *fig* witch-hunt, smear campaign
nagość *f* (*-ści*; *no pl*) **1.** nudity, nakedness **2.** *ścian*: bareness
nagotować *v/p* (*-tuję*) cook (a lot of)
nagrać *v/p* → ***nagrywać***
nagradzać ⟨**-rodzić**⟩ (*-dzam*) **1.** (*dać nagrodę*) reward **2.** *medalem, premią*: award (*I* with)
nagranie *n* (*-nia*; *-nia*) recording
nagrobek *m* (*-bka*; *-bki*) gravestone; **nagrobkow|y** *adj* tomb; ***płyta ~a*** gravestone
nagrod|a *f* (*-dy*; *-dy*) **1.** (*w zawodach, w konkursie*) prize; ***~a pocieszenia*** consolation prize **2.** (*za twórczość, naukę*) award, prize; ***≈a Nobla*** the Nobel Prize **3.** (*w podzięce*) reward; ***w ~ę za*** *A* (as a reward) for
nagrodzić *v/p* → ***nagradzać***
nagrodzony *adj film, książka*: prize-winning
nagromadzenie *n* (*-nia*; *no pl*) accumulation; **nagromadzić** *v/p* → ***gromadzić***
nagrywać ⟨**-rać**⟩ (*-wam*) **1.** record **2.** (*na taśmę*) tape **3.** (*na dysk*) copy (**na** *A* to); ***nagrywać się*** **1.** (*nagrywać swój głos*) record oneself; ***~ się na sekretarkę*** leave a message **2.** (*zostać nagranym*) get recorded
nagryzmolić *v/p* (*-lę*) scribble
nagrzewać ⟨**-rzać**⟩ (*-wam*) heat (up); ***nagrzewać się*** heat up
nagus *m* (*-sa*; *-sy*) naked person; **nagusek** *m* (*-ska*; *-ski*) naked baby; **nagusieńki** *adj dim* completely naked
naigrawać się *v/im* (*-wam*) mock (**z** *I*)
naiwniak *m* (*-ka*; *-niacy*/*-ki*), **-niaczka** *f* (*-ki*; *-ki*) *infml* sucker
naiwność *f* (*-ści*; *no pl*) naivety; **naiwny** *adj* naive
najadać się ⟨**-jeść**⟩ (*-dam*) eat one's fill (*G* of), have enough (*G* of); → ***najeść się***
najazd *m* (*-du*; *-dy*) invasion
nająć *v/p* → ***najmować***
najbardziej *adv superl* → **bardzo** most; ***~ szalony*** craziest; ***jak ~!*** of course!
najbliżej *adv superl* → ***blisko*** (the) closest, (the) nearest; ***~ położony*** (the) nearest; ***jak ~*** as close as possible; **najbliższy** *adj superl* → ***bliski*** (the) closest, (the) nearest; ***w ~ piątek*** this Friday

najczęściej *adv superl* → **często** most often
najdalej *adv superl* → ***daleko*** **1.** (the) farthest **2.** (*najpóźniej*) at the latest; **najdalszy** *adj superl* → ***daleki*** **1.** (the) farthest **2.** *termin*: (the) latest
najdłuższy *adj superl* → ***długi*** (the) longest
najechać *v/p* → ***najeżdżać***
najedzony *adj* full (up)
naj|em *m* (*-jmu*; *no pl*) lease, rental; ***brać w ~em*** lease, rent; ***umowa ~mu*** lease agreement
najemca *m* (*-cy*; *-cy*) **1.** lessee **2.** (*lokalu*) tenant
najemnik *m* (*-ka*; *-nicy*) (*żołnierz*) mercenary
najemn|y *adj robotnik, praca*: hired; ***~y żołnierz*** mercenary; ***~y morderca*** hit man; ***wojsko ~e*** mercenary troops
najeść się *v/p* (*-jem*): ***~ wstydu*** be deeply ashamed; ***~ strachu*** be really frightened; → ***najadać się***
najeździć się *v/p* (*-jeżdżę*) **1.** (*podróżować*) travel a lot; ***~ po świecie*** travel a lot (around the world) **2.** (*zmęczyć się*) ***~ samochodem*** (***rowerem***) be tired of driving (riding)
najeźdźca *m* (*-cy*; *-cy*) invader
najeżać ⟨**-żyć**⟩ (*-żam*): ***~ sierść*** bristle; ***najeżać się*** bristle
najeżdżać ⟨**-jechać**⟩ (*-dżam*) **1.** (*na kraj*) invade (**na** *A*) **2.** (*na drzewo*) run (**na** *A* into) **3.** (*na krawężnik*) run (**na** *A* into/over) **4.** *kursorem*: place, move (**na** *A* over) **5.** (*krytykować*) *infml* knock (**na** *A*)
najeżony *adj* **1.** *sierść*: bristled **2.** *człowiek*: bristling; ***~ kolcami*** with spikes; ***~ błędami*** riddled with errors
najeżyć *v/p* → ***najeżać***
najęty *adj*: ***kłamać jak ~*** lie through one's teeth
najgorsze *n* (*-szego*; *no pl*) (the) worst; ***~ jest to, że*** the worst (thing) is that
najgorszy *adj superl* → **zły** (the) worst; ***w ~m razie*** at worst; **najgorzej** *adv superl* → ***źle*** (the) worst; ***nie ~*** not (too) bad
najlepiej *adv superl* → ***dobrze*** (the) best; ***zrób to ~, jak potrafisz*** do it as best you can; ***~ już idź*** it's best if you go now; ***rośliny ~ podlewać rano*** watering is best done in the morning

N

najlepsz|y *adj superl* → **dobry** (the) best; ***w ~ym razie*** at best; ***zabawa trwała w ~e*** the party was in full swing; ***wszystkiego ~ego!*** **a)** best wishes!, all the best! **b)** (*z okazji urodzin*) Happy Birthday! **c)** (*z okazji świąt Bożego Narodzenia*) Merry Christmas!

najmniej *adv superl* → **mało** **1.** (*z niepoliczalnymi*) (the) least; ***jak ~*** as little as possible **2.** (*z policzalnymi*) (the) fewest; ***co ~*** at least; **najmniejszy** *adj superl* → **mały** **1.** (the) smallest **2.** *ilość, doświadczenie*: (the) least

najmocniej *adv superl* → **mocno** **1.** *uderzyć*: hardest **2.** *świecić*: brightest **3.** *zaciskać*: tightest; ***zaciśnij pięść ~, jak potrafisz*** clench your fist as tight as you can; ***~ przepraszam*** I'm terribly sorry

najmować ⟨**-jąć**⟩ (*-muję*) **1.** (*zatrudniać*) hire **2.** (*wynajmować*) rent

najniżej *adv superl* → **nisko** (the) lowest; **najniższy** *adj superl* → **niski** **1.** (the) lowest **2.** *osoba, uczeń*: (the) shortest

najnowszy *adj superl* → **nowy** **1.** (the) newest **2.** *model, wydanie, płyta, wiadomości*: (the) latest, (the) most recent

najpierw *adv* first

najpóźniej *adv superl* → **późno** **1.** (*jako ostatni*) last **2.** (*nie później niż*) at the latest; ***~ 15 maja*** no(t) later than 15 May

najprawdopodobniej *adv superl* → **prawdopodobnie** most probably; **najprędzej** *adv superl* → **prędko** quickest; ***jak ~*** as quickly as possible

najspokojniej *adv superl* → **spokojnie**: ***~ w świecie*** with perfect composure, (as) cool as a cucumber

najstarszy *adj superl* → **stary** (the) oldest, (the) eldest

najście *n* (*-cia*; *-cia*) uninvited visit, unsolicited visit; ***przepraszam za ~*** I'm sorry to intrude

najść *v/p* → **nachodzić**

najświeższy *adj superl* → **świeży** **1.** (the) freshest **2.** *wiadomości*: (the) latest

najważniejszy *adj superl* → **ważny** (the) most important; **najwcześniej** *adv superl* → **wcześnie** earliest; ***przyjdź jak ~*** come as early as possible; **najwięcej** *adv superl* → **dużo** the most; ***przeczytaj jak ~*** read as much as possible; **największy** *adj superl* → **duży** **1.** (the) biggest, (the) largest **2.** *pisarz, odkrycie*: (the) greatest

najwidoczniej *particle* apparently

najwyraźniej *adv superl* → **wyraźnie** clearly

najwyżej *adv superl* → **wysoko** **1.** (the) highest **2.** (*nie więcej niż*) at the most; ***ona ma co ~ 20 lat*** she can't be older than 20 **3.** (*tylko*) only; **najwyższ|y** *adj superl* → **wysoki** **1.** (the) highest; ***~y czas coś zrobić***, ***~a pora coś zrobić*** it's high time to do s.th.; ***stopień ~y*** (*przymiotnika*) the superlative; ***sprawa ~ej wagi*** matter of utmost importance; ***Sąd 2y*** the Supreme Court, High Court **2.** *osoba, budynek*: (the) tallest **3.** *piętro*: top

najzupełniej *adv* absolutely, *Br* quite

nakarmić *v/p* → **karmić**

nakaz *m* (*-zu*; *-zy*) **1.** (*polecenie*) order **2.** ***~ sądowy*** JUR writ; ***~ aresztowania*** arrest warrant; ***~ rewizji*** search warrant; ***~ eksmisji*** eviction order **3.** *wewnętrzny*: imperative

nakaz|ywać ⟨**-zać**⟩ (*-zuję*) order; ***~ać komuś coś zrobić*** order s.o. to do s.th.; ***sytuacja ~uje ostrożność*** the situation requires caution

naklejać ⟨**-leić**⟩ (*-jam*) **1.** stick (***na*** *A* on) **2.** *znaczek, naklejkę*: put, stick; **naklejka** *f* (*-ki*; *-ki*) **1.** (*nalepka*) sticker **2.** (*etykieta*) label

nakład *m* (*-du*; *-dy*) **1.** (*książki*) print run; ***~ książki został wyczerpany*** the book is out of print; ***ukazać się ~em*** *G* be published by; ***ukazać się ~em własnym*** be self-published **2.** (*gazety*): circulation **3.** ***~y*** FIN expenditure; ***~y inwestycyjne*** capital expenditure **4.** ***~ pracy*** the amount of work involved, workload

nakładać ⟨**nałożyć**⟩ (*-dam*) **1.** put (***na*** *A* on) **2.** *sweter, czapkę*: put on **3.** *cło, obowiązek*: impose (***na*** *A* on) **4.** *farbę*: apply (***na*** *A* to); ***nakładać się*** (*o terminach, falach*) overlap

nakładka *f* (*-ki*; *-ki*) **1.** (*osłona*) cover; ***~ na obiektyw*** lens hood **3.** INF shell, front end

N

nakłamać *v/p* (*-mię*) lie (*D* to), tell a lot of lies (*D* to)

nakłaniać ⟨**-łonić**⟩ (*-niam*) **1.** (*próbować przekonywać*) urge; **~ kogoś do zrobienia czegoś** urge s.o. to do s.th. **2.** (*przekonać*) persuade; **nakłoniła go, by został** she persuaded him to stay

nakłaść *v/p* (*-ładę*) put (a lot of)

nakłonić *v/p* → **nakłaniać**

nakłucie *n* (*-cia*; *-cia*) **1.** prick **2.** (*ślad*) puncture, prick mark **3.** MED puncture

nakłuwać ⟨**-łuć**⟩ (*-wam*) prick, puncture; **~ coś igłą** prick s.th. with a needle

nakolannik *m* (*-ka*; *-ki*) knee guard, knee pad

nakopcić *v/p* (*-cę*): **~ w pokoju** fill a room with smoke

nakrapiany *adj* **1.** spotted **2.** *jaja*: speckled

nakraść *v/p* (*-radnę*) steal (a lot of)

nakremować *v/p* → **kremować**[2]

nakreśl|ać ⟨**-lić**⟩ (*-lam*) **1.** (*rysować*) draw, sketch; **autor ~ił obraz** *G fig* the author painted the picture of **2.** (*przedstawiać w zarysie*) outline

nakręcać ⟨**-cić**⟩ (*-cam*) **1.** *zegarek*: wind (up) **2.** *film*: shoot

nakrętka *f* (*-ki*; *-ki*) **1.** TECH nut; **~ motylkowa** wing cap **2.** (*na butelkę*) (screw) top **3.** (*na tubkę*) (screw) cap

nakroić *v/p* (*-roję*) slice, cut

nakruszyć *v/p* (*-szę*) leave breadcrumbs

nakryci|e *n* (*-cia*; *-cia*) **1.** cover; **~e głowy** headdress, headgear; **bez ~a głowy** bareheaded **2.** (*przy stole*) place setting

nakrywać ⟨**-ryć**⟩ (*-wam*) **1.** cover; **~ stół**, **~ do stołu** set the table, *Br* lay the table **2.** (*przyłapywać*) **~ kogoś na kradzieży** catch s.o. stealing; **nakrywać się** cover oneself (*I* with)

nakrzyczeć *v/p* → **krzyczeć**

nakupić *v/p* (*-pię*) buy (a lot of)

nakurzyć *v/p* (*-rzę*) (*wzbić kurz*) raise (a lot of) dust

nalać *v/p* → **nalewać**

nalany *adj twarz*: bloated

naleciałość *f* (*-ci*; *-ci*) **1.** (foreign) influence **2.** (*zapożyczenie*) borrowing

naleci|eć *v/p* (*-cę*) **1. do pokoju ~ało komarów** a lot of mosquitoes got into the room **2.** (*o wodzie z kranu*) run (**do** *G* into)

nalega|ć *v/im* (*-gam*) insist (**na** *A* on); **~ła, żeby przyszedł** she insisted that he come

nalepiać ⟨**-pić**⟩ (*-piam*) *znaczek*, *etykietę*: put, stick (**na** *A* on); **nalepka** *f* (*-ki*; *-ki*) sticker; **~ z ceną** price label

naleśnik *m* (*-ka*; *-ki*) pancake, crepe

nalewać ⟨**-lać**⟩ (*-wam*) pour (**do** *G* into); **nalał do wanny wody** he filled the bath with water

nalewka *f* (*-ki*; *-ki*) **1.** liqueur **2.** MED tincture

należ|eć *v/im* (*-żę*) **1.** belong (**do** *G* to); **firma ~y do największych w Europie** the company is one of the largest in Europe; **gruźlica ~y do chorób zakaźnych** tuberculosis is a contagious disease; **~eć do czyichś kompetencji** be within s.o.'s authority **2.** (*być członkiem*) belong (**do** *G* to), be a member (**do** *G* of) **3.** (*powinność*) **~y coś zrobić** s.th. should be done, one should do s.th.: **~y podkreślić, że** it should be stressed that; **co ~y wiedzieć o** *L* what you should know about; **decyzja ~y do ciebie** the decision is yours; **jak ~y** as it should be; **należeć się 1. ~y mu się emerytura** he is eligible for a pension, he is entitled to a pension; **~y jej się uznanie** (**szacunek**) she deserves credit (respect); **~y nam się odpoczynek** we deserve a rest **2.** (*o kwocie*) be due (*D* to); **ile się panu** (**pani**) **~y?** how much do I owe you?

należność *f* (*-ści*; *-ści*) **1.** amount due **2.** (*opłata*) charge, fee **3.** (*dług*) debt

należn|y *adj* **1.** *płatność*, *szacunek*: due; **~a kwota** the amount due **2.** *odsetki*: accrued

należycie *adv* properly, appropriately; **należyty** *adj* **1.** proper, appropriate; **w ~m stanie** in good order **2.** *staranność*, *uwaga*: due

naliczać ⟨**-czyć**⟩ (*-czam*) **1.** calculate **2.** *odsetki*: charge

nalot *m* (*-tu*; *-ty*) **1.** (*powietrzny*) air raid; **~ bombowy** bombing raid **2.** (*policyjny*) raid **3.** (*warstwa*) (thin) layer, coating **4.** (*na języku*) coating, fur **5.** (*na metalu*) tarnish; **~ patyny** thin layer of patina; **~ rdzy** (thin) film of rust

naładować *v/p* (*-duję*) **1.** load (**do** *G* into; **na** *A* onto) **2.** *baterię*: charge; ***naładować się*** (*o baterii*) charge; → ***ładować***

naładowany *adj* **1.** *ciężarówka, broń*: loaded **2.** *akumulator*: (fully) charged **3.** (*zatłoczony*) crowded, packed

nałogowiec *m* (*-wca*; *-wcy*) addict

nałogowo *adj* habitually; ***palić ~*** be a heavy smoker; ***pić ~*** be a heavy drinker; ***~ oglądać telewizję*** be a TV addict; **nałogowy** *adj* **1.** habitual; ***~ palacz*** heavy smoker, nicotine addict **2.** *gracz*: compulsive

nałożyć *v/p* → ***nakładać***

nałóg *m* (*-łogu*; *-łogi*) **1.** addiction, habit; ***wpaść w ~*** *G* become addicted to **2.** (*przyzwyczajenie*) habit

nam *pron* us; → ***my***

namacać *v/p* (*-cam*) find, grope (*A* for); **namacalny** *adj* **1.** palpable **2.** *dowody, korzyści*: tangible

namalować *v/p* → ***malować***

namaszczać ⟨***-maścić***⟩ (*-czam*) REL anoint

namaszczenie *n* (*-nia*; *no pl*) **1.** REL anointing; ***ostatnie ~*** the last rites, anointing of the sick **2.** ***z ~m*** *fig* with solemnity

namaścić *v/p* → ***namaszczać***

nam|awiać ⟨***-mówić***⟩ (*-wiam*) **1.** (*próbować przekonać*) urge, encourage; ***~awiał mnie do odejścia*** he tried to talk me into quitting; ***~awiać do przemocy*** instigate violence **2.** (*przekonać*) talk, persuade; ***~ówiłem ją, żeby przyszła*** I persuaded her to come; ***dała się ~ówić na kino*** she agreed to go to the cinema; ***~ówiła mnie na kino*** she talked me into going to the cinema (with her); ***namawiać się*** plot, conspire

namącić *v/p* (*-cę*) stir things up; ***~ komuś w głowie*** confuse s.o.

namęczyć się *v/p* (*-czę*) get tired; ***namęczyłem się, żeby go przekonać*** I had a hard job convincing him

nami *pron* us: ***z ~*** with us; ***nad ~*** **a)** (*nad głowami*) over our heads **b)** (*piętro wyżej*) upstairs (from us); → ***my***

namiar *m* (*-ru*; *-ry*) **1.** bearing(s), position **2.** ***~y*** *infml* details, (s.o.'s) phone number and address

namiastka *f* (*-ki*; *-ki*) (poor) substitute

namierzać ⟨***-rzyć***⟩ (*-rzam*) locate, take bearings of

namiestnik *m* (*-ka*; *-nicy*) HIST governor

namieszać *v/p* → ***mieszać***

namięk|ać ⟨***-knąć***⟩ (*-kam*): ***zalać fasolę wodą, żeby ~ła*** soak beans in water to make them soft

namiętność *f* (*-ści*; *-ści*) passion; ***namiętny*** *adj* **1.** passionate **2.** *czytelnik, kolekcjoner*: avid, passionate

namiot *m* (*-tu*; *-ty*) tent; ***jechać pod ~*** go camping

namoczyć *v/p* (*-czę*) soak; ***namoczyć się*** soak

namokły *adj* wet, soaked; **namoknąć** *v/p* (*-nę*) (*o butach*) get soaked

namolny *adj infml* importunate, pushy

namow|a *f* (*-wy*; *-wy*): ***ulec czyimś ~om*** yield to s.o.'s persuasion; ***za jego ~ą*** at his suggestion

namówić *v/p* → ***namawiać***

namydlać ⟨***-lić***⟩ (*-lam*) soap

namy|sł *m* (*-łu*; *-ły*) thought, reflection; ***po ~śle*** on reflection; ***po ~śle zdecydowała się zostać*** *Br* on second thoughts she decided to stay, *Am* on second thought she decided to stay; ***zrobić coś bez ~słu*** do s.th. without thinking, do s.th. on the spur of the moment; ***potrzebuję czasu do ~słu*** I need time to think it over

namyślać się ⟨***-lić***⟩ (*-lam*) **1.** think (***nad*** *I* about); ***muszę się namyślić*** I must think it over **2.** (*zdecydować się*) make up one's mind

nanieść *v/p* (*-niosę*) **1.** bring (a lot of) **2.** *błota*: carry in (a lot of); → ***nanosić***

nanizać *v/p* (*-nizę*) thread (**na** *A* onto)

nanosić ⟨***-nieść***⟩ (*-szę*) **1.** *poprawki*: make **2.** (*zaznaczać*) mark

naobiecywać *v/p* (*-cuję*) promise a lot

naocznie *adv* with one's eyes; ***przekonać się o czymś ~*** see s.th. for oneself; **naoczny** *adj* *dowód*: clear; ***~ świadek*** eyewitness

naokoło **I** *prep* (*G*) (a)round **II** *adv* **1.** (a)round **2.** (*ze wszystkich stron, na wszystkie strony*) all around

naoliwiać ⟨***-wić***⟩ (*-wiam*) oil

naopowiada|ć *v/p* (*-dam*) tell a lot of; ***co ci znów ~ł?*** what's he been telling you now?

N

napad *m* (*-du*; *-dy*) **1.** assault, attack; **~ *na bank*** bank robbery, bank raid; **~ *rabunkowy*** robbery; **~ *z bronią w ręku*** armed robbery, hold-up **2.** MED fit, attack; **~ *kaszlu*** coughing fit; **~ *padaczki*** epileptic seizure **3.** *złości*: outburst; ***dostać ~u złości*** throw a tantrum **4.** *śmiechu*: burst **5.** SPORT attack

napad|ać[1]⟨**-paść**⟩ (*-dam*) **1.** attack (***na*** *A*); ***~li na bank*** they robbed a bank; ***został ~nięty na ulicy*** he was mugged in the street; ***co cię ~ło?*** *infml* what's come over you? **2.** *kraj*: invade, attack (***na*** *A*)

napad|ać[2] *v/p*: ***~ało dużo śniegu*** there was a heavy snowfall

napakować *v/p* (*-kuję*) pack (a lot of); **napakowany** *adj* **1.** packed **2.** (*umięśniony*) *infml* muscle-bound, beefy

napalić *v/p* (*-lę*) **1.** (*w piecu*) start a fire (***w*** *L* in) **2.** (*w pokoju*) heat (***w*** *L*); ***napalić się*** *pot*: **~ *się na*** *A* be set for; ***napaliła się na niego*** she has the hots for him *pot*

napalm *m* (*-mu*; *no pl*) napalm

napalony *adj infml* **1.** set (***na*** *A* on) **2.** (*seksualnie*) horny; ***jest na nią ~*** he has the hots for her *infml*

napar *m* (*-ru*; *-ry*) infusion

naparstek *m* (*-tka*; *-tki*) thimble

naparzon|y *adj*: ***świeżo ~a kawa*** freshly brewed coffee

N

napaskudzić *v/p* (*-dzę*) *infml* make a mess

napastliwy *adj* **1.** *krytyka*: virulent **2.** *ton*, *osobnik*: aggressive

napastnik *m* (*-ka*; *-nicy*) **1.** assailant **2.** SPORT striker, forward

napastować *v/im* (*-tuję*) **1.** (*seksualnie*) abuse, harass **2.** (*dręczyć*) pester **3.** (*zaczepiać*) accost

napaść[1] *v/p* → ***napadać***[1]

napaść[2] *v/p* (*-pasę*) *krowy, gęsi*: feed

napaść[3] *f* (*-ści*; *-ści*) **1.** attack **2.** (*inwazja*) aggression

napatoczyć się *v/p* (*-czę*) *infml* turn up (unexpectedly)

napatrzeć się *v/p*: ***nie mógł się na nią ~*** he couldn't take his eyes off her; ***napatrzyłem się już na takie filmy*** I've seen more than enough of such films

napawać *v/im* (*-wam*) *lit dumą, radością*: fill (*I* with); ***napawać się***: **~ *widokiem*** *G* feast one's eyes on; **~ *się czyimś cierpieniem*** (***własnym sukcesem***) gloat over s.o.'s suffering (one's success); **~ *się myślą o*** *L* relish the thought of

napchać *v/p* → ***napychać***

napełniać⟨**-nić**⟩ (*-niam*) **1.** fill (*I* with) **2.** *magazynek*: load

napęd *m* (*-du*; *-dy*) **1.** drive; **~ *na cztery koła*** four-wheel drive **2.** *odrzutowy*, *jądrowy*: propulsion; ***z ~em odrzutowym*** jet-propelled; **napędowy** *adj* **1.** *siła*: driving **2.** *wał*: drive; ***olej ~*** diesel (fuel), diesel (oil)

napędzać⟨**-dzić**⟩ (*-dzam*) **1.** *koniunkturę*: give a boost to, fuel **2.** TECH propel, drive **3.** (*o wietrze*) blow in **4.** **~ *komuś stracha*** give s.o. a fright

napędzany *adj*: **~ *energią słoneczną*** solar-powered; **~ *energią jądrową*** nuclear-powered

napiąć *v/p* → ***napinać***

napić się **1.** *wody*, *piwa*: drink; **~ *czegoś zimnego*** have a cold drink; ***czego się napijesz?*** what would you like to drink? **2.** have a drink

napierać⟨**-przeć**⟩ (*-ram*) **1.** push (***na*** *A* at/against) **2.** (*o tłumie*) push (forward) **3.** (*wywierać presję*) press; **~ *na kogoś, żeby coś zrobił*** press s.o. to do s.th. **4.** (*o wojsku*) advance

napięcie *n* (*-cia*; *-cia*) **1.** tension; **~ *rośnie*** FILM the tension builds **2.** PHYS voltage **3.** *mięśniowe*: tone

napięty *adj* **1.** tense **2.** *harmonogram*, *terminy*: tight **3.** *program*: busy

napinać⟨**-piąć**⟩ (*-nam*) **1.** *linę*: tighten **2.** *tkaninę*: stretch **3.** *mięśnie*: tense, flex **4.** *łuk*: draw; ***napinać się*** **1.** (*o linie*) tighten **2.** (*o tkaninie*) stretch **3.** (*wysilać się*) strain

napis *m* (*-su*; *-sy*) **1.** (*informacja*) notice **2.** (*wyryty*) inscription **3.** (*na murze*) graffiti, writing **4.** (*słowa*) words *pl* **5.** **~*y*** FILM **a)** (*początkowe lub końcowe*) credits, titles **b)** (*dialogi*) subtitles

napisać *v/p* → ***pisać***

napiwek *m* (*-wku*; *-wki*) tip, *form* gratuity

napleść *v/p* (*-lotę*) *infml*: **~ *głupot*** say a lot of nonsense; ***kto ci naplótł takich bzdur?*** who told you all that nonsense?

napletek *m* (*-tka*; *-tki*) foreskin
napłynąć *v/p* → **napływać**
napływ *m* (*-wu*; *no pl*) **1.** *uchodźców, kapitału*: inflow, influx **2.** *energii*: surge, onrush **3.** **~ krwi do twarzy** rush of blood to the face **4.** **~ pomocy** outpouring of support
napły|wać ⟨**-łynąć**⟩ (*-wam*) **1.** flow (in) (**do** *G* into), come (**do** *G* into); **jej oczy ~nęły łzami** her eyes filled with tears; **jego twarz ~nęła krwią** his face flushed with blood **2.** (*o tłumie*) flock (in) **3.** (*o listach*) come
napływowy *adj ludność*: immigrant, incoming
napocić się *v/p* (*-cę*) sweat (blood) (**nad** *I* over)
napoczynać ⟨**-cząć**⟩ (*-nam*) **1.** *butelkę*: start (a new) **1.** *bochenek*: cut into
napoleonka *f* (*-ki*; *-ki*) cream slice
napominać ⟨**-mnieć**⟩ (*-nam*) admonish
napomknąć *v/p* → **napomykać**; **napomknienie** *n* (*-nia*; *-nia*) mention
napomnieć *v/p* → **napominać**; **napomnienie** *n* (*-nia*; *-nia*) admonition, reprimand
napomykać ⟨**-mknąć**⟩ (*-kam*) **1.** mention (**o** *L*) **2.** (*robić aluzję*) hint (**o** *L* at)
napotkać *v/p* → **napotykać**
napotny *adj* diaphoretic; **środek ~** diaphoretic
napotykać ⟨**-tkać**⟩ (*-kam*) **1.** *osobę*: meet; **~ czyjeś spojrzenie** meet s.o.'s eyes **2.** *trudności*: run into **3.** *opór*: meet with, face
napowietrzny *adj kolejka*: overhead
napożyczać *v/p* (*-czam*) (*od kogoś*) borrow (a lot of)
nap|ój *m* (*-poju*; *-poje*) drink; **~oje alkoholowe** alcoholic beverages
nap|ór *m* (*-poru*; *no pl*) pressure, push; **ustąpić pod ~orem** *G* yield to; **wycofać się pod ~orem wroga** retreat before the advancing enemy
napracować się *v/p* (*-cuję*) work hard
napraw|a *f* (*-wy*; *-wy*) **1.** repair; **zanieść coś do ~y** take s.th. to be repaired; **samochód jest w ~ie** the car is being repaired, the car is in for repairs **2.** (*poprawa*) improvement; **naprawczy** *adj* repair
naprawdę *particle* really; **tak ~** really, in (actual) fact; **co tak ~ o nich myślisz?** what do you really think about them?
naprawiać ⟨**-wić**⟩ (*-wiam*) **1.** repair, fix **2.** *błąd*: correct, rectify **3.** *wady, szkodę*: make good, remedy **4.** *krzywdy*: right, redress
naprędce *adv* hastily, on an ad-hoc basis; **zebranie zwołane ~** ad-hoc meeting
naprężać ⟨**-żyć**⟩ (*-żam*) **1.** *mięśnie*: tense, flex **2.** *linę*: tighten **3.** *cięciwę*: draw; **naprężać się** **1.** (*o mięśniach*) tense **2.** (*o linie*) tighten
naprężenie *n* (*-nia*; *-nia*) PHYS stress; **naprężony** *adj* **1.** *struna, lina*: taut **2.** *mięśnie*: tense(d)
napromieniować *v/p* → **napromieniowywać**
napromieniowanie *n* (*-nia*; *no pl*) **1.** exposure to radiation **2.** *żywności*: irradiation **3.** MED radiation treatment; **napromieniowan|y** *adj teren*: contaminated (with radiation); **mieszkańcy zostali ~i** local residents were exposed to radiation
napromieniowywać ⟨**-niować**⟩ (*-niowuję*) **1.** expose to radiation **2.** *żywność*: irradiate
naprostowywać ⟨**-tować**⟩ (*-towuję*) straighten out
naprowadzać ⟨**-dzić**⟩ (*-dzam*) **1.** guide (**na** *A* to) **2.** (*dać wskazówkę*) give a clue; **~ kogoś na właściwy trop** put s.o. on the right track; **~ rozmowę na temat** *G* bring the conversation around to
naprzeciw **I** *prep* (*G*) opposite, across from **II** *adv* **1.** opposite **2.** *mieszkać*: across the street; **wyjść komuś ~** go (out) to meet s.o.; **wychodząc ~ czyimś oczekiwaniom** in an effort to meet s.o.'s expectations; **naprzeciwk|o** **I** *prep* (*G*) opposite, across from **II** *adv* **1.** opposite; **nie mieć nic ~o** *D* have nothing against; **nadjeżdżać z ~a** approach from the opposite direction **2.** *mieszkać*: across the street
naprzeć *v/p* → **napierać**
naprzód *adv* **1.** forward; **iść ~** go ahead; **posuwać się ~** **a)** advance **b)** (*o pracy*) move on, progress; **~ marsz!** forward march! **2.** (*wcześniej*) ahead, in advance

N

naprzykrzać się *v/im* (*-rzam*) keep pestering
naprzynosić *v/p* (*-szę*) bring (a lot of);
naprzywozić *v/p* (*-wożę*) bring (a lot of)
napsoci|ć *v/p* (*-cę*) get up to mischief; ***co znowu ~łeś?*** what have you been up to this time?
napuchnąć *v/p* (*-nę*) swell (up); **napuchnięty** *adj* swollen
napuszczać ⟨**-puścić**⟩ (*-czam*) **1.** *wodę*: run; ***napuścić wody do wanny*** run a bath **2.** *powietrza*: let in; ***napuścił do pokoju świeżego powietrza*** he let some fresh air into the room **3.** (*podburzać*) set (**na** *A* against)
napuszony *adj* **1.** *osoba*: puffed up, pompous **2.** *styl*: bombastic, pompous; **napuszyć się** *v/p* (*-szę*) **1.** (*o ptaku*) fluff its feathers **2.** *fig* puff up
napuścić *v/p* → ***napuszczać***
napychać ⟨**-pchać**⟩ (*-cham*) stuff (*I* with; **do** *G* into); ***napychać się*** (*najadać się*) stuff oneself with food
narada *f* (*-dy*; *-dy*) meeting, council; ***~ wojenna*** council of war
naradzać się ⟨**-dzić**⟩ (*-dzam*) **1.** confer, consult (**z** *I* with) **2.** discuss (**nad** *I*), consult (**nad** *I* about)
naramiennik *m* (*-ka*; *-ki*) **1.** shoulder strap **2.** SPORT shoulder pad
narastać ⟨**-rosnąć**⟩ (*-tam*) **1.** (*wzrastać*) increase **2.** (*wyrastać*) grow **3.** (*o osadzie*) build up **4.** (*o konfliktach*, *gniewie*) get worse, grow; **narastający** *adj* **1.** (*wzrastający*) increasing **2.** (*wyrastający*) growing **3.** *konflikty*: increasing, growing
naraz *adv* **1.** (*jednocześnie*) at once, at the same time **2.** (*nagle*) all of a sudden
narażać ⟨**-razić**⟩ (*-żam*): ***~ kogoś na niebezpieczeństwo*** endanger s.o., jeopardize s.o.; ***~ życie*** (***swoją reputację***) risk one's life (reputation); ***~ kogoś na śmieszność*** expose s.o. to ridicule; ***~ kogoś na straty*** put s.o. at the risk of damage; ***narażać się*** run the risk (**na** *A* of), expose oneself (**na** *A* to); ***~ się na śmieszność*** (***krytykę***) expose oneself to ridicule (criticism); ***~ się na niebezpieczeństwo*** put oneself at risk; ***nie ~ się*** play it safe
narażenie: ***próbował ich ratować z ~m życia*** he risked his life to save them
narciarka *f* (*-ki*; *-ki*) (female) skier; **narciarsk|i** *adj* ski; ***trasa ~a*** (ski) run, piste
narciarstwo *n* (*-wa*; *no pl*) skiing; **narciarz** *m* (*-rza*; *-rze*) skier
narcyz *m* (*-za*; *-zy*) **1.** (*roślina*) narcissus **2.** (*człowiek*) *lit* narcissist; **narcyzm** *m* (*-mu*; *no pl*) narcissism
nareszcie *adv* at last
naręcze *n* (*-cza*; *-cza*) armful
narkoman *m* (*-na*; *-ni*), **~ka** *f* (*-ki*; *-ki*) drug addict
narkomania *f* (*-nii*; *no pl*) drug addiction; **narkotyczny** *adj* **1.** narcotic, drug; ***głód ~*** withdrawal symptoms **2.** *wizje*: drug induced; **narkotyk** *m* (*-ku*; *-ki*) drug
narkotyzować się *v/im* (*-zuję*) take drugs; ***~ heroiną*** be on heroin
narkoz|a *f* (*-zy*; *-zy*) *Br* anaesthesia, *Am* anesthesia; ***pod ~ą*** *Br* under anaesthetic, *Am* under anesthetic
narobi|ć *v/p* (*-bię*) **1.** make (a lot of); ***~ć komuś wstydu*** (really) embarrass s.o.; ***~ć komuś kłopotu*** give s.o. (a lot of) trouble; ***~ć wrzasku*** scream bloody murder; ***coś ty ~ł?*** what on earth have you done? **2.** *szkód*, *zamieszania*: cause **3.** *długów*: run up (big)
narodowość *f* (*-ści*; *no pl*) nationality; **narodowościowy** *adj* ethnic
narodowowyzwoleńcz|y *adj* national liberation; ***walka ~a*** struggle for national liberation
narodowy *adj* national
narodzić się *v/p* (*-dzę*) *lit* **1.** (*powstać*) originate, emerge **2.** (*urodzić się*) be born; **narodziny** *pl* (*-dzin*) birth *sing*
narosnąć *v/p* → ***narastać***
narośl *f* (*-li*; *-le*) growth
narowisty *adj* *koń*: skittish
narożnik *m* (*-ka*; *-ki*) **1.** corner **2.** (*kanapa*) corner sofa; **narożny** *adj* corner
naród *m* (*-rodu*; *-rody*) **1.** nation, people **2.** (*ludzie*) people *pl*
narracja *f* (*-ji*; *-je*) narrative, narration; **narrator** *m* (*-ra*; *-rzy*) narrator
nart|a *f* (*-ty*; *-ty*) ski; ***jeździć na ~ach*** ski; ***~y zjazdowe*** (***biegowe***) downhill (cross-country) skis

N

naruszać ⟨**-szyć**⟩ (*-szam*) **1.** *umowę, przepisy*: breach **2.** *prawa autorskie*: infringe **3.** *prawo*: break **4.** *porządek, spokój*: disturb **5.** *zapasy*: break into **6.** *terytorium*: encroach on
naruszenie *n* (*-nia*; *no pl*) **1.** *umowy, przepisów*: breach **2.** *prawa autorskiego*: infringement **3.** *porządku, spokoju*: disturbance **4.** *zapasów*: breaking into **5.** *terytorium*: encroaching on
naruszyć *v/p* → ***naruszać***
narwać *v/p* (*-wę*) *kwiatów*: pick (a lot of)
narwaniec *m* (*-wańca*; *-wańcy*) *infml* hothead; **narwany** *adj* hot-headed
narybek *m* (*-bku*; *no pl*) **1.** *BIOL* fry **2.** *fig* new blood
narząd *m* (*-du*; *-dy*) organ
narzecze *n* (*-cza*; *-cza*) dialect
narzeczeni *pl* (*-czonych*) (the) engaged couple *sing*; **narzeczona** *f* (*-nej*; *-ne*) fiancée; **narzeczony** *m* (*-nego*; *-czeni*) fiancé
narzekać *v/im* (*-kam*) complain (**na** *A* about)
narzędnik *m* (*-ka*; *-ki*) *GRAM* instrumental (case)
narzędzie *n* (*-dzia*; *-dzia*) **1.** tool **2.** *chirurgiczny*: instrument
narzucać ⟨**-cić**⟩ (*-cam*) **1.** *kapę*: throw (**na** *A* on) **2.** *płaszcz*: put on **3.** *warunki, wolę*: impose **4.** *tempo*: force; ***narzucać się*** *v/im* impose (*D* on)
narzut *m* (*-tu*; *-ty*) *COMM* mark-up
narzuta *f* (*-ty*; *-ty*) bedspread
nas *pron* us; ***nie było ~ w domu*** we weren't home; → ***my***
nasad|a *f* (*-dy*; *-dy*) *liścia, kciuka*: base; ***u ~y nosa*** above (the bridge of) the nose; ***u ~y włosów*** close to the scalp
nasadka *f* (*-ki*; *-ki*) **1.** (*na końcówkę*) attachment **2.** *pióra*: cap **3.** ***~ szerokokątna*** *PHOT* wide-angle converter lens
nasadzać ⟨**-dzić**⟩ (*-dzam*) put (on), fix
nasączać ⟨**-czyć**⟩ (*-czam*) moisten, dampen (*I* with)
nasenn|y *adj*: ***tabletki ~e*** sleeping pills
nasi *poss* → ***nasz***
nasiadówka *f* (*-ki*; *-ki*) (*kąpiel*) sitz bath
nasiąkać ⟨**-knąć**⟩ (*-kam*) **1.** become soaked (*I* with) **2.** *wodą*: soak up **3.** *zapachem*: become saturated with
nasiedzieć się *v/p*: ***dość się już nasiedziałam*** I've been sitting long enough
nasienie *n* (*-nia*; *-siona*) **1.** seed **2.** (*sperma*) semen; **nasieniowód** *m* (*-wodu*; *-wody*) *ANAT* sperm duct; **nasienny** *adj* **1.** *roślina, drzewostan*: seed **2.** *płyn*: seminal
nasilać się ⟨**-lić**⟩ (*-lam*) **1.** (*o hałasie, gorączce*) increase, grow **2.** (*o chorobie, bólu*) worsen
nasilenie *n* (*-nia*; *no pl*) **1.** (*intensywność*) intensity **2.** (*wzrost*) increase (*G* in/of) **3.** (*pogorszenie się*) worsening, deterioration; ***nastąpiło ~ objawów choroby*** the symptoms became more severe
nasilić się *v/p* → ***nasilać się***
nasiona *pl* → ***nasienie 1***
nasionko *n* (*-ka*; *-ka*) (little) seed
nasiono *n* (*-na*; *-na*) → ***nasienie 1***
naskakiwać ⟨**-skoczyć**⟩ (*-skakuję*) jump (**na** *A* on)
naskarżyć *v/p* → ***skarżyć***
naskórek *m* (*-rka*; *no pl*) epidermis
nasłać *v/p* → ***nasyłać***
nasłonecznienie *n* (*-nia*; *no pl*) sunlight; **nasłoneczniony** *adj* *pokój, ogród*: sunny
nasłuch *m* (*-chu*; *-chy*) **1.** monitoring; ***prowadzić ~ czegoś*** monitor s.th. **2.** (*audycji*) listening; **nasłuchać się** *v/p* (*-cham*) hear a lot of
nasłuchiwać *v/im* (*-chuję*) monitor
nasmarować *v/p* → ***smarować***
nastać *v/p* → ***nastawać***
nastanie *n* (*-nia*; *no pl*) **1.** (*początek*) beginning; ***z ~m nocy*** at nightfall **2.** *wiosny*: arrival, coming
nastawać ⟨**-tać**⟩ (*-taję*) **1.** (*o wiośnie, porze*) arrive, come **2.** (*o nocy, ciszy*) fall **3.** (*zagrażać*) ***~ na czyjeś życie*** be out to kill s.o., be after s.o.'s life
nastawiać ⟨**-wić**⟩ (*-wiam*) **1.** (*kierować*) turn; ***~ policzek do pocałunku*** present one's cheek for a kiss; ***~ uszu*** prick up one's ears **2.** *zegarek, złamaną rękę*: set; ***~ budzik*** set the alarm **3.** *ostrość*: adjust **4.** *płytę, zupę*: put on **5.** *kołnierz*: put up **6.** (*negatywnie usposabiać*) set (**przeciw** *D* against); ***nastawiać się*** **1.** (*oczekiwać*) anticipate (**na** *A*); ***~ się na wygraną*** have

N

one's sights on winning **2.** (*przygotowywać się*) get ready (**na** *A* for)
nastawienie *n* (*-nia*; *-nia*) (*postawa*) attitude (**do** *G* to); **nastawiony** *adj*: ***być ~m pozytywnie*** (***krytycznie***) have a positive (critical) attitude (**do** *G* to); ***przychylnie ~*** well-disposed (**wobec** *G* towards); ***~ na zysk*** profit-oriented
nastawnia *f* (*-ni*; *-nie*) (*przy torach*) *Br* signal box, *Am* switch tower
nastąpić *v/p* → ***następować***
następca *m* (*-cy*; *-cy*), **-czyni** *f* (*-ni*; *-nie*) successor; ***~ tronu*** heir to the throne
następnie *adv* next, then; ***a ~*** and then
następn|y I *adj* **1.** (the) next; ***~ego dnia*** the next day, the following day **2.** (*jeszcze jeden*) another **II** *m* (*-nego*; *-ni*), **-na** *f* (*-nej*; *-ne*) next person; ***~y proszę!*** next, please!
następować ⟨**-tąpić**⟩ (*-puję*) **1.** (*nadeptywać*) tread (**na** *A* on); ***~ komuś na nogę*** step on s.o.'s foot **2.** (*w kolejności*) follow (**po** *L*), come after (**po** *L*); ***jak następuje*** as follows **3.** (*mieć miejsce*) occur; ***musiało nastąpić nieporozumienie*** there must have been a misunderstanding
następstw|o *n* (*-wa*; *-wa*) consequence; ***w ~ie*** *G* as a result of; **następująco** *adv* as follows; **następujący** *adj* (the) following

N

nastolatek *m* (*-tka*; *-tki*), **-tka** *f* (*-ki*; *-ki*) teenager
nastrajać ⟨**-roić**⟩ (*-jam*) *fortepian*, *gitarę*: tune
nastraszyć *v/p* (*-szę*) scare, frighten
nastręcza|ć ⟨**-czyć**⟩ (*-czam*) *problemy*, *trudności*: pose, present; ***obsługa programu nie ~ żadnych kłopotów*** the program is very easy to operate
nastroić *v/p* → ***nastrajać***
nastrojowy *adj* atmospheric
nastroszony *adj* **1.** *pióra*: ruffled **2.** *włosy*: bristled
nastroszy|ć *v/p*: ***ptak ~ł pióra*** the bird ruffled its feathers; ***kot ~ł sierść*** the cat bristled; ***nastroszyć się*** **1.** (*o kocie*, *osobie*) bristle **2.** (*o ptaku*) ruffle its feathers
nastr|ój *m* (*-roju*; *-roje*) **1.** (*psychiczny*) mood; ***w dobrym ~oju*** in a good mood **2.** (*atmosfera*) atmosphere, mood
nasturcja *f* (*-ji*; *-je*) nasturtium
nasuwać ⟨**-sunąć**⟩ (*-wam*) **1.** (*naciągać*) ***~ czapkę na oczy*** pull a hat over one's eyes **2.** *wątpliwości*: raise **3.** *podejrzenia*: arouse; ***~ skojarzenia z czymś*** bring s.th. to mind; ***to nasuwa mi na myśl*** *A* it makes me think of; ***nasuwać się*** **1.** (*o myśli*, *pomyśle*) occur (*D* to) **2.** (*o wątpliwościach*, *pytaniu*) arise
nasycać ⟨**-cić**⟩ (*-cam*) **1.** CHEM saturate **2.** *głód*: satiate **3.** *pragnienie*: satisfy **4.** *rynek*: saturate; ***nasycać się*** (*zaspokajać głód*) satiate one's hunger; ***~ się widokiem*** *G* feast one's eyes on
nasycenie *n* (*-nia*; *no pl*) **1.** CHEM saturation **2.** (*sytość*) satiation **3.** *pragnienia*: satisfaction **4.** *rynku*: saturation; **nasycony** *adj* **1.** *roztwór*, *rynek*: saturated **2.** *kolor*: vivid, rich, saturated
nasyłać ⟨**-słać**⟩ (*-łam*) **1.** *morderców*: send (**na** *A* to kill) **2.** *policję*: put (**na** *A* onto)
nasyp *m* (*-pu*; *-py*) (*kolejowy*, *drogowy*) embankment; **nasypywać** ⟨**-pać**⟩ (*-puję*) **1.** pour (**do** *G* into) **2.** (*kawy do filiżanki*) add; ***nasypywać się*** (*do oczu*, *butów*) get into
nasz *poss* (*przed rzeczownikiem*) our; (*bez rzeczownika*) ours; ***jest ~ą znajomą*** she's a friend of ours; ***~ej ery*** after Christ, AD; ***przed ~ą erą*** before Christ, BC
naszkicować *v/p* → **szkicować**
naszpikować *v/p* (*-kuję*) **1.** COOK lard (*I* with) **2.** *lekarstwami*: stuff; **naszpikowany** *adj*: ***~ lekarstwami*** drugged up to the eyeballs
naszyć *v/p* → ***naszywać***
naszyjnik *m* (*-ka*; *-ki*) necklace
naszywać ⟨**-szyć**⟩ (*-wam*) sew on; **naszywka** *f* (*-ki*; *-ki*) (sewn-on) badge
naśladować *v/im* (*-duję*) **1.** imitate, copy **2.** (*udawać*) mimic
naśladowca *m* (*-cy*; *-cy*), **-czyni** *f* (*-ni*; *-nie*) imitator, follower; **naśladowczy** *adj zdolności*: imitative; **naśladownictwo** *n* (*-wa*; *no pl*) imitation
naśmiecić *v/p* (*-cę*) litter
naśmiewać się *v/im* (*-wam*) make fun (**z** *G* of)
naświetlać ⟨**-lić**⟩ (*-lam*) **1.** PHOT expose **2.** (*wyjaśniać*) clarify, shed light on

3. *guza*: treat (with radiation); **naświetlanie** *n* (*-nia*; *-nia*) PHOT exposure

natarcie *n* (*-cia*; *-cia*) attack

natarczywy *adj* 1. *osoba*, *żądania*: insistent, *form* importunate 2. *ból*: persistent

natchnąć *v/p* (*-nę*) inspire (**do** *G* to do s.th.); **natchnienie** *n* (*-nia*; *no pl*) inspiration; **natchniony** *adj* inspired

natężać ⟨**-żyć**⟩ (*-żam*): **~ *wzrok*** (**słuch**) strain one's eyes (ears); **~ *siły*** strain, make an effort; **~ *uwagę*** focus one's attention; ***natężać się*** 1. (*powiększać się*) intensify, increase 2. (*wysilać się*) strain, exert oneself

natężenie *n* (*-nia*; *-nia*) 1. intensity; **~ *ruchu*** (**ulicznego**) traffic density 2. (*dźwięku*) volume 3. FIZ *pola*: strength; **~ *prądu elektrycznego*** amperage

natka *f* (*-ki*; *-ki*) top (leaves); **~ *pietruszki*** parsley leaves

natknąć się *v/p* → ***natykać się***

natłok *m* (*-ku*; *no pl*) mass; **~ *pracy*** heavy workload; ***mieć ~ pracy*** be swamped with work; **~ *informacji*** mass of information, information flood

natłuszczać ⟨**-łuścić**⟩ (*-czam*) grease

natomiast *conj* 1. (*podczas gdy*) whereas, while 2. (*za to*) but

natrafiać ⟨**-fić**⟩ (*-fiam*) 1. find, come across (**na** *A*) 2. (*na problemy*) encounter (**na** *A*)

natręctw|o *n* (*-wa*; *-wa*) 1. obtrusiveness 2. PSYCH obsession; ***nerwica ~*** obsessive-compulsive disorder

natręt *m* (*-ta*; *-ręci*) pushy person, nuisance; ***straszny z niego ~!*** he just won't go away!; **natrętny** *adj* 1. *osoba*: *form* importunate, *infml* pushy 2. *myśli*: obsessive 3. *komar*: annoying, *infml* pesky

natrysk *m* (*-ku*; *-ki*) shower; **natryskow|y** *adj*: ***kabina ~a*** shower cubicle

natrząsać się *v/im* (*-sam*) ridicule (**z** *G*)

natrzeć *v/p* (*-rę*): **~ *komuś uszu*** *fig* give s.o. a dressing-down; → ***nacierać***

natur|a *f* (*-ry*; *-ry*) nature; ***nieśmiała z ~y*** shy by nature; ***to nie leży w jego ~ze*** it is not in his nature; ***malować z ~y*** paint from nature; ***w ~ze*** (*w towarach*) in kind; ***martwa ~a*** ART still life

naturalizacja *f* (*-ji*; *-je*) naturalization

naturalizm *m* (*-mu*; *no pl*) naturalism

naturaln|y *adj* natural; ***przyrost ~y*** population growth; ***~ej wielkości*** life-size(d)

natychmiast *adv* immediately, at once; ***zrób to ~!*** do it now!; **natychmiastowy** *adj* 1. immediate 2. *odpowiedź*: prompt, immediate

natykać się ⟨**-tknąć**⟩ (*-kam*) come across (**na** *A*)

nauczać ⟨**-czyć**⟩ (*-czam*) teach

nauczani|e *n* (*-nia*; *no pl*) teaching, education; ***program ~a*** **a)** (*konkretnego przedmiotu*) syllabus **b)** (*wszystkich przedmiotów*) curriculum

nauczk|a *f* (*-ki*; *-ki*) *fig* lesson; ***dać komuś ~ę*** teach s.o. a lesson

nauczyciel *m* (*-la*; *-le*), **~ka** *f* (*-ki*; *-ki*) teacher; **nauczycielski** *adj* 1. *praktyka*: teaching 2. *kolegium*: teacher's; ***pokój ~*** *Br* staffroom

nauczyć *v/p* → ***uczyć***

nauk|a *f* (*-ki*; *-ki*) 1. (*ścisła*) science 2. (*wiedza*) learning, knowledge 3. (*badania*) research 4. (*dyscyplina*) science; ***~i humanistyczne*** (the) humanities 5. (*uczenie się*) learning; ***garnąć sie do ~i*** be eager to learn; ***przyłożyć się do ~i*** study hard(er); ***dzień wolny od ~i*** a day off school; ***~a języków obcych*** foreign language learning; ***~a jazdy*** driving lessons, learning to drive; ***~a szkolna*** schooling, school education; ***~a zawodu*** professional training 6. (*morał*) lesson, moral

naukowiec *m* (*-wca*; *-wcy*) scientist; **naukowo** *adv* scientifically; ***pracować ~*** do research work, work as a scientist; **naukow|y** *adj* 1. scientific; ***stopień ~y***, ***tytuł ~y*** university degree, academic title; ***pomoce ~e*** study aids 2. (*badawczy*) research; ***pracownik ~y*** researcher

naumyślnie *adv* on purpose, deliberately

nauszniki *pl* (*-ków*) 1. (*część czapki*) earflaps 2. (*osłony na uszy*) ear muffs

nawa *f* (*-wy*; *-wy*): **~ *główna*** nave; **~ *boczna*** aisle

N

nawadniać ⟨**-wodnić**⟩ (*-niam*) irrigate; **nawadniający** *adj kanały*: irrigation; **nawadnianie** *n* (*-nia*; *no pl*) irrigation

nawalać ⟨**-lić**⟩ (*-lam*) **1.** (*o urządzeniu*) break down, *infml* conk out **2.** (*o osobie*) blow it *infml*, screw it up *infml*; ***nawalać się*** (*upijać się*) *infml* get trashed; **nawalony** *adj infml* trashed

nawał *m* (*-łu*; *no pl*): ***~ pracy*** heavy workload; ***mieć ~ pracy*** be swamped with work

nawałnica *f* (*-cy*; *-ce*) **1.** violent storm; ***~ śnieżna*** blizzard **2.** (*ulewa*) rainstorm

nawarstwiać się ⟨**-wić**⟩ (*-wiam*) *fig* accumulate, build up

nawet *particle* even; ***~ gdyby*** even if; ***~ się nie pożegnał*** he didn't even say goodbye; ***~, ~*** *infml* not bad

nawiać *v/p* → ***nawiewać***

nawias *m* (*-su*; *-sy*) bracket; ***w ~ie*** in brackets; ***~ okrągły*** parenthesis, round bracket; ***~ kwadratowy*** square bracket; ***~ klamrowy*** brace; ***wziąć coś w ~*** put s.th. in brackets; ***~em mówiąc*** by the way

nawiązać *v/p* → ***nawiązywać***

nawiązani|e *n* (*-nia*; *-nia*) reference; ***w ~u do*** *G* in reference to

nawiązk|a: ***odpłacić coś z ~ą*** more than repay s.th.; ***koszty zwróciły nam się z ~ą*** we have more than recouped our investment

nawiąz|ywać ⟨**-zać**⟩ (*-zuję*) **1.** *kontakty*, *współpracę*: establish **2.** *rozmowy*, *korespondencję*: enter into **3.** *kontakt*, *znajomość*: make **4.** (*wspominać*, *odsyłać*) refer (**do** *G* to); ***~ując do*** *G* in reference to **5.** (*wzorować się*) draw (**do** *G* on)

nawiedzać ⟨**-dzić**⟩ (*-dzam*) *lit* **1.** (*o katastrofie*) strike **2.** (*o duchach*) haunt; **nawiedzony** *adj* **1.** *dom*: haunted **2.** *feministka*: rabid

nawierzchni|a *f* (*-ni*; *-nie*) (road) surface; ***o twardej ~*** hard-surface

nawietrzn|y *adj*: ***strona ~a*** (the) windward side

nawiew *m* (*-wu*; *-wy*) TECH ventilation

nawiewać ⟨**nawiać**⟩ (*-wam*) **1.** (*o powietrzu*) blow **2.** (*uciekać*) *infml* do a bunk, *Br infml* bunk off (**z** *G* from)

nawieźć *v/p* → ***nawozić***

N

nawigacja *f* (*-ji*; *no pl*) navigation; **nawigacyjny** *adj* navigation; **nawigator** *m* (*-ra*; *-rzy*) navigator; **nawigować** *v/im* (*-guję*) navigate

nawijać ⟨**-winąć**⟩ (*-jam*) **1.** *nitkę*: wind **2.** (*mówić*) *infml* jaw

nawilżacz *m* (*-cza*; *-cze*) (*powietrza*) humidifier; ***żelazko z ~em*** steam iron; **nawilżać** ⟨**-żyć**⟩ (*-żam*) **1.** moisten **2.** *powietrze*: humidify **3.** *skórę*: moisturize; **nawilżający** *adj krem*: moisturizing

nawin|ąć *v/p* → ***nawijać***; ***nawinąć się*** *v/p* (*-nę*) *infml* **1.** turn up; ***~ął im się idealny kandydat*** they came across an ideal candidate; ***chwycił pierwszą rzecz, która ~ęła mu się pod rękę*** he grabbed the first thing that came to hand **2.** (*o okazji*) come one's way, turn up

nawis *m* (*-su*; *-sy*) overhang

nawlekać ⟨**-lec**⟩ (*-kam*) **1.** *igłę*: thread **2.** *paciorki*: string (**na** *A* onto)

nawodnić *v/p* → ***nawadniać***

nawodn|y *adj* **1.** *okręt*: surface **2.** *roślinność*: floating, emergent; ***część ~a statku*** aboveboard, freeboard

nawoływać *v/im* (*-łuję*) **1.** call **2.** *fig* call (**do** *G* for), urge (**do** *G* to do s.th.); ***~ lud do walki o niepodległość*** call on the people to fight for independence; ***~ do nienawiści*** incite hatred; **nawoływanie** *n* (*-nia*; *-nia*) calling

nawozić ⟨**-wieźć**⟩ (*-wożę*) fertilize; **nawożenie** *n* (*-nia*; *no pl*) fertilization; **nawóz** *m* (*-wozu*; *-wozy*) fertilizer; ***~ sztuczny*** chemical fertilizer; ***~ naturalny*** manure, dressing

nawracać ⟨**-wrócić**⟩ (*-cam*) **I** *v/t* REL convert (**na** *A* to) **II** *v/i* (*zawracać*) turn back; ***nawracać się*** be converted, convert (**na** *A* to); **nawrócenie** *n* (*-nia*; *-nia*) conversion; **nawrót** *m* (*-rotu*; *-roty*) **1.** *choroby*: recurrence, relapse **2.** *zimy*: return

nawyk *m* (*-ku*; *-ki*) habit; **nawykać** ⟨**-knąć**⟩ (*-kam*) get used (**do** *G* to), get accustomed (**do** *G* to)

nawymyślać *v/p* (*-lam*) hurl abuse (*D* at), insult

nawzajem *adv* each other, one another; ***dziękuję, ~!*** thanks, same to you!; ***wykluczać się ~*** be mutually exclusive

nazajutrz *adv lit* the following day, the day after
nazbyt *adv* too, overly
nazbierać *v/p* (*-ram*) **1.** gather **2.** *kwiatów*: pick **3.** (*zaoszczędzić*) save (up); ***nazbierać się* 1.** (*o sumie, odpadkach*) accumulate **2.** (*o kurzu*) collect
nazębn|y *adj*: ***kamień ~y*** tartar; ***płytka ~a*** (dental) plaque
naziemny *adj* **1.** *obsługa*: ground **2.** *kolej*: overground
nazistowski *adj* Nazi
naznaczać ⟨**-czyć**⟩ (*-czam*) mark; **naznaczon|y** *adj*: ***twarz ~a cierpieniem*** face marked by suffering, face worn with suffering
nazwa *f* (*-wy*; *-wy*) name
nazwać *v/p* → ***nazywać***
nazwisk|o *n* (*-ka*; *-ka*) surname, last name; ***~o panieńskie*** maiden name; ***miała na ~o Kot*** her (sur)name was Kot; ***pod własnym ~iem*** under one's own name
nazywa|ć ⟨**-zwać**⟩ (*-wam*) name, call; ***~ć rzeczy po imieniu*** *fig* call a spade a spade; ***nazywać się*** be called; ***~m się Robert*** my name's Robert; ***jak to się ~?*** what do you call it?, what's it called?
nażreć się *v/p* (*-rę*) *infml* stuff oneself (*I* with)
neandertalczyk *m* (*-ka*; *-czycy*) Neanderthal (man)
Neapol *m* (*-lu*) Naples
nefryt *m* (*-tu*; *-ty*) jade, nephrite
negacja *f* (*-cji*; *-cje*) negation
negatyw *m* (*-wu*; *-wy*) **1.** *PHOT* negative **2.** (*minus*) disadvantage; **negatywny** *adj* negative
negliż *m* (*-żu*; *-że*) undress; ***w ~u*** in a state of undress
negocjacje *pl* (*-cji*) negotiations; **negocjator** *m* (*-ra*; *-rzy*) negotiator; **negocjować** ⟨**wy-**⟩ (*-juję*) negotiate
negować ⟨**za-**⟩ (*-guję*) negate
nekrolog *m* (*-gu*; *-gi*) **1.** (*w gazecie*) obituary **2.** (*klepsydra*) death notice
nektar *m* (*-ru*; *-ry*) nectar
nektaryna *f* (*-ny*; *-ny*), **nektarynka** *f* (*-ki*; *-ki*) nectarine
nenufar *m* (*-ru*; *-ry*) (yellow) water lily
neo- (*w złożeniach*) neo-
neolit *m* (*-tu*; *no pl*) *GEOL* the Neolithic (Period)
neologizm *m* (*-zmu*; *-zmy*) neologism
neon *m* (*-nu*; *-ny*) **1.** (*napis reklamowy*) neon sign, neon light **2.** *CHEM* neon
neonazista *m* (*-ty*; *-ziści*) neo-Nazi
neonowy *adj* neon; **neonówka** *f* (*-ki*; *-ki*) neon tube, neon light
nerk|a *f* (*-ki*; *-ki*) kidney; ***jest chory na ~i*** he has a kidney problem; **nerkowaty** *adj* kidney-shaped; ***~ kształt*** kidney shape; **nerkow|y** *adj* kidney, renal; ***kamienie ~e*** kidney stones
nerw *m* (*-wu*; *-wy*) *ANAT* nerve; ***~y*** *fig* nerves; ***działać komuś na ~y*** get on s.o.'s nerves; ***tylko bez ~ów!*** take it easy!; ***mieć zszarpane ~y*** be a nervous wreck; (***cały***) ***w ~ach*** a bundle of nerves
nerwica *f* (*-cy*; *-ce*) neurosis; ***~ lękowa*** anxiety neurosis; **nerwicowy** *adj* neurotic
nerwoból *m* (*-lu*; *-le*) neuralgia; **nerwowo** *adv* nervously; ***~ chory*** neurotic; **nerwowość** *f* (*-ści*; *no pl*) nervousness; **nerwowy** *adj* nervous; **nerwówka** *f* (*-ki*; *-ki*) *infml Br* panic stations *pl*
nerwus *m* (*-sa*; *-sy*) hothead
neseser *m* (*-ru*; *-ry*) dressing case
neska *f* (*-ki*; *-ki*) instant coffee
netto *adj* net; ***waga ~*** net weight; ***cena ~*** net price; ***dochód ~*** net profit; ***pensja ~*** net pay
neuro- (*w złożeniach*) neuro-
neurochirurg *m* (*-ga*; *-rdzy*) neurosurgeon; **neurolog** *m* (*-ga*; *-lodzy*) neurologist; **neuron** *m* (*-nu*; *-ny*) *ANAT* neuron; **neurotyk** *m* (*-ka*; *-tycy*) neurotic
neutralizować ⟨**z-**⟩ (*-zuję*) neutralize; **neutralny** *adj* neutral
newralgiczny *adj MED* neuralgic; ***punkt ~*** trouble spot
nęcący *adj* **1.** tempting **2.** *głos*: alluring **3.** *zapach*: enticing **4.** *wygląd*: seductive
nęcić ⟨**z-**⟩ (*-cę*) entice, tempt (*I* with); ***nęci mnie, żeby*** I feel tempted to
nędz|a *f* (*-dzy*; *no pl*) poverty; ***skrajna ~a*** extreme poverty, *form* penury; ***dzielnice ~y*** poverty-stricken areas
nędzarz *m* (*-rza*; *-rze*), **-rka** *f* (*-ki*; *-ki*) pauper, beggar
nędzny *adj* **1.** *pensja*: *Br* meagre, *Am* meager **2.** *wygląd*: shabby **3.** *jakość*: very poor **4.** *pogoda*: ugly **5.** *literatu-*

ra: trashy **6.** *aktor*, *książka*: lousy *infml*

nękać *v/im* (*-kam*) **1.** (*o problemach*, *kontuzjach*) plague, dog **2.** (*o wierzycielach*) harass

ni *conj*: **~ to..., ~ to** it's neither... nor; **~ mniej, ~ więcej, tylko** nothing more or less than; **~ stąd, ~ zowąd**, *infml* **~ z gruszki, ~ z pietruszki** out of the blue; **~ pies, ~ wydra** neither fish nor fowl; **~ w pięć, ~ w dziesięć** without any sense whatsoever; **~ przypiął, ~ przyłatał** completely out of place; → **ani**

niańczyć *v/im* (*-czę*) nurse; **niańka** *f* (*-ki*; *-ki*) nanny

nią *pron* her; **z ~** with her; → **ona**

niby *pron* supposedly, seemingly; **robić coś na ~** pretend to be doing s.th.; **wojna na ~** pretend war, make-believe war; **~ przypadkiem** as if by accident; **~ nic, ale** it may look like nothing is wrong, but; it may look like nothing has happened, but; **~ dlaczego?** and why is that, exactly?; **~-** (*w złożeniach*) pseudo-

nic *pron* **1.** nothing; **~ a ~** not a thing, not at all; **jak gdyby nigdy ~** as if nothing had happened; **wszystko na ~** all in vain; **~ z tego** (**nie będzie**) it's no use, it's no good; **tyle co ~** next to nothing; **~ ci do tego** it's none of your business; **niczego nam nie brakuje** we've got everything we need; **on jest do niczego** *infml* he's no good; **to ~** (*nie szkodzi*) never mind; **ale to ~** but that's not a problem; **~ takiego** nothing important; **za ~** (**w świecie**) not for anything (in the world); **niczego sobie** not bad (at all); **~ tu po nas** off we go **2.** (*w pytaniach*, *przeczeniach*) anything; **na niczym mu nie zależy** he doesn't care for anything

Nicea *f* (*-cei*) Nice

nich *pron* them; **o ~** about them; **bez ~** without them; **do ~** to them; → **oni**, **one**

nici *pl* → **nić**

nicość *f* (*-ści*; *no pl*) *lit* nothingness

nicpoń *m* (*-ponia*; *-ponie*) good-for-nothing, ne'er-do-well

niczego → **nic**; **niczemu** → **nic**

niczyj *pron* nobody's, unowned; **ziemia ~a** no-man's-land; **bez ~ej pomocy** by oneself, without anyone's help

niczym *prep* (*N*) *lit* like; **była dla mnie ~ matka** she was like a mother to me; → **nic**

nić *f* (*nici*; *nici*) thread; **grubymi ~mi szyte** *fig* (as) plain as a pikestaff, thinly disguised; **nici z mojego wyjazdu** *fig* I'm not going, my plans to go fell through

Niderlandy *pl* (*-dów*) the Netherlands

niderlandzki *adj* **1.** *język*: Dutch **2.** *malarstwo*: Netherlandish

nie *particle* **1.** (*z inną częścią mowy*) not; **~ jestem głodny** I'm not hungry; **~ idź tam** don't go there; **~ dasz rady tego podnieść** you won't be able to lift it; **~ ma jej tam** she's not there; **jeszcze ~** not yet; **już ~** not any more; **~ szkodzi!** never mind!; **~ można temu zaprzeczyć** you can't deny it; **~ do wytrzymania** unbearable; **~ płacąc** without paying; **śliczne, no ~?** it's lovely, isn't it?; **co to, to ~** that's out of the question, no way; **~, bo ~** no, and that's final **2.** (*samodzielnie*) no; **– „Jesteś zajęty?" – „~, ~ jestem."** 'Are you busy?' 'No, I'm not.'

nie- (*w złożeniach*) **1.** (*z przymiotnikami, przysłówkami, rzeczownikami*) un-, in-, im-, ir-, il-; **~mądry** unwise; **~drogi** inexpensive; **~dostępność** inaccessibility; **~możliwy** impossible; **~cierpliwie** impatiently; **~racjonalny** irrational; **~legalny** illegal **2.** (*z rzeczownikami*) non-; **~agresja** non-aggression; **~wierzący** non-believer

nieaktualny *adj* **1.** *informacje*, *mapa*: out-of-date, out of date **2.** *dokument*, *bilet*: invalid, no longer valid **3.** *oferta*: unavailable, no longer available; **nieapetyczny** *adj* unappetizing, unappealing; **nieatrakcyjny** *adj* unattractive, unappealing

niebaczny *adj lit* rash, incautious; **~ na** *A* heedless of

niebawem *adv lit* soon, *dated* anon

niebezpieczeństwo *n* (*-wa*; *-wa*) danger, jeopardy; **~ wybuchu** danger of explosion

niebezpieczny *adj* **1.** dangerous; **~ dla życia** life-threatening; **~ dla środowiska** environmentally hazardous **2.** *prędkość*, *substancja*: hazardous

niebieskawy *adj* bluish

N

niebiański *adj* heavenly, celestial
niebieski *adj* **1.** *kolor*: blue; **~ ptak** *fig* layabout **2.** *REL* heavenly; ***Królestwo ~e*** the kingdom of heaven **3.** *ASTR* celestial; ***ciało ~e*** celestial body, heavenly body
niebiesko *adv*: ***pomalowy na ~*** painted blue
niebieskogranatowy *adj* dark blue; **niebieskooki** *adj* blue-eyed
niebiosa *pl* (*-bios*) *lit* heaven *sing*; ***wychwalać kogoś pod ~*** praise s.o. to the skies
nieb|o *n* (*-ba*; *no pl*) **1.** (*firmament*) sky; ***na ~ie*** in the sky; ***rozgwieżdżone ~o*** starlit sky, starry sky; ***o ~o lepszy*** far better; ***~o w gębie!*** absolutely delicious!; ***pod gołym ~em*** in the open air; ***z ~a mi spadłeś!*** *fig* you're a godsend! **2.** *REL* heaven; ***w ~ie*** in heaven
nieborak *m* (*-ka*; *-racy*/*-ki*), **-raczka** *f* (*-czki*; *-czki*) poor thing
niebosiężny *adj lit* sky-high
nieboskłon *m* (*-nu*; *no pl*) *lit* horizon
nieboszcz|yk *m* (*-ka*; *-czycy*/*-ki*), **-czka** *f* (*-ki*; *-ki*) the deceased; ***moja babka ~ka*** my late grandmother
niebotyczn|y *adj lit gmach*: sky-high; ***~a głupota*** act of monumental stupidity
niebrzydki *adj* **1.** *dziewczyna*: not bad-looking, rather pretty **2.** *okolica*: pretty nice; **niebrzydko** *adv* **1.** *grać*: pretty well **2.** *wyglądać*: pretty good
niebyt *m* (*-tu*; *no pl*) non-existence
niebywale *adv* unusually, remarkably, exceptionally; **niebywały** *adj* **1.** exceptional, (most) unusual **2.** *sukces*: tremendous, staggering
niecał|y *adj rok*, *kilometr*: less than; ***mieć ~e 15 lat*** be (just) under 15
niecelny *adj*: ***~ strzał*** miss
niecenzuralny *adj* obscene
niech I *particle* let; ***~ zaczeka*** let him wait; ***~ zobaczę*** let me see; ***~ pomyślę*** let me think; ***~ pan(i) usiądzie*** please, sit down; ***~ sobie jadą*** let them go; ***~ pan(i) pozwoli*** allow me; ***~ to pozostanie między nami*** that's between you and me; ***~ (ci) będzie!*** all right, have it your own way!; ***~ tam!*** who cares!; ***~ żyje król!*** long live the king! **II** *conj* what if; ***a ~ ktoś o to zapyta*** what if someone asks about it; **niechby** *particle*: ***~ tylko spróbował!*** just let him try!
niechcący *adv* by accident, unintentionally
niechceni|e: ***od ~a*** **a)** (*niedbale*) casually, carelessly **b)** (*bez zaangażowania*) half-heartedly **c)** (*z łatwością*) without effort, with ease
niechęć *f* (*-chęci*; *no pl*) reluctance (**do** *G* to do s.th.), aversion; (**do** *G* to do s.th.); ***okazywać komuś ~*** show one's dislike for s.o.; **niechętnie** *adv* reluctantly; **niechętny** *adj* **1.** reluctant (**do** *G* to do s.th.); ***~ do nauki*** reluctant to study **2.** (*nieprzyjazny*) unfriendly, *Br* unfavourable, *Am* unfavorable
niechlubny *adj lit* shameful, disgraceful
niechluj *m* (*-ja*; *-je*) *infml* slob; **niechlujny** *adj* sloppy; **niechlujstwo** *n* (*-wa*; *no pl*) sloppiness
niechodliwy *adj towar*: slow-moving
niechybnie *adv lit* inevitably, for sure; **niechybny** *adj lit* inevitable
nieciekawie *adv*: ***wyglądać ~*** **a)** (*nieinteresująco*) look uninteresting **b)** (*źle*) look bad; **nieciekawy** *adj* **1.** boring, not interesting **2.** *towarzystwo*: shady, bad
niecierpliwić ⟨**z-**⟩ (*-wię*) make impatient; ***niecierpliwić się*** be impatient
niecierpliwość *f* (*-ści*; *no pl*) impatience; **niecierpliwie** *adv* **1.** impatiently **2.** (*z niepokojem*) anxiously; **niecierpliwy** *adj* impatient
niecka *f* (*-ki*; *-ki*) *GEOL* basin
niecny *adj lit* wicked, ignoble
nieco *adv* somewhat, a little
niecodzienny *adj* uncommon, unusual
nieczęsto *adv* infrequently, not often; **nieczęsty** *adj* **1.** *gość*: infrequent **2.** *przypadek*: uncommon
nieczuły *adj* insensitive (**na** *A* to) **nieczynny** *adj* **1.** *sklep*, *bank*: closed **2.** *winda*: out of order **3.** *zakład*: disused **4.** *wulkan*: extinct
nieczystoś|ć *f* (*-ści*; *no pl*) (*zanieczyszczenie*) impurity; ***~ci*** **a)** waste **b)** (*ścieki*) sewage; **nieczysto** *adv* **1.** *grać*, *śpiewać*: off-key, out of tune **2.** *zagrać*: not fair, *infml* dirty; **nieczyst|y** *adj* **1.** *sumienie*: guilty **2.** *za-*

N

miary: devious, dishonest **3.** *ton*: off-key, out of tune **4.** *diament*, *myśli*: impure **5.** *interes*, *sprawa*: shady, dishonest, *infml* dirty **6.** ***~e zagranie*** *SPORT* foul **7.** *moce*: dark

nieczytelny *adj* illegible

niedaleki *adj* **1.** (*w przestrzeni*) nearby **2.** (*w czasie*) (up)coming; ***w ~ej przyszłości*** in the near future; **niedaleko** *adv* nearby, not far (*G*/**od** *G* from); ***mieszkają ~*** they live close by

niedawno *adv* recently; ***~ temu*** not long ago; **niedawn|y** *adj* **1.** recent; ***od ~a*** since recently, for a short time; ***do ~a*** until recently **2.** *wróg, idol*: former

niedbalstwo *n* (*-wa*; *no pl*) negligence; **niedbałość** *f* (*-ści*; *no pl*) **1.** negligence, carelessness **2.** *stroju*: carelessness; **niedbały** *adj* **1.** careless **2.** *styl*: careless, sloppy **3.** *gest*: casual

niedelikatny *adj* tactless

niedługi *adj* (fairly) short; **niedługo** *adv* **1.** (*krótko*) briefly, (for) a short while **2.** (*wkrótce*) soon

niedobitki *pl* (*-ków*) survivors

niedobór *m* (*-boru*; *-bory*) **1.** (*brak*) shortage, deficiency; ***~ witamin*** vitamin deficiency **2.** (*deficyt*) deficit

niedobrany *adj* mismatched

niedobr|y *adj* **1.** bad; ***~e przeczucia*** bad feelings **2.** *odpowiedź*, *wskazówka*: wrong **3.** *potrawa*: not (very) good

niedobrze *adv* badly; ***czuć się ~*** feel unwell, not feel very well; ***jest mi ~*** I feel sick; ***~ ci w tej sukience*** this dress doesn't suit you; (***jest***) ***~ z*** *I* it's bad with; ***~, że*** it's not good that; ***~ to wygląda*** it looks pretty bad

niedochodowy *adj* unprofitable

niedociągnięcie *n* (*-cia*; *-cia*) shortcoming, defect

niedoczekanie: ***~!*** that'll be the day!, never!

niedoczynność *f* (*-ści*; *no pl*) *MED* hypofunction; ***~ tarczycy*** underactive thyroid, hypothyroidism

niedogodność *f* (*-ści*; *-ści*) inconvenience; **niedogodny** *adj* inconvenient

niedogotowany *adj* undercooked, underdone

niedojrzałość *f* (*-ści*; *no pl*) immaturity; **niedojrzały** *adj* **1.** *osoba*: immature **2.** *owoc*: unripe

niedokładność *f* (*-ści*; *no pl*) **1.** (*nieprecyzyjność*) inaccuracy **2.** (*niedbalstwo*) carelessness; **niedokładny** *adj* **1.** *pomiar*: inaccurate **2.** *człowiek*: careless; **niedokarmiony** *adj* underfed, undernourished

niedokonany *adj* *czasownik*: imperfective; **niedokończony** *adj* unfinished, incomplete; **niedokrwistość** *f* (*-ści*; *no pl*) *MED* *Br* anaemia, *Am* anemia

niedokształcony *adj* undereducated, poorly educated; **niedokwasota** *f* (*-ty*; *no pl*) *MED* achlorhydria

niedola *f* (*-li*; *-le*) misery

niedołęga *f*/*m* (*-gi*; *-gi*) *infml* **1.** (*niezdarny*) clumsy oaf, *Am* klutz **2.** (*niezaradny*) failure; **niedołęstwo** *n* (*-wa*; *no pl*) **1.** (*fizyczne*) unfitness, infirmity **2.** (*starcze*) decrepitude

niedołężnieć ⟨**z-**⟩ (*-nieję*) become infirm, become decrepit; **niedołężny** *adj* **1.** (*niesprawny*) infirm **2.** *staruszek*: decrepit

niedomagać *v*/*im* (*-gam*) be in poor health; **niedomaganie** *n* (*-nia*; *-nia*) ailment, problem

niedomówie|nie: ***bez ~ń*** openly

niedonoszony *adj* *ciąża*: preterm

niedomyślny *adj* slow-witted; **niedopałek** *m* (*-łka*; *-łki*) butt, stub; **niedopatrzenie** *n* (*-nia*; *-nia*) **1.** (*zaniedbanie*) negligence **2.** (*przeoczenie*) oversight; ***przez ~*** due to (an) oversight

niedopłata *f* (*-ty*; *-ty*) underpayment; ***~ podatku*** tax underpaid; **niedopuszczalny** *adj* unacceptable, inadmissible

niedoręczeni|e: ***w razie ~a*** if undelivered

niedorosły *adj* **1.** (*niedojrzały*) immature **2.** (*niepełnoletni*) underage **3.** *zwierzę*: young; **niedorostek** *m* (*-tka*; *-tki*) youngster

niedorozwinięty *adj* underdeveloped; ***~ umysłowo*** mentally retarded; **niedorozwój** *m* (*-woju*; *no pl*) underdevelopment; ***~ umysłowy*** mental retardation

niedorzeczny *adj* nonsensical, preposterous, absurd; **niedosięgły** *adj lit* *wzór*: unattainable; **niedoskonały** *adj* imperfect, flawed

niedosłyszalny *adj* inaudible; **niedosłyszący** *adj* hearing-impaired; **nie-**

N

dosłyszeć *v/im* (*-szę*) be hard of hearing
niedosmażony *adj* underdone; **niedosolony** *adj* with not enough salt
niedostateczny I *adj* **1.** *poziom*: insufficient, inadequate **2.** *stopień*: unsatisfactory **II** *m* (*-nego*; *-ne*) fail (mark)
niedostatek *m* (*-tku*; *-tki*) want, privation; ***cierpieć ~*** live in poverty, be in need; **niedostępny** *adj* **1.** *towar*: unavailable **2.** *miejsce*: inaccessible **3.** (*zbyt drogi*) unaffordable **4.** (*wyniosły*) aloof, unapproachable; **niedostrzegalny** *adj* imperceptible, indiscernible
niedosyt *m* (*-tu*; *no pl*): ***pozostawić w kimś uczucie ~u*** leave s.o. not entirely satisfied; ***odczuwać ~*** feel unsatisfied; ***odczuwać ~*** *G* want more of
niedoszły *adj* **1.** *artysta*: would-be **2.** *samobójca*: failed **3.** *przyjęcie*: that never happened
niedościgły, ***niedościgniony*** *adj* **1.** *wzór, ideał*: unattainable **2.** *mistrz*: *Br* unequalled, *Am* unequaled; **niedoświadczony** *adj* inexperienced; **niedotarty** *adj*: ***twój motocykl jest jeszcze ~*** *AUTO* your motorcycle still needs running in; **niedotlenienie** *n* (*-nia*; *no pl*) hypoxia, oxygen deficiency
niedotrzymanie *n* (*-nia*; *no pl*): ***~ umowy*** breach of contract; **niedotykalny** *adj* untouchable; **niedouczony** *adj* undereducated, ignorant
niedowaga *f* (*-gi*; *no pl*) underweight
niedowiarek *m* (*-rka*; *-rki*/*-rkowie*) doubter, *Br* sceptic, *Am* skeptic; **niedowidzieć** *v/im* (*-dzę*) have poor eyesight
niedowierzająco *adv* disbelievingly
niedowierzanie: ***z ~m*** in disbelief
niedowład *m* (*-du*; *-dy*) *MED* paresis
niedozwolon|y *adj* **1.** forbidden; ***jechać z ~ą prędkością*** speed; ***~e zagranie*** *SPORT* foul **2.** *działalność*: unlawful, prohibited **3.** *broń*: illicit
niedożywienie *n* (*-nia*; *no pl*) malnutrition; **niedożywiony** *adj* malnourished, undernourished
niedrogo *adv* inexpensively; ***kupić naprawdę ~*** buy for a good price, buy for a reasonable price
niedrogi *adj* inexpensive, good value
niedrożność *f* (*-ści*; *no pl*) **1.** *MED* obstruction; ***~ naczyń krwionośnych*** (blood vessel) occlusion **2.** *TECH* blockage
niedużo *adv* **1.** (*z niepoliczalnymi*) not much **2.** (*z policzalnymi*) not many
nieduży *adj* rather small, not large
niedwuznaczny *adj* unambiguous
niedyskrecja *f* (*-ji*; *-je*) indiscretion; **niedyskretny** *adj* indiscreet
niedysponowany *adj form* indisposed, unwell; **niedyspozycja** *f* (*-ji*; *-je*) *form* indisposition
niedziela *f* (*-li*; *-le*) Sunday; ***Wielka ~*** Easter Sunday; ***~ Palmowa*** Palm Sunday; **niedzielny** *adj* Sunday
niedzisiejszy *adj* **1.** yesterday's **2.** *fig* old-fashioned
niedźwiadek *m* (*-dka*; *-dki*) little bear, bear cub; ***~ pluszowy*** teddy bear, *Br* teddy
niedźwiedzi *adj* **1.** bear; ***~a przysługa*** bad turn, disservice; ***~a skóra*** bearskin **2.** *łapa, głowa*: bear's; **niedźwiedzica** *f* (*-cy*; *-ce*) female bear; ***Wielka ~*** *ASTR* Ursa Major, the Great Bear; **niedźwiedziowaty** *adj* bearish
niedźwie|dź *m* (*-wiedzia*; *-wiedzie*) bear; ***~dź biały*** polar bear; ***~dź brunatny*** brown bear; ***nie dziel skóry na ~dziu*** don't count your chickens before they are hatched
nieefektowny *adj* **1.** unattractive, dull **2.** *występ, aktorstwo*: bland; **nieekonomiczny** *adj* uneconomical; **nieelegancki** *adj* inelegant; **nieestetyczny** *adj* unaesthetic, unsightly; **nieetatowy** *adj* part-time; ***pracownik ~*** part-time worker
niefachowość *f* (*-ści*; *no pl*) lack of professionalism; **niefachowy** *adj* unprofessional, incompetent; **niefart** *m* (*-tu*/*-ta*; *no pl*) *infml* tough luck, bad luck
nieforemny *adj* **1.** *kapelusz, głowa*: unshapely, shapeless **2.** *figura geometryczna*: irregular; **nieformalny** *adj* **1.** informal, unofficial **2.** (*nielegalny*) illicit, illegal
niefortunny *adj* **1.** *wybór, sformułowanie*: unfortunate **2.** *moment*: inopportune **3.** *pomysł*: ill-considered

N

niefrasobliwie *adv* **1.** light-heartedly **2.** *traktować*: lightly **3.** *postępować*: thoughtlessly; **niefrasobliwy** *adj* carefree, light-hearted; **niefunkcjonalny** *adj* impractical

niegazowany *adj* still

niegdyś *adv* once

niegłęboki *adj* shallow, not deep; **niegłupi** *adj osoba*, *pomysł*: *Br* (quite) clever, *Am* smart

niego *pron* him; ***dla ~*** for him; ***od ~*** from him; ***do ~*** to him; ***u ~*** (***w domu***) at his place; ***bez ~*** without him; → ***on***, ***ono***

niegodny *adj lit* unworthy, undeserving; ***~ zaufania*** untrustworthy, unreliable; **niegodziwiec** *m* (*-wca*; *-wcy*) *lit* rogue, villain; **niegodziwie** *adv* deplorably; ***niegodziwy*** *adj* wicked, ignoble

niegospodarny *adj* wasteful, uneconomical; **niegościnny** *adj* inhospitable, unfriendly; **niegotowy**, ***niegotów*** *adj* not ready, **niegramatyczny** *adj* ungrammatical; **niegroźny** *adj* **1.** *pogróżki*, *ukąszenie*: harmless **2.** *wypadek*: minor **3.** *pies*: not dangerous **4.** *choroba*: not serious

niegrzeczny *adj* **1.** rude **2.** *dziecko*: naughty, bad; **niegustowny** *adj* tasteless; **niehigieniczny** *adj* insanitary, *Am* unsanitary, unhygienic; **niehonorowy** *adj Br* dishonourable, *Am* dishonorable; **nieinteligentny** *adj* unintelligent; **nieingerencja** *f* (*-ji*; *-je*) non-interference, non-intervention; **nieistotny** *adj* unimportant, irrelevant

niej *pron* her; ***od ~*** from her; ***do ~*** to her; ***u ~*** (***w domu***) at her place; ***dla ~*** for her; ***bez ~*** without her; → ***ona***

niejadalny *adj* **1.** inedible **2.** (*niesmaczny*) uneatable; **niejadowity** *adj wąż*: non-venomous

niejaki *pron* a, some; ***od ~ego czasu*** for some time; ***~ pan Smith*** a Mr Smith

niejako *particle* as it were, so to speak

niejasno *adv* unclearly; ***wyrażać się ~*** be unclear; **niejasny** *adj sytuacja*: unclear, vague

niejawn|y *adj* secret; ***~e obrady*** closed proceedings

niejed|en, ***niejedna***, ***niejedno*** *pron* many, *form* many a; ***~na kobieta*** many women, *form* many a woman

niejedno *n* (*-nego*; *no pl*) a lot; ***~ już w życiu widział*** he's seen a thing or two in his life

niejednakowy *adj* different, not the same

niejednokrotnie *adv* many times, more than once; **niejednokrotny** *adj* repeated

niejednolicie *adv pomalowany*: unevenly

niejednolity *adj* **1.** not uniform, non-uniform; ***w ~ sposób*** in different ways **2.** *system*: inconsistent **3.** *grupa*: heterogenous; **niejednorodny** *adj* composite, heterogeneous; **niejednoznaczny** *adj* ambiguous, *form* equivocal

niekaralny *adj* JUR not punishable, unpunishable; **niekarany** *adj* (with) no criminal record

niekiedy *adv* sometimes, now and then

nieklarowny *adj* (*niejasny*) unclear; **niekłamany** *adj* genuine, unfeigned

niekłopotliwy *adj* **1.** *dojazd*: convenient **2.** *osoba*, *plotki*: not troublesome

niekoleżeński *adj* unfriendly, *infml* standoffish; **niekompetentny** *adj* incompetent; **niekompletny** *adj* incomplete

niekoniecznie *adv* not necessarily; **niekonieczny** *adj* unnecessary; **niekonsekwentny** *adj* inconsistent

niekończący się *adj* endless, never-ending

niekorzystn|y *adj* **1.** *Br* unfavourable, *Am* unfavorable; ***umowa na ~ych warunkach*** unfavourable deal; ***być w ~ej sytuacji*** be at a disadvantage; ***zrobić ~e wrażenie*** make a bad impression, make an unfavourable impression; ***~e działanie leków*** adverse effects of drugs **2.** *wpływ*: bad

niekorzyść *f*: ***na czyjąś ~*** to s.o.'s disadvantage; ***zmiana na ~*** change for the worse; ***wszystkie dowody przemawiają na ~ oskarżonego*** all evidence is against the defendant

niekrępujący *adj* **1.** *atmosfera*: relaxed **2.** *mieszkanie*: with a private entrance

niekształtny *adj* misshapen, shapeless
niektórzy, ***niektóre*** *pl* (*-rych*) some
niekulturalny *adj* unmannered, impolite
niekwestionowany *adj* unquestioned, indisputable
nielegalny *adj* illegal, unlawful
nieletni I *adj* underage **II** *m* (*-niego*; *-ni*), **-nia** *f* (*-niej*; *-nie*) minor, juvenile; ***przestępczość ~ch*** juvenile delinquency
nieliczny *adj* **1.** *grupa*: small, not numerous **2.** *osoby*, *wybrańcy*: few **3.** (*rzadki*) rare
nieliteracki *adj* non-literary; **nielitościwy** *adj* merciless; **nielogiczny** *adj* illogical; **nielojalny** *adj* disloyal, not loyal; **nieludzko** *adv traktować*: inhumanely; ***o tak ~ wczesnej godzinie*** at such an unearthly hour; ***~ zmęczony*** totally exhausted, *infml* dead beat; **nieludzki** *adj* **1.** inhuman **2.** *wysiłek*: superhuman
nieład *m* (*-du*; *no pl*) disorder, mess; ***w ~zie*** in (a state of) disorder, in a mess; **nieładny** *adj* **1.** ugly, unattractive **2.** *pogoda*: bad, not good
niełask|a *f* (*-ki*; *no pl*): ***popaść w ~ę u*** *G Br* fall into disfavour with, *Am* fall into disfavor with
niełatw|y *adj* (fairly) difficult, not easy; ***~e zadanie*** not an easy task; ***~y w pożyciu*** hard to get along with
nie ma: → ***być***; ***nie ma go tam*** he's not there; ***nie ma jej w domu*** she's not at home, she's out; ***na półce nie ma żadnych książek*** there aren't any books on the shelf; ***nie ma za co*** you're welcome; ***nie ma co czekać*** there's no point waiting
niemal(że) *adv* almost, nearly
niemało *adv* quite a lot; **niemały** *adj* **1.** pretty big **2.** *suma*, *majątek*: sizeable, considerable **3.** *kłopot*: serious
niematerialn|y *adj strata*: incorporeal; ***dobra ~e*** intangible goods
niemądry *adj* unwise
Niem|cy *pl* (*-miec*) (*państwo*) Germany *sing*; ***Republika Federalna ~iec*** the Federal Republic of Germany; → ***Niemiec***
niemęski *adj* unmanly
niemęskoosobowy *adj rodzaj*: nonvirile, non-masculine-human
Niem|iec *m* (*-mca*; *-mcy*) German; ***jest ~cem*** he's German
niemieck|i I *adj* German; ***język ~i*** German, the German language; ***mówić po ~u*** speak German; ***owczarek ~i*** German shepherd, Alsatian **II** *m* (*-kiego*; *no pl*) (*język*) German; ***lekcja ~iego*** German lesson, lesson of German
niemieszkalny *adj budynek*: non-residential; **niemilknący** *adj* **1.** *hałas*: incessant **2.** *brawa*: endless
niemiłosierny *adj* **1.** *traktowanie*: merciless **2.** *upał*: terrible
niemile, ***niemiło*** *adv* **1.** *zaskoczyć*: unpleasantly **2.** *przywitać*: coldly
niemiły *adj* **1.** (*nieprzyjemny*) unpleasant, disagreeable **2.** (*nieuprzejmy*) impolite
Niemk|a *f* (*-ki*; *-ki*) German (woman); ***była ~ą*** she was German
niemłody *adj* no longer young, oldish
niemnący *adj* crease-resistant, noncrease
niemniej *conj* still, however; ***~ jednak*** nevertheless
niemo *adv lit* silently
niemoc *f* (*-cy*; *no pl*) *lit* (*słabość*) weakness; ***~ płciowa*** MED impotence; ***~ twórcza*** creativity crisis
niemodny *adj* unfashionable, out-of-date; **niemoralny** *adj* immoral; **niemowa** *f/m* (*-wy*; *-wy*) mute
niemowlę *n* (*-lęcia*; *-lęta*) baby, infant; **niemowlęctwo** *n* (*-wa*; *no pl*) babyhood, infancy; **niemowlęcy** *adj* baby
niemożliwie *adv* impossibly, awfully
niemożliwość *f* (*-ści*; *no pl*) impossibility; **niemożliw|y** *adj* impossible; ***to ~e*** it's impossible; ***~y do opisania*** indescribable, impossible to describe; ***~y do zdobycia*** *twierdza*: impregnable
niemożność *f* (*-ści*; *no pl*) *lit* impossibility
niemrawy *adj osoba*, *reakcja*: sluggish
niemu → ***jemu***
niemuzykalny *adj* unmusical
niemy I *adj* **1.** *człowiek*: dumb, mute **2.** *film*: silent **3.** *fig* speechless, dumb **II** *m* (*-mego*; *-mi*), **-ma** *f* (*-mej*; *-me*) mute (person)
nienaganny *adj* impeccable
nienaruszalny *adj* inviolable

nienaruszony *adj pieczęć*: intact
nienasycony *adj* **1.** *apetyt*: insatiable **2.** CHEM unsaturated
nienaturalny *adj* unnatural
nienaukowy *adj podejście*: unscientific
nienaumyślnie *adv* unintentionally
nienawidzić ⟨**z-**⟩ (*-dzę*) hate; ***nienawidzić się*** hate each other; **nienawistny** *adj* **1.** hateful **2.** *osoba*: loathsome, hateful; **nienawiść** *f* (*-ści*; *no pl*) hatred
nienawykły *adj* unaccustomed (**do** *G* to)
nienormalny *adj* **1.** abnormal, not normal **2.** *ludzie*: insane, *infml* crazy
nienowy *adj* **1.** (fairly) old, not new **2.** *problem*: familiar, not new; **nieobcy** *adj* familiar
nieobecność *f* (*-ści*; *-ści*) absence; ***pod czyjąś ~*** in s.o.'s absence; **nieobecny** *adj* absent; ***być ~m na*** *L* be absent from
nieobliczalny *adj człowiek*, *skutki*: unpredictable; **nieobojętny** *adj*: ***~ na ludzkie cierpienie*** not indifferent to human suffering; **nieobowiązkowy** *adj zajęcia*: optional
nieobsadzony *adj stanowisko*: vacant
nieobycie *n* (*-cia*; *no pl*) **1.** (*brak ogłady*) gaucheness, lack of sophistication **2.** (*brak oswojenia*) unfamiliarity (**z** *I* with); **nieobyty** *adj* **1.** (*bez ogłady*) uncultured, unsophisticated **2.** (*bez oswojenia*) unfamiliar (**z** *I* with)
nieoceniony *adj* invaluable; **nieoczekiwany** *adj* unexpected; **nieodczuwalny** *adj* imperceptible
nieodgadniony *adj* **1.** *przyszłość*: unforeseeable **2.** *tajemnica*: impenetrable **3.** *twarz*, *postać*: inscrutable; **nieodłączny** *adj* **1.** *towarzysz*: inseparable **2.** *cecha*: inherent, intrinsic; ***~ element*** integral part; **nieodmienny** *adj* **1.** (*niezmienny*) invariable, constant **2.** *część mowy*: invariable
nieodparty *adj* **1.** *chęć*, *urok*: irresistible **2.** *argument*: irrefutable **3.** *uczucie*: overwhelming; **nieodpłatny** *adj* free (of charge); ***wstęp ~*** admission free
nieodporny *adj* susceptible (**na** *A* to); **nieodpowiedni** *adj* inappropriate, wrong; **nieodpowiedzialny** *adj* irresponsible
nieodrodny *adj*: ***jest ~m synem swojego ojca*** he's his father's son; **nieodwołalny** *adj decyzja*, *wyrok*: irrevocable; **nieodwracalny** *adj* **1.** *szkoda*: irreparable **2.** *decyzja*, *proces*: irreversible
nieodzowny *adj* **1.** *element*: indispensable; ***~ do zrobienia czegoś*** necessary to do s.th.; ***~ warunek*** (essential) prerequisite; **nieodżałowany** *adj* **1.** *strata*: much lamented, tragic **2.** *osoba*: late (and much) lamented
nieoficjalny *adj* unofficial; **nieoględny** *adj* inconsiderate; **nieograniczony** *adj* **1.** unlimited **2.** *możliwości*: limitless **3.** *zaufanie*: absolute
nieokiełznany *adj* **1.** uncontrollable **2.** *wyobraźnia*: unfettered; **nieokreślony** *adj* **1.** *lęk*, *kształt*: indefinable **2.** *przedimek*: indefinite **3.** *wiek*, *kolor*: indeterminate; ***umowa na czas ~*** open-ended contract; **nieokrzesany** *adj* uncouth, boorish; ***nieomal*** → ***niemal***
nieomylny *adj* **1.** *człowiek*: infallible **2.** *instynkt*, *przeczucie*: unerring; **nieopanowany** *adj* **1.** *człowiek*: hot-tempered **2.** *gniew*: uncontrollable, unrestrained; **nieopatrzny** *adj słowa*, *decyzja*: rash, thoughtless; **nieopisany** *adj* indescribable, inexpressible; **nieopłacalny** *adj* unprofitable
nieopodal → ***opodal***
nieorganiczny *adj* inorganic
nieosiągalny *adj* unattainable, unreachable; **nieosobowy** *adj* impersonal; **nieostrożność** *f* (*-ści*; *no pl*) carelessness; **nieostrożny** *adj* careless; **nieostry** *adj* **1.** *nóż*: blunt **2.** PHOT out of focus, fuzzy **3.** *widzenie*: blurred
nieoswojony *adj zwierzę*: untamed; **nieoszacowany** *adj zasługi*: inestimable; **nieoznakowany** *adj* unmarked; **nieożywiony** *adj* inanimate
niepalący *m* (*-cego*; *-cy*), **-ca** *f* (*-cej*; *-ce*) non-smoker; ***przedział dla ~ch*** non-smoking compartment
niepalny *adj* non-flammable, non-combustible
niepamięć *f* (*-mięci*; *no pl*) oblivion; ***puścić coś w ~*** forget about s.th., forgive and forget s.th.; ***pójść w ~*** fall into oblivion

N

niepamiętny *adj*: ***od ~ch czasów*** from time immemorial; **nieparlamentarny** *adj* unparliamentary
nieparzysty *adj* **1.** *liczba*: odd **2.** *organ*: unpaired
niepełnoletni I *adj* underage **II** *m* (*-niego*; *-ni*) **~nia** *f* (*-niej*; *-nie*) minor
niepełnosprawn|y I *adj* disabled **II** *m* (*-nego*; *-ni*), **-na** *f* (*-nej*; *-ne*) disabled person; ***~i*** the disabled; ***dla ~ych*** suitable for the disabled, suitable for wheelchairs
niepełnowartościowy *adj towary*: substandard; **niepełny** *adj* **1.** *akta*, *dane*: incomplete **2.** *szklanka*: partially filled, not full; ***w ~m wymiarze godzin*** part-time
niepewnoś|ć *f* (*-ści*; *no pl*) uncertainty; ***dręczyła go ~ć*** he was troubled by doubt; ***trzymać kogoś w ~ci*** keep s.o. in suspense; ***~ć jutra*** uncertain future, the uncertainty of the future; **niepewny** *adj* **1.** *przyszłość*, *pogoda*, *los*: uncertain **2.** *drabina*: insecure **3.** *sojusznik*: unreliable, uncertain **4.** *krok*: hesitant, uncertain **5.** *głos*: faltering
niepijący *m* (*-cego*; *-cy*), **-ca** *f* (*-cej*; *-ce*) non-drinker
niepisany *adj prawo*: unwritten
niepiśmienny *adj* illiterate; **nieplanowy** *adj* unplanned, unscheduled; **niepłatny** *adj* **1.** *dzień*: unpaid **2.** *usługa*: free (of charge); **niepłodność** *f* (*-ści*; *no pl*) infertility; **niepłodny** *adj* sterile, infertile **3.** *okres*: infertile, safe
niepochlebny *adj Br* unfavourable, *Am* unfavorable, critical; **niepocieszony** *adj* **1.** (*niezadowolony*) unhappy **2.** (*nie do pocieszenia*) inconsolable; **niepoczytalny** *adj* insane
niepodległościowy *adj* independence; **niepodległość** *f* (*-ści*; *no pl*) independence; **niepodległy** *adj* independent
niepodobieństw|o *n* (*-wa*; *no pl*) impossibility; ***coś wydaje się ~em*** s.th. seems impossible
niepodobna: ***~ o tym zapomnieć*** it's impossible to forget it
niepodobn|y *adj* dissimilar (**do** *G* to), different (**do** *G* from), unlike (**do** *G*); ***są do siebie ~i*** **a)** (*z charakteru*) they are unlike (each other) **b)** (*z wyglądu*) they don't look alike; ***to do niego ~e*** it's unlike him; **niepodpisany** *adj* unsigned; **niepodważalny** *adj* **1.** *fakt*: incontestable, indisputable **2.** *argument*, *dowód*: irrefutable **3.** *zasługi*: unquestionable **4.** *sukces*: undeniable
niepodzielny *adj* **1.** *jednostka*, *majątek*: indivisible **2.** *władza*: undivided, absolute; **niepogoda** *f* (*-dy*; *no pl*) bad weather, *form* inclement weather; **niepohamowan|y** *adj* **1.** uncontrollable **2.** *żądza*: unbridled **3.** *ciekawość*: burning; **niepojętny** *adj uczeń*: slow; **niepojęty** *adj* incomprehensible
niepokalan|y *adj lit* immaculate; ***~e poczęcie*** *REL* Immaculate Conception; **niepokaźny** *adj* inconspicuous
niepokoić ⟨**za-**⟩ (*-koję*) **1.** (*martwić*) worry **2.** (*nie dawać spokoju*) bother; ***niepokoić się*** worry (*I*/**o** *A* about/over)
niepokojący *adj* worrying, disturbing; **niepokonany** *adj* **1.** *bokser*: undefeated **2.** *armia*: invincible; **niepok|ój** *m* (*-koju*; *-koje*) anxiety (**o** *A* about); ***wyrazić ~ój o*** *A* express one's concern about; ***nie ma powodów do ~oju*** there's no cause for concern; ***~oje*** *POLIT* unrest
niepomiernie *adv lit* immensely, immeasurably; **niepomierny** *adj lit* immense, immeasurable; **niepomny** *adj lit* oblivious (*G* to); **niepomyślny** *adj okoliczności*, *decyzja*: *Br* unfavourable, *Am* unfavorable
niepopłatny *adj* unprofitable; **niepoprawny** *adj* **1.** *nazwa*, *pisownia*: incorrect, wrong **2.** *optymista*: incurable, incorrigible; **niepopularny** *adj* unpopular; **nieporadny** *adj* **1.** inept; ***~ jak dziecko*** (as) helpless as a baby **2.** (*niezdarny*) awkward; **nieporęczny** *adj* cumbersome, unwieldy; **nieporozumieni|e** *n* (*-nia*; *-nia*) misunderstanding; ***wyjaśnić ~e*** clear up a misunderstanding; ***~a*** (*spory*) differences, misunderstandings
nieporównanie *adv lit* incomparably; **nieporównany** *adj lit* incomparable; **nieporównywalny** *adj* incomparable
nieporuszony *adj* **1.** (*nieruchomy*) motionless **2.** (*niewzruszony*) unmoved; **nieporządek** *m* (*-dku*; *-dki*) disorder,

N

mess; ***w pokoju panował ~*** the room was in (a state of) disorder; **nieporządny** *adj* untidy, messy; **nieposkromiony** *adj entuzjazm*, *żądza*: unbridled

nieposłuszeństwo *n* (*-wa*; *no pl*) disobedience; ***~ obywatelskie*** civil disobedience; **nieposłuszny** *adj* **1.** disobedient **2.** *dziecko*: naughty

niepospolity *adj* uncommon, exceptional; **niepostrzeżenie** *adv* unnoticed; **nieposzanowanie** *n* (*-nia*; *no pl*) disrespect (*G* for), disregard (*G* of); **nieposzlakowany** *adj opinia*: spotless; **niepotrzebny** *adj* unnecessary; ***czuję się ~*** I feel unwanted

niepoważn|y *adj* **1.** (*lekkomyślny*) flippant **2.** (*nieodpowiedzialny*) irresponsible; ***to ~e z ich strony*** it's irresponsible of them; **niepowetowany** *adj szkoda*, *strata*: irreparable; **niepowodzenie** *n* (*-nia*; *-nia*) failure; **niepowołan|y** *adj* unauthorized; ***dostać się w ~e ręce*** fall into the wrong hands

niepowstrzymany *adj* **1.** *postęp*: unstoppable, inexorable **2.** *ciekawość*: unbridled, relentless **3.** *pragnienie*: uncontrollable, unbridled; **niepowtarzalny** *adj* unique; **niepozorny** *adj* inconspicuous; **niepożądany** *adj* **1.** undesirable **2.** *gość*, *towarzystwo*: unwelcome

N

niepraktyczny *adj* impractical

nieprawda *f* (*-dy*; *no pl*) untruth; ***to ~*** that's not true!; ***~?*** isn't that right?; ***śliczne, ~?*** beautiful, isn't it?

nieprawdopodobny *adj* **1.** improbable, unlikely **2.** (*niewiarygodny*) incredible; **nieprawdziwy** *adj* **1.** (*niezgodny z prawdą*) untrue **2.** (*sztuczny*) false, artificial

nieprawidłowo *adv* improperly, wrongly

nieprawidłowości *pl* (*-ści*) irregularities; ***~ rozwoju*** developmental abnormalities; **nieprawidłowy** *adj* incorrect, wrong

nieprawny *adj* illegal, illegitimate; **nieprawomocny** *adj* JUR invalid; **nieprawomyślny** *adj* dissident, dissenting; **niepraw|y** *adj*: ***z ~ego łoża*** illegitimate

nieprędko *adv* not soon; ***~ to się stanie*** it'll take some time before it happens; **nieproduktywny** *adj* unproductive; **nieprofesjonalny** *adj* **1.** *wykonanie*: unprofessional, amateur **2.** *aktor*: non-professional

nieproporcjonalny *adj* disproportionate (***do*** *G* to), out of proportion; (***do*** *G* to)

nieproszony *adj gość*: uninvited

nieprzebrany *adj lit* innumerable, countless; **nieprzebyty** *adj lit* impassable; **nieprzechodni** *adj czasownik*: intransitive; **nieprzeciętny** *adj* **1.** *osobowość*: outstanding **2.** *talent*: extraordinary; **nieprzejednany** *adj* **1.** uncompromising **2.** *nienawiść*: implacable; **nieprzejezdny** *adj* **1.** impassable **2.** (*zamknięty*) closed

nieprzejrzysty *adj* opaque; **nieprzekładalny** *adj* untranslatable

nieprzekonujący *adj* unconvincing

nieprzekraczalny *adj*: ***~ termin*** (strict) deadline

nieprzekupny *adj* incorruptible; **nieprzemakalny** *adj* waterproof; **nieprzemijający** *adj wartości*, *piękno*: eternal; **nieprzemyślany** *adj* rash, ill-considered

nieprzenikniony *adj* **1.** *ciemność*: impenetrable **2.** *twarz*: inscrutable; **nieprzeparty** *adj* irresistible

nieprzepisowo *adv postępować*, *parkować*: illegally; ***jeździć ~*** break the rules (of the road); ***zagrać ~*** foul; **nieprzepisow|y** *adj* illegal; ***~e zagranie*** foul; **nieprzepuszczalny** *adj* impervious, impermeable

nieprzerwany *adj* **1.** (*nieustanny*) incessant, ceaseless **2.** *sen*, *strumień*: uninterrupted

nieprzetłumaczalny *adj* untranslatable; **nieprzewidywalny** *adj* unpredictable; **nieprzewidziany** *adj* (*zaskakujący*) unexpected; **nieprzezwyciężony** *adj trudności*: insurmountable

nieprzychylny *adj* **1.** *Br* unfavourable, *Am* unfavorable **2.** *opinia*, *nastawienie*: negative, critical **3.** *okoliczności*: adverse **4.** *recenzenci*: critical; **nieprzydatny** *adj* useless (***do*** *G* for)

nieprzyjaciel *m* (*-la*; *-le*) enemy; **nieprzyjacielski** *adj* enemy; **nieprzyjazny** *adj* **1.** unfriendly **2.** (*wrogi*) hostile; **nieprzyjemności** *pl* (*-ści*) trouble *sing*; ***miała przez niego ~*** he got her

into trouble; **nieprzyjemny** *adj* unpleasant; **nieprzypadkow|y** *adj*: ***spotkanie było ~e*** the meeting wasn't accidental
nieprzystępny *adj* **1.** *osoba*: unapproachable **2.** *tekst*: unaccessible; **nieprzytomnoś|ć** *f* (*-ści*; *no pl*) unconsciousness; ***pobić kogoś do ~ci*** beat s.o. unconscious; **nieprzytomnie** *adv*: ***~ zakochany*** madly in love; **nieprzytomny** *adj* **1.** unconscious **2.** *wzrok*: blank, vacant; **nieprzyzwoity** *adj* **1.** obscene, indecent **2.** *wyrazy*, *kawały*: dirty
niepunktualny *adj* unpunctual
nieracjonalny *adj* **1.** irrational **2.** *odżywianie*: unhealthy
nierad *adj*: ***rad ~*** willy-nilly, making a virtue out of necessity
nieraz *adv* **1.** (*często*) many times, often **2.** (*czasem*) sometimes
nierdzewny *adj* stainless
nierealny *adj* **1.** unreal **2.** *plan*: unrealistic; **nieregularny** *adj* irregular; **nierentowny** *adj* unprofitable; **nierozdzielny** *adj* inseparable; **nierozerwalny** *adj* **1.** inseparable **2.** *przyjaźń*: inseparable, indissoluble; **nierozgarnięty** *adj* slow-witted, *form* obtuse
nierozłączki *pl* (*-czek*): ***papużki ~*** lovebirds; ***są jak papużki ~*** *fig* they're inseparable
nierozłączny *adj* inseparable; **nierozpoznawalny** *adj* unrecognizable; **nierozpuszczalny** *adj Br* insoluble, *Am* insolvable; **nierozsądny** *adj* unreasonable; **nierozstrzygalny** *adj Br* insoluble, *Am* insolvable; **nieroztropny** *adj lit* imprudent; **nierozumny** *adj* mindless
nierozważny *adj* **1.** (*nieostrożny*) reckless **2.** (*nierozsądny*) imprudent
nierozwiązalny *adj Br* insoluble, *Am* insolvable
nierób *m* (*-roba*; *-roby*) loafer; **nieróbstwo** *n* (*-twa*; *no pl*) loafing, idleness; ***słodkie ~*** sweet idleness
nierówno *adj* **1.** unevenly; ***grać ~*** **a)** (*o muzyku*) play out of rhythm **b)** (*o zawodniku*) not be consistent **2.** *dzielić*: unequally **3.** *bić*: irregularly **4.** *wisieć*: askew
nierównomierny *adj* **1.** uneven **2.** *podział*: unequal **3.** *puls*: irregular; **nierówność** *f* (*-ści*; *-ści*) **1.** (*nierówne prawa*) inequality **2.** (*na powierzchni*) irregularity, bump; **nierówny** *adj* **1.** uneven **2.** *podział*, *prawa*: unequal **3.** (*krzywy*) crooked, lopsided **4.** *zawodnik*: not consistent, inconsistent
nieruchawy *adj infml* sluggish
nieruchomieć ⟨**z-**⟩ (*-mieję*) freeze, stand still
nieruchomo *adv* motionless, still; **nieruchomoś|ć** *f* (*-ści*; *no pl*) **1.** (*bezruch*) immobility **2.** ***~ci*** property, *Am* real estate; ***agencja ~ci*** *Br* estate agency, *Am* real estate agency; **nieruchomy** *adj* **1.** motionless, still **2.** (*umocowany*) fixed, immobile
nierzadki *adj* fairly frequent, not infrequent; **nierzadko** *adv* fairly frequently, not infrequently
nierząd *m* (*-du*; *no pl*) *lit* prostitution
nierządny *adj*: **czyn ~** *JUR* unlawful sexual activity
nierzeczywisty *adj* unreal; **nierzetelnie** *adv*: ***~ wykonana praca*** bad work, careless work; **nierzetelny** *adj* **1.** unreliable **2.** (*nieuczciwy*) dishonest **3.** (*niedbały*) negligent **4.** (*niedokładny*) inaccurate
niesamodzielność *f* (*-ści*; *no pl*) **1.** (*życiowa*) inability to cope on one's own **2.** (*zależność*) dependence; **niesamodzielny** *adj* **1.** (*życiowo*) unable to cope on one's own **2.** (*zależny*) dependent; **niesamowity** *adj* **1.** (*ogromny*) *infml* incredible **2.** *sen*: eerie, uncanny; **niesforny** *adj* unruly; **nieskalany** *adj* spotless; **nieskazitelny** *adj* impeccable; **nieskładny** *adj* incoherent, disjointed
nieskończenie *adv* endlessly, infinitely; **nieskończoność** *f* (*-ści*; *no pl*) infinity; ***w ~*** *fig* ad infinitum; **nieskończony** *adj* endless, infinite
nieskory *adj*: ***~ do rozmowy*** (***nauki***) unwilling to talk (study); ***~ do pracy*** work-shy; ***~ do zwierzeń*** reticent
nieskromny *adj* immodest; **nieskuteczny** *adj* ineffective
niesław|a *f* (*-wy*; *no pl*) *lit* infamy; ***okryty ~ą*** infamous; **niesławny** *adj lit* infamous
niesłowny *adj* unreliable; **niesłuszny** *adj* **1.** (*błędny*) wrong **2.** (*niesprawiedliwy*) unfair **3.** (*bezpodstawny*)

N

groundless; **niesłychany** *adj* unbelievable, amazing; **niesmaczny** *adj* tasteless

niesmak *m* (*-ku*; *no pl*) *fig* distaste; ***budzić ~*** be disgusting; ***czuć ~*** be disgusted; ***z ~iem*** with disgust

niesnaski *pl* (*-sek*) *lit* dissention *sing*, disagreements

niesolidarny *adj* disloyal; **niesolidny** *adj* **1.** *firma*, *osoba*: unreliable **2.** *produkt*: poorly made **3.** *konstrukcja*: unsound; **niespecjalnie** *adv* **1.** not particularly **2.** *czuć się*: out of sorts; **niespecjaln|y** *adj* not too good, mediocre, ***książka była ~a*** the book was nothing special

niespełna *particle* less than; ***miała ~ 40 lat, gdy umarła*** she wasn't yet 40 when she died; ***~ rozumu*** out of one's mind

niespodziank|a *f* (*-ki*; *-ki*) surprise; ***zrobić komuś ~ę*** give s.o. a surprise; **niespodziewany** *adj* **1.** unexpected **2.** *atak*: surprise, unexpected; **niespokojny** *adj* **1.** restless **2.** (*zmartwiony*) anxious, uneasy **3.** *wzrok*: uneasy **4.** *czasy*: turbulent, unsettled **5.** *morze*: rough; **niespotykany** *adj* unusual; **niespożyty** *adj energia*: boundless

niesprawiedliwość *f* (*-ści*; *-ści*) injustice; **niesprawiedliwie** *adv* unfairly, unjustly; **niesprawiedliwy** *adj* unfair, unjust (**wobec**/**dla** *G* to/for)

niesprawny *adj* **1.** (*niedziałający*) out of order, broken **2.** (*wadliwy*) faulty **3.** (*fizycznie*) disabled **4.** *zarządzanie*, *urząd*: inefficient

niestały *adj* **1.** *pogoda*: changeable **2.** (*w uczuciach*) fickle; **niestaranny** *adj* careless, sloppy

niestety *particle* unfortunately

niestosowny *adj* inappropriate, improper; **niestrawność** *f* (*-ści*; *no pl*) indigestion; **niestrawny** *adj* **1.** indigestible **2.** *fig* unpalatable, hard-going; **niestrudzony** *adj bojownik*, *wysiłki*: tireless, indefatigable

niestworzon|y *adj*: ***opowiadać ~e historie*** *infml* tell stories, talk nonsense; **niesumienny** *adj* careless, unconscientious; **nieswojo** *adv czuć się*: uneasy, uncomfortable; **nieswój** *adj* out of sorts

niesymetryczny *adj* asymmetrical; **niesympatyczny** *adj osoba*, *atmosfera*: unfriendly, disagreeable; **niesystematyczny** *adj* **1.** *osoba*: disorganized **2.** *badania*: unsystematic; **nieszablonowy** *adj* **1.** original, *infml* offbeat **2.** *podejście*: unorthodox

nieszczególnie *adv* **1.** not too well; ***wyglądać ~*** not look very good **2.** (*przed przymiotnikiem*) not too; **nieszczególny** *adj* not too good, mediocre; **nieszczelny** *adj* **1.** *kran*, *dach*: leaky **2.** *okna*: *Br* draughty, *Am* drafty; **nieszczery** *adj osoba*, *uśmiech*: insincere (**wobec** *G* with)

nieszczęsny *adj* **1.** miserable, *lit* hapless **2.** (*żałosny*) pathetic; **nieszczęści|e** *n* (*-cia*; *-cia*) **1.** (*zdarzenie*) misfortune; ***na ~e*** unfortunately; ***wyglądać jak ~e*** look a sorry sight; ***~a chodzą parami*** it never rains but it pours **2.** (*stan*) unhappiness; **nieszczęśliwy** *adj* **1.** *osoba*: unhappy **2.** *mina*: miserable **3.** *zbieg okoliczności*: unfortunate; ***~ wypadek*** **a)** serious accident **b)** (*śmiertelny*) fatal accident

nieszczęśnik *m* (*-ka*; *-nicy*) poor man, poor wretch

nieszkodliwy *adj* harmless (***dla*** *G* to); ***~ dla środowiska*** environmentally friendly

nieszpory *pl* (*-rów*) REL vespers

nieścisłość *f* (*-ści*; *-ści*) inaccuracy, error; **nieścisły** *adj* inaccurate

nieść *v/im* (*niosę*) **I** *v/t* **1.** carry; ***~ kogoś na barana*** give s.o. a piggyback ride; ***~ komuś pomoc*** aid s.o., come to s.o.'s aid **2.** *nadzieję*, *ulgę*: bring **3.** *ryzyko*: entail, carry **4.** *jaja*: lay **II** *v/i* **1.** (*o broni*) carry **2.** ***fama niesie, że*** *Br* rumour has it that, *Am* rumor has it that; ***nieść się*** (*o woni*, *dźwiękach*) waft

nieślubny *adj dziecko*: illegitimate

nieśmiałość *f* (*-ści*; *no pl*) shyness; **nieśmiały** *adj* shy

nieśmiertelnik *m* (*-ka*; *-ki*) strawflower, everlasting daisy; **nieśmiertelność** *f* (*-ści*; *no pl*) immortality; **nieśmiertelny** *adj* immortal

nieśpieszno, ***niespieszno*** *adv*: ***~ mi*** I'm in no hurry

nieśpieszny, ***niespieszny*** *adj* unhurried

nieświadomoś|ć *f* (*-ści*; *no pl*) **1.** (*niewiedza*) ignorance, unawareness; ***trzymać kogoś w ~ci*** keep s.o. in the dark **2.** *PSYCH* unconsciousness

nieświadomy *adj* **1.** (*niewiedzący*) unaware (*G* of), ignorant (*G* of) **2.** *PSYCH* unconscious

nieświeży *adj* **1.** not fresh **2.** *żywność*: off, bad **3.** *chleb*, *informacje*: not fresh, stale **4.** *oddech*: bad **5.** *pościel*: dirty; **nietakt** *m* (*-tu*; *-ty*) indiscretion; **nietaktowny** *adj* tactless, indiscreet; **nieterminowy** *adj płatność*: late; **nietęg|i** *adj*: ***mieć ~ą minę*** wear a long face; **nietęgo** *adv czuć się*: out of sorts; **nietknięty** *adj* **1.** (*w doskonałym stanie*) intact **2.** *obiad*: untouched; **nietłukący** *adj* unbreakable; **nietolerancja** *f* (*-ji*; *no pl*) intolerance; **nietolerancyjny** *adj* intolerant

nietoperz *m* (*-rza*; *-rze*) bat

nietowarzyski *adj* unsociable; **nietrafny** *adj* **1.** *odpowiedź*, *decyzja*, *wybór*: wrong **2.** *zarzut*: false; **nietrudny** *adj* easy, not difficult; **nietrwały** *adj* **1.** short-lived **2.** *żywność*: perishable **3.** *kolory*: fading **4.** *uczucia*: fleeting

nietrzeźwoś|ć *f* (*-ści*; *no pl*) intoxication, drunkenness; ***w stanie ~ci*** intoxicated, drunk; **nietrzeźwy** *adj* intoxicated, drunk; ***jazda w stanie ~m*** drunk-driving, *Am* driving while intoxicated; **nietutejszy** *adj* foreign; ***jestem ~*** I'm a stranger here

nietuzinkowy *adj* extraordinary

nietykalność *f* (*-ści*; *no pl*) **1.** inviolability **2.** *POLIT* immunity; **nietykalny** *adj* **1.** (*bezpieczny*) untouchable; ***być ~m*** *POLIT* have immunity **2.** *własność*, *granice*: inviolable

nietypowy *adj* **1.** untypical, uncharacteristic **2.** *rozmiar*: non-standard; **nieubłagany** *adj* **1.** *upływ czasu*: relentless **2.** *człowiek*: implacable, relentless; **nieuchronny** *adj* inevitable; **nieuchwytny** *adj przestępca*, *cel*: elusive; ***dzwoniłam kilka razy, ale był ~*** I called several times but he didn't answer

nieuctwo *n* (*-wa*; *no pl*) ignorance; **nieuczciwość** *f* (*-ści*; *no pl*) dishonesty; **nieuczciwy** *adj* **1.** dishonest **2.** *konkurencja*: unfair; **nieudany** *adj* **1.** unsuccessful **2.** *próba*, *zamach stanu*: failed

nieudolność *f* (*-ści*; *no pl*) **1.** ineptness **2.** *rysunku*, *stylu*: clumsiness, ineptness; **nieudolny** *adj* **1.** *osoba*, *zarządzanie*: inept **2.** *próba*: ineffectual **3.** *rysunek*, *styl*: clumsy, inept

nieufność *f* (*-ści*; *no pl*) distrust, mistrust; **nieufny** *adj* distrustful, mistrustful; **nieugięty** *adj* **1.** unbending; ***pozostać ~m*** remain adamant **2.** *bojownik*: staunch **3.** *postanowienie*: firm; **nieujarzmiony** *adj natura*: uncontrollable

nieuk *m* (*-ka*; *-ki*) (*w szkole*) dunce

nieukojony *adj lit żal*: inconsolable; **nieuleczalny** *adj* incurable; **nieulękły** *adj* fearless; **nieumiarkowany** *adj* immoderate; **nieumiejętnie** *adv* **1.** ineptly, incompetently **2.** *wykonany*, *zrobiony*: badly; **nieumiejętny** *adj* **1.** inept, incompetent; ***w ~ sposób*** ineptly, incompetently **2.** *wykonanie*: bad; **nieumyśln|y** *adj* unintentional; ***~e spowodowanie śmierci*** involuntary manslaughter; **nieunikniony** *adj* inevitable, unavoidable; **nieuprzedzony** *adj* (*bezstronny*) unbiased; **nieuprzejmy** *adj* impolite

nieurodzaj *m* (*-ju*; *-je*) crop failure; **nieurodzajny** *adj* **1.** *ziemia*: infertile **2.** *rok*: lean, bad

nieustający, ***nieustanny*** *adj* constant, incessant

nieustawny *adj* difficult to arrange; **nieustępliwy** *adj* **1.** unyielding, *form* pertinacious **2.** *obrońca*: staunch; **nieustraszony** *adj* fearless, intrepid; **nieutulony** *adj*: ***~ w żalu*** inconsolable

nieuwag|a *f* (*-gi*; *no pl*) inattention; ***przez ~ę*** **a)** inadvertently **b)** (*przez niedopatrzenie*) through oversight; **nieuważny** *adj* **1.** *osoba*: inattentive **2.** *ruch*: careless; **nieuzasadniony** *adj* **1.** unjustified **2.** *roszczenia*, *zarzuty*: unfounded; **nieużyteczny** *adj* useless; **nieużytki** *pl* (*-ków*) wasteland *sing*

niewart *adj*: ***~ czegoś*** not worth s.th.; ***nic ~*** worthless; ***~ złamanego grosza*** not worth a penny

nieważkość *f* (*-ści*; *no pl*) *PHYS* weightlessness; **nieważn|y** *adj* **1.** unimportant, not important, insignificant; ***~e!*** it doesn't matter! **2.** *dokument*, *głosy*: invalid; ***mój paszport jest już***

N

~y my passport has expired **3.** *umowa*: void

niewątpliwie *adv* undoubtedly; **niewątpliwy** *adj* undoubted, unquestionable

niewczas: ***po ~ie*** too late; **niewdzięczny** *adj* **1.** *osoba*: ungrateful **2.** *zadanie*: unrewarding, thankless; **niewesoły** *adj* sad, unhappy

niewiadomy *adj* unknown; **niewiadoma** *f* (*-mej*; *-me*) *MATH* unknown (quantity); **niewiadome** *n* (*-mego*; *no pl*) the unknown

niewiara *f* (*-ry*; *no pl*) **1.** *REL* lack of belief, unbelief **2.** (*brak zaufania*) distrust, disbelief; **niewiarygodny** *adj* **1.** *historia*: implausible **2.** *informacja*: unreliable **3.** *osoba*, *firma*: unreliable untrustworthy, not credible **4.** (*nadzwyczajny*) incredible

niewidoczny *adj* not visible, invisible

niewidom|y **I** *adj* blind **II** *m* (*-mego*; *-mi*), **-ma** *f* (*-mej*; *-me*) blind person; ***jest ~y*** he's blind; ***~i*** the blind

niewidzialny *adj* invisible

niewiedza *f* (*-dzy*; *no pl*) lack of knowledge, ignorance

niewiele **I** *adj* **1.** (*z policzalnymi*) few, not many **2.** (*z niepoliczalnymi*) little, not much **II** *adv* little, not much; ***~ brakowało, a przegrałaby*** she almost lost; ***~ brakowało!*** it was a close shave! *infml*; ***~ wspólnego*** not much in common; ***~ sobie z tego robi*** he doesn't care much about it

niewielki *adj* **1.** small, not big; ***~ego wzrostu*** short **2.** *nadzieja*: little

niewierność *f* (*-ści*; *no pl*) **1.** unfaithfulness, infidelity **2.** (*nielojalność*) disloyalty; **niewierny** *adj* **1.** unfaithful **2.** (*nielojalny*) disloyal **3.** *przekład*: inaccurate

niewierzący|y **I** *adj*: ***jest osobą ~ą*** he's a non-believer, he's an atheist **II** *m* (*-cego*; *-cy*), **-ca** *f* (*-cej*; *-ce*) non-believer, atheist

niewiniątko *n* (*-ka*; *-ka*) innocent; **niewinność** *f* (*-ści*; *no pl*) innocence; **niewinn|y** *adj* *osoba*: innocent, not guilty; ***~e kłamstewko*** white lie

niewłaściwy *adj* **1.** wrong, improper **2.**: *zachowanie, moment*, *strój*: inappropriate

niewol|a *f* (*-li*; *-le*) **1.** (*odosobnienie*) captivity; ***wziąć kogoś do ~i*** capture s.o., take s.o. prisoner **2.** *form fig* bondage; **niewolnica** *f* (*-cy*; *-ce*) (female) slave; **niewolnictwo** *n* (*-wa*; *no pl*) slavery; **niewolniczy** *adj praca*: slave; **niewolnik** *m* (*-ka*; *-nicy*) slave; ***handel ~ami*** the slave trade

niewprawny *adj* **1.** *kierowca*: inexperienced, incompetent **2.** *oko*: untrained; **niewrażliwy** *adj* insensitive (***na*** *A* to); **niewskazany** *adj* inadvisable, not recommended

niewspółmierny *adj* disproportionate; **niewybaczalny** *adj* unforgivable, inexcusable; **niewybredny** *adj* **1.** *dowcip*: coarse **2.** *gust*: unrefined, undiscriminating; **niewybuch** *m* (*-chu*; *-chy*) unexploded bomb; **niewychowany** *adj* badly behaved, ill-mannered; **niewyczerpany** *adj* inexhaustible, endless

niewydarzony *adj* (*nieudany*) failed; **niewydolność** *f* (*-ści*; *no pl*) failure; **niewydolny** *adj serce*, *system*: failing

niewygoda *f* (*-dy*; *-dy*) discomfort, inconvenience; **niewygodny** *adj* **1.** uncomfortable **2.** *fakty*, *osoba*: inconvenient

niewykształcony *adj* uneducated; **niewykwalifikowany** *adj robotnik*: unskilled, unqualified; **niewymagający** *adj* undemanding; **niewymierny** *adj* **1.** immeasurable **2.** *MATH* irrational; **niewymowny** *adj cierpienie*: unspeakable; **niewymuszony** *adj wdzięk*: natural; **niewymyślny** *adj* plain, simple

niewypał *m* (*-łu*; *-ły*) **1.** (*niewybuch*) unexploded bomb **2.** *fig infml* flop, dud; **niewypłacalny** *adj* insolvent; **niewypowiedziany** *adj lit* inexpressible; **niewyraźny** *adj* **1.** *zarys*, *światło*, *głosy*: faint **2.** *kształt*: indistinct, vague **3.** (*nieswój*) out of sorts; **niewyrobiony** *adj* **1.** (*niedoświadczony*) inexperienced; ***~ towarzysko*** unsophisticated **2.** *gust*: undeveloped, unrefined

niewysłowiony *adj* inexpressible; **niewysoki** *adj* **1.** (rather) low, not very high **2.** *osoba*: (rather) short, not very tall; **niewyspany** *adj*: ***jestem ~*** I haven't slept enough; **niewystarczająco** *adv* insufficiently; **niewys-**

tarczający *adj* insufficient; **niewyszukany** *adj* simple, plain, unsophisticated; **niewytłumaczalny** *adj* inexplicable

niewyżyty *adj* unsatisfied; **~ seksualnie** sex-starved

niewzruszony *adj* **1.** *zasady*: unshakeable **2.** *spokój*: imperturbable **3.** *osoba*: immovable, adamant **4.** *twarz*: deadpan, poker; **niezaangażowany** *adj* **1.** uninvolved **2.** *państwo*: nonaligned; **niezabudowany** *adj* undeveloped; **niezachwiany** *adj wiara, przekonania*: unshak(e)able

niezadługo *adv* soon; **~ potem** before long, soon afterwards; **niezadowolenie** *n* (*-nia*; *no pl*) dissatisfaction, discontent; **niezadowolony** *adj* dissatisfied (**z** *G* with), displeased (**z** *G* with), unhappy (**z** *G* about/with); **niezakłócony** *adj* **1.** *spokój*: undisturbed **2.** *dopływ*: uninterrupted

niezależność *f* (*-ści*; *no pl*) independence; **niezależn|y** *adj* independent (**od** *G* from); **mowa ~a** direct speach

niezamężny *adj kobieta*: unmarried; **niezamierzony** *adj* unintentional; **niezamieszkały** *adj* uninhabited; **niezapominajka** *f* (*-ki*; *-ki*) forget-me-not; **niezapomniany** *adj* unforgettable; **niezaprzeczalny** *adj* undeniable; **niezaradny** *adj* helpless; **niezasłużony** *adj* undeserved

niezastąpiony *adj* **1.** irreplaceable **2.** *pomoc*: indispensible; **niezauważalny** *adj* imperceptible

niezawisłość *f* (*-ści*; *no pl*) independence; **niezawisły** *adj* independent

niezawodność *f* (*-ści*; *no pl*) reliability; **niezawodny** *adj* **1.** reliable **2.** *pamięć, metoda*: infallible **3.** *instynkt*: unerring

niezbadany *adj obszar*: unexplored; **niezbędny** *adj* essential, indispensable, vital; **niezbity** *adj* irrefutable; **niezborność** *f* (*-ści*; *no pl*) **1.** incoherence **2.** *MED* astigmatism

niezbyt *particle* **1.** (*z przymiotnikami*) not too, none too **2.** (*z czasownikami*) not too much

niezdar|a *f/m* (*-ry*; *-ry*) *infml* **1.** (*osoba niezręczna*) **być ~ą** be all thumbs **2.** (*osoba nieudolna*) loser; **niezdarny** *adj* clumsy; **niezdatny** *adj* unfit (**do** *G* for); **~ do picia** unfit to drink

niezdecydowanie *n* (*-nia*; *no pl*) **1.** indecision **2.** (*wahanie*) hesitation; **niezdecydowany** *adj* **1.** undecided **2.** (*niezdolny do decydowania*) indecisive **3.** *ruch*: hesitant

niezdolność *f* (*-ści*; *no pl*) inability, **~ do pracy** inability to work, unfitness for work; **niezdolny** *adj* unable (**do** *G* to do s.th.), incapable (**do** *G* of); **~ do pracy** unable to work, unfit for work; **~ do służby wojskowej** unfit for military service

niezdrowo *adv* **1.** unhealthily; **odżywiać się ~** eat unhealthy food; **~ się podniecać** get overexcited **2.** *wyglądać*: unwell; **niezdrowy** *adj* unhealthy; **niezdyscyplinowany** *adj* undisciplined; **niezgłębiony** *adj tajemnica*: unfathomable

niezgod|a *f* (*-dy*; *no pl*) disagreement, discord; **w ~zie z** *I* **a)** at odds with **b)** (*z przepisami*) not compliant with; **niezgodność** *f* (*-ści*; *no pl*) **1.** (*z przepisami*) lack of compliance **2.** (*brak zgody*) disagreement **3.** (*rozbieżność*) incompatibility; **~ charakterów** incompatibility; **niezgodny** *adj* **1.** (*z przepisami*) not compliant (**z** *I* with); **~ z prawem** unlawful **2.** (*rozbieżny*) incompatible **3.** (*kłótliwy*) quarrelsome; **~ z prawdą** false

niezgorszy *adj* not bad; **niezgrabny** *adj* **1.** *nogi, figura*: not shapely **2.** *ruch*: awkward **3.** *styl*: clumsy **4.** *chód*: ungainly; **nieziemski** *adj* heavenly; **niezliczony** *adj* countless, innumerable; **niezłośliwy** *adj MED* benign; **niezły** *adj* not bad, pretty good; **niezmącony** *adj* **1.** *cisza*: undisturbed **2.** *szczęście*: perfect, unalloyed

niezmienny *adj* unchanging, invariable; **niezmiernie** *adv* extremely; **niezmiern|y** *adj* immense; **~ej wagi** of utmost importance; **niezmordowany** *adj osoba*: tireless; **niezmywalny** *adj* indelible

nieznaczny *adj* **1.** slight, small **2.** *rola, różnica*: minor, insignificant **3.** *większość głosów*: narrow, slim; **nieznajomość** *f* (*-ści*; *no pl*) unfamiliarity (*G* with), ignorance (*G* of)

nieznajomy *m* (*-mego*; *-mi*), **-ma** *f* (*-mej*; *-me*) stranger

nieznany *adj* unknown; **niezniszczalny** *adj* indestructible; **nieznośny** *adj* **1.** unbearable **2.** *dziecko*: impossible; **niezobowiązujący** *adj* **1.** *propozycja*: no-commitment **2.** *seks*: casual, no-strings-attached; **niezręczny** *adj* **1.** awkward **2.** *pytanie*: inappropriate

niezrozumiały *adj* **1.** incomprehensible **2.** (*niewyraźny*) unintelligible; **niezrozumienie** *n* (*-nia*; *no pl*) incomprehension; **niezrównany** *adj Br* unequalled, *Am* unequaled, *Br* unrivalled, *Am* unrivaled; **niezrównoważony** *adj* unstable; **~ psychicznie** mentally unbalanced; **niezupełnie** *adv* not quite; **niezupełny** *adj* incomplete, partial; **niezwłoczny** *adj* immediate, prompt

niezwyciężony *adj* invincible; **niezwykle** *adv* **1.** unusually **2.** (*bardzo*) extremely; **niezwykły** *adj* **1.** unusual **2.** (*nadzwyczajny*) extraordinary

nieźle *adv* **1.** not bad, quite well **2.** (*bardzo*) quite

nieżonaty *adj* single, unmarried; **nieżyciowy** *adj* **1.** unrealistic **2.** *osoba*: out of touch with life; **nieżyczliwie** *adv* unkindly; **nieżyczliwy** *adj* unfriendly, unkind; **nieżyjący** *adj* late, dead

nieżyt *m* (*-tu*; *-ty*) MED catarrh; **~ nosa** rhinitis; **~ żołądka** gastritis

N

nieżywotny *adj rzeczownik*: inanimate

nieżywy *adj* dead

nigdy *adv* **1.** never; **~ więcej, już ~** never again; **~ więcej wojny!** no more war!; **jak ~** like never before; **jakby ~ nic** as if nothing had happened **2.** (*w pytaniu*) ever

nigdzie *adv* **1.** nowhere; **~ indziej** nowhere else; **nie móc ~ zagrzać miejsca** be always on the move **2.** (*po przeczeniu, w pytaniu*) anywhere

nijak *adv* (in) no way; **~ nie mogłem tego zrozumieć** I just couldn't understand it; **mieć się ~ do** *G* be completely at odds with

nijaki *adj* bland, dull; **rodzaj ~** the neuter; **nijako** *adv* **1.** blandly, dully **2.** *wyglądać*: bland, dull **3.** *czuć się*: out of sorts

nikczemny *adj* wicked

nikiel *m* (*-klu*; *no pl*) CHEM nickel

nikim → **nikt**

niklować *v/im* (*-luję*) nickel-plate, nickel; **niklowany** *adj* nickel-plated

nikły *adj* **1.** *szansa, nadzieja*: slim **2.** *wartość, zainteresowanie*: hardly any, little

niknąć ⟨**z-**⟩ (*-nę*) (*znikać*) fade away

nikogo → **nikt**

nikomu → **nikt**

nikotyna *f* (*-ny*; *no pl*) nicotine

nikt *pron* **1.** nobody, no one; **~ oprócz ciebie** no one but you; **~ z nich** no one of them; **nie było tam nikogo** there was nobody there; **był nikim** he was a nobody **2.** (*po przeczeniu, w pytaniu*) anybody, anyone; **nie mów nikomu** don't tell anyone

nim[1] *pron* **1.** him; **z ~** with him **2.** it; **o ~** about it; → **on, ono**

nim[2] *conj* before

nimb *m* (*-bu*; *no pl*) halo

nimfa *f* (*-fy*; *-fy*) nymph; **nimfomanka** *f* (*-ki*; *-ki*) nymphomaniac

nimi *pron* them; **z ~i** with them; → **one, oni**

niniejszy *adj form* this; **niniejszym** *adv form* hereby

nioska *f* (*-ki*; *-ki*) BIOL layer

NIP *abbr m* (*NIP-u*; *NIP-y*) (= **numer identyfikacji podatkowej**) taxpayer identification number

nirwana *f* (*-ny*; *no pl*) REL nirvana

niski *adj* **1.** low; **~ego wzrostu** short **2.** *osoba*: short; **nisko** *adv* low

niskokaloryczny *adj* low-calorie; **niskopienny** *adj drzewo*: low-growing; **niskoprocentowy** *adj napój*: low-alcohol

nisza *f* (*-szy*; *-sze*) **1.** niche; **~ kuchenna** kitchenette **2.** (*w ścianie*) recess, alcove

niszczarka *f* (*-ki*; *-ki*) shredder

niszczący *adj* destructive

niszczeć ⟨**z-**⟩ (*-czeję*) (*o budynku*) deteriorate; **niszczyciel** *m* (*-la*; *-le*) destroyer; **niszczycielski** *adj* destructive

niszczyć ⟨**z-**⟩ (*-czę*) **1.** destroy **2.** *zdrowie, karierę*: ruin **3.** *ubranie, buty*: wear out **4.** *szkodniki*: control, eradicate; **niszczyć się 1.** (*o ubraniu, butach*) wear out **2.** (*o budynku*) deteriorate

nit *m* (*-tu*; *-ty*) rivet

nitka *f* (*-ki*; *-ki*) thread; **~ dentystyczna** dental floss

nitrogliceryna *f* (*-ny*; *-ny*) *Br* nitroglycerine, *Am* nitroglycerin
niuans *m* (*-su*; *-se*) nuance
niuchać *v/im* (*-cham*) sniff
niwa *f* (*-wy*; *-wy*) (*dziedzina*) field, domain
niweczyć ⟨**z-**⟩ (*-czę*) *lit wysiłki*, *plany*: thwart, frustrate
niwelować ⟨**z-**⟩ (*-luję*) (*wyrównywać*) level; **~ różnice** *fig* bridge the gap
nizina *f* (*-ny*; *-ny*) lowland, lowlands *pl*; **nizinny** *adj* lowland
niż[1] *conj* than; **więcej ~** more than
niż[2] *m* (*-żu*; *-że*) **1.** (*w meteorologii*) low (pressure), depression **2.** (*nizina*) depression; **~ demograficzny a)** (*okres*) baby bust **b)** (*dzieci*) baby busters
niżej *adv comp* → **nisko** lower; **~ podpisany** the undersigned; **~ wymieniony** undermentioned
niżow|y *adj*: **zatoka ~a** trough of low pressure
niższoś|ć *f* (*-ści*; *no pl*) inferiority; **kompleks ~ci** inferiority complex; **niższ|y** *adj comp* → **niski 1.** lower; **~ego wzrostu** shorter **2.** *osoba*: shorter
no I *interj* **1.** (*w odpowiedzi*) *infml* yeah; **~ pewnie!** *infml* sure!, you bet!; **~ dobrze** all right; **~ nie! a)** oh, no! **b)** (*z niedowierzaniem*) come on!; **~, ~!** (*podziw*) wow! **2.** (*w nawiązaniu*) well; **~ i?** and?; **masz je, ~ nie?** you've got them, don't you? **3.** (*ponaglenie*) come on **II** *particle* **1.** (*polecenie*) **podejdź ~ tu!** come over here! **2.** (*w nawiązaniu*) **~ więc** so; **~ ale** but; **~ to co?** so what?
nobilitować *v/im* (*-tuję*) **1.** glamorize, elevate **2.** (*nadawać szlachectwo*) ennoble
noc *f* (*-cy*; *-ce*) night; **w ~y** at night; **co ~** every night; **całą ~** all night (long); **siedzieć do późna w ~** stay up late at night, stay until late at night
nochal *m* (*-la*; *-le*) *infml Br* conk, beak
nocka *f* (*-ki*; *-ki*) night (shift)
nocleg *m* (*-gu*; *-gi*) accommodation; **~i** accomodation *sing*; **noclegownia** *f* (*-ni*; *-nie*) night shelter
nocnik *m* (*-ka*; *-ki*) chamber pot, *infml* potty; **nocn|y** *adj* **1.** night; **koszula ~a** nightgown; **~e życie** nightlife; **klub ~y** nightclub; **cisza ~a** lights out; **~y marek** *fig* night owl **2.** *lampka*: bedside **3.** *zwierzę*: nocturnal
nocować ⟨**prze-**⟩ (*-cuję*) **I** *v/i* stay (overnight), spend the night **II** *v/t* put up
nog|a *f* (*-gi*; *-gi*) **1.** leg; **złamać ~ę** break one's leg; **do góry ~ami** upside down; **przewrócić coś do góry ~ami** turn s.th. upside down; **zerwać się na równe ~i** spring to one's feet; **do ~i!** heel!; **w ~i!** run for it!; **dać ~ę** *infml* leg it; **stanąć na ~i** *fig* recover **2.** (*stopa*) foot
nogawka *f* (*-ki*; *-ki*) (trouser) leg
nokaut *m* (*-tu*; *-ty*) SPORT knock-out; **nokautować** ⟨**z-**⟩ (*-tuję*) knock out
nokturn *m* (*-nu*; *-ny*) *MUS* nocturne
nomada *m* (*-dy*; *-dzi*/*-dowie*) nomad
nomenklatura *f* (*-ry*; *-ry*) **1.** (*terminologia*) terminology, nomenclature **2.** (*ludzie*) nomenklatura
nominacja *f* (*-cji*; *-cje*) nomination; **nominalny** *adj* **1.** nominal **2.** *wartość*: nominal, face; **nomina|ł** *m* (*-łu*; *-ły*) denomination; **banknot o ~le 50 złotych** *Br* 50 zloty (bank)note, *Am* 50 zloty bill
nonsens *m* (*-su*; *-sy*) nonsense
nonszalancki *adj* flippant, cavalier
nora *f* (*-ry*; *-ry*) **1.** (*zwierzęcia*) burrow, hole; **mysia ~** mousehole; **lisia ~** (fox's) earth; **borsucza ~** badger's set **2.** (*mieszkanie*) hovel
norka *f* (*-ki*; *-ki*) *BIOL* mink
norm|a *f* (*-my*; *-my*) **1.** norm, standard; **wrócić do ~y** get back to normal; **~a prawna** legal rule; **~a europejska** European standard; **~a pracy** workload **2.** *TECH* standard
normalizować ⟨**z-**⟩ (*-zuję*) *wymiary*: standardize
normalka *f* (*-ki*; *no pl*): **to ~** *infml* it's nothing new
normalny *adj* **1.** normal, *Am* regular **2.** (*zwykły*) ordinary **3.** *bilet*: full-price, full-fare **4.** *PSYCH* normal
normować ⟨**u-**⟩ (*-muję*) (*ustalać*) regulate, govern; **normować się** go back to normal, normalize
Norweg *m* (*-ga*; *-gowie*/*-wedzy*) Norwegian; **jest ~iem** he's Norwegian; **Norwegia** *f* (*-gii*) Norway; **Norweż|ka** *f* (*-ki*; *-ki*) Norwegian; **jest ~ą** she's Norwegian; **norwesk|i** *adj* Norwe-

N

gian; ***mówić po ~u*** speak Norwegian

nos *m* (*-sa*; *-sy*) **1.** nose; ***przez ~*** through one's nose; ***mruczeć pod ~em*** mumble under one's breath; ***pociągać ~em*** sniff, snuffle; ***mieć coś w ~ie*** *infml* not care about s.th.; ***zadzierać ~a*** put on airs **2.** (*buta*) toe; ***buty ze szpiczastymi ~ami*** pointy-toed shoes

nosek *m* (*-ska*; *-ski*) **1.** *dim* (little) nose **2.** (*buta*) toe **3.** (*w rowerze*) toe clip

nosiciel *m* (*-la*; *-le*), **~ka** *f* (*-ki*; *-ki*) *MED* carrier

nosić *v/im* (*-szę*) **1.** (*przenosić*) carry; ***~ kogoś na barana*** give s.o. a piggyback ride **2.** (*przy sobie*) carry, have on one **3.** *koszulę*, *okulary*: wear **4.** *brodę*: have; **nosić się 1.** (*ubierać się*) ***czegoś się już nie nosi*** s.th. is no longer fashionable **2.** (*zamierzać*) ***~ się z zamiarem zrobienia czegoś*** intend to do s.th.

nosidełko *n* (*-ka*; *-ka*) (*dla dziecka*) child carrier

nosorożec *m* (*-żca*; *-żce*) rhinoceros, *infml* rhino; **nosowy** *adj* nasal; **nosówka** *f* (*-ki*; *-ki*) **1.** *MED* distemper **2.** (*głoska*) nasal

nostalgia *f* (*-gii*; *no pl*) **1.** nostalgia **2.** (*za krajem ojczystym*) homesickness; **nostalgiczny** *adj* nostalgic

nostryfikacja *f* (*-ji*; *-je*) *dyplomu*: recognition; **nostryfikować** *v im/p* (*-kuję*): ***~ dyplom*** have one's diploma recognized

nosze *pl* (*-szy*) stretcher *sing*

nośnik *m* (*-ka*; *-ki*) carrier; ***~ danych*** *INF* data carrier, data medium

nośność *f* (*-ści*; *no pl*) **1.** *ciężarówki*, *mostu*: load capacity **2.** *statku*: deadweight (tonnage) **3.** *nawierzchni*: bearing capacity **4.** *broni*: range; **nośn|y** *adj* **1.** *ściana*, *konstrukcja*: load-bearning **2.** *metafora*: expressive **3.** ***siła ~a*** *PHYS* lift; ***rakieta ~a*** launch vehicle

nota *f* (*-ty*; *-ty*) **1.** note; ***~ redakcyjna*** editor's note, editor's comment **2.** (*ocena*) *Br* mark, *Am* grade

notabene *particle lit* incidentally

notarialny *adj* **1.** notarial **2.** *biuro*: notary's; **notariusz** *m* (*-sza*; *-sze*) notary (public)

notatk|a *f* (*-ki*; *-ki*) note; ***robić ~i*** make notes; ***~a służbowa*** memo; **notatnik** *m* (*-ka*; *-ki*) notebook; **notes** *m* (*-su*; *-sy*) notebook; **notka** *f* (*-ki*; *-ki*) **1.** note **2.** (*w prasie*) paragraph, notice, news item

notoryczny *adj* habitual; ***~ przestępca*** repeat offender

not|ować ⟨**za-**⟩ (*-tuję*) **I** *v/t* **1.** take down, write down **2.** (*rejestrować*) register; ***~uje się wzrost cen artykułów żywnościowych*** food prices are rising **II** *v/i* make notes

notowanie *n* (*-nia*; *-nia*) *giełdowe*: quotation; **notowan|y** *adj* **1.** ***był ~y*** *JUR* he has a (criminal) record; ***nie byli ~i*** *JUR* they have no (criminal) record **2.** ***~y na giełdzie*** *ECON* listed, quoted **3.** (*oceniany*) ranked

Nowa Gwinea *f* (*Nowej Gwinei*) New Guinea

nowalijki *pl* (*-jek*) early vegetables

nowator *m* (*-ra*; *-rzy*) innovator; **nowatorski** *adj* innovative

Nowa Zelandia *f* (*Nowej Zelandii*) New Zealand

nowe *n* (*-wego*; *no pl*) the new

nowela[1] *f* (*-li*; *-le*) (*utwór*) long short story

nowela[2] *f* (*-li*; *-le*) *JUR* amendment

nowelizacja *f* (*-cji*; *-cje*) *JUR* amendment; **nowelizować** ⟨**z-**⟩ (*-zuję*) amend

nowicjusz *m* (*-sza*; *-sze*), **~ka** *f* (*-ki*; *-ki*) novice; ***~ w zawodzie*** newcomer to a profession

nowina *f* (*-ny*; *-ny*) news *sing*; ***dobra ~*** *REL* the Gospel; **nowinka** *f* (*-ki*; *-ki*) **1.** (*nowość*) novelty **2.** (*wiadomość*) news *sing*

nowiutki *adj* brand new

nowobogacki *m* (*-kiego*; *-ccy*), **-ka** *f* (*-kiej*; *-kie*) nouveau riche, (social) upstart

nowoczesny *adj* modern, up-to-date; **nowofundlandczyk** *m* (*-ka*; *-ki*) Newfoundland (dog); **nowomodny** *adj* newfangled; **nowomowa** *f* (*-wy*; *no pl*) newspeak; **noworoczny** *adj* **1.** *życzenia*, *zabawa*: New Year **2.** *postanowienia*: New Year's

noworodek *m* (*-dka*; *-dki*) newborn baby, infant; **nowoś|ć** *f* (*-ści*; *-ści*) novelty; ***~ci wydawnicze*** new books, recent publications; ***żadna ~ć*** nothing new

N

nowotworow|y *adj komórka*: cancerous, cancer; ***choroba ~a*** cancer; **nowotwór** *m (-woru; -wory)* MED cancer, *Br* tumour, *Am* tumor
nowożeńcy *pl (-ców)* newlyweds
nowożytny *adj* modern
now|y *adj* new; ***Ny Rok*** New Year; ***od ~a, na ~o*** again, once more; ***co ~ego?*** what's new, what's up?
Nowy Jork *m (Nowego Jorku)* New York
nozdrza *pl (-rzy)* nostrils
nożn|y *adj* foot; ***piłka ~a*** soccer, *Br* football
nożownik *m (-ka; -nicy)* knifer
nożyce *pl (-życ)* scissors, shears; **nożyczki** *pl (-czek)* scissors; ***~ do paznokci*** nail scissors; **nożyk** *m (-ka; -ki)* **1.** (small) knife **2.** *(ostrze)* blade
nów *m (nowiu; no pl)* new moon
nóż *m (noża; noże)* knife; ***pchnąć kogoś nożem*** stab s.o. (with a knife); ***mieć ~ na gardle*** *infml* be in a tight spot
nóżk|a *f (-ki; -ki)* **1.** *dim* (little) leg; ***~i w galarecie*** COOK pig trotters in aspic **2.** *(kieliszka)* stem
np. *abbr* (=***na przykład***) e.g.
n.p.m. *abbr* (=***nad poziomem morza***) above sea level
nr *abbr* (=***numer***) No., no.
nucić ⟨**za-**⟩ *(-cę) melodię*: hum
nud|a *f (-dy; -dy)* boredom; ***z ~ów*** out of boredom; ***ta książka to straszna ~a*** the book is really boring; **nudnawy** *adj* a little boring, tame; **nudno** *adv*: ***tam jest ~*** it it boring there; ***było jej ~*** she was bored; **nudności** *pl (-ści)* nausea *sing*; **nudny** *adj* boring, dull
nudyst|a *m (-ty; -dyści)* nudist; ***plaża dla ~ów*** nudist beach
nudziarz *m (-rza; -rze)*, **-ra** *f (-ry; -ry)* *infml* bore
nudzi|ć ⟨**z-**⟩ *(-dzę)* **I** *v/t* **1.** bore; ***to mnie ~*** I find it boring; ***szybko ~ły go nowe zabawki*** he quickly got bored with new toys **2.** *(mdlić)* ***~ mnie*** I feel sick **II** *v/i (marudzić) infml* moan, whine; ***nudzić się*** be bored; ***nudzi mi się*** I'm bored
nugat *m (-tu; no pl)* nougat
nuklearny *adj* nuclear
numer *m (-ru; -ry)* **1.** number **2.** *(ubrania, butów)* size **3.** *(czasopisma)* issue, number **4.** *infml* trick; ***wyciąć komuś ~*** pull a fast one on s.o.; **numeracja** *f (-ji; -je)* **1.** numbering **2.** *(rozmiary)* sizes *pl*; **numerek** *m (-rka; -rki)* **1.** number **2.** *(w szatni)* ticket, *Am* check **3.** *(stosunek) infml* quickie; **numerować** ⟨**po-**⟩ *(-ruję)* number
nuncjusz *m (-sza; -sze)* nuncio
nur: ***dać ~a*** take a dive
nurek *m (-rka; -rkowie)* diver; **nurkować** ⟨**za-**⟩ *(-kuję)* dive; **nurkowanie** *n (-nia; no pl)* diving; **nurkowy** *adj* diving; ***lot ~*** nosedive
nurt *m (-tu; -ty)* **1.** current **2.** *(trend)* trend, current
nurt|ować *v/im (-tuję)*: ***kogoś ~ują pytania (wątpliwości)*** s.o. is troubled by questions (doubts)
nurzać się *v/im (-rzam)* wallow (***w*** *L* in)
nuta *f (-ty; -ty)* **1.** note; ***cała ~*** *Br* semibreve, *Am* whole note; ***nuty* a)** *(notacja)* music **b)** *(partytura)* score **2.** *fig* note, touch; **nutka** *f (-ki; -ki) dim* note; **nutowy** *adj zapis*: musical
nutria *f (-rii; -rie)* **1.** BIOL coypu, *Am* nutria **2.** *(futro)* nutria
nuż *particle*: ***spróbuj, a ~ się uda*** have a try, there's always a chance; ***weź to, a ~ się przyda*** take it, you might need it
nużący *adj* tiring; **nużyć** ⟨**z-**⟩ *(-żę)* tire (out)
nylon *m (-nu; no pl)* nylon; **nylonowy** *adj* nylon

O

O

o[1] *prep (L/A)* **1.** *(na temat)* about, of; ***~ czym to jest?*** what is it about?; ***mówił ~ tobie*** he talked about you; ***dyskusja ~*** *I* discussion about, discussion on **2.** *(czas)* at; ***~ czwartej*** at four (o'clock); ***~ której godzinie?*** what time?; ***~ północy*** at midnight **3.** *(cecha)* with; ***dziewczyna ~ blond włosach*** blond-haired girl; ***~ napędzie odrzutowym*** jet-propelled **4.** *(cel)*

prosić ~ *A* ask for **5.** (*ilość*) by; ***~ 10%*** by 10 per cent; ***~ dwa lata młodsza*** two years younger **6.** (*używając*) with, on; ***chodzić ~ lasce*** walk with a stick; ***~ kulach*** on crutches; ***~ własnych siłach*** on one's own **7.** (*kontakt*) against; ***oprzeć się ~ ścianę*** lean against a wall

o[2] *interj* oh; ***~ tak!*** oh, yes!

oaza *f* (*-zy*; *-zy*) oasis

oba, ***obaj*** *pron* both

obalać ⟨**-lić**⟩ (*-lam*) **1.** *rząd*: overthrow **2.** *mit*: debunk **3.** *teorię*: invalidate, disprove **4.** *drzewo*: fell **5.** *butelkę*: *infml* knock back; ***obalenie*** *n* (*-nia*; *no pl*) *rządu*: overthrow

obandażować *v/p* (*-żuję*) bandage

obarczać ⟨**-czyć**⟩ (*-czam*) burden (*D* with); ***~ kogoś winą za*** *A* blame s.o. for

obaw|a *f* (*-wy*; *-wy*) **1.** (*lęk*) fear, anxiety; ***z ~y przed*** *I* in fear of; ***zachodzi ~a, że*** there is a fear that; ***nie ma ~!*** *infml* no fear!, never fear! **2.** (*niepokój*) concern, worry; ***budzący ~y*** worrying

obawiać się *v/im* (*-wiam*) be afraid (*G* of), fear (*G*); ***obawiam się, że*** I'm afraid (that); ***~ o coś*** be concerned about s.th.; ***~ o kogoś*** be anxious for s.o.

obcas *m* (*-sa*; *-sy*) heel; ***buty na wysokich ~ach*** high-heeled shoes; ***chodzić na wysokich ~ach***, ***nosić wysokie ~y*** wear high-heels; ***kobieta na wysokich ~ach*** a woman in high heels

obcesowy *adj* **1.** *zachowanie*: abrupt, brusque **2.** *pytanie*: blunt

obcęgi *pl* (*-gów*) **1.** pincers **2.** (*kombinerki*) pliers

obchodzi|ć ⟨**-bejść**⟩ (*-dzę*) **1.** *przeszkodę*: get round **2.** *przepisy*: get round, *form* circumvent **3.** *rocznicę*: celebrate **4.** (*interesować*) concern; ***nie ~ mnie to*** I don't care about it; ***obchodzić się*** **1.** (*posługiwać się*) handle, use (**z** *I*) **2.** (*traktować*) treat (**z** *I*) **3.** (*radzić sobie*) ***~ć się bez*** *G* do without

obchód *m* (*-chodu*; *-chody*) MED round; ***obchody*** (*uroczystości*) celebrations, celebration

obciach *m* (*-chu*; *-chy*) *infml*: ***to był ~*** it was hopeless; **obciachowy** *adj infml* hopeless

obciąć *v/p* → ***obcinać***

obciągać ⟨**-gnąć**⟩ (*-gam*) **1.** (*pokrywać*) cover (*D* with) **2.** *spódnicę*: straighten **3.** *butelkę*: *infml* knock back **4.** *vulg* go down (*D* on)

obciążać ⟨**-żyć**⟩ (*-żam*) **1.** weight, load (*I* with); ***~ kogoś winą*** put the blame on s.o. **2.** *obowiązkami*: burden (*I* with) **3.** *rachunek*: debit **4.** *kosztami*: charge (*I* with) **5.** ***~ hipoteką*** ECON encumber, mortgage

obciążający *adj* JUR incriminating

obciążeni|e *n* (*-nia*; *-nia*) **1.** load; ***bez ~a*** unloaded; ***~e genetyczne*** genetic load **2.** (*obowiązek*) burden **3.** ***~e hipoteczne*** ECON encumbrance

obciera|ć ⟨**obetrzeć**⟩ (*-ram*) **1.** (*wycierać*) wipe **2.** *skórę*: chafe; ***buty mnie ~ją*** my shoes are rubbing my feet

obcinacz *m* (*-cza*; *cze*): ***~ do paznokci*** nail clippers

obcinać ⟨**-ciąć**⟩ (*-nam*) cut; ***~ włosy*** (*u fryzjera*) have one's hair cut; ***obcinać się*** (*u fryzjera*) have one's hair cut

obcisły *adj* tight-fitting, tight

obco *adv* strange; ***czuł się tam ~*** he felt a stranger there, he felt an outsider there; **obcojęzyczny** *adj* **1.** *prasa*, *napis*: foreign **2.** *książka*: foreign language; **obcokrajowiec** *m* (*-wca*; *-wcy*) foreigner

obcość *f* (*-ści*; *no pl*) **1.** strangeness **2.** (*alienacja*) alienation

obcować *v/im* (*-cuję*): ***~ z naturą*** be in contact with nature, *form* commune with nature

obc|y **I** *adj* **1.** strange, unfamiliar; ***~e ciało*** BIOL foreign body; ***chciwość była mu ~a*** greed was alien to him; ***czuła się tam ~a*** she felt an outsider there **2.** *język*, *kapitał*, *waluta*: foreign **II** *m* (*-cego*; *-cy*), **-ca** *f* (*-cej*; *-ce*) **1.** stranger **2.** (*w science fiction*) alien

obczy|zna *f* (*-ny*; *no pl*): ***na ~źnie*** in exile

obdarowywać ⟨**-rować**⟩ (*-rowuję*) give (as a gift)

obdartus *m* (*-sa*; *-sy*) *dated* ragamuffin, *Br infml* scruff; **obdarty** *adj ubranie*: ragged

O

obdarzać ⟨**-rzyć**⟩ (*-rzam*): ~ ***kogoś szacunkiem*** place one's trust in s.o.; ~ ***kogoś miłością*** give s.o. one's love; **obdarzony** *adj*: ~ ***talentem*** gifted, endowed with talent

obdrapywać ⟨**-pać**⟩ (*-puję*) scratch

obdukcja *f* (*-ji*; *-je*) **1.** forensic examination **2.** (*zwłok*) autopsy

obdzielać ⟨**-lić**⟩ (*-lam*) deal out (*D* to)

obdzierać ⟨**obedrzeć**⟩ (*-ram*) strip, rip (**z** *G* off); ~ ***ze skóry*** skin, flay

obecnie *adv* at the moment, currently, at present; **obecnoś|ć** *f* (*-ści*; *no pl*) presence; ***w czyjejś ~ci*** in s.o.'s presence; ***lista ~ci*** attendance list; ***nauczyciel sprawdził ~ć*** the teacher called the register

obecn|y **I** *adj* **1.** present; ***~y!*** here!; ***w chwili ~ej*** at the present moment, at present **2.** (*teraźniejszy*) current, present **II** *m* (*-nego*; *-ni*) (*osoba obecna*): ***~i*** those present, attendees

obedrzeć *v/p* → ***obdzierać***

obejmować ⟨**objąć**⟩ (*-muję*) **1.** (*ramionami*) embrace **2.** (*zawierać*) include **3.** (*o przepisach, obszarze*) cover **4.** *stanowisko*: take (up), assume; ~ ***prowadzenie*** take the lead **5.** *władzę*: assume **6.** (*rozprzestrzeniać się*) ***płomienie objęły dach*** the flames spread to the roof; ***obejmować się*** (*ramionami*) embrace each other

obejrzeć *v/p* → ***oglądać***

obejści|e *n* (*-cia*; *-cia*) **1.** (*gospodarstwo*) farmstead **2.** (*maniery*) manner; ***miły w ~u*** amiable

obejść się *v/p*: ***musiała ~ smakiem*** she didn't get what she wanted, she went away empty-handed; → ***obchodzić***

obelg|a *f* (*-gi*; *-gi*) insult; ***~i*** insults, abuse

obelżywy *adj* insulting, abusive

oberwać *v/p* → ***obrywać***; **oberwanie** *n* (*-nia*; *-nia*): ~ ***chmury*** cloudburst

oberwaniec *m* (*-wańca*; *-wańcy*) *infml* scruff *Br*; **oberwany** *adj* ragged

oberżnąć *v/p* → ***obrzynać***

oberżyna *f* (*-ny*; *-ny*) *Br* aubergine, *Am* eggplant

obeschnąć *v/p* → ***obsychać***

obetrzeć *v/p* → ***obcierać***

obeznanie *n* (*-nia*; *no pl*) knowledge, familiarity; **obeznany** *adj* acquainted, familiar (**z** *I* with)

obezwładniać ⟨**-nić**⟩ (*-niam*) overpower

obeżreć *v/p* → ***obżerać***

obfitoś|ć *f* (*-ści*; *no pl*) abundance, profusion; ***róg ~ci*** horn of plenty, cornucopia

obfitować *v/im* (*-tuję*) abound (**w** *A* in/with), be full (**w** *A* of); **obfity** *adj* **1.** rich, abundant **2.** (*suty, bujny*) lavish **3.** *deszcz*: heavy, abundant

obgadywać ⟨**-dać**⟩ (*-duję*) **1.** backbite, run down **2.** (*omawiać*) talk over

obgryzać ⟨**-ryźć**⟩ (*-zam*) **1.** *kość*: gnaw **2.** *paznokcie, ołówek*: chew (on)

obiad *m* (*-du*; *-dy*) dinner; ***jeść*** ~ have dinner, dine; ***na*** ~ for dinner; **obiadowy** *adj* dinner

obibok *m* (*-ka*; *-ki*) *infml* lazybones

obicie *n* (*-cia*; *-cia*) (*materiał*) upholstery, covering

obić *v/p*: ~ ***się komuś o uszy*** ring a bell with; → ***obijać***

obie → ***oba***

obiec *v/p* → ***obiegać***

obiecać *v/p* → ***obiecywać***

obiecanka *f* (*-ki*; *-ki*) empty promise, hollow promise; **obiecujący** *adj* **1.** promising **2.** *początek*: auspicious

obiecywać ⟨**-cać**⟩ (*-cuję*) promise; ~ ***sobie coś po*** *L* pin one's hopes on; ~ ***komuś złote góry*** promise s.o. the earth, promise s.o. the moon

obieg *m* (*-gu*; *no pl*) **1.** circulation; ~ ***krwi*** blood circulation **2.** ASTR revolution; ***czas ~u*** period of revolution **3.** ECON time of circulation; ***puścić w ~*** pass round; ***wycofać z ~u*** withdraw from circulation, call in; ***drugi ~*** clandestine circulation, samizdat

obiegać ⟨**obiec, -gnąć**⟩ (*-gam*) **1.** run around, circle **2.** ASTR revolve around, go around **3.** *sklepy*: scour **4.** *prasę*: hit the headlines **5.** (*o plotce*) spread around

obiegowy *adj* *opinia*: widespread, widely-held, common; ***ruch*** ~ ASTR revolution; ***pieniądz*** ~ legal tender, *Am* lawful money

obiekcje *pl* (*-ji*) objections, doubts

obiekt *m* (*-tu*; *-ty*) **1.** object; ***niezidentyfikowany ~ latający*** UFO, Unidentified Flying Object **2.** ARCHIT building **3.** *fig* facility

O

obiektyw *m* (*-wu*; *-wy*) lens
obiektywny *adj* objective, unbiased
obierać ⟨**obrać**⟩ (*-ram*) **1.** *ziemniaki*: peel **2.** *zawód, przedstawicieli*: choose; **obieralny** *adj* elective
obierki *pl* (*-rek*), **obierzyny** *pl* (*-rzyn*) *kartofli*: peelings, peel *sing*
obietnica *f* (*-cy*; *-ce*) promise
obieżyświat *m* (*-ta*; *-ty*) globetrotter
obijać ⟨**obić**⟩ (*-jam*) **1.** *talerz*: chip **2.** *krzesło*: upholster, cover; ***obijać się*** slack, hang around
objadać ⟨**-jeść**⟩ (*-dam*) sponge off, sponge on; ***objadać się*** stuff oneself (*I* with)
objaśniać ⟨**-nić**⟩ (*-niam*) explain; **objaśnienie** *n* (*-nia*; *-nia*) explanation; *form* elucidation
objaw *m* (*-wu*; *-wy*) **1.** sign, manifestation **2.** MED symptom
objawiać ⟨**-wić**⟩ (*-wiam*) manifest, show; ***objawiać się*** manifest itself, reveal oneself; **objawienie** *n* (*-nia*; *-nia*) revelation
objawow|y *adj*: ***leczenie ~e*** symptomatic treatment
objazd *m* (*-du*; *-dy*) diversion; ***ruszyć w ~*** go on tour; **objazdowy** *adj droga*: bypass; ***teatr ~*** *Br* travelling theatre, *Am* traveling theater
objąć *v/p* → ***obejmować***
objechać *v/p* → ***objeżdżać***
objeść *v/p* → ***objadać***
objeżdżać ⟨**-jechać**⟩ (*-dżam*) **1.** *przeszkodę*: go round, drive round **2.** *kraj*: travel around **3.** (*besztać*) *infml* tell off, give a tongue lashing **4.** (*składać wizytę*) visit
objęci|e *n* (*-cia*; *-cia*) **1.** *stanowiska*: assumption **2.** ***~a*** (*uściski*) embrace; ***trzymać kogoś w ~ach*** hold s.o. in one's arms
objętość *f* (*-ści*; *-ści*) **1.** volume, capacity **2.** *książki*: length **3.** (*miara*) measured volume
objuczony *adj* laden, loaded
obkładać → ***okładać***
obkuwać ⟨**-kuć**⟩ (*-wam*) hew, cut; ***obkuwać się*** *infml Br* swot up, *dated* cram
oblać *v/o od* ***oblewać***
oblamowywać ⟨**-mować**⟩ (*-mowuję*) edge, hem
oblatany *adj* (*obeznany*) well versed (**w** *L* in), clued-up
oblatywacz *m* (*-cza*; *-cze*) test pilot
oblatywać ⟨**-lecieć**⟩ (*-tuję*) **1.** fly round, run around **2.** (*o tynku, płatkach*) fall off **3.** (*o plotkach, wiadomościach*) go the rounds; ***~ sklepy*** do the rounds of the shops; ***strach go obleciał*** he's got cold feet **4.** (*w lotnictwie*) test-fly
oblegać ⟨**-lec**⟩ (*-gam*) besiege
oblekać ⟨**-lec**⟩ (*-kam*) *pościel*: put a cover on
oblepiać ⟨**-pić**⟩ (*-piam*) paste, plaster
obleśny *adj infml* sleazy, disgusting
oblewać ⟨**-lać**⟩ (*-wam*) **1.** pour **2.** *ląd*: surround **3.** (*świętować*) *infml* drink to; ***~ nowe mieszkanie*** have a house-warming party **4.** (*na egzaminie*) fail; ***~ egzamin*** fail an exam; ***oblewać się*** **1.** spill over oneself **2.** ***~ się potem*** break out in a sweat; ***~ się rumieńcem*** blush
obleźć *v/p* → ***obłazić***
oblężenie *n* (*-nia*; *-nia*) siege; **oblężony** *adj* besieged
obliczać ⟨**-czyć**⟩ (*-czam*) **1.** calculate, count **2.** (*szacować*) estimate; **obliczalny** *adj* calculable
oblicz|e *n* (*-cza*; *-cza*) *lit* countenance; ***w ~u*** *G* in the face of; ***w ~u prawa wszyscy są równi*** all citizens are equal under the law
obliczenia *pl* (*-czeń*) calculations; ***~ kosztów*** calculations of costs; **obliczeniow|y** *adj* **1.** computational **2.** ***jednostka ~a*** unit of calculation
obliczony *adj* **1.** designed (**na** *A* to) **2.** (*zamierzony*) intended (**na** *A* for)
obliczyć *v/p* → ***obliczać***
obligacja *f* (*-ji*; *-je*) FIN bond, debenture
oblizywać ⟨**-zać**⟩ (*-zuję*) lick
oblodzony *adj* icy, ice-covered
obluzowany *adj* loose
obluzowywać ⟨**-zować**⟩ (*-zowuję*) loosen, slacken; ***obluzowywać się*** loosen, come loose
obładowywać ⟨**-dować**⟩ (*-dowuję*) load
obłamywać ⟨**-mać**⟩ (*-muję*) break off; ***obłamywać się*** break off
obłapiać ⟨**-pić**⟩ (*-piam*) *infml* paw, feel up
obłaskawiać ⟨**-wić**⟩ (*-wiam*) *lit* tame; **obłaskawiony** *adj* tame, tamed

O

obława *f* (*-wy*; *-wy*) **1.** battue (hunt), hunt **2.** *policyjna*: dragnet
obławiać się ⟨**-łowić**⟩ (*-wiam*) make a fortune, line one's pockets
obłazić ⟨**obleźć**⟩ (*-łażę*) **1.** (*o robakach*) crawl over **2.** (*o farbie*) peel off, flake off
obłąkanie *n* (*-nia*; *no pl*) MED lunacy, madness; **obłąkaniec** *m* (*-kańca*; *-kańcy*) madman, loony
obłąkany I *adj* **1.** insane, *Am* mad **2.** MED demented, deranged **II** *m* (*-nego*; *-ni*) madman; **obłąkana** *f* (*-nej*; *-ne*) madwoman
obłąkańczy *adj* **1.** insane, mad **2.** MED demented; **obłąkańczo** *adv* like a madman
obłęd *m* (*-du*; *-dy*) **1.** MED paranoia **2.** *infml* madness, lunacy; **obłędny** *adj* **1.** insane, mad **2.** MED demented
obłok *m* (*-ku*; *-ki*) cloud
obłowić się *v/p* → **obławiać się**
obłożnie *adv*: **~ chory** bedridden; **obłożn|y** *adj*: **~a choroba** prostrating illness
obłożony *adj*: **~ język** coated tongue, furred tongue
obłożyć *v/p* → **okładać**
obłuda *f* (*-dy*; *no pl*) hypocrisy, duplicity; **obłudnik** *m* (*-ka*; *-nicy*), **-nica** *f* (*-cy*; *-ce*) hypocrite; **obłudny** *adj* hypocritical, duplicitous
obłupywać ⟨**-pać**⟩ (*-puję*) shell, peel
obły *adj* egg-shaped, oval
obmacywać ⟨**-cać**⟩ (*-cuję*) feel, fondle
obmarzać ⟨**-znąć**⟩ (*-zam*) freeze over
obmawiać ⟨**-mówić**⟩ (*-wiam*) backbite, badmouth
obmierzły *adj* vile, loathsome
obmowa *f* (*-wy*; *no pl*) backbiting
obmówić *v/p* → **obmawiać**
obmurowanie *n* (*-nia*; *-nia*) wall; **obmurowywać** ⟨**-rować**⟩ (*-rowuję*) wall, surround with a wall
obmyć *v/p* → **obmywać**
obmyślać ⟨**-lić**⟩ (*-lam*) contemplate, work out
obmywać ⟨**-myć**⟩ (*-wam*) *twarz*: wash
obnażać ⟨**-żyć**⟩ (*-żam*) reveal, bare; **obnażać się 1.** (*rozbierać się*) strip off **2.** (*pokazywać genitalia*) expose oneself; **obnażony** *adj* bare, uncovered
obniżać ⟨**-żyć**⟩ (*-żam*) **1.** lower; **~ loty** lower one's standards **2.** *ceny*, *koszty*: reduce **3.** *płace*: cut; **obniżać się 1.** fall **2.** (*o poziomie*, *wieku*) drop
obniżka *f* (*-ki*; *-ki*): **~ cen** cut in prices, reduction in prices; **~ kosztów** cost cuts; **~ płac** wage cuts
obnosić ⟨**-nieść**⟩ (*-noszę*) carry around, carry about; **obnosić się** parade, flaunt (**z** *I* to)
oboczność *f* (*-ści*; *-ści*) GRAM alternation
obojczyk *m* (*-ka*; *-ki*) ANAT collarbone, clavicle
oboje *pron* both
obojętnieć ⟨**z-**⟩ (*-nieję*) become indifferent (**na** *A* to); **obojętność** *f* (*-ści*; *no pl*) indifference; **obojętn|y** *adj* **1.** indifferent; **jest mi to ~e** I don't care **2.** (*neutralny*) neutral
obojnactwo *n* (*-wa*; *no pl*) BIOL hermaphroditism, androgyny; **obojnak** *m* (*-ka*; *-ki*) BIOL hermaphrodite, androgyne
obok I *prep* (*G*) by, next to; **~ siebie** next to each other **II** *adv* by, next to; **tuż ~** right next to, right by
obolały *adj* sore, achy
obopólny *adj* mutual
obora *f* (*-ry*; *-ry*) barn, cowshed; **obornik** *m* (*-ka*; *no pl*) manure
obosieczny *adj* two-edged, double-edged
obostrzać ⟨**-rzyć**⟩ (*-rzam*) tighten; **obostrzenie** *n* (*-nia*; *-nia*) restriction
obowiązany *adj* obliged; **obowiąz|ek** *m* (*-zku*; *-zki*) duty, responsibility; **~ki** duties, obligations; **pełniący ~ki dyrektora** acting director; **poczuwać się do ~ku** have a sense of duty
obowiązkowo *adv* obligatorily
obowiązkowość *f* (*-ści*; *no pl*) **1.** (*przymus*) compulsoriness **2.** (*odpowiedzialność*) responsibility **3.** (*solidność*) reliability; **obowiązkowy** *adj* **1.** *osoba*: reliable **2.** *lektura*, *zajęcia*: required, compulsory
obowiązując|y *adj* binding; **nadać czemuś moc ~ą** make s.th. legally binding
obowiązywać *v/im* (*-zuję*) be in effect; **zacząć ~** go into effect; **obowiązuje strój wieczorowy** evening dress is de rigueur
obozować *v/im* (*-zuję*) camp, encamp; **obozowisko** *n* (*-ka*; *-ka*) **1.** camp

2. *namiotowe*: *Br* campsite, *Am* campground; **obozowy** *adj* camping, camp

obój *m* (*oboju*; *oboje*) MUS oboe

obóz *m* (*obozu*; *obozy*) camp; **~ wypoczynkowy** rest camp; **~ pracy** *Br* (forced) labour camp, *Am* (forced) labor camp; **~ dla uchodźców** refugee camp; **~ koncentracyjny** concentration camp; **rozbić ~** make camp, pitch camp

obrabiać ⟨**-robić**⟩ (*-biam*) **1.** work **2.** *ziemię*: till **3.** *materiał*: hem **4.** (*obmawiać*) *infml* badmouth **5.** (*okradać*) *infml* clean out

obrabiarka *f* (*-ki*; *-ki*) machine tool

obrabowywać ⟨**-bować**⟩ (*-bowuję*) rob

obracać ⟨**-rócić**⟩ (*-cam*) **1.** turn; **~ w gruzy**, **~ w perzynę** burn to ashes; **~ w żart** make a joke (out) of **2.** *wzrok*: look (**na** *A* at) **3.** (*pójść i wrócić*) go back and forth, go to and fro **4.** *pieniędzmi*: deal in; **obracać się 1.** turn; **~ się przeciwko** *D* backfire on; **~ się na dobre** take a turn for the better **2.** (*wirować*) whirl **3.** (*wokół słońca*) revolve (**wokół** *G* around) **4.** (*bywać*) move

obrachunek *m* (*-nku*; *-nki*) FIN account

obrać *v/p* → **obierać**

obradować *v/im* (*-duję*) debate (**nad** *I*); **obrady** *pl* (*obrad*) deliberations

obradzać ⟨**-rodzić**⟩ (*-dzam*) **1.** abound (**w** *A* in) **2.** (*o drzewie*) crop well

obramowanie *n* (*-nia*; *-nia*) **1.** frame **2.** *kominka*: surround; **obramowany** *adj* framed, surrounded, bordered

obrastać ⟨**-rosnąć**⟩ (*-tam*) (*pokrywać się*): be covered, be overgrown (*I*/**w** *A* with); **~ w piórka** feather one's nest

obraz *m* (*-zu*; *-zy*) painting, picture; **święty ~** holy picture; **~ nędzy i rozpaczy** sorry sight, pitiful sight

obraza *f* (*-zy*; *no pl*) **1.** offence, insult **2.** *uczuć*: affront; **~ moralności publicznej** affront to public morality, offence against public morality

obraz|ek *m* (*-zka*; *-zki*) **1.** *dim* (small) picture; **książka z ~kami** illustrated book; **jak z ~ka** pretty as a picture; **patrzeć w kogoś jak w ~ek** think the world of s.o., dote on s.o. **2.** *fig* picture, scene

obrazić *v/p* → **obrażać**

obrazkowy *adj* picture

obrazoburczy *adj* iconoclastic; **obrazoburstwo** *n* (*-wa*; *no pl*) iconoclasm

obrazować ⟨**z-**⟩ (*-zuję*) depict, illustrate; **obrazowy** *adj* vivid

obraźliwy *adj* **1.** offensive, insulting **2.** *osoba*: touchy, thin-skinned

obrażać ⟨**-razić**⟩ (*-żam*) offend, insult; **obrażać się** be offended, *Br* take offence, *Am* take offense (**o** *A* for/at); **~ się na kogoś za** *A* take offence at s.o. for

obrażalski I *adj* huffy **II** *m* (*-kiego*; *-scy*) *hum* Mr Hypersensitive; **obrażalska** *f* (*-kiej*; *-kie*) *hum* Ms Hypersensitive

obrażeni|e *n* (*-nia*; *-nia*) injury; **~a głowy** (**ciała**) head (body) injuries

obrażony *adj* offended

obrąbek *m* (*-bka*; *-bki*) hem

obrąbywać ⟨**-bać**⟩ (*-buję*) *gałęzie*: chop off

obrączka *f* (*-ki*; *-ki*) **1.** ring **2.** *ślubna*: wedding ring

obręb *m* (*-bu*; *-by*) **1.** range; **w ~ie** *G* within; **poza ~em** *G* outside **2.** *materiału*: hem

obrębek *m* (*-bka*; *-bki*) → **obrąbek**

obrębiać ⟨**-bić**⟩ (*-biam*) hem

obręcz *f* (*-czy*; *-cze*) **1.** hoop **2.** *koła*: wheel rim **3.** *beczki*: barrel hoop, barrel band

obrobić *v/p* → **obrabiać**

obrodzić *v/p* → **obradzać**

obrok *m* (*-ku*; *no pl*) feed

obro|na *f* (*-ny*; *no pl*) *Br* defence, *Am* defense; **~na konieczna**, **~na własna** JUR *Br* defence of necessity, *Br* self-defence; **~na z urzędu** JUR *Br* court-appointed defence, *Br* public defence; **stawać w ~nie** *G*, stand up for, *Br* come to s.o.'s defence; **mieć coś na swoją ~nę** have s.th. to say for oneself; **wziąć kogoś w ~nę** stand up for s.o., *Br* come to s.o.'s defence

obronić *v/p* → **bronić**

obronny *adj* defensive

obrońca *m* (*-cy*; *-cy*), **-czyni** *f* (*-ni*; *-nie*) **1.** defender **2.** JUR *Br* defence counsel, *Am* defense attorney **3.** SPORT defender, defensive player; **obrończ|y** *adj*: **mowa ~a** JUR *Br* defence summation, *Am* defense summation

obrosnąć *v/p* → **obrastać**

obrośnięty *adj* **1.** overgrown (*I* with) **2.** (*z zarostem*) unshaven **3.** (*włochaty*) hairy

obrotność *f* (*-ści*; *no pl*) resourcefulness; **obrotny** *adj* **1.** resourceful **2.** *Am infml* savvy

obrotomierz *m* (*-rza*; *-rze*) tachometer, revolution counter

obrotow|y *adj* rotational, rotary, revolving; ***podatek ~y*** sales tax; ***środki ~e*** *ECON* current assets, floating assets

obroża *f* (*-ży*; *-że*) collar

obróbka *f* (*-ki*; *-ki*) processing, treatment

obrócić *v/p* → ***obracać***

obrót *m* (*-rotu*; *-roty*) **1.** rotation, turn; ***wziąć kogoś w obroty*** put the screws on s.o.; ***na wysokich obrotach*** in high gear, at full steam **2.** *PHYS ECON* turnover; ***~ pieniędzmi*** (***kapitałem***) money (capital) turnover; ***~ towarami*** trade, sales

obrumieniać ⟨***-nić***⟩ (*-niam*) *COOK* brown

obrus *m* (*-sa*; *-sy*) tablecloth

obruszać ⟨***-szyć***⟩ (*-szam*) **1.** *belkę*: loosen **2.** *ziemię*: dislodge; ***obruszać się*** **1.** come loose **2.** (*o ziemi*) slide **3.** (*o osobie*) become indignant, bridle

obrys *m* (*-su*; *-sy*) outline; **obrysowywać** ⟨***-sować***⟩ (*-sowuję*) outline

obryw *m* (*-wu*; *-wy*) *ziemi*: landslide, landslip

obrywać ⟨***oberwać***⟩ (*-wam*) **1.** tear off **2.** *owoce*: pick **3.** *infml* get a beating; ***obrywać się*** come off

obryzgiwać ⟨***-gać***⟩ (*-guję*) splash

obrządek *m* (*-dku*; *-dki*) **1.** (*w gospodarstwie*) chores *pl* **2.** *REL* rite

obrządzać ⟨***-dzić***⟩ (*-dzam*) *zwierzęta*: tend

obrzezanie *n* (*-nia*; *no pl*) *REL* circumcision

obrzeże *n* (*-ża*; *-ża*) *lit* edge

obrzęd *m* (*-du*; *-dy*) rite, ceremony; **obrzędowy** *adj* ritual

obrzęk *m* (*-ku*; *-ki*) *MED* swelling, *Br* oedema, *Am* edema; **obrzękać** ⟨***-knąć***⟩ (*-kam*) *MED* swell, become swollen; **obrzękły** *adj MED* **1.** swollen, puffy **2.** *brzuch*: distended

obrzmiały *adj* → ***obrzękły***; **obrzmienie** *n* (*-nia*; *-nia*) *MED* puffiness, swelling

obrzmiewać ⟨***-mieć***⟩ (*-wam*) → ***obrzękać***

obrzucać ⟨***-cić***⟩ (*-cam*) **1.** (*rzucać*) throw **2.** *fig* shower (*I* with); ***~ kogoś wzrokiem***, ***~ kogoś spojrzeniem*** cast a glance at s.o.; ***~ wyzwiskami*** hurl insults; ***~ błotem*** *fig* slander, drag through the mud **3.** (*obszyć*) overcast, whip(stitch); ***obrzucać się*** cast at each other, throw at each other

obrzydlistwo *n* (*-wa*; *-wa*) abomination, horror; **obrzydliwiec** *m* (*-wca*; *-wcy*) rotter, stinker

obrzydliwy *adj* disgusting, revolting, nasty

obrzydły *adj* disgusting, repulsive

obrzydnąć *v/p* → ***brzydnąć***

obrzydzać ⟨***-dzić***⟩ (*-dzam*) put off, spoil; **obrzydzeni|e** *n* (*-nia*; *no pl*) disgust, revulsion; ***do ~a*** ad nauseam

obrzynać ⟨***oberżnąć***⟩ (*-nam*) cut off

obsada *f* (*-dy*; *-dy*) **1.** *THEAT* cast **2.** (*załoga*) crew, team **3.** *TECH* housing, mounting; **obsadka** *f* (*-ki*; *-ki*) penholder

obsadzać ⟨***-dzić***⟩ (*-dzam*) **1.** plant (*I* with) **2.** *stanowiska*: fill (*I* with) **3.** *TECH* mount, fix **4.** *THEAT* cast

obserwacja *f* (*-ji*; *-je*) observation; **obserwacyjny** *adj* **1.** observation; ***punkt ~*** lookout (point); **2.** *system*: monitoring; **obserwator** *m* (*-ra*; *-rzy*) observer

obserwatorium *n* (*indecl*; *-ria*) observatory; ***~ astronomiczne*** astronomical observatory; ***~ meteorologiczne*** meteorological observatory

obserwować ⟨***za-***⟩ (*-rwuję*) **1.** (*patrzeć*) watch **2.** (*zauważyć*) observe **3.** (*kontrolować*) monitor

obsesj|a *f* (*-ji*; *-je*) obsession; ***mieć ~ę na punkcie*** *G* be obsessed with; **obsesyjny** *adj* obsessive

obsiać *v/p* → ***obsiewać***

obsiadać ⟨***-siąść***⟩ (*-dam*) crowd around

obsiew *m* (*-wu*; *-wy*) sowing, seeding; **obsiewać** ⟨***-siać***⟩ (*-wam*) sow, seed

obsikać *v/p* (*-kam*) *infml* piss, pee (*A* at)

obskakiwać ⟨***-skoczyć***⟩ (*-kuję*) *infml* **1.** surround **2.** (*krytykować*) jump on, leap on **3.** (*odwiedzać*) *infml* drop in, stop by

O

obskubywać → ***oskubywać***
obskurny *adj* shabby, mang(e)y, squalid
obsługa *f* (*-gi*; *no pl*) **1.** service; **~ *klientów*** customer service; **~ *samochodów*** car service station **2.** (*personel*) personnel, staff; **~ *naziemna*** (*na lotnisku*) ground crew, ground personnel
obsługiwać ⟨***-łużyć***⟩ (*-guję*) **1.** serve **2.** attend to; ***obsługiwać się*** (*samemu*) serve oneself
obsmarowywać ⟨***-rować***⟩ (*-rowuję*) **1.** smear **2.** *infml* smear, do a hatchet job on
obsmażać ⟨***-żyć***⟩ (*-żam*) brown, sear
obstawa *f* (*-wy*; *no pl*) bodyguards *pl*
obstawać *v/im* (*-taję*) insist (***przy*** *L* on)
obstawiać ⟨***-wić***⟩ (*-wiam*) **1.** surround **2.** *zwycięzcę*: back **3.** (*w zakładach*) bet on **4.** *SPORT* mark
obstępować ⟨***-tąpić***⟩ (*-puję*) gather around, crowd around
obstrukcja *f* (*-ji*; *-je*) **1.** *MED* constipation **2.** *POLIT* (parliamentary) obstruction, stonewalling
obstrzał *m* (*-łu*; *-ły*) fire
obsunąć się *v/p* → ***obsuwać się***
obsuszać ⟨***-szyć***⟩ (*-szam*) dry, dry off
obsuwać się ⟨***-sunąć***⟩ (*-wam*) **1.** slide **2.** (*upaść*) sink
obsychać ⟨***obeschnąć***⟩ (*-cham*) dry
obsypywać ⟨***-pać***⟩ (*-puję*) **1.** sprinkle (*I* with) **2.** *fig* shower (*I* with); **~ *pocałunkami*** shower with kisses; ***obsypywać się*** fall
obszar *m* (*-ru*; *-ry*) area; **~ *powietrzny*** air space; **obszarnik** *m* (*-ka*; *-nicy*) *HIST* landowner
obszarpaniec *m* (*-pańca*; *-pańcy*) *infml* guttersnipe, scruff; **obszarpany** *adj* scruffy, shabby; **obszarpywać** ⟨***-pać***⟩ (*-puję*) tear off, tear away
obszerny *adj* **1.** spacious, roomy **2.** *ubranie*: loose-fitting **3.** *tekst*: extensive, thorough
obszukiwać ⟨***-kać***⟩ (*-kuję*) search, frisk
obszycie *n* (*-cia*; *-cia*) trim, edging; **obszywać** ⟨***-szyć***⟩ (*-wam*) trim, edge (*I* with)
obtaczać ⟨***-toczyć***⟩ (*-czam*) **1.** *TECH* turn, lathe **2.** *COOK* coat; **~ *w tartej bułce*** coat with breadcrumbs
obtarcie *n* (*-cia*; *-cia*) scrape, graze
obtłuczony *adj talerz*: chipped; **obtłukiwać** ⟨***-łuc***⟩ (*-kuję*) *talerz*: chip
obtoczyć *v/p* → ***obtaczać***
obu → ***oba***
obuch *m* (*-cha*; *-chy*) **1.** *siekiery*: butt **2.** *młotka*: face
obudowa *f* (*-wy*; *-wy*) **1.** casing **2.** *komputera, zegarka*: case
obudowywać ⟨***-dować***⟩ (*-dowuję*) **1.** fit (*I* with) **2.** *BUILD* line (*I* with)
obudzić się *v/p* (*-dzę*) wake up; → ***budzić***
obumarły *adj* dead; **obumierać** ⟨***-mrzeć***⟩ (*-ram*) **1.** die **2.** *fig* die out
oburącz *adv* with both hands, in both hands
oburzać ⟨***-rzyć***⟩ (*-rzam*) shock, outrage; ***oburzać się*** be indignant, be outraged (***na*** *A* at/over/about)
oburzający *adj* shocking, outrageous; **oburzeni|e** *n* (*-nia*; *no pl*) indignation, outrage; ***ku czyjemuś ~u*** to s.o.'s indignation; **oburzony** *adj* shocked, indignant, outraged
obustronnie *adv* on both sides, mutually; **obustronny** *adj* **1.** mutual **2.** *materiał*: double-sided **3.** *MED* double
obuwie *n* (*-wia*; *no pl*) footwear, footgear; ***sklep z ~m*** shoe shop; **obuwniczy** *adj* shoe
obwałowanie *n* (*-nia*; *-nia*) embankment; **obwałowywać** ⟨***-łować***⟩ (*-łowuję*) *rzekę*: bank, dam
obwarowani|e *n* (*-nia*; *-nia*) **1.** fortification **2. *~a*** *JUR* stipulations; **obwarowany** *adj* fortified
obwarowywać ⟨***-rować***⟩ (*-rowuję*) **1.** fortify **2.** *fig* hedge around
obwarzanek *m* (*-nka*; *-nki*) bagel
obwąchiwać ⟨***-chać***⟩ (*-chuję*) sniff
obwiązywać ⟨***-zać***⟩ (*-zuję*) tie, bind (*I* with)
obwiedziony *adj* encircled, surrounded (*I* with)
obwieszczać ⟨***-wieścić***⟩ (*-czam*) announce; **obwieszczenie** *n* (*-nia*; *-nia*) announcement, declaration
obwieszony *adj* hung (*I* with)
obwieścić *v/p* → ***obwieszczać***
obwieźć *v/p* → ***obwozić***
obwiniać ⟨***-nić***⟩ (*-niam*) accuse (***o*** *A* of), blame (***o*** *A* for); **obwiniony** *adj* accused

obwisać ⟨**-snąć**⟩ (*-sam*) droop, sag
obwisł|y *adj* droopy, sagging; ***~e piersi*** pendulous breasts
obwodnica *f* (*-cy*; *-ce*) ring road, beltway; **obwodow|y** *adj* **1.** district; ***droga ~a*** ring road **2.** *układ nerwowy*: peripheral
obwoluta *f* (*-ty*; *-ty*) dust jacket, wrapper
obwoływać ⟨**-łać**⟩ (*-łuję*) proclaim, acclaim, hail
obwozić ⟨**-wieźć**⟩ (*-wożę*) take for a ride; ***~ po mieście*** drive around town
obwoźny *adj*: ***prowadzić handel ~*** sell door-to-door
obwód *m* (*-wodu*; *-wody*) **1.** size; ***~ bioder*** hip size; ***~ biustu*** bust size **2.** (*rejon*) district; ***~ wyborczy*** voting district, electoral district **3.** *MATH* perimeter **4.** *TECH* circuit; ***~ scalony*** integrated circuit
obwódk|a *f* (*-ki*; *-ki*) edge, rim
oby *particle* may; ***~ś był szczęśliwy!*** may you be happy!; ***~ tak dalej!*** let's keep it that way
obycie *n* (*-cia*; *no pl*) **1.** familiarity, experience (**z** *I* with) **2.** (*maniery*) refinement, polish, urbanity
obyczaj *m* (*-ju*; *-je*) **1.** (*zwyczaj*) custom **2.** (*tradycja*) tradition; ***starym ~em*** according to an old tradition **3.** ***~e*** morals, mores; ***zepsucie ~ów*** corruption of morals
obyczajowość *f* (*-ści*; *no pl*) **1.** mores *pl*, customs *pl* **2.** (*moralność*) morals *pl*, morality; **obyczajow|y** *adj* **1.** ***powieść ~a*** novel of manners **2.** *temat*: social
obyć się *v/p* → ***obywać się***
obydwa, ***obydwaj***, ***obydwie***, ***obydwoje*** → ***oba***, ***oboje***
obyty *adj* **1.** experienced, familiar (**z** *I* with); ***~ w świecie*** cultured, urbane **2.** *towarzysko*: refined; ***mało ~*** socially awkward
obywać się ⟨**obejść**⟩ (*-wam*) go (**bez** *G* without), do (**bez** *G* without), make do (**bez** *G* without); ***obyło się bez kłótni*** a row was avoided
obywatel *m* (*-la*; *-le*), **~ka** *f* (*-ki*; *-ki*) citizen; ***honorowy ~*** honorary citizen; **obywatelski** *adj* civil, civic; **obywatelstwo** *n* (*-wa*; *no pl*) citizenship
obżarstwo *n* (*-wa*; *no pl*) gluttony; **obżartuch** *m* (*-cha*; *-chy*) *infml* glutton, gannet
obżerać ⟨**obeżreć**⟩ (*-ram*) *infml* **1.** gnaw **2.** ***~ kogoś*** scrounge food from s.o., scrounge food off s.o.; ***obżerać się*** gorge oneself, pig out
ocalać ⟨**-lić**⟩ (*-lam*) rescue, save (**od** *G* from); ***~ komuś życie*** save s.o.'s life
ocalały **I** *adj* **1.** rescued **2.** *rzecz*: intact **II** *m* (*-łego*; *-lali*), **-ła** *f* (*-łej*; *-łe*) survivor
ocaleć *v/p* (*-leję*) **1.** survive; ***~ od śmierci*** escape death **2.** (*o rzeczy*) remain intact, be extant; **ocaleni|e** *n* (*-nia*; *no pl*) rescue, survival; ***nie do ~a*** beyond recovery
ocalić *v/p* → ***ocalać***
ocean *m* (*-nu*; *-ny*) ocean; ***≈ Spokojny*** the Pacific Ocean; ***za ~em*** overseas; **oceaniczny** *adj* ocean, oceanic; ***statek ~*** ocean-going ship
ocen|a *f* (*-ny*; *-ny*) **1.** assessment, appraisal; ***dać do ~y*** get an expert's opinion on **2.** (*wycena*) estimation, evaluation **3.** (*w szkole*) *Br* mark, *Am* grade
oceniać ⟨**-nić**⟩ (*-niam*) **1.** assess, judge **2.** (*szacować*) assess, estimate **3.** (*w szkole*) assess
ocet *m* (*octu*; *no pl*) vinegar; ***w occie*** in vinegar, pickled
ochlapywać ⟨**-pać**⟩ (*-puję*) splash, splatter; ***ochlapać się*** **1.** splash oneself **2.** (*poplamić ubranie*) stain one's clothing
ochładzać ⟨**-łodzić**⟩ (*-dzam*) cool (down), freshen; ***ochładzać się*** cool off, cool down; ***ochłodziło się*** it got colder
ochłapy *pl* (*-pów*) **1.** scraps **2.** *fig* leftovers
ochłod|a *f* (*-dy*; *no pl*) refreshment; ***dla ~y*** to refresh oneself; **ochłodzenie** *n* (*-nia*; *-nia*) cooler weather
ochłodzić *v/p* → **ochładzać**
ochłonąć *v/p* (*-nę*) cool down, simmer down (**z** *G* after)
ochoczo *adv* willingly, enthusiastically; **ochoczy** *adj* willing, eager, cheerful; ***~ do rozmowy*** eager to talk
ochot|a *f* (*-ty*; *no pl*) willingness (**na** *A*/**do** *G* to do s.th.); ***mieć ~ę na lody*** feel like having some ice cream;

~a do życia will to live; **odeszła mnie ~a do tańca** I don't feel like dancing anymore; **z ~ą** willingly
ochotniczka *f* (*-ki*; *-ki*) volunteer; **ochotniczo** *adv* voluntarily; **ochotniczy** *adj* voluntary; **ochotnik** *m* (*-ka*; *-nicy*) volunteer; **na ~a** voluntarily
ochra *f* (*-ry*; *no pl*) *Br* ochre, *Am* ocher
ochraniacz *m* (*-cza*; *-cze*) guard, pad, patch; **~ na kolana** knee pad
ochraniać ⟨**-ronić**⟩ (*-niam*) protect (**przed** *I*/**od** *G* from); **ochraniać się** protect oneself
ochron|a *f* (*-ny*; *no pl*) protection, preservation; **~a środowiska** environmental protection; **~a przeciwpożarowa** fire protection; **~a przeciwlotnicza** anti-aircraft protection; **~a zabytków** conservation; **~a osobista** personal security; **pracownik ~y** security guard; **być pod ~ą** be protected
ochroniarz *m* (*-rza*; *-rze*) security guard, bodyguard
ochronić *v/p* → **ochraniać**
ochronn|y *adj* protective; **szczepienia ~e** (preventive) vaccination
ochrypły *adj* hoarse, husky
ochrypnąć *v/p* (*-nę*) shout oneself hoarse, become hoarse
ochrzan *m* (*-nu*; *no pl*) *infml* telling-off; **ochrzaniać** ⟨**-nić**⟩ (*-niam*) *infml* tell off, dress down
ochrzcić *v/p* → **chrzcić**
ociąga|ć się *v/im* (*-gam*) dally, linger (**z** *I* over); **~jąc się** reluctantly
ociągani|e *n* (*-nia*; *no pl*): **bez ~a** without hesitation; **z ~em** with reluctance
ociekać ⟨**-knąć**⟩ (*-kam*) **1.** drip; **~ krwią** drip with blood; **~ potem** sweat profusely **2.** (*schnąć*) drain
ociekający *adj krwią*: dripping (*I* with)
ocielić się *v/p* → **cielić się**
ociemniały *adj* blind; **zakład dla ~ch** school for the blind
ocieplać ⟨**-lić**⟩ (*-lam*) (*przed zimnem*) insulate; **ocieplać się** warm (up); **ociepliło się** it got warmer
ocieplany *adj kurtka*: quilted, padded; **ocieplenie** *n* (*-nia*; *-nia*) **1.** *klimatu*: warming **2.** TECH insulation
ocierać ⟨**otrzeć**⟩ (*-ram*) **1.** wipe **2.** *skórę*: rub, chafe; **ocierać się 1.** wipe, rub **2.** (*stykać się*) come into contact (**o** *A* with)
ociężały *adj* ponderous, lumbering; **~ umysłowo** dull, dim-witted
ociosywać ⟨**-sać**⟩ (*-suję*) hew
ocipieć *v/p* (*-pieję*) *infml* go bonkers, be off one's nut
ociupinę *adv* a bit
ocknąć się *v/p* (*-nę*) awake
ocleni|e *n* (*-nia*; *no pl*) customs clearance; **podlegający ~u** subject to customs duty, dutiable; **nie mieć nic do ~a** have nothing to declare; **oclić** *v/p* → **clić**; **oclony** *adj* duty-paid
octan *m* (*-nu*; *-ny*) CHEM acetate; **octowy** *adj* acetic
ocucić *v/p* → **cucić**
ocyganić *v/p* (*-nię*) *infml* diddle, con
ocynkować *v/p* → **cynkować**
oczarowanie *n* (*-nia*; *no pl*) bewitchment, enchantment
oczarowywać ⟨**-rować**⟩ (*-rowuję*) bewitch, enchant
oczekiwać *v/im* (*-kuję*) expect (*G*/**na** *A*), wait (*G*/**na** *A* for); **~ po kimś** *G* expect s.o. to do s.th.; **~ dziecka** expect a baby
oczekiwani|e *n* (*-nia*; *-nia*) expectation; **wbrew ~om** contrary to expectations; **zgodnie z ~ami** as expected; **oczekiwany** *adj* expected
oczerniać ⟨**-nić**⟩ (*-niam*) slander
oczęta *pl* (*ocząt*) *hum* eyes
oczk|o *n* (*-ka*; *-ka*) **1.** *dim* eye; **~o w głowie** *fig* the apple of s.o.'s eye **2.** (*w pierścionku*) gem, stone **3.** (*na kostce do gry*) pip **4.** (*w kartoflu*) eye **5.** (*w pończosze*) run, *Br* ladder **6.** (*przy robieniu na drutach*) stitch **7.** (*gra*) blackjack **8.** (*w sieci*) mesh **9. ~a** (*w rosole*) eyes of fat
oczny *adj* optic, eye
oczodół *m* (*-dołu*; *-doły*) socket, orbit
oczopląs *m* (*-su*; *no pl*) MED nystagmus; **można dostać ~u** *fig* it's so garish one's eyes get sore
oczy *pl* → **oko**
oczyszczać ⟨**oczyścić**⟩ (*-czam*) **1.** cleanse, clear, purify **2.** *fig* cleanse, rid (**z** *G* of)
oczyszczalnia *f* (*-ni*; *-nie*) *ścieków*: sewage treatment plant, purification plant; **oczyszczenie** *n* (*-nia*; *no pl*) purification
oczyścić *v/p* → **oczyszczać**

oczytanie *n* (*-nia*; *no pl*) (wide) reading; **oczytany** *adj* well-read

oczywist|y *adj* obvious, self-evident; ***to ~e, że*** it's obvious that; ***rzecz ~a*** an obvious thing; **oczywiście** *adv* of course, certainly

od *prep* (*G*) **1.** from; ***~ morza*** from the sea; ***płatny ~ godziny*** paid by the hour; ***~ ręki*** on the spot; ***~ sztuki*** apiece; ***~ zaraz*** right away, immediately, as from now; ***~ stu złotych w górę*** from 100 zlotys up(wards) **2.** (*przynależność*) to; ***dziurka ~ klucza*** keyhole; ***klucze ~ mieszkania*** keys to the flat **3.** (*w czasie*) since, for; ***~ rana do wieczora*** from morning till night; ***~ 20 lat*** for 20 years **4.** (*niż*) than; ***starszy ~e mnie*** older than me **5.** (*przeciw*) against; ***syrop ~ kaszlu*** cough syrup; ***ubezpieczenie ~ kradzieży*** insurance against theft

oda *f* (*ody*; *ody*) ode

odautorski *adj* author's

odąć *v/p* → ***odymać***

odb. *abbr* (= **odbiorca**) *listu*: recipient

odbarwiać 〈***-wić***〉 (*-wiam*) fade, bleach; ***odbarwiać się*** fade, bleach

odbezpieczać 〈***-czyć***〉 (*-czam*) *broń*: release the safety catch of, arm

odbębniać 〈***-nić***〉 (*-niam*) *infml* **1.** *godziny pracy*: sit out **2.** *zajęcia*: rattle off, botch up **3.** *utwór*, *wiersz*: bang out

odbici|e *n* (*-cia*; *-cia*) **1.** (*w lustrze*) reflection, image; ***~e światła*** reflection of light; ***mieć ~a*** *infml* be a weirdo, behave strangely **2.** (*odzwierciedlenie*) reflection, impression **3.** (*odcisk*) impression

odbić *v/p* → ***odbijać***

odbiegać 〈***-biec***〉 (*-gam*) **1.** run away (**od** *G* from) **2.** *od normy*, *rzeczywistości*: diverge, differ (**od** *G* from); ***~ od tematu*** digress from the subject; ***odbiegł go sen*** he couldn't sleep anymore; ***odbiegła ją chęć do spania*** she didn't feel like sleeping anymore

odbierać 〈***odebrać***〉 (*-ram*) **1.** (*zabierać*) take back; ***~ sobie życie*** take one's own life **2.** *poród*: deliver **3.** *list*, *paczkę*: receive **4.** *telefon*: pick up; ***~ dzicoko z przedszkola*** pick up a child from kindergarten; ***~ z lotniska*** pick up from the airport **5.** *bagaż*: collect **6.** *prawo*, *przywilej*: deprive of, divest of; ***~ sen*** deprive of sleep **7.** *słowa*: construe, interpret (***jako*** *A* as) **8.** *RADIO* receive

odbijać 〈***-bić***〉 (*-jam*) **I** *v/t* **1.** *światło*: reflect **2.** *pieczęć*: stamp, impress **3.** *deseń*: print, copy **4.** (*odłupywać*) chip (off) **5.** *piłkę*, *atak*: deflect, return **6.** *zakładników*: rescue **7.** *dziewczynę*: take away **II** *v/i* (*o statku*) push off; ***odbija mu*** *infml* he's nuts; ***odbijać się*** **1.** (*w lustrze*) be mirrored, be reflected **2.** (*o głosie*) reflect **3.** (*o piłce*) rebound **4.** *rękami*: push oneself off **5.** (*o śladach*) be impressed **6.** *fig* affect (**na** *L*) **7.** ***odbiło mu się*** he belched; ***~ się od dna*** *fig* things can only get better

odbior|ca *m* (*-cy*; *-cy*), **-czyni** *f* (*-ni*; *-nie*) **1.** *listu*: recipient **2.** *towaru*, *gazu*: consumer **3.** ***~cy*** audience

odbiorczy *adj* *RADIO* receiving; **odbiornik** *m* (*-ka*; *-ki*) *RADIO* receiver

odbiór *m* (*-bioru*; *no pl*) **1.** *nagrody*, *przesyłki*: receipt, collection; ***~ bagażu*** baggage reclaim **2.** *obiektu*: acceptance **3.** *utworu*: reception **4.** *RADIO* reception, pickup

odbitka *f* (*-ki*; *-ki*) *PHOT* copy, print; ***~ ksero*** a xerox copy; **odbity** *adj* *światło*: reflected

odblask *m* (*-ku*; *-ki*) reflected light, gleam; **odblaskow|y** *adj* fluorescent; ***światła ~e*** *AUTO* reflectors; ***trójkąt ~y*** *AUTO* warning triangle

odblokowywać 〈***-kować***〉 (*-kowuję*) **1.** *drogę*: clear **2.** *granicę*: reopen **3.** *konto*: unblock **4.** ***~ kierownicę*** unlock the steering wheel

odbudow|a *f* (*-wy*; *no pl*) *BUILD* reconstruction, rebuilding, restoration; ***być w ~ie*** be reconstructed

odbudowywać 〈***-wać***〉 (*-dowuję*) **1.** *BUILD* rebuild, reconstruct **2.** *fig* rebuild, restore

odburkiwać 〈***-knąć***〉 (*-kuję*) snap (out)

odbyć *v/p* → ***odbywać***

odbyt *m* (*-tu*; *-ty*) *ANAT* anus; **odbytnica** *f* (*-cy*; *-ce*) *ANAT* rectum

odbywać 〈***-być***〉 (*-wam*) **1.** *rozmowę*, *zebranie*: hold **2.** *szkolenie*: undergo **3.** *służbę*, *karę*: serve **4.** *podróż*: make; ***odbywać się*** take place, be held

O

odc. *abbr* (=**odcinek**) part, episode
odcedzać ⟨**-dzić**⟩ (*-dzam*) *kartofle, kluski*: drain (off), strain
odchodne: ***na ~***, ***na odchodnym*** on parting
odchody *pl* (*-dów*) excrement *sing*, faeces, *Am* feces
odchodzić ⟨**odejść**⟩ (*-dzę*) **1.** walk away, wander off; ***~ na emeryturę*** retire; ***~ od tematu*** digress from the topic, stray from the topic; ***~ od zmysłów*** *fig* be going out of one's mind, be beside oneself **2.** (*o pociągu*) leave, depart **3.** (*o farbie*) come off, peel off **4.** (*o podeszwie*) come off **5.** (*opuszczać*) leave, abandon **6.** (*o ulicy*) diverge, branch off
odchorowywać ⟨**-rować**⟩ (*-rowuję*) fall ill (as a result of)
odchować *v/p* (*-wam*) bring up, raise
odchrząkiwać ⟨**-knąć**⟩ (*-kuję*) clear one's throat, hawk
odchudzać się ⟨**-dzić**⟩ (*-dzam*) go on a diet, lose weight; **odchudzający** *adj* slimming, low-fat; **odchudzanie** (**się**) *n* (*-nia*; *no pl*) slimming
odchwaszczać ⟨**-waścić**⟩ (*-czam*) weed
odchylać ⟨**-lić**⟩ (*-lam*) **1.** *głowę*: tilt **2.** *firankę*: draw aside, pull aside; **odchylać się 1.** lean **2.** (*przechylać się*) tilt **3.** *od normy*: deviate
odchylenie *n* (*-nia*; *-nia*) deviation
odciąć *v/p*: ***~ od świata*** cut off from the outside world; → ***odcinać***
odciągać ⟨**-gnąć**⟩ (*-gam*) **1.** pull away, drag away **2.** *płyn*: draw (off) **3.** (*odwlekać*) defer, postpone **4.** *fig* draw away, entice away (**od** *G* from); ***~ uwagę*** draw attention; ***~ śmietanę z mleka*** skim milk
odciążać ⟨**-żyć**⟩ (*-żam*) relieve
odciekać ⟨**-ciec**, **-knąć**⟩ (*-kam*) drain
odcień *m* (*-nia*; *-nie*) shade, hue, tint, tinge; ***~ niebieskawy*** bluish tinge
odcierpieć *v/p* (*-pię*) **1.** endure, bear **2.** (*odpokutować*) expiate, atone (**za** *A* for); ***~ za swoje*** receive one's just deserts
odcięty *adj* cut-off; **odcięta** *f* (*-tej*; *-te*) *MATH* abscissa
odcinać ⟨**-ciąć**⟩ (*-nam*) cut off, cut away; **odcinać się 1.** (*odpowiadać*) answer back **2.** (*wypierać się*) dissociate oneself (**od** *G* from) **3.** (*zrywać kontakty*) cut oneself off (**od** *G* from) **4.** (*na tle*) show up, stand out (against)
odcin|ek *m* (*-nka*; *-nki*) **1.** section; ***~ek czasu*** length of time **2.** *filmu*, *powieści*: episode, part; ***powieść w ~kach*** a novel in instalments **3.** *MATH* segment
odcisk *m* (*-ku*; *-ki*) **1.** imprint; ***~i palców*** fingerprints **2.** *MED* callus, corn; ***nadepnąć komuś na ~*** *fig* step on s.o.'s toes
odciskać ⟨**-snąć**⟩ (*-kam*) **1.** *pieczęć*: impress **2.** *sok*: squeeze **3.** *ślad*: leave; **odciskać się 1.** be impressed, be imprinted **2.** *fig* impress
odcumowywać ⟨**-mować**⟩ (*-mowuję*) unmoor, cast off
odcyfrowywać ⟨**-rować**⟩ (*-rowuję*) decipher, decode
odczekać *v/p* (*-kam*) wait
odczepiać ⟨**-pić**⟩ (*-piam*) unfasten, unhook; **odczepiać się 1.** become unfixed **2.** (*odłączać*) uncouple **3.** ***odczep się!*** leave me alone!
odczepn|y: ***na ~ego*** offhandedly, for the sake of peace and quiet
odczuci|e *n* (*-cia*; *-cia*) feeling, impression; ***~a zmysłowe*** sensations
odczuwać ⟨**-czuć**⟩ (*-wam*) feel, sense; ***dać komuś odczuć*** make s.o. feel; ***dać się odczuć*** be felt
odczuwalny *adj* perceptible, discernible
odczyn *m* (*-nu*; *-ny*) *CHEM* reaction
odczyszczać ⟨**-czyścić**⟩ (*-czam*) get s.th. clean
odczyt *m* (*-tu*; *-ty*) **1.** lecture **2.** *TECH* reading
odczytywać ⟨**-tać**⟩ (*-tuję*) **1.** decipher **2.** (*na głos*) read out **3.** *licznik*: read off **4.** (*interpretować*) interpret **5.** *INF* read
oddać *v/p* → ***oddawać***
oddalać ⟨**-lić**⟩ (*-lam*) **1.** move away **2.** (*odwlekać*) put off **3.** *wniosek*: dismiss; **oddalać się 1.** walk away, wander off (**od** *G* from) **2.** *fig* grow apart, drift apart
oddalenie *n* (*-nia*; *no pl*) **1.** distance **2.** *wniosku*: dismissal; **oddalony** *adj* remote, distant (**od** *G* from); ***~ o dwa kilometry od*** *G* two kilometres away from

O

oddanie *n* (*-nia*; *no pl*) devotion, dedication; **~ *do eksploatacji*** putting into operation, putting into use; ***z ~m*** devotedly; **oddany** *adj* devoted, committed

oddawać ⟨**-dać**⟩ (*-daję*) **1.** give back; ***oddaję panu głos*** the floor is yours; **~ *głos na*** *A* POLIT vote for; **~ *mocz*** urinate; **~ *pod sąd*** bring to justice; **~ *pod opiekę*** leave in s.o.'s care; **~*przysługę*** do a favour; **~*życie*** sacrifice one's life; **~ *krew*** donate blood; **~ *do użytku*** put into operation; **~ *do dyspozycji*** put at s.o.'s disposal; **~ *do naprawy*** have repaired **2.** (*zwracać*) return **3.** (*ofiarowywać*) give, hand over **4.** *cześć*: pay **5.** *pocałunki*: return **6.** *sens*, *nastrój*: render; ***oddawać się*** **1.** *zajęciu*: devote oneself (*D* to); **~ *się w ręce policji*** turn oneself in (to the police) **2.** (*o kobiecie*) give oneself

oddawca *m* (*-cy*; *-cy*), **-czyni** *f* (*-ni*; *-nie*) *form* deliverer

oddech *m* (*-chu*; *-chy*) breathing, breath; ***świeży*** **~** fresh breath; ***nieświeży*** **~** bad breath; **oddechowy** *adj* respiratory

oddelegowywać ⟨**-gować**⟩ (*-gowuję*) *pracownika*: assign (**do** *G* to)

oddłużenie *n* (*-nia*; *no pl*) abatement of debts

oddolny *adj* grass-roots

oddychać *v/im* (*-cham*) breathe; **~ *głęboko*** breathe deeply; **~ *świeżym powietrzem*** breathe fresh air

oddychanie *n* (*-nia*; *no pl*) breathing; ***sztuczne*** **~** artificial respiration

oddział *m* (*-łu*; *-ły*) **1.** department; **~ *karny*** JUR criminal division **2.** (*filia*) branch **3.** (*w szpitalu*) ward; **~ *intensywnej opieki*** intensive care unit **4.** (*w wojsku*) unit, troop

oddziałowa *f* (*-wej*; *-we*) (*w szpitalu*) ward sister

oddziałowy **I** *adj* **1.** department **2.** (*w szpitalu*) ward **II** *m* (*-wego*; *-wi*) ward nurse

oddziaływać ⟨**-łać**⟩ (*-łuję*/*-wam*) **1.** have an influence (***na*** *A* on) **2.** (*wpływać*) affect **3.** CHEM interact

oddzielać ⟨**-lić**⟩ (*-lam*) separate; ***oddzielać się*** separate; **oddzielny** *adj* separate, individual

oddzierać ⟨**odedrzeć**⟩ (*-ram*) tear off, tear away

oddzwaniać ⟨**-dzwonić**⟩ (*-niam*) call back, ring back, return a call

oddźwięk *m* (*-ku*; *-ki*) *fig* response, reaction

ode *prep*: **~ *mnie*** from me; → ***od***

odebrać *v/p* → ***odbierać***

odechciewać się ⟨**-cieć**⟩: ***odechciało mu się jeść*** he didn't feel like eating anymore

odedrzeć *v/p* → ***oddzierać***

odegnać *v/p* → ***odganiać***

odegrać *v/p* → ***odgrywać***

odejmować ⟨**odjąć**⟩ (*-muję*) **1.** (*odłączać*) take away, remove; **~ *sobie lat*** never declare one's true age, pretend to be younger; **~ *coś sobie od ust*** deprive oneself of s.th. **2.** MATH subtract, deduct

odejmowanie *n* (*-nia*; *no pl*) MATH subtraction

odejście *n* (*-cia*; *no pl*) **1.** departure **2.** (*odchylenie*) deviation **3.** (*rozbieżność*) divergence

odejść *v/p* (*-jdę*): **~ *z kwitkiem*** go empty-handed; → ***odchodzić***

odemknąć *v/p* → ***odmykać***

odepchnąć *v/p* → ***odpychać***

odeprzeć *v/p* (*-rę*) drive back, repel; → ***odpierać***

oderwać *v/p* → ***odrywać***

oderwan|ie *n* (*-nia*; *no pl*) detachment; separation; ***w ~iu od*** *G* in isolation from, separately from; ***w ~iu od rzeczywistości*** out of touch with reality

oderwany *adj* unconnected; **~ *od rzeczywistości*** unrealistic, out of touch with reality

oderżnąć *v/p* → ***odrzynać***

odesłać *v/p* → ***odsyłać***

odespać *v/p* → ***odsypiać***

odetchnąć *v/p* (*-nę*) breathe; **~ *świeżym powietrzem*** get a breath of fresh air; **~ *z ulgą*** breathe a sigh of relief

odetkać *v/p* → ***odtykać***

odezwa *f* (*-wy*; *-wy*) appeal, proclamation

odezwać się *v/p* → ***odzywać się***

odęty *adj* **1.** thick, distended **2.** *fig* sulky, sullen

odfajkowywać ⟨**-kować**⟩ (*-kowuję*) *infml* tick off, check off

odfruwać ⟨**-runąć**⟩ (*-wam*) fly away

odgadywać ⟨**-dnąć**⟩ (*-duję*) **1.** guess **2.** *zagadkę*: puzzle out
odgałęziać się ⟨**-zić**⟩ (*-ziam*) branch off; **odgałęzienie** *n* (*-nia*; *-nia*) **1.** branch **2.** *drogi*: turn-off
odganiać ⟨**-gonić**, **odegnać**⟩ (*-niam*) **1.** drive off, drive away **2.** *fig* ward off **3.** *muchy*: chase away
odgarniać ⟨**-nąć**⟩ (*-niam*) **1.** sweep aside, brush aside **2.** *śnieg*: clear off
odginać ⟨**-giąć**⟩ (*-nam*) (*wyprostować*) straighten, bend back
odgłos *m* (*-su*; *-sy*) sound, noise; **~y** sounds
odgniatać ⟨**-nieść**⟩ (*-tam*) impress; **~ sobie stopy** get calluses on the feet; **odgniatać się** bruise
odgonić *v/p* → **odganiać**
odgórny *adj* POLIT top-down
odgradzać ⟨**-rodzić**⟩ (*-dzam*) **1.** separate **2.** *płotem*: fence off; **odgradzać się** **1.** (*izolować się*) isolate oneself (**od** *G* from) **2.** (*separować się*) shut oneself off (**od** *G* from)
odgraniczać ⟨**-czyć**⟩ (*-czam*) separate, divide; **odgraniczać się** differ
odgrażać się *v/im* (*-żam*) threaten
odgrodzić *v/p* → **odgradzać**
odgruzowywać ⟨**-zować**⟩ (*-zowuję*) clear s.th. of rubble
odgrywać ⟨**odegrać**⟩ (*-wam*) **1.** *sztukę*: play, act; **~ głupiego** play a fool; **~ rolę** act out a role **2.** (*w kartach*) win back; **odgrywać się** get even
odgryzać ⟨**-ryźć**⟩ (*-zam*) bite off; **odgryzać się** snap back, strike back
odgrzać *v/p* → **odgrzewać**
odgrzebywać ⟨**-bać**⟩ (*-buję*) **1.** dig up **2.** *zasypanych*: dig out
odgrzewać ⟨**-rzać**⟩ (*-wam*) warm up, heat up
odgwizdywać ⟨**-dać**⟩ (*-duję*) SPORT whistle
odhaczać ⟨**-czyć**⟩ (*-czam*) tick off
odholować *v/p* (*-luję*) tow away, haul away
odizolować *v/p* → **izolować**
odjazd *m* (*-du*; *-dy*) *pociągu*: departure; **odjazdowy** *adj infml* cool
odjąć *v/p*: **odjęło mu mowę** he was left speechless; **odjęło mu rozum** he lost his mind; **cztery ~ dwa** four minus two; → **odejmować**
odjechać *v/p* → **odjeżdżać**
odjemna *f* (*-nej*; *-ne*) MATH minuend; **odjemnik** *m* (*-ka*; *-ki*) MATH subtrahend
odjezdne: **na odjezdym** on the point of leaving, on departure
odjeżdżać ⟨**-jechać**⟩ (*-dżam*) leave, go away (**do** *G* to)
odkarmiać ⟨**-mić**⟩ (*-miam*) feed up
odkarmiony *adj* well-fed
odkażać ⟨**-kazić**⟩ (*-żam*) **1.** disinfect **2.** *teren*: decontaminate; **odkażający** *adj* antiseptic
odkąd *pron* **1.** since **2.** (*od kiedy*) since when **3.** (*od jakiegoś miejsca*) where from
odklejać ⟨**-leić**⟩ (*-jam*) *znaczek*: unstick; **odklejać się** come unstuck, come unglued
odklepywać ⟨**-pać**⟩ (*-puję*) rattle off
odkładać ⟨**odłożyć**⟩ (*-dam*) **1.** put aside, put back **2.** *słuchawkę*: hang up **3.** *zebranie*: put off **4.** (*oszczędzać*) save; **~ na czarną godzinę** save for a rainy day; **odkładać się** accumulate
odkłaniać się ⟨**-łonić**⟩ (*-niam*) return s.o.'s greeting
odkochiwać się ⟨**-chać**⟩ (*-chuję*) fall out of love
odkomenderować *v/p* (*-ruję*) detach, detail
odkopywać ⟨**-pać**⟩ (*-puję*) **1.** dig up **2.** *zasypanych*: dig out **3.** ⟨**-pnąć**⟩ *piłkę*: kick back
odkorkowywać ⟨**-kować**⟩ (*-kowuję*) uncork, unplug
odkrajać ⟨**-roić**⟩ (*-jam*) slice off
odkrawać ⟨**-roić**⟩ (*-wam*) → **odkrajać**
odkręcać ⟨**-cić**⟩ (*-cam*) **1.** unscrew, twist off **2.** *kurek*: open **3.** (*odwołać*) call off; **odkręcać się** come loose, unscrew
odkroić *v/p* → **odkrajać**
odkrycie *n* (*-cia*; *-cia*) discovery
odkryt|y *adj* **1.** open, outdoor; **z ~ą głową** bareheaded **2.** *kontynent*: discovered
odkrywać ⟨**-ryć**⟩ (*-wam*) **1.** discover; **~ Amerykę** *fig* reinvent the wheel **2.** *tajemnicę*: discover, unravel **3.** *ramiona*: bare **4.** (*wyjawiać*) lay bare; **odkrywać się** **1.** uncover oneself **2.** (*zdradzać się*) lay one's designs bare, unmask oneself

O

odkrywca *m* (*-cy*; *-cy*), **-czyni** *f* (*-ni*; *-nie*) discoverer, explorer
odkrywcz|y *adj* revealing, innovative; **~a wyprawa** exploratory expedition; **~y umysł** creative mind; **odkrywka** *f* (*-ki*; *-ki*) MIN opencast mine
odkrztuszać ⟨**-sić**⟩ (*-szam*) **1.** cough up **2.** MED expectorate
odkrzykiwać ⟨**-knąć**⟩ (*-kuję*) shout back
odkształcać ⟨**-cić**⟩ (*-cam*) deform; **odkształcać się** become deformed, lose shape
odkuć *v/p* → **odkuwać**
odkup *m* (*-pu*; *no pl*) redemption; **prawo ~u** power of redemption
Odkupiciel *m* (*-la*; *no pl*) REL Redeemer, *Br* Saviour, *Am* Savior
odkupić *v/p* → **odkupywać**
odkupienie *n* (*-nia*; *no pl*) REL redemption
odkupywać ⟨**-pić**⟩ (*-puję*) **1.** buy, purchase (**od** *G* from) **2.** (*z powrotem*) buy back, repurchase (**od** *G* from) **3.** *stratę*: replace **4.** *winę*: expiate, atone for
odkurzacz *m* (*-cza*; *-cze*) vacuum cleaner, *Br* Hoover®; **odkurzać** ⟨**-rzyć**⟩ (*-rzam*) **1.** dust **2.** (*odkurzaczem*) vacuum, *Br* hoover **3.** *fig* dust off
odkuwać ⟨**-kuć**⟩ (*-wam*) **1.** forge **2.** (*odłupać*) knock; **odkuwać się** *infml* recover financially
odlać *v/p* → **odlewać**
odlatywać ⟨**-lecieć**⟩ (*-tuję*) **1.** (*o osobie*) depart **2.** (*o samolocie*) take off **3.** (*o ptakach*) fly away **4.** (*odpadać*) come off
odległość *f* (*-ści*; *-ści*) distance; **odległ|y** *adj* distant, remote; **~y o pięć kilometrów** five kilometres away; **~a przeszłość** distant past
odlepiać ⟨**-pić**⟩ (*-piam*) unglue, unstick
odlew[1] *m* (*-wu*; *-wy*) cast, casting
odlew[2]: **uderzać na ~** strike backhanded, bash
odlewać ⟨**-lać**⟩ (*-wam*) **1.** pour out, strain **2.** TECH cast; **odlewać się** *infml* have a piss, take a piss
odlewnia *f* (*-ni*; *-nie*) foundry; **odlewniczy** *adj* casting
odleżeć *v/p* (*-żę*) **1.** *chorobę*: stay in bed, rest **2. ~ sobie plecy** get bedsores on one's back; **odleżeć się** (*o owocach*) mellow
odleżyny *pl* (*-żyn*) MED bedsores
odliczać ⟨**-czyć**⟩ (*-czam*) **1.** count out **2.** FIN deduct; **odliczanie** *n* (*-nia*; *no pl*) countdown; **odliczeni|e** *n* (*-nia*; *-nia*) FIN deduction; **po ~u podatku** post-tax
odlot *m* (*-tu*; *-ty*) departure; **czas ~u** departure time; **odlotowy** *adj infml* cool
odludek *m* (*-dka*; *-dki*) recluse, solitary; **odludny** *adj* remote, deserted; **odludzi|e** *n* (*-dzia*; *-dzia*) remote place, backwoods *pl*; **na ~u** in the middle of nowhere
odłam *m* (*-mu*; *-my*) POLIT faction; **odłamek** *m* (*-mka*; *-mki*) **1.** chip; **~ szkła** chip of glass **2.** *pocisku*: shrapnel; **~ granatu** grenade shrapnel
odłamywać ⟨**-mać**⟩ (*-muję*) break off; **odłamywać się** break off
odłączać ⟨**-czyć**⟩ (*-czam*) **1.** uncouple, detach **2.** *osoby*: separate **3.** TECH disconnect; **odłączać się 1.** detach, come off **2.** (*o osobach*) wander off, separate oneself
odłogi *pl* (*-gów*) fallow land *sing*; **leżeć ~em** lie fallow
odłożyć *v/p* → **odkładać**
odłupywać ⟨**-pać**⟩ (*-puję*) chip away, flake; **odłupywać się** chip off, flake off
odma *f* (*-my*; *no pl*) MED emphysema, pneumothorax
odmachiwać ⟨**-chać**, **-chnąć**⟩ (*-chuję*) wave back
odmaczać ⟨**-moczyć**⟩ (*-czam*) soak off; **odmaczać się** soak off
odmalowywać ⟨**-lować**⟩ (*-lowuję*) **1.** repaint **2.** *fig* describe; **odmalowywać się** be shown, be seen
odmarzać ⟨**-znąć**⟩ (*-zam*) thaw (off), defrost
odmaszerowywać ⟨**-rować**⟩ (*-rowuję*) march off, march away
odmawiać ⟨**-mówić**⟩ (*-wiam*) **1.** refuse, decline, deny; **~ sobie** deny oneself; **~ służby wojskowej** refuse to enter military service; **~ pomocy** refuse to help; **~ komuś posłuszeństwa** rebel against s.o.; **~ posłuszeństwa** TECH fail **2.** *wizytę*: cancel **3.** *modlitwę*: say

odmeldowywać się ⟨**-dować**⟩ (*-dowuję*) report one's departure
odmęt *m* (*-tu*; *-ty*) **1.** the deep, abyss **2.** *fig* turmoil, whirlpool
odmian|a *f* (*-ny*; *-ny*) **1.** change; ***dla ~y, na ~ę*** for a change **2.** (*postać*) variant **3.** *BIOL* variety **4.** *GRAM* inflection
odmieniać ⟨**-nić**⟩ (*-niam*) **1.** change **2.** *GRAM* inflect; ***odmieniać się*** **1.** change **2.** *GRAM* inflect
odmieniec *m* (*-mieńca*; *-mieńcy*) misfit
odmienność *f* (*-ści*; *no pl*) dissimilarity, otherness; ***~ poglądów*** difference of opinions; **odmienny** *adj* **1.** different, disparate **2.** *GRAM* inflected
odmierzać ⟨**-rzyć**⟩ (*-rzam*) **1.** measure out **2.** *godziny*: count
odmładzać ⟨**-łodzić**⟩ (*-dzam*) rejuvenate, regenerate
odmładzający *adj* rejuvenating
odmłodnieć *v/p* → ***młodnieć***
odmłodzić *v/p* → ***odmładzać***
odmoczyć *v/p* → ***odmaczać***
odmowa *f* (*-wy*; *-wy*) refusal; ***~ pomocy*** *JUR* failure to render assistance; **odmowny** *adj odpowiedź*: negative
odmówić *v/p* → ***odmawiać***
odmrażacz *m* (*-cza*; *-cze*) defroster
odmrażać ⟨**-rozić**⟩ (*-żam*) **1.** *szybę*, *lodówkę*: defrost **2.** *mrożonkę*: thaw **3.** ***odmrozić sobie palce*** injure one's fingers by frostbite
odmrożenie *n* (*-nia*; *-nia*) *MED* frostbite
odmrukiwać ⟨**-knąć**⟩ (*-kuję*) mumble
odmykać ⟨**odemknąć**⟩ (*-kam*) **1.** open **2.** *zamek*: unlock
odnająć *v/p* → ***odnajmować***
odnajdywać ⟨**-naleźć**⟩ (*-duję*) find, track down; ***odnajdywać się*** **1.** turn up **2.** *fig* pull oneself together
odnajmować ⟨**-jąć**⟩ (*-muję*) **1.** (*komuś*) let out, rent out **2.** (*od kogoś*) rent
odnaleźć *v/p* → ***odnajdywać***
odnawiać ⟨**-nowić**⟩ (*-wiam*) **1.** *mieszkanie*: renovate **2.** *kontakty*: renew; ***odnawiać się*** **1.** improve **2.** (*o kontaktach*) be renewed **3.** (*o chorobie*) recur **4.** (*o ranie*) open up
odniesieni|e *n* (*-nia*; *-nia*): reference; ***w ~u do*** *G* with reference to; ***punkt ~a*** point of reference
odnieść *v/p* → ***odnosić***
odnoga *f* (*-gi*; *-gi*) **1.** *rzeki*: branch **2.** *górska*: mountain range
odnosić ⟨**-nieść**⟩ (*-szę*) **1.** take back, carry back **2.** *sukces*: achieve; ***~ korzyść*** profit **3.** *zwycięstwo*: achieve, gain **4.** *szkodę*: suffer **5.** *rany*: sustain; ***odnosić się*** **1.** treat **2.** concern
odnośnie: ***~*** *G* in relation to, with reference to
odnośnik *m* (*-ka*; *-ki*) **1.** footnote, note **2.** (*znak*) reference mark
odnośny *adj* relevant, pertinent
odnotowywać ⟨**-tować**⟩ (*-towuję*) **1.** make a note of **2.** *fig* take note of
odnowić *v/p* → ***odnawiać***
odnowienie *n* (*-nia*; *no pl*) **1.** *mieszkania*: renovation **2.** *kontaktów*: renewal
odnóża *pl* (*-ży*) *BIOL* limbs
odosabniać ⟨**-sobnić**⟩ (*-niam*) isolate; ***odosabniać się*** isolate oneself
odosobnienie *n* (*-nia*; *no pl*) isolation, seclusion; **odosobniony** *adj* **1.** *miejsce*: secluded **2.** *przypadek*: isolated
odór *m* (*odoru*; *odory*) *Br* odour, *Am* odor, stench
odpadać ⟨**-paść**⟩ (*-dam*) **1.** (*o tynku*) come off **2.** (*zostać wyeliminowanym*) drop out **3.** ***odpada!*** it's out of the question!
odpadki *pl* (*-ków*) scraps; ***~ spożywcze*** kitchen waste; **odpadkowy** *adj* waste
odpady *pl* (*-dów*) **1.** waste *sing*; ***~ radioaktywne*** radioactive waste **2.** *dzianiny*: clippings, scraps
odpalać ⟨**-lić**⟩ (*-lam*) **1.** fire **2.** *papierosa*: light from another **3.** (*odpowiadać*) *infml* answer back **4.** (*dać*) *infml* spare
odparci|e *n* (*-cia*; *no pl*) **1.** *ataku*: repulse **2.** *zarzutu*: refutation; ***nie do ~a*** *argument*: irrefutable
odparowywać ⟨**-rować**⟩ (*-rowuję*) **1.** evaporate **2.** (*odpowiadać*) retort
odparz|ać ⟨**-rzyć**⟩ (*-rzam*) chafe, irritate; ***~yłam sobie stopy*** my feet are chafed
odpasywać ⟨**-sać**⟩ (*-suję*): ***~ coś*** take s.th. off the belt
odpaść *v/p* → ***odpadać***
odpędzać ⟨**-dzić**⟩ (*-dzam*) **1.** drive away, force back **2.** *owady*: chase off
odpiąć *v/p* → ***odpinać***
odpieczętowywać ⟨**-tować**⟩ (*-towuję*) unseal
odpierać ⟨**odeprzeć**⟩ (*-ram*) **1.** *wroga*:

drive back **2.** *cios*: parry **3.** *zarzut*, *argument*: refute **4.** *atak*: repulse
odpiłowywać ⟨**-łować**⟩ (*-łowuję*) saw off
odpinać ⟨**-piąć**⟩ (*-nam*) **1.** *kaptur*: detach **2.** *guzik*, *kurtkę*: unfasten; ***odpinać się*** (*o agrafce*) come undone
odpis *m* (*-su*; *-sy*) **1.** *dokumentu*: copy **2.** FIN deduction
odpisywać ⟨**-sać**⟩ (*-suję*) **1.** answer **2.** (*ściągać*) copy, crib (**od** *G* from) **3.** *własność*: cede, transfer **4.** FIN deduct; ***~ coś od podatku*** deduct s.th. from tax
odplamiacz *m* (*-cza*; *-cze*) stain remover
odpłacać ⟨**-cić**⟩ (*-cam*) pay back; ***~ pięknym za nadobne*** give tit for tat; ***odpłacać się*** repay
odpłatny *adj* chargeable, payable
odpłynąć *v/p* → ***odpływać***
odpływ *m* (*-wu*; *-wy*) **1.** outflow; ***~ kapitału*** capital outflow **2.** GEOGR ebb, low tide
odpływać ⟨**-łynąć**⟩ (*-wam*) **1.** (*o osobie*) swim away **2.** (*o statku*) sail away **3.** (*o cieczy*) run off, drain off; **odpływowy** *adj* **1.** outflow **2.** GEOGR (low) tidal
odpoczyn|ek *m* (*-nku*; *-nki*) rest; ***chwila ~ku*** break
odpoczywać ⟨**-cząć**⟩ (*-wam*) rest, take a rest, have a rest
odpokutować *v/p* (*-tuję*) atone, do penance
odpompowywać ⟨**-pować**⟩ (*-powuję*) pump out
odpornościowy *adj*: ***układ ~*** immunological system
odporność *f* (*-ści*; *no pl*) **1.** (*psychiczna*) resilience **2.** MED immunity **3.** BIOL TECH resistance
odporny *adj* **1.** BIOL TECH resistant (**na** *A* to); ***~ na wpływy atmosferyczne*** weatherproof; ***~ na zimno*** immune to cold, frost-resistant; ***~ na wstrząsy*** shock-resistant **2.** MED immune
odpowiadać ⟨**-wiedzieć**⟩ (*-dam*) **1.** answer, reply, respond (**na** *A*); ***telefon nie odpowiada*** nobody answers the phone; ***~ przed sądem*** be brought to trial, be tried **2.** (*być odpowiedzialnym*) be responsible (**za** *A* for) **3.** (*zgadzać się*) match, correspond (*D* to) **4.** (*pasować*) ***~ komuś*** suit s.o.
odpowiedni *adj* suitable, right, appropriate
odpowiednik *m* (*-ka*; *-ki*) counterpart, equivalent
odpowiedzialność *f* (*-ści*; *no pl*) responsibility; ***~ cywilna*** JUR civil liability; ***~ karna*** JUR criminal responsibility
odpowiedzialny *adj* **1.** (*rzetelny*) reliable **2.** (*winny*): responsible (**za** *A* for)
odpowiedzieć *v/p* → ***odpowiadać***; **odpowiedź** *f* (*-dzi*; *-dzi*) answer, response, reply
odpowietrzać ⟨**-rzyć**⟩ (*-rzam*) bleed; **odpowietrznik** *m* (*-ka*; *-ki*) air vent
odpór *m* (*-poru*; *no pl*) resistance
odpracowywać ⟨**-cować**⟩ (*-cowuję*) work off
odprawa *f* (*-wy*; *-wy*) **1.** briefing **2.** (*replika*) rebuff **3.** (*zapłata*) gratuity **4.** (*załatwianie formalności*) clearance; ***~ bagażu*** luggage clearance; ***~ celna*** customs clearance
odprawiać ⟨**-wić**⟩ (*-wiam*) **1.** send away, dismiss; ***~ kogoś z kwitkiem*** send s.o. away empty-handed **2.** *towar*: clear **3.** *mszę*: celebrate
odprężać ⟨**-żyć**⟩ (*-żam*) relax; ***odprężać się*** relax, unwind; **odprężenie** *n* (*-nia*; *no pl*) relaxation
odprowadzać ⟨**-dzić**⟩ (*-dzam*) **1.** accompany, see off; ***~ kogoś na dworzec*** see s.o. to the station; ***~ wzrokiem*** follow s.o. with one's eyes **2.** *gaz*, *wodę*: channel **3.** *towar*: carry **4.** *więźnia*: escort
odpruwać ⟨**-ruć**⟩ (*-wam*) unstitch, unpick; ***odpruwać się*** come unstitched, come off
odprysk *m* (*-ku*; *-ki*) **1.** *szkła*: splinter **2.** *farby*: chip
odpryskiwać ⟨**-snąć**⟩ (*-kuję*) chip off, flake off
odpukiwać ⟨**-kać**⟩ (*-kuję*) knock back; ***odpukać (w niemalowane drewno)*** *Br* touch wood
odpust *m* (*-tu*; *-ty*) **1.** (*festyn*) church fair **2.** REL indulgence, pardon; **odpustowy** *adj* **1.** (*tandetny*) trashy, garish **2.** REL indulgence, pardon
odpuszczać ⟨**-puścić**⟩ (*-czam*) **1.** *winy*: forgive, absolve of **2.** ***~ sobie*** *infml* ease up, ease off

odpychać ⟨**odepchnąć**⟩ (*-cham*) **1.** push, shove, push away **2.** *fig* repel, repulse; **odpychać się** *PHYS* repel each other
odpychający *adj* repulsive
odpytywać ⟨**-tać**⟩ (*-tuję*) *ucznia*: question, test
Odra *f* (*-ry*) Oder
odra *f* (*-ry*; *no pl*) *MED* measles *sing*
odrabiać ⟨**-robić**⟩ (*-biam*) *dług*, *zaległości*, *błędy*: make up for; **~ lekcje** do one's homework
odraczać ⟨**-roczyć**⟩ (*-czam*) postpone, adjourn
odradzać ⟨**-radzić**⟩ (*-dzam*) advise (against)
odradzać się ⟨**-rodzić**⟩ (*-dzam*) revive, regenerate
odrapany *adj* *budynek*: shabby-looking
odrapywać ⟨**-pać**⟩ (*-puję*) scrape off
odrastać ⟨**-rosnąć**⟩ (*-tam*) grow again, regenerate
odratowywać ⟨**-tować**⟩ (*-towuję*) bring back to life
odraza *f* (*-zy*; *no pl*) **1.** disgust **2.** aversion; **odrażający** *adj* revolting, repugnant
odrąbywać ⟨**-bać**⟩ (*-buję*) chop off, hack off
odreagowywać ⟨**-gować**⟩ (*-gowuję*) *stress*: release, *form* abreact
odredakcyjny *adj* editorial
odremontować *v/p* → **remontować**
odremontowany *adj* renovated
odrestaurowywać ⟨**-rować**⟩ (*-rowuję*) restore, renovate
odrębny *adj* **1.** (*odmienny*) separate **2.** (*różny*) separate, distinct
odręczny *adj* **1.** *podpis*: handwritten **2.** *naprawa*: instant, make-do
odrętwiały *adj* numb
odrętwieć *v/p* (*-wieję*) go numb
odrętwienie *n* (*-nia*; *no pl*) **1.** *rąk*: numbness, torpor **2.** *fig* stupor, apathy
odrobić *v/p* → **odrabiać**
odrobina *f* (*-ny*; *-ny*) **1.** bit, drop **2.** *fig* grain
odroczenie *n* (*-nia*; *-nia*): **~ kary** respite of the sentence; **~ od służby wojskowej** (draft) deferment
odroczyć *v/p* → **odraczać**
odrodzenie *n* (*-nia*; *no pl*) revival, rebirth; **≈** *ART* the Renaissance
odrodzić się *v/p* → **odradzać się**
odrosnąć *v/p* → **odrastać**
odrost *m* (*-tu*; *-ty*) *BIOL* shoot, sucker
odrosty *pl* (*-tów*) (*po farbowaniu włosów*) roots
odróżniać ⟨**-nić**⟩ (*-niam*) **1.** distinguish (**kogoś od** *G* s.o. from) **2.** (*rozróżniać*) differentiate; **odróżniać się** differ; **~ się od siebie** differ from each other
odróżnieni|e *n* (*-nia*; *no pl*) differentiation; **w ~u od** *G* unlike, as opposed to; **nie do ~a** indistinguishable
odruch *m* (*-chu*; *-chy*) **1.** *BIOL* reflex; **~ *warunkowy*** conditioned reflex, conditioned response; **~ *bezwarunkowy*** unconditioned reflex, unconditioned response; **~ *wymiotny*** retching reflex; **~ *ssania*** sucking reflex **2.** (*nawyk*) reaction, impulse; ***ludzki* ~** human kindness
odruchowy *adj* **1.** involuntary, spontaneous, impulsive **2.** *BIOL* reflex
odryglowywać ⟨**-lować**⟩ (*-lowuję*) unbolt, unlock
odrysowywać ⟨**-sować**⟩ (*-sowuję*) copy
odrywać ⟨**oderwać**⟩ (*-wam*) **1.** tear off **2.** (*wyrywać*) tear out **3. ~ wzrok od** *G* tear one's eyes from **4.** (*przeszkadzać*) tear away (**kogoś od** *G* s.o. from); **odrywać się 1.** come off **2.** (*oddzielać się*) break away **3.** (*od pracy*) make a break
odrzec *v/p* (*-rzeknę*) *lit* reply, answer
odrzucać ⟨**-cić**⟩ (*-cę*) **1.** (*z powrotem*) throw back **2.** (*wyrzucać*) throw away **3.** *ofertę*: reject **4.** *kandydaturę*, *skargę*: turn down
odrzut *m* (*-tu*; *-ty*) recoil, kick; **odrzutowiec** *m* (*-wca*; *-wce*) jet (aircraft)
odrzynać ⟨**-derżnąć**⟩ (*-nam*) **1.** cut off **2.** (*piłą*) saw off
odsalanie *n* (*-nia*; *no pl*) desalination
odsapka *f* (*-ki*; *-ki*) *infml* breather, rest
odsapnąć *v/p* (*-nę*) stop for a breather
odsączać ⟨**-czyć**⟩ (*-czam*) drain, strain, filter
odsądzać ⟨**-dzić**⟩ (*-dzam*) deny; **~ kogoś od czci i wiary** call s.o. every name under the sun
odseparowywać ⟨**-rować**⟩ (*-rowuję*) isolate, segregate; **odseparować się** isolate oneself, seclude oneself

odset|ek *m* (*-tka*; *-tki*) percentage, proportion; **~ki** FIN interest; **~ki za zwłokę** interest for late payment
odsiać *v/p* → **odsiewać**
odsiadywać ⟨**-siedzieć**⟩ (*-duję*) **1.** *godziny*: sit out one's time **2.** *karę*: serve one's time, do time
odsiecz *f* (*-czy*; *-cze*) relief
odsiedzieć *v/p* → **odsiadywać**
odsiewać ⟨**-siać**⟩ (*-wam*) **1.** *mąkę*: sift, sieve **2.** *fig* screen, winnow out
odskakiwać ⟨**-skoczyć**⟩ (*-kuję*) **1.** jump away (**od** *G* from) **2.** (*o piłce*) bounce; **odskocznia** *f* (*-ni*; *-nie*) **1.** springboard **2.** *fig* stepping stone **3.** (*odpoczynek*) escape
odsłaniać ⟨**-łonić**⟩ (*-niam*) **1.** uncover **2.** *firankę*: draw back **3.** *pomnik*: unveil **4.** *prawdę*: reveal **5.** *piersi*: bare; **odsłaniać się** *fig* reveal one's designs
odsłona *f* (*-ny*; *-ny*) THEAT scene
odsłonić *v/p* → **odsłaniać**
odsłonięcie *n* (*-cia*; *no pl*) (*pomnika*) unveiling
odsłonięty *adj* **1.** *miejsce*: exposed, open **2.** *piersi*: bare, exposed
odsługiwać ⟨**-łużyć**⟩ (*-guję*): **~ wojsko** serve in the army; **odsługiwać się** *Br* return a favour, *Am* return a favor
odsmażać ⟨**-żyć**⟩ (*-żam*) refry
odsprzedawać ⟨**-dać**⟩ (*-daję*) resell
odstać *v/p* (*-toję*) **1.** stand **2.** (*o płynie*) settle
odstający *adj uszy*: protruding
odstawać *v/im* (*-taję*) **1.** (*o kołnierzu*) stick out **2.** *fig* diverge, stand out
odstawiać ⟨**-wić**⟩ (*-wiam*) **1.** put away, put back; **~ niemowlę** (**od piersi**) wean a baby; **~ komuś numer** *infml* pull a fast one on s.o.; **~ ważniaka** *infml* act important **2.** *towar*: deliver **3.** *lek*: come off
odstąpić *v/p* → **odstępować**
odstąpienie *n* (*-nia*; *no pl*) waiver; **~ od umowy** withdrawal from an agreement
odstęp *m* (*-pu*; *-py*) **1.** distance, interval **2.** (*w czasie*) interval, space **3.** (*klawisz*) space
odstępca *m* (*-cy*; *-cy*) dissenter, apostate; **odstępne** *n* (*-nego*; *no pl*) compensation fee
odstępować ⟨**-tąpić**⟩ (*-puję*) **I** *v/t* **1.** give **2.** (*porzucać*) abandon **3. nie ~ kogoś na krok** dog s.o. **II** *v/i* **1.** withdraw (**od** *G* from); **~ od umowy** withdraw from an agreement **2.** (*od zasad*) renounce, abandon
odstępstwo *n* (*-wa*; *-wa*) **1.** (*od normy*) deviation **2.** (*od idei*) apostasy, dissent
odstraszać ⟨**-szyć**⟩ (*-szam*) scare off; **odstraszający** *adj* **1.** *efekt*: deterrent **2.** (*odrażający*) repellent **3.** (*przerażający*) scary
odstręczać ⟨**-czyć**⟩ (*-czam*) **1.** (*zniechęcać*) put off **2.** (*zrażać*) alienate
odstrzał *m* (*-łu*; *-ły*) cull
odsuwać ⟨**-sunąć**⟩ (*-wam*) **1.** move away, move back **2.** *zasuwkę*: slide open **3.** *firankę*: open, draw **4.** *fig* turn away, drive away, remove (**od** *G* from); **~ od władzy** remove from power; **odsuwać się 1.** move away, move aside **2.** *fig* turn away, withdraw
odsyłacz *m* (*-cza*; *-cze*) **1.** reference (mark) **2.** footnote, note
odsyłać ⟨**odesłać**⟩ (*-łam*) **1.** *list*: send back **2.** (*w tekście*) refer (**do** *G* to)
odsypiać ⟨**odespać**⟩ (*-piam*) sleep off
odsypywać ⟨**-pać**⟩ (*-puję*) pour out
odszczepieniec *m* (*-pieńca*; *-pieńcy*) dissenter, apostate, renegade
odszczurzać ⟨**-rzyć**⟩ (*-rzam*) clear of rats
odszkodowani|e *n* (*-nia*; *-nia*) compensation, damages *pl*, indemnity; **~e za przymusowe roboty** compensation for forced labour; **~a wojenne** war reparations, war indemnities
odszukiwać ⟨**-kać**⟩ (*-kuję*) seek out, find; **odszukiwać się** seek each other out, find each other, find oneself
odszyfrowywać ⟨**-rować**⟩ (*-rowuję*) decode, decipher
odszykowywać ⟨**-kować**⟩ (*-kowuję*) groom
odśnieżać ⟨**-żyć**⟩ (*-żam*) clear of snow; **odśnieżanie** *n* (*-nia*; *no pl*) clearing of snow
odśpiewać *v/p* (*-wam*) sing (through)
odśrodkowy *adj* centrifugal, decentralist
odświeżacz *m* (*-cza*; *-cze*): **~ powietrza** air-freshener; **~ do ust** mouth spray
odświeżać ⟨**-żyć**⟩ (*-żam*) **1.** freshen up **2.** *fig* renew; **odświeżać się** freshen oneself up, refresh oneself
odświętny *adj* festive

odtajać *v/p* (*-taję*) thaw (out)
odtajniony *adj* declassified
odtąd *adv* **1.** (*w czasie*) from then on, from now on, since then **2.** (*w przestrzeni*) from here, from there
odtłuszczon|y *adj* skimmed; ***mleko ~e*** skimmed milk
odtransportować *v/p* (*-tuję*) ship off
odtrącać ⟨**-cić**⟩ (*-cam*) **1.** push away **2.** *uszko*: break off **3.** *fig* reject, spurn
odtrutka *f* (*-ki*; *-ki*) antidote
odtwarzacz *m* (*-cza*; *-cze*): ***~ płyt kompaktowych*** CD player; ***~ wideo*** video player
odtwarzać ⟨**-worzyć**⟩ (*-rzam*) **1.** reconstruct, regenerate **2.** *nastrój*: reconstruct **3.** *rolę*: play, perform **4.** (*z kasety*) play (back); ***odtwarzać się*** BIOL regenerate
odtwórca *m* (*-cy*; *-cy*) performer; ***~ głównej roli*** the lead(ing man)
odtwórczy *adj* imitative; **odtwórczyni** *f* (*-ni*; *-nie*) performer; ***~ głównej roli*** the lead(ing lady)
odtykać ⟨**odetkać**⟩ (*-kam*) **1.** *odpływ*: unclog **2.** *rury*: unblock **3.** *butelkę*: uncork
oduczać ⟨**-czyć**⟩ (*-czam*) teach not to; ***oduczać się*** unlearn; ***~ się obgryzać paznokcie*** teach oneself not to bite one's nails
odurzać ⟨**-rzyć**⟩ (*-rzam*) **1.** intoxicate, drug **2.** (*otępiać*) stupefy **3.** (*oszałamiać*) daze; ***odurzać się*** take intoxicants, stupefy oneself (*I* with)
odurzając|y *adj* intoxicating, overpowering; ***środki ~e*** intoxicants; **odurzenie** *n* (*-nia*; *no pl*) intoxication, daze, stupor
odurzyć *v/p* → ***odurzać***
odwadniać ⟨**-wodnić**⟩ (*-niam*) **1.** drain **2.** MED dehydrate
odwag|a *f* (*-gi*; *no pl*) courage; ***~a cywilna*** moral courage; ***nabrać ~i, zebrać się na ~ę*** summon up one's courage
odwalać ⟨**-lić**⟩ (*-lam*) *infml* **1.** remove **2.** (*wykonać*) bash out; ***~ kawał roboty*** do a whole lot of work; ***~ robotę*** do a shoddy job **3.** ***odwal się!*** get lost!
odwar *m* (*-ru*; *-ry*) decoction
odważać ⟨**-żyć**⟩ (*-żam*) weigh out; ***odważać się*** dare (***na*** *A* to do)
odważnik *m* (*-ka*; *-ki*) weight
odważny *adj* brave, courageous
odważyć *v/p* → ***odważać***
odważyć się *v/p* → ***odważać się***
odwdzięczać się ⟨**-czyć**⟩ (*-czam*) repay (***za*** *A* for)
odwe|t *m* (*-tu*; *no pl*) revenge, retaliation; ***w ~cie za*** *A* in requital for, in retaliation for; **odwetowiec** *m* (*-wca*; *-wcy*) retaliator; **odwetowy** *adj* retaliatory
odwiązywać ⟨**-zać**⟩ (*-zuję*) undo, untie; ***odwiązywać się*** **1.** (*o osobie*) untie oneself **2.** (*o sznurowadle*) come undone
odwidzieć się *v/p* (*-dzę*) *infml* change one's mind (about)
odwieczny *adj* eternal
odwiedzać ⟨**-dzić**⟩ (*-dzam*) visit; **odwiedziny** *pl* (*-dzin*) visit *sing*; ***przyjść do kogoś w ~ do*** visit s.o.
odwiert *m* (*-tu*; *-ty*) MIN borehole, well
odwieść *v/p* → ***odwodzić***
odwieźć *v/p* → ***odwozić***
odwijać ⟨**-winąć**⟩ (*-jam*) **1.** unwrap **2.** *sznurek, nić*: unreel, unwind **3.** *rękaw*: unroll; ***odwijać się*** unreel, unwind
odwilż *f* (*-ży*; *-że*) thaw
odwinąć *v/p* → ***odwijać***
odwirowywać ⟨**-rować**⟩ (*-wuję*) *pranie*: spin-dry
odwlekać ⟨**-lec**⟩ (*-kam*) **1.** drag away **2.** (*opóźnić*) delay, put off; ***odwlekać się*** be put off
odwłok *m* (*-ka*/*-ku*; *-ki*) BIOL abdomen
odwodnić *v/p* → ***odwadniać***
odwodzić ⟨**-wieść**⟩ (*-dzę*) **1.** dissuade (***od*** *G* from) **2.** (*odprowadzić*) take aside; ***~ kogoś na stronę*** take s.o. aside
odwołać *v/p* → ***odwoływać***
odwołani|e *n* (*-nia*; *-nia*) **1.** *od decyzji*: appeal; ***aż do ~a*** until further notice **2.** (*zwolnienie*) dismissal
odwoławczy *adj komisja*: appeal
odwoływać ⟨**-łać**⟩ (*-łuję*) **1.** call (aside) **2.** *ze stanowiska*: dismiss **3.** *zarzut*: take back **4.** *spektakl, spotkanie*: cancel; ***~ zamówienie*** cancel an order **5.** *alarm*: call off; ***odwoływać się*** **1.** *do uczuć*: appeal (***do*** *G* to) **2.** (*nawiązywać*) refer (***do*** *G* to) **3.** JUR lodge an appeal
odwozić ⟨**-wieźć**⟩ (*-wożę*) take (back)

O

odwód *m* (*-wodu*; *-wody*) reserve
odwracać ⟨*-rócić*⟩ (*-cam*) **1.** turn; *~ czyjąś uwagę* distract s.o.'s attention, divert s.o.'s attention; *~ kota ogonem fig* distort the facts; *~ do góry nogami* turn upside down; *~ na lewą stronę* turn inside out **2.** *kartkę*: turn over **3.** *głowę*, *wzrok*: turn away; *odwracać się* **1.** turn **2.** *fig* turn one's back (**od** *G* on)
odwracalny *adj* reversible
odwrotnie *adv* the other way round, vice versa; *założyć ~ sweter* put the sweater inside out, put the sweater back to front; *wręcz ~* quite the opposite; *~ proporcjonalny* inversely proportional
odwrotność *f* (*-ści*; *no pl*) MATH the converse; **odwrotn|y** *adj* opposite, reverse; *~a strona* the other side, the reverse side; *~y kierunek* opposite direction
odwrócić *v/p* → *odwracać*
odwrócony *adj*: *~ tyłem do G* with one's back turned towards; *~ do góry dnem* upside down
odwrót *m* (*-rotu*; *-roty*) retreat, withdrawal; *na ~* on the contrary; *na odwrocie* on the reverse; *nie ma odwrotu* there's no going back
odwszawiać ⟨*-wić*⟩ (*-wiam*) delouse
odwykać ⟨*-knąć*⟩ (*-kam*) get out of the habit, lose the habit (**od** *G* of)
odwykły *adj* no longer accustomed (**od** *G* to), no longer used (**od** *G* to)
odwykow|y *adj*: *kuracja ~a* drying-out treatment, detoxification treatment, *infml* detox; *poradnia ~a* detoxification clinic
odwzajemniać ⟨*-nić*⟩ (*-niam*) *uczucia*: return; *odwzajemniać się* repay (*komuś za A* s.o. for)
odwzajemniony *adj* reciprocated
odymać ⟨*odąć*⟩ (*-mam*): *~ usta* pout one's lips
odyniec *m* (*odyńca*; *odyńce*) male wild boar
odzew *m* (*-wu*; *-wy*) *fig* response
odziedziczony *adj* inherited
odziedziczyć *v/p* → *dziedziczyć*
odzież *f* (*-ży*; *no pl*) clothes *pl*, clothing; *~ robocza* work clothes; *~ damska* womenswear; **odzieżowy** *adj* clothing, clothes
odznaczać ⟨*-czyć*⟩ (*-czam*) decorate, *Br* honour, *Am* honor; *odznaczać się* (*charakteryzować się*) be characterized (*I* by)
odznaczenie *n* (*-nia*; *-nia*) decoration, distinction; *~ bojowe* military decoration
odznaczyć *v/p* → *odznaczać*
odznaka *f* (*-ki*; *-ki*) badge, emblem
odzwierciedlać ⟨*-lić*⟩ (*-lam*) express, illustrate; *odzwierciedlać się* be reflected, be expressed
odzwierciedlenie *n* (*-nia*; *-nia*) reflection, image
odzwyczajać ⟨*-czaić*⟩ (*-jam*) **1.** disaccustom (*kogoś od G* s.o. from) **2.** *~ kogoś od G* (*odstawiać*) wean s.o. off from; *odzwyczajać się* disaccustom oneself (**od** *G* from), get out of the habit (**od** *G* of), give up (**od** *G*)
odzyskanie *n* (*-nia*; *no pl*) recovery
odzyskiwać ⟨*-kać*⟩ (*-kuję*) **1.** recover, regain, retrieve; *~ zdrowie* regain health, recover; *~ przytomność* regain consciousness; *~ siły* recover; *~ panowanie nad sobą* regain control of oneself **2.** TECH reclaim, recycle
odzywać się ⟨*odezwać*⟩ (*-wam*) **1.** speak **2.** (*z urlopu*) call, drop a line; *nie odzywał się* I haven't heard from him **3.** (*w kartach*) bid, call **4.** (*o dzwonku*) sound
odzywka *f* (*-ki*; *-ki*) *infml* impertinence
odżałować *v/p* (*-łuję*) **1.** get over **2.** (*poświęcić*) spare, part with
odżegnywać się ⟨*-nać*⟩ (*-nuję*) disassociate oneself (**od** *G* from)
odżywać ⟨*-żyć*⟩ (*-wam*) revive
odżywczo *adv* nourishingly; **odżywczy** *adj* nutritious, nutritional, nourishing
odżywiać ⟨*-wić*⟩ (*-wiam*) feed, nourish; *odżywiać się* **1.** (*o ludziach*) eat **2.** (*o zwierzętach*) feed (*I* on)
odżywianie (się) *n* (*-nia*; *no pl*) nutrition, diet; **odżywka** *f* (*-ki*; *-ki*): *~ do włosów* hair conditioner; *~ dla niemowląt* baby food
ofensywa *f* (*-wy*; *-wy*) offensive, attack; **ofensywny** *adj* **1.** offensive, aggressive **2.** SPORT attacking
oferent *m* (*-ta*; *-nci*) bidder, tenderer
oferma *f/m* (*-my*; *-my*) *infml* loser, moron

oferować ⟨**za-**⟩ (*-ruję*) offer; **ofert|a** *f* (*-ty*; *-ty*) offer; ***złożyć ~ę*** submit an offer; ***~a kupna*** offer to buy; ***~a sprzedaży*** offer to sell

offsetowy *adj* offset

ofiar|a *f* (*-ry*; *-ry*) **1.** victim; ***~a wypadku*** accident victim; ***~a powodzi*** flood victim; ***paść ~ą*** *G* fall victim to **2.** (*ranny*, *zabity*) casualty **3.** (*datek*) donation, contribution **4.** *infml* sucker, loser

ofiarność *f* (*-ści*; *no pl*) devotion, dedication; **ofiarny** *adj* **1.** dedicated, devoted; ***kozioł ~*** scapegoat **2.** REL sacrificial

ofiarodawca *m* (*-cy*; *-cy*), **-czyni** *f* (*-ni*; *-nie*) benefactor, donor

ofiarowywać ⟨**-rować**⟩ (*-rowuję*) **1.** give; ***~ życie*** give one's life **2.** (*darować*) donate **3.** *pomoc*: offer **4.** REL sacrifice; ***ofiarowywać się*** offer

oficer *m* (*-ra*; *-rowie*) officer; **oficerki** *pl* (*-rek*) officer's boots; **oficerski** *adj* officers'

oficjalny *adj* official, formal

oficyna *f* (*-ny*; *-ny*) **1.** annexe **2.** ***~ wydawnicza*** *lit* publishing house

ofsajd *m* (*-du*; *-dy*) SPORT offside

ofuknąć *v/p* (*-nę*) scold, reprimand

ogar *m* (*-ra*; *-ry*) hound

ogarek *m* (*-rka*; *-rki*) *świecy*: candle-end, butt

ogarniać ⟨**-nąć**⟩ (*-niam*) **1.** spread through; ***~ ramieniem*** embrace; ***~ wzrokiem*** take in **2.** (*o ogniu*, *epidemii*) engulf, sweep through **3.** (*o uczuciu*) seize, grip **4.** (*pojąć*) grasp, comprehend **5.** (*posprzątać*) *infml* tidy up

ogarnięty *adj* engulfed (*I* in)

og|ień *m* (*ognia*; *ognie*) fire; ***w ~niu*** on fire; ***krzyżowy ~ień pytań*** cross-examination; ***słomiany ~ień*** short-lived enthusiasm; ***na pierwszy ~ień*** to start with; ***na wolnym ~niu*** over low heat; ***sztuczne ~nie*** fireworks; ***zimne ~nie*** sparklers

ogier *m* (*-ra*; *-ry*) **1.** stallion **2.** *fig* stud

ogląd *m* (*-du*; *no pl*) inspection, examination

oglądać ⟨**obejrzeć**⟩ (*-dam*) **1.** *film*, *mecz*: watch; ***~ telewizję*** watch TV **2.** (*dokładnie*) examine, watch **3.** *wystawę*: see **4.** *zabytki*, *mieszkanie*: visit **5.** (*widzieć*) see; ***oglądać się*** **1.** (*w lustrze*) examine oneself **2.** (*do tyłu*) look back **3.** ***~ się na*** *A* (*zwracać uwagę*) take into account

oglądalność *f* (*-ści*; *no pl*) audience

oględność *f* (*-ści*; *no pl*) tact, diplomacy; **oględnie** *adv*: ***~ mówiąc*** to put it mildly; **oględny** *adj* reserved, moderate

oględziny *pl* (*-dzin*) examination *sing*, inspection *sing*

ogład|a *f* (*-dy*; *no pl*) *towarzyska*: polish, refinement; ***bez ~y*** uneducated, unpolished

ogłaszać ⟨**-łosić**⟩ (*-szam*) **1.** announce; ***~ stan wojenny*** declare martial law **2.** *drukiem*: publish; ***ogłaszać się*** advertise

ogłoszenie *n* (*-nia*; *-nia*) **1.** announcement, declaration **2.** (*na tablicy*, *w gazecie*) advertisement, ad; ***~ matrymonialne*** personal ad; ***~ o pracy*** job advertisement

ogłoszeniow|y *adj*: ***tablica ~a*** noticeboard; ***dział ~y*** advertisement column, personal column; ***słup ~y*** poster pillar

ogłuchnąć *v/p* (*-nę*) go deaf, become deaf

ogłupiać ⟨**-pić**⟩ (*-piam*) stupefy

ogłupiający *adj* stupefying, stultifying; **ogłupiały** *adj* stupefied; ***~ ze szczęścia*** mad with happiness; **ogłupieć** *v/p* (*-pieję*) be stupefied, become addled; ***~ ze szczętem*** become completely addled

ogłuszać ⟨**-szyć**⟩ (*-szam*) **1.** deafen **2.** (*ciosem*) knock out, knock unconscious

ogłuszający *adj* deafening

ogłuszyć *v/p* → ***ogłuszać***

ognie *pl* → ***ogień***

ognik *m* (*-ka*; *-ki*) glimmer, glow; ***~ papierosa*** cigarette glow; ***błędny ~*** will o' the wisp

ogniomistrz *m* (*-rza*; *-rze*) artillery sergeant

ognioodporny, ***ogniotrwały*** *adj* fireproof, fire-retardant

ogniow|y *adj* fire; ***straż ~a*** fire brigade; ***próba ~a*** trial by fire

ognisko *n* (*-ka*; *-ka*) **1.** campfire; ***~ domowe*** (hearth and) home **2.** (*impreza*) bonfire **3.** (*kółko*) centre **4.** PHYS MED focus

ogniskowa *f* (*-wej*; *-we*) PHYS focal length
ogniskować ⟨**z-**⟩ (*-kuję*) **1.** focus, concentrate **2.** *światło*: focus; ***ogniskować się*** focus
ognistoczerwony *adj* fiery red
ognisty *adj* **1.** fiery, fiery red **2.** *fig* fiery, passionate
ogniwo *n* (*-wa*; *-wa*) **1.** *łańcucha*, *organizacji*: link **2.** *fig* bond **3.** (*w elektryce*) cell
ogołacać ⟨**-łocić**⟩ (*-cam*): ***~ kogoś z pieniędzy*** clean s.o. out
ogołocony *adj*: ***~ z wartości*** deprived of values; ***~ z liści*** stripped of leaves
ogon *m* (*-na*; *-ny*) tail; ***koński ~*** ponytail; ***pawi ~*** peacock's tail; ***wlec się w ~ie*** fall behind; **ogon|ek** *m* (*-nka*; *-nki*) **1.** tail **2.** *liścia*: stalk **3.** (*kolejka*) *Br* queue, *Am* line; ***stać w ~ku*** *Br* queue, *Am* wait in line
ogonow|y *adj*: ***płetwa ~a*** caudal fin; ***kość ~a*** ANAT tail bone; ***zupa ~a*** oxtail soup
ogorzały *adj* suntanned
ogólnie *adv* widely, generally; ***~ biorąc***, ***~ mówiąc*** generally speaking
ogólniki *pl* (*-ków*) generalities; **ogólnikowy** *adj* vague
ogólno- (*w złożeniach*) -wide, all-
ogólnodostępny *adj* widely available; **ogólnoeuropejski** *adj* Pan-European
ogólnokształcąc|y *adj*: ***szkoła ~a*** secondary school; **ogólnopolski** *adj* all-Poland; **ogólnorozwojowy** *adj* pertaining to general development; **ogólnospołeczny** *adj* pertaining to the entire society; **ogólnoświatowy** *adj* worldwide, global
ogóln|y *adj* **1.** general; ***wykształcenie ~e*** general education; ***~e wrażenie*** general impression; ***zebranie ~e*** general meeting **2.** (*powszechny*) common **3.** (*całościowy*) total
ogół *m* (*-łu*; *no pl*) the whole, community; ***dobro ~u*** the common good; ***~em*** altogether, all in all; ***na ~*** in general, on the whole; ***w ogóle*** (***nie***) (not) at all, (not) whatsoever
ogórek *m* (*-rka*; *-rki*) cucumber; ***~ kiszony*** pickled cucumber; ***~ konserwowy*** dill pickle, dill gherkin; **ogórkowy** *adj* cucumber; ***sezon ~*** *fig* silly season
ograbiać ⟨**-bić**⟩ (*-biam*) rob, strip
ograć *v/p* → ***ogrywać***
ogradzać ⟨**-rodzić**⟩ (*-dzam*) **1.** surround, enclose **2.** (*murem*) wall (in)
ograniczać ⟨**-czyć**⟩ (*-czam*) **1.** *teren*: enclose **2.** *prędkość*, *wydatki*: limit, restrict (**do** *G* to); ***ograniczać się*** limit oneself, restrict oneself, be limited, be restricted
ogranicze|nie *n* (*-nia*; *-nia*) **1.** limitation, restriction; ***~nie prędkości*** speed limit; ***bez ~ń*** without limits **2.** (*tępota*) narrow-mindedness; **ograniczony** *adj* **1.** limited, restricted **2.** (*tępy*) dull, thick
ograniczyć *v/p* → ***ograniczać***
ograny *adj* **1.** *kawał*: stale **2.** *temat*: hackneyed
ogrodnictwo *n* (*-wa*; *no pl*) gardening, horticulture
ogrodniczki *pl* (*-czek*) dungarees, overalls
ogrodnicz|y *adj* garden, gardening; ***szkoła ~a*** gardening school; ***zakład ~y*** market-garden; ***sklep ~y*** garden centre
ogrodnik *m* (*-ka*; *-nicy*), **-niczka** *f* (*-ki*; *-ki*) gardener
ogrodowy *adj* garden
ogrodzenie *n* (*-nia*; *-nia*) fence, wall, railing
ogrodzić *v/p* → ***ogradzać***
ogrom *m* (*-mu*; *no pl*) **1.** (*wielkość*) largeness, hugeness **2.** (*ilość*) bulk (*G* of) **3.** *nieszczęść*, *pracy*: enormousness; **ogromny** *adj* **1.** huge, vast **2.** *fig* immense, tremendous
ogród *m* (*-rodu*; *-rody*) garden; ***~ owocowy*** fruit garden; ***~ warzywny*** vegetable garden; ***~ botaniczny*** botanic(al) gardens; ***~ zoologiczny*** zoological garden
ogródek *m* (*-dka*; *-dki*) **1.** garden; ***~ działkowy*** *Br* allotment; ***~ jordanowski*** children's playground **2.** *kawiarniany*: tea garden, pavement café
ogrywać ⟨**-rać**⟩ (*-wam*) (*w karty*) beat, outplay
ogryzać ⟨**-ryźć**⟩ (*-zam*) chew at, bite
ogryzek *m* (*-zka*; *-zki*) *jabłka*: core
ogryźć *v/p* → ***ogryzać***
ogrzewacz *m* (*-cza*; *-cze*) TECH heater
ogrzewać ⟨**-rzać**⟩ (*-wam*) **1.** warm, heat up **2.** *ręce*: warm **3.** *mieszkanie*:

heat; ***ogrzewać się*** **1.** warm up **2.** (*o osobie*) warm up, get warm

ogrzewanie *n* (*-nia*; *no pl*) heating; ***centralne ~*** central heating; **ogrzewczy** *adj* heating

ogumienie *n* (*-nia*; *no pl*) AUTO *Br* tyres *pl*, *Am* tires *pl*

oheblować *v/p* (*-luję*) plane

ohyda *f* (*-dy*; *no pl*) abomination; ***~!*** it's disgusting; **ohydny** *adj* atrocious

oj *interj* **1.** ow, ah, ooh **2.** (*ból*) ouch

ojciec *m* (*ojca*, *ojcowie*) father; ***~ chrzestny*** godfather; ***≈ Święty*** Holy Father; ***po ojcu*** after one's father; ***bez ojca*** fatherless

ojcobójstwo *n* (*-wa*; *-wa*) patricide; **ojcostw|o** *n* (*-wa*; *no pl*) fatherhood; ***ustalenie ~a*** establishment of paternity; ***powództwo o ustalenie ~a*** JUR paternity suit, affiliation case; **ojcowizna** *f* (*-ny*; *-ny*) patrimony; **ojcowski** *adj* father's, paternal; ***po ~u*** like a father, paternally

ojczym *m* (*-ma*; *-mowie*/*-mi*) stepfather

ojczyst|y *adj* home, native; ***język ~y*** mother tongue; ***~e strony*** fatherland; ***kraj ~y*** fatherland; **ojczyzna** *f* (*-ny*; *-ny*) **1.** home country, homeland **2.** *fig* (*kolebka*) cradle

ok. *abbr* (= **około**) c.

okalać *v/im* (*-lam*) surround, border; **okalający** *adj* surrounding

okaleczać ⟨**-czyć**⟩ (*-czam*) cripple, mutilate; **okaleczony** *adj* mutilated; ***trwale ~*** crippled; ***~ psychicznie*** mentally damaged

okaleczenie *n* (*-nia*; *-nia*) injury; ***trwałe ~*** permanent injury

okamgnieni|e: ***w ~u*** as quick as a flash; ***przez ~e*** in a second; ***na ~e*** for a second

okap *m* (*-pu*; *-py*) **1.** eaves *pl* **2.** (*w kuchni*) ventilation hood

okaz *m* (*-zu*; *-zy*) **1.** specimen; ***prawdziwy ~ głupoty*** a showpiece of stupidity; ***być ~em zdrowia*** be a picture of health **2.** *muzealny*: exhibit

okazać się *v/p* → ***okazywać się***

okazałość *f* (*-ści*; *no pl*) grandeur, *Br* splendour, *Am* splendor, magnificence; **okazały** *adj* **1.** (*duży*) impressive **2.** (*wspaniały*) magnificent, grand, sumptuous

okazanie *n* (*-nia*; *no pl*): ***~ pomocy*** assistance; ***za ~m*** on presentation

okaziciel *m* (*-la*; *-le*) *dokumentu*: bearer; ***czek na ~a*** bearer cheque

okazj|a *f* (*-ji*; *-je*) **1.** (*możliwość*) chance, opportunity; ***przy ~i*** by the way **2.** (*powód*) occasion; ***z ~i*** *G* on the occasion of; ***życzenia z ~i urodzin*** birthday wishes **3.** (*kupno*) bargain **4.** (*podwiezienie*) *infml* lift

okazjonalny *adj* occasional, incidental

okazowy *adj* display, presentation

okazyjn|y *adj kupno*, *cena*: bargain; ***po ~ej cenie*** as a bargain

okazywać ⟨**-zać**⟩ (*-zuję*) **1.** *dokumenty*: present, show **2.** (*dać wyraz*) show; ***~ komuś pomoc*** help s.o.; ***okazywać się*** turn out; ***jak się okazało*** apparently, as it turned out; ***okazuje się, że*** it turns out that

okiełznywać ⟨**-nać**⟩ (*-nuję*) **1.** *konia*: break in, curb **2.** *fig* rein in, restrain, curb

okienko *n* (*-ka*; *-ka*) **1.** *dim* (small) window **2.** (*w urzędzie*) counter, window; **okiennica** *f* (*-cy*; *-ce*) shutter; **okienny** *adj* window

oklapły, ***oklapnięty*** *adj* **1.** droopy, drooping **2.** *infml* exhausted

oklapnąć *v/p* (*-nę*) **1.** droop **2.** *infml* wilt

oklaski *pl* (*-ków*) applause; ***burzliwe ~*** thunderous applause; **oklaskiwać** *v/im* (*-kuję*) applaud

okleina *f* (*-ny*; *-ny*) veneer; **oklejać** ⟨**-leić**⟩ (*-jam*) cover, tape, veneer (*I* with)

oklep: ***na ~*** bareback

oklepany *adj infml* well worn, trite

okład *m* (*-du*; *-dy*) MED compress; ***tysiąc z ~em*** *infml* more than a thousand, over a thousand

okładać ⟨**obłożyć**⟩ (*-dam*) **1.** surround, cover **2.** *zeszyty*: cover **3.** (*bić*) bash (*I* with)

okładka *f* (*-ki*; *-ki*) *książki*, *na zeszyt*: cover; ***książka w miękkiej okładce*** paperback; ***książka w twardej okładce*** hardback

okładzina *f* (*-ny*; *-ny*) **1.** TECH facing, lining **2.** (*pokrowiec*) cover

okłamywać ⟨**-mać**⟩ (*-muję*) lie; ***okłamywać się*** deceive oneself, delude oneself

O

okn|o *n* (*-na*; *-na*) window; ***~o wystawowe*** shop window; ***~o od ulicy*** window overlooking the street; ***wyglądać przez ~o*** look through the window; ***stać w ~ie*** stand at a window

ok|o *n* **1.** (*oka*; *oczy*) eye; ***mieć ~o na*** *A* keep an eye on; ***~o za ~o*** an eye for an eye; ***na ~o*** more or less; ***na oczach*** *G* before, in front of; ***w cztery oczy*** face to face; ***na własne oczy*** with one's own eyes; ***w oczach*** rapidly; ***spod ~a*** from the corner of one's eye; ***na piękne oczy*** for s.o.'s pretty face; ***w żywe oczy*** blatantly; ***z przymrużeniem ~a*** with a pinch of salt; ***na pierwszy rzut ~a*** at first sight; ***~o w ~o*** eyeball to eyeball **2.** (*oka*; *oka*) (*w rosole*) eye of fat **3.** (*oka*; *oka*) *sieci*: mesh

okocić się *v/p* (*-cę*) (*o kotce*) kitten

okolic|a *f* (*-cy*; *-ce*) **1.** surroundings *pl*, vicinity; ***mieszkać w ładnej ~y*** live in a pretty neighbourhood; ***w ~y trzech kilometrów*** within three kilometres; ***~a dworca*** the vicinity of the station **2.** *górzysta*, *dzika*: region **3.** ***w ~y serca*** *ANAT* in the heart region

okolicznik *m* (*-ka*; *-ki*) *GRAM* adverbial (modifier)

okolicznościowy *adj* **1.** *mowa*: occasional **2.** *moneta*: commemorative

okolicznoś|ć *f* (*-ści*; *-ści*) circumstance; ***w tych ~ciach*** under the circumstances; ***~ci śmierci*** circumstances of death; ***sprzyjające ~ci*** favourable circumstances; ***~ci łagodzące*** *JUR* extenuations; ***w niewyjaśnionych ~ciach*** in unclear circumstances

okoliczny *adj* **1.** nearby **2.** *ludność*: local

okolony *adj* surrounded (*I* by)

około *prep* (*G*) (*w przybliżeniu*) about, around

okołobiegunowy *adj* *GEOGR* polar

okołoziemsk|i *adj*: ***orbita ~a*** circumterrestrial orbit

okoń *m* (*okonia*; *okonie*) perch

okop *m* (*-pu*; *-py*) trench

okopow|y *adj*: ***rośliny ~e*** bulb and root plants

okopywać ⟨**-pać**⟩ (*-puję*) earth up; ***okopywać się*** entrench oneself, dig in

okostna *f* (*-nej*; *no pl*) *ANAT* periosteum

okow|y *pl* (*-wów*) *lit* fetters, manacles; ***w ~ach lodu*** in fetters of ice

okólnik *m* (*-ka*; *-ki*) **1.** circular (letter) **2.** (*zagroda*) pen

okpiwać ⟨**-pić**⟩ (*-wam*) *infml* outwit, befool

okradać ⟨**-raść**⟩ (*-dam*) rob

okrakiem *adv* astride

okrasa *f* (*-sy*; *no pl*) *COOK pork fat seasoning*

okraszać ⟨**-sić**⟩ (*-szam*) **1.** *COOK season with fat or cream* **2.** *fig* spice up, *Br* colour, *Am* color

okraść *v/p* → **okradać**

okratować *v/p* (*-tuję*) bar; **okratowany** *adj* barred, with grating

okrawać ⟨**-roić**⟩ (*-wam*) **1.** edge, trim **2.** *fig* cut down; **okrawek** *m* (*-wka*; *-wki*) *jedzenia*: scrap

okrąg *m* (*-ręgu*; *-ręgi*) circle; **okrąglak** *m* (*-ka*; *-ki*) **1.** (*budynek*) rotunda **2.** (*drewno*) round timber; **okrąglutki** *adj dim* round, chubby

okrągł|y *adj* round; ***~y stół*** *POLIT* round table; ***na ~o*** again and again, around the clock

okrążać ⟨**-żyć**⟩ (*-żam*) **1.** go round **2.** *przeszkodę*: skirt **3.** (*okalać*) surround **4.** (*o wojsku*) encircle; **okrążenie** *n* (*-nia*; *-nia*) **1.** encirclement **2.** *SPORT* lap

okres *m* (*-su*; *-sy*) **1.** period; ***~ próbny*** probation, trial period; ***~ gwarancji*** warranty period; ***~ studiów*** duration of study, years of study; ***~ lodowcowy*** ice age, glacial period; ***przez pewien ~*** for some time; ***mieć ~*** *MED* to have one's period, to be menstruating **2.** (*sezon*, *pora*) season; ***~ świąteczny*** holiday season; ***~ ochronny*** closed season **3.** (*epoka*) era **4.** (*w szkole*) term

okresowo *adv* periodically; **okresowy** *adj* **1.** periodic; ***układ ~y pierwiastków*** *CHEM* periodic table **2.** (*tymczasowy*) temporary, passing, seasonal; ***bilet ~*** season ticket

określać ⟨**-lić**⟩ (*-lam*) **1.** determine **2.** (*nazywać*) describe; **określenie** *n* (*-nia*; *-nia*) **1.** term, expression **2.** (*nazwa*) name **3.** *GRAM* modifier; **określony** *adj* definite

okręcać ⟨**-cić**⟩ (*-cam*) **1.** (*owijać*) wrap, wind (*I* in) **2.** (*obracać*) twist, twirl; ***okręcać się*** **1.** turn round; ***~ się wokół*** *G* wind round **2.** (*zwijać się*) coil **3.** *ręcznikiem*: wrap oneself

okręg *m* (*-gu*; *-gi*) **1.** *administracyjny*: district **2.** *przemysłowy*: area **3.** *wyborczy*: constituency; **okręgowy** *adj* district

okręt *m* (*-tu*; *-ty*) ship, vessel; ***~ wojenny*** warship, man-of-war; ***~ podwodny*** submarine

okrętow|y *adj* ship; ***lina ~a*** hawser; ***dziennik ~y*** ship's log

okrężn|y *adj* circular, roundabout; ***ruch ~y*** diverted traffic, diversion; ***droga ~a*** detour; ***~a trasa*** circuitous route

okroić *v/p* → ***okrawać***

okropieństwo *n* (*-wa*; *-wa*) monstrosity

okropnoś|ć *f* (*-ści*; *-ści*) atrocity; ***~ci wojny*** disasters of war, war atrocities; ***~ć!*** how awful!

okropny *adj* **1.** horrible, dreadful **2.** (*przerażający*) ghastly, abominable, dreadful

okruch *m* (*-cha*; *-chy*) **1.** *chleba*: crumb **2.** *szkła*: sliver **3.** *fig* scrap, shred; ***~y wspomnień*** vague recollections; ***~y prawdy*** shreds of truth

okrucieństw|o *n* (*-wa*; *-wa*) cruelty, wickedness; ***~a*** atrocities

okruszyna *f* (*-ny*; *-ny*) *dim* crumb; → ***okruch***

okrutny *adj* brutal, cruel

okrycie *n* (*-cia*; *-cia*) **1.** cover **2.** (*płaszcz*) overcoat

okrywać ⟨***-ryć***⟩ (*-wam*) **1.** cover (*I* with) **2.** *kocem*: wrap; ***okrywać się*** **1.** cover oneself (*I* with); ***~ się hańbą*** *lit* disgrace oneself, dishonour oneself; ***~ się żałobą*** *lit* be plunged into mourning; ***~ się sławą*** *lit* cover oneself in glory **2.** *kocem*: wrap oneself up

okrzepły *adj* firm, firmly established; **okrzepnąć** *v/p* (*-nę*) **1.** (*twardnieć*) harden **2.** (*o osobie*) toughen **3.** (*o firmie*) become established

okrzesać *v/p* (*-szę*) hew

okrzyczany *adj* vaunted

okrzyczeć ⟨***-rzyknąć***⟩ (*-czę*) hail

okrzyk *m* (*-ku*; *-ki*) shout; ***~ radości*** shout of joy; ***~ bólu*** cry of pain

oksydować się *v/im* (*-duję*) oxidize

oktawa *f* (*-wy*; *-wy*) MUS octave

okucie *n* (*-cia*; *-cia*) **1.** fitting **2.** *laski*, *parasola*: ferrule

okuć *v/p* → ***okuwać***

okular *m* (*-ru*; *-ry*) eyepiece; **okularnica** *f* (*-cy*; *-ce*) *infml* four-eyes *sing*; **okularnik** *m* **1.** (*-ka*; *-ki*) BIOL spectacled cobra **2.** (*-ka*; *-nicy*) *infml* four-eyes *sing*

okulary *pl* (*-rów*) glasses, spectacles; ***końskie ~*** blinkers; ***on nosi ~*** he wears glasses; ***~ przeciwsłoneczne*** sun glasses

okuleć *v/p* (*-leję*) become lame

okulista *m* (*-ty*; *-liści*), **-tka** *f* (*-ki*; *-ki*) (ophthalmic) optician; **okulistyczny** *adj badanie*, *gabinet*: opthalmological; **okulistyka** *f* (*-ki*; *no pl*) opthalmology

okup *m* (*-pu*; *-py*) ransom

okupacja *f* (*-ji*; *-je*) occupation; **okupacyjny** *adj wojsko*: occupation; **okupant** *m* (*-ta*; *-nci*) occupying force(s)

okupować *v im/p* (*-puję*) occupy; ***~ telefon*** hang on the phone

okupywać ⟨***-pić***⟩ (*-puję*) **1.** *fig* pay (*I* with); ***~ życiem*** pay with one's own life **2.** *krzywdę*, *błędy*: atone for; ***okupywać się*** buy oneself out

okuwać ⟨***okuć***⟩ (*-wam*) fix metal fittings

okwiat *m* (*-tu*; *-ty*) BIOL perianth

olać *v/p* → ***olewać***

olbrzym *m* (*-ma*; *-mi*/*-my*) giant; **olbrzymi** *adj* gigantic, huge; **olbrzymka** *f* (*-ki*; *-ki*) giantess

olcha *f* (*-chy*; *-chy*) BIOL alder; **olchowy** *adj* alder

oleist|y *adj* **1.** *ziarna*: oil, oleaginous; ***roślina ~a*** oil plant **2.** *konsystencja*: oily

olej *m* (*-ju*; *-je*) **1.** COOK TECH oil; ***~ jadalny*** edible oil; ***~ słonecznikowy*** sunflower oil; ***nie mieć ~u w głowie*** not be reasonable **2.** (*obraz*) oil painting

olejarka *f* (*-ki*; *-ki*) oiler; **olejarnia** *f* (*-ni*; *-nie*) olive press, oil mill

olej|ek *m* (*-jku*; *-jki*) **1.** oil: ***~ek do opalania*** sunscreen; ***~ek różany*** rose oil; ***~ki eteryczne*** essential oils **2.** COOK *Br* flavouring, *Am* flavoring; ***~ek do ciast*** cake flavouring

olejny *adj farba*, *obraz*: oil; **olejow|y** *adj* TECH oil; ***miska ~a*** AUTO *Br* sump, *Am* oil pan

oleodruk *m* (*-ku*; *-ki*) chromolithograph

olewać ⟨**olać**⟩ (*-wam*) *infml* treat lightly, ignore

olimpiada *f* (*-dy*; *-dy*) **1.** *SPORT* the Olympic Games *pl*, the Olympics *pl*; **~ *letnia*** the summer Olympics; **~ *zimowa*** the winter Olympics **2.** (*konkurs*) contest

olimpijczyk *m* (*-ka*; *-czycy*), **-jka** *f* (*-ki*; *-ki*) **1.** Olympian **2.** *SPORT* Olympic athlete; **olimpijski** *adj* Olympic; ***znicz ~*** the Olympic torch, the Olympic flame; ***rekordzista ~*** Olympic champion, Olympic record holder

olinowanie *n* (*-nia*; *no pl*) (*w żeglarstwie*) rigging

oliwa *f* (*-wy*; *-wy*) **1.** *z oliwek*: olive oil **2.** *TECH* oil

oliwić ⟨**na-**⟩ (*-wię*) oil; **oliwka** *f* (*-ki*; *-ki*) **1.** olive **2.** (*drzewo*) olive (tree) **3.** (*kosmetyk*) baby oil; **oliwkowy** *adj* **1.** olive **2.** *kolor*: olive (green)

oliwn|y *adj* olive; ***gałązka ~a*** olive branch

olszyna *f* (*-ny*; *-ny*) **1.** alder grove **2.** (*drewno*) alder wood

olśnić *v/p* → ***olśniewać***

olśnieni|e *n* (*-nia*; *-nia*) *fig* enlightenment, inspiration, illumination; ***doznać ~a*** have a revelation, have a moment of enlightenment

olśniewać ⟨**-nić**⟩ (*-wam*) dazzle; ***olśniła mnie myśl*** I had a sudden thought; **olśniewający** *adj* **1.** dazzling **2.** *fig* brilliant

ołowiany *adj* **1.** lead **~ *żołnierzyk*** tin soldier **2.** *niebo*, *chmury*: leaden, heavy; **ołowica** *f* (*-cy*; *no pl*) *MED* lead poisoning, plumbism

ołów *m* (*ołowiu*; *no pl*) lead

ołów|ek *m* (*-wka*; *-wki*) pencil; ***~ek do brwi*** eyebrow pencil; ***kolorowy ~ek*** coloured pencil; ***żyć z ~kiem w ręku*** count every penny

ołtarz *m* (*-rza*; *-rze*) altar *m*; **ołtarzyk** *m* (*-ka*; *-ki*) altar

omal, ***omalże*** *particle* almost, nearly

omamiać ⟨**-mić**⟩ (*-miam*) beguile, delude

omamy *pl* (*-mów*) hallucinations

omaszczać ⟨**omaścić**⟩ (*-czam*) *COOK* pour liquid fat over

omasztowanie *n* (*-nia*; *no pl*) masting

omawiać ⟨**omówić**⟩ (*-wiam*) discuss, elaborate

omdlały *adj* **1.** unconscious, senseless **2.** *głos*: languid; **omdlenie** *n* (*-nia*; *-nia*) faint, *lit* swoon; **omdlewać** ⟨**-leć**⟩ (*-wam*) **1.** faint, *lit* swoon **2.** (*o rękach*) weaken, grow weary

omen *m* (*-nu*; *no pl*) omen, augury

omiatać ⟨**omieść**⟩ (*-tam*) sweep, clean

omieszkać *v/p* (*-kam*): ***nie ~*** be sure to

omieść *v/p* → ***omiatać***

omijać ⟨**ominąć**⟩ (*-jam*) **1.** pass by, walk around; ***nie ~*** *G* not miss; ***ominął ją awans*** she was passed over for promotion **2.** (*objeżdżać*) drive around **3.** *przeszkody*: bypass **4.** (*o pocisku*) miss **4.** (*unikać*) avoid, evade; ***nie ominie go kara*** he will not go unpunished

omlet *m* (*-tu*; *-ty*) *Br* omelette, *Am* omelet

omłot *m* (*-tu*; *-ty*) *BIOL* threshing

omnibus *m* (*-sa*; *-sy*) **1.** *hum* all-rounder **2.** *dated* bus

omotywać ⟨**-tać**⟩ (*-tuję*) **1.** wrap up, tie up (*I* with) **2.** *fig* inveigle, possess; ***omotywać się*** **1.** wrap oneself up (**w** *A* in) **2.** (*wplątać się*) get entangled

omowny *adj* periphrastic

omówić *v/p* → ***omawiać***

omówie|nie *n* (*-nia*; *-nia*) **1.** (*krytyka*) review, discussion **2.** (*peryfraza*) periphrasis **3.** (*sformułowanie niebezpośrednie*) *form* circumlocution; ***bez ~ń*** straightforwardly

omszony *adj* mossy

omułek *m* (*-łka*; *-łki*) blue mussel

omyć → ***obmywać***

omylny *adj* fallible; **omyłka** *f* (*-ki*; *-ki*) mistake, error; **omyłkowo** *adv* **1.** (*błędnie*) erroneously **2.** (*mylnie*) mistakenly; **omyłkowy** *adj* wrong, erroneous

omywać → ***obmywać***

on *pron* he

ona *pron* she

onanizm *m* (*-mu*; *no pl*) onanism; **onanizować się** *v/im* (*-zuję*) masturbate

ondulacja *f* (*-ji*; *-je*): ***trwała ~*** perm, permanent wave

ondulować ⟨**za-**⟩ (*-luję*) perm

one *pron* they

onegdaj, ***ongiś*** *adv lit* once, in days of yore

oni *pron* they
oniemiały *adj* speechless, dumbstruck, awestruck (**z** *G* with)
onieśmielać ⟨**-lić**⟩ (*-lam*) intimidate, overawe; **onieśmielenie** *n* (*-nia*; *no pl*) shyness, intimidation
onkologia *f* (*-gii*; *no pl*) oncology
ono *pron* it
ONZ *abbr f* (*ONZ-etu*; *no pl*) (= **Organizacja Narodów Zjednoczonych**) UN
opactwo *n* (*-wa*; *-wa*) abbey
opaczny *adj* wrong, erroneous
opad *m* (*-du*; *-dy*) **1.** precipitation; ***~y radioaktywne*** radioactive fallout **2.** *deszczu*: rainfall **3.** *śniegu*: snowfall **4.** CHEM sedimentation **5.** SPORT bend
opadać ⟨**-paść**⟩ (*-dam*) **I** *v/i* **1.** drop; ***~ z sił*** weaken, grow faint; ***~ z ciała*** grow thinner, lose weight; ***ręce mi opadają*** I give up, it's hopeless **2.** (*o liściach*) fall **3.** (*o wodzie*, *temperaturze*) fall, subside **4.** (*o terenie*) descend **5.** (*o cieście*) collapse **II** *v/t* (*otaczać*) attack, assail, beset
opadowy *adj* rain
opak *adv*: ***na ~*** mistakenly, wrongly, the wrong way
opakowani|e *n* (*-nia*; *-nia*) **1.** packaging; ***w ładnym ~u*** wrapped nicely; ***w ~u próżniowym*** vacuum-packed; ***w oryginalnym ~u*** in the original package **2.** (*pojemnik*) container
opakowywać ⟨**-kować**⟩ (*-kowuję*) wrap (up), pack
opalacz *m* (*-cza*; *-cze*) beachwear, sunsuit
opalać ⟨**-lić**⟩ (*-lam*) **1.** *pokój*: heat **2.** *twarz*: tan **3.** *sierść*: singe; ***opalać się*** sunbathe, get a (sun)tan
opalenizna *f* (*-ny*; *no pl*) (sun)tan
opalić *v/p* → ***opalać***
opalizować *v/im* (*-zuję*) opalesce
opalony *adj* **1.** (sun)tanned **2.** *pokój*: heated **3.** *brwi*: singed
opał *m* (*-łu*; *no pl*) fuel
opały *pl* (*-łów*) (*kłopoty*) plight *sing*, predicament *sing*
opałow|y *adj*: ***drewno ~e*** firewood; ***materiał ~y*** fuel; ***skład ~y*** fuel yard
opamiętać się *v/p* → ***opamiętywać się***
opamiętani|e *n* (*-nia*; *no pl*) reflection, self-control; ***bez ~a*** immoderately, with abandon
opamiętywać się ⟨**-tać**⟩ (*-tuję*) come to one's senses
opancerzony *adj* *Br* armoured *Am* armored
opanowanie *n* (*-nia*; *no pl*) self-control, composure; **opanowany** *adj* composed, controlled
opanowywać ⟨**-nować**⟩ (*-nowuję*) **1.** capture, seize **2.** *emocje*: get under control **3.** *sytuację*: control **4.** *temat*: master, learn **5.** *strach*, *pożar*: bring under control **6.** *zmęczenie*: overcome; ***opanowywać się*** control oneself
opar *m* (*-ru*; *-ry*) mist, haze; ***~y*** fumes, odours
oparci|e *n* (*-cia*; *-cia*) **1.** support **2.** *fotela*: back; ***~e dla głowy*** headrest **3.** *fig* support, basis; ***w ~u o*** *A* based on
oparty *adj fig* based, grounded, founded (**na** *L* on)
oparzelina *f* (*-ny*; *-ny*) scalding; **oparzenie** *n* (*-nia*; *-nia*) MED burn, scald
oparzony *adj* MED burnt, scalded; ***jak ~*** like a scalded cat
oparzyć *v/p* (*-rzę*) **1.** burn **2.** *płynem*, *gazem*: scald; ***oparzyć się*** **1.** get burnt **2.** *płynem*, *gazem*: get scalded
opasać *v/p* → ***opasywać***
opaska *f* (*-ki*; *-ki*) **1.** band; ***~ żałobna*** mourning band, black armband; ***~ uciskowa*** MED tourniquet **2.** (*na czoło*) headband
opasły *adj* **1.** fat, obese **2.** *tom*: bulky
opasywać ⟨**-sać**⟩ (*-suję*) **1.** gird **2.** *fig* encircle; ***opasywać się*** gird oneself
opaść *v/p* → ***opadać***
opat *m* (*-ta*; *opaci*) abbot
opatentować *v/p* (*-tuję*) patent
opatrunek *m* (*-nku*; *-nki*) MED dressing; **opatrunkowy** *adj* dressing
opatrywać ⟨**-trzyć**⟩ (*-ruję*) **1.** MED dress **2.** *okna*: seal **3.** *komentarzem*: provide (*I* with)
opatrznościowy *adj* providential; **opatrzność** *f* (*-ści*; *no pl*) providence
opatrzyć *v/p* → ***opatrywać***
opatulać ⟨**-lić**⟩ (*-lam*) bundle up, swaddle; ***opatulać się*** bundle oneself up (**w** *A* in)
opchać się *v/p* → ***opychać się***
opchnąć *v/p* (*-nę*) (*sprzedać*) *infml* palm off

O

opcja *f* (*-ji*; *-je*) option
opera *f* (*-ry*; *-ry*) **1.** opera **2.** (*budynek*) opera (house)
operacja *f* (*-ji*; *-je*) **1.** operation **2.** MED surgery; **operacyjn|y** *adj* **1.** MED operating, operation, surgical; ***sala ~a*** *Br* operating theatre, *Am* operating room; ***leczenie ~e*** surgical treatment **2.** (*zadaniowy*) operational
operator *m* (*-ra*; *-rzy*) cameraman; ***~ dźwięku*** sound technician; ***~ dźwigu*** crane operator; **operatorka** *f* (*-ki*; *-ki*) camerawoman
operatywność *f* (*-ści*; *no pl*) efficiency; **operatywny** efficient, energetic
operetka *f* (*-ki*; *-ki*) MUS operetta; **operetkowy** *adj* **1.** MUS operetta **2.** *fig* farcical
operować *v/im* ⟨**z-**⟩ (*-ruję*) **1.** operate (*A* on) **2.** *narzędziem*: use **3.** FIN circulate
operowy *adj* operatic
opędzać ⟨**-dzić**⟩ (*-dzam*) *muchy*: drive away; ***opędzać się*** drive away; ***nie mogę się opędzić od*** *G* I can't rid myself of
opętać *v/p* → ***opętywać***
opętanie *n* (*-nia*; *no pl*) obsession; **opętany** *adj* obsessed (*I* with), possessed; **opętaniec** *m* (*-tańca*; *-tańcy*) lunatic, madman; **opętańczy** *adj* crazy, frenzied
opętywać ⟨**-tać**⟩ (*-tuję*) obsess, possess
opić *v/p* → ***opijać***
opiec *v/p* → ***opiekać***
opieczętować *v/p* → ***pieczętować***
opiek|a *f* (*-ki*; *no pl*) **1.** care, attention, protection; ***~a społeczna*** **a)** social welfare **b)** (*instytucja*) welfare services; ***~a lekarska*** medical attention; ***~a nad chorymi*** nursing; ***wymagać ~i*** need care; ***pod czyjąś ~ą*** in s.o.'s care **2.** JUR custody
opiekacz *m* (*-cza*; *-cze*) toaster
opiekać ⟨**opiec**⟩ (*-kam*) **1.** grill, fry **2.** *grzanki*: toast
opiekować się ⟨**za-**⟩ (*-kuję*) **1.** take care (*I* of) **2.** *chorymi*, *zabytkami*: look after, tend
opiekun *m* (*-na*; *-nowie*), **~ka** *f* (*-ki*; *-ki*) **1.** *chorych*: minder **2.** *grupy*: carer **3.** JUR guardian **4.** ***~ka do dziecka*** babysitter
opiekuńczy *adj* **1.** protective; ***instynkt ~*** protective instinct; ***zasiłek ~*** welfare benefit **2.** JUR tutelar(y)
opielać ⟨**-lić**, **opleć**⟩ (*-lam*) weed
opieńka *f* (*-ki*; *-ki*) honey mushroom, oak mushroom
opieprz: ***dostać ~*** *infml* get a rollicking
opieprzać ⟨**-rzyć**⟩ (*-rzam*) *infml* give a dressing-down; ***opieprzać się*** *infml* laze around
opierać ⟨**oprzeć**⟩ (*-ram*) **1.** lean (***o*** *A* against) **2.** *fig* base (***na*** *L* on); ***opierać się*** **1.** lean (***o*** *A* on/against) **2.** *fig* be based (***na*** *L* on) **3.** (*bronić się*) resist, defy
opierzać się ⟨**-rzyć**⟩ (*-rzam*) BIOL fledge; **opierzony** *adj* fledged
opieszałość *f* (*-ści*; *no pl*) **1.** sluggishness, tardiness **2.** *lit* dilatoriness; **opieszały** *adj* **1.** sluggish, tardy **2.** *lit* dilatory
opiewać *v/im* (*-wam*) **I** *v/t* eulogize, extol **II** *v/i* (*o rachunku*) amount, run (***na*** *A* to)
opięty *adj* figure-hugging, tight-fitting, skintight
opijać ⟨**-pić**⟩ (*-jam*) celebrate with drink, drink to; ***opijać się*** drink too much, get drunk
opilstw|o *n* (*-wa*; *no pl*) *infml* alcohol addiction, drunkenness
opiłki *pl* (*-ków*) filings
opiłowywać ⟨**-łować**⟩ (*-łowuję*) file
opinać ⟨**opiąć**⟩ (*-nam*) hug, fit tightly
opinia *f* (*-nii*; *-nie*) **1.** opinion, view; ***~ publiczna*** public opinion; ***~ o pracowniku*** references **2.** (*reputacja*) reputation **3.** (*ekspertyza*) opinion, testimonial
opiniodawca *m* (*-cy*; *-cy*) expert; **opiniodawczy** *adj* consultative
opiniować ⟨**za-**⟩ (*-niuję*) give one's opinion on
opis *m* (*-su*; *-sy*) description; ***~ podróży*** description of a journey; **opisowy** *adj* descriptive
opisywać ⟨**-sać**⟩ (*-suję*) **1.** describe **2.** MATH circumscribe **3.** JUR inventory
opium *n indecl* opium
oplatać ⟨**-leść**⟩ (*-tam*) **1.** wind, twist around **2.** (*obejmować ramionami*) hug, embrace **3.** (*o pnączach*) entwine, cover
oplątywać ⟨**-tać**⟩ (*-tuję*) **1.** entwine **2.** *fig* ensnare, entangle

O

opleć *v/p* → ***opielać***
opleść *v/p* → ***oplatać***
opluwać ⟨**-luć**⟩ (*-wam*) **1.** spit (*A* at/on) **2.** *fig* slander
opłacać ⟨**-cić**⟩ (*-cam*) pay (*I* with); ***opłacać się* 1.** pay protection money (*D* to) **2.** pay, be profitable
opłacalność *f* (*-ści*; *no pl*) profitability, cost-effectiveness; **opłacalny** *adj* profitable, cost-effective
opłacić *v/p* → ***opłacać***
opłacony *adj* **1.** settled **2.** *list*: postpaid
opłakany *adj* miserable, pitiful; **opłakiwać** ⟨**-kać**⟩ (*-kuję*) bewail
opłat|a *f* (*-ty*; *-ty*) charge, payment; ***~a listowa*** postage; ***~a za przejazd*** fare; ***~a za doręczenie*** freight; ***za ~ą*** against payment; ***~a za gaz*** payment for gas
opłatek *m* (*-tka*; *-tki*) **1.** REL wafer **2.** (*spotkanie*) *Christmas gathering*
opłotki *pl* (*-ków*) wattle fencing *sing*
opłucna *f* (*-nej*; *-ne*) MED pleura
opłukiwać ⟨**-kać**⟩ (*-kuję*) rinse (out)
opływać ⟨**-łynąć**⟩ (*-wam*) **1.** *wyspę*: swim around **2.** (*statkiem*) circumnavigate **3.** (*żaglówką*) sail around **4.** (*o wodzie*) wash **5.** ***~ w dostatki*** live in clover
opływowy *adj kształt*: streamlined
opodal, ***nieopodal*** **I** *adv* close by **II** *prep* (*G*) near
opodatkowanie *n* (*-nia*; *no pl*) taxation; **opodatkowywać** ⟨**-kować**⟩ (*-kowuję*) tax, levy a tax on
opoka *f* (*-ki*; *no pl*) *lit* **1.** bedrock, rock **2.** (*osoba*) pillar of strength
opon|a *f* (*-ny*; *-ny*) **1.** AUTO *Br* tyre, *Am* tire **2.** ***~y mózgowe*** ANAT meninges
oponent *m* (*-ta*; *-nci*), **~ka** *f* (*-ki*; *-ki*) opponent, adversary
oponować ⟨**za-**⟩ (*-nuję*) protest (*D*/**przeciw** *D* against), oppose
opończa *f* (*-czy*; *-czy*) **1.** mantle **2.** AUTO tilt, tarpaulin
opornie *adv* **1.** (*ciężko*) with difficulty, stubbornly **2.** (*niechętnie*) unwillingly; **opornik** *m* (*-ka*; *-ki*) resistor; **oporność** *f* (*-ści*; *no pl*) **1.** *Br* wilfulness, *Am* willfulness **2.** TECH MED resistance
oporny *adj* **1.** (*uparty*) *Br* wilful, *Am* willful **2.** *osoba*: obstructive **3.** MED TECH resistant **4.** *dłużnik*: bad **5.** *choroba*: refractory
oportunista *m* (*-ty*; *-niści*), **-tka** *f* (*-ki*; *-ki*) opportunist; **oportunistyczny** *adj* opportunist
oporządzenie *n* (*-nia*; *no pl*) kit, gear
opos *m* (*-sa*; *-sy*) BIOL opossum
opowiadać ⟨**-wiedzieć**⟩ (*-dam*) talk, tell; ***opowiadać się***: ***~ się za*** *I* (**przeciw** *D*) be in favour of (against)
opowiadanie *n* (*-nia*; *-nia*) story, tale
opowiedzieć *v/p* → ***opowiadać***
opowieść *f* (*-ści*; *-ści*) story, tale
opozycja *f* (*-ji*; *-je*) opposition; **opozycjonista** *m* (*-ty*; *-niści*), **-tka** *f* (*-ki*; *-ki*) oppositionist; **opozycyjny** *adj* opposition, opposing
opój *m* (*opoja*; *opoje*) *infml* boozer, soak
opór *m* (*oporu*; *opory*) resistance; ***ruch oporu*** POLIT resistance movement; ***bez oporu*** without opposition; ***z oporem*** with difficulty, unwillingly; ***mieć opory*** have qualms
opóźniać ⟨**-nić**⟩ (*-niam*) delay, postpone; ***opóźniać się*** delay; ***pociąg opóźnia się*** the train is late
opóźnienie *n* (*-nia*; *-nia*) delay, lag; **opóźniony** *adj* **1.** *pociąg*: delayed **2.** ***~ w rozwoju*** retarded
opracowanie *n* (*-nia*; *-nia*) **1.** *tematu*: study **2.** (*rozprawa*) monograph; **opracowywać** ⟨**-cować**⟩ (*-cowuję*) work out, draw out
opraw|a *f* (*-wy*; *-wy*) **1.** *lustra*: frame; ***dać coś do ~y*** have s.th. framed **2.** *książki*: cover, binding; ***w twardej*** (***miękkiej***) ***~ie*** in hardback (paperback)
oprawca *m* (*-cy*; *-cy*) torturer, murderer, executioner
oprawiać ⟨**-wić**⟩ (*-wiam*) **1.** *książkę*: bind **2.** *obraz*: frame **3.** *siekierę*, *rubin*: set **4.** *dzika*, *rybę*: skin
oprawka *f* (*-ki*; *-ki*) **1.** frame, rim **2.** *okularów*: frames *pl* **3.** *żarówka*: socket; **oprawny** *adj* **1.** *tom*: bound **2.** *obraz*: framed **3.** *klejnot*: set
opresja *f* (*-ji*; *-je*) trouble
oprocentowanie *n* (*-nia*; *no pl*) interest; **oprocentowywać** ⟨**-tować**⟩ (*-towuję*) charge interest
oprogramowanie *n* (*-nia*; *no pl*) INF software

O

opromieniony *adj*: **~ sławą** bathed in glory
oprowadzać ⟨**-dzić**⟩ (*-dzam*) *wycieczkę*: show around; **oprowadzanie** *n* (*-nia*; *no pl*) guided tour
oprócz *prep* (*G*) apart from, aside from, except for, besides
opróżniać ⟨**-nić**⟩ (*-niam*) **1.** *kieliszek*: empty **2.** *pokój*: vacate; ***opróżniać się*** become empty
oprysk *m* (*-ku*; *-ki*) spray; **opryskiwać** ⟨**-kać**⟩ (*-kuję*) spray
opryskliwy *adj* brusque, abrupt, curt
opryszczka *f* (*-ki*; *no pl*) MED herpes
opryszek *m* (*-szka*; *-szki*) *infml* thug, hoodlum
oprzeć *v/p* → ***opierać***
oprzyrządowanie *n* (*-nia*; *-nia*) TECH gear
oprzytomnieć *v/p* (*-nieję*) **1.** regain consciousness, recover consciousness **2.** (*opamiętać się*) become sober, sober up
optować *v/im* (*-tuję*) opt (**za** *I* for)
optyczny *adj* visual, optical; **optyk** *m* (*-ka*; *-tycy*) optician; **optyka** *f* (*-ki*; *no pl*) optics
optymalizować ⟨**z-**⟩ (*-zuję*) optimize; **optymalny** *adj* optimal, optimum
optymista *m* (*-ty*; *-miści*), **-tka** *f* (*-ki*; *-ki*) optimist; **optymistyczny** *adj* optimistic
opublikowanie *n* (*-nia*; *no pl*) publication, publishing
opuchlizna *f* (*-ny*; *-ny*) swelling, puffiness; **opuchły**, ***opuchnięty*** *adj* swollen, puffy
opukiwać ⟨***opukać***⟩ (*-kuję*) tap
opust *m* (*-tu*; *-ty*) discount, reduction
opustoszały *adj* desolate, deserted; **opustoszeć** *v/p* (*-szeję*) (*o ulicy*) empty
opuszczać ⟨***opuścić***⟩ (*-czam*) **1.** lower **2.** *cenę*: reduce, lower **3.** *wyraz*: skip, omit **4.** *wykład*: miss **5.** *rodzinę*: leave; ***opuszczać się*** (*w pracy*) neglect one's duties, slack off
opuszczenie *n* (*-nia*; *-nia*) **1.** loneliness **2** (*zaniedbanie*) neglect **3.** (*w tekście*) omission; **opuszczony** *adj* **1.** lonely, abandoned **2.** (*zaniedbany*) abandoned, desolate, neglected
opuszka *f* (*-ki*; *-ki*) fingertip
opuścić *v/p* → ***opuszczać***
opychać się ⟨***opchać***⟩ (*-cham*) *infml* stuff oneself (*I* with)
opylać ⟨**-lić**⟩ (*-lam*) **1.** spray **2.** *fig infml* palm off
orać ⟨**za-**⟩ (*orzę*) **1.** *Br* plough, *Am* plow **2.** (*pracować*) *infml* drudge, slave
orangutan *m* (*-na*; *-ny*) orangutang
oranżada *f* (*-dy*; *-dy*) orangeade
oranżeria *f* (*-rii*; *-rie*) orangery, hothouse
orator *m* (*-ra*; *-rzy*) orator; **oratorski** *adj* oratorical
oraz *conj* and, as well as
orbita *f* (*-ty*; *-ty*) ASTR orbit
orchidea *f* (*-dei*; *-dee*) orchid
orczykowy *adj*: **wyciąg ~** drag lift, ski tow
order *m* (*-ru*; *-ry*) order
ordynacja *f* (*-ji*; *-je*) *wyborcza*: elections statute
ordynarny *adj* vulgar
ordynator *m* (*-ra*; *-rzy*) (*w szpitalu*) department head
ordynus *m* (*-sa*; *-sy*) *infml* lout
orędownik *m* (*-ka*; *-nicy*), **-niczka** *f* (*-ki*; *-ki*) advocate, promoter
orędzie *n* (*-dzia*; *-dzia*) address
oręż *m* (*-ża*; *no pl*) *lit* arms *pl*, weapon
organ *m* (*-nu*; *-ny*) BIOL organ
organiczny *adj* organic
organista *m* (*-ty*; *-niści*), **-tka** *f* (*-ki*; *-ki*) organist
organizacja *f* (*-ji*; *-je*) organization; ***≈ Narodów Zjednoczonych*** the United Nations; **organizacyjny** *adj* organizational
organizator *m* (*-ra*; *-rzy*), **~ka** *f* (*-ki*; *-ki*) organizer; ***~ wycieczek*** tour operator
organizm *m* (*-mu*; *-my*) BIOL POLIT organism
organizować ⟨**z-**⟩ (*-zuję*) **1.** *wycieczkę*: organize **2.** *firmę*: establish, set up
organki *pl* (*-ków*) mouth organ *sing*; **organowy** *adj* organ; **organy** *pl* (*-nów*) MUS organ *sing*
orgazm *m* (*-mu*; *-my*) orgasm
orgia *f* (*-gii*; *-gie*) orgy
orientacj|a *f* (*-ji*; *-je*) **1.** sense of direction; ***zmysł ~i*** sense of direction **2.** (*wiedza*) knowledge **3.** POLIT orientation; **orientacyjny** *cena*: approximate
orientalny *adj* oriental

O

orientować się ⟨**z-**⟩ (*-tuję*) **1.** (*w terenie*) orient(ate) oneself **2.** (*zauważać*) realize **3.** (*mieć wiedzę*) be knowledgeable (**w** *L* about)
orka[1] *f* (*-ki*; *no pl*) **1.** *Br* ploughing, *Am* plowing **2.** (*ciężka praca*) *infml* graft
orka[2] *f* (*-ki*; *-ki*) BIOL killer whale
orkiestra *f* (*-ry*; *-ry*) **1.** orchestra; **~ *symfoniczna*** symphony orchestra **2.** (*zespół*) band; **~ *jazzowa*** jazz band; **~ *dęta*** brass band; **~ *wojskowa*** military band
orlę *n* (*-lęcia*; *-lęta*) eaglet; **orl|i** *adj* eagle's; ***~e gniazdo*** eagle's nest; ***~i nos*** aquiline nose; **orlica** *f* (*-cy*; *-ce*) female eagle
Ormianin *m* (*-na*; *-mianie*), **-mianka** *f* (*-ki*; *-ki*) Armenian
ormiański *adj* Armenian
ornament *m* (*-tu*; *-ty*) ornament, design
ornat *m* (*-tu*; *-ty*) chasuble
ornitologiczny *adj* ornithological; ***stacja ~a*** ornithological station
orny *adj* arable; ***grunt ~*** arable land
orszak *m* (*-ku*; *-ki*) procession; **~ *ślubny*** wedding procession; **~ *żałobny*** funeral procession
ortodoksyjny *adj* REL orthodox
ortodontyczny *adj* orthodontic
ortografia *f* (*-fii*; *no pl*) orthography, spelling; **ortograficzny** *adj* orthographic; ***błąd ~*** spelling mistake
ortopedyczny *adj Br* orthopaedic, *Am* orthopedic
oryginalny *adj* genuine, original
oryginа|ł *m* (*-łu*; *-ły*) original; ***w ~le*** in its original version
orzec *v/p* → **orzekać**
orzech *m* (*-cha*; *-chy*) **1.** nut; **~ *włoski*** walnut; **~ *laskowy*** hazelnut; ***twardy ~ do zgryzienia*** *fig* a tough nut to crack **2.** (*drewno*) walnut; **orzechowy** **1.** nut **2.** *drewno*: walnut **3.** *kolor*: hazel
orzeczenie *n* (*-nia*; *-nia*) **1.** MED statement, certificate **2.** JUR ruling, adjudication **3.** GRAM predicate; **orzecznictwo** *n* (*-twa*; *no pl*) JUR judicature; **orzecznik** *m* (*-ka*; *-ki*) GRAM predicate
orzekać ⟨**orzec**⟩ (*-kam*) *form* **1.** state, pronounce **2.** JUR rule, adjudicate, pronounce

orzekający *adj*: ***tryb ~*** GRAM the indicative (mood)
orzeł *m* (*orła*; *orły*) **1.** eagle; **~ *czy reszka?*** heads or tails? **2.** (*zdolna osoba*) wizard, whiz
orzesz|ek *m* (*-szka*; *-szki*) *dim* (small) nut; ***~ki ziemne*** peanuts; ***~ki pistacjowe*** pistachios
orzeźwiać ⟨**-wić**⟩ (*-wiam*) refresh, invigorate; ***orzeźwiać się*** refresh oneself
orzeźwiający *adj* refreshing, invigorating; ***napój ~*** refreshing drink
orzynać ⟨**orżnąć**⟩ (*-nam*) *infml* **1.** rip off, cheat **2.** (*w karty*) rook
osa *f* (*-sy*; *-sy*) wasp; ***być cienkim*** (***w pasie***) ***jak ~*** be wasp-waisted; ***zły jak ~*** angry like a bear with a sore head
osaczać ⟨**-czyć**⟩ (*-czam*) **1.** corner **2.** *fig* assault, bombard
osad *m* (*-du*; *-dy*) **1.** deposit, residue **2.** GEOL deposit, drift
osada *f* (*-dy*; *-dy*) **1.** settlement **2.** *łodzi*: crew
osadnik[1] *m* (*-ka*; *-nicy*) settler
osadnik[2] *m* (*-ka*; *-ki*) sedimentation tank; **osadowy** *adj* GEOL sedimentary
osadzać ⟨**-dzić**⟩ (*-dzam*) **1.** fasten, plant **2.** *kolonistów*: settle **3.** *muł*: leave a deposit of **4.** *łopatę*: set **5.** *kamień*: mount **6.** **~ *w areszcie*** put in prison; ***osadzać się*** (*o kurzu*, *mule*) settle, form a deposit
osadzon|y *adj* **1.** *kamień*: mounted **2.** *fabuła*: set **3.** ***głęboko ~e oczy*** deep-set eyes
osamotnieć *v/p* (*-nieję*) become lonely; **osamotnienie** *n* (*-nia*; *no pl*) loneliness, solitude; **osamotniony** *adj* lonely
osączać ⟨**-czyć**⟩ (*-czam*) drain
osąd *m* (*-du*; *-dy*) judgement; **osądzać** ⟨**-dzić**⟩ (*-dzam*) judge, assess
oschłość *f* (*-ści*; *no pl*) dryness, coldness; **oschły** *adj* **1.** cold, dry **2.** *osoba*: hard-faced
oscylować *v/im* (*-luję*) **1.** PHYS oscillate **2.** *fig* fluctuate
osełka *f* (*-ki*; *-ki*) **1.** whetstone **2.** (*masło*) pat of butter, butterball
osesek *m* (*-ska*; *-ski*) suckling
oset *m* (*ostu*; *osty*) thistle
osiadać ⟨**osiąść**⟩ (*-dam*) settle; **~ *na mieliźnie*** be grounded

O

osiadły *adj* settled
osiągać ⟨**-gnąć**⟩ (*-gam*) **1.** achieve, attain; ~ **cel** achieve one's goal **2.** *szczyt, rozmiary*: reach
osiągalny *adj* achievable, attainable; **osiągi** *pl* (*-gów*) TECH performance *sing*; **osiągnięcie** *n* (*-cia*; *-cia*) achievement, accomplishment
osiąść *v/p* → **osiadać**
osie *pl* → **oś**
osiedlać ⟨**-lić**⟩ (*-lam*) settle; **osiedlać się** settle
osiedle *n* (*-la*; *-la*) estate; ~ **mieszkaniowe** housing estate; ~ **robotnicze** working-class housing estate; **osiedleniec** *m* (*-leńca*; *-leńcy*) settler; **osiedleńczy** *adj* settlement
osiedlić *v/p* → **osiedlać**
osiedlowy *adj* community
osiem *num* eight; **osiemdziesiąt** *num* eighty; **osiemdziesięcioletni** *adj* eighty-year-old
osiemnastka *f* (*-ki*; *-ki*) **1.** eighteen **2.** (*dziewczyna*) eighteen-year-old **3.** (*przyjęcie*) eighteenth birthday party
osiemnasto- (*w złożeniach*) eighteen-
osiemnastoletni *adj* eighteen-year-old; **osiemnastowieczny** *adj* eighteenth-century; **osiemnast|y** *adj* eighteenth; **~a** (**godzina**) six p.m., eighteen hundred hours
osiemnaście *num* eighteen; **osiemset** *num* eight hundred
osierdzie *n* (*-dzia*; *-dzia*) ANAT pericardium
osierocać ⟨**-cić**⟩ (*-cam*) orphan; **osierocieć** *v/p* (*-cieję*) be orphaned
osika *f* (*-ki*; *-ki*), **osina** *f* (*-ny*; *-ny*) **1.** aspen **2.** (*drewno*) aspen wood; **osikowy** *adj* aspen
osioł *m* (*osła*; *osły*) donkey
osiowy *adj* axial
osiwiały *adj* greyed, *Am* grayed
oskarżać ⟨**-żyć**⟩ (*-żam*) accuse (**o** *A* of); ~ **przed sądem** accuse, charge
oskarżenie *n* (*-nia*; *-nia*) **1.** accusation **2.** JUR accusation, charge; **wnieść ~ przeciw** *D* bring an accusation against, draw up charges against
oskarżony **I** *adj* accused **II** *m* (*-nego*; *-żeni*), **-na** *f* (*-nej*; *-ne*) the accused, defendant
oskarżyciel *m* (*-la*; *-le*), **~ka** *f* (*-ki*; *-ki*) prosecutor
oskarżyć *v/p* → **oskarżać**
oskrobywać ⟨**-bać**⟩ (*-buję*) **1.** scrape **2.** *marchew*: peel **3.** *rybę*: scale
oskrzel|a *pl* (*-li*) ANAT bronchi; **zapalenie ~i** bronchitis
oskubywać ⟨**-bać**⟩ (*-buję*) **1.** pick **2.** *kurę*: pluck **3.** (*oszukać*) *infml* fleece
osłabiać ⟨**-bić**⟩ (*-biam*) **1.** weaken, impair **2.** *cios*: blunt, ease, cushion; **osłabienie** *n* (*-nia*; *-nia*) **1.** weakness **2.** *organizmu*: debility; weakness; **osłabiony** *adj* debilitated, weakened
osłabnąć *v/p* → **słabnąć**
osładzać ⟨**-łodzić**⟩ (*-dzam*) **1.** sweeten **2.** *fig* sweeten, make more attractive
osłaniać ⟨**-łonić**⟩ (*-niam*) **1.** cover, screen **2.** (*chronić*) protect (**przed** *I*/**od** *G* against) **3.** SPORT cover; **osłaniać się** protect oneself
osławiony *adj gangster*: notorious, infamous
osłod|a *f* (*-dy*; *no pl*) consolation, comfort; **na ~ę** as a consolation
osłodzić *v/p* → **osładzać**
osłon|a *f* (*-ny*; *ny*) **1.** protection **2.** *fig* cover; **pod ~ą nocy** under the cover of darkness
osłonić *v/p* → **osłaniać**
osłonięty *adj*: ~ **od wiatru** sheltered
osłon|ka *f* (*-ki*; *-ki*) cover, shield; **bez ~ek** openly, outright
osłuchiwać ⟨**-chać**⟩ (*-chuję*) *chorego*: sound, auscultate
osłupiały *adj* dum(b)founded, dumbstruck
osłupieć *v/p* (*-pieję*) be dum(b)founded, be dumbstruck; **osłupienie** *n* (*-nia*; *no pl*) stupefaction; **wprawić w ~** cause to be dumbstruck
osmalać ⟨**-lić**⟩ (*-lam*) char, sear; **osmalony** *adj słońcem*: bronzed
osmarowywać → **obsmarowywać**
osnow|a *f* (*-wy*; *-wy*) **1.** *tkaniny*: warp **2.** *fig* background, fabric; **na ~ie** *G* based on
osob|a *f* (*-by*; *-by*) person; **~a fizyczna** JUR natural person; **~a prawna** JUR legal person; **~a towarzysząca** accompanying person; **na ~ę**, **od ~y** per person; **we własnej ~ie** himself, herself; **~y trzecie** third parties; **~om nieupoważnionym wstęp wzbroniony** authorized entry only

osobistość *f* (*-ści*; *-ści*) personage, personality, celebrity; **osobist|y** *adj* personal; ***dowód ~y*** identity card; ***życie ~e*** private life; ***komputer ~y*** personal computer, PC; ***ochrona ~a*** bodyguard; ***rewizja ~a*** body-search
osobliwość *f* (*-ści*; *-ści*) **1.** peculiarity, oddness **2.** *natury*: curiosity **3.** (*dziwoląg*) oddity; **osobliw|y** *adj* curious, peculiar, queer, odd; ***nic ~ego, że*** no wonder (that)
osobnik *m* **1.** (*-ka*; *-ki*) BIOL specimen **2.** (*-ka*; *-nicy*) individual, character
osobno *adv* separately, individually; **osobn|y** *adj* **1.** (*własny*) separate **2.** (*oddzielny*) separate, independent; ***z ~a*** individually **3.** (*inny*) another; ***to ~y problem*** that's another problem
osobnoś|ć: ***na ~ci*** in private
osobowość *f* (*-ści*; *-ści*) personality; ***~ prawna*** legal entity
osobow|y I *adj* **1.** personal, personnel; ***skład ~y*** members; ***akta ~e*** personal record **2.** *pociąg*: passenger **II** *m* (*-wego*; *-we*) *Br* stopping train, *Am* slow train
osocze *n* (*-cza*; *no pl*) BIOL plasma
osowiały *adj* dejected, dispirited
osóbka *f* (*-ki*; *-ki*) *hum* young person
ospa *f* (*-py*; *no pl*) pox; ***~ wietrzna*** chickenpox
ospały *adj* drowsy, languid, sluggish
ospowaty *adj* pockmarked
osprzęt *m* (*-tu*; *no pl*) accessories *pl*, fittings *pl*
ostać się *v/p* (*-toję*) *lit* withstand, survive, remain
ostatecznie I *adv* definitively **II** *particle* after all, in the end; **ostatecznoś|ć** *f* (*-ści*; *no pl*) necessity, the last resort, extremity; ***w ~ci*** as a last resort, if push comes to shove; ***doprowadzić kogoś do ~ci*** push s.o. beyond their limit
ostateczn|y *adj* **1.** conclusive, decisive **2.** (*końcowy*) final, ultimate, terminal; ***wersja ~a*** final version; ***~y wynik*** final result; ***Sąd ~y*** REL the Last Judgement
ostat|ek *m* (*-tka*; *-tki*) remains *pl*; ***do ~ka*** until the last; ***na ~ek*** last; **ostatki** *pl* (*-ków*) Shrovetide *sing*, Shrove Tuesday *sing*

ostatni *adj* last, recent; ***~mi czasy*** *lit* recently, lately; ***~ głupiec*** complete idiot; ***~ krzyk mody*** all the rage; ***~a Wieczerza*** REL the Last Supper
ostatnio *adv* recently, lately, of late
ostentacyjny *adj* ostentatious
ostępy *pl* (*-pów*) wilds, backwoods
ostoja *f* (*-toi*; *-toje*) **1.** *zwierząt*: sanctuary, refuge **2.** (*oparcie*) bastion **3.** (*podstawa*) mainstay **4.** (*wsparcie*) support
ostracyzm *m* (*-mu*; *no pl*) ostracism
ostro *adv* → **ostry**
ostroga *f* (*-gi*; *-gi*) **1.** spur **2.** (*na rzece*) groin, groyne
ostrokątny *adj* acute-angled
ostrołuk *m* (*-ku*; *-ki*) ARCHIT ogive
ostrosłup *m* (*-pa*; *-py*) MATH pyramid
ostrość *f* (*-ści*; *no pl*) **1.** sharpness **2.** *fig* severity, strictness **3.** PHOT focus
ostrożnoś|ć *f* (*-ści*; *no pl*) care, caution; ***środki ~ci*** precautions; **ostrożny** *adj* **1.** careful, cautious **2.** (*delikatny*) cautious
ostrużyny *pl* (*-żyn*) shavings, peelings
ostr|y *adj* **1.** *nóż*: sharp **2.** *wiatr*, *uwaga*: cutting **3.** (*przenikliwy*) incisive **4.** PHOT sharp, focused **5.** COOK spicy, hot **6.** (*stromy*) steep **7.** *głos*: harsh, strident **8.** *światło*, *kolor*: harsh **9.** *zapach*: sharp, pungent **10.** MED acute, severe; ***~y dyżur*** emergency ward; standby duty **11.** ***~a amunicja*** live ammunition
ostryga *f* (*-gi*; *-gi*) oyster
ostrzał *m* (*-łu*; *-ły*) (gun)fire
ostrze *n* (*-rza*; *-rza*) blade, edge
ostrzegać ⟨**-rzec**⟩ (*-gam*) alert (**przed** *I* to), warn (**przed** *I* against)
ostrzegawczy *adj* warning, danger
ostrzeliwać ⟨**-lać**⟩ (*-wuję*) fire at, shell; ***ostrzeliwać się*** fire at each other
ostrzeżenie *n* (*-nia*; *-nia*) warning, admonition
ostrzyc *v/p* (*-rzygę*) **1.** cut; ***~ sobie włosy*** cut one's hair, have one's hair cut **2.** *owcę*: shear; **ostrzyc się** *(samemu)* to cut one's hair; (*u fryzjera*) to have one's hair cut
ostrzyć ⟨**na-**⟩ (*-rzę*) **1.** grind, hone **2.** *ołówek*: sharpen; ***~ sobie zęby na*** *A* have one's eye on
ostrzyżony *adj* cropped

O

ostudzać ⟨**-dzić**⟩ (*-dzam*) cool; **ostudzać się** cool
ostukiwać → **opukiwać**
ostygnąć *v/p* (*-nę*) cool
osunąć się *v/p* → **osuwać się**
osuszać ⟨**-szyć**⟩ (*-szam*) **1.** *bagno*: drain, dry away **2.** *butelkę*: *infml* drain
osuwać się ⟨**osunąć**⟩ (*-wam*) **1.** slide, slip **2.** (*o osobie*) sink, slump; **osuwisko** *n* (*-ka*; *-ka*) landslide, landslip
oswabadzać → **oswobadzać**
oswajać ⟨**-woić**⟩ (*-jam*) **1.** accustom, habituate (**z** *I* to) **2.** *zwierzę*: tame, domesticate; **oswajać się 1.** accustom oneself, get used (**z** *I* to) **2.** (*zaznajamiać się*) become acquainted, familiarize (**z** *I* with) **3.** (*o zwierzętach*) become tamed, become domesticated
oswobadzać ⟨**-bodzić**⟩ (*-dzam*) free, liberate; **oswobadzać się** free oneself, liberate oneself (**od** *G* from)
oswobodzenie *n* (*-nia*; *no pl*) liberation; **oswobodziciel** *m* (*-la*; *-le*) liberator
oswoić *v/p* → **oswajać**
oswojony *adj* **1.** familiar (**z** *I* with) **2.** *zwierzę*: tame, domesticated
osypisko *n* (*-ka*; *-ka*) **1.** *kamienne*: scree, talus **2.** *gruzu*: heap, pile
osypywać → **obsypywać**
oszacować *v/p* → **szacować**
oszalały *adj fig* crazy, mad, frantic (**z** *G* with); **jak ~** like crazy; **oszaleć** *v/p* (*-leję*) go crazy, go mad, go wild (**na punkcie** *G* over)
oszałamiać ⟨**oszołomić**⟩ (*-miam*) **1.** intoxicate, stupefy **2.** *fig* bewilder, stun, stupefy; **oszałamiający** *adj* bewildering, staggering, stunning
oszczep *m* (*-pu*; *-py*) javelin, spear
oszczepnik *m* (*-ka*; *-nicy*), **-niczka** *f* (*-ki*; *-ki*) javelin thrower
oszczerca *m* (*-cy*; *-cy*) slanderer; **oszczerczy** *adj* defamatory, slanderous; **oszczerstwo** *n* (*-wa*; *-wa*) slander, slur
oszczędnościowy *adj* economical, economy
oszczędnoś|ć *f* (*-ści*; *-ści*) **1.** frugality, economy **2. ~ci** savings, reserves; **oszczędny** *adj* frugal, economical
oszczędzać ⟨**-dzić**⟩ (*-dzam*) **1.** economize **2.** (*odkładać pieniądze*): save, put away (**na** *A* for) **3.** (*darować życie*) spare **4.** *ubranie*: take care of; **oszczędzać się** save oneself, spare oneself
oszkalować *v/p* → **szkalować**
oszklony *adj* glazed
oszołom *m* (*-ma*; *-my*) *infml* crank, freak
oszołomić *v/p* → **oszałamiać**
oszołomienie *n* (*-nia*; *-nia*) **1.** daze, stupefaction; **~ alkoholem** alcohol intoxication **2.** (*szok*) bewilderment, daze, stupefaction; **oszołomiony** *adj* **1.** dazed, stupefied **2.** (*zaszokowany*) bewildered, dazed, stupefied
oszpecać ⟨**-cić**⟩ (*-cam*) disfigure, scar
oszroniony *adj* frosted
oszukać *v/p* → **oszukiwać**
oszukańczy *adj* fraudulent, deceitful; **oszukaństwo** *n* (*-wa*; *-wa*) deception, fraud
oszukiwać ⟨**-kać**⟩ (*-kuję*) deceive, cheat; **oszukiwać się 1.** deceive each other **2.** (*oszukiwać siebie*) deceive oneself, delude oneself
oszust *m* (*-ta*; *oszuści*), **~ka** *f* (*-ki*; *-ki*) swindler, fraudster; **oszustwo** *n* (*-wa*; *-wa*) fraud, deception; **~ podatkowe** tax fraud
oszwabiać ⟨**-bić**⟩ (*-biam*) *infml* rook, fleece
oś *f* (*osi*; *osie*) **1.** MATH axis **2.** AUTO axle **3.** TECH pivot
ościenn|y *adj Br* neighbouring, *Am* neighboring; **państwa ~e** neighbour states
oścień *m* (*-cienia*; *-cienie*) leister
oścież: **otwarty na ~** wide open
ościsty *adj* (*ryba*) bony; **ość** *f* (*ości*; *ości*) (fish)bone
oślepiać ⟨**-pić**⟩ (*-piam*) blind, dazzle; **oślepiający** *adj* blinding, dazzling
oślepnąć *v/p* (*-nę*) go blind; **oślepnięcie** *n* (*-cia*; *no pl*) blindness
ośl|i *adj* asinine, donkey; **~a łączka** nursery slope; **~e uszy** *fig* dog ears; **oślica** *f* (*-cy*; *-ce*) jenny
ośliniać ⟨**-nić**⟩ (*-niam*) drool
oślizgły, **oślizły** *adj* slimy, slippery
ośmielać ⟨**-lić**⟩ (*-lam*) encourage; **ośmielać się** dare
ośmieszać ⟨**-szyć**⟩ (*-szam*) ridicule, humiliate; **ośmieszać się** make a fool of oneself

O

ośmio- (*w złożeniach*) eight-
ośmiobok *m* (*-ku*; *-ki*) *MATH* octagon; **ośmiodniowy** *adj* eight-day; **ośmiogodzinny** *adj* eight-hour; **ośmiokąt** *m* (*-ta*; *-ty*) → ***ośmiobok***
ośmiokrotny *adj* eight-time, eightfold; **ośmioletni** *adj* eight-year-old
ośmiornica *f* (*-cy*; *-ce*) octopus
ośmioro *num* eight
ośmiu → ***osiem***; **ośmiuset** → ***osiemset***
ośnieżony *adj* snowy, snow-capped
ośrodek *m* (*-dka*; *-dki*) *Br* centre, *Am* center; ~ ***badawczy*** research centre; ~ ***szkoleniowy*** training centre; ~ ***wypoczynkowy*** resort; ~ ***zdrowia*** health centre, clinic
oświadczać ⟨**-czyć**⟩ (*-czam*) announce, declare; ***oświadczać się*** propose (marriage) (*D* to)
oświadczenie *n* (*-nia*; *-nia*) statement, pronouncement; **oświadczyny** *pl* (*-czyn*) (marriage) proposal *sing*
oświata *f* (*-ty*; *no pl*) education; **oświatowy** *adj* education, educational; ***film*** ~ educational film
oświecenie *n* (*-nia*; *no pl*) the Enlightenment; **oświecony** *adj* enlightened
oświetlać ⟨**-lić**⟩ (*-lam*) light, illuminate; **oświetlenie** *n* (*-nia*; *no pl*) lighting, illumination; **oświetleniowy** *adj* lighting
Oświęcim *m* (*-mia*) Auschwitz
ot *particle*: ~ ***tak sobie*** without reason; ~ ***co*** that's all there is to it
otaczać ⟨**otoczyć**⟩ (*-czam*) **1.** surround, encircle **2.** *murem*: enclose **3.** ~ ***kogoś ramieniem*** embrace s.o.; ***otaczać się*** surround oneself (*I* with)
otaczający *adj* surrounding
otarcie *n* (*-cia*; *-cia*) *MED* chafe, abrasion; ***na*** ~ ***łez*** as a consolation
otchłań *f* (*-ni*; *-nie*) abyss, chasm
otępiały *adj* numb; **otępieć** *v/p* (*-pieję*) feel numb; **otępienie** *n* (*-nia*; *no pl*) torpor, stupor; ~ ***starcze*** *MED* senility, dementia
otłuszczenie *n* (*-nia*; *no pl*) **1.** *MED* (*otyłość*) adiposity **2.** fatness
oto *particle*: ~ ***jest*** here is; ~ ***są*** here are; ~ ***wszystko*** that's all; ~ ***nasz dom*** this is our house; ~ ***oni*** here they are; ***w taki*** ~ ***sposób*** (in) this way; ***tak*** ~ that is how
otoczak *m* (*-ka*; *-ki*) pebble
otoczeni|e *n* (*-nia*; *no pl*) **1.** surroundings *pl* **2.** *fig* environment, *Br* neighbourhood, *Am* neighborhood; ***w*** **~*u*** *G* surrounded by
otoczka *f* (*-ki*; *-ki*) **1.** sheath, encasement **2.** *fig* circumstances *pl*, background
otoczyć *v/p* → ***otaczać***
otok *m* (*-ka*/*-ku*; *-ki*) *czapki*: hat-band
otóż *particle* so, in fact; ~ ***to*** exactly, precisely, that's it; ~ ***nie*** in fact not
otręby *pl* (*-rąb*/*-bów*) bran *sing*
otrucie *n* (*-cia*; *-cia*) poisoning
otruć *v/p* → ***truć***
otruty *adj* poisoned
otrzaskać się *v/p* (*-kam*) *infml* **1.** get the hang (**z** *I* of), be at home (**z** *I* with) **2.** (*towarzysko*) refine oneself
otrzaskany *adj* *infml* **1.** at home (**z** *I* with) **2.** (*towarzysko*) refined, worldly
otrząsać ⟨**-snąć**⟩ (*-sam*) shake off; ***otrząsać się*** **1.** shake off (**z** *G*) **2.** (*przyjść do siebie*) recover (**po** *L* from); ***otrząsnął się na myśl o*** *L* he flinched at the thought of
otrzeć *v/p* → ***ocierać***
otrzepywać ⟨**-pać**⟩ (*-puję*) shake, brush
otrzewna *f* (*-nej*; *-ne*) *ANAT* peritoneum
otrzeźwiać ⟨**-wić**⟩ (*-wiam*) **1.** sober up **2.** (*o prysznicu*, *mrozie*) refresh, invigorate **3.** *fig* disillusion
otrzeźwieć *v/p* → ***trzeźwieć***
otrzymywać ⟨**-mać**⟩ (*-muję*) receive, *form* obtain
otuch|a *f* (*-chy*; *no pl*) courage, encouragement; ***dodać komuś*** **~*y*** hearten s.o., cheer s.o. up; ***pełen*** **~*y*** uplifted, of good heart
otulać ⟨**-lić**⟩ (*-lam*) wrap up, tuck in; ***mgła otulała góry*** the mountains were shrouded in fog; ***otulać się*** wrap oneself up
otumaniać ⟨**-nić**⟩ (*-niam*) *infml* **1.** dupe, trick **2.** (*narkotykiem*) drug, dope
otwarcie[1] *adv* openly, frankly
otwarci|e[2] *n* (*-cia*; *-cia*) **1.** opening; ***godziny*** **~*a*** opening hours, business hours **2.** *fig* being receptive (***na*** *A* to)
otwartość *f* (*-ści*; *no pl*) frankness, candidness; **otwart|y** *adj* **1.** open; ***wypłynąć na*** **~*e*** ***morze*** sail into open sea; ***z*** **~*ymi*** ***rękami*** with open hands;

O

dni ~e open days; ***list ~y*** open letter **2.** (*szczery*) candid, frank **3.** (*chłonny*) open, open-minded **4.** (*publiczny*) open, public

otwieracz *m* (*-cza*; *-cze*) opener

otwierać ⟨**-worzyć**⟩ (*-ram*) **1.** *drzwi, parasol, konto*: open; ***~ dyskusję*** open a discussion; ***~ ogień*** open fire; ***~ granice*** open the borders; ***~ nawias*** open brackets; ***~ komuś oczy*** *fig* open s.o.'s eyes; ***~ usta*** open one's mouth **2.** *firmę*: open (up), establish **3.** *zamek*: unlock; **otwierać się 1.** (*o drzwiach, perspektywach*) open **2.** (*o ranie*) open (up)

otworek *m* (*-rka*; *-rki*) (small) opening, hole

otworzyć *v/p* → **otwierać**

otw|ór *m* (*-woru*; *-wory*) opening, hole; ***stać ~orem*** stand open; ***wszystko stoi przed tobą ~orem*** *fig* the world stands open before you

otyłość *f* (*-ści*; *no pl*) MED obesity

otyły *adj* obese

owa → **ów**

owacja *f* (*-ji*; *-je*) ovation, applause; **owacyjny** *adj* enthusiastic, rapturous

owad *m* (*-da*; *-dy*) insect

owadobójczy *adj*: ***środek ~*** insecticide

owadożerny *adj* BIOL insectivorous; **owadzi** *adj* insect

owal *m* (*-lu*; *-le*) oval; **owalny** *adj* oval

owca *f* (*-cy*; *-ce*) sheep; ***czarna ~*** *fig* black sheep; ***chodzić jak błędna ~*** wander around like a lost sheep

owczarek *m* (*-rka*; *-rki*) sheepdog

owczarnia *f* (*-ni*; *-nie*) sheepfold; **owczarstwo** *n* (*-wa*; *no pl*) sheep-farming; **owczarz** *m* (*-rza*; *-rze*) shepherd, sheep-farmer

owcz|y *adj* sheep; ***~y pęd*** herd instinct; ***Wyspy ⁓e*** Faroe Islands

owdowiały *adj* widowed; **owdowieć** *v/p* (*-wieję*) **1.** (*o kobiecie*) become a widow **2.** (*o mężczyźnie*) become a widower

owe → **ów**

owi → **ów**

owiać *v/p* → **owiewać**

owiany *adj*: ***~ tajemnicą*** *lit* shrouded in mystery

owieczka *f* (*-ki*; *-ki*) little sheep, lamb; ***zbłąkana ~*** *fig* stray sheep

owies *m* (*owsa*; *no pl*) oats

owiewać ⟨**owiać**⟩ (*-wam*) fan, blow gently

owijać ⟨**owinąć**⟩ (*-jam*) **1.** wrap up; ***~ (sobie) kogoś wokół palca*** *fig* wind s.o. around one's little finger **2.** (*bandażem*) wrap; **owijać się 1.** wrap up **2.** (*o bluszczu*) wind

owładnąć *v/p* (*-nę*) *lit* seize, capture; ***owładnęła mną radość*** I was overwhelmed with joy

owładnięty *adj* overwhelmed (*I* with); ***~ nienawiścią*** possessed with hate; ***~ strachem*** gripped by fear

owłosiony *adj* hairy, hirsute

owo → **ów**

owoc *m* (*-cu*; *-ce*) fruit; ***~e*** fruit; ***~e morza*** seafood; ***~e południowe*** tropical fruit; ***zakazany ~*** *fig* forbidden fruit

owocnia *f* (*-ni*; *-nie*) BIOL pericarp, seed pot; **owocny** *adj fig* fruitful; **owocować** ⟨**za-**⟩ (*-cuję*) bear fruit; **owocowy** *adj drzewo, sok*: fruit

owrzodzenie *n* (*-nia*; *-nia*) ulceration; **owrzodzony** *adj* ulcerated

owsianka *f* (*-ki*; *-ki*) *Br* porridge, *Am* oatmeal; **owsian|y** *adj* oat; ***płatki ~e*** rolled oats

owsik *m* (*-ka*; *-ki*) MED pinworm, threadworm

owszem *particle* **1.** indeed **2.** (*z pewnością*) certainly **3.** (*przeciwnie*) on the contrary

ozdabiać ⟨**-dobić**⟩ (*-biam*) ornament, embellish

ozdob|a *f* (*-by*; *-by*) **1.** ornament, decoration; ***~y choinkowe*** Christmas tree decorations; ***bez ozdób*** unadorned **2.** *fig* pride

ozdobić *v/p* → **ozdabiać**

ozdobn|y *adj* **1.** (*udekorowany, strojny*) decorative **2.** (*bogaty w ozdoby*) ornate **3.** (*będący ozdobą*) ornamental; ***rośliny ~e*** ornamentals; ***papier ~y*** gift wrap **4.** *styl*: ornate

ozdóbka *f* (*-ki*; *-ki*) ornament

ozdrowieniec *m* (*-wieńca*; *-wieńcy*) convalescent; **ozdrowieńczy** *adj* **1.** MED recuperative **2.** ECON sanative

oziębiać ⟨**-bić**⟩ (*-biam*) chill, cool; **oziębiać się** cool

oziębienie *n* (*-nia*; *-nia*) cold weather

oziębły *adj fig* cold

O

oziębnąć *v/p* (*-nę*) grow cold
ozimina *f* (*-ny*; *-ny*) winter crop; **ozimy** *adj* winter
oznaczać ⟨**-czyć**⟩ (*-czam*) **1.** mark **2.** *termin*: fix, determine **3.** (*mieć znaczenie*) mean, indicate; **oznaczenie** *n* (*-nia*; *-nia*) label, sign
oznajmiać ⟨**-mić**⟩ (*-miam*) *lit* announce, declare
oznajmienie *n* (*-nia*; *-nia*) **1.** announcement **2.** GRAM declarative sentence
oznaka *f* (*-ki*; *-ki*) **1.** indication **2.** *choroby*: symptom **3.** (*odznaka*) badge
ozonowy *adj* ozone
ozór *m* (*ozora*; *ozory*) tongue
ożaglowanie *n* (*-nia*; *no pl*) rig, sails *pl*
ożebrowanie *n* (*-nia*; *-nia*) ARCHIT (the) ribbing
ożenek *m* (*-nku*; *-nki*) marriage
ożywać ⟨**ożyć**⟩ (*-wam*) **1.** (*o osobie*) come to life **2.** (*o wspomnieniach*) come back
ożywczy *adj* invigorating, refreshing
ożywiać ⟨**-wić**⟩ (*-wiam*) **1.** revive, resuscitate **2.** *fig* enliven, liven up; **ożywiać się** **1.** (*o ulicy*) come to life **2.** (*o osobie*) cheer up, perk up
ożywienie *n* (*-nia*; *no pl*) excitement, animation; **~ gospodarcze** economic boom; **z ~m** with animation; **ożywiony** *adj* **1.** *dyskusja*: animated, lively, heated **2.** *handel*: booming, brisk **3.** *osoba*: excited, enthusiastic **4.** *materia*: animate

Ó

ósemka *f* (*-ki*; *-ki*) eight; **ósm|y** *adj* eighth; **~a** (**godzina**) eight o'clock; **o ~ej** at eight; **~y cud świata** *fig* the eighth wonder of the world
ów *pron lit* that; **w owych czasach** in those days, at that time
ówczesny *adj* of the time, contemporary

P

P

p. *abbr* **1.** (=**patrz**) v., vide, see **2.** (=**pan**) Mr. **3.** (=**pani**) Mrs., Ms. **4.** (=**punkt**) point **5.** (=**piętro**) floor
pa *interj* bye, bye-bye
pacać ⟨**-cnąć**⟩ (*-cam*) (*uderzać*) swat, whisk
pach|a *f* (*-chy*; *-chy*) **1.** ANAT armpit; **pod ~ą** under one's arm **2.** *swetra*: armhole
pachnący *adj* scented, fragrant, aromatic; **pachnieć** *v/im* (*-nę*) smell (*I* of)
pachołek *m* (*-łka*; *-łki*) **1.** lackey, stooge **2.** HIST servant **3.** (*słupek*) bollard, cone
pachwina *f* (*-ny*; *-ny*) ANAT groin
pacierz *m* (*-rza*; *-rze*) prayer
paciorek *m* (*-rka*; *-rki*) *dim* prayer
paciorki *pl* (*-ków*) beads
paciorkowce *pl* (*-ców*) BIOL streptococci
pacjent *m* (*-ta*; *-nci*), **~ka** *f* (*-ki*; *-ki*) patient
packa *f* (*-ki*; *-ki*) swat, fly swatter
pacyfikacja *f* (*-ji*; *-je*) pacification
pacyfista *m* (*-ty*; *-fiści*), **-tka** *f* (*-ki*; *-ki*) pacifist
pacykować się ⟨**wy-**⟩ (*-kuję*) *infml* daub one's face (with make-up)
pacynka *f* (*-ki*; *-ki*) hand puppet
paczka *f* (*-ki*; *-ki*) **1.** parcel, package **2.** *papierosów*: packet, pack **3.** *zapałek*: box **4.** (*prezent*) packet **5.** (*grupa*) gang, crowd; **paczkowany** *adj* pre-packed
paczuszka *f* (*-ki*; *-ki*) *dim* small parcel, small packet
paczyć ⟨**s-**⟩ (*-czę*) *charakter*: warp; **paczyć się** (*o drewnie*) warp, get warped
padaczka *f* (*-ki*; *no pl*) MED epilepsy
padać ⟨**paść**⟩ (*-dam*) **1.** fall; **~ ofiarą** *G* fall victim to; **~ sobie w ramiona**,

~ sobie w objęcia fall into each other's arms; **~ na kolana** fall to one's knees; **~ z nóg** *infml* feel dead on one's feet; **~ na nos** *infml* be dead tired; **2.** (*o zwierzętach*) die **3. pada deszcz** it's raining; **pada śnieg** it's snowing

padalec *m* (*-lca*; *-lce*) BIOL blindworm

padlina *f* (*-ny*; *-ny*) carrion, carcass

padnięty *adj infml* dead beat, zonked out

padół *m* (*-dołu*; *no pl*): **~ ziemski**, **~ łez** *lit hum* vale of tears

Padwa *f* (*-wy*) Padua

paginacja *f* (*-ji*; *no pl*) pagination

pagórek *m* (*-rka*; *-rki*) hill, knoll; **pagórkowaty** *adj* hilly, undulating

pajac *m* (*-ca*; *-ce*) **1.** (*klaun*) clown **2.** (*arlekin*) harlequin; **pajacyk** *m* (*-ka*; *-ki*) **1.** (*zabawka*) puppet clown **2.** (*ubranko*) playsuit, *Am* creepers *pl*

pająk *m* (*-ka*; *-ki*) spider

pajda *f* (*-dy*; *-dy*) thick slice

pajęczaki *pl* (*-ków*) BIOL arachnids; **pajęczyna** *f* (*-ny*; *-ny*) cobweb, spiderweb

paka *f* (*-ki*; *-ki*) **1.** chest, case **2.** (*paczka*) large parcel **3.** (*więzienie*) *infml* cooler, jug **4.** (*grupa*) *infml* gang, crowd

pakiecik *m* (*-ka*/*-ku*; *-ki*) *dim* small bundle; **pakiet** *m* (*-tu*; *-ty*) (*stos*) bundle, batch, package

Pakistan *m* (*-nu*) Pakistan; **Pakistańczyk** *m* (*-ka*; *-czycy*), **-tanka** *f* (*-ki*; *-ki*) Pakistani

pakować ⟨**s-**, **w-**⟩ (*-kuję*) **1.** pack **2.** (*upychać*) cram, stuff (**do** *G* into) **3.** *pieniądze*: sink, pour (**w** *A* into) **4.** pump iron; **pakować się 1.** pack (up) **2.** (*wpychać się*) squeeze in, barge in **3. ~ się w kłopoty** get into hot water

pakownia *f* (*-ni*; *-nie*) packing room; **pakowny** *adj* capacious; **pakowy** *adj*: **papier ~** wrapping paper

pakt *m* (*-tu*; *-ty*) pact; **~ o nieagresji** non-aggression pact; **paktować** *v/im* (*-tuję*) parley

pakuły *pl* (*-łów*/*-uł*) oakum *sing*

pakunek *m* (*-nku*; *-nki*) parcel, package

pal *m* (*-la*; *-le*) stake; **na ~ach** on stilts

palacz *m* (*-cza*; *-cze*) **1.** smoker; **~ nałogowy** heavy smoker **2.** (*pracownik*) stoker; **palaczka** *f* (*-ki*; *-ki*) smoker

palant *m* (*-ta*; *-ty*) *infml* ninny, prat

palarnia *f* (*-ni*; *-nie*) **1.** smoking room; **~ opium** opium den **2.** *kawy*: roasting plant

palący I *adj* **1.** burning, fiery hot **2.** *fig* urgent **3.** *słońce*: scorching **II** *m* (*-cego*; *-cy*), **-ca** *f* (*-cej*; *-ce*) smoker; **dla ~ch** smoking, for smokers; **przedział dla ~ch** smoking compartment, smoking coach

palcówka *f* (*-ki*; *-ki*) MUS fingering, finger exercise; **palczasty** *adj liść*: palmate

pal|ec *m* (*-lca*; *-lce*) **1.** (*u ręki*) finger; **~ec wskazujący** index finger; **~ec serdeczny** ring finger; **duży ~ec** thumb; **sam jak ~ec** all alone; **gruby na ~ec** as thick as a finger; **szeroki na ~ec** as wide as a finger; **~ec boży** an act of God; **mieć coś w małym ~cu** have s.th. at one's fingertips; **wyssany z ~ca** trumped-up; **wytykać kogoś ~cami** point a finger at; **zatłoczony, że ~ca nie da się wcisnąć** jam-packed, stuffed to the gunwales; **~ce lizać!** yum-yum!, scrumptious! **2.** (*u nogi*) toe; **na ~cach** on tiptoe

palenie *n* (*-nia*; *no pl*) **1.** *tytoniu*: smoking **2.** (*w piecu*) stoking **3.** *kawy*: roasting; **palenisko** *n* (*-ka*; *-ka*) hearth

palestra *f* (*-ry*; *no pl*) the Bar

Palestyna *f* (*-ny*) Palestine

Palestyńczyk *m* (*-ka*; *-czcy*), **-tynka** *f* (*-ki*; *-ki*) Palestinian

palestyński *adj* Palestinian

paleta *f* (*-ty*; *-ty*) palette

palić ⟨**s-**, **wy-**⟩ (*-lę*) **I** *v/i* **1.** (*w piecu*) stoke, light the fire **2.** (*o ranie*, *pieprzu*) burn **II** *v/t* **1.** *fig* burn; **s~ za sobą wszystkie mosty** burn one's bridges behind one **2.** *światło*: have a light on **3.** *papierosa*: smoke **4.** *wapno*, *cegłę*, *śmieci*: burn **5.** *kawę*: roast **6.** *zwłoki*: cremate; **palić się 1.** *fig* burn (**z** *I* with); **pali się światło** a light is on; **pali się ognisko** there is a bonfire; **pali się!** fire!; **nie pali się** *infml* there's no rush **2.** burn down

palik *m* (*-ka*; *-ki*) stake; **palikować** ⟨**o-**⟩ (*-kuję*) stake up

P

palisander *m* (*-dru*; *-dry*) rosewood; **palisandrowy** *adj* rosewood
paliwo *n* (*-wa*; *-wa*) fuel; **paliwomierz** *m* (*-rza*; *-rze*) fuel gauge, fuel indicator
palma *f* (*-my*; *-my*) palm (tree); ~ ***daktylowa*** date palm; ~ ***pierwszeństwa*** the palm; ~ ***mu odbiła*** *infml* he has (got) a screw loose; **palmow|y** *adj* palm; ***Niedziela ⁓a*** *REL* Palm Sunday
palnąć *v/p* (*-nę*) *infml* **1.** (*trzasnąć*) bang; ~ ***sobie w łeb*** shoot oneself **2.** (*powiedzieć*) blurt (out); ~ ***głupstwo*** put one's foot in it
palnik *m* (*-ka*; *-ki*) **1.** *TECH* burner, torch **2.** *kuchenki*: gas ring, burner; ***kuchenka z czterema ⁓ami*** stove with four burners
paln|y *adj* combustible, inflammable; ***broń ⁓a*** firearms
palony *adj kawa*: roasted
palowy *adj chata*: on stilts
palto *n* (*-ta*; *-ta*) (over)coat
paluch *m* (*-cha*; *-chy*) (*u nogi*) big toe; ***koślawy*** ~ *MED* hallux; **palusz|ek** *m* (*-szka*; *-szki*) *dim* **1.** (*u ręki*) finger **2.** (*u nogi*) toe **3.** ***słone ⁓ki*** salty sticks; ***⁓ki rybne*** *COOK* fish fingers
pała *f* (*-ły*; *-ły*) *infml* **1.** truncheon, club **2.** (*głowa*) nob, napper; ***łysa*** ~ baldy, slaphead
pałac *m* (*-cu*; *-ce*) palace; **pałacowy** *adj* palace, palatial; **pałacyk** *m* (*-ka*; *-ki*) (small) palace, mansion
pałać ⟨**za-**⟩ (*-łam*) *lit* burn; ~ ***nienawiścią*** burn with hatred; ~ ***gniewem*** be furious
pałaszować ⟨**s-**⟩ (*-szuję*) *infml* (*jeść*) gobble, demolish
pałąk *m* (*-ka*; *-ki*) bow-shaped handle; ***wygięty w*** ~ bow-shaped
pałeczk|a *f* (*-ki*; *-ki*) **1.** baton, wand; ***⁓a dyrygencka*** baton; ***⁓i nawozowe*** fertilizer sticks **2.** *COOK* chopstick **3.** *SPORT* baton **4.** *BIOL* bacillus
pałętać się *v/im* (*-tam*) *infml* gad about, hang around
pałka *f* (*-ki*; *-ki*) **1.** club, cudgel; ~ ***gumowa*** rubber truncheon **2.** (*uderzenie*) blow **3.** *BIOL* bulrush, reed mace
pamflet *m* (*-tu*; *-ty*) satire, lampoon
pamiątk|a *f* (*-ki*; *-ki*) **1.** keepsake **2.** *z podróży*: souvenir **3.** (*wspomnienie*) memento (**po** *I* of); ***na ⁓ę*** as a memento; **pamiątkarski** *adj* souvenir; **pamiątkowy** *adj* memorial, commemorative
pamię|ć *f* (*-mięci*; *no pl*) **1.** memory; ***⁓ć zbiorowa*** collective memory; ***⁓ć robocza***, ***⁓ć operacyjna*** *INF* random access memory; ***na ⁓ć*** by heart; ***liczyć w ⁓ci*** calculate mentally; ***świętej ⁓ci*** late; ***bez ⁓ci*** madly, head over heels; ***jeśli mnie ⁓ć nie myli*** if my memory serves me correctly **2.** *lit* remembrance
pamiętać ⟨**za-**⟩ (*-tam*) remember (**o** *L* about); **pamiętliwy** *adj* unforgiving; **pamiętnik** *m* (*-ka*; *-ki*) diary; ***⁓i*** memoirs, diaries; **pamiętny** *adj* memorable
pampers *m* (*-sa*; *-sy*) nappy, diaper
PAN *abbr m* (*PAN-u*; *no pl*) (= **Polska Akademia Nauk**) Polish Academy of Sciences
pan *m* (*-na*; *-nowie*) **1.** gentleman; ***⁓ie doktorze*** doctor; ~ ***młody*** bridegroom; ~ ***od matematyki*** maths teacher; ***⁓ Bóg*** God, Lord; ***być na ~ z*** *I* not be on the first name basis with; ***być za ~ brat z*** *I* be on familiar terms with; ***niech ~ będzie tak dobry i przyniesie mi szklankę wody*** could you be so kind as to fetch me a glass of water?; ***jak u ⁓a Boga za piecem*** very well, very comfortably **2.** (*z nazwiskiem*) Mr; ~ ***Kowalski*** Mr Kowalski **3.** (*bez nazwiska*) sir; ***proszę ⁓a, która jest godzina?*** excuse me, sir, what time is it? **4.** (*forma grzecznościowa*) you; ***jak się ~ nazywa?*** what is your name?; ***dzień dobry ⁓u!*** good morning to you! **5.** (*władca, właściciel*): master; ***być ⁓em sytuacji*** be the master of the situation; ~ ***domu*** host, master of the house
pancerny *adj Br* armoured, *Am* armored; **pancerz** *m* (*-rza*; *-rze*) *Br* armour, *Am* armor
panczenista *m* (*-ty*; *-niści*), **-tka** *f* (*-ki*; *-ki*) *SPORT* speed skater
panel *m* (*-lu*; *-le*) panel, wainscotting
pani *f* (*-ni*; *-nie*) **1.** lady; ***⁓e i panowie!*** Ladies and Gentlemen!; ~ ***od biologii*** biology teacher; ~ ***doktor*** doctor; ***być na ~ z*** *I* not be on the first name basis with **2.** (*z nazwiskiem*) Mrs

~ Nowak Mrs Nowak **3.** (*bez nazwiska*) madam, ma'am; **~ minister** (madam) Minister; **proszę ~, która jest godzina?** excuse me, ma'am, what time is it? **4.** (*forma grzecznościowa*) you; **jak się ~ nazywa?** what is your name?; **dzień dobry ~!** good morning! **5.** (*właścicielka*) mistress; **~ domu** hostess, mistress of the house

paniczny *adj* panic-stricken, in panic

panienka *f* (*-ki*; *-ki*) **1.** young lady, miss **2.** (*prostytutka*) *infml* call girl

panieński *adj*: **nazwisko ~e** maiden name

panier *m* (*-ru*; *no pl*) COOK breadcrumb, batter; **panierować** ⟨**za-**⟩ (*-ruję*) roll in breadcrumb, roll in batter

panika *f* (*-ki*; *no pl*) panic; **panikarski** *adj* panicky, alarmist; **panikarstwo** *n* (*-wa*; *no pl*) panic-mongering; **panikarz** *m* (*-rza*; *-rze*) panic-monger

pann|a *f* (*-ny*; *-ny*) **1.** (*nie mężatka*) maiden; **~a młoda** bride; **stara ~a** spinster, old maid; **być ~ą** be not married, be single; **~a z dzieckiem** an unmarried woman with a child; **~a z dobrego domu** girl of good family; **duża ~a** *hum* big girl; **Najświętsza Maria ~a** REL the Blessed Virgin Mary **2.** (*z nazwiskiem*) miss; **~a Malinowska** Miss Malinowski **3. ~a** ASTR Virgo **4.** (*stan cywilny*) single

panorama *f* (*-my*; *-my*) panorama

panoszyć się *v/im* (*-szę*) throw one's weight about, lord it

panować ⟨**za-**⟩ (*-nuję*) **1.** rule, reign (**nad** *I* over) **2.** *fig* dominate **3.** (*kontrolować*) be in control (**nad** *I* of) have control (**nad** *I* over); **~ nad sobą** exercise self-control, be self-restrained

panowanie *n* (*-nia*; *no pl*) **1.** rule, reign **2.** (*dominacja*) domination **3.** (*powszechność*) prevalence **4.** (*kontrola*) control; **~ nad sobą** self-control, self-restraint

pantera *f* (*-ry*; *-ry*) BIOL leopard, panther; **panterka** *f* (*-ki*; *-ki*) camouflage jacket

pantof|el *m* (*-fla*; *-fle*) shoe, mule; **~le damskie** ladies' shoes; **~le domowe** slippers; **być pod ~lem** *fig* be henpecked

pantofelek *m* (*-lka*; *-lki*) BIOL paramecium, slipper animalcule

pantoflarz *m* (*-rza*; *-rze*) *infml* henpecked husband

pantoflow|y *adj*: **poczta ~a** the grapevine, bush telegraph

pantomima *f* (*-my*; *-my*) mime

pańsk|i *adj* **1.** (*wyniosły*) lordly, lordlike; **po ~u** in a lordly manner **2.** (*arystokratyczny*) aristocratic **3.** (*forma grzecznościowa*) your, yours; **~i list** your letter; **czy to ~i płaszcz?** is this coat yours?

państewko *n* (*-ka*; *-ka*) small state

państwo[1] *n* (*-wa*; *-wa*) state, nation; **~ policyjne** police state; **~ opiekuńcze** welfare state

państw|o[2] *pl* (*-wa*) **1.** (*małżeństwo*) Mr and Mrs; **~o Kowalscy** Mr and Mrs Kowalski, the Kowalskis **2.** (*forma grzecznościowa*) you; **~o młodzi** newlyweds; **witamy ~a serdecznie** we welcome you cordially; **czy obejrzeli już ~o wystawę?** have you seen the exhibition?; **dokąd ~o jadą?** where are you going?; **~o pozwolą, że** please allow me to; **szanowni ~o!**, **proszę ~a!** Ladies and Gentlemen!; **czy to jest ~a syn?** is this your son?

państwowość *f* (*-ści*; *no pl*) statehood; **państwowy** *adj* state, state-owned

pańszczyzna *f* (*-ny*; *no pl*) **1.** HIST corvée **2.** (*nudna praca*) *infml* drudgery; **pańszczyźniany** *adj* corvée; **chłop ~** HIST serf, villein

PAP *abbr f indecl/m* (*PAP-u*; *no pl*) (=**Polska Agencja Prasowa**) Polish Press Agency

papa[1] *f* (*-py*; *no pl*) *dachowa*: asphalt roofing

papa[2] *f* (*-py*; *-py*) *infml* muzzle, face

papeteria *f* (*-rii*; *-rie*) stationery, letterhead

papier *m* (*-ru*; *-ry*) paper; **~ listowy** writing paper; **~ gazetowy** newsprint paper; **~ toaletowy** toilet paper; **~ ścierny** abrasive paper, sandpaper; **~ maszynowy** typing paper; **~ czerpany** handmade paper; **~ pakowy** brown paper; **~y** (*dokumenty*) documents; **~y wartościowe** ECON securities; **na ~ze** *fig* only on paper

papier|ek *m* (*-rka*; *-rki*) **1.** (piece of) paper; **~ki** *infml* documents, papers,

P

records; ***dla ~ka*** *infml* only to have a document **2.** (*po cukierku*) candy wrapping; **papierkow|y** *adj*: ***~a robota*** *infml* paperwork

papiernia *f* (*-ni*; *-nie*) paper mill; **papiernictwo** *n* (*-wa*; *no pl*) paper industry; **papierniczy** *adj* paper, stationery

papieros *m* (*-sa*; *-sy*) cigarette; **papierosek** *m* (*-ska*; *-ski*) *dim* fag; **papierośnica** *f* (*-cy*; *-ce*) cigarette case; **papierosowy** *adj* cigarette

papierowy *adj* paper; **papierówka** *f* (*-ki*; *-ki*) **1.** BIOL greening **2.** (*drewno*) pulpwood

papieski *adj* papal; **papież** *m* (*-ża*; *-że*) pope

papka *f* (*-ki*; *-ki*) mush, pulp; **papkowaty** *adj* mushy, pulpy

papla *f/m* (*-li*; *-le*) *infml* **1.** (*gaduła*) chatterbox **2.** (*plotkarz*) gossip; **paplać** *v/im* (*-lę*/*-lam*) *infml* babble; **paplanina** *f* (*-ny*; *no pl*) *infml* prattle

paprać (*-rzę*) *infml* **1.** ⟨**u-**⟩ smear **2.** ⟨**s-**⟩ (*robić niedbale*) make a mess; ***paprać się*** **1.** get dirty **2.** *fig* do a messy job **3.** (*nie goić się*) fester; ***rana się paprze*** the wound is festering, the wound is getting gangrenous

papranina *f* (*-ny*; *no pl*) *infml* mess

paproć *f* (*-roci*; *-rocie*) fern

papryka *f* (*-ki*; *-ki*) **1.** *Br* pepper, *Am* bell pepper **2.** (*w proszku*) paprika; **paprykarz** *m* (*-rza*; *-rze*) COOK pepper stew; **paprykować** *v/im* (*-kuję*) season with paprika

papuć *m* (*-pucia*; *-pucie*) *infml* slipper

P

papuga *f* (*-gi*; *-gi*) **1.** parrot **2.** *fig* copycat; **papuzi** *adj* parrot; **papużka** *f* (*-ki*; *-ki*): ***~ falista*** budgerigar

par|a[1] *f* (*-ry*; *no pl*) **1.** steam; ***pełną ~ą*** *fig* at full speed **2.** (*opary*) vapour

par|a[2] *f* (*-ry*; *-ry*) pair, couple; ***~a zakochanych*** couple of lovers; ***młoda ~a*** bride and groom; ***~a butów*** pair of shoes; ***~ami*** in pairs; ***nie do ~y*** odd; ***iść w ~ze z I*** *fig* go hand in hand with

parabola *f* (*-li*; *-le*) **1.** GEOM parabola **2.** *poetycka*: parable

parać się *v/im* (*-ram*) dabble (*I* at/in); ***~ handlem*** work in commerce

parad|a *f* (*-dy*; *-dy*) parade, show; ***wejść komuś w ~ę*** get in s.o.'s way, cross s.o.'s path; ***mieć głowę nie od ~y*** one's head is screwed on the right way

paradentoza *f* (*-zy*; *no pl*) MED periodontitis

paradny *adj* **1.** *mundur*: gala **2.** *fig* hilarious, ridiculous

paradoksalny *adj* paradoxical, contradictory

paradować *v/im* (*-duję*) **1.** parade **2.** ***~ w cylindrze*** sport a top hat

parafia *f* (*-fii*; *-fe*) parish; **parafialny** *adj* parish, parochial; **parafianin** (*-na*; *-fianie*), **-fianka** *f* (*-ki*; *-ki*) parishioner; ***parafianie*** congregation

parafina *f* (*-ny*; *no pl*) paraffin

parafraza *f* (*-zy*; *-zy*) paraphrase

paragon *m* (*-nu*; *-ny*) receipt

paragraf *m* (*-fu*; *-fy*) paragraph

Paragwaj *m* (*-ju*) Paraguay

paralela *f* (*-li*; *-le*) parallel

paralityk *m* (*-ka*; *-tycy*) paralytic, paraplegic; **paraliż** *m* (*-żu*; *no pl*) MED paralysis; **paraliżować** ⟨**s-**⟩ (*-żuję*) **1.** MED paralyze **2.** *fig* frustrate

paramilitarny *adj* paramilitary

parapet *m* (*-tu*; *-ty*) sill, windowsill; **parapetówka** *f* (*-ki*; *-ki*) *infml* housewarming party

parasol *m* (*-la*; *-le*) **1.** umbrella; ***~ ogrodowy*** garden umbrella **2.** (*od słońca*) parasol, sunshade; **parasolka** *f* (*-ki*; *-ki*) (small) umbrella

parawan *m* (*-nu*; *-ny*) **1.** screen **2.** (*przykrywka*) *fig* front

parcela *f* (*-li*; *-le*) plot of land, lot

parch *m* (*-chu*/*-cha*; *-chy*) BIOL mange

parciany *adj* sackcloth

parcie *n* (*-cia*; *no pl*) PHYS pressure, thrust; ***~ na stolec*** MED bowel movement pressure; ***~ na mocz*** MED urgency (in urinating)

parę *pron* couple, some, a few; ***~ razy*** couple of times; **paręset** *pron* a few hundreds

park *m* (*-ku*; *-ki*) park; ***~ narodowy*** national park; ***~ angielski*** English garden; ***~ maszyn*** machinery, equipment

parkan *m* (*-nu*; *-ny*) fence

parkiet *m* (*-tu*; *-ty*) **1.** (*podłoga*) parquet (floor) **2.** (*do tańca*) dance floor

parking *m* (*-gu*; *-gi*) **1.** car park, parking lot **2.** (*budynek*) multi-level car park; **~ strzeżony** attended car park; **parkometr** *m* (*-ru*; *-ry*) parking meter; **parkować** ⟨**za-**⟩ (*-kuję*) park

parkowy *adj* park

parlament *m* (*-tu*; *-ty*) Parliament; **parlamentariusz** *m* (*-sza*; *-sze*) parliamentary

parlamentarny *adj* parliamentary, parliament; **parlamentarzysta** *m* (*-ty*; *-rzyści*) MP, member of parliament

parność *f* (*-ści*; *no pl*) sultriness; **parny** *adj* sultry

parobek *m* (*-bka*; *-bcy*/*-bki*) HIST farm hand

parodia *f* (*-dii*; *-die*) parody; **parodiować** ⟨**s-**⟩ (*-diuję*) parody

parodniowy *adj* **1.** a few days', lasting a couple of days **2.** *dziecko*: a few days' old; **parogodzinny** *adj* a few hours', lasting a couple of hours

parokonny *adj* two-horse

parokrotnie *adv* repeatedly; **parokrotny** *adj* several times

paroksyzm *m* (*-mu*; *-my*) MED spasm; **~ śmiechu** paroxysm of laughter

paroletni *adj* a few years', lasting a couple of years; **paromiesięczny** *adj* a few months', lasting a couple of months; **parominutowy** *adj* a few minutes', a couple of minutes long

parotygodniow|y *adj* a few weeks', lasting a couple of weeks; **~e dziecko** infant; **parotysięczny** *adj* several thousand

parować[1] ⟨**s-**⟩ (*-ruję*) *cios*: parry

parować[2] (*-ruję*) **I** ⟨**wy-**⟩ *v/i* evaporate **II** *v/im v/t* (*gotować na parze*) steam; **parowiec** *m* (*-wca*; *-wce*) steamer; **parowóz** *m* (*-wozu*; *-wozy*) steam engine; **parowy** *adj* steam

parów *m* (*-rowu*; *-rowy*) gorge, ravine

parówka *f* (*-ki*; *-ki*) **1.** frankfurter **2.** *infml* (*łaźnia*) steam bath **3.** (*pogoda*) *infml* heat

parskać ⟨**-knąć**⟩ (*-kam*) snort; **~ śmiechem** burst into laughter, chortle

parszywy *adj* **1.** *pies*: mangy, scabby **2.** *fig* lousy, rotten

partacki *adj infml* bungling; **partactwo** *n* (*-wa*; *no pl*) *infml* botched job, bungled work; **partacz** *m* (*-cza*; *-cze*) *infml* botcher, bungler; **partaczyć** ⟨**s-**⟩ (*-czę*) *infml* botch, bungle

parter *m* (*-ru*; *-ry*) **1.** *Br* ground floor, *Am* first floor; **na ~ze** *Br* on the ground floor, *Am* on the first floor **2.** *ogrodowy*: parterre **3.** (*w teatrze*) stalls; **parterowy** *adj* **1.** *mieszkanie*: *Br* ground-floor, *Am* first-floor **2.** *dom*: one-storey

partia *f* (*-tii*; *-tie*) **1.** POLIT party **2.** (*część*) part; **~ szachów** game of chess; **dobra ~** *fig* a good match

partner *m* (*-ra*; *-rzy*), **~ka** *f* (*-ki*; *-ki*) partner; **~ w interesach** business partner; **~ do rozmowy** conversation partner; **~ seksualny** sexual partner; **~ do gry** game partner; **~ do tańca** dancing partner; **~ życiowy** partner, a person with whom one shares one's life

partnerstwo *n* (*-wa*; *no pl*) partnership

partolić ⟨**s-**⟩ (*-lę*) *infml* → **partaczyć**

partyjka *f* (*-ki*; *-ki*) *brydża*: game, round

partyjny *adj* party

partykularny *adj*: **~ interes** vested interest

partykuła *f* (*-ły*; *-ły*) GRAM particle

partytura *f* (*-ry*; *-ry*) MUS score

partyzancki *adj* guerilla, partisan; **partyzant** *m* (*-ta*; *-nci*) guerilla fighter; **partyzantka** *f* (*-ki*; *-ki*) **1.** guerilla war **2.** (*partyzanci*) guerillas *pl* **3.** (*kobieta*) woman guerilla

parujący *adj* steaming

parysk|i *adj* Paris; **bułka ~a** baguette

parytet *m* (*-tu*; *-ty*) FIN parity

Paryż *m* (*-ża*) Paris

parzyć ⟨**s-**, **po-**⟩ (*-rzę*) **1.** burn **2.** *cieczą*, *parą*: scald; **s~ sobie usta** scald one's mouth **3.** (*wypalić*) scorch **4.** COOK blanch **5.** ⟨**za-**⟩ *herbatę*, *kawę*: brew; **parzyć się 1.** burn oneself **2.** (*o herbacie*, *kawie*) brew **3.** BIOL mate

parzysty *adj* **1.** *liczba*, *numer*: even **2.** (*w parze*) paired **3.** BIOL binate

pas[1] *m* (*-sa*; *-sy*) **1.** belt; **~ startowy** runway; **~ ruchu** lane; **~ graniczny** border zone; **~ zieleni** green belt; **~y bezpieczeństwa** seat belts, safety belts **2.** (*talia*) waist; **po ~** to the waist; **w ~ie** in the waistline; **być szczupłym w ~ie** have a slim waist; **rozebrać się do ~a** undress from the waist up; **być za ~em** *fig* be coming, be closer and closer **3.** (*kawałek czegoś*) strip; **w ~y** striped

P

pas[2] *n indecl* **1.** (*w szermierce*) pass **2.** (*w tańcu*) step
pas[3] *interj* (*w kartach*) no bid!, pass!
pasaż *m* (*-żu*; *-że*) **1.** passageway; **~ handlowy** shopping mall, shopping arcade **2.** MUS passage
pasażer *m* (*-ra*; *-rowie*), **~ka** *f* (*-ki*; *-ki*) passenger; **~ na gapę** stowaway; **pasażerski** *adj* passenger
Pascha *f* (*-chy*; *no pl*) REL Passover
pasek *m* (*-ska*; *-ski*) **1.** belt **2.** *torebki, plecaka*: strap, band; **~ do zegarka** watch strap **3.** (*deseń*) strip **4.** (*naszywka*) stripe
paser *m* (*-ra*; *-rzy*), **~ka** *f* (*-ki*; *-ki*) fence; **paserstwo** *n* (*-wa*; *no pl*) fencing
pasiak *m* (*-ka*; *-ki*) (*strój więźnia*): (concentration camp) stripes *pl*; **pasiasty** *adj* striped
pasibrzuch *m* (*-cha*; *-chy*) *infml* guzzler
pasieka *f* (*-ki*; *-ki*) apiary
pasierb *m* (*-ba*; *-bowie*/*-by*) stepson; **pasierbica** *f* (*-cy*; *-ce*) stepdaughter
pasikonik *m* (*-ka*; *-ki*) grasshopper
pasj|a *f* (*-ji*; *-je*) **1.** (*zamiłowanie*) passion, love **2.** (*gniew*) fury; **wpaść w ~ę** fly into rage; **doprowadzić kogoś do ~i** drive s.o. mad; **z ~ą** passionately; furiously **3.** REL ART MUS Passion
pasjami *adv* passionately
pasjans *m* (*-sa*; *-se*) (*gra*) patience
pasjonat *m* (*-ta*; *-naci*) impulsive person, hothead
pasjonować *v/im* (*-nuję*) fascinate; **pasjnować się** be keen (*I* on)
pasjonujący *adj* fascinating, extremely interesting
paskuda *f* (*-dy*; *-dy*) ugly person; **paskudny** *adj* nasty, ugly
paskudzić ⟨**s-**⟩ (*-dzę*) **1.** foul, soil **2.** (*zepsuć, spartaczyć*) *infml* bungle; **paskudzić się** (*o ranie*) fester
paskudztw|o *n* (*-wa*; *-wa*) **1.** abomination, specimen of extreme ugliness; **~a** (*brudy*) soil **2.** (*jedzenie*) foul-tasting food
pasmanteria *f* (*-rii*; *no pl*) **1.** haberdashery **2.** (*sklep*) haberdasher's
pasmo *n* (*-ma*; *-ma*) **1.** *wełny, włosów*: strand **2.** *lasu*: stretch **3.** RADIO band **4.** **~ górskie** mountain range, ridge; **~ dymu** wisp of smoke; **~ sukcesów** winning streak, lucky streak; **~ nieszczęść** a run of bad luck
pasować[1] *v/im* (*-suję*) **1.** go (**do** *G* with); **~ do siebie** go together, be well matched; **coś mi tu nie pasuje** *infml* s.th. is wrong, s.th. stinks, I smell a rat; **~ jak wół do karety**, **~ jak pięść do nosa** be like a square peg in a round hole **2.** (*być w dobrym rozmiarze*) fit (**na** *A*); **~ jak ulał** fit like a glove **3.** (*o kolorze*) match **4.** (*o terminie*): suit **5.** **~ na rycerza** HIST knight
pasować[2] ⟨**s-**⟩ (*-suję*) (*w kartach*) pass, back out
pasożyt *m* (*-ta*; *-ty*) **1.** BIOL parasite **2.** *fig* sponger; **pasożytnicz|y** *adj* BIOL parasitic; **roślina ~a** parasitic plant; **zwierzę ~e** parasite; **pasożytować** *v/im* (*-tuję*) **1.** BIOL parasitise (**na** *L* on) **2.** *fig* sponge (**na** *I* on)
passa *f* (*-sy*; *no pl*) spell, run; **dobra ~** a lucky streak; **zła ~** a losing streak
pasta *f* (*-ty*; *-ty*) paste; **~ do butów** shoe polish; **~ do zębów** toothpaste; **~ do podłogi** floor polish
pasterka *f* (*-ki*; *-ki*) **1.** shepherdess **2.** (*gęsiarka*) gooseherd **3.** (*pasąca krowy*) cowherd **4.** REL Christmas midnight Mass; **pasterski** *adj* shepherd, pastoral
pasteryzowany *adj* pasteurised
pasterz *m* (*-rza*; *-rze*) **1.** herdsman, shepherd **2.** (*pasący krowy*) cowherd **3.** (*pasący świnie*) swineherd
pastewny *adj* *roślina*: fodder
pastor *m* (*-ra*; *-rzy*) pastor, parson
pastorał *m* (*-łu*; *-ły*) crozier
pastorałka *f* (*-ki*; *-ki*) carol
pastować ⟨**wy-**⟩ (*-tuję*) **1.** *buty*: polish **2.** *parkiet*: wax
pastuch *m* (*-cha*; *-chy*/*-chowie*) herdsman, herder
pastw|a: **paść ~ą** *G* fall prey to; **wydać kogoś na ~ę losu** leave s.o. to their own fate
pastwić się *v/im* (*-wię*) torment (**nad** *I*)
pastwisko *n* (*-ka*; *-ka*) pasture, grazing meadow
pastylka *f* (*-ki*; *-ki*) pill, lozenge
pasyjny *adj* REL Passion
pasywa *pl* (*-wów*) FIN liabilities
pasywny *adj* passive
pasza *f* (*-szy*; *-sze*) fodder

P

paszcza *f* (*-czy*; *-cze*) mouth, maw; ***lwia ~*** BIOL snapdragon
paszkwil *m* (*-lu*; *-le*) lampoon
paszport *m* (*-tu*; *-ty*) passport; **paszportow|y** *adj* passport; ***biuro ~e*** passport office
pasztecik *m* (*-ka*; *-ki*) COOK pasty, small pie; **pasztet** *m* (*-tu*; *-ty*) **1.** COOK pâté **2. *co za ~!*** *infml* what a mess!; **pasztetówka** *f* (*-ki*; *-ki*) pâté sausage
paść[1] *v/p* → ***padać***
paść[2] ⟨**u-**, **s-**⟩ (*pasę*) **1.** graze **2.** (*tuczyć*) *hum* fatten; ***paść się*** **1.** graze, pasture **2.** ***spaść się*** *hum* get fat, put on weight
pat *m* (*-tu*; *-ty*) stalemate
patałach *m* (*-cha*; *-chy*) *infml* dupe, jerk
patelnia *f* (*-ni*; *-nie*) frying pan
patent *m* (*-tu*; *-ty*) patent; **patentować** ⟨**o-**⟩ (*-tuję*) patent
patentowany *adj* patented; ***dureń ~*** complete idiot; ***leń ~*** total lazybones; **patentowy** *adj* patent, ***Urząd*** **≈** Patent and Trademark Office
patera *f* (*-ry*; *-ry*) epergne, tazza
paternoster *m indecl* reprimand, admonition
patetyczny *adj* pompous, bombastic
patka *f* (*-ki*; *-ki*) tab
patolog *m* (*-ga*; *-lodzy*/*-gowie*) pathologist; **patologiczny** *adj* pathological
patos *m* (*-su*; *no pl*) pathos, pomposity, bombast
patriarcha *m* (*-chy*; *-chowie*) patriarch; **patriarchalny** *adj* patriarchal
patriota *m* (*-ty*; *-rioci*), **-tka** *f* (*-ki*; *-ki*) patriot; **patriotyczny** *adj* patriotic
patrol *m* (*-lu*; *-le*) patrol, squad; ***~ wywiadowczy*** reconnaissance patrol, scout; **patrolować** *v/im* (*-luję*) patrol; **patrolowy** *adj* patrol
patron *m* (*-na*; *-ni*/*-nowie*) **1.** patron, protector **2.** REL patron saint; **patronat** *m* (*-tu*; *-ty*) patronage; ***pod ~em*** *G* under the auspices of
patronka *f* (*-ki*; *-ki*) **1.** patroness, protectress **2.** REL patron saint; **patronować** *v/im* (*-nuję*) be a patron of, patronize
patroszyć ⟨**wy-**⟩ (*-szę*) COOK gut, disembowel
patrzeć, ***patrzyć*** ⟨**po-**⟩ (*-rzę*) **1.** look; ***~ w lusterko*** look in the mirror; ***~ przez okno*** look through the window; ***~ łaskawym okiem na*** *A* regard s.o. with favour; ***~ krzywo na*** *A* look askance on, not like; ***jak się patrzy*** well done; ***tylko ~ jak*** it won't be long before; ***nie patrząc na*** *A* without looking at; ***~ w kogoś jak w obraz*** admire s.o. blindly; ***patrz!*** look!; ***patrzcie go!*** just look at you!; ***~ komuś na ręce*** watch s.o. closely so that he does not steal something; ***~ przez palce*** to turn a blind eye to **2.** (*oglądać*) watch **3.** (*obserwować*) observe, scrutinize
patyczkować się *v/im* (*-kuję*) *infml* handle in kid gloves (**z** *I*); ***nie patyczkując się*** without much ado
patyk *m* (*-ka*; *-ki*) stick; **patykowaty** *adj* sticklike, spindly
patyna *f* (*-ny*; *no pl*) patina
pauza *f* (*-zy*; *-zy*) pause
paw *m* (*-wia*; *-wie*) peacock; **pawi** *adj* peacock
pawilon *m* (*-nu*; *-ny*) pavilion; ***~ handlowy*** shopping centre; ***~ meblowy*** furniture shop; ***~ wystawowy*** exhibition hall
pawlacz *m* (*-cza*; *-cze*) (*pod sufitem lub nad drzwiami*) storage space
pazerny *adj* rapacious
paznok|ieć *m* (*-kcia*; *-kcie*) **1.** (*u rąk*) fingernail; ***lakier do ~ci*** nail varnish **2.** (*u nóg*) toenail
pazuch|a: ***za ~ą*** in one's bossom
pazur *m* (*-ra*; *-ry*) claw
paź *m* (*pazia*; *pazie*) HIST page; ***~ królowej*** BIOL swallowtail; ***fryzura na pazia*** bob haircut
październik *m* (*-ka*; *-ki*) October; **październikowy** *adj* October
pączek *m* (*-czka*; *-czki*) **1.** BIOL bud, gemma **2.** COOK doughnut, *Am* donut; ***czuć się jak ~ w maśle*** *fig* live in the lap ofluxury
pączkować *v/im* (*-kuję*) BIOL bud, gemmate; **pączkowanie** *n* (*-nia*; *no pl*) BIOL budding, gemmation
pączuszek *m* (*-szka*; *-szki*) *hum* chubby person
pąk *m* (*-ka*; *-ki*) bud; ***~ róży*** a rose in bud; ***wypuszczać ~i*** bud
pąsowieć ⟨**s-**⟩ (*-wieję*) *lit* redden, blush, turn puce; **pąsowy** *adj* puce, blush pink

pątnik *m* (*-ka*; *-nicy*) *lit* pilgrim
pchać ⟨**pchnąć**⟩ (*-cham*) **1.** push, shove **2.** *fig* drive (**do** *G* to); ***pchać się*** push one's way (**do** *G* to, ***przez*** *A* through); ***proszę się nie ~!*** don't push please!
pchełki *pl* (*-łek*) (*gra*) tiddlywinks
pchła *f* (*-ły*; *-ły*) flea
pchli *adj* : **~ *targ*** flea market
pchnąć *v/p* (*-nę*): **~ *kogoś nożem*** stab s.o. with a knife, knife s.o.; → ***pchać***
pchnięcie *n* (*-cia*; *-cia*) push, shove, thrust; **~ *kulą*** SPORT shot put; **~ *nożem*** stab
PCK *abbr n/m indecl* (= **Polski Czerwony Krzyż**) Polish Red Cross
PCW *abbr m/m indecl* (= **polichlorek winylu**) PVC
pecet *m* (*-ta*; *-ty*) *infml* PC, personal computer
pech *m* (*-cha*; *no pl*) bad luck; **pechowiec** *m* (*-wca*; *-wcy*) unlucky person; **pechowy** *adj* unlucky
pedagog *m* (*-ga*; *-dagodzy*/*-gowie*) teacher, educator; **pedagogiczn|y** *adj* pedagogic, pedagogical; ***ciało ~e*** teaching staff; **pedagogika** *f* (*-ki*; *no pl*) pedagogy; **~ *specjalna*** curative pedagogy
pedał[1] *m* (*-łu*; *-ły*) pedal; **~ *gazu*** accelerator
pedał[2] *m* (*-ła*; *-ły*) *infml* fag, homo, queer
pedałować *v/im* (*-łuję*) **1.** pedal **2.** (*iść*) *infml* run
pedant *m* (*-ta*; *-nci*), **~ka** *f* (*-ki*; *-ki*) pedant; **pedantyczny** *adj* pedantic
pederasta *m* (*-ty*; *-raści*) *form* pederast
pediatra *m* (*-ry*; *-rzy*) *Br* paediatrician, *Am* pediatrician; **pediatria** *f* (*-rii*; *no pl*) **1.** *Br* paediatry, *Am* pediatry **2.** (*w szpitalu*) children's ward; **pediatryczny** *adj Br* paediatric, *Am* pediatric
pedicure *m* (*-re'u*; *no pl*) pedicure
pedzio *m* (*-dzia*; *-dzie*) *infml* faggot, fag
pejcz *m* (*-cza*; *-cze*) riding whip, riding crop
pejsy *pl* (*-sów*) sidelocks
pejzaż *m* (*-żu*; *-że*) landscape
Pekin *m* (*-nu*) Peking, Beijing
pekińczyk *m* (*-ka*; *-ki*) BIOL Pekingese
peklować ⟨**za-**⟩ (*-luję*) pickle; **peklowany** *adj* pickled, corned
pelargonia *f* (*-nii*; *-nie*) geranium
peleryna *f* (*-ny*; *-ny*) cloak, cape
peleton *m* (*-nu*; *-ny*) peloton, pack
pelikan *m* (*-na*; *-ny*) pelican
pelisa *f* (*-sy*; *-sy*) fur-lined coat
pełen → ***pełny***
pełni|a *f* (*-ni*; *-nie*) *księżyca*: full moon; ***jest ~a*** the moon is full; ***w ~ lata*** in high summer; ***w ~ sezonu*** in peak season; ***być w ~ sił*** sound in body; ***~a szczęścia*** complete happiness; ***w*** (***całej***) **~** totally, absolutely
pełnić *v/im* (*-nię*) perform, *Br* fulfil, *Am* fulfill; **~ *wartę*** keep guard, stand guard; **~ *służbę*** be on duty; **~ *funkcję*** *G* hold the post of; **~ *rolę*** *G Br* fulfil the role of, *Am* fulfill the role of; **~ *obowiązki*** *G* perform the duties of; **~ *obowiązki w zastępstwie dyrektora*** be an acting director
pełno *adv* **1.** full **2.** (*po brzegi*) to the brim
pełnoetatowy *adj* full-time; **pełnokrwisty** *adj* pureblood, thoroughbred; **pełnoletni** *adj* ofage; **pełnometrażowy** *adj film*: feature
pełnomocnictwo *n* (*-wa*; *-wa*) power of attorney; **pełnomocnik** *m* (*-ka*; *-nicy*) **1.** (*przedstawiciel*) representative **2.** (*posiadający pełnomocnictwo*) holder ofa proxy **3.** (*w dyplomacji*) plenipotentiary; **pełnomocny** *adj* endowed with full power of attorney
pełnomorski *adj* oceangoing, seagoing; **pełnoprawny** *adj* rightful, having full rights; **pełnotłust|y** *adj*: ***mleko ~e*** full-cream milk, *Am* whole milk; ***ser ~y*** full-fat cheese; **pełnowartościowy** *adj* **1.** whole **2.** *dieta*: balanced; **pełnoziarnisty** *adj* wholemeal
pełn|y *adj* **1.** full; ***~ne mleko*** full-cream milk, *Am* whole milk; ***na ~nym morzu*** in high seas; ***~en nadziei*** hopeful; ***~en energii*** full of energy; ***~en podejrzeń*** mistrustful, extremely suspicious; ***do ~na*** full, full to the brim **2.** (*całkowity*) total **3.** *szczęście*, *satysfakcja*: complete **4.** (*napełniony*) filled (*G* with)
pełzać *v/im* (*-zam*), **pełznąć** *v/im* (*-nę*) creep, crawl
pełzak *m* (*-ka*; *-ki*) BIOL *Br* amoeba, *Am* ameba

P

penetracja *f* (*-ji*; *no pl*) **1.** penetration **2.** (*odkrywanie*) exploration
penicylina *f* (*-ny*; *-ny*) penicillin
penis *m* (*-sa*; *-sy*) ANAT penis
pensja *f* (*-ji*; *-je*) salary, wage
pensjonariusz *m* (*-sza*; *-sze*), **~ka** *f* (*-ki*; *-ki*) **1.** (*mieszkaniec domu starców*) inmate **2.** (*gość pensjonatu*) guest; **pensjonat** *m* (*-tu*; *-ty*) boarding house, guest house
pepitk|a: ***w ~ę*** shepherd's check
pepsyna *f* (*-ny*; *no pl*) BIOL pepsin
perełka *f* (*-ki*; *-ki*) **1.** *dim* small pearl **2.** *fig* pearl, gem
perfekcj|a *f* (*-ji*; *no pl*) perfection; ***do ~i*** to perfection; **perfekcjonista** *m* (*-ty*; *-niści*), **-tka** *f* (*-ki*; *-ki*) perfectionist
perfidny *adj* perfidious
perforacja *f* (*-ji*; *-je*) perforation
perfumeria *f* (*-rii*; *-rie*) perfumery; **perfumować** ⟨**po-**, **u-**⟩ (*-muję*) perfume; ***perfumować się*** perfume oneself, wear perfume; **perfumy** *pl* (*-fum*) perfume *sing*, scent *sing*
pergamin *m* (*-nu*; *-ny*) **1.** (*materiał*) parchment **2.** (*papier*) parchment paper; **pergaminowy** *adj* parchment
periodyczny *adj* periodical, periodic; **periodyk** *m* (*-ka*; *-ki*) periodical
perkaty *adj*: ***~ nos*** snub nose
perkusista *m* (*-ty*; *-kusiści*) drummer; **perkusja** *f* (*-ji*; *no pl*) percussion, drums *pl*
perliczka *f* (*-ki*; *-ki*) guinea fowl
perlić się *v/im* (*-lę*) bead up
perlisty *adj* **1.** pearly **2.** *śmiech*: rippling **3.** *infml* beady; **perła** *f* (*-ły*; *-ły*) pearl; **perłow|y** *adj* **1.** pearly; ***macica ~a*** mother-of-pearl **2.** (*kolor*) pearl grey
peron *m* (*-nu*; *-ny*) platform; **peronowy** **I** *adj* platform **II** *m* (*-wego*; *-wi*) platform attendant
perorować *v/im* (*-ruję*) *iron* harangue, preach
Persja *f* (*-ji*) Persia
perski *adj* Persian; ***~ dywan*** Persian rug, Persian carpet; ***kot ~*** Persian cat, Persian
personalia *pl* (*-liów*) personal data; **personaln|y** *adj* **1.** personal; ***ankieta ~a*** personal data questionnaire **2.** (*dotyczący personelu*) personnel, human resources; ***dział ~y*** HR department; **personel** *m* (*-lu*; *no pl*) personnel
perspektyw|a *f* (*-wy*; *-wy*) perspective; ***z innej ~y*** from a different angle; **perspektywiczny** *adj* perspective; ***skrót ~*** foreshortening
perswadować *v/im* (*-duję*) **1.** persuade **2.** (*łagodnie namawiać*) coax
perswazja *f* (*-ji*; *-je*) **1.** persuasion **2.** (*łagodna namowa*) coaxing
pertraktacje *pl* (*-ji*) negotiations; **pertraktować** *v/im* (*-tuję*) negotiate (**o** *L*)
perturbacje *pl* (*-ji*) commotion *sing*, turbulence *sing*, perturbation *sing*
peruka *f* (*-ki*; *-ki*) wig
perwersja *f* (*-ji*; *-je*) perversion, perversity; **perwersyjny** *adj* pervert, obscene
peryferie *pl* (*-rii*) periphery *sing*, outskirts; **peryferyjny** *adj* peripheral, suburban, marginal
peryfraza *f* (*-zy*; *-zy*) periphrasis
perypetie *pl* (*-tii*) *lit* trials and tribulations; ***~ życiowe*** complications oflif e
peryskop *m* (*-pu*; *-py*) periscope
perz *m* (*-rzu*; *no pl*) BIOL couch grass, quitch
pestka *f* (*-ki*; *-ki*) **1.** *wiśni*: stone, pit **2.** *dyni*: seed **3.** *jabłka*: pip **4.** ***to dla mnie ~!*** *fig* it's a piece ofcake for me!; **pestkow|y** *adj* drupiferous; ***owoce ~e*** drupes, stone fruits
pesymista *m* (*-ty*; *-miści*), **-tka** *f* (*-ki*; *-ki*) pessimist; **pesymistyczny** *adj* pessimistic
peszyć ⟨**s-**⟩ (*-szę*) confound, baffle; ***peszyć się*** be abashed, be disconcerted
pet *m* (*-ta*; *-ty*) *infml papierosa*: f g end, cig butt
petarda *f* (*-dy*; *-dy*) petard, firecracker
petent *m* (*-ta*; *-nci*), **~ka** *f* (*-ki*; *-ki*) **1.** client **2.** (*składający podanie*): applicant, petitioner
petrochemia *f* (*-mii*; *no pl*) petrochemistry, petrol industry
petunia *f* (*-nii*; *-nie*) petunia
petycja *f* (*-ji*; *-je*) petition
pew|ien[1] *pron* (*o osobie*) some, one, certain; ***~na ilość*** a certain amount; ***co ~ien czas*** from time to time; ***~nego dnia*** one day; ***~nego razu*** once upon a time; ***po ~nym czasie*** after some time; ***~ien pan*** a man
pewien[2] → ***pewny***
pewniak *m* (*-ka*; *-ki*) *infml* sure thing, favourite; ***na ~a*** surely, a safe bet

P

pewnie **I** *adv* **1.** (*z pewnością siebie*) confidently **2.** (*na pewno*) surely **II** *particle* sure; **– „Chciałabyś pójść do kina?” – „~!”** ‘Would you like to go to the cinema?’ ‘Sure!’
pewnik *m* (*-ka*; *-ki*) **1.** certainty, sure thing; ***można przyjąć za ~, że*** it can be assumed with certainty that **2.** *MATH PHIL* axiom
pewno *particle* surely, certainly; ***na ~*** for sure
pewnoś|ć *f* (*-ści*; *no pl*) **1.** certainty, sureness, confidence; ***~ć siebie*** self-confidence; ***z całą ~cią*** with all certainty, undoubtedly; ***z ~cią*** surely, certainly, for certain; ***dla ~ci*** just in case, to be on the safe side **2.** (*niezawodność*) reliability
pewn|y *adj* (*pewien*) **1.** sure, certain; ***~y siebie*** self-confident; ***~e zwycięstwo*** certain victory; ***~a śmierć*** *infml* certain death; ***~ym głosem*** loudly; ***być ~ym*** *G* be certain of; ***to ~e, że*** it is certain that, it is a sure thing that **2.** (*niezawodny*) reliable
pęcherz *m* (*-rza*; *-rze*) **1.** blister **2.** *MED BIOL* bladder; ***~ moczowy*** urinary bladder; ***~ płodowy*** amniotic sac; ***~ pławny*** swim bladder; **pęcherzyk** *m* (*-ka*; *-ki*) **1.** blister, bubble **2.** *MED* vesicle, follicle; ***~ żółciowy*** gall bladder
pęczak *m* (*-ku*; *no pl*) *COOK* hulled barley
pęcz|ek *m* (*-czka*; *-czki*) (*wiązka*) bunch, bundle; ***na ~ki*** *infml* in heaps, oodles
pęcznieć ⟨**na-**, **s-**⟩ (*-nieję*) swell, bloat
pęd *m* (*-du*; *-dy*) **1.** dash, rush; ***~ powietrza*** rush of air; ***~em*** in a rush, hurriedly; ***w te ~y*** this minute, immediately **2.** *BIOL* shoot, sprout **3.** *PHYS* momentum **4.** *fig* hunger, urge, craving; ***~ do wiedzy*** hunger for knowledge; ***owczy ~*** stampede, blind craze
pędrak *m* (*-ka*; *-ki*) **1.** *BIOL* grub **2.** *hum* kid, brat
pędzel *m* (*-dzla*; *-dzle*) brush, paintbrush; ***~ do golenia*** shaving brush; **pędzelek** *m* (*-lka*; *-lki*) **1.** small brush **2.** (*na uszach rysi*, *kotów*) tuft of hair
pędzić ⟨**po-**⟩ (*-dzę*) **I** *v/i* rush, scurry, run; ***~ co tchu*** run at full speed **II** *v/t* **1.** drive **2.** *spirytus*: distil **3.** ⟨**s-**⟩ (*prowadzić*) spend, lead; ***~ spokojne życie*** lead a quiet life
pędziwiatr *m* (*-ra*; *-ry*) *infml* harum-scarum
pędzlować *v/im* (*-luję*) *gardło*: swab
pęk *m* (*-ku*; *-ki*) **1.** bunch, bundle; ***~ kluczy*** bunch of keys **2.** *chrustu*: fagot
pękać ⟨**-knąć**⟩ (*-kam*) **1.** crack, split, cleave, rift **2.** (*o strunie*, *linie*) burst, snap, break **3.** (*o wargach*) chap **4.** *fig* split; ***~ ze śmiechu*** laugh one’s head off, split one’s sides; ***~ z zazdrości*** be burning with envy, be green with envy; ***~ w szwach*** rip, split at the seams
pękaty *adj* round, bulging, stocky, thickset
pęknąć *v/p* → **pękać**
pęknięcie *n* (*-cia*; *-cia*) (*szczelina*) crack, rift, burst, split; ***~ rury*** pipe burst; ***~ kości*** bone fracture
pępek *m* (*-pka*; *-pki*) navel, bellybutton; **pępowina** *f* (*-ny*; *-ny*) umbilical cord
pęta *pl* (*pęt*) **1.** (*łańcuchy*) fetters **2.** (*kajdany*) shackles **3.** *fig form* trammels
pętać ⟨**s-**⟩ (*-tam*) **1.** (*łańcuchem*) fetter **2.** (*kajdanami*) shackle **3.** *fig form* trammel; **pętać się** *infml* hang around; ***~ się pod nogami*** get in the way
pętak *m* (*-ka*; *-ki*) *infml* brat, *Am* tyke, squirt
pętelk|a *f* (*-ki*; *-ki*) loop; ***guzik z ~ą*** *infml* nought, zilch
pętla *f* (*-li*; *-le*) **1.** (*zakręt*) loop **2.** (*sznur*) noose **3.** *tramwajowa*: terminus
pęto *n* (*-ta*; *-ta*) *kiełbasy*: ring
piach *m* (*-chu*; *-chy*) sand
piać ⟨**za-**⟩ (*pieję*) crow; ***~ z radości*** howl with joy
pian|a *f* (*-ny*; *-ny*) **1.** *morska*: foam; ***toczyć ~ę*** *infml* foam at the mouth **2.** (*z mleka*, *piwa*) froth; ***piwo z ~ą*** beer with head **3.** (*z mydła*) lather; ***pokryty ~ą*** lathered **4.** (*szumowiny*) scum **5.** ***~a z białek*** *COOK* whipped egg whites
pianino *n* (*-na*; *-na*) (upright) piano
pianista *m* (*-ty*; *-niści*), **-tka** *f* (*-ki*; *-ki*) pianist
pianka *f* (*-ki*; *-ki*) foam, froth; ***~ do włosów*** styling mousse; ***~ do golenia*** shaving foam; ***~ morska*** meerschaum

P

pianow|y *adj*: ***gaśnica ~a*** foam extinguisher
piarg *m* (*-gu*; *-gi*) scree
pias|ek *m* (*-sku*; *-ski*) sand; ***lotne ~ki*** quicksand; ***budować zamki na ~ku*** build castles in the air; **piaskarka** *f* (*-ki*; *-ki*) gritter, sand spreader; **piaskowiec** *m* (*-wca*; *-wce*) sandstone; **piaskownica** *f* (*-cy*; *-ce*) sandbox; **piaskow|y** *adj* **1.** sand; ***babka ~a*** COOK pound cake **2.** (*kolor*) sandy
piasta *f* (*-ty*; *-ty*) TECH hub
piastować *v/im* (*-tuję*) *lit* **1.** *dziecko*: nurse **2.** *urząd*: hold **3.** *władzę*: wield
piaszczysty *adj* sandy
piąć się ⟨**ws-**⟩ (*pnę*) **1.** climb **2.** (*o pnączu*) creep, climb **3.** *fig* work one's way upward
piątek *m* (*-tku*; *-tki*) Friday; ***w ~*** on Friday; ***Wielki* ~** Good Friday
piątka *f* (*-ki*; *-ki*) **1.** five **2.** (*ocena*) A+
piątkowy *adj* **1.** Friday **2.** (*o uczniu*) an A pupil
piąt|y *adj* fifth; ***o ~ej*** (***godzinie***) at five (o'clock); ***~e przez dziesiąte*** bits and pieces; ***~e koło u wozu*** *fig* fifth wheel
pichcić ⟨**u-**⟩ (*-cę*) *infml* cook, concoct
pici|e *n* (*-cia*; *no pl*) drink; ***woda zdatna do ~a*** potable water; ***coś do ~a*** something to drink
pić *v/im* (*piję*) drink; ***chce mi się ~*** I'm thirsty; ***~ czyjeś zdrowie*** drink to s.o.'s health; ***~ do** G fig* allude to; ***~ na umór*** drink like there's no tomorrow; ***~ do lustra*** drink with the flies, drink alone
piec[1] *m* (*-ca*; *-ce*) **1.** (*piekarnik*) oven; ***prosto z ~a*** straight from the oven **2.** (*do wypalania*) kiln **3.** *hutniczy*: furnace **4.** *kuchenny*: stove
piec[2] ⟨**u-**⟩ (*piekę*) **1.** *ciasto*: bake **2.** *kurczaka*: roast **3.** (*na ruszcie*) grill, barbecue **4.** (*o słońcu, oczach*) burn; **piec się 1.** (*o cieście*) bake **2.** (*o pieczeni*) roast **3.** (*na grillu*) grill **4.** ***~ się na słońcu*** roast in the sun
piechot|a *f* (*-ty*; *no pl*) **1.** (*w wojsku*) infantry **2.** ***~ą, na ~ę*** on foot; ***coś ~ą nie chodzi*** s.th. does not come easily
piechur *m* (*-ra*; *-rzy*) **1.** walker **2.** (*w wojsku*) HIST infantryman
piecuch *m* (*-cha*; *-chy*) *infml* lazybones *sing*
piecyk *m* (*-ka*; *-ki*) **1.** (small) stove **2.** (*grzejnik*) heater **3.** (*piekarnik*) oven
piecz|a *f* (*-czy*; *no pl*) *lit* care; ***mieć kogoś w swojej ~y*** be responsible for s.o., be in charge ofs.o. ; ***pod czyjąś ~ą*** under s.o.'s care
pieczara *f* (*-ry*; *-ry*) cave
pieczarka *f* (*-ki*; *-ki*) button mushroom, champignon
pieczątka *f* (*-ki*; *-ki*) stamp
pieczeń *f* (*-czeni*; *-czenie*) roast; ***~ cielęca*** roast veal; ***~ wołowa*** roast beef
pieczęć *f* (*-częci*; *-częcie*) **1.** *lakowa, woskowa*: seal **2.** (*pieczątka*) stamp
pieczętować ⟨**o-, za-**⟩ (*-tuję*) **1.** (*lakować, zaklejać*) seal **2.** (*przybijać pieczątkę*) stamp
pieczołowitość *f* (*-ści*; *no pl*) assiduity; care; **pieczołowity** *adj* **1.** assiduous, careful **2.** (*skrupulatny*) painstaking
pieczony *adj* **1.** *ciasto*: baked **2.** *mięso*: roasted, roast **3.** (*na grillu*) grilled, barbecued; **pieczyste** *n* (*-tego*; *no pl*) roast
pieczywo *n* (*-wa*; *no pl*) baked goods *pl*
piedestał *m* (*-łu*; *-ły*) **1.** pedestal **2.** (*pod pomnik*) plinth **3.** (*pod popiersie*) socle
piegi *pl* (*-gów*) freckles; **piegowaty** *adj* freckled
piekarnia *f* (*-ni*; *-nie*) bakery, baker's; **piekarnik** *m* (*-ka*; *-ki*) baking oven; **piekarz** *m* (*-rza*; *-rze*) baker
piekący *adj* scorching, searing
piekielnica *f* (*-cy*; *-ce*) shrew; **piekielny** *adj* hellish, infernal, devilish; ***ogień ~*** *infml* hellfire
pieklić się *v/im* (*-lę*) *infml* fly into a rage, raise hell
piekł|o *n* (*-ła*; *-ła*) hell, inferno; ***z ~a rodem*** devilish, fiendish
pielesze *pl* (*-szy*): ***domowe ~*** the home, comforts of home
pielęgnacja *f* (*-ji*; *no pl*) **1.** care, nurturing; ***~ ciała*** bodily care; ***~ włosów*** hair care **2.** *chorych*: nursing
pielęgniarka *f* (*-ki*; *-ki*) nurse; **pielęgniarz** *m* (*-rza*; *-rze*) male nurse
pielęgnować *v/im* (*-nuję*) take care of, nurse, nurture
pielgrzym *m* (*-ma*; *-mi*) pilgrim; **pielgrzymka** *f* (*-ki*; *-ki*) pilgrimage
pielucha *f* (*-chy*; *-chy*), **pieluszka** *f* (*-ki*; *-ki*) nappy, diaper
pieluchomajtki *pl* (*-tek*) nappy pants

pieniacz *m* (*-cza*; *-cze*) barrator
pieniądz|e *pl* (*-niędzy*) money *sing*; ***wartość ~a*** *ECON* value ofmoney; ***grube ~e***, ***ciężkie ~e*** pots ofmoney, small fortune
pieniąż|ek *m* (*-żka*; *-żki*) coin; ***~ki*** *hum* money
pienić się ⟨**s-**⟩ (*-nię*) **1.** foam, froth **2.** *fig* foam at the mouth
pie|niek *m* (*pieńka*; *pieńki*) stub, stump; ***mieć na ~ńku z*** *I* be on the warpath with
pienięźn|y *adj* money, financial, monetary; ***kara ~a*** fine
pienisty *adj* foamy, frothy
pień *m* (*pnia*; *pnie*) **1.** (tree)trunk **2.** (*ścięty*) stump
pieprz *m* (*-rzu*; *no pl*) **1.** *COOK* (*mielony*) pepper; ***~ ziołowy*** herb pepper; ***suchy jak ~***, ***wyschnięty na ~*** dry as a bone; ***zwiewać gdzie ~ rośnie*** run like hell **2.** (*roślina*) peppercorn
pieprzniczka *f* (*-ki*; *-ki*) pepper shaker; **pieprznik** *m* (*-ka*; *-ki*) (*grzyb*) chanterelle; **pieprzny** *adj* **1.** peppery **2.** *kawał*: dirty, smutty
pieprznięty *adj infml* nuts
pieprzony *adj infml* bloody, frigging
pieprzówka *f* (*-ki*; *-ki*) pepper vodka
pieprzyć *v/im* (*-rzę*) **1.** *COOK* pepper, add pepper **2.** *infml* bullshit, talk bullshit **3.** (*odbywać stosunek*) *vulg* screw, shag; ***pieprzyć się*** *vulg* screw, shag
pieprzyk *m* (*-ka*; *-ki*) mole; ***z ~iem*** *fig* saucy
pierdzieć ⟨**-dnąć**⟩ (*-dzę*) *vulg* fart *infml*; ***~ w stołek*** fart around
piernaty *pl* (*-tów*) *lit hum* feather bed *sing*, bedding *sing*
piernik *m* (*-ka*; *-ki*) gingerbread; ***stary ~*** *infml* old grump; ***co ma ~ do wiatraka?*** how does that tie in?
pierogi *pl* (*-gów*) dumplings, pierogi; ***~ z serem*** *dumplings with sweet cottage cheese filling*; ***~ z kapustą*** *dumplings with cabbage filling*; ***ruskie ~*** *dumplings with salty cottage cheese and potato filling*; ***leniwe ~*** curd cheese dumplings
pierożki *pl* (*-ków*) *dim* dumplings
piersiasty *adj infml* busty, buxom; **piersiow|y** *adj* pectoral; ***klatka ~a*** ribcage, chest; **piersiówka** *f* (*-ki*; *-ki*) hip flask, chest flask
pier|ś *f* (*-rsi*; *-rsi*) breast, chest; ***~si*** (*biust*) bust, breasts *pl*; ***~ś kurczaka*** *COOK* chicken breast; ***karmić ~sią*** nurse, breast-feed; ***pełną ~sią*** to the fullest; ***co tchu w ~siach*** like a lightning, as fast as possible
pierścieniowy *adj* annular, ring-shaped; **pierścień** *m* (*-cienia*; *-cienie*) ring; **pierścionek** *m* (*-nka*; *-nki*) ring
pierwiastek *m* (*-tka*; *-tki*) **1.** *CHEM* element **2.** *MATH* root; ***~ kwadratowy*** square root; **pierwiastkować** *v/im* (*-kuję*) *MATH* extract the root
pierwiosnek *m* (*-nka*; *-nki*) cowslip, primrose
pierwo- (*w złożeniach*) first-
pierwociny *pl* (*-cin*) **1.** origins **2.** (*utwór*) early work *sing*, early writings
pierwokup *m* (*-pu*; *no pl*): ***prawo ~u*** *JUR* right ofpreemp tion
pierworodny *adj* firstborn; ***grzech ~*** *REL* original sin
pierwotniak *m* (*-ka*; *-ki*) *BIOL* protozoan
pierwotny *adj* **1.** *plan*, *zamiar*: initial, original **2.** (*prymitywny*) primitive; ***człowiek ~*** primitive man **3.** (*prehistoryczny*) prehistoric, primordial, primeval; ***~ las*** primordial forest
pierwowzór *m* (*-zoru*; *-zory*) **1.** prototype **2.** *literacki*: original
pierwszeństwo *n* (*-wa*; *no pl*) precedence, priority; ***~ przejazdu*** right of way; ***mieć ~ nad*** *I* take precedence over
pierwszo- (*w złożeniach*) first-
pierwszoklasista *m* (*-ty*; *-lasiści*), **-tka** *f* (*-ki*; *-ki*) first-former, first-grader
pierwszoligowy *adj SPORT* first-league
pierwszomajowy *adj*: ***pochód ~*** Mayday parade
pierwszoplanowy *adj* **1.** *rola*: leading **2.** *fig* crucial, main, vital, foreground
pierwszorzędny *adj* first-rate, top-class
pierwsz|y *adj* first; ***~a*** (***godzina***) one (o'clock); ***~ego maja*** on the first of May; ***po ~e*** firstly; ***po raz ~y*** for the first time; ***~a pomoc*** first aid; ***~e potrzeby*** basic needs; ***~e danie*** *COOK* first course; ***~y lepszy***, ***~y z brzegu*** whichever; ***na ~y rzut oka*** at first glance; ***z ~ej ręki*** first hand, straight from the horse's mouth; ***~a liga*** *SPORT* first league; ***na ~ym planie*** in the foreground

P

pierwszyzna: ***nie ~*** nothing new, not the first time
pierzasty *adj* **1.** feathered, feather **2.** *fig* feathery; ***~y obłok*** cirrus
pierzchać ⟨**-chnąć**⟩ (*-cham*) **1.** flee, run away **2.** (*o ptakach*) scatter **3.** (*o nastroju*) dissipate, disappear
pierzchnąć[1] *v/p* → ***pierzchać***
pierzchnąć[2] ⟨**s-**⟩ (*-nę*) (*o skórze*) chap
pierze *n* (*-rza*; *no pl*) **1.** *ptaków*: plumage, feathers *pl* **2.** (*na poduszki*) down
pierzyć się ⟨**o-**⟩ (*-rzę*) molt
pierzyna *f* (*-ny*; *-ny*) eiderdown
pies *m* (*psa*; *psy*) dog; ***~ gończy*** hound; ***pod psem*** miserable, terrible; ***pogoda pod psem*** nasty weather; ***~ z kulawą nogą*** nobody, not a soul; ***uwaga! zły ~!*** beware ofthe dog!; ***psu na budę*** ofno use, useless
piesi *pl* → ***pieszy II***
pieski *adj* dog's, dog; ***~e życie*** *infml* dog's life
pieszczoch *m* (*-cha*; *-chy*) pet, affectionate person; **pieszczoszka** *f* (*-ki*; *-ki*) pet, affectionate woman; **pieszczota** *f* (*-ty*; *-ty*) caress; **pieszczotliw|y** *adj* **1.** (*czuły*) tender; ***~e imię*** pet name **2.** (*serdeczny*) gentle **3.** (*przymilny*) cuddly
pieszo *adv* on foot
piesz|y **I** *adj* foot; ***~a wycieczka*** hike; ***ruch ~y*** pedestrian traffic **II** *m* (*-szego*; *-si*), **-sza** *f* (*-szej*; *-sze*) walker, pedestrian; ***dla ~ych*** for pedestrians
pieścić ⟨**po-**⟩ (*pieszczę*) caress, pet, fondle; ***pieścić się*** **1.** cuddle, fondle **2.** ***~ się z kimś*** pet s.o.
pieśniarz *m* (*-rza*; *-rze*), **-rka** *f* (*-ki*; *-ki*) singer, songwriter; ***~ ludowy*** folk singer
pieś|ń *f* (*-śni*; *-śni*) song; ***koniec ~ni!*** *infml* that's the end!, no more!
pietruszka *f* (*-ki*; *-ki*) parsley
pietyzm *m* (*-mu*; *no pl*) *lit* reverence; ***z ~em*** reverently
piewca *m* (*-cy*; *-cy*) *lit* eulogist, singer
pięcio- (*w złożeniach*) **1.** five- **2.** *CHEM MATH* penta-
pięcioboista *m* (*-ty*; *-boiści*) *SPORT* pentathlete; **pięciobok** *m* (*-ku*; *-ki*) *MATH* pentagon; **pięciobój** *m* (*-boju*; *-boje*) *SPORT* pentathlon
pięciodniowy *adj* five-day; **pięciogwiazdkowy** *adj hotel*: five-star; **pięciokąt** *m* (*-ta*; *-ty*) *MATH* pentagon, pentagram; **pięciokrotnie** *adv* five times; **pięciokrotny** *adj* fivefold, quintuple; **Pięcioksiąg** *m* (*-sięgu*; *no pl*) *REL* Pentateuch
pięciolecie *n* (*-cia*; *-cia*) **1.** (*rocznica*) fifth anniversary **2.** (*5 lat*) five years *pl*; **pięcioletni** *adj* five-year; **pięciolinia** *f* (*-nii*; *-nie*) *MUS* stave, staff; **pięcioraczki** *pl* (*-ków*) quintuplets; **pięcioro** *num* five
pięciuset → ***pięćset***
pięć, ***pięciu*** *num* five; ***za ~ dwunasta*** *fig* five to twelve; **pięćdziesiąt** *num* fifty; **pięćdziesiąt|y** *adj* fiftieth; ***lata ~e*** the fifties
pięćdziesięciolecie *n* (*-cia*; *-cia*) **1.** (*rocznica*) fiftieth anniversary **2.** (*50 lat*) fifty years *pl*; **pięćset** *num* five hundred
piędź *f* (*piędzi*; *piędzie*) span, the width ofhuman hand; ***walczyć o każdą ~ ziemi*** fight for every inch of ground
pięknieć ⟨**wy-**⟩ (*-nieję*) grow pretty, become more beautiful
piękniś *m* (*-nisia*; *-nisie*) popinjay, dandy
piękno *n* (*-na*; *no pl*) beauty; **pięknoduch** *m* (*-cha*; *-chy*) arty soul; imprudent person
piękność *f* (*-ści*; *no pl*) beauty; **piękny** *adj* beautiful
pięściarstwo *n* (*-wa*; *no pl*) boxing; **pięściarz** *m* (*-rza*; *-rze*) boxer
pięść *f* (*-ści*; *-ści*) fist
pięta *f* (*-ty*; *-ty*) heel; **piętka** *f* (*-ki*; *-ki*) *the end part of a loaf of bread*
piętnasto- (*z złożeniach*) fifteen-
piętnastoletni *adj* fifteen-year-old; **piętnast|y** *adj* fifteenth; (***godzina***) ***~a*** three o'clock p.m.; **piętnaście** *num* fifteen
piętno *n* (*-na*; *-na*) brand, stamp; ***~ hańby*** brand ofdishonour; **piętnować** ⟨**na-**⟩ (*-nuję*) brand, stamp, condemn
pięt|ro *n* (*-ra*; *-ra*) floor, *Br* storey, *Am* story; ***na drugim ~rze*** *Br* on the second floor/storey, *Am* on the third floor/story
piętrow|y *adj dom*: *Br* storeyed, *Am* storied; ***łóżko ~e*** bunk bed; ***autobus ~y*** double-decker
piętrzyć się ⟨**s-**⟩ (*-rzę*) **1.** pile up, accumulate **2.** (*o wodzie*) dam up, rise

P

piguła *f* (*-ły*; *-ły*) *śniegowa*: snowball; **pigułka** *f* (*-ki*; *-ki*) pill; **~ antykoncepcyjna** contraceptive pill
pigwa *f* (*-wy*; *-wy*) *BIOL* quince
pijacki *adj* drunken, boozy
pijaczyna *m* (*-ny*; *-ny*) *infml* boozer, guzzler
pijać *v/im* (*-jam*) drink; **zwykle pijam mleko** I usually have milk
pijak *m* (*-ka*; *-jacy*), **-jaczka** *f* (*-ki*; *-ki*) (heavy) drinker, alcoholic; **po ~u** *infml* while drunk
pijalnia *f* (*-ni*; *-nie*) **1.** (*w sanatorium*) pump room **2.** (*piwiarnia*) beer house
pijan|y *adj* drunk, *infml* boozed, *infml* plastered; **~y ze szczęścia** drunk with happiness; **po ~emu** under the influence ofalcohol; **~y jak bela** drunk as a lord; **~y w sztok** tight as a drum
pijaństwo *n* (*-wa*; *no pl*) alcoholism, drunkenness, *infml* boozing; **pijatyka** *f* (*-ki*; *-ki*) *infml* binge, drinking spree, bash
pijawka *f* (*-ki*; *-ki*) *BIOL* leech
pijus *m* (*-sa*; *-sy*) *infml* drunkard, *infml* wino
pik *m* (*-ka*; *-ki*) (*w kartach*) spade; **wyjść w ~i** play spades; **as ~** ace ofspades
pikać ⟨**-nąć**⟩ (*-am*) beep, beat
pikanteria *f* (*-rii*; *no pl*) piquancy, zest; **pikantny** *adj* **1.** *COOK* hot, spicy **2.** *fig* piquant
pikieta *f* (*-ty*; *-ty*) **1.** sentry **2.** *POLIT* picket, blockade
pikle *pl* (*-li*) pickles
pikling *m* (*-ga*; *-gi*) *COOK* salted and smoked fish, bloater
pikować *v/im* (*-kuję*) **1.** (*w lotnictwie*) dive, do a nose-dive **2.** *kołdrę*: quilt **3.** *rośliny*: plant out; **pikowany** *adj kołdra*: quilted
pikowy *adj* (*w kartach*) ofspade s
pilić ⟨**przy-**⟩ (*-lę*) *infml* press, rush
pilniczek *m* (*-czka*; *-czki*) (*do paznokci*) nail file; **pilnik** *m* (*-ka*; *-ki*) file
pilno *adv*: **jest mu ~ do zrobienia czegoś** he is in a hurry to do s.th., he can't wait to do s.th.
pilność *f* (*-ści*; *no pl*) **1.** diligence, care **2.** *sprawy*: urgency
pilnować ⟨**przy-**⟩ (*-nuję*) **1.** watch **2.** (*dbać*) look after, watch over, supervise; **~ dzieci** watch over the children; **~ domu** mind the house **3.** (*przestrzegać*) abide by; **pilnować się** take care ofoneself , watch oneself
pilny *adj* **1.** diligent, industrious **2.** *sprawa*: urgent, pressing
pilot[1] *m* (*-ta*; *-loci*) **1.** pilot; **drugi ~** co-pilot **2.** (*w porcie*) harbour pilot **3.** (*przewodnik*) (tourist) guide
pilot[2] *m* (*-ta*; *-ty*) **1.** *TEL* remote control **2.** (*film*) pilot
pilotaż *m* (*-żu*; *no pl*) **1.** pilotage; **nauka ~u** learining to fly a plane **2.** *statku*: piloting **3.** (*badanie*) pilot study; **pilotażowy** *adj* pilot, piloting
pilotka *f* (*-ki*; *-ki*) (*czapka*) flying cap
pilotować *v/im* (*-tuję*) **1.** *samolot*: fly **2.** *samolot, statek*: pilot **3. ~ wycieczkę** guide a tour, be a tourist guide
pilśniowy *adj* **1.** *kapelusz*: felt **2.** *BUILD* fibre
piła[1] *f* (*-ły*; *-ły*) saw
piła[2] *f* (*-ły*; *-ły*) (*ryba*) sawfish
piłeczka *f* (*-ki*; *-ki*) *tenisowa*: (tennis)-ball
piłka[1] *f* (*-ki*; *-ki*) hand saw
piłk|a[2] *f* (*-ki*; *-ki*) ball; **~a nożna** football; **~a ręczna** handball; **~a siatkowa** volleyball; **~a koszykowa** basketball; **grać w ~ę** play ball; **piłkarski** *adj* football; **piłkarz** *m* (*-rza*; *-rze*) football player, footballer
piłować *v/im* (*-łuję*) **1.** saw **2.** (*pilnikiem*) file **3.** *fig* bore
pinceta *f* (*-ty*; *-ty*) tweezers *pl*
pinda *f* (*-dy*; *-dy*) *vulg* bitch
pinezka *f* (*-ki*; *-ki*) tack, thumbtack
ping-pong *m* (*-ga*; *no pl*) table tennis
pingwin *m* (*-na*; *-ny*) penguin
piołun *m* (*-nu*; *-ny*) *BIOL* wormwood, artemisia; **piołunow|y** *adj* wormwood; **wódka ~a** absinth(e), bitters *sing*
pion *m* (*-nu*; *-ny*) **1.** vertical **2.** (*prostopadła*) perpendicular **3.** (*ciężarek na sznurku*) plumb-line **4.** *kanalizacjny*: riser, vent sack
pionek *m* (*-nka*; *-nki*) **1.** (*w szachach*) pawn **2.** (*w grach*) checker **3.** *fig* puppet
pionier *m* (*-ra*; *-rzy*) pioneer
pionowy *adj* perpendicular, vertical
piorun *m* (*-na*/*-nu*; *-ny*) thunderbolt, thunder; **uderzenie ~a** thunderclap; **burza z ~ami** thunderstorm; **~em** like a shot, as fast as you can; **jasny ~!** *infml* damn!

P

piorunochron *m* (*-nu*; *-ny*) lightning rod
piorunujący *adj* electrifying, like a thunderbolt
piosenka *f* (*-ki*;*-ki*) song
piosenkarz *m* (*-rza*; *-rze*), **-rka** *f* (*-ki*; *-ki*) singer
piórnik *m* (*-ka*; *-ki*) pencil case; **piór|o** *n* (*-ra*; *-ra*) **1.** BIOL feather **2.** (*do pisania*) pen, drawing pen; ***wieczne ~o*** fountain pen; ***gęsie ~o*** quill pen; ***mieć cięte ~o*** *fig* write in an ironic style; ***wyjść spod ~a*** *G fig* be written by **3.** *wiosła*: blade; **pióropusz** *m* (*-sza*; *-sze*) plume, crest
pipeta *f* (*-ty*; *-ty*) pipette
pipidówka *f* (*-ki*; *-ki*) *infml* place in the middle ofnowhere
piracki *adj* **1.** piratical, pirate **2.** *kopia*, *wydanie*: illegal, bootlegged, pirated; **piractwo** *n* (*-wa*; *no pl*) piracy
piramida *f* (*-dy*; *-dy*) pyramid
pirat *m* (*-ta*; *-raci*) **1.** pirate **2.** *drogowy*: road hog
Pireneje *pl* (*-jów*) the Pyrenees
piro- (*w złożeniach*) pyro-
pirs *m* (*-su*; *-sy*) pier
pisać ⟨**na-**⟩ (*-szę*) write (**do** *G* to); ***~ na maszynie*** type; ***uczyć się ~*** learn to write; ***~ na kolanie*** scribble, jot down; ***jak to się pisze?*** how do you spell it?
pisak *m* (*-ka*; *-ki*) felt-tip pen; **pisanina** *f* (*-ny*; *no pl*) *infml* scribbling, trashy text; **pisanka** *f* (*-ki*; *-ki*) Easter egg
pisan|y *adj* written; ***nie było mu ~e*** he was not meant to do s.th.; ***to jest palcem na wodzie ~e*** it is absolutely uncertain
pisarka *f* (*-ki*; *-ki*) woman writer
pisarski *adj* **1.** writer's, writing **2.** literary; **pisarstwo** *n* (*-wa*; *no pl*) **1.** literary output, oeuvre **2.** literature
pisarz *m* (*-rza*; *-rze*) writer
pisemko *n* (*-ka*; *-ka*) **1.** *dim* (official) letter **2.** (*gazeta*) small-scale newspaper; **pisemny** *adj* written, in writing
pisk *m* (*-ku*; *-ki*) **1.** squeak **2.** *opon*: screech
pisklę *n* (*-lęcia*; *-lęta*) **1.** nestling **2.** (*kurczę*) chick
piskliwy *adj* squeaky, shrill
piskorz *m* (*-rza*; *-rze*) BIOL weatherfish
pismak *m* (*-ka*; *-ki*/*-macy*) *infml* newshound
pismo *n* (*-ma*; *-ma*) **1.** writing; ***~ drukowane*** print; ***~ ręczne*** handwriting; ***~ klinowe*** cuneiform; ***≈ Święte*** the Scriptures; ***na piśmie*** in writing; ***mowa i ~*** speech and writing; ***poczuć ~ nosem*** *fig* smell a rat **2.** (*alfabet*): alphabet **3.** (*czcionka*) type **4.** (*list*) (official) letter **5.** (*czasopismo*) newspaper, magazine
pisnąć *v/p* (*-nę*): ***nie ~ ani słówka*** not say even a word, not let out a breath; → ***piszczeć***
pisownia *f* (*-ni*; *-nie*) spelling, orthography
pistacja *f* (*-ji*; *-je*) pistachio; **pistacjowy** *adj* pistachio
pistolet *m* (*-tu*; *-ty*) pistol
pisuar *m* (*-ru*; *-ry*) urinal
pisywać *v/im* (*-suję*) write from time to time; ***~ do siebie*** write to each other
piszczałka *f* (*-ki*; *-ki*) pipe; ***~ organowa*** organ-pipe
piszczeć ⟨**za-**⟩ (*-czę*) **1.** (*o myszy*) squeak **2.** (*o osobie*) squeal, screech **3.** (*o kole*) screech
piszczel *f* (*-li*; *-le*) ANAT tibia, shinbone
piśmidło *n* (*-ła*; *-ła*) *infml* **1.** tabloid **2.** (*książka*) thrash book, pulp
piśmiennictwo *n* (*-wa*; *no pl*) literature; **piśmienny** *adj* **1.** *człowiek*: literate **2.** *materiały*: stationery
pitny *adj* **1.** (*zdatny do picia*) potable, drinkable **2.** (*w postaci płynnej*) drinking; ***miód ~*** mead
pitrasić ⟨**u-**⟩ (*-szę*) *infml* cook, fix, concoct
piwiarnia *f* (*-ni*; *-nie*) beer house, pub; **piwko** *n* (*-ka*; *-ka*) *dim* beer
piwnica *f* (*-cy*; *-ce*) cellar, basement; **piwniczny** *adj* cellar, basement
piwny *adj* **1.** beer **2.** *oczy*: hazel; **piw|o** *n* (*-wa*; *-wa*) beer; ***~o z beczki*** draught beer; ***dać na ~o*** leave a tip, tip; ***nawarzyć sobie ~a*** get into hot water
piwonia *f* (*-nii*; *-nie*) paeony, peony
piwosz *m* (*-sza*; *-sze*) beer lover; **piwowarstwo** *n* (*-wa*; *no pl*) brewing industry
pizda *f* (*-dy*; *-dy*) *vulg* cunt
pizza *f* (*-zy*; *-ze*) pizza
piżama *f* (*-my*; *-my*) pyjamas *pl*
piżmak *m* (*-ka*; *-ki*) BIOL muskrat
piżmo *n* (*-ma*; *no pl*) musk

PKP *abbr n indecl* (=**Polskie Koleje Państwowe**) Polish National Railways
PKS *abbr m* (*PKS-u*; *no pl*) (=**Państwowa Komunikacja Samochodowa**) National Coach Transport Company
pkt *abbr* (=**punkt**) pt
pl. *abbr* (=**plac**) sq.
plac *m* (*-cu*; *-ce*) **1.** square; **~ targowy** market square; **~ zamkowy** castle square; **~ zabaw** playground **2.** (*parcela*) plot ofla nd, building lot **3.** (*miejsce*) site; **~ budowy** construction site
plac|ek *m* (*-cka*; *-cki*) tart, pie; **~ek śliwkowy** plum tart; **~ki ziemniaczane** potato pancakes; **masz babo ~ek!** *infml* now you've done it!
placowe *n* (*-wego*; *no pl*) yardage
placówka *f* (*-ki*; *-ki*) **1.** (*filia*) agency, branch office **2.** (*instytucja*) institution, establishment; **~ dyplomatyczna** diplomatic agency, diplomatic post **3.** (*w wojsku*) outpost
plaga *f* (*-gi*; *-gi*) plague, scourge
plagiat *m* (*-tu*; *-ty*) plagiarism
plajtować ⟨**s-**⟩ (*-tuję*) *infml* bankruptcy
plakacista *m* (*-ty*; *-ciści*) poster-designer
plakat *m* (*-tu*; *-ty*) poster
plakietka *f* (*-ki*; *-ki*) **1.** (*tabliczka*) plaque **2.** (*z nazwiskiem*) name tag, badge
plam|a *f* (*-my*; *-my*) stain, blot; **~a z tłuszczu** fat stain; **~a na czyimś honorze** *Br* stain on s.o.'s honour, *Am* stain on s.o.'s honor; **dać ~ę** *infml* screw up
plamić ⟨**po-**, **za-**, **s-**⟩ (*-mię*) **1.** stain, blot **2.** *fig* besmirch, tarnish; **plamić się 1.** soil oneself **2.** (*o obrusie*) stain **3.** *fig* tarnish one's reputation, *Br* stain one's honour, *Am* stain one's honor
plamisty *adj* flecked, speckled, dappled, mottled; **plamka** *f* (*-ki*; *-ki*) fleck, speck, spot, mottle
plan *m* (*-nu*; *-ny*) plan; **~ miasta** town plan; **na pierwszym ~ie** in the foreground; **na drugim ~ie** in the background; **zgodnie z ~em** according to plan, as planned
plandeka *f* (*-ki*; *-ki*) tarpaulin, tarp
planeta *f* (*-ty*; *-ty*) planet
planista *m* (*-ty*; *-niści*) planner; **~ przedsiębiorstwa** corporate planner
plankton *m* (*-nu*; *no pl*) plankton
planować ⟨**za-**⟩ (*-nuję*) **1.** plan **2.** (*sporządzać szkic*) draft **3.** (*projektować*) design **4.** *TECH* face, level; **planowanie** *n* (*-nia*; *no pl*) planning; **~ przestrzenne** urban planning; **planowy** *adj* planned, on schedule, scheduled
plansza *f* (*-szy*; *-sze*) **1.** (*do zdjęć, rysunków*) chart **2.** (game) board
plantacja *f* (*-ji*; *-je*) plantation; **plantator** *m* (*-ra*; *-rzy*) planter
planty *pl* (*-tów*) commons, town park *sing*
plaskać ⟨**-sknąć**⟩ (*-kam*) (*uderzyć*) smack, clap
plasować się ⟨**u-**⟩ (*-suję*) be placed on
plastelina *f* (*-ny*; *no pl*) Plasticine, modelling clay
plaster *m* (*-tra*; *-try*) **1.** *MED* Band-Aid® **2.** *COOK* (large) slice; **~ miodu** honeycomb; **plasterek** *m* (*-rka*; *-rki*) *COOK* slice; **~ kiełbasy** slice ofsausage
plastik *m* (*-ku*; *-ku*), **plastyk** *m* (*-ku*; *-ki*) plastic; **z ~u** plastic, ofplastic
plastikowy, **plastykowy** *adj* plastic, of plastic
plastyczka *f* (*-ki*; *-ki*) woman artist; **plastyczn|y** *adj* **1.** (*barwny*, *wyrazisty*) vivid, graphic; **sztuki ~e** fine arts **2.** *metal*: plastic, malleable **3.** **chirurgia ~a** plastic surgery
plastyk *m* (*-ka*; *-tycy*) artist; → **plastik**
plastyka *f* (*-ki*; *no pl*) **1.** fine arts *pl* **2.** (*barwność*, *wyrazistość*) vividness **3.** (*przedmiot szkolny*) art classes **4.** *metalu*: plasticity
platan *m* (*-na*; *-ny*) plane (tree)
platforma *f* (*-my*; *-my*) **1.** platform **2.** (*płaszczyzna*) plane **3.** *kolejowa*: lorry
platoniczny *adj* Platonic
platyna *f* (*-ny*; *no pl*) platinum; **platynowy** *adj* **1.** platinum, ofplat inum **2.** (*kolor*) platinum blond
plazma *f* (*-my*; *no pl*) *BIOL PHYS* plasm
plaż|a *f* (*-ży*; *-że*) beach; **na ~y** on the beach; **plażować** *v/im* (*-żuję*) sunbathe, lie on the beach; **plażowicz** *m* (*-cza*; *-cze*) sunbather; **plażowy** *adj* beach; **plażówka** *f* (*-ki*; *-ki*) sun dress
plądrować ⟨**s-**⟩ (*-ruję*) plunder, loot
pląsać *v/im* (*-sam*) *hum* dance; **pląsawica** *f* (*-cy*; *no pl*) *MED* chorea; **pląs|y**

P

pl (*-sów*) *hum* dancing *sing*; ***w ~ach*** capering
plątać 〈**po-**〉 (*plączę*) **1.** *nici*: tangle **2.** (*mylić*) confuse, mix up; ***plątać się* 1.** (*o niciach*) get tangled **2.** (*mylić się*) be confused; ***wszystko mu się plącze*** he can't think straight; ***plącze mu się język*** he can't find his tongue, he stutters; ***~ się w zeznaniach*** get confused, confuse things **3.** (*łazić*) hang around; ***~ się pod nogami*** get in the way **4.** (*o rzeczach*) be scattered around
plątanina *f* (*-ny*; *no pl*) tangle
plebania *f* (*-nii*; *-nie*) parsonage, rectory
plebejski *adj* plebeian, ordinary
plebiscyt *m* (*-tu*; *-ty*) *POLIT* plebiscite
plebs *m* (*-su*; *no pl*) plebs, mob, common people *pl*
plecak *m* (*-ka*; *-ki*) rucksack, backpack
plecionka *f* (*-ki*; *-ki*) braiding, plaiting, weave; **pleciony** *adj* braided, plaited, woven
pleciuch *m* (*-cha*; *-chy*), **pleciuga** *f/m* (*-gi*; *-gi*) *infml* gossip, blabbermouth
plec|y *pl* (*-ców*) **1.** *ANAT* back *sing*; ***za moimi ~ami*** *fig* behind my back; ***stać ~ami do drzwi*** with one's back to the door; ***szeroki w ~ach*** wide-shouldered **2.** *fig* friends *pl* in high places, contacts *pl*
pleć 〈**wy-**〉 (*pielę*) weed (out)
pled *m* (*-du*; *-dy*) throw, blanket
plejada *f* (*-dy*; *-dy*) pleiad; ***~ gwiazd*** pleiad ofceleb rities
plemienny *adj* tribal; **plemię** *n* (*-mienia*; *-miona*) tribe, kin
plemnik *m* (*-ka*; *-ki*) sperm (cell)
plenarny *adj* plenary
plene|r *m* (*-ru*; *-ry*) **1.** (*otwarta przestrzeń*) open air; ***w ~rze*** in the open air, en plein air; ***koncert w ~rze*** open-air concert; **2.** *FILM* location ***zdjęcia w ~rze*** filming on location; **plenerowy** *adj* open-air, plein-air
plenić się *v/im* (*-nię*) **1.** multiply **2.** (*o chwastach*) spread
plenipotencja *f* (*-ji*; *-je*) *lit* power ofattorney
plenny *adj* prolific
plenum *n* (*indecl*; *-na*) general assembly
pleść (*plotę*) **1.** 〈**u-**〉 *warkocz*: braid, plait **2.** *v/im fig* blab, blabber; ***~ bzdury***, ***~ trzy po trzy*** blabber, not talk sense
pleśniawka *f* (*-ki*; *-ki*) *MED* thrush; **pleśnieć** 〈**s-**〉 (*-nieję*) *Br* mould, *Am* mold, *Br* grow mouldy, *Am* grow moldy; **pleśniowy** *adj*: ***ser ~*** blue cheese; **pleśń** *f* (*-śni*; *-śnie*) *BIOL* mildew, *Br* mould, *Am* mold
plewy *pl* (*plew*) chaff *sing*
plik *m* (*-ku*; *-ki*) **1.** wad, bundle **2.** *INF* file
plisowany *adj* pleated
pliszka *f* (*-ki*; *-ki*) wagtail
plomba *f* (*-by*; *-by*) **1.** seal **2.** *zęba*: filling **3.** *BUILD* infill construction; **plombować** 〈**za-**〉 (*-buję*) **1.** seal **2.** *ząb*: fill
plon *m* (*-nu*; *-ny*) **1.** harvest, crop, yield; ***święto ~ów*** Harvest Day **2.** *fig* harvest
plotk|a *f* (*-ki*; *-ki*) piece ofgossip, rumour; ***~i*** gossip
plotkara *f* (*-ry*; *-ry*), **plotkarka** (*-ki*; *-ki*) gossip, blabbermouth; **plotkarski** *adj* gossipy; ***~e miasteczko*** gossipy little town; **plotkarstwo** *n* (*-wa*; *no pl*) gossiping; **plotkarz** *m* (*-rza*; *-rze*) gossip
plotkować *v/im* (*-kuję*) **1.** gossip, spread rumours (**o** *L* about) **2.** (*rozmawiać*) chat
plucha *f* (*-chy*; *-chy*) blustery weather
pluć 〈**plunąć**〉 (*pluję*) **1.** spit; cough up **2.** *fig* be through; ***~ sobie w brodę*** kick oneself
plugastwo *n* (*-wa*; *-wa*) *lit* **1.** abomination, filth **2.** (*robaki*) vermin
plugawić 〈**s-**〉 (*-wię*) *lit* defile; **plugawy** *adj* **1.** foul, filthy **2.** *język*: obscene
plujka *f* (*-ki*; *-ki*): ***mucha ~*** bluebottle (fly)
plunąć *v/p* → **pluć**
plus *m* (*-sa*; *-sy*) **1.** *MATH* plus **2.** *fig* good point, advantage; ***~y i minusy*** pros and cons; ***~ minus*** more or less
plusk *m* (*-ku*; *-ki*) **1.** splash; ***z ~iem*** with a splash **2.** *deszczu*: patter
pluskać 〈**-snąć**〉 (*-kam*/*-szczę*) **1.** splash **2.** (*o falach*) dabble **3.** (*o deszczu*) patter; ***pluskać się* 1.** (*ochlapywać się*) be splashing around **2.** (*pływać*) take a dip
pluskiewka *f* (*-ki*; *-ki*) *Am* tack, *Br* drawing pin
pluskwa *f* (*-wy*; *-wy*) *BIOL* bedbug

P

plusnąć *v/p* (*-nę*): **~ do wody** splash into the water; → **pluskać**
plusz *m* (*-szu*; *-sze*) plush
pluszcz *m* (*-cza*; *-cze*) (*ptak*) dipper, water ousel
pluszow|y *adj* plushy; **~y miś** teddy bear; **~e zabawki** soft toys
pluton[1] *m* (*-nu*; *no pl*) *CHEM* plutonium
pluton[2] *m* (*-nu*; *-ny*) (*w wojsku*) platoon; **~ egzekucyjny** firing squad; **plutonowy** *m* (*-wego*; *-wi*) sergeant
plwocina *f* (*-ny*; *-ny*) *MED* sputum, spittle
płaca *f* (*-cy*; *-ce*) pay; **~ za godzinę** wage; **~ miesięczna** salary; **~ minimalna** minimal wage
płachta *f* (*-ty*; *-ty*) cloth, sheet, tarp; **jak czerwona ~ na byka** like a red rag to a bull
płacić ⟨**za-**⟩ (*-cę*) pay (**za** *A* for, *I* with); **~ gotówką** pay cash; **~ kartą kredytową** pay by credit card; **~ wysoką cenę** *fig* pay a high price
płacowy *adj* pay
płacz *m* (*-czu*; *-cze*) cry, weep; **płacząc|y** *adj* crying, weeping; **wierzba ~a** weeping willow; **płaczka** *f* (*-ki*; *-ki*) weeper; **płaczliwy** *adj* weepy, tearful
płakać ⟨**za-**⟩ (*płaczę*) **1.** cry, *lit* weep (**z** *G* with, **nad** *I* over
płaksa *f/m* (*-sy*; *-sy*) *infml* crybaby
płask: **na ~** flat
płaski *adj* flat
płaskorzeźba *f* (*-by*; *-by*) low relief, bas-relief
płaskostopie *n* (*-pia*; *no pl*) *MED* flatfoot
płaskowyż *m* (*-żu*; *-że*) plateau
płastuga *f* (*-gi*; *-gi*) *BIOL* plaice
płaszcz *m* (*-cza*; *-cze*) **1.** coat, overcoat; **~ kąpielowy** bathrobe **2.** *TECH* mantle, casing
płaszczyć ⟨**s-**⟩ (*-czę*) flatten; **płaszczyć się** *fig* crawl, cringe (**przed** *I* to)
płaszczyk *m* (*-ka*; *-ki*) *dim* coat, cloak; **pod ~iem** *G fig* under the guise of, under the pretence of
płaszczyzna *f* (*-ny*; *-ny*) plane; **wspólna ~** common ground
płat *m* (*-ta*; *-ty*) (large) piece, sheet, slice; **~ nośny** *TECH* airfoil; **~ mózgowy** *MED* cerebral lobe
płat|ek *m* (*-tka*; *-tki*) **1.** petal; **~ek ucha** *ANAT* earlobe; **~ki śniegu** snowflakes; **~ki róży** rose petals; **~ki owsiane** oatflakes; **~ki kukurydziane** cornflakes; **jak z ~ka** smoothly **2.** (*kawałek*) piece **3.** (*plasterek*) slice
płatniczy *adj* payment; **płatnik** *m* (*-ka*; *-nicy*) payer; **~ podatku** taxpayer; **płatnoś|ć** *f* (*-ści*; *no pl*) payment; **warunki ~ci** payment terms, payment conditions; **płatny** *adj* **1.** (*wynagradzany*) paid, salaried **2.** (*do zapłacenia*) payable, due
pława *f* (*-wy*; *-wy*) buoy, float
pławić się *v/im* (*-wię*) **1.** duck **2.** *fig* bathe, wallow (**w** *L* in)
płaz *m* (*-za*; *-zy*) *BIOL* amphibian
płciow|y *adj* sexual; **dojrzałość ~a** sexual maturity; **stosunek ~y** (sexual) intercourse; **niemoc ~a** impotence; **narządy ~e** genitals; **popęd ~y** sex drive
płd. *abbr* (= **południe**, **południowy**) S
płeć *f* (*płci*; *płcie*) sex, gender
płetwa *f* (*-wy*; *-wy*) **1.** fin; **~ grzbietowa** dorsal fin; **~ rekina** shark fin **2.** *nurka*: flipper; **płetwal** *m* (*-la*; *-le*) *BIOL* blue whale; **płetwonurek** *m* (*-rka*; *-rkowie*) (scuba) diver, frogman
płn. *abbr* (= **północ**, **północny**) N
płochliwy *adj* shy, skittish
płoć *f* (*płoci*; *płocie*) *BIOL* roach
płodność *f* (*-ści*; *no pl*) **1.** fertility, fecundity **2.** *fig* productivity
płodny *adj* **1.** *kobieta*, *wyobraźnia*: fertile, fecund **2.** *pisarz*: prolific; **płodow|y** *adj Br* foetal, *Am* fetal; **wody ~e** amniotic fluid, waters; **płodozmian** *m* (*-nu*; *np pl*) crop rotation
płody *pl* → **płód**
płodzić ⟨**s-**⟩ (*-dzę*) *dziecko*: beget, breed
płomienny *adj* **1.** (*mowa*): fiery **2.** (*miłość*): ardent, passionate; **płomień** *m* (*-mienia*; *-mienie*) **1.** flame, blaze **2.** *fig* ardour, passion
płomyk *m* (*-ka*; *-ki*) (small) flame, flicker; **płomyczek** *m* (*-czka*; *-czki*) *dim* (very small) flame
płonący *adj* burning, blazing
płonąć ⟨**s-**⟩ (*-nę*) **1.** (*o świecy*) burn **2.** (*o budynku*) be in flames, be aflame, blaze **3.** (*o policzkach*) blush, flush; **~ ze wstydu** burn with shame **4. ~ żądzą zemsty** breathe revenge
płonica *f* (*-cy*; *no pl*) *MED* scarlet fever

P

płonny *adj lit* **1.** *nadzieja*: vain, futile **2.** *obawy*: groundless **3.** *dated* barren

płoszyć ⟨**s-**⟩ (*-szę*) **1.** *ptaki*: scare away **2.** *osobę*: frighten away; **płoszyć się 1.** (*o ptakach*) get scared, take flight **2.** (*o koniu*) shy **3.** (*o osobie*) flee

płot *m* (*-tu*; *-ty*) fence

płotka *f* (*-ki*; *-ki*) **1.** small fry, unimportant person **2.** BIOL roach

płotkarz *m* (*-rza*; *-rze*), **-rka** *f* (*-ki*; *-ki*) SPORT hurdler

płowieć ⟨**s-**, **wy-**⟩ (*-wieję*) **1.** fade, *Br* lose colour, *Am* lose color **2.** (*o włosach*) bleach; **płowy** *adj* **1.** tawny **2.** *włosy*: flaxen

płoza *f* (*-zy*; *-zy*) (*w saniach*) runner, skid

płócienko *n* (*-ka*; *-ka*) fine linen; **płócienny** *adj* linen

płód *m* (*płodu*; *płody*) MED *Br* foetus, *Am* fetus; **płody** *lit* fruit, brainchild; ***płody rolne*** farm produce; ***płody chorobliwej wyobraźni*** product ofa sick imagination; ***płody ziemi*** gifts of the earth

płótno *n* (*-na*; *-na*) **1.** (*materiał*) linen **2.** (*obraz*) canvas, painting

płuc|a *pl* (*płuc*) lungs; ***zapalenie ~*** pneumonia; **płucny** *adj* lung, pulmonic, pulmonary

pług *m* (*-ga*; *-gi*) *Br* plough, *Am* plow; ***~ śnieżny*** *Br* snowplough, *Am* snowplow

płukać ⟨**wy-**⟩ (*płuczę*) rinse; ***~ gardło*** gargle

płukanie *n* (*-nia*; *no pl*) rinse; ***~ żołądka*** gastric lavage

płukanka *f* (*-ki*; *-ki*) rinse; ***~ do włosów*** hair rinse; ***~ koloryzująca*** *Br* colouring rinse, *Am* coloring rinse; ***~ do ust*** mouthwash

płycizna *f* (*-ny*; *-ny*) shallows *pl*, shoal, sandbank

płyn *m* (*-nu*; *-ny*) **1.** PHYS fluid **2.** (*ciecz*) liquid; ***w ~ie*** liquid; ***~ do mycia naczyń*** washing-up liquid **3.** (*do mycia*) wash; ***~ do kąpieli*** bubble bath **4.** (*roztwór*) solution

płynąć ⟨**po-**⟩ (*-nę*) **1.** (*o wodzie, prądzie, krwi*) flow **2.** (*o czasie*) go by **3.** (*o człowieku, rybie*) swim; ***~ pod prąd*** *fig* swim against the tide; ***~ z prądem*** *fig* swim with the tide **4.** (*o statku, jachcie*) sail; ***~ łódką*** go by boat, row a boat

płynnie *adv*: ***mówić ~ po polsku*** speak fluent Polish

płynność *f* (*-ści*; *no pl*) **1.** *fig* fluidity, liquidity **2.** *ruchu*: smoothness, grace **3.** (*biegłość*) fluency **4.** ***~ środków*** FIN liquidity, solvency

płynny *adj* **1.** liquid **2.** *ruch*: smooth, graceful **3.** *kształt*, *granica*: fluid

płyta *f* (*-ty*; *-ty*) **1.** plate, panel, board, slab; ***~ pamiątkowa*** memorial plaque **2.** *gramofonowa*: record **3.** *kuchenna*: hot plate **4.** ***~ kompaktowa*** CD, compact disc

płytka *f* (*-ki*; *-ki*) **1.** plate **2.** *ceramiczna*: tile **3.** *nazębna*: plaque

płytki *adj* shallow, superficial

płytoteka *f* (*-ki*; *-ki*) record collection

pływacki *adj zawody*, *karta*: swimming

pływać *v/im* (*-wam*) **1.** swim; ***~ żabką*** swim breaststroke; ***~ statkiem*** go by ship **2.** (*o statku, łódce*) sail **3.** (*o korku*) float **4.** *fig infml* be evasive

pływak[1] *m* (*-ka*; *-wacy*), **-waczka** *f* (*-ki*; *-ki*) swimmer

pływak[2] *m* (*-ka*; *-ki*) TECH float, swimming bob; **pływalnia** *f* (*-ni*; *-nie*) **1.** swimming pool **2.** (*odkryta*) outdoor pool; **pływanie** *n* (*-nia*; *no pl*) swimming

pnący *adj* BIOL climbing; **pnącze** *n* (*-cza*; *-cza*) climber, climbing plant

pneumatyczny *adj* pneumatic, air; ***młot ~*** pneumatic drill

p.n.e. *abbr* (=***przed naszą erą***) B.C.

pniak *m* (*-ka*; *-ki*) **1.** (tree) stump **2.** (*do rąbania*) chopping block

po *prep* (*L*/*A*): ***klepać ~ ramieniu*** pat s.o.'s back; ***poznać ~ głosie*** recognize s.o.'s voice; ***kufer ~ babce*** chest (inherited) from grandmother; ***~ wojnie*** after the war; ***już ~ piątej*** it is already past five; ***~ kolana*** knee-deep; ***iść ~ chleb*** go to get bread; ***iść ~ lekarza*** go bring the doctor; ***chodzić ~ parku*** walk round the park; ***~ lewej stronie*** on the left-hand side; ***szukać ~ kieszeniach*** look in all the pockets; ***wypić ~ piwie*** drink a beer each; ***~ pracy*** after work; ***~ ile są pomidory?*** how much are tomatoes?; ***~ kolei*** one by one, in an orderly fashion; ***jeden ~ drugim*** one after another; ***butelka ~ mleku*** (empty) milk bottle; ***puszka ~ piwie*** (empty) beer can; ***~ pierwsze*** firstly;

P

~ bohatersku heroically; **~ części** partly; **mówić ~ angielsku** speak English; **co to znaczy ~ angielsku?** what does it mean in English?; **~ co?** what for?; **~ omacku** by touch, blindly, in darkness; **już ~ wszystkim** this is all

p.o. *abbr* (= **pełniący obowiązki**) acting

pobawić *v/p* (*-wię*) **1.** *gości*: entertain **2.** **~ dziecko** babysit; **pobawić się** play (**z** *I* with)

pobicie *n* (*-cia*; *-cia*) JUR assault, battery

pobić *v/p* (*-biję*) **1.** beat; **~ rekord** break a record **2.** (*pokonać*) defeat; **pobić się** have a fight, come to blows

pobiec *v/p* (*-biegnę*) run

pobielany *adj* **1.** (*posypany czymś białym*) whitened **2.** *rondel*: tinned **3.** *ściana*: whitewashed

pobierać ⟨**-brać**⟩ (*-ram*) **1.** *opłatę*: charge **2.** *pensję*: draw **3.** *energię*: consume **4.** *podatki*, *próbki*: collect; **pobierać się** get married

pobieżny *adj* cursory, perfunctory, quick

pobliski *adj* nearby, close, neighbouring

pobliż|e: **w ~u** *G* nearby, close to

pobłażać *v/im* (*-żam*) be lenient, be lax, tolerate; **pobłażliwość** *f* (*-ści*; *no pl*) leniency, laxness, tolerance; **pobłażliwy** *adj* lenient, lax, tolerant

pobłogosławić *v/p* (*-wię*) REL bless

pobłyskiwać *v/im* (*-kuję*) glimmer, shimmer, glitter

pobocze *n* (*-cza*; *-cza*) *drogi*: hard shoulder; **poboczny** *adj* secondary, minor

pobojowisko *n* (*-ka*; *-ka*) **1.** battlefield **2.** *fig* shambles *sing*

poborca *m* (*-cy*; *-cy*) collector; **~ podatkowy** tax collector

poborow|y **I** *adj* conscriptable; **komisja ~a** draft board **II** *m* (*-wego*; *-wi*) conscript

pobory *pl* → **pobór**

pobożniś *m* (*-nisia*; *-nisie*), **-nisia** *f* (*-si*; *-sie*) bigot

pobożność *f* (*-ści*; *no pl*) piety, devotion; **pobożny** *adj* pious, devout

pobór *m* (*-boru*; *-bory*) **1.** (*do wojska*) conscription draft **2.** FIN collection **3.** **pobory** salary, wages **4.** *gazu*, *energii*: consumption; **~ wody** water consumption

pobrać *v/p* → **pobierać**

pobratymiec *m* (*-mca*; *-mcy*) *lit* kin, kinsman

pobrudzić *v/p* (*-dzę*) dirty, soil

pobrzeż|e *n* (*-ża*; *-ża*) **1.** shore **2.** *morza*: seashore **3.** *rzeki*: riverside, river bank, lakeside **4.** (*skraj*) edge; **na ~u** on the outskirts

pobrzękiwać *v/im* (*-kuję*) **1.** (*brzdąkać*) strum, thrum, twang (**na** *L*) **2.** (*o kluczach*, *bransoletkach*) jangle, jingle

pobudk|a *f* (*-ki*; *-ki*) **1.** wake-up; **zrobić ~ę** give the wake up call **2.** (*w wojsku*) reveille **3.** **~i** impulse, motives

pobudliwy *adj* excitable

pobudować się *v/p* (*-duję*) build a house for oneself

pobudzać ⟨**-dzić**⟩ (*-dzam*) **1.** stimulate (**do** *G* to) **2.** (*prowokować*) incite, spur to action, provoke thinking

pobudzający *adj* stimulating, thought-provoking; **środek ~** stimulant

pobudzony *adj*: **~ seksualnie** sexually aroused

pobyć *v/p* (*-będę*) stay (somewhere) for some time

pobyt *m* (*-tu*; *-ty*) stay, sojourn; **miejsce stałego ~u** place ofpermanent residence; **~ za granicą** stay abroad

pocałunek *m* (*-nku*; *-nki*) kiss

pochewka *f* (*-ki*; *-ki*) *dim* (small) case, (small) sheath

pochlebca *m* (*-cy*; *-cy*), **-czyni** *f* (*-ni*; *-nie*) flatterer; **pochlebczy** *adj* flattering; **pochlebiać** ⟨**-bić**⟩ (*-biam*) flatter; **~ sobie** flatter oneself

pochlebny *adj* flattering, adulatory; **pochlebstwo** *n* (*-wa*; *-wa*) flattery

pochłaniacz *m* (*-cza*; *-cze*) TECH absorbent, absorber; **~ dymu** smoke absorber; **~ zapachu** odour filter

pochłaniać ⟨**-łonąć**⟩ (*-niam*) **1.** absorb; **~ wiele czasu** be time-consuming, require a lot oftime; **~ życie wielu osób** take a heavy toll **2.** **praca pochłaniała go bez reszty** he was totally preoccupied with his work **3.** *książkę*, *obiad*: devour **4.** *ciepło*: consume

pochłonięty *adj* *fig* engrossed, immersed, absorbed

pochmurnieć ⟨**s-**⟩ (*-nieję*) **1.** (*o niebie*) grow dark, become overcast **2.** (*o oso-*

P

bie) grow morose, become sullen; ***twarz mu spochmurniała*** gloom settled on his face
pochmurny *adj* **1.** cloudy, overcast **2.** *fig* gloomy, sullen
pochodna *f* (*-nej*; *-ne*) **1.** derivative **2.** MATH differential coefficient
pochodnia *f* (*-ni*; *-nie*) torch
pochodny *adj* **1.** derivative, derived; ***wyraz ~*** derivative **2.** (*wtórny*) secondary
pochodzeni|e *n* (*-nia*; *no pl*) origin, descent; ***on jest z ~a Polakiem*** he is of Polish origin; ***wyspa ~a wulkanicznego*** island of volcanic origin
pochodzić[1] *v/im* (*-dzę*) **1.** originate, come (**z** *G* from); ***~ z lat sześćdziesiątych*** come from the sixties **2.** (*o gatunku*) descend (**od** *G* from) **3.** (*o wyrazie*) derive (**od** *G* from)
pochodzić[2] *v/p* (*-dzę*) walk a little, take a stroll; → ***chodzić***
pochopny *adj* rash, hasty
pochować *v/p* → ***chować***
pochód *m* (*-chodu*; *-chody*) **1.** procession, parade **2.** (*marsz*) march; ***~ protestacyjny*** protest march
pochówek *m* (*-wku*; *-wki*) *lit* burial, interment
pochrapywać *v/im* (*-puję*) snore
pochrząkiwać *v/im* (*-kuję*) snort, grunt
pochw|a *f* (*-wy*; *-wy*) **1.** case, sheath; ***dobyć miecza z ~y*** draw the sword from its sheath **2.** ANAT vagina
pochwalać *v/im* (*-lam*) approve; ***nie ~*** disapprove; **pochwalić** *v/p* (*-lę*) praise, commend; ***pochwalić się*** boast
pochwalny *adj* laudatory, commendatory; **pochwał|a** *f* (*-ły*; *-ły*) praise; ***godny ~y*** commendable, praiseworthy
pochwycić *v/p* (*-cę*) **1.** *rękę*: catch **2.** *sens*: grasp
pochylać ⟨**-lić**⟩ (*-lam*) **1.** *głowę*: incline **2.** *drzewo*: tilt, tip; ***pochylać się*** bend oneself (down), lean (***nad*** *I* over), bow down (***przed*** *I* before)
pochylnia *f* (*-ni*; *-nie*) slipway, ramp
pochylony *adj* **1.** (*przechylony*) tilted, tipped **2.** bent, leaning (***nad*** *I* over) **3.** (*w skłonie*) bowed down (***przed*** *I* before)
pochyłość *f* (*-ści*; *-ści*) inclination, slope; **pochyły** *adj* inclined, slanting, leaning

pociąć *v/p* (*potnę*) **1.** cut up, chop, shred **2.** (*o komarach*) sting **3.** (*o molach*) shred
pociąg[1] *m* (*-gu*; *-gi*) train; ***~iem*** by train; ***~ pospieszny*** fast train; ***~ dalekobieżny*** long-distance train; ***~ osobowy*** slow train; ***~ towarowy*** freight train
pociąg[2] *m* (*-gu*, *no pl*) **1.** (*skłonność*) inclination (**do** *G* to), penchant (**do** *G* for); ***mieć ~ do*** *G* be attracted to **2.** (*upodobanie*) liking (**do** *G* for)
pociągać ⟨**-gnąć**⟩ (*-gam*) **1.** pull (**za** *A* by); ***~ kogoś do odpowiedzialności za*** *A* have s.o. account for, hold s.o. accountable for; ***~ nosem*** sniff, snivel; ***~ łyk*** take a swig; ***~ z butelki*** pull at the bottle **2.** (*za sobą*) tug **3.** (*nęcić*) draw, attract, appeal **4.** *farbą*: coat; **pociągający** *adj* **1.** appealing, attractive **2.** *myśl*: enticing, captivating
pociągły *adj twarz*: oval
pociągnąć *v/p* (*-nę*) *infml* live, last; ***on długo nie pociągnie*** he won't last long; → ***pociągać***
pociągnięcie *n* (*-cia*; *-cia*) pull, move; ***~ pędzla*** draw of a brush; ***za jednym ~m*** with one move
pociągowy *adj koń*: draught, *Am* draft
po cichu *adv* **1.** quietly **2.** *fig* secretly
pocić się ⟨**s-**⟩ (*-cę*) **1.** sweat, *form* perspire **2.** (*wysilać się*): slog away (***nad*** *I* over) **3.** (*o szkle*) steam up, fog up
pociec *v/p* (*-cieknę*), **pocieknąć** *v/p* (*-nę*) trickle, drip
pociech|a *f* (*-chy*; *-chy*) **1.** comfort, solace **2.** *infml* (*dziecko*) child, little dear; ***mieć sto ~ z*** *I infml* have many problems with
po ciemku *adv* in the dark
pociemnieć *v/p* (*-nieję*) (*o niebie*) darken, grow dark; ***pociemniało mi w oczach*** everything went black
pocierać ⟨**potrzeć**⟩ (*-ram*) rub
pocieszać ⟨**-szyć**⟩ (*-szam*) console, comfort; ***pocieszać się*** console oneself (*I* with); **pocieszający** *adj* consoling; comforting, cheering up
pocieszenie *n* (*-nia*; *-nia*) consolation; ***na ~*** as a consolation
pocieszny *adj* funny, amusing
pocieszyciel *m* (*-la*; *-le*), ***~ka*** *f* (*-ki*; *-ki*) comforter, consoler
pocieszyć *v/p* → ***pocieszać***

P

pocisk *m* (*-ku*; *-ki*) missile, shell
pocukrzyć *v/p* (*-rzę*) sweeten, add sugar
pocz|ąć *v/p* (*-cznę*) *lit* **1.** (*zrobić*) ***nie wiedzieć, co ze sobą ~ąć*** not know what to do with oneself; ***co ~ąć?*** what to do? **2.** *dziecko*: conceive; ***życie ~ęte*** begotten life; → ***poczynać***
począt|ek *m* (*-tku*; *-tki*) beginning, start; ***~ki*** (*podstawy*) rudiments; ***na ~ku***, ***z ~ku*** in the beginning; ***od ~ku*** from the outset; ***na ~ek*** as the first thing, for starters; ***w ~kach listopada*** in early November; ***z ~kiem zimy*** at the beginning ofwinter; ***brać ~ek z*** *G lit* spring from; ***dać ~ek*** *D* give rise to
początkowo *adv* in the beginning, at the outset; **początkow|y** *adj* initial; ***nauczanie ~e*** elementary education
początkujący *m* (*-cego*; *-cy*), **-ca** *f* (*-cej*; *-ce*) beginner, novice; ***dla ~ch*** for beginners
poczciwy *adj* kind-hearted, decent
poczekać *v/im* (*-kam*) **1.** wait (**z** *I* with) **2.** hold on; ***proszę chwilę ~*** hold on a moment, please
poczekalnia *f* (*-ni*; *-nie*) waiting room
poczesny *adj lit miejsce*: prominent
poczet *m* (*-cztu*; *-czty*) **1.** body; ***przyjąć w ~*** *G fig* admit among the members of, be admitted into ranks of **2.** (*świta*) retinue **3.** *sztandarowy*: colour guard
poczęcie *n* (*-cia*; *-cia*) BIOL conception; ***Niepokalane ~*** (***Maryi***) REL (Virgin Mary's) Immaculate Conception
poczęstować *v/p* (*-tuję*) treat (*I* to); **poczęstować się** help oneself(*I* to)
poczęstunek *m* (*-nku*; *-nki*) **1.** food and drinks **2.** (*przyjęcie*) a modest reception
poczt|a *f* (*-ty*; *-ty*) post office; ***~a lotnicza*** air mail; ***~a elektroniczna*** INF e-mail; ***~ą*** by post; **pocztowy** *adj* postal; ***znaczek ~*** postage stamp; ***urząd ~*** post office; **pocztówka** *f* (*-ki*; *-ki*) postcard
poczucie *n* (*-cia*; *no pl*) sense, feeling (*G* of); ***~ obowiązku*** sense ofduty; ***~ czasu*** sense oftime; ***~ honoru*** sense ofhonour; ***~ winy*** guilt; ***~ własnej wartości*** sense ofone's own worth; ***~ bezpieczeństwa*** feeling of security, feeling ofsaf ety; ***~ humoru*** sense ofhumour
poczuć *v/p* (*-czuję*) sense, feel, perceive; ***~ radość*** feel joy; ***~ się źle*** feel unwell
poczuwać się *v/im* (*-wam*) feel; ***~ do obowiązku*** feel s.th. to be one's duty; ***~ do odpowiedzialności*** feel responsible; ***~ do winy*** feel guilty
poczwarka *f* (*-ki*; *-ki*) BIOL chrysalis
poczwórny *adj* fourfold, quadruple
poczynać *v/im* (*-nam*) *lit* **1.** (*rozpoczynać*) commence; ***poczynając od*** *G* beginning with; ***śmiało sobie ~*** act boldly **2.** *dziecko*: conceive
poczynania *pl* (*-czynań*) acts, actions, enterprises
poczytać *v/p* (*-tam*) read (a little); → ***poczytywać***
poczytalność *f* (*-ści*; *no pl*) JUR soundness ofmind; **poczytalny** *adj* JUR sound in mind
poczytność *f* (*-ści*; *no pl*) *gazety*, *książki*: popularity, wide readership; **poczytny** *adj* widely-read, popular
poczytywać ⟨**-tać**⟩ (*-tuję*) *lit* consider (**za** *A*), regard (**za** *A* as); ***~ coś komuś za złe*** hold s.th. against; ***~ coś sobie za zaszczyt*** consider s.th. an honour
poćwiartować *v/p* (*-tuję*) *mięso*: quarter
poćwiczyć *v/p* (*-czę*) do (some) exercise, practise (a little), get some practice
pod *prep* (*I/A*) **1.** under; ***~ poduszką*** under a pillow; ***~ okno*** under the window; ***być ~ czyimś urokiem*** be under s.o.'s spell; ***znajdować się ~ wpływem*** *G* be under the influence of; ***zeznawać ~ przysięgą*** testify under oath; ***~ panowaniem rzymskim*** under the Romans; ***zostawić klucz ~ wycieraczką*** leave the key under the mat; ***stać ~ drzewem*** stand under a tree; ***urodzić się ~ znakiem Ryb*** be born under the star sign of Pisces; ***ma ~ sobą setkę żołnierzy*** he has a hundred soldiers under him; ***~ nadzorem rodziców*** under parental supervision **2.** (*poniżej*) below **3.** (*w przeciwnym kierunku*) against; ***~ prąd*** (***wiatr***) against the current (wind); ***~ światło*** against the light **4.** (*blisko*) to; ***podkradł się ~ drzwi*** he crawled to the door; ***odprowadzić kogoś ~ same drzwi*** see s.o. to the front door **5.** (*obok*) by; ***~ ścianą***

P

by the wall; **~ domem** by the house **6.** (*w danym miejscu*) at; **mieszkać ~ numerem piętnastym** live at number fifteen; **~ drzwiami** at the door **7.** (*blisko w czasie*) towards; **~ wieczór** towards evening **8.** (*w pobliżu*) near; **mieszkać ~ Wrocławiem** live near Wrocław **9. wpaść ~ samochód** be hit by a car; **~ warunkiem, że** on condition that; **~ karą** *G* on the penalty of; **~ postacią** *G* in the shape of; **~ nieobecność** *G* in the absence of; **mężczyzna ~ pięćdziesiątkę** a man approaching fifty; **bitwa ~ Racławicami** the battle of Racławice

podać *v/p* → **podawać**

podagra *f* (*-ry*; *no pl*) podagra

podajnik *m* (*-ka*; *-ki*) TECH *papieru*: feeder

podanie *n* (*-nia*; *-nia*) **1.** (*wniosek, prośba*) application; **~ o pracę na stanowisku** *G* application for the post of; **złożyć ~ o** *A* apply for; **złożyć ~ na piśmie** file a written application, lodge a written application **2.** (*w piłce nożnej*) pass; **przejąć ~ do** *G* intercept a pass to **3.** (*w tenisie, siatkówce*) service **4. ~ ręki** handshake; **~ się do dymisji** resignation; **~ do wiadomości** announcement; **poprosił ją o ~ adresu** he asked her to give her address **5.** (*legenda*) legend; **~ o królu Popielu** the legend of King Popiel

podarować *v/p* → **darować**

podarty *adj* torn

podarun|ek *m* (*-nku*; *-nki*) gift, present; **w ~ku** as a gift

podat|ek *m* (*-tku*; *-tki*) tax; **~ek dochodowy** income tax; **~ek obrotowy** sales tax, turnover tax; **~ek od wynagrodzeń** salary tax, pay-as-you-earn tax; **~ek od wartości dodanej** value added tax, VAT; **~ek od spadku** inheritance tax; **~ek od nieruchomości** tax on real estate; **wolny od ~ku** tax-free, exempt from taxation, tax-exempt; **ściągać** (**nakładać**) **~ki** collect (levy) taxes; **podnieść ~ki** increase taxes, raise taxes; **obniżyć ~ki** cut taxes; **uchylanie się od płacenia ~ków** tax evasion; **osoba uchylająca się od płacenia ~ków** tax dodger

podatkow|y *adj* tax; **urząd ~y** tax office, *Br* Inland Revenue; **rok ~y** tax year; **oszustwo ~e** tax fraud; **zeznanie ~e** tax return; **podatnik** *m* (*-ka*; *-nicy*) tax payer

podatność *f* (*-ści*, *no pl*): **~ na zakażenia** susceptibility to infection

podatny *adj* **1.** (*łatwo ulegający*) susceptible (**na** *A* to), prone (**na** *A* to); **~ na perswazje** (**naciski**) susceptible to persuasion (pressure); **~ na korozję** susceptible to corrosion; **~ na przeziębienia** prone to get a cold; **~ na wypadki** accident-prone **2.** (*odpowiedni*) **trafić na ~ grunt** find favourable conditions

podawać ⟨**-dać**⟩ (*-daję*) **1.** (*dawać*) **~ sobie ręce** shake hands; **~ komuś ogień** give s.o. a light; **~ komuś płaszcz** help s.o. on with a coat; **~ dalej** pass on; **~ jako powód** *G* give as the reason for; **możecie sobie podać ręce** *fig* you can shake hands, you are all the same; **~ komuś pomocną dłoń** *fig* lend s.o. a helping hand **2.** *cenę*: quote **3.** *lek*: administer **4.** *przykład*, *adres*, *termin*: give **5.** *szczegóły*: give, provide **6.** *warunki*: lay down **7.** *dania*, *napoje*, *obiad*: serve; **~ do stołu** serve at table **8.** *wyniki*: announce; **~ do wiadomości** announce **9.** *sól*, *piłkę*: pass **10. ~ do sądu** sue; **podawać się 1.** pass oneself off (**za** *A* as) **2. ~ się do dymisji** resign

podaż *f* (*-ży*; *no pl*) ECON supply; **nadwyżka ~y** excess supply; **prawo popytu i ~y** law of supply and demand

podążać ⟨**-żyć**⟩ (*-żam*) *lit* follow (**za** *I* s.o.); **~ z pomocą** come to help, offer help

podbarwiać ⟨**-wić**⟩ (*-wiam*) give a little colouring, colour slightly

podbiał *m* (*-łu*; *-ły*) BIOL coltsfoot

podbicie *n* (*-cia*; *-cia*) **1.** ANAT instep **2.** *ubrania*: lining

podbić *v/p* → **podbijać**

podbieg|ać ⟨**-biec**⟩ (*-gam*) run (**do** *G* up to), catch up; **~ać do drzwi** run up to the door; **piwnica ~ła wodą** there's water in the basement

podbiegł|y *adj*: **oczy ~e krwią** bloodshot eyes

podbiegunow|y *adj* GEOGR polar; **koło ~e północne** the Arctic Circle, **koło ~e południowe** the Antarctic Circle; **północna strefa ~a** the northern po-

P

lar regions; ***południowa strefa ~a*** the southern polar regions

podbierać ⟨**-debrać**⟩ (*-ram*) pilfer, filch (***coś*** *D* s.th. from); ***~ pieniądze z kasy*** pilfer money from the till

podbierak *m* (*-ka*; *-ki*) landing net

podbijać ⟨**-bić**⟩ (*-jam*) **1.** *państwo*: conquer **2.** *fig* win; ***podbiła jego serce*** she won his heart **3.** *piłkę*: loft, lob **4.** *cenę*: bid up, push up **5.** *buty*: sole **6.** *kurtkę*: line **7.** *legitymację*: stamp **8.** ***podbić komuś oko*** give s.o. a black eye

podbit|y *adj kraj*: conquered; ***~e ludy*** subject peoples; ***~e oko*** black eye

podbój *m* (*-boju*; *-boje*) conquest

podbramkow|y *adj* **1.** *SPORT happening in the goal area* **2.** (*krytyczny*) ***sytuacja ~a*** emergency situation; ***być w ~ej sytuacji*** be in the soup

podbródek *m* (*-dka*; *-dki*) chin

podbrzusze *n* (*-sza*; *-sza*) *ANAT* hypogastrium

podbudowa *f* (*-wy*; *-wy*) *BUILD* underpinning

podbudowywać ⟨**-dować**⟩ (*-dowuję*) **1.** *BUILD* underpin **2.** (*dokumentować*) *fig* substantiate, underpin; ***~ wywód argumentami*** underpin an exposition with arguments **3.** ***~ kogoś*** egg s.o. on, raise s.o.'s spirits

podburzać ⟨**-rzyć**⟩ (*-rzam*) incite (***przeciw*** *D* against, ***do*** *G* to)

podchmielony *adj infml* tipsy, stewed

podchody *pl* (*-dów*) **1.** (*zabawa*) hare and hounds **2.** (*podstępy*) *fig* subterfuge *sing* **3.** (*w łowiectwie*) stalking *sing*

podchodzić ⟨**-dejść**⟩ (*-dzę*) **1.** (*zbliżać się*) approach (***do*** *G*); ***~ do lądowania*** approach to land; ***~ do egzaminu*** take an exam; ***~ pod górę*** go uphill; ***serce podeszło mi do gardła*** I had my heart in my mouth **2.** (*o wodzie*) come (***do*** *G* up to); ***~ wilgocią*** become wet **3.** (*nabierać*) take in, trick **4.** (*traktować*) treat (***do*** *G* s.o.) **5.** (*w łowiectwie*) stalk

podchorąży *m* (*-żego*; *-żowie*) army cadet

podchować *v/p* → ***podchowywać***

podchowany *adj dziecko*: fairly big

podchowywać ⟨**-chować**⟩ (*-chowuję*) *dziecko, zwierzę: look after in the first stages of growth*

podchwycić *v/p* → ***podchwytywać***

podchwytliw|y *adj*: ***~e pytanie*** trick question

podchwytywać ⟨**-chwycić**⟩ (*-tuję*) **1.** *spojrzenie*: catch s.o.'s eye **2.** *temat*: pick up on; ***~ śpiew*** join in the singing

podciąć *v/p* → ***podcinać***

podciągać ⟨**-gnąć**⟩ (*-gam*) **1.** *kołdrę*: pull up **2.** *poziom*: raise, improve **3.** (*zaliczyć do jednej kategorii*) include; ***podciągać się*** **1.** (*w nauce*) improve; ***musisz podciągnąć się z rosyjskiego*** you must brush up your Russian **2.** (*na rękach*) pull oneself up

podcienia *pl* (*-ni*) *ARCHIT* arcades

podcierać ⟨**-detrzeć**⟩ (*-ram*) wipe; ***~ pupę*** *infml* wipe one's bottom

podcinać ⟨**-ciąć**⟩ (*-nam*) **1.** (*włosy*) trim **2.** (*gałęzie*) prune **3.** ***~ sobie żyły*** slash one's wrists **4.** ***~ komuś skrzydła*** *fig* clip s.o.'s wings; ***~ komuś nogi*** trip s.o. up

podciśnienie *n* (*-nia*; *no pl*) *PHYS* subatmospheric pressure, pressure below atmospheric

podczas **I** *prep* (*G*) during **II** *conj* ***~ gdy*** **a)** while **b)** (*natomiast*) whereas

podczerwon|y *adj* infrared; ***promieniowanie ~e*** infrared radiation

poddać *v/p* → ***poddawać***

poddany *m* (*-nego*; *-ni*) *HIST* subject; **poddańcz|y** *adj*: ***obowiązki ~e*** serf's duties

poddasz|e *n* (*-sza*; *-sza*) attic, loft; ***na ~u*** in the loft

poddawać ⟨**-dać**⟩ (*-daję*) **1.** surrender **2.** (*podpowiadać*) suggest **3.** ***~ działaniu pary*** steam; ***~ fermentacji*** ferment; ***~ próbie*** put to the test; ***~ krytyce*** subject to criticism; ***~ pod dyskusję*** bring for discussion; ***poddawać się*** **1.** surrender **2.** (*ulegać działaniu*) give in **3.** *leczeniu*: undergo **4.** (*rezygnować*) give up

poddostawca *m* (*-cy*; *-cy*) subsupplier

pode: ***~ mną*** under me; → ***pod***

podebrać *v/p* → ***podbierać***

podejmować ⟨**-djąć**⟩ (*-muję*) **1.** *ryzyko*: take; ***~ środki ostrożności*** take precautions; ***~ odpowiednie kroki*** take the necessary steps **2.** *walkę*: engage (in) **3.** *pracę*: take up **4.** *dyskusję*: start **5.** *temat*: pick up **6.** *gości*: receive;

~ kogoś *I* treat s.o. to **7.** *uchwałę*: adopt, pass **8.** *pieniądze*: withdraw **9.** (*podnosić*) *lit* pick up **10. ~ starania** make an effort; **~ decyzję** make a decision, take a decision; **podejmować się** undertake; **~ się zadania** take on a task; ***miejscowa firma podjęła się wykonania tej pracy*** a local business undertook the work
podejrzany I *adj* **1.** suspected; ***być ~m o*** *A* be suspected of; ***być ~m o szpiegostwo*** be suspected of espionage **2.** (*dziwny*) strange **II** *m* (*-nego*; *-ni*), **-na** *f* (*-nej*; *-ne*) suspect
podejrzeć *v/p* → ***podglądać***
podejrze|nie *n* (*-nia*; *-nia*) suspicion; ***~nie zapalenia płuc*** suspicion of pneumonia; ***wzbudzić ~nie*** arouse suspicions; ***nabrać ~ń*** become suspicious; ***nie mieć żadnych ~ń*** have no suspicions
podejrzewa|ć *v/im* (*-wam*) **1.** suspect (**o** *A* of); ***policja ~ go o dwa zamachy bombowe*** the police suspect him of carrying out two bomb attacks **2.** (*przypuszczać*) suppose; ***nigdy bym cię o to nie ~ł*** I would have never expected that of you
podejrzliwość *f* (*-ści*; *no pl*) mistrust; **podejrzliwy** *adj* suspicious, mistrustful; ***być ~m wobec*** *G* be suspicious of
podejści|e *n* (*-cia*; *-cia*) **1.** (*pod górę*) climb **2.** *fig* approach (**do** *G* to), attitude (**do** *G* to); ***w pierwszym ~u, przy pierwszym ~u*** at the first attempt
podejść *v/p* → ***podchodzić***
podekscytowany *adj* excited
podenerwowany *adj* nervous, edgy
podeprzeć *v/p* → ***podpierać***
poderwać *v/p* → ***podrywać***
poderżnąć *v/p* → ***podrzynać***
podeschnąć *v/p* → ***podsychać***
podesłać[1] *v/p* → ***podsyłać***
podesłać[2] *v/p* → ***podścielać***
podest *m* (*-tu*; *-ty*) **1.** (*dla mówcy*) podium **2.** (*między kondygnacjami*) landing
podeszły *adj wiek*: ripe; ***w ~m wieku*** advanced in age
podeszwa *f* (*-wy*; *-wy*) *buta*, *stopy*: sole
podetkać, podetknąć *v/p* → ***podtykać***
podetrzeć *v/p* → ***podcierać***
podfruwajka *f* (*-ki*; *-ki*) *hum* young lass, filly
podgardle *n* (*-la*; *-la*) COOK chap; **podgardlan|y** *adj*: ***kiszka ~a*** COOK *low quality sausage*
podgatunek *m* (*-nku*; *-nki*) BIOL subspecies
podginać ⟨**-giąć**⟩ (*-nam*) *kolana*: bend; ***podginać się*** (*o sukience*) ride up; ***podgięła ci się z tyłu sukienka*** your skirt has ridden up at the back
podglą|d *m* (*-du*; *-dy*) **1.** INF view; ***~d strony*** site view; ***~d wydruku*** print preview **2.** (*system kamer*) monitoring; ***być na ~dzie*** be under electronic surveillance, be under camera surveillance
podglądacz *m* (*-cza*; *-cze*) *infml* peeper, voyeur, Peeping Tom
podglądać ⟨**-dejrzeć**⟩ (*-dam*) peep, spy on; ***~ kogoś przez dziurkę od klucza*** peep at s.o. through the keyhole
podgłówek *m* (*-wka*; *-wki*) bolster
podgonić *v/p* (*-nię*) catch up on
podgorączkowy *adj*: ***stan ~*** MED raised temperature, subfebrile body temperature
podgórski *adj* submontane; **podgórze** *n* (*-rza*; *-rza*) foothills
podgrupa *f* (*-py*; *-py*) subgroup
podgryzać ⟨**-ryźć**⟩ (*-zam*) *korzenie*: bite
podgrzewacz *m* (*-cza*; *-cze*) heater; **podgrzewać** ⟨**-rzać**⟩ (*-wam*) heat up, warm up, warm over
podgrzybek *m* (*-bka*; *-bki*) (bay) boletus; ***~ zajączek*** yellow-cracked boletus
podhalański *adj* of Podhale (region)
podirytowany *adj*: ***~ czyimś zachowaniem*** annoyed with s.o.'s behaviour
podium *n* (*indecl*; *-dia*) **1.** (*dla orkiestry*) bandstand **2.** (*dla mówcy*) rostrum **3.** (*dla zwycięzców, dyrygenta*) podium
podjadać ⟨**-jeść**⟩ (*-dam*) **1.** *korzenie*: nibble **2.** (*jeść po trochu*) snack (between meals), munch on
podjadek *m* (*-dka*; *-dki*): ***turkuć ~*** BIOL mole cricket
podjazd *m* (*-du*; *-dy*) drive(way); **podjazdow|y** *adj*: ***wojna ~a*** guer(r)illa warfare
podjąć *v/p* → ***podejmować***
podjeść *v/p* (*-jem*): eat one's fill; → ***podjadać***

P

podjeżdżać ⟨**-jechać**⟩ (*-dżam*) come up (**do** *G* to), go (**do** *G* to); **~ pod górę** go uphill, drive uphill; **~ pod dom** arrive at the front door; **podjadę do szkoły rowerem** I'll go to school by bike

podjęcie *n* (*-cia; no pl*) *pieniędzy*: withdrawal

podjudzać ⟨**-dzić**⟩ (*-dzam*) goad (**do** *G* into doing s.th.)

podkarpacki *adj* of the Carpathians

podkasywać ⟨**-sać**⟩ (*-suję*) *nogawki, rękawy*: roll up

podklejać ⟨**-leić**⟩ (*-jam*) glue (from beneath)

podkład *m* (*-du; -dy*) **1.** *farby, lakieru*: primer, priming; **~y kolejowe** *Br* sleepers, *Am* (cross) ties **2.** MUS incidental music **3.** *pod makijaż*: foundation

podkładać ⟨**-dłożyć**⟩ (*-dam*) **1. ~ coś pod spód** put s.th. under; **~ muzykę pod tekst** provide a text with background music; **~ tekst pod muzykę** set words to a tune; **~ bombę** plant a bomb; **~ ogień pod** *A* set fire to; **~ do ogniska** add some wood to the fire; **~ komuś świnię** *infml* be malicious to s.o., do the dirty on s.o. **2.** *spodnie, spódnicę*: turn up

podkładka *f* (*-ki; -ki*) **1.** TECH washer **2.** pad; **~ pod mysz** INF mouse pad **3.** (*pod naczynie*) mat; **~ pod kufel do piwa** beer mat

podkładow|y *adj*: **farba ~a** priming paint, primer

podkochiwać się *v/im* (*-chuję*) be (a little) in love (**w** *L* with)

podkolanówki *pl* (*-wek*) knee socks

podkomendny *m* (*-nego; -ni*) subordinate; **podkomisja** *f* (*-ji; -je*) subcommittee; **podkop** *m* (*-pu; -py*) tunnel

podkopywać ⟨**-pać**⟩ (*-puję*) **1.** (*usunąć ziemię*) remove earth from under s.th. **2.** *autorytet*: undermine, undercut; **podkopywać się** dig one's way (through), dig a tunnel (**do** *G* to)

podkoszulek *m* (*-lka; -lki*) *Br* vest, *Am* undershirt

podkow|a *f* (*-wy; -wy*) horseshoe; **~y pod oczami** black rings round one's eyes; **stoły ustawione w ~ę** tables (arranged) in a semicircle

podkpiwać *v/im* (*-wam*) poke fun (**z** *G* at)

podkradać ⟨**-raść**⟩ (*-dam*) swipe, steal; **podkradać się** sneak up (**do** *G* on)

podkrążon|y *adj*: **~e oczy** black rings round one's eyes

podkreślać ⟨**-lić**⟩ (*-lam*) **1.** (*przeciągnąć kreskę*) underline **2.** (*uwypuklać*) emphasize **3.** *szczupłą talię*: accentuate; **podkreślenie** *m* (*-nia; -nia*) **1.** (*zaznaczenie*) underline **2.** (*uwypuklenie*) emphasis

podkręcać ⟨**-cić**⟩ (*-cam*) **1.** *włosy*: curl **2.** *wąsa*: twist **3.** *radio*: turn up **4.** *piłkę*: give spin (to)

podkulać ⟨**-lić**⟩ (*-lam*) **1.** *nogi*: pull up **2.** *ogon*: put its tail between its legs

podkupywać ⟨**-pić**⟩ (*-puję*) outbid

podkurczać ⟨**-czyć**⟩ (*-czam*) *kolana, nogi*: pull up

podkusić *v/im* (*-szę*) tempt; **co cię podkusiło?** what came over you?

podkuty *adj koń*: shoed

podkuwać ⟨**-kuć**⟩ (*-wam*) **1.** *konia*: shoe **2.** *buty*: hobnail **3.** (*poduczyć się*) *infml* bone up (on), swot up (on)

podlać *v/p* → **podlewać**

podlatywać ⟨**-lecieć**⟩ (*-tuję*) **1.** (*o ptakach*) fly up **2.** (*podbiegać*) run up, come running **3.** (*wznosić się*) rise

podle *adv* meanly, basely

podlec *m* (*-ca; -ce*) *infml* scoundrel

podlecieć *v/p* → **podlatywać**

podleczyć *v/im* (*-czę*) *chorobę*: partly cure, improve the condition of; **podleczyć się** improve one's condition

podlegać *v/p* (*-gam*) *instytucji*: be subordinate (*D* to); **~ czyimś wpływom** be influenced by; **~ karze** *G* be under penalty of; **~ ochronie** be protected; **~ opłacie** be liable to charge; **~ opodatkowaniu** taxable; **~ ustawie** fall within an act; **~ zmianom** undergo changes; **~ obowiązkowi** be subject to an obligation; **to nie podlega dyskusji** it is beyond doubt

podległy *adj* **1.** (*niższy rangą*) subordinate (*D* to) **2.** (*o kraju*) subjugated

podlewać ⟨**-lać**⟩ (*-wam*) **1.** *kwiaty*: water **2.** COOK baste

podliczać ⟨**-czyć**⟩ (*-czam*) add up, sum up

podlizywać się ⟨**-zać**⟩ (*-zuję*) suck up (*D* to)

podlotek *m* (*-tka; -tki*) teenage girl

P

podłamać *v/p* (*-mię*) dispirit, dishearten; ***podłamać się*** be glum (*I* about)

podłączać ⟨**-czyć**⟩ (*-czam*) connect (**do** *G* to); ***podłączać się*** join; **podłączenie** *n* (*-nia*; *-nia*) connection

podłoga *f* (*-gi*; *-gi*) floor; **podłogow|y** *adj*: ***ogrzewanie ~e*** underfloor heating; ***wykładzina ~a*** fitted carpet, carpeting

podłoś|ć *f* (*-ści*; *-ści*) **1.** (*cecha*) meanness **2.** (*postępek*) mean trick; ***dopuścić się ~ci*** commit a wicked act

podłoż|e *n* (*-ża*; *-ża*) **1.** ground; ***~e skaliste*** bedrock **2.** *fig* grounds; ***choroba o ~u nerwowym*** a nervous disorder

podłożyć *v/p* → ***podkładać***

podłużać ⟨**-żyć**⟩ (*-żam*) *ubranie*: lengthen, make longer

podłużnie *adv* lengthways, lengthwise; **podłużny** *adj* **1.** (*ciągnący się wzdłuż*) longitudinal, lengthwise; ***flet ~*** recorder; ***przekrój ~*** longitudinal (cross-)section **2.** *twarz*: oval

podłużyć *v/p* → ***podłużać***

podły *adj* **1.** *czyn*: mean, wicked **2.** (*kiepski*) lousy, wretched, rotten

podmakać ⟨**-moknąć**⟩ (*-kam*) (*o łące*) get swampy, get marshy

podmalowywać ⟨**-lować**⟩ (*-lowuję*) ground; ***podmalowywać się*** put on (a little) make-up

podmenu *m indecl* INF submenu

podmiejsk|i *adj* suburban; ***komunikacja ~a*** local transport

podminowany *adj atmosfera*: charged; **podminowywać** ⟨**-nować**⟩ (*-nowuję*) mine

podmiot *m* (*-tu*; *-ty*) **1.** GRAM subject **2.** JUR legal person, subject **3.** ***~ liryczny*** the 'I' of a poem

podmokły *adj teren*: marshy, swampy; **podmoknąć** *v/p* → ***podmakać***

podmorski *adj* submarine, undersea

podmuch *m* (*-chu*; *-chy*) gust; ***fala ~u*** blast

podmurowany *adj* BUILD underpinned; **podmurówka** *f* (*-ki*; *-ki*) BUILD underpinning, wall base

podmywać ⟨**-myć**⟩ (*-wam*) **1.** *brzeg*: undermine, wash away **2.** *chorego*: wash s.o.'s genital and anal area, wash s.o.'s private parts; ***podmywać się*** wash one's genital and anal area, wash one's private parts

podnajem *m* (*-jmu*; *no pl*) sublease, underlease; **podnajemca** *m* (*-cy*; *-cy*) subtenant; **podnajmować** ⟨**-jąć**⟩ (*-muję*) sublease, sublet

podniebieni|e *n* (*-nia*; *-nia*) ANAT palate; ***~e miękkie*** (**twarde**) soft (hard) palate; ***rozkosze ~a*** *fig* pleasures of the table, delights of the table

podniebienny *adj* palatal

podniebny *adj lit* subcelestial, sky-high

podniecać ⟨**-cić**⟩ (*-cam*) arouse, excite; ***podniecać się*** **1.** (*ekscytować się*) get excited (*I* about) **2.** (*seksualnie*) become aroused, become excited; **podniecający** *adj* exciting

podniecenie *n* (*-nia*; *no pl*) excitement, sexual arousal; **podniecony** *adj* excited, aroused, turned on

podniesienie *n* (*-nia*; *-nia*) **1.** lifting **2.** **~** REL Elevation

podnieść *v/p* → ***podnosić***

podnieta *f* (*-ty*; *-ty*) *lit* incentive, spur

podniosły *adj* elevated, solemn

podniszczony *adj ubranie*: shabby, worn-out

podnosić ⟨**-nieść**⟩ (*-szę*) **1.** *ciężar, kurtynę*: lift; ***~ na duchu*** lift s.o.'s spirits; ***~ kotwicę*** weigh anchor, raise anchor; ***~ głos*** raise one's voice; ***~ oczy*** lift one's eyes; ***~ do potęgi*** MATH raise to the power of; ***~ liczbę do kwadratu*** (**do sześcianu**) MATH square (cube) a number; ***~ rękę na*** *A* raise one's hand to, raise one's hand against; ***~ żagle*** set sail; ***~ alarm*** raise alarm **2.** *słuchawkę, z podłogi*: pick up **3.** *flagę, problem, głowę*: raise **4.** *kołnierz*: turn up **5.** *kwalifikacje*: gain **6.** *ceny*: put up, raise; ***podnosić się*** **1.** (*wstawać*) stand up, rise **2.** (*o cenach*) increase, rise **3.** (*o wietrze*) rise **4.** (*o krzyku*) be heard

podnoszenie *n* (*-nia*; *no pl*): ***~ ciężarów*** SPORT weight lifting

podnośnik *m* (*-ka*; *-ki*) AUTO elevator, lift; ***~ widłowy*** forklift

podnóż|e *n* (*-ża*; *-ża*) *góry*: foot; ***u ~a góry*** at the foot of the mountain; **podnóżek** *m* (*-żka*; *-żki*) footstool

podobać się ⟨**s-**⟩ (*-bam*) **1.** appeal (*D* to) **2.** like; ***to mi się nie podoba*** I don't like it; ***jak ci się to podoba?***

P

what do you say?; ***ile ci się (żywnie) podoba*** as much as you like
podobieństwo *n* (*-wa*; *-wa*) similarity, resemblance
podobizna *f* (*-ny*; *-ny*) effigy, image
podobnie *adv* like; **~ *jak*** just as
podobno *particle* reportedly, supposedly; ***on ~ wyjechał*** he could have left, he is said to have left; ***~ ją obraził*** he supposedly offended her
podobn|y *adj* similar (**do** *G* to); ***być ~ym do*** *G* be like, resemble; ***i tym ~e*** and the like; ***do czego to ~e?*** I never!; ***czy ~a, że*** is it possible that; ***nic ~ego!*** not at all!; ***coś ~ego!*** nothing of the sort!; ***są bardzo do siebie ~i*** they are very much alike; ***są ~i jak dwie krople wody*** they're like (two) peas in a pod
podochocony *adj* **1.** (*podpity*) tipsy, merry **2.** (*podniecony*) horny, frisky
pododdział *m* (*-łu*; *-ły*) (sub-)unit
podoficer *m* (*-ra*; *-rowie*) non-commissioned officer, non-com, NCO
podołać *v/p* (*-łam*) manage (*D*)
podomka *f* (*-ki*; *-ki*) housecoat
podopieczny *m* (*-nego*; *-ni*), **-na** *f* (*-nej*; *-ne*) charge
podorędzi|e: ***być na ~u*** be at hand
podówczas *adv lit* at the time, then
podpadać ⟨**-paść**⟩ (*-dam*) **I** *v/i* come, fall (**pod** *A* under) ***~ pod jakiś paragraf*** come under the provisions of a section **II** *v/t* ***~ komuś*** get in s.o.'s bad books
podpalacz *m* (*-cza*; *-cze*) arsonist
podpalać ⟨**-lić**⟩ (*-lam*) **I** *v/t* **1.** *dom*, *las*: set fire (to), set on fire **2.** *papierosa*: light **II** *v/i* ***~ w piecu*** make fire in the stove
podpalany *adj sierść*: bay
podpalenie *n* (*-nia*; *-nia*) arson
podpalić *v/p* → ***podpalać***
podpałk|a *f* (*-ki*; *no pl*) kindling; ***drewno na ~ę*** fire-wood
podparcie *n* (*-cia*; *no pl*) support
podpaska *f* (*-ki*; *-ki*) sanitary towel
podpaść *v/p* → ***podpadać***
podpatrywać ⟨**-trzyć**⟩ (*-ruję*) spy on; ***podpatrzyłem to u niego*** I've learned it from him, I've seen how he does it
podpełzać ⟨**-znąć**⟩ (*-zam*) **1.** (*o gadzie, owadzie*) creep (**pod** *A* up to) **2.** (*o dziecku*) crawl (**pod** *A* up to)
podpiąć *v/p* → ***podpinać***
podpić *v/im* (*-piję*): ***~ sobie*** get tipsy, get drunk
podpiekać ⟨**-piec**⟩ (*-kam*) roast briefly, sear
podpierać ⟨**-deprzeć**⟩ (*-ram*) (*wspierać*) support; ***~ ściany*** be a wallflower; ***podpierać się*** lean (**o** *A* against/on); ***~ się nosem*** be exhausted, be beat
podpinać ⟨**-piąć**⟩ (*-nam*) *włosy*: tie up;
podpin|ka *f* (*-ki*; *-ki*) **1.** *kurtki*: lining **2.** *kołdry*: duvet cover; ***na ~ce*** with the lining
podpis *m* (*-su*; *-sy*) **1.** (*autograf*) signature; ***do ~u*** to be signed **2.** *pod ilustracją*: caption; **podpisywać** ⟨**-sać**⟩ (*-suję*) *dokument*: sign; **podpisywać się** sign; ***~ się*** (***obiema rękami***) ***pod*** *I fig* subscribe to, agree totally with
podpity *adj* well oiled, tipsy
podpiwniczony *adj* BUILD (provided) with a cellar, with a basement
podpływać ⟨**-łynąć**⟩ (*-wam*) **1.** (*o człowieku*) swim (**do** *G* to) **2.** (*o łodzi*) sail (**do** *G* to)
podpora *f* (*-ry*; *-ry*) support, pillar
podporucznik *m* (*-ka*; *-nicy*) second lieutenant
podporządkowan|y *adj*: ***droga ~a*** minor road, side road; ***być ~ym*** *D* be subordinated to
podporządkowywać ⟨**-kować**⟩ (*-kowuję*) **1.** *władzy*: subordinate **2.** (*uzależniać*) subdue, subjugate; **podporządkowywać się** submit
podpowiadać ⟨**-wiedzieć**⟩ (*-dam*) **1.** (*w szkole*) prompt **2.** (*doradzać*) suggest **3.** (*szeptać*) whisper **4.** (*o intuicji, rozsądku*) tell
podpowiedź *f* (*-dzi*; *-dzi*) **1.** (*w szkole*) prompt **2.** (*wskazówka*) tip, clue
podpórka *f* (*-ki*; *-ki*) support, prop; ***~ pod sznur na bieliznę*** prop to keep the washing line up
podprowadzać ⟨**-dzić**⟩ (*-dzam*) **1.** (*towarzyszyć*) accompany (a little), take a little walk with (**do** *G* to) **2.** (*ukraść*) *infml* hook, pinch
podpucha *f* (*-chy*; *-chy*) *infml* fix, set-up
podpułkownik *m* (*-ka*; *-nicy*) lieutenant colonel
podpunkt *m* (*-tu*; *-ty*) sub-clause

podpuszczać ⟨**-puścić**⟩ (*-czam*) *infml* bully (**do** *G* into doing s.th.); **~ kogoś przeciw** *D* dare s.o. to do s.th. against, put s.o. on, set s.o. on
podpuszczka *f* (*-ki*; *no pl*) **1.** (*enzym*) rennin **2.** (*dodatek w produkcji sera*) rennet
podpuścić *v/p* → **podpuszczać**
podpytywać ⟨**-tać**⟩ (*-tuję*) sound out; **podpytywać się** ask around, sound people out
podrabiacz *m* (*-cza*; *-cze*) forger, falsifier, counterfeiter; **podrabiać** ⟨**-robić**⟩ (*-biam*) **1.** *podpis*: forge **2.** *klucze*: make a duplicate of **3.** *pieniądze, dokumenty*: counterfeit
podrapać *v/p* → **drapać**
podrasować *v/im* (*-suję*) soup up; **podrasowany** *adj* souped-up
podrastać ⟨**-rosnąć**⟩ (*-tam*) **1.** (*o dziecku*) grow up **2.** (*o włosach, rzodkiewce*) grow
podratować *v/p* (*-tuję*) (*w tarapatach*) help s.o. out, give s.o. a leg up; **~ kogoś finansowo** give s.o. a small loan
podrażać ⟨**-rożyć**⟩ (*-żam*) **1.** *koszty*: increase **2.** *towar*: raise the price of
podrażniać ⟨**-nić**⟩ (*-niam*) irritate; **podrażnienie** *n* (*-nia*; *-nia*) irritation; **podrażniony** *adj* **1.** irritated **2.** (*zdenerwowany*) vexed, irritated
podreperować *v/p* (*-ruję*) **1.** (*naprawić*) patch up, mend, fix; **~ zdrowie** get better; **~ czyjś budżet** improve s.o.'s finances **2.** *opinię*: improve, regain
podręcznik *m* (*-ka*; *-ki*) textbook; **podręczn|y** *adj bagaż*: hand; **~a apteczka** first-aid kit; **słownik ~y** concise dictionary
podrobić *v/p* → **podrabiać**
podrobiony *adj* **1.** *pieniądze, dokumenty*: counterfeit **2.** *paszport, prawo jazdy*: fake, forged **3.** *klucze*: duplicate(d)
podroby *pl* (*-bów*) COOK offal *sing*
podrosnąć *v/p* → **podrastać**
podrostek *m* (*-tka*; *-tki*) teenager
podrozdział *m* (*-łu*; *-ły*) section
podrożeć *v/p* → **drożeć**
podrożyć *v/p* → **podrażać**
podróbk|a *f* (*-ki*; *-ki*) fake, counterfeit; **~i markowej odzieży** fake designer clothing
podrównikowy *adj* equatorial
podróż *f* (*-ży*; *-że*) **1.** journey; **~ koleją** journey by train; **~ zagraniczna** journey abroad; **~ poślubna** honeymoon **2.** (*krótsza*) trip; **~ służbowa** business trip; **szczęśliwej ~y!** have a good trip! **3.** (*dłuższa*) travel; **biuro ~y** travel agency **4.** (*statkiem*) voyage
podróżnik *m* (*-ka*; *-nicy*) *Br* traveller, *Am* traveler
podróżny I *adj torba*: *Br* travelling, *Am* traveling; **czek ~** *Br* traveller's cheque, *Am* traveler's check **II** *m* (*-nego*; *-ni*), **-na** *f* (*-nej*; *-ne*) passenger
podróżować *v/im* (*-żuję*) travel (**po** *L* in/around); **~ koleją** travel by train
podrumienić *v/p* (*-nię*) roast briefly, roast golden brown
podrygi *pl* (*-gów*) *iron* twists, leaps; **ostatnie ~ a)** (*przed śmiercią*) pangs, throes **b)** (*przed dymisją*) last hurrah; **podrygiwać** *v/im* (*-guję*) (*w tańcu*) leap, hop
podrywacz *m* (*-cza*; *-cze*) woman-chaser
podrywać ⟨**-derwać**⟩ (*-wam*) **1.** (*unosić*) raise, jerk (up) **2.** *opinię, autorytet*: undermine **3.** (*uwodzić*) pick up; **podrywać się 1.** (*podskakiwać*) jump to one's feet **2.** (*o ptaku*) take wing
podrzeć *v/p* → **drzeć**
podrzędnie *adv* subordinately; **zdanie złożone ~** complex sentence; **podrzędn|y** *adj* **1.** (*mniej znaczący*) minor, secondary **2.** (*mierny*) second-rate **3.** GRAM subordinate; **zdanie ~e** subordinate clause
podrzucać ⟨**-cić**⟩ (*-cam*) **1.** (*do góry*) toss **2.** *węgla*: feed, add **3.** (*dostarczać potajemnie*) slip (**komuś** *A* s.o. s.th.) **4.** (*dostarczać*) bring; **~ kogoś do domu** (**szkoły**) give s.o. a lift home (to school)
podrzutek *m* (*-tka*; *-tki*) foundling
podrzynać ⟨**-derżnąć**⟩ (*-nam*): **~ komuś gardło** slit s.o.'s throat; **poderżnąć sobie żyły** slash one's wrists
podsadzać ⟨**-dzić**⟩ (*-dzam*) **1.** (*na mur*) help up **2.** (*na konia*) help to get on
podsądny *m* (*-nego*; *-ni*), **-na** *f* (*-nej*; *-ne*) JUR accused
podsekretarz *m* (*-rza*; *-rze*) undersecretary; **~ stanu** Undersecretary of State

podskakiwać ⟨**-skoczyć**⟩ (*-kuję*) **1.** (*do góry*) jump, leap; **~ *z radości*** jump for joy; ***podskoczyć do sklepu*** do some quick shopping; ***podskoczyć po** A* go fetch; ***podskoczę do niego*** I'll drop by him quickly; ***nie podskakuj!*** *infml* don't be so cheeky!, you'd better be careful! **2.** (*o samochodzie*) bump (along) **3.** (*o cenach*) shoot up, rocket

podskok *m* (*-ku*; *-ki*) jump, hop; ***w ~ach*** **a)** jumping **b)** *fig* hopping, on the hop

podskórn|y *adj* **1.** hypodermic **2.** *fig* skin-deep **3.** ***wody ~e*** subsoil water

podsłuch *m* (*-chu*; *-chy*) bug; ***zakładać ~ w biurze*** bug s.o.'s office; ***być na ~u*** be bugged

podsłuchiwać ⟨**-chać**⟩ (*-chuję*) **1.** (*celowo*) eavesdrop (on); **~ *pod drzwiami*** eavesdrop at the door **2.** (*przypadkiem*) overhear **3.** (*za pomocą urządzenia*) bug

podsłuchowy *adj* tapping

podsmażać ⟨**-żyć**⟩ (*-żam*) brown

podstarzały *adj* oldish, elderly

podstaw|a *f* (*-wy*; *-wy*) **1.** *BUILD* foundation **2.** (*dolna część*) base; ***~a czaszki*** *ANAT* base of the skull **3.** *pomnika*: plinth **4.** *trójkąta*: baseline **5.** *teorii*: basis; ***na ~ie** G* on the basis of **6.** (*przyczyna*) reason; ***dać ~ę do** G* give a reason for **7.** (*punkt wyjścia, założenie)* grounds *pl*; ***mieć ~ę do** G* have grounds for

podstawiać ⟨**-wić**⟩ (*-wiam*) **1.** (*podkładać*) put, place (**pod** *A* under); **~ *komuś nogę*** trip s.o. up **2.** *pociąg*: make available, put on; **~ *dodatkowe autobusy*** put on extra buses

podstawion|y *adj* ***~a osoba*** stooge

podstawka *f* (*-ki*; *-ki*) **1.** (*pod garnek*) mat **2.** (*do filiżanki*) saucer

podstawow|y *adj* basic, primary; ***szkoła ~a*** primary school, elementary school; ***badania ~e*** essential medical check-up, essential medical examination; ***~e wiadomości*** basic knowledge, elementary knowledge

podstawówka *f* (*-ki*; *-ki*) *infml* primary school, elementary school

podstemplowywać ⟨**-lować**⟩ (*-lowuję*) stamp

podstęp *m* (*-pu*; *-py*) trick; **podstępny** *adj* **1.** (*chytry*) cunning, tricky **2.** *plan*: secret

podstołeczny *adj located near the capital city*

podstrzygać ⟨**-rzyc**⟩ (*-gam*) cut s.o.'s hair (a little)

podsumowanie *f* (*-nia*; *-nia*) *fig* recapitulation, summing-up; **podsumowywać** ⟨**-mować**⟩ (*-mowuję*) **1.** (*dodać*) add up **2.** (*oceniać*) *fig* summarize, sum up; **~ *dyskusję*** sum up a discussion

podsuszać ⟨**-szyć**⟩ (*-szam*) **1.** *włosy*: dry up **2.** *pranie*, dry off

podsuwać ⟨**-sunąć**⟩ (*-wam*) **1.** (*przesuwać*) push **2.** *krzesło*: offer **3.** *myśl*: give, put into s.o.'s head; **podsuwać się** draw near (**do** *G* to)

podsycać ⟨**-cić**⟩ (*-cam*) **1.** *ogień*: fuel **2.** *nienawiść*: fan **3.** *nadzieję*: arouse, give

podsychać ⟨**-deschnąć**⟩ (*-cham*) dry a little

podsyłać ⟨**-desłać**⟩ (*-łam*) send

podszepnąć *v/p* → **podszeptywać**

podszepty *pl* (*-tów*) *fig* suggestions, instigations

podszeptywać ⟨**-pnąć**⟩ (*-tuję*) **1.** (*mówić cicho*) whisper **2.** (*doradzać*) *fig* instigate

podszew|ka *f* (*-ki*; *-ki*) *palta*: lining; ***na ~ce*** lined; ***poznać coś od ~ki*** know s.th. inside out

podszkolić *v/p* (*-lę*) train; **~ *się w** L* brush up on

podszyty *adj* lined; **~ *futrem*** fur-lined; **~ *tchórzem*** *fig* cowardly, chicken-hearted; ***wiatrem ~** kurtka*: thin

podszywać ⟨**-szyć**⟩ (*-wam*) line (*I* with); **~ *się pod** A* pretend to be

podścielać ⟨**-desłać**⟩ (*-lam*) *koc*: spread

podściółka *f* (*-ki*; *-ki*) (straw) litter

podśmiewać się *v/im* (*-wam*) scoff (**z** *G* at)

podśpiewywać *v/im* (*-piewuję*) hum (a tune)

podświadomość *f* (*-ści*; *no pl*) subconsciousness; **podświadomy** *adj* subconscious

podtekst *m* (*-tu*; *-ty*) implied meaning, deeper meaning

podtrzymywać ⟨**-mać**⟩ (*-muję*) **1.** (*wspierać*) support; **~ *kogoś na du-***

P

chu raise s.o.'s spirits **2.** *ogień*: feed **3.** *żądania*, *stosunki*: stick to **4.** *rozmowę*: maintain, keep up

podtykać ⟨**-detknąć**⟩ (*-kam*) put, place; ***~ coś komuś pod nos*** put s.th. right under s.o.'s nose

podtytuł *m* (*-łu*; *-ły*) subtitle, subheading

poducha *f* (*-chy*; *-chy*) big pillow

poduczać ⟨**-czyć**⟩ (*-czam*) **1.** give some lessons (**do** *G* in); ***~ do egzaminu*** give some lessons to prepare for the exam **2.** prepare (**do** *G* to); ***poduczać się*** **1.** improve one's knowledge (*G* of) **2.** learn some more **3.** pick up; ***~ się języka*** pick up some language

podudzie *n* (*-dzia*; *-dzia*) ANAT shank

podupadać ⟨**-paść**⟩ (*-dam*) **1.** (*marnieć*) decline, deteriorate; ***~ na duchu*** lose heart; ***ktoś podupada na zdrowiu*** s.o.'s health deteriorates; ***~ na siłach*** become weak **2.** (*materialnie*) grow poor, become impoverished

podupadły *adj* **1.** *dom*: dilapidated, rundown **2.** *materialnie*: impoverished **3.** *przedsiębiorstwo*: in decline

poduszk|a *f* (*-ki*; *-ki*) **1.** *do spania*: pillow; ***~i*** ANAT **a)** *palców*, *łap*: pads **b)** *dłoni*: palms; ***~a elektryczna*** warming cushion; ***~a powietrzna*** AUTO airbag; ***książka do ~i*** bedside book **2.** (*do stempli*) ink-pad

poduszkowiec *m* (*-wca*; *-wce*) hovercraft

podwajać ⟨**-woić**⟩ (*-jam*) double; ***podwajać się*** double

podwaliny *pl* (*-lin*) BUILD foundations; ***kłaść ~ pod*** *A fig* lay the foundations of

podważać ⟨**-żyć**⟩ (*-żam*) **1.** (*unosić*) lever; ***~ drzwi*** lift the door **2.** (*kwestionować*) challenge, question; ***nie do podważenia*** **a)** *argument*: impregnable, irrefutable **b)** *dowód*: ironclad

podwędzać ⟨**-dzić**⟩ (*-dzam*) **1.** COOK smoke (slightly) **2.** (*kraść*) *infml* pinch, nip

podwiać *v/p* → ***podwiewać***

podwiązać *v/p* → ***podwiązywać***

podwiązka *f* (*-ki*; *-ki*) garter

podwiązywać ⟨**-zać**⟩ (*-zuję*) **1.** *rośliny*: tie up **2.** *włosy*: tie **3.** MED *jajniki*: ligate, bind up

podwieczorek *m* (*-rku*; *-rki*) afternoon tea, afternoon snack

podwiewać ⟨**podwiać**⟩ **I** *v/i* (*o wietrze*) blow **II** *v/t sukienkę*: raise

podwieźć *v/p* → ***podwozić***

podwijać ⟨**-winąć**⟩ (*-jam*) **1.** *rękawy*, *spodnie*: roll up **2.** *nogi*: tuck (up) **3.** *ogon*: put between its legs

podwładny *m* (*-nego*; *-ni*), **-na** *f* (*-nej*; *-ne*) subordinate, underling

podwodn|y *adj* underwater; ***łódź ~a*** submarine

podwoić *v/p* → ***podwajać***

podwoje *pl* (*-woi*/*-jów*) *lit* (double) door *sing*; ***otworzyć swoje ~ przed*** *I fig* open the doors to

podwozić ⟨**-wieźć**⟩ (*-wożę*) give a lift

podwozie *n* (*-zia*; *-zia*) **1.** AUTO chassis **2.** (*w samolocie*) undercarriage

podwójn|y *adj porcja*, *zwycięzca*: double; ***~e obywatelstwo*** dual nationality, dual citizenship; ***~e łóżko*** double bed; ***~y agent*** double agent; ***gra ~a*** SPORT doubles; ***~a gra*** *fig* double game

podwórko *n* (*-ka*; *-ka*), **podwórze** *n* (*-rza*; *-rza*) (back)yard; ***na podwórku*** outdoors, in the open (air), outside

podwyżka *f* (*-ki*; *-ki*) *Br* rise, *Am* raise; ***~ płac*** pay rise; ***~ cen*** price increase

podwyższać ⟨**-szyć**⟩ (*-szam*) raise; ***podwyższać się*** increase

podwyższenie *n* (*-nia*; *-nia*) platform

podyktować *v/p* → ***dyktować***

podyplomow|y *adj*: ***studia ~e*** postgraduate studies

podyskutować *v/p* (*-tuję*) discuss (**o** *L*)

podzelować *v/p* (*-luję*) (re)sole

podziać *v/p* → ***podziewać***

podział *m* (*-łu*; *-ły*) division; ***~ administracyjny*** administrative division; ***~ godzin*** timetable; ***~ komórki*** BIOL cytokinesis; ***~y społeczne*** social divisions

podziałać *v/p* (*-łam*) **1.** (*mieć wpływ*) have an effect (**na** *A* on) **2.** (*poskutkować*) to work (**na** *A* against)

podziałka *f* (*-ki*; *-ki*) scale

podzielać ⟨**-lić**⟩ (*-lam*) *zdanie*, *opinię*: share

podzielić *v/p* → ***dzielić***

podzieln|y *adj* divisible; ***mieć ~ą uwagę*** be able to divide one's attention

podziemie *n* (*-mia*; *-mia*) **1.** (*piwnica*) vaults *pl* **2.** POLIT underground; **pod-**

ziemn|y *adj* underground; ***wody ~e*** underground water
podziewać ⟨**-dziać**⟩ (*-wam*) (*zagubić*) mislay; ***podziewać się* 1.** (*o rzeczy*) be mislaid; ***gdzie się podział twój zapał?*** what happened to your enthusiasm? **2.** (*o osobie*) get lost; ***gdzie on się podziewa?*** where is he nowadays?; ***nie mieć gdzie się podziać*** have nowhere to go
podzięk|ka *f* (*-ki*; *no pl*) *lit* thanks *pl*; ***słowa ~ki*** words of thanks; ***w ~ce*** by way of thanks; **podziękowani|e** *n* (*-nia*; *-nia*) thanks *pl*, gratitude; ***~e pisemne*** thank-you letter; ***słowa ~a*** words of thanks
podziurawiony *adj* perforated, full of holes
podziw *m* (*-wu*; *no pl*) admiration; ***nad ~*** admirably; ***godny ~u*** admirable; ***nie móc wyjść z ~u*** be lost in admiration; **podziwiać** *v/im* (*-wiam*) admire
podzwrotnikowy *adj* subtropical
podźwigać ⟨**-gnąć**⟩ (*-gam*) **1.** (*podnieść*) lift, heave **2.** (*z ruin*) restore, rebuild; ***podźwigać się*** stagger to one's feet, pull oneself up
podżegacz *m* (*-cza*; *-cze*), **~ka** *f* (*-ki*; *-ki*) instigator; ***~ wojenny*** warmonger
podżegać *v/im* (*-gam*) incite, put up (**do** *G* to); ***~ do wojny*** incite to war
poemat *m* (*-tu*; *-ty*) poem
poeta *m* (*-ty*; *poeci*) poet, **poetka** *f* (*-ki*; *-ki*) poetess, poet
poetycki *adj* **1.** *talent*, *proza*: poetic; ***wieczór ~*** poetry reading, poetry evening **2.** *nastrój*: lyrical; **poetyczny** *adj lit* poetic, poetical; **poezj|a** *f* (*-zji*; *no pl*) poetry; ***~e*** poems
pofałdowany *adj* **1.** *teren*: undulating **2.** *skóra*: wrinkled
pofatygować się *v/p* → ***fatygować się***
pofrunąć *v/p* → ***frunąć***
pogadać *v/p* → ***gadać***
pogadanka *f* (*-ki*; *-ki*) lecture, (less formal) talk; **pogaduszki** *pl* (*-szek*) *infml* chit-chat *sing*; ***zajść na ~*** come round to chat about this and that
poganiać ⟨**-gonić**⟩ (*-niam*) **1.** (*osobę*) urge, rush; ***~ kogoś do pracy*** urge s.o. to work **2.** *zwierzę*: drive
poganin *m* (*-na*; *-ganie*), **-nka** *f* (*-ki*; *-ki*) pagan, heathen; **pogański** *adj* pagan, heathen; **pogaństwo** *n* (*-wa*; *no pl*) heathenism, heathenry, paganism
pogar|da *f* (*-dy*; *no pl*) contempt; ***godny ~dy*** contemptible; ***mieć w ~dzie*** hold in contempt; **pogardliwie** *adv* contemptuously, scornfully; **pogardliwy** *adj* contemptuous, scornful
pogardzać ⟨**-dzić**⟩ (*-dzam*) despise, scorn (*I*)
pogarszać ⟨**-gorszyć**⟩ (*-szam*) *stosunki*, *położenie*: worsen; ***to tylko pogorszy sprawę*** it will only make things worse; ***pogarszać się*** (*o stanie zdrowia*, *pogodzie*) deteriorate; ***pogorszyło mu się*** his condition has deteriorated
pogawędka *f* (*-ki*; *-ki*) chat, chit-chat
pogląd *m* (*-du*; *-dy*) opinion, view; ***~ na świat*** outlook on life, philosophy of life; ***wymiana ~ów*** exchange of opinions
poglądowo *adv* visually
poglądow|y *adj* demonstrative, visual; ***lekcja ~a*** visual instruction, hands-on lesson
pogłębiać ⟨**-bić**⟩ (*-biam*) **1.** *dół*: deepen **2.** *rzekę*, *port*: dredge **3.** *wiedzę*: broaden, extend
pogłębiarka *f* (*-ki*; *-ki*) dredger; **pogłębienie** *n* (*-nia*; *no pl*) deepening
pogłos *m* (*-su*; *-sy*) echo, reverberation
pogłoska *f* (*-ki*; *-ki*) rumour
pogmatwany *adj* complicated, complex, intricate
pogłowie *n* (*-wia*; *no pl*) *bydła*: stock, (livestock) population
pognać *v/p* → ***gnać***
pogniewać się *v/p* → ***gniewać się***
pogod|a *f* (*-dy*; *no pl*) weather; ***mieć ~ę*** have fair weather, have nice weather; ***brzydka ~a*** nasty weather, foul weather; ***~a ducha* a)** (*nastrój*) cheerfulness, high spirits **b)** (*spokój*) serenity
pogodny *adj* **1.** *dzień*: sunny, clear **2.** *osoba*: cheerful, optimistic; ***w ~m nastroju*** cheerful, in high spirits; **pogodowy** *adj* weather
pogodynka *f* (*-ki*; *-ki*) weather report service, weather information (*phone service*)
pogodzeni|e *n* (*-nia*; *no pl*) reconciliation; ***nie do ~a z*** *I* not to be recon-

P

ciled with; ***różnice poglądów nie do ~a*** irreconcilable differences of opinion

pogodzić *v/p* → ***godzić***

pogonić *v/p* → ***poganiać***

pogoń *f* (*-goni*; *-gonie*) **1.** (*pościg*) chase, pursuit **2.** (*grupa ścigających*) persecutors, pursuers; ***~ za*** *I fig* hunt(ing) for; ***~ za sensacją*** sensationalism

pogorszenie (się) *n* (*-nia*; *no pl*) deterioration

pogorszyć *v/p* → ***pogarszać***

pogorzelec *m* (*-lca*; *-lcy*) victim of a fire; **pogorzelisko** *n* (*-ka*; *-ka*) site of a fire, fire site

pogotowi|e *n* (*-wia*; *no pl*) **1.** (*ratunkowe*) ambulance service **2.** (*samochód*) ambulance **3.** (*stan gotowości*) readiness; ***być w ~u*** be on the alert; ***~e drogowe*** breakdown emergency service; ***~e górskie*** mountain rescue service; ***~e strajkowe*** strike readiness; ***mieć coś w ~u*** have s.th. (at the) ready, have s.th. to hand

pogórze *n* (*-rza*; *-rza*) foothills

pogranicz|e *n* (*-cza*; *-cza*) borderland, frontier area, border area; ***na ~u*** on the border; **pograniczny** *adj* border

pogrąż|ać ⟨***-żyć***⟩ (*-żam*) (bring about the) ruin (of); ***jego zeznania ~yły mnie zupełnie*** his testimony brought about my ruin; ***pogrążać się*** sink (***w*** *L* in); ***~ać się materialnie*** become impoverished; ***~ać się w bólu*** (***rozpaczy***) lose oneself in anguish (despair)

pogrążony *adj fig* sunk (***w*** *L* in); ***~ w żalu*** the bereaved, in despair; ***~ w lekturze*** (***rozmyślaniach***) immersed in reading (one's thoughts); ***~ w rozmowie*** engrossed in conversation

pogrobowiec *m* (*-wca*; *-wcy*) **1.** (*urodzony po śmierci ojca*) posthumous child **2.** (*naśladowca*) epigone

pogrom *m* (*-mu*; *-my*) **1.** (*klęska*) (total) defeat **2.** (*masowy mord*) pogrom, massacre

pogromca *m* (*-cy*; *-cy*), **-czyni** *f* (*-ni*; *-nie*) conqueror, winner; ***~ zwierząt*** tamer

pogróżka *f* (*-ki*; *-ki*) threat; ***list z ~mi*** threatening letter

pogrubiać ⟨***-bić***⟩ (*-biam*) (*o ubraniu*) make (look) thicker

pogryziony *adj* **1.** (*przez psa, komary*) bitten **2.** (*przez mole*) eaten

pogryźć *v/p* → ***gryźć***

pogrzeb *m* (*-bu*; *-by*) **1.** funeral, burial **2.** (*kondukt*) funeral procession

pogrzebacz *m* (*-cza*; *-cze*) poker

pogrzebać *v/p* → ***grzebać***

pogrzebow|y *adj* funeral; ***zakład ~y*** undertaker's, *Br* funeral parlour, *Am* funeral parlor; ***uroczystości ~e*** the funeral; ***~a mina*** long face; ***mowa ~a*** funeral oration

pogubić się *v/p* → ***gubić się***

pogwałcenie *n* (*-nia*; *no pl*) breach, violation; ***~ prawa*** breach of the law; **pogwałcić** *v/p* → ***gwałcić***

pogwar *m* (*-ru*; *-ry*) *lit* din

pogwizdywać *v/im* (*-duję*) whistle

pohamować *v/p* → ***hamować***

poić ⟨***na-, u-***⟩ (*poję*) **1.** *zwierzęta*: water **2.** ***~ wódką*** ply with vodka

poinformować *v/p* → ***informować***; **poinformowany** *adj*: ***dobrze ~*** well-informed; ***źle ~*** ill-informed

poinstruować *v/p* → ***instruować***

poirytować *v/p* (*-tuję*) annoy; **poirytowany** *adj* annoyed (*I* at/with)

pojawiać się ⟨***-wić***⟩ (*-wiam*) **1.** appear **2.** (*o osobie*) turn up, show up **3.** (*o słońcu*) come out **4.** (*wyłaniać się*) emerge

pojazd *m* (*-du*; *-dy*) vehicle; ***~ kosmiczny*** spacecraft; ***~ jednośladowy*** two-wheeled vehicle

pojąć *v/p* → ***pojmować***

pojechać *v/p* (*-jadę*) go; ***~ na urlop*** go on holidays; ***~ pociągiem*** go by train → ***jechać***

pojednać się *v/p* (*-nam*) make peace (***z*** *I* with); **pojednanie** *n* (*-nia*; *-nia*) reconciliation; **pojednawczy** *adj* conciliatory

pojedyncz|y *adj* single; ***gra ~a*** SPORT singles; ***liczba ~a*** GRAM the singular; ***~y przypadek*** isolated case

pojedynek *m* (*-nku*; *-nki*) duel

pojedynk|a: ***w ~ę*** alone, single-handedly

pojedynkować się *v/im* (*-kuję*) duel

pojemnik *m* (*-ka*; *-ki*) container; ***~ na śmieci*** *Br* dustbin, rubbish bin, *Am* garbage can, trashcan

pojemność *f* (*-ści*; *no pl*) *butelki*: capacity; ***~ pamięci*** INF storage capac-

P

ity, available memory; ~ ***skokowa*** *AUTO* (engine) cubic capacity
pojemny *adj* capacious, voluminous
pojezierze *n* (*-rza*; *-rza*) lake district
pojęci|e *n* (*-cia*; *-cia*) concept, notion; ***nie do ~a*** incomprehensible, incredible; ***nie mam ~a*** I haven't (got) a clue; ***nie mieć zielonego ~a*** not have the slightest idea; **pojęciowy** *adj* conceptual
pojękiwać *v/im* (*-kuję*) groan, moan (a little)
pojętność *f* (*-ści*; *no pl*) grasp, intelligence; **pojętny** *adj* quick-witted, clever
pojmować ⟨**pojąć**⟩ (*-muję*) comprehend
pojutrze *adv* the day after tomorrow
pokarm *m* (*-mu*; *-my*) **1.** (*jedzenie*) food **2.** (*mleko matki*) (mother's) milk **3.** (*dla zwierząt*) fodder; **pokarmow|y** *adj* food; ***przewód ~y*** *ANAT* alimentary canal; ***zatrucie ~e*** food poisoning
pokaz *m* (*-zu*; *-zy*) show, display; ***~ mody*** fashion show; ***~ filmu*** showing, viewing; ***na ~*** for show
pokazow|y *adj* **1.** (*wzorowy*) showcase; ***egzemplarz ~y*** demonstration model; ***lekcja ~a*** demonstration lesson; ***proces ~y*** show trial **2.** (*bardzo dobry*) model, exemplary
pokazywać ⟨**-zać**⟩ (*-zuję*) show; ***nie ~ po sobie*** *G* not show, keep a stiff upper lip; ***~ pazurki*** show one's claws, show one's teeth; ***pokazać komuś drzwi*** show s.o. the door; ***pokazać komuś, gdzie raki zimują*** show s.o. what's what; ***ja ci pokażę!*** that'll teach you!; ***pokazywać się*** **1.** (*być obecnym*) show up; ***nie ~ się na oczy*** stay away **2.** (*odwiedzać*) come by, come round; ***~ się z najlepszej strony*** show one's best side, present oneself to the best advantage
pokaźny *adj* **1.** (*znaczny*) substantial, considerable **2.** *ilość*: fair
pokątny *adj* **1.** (*nielegalny*) unlicensed, illicit **2.** (*potajemny*) secret
poker *m* (*-ra*; *no pl*) poker; **pokerzyst|a** *m* (*-ty*; *-rzyści*) poker player; ***twarz ~y*** *fig* poker face
pokiereszowany *adj* **1.** (*ranny*) badly wounded, with multiple injuries **2.** *rzecz*: damaged

P

pokierować *v/p* → ***kierować***
pokiwać *v/p* → ***kiwać***
poklask *m* (*-ku*; *no pl*) *fig* applause; ***szukać ~u*** look for applause
poklepywać ⟨**-pać**⟩ (*-puję*) pat; ***~ kogoś po ramieniu*** pat s.o.'s shoulder, give s.o. a pat on the shoulder; ***~ kogoś po plecach*** pat s.o. on the back
pokła|d *m* (*-du*; *-dy*) **1.** *statku*: deck; ***na ~dzie*** aboard **2.** *MIN* bed; ***~dy*** (*warstwa*) strata
pokładać *v/m* (*-dam*): ***~ nadzieję*** put one's hope (***w*** *L* in); ***pokładać się*** **1.** (*zginać się*) bend **2.** (*kłaść się*) lie down, keep lying down; ***~ się ze śmiechu*** roll about laughing, double up with laughter
pokładowy *adj* **1.** *komputer*: on-board **2.** *ładunek*: on-deck **3.** *kabina*: deck; ***dziennik ~*** log(book)
pokłaść *v/p* (*-adę*) put; ***~ dzieci spać*** put the children to sleep; ***pokłaść się*** → ***pokładać się***
pokłon *m* (*-nu*; *-ny*) bow; ***oddać komuś ~*** make a deep bow to, bow down (deeply) before
pokłonić się *v/p* (*-nię*) take a bow, bow; → ***kłaniać się***
pokłosie *n* (*-sia*; *-sia*) *lit* aftermath
pokłócić *v/p* (*-cę*) divide, turn against each other; ***pokłócić się*** fall out, quarrel
pokłuć *v/p* (*-łuję*) **1.** (*pogryźć*, *użądlić*) bite all over **2.** *igłą*, *cierniem*: puncture, prick **3.** (*dźgnąć nożem*) stab (many times)
pokochać *v/p* (*-cham*) **1.** fall for, fall in love with **2.** *miasto*, *pracę*: grow very fond of, become attached to; ***pokochać się*** fall in love with each other
pokoik *m* (*-ka*; *-ki*) *dim* little room; ***~ dla dzieci*** children's room, nursery
pokojowo *adv* **1.** (*nastawiony*) peacefully **2.** (*współistnieć*) peaceably
pokojow|y[1] *adj* **1.** *POLIT* peaceful; ***misja ~a*** peace mission **2.** *atmosfera*: friendly **3.** *osoba*: peaceable
pokojow|y[2] *adj* room; ***malarz ~y*** house painter; ***temperatura ~a*** room temperature
pokojówka *f* (*-ki*; *-ki*) maid
pokolenie *n* (*-nia*; *-nia*) generation; ***konflikt pokoleń*** generation gap; ***młode ~*** rising generation

pokonani|e *n* (*-nia*; *no pl*) **1.** *trudności*: overcoming **2.** *przeciwnika*: defeat; ***nie do ~a*** **a)** *osoba*: unbeatable **b)** *armia*: invincible **c)** *trudność*, *przeszkoda*: insurmountable, insuperable

pokonan|y **I** *adj* defeated **II** *m* (*-nego*; *-konani*), **-na** *f* (*-nego*; *-konani*) defeated, beaten; ***uznać się za ~ego*** admit defeat

pokonywać ⟨**-nać**⟩ (*-nuję*) **1.** *wroga*: defeat **2.** *rywali*: beat **3.** *strach*, *nieśmiałość*: overcome **4.** *odległość*: cover **5.** *fale*: breast

pokor|a *f* (*-ry*; *no pl*) humility; ***z ~ą*** humbly; **pokornieć** ⟨**s-**⟩ (*-nieję*) grow humble; **pokorny** *adj* humble

pokos *m* (*-su*; *-sy*) **1.** (*skoszony pas*) swath(e) **2.** (*zbiór zboża*) crop

pokost *m* (*-tu*; *-ty*) varnish; **pokostować** *v/im* (*-tuję*) varnish

pokój[1] *m* (*-koju*; *no pl*) **1.** peace; ***zawrzeć ~*** make peace; ***ruch na rzecz pokoju*** peace movement; ***~ z wami!*** REL may peace be with you!; ***niech spoczywa w pokoju!*** REL may (s)he rest in peace! **2.** (*umowa*) peace treaty

pokój[2] *m* (*-koju*; *-koje*) room; ***~ dzienny*** sitting room, living room; ***~ stołowy*** dining-room; ***~ gościnny*** guestroom; ***~ dziecinny*** children's room, nursery; ***~ do pracy*** study; ***~ sypialny*** bedroom; ***~ hotelowy*** hotel room; ***~ z widokiem na morze*** room overlooking the sea, room with a sea view; ***~ nauczycielski*** staffroom; ***~ do wynajęcia*** room to let

pokpić *v/p* (*-pię*): ***~ sprawę*** bungle, mess it up

pokpiwać *v/im* (*-wam*) make fun (**z** *G* of)

pokraczny *adj* misshapen, deformed; **pokraka** *f* (*-ki*; *-ki*) hideous person, freak, monster

pokrewieństwo *n* (*-wa*; *no pl*) **1.** (*w rodzinie*) kinship; ***łączy nas bliskie*** (***dalekie***) ***~*** we are closely (distantly) related **2.** BIOL CHEM affinity **3.** *języków*: cognation; **pokrewn|y** *adj* related (*D* to); ***wyrazy ~e*** cognates; ***~e dusze*** kindred spirits, soul mates

pokręcić *v/p* (*-cę*) **1.** *gałką*: turn (for a while) **2.** *nitki*, *fakty*: muddle up; ***pokręcić się*** spin; ***~ się po*** *L* go around, walk around; ***~ się na karuzeli*** ride on a roundabout, ride on a merry-go-round

pokrętło *n* (*-ła*; *-ła*) **1.** (*do ustawiania głośności*) knob **2.** (*zaworu*) handwheel

pokrętny *adj* **1.** (*niezrozumiały*) confusing, complicated **2.** (*skomplikowany*, *nieprawdziwy*) twisted

pokroić *v/p* → **kroić**

pokropić *v/p* → **kropić**

pokrowiec *m* (*-wca*; *-wce*) **1.** *na fotel*: cover **2.** case; ***~ na gitarę*** guitar case

pokrój *m* (*-roju*; *-roje*) **1.** BIOL habit **2.** (*typ*) sort, kind; ***ludzie tego pokroju*** people of this sort

pokrótce *adv* briefly

pokryci|e *n* (*-cia*; *-cia*) **1.** *mebli*: upholstery **2.** (*na dachu*) roofing **3.** FIN cover; ***czek bez ~a*** bounced cheque; ***obietnice bez ~a*** empty promises

pokryć *v/p* → **pokrywać**

po kryjomu *adv* secretly

pokrywa *f* (*-wy*; *-wy*) **1.** (*wieko*) lid; ***~ lodu*** ice cover, ice cap **2.** TECH cover

pokrywać ⟨**-ryć**⟩ (*-wam*) **1.** (*osłaniać*) cover (*I* with); ***~ farbą*** paint, cover with paint **2.** (*materiałem*) upholster (*I* with) **3.** *koszty*: bear, cover **4.** *rachunek*: foot **5.** *długi*: pay **6.** (*o kurzu*, *lodzie*) cover **7.** BIOL cover, mount; ***pokrywać się*** **1.** (*zostać pokrytym*) be covered **2.** (*być zbieżnym*) correspond **3.** (*zachodzić na siebie*) overlap **4.** ***pokryć się*** hide; ***wszyscy się gdzieś pokryli*** all people are hiding somewhere

pokrywka *f* (*-ki*; *-ki*) *garnka*: lid

pokrzepiać ⟨**-pić**⟩ (*-piam*) **1.** (*wzmocnić*) fortify **2.** (*zachęcić*) encourage; ***pokrzepiać się*** fortify oneself (*I* with); ***~ się na duchu*** comfort oneself; ***~ się myślą o*** *L* be heartened by the thought of

pokrzepiający *adj* **1.** *trunek*: fortifying, refreshing **2.** *myśl*, *słowa*, *wiadomości*: encouraging, comforting **3.** *sen*, *prysznic*, *napój*: refreshing; **pokrzepienie** *n* (*-nia*; *no pl*) **1.** (*wzmocnienie*) invigoration **2.** (*pocieszenie*) comfort

pokrzyk *m* (*-ku*; *-ki*): ***~ wilcza jagoda*** BIOL deadly nightshade

P

pokrzykiwać *v/im* (*-kuję*) shout (every now and then); **~ na** *A* shout at, yell at
pokrzywa *f* (*-wy*; *-wy*) (stinging) nettle
pokrzywdzony **I** *adj* wronged **II** *m* (*-nego*; *-dzeni*), **-na** *f* (*-nej*; *-ne*) *JUR* aggrieved party
pokrzywka *f* (*-ki*; *no pl*) *MED* nettlerash, urticaria
pokrzywowy *adj* urticaceous
pokupny *adj towar*: sal(e)able, marketable, fast-selling
pokusa *f* (*-sy*; *-sy*) temptation
pokusić się *v/p* (*-szę*) attempt, venture (**o** *A* to do s.th.); ***pokusił się o napisanie książki*** he attempted to write a book
pokuszenie *n* (*-nia*; *no pl*) *REL* temptation
pokut|a *f* (*-ty*; *-ty*) *REL* penance; ***odprawiać ~ę*** do penance; ***w ramach ~y*** as a penance; **pokutnik** *m* (*-ka*; *-nicy*) penitent
pokutować ⟨**od-**⟩ (*-tuję*) *REL* do penance (**za** *A* for); ***wciąż pokutuje przekonanie, że*** there is a die-hard belief that
pokwapić się *v/p* → ***kwapić się***
pokwitanie *n* (*-nia*; *no pl*) puberty
pokwitowanie *n* (*-nia*; *-nia*) receipt, confirmation; ***odebrać coś za ~m*** confirm the receipt of
polać *v/p* → ***polewać***
Polak *m* (*-ka*; *-lacy*) Pole; ***jest ~iem*** he's Polish
polakierować *v/p* → ***lakierować***
polana *f* (*-ny*; *-ny*) clearing, glade
polano *n* (*-na*; *-na*) billet
polarn|y *adj* polar; ***zorza ~a*** aurora borealis, northern lights; ***noc ~a*** polar night; ***Gwiazda :a*** the Pole Star
pole *n* (*-la*; *-la*) **1.** field; ***~ bitwy*** battlefield; ***~ namiotowe*** campsite, camping ground; ***~ naftowe*** oilfield; ***~ orne*** farmland; ***~ widoczności*** field of view; ***~ karne*** *SPORT* penalty area; ***~ do popisu*** room to show one's talents off; ***wywieść kogoś w ~*** outwit s.o., outsmart s.o. **2.** *MATH* area
polec *v/p* (*-legnę*) (*na wojnie*) fall
polecać ⟨**-cić**⟩ (*-cam*) **1.** *film, książkę*: recommend; ***polecamy nasze usługi*** we remain at your service **2.** (*powierzać*) commend; ***~ czyjejś opiece*** entrust to s.o.'s care; ***polecać się**: **polecam się na przyszłość*** I hope to be of service in the future
polecający *adj*: ***list ~*** letter of recommendation
poleceni|e *n* (*-nia*; *-nia*) **1.** (*zlecenie*) order **2.** (*do zadania*) instruction; ***z ~a Piotra*** on Piotr's recommendation
polecieć *v/p* → ***lecieć***
polecony *adj*: ***list ~*** registered letter
polegać *v/im* (*-gam*) **1.** (*ufać*) depend (**na** *L* on), rely (**na** *L* on) **2.** (*zasadzać się*) consist (**na** *L* in); ***to polega na tym, że*** it consists in
poległy **I** *adj* (*na wojnie*) killed **II** *m* (*-łego*; *-gli*) casualty
polemiczny *adj* **1.** *charakter*: polemic(al) **2.** *artykuł*: critical, polemical
polemika *f* (*-ki*; *-ki*) public debate
polemizować *v/im* (*-zuję*) polemize (**z** *I* with), polemicize (**z** *I* with)
polepszać ⟨**-szyć**⟩ (*-szam*) improve; ***polepszać się*** improve; ***polepszyło mu się*** his condition has improved
polepszenie *n* (*-nia*; *no pl*) improvement
polerować ⟨**wy-**⟩ (*-ruję*) **1.** *meble*: polish **2.** *artykuł*: refine
poletko *n* (*-ka*; *-ka*) *dim* plot (of land); ***~ doświadczalne*** testing ground
polewa *f* (*-wy*; *-wy*) *COOK* glaze; **polewaczka** *f* (*-ki*; *-ki*) **1.** (*samochód*) street sprinkler **2.** (*konewka*) watering can
polewać ⟨**-lać**⟩ (*-wam*) pour; ***polewać się*** pour over oneself
poleżeć *v/p* (*-żę*) lie down for a while; → ***leżeć***
polędwica *f* (*-cy*; *-ce*) **1.** (*rodzaj mięsa*) fillet; ***~ wędzona*** smoked fillet of ham **2.** (*wędlina*) tenderloin
polibuda *f* (*-dy*; *-dy*) (*politechnika*) *infml* poly
policealn|y *adj*: ***studium ~e*** *further education college*
polichlorek *m* (*-rku*; *no pl*): ***~ winylu*** polyvinyl chloride, PVC
polichromia *f* (*-mii*; *-mie*) *ART* polychromy
policja *f* (*-ji*; *-je*) **1.** (*organ*) police **2.** (*komenda*) police station **3.** (*funkcjonariusze*) police officers *pl*, police force; ***~ drogowa*** traffic police; ***~ śledcza*** police department of criminal investigation

policjant *m* (*-ta*; *-nci*) police officer, policeman; **policjantka** *f* (*-ki*; *-ki*) police officer, policewoman
policyjny *adj* police; ***godzina policyjna*** curfew
policzalny *adj*: ***rzeczownik ~*** countable noun
policzek *m* (*-czka*; *-czki*) **1.** (*część ciała*) cheek **2.** (*uderzenie*) slap in the face; ***wymierzyć komuś ~*** slap s.o.'s face; **policzkować** ⟨**s-**⟩ (*-kuję*) slap s.o.'s face; **policzkow|y** *adj*: ***kość ~a*** ANAT cheekbone
policzyć *vp od* **liczyć**
poliester *m* (*-tru*; *-try*) polyester
poligamia *f* (*-mii*; *no pl*) polygamy
poliglota *m* (*-ty*; *-loci*) polyglot
poligon *m* (*-nu*; *-ny*) military training area
poligrafia *f* (*-fii*; *no pl*) printing industry
poliklinika *f* (*-ki*; *-ki*) policlinic
polio *n indecl* MED polio(myelitis)
polip *n* (*-pa*; *-py*) BIOL polyp
polisa *f* (*-sy*; *-sy*) policy
polistyren *m* (*-nu*; *no pl*) polystyrene
politechnika *f* (*-ki*; *-ki*) technical college, polytechnic
politologia *f* (*-gii*; *no pl*) political science
politowani|e *n* (*-nia*; *no pl*) condescending sympathy; ***z ~em*** with condescending sympathy; ***godny ~a*** pitiable, pathetic
politura *f* (*-ry*; *no pl*) (French) polish; **politurować** *v/im* (*-ruję*) polish
polityczny *adj* political
polityk *m* (*-ka*; *-tycy*) politician; **polityk|a** (*-ki*; *no pl*) **1.** (*działalność władz*) politics *sing*; ***wycofać się z ~i*** retire from politics **2.** (*zasady działania*) policy; ***~a zagraniczna*** foreign policy; ***~a podatkowa*** tax policies; ***~a personalna*** personnel policies
politykier *m* (*-ra*; *-rzy*) soapbox politician; **politykierstwo** *n* (*-wa*; *no pl*) *amateur and demagogic politicking*
politykować *v/im* (*-kuję*) politicize
Polk|a *f* (*-ki*; *-ki*) Pole; ***jest ~ą*** she's Polish
polka *f* (*-ki*; *-ki*) (*taniec*) polka
polnl|y *adj*: ***konik ~y*** grasshopper; ***~a droga*** dirt road; ***~e kwiaty*** wild flowers
polodowcowy *adj* postglacial
polon *m* (*-nu*; *no pl*) CHEM polonium *n*
polonez *m* (*-za*; *-zy*) polonaise
Polonia *f* (*-nii*; *no pl*) Polish diaspora, Polish community abroad; ***~ niemiecka*** Polish immigrant communities in Germany
polonista *m* (*-ty*; *-niści*) Polish teacher
polonistyka *f* (*-ki*; *no pl*) **1.** (*dyscyplina*) Polish studies **2.** (*wydział*) Polish department
polor *m* (*-ru*; *no pl*) *lit* good manners *pl*
polot *m* (*-tu*; *no pl*) flair; ***bez ~u*** without flair; ***z ~em*** with flair
polować ⟨**za-**⟩ (*-luję*) hunt (**na** *A* for); ***~ na męża*** *iron* try to hook a husband, go husband-hunting
polowanie *n* (*-nia*; *-nia*) hunt; ***iść na ~*** go hunting; ***~ z nagonką*** battue; ***~ na lisa*** fox hunt(ing); ***~ na grubego zwierza*** big game hunting; ***~ na czarownice*** POLIT witch-hunt
polow|y *adj* field; ***łóżko ~e*** camp bed; ***prace ~e*** work in the fields; ***mundur ~y*** combat dress; ***kuchnia ~a*** cookhouse, camp kitchen
Polska *f* (*-ki*) Poland
polsk|i I *adj* Polish; ***język ~i*** Polish; ***mówić po ~u*** speak Polish; ***co to znaczy po ~u?*** what does it mean in Polish?; ***Rzeczpospolita ~a*** the Republic of Poland **II** *m* (*-kiego*; *no pl*) Polish language
polskojęzyczny *adj* Polish-language
polskość *f* (*-ści*; *no pl*) Polish character, Polish nature
polszczyć ⟨**s-**⟩ (*-czę*) polonize
polszczyzna *f* (*-ny*; *no pl*) the Polish language
polubić *v/p* (*-bię*) come to like, take a liking to; **polubić się** come to like each other, take to each other
polubowny *adj* amicable; ***sąd ~*** court of arbitration
polucja *f* (*-ji*; *-je*) nocturnal emission
połać *f* (*-łaci*; *-łacie*) *lasu*, *pola*: (greater) part
połajanki *pl* (*-nek*) scolding *sing*, rebuke *sing*
połakomić się *v/p* → **łakomić się**
połamać *v/p* → **łamać**; **połamaniec** *m* (*-mańca*; *-mańcy*) *infml* cripple; **połaman|y** *adj* broken; ***~e kości*** fractured bones

P

połapać się *v/p* (*-pię*) look through, tumble (**w** *L* to)
połaskotać *v/p* → **łaskotać**
poławiacz *m* (*-cza*; *-cze*): **~ pereł** pearl diver; **~ wielorybów** whaler
poławiać *v/im* (*-wiam*) **1.** (*łowić ryby*) fish for **2.** *perły*: dive for
połączenie *n* (*-nia*; *-nia*) **1.** *telefoniczne*, *kolejowe*: connection **2.** *firm*: merger **3.** (*element łączący*) link; **połączon|y** *adj* connected (**z** *I* to); **~y szeregowo** arranged in series; **~e siły** common effort, combined effort
połączyć *v/p* → **łączyć**
połechtać *v/p* → **łechtać**; **połechtany** *adj*: **mile ~** flattered
połeć *m* (*-łcia*; *-łcie*): **~ słoniny** cut of pork fat
połknąć *v/p* (*-nę*): **~ haczyk** *fig* swallow the bait; → **połykać**
połogow|y *adj*: **okres ~y** puerperal period; **zakażenie ~e** puerperal fever
połow|a *f* (*-wy*; *-wy*) **1.** (*część*) half; **do ~y** half; **napełniony do ~y** half-full; **po ~ie** fifty-fifty; **~a życia** half of one's life; **kupić coś za ~ę ceny** buy s.th. half-price **2.** (*środek*) middle; **w ~ie roku** in the middle of a year **w ~ie maja** in mid May; **w ~ie drogi** halfway; **podzielić coś na ~ę** divide s.th. in half
połowica *f* (*-cy*; *-ce*) *hum* better half
połowiczn|y *adj* incomplete; **~e rozwiązanie** incomplete solution; **~y sukces** qualified success; **okres ~ego rozpadu** CHEM half-life
połowowy *adj* fishing
położeni|e *n* (*-nia*; *no pl*) **1.** (*miejsce*) location **2.** (*sytuacja*) **znaleźć się w trudnym ~u** find oneself in a difficult situation
położna *f* (*-nej*; *-ne*) midwife; **położnica** *f* (*-cy*; *-ce*) woman in childbirth; **położnictwo** *n* (*-wa*; *no pl*) obstetrics, midwifery; **położniczy** *adj* obstetric; **oddział ~** maternity ward; **położnik** *m* (*-ka*; *-nicy*) obstetrician
położyć *v/p* → **kłaść**
połóg *m* (*-łogu*; *-łogi*) puerperium
połów *m* (*-łowu*; *-łowy*) **1.** (*łowienie ryb*) fishing; **~ wielorybów** whaling **2.** (*złowione ryby*) catch
połówka *f* (*-ki*; *-ki*) **1.** (*połowa*) half **2.** (*półlitrówka wódki*) *infml* half a litre of vodka

południ|e *n* (*-nia*; *no pl*) **1.** (*pora dnia*) noon, midday; **po ~u** in the afternoon; **przed ~em** in the morning; **w ~e** at noon, at midday **2.** (*strona świata*) GEOGR the south; **na ~e od** *G* south of; **na ~u** in the south; **okno wychodzi na ~e** the window faces south; **najbardziej wysunięta na ~e część kraju** the most southerly part of the country
południk *m* (*-ka*; *-ki*) GEOGR meridian; **~ zerowy** the prime meridian; **łuk ~a** meridional arc; **południkowy** *adj* meridional
południowiec *m* (*-wca*; *-wcy*) southerner
południowo-wschodni *adj* south-east(ern)
południowo-zachodni *adj* south-west(ern)
południow|y *adj* **1.** (*o porze dnia*) midday; **w porze ~ej** at midday **2.** (*o części świata*) GEOGR BIOL south; **~y zachód** the south-west; **biegun ~y** the South Pole; **owoce ~e** citrus and tropical fruits; **~y akcent** southern accent **3.** *wiatr*: southerly
połykacz *m* (*-cza*; *-cze*): **~ ognia** fire-eater
połyka|ć ⟨**-łknąć**⟩ (*-kam*) **1.** *kęs*: swallow; **~ć łzy** *fig* gulp back the tears; **~ł ślinkę na widok** G his mouth was watering at the sight of **2.** *książkę*: devour **3.** *wiedzę*: absorb **4.** *litery*: misspell
połysk *m* (*-ku*; *no pl*) **1.** *włosów*: lustre, gloss **2.** *metalu*, *mebli*: lustre; **do ~u** till it becomes glossy; **meble na wysoki ~** high gloss furniture, highly-polished furniture
połyskiwać *v/im* (*-kuję*) **1.** (*o rzece*) shimmer **2.** (*o metalu*) glitter; **połyskliwy** *adj* **1.** *metal*: glittering **2.** *włosy*: glossy
pomacać *v/p* (*-cam*) feel
pomachać *v/p* → **machać**
pomadka *f* (*-ki*; *-ki*): **~ do ust** lipstick
pomagać ⟨**-móc**⟩ (*-gam*) **1.** (*udzielić pomocy*) help (**przy** *L*/**w** *L* with); **~ komuś coś zrobić** help s.o. (to) do s.th.; **w czym mogę pomóc?** how can I help you?; **~ biedniejszym krajom** aid poorer countries; **~ sobie** help each other **2.** (*być skutecznym*)

P

be good (**na** *A* for); ***to lekarstwo pomaga na ból głowy*** this medicine relieves headaches
pomagier *m* (*-ra*; *-rzy*) *infml* sidekick
pomaleńku, **pomalutku** *adv* **1.** (*bardzo powoli*) (very) slowly **2.** – ***„Jak leci?"*** – ***„~!"*** 'How are you doing?' 'Fine!'
pomalować *v/p* → ***malować***
pomału *adv* **1.** (*powoli*) slowly; ***~!*** slow down! **2.** – ***„Jak leci?"*** – ***„~!"*** 'How are you doing?' 'Fine!'
pomarańcza *f* (*-czy*; *-cze*) orange; **pomarańczowy** *adj* orange; **pomarańczarnia** *f* (*-ni*; *-nie*) orangery; **pomarańczowo** *adv*: ***pomalować coś na ~*** paint s.th. orange
pomarszczony *adj* **1.** *skóra*: wrinkled **2.** *owoc*: shrivelled
pomarznąć *v/p* (*-nę*) **1.** (*o roślinach*) freeze **2.** (*o ludziach*) freeze to death
pomaturalnly *adj*: ***szkoła ~a*** college
pomawiać ⟨**-mówić**⟩ (*-wiam*) JUR slander; ***~ kogoś o to, że*** unjustly accuse s.o. of
pomazać *v/p* (*-mażę*) smear (*I* with); ***~ czymś ścianę*** smear s.th. on the wall; ***pomazał twarz czekoladą*** his face got smeared with chocolate; ***pomazać się*** smear oneself
pomazaniec *m* (*-zańca*; *-zańcy*) the anointed one
pomiar *m* (*-ru*; *-ry*) measurement; ***~ kartograficzny*** cartographic measurement; ***~ temperatury*** temperature; ***robić ~y*** take measurements, make measurements, survey; **pomiarowy** *adj* measuring; ***przyrząd ~*** gauge
pomiatać *v/im* (*-tam*) push around, push about; ***nie pozwalaj mu sobą ~*** don't let him push you around; ***ich szef pomiata pracownikami*** their boss holds his employees in contempt, their boss treats his workers like dirt
pomiąć *v/p* → ***miąć***
pomidor *m* (*-ra*; *-ry*) tomato; **pomidorowy** *adj* **1.** *smak*: tomato; ***zupa pomidorowa*** tomato soup **2.** (*kolor*) tomato red
pomieszać *v/p* → ***mieszać***
pomieszanie *n* (*-nia*; *no pl*) (*zamieszanie*) confusion; ***~ z poplątaniem*** *infml* utter confusion; ***~ zmysłów*** insanity
pomieszczenie *n* (*-nia*; *-nia*) room; ***~ służbowe*** service room, staff room; ***~ biurowe*** office; ***osobne ~*** separate room
pomieszkać *v/p* (*-kam*) live for some time, dwell for some time
pomieścić *v/p* (*-mieszczę*) **1.** (*dać miejsce*) accommodate **2.** (*o zbiorniku*) hold; ***ten dzbanek może ~ litr mleka*** this jug can hold a litre of milk **3.** (*o sali*, *kinie*) seat; ***to więzienie może ~ 300 skazanych*** the jail can house over 300 prisoners; ***pomieścić się*** have enough room; ***oni się nie pomieszczą*** there isn't enough room for them
pomiędzy → ***między***
pomięty *adj* creased
pomijać ⟨**-minąć**⟩ (*-jam*) **1.** (*opuścić*) omit, *infml* skip **2.** (*nie uwzględnić*) miss out, leave out; ***pomijając***, ***pominąwszy*** to say nothing of, let alone; ***~ milczeniem*** fail to mention; ***~ kogoś przy*** *L* leave s.o. out while doing s.th.
pomimo → ***mimo***
pominąć *v/p* → ***pomijać***
pominięcie *n* (*-cia*; *no pl*) omission; ***z ~m*** *G* with the exception of
pomiot *m* (*-tu*; *-ty*) **1.** BIOL litter, offspring **2.** (*u ptaków*) brood
pomknąć *v/p* (*-nę*) run, dash
pomnażać ⟨**-nożyć**⟩ (*-żam*) multiply
pomniejszać ⟨**-szyć**⟩ (*-szam*) **1.** (*zmniejszać*) decrease **2.** *zdjęcie*: make smaller **3.** *znaczenie*: play down; ***~ znaczenie katastrofy*** play down the seriousness of the disaster; ***~ czyjeś zasługi*** belittle s.o.'s merit(s); **pomniejszy** *adj* minor, unimportant
pomnik *m* (*-ka*; *-ki*) **1.** BUILD monument **2.** (*płyta nagrobna*) gravestone, tombstone
pomnożyć *v/p* → ***pomnażać***
pomny *adj lit* mindful (*G* of); ***~ swej przysięgi*** bearing in mind his oath
pomoc *f* (*-cy*; *-ce*) **1.** help; ***~ humanitarna*** humanitarian aid; ***przyjść z ~ą*** come (*D* to) aid; ***służyć ~ą*** offer help; ***~ domowa*** domestic help, *Am* aid; ***być komuś ~ą*** be a help for; ***przy czyjejś ~y*** with s.o.'s help; ***wołanie o ~*** a cry for help; ***natychmiastowa ~*** im-

P

mediate help; ***wzywać ~y*** call for help; ***na ~!*** help! **2.** (*przedmioty, czynności*) aid: ***~e naukowe*** teaching aids; ***pierwsza ~*** first aid **3.** (*wsparcie*) support; ***~ pieniężna*** financial support, financial help **4.** ***przy ~y*** *G*, ***z ~ą*** *G* with the help of; ***za ~ą*** *G* by means of **5.** *SPORT* the defence, back (line)

pomocnica *f* (*-cy; -ce*) helper

pomocniczy *adj prace, pytanie*: auxiliary

pomocnik *m* (*-ka; -nicy*) **1.** (*osoba*) helper **2.** (*zawód*) unskilled worker, labourer **3.** *SPORT* back

pomocn|y *adj* helpful; ***być ~ym w*** *L* help with; ***podać komuś ~ą dłoń*** lend s.o. a helping hand

pomodlić się *v/p* → ***modlić się***

pomordować *v/p* (*-duję*) murder (everyone); → ***mordować***

Pomorze *n* (*-rza*) Pomerania

pomost *m* (*-tu; -ty*) **1.** (*nad jeziorem*) jetty, pier **2.** *TECH* platform; ***~ do załadunku*** loading platform

pomóc *v/p* → ***pomagać***

pomór *m* (*-moru; no pl*) plague; ***~ kur*** fowl cholera, chicken plague

pomówić *v/p* → ***pomawiać***

pomówieni|e *n* (*-nia; -nia*) **1.** *JUR* slander; ***skarżyć o ~e*** sue for slander **2.** ***mam z tobą do ~a*** I have to talk to you, I need to have a word with you

pomp|a *f* (*-py; -py*) **1.** (*urządzenie*) pump; ***~a wodna*** water pump; ***~a paliwowa*** fuel pump; ***~a główna*** master pump **2.** (*wystawność*) pomp; ***z ~ą*** with all the pomp, with great pomp and circumstance; ***przyjmować kogoś z ~ą*** receive s.o. with pomp and ceremony **3.** (*ulewa*) downpour

pompatyczny *adj* **1.** *mówca*: pompous **2.** *styl, kaznodzieja*: bombastic

pompk|a *f* (*-ki; -ki*) **1.** *rowerowa*: bicycle pump **2.** ***~i*** *SPORT Br* press-ups, *Am* push-ups

pompon *m* (*-nu; -ny*) *Br* bobble, *Am* pompom, pompon; ***czapka z ~em*** *Br* bobble hat, *Am* stocking cap

pompować ⟨***na-***⟩ (*-puję*) **1.** *materac*: pump (up) **2.** *wodę*: pump; **pompownia** *f* (*-ni; -nie*) *Br* pumping station, *Am* pump house

pomro|ka *f* (*-ki; no pl*) *lit* darkness; ***w ~ce dziejów*** in ancient history, buried in the past; ***ginąć w ~ce dziejów*** sink into oblivion

pomruk *m* (*-ku; -ki*) *burzy, bitwy*: rumble; ***~ niezadowolenia*** murmur of discontent

pomrukiwać *v/im* (*-kuję*) **1.** (*o kocie, maszynie*) purr **2.** (*o człowieku*) murmur; ***~ z zadowoleniem*** purr with satisfaction

pomstować *v/im* (*-tuję*) utter curses (***na*** *A* against), curse, execrate

pomścić *v/p* (*-mszczę*) avenge; ***~ czyjeś cierpienie*** avenge s.o.'s suffering

pomyje *pl* (*-myj*) (pig)swill *sing*

pomyleniec *m* (*-leńca; -leńcy*) madman, lunatic; **pomylony** *adj* loony *infml*, nutty *infml*

pomylić *v/p* → ***mylić***

pomyłk|a *f* (*-ki; -ki*) (*błąd*) mistake; ***przez ~ę*** by mistake; ***~a!*** (*w rozmowie telefonicznej*) wrong number!

pomysł *m* (*-łu; -ły*) idea; ***zwariowany ~*** crazy idea; ***wpaść na ~*** hit (up)on an idea, come up with an idea

pomysłodawca *m* (*-cy; -cy*) author

pomysłowy *adj* **1.** *rozwiązanie*: ingenious **2.** *człowiek*: resourceful

pomyślany *adj*: ***dobrze ~*** sensible; ***źle ~*** misconceived

pomyśleni|e: ***to jest nie do ~a*** this is unthinkable

pomyślnoś|ć *f* (*-ści; no pl*) **1.** (*szczęście w życiu*) well-being; ***życzyć wszelkiej ~ci*** wish s.o. all the best; ***~ci!*** (*toast*) good health!, here's to your health! **2.** (*dobrobyt*) prosperity; **pomyślny** *adj* **1.** *obrót sprawy*: fortunate **2.** *wiadomość, wiatr*: good **3.** *wynik egzaminu*: positive

pomywacz *m* (*-cza; -cze*), ***~ka*** *f* (*-ki; -ki*) dishwasher

ponad *prep* (*I/A*) **1.** (*miejsce*) above; ***~ głową*** above one's head; ***wzbić się ~ chmury*** soar above the clouds; ***~ miarę*** excessively; ***to jest ~ moje siły*** this is too much for me **2.** (*przekroczenie poziomu*) beyond; ***~ wszelką wątpliwość*** beyond a shadow of a doubt **3.** (*w porównaniach*) over; ***~ cztery godziny*** over four hours; ***cenić coś ~ wszystko*** value s.th. over anything else

ponad- (*w złożeniach*) **1.** (*poza przeciętność*) super-; ***~standardowy*** superstandard **2.** (*powyżej*) supra-

P

ponadczasowy *adj* **1.** *wartość*: timeless **2.** *film*: classic; **ponaddźwiękowy** *adj* supersonic; **ponadpartyjny** *adj* nonparty; **ponadklasowy** *adj* classless; **ponadprogramowy** *adj* extracurricular

ponadto *adv* furthermore, in addition, moreover

ponaglać ⟨**-lić**⟩ (*-lam*) rush (**kogoś do** *G* s.o. to); **ponaglenie** *n* (*-nia*; *-nia*) (*pismo*) reminder

ponawiać ⟨**-nowić**⟩ (*-wiam*) *próbę, prośbę*: repeat

poncz *m* (*-czu*; *-cze*) punch

ponętny *adj* **1.** *propozycja*: attractive **2.** *zapach, uśmiech*: enticing **3.** *poza*: seductive

poniedziałek *m* (*-łku*; *-łki*) Monday; **poniedziałkowy** *adj* Monday

poniekąd *particle lit* in a way

poniemiecki *adj* post-German; ***~ budynek*** building left by the Germans, building that used to be German

ponieść *v/p* (*-niosę*) (*o koniu*) bolt; ***poniósł jej torbę*** he helped her carry the bag; ***gdzie go poniosło?*** *infml* where's he gone now?; ***iść, gdzie oczy poniosą*** go wherever one wants; → ***ponosić***

ponieważ *conj* because, since

poniewczasie *adv* too late

poniewierać *v/im* (*-ram*) mistreat, ill-treat, knock about, knock around; ***poniewierać się*** **1.** (*o rzeczy*) lie about, lie around **2.** (*o osobie*) knock about, knock around

poniewierka *f* (*-ki*; *no pl*) miserable life

poniżać ⟨**-żyć**⟩ (*-żam*) humiliate; ***poniżać się*** degrade oneself

poniżając|y *adj* humiliating, degrading; ***~e traktowanie*** degrading treatment

poniżej *prep* (*G*) below; **poniżenie** *n* (*-nia*; *no pl*) humiliation; **poniższy** *adj cytat, tabela*: the following

poniżyć *v/p* → ***poniżać***

ponosić ⟨**-nieść**⟩ (*-noszę*) **1.** *koszty, ryzyko*: incur; ***~ karę*** be punished **2.** *dziecko*: carry a little; ***dać się ponieść*** get carried away; ***~ winę za*** *A* be responsible for; ***poniosło go*** he lost his temper, he got carried away **3.** *odpowiedzialność*: bear **4.** *klęskę, straty, porażkę*: suffer; ***~ śmierć*** suffer death, meet one's death

ponowić *v/p* → ***ponawiać***

ponownie *adv* **1.** again; ***~ się zakazić*** be infected again **2.** (*w złożeniach*) re-; ***~ coś reklamować*** re-advertise; ***próbować ~*** retry; **ponown|y** *adj* (*w złożeniach*) re-; ***~e zakażenie*** reinfection; ***~e małżeństwo*** remarriage

ponton *m* (*-nu*; *-ny*) **1.** (*łodź płaskodenna*) pontoon **2.** (*łódka*) (rubber) dinghy

pontyfikat *m* (*-tu*; *-ty*) REL pontificate; ***podczas ~u Jana Pawła II*** during the pontificate of Pope John Paul II

ponumerować *v/p* → ***numerować***

ponuracki *adj infml* gloomy, cheerless; **ponurak** *m* (*-ka*; *-racy*) *infml* cheerless person, *Am* sourpuss

ponuro *adv* → ***ponury***

ponurość *f* (*-ści*; *no pl*) **1.** (*nastrój*) gloom, low spirits *pl* **2.** *krajobrazu*: dreariness, bleakness

ponury *adj* **1.** *osoba*: gloomy, dismal; ***~ nastrój*** dismal mood; ***wprawić kogoś w ~ nastrój*** cast a gloom over **2.** (*krajobraz*) bleak, dreary

pończocha *f* (*-chy*; *-chy*) stocking; **pończoszniczy** *adj* hosiery; ***dział wyrobów ~ch*** hosiery department

poobiedni *adj* after-dinner

pooperacyjn|y *adj* post-operative; ***opieka ~a*** post-operative care; ***umieralność ~a*** post-operative mortality

pop[1] *m* (*-pa*; *-pi*) REL pope

pop[2] MUS **I** *adj* pop **II** *m* (*-pu*; *no pl*) pop (music)

popadać[1] ⟨**-paść**⟩ (*-dam*) fall (**w** *A* in); ***~ w przesadę*** become exaggerated; ***~ w długi*** incur debts, run up debts; ***~ w nędzę*** fall into poverty

popadać[2] *v/p*: ***popadał śnieg*** it snowed a little, some snow fell; ***popadało*** it rained a little

popamiętać *v/p* (*-tam*): ***jeszcze popamiętasz!*** I'll show you!

popar|cie *n* (*-cia*; *no pl*) support; ***udzielić komuś ~cia*** give s.o. support

poparzenie *n* (*-nia*; *-nia*) burn, scald

poparzyć *v/p* → ***parzyć***

popaść *v/p*: ***co popadnie*** whatever turns up; ***wszystko jak popadnie*** everything (without sorting out; ***gdzie popadnie*** just anywhere; ***z kim popadnie*** with anybody; → ***popadać***[1]

P

popatrzeć *v/p* → ***patrzeć***
popchnąć *v/p* → ***popychać***
popelinowy *adj* poplin
popełniać ⟨**-nić**⟩ (*-niam*) **1.** *błąd, samobójstwo*: commit **2.** *wiersz, książkę*: *iron* write **3.** *nietakt*: make
popęd *m* (*-du*; *-dy*) drive; ***~ płciowy*** sex drive, sexual drive; ***~ do hazardu*** urge for gambling
popędliwy *adj* impetuous, short-tempered
popędzać ⟨**-dzić**⟩ (*-dzam*) rush; ***~ kogoś do*** *G* hurry s.o. into; ***nie popędzaj mnie!*** don't rush me!
popędzić *v/p* (*-dzę*) rush, dash
popękany *adj* **1.** cracked **2.** *wargi*: chapped
popić *v/p* → ***popijać***
popielaty *adj Br* grey, *Am* gray
Popielec *m* (*-lca*; *-lce*) REL Ash Wednesday
popielisko *n* (*-ka*; *-ka*) ashes; **popielnica** *f* (*-cy*; *-ce*) **1.** (*większa popielniczka*) (large) ashtray **2.** ARCHIT cinerary urn; **popielniczka** *f* (*-ki*; *-ki*) ashtray; **popielnik** *m* (*-ka*; *-ki*) ash box
popierać ⟨**-przeć**⟩ (*-ram*) **1.** *wniosek*: second **2.** *prośbę, zachowanie*: back up, support **3.** *artystów*: support, help **4.** (*uzasadniać*) underpin; ***~ oskarżenie dowodami*** substantiate a charge
popiersie *n* (*-sia*; *-sia*) bust (*G* of); ***~ z marmuru*** marble bust
popijać ⟨**-pić**⟩ (*-jam*) **1.** (*pić wolno*) sip **2.** ***~ lekarstwo wodą*** wash the medicine down with water **3.** (*upijać się*) *infml* drink, tipple; ***ostatnio za dużo popija*** he has been drinking too much recently
popijawa *f* (*-wy*; *-wy*) *infml* drinking bout, bender; ***dwudniowa ~*** two-day bender
popi|ół *m* (*-piołu*; *-pioły*) **1.** (*wynik spalania*) ash; ***spalić się na ~ół*** burn to ashes; ***odradzać się z ~ołów*** rise from the ashes; ***~ół wulkaniczny*** (***z papierosa***) volcanic (cigarette) ash **2.** (*ludzkie szczątki*) ***~oły*** ashes
popis *m* (*-su*; *-sy*) show; ***pole do ~u*** opportunity to display one's talents
popisać się *v/p* → ***popisywać się***
popisow|y *adj* spectacular; ***rola ~a*** star role; ***~y numer*** star turn
popisywać się ⟨**-sać**⟩ (*-suję*) show off; ***~ bogactwem*** flaunt one's wealth; ***~ wiedzą*** parade one's knowledge; ***nie popisać się*** *iron* not to distinguish oneself
poplątać *v/p* → ***plątać***
poplecznictwo *n* (*-wa*; *no pl*) (unfair) support, connections *pl*; **poplecznik** *m* (*-ka*; *-nicy*) henchman
poplotkować *v/p* (*-kuję*) gossip a little; → ***plotkować***
popłaca|ć *v/im* (*-cam*) pay (off); ***złodziejstwo nie ~*** it does not pay to steal; ***ciężka praca ~*** hard work pays off
popłatn|y *adj* **1.** *zawód*: well-paid **2.** *interes*: profitable; ***~e zajęcie*** gainful employment
popłoch *m* (*-chu*; *no pl*) panic; ***w ~u*** in a panic; ***wpaść w ~*** panic
popołudni|e *n* (*-nia*; *-nia*) afternoon; **popołudniowy** *adj* afternoon
popołudniówka *f* (*-ki*; *-ki*) **1.** (*gazeta*) evening paper **2.** THEAT matinee
poporodow|y *adj* MED: ***depresja ~a*** post-natal depression; ***opieka ~a*** post-natal care
popracować *v/p* (*-cuję*) work a little; → ***pracować***
poprawa *f* (*-wy*; *no pl*) **1.** *pogody, stanu zdrowia*: improvement **2.** (*poprawienie oceny*) second chance, *Am* make-up
poprawczak *m* (*-ka*; *-ki*) *infml* youth custody centre, *Am* reformatory, reform school
poprawczy *adj*: ***zakład ~, dom ~*** reformatory
poprawiać ⟨**-wić**⟩ (*-wiam*) **1.** (*zmieniać na lepsze*) improve; ***~ oceny*** improve one's grades **2.** *błąd, tekst*: correct **3.** (*u krawca*) make alterations **4.** *strój*: adjust **5.** *włosy*: tidy **6.** *rekord*: better; **poprawiać się 1.** (*zmieniać się na lepsze*) improve **2.** (*tyć*) put on weight
poprawiny *pl* (*-win*) after-celebration *sing*; ***~ wesela*** (***chrzcin***) continuation of the wedding (christening party)
poprawk|a *f* (*-ki*; *-ki*) **1.** (*w tekście*) correction; ***ostateczne ~i*** final touches final adjustments **2.** (*uwzględnienie*) ***brać ~ę*** na *A* make allowances for **3.** ***~a do ustawy*** POLIT amendment

P

to the bill **4.** *ubrania*: alteration to; ***oddać coś do ~i*** take s.th. for alteration **5.** (*egzamin*) *Br* resit, *Am* make-up

poprawność *f* (*-ści*; *no pl*) correctness; **poprawny** *adj* **1.** *zdanie*: correct **2.** *strój*: proper **3.** *ocena*: sufficient

popręg *m* (*-gu*; *-gi*) girth

popromienn|y *adj*: ***choroba ~a*** radiation sickness

poprosić *v/p* → ***prosić***

poprzeczk|a *f* (*-ki*; *-ki*) **1.** (*łata*) crossbeam **2.** SPORT crossbar; ***stawiać komuś wysoko ~ę*** *fig* set s.o. a high target; **poprzeczn|y** *adj* **1.** *ulica*: cross(-wise) **2.** *belka*: cross, transverse; ***przekrój ~y*** cross section; ***przegroda ~a*** transverse bulkhead

poprzeć *v/p* → ***popierać***

poprzedni *adj* **1.** *tydzień*, *rok*: last, previous; ***w ~ch latach*** in previous years; ***~ego dnia*** the day before **2.** *pytanie*, *stwierdzenie*: previous **3.** (*były*) former; ***jej ~ chłopak*** her former boyfriend **4.** *strona*, *rozdział*: preceding, earlier; ***~e strony*** the preceding pages

poprzedni|k *m* (*-ka*; *-nicy*), **-niczka** *f* (*-ki*; *-ki*) **1.** (*na danym stanowisku*) predecessor **2.** (*mniej zaawansowany model*) forerunner; ***podobna do lutni ~czka gitary*** lute-like forerunner of the guitar

poprzednio *adv* previously, before; ***~ nieznany fakt*** previously unknown fact

poprzedzać ⟨***-dzić***⟩ (*-dzam*) **1.** (*następować wcześniej*) precede; ***obiad poprzedził występy*** the dinner preceded the show **2.** (*iść przed*) go ahead of, go before

poprzek: ***w ~*** crosswise

poprzestawać ⟨***-stać***⟩ (*-taję*) be content (***na*** *L* with); ***~ na małym*** be modest, have modest aspirations

poprzez *prep* (*A*) through

poprztykać się *v/p* (*-kam*) *infml* fall out, squabble (***o*** *A* over)

poprzyklejać *v/p* (*-jam*) glue (all over); → ***przyklejać***

poprzysięgać ⟨***-siąc***⟩ (*-gam*) *lit* swear; ***~ sobie*** swear

popstrzony *adj* speckled

popularnonaukowy *adj* popular science

popularnoś|ć *f* (*-ści*; *no pl*) popularity; ***cieszyć się ~cią wśród*** *G* be popular with; **popularny** *adj* popular; ***~ prezenter telewizyjny*** well-known TV presenter

popularyzować ⟨***s-***⟩ (*-zuję*) popularize

populistyczny *adj* populist

popuszczać ⟨***-puścić***⟩ (*-czam*) **1.** (*rozluźnić*) loosen; ***nie ~*** not yield, not give in; ***~ cugli*** *fig* allow more freedom **2.** (*o mrozie*) abate, let up

popychać ⟨***-pchnąć***⟩ (*-cham*) **1.** *wózek*: push **2.** (*ponaglać*) push (***do*** *G* to) **3.** *pracę*, *projekt*: advance, push ahead, push on (*A* with)

popychadło *n* (*-ła*; *-ła*) *infml* doormat, errand boy

popyt *m* (*-tu*; *no pl*) ECON demand (***na*** *A* for); ***cieszyć się ~em*** be in demand

por[1] *m* (*-ru*; *-ry*) ANAT pore

por[2] *m* (*-ra*; *-ry*) BIOL COOK leek

por. *abbr* **1.** (= ***porównaj***) cf. **2.** (= ***porucznik***) Lt, Lieut

por|a *f* (*-ry*; *-ry*) time; ***~a roku*** season; ***~a obiadowa*** lunchtime; ***wieczorowa ~a*** evening; ***~a odwiedzin*** visiting time; ***~a na*** *A* time for; ***w*** (***samą***) ***~ę*** (just) in time; ***przyjść nie w ~ę*** come at the wrong time; ***wizyta nie w ~ę*** ill-timed visit; ***do tej ~y*** up to now; ***o tej ~ze*** at this time; ***wczesną ~ą*** early; ***o każdej ~ze*** any time, always; ***~a wstawać!*** rise and shine!; ***nie ~a na*** *A* no time for

porabiać *v/im* (*-biam*): ***co porabiasz?*** how are things with you?

porachunki *pl* (*-ków*): ***załatwić z kimś swoje ~*** *fig* settle accounts with s.o., settle a score with s.o.; ***mieć z kimś ~*** have a bone to pick with s.o.

porad|a *f* (*-dy*; *-dy*) advice; ***~a lekarska*** medical advice; ***~a prawna*** legal advice; ***za czyjąś ~ą*** on s.o.'s advice; ***udzielić komuś ~y*** give s.o. (a piece of) advice, advise; **poradnia** *f* (*-ni*; *-nie*) clinic; ***~ małżeńska*** marriage guidance bureau

poradnictwo *n* (*-wa*; *no pl*) guidance, counselling; ***~ zawodowe*** vocational guidance; ***~ małżeńskie*** marriage counselling

poradnik *m* (*-ka*; *-ki*) (*książka*) handbook; ***~ z hasłami w porządku alfabe-***

P

tycznym alphabetically arranged handbook

poradzić *v/p* → ***radzić***

poran|ek *m* (*-nku*; *-nki*) early morning; ***o ~ku*** early in the morning; **poranny** *adj* morning

porastać ⟨***-rosnąć***⟩ (*-tam*) **1.** (*pokrywać*) become overgrown (*I* with); ***~ chwastami*** become overgrown with weeds; ***porosły mchem*** overgrown with moss **2.** (*o lesie*) cover

porażać ⟨***-razić***⟩ (*-żam*) **1.** paralyze **2.** affect

porażenie *n* (*-nia*; *no pl*) paralysis; ***~ słoneczne*** sunstroke; ***~ prądem*** electric shock

porażk|a *f* (*-ki*; *-ki*) **1.** defeat; ***doznać ~i*** suffer a defeat **2.** (*niepowodzenie*) failure; ***przyznać się do ~i*** accept failure, acknowledge failure

porażony *adj* **1.** paralyzed; ***być ~m prądem*** suffer from an electric shock, get an electric shock **2.** (*dotknięty*) affected

porcelan|a *f* (*-ny*; *no pl*) china; ***saska ~a*** Dresden (china); ***z ~y*** porcelain; **porcelanowy** *adj* **1.** (*z porcelany*) porcelain, china **2.** *cera*: fair, milky

porcj|a *f* (*-ji*; *-je*) portion; ***żelazna ~a*** emergency ration; ***na ~e*** divided in(to) portions; ***zamówić pięć ~i frytek*** order five portions of chips; ***dodatkowa ~a*** extra portion

poreperować *v/p* (*-ruję*) carry out all necessary repairs, repair; → ***reperować***

poręba *f* (*-by*; *-by*) clearing, glade (*after the trees have been felled*)

P

poręcz *f* (*-czy*; *-cze*) **1.** *schodów*: handrail, ban(n)ister **2.** *balkonu*: railing **3.** *fotela*: arm **4.** ***~e*** SPORT parallel bars

poręczać ⟨***-czyć***⟩ (*-czam*) JUR **1.** act as surety (**za** *A* for), vouch (**za** *A* for) **2.** *weksel*: guarantee

poręczenie *n* (*-nia*; *-nia*) JUR **1.** (*umowa*) assurance; ***~ majątkowe*** bail **2.** (*kaucja*) surety

poręczny *adj* handy

poręczyciel *m* (*-la*; *-le*), **~ka** *f* (*-ki*; *-ki*) JUR guarantor; **poręk|a** *f* (*-ki*; *no pl*) surety; ***z ~i*** on recommendation

pornograficzn|y *adj* pornographic; ***czasopisma*** (***filmy***) ***~e*** porno mags (movies); **pornos** *m* (*-sa*; *-sy*) *infml* porno; **porno** *adj* porn; ***film*** (***czasopismo***) ***~*** porn movie (magazine)

porodow|y *adj*: ***sala ~a*** delivery room; ***bóle ~e*** labour pains; ***oddział ~y*** delivery ward; ***izba ~a*** delivery room

porodówka *f* (*-ki*; *-ki*) *infml* maternity ward

poronić *v/p* (*-nie*) miscarry; **poronienie** *n* (*-nia*; *-nia*) miscarriage; **poroniony** *adj fig* half-baked; ***~ pomysł*** half-baked idea, non-starter

porosły *adj* overgrown (*I* with)

porosnąć *v/p* → ***porastać***

porost *m* (*-tu*; *no pl*) growth; ***środek na ~ włosów*** hair restorer

porosty *pl* (*-tów*) BIOL lichens

porowaty *adj* **1.** (*skała*) porous **2.** (*skóra*) with large pores

porozbiorowy *adj* HIST post-partition

porozumieni|e *n* (*-nia*; *-nia*) **1.** (*jednomyślność*) agreement; ***dojść do ~a*** reach an agreement, come to an agreement; ***w ~u z*** *I* by agreement with, in consultation with; ***na mocy ~a*** under the terms of the agreement **2.** (*ugoda*) settlement **3.** (*układ*) treaty; ***~e o zawieszeniu broni*** armistice

porozumiewać się ⟨***-mieć***⟩ (*-wam*) **1.** (*przekazać informację*) communicate (**z** *I* with) **2.** (*dojść do zgody*) reach an agreement

porozumiewawcz|y *adj* *spojrzenie*: knowing; ***komisja ~a*** arbitration committee

poroże *n* (*-ża*; *-ża*) *jelenia*: antlers

poród *m* (*-rodu*; *-rody*) delivery

porównani|e *n* (*-nia*; *-nia*) comparison; ***w ~u z*** *I* in comparison to, in comparison with, compared to, compared with; ***to nie był zły szpital w ~u z innymi szpitalami*** it wasn't a bad hospital, as hospitals go; ***nie do ~a*** incomparable; ***bez ~a*** far better; ***bez ~a lepszy*** incomparably better, better by far

porównawcz|y *adj* comparative; ***lingwistyka*** (***analiza***) ***~a*** comparative linguistics (analysis)

porównywać ⟨***-nać***⟩ (*-nuję*) compare (**do** *G*/**z** *I* to/with); ***tego nie da się z niczym porównać*** this is beyond compare, this is without compare; ***porównywać się*** compare oneself (**z** *I* to/with)

porównywalny *adj* comparable

poróżnić *v/p* (*-nię*) divide; **~ kogoś z** *I* set s.o. against, turn s.o. against; **poróżnić się** fall out (**z kimś o** *A* with s.o. over); **poróżniony** *adj*: **był ~ ze swoim bratem** *lit* he fell out with his brother

port *m* (*-tu*; *-ty*) **1.** *rybacki*: *Br* harbour, *Am* harbor **2.** *lotniczy*: airport **3.** (*schronienie*) *fig* refuge, shelter; **znaleźć bezpieczny ~** find safe haven; **znaleźć bezpieczny ~ dla uchodźców** provide safe havens for the refugees **4.** *drukarki*: port

portal *m* (*-lu*; *-le*) **1.** ARCH portal; **osadzony w ~u** set in a portal; **obramienie ~u** portal frame **2.** INF portal

portfel *m* (*-la*; *-le*) **1.** wallet **2.** FIN portfolio; **~ akcji** stock portfolio; **zarządzanie ~em** portfolio management; **~ zamówień (zleceń)** order book

portier *m* (*-ra*; *-rzy*) **1.** (*przy drzwiach*) doorman **2.** (*w recepcji*) receptionist

portiera *f* (*-ry*; *-ry*) portiere, door-curtain

portiernia *f* (*-ni*; *-nie*) **1.** porter's office **2.** (*w hotelu*) reception (desk)

port|ki *pl* (*-tek*) *infml* slacks, *Am* pants; **trząść ~kami**, **robić w ~ki** be scared (stiff); **chodzić bez ~ek** *fig* be very poor

portmonetka *f* (*-ki*; *-ki*) (change) purse

porto[1] *n indecl* port (wine)

porto[2] *n indecl* (letter) postage; **~ lotnicze** air mail fee; **~ za list polecony** registered letter fee

portowiec *m* (*-wca*; *-wcy*) docker, longshoreman; **portow|y** *adj Br* harbour, *Am* harbor; **władze ~e** harbour authorities

portrecista *m* (*-ty*; *-ciści*) portrait painter, portraitist

portret *m* (*-tu*; *-ty*) **1.** *malarski*: portrait **2.** (*charakterystyka*) picture; **~ pamięciowy** *Br* identikit picture, *Am* composite sketch

portretować ⟨**s-**⟩ (*-tuję*) **1.** (*wykonywać portret*) paint a portrait **2.** (*charakteryzować*) portray; **portretować się**: **dać się sportretować** have one's portrait painted

Portugalczyk *m* (*-ka*; *-czycy*) Portuguese; **Portugalia** *f* (*-lii*) Portugal; **Portugalka** *f* (*-ki*; *-ki*) Portuguese

portugalski *adj* Portuguese

portyk *m* (*-ku*; *-ki*) ARCHIT portico; **~ kolumnowy** portico of columns, colonnaded portico; **z ~iem** porticoed

porucznik *m* (*-ka*; *-nicy*) *Br* lieutenant, *Am* first lieutenant

porusz|ać ⟨**-szyć**⟩ (*-szam*) **1.** (*wprawić w ruch*) move; **~yć niebo i ziemię** move heaven and earth **2.** *kwestię*: *fig* touch (up)on; **3.** *temat*: bring up; **~ać kwestię płacy** bring up the issue of salaries **4.** TECH drive, propel; **~any siłą wiatru** propelled by wind power; **poruszać się 1.** (*wykonywać ruchy*) move; **nie ~ać się** keep still, be motionless **2.** (*rozprostować się*) stretch one's bones **3.** (*rozeznawać się*) feel at home (**w** *L* with)

poruszenie *n* (*-nia*; *-nia*) **1.** (*wzburzenie*) *fig* agitation; **ukrywać ~** conceal agitation **2.** (*zamieszanie*) stir, confusion, commotion; **cóż to za ~!** what a commotion!; **poruszony** *adj* **1.** (*wzburzony*) agitated, in a state of agitation (*I* by) **2.** (*wzruszony*) moved, touched (*I* by)

poruszyć *v/p* → **poruszać**

porwać *v/p* → **porywać**

porwanie *n* (*-nia*; *-nia*) **1.** *ludzi*: abduction, kidnapping **2.** *samolotu*: hijack, hijacking

poryw *m* (*-wu*; *-wy*): **~ wiatru** gust of wind; **w ~ie gniewu** in an outburst of anger, in a fit of rage; **w pierwszym ~ie** in the first flush

porywacz *m* (*-cza*; *-cze*), **~czka** *f* (*-ki*; *-ki*) **1.** *ludzi*: kidnapper **2.** *samolotu*: hijacker

porywać ⟨**-rwać**⟩ (*-wam*) **1.** *samolot*: hijack **2.** *osobę*: kidnap, abduct **3.** (*unieść*) carry away **4.** (*chwycić*) grab, snatch; **~ kogoś w ramiona** *fig* take s.o. in one's arms **5.** (*ogarnąć*) seize; **porwany strachem** seized by fear **6.** (*wzbudzać podziw*) captivate, hold spellbound; **porywać się** (*podejmować się*) dare (**na** *A*), make a reckless attempt (**na** *A* at); **~ się z motyką na słońce** go on a wild goose chase

porywający *adj* **1.** *wygląd*: ravishing **2.** *mówca*: rousing

porywczy *adj* impetuous, quick-tempered; **porywisty** *adj* gusty

P

porząd|ek *m* (*-dku*; *-dki*) **1.** order; ***~ek prawny***, ***~ek publiczny*** public order; ***doprowadzać coś do ~ku*** put s.th. in order; ***~ek chronologiczny*** chronological order; ***~ek dzienny***, ***~ek obrad*** agenda; ***być na ~ku dziennym*** be the order of the day, be on the agenda; ***przejść nad czymś do ~ku dziennego*** wave s.th. aside, take s.th. in one's stride; ***przywrócić*** (***utrzymywać***) ***~ek*** restore (keep) order; ***prawo i ~ek*** law and order; ***w ~ku!*** all right!; ***przywołać kogoś do ~ku*** call s.o. to order; ***zrobić ~ek z*** *I* get tough with; ***coś jest nie w ~ku*** something's wrong **2.** ***~ki*** cleaning; ***robić ~ki*** tidy (up); ***wiosenne ~ki*** spring cleaning **3.** ***~ek dorycki*** *ARCH* the Doric order

porządkować ⟨**u-**⟩ (*-kuję*) **1.** *papiery*, *myśli*: order **2.** *życie*: sort out; ***uporządkować własne życie*** sort out one's life **3.** *mieszkanie*: tidy (up), clean

porządkow|y **I** *adj* **1.** regulatory **2.** disciplinary; ***kara ~a*** disciplinary penalty **3.** reference; ***numer ~y*** reference number **4.** *GRAM* ordinal; ***liczebnik ~y*** ordinal number **II** *m* (*-wego*; *-wi*), **-wa** *f* (*-wej*; *-we*) security officer

porządn|y *adj* **1.** (*przyzwoity*, *uczciwy*) decent; ***~y obywatel*** respectable citizen **2.** (*lubiący porządek*, *czysty*) tidy **3.** *ulewa*: heavy **4.** *mróz*: severe **5.** *stół*: solid **6.** ***~y posiłek*** square meal; ***~a dawka*** hefty dose

porzeczka *f* (*-ki*; *-ki*) currant; ***biała ~*** white currant; ***czarna ~*** blackcurrant, ***czerwona ~*** redcurrant; **porzeczkowy** *adj* currant

porzekadło *n* (*-ła*; *-ła*) saying

porzucać ⟨**-cić**⟩ (*-cam*) **1.** *partnera*: leave, desert **2.** *nadzieję*: give up, abandon **3.** *pracę*: quit, resign from **4.** *szkołę*: abandon, drop out (*A* of)

posad|a *f* (*-dy*; *-dy*) post, position; ***wolna ~a*** vacancy; ***objąć ~ę*** take on a post, take up a post; ***ubiegać się o ~ę*** *G* apply for the post of; ***drżeć w ~ach*** *fig* rock to its foundations

posadzka *f* (*-ki*; *-ki*) flooring; ***~ drewniana*** (***marmurowa***) wooden (marble) flooring; ***~ z płytek*** tile(d) floor; ***~ z klepek drewnianych*** parquet floor

posadzkow|y *adj*: ***płytka ~a*** floor tile

posadzkarz *m* (*-rza*; *-rze*) floor tiler, floor layer, *Am* floorer

posag *m* (*-gu*; *-gi*) dowry

posapywać *v/im* (*-puję*) → ***sapać***

posażn|y *adj*: ***~a panna*** good match; ***ożenić się z ~ą panną*** marry a fortune

posądzać ⟨**-dzić**⟩ (*-dzam*) accuse (***kogoś o*** *A* s.o. of); **posądzenie** *n* (*-nia*; *-nia*) accusation (***o*** *A* of)

posąg *m* (*-gu*; *-gi*) statue; **posążek** *m* (*-żka*; *-żki*) statuette

poselski *adj* parliamentary; ***klub ~*** parliamentary club; ***immunitet ~*** parliamentary privilege, immunity of a parliamentary representative

poselstwo *n* (*-wa*; *-wa*) **1.** (*placówka dyplomatyczna*) legation **2.** deputation; ***przyjąć ~ rządowych urzędników*** receive a deputation of local government officials

poseł *m* (*-sła*; *-słowie*) **1.** (*do Sejmu*) deputy, (parliamentary) representative **2.** (*wysłannik*) envoy; ***~ ONZ z misją pokojową*** UN peace envoy

posesj|a *f* (*-ji*; *-je*) premises *pl*, property; ***na terenie ~i*** on the premises; ***poza terenem ~i*** off the premises

posezonow|y *adj*: ***wyprzedaż ~a*** end-of-season sale

posępnieć ⟨**s-**⟩ (*-nieję*) become gloomy

posępny *adj* **1.** *mina*, *myśli*: gloomy, cheerless **2.** *człowiek*: low-spirited **3.** *krajobraz*: bleak

posiać *v/p* → ***siać***

posiadacz *m* (*-cza*; *-cze*), **~ka** *f* (*-ki*; *-ki*) owner; ***~ akcji*** equity holder; ***~ czeku*** bearer of a cheque

posiadać *v/im* (*-dam*) **1.** *majątek*: own, possess **2.** *właściwości*: have **3.** ***nie ~ się z radości*** be over the moon

posiadani|e *n* (*-nia*; *no pl*) possession; ***stan ~a*** possessions; ***być w ~u*** *G* be in possession of; ***wziąć w ~e*** take possession of

posiadłoś|ć *f* (*-ści*; *-ści*) estate, property; ***~ci*** lands

posiąść *v/p* (*-siądę*) **1.** *umiejętność* master **2.** *kobietę*: ravish, violate

posiedzeni|e *n* (*-nia*; *-nia*) session, sitting; ***za jednym ~em*** at one sitting; ***spotkać się na nadzwyczajnym ~u***

meet in a special session; **~e sądu** sitting of a law court; **~e komisji** committee meeting; **wznawiać ~e** resume the sitting
posiew *m* (*-wu*; *-wy*) smear (test); **zrobić ~** take a smear; **~ krwi** blood culture; **~ z szyjki macicy** cervical smear
posilać się ⟨**-lić**⟩ (*-lam*) eat, have s.th. to eat
posił|ek *m* (*-łku*; *-łki*) **1.** (*jedzenie*) meal **2. ~ki** (*dodatkowe siły*) reinforcements; **posiłkowy** *adj* auxiliary; **czasownik ~** GRAM auxiliary verb
posiniaczony *adj* (beaten) black and blue
poskarżyć *v/p* → **skarżyć**
poskąpić *v/p* → **skąpić**
poskramiacz *m* (*-cza*; *-cze*) tamer
poskramiać ⟨**-romić**⟩ (*-miam*) **1.** *gniew*: curb **2.** *namiętność*, *ambicje*: restrain **3.** *zwierzęta*: tame
posłać[1] *v/p* → **posyłać**
posłać[2] → **pościelić**
posłanie[1] *n* (*-nia*; *no pl*) **1.** *filmu*, *książki*: message; **film z ~m** film with a message **2.** (*misja*) mission **3.** (*apel*) appeal
posłanie[2] *n* (*-nia*; *-nia*) bedding
posłaniec *m* (*-łańca*; *-łańcy*) messenger
posłanka *f* (*-ki*; *-ki*) deputy, (parliamentary) representative, Member of Parliament; **~ do Sejmu** Sejm deputy
posłannictwo *n* (*-wa*; *-wa*) mission
posłowie *n* (*-wia*; *-wia*) (*w książce*) afterword
posłowie *pl* → **poseł**
posłuch *m* (*-chu*; *no pl*) authority; **mieć ~ u** *G* have authority over; **dawać ~** *D* listen to; **zdobyć czyjś ~** gain the ear of s.o.
posłuchać *v/p* → **słuchać**
posług|a: **oddać komuś ostatnią ~ę** *lit* lay one's last respects to
posługiwać się ⟨**-łużyć**⟩ (*-guję*) use (*I*); **~ się językiem obcym** speak a foreign language
posłuszeństw|o *n* (*-wa*; *no pl*) obedience; **odmówić ~a** (*przestać działać*) fail, break down; **nogi odmawiają mi ~a** my feet are failing me; **silnik odmówił ~a** the engine wouldn't work; **posłuszny** *adj* obedient (**wobec** *G* to)
posłużyć *v/p* → **służyć**
posłużyć się *v/p* → **posługiwać się**
posmak *m* (*-ku*; *no pl*) **1.** (*w ustach*) aftertaste **2.** (*odcień*) smack
posoka *f* (*-ki*; *no pl*) blood, gore
pospać *v/p* (*pośpię*) sleep, nap; **~ dłużej** sleep longer, sleep in; → **spać**
pospieszać → **pośpieszać**
pospieszny → **pośpieszny**
pospolity *adj* **1.** *imię*: common **2.** *wygląd*: plain **3.** *język*: crude **4.** *zachowanie*: coarse
pospólstwo *n* (*-wa*; *no pl*) mob, populace
posprzeczać się *v/p* → **sprzeczać się**
posrebrzać ⟨**-brzyć**⟩ (*-rzam*) silverplate; **posrebrzany** *adj* silverplated
post *m* (*-tu*; *-ty*) fast; **Wielki ≈** REL Lent; **zachowywać ~** fast
posta|ć *f* (*-taci*; *-tacie*/*-taci*) **1.** (*sylwetka*) figure, silhouette; **to zmienia ~ć rzeczy** this puts a (whole) new complexion on the situation; **dorosła ~ć owada** imago **2.** (*osoba*) person; **znana ~ć** well known person **3.** (*osobistość*) celebrity **4.** (*w utworze*) character **5.** *energii*: form; **w ~ci** *G*, **pod ~cią** *G* in the form of, in the shape of
postanawiać ⟨**-nowić**⟩ (*-wiam*) decide, resolve; **~ czegoś nie robić** decide against doing s.th.; **sąd postanowił na niekorzyść oskarżonego** the judge ruled against the defendant
postanowieni|e *n* (*-nia*; *-nia*) **1.** (*uchwała*) decision **2.** (*zamiar*) resolution; **robić ~a noworoczne** make New Year's resolutions **3.** *sądu*: ruling; **ostateczne ~e sądu** the court's final ruling
postarzać ⟨**-rzyć**⟩ (*-rzam*) make look older; **powtarzać się** make oneself look older
postaw|a *f* (*-wy*; *-wy*) **1.** (*stosunek*) attitude (**wobec** *G* towards); **przyjąć ~ę obronną** adopt a defensive posture; **zmienić swoją ~ę** undergo a change of attitude **2.** (*sylwetka*) figure **3.** (*pozycja*) posture; **niedbała** (**wadliwa**) **~a** slouch (bad) posture **4.** (*poza*) stance; **przyjąć ~ę** take up a stance, assume a posture
postawić *v/p* → **stawiać**
postawn|y *adj* stout; **~a postać** portly figure; **był ~ym mężczyzną** he was a fine figure of a man

postąpić *v/p* → ***postępować***
posterun|ek *m* (*-nku*; *-nki*) **1.** (*stanowisko*) post **2.** (*osoba*) sentry, sentinel, guard **3.** (*miejsce*) guardroom, sentry box; ***~ek policji*** police station; ***~ek straży pożarnej*** *Br* fire station, *Am* fire house; ***stać na ~ku*** be on guard; **posterunkowy** *m* (*-wego*; *-wi*) **1.** (*szef posterunku*) commander of the guard **2.** (*oficer dyżurny*) constable, police officer
postękiwać *v/im* (*-kuję*) groan (quietly); → ***stękać***
postęp *m* (*-pu*; *-py*) progress; ***~y*** improvement, headway (***w*** *L* in); ***iść z ~em*** keep abreast of the times; ***robić ~y*** make headway; ***~ w informatyce*** developments in information technology; ***~ arytmetyczny*** (***geometryczny***) arithmetic (geometric) progression
postępek *m* (*-pku*; *-pki*) misdeed
postępować ⟨***-tąpić***⟩ (*-puję*) **1.** (*zachowywać się*) act; ***właściwie*** (***niewłaściwie***) ***~ z*** *I* treat s.o properly (badly); ***~ niemądrze*** act unwisely **2.** (*o pracy*) proceed, get on **3.** (*o chorobie*) develop **4.** (*kroczyć*) advance; ***~ naprzód*** go forward(s)
postępowani|e *n* (*-nia*; *-nia*) **1.** (*zachowanie*) conduct, attitude (***w stosunku do*** *G* towards); ***twoje ~e pozostawia wiele do życzenia*** your attitude leaves a lot to be desired; ***sposób ~a*** course of action **2.** *JUR* proceedings; ***~e sądowe*** legal proceedings (***przeciwko*** *D* against); ***wszcząć*** (***umorzyć***/***zawiesić***) ***~e*** start (remit/suspend) proceedings; ***~e karne*** criminal proceedings
postępowiec *m* (*-wca*; *-wcy*) progressive
postępow|y *adj* progressive; ***~i przemysłowcy*** forward-looking industrialists; ***~e idee*** innovative ideas
postępujący *adj* progressive
postkomunistyczny *adj* post-communist
postn|y *adj* *REL* *posiłek*: lenten; ***dni ~e*** maigre days; ***danie ~e*** *REL* fasting food
postojow|y *adj*: ***miejsce ~e*** parking site; ***światła ~e*** *AUTO* *Br* sidelights, *Am* parking lights
postój *m* (*-toju*; *-toje*) **1.** (*odpoczynek*) break; ***zakaz postoju*** no waiting **2.** (*przerwa w podróży*) stopover, stop-off; ***zrobić ~ we wsi*** stop off in a village; ***~ taksówek*** taxi rank, taxi stand **3.** *TECH* (*w wyniku awarii*) halt; ***~ w produkcji*** halt in production
postponować ⟨***s-***⟩ (*-nuję*) *lit* deprecate, disdain, think little (*A* of)
postrach *m* (*-chu*; *no pl*) terror, fear; ***wzbudzać ~*** terrify; ***na ~, dla ~u*** as a deterrent; ***trzymać w ~u*** hold in deterrence; ***~ studentów*** a very demanding lecturer; ***~ dzieci*** bo(o)gey man
postradać *v/p* (*-dam*) *lit* lose; ***~ zmysły*** go insane, become insane
postron|ek *m* (*-nka*; *-nki*) cord, tether, leash; ***zwierzę na ~ku*** animal on a leash; ***trzymać kozę na ~ku*** keep a goat on a tether; ***mieć nerwy jak ~ki*** have iron nerves
postronn|y *adj* **1.** ***~y obserwator*** bystander **2.** ***osoby ~e*** *JUR* third party
postrzał *m* (*-łu*; *-ły*) **1.** (*rana*) gunshot wound; ***~ w głowę*** shot in the head **2.** *MED* lumbago
postrzegać ⟨***-rzec***⟩ (*-gam*) perceive; **postrzegalny** *adj* perceptible
postrzeleniec *m* (*-leńca*; *-leńcy*) *infml* madcap
postrzel|ić *v/p* (*-lę*) shoot; ***~ono ją trzy razy w głowę*** she was shot three times in the head
postrzelony *adj* **1.** (*szalony*) crazy **2.** (*zraniony*) wounded, shot, with a gunshot wound
postrzępiony *adj* **1.** *materiał*: frayed **2.** *skała*: jagged
postsynchronizacja *f* (*-ji*; *-je*) postsynchronising
postukiwać ⟨***-kać***⟩ (*-kuję*) (*o obcasach*) knock
postulat *m* (*-tu*; *-ty*) **1.** *POLIT* demand; ***wysunąć ~*** demand **2.** *MATH* postulate; **postulować** *v/im* (*-luję*) **1.** *POLIT* demand **2.** *teorię naukową*: postulate
postument *m* (*-tu*; *-ty*) pedestal
posucha *f* (*-chy*; *no pl*) **1.** (*susza*) drought **2.** (*brak*) *fig* lack, shortage
posunąć *v/p* → ***posuwać***
posunięcie *n* (*-cia*; *-cia*) (*w grze*, *w szachach*) move; ***~ taktyczne*** tactical move; ***mądre ~*** smart move

posunięty *adj*: **daleko ~** (far) advanced
posuw *m* (*-wu*; *-wy*) TECH feed
posuwać ⟨**-sunąć**⟩ (*-wam*) **1.** *przedmiot*: move **2.** *vulg* screw, shag; **posuwać się 1.** (*przemieszczać się naprzód*) move along, advance; **~ się za daleko** *fig* go too far **2.** (*robić postępy*) progress, make progress; ***budowa posuwa się w błyskawicznym tempie*** construction is progressing very quickly; **~ *się do ostateczności*** go to extremes **2.** (*zrobić miejsce*) move **3.** (*o pracy*) go very well **4.** (*o chorobie*) progress
posyłać ⟨**-słać**⟩ (*-łam*) send (**po** *A* for); ***matka posłała mnie do piekarni po bułki*** my mother sent me to the bakery to get some bread rolls; **~ *do szkoły*** send to school; **~ *na urlop*** send on vacation, send on holiday; **~ *na śmierć*** sentence to death; ***gdzie diabeł nie może, tam babę pośle*** a woman can handle everything; **~ *komuś całusa*** blow s.o. a kiss; **~ *komuś spojrzenie*** (***uśmiech***) send s.o. a glance (smile); **~ *komuś gniewne spojrzenie*** look angrily at; **~ *piłkę do bramki*** send the ball into the goal
posyłk|a: ***chłopiec na ~i*** errand boy; ***być na ~i*** run errands, do errands
posypywać ⟨**-pać**⟩ (*-puję*) **1.** scatter, spread: **~ *ulice solą*** spread salt on streets **2. ~ *ciasto cukrem*** sprinkle sugar over the cake; **posypać się 1.** (*o liściach*) fall (in great numbers) **2.** (*o tynku*) fall off **3.** (*o iskrach*) fly **4.** (*o listach, prośbach*) pour in; ***posypały się zarzuty*** accusations flew around; ***posypały się oklaski*** rounds of applause could be heard
poszaleć *v/p* → ***szaleć***
poszanowani|e *n* (*-nia*; *no pl*) respect; ***wykazywać brak ~a dla władzy*** show a lack of respect for authority
poszarpany *adj materiał*: torn, tattered
poszczególny *adj* individual, particular
poszczęścić się *v/p*: ***poszczęściło mu się*** he was lucky, luck was on his side, he was in luck
poszedł → ***pójść***
poszerzać ⟨**-rzyć**⟩ (*-rzam*) **1.** *drogę*: widen **2.** *ubranie*, *sukienkę*: let out **3.** *horyzonty*, *wiedzę*: broaden; **poszerzać się** broaden, grow wider, become wider
poszerzenie *n* (*-nia*; *no pl*) widening
poszewka *f* (*-ki*; *-ki*) pillowcase, pillowslip
poszkodowany I *adj* (*ranny*) injured; ***być ~m w wypadku*** be injured in an accident, be a casualty; **~ *na zdrowiu*** suffering harm to one's health; ***być ~m*** be wronged; incur damage, suffer damage (**w** *L* in); ***być ~m przez los*** be wronged by fate **II** *m* (*-nego*; *-ni*), **-na** *f* (*-nej*; *-ne*) **1.** (*w wypadku*) victim **2.** (*osoba*) JUR aggrieved party, wronged party
poszlaka *f* (*-ki*; *-ki*) circumstantial evidence, indirect evidence; **poszlakowy** *adj* JUR circumstantial; ***proces ~*** trial based on circumstantial evidence, circumstantial legal case
posz|li, **~ła**, **~ło**, **~ły** → ***pójść***
poszukiwacz *m* (*-cza*; *-cze*), **~ka** *f* (*-ki*; *-ki*): **~ *złota*** gold-digger; **~ *przygód*** adventure-seeker, adventurer; **~ *pereł*** pearl diver; **~ *skarbów*** treasure hunter
poszu|kiwać *v/im* (*-kuję*) search (*G* for); ***~kiwać złota*** dig for gold; ***~kuje go policja*** he's wanted by the police
poszukiwani|e *n* (*-nia*; *-nia*) **1.** *pracy*: search, hunt; ***bezowocne ~a*** fruitless search; **w ~u** *G* in search of **2.** *złota*: digging; ***~a geologiczne*** prospecting **3. *~e prawdy*** quest for the truth **4. *~a naukowe*** research: ***~a artystyczne*** artistic search **5.** *zaginionej osoby*: search (operation)
poszukiwan|y I *adj* **1.** *zbieg*: wanted **2.** (*zaginiony*) missing **3.** *towar*: sought-after, in-demand; ***takie umiejętności są ~e na rynku*** such skills are much in demand on the market; ***bardzo ~y towar*** a highly marketable product **II** *m* (*-nego*; *-ni*), **-na** *f* (*-nej*; *-ne*) **1.** (*zbieg*) wanted person **2.** (*zaginiony*) missing person
poszukiwawczy *adj* **1.** *akcja*: search **2.** *ekspedycja*: exploratory, explorative
poszum *m* (*-mu*; *no pl*) *lit* **1.** *liści*: rustle **2.** *wiatru*: whistle, breath, hum **3.** *morza*: murmur

P

poszwa *f* (*-wy*; *-wy*) **1.** (*na kołdrę*) duvet cover, duvet case **2.** (*na poduszkę*) pillowcase

poszycie *n* (*-cia*; *no pl*) **1.** *dachu*: roofing **2.** *samolotu*: skin **3.** (*runo leśne*) undergrowth

poszywać ⟨**-szyć**⟩ (*-wam*) **1.** *dach*: cover **2.** (*kryć strzechą*) thatch

pościć *v/im* (*poszczę*) fast

pościel *f* (*-li*; *no pl*) bedding, bedclothes; ***leżeć w ~i*** lie in bed; **pościelić** *v/p* → **ścielić**; **pościelow|y** *adj* bed; ***bielizna ~a*** bed linen

pościg *m* (*-gu*; *-gi*) **1.** chase (**za** *I* after); ***~ policyjny*** police chase; ***~ samochodowy*** car chase; ***policja natychmiast wszczęła ~*** the police immediately gave chase; ***przerwać ~*** give up the chase **2.** (*pragnienie*) *fig* pursuit (**za** *I* of) **3.** (*grupa ludzi*) pursuers; **pościgow|y** *adj* pursuit, chase; ***akcja ~a*** chase; ***samolot ~y*** pursuit plane

pośladek *m* (*-dka*; *-dki*) *ANAT* buttock

pośledni *adj lit* mediocre, inferior

poślizg *m* (*-gu*; *-gi*) **1.** *AUTO* slide, skid; ***wpaść w ~*** go into a skid, skid; ***~ kontrolowany*** power slide; ***ślady po ~u*** skid marks; ***wyjść z ~u*** get out of a skid; ***niebezpieczeństwo ~u*** danger of skidding **2.** (*opóźnienie*) delay; ***z ~iem*** with a delay; ***czterogodzinny ~*** four hour delay

poślizgnąć się *v/p* (*-znę*) slip; ***noga mi się poślizgnęła*** my foot slipped; ***poślizgnęła się na lodzie*** she slipped on the ice

poślubiać ⟨**-bić**⟩ (*-biam*) *lit* wed, marry

poślubn|y *adj*: ***podróż ~a*** honeymoon; ***w noc ~ą*** on the wedding night

pośmiertn|y *adj* posthumous; ***maska ~a*** death mask; ***stężenie ~e*** *MED* rigor mortis; ***wspomnienie ~e*** obituary

pośmiewisk|o *n* (*-ka*; *no pl*) **1.** (*kpiny*) ridicule, mockery; ***wystawić na ~o*** make a laughing stock of, ridicule **2.** ***zrobić z siebie ~o*** make a laughing stock of oneself, expose oneself to ridicule; ***stać się ~iem*** become a laughing stock

pośpiech *m* (*-chu*; *no pl*) haste, hurry; ***w ~u*** in haste; ***nie ma ~u*** there is no rush; ***w wielkim ~u*** in a great hurry; ***po co ten ~?*** what's the hurry?; ***robić coś bez ~u*** do s.th. without haste

pośpieszać ⟨**-szyć**⟩ (*-szam*) (*iść*) go, rush; ***~ komuś z pomocą*** rush to the aid of s.o.; ***pośpieszyła, żeby odebrać telefon*** she hurried to answer the telephone; ***~ na ratunek*** go to the rescue; ***pośpieszyć się*** hurry up; ***pośpieszyć z*** *I fig* hasten; ***pośpiesz się!*** hurry up!

pośpieszn|y *adj* **1.** *pociąg*, *autobus*: fast **2.** (*pochopny*) (over)hasty; ***~a decyzja*** hasty decision **3.** *krok*: hasty

pośredni *adj* **1.** *wpływ*: indirect **2.** *stadium*: intermediate; ***coś ~ego między x a y*** something halfway between x and y

pośredniak *m* (*-ka*; *-ki*) *infml* job centre, employment centre

pośrednictw|o *n* (*-wa*: *no pl*) **1.** agency; ***za ~em*** *G* by the agency of, through the agency of; ***~o handlowe*** intermediate trade; ***biuro ~a pracy*** *Br* job centre, *Am* employment agency; ***biuro ~a sprzedaży nieruchomości*** real estate agency **2.** (*mediacja*) mediation; ***prosić kogoś o ~o*** ask s.o. for mediation; ***za ~em telewizji*** by means of TV

pośredniczenie *n* (*-nia*; *no pl*) mediation

pośredniczyć *v/im* (*-czę*) **1.** (*pełnić rolę rozjemcy*) mediate (**między** *I* between, **w** *L* in) **2.** **~ w** *L* be agents for

pośrednik *m* (*-ka*; *-nicy*), **-niczka** *f* (*-ki*; *-ki*) **1.** (*w sporze*) go-between **2.** *handlowy*: agent; ***~ handlu nieruchomościami*** real estate agent **3.** *POLIT* negotiator **4.** (*rozjemca*) mediator; ***pełnić rolę ~a*** act as a mediator

pośrednio *adv* → ***pośredni***

pośrodku *adv* in the middle (*G* of)

pośród *prep* (*G*) amid(st), in the midst of

poświadcz|ać ⟨**-czyć**⟩ (*-czam*) authenticate, certify, attest; ***~ono autentyczność podpisu*** the signature has been authenticated as genuine; ***~ona kopia*** certified copy

poświadczenie *n* (*-nia*; *-nia*) **1.** (*dokument*) certificate; ***~ odbioru*** proof of receipt, receipt **2.** *podpisu*: authentication, certification

poświę|cać ⟨**-cić**⟩ (*-cam*) **1.** *czas*, *wieczór*: devote (**coś** *D* s.th. to); ***być czemuś ~conym*** be devoted to; ***~cać***

więcej uwagi *D* devote more attention to; ***~cać wiele czasu*** *D* devote much time to **2.** (*dedykować*) dedicate **3.** (*udzielić błogosławieństwa*) bless **4.** *świątynię*: consecrate; **5.** (*złożyć w ofierze*) sacrifice; ***~cać życie dla*** *G* sacrifice one's life for; ***poświęcać się*** **1.** *rodzinie*, *dzieciom*: make sacrifices for **2.** *pracy*, *badaniom*: dedicate oneself to

poświęcenie *n* (*-nia*; *no pl*) **1.** (*czyn*) sacrifice; ***~ życia*** making a sacrifice of one's life **2.** (*postawa*) dedication, devotion; ***z ~m*** with dedication; ***~ się*** dedication **3.** *REL* consecration

poświst *m* (*-tu*; *-ty*) whistle, whizz

pot *m* (*-tu*; *-ty*) sweat; ***zlany ~em*** wet with sweat; ***pokryty ~em*** covered in sweat; ***spływać ~em*** dripping with sweat, dripping in sweat; ***wziąć coś na ~y*** take a diaphoretic drug; ***pracować w pocie czoła*** work in the sweat of one's brows

potajemny *adj* secret

potakiwacz *m* (*-cza*; *-cze*) yes-man; **potakiwać** *v/im* (*-kuję*) **1.** (*godzić się*) nod (in agreement) **2.** say yes, (always) agree (*D* with); **potakująco** *adv* in assent

potanieć *v/p* → ***tanieć***

potańcówka *f* (*-ki*; *-ki*) dancing party, hop

potargać *v/p* (*-gam*) *włosy*: tousle; ***z potarganymi włosami*** tousle-haired

potas *m* (*-su*; *no pl*) *CHEM* potassium

potasować *v/p* → ***tasować***

potąd *adv* up to here; ***mam tego ~!*** I've had it up to here!, I've had enough of this!; ***mam jej ~!*** I can't take her any more!

potem *adv* next, then, afterwards; ***na ~*** for later

potencja *f* (*-ji*; *no pl*) potency

potencjalny *adj* **1.** (*możliwy*) potential **2.** *klient*: prospective; **potencjał** *m* (*-łu*; *-ły*) potential; ***ten region ma ogromny ~ ekonomiczny*** the region has enormous potential for economic development

potencjometr *m* (*-ru*; *-ry*) volume control, dial

potentat *m* (*-ta*; *-ntaci*) tycoon, mogul; ***~ naftowy*** oil magnate; ***~ przemysłowy*** baron of industry

potęg|a *f* (*-gi*; *no pl*) **1.** power; ***~a militarna*** military power; **2.** *MATH* ***cztery do ~i trzeciej*** four to the power of three; ***podnieść liczbę do ~i*** raise a number to the power of; ***wykładnik ~i*** exponent, index

potęgować ⟨**s-**⟩ (*-guję*) **1.** *ból*: intensify, exacerbate **2.** *efekt*: magnify **3.** *wrażenie*: enhance **4.** *napięcie*, *panikę*: heighten **5.** *MATH* raise to the power; ***potęgować się*** **1.** (*o niepokju*) grow **2.** (*o upale*) intensify **3.** (*o panice*) heighten

potępiać ⟨**-pić**⟩ (*-piam*) **1.** (*napiętnować*) disapprove of; ***~ kogoś w czambuł*** *infml* thoroughly disapprove of **2.** condemn **3.** ***dusza potępiona*** damned soul

potępiając|y *adj* condemnatory, denunciatory; ***~a mowa*** condemnatory speech

potępieni|e *n* (*-nia*; *no pl*) **1.** (*negatywna ocena*) condemnation, disapproval; ***godne ~a zachowanie*** reprehensible conduct, contemptible behaviour **2.** *REL* damnation, perdition; ***wieczne ~e*** eternal damnation; ***~e bezbożników*** perdition of ungodly men

potępieniec *m* (*-pieńca*; *-pieńcy*) *REL lit* reprobate; ***drzeć się jak ~*** scream like one possessed

potępieńcz|y *adj lit* horrible, hellish; ***~e wrzaski*** furious yelling

potępiony I *adj REL* condemned **II** *m* (*-nego*; *-pieni*), **-na** *f* (*-nej*; *-ne*) *REL* reprobate

potężnieć ⟨**s-**⟩ (*-nieję*) gain power, gain might

potężny *adj* **1.** *cios*: mighty **2.** *człowiek*: thickset, strapping **3.** *budowla*: huge **4.** *uczucie*: intense **5.** *mocarstwo*, *organizacja*, *władca*: powerful **6.** *huk*, *wiwaty*: resounding

potknąć się *v/p* → ***potykać się***

potknięci|e *n* (*-cia*; *-cia*) stumble, trip; ***~a*** *fig* slips

potliwość *f* (*-ści*; *no pl*) perspiration

potłuczenie *n* (*-nia*; *-nia*) contusion, bruise

potnieć (*-nieję*) **1.** ⟨**s-**⟩ sweat **2.** ⟨**za-**⟩ (*o szkle*, *metalu*) mist up

potoczek *m* (*-czka*/*-czku*; *-czki*) *dim* small stream, small brook

P

potoczny *adj* **1.** *wyraz, nazwa*: colloquial; ***język ~*** informal language, colloquial language **2.** *wyobrażenie, opinia*: common; ***w ~m rozumieniu*** as people generally understand it; ***w sensie ~m*** in everyday use

potoczysty *adj język*: flowing; ***~ styl*** voluble style

potok *m* (*-ku*; *-ki*) **1.** (*woda*) stream, brook; ***górski ~*** mountain brook; ***rwący ~*** fast-flowing stream, running stream; ***~i deszczu*** torrents of rain; ***~ krwi*** rivulets of blood; ***płynąć ~iem*** *fig* flow in in large numbers; ***~ łez*** a flood of tears **2.** *słów*: torrent; ***~ wyzwisk*** hail of abuse

potomek *m* (*-mka*; *-mkowie*), **-mkini** *f* (*-ni*; *-nie*) descendant; ***potomkowie*** posterity, progeny

potomni *pl* (*-nych*) (*przyszłe pokolenia*) descendants

potomnoś|ć *f* (*-ści*; *no pl*) posterity; ***przejść do ~ci*** go down to posterity, be passed on posterity, be handed down to posterity; **potomstwo** *n* (*-wa*; *no pl*) offspring

potop *m* (*-pu*; *-py*) REL the Flood; ***prawdziwy ~, istny ~*** deluge, flood

potowy *adj*: ***gruczoł ~*** sweat gland; ***potówki*** *pl* (*-wek*) heat rash, prickly heat

potrafić *v im/p* (*-fię*) **1.** (*umieć*) be able to; ***pokaż, co potrafisz*** show us what you can do; ***najlepiej, jak potrafię*** to the best of my ability **2.** (*być zdolnym*) be capable of

potrajać ⟨**-troić**⟩ (*-jam*) triple

P

potrawa *f* (*-wy*; *-wy*) dish; ***spis potraw*** menu; ***~ z warzyw*** vegetable dish; ***~ z mięsa*** meat dish; ***~ z ryżu*** rice dish

potraw|ka *f* (*-ki*; *-ki*) fricassee; ***~ka cielęca*** veal fricassee; ***kura w ~ce*** chicken fricassee; ***~ka z zająca*** jugged hare

potrącać ⟨**-cić**⟩ (*-cam*) **1.** *mebel*: knock, push **2.** (*samochodem*) hit, knock over **3.** *temat*: touch upon, mention briefly **4.** FIN deduct (***z*** *G* from); ***~ z pensji*** check off

potrącenia *pl* (*-ceń*) **1.** FIN deduction, *Am* dockage **2.** (*wypadki*) accident involving a pedestrian

potrójn|y *adj* triple, triplex; ***~y mistrz olimpijski*** triple Olympic champion; ***~e okna*** triplex windows; ***~y kabel*** triplex cable; ***~y karton*** triplex paperboard

potrzask *m* (*-ku*; *-ki*) trap; ***znaleźć się w ~u*** *fig* be trapped, fall in a trap

potrzaskać *v/p* (*-kam*) smash, shatter

potrząsać ⟨**-snąć**⟩ (*-sam*) shake (*I* s.th.)

potrzeb|a[1] *f* (*-by*; *-by*) **1.** need; ***nagła ~a*** emergency, burning need, pressing need; ***na własne ~y*** for personal use; ***bez ~y*** unnecessarily; ***w razie ~y*** if need be; ***w miarę ~y*** if necessary; ***~y fizjologiczne***, ***~y naturalne*** physiologic(al) need; ***wyjść za ~ą*** *infml* go to the toilet; ***~a chwili*** expediency; ***nie ma ~y*** there's no need; ***w ~ie*** in need; ***~a jest matką wynalazku*** necessity is the mother of invention; ***być w ~ie*** be in need; ***opuścić kogoś w ~ie*** leave s.o. in the lurch **2.** (*rzeczy niezbędne*) necessities *pl*; ***artykuły pierwszej ~y*** articles of prime necessity; ***~y materialne*** material needs; ***podstawowe ~y*** basic needs

potrzeb|a[2] *v/irreg* ***~a mi*** *G* I need; ***do tego ~a doświadczenia*** you need experience for that; ***nie ~a, żeby*** there's no need to; ***więcej niż ~a*** more than necessary; ***~a czasu, żeby*** you need time to; ***~a mi więcej czasu*** I need more time; ***~a ci pieniędzy?*** do you need money?; ***tego właśnie mi ~a*** that's exactly what I need, that's the very thing I need

potrzebn|y *adj* necessary; ***to jest mi ~e*** I need this; ***nie być komuś ~ym*** be of no use to; ***czy jestem ci jeszcze ~y?*** do you still need me?; ***wszystko, co ~e*** all you need; ***ludzie lubią czuć się ~i*** people like to feel needed; ***~y jak dziura w moście*** I need it like (I need) a hole in the head

potrzebować *v/im* (*-buję*) need (*G* s.th.); ***nie potrzebujesz tego robić*** you don't need/have to do this; ***dziecko potrzebuje opieki*** the baby needs care

potrzebujący **I** *adj* needy, in need; ***pomoc dla najbardziej ~ch*** help for the poor; ***~ pomocy*** in need of help **II** *m* (*-cego*; *-cy*), **-ca** *f* (*-cej*; *-ce*) the needy, a person in need

potrzeć *v/p* → ***pocierać***

potulny *adj* meek, docile; ***~ jak baranek*** meek and mild, meek as a lamb

poturbowa|ć *v/p* (*-buję*) **1.** (*o zwierzęciu*) savage; ***dziecko zostało ~ne przez psa*** the child was savaged by a dog **2.** (*pobić*) rough up; ***poturbować się*** **1.** (*w wypadku*) get hurt **2.** (*w walce*) hurt each other, hurt one antoher

potwarz *f* (*-rzy*; *-rze*) calumny, slander; ***oskarżyć kogoś o ~*** bring a slander action against

potwierdza|ć ⟨**-dzić**⟩ (*-dzam*) confirm; ***fakty nie ~ją jego wersji wydarzeń*** his version of events just isn't borne out by the facts; ***~ć odbiór*** *G* acknowledge (receipt of); ***potwierdzać się*** be confirmed

potwierdzająco *adv* affirmatively; ***skinąć głową ~*** nod assent; **potwierdzenie** *n* (*-nia*; *-nia*) **1.** (*poświadczenie*) confirmation; ***pisemne ~*** written confirmation; ***~ odbioru*** notice of receipt **2.** *teorii*, *oskarżenia*: corroboration

potwierdzić *v/p* → ***potwierdzać***

potwierdzony *adj* confirmed

potworność|ć *f* (*-ści*; *-ści*) **1.** (*ohyda*) monstrosity; ***kto powiesił tę ~ć na ścianie?*** who hung that monstrosity on the wall? **2.** (*okropność*) abomination; ***uważam, że polowanie na lisa to ~ć*** I think that foxhunting is an abomination; ***~ci*** atrocities; **potworny** *adj* **1.** *krzyk*, *ból*: terrible **2.** *zbrodnia*: atrocious, hideous **3.** (*brzydki*) monstrous, dreadful; ***~ bałagan*** (***hałas***) a hell of a mess (noise) *infml*

potwór *m* (*-wora*; *-wory*) monster

potyczka *f* (*-ki*; *-ki*) skirmish; ***~ słowna*** shouting match, battle of words

potykać się ⟨**-tknąć**⟩ (*-kam*) stumble (**o** *A* over)

potylic|a *f* (*-cy*; *-ce*) *ANAT* occiput; ***strzał w ~ę*** shot in the occiput

pouczać ⟨**-czyć**⟩ (*-czam*) **1.** (*upominać*) admonish **2.** (*instruować*) instruct **3.** (*prawić kazania*) patronize

pouczając|y *adj* instructive; ***~a sztuka*** didactic play; ***~y artykuł*** informative article; **pouczenie** *n* (*-nia*; *-nia*) **1.** (*upomnienie*) admonishment **2.** (*instrukcja*) advice, information

pouczyć *v/p* → ***pouczać***

pouczyć się *v/p* (*-czę*) learn up, bone up (*G* on), learn (for some time); → ***uczyć się***

poufale *adv* → ***poufały***

poufałość *f* (*-ści*; *no pl*) **1.** (*zażyłość*) intimacy **2.** (*zachowanie*) familiarity; ***zbytnia ~*** excessive familiarity, overfamiliarity

poufał|y *adj* **1.** (*śmiały*) familiar; ***~e klepnięcie po plecach*** friendly slap on the back; ***był w stosunku do niej zbyt ~y*** he was overfamiliar with her **2.** *stosunki*: intimate; ***~a rozmowa*** intimate conversation

poufny *adj* **1.** *rozmowa*, *informacja*: confidential **2.** *sprawa*: discreet **3.** *misja*: secret **4.** *ton*: friendly

poukładać *v/p* → ***układać***

pourazowy *adj* *MED* post-traumatic; ***wstrząs ~*** post-traumatic stress disorder

pow. *abbr* **1.** (=**powierzchnia**) area **2.** (=**powiat**) district

powab *m* (*-bu*; *-by*) *lit* *osoby*: charm, appeal; ***~y świata*** attractions of the world; **powabny** *adj* *lit* charming, glamorous, attractive

powag|a *f* (*-gi*; *no pl*) **1.** *instytucji*: authority **2.** (*doniosłość*) seriousness; ***~a sytuacji*** seriousness of the situation; ***~a chwili*** significance of the moment; ***zachować ~ę*** keep a straight face; ***brak ~i*** frivolity, levity

powalać ⟨**-lić**⟩ (*-lam*) **1.** (*o chorobie*) strike down; ***choroba go powaliła*** *lit* illness struck him down **2.** (*przewracać*) knock down; ***~ na plecy*** knock down **3.** (*w walce*) fell; ***~ kogoś ciosem*** send s.o. sprawling, fell **4.** *zwierzę*: shoot dead

poważać *v/im* (*-żam*) esteem, respect

poważani|e *n* (*-nia*; *no pl*) **1.** (*uznanie*) esteem; ***cieszyć się ~em u*** *G* be held in high esteem by, be held in high esteem with, be (highly) esteemed by, be (highly) esteemed with; ***na znak ~a*** as a token of esteem **2.** (*szacunek*) respect; ***zdobyć czyjeś ~e*** earn the respect of s.o., gain the respect of s.o.; ***z ~em*** (*w listach*) yours faithfully

poważnie *adv* (*z powagą*) seriously; ***traktować ~*** take seriously; ***mówić ~*** mean it, talk seriously; ***~ chory*** seriously ill; ***~?*** *infml* are you serious?, really?; ***całkiem na ~*** in deadly earnest

P

poważnieć ⟨**s-**⟩ (*-nieję*) **1.** (*nabierać powagi*) become serious **2.** (*dorośleć*) grow up

poważn|y *adj* **1.** *zagrożenie*, *obrażenia*: serious; ***odegrać ~ą rolę*** play an important part; ***mieć ~e zamiary wobec kogoś*** be serious about marrying s.o.; ***jego stan jest bardzo ~y*** his condition is serious **2.** *problem*: grave **3.** *zarzut*: gross, heavy **4.** *polityk*: respected **5.** *firma*: reputable **6.** *muzyka*: classical

powątpiewa|ć *v/im* (*-wam*) doubt; ***~m w jego obietnice*** I'm dubious about his promises; **powątpiewający** *adj* sceptical; **powątpiewanie** *n* (*-nia*; *no pl*) doubt, dubiousness; ***z ~m*** doubtfully, doubtingly, dubiously

poweseleć *v/p* (*-leję*) cheer up, brighten (up)

powetować *v/p* (*-tuję*): ***~ sobie stratę*** make the loss up to oneself, indemnify oneself; ***~ sobie stracony czas*** make up for lost time

powiać *v/p* → ***powiewać***

powiadać *v/im* (*-dam*) *lit* say

powiadamiać ⟨***-domić***⟩ (*-miam*) notify (**o** *L* about); **powiadomienie** *n* (*-nia*; *-nia*) notification; ***pisemne ~*** written notification

powiastka *f* (*-ki*; *-ki*) story, tale; ***~ filozoficzna*** philosophical tale

powiat *m* (*-tu*; *-ty*) district; **powiatow|y** *adj* district; ***miasto ~e*** municipality

powiązać *v/p* → ***wiązać***

powiązani|e *n* (*-nia*; *-nia*) **1.** (*zależność*) connection; ***w ~u z*** *I* in connection with **2.** (*związek*) link

powiązan|y *adj*: ***być ~ym z*** *I* **a)** be connected with **b)** related to; (***nie***) ***~e ze sobą*** (un)related; ***nie ~e ze sobą fakty*** unrelated facts; ***to jest ~e z ryzykiem*** risk must be calculated here, there's risk involved in it; ***on jest ~y z mafią*** he has connections with the mafia; ***dieta i zdrowie są ze sobą ~e*** diet and health are interrelated

powi|ć *v/p* (*-wiję*) *lit* bear, give birth to; ***żona ~ła mu córkę*** his wife bore him a daughter

powidła *pl* (*-deł*) plum jam, plum confection, damson cheese

powiedzeni|e *n* (*-nia*; *-nia*) (*aforyzm*) saying; ***mieć dużo do ~a*** **a)** (*wyjaśnienie*) have a lot to say **b)** (*być decydującym*) have a (big) say; ***nie mieć nic do ~a*** have nothing to say

powiedzi|eć *v/p* (*-wiem*) **1.** say; ***~eć, że*** say that; ***nie jest ~ane, że*** it's not certain that; ***to za mało ~ane!*** that's putting it mildly **2.** (*opowiedzieć*) ***~eć komuś coś*** tell s.o. about s.th. **3.** (*mówić*) speak; ***że tak powiem*** so to speak **4.** mean; ***co chcesz przez to ~eć?*** what do you mean by that?; ***kto by ~ał, że*** who would have thought that

powiedzonko *n* (*-ka*; *-ka*) tag

powiek|a *f* (*-ki*; *-ki*) eyelid; ***bez drgnienia*** (***zmrużenia***) ***~*** without batting an eyelid (eyelash); ***spędza mu to sen z ~*** this keeps him awake; ***~i mi się same zamykają*** my eyelids are drooping

powielacz *m* (*-cza*; *-cze*) duplicator, copier

powielać ⟨**-lić**⟩ (*-lam*) **1.** (*kopiować*) duplicate, photocopy; ***~ w pięciu egzemplarzach*** make five copies **2.** (*powtarzać*) *fig* repeat the same patterns; ***~ stereotyp*** stereotype

powiernica *f* (*-cy*; *-ce*) confidante; **powiernictwo** *n* (*-wa*; *no pl*) JUR trust; **powiernik** *m* (*-ka*; *-nicy*) **1.** (*człowiek zaufany*) confidant **2.** JUR trustee, fiduciary

powierniczy|y *adj* JUR trust; ***terytorium ~e*** POLIT trust territory

powierz|ać ⟨**-rzyć**⟩ (*-rzam*) **1.** *tajemnicę*: reveal; ***~ać komuś tajemnicę*** share a secret with s.o., let s.o. in(to) a secret **2.** *zadanie*: entrust; ***~ył swoje dziecko mojej opiece*** he asked me to look after his child; ***~ono mu organizację koncertu*** he was entrusted with organizing the concert; ***~ać matce opiekę nad dzieckiem*** JUR give the mother custody of the child

powierzchni|a *f* (*-ni*; *-nie*) **1.** *wody*: surface; ***utrzymywać się na ~*** keep afloat, stay afloat; ***zetrzeć coś z ~ ziemi*** wipe s.th. out, wipe s.th. off the map; ***~a wody*** water surface **2.** *kraju*: area; ***~a użytkowa*** living space, inhabitable area **3.** MATH (surface) area; **powierzchniowy** *adj* surface

powierzchownoś|ć *f* (*-ści*; *no pl*) **1.** (*cecha*) exterior, appearance; ***osoba o***

miłej ~ci clean-cut/likeable person **2.** *zainteresowań*: superficiality, shallowness; **powierzchown|y** *adj* **1.** *rana*: slight, cutaneous **2.** *wiedza*: superficial, cursory; ***~e spojrzenie*** cursory glance
powierzyć *v/p* → ***powierzać***
powiesić *v/p* → ***wieszać***
powieszenie *n* (*-nia*; *no pl*): ***śmierć przez ~*** death by hanging
powieściopisarz *m* (*-rza*; *-rze*), **-rka** *f* (*-ki*; *-ki*) novelist; **powieściowy** *adj konwencje*: novelistic
powieść[1] *f* (*-ści*; *-ści*) novel; ***~ kryminalna*** detective novel; ***~ przygodowa*** adventure novel; ***~ rzeka*** saga; ***przerabiać na ~*** novelize; ***~ z kluczem*** roman-à-clef; ***~ w odcinkach*** serial
powieść[2] *v/p* → ***wodzić***
powieść się *v/i* (*-wiodę*) succeed, be successful; ***nie ~*** fail, be unsuccessful; ***powiodło mi się*** I made it; ***nie powiodło mu się*** he was unsuccessful, he failed
powietrz|e *n* (*-rza*; *no pl*) air; ***na*** (***świeżym***) ***~u*** in the open air, outdoors; ***wychodzić na*** (***świeże***) ***~e*** go outside; ***na wolnym ~u*** in the open, outdoors; ***wisieć w ~u*** *fig* be in the air; ***traktować kogoś jak ~e*** ignore s.o., give s.o. the cold-shoulder; ***kino na wolnym ~u*** drive-in cinema
powietrzn|y *adj* air; ***obszar ~y*** air space; ***most ~y*** airlift; ***poduszka ~a*** AUTO airbag; ***korytarz ~y*** air corridor; ***prądy ~e*** air currents, currents of air; ***trąba ~a*** whirlwind, twister
powiew *m* (*-wu*; *-wy*) breath, puff; ***lekki ~*** breath/puff of air; ***~ wiatru*** breath of wind; ***~ od morza*** gentle breeze
powi|ewać ⟨**powiać**⟩ (*-wam*) **1.** (*o wietrze*) blow; ***~ało zimnem*** a chill wind came; ***~ało spalenizną*** you could smell s.th. burning **2.** (*łopotać*) flutter, fly; ***flagi ~ewały na wietrze*** flags were fluttering in the breeze; ***flaga ~ewała w połowie masztu*** flag was flying at half-mast **3.** ***wiatr ~ewał firankami*** wind was moving the curtains **4.** (*machać*) wave; ***~ewać chusteczką*** wave a handkerchief
powiewny *adj sukienka*: flimsy
powiększać ⟨**-szyć**⟩ (*-szam*) **1.** *obszar*: extend **2.** *obraz*: enlarge; ***~ zdjęcie*** have a photograph enlarged **3.** *deficyt*, *dostawy*, *ilość*: increase; ***powiększać się*** **1.** (*o obszarze*) expand **2.** (*o grupie*) grow, increase; ***populacja powiększyła się*** population has increased
powiększając|y *adj*: ***szkło ~e*** magnifying glass
powiększalnik *m* (*-ka*; *-ki*) PHOT enlarger; **powiększenie** *n* (*-nia*; *-nia*) PHOT enlargement
powiększyć *v/p* → ***powiększać***
powijak|i: ***być w ~ach*** *fig* be in its infancy
powikłania *pl* (*-łań*) MED complications *pl*; ***mogą wystąpić ~*** complications are liable to occur
powinien *v/irreg*: ***~em*** I should, I ought to; ***~em był do niego zadzwonić*** I should have called him; ***~ zaraz wrócić*** he should be back soon; ***~ zaraz przyjechać*** he ought to be here in a moment; ***woda powinna już się zagotować*** the water should have boiled by now
powinna → ***powinno***, ***powinien***
powinność *f* (*-ści*; *-ści*) *lit* duty, obligation; ***czynić swoją ~*** do one's duty; ***czynił tylko swoją ~*** that was in the line of duty
powinowactwo *n* (*-wa*; *-wa*) kinship; ***~ chemiczne*** (chemical) affinity; **powinowaty** *adj* relative (by marriage); ***jest moim ~m*** I'm related to him
powinszowania *pl* (*-wań*) congratulations *pl*
powitać *v/p* → ***witać***
powitalny *adj* **1.** *gest*, *uśmiech*: welcoming **2.** *mowa*: opening; ***komitet ~*** welcoming committee
powitanie *n* (*-nia*; *-nia*) welcome; ***serdeczne*** (***ciepłe***) ***~*** hearty (warm) welcome; ***na ~*** in welcome; ***urządzić komuś królewskie ~*** give s.o. a royal welcome
powlec *v/p* → ***powlekać***; **powlec się** *v/p* (*-lokę*) stagger
powleczony *adj* **1.** *pościel*: freshly made bed **2.** *warstwą*: covered
powlekać ⟨**-wlec**⟩ (*-kam*) **1.** TECH coat (*I* with); ***~ farbą*** paint **2.** *poduszkę*, *kołdrę*: change; ***~ pościel*** change pillowcases; ***powlekać się*** **1.** (*pokryć się*) get covered (*I* with) **2.** (*zasnuć*

P

się) cloud over; ***niebo powlekło się chmurami*** the sky got overcast, it clouded over

powłoczka *f* (*-ki*; *-ki*) pillowcase, pillowslip; **powłok|a** *f* (*-ki*; *-ki*) **1.** *farby*: coat **2.** (*osłona*) cover **3.** (*poszwa*) quilt cover, duvet cover, duvet case; ***~a lodowa*** ice shelf, ice mantle; ***~a ozonowa*** ozone layer **4.** ***~i brzuszne*** ANAT abdominal membrane **5.** ***~a elektronowa*** TECH electron shell

powłóczyć *v/im* (*-czę*) drag (along); ***~ nogą*** drag one's leg (along); ***ledwo ~ nogami*** drag one's feet

powłóczysty *adj* **1.** *suknia*: trailing **2.** *spojrzenie*: lingering

powodować ⟨**s-**⟩ (*-duję*) **1.** *wypadek, chorobę*: cause, bring about **2.** *zmianę*: cause, produce; ***powodować się*** be driven, be motivated (*I* by)

powodzeni|e *n* (*-nia*; *no pl*) **1.** (*sukces*) success **2.** (*pomyślność*) good luck, good fortune **3.** (*sława*) fame, success; ***cieszyć się ~em*** be successful; be in (great) demand; ***mieć ~e u*** *G* be popular with; ***bez ~a*** unsuccessfully; ***z*** (***równym***) ***~em*** (just as) successfully; ***cieszący się ~em*** popular, very much in demand; ***~a!*** best of luck!, good luck!

powodzianin *m* (*-na*; *-dzianie*) flood victim

powodzi|ć się *v/i*: ***~ mu się*** (***dobrze***) he is doing well; (***nie***) ***~ mu się*** **a)** he is doing well (badly) **b)** (*finansowo*) he is well off (not well off)

powodziow|y *adj* flood; ***klęska ~a*** flood disaster; ***alarm ~y*** flood alarm; ***fala ~a*** flood wave; ***komitet ~y*** flood emergency management

powojenny *adj* postwar

powoli *adv* slowly; ***~!*** easy!; **powolny** *adj rozwój*, *ruch*, *osoba*: slow; ***~m krokiem*** walking slowly; **powolutku** *adv dim* very slowly

powołać *v/p* → ***powoływać***

powołani|e *n* (*-nia*; *-nia*) (*zamiłowanie*) vocation; ***~e do wojska*** call-up; ***z ~a*** *Br* by vocation, *Am* by calling; ***minąć się z ~em*** miss one's vocation; **powołany** *adj* **1.** (*uprawniony*) qualified (**do** *G* to) **2.** *do wojska*: called up

powoływać ⟨**-łać**⟩ (*-łuję*) *komisję*, *rząd*: appoint (**na** *A* to); ***~ kogoś na stanowisko*** *G* appoint s.o. to the post of; ***~ kogoś na ministra*** appoint s.o. (as) minister; ***~ kogoś na świadka*** JUR summon s.o. as a witness, call s.o. as a witness; ***~ coś do życia*** bring s.th. into being; ***~ do wojska*** call up; ***powoływać się*** **1.** cite (**na** *A* s.th.) **2.** make reference (**na** *A* to); ***powołując się na*** *A* with reference to, referring to

powonienie *n* (*-nia*; *no pl*) sense of smell

powozić[1] *v/im* (*-wożę*) drive (*I* s.th.)

powozić[2] *v/p* (*-wożę*) drive (a little)

po|wód[1] *m* (*-woda*; *-wody*) (*uzasadnienie*) reason (*G* for); ***z ~wodu choroby*** due to an illness; ***dać komuś ~wód do*** *G* give s.o. a reason to; ***być ~wodem*** *G* be the reason for; ***z tego ~wodu*** for that reason; ***bez żadnego ~wodu*** for no reason; ***nie ma ~wodu do paniki*** there is no reason to panic; ***nie bez ~wodu*** with good reason

powód[2] *m* (*-wodu*; *-wodowie*), **~ka** *f* (*-ki*; *-ki*) JUR plaintiff

powództwo *n* (*-wa*; *-wa*) JUR (law)suit; ***~ cywilne*** civil suit, civil action; ***sprawa z powództwa A*** A's action; ***wnieść ~ przeciwko*** *D* make a complaint against

powódź *f* (*-wodzi*; *-wodzie*) flood; ***klęska powodzi*** flooding

powój *m* (*-woju*; *-woje*) BIOL convolvulus, bindweed

powóz *m* (*-wozu*; *-wozy*) carriage

powracać ⟨**-rócić**⟩ (*-cam*) return, come back; ***~ do domu*** come back home; ***~ do zdrowia*** recover; ***~ do tematu*** get back to the subject; ***~ pamięcią do*** *G* recall, look back on

powracający *adj* recurring

powrotn|y *adj*: ***w drodze ~ej*** on one's way back; ***bilet ~y*** *Br* return ticket, *Am* round-trip ticket

powrócić *v/p* → ***powracać***

powrósło *n* (*-ła*; *-ła*) rope

powr|ót *m* (*-rotu*; *-roty*) return; ***~ót do domu*** return home; ***~ót do zdrowia*** recovery; ***~ót choroby*** relapse; ***z ~otem*** back; ***tam i z ~otem*** back and forth; ***jechać z ~otem*** go back; ***życzyć ~otu do zdrowia*** wish a quick recovery

powróz *m* (*-rozu*|*-roza*; *-rozy*) rope

powsinoga *f/m* (*-gi*; *-gi*) *infml* gadabout, loiterer
powstać *v/p* → ***powstawać***
powstanie *n* (*-nia*; *-nia*) (up)rising; **powstaniec** *m* (*-tańca*; *-tańcy*) insurgent; **powstańczy** *adj* insurgent
powstawać ⟨***-tać***⟩ (*-taję*) **1.** (*zaczynać istnieć*) come into being **2.** (*o budowli*) be built **3.** (*o firmie*) be founded, be set up **4.** (*o zamieszaniu*) come about **5.** (*wstawać*) stand up, rise; **~ z miejsca** rise from one's seat **6.** (*buntować się*) rise (**przeciw** *D* against)
powstrzymywać ⟨***-mać***⟩ (*-muję*) (*zatrzymywać*) stop; ***~ śmiech*** suppress laughter; ***~ płacz*** hold back tears; ***~ gniew*** repress anger; ***~ od*** *G*, ***~ przed*** *I* stop from, keep from, prevent from; ***powstrzymywać się*** (*hamować się*) refrain (**od** *G* from); ***~ się od alkoholu*** refrain from drinking alcohol; ***nie móc powstrzymać się od śmiechu*** can't help laughing; ***~ się z kupnem*** wait before buying s.th.; ***była taka zła, że ledwo się powstrzymywała*** she was so angry that she could hardly restrain herself
powszechnie *adv* generally; ***~ znany*** well-known; ***~ wiadomo, że*** it's common knowledge that; ***~ obowiązujący*** binding; ***~ dostępny*** freely accessible/available
powszechn|y *adj* **1.** (*rozpowszechniony*) common **2.** *radość*: general; ***historia ~a*** world history; ***literatura ~a*** world literature; ***artykuły ~ego użytku*** commodities, everyday items; ***~y spis ludności*** census **3.** *opinia*: prevailing, prevalent **4.** *prawo*: common; ***sąd ~y*** common court, court of common pleas
powszedni *adj* everyday; ***dzień ~*** weekday; ***chleb ~*** *fig* daily bread; ***zarabia na chleb ~ jako kucharz*** he earns his bread and butter as a cook
powszednieć ⟨**s-**⟩ (*-nieję*) become commonplace
powściągać ⟨***-gnąć***⟩ (*-gam*) *gniew*, *ciekawość*: restrain; ***~ język*** hold one's tongue; ***~ wybryki dzieci*** rein in children; ***powściągać się*** restrain oneself, contain oneself
powściągliwość *f* (*-ści*; *no pl*) restraint; ***zachować w czymś ~*** exercise restraint; **powściągliwy** *adj* **1.** (*z rezerwą*) restrained, reserved **2.** *krytyka*: understated
powściągnąć *v/p* → ***powściągać***
powtarzać ⟨***-tórzyć***⟩ (*-rzam*) **1.** *eksperyment*, *błąd*: repeat; ***~ klasę*** repeat a class; ***~ jak papuga*** parrot; ***~ bezkrytycznie*** repeat gullibly; ***proszę powtórzyć bratu, że*** please, tell your brother that; ***powtarzali słowa przysięgi*** they took the oath **2.** *plotki*, *sekret*: pass on **3.** (*naśladować*) copy **4.** imitate; ***powtarzał za nią ruchy*** he imitated her gestures **5.** *lekcję*, *materiał*: *Br* revise, *Am* review; ***~ trygonometrię*** (***gramatykę***) revise trigonometry (grammar); ***powtarzać się*** **1.** (*o sytuacji*) repeat oneself **2.** (*o ataku bólu*, *błędach*) recur **3.** repeat oneself
powtarzający się *adj* **1.** *ból*, *błąd*: recurring; ***~ problem z kręgosłupem*** recurring back problem; ***~ sen*** (***koszmar***) recurring dream (nightmare) **2.** (*często*) repeated; ***powtarzające się hałasy*** repeated noises; **powtarzalny** *adj* that can be repeated, that can be copied
powtórka *f* (*-ki*; *-ki*) **1.** *materiału*: *Br* revision, *Am* review **2.** (*egzamin*) retake, resit **3.** *programu*: repeat; **powtórkowy** *adj*: ***egzamin ~*** retake, resit
powtórnie *adv* again, re-; ***~ napisać*** rewrite; **powtórny** *adj* second
powtórzyć *v/p* → ***powtarzać***
powyginany *adj* bent, crooked
powypadkowy *adj* previously-damaged, damaged (in an accident)
powyżej *prep* (*G*) **1.** (*wyżej niż*) above; ***temperatura ~ zera*** positive temperature **2.** (*więcej niż*) over; **powyższy** *adj* the above
powziąć *v/p* (*-wezmę*) *lit* **1.** *decyzję*: take **2.** *podejrzenie*: conceive
powzięcie *n* (*-cia*; *no pl*): ***~ decyzji*** resolution, reaching a decision
poza[1] *f* (*-zy*; *-zy*) pose
poza[2] *prep* (I/A) **1.** (*dalej*) beyond; ***~ horyzont*** beyond the horizon; ***wyjść ~ teren*** *G* leave the area of, leave the premises of **2.** (*na zewnątrz*) outside **3.** (*oprócz*) apart from; ***~ tym*** besides; ***nikt ~ tym*** no-

P

body else; ***mieć coś ~ sobą*** be through with s.th.
pozabiurowy *adj* outside-the-office; **pozagalaktyczny** *adj* extragalactic
pozagrobow|y *adj*: ***życie ~e*** afterlife, life after death
pozakonkursowy *adj* non-competing; **pozamałżeński** *adj* extramarital; ***dziecko ~e*** illegitimate child; **pozaparlamentarny** *adj* outside-parliament
pozasłużbowy *adj* private; **pozaszkolny** *adj* extraschool, out-of-school
pozawałowy *adj* MED post-infarctional
pozazakładowy *adj* not associated with the company
pozaziemsk|i *adj* extraterrestrial; ***istota ~a*** extraterrestrial, alien
pozbawiać ⟨**-wić**⟩ (*-wiam*) deprive; ***~ nadziei*** disillusion; ***~ kogoś życia*** take s.o.'s life; ***~ kogoś snu*** deprive s.o. of sleep, cause s.o. to lose sleep; ***~ kogoś dachu nad głową*** render s.o. homeless; **pozbawiać się** deprive oneself (*G* of)
pozbawiony *adj* lacking, devoid; ***~ dachu nad głową*** homeless; ***~ środków do życia*** penniless, having nothing to live on; ***~ wszelkich wygód*** devoid of all comforts
pozbierać *v/p* → ***zbierać***
pozbywać się ⟨**-być**⟩ (*-wam*) **1.** *długów*: free oneself of **2.** *nieśmiałości*: overcome **3.** *mebli*, *ubrań*: get rid of
pozdrawiać ⟨**-rowić**⟩ (*-wiam*) greet; ***kazał cię pozdrowić*** he sends his regards; ***pozdrów go ode mnie!*** give him my (best) regards!; ***serdecznie pozdrawiam*** (*w liście*) best regards; ***pozdrawiać się*** greet each other
pozdrowieni|e *n* (*-nia*; *-nia*) greeting; ***~a*** regards; ***przekazać komuś ~a*** give one's best regards to s.o.; ***serdeczne ~a*** warm regards; ***łączę ~a*** regards
pozer *m* (*-ra*; *-rzy*) pose(u)r; **pozerstwo** *n* (*-wa*; *no pl*) posing
pozew *m* (*-zwu*; *-zwy*): ***~ sądowy*** suit; ***wnieść ~ rozwodowy*** file for a divorce; ***wnieść ~ przeciwko*** *D* file a suit against
poziom *m* (*-mu*; *-my*) **1.** (*wysokość*) level **2.** (*płaszczyzna*) plane **3.** (*piętro*) floor; ***~ wody*** water level; ***~ morza*** sea level; ***~ cukru we krwi*** MED sugar level in blood; ***~ życia*** standard of living; ***na ~ie*** classy, up to the mark, up to scratch
poziomka *f* (*-ki*; *-ki*) wild strawberry; **poziomkowy** *adj* wild strawberry
poziomnica *f* (*-cy*; *-ce*) level
poziomy *adj* level, horizontal; ***rzut ~*** ground plan
pozłacać ⟨**-łocić**⟩ (*-cam*) gold-plate; **pozłacany** *adj* **1.** *rama*: gilt **2.** (*zegarek*) gold-plated; **pozłota** *f* (*-ty*; *no pl*) gilding
poznać *v/p* → ***poznawać***
poznani|e *n* (*-nia*; *no pl*) **1.** cognition; ***nie do ~a*** out of all recognition **2.** PHIL perception
poznawać ⟨**-nać**⟩ (*-naję*) **1.** *obcy język*: learn **2.** *ludzi*: get to know; ***~ kogoś z kimś*** introduce s.o. to s.o. **3.** *świat*: see **4.** (*doświadczać*) experience **5.** (*rozpoznać*) recognise; ***~ po*** *L* recognise by; ***nie dał po sobie poznać, że*** he didn't let us feel that **6.** (*zawrzeć znajomość*) meet; ***miło mi pana/panią poznać*** pleased to meet you; ***poznawać się*** meet; ***dał się poznać jako*** we got to know him as; ***nie poznał się na niej*** he did not appreciate her; ***~ się na*** *L* (*przejrzeć*) see through
poznawalny *adj* cognizable *form*; **poznawczy** *adj* cognitive
pozorny *adj* **1.** (*z pozoru*) apparent, seeming **2.** *żal*: pretended, false
pozorować ⟨**u-**⟩ (*-ruję*) fake, feign
pozorowan|y *adj*: ***~y ból*** faked pain; ***~e działania*** fake actions
pozostać *v/p* → ***pozostawać***
pozostałość *f* (*-ści*; *-ści*) **1.** *minionej epoki*: relic **2.** CHEM remains
pozostały *adj* **1.** *część*: remaining **2.** (*inny*) the other; ***~ przy życiu*** surviving, still alive; ***~ po*** *L* left after
pozostawać ⟨**-stać**⟩ (*-taję*) **1.** (*być dalej*) remain (***w*** *L* in, ***przy*** *L* with) **2.** (*o reszcie*, *części*) be left (***po*** *L* after), remain (***po*** *L* of); ***~ w tyle*** lag behind; ***~ bez echa*** meet with no response, make no impression; ***~ w cieniu*** *fig* stay in the background, take the back seat; ***nie pozostaje mi nic innego jak*** I have no choice but to; ***to pozostawia wiele do życzenia*** this leaves a lot to be desired

P

pozostawiać ⟨**-wić**⟩ (*-wiam*) **1.** leave (behind); **~ za sobą** leave behind; **to nie pozostawia wątpliwości** it leaves no room for doubt; **~ niezapomniane wrażenie** leave a long-lasting impression; **~ otwarte drzwi** leave the door open; **~ komuś decyzję** leave s.o. to decide; **~ po sobie** leave after oneself **2.** (*w spadku*) leave (in one's last will), bequeath

pozostawiony *adj*: **~ samemu sobie** left alone

pozować *v/im* (*-zuję*) **1.** (*służyć jako model*) model (**do** *G* for) **2.** (*przybierać pozę*) pose; **~ na** *A* pose as

poz|ór *m* (*-zoru*; *-zory*) pretence; **na ~ór**, **z ~oru** apparently; **pod ~orem** *G* on the pretext of; **pod żadnym ~orem** on no account, under no circumstances; **zachowywać ~ory** keep up appearances; **stwarzać ~ory** pretend; **~ory mylą** appearances are deceptive

pozwać *v/p* → **pozywać**

pozwalać ⟨**-wolić**⟩ (*-lam*) **1.** (*zezwolić*) allow (**na** *A* to do s.th.), permit (**na** *A* s.th.) **2.** (*dopuszczać*) allow; **~ na wszystko** allow to do everything; **~ sobie na** *A* afford to do s.th.; **pozwolę sobie zapytać** I'll take the liberty of asking; **nie ~ sobie na odpoczynek** not allow oneself a rest; **nie pozwolę im, żeby** I won't allow them to; **za dużo sobie pozwalać** go too far; **jeśli pogoda pozwoli** if the weather permits, weather permitting

pozwany *m* (*-nego*; *-ni*), **-na** *f* (*-nej*; *-ne*) *JUR* defendant

pozwoleni|e *n* (*-nia*; *-nia*) **1.** (*zgoda*) permission; **za ~em!** by your leave! **2.** (*zezwolenie*) permit, licence; **bez ~a** unauthorized, without permission; **~e na budowę** construction permit; **~e na broń** gun licence

pozwolić *v/p* (*-lę*): **pozwoli pan(i), że** allow me to; **proszę, pan(i) pozwoli!** please, come in!: → **pozwalać**

pozycj|a *f* (*-cji*; *-cje*) **1.** position; **w ~i leżącej** in lying position; **utrzymać się na swoich ~ach** stand one's ground; **nowe ~e książkowe** recently published books; **bronić straconych ~i** *fig* fight for lost causes **2.** (*w spisie*) item **3.** (*w księgowości*) entry **4.** (*w społeczeństwie*) status; **mieć wysoką ~ę** have good social standing; **~a społeczna** social standing

pozycyjn|y *adj*: **światła ~e** *AUTO* running lights; **wojna ~a** positional warfare

pozyskiwać ⟨**-kać**⟩ (*-kuję*) *zaufanie*, *sprzymierzeńca*: win (**dla** *G*/**do** *G* for); **~ sobie kogoś** win s.o. over; **pozyskał sobie wszystkich** he won everybody's support

pozytyw *m* (*-wu*; *-wy*) *PHOT* positive

pozytywka *f* (*-ki*; *-ki*) musical box

pozytywny *adj* **1.** *MED* positive **2.** *wynik*: favourable

pozywać ⟨**-zwać**⟩ (*-wam*): **~ kogoś do sądu** take s.o. to court; **~ kogoś na świadka** call s.o. as a witness

pożałowani|e: **godny ~a** unfortunate

pożar *m* (*-ru*; *-ry*) fire, blaze; **ryzyko ~u** fire hazard; **pożarniczy** *adj* fire fighting; **pożarn|y** *adj*: **straż ~a** fire department; **pożarow|y** *adj* fire; **zagrożenie ~e** fire hazard/risk

pożądać *v/im* (*-dam*) desire; **pożądanie** *n* (*-nia*; *no pl*) desire; **pożądany** *adj* **1.** *wynik*, *efekt*: desired **2.** *gość*, *pomoc*: welcome; **pożądliwy** *adj* *spojrzenie*: lustful

pożegnalny *adj* **1.** *gest*: parting **2.** *list*: good-bye; **pożegnanie** *n* (*-nia*; *-nia*) **1.** (*słowa*) farewell **2.** (*chwila rozstania*) parting; **pocałować kogoś na ~** kiss s.o. goodbye

pożeracz *m* (*-cza*; *-cze*): **~ prądu** energy guzzler; **~ serc** *iron* heartbreaker; **~ książek** bookworm

pożerać ⟨**-żreć**⟩ (*-ram*) **1.** (*jeść łapczywie*) devour, gobble (up) **2.** *zwierzę*: devour **3.** *pieniądze*: cost a lot **4.** *paliwo*, *prąd*: guzzle; **~ kogoś wzrokiem** gaze lustfully at s.o.; **~ książki** devour books

pożoga *f* (*-gi*; *-gi*) *lit* conflagration; **~ wojenna** war

pożółkły *adj* yellowed

pożreć *v/p* → **pożerać**

pożyci|e *n* (*-cia*; *no pl*) life; **~e seksualne** sex life; **~e małżeńskie** married life; **trudny w ~u** difficult to live with

pożyczać ⟨**-czyć**⟩ (*-czam*) **1.** (*komuś*) lend (*D* to) **2.** (*od kogoś*) borrow (**od** *G* from)

pożyczk|a *f* (*-ki*; *-ki*) loan; **udzielić ko-**

P

muś ~i give s.o. a loan; ***dziękuję ci za ~ę*** thank you for lending the money to me; ***~a na zakup czegoś*** loan to buy s.th.
pożyczkobiorca *m* (*-cy*; *-cy*) borrower; **pożyczkodawca** *m* (*-cy*; *-cy*) lender
pożyczyć *v/p* → ***pożyczać***
pożydowski *adj* post-Jewish
pożyteczny *adj* useful; **pożyt|ek** *m* (*-tku*; *-ki*) benefit (***z*** *G* from); ***z ~kiem dla*** *G* to s.o.'s benefit, for s.o.'s benefit; ***mieć ~ek z*** *G* derive benefit from
pożywiać się ⟨***-wić***⟩ (*-wiam*) feed (*I* on)
pożywienie *n* (*-nia*; *no pl*) nourishment; **pożywka** *f* (*-ki*; *-ki*) BIOL medium; ***~ dla plotek*** *fig* fuel for gossip; **pożywny** *adj* nutritious
pójdźka *f* (*-ki*; *-ki*) (*sowa*) little owl
pójść *v/p* → ***iść***
póki *conj* as long as; ***~ co*** for the time being; ***~ czas*** before it's too late; ***~... póty*** until
pół *num* half; ***~ roku*** half a year; ***~ chleba*** half a loaf of bread; ***~ do drugiej*** half past one; ***na ~ uschły*** half dry; ***w ~ drogi*** halfway; ***za ~ ceny*** half price; ***~ na ~*** fifty-fifty; ***dzielić coś na ~*** divide s.th. in two; ***~ biedy*** it's not so bad; ***przerwać komuś w ~ słowa*** cut s.o. short
półanalfabet|a *m* (*-ty*; *-beci*) *fig* semi-illiterate person; ***być ~ą*** be semi-illiterate
półautomatyczny *adj* semi-automatic; **półbóg** *m* (*-boga*; *-bogowie*) demigod
półbuty *pl* (*-tów*) shoes *pl*; **półcień** *m* (*-cienia*; *-cienie*) **1.** (*słaby cień*) half-light **2.** (*na obrazie*) half-tone
półciężk|i *adj*: ***waga ~a*** SPORT light-heavy weight, *Br* cruiserweight
półdupek *m* (*-pka*; *-pki*) *vulg* buttock; **półdziki** *adj* half-wild, half-savage
półeczka *f* (*-ki*; *-ki*) (little) shelf
półetat *m* (*-tu*; *-ty*) part-time job; **półetatowy** *adj* part-time
półfabrykat *m* (*-tu*; *-ty*) semifinished product; **półfinał** *m* (*-łu*; *-ły*) semifinal(s)
półgębkiem: in monosyllables; ***uśmiechać się ~*** smile sheepishly
półgłosem *adv* in an undertone, under one's breath
półgłówek *m* (*-wka*; *-wki*) half-wit, nitwit
półgodzin|a: ***po ~ie*** after half an hour; ***przed ~ą*** before half an hour
półgodzinny *adj* half an hour; **półgotowy** *adj* half ready; **półgruby** *adj druk*: semibold
pół|ka *f* (*-ki*; *-ki*) shelf; ***~ka na bagaż*** rack; ***~ka na książki*** bookshelf; ***stać na ~ce*** be on a shelf; ***położyć coś na ~kę*** put s.th. (back) on the shelf; ***na ~kach księgarskch*** *fig* in bookshops
półkilogramowy *adj* half-kilogram; **półkilometrowy** *adj Br* half-kilometre, *Am* half-kilometer; **półkole** *n* (*-la*; *-la*) semicircle; **półkolem** *adv* in a half-circle
półkolisty *adj* semicircular
półkożuszek *m* (*-szka*; *-szki*) sheepskin jacket
pół|krew: ***on jest ~krwi Polakiem*** he is half Polish; ***koń ~krwi*** half-bred horse
półksiężyc *m* (*-ca*; *-ce*) crescent moon; **półkula** *f* (*-li*; *-le*) hemisphere; ***~ mózgowa*** ANAT cerebral hemisphere; **półkulisty** *adj* semicircular
półlitrowy *adj Br* half-litre, *Am* half-liter; **półlitrówka** *f* (*-ki*; *-ki*) *Br* half-litre bottle, *Am* half-liter bottle
półmetal *m* (*-lu*; *-le*) semi-metal; **półmetek** *m* (*-tka*; *-tki*) **1.** SPORT halfway stage **2.** *fig* halfway point; **półmetrowy** *adj Br* half-a-metre long, *Am* half-a-meter long
półmiesięczny *adj pensja*: half a month; **półmisek** *m* (*-ska*; *-ski*) platter, dish; **półmrok** *m* (*-ku*; *no pl*) twilight, semidarkness; ***w ~u*** in half-light; **półnagi** *adj* half-naked
północ *m* (*-cy*; *no pl*) **1.** (*pora*) midnight; ***o ~y*** at midnight **2.** GEOGR north; ***na ~y*** in the north; ***na ~*** north; ***na ~ od*** *G* north of; ***na dalekiej ~y*** in the Far North
północno-wschodni *adj* northeastern
północno-zachodni *adj* northwestern
północn|y *adj* **1.** *półkula*: northern **2.** *wiatr*: north(erly); ***Morze ≈e*** the North Sea
półnuta *f* (*-ty*; *-ty*) MUS half-note, *Br* minim; **półoficjalny** *adj* semi-

P

official; **półokrąg** *m* (*-ręgu*; *-ręgi*) *MATH* semicircle
półokrągły *adj* semicircular; **półotwarty** *adj* half-open; **półpasiec** *m* (*-paśca*; *no pl*) *MED* shingles
półpiętro *n* (*-ra*; *-ra*) landing; **półprawda** *f* (*-dy*; *-dy*) half-truth; **półprzewodnik** *m* (*-ka*; *-ki*) *PHYS* semiconductor
półprzymknięty *adj* **1.** *powieki*: half-open **2.** *drzwi*: ajar; **półprzytomny** *adj* half-conscious; *~ **z przerażenia*** terrified, frightened out of one's wits, panic-stricken, petrified; *~ **ze zmęczenia*** dead tired, exhausted
półrocze *n* (*-cza*; *-cza*) **1.** (*połowa roku*) half-year **2.** (*w szkole*) term, semester; **półroczn|y** *adj* half-yearly; ***~y pobyt*** half-a-year stay, six-month stay; ***~e dziecko*** six-month-old baby; **pół|sen** *m* (*-snu*; *no pl*) drowse; ***w ~śnie*** drowsy, half-asleep; **półsierota** *f/m* (*-ty*; *-ty*) half-orphan; **półsłodki** *adj wino*: semi-sweet
półsłówka *pl* (*-wek*) **1.** (*monosylaby*) monosyllables *pl*; ***zbywać kogoś ~mi*** answer s.o. in monosyllables **2.** (*niedopowiedzenia*) insinuations *pl*; ***mówić ~mi*** make allusions
półsłupek *m* (*-pka*; *-pki*) **1.** (*obcas*) medium heel **2.** (*ścieg*) single crochet; **półsurowy** *adj* **1.** (*niedogotowany*) half-raw **2.** (*o cieście*) half-baked
półszept: ***mówić ~em*** mutter in an undertone, whisper
półszlachetny *adj*: *kamień*, *metal*: semi-precious
półśredni *adj*: ***waga ~a*** *SPORT* welterweight
półśrodek *m* (*-dka*; *-dki*) half measure; **półświadomie** *adv* semiconsciously; **półświatek** *m* (*-tka*; *no pl*) underworld; **półtłusty** *adj ser*, *mleko*: semi-skimmed
półtor|a *num* one and a half; ***~a roku*** one and a half year; ***~ej godziny*** an hour and a half
półtoragodzinny *adj* one and a half hours'; **półtoraroczny** *adj* one and a half year
półuchem: ***słuchać czegoś ~*** listen with half an ear
półurzędowy *adj* semiofficial; **półuśmiech** *m* (*-chu*; *-chy*) half-smile
półwiecze *n* (*-cza*; *-cza*) half-century
półwiek: ***przed ~iem*** half a century ago
półwysep *m* (*-spu*; *-spy*) peninsula; **półwytrawny** *adj wino*: semi-dry
półżartem *adv* half-jokingly; **półżywy** *adj* half-dead
późnawo *adv* fairly late
późnić się *v/im* (*-nię*) (*o zegarze*) be late
później *adv comp* → ***późno*** later; ***odkładać coś na ~*** put s.th. off until later; **późniejszy** *adj comp* → ***późny*** later
późno *adv* late; ***~ w nocy*** late at night
późnogotycki *adj* late Gothic; **późnośredniowieczny** *adj* late medieval
późny *adj* late
ppłk *abbr* (= **podpułkownik**) Lt Col
ppor. *abbr* (= **podporucznik**) 2nd Lt
prababka *f* (*-ki*; *-ki*) great-grandmother
prac|a *f* (*-cy*; *-ce*) **1.** (*zajęcie*) work; ***~a zawodowa*** work; ***~a fizyczna*** physical work; ***~a umysłowa*** intellectual work; ***~a naukowa*** research; ***~a dorywcza*** off-and-on work; ***~a sezonowa*** seasonal work/labour; ***~a na zlecenie*** commissioned work; ***~a zespołowa*** team work; ***~e konserwatorskie*** restoration (works); ***~e budowlane*** construction work; ***~e wykopaliskowe*** excavation works; ***~e badawcze*** research (work); ***~e fotograficzne*** photographs; ***iść do ~y*** go to work; ***żyć z ~y*** work to live; ***~a na komputerze*** computer work; ***czas ~y*** working hours; ***~a domowa*** homework; ***~a klasowa*** test (written in class); ***~a dyplomowa*** diploma thesis; ***~a pisemna*** written work **2.** (*posada*) job; ***zwolnić z ~y*** dismiss; ***ubiegać się o ~ę*** apply for a job; ***bez ~y*** unemployed, jobless; ***~a w niepełnym wymiarze godzin*** part-time job; ***~a w pełnym wymiarze godzin*** full-time job; ***~a dodatkowa*** extra job **3.** *serca*, *nerek*: function, functioning; ***prawidłowa ~a serca*** proper heart function; ***bezawaryjna ~a silnika*** perfect engine functioning
pracobiorca *m* (*-cy*; *-cy*) employee; **pracochłonny** *adj* laborious; **pracodawca** *m* (*-cy*; *-cy*) employer; **pracoholik** *m* (*-ka*; *-licy*) workaholic

P

pracować *v/im* (*-cuję*) **1.** (*wykonywać zajęcie*) work (**dla** *G* for, **nad** *I* on); **~ całą dobę** work round the clock; **~ zawodowo** work professionally; **~ na pół etatu** work part-time; **~ naukowo** do research; **~ fizycznie** do physical work; **~ w biurze** work in an office; **~ w firmie** work in a company; **~ w fabryce** work in a factory; **~ na budowie** do construction work; **~ na kolei** work for a railway company; **~ na uczelni** work at the university; **~ jako nauczyciel** work as a teacher; **~ z trudną młodzieżą** work with troubled youth **2.** (*mieć posadę*) be employed

pracowitość *f* (*-ści*; *no pl*) diligence; **pracowity** *adj* **1.** *osoba*: diligent **2.** *życie*, *okres*: strenuous, arduous **3.** (*pracochłonny*) laborious

pracownia *f* (*-ni*; *-nie*) **1.** *malarza*: studio, atelier **2.** *fizyczna*, *chemiczna*: laboratory **3.** (*warsztat*) workshop; **~ krawiecka** tailor's shop

pracownica *f* (*-cy*; *-ce*) (female) employee; **~ fabryki** factory worker; **~ poczty** post office worker; **~ administracji** administrative worker/officer

pracownicz|y *adj* worker's; **świadczenia ~e** labour benefits; **stołówka ~a** canteen, cafeteria

pracownik *m* (*-ka*; *-nicy*) worker, employee; **~ umysłowy** white-collar worker; **~ fizyczny** blue-collar worker; **~ naukowy** researcher, research worker; **~ banku** bank worker; **~ poczty** post office worker; **~ administracji** administration worker; **długoletni ~** longtime/long-standing worker

P

pracuś *m* (*-cusia*; *-cusie*) *infml* workaholic

praczka *f* (*-ki*; *-ki*) laundress, washerwoman

praczłowiek *m* (*-ka*; *praludzie*) prehistoric man

prać ⟨**u-**, **wy-**⟩ (*piorę*) **1.** *bieliznę*: wash; **~ brudy** *fig* wash one's dirty linen in public; **~ brudne pieniądze** *fig* launder money **2.** ⟨**s-**⟩ *plamę*: wash out **3.** (*czyścić*) clean; **~ chemicznie** dry-clean

pradawny *adj lit* ancient

pradziad *m* (*-da*; *-dowie*) *lit* great grandfather; **pradziadek** *m* (*-dka*; *-dkowie*) great-grandfather; **pradziadkowie** great-grandparents; **pradzieje** *pl* (*-jów*) prehistory

Praga *f* (*-gi*) **1.** (*stolica Czech*) Prague **2.** (*dzielnica Warszawy*) Praga

pragmatyczny *adj* pragmatic

pragnąć *v/im* (*-nę*) **1.** *wolności*: desire **2.** *miłości*, *szczęścia*: long, yearn (*G* for) **3.** (*chcieć*) want **4.** *zemsty*: seek **5.** (*życzyć sobie*) wish; **pragnę powiedzieć** I wish to say, I would like to say **6.** (*pożądać*) lust (*A* for)

pragnienie *n* (*-nia*; *-nia*) **1.** thirst; **mieć ~** be thirsty **2.** (*potrzeba*) desire, longing; **zaspokajać wszystkie pragnienia** satisfy all desires; **gorące ~** burning desire; **~ miłości** thirst for love; **~ zemsty** desire for revenge; **~ śmierci** desire to die; **moim wielkim ~m jest** I have always very much desired to **3.** (*życzenie*) wish

praktyczny *adj* practical

praktyk *m* (*-ka*; *-tycy*) practictioner

prakty|ka *f* (*-ki*; *-ki*) **1.** practice; **~ka lekarska** medical practice; **~ki religijne** religious practices **2.** (*doświadczenie*) experience; **w ~ce** in practice **3.** (*czas szkolenia*) training period **4.** (*u rzemieślnika*) apprenticeship; **odbywać ~kę** serve one's apprenticeship **5.** (*w szkole*) teaching practice

praktykant (*-ta*; *-nci*), **~ka** *f* (*-ki*; *-ki*) **1.** (*w firmie*) trainee **2.** (*u rzemieślnika*) apprentice **3.** (*lekarz na praktyce*) *Br* houseman, *Am* intern

praktykować *v/im* (*-kuję*) **1.** (*szkolić się*) be in training, train **2.** (*o lekarzu*) practise **3.** (*u rzemieślnika*) be an apprentice; **tego się już nie praktykuje** it is not practiced any more

praktykujący *adj katolik*: practising

pralinka *f* (*-ki*; *-ki*) (filled) chocolate, praline

pralka *f* (*-ki*; *-ki*) washing machine; **pralnia** *f* (*-ni*; *-nie*) **1.** *chemiczna*: dry-cleaner's **2.** (*zakład*, *pomieszczenie*) laundry, laundrette

praludzie *pl* → **praczłowiek**

prałat *m* (*-ta*; *-łaci*) prelate

pramatka *f* (*-ki*; *-ki*) first mother

pranie *n* (*-nia*; *-nia*) **1.** washing; **~ wstępne** prewash; **~ mózgu** brainwashing **2.** (*ubrania*) laundry

praojciec *m* (*-jca*; *-jcowie*) *lit* forefather
prapra- (*w złożeniach*) great-great-
prapremiera *f* (*-ry*; *-ry*) world premiere
praprzodek *m* (*-dka*; *-dkowie*) primogenitor, protoplast
pras|a *f* **1.** (*-sy*; *no pl*) press; ***na łamach ~y, w ~ie*** in the press; ***~a brukowa*** tabloid press, gutter press **2.** (*-sy*; *-sy*) *TECH* the press
prasłowiański *adj* proto-Slavonic, proto-Slavic
prasowaczka *f* (*-ki*; *-ki*) ironer; **prasować** (*-suję*) **1.** ⟨**u-**⟩ *suknię*: iron **2.** ⟨**s-**⟩ *TECH* press; **prasowalnica** *f* (*-cy*; *-ce*) (clothes) press
prasowy *adj doniesienia*, *fotograf*: press; ***rzecznik ~*** spokesperson
prastary *adj* primeval, ancient
praszczur *m* (*-ra*; *-rowie*) *lit* ancestor, forefather
prawd|a *f* (*-dy*; *no pl*) truth; ***lubisz go, ~a?*** you like him, don't you?; ***czy to ~a?*** is that true?; ***nie ma w tym słowa ~y*** there isn't a grain of truth in that; ***ach, ~a!*** oh, that's true!; ***co ~a*** admittedly; ***okazać się ~ą*** prove to be true; ***~ę mówiąc*** to tell the truth, in truth, truth to tell; ***święta ~a!*** plain truth!, gospel truth!; ***mijać się z ~ą*** depart from the truth; ***powiedzieć komuś ~ę w oczy*** give s.o. a piece of one's mind
prawdomówny *adj* truthful
prawdopodobieństw|o *n* (*-wa*; *no pl*) probability; ***jakie jest ~o, że*** what is the probability that; ***według wszelkiego ~a*** in all probability
prawdopodobnie *adv* probably; **prawdopodobny** *adj* probable, likely; ***mało ~*** very unlikely
prawdziwek *m* (*-wka*; *-wki*) boletus, *Am* king bolete
prawdziwie *adv* truthfully, truly
prawdziwość *f* (*-ści*; *no pl*) **1.** *słów*: truthfulness **2.** *dokumentów*: authenticity **3.** *oferty*, *propozycji*, *emocji*: genuineness; **prawdziwy** *adj* **1.** *przyjaciel*, *historia*: true **2.** *diament*, *skóra*, *podpis*: genuine **3.** (*autentyczny*) real
prawic|a *f* (*-cy*; *no pl*) *POLIT* the Right; ***po ~y*** *lit* on the right; **prawicowy** *adj* *POLIT* right-wing, rightist
prawić *v/im* (*-wię*) *lit*: ***~ komplementy*** pay compliments; ***~ morały*** preach, sermonize
prawidło *n* (*-ła*; *-ła*) **1.** (*zasada*) rule **2.** (*do butów*) shoetree; **prawidłowy** *adj* **1.** *użycie*, *odpowiedź*: correct **2.** *rozwój*, *przemiana materii*: normal, proper **3.** (*zgodnie z przepisami*) legal
prawie *adv* almost, nearly; ***~ go nie znam*** I hardly know him; ***~ nikt*** hardly anyone, scarcely anybody; ***~ niemożliwy*** hardly possible, almost impossible
prawieki *pl* (*-ków*) time immemorial
prawniczka *f* (*-ki*; *-ki*) lawyer; **prawnicz|y** *adj* legal; ***studia ~e*** law studies; ***język ~y*** legal jargon
prawnie *adv* legally, lawfully; **prawnik** *m* (*-ka*; *-nicy*) lawyer
prawnuczek *m* (*-czka*; *-czki*/*-kowie*), **prawnuk** *m* (*-ka*; *-kowie*/*-ki*) great-grandson; **prawnuczka** *f* (*-ki*; *-ki*) great-granddaughter
prawn|y *adj* **1.** *właściciel*, *spadkobierca*: legal; ***środek ~y*** legal means; ***osoba ~a*** corporation; ***radca ~y*** legal advisor; ***moc ~a*** legal force **2.** *biuro*, *kancelaria*: law; ***podstawa ~a*** legal basis
praw|o[1] *n* (*-wa*; *-wa*) **1.** law; ***~o karne*** criminal law; ***studiować ~o*** study law; ***~a natury*** the laws of nature; ***~o jazdy*** *Br* driving licence, *Am* driver's licence; ***~o powszechnego ciążenia*** *PHYS* the law of gravity; ***w imieniu ~a*** in the name of law **2.** (*studia*) law studies **3.** (*kodeks*) code; ***~o budowlane*** the building code **4.** (*uregulowanie*) regulation; ***~o lokalowe*** housing (management) regulations **5.** (*uprawnienie*) right; ***~o wyborcze*** voting rights; ***~o autorskie*** copyright; ***~o do głosowania*** right to vote; ***mieć ~o do*** *G* have the right to; ***jakim ~em?*** by what right?; ***zgodnie z ~em*** legally
prawo[2] *adv*: ***na ~, w ~*** (to the) right
prawobrzeżny *adj* right-bank
prawodawca *m* (*-cy*; *-cy*) legislator; **prawodawstwo** *n* (*-wa*; *no pl*) legislation
prawomocny *adj* legally binding; **prawomyślny** *adj* law-abiding

praworęczny *adj* right-handed
praworządność *f* (*-ści*; *no pl*) law-abidingness; **praworządny** *adj* law-abiding
prawoskrętny *adj gwint*: right-handed; **prawoskrzydłowy** *m* (*-wego*; *-wi*) *SPORT* right-winger
prawosławny *adj* Orthodox
prawostronny *adj*: ***ruch ~*** right-hand traffic; ***u nas obowiązuje ruch ~*** we drive on the right
prawowierny *adj* orthodox; **prawowity** *adj* **1.** *małżonka*: rightful **2.** *spadkobierca*, *właściciel*: lawful; **prawoznawstwo** *n* (*-wa*; *no pl*) jurisprudence
praw|y *adj* **1.** *kierunek*: right; ***po ~ej stronie*** on the right; ***z ~a*** from the right **2.** *osoba*: honest, righteous
prawzór *m* (*-zoru*; *-zory*) prototype; **prawykonanie** *n* (*-nia*; *-nia*) premiere
prażon|y *adj migdały*: roasted; ***~a kukurydza*** popcorn
prażyć ⟨**u-**⟩ (*-żę*) **1.** (*przypiekać*) roast **2.** (*o słońcu*) beat down; ***~ się w słońcu na plaży*** sunbathe on a beach, bask in the sun on a beach
prażynki *pl* (*-nek*): ***~ ziemniaczane*** (potato) chips
prącie *n* (*-cia*; *-cia*) *ANAT* penis
prąd *m* (*-du*; *-dy*) **1.** *wody*, *powietrza*: current; ***~ stały*** *PHYS* direct current, DC; ***~ zmienny*** alternating current, AC **2.** (*nurt*) stream; ***z ~em*** with the stream; ***pod ~*** against the stream; ***płynąć pod ~*** *fig* go against the tide; ***płynąć z ~em*** *fig* go with the tide; ***z ~em czasu*** up to date
prądnica *f* (*-cy*; *-ce*) **1.** *w szpitalu*: generator **2.** *AUTO* dynamo
prątki *pl* (*-ków*): ***~ gruźlicy*** *MED* tubercle bacilli; **prątkować** *v/im* (*-kuję*) be sputum-positive
prążki *pl* (*-ków*) stripes *pl*; ***spodnie w ~*** striped trousers; **prążkowany** *adj materiał*: striped
precedens *m* (*-su*; *-sy*) precedent; ***bez ~u*** unprecedented
precel *m* (*-cla*; *-cle*), **precelek** *m* (*-lka*; *-lki*) pretzel
precyzja *f* (*-zji*; *no pl*) precision; **precyzować** ⟨**s-**⟩ (*-zuję*) state precisely, elaborate (*A* on); **precyzyjny** *adj* precise
precz *adv* away, off; ***wypędzić ~*** chase away, banish; ***pójść ~*** go away; ***~ stąd!*** go away!; ***~ z drogi!*** out of the way!; ***~ z wojną!*** stop the war!; ***~ z dyktatorem!*** down with the dictator!; ***~ z rękami!*** keep your hands off!
predestynowany *adj form* predestined (***do*** *G* for); ***być ~m do*** *G* be very suitable for
predysponować *v/p* (*-nuję*) **1.** *lit* predestine **2.** *REL* predestinate
predyspozycje *pl* (*-ji*) predisposition; ***mieć ~*** have a predisposition (***do*** *G* to/towards)
prefabrykat *m* (*-tu*; *-ty*) prefabricated element; ***dom z ~ów*** prefabricated house, prefab; **prefabrykowany** *adj* prefabricated
preferencj|a *f* (*-ji*; *-je*) preference; ***~e*** preferences, priorities
prehistoria *f* (*-rii*; *no pl*) prehistory; **prehistoryczny** *adj* prehistoric
prekursor *m* (*-ra*; *-rzy*), **~ka** *f* (*-ki*; *-ki*) precursor, forerunner
prelegent *m* (*-ta*; *-nci*), **~ka** *f* (*-ki*; *-ki*) speaker
prelekcja *f* (*-ji*; *-je*) (public) lecture
preliminarz *m* (*-rza*; *-rze*) estimate; ***~ budżetowy*** draft budget
preliminować ⟨**za-**⟩ (*-nuję*) estimate, make an estimate
preludium *n* (*indecl*, *-dia*) *MUS* prelude
premedytacj|a *f* (*-ji*; *no pl*) *JUR* premeditation, deliberation; ***morderstwo z ~ą*** premeditated murder
premia *f* (*-mii*; *-mie*) bonus
premier *m* (*-ra*; *-rzy*) prime minister, premier
premiera *f* (*-ry*; *-ry*) premiere
premiować *v/im* (*-miuję*) reward, give a bonus; **premiowy** *adj* bonus
prenumerata *f* (*-ty*; *-ty*) subscription; **prenumerator** *m* (*-ra*; *-rzy*), **~ka** *f* (*-ki*; *-ki*) subscriber; **prenumerować** ⟨**za-**⟩ (*-ruję*) subscribe; ***~ dziennik*** subscribe to a daily
preparat *m* (*-tu*; *-ty*) **1.** (*lek*, *kosmetyk*) preparation **2.** *BIOL MED* specimen; ***~ mikroskopowy*** section
preparować ⟨**s-**⟩ (*-ruję*) **1.** *BIOL MED* prepare **2.** *fakty*, *dokumenty*: fabricate
preria *f* (*-rii*; *-rie*) prairie
prerogatywa *f* (*-wy*; *-wy*) prerogative

P

presj|a *f* (*-ji*; *-je*) pressure; ***pod ~ą czasu*** against the clock
prestiż *m* (*-żu*; *no pl*) prestige
pretekst *m* (*-tu*; *-ty*) pretext; ***pod ~em*** *G* under the pretext of
pretendent *m* (*-ta*; *-nci*), **~ka** *f* (*-ki*; *-ki*) *lit* pretender; ***~ do tronu*** pretender to the throne, claimant to the throne; ***~ do ręki*** candidate for marriage
pretendować *v/im* (*-duję*) **1.** lay claim (**do** *G* to); ***~ do tronu*** lay claim to the throne, claim the throne **2.** *do roli*: aspire (**do** *G* to) **3.** *do stanowiska, tytułu*: run (**do** *G* for)
pretensj|e *pl* (*-ji*) **1.** (*roszczenia*) claim, pretension; ***wnosić ~e do*** *G* lay claim to **2.** (*uraza*) resentment; ***mieć ~e do*** *G* have a grievance against, hold a grudge against; ***nie mam do niej ~i*** I hold no grudge against her **3.** (*zarzut*) complaint
pretensjonalny *adj* pretentious
prewencyjny *adj* preventative
prezbiterium *n* (*indecl*; *-ria*) *REL* presbytery
prezencj|a *f* (*-ji*; *no pl*) presence; ***mieć ~ę*** be presentable
prezen|t *m* (*-tu*; *-ty*) gift, present; ***w ~cie*** as a gift; ***~t na urodziny*** birthday present; ***~t pod choinkę*** Christmas gift
prezenter *m* (*-ra*; *-rzy*), **~ka** *f* (*-ki*; *-ki*) **1.** *RADIO* presenter **2.** (*konferansjer*) compere
prezentować ⟨**za-**⟩ (*-tuję*) **1.** *kolekcję*: present; ***~ broń*** present arms **2.** (*przedstawiać*) introduce **3.** *film*: show **4.** *poziom*: display, exhibit **5.** *postawę*: have, adopt; ***prezentować się***; ***dobrze się ~*** look (very) presentable
prezerwatywa *f* (*-wy*; *-wy*) condom
prezes *m* (*-sa*; *-si*) chairman; ***pani ~*** chairwoman; ***~ rady ministrów*** Prime Minister
prezeska *f* (*-ki*; *-ki*) (*przewodnicząca*) chairwoman
prezesostwo[1] *n* (*-wa*; *no pl*), **prezesura** *f* (*-ry*; *no pl*) presidency, chairmanship
prezesostwo[2] *pl* (*-wa*) (*małżeństwo*) the chairman and his wife
prezesować *v/im* (*-suję*) act as the president, act as the chairperson, preside (*D* over), chair (*D* s.th.)
prezydencki *adj system*: presidential
prezydent *m* (*-ta*; *-nci*) **1.** *państwa*: president; ***wybory na ~a*** presidential election; ***pani ~*** Ms President **2.** *miasta*: mayor; **prezydentura** *f* (*-ry*; *no pl*) presidency
prezydium *n* (*indecl*; *-dia*) **1.** *parlamentu, rządu*: presidium **2.** *zebrania, sesji*: presiding committee
pręcik *m* (*-ka*; *-ki*) **1.** *dim* rod, stick **2.** **~i** *BIOL* stamens
prędki *adj* **1.** *oddech*: fast **2.** *kariera, koniec*: quick **3.** *charakter*: *infml* impulsive
prędko *adv* **1.** (*szybko*) quickly, fast **2.** (*wkrótce*) (very) soon; ***~!*** quick(ly)!
prędkościomierz *m* (*-rza*; *-rze*) speedometer
prędkość *f* (*-ści*; *-ści*) **1.** *pojazdu*: speed; ***jechać*** (***z prędkością***) ***90 km na godzinę*** drive (at) 90 km an hour; ***~ dźwięku*** *PHYS* speed of sound, acoustic velocity; ***~ światła*** *PHYS* speed of light **2.** *zmian*: pace
prędszy *adj comp* → **prędki** *nurt, koniec*: quicker
prędzej *adv comp* → **prędko** **1.** (*szybciej*) quicker; ***czym ~*** as soon as possible; ***~ czy później*** sooner or later; ***~!*** quick! **2.** (*raczej*) rather; ***~ bym się spodziewał, że*** I would rather have expected that
prędziutko *adv dim* quickly; ***~!*** quick(ly)!, hurry up!
pręga *f* (*-gi*; *-gi*) **1.** *światła, na skórze*: streak **2.** ***krwawa ~*** bloody welt, bloody wheal
pręgierz *m* (*-rza*; *-rze*) *HIST* whipping post; ***stawiać pod ~em*** be (publicly) pilloried
pręgowany *adj skóra*: striped
pręt *m* (*-ta*; *-ty*) **1.** *w ogrodzeniu*: bar; ***~ metalowy*** metal bar; ***~y w oknie*** bars **2.** (*rózga*) rod
prężność *f* (*-ści*; *no pl*) **1.** *skóry, mięśni*: suppleness **2.** *rozwoju*: quickness **3.** *ruchu*: springiness; **prężn|y** *adj* **1.** *ciało, organizacja, handel*: dynamic; ***~a gospodarka*** bouyant economy **2.** *osoba*: energetic, go-getting **3.** *krok*: springy **4.** *polityk*: vigorous
prężyć ⟨**na-**⟩ (*-żę*) *mięśnie*: flex; ***~ się do skoku*** get ready to jump

P

prima aprilis *m indecl hum* April Fools' Day; ~! April Fool!; ***zrobić komuś kawał na*** ~ play an April Fools' Day trick/prank on s.o.

priorytet *m* (*-tu*; *-ty*) priority; **priorytetowy** *adj* priority

PRiTV *abbr n indecl* (= ***Polskie Radio i Telewizja***) Polish Radio and Television

PRL *abbr m* (*PRL-u*; *no pl*) *HIST* (= ***Polska Republika Ludowa***) Polish People's Republic

probierczy *adj* test, testing; ***urząd*** ~ assay office

probierz *m* (*-rza*; *-rze*) *fig* touchstone

problem *m* (*-mu*; *-my*) problem; **problematyczny** *adj* **1.** *sprawa*: problematic **2.** (*sporny*) questionable; **problematyka** *f* (*-ki*; *no pl*) issues, problems *pl*; **problemowy** *adj* **1.** *dyskusja*, *grupa*: theme **2.** *charakter*: difficult

probostwo *n* (*-wa*; *-wa*) **1.** (*parafia*, *plebania*) presbytery, rectory **2.** (*stanowisko*) parish

proboszcz *m* (*-cza*; *-czowie*) parish priest

probówk|a *f* (*-ki*; *-ki*) test tube; ***dziecko z*** **~i** test-tube baby

proc. *abbr* (= ***procent***) per cent

proc|a *f* (*-cy*; *-ce*) *Br* catapult, *Am* slingshot; ***wylecieć jak z*** **~y** go like a rat out of a trap

proceder *m* (*-ru*; *no pl*): (**niecny**) ~ shady business, shady dealings

procedura *f* (*-ry*; *-ry*) **1.** procedure **2.** *JUR* procedure, proceedings

procent *m* (*-tu*; *-ty*) **1.** (*odsetek*) percentage; ***w stu*** **~ach** one hundred per cent; ***pewny na sto*** ~ a hundred per cent sure **2.** **~y** *FIN* interest

procentować ⟨**za-**⟩ (*-tuję*) **1.** (*przynosić zysk*) yield interest, bear interest **2.** *fig* pay (off)

procentowo *adv* as a percentage; **procentow|y** *adj* **1.** (*na procent*) interest-bearing; ***stopa*** **~a** *FIN* interest rate **2.** (*jednoprocentowy*) one per cent

proces *m* (*-su*; *-sy*) **1.** *BIOL MED* process **2.** *JUR* case; ~ ***cywilny*** (civil) lawsuit; ~ ***karny*** (criminal) trial; **procesja** *f* (*-ji*; *-je*) procession

procesor *m* (*-ra*; *-ry*) *INF* processor

procesować się *v/im* (*-suję*) (**z** *I* with), fight in court (**z** *I* s.o., **o** *G* over)

proch *m* (*-chu*; *-chy*) **1.** *strzelniczy*: gunpowder; ***beczka*** **~u** powder keg; ***siedzieć na beczce*** **~u** *fig* be sitting on a powder keg **2.** (*popiół*) ash; ***rozsypać się w*** ~ crumble to dust, disintegrate completely; ***zetrzeć kogoś na*** ~ wipe s.o. out **3.** **~y a)** (*popioły*) ashes **b)** (*leki*) *infml* medicines, drugs **c)** (*narkotyki*) *infml* dope ***być na*** **~ach** be on drugs

prochowiec *m* (*-wca*; *-wce*) trench coat; **prochownia** *f* (*-ni*; *-nie*) powder magazine

produkcja *f* (*-ji*; *no pl*) **1.** (*wytwarzanie*) manufacture **2.** (*produkty*) production; ~ ***masowa*** mass production, high-volume production; ~ ***rolna*** **a)** (*uprawa i przetwarzanie*) agricultural production **b)** (*zbiory*) produce; ~ ***samochodów*** car production; ~ ***prądu*** production of energy; ~ ***hormonów*** *BIOL* hormone production; ~ ***filmowa*** film production **3.** (*twórczość literacka*) output

produkcyjność *f* (*-ści*; *no pl*) productivity

produkcyjn|y *adj proces*, *metody*: production, manufacturing; ***zakład*** **~y** manufacturing plant; ***zdolność*** **~a** production capacity; ***wiek*** **~y** working age

produkować ⟨**wy-**⟩ (*-kuję*) **1.** *towary*: manufacture, produce **2.** *film*: make; ***produkować się*** perform

produkt *m* (*-tu*; *-ty*) product; **~*y rolne*** (agricultural) produce; ***to*** ~ ***jego wyobraźni*** that is a figment of his imagination; ~ ***krajowy brutto*** *ECON* gross domestic product; **produktywny** *adj* productive

proekologiczny *adj* ecological

prof. *abbr* (= ***profesor***) Prof.

profanacja *f* (*-ji*; *-je*) desecration, profanation; **profanować** ⟨**s-**⟩ (*-nuję*) desecrate

profesja *f* (*-ji*; *-je*) *lit* profession; **profesjonalnie** *adv* professionally; **profesjonalny** *adj* professional; ~ ***sportowiec*** professional sportsman; ***sprzęt*** ~ professional equipment

profesor *m* (*-ra*; *-rowie*/*-rzy*) **1.** (*na uniwersytecie*) professor **2.** (*nauczyciel*

P

licealny) *Br* secondary-school teacher, *Am* high-school teacher
profesorka *f* (*-ki*; *-ki*) (*nauczycielka licealna*) *Br* secondary-school teacher, *Am* high-school teacher
profesorsk|i *adj* **1.** *opinia*, *obowiązki*: professorial **2.** *tytuł*: professor's; ***nominacja ~a*** appointment to professorial position, the act of receiving professorship **3.** (*nauczycielski*) teacher's
profesura *f* (*-ry*; *no pl*) **1.** (*tytuł*) professorship, professorate **2.** (*profesorowie*) professorate
profil *m* (*-lu*; *-le*) **1.** *twarzy*, *czasopisma*, *opony*: profile; ***z ~u*** in profile; ***zdjęcie z ~u*** photograph in profile; ***klasa o ~u humanistycznym*** (school) class with an emphasis on humanities **2.** *budynku*: outline
profilaktyczn|y *adj* prophylactic; ***badania ~e*** medical check-up; ***obuwie ~e*** orthopaedic shoes; **profilaktyka** *f* (*-ki*; *no pl*) MED prevention, prophylaxis
profilow|y *adj*: ***stal ~a*** TECH profile steel
progi *pl* → ***próg***
prognoza *f* (*-zy*; *-zy*) **1.** MED prognosis **2.** ***~ pogody*** weather forecast; **prognozować** *v/im* (*-zuję*) forecast
progowy *adj dawka*: maximum
program *m* (*-mu*; *-my*) **1.** programme, *Am* program; ***~ nauczania*** curriculum; ***~ telewizyjny*** (*zestawienie audycji*) TV guide, channel guide; ***~ teatralny*** programme; ***~ wyborczy*** POLIT manifesto; ***~ rozrywkowy*** show; ***być w ~ie*** (*występować*) appear in the programme; ***zmiany w ~ie*** programme changes, programme adjustments **2.** (*plan*) plan; ***~ działania*** action plan **3.** *spotkania*, *dnia*: agenda **4.** (*audycja*) broadcast; ***~ dla dzieci*** broadcast for children **5.** RADIO channel, station
programista *m* (*-ty*; *-miści*), **-tka** *f* (*-ki*; *-ki*) INF *Br* programmer, *Am* programer
programować ⟨**za-**⟩ (*-muję*) **1.** *przebieg*: plan **2.** INF *Br* programme, *Am* program
programowy *adj* **1.** INF RADIO *Br* programme, *Am* program **2.** *teza*, *artykuł*: policy **3.** (*dotyczący programu nauczania*) curricular
progresywny *adj* progressive
prohibicja *f* (*-ji*; *no pl*) prohibition
projekcja *f* (*-ji*; *-je*) **1.** *filmu*: showing, screening, viewing **2.** *slajdów*: show **3.** PSYCH projection **4.** ***mieć dobrą projekcję głosu*** project one's voice well
projekcyjny *adj*: ***aparat ~*** picture projector; ***ekran ~*** screen
projekt *m* (*-tu*; *-ty*) **1.** (*zamierzenie*) project; ***~ ustawy*** POLIT bill; ***~y na przyszłość*** plans for the future **2.** ARCHIT TECH design; ***~ budowlany*** architectural design
projektant *m* (*-ta*; *-nci*), **~ka** *f* (*-ki*; *-ki*) **1.** *mody*: fashion designer **2.** *wnętrz*: interior designer **3.** BUILD architect
projektodawca (*-cy*; *-cy*), **-czyni** *f* (*-ni*; *-nie*) originator, initiator
projektor *m* (*-ra*; *-ry*) projector
projektować ⟨**za-**⟩ (*-tuję*) **1.** ARCHIT TECH design **2.** (*planować*) plan
projektow|y *adj zespół*: design; ***biuro ~e*** design studio
proklamować *v/im* (*-muję*) proclaim
prokurator *m* (*-ra*; *-rzy*) prosecutor; **prokuratura** *f* (*-ry*; *-ry*) *Br* Director of Public Prosecutions Office, *Am* Attorney General's Office
proletariacki *adj* proletarian; **proletariat** *m* (*-tu*; *no pl*) proletariat
proletariusz *m* (*-sza*; *-sze*), **~ka** *f* (*-ki*; *-ki*) proletarian
prolongata *f* (*-ty*; *-ty*) *form* **1.** *zapłaty*: extension **2.** FIN prolongation; **prolongować** ⟨**s-**⟩ (*-guję*) *form* **1.** *termin*: prolong **2.** FIN extend, prolong
prom *m* (*-mu*; *-my*) ferry; ***~ kosmiczny*** space shuttle
promenada *f* (*-dy*; *-dy*) promenade
promienieć *v/im* (*-nieję*) *lit* beam (*I* with) ***~ radością*** (***szczęściem***) beam with joy (happiness)
promieniotwórczy *adj* radioactive
promieniować *v/im* (*-niuję*) *ciepło*, *ból*: radiate (***na*** *A* on); ***~ radością*** radiate joy; ***promieniuje z ciebie siła*** you radiate strength
promieniowanie *n* (*-nia*: *no pl*) radiation; ***~ radioaktywne*** radioactive radiation; ***~ słoneczne*** solar radiation; ***~ cieplne*** thermal radiation

P

promienisty *adj układ*: radial
promienny *adj wzrok*: radiant
promie|ń *m* (*-mienia*; *-mienie*) **1.** *światła*: ray; **~nie rentgenowskie** PHYS X-rays; **~ń nadziei** *fig* ray of hope **2.** MATH radius; **w ~niu 30 km** within a 30 km radius, within 30 km
pro|mil *m* (*-la*; *-le*) per mill
prominentny *adj* elite
promocj|a *f* (*-ji*; *-je*) **1.** promotion; **w ~i** on special offer **2.** *doktorska*: ceremony; **~a na doktora** doctoral ceremony **3.** *ucznia*: promotion **4.** (*propagowanie*) propagation
promocyjn|y *adj* promotional; **cena ~a** promotion price, reduced price; **kampania ~a** promotion campaign
promotor *m* (*-ra*; *-rzy*) *doktoranta*: promoter
promować ⟨**wy-**⟩ (*-muję*) **1.** *ucznia*, *towar*, *projekt*: promote (**do** *G* to) **2.** (*nadawać tytuł*) confer **3.** (*opiekować się*) supervise; **promowany** *adj* promoted
promow|y *adj*: **przystań ~a** ferry port, ferry harbour
promyk *m* (*-ka*; *-ki*) *dim* ray, beam; **~ nadziei** glimmer of hope
proniemiecki *adj* pro-German
propaganda *f* (*-dy*; *no pl*) propaganda; **propagandowy** *adj* propaganda
propagandysta *m* (*-ty*; *-dyści*), **propagandzista** *m* (*-ty*; *-dziści*) propagandist; **naczelny ~** head propagandist
propagator *m* (*-ra*; *-rzy*), **~ka** *f* (*-ki*; *-ki*) propagator
propagować ⟨**roz-**⟩ (*-guję*) propagate
propan *m* (*-nu*; *no pl*) CHEM propane
proponować ⟨**za-**⟩ (*-nuję*) **1.** *rozwiązanie*, *spotkanie*: suggest, propose **2.** *towar*, *zakąskę*: offer; **~ pomoc** offer help
proporcja *f* (*-ji*; *-je*) **1.** *budowy*: proportions *pl* **2.** *składników*: proportion; **proporcjonalnie** *adv*: **~ zbudowany** well-built; **proporcjonalny** *adj* **1.** proportional; **odwrotnie ~** MATH inversely proportional **2.** *sylwetka*: well-proportioned
proporczyk *m* (*-ka*; *-ki*) pennant; **~ klubowy** club pennant; **proporzec** *m* (*-rca*; *-rce*) banner
propozycj|a *f* (*-ji*; *-je*) **1.** *wyjazdu*: suggestion **2.** (*oferta*) proposal; **odrzucić ~ę pokojową** reject a peace proposal **3.** *kupna*: offer; **~a pracy** job offer; **~a kupna** offer to buy; **zgodzić się na ~ę** accept an offer; **odrzucić ~ę** turn down an offer; **~a małżeństwa** offer of marriage, proposal of marriage
proroctwo *n* (*-wa*; *-wa*) REL prophecy
proroczy *adj* REL prophetic
prorok *m* (*-ka*; *-rocy*), **~ini** *f* (*-ni*; *-nie*) REL prophet; **fałszywy ~** *fig* false prophet; **nikt nie jest ~iem we własnym kraju** a prophet is not without honour save in his own country
prorządowy *adj* POLIT pro-government
prosektorium *n* (*indecl*; *-ria*) dissection room
proseminarium *n* (*indecl*; *-ria*) (introductory) seminar
prosiaczek *m* (*-czka*; *-czki*) *dim* (little) piglet; **prosiak** *m* (*-ka*; *-ki*) BIOL piglet
prosić ⟨**po-**⟩ (*-szę*) **1.** (*starać się skłonić*) ask (**o** *A* for); **~ kogoś do tańca** ask s.o. to dance; **(po)proszę o kawę** I'd like a cup of coffee, please; **proszę bardzo!**, **proszę uprzejmie!** **a)** (*odpowiedź na „dziękuję”*) you're welcome, don't mention it! **b)** (*podając coś*) here you are **c)** (*wyrażając zgodę*) please do, go ahead; **proszę?** pardon (me)?, excuse me?; **proszę** (**wejść**)**!** come in!; **czy mogę prosić panią Kowalską?** (*w rozmowie telefonicznej*) can I speak to Mrs Kowalska?; **proszę mi wierzyć** believe me; **co proszę?** I beg your pardon?, pardon me?; **uprzejmie proszę** (it was) a pleasure, my pleasure **2.** (*zapraszać*) ask in, invite (**na** *A* for); **~ do stołu** invite to the table; **~ kogoś do środka** ask s.o. in; **~ na herbatę** invite for tea; **~ na wesele** invite to the wedding; **dyrektor pana prosi** the manager wants to talk to you; **proszę pana, która godzina?** excuse me, what is the time?; **proszę usiąść** please, be seated, please take a seat; **prosimy nie palić** please, do not smoke; **no proszę!** (well) what do you know!; **proszę pani, chciałabym o coś zapytać** excuse me madam, I'd like to ask a question; **prosić się 1.** ask **2.** (*potrzebować*) need; **kwiaty aż proszą się o wodę** flowers desperately need watering

P

prosić się ⟨**o-**⟩ (*-szę*) *BIOL* farrow, *Am* pig
prosię *n* (*-sięcia*; *-sięta*) *BIOL* piglet; **~ pieczone** *COOK* roasted pig
proso *n* (*-sa*; *no pl*) millet
prospekt *m* (*-tu*; *-ty*) (*broszura*) prospectus, brochure
prosperować *v/im* (*-ruję*) prosper
prosta *f* (*-tej*; *-te*) *MATH* straight
prostacki *adj* **1.** *żart*, *twarz*: common **2.** *zachowanie*: coarse; **prostaczek** *m* (*-czka*; *-czkowie*) simpleton, hick; **prostaczka** *f* (*-ki*; *-ki*) churl, hick; **prostak** *m* (*-ka*; *-tacy*/*-ki*) simpleton
prostata *f* (*-ty*; *-ty*) *ANAT* prostate
prosto *adv* **1.** *jechać*: straight ahead, straight on; **~ przed siebie** straight ahead, straight on; **siedzieć ~** sit upright, sit straight; **~ do domu** directly home; **~ jak strzelił** straight ahead; **~ spod igły** brand new **2.** (*niezawile*) clearly **3.** (*niewyszukanie*) simply **4.** (*wprost*) straight, directly; **powiedzieć ~ z mostu** mouth off, speak bluntly; **mleko ~ od krowy** milk directly from the cow
prostoduszny *adj* simple-hearted
prostokąt *m* (*-ta*; *-ty*) *MATH* rectangle; **prostokątny** *adj* **1.** *plac*: rectangular **2.** *MATH* right-angled
prostolinijny *adj fig* straightforward
prostoliniowy *adj* rectilinear, straight-line; **ruch ~** *PHYS* (recti)linear motion
prostopadłościan *m* (*-nu*; *-ny*) *MATH* quadratic prism; **prostopadły** *adj* perpendicular
prostota *f* (*-ty*; *no pl*) **1.** *zachowania*: straightforwardness **2.** *stylu*, *ozdób*: simplicity
prostować (*-tuję*) **1.** ⟨**wy-**⟩ *drut*, *kartkę*: straighten out **2.** ⟨**wy-**⟩ *prąd*: rectify **3.** ⟨**s-**⟩ *błąd*, *wypowiedź*: correct; **prostować się** straighten up
prostownik *m* (*-ka*; *-ki*) **1.** *TECH* rectifier, battery charger **2.** (*mięsień*) extensor
prost|y I *adj* **1.** (*nie wygięty*) straight; **~e włosy** straight hair; **~y jak świeca** (as) straight as a (ram)rod; **100 km w linii ~ej** 100 km in a straight line **2.** (*zwykły*) simple; **po ~u** simply, merely **3.** *kąt*; right **II** *m* (*-tego*; *-te*) (*cios*) straight
prostytucja *f* (*-ji*; *no pl*) prostitution; **prostytutka** *f* (*-ki*; *-ki*) prostitute
proszący *adj* pleading
prosz|ek *m* (*-szku*; *-szki*) **1.** (*substancja*) powder; **~ek do prania** washing powder; **~ek do pieczenia** baking powder; **mleko w ~ku** powdered milk; **utrzeć na ~ek** pulverize, powder; **być w ~ku** *fig* be in pieces **2.** (*lek*) pill; **~ek przeciwbólowy** pain killer; **~ek nasenny** sleeping pill
proszkowy *adj* powder
proszony *adj* **~ obiad** dinner party; **jesteś ~ do telefonu** someone wants to speak to you on the phone
prośb|a *f* (*-by*; *-by*) **1.** (*życzenie*) request (**do** *G* of); **na własną ~ę** at one's own request; **chodzić po ~ie** beg one's bread **2.** (*podanie*) application
prościej *comp* → **prosto**
prościut(eń)ki *adj dim* **1.** (*prosty*) perfectly straight **2.** *fig* truly simple
prośny *adj maciora*: in pig
protegować ⟨**za-**⟩ (*-guję*) *lit* back
protegowana *f* (*-nej*; *-ne*) protégée; **protegowany** *m* (*-nego*; *-ni*) protégé
protekcja *f* (*-ji*; *-je*) favouritism; **protekcjonalny** *adj* patronizing, condescending
protektor[1] *m* (*-ra*; *-rzy*), **~ka** *f* (*-ki*; *-ki*) (*opiekun*) protector, patron
protektor[2] *m* (*-ra*; *-ry*) **1.** *opony*: tread **2.** (*podeszwa*) sole
protektorat *m* (*-tu*; *no pl*) **1.** (*opieka*) protection **2.** *POLIT* protectorate
protest *m* (*-tu*; *-ty*) protest; **na znak ~u** in protest; **protestacyjny** *adj* protest
protestancki *adj* Protestant
protestant *m* (*-ta*; *-nci*), **~ka** *f* (*-ki*; *-ki*) Protestant
protestować ⟨**za-**⟩ (*-tuję*) protest (**przeciw** *D* against)
protestujący *m* (*-cego*; *-cy*), **-ca** *f* (*-cej*; *-ce*) protester
protetyk *m* (*-ka*; *-tycy*), **-tyczka** *f* (*-ki*; *-ki*) prosthetician, prosthetist
proteza *f* (*-zy*; *-zy*) **1.** (*zębowa*) denture, dental prosthesis **2.** (*ortopedyczna*) artificial limb, prosthesis; **~ słuchowa** hearing aid
protokolant *m* (*-ta*; *-nci*), **~ka** *f* (*-ki*; *-ki*) **1.** (*piszący protokół*) minute taker, *Am* secretary **2.** (*w sądzie*) clerk of

P

the court, shorthand writer, stenographer

protokolarny *adj* officially recorded

protokołować ⟨**za-**⟩ (*-łuję*) **1.** (*na zebraniu*) take the minutes **2.** *rozprawę sądową*: record

protokół *m* (*-kołu*; *-koły*) **1.** POLIT protocol; **~ dyplomatyczny** diplomatic protocol **2.** (*sprawozdanie*) minutes; **~ z zebrania** meeting minutes **3.** (*zapis*) report; **~ zeznań świadków** JUR testimony, record; **~ powypadkowy** accident report; **~ szkód** damage report; **sporządzić ~** make a report

protoplasta *m* (*-ty*; *-laści*) *lit* ancestor; **protoplazma** *f* (*-my*; *no pl*) BIOL protoplasm; **prototyp** *m* (*-pu*; *-py*) TECH prototype

prowadnica *f* (*-cy*; *-ce*) TECH slide, guide(way)

prowadzący *m* (*-cego*; *-cy*), **-ca** *f* (*-cej*; *-ce*) RADIO host

prowadzenie *n* (*-nia*; *no pl*) **1.** *zakładu*: running; **~ samochodu** driving; **~ wojny** being at war **2.** SPORT lead; **objąć ~** take the lead **3.** conduct; **niemoralne ~ (się)** immoral conduct

prowadzić (*-dzę*) **I** *v/t* **1.** ⟨**za-**⟩ (*kierować, wieść*) lead; **~ kogoś za rękę** lead s.o. by the hand; **~ beztroskie życie** lead a carefree life; **~ na smyczy** walk on a leash; **~ w tańcu** lead; **to do niczego nie prowadzi** this is going nowhere **2.** ⟨**prze-**⟩ *rozmowę*: have; **~ wykład na uniwersytecie** lecture at the university **3.** *wojnę*: conduct, have **4.** ⟨**prze-**⟩ *badania*: carry out **5.** *samochód, tramwaj*: drive **6.** *samolot*: fly **7.** *zakład, hotel, restaurację*: run; **~ dom** run a house(hold); **~ gospodarstwo** run a farm **8.** *audycję*: host **II** *v/i* **1.** (*o drodze, drzwiach, schodach*) lead; **~ do** *G* lead to **2.** SPORT lead; **prowadzić się**: **źle się prowadziła** she was a women of easy virtue

prowiant *m* (*-tu*; *-ty*) provisions *pl*; **suchy ~** packed lunch

prowincja *f* (*-ji*; *-je*) province; **głucha ~** back country; **prowincjonaln|y** *adj* provincial, parochial; **miasteczko ~e** upcountry town

prowizja *f* (*-ji*; *-je*) commission

prowizorka *f* (*-ki*; *-ki*) *infml* **1.** (*budowla*) makeshift construction **2.** (*tymczasowe rozwiązanie*) quick fix; **prowizoryczn|y** *adj* **1.** *urządzenie*: makeshift; **~e rozwiązanie** quick fix

prowodyr *m* (*-ra*; *-rzy*) **1.** *bandy, szajki*: ringleader **2.** *buntu*: instigator

prowokacja *f* (*-ji*; *-je*) provocation; **prowokacyjny** *adj przemówienie, zachowanie*: provocative, provoking

prowokator *m* (*-ra*; *-rzy*) agent provocateur

prowokować ⟨**s-**⟩ (*-kuję*) provoke; **prowokujący** *adj* provocative

proz|a *f* (*-zy*; *no pl*) LIT prose; **pisać ~ą** write in prose; **~a codzienności** humdrum of life

prozaiczny *adj* **1.** *utwór*: prose **2.** *powód, zajęcie*: prosaic

prozaik *m* (*-ka*; *-zaicy*) prose writer

prozatorsk|i *adj* LIT prose; **utwór ~i** work written in prose; **twórczość ~a** prose writing

prób|a *f* (*-by*; *-by*) **1.** (*sprawdzenie*) test; **~a życiowa** personality test; **~a ciążowa** pregnancy test; **~a losowa** random sample, random selection; **~a krwi** MED blood test; **wystawić coś na ~ę** put s.th. to the test, put s.th. to the proof; **wytrzymać ~ę czasu** stand the test of time **2.** trial; **~a ogniowa** trial by fire, acid test; **na ~ę** on a trial basis; **robić coś metodą ~ i błędów** do s.th. by (the process of) trial and error **3.** (*usiłowanie*) attempt; **~a samobójcza** suicide attempt **4.** THEAT rehearsal; **~a generalna** dress rehearsal **5.** *złota, srebra*: standard

próbk|a *f* (*-ki*; *-ki*) **1.** *substancji, gleby, krwi*: sample; **~a pracy** sample of work; **dać ~ę swoich umiejętności** show what one can do; **pobrać ~ę** take a sample **2.** *powietrza, pisma*: specimen

próbnie *adv* on a trial basis; **próbnik** *m* (*-ka*; *-ki*) **1.** TECH testing set, tester **2.** ASTR cosmic probe; **próbn|y** *adj* **1.** *lot, wiercenia*: test; **zdjęcia ~e** FILM screen test **2.** *przebieg, okres*: trial **3.** *egzamin*: mock

próbować ⟨**s-**⟩ (*-buję*) **1.** (*sprawdzać*) test **2.** (*usiłować*) try; **~ szczęścia** try one's luck; **~ wszystkiego** pursue every avenue **3.** (*smakować*) try, taste

P

próchnica *f* (*-cy*; *no pl*) **1.** *MED* caries **2.** (*w rolnictwie*) humus
próchnieć ⟨**s-**⟩ (*-nieję*) **1.** (*o drewnie*) rot **2.** (*o zębie*) decay
próchno *n* **1.** (*-na*; *no pl*) (*produkt rozkładu*) rotten wood **2.** (*-na*; *-na*) (*stary człowiek*) *infml* fossil
prócz *prep* apart from, besides; **~ tego** besides
próg *m* (*progu*; *progi*) **1.** doorstep; **stać w progu** be on the doorstep; **górny ~** *fig* upper limit; **zima za progiem** winter is coming, winter is near; **u progu** *fig* very close; **progi rodzinne** *lit* family home **2.** (*granica*) threshold; **~ bólu** pain threshold; **~ słyszalności** audibility threshold, hearing threshold **3.** *SPORT* board, take-off
prószyć *v/im*: **śnieg prószy**, **prószy śniegiem** it's snowing lightly; **piach prószy w oczy** sand gets into your eyes
próżni|a *f* (*-ni*; *no pl*) **1.** *PHYS* vacuum **2.** (*pustka*) *fig* void; **padać w ~ę** fall on deaf ears, fall on stony ground; **zawisnąć w ~** be deadlocked, cease to be real; **duchowa ~a** spiritual void
próżniactwo *n* (*-wa*; *no pl*) idleness; **próżniaczy** *adj* *życie*: idle, slothful; **próżniak** *m* (*-ka*; *-niacy*/*-ki*) loafer, lazybones
próżniow|y *adj* vacuum; **opakowanie ~e** vacuum package
próżno *adv lit*: **~, na ~o** in vain
próżność *f* (*-ści*; *no pl*) vanity; **zaspokajać czyjąś ~** feed s.o.'s vanity
próżnować *v/im* (*-nuję*) loaf, be idle, laze about, laze around
próżny *adj* **1.** *butelka*: empty **2.** *nadzieja*, *wysiłki*, *człowiek*: vain **3.** *słowa*: futile, to no purpose; **przelewać z pustego w próżne** talk for talk's sake, talk for the sake of it
pruć ⟨**s-**⟩ (*pruję*) *sweter*: unravel; **~ fale** plough (through); **pruć się** (*o swetrze*) unravel
pruderyjny *adj* prudish
Prusak *m* (*-ka*; *-sacy*) *HIST* Prussian
prusak *m* (*-ka*; *-ki*) *BIOL* (German) cockroach
pruski *adj HIST* Prussian; **kwas ~** *CHEM* prussic acid; **mur ~** *ARCHIT* half-timber(ed) wall
Prusy *pl* (*Prus*) *HIST* Prussia
prychać ⟨**-chnąć**⟩ (*-cham*) snort; **~ ze złości** *fig* spit out angrily
prycza *f* (*-czy*; *-cze*) bunk
pryk *m* (*-ka*; *-ki*) *infml*: **stary ~** old fart
prym: **wieść ~** lead the way, be in the lead, make all the running
prymas *m* (*-sa*; *-si*/*-sowie*) *REL* primate
prymat *m* (*-tu*; *no pl*) *lit* **1.** (*pierwszeństwo*) primacy **2.** (*przewodzenie*) predominance; **wojna o ~ na morzu** war for predominance on the sea
prymityw[1] *m* (*-wu*; *no pl*) (*zacofanie*) primitiveness, backwardness
prymityw[2] *m* **1.** (*-wa*; *-wy*) (*prostak*) *infml* barbarian **2.** (*-wa*; *-wi*) *ART* primitive (painter)
prymitywizm *m* (*-mu*; *no pl*) **1.** (*zacofanie*) primitiveness, backwardness **2.** *ART* primitive painting
prymitywność *f* (*-ści*; *no pl*) **1.** (*pierwotność*) primitiveness, primitive character **2.** (*prostactwo*, *brutalność*) coarseness, roughness
prymitywny *adj* **1.** *narzędzia*, *metody*, *plemiona*: primitive **2.** (*brutalny*, *chamski*) coarse, rude
prymula *f* (*-li*; *-le*), **prymulka** *f* (*-ki*; *-ki*) primrose
prymus[1] *m* (*-sa*; *-si*/*-sy*), **~ka** *f* (*-ki*; *-ki*) (*osoba*) top of the class, model student, top student
prymus[2] *m* (*-sa*; *-sy*) (*kuchenka*) primus stove
pryskać ⟨**-snąć**⟩ (*-kam*) **I** *v/t* **1.** splash; **~ w twarz wodą** splash water on one's face **2.** *błotem*: splatter **3.** *szkłem*: shatter **4.** *uprawy*: spray (*I* with) **II** *v/i* **1.** (*o nastroju*) be gone, vanish **2.** (*uciec*) *Br* scarper, *Am* scram
pryskany *adj* *uprawy*: sprayed
pryszcz *m* (*-cza*; *-cze*) **1.** pimple, spot **2.** *MED* pustule **3.** (*drobnostka*) *infml* nothing; **to dla mnie ~** it's a piece of cake for me, that's nothing for me; **pryszczaty** *adj* *twarz*: spotty, pimply
pryszczyca *f* (*-cy*; *no pl*) *MED* foot-and-mouth disease, foot-and-mouth
prysznic *m* (*-ca*; *-ce*) shower; **wziąć ~** have a shower, take a shower; **zimny ~** *fig* cold water; **prysznicow|y** *adj*: **kabina ~a** shower cubicle
prywaciarz *m* (*-rza*; *-rze*) *infml* private entrepreneur
prywata *f* (*-ty*; *no pl*) *lit Am* jobbery

prywatka *f* (*-ki*; *-ki*) *infml fig* party
prywatnie *adv* privately
prywatność *f* (*-ści*; *no pl*) privacy; **prywatn|y** *adj* **1.** *życie*: private; ***zbiory ~e*** private collection; ***sprawa ~a*** private business; ***~y detektyw*** private eye, private investigator, private detective; ***szkoła ~a*** private school, *Br* public school; ***~e lekcje*** private lessons; ***osoba ~a*** private person; ***życie ~e*** private life **2.** *użytek*: personal
prywatyzacja *f* (*-ji*; *no pl*) privatisation
prywatyzować ⟨**s-**⟩ (*-zuję*) privatise
pryzm|a *f* (*-my*; *-my*) *żwiru*, *buraków*: pile, heap; ***układać w ~y*** pile
pryzmat *m* (*-tu*; *-ty*) PHYS prism; ***patrzeć na coś przez ~*** *G* look at s.th. from the angle of
przaśny *adj* **1.** *chleb*: unleavened **2.** *chłopak*: simple, unsophisticated
prządka *f* (*-ki*; *-ki*) spinner
prząść *v/im* (*przędę*) *wełnę*: spin; ***cienko ~*** *fig* live from hand to mouth, barely get by
przebaczać ⟨**-czyć**⟩ (*-czam*) forgive
przebaczenie *n* (*-nia*; *no pl*) forgiveness
przebadać *v/p* → **badać**
przebąkiwać *v/im* (*-kuję*) **1.** (*napomykać*) hint (**o** *L* at) **2.** (*mówić po kątach*) whisper
przebici|e *n* (*-cia*; *-cia*) **1.** AUTO breakdown **2.** (*otwór*) puncture; ***siła ~a*** *fig* push, wallop
przebić *v/p* → **przebijać**
przebiec *v/p* → **przebiegać**
przebieg *m* (*-gu*; *-gi*) **1.** *zdarzeń*, *obrad*: course **2.** *trasy*: route **3.** AUTO mileage
przebiegać ⟨**-biec**⟩ (*-gam*) **1.** run; ***~ przez*** *A* run across; ***~ myślą*** search one's memory; ***~ coś wzrokiem*** run one's eyes over s.th.; ***~ przez jezdnię*** run across the street; ***~ obok*** *G* run next to; ***przebiegł mnie dreszcz*** shiver went down my spine; ***granica przebiega tamtędy*** the border runs over there **2.** (*o pracy*) proceed, go; ***~ zgodnie z planem*** go according to plan
przebiegły *adj* **1.** *osoba*: crafty, cunning **2.** *uśmiech*: sly
przebierać ⟨**-brać**⟩ (*-ram*) **1.** *dziecko*: change; ***~ za*** *A* dress up as **2.** ***~ nogami*** shuffle one's feet, hop from one leg to the other **2.** *owoce*: sort (out); ***~ do woli*** pick and choose; ***nie ~ w środkach*** by hook or (by) crook; ***nie ~ w słowach*** not to mince one's words; ***przebierać się*** dress up; ***~ się za*** *A* disguise oneself as, dress up as
przebieralnia *f* (*-ni*; *-nie*) changing room
przebiera|niec *m* (*-rańca*; *-rańcy*): ***bal ~ńców*** fancy dress ball, masked ball
przebijać ⟨**-bić**⟩ (*-jam*) **1.** *igłą*, *gwoździem*: pierce; ***~ kogoś wzrokiem*** look daggers at s.o. **2.** (*wykuć*) drill, bore; ***~ dziurę*** drill a hole, bore a hole **3.** *tunel*: dig (up) **4.** (*w kartach*) trump **5.** (*o świetle*, *farbie*) show through; ***w jego głosie przebija optymizm*** (***smutek***) a note of optimism (sadness) comes through in his voice; ***przebijać się*** **1.** fight one's way (**do** *G* to); ***~ się przez*** *A* break through, get through; ***~ się przez tłum*** fight one's way through the crowd, elbow one's way through the crowd; ***~ się do zasypanych*** get through to the buried people **2.** (*odnosić sukces*) be successful **3.** (*o słońcu*, *głosie*) break through
przebijak *m* (*-ka*; *-ki*) punch
przebiśnieg *m* (*-gu*; *-gi*) BIOL snowdrop
przebitka *f* (*-ki*; *-ki*) (*kopia*) carbon copy; **przebitkowy** *adj*: ***papier ~*** copying paper
przebłagać *v/p* (*-gam*) manage to beg; ***nie dać się ~*** be merciless
przebłysk *m* (*-ku*; *-ki*) glimmer; ***~i szczęścia*** strokes of luck, some (good) luck; ***mieć ~i świadomości*** have flashes of consciousness
przebłyskiwać *v/im* (*-kuję*) **1.** (*o świetle*) glimmer **2.** (*o słońcu*) shine (a little)
przebogaty *adj* (over)abundant
przeboje *pl* → **przebój**
przebojow|y *adj osoba*: go-ahead; ***~a piosenka*** hit song; ***~y film*** blockbuster (film)
przeboleć *v/p* (*-leję*) get over; ***jeszcze tego nie przebolał*** he hasn't got over it yet
przeb|ój *m* (*-boju*; *-boje*) hit, top song; ***lista ~ojów*** hit parade; ***iść ~ojem*** *fig* be a go-getter; ***iść ~ojem przez życie***

blaze a trail for oneself, force one's way in one's life

przebrać *v/p* → **przebierać**

przebrani|e *n* (*-nia*; *-nia*) disguise; ***w ~u*** *G* disguised as; ***była w ~u*** she was in disguise; **przebrany** *adj* disguised (***za*** *A* as)

przebrnąć *v/p* (*-nę*) wade (***przez*** *A* through); ***~ przez fachowy tekst*** wade through a specialist text; ***~ przez rozmowę kwalifikacyjną*** do well in an interview

przebrzmiały *adj sława*: foregone

przebrzydły *adj* horrid, awful

przebrzmiewać ⟨**-mieć**⟩ (*-wam*) **1.** (*o melodii*) die away **2.** (*o sławie*) wane, go with the wind

przebudowa *f* (*-wy*; *-wy*) **1.** *domu*: conversion **2.** *ulicy*: rebuilding **3.** *systemu*: restructuring

przebudowywać ⟨**-dować**⟩ (*-dowuję*) **1.** *dom*: convert **2.** *ulicę*: rebuild **3.** *system*: restructure

przebudzenie (się) *n* (*-nia*; *-nia*) awakening

przebudzić *v/p* → **budzić**

przebyci|e: ***nie do ~a*** impassable, blocked; ***trudny do ~a*** hard to pass through

przebywać ⟨**-być**⟩ (*-wam*) **I** *v/t* **1.** *drogę, rzekę*: get across, cross **2.** *chorobę*: go through **3.** *próbę*: be put to **II** *v/i* (*pozostawać*) stay; ***~ na wolności*** be at large

przecedzać ⟨**-dzić**⟩ (*-dzam*) strain

przecen|a *f* (*-ny*; *-ny*) reduction (in price); ***towary z ~y*** cut price goods, discounted goods; ***kupić coś z ~y*** buy s.th. at a reduced price, buy s.th. at a discount; ***~a posezonowa*** end of season sale

przeceniać ⟨**-nić**⟩ (*-niam*) **1.** reduce the price, mark down **2.** *fig* overestimate; ***trudno przecenić*** it is hard to overestimate; ***przeceniać się*** overestimate oneself

przeceniony *adj towar*: reduced, discounted, on offer

przechadzać się *v/im* (*-dzam*) stroll (***po*** *L* around); ***~ tam i z powrotem*** stroll there and back, walk up and down

przechadzk|a *f* (*-ki*; *-ki*) stroll, saunter; ***iść na ~ę*** go for a stroll

przechładzać ⟨**-łodzić**⟩ (*-dzam*) *wodę*: cool, chill; ***przechładzać się*** (*o wodzie*) cool off

przechodni *adj* **1.** *czasownik*: transitive **2.** *puchar*: challenge **3.** *pokój*: connecting

przechodzić ⟨**przejść**⟩ (*-dzę*) **I** *v/i* **1.** (*iść*) go (***do*** *G* to); ***~ w kurtce dwie zimy*** wear one's coat for two winters; ***~ do tematu*** get to the point; ***~ do następnej klasy*** go into the next year, be promoted; ***~ w*** *A* pass into, turn into; ***~ do*** *G* pass over to; ***~ obok*** *G* pass, go past; ***~ na dietę*** go on a diet; ***~ na emeryturę*** retire; ***~ na inny język*** switch to another language; ***~ z rąk do rąk*** be passed from hand to hand; ***to nie przejdzie*** this won't work **2.** (*przebyć*) cross; ***~ przez ulicę*** cross the street; ***~ przez granicę*** cross the border **3.** (*w konkursie*) go farther, go to the next round; ***~ do następnej rundy*** get to the next round **4.** (*o świetle, głosie, kuli*) get through; ***~ przez dziurę*** get through a hole **5.** (*o trasie, linii*) cross, go through **6.** (*o deszczu*) cease, let up **7.** (*o bólu*) pass, ease (off/away), wear off **8.** REL convert (***na*** *A* to); ***~ na katolicyzm*** convert to Catholicism **II** *v/t* **1.** *biedę, chorobę*: go through; ***~ grypę*** be down with flu; ***przejść w życiu wiele*** go through a lot in one's life; ***~ badania*** undergo examinations; ***~ wilgocią*** get wet, absorb water **2.** *wyobraźnię*: be beyond **3.** *oczekiwania*: exceed, surpass; ***przejść samego siebie*** excel oneself; ***~ próbę*** be put to the test

przechodzień *m* (*-dnia*; *-dnie*) passer-by

przechodzony *adj ubranie*: worn (out)

przechorowywać ⟨**-rować**⟩ (*-rowuję*): ***przechorować całą zimę*** spend the whole winter being sick; ***bardzo przechorował porażkę*** he took the defeat very hard

przechować *v/p* → **przechowywać**

przechowalnia *f* (*-ni*; *-nie*): ***~ bagażu*** left-luggage (office)

przechowanie *n* (*-nia*; *no pl*) storing; ***na ~*** for safekeeping

przechowywać ⟨**-chować**⟩ (*-chowuję*) **1.** *pamiątki, dokumenty, zwyczaje*:

P

keep; **~ coś w pamięci** nurse the memory of, nurture the memory of; **~ w sejfie** keep in a safe **2.** *zbiega*: hide **3.** *żywność, drewno*: store; **~ w chłodnym i suchym miejscu** store in a cool and dry place, keep cool and dry; **przechowywać się** (*o zwyczaju*) be preserved

przechowywanie *n* (*-nia*; *no pl*) storage

przechrzcić *v/p* (*-czę*) rename; **przechrzcić się 1. ~ się na katolicyzm** convert to Catholicism **2.** (*zmienić imię, nazwę*) to change one's name

przechwalać się *v/im* (*-lam*) boast (*I* about)

przechwałki *pl* (*-łek*) boast, brag

przechwytywać ⟨**-chwycić**⟩ (*-tuję*) **1.** *informację, list*: intercept **2.** *władzę*: seize **3.** *samolot*: locate

przechylać ⟨**-lić**⟩ (*-lam*) *głowę, dzban*: tilt; **przechylać się 1.** (*o szafie, płocie*) tilt **2.** (*o osobie*) lean; **~ przez poręcz** lean over the railing/banister; **~ na bok** lean to one side; **~ do przodu** lean forward **3.** (*o statku*) list **4.** (*o samolocie*) bank

przechył *m* (*-łu*; *-ły*) **1.** (*przechylenie się*) tilt **2.** *statku*: list; **łódź ma ~ 10 stopni** the boat is heeling by ten degrees

przechytrzać ⟨**-rzyć**⟩ (*-rzam*) outwit

przeciąć *v/p* → **przecinać**

przeciąg *m* (*-gu*; *-gi*) **1.** *Br* draught, *Am* draft; **stać w ~u** be in the draught; **tu jest ~** it's draughty in here **2.** (*okres*) **w ~u** within; **w ~u tygodnia** within a week

przeciągać ⟨**-gnąć**⟩ (*-gam*) **I** *v/t* **1.** *nitkę*: thread (**przez** *A*) **2.** (*przesuwać*) drag, pull (**przez** *A*/**po** *L* over) **3.** *kabel*: stretch, extend **4.** *konferencję, spotkanie*: prolong, draw out, extend **5.** *sylaby*: drawl **II** *v/i* (*o pochodzie*) march past; **~ po** *L* run across, run along; **~ ręką po** *L* run one's hand across, run one's hand along; **~ strunę** *fig* overstep the mark, go too far; **przeciągać się 1.** stretch **2.** (*o konferencji, rozmowie*) drag on **3.** (*o pobycie*) stretch out

przeciągły *adj* **1.** *dźwięk, krzyk*: drawn-out, protracted **2.** *spojrzenie*: lingering

przeciążać ⟨**-żyć**⟩ (*-żam*) **1.** *pojazd*: overload **2.** *pracownika*: overburden (*I* with); **~ kogoś obowiązkami** load s.o. down with duties **3.** *serce*: overtax **4.** (*fizycznie*) overload; **przeciążać się 1.** (*fizycznie*) overtax oneself **2.** *obowiązkami*: overburden oneself (*I* with); **~ się pracą** overburden oneself with work

przeciążenie *n* (*-nia*; *no pl*) **1.** (*nadmiar*) overload **2.** *fizyczne*: G-force; **przeciążony** *adj* overloaded (*I* with)

przeciek *m* (*-ku*; *-ki*) **1.** *informacji*: leak; **z ~ów wiadomo, że** it leaked out that **2.** *paliwa*: leakage

przeciekać ⟨**-ciec**, **-knąć**⟩ (*-kam*) **1.** (*o zbiorniku, kranie, łodzi*) leak; **woda przecieka do łódki** the boat is leaking; **woda przecieka przez dach** water is leaking through the roof **2.** (*o wodzie, krwi, informacji*) leak out

przecier *m* (*-ru*; *-ry*) purée; **~ pomidorowy** tomato purée; **~ jabłkowy** apple purée; **robić ~ z** *G* COOK sieve

przecierać ⟨**przetrzeć**⟩ (*-ram*) **1.** *szklankę, okulary*: wipe; **~ oczy** wipe one's eyes; **~ szlak** *fig* pave the way, blaze a trail **2.** COOK sieve **3.** *spodnie*: wear through; **przecierać się 1.** (*o spodniach*) wear through **2.** (*o niebie*) clear up

przecierpieć *v/p* (*-pię*) **1.** *zniewagę*: bear **2.** *trudny okres*: suffer, endure; **wiele ~** go through a lot

przecież *particle* but; **~ wiesz** but you know, don't you?

przecięci|e *n* (*-cia*; *-cia*) **1.** (*miejsce*) slit **2.** *ulic, dróg*: *Br* crossroads, *Am* intersection; **punkt ~a** (point of) intersection

przeciętniak *m* (*-ka*; *-niacy*/*-ki*) *infml* ordinary man, ordinary Joe, *Am* square John

przeciętnie *adv* **1.** (*średnio*) on average **2.** *wyglądać*: plain; **przeciętna** *f* (*-nej*; *-ne*) average, mean; **powyżej** (**poniżej**) **przeciętnej** above (below) average; → **przeciętny**

przeciętn|y *adj* **1.** (*statystyczny*) average, mean; **~a pensja** average salary; **~a długość życia** life expectancy **2.** (*mierny*) mediocre; → **przeciętna**

P

przecinać ⟨**-ciąć**⟩ (*-nam*) **1.** (*rozciąć*) cut; **~ zakład** shake on a bet **2.** *drogę*: cut across **3.** *rozmowę*: cut short; ***przecinać się*** cross

przecinek *m* (*-nka*; *-nki*) **1.** (*znak*) comma **2.** *MATH* point; ***do dwóch miejsc po przecinku*** to two decimal places

przecinka *f* (*-ki*; *-ki*) cutting

przeciskać ⟨**-snąć**⟩ (*-kam*) squeeze (***przez*** *A* through); ***przeciskać się*** squeeze through

przeciw, ***przeciwko*** *prep* (*D*) against; ***nie mam nic ~ temu*** I have nothing against it

przeciw- (*w złożeniach*) anti-, counter-

przeciwbólowy *adj* painkilling, analgesic; ***środek ~*** painkiller

przeciwciało *n* (*-ła*; *-ła*) *BIOL* antibody

przeciwdeszczowy *adj*: ***płaszcz ~*** raincoat, *Br* mac

przeciwdziałać *v/im* (*-łam*) counteract (*D* s.th.)

przeciwgazow|y *adj*: ***maska ~a*** gas mask

przeciwgorączkowy *adj* temperature reducing, febrifugal

przeciwgruźliczy *adj* antituberculous

przeciwieństw|o *n* (*-wa*; *-wa*) contrast; ***w ~ie do*** *G* in contrast to, contrary to

przeciwjad *m* (*-du*; *-dy*) antivenom, antivenin

przeciwk|o *prep*: ***z ~a*** from the opposite direction; → ***przeciw***

przeciwległy *adj* opposite

przeciwlotnicz|y *adj*: ***obrona ~a*** anti-aircraft defences; ***schron ~y*** air raid shelter

przeciwmgieln|y *adj*: ***światła ~e*** *AUTO* fog lights; ***syrena ~a*** fog siren

przeciwmolowy *adj* anti-moth

przeciwnatarcie *n* (*-cia*; *-cia*) counterattack

przeciwniczka *f* (*-ki*; *-ki*) opponent, adversary

przeciwnie *particle* on the contrary; ***wręcz ~*** just the opposite, quite the opposite, quite the reverse; ***~ do ruchu wskazówek zegara*** *Br* anticlockwise, *Am* counterclockwise

przeciwnik *m* (*-ka*; *-nicy*) **1.** *SPORT* opponent **2.** (*rywal*) adversary; ***~ globalizacji*** anti-globalist; ***być ~iem kary śmierci*** be against the death penalty

przeciwności *pl* (*-ści*): ***~ losu*** adversities

przeciwn|y *adj* **1.** *zdanie*, *płeć*: opposite **2.** (*odwrotny*) contrary; ***być ~ym*** *D* be against; ***~y wiatr*** head wind, opposing wind; ***w ~ym razie*** otherwise; ***po ~ej stronie*** on the opposite side; ***w ~ym kierunku*** in the opposite direction; ***w kierunku ~ym do ruchu wskazówek zegara*** *Br* anticlockwise, *Am* counterclockwise

przeciwpancerny *adj* anti-tank; **przeciwodblaskowy** *adj* anti-glare

przeciwpowodziow|y *adj* flood; ***pogotowie ~e*** flood emergency, floodwatch, flood-warning service

przeciwpożarow|y *adj* *sprzęt*: fire; ***ochrona ~a*** fire safety measures; ***przepisy ~e*** fire (safety) regulations

przeciwskurczowy *adj* *MED* antispasmodic, spasmolytic

przeciwsłoneczn|y *adj*: ***okulary ~e*** sunglasses

przeciwstawiać ⟨**-wić**⟩ (*-wiam*) set against (*D*); ***przeciwstawiać się*** oppose (*D*), stand up (*D* to)

przeciwstawienie *n* (*-nia*; *no pl*) opposition; **przeciwstawny** *adj* opposing

przeciwtężcow|y *adj*: ***surowica ~a*** antitetanus serum

przeciwwaga *f* (*-gi*; *no pl*) *fig* counterbalance; **przeciwwskazanie** *n* (*-nia*; *-nia*) *MED* contraindication; **przeciwzapalny** *adj* *MED* anti-inflammatory

przecud(ow)ny *adj* miraculous, absolutely beautiful

przecząco *adv*: ***odpowiedzieć ~*** give a negative answer

przeczący *adj* negative

przeczekać *v/p* (*-kam*) wait out, wait for the end (*A* of); ***~ aż*** wait for the end of; ***~ burzę*** wait the storm out

przeczenie *n* (*-nia*; *-nia*) negative; ***podwójne ~*** double negation

przeczesywać ⟨**-sać**⟩ (*-suję*) **1.** *teren*: scour **2.** *włosy*: comb

przecznic|a *f* (*-cy*; *-ce*) turn; ***dwie ~e stąd*** two blocks from here

przeczucie *n* (*-cia*; *-cia*) feeling, hunch, premonition; ***złe ~*** bad feeling

przeczuć *v/p* → ***przeczuwać***

przeczulenie *n* (*-nia*; *no pl*) oversensitivity, hypersensitivity; **przeczulony** *adj* over-sensitive, touchy

przeczuwać ⟨**-czuć**⟩ (*-wam*) *koniec, śmierć*: sense
przeczyć ⟨**za-**⟩ (*-czę*) **1.** deny, negate; ***nie przeczę, że*** I shall not deny that **2.** (*być w sprzeczności*) contradict; ***~ samemu sobie*** contradict oneself
przeczyszczający *adj*: ***środek ~*** *MED* laxative; **przeczyszczenie**: ***środek na ~*** *MED* laxative
przeczytać *v/p* → ***czytać***
przeć *v/im* (*prę*) **1.** (*wywierać nacisk*) force, press **2.** (*o rodzącej*) push
przed *prep* (*I/A*) in front of; ***~ laty*** long ago; ***~ czasem*** ahead of time; ***żalić się ~*** *I* complain, moan to; ***wyciągnąć ~ siebie rękę*** stretch one's hand; ***~ naszą erą*** BC, Before Christ
przed- (*w złożeniach*) pre-
przedawkować *v/p* (*-kuję*) *MED* overdose; **przedawkowani|e** *n* (*-nia; no pl*) *MED* overdose; ***umrzeć z ~a środków nasennych*** die of an overdose of sleeping-pills
przedawniać się ⟨**-nić**⟩ (*-niam*) *JUR* lapse; **przedawnienie** *n* (*-nia; no pl*) *JUR* lapse; **przedawniony** *adj JUR* lapsed
przedbieg *m* (*-gu; -gi*) *SPORT* heat, qualifying race; ***odpaść w ~ach*** *fig* drop out in the heats, be eliminated in the heats
przeddzień: ***w ~, w przededniu*** *G* the day before, on the eve of
przede *prep*: ***~ mną*** before me; ***~ wszystkim*** first of all
przedemerytalny *adj*: ***wiek ~*** pre-retirement age
przedgórze *n* (*-rza; -rza*) *GEOGR* foreland, piedmont; **przedgwiazdkowy** *adj* pre-Christmas
przedimek *m* (*-mka; -mki*) *GRAM* article
przedkładać ⟨**-dłożyć**⟩ (*-dam*) *lit* **1.** *dokumenty*: submit **2.** *propozycję*: put forward **3.** (*woleć*) prefer, put (***nad*** *A* above)
przedłużacz *m* (*-cza; -cze*) *Br* extension lead, *Am* extension cord
przedłużać ⟨**-żyć**⟩ (*-żam*) **1.** *suknię*: lengthen, let down **2.** *wizę*: extend; ***przedłużać się*** **1.** (*o dyskusji*) drag on **2.** (*o milczeniu*) stretch on
przedłużenie *n* (*-nia; -nia*) extension
przedmałżeńsk|i *adj* pre-marriage, premarital; ***umowa ~a*** *JUR* prenuptial agreement
przedmiejski *adj* suburban; **przedmieście** *n* (*-ścia; -ścia*) suburb
przedmiot *m* (*-tu; -ty*) **1.** (*rzecz*) object **2.** *w szkole*: subject **3.** (*temat*) topic; ***~ dyskusji*** (***zainteresowań***) topic of the discussion (interest)
przedmiotowy *adj* **1.** (*tematyczny*) subject **2.** *traktowanie*: object
przedmowa *f* (*-wy; -wy*) foreword, preface
przedmówca *m* (*-cy; -cy*), **-czyni** *f* (*-ni; -nie*) the preceding speaker
przedmuchiwać ⟨**-chać**⟩ (*-chuję*) blow through
przedmurze *n* (*-rza; -rza*) bulwark
przedni *adj* **1.** front; ***~a szyba*** *AUTO Br* windscreen, *Am* windshield: ***~e zęby*** front teeth **2.** (*wyśmienity*) superior, excellent
przednów|ek: ***na ~ku*** before the harvest
przedobiedni *adj* preceding dinner; ***spacer ~*** a walk before dinner
przedostatni *adj* last but one, penultimate
przedobrzyć *v/p* (*-rzę*) *infml* overdo, gild the lily, over-egg the pudding
przedostawać się ⟨**-stać**⟩ (*-taję*) **1.** (*dojść*) find one's way (***do*** *G* to) **2.** (*o substancji*) get through **3.** (*o świetle, zapachu*) penetrate **4.** (*o informacji*) leak out
przedpłata *f* (*-ty; -ty*) down-payment
przedpokój *m* (*-koju; -koje*) hall
przedpole *n* (*-la; -la*) **1.** foreground **2.** *SPORT* area in front of the goal
przedpołudnie *n* (*-nia; -nia*) morning; **przedpołudniowy** *adj* (late) morning
przedpotopowy *adj iron* antediluvian
przedramię *n* (*-mienia; -miona*) *ANAT* forearm
przedrostek *m* (*-tka; -tki*) prefix
przedrozbiorowy *adj HIST* pre-partition, happening before the partitions (of Poland)
przedruk *m* (*-ku; -ki*) reprint; **przedrukowywać** ⟨**-kować**⟩ (*-kowuję*) reprint
przedrzeć *v/p* → ***przedzierać***
przedrzemać się *v/p* (*-mię*) take a nap
przedrzeźniać *v/im* (*-niam*) mock, mimic
przedsiębiorca *m* (*-cy; -cy*) entrepreneur, businessman; **przedsiębior-**

P

czość *f* (*-ści*; *no pl*) **1.** (*bycie przedsiębiorczym*) enterprise **2.** (*działalność gospodarcza*) enterpreneurship; **przedsiębiorczy** *adj* enterprising

przedsiębiorstwo *n* (*-wa*; *-wa*) (*firma*) enterprise, company

przedsiębrać ⟨**-sięwziąć**⟩ (*-biorę*) undertake; ***przedsięwziąć środki ostrożności*** take precautions, take protective measures

przedsięwzięcie *n* (*-cia*; *-cia*) undertaking; ***ryzykowne ~*** risky undertaking, venture

przedsionek *m* (*-nka*; *-nki*) **1.** (*pomieszczenie*) vestibule **2.** ANAT atrium

przedsmak *m* (*-ku*; *no pl*) foretaste

przedsprzedaż *f* (*-ży*; *-że*) advance sale

przedstawiać ⟨**-wić**⟩ (*-wiam*) **1.** *osobę*: introduce; ***~ sobie*** imagine; ***on nic sobą nie przedstawia*** he is a failure; ***~ wysoką wartość*** have great value, be of great value **2.** *plan*, *wniosek*, *projekt*: present, put forward **3.** *sprawę*: present, depict **4.** *dowód*: produce, provide, come up with **5.** *kandydata*: present, introduce **6.** THEAT put on; ***przedstawiać się*** **1.** (*nawzajem*) introduce each other **2.** (*siebie*) introduce oneself **3.** (*o sytuacji*, *widokach*, *sprawie*) be, present itself

przedstawiciel *m* (*-la*; *-le*), **~ka** *f* (*-ki*; *-ki*) **1.** *rządu*: representative **2.** JUR proxy

przedstawicielstwo *n* (*-wa*; *-wa*) **1.** diplomatic post **2.** (*filia*) branch

przedstawić *v/p* → ***przedstawiać***

przedstawienie *n* (*-nia*; *-nia*) THEAT performance, show

przedszkolak *m* (*-ka*; *-ki*) nursery school pupil, kindergarten pupil; **przedszkolanka** *f* (*-ki*; *-ki*) nursery school teacher

przedszkol|e *n* (*-la*; *-la*) *Br* nursery school, *Am* kindergarten; ***chodzić do ~a*** go to nursery school; **przedszkoln|y** *adj* preschool; ***wiek ~y*** preschool age; ***wychowanie ~e*** preschool education

przedślubny *adj* premarital

przedśmiertny *adj* **1.** MED agonal, premortal **2.** *spowiedź*: deathbed

przedświąteczn|y *adj* **1.** (*przed Bożym Narodzeniem*) pre-Christmas; ***okres ~y*** pre-Christmas period, time just before Christmas; ***zakupy ~e*** Christmas shopping; ***ruch ~y*** **a)** (*przed Bożym Narodzeniem*) Christmas traffic **b)** (*przed Wielkanocą*) Easter traffic **2.** (*przed świętem*) pre-holiday

przedświt *m* (*-tu*; *-ty*) **1.** *lit* daybreak, dawn **2.** *fig* harbinger

przedtem *adv* **1.** (*najpierw*) first, before; ***przyjdę, ale ~ zadzwonię*** I'll come, but I'll phone beforehand **2.** (*kiedyś*) formerly, earlier, before; ***~ był tu ogród*** there was a garden here before; ***nigdy ~*** never before; ***~ była pielęgniarką*** she was formerly a nurse

przedterminowy *adj* early; **przedwakacyjny** *adj* pre-holiday; **przedwczesny** *adj* premature, early; ***~ poród*** premature birth, premature delivery

przedwczoraj *adv* the day before yesterday

przedwczorajszy *adj* of the day before yesterday

przedwieczny *adj lit* **1.** (*bardzo stary*) ancient, as old as the hills **2.** REL eternal; **przedwieczorny** *adj* (before) evening; **przedwiośnie** *n* (*-nia*; *-nia*) early spring

przedwojenny *adj* pre-war; **przedwyborcz|y** *adj* POLIT election; ***spotkanie ~e*** election meeting

przedział *m* (*-łu*; *-ły*) **1.** *kolejowy*: compartment; ***~ dla niepalących*** nonsmoking compartment **2.** (*okres*) period; ***~ czasu*** period (of time); ***w przedziale wiekowym między 20. a 30. rokiem życia*** between 20 and 30 (years of age) **3.** MATH range; **przedziałek** *m* (*-łka*; *-łki*) *Br* parting, *Am* part; ***zrobić ~*** part one's hair; ***nosić ~ pośrodku głowy*** have a centre parting

przedzielać ⟨**-lić**⟩ (*-lam*) **1.** *wyraz*: hyphenate **2.** *pokój*: divide

przedzierać ⟨**-drzeć**⟩ (*-ram*) tear; ***przedzierać się*** **1.** (*o materiale*) tear (apart) **2.** (*o dźwięku*, *świetle*) break (**przez** *A* through) **3.** (*przedostawać się*) force one's way, struggle (**przez** *A* through); ***~ się przez blokadę*** get through the police blockade; ***~ się przez tłum*** force one's way through the crowd

P

przedzierzgać się ⟨**-gnąć**⟩ (*-gam*) *lit* transform oneself (**w** *A* into)
przedziurawiać ⟨**-wić**⟩ (*-wiam*) pierce, puncture
przedziwny *adj* **1.** (*bardzo dziwny*) weird, bizarre **2.** (*niezwykły*) wonderful
przedzwonić *v/p* (*-nię*) *infml*: **~ do kogoś** *G* give s.o. a ring; ***przedzwoń do mnie!*** call me!
przeegzaminować *v/p* → ***egzaminować***
przefaksować *v/p* → ***faksować***
przefarbować *v/p* → ***farbować***
przeflancowywać ⟨**-cować**⟩ (*-cowuję*) transplant
przeforsować *v/p* → ***forsować***
przegadać *v/p* (*-dam*) **1.** ***przegadaliśmy dwie godziny*** we spent two hours talking **2.** outtalk
przeganiać ⟨**-gonić**, **-gnać**⟩ (*-niam*) **1.** *intruza*: chase away **2.** *owce*: drive **2.** *współzawodnika*: outrun **4.** ***wiatr przegania chmury*** the wind is dispersing the clouds
przegapiać ⟨**-gapić**⟩ (*-piam*) *infml okazję*: miss
przegięcie *n* (*-cia*; *no pl*) *infml* going over the top; ***to ~!*** this is a bit over the top!
przeginać ⟨**-giąć**⟩ (*-nam*) **1.** *drut*: bend **2.** *głowę*: nod to one side **3. ~ pałę** *infml* go over the top; ***przeginać się*** bend over; ***~ w tył*** lean backwards, bend backwards
przegląd *m* (*-du*; *-dy*) **1.** *dokumentów*: review, looking through; ***~ prasy*** press review; ***~ wiadomości*** news round-up; ***~ filmów krótkometrażowych*** review of short films **2.** (*kontrola*) inspection **3.** (*zestaw*) survey **4.** *AUTO TECH* overhaul **5.** *MED* check-up **6.** *wojsk*: parade
przeglądać ⟨**przejrzeć**⟩ (*-dam*) **1.** *dokumenty*: look through **2.** *czasopismo*: go through, leaf through, skim over **3.** *TECH* check; ***przeglądać się***: ***~ się w lustrze*** examine oneself in the mirror
przeglądarka *f* (*-ki*; *-ki*) *INF* browser; ***~ do slajdów*** slide projector
przeglądow|y *adj charakter*: review; ***badania ~e*** *MED* medical check-up
przegłodzić się *v/p* (*-dzę*) be on a strict diet
przegłos *m* (*-su*; *no pl*) *GRAM* umlaut
przegłosowywać ⟨**-sować**⟩ (*-sowuję*) **1.** *ustawę*: put to a vote **2.** *kogoś*: vote down
przegnać *v/p* → ***przeganiać***
przegnić *v/p* (*-nię*) rot through, decay
przegniły *adj* rotten
przegonić *v/p* → ***przeganiać***
przegotowywać ⟨**-tować**⟩ (*-towuję*) **1.** *wodę*: boil **2.** *ziemniaki*: overcook; ***przegotowywać się*** boil
przegrać *v/p* (*-ram*): ***~ cały wieczór w karty*** spend the evening playing cards; → ***przegrywać***
przegradzać ⟨**-rodzić**⟩ (*-dzam*) partition; ***~ drogę*** bar the road, block the road
przegrana *f* (*-nej*; *-ne*) **1.** (*kwota*) loss **2.** (*porażka*) defeat
przegroda *f* (*-dy*; *-dy*) **1.** (*ściana*) partition **2.** (*zagroda*, *komora*) division
przegrodzić *v/p* → ***przegradzać***
przegródka *f* (*-ki*; *-ki*) compartment
przegrupowywać ⟨**-pować**⟩ (*-powuję*) *wojsko*: redeploy; ***przegrupowywać się*** regroup
przegrywać ⟨**-grać**⟩ (*-wam*) **1.** *wojnę*, *proces*, *pieniądze*: lose **2.** *kasetę*, *dyskietkę*: **a)** play **b)** *infml* copy
przegryzać ⟨**-gryźć**⟩ (*-zam*) **1.** *kabel*, *nitkę*: bite through **2.** (*o rdzy*) rust through **3.** (*jeść*) take a bite; ***~ piwo orzeszkami*** chase beer with peanuts; ***przegryźć się*** *infml*: ***~ się przez tekst*** wade through a text; ***sałatka się przegryzła*** the salad is mixed well
przegrzany *adj mieszkanie*, *silnik*: overheated
przegrzewać ⟨**-rzać**⟩ (*-wam*) **1.** *mieszkanie*, *silnik*: overheat **2.** *dziecko*: dress (far) too warmly; ***przegrzewać się*** (*o silniku*) overheat
przegub *m* (*-bu*; *-by*) **1.** *dłoni*: wrist **2.** *TECH* joint; **przegubowy** *adj AUTO* articulated
przehandlować *v/p* (*-luję*) flog *Br infml*
przeholowywać ⟨**-lować**⟩ (*-lowuję*) *statek*: tow; ***przeholować z*** *I* go over the top with, overdo
przehulać *v/p* (*-lam*) *pieniądze*: spend like water, squander; ***~ całą noc*** party (during) the whole night
przeinaczać ⟨**-czyć**⟩ (*-czam*) *fakty*: misrepresent

P

przeistaczać ⟨**-toczyć**⟩ (*-czam*) *lit* transform (**w** *A* into); ***przeistaczać się*** transform (oneself) (**w** *A* into)
przeistoczenie *n* (*-nia*; *-nia*) *lit* transformation
przejadać ⟨**-jeść**⟩ (*-dam*) **1.** *pensję*: spend money (on living) **2.** *zapas*: eat (up); ***przejadać się*** **1.** (*jeść za dużo*) overeat; ***przejadła mi się czekolada*** I can't eat chocolate any more, I've had enough chocolate **2.** (*nudzić się*) *infml* become boring; ***przejadły mi się kryminały*** I can't read any more crime stories, I've read enough crime stories
przejaskrawiać ⟨**-wić**⟩ (*-wiam*) exaggerate
przejaśniać się ⟨**-nić**⟩ (*-niam*) (*o niebie*) clear up; ***przejaśnia się*** it's clearing up; **przejaśnienie** *n* (*-nia*; *-nia*) sunny interval
przejaw *m* (*-wu*; *-wy*) **1.** *inteligencji, niepokoju*: sign **2.** *choroby*: symptom
przejawiać ⟨**-wić**⟩ (*-wiam*) display, show; ***przejawiać się*** manifest oneself
przejazd *m* (*-du*; *-dy*) **1.** (*samochodem*) drive; ***pierwszeństwo ~u*** right of way, priority **2.** (*przewóz*) ride; ***~ taksówką*** ride by taxi **3.** journey; ***~ koleją*** train journey **4.** passage **5.** crossing; ***~ kolejowy*** *Br* level crossing, *Am* grade crossing; ***opłata za ~*** fare; ***~em*** passing through (a place)
przejażdżka *f* (*-ki*; *-ki*) **1.** (*motocyklem*) ride **2.** (*samochodem*) drive **3.** ride; ***~ konna*** ride (on a horse)
przejąć *v/p* → ***przejmować***
przejechać *v/p* (*-jadę*): ***~ kogoś*** run s.o. over; ***przejechać się*** **1.** (*dla przyjemności*) go for a ride **2.** (*oszukać się*) *infml* to be conned; → ***przejeżdżać***
przejeść *v/p* → ***przejadać***
przejezdny I *adj droga*: passable **II** *m* (*-nego*; *-ni*), **-na** *f* (*-nej*; *-ne*) transient
przejeździć *v/p* (*-jeżdżę*) **1.** ***~ całe popołudnie na rowerze*** spend the whole afternoon biking; ***~ wszystkie pieniądze*** spend all one's money on travelling **2.** *benzynę*: use up
przejeżdżać ⟨**-jechać**⟩ (*-dżam*) **1.** *kilometr*: drive **2.** *człowieka*: run over **2.** *miejsce*: go; ***~ (przez) skrzyżowanie*** go past a crossroads; ***~ (przez) most*** go over the bridge; ***~ (przez) granicę*** cross the border; ***~ (przez) tunel*** go through the tunnel; ***~ koło*** *G* pass; ***~ przystanek*** miss one's stop; ***~ ręką po*** *L* run one's hand over
przejęcie *n* (*-cia*; *-cia*) **1.** *firmy, zwyczaju*: takeover; ***~ władzy*** seizure of power, takeover of power **2.** (*wzruszenie*) excitement; ***z ~m*** moved **3.** *piłki*: interception
przejęty *adj* moved (*I* with), excited (*I* with)
przejęzyczać się ⟨**-czyć**⟩ (*-czam*) make a slip (of the tongue)
przejęzyczenie *n* (*-nia*; *-nia*) slip (of the tongue)
przejmować ⟨**-jąć**⟩ (*-muję*) **1.** *firmę, władzę*: take over **2.** *zwyczaj*: adopt **3.** *list*: intercept **4.** (*ogarniać*) overcome; ***przejął go lęk*** he was overcome with fear; ***ten widok przejmował go lękiem*** he got scared when he saw it, fear took hold of him when he saw it; ***przejmować się*** take to heart (*I* s.th.), be worried (*I* about); ***nie przejmuj się!*** don't worry!; ***on się niczym nie przejmuje*** he is carefree, he takes everything easy
przejmujący *adj* **1.** *zimno*: biting **2.** *głos*: shrill **3.** *widok*: moving **4.** *smutek*: deep **5.** *ból*: piercing
przejrzały *adj* overripe
przejrzeć *v/p* (*-rzę*) **1.** *zamiary*: see through; ***~ (na oczy)*** find out about, see the truth, have one's eyes opened **2.** (*o niewidomym*) see the light again, recover eyesight; → ***przeglądać***
przejrzewać ⟨**-rzeć**⟩ (*-wam*) (*o owocach*) become overripe
przejrzysty *adj* **1.** (*przezroczysty*) transparent **2.** *woda, tekst*: clear **3.** *kłamstwo*: obvious
przejści|e *n* (*-cia*; *-cia*) **1.** (*droga*) crossing; ***~e dla pieszych*** pedestrian crossing; ***~e podziemne*** *Br* subway, *Am* underpass; ***~e wzbronione!*** no entry! **2.** (*miejsce*) passage; ***~e graniczne*** border crossing; ***zrobić komuś ~e*** make way for; ***stać w ~u*** stand in the way **3.** (*przeżycie*) ordeal
przejściowo *adv* temporarily; **przejściowy** *adj* temporary; ***okres ~*** transitional period; ***pokój ~*** connecting room; ***obóz ~*** transitory camp

P

przejść *v/p* (*-jdę*): **dużo ~** be through a lot; **ani by mi to przez myśl nie przeszło** I didn't even think of it; **~ do historii** go down in history; **przejść się** go for a walk (**po** *L* around); → **przechodzić**

przekabacać ⟨**-cić**⟩ (*-cam*): **~ kogoś na swoją stronę** talk s.o. round to one's side

przekarmiać ⟨**-mić**⟩ (*-miam*) overfeed

przekaz *m* (*-zu*; *-zy*) **1.** *bankowy*: order **2.** *ludowy*: account, legend **3.** *historyczny*: record **4.** *pocztowy*: order; **wysłać pieniądze ~em** remit money **5.** *informacji*: transmission **6. środki** (**masowego**) **~u** (mass) media

przekazanie *n* (*-nia*; *no pl*) *darów*: handing-over

przekazywać ⟨**-zać**⟩ (*-zuję*) **1.** *dary*: donate **2.** *pieniądze*: entrust; **~ pieniądze na konto** transfer money to a bank account **3.** *majątek*: leave in one's will **4.** *prawo*: leave **5.** *sygnał*, *pozdrowienia*: give **6.** *informacje*, *wiadomość*: pass on, give, relay; **proszę mu przekazać, że** please, could you tell him that **7.** *tradycję*: hand down **8.** *audycję*: relay, broadcast **9.** *sygnał*: transmit

przekaźnik *m* (*-ka*; *-ki*) *TECH* relay

przekąs: **z ~em** mockingly

przekąsić *v/p* (*-szę*) have a bite to eat; **~ wódkę śledziem** *infml* chase vodka with herring, eat herring following a glass of vodka

przekąsk|a *f* (*-ki*; *-ki*) snack, hors d'oeuvre; **zimne ~i** cold snacks; **~a do wódki** snack to go with vodka

przekątn|a *f* (*-nej*; *-ne*) *MATH* diagonal; **po ~ej** diagonally; **przekątny** *adj MATH* diagonal

przekimać *v/p* (*-mam*) *infml podróż*: kip (through); **przekimać się** have a kip

przekląć *v/p* → **przeklinać**

przekleństwo *n* (*-wa*; *-wa*) **1.** (*wyraz*) swearword **2.** (*klątwa*) curse

przeklęty *adj* damn, bloody

przeklinać ⟨**-ląć**⟩ (*-nam*) **I** *v/t swój los*: curse **II** *v/i* (*używać przekleństw*) swear

przekła|d *m* (*-du*; *-dy*) *tekstu*: translation; **w niemieckim ~dzie** translated into German

przekładać ⟨**przełożyć**⟩ (*-dam*) **1.** *rzecz*: rearrange; **~ nogę przez poręcz** put one's leg over the handrail **2.** *tekst*: translate **3.** *termin*: put off, postpone, reschedule **4.** *tort*: layer (*I* with) **5.** *karty*: cut

przekładaniec *m* (*-dańca*; *-dańce*) **1.** (*ciasto*) layer cake **2.** *fig* this and that

przekładnia *f* (*-ni*; *-nie*) *TECH* transmission

przekłuwać ⟨**-łuć**⟩ (*-wam*) **1.** *uszy*: pierce **2.** *balonik*: prick

przekomarzać się *v/im* (*-rzam*) banter

przekonać *v/p* → **przekonywać**

przekonani|e *n* (*-nia*; *-nia*) belief, conviction; **~a religijne** religious convictions; **nie mieć ~a do** *G* be unsure of; **dojść do ~a, że** come to believe that; **w moim ~u** in my opinion; **trafić komuś do ~a** appeal to

przekonany *adj* convinced

przekonujący, **przekonywający** *adj* **1.** *dowód*: convincing, persuasive **2.** *powód*: convincing

przekonywać ⟨**-konać**⟩ (*-nuję*/*-wam*) convince (**kogoś o** *L* s.o. of); **przekonywać się** become convinced

przekop *m* (*-pu*; *-py*) tunnel

przekopywać ⟨**-pać**⟩ (*-puję*) *grządkę*, *rów*, *tunel*: dig

przekor|a *f* (*-ry*; *no pl*) spite; **z ~y** out of spite; **przekorny** *adj* **1.** *osoba*: contrary **2.** *uśmiech*, *mina*: perverse

przekór: **na ~** *D* in defiance of

przekraczać ⟨**-roczyć**⟩ (*-czam*) **1.** *granicę*: cross; **~ próg** cross a threshold; **~ stan konta** go overdrawn, overdraw an account **2.** *prędkość*, *wiek*: exceed **3.** *prawo*, *normy*: transgress, breach

przekradać się ⟨**-raść**⟩ (*-dam*) steal (into somewhere)

przekrawać ⟨**-roić**⟩ (*-wam*) cut (in half)

przekreślać ⟨**-lić**⟩ (*-lam*) **1.** *wyraz*: cross out **2.** *marzenia*, *nadzieje*, *plany*: destroy, ruin; **to przekreśliło naszą przyjaźń** this has ruined our friendship **3.** (*uznać za niebyłe*) write off; **to go przekreśliło w moich oczach** I have written him off as a friend because of that

przekręcać ⟨**-cić**⟩ (*-cam*) **1.** *głowę*, *klucz*: turn **2.** *fakty*, *słowa*: distort **3.** *sprężynę*: turn round; **przekręcać**

się turn over; **~ się na bok** turn to one side; **~ się z boku na bok** turn from side to side; **przekręcić się** *infml* (*umrzeć*) kick the bucket

przekroczenie *n* (*-nia*; *-nia*) **1.** *granicy*: crossing **2.** *JUR* infringement; **~ prędkości** speeding; **~ kompetencji** overstepping one's authority

przekroczyć *v/p* → **przekraczać**

przekroić *v/p* → **przekrawać**

przekrój *m* (*-roju*; *-roje*): **~ podłużny** horizontal section; **~ poprzeczny** cross section, transverse section; **~ pionowy** *BUILD* vertical section; **w przekroju** in cross-section

przekrwienie *n* (*-nia*; *no pl*) *MED* plethora; **przekrwiony** *adj* *oczy*: bloodshot

przekrzykiwać ⟨**-rzyczeć**⟩ (*-kuję*) *muzykę*: shout over; **przekrzykiwać się** outshout one another

przekrzywiać ⟨**-wić**⟩ (*-wiam*) **1.** *głowę*: nod to one side **2.** *lusterko*: tilt; **przekrzywiać się 1.** (*o płocie*) tilt, start falling **2.** (*o krawacie*) become askew

przekrzywiony *adj* tilted

przekształcać ⟨**-cić**⟩ (*-cam*) **1.** (*zmieniać*) change, transform **2.** *produkcję*: restructure **3.** *rzeczywistość*: reshape **4.** *MATH* transform; **~ na** *A* transform into; **przekształcać się** transform

przekształcenie *n* (*-nia*; *-nia*) **1.** *ustrojowe, własnościowe*: transformation **2.** *zakładu*: restructuring

przekuć *v/p* → **przekuwać**

przekupka *f* (*-ki*; *-ki*) tradeswoman, peddler; **przekupny** *adj* corruptible, bribable; **przekupstwo** *n* (*-wa*; *-wa*) bribery; **przekupywać** ⟨**-pić**⟩ (*-puję*) bribe

przekuwać ⟨**-kuć**⟩ (*-wam*) **1.** *tunel*: dig, bore **2.** *ścianę*: chip through, chisel through **3.** (*nadawać nowy kształt*) hammer, forge

przekwalifikować *v/p* (*-kuję*) retrain; **przekwalifikować się** retrain; **przekwalifikowanie** *n* (*-nia*; *no pl*) retraining

przekwaterować *v/p* (*-ruję*) rehouse; *żołnierzy*: requarter, rebillet

przekwitać ⟨**-tnąć**⟩ (*-tam*) **1.** (*o kwiatach*) shed blossom, lose blossom **2.** (*o kobiecie, urodzie*) fade, wither;

przekwitanie *n* (*-nia*; *no pl*) *MED* menopause

przelać *v/p* → **przelewać**

przelatywać ⟨**-lecieć**⟩ (*-tuję*) **1.** fly (**z** *G* from, **do** *G* to, **nad** *I* over); **~ (przez) ocean** fly over the ocean; **przelecieć koło** *G* fly past, fly by **2.** *książkę*: skim **3.** *infml* screw *vulg*, *Br vulg* shag **4.** (*mijać*) pass: **te trzy tygodnie przeleciały szybko** the three weeks passed very quickly **5. ~ przez sitko** go through a sieve

przelew *m* (*-wu*; *-wy*) *FIN* transfer; **~em** by transfer; **dokonać ~u, zrealizować ~** make a transfer; **~ krwi** bloodshed

przelewać ⟨**-lać**⟩ (*-wam*) **1.** *pieniądze*: transfer, remit **2.** (*rozlać*) pour too much, spill; **~ krew** spill blood **3.** *JUR* transfer, cede; **przelewać się** (*o wodzie*) overflow; **woda przelewa się przez burtę** water is coming overboard/into the boat; **u nich się nie przelewa** *fig* they can barely make ends meet

przelewki: **to nie ~** this is no joke, this is not a joking matter

przelewowy *adj* *FIN* concerning bank transfers

przeleźć *v/p* → **przełazić**

przeleżeć *v/p* (*-żę*) (*o osobie, przedmiocie*) lie (for some time); **~ chorobę** stay in bed during an illness; **~ całą niedzielę** lie in bed the whole Sunday

przelękły *adj* frightened

przelęknąć się *v/p* (*-nę*) take a fright (*G* at), get frightened (*G* of)

przelicytowywać ⟨**-tować**⟩ (*-towuję*) outbid

przeliczać ⟨**-czyć**⟩ (*-czam*) *walutę*: convert (**na** *A* into); **~ złote na euro** convert zlotys into Euros; **przeliczać się** *fig* miscalculate; **~ się z siłami** misjudge one's abilities

przeliczeni|e *n* (*-nia*; *-nia*) conversion; **w ~u na jednego mieszkańca** (as) per inhabitant; **przeliczeniowy** *adj* conversion

przelicznik *m* (*-ka*; *-ki*) *walut*: exchange rate, conversion rate

przeliczyć *v/p* → **przeliczać**

przeliterować *v/p* (*-ruję*) spell

przelo|t *m* (*-tu*; *-ty*) **1.** *samolotu*: flight (**do** *G* to); **~t nad** *I* flight over; **być ~tem** be passing through (**w** *L* some-

P

where); ***widzieć się w ~cie*** meet each other on passing **2.** *ptaków*: passage

przelotn|y *adj* **1.** *znajomość*, *spojrzenie*: fleeting **2.** *zjawisko*, *zainteresowanie*: short-lived; ***~y deszcz*** shower; ***ptaki ~e*** birds of passage; **przelotowy** *adj trasa*, *droga*: arterial

przeludnienie *n* (*-nia*; *no pl*) overpopulation; **przeludniony** *adj* overpopulated

przeładowany *adj fig* overloaded

przeładowywać ⟨**-dować**⟩ (*-dowuję*) **1.** *towar*: reload **2.** *wóz*: overload

przeładunek *m* (*-nku*; *-nki*) reloading; **przeładunkow|y** *adj stacja*: reloading, transshipping; ***port ~y*** port of transshipment; ***punkt ~y*** place of transshipment; ***zdolność ~a*** reloading capacity

przełaj: ***iść na ~*** take a short cut

przełajowy *adj*: ***bieg ~*** SPORT cross-country run

przełamywać ⟨**-mać**⟩ (*-muję*) **1.** *gałąź*, *czekoladę*, *linię obrony*: break **2.** *niechęć*: overcome; ***~ pierwsze lody*** *fig* break the ice; ***przełamywać się*** **1.** (*złamać się*) break; **2.** (*dzielić się*) ***~ opłatkiem z*** *I* break Christmas wafer with **3.** *fig* overcome one's feelings

przełaz *m* (*-zu*; *-zy*) passage

przełazić ⟨**przeleźć**⟩ (*-łażę*) climb (***przez*** *A* over)

przełączać ⟨**-czyć**⟩ (*-czam*) switch over

przełącznik *m* (*-ka*; *-ki*) switch

przełęcz *f* (*-czy*; *-cze*) GEOGR pass

przełknąć *v/p* → ***przełykać***

przełom *m* (*-mu*; *-my*) **1.** *polityczny*: breakthrough **2.** *w życiu*, *w stosunkach*: turning point **3.** GEOGR gorge **4.** (*koniec*) turn: ***na ~ie roku*** at the turn of the year; ***na ~ie wieku*** at the turn of the century; **przełomow|y** *adj odkrycie*: ground-breaking; ***~e wydarzenia*** mould-breaking events; ***moment ~y*** turning point

przełożon|y *m* (*-nego*; *-żeni*), ***~a*** *f* (*-nej*; *-ne*) superior; ***siostra ~a*** matron; ***matka ~a*** REL Mother Superior

przełożyć *v/p* → ***przekładać***

przełyk *m* (*-ku*; *-ki*) gullet

przełykać ⟨**-łknąć**⟩ (*-kam*) swallow

przemaczać ⟨**-moczyć**⟩ (*-czam*): ***~ buty*** get one's shoes soaked through

przemagać ⟨**-móc**⟩ (*-gam*) *strach*, *niechęć*: overcome; ***przemogła go ciekawość*** his curiosity got the better of him; ***przemagać się*** overcome (one's fright/shame)

przemakać ⟨**-moknąć**⟩ (*-kam*) get soaked

przemalowywać ⟨**-lować**⟩ (*-lowuję*) **1.** *pokój*: repaint; ***~ pokój na czerwono*** (re)paint the room red **2.** *obraz*: paint over

przemarsz *m* (*-szu*; *-sze*) *wojska*: march-past

przemarzać ⟨**-znąć**⟩ (*-zam*) freeze

przemarznięty *adj* frozen

przemaszerować *v/p* (*-ruję*) march past

przemawia|ć ⟨**-mówić**⟩ (*-wiam*) make a speech, deliver a speech, speak (**do** *G* to); ***~ć za*** *I* **a)** speak up for **b)** be the proof of, support; ***~ć przeciw*** *D* speak against; ***ten argument do mnie nie ~*** the argument doesn't appeal to me; ***ten film do mnie nie ~*** I do not like/understand this film

przemądrzały *adj* big-headed, conceited

przemeblowywać ⟨**-lować**⟩ (*-lowuję*): ***~ dom*** rearrange furniture in one's house

przemeldowywać ⟨**-dować**⟩ (*-dowuję*) register; ***przemeldowywać się*** change one's address, register under a new address

przemęczać ⟨**-czyć**⟩ (*-czam*) strain; ***przemęczać się*** strain oneself, overexert oneself

przemęczenie *n* (*-nia*; *no pl*) exhaustion, fatigue; **przemęczony** *adj* exhausted, fatigued; ***~ pracą*** much overworked

przemęczyć się *v/p* (*-czę*) hold out (**w** *L* s.th.); → ***przemęczać się***

przemiał *m* (*-łu*; *no pl*) grinding

przemian: ***na ~*** alternatively

przemiana *f* (*-ny*; *-ny*) transformation; ***~ w*** *A* transformation into; ***~ materii*** BIOL metabolism

przemianowanie *n* (*-nia*; *no pl*) renaming; **przemianowywać** ⟨**-nować**⟩ (*-nowuję*) rename

przemieniać ⟨**-nić**⟩ (*-niam*) change (**w** *A* into); ***przemieniać się*** change (into)

P

przemienny *adj* alternating, changing
przemierzać ⟨**-rzyć**⟩ (*-rzam*) **1.** *kraje, pustynię, kontynent*: traverse; **~ całą Afrykę** traverse the whole of Africa; **~ świat** travel all over the world **2.** *korytarz*: go along, go down **3.** *szlak, dystans*: cover; **~ wzdłuż i wszerz** travel all over
przemieszać *v/p* (*-szam*) **1.** (*mieszać*) mix (a little) **2.** COOK stir (a little)
przemieszczać ⟨**-mieścić**⟩ (*-czam*) move; **przemieszczać się 1.** move **2.** get about, get around
przemieszkiwać ⟨**-kać**⟩ (*-kuję*) live, stay (for a while)
przemijać ⟨**-minąć**⟩ (*-jam*) **1.** (*o lecie, młodości*) go by **2.** (*o bólu*) pass
przemijający *adj* **1.** *sława*: brief **2.** *ból*: passing
przemilczać ⟨**-czeć**⟩ (*-czam*) *informację*: leave unsaid, not mention, pass over (in silence)
przemiły *adj* **1.** *osoba*: lovable, amiable **2.** *wieczór*: wonderful, most enjoyable, delightful
przeminąć *v/p* → **przemijać**
przemknąć *v/p*: **przemknęło mi przez głowę** it occurred to me; → **przemykać**
przemnażać ⟨**-nożyć**⟩ (*-żam*) multiply
przemoc *f* (*-cy; no pl*) violence; **akt ~y** act ofviolence; **użycie ~y** use violence; **~ą** by force
przemoczony *adj buty*: soaked; **~ do suchej nitki** soaked through
przemoczyć *v/p* → **przemaczać**
przemoknąć *v/p* → **przemakać**
przemoknięty, **przemokły** *adj ubranie*: soaked
przemow|a *f* (*-wy; -wy*) speech; **wygłosić ~ę** make a speech, give a speech
przemożny *adj lęk, chęć*: overpowering
przemóc *v/p* → **przemagać**
przemówić *v/p* → **przemawiać**
przemówienie *n* (*-nia; -nia*) speech
przemycać ⟨**-cić**⟩ (*-cam*) smuggle
przemyć *v/p* → **przemywać**
przemykać ⟨**-mknąć**⟩ (*-kam*) **1.** (*o pociągu, samochodzie*) shoot past **2.** (*o cieniu*) steal; **przemykać się** weave through, get by
przemysł *m* (*-łu; no pl*) industry; **~ ciężki** heavy industry; **~ górniczy** mining; **~ samochodowy** automotive industry, car industry; **~ spożywczy** food industry
przemysłowiec *m* (*-wca; -wcy*) industrialist; **przemysłowo** *adv* (*na dużą skalę*) in large numbers, on a large scale; **przemysłow|y** *adj* industrial; **miasto ~e** *Br* industrial centre, *Am* industrial center; **roślina ~a** plant for industrial purposes
przemyślany *adj* **1.** *plan*: well thought-out **2.** *działanie*: considered
przemyśleć *v/p* (*-lę*) think over, consider
przemyśliwać ⟨**-leć**⟩ (*-wuję*) think over
przemyślny *adj* **1.** *osoba*: clever, ingenious **2.** *urządzenie*: clever
przemyt *m* (*-tu; no pl*) smuggling; **towar z ~u** contraband; **przemytniczy** *adj* smuggling; **przemytnik** *m* (*-ka; -nicy*) smuggler; **~ narkotyków** drug smuggler
przemywać ⟨**-myć**⟩ (*-wam*) *ranę*: bathe
przenajświętszy *adj*: **≈ Sakrament** REL the Blessed Sacrament
przenicowywać ⟨**-cować**⟩ (*-cowuję*) **1.** *ubranie*: turn **2.** *idee*: twist, misinterpret
przeniesienie *n* (*-nia; -nia*) *zawodnika, pracownika*: transfer
przenieść *v/p* → **przenosić**
przenigdy *adv* never ever
przenikać ⟨**-knąć**⟩ (*-kam*) **1.** (*o świetle*) penetrate (**do** *G*) **2.** (*o zapachu*) waft through **3.** (*o informacji*) leak out **4.** (*o cieczy, gazie*) leak **5.** (*o wodzie*) permeate; **przenikać się 1.** (*o zapachach*) intermingle, mingle together **2.** (*o stylach*) meet
przenikliwość *f* (*-ści; no pl*) *obserwacji*: perspicacity, acumen; **przenikliwy** *adj* **1.** *zimno, ból, umysł*: penetrating, biting; **patrzeć ~m wzrokiem** gaze with a penetrating look **2.** *zapach*: sharp, strong **3.** *głos*: shrill, piercing
przeniknąć *v/p* → **przenikać**
przenocować *v/p* (*-cuję*): **~ kogoś** put s.o. up for the night; → **nocować**
przenosić ⟨**-nieść**⟩ (*-szę*) **1.** *zarazki*: transmit; **~ spojrzenie na** *A* turn one's eyes on; **~ na ekran** make into a movie **2.** *ciężar*: carry **3.** *ciężar ciała*: shift **4.** *służbowo*: transfer **5.** *zakład*: move **6.** *wyraz*: divide; **przenosić się 1.** (*o osobie*) move **2.** (*o epidemii*) spread

3. ~ się myślą do *G* start thinking of, look back on

przenośnia *f* (*-ni*; *-nie*) metaphor; **przenośnie** *adv* figuratively; **przenośny** *adj* **1.** *telewizor*: portable **2.** *znaczenie*: figurative, metaphorical; **w znaczeniu ~m** in figurative sense, figuratively

przeobrażać ⟨**-razić**⟩ (*-żam*) transform (**w** *A* into); **przeobrażać się 1.** (*zmienić się*) be transformed (**w** *A* into) **2.** BIOL metamorphose; **~ w poczwarkę** turn into chrysalis

przeobrażenie *n* (*-nia*; *-nia*) **1.** *duchowe, gospodarcze*: transformation **2.** BIOL metamorphosis

przeoczenie *n* (*-nia*; *-nia*) oversight; **przez ~** by oversight

przeoczyć *v/p* (*-czę*) **1.** *błąd*: overlook **2.** *szansę*: miss

przeogromny *adj* immense

przeokropny *adj* hideous

przeor *m* (*-ra*; *-rzy*/*-rowie*) REL prior

przeorać *v/p* → **przeorywać**

przeorganizowywać ⟨**-zować**⟩ (*-zowuję*) reorganize

przeorysza *f* (*-szy*; *-sze*) REL prioress

przeorywać ⟨**-rać**⟩ (*-ruję*) **1.** plough **2.** (*szukać*) scour

przepacać ⟨**-pocić**⟩ (*-cam*) sweat

przepad|ać ⟨**-paść**⟩ (*-dam*) **1.** (*zginąć, zniknąć*) vanish, disappear; **przepaść jak kamień w wodę** disappear into thin air; **~ać bez wieści** disappear without a trace; **~ły nam wszystkie oszczędności** all our savings are gone; **~niesz bez niego** you will not make it without him **2.** (*o szansie*) miss; **~ła mi okazja** I missed an opportunity; **~ła mi wizyta u dentysty** I missed my appointment with the dentist **3.** (*o majątku*) be forfeited; (**wszystko**) **~ło** it's all gone **4.** (*o lekcjach*) be lost **5.** (*na egzaminie*) drop out **6.** *v/im* (*uwielbiać*) be fond (**za** *I* of); **nie ~ać za** *I* dislike

przepadek *m* (*-dku*; *no pl*): **~ mienia** JUR forfeiture of property

przepadły *adj* **1.** *pieniądze*: forfeited **2.** *obraz*: lost

przepakowywać ⟨**-kować**⟩ (*-kowuję*) *plecak*: repack

przepalać ⟨**-lić**⟩ (*-lam*) *żelazko, kwas*: burn through; **~ dziurę w** *L* burn a hole; **przepalać się 1.** (*o żarówce*) burn out **2.** (*o bezpieczniku*) blow

przepasany *adj* girded up (*I* with)

przepaska *f* (*-ki*; *-ki*): **~ na włosy** hairband; **~ na oczy** blindfold; **~ na biodra** loincloth

przepasywać ⟨**-sać**⟩ (*-suję*) tie around; **przepasywać się** tie around one's waist

przepaść[1] *v/p* → **przepadać**

przepaś|ć[2] *f* (*-ści*; *-ści*/*-ście*) **1.** (*urwisko*) precipice; **runąć w ~ć** fall into precipice, go downhill; **stać nad ~cią** *fig* be on the edge ofa precipice **2.** (*różnica*) chasm, gulf, gap; **~ć nie do przebycia** unbridgeable gap

przepatrywać ⟨**-trzyć**⟩ (*-ruję*) *szuflady*: examine, inspect

przepchać, przepchnąć *v/p* → **przepychać**

przepełniać ⟨**-nić**⟩ (*-niam*) **1.** (*o osobach*) overcrowd **2.** (*o rzeczach*) overfill **3.** (*o uczuciach*) overflow

przepełnienie *n* (*-nia*; *no pl*) overcrowding

przepełniony *adj* **1.** *autobus*: crammed, overcrowded **2.** *zbiornik*: overfilled

przepędzać ⟨**-dzić**⟩ (*-dzam*) **1.** *bydło*: drive **2.** (*wyganiać*) chase away, chase out

przepici|e *n* (*-cia*; *no pl*) *fig* drinking too much, hangover; **ból głowy z ~a** headache from drinking too much

przepić *v/p* → **przepijać**

przepierać ⟨**-prać**⟩ (*-ram*) wash; **~ w ręku** handwash; **przepierka** *f* (*-ki*; *-ki*) hand wash

przepierzenie *n* (*-nia*; *-nia*) partition

przepiękny *adj* (most) beautiful, gorgeous

przepijać ⟨**-pić**⟩ (*-jam*) *pieniądze*: waste on drink; **~ do** *G* toast, drink to

przepiłowywać ⟨**-łować**⟩ (*-łowuję*) saw through

przepiórka *f* (*-ki*; *-ki*) quail

przepis *m* (*-su*; *-sy*) **1.** *kucharski*: recipe; **według starego ~u** according to an old recipe; **~ na sukces** recipe for success **2.** (*instrukcja*) instruction **3. ~y** regulations; **~y drogowe** traffic regulations; **niezgodnie z ~ami, wbrew ~om** against the law; **zgodnie z ~ami** in accordance with the regulations, according to the law **4.** (*zalece-*

P

nie) prescription; ***według ~u lekarza*** as prescribed (by the doctor); ***wydaje się z ~u lekarza*** by prescription only
przepisać *v/p* → ***przepisywać***
przepisowo *adv* **1.** (*według prawa*) legally **2.** *wykonany*: correctly **3.** *zaparkowany*: properly
przepisowy *adj* **1.** (*legalny*) legal **2.** *mundur*: regulation
przepisywać ⟨**-sać**⟩ (*-suję*) **1.** *lekarstwo*, *dietę*: prescribe **2.** *majątek*: bequeath **3.** (*ręcznie*) rewrite, copy **4.** (*na maszynie*) type out
przepity *adj* **1.** *osoba*: hungover **2.** *głos*: hoarse from drinking
przeplatać ⟨**-leść**⟩ (*-tam*) **1.** *nitki*: interlace, interweave; ***~ tekst anegdotami*** interlace the text with anecdotes **2.** *czynności*: alternate; ***przeplatać się*** *fig* be interlaced
przeplatany *adj* intertwined (*I* with)
przepłacać ⟨**-cić**⟩ (*-cam*) overpay, pay too much
przepłakać *v/p* (*-łaczę*): ***~ całą noc*** spend the whole night crying
przepłaszać ⟨**-łoszyć**⟩ (*-szam*) scare off
przepłukiwać ⟨**-kać**⟩ (*-kuję*) **1.** *bieliznę*: rinse **2.** *usta*: wash; ***~ gardło*** *infml* wet one's whistle
przepłynąć *v/p* → ***przepływać***
przepływ *m* (*-wu*; *-wy*) *wody*, *powietrza*, *kapitału*: flow
przepływać ⟨**-łynąć**⟩ (*-wam*) **1.** *jezioro*: swim across **2.** *łodzią*, *statkiem*: sail **3.** (*o wodzie*, *rzece*) flow **4.** (*o obłokach*) drift
przepocić *v/p* → ***przepacać***; **przepocony** *adj* sweaty
przepoczwarzać się ⟨**-rzyć**⟩ (*-rzam*) *BIOL* metamorphose
przepojony *adj fig* imbued (*I* with)
przepoławiać ⟨**-łowić**⟩ (*-wiam*) **1.** *masło*: halve **2.** *pokój*: partition
przepompowywać ⟨**-pować**⟩ (*-powuję*) *wodę*: pump (over)
przepona *f* (*-ny*; *-ny*) *ANAT* diaphragm
przepowiadać ⟨**-wiedzieć**⟩ (*-dam*) **1.** *nieszczęście*, *zwycięstwo*: predict; ***~ przyszłość*** foretell the future; ***~ komuś przyszłość*** tell s.o.'s fortune **2.** *pogodę*: forecast
przepowiednia *f* (*-ni*; *-nie*) prediction, prophecy
przepowiedzieć *v/p* → ***przepowiadać***

przepracowany *adj* overworked; **przepracowywać** ⟨**-cować**⟩ (*-cowuję*) serve, work; ***przepracowywać się*** work too hard, overwork
przeprać *v/p* → ***przepierać***
przepraszać ⟨**-rosić**⟩ (*-szam*) apologize (**za** *A* for); ***przepraszam!*** **a)** (*prosząc o wybaczenie*) (I'm) sorry! **b)** (*zwracając uwagę*, *wtrącając się*) excuse me; ***przepraszam, która godzina?*** excuse me, what's the time?: ***przepraszać się*** **1.** (*godzić się*) make up (**z** *I* with); ***~ się z I*** *iron* be forced to use s.th. after all **2.** (*wzajemnie*) apologize to each other
przepraszający *adj* apologetic
przepraw|a *f* (*-wy*; *-wy*) **1.** (*przeprawienie się*) crossing **2.** (*miejsce*) passage; ***~a przez góry*** (***rzekę***) passage across the mountains (the river) **3.** (*trudności*) trouble; ***mieć ~ę z*** *I* have a hard time with
przeprawiać ⟨**-wić**⟩ (*-wiam*) *uciekinierów*, *rannych*: transport, take (**przez** *A* across); ***~ przez rzekę*** transport across a river; ***przeprawiać się*** cross; ***~ się przez góry*** cross the mountains; ***~ się przez bagna*** cross the marshland
przeprosić *v/p* → ***przepraszać***
przeprosiny *pl* (*-sin*) apology; ***na ~*** as an apology; ***jesteś mi winny ~*** you owe me an apology; ***przyjąć ~*** accept an apology; ***wymamrotać ~*** mumble a few words of apology
przeproszenie *n* (*-nia*; *no pl*) **1.** (*prośba o przebaczenie*) apology **2.** ***za ~m*** pardon the expression
przeprowadzać ⟨**-dzić**⟩ (*-dzam*) **1.** *reformy*, *eksperyment*, *kontrolę*: carry out **2.** (*przekierować*) take; ***~ kogoś przez ulicę*** help s.o. across the street; ***~ kogoś przez granicę*** take s.o. across the border; ***~ statek przez cieśninę*** help a ship pass through the straits, guide a ship through the straits **3.** *kable*: lay, run **4.** *szosę*: build **5.** *tory*: lay **6.** *tunel*: dig, bore **7.** *wywiad*: conduct; ***przeprowadzać się*** move (house); ***~ się do nowego mieszkania*** move into a new flat; ***~ się do Berlina*** move to Berlin
przeprowadzk|a *f* (*-ki*; *-ki*) move; ***koszty ~i*** costs ofmoving house
przepuklina *f* (*-ny*; *no pl*) *MED* hernia

P

przepust|ka *f* (*-ki*; *-ki*) pass; ***być na ~ce*** be on a pass
przepustowość *f* (*-ści*; *no pl*) capacity
przepuszczać ⟨***-puścić***⟩ (*-czam*) **1.** *osobę*: let through; ***~ kogoś przodem*** let s.o. go first; ***~ przez maszynkę*** COOK put through a mincer **2.** *szansę*, *okazję*: miss, pass up **3.** *błędy*: overlook **4.** *światło*, *wodę*: let in **5.** *pieniądze*, *majątek*: squander
przepuszczalny *adj* permeable
przepych *m* (*-chu*; *no pl*) **1.** *barw*: magnificence **2.** (*luksus*) glamour, splendour **3.** (*dostatek*) luxury; ***żyć w ~u*** live a life of luxury
przepychać ⟨***-pchać***, ***-pchnąć***⟩ (*-cham*) **1.** *wóz*: push (***przez*** *A* through) **2.** *rurę*: unblock **3.** *ustawę*: force through; ***przepychać się*** push one's way (***przez*** *A* through), elbow one's way (***przez*** *A* through); ***~ się do wyjścia*** push one's way to the exit
przepychanka *f* (*-ki*; *-ki*) *infml* **1.** (*fizyczna*) jostle **2.** (*kłótnia*) struggle
przepyszny *adj* **1.** (*bardzo smaczny*) delicious **2.** (*wspaniały*) gorgeous, splendid **3.** (*ozdobny*) magnificent
przerabiać ⟨***-robić***⟩ (*-biam*) **1.** *tekst*: rewrite **2.** (*przetworzyć*) remodel (***na*** *A*), change (***na*** *A* into) **3.** (*zmieniać funkcję*) convert (***na*** *A* into) **4.** *sukienkę*, *palto*: alter **5.** *lekcję*: do
przeradzać się ⟨***-rodzić***⟩ (*-dzam*) turn (***w*** *A* into)
przerastać ⟨***-rosnąć***⟩ (*-tam*) **1.** (*stawać się większym*) grow taller; ***~ kogoś o głowę*** stand a head taller than **2.** *oczekiwania*, *mistrza*: surpass **3.** (*o sytuacji*, *zadaniu*) be far too difficult; ***ten problem go przerasta*** this problem is beyond his control; ***to przerasta moje możliwości*** it's beyond my capabilities
przerazić *v/p* → ***przerażać***
przeraźliwy *adj* **1.** *widok*: fearful **2.** *krzyk*: piercing **3.** *zimno*: terrible, bitter **4.** *ból*: severe, agonizing
przerażać ⟨***-razić***⟩ (*-żam*) terrify, frighten; ***przerażać się*** be terrified (*I* by); **przerażający** *adj* terrifying, horrifying
przerażenie *n* (*-nia*; *no pl*) terror; ***śmiertelne ~*** mortal fear; **przerażony** *adj* terrified
przerąbywać ⟨***-bać***⟩ (*-buję*) **1.** *pień*: chop **2.** *lód*: cut, break **3.** *lasy*: clear
przerdzewieć *v/p* (*-wieję*) rust (through)
przeredagowywać ⟨***-gować***⟩ (*-gowuję*) **1.** rewrite **2.** (*wprowadzić poprawki*) revise
przereklamowany *adj* overrated, overhyped
przerębl|el *m* (*-bla*; *-ble*) air-hole, blowhole; ***w ~lu*** in the air-hole
przerobić *v/p* (*-bię*): ***~ na swoje kopyto*** fashion after one's own mold; → ***przerabiać***
przerodzić się *v/p* → ***przeradzać się***
przerosnąć *v/p* → ***przerastać***
przerost *m* (*-tu*; *-ty*) **1.** (*nadmiar*) excess (*G* of); ***~ formy nad treścią*** excess off orm over substance **2.** MED hypertrophy; **przerośnięty** *adj* **1.** BIOL overgrown **2.** *mięso*: streaky **3.** *ciasto*: risen too much
przerób *m* (*-robu*; *no pl*) **1.** *surowca*: processing **2.** (*ilość*) output
przeróbka *f* (*-ki*; *-ki*) **1.** *płaszcza*: alteration **2.** *tekstu*: adaptation **3.** *surowca*: processing; ***dalsza ~*** further processing
przerw|a *f* (*-wy*; *-wy*) **1.** *lekcyjna*: break; ***~a obiadowa*** lunch break; ***~a na papierosa*** cigarette break; ***~a w dostawie prądu*** power cut, blackout; ***~a międzysemestralna*** winter holiday; ***~a w życiorysie*** *fig* drunken spell, blackout; ***bez ~y*** continually, nonstop **2.** THEAT *Br* interval, *Am* intermission **3.** (*luka*) gap; ***~a między zębami*** gap between one's teeth
przerwać *v/p* → ***przerywać***
przerwanie *n* (*-nia*; *no pl*) *dostaw*: interruption; ***~ ciąży*** termination ofpregn ancy, abortion; ***~ tamy*** breach ofthe dam; ***~ ciągłości*** discontinuity
przerysowywać ⟨***-sować***⟩ (*-sowuje*) **1.** *obrazek*: copy **2.** (*wyolbrzymiać*) *fig* exaggerate
przerywać ⟨***-rwać***⟩ (*-wam*) **I** *v/t* **1.** break; ***~ ciążę*** have an abortion, terminate pregnancy; ***~ studia*** **a)** take a break in one's studies **b)** drop out of studies **2.** *połączenie*: cut off **3.** *sen*, *ciszę*: interrupt; ***~ komuś w pół słowa*** cut in on; ***~ milczenie*** interrupt silence, break silence **4.** *kartkę*: rip

P

5. *groblę, blokadę*: breach **6.** (*nie skończyć*) stop **7.** *rośliny*: thin (out) **II** *v/i* (*o silniku*) splutter, stall; **przerywać się 1.** (*o linie*) be cut off **2.** (*o materiale*) rip **3.** (*o transmisji*) be interrupted

przerywany *adj* **1.** *puls, oddech*: irregular **2.** *głos*: cracked **3.** *linia*: broken

przerywnik *m* (*-ka*; *-ki*) **1.** *filmowy, muzyczny*: interlude **2.** *radiowy*: jingle

przerzedzać ⟨**-dzić**⟩ (*-dzam*) thin (out); **przerzedzać się 1.** (*o włosach*) thin **2.** (*o gronie znajomych*) diminish

przerzucać ⟨**-cić**⟩ (*-cam*) **1.** *piłkę*: throw (**przez** *A* over); **~ kurtkę przez ramię** sling a jacket over one's shoulder; **~ przez granicę a)** *ludzi*: take across the border **b)** *narkotyki*: smuggle, run across the border; **~ bieg** *AUTO* shift gear; **~ na jedynkę** (**dwójkę**) shift into first (second) **2.** *piach, ziemię*: shovel **3.** *most*: build; **~ most przez rzekę** bridge a river **4.** (*przetrząsać*) search through **5.** *odpowiedzialność*: shift (**na** *A* on); **~ na kogoś swoje obowiązki** burden s.o. with one's duties **6.** *żołnierzy, robotników*: redeploy **7.** (*kartkę*) flip over; **~ notatki** look over one's notes; **przerzucać się 1.** (*o nowotworze, ogniu*) spread (**na** *A* to) **2.** (*o osobie*) switch over (**na** *A* to) **3.** (*w kartach*) *infml* show one's card too early

przerzut *m* (*-tu*; *-ty*) **1.** *narkotyków*: smuggling **2.** *wojsk*: redeployment **3.** *MED* metastasis **4.** *SPORT* flop, cross

przerzutka *f* (*-ki*; *-ki*) *roweru*: gear(s)

przerzynać ⟨**-rżnąć**⟩ (*-nam*) **1.** *nożem*: cut in two **2.** (*przepiłować*) saw through **3.** (*odbyć stosunek*) *vulg* shag, screw, hump **4.** (*przegrać*) lose (everything)

przesad|a *f* (*-dy*; *no pl*) **1.** exaggeration **2.** (*nadmiar*) overkill; **do ~y** to a fault, to excess; **bez ~y** oh, come on!; **~a!** that's come off it!; **to lekka ~a** that's a bit ofan exaggeration, that's a bit over the top; **to gruba ~a** that's gross exaggeration; **przesadny** *adj* exaggerated, excessive; **przesadnie** *adv*: **~ ostrożny** excessively careful

przesadzać ⟨**-dzić**⟩ (*-dzam*) **1.** transplant **2.** (*do doniczki*) plant **3.** *ucznia*: move (to another seat) **4.** (*koloryzować*) *fig* exaggerate (**w** *L* about) **5.** (*robić w nadmiarze*) overdo (**w** *L*) **6.** *mur*: jump (over)

przesalać ⟨**-solić**⟩ (*-lam*) **1.** (*dodać za dużo soli*) add too much salt **2.** (*przesadzać*) *fig* overdo

przesączać ⟨**-czyć**⟩ (*-czam*) filter; **przesączać się** filter through

przesąd *m* (*-du*; *-dy*) superstition; **~y** (*uprzedzenia*) prejudice; **przesądny** *adj* superstitious

przesądzać ⟨**-dzić**⟩ (*-dzam*) **1.** (*decydować*) determine, settle (*A*/**o** *L*) **2.** ensure, secure, guarantee; **~ o zwycięstwie** secure victory; **~ o powodzeniu** ensure success **2.** (*oceniać*) prejudge; **nie móc przesądzić** be unable to decide

przesiać *v/p* → **przesiewać**

przesiadać się ⟨**-siąść**⟩ (*-dam*) **1.** (*zmieniać miejsce*) change seats **2.** (*w podróży*) change; **~ do innego stolika** sit at another table, move to another table

przesiadk|a *f* (*-ki*; *-ki*) change; **mam ~ę we Wrocławiu** I need to change in Wrocław

przesiadywa|ć ⟨**-siedzieć**⟩ (*-duję*) hang out, hang about, spend one's time; **~ł całe wieczory w kawiarniach** he spent all (his) evenings in cafes; **przesiedział całe popołudnie w bibliotece** he spent the whole afternoon in the library

przesiąkać ⟨**-knąć**⟩ (*-kam*) soak (through); **~ dymem papierosowym** become filled with cigarette smoke

przesiąknięty *adj*: **~ potem** (**krwią**) soaked with sweat (blood); **~ ideą** imbued with the idea

przesiąść się *v/p* → **przesiadać się**

przesiedlać ⟨**-lić**⟩ (*-lam*) displace; **przesiedlać się** migrate (**do** *G* to)

przesiedlenie *n* (*-nia*; *no pl*) displacement; **~ się** migration; **przesiedleniec** *m* (*-leńca*; *-leńcy*) displaced person; **przesiedleńcz|y** *adj* displacement; **prawo ~e** immigration laws

przesiedlić *v/p* → **przesiedlać**

przesiedzieć *v/p* → **przesiadywać**

przesieka *f* (*-ki*; *-ki*) clearing

przesiewać ⟨**-siać**⟩ (*-wam*) **1.** *mąkę*: sift **2.** *kandydatów*: screen

przesilać się ⟨**-lić**⟩ (*-lam*) (*o gorącze*) get over

przesilenie *n* (*-nia*; *-nia*) **1.** *choroby*: crisis **2.** **~ *letnie*** (***zimowe***) *ASTR* summer (winter) solstice

przeskakiwać ⟨**-skoczyć**⟩ (*-kuję*) **1.** jump over (***przez*** *A*); **~ *na drugą stronę*** jump to the other side; **~ *z tematu na temat*** jump from one subject to another; ***nie mów hop, póki nie przeskoczysz*** don't count your chickens before they're hatched **2.** (*przewyższyć*) *fig* outdo **3.** (*opuszczać*) skip

przeskok *m* (*-ku*; *-ki*) jump, leap (***przez*** *A* over)

przeskrobać *v/p* (*-bię*) do s.th. bad, be naughty

przesłać *v/p* → **1. przesyłać 2. prześcielać**

przesładzać ⟨**-łodzić**⟩ (*-dzam*) *COOK* add too much sugar

przesłaniać ⟨**-łonić**⟩ (*-niam*) **1.** (*zasłaniać*) cover, be in the way; ***chmura przesłoniła słońce*** the cloud darkened the sun; ***mgła przesłaniała góry*** the fog shrouded the mountains **2.** (*absorbować*) blind; ***ona przesłania mu cały świat*** she is all the world to him; ***praca przesłania mu cały świat*** he is completely absorbed by his work

przesłanie *n* (*-nia*; *-nia*) *fig* message

przesłanka *f* (*-ki*; *-ki*) premise

przesłodzić *v/p* → **przesładzać**

przesłodzony *adj* **1.** (*zbyt osłodzony*) too sweet **2.** *uśmiech*: *fig* sugary **3.** (*nadmiernie ckliwy*) cloying, syrupy

P

przesłona *f* (*-ny*; *-ny*) *PHOT* aperture

przesłonić *v/p* → **przesłaniać**

przesłuchanie *n* (*-nia*; *-nia*) **1.** *świadków*: examination **2.** *podejrzanego*: interrogation **3.** (*do roli*) audition **4.** (*przed komisją*) hearing

przesłuchiwać ⟨**-chać**⟩ (*-chuję*) **1.** *oskarżonego*: interrogate **2.** *świadka*: examine **3.** *kandydata*: interview **4.** (*do roli*) audition **5.** *płytę*: listen

przesłyszeć się *v/p* (*-szę*) mishear; ***chyba się przesłyszałem?*** did I hear you right?

przesmażać ⟨**-żyć**⟩ (*-żam*) fry (a little)

przesmyk *m* (*-ku*; *-ki*) **1.** (*pas lądu*) isthmus **2.** (*wodny*) strip, inlet **3.** (*górski*) pass

przesolić *v/p* → **przesalać**; **przesolony** *adj* too salty

przespać *v/p* → **przesypiać**

przestać[1] *v/p* (*-toję*): **~ *całą podróż*** spend the whole journey standing

przestać[2] *v/p* → **przestawać**

przestankowy *adj*: ***znak*** **~** punctuation mark

przestarzały *adj* **1.** *wyraz*: obsolete **2.** *system*: outdated, obsolete

przestawać ⟨**-stać**⟩ (*-taję*) stop; **~ *palić*** give up smoking, quit smoking; ***przestało padać*** it stopped raining; ***to przestało mieć znaczenie*** it does not matter any more; ***przestań!*** stop!

przestawiać ⟨**-wić**⟩ (*-wiam*) **1.** *stół*, *dźwignię*: move; **~ *zegarek na czas letni*** set one's watch to summer time **2.** *meble*: rearrange **3.** *wyraz*: reorder; ***przestawiać się*** switch (over) (***na*** *A* to)

przestąpić *v/p* → **przestępować**

przestępca *m* (*-cy*; *-cy*) criminal, offender; **~ *wojenny*** war criminal; ***młodociany*** **~** juvenile delinquent; **przestępczość** *f* (*-ści*; *no pl*) crime; **~ *nieletnich*** juvenile delinquency

przestępcz|y *adj* criminal; ***środowisko*** **~*e*** criminal environment; ***banda*** **~*a*** gang

przestępczyni *f* (*-ni*; *-nie*) criminal

przestępny *adj* **1.** *JUR* criminal **2.** ***rok*** **~** *ASTR* leap year

przestępować ⟨**-tąpić**⟩ (*-puję*) *próg*: cross; **~ *z nogi na nogę*** shift from foot to foot

przestępstwo *n* (*-wa*; *-wa*) crime; **~ *gospodarcze*** white-collar crime; ***popełnić*** **~** commit a crime

przestój *m* (*-toju*; *-toje*) **1.** *w pracy*: stoppage **2.** (*przetrzymanie*) demurrage

przestrach *m* (*-chu*; *no pl*) terror, fright; ***z*** **~*u*** out off right

przestrajać ⟨**-roić**⟩ (*-jam*) retune

przestraszony *adj* frightened, scared

przestraszyć *v/p* (*-szę*) frighten; ***przestraszyć się*** take fright, get scared (*G* at), be frightened (*G* of)

przestrog|a *f* (*-gi*; *-gi*) warning; ***dawać komuś*** **~*ę*** give s.o. a warning

przestronny *adj* **1.** *pokój*: spacious **2.** *plac*: large **3.** *samochód*: roomy, spacious

przestrzał *m* (*-łu*; *-ły*) (*rana*) gun-shot wound; ***otworzyć okna na ~*** open all windows

przestrzegać[1] *v/im* (*-gam*) **1.** *przepisów*: follow **2.** *regulaminu*, *prawa*: abide (*G* by) **3.** *diety*: stick to, have **4.** *tajemnicy*: keep **5.** *zwyczaju*: observe

przestrzegać[2] ⟨**-rzec**⟩ (*-gam*) warn, caution (**przed** *I* against)

przestrzelić *v/p* (*-lę*) shoot through

przestrzenn|y *adj* **1.** *forma*, *wyobraźnia*: spatial; ***planowanie ~e*** land (development) planning **2.** (*trójwymiarowy*) three-dimensional

przestrze|ń *f* (*-rzeni*; *-rzenie*) space; ***~ń kosmiczna*** (outer) space; ***~ń życiowa*** **a)** *ludzi*: living space **b)** *zwierząt*: habitat; ***~ń powietrzna*** airspace; ***~ń morza*** (open) sea; ***na ~ni kilku kilometrów*** within the range ofa few kilometres; ***na ~ni wieków*** over a span ofcenturi es; ***lęk ~ni*** fear of open spaces, agoraphobia; ***otwarta ~ń*** open space

przestudiować *v/p* (*-diuję*) study

przestudzać ⟨**-dzić**⟩ (*-dzam*) *herbatę*: cool (down); ***przestudzać się*** cool (down)

przestworza *pl* (*-rzy*) *lit* (*przestrzeń*) expanses; ***~ oceanu*** expanses ofthe ocean; ***powietrzne ~*** skies

przestygnąć *v/p* (*-nę*) (*o herbacie*) cool (down)

przesunąć *v/p* → ***przesuwać***

przesunięcie *n* (*-cia*; *-cia*) shift

przesuszać ⟨**-szyć**⟩ (*-szam*) dry (a little); ***przesuszać się*** dry

przesuwać ⟨**-sunąć**⟩ (*-wam*) **1.** *szafę*: move **2.** *spotkanie*: put off, reschedule; ***~ ręką po*** *L* run one's hand along; ***przesuwać się*** **1.** (*o osobie*) move on; ***~ się do przodu*** move forward **2.** (*o terminie*) be put off, be postponed **3.** (*o chmurach*) drift

przesuw(al)ny *adj* movable

przesycać ⟨**-cić**⟩ (*-cam*) *zapachem*: saturate

przesyłać ⟨**-słać**⟩ (*-łam*) **1.** *list*: send, post; ***~ dalej*** forward, pass on **2.** *życzenia*: send, give; ***~ komuś pozdrowienia*** give s.o. one's regards; ***moja mama przesyła ci pozdrowienia*** lots of love from my mum

przesyłka *f* (*-ki*; *-ki*) **1.** *pocztowa*: delivery **2.** *towarów*: shipment

przesypać *v/p* → ***przesypywać***

przesypiać ⟨**-spać**⟩ (*-piam*) **1.** *noc*: sleep through **2.** *zmartwienie*: sleep off **3.** (*przepuścić*) let slip, miss; ***przespać się*** get some sleep; ***przespać się z*** *I* sleep with

przesypywać ⟨**-pać**⟩ (*-puję*) pour (**do** *G* into)

przesyt *m* (*-tu*; *no pl*) satiety

przeszczep *m* (*-pu*; *-py*) MED **1.** transplant; ***~ kostny*** (***skórny***) bone (skin) graft; ***~ przyjął się*** the transplant took; ***jego organizm odrzucił ~*** his body rejected the transplant; ***~ nerki*** (***serca***) kidney (heart) transplant **2.** (*organ*) graft

przeszczepiać ⟨**-pić**⟩ (*-piam*) MED **1.** *skórę*, *kość*: graft **2.** *serce*, *nerki*: transplant

przeszeregowywać ⟨**-gować**⟩ (*-gowuję*) transfer (**do** *G* to)

przeszkadza|ć ⟨**-kodzić**⟩ (*-dzam*) **1.** (*zakłócać*) disturb (**w** *L* in); ***nie ~j mi w pracy!*** don't disturb me while I'm working!; ***to mi nie ~*** I don't mind it; ***nie ~ mu to jednak, żeby*** nevertheless, he; this does not stop him from; ***proszę sobie nie ~ć*** please don't let me disturb you; ***~ mi hałas*** the noise disturbs me **2.** (*utrudniać*) hinder; ***hałas ~ mi w koncentracji*** noise interferes with my concentration; ***uraz biodra ~ł jej w poruszaniu się*** hip injury hindered her mobility **3.** (*przerywać*) interrupt; ***choroba przeszkodziła mu w karierze*** the disease interrupted his career **4.** (*wtrącać się*) interfere

przeszkalać ⟨**-kolić**⟩ (*-lam*) train (**w** *L* in)

przeszk|oda *f* (*-dy*; *-dy*) obstacle; ***stać komuś na ~odzie*** stand in s.o.'s way; ***jeśli nic nie stanie na ~odzie*** if everything goes unimpeded; ***bez ~ód*** with no (major) obstacles

przeszkodzić *v/p* → ***przeszkadzać***

przeszkolenie *n* (*-nia*; *-nia*) training

przeszkolić *v/p* → ***przeszkalać***

przeszło *particle* over, more than

przeszłoś|ć *f* (*-ści*; *no pl*) the past; ***to należy do ~ci*** this is a thing ofthe past; ***żyć ~cią*** live in the past; ***kobieta z ~cią***

P

woman with a past; **przeszły** *adj* **1.** *zdarzenie*: past **2.** *tydzień*: last; ***czas ~*** *GRAM* the past tense, the past

przeszmuglować *v/p* → ***szmuglować***

przeszpiegi: ***chodzić na ~*** go spying

przeszukiwać ⟨***-kać***⟩ (*-kuję*) *mieszkanie, złodzieja*: search

przeszywać ⟨***-szyć***⟩ (*-wam*) **1.** (*pikować*) quilt **2.** (*fastrygować*) tack **3.** *guziki*: sew on, re-stitch **4.** (*przebić*) pierce; ***kula przeszyła jej dłoń na wylot*** the bullet went right through her hand; ***~ kogoś wzrokiem*** fix s.o. with a piercing glance, look at s.o. piercingly; ***~ powietrze*** cut through the air; ***błyskawice przeszywały niebo*** lightnings lit up the sky; ***przeszył mnie ból*** pain shot through my whole body

przeszywający *adj* **1.** *ból*: shooting, stabbing **2.** *wzrok*: piercing **3.** *zimno*: biting, bitter

prześcielać ⟨***przesłać***⟩ (*-lam*): ***~ łóżko*** make the bed

prześcieradło *n* (*-ła*; *-ła*) sheet

prześcigać ⟨***-gnąć***⟩ (*-gam*) **1.** *samochód*: overtake **2.** (*przewyższać*) outdo; ***~ się w uprzejmości*** (***komplementach***) eagerly exchange courtesies (complements) **3.** (*biec szybciej*) outrun

prześladować *v/im* (*-duję*) **1.** persecute **2.** (*dręczyć*) oppress **3.** (*o myślach, wspomnieniach*) haunt **4.** (*o chorobach*) plague; **prześladowanie** *n* (*-nia*; *-nia*) persecution

prześladowany **I** *adj* persecuted **II** *m* (*-nego*; *-ni*), **-na** *f* (*-nej*; *-ne*) persecuted person; ***~ politycznie*** persecuted for political reasons

prześladowca *m* (*-cy*; *-cy*) persecutor; **prześladowcz|y** *adj* persecution; ***mania ~a*** *MED* persecution mania

prześliczny *adj* (most) beautiful

prześlizgiwać się ⟨***-z(g)nąć***⟩ (*-guję*) **1.** (*przedostawać się*) squeeze, slip **2.** *przez studia*: slide through

prześmieszny *adj* hilarious

prześmiewać się *v/im* (*-wam*) mock (**z** *G*)

przeświadczenie *n* (*-nia*; *-nia*) conviction; **przeświadczony** *adj* convinced (**o** *L* of)

przeświecać *v/im* (*-cam*) show (**przez** *A* through)

prześwietlać ⟨***-lić***⟩ (*-lam*) **1.** *MED* X-ray **2.** *PHOT* overexpose **3.** (*starannie badać*) probe, scrutinize; ***prześwietlać się*** **1.** *MED* have an X-ray **2.** *PHOT* be overexposed

prześwietlenie *n* (*-nia*; *-nia*) *MED* X-ray; ***robić ~ stopy*** have a foot X-ray taken

prześwietny *adj lit* eminent

prześwit *m* (*-tu*; *-ty*) **1.** *między domami*: distance; ***~ w lesie*** clearing in the forest **2.** *pod mostem*: clearance

prześwitujący *adj* **1.** (*częściowo*) translucent **2.** (*całkowicie*) see-through

prześwitywać *v/im* (*-tuję*) **1.** (*o słońcu*) break through, shine through **2.** (*o materiale*) be translucent, be see-through **3.** (*być widocznym*) show through

przetaczać ⟨***-toczyć***⟩ (*-czam*) **1.** *beczki*: roll **2.** *wagony*: shunt **3.** *krew*: transfuse; ***~ komuś krew*** give s.o. a blood transfusion **4.** *piwo*: pour; ***przetaczać się*** **1.** (*o strajku, wojnie*) sweep over **2.** (*o wojsku*) trundle along, trundle through **3.** (*o chmurach*) roll

przetak *m* (*-ka*/*-ku*; *-ki*) riddle

przetańczyć *v/p* (*-czę*) **1.** *noc*: dance away **2.** *salę*: dance across

przetapiać ⟨***-topić***⟩ (*-piam*) **1.** *monety*: melt down **2.** *COOK* melt **3.** *rudę*: smelt

przetarg *m* (*-gu*; *-gi*) **1.** (*konkurs*) tender; ***ogłaszać ~ na*** *A* invite tenders for; ***kupić na ~u*** buy by tender; ***~i*** *fig* horse-trading **2.** (*aukcja*) auction

przetarty *adj* *rękaw, kołnierz*: worn through

przetasowywać ⟨***-sować***⟩ (*-sowuję*) **1.** *karty*: shuffle **2.** (*zmienić układ*) *fig* reshuffle

przeterminowan|y *adj* *czek*: expired, past the expiration date; ***mleko jest ~e*** *Br* the milk is past its use-by date, *Am* the milk is past its expiration date

przetestować *v/p* → ***testować***

przetkać *v/p* → ***przetykać***

przetłumaczyć *v/p* → ***tłumaczyć***

przetłuszczać się ⟨***-czyć***⟩ (*-czam*) (*o włosach, skórze*) be greasy

przetłuszczający się *adj* **1.** *włosy*: greasy **2.** *cera*: oily

przeto *conj lit* hence, thus

przetoczyć *v/p* → ***przetaczać***

P

przetoka *f* (*-ki*; *-ki*) MED fistula
przetopić *v/p* → **przetapiać**
przetrawiać ⟨**-wić**⟩ (*-wiam*) **1.** *posiłek*: digest **2.** *problem*: mull over **3.** *kwas*: corrode
przetrącić *v/p* (*-cę*) **1.** (*zjeść*) *infml* have a bite to eat **2.** *rękę*: break
przetrwać *v/p* (*-wam*) survive; ***~ próbę czasu*** stand the test oftime
przetrwalnik *m* (*-ka*; *-ki*) BIOL (resting) spore
przetrząsać ⟨**-snąć**⟩ (*-sam*) **1.** (*szukać*) search; ***~ wszystkie kąty w kuchni*** search the whole kitchen high and low **2.** *siano*: ted
przetrzebiać ⟨**-bić**⟩ (*-biam*) **1.** *las*: thin **2.** *zwierzęta*: kill off **3.** *ludzi*: decimate
przetrzeć *v/p* → **przecierać**
przetrzepać *v/p* (*-pię*) *chodnik*: beat; ***~ komuś skórę*** give s.o. a spanking
przetrzymywać ⟨**-mać**⟩ (*-muję*) **1.** *ból*: bear **2.** *atak*: endure **3.** *zakładników*: hold **4.** (*na policji*) be taken into custody **5.** (*ukrywać*) harbour, give shelter (*A* to) **6.** *książkę*: keep (too long/ overtime) **7.** (*wytrzymać dłużej*) outlast
przetwarzać ⟨**-worzyć**⟩ (*-rzam*) **1.** INF process **2.** convert
przetwarzanie *n* (*-nia*; *no pl*) processing; ***~ danych*** INF data processing
przetwornik *m* (*-ka*; *-ki*) converter
przetwory *pl* (*-rów*) **1.** (*własnej roboty*) preserves **2.** *przemysłowe*: products; ***~ z ryb*** fish products
przetworzyć *v/p* → **przetwarzać**
przetwórczy *adj przemysł*: processing; **przetwórnia** *f* (*-ni*; *-nie*) processing plant; **przetwórstwo** *n* (*-wa*; *no pl*) processing (industry)
przetykać ⟨**-tkać**⟩ (*-kam*) **1.** *rurę*, *zlew*: unclog **2.** *tkaninę*: interweave, interlace (*I* with)
przewag|a *f* (*-gi*; *no pl*) **1.** advantage; ***mieć ~ę nad*** *I* have the advantage over; ***uzyskiwać ~ę nad*** *I* gain the upper hand over **2.** (*wyższość*) superiority **3.** SPORT lead; ***~a 10 punktów*** ten-point lead
przewalać ⟨**-lić**⟩ (*-lam*) topple; ***przewalać się*** **1.** (*przewracać się*) topple over **2.** (*o tłumach*) throng
przeważać ⟨**-żyć**⟩ (*-żam*) **I** *v/i* **1.** (*o argumencie*, *obowiązku*) be decisive **2.** (*o kobietach*, *kolorach*) prevail; ***~ na jedną stronę*** be heavier on one side **II** *v/t* (*ważyć*) weigh
przeważający|y *adj* **1.** *większość*: vast **2.** *emocja*: predominant **3.** *siła*: overwhelming; ***~a część*** vast majority; ***w ~ym stopniu***, ***w ~ej mierze*** predominantly; **przeważnie** *particle* mostly, usually
przeważyć *v/p* → **przeważać**
przewąchiwać ⟨**-chać**⟩ (*-chuję*) sense
przewędrować *v/p* (*-ruję*) travel
przewężenie *n* (*-nia*; *-nia*) **1.** *rzeki*: narrowing **2.** *rury*: throat
przewiać *v/p* → **przewiewać**
przewiązywać ⟨**-zać**⟩ (*-zuję*) **1.** *paczkę*: tie **2.** *ranę*: tie up
przewidujący *adj* far-sighted
przewidywać ⟨**-dzieć**⟩ (*-duję*) **1.** *skutki*: predict; ***ustawa nie przewiduje, że*** the law does not provide for **2.** *przyszłość*: foresee **3.** *pogodę*: forecast **4.** (*przeczuwać*) have a premonition **5.** (*spodziewać się*) expect **6.** (*planować*) plan
przewidywa|nie *n* (*-nia*; *-nia*) anticipation; ***według wszelkich ~ń*** as anticipated, as expected; ***wbrew ~niom*** against all expectations; **przewidywany** *adj* expected
przewidzeni|e: ***to było do ~a*** it was to be expected; ***niemożliwy do ~a*** unpredictable
przewidziany *adj* **1.** (*umową*, *ustawą*) provided for **2.** (*planowany*) planned; on the agenda (**na** *A* for)
przewidzieć *v/p* → **przewidywać**
przewiercać ⟨**-cić**⟩ (*-cam*) bore through; ***~ kogoś wzrokiem*** look at s.o. piercingly
przewieszać ⟨**-sić**⟩ (*-szam*) **1.** *obraz*: move **2.** *płaszcz*: hang; ***~ płaszcz przez ramię*** sling a jacket over one's shoulder
przewietrzać ⟨**-rzyć**⟩ (*-rzam*) *pokój*: air; ***przewietrzyć się*** take some fresh air
przewiew *m* (*-wu*; *-wy*) *Br* draught, *Am* draft
przewiewać ⟨**przewiać**⟩ (*-wam*): ***przewiał nas wiatr***, ***przewiało nas*** it was so windy that we caught a cold
przewiewny *adj* **1.** *ubranie*: loose-fitting, flimsy **2.** *miejsce*: airy

przewiezienie *n* (*-nia*; *no pl*) transportation
przewieźć *v/p* → **przewozić**
przewijać 〈**-winąć**〉 (*-jam*) **1.** (*do tyłu*) rewind **2.** (*do przodu*) fast-forward **3.** *dziecko*: change **4.** *ranę*: put on new bandage, put a clean dressing **5.** INF scroll; ***przewijać się*** (*o motywie*) recur; ***przewija się tu dużo interesantów*** lots ofcustomers come and go here
przewinić *v/p* (*-nię*) *lit* be to blame
przewinienie *n* (*-nia*; *-nia*) **1.** (*wykroczenie*) offence **2.** SPORT violation, foul
przewlekać 〈**-lec**〉 (*-kam*) **1.** *nitkę*: pass through; *~ **pościel*** change sheets **2.** *obrady*, *spotkanie*: prolong, draw out **3.** *decyzję*: put off; ***przewlekać się*** (*o obradach*, *spotkaniu*) drag on
przewlekły *adj* **1.** *formalności*: protracted **2.** MED chronic
przewodni *adj rola*: key; ***motyw ~*** leitmotif; **przewodnictwo** *n* (*-wa*; *no pl*) **1.** (*zarządzanie*) leadership **2.** *obrad*: chair(manship) **3.** PHYS conduction
przewodniczący *m* (*-cego*; *-cy*), **-ca** *f* (*-cej*; *-ce*) **1.** (*kierujący obradami*) chairperson **2.** *w klasie*: class president
przewodniczka *f* (*-ki*; *-ki*) (tour) guide
przewodniczyć *v/im* (*-czę*) **1.** *obradom*: chair **2.** *zebraniu*: preside over
przewodnik[1] *m* (*-ka*; *-nicy*) **1.** *wycieczek*: guide; *~ **górski*** mountain guide; *~ **po mieście*** city guide **2.** (*przywódca*) leader
przewodnik[2] *m* (*-ka*; *-ki*) **1.** (*książka*) guide(book) **2.** PHYS conductor
przewodowy *adj* wire
przewodzić *v/im* (*-dzę*) **1.** *obradom*: chair **2.** *ciepło*; conduct **3.** (*kierować*) lead **4.** *bandzie*: be the ringleader
przewozić 〈**-wieźć**〉 (*-wożę*) transport; *~ **przez rzekę*** ferry across the river
przewozow|y *adj środki*: transport; ***przedsiębiorstwo ~e*** freight carrier; ***list ~y*** bill oflading
przewoźnik *m* (*-ka*; *-nicy*) **1.** *drogowy*: haulier **2.** *lotniczy*: carrier
przewód *m* (*-wodu*; *-wody*) **1.** (*rura*) pipe; *~ **gazowy*** gas pipe; *~ **wodociągowy*** water (supply system) pipe; *~ **kanalizacyjny*** sewerage pipe **2.** (*drut*) wire; *~ **elektryczny*** electric wire **3.** (*kanał*) canal; *~ **pokarmowy*** ANAT alimentary canal; *~ **słuchowy*** auditory canal **4.** *~ **doktorski*** PhD course; *~ **sądowy*** court proceedings; ***pod przewodem*** *G* under s.o.'s lead
przew|óz *m* (*-wozu*; *-wozy*) **1.** *osób*: transport **2.** *drogowy towarów*: haulage **3.** *lotniczy towarów*: carriage; ***koszty ~ozu*** transport(ation) costs
przewracać 〈**-rócić**〉 (*-cam*) **1.** *stołek*: overturn; ***przewracać oczami*** **a)** (*poruszać*) roll one's eyes **b)** (*flirtować*) make eyes **2.** *osobę*: knock over **3.** *kartkę*: turn over; ***przewracać kartki*** leafthrou gh a book; *~ **stronę*** turn over **4.** (*obracać*) turn; *~ **do góry nogami*** turn upside down; ***sława przewróciła mu w głowie*** fame turned his head; *~ **na lewą stronę*** turn inside out **5.** (*szperać*) search; ***przewracać się*** **1.** (*upadać*) fall over **2.** (*obracać się*) turn; *~ **się do góry dnem*** capsize; *~ **się z boku na bok*** turn over; ***przewróciłby się w grobie*** he would turn in his grave
przewrażliwiony → **przeczulony**
przewrotny *adj* **1.** (*podstępny*) perverse, scheming **2.** (*zwodniczy*) misleading
przewrócić *v/p* → **przewracać**
przewrót *m* (*-rotu*; *-roty*) **1.** (*przełom*) revolution **2.** POLIT coup d'état, coup **3.** SPORT somersault
przewyższać 〈**-szyć**〉 (*-szam*) **1.** (*być wyższym*) be taller (*A* than); *~ **o głowę*** stand a head taller than **2.** (*przekraczać*) exceed **3.** (*być lepszym*) outdo, outstrip (**w** *L* in)
przez *prep* (*A*) **1.** (*na drugą stronę lasu*, *parku*) through **2.** (*za pośrednictwem*, *ponad*) over; *~ **radio*** over the radio; *~ **telefon*** over the phone; *~ **most*** over the bridge; *~ **przypadek*** by accident; ***przeskakiwać ~ płot*** jump over a fence **3.** (*z powodu*) out of; *~ **zazdrość*** out ofjealous y **4.** (*w stronie biernej*) by; ***kochany ~ rodziców*** loved by his parents **5.** (*z określonej przyczyny*) because; *~ **to*** because ofthat ; *~ **niego*** because ofhim **6.** (*w czasie*) for, throughout, during; *~ **sekundę*** for a second; *~ **całą noc*** throughout the night; *~ **całe życie***

P

during the whole ofone's life, in all of one's days; *~ **sen*** in one's sleep; *~ **cały rok*** all year round **7.** (*na drugą stronę drogi, rzeki*) across **8.** (*przejeżdżając*) via; *~ **Poznań do Berlina*** to Berlin via Poznan

przezabawny *adj* hilarious, extremely funny

przeze *prep*: *~ **mnie*** because ofme

przezierać *v/im* (*-ram*) *lit* shine through, show through

przeziębiać ⟨**-bić**⟩ (*-biam*) give a cold; ***przeziębiać się*** catch a cold; **przeziębienie** *n* (*-nia*; *-nia*) cold; **przeziębiony** *adj*: ***być ~m*** have a cold

przezimować *v/p* → ***zimować***

przeznaczać ⟨**-czyć**⟩ (*-czam*) *pieniądze*: allocate (**na** *A* for); *~ **dla*** *G* (*ofiarować*) donate to; *~ **do czyjejś dyspozycji*** give at s.o.'s disposal; *~ **pieniądze na cele charytatywne*** give money to charity; *~ **swoje zbiory dla muzeum*** bequeath one's collection to a museum; ***to pomieszczenie przeznaczył na pracownię*** he turned this room into a workshop; ***nie było mu przeznaczone*** he was not destined for this

przeznaczeni|e *n* (*-nia*; *no pl*) **1.** (*los*) destiny; ***miejsce ~a*** destination **2.** (*zastosowanie*) (intended) use; ***zgodnie z ~em*** according to the terms ofuse; ***niezgodnie z ~em*** inconsistently with intended use **3.** (*cel*) purpose

przeznaczony *adj*: *~ **do rozbiórki*** due for demolition; *~ **na sprzedaż*** for sale; *~ **na śmierć*** to be executed

przezornie *adv* far-sightedly, wisely; **przezorność** *f* (*-ści*; *no pl*) foresight, caution; **przezorny** *adj* far-sighted

przezrocz|e, ***prześrocze*** *n* (*-cza*; *-cza*) slide; ***odczyt z ~ami*** lecture illustrated with slides, lecture with a slide show

przezroczysty *adj* **1.** *szyba*: transparent **2.** *suknia*: see-through, transparent **3.** *płyn*: clear

przezwać *v/p* → ***przezywać***

przezwisko *n* (*-ka*; *-ka*) nickname

przezwyciężać ⟨**-żyć**⟩ (*-żam*) overcome; ***przezwyciężać się*** control oneself

przezwyciężeni|e *n* (*-nia*; *no pl*) overcoming; ***nie do ~a*** impossible to overcome, not to be overcome

przezywać ⟨**-zwać**⟩ (*-wam*) **1.** (*nadawać przezwisko*) nickname **2.** (*ubliżać*) call (s.o.) names; ***przezywać się*** call each other names

przeźrocze → ***przezrocze***

przeżegnać *v/p* (*-nam*) cross; ***przeżegnać się*** cross oneself, make the sign of the cross

przeżerać ⟨**-żreć**⟩ (*-ram*) (*o rdzy, kwasie*) corrode, eat away

przeżuwacz *m* (*-cza*; *-cze*) BIOL ruminant

przeżuwać ⟨**-żuć**⟩ (*-wam*) **1.** *kęs*: chew **2.** BIOL ruminate

przeżyci|e *n* (*-cia*; *-cia*) **1.** experience; ***bogaty w ~a*** experienced **2.** ***ich ~e zależało od pogody*** their survival depended upon the weather

przeżyć *v/p* → ***przeżywać***

przeżytek *m* (*-tku*; *-tki*) anachronism; **przeżyty** *adj* outdated

przeżywać ⟨**-żyć**⟩ (*-wam*) **1.** (*doświadczać*) experience; ***przeżywał mocno film*** he took the film very emotionally; ***przeżywał egzamin*** he was very stressed out because ofhis exam; *~ **szok*** get a shock **2.** *przygodę*: have **3.** (*przetrwać*) survive **4.** (*pogodzić się*) get over, live down; *~ **kryzys*** come through a crisis; *~ **rozstanie z*** *I* be very upset after breaking up with, get over a parting with; ***przeżywał bardzo śmierć żony*** he could not get over his wife's death; ***jakoś to przeżyję!*** *iron* I shall come through this somehow! **5.** (*żyć dłużej*) outlive; ***przeżywać się*** fall out off ashion, become outdated

przędza *f* (*-dzy*; *-dzy*) yarn; *~ **dziewiarska*** knitting yarn; **przędzalnia** *f* (*-ni*; *-nie*) (*zakład*) spinning mill; **prządzarka** *f* (*-ki*;*-ki*) **1.** (*maszyna*) spinning frame **2.** (*osoba*) spinner

przęsło *n* (*-ła*; *-ła*) *mostu*: span

przodek[1] *m* (*-dka*; *-dkowie*) ancestor

przod|ek[2] *m* (*-dka*/*-dku*; *-dki*) (*w kopalni*) coalface, mine face; ***pracować na ~ku*** work at the coalface

przodować *v/im* (*-duję*) excel (**w** *L* at)

przodownictwo *n* (*-wa*; *no pl*) leadership

przodownik *m* (*-ka*; *-nicy*): *~ **pracy*** HIST *a model worker working better and much faster than others*, shock worker

przodujący *adj* leading

P

przód *m* (*przodu*; *przody*) **1.** *budynku*: front; **w ~**, **do przodu** forward; **od przodu**, **z przodu** in front; **na przodzie** at the front; **usiądź przodem do mnie!** sit facing me!; **iść przodem** lead the way; **puścić kogoś przodem** let s.o. go first; **włożyć coś tył na ~** put s.th. on back to front; **być 10 dolarów do przodu** *infml* be $10 in pocket **2.** *statku*: bow **3.** *samolotu*: nose

prztycz|ek: **dać komuś ~ka** (**w nos**) flick s.o.'s nose

prztykać ⟨**-knąć**⟩ (*-kam*): **~ palcami** snap (one's fingers)

przy *prep* (*L*) **1.** (*obok*, *podczas*) at; **~ stole** at the table; **~ tym** at the same time; **~ śniadaniu** at breakfast; **~ pracy** at work; **być ~ pieniądzach** *infml* be loaded; **~ odrobinie szczęścia** with a bit ofluck **2.** (*w okolicznościach*) by; **~ okazji** by the way; **~ świecach** by candlelight **3.** (*posiadanie*) on; **mam to ~ sobie** I have got it on me; **~ ulicy Mokotowskiej** in/on Mokotowska street **4.** (*podczas*) while; **~ czym** while; **~ goleniu** while shaving **5.** (*w obecności*) in front of, in the presence of; **~ świadkach** in the presence ofwitnesses

przybić *v/p* → **przybijać**

przybiegać ⟨**-biec**⟩ (*-gam*) come running; **~ do mety** SPORT finish the race

przybierać ⟨**-brać**⟩ (*-ram*) **I** *v/t* **1.** *stół*, *choinkę*: decorate **2.** COOK garnish **3.** *kształt*, *pozę*: assume; **sprawy przybrały zły obrót** the matters took a turn for the worse **4.** *minę*: make **II** *v/i* (*o rzece*) rise; **~ na wadze** put on weight; **~ na sile** grow stronger

przybijać ⟨**-bić**⟩ (*-jam*) **1.** *gwóźdź*: hammer, drive **2.** *tabliczkę*, *deskę*: nail **3.** *pieczęć*: put **4.** (*dopłynąć*) reach

przybitka *f* (*-ki*; *-ki*) (*na aukcji*) knockdown

przybity *adj fig* crestfallen, dejected

przyblednąć *v/p* (*-nę*) **1.** (*o osobie*) turn pale **2.** (*o kolorze*) fade

przybliżać ⟨**-żyć**⟩ (*-żam*) **1.** (*przysuwać*) bring closer (**do** *G* to) **2.** *zwycięstwo*: bring nearer **3.** (*w optyce*) magnify **4.** (*opisywać*) describe; **przybliż nam jego sylwetkę** tell us a few words about him; **przybliżać się** come closer; **~ się do siebie** *fig* get closer

przybliżeni|e *n* (*-nia*; *-nia*) approximation; **w ~u** approximately; **przybliżony** *adj data*, *wynik*: approximate

przybłąkać się *v/p* (*-kam*) (*o psie*) show up, be found

przybłęda *f/m* (*-dy*; *-dy*) **1.** (*zwierzę*) waif, stray; **pies ~** stray dog **2.** (*człowiek*) tramp, bum

przyboczn|y *adj*: **oficer ~y** adjutant; **straż ~a** lifeguard

przybornik *m* (*-ka*; *-ki*) kit; **~ do szycia** sewing kit

przybój *m* (*-boju*; *no pl*) surf

przybory *pl* (*-rów*) implements *pl*; **~ toaletowe** toiletries, toilet articles; **~ do golenia** shaving kit; **~ do pisania** writing implements, stationery; **~ do szycia** sewing kit

przybór *m* (*-boru*; *-bory*) *wody*: rise (in water level)

przybrać *v/p* → **przybierać**

przybranie *n* (*-nia*; *-nia*) **1.** COOK garnish **2.** (*ozdoba*) decoration; **kwiaty z ~m** flowers with all the trimmings

przybran|y *adj* COOK garnished (*I* with); **~e dziecko** adopted child; **~i rodzice** adoptive parents; **~e nazwisko a)** (*fałszywe*) assumed name **b)** *artysty*: stage name

przybrudzić się *v/p* (*-dzę*) (*o obrusie spodniach*) soil, dirty (a little)

przybrudzony *adj* lightly soiled

przybrzeżny *adj prąd*: nearshore coastal

przybudowywać ⟨**-dować**⟩ (*-dowuję*) BUILD build (an annex)

przybudówka *f* (*-ki*; *-ki*) BUILD *Br* annexe, *Am* annex, extension

przybyci|e *n* (*-cia*; *no pl*) *gości*, *delegacji*: arrival; **dziękuję państwu za ~e** thank you very much for coming **w chwili ~a** on arrival

przybyć *v/p* → **przybywać**

przybyły **I** *adj*: **nowo ~** newcomer, newly arrived; **właśnie ~** just arrived **II** *m* (*-łego*; *-byli*), **-ła** *f* (*-łej*; *-łe*) arrival; **nowo ~** newcomer

przybysz *m* (*-sza*; *-sze*) (new)comer; **~ kosmosu** extraterrestrial being; **~ z daleka** guest from afar

przybytek *m* (*-tku*; *-tki*) **1.** *energii*, *wagi*: increase **2.** REL church **3.** *sztuki kultury*: *Br* centre, *Am* center

P

przybywać ⟨**-być**⟩ (*-wam*) **1.** *do celu*: arrive; **~ z oficjalną wizytą** pay an official visit **2.** (*rosnąć*) increase; **przybyło nowych książek** we have more new books; **przybyło mu lat** he is getting older; **przybył mi jeden kilogram** I gained one kilogram; **przybyło wody** water level has risen; **przybyło mi kłopotów** I have got more trouble; **przybywa dnia** days are getting longer
przychodnia *f* (*-ni*; *-nie*) *zdrowia*: *Br* health centre, *Am* outpatient clinic; **~ rejonowa** community health center
przychodzić ⟨**przyjść**⟩ (*-dzę*) **1.** (*przybyć*) come (**do** *G* to); **~ po** *A* come to pick up; **~ z** *I* bring along; **~ do domu** come home; **~ na myśl** come to mind; **~ z trudem** come with difficulty; **do zdrowia** recover; **~ do siebie** come to oneself; **~ na świat** come into this world, be born; **przyszła mi ochota na coś** I feel like doing s.th. **2.** (*o liście*, *paczce*) arrive
przychód *m* (*-chodu*; *-chody*) income
przychówek *m* (*-wku*; *no pl*) **1.** (*zwierzęta*) the young **2.** (*dzieci*) *hum* small fry
przychylać się ⟨**-lić**⟩ (*-lam*) consent, accept; **~ do prośby** consent to s.o.'s request, grant s.o.'s request; **~ do propozycji** accept an offer
przychylność *f* (*-ści*; *no pl*) *Br* favour, *Am* favor; **pozyskać czyjąś ~** win s.o.'s favour; **przychylny** *adj* **1.** *osoba*: sympathetic **2.** *decyzja*, *odpowiedź*: *Br* favourable, *Am* favorable
przyciasny *adj ubranie*, *buty*: (a little) tight
przyciąć *v/p* → **przycinać**
przyciągać ⟨**-gnąć**⟩ (*-gam*) **1.** (*przysuwać*) pull closer **2.** *klientów*: attract; **~ czyjąś uwagę** attract s.o.'s attention; **przyciągać się** attract each other
przyciąganie *n* (*-nia*; *no pl*) attraction; **~ ziemskie** earth gravity
przycichać ⟨**-chnąć**⟩ (*-cham*) **1.** (*o stukocie*, *płaczu*) quiet down **2.** (*o sporach*) calm down, settle down; **afera przycichła** the scandal has calmed down, things (have) quieted down **3.** (*o deszczu*) let up
przyciemniać ⟨**-nić**⟩ (*-niam*) **1.** *kolor*: darken **2.** *światło*: turn down **3.** *włosy*: dye a little darker
przycierać ⟨**przytrzeć**⟩ (*-ram*) (*piłować*) file off; **~ komuś rogów** take s.o. down a peg
przyciężki *adj* **1.** *torba*: a little heavy **2.** *film*, *dowcip*: heavy, hard to understand
przycinać ⟨**-ciąć**⟩ (*-nam*) **1.** *materiał*: cut (to size); **przyciąć sobie język** bite one's tongue; **przyciąć sobie palec w drzwiach** catch one's finger in the door **2.** *drzewa*, *włosy*: trim **3.** taunt (*D*), jibe (*D* at)
przycinek *m* (*-nka*; *-nki*) jibe, gibe
przycisk *m* (*-ku*; *-ki*) **1.** *dzwonka*: button **2.** (*akcent*) stress; **z ~iem** *fig* with emphasis **3.** (*przedmiot*) weight; **~ do papieru** paperweight
przyciskać ⟨**-snąć**⟩ (*-kam*) **1.** *guzik*, *klamkę*: press (*A*); **~ do siebie** hug; **~ do** *G* press to **2.** (*zmuszać*) force; **~ kogoś do muru** drive s.o. to the wall
przyciszać ⟨**-szyć**⟩ (*-szam*) **1.** *głos*: lower **2.** *radio*: turn down
przyciszony *adj* **1.** *telewizor*: turned down low **2.** *głosy*: hushed, subdued
przyciszyć *v/p* → **przyciszać**
przycumować *v/p* (*-muję*) moor
przycupnąć *v/p* (*-nę*) perch; **~ na brzegu ławki** sit on the edge ofa bench
przyczajać się ⟨**-czaić**⟩ (*-jam*) **1.** (*czatować*) lie in wait **2.** (*chować się*) lurk
przyczajony *adj* lurking
przyczepa *f* (*-py*; *-py*) *samochodu*: trailer; **~ kempingowa** *Br* caravan, *Am* trailer
przyczepiać ⟨**-pić**⟩ (*-piam*) attach (**do** *G* to); **przyczepiać się 1.** (*przywrzeć*) stick (**do** *G* to) **2.** (*czepiać się*) pick on (*G* s.o.); **przyczepił się do niej jak rzep do psiego ogona** he sticks to her like a leech, he follows her about
przyczepk|a *f* (*-ki*; *-ki*) *motocykla*: sidecar; **jechać z kimś na ~ę** tag along with s.o.
przyczepność *f* (*-ści*; *no pl*) **1.** *nawierzchni*: adhesion **2.** *opon*: traction; **przyczepny** *adj* **1.** (*dający się przyczepić*) attachable **2.** AUTO adhesive
przyczerniać ⟨**-nić**⟩ (*-niam*) *włosy*: dye one's hair dark
przyczesywać się ⟨**-sać**⟩ (*-suję*) comb one's hair (quickly)
przyczołgać się *v/p* (*-gam*) come crawling

P

przyczółek *m* (*-łka*; *-łki*) **1.** (*w wojsku*) bridgehead **2.** ARCHIT gable

przyczyn|a *f* (*-ny*; *-ny*) **1.** reason; ***z tej ~y*** for that reason; ***z jakiej ~y*** why, for what reason; ***z niewiadomych ~*** for reasons unknown, for unknown reasons **2.** *choroby*, *wypadku*: cause; ***~a katastrofy*** cause ofthe disaster

przyczynek *m* (*-nku*; *-nki*) contribution

przyczyniać ⟨**-nić**⟩ (*-niam*) *zmartwień*, *radości*: bring; **przyczyniać się** contribute (**do** *G* to)

przyczynienie się *n* (*-nia*; *no pl*) contribution

przyczynowy *adj* causal; ***związek ~*** causal connection

przyćmiewać ⟨**-mić**⟩ (*-wam*) **1.** *niebo*: darken **2.** *światło*: dim **3.** (*przewyższyć*) overshadow, eclipse

przyćmiony *adj światło*: dim, subdued

przydać *v/p* → **przydawać**

przydarzać się ⟨**-rzyć**⟩ (*-rzam*) happen

przydatki *pl* (*-ków*) ANAT appendages

przydatnoś|ć *f* (*-ści*; *no pl*) usefulness; ***data ~ci do spożycia*** use-by date; ***~ć do pracy zawodowej*** suitability for work; **przydatny** *adj* useful (**do** *G* for); ***~ do spożycia*** fit to eat

przydawać ⟨**-dać**⟩ (*-daję*) *lit* lend; ***~ komuś powagi*** lend authority to; **przydawać się** come in useful, be of use (**do** *G*/**na** *A* for); ***to może się jeszcze przydać*** this may come in handy in the future; ***w podróży na pewno przyda ci się termos*** a thermos will surely be very handy during the trip; ***przydałoby się zrobić zakupy*** it would be a good idea to do the shopping; ***to mu się na niewiele przydało*** it did not help him much; ***to na nic się nie przyda*** this is useless, it won't help

przydawka *f* (*-ki*; *-ki*) GRAM attributive; **przydawkowy** *adj* attributive

przydech *m* (*-chu*; *no pl*) (*w fonetyce*) aspiration

przydeptywać ⟨**-tać**⟩ (*-tuję*) *sukienkę*, *niedopałek*: step, tread (*A* on)

przydługi *adj lekcja*: lengthy, a bit too long; **przydługo** *adv* a bit too long

przydomek *m* (*-mka*/*-mku*; *-mki*) nickname

przydomowy *adj* adjoining to the house; ***ogródek ~*** **a)** front garden **b)** back garden

przydrożn|y *adj* roadside; ***rów ~y*** roadside ditch; ***kapliczka ~a*** roadside shrine

przyduszać ⟨**-sić**⟩ (*-szam*) **1.** *do muru*: press **2.** (*przygniatać*) crush; ***~ kogoś swoim ciężarem*** crush s.o. with one's own weight **3.** *ogień*: stifle

przyduży *adj* slightly too big, a bit too large

przydybać *v/p* (*-bię*) catch (**na** *L* doing s.th.)

przydział *m* (*-łu*; *-ły*) **1.** *zadań*: assignment **2.** *pieniędzy*: allocation, allowance **3.** *żywności*: ration **4.** *do grupy*: placement

przydzielać ⟨**-lić**⟩ (*-lam*) **1.** *zajęcie*: assign **2.** *pieniądze*: allocate

przyfabryczny *adj* factory

przyfrontowy *adj* frontline

przygadywać ⟨**-dać**⟩ (*-duję*) gibe (*D* at); ***przygadać sobie dziewczynę*** chat up a girl

przygana *f* (*-ny*; *-ny*) rap

przyganiać[1] ⟨**-nić**⟩ (*-niam*) rap; ***przyganiał kocioł garnkowi*** (it's) the pot calling the kettle black

przyganiać[2] ⟨**-gnać**⟩ (*-niam*) *krowy*: drive in

przygarbić się *v/p* (*-bię*) *ze starości*: to be hunched; **przygarbiony** *adj plecy*: hunched, bent

przygarniać ⟨**-nąć**⟩ (*-niam*) **1.** (*tulić*) hug **2.** (*dać przytułek*) take in

przygasać ⟨**-snąć**⟩ (*-sam*) **1.** (*o ogniu*, *świecy*) go out **2.** (*o blasku*, *emocjach*) wane, wear off **3.** (*o popularności*, *zainteresowaniu*) wane

przygasły *adj oczy*: dimmed, cloudy, weary

przygaszać ⟨**-sić**⟩ (*-szam*) **1.** *ogień*: stifle **2.** *światło*: turn down, turn off some lights; ***~ kogoś*** *fig* stand a head above s.o., be superior

przygaszony *adj światło*, *kolor*, *osoba*: subdued

przyginać ⟨**-giąć**⟩ (*-nam*) bend

przyglądać się ⟨**przyjrzeć**⟩ (*-dam*) watch, observe (*D* s.th.); ***~ z uwagą*** look carefully (*D* at)

przygładzać ⟨**-dzić**⟩ (*-dzam*) smooth (down)

przygłuchy *adj* hard ofhearing

przygłup *m* (*-pa*; *-py*) *infml* moron, butthead

P

przygłuszać ⟨**-szyć**⟩ (*-szam*) shade, shadow
przygnać *v/p* (*-nam*) (*przybiec*) come running; → **przyganiać²**
przygnębiać ⟨**-bić**⟩ (*-biam*) depress
przygnębiający *adj* depressing; **przygnębienie** *n* (*-nia*; *no pl*) depression; **przygnębiony** *adj* **1.** (*smutny*) depressed **2.** *mina*: long, unhappy
przygniatać ⟨**-nieść**⟩ (*-tam*) **1.** *ciężarem*: crush **2.** *niedopałek*: put out **3.** *fig* overwhelm
przygniatający *adj przewaga*, *cisza*, *smutek*: overwhelming
przygnieciony *adj* overwhelmed (*I* by)
przygnieść *v/p* → **przygniatać**
przyg|oda *f* (*-dy*; *-dy*) adventure; **~oda miłosna** love affair; **pełen ~ód** adventurous
przygodny *adj* **1.** *romans*, *znajomość*: casual **2.** *świadek*, *słuchacz*: accidental
przygodowy *adj film*, *książka*: adventure
przygotować *v/p* → **przygotowywać**
przygotowania *pl* (*-wań*) preparations; **przygotowany** *adj* **1.** (*gotowy*) prepared **2.** COOK ready; **przygotowawczy** *adj* preparatory
przygotowywać ⟨**-tować**⟩ (*-towuję*) **1.** *wykład*, *przyjęcie*: prepare **2.** COOK make, cook; **~ na** *A*/**do** *G* prepare for; **przygotowywać się 1.** get ready **2.** *do egzaminu*: *Br* revise, *Am* review; **~ się do podróży** get ready for the journey; **~ się na najgorsze** prepare for the worst; **~ się na śmierć** *lit* get ready to die
przygraniczny *adj handel*, *obszar*: border
przygruby *adj* slightly too fat, on the chubby side
przygruntow|y *adj*: **~e przymrozki** ground frost
przygrywać *v/im* (*-wam*) MUS accompany
przygrywka *f* (*-ki*; *-ki*) **1.** MUS intro, introduction **2.** (*przedsmak*) prelude
przygryzać ⟨**-ryźć**⟩ (*-zam*) bite; **~ wargi** bite one's lips; **przygryźć sobie język** bite one's tongue; **~ komuś** taunt s.o.
przygrzewać ⟨**-rzać**⟩ (*-wam*) **I** *v/i* (*o słońcu*) beat down **II** *v/t* COOK heat up
przygważdżać ⟨**-woździć**⟩ (*-dżam*) nail down
przyhamowywać ⟨**-mować**⟩ (*-mowuję*) AUTO slow down
przyimek *m* (*-mka*; *-mki*) GRAM preposition; **przyimkowy** *adj* prepositional
przyjaciel *m* (*-la*; *-le*) **1.** (*zaprzyjaźniona osoba*) friend; **~ domu** friend of the family, family friend; **~ zwierząt** animal lover **2.** (*kochanek*) partner, boyfriend
przyjacielski *adj* friendly
przyjaciółka *f* (*-ki*; *-ki*) **1.** (*zaprzyjaźniona osoba*) friend; **~ od serca** special friend, best friend **2.** (*kochanka*) partner, girlfriend
przyjazd *m* (*-du*; *-dy*) *pociągu*, *gości*: arrival
przyjazn|y *adj* **1.** *atmosfera*, *osoba*: friendly; **~y dla środowiska** environment-friendly; **~a dusza** soul mate; **~a dłoń** helping hand **2.** *wiatr*: favourable
przyjaźnić się *v/im* (*-nię*) be friends (**z** *I* with)
przyjaźń *f* (*-źni*; *-źnie*) friendship
przyjąć *v/p* → **przyjmować**
przyjechać *v/p* → **przyjeżdżać**
przyjemnie *adv*: **bardzo mi ~!** very nice to meet you!; **~ pachnący** nice-smelling; → **przyjemny**
przyjemnoś|ć *f* (*-ści*; *-ści*) pleasure; **dla ~ci** for pleasure; **to sprawia mi (wielką) ~ć** I take (great) pleasure in it; **znaleźć ~ć** take pleasure (**w** *L* in); **to nie należy do ~ci**, **to średnia ~ć** it is not really enjoyable; **mam ~ć** I have the pleasure (of); **cała ~ć po mojej stronie** my pleasure, the pleasure is all mine; **z kim mam ~ć?** with whom do I have the pleasure?; **z ~cią!** with pleasure!
przyjemn|y *adj* **1.** *głos*, *osoba*, *chłód*: nice; **~ej zabawy!** have a good time!, enjoy yourself! **2.** *uczucie*, *wrażenie*, *zapach*: pleasant; **~y w smaku** tasty; **~y dla ucha** pleasing to the ear **3.** *mieszkanie*: cosy
przyjezdny I *adj* visiting **II** *m* (*-nego*; *-ni*), **-na** *f* (*-nej*; *-ne*) stranger; **dla ~ch** for visitors
przyjeżdżać ⟨**-jechać**⟩ (*-dżam*) **1.** arrive **2.** come; **~ samochodem** come by car; **~ pociągiem** come by train; **~ do kogoś z wizytą** come to visit s.o.
przyję|cie *n* (*-cia*; *-cia*) **1.** (*oficjalne*) reception; **~cie weselne** wedding recep-

tion **2.** (*towarzyskie*) party; **~cie urodzinowe** birthday party; **wydać ~cie** give a party, hold a party **3.** (*przywitanie*) welcome; **serdeczne ~cie**, **gościnne ~cie** warm welcome **4.** *do szkoły*: admission; **~cie do pracy** employment; **nie do ~cia** unacceptable; **godziny ~ć** (*u lekarza*) office hours; **izba ~ć** admission room

przyjęt|y *adj* **1.** *zwyczaj*: established; **jest ~e** it is customary **2.** *kandydat*: admitted; **~y do pracy** employed

przyjmować ⟨**-jąć**⟩ (*-muję*) **1.** *zaproszenie*, *pieniądze*, *nagrodę*: accept; **~ na siebie** take over; **~ coś do wiadomości** take note of s.th.; **książkę przyjęto do druku** the book will go to press; **~ coś za dobrą monetę** take s.th. at face value **2.** *pokarm*: take in **3.** *obywatelstwo*, *delegację*: receive **4.** *lek*, *wiadomość*: take **5.** *uchodźców*, *bezdomnych*, *nowego członka*: admit **6.** *pracownika*: employ **7.** *gościa*, *interesanta*: receive **8.** *wniosek*: adopt; **przyjmować się 1.** BIOL take root **2.** (*o przeszczepie*) take

przyjrzeć się *v/p* → **przyglądać się**

przyjście *n* (*-cia*; *no pl*) coming; **~ do zdrowia** recovery; **~ na świat** birth

przyjść *v/p* → **przychodzić**

przykaza|nie *n* (*-nia*; *-nia*) REL commandment; **dziesięć ~ń**, **dziesięcioro ~ń** REL the Ten Commandments

przykazywać ⟨**-zać**⟩ (*-zuję*) command, order; **~ coś komuś** command s.o. to do s.th.; **~ milczenie** *lit* order s.o. to be silent

P

przyklaskiwać ⟨**-snąć**⟩ (*-kuję*) *pomysłowi*, *projektowi*: applaud

przyklejać ⟨**-leić**⟩ (*-jam*) stick; **~ znaczek** put on a stamp; **przyklejać się** stick (**do** *G* to)

przyklękać ⟨**-knąć**⟩ (*-kam*) kneel down

przykład *m* (*-du*; *-dy*) (*wzór*) example; **na ~** for example, for instance; **typowy ~** typical example; **brać z kogoś ~** follow s.o.'s example; **dla ~u** as an example; **świecić ~em** *lit* set a good example; **ukarać kogoś dla ~u** punish s.o. as a warning

przykładać ⟨**przyłożyć**⟩ (*-dam*) **1.** (*zbliżyć*) put (**do** *G* against); **~ wagę do** *G* attach importance to; **ja nie przyłożę do tego ręki** *fig* I won't have anything to do with it **2.** *opatrunek*: put on; **przykładać się** apply oneself

przykładny *adj* model, exemplary

przykładowo *adv* for example; **przykładowy** *adj* **1.** *sytuacja*: hypothetical **2.** *test*: sample **3.** (*typowy*) exemplary

przykościelny *adj* church

przykracać ⟨**-rócić**⟩ (*-cam*): **~ komuś cugli** keep a tight rein on

przykręcać ⟨**-cić**⟩ (*-cam*) **1.** *śrubę*: tighten (**do** *G* on) **2.** *kran*, *gaz*: turn down; **~ komuś śrubę** *infml* tighten the screws on

przykro *adv*: **bardzo mi ~!** I'm so sorry!; **~ mi, ale** I'm sorry, but; **zrobiło mu się ~ a)** he was sorry (**za** *A* about) **b)** he felt sorry (**za siebie** for himself); **~ na to patrzeć** this is a sorry sight, it's an eyesore

przykroś|ć *f* (*-ści*; *-ści*) (*nieprzyjemność*) unpleasantness; **~ci** (*kłopoty*) trouble, distress; **sprawić komuś ~ć** make s.o. very sad; **mieć ~ci** have trouble; **z ~cią muszę stwierdzić, że** I regret to inform you that

przykrócić *v/p* → **przykracać**

przykrótki *adj* shortish

przykry *adj* **1.** *zapach*, *sytuacja*, *skutki uboczne*: unpleasant **2.** *niespodzianka*: nasty **3.** *rozmowa*, *doświadczenie*, *wspomnienia*: sad **4.** *człowiek*: ugly, ill-natured **5.** *widok*: sorry, pitiful

przykrycie *n* (*-cia*; *-cia*) **1.** (*koc*) cover **2.** (*obrus*) tablecloth; **gotować pod ~m** cook in a covered pot; **przykrywa** *f* (*-wy*; *-wy*) *garnka*: lid

przykrywać ⟨**-ryć**⟩ (*-wam*) *dziecko*: cover; **~ garnek** put a lid on a pot; **przykrywać się** cover oneself(*I* with)

przykrywk|a *f* (*-ki*; *-ki*) lid; **pod ~ą** *G fig* under the guise of

przykrzyć się *v/im*: **przykrzy mi się bez ciebie** I miss you; **przykrzy mi się** I am bored; **przykrzy mi się to długie czekanie** having to wait is so boring

przykucać ⟨**-cnąć**⟩ (*-cam*) squat crouch down

przykuć *v/p* → **przykuwać**

przykuty *adj*: **~ do łóżka** *fig* bedridden

przykuwać ⟨**-kuć**⟩ (*-wam*) **1.** *łańcuchem*: chain (**do** *G* to) **2.** *uwagę*: rivet

przylać *v/p* (*-leję*): **~ komuś** spank s.o.

przylaszczka *f* (*-ki*; *-ki*) BIOL hepatica

przylatywać ⟨**-lecieć**⟩ (*-tuję*) **1.** (*o samolocie*) arrive **2.** (*przybywać*) come

~ samolotem come by airplane; **przyleciały już bociany** storks have already come; **przyleciałeś dopiero wczoraj** you flew in only yesterday **3.** (*do karmnika*) fly in

przylądek *m* (*-dka*; *-dki*) cape, headland; **~ Północny** North Cape

przylecieć *v/p* → **przylatywać**

przylegać *v/im* (*-gam*) **1.** (*przywierać*) stick (**do** *G* to) **2.** (*graniczyć*) adjoin (**do** *G*); **~ do siebie** adjoin each other, be next to each other; **przylegający** *adj*: **~ do ciała a)** *sukienka*: clingy, clinging **b)** *ubranie*: close-fitting

przyległości *pl* (*-ści*) outbuildings and adjacent land; **przyległy** *adj pokój*: adjacent, adjoining

przylepiać ⟨**-pić**⟩ (*-piam*) stick, glue; **przylepiać się** get stuck (**do** *G* to)

przylepiec *m* (*-pca*; *-pce*) *Br* sticking plaster, *Am* Band-Aid®

przylepka *f* (*-ki*; *-ki*) *infml* (*o osobie*) sweetie; **~ chleba** heel

przylepność *f* (*-ści*; *no pl*) adhesiveness

przyleźć *v/p* → **przyłazić**

przylgnąć *v/p* (*-nę*) cling (**do** *G* to); **~ do kogoś** cuddle up to s.o., hug s.o.

przylizać *v/p* (*-liżę*): **~ włosy** slick (down) one's hair

przylot *m* (*-tu*; *-ty*) **1.** *samolotu*: arrival **2.** *ptaków*: coming

przylutowywać ⟨**-tować**⟩ (*-towuję*) solder on

przyłapywać ⟨**-pać**⟩ (*-puję*) catch (**na** *L* doing s.th.); **przyłapać kogoś na gorącym uczynku** catch s.o. red-handed; **przyłapywać się** catch oneself

przyłazić ⟨**przyleźć**⟩ (*-łażę*) *pot* come along

przyłączać ⟨**-czyć**⟩ (*-czam*) **1.** (*dodawać*) attach (**do** *G* to) **2.** *CHEM* add **3.** (*do instalacji*) connect; **przyłączać się 1.** (*dołączyć do grupy*) join; **~ się do towarzystwa** join the company **2.** *CHEM* be added

przyłączenie *n* (*-nia*; *no pl*) connection

przyłbic|a *f* (*-cy*; *-ce*) *HIST* visor; **z podniesioną ~ą** *fig* openly

przyłożyć *v/p* (*-żę*) *infml*: **~ komuś** wack s.o., wallop s.o.; → **przykładać**

przymarzać ⟨**-znąć**⟩ (*-zam*) freeze (**do** *G* to)

przymawiać ⟨**-mówić**⟩ (*-wiam*): **~ komuś** jibe at s.o.

przymglony *adj dzień*, *wzrok*: misty

przymiarka *f* (*-ki*; *-ki*) fitting

przymierać *v/p* (*-ram*): **~ głodem** starve

przymierzać ⟨**-rzyć**⟩ (*-rzam*) *spodnie*, *buty*: try on; **przymierzać się** get ready (**do** *G* for); **~ się do strzału** take aim; **przymierzalnia** *f* (*-ni*; *-nie*) fitting room

przymierz|e *n* (*-rza*; *-rza*) *POLIT* alliance; **Arka ~a** *REL* Arc ofthe Covenant

przymilać się *v/im* (*-lam*) coax (**do** *G* s.o.), endear oneself(**do** *G* to)

przymilny *adj* endearing

przymioty *pl* (*-tów*) *lit* qualities *pl*

przymiotnik *m* (*-ka*; *-ki*) adjective; **przymiotnikowy** *adj* adjectival

przymknąć *v/p* (*-nę*) leave ajar; **przymknij się!** *infml* shut up!; → **przymykać**

przymocowywać ⟨**-cować**⟩ (*-cowuję*) fasten, fix

przymówić *v/p* → **przymawiać**

przymówka *f* (*-ki*; *-ki*) sharp remark, stinging remark

przymroz|ek *m* (*-zka*; *-zki*) light frost; **przygruntowe ~ki** ground frost

przymrużać ⟨**-żyć**⟩ (*-żam*) *oczy*: squint

przymurówka *f* (*-ki*; *-ki*) *BUILD* **1.** (*przybudówka*) *Br* annexe, *Am* annex **2.** (*mur*) (extra) supporting wall

przymus *m* (*-su*; *no pl*) **1.** (*moralny*) compulsion **2.** (*naciski*) coercion **3.** (*fizyczny*) constraint **4.** *JUR* duress; **pod ~em** under duress

przymusić *v/p* → **przymuszać**

przymusow|y *adj* **1.** *pobyt*: enforced; **~e roboty** *HIST* forced labour; **~e lądowanie** forced landing; **środki ~e** *JUR* force **2.** *składka*, *leczenie*: compulsory

przymuszać ⟨**-sić**⟩ (*-szam*) force (**do** *G* to do s.th.); **przymuszać się** force oneself

przymuszony *adj* forced

przymykać ⟨**-mknąć**⟩ (*-kam*) *drzwi*, *okno*: leave ajar; **~ na coś oczy** *fig* overlook s.th., turn a blind eye to

przynaglać ⟨**-lić**⟩ (*-lam*) urge

przynajmniej *particle* at least

przynależność *f* (*-ści*; *no pl*) affiliation; **~ państwowa** nationality

przynęta *f* (*-ty*; *-ty*) bait

przynosić ⟨**-nieść**⟩ (*-szę*) **1.** *torbę*: bring; **~ ze sobą** bring along **2.** *zyski*: yield

P

przyobiecywać ⟨**-cać**⟩ (*-cuję*) *lit* promise; ~ **sobie** promise oneself

przyodziewać ⟨**-dziać**⟩ (*-wam*) *lit* clothe; **przyodziewać się** *lit* clothe

przyozdabiać ⟨**-dobić**⟩ (*-biam*) adorn

przypadać ⟨**-paść**⟩ (*-dam*) fall (**do** *G* to, **na** *A* to); **przypadło mu to do gustu** he took a liking to it; ~ **komuś w udziale** fall to; **święto przypada w czwartek** the holiday falls on Thursday; **przypadł jej do serca** she got to like him, she took to him

przypadek *m* (*-dku*; *-dki*) **1.** (*traf*) coincidence **2.** (*zdarzenie*) incident; **przez** ~ by accident; **w najlepszym przypadku** at best **3.** (*-dka*; *-dki*) GRAM case

przypadkiem *adv* by chance, by accident, accidentaly; **przypadkowo** *adv* accidentally; **przypadkowy** *adj* accidental

przypadłość *f* (*-ści*; *-ści*) ailment

przypalać ⟨**-lić**⟩ (*-lam*) **1.** *spodnie*, *włosy*: singe **2.** COOK burn **3** *papierosa*: light; **przypalać się** COOK get burnt

przypasywać ⟨**-sać**⟩ (*-suję*) **1.** *fartuch*: buckle up one's belt **2.** *miecz*: gird (on); **przypasywać się** strap oneself (**do** *G* to)

przypaść *v/p* → **przypadać**

przypatrywać się ⟨**-rzeć**⟩ (*-ruję*) → **przyglądać się**

przypełzać ⟨**-znąć**⟩ (*-zam*) (*o wężu*) come crawling

przypędzać ⟨**-dzić**⟩ (*-dzam*) **I** *v/t krowy*: drive in **II** *v/t* **przypędzić** come running

przypiąć *v/p* → **przypinać**

przypiec *v/p* → **przypiekać**

przypiecek *m* (*-cka*; *-cki*) *a bench around a stove for sitting or sleeping*

przypieczętować *v/p* (*-tuję*) seal

przypiekać ⟨**-piec**⟩ (*-kam*) **I** *v/t* **1.** *kartofle*: roast **II** *v/i* **2.** (*o słońcu*) beat down

przypieprzać ⟨**-rzyć**⟩ (*-rzam*) *infml* **1.** (*uderzyć mocno*) wallop **2.** (*pobić*) beat the shit out of; **przypieprzać się**: ~ **do** *G* get on s.o.'s back

przypierać ⟨**-przeć**⟩ (*-ram*) press (**do** *G* against/to); ~ **kogoś do muru** drive s.o. up the wall, push s.o. to the wall

przypil|ać ⟨**-lić**⟩ (*-lam*) *infml* urge; **co cię tak ~iło?** what's the sudden urge?; **~iło go** he was taken short, he was desperate for a pee

przypilnować *v/p* (*-nuję*) **1.** *dziecka*: look after (for a while) **2.** *walizki*: watch, take care of **3.** (*dopilnować*) see to

przypinać ⟨**-piąć**⟩ (*-nam*) **1.** *odznakę*, *broszkę*: pin (**do** *G* to); ~ **komuś łatkę** *fig* pigeonhole s.o., have a dig at; ~ **się pasami** strap oneself **2.** *narty*: put on

przypisek *m* (*-ska*/*-sku*; *-ski*) (*w liście*) postscript; **przypisy** *pl* (*-sów*) **1.** (*na dole tekstu*) footnote **2.** (*na końcu tekstu*) endnote **3.** (*wyjaśnienia do tekstu*) annotations *pl*

przypisywać ⟨**-sać**⟩ (*-suję*) ascribe; ~ **komuś winę** accuse s.o.

przyplątywać się ⟨**-tać**⟩ (*-tuję*) **1.** (*o osobie*) come along (uninvited); **przyplątała mu się grypa** he caught a flu **2.** (*o psie*) stray in, stray along

przypłacać ⟨**-cić**⟩ (*-cam*): ~ **coś życiem** pay with one's life for s.th.; **przypłacił sukces chorobą** illness has been the price for his success

przypłynąć *v/p* → **przypływać**

przypływ *m* (*-wu*; *-wy*) *morza*: (high) tide; **~y i odpływy** high and low tides; ~ **energii** burst ofenergy; **w ~wie radości** in a flush of joy

przypływać ⟨**-łynąć**⟩ (*-wam*) **1.** (*o osobie*) swim up; ~ **do brzegu** swim ashore **2.** (*o statku*) arrive; ~ **do brzegu** reach the shore

przypochlebiać się ⟨**-bić**⟩ (*-biam*) fawn (up) (*D* on), flatter (*D* s.o.)

przypodobać się *v/p* (*-bam*): ~ **komuś** ingratiate oneselfwith s.o., endear oneselfto s.o.

przypominać ⟨**-mnieć**⟩ (*-nam*) remind (**komuś** *A* s.o. of, **komuś o** *L* s.o. of); ~ **sobie** recall, remember; **nie przypominam sobie** I do not remember; ~ **komuś, żeby coś zrobił** remind s.o. to do s.th.; **przypominać się**: **już mi się przypomniało** I remember now; ~ **się komuś** recall oneselfto

przypomnienie *n* (*-nia*; *-nia*) reminding, reminder

przypora *f* (*-ry*; *-ry*) ARCHIT butress

przypowiastka *f* (*-ki*; *-ki*) anecdote; **przypowieść** *f* (*-ści*; *-ści*) parable

P

przypraw|a *f* (*-wy*; *-wy*) **1.** *ziołowa*: seasoning; **~a do zup** soup seasoning **2.** *korzenna*: spice; **ostre ~y** hot spices
przyprawiać ⟨**-wić**⟩ (*-wiam*) **1.** COOK spice (up) (*I* with), season; **~ do smaku** season to taste; **~ o mdłości** make s.o. sick; **~ o zawrót głowy** make s.o. dizzy; **~ komuś rogi** *fig* cuckold s.o. **2.** (*przymocować*) fix (**do** *G* to), attach; **~ sobie wąsy** stick on a false moustache
przyprostokątna *f* (*-nej*; *-ne*) MATH cathetus
przyprowadzać ⟨**-dzić**⟩ (*-dzam*) *osobę, zwierzę*: bring (along); **~ kogoś ze sobą** bring s.o. along; **~ kogoś do przedszkola** take s.o. to nursery school; **~ kogoś do domu** bring s.o. home
przyprószon|y *adj*: **~y śniegiem** snow-covered; **~y pyłem** sprinkled with dust; **włosy ~e siwizną** hoary hair, frosty hair
przyprzeć *v/p* → **przypierać**
przypudrować *v/p* (*-ruję*) *nos, czoło*: powder
przypuszczać ⟨**-puścić**⟩ (*-czam*) **I** *v/t* (*przeprowadzać*) launch; **~ szturm na** *A* launch an attack on, carry out an assault on **II** *v/i* (*snuć domysły*) suppose; **kto by przypuszczał, że** who would ever assume that; **przypuśćmy** let's say it's true; **przypuśćmy, że** let's assume that
przypuszczający *adj*: **tryb ~** GRAM conditional mood
przypuszczalny *adj* **1.** *powód*: presumable **2.** *wynik*: estimated; **~ wynik rozmów** likely outcome ofthe talks **3.** *sprawca*: suspected **4.** *kandydat*: likely; **przypuszczenie** *n* (*-nia*; *-nia*) presumption
przypuścić *v/p* → **przypuszczać**
przyrastać ⟨**-rosnąć**⟩ (*-tam*) **1.** (*do podłoża*) adhere (**do** *G* to) **2.** (*zwiększyć liczebność*) increase
przyrod|a *f* (*-dy*; *no pl*) **1.** (*natura*) nature; **ochrona ~y** nature conservation, environmental protection **2.** (*przedmiot*) natural science
przyrodni *adj*: half, step-; **~ brat** half-brother; **~a siostra** half-sister
przyrodniczy *adj* **1.** *film*: nature **2.** *nauki*: natural; **przyrodnik** *m* (*-ka*; *-nicy*) naturalist, (natural) scientist
przyrodolecznictwo *n* (*-wa*; *no pl*) physical therapy; **przyrodoznawstwo** *n* (*-wa*; *no pl*) natural history
przyrodzenie *n* (*-nia*; *-nia*) privates *pl*, privy parts *pl*
przyrodzony *adj lit* innate, inborn
przyrosnąć *v/p* → **przyrastać**
przyrost *m* (*-tu*; *-ty*) growth; **~ naturalny** population growth; **ujemny ~ naturalny** negative birth-rate
przyrostek *m* (*-tka*; *-tki*) suffix
przyrównywać ⟨**-nać**⟩ (*-nuję*) *lit* compare, liken (**do** *G* to); **przyrównywać się** compare oneself
przyrząd *m* (*-du*; *-dy*) device; **~ pomiarowy** measuring instrument, gauge; **~ gimnastyczny** gymnastics apparatus
przyrządzać ⟨**-dzić**⟩ (*-dzam*) COOK make, prepare
przyrzeczenie *n* (*-nia*; *-nia*) pledge; **przyrzekać** ⟨**-rzec**⟩ (*-kam*) promise; **~ sobie** promise oneself
przysadka *f* (*-ki*; *-ki*): **~ mózgowa** ANAT pituitary (gland)
przysadzisty *adj* stocky, dumpy
przysądzać ⟨**-dzić**⟩ (*-dzam*): **~ alimenty** JUR award alimony
przyschnięty *adj* dried off (a little)
przysiad *m* (*-du*; *-dy*) knee-bend; **robić ~y** make knee-bends; **z ~u** from squatting position
przysiadać ⟨**-siąść**⟩ (*-dam*) sit down (for a while); **~ na gałęzi** perch on a branch; **~ sobie spódnicę** sit on one's skirt; **~ z wrażenia** be flabbergasted; **przysiadać się**: **~ się do kogoś** join s.o.
przysiąc *v/p* → **przysięgać**
przysiąść *v/p* (*-siądę*): **~ fałdów** (*pilnie popracować*) buckle down; → **przysiadać**
przysięg|a *f* (*-gi*; *-gi*) oath; **pod ~ą** under oath; **~a wojskowa** military oath ofallegiance; **składać ~ę** take an oath
przysięgać ⟨**-siąc**⟩ (*-gam*) swear; **~ wierność** swear allegiance; **~ na konstytucję** swear by the constitution; **~ na Boga** swear by God; **mógłbym przysiąc** I could swear; **przysięgać się** swear
przysięgły **I** *adj tłumacz*: sworn, certified; **sędzia ~** juror **II** *m* (*-łego*; *-gli*), **-ła** *f* (*-łej*; *-łe*) juror; **ława ~ch** the jury

P

przyskakiwać ⟨**-skoczyć**⟩ (*-kuję*) jump; **~ do** *G* jump over to; **~ do drzwi** jump over to the door, run to the door
przyskrzynić *v/p* (*-nię*) *infml* **1.** (*przyłapać*) catch **2.** (*aresztować*) bust
przysłać *v/p* → **przysyłać**
przysłaniać ⟨**-łonić**⟩ (*-niam*) **1.** *twarz*: cover **2.** *lampę*: screen
przysłona *f* (*-ny*; *-ny*) *PHOT* diaphragm
przysłonić *v/p* → **przysłaniać**
przysłowie *n* (*-wia*; *-wia*) proverb; **przysłowiowy** *adj* proverbial
przysłówek *m* (*-wka*; *-wki*) adverb; **przysłówkowy** *adj* adverbial
przysłuchiwać się *v/im* (*-chuję*) *rozmowie*, *dyskusji*: listen (*D* to)
przysług|a *f* (*-gi*; *-gi*) *Br* favour, *Am* favor; **wyświadczyć komuś ~ę** do s.o. a favour; **wyświadczyć komuś niedźwiedzią ~ę** do s.o. disservice; **~a za ~ę** one good turn deserves another
przysługiwać *v/im* (*-guję*): **~ komuś** have the right (to); **przysługuje ci zniżka** you are entitled to a discount
przysłużyć się *v/p* (*-żę*) **1.** *osobie*: do s.o. a service **2.** *kulturze*: be ofservice
przysmak *m* (*-ku*; *-ki*) delicacy
przysmażać ⟨**-żyć**⟩ (*-żam*) f ry
przysnąć *v/p* → **przysypiać**
przysparzać ⟨**-porzyć**⟩ (*-rzam*) *kłopotów*: cause; **to przysporzyło mu sławy** this made him famous; **~ sobie wrogów** make enemies
przyspawać *v/p* (*-wam*) weld on
przyspieszać ⟨**-szyć**⟩ (*-szam*) **I** *v/t tempo*, *rozwój*: speed up; **~ poród** induce birth; **~ kroku** quicken one's pace **II** *v/i* (*o autobusie*) accelerate; **~ od 0 do 120 km w 10 sekund** go from 0 to 120 kph in 10 seconds
przyspieszenie *n* (*-nia*; *no pl*) **1.** *PHYS* acceleration; **~ ziemskie** gravitational acceleration, acceleration ofgravity **2.** *działań*: speeding up
przyspieszon|y *adj oddech*: quick; **~e wybory** *POLIT* early elections; **~y tryb** summary proceedings
przysporzyć *v/p* → **przysparzać**
przysposabiać ⟨**-sobić**⟩ (*-biam*) **1.** (*uczynić zdatnym*) adapt (**do** *G* for) **2.** (*przygotować*) prepare (**do** *G* for); **~ kogoś do** *G* train s.o. for; **~ do zawodu** train for a profession **3.** *JUR* adopt; **przysposabiać się** prepare (**do** *G* for)
przysposobienie *n* (*-nia*; *no pl*) *JUR* adoption; **~ zawodowe** (vocational) training
przyssać się *v/p* → **przysysać się**
przyssawka *f* (*-ki*; *-ki*) **1.** *BIOL* sucker **2.** *TECH* suction cup, sucker
przystać *v/p* → **przystawać¹**
przystanąć *v/p* → **przystawać²**
przystanek *m* (*-nku*; *-nki*) stop; **~ autobusowy** bus stop; **~ końcowy** terminus; **~ na żądanie** request stop
przystań *f* (*-tani*; *-tanie*) port, *Br* harbour, *Am* harbor; **~ dla żaglówek**, **~ jachtowa** marina; **~ promowa** ferry port
przystawać¹ ⟨**-tać**⟩ (*-taję*) **1.** (*zgadzać się*) consent (**na** *A* to) **2.** (*przylegać*) adhere (**do** *G* to); **deski przystają do siebie** the planks lie flat against each other; **okna nie przystają** the windows don't shut tight; **nie ~ do rzeczywistości** be unrealistic **3.** **jak przystało na żołnierza** as befits a soldier; **to nie przystoi** it is improper **4.** (*przyłączać się*) join
przystawać² ⟨**-tanąć**⟩ (*-taję*) (*zatrzymać się*) stop (for a while)
przystawiać ⟨**-wić**⟩ (*-wiam*) (*przysunąć*) put (**do** *G* against); **~ drabinę do ściany** put up the ladder against the wall; **przystawiać się do** *G infml* make a pitch for, make a pass at
przystawka *f* (*-ki*; *-ki*) *COOK* starter, hors d'oeuvre, appetizer
przystąpić *v/p* → **przystępować**
przystęp *m* (*-pu*; *no pl*) (*dostęp*) access; **w ~ie** *G* in a fit of; **przystępn|y** *adj* **1.** *osoba*: approachable **2.** *wykład*: accessible **3.** *język*, *styl*: plain **4.** *cena*: affordable; **po ~ej cenie** at a reasonable price
przystępować ⟨**-tąpić**⟩ (*-puję*) **1.** (*zaczynać*) begin, commence (**do** *G*); **~ do rzeczy** get down to business; **~ do komunii** *REL* go to First Communion **2.** (*przyłączyć się*) join; **~ do Unii Europejskiej** join the European Union; **~ do strajku** join the strike
przystoi → **przystawać**
przystojny *adj* handsome
przystosowanie *n* (*-nia*; *no pl*) **1.** *BIOL* adaptation **2.** *PSYCH* adjustment

P

przystosowywać ⟨**-sować**⟩ (*-wuję*) adapt (**do** *G* to); **przystosowywać się** adapt
przystrajać ⟨**-roić**⟩ (*-jam*) adorn (*I* with)
przystrzygać ⟨**-rzyc**⟩ (*-gam*) **1.** *żywopłot*: clip, trim **2.** *wąsy*: trim
przysuwać ⟨**-sunąć**⟩ (*-wam*) push nearer; **przysuwać się** move closer (**do** *G* to); **~ się do siebie** move closer to each other
przyswajać ⟨**-woić**⟩ (*-jam*) **1.** *wiedzę*: absorb **2.** *BIOL* assimilate **3.** *język*: learn **4.** *zwyczaj*: pick up; **~ sobie** *wiedzę, umiejętności*: acquire
przyswajanie *n* (*-nia*; *no pl*) *BIOL* assimilation
przyswoić *v/p* → **przyswajać**
przysyłać ⟨**-słać**⟩ (*-łam*) *kwiaty, pomoc, samochód*: send
przysypiać ⟨**-snąć**⟩ (*-piam*) nod off, drop off
przysypywać ⟨**-pać**⟩ (*-puję*) **1.** *dół*: fill up, fill in **2.** (*o lawinie, gruzach*) bury
przysysać się ⟨**przyssać**⟩ (*-sam*) cling (**do** *G* to)
przyszkolny *adj teren*: school; **przyszłoroczny** *adj* next year's
przyszłościow|y *adj*: **~e plany** plans for the future; **~y zawód** promising profession
przyszłoś|ć *f* (*-ści*; *no pl*) future; **w (niedalekiej) ~ci** in the (near) future; **plany na ~ć** plans for the future; **przyszły** *adj* **1.** *wydarzenia*: future **2.** *rok, sobota, semestr*: next; **czas ~** *GRAM* future tense
przyszywać ⟨**-szyć**⟩ (*-wam*) sew on
przyszywan|y *adj*: **~a ciocia** adoptive auntie; **~y wujek** adoptive uncle
przyśnić się *v/p* (*-nię*): **przyśniło mi się, że** I dreamt that; **przyśniła mi się babcia** I dreamt about my granny; **co ci się przyśniło?** what did you dream about?
przyśpieszać → **przyspieszać**; **przyśpieszenie** → **przyspieszenie**; **przyśpieszony** → **przyspieszony**
przyśpiewka *f* (*-ki*; *-ki*) (short) folk song; **przyśpiewywać** *v/im* (*-piewuję*): **~ sobie** croon
przyśrubowywać ⟨**-bować**⟩ (*-bowuję*) screw on
przyświeca|ć ⟨**-cić**⟩ (*-cam*): **~ć komuś** light the way for; **słońce ~** the sun is shining; **~ jej piękny cel** she has a noble purpose
przytaczać ⟨**-toczyć**⟩ (*-czam*) **1.** (*cytować*) quote; **~ źródło** refer to a source; **~ słowa** quote **2.** *przykład*: give **3.** (*wymienić*) mention, enumerate **4.** *argument*: adduce, set forth **5.** *beczkę*: roll over
przytakiwać ⟨**-knąć**⟩ (*-kuję*) **1.** (*zgadzać się*) assent, answer yes **2.** (*kiwać głową*) nod
przytakująco *adv* in assent; **kiwnąć głową ~** nod in assent
przytaszczać ⟨**-czyć**⟩ (*-czam*) lug
przytępiać ⟨**-pić**⟩ (*-piam*) *zmysły, nóż*: (make) blunt; **przytępiać się 1.** (*o nożu*) become blunt **2.** (*o słuchu, wzroku*) be dulled; **przytępił mu się słuch** he become hard ofhearing
przytępiony *adj* **1.** *nóż*: blunt **2.** *wzrok*: dull(ed)
przytknąć *v/p* → **przytykać**
przytłaczać ⟨**-łoczyć**⟩ (*-czam*) **1.** (*obciążać*) weigh down; **~ swoim ciężarem** crush with one's own weight **2.** *fig* overwhelm
przytłaczający *adj* **1.** *przewaga*: overwhelming, enormous **2.** *milczenie*: overwhelming **3.** *atmosfera*: oppressive **4.** *upał*: intense, oppressive
przytłumiać ⟨**-mić**⟩ (*-miam*) **1.** *dźwięk*: muffle **2.** *światło*: dim **3.** *płomienie*: stifle; **przytłumiony** *adj* **1.** *dźwięk*: muffled **2.** *światło*: dimmed
przytoczyć *v/p* → **przytaczać**
przytomnieć ⟨**o-**⟩ (*-nieję*) *MED* regain consciousness; **oprzytomnij!** wake up!
przytomność *f* (*-ści*; *no pl*) consciousness; **~ umysłu** presence ofmind; **stracić ~** lose consciousness, pass out; **odzyskać ~** regain consciousness
przytomny *adj* **1.** *MED* conscious **2.** (*trzeźwy*) alert, clear-headed
przytrafiać się ⟨**-fić**⟩ (*-fiam*): **~ komuś** happen to s.o.
przytrzaskiwać ⟨**-snąć**⟩ (*-kuję*): **~ sobie palce w drzwiach** jam one's fingers in the door
przytrzeć *v/p* → **przycierać**
przytrzymywać ⟨**-mać**⟩ (*-muję*) **1.** (*zatrzymać*) hold down **2.** (*potrzymać*)

stop, hold back; **przytrzymywać się** hold on (to)

przytulać ⟨**-lić**⟩ (*-lam*) *dziecko, przyjaciółkę*: hug; **~ kogoś do siebie** hug s.o.; **przytulić u siebie** take s.o. in; **przytulać się** cuddle up (**do** *G* to); **~ się do siebie** cuddle up to each other; **przytuliła się do jego ramienia** she snuggled up against his shoulder; **przytulić się u** *G* (*znaleźć schronienie*) find shelter with; **nie mieć gdzie głowy przytulić** *fig* have no place to sleep

przytulanka *f* (*-nki*; *-nki*) (*zabawka*) cuddly toy

przytulny *adj Br* cosy, *Am* cozy

przytułek *m* (*-łku*; *-łki*) shelter; **~ dla ubogich** poorhouse

przytupywać *v/im* (*-puje*) stamp one's feet

przytwierdzać ⟨**-dzić**⟩ (*-dzam*) attach, fix (**do** *G* to); **~ gwoździami** nail

przytyć *v/p* → **tyć**

przytyk *m* (*-ku*; *-ki*) sideswipe, dig (at); **~ do czyjegoś nazwiska** dig at s.o.'s name

przytykać ⟨**-tknąć**⟩ (*-kam*) put (**do** *G* against)

przyuczać ⟨**-czyć**⟩ (*-czam*) train; **~ kogoś do zawodu** train s.o. for the trade; **~ psa do** *G* train a dog to

przyuczony *adj pracownik*: semi-skilled

przywabiać ⟨**-bić**⟩ (*-biam*) **1.** (*wabić*) lure **2.** *klientów*: attract

przywalać ⟨**-lić**⟩ (*-lam*) **1.** (*o drzewie*) crush **2.** (*o lawinie, gruzach*) bury **3.** *wejście*: block **4.** (*uderzyć*) wallop; **przywalać się** *infml* make a pitch (**do** *G* for)

przywara *f* (*-ry*; *-ry*) vice

przywdziewać ⟨**-dziać**⟩ (*-wam*) *lit* don, array

przywiązanie *n* (*-nia*; *no pl*) attachment

przywiązywać ⟨**-zać**⟩ (*-zuję*) **1.** (*wiązać*) tie (**do** *G* to); **~ wagę do** *G fig* attach importance (**do** *G* to); **~ znaczenie do** *G fig* set a high value on **2.** (*zjednywać*) endear (**do** *G* to); **przywiązywać się 1.** (*wiązać się*) tie oneself(**do** *G* to) **2.** (*polubić*) become attached (**do** *G* to)

przywidzenie *n* (*-nia*; *-nia*) **1.** illusion **2.** MED hallucination

przywidzieć się *v/p*: **przywidziało ci się** you must have dreamt it, you must have been seeing things

przywierać ⟨**-wrzeć**⟩ (*-ram*) **1.** cling (**do** *G* to); **~ do ściany** flatten oneself against the wall **2.** COOK stick (**do** *G* to)

przywieść *v/p* → **przywodzić**

przywieźć *v/p* → **przywozić**

przywiędnąć *v/p* → **więdnąć**

przywilej *m* (*-ju*; *-je*) privilege; **nadać ~** grant a charter

przywitać *v/p* → **witać**

przywitanie *n* (*-nia*; *-nia*) greeting, welcome; **podnosić rękę na ~** raise one's hand in greeting

przywlekać ⟨**-lec**⟩ (*-kam*) **1.** *przedmiot*: drag **2.** *chorobę*: bring (in); **przywlec się** drag oneself, trudge

przywłaszczać ⟨**-czyć**⟩ (*-czam*) **1.** *pieniądze*: appropriate; **~ sobie** (mis)appropriate; **~ sobie czyjeś zasługi** take the credit for s.o. else's work **2.** *władzę*: usurp, seize unlawfully **3.** *tytuł*: steal, hold unlawfully

przywodzić ⟨**-wieść**⟩ (*-dzę*) *lit* **1.** (*przyprowadzić*) bring along (**do** *G* to) **2.** (*doprowadzić*) drive, bring; **~ kogoś do rozpaczy** drive s.o. to despair; **~ kogoś do szaleństwa** drive s.o. mad; **~ na myśl** bring to mind

przywoływać ⟨**-łać**⟩ (*-łuję*) **1.** (*zawołać*) call; **~ do porządku** call to order **2.** (*przypominać*) bring back **3.** (*powoływać się*) mention

przywozić ⟨**-wieźć**⟩ (*-wożę*) **1.** *osobę*: bring; **~ z podróży** bring along from a journey; **~ na pamiątkę** bring along as a souvenir **2.** *towar*: transport

przywódca *m* (*-cy*; *-cy*) leader; **~ opozycji** opposition leader; **~ duchowy** spiritual leader; **przywódcz|y** *adj talent*: commanding; **zdolności ~e** leadership

przywóz *m* (*-wozu*; *-wozy*) **1.** (*dostawa*) delivery **2.** (*import*) import

przywracać ⟨**-rócić**⟩ (*-cam*) **1.** *porządek*: restore; **~ komuś życie** bring s.o. back to life; **~ kogoś na stanowisko** reinstate s.o.; **~ do stanu używalności** *budynek*: repair, refurbish **2.** *własność*: give back

przywrzeć *v/p* → **przywierać**

przywykać ⟨**-knąć**⟩ (*-kam*) get used, get accustomed (**do** *G* to)

P

przywykły *adj* accustomed (**do** *G* to)
przyzakładow|y *adj* factory; ***stołówka ~a*** company canteen
przyziemn|y *adj sprawy, zajęcie*: mundane, everyday; ***~e powody*** down-to-earth reasons
przyznanie *n* (*-nia*; *no pl*) **1.** *stypendium*: granting **2.** *nagrody*: awarding; **przyznanie się** *n* (*-nia*; *no pl*) acknowledgement, admission; ***~ do winy*** confession of one's guilt
przyznawać ⟨**-nać**⟩ (*-naję*) **1.** *kredyt, rabat*: give **2.** *stypendium*: give **3.** *tytuł, obywatelstwo*: grant **4.** *nagrodę*: award; ***~ komuś rację*** admit that s.o. is right; ***przyznać, że*** admit that, concede that; ***przyznawać się*** **1.** own up (**do** *G* to) **2.** JUR plead guilty; ***~ się do winy*** confess one's guilt, JUR plead guilty **3.** (*wyznawać*) confess; ***przyznam się, że*** I have to confess that
przyzwalać ⟨**-wolić**⟩ (*-lam*) consent (**na** *A* to); **przyzwalający** *adj* approving
przyzwoicie *adv* → **przyzwoity**
przyzwoitka *f* (*-ki*; *-ki*) *dated* chaperone
przyzwoitoś|ć *f* (*-ści*; *no pl*) decency; ***tego wymaga ~ć*** it's common decency; ***dla ~ci*** for decency's sake; **przyzwoity** *adj osoba, pensja*: decent
przyzwolenie *n* (*-nia*; *no pl*) permission; **przyzwolić** *v/p* → **przyzwalać**
przyzwyczajać ⟨**-czaić**⟩ (*-jam*) accustom (**do** *G* to); ***przyzwyczajać się*** get used, get accustomed (**do** *G* to)
przyzwyczajeni|e *n* (*-nia*; *-nia*) habit; ***z ~a*** out ofhabit; **przyzwyczajony** *adj* accustomed (**do** *G* to)
psa → **pies**
psalm *m* (*-mu*; *-my*) psalm
psałterz *m* (*-rza*; *-rze*) psalter
pseudo- (*w złożeniach*) pseudo; ***~uczony*** pseudoscientist
pseudonim *m* (*-mu*; *-my*) pseudonym, alias
psi *adj* dog's; ***~ zaprzęg*** dog team; ***pracować za ~ grosz*** work for a mere pittance; ***kupić coś za ~ grosz*** buy s.th. dirt-cheap, buy s.th. for a song, pay peanuts for; ***to twój ~ obowiązek*** it's your bounden duty; ***~m swędem*** by a fluke
psiakość!, ***psiakrew!*** *interj* damn it!
psiarni|a *f* (*-ni*; *-nie*) kennel(s); ***zimno tu jak w ~*** it's bloody cold in here
psikus *m* (*-sa*; *-sy*) (practical) joke, prank; ***zrobić komuś ~a*** play a practical joke on
psina *f* (*-ny*; *-ny*) *dim* doggy, doggie; ***wierna ~*** faithful dog
psioczyć *v/im* (*-czę*) gripe (**na** *A* about/at)
psisko *n* (*-ka*; *-ka*) doggie; ***ogromne ~*** great big dog; ***wierne ~*** faithful dog
PSL *abbr m* (*PSL-u*; *no pl*) (= **Polskie Stronnictwo Ludowe**) Polish Peasant's Party
psocić *v/im* (*-cę*) (*o dziecku*) play tricks
psota *f* (*-ty*; *-ty*) prank, trick
psotnik *m* (*-ka*; *-nicy*), **~nica** *f* (*-cy*; *-ce*) **1.** (*psotne dziecko*) mischief **2.** (*żartowniś*) prankster; **psotny** *adj dziecko*: mischievous
pss, ***psyt*** *interj* hush
pstrąg *m* (*-ga*; *-gi*) trout
pstro *adv* gaudily; ***mieć ~ w głowie*** be light-headed
pstrokaty *adj* **1.** (*różnokolorowy*) gaudy **2.** *koń*: dappled
pstry *adj* gaudy
pstrykać ⟨**-knąć**⟩ (*-kam*): ***~ palcami*** snap one's fingers; ***~ długopisem*** play with one's pen; ***~ zdjęcia*** take snapshots
pstrzyć ⟨**u-**⟩ (*-rzę*) (*o muchach*) fleck, dapple
psu → **pies**
psubrat *m* (*-ta*; *-ty*) *lit* scoundrel, knave
psuć ⟨**po-**, **ze-**⟩ (*psuję*) **1.** *maszynę*: break, damage **2.** *nastrój, zabawę, charakter*: spoil **3.** *oczy, reputację*: ruin **4.** *powietrze*: foul up; ***psuć się*** **1.** (*o maszynie*) break down **2.** (*o jedzeniu*) go bad **3.** (*o pogodzie*) worsen **4.** (*o wzroku*) deteriorate **5.** (*o zębach*) decay **6.** (*o nastroju*) get spoilt **7.** (*o stosunkach*) become aggravated **8.** (*o charakterze*) become bad, become unpleasant
psy *pl* → **pies**
psychiatra *m* (*-ry*; *-rzy*) psychiatrist; **psychiatria** *f* (*-rii*; *no pl*) psychiatry
psychicznie *adj*: ***chory ~*** mentally ill
psychiczn|y *adj* **1.** *choroba*: mental **2.** *załamanie*: nervous; ***uraz ~y*** (psychical) trauma; ***przejść załamanie ~e*** suffer a mental breakdown; **psychika** *f* (*-ki*; *no pl*) psyche

P

psychoanalityczny *adj* psychoanalytic; **psychoanaliza** *f* (*-zy*; *no pl*) psychoanalysis

psycholog *m* (*-ga*; *-lodzy*/*-gowie*) psychologist; **psychologia** *f* (*-gii*; *no pl*) psychology; ***~ głębi*** depth psychology; **psychologiczny** *adj* psychological

psychopata *m* (*-ty*; *-paci*) psychopath; **psychosomatyczny** *adj* psychosomatic

psychoterapia *f* (*-pii*; *no pl*) psychotherapy; ***~ grupowa*** group therapy; **psychoterapeuta** *m* (*-ty*; *-peuci*) psychotherapist

psychoza *f* (*-zy*; *-zy*) psychosis

psychotropow|y *adj*: ***leki ~e*** psychotropic drugs

psykać ⟨***-knąć***⟩ (*-kam*) hush

pszczelarstwo *n* (*-wa*; *no pl*) beekeeping; **pszczelarz** *m* (*-rza*; *-rze*) beekeeper

pszczel|i *adj* bee; ***kit ~i*** bee glue; ***mleczko ~e*** royal jelly; **pszczoła** *f* (*-ły*; *-ły*) bee; ***~ robotnica*** worker bee; **pszczółka** *f* (*-ki*; *-ki*) *dim* bee

pszenica *f* (*-cy*; *no pl*) wheat

pszeniczny *adj pole*: wheat; **pszenny** *adj chleb*: wheat

pt. *abbr* (= ***pod tytułem***) entitled

ptactwo *n* (*-wa*; *no pl*) birds *pl*; ***~ domowe*** (domestic) fowl; ***dzikie ~*** wildfowl; ***~ wodne*** waterfowl

ptak *m* (*-ka*; *-ki*) bird; ***~ wędrowny*** migratory bird; ***~ drapieżny*** bird of prey; ***z lotu ~a*** from above; ***niebieski ~*** *fig* layabout

ptasi *adj ogon*, *śpiew*: bird's; ***~ móżdżek*** *fig* birdbrain; ***~e mleczko*** chocolate-covered marshmallow

ptaszarnia *f* (*-ni*; *-nie*) aviary; **ptaszek** *m* (*-szka*; *-szki*) **1.** *dim* birdie; ***ranny ~*** *fig* early bird **2.** (*znak*) *Br* tick, *Am* check **3.** (*nicpoń*) *fig* good-for-nothing **4.** (*członek*) *infml Br* willie, *Am* willy; **ptasznik** *m* **1.** (*-ka*; *-nicy*) (*hodowca*) bird breeder **2.** (*-ka*; *-ki*) (*pająk*) bird spider; **ptaszyna** *f* (*-ny*; *-ny*) *dim* birdie

PTTK *abbr n indecl* (= ***Polskie Towarzystwo Turystyczno-Krajoznawcze***) Polish Tourist Association

ptyś *m* (*ptysia*; *ptysie*) COOK cream puff

publicysta *m* (*-ty*; *-cyści*) journalist; **publicystyka** *f* (*-ki*; *no pl*) journalism

publiczność *f* (*-ści*; *no pl*) *teatralna*, *kinowa*: audience; **publiczn|y** *adj* public; ***dobro ~e*** common good; ***opinia ~a*** public opinion; ***dom ~y*** brothel; ***tajemnica ~a*** open secret; ***podać coś do ~ej wiadomości*** make s.th. publicly known

publika *f* (*-ki*; *no pl*) the audience, the public

publikować ⟨**o-**⟩ (*-kuję*) publish

puch *m* (*-chu*; *no pl*) down; ***kołdra z ~u*** eiderdown; ***śnieżny ~*** powder snow; ***rozbić w ~*** *lit* reduce to matchwood

puchacz *m* (*-cza*; *-cze*) eagle owl

puchar *m* (*-ru*; *-ry*) **1.** (*kielich*) chalice, goblet **2.** SPORT cup; **pucharowy** *adj* SPORT cup

puchlina *f* (*-ny*; *no pl*) MED edema

puchnąć ⟨**s-**⟩ (*-nę*) MED swell; ***głośno, aż uszy puchną*** this noise is ear-splitting

puchowy *adj poduszka*: down

pucołowaty *adj* chubby

pucować ⟨**wy-**⟩ (*-cuję*) shine

pucybut *m* (*-ta*; *-ty*/*-buci*) bootblack, shoe shiner

pucz *m* (*-czu*; *-cze*) coup (d'etat); ***dokonać ~u*** carry out a coup (d'etat)

pudel *m* (*-dla*; *-dle*) poodle

pudełko *n* (*-ka*; *-ka*) box; ***~ zapałek*** matchbox; ***~ po butach*** shoe box

puder *m* (*-dru*; *-dry*) powder; ***cukier ~*** *Br* caster sugar, *Am* confectioners' sugar; **puderniczka** *f* (*-ki*; *-ki*) compact

pudło *n* (*-ła*; *-ła*) **1.** *na kapelusz*: box; ***~ kartonowe*** cardboard box; ***stare ~*** *fig* old frump **2.** (*więzienie*) *infml Br* cooler, slammer, *Am* joint, stir **3.** (*strzał*) *infml* miss; ***bez pudła*** (*bezbłędnie*) spot-on

pudłować ⟨**s-**⟩ (*-łuję*) *infml* miss

pudrować ⟨**u-**, **przy-**⟩ (*-ruję*) *twarz*: powder

puf *m* (*-fu*/*-fa*; *-fy*) pouf(fe)

pukać ⟨***-knąć***⟩ (*-kam*) **1.** (*kołatać*) knock; ***~ do drzwi*** knock at the door, knock on the door **2.** (*palcami*) tap; ***~ w ścianę*** tap on the wall; ***pukać się*** tap; ***puknij się w czoło!*** you must be nuts!

pukiel *m* (*-kla*; *-kle*): ***~ włosów*** lock of hair

puknięty *adj samochód*: dented

pula *f* (*-li*; *-le*) **1.** (*ilość*) quota **2.** (*w kartach*) pool

P

pulchny *adj* **1.** *ciasto*: spongy **2.** *ziemia*: loose **3.** *ciało*: plump
pulower *m* (*-ru*/*-ra*; *-ry*) pullover
pulpet *m* (*-ta*/*-tu*; *-ty*) COOK meatball
pulpit *m* (*-tu*; *-ty*) **1.** (*do nut*) music stand **2.** TECH (control) panel
puls *m* (*-su*; *-sy*) pulse; ***zbadać ~*** take s.o.'s pulse; ***trzymać rękę na ~ie*** *fig* keep one's finger on the pulse
pulsować *v/im* (*-suję*) **1.** (*o krwi*) pulse **2.** throb; **pulsujący** *adj miasto*, *światło*: pulsating
pułap *m* (*-pu*; *-py*) **1.** (*strop*) (wooden) ceiling **2.** ceiling
pułk *m* (*-ku*; *-ki*) regiment; **pułkownik** *m* (*-ka*; *-nicy*) colonel
puma *f* (*-my*; *-my*) puma
pumeks *m* (*-su*; *-sy*) pumice
pumpy *pl* (*pump*/*-pów*) baggy trousers *pl*
punkcik *m* (*-ka*/*-ku*; *-ki*) *dim* speck, dot
punkcja *f* (*-ji*; *-je*) MED puncture
punk|t[1] *m* (*-tu*; *-ty*) **1.** point; ***~t karny*** penalty point; ***~t ciężkości*** centre ofgr avity; ***~t widzenia*** point ofv iew, viewpoint, standpoint; ***~t wyjścia*** starting point; ***~t odniesienia*** point of reference, reference point; ***w dobrym ~cie*** located conveniently; ***~t informacyjny*** information desk; ***~t obserwacyjny*** vantage point; ***~t sporny*** point at issue, moot point; ***z jego ~tu widzenia*** from his point of view **2.** matter; ***~t honoru*** matter ofh onour; ***na ~cie*** *G* concerning, regarding, with regard to; ***mieć bzika na ~cie*** *G infml* go ape over, be mad keen on; ***być wrażliwym na ~cie*** *G* be sensitive about **3.** *programu*: item **4.** *usługowy*: shop; ***~t sprzedaży*** (retail) shop
punkt[2] *particle*: ***~ ósma*** eight o'clock sharp
punktacja *f* (*-ji*; *-je*) grading scale; **punktualny** *adj* punctual
pupa *f* (*-py*; *-py*) bum; **pupcia** *f* (*-ci*; *-cie*) *dim* (little) bottom
pupil *m* (*-la*; *-le*), ***pupilek*** *m* (*-lka*; *-lki*) teacher's pet, teacher's favourite
purchawka *f* (*-ki*; *-ki*) puffball
purpura *f* (*-ry*; *no pl*) purple; **purpurowy** *adj* purple
purysta *m* (*-ty*; *-ryści*) purist; **purytanin** *m* (*-na*; *-tanie*) Puritan; **purytański** *adj* Puritan
pustak *m* (*-ka*; *-ki*) BUILD breeze block, hollow brick
pustelnia *f* (*-ni*; *-nie*) hermitage; **pustelniczy** *adj życie*: solitary; **pustelnik** *m* (*-ka*; *-nicy*) hermit
pustk|a *f* (*-ki*; *-ki*) emptiness; ***trafić w ~ę*** (*o propozycji*) fall on stony ground; ***świecić ~ami*** be completely empty; ***mam ~ę w głowie*** my mind is a blank; ***w sklepach ~i*** shops are empty; **pustkowie** *n* (*-wia*; *-wia*) wasteland
pusto *adv* → ***pusty***
pustostan *m* (*-nu*; *-ny*) uninhabited house, uninhabited flat
pustoszeć ⟨**o-**⟩ (*-szeję*) *ulica*, *sala*: become empty
pustoszyć ⟨**s-**⟩ (*-szę*) ravage, waste
pustułka *f* (*-ki*; *-ki*) common kestrel, windhover
pust|y *adj budynek*, *życie*: empty; ***na ~y żołądek*** on an empty stomach; ***~e słowa*** platitudes, meaningless phrases, empty words; ***z ~ymi rękami*** empty-handed; ***mieć ~e kieszenie*** be penniless
pustynia *f* (*-ni*; *-nie*) desert; ***~ kulturalna*** *fig* cultural desert; **pustynny** *adj* desert
puszcza *f* (*-czy*; *-cze*) primeval forest
puszczać ⟨**puścić**⟩ (*-czam*) **I** *v/t* **1.** let go; ***~ pączki*** BIOL sprout buds; ***~ korzenie*** BIOL take root; ***~ kaczki*** play ducks and drakes; ***~ w obieg*** circulate, put into circulation; ***~ coś mimo uszu*** let s.th. pass; ***~ oczko do*** *G* wink at; ***~ wodze fantazji*** give full play to fantasy; ***~ kogoś z torbami*** take s.o. to the cleaner's; ***~ pawia*** *infml* puke *infml*, throw up; ***oczko ci puściło w rajstopach*** your tights ran; ***nie ~ pary z ust*** not breathe a word; ***~ farbę*** spill the beans **2.** *radio*, *wodę*: turn on; ***~ komuś krew*** bleed s.o. **3.** *kasetę*: play **4.** *infml* ***~ bąki*** pass wind **5.** *latawca*: fly **6.** *sok*: ooze **II** *v/i* **1.** (*o mrozie*) let up **2.** (*o drzwiach*, *zamku*) burst **3.** (*o plamie*) come out **4.** (*w praniu*) run; ***puszczać się*** **1.** *infml* sleep around **2.** ***~ się biegiem*** break into run, set off at a run **3.** (*zwalniać uścisk*) let go of; ***puścił się rury*** he let go ofthe pipe
puszczalska *f* (*-kiej*; *-kie*) *infml* floozie (a bit ofa) tart, easy lay, slut
puszczyk *m* (*-ka*; *-ki*) tawny owl
puszek *m* (*-szku*/*-szka*; *-szki*) down

pusz|ka *f* (*-ki*; *-ki*) **1.** *groszku*: can, *Br* tin; ***~ka piwa*** can ofbeer; ***~ka po piwie*** beer can; ***w ~ce*** tinned, canned; ***pomidory w ~ce*** tinned tomatoes, canned tomatoes **2.** (*do kwesty*) collection box
puszkować *v/im* (*-kuję*) can, *Br* tin; **puszkowy** *adj* canned, *Br* tinned
puszyć się 〈***na-***〉 (*-szę*) **1.** (*o ptakach*) puff up, puff out (feathers) **2.** (*o osobie*) blow one's own trumpet
puszysty *adj* **1.** *włosy*: frizzy **2.** *dywan*: nappy, fluffy **3.** *śnieg*: fleecy **4.** *ogon*: bushy **5.** (*gruby*) *iron* chubby **6.** *ciasto*: light, spongy, fluffy
puścić *v/p* → ***puszczać***
puzderko *n* (*-ka*; *-ka*) casket
puzon *m* (*-nu*; *-ny*) trombone; **puzonista** *m* (*-ty*; *-niści*) trombonist
pycha *f* (*-chy*; *no pl*) pride; ***~!*** yummy!, delicious!
pykać 〈***-knąć***〉 (*-kam*): ***~ fajkę*** puff at one's pipe
pylica *f* (*-cy*; *no pl*) MED anthracosis, dust disease
pył *m* (*-łu*; *-ły*) dust; ***~ kosmiczny*** ASTR space dust; ***~ wulkaniczny*** volcanic dust; **pył|ek** *m* (*-łku*; *-łki*) **1.** (*drobina*) speck, mote **2.** BIOL pollen; ***~ki*** pollen
pypeć *m* (*-pcia*; *-pcie*) MED blot
pysk *m* (*-ka*; *-ki*) **1.** (*zwierzęcia*) muzzle **2.** *infml* gob; ***o suchym ~u*** without food or drink; ***dostać po ~u*** be punched in the face; ***padać na ~*** be beat, be exhausted; ***trzymać kogoś za ~*** keep a tight rein on s.o.; ***stul ~!*** shut your gob!; ***wyrzucić kogoś na zbity ~*** kick s.o. out; ***daj ~a!*** give us a kiss!
pyskacz *m* (*-cza*; *-cze*) *infml* loudmouth, barker; **pyskaty** *adj infml* loudmouthed, cheeky; **pyskować** *v/im* (*-kuję*) *infml* talk back; **pyskówka** *f* (*-ki*; *-ki*) *infml* row, arguing
pyszałek *m* (*-łka*; *-łki*) conceited bore, coxcomb, *Am* braggart, jackanapes; **pyszałkowaty** *adj* conceited, arrogant
pyszczek *m* (*-czka*; *-czki*) **1.** *kota*: snout **2.** (*twarz*) darling little face
pysznić się *v/im* (*-nię*) act big, show off, boast (*I* about)
pyszności *pl* (*-ści*) dainties *pl*, delicacies *pl*; ***same ~*** all is delicious; ***zupa ~!*** the soup is simply delicious!; ***~!*** delicious!, mouthwatering!
pyszn|y *adj* **1.** (*wyniosły*) proud **2.** (*smaczny*) delicious **3.** (*doskonały*) great; ***mieć się z ~a*** be in a tight situation, be in hot water
pyta|ć (się) 〈***s-, za-***〉 (*-tam*) **1.** (*informować się*) ask (**o** *A* about); ***~ć kogoś o radę*** ask s.o.'s advice; ***~ć kogoś o drogę*** ask s.o. the way, ask s.o. for directions; ***nie ~jąc o*** *A* without asking for; ***szef o ciebie ~ł*** the boss has been asking about you **2.** (*w szkole*) test (orally) (**z** *G* on), *Am* quiz (**z** *G* about), give an oral (**z** *G* in)
pytając|y *adj wzrok*: enquiring; ***zdanie ~e*** interrogative sentence; **pytajnik** *m* (*-ka*; *-ki*) question mark; **pytajny** *adj* interrogative
pytani|e *n* (*-nia*; *-nia*) question; ***mieć ~e*** have a question (**do** *G* for); ***zadać ~e*** ask a question; ***podchwytliwe ~e*** trick question; ***~e egzaminacyjne*** exam(ination) question; ***bez ~a*** without permission; (***też***) ***~!*** what a question to ask!; ***zarzucić kogoś ~ami*** flood s.o. with questions; ***sformułować ~e*** frame a question, phrase a question
pytlować *v/im* (*-luję*) *infml* chatter
pytlowy *adj*: ***chleb ~*** wholewheat bread
pyton *m* (*-na*; *-ny*) python
pyza *f* (*-zy*; *-zy*) **1.** COOK potato dumpling **2.** (*grubas*) roly-poly; **pyzaty** *adj* chubby-cheeked
PZU *abbr n/m indecl* (= ***Państwowy Zakład Ubezpieczeń***) Polish (State) Insurance Company

R

R

r. *abbr* (= ***rok***) yr.
raban *m* (*-nu*; *-ny*) fuss; ***narobić ~u*** kick up a fuss
rabarbar *m* (*-ru*; *-ry*) rhubarb
rabat *m* (*-tu*; *-ty*) discount
rabata *f* (*-ty*; *-ty*) flower bed
rabin *m* (*-na*; *-ni*) rabbi
rabować (*-buję*) **1.** 〈***ob-***〉 *bank*: rob, hold up **2.** 〈***ob-***〉 *sklepy*: loot, plunder **3.** 〈***z-***〉 *pieniądze*: steal

rabunek *m* (*-nku*; *-nki*) robbery; **rabunkow|y** *adj*: ***napad ~y*** hold-up, robbery; ***gospodarka ~a*** wasteful exploitation; ***~e wycinanie lasu*** predatory deforestation
rabuś *m* (*-busia*; *-busie*) robber
raca *f* (*-cy*; *-ce*) flare
rachityczny *adj* **1.** MED frail **2.** *krzesło*: rickety
rachub|a *f* (*-by*; *-by*): ***to nie wchodzi w ~ę*** that's out ofthe question; ***pomylić się w ~ach*** *fig* miscalculate, make a mistake; ***stracić ~ę czasu*** lose track oftime
rachun|ek *m* (*-nku*; *-nki*) **1.** (*w restauracji*) *Br* bill, *Am* check; ***~ek za telefon*** phone bill; ***~ek za gaz i elektryczność*** gas and electricity bill; ***~ek sumienia*** REL examination of one's conscience; ***pracować na własny ~ek*** work for oneself, be self-employed; ***wyrównać z kimś ~ki*** *fig* settle accounts with **2.** (*konto*) account; ***~ek bieżący*** current account; ***~ek oszczędnościowy*** savings account; ***~ek walutowy*** foreign currency account **3.** (*obliczanie*) calculation; ***~ek prawdopodobieństwa*** MATH probability theory
rachunkowość *f* (*-ści*; *no pl*) **1.** (*księgowość*) accountancy, accounting **2.** (*dział instytucji*) accounting department; **rachunkow|y** *adj* **1.** MATH arithmetic; ***błąd ~y*** miscalculation **2.** FIN account, accounting; ***księga ~a*** accounts book
racica *f* (*-cy*; *-ce*) BIOL (cloven) hoof
racj|a *f* (*-ji*; *-je*) **1.** (*słuszność*) right; ***mieć ~ę*** be right; ***przyznać komuś ~ę*** accept s.o.'s argument, cede a point to; ***~a bytu*** raison d'être; ***z jakiej ~i?*** by what right?; ***~a!*** absolutely right! **2.** (*argument*) reason; ***~e*** reasons, arguments; ***~a stanu*** POLIT reason of state; ***nie bez ~i*** not without reason **3.** *dzienna*: ration
racjonalizacja *f* (*-ji*; *no pl*) *Br* rationalisation, *Am* rationalization
racjonalizator *m* (*-ra*; *-rzy*) inventor
racjonalny *adj* **1.** (*przemyślany*) reasonable, sensible **2.** *myślenie*: rational
racjonalizować ⟨**z-**⟩ (*-zuję*) *Br* rationalise, *Am* rationalize
racjonować (*-nuję*) ration
racuch *m* (*-cha*; *-chy*) *fritter made of yeast dough*
raczej *particle* rather; ***~ ciasny*** rather cramped
raczkować *v/im* (*-kuję*) **1.** (*o dziecku*) crawl **2.** (*o nowej technologii*) *fig* be still in nappies, be in its infancy
raczyć ⟨**u-**⟩ (*-czę*) **1.** (*częstować*) treat (*I* to) **2.** ***pan raczy żartować*** you are joking, ofcou rse; ***raczyć się*** treat oneself(*I* to)
rad[1] *m* (*-du*; *no pl*) CHEM radium
rad[2] *adj lit* pleased (**z** *G* to do s.th.); ***~ bym*** I would be happy to; ***~ nierad*** willy-nilly, whether you like it or not; ***jestem ~, że widzę cię całego i zdrowego*** I'm pleased to see you safe and sound
rad|a *f* (*-dy*; *-dy*) **1.** (*porada*) (piece of) advice; ***poszedł za jej ~ą*** he followed her advice; ***dać sobie ~ę*** manage (**z** *I*); ***dać sobie ~ę bez*** *G* do without; ***na to nie ma ~y*** there's nothing we can do about it; ***nie da ~y*** no can do; ***jest na to ~a*** there's a way, we'll figure it out **2.** (*grupa*) council; ***~a nadzorcza*** board ofsu pervisors; ***~a zakładowa*** works council; ***~a pedagogiczna*** **a)** (*zebranie*) staff meeting, teachers' meeting **b)** (*nauczyciele*) teaching staff; ***~a Ministrów*** the Cabinet; ***~a Bezpieczeństwa*** Security Council
radar *m* (*-ru*; *-ry*) radar; **radarowy** *adj* radar
radca *m* (*-cy*; *-cy*) counsel; ***~ prawny*** legal counsel
radiacja *f* (*-ji*; *no pl*) PHYS radiation
radiesteta *m* (*-ty*; *-steci*) dowser, (water) diviner
radi|o *n* (*-dia*; *-dia*) radio; ***w ~u*** on the radio; ***pracować w ~u*** work for radio; ***słuchać ~a*** listen to the radio
radioabonent *m* (*-ta*; *-nci*) licensed radio listener; **radioaktywny** *adj* PHYS radioactive; ***opad ~*** fallout
radioamator *m* (*-ra*; *-rzy*) ham; **radiobiologia** *f* (*-gii*; *no pl*) radiobiology; **radiofonia** *f* (*-nii*; *no pl*) radio broadcasting
radiokomunikacja *f* (*-ji*; *no pl*) radiocommunications; **radiolatarnia** *f* (*-ni*; *-nie*) radio beacon

R

radiolog *m* (*-ga*; *-lodzy*) radiologist; **radiologia** *f* (*-gii*; *no pl*) radiology; **radiolokacja** *f* (*-ji*; *no pl*) radiolocation

radiomagnetofon *m* (*-nu*; *-ny*) radio cassette recorder; **radioodbiornik** *m* (*-ka*; *-ki*) radio (receiver); **radiopajęczarz** *m* (*-rza*; *-rze*) unlicensed listener

radiosłuchacz *m* (*-cza*; *-cze*), **~ka** *f* (*-ki*; *-ki*) (radio) listener

radiostacja *f* (*-ji*; *-je*) radio station; **radiotechnik** *m* (*-ka*; *-nicy*) radio engineer

radiotelefon *m* (*-nu*; *-ny*) radiotelephone; **radiotelegrafista** *m* (*-ty*; *-fiści*) radio(telegraph) operator; **radiotelegram** *m* (*-mu*; *-my*) radiogram

radioterapia *f* (*-pii*; *no pl*) MED radiotherapy; **radiowęzeł** *m* (*-zła*; *-zły*) *Br* radio centre, *Br* broadcasting centre, *Am* radio center, *Am* broadcasting center; **radiowóz** *m* (*-wozu*; *-wozy*) police car; **radiowy** *adj* radio

radny *m* (*-nego*; *-ni*), **-na** *f* (*-nej*; *-ne*) councillor

radoch|a *f* (*-chy*; *no pl*) *infml* fun; ***mieć ~ę z czegoś*** have a ball doing s.th.; **radosny** *adj* joyful; ***~ okrzyk*** cry of joy

radoś|ć *f* (*-ści*; *-ści*) joy; ***płakać z ~ci*** weep for joy, weep with joy; ***~ć życia*** joy of life

radośnie *adv* → ***radosny***

radować ⟨**u-**⟩ (*-duję*) *lit* gladden; ***radować się*** rejoice (*I*/**z** *G* at/in)

radykał *m* (*-ła*; *-łowie*) radical; **radykalny** *adj* radical

radzi → ***rad***[2]

radzić ⟨**po-**⟩ (*-dzę*) advise; ***~ sobie*** cope (**z** *I* with); ***~ nad*** *I lit* debate; ***nie radzę ci wracać*** I wouldn't come backif I were you, you'd better not come back; ***radzić się*** asks .o. for advice; ***nic na to nie poradzę*** I can't do anything about it

radziecki *adj* HIST Soviet

rafa *f* (*-fy*; *-fy*) reef; ***~ koralowa*** coral reef

rafineria *f* (*-rii*; *-rie*) refinery

rafinowany *adj*: ***cukier ~*** refined sugar

raj *m* (*-ju*; *no pl*) REL paradise

rajcować *v/im* (*-cuję*) **I** *v/t* (*podniecać*) give a kick, turn on **II** *v/i* (*rozmawiać*) chatter

rajd *m* (*-du*; *-dy*) **1.** *samochodowy*, *rowerowy*: rally **2.** (*w wojsku*) rally; **rajdowiec** *m* (*-wca*; *-wcy*) rally driver

rajski *adj* REL paradise; ***~ ogród*** the Garden of Eden; ***~ ptak*** bird of paradise

rajstopy *pl* (*-top*), **rajtuzy** *pl* (*-tuz*) *Br* tights *pl*, *Am* pantyhose *sing*

rak *m* (*-ka*; *-ki*) **1.** BIOL crayfish; ***spiec ~a*** turn crimson **2.** ***~i*** crampons **3.** MED cancer; ***~ płuc*** lung cancer; ***~ krtani*** cancer of the larynx; ***jest chory na ~a*** he's got cancer **4.** ***≈*** ASTR Cancer; ***zwrotnik ≈a*** the Tropic of Cancer

rakarz *m* (*-rza*; *-rze*) dogcatcher

rakieta[1] *f* (*-ty*; *-ty*) **1.** (*pocisk*) missile; ***~ balistyczna*** ballistic missile **2.** (*pojazd*) rocket; ***~ sygnalizacyjna***, ***~ świetlna*** flare

rakieta[2] *f* (*-ty*; *-ty*) *tenisowa*: racket

rakietka *f* (*-ki*; *-ki*) bat

rakietnica *f* (*-cy*; *-ce*) flare gun; **rakietow|y** *adj* rocket; ***wyrzutnia ~a*** rocket launcher; ***baza ~a*** missile base

rakotwórczy *adj* carcinogenic, cancer-causing; **rakow|y** *adj* cancerous; ***komórka ~a*** cancerous cell

rama *f* (*-my*; *-my*) **1.** (*oprawa*) frame; ***~ okienna*** window frame, sash; ***~ rowerowa*** bicycle frame **2.** (*szkielet*) framework; ***w ~ch*** *G fig* within the confines of

ramadan *m* (*-nu*; *no pl*) REL Ramadan

ramiączko *n* (*-ka*; *-ka*) **1.** *sukienki*, *stanika*: shoulder strap **2.** (*wieszak*) hanger

rami|ę *n* (*-mienia*; *-miona*) **1.** shoulder; ***przewiesić torbę przez ~ę*** sling one's bag over one's shoulder; ***szerokie ~ona*** broad shoulders; ***poklepać kogoś po ~eniu*** tap s.o. on the shoulder; ***woda sięgała mu do ~on*** the water came up to his shoulders; ***zaglądać przez ~ę*** lookover one's shoulder; ***włosy do ~on*** shoulder-length hair; ***z otwartymi ~onami*** with open arms; ***z czyjegoś ~enia*** on s.o.'s behalf; ***wzruszyć ~onami*** shrug one's shoulders **2.** arm; ***~ona ośmiornicy*** arms of an octopus; ***~ę w ~ę*** arm in arm; ***chwycić za ~ę*** catch s.o.'s arm; ***nieść kogoś na ~onach*** carry s.o. on one's arms; ***zarzuciła mu ~ona na szyję*** she threw her arms around his neck **3.** *cyrkla*: leg **4.** *świecznika*, *rzeki krzyża*: branch

ramka *f* (*-ki*; *-ki*) frame

ramol *m* (*-la*; *-le*) *infml* fogey

R

ramowy *adj plan*: framework
rampla *f* (*-py*; *-py*) ramp; **światła ~y** *THEAT* footlights
ranla *f* (*-ny*; *-ny*) wound; **~a kłuta** punctured wound; **~a cięta** cut; (**że**) **do ~y przyłóż** good and gentle; **~y boskie!** *infml* holy smoke!, holy Christ!
randka *f* (*-ki*; *-ki*) date; **~ w ciemno** blind date
ranlek *m* (*-nka*; *-nki*) *lit* morning; **wczesnym ~kiem** early morning
ranga *f* (*-gi*; *-gi*) rank; **służyć w randze kapitana** serve at the rankof captain
ranić ⟨**z-**⟩ (*-nię*) **1.** *uczucia*: hurt **2.** *kulą*: wound; **ranić się** cut oneself; **raniony** *adj żołnierz*, *zwierzę*: wounded
raniuteńko, **raniutko** *adv* in the wee hours of the morning, in the small hours
ranka *f* (*-ki*; *-ki*) *dim* (small) wound, cut
ranking *m* (*-gu*; *-gi*) ranking
rannly **I** *adj* **1.** *człowiek*, *zwierzę*: wounded, injured; **~y żołnierz** wounded soldier; **ciężko ~y** badly wounded **2.** morning; **~y ptaszek** *fig* early bird; **~e wstawanie** getting up early; **~e pantofle** slippers; **we wczesnych godzinach ~ych** in the small hours, early in the morning **II** *m* (*-nego*; *-ni*), **-na** *f* (*-nej*; *-ne*) wounded person, injured person, casualty
ranlo **I** *adv* morning; **wcześnie ~o** early in the morning; **dziś ~o** today in the morning; **jutro ~o** tomorrow morning **II** *n* (*-na*; *no pl*) morning; **z ~a** in the morning; **nad ~em** in the small hours of the morning, early in the morning
raper *m* (*-ra*; *-rzy*) rapper
raport *m* (*-tu*; *-ty*) **1.** (*sprawozdanie*) report **2.** (*w wojsku*) account; **stanąć do ~u** stand to account; **raportować** ⟨**za-**⟩ (*-tuję*) report
rapsodia *f* (*-dii*; *-die*) *MUS* rhapsody
raptem *adv* all of a sudden, suddenly; **raptowny** *adj* **1.** *zmiana*: sudden, abrupt **2.** *osoba*: impulsive, impetuous
rarytas *m* (*-sa*; *-sy*) **1.** (*przysmak*) delicacy **2.** (*rzadkość*) rarity
rasla *f* (*-sy*; *-sy*) **1.** *ludzi*: race; **~a czarna** (**biała**) the black(white) race **2.** *zwierząt*: breed; **czystej ~y** thoroughbred
rasista *m* (*-ty*; *rasiści*) racist; **rasistowski** *adj* racist
rasowly *adj* **1.** *konflikt*, *dyskryminacja*: racial **2.** *BIOL* pedigree
ratla *f* (*-ty*; *-ty*) *FIN* instalment, *Am* installment; **kupić na ~y** *Br* buy on hire purchase, *Am* buy on an installment plan; **płacić na ~y** pay by instalments; **kupno na ~y** hire purchase; **na ~y** (*nieregularnie*) by fits and starts, off and on
ratalnly *adj* instalment, *Am* installment; **sprzedaż ~a** *Br* hire purchase, *Am* installment plan
ratować ⟨**u-**⟩ (*-tuję*) rescue, save (**od** *G* from); **~ zasypanych** rescue buried people; **~ komuś życie** save s.o.'s life; **~ sytuację** *fig* save the day, salvage the situation; **~ tonącego** save a drowning man; **~ swoją skórę** save one's skin; **ratować się** save oneself; **~ się ucieczką** run for one's life, run for dear life
ratownictwo *n* (*-wa*; *no pl*) rescue; **~ morskie** lifeboat service; **~ górnicze** mine rescue service; **~ górskie** mountain rescue (service)
ratowniczy *adj akcja*, *ekipa*: rescue; **ratownik** *m* (*-ka*; *-nicy*) **1.** *górski*: rescuer **2.** (*pływak*) lifeguard
ratunlek *m* (*-nku*; *-no pl*) help; **~ku!** help!; **biec komuś na ~ek** come to s.o.'s rescue; **ratunkowly** *adj akcja*: rescue; **kamizelka ~a** life jacket; **koło ~e** life buoy
ratusz *m* (*-sza*; *-sze*) *Br* town hall, *Am* city hall; **ratuszowy** *adj Br* town hall, *Am* city hall
ratyfikacja *f* (*-ji*; *no pl*) ratification; **ratyfikować** *v/im* (*-kuję*) ratify
rausz *m* (*-szu*/*-sza*; *no pl*) drunkenness; **na ~u** tipsy, merry
raut *m* (*-tu*; *-ty*) reception
raz **I** *m* (*-zu*; *-zy*) **1.** (*okoliczność*) time; **pierwszy ~** the first time; **dwa ~y** twice, two times; **dwa ~y dwa** two times two; **ile ~y** how many times; **jeszcze ~** once more, one more time; **~ po ~** time after time; **~ na zawsze** once and for all; **za każdym ~em** every time, each time; **tym ~em** this time; **w obu ~ach** in both cases; **w ~ie** *G* in case; **w każdym ~ie** anyway; **w takim ~ie** well then, in that case; **w najlepszym ~ie** at best; **na przyszły ~** the next time; **innym ~em** some other time; **ostatnim ~em** last time; **ani ~u** not even once;

R

w **~ie czego** just in case; ***w sam ~*** just fine **2.** (*kiedyś*) once; ***pewnego ~u*** once; ***~ na jakiś czas*** once in a while; ***na ~ie*** for the time being; ***na ~ie!*** (*pożegnanie*) see you!; ***od ~u*** straight away, at once; ***~ dwa*** in no time; ***w takim ~ie*** so, in that case; ***w przeciwnym ~ie*** otherwise **II** *num* (*jeden*) one **III** *particle* first, firstly, to start with

razem *adv* together; ***wszyscy ~*** everybody, altogether; ***wszystko ~*** altogether

razić ⟨**po-**⟩ (*rażę*) **1.** (*o świetle*) dazzle; ***raziło mnie słońce*** the sun dazzled me **2.** (*o pociskach*) wound **3.** (*sprawiać przykre wrażenie*) offend; ***~ czyjeś uszy*** offend s.o.'s ears

razowiec *m* (*-wca*; *-wce*) *Br* wholemeal bread, *Am* wholewheat bread; **razowy** *adj chleb, bułka*: *Br* wholemeal, *Am* wholewheat

raźniej *adv*: ***poczuć się ~*** feel safer, feel better

raźny *adj* **1.** (*silny, zdrowy*) lively, energetic **2.** *krok*: brisk

rażący *adj* **1.** *kolor*: (too) bright, garish **2.** *światło*: dazzling, glaring **3.** *niesprawiedliwość*: flagrant, glaring **4.** *błąd*: gross, glaring **5.** *zaniedbanie*: gross

rażeni|e *n* (*-nia*; *no pl*): ***pole ~a*** field of fire; ***siła ~a*** explosive power; ***środki masowego ~a*** weapons of mass destruction

rażony *adj*: ***~ piorunem*** thunderstruck; ***~ paraliżem*** stricken with paralysis; ***~ kulą*** with a gunshot wound, wounded

rąbać (*-bię*) **1.** ⟨**na-**⟩ *drewno*: chop **2.** ⟨**z-**⟩ *drzewa*: fell, cut down **3.** ⟨**wy-**⟩ *otwór*: cut **4.** ⟨**w-**⟩ (*jeść*) *infml* wolf (down), gobble up; ***wrąbał kanapkę z kurczakiem*** he gobbled up a chicken sandwich **5.** (*grać*) *infml* strum (away); ***rąbał na swojej gitarze*** he was strumming away on his guitar

rąb|ek *m* (*-bka*; *-bki*) *spódnicy*: hem; ***uchylić ~ka tajemnicy*** unveil a secret

rąbnąć *v/p* (*-nę*) (*uderzyć*) whack, wallop; ***~ kogoś w głowę*** wacks.o. on the head; ***~ prawdę*** speakbluntly; ***rąbnąć się*** bang, hit oneself (***o*** *A* against)

rączk|a *f* (*-ki*; *-ki*) **1.** *dim* (tiny) hand; ***mieć złotą ~ę*** be a handyman **2.** (*uchwyt*) handle

rączy *adj lit rumak*: swift

rąk → **ręka**

rdza *f* (*-dzy*; *no pl*) rust; **rdzawobrunatny** *adj* russet, reddish-brown; **rdzawoczerwony** *adj* rusty; **rdzawy** *adj* rust-coloured

rdzeniowy *adj* ANAT BIOL spinal

rdzenny *adj ludność*: indigenous

rdzeń *m* (*rdzenia*; *rdzenie*) **1.** BIOL PHYS core; ***~ kręgowy*** ANAT spinal cord **2.** GRAM root

rdzewieć ⟨**za-**⟩ (*-wieję*) rust

rdzoodporny *adj* rust-proof

reagować ⟨**za-**⟩ (*-guję*) react (***na*** *A* to)

reakcja *f* (*-ji*; *-je*) reaction; ***~ jądrowa*** PHYS nuclear reaction; ***~ łańcuchowa*** CHEM chain reaction

reakcjonista *m* (*-ty*; *-niści*) reactionary

reakcyjny *adj* **1.** *poglądy*: reactionary **2.** CHEM reactive

reaktor *m* (*-ra*; *-ry*): ***~ jądrowy*** PHYS nuclear reactor

reaktywować *v/im* (*-tywuję*) reactivate

realia *pl* (*-liów*) *lit* **1.** (*rzeczywistość*) realities *pl* **2.** (*w utworze*) historical background

realist|a *m* (*-ty*; *-liści*), **-tka** *f* (*-ki*; *-ki*) realist; ***nie jesteś ~ą*** you are being unrealistic

realistyczny *adj* realistic

realizacja *f* (*-ji*; *-ji*) **1.** *marzeń*: realization, fulfilment **2.** FILM production **3.** *planu*: execution

realizator *m* (*-ra*; *-rzy*), **~ka** *f* (*-ki*; *-ki*) FILM RADIO producer; ***~em planu jest*** the plan is carried out by

realizatorsk|i *adj*: ***ekipa ~a*** FILM filmteam

realizm *m* (*-mu*; *no pl*) ART realism

realizować ⟨**z-**⟩ (*-zuję*) **1.** *marzenie*: realize **2.** *czek*: cash **3.** *receptę*: fill **4.** *plan*: carry out, execute; ***realizować się*** achieve self-realization, *Am* fulfill one self

realność *f* (*-ści*; *no pl*) reality; **realn|y** *adj* **1.** *zagrożenie*: real; ***~a płaca*** real wages; ***~a wartość*** ECON real value **2.** *plan*: feasible, *infml* doable

reanimować *v/im* (*-muję*) resuscitate; **reanimacja** *f* (*-ji*; *-je*) resuscitation

reasumować ⟨**z-**⟩ (*-muję*) *lit* recap, recapitulate

rebelia *f* (*-lii*; *-lie*) rebellion; **rebeliant** *m* (*-ta*; *-nci*) rebel

R

rebus *m* (*-su*; *-sy*) rebus, picture puzzle
recenzent *m* (*-ta*; *-nci*) reviewer; **recenzja** *f* (*-ji*; *-je*) review; **recenzować** ⟨**z-**⟩ (*-zuje*) review
recepcja *f* (*-ji*; *-je*) **1.** (*w hotelu*) reception (desk) **2.** (*odbiór*) reception; **recepcjonista** *m* (*-ty*; *-niści*) receptionist
recept|a *f* (*-ty*; *-ty*) **1.** (*od lekarza*) prescription; (**tylko**) ***na ~ę*** by prescription only, on prescription only; ***lek bez ~y*** non-prescription drug, over the counter drug **2.** (*rozwiązanie*) recipe; **receptura** *f* (*-ry*; *-ry*) recipe
recesja *f* (*-ji*; *-je*) ECON recession
rechot *m* (*-tu*; *-ty*) **1.** *żab*: croak **2.** (*śmiech*) cackle; **rechotać** ⟨**za-**⟩ (*-choczę*/*-chocę*) **1.** (*o żabie*) croak **2.** (*o osobie*) cackle
recital *m* (*-lu*; *-le*) recital
recydywa *f* (*-wy*; *-wy*) JUR recidivism; **recydywista** *m* (*-ty*; *-wiści*) JUR recidivist
recykling *m* (*-gu*; *no pl*) recycling
recytować ⟨**wy-**⟩ (*-tuję*) *wiersz*: recite
red. *abbr* (=**redaktor**) ed.
redagować ⟨**z-**⟩ (*-guję*) edit
redakcj|a *f* (*-ji*; *-je*) **1.** (*opracowanie*) editing; ***pod ~ą*** *G* edited by **2.** (*zespół dziennikarzy*) editorial staff; **redakcyjny** *adj uwagi*: editorial
redaktor *m* (*-ra*; *-rzy*) editor
redukcja *f* (*-ji*; *-je*) **1.** *zmniejszenie*: reduction; **~ płac** pay cut **2.** *zwolnienie*: redundancy; ***~ personelu*** layoff(s); ***~ etatów*** job cuts, redundancies
redukować ⟨**z-**⟩ (*-kuję*) **1.** *wydatki*: reduce, cut down on; ***~ koszty*** cut costs, reduce costs **2.** (*zwalniać*) make redundant, lay off **3.** *płace*: cut
reedukacja *f* (*-ji*; *no pl*) reeducation; **reedycja** *f* (*-ji*; *-je*) reprint
referat *m* (*-tu*; *-ty*) **1.** (*wykład*) paper **2.** (*dział*) department
referencje *pl* (*-ji*) references *pl*
referendum *n* (*indecl*; *-da*) referendum
referent *m* (*-ta*; *-nci*), **~ka** *f* (*-ki*; *-ki*) **1.** (*sprawozdawca*) speaker **2.** (*pracownik*) head of department
referować ⟨**z-**⟩ (*-ruję*) report
refleks *m* **1.** (*-su*; *no pl*) reflex; ***mieć dobry ~*** have good reflexes **2.** (*-su*; *-sy*) (*odblask*) reflection; **refleksja** *f* (*-ji*; *-je*) reflection; ***nasunęła mi się smutna ~*** it brought sad reflections; **refleksyjny** *adj* reflective
reflektor *m* (*-ra*; *-ry*) **1.** AUTO headlight **2.** (*lampa*) searchlight
reflektować *v/im* (*-tuję*) be interested (**na** *A* in); ***~ na mieszkanie*** be interested in a flat; ***reflektować się*** come to one's senses
reform|a *f* (*-my*; *-my*) reform; ***~y polityczne*** political reform; ***~a szkolnictwa*** educational reform; ***wymagający ~*** in need of reform
reformacja *f* (*-ji*; *no pl*) HIST the Reformation
reformator *m* (*-ra*; *-rzy*) reformer
reformować ⟨**z-**⟩ (*-muję*) reform
refren *m* (*-nu*; *-ny*) MUS refrain, chorus
refundacja *f* (*-ji*; *no pl*) reimbursement, refund; **refundować** ⟨**z-**⟩ (*-duję*) refund, reimburse
regał *m* (*-łu*; *-ły*) bookcase
regatowy *adj* SPORT regatta; **regaty** *pl* (*-gat*) SPORT regatta
regeneracja *f* (*-ji*; *no pl*) regeneration; **regenerować** ⟨**z-**⟩ (*-ruję*) regenerate; ***regenerować się*** regenerate
regent *m* (*-ta*; *-nci*), **~ka** *f* (*-ki*; *-ki*) regent
region *m* (*-nu*; *-ny*) region; **regionalny** *adj* regional
reglamentacja *f* (*-ji*; *no pl*) *żywności*: rationing; **reglamentować** *v/im* (*-tuję*) *żywność*: ration
regle *pl* (*-li*) subalpine forest *sing*, Tatra nappe *sing*
regres *m* (*-su*; *-sy*), ***regresja*** *f* (*-ji*; *-je*) *gospodarczy*: regression
regulacja *f* (*-ji*; *-je*) **1.** *dźwięku*, *ruchu*: control; ***~ urodzeń*** birth control **2.** *rzeki*: engineering **3.** *prawa*, *stosunków*: regulation **4.** *rachunek*: settlement
regulamin *m* (*-nu*; *-ny*) (*statut*) regulations *pl*, statute; ***~ korzystania z biblioteki*** library rules and regulations; **regulaminowy** *adj* **1.** (*zgodny z regulaminem*) statutory **2.** *ubiór*: regulation
regularny *adj połączenie*, *oddech*, *rysy*: regular; **regulator** *m* (*-ra*; *-ry*) TECH regulator; ***na cały ~*** at full blast
regulować (*-luję*) **1.** ⟨**u-**⟩ *ruch*: control **2.** ⟨**u-**⟩ *rzekę*: engineer **3.** ⟨**u-**⟩ *rachunek*: settle **4.** ⟨**u-**⟩ *stosunki*: nor-

R

malize **5.** ⟨**wy-**⟩ *odległość*, *dźwięk*: regulate

reguł|a *f* (*-ły*; *-ły*) **1.** (*przepis*) rule; ***~y gry*** rules of the game; ***~y gramatyczne*** grammar rules; ***z ~y*** as a rule; ***to nie jest ~ą*** this is not a rule; ***stać się ~ą*** become a rule **2.** *REL* principle

rehabilitacja *f* (*-ji*; *-je*) *JUR MED* rehabilitation; **rehabilitacyjn|y** *adj*: ***ośrodek ~y*** *Br* rehabilitation centre, *Am* rehabilitation center; ***ćwiczenia ~e*** physiotherapy

rehabilitant *m* (*-ta*; *-nci*), **~ka** *f* (*-ki*; *-ki*) physiotherapist

rehabilitować ⟨**z-**⟩ (*-tuję*) *JUR MED* rehabilitate

reinkarnacja *f* (*-ji*; *-je*) *REL* reincarnation

rej: ***wodzić ~*** *fig* call the tune

reja *f* (*rei*; *-je*) yard

rejestr *m* (*-ru*; *-ry*) register

rejestracj|a *f* (*-ji*; *-je*) **1.** *pacjenta*, *samochodu*: registration; ***zapisać się w ~i*** register oneself **2.** (*numer rejestracyjny*) *Br* licence plate, *Am* license plate; ***z zagraniczną ~ą*** *AUTO* with foreign plates **3.** *muzyki*: recording **4.** (*miejsce w przychodni*) reception

rejestracyjn|y *adj* *AUTO* registration; ***tablica ~a*** *Br* number plates, *Am* license plates; ***numer ~y*** number plates; ***dowód ~y*** registration; **rejestrator** *m* (*-ra*; *-ry*): ***~ lotu*** *LOTN* flight recorder, blackbox; **rejestratorka** *f* (*-ki*; *-ki*) (doctor's) assistant

rejestrować ⟨**za-**⟩ (*-ruję*) **1.** register **2.** *dźwięk*: record; ***rejestrować się*** **1.** (*u lekarza*) make an appointment **2.** (*meldować się*) register

rejon *m* (*-nu*; *-ny*) **1.** (*okolica*) region, area **2.** district, borough; **rejonowy** *adj* district

rejs *m* (*-su*; *-sy*) **1.** voyage; ***dziewiczy ~*** maiden voyage; ***gotowy do ~u*** ready to sail **2.** (*samolotem*) flight; **rejsowy** *adj*: ***lot ~*** scheduled flight

rekcja *f* (*-ji*; *-je*) *GRAM* government, case governed by a verb

rekin *m* (*-na*; *-ny*) shark

reklam|a *f* (*-my*; *-my*) advert, advertisement; ***~a telewizyjna*** commercial; ***~a prasowa*** newspaper ad; ***specjalista od ~y*** advertising consultant; ***dział ~y*** publicity department; ***zakaz ~y*** advertising forbidden; ***przerwa na ~ę*** commercial break

reklamacj|a *f* (*-ji*; *-je*) complaint; ***składać ~ę*** file a complaint

reklamować ⟨**za-**⟩ (*-muję*) **1.** (*składać reklamację*) complain **2.** (*robić reklamę*) advertise; ***~ pastę do zębów*** advertise toothpaste

reklamow|y *adj* *agencja*, *kampania*: advertising; ***tablica ~a*** *Br* hoarding, *Am* billboard

reklamówka *f* (*-ki*; *-ki*) **1.** (*film*) commercial **2.** (*broszura*) flier, flyer, leaflet **3.** (*rzecz*) promotional gift **4.** (*torba plastikowa*) plastic bag

rekolekcje *pl* (*-ji*) *REL* retreat

rekomendacj|a *f* (*-ji*; *-je*) recommendation; ***za ~ą*** *G* on s.o.'s recommendation; **rekomendować** ⟨**-za**⟩ (*-duję*) recommend

rekompensata *f* (*-ty*; *-ty*) *straty*: compensation; **rekompensować** ⟨**z-**⟩ (*-suję*) *stratę*: compensate; ***~ sobie coś*** compensate for s.th.

rekonesans *m* (*-su*; *-se*/*-sy*) reconnaissance

rekonstruować ⟨**z-**⟩ (*-ruuję*) reconstruct

rekontra *f* (*-ry*; *-ry*) redouble

rekonwalescencja *f* (*-ji*; *no pl*) convalescence; **rekonwalescent** *m* (*-ta*; *-nci*), **~ka** *f* (*-ki*; *-ki*) convalescent

rekord *m* (*-du*; *-dy*) record; ***~ halowy*** indoor record; ***~ świata*** world record; ***pobić ~*** breaka record; **rekordowy** *adj* record; ***w ~m czasie*** in record time

rekordzista *m* (*-ty*; *-dziści*), **-tka** *f* (*-ki*; *-ki*) record-holder; ***~ świata*** world record-holder

rekreacja *f* (*-ji*; *no pl*) recreation

rekreacyjn|y *adj* recreational; ***baza ~a*** leisure facilities

rekrut *m* (*-ta*; *-ruci*) recruit; **rekrutacja** *f* (*-ji*; *-je*) **1.** (*do wojska*) conscription **2.** *uczniów*, *studentów*: enrolment, recruitment

rekrutować *v*/*im* (*-tuję*) **1.** (*do wojska*) conscript **2.** *uczniów*, *studentów*: recruit; ***rekrutować się*** be recruited (***z*** *G* from)

rektor *m* (*-ra*; *-rzy*) rector

rekultywacja *f* (*-ji*; *no pl*) land reclamation

R

rekwiem *n indecl* MUS requiem
rekwirować ⟨**za-**⟩ (*-ruję*) requisition
rekwizycja *f* (*-ji*; *-je*) requisition
rekwizyt *m* (*-tu*; *-ty*) THEAT prop; **rekwizytornia** *f* (*-ni*; *-nie*) THEAT prop room, property room
relacj|a *f* (*-ji*; *-je*) **1.** (*sprawozdanie*) report; **zdać ~ę z** *G* report **2.** (*stosunek*) relationship **3.** (*połączenie kolejowe*) line; ***pociąg ~i Warszawa – Berlin*** the Warsow to Berlin train
relacjonować ⟨**z-**⟩ (*-nuję*) report
relaks *m* (*-su*; *no pl*) relaxation
relaksować ⟨**z-**⟩ (*-suję*) relax; ***relaksować się*** relax
relatywizm *m* (*-mu*; *no pl*) relativism; **relatywizować** ⟨**z-**⟩ (*-zuje*) relativize; **relatywny** *adj* relative
relegacja *f* (*-ji*; *-je*) *form* expulsion; **relegować** *v/im* (*-guje*) *form* expel
relief *m* (*-fu*; *-fy*) ART relief; ***~ płaski*** bas-relief; ***~ wypukły*** high relief
religi|a *f* (*-gii*; *-gie*) religion; ***nauka ~i*** religious instruction
religianctwo *n* (*-wa*; *no pl*) religiosity
religijność *f* (-ści; *no pl*) religiousness; **religijny** *adj osoba*, *obrzęd*: religious
religioznawstwo *n* (*-wa*; *no pl*) religious studies *pl*
relikt *m* (*-tu*; *-ty*) relict
relikwia *f* (*-wii*; *-wie*) REL relic; **relikwiarz** *m* (*-rza*; *-rze*) REL reliquary
remanent *m* (*-tu*; *-ty*) *sklepu*: stocktaking
remis *m* (*-su*; *-sy*) SPORT draw; **remisować** ⟨**z-**⟩ (*-suję*) SPORT draw; **remisowy** *adj* SPORT draw
remiza *f* (*-zy*; *-zy*): ***~ strażacka*** fire station
remon|t *m* (*-tu*; *-ty*) **1.** *maszyny*: refurbishment, repair; ***~t kapitalny*** major overhaul **2.** *mieszkania*: redecoration; ***być w ~cie*** be redecorated, be refurbished; ***~t kapitalny*** extensive redecoration
remontować ⟨**wy-**, **od-**⟩ (*-tuję*) **1.** *mieszkanie*, *budynek*: do up, redecorate **2.** *maszynę*: repair; **remontowy** *adj* redecoration, refurbishment
Ren *m* (*-nu*) the Rhine; ***nad ~em*** on the Rhine
rencista *m* (*-ty*; *-ciści*), **-tka** *f* (*-ki*; *-ki*) pensioner
renegat *m* (*-ta*; *-gaci*) *lit* renegade
renesans *m* (*-su*; *no pl*) ART the Renaissance
renifer *m* (*-ra*; *-ry*) reindeer; **reniferowy** *adj*: ***chrobotek ~*** BIOL reindeer moss
renoma *f* (*-my*; *no pl*) reputation; **renomowany** *adj* reputable
renowacja *f* (*-ji*; *-je*) *dworku*: renovation
ren|ta *f* (*-ty*; *-ty*) pension; ***~ta starcza*** old-age pension; ***być na ~cie*** be a pensioner; ***~ta inwalidzka*** disability pension
rentgen *m* (*-na*; *-ny*) **1.** (*aparat*) X-ray machine **2.** (*prześwietlenie*) X-ray; ***zrobić sobie ~*** have an X-ray taken; ***zrobić ~ szczęki*** X-ray one's jaw
rentgenogram *m* (*-mu*; *-my*) X-ray picture, roentgenogram
rentgenowski *adj* X-ray; ***zdjęcie ~e*** X-ray (picture); ***badanie ~e*** X-ray examination
rentowność *f* (*-ści*; *no pl*) profitability
rentowny *adj* profitable
reński *adj*: ***wino ~e*** *Br* hock, *Am* rhine wine
reorganizować ⟨**z-**⟩ (*-zuję*) reorganize
reparacje *pl* (*-ji*) POLIT (*zapłata*) (war) reparations
repatriacja *f* (*-ji*; *no pl*) POLIT *jeńców*: repatriation; **repatriant** *m* (*-ta*; *-nci*), **~ka** *f* (*-ki*; *-ki*) *wojenny*: repatriated person
reperacj|a *f* (*-ji*; *-je*) repair; ***to wymaga ~i*** this must be repaired
reperkusje *pl* (*-ji*) repercussions *pl*
reperować ⟨**z-**⟩ (*-ruję*) repair
repertuar *m* (*-ru*; *-ry*) repertoire
repeta *f* (*-ty*; *-ty*) *infml* second helping
repetować ⟨**za-**⟩ (*-tuję*) **1.** *broń*: repeat **2.** ***~ klasę*** repeat a class
repetytorium *m* (*indecl*; *-ria*) **1.** (*powtórzenie*) review **2.** (*podręcznik*) review coursebook
replika *f* (*-ki*; *-ki*) *lit* **1.** *obrazu*: replica **2.** (*odpowiedź*) retort **3.** (*w sądzie*) rebuttal
reportaż *m* (*-żu*; *-że*) report, reportage; ***~ telewizyjny*** screen documentary, TV coverage
reporter *m* (*-ra*; *-rzy*), **~ka** *f* (*-ki*; *-ki*) reporter; **reporterski** *adj* reporter, reporter's
represje *pl* (*-ji*) repression, repressive measures *pl*; **represyjny** *adj* repressive

reprezentacja *f* (*-ji*; *-je*) **1.** (*przedstawicielstwo*) representation **2.** SPORT team; **~ narodowa** national team; **reprezentacyjny** *adj* **1.** *fundusz*: entertainment **2.** *charakter*, *funkcja*: representation **3.** *strój*: formal
reprezentant *m* (*-ta*; *-nci*), **~ka** *f* (*-ki*; *-ki*) representative; **Izba ~ów** The House of Representatives
reprezentować *v/im* (*-tuje*) *firmę*: represent
reprodukcja *f* (*-ji*; *-je*) **1.** *obrazu*: reproduction **2.** (*ilustracja*) picture, copy
reprymenda *f* (*-dy*; *-dy*) reprimand
reprywatyzacja *f* (*-ji*; *no pl*) *Br* reprivatisation, *Am* reprivatization
republika *f* (*-ki*; *-ki*) republic; **~ Federalna Niemiec** Federal Republic of Germany
republikanin *m* (*-na*; *-kanie*), **-kanka** *f* (*-ki*; *-ki*) republican
republikański *adj* republican
reputacj|a *f* (*-ji*; *no pl*) (*opinia*) reputation; **psuć komuś ~ę** damage s.o.'s reputation
resocjalizacja *f* (*-ji*; *no pl*) rehabilitation, resocialization
resor *m* (*-ru*; *-ry*) AUTO (suspension) spring; **na ~ach** with suspension springs; **bujda na ~ach** *infml Br* fib, *Am* humbug
resorpcja *f* (*-ji*; *no pl*) BIOL reabsorbtion
resort *m* (*-tu*; *-ty*) department; **resortowy** *adj* department
respekt *m* (*-tu*; *no pl*) respect; **mieć ~** have respect (**dla** *G* for); **respektować** *v/im* (*-tuję*) respect
respirator *m* (*-ra*; *-ry*) MED respirator
respondent *m* (*-ta*; *-nci*), **~ka** *f* (*-ki*; *-ki*) respondent
restauracj|a[1] *f* (*-ji*; *-je*) (*lokal*) restaurant; **iść do ~i** go to the restaurant
restauracja[2] *f* (*-ji*; *-je*) **1.** (*odnawianie*) restoration **2.** POLIT the Restoration
restauracyjka *f* (*-ki*; *-ki*) *dim* (small) restaurant
restauracyjny *adj*: **wagon ~** dining car; **personnel ~** restaurant staff
restaurator[1] *m* (*-ra*; *-rzy*) (*konserwator*) renovator, restorer
restaurator[2] *m* (*-ra*; *-rzy*), **~ka** *f* (*-ki*; *-ki*) restaurateur

R

restaurować ⟨**od-**⟩ (*-ruję*) *zabytki*: restore
restrukturyzować *v/im* (*-zuję*) restructure
restrykcje *pl* (*-ji*) restrictions *pl*
reszka *f* (*-ki*; *-ki*) *monety*: heads; **orzeł czy ~?** heads or tails?
reszt|a *f* (*-ty*; *-ty*) **1.** (*pozostałości*) rest; **~a gości** the remaining guests; **~ę życia spędził na wsi** he spent the rest of his life in the countryside; **bez ~y** completely **2.** (*pieniądze*) change; **~y nie trzeba!** keep the change!; **resztk|a** *f* (*-ki*; *-ki*) rest; **~a sera** leftover cheese; **~i sił** remaining strength; **gonić ~ami sił** be on one's last legs; **~i materiału** remnants; **~i jedzenia** leftovers
retoryczny *adj* rhetorical
retransmisja *f* (*-ji*; *-je*) RADIO repeat, retransmission
retrospektywny *adj* retrospective; **przegląd ~** retrospective
retusz *m* (*-szu*; *-sze*) **1.** PHOT retouch **2.** *tekstu*: minor corrections *pl*; **retuszować** ⟨**wy-**⟩ (*-szuję*) PHOT retouch
rety *interj*: **~!** oh dear!
reumatyczny *adj* rheumatic; **reumatyzm** *m* (*-mu*; *no pl*) rheumatism
rewaloryzacja *f* (*-ji*; *-je*) **1.** FIN revaluation **2.** *zabytków*: restoration
rewanż *m* (*-żu*; *-że*) **1.** (*zemsta*) revenge **2.** SPORT rematch, return match **3.** (*odwzajemnienie się*) return service, return favour; **w ~u za coś** in return for s.th.
rewanżować się ⟨**z-**⟩ (*-żuję*) **1.** (*odwzajemniać się*) pay back(**za** *A* for) **2.** (*mścić się*) avenge oneself
rewanżowy *adj*: **mecz ~** SPORT return match
rewelacja *f* (*-ji*; *-je*) revelation; **rewelacyjny** *adj* sensational
rewers *m* (*-su*; *-sy*) **1.** *monety*: reverse **2.** *w bibliotece*: (borrowing) slip
rewia *f* (*-wii*; *-wie*) revue; **~ mody** fashion show
rewident *m* (*-ta*; *-nci*), **~ka** *f* (*-ki*; *-ki*) auditor
rewidować ⟨**z-**⟩ (*-duję*) **1.** *bagaż*: search **2.** *zdanie*: change, revise
rewindykacja *f* (*-ji*; *-je*) *dzieł sztuki*: claim
rewiowy *adj* revue

rewir *m* (*-ru*; *-ry*) **1.** (*w leśnictwie*) forest district **2.** (*w łowiectwie*) hunting ground **3.** (*ulubione miejsce*) stamping ground
rewizj|a *f* (*-ji*; *-je*) **1.** *mieszkania*: search; **~a osobista** personal search; **nakaz** (**dokonania**) **~i** search warrant; **przeprowadzić ~ę mieszkania** search a house **2.** *ksiąg finansowych*: audit **3.** *ustawy*: amendment **4.** *poglądów*: revision **5.** *JUR* appeal
rewizjonista *m* (*-ty*; *-niści*) *POLIT* revisionist; **rewizjonistyczny** *adj POLIT* revisionist
rewizyjn|y *adj*: **komisja ~a** board of control, auditing committee; **sąd ~y** *JUR* court of review
rewizyta *f* (*-ty*; *-ty*) return visit
rewolucj|a *f* (*-ji*; *-je*) revolution; **~a październikowa** the October Revolution; **Wielka ≈a Francuska** the French Revolution; **~a kulturalna** the Cultural Revolution; **przywódca ~i** revolution leader
rewolucjonista *m* (*-ty*; *-niści*), **-tka** *f* (*-ki*; *-ki*) revolutionary
rewolucjonizować ⟨**z-**⟩ (*-zuję*) *fig* revolutionize
rewolucyjny *adj* revolutionary
rewolwer *m* (*-ru*; *-ry*) revolver
rezerw|a *f* (*-wy*; *-wy*) **1.** (*zapas*, *dystans*) reserve; **trzymać w ~ie** keep in reserve; **z ~ą** with reserve **2.** (*wojska*) the reserves **3.** *SPORT* substitute, reserve
rezerwacj|a *f* (*-ji*; *-je*) *biletu*, *pokoju*: reservation, booking; **z ~ą** with reservation only
rezerwat *m* (*-tu*; *-ty*) *Indian*: reservation; **~ przyrody** reserve
rezerwista *m* (*-ty*; *-wiści*) reservist
rezerwować ⟨**za-**⟩ (*-wuję*) *miejsce*, *pokój*, *stolik*: book, reserve
rezerwowy *adj SPORT* reserve
rezerwuar *m* (*-ru*; *-ry*) reservoir
rezolucja *f* (*-ji*; *-je*) resolution
rezolutność *f* (*-ści*; *no pl*) cleverness; **rezolutny** *adj* clever
rezonans *m* (*-su*; *-se*) *PHYS* resonance; **rezonansowy** *adj PHYS* resonance
rezonować *v/im* (*-nuje*) resonate
rezulta|t *m* (*-tu*; *-ty*) result; **w ~cie** as a result
rezurekcja *f* (*-ji*; *-je*) *REL* Easter Sunday morning mass; **rezurekcyjn|y** *adj*: **procesja ~a** Easter procession

rezydencja *f* (*-ji*; *-je*) residence
rezydować *v/im* (*-duję*) reside
rezygnacj|a *f* (*-ji*; *-je*) resignation; **~a z urzędu** stepping down, resignation; **złożyć ~ę** hand in one's resignation, step down; **~a z** *G* abandonment of
rezygnować ⟨**z-**⟩ (*-nuję*) give up (**z** *G*); **~ ze stanowiska** resign from one's position
reżim, **reżym** *m* (*-mu*; *no pl*) **1.** *POLIT* regime **2.** (*rygor*) discipline
reżyser *m* (*-ra*; *-rzy*) director; **~ filmowy** film director; **reżyser|ia** *f* (*-rii*; *no pl*) direction; **w ~ii** *G* directed by
reżyserka *f* (*-ki*; *-ki*) **1.** (*kobieta reżyser*) female director **2.** (*pomieszczenie*) control room
reżyserować ⟨**wy-**⟩ (*-ruję*) direct
reżyserski *adj* director's
rębacz *m* (*-cza*; *-cze*) *MIN* cutter
ręce *pl* → **ręka**
ręcznie *adv* by hand; **~ robiony** handmade; **~ napisany** handwritten; **~ szyty** sewn by hand; **~ malowany** painted by hand; **~ napędzany** manually-operated; **napisać ~** write by hand; → **ręczny**
ręcznik *m* (*-ka*; *-ki*) towel; **~ kąpielowy** bath towel
ręczn|y *adj* hand; **~a robota** handmade; **~y hamulec** handbrake; **prace ~e** handicrafts; **napęd ~y** *TECH* hand drive, hand control, manual operation; **bagaż ~y** hand luggage; **piłka ~a** handball
ręczyć *v/im* (*-czę*) vouch (**za** *A* for); **ręczę ci, że** I can assure you that; **ręczę, że** I am certain that
ręk|a *f* (*-ki*, *ręce*) **1.** (*dłoń*) hand; **złamać sobie ~ę** breakone's hand; **~a w ~ę** hand in hand; **trzymać kogoś za ~ę** hold s.o. by the hand; **oddać do rąk** deliver personally; **z rąk do rąk** from hand to hand; **od ~i** while one waits, on the spot; **to jest mi nie na ~ę** it doesn't suit me; **mieć pod ~ą** have close at hand; **iść komuś na ~ę** *fig* be accommodating with; **dać komuś wolną ~ę** give s.o. a free hand; **działać na własną ~ę** act by oneself; **do rąk własnych** in person, personally; **podać komuś ~ę** shake hands with; **mieć pełne ręce roboty** have one's hands full (at work); **własnymi ~ami** with

R

one's own hands; ***ręce przy sobie!*** hands off!, keep your hands to yourself!; ***ręce do góry!*** hands up!; ***prosić kogoś o ~ę*** askfor s.o.'s hand (in marriage), propose to; ***mieć dwie lewe ręce*** be clumsy, be all thumbs; ***być w dobrych ~ach*** be in good hands; ***dostać kogoś w swoje ręce*** get one's hands on s.o. **2.** (*ramię*) arm; ***pod ~ę*** arm in arm

rękaw *m* (*-wa*; *-wy*) **1.** *koszuli*: sleeve; ***bez ~ów*** sleeveless; ***sypać jak z ~a*** produce by the dozen; ***zakasać ~y*** roll up one's sleeves **2.** (*do kierunku wiatru*) wind sock **3.** (*przejście do samolotu*) wind sleeve

rękawic|e *pl* (*-wic*) gloves *pl*; ***~e ochronne*** working gloves; ***gumowe ~e*** rubber gloves; ***~e bokserskie*** boxing gloves; ***~a kąpielowa*** washing glove

rękawicz|ki *pl* (*-czek*) gloves *pl*; ***skórzane ~ki*** leather gloves; ***~ki z jednym palcem*** mittens; ***para ~ek*** a pair of gloves; ***zmieniać jak ~ki*** change like one changes shoes; ***w białych ~kach*** *fig* in velvet gloves

rękoczyn|y *pl* (*-nów*) (*bójka*) violent actions *pl*; ***posunąć się do ~ów*** become violent, start fighting; ***doszło do ~ów*** it came to blows

rękodzielnictwo *n* (*-wa*; *no pl*) (handi)crafts; **rękodzielnik** *m* (*-ka*; *-nicy*) craftsman; **rękodzieł|o** *n* (*-ła*; *no pl*) (handi)craft; ***~a*** (handi)crafts

rękojeść *f* (*-ści*; *no pl*) **1.** *noża*: handle **2.** *broni palnej*: grip **3.** *miecza*: hilt

rękojmia *f* (*-mi*; *-mie*) **1.** *bezpieczeństwa*, *pokoju*: guarantee **2.** COMM warranty

R

rękopis *m* (*-su*; *-sy*) manuscript

RFN *abbr m* (*RFN-u*; *no pl*) (= **Republika Federalna Niemiec**) Federal Republic of Germany

ring *m* (*-gu*; *-gi*) SPORT ring

riposta *f* (*-ty*; *-ty*) *lit* retort, riposte

robactwo *n* (*-wa*; *no pl*) insects *pl*

robaczek *m* (*-czka*; *-czki*) *dim* (little) worm; ***~ świętojański*** *Br* glow-worm, *Am* lightening bug

robaczkow|y *adj*: ***wyrostek ~y*** ANAT (vermiform) appendix; ***ruchy ~e*** peristalsis, peristaltic movements; ***zapalenie wyrostka ~ego*** appendicitis

robaczyca *f* (*-cy*; *no pl*) MED helminthiasis

robaczywieć ⟨**z-**⟩ (*-wieję*) (*o owocach*, *grzybach*) become wormy, verminate; **robaczywy** *adj jabłko*, *grzyb*: wormy, worm-eaten

robak *m* (*-ka*; *-ki*) (*w jabłku*, *w mięsie*) worm; ***~i*** MED worms; ***zalewać ~a*** *infml* drown one's sorrows, hit the bottle; **robal** *m* (*-la*; *-le*) (big ugly) worm

robić ⟨**z-**⟩ (*-bię*) **1.** *obiad*, *herbatę*: make; ***~ porządki*** tidy up, clean; ***~ miny*** pull faces, make faces; ***~ użytek z*** *G* make use of; ***~ na drutach*** knit; ***~ komuś nadzieję*** raise one's hopes; ***~ sobie wrogów*** make enemies; ***~ wyjątek*** make an exception; ***nic sobie nie ~ z*** *G* not be bothered by; ***~ komuś trudności*** cause s.o. difficulties; ***~ kogoś w konia*** *infml* make a fool of, cheat; ***~ komuś na złość*** spite s.o.; ***~ komuś wstyd*** shame s.o., show s.o. up; ***~ z igły widły*** make mountains out of molehills; ***~ pieniądze*** make money; ***zrobić cztery kilometry*** travel four kilometers **2.** *lekcje*, *pranie*, *zakupy*: do; ***~ zakupy*** do the shopping; ***~ pranie*** do the washing; ***co on robi?*** what's he doing?; ***co ~?*** what shall we do?; ***to ci dobrze zrobi*** this will do you good; ***robić swoje*** do one's job; ***~ siusiu*** *infml* pee **3.** (*pracować*) *infml* work; ***robić się*** become, get; ***robi się ciepło*** it's getting warm; ***zrobiło mi się smutno*** I felt sad; ***zrobiło mi się słabo*** I felt faint; ***zrobiło mi się ciemno przed oczami*** I saw darkness; ***już się robi!*** all right, I'm doing it now!, I'll do it right away

robociarz *m* (*-rza*; *-rze*) *infml Br* labourer, *Am* worker; **robocizn|a** *f* (*-ny*; *no pl*) *Br* labour, *Am* labor; ***koszty ~y*** *Br* labour costs, *Am* labor costs

roboczodniówka *f* (*-ki*; *-ki*) manshift, day; **roboczogodzina** *f* (*-ny*; *-ny*) man-hour

robocz|y *adj ubranie*, *rękawice*: work; ***dzień ~y*** weekday; ***zespół ~y*** work team; ***wizyta ~a*** POLIT working visit; ***siła ~a*** workforce, *Br* labour force, *Am* labor force; ***pamięć ~a*** INF work memory

robol *m* (*-la*; *-le*) *infml* workhorse, *infml* prole

robot *m* (*-ta*; *-ty*) robot; **~ *kuchenny*** food processor

robot|a *f* (*-ty*; *-ty*) work; ***czarna ~a*** dirty work, donkey work; ***krecia ~a*** intrigues; ***~y drogowe*** road works; ***~y przymusowe*** *HIST* forced labour; ***po robocie*** after work; ***własnej ~y*** home-made; ***nie mieć nic do ~y*** have nothing to do

robotnica *f* (*-cy*; *-ce*) **1.** (*pracownica*) worker **2.** *BIOL* worker bee; **robotniczy** *adj ruch*, *klasa*: working; ***hotel ~*** workers' hostel; **robotnik** *m* (*-ka*; *-nicy*) worker; **~ *budowlany*** construction worker; **~ *portowy*** docker; **~ *wykwalifikowany*** skilled worker

robótk|a *f* (*-ki*; *-ki*): ***~a na drutach*** knitting; ***ręczne ~i*** needlework, handicrafts

rock *m* (*-ka*; *no pl*) *MUS* rock; **rockowy** *adj* rock

roczek *n* (*-czku*; *latka*) *dim* year; ***dziecko ma już ~*** the baby is already one year old

rocznica *f* (*-cy*; *-ce*) anniversary; ***trzecia ~ ślubu*** third wedding anniversary; **~ *śmierci*** death anniversary, anniversary of s.o.'s death; **rocznie** *adv* yearly, every year

rocznik *m* (*-ka*; *-ki*) **1.** *statystyczny*: yearbook; ***~i*** chronicle **2.** (*rok urodzenia*) year; ***który jesteś rocznik?*** when were you born? **3.** (*rok produkcji wina*) vintage

roczn|y *adj* yearly; ***~e dziecko*** one-year-old baby

rodaczka *f* (*-ki*; *-ki*) compatriot, fellow countrywoman; **rodak** *m* (*-ka*; *-dacy*) compatriot, fellow countryman

rodnik *m* (*-ka*; *-ki*) *CHEM* radical

rodn|y *adj*: ***narządy ~e*** *ANAT* reproductive organs

rododendron *m* (*-nu*; *-ny*) rhododendron

rodowity *adj* native; **~ *Polak*** trueborn Pole

rodow|ód *m* (*-wodu*; *-wody*) **1.** *utworu*, *produktu*: origin **2.** (*dzieje rodu*) lineage **3.** *konia*: pedigree; ***pies z ~odem*** pedigree dog

rodow|y *adj*: ***nazwisko ~e*** maiden name; ***szlachta ~a*** hereditary nobility; ***walki ~e*** family feuds; ***drzewo ~e*** family tree

rody *pl* → ***ród***

rodzaj *m* (*-ju*; *-je*) **1.** (*typ*) kind; ***jedyny w swoim ~u*** one of its kind, unique; ***coś w ~u*** something like **2.** *BIOL* genus; **~ *ludzki*** humankind **3.** (*w literaturoznawstwie*) genre **4.** *GRAM* gender

rodzajnik *m* (*-ka*; *-ki*) *GRAM* article

rodzajow|y *adj* ***malarstwo ~e*** genre painting

rodzeństwo *n* (*-wa*; *no pl*) brothers and sisters *pl*, siblings *pl*

rodzic *m* (*-ca*; *-ce*) parent; **rodzice** *pl* (*-ców*) parents *pl*; **~ *chrzestni*** the godparents; **~ *przybrani*** adoptive parents; **rodzicielski** *adj* parental; ***zebranie ~e*** parent-teacher meeting; ***komitet ~*** parents' council

rodzić (*-dzę*) **1.** ⟨**u-**⟩ give birth to; **~ *dziecko*** have a baby **2.** ⟨**z-**⟩ (*spowodować*) give rise to **3.** *v/im owoce*: bear; **rodzić się 1.** (*o dziecku*) be born **2.** (*pochodzić*) come into being, emerge

rodzimy *adj* **1.** *historia*, *literatura*: native; **~ *użytkownik języka*** native speaker **2.** *handel*, *przemysł*: home, domestic **3.** (*miejscowy*) local **4.** (*swojski*) familiar

rodzin|a *f* (*-ny*; *-ny*) family; ***~a wielodzietna*** large family, family with many children; ***~a zastępcza*** foster family, adoptive family; ***daleka ~a*** distant family, distant relatives; ***ojciec ~y*** head of the family; ***głowa ~y*** the head of the family; ***założyć ~ę*** start a family; ***~a zmarłego*** the bereaved; ***~a panującego*** the ruling house; ***bez ~y*** without living relatives; ***~a językowa*** language family; ***Święta ~a*** *REL* the Holy Family

rodzinka *f* (*-ki*; *-ki*) *dim* family; ***ładna ~*** *iron* nice family

rodzinn|y *adj* **1.** *uroczystość*, *pamiątki*, *osoba*: family; ***dom ~y*** family house, one's parents' house; ***w gronie ~ym*** in one's family circle; ***spotkanie ~e*** family reunion **2.** *miasto*: home; ***kraj ~y*** motherland, mother country; ***sprawy ~e*** family matters

rodzony *adj* one's own, blood

rodzynki *pl* (*-ków*/*-nek*) raisins *pl*

rogacizna *f* (*-ny*; *no pl*) horned cattle

R

rogacz *m* (*-cza*; *-cze*) **1.** *BIOL* stag **2.** (*mężczyzna*) cuckold
rogal *m* (*-la*; *-le*), **rogalik** *m* (*-ka*; *-ki*) croissant
rogatk|i *pl* (*-tek*) **1.** (*brama*) tollgate *sing*; ***za ~ami miasta*** outside the city **2.** (*na autostradzie*) toll booth
rogat|y *adj* **1.** *zwierzę*: horned; ***bydło ~e*** horned cattle **2.** *osoba*, *charakter*: stubborn
rogatywka *f* (*-ki*; *-ki*) four-cornered cap
rogi *pl* → ***róg***
rogowacieć 〈**z-**〉 (*-cieję*) (*o skórze*) become horny
rogow|y *adj*: ***okulary w ~ej oprawce*** horn-rimmed glasses
rogówka *f* (*-ki*; *-ki*) *ANAT* cornea
roić *v/im* (*roję*) (*marzyć*) dream (***o*** *L* of); ***roić się*** **1.** ***roi mu się, że*** he imagines that **2.** 〈**wy-**〉 (*o pszczołach*) swarm **3.** (*być przepełnionym*) be full (***od*** *G* of)
rojalista *m* (*-ty*; *-liści*), **-tka** *f* (*-ki*; *-ki*) royalist; **rojalistyczny** *adj* royalist
roje *pl* → ***rój***
rojno *adv* ***było ~*** there were swarms of people; **rojny** *adj plac*, *ulica*: crowded
rok *m* (*-ku*; *lata*) year; ***od ~u*** for a year; ***przed ~iem***, ***~ temu*** a year ago; ***za ~*** next year; ***raz do ~u*** once a year; ***z ~u na ~*** from year to year; ***~ w ~*** year in year out; ***~ przestępny*** leap year; ***Nowy ~*** New Year; ***do siego ~u!*** Happy New Year!; ***~ świetlny*** *ASTR* light year; ***~ akademicki*** academic year; ***zostać na drugi ~*** (*w szkole*) repeat a class
rokfor *m* (*-ra*/*-ru*; *-ry*) (*gatunek sera*) Roquefort
rokitnik *m* (*-ka*; *-ki*) *BIOL* sea-buckthorn
rokoko *n indecl* rococo; **rokokowy** *adj* rococo
rokować *v/im* (*-kuję*) *form* **1.** *POLIT* negotiate (***o*** *A*) **2.** (*zapowiadać*, *przepowiadać*) augur; ***~ nadzieje*** hold promise, promise well; ***~ sukces*** be likely to succeed; ***~ poprawę*** show improvement; ***nie ~ nic dobrego*** bode ill, augur badly
rokowani|e *n* (*-nia*; *-nia*) **1.** *MED* prognosis **2.** ***~a*** *POLIT* negotiations; ***~a pokojowe*** peace talks
rokrocznie *adv* every year
rol|a[1] *f* (*-li*; *-le*) soil; ***na ~i*** on the land
rol|a[2] *f* (*-li*; *-le*) **1.** *THEAT* role, part; ***~a tytułowa*** title role; ***w ~i głównej*** starring; ***odgrywać ~ę w*** *L* play a part in; ***to nie gra ~i*** it doesn't matter **2.** (*zwój*) roll; ***~a papieru*** roll of paper
rolada *f* (*-dy*; *-dy*) *COOK* **1.** (*ciasto*) *Br* (Swiss) roll, *Am* jelly roll **2.** (*mięso*) roulade; ***~ wołowa*** roulade of beef, beef olive
roleta *f* (*-ty*; *-ty*) roller blind
rolk|a *f* (*-ki*; *-ki*) (*zwój*) roll; ***~a papieru toaletowego*** toilet roll; ***~a nici*** spool of thread; ***~i*** roller blades
rolnictwo *n* (*-wa*; *no pl*) agriculture
rolnicz|y *adj maszyna*: agricultural; ***kółko ~e*** farmers' association
rolnik *m* (*-ka*; *-nicy*), **-niczka** *f* (*-ki*; *-ki*) farmer
roln|y *adj* agricultural; ***gospodarstwo ~e*** farm; ***produkty ~e*** farm produce; ***reforma ~a*** agrarian reform
rolować (*-luję*) **1.** 〈**z-**〉 (*zwijać*) roll **2.** 〈**wy-**〉 (*oszukiwać*) *infml* cheat
romanistyka *f* (*-ki*; *no pl*) Romance studies *pl*
romans *m* (*-su*; *-se*) **1.** (*przygoda miłosna*) (love) affair **2.** (*powieść*) love story **3.** *MUS* romance
romansidło *n* (*-ła*; *-ła*) (mawkish) love story; **romansik** *m* (*-ku*; *-ki*) *dim* (minor) love affair
romansować *v/im* (*-suję*) **1.** have an affair
romantyczność *f* (*-ści*; *no pl*) *fig* romance; **romantyczny** *adj* romantic
romantyk *m* (*-ka*; *-tycy*), **-tyczka** *f* (*-ki*; *-ki*) **1.** romantic **2.** (*w literaturze*) romanticist
romantyzm *m* (*-mu*; *no pl*) romanticism
romański *adj* **1.** *język*: Romance **2.** *ARCHIT* Romanesque
romb *m* (*-bu*; *-by*) rhombus
rondel *m* (*-dla*; *-dle*) saucepan
rondo *n* (*-da*; *-da*) **1.** (*skrzyżowanie*) *Br* roundabout, *Am* traffic circle; ***objechać ~*** go round a traffic circle **2.** *kapelusza*: brim **3.** *MUS* rondo
ronić (*-nię*) **1.** 〈**u-**〉 ***~ kroplę*** *lit* spill a drop **2.** 〈**u-**〉 ***~ łzy*** *lit* shed tears **3.** 〈**po-**〉 *MED* miscarry, have a miscarriage
ropa *f* (*-py*; *no pl*) **1.** *MED* pus **2.** *AUTO* diesel (oil); ***~ naftowa*** (crude) oil, petroleum

R

ropieć ⟨**za-**⟩ (*-pieję*) (*o ranie*) suppurate
ropień *m* (*-pnia*; *-pnie*) MED abscess; **ropn|y** *adj* MED purulent, suppurative; **złoża ~e** oil fields
roponośny *adj* oil-bearing
ropucha *f* (*-chy*; *-chy*) toad
roraty *pl* (*-rat*/*-tów*) REL *early morning Advent mass*
ros|a *f* (*-sy*; *no pl*) dew; **poranna ~a** morning dew; **chodzić po ~ie** walk on dew
rosiczka *f* (*-ki*; *-ki*) BIOL sundew
rosić ⟨**z-**⟩ (*-szę*) *lit* spray; **pot zrosił mu twarz** his face is covered in sweat, sweat ran down his face
Rosja *f* (*-ji*) Russia; **Rosjanin** *m* (*-na*; *-janie*), **-janka** *f* (*-ki*; *-ki*) Russian
rosły *adj* strapping
rosnąć ⟨**u-**⟩ (*-nę*) **1.** grow; **~ jak na drożdżach** grow very quickly **2.** (*wychowywać się*) grow up **3.** (*o cenach, bezrobociu*) rise
rosochaty *adj wierzba*: (bi)furcate, branchy
rosołow|y *adj*: **kostka ~a** *Br* stockcube, *Am* bullion cube
rosół *m* (*-sołu*; *-soły*) broth; **~ z kury** chicken consommé; **rozebrany do rosołu** stark naked, completely naked, starkers
rostbef *m* (*-fu*; *-fy*) roast beef
rosyjsk|i *adj* Russian; **język ~i** Russian; **~a ruletka** Russian roulette
roszczenia *pl* (*-czeń*) claims *pl*; **wysunąć ~** lay claims (**o** *A* to)
rościć *v/im* (*roszczę*): **~ (sobie) prawo do** *G* claim the right to; **~ niesłuszne pretensje do** *G* not have the right to
roślejszy *comp* → **rosły**
roślin|a *f* (*-ny*; *-ny*) plant; **~a ozdobna** ornamental plant; **~a lecznicza** medicinal plant; **~a pnąca** climbing plant, vine; **~a pastewna** fodder plant; **~y okopowe** root plants; **~a wieloletnia** perennial; **roślinka** *f* (*-ki*; *-ki*) *dim* (little) plant; **roślinność** *f* (*-ści*; *no pl*) vegetation, plantlife
roślinny *adj* **1.** *olej, tłuszcz*: vegetable **2.** *świat*: plant; **roślinożerny** *adj* herbivorous
rota *f* (*-ty*; *-ty*): **~ przysięgi** oath
rotacja *f* (*-ji*; *-je*) **1.** (*zmiana*) change; **~ pracowników** staff rotation **2.** (*ruch*) rotation
rotunda *f* (*-dy*; *-dy*) rotunda
rowek *m* (*-wka*; *-wki*) groove
rowe|r *m* (*-ru*; *-ry*) bicycle, bike; **~r wyścigowy** racing bicycle, racer; **~r górski** mountain bike; **~r wodny** pedal boat; **jeździć na ~rze** ride a bicycle, cycle; **rowerow|y** *adj* cycling, bicycle; **wycieczka ~a** (*ćwiczenie*) cycling trip
rowerek *m* (*-rka*/*-rku*; *-rki*) **1.** *dim* (little) bike **2.** (*ćwiczenie*) cycling
rowerzysta *m* (*-ty*; *-rzyści*), **-tka** *f* (*-ki*; *-ki*) cyclist
rowkować *v/im* (*-kuje*) *blachę*: groove; **rowkowanie** *f* (*-nia*; *no pl*) grooving; **rowkowany** *adj blacha*: grooved, fluted
rowy *pl* → **rów**
rozanielony *adj* overjoyed, beaming, over the moon
rozbabrać *v/p* (*-brzę*) *infml* **1.** (*nie skończyć*) make a mess of; **~ jedzenie** hardly start eating and leave it **2.** (*źle zrobić*) bungle, botch (up) **3.** (*porozrzucać*) dig up, scatter
rozbawiać ⟨**-wić**⟩ (*-wiam*) amuse; **rozbawiać się** start enjoying oneself
rozbawienie *n* (*-nia*; *no pl*) amusement; **z ~m** amused
rozbawiony *adj* **1.** *osoba*: amused **2.** *spojrzenie, mina*: amused
rozbeczeć się *v/p* (*-czę*) *infml* burst into tears
rozbełtywać ⟨**-tać**⟩ (*-tuję*) *jajko*: whisk
rozbestwiać ⟨**-wić**⟩ (*-wiam*) make furious, make aggressive; **rozbestwiać się** get out of hand; **rozbestwiony** *adj* (*niezdyscyplinowany*) unruly, uncontrollable
rozbicie *n* (*-cia*; *no pl*): **~ samolotu** plane crash; **~ okrętu** shipwreck
rozbić *v/p* → **rozbijać**
rozbiec się *v/p* → **rozbiegać się**
rozbieg *m* (*-gu*; *-gi*) **1.** SPORT run-up **2.** (*w lotnictwie*) take off run
rozbiegać się ⟨**-biec**⟩ (*-gam*) **1.** (*o osobach*) disperse **2.** SPORT take a run-up **3.** (*o drogach*) diverge, fork
rozbiegany *adj* **1.** *oczy, myśli*: anxious, restless **2.** *ludzie*: busy, running
rozbierać ⟨**-zebrać**⟩ (*-ram*) **1.** undress **2.** *aparat*: take apart, dismantle **3.** *budynek*: pull down **4. rozbiera mnie choroba** I am getting ill; **rozbierać**

się undress, get undressed; **~ się do naga** strip naked, undress completely
rozbieralnia *f* (*-ni*; *-nie*) changing-room
rozbieran|y *adj*: **~e zdjęcie** nude photograph
rozbieżność *f* (*-ści*; *-ści*) discrepancy; **~ zdań** dissent, difference in opinion; **rozbieżn|y** *adj oceny*, *wyniki*, *zdania*: divergent; **zdania są ~e** opinions differ
rozbijać ⟨**-bić**⟩ (*-jam*) **1.** *talerz*, *szybę*, *jajko*: break; **~ sobie nos** breakone's nose; **~ bank** breakthe bank **2.** *małżeństwo*: breakup **3.** *mięso*: tenderize, beat **4.** *nieprzyjaciela*: defeat **5.** (*podzielić*) divide (up) (**na** *A* in) **6.** *głowę*: hurt **7.** *samochód*: crash **8.** *namiot*, *obóz*: pitch; **rozbijać się 1.** (*o talerzu*, *szybie*) break; **~ się na kawałki** break to pieces **2.** (*jeździć*) ride around; **~ się taksówkami** ride around the town by taxi **3.** (*podróżować*) drive around; **~ się samochodem** drive around by car **4.** (*o samolocie*) crash; **~ się o skałę** crash against the rock **5.** (*o planach*) fall through
rozbiór *m* (*-bioru*; *-biory*): **~ zdania** *GRAM* parsing of a sentence; **~ Polski** *HIST* partition of Poland; **rozbiórka** *f* (*-ki*; *-ki*) *budynku*: demolition
rozbisurmanić *v/p* (*-nię*) *infml dziecko*: spoil; **rozbisurmanić się** (*o dziecku*) become naughty, run wild
rozbitek *m* (*-tka*; *-tkowie*) castaway; **~ życiowy** loser
rozbity *adj* **1.** *dzban*: broken **2.** *oddziały*: defeated **3.** *osoba*: depressed, worn out and weak
rozbłyskiwać ⟨**-snąć**⟩ (*-kuję*) flash
rozboleć *v/p*: **rozbolała mnie głowa** I've got a headache, my head has started to hurt
rozbój *m* (*-boju*; *-boje*) robbery; **~ w biały dzień** daylight robbery
rozbójnik *m* (*-ka*; *-nicy*) highwayman; **~ morski** pirate
rozbrajać ⟨**-roić**⟩ (*-jam*) **1.** *osobę*: disarm **2.** *bombę*: defuse; **rozbrajać się** *POLIT* disarm
rozbrajający *adj fig* disarming
rozbrat *m* (*-tu*; *no pl*) *lit* breach, rupture; **brać ~ z** *I fig* part with, abandon, give up
rozbroić *v/p* → **rozbrajać**
rozbrojenie *n* (*-nia*; *no pl*) **1.** *państwa*: disarmament **2.** *bomby*: defusing; **rozbrojeniowy** *adj POLIT* disarmament
rozbrykany *adj dziecko*: frisky
rozbryzgiwać ⟨**-gać**⟩ (*-guję*) *błoto*: splash
rozbrzmiewa|ć ⟨**-mieć**⟩ (*-wam*) resound; **sala ~ oklaskami** the hall resounds with applause, thunderous applause can be heard in the hall
rozbudowa *f* (*-wy*; *-wy*) *BUILD* extension; **rozbudowywać** ⟨**-dować**⟩ (*-duję*) *BUILD* extend
rozbudzać ⟨**-dzić**⟩ (*-dzam*) *fig* arouse; **rozbudzać się** (*o dziecku*) become awake
rozbujać → **rozhuśtać**
rozchełstan|y *adj* **1.** *osoba*: scruffy **2.** *strój*: undone; **w ~ej koszuli** in an unbuttoned shirt
rozchlapywać ⟨**-pać**⟩ (*-puję*) *błoto*, *wodę*: splash
rozchmurzać się ⟨**-rzyć**⟩ (*-rzam*) **1.** (*o niebie*) clear (up); **rozchmurzyło się** it's cleared up **2.** (*o osobie*) cheer up
rozchodzić *v/p* (*-dzę*) *buty*: breakin
rozchodzić się ⟨**-zejść**⟩ (*-dzę*) **1.** (*o tłumie*) disperse **2.** (*o małżeństwie*) breakup **3.** (*o drogach*) diverge **4.** (*o zapachu*, *wieściach*) spread **5.** (*o cieple*) radiate **6.** (*o dźwięku*) travel **7.** (*o materiale*) come apart **8.** (*o towarze*) sell well **9.** (*o pieniądzach*) disappear
rozchorować się *v/p* (*-ruję*) fall ill, be taken ill
rozchód *m* (*-chodu*; *-chody*) **1.** (*wydatki*) expenses *pl* **2.** *FIN* expenditure
rozchwiany *adj* **1.** *kładka*: unsteady **2.** *osoba*: changeable, unstable
rozchwytywać *v/im* (*-tuję*) be sold out; **rozchwytywany** *adj* sought-after; **być ~m** be in demand
rozchybotany *adj* wobbly
rozchylać ⟨**-lić**⟩ (*-lam*) **1.** *usta*, *okiennice*: open (a little) **2.** *gałęzie*: draw aside; **rozchylać się** (*o płatkach*) (half-)open; **rozchylony** *adj usta*: half-opened
rozciąć *v/p* → **rozcinać**
rozciągać ⟨**-gnąć**⟩ (*-gam*) **1.** *gumę*, *sweter*, *mięśnie*: stretch **2.** *kontrolę*, *wpływy*: extend (**na** *A* on); **rozciągać się 1.** (*o gumie*, *swetrze*) stretch; **~ się na łóżku** sprawl out on one's bed

R

2. (*o lasach, widoku*) spread out **3.** (*o działalności*) include (***na*** *A*)
rozciągliwy *adj* stretchy
rozciągłoś|ć: ***w całej ~ci*** **a)** (fully) stretched out **b)** *fig* to its full extent
rozcieńczać ⟨**-czyć**⟩ (*-czam*) dilute
rozcieńczalnik *m* (*-ka*; *-ki*) thinner
rozcierać ⟨**-zetrzeć**⟩ (*-ram*) **1.** *stopy, ręce, maść*: rub (over) **2.** *żółtka*: mix **3.** *czosnek*: crush, pulp; ***~ na proch*** grind to powder, pulverize
rozcięcie *n* (*-cia*; *-cia*) **1.** (*rana*) cut **2.** *w sukience*: slit; **rozcinać** ⟨**-ciąć**⟩ (*-nam*) cut; ***~ na połowę*** cut in half
rozczapierzać ⟨**-rzyć**⟩ (*-rzam*) *palce*: spread
rozczarowanie *n* (*-nia*; *-nia*) disappointment; **rozczarowany** *adj* disappointed
rozczarowywać ⟨**-rować**⟩ (*-rowuję*) disappoint; ***rozczarowywać się*** become disillusioned, become disappointed
rozczepiać ⟨**-pić**⟩ (*-piam*) *wagony*: detach
rozczesywać ⟨**-sać**⟩ (*-suję*) *włosy*: comb (out)
rozczłonkowywać ⟨**-kować**⟩ (*-kowuję*) dismember
rozczochrany *adj* unkempt, tousled
rozczulać ⟨**-lić**⟩ (*-lam*) *widok, opowieść*: touch, move; ***~ do łez*** move to tears; ***rozczulać się*** become sentimental, become maudlin; ***~ się nad*** *I fig* dote on; ***~ się nad sobą*** wallow in self-pity
rozczulający *adj* touching
rozczulenie *n* (*-nia*; *no pl*) emotion, melting mood; ***z ~m*** moved, with sentiment
rozczulić *v/p* → ***rozczulać***
rozczyn *m* (*-nu*; *-ny*) leaven
rozczyniać ⟨**-nić**⟩ (*-niam*): ***~ ciasto*** blend yeast with flour (***na*** *A* for)
rozczytać *v/p* (*-tam*) be able to decipher (**w** *L*)
rozczytywać się *v/im* (*-tuję*) spend (a lot of) time reading (**w** *L*)
rozdać *v/p* → ***rozdawać***; **rozdanie** *n* (*-nia*; *-nia*) (*w kartach*) hand
rozdarcie *n* (*-cia*; *-cia*) **1.** *koszuli*: rip **2.** *fig* dilemma
rozdawać ⟨**-dać**⟩ (*-daję*) **1.** *ulotki*: give out **2.** *nagrody*: hand out **3.** *karty*: deal **4.** *autografy*: give **5.** *pieniądze*: give away; ***~ pomiędzy*** *A* give out to; ***~ majątek między ubogich*** give one's fortune away to the poor; ***~ uczniom zeszyty*** give out notebooks to students
rozdąć *v/p* → ***rozdymać***
rozdeptany *adj* **1.** *buty*: worn out **2.** *niedopałek*: trampled on
rozdeptywać ⟨**-tać**⟩ (*-tuję*) *niedopałek*: trample on; ***~ błoto po podłodze*** track mud all over the floor
rozdęty *adj brzuch*: bloated
rozdłubywać ⟨**-bać**⟩ (*-buję*) *dziurę*: poke open
rozdmuchiwać ⟨**-chać**⟩ (*-chuję*) **1.** *liście*: blow about **2.** *ogień*: fan **3.** *sprawę*: blow up
rozdrabniać ⟨**-robnić**⟩ (*-niam*) **1.** *chleb*: crumble **2.** *pokarm*: chop (up); ***rozdrabniać się*** crumble; ***nie rozdrabniaj się*** don't get bogged down (in details)
rozdrapywać ⟨**-pać**⟩ (*-puję*) **1.** *ranę*: scratch; ***rozdrapywać*** (***stare***) ***rany*** *fig* rake the ashes **2.** *majątek, towar*: snatch (away)
rozdrażniać ⟨**-nić**⟩ (*-niam*) irritate
rozdrażnienie *n* (*-nia*; *no pl*) irritation; **rozdrażniony** *adj* irritated
rozdrobnić *v/p* → ***rozdrabniać***
rozdroż|e *n* (*-ża*; *-ża*) crossroads *pl*; ***stanąć na ~u*** *fig* be at the crossroads
rozdwajać się ⟨**-woić**⟩ (*-jam*) (*o włosach, paznokciach*) split; ***przecież się nie rozdwoję!*** I can't go out of my way!, I can't be in two places at once
rozdwojenie *n* (*-nia*; *no pl*): ***~ jaźni*** MED split personality
rozdygotany *adj* shaking, tottery
rozdymać ⟨**-dąć**⟩ (*-mam*) **1.** *żagle*: swell, puff out **2.** *brzuch*: distend
rozdz. *abbr* (= ***rozdział***) ch.
rozdział *m* (*-łu*; *-ły*) **1.** *książki*: chapter **2.** (*podział*) distribution **3.** (*oddzielenie*) separation; ***~ kościoła od państwa*** the separation of Church and State
rozdziawiać ⟨**-wić**⟩ (*-wiam*) *usta*: open wide
rozdzielać ⟨**-lić**⟩ (*-lam*) **1.** (*rozdawać*) give out, distribute **2.** (*oddzielać*) separate; ***rozdzielać się*** **1.** (*o osobach*) split up **2.** (*o drodze*) fork, diverge

rozdzielcz|y *adj punkt*: distribution; ***tablica ~a*** control panel; ***deska ~a*** AUTO dashboard
rozdzielnia *f* (*-ni*; *-nie*) TECH switchboard
rozdzielnik *m* (*-ka*; *-ki*) supply list, distribution list; ***według ~a*** by the supply list
rozdzielny *adj pisownia*: separate
rozdzierać ⟨***-zedrzeć***⟩ (*-ram*) **1.** *kartkę*: tear; ***rozedrzeć sobie spodnie*** tear one's trousers; ***to rozedrze mu serce*** this will breakhis heart **2.** *na części*: tear apart; ***rozdzierać się*** **1.** (*o materiale*) tear **2.** (*o osobie*) start screaming, start yelling
rozdzierający *adj* **1.** *krzyk*: piercing **2.** *widok*: heart-rending **3.** *ból*: excruciating
rozdźwięk *m* (*-ku*; *-ki*) *fig* **1.** (*różnica*) discrepancy **2.** (*konflikt*) discord, conflict
rozebrać *v/p* → ***rozbierać***
rozedrzeć *v/p* → ***rozdzierać***
rozegnać *v/p* → ***rozganiać***
rozegrać *v/p* → ***rozgrywać***
rozejm *m* (*-mu*; *-my*) truce
rozejrzeć się *v/p* → ***rozglądać się***
rozejść się *v/p* → ***rozchodzić się***
rozepchany *adj kieszeń*: stretched, baggy; **rozepchnąć** *v/p* ***rozpychać***
rozeprzeć *v/p* → ***rozpierać***
rozerwać *v/p* → ***rozrywać***; **rozerwany** *adj* torn
rozerżnąć *v/p* → ***rozrzynać***
rozeschnąć się *v/p* → ***rozsychać się***
rozesłać[1] *v/p* → ***rozsyłać***
rozesłać[2] *v/p* → ***rozścielać***
rozespany *adj* sleepy, drowsy, half asleep
roześmiać się *v/p* (*-mieję*) burst out laughing; ***~ głośno*** laugh out loud
roześmiany *adj* **1.** *twarz*: happy **2.** *głos*: laughing
rozeta *f* (*-ty*; *-ty*) ARCHIT **1.** (*motyw*) rosette **2.** (*okno*) rose window
rozetrzeć *v/p* → ***rozcierać***
rozewrzeć *v/p* → ***rozwierać***
rozeznać się *v/p* → ***rozeznawać się***
rozeznani|e *n* (*-nia*; *no pl*): ***mieć*** (***dobre***) ***~e w*** *L* feel at home with, know all about; ***nie mieć ~a w*** *L* know nothing about; ***stracić ~e*** (***w sytuacji***) lose control (of the situation), lose touch (with the situation); ***brak ~a w*** *L* lack of understanding
rozeznawać się ⟨***-znać***⟩ (*-naję*) find one's bearings (***w*** *L* with), find one's way around; ***~ w sytuacji*** know where one stands
rozeźlony *adj* angry
rozgadywać ⟨***-dać***⟩ (*-duję*) tell everyone, babble (out); ***rozgadywać się*** start chattering (away)
rozgałęziacz *m* (*-cza*; *-cze*) **1.** (*prądu*) adapter **2.** (*do monitorów*) splitter
rozgałęziać się ⟨***-zić***⟩ (*-ziam*) **1.** (*o drodze*) fork, diverge **2.** (*o drzewie*) branch **3.** (*o przewodach*) split
rozgałęzienie *n* (*-nia*; *-nia*) branch; ***~ dróg*** fork; ***~ rzeki*** branch of a river
rozgałęziony *adj* **1.** *droga*: forked **2.** *drzewo*: branchy
rozganiać ⟨***-gonić***, ***-zegnać***⟩ (*-niam*) **1.** *manifestantów*: disperse **2.** *chmury*: clear
rozgardiasz *m* (*-szu*; *no pl*) commotion, bustle, confusion
rozgarniać ⟨***-nąć***⟩ (*-niam*) **1.** *piasek, ziemię*: clear aside **2.** *trawę, włosy*: part
rozgarnięty *adj* sharp-witted
rozginać ⟨***-giąć***⟩ (*-nam*) unbend
rozglądać się ⟨***-zejrzeć***⟩ (*-dam*) (have a) look(***po*** *L* around); ***~ za*** *I fig* look out for
rozgłaszać ⟨***-łosić***⟩ (*-szam*) **1.** *nowinę*: announce, make known **2.** *plotki*: spread **3.** *tajemnicę*: give away, reveal
rozgłos *m* (*-su*; *no pl*) **1.** publicity; ***nabrać ~u*** attract publicity; ***bez ~u*** without publicity; ***zdobywać ~*** gain publicity, become well-known; ***nadać ~*** give (wide) publicity **2.** (*zła sława*) notoriety
rozgłosić *v/p* → ***rozgłaszać***
rozgłośnia *f* (*-ni*; *-nie*) broadcasting station
rozgniatać ⟨***-nieść***⟩ (*-tam*) **1.** *puszkę, czosnek*: crush **2.** *orzech*: crack **3.** *robaka*: squash **4.** *niedopałek*: stub out, stamp out
rozgniewać *v/p* (*-wam*) make angry, anger; ***rozgniewać się*** get angry (***na*** *A* with)
rozgniewany *adj* angry
rozgonić *v/p* → ***rozganiać***

R

rozgorączkowanie *n* (*-nia*; *no pl*) agitation; **rozgorączkowany** *adj* **a)** frantic **b)** *MED* feverish; ***być ~m*** **a)** be feverish **b)** *MED* have a temperature, have a fever
rozgoryczenie *n* (*-nia*; *no pl*) bitterness; **rozgoryczony** *adj* embittered
rozgorzeć *v/p* (*-rzeje*) (*o walce*, *sporach*) flare up, start; ***~ miłością do** G lit* fall passionately in love with; ***~ gniewem** lit* be burning with anger; ***~ namiętnością** lit* be inflamed with desire
rozgościć się *v/p* (*-goszczę*) make oneself comfortable; ***proszę się rozgościć!*** make yourself at home!
rozgotowywać ⟨***-tować***⟩ (*-towuję*) overcook; ***rozgotowywać się*** be(come) overdone
rozgrabić *v/p* (*-bię*) steal, plunder
rozgraniczać ⟨***-czyć***⟩ (*-czam*) **1.** (*wytyczyć*) delimit **2.** (*rozróżniać*) differentiate
rozgromić *v/p* (*-mię*) rout
rozgrymaszony *adj dziecko*: spoilt
rozgrywać ⟨***-zegrać***⟩ (*-wam*) *mecz*, *partię*: play; ***rozgrywać się*** (*o wypadkach*) take place; ***akcja filmu rozgrywa się w*** the film is set in
rozgrywki *pl* (*-wek*) *SPORT* games *pl*; ***~ o władzę*** *POLIT* struggle for power, power struggle
rozgryzać ⟨***-gryźć***⟩ (*-zam*) *orzech*, *pestki*: crack; ***rozgryźć zagadkę*** crack a riddle; ***nie móc rozgryźć*** not be able to figure out
rozgrzać *v/p* → ***rozgrzewać***
rozgrzany *adj piec*: hot; ***~ do czerwoności*** red-hot
rozgrzebywać ⟨***-bać***⟩ (*-buję*) **1.** *ziemię*: dig up **2.** *papiery*: turn upside down **3.** *pracę*: leave in a mess
rozgrzeszać ⟨***-szyć***⟩ (*-szam*) *REL* absolve (***kogoś z*** *G* s.o. of)
rozgrzeszenie *n* (*-nia*; *-nia*) *REL* absolution
rozgrzewać ⟨***-rzać***⟩ (*-wam*) *dłonie*, *silnik*: warm (up); ***rozgrzewać się*** **1.** (*o osobie*) warm oneself up; ***~ się herbatą*** have some tea to warm oneself up, warm oneself with a cup of tea; ***~ się biegiem*** run a little to warm up, warm oneself up by running **2.** (*o silniku*) warm up **3.** (*o piecu*) become warm
rozgrzewk|a *f* (*-ki*; *-ki*) *SPORT* warm-up; ***dla ~i*** to warm up
rozgwiazda *f* (*-dy*; *-dy*) starfish
rozgwieżdżon|y *adj* starlit; ***~e niebo*** starlit sky
rozharatać *v/p* (*-tam*) wound badly, mangle
rozhukany *adj dzieci*, *konie*: unruly, unbridled
rozhuśtać *v/p* (*-tam*) set swinging, swing; ***rozhuśtać się*** **1.** (*o łódce*) roll **2.** (*o huśtawce*) swing
rozjarzony *adj* **1.** *światłami*: lit up **2.** (*żarzący się*) glowing
rozjaśniacz *m* (*-cza*; *-cze*) bleach
rozjaśniać ⟨***-nić***⟩ (*-niam*) **1.** brighten; ***uśmiech rozjaśnił mu twarz*** a smile lit up his face **2.** *włosy*: bleach
rozjazd *m* (*-du*; *-dy*) junction; ***być w ~ach*** be out of town, be away
rozjątrzać ⟨***-rzyć***⟩ (*-rzam*) **1.** *osobę*: make angry **2.** *spór*: inflame; ***rozjątrzać się*** **1.** (*o ranie*) irritate **2.** (*o sporze*) worsen, aggravate
rozjechać *v/p* (*-jadę*) run over; → ***rozjeżdżać się***
rozjemca *m* (*-cy*; *-cy*) **1.** *POL* peace-envoy **2.** *PRAW* arbitrator; **rozjemczy** *adj* arbitration
rozjeżdżać się ⟨***-jechać***⟩ (*-dżam*) (*o gościach*) leave; ***~ na wakacje*** go on holiday
rozjuszony *adj* furious
rozkapryszony *adj dziecko*: capricious
rozkaz *m* (*-zu*; *-zy*) order; ***być pod ~ami** G* serve under; ***~!*** yes sir!
rozkazać *v/p* → ***rozkazywać***
rozkazujący *adj* commanding; ***~ ton*** commanding tone; ***tryb ~*** *GRAM* the imperative, imperative mood; ***powiedzieć coś ~m tonem*** say s.th. in a commanding tone
rozkazywać ⟨***-zać***⟩ (*-zuję*) order
rozkiełznać *v/p* (*-nam*) *konia*: unbridle; **rozkiełznany** *adj koń*: unbridled
rozklejać ⟨***-leić***⟩ (*-jam*) **1.** *plakaty*: paste up, put up **2.** (*rozdzielać*) unstick; ***rozklejać się*** **1.** (*rozlecieć się*) come unstuck, come apart **2.** (*rozpłakać się*) start crying **3.** (*załamać się*) go to pieces
rozklekotan|y *adj* **1.** *stół*: rickety **2.** *budynek*: ramshackle; ***~y samochód*** rattletrap, jalopy, oldbanger; ***mieć ~e***

R

nerwy be all nerves, be a bundle of nerves

rozkład *m* (*-du*; *-dy*) **1.** *obowiązków*, *kosztów*, *jazdy*: timetable; ***według ~u*** according to plan, according to the timetable, as planned **2.** (*plan*) schedule; ***~ dnia*** schedule for the day **3.** (*program zajęć*) curriculum; ***~ materiału*** year programme, curriculum (for one year) **4.** *ustroju*, *rodziny*: breakup **5.** CHEM BIOL decomposition **6.** *ciała*: decay **7.** *mieszkania*: layout

rozkładać ⟨**-złożyć**⟩ (*-dam*) **1.** *koc*, *nogi*: spread; ***~ ręce*** *fig* spread one's arms; ***~ na raty*** arrange into instalments; ***rozłożyła mnie choroba*** I fell ill **2.** *gazetę*: unfold **3.** *łóżko*: unfold **4.** *parasol*: open **5.** *namiot*: put up, pitch **6.** *pracę*: divide (up) **7.** *koszty*, *obowiązki*: divide, share **8.** *maszynę*: take apart, dismantle **9.** *towar*: put out, lay out **10.** BIOL CHEM decompose; ***rozkładać się*** **1.** *na kocu*, *na łóżku*: stretch out **2.** (*ulokować się*) be laid out **3.** BIOL CHEM decompose **4.** (*o ciele*) decay **5.** (*o kanapie*) unfold **6.** ***~ się równo*** be equally divided

rozkładan|y *adj* **1.** *tapczan*: folding; ***~e krzesło*** folding chair **2.** *stół*: extendable, drop-leaf

rozkładowy *adj* **1.** *mieszkanie*: well-planned **2.** BIOL decomposition

rozkochany *adj lit* **1.** *osoba*: deeply in love (***w*** *L* with) **2.** *spojrzenie*: loving; ***~ w Grecji*** in love with Greece

rozkochiwać ⟨**-chać**⟩ (*-chuję*) *lit* inspire with love, *Br* enamour, *Am* enamor; ***~ kogoś w sztuce*** inspire s.o. with a love for art; ***rozkochała go w /FONT› sobie*** *lit* he became infatuated with her, he fell head over heels for her; ***rozkochiwać się*** fall in love (***w*** *L* with)

rozkodować *v/p* (*-duję*) decode

rozkojarzony *adj* absent-minded

rozkołysać *v/p* (*-szę*) set swinging; ***rozkołysać się*** **1.** (*o łódce*) rock, roll **2.** (*o moście*, *drzewach*) sway, swing

rozkołysany *adj* **1.** *łódka*: rocking **2.** *morze*: rolling **3.** *trawy*, *most*: swaying

rozkopywać ⟨**-pać**⟩ (*-puję*) *ulicę*: dig (up); ***~ pościel*** kick one's bedclothes off

rozkosz *f* (*-szy*; *-sze*) **1.** (*szczęście*) bliss **2.** (*przyjemność*) pleasure **3.** *zmysłowa*: voluptuousness, sensuality; ***~e*** pleasures; ***z ~ą*** with relish, with delight; ***~e podniebienia*** real treat; ***~ dla oka*** sight for sore eyes

rozkoszny *adj* **1.** *posiłek*, *osoba*: delightful **2.** *dziecko*: charming

rozkoszować się *v/im* (*-szuję*) delight (*I* in); ***~ myślą*** relish the thought; ***~ winem*** enjoy one's fill of wine; ***~ pięknym widokiem*** feast one's eyes on a beautiful view; ***~ wolnością*** revel in one's freedom

rozkraczać się ⟨**-czyć**⟩ (*-czam*) **1.** (*rozsuwać nogi*) straddle **2.** (*psuć się*) *infml* conk out

rozkraczony *adj* straddling

rozkradać ⟨**-raść**⟩ (*-dam*) steal away, steal (everything)

rozkręcać ⟨**-cić**⟩ (*-cam*) **1.** (*rozebrać*) take apart, take to pieces **2.** *interes*, *produkcję*: start up **3.** *towarzystwo*: get going; ***rozkręcać się*** **1.** (*o zabawie*, *towarzystwie*) (slowly) pickup steam, get the party moving **2.** (*o produkcji*) increase **3.** (*o interesie*) become thriving

rozkroić *v/p* (*-roję*) cut; ***~ na połowę*** cut in two

rozkrok *m* (*-ku*; *-ki*) SPORT straddle; ***stawać w ~u*** stand astride, stand with one's legs apart

rozkruszać ⟨**-szyć**⟩ (*-szam*) crumble, crush; ***rozkruszać się*** crumble, crush

rozkrwawić *v/p* (*-wię*): ***~ coś sobie*** make s.th. bleed

rozkrzewiać ⟨**-wić**⟩ (*-wiam*) (*propagować*) spread, propagate; ***rozkrzewiać się*** **1.** BIOL develop **2.** (*upowszechniać się*) spread (out)

rozkrzyżować *v/p* (*-żuję*): ***~ ramiona*** spread out one's arms

rozkuć *v/p* → ***rozkuwać***

rozkulbaczyć *v/p* (*-czę*) *konia*: unsaddle

rozkupywać ⟨**-pić**⟩ (*-puję*) buy up

rozkurczać ⟨**-czyć**⟩ (*-czam*) **1.** *palce*, *mięśnie*: loosen (up) **2.** *pięści*: unclench; ***~ nogi*** stretch one's legs

rozkurczow|y *adj* MED relaxant; ***ciśnienie ~e*** diastolic pressure

rozkurczyć *v/p* → ***rozkurczać***

rozkuwać ⟨**-kuć**⟩ (*-wam*): ***~ z kajdan*** unchain, unshackle

R

rozkwi|t *m* (*-tu; no pl*) **1.** *BIOL* blossom; ***w pełni ~tu*** in full bloom **2.** (*rozwój*) heyday, prime; ***w ~cie*** in its heyday
rozkwitać ⟨**-tnąć**⟩ (*-tam*) *BIOL* **1.** (*o drzewach*) blossom **2.** (*o kwiatach*) bloom **3.** (*o przemyśle*) flourish, bloom
rozlać *v/p* → ***rozlewać***
rozlany *adj* **1.** *pismo, litery*: blurred **2.** *fotografia*: hazy, blurred **3.** (*otyły*) fat, obese
rozlatywać się ⟨**-lecieć**⟩ (*-tuję*) **1.** (*o ptakach, owadach*) fly away in different directions **2.** (*o osobach*) scatter **3.** (*o butach, książkach*) fall to pieces, fall apart
rozlazły *adj* **1.** (*niemrawy*) sluggish **2.** *chód*: slouching, shuffling
rozlegać się ⟨**-lec**⟩ (*-gam*) **1.** (*o dźwięku*) ring (out), be heard, reverberate; ***rozległ się kobiecy śmiech*** woman's laughter reverberated **2.** (*o dzwonku*) ring **3.** (*o proteście*) be organized, be staged
rozlegle *adv* → ***rozległy***
rozległość *f* (*-ści; no pl*) extent; **rozległy** *adj* **1.** (*szeroki*) wide **2.** *plany*: extensive
rozleniwiać ⟨**-wić**⟩ (*-wiam*) make lazy; ***rozleniwiać się*** become lazy
rozleniwienie *n* (*-nia; no pl*) laziness, sluggishness; **rozleniwiony** *adj* lazy
rozlepiać ⟨**-pić**⟩ (*-piam*) *plakaty*: paste, post
rozlewać ⟨**-lać**⟩ (*-wam*) **I** *v/t* **1.** (*przez nieuwagę*) spill **2.** *herbatę, zupę*: pour; **~** (***do kieliszków***) pour (out) (in to glasses); ***~ do butelek*** bottle **II** *v/i* (*o rzece*) flood, burst (its) banks; ***rozlewać się*** (*o herbacie*) spill
rozlewisko *n* (*-ka; -ka*) flood plain
rozlewnia *f* (*-ni; -nie*) bottling plant
rozleźć się *v/p* → ***rozłazić się***
rozliczać ⟨**-czyć**⟩ (*-czam*) balance, clear; ***rozliczać się*** account (**z** *G* for); ***~ się z*** *I* settle accounts with
rozliczenie *n* (*-nia; -nia*) *FIN* settlement (of accounts); ***~ podatkowe*** tax payment; ***~ z przeszłością*** coming to terms with the past; **rozliczeniowy** *adj FIN* accounting
rozliczny *adj* **1.** (*rozmaity*) manifold **2.** (*liczny*) numerous
rozlokowywać ⟨**-kować**⟩ (*-kowuję*) **1.** *gości*: quarter **2.** (*rzeczy*) arrange, put; ***rozlokowywać się*** **1.** (*zamieszkać*) settle **2.** (*rozgościć się*) make oneself comfortable
rozlosowywać ⟨**-sować**⟩ (*-sowuję*) distribute by lot; ***~ nagrody*** draw prizes
rozluźniać ⟨**-nić**⟩ (*-niam*) **1.** *krawat*: loosen **2.** *atmosferę, obyczaje*: make more relaxed **3.** *mięśnie*: relax; ***rozluźniać się*** **1.** (*o sznurku, normach*) loosen **2.** (*o atmosferze*) become relaxed **3.** (*o osobie*) relax, loosen up **4.** (*o wagonie*) become less crowded; ***rozluźniło się*** there are fewer people
rozluźniony *adj* **1.** *krawat*: loosened **2.** *mięśnie, osoba, atmosfera*: relaxed
rozładowywać ⟨**-dować**⟩ (*-dowuję*) **1.** *towar, ciężarówkę*: unload; ***~ broń*** unload a firearm; ***~ napięcie*** relieve the tension **2.** *kondensator*: discharge; ***~ złość*** vent one's anger (**na** *L* on); ***rozładowywać się*** **1.** (*o atmosferze*) become relxed; ***napięcie się rozładowało*** the tension was defused **2.** (*o akumulatorze, baterii*) go flat, go dead
rozładunek *m* (*-nku; -nki*) unloading; **rozładunkowy** *adj* unloading
rozłam *m* (*-mu; -my*) split
rozłazić się ⟨**rozleźć**⟩ **1.** (*o owadach*) spread, crawl in different directions **2.** (*o osobach*) disperse (**po** *L* all over) **3.** (*o butach*) fall apart
rozłączać ⟨**-czyć**⟩ (*-czam*) **1.** *kable*: disconnect **2.** *zakochanych, walczących*: separate; ***rozłączać się*** disconnect; ***poszę się nie rozłączać!*** (*w telefonie*) please don't hang up, hold the line, please; ***coś nas rozłączyło*** (*w telefonie*) we were disconnected
rozłącznie *adv* ***pisany ~*** written separately, written as two words; **rozłączny** *adj pisownia*: separate
rozłąk|a *f* (*-ki; -ki*) separation; ***dodatek za ~ę*** separation allowance; **rozłąkowe** *n* (*-wego; no pl*) separation allowance
rozłożenie *n* (*-nia; no pl*) spreading, distribution
rozłożyć *v/p* → ***rozkładać***
rozłożysty *adj drzewo*: branchy, branching
rozłupywać ⟨**-pać**⟩ (*-puję*) **1.** *orzechy*: crack **2.** *drewno*: split
rozmach *m* (*-chu; no pl*) **1.** (*zamach*) swing; ***wziąć ~*** take a swing **2.** (*impet*)

force, momentum; ***nabierać ~u*** gather momentum; ***z ~em*** with a flourish
rozmaczać ⟨***-moczyć***⟩ (*-czam*) *chleb*: soak
rozmagnesowywać ⟨***-sować***⟩ (*-sowuję*) demagnetize
rozmaicie *adv* → ***rozmaity***
rozmaito|ść *f* (*-ści*; *no pl*) variety; ***~ści*** *pl* (*-ści*) miscellany; **rozmaity** *adj* various, diverse
rozmakać ⟨***-moknąć***⟩ (*-kam*) get soaked, become soaked
rozmamłany *adj infml* sluggish
rozmaryn *m* (*-nu*; *-ny*) rosemary
rozmarzać[1] ⟨***-znąć***⟩ (*-zam*) thaw
rozmarzać[2] ⟨***-rzyć***⟩ (*-rzam*) make dreamy, put into a dreamy mood; ***rozmarzać się*** fall into a reverie
rozmarzony *adj oczy*, *twarz*: dreamy, daydreaming; ***być ~m*** be daydreaming
rozmarzyć *v/p* → ***rozmarzać***[2]
rozmawiać *v/im* (*-wiam*) **1.** (*prowadzić rozmowę*) talk(***o*** *L* about); ***~ przez telefon*** talkon the phone; ***~ po niemiecku*** talkin German **2.** (*mówić*) speak (***o*** *L* about); ***nie rozmawiamy ze sobą*** we're not on speaking terms
rozmaz *m* (*-zu*; *-zy*) *MED* smear; **rozmazany** *adj litery*, *obraz*: blurred
rozmazywać ⟨***-zać***⟩ (*-zuje*) **1.** *tusz*, *litery*: smudge **2.** *brud*: smear; ***rozmazywać się*** **1.** (*o kształtach*) blur **2.** (*o tuszu*) smudge
rozmiar *m* (*-ru*; *-ry*) **1.** (*wielkość*) size; ***~ ubrania*** clothes size; ***~ butów*** shoe size **2.** *szkód*: extent
rozmieniać ⟨***-nić***⟩ (*-niam*) *pieniądze*: change, break; ***~ się na drobne*** *fig* focus on many unimportant things
rozmieszać *v/p* (*-szam*) mix, stir
rozmieszczać ⟨***-mieścić***⟩ (*-czam*) **1.** *osoby*: place **2.** *oddziały*, *pionki*: deploy **3.** *książki*: arrange **4.** *gości*: seat; ***rozmieszczać się*** **1.** (*o gościach*) take seats **2.** (*o żołnierzach*) deploy
rozmieszczenie *n* (*-nia*; *no pl*) **1.** (*umieszczenie*) placement **2.** (*położenie*) location, position **3.** *oddziałów*: deployment; **rozmieszczony** *adj* put in place, arranged
rozmieścić *v/p* → ***rozmieszczać***
rozmiękać ⟨***-knąć***⟩ (*-kam*) soften
rozmiękczać ⟨***-czyć***⟩ (*-czam*) soften; ***~ czyjeś serce*** soften s.o.'s heart
rozmięknąć *v/p* → ***rozmiękać***
rozmijać się ⟨***-minąć***⟩ (*-jam*) **1.** (*odchodzić*) deviate; ***~ z prawdą*** deviate from the truth **2.** (*nie spotkać się*) miss each other
rozmiłowanie *n* (*-nia*; *no pl*) love, enthusiasm (***w*** *L* for); **rozmiłowany** *adj*: ***być ~m w*** *L* be an ardent lover of
rozminąć się *v/p* → ***rozmijać się***
rozminowywać ⟨***-nować***⟩ (*-nowuję*) clear of mines
rozmnażać ⟨***-nożyć***⟩ (*-żam*) **1.** *BIOL* breed **2.** *majątek*: grow; ***rozmnażać się*** *BIOL* reproduce
rozmnażanie *n* (*-nia*; *no pl*) reproduction; ***~*** (***się***) reproduction
rozmnożyć *v/p* → ***rozmnażać***
rozmoczyć *v/p* → ***rozmaczać***
rozmoknąć *v/p* → ***rozmakać***
rozmontowywać ⟨***-tować***⟩ (*-towuję*) take apart, disassemble
rozmotać *v/p* (*-tam*) *nici*: disentangle
rozmow|a *f* (*-wy*; *-wy*) **1.** (*konwersacja*) conversation; ***~a kwalifikacyjna*** interview **2.** (*dyskusja*) discussion **3.** ***~y*** *POLIT* talks, negotiations **4.** *telefoniczna*: call; ***~a miejscowa*** local call; ***~a zamiejscowa*** long distance call; **rozmowny** *adj* talkative
rozmówca *m* (*-cy*; *-cy*), **-czyni** *f* (*-ni*; *-nie*) interlocutor
rozmówić się *v/p* (*-wię*) have a word (***z*** *I* with)
rozmówki *pl* (*-wek*) phrase book
rozmównica *f* (*-cy*; *-ce*) **1.** (*w więzieniu*) *Br* parlour, *Am* parlor **2.** (*budka telefoniczna*) telephone booth
rozmrażać ⟨***-rozić***⟩ (*-żam*) *lodówkę*, *mięso*, *zamek*: defrost
rozmyć *v/p* → ***rozmywać***
rozmysł: ***z ~em*** with intent, on purpose
rozmyślać *v/im* (*-lam*) ponder; ***~ głęboko*** meditate (***nad*** *I* on), thinkintensively (***nad*** *I* about)
rozmyślani|e *n* (*-nia*; *-nia*): ***~a*** meditations
rozmyślić się *v/p* (*-lę*) change one's mind
rozmyślny *adj* **1.** *zabójstwo*: premeditated **2.** *czyn*: deliberate, intentional
rozmyty *adj* **1.** *brzeg*: washed out **2.** *kształt*: blurred
rozmywać ⟨***-myć***⟩ (*-wam*) **1.** *ślady*: blot out **2.** *litery*: blur **3.** *brzeg*: wash out; ***rozmywać się*** *fig* blur

R

roznamiętniać ⟨**-nić**⟩ (*-niam*) impassion, inflame (**do** *G* for); ***roznamiętniać się*** become turned on
roznamiętniony *adj* inflamed, turned on
rozneglizowany *adj* skimpity dessed
rozniecać ⟨**-cić**⟩ (*-cam*) **1.** *entuzjazm, ogień*: kindle **2.** *zapał, gniew*: stir up
roznieść *v/p* → ***roznosić***
roznosiciel *m* (*-la*; *-le*): delivery boy, delivery man; ~ ***gazet*** paper boy; ~ ***mleka*** milkman; ~ ***zarazków*** germ carrier
roznosicielka *f* (*-ki*; *-ki*): delivery woman; ~ ***gazet*** paper girl; ~ ***mleka*** milkwoman
roznosić ⟨**-nieść**⟩ (*-szę*) **1.** *gazety, pocztę*: deliver; ~ ***po*** *L* deliver to; ***roznosi go energia*** he is full of energy **2.** *zarazki*: carry **3.** *plotki*: spread **4.** (*zniszczyć*) destroy **5.** *armię*: rout; ***roznosić się*** (*o wiadomościach, plotkach*) spread; ***roznosi się zapach lawendy*** scent of lavender is wafting through the air; ***roznosi się zapach świeżego chleba*** you can smell freshly baked bread
rozochocić się *v/p* (*-cę*) liven up, become animated
rozochocony *adj* **1.** *osoba*: animated, livened up **2.** *głos*: excited
rozogniać się ⟨**-nić**⟩ (*-niam*) **1.** (*o ranie*) start to fester **2.** (*o konflikcie*) inflame
rozogniony *adj* MED feverish
rozpacz *f* (*-czy*; *no pl*) despair; ***doprowadzać kogoś do ~y*** drive s.o. to despair; ***popadać w ~*** fall into despair; ***~ po czyjejś śmierci*** grief after s.o.'s death; ***czarna ~*** utter despair
rozpaczać *v/im* (*-czam*) despair; ***~ po śmierci*** *G* mourn; ***~ po stracie*** *G* grieve over the loss of; ***nie rozpaczaj!*** don't despair!
rozpaczliwy *adj* desperate
rozpad *m* (*-du*; *no pl*) **1.** *rodziny*: break-up **2.** *systemu*: fall, collapse **3.** PHYS CHEM disintegration; ***okres połowicznego ~u*** half-life
rozpadać się[1] ⟨**-paść**⟩ (*-dam*) **1.** (*o systemie*) fall **2.** (*o związku, małżeństwie*) breakup **3.** (*o budynku*) collapse **4.** (*psuć się*) fall apart **4.** CHEM PHYS disintegrate
rozpadać się[2] *v/p*: ***rozpadało się*** it started raining for good
rozpadlina *f* (*-ny*; *-ny*): ***~ skalna*** fissure
rozpakowywać ⟨**-kować**⟩ (*-kowuję*) **1.** *plecak*: unpack **2.** *prezent*: unwrap; ***rozpakowywać się*** unpack
rozpalać ⟨**-lić**⟩ (*-lam*) **1.** *ogień*: light; ***~ w piecu*** start fire in the stove; ***~ coś do czerwoności*** heat up till s.th. is red hot **2.** *namiętność, gniew*: kindle; ***rozpalać się*** **1.** (*o ogniu*) start (burning) **2.** (*o konflikcie, kłótni*) flare up
rozpalony *adj* **1.** *kamienie*: red-hot **2.** (*w gorączce*) feverish **3.** *twarz*: burning
rozpałk|a: ***drewno na ~ę*** kindling
rozpamiętywać *v/im* (*-tuję*) brood (*A* on)
rozpaplać *v/p* (*-lę*/*-lam*) babble out
rozpaprać *v/p* (*-rzę*) leave unfinished
rozparcelowywać ⟨**-lować**⟩ (*-lowuję*) parcel out
rozpasanie *n* (*-nia*; *no pl*) debauchery; ***~ obyczajów*** immorality, complete lackof morals; **rozpasany** *adj* unbridled, unrestrained
rozpaść się *v/p* → ***rozpadać się***[1]
rozpatrywać ⟨**-rzyć**⟩ (*-ruję*) *prośbę, możliwości*: consider; ***prośba została rozpatrzona pozytywnie*** the request has been accepted; ***rozpatrzyć podanie negatywnie*** turn down an application; ***rozpatrywać się*** consider (**w** *L*)
rozpatrzeni|e *n* (*-nia*; *no pl*): ***po uważnym ~u*** after due consideration
rozpęd *m* (*-du*; *no pl*): ***nabierać ~u*** gather momentum
rozpędzać ⟨**-dzić**⟩ (*-dzam*) **1.** *demonstrantów*: disperse, scatter; ***~ na cztery wiatry*** scatter to the four winds, break up **2.** *złe myśli, zmartwienia*: dispel **3.** *pojazd*: speed up; ***rozpędzać się*** AUTO accelerate, pickup speed; ***tylko się tak nie rozpędzaj!*** hey, hold it!
rozpętywać ⟨**-tać**⟩ (*-tuję*) **1.** *wojnę, dyskusję*: sparkoff **2.** *piekło*: unleash; ***rozpętać się*** **1.** (*o burzy*) breakout **2.** (*o dyskusji*) start, flare up
rozpiąć *v/p* → ***rozpinać***
rozpić *v/p* → ***rozpijać***
rozpieczętowywać ⟨**-tować**⟩ (*-tuję*) *list*: open, unseal

R

rozpieprzać ⟨**-rzyć**⟩ (*-rzam*) *vulg* fuck up; ***rozpieprzać się*** fuckup

rozpiera|ć ⟨**-zeprzeć**⟩ (*-ram*): ***~ go duma*** he is bursting with pride; ***~ go ciekawość*** he is burning with curiosity; ***~ go energia*** he is full of energy; ***~ go radość*** he is burning with joy; ***~ć się*** sit back, lounge

rozpierzchać się ⟨**-chnąć**⟩ (*-cham*) disperse

rozpieszczać ⟨**-pieścić**⟩ (*-czam*) *dziecko*: spoil; **rozpieszczony** *adj* spoilt

rozpiętość *f* (*-ści*; *no pl*) span; **~ cen** price range

rozpijaczony *adj* drinking heavily

rozpijać ⟨**-pić**⟩ (*-jam*) *młodzież*: push into drinking; ***rozpijać się*** take to drink, drink heavily

rozpiłowywać ⟨**-łować**⟩ (*-łowuję*) saw through

rozpinać ⟨**-piąć**⟩ (*-nam*) **1.** *płaszcz*: unbutton **2.** *guziki*: undo **3.** *pasek*: unbuckle **4.** *suwak*: unzip **5.** *płótno, skrzydła*: spread **6.** *pasy*: AUTO unfasten **7.** ***~ żagle*** set sail; ***rozpinać się*** **1.** (*o osobie*) stretch **2.** (*o agrafce*) come undone

rozpisanie *n* (*-nia*; *no pl*) *konkursu*: announcement

rozpisywać ⟨**-sać**⟩ (*-suję*) **1.** *wybory*: call **2.** *konkurs*: invite entries for; ***rozpisywać się*** write at length, expatiate; ***gazety rozpisują się o*** *L* every newspaper writes about

rozplanowywać ⟨**-nować**⟩ (*-nowuję*) **1.** *zajęcia*: plan; ***~ sobie czas*** plan (out) one's time **2.** *przestrzeń*: design **3.** *układ ulic, miasto*: lay out

rozplatać ⟨**-leść**⟩ (*-tam*) *warkocze*: unbraid

rozplątywać ⟨**-tać**⟩ (*-tuję*) **1.** *węzeł*: untangle **2.** *zagadkę*: unravel

rozpleniać się ⟨**-nić**⟩ (*-niam*) **1.** BIOL spread **2.** (*o prostytucji*) proliferate

rozpleść *v/p* → ***rozplatać***

rozpłakać się *v/p* (*-łaczę*) burst into tears

rozpłaszczać ⟨**-czyć**⟩ (*-czam*) flatten out; ***rozpłaszczać się*** **1.** flatten oneself **2.** *infml* take off one's overcoat; **rozpłaszczony** *adj* flattened out

rozpłatać *v/p* (*-tam*) slash

rozpłodnik *m* (*-ka*; *-ki*) BIOL breeder; **rozpłodowy** *adj* BIOL breeding; ***ogier ~*** stud

rozpłód *m* (*-łodu*; *no pl*) BIOL breeding, reproduction

rozpływać się ⟨**-łynąć**⟩ (*-wam*) **1.** (*topić się*) melt; ***rozpłynąć się w powietrzu*** vanish into thin air; ***rozpływać się nad*** *I* revel in; ***rozpływać się w ustach*** melt in one's mouth; ***rozpływać się w zachwytach*** revel in admiration, go into raptures; ***rozpływać się w podziękowaniach*** be very thankful **2.** (*o plamie, farbie*) spread out **3.** (*o kształtach*) blur **4.** (*o tłumie*) disperse

rozpocząć *v/p* → ***rozpoczynać***

rozpoczęcie *n* (*-cia*; *no pl*) start, beginning; ***~ roku szkolnego*** beginning of the school year

rozpoczynać ⟨**-cząć**⟩ (*-nam*) start, begin; ***rozpoczynać się*** start, begin

rozpogadzać się ⟨**-godzić**⟩ (*-dzam*) **1.** (*o niebie*) clear up **2.** (*o osobie*) cheer up

rozpogodzenie *n* (*-nia*; *-nia*) bright spell, sunny spell

rozpolitykowany *adj* politically minded

rozpoławiać ⟨**-łowić**⟩ (*-wiam*) halve; ***rozpoławiać się*** divide into two halves

rozporek *m* (*-rka*; *-rki*) **1.** (*w spodniach męskich*) fly **2.** (*w spódnicy*) zip **3.** (*rozcięcie w spódnicy*) slit

rozporządzać ⟨**-dzić**⟩ (*-dzam*) **1.** order **2.** (*zarządzać*) manage (*I*) **3.** (*dysponować*) dispose of; ***rozporządzać się*** decide by oneself (without permission) (*I* about)

rozporządzenie *n* (*-nia*; *-nia*) **1.** decree **2.** (*polecenie*) order

rozpostarty *adj* stretched

rozpościerać ⟨**-postrzeć**⟩ (*-ram*) *koc*: spread; ***rozpościerać się*** (*o widoku, lasach*) stretch

rozpowiadać ⟨**-wiedzieć**⟩ (*-dam*) *plotki*: put around, spread

rozpowszechniać ⟨**-nić**⟩ (*-niam*) **1.** *zwyczaj*: spread **2.** *film*: distribute; ***rozpowszechniać się*** (*o zwyczaju*) (be) spread

rozpowszechnianie *n* (*-nia*; *no pl*) *filmu*: distribution; **rozpowszechniony** *adj zwyczaj, opinia*: widespread

rozpoznać *v/p* → ***rozpoznawać***

rozpoznanie *n* (*-nia*; *-nia*) **1.** *przestępcy*: identification **2.** *miejsca*: recognition **3.** *MED* diagnosis **4.** *JUR* examination (of a case); **~ ciała** body identification **5.** (*w wojsku*) reconnaissance

rozpoznawać ⟨**-nać**⟩ (*-naję*) **1.** *twarze, miejsca*: recognize (**po** *L* by) **2.** *przestępcę*: identify **3.** *JUR* lookinto, examine; ***rozpoznawać się*** recognize each other

rozpoznawalny *adj* recognizable; **rozpoznawcz|y** *adj* **1.** *znak*: identification **2.** ***hasło ~e*** password; ***lot ~y*** reconnaissance flight; ***samolot ~y*** spotter

rozpracowywać ⟨**-cować**⟩ (*-cowuję*) **1.** *osobę*: expose **2.** *szajkę*: dismantle **3.** *szyfr*: crack

rozpraszać ⟨**-roszyć**⟩ (*-szam*) **1.** *osobę*: distract, put off **2.** *ciemności*: *lit* disperse **3.** *wątpliwości*: dispel **4.** *tłum*: breakup; ***rozpraszać się*** **1.** (*o tłumie*) disperse **2.** be distracted **3.** (*o chmurach*) clear

rozpraw|a *f* (*-wy*; *-wy*) **1.** *JUR* trial; ***sala ~*** courtroom; ***otworzyć ~ę*** open a trial; ***odroczyć ~ę*** adjourn a trial; ***zamknąć ~ę*** close a trial **2.** (*traktat*) dissertation; ***~y*** debate; ***~a doktorska*** doctoral thesis, doctoral dissertation

rozprawiać *v/im* (*-wiam*) speakat length (**o** *L* about)

rozprawiać się ⟨**-wić**⟩ (*-wiam*) **1.** crack down (**z** *I* on) **2.** (*wyrównać porachunki*) get even (**z** *I* with); ***szybko się rozprawić z*** *I* deal quickly with

rozprawka *f* (*-ki*; *-ki*) argumentative essay, discursive essay

rozprężać ⟨**-żyć**⟩ (*-żam*) *mięśnie*: relax; ***rozprężać się*** relax

rozpromieniać się ⟨**-nić**⟩ (*-niam*) brighten up

rozpromieniony *adj* radiant, beaming

rozprostowywać ⟨**-tować**⟩ (*-towuję*) **1.** *drut*: straighten **2.** *plecy*: sit up, stop slouching; ***~ kości*** stretch one's legs; ***rozprostowywać się*** stretch

rozproszenie *n* (*-nia*; *no pl*) **1.** (*rozsypka*) dispersion **2.** (*brak koncentracji*) distraction; **rozproszony** *adj* **1.** *miasta*: away from each other **2.** *rodzina*: in different places **3.** *osoba*: distracted **4.** *światło*: diffused

rozproszyć *v/p* → ***rozpraszać***

rozprowadzać ⟨**-dzić**⟩ (*-dzam*) **1.** *towar*: distribute, send out **2.** *farbę*: spread **3.** *krem*: apply **4.** (*rozcieńczać*) dilute (*I* with)

rozpruwać ⟨**-ruć**⟩ (*-wam*) **1.** (*przypadkiem*) rip; ***~ sukienkę*** rip a dress **2.** *szew*: unpick **3.** *brzuch*: slash **4.** *kasę*: crackopen; ***rozpruwać się*** (*o szwie*) rip, get unstitched; ***sukienka się rozpruła*** the dress got unstitched

rozpryskać *v/p* → ***rozpryskiwać***

rozpryskiwacz *m* (*-cza*; *-cze*) sprayer, sprinkler

rozpryskiwać ⟨**-kać**, **-snąć**⟩ (*-kuję*) **1.** *ciecz*: spatter, splatter **2.** *dżem, błoto*: splatter; ***rozpryskiwać się*** spatter; ***talerz rozprysnął się (na kawałki)*** the plate shattered

rozprząc *v/p* → ***rozprzęgać***

rozprzedawać ⟨**-dać**⟩ (*-daję*) sell out

rozprzedaż *f* (*-ży*; *-że*) sale

rozprzestrzeniać ⟨**-nić**⟩ (*-niam*) (*rozpowszechniać*) spread, propagate, disseminate; ***rozprzestrzeniać się*** (*o epidemii, ogniu*) spread (**na** *A* onto)

rozprzęgać ⟨**-gnąć**, **-rząc**⟩ (*-gam*) **1.** *konia*: unharness **2.** *ład*: upset, disturb; ***rozprzęgać się*** (*o ładzie, strukturze*) become chaotic

rozprzężenie *n* (*-nia*; *no pl*) disorder, anarchy; ***~ dyscypliny*** indiscipline; ***~ obyczajów*** relaxation of morals, moral decline

rozpuk: ***śmiać się do ~u*** roar with laughter

rozpulchniać ⟨**-nić**⟩ (*-niam*) **1.** *ziemię*: loosen **2.** *ciasto*: leaven **3.** *skórę*: soften, soak

rozpu|sta *f* (*-ty*; *no pl*) debauchery; ***oddawać się ~ście*** lead a debauched lifestyle; ***gniazdo ~sty*** den of iniquity; **rozpustn|y** *adj* debauched, licentious; ***~e życie*** indulgent lifestyle

rozpuszczać ⟨**-puścić**⟩ (*-czam*) **1.** *tabletkę*: dissolve **2.** ***~ włosy*** let one's hair loose **3.** *COOK* melt **4.** *plotkę*: spread **5.** *dzieci*: spoil; ***chłopak jest rozpuszczony jak dziadowski bicz*** the boy is spoiled rotten **6.** *pieniądze*: squander; ***rozpuszczać się*** **1.** (*o cukrze, tabletce*) dissolve **2.** (*o śniegu, czekoladzie, lodach*) melt **3.** (*o dziecku*) become spoilt

rozpuszczalnik *m* (*-ka*; *-ki*) solvent, thinner; **rozpuszczaln|y** *adj* soluble;

R

kawa ~a instant coffee; ***~y w wodzie*** soluble in water
rozpuszczon|y *adj* **1.** *dziecko*: spoilt **2.** *włosy*: loose; ***nosić ~e włosy*** wear one's hair loose
rozpuścić *v/p* → ***rozpuszczać***
rozpychać ⟨**-zepchnąć**⟩ (*-cham*) *kieszeń*, *spodnie*: stretch; ***rozpychać się*** get stretched; ***rozpychać się łokciami*** *fig* jostle
rozpylacz *m* (*-cza*; *-cze*) atomizer; ***w ~u*** in spray
rozpylać ⟨**-lić**⟩ (*-lam*) spray
rozpytywać ⟨**-tać**⟩ (*-tuję*) askaround; ***rozpytywać się*** askaroun d (**o** *A* about)
rozrabiać ⟨**-robić**⟩ (*-biam*) **1.** *farbę*: mix together **2.** (*rozcieńczać*) dilute **3.** (*awanturować się*) stir things up, make a row **4.** (*o dziecku*) be naughty
rozrabiaka *m* (*-ki*; *-ki*) *infml* little rascal, troublemaker, hooligan
rozrachun|ek *m* (*-nku*; *-nki*) **1.** (*podsumowanie*) *fig* final analysis; ***dokonać ~ku z przeszłością*** square up the past, come to terms with the past; ***w ostatecznym ~ku*** *fig* in the final analysis **2.** *FIN* settlement; **rozrachunkowy** *adj* clearance, clearing
rozradowany *adj* joyous
rozrastać się ⟨**-rosnąć**⟩ (*-tam*) **1.** *BIOL MED* grow **2.** (*o rodzinie*, *majątku*) increase **3.** (*o mieście*) expand, grow bigger
rozrąbać *v/p* (*-bię*) cleave, chop up
rozregulowany *adj żołądek*: upset, sick
rozregulowywać ⟨**-lować**⟩ (*-lowuję*) **1.** *TECH* put out of order **2.** (*rozstrajać*) *fig* upset; ***rozregulowywać się*** **1.** *TECH* get out of order **2.** (*rozstrajać się*) *fig* lose balance, go out of tune
rozrobić *v/p* → ***rozrabiać***
rozrodczość *f* (-ści; *no pl*) reproduction capacity; **rozrodcz|y** *adj funkcje*: reproductive; ***narządy ~e*** reproductive organs; ***wiek ~y*** reproductive age
rozrosnąć się *v/p* → ***rozrastać się***
rozrób|a *f* (*-by*; *-by*) brawl; ***zrobić ~ę*** start a brawl
rozród *m* (*-rodu*; *no pl*) *BIOL* reproduction
rozróżniać ⟨**-nić**⟩ (*-niam*) distinguish; **rozróżnienie** *n* (*-nia*; *-nia*) distinction
rozruch *m* (*-chu*; *-chy*) **1.** *TECH* starting; ***~ próbny*** test run, test starting **2.** *produkcji*: start **3.** ***~y*** *POLIT* riots
rozruszać *v/p* (*-szam*) **1.** ***~ palce*** work off the stiffness in one's fingers; ***~ nogi*** get some exercise **2.** *silnik*: start, ignite **3.** *towarzystwo*: liven up; ***rozruszać się*** **1.** (*poćwiczyć*) get some exercise **2.** (*o towarzystwie*) liven up
rozrusznik *m* (*-ka*; *-ki*) *AUTO* starter; ***~ serca*** *MED* pacemaker
rozrywać ⟨**-zerwać**⟩ (*-wam*) **1.** (*rozdzierać*) tear apart, rip **2.** (*zabawiać*) entertain; ***rozrywać się*** tear, get torn
rozrywany *adj* sought-after
rozrywk|a *f* (*-ki*; *-ki*) entertainment; ***dla ~i*** for fun; ***~i*** entertainment; ***~i sportowe*** games; ***ulubiona ~a*** favourite pastime; **rozrywkowy** *adj program*: entertainment
rozrządow|y *adj*: ***górka ~a*** hump
rozrzedzać ⟨**-dzić**⟩ (*-dzam*) dilute; ***rozrzedzać się*** (*o tłumie*) thin (out); **rozrzedzony** *adj* **1.** *płyn*: diluted **2.** *powietrze*: rarefied
rozrzewniać ⟨**-nić**⟩ (*-niam*) move; ***rozrzewniać się*** be moved (to tears); **rozrzewniający** *adj* moving, touching; **rozrzewnienie** *n* (*-nia*; *no pl*) emotion; ***wspominać coś z ~m*** have fond memories of s.th.
rozrzucać ⟨**-cić**⟩ (*-cam*) **1.** *zabawki*: scatter **2.** *ulotki*: drop **3.** *nawóz*: spread
rozrzutnik *m* (*-ka*; *-nicy*), **-nica** *f* (*-cy*; *-ce*) spendthrift, squanderer
rozrzutność *f* (*-ści*; *no pl*) extravagance; **rozrzutny** *adj* **1.** *osoba*: extravagant **2.** *praktyki*, *naród*: wasteful
rozrzynać ⟨**-zerżnąć**⟩ (*-nam*) saw through
rozsada *f* (*-dy*; *-dy*) seedling; **rozsadnik** *m* (*-ka*; *-ki*) cold frame, seedbed
rozsadzać ⟨**-dzić**⟩ (*-dzam*) **1.** *rośliny*: plant, put around **2.** *uczniów*: separate **3.** *skałę*: blow up **4.** *gości*: seat
rozsądek *m* (*-dku*; *no pl*) reason; ***zdrowy ~*** common sense; ***przemówić komuś do ~u*** talksome sense into s.o.; **rozsądny** *adj* reasonable, sensible
rozsądzać ⟨**-dzić**⟩ (*-dzam*) **1.** *spór*: settle (by arbitration) **2.** (*wydać formalną decyzję*) adjudicate (*A* upon)
rozsiać *v/p* → ***rozsiewać***

R

rozsiadać się ⟨**-siąść**⟩ (*-dam*) (*siadać wygodnie*) sit (down comfortably), sit back **2.** (*zajmować dużo miejsca*) spread out, sprawl all over (the place)
rozsian|y *adj domy, osoby*: scattered; ***~i po całym świecie*** scattered all over the world
rozsiąść się *v/p* → ***rozsiadać się***
rozsierdzić *v/p* (*-dzę*) anger; **rozsierdzony** *adj* angry
rozsiew *m* (*-wu*; *no pl*) sowing
rozsiewać ⟨**-siać**⟩ (*-wam*) **1.** sow **2.** *plotki*, *zarazki*: spread
rozsiodływać ⟨**-łać**⟩ (*-łuję*) unsaddle
rozsławiać ⟨**-wić**⟩ (*-wiam*) make famous; ***~ na całym świecie*** make famous all over the world
rozsmakowywać się ⟨**-kować**⟩ (*-kowuję*) acquire a taste (***w*** *L* for)
rozsmarowywać ⟨**-rować**⟩ (*-rowuję*) *krem*: spread
rozstać się *v/p* → ***rozstawać się***
rozstaj *m* (*-ju*; *-je*) crossroads *pl*; ***na ~u*** *fig* at a crossroads; **rozstanie** *n* (*-nia*; *-nia*) parting
rozstaw *m* (*-wu*; *-wy*) TECH span, distance; ***~ kół*** AUTO wheelbase
rozstawać się ⟨**-tać**⟩ (*-taję*) **1.** (*pożegnać się*) part (***z*** *I* with); ***nie ~*** never part (***z*** *I* with) **2.** (*z chłopakiem*) split up, breakup
rozstawiać ⟨**-wić**⟩ (*-wiam*) **1.** *krzesła*: arrangel; ***~ po kątach*** *fig* whip into line **2.** *zawodników*: line up **3.** *kieliszki*: put, place **4.** *talerze*: lay out **5.** *nogi*: spread **6.** (*rozkładać*) set up; ***rozstawiać się*** take one's stand
rozstawienie *n* (*-nia*; *-nia*) **1.** (*ustawienie*) arrangement **2.** *zawodników*: line-up **3.** (*odległość*) distance
rozstęp *m* (*-pu*; *-py*) (*przestrzeń*) gap; ***~ skalny*** crevice; ***~y*** (**skórne**) stretch marks
rozstępować się ⟨**-tąpić**⟩ (*-puję*) **1.** (*o tłumie*) part **2.** (*o ziemi*) open (up) **3.** (*o skale*) come apart, break
rozstrajać ⟨**-roić**⟩ (*-jam*) **1.** MUS put out of tune **2.** *nerwy*: fray; ***rozstrajać się*** go out of tune
rozstrój *m* (*-roju*; *-roje*) breakdown, disorder; ***~ żołądka*** stomach upset, (minor) indigestion; ***~ nerwowy*** nervous breakdown
rozstrzelanie *n* (*-nia*; *no pl*) execution (by firing squad); **rozstrzelany** *adj* executed (by firing squad)
rozstrzeliwać[1] ⟨**-lać**⟩ (*-wuję*) (*dokonać egzekucji*) execute by firing squad, put before the firing squad
rozstrzeliwać[2] ⟨**-lić**⟩ (*-wuję*) *litery*: space out
rozstrzelony *adj litery*: spaced-out
rozstrzygać ⟨**-gnąć**⟩ (*-gam*) **1.** (*rozsądzać*) decide (**o** *L*); ***teraz rozstrzygają się jego losy*** his fate is now being decided **2.** *wątpliwości*: clear up **3.** *problem*: resolve **4.** *spór*: settle
rozstrzygający *adj* decisive; ***~ głos*** casting vote; **rozstrzygnięcie** *n* (*-cia*; *-cia*) decision
rozsunąć *v/p* → ***rozsuwać***
rozsupływać ⟨**-łać**⟩ (*-łuję*) disentangle, untangle
rozsuwać ⟨**-sunąć**⟩ (*-wam*) **1.** (*rozdzielać*) separate **2.** *stół*: extend, put out **3.** *zasłony*: draw (apart) **4.** *drabinę*: extend; ***rozsuwać się*** **1.** (*zrobić miejsce*) step aside **2.** (*o kurtynie*) draw aside
rozsuwan|y *adj* **1.** *stół*: extendible **2.** *antena*: telescopic; ***~a drabina*** extension ladder; ***~e drzwi*** sliding door
rozsychać się ⟨**-zeschnąć**⟩ (*-cham*) (*o deskach*) dry up, dry out
rozsyłać ⟨**-zesłać**⟩ (*-łam*) **1.** *kurierów*: dispatch **2.** *listy*: send
rozsyp|ka: ***uciekać w ~ce*** flee in confusion; ***pójść w ~kę*** be dispersed
rozsypywać ⟨**-pać**⟩ (*-puję*) *sól*, *cukier*: spill; ***rozsypywać się*** **1.** (*o soli*, *cukrze*) spill **2.** (*o budynku*) dilapidate **3.** (*o murze*) crumble
rozszarpywać ⟨**-pać**⟩ (*-puję*) (*o granacie*, *zwierzęciu*) tear to pieces
rozszczepiać ⟨**-pić**⟩ (*-piam*) **1.** PHYS CHEM split **2.** *światło*: disperse **3.** *drewno*: splinter; ***rozszczepiać się*** **1.** (*pękać*) split, cleave **2.** PHYS CHEM split, break
rozszczepienie *n* (*-nia*; *no pl*) (*rozłączenie*) split, cleft; ***~ atomu*** PHYS atomic fission; ***~ osobowości***, ***~ jaźni*** PSYCH multiple personality; **rozszczepialny** *adj* PHYS fissile
rozszerzać ⟨**-rzyć**⟩ (*-rzam*) **1.** broaden; ***~ swoje horyzonty*** broaden one's horizons **2.** extend; ***~ czyjeś uprawnienia***

R

extend s.o.'s powers **3.** *rzekę*, *drogę*, *szczelinę*: widen; ***rozszerzać się*** **1.** (*stawać się szerszym*) broaden **2.** (*o źrenicach*) dilate **3.** (*o ogniu*, *epidemii*) spread (**na** *A* onto)
rozszerzany *adj* flared
rozszerzenie *n* (*-nia*; *no pl*) **1.** *drogi*, *rzeki*: widening **2.** *pliku*: extension **3.** *wiedzy*, *horyzontów*: broadening; **rozszerzony** *adj* extended, broadened
rozsznurowywać ⟨**-rować**⟩ (*-rowuję*) **1.** *buty*: undo **2.** *gorset*: unlace; ***rozsznurowywać się*** come undone
rozszyfrowywać ⟨**-rować**⟩ (*-rowuję*) **1.** *depeszę*, *napis*: decipher **2.** *tajemnicę*, *zagadkę*: unravel **3.** *zamiary*, *charakter*, *osobę*: see through
rozścielać ⟨**-zesłać**⟩ (*-lam*) *koc*, *prześcieradło*: spread
rozśmieszać ⟨**-szyć**⟩ (*-szam*) make laugh
rozśpiewać się *v/m* (*-wam*) start singing, find pleasure in singing
rozświecać ⟨**-cić**⟩ (*-cam*) light up, illuminate
rozświetlać ⟨**-lić**⟩ (*-lam*) light up, illuminate; ***rozświetlać się*** light up
roztaczać ⟨**-toczyć**⟩ (*-czam*) **1.** *plan*, *wizje*: unfold; ***~ opiekę nad kimś*** have s.o. under one's protection **2.** *zapach*, *światło*: spread; ***roztaczać się*** **1.** (*o dolinie*) extend, stretch **2.** (*o widoku*) open out, stretch
roztańczyć się *v/p* (*-czę*) start dancing
roztapiać ⟨**-topić**⟩ (*-piam*) **1.** *śnieg*: melt **2.** COOK melt (in the pan); ***roztapiać się*** (*o śniegu*) melt, thaw
roztargnienie *n* (*-nia*; *no pl*) absent-mindedness; ***zrobić coś przez ~*** do s.th. absent-mindedly; ***z ~m*** absent-mindedly
roztargniony *adj* absent-minded
rozter|ka *f* (*-ki*; *-ki*) indecision, quandary; ***w ~ce*** in a quandary
roztkliwiać ⟨**-wić**⟩ (*-wiam*) move; ***roztkliwiać się*** get sentimental; ***~ się nad sobą*** feel sorry for oneself
roztłuc *v/p* → **tłuc**
roztocza *pl* (*-czy*) BIOL saprophyte *sing*
roztoczyć *v/p* → ***roztaczać***
roztopić *v/p* → ***roztapiać***
roztopy *pl* (*-pów*) thaw; ***wiosenne ~*** thaw

roztrąbić *v/p* (*-bię*) *infml* spread, retail; ***~ coś na cały świat*** shout s.th. from the rooftops
roztrącać ⟨**-cić**⟩ (*-cam*) jostle, push
roztropność *f* (-ści; *no pl*) prudence; **roztropny** *adj* **1.** *osoba*: prudent **2.** *dziecko*: bright **3.** *plan*, *spojrzenie*: clever
roztrwaniać ⟨**-wonić**⟩ (*-niam*) **1.** *pieniądze*: squander **2.** *talent*, *czas*: waste, dissipate
roztrzaskiwać ⟨**-kać**⟩ (*-kuję*) smash up; ***roztrzaskiwać się*** **1.** (*o okręcie*) be wrecked **2.** (*o samolocie*) crash **3.** (*o wazonie*) break
roztrząsać ⟨**-snąć**⟩ (*-sam*) **1.** *nawóz*: spread **2.** (*myśleć*) mull over **3.** (*omawiać*) thrash out, discuss in detail
roztrzepanie *n* (*-nia*; *no pl*) scatter-brainedness, absent-mindedness; **roztrzepany** *adj* scatterbrained
roztrzepywać ⟨**-pać**⟩ (*-puję*) COOK whisk, whip
roztrzęsiony *adj* **1.** *osoba*: jittery, distressed **2.** *głos*: trembling **3.** *ręce*: shaking; ***być ~m*** be jittery
roztwór *m* (*-woru*; *-wory*) CHEM solution; ***~ soli*** **a)** CHEM salt solution **b)** COOK salt water
roztyć się *v/p* (*-tyję*) grow fat
rozum *m* (*-mu*; *-my*) **1.** (*umysł*) mind; ***ty chyba straciłeś ~*** you must have lost your mind **2.** (*rozsądek*) reason **3.** (*rozumowanie*) sense; ***chłopski ~*** common sense; ***na zdrowy ~*** common sense suggests that; ***mieć swój ~*** to know one's own mind, be in one's right senses; ***nauczyć kogoś ~u*** teach s.o. a lesson; ***mieć więcej szczęścia niż ~u*** succeed by a fluke, have more luck than sense; ***być niespełna ~u*** be nuts, be crazy; ***pójść po ~ do głowy*** find a reasonable solution to a problem, think of s.th. sensible; ***pozjadać wszystkie ~y*** be such a smart aleck
rozumieć ⟨**z-**⟩ (*-miem*) **1.** understand; ***nic nie rozumiem*** I can't understand anything; ***~ po niemiecku*** understand German; ***doskonale to rozumiem*** I can understand it very well; ***nie rozumiem twojej decyzji*** I can't understand your decision **2.** (*mieć na myśli*) mean; ***co przez to rozumiesz?*** wha

do you mean?; **rozumieć się** understand each other; **~ się bez słów** be on the same wavelength; **to się rozumie samo przez się** it goes without saying; **ma się ~** yes, of course

rozumny *adj lit* **1.** *osoba*: clever **2.** *wybór*: wise **3.** *istota*, *stworzenie*: intelligent; **człowiek ~** Homo sapiens **4.** (*rozsądny*) sensible

rozumować *v/im* (*-muję*) reason; **~ błędnie** thinker roneously, think incorrectly; **~ logicznie** thinklo gically

rozumowani|e *n* (*-nia*; *-nia*) reasoning; **tok ~a** line of reasoning; **sposób ~a** way of reasoning

rozumowy *adj* rational

rozwadniać ⟨**-wodnić**⟩ (*-niam*) dilute, water down

rozwag|a *f* (*-gi*; *no pl*) prudence; **brać pod ~ę** take s.th. into consideration; **nie brać pod ~ę** not pay attention to, ignore

rozwalać ⟨**-lić**⟩ (*-lam*) *infml* **1.** (*rozbić*) smash (up); **~ sobie kolano** hurt one's knee; **~ samochód** crash a car **2.** *dom*: pull down **3.** (*rozrzucać*) scatter, throw about; **rozwalać się 1.** (*rozlatywać się*) get shattered, breakinto pieces **2.** (*rozsiadać się*) loll, sprawl (all over the place)

rozwalniając|y *adj*: **środek ~y** *MED* laxative

rozwałkowywać ⟨**-kować**⟩ (*-kowuję*) **1.** *ciasto*: roll (out) **2.** *temat*: dwell (on)

rozwarstwienie *n* (*-nia*; *-nia*) **1.** *społeczeństwa*: stratification **2.** *paznokci*: splitting

rozwarty *adj* (wide) open; **kąt ~** *MATH* obtuse angle

rozważać ⟨**-żyć**⟩ (*-żam*) **1.** *możliwości*, *rozwiązania*: consider, thinkabout ; **~ za i przeciw** consider all the pros and cons **2.** *towar*: weigh out

rozważania *pl* (*-żań*) reflections *pl*, ruminations *pl* (**nad** *I* on)

rozważny *adj* **1.** *osoba*: thoughtful **2.** *krok*, *czyn*: prudent, considerate

rozweselać ⟨**-lić**⟩ (*-lam*) cheer up; **rozweselić się** cheer up

rozweselony *adj* joyous

rozwiać *v/p* → **rozwiewać**

rozwiązać *v/p* → **rozwiązywać**

rozwiązanie *n* (*-nia*; *-nia*) **1.** *umowy*: termination **2.** *parlamentu*: dissolution **3.** *problemu*, *zagadki*, *techniczne*: solution **4.** (*poród*) *lit* delivery

rozwiązły *adj* **1.** *człowiek*: promiscuous, dissolute; **~ tryb życia** dissolute life(style) **2.** *obyczaje*: lax

rozwiązywać ⟨**-zać**⟩ (*-zuję*) **1.** *problem*, *zadanie*: solve **2.** *supeł*: undo, untie **3.** *zgromadzenie*: dissolve **4.** *firmę*: close down

rozwichrzony *adj* *włosy*: tousled, disheveled

rozwidlać się ⟨**-lić**⟩ (*-lam*) *droga*: fork

rozwidlenie *n* (*-nia*; *-nia*) fork

rozwidniać się: **zaczyna ~** the day is breaking

rozwiedziony *adj* divorced

rozwielitka *f* (*-ki*; *-ki*) *BIOL* daphnia

rozwierać ⟨**-zewrzeć**⟩ (*-ram*) open; **rozwierać się** open

rozwieszać ⟨**-sić**⟩ (*-szam*) *bieliznę*: hang out

rozwieść *v/p* → **rozwodzić**

rozwiewać ⟨**-zwiać**⟩ (*-wam*) **1.** *liście*: blow away, scatter **2.** *włosy*: blow through **3.** *obawy*, *wątpliwości*: dispel **4.** *marzenia*: ruin, put an end to **5.** *dym*, *mgłę*: clear; **rozwiewać się** (*o marzeniach*, *planach*) be ruined, be dispelled

rozwieźć *v/p* → **rozwozić**

rozwijać ⟨**-winąć**⟩ (*-jam*) **1.** *paczkę*, *prezent*, *cukierki*: unwrap; **~ pączki** *BIOL* be budding; **~ swoje myśli** develop one's thoughts; **~ w sobie odpowiedzialność** become more responsible; **~ w dziecku ciekawość** arouse curiosity in a child; **~ w dziecku samodzielność** instil a sense of self-reliance in a child **2.** *działalność*, *usługi*: expand **3.** *zwój*: unroll **4.** *skrzydła*: spread **5.** *sztandar*: unfurl **6.** *prędkość*: pickup **7.** *zainteresowania*, *temat*: develop **8.** *żagle*: set; **rozwijać się 1.** (*o talencie*, *osobowości*, *kraju*) develop; **~ się bardzo dobrze** thrive

2. (*o sytuacji*, *zdarzeniach*) progress

rozwijający się *adj*: **kraj ~** developing country

rozwikływać ⟨**-łać**⟩ (*-łuję*) **1.** *supeł*: disentangle **2.** *zagadkę*: solve, figure out

rozwinąć *v/p* → **rozwijać**

R

rozwinięty *adj* **1.** (*w pełni rozwoju*) developed; ***wysoko ~*** highly developed; ***w pełni ~*** fully developed; ***słabo ~*** underdeveloped; ***~ nad wiek*** precocious **2.** *kwiaty*: open, fully-blown **3.** *mięśnie*: strong
rozwlekać ⟨**-lec**⟩ (*-kam*) **1.** (*rozrzucać*) scatter, spread (***po*** *L* all over) **2.** *przemówienie*: string out, stretch out
rozwlekły *adj* wordy, verbose
rozwłóczyć *v/p* (*-czę*) scatter, spread (***po*** *L* all over)
rozwodnić *v/p* → ***rozwadniać***
rozwodnik *m* (*-ka*; *-nicy*) divorcee; ***on jest ~iem*** he is a divorcee
rozwodniony *adj* diluted, watered down
rozwodowy *adj* JUR divorce
rozwodzić się ⟨**-wieść**⟩ (*-dzę*) **1.** (*uzyskiwać rozwód*) divorce (***z*** *I* s.o.) **2.** (*mówić szczegółowo*) talkat length, dwell (***nad*** *I* upon) **3.** (*pisać szczegółowo*) write at length, dwell (***nad*** *I* upon)
rozwojowy *adj* BIOL developmental; ***cykl ~*** developmental cycle
rozwolnienie *n* (*-nia*; *-nia*) MED diarrhoea
rozwozić ⟨**-wieźć**⟩ (*-wożę*) *towar*, *mleko*: deliver; ***~ po domach*** deliver home
rozwód *m* (*-wodu*; *-wody*) divorce; ***brać ~*** divorce; **rozwódk|a** *f* (*-ki*; *-ki*) divorcee; ***ona jest ~ą*** she is a divorcee
rozw|ój *m* (*-woju*; *no pl*) development; ***~ój choroby*** course of an illness; ***~ój wypadków*** turn of events; ***stadium ~oju*** stage of development; ***tempo ~oju*** pace of development; ***opóźniony w ~oju*** MED retarded; ***~ój gospodarczy*** economic progress, economic growth
rozwrzeszczany *adj* screaming, bawling
rozwrzeszczeć się *v/p* (*-czę*) start bawling
rozwścieczyć *v/p* (*-czę*) enrage, infuriate; ***rozwścieczyć się*** get mad, flare up
rozwścieczony *adj* enraged (*I* by/at)
rozwydrzenie *n* (*-nia*; *no pl*) waywardness, unruliness; **rozwydrzony** *adj* **1.** *dziecko*: unruly, spoilt **2.** *tłum*: rowdy
rozzłoszczony *adj* irritated, vexed
rozzłościć *v/p* (*-łoszczę*) anger; ***rozzłościć się*** get angry (***na*** *A* with)
rozzuchwalać się ⟨**-lić**⟩ (*-lam*) grow impudent, grow cheeky, get insolent, get arogant
rozzuchwalony *adj* impudent, cheeky
rozżalać ⟨**-lić**⟩ (*-lam*) **1.** offend, hurt s.o.'s feelings **2.** (*rozczulić*) move, touch; ***rozżalać się*** get embittered, become embittered; ***~ się na*** *A* complain about; ***~ się nad sobą*** feel sorry for oneself; ***~ się nad swoim losem*** pity one's life
rozżalenie *n* (*-nia*; *no pl*) bitterness, sorrow; ***z ~m*** bitterly, with bitterness
rozżalony *adj* embittered; ***rozżalony na*** *A* bitter about
rozżarzać ⟨**-rzyć**⟩ (*-rzam*) incandesce; ***rozżarzać się*** incandesce; ***~ się do czerwoności*** become red-hot
rozżarzony *adj* incandescent, glowing; ***~ do czerwoności*** red hot; ***~ do białości*** white hot
rożek *m* (*-żka*; *-żki*) COOK **1.** (*rogalik*) croissant **2.** (*wafel*) cone **3.** ***~ki***, ***różki*** *ślimaka*: tentacles
roż|en *m* (*-żna*; *-żny*) (*pręt*) (roasting-)spit; ***z ~na*** COOK spitroasted; ***kurczak z ~na*** (spit) roasted chicken; ***nabić na ~en*** skewer
rożny *adj*: ***rzut ~*** SPORT corner kick, corner
ród *m* (*rodu*; *rody*) **1.** (*rodzina*) family; ***ona jest rodem z*** she and her family come from; ***ktoś z piekła rodem*** (one) hell of a person; ***pomysł z piekła rodem*** fiendish idea **2.** (*dynastia*) house; ***~ szlachecki*** noble family; ***~ królewski*** royal family; ***~ Jagiellonów*** The House of Jagiellon
róg *m* (*rogu*; *rogi*) **1.** *pokoju*, *kartki*, *stołu*: corner; ***w rogu*** in the corner; ***miejsce w rogu*** seat in the corner; ***na rogu*** on the corner; ***za rogiem*** round the corner; ***mieszkać za rogiem*** live round the corner ***zapędzać kogoś w kozi ~*** drive s.o. into a corner, show s.o. one's supremacy; ***przyprawiać komuś rogi*** cuckold s.o. **2.** *zwierzęcia* horn; ***~ obfitości*** horn of plenty; ***grzebień z rogu*** horn comb **3.** ***rogi*** **a)** *byka*, *barana*: horns **b)** *jelenia*: antlers **c)** *ślimaka*: tentacles **4.** MUS horn

R

rój *m* (*roju*; *roje*) swarm; **~ pszczół** swarm of bees; **~ dzieci** swarm of children

rów *m* (*rowu*; *rowy*) **1.** *melioracyjny*: ditch **2.** *oceaniczny*: trench

rówieśnik *m* (*-ka*; *-nicy*), **-nica** *f* (*-cy*; *-ce*) peer; **on jest moim ~iem** we are the same age; **lubiana wśród ~ów** popular among her peers

równać ⟨**wy-**⟩ (*-nam*) **1.** *teren*, *plac*: level **2.** *prawa*, *obowiązki*: equalize; **równać się 1.** (*w szeregu*) fall into line **2.** (*być równym*) come up (**z** *I* to), equal (**z** *I* s.o.); **nie móc się ~ z** *I* not be a match for; **osiem minus cztery równa się cztery** eight minus four equals four; **równaj krok!** keep in step!

równanie *n* (*-nia*; *-nia*) MATH equation; **układ równań** set of equations

równi|a *f* (*-ni*; *-nie*): **~a pochyła** PHYS inclined plane; **staczać się po ~ pochyłej** *fig* be going steadily downhill; **na ~ z** *I* on a par with; **traktować na ~ z** *I* treat on a par with, treat as equal to

równie *adv* equally; **~ dobrze możesz nic nie robić** you might just as well do nothing; **coś ~ pięknego** s.th. as beautiful as; **również** *particle* also, as well

równik *m* (*-ka*; *no pl*) GEOGR equator; **równikowy** *adj* GEOGR equatorial; **las ~** (equatorial) rain forest

równina *f* (*-ny*; *-ny*) plain; **równinny** *adj* GEOGR flat, plain; **~ teren** plain area, plain country, lowlands

równiusieńki *adj dim* straight as a die, dead straight, as flat as can be

równo *adv* → **równy**

równoboczny *adj*: **trójkąt ~** MATH equilateral triangle

równobrzmiący *adj* identical, verbatim; **równoczesny** *adj* simultaneous; **równoległa** *f* (*-łej*; *-łe*) MATH parallel line

równoległobok *m* (*-ku*; *-ki*) MATH parallelogram; **równoległościan** *m* (*-nu*; *-ny*) MATH parallelepiped

równoległ|y *adj* parallel; **~a klasa** parallel form

równoleżnik *m* (*-ka*; *-ki*) GEOGR parallel (of latitude); **równomierny** *adj* even, steady, regular; **równonoc** *f* (*-cy*; *-ce*) ASTR equinox

równoprawny *adj* equal

równoramienny *adj*: **trójkąt ~** MATH isosceles triangle

równorzędny *adj* **1.** *stanowisko*, *nagroda*: equally good, equivalent **2.** *partner*: equal; **~ przeciwnik** equal enemy, match

równoś|ć *f* (*-ści*; *no pl*) *szans*, *społeczna*: equality; **znak ~ci** MATH equals sign; **~ć wobec prawa** equality before the law; **stawiać znak ~ci między** *I fig* equal s.th. with

równouprawnienie *n* (*-nia*; *no pl*) equal rights *pl*; **~ kobiet** equal rights for women

równowag|a *f* (*-gi*; *no pl*) balance; **wyprowadzić kogoś z ~i** *fig* throw s.o. off balance; **stracić ~ę** lose one's balance; **odzyskać ~ę** regain one's balance; **utrzymać ~ę** keep balance; **~a psychiczna** spiritual balance; **~a ekologiczna** ecological balance

równowartościowy *adj* equivalent; **równoważnia** *f* (*-ni*; *-nie*) SPORT beam; **równoważnik** *m* (*-ka*; *-ki*) *zdania*: equivalent; **równoważny** *adj* equivalent, equal

równoważyć ⟨**z-**⟩ (*-żę*) (counter) balance; **równoważyć się** (be in) balance

równoznaczny *adj* **1.** (*mający jednakowe znaczenie*) equivalent (**z** *I* to) **2.** *słowo*: synonymous

równy *adj* **1.** (*gładki*) flat, smooth; **stopień ~** GRAM positive degree, the positive; **w ~m wieku** the same age; **~ gość** *infml* cool dude, cool guy; **jak z ~m sobie** on equal terms **2.** (*płaski*) flat, even **3.** (*prosty*) straight **4.** (*jednakowy*) equal **5.** *oddech*: even **6.** *krok*: regular, steady

rózg|a *f* (*-gi*; *-gi*) cane; **~i** hiding, beating

róż *m* (*-żu*; *-że*) **1.** (*kosmetyk*) blush, blusher **2.** (*kolor*) pink

róż|a *f* (*-ży*; *-że*) **1.** (*kwiat*) rose; **dzika ~a** BIOL wild rose; **bukiet ~** bunch of roses **2.** MED erysipelas

różaniec *m* (*-żańca*; *-żańce*) REL rosary; **odmawiać ~** say one's rosary

różany *adj* **1.** *aleja*, *olejek*: rose **2.** *policzki*: rosy

różdżk|a *f* (*-ki*; *-ki*) **1.** (*przyrząd różdżkarza*) divining rod **2.** *czarodzieja*: wand; **~a czarodziejska** magic wand;

jak za dotknięciem czarodziejskiej ~i as if by magic; **różdżkarz** *m* (*-rza*; *-rze*) water-diviner
różne → ***różny***
różnic|a *f* (*-cy*; *-ce*) **1.** (*nierówność*, *niezgodność*) difference; ***~a wieku*** age difference; ***~a zdań*** difference of opinion, disagreement; ***to nie robi ~y*** it doesn't make any difference, it makes no difference **2.** *MATH* remainder **3.** *terenu*: slope, incline
różnicować ⟨**z-**⟩ (*-cuję*) differentiate; ***różnicować się*** become different
różniczkowy *adj*: ***rachunek ~*** *MATH* differential calculus
różnić *v/im* (*-nię*) distinguish, differ (**od** *G* from); ***różnić się*** differ (*I* in, **od** *G* from); ***~ się pod względem*** *G* differ in; ***~ się między sobą*** be different
różnobarwny *adj Br* multicoloured, *Am* multicolored, *Br* varicoloured, *Am* varicolored; **różnojęzyczny** *adj* **1.** *osoba*: polyglot **2.** *kraj*: multilingual; **różnokolorowy** → ***różnobarwny***
różnoraki *adj* varied, diverse
różnorodny *adj* diverse, manifold
różnoś|ć *f* (-ści; *no pl*) variety, diversity; (**różne**) ***~ci*** *pl* (*-ści*) bits and bobs, bits and pieces, various things
różn|y *adj* (*odmienny*) different; ***liczba ~a od zera*** number other than zero
różowawy *adj* delicate pink, pinkish
różowieć ⟨**za-**⟩ (*-wieję*) (*o policzkach*) turn rosy, become rosy
różow|y *adj* **1.** *kolor*: pink **2.** *policzki*, *skóra*: rosy; ***patrzeć na coś przez ~e okulary*** see s.th. through rose-colored spectacles
różyczka *f* (*-ki*; *no pl*) *MED* German measles
RP *abbr f indecl* (= **Rzeczpospolita Polska**) the Republic of Poland
rtęć *f* (*rtęci*; *no pl*) *CHEM* mercury
rubaszny *adj humor*, *język*: coarse
rubieże *pl* (*-ży*) *lit* borderland *sing*, frontier *sing*
rubin *m* (*-nu*; *-ny*) ruby; **rubinowy** *adj minerał*, *kolor*: ruby
rubryka *f* (*-ki*; *-ki*) **1.** (*w formularzu*) blank (space) **2.** (*w gazecie*) column, section; ***~ ogłoszeń*** ads, advertisement section
ruch *m* (*-chu*; *-chy*) **1.** movement; ***~ polityczny*** political movement; ***~ oporu*** Resistance; ***~ ręki*** movement of the hand, gesture; ***~ w obronie pokoju*** *POLIT* peace movement; ***~ ekologiczny*** ecological movement; ***~ literacki*** literary movement; ***bez ~u*** still; ***zgodnie z ~em wskazówek zegara*** clockwise **2.** (*działanie*) motion; ***puścić w ~*** set in motion; ***~ jednostajny*** *PHYS* uniform motion; ***~ jednostajnie opóźniony*** *PHYS* uniformly retarded motion; ***~ jednostajnie przyśpieszony*** *PHYS* uniformly accelerated motion; ***być w ~u*** **a)** (*śpieszyć się*) be on the run **b)** *TECH* be in motion **3.** (*ćwiczenia fizyczne*) exercise; ***~ na świeżym powietrzu*** exercise in the open air **4.** *drogowy*, *uliczny*: traffic; ***regulować ~*** control the traffic; ***panuje tu duży ~*** there's heavy traffic here **5.** (*w grze*) move, turn; ***teraz twój ~*** it's your turn now **6.** (*ożywienie*) boom
ruchliwość *f* (*-ści*; *no pl*) mobility; ***~ zawodowa*** professional mobility; ***~ ulic*** traffic (in the streets); ***~ dziecka*** liveliness (of a child)
ruchliwy *adj* **1.** *ulica*, *plac*: busy **2.** *dziecko*: lively, active **3.** (*o rękach*, *oczach*) restless **4.** *staruszek*: active, vivacious **5.** (*rzutki*) active **6.** (*ruchomy*) mobile
ruchomo *adv* → ***ruchomy***
ruchomoś|ć *f* (*-ści*; *no pl*) **1.** (*zdolność poruszania się*) movability, mobility **2.** (*majątek ruchomy*) *JUR* personal property; ***~ci*** movables **3.** *akcentu*: shifting
ruchom|y *adj cel*, *ręka*: moving; ***schody ~e*** escalator; ***~e święto*** movable feast; ***~a scena*** revolving stage; ***majątek ~y*** *JUR* personal property, movables; ***~e wydmy*** migrating dunes, mobile dunes
ruchowo *adv*: ***sprawny ~*** adroit, nimble, physically talented; ***niesprawny ~*** physically handicapped; **ruchow|y** *adj* **1.** *nerwy*: motor **2.** (*związany z ruchem*) physical; ***zabawy ~e*** outdoor activities, outdoor games
ruda *f* (*-dy*; *-dy*) ore; ***~ żelaza*** iron ore
rudawy *adj* reddish, ginger
rudera *f* (*-ry*; *-ry*) ruin, rundown place

R

rudo *adv* → **rudy**
rudoblond *adj* reddish; **rudobrunatny** *adj* reddish brown, chestnut; **rudowłosy** *adj* redheaded, red-haired
rudy I *adj* **1.** *kolor, włosy*: red, ginger **2.** (*rudowłosy*) red-haired **II** *m* (*-dego; -dzi*), **-da** *f* (*-dej; -de*) redhead
rudzielec *m* (*-lca; -lcy*) *infml* carrot-head, carrot-top; **rudzik** *m* (*-ka; -ki*) BIOL robin
ruf\|a *f* (*-fy; -fy*) stern; ***na ~ie*** aft
rugać ⟨**z-**⟩ (*-gam*) tell off
rugbista *m* (*-ty; -biści*) rugby player
rugować ⟨**wy-**⟩ (*-guję*) **1.** (*wysiedlać*) displace **2.** (*wypierać*) eliminate
ruin\|a *f* (*-ny; -ny*) ruin; ***~y zamku*** ruins of a castle; ***doprowadzić do ~y*** bring to ruin; ***doprowadzić swoje zdrowie do ~y*** ruin one's health; ***~a człowieka*** *fig* wreck of a person
ruj\|a *f* (*rui; no pl*) rut, heat; ***suka ma ~ę*** the bitch is in heat
rujnować ⟨**z-**⟩ (*-nuję*) **1.** *zdrowie, nerwy, osobę*: ruin; ***~ finansowo*** ruin financially **2.** *miasto, domy*: devastate, destroy; ***rujnować się*** go bankrupt
ruletka *f* (*-ki; -ki*) roulette; ***rosyjska ~*** Russian roulette
rulon *m* (*-nu; -ny*) *papieru*: roll
rum *m* (*-mu; no pl*) rum
rumak *m* (*-ka; -ki*) *lit* steed
rumianek *m* (*-nku; -nki*) **1.** BIOL camomile **2.** (*napar*) camomile tea; **rumiankowy** *adj* camomile
rumiany *adj* **1.** *twarz, dziecko*: ruddy **2.** *jabłko*: red **3.** *pieczeń*: golden brown
rumienić ⟨**przy-**, **z-**, **za-**⟩ COOK brown; ***rumienić się*** blush; ***w sadzie rumienią się jabłka*** apples are glowing ripe in the orchard
rumie\|niec *m* (*-mieńca; -mieńce*) *twarzy*: blush; ***pokryć się ~ńcem wstydu*** blush with shame; ***nabrać ~ńców*** start looking good, start looking healthy; ***na jej twarz wystąpił ~niec*** she blushed, she turned red in the face; ***z ~ńcem wstydu na twarzy*** red in the face; ***mieć ~ńce na policzkach*** have red cheeks
rumor *m* (*-ru; -ry*) clatter
rumowisko *n* (*-ka; -ka*) rubble
rumsztyk *m* (*-ku; -ki*) rump steak

Rumun *m* (*-na; -ni*), **~ka** *f* (*-ki; -ki*) Romanian, Rumanian; **Rumunia** *f* (*-nii*) Romania, Rumania; **rumuński** *adj* Romanian, Rumanian
runąć *v/p* (*-nę*) **1.** (*o drzewie, osobie*) fall down **2.** (*o samolocie*) plummet **3.** (*zawalić się*) collapse **4.** (*o suficie, dachu*) cave in **5.** (*o planach*) fall through **6.** ***~ do wyjścia*** rush to the exit
rund\|a *f* (*-dy; -dy*) SPORT round; ***~a negocjacji*** POLIT round of negotiations; ***~a honorowa*** lap of honor; ***zrobić ~ę po mieście*** take a stroll around the town
runo *n* (*-na; no pl*) fleece; ***~ leśne*** (lowest) undergrowth, underbrush
rupieciarnia *f* (*-ni; -nie*) lumber room
rupiecie *pl* (*-ci*) junk *sing*, lumber *sing*
rur\|a *f* (*-ry; -ry*) **1.** (*przewód*) pipe; ***~y wodociągowe*** water pipes; ***~a wydechowa*** AUTO exhaust pipe; ***walić z grubej ~y*** say bluntly, not pull one's punches **2.** (*kobieta*) *vulg* piece of ass; ***niezła z niej ~a*** she's a fuckable chick
rurk\|a *f* (*-ki; -ki*) (little) pipe; ***~a z kremem*** COOK cream horn; ***zwinąć coś w ~ę*** roll, make a roll of; ***makaron ~i*** rigatoni; **rurkowaty** *adj* pipelike, tubular
rurociąg *m* (*-gu; -gi*) pipeline; ***~ gazowy*** gas pipeline
rusałka *f* (*-ki; -ki*) water nymph
ruski I *adj* **1.** (*dotyczący Rusi*) HIST Ruthenian **2.** *infml* Russian; ***~e pierogi*** COOK *cheese-and-potato-filled pierogi, pirozhki* **II Ruski** *m* (*-kiego; -scy*) *infml* Russki, Russky
rusycystyka *f* (*-ki; no pl*) Russian studies *pl*
ruszać ⟨**-szyć**⟩ (*-szam*) **I** *v/t* **1.** *rzeczy*: touch; ***nie ruszaj tego!*** keep your hands off!, don't touch it!; ***~ sprawę*** get things moving; ***to mnie nie rusza*** I don't care **2.** *zapasy*: start on **3.** (*poruszyć*) move; ***~ ręką*** move one's hand; ***co rusz*** every second, again and again **II** *v/i* **1.** set off; ***~ w drogę*** set off, begin a journey; ***~ w drogę powrotną*** head for home, start the journey back; ***~ w dalszą podróż*** continue one's journey; ***~ z kopyta*** *infml* shoot, get cracking; ***~ głową*** use

R

one's head **2.** (*samochodem*) start, drive off, pull out **3.** (*o fabryce, produkcji*) start, get off the ground **4.** (*o silniku*) start; ***ruszać się* 1.** (*o osobie*) move; ***nie ~ się z domu*** stay at home (all the time); ***nie ~ się z miejsca*** stay put; ***~ się jak mucha w smole*** move at a snail's pace **2.** (*o zębie, półce*) be loose

rusznikarz *m* (*-rza; -rze*) gunsmith

ruszt *m* (*-tu; -ty*) **1.** (*do smażenia*) grill; ***z ~u*** *COOK* grilled **2.** (*w piecu*) grate

rusztowanie *n* (*-nia; -nia*) *BUILD* scaffolding

ruszyć *v/p* (*-szę*): ***nie ~ palcem*** not lift a finger; ***sumienie go ruszyło*** his conscience began to nag him; ***~ sprawę z miejsca*** get things going; ***nie dać się ~ z miejsca*** not move an inch; → ***ruszać***

ruta *f* (*-ty; -ty*) *BIOL* rue

rutyn|a *f* (*-ny; no pl*) **1.** (*doświadczenie*) experience **2.** (*rutyniarstwo*) routine, rut; ***popaść w ~ę*** move in a rut; ***mieć ~ę*** be experienced, know the ropes

rutyniarstwo *n* (*-wa; no pl*) routine; **rutyniarz** *m* (*-rza; -rze*) (old) stager, old hand, experienced person

rutynowany *adj* experienced, seasoned; **rutynowo** *adv* routinely; **rutynow|y** *adj* routine, standard; ***~a kontrola*** routine inspection; ***~e pytanie*** routine question

rwać (*rwę*) **I** *v/t* **1.** ⟨**po-**⟩ *materiał*: tear (apart), rip; ***~ sobie włosy z głowy*** *fig* tear one's hair (out) **2.** ⟨**ze-**⟩ *owoce, kwiaty*: pick **3.** ⟨**wy-**⟩ *ząb*: pull out; ***~ chwasty*** weed (out) **II** *v/i* **1.** (*biec*) run, rush **2.** ***ząb mnie rwie*** I have a shooting pain in my tooth; ***rwać się* 1.** (*o materiale*) tear, rip; ***porwały mi się rajstopy*** I ripped my tights **2.** (*o rozmowie, głosie*) break off **3.** (*pragnąć*) be dying (***do*** *G* for)

rwanie *n* (*-nia; no pl*) **1.** (*podnoszenie ciężarów*) snatch **2.** *owoców*: picking **3.** (*ból*) shooting pain

rwący *adj* **1.** *potok*: swift, rapid **2.** *ból*: shooting, acute

rwetes *m* (*-su; no pl*) hubbub, bustle

ryb|a *f* (*-by; -by*) **1.** fish; ***~a morska*** sea fish; ***~a słodkowodna*** freshwater fish; ***~a drapieżna*** preditor fish; ***~a smażona*** fried fish; ***~a wędzona*** smoked fish; ***gruba ~a*** *fig* bigwig, big shot; ***iść na ~y*** go fishing, go angling; ***łowić ~y*** fish; ***~a bierze*** the fish bites; ***zdrowy jak ~a*** (as) fit as a fiddle, (as) right as rain; ***czuć się jak ~a w wodzie*** be in one's element; ***łowić ~y w mętnej wodzie*** *fig* fish in troubled waters; **2.** ***~y*** *ASTR* Pisces

ryback|i *adj* fishing; ***wioska ~a*** fishing village; ***kuter ~i*** fishing boat; **rybactwo** *n* (*-wa; no pl*) fishery, fishing

rybaczki *pl* (*-czek*) pedal pushers

rybałt *m* (*-ta; -bałci*) *HIST* minstrel

rybak *m* (*-ka; -bacy*) fisherman; **rybi** *adj* **1.** *mięso, łuska*: fish **2.** *smak, zapach*: fishy

rybitwa *f* (*-wy; -wy*) tern

rybk|a *f* (*-ki; -ki*) *dim* (little) fish; ***złota ~a*** goldfish; ***moja ~o!*** honey!, baby!

rybn|y *adj danie*: fish; ***sklep ~y*** fishmonger's (shop); ***mączka ~a*** fish meal

rybołówstwo *n* (*-wa; no pl*) fishery

ryc. *abbr* (=**rycina**) pic

rycersk|i *adj* **1.** (*uprzejmy*) *fig* courteous, chivalrous **2.** *przygody, turnieje, przymioty*: knightly; ***zbroja ~a*** knight's armour

rycerstwo *n* (*-wa; no pl*) knighthood; **rycerz** *m* (*-rza; -rze*) knight; ***błędny ~*** knight errant

rychło *adv lit* soon; ***~ w czas*** *iron* (way) too late; ***~ patrzeć jak*** any time now; **rychły** *adj lit* **1.** *zwycięstwo*: forthcoming **2.** *koniec*: impending

rycina *f* (*-ny; -ny*) **1.** (*obraz*) print **2.** (*ilustracja w książce*) picture, illustration; ***ozdobiony ~mi*** illustrated

rycynowy *adj*: ***olej ~*** castor oil

ryczałt *m* (*-tu; -ty*) *FIN* lump sum, flat rate; ***~em*** in the lump, globally; **ryczałtowy** *adj* flat-rate; ***pobierać za coś opłatę zryczałtowaną*** charge a flat rate on s.th.

ryczeć ⟨***ryknąć***⟩ (*-czę*) **1.** (*o lwie, morzu*) roar **2.** (*krzyczeć*) yell (***na*** *A* at) **3.** (*o krowie*) moo, low **4.** (*o ośle*) bray **4.** (*o syrenie, radiu*) blare

ryć (*ryję*) **1.** ⟨**wy-**⟩ (*w drewnie, kamieniu*) carve **2.** ⟨**wy-**⟩ (*w metalu*) engrave **3.** *v/im* (*uczyć się, kuć*) grind cram, *Br* swot **4.** ⟨**z-**⟩ (*kopać*) dig **5.** ⟨**z-**⟩ (*o świni*) root **6.** *v/im* (*zaśmie-*

R

wać się) laugh out loud (**z** *G* at); **~ ze śmiechu** roar with laughter
rydwan *m* (*-nu*; *-ny*) chariot
rydz *m* (*-dza*; *-dze*) BIOL rufous milk-cap; **zdrów jak ~** as sound as a bell
Ryga *f* (*-gi*) Riga
rygiel *m* (*-gla*; *-gle*) latch, bolt
ryglować ⟨**za-**⟩ (*-luję*) *drzwi*: bolt
rygor *m* (*-ru*; *-ry*) *Br* rigour, *Am* rigor, (strict) discipline; **utrzymywać ~** maintain discipline; **pod ~em** *G* JUR under penalty of; **rygorystyczny** *adj* rigorous
ryj *m* (*-ja*; *-je*) **1.** *świni*: snout **2.** (*twarz*) *vulg* mug, muzzle; **zamknij ~** shut your trap, shut your gob; **ryjek** *m* (*-jka*; *-jki*) **1.** *dim* (little) snout **2.** *owada*: proboscis *pl* **3.** (*zwinięte wargi*) pursed lips *pl*; **ryjówka** *f* (*-ki*; *-ki*) BIOL shrew, shrewmouse
ryk *m* (*-ku*; *-ki*) **1.** *lwa*, *silnika*, *morza*: roar **2.** *krowy*: lowing, moo **3.** *syreny*: blare **4.** (*wrzask*) scream, yell **5.** (*płacz*) howl, *Am* boohoo
ryknąć *v/p* → **ryczeć**
rykoszet: **odbić się ~em** ricochet, rebound
rykowisko *n* (*-ka*; *-ka*) **1.** (*miejsce*) rutting area **2.** (*czas*) rutting season
ryksza *f* (*-szy*; *-szy*) rickshaw
rym *m* (*-mu*; *-my*) rhyme
rymarz *m* (*-rza*; *-rze*) saddler
rymować ⟨**z-**⟩ (*-muję*) rhyme; **rymować się** rhyme
rynek *m* (*-nku*; *-nki*) **1.** ECON market; **~ krajowy** domestic market; **~ pracy** *Br* labour market, *Am* labor market; **~ zbytu** outlet; **wolny ~** free market; **czarny ~** black market; **wypuszczać coś na ~** put s.th. on the market **2.** (*w mieście*) market square **3.** (*targowisko*) marketplace, bazaar
rynienka *f* (*-ki*; *-ki*) stewpan
rynkow|y *adj* ECON market; **cena ~a** market price
rynna *f* (*-ny*; *-ny*) rainwater pipe
rynsztok *m* (*-ka*; *-ki*) gutter; **stoczyć się do ~a** *fig* end up in the gutter
rynsztun|ek *m* (*-nku*; *-nki*) **1.** (*wyposażenie żołnierza*) (combat) kit; **w pełnym ~ku** in full gear **2.** *iron* clothes *pl*; **w pełnym ~ku** fully clothed
rypnąć *v/p* (*-nę*) whack, slam (down), bang (down); **rypnąć się 1.** (*zrobić błąd*) make a goof (**w** *L* in) **2.** (*uderzyć się*) knock (oneself), bump (oneself) (**w** *A* against)
rys *m* (*-su*; *-sy*) **1.** (*zarys*) outline **2.** (*cecha*) trait, feature; **~ charakteru** character trait; **~y twarzy** features
rys. *abbr* (= **rysunek**) fig., pic
rysa *f* (*-sy*; *-sy*) **1.** (*zadrapanie*) scratch **2.** (*pęknięcie*) crack
rysi *adj* lynx
rysik *m* (*-ka*; *-ki*) **1.** (*wkład grafitowy*) lead **2.** (*do pisania na tabliczkach łupkowych*) slate pencil **3.** (*rylec*) stylus
rysopis *m* (*-su*; *-sy*) description; **odpowiadać ~owi** fit the description
rysować (*-suję*) **1.** ⟨**na-**⟩ (*kreślić*) draw (*I* with) **2.** ⟨**po-**⟩ (*robić rysy*) scratch (*I* with); **~ powierzchnię** scratch the surface **3.** ⟨**na-**⟩ (*szkicować*) sketch; **~ z natury** draw from life; **~ z pamięci** draw from memory; **rysować się 1.** (*o sylwetce*, *przyszłości*) appear, take shape; **~ się na tle** *G* **a)** (*przedstawiać się*) appear against the backdrop of, be seen against **b)** (*o konturach*) stand out against, be sharply defined against, show clearly against **2.** (*pękać*) crack **3.** (*pokrywać się rysami*) get scratched
rysownica *f* (*-cy*; *-ce*) drawing board
rysownik *m* (*-ka*; *-nicy*) *Br* draughtsman, *Am* draftsman; **rysowniczka** *f* (*-ki*; *-ki*) *Br* draughtswoman, *Am* draftswoman
rysun|ek *m* (*-nku*; *-nki*) **1.** drawing; **~ek ołówkiem** pencil drawing; **~ek piórkiem** pen drawing; **~ek węglem** charcoal drawing; **~ek na szkle** painting on glass **2.** *ust*, *oczu*: outline **3. ~ki** (*w szkole*) art classes; **nauka ~ku** drawing lessons
rysunkowy *adj blok*, *kredki*: drawing; **film ~** (animated) cartoon, cartoon film
ryś *m* (*rysia*; *rysie*) lynx
rytm *m* (*-mu*; *-my*) MUS rhythm; **wyczucie ~u** sense of rhythm; **do ~u** *G* to the beat of, to the rhythm of; **zaburzenia ~u serca** irregular heartbeat; **wybić kogoś z ~u** put s.o. off their stroke; **rytmiczny** *adj* rhythmic, rhythmical; **rytmika** *f* (*-ki*; *no pl*) rhythmic gymnastics

rytować *v/im* (*-tuję*) engrave; **rytownik** *m* (*-ka*; *-nicy*) engraver

rytualny *adj* ritual; **rytuał** *m* (*-łu*; *-ły*) rite, ritual; **~ *inicjacyjny*** rite of passage

ryty *adj* engraved

rywal *m* (*-la*; *-le*), **~ka** *f* (*-ki*; *-ki*) **1.** (*konkurent*) rival **2.** *SPORT* competitor; **rywalizacja** *f* (*-ji*; *-je*) **1.** rivalry **2.** *SPORT* competition

rywalizować *v/im* (*-zuję*) compete (**z** *I* with, **o** *A* for) **~ ze sobą o** *A* compete with each other for

ryzykancki *adj* (*brawurowy*) reckless; **ryzykanctwo** *n* (*-wa*; *no pl*) recklessness; **ryzykant** *m* (*-ta*; *-nci*) risk-taker

ryzyk-fizyk *adv infml* sink or swim

ryzyko *n* (*-ka*; *no pl*) risk; ***lubić ~*** be a risk-taker, be daring; ***~ zawodowe*** occupational hazard; ***na własne ~*** at one's own risk, at one's own peril; ***narażać się na ~*** *G* run the risk of; ***~ dla zdrowia*** health hazard

ryzykować ⟨**za-**⟩ (*-kuję*) **1.** (*narażać się*) take risks, take chances; ***~ życiem*** risk one's life **2.** (*odważać się*) risk, venture; **ryzykowny** *adj* **1.** *przedsięwzięcie*: risky, chancy **2.** *twierdzenie*: bold

ryż *m* (*-żu*; *no pl*) rice; ***~ na mleku*** rice pudding; **ryżow|y** *adj potrawa*, *pole*: rice; ***szczotka ~a*** scrubbing brush; ***pole ~e*** paddy (field), ricefield

ryży → ***rudy***

rz. *abbr* (= **rzeka**) R.

rzadk|i *adj* **1.** *płyn*, *zupa*, *las*: thin **2.** *włosy*: thinning **3.** *powietrze*: rare, rarefied **4.** (*nieczęsto spotykany*) rare; ***z ~a*** (*nieczęsto*) rarely, rather seldom

R

rzadko *adv* rarely, seldom; ***~ zaludniony*** thinly populated; ***~ kto*** (very) few people, hardly anyone; ***~ kiedy*** hardly ever

rzadkość *f* (*-ści*; *no pl*) rarity

rzadziej *comp* → ***rzadko***

rząd[1] *m* (*rzędu*; *rzędy*) **1.** (*szereg*) row; ***z rzędu*, *pod ~*** in a row; ***dwa lata pod ~*** two years running; ***iść rzędem*** walk one after another; ***drugi z rzędu*** the next; ***w pierwszym rzędzie*** *fig* first and foremost, in the first place; ***wydatki rzędu*** expenses to the tune of; ***suma rzędu*** sum in the region of; ***drugiego rzędu*** **a)** (*mniej ważny*) of secondary importance **b)** (*gorszy jakościowo*) second rate **2.** *BIOL* order

rząd[2] *m* (*-du*; *-dy*) **1.** *POLIT* government; ***~y*** government, rule; ***sprawować ~y*** be in government; ***~y absolutne*** absolute rule; ***zmiana ~u*** change of government; ***objąć ~y*** assume power, take over power **2.** ***związek ~u*** *GRAM* government

rządca *m* (*-cy*; *-cy*) estate manager

rządek *m* (*-dka*; *-dki*) *dim* row

rządowy *adj POLIT* **1.** *program*: government **2.** *organizacja*: governmental

rządzący **I** *adj partia*: ruling **II** *m* (*-cego*; *-cy*) (*osoba u władzy*) the one in power, the government

rządzi|ć *v/im* (*-dzę*) **1.** (*sprawować rządy*) govern (*I*), be in government **2.** (*kierować*) manage (*I*), be in charge (*I* of); ***kto tu ~?*** who's in charge?; ***kto w tym domu ~?*** who's the boss in this house? **3.** (*o prawach*, *regułach*) govern, be valid; ***rządzić się*** (*panoszyć się*) boss the show, rule the roost; ***~ się jak szara gęś*** act like s.o. owns the place

rzec *v/p* (*rzeknę*) *lit* say; ***jak(o) się rzekło*** as has been said; ***~ można*** one could say; ***słowo się rzekło*** no sooner said than done; ***by nie ~*** not to say; ***rzekłbyś*** one could say; ***nie rzekłszy słowa*** without saying a (single) word

rzecz *f* (*-czy*; *-czy*) **1.** (*przedmiot*) thing; ***~y*** things, belongings; ***~y osobiste*** personal belongings, personal possessions; ***biuro ~y znalezionych*** lost property office **2.** (*sprawa*) matter, problem; ***ogólnie ~ biorąc*** generally speaking; ***~ w tym, że*** the problem is that; ***w czym ~?*** what's the matter?; ***na ~*** *G* in favour of, for the benefit of, in aid of; ***przekazać darowiznę na ~ instytucji*** make a donation to an institution; ***na ~ pokoju*** for peace; ***na ~ ochrony środowiska*** for the protection of the natural environment; ***mówić do*** (***od***) ***~y*** talk sense (nonsense); (***przystąpić***) ***do ~y*** get to the point, address the issue; ***co to ma do ~y?*** what does that have to do with the matter at hand?; ***to nie ma nic do ~y*** that's irrelevant, it's neither here nor there; ***wielkie mi ~y!*** big deal!;

ładne ~y! a pretty kettle of fish!; ***być do ~y*** all right; ***jest ~ą wiadomą, że*** it's common knowledge that; ***~ jasna*** of course, needless to say; ***w gruncie ~y***, ***w istocie ~y*** essentially, indeed, as a matter of fact; ***~ gustu*** matter of taste; ***to nie moja ~*** this is none of my business; ***nie od ~y byłoby*** *lit* it would be reasonable

rzeczka *f* (*-ki*; *-ki*) *dim* rivulet, creek

rzecznik *m* (*-ka*; *-nicy*), **-niczka** *f* (*-ki*; *-ki*) (*zwolennik*) advocate, supporter; ***~ rządu*** *POLIT* government spokesperson; ***~ praw obywatelskich*** ombudsman, *Br* the Parliamentary Commissioner

rzeczny *adj* **1.** *port*: river **2.** *muł*, *piasek*: fluvial

rzeczony *adj lit* aforesaid, aforementioned

rzeczownik *m* (*-ka*; *-ki*) noun, substantive; ***~ pospolity*** common noun; ***~ rodzaju męskiego*** masculine noun

rzeczowo *adv* succinctly, matter-of-fact

rzeczowość *f* (*-ści*; *no pl*) matter-of-factness, objectivity; **rzeczow|y** *adj* **1.** *argument*: succinct, concrete **2.** (*obiektywny*) factual, tangible **3.** material; ***nagroda ~a*** (material) prize, prize item; ***dowód ~y*** *JUR* material proof, exhibit

rzeczoznawca *m* (*-cy*; *-cy*) expert

Rzeczpospolita *f* (*-tej*; *no pl*): ***~ Polska*** the Republic of Poland; ***Polska ~ Ludowa*** *HIST* the Polish People's Republic; ***~ szlachecka*** *HIST* democracy of nobles, the kingdom of Poland

rzeczywistoś|ć *f* (*-ści*; *no pl*) reality; ***w ~ci*** in reality, in fact; ***oderwany od ~ci*** having no sense of reality, out of touch, unrealistic; ***to nie odpowiada ~ci*** it doesn't correspond with the facts

rzeczywist|y *adj* real; ***członek ~y*** real member; ***wartość ~a*** *ECON* real value

rzeczywiście *particle* really, in fact

rzednąć ⟨**z-**⟩ (*-nę*) **1.** (*stawać się rzadszym*) become thin, get thin; ***mina mu zrzedła*** his face fell **2.** (*o włosach*) be thinning **3.** (*o mgle*) lift, clear

rzek|a *f* (*-ki*; *-ki*) river; ***w dół*** (***górę***) ***~i*** down (up) the river; ***w rzece*** in the river; ***nad ~ą*** on the river, by the river

rzekomo *particle* allegedly; ***~ nic nie wiedział*** he allegedly knew nothing, he's alleged to have known nothing

rzekom|y *adj* alleged, would-be; ***owoc ~y*** spurious fruit; ***ciąża ~a*** phantom pregnancy, false pregnancy

rzemienny *adj* leather

rzemień *m* (*-mienia*; *-mienie*) strap, thong

rzemieślnicz|y *adj*: ***wyroby ~e*** handicrafts; ***zakład ~y*** workshop; ***izba ~a*** craft council; **rzemieślnik** *m* (*-ka*; *-nicy*) artisan, craftsman

rzemiosło *n* (*-ła*; *-ła*) **1.** (*twórczość*) craftsmanship **2.** (*zawód*) trade; ***~ artystyczne*** handicraft, arts and crafts

rzemyk *m* (*-ka*; *-ki*) thong

rzep *m* (*-pa*; *-py*) **1.** *BIOL* bur(r); ***przyczepić się do kogoś jak ~ do psiego ogona*** *infml* cling to s.o. like a barnacle **2.** (*zapięcie*) Velcro® fastener

rzepa *f* (*-py*; *-py*) *BIOL* turnip

rzepak *m* (*-ku*; *no pl*) *BIOL* (oilseed) rape; **rzepakowy** *adj BIOL* rape(seed); ***olej ~*** rape(seed) oil

rzepk|a *f* (*-ki*; *-ki*) *ANAT* kneecap, patella; ***każdy sobie ~ę skrobie*** every man for himself, everybody has an axe to grind

rzesz|a *f* (*-szy*; *-sze*) **1.** ***~e*** *G* crowds of, throng of **2.** ***Trzecia ~a*** *HIST* the Third Reich

rześki *adj* **1.** *osoba*: refreshed, lively, *Am* chipper **2.** *powietrze*: brisk, bracing **3.** *ranek*: fresh, chilly

rzeteln|y *adj* **1.** *osoba*: thorough, reliable **2.** *praca*: solid, thorough; ***~a robota*** good piece of work **3.** *wiedza*: genuine, thorough, sound

rzewny *adj* **1.** (*żałosny*) doleful; ***płakać ~mi łzami*** weep bitter tears **2.** (*nostalgiczny*) wistful, nostalgic

rzeź *f* (*rzezi*; *rzezie*) **1.** (*ubój*) slaughter; ***bydło na ~*** beef cattle; ***prowadzić na ~*** take to be slaughtered **2.** (*masowe zabijanie*) massacre, butchery; ***~ Niewiniątek*** *REL* the massacre of the Innocents

rzeźba *f* (*-by*; *-by*) sculpture; ***~ w brązie*** sculpture in bronze; ***~ marmurowa*** marble sculpture; ***~ drewniana*** woodcarving; ***~ monumentalna*** monumental sculpture; ***~ Henry'ego Moore'a*** sculpture by Henry Moore; ***~ przed-***

stawiająca konia sculpture of a horse; **~ *naturalnej wielkości*** life-sized sculpture; **~ *terenu*** *GEOL* the features of the landscape, relief; **~ *bieżnika*** *AUTO* tread pattern

rzeźbiarka *f* (*-ki*; *-ki*) sculptor; **rzeźbiarski** *adj* **1.** *pracownia*: sculptor's; **~ *talent*** talent for sculpting **2.** *prace*: sculptural; **rzeźbiarstwo** *n* (*-wa*; *no pl*) **1.** (*dziedzina sztuki*) sculpture **2.** (*snycerka*) carving

rzeźbiarz *m* (*-rza*; *-rze*) sculptor

rzeźbić ⟨**wy-**⟩ (*-bię*) **1.** (*wykonywać rzeźby*) sculpt **2.** (*w drewnie*) carve **3.** *GEOL* form, sculpture

rzeźnia *f* (*-ni*; *-nie*) *Br* abattoir, *Am* slaughterhouse; **rzeźniczy** *adj*: ***tasak* ~** cleaver, meat-axe; **rzeźnik** *m* (*-ka*; *-nicy*) **1.** (*rzemieślnik*) butcher **2.** (*sklep*) butcher's (shop); **rzeźn|y** *adj*: ***zwierzęta* ~e** animals fit for slaughter

rzeźwy *adj lit* **1.** *osoba*: brisk, fresh, refreshed **2.** *powietrze*, *poranek*: fresh, bracing

rzeżączka *f* (*-ki*; *no pl*) *MED* gonorrh(o)ea

rzeżucha *f* (*-chy*; *no pl*) *BIOL* bittercress

rzędn|a *f* (*-nej*; *-ne*) *MATH* ordinate; ***oś* ~ych** the ordinate axis, y-axis, the axis of ordinates

rzędy *pl* → **rząd**[1]

rzępolić *v/im* (*-lę*) plonk

rzęsa *f* (*-sy*; *-sy*) eyelash; **~ *wodna*** *BIOL* duckweed; ***stawać na* ~ch** *infml* do one's utmost, go to great lengths, redouble one's efforts; ***chodzić na* ~ch** *infml* **a)** (*być zmęczonym*) be dead tired **b)** (*dobrze się bawić*) paint the town red

rzęsisty *adj lit* **1.** *deszcz*: pouring; ***padał* ~ *deszcz*** it was pouring down **2.** *brawa*: rapturous **3.** *światła*: bright

rzęzić *v/im* (*rzężę*) wheeze; **rzężenie** *n* (*-nia*; *no pl*) wheeze

rzodkiew|ka *f* (*-ki*; *-ki*) radish; ***pęczek* ~ek** bunch of radishes

rzucać ⟨**-cić**⟩ (*-cam*) **1.** *piłkę*, *kamień*: throw; ***rzucało samochodem*** the ride was very bumpy; ***losy rzuciły go tu*** he found himself here; **~ *kogoś na kolana*** *fig* bring s.o. to his knees; ***nie rzucać słów na wiatr*** not speak idly; ***rzucać grochem o ścianę*** *fig* waste one's breath; ***rzucać komuś kłody pod nogi*** put a spoke in s.o.'s wheel **2.** (*kości*, *sieć*, *oszczerstwa*) cast; **~ *kotwicę*** cast anchor, drop anchor; **~ *cień*** cast a shadow, throw a shadow; **~ *spojrzenie na*** *A*, **~ *okiem na*** *A* cast a glance at, take a glance at; **~ *czar na*** *A* cast a spell on **3.** *piłkę baseballową*, *kamień*: pitch **4.** *rodzinę*: forsake **5.** *chłopaka*: abandon, dump **6.** *palenie*: give up, quit; **~ *studia*** drop out of college **7.** *uwagę*: drop, make; **~ *mięsem*** *infml* curse, use four-letter words **8.** (*ciskać*) fling, hurl; ***rzucać się*** **1.** (*skoczyć*) throw oneself; **~ *się na ziemię*** throw oneself onto the ground; **~ *się na łóżko*** fall on the bed; **~ *się pod pociąg*** throw oneself under a train; **~ *się komuś na szyję*** fling oneself into s.o.'s arms; **~ *się sobie w ramiona*** hug each other; **~ *się w oczy*** stand out **2.** (*miotać się*) thrash about, thrash around **3.** (*rozrabiać*) kick up a row **4.** (*pędzić*) dart, dash; **~ *się do ucieczki*** bolt, dart away; **~ *się do drzwi*** dash to the door, rush to the door

rzut *m* (*-tu*; *-ty*) throw, cast; **~ *wolny*** free kick; **~ *karny*** penalty kick; **~ *rożny*** corner kick, corner; **~ *dyskiem*** *SPORT* the discus; **~ *oszczepem*** *SPORT* javelin throw; **~ *młotem*** *SPORT* hammer throw; **~ *poziomy* (*pionowy*)** *ARCHIT* floor (vertical) projection; ***na pierwszy* ~ *oka*** at a (single) glance

rzutki *adj* **1.** *osoba*: enterprising, agile go-ahead **2.** *umysł*: active, alert; **rzutkość** *f* (*-ści*; *no pl*) enterprise agility

rzutnik *m* (*-ka*; *-ki*) overhead projector

rzutować *v/im* (*-tuję*) **I** *v/i* (*mieć wpływ*) influence (***na*** *A*) **II** *v/t* *MATH* project

rzygać ⟨**-gnąć**, **wy-**⟩ (*-gam*) *infml* puke (up); **~ *się chce*** it makes me puke; **rzygowiny** *pl* (*-win*) *infml* puke *sing*

Rzym *m* (*-mu*) Rome

Rzymianin *m* (*-na*; *-mianie*), **-mianka** (*-ki*; *-ki*) Roman

R

rzymsk|i *adj* Roman; ***cesarstwo ~ie***, ***imperium ~ie*** the Roman Empire; ***pieczeń ~a*** *COOK* meat loaf
rzymskokatolicki *adj REL* Roman Catholic
rżeć ⟨**za-**⟩ (*rżę*) **1.** (*o koniu*) neigh **2.** (*śmiać się*) guffaw
rżnąć *v/im* (*rżnę*) **1.** *drewno*: saw **2.** *bydło*: slaughter **3.** *szkło*: cut **4.** *vulg* screw, fuck, shag **5.** ***~ w karty*** *infml* play cards with gusto **6.** ***~ głupka*** *infml* act the fool
rżnięty *adj szkło*: cut
rżysko *n* (*-ka*; *-ka*) stubble

S

s. *abbr* **1.** (= ***strona***) p. **2.** (= ***strony***) pp.
SA *abbr* (= ***Spółka Akcyjna***) PLC
sabat *m* (*-tu*; *-ty*): ***~ czarownic*** sabbath, sabbat
sabotaż *m* (*-żu*; *-że*) sabotage; **sabotażysta** *m* (*-ty*; *-żyści*), **-tka** *f* (*-ki*; *-ki*) saboteur; **sabotować** *v/im* (*-tuję*) sabotage
sacharyna *f* (*-ny*; *no pl*) saccharin
sad *m* (*-du*; *-dy*) orchard; ***~ jabłkowy*** apple tree orchard
sadło *n* (*-ła*; *no pl*) *COOK* fat; ***obrastać w ~*** run to fat
sadomasochizm *m* (*-mu*; *no pl*) sadomasochism
sadowić się ⟨**u-**⟩ (*-wię*) settle oneself
sadownictwo *n* (*-wa*; *no pl*) fruit-growing, fruit-farming; **sadownik** *m* (*-ka*; *-nicy*) fruit grower
sadysta *m* (*-ty*; *-dyści*), **-tka** *f* (*-ki*; *-ki*) sadist; **sadystyczny** *adj* sadistic
sadza *f* (*-dzy*; *-dze*) soot
sadzać ⟨**posadzić**⟩ (*-dzam*) *gości*: seat; ***~ kogoś do więzienia*** put s.o behind bars
sadzawka *f* (*-ki*; *-ki*) pool, pond
sadzeniaki *pl* (*-ków*) seed potatoes
sadzić ⟨**po-**⟩ (*-dzę*) plant; ***~ wielkimi susami*** stride; ***~ dowcipami*** crack jokes; ***~ błędy*** make mistakes; ***sadzić się*** exert oneself, spare no effort (***na*** *A* to do s.th.); ***~ się na dowcipy*** try to be funny; ***~ się na uprzejmość*** try to be polite
sadzonka *f* (*-ki*; *-ki*) **1.** (*rozsada*) seedling **2.** *drzewek*: sapling **3.** (*pęd*) cutting
sadzon|y *adj*: ***jajko ~e*** *Br* fried egg, *Am* egg made sunny-side up
sadź *f* (*-dzi*; *no pl*) rime(-frost)
safanduła *m/f* (*-ły*; *-ły*) bungler, duffer, oaf
saga *f* (*-gi*; *-gi*) saga
sagan *m* (*-na*; *-ny*) (large) cooking pot
sakralny *adj* sacral; **sakrament** *m* (*-tu*; *-ty*) *REL* sacrament; ***ostatni ~*** Last Sacrament, viaticum
saksofon *m* (*-nu*; *-ny*) saxophone
saksofonista *m* (*-ty*; *-niści*), **-tka** *f* (*-ki*; *-ki*) saxophonist
saksy *pl*: ***wyjechać na ~*** *infml* undertake seasonal labour abroad
sakw|a *f* (*-wy*; *-wy*): ***~y rowerowe*** panniers
sala *f* (*-li*; *-le*) **1.** *koncertowa*: hall; ***~ gimnastyczna*** gymnasium, gym; ***~ wykładowa*** lecture hall; ***~ posiedzeń*** sessions chamber **2.** (*publiczność*) audience **3.** *w szpitalu*: (hospital) ward, sick bay; ***~ porodowa*** delivery room
salamandra *f* (*-ry*; *-ry*) *BIOL* salamander
salami *n indecl COOK* salami
salaterka *f* (*-ki*; *-ki*) salad bowl
salceson *m* (*-nu*; *-ny*) *COOK Br* brawn, *Am* headcheese; ***czarny ~*** black pudding
saletra *f* (*-ry*; *no pl*) *CHEM* nitrate
salmonella *f* (*-li*; *-le*) *BIOL* salmonella
salomonowy *adj*: ***~ wyrok*** the judgment of Solomon
salon *m* (*-nu*; *-ny*) **1.** (*duży pokój*) living room, drawing room **2.** (*towarzystwo*, *sklep*) salon; ***~ fryzjerski*** hair salon; ***~ piękności*** *Br* beauty parlour, *Am* beauty parlor, beauty salon; ***~ gier*** *Br* video arcade, amusement arcade, *Am* penny arcade, house of games; ***~ literacki*** literary salon; ***~ meblowy*** furniture shop
salonowy *adj* **1.** (*wykwintny*) refined **2.** *muzyka*: chamber **3.** ***lew ~*** lady's man, man of the world, lounge lizard
salowa *f* (*-wej*; *-we*) *MED* orderly
salut *m* (*-tu*; *-ty*) salute; ***oddać ~*** give a salute, fire a salut

salutować ⟨**za-**⟩ (*-tuję*) salute
salw|a *f* (*-wy*; *-wy*) salvo, volley; ***~a honorowa*** salute; ***~y śmiechu*** rounds of laughter
sałat|a *f* (*-ty*; *-ty*) BIOL lettuce; ***~a głowiasta*** head lettuce, cabbage lettuce; ***dwie główki ~y*** two lettuce heads
sałatka *f* (*-ki*; *-ki*) COOK salad; ***~ jarzynowa*** vegetable salad; ***~ śledziowa*** herring salad; **sałatkowy** *adj ogórek, komplet*: salad; ***bar ~*** salad bar
sam I *pron* **1.** (*samodzielny*) by himself, by herself, by itself; ***~ to zrobił*** he did it himself, he did it on his own; ***dziecko już ~o chodzi*** the child can walk by itself; ***problem ~ się rozwiązał*** the problem solved itself **2.** (*samotny*) alone; ***dzieci zostały ~e w domu*** the children were alone at home **3.** (*tylko*) nothing but; ***miała z nim ~e kłopoty*** she had nothing but trouble with him **4.** (*wzmocnienie*) very; ***do ~ej ziemi*** to the very bottom; ***nad ~ym morzem*** right by the sea; ***do ~ego rana*** till the early morning; ***w ~ą porę*** just in time, in the nick of time; ***w ~ raz dla mnie*** just right for me; ***w ~ym środku*** right in the middle; ***nie miał czasu dla ~ego siebie*** he did not have time even for himself; ***pan przeczy ~emu sobie*** you contradict yourself; ***to mówi ~o za siebie*** the facts speak for themselves; ***~ w sobie*** by itself; ***~ jeden*** all alone; ***ten ~, ta ~a, to ~o*** the same, one and the same; ***tym ~ym*** thus, thereby, this is why; ***na ~ widok*** *G* at the very sight of; ***na ~ą myśl*** at the (very) thought; ***~ prezydent*** the president himself; ***~ przez się*** by himself; ***tak ~o*** exactly the same way, ***tyle ~o*** just as much, just as many; ***~ na ~*** in private, tête-à-tête **II** *m* (*-mu*; *-my*) (*sklep*) supermarket
sama → ***sam I***
samarytanin *m* (*-na*; *-tanie*), **-tanka** *f* (*-ki*; *-ki*) *lit* Samaritan
samczyk *m* (*-ka*; *-ki*) BIOL (*ryba, ptak*) male
same → ***sam I***
sami → ***sam I***
samica *f* (*-cy*; *-ce*) **1.** female **2.** *jelenia*: doe **3.** *słonia*: cow **4.** *psa, wilka*: bitch
samiczka *f* (*-ki*; *-ki*) BIOL female
samiec *m* (*-mca*; *-mce*) **1.** male **2.** *dużych zwierząt*: bull **3.** *owcy*: ram **4.** *ptaków*: cock **5.** (*mężczyzna*) *infml* macho
samiuteńki, ***samiutki*** *adj dim* all alone, all on one's own
samo → ***sam I***
samo- (*w złożeniach*) self-, auto-; ***~zatrudnienie*** self-employment
samobójca *m* (*-cy*; *-cy*), **-czyni** *f* (*-ni*; *-nie*) suicide
samobójcz|y *adj* suicidal; ***gol ~y, bramka ~a*** SPORT own goal; ***myśli ~e*** suicidal thoughts; ***mieć myśli ~e*** be contemplating suicide; ***próba ~a*** suicide attempt
samobójstwo *n* (*-wa*; *-wa*) suicide; ***popełnić ~*** commit suicide; ***usiłować popełnić ~*** attempt suicide
samochodow|y *adj* **1.** *przemysł*: *Br* car, *Am* automotive; ***warsztat ~y*** garage; ***wyścigi ~e*** motor racing **2.** *mapa*: road **3.** *wypadek*: car; **samochodziarz** *m* (*-rza*; *-rze*) car freak; **samochodzik** *m* (*-ka*; *-ki*) (*zabawka*) toy-car; ***zasuwać jak mały ~*** **a)** (*biec*) run very quickly **b)** (*pracować*) work like crazy
samoch|ód *m* (*-chodu*; *-chody*) car; ***~ód osobowy*** (motor) car, *Am* automobile; ***~ód ciężarowy*** *Br* lorry, *Am* truck; ***~ód dostawczy*** delivery van; ***~ód pułapka*** booby-trap(ped) car; ***~od z automatyczną skrzynią biegów*** automatic; ***~ód kombi*** *Br* estate car, *Am* station wagon; ***prowadzić ~ód*** drive a car; ***jesteś ~odem?*** did you come by car?
samochwalczy *adj* boastful, showy; **samochwalstwo** *n* (*-wa*; *no pl*) boastfulness
samochwała *f/m* (*-ły*; *-ły*) braggart, bigmouth
samoczynny *adj* TECH automatic
samodzielność *f* (*-ści*; *no pl*) independence; **samodzielny** *adj* **1.** *dziecko*: independent **2.** *praca, myślenie*: individualistic, free **3.** (*niezależny*) independent, self-sufficient **4.** (*odrębny*) autonomous
samogłoska *f* (*-ki*; *-ki*) vowel; ***~ nosowa*** nasal vowel; **samogłoskowy** *adj* vowel
samogon *m* (*-nu*; *no pl*) moonshine, *Am* hooch

S

samogwałt *m* (*-tu*; *no pl*) masturbation; ***uprawiać ~*** masturbate
samoistnie *adv* spontaneously, by itself; **samoistn|y** *adj* **1.** (*samodzielny*) spontaneous **2.** (*odrębny*) independent; ***~e wyleczenie*** MED idiopathic recovery
samokontrola *f* (*-li*; *no pl*) self-control
samokrytyczny *adj* self-critical; **samokrytyk|a** *f* (*-ki*; *no pl*) self-criticism; ***złożyć ~ę*** do a self-critique
samokształcenie *n* (*-nia*; *no pl*) self-education, self-study
samolot *m* (*-tu*; *-ty*) *Br* (aero)plane, *Am* (air)plane; ***~ pasażerski*** passenger plane; ***~ bojowy*** fighter aircraft, warplane; ***lecieć ~em*** go by plane, fly
samolub *m* (*-ba*; *-by*) egotist, egoist; **samolubny** *adj* selfish, egoistic; **samolubstwo** *n* (*-wa*; *no pl*) selfishness, egoism
samoobron|a *f* (*-ny*; *no pl*) *Br* self-defence, *Am* self-defense; ***w ~ie*** in self-defense
samoobsługa *f* (*-gi*; *no pl*) self-service; **samoobsługowy** *adj*: ***sklep ~*** self-service shop
samookaleczenie *n* (*-nia*; *-nia*) self-mutilation, self-harm; **samoopalacz** *m* (*-cza*; *-cze*) tanning foam, tanning cream; **samooskarżenie** *n* (*-nia*; *-nia*) self-accusation
samopas *adv lit* on one's own; ***zostawić ~*** leave unattended, leave without anyone to look after
samopoczucie *n* (*-cia*; *no pl*) frame of mind, mood; ***dobre ~*** comfort; ***złe ~*** discomfort; ***mieć dobre ~*** **a)** (*psychiczne*) be in a good mood **b)** (*fizyczne*) feel well; **samopomoc** *f* (*-cy*; *no pl*) mutual aid
samoprzylepny *adj* self-adhesive, stick-on; **samorodny** *adj* **1.** *talent*: natural, inborn **2.** *artysta*: born
samorząd *m* (*-du*; *-dy*) self-government; ***~ gminny*** parish council, parish government; ***~ miejski*** *Br* town council, *Am* municipal government; **samorządny** *adj* self-governing, autonomous, independent; **samorządowy** *adj* council; ***okręg ~*** municipality
samorzutny *adj akcja*: spontaneous; ***~ wybuch*** spontaneous explosion;
samosąd *m* (*-du*; *-dy*) lynching; ***dokonywać ~u na kimś*** lynch s.o.; **samosiejka** *f* (*-ki*; *-ki*) self-sown plant; **samospalenie** *n* (*-nia*; *-nia*) self-immolation, self-burning
samostanowienie *n* (*-nia*; *no pl*) POLIT autonomy
samotnia *f* (*-ni*; *-nie*) retreat, hermitage; **samotniczy** *adj* reclusive, solitary; **samotnie** *adv* alone; ***~ podróżować*** travel alone, travel by oneself; ***kobieta ~ wychowująca dziecko*** single mother; **samotnik** *m* (*-ka*; *-nicy*), **-nica** *f* (*-cy*; *-ce*) loner, recluse
samotnoś|ć *f* (*-ści*; *no pl*) **1.** loneliness **2.** solitude; ***żyć w ~ci*** live in solitude;
samotn|y **I** *adj* **1.** *osoba*, *drzewo*: solitary **2.** (*sam*) lonely; ***~a kobieta*** single woman, unmarried woman, spinster; ***~y mężczyzna*** single man, unmarried man, bachelor; ***~y podróżny*** unaccompanied traveller **II** *m* (*-nego*; *-ni*), **-na** *f* (*-nej*; *-ne*) single person; ***wigilia dla ~ych*** Christmas Eve for lonely people
samouczek *m* (*-czka*; *-czki*) 'teach-yourself' book; **samouk** *m* (*-ka*; *-ki*/*-moucy*) self-taught person
samowar *m* (*-ra*; *-ry*) samovar
samowładca *m* (*-cy*; *-cy*) autocrat; **samowładztwo** *n* (*-wa*; *no pl*) autocracy
samowol|a *f* (*-li*; *no pl*) lawlessness; ***akt ~i*** lawless act; **samowolny** *adj* **1.** *decyzja*: arbitrary, lawless **2.** (*nieposłuszny*) *Br* wilful, *Am* willful, self-willed
samowystarczalny *adj* **1.** *kraj*: self-sufficient **2.** *finansowo*: self-supporting
samowyzwalacz *m* (*-cza*; *-cze*) PHOT self-timer
samozachowawczy *adj*: ***instynkt ~*** self-preservation instinct
samozadowolenie *n* (*-nia*; *no pl*) self-satisfaction; **samozaparcie** *n* (*-cia*; *no pl*) perseverance, persistence; ***z ~m*** persistently, with perseverance
samozapłon *m* (*-nu*; *no pl*) **1.** AUTO self-ignition **2.** PHYS spontaneous ignition
samozapylenie *n* (*-nia*; *no pl*) BIOL self-pollination
samozwaniec *m* (*-wańca*; *-wańcy*) usurper; **samozwańczy** *adj władca*: self-proclaimed

sanacja *f* (*-ji*; *no pl*) *fig* *HIST* moral cleansing policy
sanatorium *n* (*indecl*; *-ria*) sanatorium
sandacz *m* (*-cza*; *-cze*) pikeperch
sandałowy *adj* sandalwood
sandały *pl* (*-łów*) sandals
saneczkarstwo *n* (*-wa*; *no pl*) *SPORT* tobogganing
saneczkarz *m* (*-rza*; *-rze*), **-rka** *f* (*-ki*; *-ki*) *SPORT* tobogganist
sanie *pl* (*sań*) sleigh *sing*
sanitariusz *m* (*-sza*; *-sze*), **~ka** *f* (*-ki*; *-ki*) **1.** (*w karetce*) paramedic **2.** (*w wojsku*) medic, stretcher-bearer
sanitarn|y *adj* *warunki*: sanitary; ***punkt ~y*** first-aid station; ***urządzenia ~e*** sanitary facilities
sankcj|a *f* (*-ji*; *-je*) sanction; ***nakładać ~e na*** *A* impose sanctions on, impose sanctions against
sankcjonować *v/im* (*-nuję*) (*nadawać moc prawną*) authorize, sanction
sanki *pl* (*-nek*) toboggan *sing*, *Br* sledge *sing*, *Am* sled *sing*; **sanna** *f* (*-ny*; *no pl*) sleighing
sapać ⟨**-pnąć**⟩ (*-pię*) pant
saper *m* (*-ra*; *-rzy*) **1.** (*osoba rozbrajająca miny*) sapper **2.** (*budujący mosty*) engineer; **saperka** *f* (*-ki*; *-ki*) camp shovel; **saperki** *pl* (*-rek*) boots
sapka *f* (*-ki*; *no pl*) *MED* the snuffles
sapnąć *v/p* → ***sapać***
Sardynia *f* (*-nii*) Sardinia
sardynka *f* (*-ki*; *-ki*) sardine
sarenka *f* (*-ki*; *-ki*) *dim* → ***sarna***
sarkać ⟨**-knąć**⟩ (*-kam*) grumble (**na** *A* about)
sarkastyczny *adj* sarcastic
sarknąć *v/p* → ***sarkać***
sarkofag *m* (*-gu*; *-gi*) sarcophagus
sarna *f* (*-ny*; *-ny*) roe (deer); **sarni** *adj* roe deer's; **sarnina** *f* (*-ny*; *no pl*) *COOK* venison
sasanka *f* (*-ki*; *-ki*) *BIOL* pasque-flower
saszetka *f* (*-ki*; *-ki*) **1.** (*torebka*) travel document organizer **2.** (*przy pasie*) *Br* bumbag, *Am* fanny pack **3.** (*opakowanie*) sachet; ***herbata w ~ch*** tea bags
sataniczny *adj* satanic; **satanizm** *m* (*-mu*; *no pl*) Satanism
satelicki *adj*: ***państwo ~e*** *POLIT* satellite country
satelita *m* (*-ty*; *-ty*) *ASTR* satellite; **satelitarny** *adj* *RADIO* satellite
Saturn *m* (*-na*) *ASTR* Saturn
satyna *f* (*-ny*; *no pl*) satin; **satynowy** *adj* satin
satyra *f* (*-ry*; *-ry*) satire; **satyryczny** *adj* satiric, satirical; ***program ~*** comedy show
satyryk *m* (*-ka*; *-rycy*) **1.** (*pisarz*) satirist **2.** *kabaretowy*: comic
satysfakcj|a *f* (*-ji*; *no pl*) satisfaction; ***złośliwa ~a*** malicious glee, gloating; ***~a seksualna*** sexual satisfaction; ***mieć ~ę*** be pleased; ***mieć ~ę z pracy*** find one's job rewarding; ***dawać komuś ~ę*** give satisfaction to
satysfakcjonować ⟨**u-**⟩ (*-nuję*) satisfy
saudyjsk|i *adj* Saudi (Arabian); ***Arabia 2a*** Saudi Arabia
są → ***być***
sączek *m* (*-czka*; *-czki*) **1.** *CHEM* filter **2.** *MED* drain
sączyć (*-czę*) **1.** *v/im* (*pić powoli*) sip **2.** ⟨**prze-**⟩ (*wlewać*) trickle (**do** *G* into); **sączyć się** ⟨**prze-**⟩ **1.** (*o wodzie*) ooze, trickle **2.** (*o świetle*) shimmer through, come through
sąd *m* (*-du*; *-dy*) **1.** *JUR* court of law, court of justice; ***~ dla nieletnich*** juvenile court; ***~ doraźny*** summary court; ***~ polowy***, ***~ wojenny*** court martial; ***2 Najwyższy*** *Br* the High Court, *Am* Supreme Court; ***2 Ostateczny*** *REL* the Last Judgement; ***podać kogoś do ~u*** sue s.o., take s.o. to court; ***stanąć przed ~em*** stand trial **2.** (*proces*) trial **3.** (*budynek*) court(house) **4.** (*ocena*) judg(e)ment; ***wydać ~ o*** *L* make a judgement about; ***wyrobić sobie ~*** form an opinion (**o** *L* about)
sądny *adj*: ***~ dzień*** doomsday
sądownictwo *n* (*-wa*; *no pl*) judiciary
sądownie *adv* *dochodzić*: through legal action, in court; **sądow|y** *adj* **1.** *akta*: court; ***w drodze ~ej*** through legal action; ***rozprawa ~a*** trial **2.** *medycyna*: forensic
sądzić *v/im* (*-dzę*) **I** *v/t* *JUR* judge, try **II** *v/i* **1.** (*oceniać*) judge **2.** (*mieć określoną opinię*) think (**o** *L* about); ***sądzę, że*** I believe that; ***sądząc*** judging (**po** *L* by, **z** *G* from); ***co o tym sądzisz?*** what do you think about it?; ***jak sądzisz?*** what's your opin-

S

ion?; ***nie sądzę*** I don't think so; ***chciał, jak sądzę, tu przyjść*** I believe he wanted to come here
sądzon|y: *adj* ***nie było mu ~e*** *lit* this was not destined for him
sąsiad *m* (*-da*; *-siedzi*), **~ka** *f* (*-ki*; *-ki*) *Br* neighbour, *Am* neighbor; ***~ przy stole*** the person sitting next to s.o. at the table; ***dziecko ~ów*** our neighbour's child; ***~ zza ściany*** next door neighbour
sąsiadować *v/im* (*-duję*) **1.** live next door (**z** *I* to), *Br* be neighbours, *Am* be neighbors (**z** *I* with); ***sąsiaduje z nami młoda rodzina*** we live next door to a young family; ***~ (ze sobą)*** be (next door) neighbours **2.** (*o kraju, domu*) *Br* neighbour, *Am* neighbor (**z** *I* on)
sąsiedni *adj* **1.** *kraj, miasto*: *Br* neighbouring, *Am* neighboring **2.** *dom, mieszkanie*: next-door **3.** *pokój*: adjoining
sąsiedzi *pl* → **sąsiad**
sąsiedzk|i *adj* **1.** *troska*: *Br* neighbourly, *Am* neighborly; ***~a pomoc*** *Br* neighbourly help **2.** (*z sąsiadami*) *Br* between neighbours, *Am* between neighbors; ***~ie spory*** *Br* rows between neighbours; ***mieszkać po ~u*** live next-door, *Br* be next-door neighbours;
sąsiedztw|o *n* (*-wa*; *no pl*) *Br* neighbourhood, *Am* neighborhood; ***w ~ie*** *G* in the neighbourhood of, in the vicinity of
sążnisty *adj artykuł, list*: lengthy
scalać ⟨**-lić**⟩ (*-lę*) **1.** *politycznie*: integrate **2.** *informacje*: collate **3.** *firmy, pliki*: merge **4.** (*łączyć*) connect; ***scalać się*** *fig* unite, integrate
scalenie *n* (*-nia*; *no pl*) integration
scalony *adj*: ***układ ~*** integrated circuit
scen|a *f* (*-ny*; *-ny*) **1.** (*w teatrze*) stage **2.** *dramatu, filmu*: scene; ***~a miłosna*** love scene; ***zrobić ~ę*** *fig* make a scene; ***~a wydarzeń*** scene; ***~a polityczna*** political arena, political scene
scenariusz *m* (*-sza*; *-sze*) **1.** *filmu, sztuki, audycji*: script **2.** *filmu*: screenplay **3.** *wydarzeń*: scenario
scenarzysta *m* (*-ty*; *-rzyści*), **-tka** *f* (*-ki*; *-ki*) scriptwriter
sceneria *f* (*-rii*; *-rie*) scenery, setting
sceniczny *adj utwór*: stage
scenograf *m* (*-fa*; *-fowie*) set designer; **scenografia** *f* (*-fii*; *no pl*) set design; **scenopisarstwo** *n* (*-wa*; *no pl*) scriptwriting
sceptyczny *adj* sceptical; **sceptyk** *m* (*-ka*; *-tycy*) sceptic
schab *m* (*-bu*; *-by*) COOK (*mięso*) joint of pork
schabowy *adj*: ***kotlet ~*** COOK pork chop
schadzka *f* (*-ki*; *ki*) *lit* tryst
schamieć *v/p* (*-mieję*) become boorish, become brutalized, coarsen
schemat *m* (*-tu*; *-ty*) **1.** (*zarys*) outline **2.** (*rysunek*) schematic, diagram; ***~ elektryczny*** circuit diagram; ***~ myślowy*** (fixed) manner of thinking; **schematyczny** *adj* **1.** (*uproszczony*) schematic **2.** (*nieoryginalny*) conventional
schizofrenia *f* (*-nii*; *no pl*) schizophrenia; **schizofrenik** *m* (*-ka*; *-nicy*), **-niczka** *f* (*-ki*; *-ki*) schizophrenic
schlać się *v/p* (*-leję*) *infml* get loaded, get tanked up; **schlany** *adj infml* tight, loaded, pissed
schlebiać *v/im* (*-biam*) flatter (*D*); ***schlebia mi, że*** it flatters me that
schludnie *adv* neatly; ***wyglądał ~*** he was looking spruce; **schludny** *adj* neat, tidy
schładzać ⟨**-łodzić**⟩ (*-dzam*) *napoje*: chill; **schłodzony** *adj* chilled
schnąć ⟨**wy-**⟩ (*-nę*) **1.** (*o bieliźnie, farbie*) dry; ***~ z tęsknoty*** pine (**za** *I* for) **2.** (*o roślinie*) wither **3.** (*o pieczywie*) become stale
schod|ek *m* (*-dka*; *-dki*) step; ***~ki*** small stairs
schodow|y *adj*: ***klatka ~a*** staircase, stairway
schod|y *pl* (*-dów*) stairs; ***~y ruchome*** escalator; ***kręcone ~y*** spiral staircase; ***zejść po ~ach*** go downstairs
schodzić ⟨**zejść**⟩ (*-dzę*) **1.** (*o osobie, temperaturze*) go down; ***~ na bok*** stand aside; ***~ z kursu*** deviate from the course; ***~ komuś z drogi*** *fig* get out of s.o.'s way; ***~ na ląd*** disembark, go ashore; ***~ do lądowania*** descend; ***~ z konia*** dismount from a horse; ***~ z roweru*** get off a bike; ***~ do podziemia*** POLIT go underground; ***~ na psy*** *infml* go to the dogs; ***film zszedł***

S

z ekranu the film is not on any more; ***~ na dalszy plan*** *fig* recede into the background; ***~ na złą drogę*** go astray; ***towar dobrze schodzi*** the goods sell well; **schodzić buty** wear out one's shoes **2.** (*o skórze*) peel **3.** (*o plamie*) come off **4.** (*o opuchliznie*) subside, go down **5.** (*o czasie*) take; ***zeszło mi na tym sporo czasu*** it took me a lot of time; **schodzić się 1.** (*o osobach*) gather **2.** (*o liniach*) converge, meet **3.** (*o rocznicy*, *zdarzeniach*) coincide (**z** *I* with)
scholastyczny *adj* scholastic
schorowany *adj* ailing, sick
schorzenie *m* (*-nia*; *-nia*): ***~ nerek*** kidney disease, kidney trouble; ***~ serca*** heart condition; ***~ reumatyczne*** rheumatism, rheumatic disease
schować *v/p* → **chować**
schowek *m* (*-wka*; *-wki*) **1.** (*skrytka*) hiding place **2.** (*w samochodzie*) glove compartment
schron *m* (*-nu*; *-ny*) shelter; ***~ przeciwlotniczy*** air-raid shelter
schronić się *v/p* → **chronić się**
schronienie *n* (*-nia*; *-nia*) shelter; **schronisko** *n* (*-ka*; *-ka*) **1.** *młodzieżowe*: hostel **2.** *górskie*: hut, lodge **3.** (*dla zwierząt*) animal shelter
schrypnięty *adj* hoarse
schudnąć *v/p* → **chudnąć**; **schudnięcie** *n* (*-cia*; *no pl*) weight loss
schwał: ***chłop na ~*** great guy
schwytać (*-tam*), **schwycić** (*-cę*): ***~ kogoś na gorącym uczynku*** catch s.o. red-handed; → **chwytać**
schylać ⟨**-lić**⟩ (*-lam*) **1.** *głowę*: lower **2.** *gałęzie*: bend down; **schylać się** bend
schył|ek *m* (*-łku*; *no pl*) *lit epoki*, *kariery*: decline, twilight; ***u ~ku kariery*** at the end of one's career, in the twilight of one's career; ***~ek życia*** the autumn of one's life; ***~ek wieku*** end of century; ***dzień miał się ku ~kowi*** the day was drawing to a close; **schyłkowy** *adj faza*, *pisarz*, *tendencje*: decadent
scukrzyć się *v/p* (*-rzę*) (*o miodzie*) set
scysja *f* (*-ji*; *-je*) altercation, brush
scyzoryk *m* (*-ka*; *-ki*) penknife
sczepiać ⟨**-pić**⟩ (*-piam*) **1.** *wagony*: couple together, link up **2.** *kartki*: staple; **sczepiać się**: ***sczepili się nartami*** their skis got caught up
sczernieć *v/p* → **czernieć**
sczerstwieć *v/p* → **czerstwieć**
seans *m* (*-su*; *-se*) **1.** *filmowy*: showing, viewing **2.** *psychoanalityczny*: session; ***~ spirytystyczny*** séance
secesyjn|y *adj*: ***styl ~y*** Art Nouveau; ***wojna ~a*** *HIST* the American Civil War
sedes *m* (*-su*; *-sy*) toilet; **sedesow|y** *adj*: ***deska ~a*** toilet seat
sedno *n* (*-na*; *no pl*) essence; ***~ sprawy*** heart of the matter, crux of the matter; ***trafić w ~*** hit the nail on the head
segment *m* (*-tu*; *-ty*) **1.** (*część*) segment **2.** *pokojowy*: unit **3.** *kuchenny*: fitted kitchen **4.** (*dom*) *Br* terraced house, *Am* row house
segmentow|y *adj* segmented; ***kuchenne meble ~e*** fitted kitchen
segregacja *f* (*-ji*; *no pl*) segregation; ***~ śmieci*** waste sorting; ***~ rasowa*** racial segregation
segregator *m* (*-ra*; *-ry*) binder, file
segregować ⟨**po-**⟩ (*-guję*) *Br* categorise, *Am* categorize, sort out
sejf *m* (*-fu*; *-fy*) safe
Sejm *m* (*-mu*; *-my*) *POLIT* (*the lower chamber of the Polish parliament*) the Sejm; **sejmik** *m* (*-ku*; *-ki*) *HIST* assembly; **sejmowy** *adj POLIT* parliamentary
sejsmiczny *adj* seismic
sekator *m* (*-ra*; *-ry*) secateurs *pl*, pruning shears *pl*
sekciarstwo *n* (*-wa*; *no pl*) *POLIT REL* sectarianism; **sekciarz** *m* (*-rza*; *-rze*) *POLIT REL* sectarian
sekcja *f* (*-ji*; *-je*) section; ***~ zwłok*** *MED* autopsy
sekre|t *m* (*-tu*; *-ty*) secret; ***w ~cie*** in secret
sekretariat *m* (*-tu*; *-ty*) (secretarial) office, secretary's office; **sekretarka** *f* (*-ki*; *-ki*) secretary; ***automatyczna ~*** answering machine, *Am* answerphone
sekretarz *m* (*-rza*; *-rze*) *POLIT* secretary; ***~ stanu*** Secratary of State; **sekretarzyk** *m* (*-ka*; *-ki*) (*mebel*) secretaire
sekretny *adj schody*, *drzwi*: secret
seks *m* (*-su*; *no pl*) sex; ***bezpieczny ~*** safe sex; **seksowny** *adj* sexy

sekstet *m* (*-tu*; *-ty*) *MUS* sextet
seksualność *f* (-ści; *no pl*) sexuality; **seksualn|y** *adj* sexual; ***wychowanie ~e*** sex education; ***morderstwo na tle ~ym*** *JUR* sex-related murder
sekta *f* (*-ty*; *-ty*) *REL* sect; **sektor** *m* (*-ra*; *-ry*) **1.** *widowni*: section **2.** *gospodarki*: sector
sekund|a *f* (*-dy*; *-dy*) second; ***co do ~y*** to the second; ***wpaść do kogoś na ~ę*** call on s.o. for a moment
sekundant *m* (*-ta*; *-nci*) second
sekundnik *m* (*-ka*; *-ki*) second hand
sekundować *v/im* (*-duję*) second (***komuś w*** *L* s.o. in); ***~ w pojedynku*** be s.o.'s second in a duel
sekutnica *f* (*-cy*; *-ce*) *lit* shrew
Sekwana *f* (*-ny*) the Seine
sekwencja *f* (*-ji*; *-je*) *filmowa*: sequence; **sekwens** *m* (*-su*; *-sy*) **1.** (*w kartach*) sequence, run **2.** (*w pokerze*) straight (flush)
sekwoja *f* (*-woi*; *-je*) *BIOL* sequoia
seledynowy *adj* celadon
selekcja *f* (*-ji*; *no pl*) selection; ***~ naturalna*** *BIOL* natural selection; **selekcjoner** *m* (*-ra*; *-rzy*) *SPORT* selector, (team) manager
selekcjonować ⟨**wy-**⟩ (*-nuję*) select
selektywny *adj* selective
seler *m* (*-ra*; *-ry*) **1.** (*korzeniowy*) celeriac **2.** (*naciowy*) celery
semafor *m* (*-ra*; *-ry*) semaphore
semantyczny *adj* semantic
semestr *m* (*-ru*; *-ry*) term, semester; ***~ letni*** summer semester, summer term; ***~ zimowy*** winter semester, winter term; ***na pierwszym ~ze*** in the first semester
semestraln|y *adj* term, semester; ***zaliczenie ~e*** term credit; ***kolokwium ~e*** end-of-term test; ***praca ~a*** term paper
seminarium *n* (*indecl*; *-ria*) **1.** (*zajęcia*, *dyskusja*) seminar **2.** (*szkoła*): ***~ duchowne*** seminary; **seminarzysta** *m* (*-ty*; *-rzyści*) (*duchowny*) seminarist
sen *m* (*snu*, *sny*) **1.** (*marzenie senne*) dream; ***~ na jawie*** daydream; ***ujrzeć coś we śnie*** see s.th. in a dream; ***pamiętać coś jak przez ~*** have a dim recollection of s.th.; ***koszmarne sny*** nightmares; ***kolorowych snów!*** sweet dreams! **2.** (*spanie*) sleep; ***~ zimowy*** *BIOL* hibernation; ***układać do snu*** put to bed; ***mówić przez ~*** talk in one's sleep
senacki *adj* **1.** *dom*: Senate **2.** *immunitet*, *dekret*: senatorial
senat *m* (*-tu*; *-ty*) *POLIT* senate; ***wybory do ~u*** senatorial elections; **senator** *m* (*-ra*; *-rzy*/*-rowie*) senator
senior *m* (*-ra*; *-rzy*), **~ka** *f* (*-ki*; *-ki*) senior
sennie *adv* sleepily, drowsily; ***nastrajać kogoś ~*** make s.o. sleepy, make s.o. drowsy; **sennik** *m* (*-ka*; *-ki*) book of dream interpretation, dream book; **senność** *f* (*-ści*; *no pl*) sleepiness, drowsines
senn|y *adj* **1.** *osoba*, *oczy*, *głos*: drowsy, sleepy; ***marzenie ~e*** dream; ***~e miasteczko*** sleepy town **2.** *atmosfera*: torpid
sens *m* (*-su*; *-sy*) **1.** (*znaczenie*, *waga*) sense; ***nie ma ~u*** there is no point; ***z ~em*** sensibly; ***bez ~u*** make no sense; ***w pewnym ~ie*** in a sense; ***coś w tym ~ie*** something like that **2.** *gestu*, *słowa*: meaning
sensacj|a *f* (*-ji*; *-je*) sensation; ***wywołać ~ę*** cause a sensation, create a sensation; ***~e żołądkowe*** stomach upset, stomach trouble
sensacyjn|y *adj* sensational; ***film ~y***, ***powieść ~a*** thriller
sensat *m* (*-ta*; *-saci*), **~ka** *f* (*-ki*; *-ki*) sobersides
sensowny *adj* *zajęcie*, *decyzja*, *osoba*: reasonable, sensible
sentencja *f* (*-ji*; *-je*) maxim, saying
sentyment *m* (*-tu*; *-ty*) fondness; ***bez ~ów*** unsentimental; ***nie bawić się w ~y*** be hard-headed; **sentymentalny** *adj* sentimental
separacj|a *f* (*-ji*; *-je*) *JUR* (legal) separation; ***żyć w ~i*** be separated; **separatka** *f* (*-ki*; *-ki*) **1.** (*w więzieniu*) separate cell **2.** (*w szpitalu*) private room, sickbay
separatysta *m* (*-ty*; *-ratyści*) *POLIT* separatist
separować ⟨**od-**⟩ (*-ruję*) isolate, separate (**od** *G* from); ***separować się*** separate, remain detached
sepia *f* (*-pii*; *no pl*) (*kolor*) sepia
seplenić *v/im* (*-nię*) lisp

S

ser *m* (*-ra*; *-ry*) cheese; **~ *żółty*** (hard) cheese; **~ *biały*** cottage cheese; **~ *owczy*** sheep's milk cheese

Serb *m* (*-ba*; *-bowie*), **~ka** *f* (*-ki*; *-ki*) Serb; **Serbia** *f* (*-bii*) Serbia; **serbski** *adj* Serbian; **serbsko-chorwacki** *adj* Serbo-Croat(ian)

serc|e *n* (*-ca*; *-ca*) **1.** ANAT heart; ***być chorym na ~e*** have a heart disease, have a heart condition; ***brak ~a*** heartlessness; ***być bez ~a, nie mieć ~a*** have no heart, be heartless; ***brać coś sobie do ~a*** take s.th. to heart; ***coś przypadło komuś do ~a*** s.o. took a liking to s.th.; ***z całego ~a*** with all one's heart; ***z ciężkim ~em*** with a heavy heart; ***z ręką na ~u*** frankly, to be frank; ***okazywać ~e*** show kindness **2.** *dzwonu*: clapper

sercowaty *adj* heart-shaped; **sercowiec** *m* (*-wca*; *-wcy*) cardiac; **sercowy** *adj* **1.** MED cardiac **2.** (*miłosny*) love

serdak *m* (*-ka*; *-ki*) jerkin

serdecznie *adv* cordially, warmly; **~ *dziękuję*** many thanks indeed; ***ubawić się ~*** have a (jolly) good laugh; ***śmiać się ~*** laugh heartily; ***mam tego ~ dosyć!*** I've had enough of this!, I'm fed up with this!

serdeczność *f* (*-ści*; *no pl*) warmth, friendliness; **serdeczn|y** *adj* **1.** *list*: warm, friendly **2.** *śmiech*: hearty; ***~y przyjaciel*** bosom friend; ***~y palec*** ring finger; ***~e pozdrowienia*** best regards

serdelek *m* (*-lka*; *-lki*) frankfurter, small pork sausage

serdelow|y *adj*: ***kiełbasa ~a*** mincedmeat sausage

serduszko *n* (*-ka*; *-ka*) *dim* (little) heart; ***moje ~!*** my sweetheart!

S

serek *m* (*-rka*; *-rki*) *dim* cheese; **~ *topiony*** cheese spread, processed cheese; **~ *homogenizowany*** smooth cottage cheese, cream cheese; **~ *waniliowy*** vanilla cream cheese; ***dekolt w ~*** V-neck

seri|a *f* (*-rii*; *-rie*) **1.** (*ciąg*) series; ***~a znaczków*** set of stamps; ***film z ~i*** G another episode of **2.** (*z karabinu*) round **3.** *antybiotyku*: course; **serial** *m* (*-lu*; *-le*) **1.** series **2.** (*niezależne odcinki*) serial

serio *adv*: (***na***) **~** seriously; ***traktować ~*** treat seriously; ***~?*** really?

sernik *m* (*-ka*; *-ki*) cheesecake

serowarstwo *n* (*-wa*; *no pl*) cheese making

serpentyna *f* (*-ny*; *-ny*) **1.** (*droga*) road with hairpin bends **2.** (*wstęga*) streamer

serw *m* (*-wu*; *-wy*) SPORT serve, service

serwantka *f* (*-ki*; *-ki*) glass cabinet, glass case

serwatka *f* (*-ki*; *-ki*) whey

serweta *f* (*-ty*; *-ty*) tablecloth; **serwetka** *f* (*-ki*; *-ki*) napkin; **~ *papierowa*** paper napkin

serwis *m* (*-su*; *-sy*) **1.** (*naczynia*) service, set; **~ *do kawy*** coffee service, coffee set **2.** (*usługi*) service; **~ *gwarancyjny*** repair under guarantee **3.** SPORT serve, service **4.** **~ *informacyjny*** (*wiadomości*) the news, headlines; **~ *prasowy*** news service; **~ *sportowy*** sportsnews

serwisowy *adj*: ***punkt ~*** service (station), repair shop

serwować ⟨**za-**⟩ (*-rwuję*) serve; **~ *dowcipy*** tell jokes

seryjny *adj* **1.** *produkcja*: mass **2.** *film, morderstwo*: serial

sesja *f* (*-ji*; *-je*) *naukowa*: session; **~ *egzaminacyjna*** end-of-term examinations, semester finals; **~ *zdjęciowa*** shoot(ing); **~ *nagraniowa*** recording session

set *m* (*-ta*; *-ty*) SPORT set

setk|a *f* (*-ki*; *-ki*) **1.** (*100*) one hundred, a hundred; ***dożyć ~i*** live to be a hundred; ***jechać ~ą*** be doing 100 km per hour; ***~i ludzi*** hundreds of people **2.** (*banknot*) *Br* ton, *Am* century **3.** (*wódka*) jigger, shot **4.** (*bieg*) *Br* the hundred metres, *Am* the hundred meters

setnie *adv*: ***bawić się ~*** have jolly good fun

setn|y *adj* **1.** (*z kolei*) hundredth; ***jedna ~a*** one hundredth; ***~a część*** one per cent, one hundredth **2.** (*wyborny*) great, jolly good

sezon *m* (*-nu*; *-ny*) **1.** *turystyczny*: season; **~ *letni*** (***zimowy***) holiday (winter) season; **~ *grzewczy*** heating period; **~ *ogórkowy*** *fig* silly season; ***w ~ie*** in season; ***po ~ie*** off season; ***pełnia ~u*** high season

sezonowo *adv* seasonally; **sezonow|y** *adj owoce*, *robotnik*: seasonal; ***praca ~a*** seasonal labour
sędzi|a[1] *m* (*-dziego*; *-dziowie*) **1.** JUR judge; ***~a dla nieletnich*** juvenile court judge; ***~a sądu powiatowego*** district judge; ***mianować ~ą***, ***powołać na ~ego*** appoint a judge **2.** (*w futbolu*) referee **3.** (*w tenisie*) umpire
sędzia[2] *f* (*-dzi*; *-dzie*) (*kobieta*) JUR judge; **sędzina** *f* (*-ny*; *-ny*) JUR judge
sędziować *v/im* (*-dziuję*) **1.** JUR be a judge **2.** SPORT referee
sędziowski *adj* **1.** JUR judge's **2.** SPORT referee's, umpire's
sędziwy *adj* aged; ***~ wiek*** ripe old age
sęk *m* (*-ka*; *-ki*) knot; ***~ w tym, że*** the snag is that, the hitch is that; ***drewno bez ~ów*** wood without (any) knots; **sękaty** *adj drzewo*, *kij*: knotty
sęp *m* (*-pa*; *-py*) BIOL vulture; **sępi** *adj* BIOL **1.** *gniazdo*: vulture's **2.** *profil*: vulturine
sfałdować *v/p* → ***fałdować***
sfałszować *v/p* → ***fałszować***
sfastrygować *v/p* → ***fastrygować***
sfer|a *f* (*-ry*; *-ry*) **1.** (*zakres*) sphere **2.** (*środowisko*) ***~y*** circles; ***~a klimatyczna*** climatic zone; ***~a podzwrotnikowa*** subtropical zone; ***~a prywatności*** privacy; ***~a wpływów*** sphere of influence; ***~a działalności*** sphere of activity; ***wyższe ~y*** upper classes; ***niższe ~y*** lower classes; ***~y rządowe*** government circles **3.** ***~a niebieska*** ASTR celestial sphere; ***muzyka ~ (niebieskich)*** music of the spheres
sfilcowany *adj* felted
sfilmować *v/p* → ***filmować***; **sfilmowanie** *n* (*-nia*; *no pl*) screen adaptation, film version; ***~ powieści*** screen adaptation of a novel, film version of a novel
sfinalizować *v/p* → ***finalizować***
sfingować *v/p* → ***fingować***
sfinks *m* (*-sa*; *-sy*) sphinx
sflaczały *adj skóra*: flabby; **sflaczeć** *v/p* → ***flaczeć***
sfora *f* (*-ry*; *-ry*) *psów*: pack
sformatować *v/p* → ***formatować***; **sformatowany** *adj* INF formatted
sformować *v/p* → ***formować***
sformułować *v/p* → ***formułować***; **sformułowanie** *n* (*-nia*; *-nia*) wording, expression; ***niefortunne ~*** infelicity, inappropriate expression
sforsować *v/p* → ***forsować***
sfotografować *v/p* → ***fotografować***
sfrunąć *v/p* → ***sfruwać***
sfrustrować *v/p* → ***frustrować***; **sfrustrowany** *adj* frustrated
sfruwać ⟨**-runąć**⟩ (*-wam*) **1.** (*odfrunąć*) fly away **2.** *na ziemię*: fly down
siać ⟨**za-**, **po-**⟩ (*sieję*) **1.** sow; ***~ niezgodę*** sow dissension, spread discord **2.** *nawóz*: scatter **3.** *zamęt*: raise, cause; ***~ zgorszenie*** cause scandals **4.** *nienawiść*, *niepokój*, *strach*: arouse **5.** *panikę*: spread, cause
siad *m* (*-du*; *-dy*) SPORT squat; ***~!*** sit!
siadać ⟨**siąść**, **usiąść**⟩ (*-dam*) **1.** (*na kanapie*) sit down (***na*** *L* on; ***przy*** *L* at); ***~ do stołu*** take one's place at the table; ***~ na krześle*** sit (down) on a chair; ***~ w fotelu*** sit in an armchair; ***~ do obiadu*** sit down to dinner; ***~ do pracy*** get down to work; ***~ do komputera*** start working on the computer; ***~ za biurkiem***, ***~ przy biurku*** sit at the desk **2.** (*do pociągu*, *autobusu*) get on **3.** (*do samochodu*) get in **4.** (*do samolotu*) board **5.** (*o ptaku*) perch, rest **6.** (*psuć się*) *infml* break down
siadywa|ć *v/im* (*-duje*) sit (often/from time to time); ***często ~ł w ogrodzie*** he would often sit in the garden
siano *n* (*-na*; *no pl*) hay; **sianokosy** *pl* (*-sów*) haymaking
siara *f* (*-ry*; *no pl*) **1.** *kobiety*: colostrum **2.** (*niepowodzenie*, *wstyd*) *infml* shame, come-down, fuckup
siarczan *m* (*-nu*; *-ny*) CHEM *Br* sulphate, *Am* sulfate; **siarczyn** *m* (*-nu*; *-ny*) CHEM *Br* sulphite, *Am* sulfite
siarczyst|y *adj* **1.** *mróz*: biting, bitter; ***~e przekleństwo*** strong swear word **2.** *klaps*: resounding, powerful **3.** *pocałunek*: powerful; **siarczyście** *adv*: ***kląć ~*** swear like a trooper
siarka *f* (*-ki*; *no pl*) CHEM *Br* sulphur, *Am* sulfur
siarkowodór *m* (*-doru*; *no pl*) CHEM *Br* hydrogen sulphide, sulphuretted hydrogen, *Am* hydrogen sulfide, sulfuretted hydrogen; **siarkowy** *adj* CHEM Br sulphuric, *Am* sulfuric; ***kwas ~*** sulfuric acid, sulphuric acid

siatka *f* (*-ki*; *-ki*) **1.** (*plecionka*) net; **~ na zakupy** shopping bag; **2.** (*ogrodzenie*) wire netting, wire fence **3.** (*piłka siatkowa*) *infml* volleyball **4.** (*przeciw komarom*) screen
siatkarz *m* (*-rza*; *-rze*), **-rka** *f* (*-ki*; *-ki*) volleyball player
siatkow|y *adj* net; **piłka ~a** volleyball
siatkówka *f* **1.** (*-ki*; *-ki*) *ANAT* retina **2.** (*-ki*; *no pl*) *SPORT* volleyball
siąkać ⟨**-knąć**⟩ (*-kam*): **~ nosem** sniff
siąpić *v/im*: **siąpi** it's drizzling
siąść *v/p* → **siadać**
sidła *pl* (*-deł*) (*pułapka*) snare *sing*; **zastawić ~** set a snare; **wpaść w czyjeś ~** *fig* fall into s.o.'s trap
siebie *pron* oneself; **dla ~** for oneself; **wracać do ~ a)** (*odzyskiwać przytomność*) come to **b)** (*do domu*) come back to one's place; **mieć coś przy sobie** have s.th. on oneself; **następować po sobie** come one after another; **pod sobą** under oneself; **przed sobą** before oneself; **przed ~** straight on, straight ahead; **mieć coś na sobie** be wearing, have s.th. on; **zrobić sobie herbatę** make the tea; **widzieć ~ w lustrze** see oneself in the mirror; **rozmawiać ze sobą** talk to each other; **podzielić między ~** share among themselves; **patrzeć za ~** look back; **blisko ~** side by side
siec *v/im* (*siekę*) *szablą*, *mieczem*: slash; **siecze deszcz** the rain is lashing down, it's pelting down (with rain)
sieciowy *adj* net, network
sieczka *f* (*-ki*; *no pl*) chaff; **sieczkarnia** *f* (*-ni*; *-nie*) chaff-cutter
sieczn|y *adj*: **broń ~a** side arms
sieć *f* (*sieci*; *sieci*) **1.** *rybacka*: (fishing) net **2.** *dystrybutorów*: network **3.** *pajęcza*: web, cobweb
siedem *num* seven
siedemdziesiąt *num* seventy; **siedemdziesiąt|y** *adj* seventieth; **lata ~e** the seventies; **siedemdziesięcioletni** *adj* seventy-year-old
siedemnastka *f* (*-ki*; *-ki*) seventeen; **siedemnastolatek** *m* (*-tka*; *-tki*/*-tkowie*), **-tka** *f* (*-ki*; *-ki*) seventeen-year-old; **siedemnastoletni** *adj* seventeen-year-old, of seventeen; **siedemnastowieczny** *adj* seventeenth-century, from the seventeenth century
siedemnast|y *adj* seventeenth; **~a** (**godzina**) five o'clock p.m.; **siedemnaście** *num* seventeen
siedemset *num* seven hundred
siedlisko *n* (*-ka*; *-ka*) **1.** *zwierząt*: habitat; **~ chorób** hotbed of disease, pesthole **2.** *ludzi*: settlement
siedmio- (*w złożeniach*) seven-; **świecznik ~ramienny** seven-branched candelabrum
Siedmiogród *m* (*-rodu*) Transylvania
siedmiokrotny *adj* sevenfold; **siedmioletni** *adj* **1.** *okres*: seven-year **2.** *dziecko*: seven-year-old; **siedmiomiesięczny** *adj* **1.** (*trwający siedem miesięcy*) seven-month **2.** *dziecko*: seven-month-old; **siedmioro**, **siedmiu** *num* seven
siedząco: **na ~** in a sitting position, in a reclining position
siedząc|y *adj*: **miejsce ~e** seat; **pozycja ~a** sitting position, reclining position; **~a praca** sedentary work
siedzenie *n* (*-nia*; *-nia*) **1.** (*miejsce*) seat **2.** (*pupa*) bottom
siedziba *f* (*-by*; *-by*) *rządu*, *firmy*: seat; **główna ~** the headquarters
siedzieć *v/im* (*-dzę*) sit (**na** *L* on); **~ przy stole** sit at the table; **~ za biurkiem** sit at the desk; **~ nad** *I fig* work on; **~ w** *L fig* know all about; **~ w więzieniu** do time; **~ na jajach** *BIOL* sit on eggs, brood; **~ w domu** stay at home; **~ w długach** (**po uszy**) be in debt (up to one's eyeballs); **~ jak na szpilkach** shake in one's shoes; **siedź cicho!** be quiet!
siekacz *m* (*-cza*; *-cze*) *ANAT* incisor (tooth)
siekać ⟨**po-**⟩ (*-kam*) *COOK* chop
siekany *adj COOK* chopped
siekier|a *f* (*-ry*; *-ry*) axe; **tak tu nadymione, że ~ę można powiesić** it's so horribly smoky in here
sielanka *f* (*-ki*; *no pl*) *lit* idyll; **sielankowy** *adj atmosfera*: idyllic
sielski *adj lit* idyllic
siemię *n* (*-mienia*; *no pl*): **~ lniane** linseed
siennik *m* (*-ka*; *-ki*) straw mattress
sienny *adj*: **katar ~** *MED* hay fever
sień *f* (*sieni*; *sienie*) (hall)way
siepacze *pl* (*-czy*) *lit* henchmen, myrmidons

sieroc|y *adj renta*, *dola*: orphan('s); **choroba ~a** MED hospitalism
sierot|a *f* (*-ty*; *-ty*) **1.** (*dziecko bez rodziców*) orphan; **dom ~** orphanage **2.** (*oferma*) *infml* dupe, wimp
sierp *m* (*-pa*; *-py*) **1.** (*narzędzie rolnicze*) sickle; **~ księżyca** crescent **2.** *SPORT* hook
sierpień *m* (*-pnia*; *-pnie*) August; **sierpniowy** *adj* August
sierpowy *m* (*-wego*; *-we*) *SPORT* hook
sierść *f* (*-ści*; *no pl*) *psa*, *kota*: fur
sierżant *m* (*-ta*; *-nci*) sergeant
siew *m* (*-wu*; *-wy*) seed time; **siewca** *m* (*-cy*; *-cy*) sower; **~ niezgody** fomenter of discord, troublemaker
siewka *f* (*-ki*; *-ki*) **1.** (*sadzonka*) seedling **2.** (*ptak*) plover
siewnik *m* (*-ka*; *-ki*) seeder; **siewn|y** *adj* seed; **ziarno ~e** seeds
się *pron* **1.** (*w czasownikach zwrotnych*) oneself; ***on ~ myje*** he's washing (himself); ***myj ~!*** wash yourself!; ***jeśli ~ chce*** if you want; ***nigdy ~ nie wie*** you never know; ***chce mi ~ spać*** I'm sleepy; ***chce mi ~ pić*** I'm thirsty; ***tu dobrze ~ mieszka*** it's a good place to live; ***wygodnie ci ~ siedzi?*** are you comfortable?; ***widział ~ w lustrze*** he saw himself in the mirror **2.** (*w stronie biernej*) ***obok buduje ~ nowy hotel*** a new hotel is being built nearby; ***dużo ~ o tym mówi*** people talk about it a lot **3.** (*siebie nawzajem*) each other, one another; ***oni bardzo się lubią*** they like each other a lot
sięgać ⟨**-gnąć**⟩ (*-gam*) **I** *v/t* (*dosięgnąć*) reach (**po** *A*); ***ona sięga do klamki*** she can reach the door handle **II** *v/i* **1.** (*dochodzić*) reach; ***~ do kolan*** reach up to one's knees; ***~ po*** *A fig* reach (out) for; ***~ po klucze*** reach out for the keys; ***~ po papierosa*** reach for cigarettes; ***~ po narkotyki*** take drugs; ***~ po władzę*** seize power; ***~ po pióro*** *fig* start writing; ***~ pamięcią do*** *G* go back (in one's mind) to; ***~ po cudze*** steal; **2.** (*o tradycji*, *historii*) date back (*G* to), date (*G* from); ***jak okiem sięgnąć*** as far as the eye can see; ***historia miasta sięga wczesnego średniowiecza*** the history of the town dates back to the early Middle Ages; ***bezrobocie sięga dwudziestu procent*** unemployment runs to twenty per-cent
sikacz *m* (*-cza*; *-cze*) *infml* plonk, cheap wine
sikać ⟨**-knąć**⟩ (*-kam*) **1.** *infml* pee, piddle **2.** (*o krwi*) gush, spurt
sikawka *f* (*-ki*; *-ki*) (hand-powered) fire pump
siknąć *v/p* → **sikać**
sikora *f* (*-ry*; *-ry*), **sikorka** *f* (*-ki*; *-ki*) tit; ***~ bogatka*** great tit
siksa *f* (*-sy*; *-sy*) *infml* minx
siku: ***robić ~*** *infml* pee, piddle
silić się ⟨**wy-**⟩ (*-lę*): ***~ na uprzejmość*** try hard to be polite; ***~ na uśmiech*** force a smile; ***nie ~*** not exert oneself
silnie *adv* → **silny**
silnik *m* (*-ka*; *-ki*) *TECH AUTO* engine; ***~ spalinowy*** combustion engine; ***~ elektryczny*** electric motor; **silnikowy** *adj olej*: engine, motor
siln|y *adj* **1.** (*mocny*) strong; ***mieć ~ą wolę*** be strong willed **2.** *uderzenie*: mighty, heavy **3.** *gorączka*: high **4.** *mróz*: bitter, severe **5.** *ból*: intense, severe **6.** *akcent*: broad, marked
silos *m* (*-su*; *-sy*) silo
sił|a *f* (*-ły*; *-ły*) **1.** (*moc*, *energia*) strength; ***~a fizyczna*** physical strength; ***nabierać ~*** regain one's strength (after an illness); ***w sile wieku*** in one's prime (time of life); ***pracować ponad ~y*** work too hard, overwork **2.** (*energia fizyczna*) force; ***~a ciężkości*** the force of gravity; ***~ą*** by force; ***użyć ~y*** use force; ***bez użycia ~y*** without using force, peacefully; ***~ą rzeczy*** perforce, necessarily **3.** (*potęga*) power; ***~a wiatru*** wind power **4.** (*natężenie*) intensity; **5.** (*grupa ludzi*) force; ***~a robocza*** labour force, workforce; ***~y zbrojne*** armed forces
siłacz *m* (*-cza*; *-cze*) strongman
siłować się *v/im* (*-łuje*) wrestle, struggle (**z** *I* with); ***~ z zamkiem*** struggle with a lock
siłownia *f* (*-ni*; *-nie*) **1.** *SPORT* gym **2.** (*elektrownia*) power plant; ***~ wiatrowa*** wind power station; **siłowy** *adj sport*, *trening*: strength
sinawy *adj* bluish, livid
siniak *m* (*-ka*; *-ki*), **siniec** *m* (*sińca*; *sińce*) bruise; ***sińce pod oczami*** dark circles under one's eyes

S

sinieć ⟨**z-**⟩ (*-nieję*) *skóra*, *wargi*: become blue
siny *adj* livid, blue; ***był ~ z zimna*** he was blue with cold
siodełko *n* (*-ka*; *-ka*) *roweru*: saddle; **siodełkowy** *adj*: ***wyciąg ~*** chairlift
siodłać ⟨**o-**⟩ (*-łam*) saddle
siod|ło *n* (*-ła*; *-ła*) saddle; ***siedzieć mocno w ~le*** *fig* be in the saddle
siorbać *v/im* (*-bię*) *zupę*: slurp
siostra *f* (*-ry*; *-ry*) sister; ***~ cioteczna*** cousin; ***~ bliźniaczka*** twin-sister; ***~ przyrodnia*** step-sister; ***~ zakonna*** nun; ***~ oddziałowa*** ward nurse
siostrzany *adj* sisterly
siostrzenica *f* (*-cy*; *-ce*) niece; **siostrzeniec** *m* (*-rzeńca*; *-rzeńcy*) nephew
siostrzyczka *f* (*-ki*; *-ki*) *dim* little sister
siódemka *f* (*-ki*; *-ki*) seven; **siódm|y** *adj* seventh; ***być w ~ym niebie*** be in seventh heaven; ***wyciskać z kogoś ~e poty*** make s.o. sweat blood; ***jest ~a*** it's seven (o'clock)
sitko *n* (*-ka*; *-ka*) (little) strainer, sieve
sito *n* (*-ta*; *-ta*) strainer, sieve; ***przejść przez ~ egzaminacyjne*** be successful in an examination
sitowie *n* (*-wia*; *no pl*) bulrush
sitwa *f* (*-wy*; *-wy*) clique, coterie
siurek *m* (*-rka*; *-rki*), **siusiak** *m* (*-ka*; *-ki*) *infml* willie
siusiać *v/im* (*-siam*) *infml* pee, wee
siusiu: ***robić ~*** *infml* pee, wee
siwawy *adj włosy*: *Br* greyish, *Am* grayish; ***on jest już ~*** he has already gone grey; **siwek** *m* (*-wka*; *-wki*) *Br* grey (horse), *Am* gray (horse)
siwieć *v/im* ⟨**o-**⟩ (*-wieję*) *Br* turn grey, go grey, *Am* turn gray, go gray
siwiuteńki *adj dim Br* grey(-haired), *Am* gray(-haired); **siwizna** *f* (*-ny*; *no pl*) *Br* grey hair, *Am* gray hair
siwobrody *adj Br* grey-bearded, *Am* gray-bearded; **siwowłosy** *adj Br* grey-haired, *Am* gray-haired
siwucha *f* (*-chy*; *-chy*) *infml* cheap vodka
siwy *adj* **1.** *kolor*, *włosy*: *Br* grey, *Am* gray **2.** *osoba*: *Br* grey-haired, *Am* gray-haired
ska, ***s-ka*** *abbr* (= **spółka**) Co.
skacowany *adj* hungover
skafander *m* (*-dra*; *-dry*) **1.** (*kurtka z kapturem*) anorak, winter jacket **2.** *astronauty*: space suit
skaj *m* (*-ju*; *no pl*) leatherette, *Am* American cloth
skakać ⟨**skoczyć**⟩ (*skaczę*) **1.** (*w dal*) jump; ***~ komuś do gardła*** jump at s.o.'s throat; ***~ koło kogoś*** be all over s.o., fawn (up)on s.o.; ***~ z tematu na temat*** jump from one topic to another; ***~ na równe nogi*** jump to one's feet; ***skocz po gazetę!*** go and get a newspaper!; ***skoczyłby za nią w ogień*** he would go through fire and water for her **2.** (*podskakiwać*) spring; ***~ z radości*** jump (up and down) for joy, hop up and down with delight
skakan|ka *f* (*-ki*; *-ki*) *Br* skipping rope, *Am* jump rope; ***skakać na ~ce*** play with a skipping rope, play with a jump rope
skal|a *f* (*-li*; *-le*) (*podziałka*) scale; ***~a głosu*** range of voice; ***~a wartości*** set of values; ***~a podatkowa*** tax scale; ***zakrojony na szeroką ~ę*** on a large scale
skalany *adj lit fig* defiled; ***~ krwią*** sullied with blood
skaleczenie *n* (*-nia*; *-nia*) cut; **skaleczony** *adj* cut; **skaleczyć** *v/p* → **kaleczyć**
skalisty *adj* rocky; **skalny** *adj blok*, *ściana*: rock; ***odłamek ~*** stone chipping; ***ogród ~*** rock garden, rockery
skalować ⟨**wy-**⟩ (*-luje*) calibrate
skalpel *m* (*-la*; *-le*) scalpel
skała *f* (*-ły*; *-ły*) rock; ***~ wulkaniczna*** volcanic rock; ***~ podwodna*** underwater rock
skamieliny *pl* (*-lin*), ***skamieniałości*** *pl* (*-ści*) GEOL fossils
skamieniały *adj* GEOL petrified
skamlać (*-lam*), **skamleć** ⟨**za-**⟩ (*-lę*) (*o psie*) yelp, whimper
skandal *m* (*-lu*; *-le*) scandal; **skandaliczny** *adj* scandalous, disgraceful
skandować *v/im* (*-duję*) chant
skandynawski *adj* Scandinavian
skaner *m* (*-ra*; *-ry*) INF scanner; **skanować** ⟨**ze-**⟩ (*-nuję*) INF scan
skansen *m* (*-nu*; *-ny*) open-air ethnographic museum
skapitulować *v/p* → **kapitulować**
skapnąć *v/p* → **skapywać**

S

skapować *v/p* → ***kapować***
skapywać ⟨**-pnąć**⟩ (*-puję*) dribble, drip
skarabeusz *m* (*-sza*; *-sze*) BIOL scarab
skarb *m* (*-bu*; *-by*) treasure; ***~ państwa*** the Treasury; ***~ie!*** sweetheart!, darling!
skarbiec *m* (*-bca*; *-bce*) treasury, vault; ***~ bankowy*** strongroom; ***~ koronny*** royal treasures; **skarbnica** *f* (*-cy*; *-ce*) strongroom; ***~ wiedzy*** the fount of (all) knowledge, repository of knowledge; ***~ doświadczeń*** fount of experience
skarbnik *m* (*-ka*; *-nicy*), **-niczka** *f* (*-ki*; *-ki*) treasurer
skarbonka *f* (*-ki*; *-ki*) money-box, piggy-bank
skarbowy *adj*: ***urząd ~*** *Br* Inland Revenue, *Am* the Internal Revenue Service; ***znaczek ~*** revenue stamp
skarcić *v/p* → ***karcić***
skarg|a *f* (*-gi*; *-gi*) complaint (***na*** *A* against); ***wnieść ~ę na*** *A* JUR lodge a complaint against
skarlały, **skarłowaciały** *adj* *róża*: stunted
skarłowacieć *v/p* → ***karłowacieć***
skarpa *f* (*-py*; *-py*) escarpment, scarp
skarpeta *f* (*-ty*; *-ty*), **skarpetka** *f* (*-ki*; *-ki*) sock
skarykaturować *v/p* → ***karykaturować***
skarżyć (*-żę*) **1.** ⟨**na-**, **po-**⟩ (*narzekać*) complain **2.** ⟨**za-**⟩ JUR sue (***o*** *A* for); ***skarżyć się*** complain (***na*** *A* about); ***~ się na ból serca*** complain about heart pain
skarżypyta *f/m* (*-ty*; *-ty*) tall tale
skasować *v/p* → ***kasować***
skatalogować *v/p* → ***katalogować***
skatować *v/p* → ***katować***
skauting *m* (*-gu*; *no pl*) scouting
skaz|a *f* (*-zy*; *-zy*) (*na powierzchni*) flaw; ***~a białkowa*** MED (protein) diathesis; ***bez ~y*** *fig* flawless; ***~a na honorze*** *Br* blemish on s.o.'s honour, *Am* blemish on s.o.'s honor
skazać *v/p* → ***skazywać***
skazanie *n* (*-nia*; *no pl*): ***~ na śmierć*** JUR death sentence
skazaniec *m* (*-zańca*; *-zańcy*) convict
skazany **I** *adj* JUR convicted (***na*** *A* of); ***~ na porażkę*** doomed to failure **II** *m* (*-nego*; *-ni*), **-na** *f* (*-nej*; *-ne*): ***~ na śmierć*** sentenced to death
skazić *v/p* (*skażę*) contaminate
skazywać ⟨**-zać**⟩ (*skażę*) sentence; ***~ na sześć lat pozbawienia wolności*** sentence to six years' imprisonment
skażenie *n* (*-nia*; *no pl*) pollution; ***~ radioaktywne*** contamination; **skażony** *adj* **1.** (*zanieczyszczony*) polluted **2.** (*zatruty*) contaminated
skąd *pron* where from, whence; **skądinąd** *pron* **1.** (*z innego miejsca*) from somewhere else **2.** (*z innego źródła*) from other sources
skądże *pron* **1.** (*skąd*) where from; ***~ miałbym to wiedzieć?*** how should I know it? **2.** (*wcale*) not at all
skąpany *adj*: ***~ w słońcu*** bathed in sunlight
skąpić ⟨**po-**⟩ (*-pię*) stint (*G* on), grudge (***komuś*** *G* s.o. s.th.); ***nie ~ komuś pochwał*** shower praise on s.o.
skąpiec *m* (*-pca*; *-pcy*) miser
skąpo *adv* → ***skąpy***
skąpstwo *n* (*-wa*; *no pl*) stinginess, meanness, miserliness
skąpy *adj* **1.** (*nadmiernie oszczędny*) mean, stingy; ***~ w słowach*** sparing with words **2.** *informacje*, *oświetlenie*, *roślinność*, *posiłek*: scanty **3.** *posiłek*, *ubranie*: skimpy
skiba *f* (*-by*; *-by*) **1.** *gleby*: ridge **2.** *chleba*: slice
skierować *v/p* → ***kierować***
skierowanie *n* (*-nia*; *-nia*) (*do lekarza*) referral; ***dostałem ~ do laryngologa*** I've been referred to a laryngologist; ***~ na badania*** laboratory order; ***~ do szpitala*** referral to hospital
skin *m* (*-na*; *-ni*) *infml* skinhead
skinąć *v/p* (*-nę*) **1.** *głową*: nod **2.** (*przywoływać*) beckon (***na*** *A* to)
skinienie *n* (*-nia*; *-nia*) **1.** *ręki*: wave; ***być gotowym na czyjeś każde ~*** be at sb's beck and call **2.** *głowy*: nod
skisły *adj* COOK sour
skisnąć *v/p* → ***kisnąć***
skląć *v/p* (*-lnę*) swear at
sklecić *v/p* → ***klecić***
sklejać ⟨**-leić**⟩ (*-jam*) glue together; ***dobry tusz nie skleja rzęs*** good mascara won't make eyelashes stick together
sklejka *f* (*-ki*; *-ki*) plywood
sklep *m* (*-pu*; *-py*) *Br* shop, *Am* store; ***~ spożywczy*** grocery, grocer's shop,

grocer's store; **~ obuwniczy** shoe shop

sklepienie *n* (*-nia*; *-nia*) vault; **~ czaszki** ANAT the cranial vault; **~ niebieskie** *lit* the heavenly vault; **~ beczkowe**, **~ kolebkowe** barrel vault, wagon vault, tunnel vault; **~ gwiaździste** stellar vault; **~ klasztorne** cloister vault; **~ krzyżowe** groin vault; **~ krzyżowo-żebrowe** rib vault; **~ nieckowe** trough vault; **~ sieciowe** net vault; **~ wachlarzowe** fan vault; **~ zwierciadlane** cavetto vault

sklepikarz *m* (*-rza*; *-rze*), **-rka** *f* (*-ki*; *-ki*) shopkeeper

sklepion|y *adj* ARCHIT vaulted; **wysoko ~e czoło** high forehead

sklepowa *f* (*-wej*; *-we*) *Br* shop assistant, *Am* salesclerk; **sklepow|y** *adj* shop; **kasa ~a** cash register; **wystawa ~a** shop window

sklerotyczny *adj* sclerotic; **skleroza** (*-zy*; *no pl*) *f* sclerosis; **mieć sklerozę** be senile, *fig* be forgetful

sklonować *v/p* → **klonować**

skład *m* (*-du*; *-dy*) **1.** (*zbiór elementów*) composition; (**nie**) **mieć na ~zie** (not) have in stock; **~ komisji** makeup; **~ rządu** cabinet; **~ amunicji** ammunition depot **2.** COOK ingredients *pl* **3.** *drużyny*: lineup; **wchodzić w ~** *G* be a member of; **w pełnym ~zie** at full strength **4.** *węgla*: yard **5.** *żywności*: store **6.** (*w drukarstwie*) typesetting

składacz *m* (*-cza*; *-cze*) type setter

składać ⟨**złożyć**⟩ (*-dam*) **1.** *serwetkę*, *ubranie*, *leżak*: fold; **~ fałszywe zeznanie** give false testimony; **~ hołd** pay homage; **~ listy uwierzytelniające** present one's credentials; **~ ikrę** spawn; **złożyć swoj los w czyjeś ręce** place one's life in s.o.'s hands **2.** *parasol*: furl **3.** *namiot*: put down **4.** (*zestawiać*) assemble **5.** *pieniądze*: save up, put aside **6.** *wieniec*: lay **7.** *urząd*: step down, resign **8.** *przysięgę*, *egzamin*: take; **składać się 1.** (*o łóżku*, *krześle*) fold **2.** (*zbierać pieniądze*) club together **3.** (*być składową*) make up; **~ się z** G be made up of, be composed of **4.** (*zdarzyć się*) happen; **tak się składa, że** it happens that; **dobrze się złożyło,że** it was fortunate that

składak *m* (*-ka*; *-ki*) **1.** (*kajak*) folding canoe **2.** (*rower*) folding bike **3.** (*komputer*) self-assembled computer

składanka *f* (*-ki*; *-ki*) **1.** *muzyczna*: medley **2.** *estradowa*, *kabaretowa*: variety act

składankowy *adj*: **album ~** miscellaneous album

składany *adj* **1.** *kajak*, *krzesło*: collapsible, fold-up **2.** *rower*: folding **3.** *łóżko*, *stół*: foldaway **4.** *komputer*: self-assembled

składka *f* (*-ki*; *-ki*) **1.** (*zbiórka*) collection **2.** (*kwota dołożona*) contribution; **~ członkowska** membership fee; **~ ubezpieczeniowa** insurance premium; **~ na fundusz emerytalny** pension (fund) contribution; **ze składek publicznych** by public subscription

składnia *f* (*-ni*; *-nie*) syntax; **składniowy** *adj* syntax

składnik *m* (*-ka*; *-ki*) **1.** *potrawy*: ingredient **2.** (*element*) component **3.** MATH element

składnica *f* (*-cy*; *-ce*) (*magazyn*) storehouse

składowa *f* (*-wej*; *-we*): **~ wektora** MATH vector element, vector component

składować *v/im* (*-duję*) store

składowe *n* (*-wego*; *no pl*) storage payment, storage charges *pl*

składowisko *n* (*-ka*; *-ka*) **1.** (*ilość składowanych rzeczy*) stockpile **2.** (*miejsce składowania*) storage yard; **~ odpadów** landfill site; **~ złomu** scrapyard; **~ atomowe** nuclear waste storage, radioactive waste storage

składow|y *adj*: **część ~a** element, component

skłamać *v/p* → **kłamać**

skłaniać ⟨**-łonić**⟩ (*-niam*) **1.** (*o okolicznościach*, *faktach*) induce (**do** *G* to do s.th.); **co cię do tego skłoniło?** what induced you to do that? **2.** *głowę*: bend, lower; **skłaniać się 1.** incline, lean (**do** *G*/**ku** *D* towards/to); **John skłania się ku ubraniom włoskim** John has an inclination for Italian clothes; **dzień skłaniał się ku końcowi** *lit* the day was drawing to a close; **słońce skłaniało się ku zachodowi** *lit* the sun was going down **2.** (*ukłonić się*) bow

S

skłon *m* (*-nu*; *-ny*) *tułowia*: bend
skłonić *v/p* → **skłaniać**
skłonnoś|ć *f* (*-ści*; *-ści*) **1.** (*upodobanie*) tendency, inclination (**do** *G* for/to); **~ć do tycia** tendency to put on weight **2.** (*podatność*) susceptibility (**do** *G* to) **3.** *wrodzona*: disposition
skłonny *adj* **1.** MED susceptible, prone (**do** *G* to) **2.** willing (**do** *G* to do s.th.); **~ do kompromisu** willing to compromise; **~ do gniewu** quick-tempered; **~ do poświęceń** ready to make sacrifices
skłócać ⟨**-cić**⟩ (*-cam*) *kolegów*: divide; **jej małżeństwo skłóciło braci** her marriage caused a rift between the brothers
skłócony *adj* on very bad terms (**z** *I* with)
sknera *f/m* (*-ry*; *-ry*) skinflint, miser, scrooge; **sknerstwo** *n* (*-wa*; *no pl*) stinginess, meanness
sknocić *v/p* → **knocić**
skobel *m* (*-bla*; *-ble*) hasp
skoczek[1] *m* (*-czka*; *-czkowie*) **1.** *narciarski*: ski jumper; **~ w dal** long jumper; **~ wzwyż** high jumper **2.** *spadochronowy*: parachutist **3.** (*w cyrku*) acrobat, *Am* aerialist
skoczek[2] *m* (*-czka*; *-czki*) (*w szachach*) knight
skocznia *f* (*-ni*; *-nie*): **~ narciarska** ski jump
skoczny *adj* **1.** *melodia*, *taniec*: lively **2.** *sprawny*: agile, nimble
skoczyć *v/p* → **skakać**
skodyfikować *v/p* → **kodyfikować**
skojarzenie *n* (*-nia*; *-nia*) association; **skojarzeniowy** *adj* **1.** *pamięć*: associative **2.** *test*: association
skojarzyć *v/p* → **kojarzyć**
skok *m* (*-ku*; *-ki*) jump; **~ w dal** SPORT long jump; **~ wzwyż** SPORT high jump; **~ o tyczce** SPORT pole-vault; **~i narciarskie** SPORT ski-jumping; **~ na bank** *infml* hold-up; **~i cen** fluctuation in prices, price fluctuations; **~i temperatury** variations in temperature, changes in temperature; **jednym ~iem** in one leap; **~ w bok** one-night stand; **~ gwintu** pitch of thread
skokow|y *adj*: **staw ~y** ANAT ankle joint; **pojemność ~a** AUTO engine cubic capacity
skoligacony *adj* related by marriage, connected by marriage
skolonizować *v/p* → **kolonizować**
skołatany *adj* **1.** *osoba*: troubled (*I* with) **2.** *nerwy*: shattered, in ruins
skołowacieć *v/p* → **kołowacieć**
skołować *v/p* (*-łuję*) wangle, get (illegally)
skołowany *adj* confused, baffled
skombinować → **skołować**
skomentować *v/p* → **komentować**
skomleć, **skomlić** ⟨**za-**⟩ (*-lę*) (*o psie*) whimper, whine
skomplikować *v/p* → **komplikować**
skomplikowany *adj* complicated
skomponować *v/p* → **komponować**
skompromitować *v/p* → **kompromitować**
skompromitowany *adj* discredited
skomputeryzować *v/p* → **komputeryzować**
skonać *v/p* (*-nam*) die
skonany *adj infml* dog-tired, beat
skoncentrować *v/p* → **koncentrować**
skoncentrowany *adj* concentrated
skondensowan|y *adj* condensed; **mleko ~e** condensed milk, evaporated milk
skonfiskować *v/p* → **konfiskować**
skonfrontować *v/p* → **konfrontować**
skonkretyzować *v/p* → **konkretyzować**
skonsternowany *adj* disconcerted, confused
skonstatować *v/p* → **konstatować**
skonstruować *v/p* → **konstruować**
skonsultować *v/p* → **konsultować**
skonsumować *v/p* → **konsumować**
skontaktować *v/p* → **kontaktować**
skontrolować *v/p* → **kontrolować**
skontrować *v/p* → **kontrować**
skończon|y *adj* **1.** (*bez przyszłości*) finished; **między nami wszystko ~e** it is all over between us **2.** (*doskonały*) absolute, perfect **3.** (*całkowity*) complete, utter; **~y dureń** complete fool
skończyć *v/p* → **kończyć**
skoordynować *v/p* → **koordynować**
skopiować *v/p* → **kopiować**
skorek *m* (*-rka*; *-rki*) BIOL earwig
skoro *conj* **1.** (*kiedy*) as soon as; **~ świt** at the break of the day, at daybreak, early morning **2.** (*ponieważ*) since

skorodować *v/p* → ***korodować***
skoroszyt *m* (*-tu*; *-ty*) folder, ring binder; **skorowidz** *m* (*-dza*; *-dze*) index; ~ ***rzeczowy*** subject index
skorpion *m* (*-na*; *-ny*) **1.** *BIOL* scorpion **2.** ~ *ASTR* Scorpio, *infml* the Scorpion
skorumpować *v/p* → ***korumpować***
skorumpowany *adj* corrupt
skorupa *f* (*-py*; *-py*) **1.** *jaja*, *orzecha*, *żółwia*: shell; ~ ***ślimaka*** snail's shell **2.** (*powłoka*) crust; ~ ***lodu*** crust of ice; ~ ***ziemska*** the Earth's crust
skorupiaki *pl* (*-ków*) *BIOL* crustaceans
skorupka *f* (*-ki*; *-ki*) *dim* shell; ~ ***jajka*** eggshell; ~ ***ślimaka*** snail's shell
skory *adj*: ~ ***do pomocy*** willing to help; ~ ***do kłótni*** quick to anger, bad-tempered; ***być ~m do śmiechu*** laugh eagerly
skorygować *v/p* → ***korygować***
skorzy → ***skory***
skorzystać *v/p* → ***korzystać***
skos: ***na ~***, ***w ~*** on a slant, at a slant, diagonally
skosić *v/p* → ***kosić***
skostniały *adj* **1.** (*sztywny*) *fig* stiff; ~ ***z zimna*** numb with cold **2.** *MED* ossified
skostnieć *v/p* → ***kostnieć***
skostnienie *n* (*-nia*; *-nia*) **1.** *MED* ossification **2.** (*sztywność*) stiffness
skosztować *v/p* → ***kosztować II***
skośn|y *adj*: ***~e oczy*** slanting eyes
skowron|ek *m* (*-nka*; *-nki*) lark; ***cały w ~kach*** very happy, in seventh heaven, on cloud nine
skowyczeć *v/im* (*-czę*) (*o psie*) yelp
skowyt *m* (*-tu*; *no pl*) yelp
skór|a *f* (*-ry*; *-ry*) **1.** skin; ***dać komuś w ~ę*** give s.o. a hiding, tan s.o.'s hide; ***~a i kości*** *fig* bag of bones, skin and bones; ***dobrać się komuś do ~y*** crack down on s.o.; ***dobiorą mu się do ~y*** he will get his comeuppance; ***nie chciałbym być w jego ~ze*** I wouldn't like to be in his shoes **2.** leather; ***rękawice ze ~y*** leather gloves **3.** *zwierzęcia*: hide
skórk|a *f* (*-ki*; *-ki*) *dim* **1.** skin; ***gęsia ~a*** *fig* gooseflesh, *Br* goose bumps, *Am* goose-pimples **2.** *zwierzęcia futerkowego*: pelt **3.** (*przy paznokciu*) cuticle **4.** *chleba*: crust **5.** *cytryny*, *banana*: peel; ***obierać ze ~i*** peel, skin; **skórkowy** *adj* leather; **skórny** *adj* skin
skóropodobny *adj* leathery
skórzany *adj* leather; **skórzasty** *adj* *BIOL* coriaceous
skra *f* (*-ry*; *-ry*) *lit* spark
skracać ⟨**-rócić**⟩ (*-cam*) **1.** *sukienkę*: turn up; ~ ***sobie czas robiąc coś*** while away the time doing s.th. **2.** *artykuł*, *sznur*: shorten **3.** *wyraz*: abbreviate **4.** *drogę*: take a short cut **5.** *ułamek*: cancel; ***skracać się*** (*w praniu*) shrink; ***skracaj się!*** be brief!
skradać się *v/im* (*-dam*) sneak (**do** *G* into)
skradziony *adj* stolen
skraj *m* (*-ju*; *-je*) *miasta*, *lasu*: edge; ***na ~u*** on the edge; ***na ~u nędzy*** (***rozpaczy***) on the brink of poverty (despair)
skrajność *f* (*-ści*; *-ści*) extremity; **skrajny** *adj* extreme
skrapiać ⟨**-ropić**⟩ (*-piam*) sprinkle
skraplać ⟨**-roplić**⟩ (*-lam*) *CHEM* condense; ***skraplać się*** condense (into a liquid)
skraść *v/p* → ***kraść***
skrawać ⟨**-roić**⟩ (*-wam*) **1.** *ubranie*: tailor **2.** *szynkę*: cut **3.** *TECH* machine
skraw|ek *m* (*-wka*; *-wki*) scrap; ***~ki papieru*** paper scraps; ***~ki materiału*** cloth scraps; ***~ek ziemi*** patch of land
skreślać ⟨**-lić**⟩ (*-lam*) **1.** (*wykreślać*) cross out **2.** (*wykluczyć*) exclude; ~ ***z listy*** cross off a list; ***skreślić parę słów do kogoś*** drop s.o. a line
skręcać ⟨**-cić**⟩ (*-cam*) **I** *v/t* **1.** *kabel*, *sznurek*: weave **2.** *papierosa*: roll **3.** (*montować*) assemble **4.** *nogę*: sprain **II** *v/i* **1.** (*o pojeździe*, *drodze*) turn; ~ ***w lewo*** turn left; ~ ***za rogiem*** turn round the corner; ***skręcić kark*** break one's neck; ***skręcać się***: ~ ***się ze śmiechu*** convulse with laughter, roll about laughing; ~ ***się z bólu*** writhe in pain; ~ ***się z zazdrości*** feel fierce jealousy, feel horrible pangs of jealousy
skręcenie *n* (*-nia*; *-nia*) *MED* sprain
skrępowani|e *n* (*-nia*; *no pl*) **1.** (*zakłopotanie*) embarrassment; ***bez ~a*** self-assuredly, free of any inhibitions, freely **2.** (*ograniczenie*) restraint, restriction; **skrępowany** *adj* **1.** *nogi*, *ręce*: tied up **2.** (*ograniczony*) ham-

pered (*I* by); ***nieskrępowany dostęp*** free access **3.** *zakłopotany*: embarrassed

skręt[1] *m* (*-tu*; *-ty*) **1.** (*ruch*) turn; ***wykonać ~*** (***w prawo***) AUTO take a (right) turn; ***~ kiszek*** MED intestinal volvulus **2.** *rzeki*, *drogi*: bend **3.** PHYS spin **4.** *tułowia*: turn

skręt[2] *m* (*-ta*; *-ty*) *infml* **1.** (*papieros*) *Br* roll-up, rollie, *Am* roll-your-own **2.** (*z marihuany*) joint, spliff

skrobaczka *f* (*-ki*; *-ki*) **1.** (*do warzyw*) peeler **2.** (*do szyb*) scraper

skrobać ⟨**-bnąć**⟩ (*-bię*) **1.** (*zdrapywać*) scrape off **2.** *warzywa*: peel, scrape; ***~ marchewki*** scrape carrots **3.** *rybę*: scale **4.** (*drapać*) scratch **5.** (*pisać*) scribble; ***skrobać się*** scratch oneself

skrobanka *f* (*-ki*; *-ki*) *infml* abortion

skrobia *f* (*-bi*; *no pl*) BIOL CHEM starch; **skrobiowy** *adj* starchy, starch

skrobnąć *v/p* → ***skrobać***

skroić *v/p* (*-roję*): ***~ cały chleb*** slice all the bread, slice a whole loaf of bread; ***~ resztę sera*** slice the rest of the cheese; → ***skrawać***

skrojony *adj materiał*: tailored, cut; ***~ na miarę*** tailored to measure, cut to measure

skromnisia *f* (*-si*; *-sie*) Miss Prim and Proper

skromność *f* (*-ści*; *no pl*) modesty; **skromny** *adj* **1.** *osoba*: modest **2.** *mieszkanie*: simple **3.** *dochody*: *Br* meagre, *Am* meager **4.** (*niewyszukany*) simple, plain

skroń *f* (*-roni*; *-ronie*) temple

skropić *v/p* → ***skrapiać***

skroplić *v/p* → ***skraplać***

skroplony *adj* liquefied

skrócić *v/p* → ***skracać***

skrócony *adj* **1.** *spodnie*: shortened **2.** *wersja*: abridged **3.** *nazwa*: abbreviated

skró|t *m* (*-tu*; *-ty*) **1.** *nazwy*: abbreviation; ***~t perspektywiczny*** foreshortening **2.** *tekstu*: summary; ***w ~cie*** in short; ***wiadomości w ~cie*** news headlines **3.** (*skrócenie*) abridgement **4.** (*droga*) short cut; ***iść na ~ty*** take a short cut

skrótowiec *m* (*-wca*; *-wce*) GRAM acronym

skrótowo *adv* in short, in brief; **skrótowy** *adj* brief, short

skruch|a *f* (*-chy*; *no pl*) repentance; ***ze ~ą*** repentantly

skrupiać się ⟨**-pić**⟩ (*-pię*): ***wszystko skrupiło się na mnie*** I took the brunt; ***jego gniew skrupia się na dzieciach*** he lets all his anger out on the children

skrupulatny *adj* **1.** *osoba*: meticulous, painstaking **2.** *badania*: thorough

skrupuł|y *pl* (*-łów*) scruples; ***robić coś bez ~ów*** not have scruples about doing s.th.

skruszeć *v/p* → ***kruszeć***

skruszony *adj osoba*, *mina*: apologetic

skruszyć *v/p* (*-szę*) **1.** *skałę*: crush **2.** *serce*, *osobę*: soften; ***skruszyć się*** **1.** (*o skale*, *murze*) crumble, be crushed **2.** (*o osobie*) repent

skrutacyjn|y *adj*: ***komisja ~a*** returning committee

skrwawiony *adj* covered with blood

skrycie *adv* secretly

skryć *v/p* → ***skrywać***

skrypt *m* (*-tu*; *-ty*) textbook

skrytka *f* (*-ki*; *-ki*) hiding place; ***~ pocztowa*** post office box, PO box

skrytobójca *m* (*-cy*; *-cy*) treacherous killer; **skrytobójstwo** *n* (*-wa*; *-wa*) treacherous killing

skrytoś|ć *f* (*-ści*; *no pl*) secretiveness; ***w ~ci ducha*** in one's heart of hearts; **skryty** *adj* **1.** *osoba*: secretive **2.** (*tajemny*) secret

skrywać ⟨**-ryć**⟩ (*-wam*) **1.** (*chować*) hide **2.** (*zatajać*) keep secret; ***skrywać się*** hide

skrzat *m* (*-ta*; *-ty*) **1.** (*krasnal*) brownie **2.** (*dziecko*) sprat, tot

skrzeczeć ⟨**za-**⟩ (*-czę*) **1.** (*o żabie*) croak **2.** (*o sroce*) caw **3.** (*o osobie*) croak, screech

skrzek *m* (*-ku*; *no pl*) **1.** BIOL spawn **2.** (*głos*) croak; screech; **skrzekliwy** *adj głos*: croaky, screechy

skrzela, ***skrzele*** *pl* (*-li*) gills

skrzep *m* (*-pu*; *-py*) MED clot

skrzepnąć *v/p* → ***krzepnąć***

skrzepnięty, ***skrzepły*** *adj* **1.** *krew*: clotted **2.** *błoto*: set, hard

skrzętny *adj* assiduous, hard-working

skrzyć się *v/im* (*-rzę*) sparkle

S

skrzydełk|o *n* (*-ka*; *-ka*) **1.** *dim* winglet **2.** *książki*: flap; ***tekst na ~u*** blurb
skrzydlaty *adj* winged
skrzyd|ło *n* (*-ła*; *-ła*) **1.** wing; ***~ła drzwi*** door leaves; ***~ło domu*** wing of a house; ***biec jak na ~łach*** run like the wind; ***dodać komuś ~eł*** lend wings to s.o. **2.** (*w wojsku*) flank
skrzydłowy I *adj* wing **II** *m* (*-wego*; *-wi*) *SPORT* winger, wing
skrzykiwać ⟨**-knąć**⟩ (*-kuję*) muster, call together; ***skrzykiwać się*** get together, come together
skrzynia *f* (*-ni*; *-nie*) **1.** (*kufer*) chest; ***~ biegów*** *AUTO* gear box **2.** (*na butelki*) crate **3.** *SPORT* box
skrzynka *f* (*-ki*; *-ki*) box; ***~ pocztowa*** letter box; ***~ poczty elektronicznej*** mailbox; ***~ z narzędziami*** tool-box; ***czarna ~*** black box, flight recorder
skrzyp *m* (*-pu*; *-py*) *BIOL* horsetail, scouring rush
skrzypaczka *f* (*-ki*; *-ki*) violinist
skrzypce *pl* (*-piec*) violin *sing*; ***grać pierwsze ~*** *fig* play first fiddle; **skrzypcowy** *adj* violin; **skrzypek** *m* (*-pka*; *-pkowie*) violinist
skrzypieć ⟨**-pnąć**⟩ (*-pię*) **1.** (*o łóżku, schodach, podłodze*) creak **2.** (*o drzwiach, zawiasach*) screech **3.** (*o śniegu*) crunch
skrzywdzić *v/p* → ***krzywdzić***
skrzywdzony *adj* wronged, harmed; ***~ przez los*** suffering from a terrible stroke of fate
skrzywić *v/p* → ***krzywić***
skrzywienie *n* (*-nia*; *-nia*) **1.** (*zgięcie*) bend **2.** (*grymas*) wry face; ***~ kręgosłupa*** *MED* curvature of the spine, spinal deformity; ***~ psychiczne*** psychological disorder; ***to u niego ~ zawodowe*** this is his professional bent
skrzywiony *adj* **1.** *mina*: wry **2.** *usta*: deformed; ***~ psychicznie*** psychologically disturbed
skrzyżować *v/p* → ***krzyżować***
skrzyżowani|e *n* (*-nia*; *-nia*) **1.** *dróg*: (road) junction, *Am* intersection; ***na ~u*** at a (road) junction **2.** *BIOL* cross
skubać ⟨**-bnąć**⟩ (*-bię*) **1.** pluck; ***~ kurę*** pluck a chicken; ***~ brwi*** pluck eyebrows **2.** *trawę*: nibble
skuć *v/p* → ***skuwać***
skudłacić *v/p* → ***kudłacić***
skulić *v/p* → ***kulić***
skumać się *v/p* → ***kumać się***
skunks *m* (*-sa*; *-sy*) *BIOL* (striped) skunk
skup *m* (*-pu*; *-py*) purchase, buying; ***~ butelek*** bottle return
skupiać ⟨**-pić**⟩ (*-piam*) **1.** *osoby*: gather **2.** *władzę*: hold; ***skupiać się*** **1.** (*gromadzić się*) gather **2.** (*koncentrować się*) concentrate, focus (***na*** *L* on)
skupić *v/p* → ***skupować***
skupieni|e *n* (*-nia*; *-nia*) concentration; ***stan ~a*** *PHYS* state of aggregation; ***w ~u*** with concentration
skupiony 1. *osoby*: gathered **2.** *uwaga*: focused **3.** (*uważny*) concentrated **4.** (*zwarty*) dense **5.** *siły*: joined
skupisko *n* (*-ka*; *-ka*) accumulation, cluster
skupować ⟨**-pić**⟩ (*-puję*) buy, purchase
skurcz *m* (*-czu*; *-cze*): ***~ mięśni*** muscular contraction; ***~e porodowe*** labour pains
skurczybyk *m* (*-ka*; *-ki*) *infml* son of a gun, bastard, rotter; **skurwysyn** *m* (*-na*; *-ny*) *vulg* son of a bitch
skurczyć *v/p* → ***kurczyć***
skusić *v/p* (*-szę*) tempt; ***skusić się***: ***skuszę się na ciastko*** I'll have a piece of cake; ***co cię skusiło?*** what made you do that?
skuteczność *f* (*-ści*; *no pl*) effectiveness; **skuteczny** *adj* effective
skut|ek *m* (*-tku*; *-tki*) effect, result; ***~ek odwrotny od zamierzonego*** opposite effect; ***~ek prawny*** *JUR* legal effect; ***~ek uboczny*** side effect; ***nie odnieść ~ku*** come to nothing, have no effect; ***bez ~ku*** to no effect; (***aż***) ***do ~ku*** to the bitter end; ***dramatyczny w ~kach*** with dramatic results; ***na ~ek*** *G* as a result of
skuter *m* (*-ra*; *-ry*) motor scooter
skutkować ⟨**po-**⟩ (*-kuję*) **1.** (*pociągać coś za sobą*) result in **2.** (*o lekarstwie*) work; **skutkow|y** *adj*: ***zdanie ~e*** *GRAM* consecutive clause
skuty *adj*: ***~ lodem*** ice-bound, ice-covered, frozen solid
skuwać ⟨**-kuć**⟩ (*-wam*) *elementy*: forge together; ***~ kogoś kajdankami*** (hand)cuff s.o.; ***~ łańcuchem*** chain

S

skuwka *f* (*-ki*; *-ki*) (*do pióra*) cap, top; (*laski*) ferrule
skwapliwy *adj* eager
skwar *m* (*-ru*; *-ry*) scorching heat
skwarki *pl* (*-rek*) crackling *sing*, pork scratchings
skwarny *adj dzień*: sweltering, scorching
skwasić się *v/p* (*-szę*) COOK turn sour
skwaszony *adj osoba*, *mina*: sour
skwaśnieć *v/p* → ***kwaśnieć***
skwer *m* (*-ru*; *-ry*) square
skwierczeć *v/im* (*-czę*) (*o tłuszczu*) sizzle
skwitować *v/p* → ***kwitować***
slajdy *pl* (*-dów*) slides
slalom *m* (*-mu*; *-my*) SPORT slalom; ***~ gigant*** giant slalom
slams|y *pl* (*-sów*) slums; ***dzielnica ~ów*** the slums
slang *m* (*-gu*; *-gi*) slang; ***~ młodzieżowy*** teenage slang
slawista *m* (*-ty*; *-wiści*), **-tka** *f* (*-ki*; *-ki*) Slavicist; **slawistyka** *f* (*-ki*; *no pl*) *Br* Slavonic studies *pl*, *Am* Slavic studies *pl*
slipy *pl* (*-pów*) briefs
slogan *m* (*-nu*; *-ny*) slogan; ***~ wyborczy*** election slogan, election motto; ***~ reklamowy*** advertising slogan; **sloganowy** *adj* meaningless, stereotyped
słabeusz *m* (*-sza*; *-sze*) **1.** (*człowiek słaby*) weakling **2.** (*uczeń*) very poor student
słabiusieńki, ***słabiutki*** *adj dim* feeble, faint
słabizna *f* (*-ny*; *-ny*) *infml* **1.** (*film*) poor stuff **2.** (*pachwina*) groin
słabnąć (*-nę*) **1.** ⟨**o-**, **za-**⟩ (*o osobie*) weaken, grow weak **2.** ⟨**o-**⟩ (*o pozycji*, *walucie*) weaken **3.** ⟨**o-**⟩ (*o wietrze*, *głosie*, *wsparciu*) waver **4.** ⟨**o-**⟩ (*o bólu*) ease off **5.** ⟨**o-**⟩ (*o zainteresowaniu*, *ruchu*) decline, diminish **6.** ⟨**o-**⟩ (*o wzroku*) deteriorate
słabo *adv* **1.** (*niemocno*) feebly, faintly; ***~ widzieć*** have poor eyesight; ***~ widoczny*** hard to see; ***~ zaludniony*** underpopulated, thinly populated; ***~ mi*** I feel faint **2.** (*marnie*) poorly
słabostka *f* (*-ki*; *-ki*) *fig* (small) weakness
słabość *f* (*-ści*; *-ści*) weakness; ***mieć ~ do*** *G* have a weakness for; **słabowity** *adj* frail; **słab|y** *adj* **1.** *napój*, *konstrukcja*: weak; ***mieć ~ą głowę*** not hold (one's) liquor well **2.** *światło*: faint **3.** (*marny*) poor **4.** *mróz*: light
słać[1] *v/im* (*ślę*) *lit* send
słać[2] ⟨**po-**⟩ (*ścielę*): ***~ łóżko*** **a)** (*na noc*) make the bed **b)** (*na dzień*) do the bed
słać się *v/im* (*ścielę*) (*o dymie*, *mgle*) float
słaniać się *v/im* (*-niam*) stagger
sław|a *f* (*-wy*; *no pl*) **1.** (*rozgłos*) fame; ***zdobywać ~ę*** win fame; ***światowej ~y*** world-famous **2.** (*opinia*) reputation; ***cieszyć się dobrą (złą) ~ą*** have a good (bad) reputation **3.** (*osoba*) celebrity, star; **sławetny** *adj lit* famous
sławić *v/im* (*-wię*) **1.** (*wychwalać*) extol **2.** *Boga*: praise
sławny *adj* famous
słodkawy *adj* sweetish
słodk|i *adj* sweet; ***~a woda*** fresh water; ***~a kapusta*** (white) cabbage; ***~ie mleko*** sweet milk; ***~a idiotka*** *infml* bimbo; ***~ie słówka*** sweet talking; ***robić ~ie oczy do*** *G* make sheep's eyes at
słodko-kwaśny *adj* sweet-and-sour
słodkości *pl* (*-ści*) sweets
słodkowodny *adj* freshwater
słodow|y *adj*: ***piwo ~e*** (low-alcohol) malt beer
słodycz *f* (*-czy*; *no pl*) sweetness; **słodycze** *pl* (*-czy*) *Br* sweets, *Am* candies; **słodzić** ⟨**po-**⟩ (*-dzę*) sweeten; **słodzik** *m* (*-ka*; *-ki*) sweetener; **słodziutki** *adj dim potrawa*, *osoba*: very sweet
słoiczek *m* (*-czka*; *-czki*) *dim* → ***słoik***
słoik *m* (*-ka*; *-ki*) jar; ***~ dżemu*** jar of jam; ***~ ogórków*** jar of gherkins
słoje *pl* → ***słój***
słojowanie *n* (*-nia*; *no pl*) graining, grain
słom|a *f* (*-my*; *no pl*) straw; ***kryty ~ą*** thatched
słomianka *f* (*-ki*; *-ki*) straw mat; **słomian|y** *adj* straw; ***~a wdowa*** *iron* grass widow; ***~y ogień*** *fig* flash in the pan, short-lived enthusiasm
słomka *f* (*-ki*; *-ki*) straw; **słomkowy** *adj kapelusz*, *kolor*: straw
słonawy *adj smak*: saltish

słoneczko *n* (*-ka*; *-ka*) *dim* **1.** (*słońce*) sun; ***moje ~!*** sweetheart!, sugar! **2.** (*do ogrzewania*) electric heater
słonecznik *m* (*-ka*; *-ki*) **1.** (*kwiat*) sunflower **2.** (*ziarna*) sunflower seeds *pl*; **słonecznikowy** *adj olej, pestki*: sunflower
słoneczn|y *adj* **1.** *ciepło, energia*: solar; ***zegar ~y*** sundial; ***udar ~y, porażenie ~e*** *MED* heatstroke; ***Układ Ꞩy*** *ASTR* solar system **2.** *dzień, miejsce*: sunny; ***~a pogoda*** sunny weather
słoniątko *n* (*-ka*; *-ka*) *dim* baby elephant; **słonik** *m* (*-ka*; *-ki*) **1.** *BIOL* baby elephant **2.** (*rzecz*) elephant; **słonica** *f* (*-cy*; *-ce*) female elephant, cow elephant
słonin|a *f* (*-ny*; *no pl*) *COOK* pork fat; ***buty na ~ie*** crepe-soled shoes
słoniowaty *adj* **1.** *osoba, chód*: elephantine **2.** *udo*: fat; **słoniow|y** *adj* elephant's; ***kość ~a*** ivory
słonko *n* (*-ka*; *-ka*) *dim* sun; ***moje ~!*** my sunshine!
słono *adv* saltily; ***~ zapłacić za*** *A* pay through the nose for; **słoność** *f* (*-ści*; *no pl*) saltiness; **słonowodny** *adj ryby*: saltwater
słony *adj* **1.** *żywność*: salty **2.** *cena*: steep, exorbitant **3.** *dowcip*: spicy
słoń *m* (*słonia*; *słonie*) elephant; ***~ morski*** elephant seal, sea elephant; ***poruszać się jak ~ w składzie porcelany*** move around like a bull in a china shop; ***~ nadepnął mu na ucho*** he's tone-deaf
słońc|e *n* (*-ca*; *-ca*) sun; ***Ꞩe*** *ASTR* the Sun; ***leżeć na ~u*** sunbathe, lie in the sun; ***jasne jak ~e*** crystal clear; ***pod ~e*** against the sun; ***porywać się z motyką na ~e*** try to square the circle, bite off more than one can chew
słota *f* (*-ty*; *no pl*) rainy weather; **słotny** *adj* rainy
Słowacja *f* (*-ji*) Slovakia; **słowacki** *adj* Slovak, Slovakian; **Słowak** *m* (*-ka*; *-wacy*), **-waczka** *f* (*-ki*; *-ki*) Slovak
Słowenia *f* (*-ii*) Slovenia; **Słoweniec** *m* (*-wenca*; *-wency*), **-wenka** *f* (*-ki*; *-ki*) Slovenian; **słoweński** *adj* Slovene, Slovenian
Słowianin *m* (*-na*; *-wianie*), **-wianka** *f* (*-ki*; *-ki*) Slav

S

słowiański *adj Br* Slavonic, *Am* Slavic; **słowiańszczyzna** *f* (*-ny*; *no pl*) the Slavs *pl*
słowiczy *adj*: ***~ śpiew*** nightingale's singing
słowik *m* (*-ka*; *-ki*) nightingale
słownictwo *n* (*-wa*; *no pl*) vocabulary; ***~ fachowe*** professional jargon; **słowniczek** *m* (*-czka*; *-czki*) mini-dictionary; **słownie** *adv* in words
słownik *m* (*-ka*; *-ki*) **1.** dictionary; ***~ polsko-niemiecki*** Polish-German dictionary; ***~ wyrazów obcych*** dictionary of foreign words; ***~ kieszonkowy*** pocket dictionary **2.** (*słownictwo*) vocabulary; **słownikowy** *adj* dictionary
słowny *adj* **1.** (*wyrażony mową*) verbal **2.** *człowiek*: reliable
słow|o *n* (*-wa*; *-wa*) word; ***~o wstępne*** foreword; ***~a*** (***piosenki***) lyrics; ***~o boże*** *REL* God's Word, the Word of God; ***~o w ~o*** word for word; ***co do ~a*** literally; ***nie mogłem dojść do ~a*** I couldn't get a word in edgeways; ***w całym tego ~a znaczeniu*** par excellence; ***menedżer w całym tego ~a znaczeniu*** manager par excellence; ***trzymać kogoś za ~o*** hold s.o. to their promise; ***dotrzymać ~a*** keep one's word; ***liczyć się ze ~ami*** mind what one says; ***swoimi ~ami*** in one's own words; ***innymi ~y*** in other words; ***w krótkich ~ach*** in short, briefly; ***~em*** in one word; ***brak mi słów*** I'm lost/at a loss for words, I'm speechless; ***szkoda słów*** it's a waste of breath
słowotwórstwo *n* (*-wa*; *no pl*) word-formation
słód *m* (*słodu*; *no pl*) malt
słój *m* (*słoja*; *słoje*) jar; ***~ miodu*** jarful of honey; **słoje** *BIOL* rings
słów|ko *n* (*-ka*; *-ka*) word; ***~ka*** vocabulary; ***uczyć się ~ek*** learn vocabulary, learn new words; ***piękne ~ka*** lip service; ***czułe ~ka*** sweet nothings, flattery
słuch *m* (*-chu*; *-chy*) **1.** hearing; ***stracić ~*** lose one's hearing ability; ***wada ~u*** hearing defect, impaired hearing; ***zamienić się w ~*** be all ears; ***~ o nim zaginął*** he disappeared without trace; ***ze ~u*** *MUS* by ear; ***~ muzyczny*** *MUS*

good ear for music; ***chodzą ~y, że*** rumour has it that; ***doszły mnie ~y, że*** I have heard that; ***powiedzieć komuś do ~u*** give s.o. a piece of one's mind **2. *~y zająca*** hare's ears
słuchacz *m* (*-cza*; *-cze*), **~ka** *f* (*-ki*; *-ki*) **1.** (*słuchający*) listener; ***~ radiowy*** radio listener **2.** (*student*) student; ***wolny ~*** auditor
słuchać ⟨**po-**⟩ (*-cham*) listen (*G* to); ***~ uważnie*** listen carefully; ***~ muzyki*** listen to music; ***~ radia*** listen to the radio; ***~ wykładu*** listen to a lecture; *~ G* (*być posłusznym*) listen to; ***~ rady*** take s.o.'s advice; ***~ rozkazów*** follow orders; ***nie mogę już ~ jego pochwał*** I can't listen to his praises any more; ***~ jednym uchem*** (***a drugim wypuszczać***) listen with half an ear; ***słucham? a)*** (*niedosłyszałem*) pardon me? **b)** (*przez telefon*) hallo?; ***słucham pana?*** what can I do for you?; ***słuchaj!*** listen!; ***słucham?!*** what?!; ***posłuchaj mnie!*** listen to me!
słuchawk|a *f* (*-ki*; *-ki*) **1.** *telefonu*: receiver; ***podnosić ~ę*** pick up the phone, answer the phone; ***odkładać ~ę*** hang up **2. *~i*** (*radiowe*) headphones **3.** *MED* stethoscope
słuchowisko *n* (*-ka*; *-ka*) radio drama, radio play
słuchowy *adj* **1.** *zasięg*, *układ*: auditory **2.** *efekty*, *materiał*: aural; ***aparat ~*** *MED* hearing aid
sługus *m* (*-sa*; *-sy*/*-si*) minion, lackey
słup *m* (*-pa*; *-py*) pole; ***~ wysokiego napięcia*** pylon; ***~ ogłoszeniowy*** advertising pillar; ***~ ognia*** pillar of fire; ***~ graniczny*** boundary post; ***stać jak ~*** be rooted to the spot; ***postawić oczy w ~*** look with a fixed stare
słupek *m* (*-pka*; *-pki*) **1.** *dim* post, pole; ***stanąć słupka*** sit up, stand on hind legs; ***~ startowy*** *SPORT* starting block; ***robić słupki*** do one's sums in columns; ***~ kilometrowy*** *AUTO* milestone **2.** *BIOL* pistil **3.** (*obcas*) heel **4.** (*w termometrze*) column
słusznie *adv* rightly, justly; ***~!*** right!; → ***słuszny***
słusznoś|ć *f* (*-ści*; *no pl*) rightness, soundness; ***mieć ~ć*** be right; ***nie mieć ~ci*** be wrong; **słuszn|y** *adj* **1.** (*właściwy*) right, correct **2.** (*uzasadniony*, *sprawiedliwy*) just, fair; ***~ego wzrostu*** *lit* of substantial height
służalczy *adj* servile, obsequious
służalec *m* (*-lca*; *-lcy*) flunkey, cringer
służąca *f* (*-cej*; *-ce*) maid, servant; **służący** *m* (*-cego*; *-cy*) servant
służb|a *f* (*-by*; *-by*) **1.** service; ***~a drogowa*** public road maintenance service; ***~a holownicza*** tow service; ***~y specjalne*** secret service; ***~y porządkowe*** security agency; ***~a zdrowia*** (national) health service; (***zasadnicza***) ***~a wojskowa*** compulsory military service, obligatory military service; ***zastępcza ~a wojskowa*** alternative service (in lieu of military service); ***zdolny do ~y*** fit for service, fit for duty; ***w ~ie idei*** in the service of an ideal **2.** (*personel*) servants *pl* **3.** (*dyżur*) duty; ***pełniący ~ę***, ***na ~ie*** on duty; ***po ~ie*** off duty
służbista *m* (*-ty*; *-biści*), **-tka** *f* (*-ki*; *-ki*) (*urzędnik*) martinet, stickler for authority, jack-in-office
służbowo *adv* on business; **służbow|y** *adj* **1.** *samochód*: company **2.** *podróż*, *tajemnica*: business; ***na drodze ~ej*** through official channels
służbówka *f* (*-ki*; *-ki*) duty room
służyć ⟨**po-**⟩ (*-żę*) **1.** (*pełnić usługi*) serve (*D*); ***~ do mszy*** *REL* serve at Mass; ***~ za*** *A* serve as; ***~ w wojsku*** serve in the army; ***~ za wzór***, ***~ za przykład*** set an example, give a lead; ***~ radą i pomocą*** offer one's help and advice; ***czym mogę ~?*** what can I do for you? **2.** (*wpływać dodatnio*) do good; ***powietrze morskie bardzo mi służy*** sea air agrees with me; ***mocna kawa mi nie służy*** strong coffee doesn't agree with me; ***zdrowie mu służy*** he is in good health **3.** (*o psie*) beg
słychać *v*/*irreg* be heard; ***słabo ~ dzwonek*** the bell is hardly audible; ***czy mnie ~?*** can you hear me?; ***nic nie ~*** we can't hear anything; ***było ~ krzyk*** a cry could be heard; ***nie ~ o*** *L fig* there is no news about; ***co ~ w sprawie twojego awansu?*** is there any news concerning your promotion?; ***co ~*** (***u ciebie***)***?*** what have you been up to?, what's up?, what's new?; ***co nowego ~?*** what's new?

słynąć ⟨**za-**⟩ (*-nę*) be famous (**z** *G* for)
słynny *adj* famous; **~ na cały świat** world-famous
słyszalnoś|ć *f* (*-ści*; *no pl*) audibility; **próg ~ci** audibility threshold; **słyszalny** *adj* audible
słyszeć ⟨**u-**⟩ (*-szę*) hear; **słabo ~** be hard of hearing; **słyszałem, że** I've heard that; **pierwsze słyszę** that's a new one on me!, it's the first time I've heard of it!, it's news to me!; **kto to słyszał!** that's incredible!; **nie chcę o tym ~!** that's out of the question!
smacznie *adv* tasty; **jeść ~** eat with relish; **smaczn|y** *adj* **1.** tasty; **~y kąsek** *fig* titbit; **~ego!** enjoy your meal! **2.** *sen*: sound
smagać ⟨**-gnąć**⟩ (*-gam*) **1.** (*bić*) whip, flog **2.** (*o deszczu*) lash (down)
smagły *adj skóra*: swarthy, dusky
smagnąć *v/p* **smagać**
smak *m* (*-ku*; *-ki*) taste; **ze ~iem a)** *jeść*: with relish **b)** *fig* tastefully; **bez ~u** tasteless; **o ~u waniliowym** vanilla flavour; **przyprawiać do ~u** add spices to taste; **być komuś nie w ~** not be to one's liking
smakołyk *m* (*-ka*; *-ki*) *Br* titbit, *Am* tidbit
smakosz *m* (*-sza*; *-sze*) gourmet
smakować ⟨**po-**⟩ (*-kuję*) taste; **bardzo mi smakuje** I enjoy the food a lot; **jak ci smakuje zupa?** do you like the soup?
smakowi|ty *adj* delicious, dainty, mouth-watering; **smakow|y** *adj wrażenia*: gustatory; **dodatki ~e** flavour enhancers; **kubki ~e** ANAT taste buds
smalec *m* (*-lcu*; *no pl*) lard
smalić *v/im* (*-lę*): **~ cholewki do** *G* court s.o.
smar *m* (*-ru*; *-ry*) grease; **~ do nart** ski wax
smardz *m* (*-dza*; *-dze*) BIOL morel
smarkacz *m* (*-cza*; *-cze*) *infml* snot(nose), whippersnapper
smarkać ⟨**-knąć**⟩ (*-kam*/*-rczę*) *infml* blow one's nose
smarkateria *f* (*-rii*; *no pl*) *infml* whippersnappers *pl*, whipsters *pl*; **smarkaty** *adj infml* wet behind the ears
smarknąć *v/p* → **smarkać**
smarkula *f* (*-li*; *-le*) *infml* chit, snotnose
smarować ⟨**po-**, **na-**, **u-**, **wy-**⟩ (*-ruję*) **1.** *chleb*: spread (*I* with) **2.** *plecy*, *stopy*: rub (*I* with); **~ kremem czyjeś plecy** put cream on s.o.'s back, cream s.o.'s back **3.** (*dać łapówkę*) grease s.o.'s palm **4.** *zawiasy*: grease, lubricate **5.** (*zabrudzić*) soil, dirty; **smarować się 1.** put on (*I*); **~ się kremem** put on cream; **masło dobrze się smaruje** butter spreads well **2.** (*brudzić się*) get besmeared, get soiled
smarowidło *n* (*-ła*; *-ła*) **1.** (*smar*) lubricant, grease **2.** (*maść*) ointment
smażalnia *f* (*-ni*; *-nie*) fish-and-chip shop, fish-and-chip stand
smażony *adj* fried
smażyć ⟨**u-**⟩ (*-żę*) *kartofle*, *rybę*: **a)** (*z panierką*) fry **b)** (*bez panierki*) sauté; **~ na głębokim tłuszczu** deep-fry; **~ jajecznicę** make scrambled eggs; **~ konfitury** make preserves; **smażyć się** be fried; **~ się na słońcu** bake in the sun
smętny *adj lit* **1.** (*melancholijny*) wistful, doleful **2.** *widok*: sorry **3.** *melodia*: sad **4.** (*smutny*) cheerless
smoczek *m* (*-czka*; *-czki*) **1.** (*do ssania*) *Br* dummy, *Am* pacifier **2.** (*na butelkę*) *Br* teat, *Am* nipple
smoczy *adj* dragon's
smog *m* (*-gu*; *no pl*) smog
smok *m* (*-ka*; *-ki*) dragon
smoking *m* (*-gu*; *-gi*) *Br* dinner jacket, *Am* tuxedo
smolisty *adj* **1.** *substancja*: tarry **2.** (*czarny*) pitch-black; **smolny** *adj drewno*: pitchy, tarry
smoła *f* (*-ły*; *no pl*) tar, pitch; **czarny jak ~** pitch-black; **smołować** ⟨**wy-**⟩ (*-łuję*) tar, pitch
smrodliwy *adj* stinking
smrodzić (*-dzę*) give off a stench
smród *m* (*-rodu*; *-rody*) stench
SMS *m* (*SMS-a*; *SMS-y*) text (message)
smucić ⟨**za-**⟩ (*-cę*) sadden, grieve; **smucić się** be sad; **za~ się** become sad, grow sad
smuga *f* (*-gi*; *-gi*): **~ światła** streak of light; **~ dymu** plume of smoke, smoke trail
smukły *adj* slender
smutas *m* (*-sa*; *-sy*) *infml* sourpuss, wet blanket

smut|ek *m* (*-tku*; *-tki*) sadness; ***~ki*** worries; ***pogrążony w ~ku*** grief-stricken
smutnieć ⟨**po-**⟩ (*-nieję*) become sad, sadden
smutn|y *adj* sad; ***~y widok*** sorry sight; ***~o mi*** I'm sad; ***to ~e, że*** it is sad that
smużka *f* (*-ki*; *-ki*) *dim*: ***~ światła*** small streak of light; ***~ dymu*** little plume of smoke
smycz *f* (*-czy*; *-cze*) lead, leash; ***na ~y*** on a leash; ***pies zerwał się ze ~y*** the dog broke the leash
smyczek *m* (*-czka*; *-czki*) MUS bow; **smyczkowy** *adj* MUS **1.** *kwartet*: string **2.** *instrument*: stringed
smyk *m* (*-ka*; *-ki*) *infml* kid
smykałk|a *f* (*-ki*; *no pl*); ***mieć ~ę do*** *G* have a flair for, have a knack for
snach, ***snami*** → ***sen***
snajper *m* (*-ra*; *-rzy*) sniper, marksman
snąć *v/p* (*snę*) (*o rybie*) die
snem → ***sen***
snob *m* (*-ba*; *-by*) snob; **snobistyczny** *adj* snobbish
snop *m* (*-pa*; *-py*) sheaf; ***~ światła*** beam of light, pencil of rays; **snopowiązałka** *f* (*-ki*; *-ki*) sheaf-binder, (reaper) binder
snowboard *m* (*-du*; *-dy*) snowboard
snów, ***snu*** → ***sen***
snuć *v/im* (*snuję*) **1.** *przędzę*, *pajęczynę*: spin; ***~ domysły*** speculate; ***~ intrygi*** intrigue; ***~ marzenia*** dream **2.** *plany*: devise, make; **snuć się 1.** (*o mgle*) drift, swirl **2.** (*o babim lecie*) float **3.** (*o zapachu*) waft **4.** (*o dymie*) trail **5.** (*o osobie*) mope about; ***snują mi się różne myśli po głowie*** I've got all sorts of thoughts in my head
sny *pl* → ***sen***
snycerstwo *n* (*-wa*; *no pl*) woodcarving
sobą → ***siebie***
sobek *m* (*-bka*; *-bki*) *infml* egoist, self-seeker
sobie *pron*: ***był ~*** there was once; ***niczego ~*** quite all right; ***żartujesz ~!*** you must be joking!; ***pospać ~*** sleep in; → ***siebie***
sobiepański *adj* high-handed; **sobiepaństwo** *n* (*-wa*; *no pl*) high-handedness
sobkostwo *n* (*-wa*; *no pl*) egoism, self-seeking
sobole *pl* → ***soból***
soboli, ***sobolowy*** *adj* sable
sobot|a *f* (*-ty*; *-ty*) Saturday; ***w ~ę*** on Saturday; ***Wielka ~a*** REL Holy Saturday; **sobotni** *adj* Saturday; ***~ wieczór*** Saturday evening
sobowtór *m* (*-ra*; *-ry*) double, lookalike
soból *m* (*-bola*; *-bole*) sable
sobór *m* (*-boru*; *-bory*) REL **1.** *watykański*: council **2.** (*cerkiew*) cathedral
sobótka *f* (*-ki*; *-ki*) Midsummer
socjaldemokratyczny *adj* Social Democratic
socjalistyczny *adj* socialist
socjalizacja *f* (*-ji*; *no pl*) socialization
socjalizm *m* (*-mu*; *no pl*) socialism
socjaln|y *adj* social; ***minimum ~e*** poverty line, subsistence level; ***świadczenia ~e*** social services, social security contributions, fringe benefits; ***pracownik ~y*** social worker
socjolog *m* (*-ga*; *-gowie*/*-lodzy*) sociologist; **socjologia** *f* (*-gii*; *no pl*) sociology; **socjologiczny** *adj* sociological
socrealizm *m* (*-mu*; *no pl*) HIST socialist realism
soczewica *f* (*-cy*; *no pl*) BIOL lentils *pl*
soczewk|a *f* (*-ki*; *-ki*) PHYS PHOT lens; ***~i kontaktowe*** contact lenses
soczysty *adj* **1.** *owoc*: juicy, sappy **2.** *barwa*: rich **3.** *dowcip*: spicy
soda *f* (*-dy*; *no pl*) CHEM soda; ***~ oczyszczona*** sodium bicarbonate, baking soda; ***~ żrąca*** caustic soda
sodoma: ***~ i gomora*** Sodom and Gomorrah
sodomia *f* (*-mii*; *no pl*) zoophilia
sodow|y *adj*: ***woda ~a*** soda water
sofa *f* (*-fy*; *-fy*) sofa
soja *f* (*soi*; *no pl*) **1.** BIOL soya bean **2.** COOK soya beans *pl*; **sojowy** *adj* COOK soya
sojusz *m* (*-szu*; *-sze*) alliance; **sojuszni|czy** *adj* POLIT *siły*, *państwa*, *ofensywa*: allied; ***umowa ~a*** alliance
sojusznik *m* (*-ka*; *-nicy*), **-niczka** *f* (*-ki*; *-ki*) POLIT ally
sok *m* (*-ku*; *-ki*) **1.** *owocowy*, *warzywny*: juice; ***~ żołądkowy*** ANAT gastric juice **2.** *zagęszczany*: syrup
sokoli *adj* falcon's; ***~ wzrok*** *fig* eagle eye; **sokolnik** *m* (*-ka*; *-nicy*) falconer
sokowirówka *f* (*-ki*; *-ki*) juice extractor, *Am* juicer

sokół *m* (*-koła*; *-koły*) falcon
sola *f* (*-li*; *-le*) BIOL sole
solanka *f* (*-ki*; *-ki*) **1.** (*roztwór*) brine **2.** (*źródło*) saline spring, saline
solankowy *adj kąpiel*: saline
solarium *n* (*indecl*; *-ria*) solarium; **solarny** *adj* solar
sole *pl* → ***sól***
solenizant *m* (*-ta*; *-nci*), **~ka** *f* (*-ki*; *-ki*) person celebrating their birthday, person celebrating their nameday; ***być ~em*** have one's birthday, have one's nameday
solennie *adv*: ***przyrzec ~*** give a solemn promise; **solenny** *adj lit zapewnienie*: solemn
solić ⟨**o-**, **po-**⟩ (*-lę*) add salt, salt
solidarnościowiec *m* (*-wca*; *-wcy*) HIST *a member of the trade union "Solidarność"*
solidarnościowy *adj strajk*: sympathy
solidarność *f* (*-ści*; *no pl*) solidarity; **solidarny** *adj* solidary
solidaryzować się *v/im* (*-zuję*) *Br* sympathise, *Am* sympathize
solidny *adj* **1.** *osoba*, *firma*: reliable, solid **2.** *wiedza*: sound **3.** *wykształcenie*: good **4.** *materiał*, *konstrukcja*: solid **5.** *porcja*: big
solista *m* (*-ty*; *-liści*), **-tka** *f* (*-ki*; *-ki*) soloist
solniczka *f* (*-ki*; *-ki*) *Br* saltcellar, *Am* saltshaker
solny *adj* salt; ***kwas ~*** CHEM hydrochloric acid
solony *orzeszki*, *masło*: salted
solowy *adj* MUS solo; **solówka** *f* (*-ki*; *-ki*) solo
sołectwo *n* (*-wa*; *-wa*) *the smallest administrative unit in Poland*; **sołtys** *m* (*-sa*; *-si*) *(elected) chair of the village council*
somnambulik *m* (*-ka*; *-licy*) sleepwalker, somnambulist; **somnambulizm** *m* (*-mu*; *no pl*) somnambulism, sleep walking
sonata *f* (*-ty*; *-ty*) MUS sonata
sonda *f* (*-dy*; *-dy*) **1.** probe; ***~ kosmiczna*** ASTR space probe; ***~ głębinowa*** deep-sea lead, sounding line; ***~ żołądka*** stomach probe **2.** (*sondaż*) opinion poll
sondaż *m* (*-żu*; *-że*) **1.** (*sondowanie*) probing, sounding **2.** (*badanie opinii*) opinion poll; ***~ przedwyborczy*** pre-election opinion poll
sondować ⟨**wy-**⟩ (*-duję*) **1.** TECH MED probe; ***~ żołądek*** probe s.o.'s stomach **2.** *opinię publiczną*: sound out
sonet *m* (*-tu*; *-ty*) sonnet
sopel *m* (*-pla*; *-ple*) icicle; ***ręce jak ~*** hands like ice
sopran *m* (*-nu*; *-ny*) (*głos*, *śpiewak*) soprano; **sopranista** *m* (*-ty*; *-niści*), **-tka** *f* (*-ki*; *-ki*) soprano; **sopranowy** *adj partia*: soprano
sortować ⟨**po-**⟩ (*-tuję*) sort (out)
sos *m* (*-su*; *-sy*) COOK sauce; ***~ pieczarkowy*** mushroom sauce; ***być nie w ~ie*** *fig* be out of sorts; **sosjerka** *f* (*-ki*; *-ki*) gravy boat, sauce boat
sosna *f* (*-ny*; *-ny*) **1.** BIOL pine (tree) **2.** (*drewno*) pine wood; **sosnowy** *adj* pine
sowa *f* (*-wy*; *-wy*) owl; **sowi** *adj* **1.** *dziupla*: owl's **2.** *fig* owlish
sowiecki *adj* Soviet
sowity *adj napiwek*, *porcja*: generous
sód *m* (*sodu*; *no pl*) CHEM sodium
sójka *f* (*-ki*; *-ki*) BIOL Eurasian jay; ***wybierać się jak ~ za morze*** delay one's trip all the time, keep putting one's trip off
sól *f* (*soli*; *sole*) salt; ***~ kuchenna*** table salt; ***~ morska*** sea salt; ***sole mineralne*** mineral nutrients; ***być komuś solą w oku*** be a thorn in s.o.'s side; ***~ ziemi*** *fig* the salt of the earth
spacer *m* (*-ru*; *-ry*) walk; ***iść na ~*** go for a walk; ***~ po mieście*** stroll around the city; ***iść ~em*** stroll
spacerować ⟨**po-**⟩ (*-ruję*) walk, stroll; ***~ po mieście*** stroll around the city
spacerowicz *m* (*-cza*; *-cze*), **~ka** *f* (*-ki*; *-ki*) stroller, walker
spacerowy *adj droga*: walking; ***wózek ~*** *Br* pushchair, *Am* stroller; ***iść ~m krokiem*** walk slowly, stroll
spacerówka *f* (*-ki*; *-ki*) *Br* pushchair, *Am* stroller
spacj|a *f* (*-ji*; *-je*) space; ***klawisz ~*** space bar
spaczony *adj drewno*: warp
spaczyć *v/p* → ***paczyć***
spać *v/im* (*śpię*) sleep (**z** *I* with); ***~ jak kamień*** sleep like a log, be sound asleep; ***~ na pieniądzach*** *fig* be rolling in money; ***chce mi się ~*** I'm slee-

py; ***to nie daje mi ~*** that keeps me awake; ***konkurencja nie śpi*** competition is alert; ***~ ze sobą*** sleep with each other

spad *m* (*-du*; *-dy*) *terenu*, *dachu*: slope; ***~y*** windfall

spadać ⟨**spaść**⟩ (*-dam*) **1.** (*o liściach*, *temperaturze*) fall (down) (***z*** *G* from) **2.** (*o cenach*) go down **3.** (*o terenie*) slope **4.** (*o ciosach*, *nieszczęściu*, *winie*) come down (***na*** *A* on) **5.** ***spadaj!*** *infml* get lost!

spad|ek[1] *m* (*-dku*; *-dki*) *JUR* inheritance; ***otrzymać w ~ku po*** *L* inherit from; ***zostawić coś komuś w ~ku*** bequeath s.o. s.th., leave s.o. s.th.

spadek[2] *m* (*-dku*; *-dki*) **1.** *temperatury*, *cen*, *urodzeń*: fall, drop; ***~ ciśnienia*** drop in pressure **2.** decline; ***~ na giełdzie*** *FIN* decline in prices **3.** *terenu*: slope

spadkobierca *m* (*-cy*; *-cy*) *JUR* heir, inheritor; **spadkobierczyni** *f* (*-ni*; *-nie*) *JUR* heiress; inheritress

spadkowy[1] *adj JUR* inheritance

spadkow|y[2] *adj*: ***tendencje ~e*** downward tendency

spadochron *m* (*-nu*; *-ny*) parachute; ***skakać na ~ie*** parachute; **spadochroniarstwo** *n* (*-wa*; *no pl*) parachuting

spadochroniarz *m* (*-rza*; *-rze*), **-rka** *f* (*-ki*; *-ki*) **1.** *SPORT* parachutist, *Am* parachuter **2.** (*w wojsku*) paratrooper; **spadochronowy** *adj* parachuting

spadzisty *adj* **1.** (*nachylony*) sloping, tilting **2.** (*stromy*) steep

spajać ⟨**spoić**⟩ (*-jam*) *TECH* join, connect

spakować *v/p* → ***pakować***

spalać ⟨**-lić**⟩ (*-lam*) **1.** *listy*, *śmieci*: burn **2.** *zwłoki*: cremate, burn **3.** (*zużywać*) burn (up), use up; ***spalić na panewce*** come to nothing; ***spalać się*** **1.** (*tracić energię*) burn out; ***spalić się doszczętnie*** burn up, burn down; ***spaliłby się ze wstydu*** he would blush for shame **2.** *BIOL* oxidize, oxidate **3.** (*na słońcu*) get sunburnt, get a sunburn **4.** *KULIN* burn **5.** (*o bezpieczniku*) blow out **6.** (*o żarówce*) burn out

spalanie *n* (*-nia*; *no pl*) **1.** (*w silniku*) combustion; ***~ śmieci*** incineration **2.** *zwłok*: cremation

spalarnia *f* (*-ni*; *-nie*): ***~ odpadków*** incinerating plant

spalenizn|a *f* (*-ny*; *no pl*) smell of s.th. burning; ***czuję ~ę*** I can smell something burning

spalić *v/p* → **1.** ***spalać*** **2.** ***palić***

spalinowy *adj*: ***silnik ~*** *AUTO* internal-combustion engine

spaliny *pl* (*-lin*) fumes, combustion gases

spalony **I** *adj* **1.** burnt **2.** *SPORT* disqualified **3.** (*opalony*) sunburnt **II** *m* (*-nego*; *-ne*) *SPORT* offside

spałaszować *v/p* → ***pałaszować***

spanie *n* **1.** (*-nia*; *no pl*) (*czynność*) sleeping **2.** (*-nia*; *-nia*) (*miejsce*) *infml* place to sleep, bed

spanikować *v/p* (*-kuję*) **1.** (*wpaść w panikę*) panic **2.** (*wystraszyć się*) chicken out

spaprać *v/p* → ***paprać***

sparaliżować *v/p* → ***paraliżować***

sparaliżowany *adj MED* palsied, paralyzed

sparciały *adj* **1.** *owoce*, *warzywa*: unfresh, shrivelled **2.** *guma*: damaged, rotten

sparcieć *v/p* (*-cieję*) **1.** (*o owocach*) become stringy, become spongy, become unfresh **2.** (*o skórze*, *sznurku*) become rotten

sparodiować *v/p* → ***parodiować***

sparować *v/p* → ***parować***[1]

spartaczyć *v/p* → ***partaczyć***

spartakiada *f* (*-dy*; *-dy*) *SPORT* athletic meet

spartańsk|i *adj* Spartan; ***żyć po ~u*** *fig* have a spartan lifestyle, live rough

sparzyć się *v/p* (*-rzę*) ***~ na*** *L fig* burn one's fingers by, have one's fingers burnt by→ ***parzyć***

spasiony, ***spasły*** *adj* **1.** (*utuczony*) fattened **2.** (*gruby*) *fig* fat

spasować *v/p* → ***pasować***[2]

spastyczny *adj* spastic

spaść[1] *v/p* (*spadnę*) ***spadł śnieg*** it snowed, it has been snowing; ***z byka spadłeś?*** *infml* are you out of your mind?; → ***spadać***

spaść[2] *v/p* → ***paść***[2]

spaw *m* (*-wu*; *-wy*) weld; **spawacz** *m* (*-cza*; *-cze*) welder; **spawać** ⟨**ze-**⟩ (*-wam*) weld; **spawany** *adj* welded; **spawarka** *f* (*-ki*; *-ki*) welder

spazm *m* (*-mu*; *-my*) *MED* spasm, convulsion; **~y** (convulsive) sobbing; **spazmatyczny** *adj* **1.** *MED* spasmodic **2.** *śmiech*: hysterical; **~ płacz** convulsive sobbing; **spazmować** *v/im* (*-muję*) convulse, blubber
spąsowieć *v/p* → **pąsowieć**
spec *m* (*-ca*; *-ce*) expert, master hand, whiz
specjalista *m* (*-ty*; *-liści*), **-tka** *f* (*-ki*; *-ki*) expert, specialist; **lekarz ~** specialist; **specjalistyczny** *adj* **1.** *literatura*, *wiedza*: specialist **2.** *sprzęt*: special
specjalizacja *f* (*-ji*; *-je*) **1.** (*ścisły podział*) specialization **2.** *MED* specialty
specjalizować się ⟨**wy-**⟩ (*-zuję*) specialize
specjalnie *adv* **1.** (*w sposób wyjątkowy*) especially, particularly **2.** (*umyślnie*) intentionally, on purpose; **nie ~** not exactly
specjalność *f* (*-ści*; *-ści*) **1.** (*dziedzina*) *Br* speciality, *Am* specialty; **~ zakładu** *COOK* speciality of the house, specialty of the house
specjaln|y *adj* **1.** (*szczególny*) special **2.** *nagroda*, *zadanie*: extra; **nic ~ego** nothing special; **pedagogika ~a** special education, special pedagogics; **szkoła ~a** special school, school for children with special needs
specjały *pl* (*-łów*) delicacies
specyficzny *adj* **1.** (*charakterystyczny*) specific, characteristic **2.** (*swoisty*) peculiar; **specyfik** *m* (*-ku*; *-ki*) *MED* medicine, remedy
specyfika *f* (*-ki*; *no pl*) peculiarity, specificity; **specyfikacja** *f* (*-ji*; *no pl*) specification
spedycja *f* (*-ji*; *no pl*) shipment, shipping; **spedytor** *m* (*-ra*; *-rzy*) (*firma*) shipping agent, shipper
spektakl *m* (*-lu*; *-le*) *THEAT* performance, show
spekulacj|a *f* (*-ji*; *-je*) **1.** (*nieuczciwa*) black market trading, profiteering **2.** *FIN* speculation; **~e na giełdzie** agiotage **3.** (*przypuszczenie*) speculation, guesswork
spekulant *m* (*-ta*; *-nci*) profiteer
spekulować *v/im* (*-luję*) **1.** (*handlować nielegalnie*) operate on the black market, profiteer; **~ na** *L* speculate in **2.** (*myśleć*) *lit* speculate

S

spelunka *f* (*-ki*; *-ki*) dive, joint
spełniać ⟨**-nić**⟩ (*-niam*) **1.** *życzenie*, *zadanie*: *Br* fulfil, *Am* fulfill; **~ swój cel** serve one's purpose; **spełniać się** **1.** (*o marzeniach*) be fulfilled, come true **2.** (*o przeczuciach*, *obawach*) come true **3.** (*o osobie*) be fulfilled, self-actualize, achieve self-actualization
spełnienie *n* (*-nia*; *no pl*) **1.** *marzeń*, *życzeń*: *Br* fulfilment, *Am* fulfillment **2.** *zawodowe*, *osobiste*: (self-)realization, fulfilment
spełznąć *v/p* (*-nę*) **~ na niczym** misfire, come to nothing
sperma *f* (*-my*; *no pl*) sperm
speszony *adj* disconcerted, abashed
speszyć *v/p* → **peszyć**
spęczniały *adj* swollen
spęcznieć *v/p* → **pęcznieć**
spęd *m* (*-du*; *-dy*): **~ bydła** round-up (of cattle)
spędzać ⟨**-dzić**⟩ (*-dzam*) **1.** *czas*, *rok*, *urlop*: spend **2.** *bydło*: round up
spękany *adj wargi*: chapped
spętać *v/p* → **pętać**
spętany *adj* tied up
spiąć się *v/p* (*zepnę*) *infml* brace oneself up, get it all together; → **spinać**
spichlerz *m* (*-rza*; *-rze*), **spichrz** *m* (*-rza*; *-rze*) granary
spiczasty *adj* peaked
spić *v/p* (*spiję*) *infml*: prime (**kogoś** *I* s.o. with); **spić się** get drunk, get sloshed; → **spijać**
spiec *v/p* (*spiekę*): **~ sobie plecy** get a sunburn on one's back; **~ się na słońcu** get sunburnt
spieczony *adj* **1.** *wargi*: dry, chapped **2.** *ziemia*: arid **3.** *COOK* scorched
spiekota *f* (*-ty*; *-ty*) scorching heat, swelter
spienić się *v/p* → **pienić się**
spieniężać ⟨**-żyć**⟩ (*-żam*) cash, sell
spieniony *adj* **1.** *fala*: foamed **2.** *napój*: frothy
spieprzać ⟨**-rzyć**⟩ (*-rzam*) *infml* **1.** (*uciekać*) clear off, push off; **spieprzaj!** *Br* bugger off!, fuck off! **2.** **spieprzyć coś** fuck s.th. up, screw s.th. up; **spieprzyć się** (*zepsuć się*) get screwed up, break (fucking) down
spierać ⟨**sprać**⟩ (*-ram*) **1.** *plamę*: wash off, remove; **spierać się** **1.** (*o plamie*)

be removed, come off **2.** (*kłócić się*) quarrel, argue (**z** *I* with, **o** *A* about)
spierzchnąć *v/p* → **pierzchnąć²**
spierzchnięty *adj* **1.** *wargi*: chapped **2.** *ręce*: dry, rough
spieszczać ⟨**-pieścić**⟩ (*-czam*) *GRAM* use diminutive form(s)
spieszczenie *n* (*-nia*; *-nia*) *GRAM* diminutive; **~ imienia** pet name
spieszczon|y *adj* diminutive; **~y wyraz** diminutive; **~a forma imienia** pet name
spieszny → **śpieszny**
spieszyć → **śpieszyć**
spięcie *n* (*-cia*; *-cia*) **1.** (*połączenie*) clasp, brace **2.** *TECH* short circuit **3.** (*niewielka kłótnia*) clash
spiętrzać ⟨**-rzyć**⟩ (*-rzam*) **1.** (*akumulować*) tower, heap **2.** *wodę*: dam (up)
spiętrzenie *n* (*-nia*; *-nia*) **1.** (*stos*) heap; **~ kry** ice jam **2.** (*nagromadzenie*) accumulation **3.** (*tama*) dam
spiętrzony *adj* **1.** *rzeczy*: piled up **2.** *woda*: rough, dammed
spięty *adj* tense, inhibited
spijać ⟨**spić**⟩ (*-jam*) *piankę*: drink (off)
spiker *m* (*-ra*; *-rzy*), **~ka** *f* (*-ki*; *-ki*) *RADIO* announcer, presenter
spiknąć *v/p* (*-nę*) *infml osoby*: fix up, unite; **spiknąć się** come together, get together, be in cahoots
spiłowywać ⟨**-łować**⟩ (*-łowuję*) file off
spinacz *m* (*-cza*; *-cze*) **1.** (*do papieru*) (paper) clip **2.** (*do bielizny*) peg
spinać ⟨**spiąć**⟩ (*-nam*) **1.** *kartki*: clip together **2.** *włosy*: pin up; **~ konia ostrogami** spur a horse
spinka *f* (*-ki*; *-ki*): **~ do włosów** clip, hairpin; **~ do mankietów** cuff-link; **~ do krawata** tiepin
spirala *f* (*-li*; *-le*) **1.** (*zwój*) spiral; **~ przemocy** spiral of violence; **2.** (*wkładka domaciczna*) coil; **spiralny** *adj* spiral
spirytus *m* (*-su*; *-sy*) spirit; **spirytusowy** *adj* spirit
spirytystyczny *adj*: **seans ~** séance
spis *m* (*-su*; *-sy*) **1.** list; **~ ludności** census; **~ potraw** menu **2.** *haseł*, *ulic*: directory; **~ treści** (table of) contents **3.** (*czynność*) registration
spisać *v/p* → **spisywać**
spisek *m* (*-sku*; *-ski*) *POLIT* conspiracy, plot; **spiskować** *v/im* (*-kuję*) conspire, plot; **spiskowiec** *m* (*-wca*; *-wcy*) conspirator
spisywać ⟨**-sać**⟩ (*-suję*) **1.** (*zamieszczać na liście*) add to a list, make a list **2.** *protokół*: make; **~ umowę** conclude a contract, make a contract; **~ testament** make one's last will; **~ na straty** *fig* write off **3.** *wspomnienia*, *wrażenia*: write down **4.** (*przepisać*) copy; **spisywać się 1.** (*o osobie*) perform well, do well; **~ się dobrze** (**źle**) do well (badly) **2.** (*o rzeczy*) work good, run good
spity *adj* drunk
spiż *m* (*-żu*; *no pl*) bronze
spiżarka *f* (*-ki*; *-ki*) larder, pantry; **spiżarnia** *f* (*-ni*; *-nie*) store room
spiżowy *adj* bronze
splajtować *v/p* → **plajtować**
splamić *v/p* → **plamić**
splatać ⟨**-leść**⟩ (*-tam*) **1.** *warkocz*: *Br* plait, *Am* braid **2.** *sznur*: twist, twine **3.** (*palce*) interlock; **~ dłonie** clasp one's hands; **~ się w uścisku** hug, embrace each other
splądrować *v/p* → **plądrować**
splątany *adj* entangled, tangled
splendor *m* (*-ru*; *-ry*) *lit Br* splendour, *Am* splendor, *Br* glamour, *Am* glamor
spleśniały *adj* **1.** *chleb*: *Br* mouldy, *Am* moldy **2.** *ciecz*: musty
spleśnieć *v/p* → **pleśnieć**
splot *m* (*-tu*; *-ty*) **1.** *lin*: coil, braid; **~ wydarzeń** chain of events, coincidence; **~ słoneczny** *ANAT* solar plexus **2.** *gałęzi*: tangle **3.** *materiału*: weave **4.** *włosów*: plait, lock
splugawić *v/p* → **plugawić**
splunąć *v/p* → **spluwać**
spluwa *f* (*-wy*; *-wy*) *infml* piece, gat
spluwaczka *f* (*-ki*; *-ki*) (*u dentysty*) spittoon, *Am* cuspidor
spluwać ⟨**-lunąć**⟩ (*-wam*) spit (out)
spłacać ⟨**-cić**⟩ (*-cam*) pay off, repay
spłakany *adj* all in tears, weeping
spłaszczać ⟨**-czyć**⟩ (*-czam*) **1.** *rzecz*: flatten **2.** *problem*: simplify
spłaszczony *adj* **1.** (*płaski*) flat **2.** (*nadmiernie uproszczony*) shallow, (over)-simplified
spłat|a *f* (*-ty*; *-ty*) payment, repayment; **~y** payments; **kupić coś na ~y** *Br* buy s.th. on hire purchase, *Am* buy s.th. on the instalment plan

spłatać *v/p* (*-tam*): **~ komuś figla** play a (practical) joke on
spław *m* (*-wu*; *no pl*) floating (of timber) down the river, rafting
spławiać ⟨**-wić**⟩ (*-wiam*) **1.** *drzewo*: float **2.** *infml* get rid of
spławik *m* (*-ka*; *-ki*) *wędki*: float, *Am* bob
spławny *adj* navigable
spłodzić *v/p* → **płodzić**
spłonąć *v/p* (*-nę*) **1.** (*o domu*) burn down **2.** (*o osobie*) burn up, die in flames; **~ rumieńcem** *lit* blush, redden
spłonka *f* (*-ki*; *-ki*) primer, detonator
spłowiały *adj* pale, faded
spłuczka *f* (*-ki*; *-ki*) *ubikacji*: flusher
spłukać się *v/p* (*-łuczę*) *infml* go broke, go bust; → **spłukiwać**
spłukany *adj infml* broke, hard up
spłukiwać ⟨**-kać**⟩ (*-kuję*) *włosy*: rinse; → **spłukać się**
spłycać ⟨**-cić**⟩ (*-cam*) oversimplify, trivialize
spłynąć *v/p* → **spływać**
spływ *m* (*-wu*; *-wy*) *kajakowy*: canoeing trip, canoeing rally; **~ tratwą** rafting trip
spływać ⟨**-łynąć**⟩ (*-wam*) **1.** (*o wodzie*) flow **2.** (*o pocie*, *łzach*) run down, stream **3.** (*o tratwie*, *łodzi*) drift, float; **~ krwią** run with blood; **spływać potem** be streaming, be pouring with sweat; **spływaj!** *infml* get lost!, beat it!, buzz off!
spochmurnieć *v/p* → **pochmurnieć**
spocić się *v/p* → **pocić się**
spocony *adj* sweaty
spocząć *v/p* (*-cznę*) **1.** (*o wzroku*) rest (**na** *L* on); **~ na laurach** rest on one's laurels; **nie spocznę, dopóki** I shall know no rest until; **spocznij!** at ease! **2.** (*usiąść*) sit down; **proszę ~!** take a seat please!, sit down please!, do sit down!; → **spoczywać**
spoczyn|ek *m* (*-nku*; *no pl*) *lit* rest, repose; **stan ~ku a)** PHYS standstill **b)** (*emerytura*) retirement; **chwila ~ku** break, rest; **nocny ~ek** night's rest; **udać się na ~ek** *lit* retire (for the night); **miejsce wiecznego ~ku** last resting place; **w stanie ~ku** retired; **przejść w stan ~ku** retire
spoczywać ⟨**-cząć**⟩ (*-wam*) **1.** (*o osobie*) have a rest, take a rest **2.** (*o rzeczach*) rest (**na** *L* on), lie (**na** *L* on); **cała odpowiedzialność spoczywa na jej barkach** the whole responsibility rests on her (shoulders); **~ w grobie** lie in one's grave; **tu spoczywa w Bogu** here rests in peace
spod *prep* (*G*) **1.** *wyciągnąć*: from under; **~ spodu** from underneath **2.** (*z okolicy*) from somewhere around of, from the area of; **być ~ znaku Wagi** ASTR be a Libra; **uwolnić się ~** *G* free oneself from
spode: **patrzeć ~ łba na** *A* look askance at; → **spod**
spodek *m* (*-dka*; *-dki*) saucer
spodenki *pl* (*-nek*) shorts; **~ kąpielowe** bathing-trunks
spodlić *v/p* (*-lę*) (*uczynić podłym*) degrade, debase; **spodlić się** (*stać się podłym*) turn vile, turn mean
spodni *adj* bottom; **~a strona** bottom side
spodnie *pl* (*-ni*) *Br* trousers, *Am* pants; **~ narciarskie** salopettes; **spuścić ~** drop one's pants
spodobać się *v/p* (*-bam*) appeal (*D* to); **spodobał się jej** she took fancy/a liking to him
spody *pl* → **spód**
spodziewać się *v/im* (*-wam*) expect (**po** *L* from); **~ dziecka** be expecting a baby; **nie ~ niczego złego** not suspect anything bad; **kto by się spodziewał!** who would have thought it!; **można się po nim wszystkiego spodziewać** he's capable of anything, you would expect anything of him; **spodziewam się, że** I hope
spoglądać ⟨**spojrzeć**⟩ (*-dam*) glance, look (**na** *A* at); **~ w lustro** look in the mirror; **~ na zegarek** glance at the watch; **~ w górę** look up; **~ z góry na** *A fig* look down on; **~ po sobie** glance at each other
spoić[1] *v/p* → **spajać**
spoić[2] *v/p* (*spoję*) make drunk, get drunk
spoina *f* (*-ny*; *-ny*) **1.** (*między cegłami*) joint **2.** (*przy spawaniu*) seam, weld
spoisty *adj* **1.** *masa*: cohesive **2.** *tekst* coherent; **spoiwo** *n* (*-wa*; *-wa*) **1.** TECH binder **2.** *spawalnicze*: filler metal; **~ farby** paint vehicle
spojówka *f* (*-ki*; *-ki*) ANAT conjunctiva

S

spojrzeć *v/p* (*-rzę*): **~ prawdzie w oczy** face the truth; **~ śmierci w oczy** look death in the face; **~ komuś prosto w oczy** look s.o. straight in the eyes; → **spoglądać**

spojrzenie *n* (*-nia*; *-nia*) glance, look; **uporczywe ~** gaze; **groźne ~** glower look; **przelotne ~** glimpse, furtive glance; **nieobecne ~** faraway look; **mieć trzeźwe ~ na coś** consider s.th. soberly, have a sober attitude towards s.th.

spoko *adv infml*: **~!** don't worry!, cool!, sure!

spokojnie *adv* calmly, composedly; **~ zrezygnować** resign safely; (**tylko**) **~!** stay calm!, calm down!, steady!

spokojny *adj* **1.** *osoba*: calm, quiet **2.** *dzielnica*, *morze*, *życie*: quiet; **Ocean ~** the Pacific Ocean **3.** *kolor*: mellow **4.** *demonstracja*: peaceful; **być ~m o** *A* not worry about; **bądź ~!** don't worry!

spokornieć *v/p* → **pokornieć**

spok|ój *m* (*-koju*; *no pl*) **1.** (*równowaga*) quiet, calmness **2.** (*zgoda*) peace; **~ój ducha** peace of mind; **daj mi ~ój!** leave me alone!; **żyć w ~oju** live in peace; **zachować ~ój** stay calm, stay cool

spokrewniony *adj* related (**z** *I* to)

spolaryzowany *adj* polarized

spoliczkować *v/p* → **policzkować**

spolszczać ⟨**-czyć**⟩ (*-czam*) **1.** (*polonizować*) *Br* polonise, *Am* polonize **2.** (*tłumaczyć*) translate into Polish; **spolszczony** *adj nazwisko*, *wymowa*: *Br* polonised, *Am* polonized

społeczeństwo *n* (*-wa*; *-wa*) **1.** (*ogół ludzi*) society **2.** (*opinia publiczna*) public opinion

społecznik *m* (*-ka*; *-nicy*) social activist; **pracować jako ~** do welfare work

społecznie *adv*: **pracować ~** do community work; **społeczność** *f* (*-ści*; *-ści*) community

społeczn|y *adj* **1.** (*socjalny*) social **2.** *mienie*, *dobro*: public **3.** *organizacja*: voluntary **4.** (*komunalny*) communal; **nauki ~e** social sciences; **reakcje ~e** public opinion; **praca ~a** community work, welfare work; **ubezpieczenia ~e** *Br* national insurance, *Am* social security; **przedszkole ~e** *Br* nursery school, *Am* kindergarten

spomiędzy *prep* (*G*) from among, from between

sponad *prep* (*G*) from above

sponiewierany *adj osoba*: ill-treated, maltreated

sponsorować ⟨**za-**⟩ (*-ruję*) sponsor

spontaniczny *adj* spontaneous

spopielać ⟨**-lić**⟩ (*-lam*) (*zamienić w popiół*) incinerate, burn to ashes

spopielony *adj* **1.** (*spalony*) burnt to ashes **2.** *ziemia*: parched

spopularyzować *v/p* → **popularyzować**

sporadyczny *adj* **1.** *wypadek*, *zjawisko*: sporadic, occasional, infrequent **2.** *deszcz*: occasional

sporn|y *adj* controversial, debatable; **kwestia ~a** disputable issue, moot point

sporo *adv* quite a lot, a great deal

sport *m* (*-tu*; *-ty*) sport; **~y zimowe** winter sports; **~y wodne** water sports; **~ wyczynowy** professional sport; **uprawiać ~** do a sport, practice sports

sportowiec *m* (*-wca*; *-wcy*) **a)** (*mężczyzna*) sportsman **b)** (*kobieta*) sportswoman; **sportowo** *adv* sportily; **ubrany na ~** casually dressed

sportow|y *adj* **1.** *klub*, *dyscyplina*, *samochód*: sports; **wydarzenie ~e** sports event, sporting event; **~e zachowanie** sportsmanship **2.** *ubranie*: casual; **bluza ~a** sweatshirt; **odzież ~a** sportswear

sportretować *v/p* → **portretować**

spor|y[1] *adj* pretty big, quite large; **~y kawał drogi** quite a distance; **~y dochód** handsome income; **~a ilość** considerable amount; **~a porcja** generous portion

spory[2] *pl* → **spór**

sporysz *m* (*-szu*; *-sze*) BIOL ergot

sporządzać ⟨**-dzić**⟩ (*-dzam*) **1.** *plany*, *listę*, *testament*: make; **~ protokół z** *G* take minutes of **2.** *umowę*: prepare, draw up **3.** *notatki*: write, make **4.** COOK prepare

sposępnieć *v/p* → **posępnieć**

sposobnoś|ć *f* (*-ści*; *-ści*) occasion, opportunity; **przy każdej ~ci** on every occasion; **nadarzyła się ~ć** an opportunity presented itself

spos|ób *m* (*-sobu*; *-soby*) **1.** manner; **~ób mówienia** manner of speaking,

S

turn of phrase; **~ób bycia** manners; **mieć ujmujący ~ób bycia** have prepossessing manners, be charming **2.** way; **~ób myślenia** way of thinking; **w ten ~ób** in this way; **w grzeczny ~ób** in a polite way; **na swój ~ób** in a way; **w następujący ~ób** like this; **w pewien ~ób** in a way; **dziwnym ~obem** in a strange way; **w istotny ~ób** considerably **3.** means *pl*; **wszelkimi ~obami** by all means, using all methods; **w żaden ~ób** no way, by no means; **nie ~ób (jest)** it's impossible

spostponować *v/p* → **postponować**

spostrzegać ⟨**-rzec**⟩ (*-gam*) **1.** (*zauważyć*) notice, catch sight (*A* of) **2.** (*odczuć*) become aware (*A* of), realize

spostrzegawczoś|ć *f* (*-ści*; *no pl*) perceptiveness; **wykazywać się dużą ~cią** be very insightful; **spostrzegawczy** *adj* perceptive; **być ~m** be perceptive

spostrzeżeni|e *n* (*-nia*; *-nia*) **1.** awareness **2.** (*uwaga*) remark; **dzielić się ~ami z** *I* share one's observations with

spośród → **spomiędzy**

spotęgować *v/p* → **potęgować**

spotężnieć *v/p* → **potężnieć**

spotkać *v/p* → **spotykać**

spotkanie *n* (*-nia*; *-nia*) **1.** meeting; **wyjść komuś na ~** (go to) meet s.o. **2.** appointment; **nie przyjść na ~** break an appointment, miss an appointment **3.** encounter **4.** (*towarzyskie*) get-together, party

spotniały *adj* **1.** *człowiek*: perspiring, sweaty **2.** *okulary*, *szyba*: misted over, steamy

spotnieć *v/p* → **potnieć**

spotwarzać ⟨**-rzyć**⟩ (*-rzam*) slander, defame

S

spotykać ⟨**-tkać**⟩ (*-kam*) **1.** (*zobaczyć*, *poznać*) meet **2.** (*natknąć się*) come across **3.** (*stawać się czyimś udziałem*) happen; **spotkało go nieszczęście** he met with misfortune; **spotkała go kara** he was punished; **spotkała go śmierć** he was killed, he died; **spotykać się** meet; **~ się z uznaniem** meet with approval; **~ się z dobrym przyjęciem** meet with warm reception; **~ się z trudnościami** meet with difficulties; **to się często spotyka** it's quite common; **~ się ponownie** meet again

spoufalać się ⟨**-lić**⟩ (*-lam*) get (too) familiar (**z** *I* with)

spowalniać ⟨**-wolnić**⟩ (*-niam*) slow down

spowiadać ⟨**wy-**⟩ (*-dam*) hear confession; **spowiadać się** confess (**z** *G*)

spowiednik *m* (*-ka*; *-nicy*) confessor

spowie|dź *f* (*-dzi*; *-dzi*) REL confession; **iść do ~dzi** go to confession

spowinowacony *adj* related (by marriage)

spowodować *v/p* → **powodować**

spowodowany *adj* caused (*I* by), due (*I* to)

spowolnić *v/p* → **spowalniać**

spowszedniały *adj* commonplace

spowszednieć *v/p* → **powszednieć**

spoza *prep* (*G*) from behind, from beyond, from outside

spozierać *v/im* (*-ram*) → **spoglądać**

spożyci|e *n* (*-cia*; *no pl*) consumption; **termin przydatności do ~a** best before date

spożywać ⟨**-żyć**⟩ (*-wam*) consume; **~ alkohol w nadmiarze** drink too much alcohol; **~ śniadanie** *lit* have breakfast

spożywca *m* (*-cy*; *-cy*) consumer; **spożywcz|y** *adj* food; **sklep ~y** the grocer's, grocery; **artykuły ~e** foodstuffs, groceries, food

spód *m* (*spodu*; *spody*) **1.** (*dno*) bottom; **na (samym) spodzie** at the very bottom; **pod spodem** underneath **2.** *materiału*: foundation **3.** COOK base **4.** (*podeszwa*) sole

spódnica *f* (*-cy*; *-ce*), **spódniczka** *f* (*-ki*; *-ki*) skirt

spójnik *m* (*-ka*; *-ki*) conjunction

spójny *adj* coherent

spółdzielca *m* (*-cy*; *-cy*) member of a co-operative; **spółdzielczy** *adj* co-operative; **spółdzielnia** *f* (*-ni*; *-nie*) co-operative (society); **~ mieszkaniowa** *Br* housing co-operative, building society, *Am* co-operative apartment corporation; **studencka ~ pracy** students' working co-operative

spółgłoska *f* (*-ki*; *-ki*) consonant

spółk|a *f* (*-ki*; *-ki*) ECON partnership; **~a akcyjna** joint stock company; **~a z ograniczoną odpowiedzialnością**

limited liability company; ***do ~i*** jointly; ***robić coś do ~i z*** *I* do s.th. together with

spółkować *v/im* (*-kuję*) copulate; **spółkowanie** *n* (*-nia*; *no pl*) copulation

spór *m* (*sporu*; *spory*) **1.** (*polemika*) dispute, controversy (**o** *A* over); ***spory*** controversies **2.** (*zatarg*) argument, quarrel (***z powodu*** *G* because of) **3.** JUR litigation; ***być przedmiotem sporu*** be the subject of litigation

spóźniać się ⟨**-nić**⟩ (*-niam*) **1.** (*przychodzić za późno*) be late, come late **2.** (*nie zdążać*) miss; ***~ na pociąg*** miss the train **3.** (*o zegarku*) be late; ***~ pięć minut*** to lose five minutes **4.** (*z płatnością*) be overdue

spóźnialski *m* (*-kiego*; *-scy*), **-ka** *f* (*-kiej*; *-kie*) *infml* **1.** (*osoba*) latecomer **2.** *fig* laggard

spóźnienie *n* (*-nia*; *-nia*) delay; **spóźnion|y** *adj* **1.** *osoba*: late **2.** *start*, *reakcja*, *odjazd*: delayed **3.** *próba*, *obchody*: belated; ***~e życzenia*** belated wishes

spracować się *v/p* (*-cuję*) exhaust oneself, tire oneself out; **spracowany** *adj* exhausted, tired out

sprać *v/p* (*spiorę*) (*zbić*) *infml* beat; → ***spierać***

spragniony *adj* thirsty; ***~ przygód*** thirsty for adventure; ***~ miłości*** craving for love; ***~ wiedzy*** eager for knowledge

sprasować *v/p* → ***prasować***

spraszać ⟨**-rosić**⟩ (*-szam*): ***~ gości*** invite guests

spraw|a *f* (*-wy*; *-wy*) **1.** (*fakt*, *wydarzenie*) matter; ***to ~a trzech dni*** this is a matter of three days; ***w tej ~ie*** in this matter; ***gorsza ~a, że*** it's worse that; ***na dobrą ~ę*** as a matter of fact; ***zdać ~ę z*** *G* give an account of; ***zdawać sobie ~ę z*** *G* realize; ***nie ma ~y!*** no problem!; ***w ~ie*** *G* regarding; ***za ~ą*** *G* because of **2.** business; ***to nie moja ~a*** it's none of my business **3.** JUR case **4.** (*kwestia*) question

sprawc|a *m* (*-cy*; *-cy*), **-czyni** *f* (*-ni*; *-nie*) JUR perpetrator; ***przeciw(ko) nieznanemu ~y*** JUR against an unidentified perpetrator; ***~a wypadku*** the guilty party

sprawdzać ⟨**-dzić**⟩ (*-dzam*) **1.** (*kontrolować*, *badać*) check (up); ***~ podwójnie*** double check **2.** (*w książce telefonicznej*, *słowniku*) look up; ***~ pisownię*** spell-check **3.** *obecność*, *bilety*, *paszport*: check **4.** *lekcje*, *zadanie*: correct; ***sprawdzać się*** **1.** (*okazać się przydatnym*) prove useful **2.** (*o przepowiedni*, *słowach*) come true **3.** (*wykazać się*) prove oneself

sprawdzalny *adj* verifiable

sprawdzian *m* (*-nu*; *-ny*) **1.** (*dłuższy*) test **2.** (*krótszy*) quiz

sprawdzić *v/p* → ***sprawdzać***

sprawdzony *adj* **1.** *lek*, *środek*: tested **2.** *skuteczność*: proven **3.** (*godny zaufania*) sure, reliable

sprawiać ⟨**-wić**⟩ (*-wiam*) **1.** (*powodować*) cause, bring about **2.** (*kupować*) buy, purchase; ***~ sobie nowe buty*** buy new shoes **3.** *radość*, *kłopot*, *wrażenie*: give; ***~ lanie*** give a thrashing; ***~ komuś zawód*** let s.o. down **4.** *różnicę*: make

sprawiedliwoś|ć *f* (*-ści*; *no pl*) **1.** (*sprawiedliwe traktowanie*) fairness **2.** (*sądownictwo*) justice; ***ministerstwo ~ci*** the Ministry of Justice; ***wymiar ~ci*** the judiciary; ***oddać komuś ~ć*** do justice to s.o.

sprawiedliwy *adj* **1.** (*uczciwy*) just, fair **2.** *kara*: deserved

sprawka *f* (*-ki*; *-ki*) doing; ***to twoja ~*** this is your doing

sprawność *f* (*-ści*; *no pl*) **1.** (*zdolność*) ability; ***~ fizyczna*** fitness; ***~ umysłowa*** mental ability, intellectual ability **2.** TECH efficiency

sprawnościowy *adj*: ***test ~*** fitness test

sprawny *adj* **1.** fit; ***~ fizycznie*** physically fit **2.** TECH in running order **3.** *system*, *pracownik*: efficient **4.** *ruchy*: dexterous, dextrous

sprawować *v/im* (*-rawuję*) **1.** *urząd*: hold; ***~ władzę*** be in authority; ***~ nadzór*** supervise; ***~ opiekę nad*** *I* look after; ***~ rządy*** govern **2.** *kontrolę*: exercise; ***sprawować się*** behave

sprawowanie (się) *n* (*-nia*; *no pl*) behaviour, conduct; ***dobre*** (***złe***) ***~*** good (bad) conduct

sprawozdanie *n* (*-nia*; *-nia*) report; ***~ z działalności*** *G* report on; ***~ z meczu*** game coverage, game commentary

sprawozdawca *m* (*-cy*; *-cy*), **-czyni** *f* (*-ni*; *-nie*) reporter; **~ sportowy** sports commentator; **~ zagraniczny** foreign correspondent
sprawozdawczy *adj dział*, *zespół*: reporting; **referat ~** report
sprecyzować *v/p* → **precyzować**
spreparować *v/p* → **preparować**
sprężać ⟨**-żyć**⟩ (*-żam*) TECH compress; **sprężać się 1.** (*mobilizować się*) get oneself together, pull one's socks up **2.** (*o gazie*) undergo compression, become compressed
sprężarka *f* (*-ki*; *-ki*) TECH air-compressor; **sprężony** *adj* compressed
sprężyna *f* (*-ny*; *-ny*) **1.** TECH spring **2.** *fig* mover
sprężynować *v/im* (*-nuję*) spring (back)
sprężynowy *adj napęd*, *zegar*: spring; **nóż ~** *Br* flick knife, *Am* switchblade (knife); **materac ~** TECH inner-spring mattress, interior-sprung mattress
sprężystość *f* (*-ści*; *no pl*) **1.** *materaca*: springiness **2.** *ruchów*: nimbleness **3.** TECH resilience **4.** PHYS elasticity
sprężysty *adj* **1.** *materac*, *krok*: springy **2.** (*giętki*) elastic **3.** (*elastyczny*) resilient **4.** *ruchy*: nimble **5.** *skóra*: supple
sprint *m* (*-tu*; *-ty*) sprint
sprinter *m* (*-ra*; *-rzy*), **~ka** *f* (*-ki*; *-ki*) sprinter
sprofanować *v/p* → **profanować**
sprolongować *v/p* → **prolongować**
sprosić *v/p* → **spraszać**
sprostać *v/p* (*-tam*) **1.** *trudnościom*: cope (*D* with) **2.** (*dorównać*) be equal (*D* to); **~ komuś** be a match for s.o., come up to s.o.; **~ czyimś oczekiwaniom** live up to s.o.'s expectations **3.** (*podołać*) manage (*D*)
sprostować *v/p* → **prostować**
sprostowanie *n* (*-nia*; *-nia*) correction
sproszkowany *adj* powdered
sprośny *adj żart*: ribald
sprowadzać ⟨**-dzić**⟩ (*-dzam*) **1.** *osobę*, *pomoc*: bring, get; **co cię tu sprowadza?** what brings you here?; **~ kogoś na złą drogę** lead s.o. astray; **~ rozmowę na inne tory** switch the conversation to another topic, change topic **2.** *towar*: import **3.** (*pociągać za sobą*) cause, bring about **4.** (*z góry*) lead downstairs, lead down **5.** (*ograniczać*) reduce (**do** *G* to); **sprowadzać się 1.** (*ograniczać się*) boil down (**do** *G* to), resolve itself (**do** *G* into); **wszystko sprowadza się do tego, że** what it comes down to is that; **wszystko sprowadza się do wyborów** it all comes down to choice **2.** (*osiedlać się*) move in
sprowokować *v/p* → **prowokować**
spróbować *v/p* (*-buję*) **1.** (*eksperymentować*) try **2.** (*usiłować*) attempt **3.** COOK taste
spróchniały *adj* **1.** *dach*: rotten **2.** *ząb*: decayed, carious
spróchnieć *v/p* → **próchnieć**
spruć *v/p* → **pruć**
spryciara *f* (*-ry*; *-ry*) *infml* artful lass, cunning lass; **spryciarz** *m* (*-rza*; *-rze*) *infml* sly fox, smart cookie
spryskać *v/p* → **spryskiwać**
spryskiwacz *m* (*-cza*; *-cze*) **1.** sprayer; **żelazko ze ~em** iron with automatic water spray (function) **2.** AUTO windscreen washer
spryskiwać ⟨**-kać**⟩ (*-kuję*) **1.** *rośliny*: spray **2.** *bieliznę*: sprinkle
spryt *m* (*-tu*; *no pl*) quick wit, smartness, cunning; **sprytny** *adj osoba*, *rozwiazanie*: clever
sprząc *v/p* → **sprzęgać**
sprzączka *f* (*-ki*; *-ki*) **1.** *paska*: buckle **2.** *torebki*: clasp
sprzątaczka *f* (*-ki*; *-ki*) charwoman, cleaning lady
sprzątać ⟨**-tnąć**⟩ (*-tam*) **1.** (*porządkować*) clean, tidy up **2.** (*usunąć*) remove, take away; **~ ze stołu** clear the table; **~ komuś coś sprzed nosa** take s.th. from under s.o.'s nose **3.** (*zabić*) *infml* erase, do in
sprzątanie *n* (*-nia*; *no pl*) cleaning
sprzeciw *m* (*-wu*; *-wy*) **1.** (*niezgadzanie się*) objection **2.** JUR demur; **wnosić ~ przeciw** *D* object to, raise an objection against
sprzeciwiać się ⟨**-wić**⟩ (*-wiam*) oppose (*D*), object (*D* to)
sprzeczać się ⟨**po-**⟩ (*-czam*) argue (**o** *A* about), quarrel (**o** *A* about)
sprzeczka *f* (*-ki*; *-ki*) squabble, argument
sprzecznoś|ć *f* (*-ści*; *-ści*) discrepancy, contradiction; **~ć interesów** conflic

S

of interests; ***stać w ~ci do*** *G* be at variance with

sprzeczny *adj* **1.** *emocje*: conflicting **2.** *informacje*: contradictory (**z** *I* to) **3.** *interesy*: competing, contradictory; ***~ z prawem*** against the law

sprzed *prep* (*G*) from before

sprzedać *v/p* → ***sprzedawać***

sprzedający *m* (*-cego*; *-cy*), **-ca** *f* (*-cej*; *-ce*) seller

sprzedajny *adj* corrupt, corruptible

sprzedani|e *n*: ***do ~a*** for sale

sprzedawać ⟨**-dać**, **po-**⟩ (*-daję*) sell; ***sprzedawać się*** **1.** (*o osobie*) sell out **2.** (*o towarze*) sell **3.** prostitute oneself

sprzedawca *m* (*-cy*; *-cy*) **1.** (*handlowiec*) salesman **2.** (*w sklepie*) *Br* shop assistant, *Am* salesclerk

sprzedawczyk *m* (*-ka*; *-ki*) traitor, renegade

sprzedawczyni *f* (*-ni*; *-nie*) **1.** (*handlowiec*) saleswoman **2.** (*w sklepie*) *Br* shop assistant, *Am* salesclerk

sprzedaż *f* (*-ży*; *no pl*) sale; ***~ detaliczna*** retail; ***~ hurtowa*** wholesale; ***~ wysyłkowa*** mail-order; ***na ~*** for sale; **sprzedażny** *adj cena*: selling

sprzeniewierzać ⟨**-rzyć**⟩ (*-rzam*) embezzle; ***sprzeniewierzać się*** betray (*D*)

sprzeniewierzenie *n* (*-nia*; *no pl*) embezzlement; **sprzeniewierzenie się** *n* (*-nia*; *no pl*) betrayal, disloyalty

sprzęgać ⟨**-gnąć**, **-rząc**⟩ (*-gam*) connect, couple

sprzęgło *n* (*-ła*; *-ła*) AUTO clutch; ***włączyć ~*** apply the clutch; ***wyłączyć ~*** declutch

sprzęgnąć *v/p* → ***sprzęgać***

sprzęt[1] *m* (*-tu*; *-ty*) equipment; ***~ sportowy*** sports equipment; ***~ komputerowy*** hardware; ***~y domowe*** furniture

sprzęt[2] *m* (*-tu*; *no pl*) (*w rolnictwie*) harvesting, gathering (of crops)

sprzężenie *n* (*-nia*; *no pl*) coupling; ***~ zwrotne*** feedback; **sprzężony** *adj* TECH coupled (**z** *I* with)

sprzyjać *v/im* (*-jam*) be friendly (*D* to), further, promote (*D*); ***~ komuś*** favour s.o.; ***pogoda sprzyja*** the weather is favourable; ***zdrowie mu sprzyja mimo wieku*** he is in good health despite his age

sprzyjający *adj Br* favourable, *Am* favorable; ***~ moment*** propitious moment

sprzykrzyć się *v/p*: ***sprzykrzyło mu się czekanie*** he was tired of waiting

sprzymierzać się ⟨**-rzyć**⟩ (*-rzam*) ally oneself (**z** *I* with)

sprzymierzeniec *m* (*-rzeńca*; *-rzeńcy*) ally; **sprzymierzony** *adj* allied, confederate

sprzymierzyć się *v/p* → ***sprzymierzać się***

sprzysięgać się ⟨**-siąc**⟩ (*-gam*) conspire, plot (**przeciw** *D* against)

sprzysiężenie *n* (*-nia*; *-nia*) conspiracy, plot

spuchnąć *v/p* → ***puchnąć***

spuchnięty *adj* swollen

spudłować *v/p* → ***pudłować***

spulchniać ⟨**-nić**⟩ (*-niam*) *glebę*: cultivate

spust *m* (*-tu*; *-ty*) **1.** *broni*: trigger; ***~ migawki*** shutter release; ***mieć ~*** *infml* be a heavy eater **2.** *cieczy*: escape

spustoszenie *n* (*-nia*; *-nia*) devastation; ***siać ~*** wreak havoc

spuszczać ⟨**spuścić**⟩ (*-czam*) **1.** (*upuszczać*) drop; ***~ psa z łańcucha*** let a dog loose; ***~ psa ze smyczy*** unleash a dog; ***~ statek na wodę*** launch a ship; ***~ z ceny*** reduce the price, lower the price, bring down the price; ***nie ~ kogoś z oczu*** not let s.o. out of one's sight; ***~ z tonu*** come down a peg (or two); ***~ komuś lanie*** give s.o. a thrashing; ***~ wodę*** (*w toalecie*) flush the toilet **2.** *żaluzje*: let down; ***~ głowę*** droop one's head; ***~ wzrok***, ***~ oczy*** cast down one's eyes **3.** *płyn*, *powietrze*: let out; ***spuszczać się*** **1.** (*zniżać się*) let oneself down, lower oneself **2.** (*powodować wytrysk nasienia*) *vulg* shoot one's load

spuścizna *f* (*-ny*; *-ny*) **1.** *twórcy*: output **2.** (*spadek*) heritage, legacy

spychacz *m* (*-cza*; *-cze*) bulldozer

spychać ⟨**zepchnąć**⟩ (*-cham*) push down; ***~ na kogoś odpowiedzialność*** *fig* shift responsibility upon s.o.; ***~ w bok*** push aside; ***~ kogoś ze schodów*** push s.o. down the stairs

spycharka *f* (*-ki*; *-ki*) → ***spychacz***

spytać *v/p* → ***pytać***

spytki: ***brać kogoś na ~*** pump s.o.

sp. z o.o. *abbr* (= **spółka z ograniczoną odpowiedzialnością**) Ltd.
sraczk|a *f* (*-ki*; *-ki*) *vulg* the shits, the runs; ***dostałem ~i od tych pomidorów*** those tomatoes gave me the shits
srać *v/im* (*sram*) *vulg* shit; ***~ na** A fig* not give a shit about, not give a damn about
srebrnoszary *adj* silver-grey
srebrn|y *adj* silver; ***~e wesele*** silver wedding (anniversary); **srebro** *n* (*-ra*; *-ra*) silver; ***srebra*** silverware; ***żywe ~*** quicksilver
srebrzyć ⟨**po-**⟩ (*-rzę*) silver; ***srebrzyć się*** shine like silver
srebrzysty *adj* silvery
sroczy *adj* magpie's
srodze *adv lit* badly
srog|i *adj lit* **1.** *osoba*: strict, severe; ***~a mina*** stern face **2.** *kara*, *los*: cruel **3.** *zima*, *mróz*: bitter, severe; **srogość** *f* (*-ści*; *no pl*) *lit* severity, sternness
sroka *f* (*-ki*; *-ki*) magpie
srokaty *adj koń*: piebald, pied
srom *m* (*-mu*; *-my*) *ANAT* vulva
sromotn|y *adj lit* shameful, ignominious, disgraceful; ***~a klęska*** overwhelming defeat
sromow|y *adj*: ***wargi ~e*** *ANAT* labia
sroższy *comp* → ***srogi***
ssać *v/im* (*ssę*) *cukierek*, *tabletkę*: suck; ***~ pierś matki*** nurse, suck one's mother's breast; ***~ palec*** suck one's thumb
ssak *m* (*-ka*; *-ki*) mammal
ssący *adj* **1.** *organy*: suctorial **2.** *pompa*: suction
stabilizacja *f* (*-ji*; *no pl*) *Br* stabilisation, *Am* stabilization
stabilizować ⟨**u-**⟩ (*-zuję*) *sytuację*, *gospodarkę*: *Br* stabilise, *Am* stabilize; ***stabilizować się*** (*o sytuacji*, *pogodzie*) *Br* stabilise, *Am* stabilize
stabilny *adj* stable, firm
stacja *f* (*-ji*; *-je*) station; ***~ kolejowa*** railway station; ***~ metra*** *Br* tube station, *Am* subway station; ***~ końcowa*** terminus, terminal station; ***~ benzynowa*** *Br* filling station, *Br* petrol station, *Am* gas station; ***~ meteorologiczna*** weather station; ***~ nadawcza*** *RADIO* broadcasting station; ***~ satelitarna*** *ASTR* satellite station; ***~ dysków*** *INF* disc drive
stacjonarn|y *adj*: ***studia ~e*** intramural studies, full-time studies; ***komputer ~y*** desktop computer, PC
stacjonować *v/im* (*-nuję*) be stationed
stacyjka *f* (*-ki*; *-ki*) **1.** *dim* little station **2.** *AUTO* ignition switch, ignition lock
staczać ⟨**stoczyć**⟩ (*-czam*) *belki*: roll; ***staczać się*** **1.** (*sturlać się*) roll down **2.** *fig* go downhill; ***~ się na dno*** go to the dogs, hit rock bottom
stać[1] *v/im* (*stoję*) **1.** (*o osobie*, *rzeczy*) stand; ***~ prosto*** stand straight; ***~ w korku*** be stuck in a traffic jam; ***~ na głowie*** *SPORT* stand on one's head; ***~ na warcie*** keep guard, keep watch, *Am* stand sentry; ***~ w miejscu*** stand still; ***~!***, ***stój!*** halt!; hold it!; ***jak sprawy stoją?*** how are things?; ***po czyjej stoisz stronie?*** which side are you on? **2.** (*o zegarku*) have stopped **3.** (*o windzie*) stand still **4.** (*o maszynie*, *zakładzie*) be at a standstill
stać[2] *v/irreg*: ***~ go na hotel*** he can afford a hotel; ***nie ~ mnie na to*** I can't afford it
stać się *v/p* (*staję*) (*zajść*) happen; ***co się stało?*** what's the matter?; ***co się stało z...?*** what happened with...?; ***nic ci się nie stanie*** nothing's going to happen to you, you'll be ok; ***stało się coś złego*** something bad has happened; ***dobrze się stało, że*** it's a good thing that; ***stał się cud*** it was a miracle; → ***stawać się***
stadion *m* (*-nu*; *-ny*) stadium
stadnina *f* (*-ny*; *-ny*) stud (farm)
stadn|y *adj*: ***instynkt ~y*** herd instinct; ***zwierzę ~e*** gregarious animal, herd animal; ***prowadzić ~y tryb życia*** live in a herd
stado *n* (*-da*; *-da*) **1.** *owiec*, *ptaków*: flock **2.** *wilków*: pack **3.** *lwów*: pride **4.** *bydła*, *słoni*: herd
stagnacja *f* (*-ji*; *no pl*) stagnation
stajać *v/p* → ***tajać***
stajnia *f* (*-ni*; *-nie*) stable
stal *f* (*-li*; *no pl*) steel; ***twardy jak ~*** as hard as nails, as hard as steel
stale *adv* constantly, incessantly
stali → ***stały***
stalinowski *adj* Stalinist
stalownia *f* (*-ni*; *-nie*) steelworks *sing*; **stalowoszary** *adj Br* steel-grey, *Am* steel-gray; **stalow|y** *adj* **1.** (*ze stali*)

steel; **~e nerwy** nerves of steel **2.** *kolor*: *Br* steel-grey, *Am* steel-gray
stalówka *f* (*-ki*; *-ki*) nib
stała *f* (*-łej*; *-łe*) *MATH* constant
stało się → ***stawać się***
stałociepln|y *adj* *BIOL* warm-blooded, homothermal; ***zwierzę ~e*** warm-blooded animal, endotherm
stałość *f* (*-ści*; *no pl*) constancy
stał|y *adj* **1.** *PHYS* solid; ***~y ląd*** mainland; ***prąd ~y*** *PHYS* direct current **2.** *temperatura*, *wartość*, *postęp*: constant **3.** *uczucie*, *charakter*, *pogoda*: stable **4.** *dochód*, *posada*, *współpracownik*, *adres*: permanent; ***mieć ~ą posadę*** have a permanent job; ***na ~e*** for good; ***~e miejsce zamieszkania*** permanent address; ***bez ~ego miejsca zamieszkania*** of no fixed abode **5.** *cena*, *koszty*: fixed **6.** *komisja*, *zaproszenie*: standing **7.** *gość*, *klient*, *publiczność*: regular
stamtąd *pron* from there
stan *m* (*-nu*; *-ny*) **1.** (*forma*, *postać*) state; ***~ zdrowia*** health condition; ***~ duchowy*** state of mind; ***~ pogody*** weather conditions; ***~ wody*** water level; ***~ średni*** *HIST* middle class; ***~ kasy*** balance in hand, cash in balance, cash in hand; ***~ rzeczy*** circumstance, matter of fact; ***w dobrym ~ie*** in good condition; ***być w ~ie*** be able to; ***żyć ponad ~*** live beyond one's means; ***~ cywilny*** marital status; ***~ konta*** *FIN* account balance; ***być w odmiennym ~ie*** be expecting, be in the family way **2.** (*talia*) waist **3.** (*tułów*) trunk
stanąć *v/p* (*staję*) (*o rzece*) freeze; ***stanęło na tym, że*** it was decided that, ***na czym stanęliśmy?*** where did we leave off?; ***~ na wysokości zadania*** rise to the occasion; ***~ w ogniu*** be on fire; ***~ w martwym punkcie*** get to a dead end, come to a standstill; → ***stawać***
stancj|a *f* (*-ji*; *-je*) lodgings *pl*, *Br* digs *pl*; ***mieszkać na ~i*** live in digs, live in lodgings
standard *m* (*-du*; *-dy*) standard; ***~ życia*** standard of living; **standardowy** *adj* standard
standaryzacja (*-ji*; *no pl*) *Br* standardisation, *Am* standardization
standaryzować *v/im* (*-zuję*) *Br* standardise, *Am* standardize
stanieć *v/p* → ***tanieć***
stanik *m* (*-ka*; *-ki*) **1.** (*biustonosz*) bra, brassiere **2.** (*część stroju*) bodice
staniol *m* (*-lu*; *no pl*) tinfoil, silver-paper
stanowczo *adv* firmly; → ***stanowczy***
stanowczość *f* (*-ści*; *no pl*) firmness
stanowczy *adj* **1.** *osoba*, *decyzja*: firm **2.** *odmowa*, *sprzeciw*: outright, flat, blunt **3.** *ton*: commanding, firm
stanowić (*-wię*) **1.** *problem*, *zagrożenie*: present, be **2.** *wyjątek*: constitute **3.** (*decydować*) determine **4.** ⟨**u-**⟩ (*ustanawiać*) make; ***~ prawo*** make law
stanowisk|o *n* (*-ka*; *-ka*) **1.** (*posada*) position, post; ***~o pracy*** place of work; ***~o kierownicze*** managerial position; ***wysokie ~o*** high-ranking position; ***objąć ~o*** take up a position **2.** (*pogląd*) point of view, standpoint; ***stać na ~u, że*** take the view that **3.** location; ***~o słoneczne*** sunny place
stanowy *adj* **1.** *HIST* class **2.** *POLIT* state
Stany *pl* (*-nów*): ***~ Zjednoczone*** the United States
stapiać ⟨**stopić**⟩ (*-piam*) **1.** *śnieg*: thaw **2.** *masło*: melt **3.** *TECH* fuse together; ***stapiać się*** (*o śniegu*) thaw
starać się ⟨**po-**⟩ (*-ram*) try; ***~ o*** *A* apply for; ***on stara się o pracę*** he's looking for a job
stara|nia *pl* (*-rań*) efforts, *Br* endeavours, *Am* endeavors; ***dołożyć wszelkich ~ń, żeby*** make every effort to, do one's best to; ***nie szczędzić ~ń*** spare no pains; ***czynić ~nia*** seek, try
staranność *f* (*-ści*; *no pl*) care, accuracy; **staranny** *adj* **1.** (*dbały*, *sumienny*) careful, conscientious **2.** *ubiór*, *język*: neat
starcie *n* (*-cia*; *-cia*) **1.** (*bitwa*) clash, scuffle **2.** (*sprzeczka*) squabble **3.** *SPORT* round **4.** *MED* abrasion
starcy *pl* → ***starzec***
starczać ⟨**-czyć**⟩ (*-czam*) suffice
starcz|y *adj* senile; ***niedołęstwo ~e*** senility
starczyć *v/p* → ***starczać***
stare *n* (*-rego*; *no pl*): ***wszystko po ~mu*** everything is as before; ***po ~mu*** as before, as usual

staro *adv* old; ***wyglądać ~*** look old
starocerkiewny *adj* Old Church
staro|ć *f* (*-roci*; *-rocie*) junk, old stuff; ***targ ~ci*** antiques fair
starodawny *adj* ancient; **starodruk** *m* (*-ku*; *-ki*) old print; **starodrzew** *m* (*-wu*; *-wy*) old trees *pl*, old-growth forest
starogrecki *adj* ancient Greek, classical Greek
starokawalerski *adj* old-bachelorish; **staromiejski** *adj* old town; **staromodny** *adj* old-fashioned; **staropanieński** *adj* old-maidish
staropolsk|i *adj* Old Polish; ***po ~u*** in the Old Polish manner
starorzecze *n* (*-cza*; *-cza*) oxbow (lake)
starosta *m* (*-ty*; *-towie*) **1.** district governor **2.** *grupy*: foreman **3.** HIST starost; **starościna** *f* (*-ny*; *-ny*) **1.** *grupy*: forewoman **2.** HIST starost's wife
staroś|ć *f* (*-ści*; *no pl*) old age; ***późna ~ć*** advanced age, old age; ***na ~ć*** for old age, in one's old age; ***do późnej ~ci*** till old age; ***ze ~ci*** of old age; ***spłowiały ze ~ci*** faded with age
staroświecki *adj* old-fashioned
starowina *f/m* (*-ny*; *-ny*), **starowinka** *f/m* (*-ki*; *-ki*) **1.** (*staruszka*) old woman, granny **2.** (*staruszek*) old man
starozakonny *adj* Old Testament
starożytność *f* (*-ści*; *no pl*) antiquity; **starożytny** *adj* **1.** antique **2.** (*stary*) ancient
starówka *f* (*-ki*; *-ki*) Old Town
starsi → ***starszy***
starszak *m* (*-ka*; *-ki*) preschooler, *Am* senior kindergarten pupil; **starszaw|y** *adj* elderly, oldish; ***~a osoba*** elderly person
starszeństw|o *n* (*-wa*; *no pl*) seniority; ***według ~a*** according to age
starsz|y **I** *adj comp* → ***stary*** **1.** older; ***moja ~a siostra*** my elder sister **2.** (*w hierarchii*) superior **II** *m* (*-szego*; *-si*) elder
starszyzna *f* (*-ny*; *no pl*) the elders *pl*
start *m* (*-tu*; *-ty*) **1.** start; ***na miejsca, gotowi, ~!*** on your marks, get set, go!; ready, steady, go! **2.** *samolotu*: take-off
starter[1] *m* (*-ra*; *-rzy*) SPORT starter
starter[2] *m* (*-ra*; *-ry*) AUTO starter
startować ⟨**wy-**⟩ (*-tuję*) **1.** start **2.** (*o samolocie*) take off; ***~ do G*** *infml* try to pick s.o. up
startowy *adj* starting; ***pas ~*** runway
starty *adj* **1.** *warzywa*, *ser*: grated **2.** *buty*: worn out **3.** *rysunek*, *napis*: rubbed off, rubbed out, worn off
starusz|ek *m* (*-szka*; *-szkowie*) old man; ***~kowie*** *infml* old couple; **staruszka** *f* (*-ki*; *-ki*) old woman, old lady
star|y *adj* old; ***~e miasto*** Old Town; ***~y jak świat*** (as) old as the hills; ***~y koń*** *fig* old chap; ***~y znajomy*** old friend; ***S~y Testament*** REL Old Testament
starzec *m* (*starca*; *starcy*) old man
starzeć się ⟨**po-**, **ze-**⟩ (*-rzeję*) (*o osobie*) grow old, get old; ***starzejące się społeczeństwo*** aging society **2.** TECH wear out **3.** (*dezaktualizować się*) expire, become outdated
starzej *adv comp* → ***staro*** older
starzenie (się) *n* (*-nia*; *no pl*) growing old
starzy → ***stary***
starzyzn|a *f* (*-ny*; *no pl*) junk, rubbish; ***handlarz ~ą*** junk-dealer, old-clothesman; ***sklep ze ~ą*** junk shop, junk store
stateczny *adj* **1.** *osoba*: sedate, staid **2.** *życie*: orderly, peaceful **3.** *łódź*: stable
stat|ek *m* (*-tku*; *-tki*) ship; ***~ek handlowy*** merchant, trader; ***~ek dalekomorski*** deep-sea ship; ***na ~ku*** aboard, on board; ***~kiem*** by ship
statua *f* (*-tuy*/*-tui*; *-tuy*) statue; **statuetka** *f* (*-ki*; *-ki*) statuette
statut *m* (*-tu*; *-ty*) statutes *pl*, rules and regulations *pl*; **statutowy** *adj* statutory
statyczny *adj* static; **statyka** *f* (*-ki*; *no pl*) statics *sing*
statysta *m* (*-ty*; *statyści*), **-tka** *f* (*-ki*; *-ki*) FILM extra
statystyczny *adj* statistic; **statystyka** *f* (*-ki*; *-ki*) statistics *sing*
statyw *m* (*-wu*; *-wy*) PHOT tripod
staw *m* (*-wu*; *-wy*) **1.** (*z rybami*) pond; ***~ hodowlany*** **a)** fishpond **b)** (*do hodowli narybku*) nursery **2.** ANAT joint; ***ból w ~ach*** pain in the joints
stawać ⟨**stanąć**⟩ (*staję*) **1.** (*podnosić się*) stand up; ***~ oko w oko z kimś*** con

S

front s.o.; ***noga ludzka tu nigdy nie stanęła*** no human foot has ever trodden on this land; **~ *na palcach*** stand on one's toes; **~ *w rozkroku*** stand astride, stand with one's legs apart; **~ *przed*** *I*, **~ *wobec*** *G fig* face; **~ *komuś na przeszkodzie*** *fig* stand in s.o.'s way; **~ *na głowie*** *fig* do one's best, do all one can; **~ *okoniem*** *fig* refuse firmly, *Am* stand pat, stand one's ground **2.** (*zatrzymać się*) stop **3.** (*o produkcji*) stop, stand idle **4.** (*o budynku*) be built, be erected **5.** (*nadepnąć*) step (***na*** *A* on)

stawać się ⟨**-tać**⟩ (*-taję*) become

stawiać ⟨**postawić**⟩ (*-wiam*) **1.** (*kłaść*) put; **~ *na swoim*** have one's way; **~ *coś pod zakiem zapytania*** call s.th. into question; **~ *kogoś w trudnej sytuacji*** put s.o. on the spot, put s.o. out; **~ *sprawę na ostrzu noża*** bring matters to a head; **~ *kogoś przed faktem dokonanym*** present s.o. with a fait accompli **2.** (*podnosić*) raise **3.** (*budować*) put up, build **4.** *warunki*: impose, lay down **5.** *diagnozę*: make, give **6.** *tezę*: advance **7.** *samochód*: park **8.** *pomnik*: put up, erect **9.** *kołnierz*: turn up, raise **10.** *przecinek*: put **11.** *żagle*: set **12.** (*fundować*) stand, treat (***komuś*** *A* s.o. to); **~ *kolejkę*** stand a round; ***stawiać się*** **1.** (*sprzeciwiać się*) put one's foot down **2.** (*budować*) build a house

stawić *v/p* (*-wię*): **~ *komuś czoła*** confront s.o., stand up to s.o.

stawić się *v/p* (*-wię*) appear

stawiennictw|o *n* (*-wa*; *no pl*) appearance; ***nakaz ~a*** summons

stawk|a *f* (*-ki*; *-ki*) **1.** (*w grze*) stake; ***~ą jest jego życie*** *fig* his life is at stake **2.** (*suma*) rate; ***~a za godzinę*** hourly rate; ***~a podatkowa*** rate of taxation

stawow|y *adj* ANAT articular; ***maź ~a*** synovia

staż *m* (*-żu*; *-że*) **1.** (*praktyka*) internship **2.** *nauczycielski*: training; **~ *naukowy*** research fellowship **3.** (*okres pracy*): **~ *pracy*** seniority; ***na podstawie ~u pracy*** on the basis of seniority, by seniority

stażysta *m* (*-ty*; *-żyści*), **-tka** *f* (*-ki*; *-ki*) **1.** (*nauczyciel*, *elektryk*, *dentysta*) trainee **2.** (*lekarz*, *dziennikarz*, *urzędnik*) intern

stąd **I** *pron* from here **II** *conj* (*dlatego*) hence

stąpać *v/im* (*-pam*) *lit* tread, step; **~ *na palcach*** walk on tiptoe(s); ***mocno ~ po ziemi*** have one's feet (firmly) on the ground

stąpnąć *v/p* → ***stąpać***

stchórzyć *v/p* → ***tchórzyć***

stearynowy *adj* stearic

stebnować → ***stębnować***; **stebnowany** → ***stębnowany***

stek *m* (*-ku*; *-ki*) COOK steak; **~ *kłamstw*** pack of lies; **~ *wyzwisk*** torrent of abuse

stelaż *m* (*-żu*; *-że*) **1.** (*rama*) frame, rack; ***plecak ze ~em*** *Br* external-frame rucksack, *Am* external-frame backpack **2.** (*podstawka*) (music-) stand

stempel *m* (*-pla*; *-ple*) **1.** (*do pieczątek*) stamp; **~ *pocztowy*** postmark **2.** MIN prop; **stemplować** ⟨**o-**⟩ (*-luję*) stamp

stenograf *m* (*-fa*; *-fowie*) stenographer; **stenografować** *v/im* (*-fuję*) take down in shorthand, stenograph

step *m* (*-pu*; *-py*) steppe

ster *m* (*-ru*; *-ry*) rudder; ***być u ~u*** *fig* be at the helm, be the leader

sterany *adj* **1.** (*zapracowany*) jaded, worn out by work **2.** *zdrowie*: broken, ruined

sterczący *adj* **1.** *wydatny*: protruding, sticking out **2.** *uszy*, *brzuch*: sticking out **3.** (*wystający*) sticking out; ***chusteczka stercząca z kieszeni marynarki*** handkerchief sticking out of his jacket pocket

sterczeć *v/im* (*-czę*) **1.** (*o uszach*, *nogach*) stick out **2.** (*o brzegu*, *zębach*) protrude

stereofoniczny *adj* stereophonic

stereotypowy *adj* stereotypical

sternik *m* (*-ka*; *-nicy*) helmsman; **~ *automatyczny*** **a)** (*w samolocie*) automatic pilot **b)** (*na statku*) gyropilot

sterować *v/im* (*-ruję*) **1.** *statkiem*: helm **2.** *samolotem*: pilot **3.** (*kierować*) steer **4.** *gospodarką*: control

sterowanie *n* (*-nia*; *no pl*) steering; ***zdalne*** **~** remote control

sterowany *adj*: ***zdalnie ~*** remote controlled; ***ręcznie ~*** manually controlled
sterownia *f (-ni; -nie)* **1.** *(na statku)* pilot house **2.** *(w fabryce)* control room; **sterowniczy** *adj*: ***pulpit ~*** control panel; **sterownik** *m (-ka; -ki)* INF driver; **sterowny** *adj* navigable, controllable
sterroryzować *v/p* → ***terroryzować***
sterta *f (-ty; -ty)* **1.** *śmieci*: heap **2.** *trocin, bagażu, papierów*: pile **3.** *siana*: mow **4.** *gnoju*: midden, hill **5.** *gazet, przesądów, monet*: stack
sterylizacja *m (-ji; no pl)* sterilization; **sterylizować** ⟨**wy-**⟩ *(-zuję)* sterilize
sterylny *adj* sterile
stetryczały *adj* grumpy, surly, ill-tempered
steward *m (-da; -dzi)* steward, flight attendant; **stewardessa** *f (-sy; -sy)* stewardess, flight attendant
stębnować, ***stebnować*** ⟨**o-**⟩ *(-nuję)* *materiał*: quilt
stębnowany, ***stębnowany*** *adj* quilted
stęchlizn|a *f (-ny; no pl)* fustiness, *Br* mouldiness, *Am* moldiness, must; ***czuć ~ą*** it smells of fustiness; **stęchły** *adj* fusty, musty; **stęchnąć** *v/p (-nę)* grow fusty, become fusty
stękać ⟨**-knąć**⟩ *(-kam)* groan, moan; **stęknięcie** *n (-cia; -cia)* groan, moan
stęp *m (-pa; no pl) konia*: walk; ***jechać ~a*** walk
stępiać ⟨**-pić**⟩ *(-piam)* blunt
stępieć *v/p* → ***tępieć***
stępiony *adj* blunt
stęsknić się *v/p (-nię)* long (**za** *I* for), hanker (**za** *I* after); ***stęsknił się za nią*** he misses her a lot; **stęskniony** *adj* longing, hankering
stężały *adj* hardened
stężeć *v/p* → ***tężeć***
stężenie *n (-nia; no pl)* CHEM concentration; ***~ pośmiertne*** rigor mortis; **stężony** CHEM concentrated
stiuk *m (-ku; -ki)* ARCHIT stucco
stłamsić *v/p* → ***tłamsić***
stłocz|ony *adj*: ***ludzie ~eni w tramwaju*** people cooped up in a tram; ***ludzie ~eni w windzie*** people crammed in a lift
stłoczyć *v/p (-czę)* cram, coop up
stłuc *v/p* → ***tłuc***
stłuczenie *n (-nia; -nia)* MED bruise, contusion
stłuczka *f (-ki; -ki)* **1.** AUTO bump, fender bender **2.** *(stłuczone szkło)* cullet **3.** *(przedmiot)* breakages *pl*
stłumić *v/p* → ***tłumić***
stłumiony *adj* **1.** *głos*: muffled **2.** *kolor, światło*: subdued
sto *num* a hundred, one hundred; ***na ~ procent*** one hundred percent, for sure; ***~ razy*** a hundred times; ***na ~ dwa*** first-rate, A-one perfect; ***~ lat!*** many happy returns (of the day)!
stocznia *f (-ni; -nie)* shipyard; **stoczniowiec** *m (-wca; -wcy)* shipyard worker; **stoczniowy** *adj przemysł*: shipbuilding
stoczyć *v/p (-czę)*: ***~ bitwę*** fight a battle; → ***staczać***
stodoła *f (-ły; -ły)* barn
stogi *pl* → ***stóg***
stoi → ***stać***[1]
stoicki *adj*: ***~ spokój*** stoical attitude
stoisko *n (-ka; -ka)* **1.** *(dział sklepu)* department **2.** *(na kiermaszu)* stand, stall; ***~ z książkami*** bookstall; ***~ z warzywami*** greengrocery
stojak *m (-ka; -ki)* stand; ***~ na kwiaty*** flower stand; ***~ na rowery*** (cycle) rack
stojąco *adv*: ***na ~*** standing (up)
stojąc|y *adj* **1.** *(na stojąco)* standing; ***woda ~a*** stagnant water; ***mieć ~ą pracę*** have a job in which you need to stand a lot; ***miejsca ~e*** *(w autobusie)* standing room; ***zegar ~y*** grandfather clock **2.** *pozycja*: upright
stok *m (-ku; -ki)* slope
stokrotka *f (-ki; -ki)* daisy
stokrotn|y *adj* hundredfold; ***~e dzięki!*** thanks a million!
stolarka *f (-ki; no pl)* **1.** *(rzemiosło)* carpentry **2.** *budowlana*: woodwork; **stolarnia** *f (-ni; -nie)* carpenter's workshop; **stolarstwo** *n (-wa; no pl)* carpentry; **stolarz** *m (-rza; -rze)* carpenter
stolcow|y *adj*: ***kiszka ~a*** ANAT rectum
stolec *m (-lca; -lce)* MED stool; ***oddać ~ do badania*** have one's stool examined; ***regularny ~*** regular stool
stolica *f (-cy; -ce)* capital; ***~ Apostolska*** the Holy See
stolik *m (-ka; -ki) dim* (small) table; ***zarezerwować ~*** book a table; ***~ pod telewizor*** TV table

stolnica *f* (*-cy*; *-ce*) pastry board
stołeczny *adj* capital
stołek (*-łka*; *-łki*) stool; **~ barowy** bar stool
stołować *v/im* (*-łuję*) *gości*: board; **stołować się** board (**u** *G* at/with); **~ się w pensjonacie** eat one's meals in a guest-house
stołow|y **I** *adj* **1.** *noga*, *nakrycie*: table; **łyżka ~a** tablespoon; **zastawa ~a** tableware **2.** *pokój*: dining **II** *m* (*-wego*; *-we*) (*pokój stołowy*) dining room
stołówka *f* (*-ki*; *-ki*) *zakładowa*: canteen
stoły *pl* → **stół**
stomatologia *f* (*-gii*; *no pl*) dentistry
stomatologiczn|y *adj* dental; **przychodnia ~a** dental clinic; **fotel ~y** dental chair; **studia ~e** dentistry; **gabinet ~y** dentist's (surgery)
stonka *f* (*-ki*; *-ki*): **~ ziemniaczana** Colorado beetle
stonoga *f* (*-gi*; *-gi*) woodlouse
stonowany *adj kolor*, *światło*: subdued
stop[1] *m* (*-pu*; *-py*) alloy
stop[2]: **~!** hold it!, stop!; **jechać ~em** *infml* hitchhike
stop|a *f* (*-py*; *-py*) **1.** *ANAT* foot; **~a metryczna** foot; **u stóp góry** at the foot of the mountain; **od stóp do głów** from head to toe; **na ~ie koleżeńskiej** on friendly terms; **żyć na wojennej ~ie** be on bad terms; **paść komuś do stóp** fall at s.o.'s feet **2.** *ECON* rate; **~a życiowa** standard of living; **~a procentowa** interest rate
stoper *m* (*-ra*; *-ry*) stopwatch
stopić *v/p* → **stapiać**
stop|ień *m* (*-pnia*; *-pnie*) **1.** *schodów*: stair, step **2.** (*ocena*) *Br* mark, *Am* grade **3.** (*jednostka miary*) degree; **~ień naukowy** degree; **~ień wyższy** comparative degree, the comparative; **~ień najwyższy** superlative degree, the superlative; **poparzenie pierwszego** (**drugiego**) **~nia** *MED* first-degree (second-degree) burn; **do tego ~nia, że** to such a degree that **4.** (*ranga*) rank **5.** (*rozmiar*) extent; **w dużym ~niu** to a large extent; **w mniejszym ~niu** to a lesser extent; **w pewnym ~niu** to a certain extent, to a certain degree **6.** (*poziom*) level; **~ień rozwoju** development phase; **~ień trudności** level of difficulty
stopiony *adj masło*: melted
stopka *f* (*-ki*; *-ki*) copyright note
stopniały *adj śnieg*, *lód*: thawed, melted
stopniować *v/im* (*-niuję*) **1.** *trudności*, *wymagania*: (gradually) increase **2.** *przymiotniki*: compare **3.** *kolor*: gradate
stopniowo *adv* gradually; **stopniowy** *adj* gradual
stopować ⟨**za-**⟩ (*-puję*) put paid (*A* to), stop
storczyk *m* (*-ka*; *-ki*) orchid
stornować *v/p* (*-nuję*) (*poprawiać błąd w księgach*) correct
storpedować *v/p* → **torpedować**
story *pl* (*stor*) blinds, curtains
stos *m* (*-su*; *-sy*) **1.** (*kupa*) heap, pile **2.** (*ułożony*) stack; **układać w ~** stack **3.** (*do spalenia*) pyre **4.** *HIST* stake; **spalić kogoś na ~ie** burn s.o. at the stake
stosować ⟨**za-**⟩ (*-suję*) **1.** *metody*, *leczenie*: apply **2.** *przemoc*: resort (*A* to) **3.** (*używać*) use **4.** *taktykę*, *metodę*: employ; **stosować się 1.** (*przestrzegać*) comply (**do** *G* with) **2.** (*odnosić się*) apply (**do** *G* to)
stosowany *adj sztuka*, *nauka*: applied
stosownie *adv* **1.** (*odpowiednio*) appropriately, suitably; **~ wykształcony** appropriately educated; **~ do wymogów** as required **2.** (*przyzwoicie*) properly; **stosown|y** *adj* appropriate; **w ~ej chwili** in the suitable instant; **uważać za ~e** see fit, think fit
stosun|ek *m* (*-nku*; *-nki*) **1.** (*relacja*) relationship; **~ki a)** (*warunki*) conditions **b)** (*kontakty*) connections **c)** (*relacje*) relationships; **mieć ~ki** have connections; **~ek płciowy** sexual intercourse, sex act; **~ek przerywany** coitus interruptus; **w ~ku do** *G* in relation to; **w ~ku do mnie** towards me; **być w dobrych ~kach z** *I* have a good relationship with, be on good terms with, get on well with **2.** (*nastawienie*) attitude (**do** *G* to/towards)
stosunkowy *adj* relative
stowarzyszać się ⟨**-szyć**⟩ (*-szam*) associate, form an association
stowarzyszenie *n* (*-nia*; *-nia*) association; **~ przedsiębiorców** trade association; **tajne ~** secret association;

S

stowarzyszony *adj* organized (***w*** *A* in); ***członek ~*** associate member
stożek *m* (*-żka*; *-żki*) cone; ***~ wulkaniczny*** volcanic cone; **stożkowaty** *adj* cone-shaped, conical
stóg *m* (*stogu*; *stogi*) stack; ***~ siana*** haystack, hayrick
stój → ***stać***[1]
stójka *f* (*-ki*; *-ki*) standing collar, stand-up collar
stół *m* (*stołu*; *stoły*) table; ***~ biesiadny*** banquet table; ***~ weselny*** wedding table; ***~ operacyjny*** operating table; ***przy stole*** at the table
stówa *f* (*-wy*; *-wy*), **stówka** *f* (*-ki*; *-ki*) *infml* a hundred
str. *abbr* **1.** (= **strona**) p., pg. **2.** (= **strony**) pp.
strace|nie *n* (*-nia*; *-nia*) execution; ***miejsce ~ń*** place of execution; ***nie mieć nic do ~nia*** have nothing to lose; ***nie mieć czasu do ~nia*** have no time to lose
strace|niec *m* (*-ceńca*; *-ceńcy*) desperado; ***oddział ~ńców*** suicide squad; **straceńcz|y** *adj* foolhardy, undaunted by death
strach *m* (*-chu*; *-chy*) fear; ***śmiertelny ~*** mortal fear; ***~y*** (*zjawy*) *Br* spectres, *Am* specters, ghosts; ***~ na wróble*** scarecrow; ***ze ~u*** with fear; ***~ było patrzeć*** one was afraid to look; ***aż ~ pomyśleć*** I shudder to think; ***mieć ~a*** have cold feet; ***robić w portki ze ~u*** *infml* shit one's pants with fear
strachliwy *adj* faint-hearted, timid
stracić *v/p* → ***tracić***
stracon|y *adj* **1.** (*zagubiony*) lost; ***jeszcze nic ~ego*** all is not yet lost **2.** (*skazany*) executed
stragan *m* (*-nu*; *-ny*) stall, stand; ***~ z kwiatami*** flower stall; ***~ z warzywami*** vegetable stall, greengrocery
straganiarka *f* (*-ki*; *-ki*), **~niarz** *m* (*-rza*; *-rze*) stallholder
strajk *m* (*-ku*; *-ki*) strike; ***~ głodowy*** hunger strike; ***~ powszechny*** general strike; ***~ ostrzegawczy*** warning strike, token strike
strajkować ⟨**za-**⟩ (*-kuję*) strike
strajkowy *adj* strike
strajkujący **I** *adj* striking **II** *m* (*-cego*; *-cy*), **-ca** *f* (*-cej*; *-ce*) striker
strapić *v/p* → ***trapić***
strapienie *n* (*-nia*; *-nia*) *lit* grief; **strapiony** *adj* gloomy, distressed
straszak *m* (*-ka*; *-ki*) (*pistolet*) toy gun
straszliwy *adj* dreadful, terrible, awful
straszn|y *adj* dreadful, terrible, horrible; ***~e pieniądze*** a hell of a lot of money; ***nie taki diabeł ~y, jak go malują*** the devil is not so black as he is painted
straszyć ⟨**po-**⟩ (*-szę*) frighten, scare; ***tu straszy*** the place is haunted
straszydło *n* (*-ła*; *-ła*) fright, monster; ***wyglądać jak ~*** look a fright
strat|a *f* (*-ty*; *-ty*) **1.** loss; ***~y finansowe*** financial loss; ***~y materialne*** material losses; ***ze ~ą*** *FIN* at a loss; ***ponieść ~ę*** suffer a loss; ***po stracie ojca*** after losing one's father; ***~y w ludziach*** casualties **2.** *czasu*, *pieniędzy*: waste
strategia *f* (*-gii*; *-gie*) strategy; **strategiczny** *adj* strategic
stratny *adj*: ***być ~m*** *FIN* make a loss
stratować *v/p* → ***tratować***
strawa *f* (*-wy*; *no pl*): ***~ duchowa*** food for thought, intellectual nourishment
strawić *v/p* → ***trawić***
strawny *adj*: ***lekko~*** easy to digest; ***ciężko~*** difficult to digest
straż *f* (*-ży*; *-że*) guard, *Am* sentry; ***~ pożarna*** fire brigade; ***~ graniczna*** border guard; ***~ przyboczna*** personal guard; ***~ przednia*** advance guard, ***~ tylna*** rear guard; ***trzymać ~*** be on guard, keep guard; ***trzymać pod ~ą*** keep under guard
strażack|i *adj* fireman's; ***wóz ~i*** fire engine; ***remiza ~a*** fire station
strażak *m* (*-ka*; *-żacy*) fireman
strażnica *f* (*-cy*; *-ce*) watchtower; ***~ zamkowa*** *HIST* castle watchtower
strażniczka *f* (*-ki*; *-ki*) *więzienna*: wardress, prison guard; **strażnik** *m* (*-ka -nicy*) *więzienny*: warder, prison guard; ***~ graniczny*** border guard
strącać ⟨**-cić**⟩ (*-cam*) **1.** (*strząsać*) shake off **2.** *samolot*: shoot down
strączek *m* (*-czka*; *-czki*) pod, legume
strączkow|y *adj*: ***rośliny ~e*** legumes, leguminous plants
strąk *m* (*-ka*; *-ki*) pod, legume
strefa *f* (*-fy*; *-fy*) *klimatyczna*, *przygraniczna*, *czasowa*: zone; ***szara ~*** *fig* black economy, (economic) twilight

S

zone; ~ ***działań wojennych*** military operations zone; **strefowy** *adj* zonal

stremowany *adj* nervous, jittery

stres *m* (*-su*; *-sy*) stress

stresować ⟨**ze-**⟩ (*-suję*) stress, put under stress; **stresowy** *adj sytuacja*: stressful; **stresujący** *adj* stressful

streszczać ⟨**-reścić**⟩ (*-czam*) *Br* summarise, *Am* summarize; ***streszczać się*** be brief, cut a long story short; ***streszczaj się!*** keep it short!, be brief!

streszczenie *n* (*-nia*; *-nia*) **1.** *sytuacji*: summary **2.** *wydarzeń*: résumé **3.** *filmu*: synopsis **4.** *publikacji naukowej*: abstract

streścić *v/p* → ***streszczać***

stręczyciel *m* (*-la*; *-le*) pimp; **stręczycielstwo** *n* (*-wa*; *no pl*) procuration, pimping

striptiz *m* (*-zu*; *-zy*) striptease; **striptizerka** *f* (*-ki*; *-ki*) stripper

strofa *f* (*-fy*; *-fy*) *lit* stanza, verse

strofować *v/im* (*-fuję*) scold, rebuke

stroiciel *m* (*-la*; *-le*) MUS tuner

stroić ⟨**wy-**⟩ (*-roję*) **1.** (*ubierać*) dress up; ~ ***miny*** make faces, pull faces; ~ ***sobie żarty z*** *G* make fun of **2.** (*dekorować*) decorate, embellish **3.** MUS RADIO tune; ***stroić się*** dress up; ***wystroić się*** get spruced up

stroik *m* (*-ka*; *-ki*) **1.** (*na stole*) table decoration **2.** (*na głowie*) headdress **3.** MUS reed

stroje *pl* → ***strój***

strojnisia *f* (*-si*; *-sie*) *Br* glamour puss; **strojniś** *m* (*-nisia*; *-nisie*) dandy, clotheshorse

strojny *adj lit* decorated, chic

stromizna *f* (*-ny*; *-ny*) *zbocza*: steep slope

stromy *adj* steep

stron|a *f* (*-ny*; *-ny*) **1.** (*bok*) side; ~***a świata*** quarter of the world; ~***y rodzinne*** homeland; ***dalekie*** ~***y*** a long way off; ***z naszych*** ~ from where we live; ***udać się na*** ~***ę*** (*do toalety*) go to relieve oneself; ***ze*** ~***y*** on the part of, from; ***w*** ~***ę*** *G* in the direction of; ***z jednej*** ~***y... z drugiej*** ~***y*** on the one hand... on the other hand **2.** page; ~***a internetowa*** web page **3.** JUR party **4.** GRAM voice; ~***a czynna*** active voice; ~***a bierna*** passive voice

stronica *f* (*-cy*; *-ce*) *lit książki*: page

stronić *v/im* (*-nię*) shun (**od** *G*); ***nie stroni od alkoholu*** he is partial to alcohol

stronnictwo *n* (*-wa*; *-wa*) POLIT party; **stronniczka** *f* (*-ki*; *-ki*) backer, supporter; **stronniczość** *f* (*-ści*; *no pl*) bias, partiality; **stronniczy** *adj* partial, prejudiced, bias(s)ed; **stronnik** *m* (*-ka*; *-nicy*) follower, supporter

stront *m* (*-tu*; *no pl*) CHEM strontium

strop *m* (*-pu*; *-py*) BUILD ceiling

stropić *v/p* (*-pię*) *lit* abash, disconcert; ***stropić się*** become abashed

stropiony *adj lit* abashed, disconcerted

stroskany *adj lit* sorrowful, troubled

stroszyć ⟨**na-**⟩ (*-szę*) *pióra*: ruffle

strój *m* (*-roju*; *-roje*) attire, dress; ~ ***ludowy*** national dress, national costume; ~ ***wieczorowy*** evening dress, evening wear; ~ ***żałobny*** mourning clothes; ~ ***kąpielowy*** *Br* swimsuit, swimming costume, *Am* bathing suit

stróż *m* (*-ża*; *-że*) **1.** (*strażnik*) guard; ***anioł*** ~ REL guardian angel **2.** (*dozorca*) caretaker; ~ ***nocny*** night watchman; **stróżówka** *f* (*-ki*; *-ki*) lodge, gatehouse

struchlały *adj lit* petrified (with horror), terrified

struchleć *v/p* → ***truchleć***

strucla *f* (*-li*; *-le*) COOK stollen (loaf)

strudzony *adj* fatigued, wearied

strug *m* (*-ga*; *-gi*) plane

struga *f* (*-gi*; *-gi*): ~ ***wody*** stream of water; ~ ***światła*** ray of light; ***płynąć*** ~***mi*** flow heavily; ***deszcz leje*** ~***mi*** the rain is coming down in buckets, it is pouring down; ***w*** ~***ch deszczu*** in pouring rain

strugaczka *f* (*-ki*; *-ki*) sharpener

strugać (*-gam*) **1.** ⟨**za-**⟩ *ołówek*: sharpen; ~ ***wariata*** play dumb, play the fool **2.** (*rzeźbić*) carve **3.** TECH plane

struktura *f* (*-ry*; *-ry*) structure; **strukturalny** *adj* structural

strumie|ń *m* (*-mienia*; *-mienie*) (*potok*) stream; ~***ń wody*** jet of water; ~***ń światła*** ray of light; ~***ń powietrza*** current of air; ~***niami*** in sheets

strumyczek *m* (*-czka*; *-czki*), **strumyk** *m* (*-ka*; *-ka*) rill, streamlet, rivulet

strun|a *f* (*-ny*; *-ny*) MUS string; ~***y głosowe*** ANAT vocal chords; ***wyprostowany***

jak ~a bolt upright, stiff as a poker; **strunowy** *adj* MUS stringed
strup *m* (*-pa*; *-py*) scab; **strupek** *m* (*-pka*; *-pki*) crust
strusi *adj* BIOL ostrich; ***~a polityka*** *fig* ostrich policy
struś *m* (*-rusia*; *-rusie*) BIOL ostrich
struty *adj*: ***chodzić jak ~*** *fig* be disheartened
strużyny *pl* (*-żyn*) (wood) shavings
strwożony *adj* scared
strych *m* (*-chu*; *-chy*) attic, loft
strycz|ek *m* (*-czka*; *-czki*) halter, noose, rope; ***zadyndać na ~ku*** dance on air
stryj *m* (*-ja*; *-jowie*) (paternal) uncle
stryjeczn|y *adj*: ***brat ~y*** first cousin, full cousin; ***siostra ~a*** first cousin, full cousin
stryjenka *f* (*-ki*; *-ki*) (paternal) uncle's wife
strzał *m* (*-łu*; *-ły*) shot; ***celny ~*** hit; ***gotowy do ~u*** ready to fire; ***~ w dziesiątkę*** *fig* bull's-eye
strzała *f* (*-ły*; *-ły*) arrow; **strzałka** *f* (*-ki*; *-ki*) **1.** (*znak*) arrow **2.** (*igła*) pointer; ***~ wodna*** BIOL arrowhead
strząsać ⟨**-snąć**⟩ (*-sam*) shake off
strzec *v/im* (*-rzegę*) **1.** *tajemnicy*: keep **2.** *domu*, *trzody*: guard; ***~ jak oka w głowie*** guard like the apple of one's eye **3.** (*chronić*) protect **4.** *granicy*: keep watch; ***strzec się*** watch out (*G* for), beware (*G* of)
strzech|a *f* (*-chy*; *-chy*) thatched roof, thatch; ***kryty ~ą*** thatched
strzelać ⟨**-lić**⟩ (*-lam*) **1.** shoot (**do** *G* at) **2.** (*o sztucznych ogniach*) go off, explode **3.** (*o korkach*) pop, shoot; ***strzelają korki od szampana*** champagne bottles are being popped open; ***~ z*** *G* shoot with; ***~ w tłum***, ***~ do tłumu*** shoot at the crowd; ***~ w górę*** *fig* shoot up, shoot in the air; ***~ z bicza*** crack one's whip; ***~ piłkę do bramki*** kick the ball into a goal; ***strzelić kogoś w twarz*** *infml* punch s.o. in the face, slap s.o. in the face
strzelanina *f* (*-ny*; *-ny*) shooting; **strzelba** *f* (*-by*; *-by*) shotgun, rifle
strzelec *m* (*-lca*; *-lcy*) **1.** (*strzelający*) shot, rifleman; ***~ wyborowy*** marksman **2.** (*zdobywca bramki*) shooter, scorer **3.** ***&*** ASTR Sagittarius
strzeleck|i *adj* shooting; ***związek ~i*** rifle club; ***broń ~a*** shotguns **strzelectwo** *n* (*-wa*; *no pl*) shooting
strzelić *v/p* → **strzelać**
strzelisty *adj drzewo*, *wieża*: tapering
strzelnica *f* (*-cy*; *-ce*) **1.** (*na wolnym powietrzu*) target range **2.** (*na jarmarku*) shooting gallery; **strzelnicz|y** *adj* shooting; ***proch ~y*** gunpowder; ***tarcza ~a*** target
strzemienne *n* (*-nego*; *no pl*) one for the road; **strzemię** *n* (*-mienia*; *-miona*) stirrup
strzepywać ⟨**-pnąć**⟩ (*-puję*) *kurz*, *śnieg*: shake off, flick off
strzeżony *adj*: ***parking ~*** *Br* attended car park, *Am* attended parking lot
strzęp *m* (*-pu*; *-py*) *materiału*, *papieru*: scrap; ***~y rozmowy*** snatches of conversation; ***~y wspomnień*** snatches of memories; ***w ~ach*** in rags, in tatters; ***rozrywać kogoś na ~y*** tear s.o. limb from limb; ***został z niego ~ człowieka*** he's a wreck of a man
strzępek *m* (*-pku*; *-pki*) *dim* → **strzęp**
strzępiasty *adj* **1.** (*z nierównymi brzegami*) jagged **2.** *liść*: lacerate **3.** *chmura*: fringed
strzępić ⟨**wy-**⟩ (*-pię*): ***~ sobie język*** waste one's breath; ***strzępić się*** fray
strzyc ⟨**o-**⟩ (*-rzygę*) **1.** *włosy*: cut; ***~ uszami*** prick its ears **2.** *owce*: shear **3.** *trawę*: mow, cut **4.** *żywopłot*: trim; ***strzyc się*** have one's hair cut
strzyga *f* (*-gi*; *-gi*) lamia, vampire
strzyka|ć ⟨**-knąć**⟩ (*-kam*) **1.** (*boleć*) crick; ***~ mi w kościach*** I feel a crick in my bones **2.** (*tryskać*) spurt
strzykawka *f* (*-ki*; *-ki*) syringe
strzyknąć *v/p* → **strzykać**
strzyżenie *n* (*-nia*; *no pl*) **1.** (*obcinanie włosów*) haircut **2.** *owiec*: shearing; **strzyżony** *adj* **1.** *włosy*: cut **2.** *trawnik*: mown
strzyżyk *m* (*-ka*; *-ki*) BIOL wren
stu → **sto**
stu- (*w złożeniach*) **1.** (*żyjący sto lat*) hundred-year-old; ***~letnie drzewa*** hundred-year-old trees **2.** (*trwający sto lat*) hundred-year
studencki *adj* student, students'; ***dom ~*** *Br* hall of residence, *Am* dormitory
student *m* (*-ta*; *-nci*), **~ka** *f* (*-ki*; *-ki*) student; ***~ medycyny*** medical student;

~ *germanistyki* student of German; **~ *pierwszego roku*** first year student, fresher, freshman
studia *pl* (*-diów*) **1.** (*wyższe*) studies; **~ *medyczne*** medical studies; **~ *dzienne*** full-time studies; **~ *eksternistyczne*** auditing students' academic programme; **~ *zaoczne*** part-time studies, extramural studies; ***na ~ch*** during one's studies, at university; **~ *na uniwersytecie*** studies at university; ***być na ~ch*** study **2.** (*badania*) research
studio *n* (*-dia*; *-dia*) *RADIO* studio; **~ *nagrań*** recording studio
studiować *v/im* (*-diuję*) study; **studium** *n* (*indecl*; *-dia*) (*badanie*) study
studnia *f* (*-ni*; *-nie*) well; **~ *bez dna*** *fig* black hole
studniowy *adj* hundred-day; **studniówka** *f* (*-ki*; *-ki*) pre-graduation ball
studyjny *adj kino*, *teatr*: studio
studzić ⟨**o-**⟩ (*-dzę*) cool down, cool off; ***studzić się*** cool down, cool off
studzienka *f* (*-ki*; *-ki*) **1.** (*studnia*) well **2.** *kanalizacyjna*, *ściekowa*: drain; **studzienny** *adj* well
stugramowy *adj* hundred gram, hundred gramme
stuk *m* (*-ku*; *-ki*) **1.** *maszyny do pisania*, *kopyt*: clatter **2.** *kół*, *karabinu*, *kości*: rattle **3.** *obcasów*, *myszki*, *przycisków*: click
stukać ⟨**-knąć**⟩ (*-kam*) knock; **~ *do drzwi*** knock on the door, knock at the door; ***stukać na maszynie*** clatter at the typewriter; ***stuknąć w drzewo*** *infml* bump into a tree; ***stuknąć kogoś*** *infml* hit s.o.; ***stuknęła mu trzydziestka*** *infml* he's past (the magic) thirty; ***stukać się*** hit oneself; ***stuknij się w czoło!*** *infml* get wise!
stukanie *n* (*-nia*; *no pl*); **~ *do drzwi*** knocking at the door
stuknięty *adj infml* **1.** *osoba*: bonkers, nutty **2.** *samochód*: bumped
stukot *m* (*-tu*; *-ty*) → ***stuk***
stukotać *v/im* (*-koczę*/*-kocę*) **1.** (*o kołach*, *kopytach*) clatter **2.** (*o deszczu*) patter
stulać ⟨**-lić**⟩ (*-lam*) *płatki*: close
stulecie *n* (*-cia*; *-cia*) **1.** (*jubiluesz*) centenary **2.** (*wiek*) century
stulejka *f* (*-ki*; *-ki*) *MED* phimosis
stuletni *adj* **1.** *rządy*: hundred-year **2.** *drzewa*: hundred-year-old
stulić *v/p* → ***stulać***
stuła *f* (*-ły*; *-ły*) *REL* stole
stułbia *f* (*-bi*; *-bie*) *BIOL* hydra
stuprocentowy *adj* **1.** (*pewny*) one hundred per cent **2.** *wełna*: pure; **stutysięczny** *adj* **1.** (*z kolei*) one hundred thousandth **2.** *armia*: one hundred thousand
stwardniały *adj* hard, hardened
stwardnieć *v/p* → ***twardnieć***
stwardnienie *n* (*-nia*; *-nia*) *skóry*: callosity; **~ *rozsiane*** *MED* multiple sclerosis
stwarzać ⟨**-worzyć**⟩ (*-rzam*) **1.** *warunki*, *atmosferę*: offer **2.** *dzieło*: create; **~ *wrażenie*** look like; **~ *zagrożenie dla*** *G* pose a threat to, present a threat to; **~ *pozory*** *G* put on a show of
stwierdz|ać ⟨**-dzić**⟩ (*-dzam*) state; ***lekarz ~ił jego zgon*** the doctor pronounced him dead
stwierdzenie *n* (*-nia*; *-nia*) statement
stworzenie *n* **1.** (*-nia*; *no pl*) (*powołanie do życia*) creation **2.** (*-nia*; *-nia*) (*osobnik*) creature
stworzonko *n* (*-ka*; *-ka*) little creature
stworzony *adj*: ***jakby ~*** made out, cut out (**do**/**dla** *G* for)
Stworzyciel *m* (*-la*; *no pl*) *REL* the Creator
stworzyć *v/p* → ***stwarzać***
stwór *m* (*-wora*; *-wory*) creature; **Stwórca** *m* (*-cy*; *no pl*) the Creator
styczeń *m* (*-cznia*; *-cznie*) January
styczna *f* (*-nej*; *-ne*) *MATH* tangent
styczniowy *adj* January
styczność *f* (*-ści*; *no pl*) contact; ***mieć ~ z*** *I* be in contact with, be in touch with; **styczn|y** *adj poglądy*: similar; ***punkty ~e*** **a)** *fig* things in common **b)** *MATH* tangential points
stygmat *m* (*-tu*; *-ty*) *lit* stigma; ***~y*** *REL* stigmas
stygnąć ⟨**o-**⟩ (*-nę*) cool down
styk *m* (*-ku*; *-ki*) **1.** (*przyleganie*) adjacency **2.** (*kontakt*) contact; ***na ~u*** *G fig* at the meeting point of
stykać ⟨**zetknąć**⟩ (*-kam*) **1.** *końce*: connect **2.** *osoby*: contact (**z** *I* with), put in touch (**z** *I* with); ***stykać się*** **1.** (*o końcach*, *palcach*) touch, have contact **2.** (*o osobach*) encounter,

S

meet (**z** *I*) **3.** (*dotykać*) touch (**z** *I*) **4.** (*spotykać*) encounter (**z** *I*)

styl *m* (*-lu*; *-le*) style; **~ dowolny** SPORT free style; **stylistyczny** *adj analiza, błąd*: stylistic

stylizować ⟨**u-**, **wy-**⟩ (*-zuję*) stylize, *Br* stylise; **stylizowany** *adj* stylized, *Br* stylised

stylowy *adj* **1.** *cecha*: style, stylistic, of style **2.** (*autentyczny*) period **3.** (*gustowny*) stylish

stymulator *m* (*-ra*; *-ry*) *wzrostu*: stimulator; **~ serca** pacemaker

stymulować *v/im* (*-luję*) stimulate

stypa *f* (*-py*; *-py*) funeral banquet, wake

stypendialny *adj* scholarship; **stypendium** *n* (*indecl*; *-dia*) **1.** (*studia*) scholarship; **~ naukowe** grant; **~ doktoranckie** doctoral scholarship **2.** (*pobyt w trakcie studiów*) study period

stypendysta *m* (*-ty*; *-dyści*), **-tka** *f* (*-ki*; *-ki*) scholarship holder

styropian *m* (*-nu*; *no pl*) polystyrene foam, Styrofoam®

subiektywny *adj* subjective

sublimacja *f* (*-ji*; *no pl*) PSYCH FIZ sublimation

subkultura *f* (*-ry*; *-ry*) subculture

sublimować *v/im* (*-muję*) PSYCH PHYS sublimate, sublime

sublokator *m* (*-ra*; *-rzy*), **~ka** *f* (*-ki*; *-ki*) lodger, *Am* subtenant, roomer; **być ~em** share a room, be a roomer, be a lodger

sublokatorski *adj* subtenant: **pokój ~** shared room

subordynacja *f* (*-ji*; *no pl*) obedience, discipline

subskrypcja *f* (*-ji*; *-je*) subscription

substancja *f* (*-ji*; *-je*) substance

subtelny *adj* **1.** *osoba*: delicate **2.** *charakter*: gentle **3.** *rysy, uroda, zapach*: subtle **4.** *sprawa*: touchy **5.** *różnica*: fine **6.** *dowcip*: refined

subwencja *f* (*-ji*; *-je*) subvention

subwencjonować *v/im* (*-nuję*) subsidize *fig*

suchar *m* (*-ra*; *-ry*) **1.** (*pieczywo*) rusk, very hard biscuit **2.** (*chudzielec*) *fig* scrag

sucho *adv* → **suchy**

suchość *f* (*-ści*; *no pl*) dryness; **~ w ustach** MED dry mouth

suchuteńki, **suchutki** *adj dim* (perfectly) dry

suchy *adj* dry

suczka *f* (*-ki*; *-ki*) *dim* bitch

Sudety *pl* (*-tów*) the Sudety

sufiks *m* (*-su*; *-sy*) suffix

sufi|t *m* (*-tu*; *-ty*) ceiling; **na ~cie** on the ceiling

sufler *m* (*-ra*; *-rzy*), **~ka** *f* (*-ki*; *-ki*) prompter

sugerować ⟨**za-**⟩ (*-ruję*) **1.** (*proponować*) suggest **2.** (*dawać do zrozumienia*) imply; **sugerować się** be influenced

sugesti|a *f* (*-tii*; *-tie*) suggestion; **ulegać ~i** succumb to a suggestion, act on a suggestion; **sugestywny** *adj* evocative

suita *f* (*-ty*; *-ty*) MUS suite

suka *f* (*-ki*; *-ki*) **1.** BIOL bitch **2.** (*samochód policyjny*) *Br* Black Maria, *Am* paddy wagon

sukces *m* (*-su*; *-sy*) success; **odnieść ~** be a success, be successful

sukcesja *f* (*-ji*; *-je*) succession

sukcesor *m* (*-ra*; *-rzy*) successor; **sukcesorka** *f* (*-ki*; *-ki*) heiress

sukcesywny *adj* gradual, successive

sukienka *f* (*-ki*; *-ki*) dress

sukiennice *pl* (*-nic*) HIST cloth halls

sukinsyn *m* (*-na*; *-ny*) *infml* bastard

suknia *f* (*-ni*; *-nie*) dress; **~ balowa** ball dress; **~ ślubna** wedding dress

sukno *n* (*-na*; *-na*) (*materiał*) cloth

sułtan (*-na*; *-nowie*/*-ni*) sultan

sum (*-ma*; *-my*) BIOL catfish

sum|a *f* (*-my*; *-my*) **1.** MATH sum; **w ~ie** all things considered, all in all **2.** (*kwota*) amount **3.** REL High Mass

sumaryczny *adj* summary

sumiast|y *adj*: **~e wąsy** bushy moustache

sumieni|e *n* (*-nia*; *-nia*) conscience; **mieć na ~u** have on one's conscience; **mieć czyste ~e** have clear conscience; **mieć wyrzuty ~a** have pangs of conscience, have qualms of conscience; **nie mieć ~a**, **być bez ~a** be utterly ruthless; **gryzie go ~e** his conscience pricks him, he has bad conscience

sumienny *adj* conscientious, diligent

sumka *f* (*-ki*; *-ki*) *dim* sum; **niezła ~** substantial amount of money

S

sumować⟨**z-**⟩ (*-muję*) MATH add up, total up; ***sumując*** to sum up, summing up; ***sumować się*** add up, sum up
sunąć *v/im* (*-nę*) **I** *v/i* **1.** (*przesuwać się*) glide (**po** *L* over) **2.** (*o aucie*) roll down **II** *v/t* (*przesuwać*) push
supeł *m* (*-pła*; *-pły*) knot; **supełek** *m* (*-ka*; *-ki*) *dim* (small) knot
super- (*w złożeniach*) super-; ***~nowoczesny*** ultra-modern
super *adj*, *adv infml* super
superata *f* (*-ty*; *-ty*) FIN surplus
supersam *m* (*-mu*; *-my*) supermarket
supłać *v/im* (*-łam*) make knots (*A* on), tie knots (*A* in); ***supłać się*** tangle
surfing *m* (*-gu*; *no pl*) surfing
surfingow|y *adj* surfing; ***deska ~a*** surfboard
surogat *m* (*-tu*; *-ty*) **1.** (*zastępstwo*) substitute **2.** (*namiastka*) *fig* surrogate
surowcowy *adj* raw material
surowica *f* (*-cy*; *-ce*) BIOL MED serum; **surowiczy** *adj* MED serous
surow|iec *m* (*-wca*; *-wce*) raw material; ***~ce wtórne*** recyclable materials
surowo *adv* severely, strictly; → ***surowy***
surowość *f* (*-ści*; *no pl*) **1.** *klimatu*: harshness, severity **2.** *budynku*: austerity **3.** *osoby*, *przepisów*: strictness; **surowy** *adj* **1.** COOK raw **2.** *klimat*: harsh, severe **3.** *osoba*: strict **4.** *drewno*: unseasoned; ***budynek w stanie ~m*** BUILD shell of a building
surówka *f* (*-ki*; *-ki*) **1.** COOK salad; ***~ z białej kapusty*** coleslaw **2.** TECH pig-iron **3.** *lniana*: unbleached linen
sus *m* (*-sa*; *-sy*) leap, bound
suseł *m* (*-sła*; *-sły*) BIOL gopher; ***spać jak ~*** sleep like a log
susi → ***suchy***
susz *m* (*-szu*; *-sze*) **1.** (*owoce*) dried fruit **2.** (*warzywa*) dried vegetables
susza *f* (*-szy*; *-sze*) drought
suszarka *f* (*-ki*; *-ki*) **1.** (*do włosów*) hairdryer **2.** (*do naczyń*) dish drainer **3.** (*do prania*) tumble dryer **4.** (*do rąk*) hand drier; **suszarnia** *f* (*-ni*; *-nie*) **1.** *bielizny*: drying room **2.** *tytoniu*: drying plant
suszony *adj* dried
suszyć⟨**wy-**⟩ (*-szę*) dry; ***~ na powietrzu*** dry in the open air; ***~ komuś głowę*** *fig* pester s.o.; ***suszyć się*** dry, get dry
sutanna *f* (*-ny*; *-ny*) cassock
sutek *m* (*-tka*; *-tki*) nipple
sutener *m* (*-ra*; *-rzy*) pimp, procurer; **sutenerstwo** *n* (*-wa*; *no pl*) pimping
suterena *f* (*-ny*; *-ny*) basement
suto *adv* richly; ***~ zastawiony stół*** table laden with food; ***~ zdobiony*** richly decorated
suty *adj* **1.** *posiłek*: lavish, sumptuous **2.** *zapłata*: generous
suwak *m* (*-ka*; *-ki*) zip, *Am* zipper; ***~ logarytmiczny*** slide rule
suwerenność *f* (*-ści*; *no pl*) POLIT sovereignty, independence; **suwerenny** *adj* sovereign, independent
swa → ***swój***
swad|a *f* (*-dy*; *no pl*) fluency, volubility; ***mówić ze ~ą*** speak eloquently, speak volubly
swary *pl* (*-rów*) *lit* squabbles
swastyka *f* (*-ki*; *-ki*) swastika
swawola *f* (*-li*; *-le*) *lit* **1.** (*zabawa*, *dokazywanie*) frolicking **2.** (*samowola*) *Br* licence, *Am* license
swawolić *v/im* (*-lę*) *lit* (*dokazywać*) romp, frolic
swawolny *adj lit* frolicsome, playful
swąd *m* (*-wędu*; *no pl*) smell of burning
swe → ***swój***
sweter *m* (*-tra*; *-try*) sweater, *Br* jumper; ***~ rozpinany*** cardigan
swędzenie *n* (*-nia*; *no pl*) itching
swędzieć ⟨**za-**⟩ (*-dzę*) itch
swobod|a *f* (*-dy*; *-dy*) **1.** (*wolność*) freedom; ***~y obywatelskie*** civil liberties; ***~a działania*** free hand; ***~a ruchów*** liberty of movement **2.** (*niewymuszoność*) ease; **swobodny** *adj* **1.** (*wolny*) free **2.** (*niewymuszony*) unconstrained, free **3.** *ubranie*: casual, informal
swoi → ***swój II***
swoisty *adj* **1.** (*specyficzny*) peculiar **2.** (*charakterystyczny*) characteristic
swoja → ***swój***
swoje[1] → ***swój I***
swo|je[2] *n* (*-jego*; *no pl*) one's own; ***obstawać przy ~im*** stick to one's guns; ***postawić na ~im*** have it one's way; ***robić ~je*** do one's job; ***wiedzieć ~je*** have one's opinion; ***wyjść na ~je*** come out on top; ***dostawać za ~je*** be taught a lesson; ***być pewnym swego*** be sure one is right

S

swojsk|i *adj* **1.** (*rodzimy*) familiar; ***czuć się ~o*** feel at home **2.** (*domowej roboty*) home-made

swój I *poss* one's, one's own; ***tu mam swoje rzeczy*** I have my things here; ***czy lubisz swoją pracę?*** do you like your job?; ***tam poznał swoją żonę*** he met his wife there; ***wynajęła swoje mieszkanie*** she let out her flat; ***swoimi słowami*** in one's own words; ***chodzić swoimi drogami*** follow one's own path; ***to ~ chłop*** he's a good guy **II** *m* (*swojego*; *swoi*) **1.** (*krewny*) relative, *Am* one's folk **2.** (*rodak*) fellow countryman; **swoi a)** (*rodzina*) family **b)** (*rodacy*) fellow countrymen **c)** (*znajomi*) friends

sybaryta *m* (*-ty*; *-ryci*) *lit* sybarite

Syberia *f* (*-rii*) Siberia

syberyjski *adj* Siberian

sycić ⟨***na-***⟩ (*-cę*) satiate, fill up; ***~ głód*** satisfy one's hunger; ***syciliśmy oczy tym widokiem*** *lit* we feasted our eyes on the sight; **sycić się 1.** (*karmić do syta*) sate oneself (*I* on) **2.** (*upajać się*) take delight (*I* in)

Sycylia *f* (*-lii*) Sicily

sycylijski *adj* Sicilian

syczeć ⟨***syknąć***⟩ (*-czę*) hiss

syfilis *m* (*-su*; *no pl*) MED syphilis

syfon *m* (*-nu*; *-ny*) soda siphon, siphon, *Am* siphon bottle

sygnalista *m* (*-ty*; *-liści*) signalman; **sygnalizacja** *f* (*-ji*; *no pl*) signalling; ***~ świetlna*** traffic lights; ***~ alarmowa*** alarm system

sygnalizator *m* (*-ra*; *-ry*) signalling equipment, signalling device; ***~ świetlny*** light signal, flashing lights; ***~ alarmowy*** alarm signal

sygnalizować ⟨***za-***⟩ (*-zuję*) **1.** (*dawać sygnał*) signal **2.** *problem*: indicate

sygna|ł *m* (*-łu*; *-ły*) signal; ***~ł alarmowy*** alarm signal; ***~ł świetlny*** light signal, flashing lights; ***na ~le*** with the siren going

sygnatariusz *m* (*-sza*; *-sze*) POLIT (*państwo*) signatory; **sygnatura** *f* (*-ry*; *-ry*) shelf mark, catalogue number

sygnet *m* (*-tu*; *-ty*) signet ring

sygnować *v/im* (*-nuje*) sign

syjamski *adj* Siamese; ***bliźnięta ~e*** Siamese twins; ***kot ~*** Siamese cat

syjonista *m* (*-ty*; *-niści*) Zionist; **syjonistyczny** *adj* Zionist, Zionistic

syk *m* (*-ku*; *-ki*) hiss

syknąć *v/p* → **syczeć**

sylaba *f* (*-by*; *-by*) syllable; **sylabizować** *v/im* (*-zuję*) **1.** (*artykułować sylaby*) read syllable by syllable **2.** (*czytać z trudem*) read haltingly

sylwester *m* (*-tra*; *-try*) **1.** (*koniec roku*) New Year's Eve **2.** (*zabawa*) New Year's Eve party; **sylwestrowy** *adj* New Year's Eve

sylwetka *f* (*-ki*; *-ki*) **1.** (*zarys*) silhouette **2.** (*charakterystyka*) profile

symbol *m* (*-lu*; *-le*) symbol; **symboliczny** *adj* symbolic

symbolizować *v/im* (*-zuję*) *Br* symbolise, symbolize

symetria *f* (*-rii*; *no pl*) symmetry; **symetryczny** *adj* symmetric, symmetrical

symfonia *f* (*-nii*; *-nie*) symphony; **symfoniczn|y** *adj* symphony, symphonic; ***orkiestra ~a*** symphony orchestra

sympati|a *f* (*-tii*; *-tie*) **1.** (*uczucie*) liking; ***czuć ~ę do*** *G* feel attracted to **2.** (*dziewczyna*) girlfriend **3.** (*chłopak*) boyfriend

sympatyczka *f* (*-ki*; *-ki*) sympathizer

sympatyczny *adj* nice, friendly

sympatyk *m* (*-ka*; *-tycy*) sympathizer

sympatyzować *v/im* (*-zuję*) *Br* sympathise, sympathize (**z** *I* with)

symptom *m* (*-mu*; *-my*) symptom

symulant *m* (*-ta*; *-nci*), **~ka** *f* (*-ki*; *-ki*) malingerer

symulator *m* (*-ra*; *-ry*) TECH simulator; ***~ lotu*** flight simulator

symulować *v/im* (*-luję*) *chorobę*: simulate, feign

symultana *f* (*-ny*; *-ny*) simultaneous chess competition, simultaneous chess play; **symultaniczny** *adj* simultaneous; ***tłumacz ~*** simultaneous interpreter

syn *m* (*-na*; *-nowie*) son; ***~ chrzestny*** godson; ***~ marnotrawny*** REL prodigal son; ***≈ Boży*** Son of God

synagoga *f* (*-gi*; *-gi*) synagogue

synchroniczn|y *adj* synchronic, synchronous; ***pływanie ~e*** SPORT synchronized swimming

synchronizować ⟨***z-***⟩ (*-zuję*) *Br* synchronise, synchronize

S

syndyk *m* (*-ka*; *-dycy*/*-kowie*) **1.** (*zarządca*) official receiver; **~ *masy upadłościowej*** receiver in bankruptcy **2.** *JUR* syndic; **syndykat** *m* (*-tu*; *-ty*) *ECON* syndicate

synek *m* (*-nka*; *-nkowie*) *dim* (little) son

synod *m* (*-du*; *-dy*) synod

synonim *m* (*-mu*; *-my*) synonym; **synonimiczny** *adj* synonymous

synoptyczny *adj* synoptic; **synoptyk** *m* (*-ka*; *-tycy*) weather forecaster, weatherman

synowa *f* (*-wej*; *-we*) daughter-in-law

syntaktyczny *adj* syntactic

syntetycznie *adv* (*sztucznie*) synthetically; **syntetyczn|y** *adj* (*sztuczny*) synthetic; ***włókno ~e*** *Br* synthetic fibre, *Am* synthetic fiber

syntetyk *m* (*-ku*; *-ki*) (*materiał*) synthetic; **synteza** *f* (*-zy*; *-zy*) synthesis; **syntezator** *m* (*-ra*; *-ry*) *MUS* synthesizer

sypać ⟨**-pnąć**⟩ (*-pię*) **1.** (*wsypywać*) pour (**do** *G* into); **~ *piasek*** pour sand; **~ *dowcipami*** crack jokes all the time; **~ *pochwałami*** be lavish with praises; **~ *pieniędzmi*** scatter one's money around; ***sypie*** (***śnieg***) it's snowing (heavily); ***wiatr sypie piaskiem w oczy*** the wind is blowing sand in our faces **2.** (*donieść*) *infml* inform, squeal (*A* on) **3.** *wał*, *kopiec*: build, raise; ***sypać się*** **1.** (*o tynku*) come off **2.** (*o iskrach*) fly **3.** (*o wąsach*) sprout **4.** (*rozpadać się*) fall apart, fall to pieces **5.** (*o pochwałach*, *nagrodach*) shower down

sypiać *v/im* (*-piam*) sleep (**z** *I* with); **~ *ze sobą*** be lovers; **~ *przy otwartym oknie*** sleep by an open window; ***nie ~*** have problems falling asleep

sypialnia *f* (*-ni*; *-nie*) bedroom

sypialny *adj*: ***wagon ~*** sleeping car, sleeper; ***pokój ~*** bedroom

sypk|i *adj* **1.** loose; ***skała ~a*** *GEOL* detached rock **2.** *śnieg*: powdery

sypko *adv*: ***gotować ryż na ~*** prepare al dente rice

sypnąć *v/p* → ***sypać***

syrena *f* (*-ny*; *-ny*) **1.** *alarmowa*, *strażacka*, *okrętowa*: siren **2.** (*w bajkach*) mermaid **3.** (*ssak*) sirenian

syreni *adj*: **~ *śpiew*** siren song

Syria *f* (*-rii*) Syria

syrop *m* (*-pu*; *-py*) syrup, *Am* sirup; **~ *od kaszlu*** cough syrup, cough mixture

Syryjczyk *m* (*-ka*; *-czycy*), **~ryjka** *f* (*-ki*; *-ki*) Syrian; **syryjski** *adj* Syrian

system *m* (*-mu*; *-my*) system; **~ *operacyjny*** *INF* operating system

systematyczność *f* (*-ści*; *no pl*) regularity, method; ***cechuje go ogromna ~*** he is very methodical; **systematyczny** *adj* (*planowy*) systematic, methodical

sytość *f* (*-ści*; *no pl*) repletion, satiety

sytuacja *f* (*-ji*; *-je*) situation; **sytuacyjny** *adj* **1.** *komizm*: situation **2.** *plan*: general **3.** *kryzys*, *stres*: situational

sytuować ⟨**u-**⟩ (*-tuuję*) locate, place

sytuowany *adj*: ***dobrze*** (***źle***) **~** well (badly) off

syty *adj* replete, full; **~ *sławy*** famous enough

syzyfow|y *adj*: ***~a praca*** Sisyphean task

szabas *m* (*-su*; *-sy*) *REL* Sabbath

szaber *m* (*-bru*; *no pl*) looting

szabla *f* (*-li*; *-le*) *Br* sabre, *Am* saber

szablon *m* (*-nu*; *-ny*) template; **szablonowy** *adj* routine, stereotypical

szabrować ⟨**wy-**⟩ (*-ruję*) loot, pillage

szach[1] *m* (*-cha*; *-chowie*) shah

szach[2] *m* (*-chu*/*-cha*; *no pl*) (*w szachach*) check; ***dać ~a*** check (the king); ***~-mat!*** checkmate!

szachista *m* (*-ty*; *-chiści*), **-tka** *f* (*-ki*; *-ki*) chess player

szachownic|a *f* (*-cy*; *-ce*) (*plansza*) chessboard; ***w ~ę*** chequered, *Am* checked

szachraj *m* (*-ja*; *-je*), **~ka** *f* (*-ki*; *-ki*) cheat, swindler; **szachrajstwo** *n* (*-wa*; *-wa*) swindle; **szachrować** *v/im* (*-ruję*) cheat, flimflam

szachy *pl* (*-chów*) chess; ***grać w ~*** play chess

szacować ⟨**o-**⟩ (*-cuję*) *straty*, *ilość*: assess, estimate

szacowny *adj lit* **1.** *osoba*, *insytucja*: venerable **2.** *nazwisko*: respectable **3.** *firma*: reputable

szacun|ek *m* (*-nku*; *no pl*) **1.** (*poważanie*) respect; ***mieć ~ek dla*** *G* have high regard for, have great respect for, respect; ***brak ~ku*** disrespectfulness; ***pełen ~ku*** respectful; ***przez***

S

~ek out of respect **2.** (*ocena*) estimate, assessment

szacunkowo *adv* approximately; **szacunkowy** *adj* approximate

szadź *f* (*szadzi*; *no pl*) rime frost, hoar frost

szafa *f* (*-fy*; *-fy*) **1.** (*kredens*) cupboard; **~ na ubrania** wardrobe; **~ z lustrem** mirrored wardrobe; **~ ścienna** closet; **~ pancerna** strongbox, safe; **~ grająca** jukebox **2.** (*na książki*) bookcase **3.** (*na akta*) cabinet

szafir *m* (*-ru*/*-ra*; *-ry*) sapphire; **szafirowy** *adj* sapphire (blue)

szafka *f* (*-ki*; *-ki*) **1.** *kuchenna*: cupboard, (kitchen) unit; **~ nocna** bedside table; **~ na buty** shoe cabinet **2.** (*osobista*) locker

szafot *m* (*-tu*; *-ty*) scaffold

szafować *v/im* (*-fuję*) be liberal, be lavish (*I* with); **~ pieniędzmi** squander money

szafran *m* (*-nu*; *-ny*) saffron; **szafranowy** *adj* saffron

szajba *infml*: **~ mu odbiła** he's got a screw loose

szajka *f* (*-ki*; *-ki*) gang, ring

szakal *m* (*-la*; *-le*) jackal

szal *m* (*-la*; *-le*) shawl

szala *f* (*-li*; *-le*) scale

szalbierstwo *n* (*-wa*; *-wa*) fraud, swindle; **szalbierz** *m* (*-rza*; *-rze*) swindler, fraud

szaleć ⟨**po-**⟩ (*-leję*) **1.** (*wariować*) go crazy; **~ za** *I* be mad about; **~ na rolkach** romp on the roller-skates; **~ z zakupami** go on a shopping spree; **~ z radości** be delirious with joy; **~ ze strachu** be frantic with fear, be petrified; **~ z miłości** be frantic with love **2.** (*złościć się*) rage, be mad; **~ z gniewu** be frantic with anger **3.** (*o burzy, grypie, pożarze, wojnie*) rage **4.** (*bawić się hałaśliwie*) romp **5.** (*hulać*) revel; **~ całą noc** revel the whole night

szalenie *adv* extremely, exceedingly, mighty; **szaleniec** *m* (*-leńca*; *-leńcy*) madman

szaleńcz|y *adj* **1.** *plan, śmiech*: mad; **~y pomysł** mad scheme, manic idea; **~a odwaga** great courage **2.** *tempo*: frantic, breakneck **3.** *taniec, rytm*: wild, furious **4.** (*ryzykancki*) foolhardy; **szaleństwo** *n* (*-wa*; *-wa*) **1.** MED madness **2.** (*wybryk, lekkomyślność*) lunacy, revel; **to czyste ~** this is pure folly, this is sheer madness

szalet *m* (*-tu*; *-ty*) *Br* public convenience, *Br* public toilet, *Am* comfort station, outdoor toilet

szalik *m* (*-ka*; *-ki*) scarf

szalon|y *adj* **1.** (*zwariowany*) crazy; **jak ~y** like crazy; **choroba ~ych krów** BSE, bovine spongiform encephalopathy **2.** (*opętany*) mad **3.** *tempo*: breakneck **4.** *taniec, zabawa, namiętność*: wild **5.** (*niesamowity*) unbelievable, extraordinary; **mieć ~e szczęście** be extremely lucky **6.** *czyn*: mad; **~y pomysł** mad scheme, mad idea

szalować ⟨**o-**⟩ (*-luję*) board

szalupa *f* (*-py*; *-py*) cockboat; **~ ratunkowa** lifeboat

szał *m* (*-łu*; *no pl*) madness; **~ miłosny** mad love; **~ zakupów** compulsive buying, shopping binge; **~ bojowy** combat madness; **wpaść w ~** go wild, fly into a fury; **doprowadzać kogoś do ~u** drive s.o. mad

szałas *m* (*-su*; *-sy*) shelter, shanty

szałowy *adj* awesome, cool

szałwia *f* (*-wii*; *-wie*) sage

szaman *m* (*-na*; *-ni*) shaman, witch doctor

szambo *n* (*-ba*; *-ba*) cesspool

szamotać *v/im* (*-moczę*/*-mocę*) *wiatr*: move violently; **szamotać się** tussle (**z** *I* with); **~ się z zamkiem** struggle with the lock

szampan *m* (*-na*; *-ny*) champagne

szampański *adj* *zabawa*: sparkling; **~ nastrój** hectic spirit, sparkling good time

szampon *m* (*-nu*; *-ny*) shampoo

szanować ⟨**u-**⟩ (*-nuję*) **1.** *osobę, poglądy*: respect **2.** *ubranie, zdrowie*: take care (*A* of); **szanować się** take care of oneself; **szanująca się gazeta** self-respecting newspaper; **szanujący się fachowiec** self-respecting professional, self-respecting expert

szanowany *adj* respectable; **szanown|y** *adj* *jubilat*: *Br* honourable, *Am* honorable; **~i Państwo!** Ladies and Gentleman!

S

szansa *f* (*-sy*; *-se*) chance; **~ życiowa** the chance of a lifetime
szantaż *m* (*-żu*; *-że*) blackmail; **szantażować** *v/im* (*-żuję*) blackmail; **szantażysta** *m* (*-ty*; *-żyści*), **-tka** *f* (*-ki*; *-ki*) blackmailer
szarada *f* (*-dy*; *-dy*) charade
szarak *m* (*-ka*; *-ki*) BIOL hare
szarańcza (*-czy*; *-cze*) **1.** BIOL locust **2.** *fig* swarm
szarawy *adj Br* greyish, *Am* grayish
szarfa *f* (*-fy*; *-fy*) sash
szargać *v/im* (*-gam*) *lit fig* slander; **~ czyjeś dobre imię** tarnish s.o.'s good name
szarlatan *m* (*-na*; *-ni*) charlatan
szarlataneria *f* (*-rii*; *no pl*), **szarlataństwo** *f* (*-wa*; *no pl*) charlatanry
szarlotka *f* (*-ki*; *-ki*) apple-pie
szarmancki *adj mężczyzna*: gallant
szaro *adv*: **zrobić kogoś na ~** *infml* cheat s.o., take s.o. in, frame s.o.; **zrobiło się ~** it grew dark
szarotka *f* (*-ki*; *-ki*) BIOL edelweiss
szarozielony *adj Br* grey-green, *Am* gray-green
szarówka *f* (*-ki*; *-ki*) **1.** (*wieczorem*) dusk **2.** (*rano*) morning twilight
szarpać ⟨**-pnąć**⟩ (*-pię*) **1.** *zamek*, *klamkę*: jerk **2.** (*strunę*) pick, pluck **3.** *osobę*: pull (**za** *A* at); **~ za smycz** (**sznurek**) yank at the leash (cord) **4.** (*rozdzierać*) tear; **~ sobie nerwy** fray one's nerves; **szarpać się 1.** tussle (**za** *A* with) **2.** *fig* struggle (**z** *A* with); **~ się z zamkiem** (*usiłować otworzyć*) struggle with the lock **3. szarpnąć się na** *A infml* spend a lot of money on
szarpnięcie *n* (*-cia*; *-cia*) jerk, yank *infml*
szaruga *f* (*-gi*; *-gi*) spell of foul weather, rainy day
szar|y *adj* **1.** *kolor*: grey, *Am* gray; **~y człowiek** *fig* the man in the street, everyman; **~a eminencja** éminence grise, grey eminence; **~a strefa** ECON grey zone, grey area; **na ~ym końcu** at the very end; **~e komórki** grey matter, grey cells **2.** *cera*: ashen, ash-coloured **3.** *dzień*: gloomy **4.** (*monotonny*) dull
szarzeć ⟨**po-**, **z-**⟩ (*-rzeję*) **1.** (*o niebie*) grow grey; **szarzeje** it is getting dark **2.** (*o materiale*) show grey
szarzy → **szary**
szarzyzna *f* (*-ny*; *no pl*) *fig* drabness, monotony
szarża *f* (*-ży*; *-że*) charge
szarżować *v/im* (*-żuję*) (*przypuszczać atak*) charge; **~ samochodem** drive too fast, drive recklessly
szastać *v/im* (*-tam*): **~ pieniędzmi** squander one's money, be very careless with one's money
szaszłyk *m* (*-ka*; *-ki*) shashlik
szata *f* (*-ty*; *-ty*) *lit* garment; **~ graficzna** layout; **~ roślina** plant cover
szatan *m* **1.** (*-na*; *-ny*/*-ni*) REL Satan **2.** (*-na*; *-ny*) BIOL satan's bolete; **szatański** *adj* satanic
szatkować ⟨**po-**⟩ (*-kuję*): **~ kapustę** shred the cabbage
szatni|a *f* (*-ni*; *-nie*) cloak-room; **w ~** in the cloak-room; **szatniarz** *m* (*-rza*; *-rze*), **~rka** *f* (*-ki*; *-ki*) cloak-room attendant
szatyn *m* (*-na*; *-ni*), **~ka** (*-ki*; *-ki*) auburn-haired person, brown-haired person, chestnut-haired person
szczać *v/im* (*-czę*) *infml* piss
szczapa *f* (*-py*; *-py*) chip; **chudy jak ~** as thin as a lath
szczaw *m* (*-wiu*; *-wie*) sorrel; **szczawiow|y** *adj*: **zupa ~a** sorrel soup
szczątki *pl* (*-ków*) **1.** *samolotu*: wreckage *sing*; **2.** (*o zmarłym*) remains **3.** *statku*: **a)** (*pod wodą*) wreckage *sing* **b)** (*pływające na wodzie*) flotsams **4.** *budowli*: ruins, remains
szczątkowy *adj* **1.** ANAT vestigial **2.** *informacja*: fragmentary **3.** *ślady*: residual
szczeb|el *m* (*-bla*; *-ble*) **1.** (*drabiny*) rung **2.** *fig* level; **na ~lu centralnym** POLIT at the central level; **na najwyższym ~lu** POLIT top-level, at high level; **piąć się po ~lach kariery** move up the ladder, go up the ladder
szczebiot *m* (*-tu*; *-ty*) **1.** *ptaków*: chirp, chirping **2.** *dziecka*: babble; **szczebiotać** *v/im* (*-bioczę*/*-biocę*) **1.** (*o ptakach*) chirp **2.** (*o dziecku*) babble
szczecina *f* (*-ny*; *no pl*) **1.** *zwierzęcia*: bristles *pl* **2.** (*zarost*) stubble; **szczeciniasty** *adj* bristly, stubbly
szczególnie *particle* particularly, specially; **szczególnoś|ć** (*-ści*; *no pl*): **w ~ci** particulary; **szczególn|y**

adj special; **nic ~ego** nothing special; **znaki ~e** distinguishing marks
szczegół *m* (*-łu*; *-ły*) detail; **szczegółowo** *adv* in detail; **szczegółow|y** *adj* detailed; **mapa ~a** detailed map
szczekać ⟨**-knąć**⟩ (*-kam*) bark
szczelina *f* (*-ny*; *-ny*) **1.** (*odstęp*) gap **2.** (*między deskami*) slit **3.** GEOL crevice **4.** (*pęknięcie*) crack, chink; **szczelinow|y** *adj*: ***spółgłoska ~a*** fricative
szczelny *adj* tight, hermetic
szczeniacki *adj* infantile, puppy; **szczeniak** *m* (*-ka*; *-ki*) **1.** BIOL puppy **2.** *infml* pup(py); **szczenić się** ⟨**o-**⟩ (*-nię*) (*o suce*) pup, have puppies
szczenię *m* (*-nięcia*; *-nięta*) pup; **szczenięc|y** *adj*: ***~e lata*** puppy years, cub years; ***~y*** *iron* puppyish
szczenny *adj suka*: in pup
szczep *m* (*-pu*; *-py*) **1.** *afrykański*: tribe **2.** BOT graft; ***~ winny*** grapevine (graft)
szczepić ⟨**za-**⟩ (*-pię*) **1.** MED vaccinate (**przeciw** *D* against) **2.** *rośliny*: graft; **szczepić się** MED vaccinate
szczepienie *f* (*-nia*; *-nia*) **1.** MED vaccination; ***~ przeciw ospie*** vaccination against smallpox **2.** *roślin*: grafting; **szczepionka** *f* (*-ki*; *-ki*) vaccine
szczerba *f* (*-by*; *-by*) **1.** (*w murze*, *uzębieniu*) gap **2.** (*w ostrzu*) nick **3.** (*nacięcie*) notch; **szczerbaty** *adj dziecko*, *staruszek*: gap-toothed
szczerość *f* (*-ści*; *no pl*) sincerity, *Am* frankness
szczerozłoty *adj* made of pure gold
szczer|y *adj* **1.** sincere, frank; ***~a prawda*** naked truth; ***w ~ym polu*** in the open (country); ***mieć ~e chęci*** mean well, have a genuine desire; ***jeśli mam być ~y*** to tell you the truth, truth to tell **2.** *złoto*, *srebro*: pure; **szczerze** *adv*; sincerely, frankly; ***~ mówiąc*** frankly speaking
szczerzyć ⟨**wy-**⟩ (*-rzę*): ***~ zęby*** grin (**do** *G* at)
szczeżuja *f* (*-żui*; *-je*) swan mussel
szczędzić *v/im* (*-dzę*): ***nie ~ trudu*** spare no effort; ***nie ~ pieniędzy*** spare no money; ***nie ~ pochwał*** be full of praise (*D* for)
szczęk *m* (*-ku*; *no pl*) **1.** *kluczy*, *łańcucha*: jangle **2.** *zbroi*, *broni*: clash, clang **3.** *talerzy*, *filiżanek*: rattle
szczęka *f* (*-ki*; *-ki*) jaw; ***dolna*** (***górna***) ***~*** lower (upper) jaw; ***sztuczna ~*** false teeth, dentures *pl*; ***~ mu opadła*** *fig* his jaw dropped
szczęka|ć ⟨**-knąć**⟩ (*-kam*) **I** *v/i* **1.** (*o łańcuchu*, *kluczach*) jangle **2.** (*o broni*) clang **3.** (*o mieczach*) clash **4.** (*o naczyniach*, *kościach*) rattle **II** *v/t* ***ktoś ~zębami*** s.o.'s teeth chatter
szczękościsk *m* (*-ku*; *no pl*) lock-jaw, trismus; **szczękow|y** *adj*: ***kość ~a*** jawbone; ***chirurgia ~a*** jaw surgery; ***hamulec ~y*** AUTO shoe brake
szczęściara *f* (*-ry*; *-ry*) lucky girl; **szczęściarz** *m* (*-rza*; *-rze*) lucky boy
szczęścić się *v/im*: ***we wszystkim mu się szczęści*** he is lucky in everything; ***nie szczęściło mu się ostatnio*** he's been out of luck recently, he's been down on his luck lately; ***nie szczęści mu się w pracy*** he is unsuccessful at work
szczęści|e *n* (*-cia*; *no pl*) **1.** (*uczucie zadowolenia*) happiness; ***~e rodzinne*** family happiness; ***dać komuś ~e*** make s.o. happy **2.** (*powodzenie*) luck, success; ***na ~e*** fortunately, luckily; ***przynoszący ~e*** lucky; ***przynosić ~e*** bring good luck; ***całe ~e, że*** how lucky that, fortunately; ***~e w nieszczęściu, że*** just as well that; ***próbować ~a*** try one's luck; ***dał mi na ~e łańcuszek*** he gave me a little chain for luck
szczęść: ***~ Boże!*** God bless (you)!
szczęśliwiec *m* (*-wca*; *-wcy*) lucky person, lucky man
szczęśliw|y *adj* **1.** (*zadowolony z życia*) happy; ***bardzo ~e małżeństwo*** very happy marriage; ***wyglądać na ~ego*** look happy; ***Ƨego Nowego Roku!*** Happy New Year **2.** (*pomyślny*) lucky, successful; ***~ej podróży!*** happy journey!, have a safe journey!; ***mieć ~ą rękę*** have a lucky hand **3.** (*pomyślny*, *sprzyjający*) fortunate; ***~y przypadek*** fortunate incident
szczęt: ***do ~u*** completely, utterly
szczodry *adj* generous
szczoteczka *f* (*-ki*; *-ki*): ***~ do zębów*** toothbrush
szczotka *f* (*-ki*; *-ki*) brush; ***~ do włosów*** hair-brush; ***~ do butów*** shoe-brush; ***~ do zamiatania*** broom; ***~ do mycia podłogi*** floor-polisher

S

szczotkować ⟨**wy-**⟩ (*-kuję*) **1.** *włosy, buty*: brush **2.** *konia*: brush down
szczuć ⟨**po-**⟩ (*-czuję*): **~ *kogoś psami*** set dogs on s.o.
szczudła *pl* (*-deł*): ***chodzić na ~ch*** walk on stilts
szczupak *m* (*-ka*; *-ki*) pike
szczupleć ⟨**wy-**, **ze-**⟩ (*-leję*) **1.** slim **2.** (*o zapasach, dochodach*) diminish, shrink
szczuplutki *adj dim* very slim; **szczupłość** *f* (*-ści*; *no pl*) slimness
szczupły *adj* **1.** slim **2.** *dłonie*: lean **3.** *zapasy*: scanty, *Br* meagre, *Am* meager **4.** *grono*: small
szczur *m* (*-ra*; *-ry*) rat; ***trutka na ~y*** rat poison; **~ *lądowy*** landlubber; **szczurzy** *adj* rat's
szczwany *adj* sly, cunning; **~ *lis*** cunning (old) fox
szczycić się ⟨**po-**⟩ (*-cę*) **1.** take pride (*I* in) **2.** (*posiadać*) boast; ***Polska może ~ pięknymi plażami*** Poland boasts beautiful beaches
szczygieł *m* (*-gła*; *-gły*) goldfinch
szczyp|ać ⟨**-pnąć**⟩ (*-pię*) **I** *v/t* pinch; ***~ać trawę*** browse on grass; ***dym ~ał nas w oczy*** the smoke was stinging our eyes **II** *v/i* **1.** (*o oczach*) sting, bite; ***oczy mnie ~ią*** my eyes are stinging; ***szampan ~ie w język*** the champagne tickles my tongue **2.** (*o mrozie*) nip; ***mróz ~ie*** it's nipping; **szczypać się** (*siebie*) pinch oneself
szczypawka *f* (*-ki*; *-ki*) BIOL earwig
szczypce *pl* (*-piec*) **1.** TECH pincers, pliers **2.** (*kraba*) pincers; **szczypczyki** *pl* (*-ków*) tweezers
szczypiorek *m* (*-rku*; *no pl*) chive
szczypnąć *v/p* → **szczypać**
szczypta *f* (*-ty*; *-ty*) *soli*, *pieprzu*: pinch; **~ *szczęścia*** a piece of luck
szczy|t *m* (*-tu*; *-ty*) **1.** *góry*: summit, peak; ***godziny ~tu*** rush hours; ***spotkanie na ~cie*** POLIT summit (meeting); ***u ~tu sławy*** at the (very) height of one's fame; ***to ~t wszystkiego!*** *infml* that beats everything! **2.** *drzewa*, *wieży*: top **3.** BUILD gable
szczytny *adj* **1.** *ideały*: lofty **2.** *cele*: noble
szczytowanie *n* (*-nia*; *-nia*) orgasm
szczytow|y *adj* **1.** *forma*: top, excellent **2.** *osiągnięcie*: greatest **3.** *partia*: upper **4.** (*dotyczący szczytu budynku*) ***ściana ~a*** BUILD gable
szedł → ***iść***
szedłem → ***iść***
szef *m* (*-fa*; *-fowie*) boss, manager; **~ *sztabu*** chief of staff; **~ *kuchni*** chef; **szefostwo** *n* (*-wa*; *no pl*) management; **szefowa** *f* (*-wej*; *-we*) manageress, boss
szejk *m* (*-ka*; *-kowie*) sheik
szelest *m* (*-tu*; *-ty*) rustle
szeleścić ⟨**za-**⟩ (*-leszczę*) rustle
szelf *m* (*-fu*; *-fy*) GEOGR shelf
szelk|i *pl* (*-lek*) *Br* braces, *Am* suspenders; ***spódnica na ~ach*** skirt with straps
szelma *f/m* (*-my*; *-my*) rogue, rascal; **szelmowski** *adj* **1.** (*łotrowski*) roguish; **~ *postępek*** roguish act **2.** *uśmiech*: skittish **3.** *hum* impish
szemrać *v/im* (*-rzę*) murmur
szepnąć *v/p* → ***szeptać***
szept *m* (*-tu*; *-ty*) whisper; ***rozmawiać ~em*** whisper, speak in a whisper; ***~y*** *fig* gossip, rumour
szeptać ⟨**-pnąć**⟩ (*-pczę/-pcę*) whisper; **~ *komuś do ucha*** whisper into s.o.'s ear
szeptanina *f* (*-ny*; *no pl*) whispers *pl*, whispering; **szeptany** *adj propaganda*: whispered
szereg *m* (*-gu*; *-gi*) row; ***~i*** *fig* ranks; ***ustawić się w ~u*** line up, form a row
szeregować ⟨**u-**⟩ (*-guję*) rank, classify
szeregowiec *m* (*-wca*; *-wcy*) private (soldier); ***starszy ~*** *Br* lance corporal, *Am* private first class
szeregowy **I** *adj* **1.** *zabudowa*: terraced **2.** *połączenie*: serial **3.** (*przeciętny*) ordinary, regular **II** *m* (*-wego*; *-wi*) (*w wojsku*) private
szermierka[1] *f* (*-ki*; *no pl*) (*sport*) fencing; **~ *słowna*** sword-play, verbal sparring
szermierka[2] *f* (*-ki*; *-ki*) (*kobieta*) (female) fencer
szermierz *m* (*-rza*; *-rze*) fencer
szerok|i *adj* **1.** broad, wide; ***~i na 2 metry*** 2 metres wide; ***~i w barach*** broad-shouldered, broad-chested; ***~i uśmiech*** broad smile; ***mieć ~i gest*** be generous; ***mieć ~ie horyzonty*** be broad-minded; ***na ~ą skalę*** on a large scale; ***jak kraj długi i ~i*** all across the

S

country, throughout the country; ***~iej drogi!*** have a safe journey!; ***w ~im świecie*** in the wide world **2.** *rzeka, droga, asortyment, publiczność*: wide **3.** *ubranie*: loose, baggy

szeroko *adv* widely; ***~ rozpowszechniony*** widespread; ***~ otwarty*** wide open

szerokość *f* (*-ści*; *no pl*) breadth, width; ***~ geograficzna*** latitude

szerszeń *m* (*-szenia*; *-szenie*) hornet

szerszy *comp* → **szeroki**

szerzej *comp* → **szeroko**

szerzyć *v/im* (*-rzę*) propagate, spread; ***szerzyć się*** spread

szesnastka *f* (*-ki*; *-ki*) **1.** (number) sixteen **2.** (*dziewczyna*) *infml* sixteen-year-old

szesnastoletni *adj* **1.** *chłopak, samochód*: sixteen-year-old **2.** *okres*: sixteen-year, of sixteen years; **szesnastowieczny** *adj* sixteenth-century

szesnast|y *adj* sixteenth; ***o ~ej*** at four o'clock p.m.

szesnaście *num* sixteen

sześcian *m* (*-nu*; *-ny*) MATH cube; ***podnieść do ~u*** cube, raise to the power of three; **sześcienny** *adj* cubic

sześcio- (*w złożeniach*) six-, hexa-; ***~letnia dziewczyna*** six-year-old girl, ***~boczny*** hexagonal

sześciobok *m* (*-ku*; *-ki*) MATH hexagon; **sześciokrotny** *adj* **1.** *mistrz*: six-time **2.** *wzrost*: sixfold

sześciolatek *m* (*-tka*; *-tki*) sixteen-year-old, boy of six; **sześciolatka** *f* (*-ki*; *-ki*) sixteen-year-old, girl of six

sześciolecie *n* (*-cia*; *-cia*) **1.** (*okres*) six-year period **2.** (*rocznica*) sixth anniversary; **sześcioletni** *adj* **1.** *dziecko, samochód*: six-year-old **2.** *okres*: six-year, of six years; **sześciomiesięczny** *adj* **1.** *dziecko*: six-month-old **2.** *okres*: six-year, of six years

sześcioro, ***sześciu, sześć*** *num* six

sześćdziesiąt *num* sixty; **sześćdziesiąt|y** *adj* sixtieth; ***lata ~e*** the sixties

sześćdziesięcioletni *adj* **1.** sixty-year-old **2.** *okres*: sixty-year, of sixty years; **sześćset** *num* six hundred

szew *m* (*szwu*; *szwy*) stitch; ***zdjąć szwy*** take out the stitches, remove the stitches; ***bez szwu*** seamless

szewc *m* (*-ca*; *-cy*) shoemaker, cobbler; **szewsk|i** *adj* shoemaker's, cobbler's; ***~a pasja*** fury

szkalować ⟨**o-**⟩ (*-luję*) slander, vilify

szkapa *f* (*-py*; *-py*) nag, hack

szkaradny *adj* hideous

szkarlatyna *f* (*-ny*; *no pl*) MED scarlet fever

szkarłat *m* (*-tu*; *-ty*) scarlet; **szkarłatny** *adj* scarlet

szkatułka *f* (*-ki*; *-ki*) casket

szkic *m* (*-cu*; *-ce*) **1.** (*projekt*) draft **2.** (*do obrazu*) sketch

szkicować ⟨**na-**⟩ (*-cuję*) **1.** (*rysować*) sketch **2.** (*przedstawiać w zarysie*) outline

szkicownik *m* (*-ka*; *-ki*) sketch-book, sketch-block; **szkicowo** *adv* **1.** (*niekompletnie*) sketchily **2.** (*w przybliżeniu*) roughly

szkielet *m* (*-tu*; *-ty*) **1.** ANAT skeleton **2.** BUILD framework

szkiełko *n* (*-ka*; *-ka*) glass; ***~ od zegarka*** watch glass

szklanka *f* (*-ki*; *-ki*) **1.** (*naczynie*) glass; ***~ mleka*** glass of milk **2.** (*gołoledź*) glazed frost, glaze ice; **szklany** *adj* **1.** glass **2.** *oczy, wzrok*: glassy

szklarnia *f* (*-ni*; *-nie*) greenhouse; **szklarniowy** *adj* greenhouse

szklarski *adj* glazier's; **szklarz** *m* (*-rza*; *-rze*) glazier

szklić ⟨**o-**⟩ (*-lę*) glaze

szklisty *adj* glassy; **szkliwo** *n* (*-wa*; *no pl*) **1.** *ceramiczne*: glaze **2.** ANAT enamel

szkł|o *n* (*-ła*; *-ła*) **1.** glass; ***~o kuloodporne*** bulletproof glass; ***rżnięte ~o*** cut glass; ***~o artystyczne*** artistic glass; ***~o powiększające*** magnifying glass; ***za ~em*** under glass; ***pod ~em*** AGR under glass, in a greenhouse **2.** (*soczewka*) lens; ***~a kontaktowe*** contact lenses **3.** (*naczynia*) glassware **4.** (*odpryski*) splinters *pl*, chips *pl*

Szkocja *f* (*-ji*) Scotland

szkocki *adj* Scottish

szkod|a **I** *f* (*-dy*; *-dy*) (*strata*) damage, loss; ***~y spowodowane pożarem*** fire damage; ***na ~ę*** *G*, ***ze ~ą dla*** *G* to the detriment of **II** *adv* ***~a mi go*** I pity him, I'm sorry for him; ***~a!*** what a pity!; ***~a, że*** it's a pity that; ***jaka ~a!***

S

what a pity!, what a shame!; **~a nam było wyjeżdżać** we wished we could have stayed; **~a twojego czasu** you're wasting your time, it's a waste of your time; **~a słów** waste of breath

szkodliwość *f* (*-ści*; *no pl*) harmfulness; **~ społeczna** damage to society; **szkodliwy** *adj* **1.** harmful, bad; **~ dla zdrowia** harmful to one's health; **~ dla środowiska** environmentally unfriendly **2.** *klimat*: unwholesome

szkodnik *m* (*-ka*; *-ki*) pest; **~i** pests, vermin

szkodzi|ć ⟨**za-**⟩ (*-dzę*) be harmful, do harm (*D* to); **co to ~?** what harm is there in that?; **nie ~!** never mind!; **co ci ~ zapytać go o to?** why don't you ask him about it?

szkolenie *n* (*-nia*; *-nia*) training (course); **~ zawodowe** professional training; **szkoleniowiec** *m* (*-wca*; *-wcy*) **1.** (*nauczyciel*) trainer, instructor **2.** (*trener*) coach; **szkoleniowy** *adj kurs*: training

szkolić ⟨**wy-**⟩ (*-lę*) *zawodowo*: train; **szkolić się** receive training (**w** *L* in), undergo training (**w** *L* in)

szkolnictwo *n* (*-wa*; *no pl*) education, educational system; **~ wyższe** higher education

szkolny *adj* school; **podręcznik ~** school handbook; **~ kolega** schoolmate; **dzieci w wieku ~m** school-age children; **był w wieku ~m** he was at school age

szkoł|a *f* (*-ły*; *-ły*) school; **chodzić do ~y** go to school, attend school; **~a podstawowa** *Br* primary school, *Am* elementary school; **~a średnia** *Br* secondary school, *Am* high school; **~a wyższa** higher education institution, *Am* tertiary-level school, college; **~a zawodowa** vocational school; **~a baletowa** ballet school; **~a przetrwania** survival school; **~a rodzenia** antenatal classes; **iść do ~y w wieku sześciu lat** go to school at the age of six

szkopuł *m* (*-łu*; *-ły*) *lit* hitch; **~ w tym, że** the problem is that, the hitch is that

szkorbut *m* (*-tu*; *no pl*) MED scurvy

Szkot *m* (*-ta*; *Szkoci*) Scotsman, Scot; **Szkotka** *f* (*-ki*; *-ki*) Scotswoman, Scot

szkółka *f* (*-ki*; *-ki*) *dim* school; **~ leśna** nursery; **~ narciarska** ski school; **~ niedzielna** Sunday school

szkrab *m* (*-ba*; *-by*) tot, toddler

szkutnictwo *n* (*-wa*; *no pl*) boatbuilding; **szkutnik** *m* (*-ka*; *-nicy*) boatbuilder

szkwał *m* (*-łu*; *-ły*) squall

szlaban *m* (*-nu*; *-ny*) barrier; **mieć ~** *infml* be grounded (**na** *A* for)

szlachcic *m* (*-ca*; *-ce*) HIST nobleman, gentleman; **~ zagrodowy** yeoman; **szlachcianka** *f* (*-ki*; *-ki*) HIST noblewoman

szlachecki *adj* nobleman's, gentleman's; **szlachectwo** *n* (*-wa*; *no pl*) HIST nobility; **nadać ~ a)** HIST ennoble **b)** (*współcześnie*) knight; **Beatlesom nadano ~** the Beatles were knighted

szlachetność *f* (*-ści*; *no pl*) **1.** *czynu*: nobleness, high-mindedness **2.** *rysów*: refinement, dignity; **szlachetny** *adj* **1.** noble **2.** *rysy*, *proporcje*: noble, refined, dignified **3.** *kamień*: precious

szlachta *f* (*-ty*; *no pl*) HIST nobility; **~ zaściankowa** HIST yeomanry; **~ rodowa** nobility

szlafrok *m* (*-ka*; *-ki*) *Br* dressing-gown, *Am* (bath)robe; **~ kąpielowy** bathrobe

szlag *infml*: **~ mnie trafia** I'm furious, it gets my goat

szlagier *m* (*-ru*; *-ry*) **1.** (*piosenka*) hit; **wielki ~** smash hit; **~ sezonu** hit of the season **2.** (*książka*, *film*) blockbuster **3.** (*książka*) bestseller

szlajać się *v/im* (*-jam*) *infml* gallivant, hang around

szlak *m* (*-ku*; *-ki*) **1.** route; **~ handlowy** trade route; **~ komunikacyjny** communication route; **~ morski** sea route, sea lane; **~ bursztynowy** HIST amber route **2.** (*dla turystów*) trail, track; **~ turystyczny**, **~ wędrowny** hiking trail, track; **~ rowerowy** bicycle track **3.** (*na tkaninie*) border

szlam *m* (*-mu*; *-my*) silt, mud

szli → **iść**

szlif *m* (*-fu*; *-fy*) cut; **ostatni ~** *fig* the finishing touch(es)

szlifierka *f* (*-ki*; *-ki*) grinding machine; **szlifierski** *adj* grinding; **kamień ~**

S

grindstone; **szlifierz** *m* (*-rza*; *-rze*) grinder; **~ diamentów** diamond cutter
szlifować ⟨**o-**⟩ (*-fuję*) **1.** (*obrabiać*) grind **2.** *diamenty, szkło*: cut **3.** (*polerować*) polish **4.** *fig* polish (up)
szloch *m* (*-chu*; *-chy*) sob
szlochać ⟨**za-**⟩ (*-cham*) sob
szlufka *f* (*-ki*; *-ki*) *Br* belt loop, *Am* belt carrier
szła → ***iść***
szłam → ***iść***
szmacian|y *adj*: ***lalka ~a*** rag doll
szmal *m* (*-lu*; *no pl*) *infml* dough
szmaragd *m* (*-du*; *-dy*) emerald; **szmaragdowy** *adj* **1.** (*ze szmaragdu*) emerald **2.** (*o kolorze*) emerald-green
szmat: ***~ drogi*** a very long way; ***~ czasu*** a very long time
szmat|a *f* (*-ty*; *-ty*) **1.** rag; ***~a do podłogi*** floor rag **2.** (*o człowieku*) *infml* piece of shit **3.** (*kobieta*) *infml* slut; **szmatk|a** *f* (*-ki*; *-ki*) (*ściereczka*) cloth; ***~i*** *fig* clothes
szmatławiec *m* (*-wca*; *-wce*) *infml* rag
szmelc *m* (*-cu*; *no pl*) scrap, junk
szmer *m* (*-ru*; *-ry*) murmur; ***~y w sercu*** heart murmurs
szmergl|iel: ***mieć ~la na punkcie*** *G infml* be crazy about
szminka *f* (*-ki*; *-ki*) **1.** (*do ust*) lipstick **2.** THEAT greasepaint
szminkować ⟨**wy-**, **u-**⟩ (*-kuję*): ***~ usta*** put on lipstick; ***szminkować się*** put on lipstick
szmira *f* (*-ry*; *-ry*) trash
szmugiel *m* (*-glu*; *no pl*) smuggling, contraband
szmuglować ⟨**prze-**⟩ (*-luję*) smuggle
sznur *m* (*-ra*; *-ry*) rope, line; ***~ do bielizny*** clothes-line; ***~ pereł*** string of pearls; ***~ ptaków*** string of birds; **sznurek** *m* (*-rka*; *-rki*) string
sznurować ⟨**za-**⟩ (*-ruję*) lace (up)
sznurowadło *n* (*-ła*; *-ła*) *Br* (shoe)lace, *Am* shoestring
sznurow|y *adj*: ***drabinka ~a*** rope-ladder
sznurówka *f* (*-ki*; *-ki*) → ***sznurowadło***
sznycel *m* (*-cla*; *-cle*) schnitzel, veal cutlet
szofer *m* (*-ra*; *-rzy*) **1.** (*prywatny kierowca*) chauffeur **2.** (*kierowca*) driver; **szoferka** *f* (*-ki*; *-ki*) cab
szok *m* (*-ku*; *no pl*) shock; ***w ~u*** in shock, shocked; ***doznać ~u*** get a shock; ***~ na giełdzie*** FIN stock market shock
szokować ⟨**za-**⟩ (*-kuję*) shock; **szokujący** *adj* shocking
szop *m* (*-pa*; *-py*) raccoon
szopa *f* (*-py*; *-py*) shed; **szopka** *f* (*-ki*; *-ki*) **1.** REL nativity scene, *Am* creche **2.** (*farsa, błazenada*) farce
szorować ⟨**wy-**⟩ (*-ruję*) **1.** *ręce, podłogę*: scrub; ***szoruj stąd!*** *infml* off you go!, *Am* beat it! **2.** *zlew, garnki*: scour
szorstki *adj* **1.** *powierzchnia*: rough **2.** (*obcesowy*) brusque, curt
szorty *pl* (*-tów*) shorts
szosa *f* (*-sy*; *-sy*) road, highway; **szosow|y** *adj*: ***kolarstwo ~e*** road racing
szot *m* (*-tu*; *-ty*) (*zespół lin i bloków*) sheet
szowinista *m* (*-ty*; *-niści*) chauvinist; **szowinistyczny** *adj* chauvinistic
szóstk|a *f* (*-ki*; *-ki*) six; ***mieszkać pod ~ą*** live at number six; ***~a pik*** six of spades; ***pojechał ~ą*** he took the tram number six; **szóst|y** *adj* sixth; ***o ~ej*** (***godzinie***) at six (o'clock)
szpachla *f* (*-li*; *-le*) **1.** (*narzędzie*) putty knife **2.** (*masa*) putty; **szpachlować** ⟨**wy-**⟩ (*-luję*) putty, fill with putty; **szpachlówka** *f* (*-ki*; *-ki*) (painter's) putty
szpada *f* (*-dy*; *-dy*) **1.** sword, rapier **2.** SPORT épée
szpadel *m* (*-dla*; *-dle*) spade
szpagat *m* (*-tu*; *-ty*) **1.** SPORT splits; ***robić ~*** do the splits **2.** (*sznurek*) twine
szpak *m* (*-ka*; *-ki*) BIOL starling
szpakowaty *adj* *włosy*: pepper-and-salt, touched with grey
szpaler *m* (*-ru*; *-ry*) double row
szpalta *f* (*-ty*; *-ty*) column
szpan *infml*: ***dla ~u*** for show, to show off
szpaner *m* (*-ra*; *-rzy*), ***~ka*** *f* (*-ki*; *-ki*) *infml* show-off; **szpanerstwo** *n* (*-wa*; *no pl*) *infml* showing off; **szpanerski** *adj* *infml* swanky, showy
szpanować ⟨**za-**⟩ (*-nuję*) *infml* show off, swank
szpara *f* (*-ry*; *-ry*) **1.** (*szczelina*) slit **2.** (*w drzwiach*) gap
szparagi *pl* (*-gów*) asparagus *sing*
szparagow|y *adj* asparagus; ***fasolka ~a*** *Br* French beans, *Am* string beans
szpargały *pl* (*-łów*) old papers

S

szparka *f* (*-ki*; *-ki*) slit, chink
szpecić ⟨**o-**⟩ (*-cę*) **1.** *osobę*, *wygląd*: disfigure **2.** *widok*: mar, spoil
szperać *v/im* (*-ram*) rummage (**w** *L* through); **~ w cudzych rzeczach** poke around in s.o. else's stuff
szpetny *adj* ugly, unsightly; **szpetota** *f* (*-ty*; *no pl*) ugliness
szpic *m* (*-ca*; *-ce*) point; **w ~** pointed; **dekolt w ~** V-neck; **~ na choinkę** christmas tree peak
szpicel *m* (*-cla*; *-cle*) rat, snoop(er)
szpiclować *v/im* (*-luję*) **1.** (*szpiegować*) spy **2.** (*donosić*) grass (*G* on) **3.** (*poszukiwać informacji*) snoop (around)
szpicruta *f* (*-ty*; *-ty*) riding crop
szpieg *m* (*-ga*; *-piedzy*) spy; **szpiegostwo** *n* (*-wa*; *no pl*) espionage, spying; **szpiegować** *v/im* (*-guję*) spy; **szpiegowski** *adj* spy
szpik *m* (*-ku*; *no pl*): **~ kostny** ANAT bone marrow; **zepsuty do ~u kości** *fig* rotten to the core; **zmarznąć do ~u kości** be chilled to the marrow
szpikować ⟨**na-**⟩ (*-kuję*) COOK lard (*I* with); **~ cytatami** lard with quotations; **~ lekarstwami** stuff with drugs
szpikulec *m* (*-lca*; *-lce*) **1.** spike **2.** (*do pieczenia*) skewer, spit
szpilk|a *f* (*-ki*; *-ki*) pin; **~a do włosów** hairpin; **~a do krawata** tie-pin; **~i** stilettos, stiletto heels; **nosić ~i** wear high heels; **siedzieć jak na ~ach** be on tenterhooks, *Am* be on pins and needles
szpinak *m* (*-ku*; *no pl*) spinach
szpital *m* (*-la*; *-le*) hospital; **~ dla umysłowo chorych** mental hospital; **~ polowy** field hospital; **szpitalny** *adj* hospital
szpony *pl* (*-nów*) **1.** (*ptaków*) talons; **orzeł zatopił ~ w króliku** the eagle sank its talons into the rabbit **2.** (*ssaków drapieżnych*) claws; **dostać się w czyjeś ~** *fig* fall into s.o.'s clutches
szprotka *f* (*-ki*; *-ki*) sprat
szprycha *f* (*-chy*; *-chy*) **1.** (*rowerowa*) spoke **2.** (*dziewczyna*) *infml* chick
szprycować ⟨**na-**⟩ (*-cuję*): **~ lekarstwami** stuff with drugs; **szprycować się** *infml* shoot up; **ona się szprycuje** she is a junkie
szpula *f* (*-li*; *-le*) spool, reel; **szpulka** *f* (*-ki*; *-ki*) *nici*: bobbin
szrama *f* (*-my*; *-my*) scar
szreń *f* (*-reni*; *no pl*) névé, firn
szron *m* (*-nu*; *no pl*) hoar frost, *lit* rime
sztab *m* (*-bu*; *-by*) *batalionu*: staff; **~ doradców** board of advisors; **~ główny** general staff; **~ ekspertów** panel of experts
sztaba *f* (*-by*; *-by*) bar; **~ złota** goldbar
sztabka *f* (*-ki*; *-ki*) *dim* → **sztaba**
sztabowy *adj oficer*: staff
sztacheta *f* (*-ty*; *-ty*) picket
sztafeta *f* (*-ty*; *-ty*) SPORT relay race; **sztafetowy** *adj bieg*, *pałeczka*: relay
sztalugi *pl* (*-lug*) easel *sing*; **sztalugow|y** *adj*: **malarstwo ~e** easel painting
sztam|a: **trzymać ~ę** keep in good (**z** *I* with), be as thick as thieves (**z** *I* with)
sztampa *f* (*-py*; *no pl*) set pattern; **sztampowy** *adj sposób*, *finał*, *tytuł*: hackneyed, run-of-the-mill
sztanca *f* (*-cy*; *-ce*) die
sztandar *m* (*-ru*; *-ry*) **1.** banner **2.** *szkolny*: standard; **sztandarowy** *adj* (*reprezentatywny*) representative, leading; **~ przykład** representative example; **poczet ~** colour guard
sztanga *f* (*-gi*; *-gi*) SPORT barbell; **sztangista** *m* (*-ty*; *-giści*) weightlifter
Sztokholm *m* (*-mu*) Stockholm
sztolnia *f* (*-ni*; *-nie*) MIN gallery, drift
sztorc: **na ~**, **~em** on end
sztorcować ⟨**ob-**⟩ (*-cuję*) *infml* give s.o. a dressing down, bawl s.o. out
sztorm *m* (*-mu*; *-my*) storm; **sztormiak** *m* (*-ka*; *-ki*) **1.** (*kurtka*) sailing jacket **2.** (*komplet*) sailing suit; **sztormowy** *adj* stormy
sztruksowy *adj spodnie*, *kurtka*: cord, corduroy; **sztruksy** *pl* (*-sów*) cords, corduroys
sztuback|i *adj*: **~i kawał** schoolboy's joke; **~a miłość** school love, puppy love
sztucer *m* (*-ra*; *-ry*) rifle
sztuczka *f* (*-ki*; *-ki*) trick
sztuczn|y *adj oddychanie*, *lodowisko*: artificial; **włókno ~e** *Br* synthetic fibre, *Am* synthetic fiber; **~e ognie** fireworks
sztućce *pl* (*-ców*) cutlery *sing*
sztufada *f* (*-dy*; *-dy*) COOK larded beef roast, stewed beef
sztuk|a *f* (*ki*; *-ki*) **1.** art; **~a kulinarna** the art of cooking; **~i piękne** fine arts;

S

~a współczesna modern art; **historia ~i** the history of art; **do trzech razy ~a** third time lucky; **to nie ~a** there's nothing to it **2.** THEAT play **3.** (*egzemplarz*) piece, item; **sprzedawać na ~i** sell by the piece

sztukateria *f* (*-rii*; *-rie*) ARCHIT stucco (work)

sztukmistrz *m* (*-rza*; *-rzowie*) conjurer, magician

sztukować ⟨**do-**, **ze-**⟩ (*-kuję*) lengthen

szturchać ⟨**-chnąć**⟩ (*-cham*) nudge; **szturchaniec** *m* (*-chańca*; *-chańce*) nudge

szturm *m* (*-mu*; *-my*) storm; **przypuścić ~ na** *A* storm; **wziąć coś ~em** take s.th. by storm; **szturmować** *v/im* (*-muję*) storm

sztych *m* (*-chu*; *-chy*) (*rycina*) engraving

sztyf|t **dezodorant w ~cie** deostick, stick deodorant

sztygar *m* (*-ra*; *-rzy*) MIN foreman

sztylet *m* (*-tu*; *-ty*) dagger

sztywniak *m* (*-ka*; *-niacy*/*-ki*) *infml* stuff shirt, *infml* stiff

sztywnieć ⟨**ze-**⟩ (*-nieję*) *kark*, *palce*: stiffen, get stiff; **~ ze strachu** be petrified

sztywn|y *adj* **1.** stiff **2.** *przepisy*, *reguły*, *struktura*, *interpretacja*: rigid **3.** *ruchy*: wooden, angular **4.** *okładka*: hard; **książka w ~ej okładce** harback **5.** *cena*: fixed

szubienica *f* (*-cy*; *-ce*) gallows *sing*

szubrawiec *m* (*-wca*; *-wcy*) scoundrel, rogue

szufelka *f* (*-ki*; *-ki*) **1.** (*do śmieci*) dustpan **2.** (*do węgla*, *koksu*) (little) shovel; **szufla** *f* (*-li*; *-le*) shovel

szuflada *f* (*-dy*; *-dy*) drawer; **szufladkować** ⟨**za-**⟩ (*-kuję*) *fig* pigeon-hole

szuflować *v/im* (*-luję*) shovel

szuja *f/m* (*szui*; *-je*) rascal, scum

szukać *v/im* (*-kam*) look for, seek; **~ pracy** look for a job; **~ guza** be looking for trouble; **~ kompromisu** search for a compromise; **~ pomocy** (**porady fachowej**) seek help (professional advice); **szukałem wszędzie** I've looked everywhere; **~ czegoś po omacku** grope for s.th.; **~ czegoś w słowniku** look s.th. up in a dictionary; **~ igły w stogu siana** *fig* look for a needle in a haystack; **szukaj!** search for it!

S

szukanie *n* (*-nia*; *no pl*) search; **~ pracy** job hunting, looking for a job; **~ mieszkania** flat hunting

szuler *m* (*-ra*; *-rzy*) cardsharp(er)

szum *m* (*-mu*; *-my*) **1.** hum; **~ w uszach** buzzing in the ears; **narobić ~u** *fig* hype (**wokół** *G*), make a big fuss (**wokół** *G* about) **2.** *fal*, *strumienia*: murmur **3.** *wiatru*, *drzew*: sough, murmur **4.** *wentylatora*, *skrzydeł*: whirr **5. ~y** RADIO static

szumi|eć *v/im* (*-mię*) **1.** hum; **~ało mi w uszach** my ears buzzed; **~ało nam w głowach** (*po alkoholu*) we were tipsy **2.** (*o falach*, *strumieniu*) murmur **3.** (*o wietrze*, *drzewach*) sough, murmur **4.** (*o piwie*, *szampanie*) sparkle **5.** (*o wentylatorze*, *suszarce*) whirr

szumny *adj* **1.** *zapowiedź*, *nazwa*: grand-sounding **2.** *słowa*: pompous, bombastic

szumowiny *pl* (*-win*) **1.** COOK scum *sing* **2.** (*ludzie*) dregs (of society), riff-raff *sing*

szurać ⟨**-rnąć**⟩ (*-ram*) make a scraping sound: **~ nogami** shuffle one's feet

szurnięty *adj infml* nuts, crazy, loony

szuwary *pl* (*-rów*) rush *sing*, rushes

szwab *m* (*-ba*; *-by*), **~ka** *f* (*-ki*; *-ki*) *infml* Kraut, Fritz; **szwabski** *adj infml* Kraut

szwaczka *f* (*-ki*; *-ki*) seamstress

szwadron *m* (*-nu*; *-ny*) squadron

szwagier *m* (*-gra*; *-growie*) brother-in-law; **szwagierka** *f* (*-ki*; *-ki*) sister-in-law

Szwajcar *m* (*-ra*; *-rzy*) Swiss; **Szwajcaria** *f* (*-rii*) Switzerland; **Szwajcarka** *f* (*-ki*; *-ki*) Swiss; **szwajcarski** *adj* Swiss

szwalnia *f* (*-ni*; *-nie*) sewing (work)-shop

szwank *m* (*-ku*; *no pl*) injury, loss; **narazić kogoś na ~** jeopardize s.o., put s.o. in jeopardy; **wyjść z czegoś bez ~u** come through s.th. unscathed, escape s.th. unharmed

szwank|ować *v/im* (*-kuję*) be failing, not work well; **czyjeś zdrowie ~uje** s.o.'s health is failing

szwargotać *v/im* (*-goczę*/*-gocę*) jabber, gibber

Szwecja *f* (*-ji*) Sweden; **Szwed** *m* (*-da*; *-dzi*) Swede; **Szwedka** *f* (*-ki*; *-ki*) Swede, Swedish woman

szwedzki *adj* Swedish; **stół ~** all-you-can-eat buffet, smorgasbord
szwendać się *v/im* (*-dam*) gad about, hang around
szwindel *m* (*-dlu*; *-dle*) swindle
szwu → **szew**
szwy *pl* → **szew**
szyb *m* (*-bu*; *-by*) shaft; **~ wentylacyjny** ventilation shaft; **~ górniczy** mineshaft, coal pit; **~ naftowy** oil well
szyba *f* (*-by*; *-by*) **1.** (window)pane **2.** *AUTO Br* windscreen, *Am* windshield
szyberdach *m* (*-chu*; *-chy*) sunroof
szybka *f* (*-ki*; *-ki*) (small) pane
szybki *adj* **1.** quick, fast; **~e czytanie** speed reading; **~ zysk** quick profit **2.** *jazda*: fast **3.** *oddech*, *spojrzenie*: quick **4.** *tempo*: fast, *zmiany*: rapid, fast
szybkobieżny *adj* **1.** *autobus*: fast, express **2.** *winda*: high-speed; **szybkostrzelny** *adj*: **pistolet ~** quick-firing gun
szybkościomierz *m* (*-rza*; *-rze*) *AUTO* speedometer
szybkość *f* (*-ści*; *-ści*) **1.** (*prędkość*) speed; **zwiększać ~** accelerate **2.** *decyzji*, *odpowiedzi*: promptness, quickness
szybkowar *m* (*-ru*; *-ry*) pressure cooker
szybować ⟨**po-**⟩ (*-buję*) soar, glide
szybowcowy *adj*: **lot ~** glider flight
szybowiec *m* (*-wca*; *-wce*) glider; **szybownictwo** *n* (*-wa*; *no pl*) gliding; **szybownik** *m* (*-ka*; *-nicy*) glider pilot
szybowy *adj MIN* shaft
szybsi → **szybki**
szybszy *comp* → **szybki**
szycha *f* (*-chy*; *-chy*) *infml* big fish, big shot, bigwig
szyci|e *n* (*-cia*; *no pl*) **1.** sewing; **maszyna do ~a** sewing machine **2.** (*ręczne*) needlework
szyć ⟨**u-**⟩ (*szyję*) **1.** sew; **dać coś do szycia**, **uszyć sobie coś** have s.th. made **2.** *ranę*: stitch (up)
szydełk|o *n* (*-ka*; *-ka*) crochet hook; **robić ~iem** crochet; **szydełkować** *v/im* (*-kuję*) crochet; **szydełkowy** *adj* crochet
szyderca *m* (*-cy*; *-cy*) scoffer, jeerer; **szyderczo** *adv*: **uśmiechać się ~** sneer; **szyderczy** *adj* derisive, scoffing; **~ uśmieszek** sneer; **szyderstwo** *n* (*-wa*; *-wa*) **1.** (*szyderczy stosunek*) derision **2.** (*komentarz*) scoff, sneer
szydło *n* (*-ła*; *-ła*) awl; **wyszło ~ z worka** the cat is out of the bag, the truth has come out
szydzić *v/im* (*-dzę*) scoff, sneer (**z** *G* at)
szyfon *m* (*-nu*; *-ny*) chiffon
szyfr *m* (*-ru*; *-ry*) code, cipher; **szyfrować** ⟨**za-**⟩ (*-ruję*) code, cipher; **szyfrowy** *adj* code; **zamek ~** combination lock
szyja *f* (*szyi*; *-je*) neck; **łabędzia ~** *fig* swan-neck
szyjk|a *f* (*-ki*; *-ki*) *dim* neck; **~a butelki** neck of the bottle, bottle's neck; **~a macicy** *ANAT* cervix; **zapalenie ~i macicy** cervicitis
szyjn|y *adj*: **kręgi ~e** *ANAT* cervical vertebrae
szyk[1] *m* (*-ku*; *no pl*) chic, style; **z ~iem** elegantly
szyk[2] *m* (*-ku*; *no pl*) **1.** formation; **~ marszowy** march formation; **~ bitewny** battle order; **popsuć komuś ~i** *fig* thwart s.o.'s plans **2.** *GRAM* **~ zdania** word order; **~ przestawny** inversion
szykanować *v/im* (*-nuję*) harass; **szykany** *pl* (*-kan*) harassment *sing*
szykować ⟨**przy-**, **u-**⟩ (*-kuję*) **1.** prepare **2.** (*gotować*) cook; **szykować się** get ready, prepare (**do** *G*/**na** *A* for); **~ się do podróży** get ready for a journey; **~ się do skoku** prepare for one's jump
szyld *m* (*-du*; *-dy*) signboard; **działać pod ~em** *G* act under the aegis of, operate behind the facade of
szyling *m* (*-ga*; *-gi*) **1.** (*brytyjski*) shilling **2.** (*austriacki*) schilling
szylkret *m* (*-tu*; *no pl*) tortoiseshell
szympans *m* (*-sa*; *-sy*) chimpanzee, *infml* chimp
szyn|a *f* (*-ny*; *-ny*) **1.** (*kolejowa*) rail; **~y** rail tracks **2.** *MED* splint
szynka *f* (*-ki*; *-ki*) ham
szynowy *adj transport*: rail
szyper *m* (*-pra*; *-prowie*) skipper
szypułkować *v/im* (*-kuje*): **~ truskawki** remove stems from strawberries
szyszka *f* (*-ki*; *-ki*) cone
szyty *adj*: **~ na miarę** made-to-measure

S

ścian|a *f* (*-ny*; *-ny*) **1.** wall; **~a działowa** partition wall; **mieszkać przez ~ę** live next door; **w czterech ~ach** in four walls **2.** *skrzyni*, *szafy*: side; **ścianka** *f* (*-ki*; *-ki*) *skrzyni*, *szafy*: side; **~ działowa** partition wall

ściąć *v/p* → **ścinać**

ściąga *f* (*-gi*; *-gi*) *infml* crib, cheat sheet

ściągacz *m* (*-cza*; *-cze*) (*przy rękawie*) ribbed cuff

ściągać ⟨**-gnąć**⟩ (*-gam*) **I** *v/t* **1.** *buty*, *ubranie*, *pierścionek*: take off **2.** *podatki*: collect **3.** (*sprowadzać*) bring, get; **~ komuś coś na kark** lumber s.o. with s.th.; **~ sobie coś na kark** be saddled with s.th., get lumped with s.th.; **~ na siebie uwagę** draw attention to oneself; **~ na siebie czyjś gniew** turn s.o.'s anger upon oneself; **~ kogoś z łóżka** drag s.o. out of bed **4.** *skórę*: remove; **~ skórę z pomidorów** (**świni**) skin tomatoes (pig) **5.** *wino*: rack **6.** *flagę*: take down **7.** *brwi*: knit **8.** (*odpisywać*) cheat, copy **9.** INF download **II** *v/i* (*zbierać się*) come flocking, gather; **ściągać się** (*kurczyć się*) contract; **~ się pasem** tighten one's belt

ściągawka *f* (*-ki*; *-ki*) crib, cheat sheet

ściągnąć *v/p* → **ściągać**

ścichać ⟨**-chnąć**⟩ (*-cham*) **1.** *gwar*, *odgłosy*: become quiet **2.** (*powoli*) die away

ścieg *m* (*-gu*; *-gi*) stitch; **~ łańcuszkowy** chain stitch

ściek *m* (*-ku*; *-ki*) (*kanał*) sewer; **~i** (*zanieczyszczenia*) sewage, waste

ściekać ⟨**-knąć**⟩ (*-kam*) (*o wodzie*, *pocie*) trickle (down)

ściekow|y *adj* sewage; **studzienka ~a**, **kratka ~a** drain

ścielić ⟨**po-**⟩ (*-lę*): **~ łóżko** make the bed

ściemniać ⟨**-nić**⟩ (*-niam*) **1.** *światło*: darken **2.** (*zmyślać*) *infml* pile it on, lay it on thick; **ściemnia się** it's getting dark

ściemnieć *v/p* → **ciemnieć**

ścienn|y *adj lustro*, *zegar*: wall; **malowidło ~e** mural

ścierać ⟨**zetrzeć**⟩ (*-ram*) **1.** *skórę*: scrape, abrade **2.** (*gumką*) *Br* rub out, *Am* erase; **~ kurze z** *G* dust **3.** COOK grate **4.** *napis*: wipe off **5.** *tablicę*: clean, erase **6.** *podłogę*: clean, wash; **ścierać się 1.** (*o materiale*) wear out **2.** (*o napisie*) wear off **3.** (*o wojsku*, *poglądach*) clash **4.** (*o farbie*) wear thin

ściereczka *f* (*-ki*; *-ki*) *dim* → **ścierka**

ścierka *f* (*-ki*; *-ki*) cloth; **~ do naczyń** *Br* tea towel, *Am* dish towel; **~ do kurzu** duster; **~ do podłogi** floor cloth

ściernisko *n* (*-ka*; *-ka*) stubble field

ścierny *adj*: **papier ~** sandpaper

ścierpieć *v/p*: **ktoś nie może czegoś ~** s.o. can't stand s.th.

ścierpnąć *v/p* → **cierpnąć**

ścierwo *n* (*-wa*; *-wa*) **1.** (*padlina*) carcass, carrion **2.** (*sukinsyn*) *vulg* scum

ścieśniać ⟨**-nić**⟩ (*-niam*): **~ litery** squeeze (one's) letters together; **~ krzesła** put the chairs closer to each other; **~ szeregi** move in closer; **ścieśniać się 1.** (*o ludziach*) squeeze up **2.** (*zwężać się*) narrow

ścieżka *f* (*-ki*; *-ki*) path; **~ rowerowa** bicycle path, bicycle lane; **~ dźwiękowa** soundtrack; **~ zdrowia** keep-fit trail, fitness trail

ścięcie *n* (*-cia*; *-cia*) **1.** (*egzekucja*) beheading **2.** (*w tenisie*) smash **3.** (*w siatkówce*) spike

ścięgno *n* (*-na*; *-na*) ANAT tendon; **~ Achillesa** Achilles tendon

ścięty *adj* **1. buty ze ~m noskiem** flat-pointed shoes **2.** MATH truncated; **stożek ~** truncated cone **3.** *drzewo*: felled **4.** *dach*: sloping **5.** *galaretka*: set

ścigać *v/im* (*-gam*) **1.** (*gonić*) chase, pursue **2.** JUR prosecute; **ścigać się** race (**z** *I* against)

ścinać ⟨**ściąć**⟩ (*-nam*) **1.** cut; **ściąć kogoś z nóg** bowl s.o. over, knock s.o. sideways, knock s.o. back **2.** *drzewo*: fell, cut down **3.** (*w tenisie*) smash **4.** (*w siatkówce*) spike **5.** *skazańca*: behead **6.** *białko*: coagulate; **ścinać się 1.** (*o krwi*, *białku*) congeal **2.** (*o galaretce*) set

ścinki *pl* (*-ków*) *papieru*, *materiału*: scraps

ściółka *f* (*-ki*; *no pl*) **1.** (*leśna*) forest bed **2.** *AGR* bedding, litter
ścisk *m* (*-ku*; *no pl*) **1.** crush **2.** (*tłum*) crowd
ściskać ⟨**-snąć**⟩ (*-kam*) **1.** (*zgniatać*) squeeze; **~ komuś dłoń** squeeze s.o.'s hand; **~ coś sznurkiem** tie the string tightly around s.th.; **mróz ściska** *fig* it is freezing; **strach ścisnął go za gardło** he was scared stiff; **ściska mnie w żołądku** I have butterflies in my stomach **2.** (*chwytać*) clasp, grip; **~ coś w dłoni** clasp s.th. in one's hand **3.** (*obejmować ramionami*) hug, embrace; **ściskać się 1.** (*obejmować się*) hug each other **2.** (*tłoczyć się*) squeeze up **3.** (*opasywać się*) **~ się paskiem** tighten one's belt
ścisłoś|ć *f* (*-ści*; *no pl*) (*dokładność*) accuracy; **dla ~ci** to be precise
ścisł|y *adj* **1.** *stosunki*, *współpraca*, *związek*: close; **~e grono przyjaciół** the inner circle of friends **2.** *dieta*, *sens*: strict; **w ~ym tego słowa znaczeniu** in the strict sense of the word **3.** *informacja*, *dane*: accurate, precise **4.** *nauki*: exact; **nauki ~e i przyrodnicze** science **5.** *pismo*: dense **6.** *materiał*: compact **7.** *tajemnica*: top
ścisnąć *v/p* → **ściskać**
ściszać ⟨**-szyć**⟩ (*-szam*) **1.** *głos*: lower **2.** *radio*: turn down
ściśle *adv*: **~ biorąc** as a matter of fact; **~ tajne** top secret, strictly confidential; → **ścisły**
ściślejszy *comp* → **ścisły**
ślad *m* (*-du*; *-dy*) **1.** mark; **czyjeś palce zostawiają ~y na stole** s.o.'s fingers leave marks on the table; **~ stopy** footprint; **~ kopyta** hoof-print **2.** (*pozostałość*) trace; **zniknąć bez ~u** disappear without trace; **ani ~u** no trace (*G* of) **3.** (*trop*) trail; **iść ~em** follow (*G*); **iść w czyjeś ~y** follow in s.o.'s footsteps
śladow|y *adj* trace; **~e ilości** trace quantities; **pierwiastki ~e** trace elements
ślamazara *f/m* (*-ry*; *-ry*) sluggard, sluggish person
ślamazarny *adj* sluggish; **w ~m tempie** sluggishly
ślaz *m* (*-zu*; *-zy*) mallow
Śląsk *m* (*-ka*) Silesia
śląski *adj* Silesian
Ślązak *m* (*-ka*; *-zacy*), **-zaczka** *f* (*-ki*; *-ki*) Silesian
śledczy *adj* investigative; **oficer ~** investigator, investigative officer
śledzić ⟨**prze-**, **wy-**⟩ (*-dzę*) *osobę*, *przebieg*: follow
śledziona *f* (*-ny*; *-ny*) *ANAT* spleen
śledziowy *adj* *COOK* herring
śledztwo *n* (*-wa*; *-wa*) investigation
śledź *m* (*-dzia*; *-dzie*) **1.** herring; **~ wędzony** smoked herring **2.** (*do namiotu*) tent peg
ślepia *pl* (*-piów*/*-pi*) **1.** (*u człowieka*) *infml* peepers; **wytrzeszczać ~** stare **2.** (*u zwierząt*) eyes
ślepiec *m* (*-pca*; *-pcy*) blind man
ślepnąć ⟨**o-**⟩ (*-nę*) go blind
ślepo *adv* *fig* blindly; **na ~** blindly; **ślepota** *f* (*-ty*; *no pl*) blindness; **kurza ~** night blindness
ślep|y **I** *adj* blind (**na** *A* to); **~a kiszka** *ANAT* appendix; **~y nabój** blank (cartridge); **~a uliczka a)** blind alley, cul-de-sac **b)** *fig* dead end **II** *m* (*-pego*; *-pi*) blind man; **ślepa** *f* (*-pej*; *-pe*) blind woman
ślęczeć *v/im* (*-czę*) pore (**nad** *I* over)
ślicznotka *f* (*-ki*; *-ki*) pretty face, baby doll; **śliczny** *adj* lovely, cute
ślimacznica *f* (*-cy*; *-ce*) *ARCHIT* volute, helix; **ślimaczy** *adj* snail's
ślimak *m* (*-ka*; *-ki*) **1.** (*ze skorupą*) snail **2.** (*bez skorupy*) slug **3.** (*skrzyżowanie*) cloverleaf
ślina *f* (*-ny*; *no pl*) saliva
śliniaczek *m* (*-czka*; *-czki*) *dim* → **śliniak**
śliniak *m* (*-ka*; *-ki*) bib; **ślinianki** *pl* (*-nek*) *ANAT* salivary glands
ślinić ⟨**po-**⟩ (*-nię*) lick, moisten (with saliva); **ślinić się 1.** dribble, drool **2.** (*podniecać się*) drool (**na widok** *G* over)
ślinka *f* (*-ki*; *no pl*): **na widok czegoś cieknie komuś ~** it makes s.o.'s mouth water, s.o.'s mouth waters when they see s.th.
ślinow|y *adj*: **gruczoły ~e** *ANAT* salivary glands
śliski *adj* slippery
śliwa *f* (*-wy*; *-wy*) plum, **śliwka** *f* (*-ki*; *-ki*) plum; **~ suszona** prune; **śliwko-**

wy *adj* **1.** *dżem*: plume **2.** *kolor, smak*: plummy; **śliwowica** *f* (*-cy; no pl*) slivovitz

ślizgacz *m* (*-cza; -cze*) speedboat

ślizgać się *v/im* (*-gam*) **1.** (*na lodzie, na butach*) slide; ***~ na łyżwach*** skate **2.** (*o samochodzie*) skid

ślizgawica *f* (*-cy; no pl*) icy roads, icy conditions; **ślizgawka** *f* (*-ki; -ki*) slide

ślub *m* (*-bu; -by*) **1.** wedding; ***~ cywilny*** civil marriage; ***~ kościelny*** church wedding; ***brać ~*** get married; ***ich ~ odbędzie się w przyszłym miesiącu*** they're getting married next month; ***dawać komuś ~, udzielać komuś ~u*** marry s.o. **2.** ***~y zakonne*** REL holy orders; ***złożyć ~y zakonne*** REL take vows

ślubn|y *adj* **1.** wedding; ***suknia ~a*** wedding dress; ***~e obrączki*** wedding rings **2.** *dziecko*: legitimate

ślubować *v/im* (*-buję*) pledge, make a pledge; **ślubowanie** *n* (*-nia; -nia*) **1.** (*przysięga*) oath, pledge; ***złożyć ~*** take an oath **2.** REL vow

ślusarnia *f* (*-ni; -nie*) locksmith's (work)shop; **ślusarz** *m* (*-rza; -rze*) locksmith

śluz *m* (*-zu; no pl*) mucus

śluza *f* (*-zy; -zy*) **1.** (*zapora*) sluice (gate) **2.** (*na szlaku wodnym*) lock **3.** (*w porcie*) tide lock

śluzow|y *adj* mucous; ***błona ~a*** mucous membrane; **śluzówka** *f* (*-ki; -ki*) ANAT mucosa

śmiać się ⟨**za-**⟩ (*śmieję*) laugh (**z** *G* at); ***~ przez łzy*** laugh through tears; ***~ do rozpuku*** split one's sides with laughter

śmiałek *m* (*-łka; -łkowie*) daredevil

śmiało *adv* **1.** boldly; ***~!*** come on!, go ahead!; ***można ~ powiedzieć, że*** one can safely say that **2.** (*z łatwością*) *infml* easily; → ***śmiały***

śmiałość *f* (*-ści; no pl*) **1.** (*odwaga*) boldness **2.** (*pewność siebie*) self-confidence; **śmiały** *adj* **1.** *osoba, plan, decyzja*: bold, daring **2.** (*pewny siebie*) self-assured, self-confident

śmiech *m* (*-chu; -chy*) laughter; ***nie było nam do ~u*** we did not feel like laughing; ***być ~u wartym*** be ridiculous; ***narazić się na ~*** make a laughing stock of oneself, expose oneself to ridicule

śmieciarka *f* (*-ki; -ki*) *Br* dustcart, *Am* garbage truck; **śmieciarz** *m* (*-rza; -rze*) **1.** (*robotnik*) *Br* dustman, *Am* garbage man **2.** (*grzebiący w śmietnikach*) scavenger

śmiecić ⟨**za-**⟩ (*-cę*) litter

śmieć[1] *v/im* (*śmiem*) *lit* dare; ***jak śmiesz!*** how dare you!; ***śmiem wątpić*** I doubt it

śmieć[2] *m* (*śmiecia; śmieci/śmiecie*) **2.** piece of junk; ***śmieci*** *Br* rubbish, *Am* garbage; ***wyrzucać coś do śmieci*** throw s.th. into a dust bin

śmielej *comp* → ***śmiało***

śmielszy *comp* → ***śmiały***

śmiercionośny *adj* **1.** *broń, substancja*: lethal **2.** *cios, spojrzenie*: deadly

śmier|ć *f* (*-ci; no pl*) death; ***~ć głodowa*** starvation, death from starvation; ***~ć samobójcza*** suicidal death, suicide; ***walczyć na ~ć i życie*** fight to the death; ***zapić się na ~ć*** drink oneself to death; ***zapomniałam na ~ć!*** *infml* I clean forgot!; ***wyrok ~ci*** death sentence

śmierdzący *adj* stinking; ***~ leń*** lazy bones

śmierdzi|eć *v/im* (*-dzę*) stink (*I* of); ***tu ~*** it stinks here; ***~ od niego wódką*** he reeks of vodka

śmierdziel *m* (*-la; -le*) *infml* stinker

śmiertelnik *m* (*-ka; -nicy*), **-niczka** *f* (*-ki; -ki*) mortal

śmiertelność *f* (*-ści; no pl*) mortality; ***~ niemowląt*** infant mortality (rate); **śmiertelnie** *adv*: ***nudzić się ~*** be deadly bored; **śmiertelny|y** *adj* mortal; ***~a cisza*** deathly silence; ***~e niebezpieczeństwo*** deadly danger, mortal danger; ***~y wróg*** deadly enemy

śmieszka *f* (*-ki; -ki*) giggler; ***mewa ~*** BIOL black-headed gull

śmiesznie *adv* comically; ***~ niska cena*** ridiculously low price; ***~ tani*** ridiculously cheap; → ***śmieszny***

śmiesznostki *pl* (*-tek*) trivialities, trifles

śmieszność *f* (*-ści; no pl*) ridiculousness; ***narazić się na ~*** make a laughing stock of oneself, expose oneself to ridicule; **śmieszny** *adj* **1.** (*zabawny*) funny, amusing **2.** (*absurdalny*) ridiculous

śmieszyć *v/im* (*-szę*) amuse

śmietana *f* (*-ny*; *no pl*) cream; ***bita ~*** whipped cream; **śmietank|a** *f* (*-ki*; *no pl*) cream; ***kawa ze ~ą*** coffee with cream; ***~a kosmetyczna*** cleansing cream; ***~a towarzyska*** *fig* the cream of society; **śmietankowy** *adj* cream, creamy

śmietniczka *f* (*-ki*; *-ki*) litter bin; **śmietnik** *m* (*-ka*; *-ki*) **1.** (*w domu*) *Br* dustbin, *Am* garbage can **2.** (*przed domem*) *Br* skip, *Am* dumpster **3.** (*bałagan*) *infml* mess **4.** (*brudne miejsce*) *infml* dump; **śmietnisko** *n* (*-ka*; *-ka*) *Br* rubbish dump, *Am* garbage dump

śmigać ⟨**-gnąć**⟩ (*-gam*) **1.** (*o latawcu, samochodzie*) whoosh, whizz **2.** (*o osobie*) dart

śmigło *n* (*-ła*; *-ła*) propeller; **śmigłowiec** *m* (*-wca*; *-wce*) helicopter, *infml* chopper

śniadanie *n* (*-nia*; *-nia*) breakfast; ***jeść ~*** have breakfast; ***drugie ~*** *Br* elevenses, *Am* midmorning snack; **śniadaniowy** *adj* breakfast; ***papier ~*** sandwich paper

śniadanko *n* (*-ka*; *-ka*) *dim* → **śniadanie**

śniady *adj cera*: dark, swarthy

śnić *v/im* (*śnię*) dream (**o** *L* of/about); ***śniło mi się, że*** I dreamt that; ***śniły mi się koszmary*** I had nightmares; ***śnił mi się mój stary przyjaciel*** I had a dream about an old friend of mine; ***co ci się dzisiaj śniło?*** what did you dream about last night?; ***śni mu się daleka podróż*** he's dreaming of a long journey; ***ani mi się śni!*** no way!; ***nawet mu się to nie śniło*** he wouldn't even dream about it; ***~ na jawie*** daydream

śniedzieć ⟨**za-**⟩ (*-dzieję*) acquire patina, become patinated

śnie|dź *f* (*-dzi*; *no pl*) patina, verdigris; ***pokryty ~dzią*** patinated, verdigrised

śnieg *m* (*-gu*; *-gi*) snow; ***pada ~*** it's snowing; ***biały jak ~*** (as) white as snow; ***pokryty ~iem*** snow-covered; ***zasypany ~iem*** snowbound

śniegowy *adj* snow

śnieguliczka *f* (*-ki*; *-ki*) BIOL snowberry

śnieżek *m* (*-żku*; *no pl*) *dim* light snow; **śnieżka** *f* (*-ki*; *-ki*) snowball; **śnieżnobiały** *adj* snow-white

śnieżny *adj* snow; **śnieżyca** *f* (*-cy*; *-ce*) blizzard, snowstorm; **śnieżyczka** *f* (*-ki*; *-ki*) BIOL snowdrop; **śnieżynki** *pl* (*-nek*) snowflakes

śnięty *adj ryba*: dead

śp. *abbr* (= ***świętej pamięci***) (*przed nazwiskiem*) the late

śpiąc|y *adj* **1.** (*senny*) sleepy **2.** (*pogrążony we śnie*) sleeping; ***Ša Królewna*** Sleeping Beauty

śpiączka *f* (*-ki*; *-ki*) MED coma; ***~ afrykańska*** sleeping sickness

śpiesznie, ***spiesznie*** *adv* hurriedly, quickly

śpieszno, ***spieszno*** *adv*: ***~ jej było do wyjścia*** she was in a hurry to leave

śpieszny, ***spieszny*** *adj* hurried, hasty; ***~m krokiem*** hurriedly

śpieszyć, ***spieszyć*** ⟨**po-**⟩ (*-szę*) hurry; ***~ komuś na ratunek*** go to s.o.'s rescue; ***śpieszyć się*** **1.** (*o osobie*) (be in a) hurry; ***~ się z*** *I* be in a hurry with; ***śpieszy mi się*** I'm in a hurry; ***śpieszy mu się do domu*** he is in a hurry to get home; ***nie ~ się z*** take one's time doing s.th. **2.** (*o zegarze*) be fast

śpiew *m* (*-wu*; *-wy*) singing; ***~ słowika*** nightingale's song; **śpiewaczka** *f* (*-ki*; *-ki*) (female) singer; ***~ operowa*** opera singer

śpiewać ⟨**za-**, **wy-**⟩ (*-wam*) sing; ***~ komuś do snu*** sing s.o. to sleep

śpiewająco *adv* easily; ***zdała egzamin ~*** she passed the exam with flying colours; **śpiewający** *adj* singing; ***ptak ~*** singing bird, songbird

śpiewak *m* (*-ka*; *-wacy*) singer; ***~ operowy*** opera singer; **śpiewka** *f* (*-ki*; *-ki*) song; ***ta sama ~*** the same old story

śpiewnik *m* (*-ka*; *-ki*) **1.** (*zbiór piosenek*) songbook **2.** (*z hymnami religijnymi*) hymnal; **śpiewny** *adj* **1.** *wymowa*: singsong **2.** *głos*: melodious

śpioch *m* (*-cha*; *-chy*) sleepyhead; **śpiochy** *pl* (*-chów*) **1.** (*ubiór*) rompers **2.** (*w oczach rano*) *infml* sleepy sand *sing*, crusties

śpioszek *m* (*-szka*; *-szki*) *dim* → **śpioch**

śpioszki *pl* (*-ków*) *dim* → **śpiochy**

śpiwór *m* (*-wora*; *-wory*) sleeping bag

średni *adj* **1.** average; ***to ~a przyjemność*** you wouldn't call it a pleasure **2.** *rozmiar*: medium **3.** *wiek*: middle;

Ś

w ~m wieku middle-aged **4.** *wykształcenie*: secondary

średnia *f* (*-niej*; *-nie*) **1.** average, mean; ***~ wieku*** average age; ***~ życia*** average life expectancy **2.** *MATH* mean

średnica *f* (*-cy*; *-ce*) diameter; **średnik** *m* (*-ka*; *-ki*) semicolon; **średnio** *adv* **1.** (*przeciętnie*) on average **2.** (*słabo*) not very; ***~ ciekawy*** not very interesting

średniodystansowiec *m* (*-wca*; *-wcy*) *SPORT* middle-distance runner; **średnioroczny** *adj opady*, *tempertura*: average yearly

średniowiecze *n* (*-cza*; *no pl*) Middle Ages *pl*; **średniowieczny** *adj* medieval

średniozamożny *adj* quite well-off

środa *f* (*-dy*; *-dy*) Wednesday; ***~ popielcowa*** *REL* Ash Wednesday

środ|ek *m* (*-dka*; *-dki*) **1.** (*punkt centralny*) middle; *Br* centre, *Am* center; ***~ek ciężkości*** *PHYS* the centre of gravity; ***na ~ku pokoju*** in the middle of the room; ***wchodzić do ~ka*** come in(side); ***w ~ku*** in the middle (*G* of) **2.** (*wnętrze*) inside; ***zaglądać do ~ka*** look inside; ***od ~ka*** from inside **3.** (*sposób*) means, measure; ***~ki do życia*** livelihood; ***bez ~ków do życia*** penniless, *form* impecunious; ***wszelkimi ~kami*** by all means available; ***~ek piorący*** washing agent; ***~ki zaradcze*** **a)** (*zapobiegające*) prevent(at)ive measures **b)** (*usuwające skutki*) remedial measures; ***~ki ostrożności*** precautions; ***~ek płatniczy*** legal tender; ***~ek prawny*** legal remedy; ***~ek lokomocji*** *Br* means of transport, *Am* means of transportation; ***~ki masowego przekazu*** the mass media; ***~ki wyrazu*** forms of expression; ***~ki trwałe*** *ECON* fixed assets **4.** *MED* remedy; ***~ek przeciwbólowy*** painkiller; ***~ek antykoncepcyjny*** contraceptive

środkowoeuropejski *adj* Central European

środkow|y *adj* middle, central; ***palec ~y*** middle finger; ***Europa ~a*** Central Europe

środowisk|o *n* (*-ka*; *-ka*) **1.** (*otoczenie*) environment; ***~o naturalne*** the natural environment; ***~o przestępcze*** the criminal environment, criminal underworld; ***zanieczyszczenie ~a*** environmental pollution **2.** *BIOL* (*miejsce występowania*) habitat

środowiskow|y *adj* environmental; ***pielęgniarka ~a*** community nurse; ***wywiad ~y*** community interview

środowy *adj* Wednesday

śródlądow|y *adj* inland; ***żegluga ~a*** inland navigation

śródmiejski *adj* central, downtown; **śródmieście** *n* (*-cia*; *-cia*) *Br* city centre, *Am* city center, downtown

śródziemnomorski *adj* Mediterranean

śruba *f* (*-by*; *-by*) **1.** bolt **2.** (*okrętowa*) screw propeller; **śrubka** *f* (*-ki*; *-ki*) (little) screw

śrubokręt *m* (*-tu*; *-ty*) screwdriver

śrubować *v/im* (*-buję*) *ceny*, *wymagania*: jack up

śrubowy *adj* **1.** bolt **2.** *napęd*: screw

śrut *m* (*-tu*; *no pl*) shot; **śrutowy** *adj* shot

św. *abbr* (= ***święty***) St

świadczenia *pl* (*-czeń*) **1.** (*zobowiązania*) benefits; ***~ socjalne*** social benefits, welfare benefits **2.** (*usługi*) services

świadczenie *n* (*-nia*; *no pl*) *usług*: rendering

świadczyć ⟨**za-**⟩ (*-czę*) **1.** (*zeznawać*) testify; ***~ przeciw*** *D* give evidence against, testify against; ***~ na korzyść*** *G* give evidence in favour of, testify in favour of **2.** *usługi*: provide **3.** (*wskazywać*) testify to, indicate **4.** (*być dowodem*) ***coś dobrze*** (***źle***) ***o kimś świadczy*** s.th. reflects well (badly) on s.o.; ***o czym to świadczy?*** what does it mean?

świadectwo *n* (*-wa*; *-wa*) **1.** (*szkolne*) report; ***~ dojrzałości*** certificate of secondary education, *Br* General Certificate of Secondary Education, GCSE, *Am* High School Diploma **2.** (*ukończenia kursu*) certificate **3.** (*dowód*) testimony; ***dawać ~*** *fig* testify (*D* to)

świad|ek *m* (*-dka*; *-dkowie*) *JUR* witness; ***naoczny ~ek*** eyewitness; ***być ~kiem czegoś*** witness s.th.; ***przy ~kach*** in the presence of witnesses; ***być ~kiem koronnym*** *JUR* *Br* turn Queen's evidence, turn King's evidence, *Am* turn State's evidence

świadom → ***świadomy***

Ś

świadomość *f* (*-ści*; *no pl*) **1.** (*wiedza*) awareness; ***mieć ~*** *G* be aware of **2.** (*przytomność*) consciousness; **świadomy** *adj* **1.** (*zdający sobie sprawę*) aware (**z** *G* of) **2.** (*przytomny*) conscious **3.** *decyzja*, *wybór*: conscious

świ|at *m* (*-ta*; *-ty*) (the) world; ***na całym ~ecie*** all over the world; ***podróż dookoła ~ata*** journey around the world; ***jeździć po ~ecie*** travel around the world; ***najlepsze wino na ~ecie*** the best wine in the world; ***tamten ~at*** REL the next world; ***Trzeci Ŝat*** the Third World; ***~at stoi przed tobą otworem*** the world is your oyster; ***ktoś ~ata nie widzi poza czymś*** s.th. is all the world to s.o.; ***za nic w ~ecie*** not for the whole world; ***przejechać się na tamten ~at*** pay one's debt to nature; ***jak ~at ~atem*** **a)** (*nigdy*) never **b)** (*zawsze*) always, from time immemorial; ***kląć na czym ~at stoi*** swear like a trooper; ***pępek ~ata*** the hub of the universe

światek *m* (*-tka*; *no pl*) circle, community; ***~ przestępczy*** the criminal world

światełko *n* (*-ka*; *-ka*) (little) light

światł|o *n* (*-ła*; *-ła*) **1.** light; ***~o słoneczne*** sunlight; ***~o dzienne*** daylight; ***pod ~o*** against the light; ***w świetle księżyca*** by moonlight; ***w świetle*** *G fig* in the light of.; ***ujrzeć ~o dzienne*** see the light of day; ***rzucać nowe ~o na*** *A fig* throw new light on; ***przedstawić coś w dobrym świetle*** show s.th. in a good light **2.** AUTO light; ***~a przednie*** headlights; ***~a tylne*** *Br* rear lights, *Am* tail lights; ***~a długie*** *Br* full beam headlights, *Am* high beams; ***~a krótkie***, ***~a mijania*** low beams, *Br* dipped headlights; ***~a postojowe*** parking lights, *Am* sidelights; ***~a awaryjne*** hazard lights; ***~a cofania*** backup light; ***~a skrzyżowania*** traffic lights; ***stać na ~ach*** wait at the lights, wait for the lights to change; ***przejechać na czerwonym świetle*** jump the red light **3.** (*przekrój*) inside diameter

światłocień *m* (*-cienia*; *-cienie*) chiaroscuro; **światłoczuły** *adj* photosensitive

światłolubny *adj* light-loving

światłomierz *m* (*-rza*; *-rze*) light meter; **światłość** *f* (*-ści*; *no pl*) *lit* light; **światłowstręt** *m* (*-tu*; *no pl*) photophobia; **światły** *adj* enlightened

światopogląd *m* (*-du*; *-dy*) outlook (on life), world view; **światowiec** *m* (*-wca*; *-wcy*) man of the world, worldling; **światow|y** *adj* **1.** world, global; ***~ej sławy*** world-famous **2.** (*obyty*) cultivated

świąd *m* (*-du*; *no pl*) itch(ing)

świąteczn|y *adj* **1.** (*bożonarodzeniowy*) Christmas; ***okres ~y*** Christmastime; ***~a kartka*** Christmas card **2.** (*wielkanocny*) Easter **3.** (*odświętny*) festive

świątek *m* (*-tka*; *-tki*) holy image; ***~ i piątek*** seven days a week; day in, day out

świątobliwy *adj* saintly; **świątynia** *f* (*-ni*; *-nie*) temple; ***~ sztuki*** temple of the arts

świder *m* (*-dra*; *-dry*) **1.** (*mechaniczny*) drill **2.** (*ręczny*) gimlet

świdrować *v/im* (*-ruję*): ***~ kogoś spojrzeniem*** look piercingly at s.o., bore one's eyes into s.o.; **świdrujący** *adj spojrzenie*: piercing

świec|a *f* (*-cy*; *-ce*) **1.** candle; ***przy ~ach*** by candlelight; ***ze ~ą kogoś szukać*** s.o. is very hard to find **2.** ***~a zapłonowa*** AUTO spark plug **3.** SPORT shoulder stand

świecić *v/im* (*-cę*) **1.** (*o słońcu*, *księżycu*) shine; ***dom świecił pustkami*** *fig* the house was (almost) empty; ***półki świecą pustkami*** *fig* the shelves are (almost) empty; ***~ oczami za kogoś*** blush for s.o. **2.** (*o lampie*, *latarni*) be on **3.** (*o świecy*) burn; **świecić się 1.** (*o świetle*) be on; ***w jednym oknie jeszcze się świeciło*** in one window the light was still on; ***dlaczego w kuchni się świeci?*** why is the light in the kitchen on? **2.** (*o oczach*) glitter, gleam **3.** (*błyszczeć*) shine; ***podłoga się świeciła*** the floor was shining

świecidełka *pl* (*-łek*) trinkets

świeck|i *adj* lay, laic; ***~a osoba*** lay person

świeczka *f* (*-ki*; *-ki*) candle; **świecznik** *m* (*-ka*; *-ki*) candlestick; ***być na ~u*** *fig* be in the limelight, be in the spotlight

świergot *m* (*-tu*; *-ty*) twitter; **świergotać** *v/im* (*-goczę*) twitter

świerk *m* (*-ku*; *-ki*) spruce

świerszcz *m* (*-cza*; *-cze*) BIOL cricket

świerszczyk *m* (*-ka*; *-ki*) **1.** blue magazine, porn magazine **2.** *dim* → ***świerszcz***

świerzb *m* (*-bu*; *no pl*) MED scabies

świerzbić *v/im* (*-bię*) itch; ***język mnie świerzbił, żeby to powiedzieć*** I was itching to say that

świetlany *adj przyszłość*: bright

świetlica *m* (*-cy*; *-ce*) (*w szkole*) common room

świetliczanka *f* (*-ki*; *-ki*) common room supervisor

świetlik *m* (*-ka*; *-ki*) **1.** (*owad*) glow-worm **2.** (*roślina*) eyebright **3.** BUILD skylight

świetlisty *adj* luminous, bright; **świetlny** *adj* light; **świetlówka** *f* (*-ki*; *-ki*) fluorescent tube

świetność (*-ści*; *no pl*) (*czas*) *Br* splendour, *Am* splendor, glory; **świetny** *adj* excellent; ***być w ~m humorze*** be in a very good mood

świeżo *adv* freshly; ***~ upieczony*** *fig* freshly graduated, freshly qualified; ***~ malowane!*** wet paint!; **świeżość** *f* (*-ści*; *no pl*) freshness; **świeżutki** *adj dim* fresh

świeży *adj* fresh

święcenia *pl* (*-ceń*): ***~ kapłańskie*** (holy) orders, ordination

święcić ⟨**po-**⟩ (*-cę*) **1.** *kościół*: consecrate **2.** *potrawy*: bless **3.** ***~ triumfy*** enjoy great success, be riding high; ***coś się święci*** there's s.th. in the wind, s.th. is coming

święcie *adv*: ***~ przekonany*** deeply convinced, absolutely sure; ***~ w coś wierzyć*** firmly believe in s.th.

święconka *f* (*-ki*; *-ki*) *blessed food* (*usually eggs, bread and meat*) *eaten on Easter day*

święcony *adj* **1.** *woda*: holy **2.** *jajko, chleb*: blessed

święt|o *n* (*-ta*; *-ta*) holiday; ***~o państwowe*** national holiday; ***~o kościelne*** feast (day), church holiday; ***pociąg nie kursuje w ~a*** the train does not run on holidays; ***~a*** **a)** (*Boże Narodzenie*) Christmas **b)** (*Wielkanoc*) Easter; ***Ṡo Zmarłych*** All Saints Day

świętojańsk|i *adj*: ***robaczek ~i*** BIOL glow-worm; ***noc ~a*** St John's Eve

świętokradztwo *n* (*-wa*; *-wa*) sacrilege; ***popełnić ~*** commit sacrilege

świętoszek *m* (*-szka*; *-szki*), **-szka** *f* (*-ki*; *-ki*) hypocrite, goody-goody; **świętoszkowaty** *adj* prudish, goody-goody

świętoś|ć *f* (*-ści*; *-ści*) **1.** holiness; ***przysięgać na wszystkie ~ci*** swear by all one holds sacred **2.** (*bycie świętym*) sainthood **3.** *życia*: sanctity **4.** (*przedmiot*) sacred object

świętować *v/im* (*-tuję*) celebrate

święt|y **I** *adj* **1.** holy; ***Pismo Ṡe*** the (Holy) Bible, the Scriptures; ***Ṡy Mikołaj*** *infml* Santa Clause; ***katedra ~ej Marii Magdaleny*** St Mary Magdalene's Cathedral; ***daj mi ~y spokój!*** leave me alone!; ***dla ~ego spokoju*** just in case, for s.o.'s peace of mind; ***~a cierpliwość*** the patience of a saint; ***~a racja!*** absolutely right!; ***~e oburzenie*** virtuous indignation **2.** (*nietykalny, nienaruszalny*) sacred; ***~e wspomnienia*** sacred memories; ***to, co mówił, było dla nas ~e*** what he said was sacred for us **II** *m* (*-tego*; *święci*) saint; ***Wszystkich Ṡych*** All Saints' Day

świnia *f* (*-ni*; *-nie*) BIOL pig; **świniak** *m* (*-ka*; *-ki*) (*prosiak*) pig, piglet

świnić ⟨**za-**⟩ (*-nię*) mess up, muck up

świnka *f* (*-ki*; *-ki*) *dim* **1.** (little) pig; ***~ morska*** guinea-pig **2.** MED mumps

świntuch *m* (*-cha*; *-chy*) **1.** (*lubieżnik*) lecher; ***stary ~*** dirty old man **2.** (*brudas*) (dirty) pig

świntuszyć *v/im* (*-szę*) **1.** (*mówić o świństwach*) talk dirty **2.** (*brudzić*) make a mess

świńsk|i *adj* **1.** ***~a skóra*** pigskin **2.** *zachowanie, dowcip*: dirty

świństw|o *n* (*-wa*; *-wa*) **1.** (*czyn*) dirty trick; ***zrobić komuś ~o*** play a dirty trick on s.o. **2.** (*jedzenie*) crappy food, *infml* muck **3.** (*komentarz*) ***~a*** dirty talk

świr *m* (*-ra*; *-ry*) *infml* nut, psycho; ***dostać ~a*** go nuts; ***mieć ~a na punkcie*** *G* be nuts about

Ś

świrować *v/im* (*-ruję*) *infml* go nuts
świst *m* (*-tu*; *-ty*) **1.** *wiatru*, *kul*: whistle **2.** *szpady*: swish; **świstać** ⟨**-nąć**⟩ (*-szczę*) *kule*, *wiatr*: whistle
świstak *m* (*-ka*; *-ki*) marmot
świ|t *m* (*-tu*; *-ty*) dawn; ***o ~cie*** at dawn, at daybreak
świta *f* (*-ty*; *-ty*) entourage
świta|ć *v/im*: **~** dawn is breaking; ***~ mi, że*** it dawns on me that

T

t *abbr* (=**tona**) t., metric ton
t. *abbr* (=**tom**) vol.
ta → ***ten***
tabaka *f* (*-ki*; *-ki*) snuff; **tabakierka** *f* (*-ki*; *-ki*), ***tabakiera*** *f* (*-ry*; *-ry*) snuff box
tabela *f* (*-li*; *-le*) table; **tabelaryczny** *adj* tabular
tabletka *f* (*-ki*; *-ki*) pill, tablet
tablica *f* (*-cy*; *-ce*) **1.** (*informacyjna*) board; ***~ ogłoszeń*** noticeboard **2.** (*pamiątkowa*) plaque, (memorial) tablet **3.** (*w szkole*) blackboard, whiteboard **4.** ***~ rejestracyjna*** AUTO *Br* number plate, *Am* license plate **5.** (*kamienna*) slab
tabliczka *f* (*-ki*; *-ki*): ***~ czekolady*** bar of chocolate; ***~ mnożenia*** multiplication table; ***~ z nazwiskiem*** nameplate
tabor *m* (*-ru*; *-ry*): ***~ cygański*** **a)** (*grupa*) band of travelling gypsies **b)** (*obóz*) gypsy camp; ***~ kolejowy*** rolling stock
taboret *m* (*-tu*; *-ty*) stool
tabu *n indecl* taboo; ***temat ~*** taboo subject
tabulator *m* (*-ra*; *-ry*) INF tabulator
tabun *m* (*-nu*; *-ny*): ***~ koni*** herd of horses
tac|a *f* (*-cy*; *-ce*) **1.** tray **2.** REL plate; ***zbierać na ~ę, chodzić z ~ą*** take collection
tachać ⟨**przy-**⟩ (*-cham*) lug
tacka *f* (*-ki*; *-ki*) *dim* (small) tray
tacy → ***taki***
taczka *f* (*-ki*; *-ki*) wheelbarrow
tafla *f* (*-li*; *-le*) **1.** *lodu*, *jeziora*: sheet **2.** *lustra*, *szkła*: pane **3.** *wody*: surface
tafta *f* (*-ty*; *no pl*) taffeta
taić *v/im* (*taję*) *lit* hide, conceal; ***nie ~*** make no secret (*G* of); ***nie taił, że*** he didn't hide the fact that
tajać ⟨**s-**⟩ (*-ję*) thaw
tajemnic|a *m* (*-cy*; *-ce*) **1.** (*sekret*) secret; ***~a zawodowa***, ***~a handlowa*** trade secret; ***~a państwowa*** state secret; ***w ~y*** in secret; ***trzymać coś w ~y*** keep s.th. secret; ***~a spowiedzi*** seal of confession **2.** (*rzecz tajemnicza*) mystery
tajemniczy *adj* **1.** (*zagadkowy*) mysterious **2.** (*skryty*) secretive
tajemn|y *adj* **1.** (*tajny*) secret; ***~e przejście*** secret passage **2.** (*magiczny*) magic; ***wiedza ~a*** esoteric knowledge
tajfun *m* (*-nu*; *-ny*) typhoon
tajga *f* (*-gi*; *-gi*) the taiga
tajniak *m* (*-ka*; *-niacy*) undercover agent
tajniki *pl* (*-ków*) secrets
tajność *f* (*-ści*; *no pl*) secrecy; **tajn|y** *adj* secret; ***~e głosowanie*** secret vote, (secret) ballot; ***ściśle ~e*** top secret
tak I *particle* yes; ***~ jest!*** yes sir!; – ***„Czy Kasia lubi pstrągi?"*** – ***„~."*** 'Does Kasia like trout?' 'Yes, she does.' **II** *adv* ***~ daleko*** (***dużo***) so far (much); ***~ bardzo*** so much; ***~ zwany*** so-called; ***i ~ dalej*** and so on; ***~ że*** so that; ***i ~ nie wygrają*** they won't win anyway; ***~ samo*** in the same way; ***~ sobie*** so-so; ***~... jak i*** both... and; ***~ czy inaczej*** one way or another; ***to było ~*** it went like this; ***nie lubię brzoskwiń, ale morele ~*** I don't like peaches, but I do like apricots; ***był ~ zadowolony z siebie, że położył się spać*** he was so pleased with himself that he went to sleep; ***zróbmy ~*** let's do it this way
taki *pron* **1.** (*przed rzeczownikiem*) such; ***~ pies*** such a dog **2.** (*przed przymiotnikiem*) so; ***~ piękny*** so beautiful **3.** ***~ sam*** the same; ***~ sobie*** so-so; ***nic ~ego*** **a)** (*nic podobnego*) nothing of the sort **b)** (*nie ma problemu*) no big deal; ***ty ~ owaki!*** you so-and-so!, ***interes jako ~*** business as such

takielunek *m* (*-nku*; *-nki*) rigging
taksiarz *m* (*-rza*; *-rze*) *infml* → ***taksówkarz***
taksometr *m* (*-ru*; *-ry*) taximeter
taksować ⟨**o-**⟩ (*-suję*) *straty*: estimate; ***~ kogoś wzrokiem*** eye s.o. up
taksówka *f* (*-ki*; *-ki*) taxi, *Am* cab; **taksówkarz** *m* (*-rza*; *-rze*) taxi-driver, *Am* cab driver
takt[1] *m* (*-tu*; *no pl*) (*wyczucie*, *delikatność*) tact; ***z ~em*** tactfully
takt[2] (*-tu*; *-ty*) **1.** (*jednostka metryczna*) *Br* bar, *Am* measure **2.** (*rytm*) beat; **taktomierz** *m* (*-rza*; *-rze*) metronome
taktowny *adj* tactful
taktyczny *adj* tactical; **taktyk** (*-ka*; *-tycy*) tactician; **taktyka** *f* (*-ki*; *no pl*) tactic
także *particle* also, as well, too
talent *m* (*-tu*; *-ty*) talent; ***mieć ~ do języków*** have a gift for languages
talerz *m* (*-rza*; *-rze*) **1.** plate; ***latający ~*** *fig* flying saucer **2.** ***~e*** MUS cymbals
tali|a *f* (*-lii*; *-lie*) **1.** (*pas*) waist; ***wcięty w ~i*** narrow in the waist, slim; ***mieć ~ę osy*** have a wasp waist **2.** *kart*: *Br* pack, *Am* deck
talizman *m* (*-nu*; *-ny*) talisman, charm
talk *m* (*-ku*; *no pl*) **1.** talc **2.** (*kosmetyk*) talcum powder, talc
talon *m* (*-nu*; *-ny*) coupon
tałatajstwo *n* (*-wa*; *no pl*) *infml* riff-raff, rabble
tam **I** *pron* **1.** there; ***kto ~?*** who's there?; ***tu i ~*** here and there; ***~, gdzie*** where; ***~ i z powrotem*** there and back; ***bilet ~ i z powrotem*** *Br* return ticket, *Am* round-trip ticket **2.** (*z towarzyszącym gestem*) over there **II** *particle* ***co ~ słychać?*** how are you doing?; ***jak ~ studia?*** how are your studies?; ***jak ~ było?*** how was it?; ***jaki ~ z niego*** he is no; ***jak mu ~*** what's his name
tama *f* (*-my*; *-my*) dam
tamci → ***tamten***
tamować ⟨**za-**⟩ (*-muję*) **1.** *krwotok*: stem, staunch **2.** *ruch*: block **3.** *rozwój*: hinder
tampon *m* (*-nu*; *-ny*) tampon
tamta, ***tamte*** → ***tamten***
tamtej|szy *adj* local; ***~sze biuro*** the local office, the office there; ***~si ludzie*** the local people
tamt|en *pron* **1.** that; ***z ~ej strony***, ***po ~ej stronie*** (*z drugiej strony*) on the other side; ***w ~ych czasach*** in those days; ***na ~ym świecie*** on the other side **2.** (*zamiast rzeczownika*) that one
tamtędy *pron* (down) that way
tamto: ***to i ~*** this and that; → ***tamten***
tamże *pron* there, in that place
tancer|z *m* (*-rza*; *-rze*), **-rka** *f* (*-ki*; *-ki*) dancer; ***~ka rewiowa*** showgirl
tandem *m* (*-mu*; *-my*) tandem
tandeta *f* (*-ty*; *no pl*) trash; **tandetny** *adj* trashy, *infml* tacky
taneczny *adj* *muzyka*: dance; ***~m krokiem*** gracefully
tango *m* (*-ga*; *-ga*) tango
tani *adj* cheap; ***za ~e pieniądze*** cheaply; ***~m kosztem*** cheaply, at a low cost
taniec *m* (*tańca*; *tańce*) dance; ***~ brzucha*** belly dance; ***poprosić kogoś do tańca*** ask s.o. to dance; ***iść na tańce*** go to a dance, go dancing
tanieć ⟨**po-**, **s-**⟩ (*-nieję*) get cheaper
tanio *adv* cheaply; **taniocha** *f* (*-chy*; *no pl*) *infml* dirt-cheap stuff, cheapo; ***to ~*** it's dirt-cheap
tankować ⟨**za-**⟩ (*-kuję*) **1.** fill up, get fuel **2.** (*o samolocie*) refuel **3.** (*pić alkohol*) *infml* booze, tank up
tankowiec *m* (*-wca*; *-wce*) (oil) tanker
tantiemy *pl* (*-tiem*) royalties
tańce *pl* → ***taniec***
tańczyć ⟨**za-**⟩ (*-czę*) dance
tapczan *m* (*-nu*; *-ny*) *Br* divan (bed), bed
tapet|a *f* (*-ty*; *-ty*) wallpaper; ***położyć ~ę w pokoju*** (wall)paper a room
tapetować ⟨**wy-**⟩ (*-tuję*) (wall)paper
tapicer *m* (*-ra*; *-rzy*) upholsterer; **tapicerka** *f* (*-ki*; *no pl*) upholstery; **tapicerski** *adj* *zakład*: upholstery
tapirować ⟨**u-**⟩ (*-ruję*) *Br* backcomb, *Am* tease
tarabanić się *v/im* (*-nię*) clamber
tarantula *f* (*-li*; *-le*) (European) tarantula, wolf spider
tarapat|y *pl* (*-tów*) trouble *sing*; ***wpaść w ~y*** get in trouble; ***być w ~ach*** be in trouble
taras *m* (*-su*; *-sy*) terrace; ***~ widokowy*** observation deck
tarasować ⟨**za-**⟩ (*-suję*) **1.** *drogę*, *przejście*: block **2.** *drzwi*: bar

tarcica *f* (*-cy*; *-ce*) *Br* (sawn) timber, *Am* (sawn) lumber
tarcie *m* (*-cia*; *-cia*) friction
tarcza *f* (*-czy*; *-cze*) **1.** shield **2.** *zegara*: dial, face **3.** (*strzelecka*) target **4.** (*szkolna*) (school) badge **5.** *telefonu*: dial **6.** *słońca*, *księżyca*: disc
tarczow|y *adj*: ***piła ~a*** circular saw; ***hamulce ~e*** disc brakes
tarczyca *f* (*-cy*; *-ce*) ANAT thyroid (gland)
targ *m* (*-gu*; *-gi*) market; ***~i*** COMM fair, exhibition; ***~i książki*** book fair; ***~i samochodowe*** car show; ***pchli ~*** flea market; ***dobić ~u*** strike a bargain; ***po długich ~ach*** after much bargaining, after long negotiations
targa|ć ⟨**-gnąć**⟩ (*-gam*) **1.** (*nieść*) lug **2.** (*ciągnąć*) tug; ***~ły nim wątpliwości*** *fig* he was torn by doubt, he was tormented by doubt **3.** (*czochrać*) ruffle
targnąć się *v/p* (*-nę*): ***~ na swoje*** (***czyjeś***) ***życie*** make an attempt on one's own (s.o.'s) life
targować się *v/im* (*-guję*) bargain, haggle (**o** *A* over); **targowisko** *n* (*-ka*; *-ka*) market(place); **targowy** *adj* **1.** *dzień*: market **2.** *hale*, *pawilony*: fair, exhibition
tarka *f* (*-ki*; *-ki*) grater
tarlisko *n* (*-ka*; *-ka*) spawning ground; **tarło** *n* (*-ła*, *no pl*) **1.** spawning; ***odbywać ~*** spawn **2.** (*okres*) spawning season
tarmosić *v/im* (*-szę*) **1.** *włosy*: ruffle **2.** (*za rękaw*) tug (**za** *A* at)
tarnina *f* (*-ny*; *-ny*) **1.** (*krzew*) blackthorn, sloe **2.** (*owoce*) sloe
tartak *m* (*-ku*; *-ki*) sawmill
tart|y *adj* COOK grated; ***bułka ~a*** breadcrumbs
taryf|a *f* (*-fy*; *-fy*) rate; ***stosować ~ę ulgową wobec kogoś*** *fig* be lenient with s.o.; **taryfikator** *m* (*-ra*; *-ry*) **1.** (*opłat*) table of rates, tariff of charges **2.** (*płac*) salary scale
tarzać ⟨**wy-**⟩ (*-rzam*) roll; ***tarzać się*** **1.** roll (around); ***~ w śniegu*** roll around in the snow; ***~ ze śmiechu*** be rolling with laughter, be in stitches **2.** (*w błocie*, *wodzie*) wallow
tasak *m* (*-ka*; *-ki*) chopper, cleaver
tasiemiec *m* (*-mca*; *-mce*) BIOL tapeworm; **tasiemcowy** *adj fig* very long, lengthy
tasiemka *f* (*-ki*; *-ki*) ribbon
tasować ⟨**po-**⟩ (*-suję*) *karty*: shuffle
taśm|a *f* (*-my*; *-my*) **1.** tape; ***~a klejąca*** sticky tape, *Am* Scotch® tape; ***~a samoprzylepna*** adhesive tape; ***~a wideo*** videotape; ***~a filmowa*** film **2.** ***~a produkcyjna***, ***~a montażowa*** TECH assembly line; ***pracować przy ~ie*** work at an assembly line
taśmociąg *m* (*-gu*; *-gi*) conveyor system; **taśmow|y** *adj* ***produkcja ~a*** **a)** assembly-line **b)** *fig* churning out, knocking off
tata *m* (*-ty*; *-towie*) → ***tatuś***
Tatar *m* (*-ra*; *-rzy*) Tatar
tatarak (*-ku*; *-ki*) BIOL sweet flag, sweet rush
tatarski *adj* Tatar; ***sos ~*** tartare sauce
taternictwo *n* (*-wa*; *no pl*) mountaineering; **taternik** *m* (*-ka*; *-nicy*) mountaineer
tato *m* (*-ty*; *-towie*) → ***tatuś***
Tatry *pl* (*Tatr*) the Tatra Mountains
tatrzański *adj* Tatra
tatuaż *m* (*-żu*; *-że*) tattoo; **tatuować** ⟨**wy-**⟩ (*-tuuję*) tattoo
tatuś *m* (*-tusia*; *-tusiowie*) *dim* daddy
taxi *n indecl* taxi; ***radio ~*** radiotaxi
tą → ***ten***
tąpnięcie *n* (*-cia*; *-cia*) **1.** GEOL rockburst **2.** MIN crump
tchawica *f* (*-cy*; *-ce*) ANAT trachea, windpipe
tchem → ***dech***
tchnąć *v/p* (*-nę*): ***~ życie w*** *A lit* breathe life into; ***~ spokojem*** exude calm; ***tchnęło stęchlizną*** the air was mouldy
tchnienie *n* (*-nia*; *-nia*) *lit* breath; ***wydać ostatnie ~*** breathe one's last
tchórz *m* (*-rza*; *-rze*) **1.** (*osoba*) coward **2.** BIOL polecat; **tchórzliwie** *adv* cowardly, in cowardly fashion; **tchórzliwy** *adj* cowardly; **tchórzostwo** *n* (*-wa*; *no pl*) cowardice
tchórzyć ⟨**s-**⟩ (*-rzę*) chicken out
tchu → ***dech***
te → ***ten***
teatr *m* (*-ru*; *-ry*) *Br* theatre, *Am* theater; ***~ lalek*** *Br* puppet theatre, *Am* puppet theater; **teatralny** *adj*

theatrical; ***krytyk ~*** *Br* theatre critic, *Am* theater critic
teatrologia *f* (*-gii*; *no pl*) theatrology
teatroman *m* (*-na*; *-ni*), **~ka** *f* (*-ki*; *-ki*) *Br* theatregoer, *Am* theatergoer
techniczn|y *adj* **1.** technical; ***kalka ~a*** tracing paper; ***pismo ~e*** lettering **2.** *postęp*, *rewolucja*: technological
technik *m* (*-ka*; *-nicy*) technician; ***~ dentystyczny*** dental technician; **technika** *f* (*-ki*; *-ki*) **1.** (*metoda*, *umiejętność*) technique **2.** (*wiedza i technologia*) engineering, technology
technikum *n* (*indecl*; *-ka*) vocational secondary school
techno *n indecl* MUS techno
technokracja *f* (*-ji*; *no pl*) technocracy; **technologia** *f* (*-gii*; *-gie*) technology
teczka *f* (*-ki*; *-ki*) **1.** (*torba*) briefcase; ***~ szkolna*** school bag **2.** (*okładka*) folder
teflon *n* (*-nu*; *no pl*) Teflon®; **teflonow|y** *adj* non-stick, Teflon®; ***patelnia ~a*** non-stick frying pan
tego → ***ten***, ***to I***
tegoroczny *adj* this year's
tej → ***ten***
teka *f* (*-ki*; *-ki*) portfolio; ***~ ministerialna*** minister's portfolio
tekst *m* (*-tu*; *-ty*) text; **tekstowy** *adj* textual; ***plik ~*** text file
tekstylia *pl* (*-liów*) textiles; **tekstylny** *adj* textile
tektoniczny *adj* GEOL tectonic
tektura *f* (*-ry*; *no pl*) cardboard; **tekturowy** *adj* cardboard
tel. *abbr* (= ***telefon***) tel.
telebim *m* (*-mu*; *-my*) (large) outdoor screen; **teledysk** *m* (*-ku*; *-ki*) video; **telefaks** (*-su*; *-sy*) Telefax®
telefon *m* (*-nu*; *-ny*) **1.** (*aparat*) (tele-)phone; ***~ komórkowy*** *Br* mobile phone, *Am* cell phone; ***~ bezprzewodowy*** cordless telephone; ***~ zaufania*** helpline; ***odebrać ~*** answer the phone; ***rozmawiać przez ~*** talk on the phone, be on the phone; ***zarezerwować coś przez ~*** book s.th. by phone; ***Opaliński przy ~ie*** Opaliński speaking; ***~y się urywały*** the phones kept ringing off the hooks **2.** (*rozmowa*) (phone) call; ***czy były do mnie jakieś ~y?*** did anyone call me?
telefoniczn|y *adj* (tele)phone; ***rozmowa ~a*** phone call; ***budka ~a*** phone booth, *Br* phone box; ***książka ~a*** telephone directory, phone book; ***słuchawka ~a*** receiver
telefonista *m* (*-ty*; *-niści*), **-tka** *f* (*-ki*; *-ki*) phone operator
telefonować ⟨**za-**⟩ (*-nuję*) telephone
telegazeta *f* (*-ty*; *-ty*) teletext
telegraficzny *adj* telegraphic; ***w ~m skrócie*** *fig* briefly, in a nutshell
telegram *m* (*-mu*; *-my*) telegram; **telekomunikacja** *f* (*-ji*; *no pl*) telecommunications *sing*
telenowela *f* (*-li*; *-le*) soap opera
telepać się *v/im* (*-pię*) **1.** (*trząść się*) shake **2.** (*podróżować*) bump along; ***~ autobusem*** bump along in a bus
telepatia *f* (*-tii*; *no pl*) telepathy; **telepatyczny** *adj* telepathic; **teleskop** *m* (*-pu*; *-py*) **1.** (*przyrząd optyczny*) telescope **2.** (*amortyzator*) shock absorber
teleturniej *m* (*-ju*; *-je*) quiz (show); **telewidz** *m* (*-dza*; *-dzowie*) viewer
telewizj|a *f* (*-ji*; *-je*) television, TV; ***oglądać ~ę*** watch television, watch TV; **telewizor** *m* (*-ra*; *-ry*) television (set), TV (set); **telewizyjny** *adj* television, TV
temat *m* (*-tu*; *-ty*) **1.** subject, topic; ***mówić na ~*** *G* speak about; ***nie na ~*** beside the point, off the point; ***~ do dyskusji*** discussion topic, point to discuss **2.** (*część wyrazu*) stem **3.** *muzyczny*: theme; **tematyczny** *adj* *podejście*: thematic
temblak *m* (*-ku*; *-ki*) sling
temperament *m* (*-tu*; *-ty*) temperament; ***ognisty ~*** fiery temperament
temperatur|a *f* (*-ry*; *-ry*) temperature; ***~a pokojowa*** room temperature; ***~a ciała*** body temperature; ***~a wrzenia*** PHYS boiling point; ***mieć ~ę*** have a temperature; ***minusowe ~y*** temperatures below zero
temperować ⟨**za-**, **u-**⟩ (*-ruję*) **1.** *ołówek*: sharpen **2.** *fig* restrain
temperówka *f* (*-ki*; *-ki*) pencil-sharpener
temp|o *f* (*-pa*; *no pl*) **1.** (*szybkość*) pace; ***~o pracy wzrosło*** the pace of work is faster; ***w zwolnionym ~ie*** in slow motion **2.** MUS tempo

temu[1] → **ten, to I**
temu[2]: ***dwa lata ~*** two years ago; ***dawno ~*** long ago, a long time ago
ten *pron* this; ***~ i ów*** someone or other; ***~ i ten*** this and that; ***~ sam*** the same; ***~ mnie interesuje*** I want this one
tendencja *f (-ji; -je)* tendency, trend; **tendencyjny** *adj* bias(s)ed, tendentious
tenis *m (-sa; no pl)* tennis; ***~ stołowy*** table tennis
tenisista *m (-ty; -siści)*, **-tka** *f (-ki; -ki)* tennis player
tenisowy *adj* tennis
tenor *m* **1.** *(-ru; -ry)* (*głos*) tenor **2.** *(-ra; -rzy)* (*śpiewak*) tenor
tenże *pron* this one
teolog *m (-ga; -gowie/-lodzy)* theologian; **teologia** *f (-gii; no pl)* theology; **teologiczny** *adj* theological
teoretyczny *adj* theoretical; **teoretyk** *m (-ka; -tycy)* theorist, theoretician
teoretyzować *v/im (-zuję)* theorize
teoria *f (-rii; -rie)* theory; ***~ względności*** PHYS the theory of relativity; **teoryjka** *f (-ki; -ki)* (little) theory
terakota *f (-ty; no pl)* **1.** terracotta **2.** (*płytki podłogowe*) floor tiles
terapeuta *m (-ty; -peuci)*, **-tka** *f (-ki; -ki)* therapist; **terapeutyczny** *adj* therapeutic
terapia *f (-pii; -pie)* therapy; ***~ grupowa*** group therapy
teraz *adv* now; ***od ~*** from now on; ***i co ~?*** now what?
teraźniejszość *f (-ści; no pl)* the present; **teraźniejszy** *adj* present; ***czas ~*** GRAM the present tense
tercet *m (-tu; -ty)* (vocal) trio; **tercja** *f (-ji; -je)* **1.** (*w hokeju*) period **2.** (*w muzyce*) third
teren *m (-nu; -ny)* **1.** area; ***~ budowy*** construction site; ***~y zielone*** parklands; ***~y zabudowane*** built-up areas; ***~ szkoły*** school grounds; ***~ zakładu*** factory premises; ***~ łowiecki*** hunting ground; ***~y połowów*** fishery; ***pracować w ~ie*** work in the field **2.** (*naturalny*) terrain; ***~ górzysty*** mountainous terrain; **terenow|y** *adj* **1.** *władze*: local **2.** ***samochód ~y*** AUTO off-road vehicle **3.** ***badania ~e*** fieldwork **4.** *ćwiczenia, gry*: outdoor

terkot *m (-tu; no pl)* **1.** *maszyny*: clatter **2.** *budzika*: rattle **3.** *kutra*: chug
terkotać *v/im (-koczę/-kocę)* **1.** (*o maszynie*) clatter **2.** (*o budziku*) rattle **3.** (*o kutrze*) chug **4.** (*gadać, paplać*) chatter, babble
term|a *f (-my; -my)* **1.** TECH water heater **2.** (*źródło*) hot spring, thermal spring **3.** ***~y*** HIST therms; **termiczny** *adj* thermal; ***szok ~*** thermal shock
termin *m (-nu; -ny)* **1.** (*okres czasu*) period; ***w ~ie*** on time; ***przed ~em*** ahead of time; ***po ~ie*** too late **2.** (*data*) date; ***~ dostawy*** delivery date; ***~ wyborów*** election date **3.** (*ostateczna data*) deadline; ***dotrzymywać ~u*** meet the deadline; ***przekroczyć ~*** miss the deadline **4.** (*wyraz*) term
terminal *m (-lu/-la; -le)* terminal
terminarz *m (-rza; -rze)* **1.** (*kalendarz*) diary **2.** (*rozkład, plan*) schedule
terminowo *adv* on time; **terminowość** *f (-ści; no pl)* punctuality; **terminowy** *adj* punctual, on time
termit *m (-tu; -ty)* BIOL termite
termo- (*w złożeniach*) thermo-, thermal; **termodynamiczny** *adj* thermodynamic; **termoizolacja** *m (-ji; -je)* thermal insulation
termofor *m (-ru; -ry)* hot-water bottle; **termojądrowy** *adj* thermonuclear; **termometr** *m (-ru; -ry)* thermometer
termos *m (-su; -sy)* *Br* vacuum flask, Thermos® flask, *Am* vacuum bottle
terpentyna *f (-ny; no pl)* turpentine
terror *m (-ru; no pl)* POLIT terror
terrorysta *m (-ty; -ryści)*, **-tka** *f (-ki; -ki)* terrorist
terrorystyczny *adj* terrorist; ***zamach ~*** terrorist attack; **terroryzm** *m (-mu; no pl)* terrorism; ***akt ~u*** act of terrorism
terroryzować ⟨**s-**⟩ *(-zuję)* terrorize
terytorialn|y *adj* POLIT territorial; ***wody ~e*** territorial waters; **terytorium** *n (indecl; -ria)* territory
test *m (-tu; -ty)* test; ***~ na inteligencję*** intelligence test, IQ test; ***~ ciążowy*** pregnancy test
testament *m (-tu; -ty)* will, testament; ***Nowy ~*** the New Testament; ***Stary ~*** the Old Testament; **testamentowy** *adj* testamentary
testować ⟨***prze-***⟩ *(-tuję)* test

T

testowan|y *adj* tested; ***osoba ~a*** (test) subject; ***nietestowany na zwierzętach*** not tested on animals
teściowa *f* (*-wej*; *-we*) mother-in-law; **teść** *m* (*-ścia*; *-ściowie*) father-in-law; **teściowie** *pl* (*teściów*) in-laws
teza *f* (*-zy*; *-zy*) thesis
też *particle* also, too; ***to ~ jest złe*** this is also bad; ***jak ~*** as well as; ***~ (mi) pytanie!*** what a question!; ***~ coś!*** well, I never!
tę → ***ten***
tęchnąć ⟨**s-**⟩ (*-nę*) (*pleśnieć*) *Br* grow mouldy, *Am* go moldy
tęcz|a *f* (*-czy*; *-cze*) rainbow; ***wpatrywać się w kogoś jak w ~ę*** gaze at s.o. adoringly
tęczow|y *adj Br* rainbow-coloured, *Am* rainbow-colored; ***~e kolory*** colours of the rainbow; **tęczówka** *f* (*-ki*; *-ki*) *ANAT* iris
tędy *pron* this way; ***~ i owędy*** here and there
tęgawy *adj* stout
tęg|i *adj* **1.** (*gruby*) stout **2.** (*silnie zbudowany*) sturdy **3.** (*mocny*) huge; ***dostać ~ie lanie*** get a sound thrashing **4.** (*zdolny*): ***~a z niego głowa*** he has a good head on his shoulders **5.** *zima*: severe
tępak *m* (*-ka*; *-ki*) moron
tępić ⟨**wy-**, **s-**⟩ (*-pię*) **1.** *szkodniki, chwasty*: kill, control **2.** *zło, opozycję*: fight, combat **3.** *nóż*: blunt **4.** *gatunek*: exterminate **5.** (*prześladować*) persecute; ***tępić się*** (*o nożu*) go blunt; ***~ się nawzajem*** fight each other
tępieć ⟨**s-**⟩ (*-pieję*) **1.** *nóż*: go blunt **2.** *słuch*: dull, weaken
tępo *adv* → ***tępy***
tępota *f* (*-ty*; *no pl*) **1.** (*brak inteligencji*) dullness, *form* obtuseness **2.** (*apatia*) apathy
tępy *adj* **1.** *nóż, zakończenie*: blunt **2.** (*głupi*) dull, *form* obtuse **3.** *ból, odgłos*: dull **4.** *spojrzenie, wzrok*: blank, vacant
tęsknić ⟨**za-**⟩ (*-nię*) **1.** (*odczuwać brak*) miss (**za** *I*/**do** *G*), hanker (**za** *I*/**do** *G* after); ***~ za krajem***, ***~ za domem*** be homesick **2.** (*pragnąć*) long (**za** *I*/**do** *G* for), yearn (**za** *I*/**do** *G* for)
tęskno *adv*: ***jest mi ~ za tobą*** I long for you, I miss you; → ***tęskny***
tęsknot|a *f* (*-ty*; *-ty*) longing; ***~a za domem***, ***~a za krajem*** homesickness; ***pełen ~y*** longing, wistful; **tęskny** *adj* wistful, longing
tętent *m* (*-tu*; *no pl*) *kopyt*: clatter, drumming
tętnica *f* (*-cy*; *-ce*) *ANAT* artery; **tętniczy** *adj ANAT* arterial
tętni|ć *v/im* (*-nię*) **1.** *fig* ***~ć życiem*** be teeming with life, be bustling with life; ***~ące życiem miasto*** vibrant city **2.** (*o krwi*) pulsate
tętno *n* (*-na*; *-na*) pulse
tężec *m* (*-żca*; *no pl*) tetanus
tężeć ⟨**s-**⟩ (*-żeję*) **1.** *galaretka, gips*: set **2.** *twarz*: freeze, stiffen
tężyzna *f* (*-ny*; *no pl*) **1.** (*siła*) brawn, strength **2.** (*sprawność*) fitness
tfu *interj*: ***~!*** *infml* ugh!, yuck!
tik *m* (*-ku*; *-ki*) tic
tiul *m* (*-lu*; *-le*) tulle
tj. *abbr* (= ***to jest***) i.e.
tkacki *adj* weaving; ***warsztat ~*** loom; **tkactwo** *n* (*-wa*; *no pl*) weaving
tkacz *m* (*-cza*; *-cze*), **~ka** *f* (*-ki*; *-ki*) weaver
tkać ⟨**u-**⟩ (*tkam*) weave
tkalnia *f* (*-ni*; *-nie*) **1.** (*warsztat*) weaver's shop **2.** (*fabryka*) weaving mill
tkanina *f* (*-ny*; *-ny*) fabric, cloth
tkanka *f* (*-ki*; *-ki*) *BIOL* tissue; ***~ łączna*** connective tissue
tkany *adj* woven
tkliwość *f* (*-ści*; *no pl*) affection; **tkliwy** *adj* affectionate, loving
tknąć *v/p* (*-nę*) ***coś mnie tknęło*** I had a hunch; ***coś mnie tknęło, żeby otworzyć drzwi*** something told me to open the door; → ***tykać***[2]
tknięty *adj*: ***~ trwogą*** terror-stricken
tkwić ⟨**u-**⟩ (*-wię*) **1.** be stuck (**w** *L* in); ***~ w korku*** be stuck in traffic; ***utkwić w czyjejś pamięci*** remain etched in s.o.'s memory, be imprinted on s.o.'s mind; ***tkwimy tu już od dwóch godzin*** we've been pinned down here for two hours now **2.** (*o przyczynach*) lie
tlący się *adj Br* smouldering, *Am* smoldering

T

tlen *m* (*-nu*; *no pl*) oxygen; **tlenek** *m* (*-nku*; *-nki*) oxide; **~ węgla** carbon monoxide
tlenić ⟨**u-**⟩ (*-nię*) *włosy*: bleach
tlenion|y *adj* bleached; **~a blondynka** peroxide blonde; **tlenowy** *adj* oxygen
tlić się *v/im* (*tlę*) *Br* smoulder, *Am* smolder; ***tliła się w nim iskierka nadziei*** hope still lingered in his heart
tłamsić ⟨**s-**⟩ (*-szę*) **1.** (*gnębić*) suppress **2.** *uczucia*: hold back, suppress
tło *n* (*tła*; *tła*) background; ***w tle*** in the background; ***na białym tle*** against a white background; ***morderstwo na tle rabunkowym*** murder and robbery; ***konflikty na tle etnicznym*** ethnic conflicts
tłocznia *f* (*-ni*; *-nie*) TECH press
tłoczno *adv*: ***w pociągu było ~*** the train was packed
tłoczny *adj* **1.** *tramwaj*: crowded, packed **2.** *ulica*: busy
tłoczony *adj* **1.** *druk*: embossed **2.** *olej*: pressed
tłoczyć *v/im* (*-czę*) **1.** *olej*: press **2.** *powietrze*, *wodę*: pump **3.** (*ozdabiać*) emboss; **tłoczyć się** crowd
tłok[1] *m* (*-ku*; *no pl*) (*ścisk*) crowd
tłok[2] *m* (*-ka*; *-ki*) TECH piston
tłuc (*tłukę*) **I** *v/t* **1.** ⟨**s-**⟩ (*rozbijać*) break **2.** ⟨**roz-**⟩ (*miażdżyć*) crush **3.** ⟨**u-**⟩ *kartofle*: mash **4.** ***stłuc sobie kolano*** bruise one's knee **5.** ⟨**u-**⟩ *mięso*: beat **II** *v/i* **1.** (*łomotać*) *infml* bang **2.** (*bić*) *infml* beat **3.** (*o sercu*) hammer; **tłuc się** **1.** (*o szkle*) break **2.** (*bić się*) *infml* fight **3.** (*hałasować*) *infml* bang around **4.** (*jechać*) *infml* ***~ się autobusem*** bump along in a bus
tłuczek *m* (*-czka*; *-czki*) **1.** (*do kartofli*) (potato) masher **2.** (*do mięsa*) mallet
tłuczeń *m* (*-cznia*; *no pl*) crushed stone
tłuczon|y *adj*: ***~e kartofle*** mashed potatoes
tłuk *m* (*-ka*; *-ki*) *infml* moron, *Am* schmuck
tłum *m* (*-mu*; *-my*) crowd; ***~y turystów*** crowds of tourists; ***~y kibiców*** crowds of fans; ***w ~ie*** in the crowd
tłumacz *m* (*-cza*; *-cze*) **1.** (*pisemny*) translator; ***~ przysięgły*** certified translator, sworn translator **2.** (*ustny*) interpreter; ***~ w sądzie*** court interpreter
tłumaczenie *n* (*-nia*; *-nia*) **1.** translation; ***~ na niemiecki*** translation into German; ***wolne ~*** free translation **2.** (*ustne*) interpreting, interpretation; ***~ symultaniczne*** simultaneous translation **3.** (*wyjaśnienie*) explanation **4.** (*usprawiedliwienie*) excuse **5.** (*uzasadnienie*) justification
tłumaczka *f* (*-ki*; *-ki*) **1.** (female) translator **2.** (*ustna*) (female) interpreter
tłumaczyć (*-czę*) **1.** ⟨**wy-**⟩ (*wyjaśniać*) explain; ***nie da sobie nic wytłumaczyć*** he won't listen to anybody **2.** ⟨**wy-**⟩ (*uzasadniać*) justify **3.** ⟨**wy-**⟩ (*usprawiedliwiać*) excuse **4.** ⟨**prze-**⟩ (*przekładać*) translate; ***~ z niemieckiego na polski*** translate from German into Polish **5.** ⟨**prze-**⟩ (*przekładać ustnie*) interpret; **tłumaczyć się** excuse oneself
tłumić ⟨**s-**⟩ (*-mię*) **1.** *bunt*, *powstanie*: suppress, quell **2.** *płacz*, *śmiech*, *ziewnięcie*: stifle **3.** *gniew*, *łzy*: contain **4.** *głos*, *dźwięk*: muffle **5.** (*amortyzować*) dampen **6.** *poczucie winy*: smother **7.** *ogień*: put out, extinguish
tłumik *m* (*-ka*; *-ki*) **1.** AUTO *Br* silencer, *Am* muffler **2.** (*broni*) silencer **3.** (*saksofonu*, *trąbki*) mute
tłumnie *adv* in great numbers, in crowds; **tłumny** *adj*: ***pogrzeb był ~*** a great number of people took part in the funeral
tłumoczek *m* (*-czka*; *-czki*) *dim* little bundle; **tłumok** *m* (*-ka*; *-ki*) **1.** (*bagaż*) bundle **2.** (*osoba*) *infml* moron
tłust|y *adj* **1.** fat; ***~y czwartek*** *the last Thursday before Lent*, the Fat Thursday **2.** *żywność*: fat, fatty; ***~e mleko*** whole milk **3.** *włosy*, *cera*, *plama*: greasy **4.** ***~ym drukiem*** in bold (type)
tłuszcz *m* (*-czu*; *-cze*) fat, grease; **tłuszczowy** *adj* *tkanka*, *związek*: fatty, fat
tłuścić ⟨**za-**⟩ (*tłuszczę*) grease; **tłuścić się** become greasy
tłuścioch *m* (*-cha*; *-chy*) *infml* fatty; **tłuścioszek** *m* (*-szka*; *-szki*) *infml* *dim* fatty
tłuściutki *adj* *dim* plump
tnę → **ciąć**
to **I** *pron* **1.** it; ***jak ~ się nazywa?*** what is it called?, what do you call it?; ***~ mi się podoba*** I like it; ***co ty na ~?*** how about it?, what do you think about

T

it?; ***dajmy na ~*** say; ***przez ~*** because of it; ***~ ciekawe*** that's interesting **2.** (*nie tamto*) this; ***co ~ jest?*** what's this? ***kto ~?*** who's that?; ***~ mój mąż*** this is my husband; ***popatrz na ~!*** look at this! **3.** (*zamiast czasownika*) ***czas ~ pieniądz*** time is money; ***~ miło z jej strony*** that's nice of her; ***~ ja*** it's me; ***~ fakt*** it's true; ***~ prawda*** it's true, that's right; ***co ~ za jeden?*** who is he?; ***co ~ za hałas?!*** what's that noise?! **II** *conj* ***jak chcesz, ~ przyjdź po to*** if you want, come and get it; ***jak skończysz, ~ posprzątaj*** clean up when you're finished **III** *particle* ***no ~ co?*** so what? ***~ nic*** never mind, it's all right; ***jak ~*** how come?

toaleta *f* (*-ty*; *-ty*) toilet; **toaletka** *f* (*-ki*; *-ki*) dressing table; **toaletowy** *adj* toilet; ***papier ~*** toilet paper

toast *m* (*-tu*; *-ty*) toast; ***wznieść ~*** raise a toast (***na cześć*** *G* to), propose a toast (***na cześć*** *G* to)

tobą *pron* you; ***z ~*** with you; → ***ty***

tobie *pron* you; ***o ~*** about you; → ***ty***

tobół *m* (*-bołu*; *-boły*) → ***tłumok***

toczek *m* (*-czka*; *-czki*) toque

toczn|y *adj*: ***łożysko ~e*** roller bearing; **toczony** *adj* **1.** (*z drewna*) turned **2.** (*z gliny*) thrown

toczyć *v/im* (*-czę*) **1.** (*po powierzchni*) roll **2.** *dyskusję*: conduct, carry on **3.** *spory*: have **4.** *wojnę*: fight **5.** (*na kole garncarskim*) throw, fashion **6.** (*na tokarce*) turn **7.** ***drewno toczone przez robaki*** worm-eaten timber; ***toczyć się*** **1.** (*po powierzchni*) roll **2.** (*trwać*) go on, be in progress; ***życie toczy się dalej*** life goes on **3.** (*o akcji*) take place

toga *f* (*-gi*; *-gi*) **1.** gown **2.** (*w starożytnym Rzymie*) toga

tojad *m* (*-du*; *-dy*) BIOL aconite

tok *m* (*-ku*; *no pl*) **1.** course; ***być w ~u*** be in progress, be underway; ***~ myśli*** train of thought; ***codzienny ~ dnia*** daily routine **2.** (*cietrzewia*) toot, mating call

tokarka *f* (*-ki*; *-ki*) lathe; **tokarski** *adj*: ***warsztat ~***, ***wyroby ~e*** turnery; **tokarz** *m* (*-rza*; *-rze*) turner

tokować *v/im* (*-kuję*) (*o ptakach*) toot

toksyczny *adj* toxic

tolerancja *f* (*-ji*; *no pl*) tolerance; **tolerancyjny** *adj* tolerant; **tolerować** *v/im* (*-ruję*) tolerate

tom *m* (*-mu*; *-my*) volume; ***w dwóch ~ach*** in two volumes

tomik *m* (*-ku*; *-ki*): ***~ poezji*** book of poetry

tomisko *n* (*-ka*; *-ka*) hefty volume

tomografia *f* (*-fii*; *no pl*) **1.** (*metoda*) tomography, (CAT) scanning **2.** (*badanie*) (CAT) scan

ton *m* (*-nu*; *-ny*) **1.** tone; ***w złym ~ie*** not the done thing; ***należeć do dobrego ~u*** be good form, be the done thing; ***nadawać ~*** set the tone **2.** (*odcień*) tint

tona *f* (*-ny*; *-ny*) tonne

tonacj|a *f* (*-ji*; *-je*) **1.** MUS key; ***w ~i d-moll*** in D minor **2.** (*koloryt*) tones *pl*, shades *pl*; ***utrzymany w jasnej ~i*** in light tones, in light shades; ***w pastelowej ~i*** in pastel shades; ***~a głosu*** pitch of voice

tonaż *m* (*-żu*; *no pl*) tonnage

tonąca *f* (*-cej*; *-ce*) drowning woman; **tonący** *f* (*-cego*; *-cy*) drowning man

tonąć (*-nę*) **1.** ⟨**u-**⟩ (*o osobie*) drown; ***~ w długach*** *fig* be up to one's ears in debt; ***~ we łzach*** be in floods of tears, be flooded with tears; ***~ w mroku*** *fig* be enveloped in darkness **2.** ⟨**za-**⟩ (*o statku*) sink, go under

tonik *m* (*-ku*; *-ki*) **1.** (*napój*) tonic (water) **2.** (*kosmetyk*) (skin) tonic

toń *f* (*toni*; *tonie*) *lit* (the) depths *pl*

topaz *m* (*-zu*; *-zy*) topaz

topić (*-pię*) **1.** ⟨**u-**⟩ (*zabijać*) drown; ***~ smutki w alkoholu*** *fig* drown one's sorrows **2.** ⟨**roz-**⟩ (*roztapiać*) melt **3.** ⟨**za-**⟩ *statek*: sink **4.** ⟨**u-**⟩ *pieniądze*: lose, *infml* blow; ***topić się*** **1.** (*o osobie*) drown **3.** (*o metalu*, *serze*) melt **2.** (*o śniegu*, *lodzie*) melt, thaw

topiel *f* (*-li*; *-le*) *lit* **1.** deep water **2.** (*wir*) whirlpool, vortex

topielec *m* (*-lca*; *-lcy*) drowned man, drowned body; **topielica** *f* (*-cy*; *-ce*) drowned woman

topik *m* **1.** (*-ka*; *-ki*) BIOL water spider **2.** (*-ku*; *-ki*) PHYS fuse link, fusible link

topiony *adj*: ***~ ser*** processed cheese

toples(s) *adj* topless

topliwy *adj*: ***łatwo ~*** TECH easily fusible, low melting point

topnieć ⟨**s-**⟩ (*-nieję*) **1.** (*o metalu*) melt **2.** (*o śniegu, lodzie*) melt, thaw **3.** (*o zapasach, oszczędnościach*) dwindle (away), melt away **4.** (*o poparciu*) ebb away

topograficzny *adj* topographic(al)

topola *f* (*-li*; *-le*) poplar; **topolowy** *adj* poplar

toporek *m* (*-rka*; *-rki*) hatchet

toporny *adj* **1.** clumsy, graceless **2.** (*grubo ciosany*) crude, rough

topór *m* (*-pora*; *-pory*) **1.** *Br* axe, *Am* ax **2.** (*mały*) hatchet **3.** (*broń*) *Br* battle-axe, *Am* battleax

tor *m* (*-ru*; *-ry*) **1.** course; **~ wyścigowy** *SPORT* *Br* racecourse, *Am* racetrack; **~ przeszkód a)** assault course **b)** (*w wyścigach konnych*) jump course; **~ wodny** fairway **2.** (*kolejowy*) railway track; **boczny ~** sidetrack **3.** *saneczkowy*: run **4.** (*droga*) path; **~ lotu** trajectory

torba *f* (*-by*; *-by*) **1.** bag; **~ na zakupy** *Br* carrier bag, *Am* shopping bag; **~ podróżna** travel bag; **puścić kogoś z ~mi** reduce s.o. to beggary, milk s.o. dry **2.** *BIOL* pouch; **torbacz** *m* (*-cza*; *-cze*) *BIOL* marsupial

torbiel *f* (*-li*; *-le*) cyst

torebka *f* (*-ki*; *-ki*) bag; **~ damska** handbag; **~ foliowa** plastic bag

torf *m* (*-fu*; *-fy*) peat; **torfowisko** *n* (*-ka*; *-ka*) peat bog; **torfowy** *adj* peat

tornister *m* (*-tra*; *-try*) satchel, school bag

torować ⟨**u-**⟩ (*-ruję*): **~ sobie drogę** elbow one's way, clear one's way; **~ drogę** *fig* pave the way (*D* for)

torpeda *f* (*-dy*; *-dy*) torpedo; **torpedo** *n* (*-da*; *-da*) hub brake

torpedować ⟨**s-**⟩ (*-duję*) torpedo

torpedowiec *m* (*-wca*; *-wce*) torpedo boat; **torpedowy** *adj* torpedo

tors *m* (*-su*; *-sy*) **1.** (*część ciała*) trunk **2.** (*rzeźba*) torso

torsj|e *pl* (*-ji*) vomiting *sing*; **mieć ~e** vomit; **dostać ~i** start vomiting

tort *m* (*-tu*; *-ty*) (layer) cake; **~ urodzinowy** birthday cake; **tortownica** *f* (*-cy*; *-ce*) springform pan; **tortowy** *adj* cake

tortur|a *f* (*-ry*; *-ry*) **1.** torture; **~y** torture; **narzędzia ~** instruments of torture **2.** (*udręka*) torture, torment

torturować *v/im* (*-ruję*) **1.** torture **2.** *fig* torture, torment

tost *m* (*-tu*; *-ty*) *COOK* toast; **toster** *m* (*-ra*; *-ry*) toaster

totalitarny *adj* *POLIT* totalitarian; **totalitaryzm** *m* (*-mu*; *-my*) *POLIT* totalitarianism

totalny *adj* **1.** total **2.** *POLIT* totalitarian

totek *m* (*-tka*; *-tki*) lottery

toteż *conj lit* so that, therefore

totolotek *m* (*-tka*; *no pl*) (national) lottery

Tow. *abbr* (= **Towarzystwo**) Soc., Assoc.

towar *m* (*-ru*; *-ry*) **1.** (*wytwór*) commodity; **~y** goods, merchandise **2.** (*wytwory*) goods; **dostarczać ~** supply goods **3.** (*dziewczyna*) *infml* dish

towarow|y I *adj* **1.** goods; **dom ~y** department store; **wymiana ~a** barter; **znak ~y** trademark **2.** (*dotyczący transportu towarów*) freight; **pociąg ~y** freight train, *Br* goods train; **statek ~y, samolot ~y** freighter **II** *m* (*-wego*; *-we*) freight train, *Br* goods train

towarzysk|i *adj* **1.** *osoba*: sociable **2.** *spotkanie, życie, skandal*: social; **formy ~ie** social manners **3.** *SPORT* **spotkanie ~ie** friendly match **4. agencja ~a** escort agency **5. kronika ~a** gossip column

towarzystw|o *n* (*-wa*; *-wa*) **1.** company; **dotrzymywać komuś ~a** keep s.o. company; **dla ~a** for company; **unikać czyjegoś ~a** avoid s.o.'s company; **wpaść w złe ~o** get into bad company, fall in with bad company; **przyjść w ~ie kogoś** come with s.o. **2.** (*organizacja*) society

towarzysz *m* (*-sza*; *-sze*), **~ka** *f* (*-ki*; *-ki*) **1.** companion; **~ podróży** travelling companion; **~ zabaw** playmate; **~ życia** life companion; **~ niedoli** companion in misery; **~ broni** brother in arms **2.** *POLIT* comrade

towarzysząc|y *adj* accompanying: **osoba ~a** partner; **imprezy ~e** accompanying events

towarzyszyć (*-szę*) accompany; **~ komuś** accompany s.o., keep s.o. company

tożsamoś|ć *f* (*-ści*; *no pl*) identity; **dowód ~ci** ID, identity card; **tożsamy** *adj lit* identical

T

tracić ⟨**s-**⟩ (*-cę*) **1.** lose; **~ na wadze** lose weight; **~ z oczu** lose sight (*A* of); **~ głowę** lose one's head; **~ grunt pod nogami** lose one's footing, be out of one's depth **2.** (*marnować*) waste

tradycja *f* (*-ji*; *-je*) tradition; **tradycyjny** *adj* traditional

traf *m* (*-fu*; *-fy*) chance; ***ślepy* ~** pure chance; ***szczęśliwy* ~** a stroke of luck; ***szczęśliwym ~em*** luckily; ***dziwnym ~em*** by a bizarre twist of fate, ***~ chciał, że*** as luck would have it

trafiać ⟨**-fić**⟩ (*-fiam*) **1.** (*do celu*) hit the target; ***~ w coś*** hit s.th.; ***nie ~*** miss; ***~ w dziesiątkę*** hit the bull's eye; ***~ kluczem do zamka*** find the keyhole; ***piłka trafiła do bramki*** the ball flew into the net, a goal was scored; ***na chybił trafił*** at random, hit-or-miss; ***trafiło na niego*** *fig* he had the bad luck; ***~ komuś do przekonania*** *fig* convince s.o. **2.** (*znajdować*) come across (**na** *A*), encounter (**na** *A*); ***trafiłem na zabawny artykuł*** I came across an amusing article; ***dobrze ~*** **a)** (*spotkać właściwą osobę*) find the right person **b)** (*znaleźć się we właściwym miejscu*) find the right place **3.** (*spotykać*) come across (**na** *A*), run into (**na** *A*); ***trafić na złą pogodę*** have bad weather, encounter bad weather **4.** (*znajdować drogę*) find one's way; ***~ do środka*** find one's way inside; ***~ do domu*** find one's way home; ***trafić za kratki*** end up in jail; ***trafić do szpitala*** land in hospital, be hospitalized; ***dokument trafił w jego ręce*** the document fell into his hands; ***jak tam trafić?*** how to get there?; ***czy dobrze trafiłam?*** am I in the right place?; ***trafić na pierwsze strony gazet*** hit the headlines; ***ten argument do niego nie trafia*** he doesn't accept this argument; ***trafiło do mnie, że*** *fig* I realized that **5.** (*wygrywać*) ***trafić w totolotka*** win the lottery; ***trafiać się*** **1.** (*o okazji*) come up, arise **2.** (*o kupcu*) come up **3.** (*przydarzać się*) happen; ***tacy dobrzy dentyści trafiają się rzadko*** it's quite unusual to come across such a good dentist

trafienie *n* (*-nia*; *-nia*) **1.** hit **2.** (*w totolotku*) lucky number(s)

trafiony *adj* **1.** hit; ***~ kulą*** hit by a bullet **2.** *inwestycja*, *zakup*: good **3.** *decyzja*: right

trafność *f* (*-ści*; *no pl*) accuracy; **trafny** *adj* **1.** *diagnoza*, *strzał*: accurate **2.** *inwestycja*, *wybór*: good **3.** *nazwa*: appropriate, apt **4.** *ocena*, *krytyka*: apt **5.** *pytanie*, *uwaga*: apt, pertinent **6.** *odpowiedź*, *decyzja*: right

tragarz *m* (*-rza*; *-rze*) **1.** (*podczas ekspedycji*) carrier **2.** (*bagażowy*) porter

tragedi|a *f* (*-dii*; *-die*) tragedy; ***robić z czegoś ~ę*** dramatize s.th., make a drama out of s.th.

tragiczka *f* (*-ki*; *-ki*) THEAT tragic actress; **tragik** *m* (*-ka*; *-gicy*) THEAT **1.** (*autor*) tragedian **2.** (*aktor*) tragic actor, tragedian

tragiczn|y *adj* **1.** tragic; ***~y wypadek*** tragic accident; ***~y w skutkach*** disastrous; ***zginąć śmiercią ~ą*** die a violent death; ***aktor ~y*** tragic actor **2.** (*fatalny*, *okropny*) terrible, awful

tragikomiczny *adj* tragicomic(al)

trajkot *m* (*-tu*; *no pl*) chatter, *infml* gabble; **trajkotać** *v/im* (*-koczę*/*-kocę*) chatter, *infml* gabble

trajlować *v/im* (*-luję*) → ***trajkotać***

trakcja *f* (*-ji*; *-je*) **1.** (*trasa*) route **2.** (*napęd*) traction

trak|t *m* (*-tu*; *-ty*) **1.** ***w ~cie*** *G* during, in the course of **2.** (*szlak*) route **3.** (*droga*) road

traktat *m* (*-tu*; *-ty*) **1.** POLIT treaty; ***~ pokojowy*** peace treaty **2.** (*rozprawa*) treatise

traktor *m* (*-ra*; *-ry*) tractor; **traktorzysta** *m* (*-ty*; *-ryści*), **-tka** *f* (*-ki*; *-ki*) tractor driver

traktować ⟨**po-**⟩ (*-tuję*) **1.** treat; ***~ coś poważnie*** take s.th. seriously; ***~ kogoś z góry*** patronize s.o., look down on s.o.; ***~ kogoś jak powietrze*** ignore s.o., cut s.o. dead; ***potraktowano nas po królewsku*** we were treated like royalty **2.** (*omawiać*) deal (**o** *L* with), treat (**o** *L* of)

trałm *m* (*-łu*; *-ły*) (*sieć*) trawl; **trałowiec** *m* (*-wca*; *-wce*) minesweeper

trampki *pl* (*-pek*) *Br* gym shoes, plimsolls, *Am* sneakers

trampolina *f* (*-ny*; *-ny*) **1.** (*odskocznia*) springboard **2.** (*na basenie*) spring-

T

board, diving board **3.** (*batut*) trampoline

tramwaj *m* (*-ju*; *-je*) *Br* tram, *Am* streetcar; **tramwajarz** *m* (*-rza*; *-rze*) *Br* tram driver, *Am* streetcar driver; **tramwajowy** *adj Br* tram, *Am* streetcar

tran *m* (*-nu*; *no pl*) (*z dorsza*) cod-liver oil

trans *m* (*-su*; *-sy*) trance

transakcj|a *f* (*-ji*; *-je*) transaction, deal; ***~a walutowa*** foreign currency transaction; ***sfinalizować ~ę*** complete a transaction, close a deal

transatlantycki *adj* transatlantic; **transatlantyk** *m* (*-ku*; *-ki*) transatlantic (liner)

transfer *m* (*-ru*; *-ry*) transfer

transformacja *f* (*-ji*; *-je*) transformation; **transformator** *m* (*-ra*; *-ry*) transformer; **transfuzja** *f* (*-ji*; *-je*) *krwi*: transfusion

transkrybować ⟨**s-**⟩ (*-buję*) transcribe

transkrypcja *f* (*-ji*; *-je*) transcription; ***~ fonetyczna*** phonetic transcription

transmisja *f* (*-ji*; *-je*) **1.** transmission **2.** RADIO TEL broadcast, transmission; ***~ bezpośrednia***, ***~ na żywo*** live coverage, live broadcast

transmitować *v/im* (*-tuję*) RADIO TEL broadcast, transmit; ***~ coś na żywo*** broadcast s.th. live

transparent *m* (*-tu*; *-ty*) banner

transplantacja *f* (*-ji*; *-je*) transplant, transplantation; ***~ skóry*** skin graft

transport *m* (*-tu*; *-ty*) **1.** *Br* transport, *Am* transportation **2.** (*towar*) shipment; **transporter** *m* (*-ra*; *-ry*) **1.** (*przenośnik*) conveyor **2.** (*wóz bojowy*) personnel carrier

transportować ⟨**prze-**⟩ (*-tuję*) transport

transportowiec *m* (*-wca*; *-wce*) **1.** (*pracownik*) *Br* transport worker, *Am* transportation worker **2.** (*samolot transportowy*) cargo plane, freighter **3.** (*statek*) cargo ship, freighter **4.** (*samolot wojskowy*) transport plane; **transportowy** *adj* **1.** *Br* transport, *Am* transportation **2.** *firma*: shipping **3.** *statek*, *samolot*: cargo

transwestyta *m* (*-ty*; *-styci*), **-tka** *f* (*-ki*; *-ki*) transvestite

tranzystorowy *adj* transistor

tranzyt *m* (*-tu*; *no pl*) transit; ***jechać ~em przez*** *A* go via, go through; **tranzytowy** *adj* transit

traper *m* (*-ra*; *-rzy*) trapper

trapez *m* (*-zu*; *-zy*) **1.** (*figura*) *Br* trapezium, *Am* trapezoid **2.** SPORT trapeze

trapi|ć ⟨**s-**⟩ (*-pię*) *lit* trouble, plague; ***~ły go kontuzje*** he was plagued by injuries, he was dogged by injuries; ***~ mnie to, że*** it bothers me that; ***trapić się*** be worried (*I* about)

tras|a *f* (*-sy*; *-sy*) route; ***autobus kursuje na ~ie Warszawa – Berlin*** the bus runs from Warsaw to Berlin; ***~a szybkiego ruchu*** *Br* dual carriageway, *Am* divided highway; ***~a koncertowa*** concert tour; ***~a narciarska*** ski run

traszka *f* (*-ki*; *-ki*) BIOL newt

tratować ⟨**s-**⟩ (*-tuję*) trample; ***stratować kogoś na śmierć*** trample s.o. to death

tratwa *f* (*-wy*; *-wy*) raft; ***~ ratunkowa*** life raft

traumatyczny *adj* traumatic

traw|a *f* (*-wy*; *-wy*) grass; ***leżeć na ~ie*** lie on the grass; ***wiedzieć, co w ~ie piszczy*** *fig* know which way the wind is blowing, know what's what

trawestacja *f* (*-ji*; *-je*) *lit* travesty

trawiasty *adj* **1.** *kort*: grass **2.** *kolor*: grass-green

trawi|ć (*-wię*) **1.** ⟨**s-**⟩ digest **2.** ⟨**s-**⟩ *fig* ***nie ~ę go*** I don't like him, I can't stand him **2.** ⟨**s-**⟩ (*o niepokoju*, *niepewności*, *chorobie*, *ogniu*) consume **3.** ⟨**s-**⟩ *czas*: spend; ***~ czas na*** *L* spend one's time doing s.th. **4.** ⟨**wy-**⟩ *metal*: etch, pickle

trawienie *n* (*-nia*; *no pl*) digestion; **trawienn|y** *adj* digestive; ***układ ~y*** digestive system; ***soki ~e*** digestive juices

trawka *f* (*-ki*; *no pl*) *dim* **1.** grass **2.** (*źdźbło*) blade of grass; **trawnik** *m* (*-ka*; *-ki*) lawn

trąb|a *f* (*-by*; *-by*) **1.** MUS trumpet **2.** (*słonia*) trunk **3.** ***~a powietrzna*** whirlwind, twister **4.** (*fujara*) *infml* bungler, loser; ***zrobić kogoś w ~ę*** take s.o. for a ride, take s.o. in

trąbić ⟨**za-**⟩ (*-bię*) **I** *v/i* **1.** blow the trumpet; ***~ na alarm*** sound the alarm **2.** AUTO honk (the horn) (***na*** *A* at), *Br* hoot (the horn) (***na*** *A* at) **3.** (*o słoniu*)

T

trumpet **4.** (*rozgłaszać*) trumpet (**o** *L*); **~ na wszystkie strony o** *L* shout from the rooftops about

trąbk|a *f* (*-ki*; *-ki*) **1.** *MUS* trumpet **2.** (*sygnałowa*) bugle **3. ~a Eustachiusza** *ANAT* Eustachian tube **4.** (*rurka*) tube; **zwinąć w ~ę** roll up

trącać ⟨**-cić**⟩ (*-cam*) **1.** (*uderzać*) nudge **2.** *strunę*: pluck; **trącać się**: **~ się** (**kieliszkami**) clink one's glasses, chink one's glasses

trącić *v/im* (*-cę*) **1.** (*cuchnąć*) smell (*I* of) **2.** *fig* **~ czymś** smack of s.th.; **~ myszką** be behind the times, be old hat; → **trącać**

trąd *m* (*-du*; *no pl*) *MED* leprosy

trądzik *m* (*-ku*; *no pl*) acne

trefl *m* (*-la*; *-le*) (*w kartach*) clubs; **as ~** ace of clubs; **treflowy** *adj król, dama*: of clubs

trefny *adj* **1.** (*kradziony*) *infml* hot **2.** (*wadliwy*) *infml* dud **3.** (*niekoszerny*) tref, not kosher

trele *pl* (*-li*/*-lów*): **słowicze ~** nightingale trills

trema *f* (*-my*; *no pl*) stage fright

tren[1] *m* (*-nu*; *-ny*) (*utwór*) threnody

tren[2] *m* (*-nu*; *-ny*) *sukni*: train

trener *m* (*-ra*; *-rzy*), **~ka** *f* (*-ki*; *-ki*) coach, trainer

trening *m* (*-gu*; *-gi*) practice, training; **chodzę na ~ dwa razy w tygodniu** I have practice twice a week; **treningowy** *adj* **1.** practice, training; **worek ~** *Br* punchbag, *Am* punching bag **2.** *rower*: exercise

trenować ⟨**wy-**⟩ (*-nuję*) **1.** train; **~ przed biegiem** be in training for a race **2.** (*ćwiczyć*) *Br* practise, *Am* practice

treska *f* (*-ki*; *-ki*) hairpiece

tresować ⟨**wy-**⟩ (*-suję*) **1.** *konia*: break in, train **2.** *psa*: train **3.** *fig* drill; **tresura** *f* (*-ry*; *no pl*) training; **~ lwów** lion taming

treściow|y *adj* content; **zawartość ~a** content; **treściwy** *adj* **1.** (*zwięzły*) pithy **2.** *pokarm*: nutritious

treś|ć *f* (*-ści*; *-ści*) **1.** *książki, wypowiedzi*: content; **zawierać niewiele ~ci** lack content **2. ~ć żołądka** stomach contents **3.** (*sens*) meaning

trębacz *m* (*-cza*; *-cze*) **1.** trumpeter **2.** (*w wojsku*) bugler

trędowaty I *adj* leprous **II** *m* (*-tego*; *-waci*), **-ta** *f* (*-tej*; *-te*) leper

triatlon *m* (*-nu*; *-ny*) *SPORT* triathlon

trick, trik *m* (*-ku*; *-ki*) trick; **trikowy** *adj* trick

trio *n* (*tria*; *tria*) *MUS* trio

triumf *m* (*-fu*; *-fy*) triumph; **triumfalny** *adj* **1.** *okrzyk, gest*: triumphant **2.** *łuk, powrót*: triumphal

triumfować ⟨**za-**⟩ (*-fuję*) triumph (**nad** *I* over)

trochę *adv* **1.** (*przed przymiotnikiem*) a little, a bit; **~ zmęczony** a little tired; **ani ~** not a bit **2.** (*przed rzeczownikiem*) some; **~ wina** some wine **3.** (*chwilę*) for a while, for a moment

trociny *pl* (*-cin*) sawdust *sing*

troczki *pl* (*-ków*) straps

troć *f* (*troci*; *trocie*) brown trout, sea trout

trofeum *n* (*indecl*; *-fea*) trophy

troić się *v/im* (*troję*) triple

trojaczki *pl* (*-ków*) triplets; **trojaki** *adj* triple

troje *num* three; **~ dzieci** three children

trolejbus *m* (*-su*; *-sy*) *Br* trolleybus, *Am* trackless trolley

trombocyty *pl* (*-tów*) *ANAT* thrombocytes

tron *m* (*-nu*; *-ny*) throne; **zasiąść na ~ie** ascend to the throne; **zasiadać na ~ie** (*rządzić*) rule; **tronowy** *adj* throne

trop *m* (*-pu*; *-py*) **1.** (*ślad*) track, trail; **być na** (**właściwym**) **~ie** be on the right track; **być na fałszywym ~ie** be on the wrong track; **naprowadzać kogoś na ~** put s.o. on the trail; **iść czyimś ~em** follow s.o.; **wpaść na ~** pick up the trail (*G* of) **2.** (*literacki*) trope

tropiciel *m* (*-la*; *-le*) **1.** tracker; **pies ~** tracker dog **2.** (*poszukiwacz*) hunter, seeker

tropić ⟨**wy-**⟩ (*-pię*) **1.** *zwierzę*: track, trail **2.** *przestępców*: track down, hunt down

tropik *m* (*-ku*; *-ki*) (*pokrycie namiotu*) flysheet; **tropiki** *pl* (*-ków*) the tropics

tropikalny *adj* tropical

tros|ka *f* (*-ki*; *-ki*) **1.** (*zmartwienie*) worry; **wolny od ~k** carefree **2.** (*niepokój*) concern; **wyrazić ~kę o** *A* express concern about **3.** (*dbałość*) care,

T

concern; ***z ~ką*** with care; ***~ka o dziecko*** concern for one's child; ***~ka o bezpieczeństwo*** concern for safety; ***~ka o szczegóły*** concern for details; ***otoczyć kogoś ~ką*** take good care of s.o.; ***wymagać ~ki*** require care; ***w ~ce o*** *A* out of concern for; ***dzieci specjalnej ~ki*** children with special needs

troskliwy *adj* **1.** caring **2.** *opieka*: good

troszcz|yć się ⟨**za-**⟩ (*-czę*) **1.** (*opiekować się*) take care (**o** *A* of), look after (**o** *A*) **2.** (*dbać*) care (**o** *A* about); ***nikt się o to nie ~y*** nobody cares about it **3.** (*niepokoić się*) worry, be worried (**o** *A* about); ***nie ~ąc się o*** *A* without regard to

troszeczkę, ***troszkę*** *dim* → ***trochę***

trój- (*w złożeniach*) three-, tri-; ***~kołowy*** three-wheeled; ***~boista*** triathlete

trója *f* (*trói*; *-je*) (*ocena*) C, satisfactory

trójbarwny *adj Br* tricolour, three-coloured, *Am* tricolor, three-colored; **trójbój** *m* (*-boju*; *-boje*) SPORT triathlon

trójca *f* (*-cy*; *-ce*) trio; ***⁓ Święta*** REL the Holy Trinity

trójk|a *f* (*-ki*; *-ki*) **1.** three; ***~a koni*** three horses; ***~a rodzeństwa*** three siblings; ***w ~ę zjedliśmy obiad*** the three of us had dinner; ***~ami*** in threes **2.** (*w kartach*) the three **3.** (*tramwaj*, *mieszkanie*) number three **4.** (*bieg*) the third (gear); ***wrzucić ~ę*** put the car into third

trójkąt *m* (*-ta*; *-ty*) triangle; ***~ ostrzegawczy***, ***~ odblaskowy*** AUTO warning triangle; ***~ małżeński*** love triangle; **trójkątny** *adj* triangular

trójkolorowy *adj Br* tricolour, three-coloured, *Am* tricolor, three-colored

trójnasób: ***w ~*** threefold

trójnóg *m* (*-nogu*; *-nogi*) tripod; **trójpasmowy** *adj* three-lane; **trójskok** *m* (*-ku*; *no pl*) SPORT triple jump

trójszereg *m* (*-gu*; *-gi*) three rows *pl*

trójwymiarowy *adj* three-dimensional, 3D; **trójząb** *m* (*-zębu*; *-zęby*) trident

truchleć ⟨**s-**⟩ (*-leję*) **1.** (*bać się*) *lit* quail; ***~ ze strachu*** quail with fear; ***~ na myśl o*** *L* quail at the thought of **2.** (*drętwieć ze strachu*) be petrified

trucht *m* (*-tu*; *no pl*) **1.** (*konia*) jog trot **2.** (*człowieka*) jog, trot; ***biec ~em*** jog, trot; **truchtać** *v/im* (*-tam*) trot

truciciel *m* (*-la*; *-le*), ***~ka*** *f* (*-ki*; *-ki*) poisoner

trucizna *f* (*-ny*; *-ny*) poison

truć ⟨**za-**, **o-**⟩ (*truję*) **I** *v/t* (*mordować*) poison **II** *v/i* **1.** (*narzekać*) *infml* gripe, *Br* whinge **2.** (*zamęczać prośbami*) nag

trud *m* (*-du*; *-dy*) **1.** (*wysiłek*) effort, trouble; ***z ~em*** with difficulty; ***bez ~u*** easily, effortlessly; ***zadać sobie ~, żeby coś zrobić*** take the trouble to do s.th.; ***nie szczędzić ~ów, by coś zrobić*** go to a lot of trouble to do s.th., go to great lengths to do s.th.; ***nie zadał sobie ~u, żeby to sprawdzić*** he didn't bother to check it **2.** (*ciężkie warunki*) hardship; ***~y podróży*** hardships of a journey

trudnić się *v/im* (*-nię*): ***~ czymś*** do s.th. for a living; ***~ handlem*** be in trade; ***trudnił się przemytem*** he was a smuggler

trudno *adv* hard; ***~ powiedzieć*** it's hard to tell, it's difficult to tell; ***~ mi to zrozumieć*** I can hardly understand it; ***~ w to uwierzyć*** it's hard to believe; ***~ się dziwić, że*** no wonder (that); ***~ nam było wyjeżdżać*** it was hard for us to leave; ***~ o dobrą pracę*** it's hard to find a good job; ***~ o dobrego lekarza*** a good doctor is hard to find; (***no to***) ***~!*** tough luck!; ***ta książka jest ~ dostępna*** the book is difficult to obtain

trudnoś|ć *f* (*-ści*; *-ści*) difficulty, problem; ***bez ~ci*** without difficulty, easily; ***z ~cią*** with difficulty; ***~ci*** difficulties, problems; ***miał ~ci z otwarciem drzwi*** he had difficulty opening the door; ***miała ~ci z zaśnięciem*** she had trouble falling asleep; ***mówienie o tym zawsze przychodziło mi z ~cią*** I've always found it difficult to talk about it; ***sprawiać ~ci*** cause difficulties; ***czy nie sprawi ci ~ć, jeśli*** would it put you out if

trudn|y *adj* difficult, hard; ***~y do zrozumienia*** difficult to understand, hard to understand; ***~e dzieciństwo*** tough childhood, difficult childhood; ***~a młodzież*** difficult youth; ***~y w poży-***

ciu difficult to get on with, difficult to deal with; **~a rada!** there is nothing to be done!
trudzić *v/im* (*-dzę*) (*fatygować*) trouble, bother; **trudzić się 1.** (*męczyć się*) toil, take pains; **~ się nad** *I* toil away at **2.** (*fatygować się*) trouble, bother; **niepotrzebnie się pani trudziła** you needn't have troubled
trufla *f* (*-li*; *-le*) truffle
trujący *adj* **1.** poisonous; **gaz ~** poison gas, poisonous gas **2.** (*toksyczny*) toxic
trumienny *adj Br* coffin, *Am* casket: **portret ~** *ART* coffin portrait
trumna *f* (*-ny*; *-ny*) *Br* coffin, *Am* casket
trunek *m* (*-nku*; *-nki*) *lit* alcoholic beverage; **trunkowy** *adj lit* fond of drink
trup *m* (*-pa*; *-py*) dead body, corpse; **paść ~em** drop dead; **dążyć do czegoś po ~ach** *fig* try to do s.th. at any cost; **po moim ~ie!** *infml* over my dead body!; **zalać się w ~a** *infml* get blind drunk; **~ słał się gęsto** people were dying in large numbers
trupi *adj* **1. ~a czaszka** skull (and crossbones) **2.** *zapach*: putrid **3.** *cera*: deathly pale, pallid; **trupiarnia** *f* (*-ni*; *-nie*) *infml Br* morgue, *Am* mortuary; **trupio** *adv*: **~ blady** (as) white as a sheet
trusia: **siedzieć jak ~** be as quiet as a mouse
truskawka *f* (*-ki*; *-ki*) strawberry; **truskawkowy** *adj* strawberry
truteń *m* (*-tnia*; *-tnie*) drone
trutka *f* (*-ki*; *-ki*) poison; **~ na szczury** rat poison
trwa|ć ⟨**po-**⟩ (*-wam*) **1.** last; **film ~ dwie godziny** the film lasts two hours, the film is two hours long; **prace budowlane wciąż ~ją** construction work is still in progress; **negocjacje ~ją** negotiations are underway; **jak długo to ~?** how long has this been going on? **2.** (*pozostawać*) stay, remain: **~ć w tej samej pozycji** remain motionless; **~ć w milczeniu** remain silent **3.** (*obstawać*) stick (**przy** *L* to); **~ć przy swoim zdaniu** stick to one's opinion; **~ć przy swojej decyzji** stick by one's decision
trwale *adv* permanently
trwałość *f* (*-ści*; *no pl*) durability

T

trwał|y *adj* **1.** *związek*, *uczucie*: (long-) lasting **2.** *materiał*, *produkt*: durable **3.** *kalectwo*, *pokój*, *ślad*: permanent; **pozostawić po sobie ~y ślad** *fig* earn one's place in history; **na ~e** permanently; **trwała** *f* (*-łej*; *-łe*) (*fryzura*) perm
trwanie *n* (*-nia*; *no pl*) duration
trwog|a *f* (*-gi*; *no pl*) *lit* terror; **z ~ą** in terror; **bić na ~ę** *fig* raise the alarm
trwonić ⟨**roz-**⟩ (*-nię*) waste, squander, fritter away
trwożliwy, **trwożny** *adj lit* fearful, faint-hearted
trwożyć ⟨**s-**⟩ (*-żę*) *lit* frighten; **trwożyć się** be frightened
tryb *m* (*-bu*; *-by*) **1.** (*sposób*) mode, method; **~ życia** lifestyle; **~ postępowania** course of action; **~ działania** mode of operation; **iść swoim ~em** run one's course; **w ~ie przyśpieszonym** *JUR* summarily **2.** *GRAM* mood; **~ oznajmujący** the indicative (mood); **~ rozkazujący** the imperative (mood) **3.** (*ząb na kole zębatym*) cog; **~y** *fig* machine; **trybiki** *pl* (*-ków*) *TECH* cogs
trybuna *f* (*-ny*; *-ny*) **1.** (*mównica*) tribune, rostrum **2.** (*podwyższenie*) parade platform, parade stand **3.** *SPORT* stand
trybunał *m* (*-łu*; *-ły*) *JUR* tribunal
trygonometria *f* (*-rii*; *no pl*) trigonometry
tryk *m* (*-ka*; *-ki*) ram
trykot *m* (*-tu*; *-ty*) **1.** (*tkanina*) tricot **2.** (*ubranie*) leotard
trykotowy *adj koszulka*: tricot
trylogia *f* (*-gii*; *-gie*) trilogy; **trymestr** *m* (*-ru*; *-ry*) **1.** *Br* term, *Am* trimester **2.** *MED* trimester
tryper *m* (*-pra*; *no pl*) *infml* (the) clap
tryptyk *m* (*-ku*; *-ki*) *ART THEAT* triptych
tryskać ⟨**-snąć**⟩ (*-kam*) **I** *v/i* **1.** (*o wodzie*, *krwi*, *źródle*) gush (out), spout **2.** (*o iskrach*) fly **II** *v/t* **~ zdrowiem** be bursting with health; **~ energią** be bursting with energy
trywialny *adj* trivial
trzask *m* (*-ku*; *-ki*) **1.** *kry*, *bata*, *gałęzi*: crack **2.** *drzwi*: slam, bang; **z ~iem** with a bang **3.** *ognia*: crackle **4.** (*przy łamaniu*) snap, crack; **~ prask** *infml* suddenly, all of a sudden **5. ~i** *RADIO* static

trzaskać ⟨**-snąć**⟩ (*-kam*) **I** *v/i* **1.** (*o gałęzi, lodzie*) crack **2.** (*o drzwiach*) bang (shut), slam (shut) **3.** (*o ogniu*) crackle **4.** (*o piorunach*) boom, burst **5.** *~ z bata* crack a whip **II** *v/t* **1.** *drzwiami*: bang (shut), slam (shut) **2.** *słuchawką*: slam down **3.** (*robić szybko*) *infml* knock off; *~ zdjęcia* take shot after shot

trzaskający *adj*: *~ mróz* crackling cold

trzasnąć *v/p* → ***trzaskać***

trząść ⟨**za-**⟩ (*trzęsę*) shake; *~ portkami infml* be scared stiff; ***samochód trząsł na wyboistej drodze*** the car bounced along a bumpy road; ***ona trzęsie całym instytutem*** *fig* she keeps a firm grip on the whole department, she bosses the whole department around; ***trząść się*** shake, tremble; *~ się z zimna* be shivering with cold; *~ się ze strachu* (*gniewu*) tremble with fear (anger); *~ się jak osika* be shaking like a leaf; ***głos mu się trząsł*** his voice was shaking, his voice was trembling

trzcina *f* (*-ny*; *-ny*) reed; *~ cukrowa* sugar cane

trzeba *v/irreg*: *~ to zrobić* it's necessary to do that, that needs to be done; ***do tego nie ~ dużo pieniędzy*** you don't need a lot of money to do that; ***jak ~, jeśli ~*** if necessary; ***to jest wszystko, czego ci ~*** that's all you need; ***niczego więcej mi nie ~*** that's all I need; *~ było wyjść wcześniej* you should have left earlier; *~ było wiele cierpliwości* one needed to be very patient; *~ przyznać, że* I must admit that, admittedly; *~ mi odpoczynku* I need a rest; *~ ci wiedzieć, że* you should know that; ***dziękuję, nie ~!*** no thanks

trzebić ⟨**wy-**⟩ (*-bię*) **1.** *zwierzęta*: kill **2.** *lasy*: thin out

trzech *num* three; ***Święto ~ Króli*** the Epiphany; → ***trzy***

trzechsetlecie *n* (*-cia*; *-cia*) (*rocznica*) tercentenary

trzeci *adj* (the) third; ***po ~e*** third(ly); ***jedna ~a*** one third; ***o ~ej*** at three

trzeciorzędny *adj* third-rate

trzeć ⟨**po-**, **ze-**⟩ (*trę*) **1.** rub (**o** *A* against); *~ oczy* rub one's eyes **2.** COOK grate; ***trzeć się*** rub (oneself) (**o** *A* against)

trzej *num* three

trzepaczka *f* (*-ki*; *-ki*): *~ do dywanów* carpet beater; *~ do jajek* egg beater, egg whisk

trzepać ⟨**wy-**, **-pnąć**⟩ (*-pię*) **1.** *dywan*: beat **2.** (*uderzać*) hit; *~ językiem infml* prattle, blabber

trzepnięty *adj infml* nuts, cracked; **trzepot** *m* (*-tu*; *no pl*) flutter

trzepotać ⟨**za-**⟩ (*-poczę*/*-pocę*) **I** *v/i* flutter; *~ na wietrze* flutter in the wind **II** *v/t* flutter; *~ skrzydłami* flutter one's wings, flap one's wings; ***trzepotać się*** (*w sieci*) flip about, flop about

trzeszczeć ⟨**za-**⟩ (*-czę*) **1.** (*o podłodze, schodach*) creak **2.** (*o lodzie, gałęzi*) crack **3.** (*o radiu, telefonie*) crackle **4** *fig ~ w szwach* be bursting at the seams

trzewia *pl* (*-wi*) entrails, guts

trzewiki *pl* (*-ków*) (laced) ankle boots

trzeźwić ⟨**o-**⟩ (*-wię*) try to bring round

trzeźwieć ⟨**wy-**, **o-**⟩ (*-wieję*) sober up

trzeźwy *adj* sober

trzęsawisko *n* (*-ka*; *-ka*) bog, swamp, quagmire

trzęsienie *n* (*-nia*; *-nia*): *~ ziemi* earthquake

trzmiel *m* (*-la*; *-le*) bumblebee

trznadel *m* (*-dla*; *-dle*) yellowhammer

trzod|a *f* (*-dy*; *-dy*) **1.** *~a chlewna* pigs; ***hodowla ~y chlewnej*** pig farming **2.** (*gromada zwierząt*) herd

trzon *m* (*-nu*; *-ny*) **1.** (*rdzeń*) core **2.** *grzyba*: stem **3.** *kolumny*: shaft **4.** *macicy*: body **5.** *zespołu*: backbone; **trzonek** *m* (*-nka*; *-nki*) *młotka, motyki*: handle

trzonowy *adj*: ***ząb ~*** molar

trzpień *m* (*-pienia*; *-pienie*) **1.** (*pręt*) rod **2.** *śruby, gwoździa*: shank **3.** (*tokarski*) mandrel, arbor

trzpiot *m* (*-ta*; *-ty*), **~ka** *f* (*-ki*; *-ki*) *lit* butterfly, flibbertigibbet; **trzpiotowaty** *adj* **1.** (*beztroski*) light-hearted **2.** (*roztrzepany*) scatterbrained

trzustka *f* (*-ki*; *-ki*) ANAT pancreas

trzy *num* three

trzycyfrowy *adj* three-digit; **trzyczęściowy** *adj* **1.** three-part **2.** *garnitur*: three-piece; **trzydrzwiowy** *adj* three-door

trzydziest|ka *f* (*-ki*; *-ki*) **1.** thirty; ***on jest po ~ce*** he's in his early thirties, he's thirty-something; ***jechaliśmy ~ką*** we were doing 30 (kph) **2.** (*mieszkanie, tramwaj*) number 30

trzydziestolatek *m* (*-tka*; *-tkowie*), **-tka** *f* (*-ki*; *-ki*) thirty-year-old

trzydziestolecie *n* (*-cia*; *-cia*) **1.** (*rocznica*) thirtieth anniversary **2.** (*okres czasu*) period of thirty years; **trzydziestoletni** *adj* **1.** *mężczyzna*: thirty-year-old **2.** *okres, doświadczenie, pożycie*: thirty-year

trzydziest|y *adj* (the) thirtieth; ***lata ~e*** the thirties, the 30s; **trzydzieści** *num* thirty

trzykołowy *adj* three-wheel

trzykroć: ***po ~*** *lit* thrice, three times

trzykrotny *adj* **1.** *wzrost, spadek*: three-fold **2** *mistrz, zwycięzca*: triple, three-time

trzylatek *m* (*-tka*; *-tki*), **-tka** *f* (*-ki*; *-ki*) three-year-old

trzyletni *adj* **1.** *dziecko, samochód*: three-year-old **2.** *plan, okres*: three-year

trzymać ⟨**po-**⟩ (*-mam*) **1.** hold; ***~ kogoś za rękę*** hold s.o. by the hand; ***~ coś w ręku*** hold s.th. in one's hand; ***~ na ręku dziecko*** hold a baby in one's arms; ***trzymała ręce w kieszeniach*** she had her hands in her pockets; ***~ coś w tajemnicy*** keep s.th. secret; ***~ kogoś w niepewności*** keep s.o. in suspense; ***trzymała go do chrztu*** she's his godmother; ***~ kurs*** stay on course; ***~ linię*** watch one's weight; ***trzymaj za mnie kciuki!*** keep your fingers crossed for me!; ***~ język za zębami*** hold one's tongue **2.** (*przechowywać, zatrzymywać*) keep; ***~ kogoś w areszcie*** keep s.o. in custody; ***trzymać się*** **1.** hold on (***za*** *A* to); ***trzymali się za ręce*** they were holding each other's hands; ***~ się razem*** stick together; ***~ się tematu*** keep to the point; ***~ się z dala od*** *G* stay away from; ***~ się kierunku*** keep the right direction; ***żarty się go trzymają*** he's joking **2.** (*być w określonym stanie*) *fig* remain, keep; ***dobrze się trzymać*** be in good shape; ***~ się prosto*** hold oneself straight; ***~ się przy życiu*** stay alive; ***~ się dzielnie*** be brave; ***trzymaj się!*** take care!

trzymank|a: ***jechać bez ~i*** ride without holding (on) the handlebars

trzymiesięczny *adj* **1.** *dziecko*: three-month-old **2.** *kurs, okres*: three-month **3.** *wypowiedzenie*: three-month's; **trzyminutowy** *adj* three-minute

trzynastka *f* (*-ki*; *-ki*) **1.** thirteen **2.** (*tramwaj, mieszkanie*) number 13 **3.** (*pensja*) annual bonus

trzynastoletni *adj* **1.** *dziecko, samochód*: thirteen-year-old **2.** *okres*: thirteen-year; **trzynastowieczny** *adj* thirteenth-century; **trzynast|y** *adj* thirteenth; ***o ~ej*** at one (o'clock) p.m.

trzynaście *num* thirteen

trzyosobowy *adj* **1.** *zespół, grupa*: three-person, of three persons **2.** *pokój*: triple; **trzypiętrowy** *adj budynek*: *Br* four-storey, *Am* four-story; **trzypokojowy** *adj* three-room; **trzysta** *num* three hundred

trzytomowy *adj* three-volume; **trzytygodniowy** *adj* **1.** *okres, kurs*: three-week **2.** *dziecko*: three-week-old; **trzyzmianow|y** *adj* three-shift; ***praca ~a*** three-shift work

tu I *pron* (*tutaj*) here; ***~ i tam, ~ i ówdzie*** here and there; ***co ~ się dzieje?*** what is going on here?; ***połóż to ~*** put it (in) here **II** *particle* **1.** (*przedstawianie się*) ***~ Ania, czy mogę rozmawiać z Markiem?*** this is Ania, can I speak to Marek? **2.** (*ekspresywnie*) ***aż ~ nagle*** and all of a sudden

tuba *f* (*-by*; *-by*) **1.** (*opakowanie*) tube **2.** MUS tuba; **tubalny** *adj głos*: booming, stentorian

tubka *f* (*-ki*; *-ki*) tube; ***~ pasty do zębów*** tube of toothpaste

tubylczy *adj ludność, zwyczaje*: native, local, indigenous; **tubylec** *m* (*-lca*; *-lcy*) native, local

tucząc|y *adj* fattening; ***czekolada jest ~a*** chocolate is fattening

tucznik *m* (*-ka*; *-ki*) porker; **tuczny** *adj* fattening

tucz|yć ⟨**u-**⟩ (*-czę*) **I** *v/t* **1.** *zwierzęta*: fatten up **2.** *dzieci*: overfeed **II** *v/i* ***słodycze ~ą*** sweets make you fat; ***tuczyć się*** grow fat

tudzież *conj lit* also, as well

tuja *f* (*tui*; *-je*) BIOL thuja, thuya

T

tuleja *f* (*-lei*; *-je*) **1.** (*osłona*) sleeve **2.** (*gwintowana końcówka*) tailpiece **3.** (*opakowanie*) cornet; **tulejka** *f* (*-ki*; *-ki*) **1.** (*osłona*) sleeve **2.** (*opakowanie*) (small) cornet

tulić ⟨**s-**, **przy-**⟩ (*-lę*): **~** (**do siebie**) hug; **~ głowę do poduszki** bury one's head into a pillow; **~ ogon** tuck one's tail between one's legs; **~ płatki** fold one's petals; **tulić się** cuddle up (**do** *G* to); **~ do siebie** cuddle up to each other

tulipan *m* (*-na*; *-ny*) tulip

tułacz *m* (*-cza*; *-cze*) wanderer; **tułaczka** *f* (*-ki*; *-ki*) **1.** (*wędrowanie*) wandering, wanderings *pl* **2.** (*wygnanie*) exile **3.** (*kobieta*) wanderer; **tułacz|y** *adj*: **~e życie** life of wandering, wanderer's life

tułać się *v/im* (*-łam*) wander, rove; **~ po świecie** wander (around) the world

tułów *m* (*-łowia*; *-łowie*) **1.** torso, trunk **2.** (*zwierzęcia*) trunk

tuman *m* (*-nu*; *-ny*) **1.** (*chmura*) cloud; **~y kurzu** clouds of dust **2.** (*matoł*) *infml* moron, dunce

tumanić ⟨**o-**⟩ (*-nię*) **1.** (*oszukiwać*) fool **2.** (*mamić*) tempt; **~ kogoś obietnicami** tempt s.o. with promises

tundra *f* (*-ry*; *-ry*) (the) tundra

tunel *m* (*-lu*; *-le*) tunnel; **~ aerodynamiczny** wind tunnel; **~ foliowy** plastic tunnel; **~ powietrzny** INF air duct

Tunezja *f* (*-ji*) Tunisia

Tunezyjczyk *m* (*-ka*; *-czycy*), **-yjka** (*-ki*; *-ki*) Tunesian; **tunezyjski** *adj* Tunisian

tuńczyk *m* (*-ka*; *-ki*) tuna; **sałatka z ~a** tuna salad

tupać ⟨**-pnąć**⟩ (*-pię*) stamp one's feet

tupet *m* (*-tu*; *no pl*) *Br* cheek, *infml* nerve; **ale ~!** what a cheek!, what a nerve!; **mieć ~ coś zrobić** have the cheek to do s.th., have the nerve to do s.th.

tupnąć *v/p* → **tupać**

tupot *m* (*-tu*; *no pl*) patter; **~ nóg** patter of feet; **tupotać** *v/im* (*-poczę*/*-pocę*) patter

tur *m* (*-ra*; *-ry*) BIOL aurochs; **silny jak ~** (as) strong as an ox

tura *f* (*-ry*; *-ry*) **1.** POLIT SPORT round; **druga ~ wyborów** run-off election **2.** (*grupa*) group, party

turban *m* (*-nu*; *-ny*) turban

turbina *f* (*-ny*; *-ny*) turbine; **turbinowy** *adj* turbine

Turcja *f* (*-ji*) Turkey

Turczynk|a *f* (*-ki*; *-ki*) Turk, Turkish woman; **jest ~ą** she's Turkish

tureck|i *adj* Turkish; **mówić po ~u** speak Turkish; **kawa po ~u** Turkish coffee; **siedzieć po ~u** sit cross-legged; **siedziałem jak na ~im kazaniu** *fig* it was all Greek to me

Turek *m* (*-rka*; *-rcy*) Turk

turkot *m* (*-tu*; *no pl*) rattle; **turkotać** ⟨**za-**⟩ (*-koczę*/*-kocę*) (*o kole*, *maszynie*) rattle

turkusowy *adj* turquoise

turlać ⟨**po-**⟩ (*-lam*) roll; **turlać się** roll (about)

turnia *f* (*-ni*; *-nie*) crag

turniej *m* (*-ju*; *-je*) tournament; **~ telewizyjny** quiz show

turnus *m* (*-su*; *-sy*) **1.** (*wczasowicze*) *Br* group (of holiday-makers), *Am* group (of vacationers) **2.** (*czas*) period

Turyngia *f* (*-gii*) GEOGR Thuringia

turysta *m* (*-ty*; *-ryści*), **-tka** *f* (*-ki*; *-ki*) tourist; **~ indywidualny** individual tourist

turystyczny *adj* tourist; **ruch ~** tourist traffic; **turystyka** *f* (*-ki*; *no pl*) tourism; **~ masowa** mass tourism; **~ piesza** hiking

tusz *m* (*-szu*; *-sze*) ink; **~ do rzęs** mascara

tusza *f* **1.** (*-szy*; *no pl*) (*otyłość*) corpulence **2.** (*-szy*; *-sze*) (*zwierzę*) carcass

tutaj → **tu**

tutejszy *adj* local

tuzin *m* (*-na*; *-ny*) dozen; **dwa ~y** two dozen

tuż *particle* **1.** (*w czasie*) just: **~ przed** just before; **~ po** just after: **lato ~, ~** summer's just around the corner; **~ potem** shortly after **2.** (*w przestrzeni*) right, just: **~ za** *I* right behind; **~ przed** *I* right in front of; **~ obok** *G*, **~ przy** *L* right next to; **~ nad** *I* just above; **~ za linią** (*w tenisie*) **a)** (*za linią boczną*) just wide **b)** (*za linią końcową*) just long

TVP *abbr f indecl* (= **Telewizja Polska**) Polish Television

twa → **twój**

twardnieć ⟨**s-**⟩ (*-nieję*) harden

twardo *adv*: **jajko na ~** hard-boiled egg; **~ obstawać przy swoim** stick firmly to one's opinion
twardogłowy *m* (*-wego*; *-wi*) hard-liner
twardość *f* (*-ści*; *no pl*) **1.** *materiału*: hardness **2.** *osoby*: toughness
tward|y *adj* **1.** hard; **dysk ~y** hard disk; **~a woda** hard water; **książka w ~ej okładce** hardback; **~y jak kamień** hard as a rock **2.** *osoba*, *mięso*: tough **3.** *sen*: sound
twardziel *m* (*-la*; *-le*) *infml* **1.** tough guy **2.** *INF* hard disk
twarożek *m* (*-żka*; *-żki*) *dim* cottage cheese; **~ waniliowy** vanilla-flavoured cottage cheese
twaróg *m* (*-rogu*; *-rogi*) cottage cheese
twarz *f* (*-rzy*; *-rze*) face; **odwrócić się ~ą do ściany** turn to face the wall; **jest ci w tym kolorze do ~y** this colour suits you; **w tej bluzce jest ci do ~y** you look good in this blouse; **~ą w ~** face to face; **stracić ~** lose face; **roześmiać się komuś w ~** laugh in s.o.'s face
twarzowy *adj* **1.** *ANAT* facial **2.** *kapelusz*: becoming
twe → **twój**
twierdza *f* (*-dzy*; *-dze*) fortress, stronghold
twierdzący *adj* **1.** affirmative **2.** *odpowiedź*: positive, affirmative; **twierdzenie** *n* (*-nia*; *-nia*) **1.** (*zdanie*) statement **2.** *MATH* theorem
twierdzić ⟨**s-**⟩ (*-dzę*) claim, maintain, say
twoi, **twoja**, **twoje** → **twój**
tworzyć ⟨**u-**⟩ (*-rzę*) **1.** *dzieło*, *muzykę*: create **2.** *koło*, *parę*, *nowy rząd*: form; **~ dobraną parę** make a good couple **3.** (*zakładać*) set up, establish; **tworzyć się** form
tworzywo *n* (*-wa*; *-wa*) material; **~ sztuczne** plastic
twój *poss* **1.** (*przed rzeczownikiem*) your **2.** (*bez rzeczownika*) yours; **to jest mój pokój, a to ~** this is my room and that is yours
twór *m* (*tworu*; *twory*) **1.** (*istota żywa*) creature **2.** (*dzieło*) creation, work **3.** *wyobraźni*: product, figment **4.** *GEOL* formation
twórc|a *m* (*-cy*; *-cy*), **-czyni** *f* (*-ni*; *-nie*) **1.** (*artysta*) artist; **młodzi ~y** young artists; **~a ludowy** folk artist **2.** *obrazu*, *utworu*, *budowli*: creator **3.** *teorii*: author, founder
twórczo *adv* → **twórczy**
twórczoś|ć *f* (*-ści*; *no pl*) **1.** (*praca twórcza*) (artistic) work **2.** (*dzieła*) work, (creative) output; **życie i ~ć** life and work; **nagroda za całokształt ~ci** lifetime achievement award
twórczy *adj* **1.** *akt*, *praca*, *osoba*: creative **2.** *dorobek*, *środowiska*: artistic
ty *pron* you; **być na ~ z** *I* be on first-name terms with
tych → **ten**, **to I**
tyci *adj* tiny
tyczka *f* (*-ki*; *-ki*) pole; **~ fasoli** beanpole; **chudy jak ~** (as) thin as a beanpole; **tyczkarz** *m* (*-rza*; *-rze*) *SPORT* pole-vaulter
tyczyć się *v/im*: **co się tyczy** *G* as for, as regards
tyć ⟨**u-**, **przy-**⟩ (*tyję*) put on weight, gain weight
tydzień *m* (*tygodnia*; *tygodnie*) week; **w tym tygodniu** this week; **za ~** in a week, in one week; **~ temu** a week ago; **od tygodnia** for a week; **raz na ~** once a week; **w tygodniu** during the week; **tygodniami** for weeks
tyfus *m* (*-su*; *no pl*) *MED* typhus; **~ plamisty** typhus fever, spotted fever; **~ brzuszny** typhoid (fever)
tygiel *m* (*-gla*; *-gle*) melting pot
tygodnie *pl* → **tydzień**
tygodnik *m* (*-ka*; *-ki*) weekly
tygodniowy *adj* **1.** *okres*: one-week **2.** *dziecko*: one-week-old **3.** *urlop*: week-long, one-week **4.** *zarobki*: weekly
tygodniówka *f* (*-ki*; *-ki*) (weekly) wage
tygrys *m* (*-sa*; *-sy*) tiger; **tygrysica** *f* (*-cy*; *-ce*) tigress
tyka *f* (*-ki*; *-ki*): **~ fasoli** beanpole
tykać[1] *v/im* (*-kam*) (*o zegarze*) tick
tykać[2] ⟨**tknąć**⟩ (*-kam*) touch
tykać[3] *v/im* (*-kam*) *infml* be on first-name terms with
tykanie *n* (*-nia*; *no pl*) *zegara*: ticking
tykowaty *adj* *chłopak*: lanky
tylda *f* (*-dy*; *-dy*) tilde
tyle I *pron* **1.** (*przed rzeczownikami policzalnymi*) so many; **~ samo figur** the same number of figures, just as many figures **2.** (*przed rzeczownikami niepoliczalnymi*) so much, that much;

~ samo pieniędzy the same amount of money, just as much money; **dwa razy ~**, **drugie ~** twice as much; **~ co nic** next to nothing; **nie znam tej książki na ~, żeby się wypowiadać** I don't know the book well enough to comment **II** *adv* **nie ~..., ile** not so much... as; **~ że**, **~ tylko, że** except that

tylekroć *pron lit* so many times; **ilekroć ją prosił, ~ odmawiała** whenever he asked her, she'd always say 'no'

tylko I *particle* only; **~ pomyśl** just think; **nic nie robią, ~ jedzą i śpią** they do nothing but eat and sleep; **gdybym ~ wiedziała** if only I had known; **~ spokojnie!** stay calm! **II** *conj* **jeśli ~**, **gdyby ~** if only; **jak ~** as soon as; **nie ~..., ale** not only..., but also; **~ że** only **III** *adv* only; **co ~ zechcesz** whatever you want; **~ co** only just

tylnojęzykowy *adj* velar

tyln|y *adj* **1.** back; **~a kieszeń** back pocket; **~e siedzenie** back seat, rear seat; **straż ~a** rearguard **2.** *łapy*: hind **3.** *światła*: *Br* rear, *Am* tail **4.** *koło*, *szyba*: rear

tylokrotnie *adv* (*wielokrotnie*) so many times; **tylokrotny** *adj próby*: recurring

tylu → **tyle**

tył *m* (*-łu*; *-ły*) **1.** (the) back; **~ głowy** the back of the head; **zrobić krok do ~u**, **zrobić krok w ~** take a step backwards; **czytać coś od ~u** read s.th. backwards; **zaatakować kogoś od ~u** attack s.o. from behind; **stać ~em do** *G* stand with one's back to; **wyjechać ~em** reverse, back; **przestawić zegarki o godzinę do ~u** set the clocks back one hour; **założyć coś ~ na przód** *Br* put s.th. on back to front, *Am* put s.th. on backwards; **pozostawać w tyle za** *I* lag behind; **być do ~u z pracą** *infml* be behind with one's work; **zostawić kogoś w tyle** leave s.o. behind; **na ~ach wroga** behind enemy lines; **~em do kierunku jazdy** (*w pociągu*) with one's back to the engine **2.** *budynku*, *samochodu*, *ciężarówki*: (the) back, (the) rear; **na ~ach pałacu** at the back of the palace, at the rear of the palace

tyłek *m* (*-łka*; *-łki*) *infml* backside, behind, *Br* bottom, *Am* butt; **rusz ~!** get off your backside!; **wypinać ~** *Br* stick out one's bum, *Am* stick out one's butt

tym: **im starszy, ~ mądrzejszy** the older, the wiser; → **ten**, **to I**

tymczasem *adv* **1.** meanwhile, in the meantime; **ona ~ opiekowała się dziećmi** she, meanwhile, took care of the children, in the meantime she took care of the children **2.** (*ale*) yet **3.** (*na razie*) see you

tymczasowość *f* (*-ści*; *no pl*) temporariness; **tymczasowy** *adj* **1.** temporary **2.** *rząd*: interim, transitional **3.** *środki*: interim, temporary **4.** *kierownik*: acting

tymi → **ten**, **to I**

tymianek *m* (*-nku*; *-nki*) thyme

tynk *m* (*-ku*; *-ki*) BUILD plaster

tynkować ⟨**o-**⟩ (*-kuję*) plaster

tynkowany *adj* plastered

typ[1] *m* (*-pu*; *-py*) **1.** (*rodzaj*) type, kind; **laser nowego ~u** a new type of laser; **ludzie tego ~u** people of that sort **2.** PSYCH type **3.** BIOL phylum

typ[2] *m* (*-pa*; *-py*), **typek** *m* (*-pka*; *-pki*) (*osobnik*) *infml* character; **~ spod ciemnej gwiazdy** shady character

typografia *f* (*-fii*; *no pl*) typography

typowa|ć ⟨**wy-**⟩ (*-puję*) **1.** (*wybierać*) select **2.** (*wyznaczać*) nominate **3.** (*przewidywać*) predict; **~ć zwycięzcę** predict who is going to win, predict a winner; **jest ~ny na zwycięzcę turnieju** he is tipped to win the tournament

typowość *f* (*-ści*; *no pl*) typical character

typowy *adj* typical (**dla** *G* of)

tyrać *v/im* (*-ram*) *infml* slave (away)

tyran *m* (*-na*; *-ni*) **1.** tyrant **2.** *fig* tyrant, despot; **tyrania** *f* (*-nii*; *no pl*) tyranny

tyranizować *v/im* (*-zuję*) tyrannize

tys. *abbr* (=**tysiąc**) thousand

tysiąc *m* (*-ca*; *-ce*) thousand; **dwa ~e** two thousand; **~ami** in thousands

tysiąclecie *n* (*-cia*; *-cia*) (*rocznica*) millennium; **tysiącletni** *adj* **1.** *dąb*, *tradycja*, *państwo*: thousand-year-old **2.** *okres*: millennial, thousand-year; **~e królestwo** REL millennial kingdom

tysięczn|y *adj* **1.** (*z kolei*) thousandth **2.** **~e tłumy** *fig* thousands of people

tytan[1] *m* (*-nu*; *no pl*) CHEM titanium

T

tytan² *m* (*-na*; *-ni*) (*w mitologii*) Titan; **~ pracy** *fig* demon for work
tytoniowy *adj* tobacco
tytoń *m* (*-toniu*; *-tonie*) tobacco
tytuł *m* (*-łu*; *-ły*) **1.** title; **pod ~em** entitled; **~ naukowy** academic title; **~ mistrzowski** SPORT championship title; **~ własności** title deed **2.** (*powód*, *źródło*) **~em wyjaśnienia** by way of explanation; **dochód z ~u** *G* income from; **roszczenia z ~u** *G* claims arising from; **odszkodowanie z ~u szkód** compensation for damages; **świadczenie z ~u renty** pension benefit
tytułować ⟨**za-**⟩ (*-łuję*) **1.** (*nadawać tytuł*) (en)title **2.** (*zwracać się*) address (*I* as)
tytułowy *adj* title
tzn. *abbr* (= **to znaczy**) i.e.
tzw. *abbr* (= **tak zwany**) so-called

U

u *prep* (*G*) **1.** (*miejsce*) at; **~ mnie** at my place; **~ Pawła** at Paweł's (place); **~ lekarza** at the doctor's; **zatrzymać się ~ znajomych** stay with one's friends; **~ góry strony** at the top of the page; **~ czyjegoś boku** by s.o.'s side **2.** (*część*) of; **palce ~ nóg** toes; **paznokcie ~ rąk** fingernails **3.** (*cecha*) in, of; **infekcje ~ niemowląt** infections in infants; **~ władzy** in power
uaktualniać ⟨**-nić**⟩ (*-niam*) update
uaktywniać ⟨**-nić**⟩ (*-niam*) **1.** *proces*, *gen*: activate **2.** *ludzi*: encourage to action, mobilize **3.** INF enable
uatrakcyjniać ⟨**-nić**⟩ (*-niam*) make more attractive, enhance
ub. *abbr* (= **ubiegły**) last
ubarwiać ⟨**-wić**⟩ (*-wiam*) *historię*, *opowieść*: embellish
ubarwienie *n* (*-nia*; *no pl*) coloration, *Br* colouring, *Am* coloring
ubaw *m* (*-wu*; *-wy*) *infml* **1.** (*radość*) a good laugh, (good) fun; **mieliśmy niezły ~** we had a good laugh **2.** (*zabawne wydarzenie*, *osoba*) riot
ubawić *v/im* (*-wię*) amuse; **ubawić się** have a good laugh, have (good) fun
ubezpieczać ⟨**-czyć**⟩ (*-czam*) **1.** insure **2.** (*kryć*, *osłaniać*) cover **3.** (*przy wspinaczce*) belay; **ubezpieczać się** insure oneself (**od** *G* against)
ubezpieczenie *n* (*-nia*; *-nia*) insurance; **~ społeczne** *Br* national insurance, *Am* social security; **~ na życie** life insurance; **~ od kradzieży** theft insurance; **~ od odpowiedzialności cywilnej** third-party insurance; **ubezpieczeniowy** *adj* insurance
ubezpieczony **I** *adj* insured (**od** *G*/**na wypadek** *G* against); **~ społecznie** *Br* covered under national insurance, *Am* covered under social security **II** *m* (*-nego*; *-czeni*), **-na** *f* (*-nej*; *-ne*) the insured (person)
ubezpieczyciel *m* (*-la*; *-le*) (*instytucja*) insurer
ubezpieczyć *v/p* → **ubezpieczać**
ubić *v/p* → **ubijać**
ubieg|ać ⟨**ubiec**⟩ (*-gam*) **1.** *osobę*: beat, be faster (*A* than); **~łem go** I beat him to it **2.** *prośbę*: anticipate **3.** (*przebiegać*) **~ł dwadzieścia metrów i zatrzymał się** he ran twenty metres and stopped; **ubiegać się 1.** *o pracę*, *kredyt*: apply (**o** *A* for) **2.** *o prezydenturę*: run (**o** *A* for) **3.** (*współzawodniczyć*) compete (**o** *A* for) **4.** *o azyl*: seek **5. ~ się o czyjąś rękę** seek s.o.'s hand in marriage, court s.o.
ubiegłoroczny *adj* last year's
ubiegły *adj miesiąc*, *rok*: last
ubierać ⟨**ubrać**⟩ (*-ram*) **1.** *dziecko*, *chorego*: dress (**w** *A* in) **2.** *spodnie*, *bluzkę*: put on **3.** *choinkę*: decorate **4. ~ coś w słowa** *lit* put s.th. into words; **ubierać się 1.** (*zakładać ubranie*) get dressed, dress (oneself); **~ się w koszulę** put on a shirt; **nie mieć się w co ubrać** have nothing to wear **2.** (*mieć określony styl*) dress; **~ się modnie** dress fashionably; **~ się sportowo** wear sports clothes, dress casually; **~ się na czarno** wear black; **~ się u Armaniego** wear Armani

ubijać⟨**ubić**⟩ (*-jam*) **1.** (*ugniatać*) compact, compress **2.** *białka*, *śmietanę*: beat, whip; **~ *trzepaczką*** whisk **3.** *masło*: churn **4.** *wieprza*: slaughter, kill **5.** **~ *interes*** *fig* strike a deal
ubijak *m* (*-ka*; *-ki*) **1.** (*do ziemniaków*) masher **2.** (*do ziemi*) rammer
ubikacja *f* (*-ji*; *-je*) toilet
ubiór *m* (*ubioru*; *ubiory*) clothes *pl*, clothing, dress; ***ubiory męskie*** (***damskie***) men's (women's) clothing, menswear (womenswear)
ubliżać ⟨**-żyć**⟩ (*-żam*) insult, offend; **~ *ludzkiej godności*** be an affront to human dignity; **ubliżający** *adj* insulting, offending
ubłocony *adj* muddied
uboczle (***położony***) ***na ~u*** out-of-the-way, off the beaten track; ***trzymać się na ~u*** keep oneself in the background, stay on the sidelines
uboczn|y *adj* **1.** *kwestia*, *rola*: side, secondary **2.** *wątek*, *objaw*: secondary; ***działanie ~e***, ***efekt ~y*** side effect; ***produkt ~y*** by-product; ***zajęcia ~e*** sidelines
ubo|gi I *adj* **1.** poor; ***~gi w witaminy*** low in vitamins **2.** *ubranie*: shabby, poor **II** *m* (*-giego*; *ubodzy*), **-ga** *f* (*-giej*; *-gie*) poor person; ***~dzy*** the poor
ubogo *adv* → ***ubogi***
ubolewać *v/im* (*-wam*) **1.** (*żałować*) regret (***nad*** *I*), lament (***nad*** *I*); ***ubolewam, że*** I regret that; **~ *nad faktem, że*** *form* bemoan the fact that **2.** (*potępiać*) deplore (***nad*** *I*)
ubolewani|e *n* (*-nia*; *no pl*) **1.** (*współczucie*) sympathy; ***wyrazy głębokiego ~a*** deepest sympathy, deepest condolences **2.** (*żal*) regret; ***wyrazić ~e*** express one's regret; ***godny ~a*** regrettable, lamentable
ubożeć ⟨**z-**⟩ (*-żeję*) become impoverished
uboższej *comp* → ***ubogo***
uboższy *comp* → ***ubogi***
ubożyć ⟨**z-**⟩ (*-żę*) impoverish
ubój *m* (*uboju*; *uboje*) slaughter
ubóstwiać *v/im* (*-wiam*) **1.** (*uwielbiać*) adore, worship **2.** REL worship
ubóstwo *n* (*-wa*; *no pl*) poverty
ubrać *v/p* → ***ubierać***
ubrani|e *n* (*-nia*; *-nia*) **1.** (*ubiór*) clothes *pl*, clothing; ***~e robocze*** work clothes; ***bez ~a*** with no clothes on **2.** (*część garderoby*) item of clothing, garment
ubran|y *adj* dressed; ***być ~ym w*** *A* wear, be wearing; ***była ~a na czarno*** she was dressed in black
ubrda|ć *v/p* (*-dam*): ***~ł sobie, że*** *infml* he got the idea into his head that, he got the crazy idea that
ubrudzić *v/p* → ***brudzić***
ubyć *v/p* → ***ubywać***
ubytek *m* (*-tku*; *-tki*) **1.** (*strata*) loss; ***~ na wadze*** weight loss, loss of weight **2.** (*w zębie*) cavity
ubywa|ć ⟨**ubyć**⟩ (*-wam*): ***ubyło jej trzy kilo*** she lost three kilos; ***ubyło mi na wadze*** I've lost some weight; ***~ mu sił*** he is getting weaker; ***~ zapasów*** the supplies are dwindling; ***ubyło wody w rzece*** the water level in the river has dropped; ***~ dnia*** the days are closing in; ***~ uczniów*** the number of pupils is falling; ***nic ci nie ubędzie!*** *infml* it won't hurt you!
ubzdryngolony *adj* *infml* plastered, sloshed
ucałować *v/p* → ***całować***
ucałowania *pl* (*-wań*) *lit* kisses; ***przesyłam ~*** (many) kisses
ucharakteryzować *v/p* → ***charakteryzować***
uchlać się *v/p* (*-lam*) *infml* get plastered, get sloshed
uchlany *adj* *infml* plastered, sloshed
uch|o[1] *n* (*ucha*; *uszy*) **1.** (*część ciała*) ear; ***bolało mnie ~o*** I had (an) earache; ***głuchy na jedno ~o*** deaf in one ear; ***odstające uszy*** protruding ears, bat ears; ***powiedzieć coś komuś na ~o*** whisper s.th. to s.o.'s ear; ***usłyszeć coś na własne uszy*** hear s.th. with one's own ears; ***dzwoni mi w uszach*** my ears are ringing; ***obiło mi się o uszy, że*** I've heard that; ***po uszy w długach*** up to one's ears in debt; ***zakochany po uszy*** head over heels in love; ***mieć czegoś powyżej uszu*** be fed up with s.th.; ***uśmiechnięty od ~a do ~a*** smiling from ear to ear; ***dać komuś w ~o*** *infml* give s.o. a clip on the ear **2.** (*część czapki*) (ear)flap; ***czapka z uszami*** cap with earflaps

ucho[2] *n* (*ucha*; *ucha*) **1.** *dzbanka*, *kubka*: handle **2.** *igły*: eye

uchodzić ⟨**ujść**⟩ (*-dzę*) **1.** escape; ***ujść z życiem***, ***ujść cało*** escape with one's life, survive; ***ledwo uszli z życiem*** they narrowly escaped death; ***nie ujdzie ci to na sucho!*** you won't get away with it!; ***coś uszło czyjejś uwagi*** s.th. escaped s.o.'s attention: ***to nie uchodzi*** it's not the done thing, it's not done; ***ujdzie*** (***w tłoku***) *infml* it's fine, it will do **2.** (*być uznawanym*) pass (**za** *A* as) **3.** (*o rzece*) flow, *lit* disgorge (**do** *G* into)

uchodźc|a *m* (*-cy*; *-cy*) refugee; ***obóz dla ~ów*** refugee camp; ***~a polityczny*** political refugee; **uchodźstw|o** *n* (*-wa*; *no pl*) exile; ***na ~ie*** in exile

uchować *v/p* (*-wam*) *lit* save (***przed*** *I* from); ***uchować się*** survive; ***nic się przed nim nie da ~*** nothing is safe from him

uchronić *v/p* (*-nię*) save (**od** *G*/***przed*** *I* from); ***~ coś od zapomnienia*** save s.th. from oblivion

uchwalać ⟨**-lić**⟩ (*-lam*) *ustawę*, *rezolucję*: pass

uchwała *f* (*-ły*; *-ły*) POLIT resolution

uchwycić *v/p* (*-cę*) **1.** seize **2.** *sens*, *myśl*: grasp **3.** *podobieństwo*, *nastrój*: capture; ***uchwycić się*** **1.** *gałęzi*: catch hold of, grab hold of **2.** *fig myśli*: cling to

uchwyt *m* (*-tu*; *-ty*) **1.** handle **2.** (*uchwycenie ręką*) grip **3.** (*rakiety tenisowej*) grip; **uchwytny** *adj* **1.** (*dostrzegalny*) noticeable, perceptible; ***ledwie ~*** barely noticeable, barely perceptible **2.** (*o osobie*) reachable

uchybiać ⟨**-bić**⟩ (*-biam*) **1.** *przepisom*, *prawu*, *warunkom*: be in breach of, transgress **2.** *etykiecie*, *protokołowi*, *obowiązkom*: breach

uchybienie *n* (*-nia*; *-nia*) **1.** (*wada*) flaw **2.** (*błąd*) ***~ w sztuce lekarskiej*** medical malpractice **3.** *przepisom*, *obowiązkom*, *etykiecie*: breach **4.** *przepisom*, *zasadom*: breach, transgression

uchylać ⟨**-lić**⟩ (*-lam*) **1.** *drzwi*, *okno*: open slightly, open a little **2.** *zasłonę*: open a little **3.** *wyrok*: overturn, quash, revoke **4.** *decyzję*: reverse, overturn **5.** *przepis*: repeal **6.** ***uchylić rąbka tajemnicy*** *fig* partly lift the veil of secrecy; ***uchylać się*** **1.** (*o oknie*, *drzwiach*) open slightly, open a little **2.** (*unikać*) evade (**od** *G*); ***~ się od odpowiedzialności*** shirk responsibility, evade responsibility; ***~ się od płacenia podatków*** evade taxes; ***~ się od służby wojskowej*** dodge military service, evade military service **3.** (*robić unik*) dodge (***przed*** *I*)

uchylony *adj* **1.** *drzwi*: ajar, slightly open **2.** *okno*: slightly open **3.** *powieki*: half-open

uciąć *v/p* (*utnę*): ***~ w pół zdania*** break off in mid-sentence; ***dać sobie za kogoś rękę ~*** *fig* put one's hand into the fire for s.o.; ***~ sobie drzemkę*** have a nap; ***~ sobie pogawędkę*** have a chat; → ***ucinać***

uciążliwy *adj* **1.** *warunki*: hard **2.** *podróż*: arduous **3.** *osoba*, *hałas*: troublesome; ***być ~m dla*** *G* be a nuisance for **4.** *obowiązek*: burdensome, onerous **5.** *upał*: oppressive

ucichnąć *v/p* → ***cichnąć***

uciec *v/p* → ***uciekać***

ucie|cha *f* (*-chy*; *-chy*) **1.** (*radość*) joy, fun; ***pisnąć*** (***klasnąć***) ***z ~chy*** squeal (clap one's hands) with delight; ***ku czyjejś ~sze*** to s.o.'s amusement **2.** (*przyjemność*) ***~chy*** pleasures

ucieczk|a *f* (*-ki*; *-ki*) **1.** escape; ***~a z miejsca wypadku*** fleeing from the scene of the accident, hit-and-run offence; ***salwować się ~ą*** take flight **2.** (*z więzienia*) breakout, jailbreak **3.** (*z miejsca przestępstwa*) getaway **4.** SPORT breakaway

uciekać ⟨**uciec**⟩ (*-kam*) **1.** run away, escape (**od** *G* from); ***~ z więzienia*** escape from prison, break jail; ***~ z lekcji*** skip lessons; ***~ z domu*** run away from home; ***uciekli do Brazylii*** they fled to Brasil **2.** (*o czasie*) ***czas ucieka*** time is short, we're running out of time **3.** (*odjeżdżać*) ***autobus mi uciekł*** I missed the bus; ***uciekać się*** resort (**do** *G* to)

uciekinier *m* (*-ra*; *-rzy*), ***~ka*** *f* (*-ki*; *-ki*) **1.** (*z więzienia*, *z obozu*) runaway, fugitive **2.** (*uchodźca*) refugee

ucieleśniać ⟨**-nić**⟩ (*-niam*) (*uosabiać*) embody; ***ucieleśniać się*** materialize

U

ucierać ⟨**utrzeć**⟩ (*-ram*) **1.** *marchew, ser*: grate **2.** *żółtka*: mix
ucierpieć *v/p* (*-pię*) **1.** (*w wypadku*) be hurt **2.** (*o reputacji, zdrowiu*) suffer **3.** (*być dotkniętym*) be affected
ucieszny *adj* amusing
ucieszyć *v/p* → ***cieszyć***
ucinać ⟨**uciąć**⟩ (*-nam*) **1.** *sznurek, gałąź*: cut (off) **2.** *fundusze*: cut **3.** *dyskusję*: cut short
ucisk *m* (*-ku; no pl*) **1.** (*nacisk*) pressure **2.** (*w piersiach, gardle*) tightness **3.** (*w żołądku, gardle*) knot **4.** (*gnębienie*) oppression
uciskać ⟨**-snąć**⟩ (*-kam*) **1.** (*naciskać*) press **2.** (*o butach*) pinch (one's feet) **3.** (*gnębić*) oppress
uciskany *adj lud*: oppressed
uciskowy *adj*: ***opatrunek ~*** pressure dressing
ucisnąć *v/p* → ***uciskać***
uciszać ⟨**-szyć**⟩ (*-szam*) **1.** *dzieci, uczniów*: quiet, silence **2.** *opozycję, sumienie*: silence; ***uciszać się*** **1.** (*o mrozu*) calm down **2.** (*o hałasie, wietrze*) die down; ***uciszyło się*** it got quiet **3.** (*o osobie*) fall silent; ***ucisz się!*** be quiet!
uciśniony *adj* oppressed
uciułać *v/p* → ***ciułać***
ucywilizować *v/p* (*-zuję*) civilize
uczcić *v/p* (*uczczę*) *rocznicę*: celebrate; → ***czcić***
uczciwość *f* (*-ści; no pl*) honesty; ***~ zawodowa*** professional integrity; **uczciwy** *adj* **1.** honest **2.** *proces, rywalizacja, oferta*: fair
uczelnia *f* (*-ni; -nie*) **1.** (*wyższa*) school (of higher education), *Am* college **2.** (*uniwersytet*) university, *infml* uni
uczenie *adv* learnedly
uczennica *f* (*-cy; -ce*) schoolgirl, *Br* pupil; → ***uczeń***
uczeń *m* (*ucznia; uczniowie*) **1.** (*w szkole podstawowej*) schoolboy, *Br* pupil; ***~ pierwszej klasy*** *Br* first-class pupil, *Am* first-grader **2.** (*w szkole średniej*) student **3.** (*rzemieślnika*) apprentice **4.** (*mistrza*) disciple, follower
uczepić się *v/p* (*-pię*) **1.** (*chwycić się*) clutch, grab hold of **2.** (*krytykować*) pick on
uczesać *v/p* → ***czesać***
uczesanie *n* (*-nia; -nia*) hairstyle, *infml* hairdo
uczestnictwo *n* (*-wa; no pl*) participation; **uczestniczka** *f* (*-ki; -ki*) participant; ***~ konferencji*** conference participant
uczestniczyć *v/im* (*-czę*) **1.** participate (**w** *L* in), take part (**w** *L* in); ***~ w przygotowaniach*** take part in the preparations **2.** (*w spotkaniu, konferencji, uroczystości*) attend (**w** *L*) **3.** (*w dochodach*) share (**w** *L* in)
uczestnik *m* (*-ka; -nicy*) participant; ***~ konferencji*** conference participant
uczęszczać *v/im* (*-czam*) attend (**do** *G*/**na** *A*); ***~ do szkoły*** attend school; ***~ na kurs niemieckiego*** attend a course of the German language
uczęszczany *adj* **1.** *kawiarnia, kino*: (much) frequented **2.** *droga, trasa*: busy
uczłowieczać ⟨**-czyć**⟩ (*-czam*) humanize
uczniak *m* (*-ka; -ki/-niacy*) *iron* schoolboy; **uczniowski** *adj* **1.** student, *Br* pupil **2.** *mundurek*: school
uczoność *f* (*-ści; no pl*) learnedness
uczony **I** *adj człowiek, wywody*: learned, erudite **II** *m* (*-nego; uczeni*), **-na** *f* (*-nej; -ne*) **1.** (*naukowiec*) scientist **2.** (*humanista*) scholar
uczta *f* (*-ty; -ty*) feast
ucztować *v/im* (*-tuję*) feast
uczuci|e *n* (*-cia; -cia*) **1.** feeling; ***odwzajemniać czyjeś ~a*** reciprocate s.o.'s feelings; ***z mieszanymi ~ami*** with mixed feelings; ***mieć ~e, że*** have a feeling that **2.** (*miłość, sympatia*) affection; ***z ~em*** with affection **3.** (*fizyczne doznanie*) sensation, feeling; ***~e głodu*** (sensation of) hunger, (feeling of) hunger
uczuciowość *f* (*-ści; no pl*) emotionality; **uczuciowy** *adj* emotional; ***~ człowiek*** emotional person
uczulać ⟨**-lić**⟩ (*-lam*) **1.** (*wywoływać alergię*) cause allergy **2.** (*uwrażliwiać*) sensitize (**na** *A* to), make s.o. (more) aware (**na** *A* of); **uczulający** *adj* sensitizing; ***czynnik ~*** sensitizing agent, allergen
uczulenie *n* (*-nia; -nia*) allergy (**na** *A* to); ***~ na pyłki*** pollen allergy; **uczuleniowy** *adj* **1.** *reakcja*: allergic **2.** *testy*:

allergy; **uczulony** *adj* allergic (**na** *A* to)

uczyć ⟨**na-**⟩ (*uczę*) teach; **~ *kogoś pływać*** teach s.o. (how) to swim; **~ *języka francuskiego*** teach French; ***ona uczy mnie gry na gitarze*** she gives me guitar lessons; ***uczyć się*** **1.** (*poświęcać czas na naukę*) study; **~ *się pilnie*** study hard; **~ *się do egzaminu*** study for an exam **2.** (*zdobywać określoną wiedzę*) learn; **~ *się języka niemieckiego*** learn (to speak) German; **~ *się czegoś na pamięć*** learn s.th. by heart, memorize s.th.; ***sam nauczył się grać na trąbce*** he taught himself (to play) the trumpet; **~ *się na błędach*** learn from one's mistakes

uczyn|ek *m* (*-nku*; *-nki*) deed; ***dobry ~ek*** good deed, act of kindness; ***przyłapać kogoś na gorącym ~ku*** catch s.o. red-handed

uczynić *v/p* → **czynić**

uczynność *f* (*-ści*; *no pl*) helpfulness; **uczynny** *adj* helpful

udać *v/p* → **udawać**

udan|y *adj* **1.** *próba*, *kampania*, *małżeństwo*, *rok*: successful **2.** *wakacje*, *wieczór*: enjoyable, successful; ***wieczór był ~y*** the evening was a success; ***nasze wakacje były bardzo ~e*** our holidays were a great success **3.** *projekt*: good **4.** *produkt*: good, well-designed, well-engineered

udar *m* (*-ru*; *-ry*) MED stroke: **~ *słoneczny*** sunstroke; **~ *mózgu*** (cerebral) stroke; **~ *cieplny*** heat stroke

udaremniać ⟨**-nić**⟩ (*-niam*) *plany*, *próbę*: thwart

udawać ⟨**udać**⟩ (*udaję*) **1.** pretend; **~ *zdziwienie*** (***zainteresowanie***) pretend to be surprised (interested), fake surprise (interest); ***udawał, że jej nie zna*** he pretended not to know her, he pretended he didn't know her; **~ *martwego*** play dead; **~ *głupiego*** play dumb **2.** *chorobę*: fake, feign; ***udaje, że jest chora*** she's malingering, she's faking illness **3.** *orgazm*: fake **4.** (*imitować*) imitate **5.** (*podawać się za*) pretend to be; ***przestępcy udawali policjantów*** the criminals pretended to be policemen **6.** (*parodiować*) take off; ***udawać się*** **1.** succeed; ***jemu wszystko się udaje*** he's successful in everything he does, he's always successful; ***udało mi się ją przekonać*** I managed to convince her **2.** (*o przyjęciu*, *eksperymencie*, *spotkaniu*) be a success, be successful **3.** (*o cieście*, *zdjęciu*) turn out well, come out well **4.** (*o dzieciach*) turn out well **5.** (*poszczęścić się*) ***udało nam się*** we've been lucky **6.** (*wybierać się*) *lit* go; ***udać się do kogoś z wizytą*** pay s.o. a visit

udawany *adj współczucie*: feigned, fake

udeptywać ⟨**-tać**⟩ (*-tuję*) tramp down

uderzać ⟨**-rzyć**⟩ (*-rzam*) **1.** hit; ***uderzyć kogoś w głowę*** hit s.o. on the head; ***uderzyć kogoś w twarz*** punch s.o. in the face; ***samochód uderzył w drzewo*** the car crashed into a tree, the car hit a tree; ***uderzyć pięścią w stół*** thump the table, slam one's fist against the table; ***uderzyło mnie, że*** *fig* it struck me that **2.** (*pięścią*) punch **3.** (*otwartą dłonią*) slap **4.** (*głową*) butt **5.** (*o piorunie*, *meteorycie*) strike (**w** *A*) **6.** (*atakować*) strike (**na** *A*), attack (**na** *A*); ***uderzać się*** hit; ***uderzyłem się w kolano*** I bumped my knee; ***uderzył się głową o kant*** he banged his head against the edge

uderzający *adj podobieństwo*: striking

uderzenie *n* (*-nia*; *-nia*) **1.** hit; **~ *pioruna*** stroke of lightning, thunderbolt **2.** (*cios*) blow; **~ *w głowę*** blow on the head **3.** (*atak*) strike, attack

uderzeniow|y *adj* **1.** *fala*, *dawka*: shock **2.** ***grupa ~a*** strike force

uderzyć *v/p* → **uderzać**

udk|o *n* (*-ka*; *-ka*) COOK ***kurze ~o*** thigh; ***żabie ~a*** frogs' legs

udławić się *v/p* (*-wię*) choke (*I* on); **~ *ością*** choke on a fish bone; ***nie jedz tak szybko, bo się udławisz!*** don't eat so fast or you'll choke!

udo *n* (*uda*; *uda*) ANAT thigh; ***mięśnie ud*** thigh muscles

udobruchać *v/p* (*-cham*) placate, mollify; ***udobruchać się*** be placated, be mollified

udogadniać ⟨**-nić**⟩ (*-nię*) **1.** (*ułatwiać*) facilitate **2.** (*poprawiać*) improve

udogodnieni|e *n* (*-nia*; *-nia*) **1.** (*ulepszenie*) improvement **2.** (*dla niepeł-*

nosprawnych, gości hotelowych) facility **3.** (*wygoda*) convenience; ***pokoje z wszelkimi ~ami*** rooms with all the modern conveniences, *Br infml* rooms with all mod cons

udokumentować *v/p* → ***dokumentować***

udoskonalać ⟨**-lić**⟩ (*-lam*) improve; **udoskonalenie** *n* (*-nia*; *-nia*) improvement; **udoskonalony** *adj* improved

udostępni|ać ⟨**-nić**⟩ (*-niam*) **1.** make available; ***zbiory zostały ~one publiczności*** the collection was opened to the public **2.** (*ujawniać*) disclose

udowadniać ⟨**-wodnić**⟩ (*-niam*) prove; ***~ komuś winę*** prove s.o. guilty, prove s.o.'s guilt

udow|y *adj* thigh; ***kość ~a*** ANAT femur, thigh bone

udój *m* (*udoju*; *udoje*) **1.** (*dojenie*) milking **2.** (*ilość mleka*) milk yield

udrapować *v/p* → ***drapować***

udręczenie *n* (*-nia*; *-nia*), **udręka** *f* (*-ki*; *-ki*) distress; **udręczony** *adj* distressed

uduchowiony *adj* soulful

udupić *v/p* (*-pię*) *vulg* **1.** (*rozprawić się*) fuck (over) **2.** (*załatwiać*) ***~ kogoś*** *Br* nail s.o.'s arse, *Am* nail s.o.'s ass

udusić *v/p* (*-szę*) **1.** (*za szyję*) strangle, choke **2.** (*zakrywając twarz*) smother, suffocate **3.** COOK stew; ***udusić się*** **1.** (*umrzeć*) suffocate **2.** COOK stew

uduszenie *n* (*-nia*; *no pl*) **1.** suffocation; ***śmierć przez ~*** death from suffocation **2.** (*za szyję*) strangulation

udział *m* (*-łu*; *-ły*) **1.** (*uczestnictwo*) participation; ***brać ~ w*** *L* take part in, participate in **2.** (*wkład*) ECON share; ***mieć 50% ~ów w spółce*** have a 50 per cent stake in a company **3.** (*w zyskach, rynku*) share **4.** (*w zbrodni*) complicity

udziałowiec *m* (*-wca*; *-wcy*) ECON shareholder; **udziałow|y** *adj*: ***świadectwo ~e*** ECON share certificate; ***kapitał ~y*** ECON share capital, equity

udziec *m* (*udźca*; *udźce*) COOK haunch, leg

udzielać ⟨**-lić**⟩ (*-lam*) **1.** give; ***~ komuś rady*** give s.o. a piece of advice; ***~ wywiadu*** give an interview; ***~ komuś pomocy*** help s.o.; ***~ komuś pierwszej pomocy*** give s.o. first aid; ***~ komuś korepetycji*** give s.o. private lessons, coach s.o.; ***~ komuś ślubu*** officiate at s.o.'s wedding **2.** *informacji*: give, provide; ***~ komuś informacji*** give s.o. information, provide s.o. with information **3.** *azylu, audiencji, koncesji*: grant **4.** *kredytu*: give, extend; ***udzielać się*** **1.** (*o nastroju*) spread (*D* to) **2.** (*o entuzjazmie*) rub off (*D* on) **3.** (*uczestniczyć*) ***~ się towarzysko*** have an active social life **4.** (*pracować*) work; ***~ się społecznie*** work for the community

udziwniony *adj* bizarre

udźwiękowiać ⟨**-wić**⟩ (*-wiam*) record sound for

udźwig *m* (*-gu*; *no pl*) (*dźwigu*) lifting capacity

udźwignąć *v/p* (*-nę*) lift

uf, ***uff*** *interj* whew!, *Br* phew!

ufać ⟨**za-**⟩ (*ufam*) **1.** trust; ***ufam, że*** I trust that; ***~ własnym siłom*** be self-confident, be confident of one's ability; ***~ w swoją szczęśliwą gwiazdę*** trust one's lucky star **2.** (*wierzyć*) believe

ufarbować *v/p* → ***farbować***

ufnoś|ć *f* (*-ści*; *no pl*) trust, confidence; ***z ~cią*** trustingly

ufny *adj* trusting, trustful; ***~ we własne siły*** self-confident, confident of one's ability

ufoludek *m* (*-dka*; *-dki*) *iron* alien

uformować *v/p* → ***formować***

ufundować *v/p* → ***fundować***

uganiać się *v/im* (*-niam*): ***~ za przyjemnościami*** seek pleasure; ***~ za pieniędzmi*** be out for money, seek money; ***~ za spódniczkami*** *infml* chase skirts

ugasić *v/p* (*-szę*) **1.** *pożar*: put out, extinguish **2.** ***~ pragnienie*** quench one's thirst

ugaszczać ⟨**ugościć**⟩ (*-czam*): ***~ kogoś obiadem*** host a dinner for s.o.

uginać ⟨**ugiąć**⟩ (*-nam*) bend; ***uginać się*** **1.** (*o gałęzi*) bend; ***drzewa uginają się pod ciężarem owoców*** the trees are weighed down with fruit; ***nogi się pode mną ugięły*** my legs went from under me; ***stół się ugina*** (***pod ciężarem jadła***) *fig* the table is groaning with food, the table is piled with food **2.** (*o materacu*) yield

ugłaskiwać ⟨**-kać**⟩ (*-kuję*) placate

ugniatać ⟨**-nieść**⟩ (*-tam*) **1.** *ciasto*: knead **2.** (*ziemię ręką*) firm **3.** (*uwierać*) dig into, pinch

ugoda *f* (*-dy*; *-dy*) **1.** JUR settlement **2.** (*porozumienie*) agreement **3.** (*kompromis*) compromise

ugodowiec *m* (*-wca*; *-wcy*) advocate of compromise; **ugodow|y** *adj* conciliatory; ***polityka ~a*** policy of conciliation

ugodzić *v/p* (*-dzę*) *lit* (*trafić*) hit, strike; ***~ kogoś nożem*** stab s.o. with a knife

ugościć *v/p* → ***ugaszczać***

ugór *m* (*ugoru*; *ugory*) AGR fallow (land); ***leżeć ugorem*** lie fallow

ugruntowywać ⟨**-tować**⟩ (*-towuję*) *pozycję, władzę*: strengthen

ugrupowani|e *n* (*-nia*; *-nie*) **1.** (*grupa*) group; ***~a polityczne*** political groupings, political groups **2.** (*partia*) party **3.** (*organizacja*) organization

ugryźć *v/p* (*-ryzę*) **1.** (*o komarze, psie*) bite **2.** (*o osie*) sting

ugrząźć, ***ugrzęznąć*** *v/p* → ***grzęznąć***

ugrzeczniony *adj* obsequious, overly polite

uiszczać ⟨**uiścić**⟩ (*-czam*) *form* pay

ujadać *v/im* (*-dam*) (*o psie*) bark (furiously)

ujarzmiać ⟨**-mić**⟩ (*-miam*) **1.** *naród*: subjugate **2.** *siły przyrody*: harness

ujawniać ⟨**-nić**⟩ (*-niam*) **1.** reveal, disclose; ***~, że*** reveal that, disclose that **2.** *aferę*: bring to light, reveal **3.** *talent*: show; ***ujawniać się*** **1.** (*wychodzić na jaw*) come to light **2.** (*dekonspirować się*) reveal one's identity; ***był homoseksualistą, ale się z tym nie ujawniał*** he was gay but didn't come out **3.** (*o talencie, zdolnościach*) reveal itself, become apparent

ujawnienie *n* (*-nia*; *no pl*) *danych, faktów*: disclosure

ująć *v/p* → ***ujmować***

ujechać *v/p* (*ujadę*): ***~ parę kilometrów*** drive a few miles

ujednolicać ⟨**-cić**⟩ (*-cam*) **1.** *system*: standardize, make uniform **2.** *przepisy*: unify

ujemny *adj* **1.** negative; ***wynik ~*** negative result **2.** *temperatura*: sub-zero

ujeżdżać ⟨**ujeździć**⟩ (*-dżam*) *konia*: break in

ujeżdżalnia *f* (*-ni*; *-nie*) riding arena, schooling arena

ujęcie *n* (*-cia*; *-cia*) **1.** FILM shot, take **2.** PHOT shot; ***~ z profilu*** profile **3.** *tematu*: take (*G* on), approach (*G* to) **4.** *wody*: intake

ujęty *adj* **1.** *przestępca*: apprehended **2.** *uciekinier*: captured

ujm|a *f* (*-my*; *-my*) *lit* discredit; ***przynosić komuś ~ę*** be a disgrace to s.o.; ***~a dla czyjegoś honoru*** a blot on s.o.'s honour

ujmować ⟨**ująć**⟩ (*-muję*) **1.** (*ręką*) take hold of **2.** (*przedstawiać*) present **3.** (*zjednywać sobie*) ***ujął wszystkich swoim ciepłem*** he endeared himself to everyone with his warmth; ***ujęła mnie jej prostota*** I was charmed by her simplicity **4.** (*odejmować*) take away, take off; ***ujmować się za*** *I* (*wstawiać się*) stand up for

ujmujący *adj* *uśmiech, osoba*: charming, winning

ujrzeć *v/p* (*-rzę*) *lit* see, catch sight of

ujście *n* (*-cia*; *-cia*) **1.** *rzeki*: estuary, mouth **2.** *fig* outlet, vent; ***dać ~ swoim emocjom*** give vent to one's emotions

ujść *v/p* (*ujdę*): ***~ dwa kilometry*** go two kilometres; → ***uchodzić***

ukamienować *v/p* → ***kamienować***

ukamienowanie *n* (*-nia*; *-nia*) HIST stoning (to death), *Am* lapidation

ukarać *v/p* → ***karać***

ukartowan|y *adj*: ***to wszystko zostało ~e*** *Br* it's a put-up job, it's all cooked up

ukatrupić *v/p* (*-pię*) *infml* do in, *Am* rub out

ukazanie *n* (*-nia*; *no pl*) (*prezentacja*) presentation; ***ukazanie się*** *książki, czasopisma*: publication

ukazywać ⟨**-zać**⟩ (*-zuję*) show, reveal; ***ukazywać się*** **1.** (*o książce, czasopiśmie*) come out, be published **2.** (*o widoku*) come into view **3.** (*we śnie*) appear

ukąsić *v/p* → ***kąsać***

ukąszenie *n* (*-nia*; *-nia*) *żmji, komara*: bite

UKF *abbr m* (*UKF-u*; *no pl*) (= ***ultrakrótkie fale***) UHF

ukisić *v/p* → **kisić**
ukleja *f* (*-lei*; *-je*) BIOL bleak
uklęknąć *v/p* (*-nę*) kneel down
układ *m* (*-du*; *-dy*) **1.** (*rozmieszczenie, rozkład*) arrangement; **~ sił** POLIT balance of power **2.** (*plan*) layout **3.** system; **≈ Słoneczny** ASTR the Solar System; **~ nerwowy** ANAT the nervous system; **~ pokarmowy** ANAT the alimentary system **4. ~ scalony** INF chip, integrated circuit **5.** (*umowa*) agreement; **zbiorowy ~ pracy** collective bargaining agreement **6.** (*traktat*) treaty **7.** (*znajomość*) **~y** connections
układać ⟨**ułożyć**, **po-**⟩ (*-dam*) **1.** arrange; **~ coś według alfabetu** arrange s.th. in alphabetical order; **~ kogoś do snu** put s.o. to bed; **~ coś z klocków** build s.th. with blocks; **~ coś w fałdy** drape sth. **2.** *chorego*, *rannego*: lay down **3.** *parkiet*: lay **4.** *pasjansa*: play **5.** *włosy*: do **6.** *tekst*, *wiersz*: write **7.** *plan*: make, devise **8.** *jadłospis*, *pytania*: prepare **9.** *melodię*: make up; **układać się 1.** (*kłaść się*) lie (down); **~ się do snu** lie down to sleep **2.** (*przebiegać*) **dobrze mi się układa** I'm doing fine; **wszystko się jakoś ułoży!** everything is going to be alright! **3.** (*formować się*) **włosy układają się jej w loki** her hair curles **4.** (*o stosunkach*) **~ się dobrze** be good **5.** (*negocjować*) negotiate, bargain
układanka *f* (*-ki*; *-ki*) puzzle, *Br* jigsaw (puzzle)
układny *adj* courteous, polite
ukłon *m* (*-nu*; *-ny*) **1.** bow; **złożyć ~** bow; **~ w stronę** *G fig* gesture of respect for **2.** (*pozdrowienie*) **~y** regards, *form* compliments
ukłonić się *v/p* → **kłaniać się**
ukłucie *n* (*-cia*; *-cia*) **1.** (*igły*) prick **2.** (*komara*) bite **3.** (*osy*) sting
ukłuć *v/p* → **kłuć**
uknuć *v/p* → **knuć**
ukochany I *adj* beloved, sweetheart **II** *m* (*-nego*; *-ni*), **-na** *f* (*-nej*; *-ne*) beloved, love, sweetheart
ukoić *v/p* → **koić**
ukojenie *n* (*-nia*; *no pl*) *lit* **1.** (*ulga*) relief **2.** (*pociecha*) consolation, *lit* solace
ukołysać *v/p* (*-szę*) rock to sleep
ukonstytuować *v/p* → **konstytuować**
ukończeni|e *n* (*-nia*; *no pl*) **1.** completion; **~e budowy** the completion of construction; **budowa jest na ~u** the construction is nearing completion **2. ~e szkoły wyższej** graduation
ukończyć *v/p* (*-czę*) *lit* **1.** finish; **~ osiemnaście lat** turn eighteen **2.** *szkołę wyższą*: graduate (*A* from) **3.** *szkołę średnią*: finish, complete, leave
ukoronować *v/p* → **koronować**
ukoronowanie *n* (*-nia*; *no pl*) *fig* crowning achievement
ukorzeniać się ⟨**-nić**⟩ (*-niam*) take root; **ukorzeniony** *adj* rooted
ukorzyć się *v/p* → **korzyć się**
ukos: **na ~** obliquely, aslant, diagonally; **patrzeć z ~a na** *A* look askance at, frown upon
ukośny *adj* oblique, diagonal
ukradkiem *adv* stealthily, furtively; **spojrzeć ~ na** *A* cast a furtive glance at; **wymknąć się ~ z** *G* sneak out of; **ukradkowy** *adj spojrzenie*: furtive
ukradzion|y *adj* stolen; **~e mienie** stolen goods
Ukraina *f* (*-ny*) Ukraine
Ukrainiec *m* (*-raińca*; *-raińcy*), **-nka** *f* (*-ki*; *-ki*) Ukrainian; **ukraiński** *adj* Ukrainian
ukraść *v/p* → **kraść**
ukręcić *v/p* (*-cę*) **1.** *żółtka*, *krem*: mix **2.** *sznur*: twist **3.** (*urwać*) twist off, wrench off
ukroić *v/p* (*-roję*) cut; **~ kromkę chleba** cut a slice of bread
ukrop *m* (*-pu*; *no pl*) boiling water; **uwijać się jak w ~ie** work like crazy, bustle about feverishly
ukrócić *v/p* (*-cę*) put an end to
ukryci|e *n* (*-cia*; *no pl*) hiding (place); **w ~u** in hiding; **strzelać z ~a** snipe; **ukryty** *adj* hidden
ukrywać ⟨**-ryć**⟩ (*-wam*) **1.** hide; **ukryć twarz w dłoniach** bury one's face in one's hands; **nie ukrywam, że** I'm not denying that **2.** *myśli*, *zamiary*, *prawdę*: conceal; **~ coś przed** *I* conceal s.th. from; **ukrywać się** hide; **nie da się ukryć, że** there's no denying that
ukrzyżować *v/p* → **krzyżować**

ukrzyżowanie *n* (*-nia*; *no pl*) *REL* crucifixion
ukształtować *v/p* → ***kształtować***
ukształtowanie *n* (*-nia*; *no pl*): ***~ terenu*** *GEOGR Br* the lie of the land; *Am* the lay of the land, topography
ukuć *v/p* (*ukuję*) *nazwę*, *termin*: coin
ukwasić *v/p* → ***kwasić***
ukwiał *m* (*-ła*/*-łu*; *-ły*) *BIOL* sea anemone
ukwiecony *adj* flowery
ul *m* (*-la*; *-le*) (bee) hive; ***tu jest jak w ~u*** this place is a (bee)hive of activity
ul. *abbr* (= ***ulica***) St.
ulać *v/p* → ***ulewać***
ulał: ***leżeć jak ~*** fit perfectly, be a perfect fit
ulatniać się ⟨***ulotnić***⟩ (*-niam*) **1.** (*o gazie*) escape, leak **2.** (*wyparowywać*) evaporate **3.** (*o zapachu*) wear off **4.** (*o nastroju*) evaporate, vanish **5.** (*o osobie*) *infml* disappear; ***ulotnić się z przyjęcie*** sneak out of a party, slip out of a party **6.** (*o przedmiotach*) vanish, disappear
ulatywać ⟨***ulecieć***⟩ (*-tuję*) **1.** (*odlecieć*) fly away **2.** (*o cieple*) escape, leak **3.** ***uleciało mi to z pamięci*** *fig* it slipped my mind
ulec *v/p* ***ulegać***
uleczalny *adj* curable
uleczyć *v/p* (*-czę*) cure, heal (**z** *G* of)
ulegać ⟨***ulec***⟩ (*-gam*) **1.** (*zostać pokonanym*) be defeated **2.** (*ustępować*) give in (*D* to), succumb (*D* to); ***~ naciskom*** give in to pressure; ***uległ jej prośbom*** he yielded to her requests **3.** (*poddawać się*) ***~ wpływom*** *G* be influenced by; ***~ zmianom*** undergo changes, be changed; ***~ pokusie*** yield to temptation, give in to temptation; ***~ zapomnieniu*** fall into oblivion; ***sprawa uległa przedawnieniu*** *JUR* the statute of limitations for the offence has expired; ***~ zepsuciu*** go off; ***~ pogorszeniu*** deteriorate; ***nie ulega wątpliwości, że*** there is no doubt that **4.** *wypadkowi*: have
uległoś|ć *f* (*-ści*; *no pl*) submissiveness, pliability; ***zmusić kogoś do ~ci*** force s.o. into submission
uległy *adj* submissive, pliant
ulepić *v/p* → ***lepić***

U

ulepszać ⟨***-szyć***⟩ (*-szam*) improve; **ulepszenie** *n* (*-nia*; *-nia*) improvement
ulewa *f* (*-wy*; *-wy*) downpour
ulewać ⟨***ulać***⟩ (*-wam*) pour off
ulewny *adj deszcz*: pouring, torrential
uleżeć *v/p* (*-żę*): ***nie móc ~ w łóżku*** not be able to stay in bed
ulęgałka *f* (*-ki*; *-ki*) wild pear, common pear; ***przebierać jak w ~ch*** pick and choose
ulg|a *f* (*-gi*; *-gi*) **1.** (*odprężenie*) relief; ***odetchnąć z ~ą*** heave a sigh of relief **2.** (*zniżka*) reduction, discount; ***~a podatkowa*** tax relief
ulgowo *adv kupić*: at a discount; ***traktować kogoś ~*** give s.o. preferential treatment, *infml* go easy on s.o.
ulgow|y **I** *adj* **1.** *bilet*, *opłata*: discounted, *Br* concessionary **2.** ***taryfa ~a*** *fig* preferential treatment **II** *m* (*-wego*; *-we*) (*bilet*) discounted ticket
ulic|a *f* (*-cy*; *-ce*) street; ***mieszkać na ~y Orzechowej*** *Br* live in Orzechowa street, *Am* live on Orzechowa Street; ***sklep przy ~y Pomorskiej*** *Br* a shop in Pomorska street, *Am* a shop on Pomorska Street; ***przejść przez ~ę*** cross the street; ***ślepa ~a*** dead end (street), cul-de-sac
uliczka *f* (*-ki*; *-ki*) by-street, backstreet; ***ślepa ~*** dead end, blind alley, cul-de-sac; **uliczny** *adj* street; ***ruch ~*** traffic; ***artysta ~*** street entertainer
ulokować *v/p* → ***lokować***
ulokowanie *n* (*-nia*; *no pl*) **1.** (*zakwaterowanie*) accommodation **2.** (*inwestycja*) investment
ulotka *f* (*-ki*; *-ki*) **1.** flyer, leaflet **2.** *POLIT* leaflet
ulotnić się *v/p* → ***ulatniać się***
ultradźwiękowy *adj* ultrasonic, ultrasound; **ultrafioletowy** *adj* ultraviolet
ultrakrótki *adj*: ***fale ~e*** VHF
ultramaryna *f* (*-ny*; *no pl*) ultramarine (blue); **ultranowoczesny** *adj* ultramodern; **ultraprawicowy** *adj partia*: extreme right, far right
ulubieniec *m* (*-bieńca*; *-bieńcy*), **-nica** *f* (*-cy*; *-ce*) *Br* favourite, *Am* favorite
ulubiony *adj Br* favourite, *Am* favorite
ulżyć *v/p* (*-żę*): ***~ komuś w pracy*** reduce s.o.'s workload; ***~ czyimś cierpieniom*** alleviate s.o.'s suffering; ***ulżyło***

mi (***na sercu***) I was relieved; ***~ sobie*** **a)** (*nawymyślać komuś*) *infml* blow off steam **b)** (*załatwić się*) relieve oneself

ułamać *v/p* → ***ułamywać***

ułamek *m* (*-mka*; *-mki*) fraction; ***przez ~ sekundy*** for a split second, for a fraction of a second

ułamywać ⟨***-mać***⟩ (*-muję*) break off

ułan *m* (*-na*; *-ni*) *HIST* uhlan, (light) cavalryman

ułaskawiać ⟨***-wić***⟩ (*-wiam*) pardon; **ułaskawienie** *n* (*-nia*; *-nia*) pardon

ułatwiać ⟨***-wić***⟩ (*-wiam*) make easier, facilitate

ułatwie|nie *n* (*-nia*; *-nia*) **1.** (*uczynienie łatwiejszym*) facilitation **2.** (*pomoc*) help; ***być*** (***dużym***) ***~niem w pracy*** make work (much) easier; ***wprowadzić kilka ~ń w pracy*** to introduce a few changes to make work easier

ułomność *f* (*-ści*; *-ści*) **1.** (*kalectwo*) disability, handicap **2.** (*wada*) *fig* flaw, defect; **ułomny** *adj* disabled, handicapped

ułożenie *n* (*-nia*; *-nia*) **1.** (*układ*) arrangement **2.** (*dobre maniery*) good manners *pl*

ułożony *adj*: ***dobrze ~*** (*mający dobre maniery*) well-mannered

ułożyć *v/p* → ***układać***

ułuda *f* (*-dy*; *no pl*) *lit* delusion

umacniać ⟨***umocnić***⟩ (*-niam*) **1.** strengthen; ***~ kogoś w przekonaniu, że*** confirm s.o. in their belief that, reinforce s.o.'s belief that **2.** *pozycję, władzę*: consolidate, strengthen, reinforce **3.** (*fortyfikować*) fortify; ***umacniać się*** strengthen; ***~ się w przekonaniu, że*** become confirmed in one's belief that

umalować *v/p* → ***malować***

umar|ły *m* (*-łego*; *-rli*) dead person, *form* the deceased; ***~li*** the dead, *form* the deceased

umartwiać się ⟨***-wić***⟩ (*-wiam*) mortify one's body; **umartwienie** *n* (*-nia*; *-nia*) mortification

umarzać ⟨***umorzyć***⟩ (*-rzam*) **1.** *dług, podatek, karę*: remit **2.** *sprawę*: dismiss **3.** *dochodzenie*: discontinue **4.** *kredyt*: write off **5.** *środki trwałe*: depreciate

umasawiać ⟨***-sowić***⟩ (*-wiam*) popularize, make widely available; **umasowienie** *n* (*-nia*; *no pl*) popularization, making widely available

umawiać ⟨***umówić***⟩ (*-wiam*) (*ustalać spotkanie*) make an appointment for; ***umówiła ich ze sobą*** (*na randkę*) she arranged a date between them; ***umawiać się*** **1.** (*na spotkanie*) arrange to meet; ***umówił się z nią*** (*na randkę*) he has a date with her; ***~ się na piątą*** make an appointment for five **2.** (*ustalić*) agree, arrange, ***~ się co do*** *G* agree on

umazać *v/p* → ***mazać***

umeblować *v/p* → ***meblować***

umeblowanie *n* (*-nia*; *no pl*) furniture, furnishings *pl*

umęczony *adj* exhausted, dead tired; **umęczyć** *v/p* (*-czę*) exhaust, tire out; ***umęczyć się*** exhaust oneself, become exhausted

umiar *m* (*-ru*; *no pl*) moderation, restraint; ***z ~em*** in moderation; ***zachować ~*** exercise restraint; ***bez ~u*** immoderately

umiarkowanie[1] *n* (*-nia*; *no pl*) → ***umiar***

umiarkowanie[2] *adv* **1.** moderately **2.** *zainteresowany*: mildly, moderately; **umiarkowany** *adj* **1.** moderate **2.** *osoba*: restrained **3.** *ceny*: reasonable, moderate **4.** *poglądy*: moderate, middle-of-the-road **5.** *klimat*: temperate, mild

umie|ć *v/im* (*umiem*) **1.** (*potrafić*) can; ***ona ~ pływać*** she can swim; ***czy ~sz gotować?*** can you cook? **2.** (*znać*) know; ***~ć coś na pamięć*** know s.th. by heart; ***~ć sobie poradzić z*** *I* be able to manage, be able to cope with; ***~ć się bawić*** have a sense of fun

umiejętnoś|ć *f* (*-ści*; *-ści*) skill, ability; ***rozwijać swoje ~ci*** develop one's skills; ***~ć kojarzenia faktów*** ability to put facts together; ***~ć obsługi komputera*** computer literacy; **umiejętny** *adj Br* skilful, *Am* skillful

umiejscawiać ⟨***-cowić***⟩ (*-wiam*) locate; ***~ coś czasowo*** locate s.th. in time; **umiejscowienie** *n* (*-nia*; *no pl*) location

umierać ⟨***umrzeć***⟩ (*-ram*) die; ***~ na raka*** die of cancer; ***~ z głodu*** starve to death, die of starvation; ***~ śmiercią***

naturalną die a natural death, die of natural causes; **~ *nagle*** die a sudden death

umierający **I** *adj* dying **II** *m* (*-cego*; *-cy*), **-ca** *f* (*-cej*; *-ce*) dying person

umieralność *f* (*-ści*; *no pl*) mortality (rate); **~ *niemowląt*** infant mortality (rate)

umieszcz|ać ⟨**umieścić**⟩ (*-czam*) place, put; ***~ać coś na liście*** put s.th. on a list; ***~ać kogoś w szpitalu*** hospitalize s.o., put s.o. in hospital; ***akcję filmu ~ono w*** *L* the movie is set in

umięśniony *adj* muscular

umila|ć ⟨**-lić**⟩ (*-lam*): ***~liśmy sobie czas śpiewając*** we whiled away the time singing; ***~ła sobie czas oglądając film*** she kept herself amused by watching movie

umilk|nąć *v/p* (*-nę*) fall silent; ***wszyscy nagle ~li*** there was a sudden silence

umiłowanie *n* (*-nia*; *no pl*) *lit* love; **~ *wolności*** (***sztuki***) love of freedom (art)

umiłowany *adj lit* beloved

umizgać się *v/im* (*-gam*) woo, court (**do** *G*); **umizgi** *pl* (*-gów*) courtship *sing*, wooing *sing*

umknąć *v/p* → ***umykać***

umniejszać ⟨**-szyć**⟩ (*-szam*) belittle, play down; **~ *czyjeś osiągnięcia*** belittle s.o.'s achievements

umocnić *v/p* → ***umacniać***

umocnienie *n* (*-nia*; *-nia*) **1.** strengthening **2.** (*fortyfikacja*) fortification

umocowywać ⟨**-cować**⟩ (*-cowuję*) fasten, fix

umoczyć *v/p* (*-czę*) **I** *v/t* **1.** (*w cieczy*) dip, immerse; **~ *usta w szampanie*** take a sip of champagne **2.** (*zrobić źle*) *infml* screw up **II** *v/i* (*zepsuć*) *infml* screw up

umoralniać ⟨**-nić**⟩ (*-niam*) edify

umorusać się *v/p* (*-sam*) get soiled, get dirty; **umorusany** *adj dziecko*, *twarz*: grimy, dirty

umorzyć *v/p* → ***umarzać***

umotywować *v/p* → ***motywować***

umotywowanie *n* (*-nia*; *no pl*) justification

umow|a *f* (*-wy*; *-wy*) **1.** (*dokument*) agreement, contract; ***~a sprzedaży***, ***~a kupna*** contract of sale, contract of purchase; ***~a najmu*** lease agreement, tenancy agreement; ***~a o pracę*** contract of employment, employment contract; ***~a o dzieło*** contract for work, contract for a specific task; ***~a o wymianie handlowej*** trade agreement; ***zgodnie z ~ą*** in accordance with the agreement, under the agreement **2.** (*umówienie się*) agreement

umown|y *adj* **1.** (*dotyczący umowy*) contractual; ***kara ~a*** contract penalty **2.** (*konwencjonalny*) conventional; ***kwestia ~a*** matter of convention **3.** (*fikcyjny*) fictional

umożliwiać ⟨**-wić**⟩ (*-wiam*) make possible, enable

umówić *v/p* → ***umawiać***

umówi|ony *adj* **1.** (*na spotkanie*) ***jestem z nim ~ony na jutro*** I've arranged to meet him tomorrow; ***jestem z nim ~ony na kawę*** I've arranged to have coffee with him; ***jesteśmy ~eni do kina*** we're going to the cinema together, we have a date to see a movie **2.** (*ustalony*) agreed, arranged

umrzeć *v/p* → ***umierać***

umundurowanie *n* (*-nia*; *no pl*) uniform; **umundurowany** *adj* uniformed

umyć *v/p* → ***myć***

umykać ⟨**umknąć**⟩ (*-kam*) (*uciekać*) make off, flee; **~ *czyjejś uwadze*** escape s.o.'s notice

umy|sł *m* (*-łu*; *-ły*) mind; ***krytyczny ~sł*** critical mind; ***zdrowy na ~śle*** sane, in one's right mind; ***chory na ~śle*** insane, brain-sick

umysłowość *f* (*-ści*; *no pl*) mind, way of thinking

umysłow|y *adj* **1.** ***praca ~a*** **a)** intellectual work **b)** (*urzędnicza*) white-collar work **2.** *choroba*: mental

umyślny *adj* **1.** intentional, deliberate **2.** JUR premeditated

umywać ⟨**umyć**⟩ (*-wam*): **~ *ręce*** *fig* wash one's hands (**od** *G* of); ***nie ~ się do*** *G* not compare to, *infml* not be a patch on

umywalka *f* (*-ki*; *-ki*) washbasin; **umywalnia** *f* (*-ni*; *-nie*) washroom, bathroom

unaoczniać ⟨**-nić**⟩ (*-niam*) reveal, demonstrate, make aware (*A* of)

unia *f* (*unii*; *unie*) union

unicestwiać ⟨**-wić**⟩ (*-wiam*) (*niszczyć*) annihilate, destroy

unicki *adj* REL Uniate

uniemożliwi|ać ⟨**-wić**⟩ (*-wiam*) make impossible, prevent; ***to ~ło mu przyjazd do Polski*** this prevented him from coming to Poland; ***to ~a wciśnięcie dwóch klawiszy równocześnie*** this makes it impossible to press two keys at the same time

unieruchami|ać ⟨**-chomić**⟩ (*-miam*) **1.** (*uczynić nieruchomym*) immobilize; ***~ać złamaną rękę*** immobilize a broken arm; ***choroba ~ła go w łóżku*** the illness confined him to bed **2.** (*zatrzymywać*) stop

uniesieni|e *n* (*-nia*; *-nia*) *lit* rapture; ***w miłosnym ~niu*** in the throes of passion

unieszczęśliwiać ⟨**-wić**⟩ (*-wiam*) make unhappy

unieszkodliwiać ⟨**-wić**⟩ (*-wiam*) **1.** *truciznę*: neutralize **2.** *napastnika*: render helpless **3.** *bombę*: defuse

unieść *v/p* → ***unosić***

unieśmiertelniać ⟨**-nić**⟩ (*-niam*) immortalize

unieważniać ⟨**-nić**⟩ (*-niam*) **1.** *umowę*, *zamówienie*: cancel **2.** *małżeństwo*: annul **3.** *decyzję*, *wyrok*: revoke **4.** *wybory*: declare invalid, invalidate

unieważnienie *n* (*-nia*; *-nia*) **1.** *umowy*, *zamówienia*: cancellation **2.** *małżeństwa*: annulment **3.** *decyzji*, *wyroku*: revocation **4.** *aktu*, *wyborów*: invalidation

uniewinniać ⟨**-nić**⟩ (*-niam*) *oskarżonego*: acquit; **uniewinniający** *adj*: ***wyrok ~*** acquittal

uniewinnienie *n* (*-nia*; *-nia*) acquittal

uniezależniać ⟨**-nić**⟩ (*-niam*) make independent (**od** *G* of); ***uniezależniać się*** become independent; ***~ materialnie*** become independent financially (**od** *G* of)

unifikować ⟨**z-**⟩ (*-kuję*) **1.** unify, make uniform **2.** *przepisy*: standardize

uniform *m* (*-mu*; *-my*) uniform; ***w ~ie*** in uniform

unik *m* (*-ku*; *-ki*): ***zrobić ~*** dodge (**przed** *I*), duck (**przed** *I*); ***zrobić ~ w bok*** dodge to the side, duck to the side; ***~i*** *fig* dodges, dodging; ***stosować ~i*** *fig* be evasive

unikać ⟨**-knąć**⟩ (*-kam*) **1.** avoid; ***~ czyjegoś wzroku*** avoid one's eyes; ***~ czegoś jak ognia*** avoid s.th. like the plague **2.** *tematu*, *odpowiedzi*: avoid, evade; ***~ odpowiedzi na pytanie*** avoid answering a question, sidestep a question; → ***uniknąć***

unikalny *adj* unique

uniknąć *v/p* (*-nę*) **1.** avoid; ***~ kary za*** *A* get away with **2.** *kontroli*, *aresztowania*, *śmierci*: escape **3.** *ciosu*: dodge; → ***unikać***

uniknięci|e *n* (*-cia*; *no pl*): ***to nie do ~a*** it's unavoidable, it cannot be helped

uniwerek *m* (*-rku*; *-rki*) *infml* uni

uniwersalny *adj* **1.** *metoda*: universal **2.** *urządzenie*: all-purpose, multi-purpose

uniwersytecki *adj* university, academic; **uniwersytet** *m* (*-tu*; *-ty*) university

uniżony *adj* **1.** (*służalczy*) servile, obsequious **2.** *sługa*: humble

unosić ⟨**unieść**⟩ (*-szę*) **1.** raise **2.** (*dźwigać*) lift **3.** *głowę*, *wzrok*: lift, raise **4.** (*o wietrze*, *rzece*) carry away; ***unosić się*** **1.** (*o osobie*, *dymie*) rise **2.** (*rozgniewać się*) ***~ się gniewem*** lose one's temper **3.** (*w powietrzu*) float; ***w powietrzu unosi się balon*** a balloon is floating in the air; ***w powietrzu unosił się zapach róż*** there was a scent of roses in the air **4.** (*na wodzie*) float, drift **5.** (*o oparach*, *mgle*) hang

unowocześniać ⟨**-nić**⟩ (*-niam*) modernize

uodparniać, ***uodporniać*** ⟨**-pornić**⟩ (*-niam*) **1.** immunize (**na** *A* against) **2.** (*czynić niewrażliwym*) toughen, harden; ***uodparniać się***, ***uodporniać się*** **1.** (*na chorobę*) become immune (**na** *A* against) **2.** (*stawać się niewrażliwym*) toughen, harden

uogólniać ⟨**-nić**⟩ (*-niam*) generalize; **uogólnienie** *n* (*-nia*; *-nia*) generalization

UOP *abbr m* (*UOP-u*; *no pl*) (= ***Urząd Ochrony Państwa***) the Office for State Protection

uosabiać ⟨**-sobić**⟩ (*-biam*) embody, personify; **uosobienie** *n* (*-nia*; *-nia*) embodiment, personification

upadać ⟨**upaść**⟩ (*-dam*) **1.** (*przewracać się*) fall (down), fall (over); **~ na** *A* fall on; **~ na ziemię** fall to the ground; **~ na kolana** fall to one's knees; **~ na fotel** collapse into the armchair; **~ na duchu** *fig* lose one's hope **2.** (*o rządzie, fortecy*) fall **3.** (*bankrutować*) go bankrupt, collapse, *infml* go under **4.** (*o gospodarce, kulturze*) decline **5.** (*o wniosku*) be rejected, be voted down **6.** (*o powstaniu, rewolucji*) fail, collapse **7.** (*o projekcie*) come to nothing

upadek *m* (*-dku; -dki*) **1.** fall; **~ obyczajów** moral decline **2.** *kultury*: decline **3.** *gospodarki*: collapse

upadlać ⟨**upodlić**⟩ (*-lam*) disgrace, debase; **upadlać się** disgrace oneself, debase oneself

upadłościow|y *adj*: **postępowanie ~e** bankruptcy proceedings; **masa ~a** bankrupt's estate

upadłość *f* (*-ści; no pl*) bankruptcy; **ogłosić ~** declare bankruptcy

upadł|y *adj* **1.** *firma*: bankrupt **2.** *fig* fallen; **walczyć do ~ego** struggle to the bitter end

upajać ⟨**upoić**⟩ (*-jam*) intoxicate, inebriate, make drunk; **upajać się** **1.** get intoxicated, get inebriated **2.** *fig* relish (*I*), delight (*I* in); **upajający** *adj* intoxicating

upalny *adj lato, dzień*: sweltering, scorching

upał *m* (*-łu; -ły*) heat; **był straszny ~** it was scorching hot

upamiętniać ⟨**-nić**⟩ (*-niam*) commemorate; **upamiętniając|y** *adj*: **tablica ~a** commemorative plaque, memorial tablet; **upamiętnieni|e**: **dla ~a** *G* in remembrance of, in commemoration of

upaństwowić *v/p* (*-wię*) nationalize

upaprać *v/p* → **paprać**

uparcie *adv* → **uparty**

uparciuch *m* (*-cha; -chy*) (stubborn) mule

U

upart|y *adj* stubborn; **na ~ego** *Br infml* at a push

upaść[1] *v/p* (*upadnę*): **~ na głowę** lose one's mind, lose one's senses; **chyba upadłaś na głowę!** you must be out of your mind!; → **upadać**

upaść[2] *v/p* → **paść**[2]

upatrywać ⟨**-trzyć**⟩ (*-ruję*) **1.** see (**w** *L* in) **2.** (*wybierać*) **~ sobie** choose

upchać, **upchnąć** *v/p* → **upychać**

upełnomocnić *v/p* (*-nię*) authorize, empower (**do** *G* to do s.th.)

uperfumować *v/p* → **perfumować**

uperfumowany *adj* scented

upewniać ⟨**-nić**⟩ (*-niam*) assure; **upewniać się** make sure (**że** that)

upiąć *v/p* → **upinać**

upichcić *v/p* → **pichcić**

upić *v/p* → **upijać**

upiec *v/p* (*upiekę*): **upiekło mu się** *infml* he got off scot-free; **~ dwie pieczenie na jednym ogniu** kill two birds with one stone; → **piec**[2]

upieczony *adj*: **świeżo ~ a)** *chleb*: newly baked **b)** *inżynier*: newly minted, newly graduated

upierać się ⟨**uprzeć**⟩ (*-ram*) insist (**przy** *L* on)

upierdliwy *adj infml* pesky; **być ~m** *Br* be a pain in the arse, *Am* be a pain in the ass

upierzenie *n* (*-nia; no pl*) plumage

upiększać ⟨**-szyć**⟩ (*-szam*) **1.** beautify, make beautiful **2.** *fakty*: embellish **3.** *przeszłość*: glorify; **upiększać się** make oneself beautiful; **upiększający** *adj zabiegi*: cosmetic

upijać ⟨**upić**⟩ (*-jam*) get drunk; **upijać się** get drunk; **~ się jak świnia** get blind drunk

upinać ⟨**upiąć**⟩ (*-nam*) **1.** *włosy*: do up, pin up **2.** *materiał*: drape

upiorny *adj* **1.** *głos, postać*: ghostly **2.** *pogoda*: ghastly

upiór *m* (*upiora; upiory*) ghost, phantom

upitrasić *v/p* → **pitrasić**

uplasować się *v/p* → **plasować się**

upleść *v/p* → **pleść**

upławy *pl* (*-wów*) MED vaginal discharge *sing*

upłynąć *v/p* → **upływać**

upłynniać ⟨**-nić**⟩ (*-niam*) *towar*: sell off

upływ *m* (*-wu; no pl*): **~ czasu** the passage of time; **z ~em czasu** over time; **w miarę ~u czasu** in the course of time; **z ~em lat**, **w miarę ~u lat** over the years; **po ~ie roku** after a year; **po ~ie terminu** after the deadline; **~ krwi** loss of blood

upływa|ć ⟨**-łynąć**⟩ (*-wam*) **1.** (*o czasie*) pass, go by **2.** (*o terminie*) expire; ***termin nadsyłania esejów ~ piętnastego sierpnia*** the deadline for sending in essays is 15th August
upodabniać ⟨**-dobnić**⟩ (*-niam*) make resemble (**do** *G*); ***upodabniać się*** become similar (**do** *G* to), become like (**do** *G*); ***~ się do siebie*** become alike, become similar
upodlenie *n* (*-nia*; *no pl*) debasement, degradation
upodlić *v/p* → ***upadlać***
upodobać *v/p* (*-bam*): ***~ sobie*** *lit* take a liking (*A* to), take a fancy (*A* for/to)
upodoba|nie *n* (*-nia*; *-nia*) **1.** (*lubienie*) liking, fondness, *form* predilection; ***znajdować w czymś ~nie*** relish s.th., enjoy s.th., have a liking for s.th.; ***z ~niem*** with relish, with great pleasure **2.** (*gust*) taste; ***według swoich ~ń*** according to one's taste, according to one's preference
upodobnić *v/p* → ***upodabniać***
upoić *v/p* → ***upajać***
upojeni|e *n* (*-nia*; *no pl*) **1.** (*alkoholowe*) (alcoholic) intoxication, drunkenness; ***w stanie ~a alkoholowego*** intoxicated, drunk **2.** (*ekstaza*) elation, ecstasy; **upojny** *adj* **1.** *zapach*: intoxicating **2.** *chwile*, *lato*: blissful
upokarzać ⟨**-korzyć**⟩ (*-rzam*) humiliate; ***upokarzać się*** humiliate oneself; **upokarzający** *adj* humiliating
upokorzyć *v/p* → ***upokarzać***
upolityczniać ⟨**-nić**⟩ (*-niam*) politicize; ***upolityczniać się*** become politicized
upolityczniony *adj* politicized
upolować *v/p* (*-luję*) **1.** (*zastrzelić*) shoot **2.** (*zabić*) kill **3.** *towar*: hunt down **4.** *męża*: hook
upominać ⟨**-mnieć**⟩ (*-nam*) reprimand, rebuke; ***upominać się*** demand (**o** *A*); ***~ się o zwrot długu*** demand payment of a debt
upominek *m* (*-nku*; *-nki*) gift, present
upomnieć *v/p* → ***upominać***
upomnieni|e *n* (*-nia*; *-nia*) **1.** (*krytyka*) reprimand, admonition; ***udzielić komuś ~a*** reprimand s.o., admonish s.o. **2.** (*pismo*) reminder; ***wysłać ~e*** send a reminder
uporać się *v/p* (*-ram*) manage (**z** *I* to do s.th.)
uporczywy *adj* **1.** persistent; ***~ ból*** persistent pain **2.** *milczenie*: stubborn, obstinate
uporządkować *v/p* (*-kuję*) **1.** *mieszkanie*, *biurko*: tidy (up) **2.** *dokumenty*, *fakty*: put in order **3.** *sprawy osobiste*, *życie*: sort out
uposażeni|e *n* (*-nia*; *-nia*) pay, salary
upośledzenie *n* (*-nia*; *-nia*): ***~ fizyczne*** physical disabilty, physical handicap; ***~ umysłowe*** mental handicap; ***~ słuchu*** hearing impairment; ***~ wzroku*** visual impairment; **upośledzony** *adj* handicapped, disabled; ***ciężko ~*** seriously disabled; ***~ umysłowo*** mentally handicapped
upoważniać ⟨**-nić**⟩ (*-niam*) authorize (**do** *G* to)
upoważnieni|e *n* (*-nia*; *-nia*) authorization; ***z ~a*** *G* on behalf of
upoważniony *adj*: ***być ~m*** be authorized (**do** *G* to do s.th.)
upowszechniać ⟨**-nić**⟩ (*-niam*) **1.** *kulturę*, *sport*: promote, popularize **2.** *informacje*: spread, disseminate; ***upowszechniać się*** become widespread
upozorować *v/p* (*-ruję*) *wypadek*, *włamanie*: stage
upozorowanie *n* (*-nia*; *no pl*) *wypadku*, *włamania*: staging; **upozorowany** *adj* *wypadek*, *włamanie*: staged
upór *m* (*uporu*; *no pl*) **1.** obstinacy, stubbornness; ***z uporem*** stubbornly, obstinately **2.** (*determinacja*) determination
uprać *v/p* → ***prać***
upragniony *adj* longed-for, desired, long-awaited
upraszа|ć ⟨**-rosić**⟩ (*-szam*) ask; ***~ się o niepalenie*** smoking prohibited; ***~ się o ciszę*** silence, please
upraszczać ⟨**-rościć**⟩ (*-czam*) simplify
uprawa *f* (*-wy*; *no pl*) **1.** (*ziemi*) cultivation **2.** (*roślin*) cultivation, growing; ***~ warzyw*** cultivation of vegetables; ***~ zboża*** corn growing; ***~ tytoniu*** tobacco growing
uprawiać *v/im* (*-wiam*) **1.** *ziemię*: cultivate **2.** *warzywa*, *zboże*: grow **3.** *sport*: do, play **4.** *seks*: have **5.** ***~ hazard*** gamble **6.** ***~ turystykę*** travel
uprawianie *n* (*-nia*; *no pl*): ***~ sportu*** (doing) sport; ***~ turystyki*** *Br* travelling, *Am* traveling

U

uprawniać ⟨**-nić**⟩ (*-niam*) authorize (**do** *G* to do s.th.), entitle (**do** *G* to)
uprawnienia *pl* (*-wnień*) **1.** authority *sing* **2.** *rządu*: powers **3.** (*kwalifikacje*) qualifications **4.** (*prawa*) rights; **uprawniony** *adj* entitled, authorized; **~ do głosowania** eligible to vote
uprawn|y *adj* **1.** *rośliny*: cultivated **2.** *ziemia*: arable, cultivable; **pola ~e** farmland, arable land
uprawomocnić się *v/p* (*-nię*) become effective, become valid
uprosić *v/p* → **upraszać**
uproszczenie *n* (*-nia*; *-nia*) simplification
uprościć *v/p* → **upraszczać**
uprowadzać ⟨**-dzić**⟩ (*-dzam*) **1.** *osobę*: kidnap, abduct **2.** *samolot*, *pojazd*: hijack
uprowadzenie *n* (*-nia*; *-nia*) **1.** *osoby*: kidnapping, abduction **2.** *samolotu*: hijacking
uprząż *f* (*-rzęży*; *-rzęże*) harness
uprzeć się *v/p* → **upierać się**
uprzedni *adj* previous, prior; **uprzednio** *adv* previously, earlier
uprzedzać ⟨**-dzić**⟩ (*-dzam*) **1.** (*ostrzegać*) warn (**o** *L* about) **2.** (*informować*) inform (**o** *L* of) **3.** (*ubiec*) forestall **4.** *pytanie*, *życzenie*: anticipate; **~ czyjeś wszystkie życzenia** anticipate s.o.'s every wish **5. ~ fakty** speculate; **uprzedzać się** become prejudiced (**do** *G* against)
uprzedzająco *adv*: **~ grzeczny** exceedingly polite
uprzedze|nie *n* (*-nia*; *-nia*) prejudice, bias; **~nia rasowe** racial prejudice; **bez ~ń**, **wolny od ~ń** unprejudiced, unbiased; **mieć ~nia do** *G* be prejudiced against
uprzedzić *v/p* → **uprzedzać**
uprzedzony *adj* prejudiced, bias(s)ed
uprzejmie *adv*: **proszę ~ a)** (*odpowiadając na podziękowanie*) you're welcome, my pleasure **b)** (*podając coś*) here you are; **dziękuję ~** thank you very much; → **uprzejmy**
uprzejmoś|ć *f* (*-ści*; *-ści*) **1.** (*grzeczność*) politeness, courtesy; **wymienić ~ci** exchange courtesies **2.** (*przysługa*) *Br* favour, *Am* favor; **wyświadczyć komuś ~ć** do s.o. a favour
uprzejm|y *adj* polite (**dla**/**wobec** *G* to/towards); **bądź tak ~y i zrób to** would you be so kind as to do it?; **czy byłby pan ~y przypomnieć mi jutro o tym?** could you remind me of that tomorrow, please?; **była ~a na mnie zaczekać** she was kind enough to wait for me
uprzemysłowienie *n* (*-nia*; *no pl*) industrialization; **uprzemysłowiony** *adj* industrialized; **wysoko ~** highly industrialized
uprzyjemniać ⟨**-nić**⟩ (*-niam*) make enjoyable, make more fun; **~ sobie czas rozmową** while away the time talking
uprzykrzać ⟨**-rzyć**⟩ (*-rzam*) spoil, make unpleasant; **~ komuś życie** be a pain in the neck for s.o., be a nuisance for s.o.; **uprzykrzyło mu się czekanie** he got bored waiting
uprzykrzony *adj* irritating
uprzytamniać ⟨**-tomnić**⟩ (*-niam*): **~ komuś, że** make s.o. aware that; **~ sobie, że** realize that
uprzywilejowany *adj* **1.** privileged **2.** *pojazd*: emergency
upust *m* (*-tu*; *-ty*) **1.** *cen*: discount, reduction **2. dać ~** *fig* give vent (*D* to)
upuszczać ⟨**upuścić**⟩ (*-czam*) drop
upychać ⟨**upchać**, **upchnąć**⟩ (*-cham*) stuff
ur. *abbr* (= **urodzony**) b.
urabiać ⟨**urobić**⟩ (*-biam*) **1.** *glinę*: work, form **2.** *charakter*: form, *Br* mould, *Am* mold **3.** *ciasto*: knead **4. ~ sobie ręce po łokcie** *fig* work one's hands to the bone
uraczyć *v/p* (*-czę*): treat (*I* to); → **raczyć**
uradowany *adj lit* delighted, overjoyed
uradzać ⟨**-dzić**⟩ (*-dzam*) *lit* agree
uran *m* (*-nu*; *no pl*) CHEM uranium; **uranowy** *adj* uranium
Uran *m* (*-na*; *no pl*): **~** ASTR Uranus
urastać *v/im* (*-tam*): **~ do rozmiarów** *G* *fig* take on the proportions of
uratować *v/p* → **ratować**
uraz *m* (*-zu*; *-zy*) **1.** injury **2.** PSYCH trauma
uraz|a *f* (*-zy*; *-zy*) resentment, grudge; **dawne ~y** old grudge; **żywić ~ę do** *G* have a grudge against, nurse a grudge against
urazić *v/p* → **urażać**

U

urazow|y *adj* traumatic; ***chirurgia ~a*** traumatology; ***oddział ~y*** trauma ward
urażać ⟨***urazić***⟩ (*-żam*) hurt; ***uraził ją swoją uwagą*** he hurt her with his remark, she was piqued by his remark
urażony *adj* **1.** *osoba, mina*: offended **2.** *duma, ambicja*: hurt
urągać *v/im* (*-gam*) offend; ***~ zdrowemu rozsądkowi*** defy common sense
urbanista *m* (*-ty*; *-niści*) urban planner, city planner
urbanistyczny *adj* urban; **urbanistyka** *f* (*-ki*; *no pl*) urban planning, city planning
urealniać ⟨***-nić***⟩ (*-niam*) make real
uregulować *v/p* → ***regulować***
uregulowanie *n* (*-nia*; *-nia*) JUR regulation; **uregulowany** *adj* regulated, controlled
urlop *m* (*-pu*; *-py*) *Br* holiday, *Am* vacation; ***być na ~ie*** *Br* be on holiday, *Am* be on vacation; ***jechać na ~*** *Br* go on holiday, *Am* go on vacation; ***wziąć ~*** take leave; ***~ macierzyński*** maternity leave
urlopowicz *m* (*-cza*; *-cze*), **~ka** *f* (*-ki*; *-ki*) *Br* holiday-maker, *Am* vacationer
urlopowy *adj przerwa, sezon*: holiday
urna *f* (*-ny*; *-ny*) urn; ***~ wyborcza*** ballot box
urobić *v/p* (*-bię*): ***urobić się*** work one's hands to the bone, work very hard; → ***urabiać***
uroczy *adj* charming, adorable
uroczystość *f* (*-ści*; *-ści*) ceremony, celebration; ***~ rodzinna*** family celebration, family gathering; ***~ rocznicowa*** anniversary ceremony; ***~ pogrzebowa*** funeral ceremony; ***~ otwarcia*** opening ceremony
uroczysty *adj* **1.** solemn **2.** *strój*: formal
urod|a *f* (*-dy*; *no pl*) **1.** (*piękno*) beauty **2.** (*wygląd*) appearance; ***mieć dziewczęcą ~ę*** look like a girl
urodzaj *m* (*-ju*; *-je*) bumper crop; ***~ na owoce*** a good year for fruit; **urodzajny** *adj* **1.** *rok*: good **2.** *ziemia*: fertile
urodzeni|e: ***od ~a*** since birth; ***zaraz po ~u*** just after birth; ***rok ~a*** year of birth
urodzić *v/p* → ***rodzić***
urodzinowy *adj* birthday
urodziny *pl* (*-dzin*) **1.** (*rocznica*) birthday *sing*; ***obchodzić ~*** celebrate one's birthday **2.** (*przyjęcie*) birthday party **3.** (*narodziny*) birth
urodziwy *adj lit* comely, pretty
urodzony *adj* born; ***w czepku ~*** *fig* born with a silver spoon in one's mouth; ***szlachetnie ~*** of noble birth
urojenia *pl* (*-jeń*) delusions
urojony *adj* imaginary
urok *m* (*-ku*; *-ki*) **1.** (*wdzięk*) charm; ***pełen ~u*** charming; ***był pod jej ~iem*** he was under her spell **2.** (*zaklęcie*) spell; ***rzucić ~ na*** *A* cast a spell on
urolog *m* (*-ga*; *-lodzy*) urologist
urosnąć *v/p* → ***rosnąć***
urozmaicać ⟨***-cić***⟩ (*-cam*) add variety to
urozmaiceni|e *n* (*-nia*; *-nia*) variety, diversity; ***dla ~a*** for a change; **urozmaicony** *adj* varied, diversified
uruchamiać ⟨***-chomić***⟩ (*-miam*) **1.** start (up), get going, set in motion **2.** *silnik, produkcję*: start **3.** *fabrykę*: open
urwać *v/p* (*-wę*) ***urwać się***: ***urwał się z choinki*** *fig* he's on another planet; → ***urywać***
urwanie: ***mieć ~ głowy*** have a hectic time
urwis *m* (*-sa*; *-sy*) urchin
urwisk|o *n* (*-ka*; *-ka*) precipice, cliff; ***nad ~iem*** on the edge of a cliff; **urwisty** *adj zbocze*: precipitous
urynkowienie *n* (*-nia*; *no pl*) ECON inclusion in the free market
urywać ⟨***urwać***⟩ (*-wam*) **1.** (*odrywać*) tear off **2.** (*przerwać*) break; ***~ w połowie zdania*** break off in mid-sentence, break off in the middle of a sentence; ***urywać się*** **1.** (*odrywać się*) come off; ***upił się tak, że film mu się urwał*** *infml* he got so drunk that he passed out **2.** (*o głosie*) break off **3.** (*z pracy*) *infml* get off (***z*** *G*)
uryw|ek *m* (*-wka*/*-wku*; *-wki*) **1.** fragment; ***~ki rozmowy*** fragments of conversation, snatches of conversation **2.** *tekstu*: fragment, excerpt; **urywkowy** *adj* fragmentary
urząd *m* (*urzędu*; *urzędy*) office; ***~ pocztowy*** post office; ***~ stanu cywilnego*** registry office; ***z urzędu*** officially, ex officio; ***obrońca z urzędu***

Br court-appointed defence lawyer, *Am* public defender

urządzać ⟨**-dzić**⟩ (*-dzam*) **1.** *mieszkanie, pokój*: furnish **2.** *przyjęcie, imprezę*: organize **3.** *urodziny, imieniny*: celebrate **4.** (*pasować*) suit; ***to mnie nie urządza*** *infml* it doesn't suit me **5.** *scenę*: *infml* make **6.** (*pomóc zagospodarować się*) ***urządzić kogoś*** fix s.o.; **urządzać się 1.** (*osiadać*) settle **2.** (*robić sobie kłopot*) *infml* get into a mess

urządzeni|e *n* (*-nia*; *-nia*) device; ***~a*** equipment; ***~e klimatyzacyjne*** air-conditioning unit; ***~e alarmowe*** alarm device

urządzić *v/p* → **urządzać**

urzec *v/p* → **urzekać**

urzeczony *adj* spell-bound, bewitched

urzeczywistniać ⟨**-nić**⟩ (*-niam*) **1.** *marzenia*: realize, *Br* fulfil, *Am* fulfill **2.** *plany*: carry out; **urzeczywistniać się** (*o marzeniach*) come true

urzekać ⟨**urzec**⟩ (*-kam*) **1.** (*rzucić czar*) bewitch **2.** (*zachwycić*) captivate; **urzekający** *adj* fascinating, captivating

urzędas *m* (*-sa*; *-sy*) *infml* bureaucrat, *Br infml* pen-pusher, *Am infml* pencil-pusher

urzędniczy *adj* clerical

urzędnik *m* (*-ka*; *-nicy*), **-niczka** *f* (*-ki*; *-ki*) **1.** clerk, office worker; ***~ pocztowy*** post office worker **2.** (*państwowy*) civil servant; ***~ stanu cywilnego*** registrar

urzędować *v/im* (*-duję*) **1.** (*w biurze*) work **2.** (*piastować stanowisko*) hold an office; **urzędowani|e**: ***godziny ~a*** office hours

urzędow|y *adj* official; ***język ~y*** official language; ***pismo ~e*** official letter

urzędy *pl* → **urząd**

urżnąć *v/p* (*-nę*) cut off; ***urżnąć się*** *infml* get drunk; **urżnięty** *adj* drunk as a skunk

usadawiać ⟨**-dowić**⟩ (*-wiam*) *dziecko*: place; ***usadawiać się*** (*w fotelu*) make oneself comfortable

usadzać ⟨**-dzić**⟩ (*-dzam*) **1.** (*sadzać*) seat **2. usadzić kogoś** *infml* take s.o. a peg or two

usamodzielniać się ⟨**-nić**⟩ (*-niam*) become independent

usatysfakcjonować *v/p* → **satysfakcjonować**

USC *abbr m/n indecl* (= **Urząd Stanu Cywilnego**) *Br* registry office, register office

uschnąć *v/p* → **usychać**

USG *abbr n indecl* (= **ultrasonografia**) ultrasound, US

usiany *adj* dotted (*I* with)

usiąść *v/p* → **siadać**

usidlać ⟨**-lić**⟩ (*-lam*) ensnare

usiedzieć *v/p*: ***nie móc ~*** be restless, *infml* have ants in one's pants

usilny *adj* **1.** *prośba*: insistent **2.** *starania*: insistent, strenuous

usiłować *v/im* (*-łuję*) attempt, strive; **usiłowanie** *n* (*-nia*; *-nia*) attempt; ***~ zabójstwa*** attempted murder

uskakiwać ⟨**uskoczyć**⟩ (*-kuję*) dodge (**przed** *I*)

uskarżać się *v/im* (*-żam*) complain (**na** *A* about/of)

uskładać *v/p* (*-dam*) *pieniądze*: put aside, save up

uskoczyć *v/p* → **uskakiwać**

uskok *m* (*-ku*; *-ki*) **1.** GEOL fault **2.** (*unik*) dodge; ***~ w lewo*** dodge to the left **3.** (*w ścianie*) offset

uskrzydlać ⟨**-lić**⟩ (*-lam*): ***~ kogoś*** give s.o. wings, boost s.o.'s confidence

usłany *adj* covered, strewn (*I* with); ***~ różami*** paved with roses

usług|a *f* (*-gi*; *-gi*) ECON service; ***~i*** services; ***~i gwarancyjne*** warranty service; ***~i krawieckie*** sewing services; ***~i pogrzebowe*** funeral services; ***być na czyichś ~ach*** be at s.o.'s service

usługiwać *v/im* (*-guję*) serve; ***~ komuś przy stole*** wait the table for s.o.

usługobiorca *m* (*-cy*; *-cy*) customer, client; **usługodawca** *m* (*-cy*; *-cy*) service provider

usługow|y *adj*: ***działalność ~a*** (provision of) services; ***punkt ~y*** shop, *Br* service centre, *Am* service center

usłużny *adj* attentive, obliging

usłyszeć *v/p* (*-szę*) hear

usmarkany *adj* with snot all over one's face

usmarować *v/p* (*-ruję*) **1.** smear **2.** (*ubrudzić*) soil; ***usmarować się*** **1.** smear oneself **2.** (*ubrudzić się*) soil oneself

usmażyć *v/p* → **smażyć**

usnąć *v/p* → **usypiać**
uspokajać ⟨**-koić**⟩ (*-jam*) calm down; **~ sumienie** ease one's conscience, *form* salve one's conscience; **uspokajać się 1.** (*o osobie*) calm down **2.** (*o wietrze*) die down
uspokajając|y *adj*: **środki ~e** tranquillizers, *Am* tranquilizers
uspokoić *v/p* → **uspokajać**
uspołeczniać ⟨**-nić**⟩ (*-niam*) nationalize; **uspołeczniać się** become nationalized
usposobienie *n* (*-nia*; *no pl*) disposition, nature; **pogodne ~** cheerful disposition, sunny disposition; **mieć miłe ~** be nice-tempered, be good-natured
usposobiony *adj* disposed (**do** *G* to/towards); **przyjaźnie ~** friendly, well-disposed; **wrogo ~** ill-disposed
usprawiedliwiać ⟨**-wić**⟩ (*-wiam*) justify; **usprawiedliwiać się** excuse oneself
usprawiedliwienie *n* (*-nia*; *-nia*) **1.** (*uzasadnienie*) justification **2.** (*pisemne wyjaśnienie*) excuse note
usprawniać ⟨**-nić**⟩ (*-niam*) improve, rationalize
ust|a *pl* (*ust*) lips, mouth *sing*; **pełne ~a** full lips; **wąskie ~a** narrow lips; **mówić z pełnymi ~ami** talk with one's mouth full; **pocałować kogoś w ~a** kiss s.o. on the lips; **otworzyć ~a** open one's mouth; **być na ~ach wszystkich** *fig* be on everyone's tongue; **~a mu się nie zamykały** he couldn't stop talking; **przekazywany z ~ do ~** passed by word of mouth; **cały dzień nie miał nic w ~ach** he didn't eat anything for the whole day; **rozpływać się w ~ach** melt in one's mouth; **metoda ~a-~a** mouth-to-mouth resuscitation, the kiss of life; **nie mieć do kogo ~ otworzyć** have no one to talk to
ustać[1] *v/p* → **ustawać**
ustać[2] *v/p* (*-toję*): **on nie może ~ a)** he can hardly stand **b)** (*ze zmęczenia*) he's on his last legs; **ustać się** (*o płynie*) settle
ustalać ⟨**-lić**⟩ (*-lam*) **1.** *warunki*: set **2.** *termin, cenę, plan*: fix **3.** *fakty*: establish; **ustalić czyjąś tożsamość** establish s.o.'s identity, identify s.o.; **ustalić, że** establish that **4.** *kierunek*: find; **ustalać się** (*o pogodzie*) settle (down)
ustalenie *n* (*-nia*; *-nia*) **1.** (*postanowienie*) decision, arrangement **2.** (*wynik śledztwa*) finding **3. ~ tożsamości** identification
ustalić *v/p* → **ustalać**
ustanawiać ⟨**-nowić**⟩ (*-wiam*) **1.** *prawa*: make, lay down **2.** *rekord*: set **3.** *spadkobiercę*: name as one's heir **4.** *święto*: establish
ustan|ek: **bez ~ku** ceaselessly
ustatkować się *v/p* (*-kuję*) settle down
ustawa *f* (*-wy*; *-wy*) act, law; **~ zasadnicza** constitution
ustawać ⟨**-tać**⟩ (*-taję*) **1.** stop; **nie ustawać w wysiłkach** keep trying, persist in one's efforts **2.** (*o wietrze, burzy*) die down; **deszcz ustał** it stopped raining **3.** (*o bólu*) subside
ustawiać ⟨**-wić**⟩ (*-wiam*) **1.** (*układać*) put, place **2.** *rusztowanie*: mount, put up **3.** *ostrość, głośność*: adjust; **ustawiać się 1.** (*w kolejce, szeregu*) line up **2.** (*w szyku*) form ranks
ustawiczny *adj* constant, incessant
ustawny *adj mieszkanie, pokój*: easy to furnish
ustawodawca *m* (*-cy*; *-cy*) legislator; **ustawodawcz|y** *adj* legislative; **władza ~a** legislative power, the legislative; **ustawodawstwo** *n* (*-wa*; *no pl*) legislation
ustawowo *adv* by law, statutorily; **ustawowy** *adj* statutory
ustąpić *v/p* (*-pię*): **~ komuś pola** give ground to s.o.; → **ustępować**
ustąpienie *n* (*-nia*; *no pl*): **~** (**ze stanowiska**) resignation
uster|ka *f* (*-ki*; *-ki*) TECH fault, defect; **bez ~ek** faultless
ustęp *m* (*-pu*; *-py*) **1.** (*tekstu*) passage **2.** (*ubikacja*) lavatory
ustępliwy *adj* compliant
ustępować ⟨**-tąpić**⟩ (*-puję*) **1.** yield, give in (**przed** *I* to); **~ komuś miejsca** give up one's seat to s.o.; **~ z drogi** give way; **~ ze stanowiska** resign **2.** (*nie dorównywać*) not be as good as, not be a match for; **nie ustępować komuś w** *L* not be second to s.o. in **3.** (*o bólu, gorączce*) subside **4.** (*o mrozie*) relent, abate

ustępstwa *pl*: ***iść na ~*** make concessions
ustnik *m* (*-ka*; *-ki*) mouthpiece; **ustn|y** *adj* oral; ***jama ~a*** oral cavity; ***głoska ~a*** oral sound
ustosunkowany *adj* well-connected
ustosunkowywać się ⟨**-kować**⟩ (*-kowuję*) take a position (**do** *G* on); ***~ krytycznie*** be critical (**do** *G* of)
ustrojow|y *adj* **1.** *zmiany*: political **2.** ***płyny ~e*** body fluids
ustronie *n* (*-nia*; *-nia*) retreat
ustronny *adj* secluded
ustrój *m* (*-roju*; *-roje*) **1.** POLIT (political) system **2.** BIOL system
ustrzec *v/p* (*-rzegę*) protect (**przed** *I* from); **ustrzec się** avoid (**przed** *I* **od** *G*)
usunąć *v/p* → **usuwać**
usunięcie *n* (*-cia*; *-cia*) removal; ***~ ciąży*** abortion
usuwać ⟨**usunąć**⟩ (*-wam*) **1.** remove; ***~ ciążę*** **a)** (*o kobiecie*) have an abortion **b)** (*o lekarzu*) perform an abortion **2.** *ząb*: extract, pull out **3.** *awarię*: repair **4.** *śnieg*: clear; **usuwać się** step aside
usychać ⟨**-schnąć**⟩ (*-cham*) **1.** (*o roślinie*) wither **2.** (*o osobie*) ***~ z tęsknoty za*** *I* pine for
usynawiać ⟨**-nowić**⟩ (*-wiam*) adopt
usynowienie *n* (*-nia*; *-nia*) adoption
usypać *v/p* → **usypywać**
usypiać (*-piam*) **I** ⟨**usnąć**⟩ *v/i* (*zasypiać*) fall asleep **II** ⟨**uśpić**⟩ *v/t* **1.** *dziecko*: put to sleep **2.** *zwierzę*: put down **3.** *pacjenta*: *Br* anaesthetize, *Am* anesthetize
usypiający *adj* **1.** *tabletka*: sleeping **2.** *głos*: soporific
usypisko *n* (*-ka*; *-ka*) **1.** mound, pile **2.** GEOL scree
usypywać ⟨**-pać**⟩ (*-puję*) build, raise
usystematyzować *v/p* (*-zuję*) systematize
usytuować *v/p* → **sytuować**
usytuowanie *n* (*-nia*; *no pl*) location; **usytuowany** *adj* situated, located
uszanowanie *n* (*-nia*; *no pl*) respect
uszczelka *f* (*-ki*; *-ki*) TECH gasket, washer
uszczelniać ⟨**-nić**⟩ (*-niam*) seal
uszczerb|ek *m* (*-bku*; *no pl*) **1.** (*na zdrowiu*) ***z ~kiem dla zdrowia*** to the detriment of one's health; ***bez ~ku dla zdrowia*** without detriment to one's health **2.** (*szkoda materialna*) ***doznać ~ku*** suffer damage; ***nie przynosić ~ku*** bring no harm
uszczęśliwiać ⟨**-wić**⟩ (*-wiam*) make happy; ***~ kogoś na siłę*** make s.o. happy whether they like it or not
uszczknąć *v/p* (*-nę*) nip off
uszczuplać ⟨**-lić**⟩ (*-lam*) diminish, deplete
uszczypliwy *adj* **1.** *uwaga*: cutting, biting **2.** *osoba*: sharp-tongued
uszczypnąć *v/p* (*-nę*) pinch; **uszczypnąć się** pinch oneself
uszkadzać ⟨**-kodzić**⟩ (*-dzam*) **1.** (*niszczyć*) damage **2.** (*ranić*) injure
uszko *n* (*-ka*; *-ka*) *dim* **1.** (*ucho*) (small) ear **2.** *igły*: eye **3.** *filiżanki*: handle **4.** COOK stuffed dough pocket
uszkodzenie *n* (*-nia*; *-nia*) damage; ***~ ciała*** injury, (bodily) harm
uszkodzić *v/p* → **uszkadzać**
uszkodzony *adj* **1.** damaged **2.** (*niedziałający*) out of order
uszlachetniać ⟨**-nić**⟩ (*-niam*) **1.** *surowiec*: purify **2.** *olej*: refine **3.** (*udoskonalać*) improve, refine
uszminkować *v/p* → **szminkować**
uszn|y *adj* ANAT ear; ***małżowina ~a*** auricle
usztywniać ⟨**-nić**⟩ (*-niam*) **1.** stiffen **2.** (*unieruchamiać*) immobilize
uszy *pl* → **ucho**[1]
uszyć *v/p* → **szyć**
uścisk *m* (*-ku*; *-ki*) **1.** (*ramionami*) embrace, hug; ***przesyłać ~i*** send love **2.** (*dłonią*) grip, clasp; ***~ dłoni*** handshake
uściskać *v/p* (*-kam*) **1.** (*obejmować*) hug, embrace; ***uściskaj go ode mnie*** send my love to him **2.** (*ściskać*) ***~ komuś dłoń*** shake hands with s.o.
uściślać ⟨**-lić**⟩ (*-lam*) **1.** (*precyzować*) state (more) precisely **2.** (*określać*) specify
uśmiać się *v/p* (*-mieję*) have a good laugh; ***~ do łez*** cry with laughter, laugh to tears; ***koń by się uśmiał*** don't make me laugh, it would make a cat laugh
uśmiech *m* (*-chu*; *-chy*) smile; ***szyderczy ~*** sneer; ***~ losu*** a stroke of luck, a lucky turn of fortune

U

uśmiechać się ⟨**-chnąć**⟩ (*-cham*) smile (**do** *G* to); **~ szyderczo** sneer; **~ pod nosem**, **~ pod wąsem** crack a smile; **coś się komuś nie uśmiecha** *fig* s.o. doesn't like the idea of s.th., s.o. is not happy about s.th.
uśmiechnięty *adj* smiling
uśmiercać ⟨**-cić**⟩ (*-cam*) kill, put to death
uśmierzać ⟨**-rzyć**⟩ (*-rzam*) *ból*: relieve, soothe; **uśmierzając|y** *adj*: **środki ~e ból** painkillers
uśmieszek *m* (*-szku*; *-szki*) **1.** (*pełen wyższości*) smirk **2.** (*złośliwy*) sneer
uśpić *v/p* → **usypiać**
uświadamiać ⟨**-domić**⟩ (*-miam*) make aware, inform; **~ sobie, że** realize that, come to the realization that; **~ kogoś seksualnie** give sex education to s.o., explain the facts of life to s.o.
uświadomiony *adj*: **on jest ~ seksualnie** he knows the facts of life; **uświadomienie** *n* (*-nia*; *no pl*) (*wiedza*) awareness, consciousness
uświetniać ⟨**-nić**⟩ (*-niam*) *Br* add splendour to, *Am* add splendor to
uświęcony *adj*: **~ tradycją**, **~ zwyczajem** sanctified, *Br* time-honoured, *Am* time honored
utajniony *adj* classified
utajony *adj* latent
utalentowany *adj* talented, gifted
utarczka *f* (*-ki*; *-ki*) (*słowna*) squabble
utarg *m* (*-gu*; *-gi*) takings *pl*; **~ dzienny** day's takings
utargować *v/p* (*-guję*) knock (the price) down, beat down
utarty *adj*: **~m zwyczajem** traditionally; **~ zwrot** set phrase
utemperować *v/p* → **temperować**
utensylia *pl* (*-liów*) utensils
utęsknienie: **z ~m** longingly
utkać *v/p* → **tkać**
utknąć *v/p* (*-nę*): **~ w martwym punkcie** come to a standstill; → **utykać**[1]
utkwić *v/p* (*-wię*) (*o drazdze, ości*) stick; **~ w pamięci** stick in s.o.'s mind; **~ wzrok w** *L* fix one's eyes on
utleniacz *m* (*-cza*; *-cze*) **1.** CHEM oxidant **2.** (*do włosów*) bleach; **utleniać** ⟨**-nić**⟩ (*-niam*) CHEM oxidate; **utlenianie** *n* (*-nia*; *no pl*) CHEM oxidation
utlenić *v/p* → **1. tlenić 2. utleniać**
utlenion|y *adj* **1.** *włosy*: bleached **2.** *blondynka*: peroxide **3. woda ~a** hydrogen peroxide, oxygenated water
utłuc *v/p* → **tłuc**
utonąć *v/p* → **tonąć**
utopia *f* (*-pii*; *-pie*) utopia
utopić *v/p* (*-pię*) drown; **utopiłby ją w łyżce wody** *fig* he wouldn't spit on her if she were on fire; **utopić się** drown; → **topić się**
utopijny *adj* utopian
utorować *v/p* → **torować**
utożsamiać ⟨**-mić**⟩ (*-miam*) identify; **utożsamiać się** identify (**z** *I* with)
utracić *v/p* (*-cę*) *lit* lose
utrapienie *n* (*-nia*; *-nia*) nuisance, pain in the neck, trouble
utrat|a *f* (*-ty*; *no pl*) loss; **~a ciepła** heat loss; **~a wzroku** loss of sight; **do ~y tchu** until one drops
utrącić *v/p* (*-cę*) *uszko*: knock off
utrudniać ⟨**-nić**⟩ (*-niam*) **1.** make difficult, complicate **2.** *przejazd*: hinder
utrudnienie *n* (*-nia*; *-nia*) difficulty, hindrance
utrudzić się *v/p* (*-dzę*) become weary
utrwalacz *m* (*-cza*; *-cze*) **1.** PHOT fixer **2. ~ fryzjerski** hair fixative
utrwalać ⟨**-lić**⟩ (*-lam*) **1.** *przyjaźń*: cement, solidify **2.** (*upamiętniać*) preserve; **~ coś na zdjęciu** photograph s.th.; **utrwalać się** become established, take root
utrzeć *v/p* → **ucierać**
utrzymać *v/p* → **utrzymywać**
utrzymani|e *n* (*-nia*; *no pl*) **1.** TECH maintenance **2. koszty ~a** cost of living; **mieć kogoś na ~u** provide for s.o.; **całodzienne ~e** full board, board and lodging
utrzymany *adj*: **dobrze ~** well-kept; **~ w dobrym stanie** in good condition; **~ w jasnej tonacji** predominantly light, in light tones; **~ w uroczystym tonie** solemn
utrzymywać ⟨**-mać**⟩ (*-muję*) **1.** hold; **~ kogoś przy życiu** keep s.o. alive; **~ kontakt z** *I* stay in touch with, have contact with **2.** *równowagę*, *kochankę*: keep; **~ porządek w pokoju** keep a room tidy **3.** *dziecko*: provide for, support; **~ rodzinę** provide for one's family, support one's family; **utrzy-**

mywać się 1. (*zarabiać*) earn a living; **z czego się utrzymujesz?** what do you do for a living? **2.** (*pozostawać*) remain **3.** (*o zwyczaju*) be alive

utuczyć *v/p* → **tuczyć**

utulać ⟨**-lić**⟩ (*-lam*): **~ kogoś do snu** lull s.o. to sleep

utwardzać ⟨**-dzić**⟩ (*-dzam*) *drogę*: harden

utwierdzać się ⟨**-dzić**⟩ (*-dzam*): **~ w** *L* strengthen oneself in; **~ w przekonaniu, że** strengthen one's conviction that

utworzyć *v/p* → **tworzyć**

utwór *m* (*-woru*; *-wory*) **1.** (*dzieło*) work **2.** MUS piece, work

utycie *n* (*-cia*; *no pl*) weight gain

utyć *v/p* → **tyć**

utykać[1] ⟨**utknąć**⟩ (*-kam*) (*zatrzymywać się*) get stuck

utykać[2] *v/im* (*-kam*) (*kuleć*) limp; **~ na lewą nogę** have a limp in one's left leg

utylizacja *f* (*-cji*; *no pl*) utilization, recycling; **~ śmieci** (waste) recycling

utyskiwać *v/im* (*-kuję*) grumble (**na** *A* about), *infml* gripe (**na** *A* about)

uwa|ga *f* (*-gi*; *-gi*) **1.** (*koncentracja*) attention; **~ga!** look out!, be careful!; **rozproszona ~ga** distracted attention; **brać coś pod ~gę** consider s.th., take s.th. into consideration; **skupić ~gę na** *L* focus (one's) attention on; **zwrócić komuś ~gę na** *A* point to; **zwrócić ~gę na** *A* draw attention to; **zwracić na siebie ~gę** attract attention; **proszę zwrócić** (**szczególną**) **~gę na** *A* please, pay (special) attention to; **nie zwracać ~gi na** *A* **a)** take no notice of, overlook **b)** (*celowo przymykać oko*) overlook; **z ~gi na** *A* in view of, in consideration of; **mieć na ~dze** remember, bear in mind; **godny ~gi, zasługujący na ~gę** noteworthy, remarkable; **z ~gą** attentively, intently; **przykuwający ~gę** riveting, attention-drawing; **odwrócić czyjąś ~gę** divert s.o.'s attention, distract s.o.'s attention (**od** *G* from); **w centrum ~gi** in the focus of attention, in the limelight; **to uszło jego ~dze** it slipped his attention, he didn't notice it; **zwrócił moją ~gę na** *A* he drew my attention to **2.** (*spostrzeżenie*) comment, remark, observation; **robić ~gi** remark (**na temat** *G* on) **3.** (*pouczenie*) reproof; **zwrócić komuś ~gę** reprove s.o., admonish s.o. **4.** (*do zeszytu, dziennika*) note

uwalniać ⟨**uwolnić**⟩ (*-niam*) release, free; **~ kogoś od obowiązków** exempt s.o. from their duties; **uwalniać się** rid oneself (**od** *G* of)

uwarunkowany *adj* **1.** conditioned (*I* by) **2.** *genetycznie*: determined

uważa|ć *v/im* (*-żam*) **1.** (*być ostrożnym*) be careful; **~ć na** *A* watch out for; **~j!** look out!, watch out!; **~ć na siebie** take care of oneself; **~ć na dziecko** *Br* mind a child, *Am* watch a child **2.** (*sądzić*) think, believe; **~m, że** I think that; **~ć kogoś** (**coś**) **za** *A* regard s.o. (s.th.) as; **~ć coś za swój obowiązek** consider s.th. (to be) one's duty; **jak pan ~** as you wish; **uważać się**: **~ć się za** *A* regard oneself as

uważany *adj*: **~ za** *A* regarded as

uważny *adj* attentive, careful

uwertura *f* (*-ry*; *-ry*) MUS overture (**do** *G* to)

uwędzić *v/p* → **wędzić**

uwiąd *m* (*-du*; *no pl*): **~ starczy** senile decay, decrepitude

uwiązany *adj* **1.** (*w domu*) *fig* stuck **2.** (*do płotu*) tied up

uwiązywać ⟨**-zać**⟩ (*-zuję*) tie (**do** *G* to); **~ psa na łańcuchu** chain a dog

uwić *v/p* → **wić**[1]

uwidaczniać ⟨**-docznić**⟩ (*-niam*) demonstrate, show; **uwidaczniać się** become visible

uwieczniać ⟨**-nić**⟩ (*-niam*) immortalize; **uwieczniać się** immortalize oneself

uwielbiać *v/im* (*-biam*) adore, worship; **uwielbienie** *n* (*-nia*; *no pl*) adoration, worship

uwieńczony *adj*: **~ sukcesem** crowned with success, succesful

uwierać *v/im* (*-ram*) (*o bucie*) pinch

uwierzyć *v/p* → **wierzyć**

uwierzytelniać ⟨**-nić**⟩ (*-niam*) **1.** authenticate **2.** (*notarialnie*) notarize; **uwierzytelnienie** *n* (*-nia*; *no pl*) **1.** authentication **2.** (*notarialne*) notarization

uwiesić się *v/p* (*-szę*): **~ komuś na szyi** hang on s.o.'s neck
uwieść *v/p* → **uwodzić**
uwięzić *v/p* (*uwiężę*) imprison, incarcerate
uwięzienie *n* (*-nia*; *-nia*) imprisonment, incarceration; **uwięziony** *adj* imprisoned, incarcerated; **~ w lodach statek** icebound ship
uwięznąć *v/p* → **więznąć**
uwię|ź: **na ~zi a)** (*na smyczy*) on a leash **b)** (*na łańcuchu*) chained; **spuścić psa z ~zi** unleash a dog; **trzymać psa na ~zi** hold a dog on leash
uwijać się 〈**uwinąć**〉 (*-jam*) bustle (**z** *I* about)
uwikłać *v/p* → **wikłać**
uwinąć się *v/p* (*-nę*) make short work (**z** *I* of)
uwłacza|ć *v/im* (*-czam*) *lit* be an affront to; **to ~ jego godności** it's beneath his dignity; **uwłaczający** *adj* humiliating, degrading
uwłaszczenie *n* (*-nia*; *no pl*) enfranchisement
uwodziciel *m* (*-la*; *-le*), **~ka** *f* (*-ki*; *-ki*) seducer; **uwodzicielski** *adj* seductive
uwodzić 〈**uwieść**〉 (*-dzę*) seduce
uwolnić *v/p* → **uwalniać**
uwolnienie *n* (*-nia*; *no pl*) **1.** *więźniów*: release **2.** *od ograniczeń*, *cierpień*: liberation (**od** *G* from)
uwrażliwienie *n* (*-nia*; *no pl*) sensitization
uwspółcześniony *adj* modernized
uwstecznion|y *adj* **1.** (*opóźniony*) backward **2.** BIOL reduced; **~e płetwy ogonowe** reduced tail fins
uwydatniać 〈**-nić**〉 (*-niam*) **1.** (*podkreślać*) emphasize **2.** *kształty*: accentuate
uwypuklać 〈**-lić**〉 (*-lam*) → **uwydatniać**
uwzględniać 〈**-nić**〉 (*-niam*) **1.** (*brać pod uwagę*) consider, take into consideration **2.** *prośbę*, *żądanie*: meet; **uwzględnienie** *n* (*-nia*; *no pl*) consideration; **z ~m** *G* **a)** taking account of **b)** (*włączając*) including
uwziąć się *v/p* (*uwezmę*) have it in (**na** *A* for)
uzależniać 〈**-nić**〉 (*-niam*) make dependent (**od** *G* on); **uzależniać się 1.** become dependent (**od** *G* on) **2.** *od alkoholu*, *narkotyków*: become addicted (**od** *G* to)
uzależnienie *n* (*-nia*; *-nia*) **1.** (*finansowe*) dependence **2.** MED addiction; **~ od alkoholu** alcohol addiction; **~ od narkotyków** drug addiction
uzależniony I *adj* **1.** (*niesamodzielny*) dependent **2.** addicted (**od** *G* to); **~ od alkoholu** addicted to alcohol; **~ od narkotyków** addicted to drugs **II** *m* (*-nego*; *-żnieni*), **-na** *f* (*-nej*; *-ne*) addict; **~ od alkoholu** alcohol addict; **~ od narkotyków** drug addict
uzasadniać 〈**-nić**〉 (*-niam*) justify, substantiate
uzasadnienie *n* (*-nia*; *-nia*) justification; **uzasadniony** *adj* **1.** *zarzut*, *wyrok*: justified, substantiated **2.** *pretensja*, *obawa*, *żal*: reasonable
uzbierać *v/p* (*-ram*) **1.** *grzybów*: pick **2.** *pieniędzy*: put aside
uzbrajać 〈**-roić**〉 (*-jam*) arm; **uzbrajać się** arm oneself; **uzbroić się w cierpliwość** have patience; **musisz uzbroić się w cierpliwość** you're in for a long wait
uzbrojenie *n* (*-nia*; *no pl*) **1.** (*broń*) weapons *pl*, armament **2.** BUILD utilities *pl*, service infrastructure; **uzbrojony** *adj* (*posiadający broń*) armed (**w** *A* with)
uzda *f* (*-dy*; *-dy*) bridle
uzdatniać 〈**-nić**〉 (*-niam*) *wodę*: treat
uzdolnienie *n* (*-nia*; *-nia*) gift, talent; **uzdolniony** *adj* gifted
uzdrawiać 〈**-rowić**〉 (*-wiam*) **1.** *chorego*: heal **2.** *gospodarkę*: improve **3.** *stosunki*: restore, repair; **uzdrawiający** *adj właściwości*: healing, restorative
uzdrowiciel *m* (*-la*; *-le*), **~ka** *f* (*-ki*; *-ki*) healer
uzdrowić *v/p* → **uzdrawiać**
uzdrowienie *n* (*-nia*; *-nia*) healing; **cudowne ~** miraculous healing, miraculous recovery; **uzdrowisko** *n* (*-ka*; *-ka*) spa, health resort
uzewnętrzniać 〈**-nić**〉 (*-niam*) *uczucia*: manifest, express; **uzewnętrzniać się** manifest itself
uzębienie *n* (*-nia*; *no pl*) teeth *pl*, dentition

uzgadniać ⟨**-godnić**⟩ (*-niam*) **1.** (*wyrażać zgodę*) agree on **2.** (*ustalać*) set **3.** (*dopasowywać*) fit
uziemiać ⟨**-mić**⟩ (*-miam*) *Br* earth, *Am* ground
uziemienie *n* (*-nia*; *-nia*) *Br* earthing, *Am* grounding; **uziemiony** *adj fig Br* earthed, *Am* grounded
uzmysławiać ⟨**-łowić**⟩ (*-wiam*) make aware; **~ *sobie*** realize
uznać *v/p* → ***uznawać***
uznani|e *n* (*-nia*; *no pl*) respect, regard; ***spotkać się z ~em*** receive recognition, win critical acclaim; ***według własnego ~a*** at one's own discretion; ***zależeć od czyjegoś ~a*** be at s.o.'s discretion
uznany *adj* recognized, *Br* recognised
uznawać ⟨**-nać**⟩ (*-naję*) **1.** (*akceptować*) acknowledge, recognize, *Br* recognise **2.** (*uważać*) regard; **~ *coś za*** *A* regard s.th. as; **~ *coś za konieczne*** consider s.th. necessary **3.** (*stwierdzać*) ***uznał, że*** he decided that; **~ *uznał swój błąd*** he admitted his mistake, he admitted he was wrong; ***uznać kogoś za zmarłego*** find s.o. dead; ***uznać kogoś winnym*** find s.o. guilty; ***uznać dziecko*** acknowledge a child as one's; ***uznawać się***: **~ *się za*** *A* consider oneself; **~ *się za pokonanego*** admit one's defeat
uzupełniać ⟨**-nić**⟩ (*-niam*) **1.** supplement **2.** *zapas*: replenish; **~ *coś wodą*** fill s.th. up with water, top s.th. up with water **3.** *braki*, *brakujące części*: fill in; ***uzupełniać się*** complement each other
uzupełniając|y *adj* complementary, supplementary; ***wybory ~e*** by-election
uzupełnienie *n* (*-nia*; *-nia*) **1.** *diety*: supplement **2.** *zapasów*: replenishment
uzurpować *v/im* (*-puję*) usurp; **~ *sobie prawo*** usurp the right
uzwojenie *n* (*-nia*; *-nia*) winding
uzyskiwać ⟨**-kać**⟩ (*-kuję*) **1.** obtain, get **2.** *stypendium*, *dyplom*: receive **3.** *dostęp*: gain **4.** *wyniki*, *rezultaty*: achieve
użalać się ⟨**-lić**⟩ (*-lam*) complain (***na*** *A* about); **~ *nad kimś*** pity s.o.; **~ *nad sobą*** pity oneself
użądlić *v/p* (*-lam*) sting
użerać się *v/im* (*-ram*) *infml* wrangle (***z*** *I* with)
użyci|e *n* (*-cia*; *-cia*) **1.** use; ***sposób ~a*** instructions for use; ***wygodny w ~u*** easy to use; ***gotowy do ~a*** ready for use; ***być w ~u*** be in use; ***wyjść z ~a*** go out of use; ***przy ~u*** *G* using, with the use of **2.** (*zużycie*) usage
użyczać ⟨**-czyć**⟩ (*-czam*) lend; **~ *komuś gościny*** offer s.o. one's hospitality
użyć *v/p* → ***używać***
użyteczność|ć *f* (*-ści*; *no pl*) usefulness; ***budynek ~ci publicznej*** public building; **użyteczny** *adj* useful
użyt|ek *m* (*-tku*; *-tki*) **1.** use; ***robić ~ek z*** *G* make use of; ***do ~ku zewnętrznego*** for external use; ***do ~ku domowego*** for home use; ***na własny ~ek*** for personal use, for one's own use; ***jednorazowego ~ku*** disposable **2.** ***~ki*** AGR arable land
użytkować ⟨**z-**⟩ (*-kuję*) use; **użytkowanie** *n* (*-nia*; *no pl*) use; **~ *wieczyste*** perpetual lease, perpetual usufruct
użytkownik *m* (*-ka*; *-nicy*), **-niczka** *f* (*-ki*; *-ki*) user; ***rodzimy ~ języka*** native speaker
użytkow|y *adj przedmiot*, *sztuka*: functional; ***powierzchnia ~a*** usable floor space, usable floor area; ***program ~y*** INF application; ***sztuka ~a*** functional art, applied art; ***lokal ~y*** (business) premises
używać ⟨**użyć**⟩ (*-wam*) **1.** use **2.** *wolności*: enjoy; **~ *życia*** enjoy life, *infml* live it up **3.** *alkoholu*: drink
używalnoś|ć *f* (*-ści*; *no pl*) usability; ***w stanie ~ci*** ready to use; **używalny** *adj* in working order, usable
używan|y *adj* used, second-hand; ***~y samochód*** used car, second-hand car; ***~e ubrania*** second-hand clothes; ***nie ~y*** new
używka *f* (*-ki*; *-ki*) stimulant, psychoactive substance
użyźniać ⟨**-nić**⟩ (*-niam*) fertilize

V

VAT *abbr m* (*VAT-u*; *no pl*) (= ***podatek od wartości dodanej***) VAT

verte *interj* PTO, please turn over

video → ***wideo***

W

w *prep* (*L*/*A*) **1.** (*miejsce*) in, at; ***~ mieszkaniu*** in a flat; ***w domu*** at home; ***~ biurze*** at the office; ***~ gazecie*** in a newspaper; ***~ Madrycie*** in Madrid; ***~ Polsce*** in Poland; ***~ górach*** in the mountains; ***~ oddali*** in the distance **2.** (*charakterystyka*) in; ***być ~ okularach*** be wearing glasses; ***mleko ~ proszku*** powdered milk; ***~ dwóch tomach*** in two volumes; ***mydło ~ płynie*** liquid soap; ***cukier ~ kostkach*** cube sugar; ***~ gotówce*** in cash; ***~ paski*** striped; ***~ poprzek*** crosswise **3.** (*kierunek*) to; ***jechać ~ góry*** go to the mountains; ***skręcić ~ prawo*** turn right **4.** (*czas*) in, at, on; ***~ roku 2000*** in 2000; ***we wtorek*** on Tuesday; ***~ lipcu*** in July; ***~ lecie*** in (the) summer; ***~ dzień*** during the day, by day; ***~ nocy*** at night; ***~ czasie*** *G* during; ***~ święta*** during holidays; ***~ dniu czyichś urodzin*** on s.o.'s birthday

w. *abbr* (= ***wiek***) c.

wab: ***na ~ia*** as a decoy

wabić *v/im* (*-bię*) **1.** attract, entice (*I* with) **2.** (*wołać*) call **3.** (*karmą*) lure; ***wabić się*** (*o psie*) be called; ***jak się wabi twój pies?*** what's your dog's name?

wabik *m* (*-ka*; *-ki*) *fig* decoy, hook

wachlarz *m* (*-rza*; *-rze*) **1.** fan **2.** *kolorów*, *zainteresowań*: array **3.** *możliwości*: range

wachlować *v/im* (*-luję*) fan (*I* with); ***wachlować się*** fan oneself

wachta *f* (*-ty*; *-ty*) watch

waciak *m* (*-ka*; *-ki*) quilted jacket

wacik *m* (*-ka*; *-ki*) cotton pad

wada *f* (*-dy*; *-dy*) **1.** (*minus*) drawback, shortcoming **2.** *charakteru*, *osoby*: fault, shortcoming **3.** *urządzenia*, *produktu*: flaw, fault **4.** *MED* defect; ***~ serca*** cardiac defect; ***~ wymowy*** speech impediment

wadium *n* (*indecl*; *-dia*) bid bond

wadliwie *adv* defectively, faultily; **wadliwy** *adj* defective, faulty

wafel *m* (*-fla*; *-fle*) **1.** wafer **2.** (*na lody*) cornet

wa|ga *f* (*-gi*; *-gi*) **1.** (*przyrząd*) scales **2.** (*ciężar*) weight; ***sprzedawać coś na ~gę*** sell s.th. by weight; ***przybrać na ~dze*** put on weight, gain weight; ***stracić na ~dze*** lose weight **3.** (*ważność*) importance; ***przywiązywać wielką ~gę do*** *G* attach importance to; ***sprawa najwyższej ~gi*** matter of paramount importance **4.** ***≈ga*** *ASTR* Libra, the Scales

wagarować *v/im* (*-ruję*) skip school, *Br infml* bunk off, *Br infml* skive; **wagarowicz** *m* (*-cza*; *-cze*) *Br* truant; **wagary** *pl* (*-rów*): ***iść na ~*** skip school, *Br infml* bunk off, *Br infml* skive

wagon *m* (*-nu*; *-ny*) *Br* carriage, *Am* car; ***~ sypialny*** sleeping car, sleeper; ***~ restauracyjny*** dining car, *Br* restaurant car

wahać się ⟨**za-**⟩ (*-ham*) **1.** (*być niezdecydowanym*) hesitate (***między*** *I* between); ***nie ~ przed*** *I* not hesitate to do s.th. **2.** (*o cenie*, *temperaturze*) fluctuate **3.** (*o wahadle*) sway

wahadło *n* (*-dła*; *-dła*) pendulum; **wahadłowiec** *m* (*-wca*; *-wce*) space shuttle

wahadłowo *adv* **1.** ***kursować ~*** shuttle **2.** ***ruch odbywający się ~*** *AUTO* alternating traffic (flow)

wahadłowy *adj* **1.** ***ruch ~*** **a)** swinging motion **b)** *AUTO* alternating traffic (flow) **2.** *drzwi*: swinging

wahani|e *n* (*-nia*; *-nia*) **1.** (*niezdecydowanie*) hesitation; ***bez ~a*** without hesitation **2.** *temperatury*, *cen*: fluctuation

wakacje *pl* (*-ji*) *Br* (summer) holiday(s), *Am* (summer) vacation *sing*; **wakacyjny** *adj Br* holiday, *Am* vacation

wakat *m* (*-tu*; *-ty*) vacancy
wakować *v/im* (*-kuję*) be vacant
walać ⟨**u-**⟩ (*-lam*) dirty; ***walać się*** **1.** (*poniewierać się*) lie about **2.** (*brudzić się*) soil oneself, get dirty
walc *m* (*-ca*; *-ce*) waltz
walcować *v/im* (*-cuję*) *blachę*: roll
walcowany *adj blacha*: rolled; **walcowaty** *adj* cylindrical; ***mieć ~ kształt*** be cylindrical; **walcownia** *f* (*-ni*; *-nie*) rolling mill
walczyć *v/im* (*-czę*) fight (***z*** *I* against; ***o*** *A* for); ***~ o swoje prawa*** fight for one's rights; ***~ za ojczyznę*** fight for one's country; ***~ o lepszą przyszłość*** fight for a better future; ***~ ze snem*** struggled to remain awake, fight off sleep; ***~ ze śmiercią*** be fighting with death
walec *m* (*-lca*; *-lce*) **1.** (*drogowy*) road roller **2.** MATH cylinder
waleczność *f* (*-ści*; *no pl*) bravery, *form* gallantry; **waleczny** *adj* **1.** *żołnierz*: brave **2.** *czyn*: brave, valiant
walenie *pl* (*-ni*) BIOL cetaceans
waleriana *f* (*-ny*; *no pl*) BIOL MED valerian; **walerianow|y** *adj* valerian; ***krople ~e*** valerian (drops)
walet *m* (*-ta*; *-ty*) **1.** (*w kartach*) jack; ***~ kier*** jack of hearts **2.** ***na ~a*** (*nago*) *infml* naked; ***kąpać się na ~a*** skinny-dip
walić ⟨**-lnąć**⟩ (*-lę*) **1.** hit; ***walnąć pięścią w stół*** slam one's fist down on the table; ***~ w drzwi*** bang on the door; ***wal śmiało!*** *infml* go ahead, lay it on me!; ***~ konia*** *vulg* jerk off, *Br* wank, *Br* toss off **2.** (*pięścią*) punch **3.** (*o sercu*) pound; ***serce mi waliło*** my heart was pounding; ***walić się*** **1.** (*rozpadać się*) fall apart, crumble **2.** (*zawalać się*) collapse **3.** (*o drzewach*) fall over **4.** (*na sofę, fotel*) collapse; ***walnąć się*** (*uderzyć się*) bash (oneself); ***~ się w głowę*** bash one's head
walizka *f* (*-ki*; *-ki*) suitcase; ***żyć na ~ch*** live out of a suitcase
walizkowy *adj* portable
walka *f* (*-ki*; *-ki*) **1.** fight; ***~ wręcz*** hand-to-hand combat, unarmed combat; ***~ o byt*** struggle for life; ***~ byków*** bullfight; ***~ ze szkodnikami*** pest control **2.** (*o władzę*) struggle (***o*** *A* for) **3.** (*na pięści*) fistfight
walkman *m* (*-na*; *-ny*) Walkman®
walkower: ***wygrać ~em*** win by default
walnąć *v/p* → ***walić***
walnięty *adj infml* nuts, psycho
walny *adj* **1.** *zebranie*: general **2.** *bitwa*: decisive
walonki *pl* (*-nek*) felt boots
walor *m* (*-ru*; *-ry*) **1.** (*wartość*) value; ***~y artystyczne*** (***literackie***) artistic (literary) merit; ***~y smakowe*** (good) taste; ***~ nowości*** novelty value **2.** ***~y*** FIN securities
waluta *f* (*-ty*; *-ty*) currency; ***obca ~*** foreign currency; **walutowy** *adj* **1.** *rynek, rezerwy*: foreign exchange **2.** *kursy*: exchange **3.** *rachunek*: foreign currency **4.** *kryzys*: currency **5.** *fundusz, polityka*: monetary
wał *m* (*-łu*; *-ły*) **1.** (*usypisko*) embankment; ***~ przeciwpowodziowy*** floodbank, levee **2.** TECH shaft; ***~ napędowy*** drive shaft; ***~ korbowy*** crankshaft **3.** ***takiego ~a!*** *vulg* up yours!
wał|ek *m* (*-łka*; *-łki*) **1.** roller; ***~ek do ciasta*** rolling pin; ***~ki tłuszczu*** rolls of fat; ***w kształcie ~ka*** roller-shaped **2.** (*do włosów*) curler, roller **3.** (*podgłówek*) bolster
wałęsa|ć się *v/im* (*-sam*) wander around; ***~jący się pies*** stray dog
wałkonić się *v/im* (*-nię*) loaf around, *infml* bum around; **wałkoń** *m* (*-konia*; *-konie*) loafer
wałkować *v/im* (*-kuję*) **1.** *ciasto*: roll out **2.** ***~ temat*** *Br* labour the point, *Am* labor the point
wałówka *f* (*-ki*; *-ki*) **1.** provisions *pl* **2.** (*do pracy, szkoły*) *Br* packed lunch, *Am* bag lunch
wam *pron* you; ***z ~i*** with you; → ***wy***
wampir *m* (*-ra*; *-ry*) vampire
wandal *m* (*-la*; *-le*) vandal; ***2owie*** HIST Vandals
wanienka *f* (*-ki*; *-ki*) **1.** small bath **2.** (*do kąpania niemowląt*) baby bath
wanilia *f* (*-lii*; *no pl*) vanilla; **waniliowy** *adj* vanilla
wanna *f* (*-ny*; *-ny*) **1.** (*w łazience*) bath (-tub) **2.** (*zbiornik*) tank
wapienn|y *adj* **1.** limestone; ***kamień ~y*** limestone **2.** *skały*: calcareous **3.** *za-*

W

prawa: lime **4.** ***woda ~a*** CHEM limewater
wapień *m* (*-pienia*; *-pienie*) limestone
wapniak *m* (*-ka*; *-ki*) *infml* oldie, fossil
wapnieć ⟨**z-**⟩ (*-nieję*) calcify
wapno *n* (*-na*; *no pl*) **1.** lime **2.** MED calcium
wapń *m* (*-pnia*; *no pl*) CHEM calcium
wara *interj*: ***~ od*** *G* hands off
warcaby *pl* (*-ców*) *Br* draughts, *Am* checkers; ***grać w ~*** play checkers
warchlak *m* (*-ka*; *-ki*) piglet
warchoł *m* (*-ła*; *-ły*) (*awanturnik*) *lit* brawler
warczeć *v/i* ⟨**-rknąć**⟩ (*-czę*) **1.** (*o psie*) growl, snarl **2.** (*o osobie*) snap (**na** *A* at) **3.** (*o maszynie*) whirr
warg|a *f* (*-gi*; *-gi*) lip; ***górna ~a*** upper lip; ***dolna ~a*** lower lip; ***zajęcza ~a*** harelip; ***~i sromowe*** labia
wariacje *pl* (*-ji*) MUS variations
wariacki *adj* crazy; ***w ~m tempie*** at break-neck speed, at break-neck pace; **wariactwo** *n* (*-wa*; *-wa*) **1.** folly **2.** *dated* madness
wariant *m* (*-tu*; *-ty*) version
wariat *m* (*-ta*; *-riaci*), **~ka** *f* (*-ki*; *-ki*) **1.** madman **2.** *fig* lunatic; ***to ~!*** he's crazy!; ***jak ~*** like crazy; ***robić ~a z*** *G* make a fool of
wariatkowo *n* (*-wa*; *no pl*) *infml* nuthouse
wariować ⟨**z-**⟩ (*-riuję*) **1.** go mad; ***~ na punkcie*** *G* be crazy about **2.** (*wygłupiać się*) *infml* fool around
warknąć *v/p* → ***warczeć***
warkocz *m* (*-cza*; *-cze*) **1.** *Br* plait, *Am* braid **2.** *komety*: tail
warkot *m* (*-tu*; *no pl*) whirr; **warkotać** *v/im* (*-koczę*/*-kocę*) whirr
warować *v/im* (*-ruję*) **1.** (*o psie*) lie down **2.** *fig* keep guard
warownia *f* (*-ni*; *-nie*) stronghold; **warowny** *adj* fortified
warstewka *f* (*-ki*; *-ki*) *dim* (thin) layer; **warstwa** *f* (*-wy*; *-wy*) **1.** layer; ***~ ozonowa*** the ozone layer **2.** *farby*: coat **3.** *społeczna*: stratum; **warstwowo** *adv* in layers
Warszawa *f* (*-wy*) Warsaw
warsztat *m* (*-tu*; *-ty*) **1.** workshop; ***~ samochodowy*** garage; ***~ blacharski*** body shop; ***~ pracy*** workplace **2.** ***~y*** (*zajęcia*) workshop **3.** (*techniku*) technique; **warsztatowy** *adj* workshop; ***stół ~*** workbench
wart *adj* worth; ***~ zobaczenia*** worth seeing; ***to nic nie ~e, to śmiechu ~e*** *infml* that's rubbish; ***~ zachodu*** worth the trouble
war|ta *f* (*-ty*; *-ty*) guard; ***stać na ~cie*** be on guard; ***zmiana ~ty*** the changing of the guard; ***~ta honorowa*** *Br* guard of honour, *Am* honor guard
wartki *adj* **1.** *nurt*, *strumień*: rapid **2.** *akcja*: lively
warto *v/irreg* worth; ***nie ~ o tym mówić*** it's not worth talking about; ***czy ~?*** is it worth it?; ***~ było*** it was worth it; ***~ by było założyć firmę*** it would be a good idea to start a company; ***~ dodać, że*** it is worth mentioning that
wartościować *v/im* (*-ciuję*) judge
wartościow|y *adj* **1.** valuable; ***papiery ~e*** FIN securities **2.** *pokarm*: nutritious **3.** *książka*: quality
wartościujący *adj* **1.** evaluative **2.** *sąd*: value
wartoś|ć *f* (*-ści*; *-ści*) **1.** value; ***bez ~ci*** worthless, of no value; ***~ć odżywcza*** nutritional value; ***poczucie własnej ~ci*** self-esteem; ***umowa o ~ci 3 mln dolarów*** a $3 million contract; ***kredyt o ~ci 100 000 zł*** a loan of PLN 100,000 **2.** *artystyczna*: merit, value
wartownia *f* (*-ni*; *-nie*) **1.** (*pomieszczenie*) guardroom **2.** (*budowla*) guardhouse; **wartownik** *m* (*-ka*; *-nicy*) guard
warun|ek *m* (*-nku*; *-nki*) **1.** condition; ***~ki życia*** living conditions; ***pod ~kiem, że*** on condition that, provided that; ***~ki umowy*** terms and conditions of a contract; ***zgodnie z ~kami umowy*** as per the agreement, under the agreement; ***na dogodnych ~kach*** on easy terms; ***pod żadnym ~kiem*** on no account **2.** (*postanowienie*) provision
warunkować *v/im* (*-kuję*) condition
warunkowo *adv* **1.** conditionally **2.** ***zostać zwolnionym ~*** JUR be released on parole, be paroled
warunkow|y *adj* conditional; ***tryb ~y*** GRAM the conditional (mood); ***zdanie ~e*** GRAM conditional clause; ***odruch ~y*** conditional reflex

W

warząchew *f* (*-chwi*; *-chwie*) large wooden spoon
warzelnia *f* (*-ni*; *-nie*): **~ piwa** brew house
warzyć *v/im* (*-rzę*) **1.** *piwo*: brew **2.** *sól*: make; **warzyć się** ⟨**z-**⟩ (*o mleku*) curdle
warzywniak *m* (*-ka*; *-ki*) **1.** (*sklep*) greengrocer's (shop) **2.** (*ogród*) vegetable garden
warzywnictwo *n* (*-wa*; *no pl*) *Br* market gardening, *Am* truck farming; **warzywniczy** *adj uprawy*: *Br* market gardening, *Am* truck farming; **warzywny** *adj* vegetable
warzywo *n* (*-wa*; *-wa*) vegetable
was *pron* you; → **wy**
wasal *m* (*-la*; *-le*) HIST vassal, liege
wasz *poss* **1.** (*przed rzeczownikiem*) your **2.** (*bez rzeczownika*) yours; ***to jest mój namiot, a to ~*** this is my tent and that's yours
waśnie *pl* (*-ni*) discord *sing*, strife *sing*
wat *m* (*-ta*; *-ty*) watt
wat|a *f* (*-ty*; *no pl*) *Br* cotton wool, *Am* cotton; ***~a cukrowa*** *Br* candyfloss, *Am* cotton candy; ***~a szklana*** glass wool; ***miałem nogi jak z ~y*** my legs felt like jelly
wataha *f* (*-hy*; *-hy*) **1.** band, gang **2.** *wilków*: pack
watka *f* (*-ki*; *-ki*) **1.** (*kulista*) *Br* cotton wool ball, *Am* cotton ball **2.** (*spłaszczona*) *Br* cotton wool pad, *Am* cotton pad
watolina *f* (*-ny*; *no pl*) wadding; **watować** ⟨**wy-**⟩ (*-tuję*) wad; **watowany** *adj* wadded
Watykan *m* (*-nu*) the Vatican
wawrzyn *m* (*-nu*; *-ny*) laurel
waza *f* (*-zy*; *-zy*) **1.** ART vase **2.** (*na zupę*) tureen
wazelina *f* (*-ny*; *no pl*) **1.** (*substancja*) vaseline **2.** (*lizus*) *infml* toady; **wazeliniarstwo** *n* (*-wa*; *no pl*) *infml* toadying; **wazeliniarz** *m* (*-rza*; *-rze*) *infml* toady, *Am* apple polisher
wazon *m* (*-nu*; *-ny*) vase
ważka *f* (*-ki*; *-ki*) dragon-fly
ważki *adj* important, weighty
ważniactwo *n* (*-wa*; *no pl*) big-headedness; **ważniak** *m* (*-ka*; *-niacy*/*-ki*) *infml* **1.** (*zarozumialec*) big-head **2.** (*na wysokim stanowisku*) big shot
ważniejsz|y *adj comp* → **ważny** more important; **co ~e** more importantly
ważnoś|ć *f* (*-ści*; *no pl*) **1.** importance **2.** (*aktualność*) validity; ***data ~ci*** *Br* expiry date, *Am* expiration date; ***tracić ~ć*** expire; **ważn|y** *adj* **1.** important **2.** (*aktualny*) valid; ***paszport ~y do 2006 roku*** a passport valid until 2006
ważyć ⟨**z-**⟩ (*-żę*) weigh; **~ *słowa*** weigh one's words; **ważyć się 1.** (*na wadze*) weigh oneself **2.** ***ważą się jego losy*** *fig* his fate is being decided **3.** (*śmieć*) *lit* dare (**na** *A* (to) do s.th.); ***ani mi się waż!*** don't you dare!
wąchać ⟨**po-**⟩ (*-cham*) **1.** smell, sniff; **~ *kwiatki od spodu*** *infml* push up the daisies **2.** (*narkotyzować się*) sniff
wądół *m* (*-dołu*; *-doły*) ravine
wąglik *m* (*-ka*; *-ki*) MED anthrax
wągrowaty *adj cera*, *twarz*: covered with blackheads
wągry *pl* (*-rów*) **1.** blackheads **2.** (*larwy*) bladder worms
wąsacz *m* (*-cza*; *-cze*), **wąsal** *m* (*-la*; *-le*) **1.** *Br* moustached man, *Am* mustached man **2.** (*z długimi*, *podkręconymi wąsami*) mustachioed man
wąsaty *adj* **1.** (*o mężczyźnie*) *Br* moustached, *Am* mustached **2.** *kot*: whiskered
wąsk|i *adj* **1.** narrow; ***~a uliczka*** narrow street; ***~ie grono przyjaciół*** a small circle of friends; ***w ~im zakresie*** to a limited extent **2.** *wargi*: thin **3.** (*obcisły*) tight
wąskotorow|y *adj* narrow-gauge; ***kolej ~a*** narrow-gauge railway
wąsy *pl* (*-sów*) **1.** (*u mężczyzny*) *Br* moustache, *Am* mustache **2.** (*u kota*) whiskers **3.** (*u roślin*) tendrils
wątek *m* (*-tku*; *-tki*) **1.** *rozmowy*, *fabuły*: thread; **zgubić ~** (*oglądając film*) lose the plot **2.** (*myśli*) train; **stracić ~** (*mówiąc*) lose one's train of thought **3.** (*motyw*) motive, theme
wątł|y *adj* **1.** *osoba*, *ciało*, *roślina*: frail **2.** *budowa ciała*: slight; ***~ej budowy*** of slight build **3.** *zdrowie*: fragile, poor; ***~ego zdrowia*** of fragile health **4.** *nadzieja*, *światło*: faint **5.** *konstrukcja*: fragile, flimsy
wątpiący *adj* doubting; **wątpić** ⟨**z-**⟩ (*-pię*) doubt (**w** *A*); **wątpieni|e**:

W

bez ~a without (a) doubt, undoubtedly
wątpliwie *adv* → ***wątpliwy***
wątpliwoś|ć *f* (*-ści*; *-ści*) doubt; ***to nie ulega ~ci*** there is no doubt about it; ***ponad wszelką ~ć*** beyond all doubt; ***podać coś w ~ć*** question s.th., call s.th. into question
wątpliwy *adj* questionable, doubtful
wątroba *f* (*-by*; *-by*) liver; **wątrobianka** *f* (*-ki*; *-ki*) *Br* liver sausage, *Am* liverwurst; **wątróbka** *f* (*-ki*; *-ki*) liver
wąwóz *m* (*-wozu*; *-wozy*) ravine
wąż *m* (*węża*; *węże*) **1.** (*zwierzę*) snake; ***mieć węża w kieszeni*** *fig* be stingy, be tight-fisted **2.** (*przewód*) hose **3.** *samochodów*: string
wbić *v/p* (*wbiję*): ***~ sobie coś do głowy*** get s.th. into one's head; → ***wbijać***
wbiegać ⟨**wbiec**⟩ (*-gam*) run (**do** *G* into); ***~ do pokoju*** run into a room; ***~ po schodach*** run upstairs
wbijać ⟨**wbić**⟩ (*-jam*) **1.** *gwóźdź, hak*: hammer, drive in **2.** *pal*: ram **3.** *klin*: drive **4.** *igłę*: stick **5.** *paznokcie*: dig **6.** *nóż*: plunge **7.** *zęby*: sink **8.** ***~ sobie drzazgę*** get a splinter **9.** ***~ piłkę do bramki*** score a goal **10.** ***~ wzrok w*** *A* fix one's eyes on; ***wbijać się*** (*o gwoździu*) stick in; ***wbiła mu się drzazga*** he got a splinter
wbrew *prep* (*D*) against, contrary to; ***~ jego woli*** against his will; ***~ (wszelkim) oczekiwaniom*** contrary to (all) expectation
wbudowywać ⟨**-dować**⟩ (*-dowuję*) build in; ***~ coś w ścianę*** build s.th. into a wall
wcale *particle*: ***~ nie*** not at all; ***~ nie twierdzę, że*** I don't claim that; ***~ niezły*** quite good; ***~, ~*** not bad at all
wchłaniać ⟨**-łonąć**⟩ (*-niam*) **1.** absorb **2.** *wiedzę*: take in, drink in; ***wchłaniać się*** (*o kremie*) absorb
wchodzić ⟨**wejść**⟩ (*-dzę*) **1.** go, walk (**do** *G* into), enter (**do** *G*); ***proszę wejść!*** come in!; ***~ bez pukania*** come in without knocking; ***~ po schodach*** go upstairs; ***~ po drabinie*** climb a ladder; ***~ w zakręt*** go into a bend; ***~ w kałużę*** step into a puddle; ***~ na ekrany*** be released; ***~ do portu*** call at a port; ***~ w zwyczaj*** become customary; ***~ w kontakt*** come into contact; ***~ do finału*** SPORT reach the final; ***~ w życie*** (*o przepisie*) come into force, come into effect; ***~ w szczegóły*** go into detail(s); ***wchodzę w to!*** *infml* I'm in! **2.** (*mieścić się*) fit (**do** *G* into) **3.** (*w modę*) come (**w** *A* into) **4.** (*na rynek*) enter (**na** *A*)
wciąć *v/p*: ***wcięło go*** *infml* he disappeared; → ***wcinać***
wciągać ⟨**-gnąć**⟩ (*-gam*) **1.** pull (**do** *G* into); ***~ kogoś na listę*** enter s.o.'s name on a list **2.** *brzuch*: pull in **3.** *powietrze*: breathe in, inhale **4.** *flagę*: hang out **5.** *w zasadzkę*: draw (**w** *A* into); ***wciągać się*** get into the swing
wciąż *adv* **1.** (*nadal*) still **2.** (*cały czas*) constantly, again and again
wcielać ⟨**-lić**⟩ (*-lam*) incorporate (**do** *G* into); ***~ coś w życie*** put s.th. into effect; ***~ słowa w czyn*** put words into action; ***~ kogoś do wojska*** enlist s.o.; ***~ się w postać*** *G* (*o aktorze*) portray
wcielenie *n* (*-nia*; *-nia*) embodiment, incarnation
wcielony *adj* incarnate; ***diabeł ~*** the devil incarnate
wcierać ⟨**wetrzeć**⟩ (*-ram*) rub in; ***~ krem w skórę*** rub cream into the skin
wcięcie *n* (*-cia*; *-cia*) **1.** (*w tekście*) indentation **2.** ***~ w talii*** waistline
wcięt|y *adj* **1.** *sukienka*: waisted **2.** ***mieć ~ą talię*** have a slim waist
wcinać ⟨**wciąć**⟩ (*-nam*) *tekst*: indent; ***wcinać się*** (*w rozmowę*) *infml* cut in
wciry: ***dać komuś ~*** *infml* beat s.o. up
wciskać ⟨**-snąć**⟩ (*-kam*) **1.** (*wpychać*) squeeze (in), jam; ***~ komuś coś do ręki*** press s.th. into s.o.'s hand **2.** *towar*: palm off; ***~ komuś wadliwy towar*** palm s.o. with faulty goods **3.** *klawisz*: press **4.** (*naciągać*) pull (**na** *A* over); ***~ czapkę na oczy*** pull one's hat over one's eyes **5.** ***~ komuś ciemnotę, ~ komuś kit*** *infml* bullshit s.o.; ***wciskać się*** **1.** (*wpychać się*) squeeze in, push in; ***~ się do samochodu*** squash into a car **2.** (*zakładać*) get (**w** *A* into), squeeze (**w** *A* into)
wciśnięty *adj* **1.** *rzeczy*: squeezed **2.** *guzik*: pressed **3.** *czapka*: pulled (down)
wczasowicz *m* (*-cza*; *-cze*), **~ka** *f* (*-ki*; *-ki*) *Br* holidaymaker, *Am* vacationer

wczasowy *adj* holiday; ***ośrodek ~*** holiday resort
wczas|y *pl* (*-sów*) *Br* holiday *sing*, *Am* vacation *sing*; ***na ~ach*** on holiday; ***jechać gdzieś na ~y*** go somewhere for one's holiday; ***~y w siodle*** horse riding holiday; ***~y zorganizowane*** package holiday; ***dopłaty do ~ów*** holiday bonus
wczepiać się ⟨***-pić***⟩ (*-piam*) **1.** (*o kocie*) sink its claws (***w*** *A* into) **2.** (*o rzepie*) cling (***w*** *A* to)
wczesno- (*w złożeniach*) early; ***środek ~poronny*** the morning-after pill
wczesny *adj* early
wcześniactwo *n* (*-wa*; *no pl*) prematurity; **wcześniak** *m* (*-ka*; *-ki*) premature baby; ***urodzić się jako ~*** *Am infml* be born a preemie
wcześnie *adv* early; **wcześniejszy** *adj comp* → **wczesny** **1.** earlier **2.** (*poprzedni*) previous
wczoraj *adv* yesterday; **wczorajsz|y** *adj* yesterday, yesterday's; ***~e pieczywo*** yesterday's bread
wczuwać się ⟨***-czuć***⟩ (*-wam*) identify (***w*** *A* with), empathize (***w*** *A* with)
wczytywać ⟨***-tać***⟩ (*-tuję*) INF load, read in; ***wczytywać się*** **1.** (*czytać uważnie*) read carefully (***w*** *A*) **2.** (*o programie, danych*) INF load **3.** (*o danych*) INF be read in
wdawać się ⟨**wdać**⟩ (*wdaję*) **1.** (*brać udział*) get (***w*** *A* into); ***~ w bójkę*** get into a fight; ***nie wdając się w szczegóły*** without going into details; ***~ w złe towarzystwo*** get into bad company, *infml* fall in with a bad crowd **2.** (*w dyskusję*) enter (***w*** *A* into), embark (***w*** *A* on) **3.** ***wdał się w swego ojca*** he takes after his father
wdech *m* (*-chu*; *-chy*) inhalation; ***zrobić ~*** breathe in, inhale
wdepnąć *v/p* (*-nę*) **1.** step (***w*** *A* into); ***~ w gówno*** *vulg fig* get into deep shit **2.** (*wstąpić*) *infml* drop in, come by
wdeptywać ⟨***-tać***⟩ (*-tuję*): ***~ coś w ziemię*** tread s.th. into the ground
wdmuchiwać ⟨***-chnąć***, ***-chać***⟩ (*-chuję*) blow (***w*** *A* into)
wdowa *f* (*-wy*; *-wy*) widow; ***słomiana ~*** grass widow; **wdowi** *adj* widow, widow's; ***~ grosz*** widow's mite; **wdowiec** *m* (*-wca*; *-wcy*) widower; ***słomiany ~*** grass widower; **wdowieństwo** *n* (*-wa*; *no pl*) widowhood
wdrapywać się ⟨***-pać***⟩ (*-puję*) climb (***na*** *A* up), clamber (***na*** *A* up)
wdrażać ⟨***-rożyć***⟩ (*-żam*) **1.** *technologię*, *system*: implement, introduce **2.** (*przyuczać*) train (***do*** *G* to do s.th.); ***wdrażać się*** get used (***do*** *G* to)
wdychać *v/im* (*-cham*) breathe in, inhale
wdzianko *n* (*-ka*; *-ka*) outfit
wdzierać się ⟨**wedrzeć**⟩ (*-ram*) (*wtargnąć*) force one's way (***do*** *G* into); ***wdarli się do miasta*** they invaded the city
wdzięcznoś|ć *f* (*-ści*; *no pl*) gratitude, appreciation; ***mieć dług ~ci wobec*** *G* be indebted to; **wdzięczny** *adj* **1.** grateful; ***byłbym ~ za pomoc*** I'd appreciate some help **2.** (*uroczy*) graceful
wdzięczyć się *v/im* (*-czę*): ***~ do*** *G* flirt with, make eyes at
wdzięk *m* (*-ku*; *no pl*) grace; ***z ~iem*** gracefully, with grace; ***~i kobiece*** female charms
we *prep* (*L*/*A*) in; ***~ Wrocławiu*** in Wrocław; ***~ śnie*** in one's sleep; ***~ krwi*** in blood; → ***w***
według *prep* (*G*) according to; ***~ planu*** according to plan; ***~ mnie*** in my opinion; ***~ alfabetu*** alphabetically
wedrzeć się *v/p* → **wdzierać się**
weekend *m* (*-du*; *-dy*) weekend; **weekendowy** *adj* weekend
wegetacja *f* (*-ji*; *no pl*) **1.** BIOL growth **2.** (*egzystencja*) vegetation
wegetarianin *m* (*-na*; *-ranie*) vegetarian; **wegetarianizm** *m* (*-mu*; *no pl*) vegetarianism; ***przejść na ~*** become a vegetarian, turn vegetarian; **wegetarianka** *f* (*-ki*; *-ki*) (female) vegetarian; **wegetariański** *adj* vegetarian
wegetatywny *adj* vegetative; **wegetować** *v/im* (*-tuję*) (*egzystować*) vegetate
wejrzeni|e: ***miłość od pierwszego ~a*** love at first sight
wejście *n* (*-cia*; *-cia*) **1.** (*do budynku*) entrance **2.** (*wstęp*) entry **3.** INF input; **wejściowy** *adj* **1.** *drzwi*: entrance **2.** *dane*, *sygnał*: input; **wejściówka** *f* (*-ki*; *-ki*) (*bilet*) standing ticket

wejść *v/p* (*wejdę*): **~ komuś w krew** become second nature to s.o.; → **wchodzić**
wek *m* (*-ka*/*-ku*; *-ki*) (preserving) jar; **wekować** ⟨**za-**⟩ (*-kuję*) preserve, put into jars
weksel *m* (*-sla*; *-sle*) FIN bill (of exchange); **~ własny** promissory note; **wekslowy** *adj* bill of exchange
wektor *m* (*-ra*; *-ry*) MATH vector
welon *m* (*-nu*; *-ny*) veil; **~ ślubny** wedding veil
welur *m* (*-ru*; *-ry*) velour
welwet *m* (*-tu*; *-ty*) velveteen
wełna *f* (*-ny*; *-ny*) **1.** wool; **czysta ~** pure wool **2.** (*sierść*) fleece; **wełniany** *adj* *Br* woollen, *Am* woolen; **wełnisty** *adj* woolly
wena *f* (*-ny*; *no pl*) *lit* inspiration
wendeta *f* (*-ty*; *-ty*) vendetta
Wenecja *f* (*-ji*) Venice
weneryczn|y *adj*: **choroba ~a** venereal disease
wentyl *m* (*-la*; *-le*) valve
wentylacja *f* (*-ji*; *no pl*) ventilation; **wentylacyjny** *adj* ventilation; **wentylator** *m* (*-ra*; *-ry*) fan
Wenus *f indecl* ASTR Venus
wepchnąć *v/p* → **wpychać**
weprzeć *v/p* → **wpierać**
weranda *f* (*-dy*; *-dy*) veranda, *Am* porch
werbalny *adj* verbal
werbel *m* (*-bla*; *-ble*) snare drum
werbować ⟨**z-**⟩ (*-buję*) recruit; **werbunek** *m* (*-nku*; *-nki*) recruitment
werdykt *m* (*-tu*; *-ty*) verdict
wermiszel *m* (*-lu*; *no pl*) vermicelli
wermut *m* (*-tu*; *-ty*) vermouth
wernisaż *m* (*-żu*; *-że*) opening
wers *m* (*-su*; *-sy*) *lit* line, verse
wersalka *f* (*-ki*; *-ki*) sofa bed
wersja *f* (*-ji*; *-je*) version; **~ ostateczna** final version
wertepy *pl* (*-pów*) rough terrain
wertować ⟨**prze-**⟩ (*-tuję*) *książkę*: browse through
werw|a *f* (*-wy*; *no pl*) verve; **pełen ~y** full of verve; **z ~ą** with verve
weryfikacja *f* (*-ji*; *-je*) **1.** (*sprawdzenie*) verification **2.** (*sprawdzenie i poprawienie*) review **3.** *osoby*: screening, *Br* vetting; **weryfikować** ⟨**z-**⟩ (*-kuję*) **1.** (*sprawdzać*) verify **2.** (*sprawdzać i poprawiać*) review
werznąć się, **werżnąć się** *v/p* → **wrzynać się**
wesele *n* (*-la*; *-la*) wedding
weselej *comp* → **wesoło**
weselszy *comp* → **wesoły**
wesołek *m* (*-łka*; *-łki*) joker
wesoło *adv* cheerfully, merrily: **było bardzo ~** there was a lot of fun, we had a lot of fun; **wesołość** *f* (*-ści*; *no pl*) cheerfulness
wesoł|y *adj* **1.** cheerful; **~e miasteczko** *Br* funfair, *Am* amusement park; **~ej zabawy!** have fun!; **~ych Świąt! a)** (*Bożego Narodzenia*) Merry Christmas! **b)** (*Wielkanocnych*) Happy Easter! **2.** *kolor*, *muzyka*: lively
wesprzeć *v/p* → **wspierać**
wessać *v/p* → **wsysać**
westchnąć *v/p* → **wzdychać**
westchnienie *n* (*-nia*; *-nia*) sigh
wesz *f* (*wszy*; *wszy*) louse; **złapać wszy** become infested with lice
wet: **oddać ~ za ~** do tit for tat
weteran *m* (*-na*; *-ni*) veteran
weterynaria *f* (*-rii*; *no pl*) veterinary medicine; **weterynarz** *m* (*-rza*; *-rze*) vet, *Am* veterinarian, *Br* veterinary surgeon
wetknąć *v/p* → **wtykać**
weto *n* (*-ta*; *-ta*) veto; **złożyć ~** exercise a veto
wetrzeć *v/p* → **wcierać**
wew. *abbr* (= **numer wewnętrzny**) ext.
wewnątrz I *adv* **1.** inside; **od ~** from the inside; **do ~** inwards **2.** (*w budynku*) indoors **II** *prep* (*G*) inside
wewnętrznie *adv* internally; **wewnętrzny** *adj* **1.** internal; **numer ~** TEL extension number **2.** *kieszeń*, *tor*: inside **3.** *ucho*, *dziedziniec*: inner
wezbrać *v/p* → **wzbierać**
wezbrany *adj* *rzeka*: swollen
wezgłowi|e *n* (*-wia*; *-wia*) *łóżka*: (bed-)head; **u ~a czyjegoś łóżka** at the head of s.o.'s bed
Wezuwiusz *m* (*-sza*) Vesuvius
wezwać *v/p* → **wzywać**
wezwanie *n* (*-nia*; *-nia*) **1.** (*pismo*) summons *sing*; **~ do sądu** summons (to appear in court), *Am* citation; **~ do wojska** call-up papers **2.** (*apel*)

call **3. kościół pod ~m Św. Jana** St John's Church
weżreć się *v/p* → **wżerać się**
węch *m* (*-chu*; *no pl*) (the sense of) smell; **węchowy** *adj* olfactory
wędka *f* (*-ki*; *-ki*) fishing rod, *Am* fishing pole; **wędkarsk|i** *adj* angling, fishing; **sprzęt ~i** fishing tackle; **żyłka ~a** fishing line; **wędkarstwo** *n* (*-wa*; *no pl*) angling, fishing; **wędkarz** *m* (*-rza*; *-rze*) angler
wędlina *f* (*-ny*; *-ny*) cold meat; **półmisek z ~mi** platter of cold cuts (and sausages)
wędrować ⟨**po-**⟩ (*-ruję*) **1.** (*o turyście*) hike **2.** (*podróżować*) travel **3.** (*spacerować*) wander **4.** (*o zwierzętach*) migrate
wędrowiec *m* (*-wca*; *-wcy*) **1.** (*podróżnik*) *Br* traveller, *Am* traveler **2.** (*turysta pieszy*) hiker; **wędrowny** *adj* **1.** *plemię*: nomadic **2.** *ptak*: migratory **3.** *kaznodzieja*, *handlarz*: itinerant **4.** *cyrk*, *teatr*: *Br* travelling, *Am* traveling
wędrówka *f* (*-ki*; *-ki*) **1.** (*wycieczka piesza*) hike **2.** (*podróż*) travel **3.** HIST migration; **~ ludów** migration of peoples
wędzarnia *f* (*-ni*; *-nie*) smokehouse; **wędzić** ⟨**u-**⟩ (*-dzę*) smoke
wędzidło *n* (*-ła*; *-ła*) (horse) bit
wędzisko *n* (*-ka*; *-ka*) rod
wędzonka *f* (*-ki*; *-ki*) smoked bacon; **wędzony** *adj* smoked
węgiel *m* (*-gla*; *-gle*) **1.** coal; **~ kamienny** hard coal; **~ brunatny** brown coal; **~ drzewny** charcoal; **spalić coś na ~** burn s.th. black **2.** CHEM carbon **3.** (*do rysowania*) charcoal
węg|ieł *m* (*-gła*; *-gły*) corner; **zza ~ła** from around the corner
Węgier *m* (*-gra*; *-grzy*), **~ka** *f* (*-ki*; *-ki*) Hungarian
węgierka *f* (*-ki*; *-ki*) (*śliwka*) plum
węgierski *adj* Hungarian
węglan *m* (*-nu*; *-ny*) CHEM carbonate; **węglowodany** *pl* (*-nów*) CHEM carbohydrates; **węglowodór** *m* (*-doru*; *-dory*) CHEM hydrocarbon; **węglowy** *adj* **1.** *górnictwo*, *pył*: coal **2.** *stal*: carbon **3.** *kwas*: carbonic
węgorz *m* (*-rza*; *-rze*) eel
Węgry *pl* (*-gier*) Hungary
węszyć ⟨**wy-**⟩ (*-szę*) **1.** (*o zwierzęciu*) sniff **2.** (*śledzić*) nose around, sniff around
węz|eł *m* (*-zła*; *-zły*) **1.** knot; **zawiązać ~eł** tie a knot **2.** *komunikacyjny*: hub; **~eł kolejowy** rail hub **3.** MATH INF node **4. ~ły chłonne** ANAT lymph glands, lymph nodes
węzełek *m* (*-łka*; *-łki*) **1.** (*supełek*) (small) knot **2.** (*zawiniątko*) bundle
węzłowato *adv*: **krótko i ~** briefly and to the point, in a nutshell
węzłowy *adj* **1.** *zagadnienie*: crucial, key **2.** *stacja*: junction
węże *pl* → **wąż**
wężowaty *adj* **1.** *ruch*: snake-like **2.** *droga*: serpentine
wężowisko *n* (*-ka*; *-ka*) **1.** nest of snakes **2.** (*plątanina*) tangle; **wężownica** *f* (*-cy*; *-ce*) TECH coil; **wężow|y** *adj* **1. ~a skóra** snakeskin **2.** *torebka*: snakeskin **3.** *ruchy*: snake-like
węższy *comp* → **wąski**
wężyk *m* (*-ka*; *-ki*) **1.** (*linia*) wavy line **2.** (*zygzak*) zigzag
WF *abbr m* (*WF-u*; *WF-y*) (=**wychowanie fizyczne**) PE, physical education
wg *abbr* (=**według**) **1.** (*w określonej kolejności*) by; **~ nazw** by name **2.** (*zgodnie z*) according to
wgiąć *v/p* → **wginać**
wgięcie *n* (*-cia*; *-cia*) dent; **wgięty** *adj* dented
wginać ⟨**wgiąć**⟩ (*-nam*) dent; *wginać się* get dented, be dented
wgląd *m* (*-du*; *no pl*) **1.** (*dostęp*) access; **mieć ~ w coś** have the right to inspect s.th.; **do ~u** available (for inspection) **2.** (*zrozumienie*) insight
wgłębiać się ⟨**-bić**⟩ (*-biam*) (*badać*) go (**w** *A* into), delve (**w** *A* into); **wgłębienie** *n* (*-nia*; *-nia*) hollow
wgniatać ⟨**-nieść**⟩ (*-tam*) **1.** (*wginać*) dent **2.** (*naciskać*) press (down); **wgniatać się** (*o błotniku*) get dented, be dented; **wgniecenie** *n* (*-nia*; *-nia*) (*w błotniku*) dent
wgryzać się ⟨**-ryźć się**⟩ (*-zam*) **1.** (*w jabłko*) bite (**w** *A* into) **2.** (*wżerać się*) eat (**w** *A* into) **3.** (*badać*) go (**w** *A* into), look (**w** *A* into)
wiać *v/im* (*wieję*) **1.** blow; **mocno wieje** it's very windy; **wieje** (*o przeciągu*) it's

draughty **2.** (*uciekać*) *infml* run away, bolt
wiaderko *n* (*-ka*; *-ka*) *dim* (small) bucket
wiadomo *v/irreg* it's a known fact, everybody knows; ***nie ~*** nobody knows; ***czy ~ coś o nim?*** is there any information about him?, has there been any news of him?; ***było ~, że*** everybody knew that; ***nic mi o tym nie ~*** I know nothing about it; ***nigdy nie ~*** you never know; ***jak ~*** as everybody knows; ***powszechnie ~, że*** it is common knowledge that; ***nie ~ kiedy*** nobody knows when; ***o ile mi ~*** as far as I know; ***wszystkim było ~, że*** everybody knew that
wiadomoś|ć *f* (*-ści*; *-ści*) (piece of) news *sing*; ***~ci*** news; ***podać coś do publicznej ~ci*** make s.th. public; ***przyjąć coś do ~ci*** take note of s.th.; ***zostawić komuś ~ć*** leave s.o. a message
wiadom|y *adj* known; ***z ~ych powodów*** for obvious reasons; ***~a rzecz!*** sure!
wiadro *n* (*-ra*; *-ra*) bucket; ***~ wody*** bucket of water; ***~ na śmieci*** *Br* litter bin, *Am* trash can
wianek *m* (*-nka*; *-nki*) **1.** (*na głowie*) garland **2.** *czosnku*, *grzybów*: string; **wianuszek** *m* (*-szka*; *-szki*) *dim* (little) garland
wiar|a *f* (*-ry*; *no pl*) faith; ***~a w siebie*** self-confidence; ***nie do ~y*** unbelievable; ***w dobrej wierze*** in good faith; ***w złej wierze*** in bad faith; ***dawać czemuś ~ę*** believe s.th.; ***dochować komuś ~y*** remain faithful to s.o.; ***przyjmować coś na ~ę*** take s.th. on trust
wiarołomny *adj lit* faithless, unfaithful **wiarołomstwo** *n* (*-wa*; *-wa*) *lit* faithlessness
wiarus *m* (*-sa*; *-sy*) old comrade
wiarygodność *f* (*-ści*; *no pl*) credibility, reliability; **wiarygodny** *adj* credible, reliable
wiata *f* (*-ty*; *-ty*) *tramwajowa*: shelter
wiaterek *m* (*-rku*; *-rki*) (gentle) breeze
wiatr *m* (*-ru*; *-ry*) wind; ***na wietrze*** in the wind; ***pod ~*** against the wind, upwind; ***z ~em*** with the wind, downwind; ***~ od morza*** onshore wind; ***~ w plecy*** tailwind; ***pomyślne ~y*** *fig* fair winds; ***rozpędzić coś na cztery ~y*** chase s.th. away; ***być jak chorągiewka na wietrze*** be as changeable as a weathercock
wiatraczek *m* (*-czka*; *-czki*) fan; **wiatrak** *m* (*-ka*; *-ki*) **1.** (*młyn*) windmill; ***walczyć z ~ami*** tilt at windmills **2.** TECH fan
wiatropylny *adj* wind-pollinated
wiatrówka *f* (*-ki*; *-ki*) **1.** (*kurtka*) *Br* windcheater, *Am* windbreaker **2.** (*broń*) air gun, air rifle
wiąz *m* (*-zu*; *-zy*) elm
wiązać ⟨**z-**, **za-**, **po-**⟩ (*wiążę*) **I** *v/t* **1.** (*przywiązywać*) tie **2.** (*związywać*) tie up; ***~ jeńców*** tie up one's captives; ***wiązać coś w snopy*** bind s.th. into sheaves; ***~ buty*** lace up one's shoes **3.** (*łączyć*) combine (***coś z*** *I* s.th. with); ***~ nadzieje z*** *I* pin one's hopes on; ***ledwo ~ koniec z końcem*** hardly make ends meet **4.** (*kojarzyć*) associate (**z** *I* with) **II** *v/i* (*twardnieć*) set; ***wiązać się*** **1.** (*pociągać za sobą*) involve (**z** *I*) **2.** (*tworzyć związek*) become involved (**z** *I* with), get into a relationship (**z** *I* with); ***z nikim się nie ~*** not get involved with anybody **3.** CHEM bind; ***atomy węgla wiążą się z tlenem*** carbon atoms bind with oxygen
wiązanie *n* (*-nia*; *-nia*) **1.** SPORT (ski) binding **2.** CHEM bond **3.** BUILD truss; **wiązanka** *f* (*-ki*; *-ki*) **1.** *kwiatów*: bouquet **2.** MUS medley
wiązan|y *adj* **1.** *buty*: lace-up **2.** ***sprzedaż ~a*** hand package deal **3.** ***mowa ~a*** poetry
wiązka *f* (*-ki*; *-ki*) **1.** bundle **2.** *światła*: light beam
wiążący *adj decyzja*, *umowa*: binding
wibracja *f* (*-ji*; *-je*) vibration; **wibrator** *m* (*-ra*; *-ry*) vibrator; **wibrować** *v/im* (*-ruję*) vibrate
wice- (*w złożeniach*) vice; ***~prezes*** vice-chairman
wiceadmirał *m* (*-ła*; *-łowie*) vice-admiral; **wicedyrektor** *m* (*-ra*; *-rzy*) deputy director, deputy head; **wiceminister** *m* (*-tra*; *-trowie*) deputy minister
wicemistrz *m* (*-rza*; *-rzowie*), **~yni** *f* (*ni*; *nie*) SPORT runner-up, vice-champion

wicepremier *m* (*-ra*; *-rzy*) deputy prime minister; **wiceprezydent** *m* (*-ta*; *-nci*) **1.** (*państwa*) vice-president **2.** (*miasta*) deputy mayor
wichrzyciel *m* (*-la*; *-le*) troublemaker; **wichrzycielski** *adj* troublemaking, incendiary; **wichrzycielstwo** *n* (*-wa*; *no pl*) troublemaking, incendiarism
wichrzyć ⟨**z-**⟩ (*-rzę*) **1.** (*podburzać*) stir up trouble **2.** *włosy*: ruffle
wichura *f* (*-ry*; *-ry*) gale, storm wind
wić[1] ⟨**u-**⟩ (*wiję*) **1.** *wianek*: weave **2.** *gniazdo*: build; ***wić się*** **1.** (*o żmii*) slither **2.** (*o drodze*) meander, wind **3.** (*o włosach*) wave **4.** (*o osobie*) writhe: ***~ się z bólu*** writhe with pain; ***~ się jak piskorz*** *fig* wriggle like an eel
wić[2] *f* (*wici*; *wici*) *BIOL* flagellum
widać *v/irreg*: ***było ~ gwiazdy na niebie*** there were stars in the sky; ***ledwo było ją ~*** you could hardly see her, she was hardly visible; ***nic nie ~*** you can't see anything; ***jak ~*** as you can see; ***nie ~ końca*** there's still no end in sight; ***~ jej stanik*** her bra is showing; ***~ było po nim zdenerwowanie*** his nervousness showed; ***~ był zmęczony*** he must have been tired
widelec *m* (*-lca*; *-lce*) fork; **widelczyk** *m* (*-ka*; *-ki*) (small) fork
widełki *pl* (*-łek*) **1.** *TECH* fork **2.** *telefonu*: cradle **3.** ***~ stawek płacowych*** wage differentials
wideo I *n indecl* **1.** video **2.** (*odtwarzacz*) VCR, *Br* video **II** *adj* video; ***film ~*** video; ***wypożyczalnia kaset ~*** video rental, video shop
wideokaseta *f* (*-ty*; *-ty*) video cassette, videotape; **wideoklip** *m* (*-pu*; *-py*) videoclip; **wideoteka** *f* (*-ki*; *-ki*) video library
widłak *m* (*-ka*; *-ki*) (*roślina*) clubmoss, lycopod
widły *pl* (*-deł*) pitchfork *sing*; ***robić z igły ~*** make a mountain out of a molehill
widmo *n* (*-ma*; *-ma*) **1.** (*zjawa*) phantom, *Br* spectre, *Am* specter; ***~ głodu*** the spectre of hunger; ***~ wojny*** the spectre of war **2.** *PHYS* spectrum; **widmowo** *adv* ghostly; **widmowy** *adj* **1.** ghostly **2.** *analiza*: spectral
widnieć *v/im* (*-nieję*) **1.** (*być widocznym*) be visible; ***widnieje napis*** there is an inscription **2.** (*świtać*) dawn
widno *adv*: ***jest ~*** it's light
widnokr|ąg *m* (*-kręgu*; *no pl*) horizon; ***na ~ęgu*** on the horizon; **widny** *adj dzień*, *pokój*: bright, light
widocznie *adv* apparently, clearly
widoczność *f* (*-ści*; *no pl*) visibility; **widoczny** *adj* **1.** visible; ***~ gołym okiem*** visible to the naked eye **2.** (*wyraźny*) clear, noticeable
widok *m* (*-ku*; *-ki*) **1.** (*krajobraz*) view (***na*** *A* of) **2.** *osoby*, *rzeczy*: sight; ***~i*** (*perspektywy*) prospects (***na*** *A* for); ***z ~iem na morze*** with a view of the sea; ***mieć coś na ~u*** have s.th. in view, have one's eye on s.th.
widokowy *adj taras*, *wieża*: observation; **widokówka** *f* (*-ki*; *-ki*) postcard
widomy *adj lit* **1.** (*widoczny*) visible; ***~ znak*** visible sign **2.** (*oczywisty*) evident; **widowisko** *n* (*-ka*; *-ka*) (*impreza*) show, spectacle; ***robić z siebie ~*** make a spectacle of oneself
widownia *f* (*-ni*; *-nie*) **1.** (*miejsca*) seats, audience **2.** (*oglądający*) audience
widywać *v/im* (*-duję*) see occasionally; ***~ często*** see often; ***widywać się*** see each other; ***~ się często*** meet each other very often
widz *m* (*-dza*; *-dzowie*) **1.** (*gap*) onlooker, bystander **2.** (*telewizyjny*, *kinowy*) viewer **3.** (*w teatrze*, *na stadionie*) spectator
widzeni|e *n* (*-nia*; *-nia*) **1.** (*wizja*) vision; ***znać kogoś z ~a*** know s.o. by sight; ***do ~a!*** good bye! **2.** (*we śnie*) dream, hallucination **3.** (*w więzieniu*) visit; ***zezwolenie na ~e*** visit permit
widziadła *pl* (*-deł*) **1.** (*zjawy*) apparitions **2.** (*koszmary*) nightmares
widzialność *f* (*-ści*; *no pl*) visibility; **widzialny** *adj* visible; **widziany** *adj*: ***mile ~*** welcome; ***źle ~*** unwelcome
widzieć *v/im* (*-dzę*) see; ***widzę ją*** I can see her; ***źle ~*** have poor sight; ***widzę to inaczej*** I see it differently; ***kogo widzę!*** is it you I see?; ***a widzisz!*** you see!; ***widział to kto!*** that's unbelievable!; ***nie ~ dalej niż czubek własnego nosa*** not see beyond the end of one's nose; ***widzieć się*** see oneself
widzimisię *n indecl* whim

wiec *m* (*-cu*; *-ce*) rally
wiecha *f* (*-chy*; *-chy*) *słomy*: bunch
wieczerza *f* (*-rzy*; *-rze*): ***~ wigilijna*** Christmas Eve dinner; ***Ostatnia ~*** the Last Supper
wieczko *n* (*-czka*; *-czka*) (*puderniczki*, *szkatułki*) lid, top
wieczność *f* (*-ści*; *no pl*) eternity; **wieczn|y** *adj* **1.** (*bez końca*) eternal; ***życie ~e*** eternal life; ***po ~e czasy*** *lit* forever; ***~e pióro*** fountain pen **2.** (*ciągły*) endless; ***~y student*** *fig* eternal student
wieczor|ek *m* (*-rku*; *-rki*) evening, soirée; ***~kiem*** in the evening; ***~ek zapoznawczy*** ice-breaking event, ice-breaking party
wieczorem → ***wieczór***
wieczorny *adj* evening; **wieczorow|y** *adj strój*, *szkoła*: evening; ***~ą porą*** in the evening
wieczorówka *f* (*-ki*; *-ki*) *infml* evening classes, *dated* night school
wiecz|ór *m* (*-czoru*; *-czory*) evening, night; ***dobry ~ór!*** good evening!; ***~orem*** in the evening; ***jutro ~orem*** tomorrow evening; ***pod ~ór*** towards the evening; ***co ~ór*** every evening; ***od rana do ~ora*** from morning till evening; ***~ór poetycki*** poetry reading; ***~ór kawalerski*** *Br* stag party, *Am* bachelor party; ***miłego ~oru!*** have a nice evening!
wieczyst|y *adj* **1.** *lit* eternal, perpetual **2.** ***dzierżawa ~a*** ECON perpetual usufruct; ***księga ~a*** ECON the land and mortgage register
Wiedeń *m* (*-dnia*) Vienna
wiedeński *adj* Viennese
wiedz|a *f* (*-dzy*; *no pl*) knowledge; ***~a fachowa*** expert knowledge, expertise; ***bez jego ~y*** without his knowledge, behind his back; ***za jego ~ą*** with his knowledge
wiedzieć *v/im* (*wiem*) know (***o*** *L* about); ***o ile wiem*** as far as I know; ***kto wie*** who knows; ***nie chcieć nic ~*** not want to know anything; ***wiesz co?*** you know what?; ***bo ja wiem*** well, I don't know; ***skąd wiesz?*** how do you know?; ***nie ~ czemu*** *lit* God only knows why; ***cholera wie*** who the hell knows
wiedźma *f* (*-my*; *-my*) witch
wiejski *adj* **1.** *życie*, *powietrze*: country, countryside **2.** *okolica*, *młodzież*, *społeczność*: rural **3.** *kościół*: village **4.** *chleb*: farmhouse
wiek *m* (*-ku*; *-ki*) **1.** age; ***w ~u dwudziestu lat*** at the age of twenty; ***osoba w średnim ~u*** a middle-aged person; ***dzieci w ~u szkolnym*** school-age children, children of school age; ***osoby w ~u emerytalnym*** people of retirement age, people of pensionable age; ***~ produkcyjny*** working age; ***on jest w moim ~u*** he is my age; ***z ~iem*** with age; ***w kwiecie ~u*** *lit* in one's prime **2.** (*stulecie*) century; ***~i*** centuries; ***~i średnie*** the Middle Ages; ***na ~i*** for centuries; ***od ~ów*** for centuries
wieko *n* (*-ka*; *-ka*) lid
wiekopomny *adj dzieło*: immortal; **wiekowo** *adv*: ***grupa mieszana ~*** a mixed-age group; ***wyglądać ~*** look old, look ancient; **wiekowy** *adj* **1.** ancient, old **2.** *grupa*: age
wiekuisty *adj* eternal
wielbiciel *m* (*-la*; *-le*), **~ka** (*-ki*; *-ki*) **1.** (*adorator*) admirer **2.** *talentu*, *twórczości*: enthusiast **3.** *muzyki*: lover
wielbić *v/im* (*-bię*) *lit* **1.** (*uwielbiać*) adore **2.** (*oddawać cześć*) worship
wielbłąd *m* (*-da*; *-dy*) camel; **wielbłądzi** *adj*: ***~a wełna*** camel hair, camel; ***płaszcz z ~ej wełny*** camel-hair coat
wielce *adv lit* greatly
wielcy → ***wielki***
wiel|e **I** *pron* **1.** a lot of, a great deal of; ***~e czasu*** a lot of time **2.** (*z policzalnymi*) many; ***z ~u powodów*** for many reasons **3.** (*z niepoliczalnymi*) much **II** *adv* a lot, much; ***mieć ~e wspólnego z*** *I* have a lot in common with; ***mieć ~e do powiedzenia*** have a lot to say; ***o ~e za dużo*** far too much; ***o ~e za wcześnie*** much too early; ***tego już za ~e!*** this is enough!
wielekroć *pron lit* many a time
wielgachny *adj infml* whopping, huge
Wielkanoc *f* (*-cy*/*-kiejnocy*; *-ce*) Easter; ***na ~*** at Easter; ***kartka na ~*** Easter card; **wielkanocn|y** *adj* Easter; ***życzenia ~e*** Easter greetings
wielk|i *adj* **1.** great; ***~ie litery*** capital letters; ***~i palec*** big toe; ***~a woda*** flood; ***2i Tydzień*** Easter Week, Passion

Week; **~i Piątek** Good Friday; **Aleksander ~i** Alexander the Great; **~a Brytania** Great Britain **2.** (*bardzo duży*) huge, great

wielkoduszny *adj* magnanimous; **wielkolud** *m* (*-da*; *-dy*) giant; **wielkomiejski** *adj* big-city, metropolitan; **wielkomocarstwowy** *adj* imperialistic; **wielkopański** *adj* lordly; **wielkopłytowy** *adj* prefab concrete

Wielkopolska *f* (*-ki*) Great Poland

wielkoś|ć *f* (*-ści*; *-ści*) **1.** (*rozmiar*) size; ***jednakowej ~ci*** of the same size **2.** MATH quantity **3.** *człowieka*: greatness **4.** (*ogrom*) enormity

wielkoświatowy *adj* refined; ***~ człowiek*** a man of the world

wieloaspektowy *adj* multifaceted, many-sided; **wielobarwny** *adj Br* colourful, *Am* colorful, *Br* multicoloured, *Am* multicolored; **wielobój** *m* (*-boju*; *-boje*) multi-discipline event; **wieloczęściowy** *adj* multipartite

wielodniowy *adj* of many days; **wielodzietny** *adj* large, with many children; **wielofunkcyjny** *adj* multifunctional, multipurpose

wielojęzyczny *adj* multilingual; **wielokąt** *m* (*-ta*; *-ty*) polygon; **wielokomórkowy** *adj* multicellular, metazoan; **wielokropek** *m* (*-pka*; *-pki*) ellipsis, suspension points

wielokrotnie *adv* repeatedly; **wielokrotny** *adj* **1.** *próby*: repeated **2.** *morderca*, *gwałciciel*: serial; ***~ przestępca*** habitual offender

wieloletni *adj* **1.** of many years **2.** ***~e badania*** many years of research **3.** *przyjaźń*, *związek*: long-standing **4.** *roślina*: perennial

wielomilionowy *adj* multi-million; **wielonarodowy** *adj państwo*: multinational; **wieloosobowy** *adj pokój*: shared; **wielopartyjny** *adj* multiparty; **wielopasmowy** *adj droga*: multilane; **wielopiętrowy** *adj* multi-storey

wielopłaszczyznowy *adj* many-sided, multifaceted, complex; **wielopostaciowy** *adj* polymorphous; **wielorako** *adv* in many ways; **wieloraki** *adj* multiple

wieloryb *m* (*-ba*; *-by*) whale; **wielorybi** *adj* whale; **wielorybnictwo** *n* (*-wa*; *no pl*) whaling; **wielorybniczy** *adj* whaling; ***statek ~*** whaling ship, whaler; **wielorybnik** *m* (*-ka*; *-nicy*) whaler

wielostopniowy *adj* multistage; **wielostronny** *adj* **1.** *analiza*: multifaceted **2.** *zainteresowania*: multiple **3.** *umowa*: multilateral; **wielościan** *m* (*-nu*; *-ny*) polyhedron; **wielość** *f* (*-ści*; *no pl*) multitude

wielotomowy *adj* multi-volume; **wielotonowy** *adj* of many tons, multitonne; **wielotysięczny** *adj tłum*: of many thousands; **wielowarstwowy** *adj* **1.** multilayered **2.** *fig* multifaceted; **wielowiekowy** *adj* centuries-old, of many centuries

wielowymiarowy *adj* multidimensional; **wieloznaczność** *f* (*-ści*; *no pl*) ambiguity; **wieloznaczny** *adj* ambiguous; **wielożeństwo** *n* (*-wa*; *no pl*) polygamy

wielu → ***wiele***

wieniec *m* (*wieńca*; *wieńce*) wreath

wieńcow|y *adj* coronary; ***naczynia ~e*** coronary arteries; ***choroba ~a*** angina pectoris

wieńczyć ⟨**z-**⟩ (*-czę*) crown

wieprz *m* (*-rza*; *-rze*) porker, *Am* hog; **wieprzowina** *f* (*-ny*; *no pl*) pork; **wieprzowy** *adj* pork

wiercenia *pl* (*-ceń*) drillings; ***~ próbne*** test drillings

wiercić ⟨**wy-**⟩ (*-cę*) drill, bore; ***~ komuś dziurę w brzuchu*** pester s.o.; ***wiercić się*** fidget

wiercipięta *f/m* (*-ty*; *-ty*) fidget

wiernopoddańczy *adj* servile

wierność *f* (*-ści*; *no pl*) fidelity, faithfulness; ***wysoka ~ odtwarzania*** high fidelity

wiern|y *adj* **1.** *sługa*, *kopia*: faithful **2.** *kopia*: accurate **3.** ***~i*** REL believers; (*zgromadzeni*) congregation

wiersz *m* (*-sza*; *-sze*) **1.** (*utwór*) poem; ***pisać ~e*** write poems; ***~e dla dzieci*** children's poems **2.** (*wers*) line; ***pisać od nowego ~a*** start a new line; ***między ~ami*** *fig* between the lines

wierszokleta *m* (*-ty*; *-leci*) rhymester

wierszówka *f* (*-ki*; *-ki*) linage

wiertarka *f* (*-ki*; *-ki*) drill; **wiertło** *n* (*-ła*; *-ła*) drill bit; **wiertnicz|y** *adj* drilling; ***platforma ~a*** drilling platform, drilling rig, oil rig; ***otwór ~y*** bore, borehole; ***wieża ~a*** derrick

wierutny *adj lit* **1.** *bzdura*: utter **2.** *kłamstwo*: outright
wierzący I *adj* believing **II** *m* (*-cego*; *-cy*), **-ca** *f* (*-cej*; *-ce*) believer
wierzba *f* (*-by*; *-by*) willow; **~ płacząca** weeping willow
wierzch *m* (*-chu*; *-chy*) **1.** (*górna część*) top; **na ~u** on top; **na ~** on top: **jechać ~em** ride on horseback; **prawda wyjdzie na ~** the truth will come out **2.** (*zewnętrzna część*) the outside; **~ dłoni** the back of the hand; **założyć coś na ~** put s.th. on top; **oczy wyszły mu na ~** his eyes popped out (of his head)
wierzchni *adj* outer, top; **~a warstwa** outer coat; **~e okrycie** outerwear
wierzchołek *m* (*-łka*; *-łki*) **1.** *góry*: summit, peak **2.** *drzewa*: top **3.** *MATH* vertex; **wierzchowiec** *m* (*-wca*; *-wce*) saddle horse, hack
wierzenia *pl* (*-rzeń*) beliefs; **~ ludowe** folk beliefs
wierzgać 〈**-gnąć**〉 (*-gam*) (*o koniu*) kick, buck
wierzyciel *m* (*-la*; *-le*) creditor
wierzyć 〈**u-**〉 (*-rzę*) **I** *v/i* believe (**w** *A* in, **że** that) **II** *v/t* believe; **~ komuś na słowo** take s.o.'s word for it; **nie ~ swoim oczom** not believe one's eyes; **~ się nie chce** this is unbelievable
wierzytelność *f* (*-ści*; *-ści*) liability, debt
wieszać 〈**powiesić**〉 (*-szam*) hang (**na** *L* on); **powiesiła obrazek na ścianie** she hung a picture on the wall; **powieszono go o świcie** he was hanged at dawn; **~ psy na kimś** badmouth s.o., fiercely criticize s.o.; **wieszać się 1.** hang oneself (**na** *L* on) **2.** (*o komputerze*) lock up
wieszak *m* (*-ka*; *-ki*) **1.** (*ramiączko*) (coat) hanger **2.** (*stojący*) coat stand **3.** (*hak*) (coat) hook; **powiesić płaszcz na ~u** hang a coat up (on a hook) **4.** (*kołek*) peg **5. ~ na ręczniki** towel rail
wieszcz *m* (*-cza*; *-cze*) *lit* **1.** (*wróżbita*) seer, prophet **2.** (*poeta*) bard; **wieszczka** *f* (*-ki*; *-ki*) prophetess; **wieszczy** *adj* prophetic
wieś *f* (*wsi*; *wsie*) **1.** (*miejscowość*) village; **we wsi** in a village **2.** (*teren poza miastem*) the country(side); **na wsi** in the country(side); **pojechać na ~** go to the country(side); **życie na wsi** life in the country(side); **~ zabita dechami** backwater village, the backwoods
wieś|ć[1] *f* (*-ści*; *-ści*) **1.** news *sing*; **przepaść bez ~ci** vanish without a trace **2.** (*plotka*) *Br* rumour, *Am* rumor
wieść[2] 〈**po-**〉 (*wiodę*) *lit* **1.** (*prowadzić*) lead; **~ spokojne życie** live a peaceful life **2.** *spór*: have, be involved in, be in; **~ spór z** *I* have a dispute with, be in dispute with; **wieść się**: **wiedzie im się dobrze a)** (*odnoszą sukcesy*) they're doing well **b)** (*są w dobrej sytuacji finansowej*) they're well off; **jak im się wiedzie?** how are they doing?; **nie wiodło mu się w interesach** his business wasn't doing well
wieśniak *m* (*-ka*; *-niacy*), **-niaczka** *f* (*-ki*; *-ki*) **1.** (*mieszkaniec wsi*) villager **2.** (*chłop*) peasant **3.** (*prostak*) country bumpkin, *Am* hick
wietrzeć 〈**z-**〉 (*-rzeję*) **1.** *GEOL* erode, weather **2.** (*o perfumach*) lose its fragrance
wietrzenie *n* (*-nia*; *-nia*) **1.** *mieszkania*, *pościeli*: airing **2.** *GEOL* erosion
wietrzn|y *adj* **1.** windy **2. ospa ~a** chickenpox
wietrzyć 〈**wy-**, **z-**〉 (*-rzę*) **1.** *pokój*, *pościel*: air **2. ~ podstęp** smell a rat; **wietrzyć się** be aired, air
wietrzyk *m* (*-ka*; *-ki*) breeze
wiewiórka *f* (*-ki*; *-ki*) squirrel
wieźć *v/im* (*wiozę*) **1.** carry **2.** (*transportować*) transport
wieża *f* (*-ży*; *-że*) **1.** tower; **~ kościelna** church tower, steeple; **~ ciśnień** water tower; **~ wiertnicza** drilling rig, derrick; **~ artyleryjska** turret; **~ obserwacyjna** watchtower; **Ꞩ Babel** the Tower of Babel; **~ Eiffla** the Eiffel tower; **krzywa ~ w Pizie** the leaning tower of Pisa; **bliźniacze wieże Światowego Centrum Handlowego** the twin towers of the World Trade Center; **~ z kości słoniowej** *fig* ivory tower **2.** *MUS* (stereo) system **3.** (*w szachach*) rook **4.** (*do skoków do wody*) diving platform **5.** *INF* tower case
wieżowiec *m* (*-wca*; *-wce*) **1.** tower block, high-rise **2.** (*drapacz chmur*) skyscraper; **wieżyczka** *f* (*-ki*; *-ki*) *dim* turret

W

więc **I** *conj* so; ***poczuła się senna, ~ poszła spać*** she felt sleepy, so she went to bed **II** *particle* so; (***a***) **~** so, therefore; (***no***) ***~?*** so?; ***tak ~*** therefore

więcej *adv comp* → ***dużo*** more; ***co ~*** what is more; ***coraz ~*** more and more; ***nic ~*** nothing more, nothing else; ***nigdy ~*** never again; ***mniej ~*** about, more or less

więdnąć ⟨***z-***, ***przy-***⟩ (*-nę*) **1.** wilt, wither **2.** (*o urodzie*) fade

większoś|ć *f* (*-ści*; *no pl*) majority; ***~ć ludzi*** most people; ***w ~ci przypadków*** in most cases, in the majority of cases; ***być w ~ci*** be in the majority; ***~cią głosów*** by a majority of votes; ***bezwzględna ~ć*** absolute majority; ***kwalifikowana ~ć*** qualified majority

większ|y *adj comp* → ***duży*** **1.** bigger, larger; ***~y od*** *G*, ***~y niż*** *N* bigger than, larger than; ***~a część*** majority, bigger part **2.** *zakupy*, *wydatki*: major

więzić ⟨***u-***⟩ (*więżę*) hold prisoner, keep in prison

więzieni|e *n* (*-nia*; *-nia*) **1.** (*zakład karny*) prison **2.** (*kara*) imprisonment; ***zostać skazanym na karę dożywotniego ~a*** be sentenced to life imprisonment

więziennictwo *n* (*-wa*; *no pl*) the prison system; **więzienny** *adj* prison; ***strój ~*** prison uniform

więzień *m* (*więźnia*; *więźniowie*) inmate, prisoner; ***~ polityczny*** political prisoner, political detainee; ***~ obozu koncentracyjnego*** concentration camp prisoner

więznąć ⟨***u-***⟩ (*-nę*) get stuck; ***głos wiązł mu w gardle*** words stuck in his throat

więzy *pl* (*-zów*) **1.** *fig* ties, bonds; ***~ rodzinne*** family ties **2.** (*pęta*) fetters, chains

więź *f* (*więzi*; *więzi*) *emocjonalna*, *społeczna*: bond

więźniarka *f* (*-ki*; *-ki*) **1.** (*w zakładzie karnym*) prisoner, inmate **2.** (*w obozie*) prisoner; ***~ obozu koncentracyjnego*** concentration camp prisoner

wigilia *f* (*-lii*; *-lie*) (*przeddzień*) eve; ***Ꞩ*** (***Bożego Narodzenia***) Christmas Eve

wigilijny *adj* Christmas Eve; ***wieczór ~*** Christmas Eve

wigor *m* (*-ru*; *no pl*) *Br* vigour, *Am* vigor; ***pełen ~u*** full of vigour

wikariusz *m* (*-sza*; *-sze*) (*w kościele katolickim*) curate

wiklina *f* (*-ny*; *no pl*) **1.** (*wierzba*) (purple) osier **2.** (*surowiec*) wicker **3.** (*wyroby*) wickerwork; **wiklinow|y** *adj* wicker; ***kosz ~y*** wicker basket; ***wyroby ~e*** wickerwork

wikłać ⟨***za-***⟩ (*-łam*) (*wplątywać*) entangle, *lit* embroil; ***wikłać się*** **1.** ⟨***u-***⟩ (*wplątać się*) become entangled, *lit* become embroiled **2.** (*komplikować się*) become tangled

wikt *m* (*-tu*; *no pl*) board

wilczek *m* (*-czka*; *-czki*) **1.** (*wilk*) wolf cub **2.** (*pies*) Alsatian pup; **wilczur** *m* (*-ra*; *-ry*) *infml* German shepherd, Alsatian

wilcz|y *adj* lupine; ***mieć ~y apetyt*** eat like a horse; ***~a jagoda*** belladonna, deadly nightshade; **wilczyca** *f* (*-cy*; *-ce*) (*samica wilka*) she-wolf

wilga *f* (*-gi*; *-gi*) golden oriole

wilgoć *f* (*-goci*; *no pl*) **1.** (*w ścianach*, *piwnicy*) dampness, *Br* damp **2.** (*w powietrzu*, *ziemi*) moisture; **wilgotnawy** *adj* *włosy*, *ściereczka*: dampish, slightly wet

wilgotnieć ⟨***z-***⟩ (*-nieję*) get wet, get damp; **wilgotno** *adv* wet, damp; **wilgotność** *f* (*-ści*; *no pl*) **1.** moisture **2.** *powietrza*: humidity; **wilgotny** *adj* **1.** *ubranie*, *szmatka*: damp, wet **2.** *pokój*: damp **3.** *powietrze*: humid **4.** *gleba*: moist

wilk *m* (*-ka*; *-ki*) **1.** wolf; ***być głodnym jak ~*** be starving, be (as) hungry as a horse; ***~ w owczej skórze*** a wolf in sheep's clothing; ***patrzeć na kogoś ~iem*** glower at s.o.; ***o ~u mowa*** speak of the devil; ***nie wywołuj ~a z lasu*** let sleeping dogs lie; ***~ morski*** old dog **2.** (*owczarek*) German shepherd, *Br* Alsatian

wilkołak *m* (*-ka*; *-ki*) werewolf

willa *f* (*-li*; *-le*) villa, detached house; **willow|y** *adj*: ***dzielnica ~a*** residental district

win|a *f* (*-ny*; *-ny*) fault, guilt, blame; ***to jego ~a*** it's his fault; ***to nie twoja ~a*** it's not your fault; ***~ę ponoszą organizatorzy*** the fault is with the organizers; ***ponosić ~ę za*** *A* be to blame for; ***z własnej ~y*** through one's own fault; ***poczuwać się do ~y*** feel guilty;

W

poczucie ~y a sense of guilt; ***dowieść czyjejś ~y*** prove s.o.'s guilt; ***przyznawać się do ~y*** **a)** admit one's guilt **b)** (*w sądzie*) plead guilty; ***zwalać ~ę na*** *A* shift the blame on, pin the blame on; ***wziąć ~ę na siebie*** take the blame

winda *f* (*-dy*; *-dy*) *Br* lift, *Am* elevator

windykacja *f* (*-ji*; *no pl*): ***~ długów*** debt collection

windziarz *m* (*-rza*; *-rze*) *Br* lift attendant, *Am* elevator man

winiak *m* (*-ku*; *-ki*) brandy; **winiarnia** *f* (*-ni*; *-nie*) **1.** (*lokal*) wine bar, wine vault **2.** (*wytwórnia*) winery

winić *v/im* (*-nię*) blame (***kogoś o*** *A* s.o. for), put the blame (***kogoś o*** *A* on s.o. for)

winien[1] *adj* **1.** (*ponoszący winę*): ***kto jest temu ~?*** whose fault is it?, who is to blame for it?; ***sam sobie jesteś ~*** it's your own fault **2.** (*mający dług*): ***jestem mu ~ sto złotych*** I owe him 100 zlotys; ***ile jestem panu ~?*** how much do I owe you?; ***jesteś mi ~ wyjaśnienie*** you owe me an explanation

winien[2] *v/irreg*: ***~em to zrobić*** *lit* I ought to do it; ***~eś był przyjść*** *lit* you ought to have come

winieta *f* (*-ty*; *-ty*) **1.** AUTO toll sticker **2.** (*w książce*) vignette

winnica *f* (*-cy*; *-ce*) vineyard

winniczek *m* (*-czka*; *-czki*) Roman snail

winno → ***winien***, ***powinno***

winn|y[1] **I** *adj*: ***być komuś coś ~ym*** owe s.o. s.th.; → ***winien***[1] **II** *m* (*-nego*; *-ni*), ***~a*** *f* (*-nej*; *-ne*) culprit; ***uznać kogoś za ~ego*** find s.o. guilty

winny[2] *adj* **1.** *ocet*, *drożdże*: wine **2.** ***krzew ~*** (grape)vine **3.** *smak*: slightly tart

wino *n* (*-na*; *-na*) wine; ***czerwone ~*** red wine; ***grzane ~*** mulled wine; ***~ musujące*** sparkling wine; **winobranie** *n* (*-nia*; *-nia*) grape harvest, vintage; ***pojechać na ~*** go grape picking

winogrona *pl* (*-ron*) grapes; **winogronowy** *adj sok*: grape

winorośl *f* (*-li*; *-le*) (grape)vine; ***uprawa ~i*** wine growing

winowajca *m* (*-cy*; *-cy*), **-czyni** *f* (*-ni*; *-nie*) culprit

winszować ⟨**po-**⟩ (*-szuję*) congratulate (***komuś z okazji*** *G* s.o. on); ***~ komuś z okazji ślubu*** congratulate s.o. on their marriage

wiocha *f* (*-chy*; *-chy*) *infml* **1.** ***zapadła ~*** backwoods village **2.** *fig* crappy stuff

wiodący *adj fig* leading

wiodę → ***wieść***[2]

wiolinowy *adj klucz*: treble

wiolonczela *f* (*-li*; *-le*) cello

wiolonczelista *m* (*-ty*; *-liści*), **-tka** *f* (*-ki*; *-ki*) cellist

wiosenn|y *adj* spring; ***~e roztopy*** spring thaw; ***robić ~e porządki*** spring-clean

wioska *f* (*-ki*; *-ki*) village; ***~ rybacka*** fishing village; ***~ olimpijska*** olympic village

wiosło *n* (*-ła*; *-ła*) **1.** (*łodzi*) oar **2.** (*kajaka*) paddle; **wiosłować** *v/im* (*-łuję*) **1.** (*w łodzi*) row **2.** (*w kajaku*) paddle; **wiosłow|y** *adj*: ***łódź ~a*** rowboat

wiosn|a *f* (*-ny*; *-ny*) spring; ***na ~ę*** in the spring(time)

wioślarz *f* (*-rza*; *-rze*), **-rka** *f* (*-ki*; *-ki*) rower, oarsman; **wioślarstwo** *n* (*-wa*; *no pl*) rowing

wiotczeć ⟨**z-**⟩ (*-czeję*) **1.** (*o ciele*) get limp **2.** (*o skórze*) become slack **3.** (*o mięśniach*) go slack, become flabby

wiotki *adj* **1.** *ciało*: limp **2.** *skóra*, *mięśnie*: slack **3.** *mięśnie*: flabby **4.** *kibić*: tiny, slender

wiozę → ***wieźć***

wiórki *pl* (*-ków*): ***~ kokosowe*** desiccated coconut; ***~ czekoladowe*** chocolate shavings

wiórkować ⟨**wy-**⟩ (*-kuję*) *podłogę*: scrub with steel wool

wiórow|y *adj*: ***płyta ~a*** chipboard

wiór|y *pl* (*-rów*) shavings, chips; ***suchy jak ~*** bone dry, (as) dry as a bone

wir *m* (*-ru*; *-ry*) **1.** (*wody*) whirlpool; ***rzucić się w ~ pracy*** throw oneself into (one's) work; ***w ~ze walki*** in the thick of the action, in the thick of the fighting **2.** (*powietrza*) whirl, eddy

wiraż *m* (*-żu*; *-że*) **1.** (*zakręt*) bend **2.** (*skręt*) turn

wirnik *m* (*-ka*; *-ki*) rotor

wirować ⟨**za-**, **od-**⟩ (*-ruję*) **I** *v/i* **1.** (*o płatkach śniegu, kurzu*) whirl, swirl

(around) **2.** (*o tancerzu*) whirl, spin (around) **3.** *TECH* spin **4.** ***wiruje mi w głowie*** my head is spinning **II** *v/t pranie*: spin, *Br* spin-dry
wirowy *adj* rotary; ***ruch ~*** rotary motion
wirówka *f* (*-ki*; *-ki*) **1.** (*w pralce*) spin dryer **2.** (*laboratoryjna*) centrifuge **3.** (*do mleka*) cream separator
wirtualny *adj* virtual
wirtuoz *m* (*-za*; *-zi*) virtuoso; **wirtuozerski** *adj* virtuoso, masterly
wirus *m* (*-sa*; *-sy*) virus; **wirusowy** *adj* viral
wisieć *v/im* (*-szę*) hang (***nad*** *I* above); ***~ na telefonie*** *infml* be hogging the phone (line); ***~ w powietrzu*** *fig* be in the air, be in the offing; ***~ na włosku*** *fig* be hanging by a thread
wisielczy *adj*: ***~ humor*** *Br* gallows humour, *Am* gallows humor; **wisielec** *m* (*-lca*; *-lcy*) hanged man;
wisiorek *m* (*-rka*; *-rki*) pendant
Wisła *f* (*-ły*) the Vistula (river)
wiszący *adj*: ***most ~*** suspension bridge; → ***wisieć***
wiślany *adj* **1.** *brzeg*: Vistula's **2.** *żegluga*: on the Vistula
wiśnia *f* (*-ni*; *-nie*) **1.** (sour) cherry **2.** (*drzewo*) (sour) cherry tree; **wiśniak** *m* (*-ku*; *-ki*) cherry brandy
witać ⟨***przy-***, ***po-***⟩ (*-tam*) welcome, greet; ***witam*** (***serdecznie***)***!*** welcome!; ***witaj!*** hello!, hi!; ***witać się*** greet each other; ***~ się z*** *I* greet
witalny *adj* vital
witamina *f* (*-ny*; *-ny*) vitamin; **witaminowy** *adj* vitamin
witraż *m* (*-ża*/*-żu*; *-że*) **1.** (*okno*) stained glass window **2.** (*kompozycja*) stained glass
witryna *f* (*-ny*; *-ny*) **1.** (*wystawa sklepowa*) shop window **2.** (*gablota*) display case, show case **3.** *INF* website
wiwat *m* (*-tu*; *-ty*): ***~!*** cheer!; ***~y*** cheers; ***strzelać na ~*** shoot in the air; ***dać komuś do ~u*** give s.o. a hard time; **wiwatować** *v/im* (*-tuję*) cheer (***na cześć*** *G*)
wiza *f* (*-zy*; *-zy*) visa; ***~ tranzytowa*** transit visa
wizażysta *m* (*-ty*; *-żyści*), **-tka** *f* (*-ki*; *-ki*) make-up artist
wizerunek *m* (*-nku*; *-nki*) **1.** image; ***~ firmy*** corporate image **2.** *ART* picture, portrait
wizj|a *f* (*-ji*; *-je*) vision; ***~a lokalna*** visit to the scene of a crime; ***być na ~i*** be on camera
wizjer *m* (*-ra*; *-ry*) **1.** (*w drzwiach*) peephole **2.** *PHOT* view-finder
wizjonerski *adj* visionary
wizować *v/im* (*-zuję*): ***~ paszport*** stamp a visa in a passport
wizualny *adj* visual; **wizyjny** *adj sygnał*, *system*: video
wizyt|a *f* (*-ty*; *-ty*) visit; ***~a u lekarza*** appointment with a doctor; ***~a domowa lekarza*** home visit; ***przyjechać do kogoś z ~ą*** come to visit s.o.; ***złożyć komuś ~ę*** pay s.o. a visit; ***umówić się na ~ę u lekarza*** make an appointment with a doctor
wizytacja *f* (*-cji*; *-cje*) inspection; **wizytator** *m* (*-ra*; *-rzy*) inspector; **wizytować** *v/im* (*-tuję*) inspect
wizytowy *adj*: ***strój ~*** formal dress
wizytówka *f* (*-ki*; *-ki*) **1.** (*służbowa*) (business) card **2.** (*prywatna*) *Br* (visiting) card, *Am* (calling) card **3.** (*na drzwiach*) nameplate **4.** *fig* showpiece
wjazd *m* (*-du*; *-dy*) **1.** (*brama*) entrance (gate) **2.** (*podjazd*) drive, driveway **3.** (*do kraju*, *miasta*) entry **4.** ***~ na autostradę*** *Br* slip-road, *Am* entrance ramp; **wjazdowy** *adj* **1.** *brama*: entrance **2.** *wiza*: entry
wjeżdżać ⟨***wjechać***⟩ (*-dżam*) **1.** (*o samochodzie*) drive (***do*** *G* into) **2.** ***~ na peron*** (*o pociągu*) pull in **3.** (*na górę*) go up **4.** ***~ na kogoś*** *Br infml* slag s.o. off, *Am infml* dump on s.o.
wklejać ⟨***-leić***⟩ (*-jam*) paste (in)
wklejka *f* (*-ki*; *-ki*) (*w książce*) plate
wklęsły *adj* **1.** concave **2.** *policzki*: hollow, sunken
wkład *m* (*-du*; *-dy*) **1.** contribution; ***~ pracy*** contribution (of work) **2.** (*w banku*) deposit **3.** (*wymienny element*) refill; ***~ do długopisu*** ball pen refill **4.** (*do drukarki*) cartridge
wkładać ⟨***włożyć***⟩ (*-dam*) **1.** put (***do*** *G* into); ***włożyć w coś wiele pracy*** put a lot of work into s.th.; ***włożyć w coś wiele wysiłku*** put a lot of effort into s.th.; ***włożyć klucz do zamka*** put

a key in a keyhole, insert a key into a keyhole **2.** *suknię, pierścień, okulary*: put on **3.** *kapitał*: put, pour (**w** *A* into)
wkładka *f* (*-ki*; *-ki*) **1.** (*do gazety*) insert **2.** (*do butów*) insole **3.** (*domaciczna*) intrauterine device, IUD **4.** (*w zupie*) (pieces of) meat
wkoło → ***wokół***
wkopywać ⟨**-pać**⟩ (*-puję*) **1.** (*w ziemię*) sink into the ground **2.** *roślinę*: plant **3.** *fig* get into trouble; ***wkopywać się*** **1.** (*w ziemię*) dig oneself **2.** (*zdradzić się*) give oneself away
wkraczać ⟨**-roczyć**⟩ (*-czam*) **1.** (*wchodzić*) enter (**do** *G*); ***~ w ostatnią fazę*** enter the last phase **2.** (*interweniować*) step in
wkradać się ⟨**-raść**⟩ (*-dam*) sneak in, slip in; ***wkraść się do domu*** steal into a house; ***wkraść się w czyjeś łaski*** insinuate oneself into s.o.'s favour
wkrapiać ⟨**-ropić**⟩ (*-piam*) (*zbić*) *infml* beat up
wkraplać ⟨**-roplić**⟩ (*-lam*) *Br* instil, *Am* instill (**do** *G* into)
wkraść się *v/p* → ***wkradać się***
wkręcać ⟨**-cić**⟩ (*-cam*) **1.** *śrubę*: drive **2.** *żarówkę*: screw in; ***wkręcać się*** (*o nogawce, włosach*) get caught
wkręt *m* (*-tu*; *-ty*) screw
wkroczyć *v/p* → ***wkraczać***
wkroplić *v/p* → ***wkraplać***
wkrótce *adv* soon; ***~ po*** *L* soon after; ***~ potem*** soon after, soon afterwards
wkupywać się ⟨**-pić**⟩ (*-puję*) buy one's way (**w** *A* into); ***~ w czyjeś łaski*** gain favour with s.o.
wkurzać ⟨**-rzyć**⟩ (*-rzam*) → ***wnerwiać***
wkurzony *adj infml* pissed (off)
wkuwać *v im/p* (*-wam*) *infml* **I** *v/t* bone up (*A* on), *Br* swot up (*A* on) **II** *v/i* cram; ***~ do egzaminu*** cram for an exam
wlać *v/p* (*wleję*): ***~ komuś*** *infml* beat s.o. up, give s.o. a hiding; → ***wlewać***
wlatywać ⟨**wlecieć**⟩ (*-tuję*) **1.** (*o ptaku, komarze*) fly in; ***wlecieć do pokoju*** fly into a room **2.** (*wpadać*) fall in; ***wlecieć do wody*** fall into the water **3.** (*wbiegać*) *infml* run (**do** *G* into), burst (**do** *G* into)
wlec ⟨**po-**⟩ (*wlokę*) drag; ***~ coś za sobą*** drag s.th. behind one; ***~ kogoś*** drag s.o. along; ***wszędzie ~ ze sobą coś*** cart s.th. around; ***wlec się*** **1.** (*ciągnąć się*) drag, trail; ***~ się po ziemi*** trail along **2.** (*zostawać w tyle*) lag behind **3.** (*dłużyć się*) drag on, drag; ***~ się bez końca*** drag on endlessly
wlecieć *v/p* → ***wlatywać***
wlepiać ⟨**-pić**⟩ (*-piam*) stick (**do** *G* into); ***~ komuś mandat*** *infml* give s.o. a ticket; ***~ gały w*** *A infml* gawk at
wlew *m* (*-wu*; *-wy*) (*otwór*) intake, inlet; ***korek ~u paliwa*** fuel cap
wlewać ⟨**wlać**⟩ (*-wam*) pour (**do** *G* into/in)
wleźć *v/p* → ***włazić***
wliczać ⟨**-czyć**⟩ (*-czam*) include (**do** *G* in)
wliczony *adj* included; ***~ w cenę*** included in the price
wlotowy *adj*: ***otwór ~*** inlet
władać *v/im* (*-dam*) **1.** *państwem*: rule **2.** (*językiem*) ***~ angielskim*** have a good command of English **3.** *bronią*: wield
władca *m* (*-cy*; *-cy*), **-czyni** *f* (*-ni*; *-nie*) ruler
władczy *adj lit ton, gest*: commanding
władz|a *f* (*-dzy*; *-dze*) **1.** (*rządzenie*) power; ***dojść do ~y*** come to power; ***być u ~y*** be in power **2.** (*instytucje*) the authorities *pl*; ***~e*** the authorities; ***~e państwowe*** state authorities **3.** (*kontrola*) control; ***stracić ~ę nad sobą*** lose control; ***~a rodzicielska*** custody; ***stracić ~ę w nogach*** lose the use of one's legs; ***w pełni ~ umysłowych*** in full possession of one's (mental) faculties
włamać się *v/p* → ***włamywać się***
włamanie *n* (*-nia*; *-nia*) burglary, break-in, forced entry; ***~ miało miejsce między północą a szóstą rano*** the break-in occurred between midnight and six in the morning; **włamywacz** *m* (*-cza*; *-cze*) burglar
włamywać się ⟨**-mać**⟩ (*-muję*) break in; ***włamano się do jej mieszkania*** her flat has been broken into
własnoręczny *adj podpis*: own, personal
własnościow|y *adj* privately owned; ***mieszkanie ~e*** privately owned flat; ***przekształcenia ~e*** ownership transformation; ***rozdrobniona struktura ~a*** fragmented ownership

własność *f* (*-ści*; *no pl*) **1.** (*prawo*) ownership; ***posiadać coś na ~*** own s.th., be the owner of s.th. **2.** (*majątek*) property

własn|y *adj* (s.o.'s) own; ***z ~ej woli*** of one's own free will; ***z ~ej inicjatywy*** on one's own initiative; ***na ~ą rękę*** on one's own; ***w obronie ~ej*** in self defence; ***we ~ej osobie*** in person; ***~ej roboty*** home-made; ***nazwa ~a*** proper name

właściciel *m* (*-la*; *-le*), **~ka** *f* (*-ki*; *-ki*) owner; ***~ psa*** dog owner; ***~ akcji*** shareholder

właściwie **I** *particle* (*w gruncie rzeczy*) actually, in fact **II** *adv* **1.** (*odpowiednio*) properly **2.** (*poprawnie*) correctly; → ***właściwy***

właściwoś|ć *f* (*-ści*; *-ści*) property; ***~ci*** properties

właściw|y *adj* **1.** (*odpowiedni*) right, proper; ***we ~ym czasie*** in due time **2.** (*poprawny*) correct; ***~a odpowiedź*** correct answer **3.** (*charakterysyczny*) typical (**dla** *G* of) **4. *ciężar ~y*** *CHEM PHYS* specific gravity **5.** *sąd*: competent

właśnie **I** *adv* just; ***~ wyszła*** she's just left; ***~ miałem to zrobić*** I was just about to do it **II** *particle* just, exactly; ***tego mi ~ potrzeba*** that's just what I need; ***to ~ chcę zrobić*** that's exactly what I want to do, that's just what I want to do **III** *interj* exactly

właz *m* (*-zu*; *-zy*) **1.** (*kanału*) manhole **2.** (*czołgu*) hatch

włazić ⟨**wleźć**⟩ (*-łażę*) **1.** (*do środka*) get (**do** *G* in/into) **2.** (*na górę*) climb (**na** *A* up) **3.** (*pod spód*) get (**pod** *A* under) **4.** (*w kałużę*) step (**w** *A* into) **5.** (*mieścić się*) go (**do** *G* into) **6. *ile wlezie*** as much as possible; ***jedz, ile wlezie*** eat as much as you can

włączać ⟨**-czyć**⟩ (*-czam*) **1.** *światło*, *telewizor*: turn on, switch on **2.** *bieg*: shift into, put into **3.** (*przyłączać*) include; ***włączać się*** join (**do** *G*)

włącznie *adv* inclusive; ***~ ze środą*** Wednesday inclusive

Włoch *m* (*-cha*; *Włosi*) Italian; ***jest ~em*** he's Italian

włochaty *adj* **1.** *pies*: shaggy **2.** *tkanina*: fuzzy **3.** *łodyga*, *liść*: fuzzy, hairy

Włochy *pl* (*Włoch*) Italy *sing*

włos *m* (*-sa*; *-sy*) hair; ***~y*** hair; ***głaskać kota pod ~*** stroke a cat the wrong way; ***ani o ~*** not an inch; ***o*** (***mały***) ***~*** by a hair's breadth; ***rwać sobie ~y z głowy*** tear one's hair out; ***dzielić ~ na czworo*** split hairs; ***suszarka do ~ów*** hairdryer; ***lakier do ~ów*** hairspray; ***~y anielskie*** tinsel

włosie *n* (*-sia*; *no pl*) **1.** (*końskie*) horsehair **2.** (*dywanu*) pile; ***dywany z grubym ~m*** deep-pile carpets

włosień *m* (*-sienia*/*włośnia*; *-sienie*/*włośnie*) *BIOL* trichina

włoski[1] *pl* (*-ków*) *dim* **1.** (fine) hair *sing* **2.** (*meszek*) fuzz *sing*

włosk|i[2] *adj* Italian; ***orzech ~i*** walnut; ***kapusta ~a*** savoy cabbage

włosowat|y *adj*: ***naczynia ~e*** *ANAT* capillary vessels, capillaries

włoszczyzna *f* (*-ny*; *no pl*) (mixed) soup vegetables

Włoszk|a *f* (*-ki*; *-ki*) Italian; ***jest ~ą*** she's Italian

włośnica *f* (*-cy*; *no pl*) *MED* trichinosis

włożyć *v/p* → ***wkładać***

włóczęga[1] *f* (*-gi*; *-gi*) (*wędrowanie*) roaming **2.** (*piesza wycieczka*) hike, *Br* ramble

włóczęga[2] *m* (*-gi*; *-gi*/*-czędzy*) vagabond, tramp; **włóczęgostwo** *n* (*-wa*; *no pl*) vagrancy

włóczka *f* (*-ki*; *-ki*) (knitting) wool; **włóczkowy** *adj* knitted

włócznia *f* (*-ni*; *-nie*) spear

włóczyć *v/im* (*-czę*) drag; ***~ kogoś*** drag s.o. along; ***włóczyć się*** roam (about); ***~ się po knajpach*** crawl from bar to bar

włóczykij *m* (*-ja*; *-je*) rolling stone

włókiennictwo *n* (*-wa*; *no pl*) the textile industry; **włókienniczy** *adj* textile

włókniarz *m* (*-rza*; *-rze*), **-rka** *f* (*-ki*; *-ki*) textile worker

włóknisty *adj* fibrous; **włókno** *n* (*-na*; *-na*) *Br* fibre, *Am* fiber; ***~ syntetyczne*** synthetic fibre

wmawiać ⟨**wmówić**⟩ (*-wiam*) persuade; ***wmówić komuś, że*** make s.o. believe that; ***~ sobie, że*** kid oneself into believing that

wmontowywać ⟨**-tować**⟩ (*-towuję*) fit (in), build in

wmówić *v/p* → ***wmawiać***

W

wmurowywać ⟨**-rować**⟩ (*-rowuję*) build in, set in
wmuszać ⟨**-sić**⟩ (*-szam*): **~ *komuś jedzenie*** force s.o. to eat
wnerwiać ⟨**-wić**⟩ (*-wiam*): **~ *kogoś*** *infml* bug s.o., get on s.o.'s nerves; ***wnerwiać się*** *infml* get peeved
wnerwiony *adj infml* peeved
wnet *adv lit* soon, anon
wnęka *f* (*-ki*; *-ki*) alcove; **~ *kuchenna*** kitchenette
wnętrz|e *n* (*-rza*; *-rza*) **1.** inside; ***zajrzeć do ~a*** look inside **2.** ARCHIT interior; ***architektura ~*** interior design **3.** PSYCH inner life
wnętrzności *pl* (*-ści*) entrails, intestines
wniebogłosy *adv* at the top of one's voice; ***drzeć się ~*** scream at the top of one's voice, shout one's head off
Wniebowstąpienie *n* (*-nia*; *no pl*) REL Ascension; **Wniebowzięcie** *n* (*-cia*; *no pl*) REL Assumption
wniebowzięty *adj* ecstatic, *infml* on cloud nine
wnieść *v/p* → ***wnosić***
wnikać ⟨**-knąć**⟩ (*-kam*) penetrate (**w** *A*); ***nie wnikając w szczegóły*** without going into details
wnikliwy *adj* **1.** *umysł, obserwator*: astute **2.** *analiza*, *badania*: thorough, insightful **3.** *spojrzenie*: piercing, penetrating
wniknąć *v/p* → ***wnikać***
wnios|ek *m* (*-sku*; *-ski*) **1.** (*konkluzja*) conclusion; ***dojść do ~ku, że*** come to the conclusion that; ***wyciągać pochopne ~ki*** jump to conclusions **2.** (*propozycja*) proposal **3.** (*na zebraniu*) motion; ***przyjąć ~ek*** accept a motion; ***odrzucić ~ek*** reject a motion; ***zgłosić ~ek*** put forward a motion; ***poprzeć ~ek*** second a motion **4.** (*podanie*) application; ***złożyć ~ek o*** *A* apply for
wnioskodawca *m* (*-cy*; *-cy*), **-czyni** *f* (*-ni*; *-nie*) **1.** applicant, petitioner **2.** (*autor*) author
wnioskować ⟨**wy-**⟩ (*-kuję*) **1.** (*wyciągać wnioski*) conclude (**z** *G* from) **2.** (*zgłaszać wniosek*) **~ o** *A* put forward a motion to do s.th.
wniwecz: ***obrócić ~ czyjeś plany*** *lit* shatter s.o.'s plans
wnosić ⟨**wnieść**⟩ (*-szę*) **1.** (*do środka*) carry in, bring in; **~ *coś do pokoju*** carry s.th. into a room **2.** (*na górę*) carry up, bring up **3.** *skargę*, *opłatę*: make **4.** *skargę*, *protest*: lodge **5.** *pozew*: file; **~ *o rozwód*** file for divorce **6.** **~ *wkład do*** *G* contribute to, make a contribution to **7.** (*zgłaszać wniosek*) put forward a motion (**o** *A* to do s.th.) **8.** (*dochodzić do wniosku*) conclude, gather
wnuczek *m* (*-czka*; *-czkowie*) grandson; **wnuczka** *f* (*-ki*; *-ki*) granddaughter; **wnuczęta** *pl* (*-cząt*) grandchildren
wnuk *m* (*-ka*; *-kowie*/*-ki*) grandson; **~i** grandchildren
wnusia *f* (*-si*; *-sie*) *dim* (little) granddaughter; **wnuś** *m* (*wnusia*; *wnusie*/*wnusiowie*) *dim* (little) grandson
wnyki *pl* (*-ków*) (*sidła*) snare *sing*
woalka *f* (*-ki*; *-ki*) veil
wobec *prep* (*G*) **1.** (*względem*) to, toward(s); **~ *niej był miły*** he was nice to her; ***stanąć ~ zagrożenia*** be confronted with danger, be in danger **2.** (*z powodu*) because of, due to; **~ *tego, że*** because; **~ *tego*** in that case, for that reason **3.** (*w porównaniu*) compared to, in comparison with **4.** (*w obecności*) in the presence of; ***wszem i ~*** to all and sundry
wod|a *f* (*-dy*; *-dy*) water; ***~a pitna*** drinking water; ***bieżąca ~a*** running water, tap water; ***słodka ~a*** fresh water; ***~a mineralna*** mineral water; ***~a święcona*** holy water; ***~a kolońska*** cologne, eau de Cologne; ***~y gruntowe*** ground water; ***~y terytorialne*** territorial waters; ***~y płodowe*** amniotic fluid, *infml* the waters; ***nastawić ~ę na herbatę*** put the kettle on; ***z ~y*** COOK boiled; ***cicha ~a brzegi rwie*** still waters run deep; ***to ~a na ich młyn*** that's all grist to their mill; ***~a sodowa uderzyła mu do głowy*** success has gone to his head
wodewil *m* (*-lu*; *-le*) THEAT vaudeville
wodniactwo *n* (*-wa*; *no pl*) water sports *pl*
wodnik *m* (*-ka*; *-ki*) **1.** (*w baśniach*) water sprite, water-elf **2.** **≈** ASTR Aquarius

wodnisty *adj* watery; **wodn|y** *adj* **1.** water; ***para ~a*** steam; ***roślina ~a*** water plant; ***łóżko ~e*** waterbed; ***rower ~y*** pedal boat; ***znak ~y*** watermark; ***elektrownia ~a*** hydroelectric power plant **2.** *roztwór*: aqueous, water **3.** *flora*: aquactic, water
wodociąg *m* (*-gu*; *-gi*) waterworks *pl*; **wodociągow|y** *adj*: ***sieć ~a*** water supply system
wodogłowie *n* (*-wia*; *no pl*) hydrocephalus, *infml* water on the brain; **wodolecznictwo** *n* (*-wa*; *no pl*) hydrotherapy; **wodolejstwo** *n* (*-wa*; *no pl*) wordiness, *Br infml* waffle; **wodolot** *m* (*-tu*; *-ty*) hydrofoil; **wodołaz** *m* (*-za*; *-zy*) (*pies*) Newfoundland (dog)
wodoodporny *adj* **1.** waterproof **2.** *zegarek*: water-resistant; **wodopój** *m* (*-poju*; *-poje*) watering place; **wodorost** *m* (*-tu*; *-ty*) seaweed
wodorowy *adj* hydrogen
wodospad *m* (*-du*; *-dy*) waterfall; **wodoszczelny** *adj* **1.** watertight **2.** *warstwa*: waterproof; **wodotrysk** *m* (*-ku*; *-ki*) fountain
wodować ⟨**z-**⟩ (*-duję*) launch
wodór *m* (*-doru*; *no pl*) CHEM hydrogen
wodz|e *pl* (*-dzy*) reins; ***trzymać nerwy na ~y*** stay cool; ***puszczać ~e fantazji*** let one's imagination run free
wodzić *v/im* (*-dzę*): **~ *wzrokiem za*** *I* follow s.o. with one's eyes; **~ *kogoś za nos*** lead s.o. by the nose; **~ *palcem po*** *L* run one's finger over, move one's finger over
wodzowie *pl* → ***wódz***
woj. *abbr* (= **województwo**) province, voivodeship
wojak *m* (*-ka*; *-jacy*) soldier
wojaż *m* (*-żu*; *-że*) *dated* voyage, journey; ***~e*** travels
wojenn|y *adj* war; ***jeniec ~y*** prisoner of war; ***stan ~y*** martial law; ***wspomnienia ~e*** wartime memories; ***okręt ~y*** warship; ***sąd ~y*** court martial
wojewoda *m* (*-dy*; *-dowie*) **1.** (provincial) governor, voivod(e) **2.** HIST voivod(e)
wojewódzki *adj* provincial; **województwo** *n* (*-wa*; *-wa*) province, voivodeship
wojłok *m* (*-ku*; *-ki*) (low-quality) felt
wojn|a *f* (*-ny*; *-ny*) war; ***~a domowa*** civil war; ***druga ~a światowa*** World War II, the Second World War; ***zimna ~a*** the Cold War, the cold war; ***święta ~a*** holy war; ***iść na ~ę*** go to war; ***zginąć na ~ie*** die in the war; ***wypowiedzieć komuś ~ę*** declare war on s.o.; ***w czasie ~y*** during the war; ***gdy wybuchła ~a*** when the war broke out
wojować *v/im* (*-juję*) *fig* fight (**z** *I*), combat (**z** *I*)
wojowniczy *adj* **1.** *naród*: warlike **2.** *nastrój*, *osoba*: combative **3.** *nastawienie*: belligerent; **wojownik** *m* (*-ka*; *-nicy*) warrior
wojsk|o *n* (*-ka*; *-ka*) **1.** (*siły zbrojne*) army, armed forces *pl*; ***~a lądowe*** the army; ***~a lotnicze*** the air force; ***zaciągnąć się do ~a*** enlist in the army **2.** (*służba wojskowa*) military service **3.** (*żołnierze*) soldiers *pl* **4.** (*oddziały*) troops *pl*
wojskowo *adv* militarily; ***został przeszkolony ~*** he received military training
wojskow|y **I** *adj* military; ***służba ~a*** military service; ***cmentarz ~y*** military cemetery; ***odmowa służby ~ej*** **a)** refusal to serve in the army **b)** (*z pobudek moralnych*) conscientious objection **II** *m* (*-wego*; *-wi*) serviceman, soldier
wokalny *adj* vocal
wokand|a *f* (*-dy*; *-dy*): ***sprawa wchodzi na ~ę*** the case comes up for trial
wokół, ***wokoło***, ***wkoło*** **I** *adv* around; ***wszędzie ~*** all around **II** *prep* (*G*) around
wol|a *f* (*-li*; *no pl*) will; ***mimo ~i*** involuntarily; ***z własnej ~i*** of one's own free will; ***do ~i*** at will; ***dobra ~a*** goodwill; ***gest dobrej ~i*** goodwill gesture; ***zła ~a*** ill will; ***wolna ~a*** free will; ***ostatnia ~a*** last will (and testament); ***silna ~a*** strong will, willpower
wole *n* (*-la*; *-la*) (*u ptaka*) crop
woleć *v/im* (*-lę*) prefer (**coś niż** *A* s.th. to); ***wolę te czerwone*** I prefer the red ones; ***wolałbym zostać*** I'd rather stay, I'd prefer to stay
wolfram *m* (*-mu*; *no pl*) CHEM tungsten, wolfram
wol|i *adj* ox; ***~a skóra*** oxhide

wolne *n* (*-nego*; *no pl*) time off; ***mieć tydzień ~go*** have a week off
wolniutki *adj dim* very slow
wolno[1] *adv* slowly, *infml* slow; ***puścić kogoś ~*** let s.o. go; ***dom ~ stojący*** detached house; ***wanna ~ stojąca*** free-standing bath
wolno[2] *v/irreg*: ***tu nie ~ palić*** smoking is not allowed here; ***nie ~ ci wyjść*** you are not allowed to leave; ***wszystko mu ~*** he's allowed to do anything he wants; ***czy ~ zapytać*** may I ask; ***nie ~ ci o tym zapominać*** you mustn't forget it, you shouldn't forget it
wolnocłowy *adj* duty-free; ***sklep ~*** duty-free shop; **wolnomularstwo** *n* (*-wa*; *no pl*) freemasonry; **wolnomyśliciel** *m* (*-la*; *-le*) freethinker
wolnorynkow|y *adj* free-market; ***gospodarka ~a*** free-market economy
wolnościowy *adj* liberation, freedom
wolnoś|ć *f* (*-ści*; *no pl*) freedom, liberty; ***~ć słowa*** freedom of speech; ***~ć wyznania*** freedom of religion; ***~ć wypowiedzi artystycznej*** freedom of artistic expression; ***być na ~ci*** be free; ***zwierzęta żyjące na ~ci*** animals living in the wild; ***wypuścić kogoś na ~ć*** free s.o., release s.o.; ***wyjść na ~ć*** be released
woln|y[1] *adj* **1.** free (**od** *G* from); ***~y etat*** vacancy; ***~y od opłat*** free of charge; ***~y od podatku*** tax-free; ***na ~ym powietrzu*** outdoors; ***czas ~y*** free time, leisure; ***wstęp ~y*** free admission; ***~e tłumaczenie*** free translation; ***rzut ~y*** SPORT free kick; ***~y zawód*** freelance occupation; ***~y słuchacz*** auditing student, *Am* auditor; ***~e rodniki*** free radicals **2.** *mężczyzna*, *kobieta*: single; ***stanu ~ego*** single
woln|y[2] *adj* (*powolny*) slow; ***iść ~ym krokiem*** walk slowly, walk at a slow pace; ***z ~a*** slowly, little by little; ***na ~ym ogniu*** over low heat; ***~ego!*** not so fast!
wolontariusz *m* (*-sza*; *-sze*), **~ka** *f* (*-ki*; *-ki*) volunteer
woltomierz *m* (*-rza*; *-rze*) voltmeter
woltyżer *m* (*-ra*; *-rzy*/*-rowie*), **~ka** *f* (*-ki*; *-ki*) circus rider
woltyzerka *f* (*-ki*; *no pl*) equestrian vaulting
wołacz *m* (*-cza*; *-cze*) GRAM vocative
wołać ⟨**za-**⟩ (*-łam*) call; **~ do** *G* shout to; ***~ o pomoc*** cry for help; ***wołają na niego „Jojo"*** they call him 'Jojo'; ***zawołała go do telefonu*** she told him he was wanted on the phone; ***~ o pomstę do nieba*** be outrageous
wołanie *n* (*-nia*; *-nia*) **1.** (*okrzyk*) call; ***~ o pomoc*** cry for help **2.** (*okrzyki*) calling, calls *pl*
wołek *m* (*-łka*; *-łki*): ***~ zbożowy*** grain weevil
wołowina *f* (*-ny*; *no pl*) beef; **wołow|y** *adj* beef; ***dupa ~a*** *vulg* loser
woły *pl* → ***wół***
wonny *adj lit* fragrant
woń *f* (*woni*; *wonie*) *lit* **1.** smell; ***przykra ~*** *Br* unpleasant odour, *Am* unpleasant odor **2.** *kwiatów*: scent, fragrance
WOP *abbr m* (*WOP-u*; *no pl*) (= ***Wojska Ochrony Pogranicza***) (Polish) Border Guard
wopista *m* (*-ty*; *-piści*) border guard
WOPR *abbr m* (*WOPR-u*; *no pl*) (= ***Wodne Ochotnicze Pogotowie Ratunkowe***) Volunteer Lifeguards Association
woreczek *m* (*-czka*; *-czki*) *dim* (small) bag; ***~ żółciowy*** ANAT gall bladder
wor|ek *m* (*-rka*; *-rki*) sack; ***~ek plastikowy*** (***na śmieci***) plastic (refuse) bag; ***~ki pod oczami*** bags under one's eyes; ***~ek z piachem*** sandbag; ***~ek treningowy*** punching bag; ***wrzucać coś do jednego ~ka*** lump s.th. together
workowaty *adj* **1.** *spódnica*: baggy **2. *wilk ~*** Tasmanian wolf, thylacine
wory *pl* → ***wór***
wosk *m* (*-ku*; *-ki*) wax; ***~ pszczeli*** beeswax; ***~ do podłóg*** floor polish; **woskować** ⟨**na-**⟩ (*-kuję*) *podłogę*: wax
woskowina *f* (*-ny*; *no pl*) earwax; **woskow|y** *adj* **1.** (*z wosku*) wax; ***figura ~a*** waxwork; ***gabinet figur ~ych*** *Br* waxworks, *Am* wax museum **2.** *cera*: waxen
wotum *n* (*indecl*; *-ta*) **1. *~ zaufania*** POLIT vote of confidence; ***~ nieufności*** POLIT vote of no confidence **2.** REL votive offering
wozić *v/im* (*wożę*) carry, drive, take; ***~ dzieci do szkoły*** take children to school; ***~ ze sobą*** take along (with one)

wozy *pl* → **wóz**
woźna *f* (*-nej*; *-ne*) *Br* (female) caretaker, *Am* (female) janitor
woźnica *m* (*-cy*; *-ce*) **1.** (*furman*) (cart) driver **2.** (*powozu*) coachman
woźny *m* (*-nego*; *-ni*) *Br* caretaker, *Am* janitor
wódeczka *f* (*-ki*; *-ki*) *dim* vodka
wódk|a *f* (*-ki*; *-ki*) vodka; **~a czysta** (pure) vodka; **butelka ~i** a bottle of vodka; **kieliszek ~i** a glass of vodka; **~i gatunkowe** *Br* flavoured vodkas, *Am* flavored vodkas; **iść na ~ę** go out for a drink
wódz *m* (*wodza*; *wodzowie*) **1.** (*przywódca*) leader **2.** *plemienia*: chief **3.** **~ naczelny** commander-in-chief
wójt *m* (*-ta*; *-towie*) borough administrator, commune head
wół *m* (*wołu*; *woły*) ox; **~ roboczy** *fig* drudge; **pracować jak ~** work like a horse, work one's fingers to the bone; **tu stoi napisane jak ~** it's here written in black and white
wór *m* (*wora*; *wory*) (big) sack
wówczas *adv lit* then, at the time
wóz *m* (*wozu*; *wozy*) **1.** (*samochód*) car; **~ policyjny** police car; **~ dostawczy** delivery van; **~ strażacki** fire engine **2.** (*furmanka*) cart, wagon, *Br* waggon; **raz na wozie raz pod wozem** *fig* some you win, some you lose **3.** (*zawartość wozu*) cartful; **~ węgla** cartful of coal
wóz|ek *m* (*-zka*; *-zki*) **1.** (*na zakupy*, *na bagaż*, *w szpitalu*) trolley **2.** (*dziecięcy*) *Br* pram, *Am* baby carriage; **~ek spacerowy** *Br* pushchair, *Am* stroller; **~ek dla lalek** toy pram **3.** (*inwalidzki*) wheelchair; **poruszać się na ~ku** use a wheelchair **4.** **~ek widłowy**, **~ek podnośnikowy** forklift truck **5.** (*ciągnięty przez konia*, *człowieka*) cart; **jechać na tym samym ~ku** *fig* be in the same boat
wózkowy *m* (*-wego*; *-wi*) (forklift truck) driver
WP *abbr* **1.** (= **Wojsko Polskie**) the Polish Army **2.** (= **wielmożny pan**) Mr **3.** (= **wielmożna pani**) Mrs **4.** (= **wielmożni państwo**) Mr and Mrs
wpadać ⟨**wpaść**⟩ (*-dam*) **1.** (*w dół*) fall (**w** *A* into); **~ komuś do oka** get into s.o.'s eye; **~ w pułapkę** fall into a trap; **~ w komuś ręce** fall into s.o.'s hands; **~ do morza** (*o rzece*) flow into the sea; **~ na pomysł** *infml* hit (up)on an idea; **~ na ślad** find a trace **2.** (*o powietrzu*) come in; **przez otwarte okno wpadało zimne powietrze** cold air was coming through the open window **3.** (*wbiegać*) rush in, storm in; **wpaść do pokoju** rush into a room **4.** (*odwiedzać*) drop in (**do** *G* on), *Am* come by and see (**do** *G*) **5.** (*zostawać wykrytym*) be caught **6.** (*o szpiegu*) be exposed **7.** (*znajdować się w określonej sytuacji*) get into; **~ w kłopoty** get into trouble; **~ w nałóg** get into a habit, get addicted; **~ w poślizg** go into a skid **8.** (*zderzać się*) **~ na** *A* **a)** (*jadąc*, *biegnąc*) run into **b)** (*idąc*) bump into; **samochód wpadł na drzewo** the car hit a tree; **~ pod samochód** be knocked down by a car
wpadk|a *f* (*-ki*; *-ki*) **1.** (*przestępcy*) bust; **mieć ~ę** be bust **2.** (*wykrycie agenta*) exposure **3.** (*pomyłka*) slip-up, blunder **4.** (*zajście w ciążę*) unwanted pregnancy
wpajać ⟨**wpoić**⟩ (*-jam*) *Br* instil, *Am* instill (**coś** *D* s.th. in)
wpakować *v/p* (*-kuję*) *rzeczy*: stuff, cram (**do** *G* in); **~ kogoś do samochodu** get s.o. into a car; **~ kogoś do więzienia** put s.o. away; **~ komuś kulę w pierś** put a bullet into s.o.'s chest; **wpakować się 1.** (*wpaść*) get (**na** *A* into); **~ się w kłopoty** get into trouble; **~ się na drzewo** run into a tree **2.** (*wcisnąć się*) cram (**do** *G* into)
wparować *v/p* (*-ruję*) (*wejść*) *infml* rush in; **~ do kuchni** rush into the kitchen
wpaść *v/p* (*wpadnę*): **~ jak śliwka w kompot** get into hot water, get into serious trouble; → **wpadać**
wpatrywać się *v/i* (*-ruję*) gaze (**w** *A* at), stare (**w** *A* at); **wpatrzony** *adj*: **być ~m w** *A* gaze at, have one's eyes fixed on
wpełzać ⟨**-znąć**⟩ (*-zam*) crawl in, creep in
wpędzać ⟨**-dzić**⟩ (*-dzam*): **~ kogoś w rozpacz** drive s.o. to despair; **~ kogoś w kompleksy** give s.o. a complex; **~ kogoś w kłopoty** get s.o. into trouble;

~ kogoś w chorobę make s.o. ill; **~ się w chorobę** make oneself ill
wpiąć *v/p* → **wpinać**
wpić *v/p* → **wpijać**
wpieniać ⟨**-nić**⟩ (*-niam*) *infml* piss off, *Br infml* hack off, *Am infml* tick off; **wpieniać się** *infml* get pissed (off), *Br infml* get hacked off, *Am infml* get ticked off; **wpieniony** *adj infml* pissed (off), *Br infml* hacked off, *Am infml* ticked off
wpieprzać ⟨**-rzyć**⟩ (*-rzam*) **1.** (*bić*) beat up **2.** (*jeść*) gobble up
wpierać ⟨**weprzeć**⟩ (*-ram*): **~ komuś, że** try hard to convince s.o. that
wpierw *adv lit* first
wpijać ⟨**wpić**⟩ (*-jam*) dig, sink; **~ paznokcie w** *A* dig one's nails into; **~ zęby w** *A* sink one's teeth into; **wpijać się 1. ~ się paznokciami w** *A* dig one's nails into; **~ się zębami w** *A* sink one's teeth into **2.** (*cisnąć*) dig **3.** (*o kleszczu*) burrow (**w** *A* into)
wpinać ⟨**-piąć**⟩ (*-nam*) **1.** *kartkę, dokument*: file, put (**do** *G* in) **2.** *spinkę*: stick (**w** *A* in)
wpis *m* (*-su*; *-sy*) entry; **wpisowy** *adj opłata*: registration
wpisywać ⟨**-sać**⟩ (*-suję*) **1.** (*w rubrykę*) write (**do** *G* in) **2.** (*do komputera*) enter (**do** *G* in) **3.** (*na listę*) put (**na** *A* on); **wpisany na listę** listed **4.** (*w okrąg*) inscribe (**coś w** *A* s.th. within); **wpisywać się** sign up; **~ się na listę** put one's name on a list
wplatać ⟨**-leść**⟩ (*-tam*) weave in; **~ kwiaty we włosy** weave flowers into s.o.'s hair
wplątywać ⟨**-tać**⟩ (*-tuję*) *fig* involve, entangle; **być wplątanym w spisek** be involved in a conspiracy; **wplątywać się 1.** *fig* get involved, become entangled (**w** *A* in) **2.** (*we włosy*) get tangled
wpleść *v/p* → **wplatać**
wpłacać ⟨**-cić**⟩ (*-cam*) pay; **wpłata** *f* (*-ty*; *-ty*) payment
wpław *adv*: **przepłynąć rzekę ~** swim across the river
wpłynąć *v/p* → **wpływać**
wpływ *m* (*-wu*; *-wy*) **1.** influence, impact; **wywierać ~** influence (**na** *A*), exert influence (**na** *A* on); **pod ~em alkoholu** under the influence of alcohol; **mieć ~y** have connections **2. ~y** FIN income; **~y ze sprzedaży** FIN (sale) proceeds
wpływać *v/i* ⟨**-łynąć**⟩ (*-wam*) **1.** (*mieć wpływ*) influence (**na** *A*), affect (**na** *A*); **~ na czyjąś decyzję** influence s.o.'s decision; **dobrze** (**źle**) **~ na** *A* have a good (bad) influence on **2.** (*do portu*) sail (**do** *G* into), arrive (**do** *G* at) **3.** (*o kwocie, przelewie*) come in, be received **4.** (*o rzece*) flow (**do** *G* into) **5.** (*dostawać się*) get in
wpływowy *adj* influential
wpoić *v/p* → **wpajać**
wpół *adv*: **~ do drugiej** half past one; **o ~ do czwartej** at half past three; **objąć kogoś ~** put one's arms around s.o.'s waist; **złożony ~** folded in half, folded in two; **zgiąć się ~** bend double; **na ~ przytomny** half-conscious
wpółotwarty → **półotwarty**
wpółprzytomny → **półprzytomny**
wpółsurowy → **półsurowy**
wpółżywy *adj* half dead
wpraszać się ⟨**-rosić**⟩ (*-szam*) invite oneself (**do** *G* to)
wpraw|a *f* (*-wy*; *no pl*) skill; **wyjść z ~y** get out of practice; **wyszła z ~y** she's out of practice; **z ~ą** *Br* skilfully, *Am* skillfully; **dla ~y** to get practice; **żeby nie wyjść z ~y** to keep in practice
wprawdzie *particle* admittedly, indeed
wprawiać ⟨**-wić**⟩ (*-wiam*) **1.** (*mocować*) set; **wprawić szybę** replace a window pane **2.** (*wywoływać*) **~ kogoś w dobry nastrój** put s.o. in a good mood, cheer s.o. up; **~ kogoś w podziw** impress s.o. greatly; **~ coś w ruch** set s.th. in motion; **~ kogoś w zakłopotanie** embarrass s.o.; **wprawiać się**: **~ się w** *L* improve one's skills in, *Br* practise, *Am* practice
wprawka *f* (*-ki*; *-ki*) exercise; **wprawny** *adj* **1.** *osoba, ruchy*: *Br* skilful, *Am* skillful **2.** *oko*: trained
wprosić się *v/p* → **wpraszać się**
wprost *particle* **1.** (*bezpośrednio*) directly; **~ przeciwnie** just the opposite; **na ~** *G* directly opposite **2.** (*prosto*) straight; **~ przed siebie** straight ahead **3.** (*wręcz*) simply **4.** (*otwarcie*) straight, openly
wprowadzać ⟨**-dzić**⟩ (*-dzam*) **1.** introduce; **~ kogoś w błąd** misinform s.o.,

mislead s.o.; **~ coś w życie** bring s.th. into effect; **~ produkt na rynek** launch a product; **~ kogoś w dobry humor** put s.o. in a good mood; **~ samochód do garażu** drive a car into a garage **2.** *osobę*: lead in; **~ kogoś do pokoju** lead s.o. into a room **3.** *hasło*: enter **4.** *rurkę*: insert; **wprowadzać się 1.** (*przeprowadzać się*) move in; **~ się do młodszej kobiety** move in with a younger woman **2.** (*wywoływać*) **~ się w dobry humor** put oneself in a good mood

wprowadzenie *n* (*-nia*; *-nia*) **1.** (*wstęp*) introduction **2.** *danych*: input; **~ się** moving in

wprzęgać ⟨**-gnąć**, **-rząc**⟩ (*-gam*) harness

wpust *m* (*-tu*; *-ty*) **1.** (*w desce*) rabbet **2.** (*otwór*) inlet; **~ ściekowy** gully, storm inlet **3.** ANAT cardia

wpuszczać ⟨**wpuścić**⟩ (*-czam*) let in; **~ kogoś do domu** let s.o. into the house; **~ kogoś w maliny** *infml* mislead s.o., take s.o. for a ride, lead s.o. up the garden path; **~ nogawki do butów** tuck one's trousers into one's boots

wpychać ⟨**wepchnąć**⟩ (*-cham*) **1.** (*wciskać*) push, cram; **~ coś w kogoś** (*dawać jeść*) force s.o. to eat s.th. **2.** (*sprzedawać*) palm off; **wpychać się** squeeze; **~ się do kolejki** *Br* jump the queue, *Am* jump the line

wracać ⟨**wrócić**⟩ (*-cam*) **1.** return, come back; **wrócić do zdrowia** recover; **~ myślami do** *G* recall; **~ do równowagi** recover one's mental equilibrium; **ale wracając do** *G* but getting back to **2.** (*o dziełach sztuki*) be returned **3.** (*o modzie*, *myślach*) come back

wrak *m* (*-ku*; *-ki*) wreck; **~ człowieka** wreck of a man

wrastać ⟨**wrosnąć**⟩ (*-tam*) **1.** (*o roślinach*) take root **2.** (*o paznokciach*) grow in; **~ w skórę** grow into the skin **3.** (*stać się częścią*) become part (**w** *A* of), blend (**w** *A* into)

wraz *particle*: **~ z** *I* together with, along with

W

wrażeni|e *n* (*-nia*; *-nia*) impression; **~a wzrokowe** visual impressions; **odnieść ~e, że** have the impression that; **robić ~e**, **wywierać ~e** make an impression; **być pod ~m** be impressed; **sprawiać ~e zdenerwowanego** seem nervous

wrażliwość *f* (*-ści*; *no pl*) sensitivity (**na** *A* to); **wrażliwy** *adj* sensitive (**na** *A* to); **~ na zimno** sensitive to cold, susceptible to cold; **~ na zmiany pogody** sensitive to changes in the weather; **przesadnie ~** oversensitive

wrąb *m* (*wrębu*; *wręby*) groove, rabbet

wrąbać *v/p* (*-bię*) (*zjeść*) *infml* scoff down, gobble down

wre → **wrzeć**

wreszcie *adv* at last, finally; **~!** at last!

wręcz I *particle* even; **~ przeciwnie** quite the reverse, just the opposite **II** *adv* openly, straight; **walka ~** hand-to-hand combat

wręczać ⟨**-czyć**⟩ (*-czam*) **1.** give **2.** (*do ręki*) hand **3.** *wymówienie*: hand in

wrodzić się *v im/p* (*-dzę*): **wrodził się w ojca** he takes after his father

wrodzony *adj* **1.** inborn, innate **2.** *wada*: congenital

wrogi *adj* **1.** hostile **2.** *oddziały*, *armia*: enemy; **wrogo** *adv* with hostility; **~ nastawiony** hostile (**do** *G* towards/to); **wrogość** *f* (*-ści*; *no pl*) hostility; **wrogowie** *pl* → **wróg**

wron|a *f* (*-ny*; *-ny*) crow; **jeśli wejdziesz między ~y, musisz krakać jak i one** when in Rome, do as the Romans do; **wroni** *adj* crow, crow's

wrosnąć *v/p* → **wrastać**

wrota *pl* (*wrót*) *lit* **1.** (*do zamku*) gates **2.** *fig* gateway *sing* (**do** *G* to); **~ do sukcesu** gateway to success

wrotk|i *pl* (*-tek*) roller skates; **jeździć na ~ach** roller skate

wróbel *m* (*-bla*; *-ble*) sparrow; **lepszy ~ w garści niż gołąb na dachu** one bird in the hand is worth two in the bush; **wróbelek** *m* (*-lka*; *-lki*) *dim* (little) sparrow

wrócić *v/p* → **wracać**

wróg *m* (*wroga*; *wrogowie*) enemy

wróżb|a *f* (*-by*; *-by*) **1.** (*przepowiednia*) prediction, prophecy **2.** (*znak*) omen; **dobra ~a** good omen; **zła ~a** bad omen; **być dobrą ~ą na przyszłość** bode well for the future

wróżbiarstwo *n* (*-wa*; *no pl*) fortune-telling, divination

wróżbita *m* (*-ty*; *-bici*) fortune-teller; **wróżebny** *adj* prophetic; **wróżka** *f* (*-ki*; *-ki*) **1.** (*przepowiadająca przyszłość*) fortune-teller **2.** (*w baśni*) fairy godmother; ***dobra ~*** good witch; ***zła ~*** bad witch

wróżyć ⟨**po-**, **wy-**⟩ (*-żę*) **I** *v/i* **1.** (*przepowiadać przyszłość*) tell fortunes; ***~ z kart*** read the cards; ***to jest wróżenie z fusów*** *fig* this is pure guesswork **2.** (*zapowiadać*) bode, *form* augur; ***~ źle*** bode ill, be a bad sign; ***~ dobrze*** bode well, be a good sign **II** *v/t* **1.** (*przepowiadać*) foretell; ***~ komuś z ręki*** read s.o.'s palm **2.** (*być zapowiedzią*) indicate, be a harbinger of; ***~ dobrą pogodę*** indicate fine weather

wryć się *v/p* (*wryję*) sink (**w** *A* in); ***coś wryło się komuś w pamięć*** s.th. is engraved in s.o.'s memory

wryty: ***stanąć jak ~*** stop dead

wrzask *m* (*-ku*; *-ki*) **1.** screaming **2.** (*okrzyk*) scream; **wrzaskliwy** *adj* noisy; **wrzasnąć** *v/p* → **wrzeszczeć**

wrzaw|a *f* (*-wy*; *no pl*) din, racket; ***wywołać ~ę*** *fig* make a racket, create an uproar

wrzący *adj* boiling; **wrzątek** *m* (*-tku*; *no pl*) boiling water

wrzeciono *n* (*-na*; *-na*) spindle

wrzeć *v/im* (*wrę*) boil; ***praca wre*** the work is in full swing; ***w mieście wrzało od plotek*** the town was abuzz with gossip; ***w biurze wrzało jak w ulu*** the office was buzzing with activity; ***~ z gniewu*** be seething (with anger)

wrzeni|e *n* (*-nia*; *no pl*) **1.** boiling; ***temperatura ~a*** boiling point; ***doprowadzić coś do ~a*** *Br* bring s.th. to the boil, *Am* bring s.th. to a boil **2.** (*polityczne*) turmoil

wrzesień *m* (*września*; *wrześnie*) September

wrzeszczeć ⟨**wrzasnąć**⟩ (*-czę*) scream (**na** *A* at), yell (**na** *A* at)

wrześniowy *adj* September

wrzodow|y *adj*: ***choroba ~a*** peptic ulcer disease

wrzos *m* (*-su*; *-sy*) heather; **wrzosowisko** *n* (*-ka*; *-ka*) moorland; **wrzosowy** *adj* heather

wrzód *m* (*wrzodu*; *wrzody*) **1.** (*na żołądku*) ulcer **2.** (*czyrak*) boil, ulcer

wrzucać ⟨**-cić**⟩ (*-cam*) throw (**do** *G* into), put (**do** *G* into); ***~ coś na siebie*** throw s.th. on; ***~ bieg*** shift into gear

wrzynać się ⟨**werżnąć się**⟩ (*-nam*) dig into, cut in; ***~ w skórę*** dig into the skin, cut into the skin

wsadzać ⟨**-dzić**⟩ (*-dzam*) **1.** (*wciskać*) put, stick; ***~ ręce do kieszeni*** put one's hands in one's pockets; ***~ kogoś do pociągu*** put s.o. on a train; ***~ nos w nie swoje sprawy*** poke one's nose into other people's affairs **2.** (*do więzienia*) *infml* put away

wsch. *abbr* (= **wschód, wschodni**) E

wschodni *adj* **1.** eastern, east **2.** *wiatr*: easterly **3.** *muzyka*, *kultura*: Eastern; ***Europa ~a*** Eastern Europe

wschodnioeuropejski *adj* East(ern) Europe(an)

wschodzić ⟨**wzejść**⟩ (*-dzę*) **1.** (*o słońcu*, *księżycu*) rise **2.** (*o roślinie*) sprout

wschód *m* (*-chodu*; *-chody*) **1.** GEOGR (the) east; ***na wschodzie*** in the east; ***ze wschodu*** from the east; ***na ~ od*** *G* to the east of; ***Bliski ~*** the Near East; ***Środkowy ~*** the Middle East; ***Daleki ~*** the Far East **2.** *słońca*: sunrise; ***o wschodzie słońca*** at sunrise

wsi → ***wieś***

wsiadać ⟨**wsiąść**⟩ (*-dam*) **1.** (*do samochodu*) get (**do** *G* into) **2.** (*do autobusu*, *pociągu*, *samolotu*) get (**do** *G* on) **3.** (*na rower*) get (**na** *A* on) **4.** (*na statek*, *do samolotu*) board (**na** *A*, **do** *G*) **5.** (*na konia*) mount (**na** *A*) **6.** ***~ na kogoś*** *infml* lay into s.o., tell s.o. off

wsiąkać ⟨**-knąć**⟩ (*-kam*) **1.** soak in; ***~ w ziemię*** soak into the ground **2.** (*znikać*) *infml* disappear

wsiąść *v/p* → ***wsiadać***

wsie *pl* → ***wieś***

wsioch *m* (*-cha*; *-chy*) *infml* (country) bumpkin, *Am* hick

wsiowy *adj* village

wskakiwać ⟨**wskoczyć**⟩ (*-kuję*) **1.** (*do samochodu*) jump (**do** *G* into); ***~ do wody*** **a)** jump into the water **b)** (*na główkę*) dive into the water **2.** (*na rower*, *scenę*) jump (**na** *A* on) **3.** (*do pociągu*) hop (**do** *G* on) **4.** ***~ w inne ubranie*** *infml* change clothes quickly

wskazać *v/p* → ***wskazywać***

wskaza|nie *n* (*-nia*; *-nia*) **1.** recommendation; ***~nia lekarza*** doctor's orders; ***według ~ń lekarza*** as recommended by the doctor, as indicated by the doctor **2.** (*przyrządu pomiarowego*) reading

wskazany *adj* advisable, recommended; ***pod ~m adresem*** at the address given; **wskazówk|a** *f* (*-ki*; *-ki*) **1.** (*informacja*) tip, clue, hint; ***~i*** **a)** (*rady*) advice **b)** (*polecenia*) instructions **3.** (*zegara*) hand **4.** (*zalecenie*) recommendation **5.** (*znak*) sign

wskazujący *adj* **1.** ***palec ~*** index finger **2.** *zaimek*: demonstrative

wskazywać ⟨***-zać***⟩ (*-zuję*) **1.** show, indicate; ***~ komuś drogę do*** *G* show s.o. the way to, give s.o. directions how to get to; ***~ komuś miejsce*** (*przy stole*) seat s.o., show s.o. to their seat **2.** (*palcem*) point (***na*** *A* to) **3.** (*o zegarze*) say **4.** (*następcę*) name

wskaźnik *m* (*-ka*; *-ki*) **1.** (*liczba*) index, indicator, rate; ***~ cen*** price index; ***~i finansowe*** financial indicators; ***~ urodzeń*** birth rate; ***~ bezrobocia*** unemployment rate; ***~i oglądalności*** viewer ratings, audience ratings **2.** (*przyrząd*) gauge; ***~ paliwa*** fuel gauge **3.** (*wskazówka, dioda*) indicator **4.** (*nauczyciela*) pointer

wskoczyć *v/p* → ***wskakiwać***

wskórać *v/p* (*-ram*): ***nic nie ~*** get nowhere; ***tym nic nie wskórasz*** it won't help, it'll get you nowhere; ***niewiele ~*** not get far

wskroś: ***na ~*** thoroughly, through and through; ***na ~ uczciwy*** perfectly honest, honest to the bone

wskrzeszać ⟨***-sić***⟩ (*-szam*) **1.** *zmarłego*: resurrect, raise from the dead **2.** *fig* revive

wskutek *prep* (*G*) as a result of; ***~ tego*** as a result, consequently; ***~ czego*** as a result of which

wsławiać się ⟨***-wić***⟩ (*-wiam*) become famous (*I* for)

wsłuch|iwać się ⟨***-chać***⟩ (*-chuję*) listen intently (***w*** *A* to); ***~aj się w siebie*** listen to your inner voice

wspak: ***czytać coś*** (***na***) ***~*** read s.th. backwards

wspaniale *adv*: ***czuć się ~*** feel great; ***~!*** that's fantastic!, that's great!

wspaniałomyślność *f* (*-ści*; *no pl*) magnanimity, generosity; **wspaniałomyślny** *adj* magnanimous, generous

wspaniały *adj* **1.** (*budzący zachwyt*) wonderful, *Br* marvellous, *Am* marvelous, great **2.** *wynik*: brilliant, great **3.** *przyjęcie*: grand, great

wsparcie *n* (*-cia*; *no pl*) support

wspiąć się *v/p* → ***wspinać się***

wspierać ⟨***wesprzeć***⟩ (*-ram*) **1.** support; ***wsparty na słupach*** supported by posts; ***~ głowę na ręce*** rest one's head on one's hand **2.** (*popierać*) back (up), support **3.** (*finansowo*) support, assist; ***wspierać się*** **1.** (*pomagać sobie*) support each other **2.** (*opierać się*) lean (***na*** *L* on)

wspinacz *m* (*-cza*; *-cze*) climber, mountaineer; **wspinaczka** *f* (*-ki*; *-ki*) climbing; ***~ wysokogórska*** mountaineering

wspinać się ⟨***-piąć***⟩ (*-nam*) climb; ***~ na górę*** climb (up) a mountain; ***~ na szczyt*** climb to the top; ***~ na palce*** stand on one's toes

wspomagać ⟨***-móc***⟩ (*-gam*) help, support; **wspomaganie** *n* (*-nia*; *-nia*): ***~ kierownicy*** power steering

wspominać ⟨***-mnieć***⟩ (*-nam*) mention (***o*** *L*); ***nie wspominając o*** *L* not to mention; ***~ stare, dobre czasy*** remember the good old times; ***wspomnisz moje słowa*** mark my words

wspomniany *adj* **1.** (*powyżej*) above-mentioned **2.** JUR said

wspomnieni|e *n* (*-nia*; *-nia*) memory, recollection; ***~a*** memories; ***~e pośmiertne*** obituary; ***na samo ~e o*** *L* at the mere mention of

wspomóc *v/p* → ***wspomagać***

wspólnictwo *n* (*-wa*; *no pl*) **1.** (*w przestępstwie*) complicity **2.** (*partnerstwo*) partnership; **wspólniczka** *f* (*-ki*; *-ki*) **1.** ECON partner **2.** (*przestępczyni*) accomplice; **wspólnik** *m* (*-ka*; *-nicy*) **1.** ECON partner **2.** (*przestępca*) accomplice

wspólnota *f* (*-ty*; *-ty*) community; ***~ interesów*** common goals, community of interests; ***~ majątkowa*** joint property; ***~ pierwotna*** primitive community; ***Ꮭ Narodów*** the Commonwealth of Nations

W

wspóln|y *adj* **1.** common; ***~y wróg*** common enemy; ***~a mogiła*** mass grave; ***robić coś ~ymi siłami*** join forces to do s.th., make a joint effort to do s.th.; ***nie mieć nic ~ego z*** *I* have nothing to do with; ***co to ma z nią ~ego?*** what does it have to do with her?; ***znajdować z kimś ~y język*** be on the same wavelength with **2.** *mieszkanie, pogląd*: shared; ***~y pogląd*** shared viewpoint

współautor *m* (*-ra*; *-rzy*), **~ka** *f* (*-ki*; *-ki*) co-author; **współautorstwo** *n* (*-wa*; *no pl*) co-authorship, joint authorship

współczesność *f* (*-ści*; *no pl*) the present (day); **współczesny** *adj* **1.** *pisarz, sztuka*: contemporary **2.** *fizyka, technika, historia, sztuka*: modern; **współcześni** *pl* (*-czesnych*) contemporaries; **współcześnie** *adv* (*obecnie*) today, in our times

współczuci|e *n* (*-cia*; *no pl*) compassion, sympathy; ***złożyć komuś wyrazy ~a*** offer one's condolences to s.o.; ***godny ~a*** deserving of compassion

współczuć *v/im* (*-czuję*) feel sorry (*D* for), sympathize (*D* with); **współczująco** *adv* compassionately

współczynnik *m* (*-ka*; *-ki*) **1.** *ECON* ratio, rate; ***~ inflacji*** rate of inflation **2.** *PHYS MATH* coefficient

współdecydować *v/im* (*-duję*) decide together, make joint decisions (**o** *L* on)

współdziałać *v/im* (*-łam*) cooperate; **współdziałanie** *n* (*-nia*; *no pl*) cooperation

współgrać *v/im* (*-ram*) harmonize, correspond (**z** *I* with)

współistnienie *n* (*-nia*; *no pl*) coexistence

współlokator *m* (*-ra*; *-rzy*), **~ka** *f* (*-ki*; *-ki*) **1.** (*w mieszkaniu*) *Br* flatmate, *Am* room-mate **2.** (*w pokoju*) roommate

współmałżonek *m* (*-nka*; *-nkowie*), **-nka** *f* (*-ki*; *-ki*) spouse

współmierny *adj* commensurate (**do** *G* with)

współobywatel *m* (*-la*; *-le*), **~ka** *f* (*-ki*; *-ki*) fellow citizen

współodpowiedzialny *adj* jointly responsible (**za** *A* for)

współoskarżony *m* (*-nego*; *-żeni*), **-na** *f* (*-nej*; *-ne*) *JUR* co-defendant

współpasażer *m* (*-ra*; *-rowie*), **~ka** *f* (*-ki*; *-ki*) fellow passenger

współpraca *f* (*-cy*; *no pl*) cooperation, collaboration

współpracować *v/im* (*-cuję*) cooperate, collaborate (**z** *I* with)

współpracownik *m* (*-ka*; *-nicy*), **-niczka** *f* (*-ki*; *-ki*) **1.** collaborator **2.** (*w miejscu pracy*) co-worker **3.** (*partner*) partner

współrządzić *v/im* (*-dzę*) share political power, govern together

współrzędna *f* (*-nej*; *-ne*) *MATH* coordinate

współsprawca *m* (*-cy*; *-cy*), **-czyni** *f* (*-ni*; *-nie*) *JUR* accomplice

współuczestnictwo *n* (*-wa*; *no pl*) participation; **współuczestniczyć** *v/im* (*-czę*) participate; **współuczestnik** *m* (*-ka*; *-nicy*), **-niczka** *f* (*-ki*; *-ki*) participant

współudział *m* (*-łu*; *no pl*) **1.** participation **2.** (*w przestępstwie*) complicity

współwięzień *m* (*-więźnia*; *-więźniowie*), **-więźniarka** *f* (*-ki*; *-ki*) **1.** fellow inmate, fellow prisoner **2.** (*w jednej celi*) cellmate

współwinny **I** *adj* ***być ~m*** *G* be an accomplice to, be an accessory to **II** *n* (*-nego*; *-ni*) accomplice, accessory; ***~ przestępstwa*** accomplice, partner in crime

współwłasność *f* (*-ści*; *no pl*) **1.** (*majątek*) joint property **2.** (*prawo własności*) joint ownership; **współwłaściciel** *m* (*-la*; *-le*), **~ka** *f* (*-ki*; *-ki*) co-owner, joint owner

współwyznawca *m* (*-cy*; *-cy*) fellow believer, co-religionist

współzależność *f* (*-ści*; *no pl*) correlation

współzawodnictwo *n* (*-wa*; *no pl*) rivalry, competition; **współzawodniczyć** *v/im* (*-czę*) compete (**z** *I* with, **o** *A* for)

współżycie *n* (*-cia*; *no pl*) coexistance; ***~ seksualne*** sex life; ***rozpocząć ~*** become sexually active; **współżyć** *v/im* (*-żyję*) **1.** live together **2.** (*seksualnie*) have sex, have intercourse

wstawać ⟨**-tać**⟩ (*-taję*) get up; ***wcześnie ~*** get up early; ***~ od stołu*** rise from the table
wstawiać ⟨**-wić**⟩ (*-wiam*) **1.** put; ***~ wodę na herbatę*** put the kettle on; ***~ brakujące słowa*** fill in the gaps **2.** *szybę*: replace; **wstawiać się 1.** (*ujmować się*) stand up (**za** *I* for), intercede (**za** *I* for/in behalf of) **2.** (*upić się*) *infml* get tipsy
wstawiennictw|o *n* (*-wa*; *no pl*) intercession; ***za czyimś ~em*** through s.o.'s intercession
wstawiony *adj infml* tipsy
wstawka *f* (*-ki*; *-ki*) **1.** (*dygresja*) digression **2.** (*przerywnik*) interlude **3.** (*w ubraniu*) gusset **4.** (*uzupełnienie*) insertion
wstąpić *v/p* → ***wstępować***
wstąpienie *n* (*-nia*; *no pl*): ***~ do wojska*** joining the army; ***~ w związek małżeński*** getting married; ***~ na tron*** ascension to the throne
wstążeczka *f* (*-ki*; *-ki*) *dim* ribbon; **wstążka** *f* (*-ki*; *-ki*) ribbon
wstecz *adv* backwards; ***spoglądać ~ na*** *A fig* look back on; ***działać ~*** retroact; ***cała ~!*** full speed astern!
wstecznictwo *n* (*-wa*; *no pl*) reactionary attitudes *pl*, reactionarism; **wstecznik** *m* (*-ka*; *-nicy*) reactionary; **wsteczny** *adj* **1.** *poglądy*: reactionary **2.** ***bieg ~*** AUTO reverse (gear) **3.** *lusterko*: rear-view **4.** *moc*: retroactive
wstęg|a *f* (*-gi*; *-gi*) ribbon; ***przeciąć ~ę*** cut the ribbon
wstęp *m* (*-pu*; *-py*) **1.** (*wejście*) entry, admission; ***~ wzbroniony*** no entry; ***~ wolny*** admission free; ***bilet ~u*** admission ticket, entrance ticket; ***ile kosztuje ~?*** how much is it to get in?, what's the admission?; ***~ od godziny ósmej*** admission from 8 o'clock **2.** (*wprowadzenie*) introduction; ***na ~ie*** to begin with, to start with
wstępn|y *adj* **1.** *wyniki*, *rozmowy*: preliminary, initial **2.** *uwagi*, *kurs*: introductory **3.** *egzamin*: entrance **4.** ***słowo ~e*** preface, foreword **5.** ***artykuł ~y*** editorial, *Br* leading article
wstępować ⟨**-tąpić**⟩ (*-puję*) (**do** *G*) **1.** (*przystępować*) join, enter; ***~ do klubu*** join a club; ***~ do zakonu*** enter a convent; ***~ do armii*** join the army; ***~ w związek małżeński*** get married, *lit* enter into matrimony; ***~ na uniwersytet*** *Br* enrol at a university, *Am* enroll in a university **2.** (*zachodzić*) stop by, drop in; ***~ do kogoś*** stop by to see s.o., drop in on s.o.; ***~ do kawiarni*** stop by a coffee shop; ***~ na kawę*** stop by for (a) coffee, drop in for a cup of coffee **3.** (*wchodzić*) step (**na** *A* on); ***~ na tron*** *fig* take the throne, ascend the throne **4.** *fig* fill (**w** *A*); ***wstąpiła w nas nadzieja*** hope filled our hearts, we were filled with hope; ***wstąpiła w niego nowa energia*** he got his second wind
wstręt *m* (*-tu*; *no pl*) disgust, revulsion, repulsion; ***czuć ~ do kogoś*** find s.o. repulsive, be disgusted by s.o.; ***wzbudzający ~*** disgusting, repulsive; ***ze ~em*** with disgust, with revulsion; ***robić komuś ~y*** place obstacles in s.o.'s way; **wstrętny** *adj* **1.** disgusting, repulsive **2.** *jedzenie*: awful, disgusting
wstrząs *m* (*-su*; *-sy*) shock; ***~ mózgu*** concussion; ***~y sejsmiczne*** seismic activity, seismic shaking; ***łagodne ~y*** (*sejsmiczne*) tectonic tremors; ***bez ~ów*** **a)** (*gładko*) smoothly **b)** (*spokojnie*) peacefully
wstrząsać ⟨**-snąć**⟩ (*-sam*) **1.** shake; ***wstrząsały nim dreszcze*** he was shaking **2.** *fig* shock; **wstrząsający** *adj* shocking; **wstrząsow|y** *adj*: ***terapia ~a*** shock treatment, shock therapy; **wstrząśnięty** *adj fig* shocked
wstrzemięźliwie *adv lit* moderately, *lit* abstemiously
wstrzemięźliwy *adj* **1.** *lit* abstemious; ***~ seksualnie*** *form* continent **2.** (*powściągliwy*) restrained
wstrzykiwać ⟨**-knąć**⟩ (*-kuję*) inject
wstrzymywać ⟨**-mać**⟩ (*-muję*) **1.** stop **2.** *oddech*: hold; **wstrzymywać się** put off (**z** *I*), defer (**z** *I*); ***~ się od*** *G* refrain from; ***~ się od głosu*** abstain (from voting); ***nie mógł wstrzymać się od śmiechu*** he couldn't help laughing, he couldn't keep a straight face
wstyd *m* (*-du*; *no pl*) **1.** shame; ***~ mi*** I am ashamed (**za** *A* of); ***zrobiło mi się ~*** I felt ashamed; (**to**) ***~, że*** it's a shame that, it's a disgrace that; ***to ża-***

den ~ it's nothing to be ashamed of; (**to**) **~!** it's a shame!, it's a disgrace!; ***nie mieć ~u*** have no shame; ***przynosić komuś ~*** bring shame on s.o., disgrace s.o. **2.** (*onieśmielenie*) embarrassment; ***czerwienić się ze ~u*** blush with embarrassment

wstydliwie *adv* shyly

wstydliwy *adj* **1.** *osoba*: shy, bashful **2.** *uśmiech*: embarrassed, bashful **3.** *temat*: embarrassing, awkward

wstydzić się *v/im* (*-dzę*) **1.** be ashamed (*G* of) **2.** (*być nieśmiałym*) be shy

wsuwać ⟨**wsunąć**⟩ (*-wam*) slip, put; ***~ coś do kieszeni*** slip s.th. into one's pocket; ***~ coś komuś do ręki*** slip s.th. into s.o.'s hand; ***wsuwać się*** slip, slide (**pod** *A* under)

wsuwka *f* (*-ki*; *-ki*) (*do włosów*) hairpin

wsypa *f* (*-py*; *-py*) (*wpadka*) *infml* bust

wsypywać ⟨**-pać**⟩ (*-puję*) **1.** pour (**do** in/into) **2.** (*zdradzać*) *infml* rat (*A* on); *Br infml* grass (*A* on); ***wsypywać się*** get (**do** *G* into)

wsysać ⟨**wessać**⟩ (*-sam*) suck in, suck up

wszcząć *v/p* → ***wszczynać***

wszczepiać ⟨**-pić**⟩ (*-piam*) **1.** *elektrodę, organ*: implant **2.** (*w łodygę, pień*) graft **3.** ***~ coś komuś*** *fig Br* instil s.o. with s.th., *Am* instill s.o. with s.th., inculcate s.th. in s.o., inculcate s.o. with s.th.

wszczynać ⟨**-cząć**⟩ (*-nam*) **1.** start **2.** *postępowanie*: initiate, instigate **3.** *śledztwo, dochodzenie*: launch, initiate

wszechmoc *f* (*-cy*; *no pl*) omnipotence; **wszechmocny** *adj* almighty, omnipotent; **wszechnica** *f* (*-cy*; *-ce*) **1.** *lit* university **2.** (*kurs*) series of lectures

wszechobecny *adj* ubiquitous, omnipresent; **wszechogarniający** *adj* overwhelming, overpowering, all-embracing; **wszechstronny** *adj* **1.** *artysta, zawodnik*: versatile, all-round **2.** *wykształcenie*: broad, comprehensive **3.** *analiza, studium*: thorough **4.** *zainteresowania*: wide-ranging

wszechświat *m* (*-ta*; *no pl*) the universe; **wszechwiedzący** *adj* omniscient, all-knowing; **wszechwładny** *adj* all-powerful, omnipotent

wszelk|i *pron* all, every, any; ***za ~ą cenę*** at all costs, at any cost; ***na ~i wypadek*** just in case, just to be on the safe side, ***~imi sposobami*** by all possible means; ***~iego rodzaju*** all kinds of, of all kinds; ***ponad ~ą wątpliwość*** beyond any doubt

wszerz *adv* across, in width

wszędobylski *adj* ubiquitous

wszędzie *adv* everywhere

wszy *pl* → ***wesz***

wszyć *v/p* → ***wszywać***

wszyscy *pron* all, everybody

wszyst|ek *pron* all, every; ***ze ~kich sił*** with all one's strength; ***po ~kie czasy*** forever

wszystkie *pron* all, every

wszystk|o *pron* everything, all; ***robimy ~o, co w naszej mocy*** we're doing everything we can; ***to ~o*** that's all; ***przede ~im***, ***nade ~o*** above all, first of all; ***już po ~im*** it's all over; ***~o jedno*** it's all the same, it doesn't matter; ***mimo ~o*** after all; ***~iego najlepszego!*** all the best!; ***~iego najlepszego z okazji urodzin!*** many happy returns!

wszystkowiedzący *adj* omniscient; all-knowing

wszystkożerny *adj* omnivorous

wszyściuteńko, **wszyściutko** *pron dim* absolutely everything

wszywać ⟨**wszyć**⟩ (*-wam*) **1.** *klin, rękaw*: sew in **2.** *esperal*: implant

wścibiać ⟨**-bić**⟩ (*-biam*): ***~ nos w nie swoje sprawy*** poke one's nose into other people's affairs

wścibski *adj* **1.** *sąsiadka, pytania*: nosy, inquisitive **2.** *spojrzenie*: inquisitive

wściekać ⟨**-ciec**⟩ (*-kam*) make mad, make furious; ***wściekać się*** get mad; ***wściec się można!*** it's enough to drive you up the wall!

wściekle *adv*: ***spojrzeć ~ na kogoś*** look ferociously at s.o.; ***~ głodny*** voraciously hungry, ravenous; ***~ różowa bluzka*** a shocking pink top

wściekli|zna *f* (*-ny*; *no pl*) MED rabies *sing*; ***szczepionka przeciw ~źnie*** rabies vaccine

wściekłoś|ć *f* (*-ści*; *no pl*) rage, fury; ***doprowadzić kogoś do ~ci*** infuriate s.o., drive s.o. mad; ***wpaść***

we ~ć fly into a rage, become furious

wściekły *adj* **1.** *osoba*, *spojrzenie*: furious **2.** *osoba*: *Am infml* mad **3.** *pies*, *lis*: rabid **4.** *róż*: shocking **5.** *wiatr*: fierce **6.** *ból*: excruciating

wślizgiwać się ⟨***-znąć***, ***-gnąć***⟩ (*-guję*) **1.** (*do środka*) slip in; ***~ do pokoju*** slip into a room **2.** (*pod kołdrę*) slip (***pod*** *A* under) **3.** (*o wężu*) creep in, slither in

wśród *prep* (*G*) among, in the middle of; ***dom ~ drzew*** a house among the trees; ***~ gromkich braw*** amid thunderous applause

wtaczać ⟨**wtoczyć**⟩ (*-czam*) **1.** roll in **2.** (*pod górę*) roll up **3.** *wózek*: push in, wheel in; ***~ wózek do pokoju*** push a wheelchair into a room; ***wtaczać się*** **1.** roll (***do*** *G* into) **2.** (*o osobie*) *infml* lumber (***do*** *G* into)

wtajemniczać ⟨***-czyć***⟩ (*-czam*) **1.** (*w tajniki*) initiate (***w*** *A* into) **2.** (*w plan*) let in (***w*** *A* on)

wtajemniczony I *adj* initiated **II** *m* (*-nego*; *-czeni*), **-na** *f* (*-nej*; *-ne*) **1.** initiate; ***~eni*** the initiated **2.** (*mający dostęp do poufnych informacji*) insider

wtapiać ⟨**wtopić**⟩ (*-piam*) set (***w*** *A* in); ***wtapiać się*** *fig* blend (***w*** *A* in); ***~ się w tłum*** melt into the crowd

wtargnąć *v/p* (*-nę*) **1.** (*do pomieszczenia*) barge (***do*** *G* into) **2.** (*do miasta*, *kraju*) invade (***do*** *G*)

wtedy *adv* then, at that time; ***i co ~?*** and then what?

wtem *adv* suddenly, all of a sudden

wtłaczać ⟨***-łoczyć***⟩ (*-czam*) **1.** *wodę*, *gaz*: pump (***do*** *G* into) **2.** *gaz*: force **3.** *pasażerów*: cram, pack; ***wtłaczać się*** cram, crowd

wtoczyć *v/p* → ***wtaczać***

wtorek *m* (*-rku*; *-rki*) Tuesday; ***we ~*** on Tuesday; **wtorkowy** *adj* **1.** *wieczór*: Tuesday **2.** *lekcja*: Tuesday's

wtór: ***przy ~ze*** *G* to the accompaniment of

wtórn|y *adj* **1.** secondary; ***rynek ~y*** the secondary market; ***surowce ~e*** recyclable materials, recyclables; ***~y analfabetyzm*** loss of literacy **2.** (*nieoryginalny*) derivative

wtórować ⟨***za-***⟩ (*-ruję*) **1.** accompany (***komuś na*** *L* s.o. on) **2.** (*powtarzać*) echo

wtór|y: ***po ~e*** secondly; ***po raz ~y*** for the second time

wtrącać ⟨***-cić***⟩ (*-cam*) **1.** (*do więzienia*) throw (***do*** *G* in) **2.** *uwagę*: interject; ***wtrącać się*** **1.** (*do rozmowy*) cut in, butt in (***do*** *G* on) **2.** (*do spraw*) meddle (***do*** *G* in), interfere (***do*** *G* with), butt in (***do*** *G* on); ***nie wtrącaj się!*** it's none of your business!, mind your own business!

wtrącenie *n* (*-nia*; *-nia*) interjection, aside

wtryniać ⟨***-nić***⟩ (*-niam*) (*zapodziać*) *infml* mislay; ***wtryniać się*** barge in

wtryskarka *f* (*-ki*; *-ki*) *Br* injection moulding machine, *Am* injection molding machine

wtryskiwać ⟨***-snąć***⟩ (*-kuję*) inject

wtulać ⟨***-lić***⟩ (*-lam*): ***~ twarz w poduszkę*** nestle one's head into a pillow; ***~ głowę w ramiona*** lower one's head and hunch one's shoulders; ***wtulać się*** snuggle, nestle (***w*** *A* in/into)

wtulony *adj* snuggled, nestled; ***~ w poduszkę*** nestling one's head on a pillow

wtyczka *f* (*-ki*; *-ki*) **1.** plug **2.** (*osoba*) *infml* plant, mole; **wtyczkow|y** *adj*: ***gniazdo ~e*** socket, *Am* outlet

wtykać ⟨**wetknąć**⟩ (*-kam*) **1.** put (***do*** *G* into/in) **2.** (*do zamka*, *kieszeni*) stick (***do*** *G* in/into)

wuj *m* (*-ja*; *-jowie*), ***wujek*** *m* (*-jka*; *-jkowie*) uncle

wulgarny *adj* vulgar, crude

wulkan *m* (*-nu*; *-ny*) volcano; ***~ energii*** powerhouse; **wulkaniczny** *adj* volcanic

wulkanizować ⟨***z-***⟩ (*-zuję*) vulcanize

ww. *abbr* (= ***wyżej wymieniony***) abovementioned

W-wa *abbr f* (*W-wy*) (= **Warszawa**) Warsaw

wwozić ⟨**wwieźć**⟩ (*wwożę*) (*z zagranicy*) bring (in); ***~ coś do kraju*** bring s.th. into a country

wwóz *m* (*wwozu*; *no pl*) importation

wy *pron* you

wybaczać ⟨***-czyć***⟩ (*-czam*) forgive

wybaczalny *adj* forgivable, excusable; **wybaczeni|e** *n* (*-nia*; *no pl*) forgiveness; ***nie do ~a*** unforgivable, inexcusable

wybaczyć *v/p* (*-czę*) forgive; ***proszę mi ~, pan wybaczy*** pardon me, I beg your pardon
wybadać *v/p* (*-dam*) sound out; ***~ grunt*** *fig* spy out the land
wybałuszać ⟨**-szyć**⟩ (*-szam*): ***~ oczy na*** *A* goggle at
wybawca *m* (*-cy*; *-cy*), **-czyni** *f* (*-ni*; *-nie*) *Br* saviour, *Am* savior
wybawiać ⟨**-wić**⟩ (*-wiam*) save, rescue; ***~ kogoś od śmierci*** save s.o. from death; ***~ kogoś z kłopotu*** get s.o. out of trouble
wybawiciel *m* (*-la*; *-le*), **~ka** *f* (*-ki*; *-ki*) *Br* saviour, *Am* savior
wybawienie *n* (*-nia*; *no pl*) **1.** (*ratunek*) salvation, rescue **2.** REL salvation
wybąkać *v/p* (*-kam*) mumble
wybić *v/p* (*-biję*): ***~ coś sobie z głowy*** get an idea out of one's head; → ***wybijać***
wybiec *v/p* → ***wybiegać***
wybieg *m* (*-gu*; *-gi*) **1.** (*w zoo*) (outdoor) enclosure **2.** (*dla koni*) paddock **3.** (*dla bydła*) corral **4.** (*dla modelek*) catwalk **5.** *fig* ploy, trick; ***posłużyć się ~iem*** use a trick
wybiegać ⟨**-biec**⟩ (*-gam*) run out (***z*** *G* of); ***~ za*** *I* run after; ***~ komuś na spotkanie*** run out to meet s.o.; (***nie***) ***~ poza*** *A fig* (not) go beyond; ***~ myślą w przyszłość*** think ahead, take the long view; ***wybiegać się***: ***psy muszą się ~*** dogs need to run a lot
wybielać ⟨**-lić**⟩ (*-lam*) **1.** *bieliznę*, *tkaninę*: bleach **2.** *zęby*: whiten **3.** *osobę*: whitewash; ***wybielać się*** *fig* whitewash oneself
wybierać ⟨**-brać**⟩ (*-ram*) **1.** choose, select; ***jest w czym ~*** there's a lot to choose from **2.** *numer*: dial **3.** *pieniądze*: withdraw **4.** *prezydenta*, *przewodniczącego*: elect **5.** *wodę*: draw **6.** *sieci*: haul in; ***wybierać się*** go; ***wybrać się w podróż*** set out on a journey; ***wybrać się do kogoś z wizytą*** pay s.o. a visit; ***wybrać się na spacer*** go for a walk; ***wybrać się do teatru*** go to the theatre
wybieralny *adj* elective
wybijać ⟨**-bić**⟩ (*-jam*) **1.** *szybę*: break, smash **2.** *dziurę w ścianie*: knock **3.** *ząb*: knock out **4.** *oko*: poke out **5.** *godzinę*, *północ*: strike **6.** *rytm*: beat (out) **7.** *mieszkańców*, *zwierzęta*: kill off, wipe out **8.** *medal*: mint **9.** ***obrońca wybił piłkę na aut*** the defender knocked the ball out of bounds; ***wybijać się*** **1.** (*osiągać znaczenie*, *sławę*) make a mark, make one's mark **2.** (*wyróżniać się*) stand out **3.** ***wybić się z rytmu*** *fig* lose one's rhythm **4.** ***wybić się ze snu*** be unable to fall asleep, become wide awake
wybiórczo *adv* selectively; **wybiórczy** *adj* selective
wybitnie *adv* **1.** remarkably **2.** *uzdolniony*: highly; **wybitny** *adj* **1.** *osoba*, *zdolności*: outstanding **2.** *kariera*: remarkable
wyblakły *adj* faded; **wyblaknąć** *v/p* → ***blaknąć***
wybłagać *v/p* (*-gam*) get by begging (***u*** *G* from)
wyboisty *adj* bumpy
wyboje *pl* (*-jów*/*-boi*) potholes
wyborca *m* (*-cy*; *-cy*) voter; **wyborcz|y** *adj* election; ***kampania ~a*** election campaign; ***lokal ~y*** polling station; ***urna ~a*** ballot box
wyborny *adj* excellent, exquisite
wyborow|y *adj* **1.** select, choice; ***strzelec ~y*** sharpshooter, marksman **2.** *wódka*: premium
wyb|ór *m* (*-boru*; *-bory*) **1.** choice, selection; ***dokonać ~oru*** make a choice; ***nie mieć ~oru*** have no choice; ***do ~oru*** to choose from; ***z ~oru*** by choice; ***~ory*** POLIT election(s); ***~ory do parlamentu*** parliamentary election(s); ***~ory uzupełniające*** by-election; ***~ór na stanowisko premiera*** appointment to the post of prime minister, appointment as prime minister; ***~ór na nowego lidera partii*** election as the new party leader; ***czegoś jest do ~oru do koloru*** there is a wide selection of s.th. **2.** *utworów*: selection
wybrać *v/p* → ***wybierać***
wybrakowany *adj* faulty, defective; ***egzemplarz ~*** faulty item, defective item
wybranek *m* (*-nka*; *-nkowie*) *lit* beloved, sweetheart
wybraniać ⟨**-ronić**⟩ (*-niam*) defend (***od*** *G* from), rescue (***od*** *G* from)
wybraniec *m* (*-rańca*; *-rańcy*) the chosen one; ***~ losu*** fortune's darling

wybrany **I** *adj* chosen, selected **II** *m* (*-nego*; *-ni*), **-na** *f* (*-nej*; *-ne*) the chosen one; **~i** the chosen few

wybredny *adj* **1.** picky, fussy **2.** *gust*: discriminating

wybrnąć *v/p* (*-nę*) get out (**z** *G* of); **~ z długów** get out of debt

wybronić *v/p* → **wybraniać**

wybrudzić *v/p* → **brudzić**

wybrukować *v/p* → **brukować**

wybryk *m* (*-ku*; *-ki*) prank; **chuligańskie ~i** acts of hooliganism; **~ młodości** youthful escapade; **~ natury** freak of nature

wybrzeż|e *n* (*-ża*; *-ża*) coast; **pojechać na ~e** go to the seaside; **mieszkać na ~u** live at the seaside

wybrzuszać się ⟨**-szyć**⟩ (*-szam*) (*o deskach*) swell up

wybrzydzać *v/im* (*-dzam*) **1.** be fussy **2.** (*narzekać*) gripe (**na** *A* about)

wybuch *m* (*-chu*; *-chy*) **1.** *bomby*: explosion **2.** *wojny*, *epidemii*: outbreak **3.** *gniewu*: outburst **4.** *wulkanu*: eruption; **~y wulkanów** volcanic eruptions

wybuchać ⟨**-chnąć**⟩ (*-cham*) **1.** explode, go off **2.** (*o wojnie*, *epidemii*, *panice*) break out **3.** (*o wulkanie*) erupt **4. ~ śmiechem** burst out laughing; **~ płaczem** burst into tears; **~ gniewem** flare up in anger

wybuchowy *adj* **1.** *ładunek*: explosive; **materiał ~** explosive **2.** *osoba*: hot-tempered, short-tempered

wybudować *v/p* → **budować**

wybujały *adj* **1.** *ambicja*: excessive **2.** *fantazja*: wild, vivid **3.** *roślinność*: exuberant, lush

wybulić *v/p* → **bulić**

wyburzać ⟨**-rzyć**⟩ (*-rzam*) knock down, pull down

wybywać ⟨**-być**⟩ (*-wam*) *infml* go off

wycałować *v/p* (*-łuję*) kiss (repeatedly)

wycelować *v/p* → **celować**[1]

wycena *f* (*-ny*; *-ny*) valuation, appraisal; **wyceniać** ⟨**-nić**⟩ (*-niam*) value (**na** *A* at), price (**na** *A* at)

wychlać *v/p* (*-lam*) *infml* guzzle

wychładzać ⟨**-łodzić**⟩ (*-dzam*) cool (down)

wychodek *m* (*-dka*; *-dki*) privy, *Am* outhouse

wychodn|e *n* (*-nego*; *no pl*) time off; **mieć ~e** to have time off; **na ~ym** on leaving

wychodzić ⟨**wyjść**⟩ (*-dzę*) **1.** leave (**z** *G*), go out (**z** *G* of), come out (**z** *G* of); **~ spod** *G* come (out) from under; **~ zza chmur** come out from behind the clouds; **okna wychodzą na ulicę** the windows look out on a street; **~ z mody** go out of fashion; **~ z użycia** (*o słowie*) fall out of use; **~ z więzienia** be released from prison; **~ poza** *A fig* go beyond; **~ za mąż** get married; **~ za mąż za kogoś** marry s.o.; **~ z inicjatywą** put forward a proposal, put forward an initiative; **~ komuś na dobre**, **~ komuś na zdrowie** do s.o. good; **~ z założenia, że** assume that; **~ dobrze na zdjęciu** come out well on a photograph; **~ komuś naprzeciw** *fig* meet s.o. half-way; **~ na swoje** break even, make a profit; **~ na czysto** break even; **~ dobrze na** *L* (*zyskać*) make a profit on; **to na jedno wychodzi** it's all the same; **~ w morze** put out to sea **2.** (*o zarządzeniu*) be issued, come out **3.** (*o włosach*) fall out **4.** (*udać się*) come out; **zdjęcia wyszły dobrze** photos came out well; **jak wyszło ciasto?** how did the cake turn out?; **nic z tego nie wyszło** it came to nothing **5.** (*o gazecie, książce*) come out, be published

wychodźca *m* (*-cy*; *-cy*) *lit* emigrant; **wychodźstwo** *n* (*-wa*; *no pl*) *lit* emigration

wychować *v/p* → **wychowywać**

wychowanek *m* (*-nka*; *-nkowie*), **-nka** *f* (*-ki*; *-ki*) **1.** (*podopieczny*) foster child; **~ domu dziecka** child brought up in a children's home **2.** (*absolwent*) alumnus

wychowanie *n* (*-nia*; *no pl*) **1.** (*kształcenie*) education; **~ fizyczne** physical education **2.** (*opieka*) **wziąć kogoś na ~** take s.o. in **3.** (*ogłada*) (good) manners *pl*

wychowany *adj*: **dobrze ~** well-brought up, well-mannered; **źle ~** ill-mannered, bad-mannered

wychowawca *m* (*-cy*; *-cy*), **-czyni** *f* (*-ni*; *-nie*) **1.** (*w szkole*) *Br* class tutor, form teacher, *Am* home-room teacher

2. (*na kolonii*) *Am* counselor **3.** (*w domu dziecka*) carer **4.** (*w przedszkolu*) *Br* nursery (school) teacher, *Am* pre-school teacher

wychowawcz|y *adj*: ***metody ~e*** educational methods; ***urlop ~y*** parental leave; ***zakład ~y*** *Br* childcare centre, *Am* childcare center; ***zasiłek ~y*** maternity benefit

wychowywać ⟨**-chować**⟩ (*-chowuję*) **1.** (*zapewniać opiekę*) bring up, rear **2.** (*kształcić*) educate, train; ***wychowywać się*** be brought up, be reared

wychuchany *adj* **1.** *mieszkanie*: spotless, spick-and-span **2.** *dziecko*: pampered

wychudły *adj* emaciated, gaunt, scrawny

wychudnąć *v/p* (*-nę*) lose a lot of weight

wychwalać *v/im* (*-lam*) praise, *form* extol

wychwytywać ⟨**-chwycić**⟩ (*-tuję*) *błąd*: pick up, find, notice

wychylać ⟨**-lić**⟩ (*-lam*) **1.** (*przez okno*) lean out; ***wychylił głowę za okno*** he leaned his head out (of) the window **2.** *kieliszek*: down, knock back; ***wychylać się*** **1.** (*z okna*) lean out; ***~ się z okna*** lean out (of) a window **2.** (*zza chmur*) emerge (**zza** *G* from behind) **3.** (*zza zakrętu*, *rogu*) appear (**zza** *G* from behind) **4.** ***~ się do przodu*** lean forward **5.** *fig* stick one's neck out

wyciąć *v/p* (*wytnę*): ***~ komuś numer*** *infml* pull a fast one on s.o.; → ***wycinać***

wyciąg *m* (*-gu*; *-gi*) **1.** (*w górach*) ***~ narciarski*** ski lift; ***~ krzesełkowy*** chairlift **2.** *FIN* statement; ***~ z konta*** bank statement **3.** (*ekstrakt*) extract **4.** (*fragment*) excerpt, extract **5.** (*skrót*) abstract **6.** *MED* traction **7.** (*okap*) ventilation hood

wyciągać ⟨**-gnąć**⟩ (*-gam*) **1.** take out, pull out, get out; ***~ coś z kieszeni*** take s.th. out of one's pocket; ***~ z kogoś informacje*** get information out of s.o.; ***~ od kogoś pieniądze*** sponge off s.o., sponge on s.o.; ***~ rękę do zgody*** *fig* hold out one's hand, hold out an olive branch; ***jego samochód wyciąga 220 km/h*** his car does 220 kph, *infml* his car maxes out at 220 kph; ***~ konsekwencje z czegoś*** not let s.th. pass **2.** (*prostować*) stretch out; ***~ nogi*** stretch out one's legs; ***wyciągnąć kopyta*** *infml* kick the bucket **3.** *szyję*: crane **4.** *wnioski*: draw **5.** (*z domu*, *łóżka*) *infml* drag out; ***wyciągnąć kogoś do kina*** drag s.o. out to the cinema, drag s.o. out to see a movie; ***~ kogoś z łóżka*** get s.o. out of bed; ***wyciągać się*** **1.** (*o osobie*) strech out **2.** (*o swetrze*) strech (out of shape)

wycie *n* (*-cia*; *-cia*) **1.** (*wilka*, *psa*) howling **2.** (*syreny*, *człowieka*) wailing

wyciec *v/p* → ***wyciekać***

wycieczk|a *f* (*-ki*; *-ki*) **1.** trip, excursion; ***~a klasowa*** class trip; ***jechać na ~ę*** go on a trip **2.** (*objazdowa*) tour **3.** (*piesza*) hike **4.** (*grupa*) party

wycieczkowicz *m* (*-cza*; *-cze*) *Br* tripper, sightseer; **wycieczkowy** *adj* **1.** *sezon*: holiday; ***rejs ~*** cruise; ***statek ~*** pleasure boat **2.** *autobus*: sightseeing

wyciek *m* (*-ku*; *-ki*) leak; **wyciekać** ⟨**-ciec**⟩ (*-kam*) leak

wycieńczać ⟨**-czyć**⟩ (*-czam*) exhaust, wear out; **wycieńczenie** *n* (*-nia*; *no pl*) exhaustion; **wycieńczony** *adj* exhausted

wycieraczka *f* (*-ki*; *-ki*) **1.** (*przed drzwiami*) doormat **2.** (*w samochodzie*) wiper; ***~ przednia*** *Br* windscreen wiper, *Am* windshield wiper

wycierać ⟨**wytrzeć**⟩ (*-ram*) **1.** wipe (**coś z** *G* s.th. off); ***~ twarz*** wipe one's face, dry one's face; ***~ nos*** blow one's nose; ***~ kurz z*** *G* dust; ***wytarła kurze*** she did the dusting **2.** *tablicę*: clean, erase **3.** (*gumką*) rub out **4.** (*zużywać*) wear out; ***wycierać się*** **1.** (*po kąpieli*) dry oneself **2.** (*o ubraniu*) wear out

wycierpieć *v/p* (*-pię*): ***wiele ~*** suffer a lot

wycięcie *n* (*-cia*; *-cia*) **1.** (*wycięte miejsce*) notch, nick **2.** (*dekolt*) neckline **3.** *lasu*: clearance

wycinać ⟨**-ciąć**⟩ (*-nam*) **1.** (*z materiału*) cut out **2.** (*z organizmu*) remove **3.** (*ścinać*) cut down, fell

wycinanka *f* (*-ki*; *-ki*) paper cut-out; **wycinek** *m* (*-nka*; *-nki*) **1.** (*część*) part, section **2.** (*z gazety*) (press) clipping, *Br* (press) cutting **3.** *koła*, *kuli*: segment **4.** (*do badania*) sample; **wycinkowy** *adj* fragmentary

wyciosywać ⟨**-sać**⟩ (*-suję*) carve, chisel (**z** *G* out of)

wycisk: ***dać komuś ~*** *infml* give s.o. a hard time

wyciskacz *m* (*-cza*; *-cze*) squeezer; ***~ do cytryn*** lemon squeezer; ***~ łez*** *infml* tear jerker

wyciskać ⟨**-snąć**⟩ (*-kam*) **1.** squeeze; ***~ swoje piętno na*** *L* leave one's mark on, have an impact on **2.** *prawdę*: pull, wring (**coś z** *G* s.th. out of) **3.** *pieczęć*, *wzór*: emboss

wyciszać ⟨**-szyć**⟩ (*-szam*) *pokój*: soundproof: ***wyciszać się*** *fig* calm (oneself) down

wycofywać ⟨**-fać**⟩ (*-fuję*) **1.** withdraw (**z** *G* from) **2.** *samochód*: reverse; ***wycofywać się*** **1.** (*o wojsku*) retreat **2.** (*z obietnicy*) back out (**z** *G* on) **3.** (*z wyścigu*) withdraw (**z** *G* from)

wycwanić się *v/p* (*-nię*) *infml* get smart

wycyganiać ⟨**-nić**⟩ (*-niam*) *infml* con (**coś od kogoś** s.o. out of s.th.), wheedle (**coś od kogoś** s.th. out of s.o.)

wycyklinować *v/p* → **cyklinować**

wyczekiwać ⟨**-kać**⟩ (*-kuję*) **1.** wait (*G* for) **2.** (*niecierpliwie*) look forward (*G*/**na** *A* to), await (*G*/**na** *A*)

wyczekując|y *adj* **1.** *spojrzenie*: expectant **2.** ***~a postawa*** wait-and-see attitude

wyczerpać *v/p* → **wyczerpywać**

wyczerpani|e *n* (*-nia*; *no pl*) exhaustion; ***być na ~u*** **a)** (*o zapasach*) be running out **b)** (*o cierpliwości*) be wearing thin; **wyczerpan|y** *adj* **1.** *człowiek*: exhausted; ***być ~ym nerwowo*** be a nervous wreck **2.** ***nakład książki został ~*** the book is out of print

wyczerpujący *adj* **1.** *odpowiedź*, *informacja*: exhaustive, in-depth **2.** *praca*: exhausting

wyczerpywać ⟨**-pać**⟩ (*-puję*) **1.** *osobę*, *temat*: exhaust **2.** *możliwości*, *środki*: run out of **3.** *zapasy*: use up; ***wyczerpywać się*** **1.** (*o środkach*, *zapasach*) run out **2.** (*o cierpliwości*) wear thin; ***jej cierpliwość się wyczerpała*** she's lost patience **3.** (*o baterii*) go flat, go dead **4.** (*o temacie*, *człowieku*) be exhausted **5.** ***nakład książki wyczerpał się*** the book is out of print

wyczesywać ⟨**-sać**⟩ (*-suję*) comb out

wyczuci|e *n* (*-cia*; *no pl*) **1.** sense; ***~e rytmu*** sense of rhythm; ***~e językowe*** feel for language; ***~e czasu*** (good) timing; ***robić coś na ~e*** do s.th. by following one's nose **2.** (*takt*) tact; ***z ~em*** with tact, tactfully; ***bez ~a*** tactlessly

wyczulony *adj* sensitive (**na** *A* to)

wyczuwać ⟨**-czuć**⟩ (*-wam*) **1.** (*uświadamiać sobie*) sense; ***~ niebezpieczeństwo*** sense danger; ***~ napięcie*** feel the tension; ***wyczuła, że coś jest nie tak*** she felt that something was wrong, she sensed that something was wrong **2.** (*dotykiem*) feel **3.** *zapach*: smell **4.** *samochód*: get the feel of

wyczuwalny *adj* **1.** perceptible **2.** *napięcie*: palpable

wyczyn *m* (*-nu*; *-ny*) feat, exploit; ***~y akrobatyczne*** acrobatic feats; ***nie lada ~*** no mean feat

wyczyniać *v/im* (*-niam*): ***~ cuda*** do amazing things, do wonders; ***co ty wyczyniasz?*** what (on earth) are you doing?

wyczynowiec *m* (*-wca*; *-wcy*) competitive sportsman; **wyczynowy** *adj* *sport*: competitive

wyczyścić *v/p* → **czyścić**

wyczytywać ⟨**-tać**⟩ (*-tuję*) **1.** (*dowiadywać się*) read **2.** (*na głos*) read out **3.** (*zauważać*) read, see

wyć ⟨**za-**⟩ (*wyję*) **1.** (*o psie*, *wietrze*) howl **2.** (*krzyczeć*) cry, yell; ***~ z bólu*** howl in pain **3.** (*płakać*) wail, cry **4.** (*o syrenie*) wail

wyćwiczony *adj* **1.** *osoba*: skilled **2.** *mięśnie*: developed **3.** *umiejętność*: *Br* practised, *Am* practiced

wyćwiczyć *v/p* → **ćwiczyć**

wydać *v/p* → **wydawać**

wydajność *f* (*-ści*; *no pl*) **1.** productivity, efficiency; ***~ z hektara*** (crop) yield per hectare **2.** (*produkcja*) output **3.** INF performance; **wydajny** *adj* **1.** *proces*, *pracownik*: efficient **2.** *procesor*, *karta graficzna*: high-performance

wydalać ⟨**-lić**⟩ (*-lam*) **1.** (*z kraju*) expel, deport; ***imigranci zostali wydaleni***

z USA the immigrants were expelled from the US **2.** (*ze szkoły*) expel **3.** (*z pracy*) dismiss **4.** BIOL excrete

wydalenie *n* (*-nia*; *no pl*) **1.** (*z kraju*) deportation **2.** (*ze szkoły*) expulsion **3.** (*z pracy*) dismissal **4.** BIOL excretion

wydalić *v/p* → ***wydalać***

wydanie *n* (*-nia*) **1.** (*edycja*) edition **2.** (*numer*) issue **3.** (*opublikowanie*) publishing **4.** *zaświadczenia*: issuance

wydarzać się ⟨***-rzyć***⟩ (*-rzam*) happen, take place; **wydarzenie** *n* (*-nia*; *-nia*) event

wydatek *m* (*-tku*; *-tki*) expense

wydatkować *v/p* (*-kuję*) spend

wydatny *adj* **1.** *usta*: prominent **2.** *wkład*: considerable, significant

wydawać ⟨***-dać***⟩ (*-daję*) **1.** *sumę*: spend **2.** *rzeczy*: give out **3.** *okrzyk, przyjęcie, rozkaz, opinię*: give **4.** *zaświadczenie, dekret*: issue **5.** *wyrok*: pass **6.** *książkę*: publish **7.** *zapach*: give off **8.** *przestępcę*: turn in **9.** *sekret*: give away, reveal **10.** ***~ kogoś na świat*** give birth to s.o.; ***wydawać się*** **1.** (*sprawiać wrażenie*) seem, appear; ***wydawało się, że samochód zwalnia*** the car appeared to be slowing down **2.** (*wyjść na jaw*) come out, be revealed **3.** (*zdradzić się*) give oneself away

wydawca *m* (*-cy*; *-cy*) publisher; **wydawnictwo** *n* (*-wa -wa*) publishing company, publishing house; **wydawniczy** *adj* **1.** publishing **2.** *sukces*: commercial

wydąć *v/p* → ***wydymać***

wydech *m* (*-chu*; *-chy*) exhalation; ***zrobić ~*** breathe out, exhale; **wydechowy** *adj rura*: exhaust

wydekoltować się *v/p* → ***dekoltować się***; **wydekoltowan|y** *adj* **1.** *bluzka*: low-cut **2.** ***~a kobieta*** a woman in a low-cut dress

wydelegować *v/p* → ***delegować***

wydelikacony *adj dłonie, skóra*: very delicate, sensitive

wydepilować *v/p* → ***depilować***

wydeptywać ⟨***-tać***⟩ (*-tuję*) *ścieżkę*: wear

wydębić *v/p* (*-bię*) *pieniądze, notatki*: wangle (***coś od*** *G* s.th. out of), get (***coś od*** *G* s.th. from)

wydęty *adj wargi*: pouting

wydłubywać ⟨***-bać***⟩ (*-buję*) **1.** *ziarna, rodzynki*: pick out **2.** *oczy*: poke out

wydłużać ⟨***-żyć***⟩ (*-żam*) **1.** extend **2.** *podróż*: prolong; ***wydłużać się*** lengthen

wydłużony *adj kształt*: elongated

wydm|a *f* (*-my*; *-my*) dune; ***ruchome ~y*** shifting dunes; **wydmowy** *adj* dune

wydmuchiwać ⟨***-chać***⟩ (*-chuję*) blow; ***~ nos*** blow one's nose

wydmuszka *f* (*-ki*; *-ki*) blown egg

wydobycie *n* (*-cia*; *no pl*) **1.** *surowców, kopalin*: mining, extraction; ***~ diamentów*** diamond mining **2.** (*wydobyta ilość*) output **3.** (*ciała z wody, spod gruzów*) recovery

wydobywać ⟨***-być***⟩ (*-wam*) **1.** (*wyjmować*) take out, bring out; ***~ coś na światło dzienne*** bring s.th. to light **2.** *węgiel, sól, złoto*: mine **3.** *ropę*: extract **4.** *dźwięk*: make; ***wydobywać się*** **1.** (*wydostawać się*) get out **2.** (*o gazie*) escape

wydobywcz|y *adj* mining; ***przemysł ~y*** the mining industry; ***platforma ~a*** mining platform, drilling platform

wydoić *v/p* → ***doić***

wydolność *f* (*-ści*; *no pl*) **1.** MED function **2.** (*sprawność*) efficiency; **wydolny** *adj* **1.** healthy **2.** (*sprawny*) functioning properly

wydołać *v/p* (*-łam*): ***nie ~*** *infml* fail

wydorośleć *v/p* → ***dorośleć***

wydostawać ⟨***-tać***⟩ (*-taję*) **1.** (*wyjąć*) take out, get out; ***~ kogoś*** get s.o. out; ***wydostać coś od kogoś*** get s.th. out of s.o.; ***wydostawać się*** **1.** (*z wnętrza*) get out **2.** (*o gazie*) escape

wydra *f* (*-ry*; *-ry*) **1.** (*zwierzę*) otter **2.** (*kobieta*) vixen

wydrapywać ⟨***-pać***⟩ (*-puję*) **1.** (*ryć*) carve **2.** ***~ komuś oczy*** scratch s.o.'s eyes out

wydrążać ⟨***-żyć***⟩ (*-żam*) **1.** *dziurę*: bore, drill **2.** *owoce*: stone, pit **3.** *tunel*: drive, cut

wydrążony *adj* hollowed-out

wydruk *m* (*-ku*; *-ki*) printout

wydrwiwać ⟨***-rwić***⟩ (*-wam*) scoff, mock

wydrzeć *v/p* → ***wydzierać***

wydusić *v/p* (*-szę*) **1.** squeeze **2.** *informacje*: get (***coś z kogoś*** s.th. out of s.o.), extort (**coś z kogoś** s.th. from s.o.) **3.** *słowo*: stammer out; ***nie mogła z siebie ~ ani słowa*** she couldn't get a word out **4.** (*zabić*) strangle

wydychać *v/im* (*-cham*) breathe out, exhale

wydymać ⟨**-dąć**⟩ (*-mam*) **1.** *firankę, żagle*: fill **2.** *usta*: pout **3.** *vulg* screw, shag

wydział *m* (*-łu; -ły*) **1.** *urzędu*: department **2.** *uniwersytetu*: faculty, department

wydziedziczać ⟨**-czyć**⟩ (*-czam*) disinherit

wydzielać ⟨**-lić**⟩ (*-lam*) **1.** *sok, enzymy*: secrete **2.** *ciepło, zapach*: give off **3.** *energię*: generate **4.** *miejsce, teren*: mark off; ***wydzielać się*** **1.** (*o soku, enzymach*) be secreted **2.** (*o cieple*) be given off **3.** (*o energii*) be generated

wydzielina *f* (*-ny; -ny*) secretion; ***~ ropna*** pus

wydzierać ⟨**-drzeć**⟩ (*-ram*) **1.** *kartkę*: tear (out) **2.** (*z rąk*) grab, snatch **3.** *tajemnicę*: wrest (**coś** *D* s.th. from); ***wydzierać się*** (*krzyczeć*) yell, scream

wydzierżawiać ⟨**-wić**⟩ (*-wiam*) lease

wydziobywać ⟨**-bać**⟩ (*-buję*) peck out

wydziwiać ⟨**na-**⟩ (*-wiam*) (*narzekać*) *infml* gripe

wydzwaniać *v/im* (*-niam*): ***~ do kogoś*** keep calling s.o., *Br* keep ringing s.o. up

wydźwięk *m* (*-ku; no pl*) *fig* overtones *pl*, implications *pl*

wyegzekwować *v/p* → ***egzekwować***

wyeksmitować *v/p* → ***eksmitować***

wyekspediować *v/p* → ***ekspediować***

wyeksploatować *v/p* → ***eksploatować***

wyeksponować *v/p* → ***eksponować***

wyeksportować *v/p* → ***eksportować***

wyeliminować *v/p* → ***eliminować***

wyemigrować *v/p* → ***emigrować***

wyfiokowany *adj dziewczyna*: dolled-up

wyfroterować *v/p* → ***froterować***

wyfruwać ⟨**-runąć**⟩ (*-wam*) (*o ptaku*) fly out (**z** *G* of)

wyga *m* (*-gi; -gi*): ***stary ~*** old hand

wygadać *v/p* (*-dam*) let out, blurt out; ***wygadać się*** spill the beans, *infml* blab

wygadany *adj* smooth-tongued, glib; ***być ~m*** *Br* have the gift of the gab, *Am* have a gift of gab

wygadywać *v/im* (*-duję*): ***~ głupstwa*** talk rubbish; ***co ty wygadujesz?*** what (on earth) are you talking about?

wygájać ⟨**-goić**⟩ (*-jam*) heal; ***wygajać się*** heal up

wygalać ⟨**-golić**⟩ (*-lam*) shave (off)

wyganiać ⟨**-gonić, -gnać**⟩ (*-niam*) **1.** (*przeganiać*) chase out **2.** (*wyrzucać*) throw out; ***~ kogoś z domu*** throw s.o. out of one's home

wygarbować *v/p* → ***garbować***

wygarniać ⟨**-nąć**⟩ (*-niam*) **1.** *popiół*: rake (out), take (out) **2.** (*spod łóżka*) get (**z** *G* from under) **3.** ***wygarnąć komuś*** *infml* give it to s.o. straight, give s.o. a piece of one's mind

wygasać ⟨**-snąć**⟩ (*-sam*) **1.** (*o ogniu*) go out, die out **2.** (*o wulkanie*) become extinct **3.** (*o miłości*) die **4.** (*o epidemii, entuzjazmie*) die down **5.** (*o umowie*) expire

wygasić *v/p* → ***wygaszać***

wygasły *adj* **1.** *wulkan, ród*: extinct **2.** *miłość, ognisko*: dead **3.** *umowa*: expired

wygasnąć *v/p* → ***wygasać***

wygaszać ⟨**-sić**⟩ (*-szam*) **1.** *ogień*: put out **2.** *światła*: put out, switch off **3.** *monitor*: blank

wygiąć *v/p* → ***wyginać***

wygibasy *pl* (*-sów*) (*ruchy*) contortions, twists and turns

wygięcie *n* (*-cia; -cia*) curve, bend; **wygięty** *adj* bent

wygimnastykowany *adj* supple

wyginać ⟨**-giąć**⟩ (*-nam*) bend; ***wyginać się*** bend

wyginąć *v/p* (*-nę*) become extinct

wygląd *m* (*-du; no pl*) **1.** *przedmiotu*: appearance **2.** *osoby*: looks *pl*, appearance; ***dbać o ~*** take care of one's appearance; ***przypominać kogoś z ~u*** look like s.o.

wyglądać *v/im* (*-dam*) **1.** (*mieć wygląd*) look; ***~ młodo*** look young; ***~ zdrowo*** look healthy; ***~ na artystę*** look like an artist; ***~ zza chmur*** appear from behind the clouds; ***~ na swoje lata*** look one's age; ***wygląda na to, że*** it looks like **2.** (*patrzeć*) look (**przez** *A* out); ***~ przez okno*** look out of the window

W

3. (*oczekiwać*) look forward to, await

wygładzać ⟨**-dzić**⟩ (*-dzam*) **1.** *materiał, piórka*: smooth (out) **2.** *zmarszczki*: smooth away, reduce **3.** (*strugiem*) plane **4.** (*papierem ściernym*) polish **5.** *fig* polish (up); ***wygładzać się*** smooth (out), become smooth

wygłaszać ⟨**-łosić**⟩ (*-szam*) **1.** *mowę, referat*: give, deliver **2.** *opinię*: express, voice **3.** *kazanie*: preach **4.** *uwagę*: make **5.** *litanię*: recite

wygłodzić *v/p* (*-dzę*) starve; ***wygłodzić się*** starve oneself; **wygłodzony** *adj* starving, ravenous

wygłos *m* (*-su*; *-sy*): ***ubezdźwięcznianie w ~ie*** final devoicing

wygłosić *v/p* → ***wygłaszać***

wygłup *m* (*-pu*; *-py*): *infml* ***~y*** antics; ***co to za ~y!*** stop clowning around!

wygłupiać się *v/im* (*-piam*) *infml* fool around, clown (around), play a fool; ***nie wygłupiaj się!*** (*nie żartuj*) don't try to be funny!, stop joking like that!

wygnać *v/p* → ***wyganiać***

wygnani|e *n* (*-nia*; *no pl*) exile, banishment; ***na ~u*** in exile; **wygnaniec** *m* (*-gnańca*; *-gnańcy*) exile

wygniatać ⟨**-nieść**⟩ (*-tam*) **1.** *ubranie*: crumple **2.** *ciasto*: knead **3.** *kapustę*: squeeze; ***wygnieść się*** (*o ubraniu*) crumple, crease

wygnieciony *adj* **1.** *ubranie, kartka*: crumpled **2.** *trawa*: trampled

wygod|a *f* (*-dy*; *-dy*) comfort; ***dla ~y*** for convenience; ***być dużą ~ą*** be very convenient; ***mieszkanie z ~ami*** apartment with modern coveniences, apartment with all mod cons; ***w domu brakuje podstawowych wygód*** the house is lacking in basic amenities

wygodnicki *adj* comfort-loving; ***jest ~*** **a)** (*lubi wygody*) he likes his comforts **b)** (*unika pracy*) he's lazy

wygodnictwo *n* (*-wa*; *no pl*) comfort-loving nature, love of comfort

wygodnie *adv* comfortably; ***jest ci ~?*** are you comfortable?; ***usiądź ~*** sit down and make yourself comfortable

wygodn|y *adj* **1.** comfortable, *infml* comfy; ***~y w użyciu*** handy; ***~e życie na Bahamach*** easy life in the Bahamas; ***~y sposób poruszania się po mieście*** convenient way of getting around the town **2.** (*lubiący wygody*) comfort-loving **3.** (*leniwy*) lazy

wygoić *v/p* → ***wygajać***

wygolić *v/p* → ***wygalać***

wygolony *adj* shaven

wygonić *v/p* → ***wyganiać***

wygospodarować *v/p* (*-ruję*) (*znajdować*) find

wygotowywać ⟨**-tować**⟩ (*-towuję*) **1.** boil **2.** (*gotować za długo*) overcook; ***wygotowywać się*** boil away; ***woda w czajniku wygotowała się*** the kettle has boiled dry

wygódka *f* (*-ki*; *-ki*) privy

wygórowan|y *adj* **1.** *cena, podatki*: unreasonable, excessive, *infml* steep; ***mieć ~ą cenę*** be too expensive; ***bardzo ~e ceny*** exorbitant prices, *form* extortionate prices **2.** *ambicja, żądania*: unreasonable, excessive; ***mieć ~e mniemanie o sobie*** be too big for one's shoes; ***~e ambicje polityczne*** vaulting political ambitions

wygrać *v/p* → ***wygrywać***

wygramolić się *v/im* (*-lę*) **1.** (*wydostać się*) scramble out (***z*** *G* of) **2.** (*wdrapać się*) clamber (***na*** *A* onto)

wygran|a *f* (*-nej*; *-ne*) **1.** win, victory; ***dać za ~ą*** give in, give up; ***łatwa ~a*** walkover **2.** (*rzecz, kwota*) prize; ***główna ~a*** main prize; ***wygrać główną ~ą*** win the main prize, hit the jackpot **3.** (*pieniądze*) winnings *pl*

wygrażać *v/im* (*-żam*) threaten

wygrywać ⟨**-rać**⟩ (*-wam*) win; ***~ z*** *I* beat

wygryzać ⟨**-ryźć**⟩ (*-zam*) **1.** *dziurę*: gnaw **2.** *fig* oust

wygrzać się *v/p* → ***wygrzewać się***

wygrzebywać ⟨**-bać**⟩ (*-buję*) dig out; ***wygrzebać się*** **1.** (*być gotowym*) (finally) get ready **2.** (*z łóżka*) drag oneself out (***z*** *G* of)

wygrzewać się ⟨**-rzać**⟩ (*-wam*) warm up, warm oneself; ***~ na słońcu*** bask in the sun

wygwizd|ów *m* (*-dowa*; *no pl*): ***mieszkać na ~owie*** live in the middle of nowhere

wygwizdywać ⟨**-dać**⟩ (*-duję*) **1.** *melodię*: whistle **2.** *aktora, sztukę*: hiss, boo

wyhaftować *v/p* → ***haftować***

wyhamowywać ⟨**-mować**⟩ (*-mowuję*) brake, apply the brake

wyheblować *v/p* → ***heblować***
wyhodować *v/p* → ***hodować***
wyidealizowany *adj* idealized
wyimaginowany *adj* (*urojony*) imaginary, fictitious
wyjadacz *m* (*-cza*; *-cze*): ***stary ~*** old hand
wyjadać ⟨***-jeść***⟩ (*-dam*) eat up
wyjaławiać ⟨***-łowić***⟩ (*-wiam*) **1.** *narzędzia*: sterilize **2.** *ziemię*: impoverish
wyjaśniać ⟨***-nić***⟩ (*-niam*) **1.** explain (**coś** *D* s.th. to); ***~ komuś, jak coś zrobić*** tell s.o. how to do s.th. **2.** *wątpliwości*: clarify, clear up **3.** *nieporozumienie*: clear up; ***wyjaśniać się*** become clear
wyjaśnienie *n* (*-nia*; *-nia*) explanation
wyjawiać ⟨***-wić***⟩ (*-wiam*) reveal
wyjazd *m* (*-du*; *-dy*) **1.** (*odjazd*) departure **2.** (*podróż*) trip, journey; ***~ służbowy*** business trip; ***~ za granicę*** trip abroad; ***~ na wieś*** trip to the country; ***~ za miasto*** trip out of town; ***na wyjeździe*** away (from home); **wyjazdowy** *adj* **1.** *droga*, *wiza*: exit **2.** *mecz*: away
wyjąć *v/p* → ***wyjmować***
wyjąkać *v/p* (*-kam*) stammer out, stutter out
wyjąt|ek *m* (*-tku*; *-tki*) **1.** exception (**od** *G* to); ***bez ~ku*** without exception; ***z ~kiem*** except, with the exception of; ***w drodze ~ku*** by way of exception, as an exception; ***chlubny ~ek*** notable exception **2.** (*fragment*) excerpt, extract
wyjątkowo *adv* **1.** exceptionally **2.** (*szczególnie*, *zwłaszcza*) particularly; ***~ interesujący*** particularly interesting **3.** (*w wybranych przypadkach*) in exceptional cases; **wyjątkowy** *adj* **1.** exceptional; ***stan ~*** POLIT state of emergency **2.** *szansa*: exceptional, rare **3.** *okazja*, *dzień*: special, exceptional
wyjechać *v/p* → ***wyjeżdżać***
wyjednywać ⟨***-nać***⟩ (*-nuję*) (manage to) obtain
wyjeść *v/p* → ***wyjadać***
wyjezdn|e: ***na ~ym*** just before one's departure
wyjeżdżać ⟨***-jechać***⟩ (*-dżam*) **1.** (*z miasta*, *kraju*) leave (**z** *G*); ***~ na urlop*** go on holiday; ***~ za granicę*** go abroad; ***wyjechali*** they're away **2.** (*z garażu*) drive out (**z** *G* of) **3.** (*na ulicę*) drive (**na** *A* into) **4.** (*powiedzieć*) *infml* come out (**z** *I* with); ***~ z głupimi uwagami*** make some stupid comments, come out with some stupid comments
wyjeżdżony *adj droga*: rutty
wyjęczeć *v/p* (*-czę*) moan out, groan out; → ***jęczeć***
wyjęty *adj*: ***~ z kontekstu*** (taken) out of context; ***~ spod prawa*** HIST outlaw
wyjmować ⟨***-jąć***⟩ (*-muję*) **1.** take out (**z** *G* of) **2.** *kleszcza*, *drzazgę*: remove, extract
wyjrzeć *v/p* (*-rzę*) **1.** (*o osobie*) look out; ***~ przez okno*** look out (of) a window **2.** (*o słońcu*) peek out, appear; ***~ zza chmur*** peek out from behind the clouds, appear from behind the clouds
wyjści|e *n* (*-cia*; *-cia*) **1.** (*w budynku*) exit; ***~e awaryjne*** emergency exit; ***~e przeciwpożarowe*** fire escape; ***tylne ~e*** back door, rear exit **2.** (*z trudnej sytuacji*) way out, solution; ***to sytuacja bez ~a*** there is no way out; ***nie mam ~a*** I have no choice **3.** (*wychodzenie*) departure, leaving **4.** INF output
wyjściow|y *adj* **1.** *drzwi*: exit **2.** *pozycja*, *cena*: starting **3.** *sytuacja*, *cena*: initial **4.** *sygnał*, *urządzenie*: output **5.** ***ubranie ~e*** one's Sunday clothes, one's best clothes
wyjść *v/p* (*-jdę*) (*udać się*) come out (well); ***próbowałem, ale nie wyszło*** I tried but failed, I tried but it didn't work; → ***wychodzić***
wyka *f* (*-ki*; *no pl*) (*roślina*) vetch
wykałaczka *f* (*-ki*; *-ki*) toothpick
wykańczać ⟨***-kończyć***⟩ (*-czam*) **1.** *dom*: decorate **2.** *zapasy*: use up **3.** *materiał*: hem, trim; ***~ coś koronką*** trim s.th. with lace **4.** (*zabijać*) *infml* do in **5.** (*męczyć*) *infml* wear out, tire out; ***wykańczać się*** **1.** (*męczyć się*) wear oneself out; ***wykończyć się nerwowo*** become a nervous wreck **2.** (*o zapasach*) run out
wykapany *adj*: ***~ ojciec*** *infml* the picture of his father, the spitting image of his father, a chip off the old block

wykaraskać się *v/ip* (*-kam*) get out of trouble; **~ z długów** get out of debt
wykarczować *v/p* → **karczować**
wykarmiać ⟨**-mić**⟩ (*-miam*) **1.** feed **2.** *dziecko piersią*: breastfeed, nurse **3.** *zwierzę piersią*: suckle
wykaz *m* (*-zu*; *-zy*) list
wykazywać ⟨**-zać**⟩ (*-zuję*) **1.** demonstrate **2.** (*o śledztwie*) reveal, show, conclude **3. ~ podobieństwo do** *G* resemble, bear a resemblance to; **wykazywać się 1.** (*pokazać*): **~ się zdolnościami organizacyjnymi** demonstrate organizational skills; **~ się dogłębną znajomością rynku** demonstrate an in-depth understanding of the market **2.** (*udowadniać swoją wartość*) prove oneself
wykidajło *m* (*-ły*; *-ły*/*-ła*) *infml* bouncer
wykiełkować *v/p* → **kiełkować**
wykipieć *v/p* (*-pię*) boil over
wykitować *v/p* (*-tuję*) *infml* kick the bucket, peg out
wykiwać *v/p* (*-wam*) *infml* dupe, trick
wyklarować *v/p* → **klarować**
wykląć *v/p* → **wyklinać**
wyklejać ⟨**-leić**⟩ (*-jam*) **1.** *ściany*: paper **2.** *wnętrze pudełka*: line; **wyklejka** *f* (*-ki*; *-ki*) endpaper
wyklęty *adj* **1.** excommunicated **2.** (*przez rodzica*) cursed
wyklinać ⟨**-ląć**⟩ (*-nam*) **1.** excommunicate **2.** *dziecko*: curse
wykluczać ⟨**-czyć**⟩ (*-czam*) **1.** rule out, exclude; **policja wykluczyła morderstwo** the police have ruled out murder **2.** (*z organizacji*) expel (**z** *G* from); **wykluczać się**: **~ się wzajemnie** be mutually exclusive
wykluczony *adj* out of the question, impossible
wykluwać się ⟨**-luć**⟩ (*-wam*) hatch
wykład *m* (*-du*; *-dy*) lecture
wykładać ⟨**wyłożyć**⟩ (*-dam*) **1.** *towar*: lay out **2.** (*pokrywać*) cover (*I* with); **~ ściany kafelkami** tile the walls, **~ schody dywanem** carpet the stairs **3.** *pieniądze*: put up **4.** (*uczyć*) lecture; **~ na uniwersytecie** be a university lecturer; **~ nauki ścisłe** lecture in science **5.** *pogląd*: expound
wykładnia *f* (*-ni*; *-nie*) interpretation; **wykładnik** *m* (*-ka*; *-ki*) **1.** *fig* indicator **2.** *MATH* exponent
wykładowca *m* (*-cy*; *-cy*) **1.** (*na uniwersytecie*) lecturer **2.** (*na kursach*) instructor
wykładow|y *adj*: **sala ~a** lecture room; **język ~y** language of instruction
wykładzina *f* (*-ny*; *-ny*): **~ dywanowa** carpeting, fitted carpet
wykłócać się ⟨**-cić**⟩ (*-cam*) argue (**o** *A* over/about)
wykłuwać ⟨**-łuć**⟩ (*-wam*) *oczy*: poke out
wykolegować *v/p* (*-guję*) *infml* shortchange
wykolejać ⟨**-leić**⟩ (*-jam*) *pociąg*: derail; **wykolejać się 1.** (*o pociągu, tramwaju*) derail **2.** *fig* become demoralized
wykolejenie *n* (*-nia*; *no pl*) **1.** *pociągu, tramwaju*: derailment **2.** *fig* demoralization; **wykolejeniec** *m* (*-jeńca*; *-jeńcy*) *infml* demoralized man; **~ życiowy** derelict; **wykolejony** *adj fig* demoralized
wykombinować *v/p* (*-nuję*) **1.** (*załatwić*) (manage to) get **2.** (*wywnioskować*) figure out, work out
wykonać *v/p* → **wykonywać**
wykonaln|y *adj* feasible, workable, practicable; **technicznie ~y** technically feasible
wykonani|e *n* (*-nia*; *-nia*) **1. pierwsze ~e kwartetu** *MUS* the first performance of a quartet; **jego ~e** *THEAT* his interpretation, his rendition; **piosenka w ~u** *G* a song performed by, a song sung by **2.** (*robocizna*) workmanship; **wysoka jakość ~a** good workmanship **3.** *projektu*, *planu*: completion, implementation **4.** *wyroku*: execution, carrying out
wykonawca *m* (*-cy*; *-cy*), **-czyni** *f* (*-ni*; *-nie*) **1.** (*aktor*, *muzyk*) performer, artist **2.** (*robót*) contractor, builder **3.** *testamentu*: executor; **wykonawcz|y** *adj* **1.** *władza*, *klauzula*, *komitet*: executive; **władza ~a a)** executive power **b)** (*instytucje*) the executive (branch) **2.** *styl*: performing
wykonawstwo *n* (*-wa*; *no pl*) *BUILD* construction work
wykonywać ⟨**-nać**⟩ (*-nuję*) **1.** (*produkować*) make **2.** *polecenie*, *rozkaz*, *zadanie*, *eksperyment*: carry out **3.** *projekt*: make, produce **4.** *ćwicze-*

W

nie, pracę: do **5. ~ zawód nauczyciela** work as a teacher **6.** *wyrok*: execute, carry out **7.** *rolę, utwór*: play

wykończeni|e *n* (*-nia*; *-nia*) **1.** (*brzeg ubrania*) trimming, trim **2.** (*jakość wykonania*) workmanship **3.** (*wnętrz*) decoration **4. nasze zapasy są na ~u** our supplies are running out; **wykończeniow|y** *adj*: **prace ~e** decoration

wykończony *adj infml* dead beat, *Br infml* fagged (out)

wykończyć *v/p* → **wykańczać**

wykop *m* (*-pu*; *-py*) BUILD excavation, trench; **wykopalisk|o** *n* (*-ka*; *-ka*) **1.** (*teren*) excavation **2.** (*rzecz*) find; **wykopaliskow|y** *adj* excavation; **stanowisko ~e** excavation site; **prace ~e** excavations

wykopki *pl* (*-ków*) **1.** (*ziemniaków*) potato-lifting **2.** (*buraków*) beet-lifting

wykopywać ⟨**-pać**⟩ (*-puję*) **1.** *dół, rów, tunel*: dig **2.** *studnię*: dig, sink **3.** *rzecz*: dig out **4.** *szczątki ludzkie*: unearth

wykorkować *v/p* (*-kuję*) *infml* kick the bucket

wykorzeniać ⟨**-nić**⟩ (*-niam*) **1.** *fig* eradicate **2.** *drzewa*: uproot, eradicate

wykorzystywać ⟨**-tać**⟩ (*-tuję*) **1.** use, utilize **2.** *okazję*: take, use; **~ sposobność** take an opportunity; **chciałbym wykorzystać tę okazję, aby wam podziękować** I'd like to take the opportunity to thank you **3.** *pracowników, luki prawne, ludzkie lęki*: exploit **4.** *swoją przewagę, czyjąś nieobecność, czyjąś hojność*: take advantage of **5.** *seksualnie*: abuse **6.** *odpady*: utilize; **~ coś ponownie** reuse s.th.

wykosztowywać się ⟨**-tować**⟩ (*-towuję*) spend a lot (**na** *A* on), *infml* shell out (**na** *A* for)

wykpiwać ⟨**-pić**⟩ (*-wam*) ridicule, mock; **wykpiwać się** avoid (**od** *G*), get out (**od** *G* of)

wykracza|ć ⟨**-roczyć**⟩ (*-czam*) **1.** (*wychodzić*) go beyond (**poza** *A*); **to ~ poza jej obowiązki** this goes beyond her duties; **~ć poza bariery kulturowe** transcend cultural barriers **2.** (*przeciw prawu*) violate (**przeciw** *D*)

wykradać ⟨**-raść**⟩ (*-dam*) **1.** steal **2.** *dziecko*: kidnap; **wykradać się** steal out (**z** *G* of), steal away (**z** *G* from)

wykra|kać *v/p*: **nie mów tak, bo ~czesz** don't say that, or it might come true

wykraść *v/p* → **wykradać**

wykrawać ⟨**-roić**⟩ (*-wam*) cut out

wykres *m* (*-su*; *-sy*) chart, graph, diagram; **~ kolumnowy** bar chart, histogram; **~ kołowy** pie chart; **~ funkcji** graph of a function

wykreślać ⟨**-lić**⟩ (*-lam*) **1.** (*z listy*) cross off (**z** *G*) **2.** (*rysować*) draw, plot

wykręcać ⟨**-cić**⟩ (*-cam*) **1.** *śrubę, żarówkę*: unscrew, take out **2.** *bieliznę*: wring (out) **3.** *rękę*: twist **4.** *numer*: dial; **~ komuś numer** *infml* take s.o. for a ride; **wykręcać się** *fig* weasel out (**od** *G* of), get out (**od** *G* of); **~ się od swoich obowiązków** shirk one's duties; **~ się od odpowiedzi na pytanie** evade (answering) a question

wykręt *m* (*-tu*; *-ty*) excuse; **wykrętny** *adj odpowiedź*: evasive

wykroczenie *n* (*-nia*; *-nia*) JUR *Br* offence, *Am* offense, *Br* misdemeanour, *Am* misdemeanor

wykroczyć *v/p* → **wykraczać**

wykroić *v/p* → **wykrawać**

wykrojon|y *adj*: **ładnie ~e usta** nicely shaped mouth

wykrok *m* (*-ku*; *-ki*) SPORT step forward, lunge

wykropkowywać ⟨**-kować**⟩ (*-kowuję*) dot (out)

wykrot *m* (*-tu*; *-ty*) (*w ziemi*) hollow (left by a fallen tree)

wykrój *m* (*-roju*; *-roje*) **1.** (*krawiecki*) pattern **2.** (*kształt*) shape

wykruszać się ⟨**-szyć**⟩ (*-szam*) **1.** (*o ludziach*) drop out **2.** (*odpadać*) crumble out, fall off

wykrwawić się *v/p* (*-wię*) lose a lot of blood; **~ na śmierć** bleed to death

wykrycie *n* (*-cia*; *no pl*) **1.** detection **2.** *spisku*: uncovering

wykryć *v/p* → **wykrywać**

wykrywacz *m* (*-cza*; *-cze*) detector; **~ min** mine detector; **~ kłamstw** lie detector, polygraph

wykrywać ⟨**-ryć**⟩ (*-wam*) **1.** detect **2.** *spisek*: uncover **3.** *błąd, winnych*: find **4.** (*odkrywać*) discover

wykrywalność *f* (*-ści*; *no pl*): **~ przestępstw** crime detection rate; **wykrywalny** *adj* detectable

wykrzesać *v/p* (*-szę*) **1.** *energię*: summon up **2.** *entuzjazm, siłę*: muster; **~ siły** muster strength **3.** *ogień*: strike

wykrztusić *v/p* (*-szę*) **1.** (*odkaszlnąć*) cough up **2.** (*powiedzieć*) stammer out; ***nie mógł ~ słowa*** he couldn't get a word out; **wykrztuśny** *adj* expectorant

wykrzykiwać ⟨**-rzyczeć**⟩ (*-kuję*) yell out, shout out

wykrzyknik *m* (*-ka*; *-ki*) **1.** (*w interpunkcji*) exclamation mark **2.** (*część mowy*) interjection

wykrzywiać ⟨**-wić**⟩ (*-wiam*) twist; **wykrzywiać się** **1.** (*o twarzy*) twist **2.** (*o słupie*) bend **3.** (*o półce*) warp

wykrzywion|y *adj* **1.** *twarz*: contorted, twisted; ***~y z bólu*** contorted with pain **2.** *usta*: twisted, curled; ***usta ~e w szyderczym uśmiechu*** lips curled in a sneering smile **3.** *słup, ząb*: crooked **4.** *palce*: gnarled **5.** *fig* distorted; ***~y obraz islamu*** a distorted picture of Islam

wykształcać ⟨**-cić**⟩ (*-cam*) **1.** *zdolności, mięśnie*: develop **2.** *dzieci*: educate **3.** *specjalistów*: train; **wykształcać się** (*rozwijać się*) develop

wykształcenie *n* (*-nia*; *no pl*) education; ***~ wyższe*** higher education; ***mieć wyższe ~*** have a degree; ***wszechstronne ~*** comprehensive education; ***~ zawodowe*** vocational education

wykształcon|y *adj* **1.** (*mający wykształcenie*) educated; ***jest ~a*** she's well-educated; ***wszechstronnie ~y*** comprehensively educated; ***inżynier ~y na Zachodzie*** Western-educated engineer **2.** (*rozwinięty*) developed, formed; ***dobrze ~y zmysł zapachu*** highly developed sense of smell

wykuć *v/p* → **wykuwać**

wykup *m* (*-pu*; *-py*) **1.** repurchase; ***~ akcji*** buyout; ***~ menedżerski*** management buyout; ***~ lewarowany*** leveraged buyout; ***~ obligacji*** bond redemption; ***masowy ~ towarów*** panic buying **2.** *zakładników*: ransoming

wykupywać ⟨**-pić**⟩ (*-puję*) **1.** (*kupować wszystko*) buy up **2.** (*odkupować*) repurchase **3.** (*kupować*) buy; ***~ receptę*** have one's prescription filled **4.** *firmę*: buy out **5.** *obligacje*: redeem **6.** *zakładników*: ransom; **wykupywać się** buy oneself out

wykurować *v/p* (*-ruję*) cure; **wykurować się** recover

wykurzać ⟨**-rzyć**⟩ (*-rzam*) **1.** (*wyganiać*) drive out **2.** (*dymem*) smoke out

wykusz *m* (*-sza*; *-sze*) ARCHIT bay window

wykuwać ⟨**-kuć**⟩ (*-wam*) **1.** (*w metalu*) forge **2.** (*w kamieniu*) sculpt **3.** *otwór*: cut **4.** (*uczyć się*) *infml* learn by rote

wykwalifikowany *adj* **1.** *robotnik, rzemieślnik*: skilled **2.** *pielęgniarka*: qualified

wykwaterowywać ⟨**-rować**⟩ (*-rowuję*) relocate

wykwint *m* (*-tu*; *no pl*) refinement, (refined) elegance; **wykwintny** *adj* **1.** *danie, wino*: exquisite **2.** *styl, maniery*: refined

wylać *v/p* → **wylewać**

wylanie *n* (*-nia*; *no pl*) (*z pracy*) *infml* sacking, firing

wylatywać ⟨**-lecieć**⟩ (*-tuję*) **1.** (*o ptaku, owadzie*) fly out, fly off **2.** (*o samolocie*) take off **3.** (*o gazie, powietrzu*) escape, come out **4.** (*wybiegać*) *infml* rush out **5.** (*z pracy*) *infml* get the sack, be sacked, be fired **6.** ***~ w powietrze*** blow up, explode **7.** ***wyleciało mi to z głowy*** it slipped my mind

wyląc się *v/p* → **wylęgać się**

wylądować *v/p* → **lądować**

wyląg *m* (*-lęgu*; *-lęgi*) **1.** (*wykluwanie się*) hatching **2.** (*pisklęta*) brood, hatch

wylec *v/p* → **wylegać**

wylecieć *v/p* → **wylatywać**

wyleczyć *v/p* (*-czę*) cure; **wyleczyć się** recover: ***~ się z*** *G* get over, recover from; → **leczyć się**

wylegać ⟨**-lec**⟩ (*-gam*) (*o ludziach, tłumach*) pour (out) (**na** *A* onto); ***~ na ulice*** pour onto the streets

wylegitymować *v/p* → **legitymować**

wylegiwać się *v/im* (*-guję*) lie, loll; ***~ w łóżku do południa*** lie in till noon

wylepiać ⟨**-pić**⟩ (*-piam*) paste

wyletniać się ⟨**-nić**⟩ (*-niam*) dress too lightly

wylew *m* (*-wu*; *-wy*) **1.** (*krwotok*) *Br* haemorrhage, *Am* hemorrhage;

~ ***krwi do mózgu*** cerebral haemorrhage **2.** (*udar*) stroke **3.** *cieczy, rzeki*: overflow

wylewać ⟨**-lać**⟩ (*-wam*) **1.** pour out (**z** *G* of) **2.** (*niechcący*) spill **3.** (*z pracy*) *infml* sack, fire **4.** (*o rzece*) overflow **5.** (*pokrywać*) cover; ***wylewać się*** **1.** (*o cieczy*) spill **2.** (*o tłumach*) overflow

wylewny *adj* **1.** *osoba, powitanie*: effusive **2.** *podziękowanie, przeprosiny*: profuse

wyleźć *v/p* → ***wyłazić***

wyleżeć *v/p*: ***nie mogę ~ w łóżku*** I can't stay in bed

wylęg → ***wyląg***

wylęgać się ⟨**-gnąć**⟩ (*-gam*) hatch

wylęgani|e *n* (*-nia*; *no pl*): ***okres ~a*** incubation period

wylęgarnia *f* (*-ni*; *-nie*) **1.** (*hodowla*) hatchery **2.** *szczurów, bakterii*: breeding ground **3.** *fig* breeding ground, hotbed; ***~ przestępców*** hotbed of crime; ***~ talentów*** breeding ground for talents, incubator for talents

wylęgnąć się *v/p* → ***wylęgać się***

wylękniony *adj* fearful

wyliczać ⟨**-czyć**⟩ (*-czam*) **1.** (*wymieniać*) enumerate, list **2.** (*obliczać*) calculate, work out **3.** (*odliczać*) count out; **wyliczanka** *f* (*-ki*; *-ki*) counting-out rhyme, rhyme

wyliniały *adj* **1.** *tkanina, futro*: threadbare, worn-out **2.** *pies, kot*: bald

wylinieć *v/p* → ***linieć***

wylizywać ⟨**-zać**⟩ (*-zuję*) lick clean; ***wylizywać się*** *fig* pull through, get over (**z** *G*)

wylosowywać ⟨**-sować**⟩ (*-sowuję*) **1.** (*wyciągać*) draw **2.** (*wygrywać*) win

wylot *m* (*-tu*; *-ty*) **1.** *tunelu*: mouth **2.** *ulicy*: exit **3.** *rury*: outlet **4.** *węża*: spout **5.** *lufy*: muzzle **6.** (*odlot*) take-off, departure **7.** ***na ~*** (*na wskroś*) through; ***kula przebiła ścianę na ~*** the bullet came through the wall; ***znać kogoś na ~*** *fig* know s.o. inside out

wylotow|y *adj*: ***ulica ~a*** access road; ***otwór ~y*** outlet

wyludnienie *n* (*-nia*; *no pl*) depopulation; **wyludniony** *adj* **1.** *ulica, dom*: deserted **2.** *teren*: depopulated; **wyludniać** ⟨**-nić**⟩ (*-niam*) depopulate; ***wyludniać się*** **1.** (*o ulicach*) become deserted **2.** (*o terenie*) become depopulated

wyładnieć *v/p* → ***ładnieć***

wyładowani|e *n* (*-nia*; *-nia*) **1.** PHYS discharge; ***~a atmosferyczne*** atmospheric discharges, lightning **2.** *towaru*: unloading

wyładowywać ⟨**-dować**⟩ (*-dowuję*) **1.** unload **2.** *złość, zły nastrój*: vent (***na*** *A* on); ***wyładowywać się*** **1.** (*o baterii*) go flat, go dead **2.** (*o kondensatorze*) discharge **3.** (*o osobie*) let off steam; ***~ się na*** *L* take it out on

wyładunek *m* (*-nku*; *-nki*) **1.** unloading **2.** (*ze statku*) discharge

wyłamywać ⟨**-mać**⟩ (*-muję*) **1.** break; ***~ palce*** *fig* crack one's knuckles **2.** *drzwi*: break down; ***wyłamywać się*** *fig* get out of line, step out of line

wyłaniać ⟨**-łonić**⟩ (*-niam*) **1.** *komisję, delegację*: appoint **2.** *kandydata*: nominate **3.** *zwycięzcę*: determine; ***wyłaniać się*** **1.** appear, loom into view (**z** *G* out of) **2.** (*o kwestii, sprawie*) arise, emerge

wyłapywać ⟨**-pać**⟩ (*-puję*) **1.** *ludzi, zwierzęta*: catch **2.** *błędy*: spot, pick out

wyławiać ⟨**-łowić**⟩ (*-wiam*) **1.** *ryby*: catch **2.** *ciało*: pull out (**z** *G* of) **3.** *fig* find, pick out; ***~ uzdolnionych uczniów*** find gifted students

wyłazić ⟨**wyleźć**⟩ (*-łażę*) **1.** get out, clamber out (***spod*** *G* from under); ***~ ze skóry*** *fig* fall over oneself **2.** (*o włosach*) come out **3.** *fig* come out, show

wyłączać ⟨**-czyć**⟩ (*-czam*) **1.** *światło, telewizor*: switch off, turn off **2.** *silnik*: turn off, stop **3.** *sprzęgło*: let off **4.** *prąd*: cut off **5.** *wodę*: shut off **6.** (*z prądu*) unplug **7.** (*wykluczać*) exclude **8.** (*pomijać*) leave out (**z** *G* of); ***wyłączać się*** **1.** (*o telewizorze, świetle*) switch off **2.** (*o ogrzewaniu*) go off **3.** (*nie uważać*) tune out **4.** (*odkładać słuchawkę*) hang up **5.** (*wycofywać się*) withdraw **6.** ***nie wyłączając*** *G* including

wyłączenie *n* (*-nia*; *-nia*) **1.** *urządzenia*: switching off **2.** *prądu*: power cut **3.** (*wykluczenie*) exclusion; ***z ~m*** *G* excluding

W

wyłącznie *particle* only, exclusively, solely
wyłącznik *m* (*-ka*; *-ki*) switch
wyłączny *adj* **1.** *dystrybutor*, *importer*: exclusive, sole **2.** *prawo*: exclusive **3.** *spadkobierca*: sole
wyłogi *pl* (*-gów*) facings
wyłom *m* (*-mu*; *-my*) **1.** breach, hole; **~ w murze** breach in a wall **2.** *fig* break
wyłonić *v/p* → **wyłaniać**
wyłowić *v/p* → **wyławiać**
wyłożyć *v/p* → **wykładać**
wyłudzać ⟨**-dzić**⟩ (*-dzam*) **1.** (*podstępem*) swindle (**od** *G* out of) **2.** (*szantażem*) extort (**od** *G* from)
wyłupać *v/p* → **wyłupywać**
wyłupiać ⟨**-pić**⟩ (*-piam*) *oczy*: gouge out, poke out
wyłupiasty *adj oczy*: bulging
wyłupić *v/p* → **wyłupiać**
wyłupywać ⟨**-pać**⟩ (*-puję*) *oczy*: gouge out, poke out
wyłuskiwać ⟨**-kać**⟩ (*-kuję*) **1.** *nasiona*: husk **2.** *orzechy*: shell **3.** (*wydobywać*) pull out, fish out **4.** *sens*: extract
wyłuszczać ⟨**-czyć**⟩ (*-czam*) **1.** *problem*, *poglądy*, *przyczyny*: lay out **2.** *poglądy*: expound
wyłysiały *adj* bald
wyłysieć *v/p* → **łysieć**
wymacać *v/p* (*-cam*) (*znaleźć*) find; → **wymacywać**
wymachiwa|ć *v/im* (*-chuję*) **1.** wave (around); **~ła rękami** she was waving her arms around **2.** *skrzydłami*: flap **3.** *batem*: swing
wymacywać ⟨**-cać**⟩ (*-cuję*) feel, grope
wymaga|ć *v/im* (*-gam*) **1.** require, need; **sytuacja ~ła natychmiastowego działania** the situation required immediate action; **~ć dużo wysiłku** require a lot of effort, take a lot of effort; **~ć systematyczności** require systematic effort; **samochód ~ naprawy** the car needs to be repaired; **~ć od kogoś kreatywności** require s.o. to be creative **2.** (*żądać*) demand
wymagając|y *adj* **1.** *szef*, *nauczyciel*: demanding **2.** **osoby ~e opieki medycznej** people in need of medical care, people who require medical care
wymagani|e *n* (*-nia*; *-nia*) **1.** requirement; **mieć wysokie ~a** be very demanding **2.** (*warunek*) condition **3.** (*żądanie*) demand; **wymagany** *adj* required
wymaglować *v/p* → **maglować**
wymalowany *adj* painted
wymamrotać *v/p* (*-roczę*/*-rocę*) mutter, mumble
wymarci|e: **na ~u** endangered, threatened with extinction; **wymarły** *adj* **1.** *gatunek*: extinct **2.** *ulice*, *dom*: deserted **3.** *miasto*: dead
wymarsz *m* (*-szu*; *-sze*) marching out, departure
wymarzać ⟨**-znąć**⟩ (*-zam*) **1.** (*o roślinach*) be killed by frost **2.** (*o osobie*) freeze
wymarzony *adj* **1.** *dom*, *kandydat*: dream **2.** *pogoda*: perfect
wymarzyć *v/p* (*-rzę*) dream (up); **wszystko, co można sobie ~** everything you could dream of
wymasować *v/p* → **masować**
wymaszerować *v/p* (*-ruję*) march off
wymawiać ⟨**-mówić**⟩ (*-wiam*) **1.** (*artykułować*) pronounce; **źle ~** mispronounce **2.** (*wyrażać*) utter, say **3.** (*zrywać umowę*) **~ komuś pracę** give s.o. notice; **wymawiać się 1.** (*wykręcać się*) excuse oneself (**od** *G* from) **2.** (*być artykułowanym*) **jak to się wymawia?** how do you pronounce it?
wymaz *m* (*-zu*; *-zy*) smear (test)
wymazywać ⟨**-zać**⟩ (*-zuję*) **1.** (*ścierać gumką*) rub out, erase **2.** (*ścierać gąbką*) clean, erase; **~ coś z pamięci** block s.th. out of one's memory; **wymazywać się** (*brudzić się*) smear oneself (*I* with)
wymądrzać się *v/im* (*-rzam*) play the smart guy
wymeldowywać ⟨**-dować**⟩ (*-dowuję*): **~ kogoś** notify the authorities of s.o.'s change of address, notify the authorities that s.o. has moved out; **wymeldowywać się 1.** (*z miejsca zamieszkania*) notify the authorities of one's change of address **2.** (*z hotelu*) check out
wymęczyć *v/p* (*-czę*) tire out, exhaust; **~ odpowiedź** answer a question with

great difficulty; **~ zwycięstwo** *Br* labour one's way to victory

wymiana *f* (*-ny*; *-ny*) **1.** exchange; **~ gospodarcza** business exchange; **~ ognia** exchange of fire; **~ doświadczeń** experience sharing, skill-sharing; **~ myśli** exchange of ideas; **gwałtowna ~ zdań** angry exchange **2.** *oleju*: change **3.** *części*: change, replacement

wymia|r *m* (*-ru*; *-ry*) **1.** (*wielkość*) measurement, size; **~ry** measurements; **pracować w pełnym ~rze godzin** have a full-time job; **pracować w niepełnym ~rze godzin** have a part-time job; **~r kary** sentence; **najwyższy ~r kary** the maximum sentence; **poprosić o łagodny ~r kary** appeal for clemency; **~r podatku** tax rate **2.** PHYS MATH dimension; **czwarty ~r** the fourth dimension; **całkowicie nowy ~r** *fig* a whole new dimension **3. ~r sprawiedliwości** JUR the judiciary, justice

wymiatać ⟨**-mieść**⟩ (*-tam*) sweep (out) (**spod** *G* from under)

wymieniać ⟨**-nić**⟩ (*-niam*) **1.** *towary*, *myśli*, *pieniądze*: exchange (**na** *A* for) **2.** *pieniądze*, *olej*: change; **~ złotówki na dolary** change zlotys into dollars **3.** (*zastępować*) replace (**coś** *I* s.th. with) **4.** (*wyliczać*) list, name **5.** *nazwisko*: mention **6.** *cenę*: give, quote; **wymieniać się 1.** exchange, swap; **~ się adresami** exchange addresses; **~ się koszulkami** swap shirts **2.** (*zastępować*) change

wymienialny *adj waluta*: convertible

wymienić *v/p* → **wymieniać**

wymieniony *adj* (*wspomniany*) said, mentioned; **wyżej ~** above-mentioned, aforementioned

wymienny *adj* **1.** *element*: replaceable **2.** *transakcja*: exchange; **handel ~** barter

wymierać ⟨**-mrzeć**⟩ (*-ram*) **1.** (*o gatunku*) become extinct **2.** (*o potomkach*) die out **3.** (*o ulicach*) become deserted

wymiern|y *adj* **1.** measurable **2. liczby ~e** MATH rational numbers

W

wymierzać ⟨**-rzyć**⟩ (*-rzam*) **1.** *długość*, *działkę*: measure **2.** *karę*: inflict, mete out **3.** *sprawiedliwość*: administer **4.** (*celować*) aim: **wymierzyć do kogoś z karabinu** aim one's gun at s.o. **5.** (*uderzać*) **~ komuś policzek** slap s.o. in the face; **~ komuś cios** deal s.o. a blow

wymierzon|y *adj* directed, aimed; **ataki ~e w USA** attacks against the US

wymieszać *v/p* → **mieszać**

wymieść *v/p* → **wymiatać**

wymię *n* (*-mienia*; *-miona*) udder

wymięty *adj* **1.** (*pognieciony*) crumpled **2.** (*zmęczony*) *fig* haggard, worn out

wymigiwać się ⟨**-gać**⟩ (*-guję*) wriggle (**od** *G* out of), duck (**od** *G*)

wymijać ⟨**-minąć**⟩ (*-jam*) **1.** (*omijać*) pass, go past **2.** (*wyprzedzać*) *Br* overtake, *Am* pass; **wymijać się** pass each other; **wymijający** *adj* evasive

wymijanie *n* (*-nia*; *no pl*) **1.** (*omijanie*) passing **2.** (*wyprzedzanie*) *Br* overtaking, *Am* passing

wyminąć *v/p* → **wymijać**

wymiociny *pl* (*-cin*) vomit *sing*; **wymiotny** *adj*: **odruch ~** vomiting reflex; **środek ~** emetic; **wywoływać u kogoś odruch ~ a)** make s.o. retch **b)** *fig* make s.o. nauseous

wymiotować ⟨**z-**⟩ (*-tuję*) vomit, throw up

wymioty *pl* (*-tów*) **1.** (*wymiotowanie*) vomiting *sing*; **zbiera mi się na ~** I'm nauseous, I feel sick **2.** (*wymiociny*) vomit *sing*

wymknąć się *v/p* → **wymykać się**

wymłócić *v/p* (*-cę*) **1.** *zboże*: thresh **2.** *fig* batter

wymoczek *m* (*-czka*; *-czki*) *infml* weakling

wymoczyć *v/p* (*-czę*) soak

wymodelować *v/p* → **modelować**

wymodzić *v/p* (*-dzę*) *infml* **1.** (*wymyślić*) come up with **2.** (*zrobić*) do

wymog|i *pl* (*-gów*) requirements; **ubrany zgodnie z ~ami mody** dressed in the latest fashion

wymontowywać ⟨**-tować**⟩ (*-towuję*) remove, take out

wymordować *v/p* (*-duję*) kill, slaughter; **wymordować się** kill each other

wymościć *v/p* → **mościć**

wymow|a *f* (*-wy*; *no pl*) **1.** pronunciation **2.** *fig* significance **3. dar ~y** *lit* eloquence; **wymowny** *adj* **1.** *gest*, *spojrzenie*: meaningful **2.** *tytuł*: telling **3.** *osoba*: eloquent

wymóc *v/p* (*-mogę*): **~ na kimś zgodę na** *A* make s.o. agree to; **~ na kimś obietnicę** *G* force s.o. promise
wymówić *v/p* → **wymawiać**
wymówieni|e *n* (*-nia*; *-nia*) **1.** (*zawiadomienie o zwolnieniu*) notice; **dostać ~e** be given notice; **złożyć ~e** hand in one's notice **2.** (*artykulacja*) **nie do ~a** unpronounceable
wymówk|a *f* (*-ki*; *-ki*) **1.** excuse **2. ~i** (*wyrzuty*) reproaches
wymrażać ⟨**-rozić**⟩ (*-żam*) freeze; **wymrozić się** (*o osobie*) *infml* freeze
wymrzeć *v/p* → **wymierać**
wymurować *v/p* → **murować**
wymusić *v/p* → **wymuszać**
wymuskany *adj* spruce, well-groomed; **mieć ~ wygląd** be all spruced up
wymuszać ⟨**-sić**⟩ (*-szam*) **1.** *okup*, *haracz*: extort **2.** (*zmuszać*) **~ na kimś przyznanie się do winy** force s.o. to plead guilty, coerce s.o. into pleading guilty **3. wymusić pierwszeństwo przejazdu na** *L* fail to yield right of way to
wymuszenie *n* (*-nia*; *-nia*) **1.** *okupu*, *haraczu*: extortion **2.** *JUR* coercion; **wymuszony** *adj* forced
wymyć *v/p* → **wymywać**
wymykać się ⟨**-mknąć**⟩ (*-kam*) (*uciekać*) slip out (**z** *G* of), sneak out (**z** *G* of); **~ spod kontroli** get out of control; **wymknęło mu się, że** he let it slip that; **~ śmierci** escape death; **~ definicjom** defy any definition
wymysł *m* (*-łu*; *-ły*) **1.** invention, fabrication; **to nie jest ~em mediów** this is not a fiction created by the media **2.** (*kaprys*) whim
wymyślać ⟨**-lić**⟩ (*-lam*) **1.** (*wpadać na pomysł*) invent, come up with **2.** (*wynajdować*) invent **3.** (*ubliżać*) swear, hurl abuse (*D* at)
wymyślny *adj* sophisticated, fancy
wymywać ⟨**-myć**⟩ (*-wam*) **1.** *wąwóz*, *jar*: carve **2.** *złoto*: wash (**z** *G* out of)
wynagradzać ⟨**-rodzić**⟩ (*-dzam*) **1.** (*dawać nagrodę*) reward (**za** *A* for) **2.** (*dawać zapłatę*) pay, *form* remunerate (**za** *A* for) **3.** *stratę*, *krzywdę*: compensate for, make up for; **~ komuś krzywdę** make amends to s.o., redress s.o.'s grievance; **jak mogę ci to wynagrodzić?** how can I make it up to you?
wynagrodzeni|e *n* (*-nia*; *no pl*) **1.** (*płaca*) pay, *form* remuneration; **~e zasadnicze** basic pay, base salary; **praca bez ~a** unpaid work; **praca za ~em** paid work; **dostawać zbyt wysokie ~e** be overpaid **2.** *szkody*: compensation (*G* for) **3.** (*nagroda*) reward
wynagrodzić *v/p* → **wynagradzać**
wynająć *v/p* → **wynajmować**
wynajdywać ⟨**-naleźć**⟩ (*-duję*) **1.** (*wymyślać*) invent **2.** (*wyszukiwać*) find
wynaj|em *m* (*-jmu*; *no pl*) **1.** *mieszkania*, *domu*: renting **2.** *samochodu*, *sprzętu*: rental, hire; **firma zajmująca się ~mem samochodów** car rental company **3.** *jachtów*, *samolotów*: charter
wynajęci|e *n* (*-cia*; *no pl*): **pokoje do ~a** rooms to let, rooms for rent; **samochody do ~a** cars for hire
wynajmować ⟨**-jąć**⟩ (*-muję*) **1.** *mieszkanie*, *pokój*: rent; **~ swój dom na lato** let out one's house for the summer; **~ z kimś pokój** *Am* room with s.o.; **~ wspólnie pokój** *Am* room together **2.** *samochód*, *robotnika*, *mordercę*: hire **3.** *jacht*, *samolot*: charter
wynalazca *m* (*-cy*; *-cy*) inventor; **wynalazczość** *f* (*-ści*; *no pl*) inventiveness; **wynalazczy** *adj* inventive; **wynalazczyni** *f* (*-ni*; *-nie*) (female) inventor; **wynalazek** *m* (*-zku*; *-zki*) invention
wynaleźć *v/p* → **wynajdywać**
wynaturzenie *n* (*-nia*; *-nia*) abnormality, degeneration; **wynaturzony** *adj* abnormal, degenerated
wynegocjować *v/p* → **negocjować**
wynędzniały *adj* emaciated, wasted
wynieść *v/p* → **wynosić**
wynik *m* (*-ku*; *-ki*) **1.** result; **w ~u** *G* as a result of, because of, due to; **~i badań a)** (*w nauce*) research findings **b)** *MED* test results; **pomyślny ~ negocjacji** success of negotiations; **~i pracy** performance **2.** *SPORT* score, result **3.** *dyskusji*, *zebrania*, *wyborów*: outcome **4.** (*konsekwencje*) effect, aftermath **5.** (*wniosek*) conclusion
wynikać ⟨**-knąć**⟩ (*-kam*) result (**z** *G* from); **z badań wynika, że** the research shows that

wyniosłość *f* (*-ści*; *-ści*) **1.** (*zachowanie*) haughtiness, superciliousness **2.** (*wzniesienie*) *form* elevation

wyniosły *adj* **1.** (*dumny*) haughty, supercilious **2.** (*wysoki*) towering, soaring

wyniszczać ⟨**-czyć**⟩ (*-czam*) **1.** *zdrowie*: ruin **2.** *kraj*: devastate **3.** *szkodniki*: destroy **4.** *gatunek*, *plemiona*: exterminate

wyniszczony *adj*: ***~ wojną kraj*** war-ravaged country; ***~ chorobą*** wasted by disease; ***~ głodem*** starved

wyniuchać *v/p* (*-cham*) *fig* nose out

wynocha *interj*: ***~!*** get out!, out!

wynos: ***na ~*** to go, *Br* to take away; ***danie na ~*** *Br* takeaway, *Am* takeout

wynosić ⟨**-nieść**⟩ (*-szę*) **1.** carry; ***~ kogoś pod niebiosa*** praise s.o. to the skies; ***~ kogoś na tron*** put s.o. on the throne; ***wyniosła to z domu*** *fig* she was brought up that way; ***~ naukę z*** *G* learn a lesson from **2.** *śmieci*: take out, take away **3.** (*na górę*) carry upstairs, carry up **4.** *wiedzę*, *doświadczenia*: gain **5.** (*o sumie*, *ilości*) amount to **6.** (*o kosztach*, *stratach*) total, amount to; ***wynosić się*** **1.** (*wychodzić*) go out, leave; ***wynoś się!*** get out! **2.** (*wywyższać się*) look down (***ponad*** *A* on)

wynurzać ⟨**-rzyć**⟩ (*-rzam*): ***~ głowę z wody*** raise one's head out of the water; ***~ wiosła z wody*** take the oars out of the water; ***wynurzać się*** **1.** come to the surface, surface **2.** *fig* appear, emerge

wynurzenia *pl* (*-rzeń*) (*zwierzenia*) confessions

wyobcowanie *n* (*-nia*; *no pl*) alienation; **wyobcowany** *adj* alienated

wyobrazić *v/p* → ***wyobrażać***

wyobraźni|a *f* (*-ni*; *no pl*) imagination; ***mieć ~ę*** be imaginative; ***pozbawiony ~*** unimaginative

wyobra|żać ⟨**-razić**⟩ (*-żam*) **1.** (*wizualnie*) represent; ***ten obraz ~ża św. Jerzego, który zabija smoka*** the painting represents St George killing the dragon **2.** (*umysłowo*): ***~żać sobie*** imagine, picture; ***~ź sobie, że jesteś w dżungli*** imagine (that) you're in a jungle; ***nie ~żam sobie życia bez tańca*** I can't imagine life without dancing; ***trudno to sobie ~zić*** it's difficult to imagine; ***wciąż ~ża sobie, że jestem dwulatkiem*** he still conceives of me as a two-year-old

wyobrażeni|e *n* (*-nia*; *-nia*) **1.** (*pojęcie*, *pogląd*) idea; ***nie mieć o czymś ~a*** have no idea about s.th.; ***mieć błędne ~e o*** *L* have mistaken beliefs about; ***~e o świecie*** conception of the world; ***~e o sobie*** one's self-image **2.** (*wizualne*) image, representation; ***~e Wenus*** representation of Venus

wyodrębniać ⟨**-nić**⟩ (*-niam*) **1.** (*oddzielać*) separate, mark off **2.** (*wyróżniać*) distinguish **3.** CHEM BIOL isolate, separate; ***wyodrębniać się*** be separated

wyolbrzymiać ⟨**-mić**⟩ (*-miam*) exaggerate, overstate, play up

wyostrzony *adj* *świadomość*, *zmysły*: sharpened

wypacać ⟨**-pocić**⟩ (*-cam*) *toksyny*: sweat out; ***wypacać się*** sweat a lot

wypacykować się *v/p* → ***pacykować się***

wypaczać ⟨**-czyć**⟩ (*-czam*) **1.** *charakter*, *drzwi*: warp **2.** *sens*, *obraz*: distort; ***wypaczać się*** **1.** (*o drewnie*) warp **2.** (*o charakterze*) get warped

wypad *m* (*-du*; *-dy*) **1.** (*wycieczka*) trip, outing; ***~ za miasto*** trip out of town; ***zrobić ~ do miasta*** go into town **2.** (*atak*) foray; ***~ na terytorium nieprzyjaciela*** foray into enemy territory

wypadać ⟨**-paść**⟩ (*-dam*) **1.** (*wylatywać*) fall out; ***~ z wózka*** fall out of a pram; ***~ z ręki*** drop out of s.o.'s hand; ***wypadło mi z głowy*** it slipped my mind **2.** *włosy*, *zęby*: come out **3.** (*zdarzać się*) ***może coś mu wypadło?*** something might have come up; ***tak wypadło*** it so happened **4.** (*przypadać*) fall; ***~ w niedzielę*** fall on Sunday **5.** (*sprawiać wrażenie*) come across; ***bardzo dobrze wypadła*** she came across very well; ***dobrze wypadł na rozmowie kwalifikacyjnej*** he did well in the interview **6.** (*nagle wybiegać*) rush out, burst out **7.** (*być właściwym*) ***komuś nie wypada czegoś robić*** it is unbecoming of s.o. to do s.th., s.o. should not do s.th.;

wypadałoby ich odwiedzić we should visit them; ***to nie wypada*** it's bad manners, it's not done
wypad|ek *m* (*-dku*; *-dki*) **1.** accident; ***~ek drogowy*** traffic accident, road accident; ***~ek samochodowy*** car accident, car crash; ***~ek przy pracy*** accident at work; ***nagły ~ek*** emergency; ***w nagłych ~kach*** in case of emergency; ***zginąć w ~ku*** be killed in an accident **2.** (*przypadek*) case, instance; ***na wszelki ~ek*** just in case; ***na ~ek*** *G* in case of; ***w najlepszym ~ku*** at best; ***w najgorszym ~ku*** at worst; ***w żadnym ~ku*** on no account; ***w przeciwnym ~ku*** otherwise, or else **3.** ***~ki*** (*zdarzenia*) events
wypal|ać ⟨**-lić**⟩ (*-lam*) **I** *v/t* **1.** *dziurę, piętno*: burn **2.** *papierosa*: smoke **3.** *cegły*: bake **4.** *kurzajkę*: burn off **II** *v/i* **1.** (*z pistoletu*) fire **2.** (*udać się*) *infml* come off; ***plan nie ~ił*** the plan didn't come off, the plan flopped; ***wypalać się*** **1.** (*o świecy, ognisku, zawodniku*) burn out **2.** (*o romansie, przyjaźni*) come to an end, *infml* fizzle out
wypaplać *v/p* (*-lam*/*-lę*) blab (**komuś** *A* to s.o. about)
wyparowywać ⟨**-rować**⟩ (*-rowuję*) **1.** evaporate **2.** *fig* vanish into thin air
wyparty *adj uczucia*: repressed
wyparzać ⟨**-rzyć**⟩ (*-rzam*) scald
wypasiony *adj* **1.** (*gruby*) fat **2.** *infml* cool
wypastować *v/p* → ***pastować***
wypaść *v/p*: ***nie wypadł sroce spod ogona*** he's not just anybody; → ***wypadać***
wypatrywać *v/im* (*-ruję*) look out for; ***~ okazji*** look out for an opportunity; → ***wypatrzyć***
wypatrzyć *v/p* (*-rzę*) **1.** (*zauważyć*) spot, see **2.** (*znajdować*) find
wypchać *v/p* → ***wypychać***
wypchany *adj* **1.** *torba*: bulging, stuffed (*I* with) **2.** *autobus*: jam-packed **3.** *kolana*: baggy **4.** *zwierzę*: stuffed
wypchnąć *v/p* → ***wypychać***
wypełniać ⟨**-nić**⟩ (*-niam*) **1.** *naczynie, stadion*: fill (up) **2.** *lukę, szczelinę*: fill in **3.** *formularz*: fill in, *Am* fill out **4.** *obietnice*: *Br* fulfil, *Am* fulfill; ***~ obietnice wyborcze*** hold to one's election promises **5.** *zadanie*: complete **6.** *rozkazy*: carry out; ***wypełniać się*** (*o naczyniu*) fill up; ***~ się łzami*** fill with tears, fill up
wypełniony *adj* full (*I* of)
wypełzać ⟨**-znąć**⟩ (*-zam*) crawl out, creep out (**z** *G* of)
wyperfumować się *v/p* → ***perfumować się***
wyperswadować *v/p* → ***perswadować***
wypędz|ać ⟨**-dzić**⟩ (*-dzam*) **1.** (*wyganiać*) chase out; throw out; ***~ił psa z ogrodu*** he chased the dog out of the garden; ***mąż ~ił ją z domu*** her husband turned her out of their home **2.** (*z kraju*) expel **3.** *szatana*: cast out
wypędzony **I** *adj* *POLIT* expelled, displaced **II** *m* (*-nego*; *-dzeni*), **-na** *f* (*-nej*; *-ne*) *POLIT* expelled person, displaced person; ***~eni*** the expelled
wypiąć *v/p* → ***wypinać***
wypić *v/p* (*-piję*) drink (up); ***~ sobie trochę*** *infml* have some drinks; ***~ czyjeś zdrowie*** drink to s.o.'s health; ***~ piwo, którego się nawarzyło*** face the music; → ***wypijać***
wypieczony *adj* brown-crusted, crusty
wypiek *m* (*-ku*; *-ki*) **1.** ***~i*** (*pieczywo, ciasta*) baked goods; ***słodkie ~i*** patisserie; ***domowe ~i*** home-made cakes **2.** (*pieczenie*) baking; ***~ chleba*** bread baking, bread making; ***własnego ~u, domowego ~u*** home-baked, home-made **3.** ***~i*** (*na twarzy*) flush; ***z ~ami na twarzy*** with flushed cheeks
wypielęgnować *v/p* → ***pielęgnować***
wypielić *v/p* → ***pielić***
wypieprzyć *v/p* (*-rzę*) **1.** (*wyrzucić*) *infml* chuck out **2.** (*odbyć stosunek*) *vulg* screw, shag; ***wypieprzyć się*** (*upaść*) *infml* take a spill; ***~ się na rowerze*** take a spill off one's bike
wypierać ⟨**-przeć**⟩ (*-ram*) **1.** drive out, force out; ***wyparli nieprzyjaciela z miasta*** they drove the enemy from the town **2.** *najeźdźców*: oust **3.** (*zastępować*) displace, supplant **4.** *uczucia*: repress **5.** *rośliny*: crowd out; ***wypierać się*** **1.** deny; ***~ się jakichkolwiek związków z*** *I* deny any connection with **2.** *wiary*: renounce **3.** *syna, córki*: disown

wypieszczony *adj* **1.** *dziecko*: pampered **2.** *mieszkanie*: spotless, shipshape

wypięknieć *v/p* → **pięknieć**

wypijać ⟨**-pić**⟩ (*-jam*) drink; **~ coś do dna** drink s.th. in one go

wypinać ⟨**-piąć**⟩ (*-nam*) **1.** (*wystawiać*) stick out; **~ tyłek** *infml* stick one's bottom out, stick one's bottom in the air **2.** (*wyciągać*) take out; ***wypinać się*** *fig* turn one's back (**na** *A* on)

wypindrzyć się *v/p* (*-rzę*) *infml* get dolled up

wypis *m* (*-su*; *-sy*) **1.** (*z dokumentu*) extract **2.** (*ze szpitala*) discharge note **3. ~y** (*podręcznik*) reader

wypisywać ⟨**-sać**⟩ (*-suję*) **1.** (*spisywać*) write out **2.** *czek*: write out, make out **3.** *receptę*: write, write out **4.** *bzdury*: write **5.** *długopis*: use up **6.** (*przepisywać*) copy **7.** (*ze szpitala*) discharge **8.** (*ze szkoły*) remove **9.** ***wypisz, wymaluj ojciec*** he's the picture of his father, he is the spitting image of his father; ***wypisywać się*** **1.** (*z klubu*) leave, quit (**z** *G*) **2.** (*ze szpitala*) discharge oneself (**ze** *G* from) **3.** (*o wkładzie*) run out

wyplatać ⟨**-leść**⟩ (*-tam*) *kosze*: weave, plait; **wyplatany** *adj* **1.** *meble*: wicker **2.** *kosz*: woven

wyplątywać ⟨**-tać**⟩ (*-tuję*) free, disentangle; ***wyplątywać się*** **1.** free oneself, disentangle oneself (**z** *G* from) **2.** *fig* extricate oneself (**z** *G* from)

wypleć *v/p* → **pleć**

wypleniać ⟨**-nić**⟩ (*-niam*) **1.** *fig* root out, eradicate **2.** *chwasty*: kill off

wypluć *v/p* → **wypluwać**

wypluty *adj infml* dead beat, *Am infml* pooped

wypluwać ⟨**-luć**⟩ (*-wam*) spit out; ***wypluj to słowo!*** don't even think about it!, touch wood!

wypłacać ⟨**-cić**⟩ (*-cam*) **1.** (*wydawać*) pay out **2.** (*o bankomacie*) dispense, give **3.** (*pobierać*) withdraw

wypłacalny *adj* solvent

wypłacić *v/p* → **wypłacać**

wypłakiwać ⟨**-kać**⟩ (*-kuję*): **~ oczy** cry one's eyes out; ***wypłakiwać się*** have a good cry; ***~ się na czyimś ramieniu*** cry on s.o.'s shoulder

wypłaszać ⟨**-łoszyć**⟩ (*-szam*) flush out

wypłat|a *f* (*-ty*; *-ty*) **1.** (*wypłacenie, wypłacana suma*) payment; ***kwota do ~y*** amount to be paid **2.** (*wypłacenie z konta*) withdrawal; ***dokonać ~y*** make a withdrawal **3.** (*pensja*) pay, salary; ***dzień ~y*** pay day

wypłoszyć *v/p* → **wypłaszać**

wypłowiały *adj kolor, materiał*: faded

wypłowieć *v/p* → **płowieć**

wypłukiwać ⟨**-kać**⟩ (*-kuję*) **1.** rinse; ***wypłukać usta*** rinse one's mouth; ***wypłukać gardło*** gargle **2.** *wąwóz, jar*: carve (out) **3. ~ złoto** pan for gold

wypływać ⟨**-łynąć**⟩ (*-wam*) **1.** (*o statku*) sail out **2.** (*o promie*) depart **3.** (*o pływaku*) set off, start swimming **4.** *łodzią*: go out (*I* by) **5.** (*wynurzać się*) come to the surface, surface **6.** (*o płynie*) flow out **7.** (*wynikać*) result (**z** *G* from) **8.** (*odnosić sukces*) *infml* make it **9.** (*o źródle*) rise

wypocić *v/p* → **wypacać**

wypociny *pl* (*-cin*) *infml* garbage *sing*, *Br* rubbish *sing*

wypocząć *v/p* → **wypoczywać**

wypoczęty *adj* (well-)rested

wypoczynek *m* (*-nku*; *no pl*) **1.** (*wakacje*) *Br* holidays *pl*, *Am* vacation **2.** (*odpoczynek*) rest; ***aktywny ~*** active leisure; **wypoczynkow|y** *adj* ***miejscowość ~a*** holiday resort; ***meble ~e*** living-room suite, lounge suite

wypocz|ywać ⟨**-cząć**⟩ (*-wam*) **1.** (*być na wakacjach*) *Br* be on holiday, *Am* be on vacation **2.** (*odpoczywać*) rest; ***powinnaś ~ąć*** you need a rest

wypogadzać się ⟨**-godzić**⟩ (*-dzam*) (*o niebie*) clear up, brighten up; ***wypogadza się*** it's clearing up

wypolerować *v/p* → **polerować**

wypominać ⟨**-mnieć**⟩ (*-nam*): ***~ coś komuś*** keep throwing s.th. back at s.o., rub s.o.'s nose in s.th.; ***nie musisz mi tego ~*** you don't have to rub it in

wypompowany *adj* (*zmęczony*) *Am infml* pooped

wyporność *f* (*-ści*; *no pl*) displacement

wyposażać ⟨**-żyć**⟩ (*-żam*) equip (**coś w** *A* s.th. with, **kogoś w** *A* s.o. in); ***~ szkołę w coś*** equip a school with s.th., resource a school with s.th.; **wyposażenie** *n* (*-nia*; *no pl*) (*sprzęt*) equipment; **~ kuchni** (**łazienki**) kitchen (bathroom) fittings; **~ mieszkania** furnishings; **~ kościoła** church furnishings

wypowiadać 〈**-wiedzieć**〉 (*-dam*) **1.** *słowo*: say, utter; ***nie dać się wypowiedzieć*** (*o słowie*) be unpronounceable **2.** *opinię*: express **3. *~ komuś pracę*** give s.o. notice **4.** *wojnę*: declare; ***wypowiadać się*** **1.** express one's opinion (***na temat*** *G* on/about); ***~ się za*** *I* speak up for; ***~ przeciwko*** *D* speak out against **2.** (*komentować*) comment (***na temat*** *G* on)

wypowiedzenie *n* (*-nia*; *-nia*) **1.** *pracy, najmu*: notice; ***wręczać ~*** hand in one's notice **2.** *umowy*: notice (of termination) **3.** (*artykulacja*) utterance **4.** *wojny*: declaration

wypowiedź *f* (*-dzi*; *-dzi*) statement, comment

wypożyczać 〈**-czyć**〉 (*-czam*) **1.** (*komuś*) lend (*D* to), loan (*D* to); ***w tej bibliotece można ~ płyty kompaktowe*** this library loans CDs **2.** (*od kogoś*) borrow (***od*** *G* from) **3.** *rowery, sprzęt*: hire, rent

wypożyczalnia *f* (*-ni*; *-nie*) **1. *~ kaset wideo*** *Br* video rental shop, *Am* video rental store **2. *~ samochodów*** *Br* car hire (agency), *Am* car rental (agency) **3.** (*biblioteka*) library

wypożyczyć *v/p* → ***wypożyczać***

wypracować *v/p* → ***wypracowywać***

wypracowanie *n* (*-nia*; *-nia*) essay, composition

wypracow|ywać 〈**-cować**〉 (*-cowuję*) **1.** *metodę, technikę*: work out **2.** *zysk*: make, earn **3. *~aliśmy sobie tę pozycję*** we've worked hard to achieve this position

wyprać *v/p* → ***prać***

wypraszać 〈**-rosić**〉 (*-szam*) **1.** (*wybłagać*) wheedle out **2.** (*kazać wyjść*) ask to leave (**z** *G*); ***~ kogoś za drzwi*** show s.o. the door **3. *wypraszam sobie*** I beg your pardon

wyprawa *f* (*-wy*; *-wy*) expedition; ***~ badawcza*** scientific expedition; ***~ krzyżowa*** crusade

wyprawiać 〈**-wić**〉 (*-wiam*) **1.** (*wysyłać*) send (***do*** *G* to); ***~ kogoś na tamten świat*** dispatch s.o. **2.** (*organizować, robić*) give; ***~ urodziny*** throw a birthday party; ***~ awantury*** kick up a fuss; ***co ty wyprawiasz?*** what do you think you are doing? **3.** (*garbować*) tan

wyprawka *f* (*-ki*; *-ki*) (*dla niemowlaka*) layette

wyprężać 〈**-żyć**〉 (*-żam*) *pierś*: throw out; ***wyprężać się*** draw oneself up

wyprodukować *v/p* → ***produkować***

wyprosić *v/p* → ***wypraszać***

wyprostować *v/p* → ***prostować***; **wyprostowany** *adj* straight; ***stał ~*** he stood erect, he stood upright

wyprowadzać 〈**-dzić**〉 (*-dzam*) **1.** (*na spacer, z garażu*) take (out); ***~ psa na spacer*** take a dog for a walk, walk a dog; ***~ samochód z garażu*** take a car out of a garage **2.** (*z pomieszczenia*) lead out; ***~ oskarżonego z sali sądowej*** escort a defendant out of a courtroom; ***~ kogoś siłą z pokoju*** frogmarch s.o. out of a room **3.** *wzór*: derive **4. *~ kogoś z równowagi*** (*denerwować*) make s.o. angry, get on s.o.'s nerves; ***dawać się łatwo wyprowadzić z równowagi*** *fig* have a short fuse; ***~ kogoś z błędu*** put s.o. right, set s.o. straight; ***wyprowadzać się*** move (out); ***~ się z mieszkania*** move out of a flat

wyprowadzka *f* (*-ki*; *-ki*) *infml* **1.** move **2.** (*przenoszenie rzeczy*) *Br* removal

wypróbować *v/p* → ***wypróbowywać***

wypróbowany *adj* **1.** *metody*: *Br* tried and tested, *Am* tried and true **2.** *pracownik*: reliable

wypróbowywać 〈**-bować**〉 (*-bowuję*) try out, test

wypróżnia|ć 〈**-nić**〉 (*-niam*) empty; ***wypróżniać się*** defecate, move one's bowels, *form* evacuate; ***czy ~ł się pan dzisiaj?*** have you moved your bowels today?

wypróżnienie *n* (*-nia*; *-nia*) defecation, bowel movement, *form* evacuation

wypruwać 〈**-ruć**〉 (*-wam*) unpick, undo; ***~ sobie żyły*** *infml* sweat one's guts out, slog one's guts out

wyprysk *m* (*-ku*; *-ki*) (*pryszcz*) pimple, spot

wyprząc *v/p* → ***wyprzęgać***

wyprzeć *v/p* → ***wypierać***

wyprzedać *v/p* → ***wyprzedawać***

wyprzedany → ***wysprzedany***

W

wyprzeda|wać ⟨**-dać**⟩ (*-daję*) sell (off); **~wać zapasy** clear the stock; **wszystko ~liśmy** we've sold out of everything

wyprzedaż *f* (*-ży*; *-że*) sale; **~ letnia** summer sale; **~ zimowa** winter sale; **posezonowa ~** seasonal sale; **kupić coś na ~y** buy s.th. on sale, *Br* buy s.th. in the sales

wyprzedzać ⟨**-dzić**⟩ (*-dzam*) overtake, pass; **patrz w lusterko, zanim zaczniesz ~** check your rear-view mirror before you overtake; **wyprzedzić konkurencję** get ahead of the competition; **zostać wyprzedzonym** *fig* be left behind; **~ swoją epokę** be ahead of one's time

wyprzedzenie *n* (*-nia*; *no pl*): **z ~m** in advance, ahead of time; **z tygodniowym ~m** a week in advance

wyprzedzić *v/p* → **wyprzedzać**

wyprzęgać ⟨**-rząc**⟩ (*-gam*) *konia*: unharness

wypsnąć się *v/p infml*: **coś się komuś wypsnęło** s.o. let s.th. slip; **tak mi się wypsnęło** it just slipped out

wypucować *v/p* → **pucować**

wypukłość *f* (*-ści*; *-ści*) bulge; **wypukły** *adj* **1.** *kształt*, *soczewka*: convex **2.** *brzuch*, *czoło*: bulging, prominent

wypunktować *v/p* (*-tuję*) list, itemize

wypustka *f* (*-ki*; *-ki*) BIOL projection

wypuszczać ⟨**-puścić**⟩ (*-czam*) **1.** (*rozluźniać uchwyt*) let go; **~ z rąk linę** let a rope go, let go of a rope **2.** (*na ziemię*) drop; **~ z rąk pistolet** drop a gun **3.** (*z pomieszczenia*, *pojemnika*) let out; **wypuście mnie!** let me out!; **~ wodę z wanny** drain the water from a bathtub **4.** (*uwalniać*) set free, release **5.** *ścieki*: discharge **6. ~ coś na rynek** launch s.th., put s.th. on the market **7.** (*spuszczać*): **wypuścić powietrze z kół** (completely) deflate the tyres, *Br* let the tyres down; **~ trochę powietrza z koła** deflate a tyre a bit **8.** *liście*: put out; **~ pąki** bud, put out buds **9.** *banknoty*: issue **10. ~ strzałę z łuku** release an arrow, shoot an arrow **11.** *chmurę dymu*: puff **12.** *rakietę*: launch; **wypuszczać się** (*wyjechać*) set out, set off, venture; **~ się w podróż** set out on a journey

wypuszczenie *n* (*-nia*; *no pl*): **~ (na wolność)** release

wypychać ⟨**-pchać**, **-pchnąć**⟩ (*-cham*) **1.** *zwierzęta*, *poduszki*: stuff **2.** *osobę*: push out, force out **3. spodnie wypchane na kolanach** trousers bagging at the knees; **wypychać się 1.** (*o ubraniu*) bag; **~ się na kolanach** bag at the knees **2. wypchaj się!** *infml* get stuffed!, go fly a kite!

wypytywać ⟨**-tać**⟩ (*-tuję*) **1.** question (**o** *A* about) **2.** (*wiele osób*) ask around

wyrabiać ⟨**-robić**⟩ (*-biam*) **1.** (*wytwarzać*, *robić*) make; **co ty wyrabiasz?** *infml* what do you think you're doing? **2.** (*rozwijać*) develop; **~ mięśnie a)** (*rozbudowywać*) build one's muscles **b)** (*wzmacniać*) tone one's muscles; **~ sobie zdanie na temat** *G* form an opinion about; **~ sobie markę jako** *N* make a name as; **~ w dzieciach samodzielność** teach (your) children to be independent; **~ sobie złą opinię** gain a bad reputation **3.** (*uzyskiwać*) get; **~ sobe paszport** get a passport **4.** (*ugniatać*) knead; **wyrabiać się 1.** (*na czas*) *infml* make it: **nie wyrobię się** *infml* I won't make it; **ledwo wyrobiłem się w terminie** I just managed to meet the deadline **2.** (*o cesze*) develop, form **3.** (*poprawiać się*) improve; **~ się towarzysko** improve one's social skills

wyrachowanie *n* (*-nia*; *no pl*) calculation; **wyrachowany** *adj* calculating

wyradzać się ⟨**-rodzić**⟩ (*-dzam*): **wyrodził się ze swojej rodziny** he's a disgrace to his family

wyrafinowanie *n* (*-nia*; *no pl*) refinement, sophistication; **wyrafinowany** *adj* refined, sophisticated

wyrastać ⟨**-rosnąć**⟩ (*-stam*) **1.** grow; **~ z ubrania** grow out of one's clothes, outgrow one's clothes; **~ z** *G fig* grow out of **2.** (*o pędach*) shoot up **3.** (*o cieście*, *budynku*) rise **4.** (*wychowywać się*) grow up; **~ na przystojnego młodzieńca** grow up to be a handsome young man

wyraz *m* (*-zu*; *-zy*) **1.** (*słowo*) word; **obcy ~** foreign word; **~y złożone** compounds; **moje ~y współczucia** my condolences **2.** *fig* expression; **dać ~ czemuś** express s.th.; **~ twarzy** facial expression; ***bez ~u*** blank; ***pełen ~u*** very expressive; ***nad ~*** exceedingly; ***środki ~u*** means of expression; ***z ~ami szacunku*** yours truly, yours faithfully

wyraziciel *m* (*-la*; *-le*) *lit* exponent

wyrazić *v/p* → ***wyrażać***

wyrazistość *f* (*-ści*; *no pl*) **1.** (*wyraz*) expressiveness **2.** (*klarowność*) clarity **3.** (*odznaczanie się wyrazistymi cechami*) distinctiveness

wyrazisty *adj* **1.** (*pełen wyrazu*) expressive **2.** (*wyraźny*) distinctive

wyraźnie *adv* clearly, distinctly; **wyraźn|y** *adj* **1.** clear, distinct; ***bez ~ego powodu*** for no apparent reason **2.** *wzrost*, *spadek*, *poprawa*: noticeable, marked **3.** *wskazówki*: clear, explicit **4.** *pismo*: legible **5.** *błąd*: obvious **6.** *kontrast*: marked **7.** *akcent*: distinct, pronounced **8.** *obraz*: sharp

wyrażać ⟨**-razić**⟩ (*-żam*) express; ***~ opinię*** express one's opinion; ***~ zgodę*** agree (***na*** *A* to), consent (***na*** *A* to); ***~ sprzeciw*** object; ***~ aprobatę*** give one's approval, express one's approval; ***~ niezadowolenie*** express one's dissatisfaction, show one's dissatisfaction; ***~ coś słowami*** verbalize s.th., put s.th. in words; ***wyrażać się*** **1.** (*mówić*) speak (***o*** *L* of); ***~ się o kimś pozytywnie*** (***negatywnie***) speak well (ill) of s.o.; ***~ się o kimś w samych superlatywach*** speak very highly of s.o.; ***że się tak wyrażę*** so to speak **2.** (*wyrażać opinie*) ***eksperci wyrażają się pochlebnie o*** *L* the experts speak in favour of, the experts are in favour of **3.** (*znajdować odbicie*) manifest itself, be reflected **4.** (*przeklinać*) use foul language, swear

wyrażenie *n* (*-nia*; *-nia*) expression; ***~ zgody*** agreement, consent; ***~ potoczne*** colloquialism; ***przepraszam za ~*** if you'll pardon the expression; ***raczej niefortunne ~*** a rather unfortunate expression, a rather unfortunate choice of words

wyrąb *m* (*-rębu*; *-ręby*) clearing; ***~ lasów*** forest clearing

wyrąbywać ⟨**-bać**⟩ (*-buję*) **1.** *drzewa*: cut down, fell **2.** *lasy*: clear **3.** *otwór*: hack

wyrecytować *v/p* → ***recytować***

wyremontować *v/p* → ***remontować***

wyretuszować *v/p* → ***retuszować***

wyreżyserować *v/p* → ***reżyserować***

wyręczać ⟨**-czyć**⟩ (*-czam*): ***~ kogoś w czymś*** relieve s.o. of s.th., help s.o. by doing s.th.; ***~ kogoś w myśleniu*** do the thinking for s.o.; ***wyręczać się***: ***~ się kimś*** have s.o. do s.th.

wyrko *n* (*-ka*; *-ka*) *infml* sack

wyrobić *v/p* (*-bię*): ***nie ~ się na pociąg*** miss a train, be late for a train; → ***wyrabiać***

wyrobienie *n* (*-nia*; *no pl*) **1.** (*ogłada*) sophistication **2.** *paszportu*, *dowodu*: *infml* getting **3.** *nawyku*: formation; ***~ nawyku wczesnego wstawania*** getting into the habit of getting up early **4.** *stylu*, *umiejętności*: development; **wyrobion|y** *adj* **1.** *osoba*, *gust*: sophisticated, refined; ***~y towarzysko*** socially cultured, sophisticated **2.** *styl*, *publiczność*: sophisticated **3.** *ciasto*: well-kneaded **4.** *mięśnie*: well-toned **5.** *pozycja*: established **6.** ***mieć ~e zdanie na temat*** *G* have an opinion about, have definite views on

wyrobisko *n* (*-ka*; *-ka*) excavation

wyroby *pl* → ***wyrób***

wyrocznia *f* (*-ni*; *-nie*) **1.** oracle **2.** *fig* authority; ***~ w sprawach dobrego smaku*** arbiter of taste

wyrodek *m* (*-dka*; *-dki*) black sheep

wyrodnieć ⟨**z-**⟩ (*-nieję*) degenerate

wyrodny *adj matka*: heartless

wyrodzić się *v/p* → ***wyradzać się***

wyroić się *v/p* → ***roić się***

wyrok *m* (*-ku*; *-ki*) **1.** (*kara*) sentence; ***wydawać ~ na*** *A* pass sentence on; ***~ śmierci*** death sentence; ***~ dożywotniego więzienia*** life imprisonment; ***odbywać ~ więzienia*** serve a jail sentence, serve time **2.** (*orzeczenie sądu*) verdict; ***~ skazujący*** guilty verdict, verdict of guilty; ***~ uniewinniający*** innocent verdict; ***podpisywać na siebie ~*** *fig* sign one's own death warrant

wyrokować ⟨**za-**⟩ (*-kuję*) (*rozstrzygać*) determine (***o*** *L*)

wyrolować *v/p* (*-luję*): ***~ kogoś*** *infml* dupe s.o., pull a fast one on s.o.

wyrosnąć *v/p* → ***wyrastać***

wyrost: ***na ~* a)** *ubrania*: with room to grow **b)** *plany*, *zmartwienie*: premature **c)** *słowa*: exaggerated

wyrost|ek *m* (*-tka*; *-tki*) **1.** (*chłopiec*) youngster **2.** ***~ek robaczkowy*** ANAT appendix; ***zapalenia ~ka robaczkowego*** MED appendicitis

wyrozumiałość *f* (*-ści*; *no pl*) understanding

wyrozumiały *adj* understanding

wyr|ób *m* (*-robu*; *-roby*) **1.** (*przedmiot*) product; ***~oby*** goods; ***~oby skórzane*** leather goods; ***~oby cukiernicze*** confectionery; ***~oby tekstylne*** textiles; ***~oby szklane*** glassware; ***~oby gotowe*** finished goods **2.** (*produkcja*) production, manufacture

wyrównać *v/p* → ***wyrównywać***

wyrównanie *n* (*-nia*; *-nia*) **1.** (*rekompensata*) compensation **2.** *tekstu*: alignment **3.** *podłoża*, *podłogi*: *Br* levelling, *Am* leveling **4.** (*równe ustawienie*) adjustment **5.** (*bramka*, *punkt*) equalizer **6.** (*zrównanie szans w sporcie*) handicap **7.** ***~ rachunków*** *fig* settling the score

wyrównany *adj* **1.** *powierzchnia*: *Br* levelled, *Am* leveled, even **2.** *poziom*: comparable, even **3.** *szanse*: even **4.** *mecz*: even, closely fought; ***mecz był bardzo ~*** the game could have gone either way

wyrównawczy *adj* **1.** *zajęcia*: catch-up, compensatory **2.** ***dodatek ~*** compensatory allowance

wyrównywać ⟨***-nać***⟩ (*-nuję*) **1.** level, even out; ***~ podłogę*** level the floor; ***~ tekst*** align a text; ***~ szanse*** level the playing field; ***~ rachunki*** *fig* even the score, get even; ***~ krzywdy*** make amends **2.** (*wygładzać*) smooth **3.** (*doprowadzać do remisu*) equalize, even the score; ***wyrównywać się*** **1.** (*o poziomie*) even out **2.** (*o ciśnieniu*) become even **3.** (*o pulsie*) become steady

wyróżniać ⟨***-nić***⟩ (*-niam*) **1.** (*faworyzować*) *Br* favour, *Am* favor **2.** (*wyodrębniać*) distinguish **3.** (*podkreślać*) emphasize; ***wyróżniać się*** stand out; ***~*** *I* be distinguished by

wyróżnienie *n* (*-nia*; *-nia*) **1.** (*w konkursie*) *Br* honourable mention, *Am* honorable mention; ***zdobywać ~*** win an honourable mention **2.** *pieniężne*: reward, award **3.** (*za wyniki w nauce*) distinction; ***dyplom z ~m*** diploma with distinction

wyróżnik *m* (*-ka*; *-ki*) **1.** (*cecha*) distinguishing feature, hallmark **2.** MATH discriminant

wyruszać ⟨***-szyć***⟩ (*-szam*) set out, set off; ***~ w podróż*** set out on a journey; ***~ w drogę*** set off, *infml* hit the road; ***~ na wojnę*** go to war

wyrwa *f* (*-wy*; *-wy*) **1.** hole; ***~ po bombie*** shell hole **2.** (*w murze*) breach

wyrwać *v/p* → ***wyrywać***

wyrwany *adj*: ***~ z kontekstu*** (taken) out of context

wyryć *v/p*: → ***ryć***; **wyryt|y** *adj*: ***data ~a w kamieniu*** date etched in stone

wyrywać ⟨***-rwać***⟩ (*-wam*) **I** *v/t* **1.** tear out; ***~ kartkę z notesu*** tear a page out of one's notebook; ***~ komuś torebkę*** snatch s.o.'s handbag; ***~ drzewo z korzeniami*** uproot a tree; ***~ kogoś ze snu*** rouse s.o. from sleep; ***~ kogoś do odpowiedzi*** call s.o. to the board **2.** *ząb*: pull out **3.** (*podrywać*) *infml* pick up **II** *v/i* (*uciekać*) *infml* bolt; ***wyrywać się*** **1.** (*wyswobadzać się*) break free, break away; ***~ się strażnikom*** break away from one's guards **3.** (*wyjeżdżać*) *infml* get away **2.** (*wypowiadać*) *infml* come out (**z** *I* with), blurt out; ***wyrwało mi się*** well, I shouldn't have said that

wyrywki: ***na ~*** (*losowo*) at random; ***znać coś na ~*** know s.th. off pat, *Am* know s.th. down pat

wyrywkowy *adj* **1.** (*losowy*) random; ***kontrola ~a*** spot check, random check **2.** *obserwacje*: sample

wyrządzać ⟨***-dzić***⟩ (*-dzam*): ***~ komuś krzywdę*** hurt s.o.; ***~ szkody*** do damage

wyrzec *v/p* (*-rzeknę*) *lit* utter, say; ***wyrzec się*** *v/p* → ***wyrzekać się***

wyrzeczenie *n* (*-nia*; *-nia*) sacrifice; **wyrzeczenie się** *n* (*-nia*; *no pl*) **1.** renunciation **2.** *syna*, *córki*: disowning

wyrzekać się ⟨***-rzec***⟩ (*-kam*) **1.** renounce **2.** *syna*, *córki*: disown

wyrzeźbić *v/p* → ***rzeźbić***

wyrzucać ⟨***-cić***⟩ (*-cam*) **1.** (*pozbywać się*) throw out; ***~ śmieci*** *Br* take out

W

the rubbish, *Am* take out the garbage; **~ coś do kosza** throw s.th. in(to) a bin; **~ coś przez okno** throw s.th. out (of) the window; **~ kogoś za drzwi** kick s.o. out; **~ pieniądze w błoto** throw money down the drain **2.** (*robić wyrzuty*) reproach; **~ sobie coś** blame oneself for s.th. **3.** (*eksmitować*) turn out, throw out **4.** (*ze szkoły*) expel **5.** (*zwalniać z pracy*) *infml* sack, fire **6.** *pasażera*: *infml* drop off

wyrzut *m* (*-tu*; *-ty*) **1.** (*pretensja*) reproach; **z ~em** reproachfully **2. ~y sumienia** remorse, pricks of conscience **3.** (*rzucenie*) throw **4.** (*rzucenie do góry*) toss; **wyrzutek** *m* (*-tka*; *-tki*) outcast; **~ społeczeństwa** social outcast; **wyrzutnia** *f* (*-ni*; *-nie*) TECH launcher

wyrzygać *v/p* → **rzygać**

wyrzynać ⟨**-rżnąć**⟩ (*-nam*) (*mordować*) slaughter, massacre; → **wyrżnąć**; **wyrzynać się 1.** (*wyrastać*) **dziecku wyrzynają się ząbki** the baby is teething **2.** (*mordować się*) slaughter each other

wyrżną|ć *v/p* (*-nę*) **1.** (*wycinać*) carve, cut out **2.** (*upadać*) *infml* fall over **3.** (*uderzać*) *infml* bang; **~ć głową o** *A* bang one's head against; **samochód ~ł w drzewo** the car slammed into a tree; → **wyrzynać**

wys. *abbr* (= **wysokość**) **1.** *przedmiotu*: h, ht **2.** (*nad poziomem morza*) alt.

wysadzać ⟨**-dzić**⟩ (*-dzam*) **1.** (*z samochodu, statku*) drop off, let off; **~ kogoś na ląd** let s.o. off on the shore **2.** (*sadzić*) plant **3.** (*w powietrze*) blow up

wysadzany *adj*: **~ diamentami** set with diamonds, inset with diamonds; **~ drzewami** lined with trees

wysączać ⟨**-czyć**⟩ (*-czam*) (*wypijać*) sip up, drain; **wysączać się** (*wylewać się*) trickle

wyschnąć *v/p* → **wysychać**

wyselekcjonować *v/p* → **selekcjonować**

wysepka *f* (*-ki*; *-ki*) **1.** (*mała wyspa*) (small) island, islet **2.** (*na jezdni*) *Br* (traffic) island, refuge, *Am* safety island

wysiać *v/p* → **wysiewać**

wysiadać ⟨**-siąść**⟩ (*-dam*) **1.** (*z samochodu*) get out (**z** *G* of) **2.** (*z pociągu, autobusu*) get off (**z** *G*) **3.** (*ze statku*) get off, disembark (**z** *G*) **4.** (*o urządzeniu, organie*) *infml* conk out

wysiadka: **~!** everybody out!

wysiadywać ⟨**-siedzieć**⟩ (*-duję*) **1.** *jaja*: incubate **2.** (*spędzać czas*) spend hours, sit (around)

wysiąść *v/p* → **wysiadać**

wysiedlać ⟨**-lić**⟩ (*-lam*) displace

wysiedlenie (*-nia*; *no pl*) displacement; **wysiedle|niec** *m* (*-leńca*; *-leńcy*) displaced person, refugee; **~ńcy** the displaced, refugees

wysiedzieć: **nie móc ~ w domu** be too restless to stay at home; → **wysiadywać**

wysiew *m* (*-wu*; *-wy*) sowing

wysiewać ⟨**-siać**⟩ (*-wam*) sow

wysięgnik *m* (*-ka*; *-ki*) **1.** *dźwigu*: jib **2.** *kamery, mikrofonu*: boom **3.** *lampy, monitora*: extension arm

wysięk *m* (*-ku*; *-ki*) effusion

wysilać ⟨**-lić**⟩ (*-lam*) strain; **wysilać się** make an effort; **~ się żeby, coś zrobić**, **~ się na coś** make an effort to do s.th.; **bardzo się wysilić** exert oneself

wysił|ek *m* (*-łku*; *-łki*) effort; **włożyć w coś wiele ~ku** put a lot of effort into s.th.; **bez ~ku** without effort, effortlessly; **robić coś z ~kiem** struggle to do s.th.

wysiudać *v/d* (*-dam*) *infml* get rid of

wyskakiwać ⟨**-skoczyć**⟩ (*-kuję*) **1.** jump out (**z** *G* of); **~ z łóżka** jump out of bed; **~ z pociągu** jump out of a train; **~ przez okno** jump out (of) a window; **~ z szyn** come off the track **2.** (*o pryszczu*) *infml* pop out, appear **3.** (*wychodzić na chwilę*) *infml* pop out (**po** *A* for) **4.** (*z pomysłem*) *infml* come out (**z** *I* with)

wyskok *m* (*-ku*; *-ki*) **1. ~i** (*wygłupy*) *infml* excesses **2.** (*w górę*) jump **3.** (*wypad*) *infml* jaunt

wyskokow|y *adj*: **napoje ~e** alcoholic beverages, *infml* booze

wyskrobywać ⟨**-bać**⟩ (*-buję*) **1.** scrape out **2.** *naczynie*: scrape clean **3.** (*wydrapywać*) scratch

wyskubywać ⟨**-bać**⟩ (*-buję*) pluck (out)
wysłać[1] *v/p* → ***wysyłać***
wysłać[2] *v/p* → ***wyściełać***
wysłannik *m* (*-ka*; *-nicy*), **-niczka** *f* (*-ki*; *-ki*) **1.** (*polityczny*) envoy **2.** (*korespondent*) correspondent
wysławiać[1] *v/im* (*-wiam*) glorify, *Br* extol, *Am* extoll
wysławiać[2] ⟨**-łowić**⟩ (*-wiam*) express (in words), articulate; ***wysławiać się*** express oneself
wysłuchiwać ⟨**-chać**⟩ (*-chuję*) **1.** *koncertu*: listen (*G* to) **2.** *osoby*: hear out **3.** *modlitw*: answer
wysługa *f* (*-gi*; *no pl*): ***~ lat*** seniority
wysługiwać się *v/im* (*-guję*) **1.** (*służyć komuś*) serve **2.** (*wyręczać się kimś*) use
wysłużony *adj* well-worn
wysmarkać *v/p* (*-kam*): ***~ nos*** blow one's nose; ***wysmarkać się*** blow one's nose
wysmarować *v/p* → ***smarować***
wysmołować *v/p* → ***smołować***
wysmukły *adj* slender
wysnuwać ⟨**-nuć**⟩ (*-wam*) *wnioski*: draw
wysoce *adv* highly; ***~ uzdolniony*** highly talented; ***~ ceniony*** highly valued, greatly valued; ***~ sobie cenić*** *A* think highly of
wysok|i *adj* **1.** high; ***~i na dwa metry*** *Br* 2 metres high, *Am* 2 meters high; ***~a jakość*** high quality; ***~ie napięcie*** high voltage; ***buty na ~ich obcasach*** high-heeled shoes, high heels; ***z ~a*** from (high) above **2.** *osoba*, *drzewo*, *budynek*: tall; ***~i na dwadzieścia metrów*** *Br* 20 metres tall, *Am* 20 meters tall **3.** *wyrok*: harsh, heavy **4.** *urzędnik*, *stanowisko*: senior
wysoko *adv* **1.** high; ***mierzyć ~*** aim high **2.** (*wysoce*) highly; ***~ płatna praca*** highly paid job
wysoko- (*w złożeniach*) high-; ***~ciśnieniowy*** high-pressure; ***~kaloryczny*** high-calorie; ***~oprocentowany*** high-interest
wysokogatunkowy *adj* high-quality; **wysokogórsk|i** *adj* mountain, alpine; ***wspinaczka ~a*** mountain climbing; **wysokoobrotowy** *adj* high-speed
wysokonakładowy *adj* high-circulation; **wysokopienny** *adj las*: high; **wysokoprężny** *adj silnik*: diesel; **wysokoprocentowy** *adj* **1.** *alkohol*: high-proof **2.** *ruda*: high-grade
wysokościomierz *m* (*-rza*; *-rze*) altimeter; **wysokościowiec** *m* (*-wca*; *-wce*) high-rise; **wysokościow|y** *adj*: ***prace ~e*** work at heights; ***choroba ~a*** altitude sickness
wysokoś|ć *f* (*-ści*; *no pl*) **1.** height; ***mieć cztery metry ~ci*** *Br* be 4 metres high, *Am* be 4 meters high; ***nabierać ~ci*** gain height **2.** (*nad poziomem morza*) altitude; ***na dużej ~ci*** at high altitude **3.** (*kwota*) amount; ***zysk w ~ci 2 mln zł*** profit of PLN 200 million, PLN 200m profit
wysondować *v/p* → ***sondować***
wyspa *f* (*-py*; *-py*) island; ***~ koralowa*** coral island
wyspać się *v/p* → ***wysypiać się***
wyspany *adj*: ***jestem ~*** I've had a good night's sleep; ***nie jestem ~*** I haven't slept well, I haven't had enough sleep
wyspecjalizować się *v/p* → ***specjalizować się***
wyspiarka *f* (*-ki*; *-ki*) (female) islander; **wyspiarski** *adj* island; **wyspiarz** *m* (*-rza*; *-rze*) islander
wysportowany *adj* athletic
wyspowiadać się *v/p* → ***spowiadać się***
wysprzedany *adj* sold out
wyssać *v/p* → ***wysysać***
wystający *adj* **1.** protruding, jutting **2.** *kości policzkowe*: high, prominent **3.** *brzuch*: protruding, prominent
wystarać się *v/im* (*-ram*) (manage to) get (**o** *A*), arrange (**o** *A*)
wystarcz|ać ⟨**-czyć**⟩ (*-czam*) be enough, *form* suffice; ***to ~y*** that will do; ***nie ~a im pieniędzy*** they don't have enough money; ***tortu ~y dla wszystkich*** there is enough cake for everyone; ***~y mi mały pokój*** a small room will be enough for me; ***~y nam 2 dni na skończenie pracy*** it'll take us 2 days to get the job done, it won't take us more than 2 days to get the job done; ***~y spojrzeć*** it's enough to take a look; ***~y, że zadzwonisz*** it's enough to make a phone call; ***~y!*** that's enough!
wystarczający *adj* sufficient
wystarczyć *v/p* → ***wystarczać***

W

wystartować *v/p* → ***startować***
wystaw|a *f* (*-wy*; *-wy*) **1.** *ART* exhibition; ***~a sztuki*** art exhibition **2.** *kwiatów, psów*: show **3.** (*witryna*) (shop) window; ***na ~ie*** in the window
wystawać *v/im* (*-taję*) **1.** protrude, stick out (**z** *G*/**spod** *G* from) **2.** (*o koszuli, ramiączku*) show
wystawca *m* (*-cy*; *-cy*) **1.** (*na targach*) exhibitor **2.** *czeku*: drawer
wystawiać 〈**-wić**〉 (*-wiam*) **1.** (*na zewnątrz*) put out; ***~ głowę przez okno*** stick one's head out (of) a window; ***~ kogoś na próbę*** put s.o. to the test, put s.o. through his paces; ***~ coś na sprzedaż*** put s.th. up for sale; ***~ coś na widok publiczny*** put s.th. on public display, display s.th. in public; ***~ kogoś na niebezpieczeństwo*** expose s.o. to danger; ***~ kogoś do wiatru*** *infml* take s.o. for a ride **2.** (*na targach, na wystawie*) exhibit **3.** (*na półkach*) display **4.** *rachunek, czek*: make out **5.** *sztukę*: stage **6.** (*dawać*) give; ***nauczycielka wystawiła jej piątkę*** the teacher gave her an A; ***wystawiać się***: ***~ na*** *A* expose oneself to; ***~ się na niebezpieczeństwo*** expose oneself to danger; ***~ się na pośmiewisko*** make a fool of oneself, expose oneself to ridicule
wystawn|y *adj* **1.** *uczta, życie*: lavish; ***prowadzić ~e życie*** live in luxury **2.** *uczta*: sumptuous
wystawow|y *adj* **1.** exhibition; ***gablota ~a*** display case, display cabinet **2.** *okno*: shop
wystąpić *v/p* → ***występować***
wystąpienie *n* (*-nia*; *-nia*) **1.** (*przemowa*) speech, (public) address **2.** (*pojawienie się*) occurrence
wysterylizować *v/p* → ***sterylizować***
występ *m* (*-pu*; *-py*) **1.** performance; ***~ solowy*** solo performance; ***~ Chippendalesów*** Chippendales show **2.** (*koncert*) show, concert **3.** (*udział w programie*) appearance; ***~ telewizyjny*** television appearance **4.** (*wystająca część*) projection; ***~ skalny*** ledge
występek *m* (*-pku*; *-pki*) misdeed; **występny** *adj* wicked
występować 〈**-tąpić**〉 (*-puję*) **1.** (*o muzykach, artystach scenicznych*) perform; ***~ z koncertem*** give a concert **2.** (*o aktorach*) appear, star; ***~ w roli*** *G* play; ***wystąpiła w „Drakuli"*** **a)** she appeared in 'Dracula' **b)** (*w jednej z głównych ról*) she starred in 'Dracula' **3.** (*w programie*) appear **4.** (*wychodzić*) step out (**z** *G* of); ***rzeka wystąpiła z brzegów*** the river burst its banks **5.** (*podejmować działanie*) ***~ w czyjejś obronie*** stand up for s.o.; ***~ z wnioskiem*** put forward a motion; ***~ o*** *A*, ***~ z prośbą o*** *A* ask for, apply for **6.** (*o złożach, roślinach*) occur
występowani|e *n* (*-nia*; *no pl*) **1.** *złóż, gatunku, choroby, przestępstw*: occurrence; ***częstość ~a astmy*** incidence of asthma **2.** *objawów*: appearance
wystosować *v/p* (*-suję*) *pismo, protest*: submit (**do** *G* to)
wystraszyć *v/p* (*-szę*) **1.** (*przestraszyć*) scare, frighten **2.** (*wypłoszyć*) scare away; ***wystraszyć się*** get scared, get frightened
wystroić *v/p* → ***stroić***
wystrojony *adj* **1.** (*udekorowany*) decorated **2.** (*elegancko ubrany*) dressed up, spruced up
wystrzał *m* (*-łu*; *-ły*) (gun)shot; **wystrzałow|y** *adj infml* sensational; ***~a dziewczyna***, ***~y samochód*** knockout, stunner
wystrzegać się *v/im* (*-gam*) beware (*G* of)
wystrzelać *v/p* (*-lam*) **1.** shoot dead **2.** *amunicję*: use up
wystrzelić *v/p* (*-lę*) **1.** fire; ***~ z pistoletu*** fire a gun; ***~ w górę*** shoot up **2.** *rakietę*: launch
wystrzępiony *adj* frayed
wystukiwać 〈**-kać**〉 (*-kuję*) **1.** *rytm*: beat out, tap out **2.** (*na maszynie*) *infml* type
wystylizować *v/p* → ***stylizować***
wysunąć *v/p* → ***wysuwać***
wysunięty *adj* (*wystający*) protruding; ***najdalej ~ na zachód*** (***wschód***) the westernmost (easternmost)
wysuszony *adj* dry; ***~ na słońcu*** dried in the sun; **wysuszyć** *v/p* → ***suszyć***
wysuwać 〈**-sunąć**〉 (*-wam*) **1.** (*wyciągać, wystawiać*); ***~ szufladę*** pull out a drawer: ***~ głowę za okno*** stick one's head out (of) the window; ***~ głowę***

zza zasłony poke one's head from behind a curtain **2.** (*przesuwać*) ***~ coś na środek pokoju*** move s.th. to the middle of a room; ***~ krzesło*** pull out a chair **3.** *propozycję*, *wniosek*, *kandydaturę*: put forward; ***wysunięto jego kandydaturę na prezydenta*** he's been nominated for the presidency **4.** *żądania*: make **5.** *kandydata*: put up; ***wysuwać się*** **1.** (*wypadać*) slip out **2.** (*przesuwać się*) come out; ***~ się na prowadzenie*** take the lead

wyswobadzać ⟨***-bodzić***⟩ (*-dzam*) free; ***wyswobadzać się*** free oneself; ***wyswobodzić się z więzów*** free oneself from one's bonds

wysycha|ć ⟨***-schnąć***⟩ (*-cham*) dry; ***rzeki ~ją*** rivers are running dry

wysyłać ⟨***-słać***⟩ (*-łam*) **1.** send; ***~ coś pocztą*** *Br* post s.th., send s.th. by post, *Am* mail s.th.; ***~ kogoś po gazetę*** send s.o. to buy a newspaper, tell s.o. to buy a newspaper; ***~ kogoś na zakupy*** send s.o. to do the shopping; ***~ kogoś na obóz letni*** send s.o. to a summer camp; ***~ na szkolenie*** send s.o. for training **2.** *sygnały*: send (out), emit

wysyłka *f* (*-ki*; *-ki*) shipment, dispatch; **wysyłkow|y** *adj* mail-order; ***katalog sprzedaży ~ej*** *Br* mail-order catalogue, *Am* mail-order catalog

wysypać *v/p* → ***wysypywać***

wysypiać się ⟨***-spać***⟩ (*-piam*) get enough sleep

wysypisko *n* (*-ka*; *-ka*): ***~ śmieci*** dump

wysypka *f* (*-ki*; *-ki*) rash

wysypywać ⟨***-pać***⟩ (*-puję*) **1.** pour out, empty out **2.** (*przypadkowo*) spill; ***wysypywać się*** spill out

wysysać ⟨***-ssać***⟩ (*-sam*) suck (out)

wyszaleć się *v/im* (*-leję*) let off steam

wyszarpywać ⟨***-pnąć***⟩ (*-puję*) tear out, snatch

wyszczególniać ⟨***-nić***⟩ (*-niam*) specify; **wyszczególnienie** *n* (*-nia*; *-nia*) **1.** (*lista*) (detailed) list **2.** (*określenie*) specification

wyszczerbiony *adj* *ostrze*, *talerz*: chipped

wyszczerzać ⟨***-rzyć***⟩ (*-rzam*): ***~ zęby*** **a)** bare one's teeth **b)** (*w uśmiechu*) grin

wyszczotkować *v/p* → ***szczotkować***

wyszczupleć *v/p* → ***szczupleć***

wyszkolić *v/p* → ***szkolić***

wyszperać *v/p* (*-ram*) dig out

wyszpiegować *v/p* (*-guję*) find out

wyszukany *adj* **1.** *język*, *potrawy*: sophisticated, refined **2.** *gust*: discriminating, sophisticated **3.** (*znaleziony*) found; **wyszukiwać** ⟨***-kać***⟩ (*-kuję*) seek out, search out, find

wyszumieć się *v/p* (*-mię*) let off steam

wyszyć *v/p* → ***wyszywać***

wyszydzać ⟨***-dzić***⟩ (*-dzam*) ridicule, scoff (*A* at)

wyszykować *v/p* (*-kuję*) prepare; ***~ kogoś do szkoły*** get s.o. ready for school; → ***szykować***

wyszynk *m* (*-ku*; *no pl*) **1.** (*sprzedaż*) sale of alcoholic beverages; ***~ wina*** sale of wine **2.** (*pozwolenie*) alcohol licence; ***restauracja z ~iem*** licensed restaurant

wyszywać ⟨***-szyć***⟩ (*-wam*) embroider; **wyszywanka** *f* (*-ki*; *-ki*) embroidery; **wyszywany** *adj* embroidered

wyściełać ⟨***wysłać***⟩ (*-łam*) line, pad; **wyściełany** *adj* lined, padded

wyścig *m* (*-gu*; *-gi*) race; ***~i konne*** horse racing; ***~ zbrojeń*** the arms race; ***~ z czasem*** race against time, race against the clock; ***robić coś na ~i*** race with each other to do s.th.

wyścigowy *adj* racing; **wyścigówka** *f* (*-ki*; *-ki*) **1.** (*samochód*) racing car **2.** (*rower*) racing bike

wyściółka *f* (*-ki*; *-ki*) lining, padding

wyśledzić *v/p* (*-dzę*) track down

wyślizgiwać się ⟨***-znąć***, ***-gnąć***⟩ (*-guję*) slip out; ***~ komuś z ręki*** slip from one's hand

wyśmiać *v/p* → ***wyśmiewać***

wyśmienicie *adv*: ***to pachnie ~*** it smells delicious; ***czuję się ~*** I feel great; **wyśmienity** *adj* **1.** *potrawa*: delicious **2.** *pogoda*, *muzyka*: excellent

wyśmiewać ⟨***-miać***⟩ (*-wam*) laugh at, ridicule; ***wyśmiewać się*** make fun (**z** *G* of)

wyśniony *adj* dream

wyśpiewywać ⟨***-wać***⟩ (*-piewuję*) **1.** (*śpiewać*) sing **2.** (*zdradzać*) *infml* give away; ***wyśpiewać wszystko*** spill the beans

W

wyświadczać ⟨**-czyć**⟩ (*-czam*): **~ komuś przysługę** *Br* do s.o. a favour, *Am* do s.o. a favor
wyświechtany *adj fig* hackneyed; **~ frazes** cliché
wyświetlacz *m* (*-cza*; *-cze*) display
wyświetlać ⟨**-lić**⟩ (*-lam*) **1.** *komunikat*: display **2.** *film*: show, screen **3.** *prze-źrocza*: show, project
wyświęcać ⟨**-cić**⟩ (*-cam*) ordain; **~ kogoś na kapłana** ordain s.o. a priest
wytaczać ⟨**-toczyć**⟩ (*-czam*) **1.** *beczkę*: roll out **2.** *armatę*: wheel out **3.** (*na tokarce*) turn **4.** (*na kole garncarskim*) throw **5.** (*wszczynać*) **~ komuś proces** bring a legal action against s.o.; **wytaczać się 1.** (*o samochodzie, pociągu*) roll **2.** (*o osobie nietrzeźwej*) stagger out
wytapetować *v/p* → **tapetować**
wytapiać ⟨**-topić**⟩ (*-piam*) **1.** *tłuszcz*: melt **2.** *metal*: smelt
wytargować *v/p* (*-guję*) **1.** bargain off the price; **wytargował 20 złotych** he bargained 20 zlotys off the price; **~ niższą cenę** beat a price down **2.** *ustępstwa*: manage to gain
wytarty → **wyświechtany**
wytatuować *v/p* → **tatuować**
wytchnąć *v/p* (*-nę*): **~ chwilę** rest for a while; **wytchnieni|e** *n* (*-nia*; *no pl*) **1.** (*odpoczynek*) rest; **bez ~a** without rest; **pracować bez ~a** keep one's nose to the grindstone **2.** (*przerwa*) break
wytępić *v/p* (*-pię*) **1.** *szkodniki, zwierzęta*: kill off **2.** *poglądy*: eradicate; → **tępić**; **wytępienie** *n* (*-nia*; *no pl*) extermination
wytęskniony *adj* longed-for, dream
wytężać ⟨**-żyć**⟩ (*-żam*): **~ wzrok** look hard; **~ słuch** prick up one's ears; **~ wszystkie siły** summon all one's strength; **~ umysł** think hard, rack one's brains; **wytężony** *adj* **1.** *wysiłek*: strenuous **2.** *praca*: hard, intensive
wytknąć *v/p* → **wytykać**
wytłaczać ⟨**-łoczyć**⟩ (*-czam*) **1.** *olej, sok*: press, extract **2.** *płyty*: press **3.** *napis, wzór*: emboss
wytłuc *v/p* (*-łukę*) (*wymordować*) *infml* kill off, slaughter
wytłumaczenie *n* (*-nia*; *-nia*) **1.** (*wyjaśnienie*) explanation **2.** (*usprawiedliwienie, wymówka*) excuse; **wytłumaczyć** *v/p* → **tłumaczyć**
wytłuszczać ⟨**-łuścić**⟩ (*-czam*) **1.** (*brudzić*) grease **2.** INF put in bold
wytoczyć *v/p* → **wytaczać**
wytopić *v/p* → **wytapiać**
wytracać ⟨**-cić**⟩ (*-cam*) *szybkość*: lose
wytrawny *adj* **1.** *gracz*: expert **2.** *znawca*: experienced **3.** *wino*: dry
wytrąbić *v/p* (*-bię*) (*wypić*) *infml* guzzle
wytrącać ⟨**-cić**⟩ (*-cam*) (*z ręki*) knock out (**z** *G* of); **~ kogoś z równowagi** (*denerwować*) make s.o. angry, get on s.o.'s nerves; **wytrącać się** precipitate
wytrenować *v/p* → **trenować**
wytresować *v/p* → **tresować**
wytresowany *adj pies*: trained
wytropić *v/p* (*-pię*) track down; → **tropić**
wytruć *v/p* (*-ruję*) poison
wytrwać *v/p* (*-wam*) **1.** (*kontynuować*) persevere (**w** *L* in); **~ w wierze** (**walce**) keep believing (fighting) **2.** (*wytrzymać*) hold out, endure; **~ do końca** hold out till the end
wytrwałość *f* (*-ści*; *no pl*) persistence, perseverance; **wytrwały** *adj* **1.** *osoba*: persistent, persevering, gritty; **~ w** *L* persistent in **2.** *praca*: tenacious
wytrych *m* (*-cha*/*-chu*; *-chy*) skeleton key, picklock
wytrysk *m* (*-ku*; *-ki*) **1.** *nasienia*: ejaculation; **przedwczesny ~** premature ejaculation; **mieć ~** ejaculate **2.** *ropy*: spurt
wytryskiwać ⟨**-snąć**⟩ (*-kuję*) gush, spurt (out)
wytrzasną|ć *v/p*: **skąd to ~łeś?** *infml* where did you get it?
wytrząsać ⟨**-snąć, -trząść**⟩ (*-sam*) shake out (**z** *G* of)
wytrzebić *v/p* → **trzebić**
wytrzeć *v/p* → **wycierać**
wytrzepywać ⟨**-pać**⟩ (*-puję*) **1.** *dywan*: beat **2.** *ubranie*: dust **3.** *obrus*: shake out
wytrzeszczać ⟨**-czyć**⟩ (*-czam*): **~ oczy na** *A*, **~ gały na** *A infml* goggle at
wytrzeźwieć *v/p* → **trzeźwieć**
wytrzymać *v/p* → **wytrzymywać**
wytrzymałoś|ć *f* (*-ści*; *no pl*) **1.** *fizyczna, psychiczna*: stamina, endurance; **u kresu ~ci nerwowej** on the verge of

a nervous breakdown **2.** *na choroby, zimno*: resistance **3.** *na ból*: resistance, tolerance **4.** (*trwałość*) durability **5.** *TECH* strength

wytrzymały *adj* **1.** (*odporny na działanie czynników fizycznych*) resistant (**na** *A* to); **~ *na mróz*** frost-resistant; **~ *na wysoką temperaturę*** heat-resistant; **~ *na rozciąganie*** resistant to stretching **2.** (*trwały*) durable, heavy-duty **3.** (*odporny fizycznie lub psychcznie*) tough, hardy **4.** *na ból*: tolerant (**na** *A* of) **5.** *roślina*: hardy

wytrzym|ywać ⟨***-mać***⟩ (*-muję*) **1.** (*znosić*) stand, endure; ***nie mogła tego ~ać*** she couldn't stand it; ***~ywać z kimś*** put up with s.o.; ***~ać do końca*** hold out till the end; ***nie ~ać próby czasu*** not stand the test of time **2.** (*nie poddawać się*) hold out, hold on **3.** *napór, obciążenie*: withstand **4.** (*o linie*) hold

wytwarzać ⟨***-worzyć***⟩ (*-rzam*) **1.** produce, manufacture, make **2.** *przeciwciała, enzymy, hormony*: produce **3.** *prąd, pole magnetyczne*: generate

wytworny *adj* **1.** elegant **2.** *maniery*: refined

wytworzyć *v/p* → ***wytwarzać***

wytwór *m* (*-woru*; *-wory*): **~ *czyjejś wyobraźni*** figment of s.o.'s imagination; **~ *chorej wyobraźni*** product of a twisted mind; **wytwórca** *m* (*-cy*; *-cy*) producer, manufacturer, maker

wytwórczość *f* (*-ści*; *no pl*) production; ***drobna ~*** small-scale production; **wytwórczy** *adj*: ***zakład ~*** manufacturing plant

wytwórnia *f* (*-ni*; *-nie*) **1.** (*przedsiębiorstwo*) company, maker; **~ *filmowa*** film studio; **~ *płytowa*** record company **2.** (*zakład*) plant

wytyczać ⟨***-czyć***⟩ (*-czam*) **1.** *drogę, działkę*: mark out **2.** *cele*: set **3.** *granicę*: delimit, define **4.** *trasę wycieczki*: plan (out)

wytyczne *pl* (*-nych*) **1.** (*wskazówki*) guidelines **2.** *POLIT* directives

wytyczyć *v/p* → ***wytyczać***

wytykać ⟨***-tknąć***⟩ (*-kam*): **~ *kogoś palcami*** *fig* point the finger at s.o.; **~ *komuś błędy*** point out mistakes to s.o.

wytypować *v/p* → ***typować***

wyuczon|y *adj*: ***zawód ~y*** trade, profession; ***~a reakcja*** learned response; ***~y na pamięć*** memorized

wyuczyć się *v/p* (*-czę*) learn; **~ *stolarki*** learn carpentry, train as a carpenter

wyuzdanie *n* (*-nia*; *no pl*) debauchery, wantonness; **wyuzdany** *adj* debauched, wanton

wywabiacz *m* (*-cza*; *-cze*): **~ *plam*** stain remover

wywabiać ⟨***-bić***⟩ (*-biam*) **1.** *plamę*: remove **2.** (*z ukrycia*) lure out (**z** *G* of)

wywalać ⟨***-lić***⟩ (*-lam*) **1.** (*wyrzucać*) throw out; **~ *gały*** *infml* goggle, gawk **2.** (*wykopywać*) kick out, boot out **3.** *drzwi*: break down, force open **4.** *język*: stick out; ***wywalać się*** *infml* fall over; ***wywalił się na rowerze*** *infml* he took a spill off his bike

wywalczyć *v/p* (*-czę*) secure, gain

wywalić *v/p* → ***wywalać***

wywar *m* (*-ru*; *-ry*) stock; **~ *z jarzyn*** vegetable stock

wyważony *adj fig* balanced

wywęszyć *v/p* (*-szę*) scent

wywiać *v/p* → ***wywiewać***

wywiad *m* (*-du*; *-dy*) **1.** (*z aktorem, politykiem*) interview; ***udzielić ~u*** give an interview **2.** (*instytucja*) secret service, intelligence **3.** (*działalność*) intelligence, espionage; **~ *przemysłowy*** industrial espionage **4.** (*historia choroby*) medical history

wywiadowca *m* (*-cy*; *-cy*) *POLIT* intelligence agent

wywierać ⟨***-wrzeć***⟩ (*-ram*): **~ *na kogoś nacisk*** put pressure on s.o., exert pressure on s.o.; **~ *na kimś wrażenie*** impress s.o., make an impression on s.o.

wywiercić *v/p* (*-cę*) drill; → ***wiercić***

wywieszać ⟨***-sić***⟩ (*-szam*) **1.** *pranie*: hang out **2.** *kartkę, ogłoszenie*: put up, display; **wywieszka** *f* (*-ki*; *-ki*) notice

wywieść *v/p* (*-wiodę*): **~ *kogoś w pole*** *fig* lead s.o. down the garden path; → ***wywodzić***

wywietrznik *m* (*-ka*; *-ki*) **1.** (*urządzenie*) ventilator **2.** (*lufcik*) window vent

wywietrzyć *v/p* → ***wietrzyć***

wywiewać ⟨***wywiać***⟩ (*wywiewam*) blow off; ***wywiać coś za okno*** blow s.o. out (of) a window

wywieźć *v/p* → **wywozić**

wywijać ⟨**-winąć**⟩ (*-jam*) **1.** *szablą*: brandish, *lit* flourish **2.** *kołnierz*: turn down **3.** *mankiety*: turn up **4.** **~ rękami** flail one's arms

wywinąć się *v/p* (*-nę*): **~ od odpowiedzialności** *infml* shirk responsibility; **udało im się z tego wywinąć** *infml* they managed to wiggle out of it; → **wywijać**

wywiórkować *v/p* → **wiórkować**

wywlekać ⟨**-lec**⟩ (*-kam*) drag out

wywłaszczać ⟨**-czyć**⟩ (*-czam*) **1.** *osobę*: dispossess **2.** *tereny*: expropriate

wywłoka *f* (*-ki*; *-ki*) *infml* **1.** (*przykra osoba*) rat bag **2.** (*kobieta rozwiązła*) slut, *Br* slapper

wywnioskować *v/p* → **wnioskować**

wywodzić ⟨**-wieść**⟩ (*-dzę*): **~ swoją nazwę od** *G* derive one's name from; **wywodzić się** come from

wywołać *v/p* → **wywoływać**

wywoławcz|y *adj*: **cena ~a** starting price

wywoływać ⟨**-łać**⟩ (*-łuję*) **1.** *osobę*: call (out); **~ ucznia do tablicy** call a student to the board **2.** *protest*, *dyskusję*, *reakcję alergiczną*: provoke **3.** *niezadowolenie*: cause **4.** *zainteresowanie*: arouse, pique **5.** *skutki*: have **6.** *duchy*: conjure up **7.** *film*: develop

wywozić ⟨**-wieźć**⟩ (*-wożę*) **1.** take away; **~ coś z kraju** take s.th. out of the country; **~ kogoś na wieś** take s.o. to the country **2.** *śmieci spod domu*: collect **3.** *śmieci na wysypisko*: take, haul **4.** (*deportować*) send, deport; **wywieźli go na Syberię** he was sent to Siberia, he was deported to Siberia

wywóz *m* (*-wozu*; *-wozy*) **1.** (*wywożenie*) transport; **~ śmieci** waste disposal, *Am* garbage collection **2.** (*eksport*) export

wywózka *f* (*-ki*; *-ki*) **1.** (*wywożenie*) transport; **~ śmieci** waste disposal, *Am* garbage collection **2.** (*deportacja*) deportation; **~ na wschód** deportation to the East

wywracać ⟨**-rócić**⟩ (*-cam*) **1.** (*przewracać*) knock over **2.** (*odwracać*) **~ coś na lewą stronę** turn s.th. inside out; **wywracać się 1.** (*o osobie*, *drzewie*) topple over, fall over **2.** (*o łodzi*) capsize **3.** (*o samochodzie*) overturn **4.** (*o motocyklu*) tip over

wywrotk|a *f* (*-ki*; *-ki*) **1.** (*pojazd*) *Br* dumper truck, *Am* dump truck **2.** (*upadek*) fall; **miał ~ę na rowerze** he fell off his bike **3.** (*samochodu*) rollover **4.** (*łodzi*) capsizing; **mieć ~ę** capsize, keel over

wywrotowiec *m* (*-wca*; *-wcy*) subversive; **wywrotowy** *adj* subversive

wywrócić *v/p* → **wywracać**

wywróżyć *v/p* → **wróżyć**

wywrzeć *v/p* → **wywierać**

wywyższać się ⟨**-szyć**⟩ (*-szam*) put on airs; **~ nad** *A* be patronizing towards

wyzbywać się ⟨**-być**⟩ (*-wam*) **1.** get rid of, dispose of **2.** *nawyku*: stop

wyzdrowieć *v/p* (*-wieję*) recover

wyzdrowienie *n* (*-nia*; *no pl*) recovery

wyziewy *pl* (*-wów*) fumes

wyznaczać ⟨**-czyć**⟩ (*-czam*) **1.** *cenę*, *termin*: set, fix **2.** *trasę wycieczki*: plan (out) **3.** *przywódcę*: appoint **4.** *nagrodę*: offer; **wyznaczony** *adj termin*: set, fixed

wyznać *v/p* → **wyznawać**

wyznani|e *n* (*-nia*; *-nia*) **1.** (*wiara*) denomination, faith; **wolność ~a** freedom of religion; **~e wiary a)** confession of faith **b)** *artysty*, *filozofa*: profession of faith **2.** (*zwierzenie*) confession; **~a miłosne** declarations of love; **wyznaniowy** *adj różnice*: religious

wyznawać ⟨**-nać**⟩ (*-naję*) **1.** confess; **~ swoje grzechy** confess one's sins; **~ winę** confess one's guilt; **~ zasadę, że**, **~ pogląd, że** believe that **2.** *prawdę*: tell **3.** *tajemnicę*: reveal **4.** *wartości*: hold, subscribe to; **~ te same wartości** share the same values **5.** (*być wyznawcą*) **wyznaje buddyzm** he's a Buddhist; **wyznają islam** they're Muslims

wyznawca *m* (*-cy*; *-cy*), **-czyni** *f* (*-ni*; *-nie*) **1.** REL believer, follower; **~ islamu** Muslim, follower of Islam; **~ buddyzmu** Buddhist, follower of Buddhism; **~ chrześcijaństwa** Christian **2.** (*zwolennik*) follower, supporter

wyzuty *adj lit* devoid (**z** *G* of): **~ z wszelkich uczuć** devoid of human feelings, cold as a stone

wyzwać *v/p* → **wyzywać**
wyzwalać ⟨**-wolić**⟩ (*-lam*) **1.** (*uwalniać*) liberate, free **2.** *energię*: release
wyzwanie *n* (*-nia*; *-nia*) challenge
wyzwiska *pl* (*-wisk*) abuse *sing*, abusive language *sing*; ***obrzucić kogoś ~mi*** hurl abuse at s.o.
wyzwolenie *n* (*-nia*; *-nia*) liberation; **wyzwoliciel** *m* (*-la*; *-le*) liberator; **wyzwolony** *adj* **1.** *kraj*, *osoba*: liberated **2.** *sztuki*: liberal
wyzwolić *v/p* → **wyzwalać**
wyzysk *m* (*-ku*; *no pl*) exploitation; **wyzyskiwacz** *m* (*-cza*; *-cze*) exploiter; **wyzyskiwać** ⟨**-kać**⟩ (*-kuję*) exploit
wyzywać ⟨**-zwać**⟩ (*-wam*) **1.** (*zmuszać do udziału*) challenge: ***~ kogoś do walki*** challenge s.o.; ***~ kogoś na pojedynek*** challenge s.o. to a duel **2.** (*ubliżać*) call names; ***~ kogoś od najgorszych*** call s.o. foul names
wyzywający *adj* provocative
wyż *m* (*-żu*; *-że*) **1.** (*w metereologii*) high-pressure area, high **2.** ***~ demograficzny*** baby boom
wyżalać się ⟨**-lić**⟩ (*-lam*): ***~ przed*** *I* pour one's troubles to
wyżąć *v/p* → **wyżymać**
wyżebrać *v/p* → **żebrać**
wyżej *adv* higher; ***~ wymieniony*** above-mentioned
wyżeł *m* (*-żła*; *-żły*) pointer
wyżerać ⟨**-żreć**⟩ (*-ram*) **1.** (*o osobie*) gobble (down) **2.** (*o zwierzęciu*) devour **3.** (*o rdzy*) eat away
wyżerka *f* (*-ki*; *-ki*) *infml* blow-out, *Br* nosh-up
wyżłabiać ⟨**-łobić**⟩ (*-biam*) carve; → **żłobić**
wyżłobienie *n* (*-nia*; *-nia*) groove
wyżłopać *v/p* → **żłopać**
wyżowy *adj* high-pressure
wyżreć *v/p* → **wyżerać**
wyższoś|ć *f* (*-ści*; *no pl*) superiority; ***z ~cią*** with superiority, condescendingly
wyższ|y *adj comp* → **wysoki** **1.** higher; ***~a uczelnia*** university, college; ***szkolnictwo ~e*** higher education; ***mieć ~e wykształcenie*** have a degree, have a university degree; ***stopień ~y*** GRAM the comparative; ***siła ~a*** force majeure, act of God **2.** *osoba*, *drzewo*, *budynek*: taller; ***jest od niej ~y*** he's taller than her
wyżyć *v/p* (*-żyję*) **1.** (*przeżywać*) survive **2.** (*utrzymywać się*) ***~ z jednej pensji*** *infml* live off one salary; ***wyżyć się*** *v/p* → ***wyżywać się***
wyżymać ⟨**-żąć**⟩ (*-mam*) *bieliznę*: wring
wyżyn|a *f* (*-ny*; *-ny*) upland; ***~y*** uplands; **wyżynny** *adj* upland
wyżywać się ⟨**-żyć**⟩ (*-wam*) have one's fling, let off steam; ***~ na*** *L* take one's anger out on
wyżywić *v/p* (*-wię*) feed; ***wyżywić się*** feed oneself
wyżywienie *n* (*-nia*; *no pl*) food; ***całodzienne ~*** full board; ***pokój z ~m*** board and lodging; ***~ we własnym zakresie*** self-catering
wzajemnie *adv* one another, each other; ***nienawidzą się ~*** they hate each other; ***~ się wykluczające*** mutually exclusive
wzajemnoś|ć *f* (*-ści*; *no pl*) mutuality, reciprocity; ***miłość bez ~ci*** unrequited love; ***kochała go z ~cią*** her love was reciprocated; **wzajemny** *adj* mutual, reciprocal; ***~ stosunek*** interrelation
wzbić *v/p* → **wzbijać**
wzbierać ⟨**wezbrać**⟩ (*-ram*) **1.** (*o rzece*) swell **2.** (*o wodzie*) rise **3.** (*o gniewie*) well up
wzbijać ⟨**-bić**⟩ (*-jam*) *kurz*: raise; **wzbijać się** rise
wzbogacać ⟨**-cić**⟩ (*-cam*) enrich; ***wzbogacać się*** become rich, make one's fortune; **wzbogacenie** *n* (*-nia*; *no pl*) enrichment, enhancement; ***wzbogacenie się*** becoming rich
wzbraniać się *v/im* (*-niam*) shrink (***przed*** *I* from)
wzbronion|y *adj* prohibited, forbidden; ***kąpiel ~a*** no swimming; ***palenie ~e*** no smoking; ***nieupoważnionym wstęp ~y*** staff only
wzbudzać ⟨**-dzić**⟩ (*-dzam*) **1.** *strach*, *podejrzenia*: arouse **2.** *sensację*: cause **3.** *zazdrość*, *zaufanie*: inspire **4.** *niezadowolenie*: stir up **5.** ***~ sympatię*** be likeable
wzburzać ⟨**-rzyć**⟩ (*-rzam*) **1.** agitate **2.** (*wściekać*) outrage; **wzburzać się** be agitated

W

wzburzenie *n* (*-nia*; *no pl*) **1.** anger, outrage **2.** (*publiczne*) outrage, uproar; **wzburzony** *adj* **1.** (*zdenerwowany*) outraged **2.** (*spieniony*) rough

wzdąć *v/p* → ***wzdymać***

wzdęcie *n* (*-cia*; *-cia*) flatulence; **wzdęty** *adj* bloated, flatulent

wzdłuż I *prep* (*G*) along **II** *adv przeciąć*: lengthwise

wzdrygać się ⟨**-gnąć**⟩ (*-gam*) flinch, wince; ***~ na myśl o*** *L* wince at the thought of; ***~ na dźwięk*** *G* start at the sound of

wzdychać ⟨**westchnąć**⟩ (*-cham*) sigh; ***~ z ulgą*** breathe a sigh of relief; ***~ do kogoś*** pine for s.o.

wzdymać ⟨**-dąć**⟩ (*-mam*) *żagle*: swell

wzejść *v/p* → ***wschodzić***

wzgard|a *f* (*-dy*; *no pl*) contempt, disdain; ***ze ~ą*** contemptuously, disdainfully; **wzgardliwy** *adj* contemptuous, disdainful, scornful; **wzgardzić** *v/p* (*-dzę*) spurn

wzgl|ąd *m* (*-lędu*; *-lędy*) **1.** consideration, regard; ***mieć na ~ędzie*** bear in mind, consider; ***ze ~ędu na*** *A* because of, on account of; ***bez ~ędu na*** *A* irrespective of, regardless of; ***pod tym ~ędem*** in this respect, from that point of view; ***pod ~ędem*** *G* as regards; ***ze ~ędu na ciebie*** because of you; ***~ędy bezpieczeństwa*** safety reasons; ***ze ~ędów zdrowotnych*** because of healthy reasons; ***pod wieloma ~ędami*** in many respects **2.** ***~ędy*** (*sympatia*) *Br* favour, *Am* favor; ***zabiegać o czyjeś ~ędy*** **a)** (*zabiegać o życzliwość*) *Br* try to win s.o.'s favour, *Am* try to win s.o.'s favor **b)** (*zalecać się*) court s.o.; ***cieszyć się czyimiś ~ędami*** be in s.o.'s good graces

względem *prep* (*G*) in relation to; ***~ siebie*** to each other

względnie *adv* relatively; **względny** *adj* **1.** (*relatywny*) relative **2.** (*dość dobry*) reasonable, tolerably good

względy *pl* → ***wzgląd***

wzgórek *m* (*-rka*; *-rki*) hillock, hill; ***~łonowy*** ANAT **a)** mons pubis **b)** (*u kobiety*) mons veneris

wziąć *v/p* → ***brać***[2]

wziernik *m* (*-ka*; *-ki*) MED endoscope

wzięci|e *n* (*-cia*; *no pl*): ***mieć ~e u kobiet*** be popular with the ladies; ***być do ~a*** be available, be single; ***cieszyć się ~em*** be very popular, be in great demand; ***ten produkt cieszy się ~em*** this product is in demand; ***~e do niewoli*** capture

wzięty *adj* in demand, popular, well-known

wzlatywać ⟨**-lecieć**⟩ (*-tuję*) fly up

wzlot *m* (*-tu*; *-ty*) *samolotu*, *balonu*: ascent; ***~y i upadki*** *fig* ups and downs

wzmacniacz *m* (*-cza*; *-cze*) amplifier; **wzmacniać** ⟨**-mocnić**⟩ (*-niam*) **1.** strengthen **2.** *więź*: consolidate **3.** *sygnał*: amplify **4.** *straż*: reinforce; ***wzmacniać się*** get stronger; **wzmacniający** *adj* **1.** strengthening **2.** *szampon*: restorative

wzmagać ⟨**-móc**⟩ (*-gam*) increase, deepen; ***wzmagać się*** increase, deepen

wzmianka *f* (*-ki*; *-ki*) mention

wzmocnić *v/p* → ***wzmacniać***

wzmocnienie *n* (*-nia*; *-nia*) **1.** (*konstrukcji*) reinforcement **2.** (*dźwięku*) amplification; ***środek na ~*** pick-me-up

wzmożony *adj* increased

wzmóc *v/p* → ***wzmagać***

wznak: ***leżeć na ~*** lie (flat) on one's back

wznawiać ⟨**-nowić**⟩ (*-wiam*) **1.** *pracę*: resume **2.** *książkę*: reissue

wzniecać ⟨**-cić**⟩ (*-cam*) **1.** *pożar*: start **2.** *ogień*: kindle **3.** *nienawiść*: arouse **4.** *pył*: stir up

wzniesienie *n* (*-nia*; *-nia*) **1.** (*pagórek*) hill **2.** (*nad poziom morza*) elevation

wznieść *v/p* → ***wznosić***

wzniosły *adj* **1.** lofty, sublime **2.** *cel*: noble

wznosić ⟨**-nieść**⟩ (*-noszę*) **1.** (*unosić*) lift, raise; ***~ toast*** raise one's glass, propose a toast; ***~ toast za jego zdrowie*** propose a toast to his health **2.** *dom*, *pomnik*: erect, build **3.** *kurz*: raise **4.** ***~ okrzyki na czyjąś cześć*** cheer s.o.; ***wznosić się*** (*o ptaku*, *samolocie*) rise; ***~ się ponad*** *A* rise above

wznowić *v/p* → ***wznawiać***

wznowienie *n* (*-nia*; *-nia*) **1.** *książki*: reissue **2.** *rozmów*: resumption

wzorcowy *adj* model
wzorek *m* (*-rku*; *-rki*) pattern; **wzornictwo** *n* (*-wa*; *no pl*) design; **~ przemysłowe** industrial design
wzorować się *v/im* (*-ruję*) model oneself (**na** *L* on)
wzorowany *adj*: **~ na** *L* based on, *Br* modelled on, *Am* modeled on
wzorowy *adj* exemplary, model, perfect
wzory *pl* → **wzór**
wzorzec *m* (*-rca*; *-rce*) **1.** (*pierwowzór*) prototype **2.** (*model*) model; **~ osobowy** role model **3.** (*zespół cech, wzór*) pattern **4.** TECH standard; **~ miary** standard of measure; **~ wagi** standard weight
wzorzysty *adj Br* colourful, *Am* colorful, patterned
wzór *m* (*wzoru*; *wzory*) **1.** (*model, przykład*) model; **brać kogoś za ~** follow s.o.'s example; **stawiać kogoś za ~** hold s.o. up as a model **2.** (*deseń*) pattern, design **3.** (*zespół cech, wzorzec*) pattern; **~ podpisu** specimen signature; **na ~** *G* based on, *Br* modelled on, *Am* modeled on **4.** *cnót, skromności*: paragon **5.** MATH CHEM formula
wzrastać ⟨**-rosnąć**⟩ (*-tam*) **1.** (*o wydatkach, gorączce*) rise, increase **2.** (*o popularności*) grow, increase
wzrastający *adj* growing, increasing, rising
wzrok *m* (*-ku*; *no pl*) (eye)sight, vision; **stracić ~** lose one's sight; **odzyskać ~** regain one's sight; **mieć dobry ~** have good eyesight; **mieć słaby ~** have poor eyesight; **badać ~iem** scrutinize; **mieć sokoli ~** *fig* be eagle-eyed
wzrokowiec *m* (*-wca*; *-wcy*) visualizer
wzrokowy *adj* **1.** visual **2.** *kontakt*: eye **3.** *nerw*: optic
wzrosnąć *v/p* → **wzrastać**
wzrost *m* (*-tu*; *no pl*) **1.** (*wysokość*) height; **średniego ~u** of medium height; **wysokiego ~u** tall; **niskiego ~u** short; **ile masz ~u?** how tall are you? **2.** (*rośnięcie*) growth **3.** *fig* increase, rise; **~ cen** rise in prices, increase of prices; **~ zainteresowania** increased interest, rise of interest; **~ gospodarczy** economic growth; **~ płac** salary increase
wzrusz|ać ⟨**-szyć**⟩ (*-szam*) **1.** *osobę*: move **2.** *ramionami*: shrug; **~yła ramionami** she shrugged her shoulders **3.** *ziemię*: loosen
wzruszający *adj* moving, touching; **wzruszenie** *n* (*-nia*; *no pl*) emotion; **wzruszony** *adj* moved, touched
wzwód *m* (*-wodu*; *-wody*) erection
wzwyż *adv* up, upwards; **od 12 ~** 12 and over; **skok ~** SPORT high jump
wzywać ⟨**wezwać**⟩ (*-wam*) call; **~ pomocy** call for help; **~ kogoś** (*wywoływać*) call s.o. out; **~ kogoś do zrobienia czegoś** call on s.o. to do s.th.; **~ kogoś do sądu** summon s.o. (to appear in court), cite s.o. (to appear in court); **~ na świadka** summon as a witness; **~ przez megafon** call over a megaphone
wżenić się *v/p* (*-nię*) marry (**w** *A* into)
wżerać się ⟨**wеżreć**⟩ (*-ram*) (*o rdzy*) eat away at, eat into

Z

z *prep* (*G*) **1.** (*miejsce, źródło, czas*) from; **pochodzić ~ Polski** come from Poland; **~ Londynu** from London; **~ domu** from home; **~ pracy** from work; **weź to ~ półki!** take it from the shelf; **wyjąć coś ~ pudełka** take s.th. out of a box; **wysiadać ~ autobusu** get off a bus; **ścierać wodę ~ twarzy** wipe water off one's face; **~ tyłu** in the back, behind **2.** (*składnik, dodatek, grupa, środowisko*) of, from, and, with; **~ cukrem** with sugar; **sałatka ~ pomidorów** tomato salad; **sok ~ marchwi** carrot juice; **razem ~ nami** with us; **~e mną** with me; **być ~ kimś** be with s.o.; **każdy ~ nas** each of us; **~e srebra** silver, made of silver; **~e skóry** leather, made of leather; **wielu ~ nich** many of them; **zrób coś ~ tym!** do something about that! **3.** (*powód, przyczyna*) (out) of; **~ radości** for joy; **drżeć ~ zimna** shiver with cold

4. (*stan, nasilenie, okoliczności, skutek*) with; ~ ***trudem*** with difficulty; ~ ***uwagą*** carefully; ~ ***dobrymi wynikami*** with good results; ~***e śpiewem*** singing; ***ni ~ tego, ni ~ owego*** all of a sudden **5.** (*przybliżenie*) about; ~ ***pięć*** about five; ~ ***godzinę*** about one hour

za[1] *prep* (*I/A*) **1.** (*miejsce*) behind, after; ***stań ~ nim*** stand behind him; ~ ***domem*** behind the house; ~ ***mną*** behind me; ~ ***granicą*** abroad; ***trzymać ~ rękę*** hold by the hand; ***siedzieć ~ stołem*** sit at the table; ~ ***biurkiem*** at the desk; ~ ***rogiem*** round the corner; ***biec ~ kimś*** run after s.o., chase s.o. **2.** (*czas*) in; ~ ***moich czasów*** in my time; ~ ***panowania*** *G* during the reign of, under; ***jest ~ dziesięć czwarta*** it's ten to four; ~ ***pięć minut*** in five minutes; ~ ***rok*** in one year; ~ ***godzinę*** in an hour, in an hour's time **3.** (*cel*) at, by, for; ~ ***wszelką cenę*** at all costs; ~ ***nic*** for nothing; ~ ***pomocą*** *G* by means of, using; ***walczyć ~ wolność*** fight for freedom **4.** (*następowanie*) after, by; ***jeden ~ drugim*** one after another, one by one **5.** (*powód, przyczyna*) for; ~ ***kradzież*** for theft; ~ ***dobre wyniki*** for good results **6.** (*funkcja*) as; ***służyć ~*** *A* serve as **7.** (*zastępowanie*) as, for; ***przebrać się ~*** *A* dress up as; ~ ***sto złotych*** for a hundred zlotys

za[2] *adv* (*nasilenie*) ***co to ~ szczęście!*** what joy this is!; ***co ~ dzień!*** what a day!; ***tego już ~ wiele!*** this is too much, that's the last straw!; ~ ***ciężki*** too heavy; ~ ***drogi*** too expensive; ~ ***dużo rzeczy*** too many things; ~ ***późno*** too late

zaabsorbować *v/p* → ***absorbować***

zaadaptować *v/p* → ***adaptować***

zaadoptować *v/p* → ***adoptować***

zaadresować *v/p* → ***adresować***

zaaferowany *adj* preoccupied (*I* with), engrossed (*I* in)

zaakcentować *v/p* → ***akcentować***

zaakceptować *v/p* → ***akceptować***

zaaklimatyzować się *v/p* → ***aklimatyzować się***

zaalarmować *v/p* → ***alarmować***

zaanektować *v/p* → ***anektować***

zaangażować *v/p* → ***angażować***

zaangażowanie *n* (*-nia; no pl*) involvement (**w** *A* in); **zaangażowany** *adj* involved (**w** *A* in), committed (**w** *A* to)

zaapelować *v/p* → ***apelować***

zaaplikować *v/p* → ***aplikować***

zaaprobować *v/p* → ***aprobować***

zaaranżować *v/p* → ***aranżować***

zaaresztować *v/p* → ***aresztować***

zaatakować *v/p* → ***atakować***

zaawansowan|y I *adj* advanced; ~***a ciąża*** advanced pregnancy **II** *m* (*-nego; -ni*), **-na** *f* (*-nej; -ne*) advanced student; ***dla ~ych*** for advanced learners

zaawizować *v/p* → ***awizować***

zababrać *v/p* → ***babrać***

zabalsamować *v/p* → ***balsamować***

zabandażować *v/p* → ***bandażować***

zabarwiać ⟨**-wić**⟩ (*-wiam*) *Br* colour, *Am* color, dye; ~ ***coś na czerwono*** dye s.th. red; **zabarwiać się** turn; ~ ***się na czerwono*** turn red; **zabarwienie** *n* (*-nia; no pl*) **1.** (*kolor*) *Br* colour, *Am* color **2.** (*odcień*) tint

zabarykadować *v/p* → ***barykadować***

zabaw|a *f* (*-wy; -wy*) **1.** (*przyjemność*) fun, entertainment; ***dla ~y*** for fun; ***przyjemnej ~y!*** have fun!, have a good time! **2.** (*gra*) game **3.** (*tańce*) dance

zabawiać ⟨**-wić**⟩ (*-wiam*) **1.** amuse **2.** *gości*: entertain; → ***bawić***

zabawka *f* (*-ki; -ki*) toy; ***sklep z ~mi*** toy shop; **zabawn|y** *adj* amusing, funny; ~***e, że*** it's funny that

zabeczeć *v/p* → ***beczeć***

zabejcować *v/p* → ***bejcować***

zabetonować *v/p* → ***betonować***

zabezpieczać ⟨**-czyć**⟩ (*-czam*) **1.** secure **2.** (*chronić*) protect (***przed*** *I* from); **zabezpieczać się 1.** (*chronić się*) secure oneself, protect oneself; ~ ***się na przyszłość*** secure one's future; ~ ***się na starość*** provide for one's old age, make provisions for old age **2.** (*stosować antykoncepcję*) use contraceptives

zabezpiecze|nie *n* (*-nia; -nia*) **1.** (*ochrona*) protection; ***system ~ń*** security system **2.** FIN security, guarantee; ~***nie kredytu*** loan collateral; **zabezpieczony** *adj* protected, secured

zabezpieczyć *v/p* → ***zabezpieczać***

zabici|e *n* (*-cia; no pl*) homicide, killing; ***dla ~a czasu*** to kill time

Z

zabić *v/p* (*-biję*): ***serce zabiło mu mocniej*** his heart started beating faster; → ***zabijać***
zabiec *v/p* → ***zabiegać***
zabiedzony *adj* emaciated
zabieg *m* (*-gu*; *-gi*) **1.** (*operacja*) minor surgery; ~ ***kosmetyczny*** cosmetic surgery **2.** (*przerwanie ciąży*) *infml* abortion **3.** **~i** (*wysiłki*) *Br* endeavours, *Am* endeavors
zabiegać ⟨**-biec**⟩ (*-gam*): ~ ***komuś drogę*** bar s.o.'s way; ~ **o** *A* try to get, seek; ~ ***o głosy*** canvass for votes; ~ ***o czyjeś względy*** **a)** (*zabiegać o życzliwość*) *Br* try to win s.o.'s favour, *Am* try to win s.o.'s favor **b)** (*zalecać się*) court s.o.
zabiegany *adj* busy
zabiegowy *adj*: ***gabinet*** ~ treatment room; ***stół*** ~ operating table
zabielać ⟨**-lić**⟩ (*-lam*) (*dodawać śmietanę*) add cream to
zabierać ⟨**-brać**⟩ (*-ram*) take; ~ ***ze sobą*** take; ~ ***głos*** speak, take the floor; ~ ***komuś czas*** take up s.o.'s time; ~ ***dużo miejsca*** take up a lot of space; ***zabrało jej to tydzień*** it took her a week; ~ ***na obiad*** take out to dinner; ***zabierać się*** **1.** (*wychodzić*) get out; ***zabieraj się stąd!*** get out of here! **2.** (*do pracy*) get down (**do** *G* to), set (**do** *G* to)
zabijać ⟨**-bić**⟩ (*-jam*) **1.** kill; ***zabił go samochód*** he was killed by a car **2.** ~ ***gwoździami*** nail up; ***zabijać się*** commit suicide; ~ ***się*** **o** *A* fight for
zabijaka *m* (*-ki*; *-ki*) brawler
zabit|y **I** *adj* **1.** (*martwy*) killed **2.** ***~e dechami okna*** boarded windows **II** *m* (*-tego*; *-bici*), **-ta** *f* (*-tej*; *-te*): ***jeden ~y, dwóch rannych*** one dead, two wounded; ***spać jak ~y*** sleep like a log
zabliźniać się ⟨**-nić**⟩ (*-niam*) (*o ranie*) heal, close up
zablokować *v/p* → ***blokować***
zabłądzić *v/p* (*-dzę*) get lost, lose one's way
zabłąkać się *v/p* (*-kam*) get lost, lose one's way; **zabłąkany** *adj* **1.** (*zgubiony*) lost **2.** *kula*, *pies*: stray
zabłocić *v/p* → ***błocić***; **zabłocony** *adj buty*, *podłoga*: muddy
zabobon *m* (*-nu*; *-ny*) superstition; **zabobonny** *adj* superstitious
zaborca *m* (*-cy*; *-cy*) partitioner; **zaborczy** *adj* possessive
zabój: ***być zakochanym w kimś na*** ~ be madly in love with s.o., be head over heels in love with s.o.; ***zakochać się w kimś na*** ~ fall head over heels in love with s.o.
zabójca *m* (*-cy*; *-cy*) **1.** killer **2.** (*morderca*) murderer **3.** (*zamachowiec*) assassin
zabójcz|y *adj* **1.** (*śmiertelny*) fatal, lethal **2.** (*szkodliwy*, *nieznośny*) killing, murderous; ***~y klimat*** murderous climate: ***~y styl życia*** destructive lifestyle **3.** (*zalotny*) ***~e spojrzenie*** seductive look
zabójczyni *f* (*-ni*; *-nie*) **1.** killer **2.** (*morderczyni*) murderess **3.** (*zamachowiec*) assassin
zabójstwo *n* (*-wa*; *-wa*) **1.** homicide, killing **2.** (*morderstwo*) murder **3.** (*w zamachu*) assassination
zabór *m* (*-boru*; *-bory*) **1.** JUR seizure **2.** (*terytorium*) annexed territory **3.** (*przejęcie terytorium*) annexation
zabrać *v/p* → ***zabierać***
zabraknąć: ***zabrakło nam pieniędzy*** we didn't have enough money; ***zabrakło nam jednego dnia*** we needed one more day; ***zabrakło nam farby*** we ran out of paint; ***nie może cię tam*** ~ you must be there
zabraniać ⟨**-ronić**⟩ (*-niam*) forbid, prohibit; **zabroniony** *adj* forbidden, prohibited
zabronować *v/p* → ***bronować***
zabrudzić *v/p* → ***brudzić***; **zabrudzony** *adj* dirty
zabryzgać *v/p* (*-gam*) splash
zabrzmieć *v/p* → ***brzmieć***
zabuczeć *v/p* → ***buczeć***
zabudowa *f* (*-wy*; *no pl*) buildings *pl*; **zabudowania** *pl* (*-wań*) buildings; ~ ***fabryczne*** factory buildings; **zabudowywać** ⟨**-dować**⟩ (*-dowuję*) **1.** *teren*: develop **2.** *kuchnię*: furnish
zabukować → ***rezerwować***
zabuksować *v/p* → ***buksować***
zabulić *v/p* → ***bulić***
zaburzać ⟨**-rzyć**⟩ (*-rzam*) **1.** disturb **2.** *równowagę*: upset
zaburzenia *pl* (*-rzeń*) disorders; ~ ***snu*** sleep disorders; ~ ***oddychania*** breathing disorders

zabyt|ek *m* (*-tku*; *-tki*) **1.** (*budynek, pomnik, obiekt przyrody*) monument; **~ek architektoniczny** monument of architecture; **ochrona ~ków** (heritage) conservation; **~ki przyrody** natural monuments **2.** (*budynek*) historic building, monument **3.** (*literacki*) relic **4.** (*przedmiot*) period piece, historic artefact **5.** *fig* museum piece
zabytkow|y *adj* historic; **~a część miasta** historic part of a city; **~y przedmiot** antique object, period piece
zacementować *v/p* → **cementować**
zacerować *v/p* → **cerować**
zach. *abbr* (= **zachód**, **zachodni**) W
zachcianka *f* (*-ki*; *-ki*) whim
zachciewać się ⟨**-cieć**⟩: **zachciało mi się pić** I felt thirsty: **zachciało mu się lodów** he felt like having some ice-cream
zachęcać ⟨**-cić**⟩ (*-cam*) encourage; **zachęcająco** *adv*: **to brzmi ~** it sounds promising; **zachęcający** *adj* encouraging; **zachęta** *f* (*-ty*; *-ty*) encouragement
zachłanność *f* (*-ści*; *no pl*) greed; **zachłanny** *adj* greedy
zachłystywać się ⟨**-snąć**⟩ (*-tuję*) choke (*I* on)
zachmurzać się ⟨**-rzyć**⟩ (*-rzam*) cloud over; **zachmurzenie** *n* (*-nia*; *-nia*) clouds *pl*; **~ duże** heavy clouds; **zachmurzony** *adj* cloudy
zachodni *adj* **1.** west, western; **Europa Ƶa** Western Europe **2.** *wiatr*: westerly, west
zachodnioeuropejski *adj* West European
zachodzić ⟨**zajść**⟩ (*-dzę*) **1.** (*dochodzić*) get (**do** *G* to), reach (**do** *G*); **~ daleko** *fig* go far; **~ w ciążę** get pregnant; **~ na siebie** overlap **2.** (*odwiedzać*) drop in, come by **3.** (*o słońcu*) set **4.** (*zdarzać się*) occur; **zaszła pomyłka** there's been a mistake; **zaszło nieporozumienie** there's been a misunderstanding **5.** (*pokrywać się*) **~ parą** mist over
zachomikować *v/p* → **chomikować**
zachorować *v/p* (*-ruję*) fall ill
zachowanie *n* (*-nia*; *-nia*) *Br* behaviour, *Am* behavior
zachowany *adj*: **dobrze ~** well preserved
zachowawczy *adj* conservative
zachowywać ⟨**-chować**⟩ (*-chowuję*) **1.** (*zatrzymywać*) keep, retain; **~ przy życiu** keep alive; **~ dla siebie** keep to oneself; **~ dystans do** *G* keep one's distance from; **~ spokój** remain calm; **~ zimną krew** keep cool; **~ milczenie** remain silent; **~ pozory** keep up appearances; **~ w pamięci** remember **2.** (*przechowywać*) store, keep **3.** *obyczaje, tradycje*: observe **4.** *dietę*: stick to; **zachowywać się** behave, act
zachód *m* (*-chodu*; *-chody*) **1.** GEOGR (the) west; **na zachodzie** in the west; **na ~ od** *G* to the west of; **południowy ~** (the) South-West; **Ƶ** (*krąg kulturowy*) the West **2.** *słońca*: sunset **3.** (*fatyga*) **szkoda zachodu** it's not worth the trouble; **warty zachodu** worth one's while
zachrypnięty *adj* hoarse
zachwalać *v/im* (*-lam*) praise
zachwaszczony *adj* weedy
zachwiać *v/p* (*-wieję*) shake, rock; **zachwiać się** shake, rock
zachwycać ⟨**-cić**⟩ (*-cam*) delight; **zachwycać się** admire (*I*), enthuse (*I* about); **zachwycający** *adj* delightful; **zachwyt** *m* (*-tu*; *-ty*) **1.** (*podziw*) admiration **2.** (*radość*) delight; **z ~em** with delight
zachybotać *v/p* → **chybotać**
zaciąć *v/p* → **zacinać**
zaciągać ⟨**-gnąć**⟩ (*-gam*) **1.** *osobę*: drag **2.** *zasłonę*: draw **3.** *kredyt, pożyczkę*: raise; **zaciągać się 1.** (*papierosem*) draw on **2.** (*do wojska*) enlist (**do** *G* in)
zaciekawić *v/p* → **ciekawić**; **zaciekawienie** *n* (*-nia*; *no pl*) interest, curiosity
zacieki *pl* (*-ków*) (*na ścianach*) damp patches
zaciekły *adj* **1.** *walka*: fierce **2.** *wróg*: bitter
zaciemniać ⟨**-nić**⟩ (*-niam*) (*pomieszczenie*) darken
zaciemnienie *n* (*-nia*; *-nia*) blackout
zacieniony *adj* shady
zacier *m* (*-ru*; *-ry*) (*na bimber*) mash
zacierać ⟨**zatrzeć**⟩ (*-ram*) **1.** *ślady*: cover up **2.** *granicę, różnice*: blur **3.** *silnik*: seize **4.** **~ ręce** rub one's hands; **zacierać się 1.** (*w pamięci*)

fade away; **coś ~ się w pamięci** the memory of s.th. fades away **2.** (*o napisie*) wear away **3.** (*o granicach, różnicach*) blur **4.** (*o silniku*) seize up
zacieśniać ⟨**-nić**⟩ (*-niam*) tighten; **zacieśniać się** (*o współpracy*) develop
zacietrzewiać się ⟨**-wić**⟩ (*-wiam*) get heated; **zacietrzewiony** *adj* heated, frenzied
zacięcie *n* (*-cia*; *-cia*) **1.** (*zapał, zaangażowanie*) involvement, passion; **mieć ~ do wędkarstwa** be an eager angler **2.** (*rowek*) cut
zacięty *adj* **1.** *walka, spory*: fierce **2.** *osoba*: determined, tenacious **3.** *wróg*: bitter
zacinać ⟨**-ciąć**⟩ (*-nam*) **1.** (*kaleczyć*) cut **2.** (*o deszczu*) slant down **3.** (*w wędkarstwie*) strike; **zacinać się 1.** (*kaleczyć się*) cut oneself **2.** (*jąkać się*) stammer, stutter **3.** (*o zamku*) jam
zacisk *m* (*-ku*; *-ki*) clamp
zaciskać ⟨**-snąć**⟩ (*-kam*) **1.** (*ścieśniać*) tighten; **~ pętlę na czyjejś szyi** tighten the noose around s.o.'s neck **2.** *pięści*: clench **3.** *wargi*: purse **4.** *zęby*: grit **5. zaciśnięte powieki** tightly closed lids
zacisz|e *n* (*-sza*; *-sza*) retreat; **w domowym ~u** in the privacy of one's home
zaciszny *adj* **1.** (*osłonięty od wiatru*) sheltered **2.** (*spokojny*) calm **3.** (*przytulny*) snug
zacny *adj* good, kind
zacofanie *n* (*-nia*; *no pl*) backwardness; **zacofany** *adj* backward
zacumować *v/p* → **cumować**
zacytować *v/p* → **cytować**
zaczadzony *adj* asphyxiated
zaczajać się ⟨**-czaić**⟩ (*-jam*): **~ na** *A* lie in wait for
zaczarować *v/p* (*-ruję*) put a spell on, enchant; **zaczarowany** *adj* enchanted
zacząć *v/p* → **zaczynać**
zaczątek *m* (*-tku*; *-tki*) beginning
zaczekać *v/p* → **czekać**
zaczepiać ⟨**-pić**⟩ (*-piam*) **1.** (*przypadkiem zahaczać*) catch (**o** *A* on) **2.** (*przymocowywać*) fasten (**o** *A* to) **3.** (*zagadywać*) accost **4.** (*prowokować*) provoke; **zaczepiać się 1.** (*zahaczać*) get caught (**o** *A* in) **2.** (*szukać zaczepki*) look for a fight
zaczepk|a *f* (*-ki*; *-ki*): **szukać ~i** look for a fight; **zaczepny** *adj* **1.** (*agresywny*) aggressive **2.** *spojrzenie, ton*: provocative
zaczerpnąć *v/p* (*-nę*) **1.** scoop up; **~ wody** draw some water; **~ informacji o** *L* find out about **2.** *motyw, cytat*: take; **~ powietrza** take a breath
zaczerwienić się *v/p* → **czerwienić się**
zaczerwienienie *n* (*-nia*; *-nia*) reddening; **zaczerwieniony** *adj* red
zaczesywać ⟨**-sać**⟩ (*-suję*) comb; **~ włosy do tyłu** comb one's hair back
zaczęty *adj paczka, butelka*: opened, open
zaczyn *m* (*-nu*; *-ny*) leaven
zaczynać ⟨**-cząć**⟩ (*-nam*) start, begin; **~ od** *G* start with; **zaczęło padać** it started raining; **~ od nowa** start anew, start again; **zaczynać się** start, begin; **~ się na literę A** start with the letter A
zaczyniać ⟨**-nić**⟩ (*-niam*) leaven
zaczytywać się *v/im* (*-tuję*) read a lot (**w** *L* of)
zaćma *f* (*-my*; *-my*) cataract
zaćmienie *n* (*-nia*; *-nia*) eclipse; **~ Słońca** solar eclipse; **~ Księżyca** lunar eclipse; **zaćmiewać** ⟨**-mić**⟩ (*-wam*) (*przewyższać*) eclipse, overshadow
zad *m* (*-du*; *-dy*) rump
zadać *v/p* → **zadawać**
zadanie *n* (*-nia*; *-nia*) task; **~ domowe** homework; **~ z fizyki** physics problem
zadarty *adj nos*: snub; **z ~m nosem** snub-nosed
zadat|ek *m* (*-tku*; *-tki*) **1.** (*kwota*) deposit **2. ~ki** (*predyspozycja*) makings; **mieć ~ki na** *A* have all the makings of
zadawać ⟨**-dać**⟩ (*-daję*) **1.** *pytanie*: ask **2.** *zadanie*: give, assign **3.** *cios*: deal **4.** (*powodować*) **~ komuś ból** make s.o. suffer, inflict pain on s.o.: **~ wrogowi klęskę** defeat the enemy; **~ czemuś kłam** *lit* give the lie to s.th.; **~ sobie trud, by coś zrobić** take the trouble to do s.th.; **~ komuś śmierć** take s.o.'s life; **zadawać się** mix (**z** *I* with)
zadawniony *adj* **1.** *konflikt*: long-standing **2.** *wrogość, nienawiść*: inveterate
zadąć *v/p* → **dąć**
zadbać *v/p* → **dbać**

zadbany *adj* **1.** *osoba, wygląd, zwierzę*: well-groomed **2.** *włosy*: neat **3.** *paznokcie*: (well-)manicured **4.** *ogródek*: tidy, well-maintained
zadebiutować *v/p* → **debiutować**
zadecydować *v/p* → **decydować**
zadedykować *v/p* → **dedykować**
zadek *m* (*-dka*; *-dki*) *infml* backside, rump
zadeklamować *v/p* → **deklamować**
zadeklarować *v/p* → **deklarować**
zadekować *v/p* → **dekować**
zademonstrować *v/p* → **demonstrować**
zadenuncjować *v/p* → **denuncjować**
zadeptywać ⟨**-tać**⟩ (*-tuję*) **1.** trample; **~ ogień** stamp out the fire **2.** (*brudzić*) soil
zadłużać się ⟨**-żyć**⟩ (*-żam*) get into debt (**u** *G* with); **zadłużenie** *n* (*-nia*; *no pl*) debt; **zadłużony** *adj*: **być ~m** be in debt
zadomowić się *v/p* (*-wię*) settle (in)
zadość: **uczynić ~ czyjejś prośbie** *lit* satisfy s.o.'s request; **uczynić ~ prawu** *lit* comply with the law; **sprawiedliwości stało się ~** justice has been done
zadośćuczynić *v/p* (*-nię*) *prośbie*, *wymaganiom*: *lit* satisfy, comply with
zadośćuczynienie *n* (*-nia*; *no pl*) **1.** redress **2.** (*pieniężne*) compensation
zadowalać ⟨**-wolić**⟩ (*-lam*) satisfy; **~ kogoś seksualnie** satisfy s.o. sexually; **zadowalać się** make do with, settle for
zadowalający *adj* satisfactory; **zadowolenie** *n* (*-nia*; *no pl*) satisfaction; **~ z pracy** job satisfaction; **robić coś z ~m** take pleasure in doing s.th.; **zadowolony** *adj* satisfied, glad, happy, pleased (**z** *G* with); **~ z siebie** self-satisfied
zadra *f* (*-ry*; *-ry*) splinter
zadrapać *v/p* (*-pię*), **zadrasnąć** *v/p* (*-nę*) scratch
zadrażnienia *pl* (*-nień*) friction *sing*
zadręczać ⟨**-czyć**⟩ (*-czam*) torment, pester; **~ kogoś pytaniami** pester s.o. with questions; **zadręczać się** agonize (*I* over)
zadrukowany *adj* printed
zadrzeć *v/p* → **zadzierać**
zadrzewiać ⟨**-wić**⟩ (*-wiam*) afforest
zaduch *m* (*-chu*; *no pl*) stuffiness; **tu jest straszny ~** *infml* it's awfully stuffy in here
zadufany *adj*: **~ (w sobie)** self-assured
zadum|a *f* (*-my*; *no pl*) reverie, meditation; **być pogrążonym w głębokiej ~ie** be deep in reverie, be deep in meditation; **wyrwać kogoś z ~y** bring s.o. out of his reverie
zadumać się *v/p* (*-mam*) *lit* become pensive, fall into a reverie
zadumany *adj* pensive, thoughtful, lost in thought
zadupi|e *n* (*-pia*; *-pia*) *infml* hole in the middle of nowhere, godforsaken hole; **mieszkać na ~u** live out in the sticks
zadurzony *adj* infatuated (**w** *L* with)
zadusić *v/p* → **dusić**
Zaduszki *pl* (*-szek*) *REL* All Souls' Day *sing*
zaduszny *adj*: **Dzień ~** *REL* All Soul's Day
zadyma *f* (*-my*; *-my*) *infml* trouble
zadymiać ⟨**-mić**⟩ (*-miam*) fill with smoke
zadymiarz *m* (*-rza*; *-rze*) *infml* troublemaker, *Br infml* yob; **wrzeszczący ~e z ogolonymi głowami** loud-mouthed yobs with shaven heads
zadymiony *adj* smoky
zadymka *f* (*-ki*; *-ki*) snowstorm, blizzard
zadyszany, **zdyszany** *adj* out of breath, breathless
zadyszk|a *f* (*-ki*; *-ki*) short breath, breathlessness; **dostawać ~i** lose one's breath, get winded
zadzierać ⟨**-drzeć**⟩ (*-ram*) **1.** *spódnicę*: pull up, hike up **2. ~ głowę** crane one's neck **3. ~ nosa** *fig* be toffee-nosed, put on airs **4.** *paznokieć*: chip **5.** (*zaczepiać*) mess (**z** *I* with)
zadziora *f/m* (*-ry*; *-ry*) (*osoba*) brawler
zadziorny *adj* aggressive, quarrelsome
zadziwiać ⟨**-wić**⟩ (*-wiam*) astonish; **zadziwiający** *adj* astonishing
zadzwonić *v/p* → **dzwonić**
zadźgać *v/p* (*-gam*) stab to death
zadżumiony *adj* plague-stricken
zafarbować *v/p* → **farbować**
zafascynować *v/p* → **fascynować**
zafascynowany *adj* fascinated (*I* by)
zafundować *v/p* → **fundować**

zagadać *v/p* → ***zagadywać***
zagadk|a *f* (*-ki*; *-ki*) **1.** riddle **2.** (*tajemnica*) mystery, riddle; ***coś jest wciąż ~ą dla naukowców*** s.th. still baffles the scientists
zagadkowy *adj* enigmatic, mysterious
zagadnienie *n* (*-nia*; *-nia*) problem, issue
zagadywać 〈**-dać**〉 (*-duję*) **1.** (*zacząć mówić*) start talking; ***spędzić wieczór zagadując dziewczyny*** *infml* spend an evening chatting up girls **2.** (*zagłuszyć mówieniem*) talk down
zagajać 〈**-gaić**〉 (*-jam*) *zebranie*, *dyskusję*: open
zagajnik *m* (*-ka*; *-ki*) coppice
zagalopować się *v/p* (*-puję*) overstep the mark; ***~ w wydatkach*** spend way too much
zaganiać 〈**-gnać**, **-gonić**〉 (*-niam*) drive
zaganiany *adj* busy
zagapić się *v/p* (*-pię*) stare; ***zagapiłem się*** I wasn't looking
zagarniać 〈**-nąć**〉 (*-niam*) **1.** (*przyciągnąć do siebie*) gather, sweep up; ***~ coś do torby*** sweep s.th. into one's bag **2.** (*przywłaszczać sobie*) seize
zagazować *v/p* (*-zuję*) gas
zagęszczać 〈**-gęścić**〉 (*-czam*) *sos*, *farbę*: thicken; ***zagęszczać się*** thicken
zagiąć *v/p* → ***zaginać***
zagięcie *n* (*-cia*; *-cia*) **1.** bend **2.** (*materiału*) fold
zaginać 〈**-giąć**〉 (*-nam*) **1.** *drut*: bend **2.** *kartki*: fold **3.** (*zadawać trudne pytanie*) *infml* stump, get; ***tu cię zagiąłem*** I stumped you on that one; ***zaginać się*** bend
zaginąć *v/p* (*-nę*) go missing, disappear; ***ślad po nim zaginął*** there's no trace of him
zaginiony *adj* **1.** *osoba*: missing **2.** *przedmiot*, *skarb*: lost; ***dawno ~*** long-lost
zagipsować *v/p* → ***gipsować***
zaglądać 〈**zajrzeć**〉 (*-dam*) **1.** (*spoglądać*) look (**do** *G* in/into); ***~ przez dziurkę od klucza*** peep through a keyhole; ***~ przez okno*** look in through a window; ***zamknij oczy i nie zaglądaj*** close your eyes and don't peek; ***~ do notatek*** refer to one's notes **2.** (*odwiedzać*) drop in, come by; ***lubić ~ do kieliszka*** *fig* be fond of drink; ***zacząć ~ do kieliszka*** *fig* take to the bottle; ***darowanemu koniowi nie zagląda się w zęby*** never look a gift horse in the mouth, beggars can't be choosers
zagłada *f* (*-dy*; *no pl*) extermination
zagłębiać 〈**-bić**〉 (*-biam*) *zęby*: sink; ***zagłębiać się*** **1.** (*dostawać się*) get deep, go deep; ***~ się w fotelu*** sink in an armchair **2.** (*zajmować się*) ***~ się w pracy*** immerse oneself in one's work; ***~ się w myślach*** become lost in thought, immerse oneself in thought
zagłębie *n* (*-bia*; *-bia*) region; ***~ węglowe*** coal-mining region; ***~ naftowe*** oil-producing region
zagłębienie *n* (*-nia*; *-nia*) hollow
zagłodzić *v/p* (*-dzę*) starve; ***~ kogoś na śmierć*** starve s.o. to death; ***zagłodzić się*** starve oneself; → ***głodzić się***
zagłosować *v/p* → ***głosować***
zagłówek *m* (*-wka*; *-wki*) **1.** (*w samochodzie*) headrest **2.** (*na łóżku*) bolster
zagłuszać 〈**-szyć**〉 (*-szam*) **1.** *hałas*: drown out **2.** *stację radiową*: jam **3.** *wyrzuty sumienia*: stifle
zagmatwać *v/p* → ***gmatwać***; ***zagmatwany*** *adj* complicated, tangled
zagnać *v/p* → ***zaganiać***
zagniewany *adj* angry, cross
zagnieżdżać się 〈**-nieździć**〉 (*-dżam*) nest
zagoić *v/p* → ***goić***
zagon *m* (*-nu*; *-ny*) patch
zagonić *v/p* → ***zaganiać***
zagoniony → ***zaganiany***
zagorzały *adj* **1.** *zwolennik*, *przeciwnik*: fervent, ardent **2.** *dyskusja*: heated
zagospodarowywać 〈**-rować**〉 (*-rowuję*) **1.** (*zabudować*) develop **2.** (*rozpoczynać uprawę*) bring under cultivation **3.** (*czynić produktywnym*) make productive **4.** *czas*: make good use of; ***zagospodarowywać się*** settle in
zagotować *v/p* (*-tuję*) boil; ***~ wodę na herbatę*** boil some water for tea; → ***gotować***
zagrabiać 〈**-bić**〉 (*-biam*) **1.** (*grabiami*) rake (up) **2.** (*zabierać*) seize; → ***grabić***

zagrać *v/p* → ***grać***
zagradzać ⟨***-rodzić***⟩ (*-dzam*) **1.** block; ***~ komuś drogę*** bar s.o.'s way **2.** (*płotem*) fence off
zagranic|a *f* (*-cy*; *no pl*) foreign countries *pl*; ***wrócić z ~y*** return from abroad; ***turyści z ~y*** foreign tourists; ***kontakty z ~ą*** international contacts; **zagraniczniak** *m* (*-ka*; *-niacy*) *infml* foreigner
zagraniczn|y *adj* **1.** foreign; ***podróż ~a*** trip abroad **2.** *kontakty*: international
zagraża|ć ⟨***-rozić***⟩ (*-żam*) threaten; ***~ mu niebezpieczeństwo*** he's in danger
zagroda *f* (*-dy*; *-dy*) **1.** (*zabudowania z podwórzem*) farmstead **2.** (*dla zwierząt*) enclosure, pen
zagrodzić *v/p* → ***zagradzać***
zagrozić *v/p* → ***zagrażać***; **zagrożenie** *n* (*-nia*; *-nia*) risk, threat, hazard; ***stanowić ~ dla życia*** be life-threatening
zagruntować *v/p* → ***gruntować***
zagrych|a *f* (*-chy*; *-chy*) *infml* snack; ***ogórek na ~ę*** cucumber for a snack
zagrywka *f* (*-ki*; *-ki*) **1.** SPORT serve **2.** (*posunięcie*) *infml* move
zagryzać ⟨***-ryźć***⟩ (*-zam*) **1.** (*zabić*) bite to death **2.** ***~ wargi*** bite one's lips **3.** (*po wódce*) ***zagryzł wódkę śledziem*** he followed the vodka with a piece of herring
zagrzać *v/p* (*-rzeję*): (***nigdzie***) ***nie ~ miejsca*** not stay long (anywhere); ***zagrzać się*** get warm
zagrzebywać ⟨***-bać***⟩ (*-buję*) bury; ***zagrzebywać się*** (*o zwierzęciu*) bury oneself
zagwarantować *v/p* → ***gwarantować***
zahaczać ⟨***-czyć***⟩ (*-czam*) hook; ***~ o*** *A* catch on
zahamować *v/p* → ***hamować***
zahamowa|nie *pl* (*-wań*) PSYCH inhibition; ***mieć ~nia*** be inhibited; ***bez ~ń*** with no inhibitions
zaharowany *adj* overworked
zahartować *v/p* → ***hartować***; **zahartowany** *adj* **1.** (*silny*) strong **2.** ***~ w bojach*** battle-hardened
zahipnotyzować *v/p* → ***hipnotyzować***; **zahipnotyzowany** *adj* hypnotized
zahukany *adj* cowed
zaimek *m* (*-mka*; *-mki*) pronoun
zaimponować *v/p* → ***imponować***
zaimprowizowany *adj* improvized
zainaugurować *v/p* → ***inaugurować***
zainfekować *v/p* → ***infekować***
zaingerować *v/p* → ***ingerować***
zainicjować *v/p* → ***inicjować***
zainkasować *v/p* → ***inkasować***
zainspirować *v/p* → ***inspirować***
zainstalować *v/p* → ***instalować***
zainteresować *v/p* → ***interesować***
zainteresowani|e *n* (*-nia*; *-nia*) interest; ***~a*** (*zamiłownia*) interests, hobbies; **zainteresowan|y** *adj* interested (*I* in); ***~e strony*** the interested parties
zaintonować *v/p* → ***intonować***
zaintrygować *v/p* → ***intrygować***
zainwestować *v/p* → ***inwestować***
zaistnieć *v/p* (*-nieję*) come into being, arise
zaizolować *v/p* → ***izolować***
zajad *m* (*-du*; *-dy*) lip sore
zajadać *v/im* (*-dam*) eat heartily; ***zajadać się*** gorge oneself on
zajadły *adj* **1.** *walka*: fierce **2.** *wróg*: bitter **3.** *spór*: heated
zajazd *m* (*-du*; *-dy*) inn
zając *m* (*-ca*; *-ce*) hare
zająć *v/p* → ***zajmować***
zająknąć się *v/p* (*-nę*) stammer, falter; ***ani ~ o*** *L* not mention, never mention
zająknieni|e *n* (*-nia*; *-nia*), **zająknięcie** *n* (*-cia*; *-cia*): ***bez ~a*** without faltering; ***wyrecytować coś bez ~a*** recite s.th. without a hitch
zajechać *v/p* → ***zajeżdżać***
zajezdnia *f* (*-ni*; *-nie*) depot
zajeżdżać ⟨***-jechać***⟩ (*-dżam*) **1.** (*dojeżdżać*) arrive; ***~ przed*** *A* pull up outside **2.** (*śmierdzieć*) *infml* stink (*I* of)
zajęci → ***zajęty***
zajęci|e *n* (*-cia*; *-cia*) (*praca*) job, occupation; ***~a*** **a)** (*w szkole*) lessons **b)** (*na uczelni*) classes
zajęcz|y *adj* hare's; ***~a warga*** harelip
zajęty *adj* **1.** *osoba*: busy **2.** *miejsce*: taken, occupied **3.** *telefon*: busy, engaged
zajmować ⟨***-jąć***⟩ (*-muję*) **1.** (*miejsce*) take up; ***~ miejsce*** (*siadać*) take a seat; ***~ drugie miejsce*** SPORT be second, come second; ***~ stanowisko*** **a)** (*wypowiadać się*) take a stance **b)** (*w firmie*) hold a position, have a position **2.** *czas*: take; ***~ dużo czasu***

take a lot of time; ***ile czasu ci to zajęło?*** how much time did it take you? **3.** *miasto, twierdzę*: capture **4.** (*absorbować*) absorb **5.** (*rezerwować*) keep; **zajmować się 1.** (*opiekować się*) take care of, look after **2.** (*interesować się*) be interested in **3.** *gośćmi*: entertain **4.** (*wykonywać czynność*) be busy (*I* doing s.th.) **5.** (*mieć zawód*) ***czym się pan zajmuje?*** what do you do?

zajmujący *adj* engrossing, interesting, absorbing

zajrzeć *v/p* → ***zaglądać***

zajście *n* (*-cia*; *-cia*) incident

zajść *v/p* → ***zachodzić***

zakalec *m* (*-lca*; *-lce*) half-baked cake

zakała *f/m* (*-ły*; *-ły*) *fig* disgrace

zakamar|ek *m* (*-rka*; *-rki*) nook; ***wszyskie ~ki*** every nook and cranny

zakamuflować *v/p* → ***kamuflować***; **zakamuflowany** *adj* disguised, camouflaged

zakańczać ⟨**-kończyć**⟩ (*-czam*) end, finish; **zakańczać się** end, finish

zakapować *v/p* → ***kapować***

zakasłać *v/p* (*-szlę*) cough; → ***kasłać***

zakasować *v/p* (*-suję*) *infml* top

zakasywać ⟨**-sać**⟩ (*-suję*) roll up; ***~ rękawy*** *fig* put one's shoulder to the wheel

zakaszleć → ***zakasłać***

zakatarzony *adj*: ***być ~m*** have a cold, have a runny nose

zakatrupić *v/p* (*-pię*) *infml* do in

zakaz *m* (*-zu*; *-zy*) ban, prohibition; ***„~ wstępu"*** 'no entry'; ***„~ palenia"*** 'no smoking'; ***„~ postoju"*** 'no waiting'; **zakazać** *v/p* → ***zakazywać***

zakazany *adj* prohibited, forbidden; ***~ owoc*** forbidden fruit

zakazić *v/p* → ***zakażać***

zakazywać ⟨**-zać**⟩ (*-zuję*) forbid, ban

zakaźnie *adv*: ***być ~ chorym*** suffer from an infectious disease

zakaźn|y *adj* infectious; ***choroba ~a*** infectious disease, contagious disease; ***szpital chorób ~ych*** isolation hospital

zakażać ⟨**-kazić**⟩ (*-żam*) infect; **zakażać się** become infected; **zakażenie** *n* (*-nia*; *-nia*) infection; ***~ krwi*** blood infection; **zakażony** *adj* infected (*I* with)

zakąsić *v/p* (*-szę*): ***wypił wódkę i zakąsił śledziem*** he followed the vodka with a piece of herring

zakąsk|a *f* (*-ki*; *-ki*) starter, appetizer, snack; ***zimne ~i*** cold refreshments; ***~i na gorąco*** hot refreshments; ***na ~ę*** for a snack

zakąt|ek *m* (*-tka*; *-tki*) corner, nook; ***malowniczy ~ek*** beauty spot, picturesque corner; ***w najdalszych ~kach świata*** in the most remote corners of the world; ***każdy ~ek*** every nook and cranny

zakichany *adj infml* pesky, darn

zakisić *v/p* (*-szę*) **1.** *ogórki*: pickle **2.** *kapustę*: sour

zakitować *v/p* → ***kitować***

zaklajstrować *v/p* → ***klajstrować***

zaklasyfikować *v/p* → ***klasyfikować***

zakląć *v/p* (*-lnę*) swear; → ***zaklinać***

zaklejać ⟨**-leić**⟩ (*-jam*) **1.** *kopertę*: seal **2.** *dętkę*: patch, fix **3.** *folią*: cover (*I* with)

zaklepać *v/p* (*-pię*) **1.** flatten **2.** (*zarezerwować*) *infml* ***~ sobie*** book

zakleszczony *adj* jammed, stuck

zaklęcie *n* (*-cia*; *-cia*) spell; **zaklęty** *adj* **1.** enchanted; ***milczeć jak ~*** be (as) silent as the grave **2.** *krąg*: charmed

zaklinacz *m* (*-cza*; *-cze*): ***~ węży*** snake charmer

zaklinać ⟨**-ląć**⟩ (*-nam*) **1.** (*czarować*) charm **2.** (*błagać*) implore; **zaklinać się** swear

zaklinować *v/p* (*-nuję*) jam, block; **zaklinować się** get stuck

zakład *m* (*-du*; *-dy*) **1.** (*przedsiębiorstwo*) company; ***~ produkcyjny*** production plant, factory; ***~ fryzjerski*** **a)** (*męski*) barber's **b)** (*damski*) hairdresser's; ***~ wulkanizacyjny*** tyre repair shop; ***~ pracy chronionej*** sheltered workshop; ***~ utylizacji odpadów*** reprocessing plant **2.** (*instytucja*) institution; ***~ karny*** penal institution, *Am* penitentiary; ***~ poprawczy*** young offenders' institution **3.** (*założenie się*) bet; ***iść o ~*** bet; ***~?*** is it a bet?

zakładać ⟨**założyć**⟩ (*-dam*) **1.** (*umieszczać*) ***~ sukienkę*** put on a dress; ***~ okulary*** put on one's glasses; ***~ kaptur*** put up one's hood; ***~ nogę na nogę*** cross one's legs: ***~ plombę*** put in a filling; **~ komuś szwy** stitch up s.o. **2.** (*instalować*) install, fit; **~ prąd** install electricity; **~ podsłuch na telefonie** bug a phone **3.** *firmę*: start, set up, establish **4.** *zespół muzyczny*, *rodzinę*: start **5.** *miasto*: found **6.** *konto*: open **7.** (*przyjmować*) assume; **zakładam, że** I assume that; **załóżmy, że** let's assume that; **zakładać się** (*iść o zakład*) bet (**o** *A*); **~ się z kimś o coś** bet s.o. s.th.

zakładka *f* (*-ki*; *-ki*) **1.** (*w książce*, *przeglądarce*) bookmark **2.** (*w oknie programu*) tab

zakładnik *m* (*-ka*; *-nicy*), **-niczka** *f* (*-ki*; *-ki*) hostage; **wziąć kogoś jako ~a** take s.o. hostage

zakładow|y *adj* company; **lekarz ~y** company doctor; **stołówka ~a** company canteen; **kapitał ~y** share capital

zakłamanie *n* (*-nia*; *no pl*) hypocrisy; **zakłamany** *adj* hypocritical

zakłopotanie *n* (*-nia*; *no pl*) embarrassment; **wprawiać w ~** embarrass; **zakłopotany** *adj* embarrassed

zakłócać 〈**-cić**〉 (*-cam*) (*przeszkadzać*) disturb, disrupt; **~ czyjąś prywatność** invade s.o.'s privacy; **~ czyjąś karierę** disrupt s.o.'s career

zakłóceni|e *n* (*-nia*; *-nia*) **1.** (*naruszenie porządku*) disturbance, disruption; **~a komunikacyjne**, **~a w ruchu** traffic disturbances; **~e porządku publicznego** breach of the peace **2.** (*w eterze*) interference, noise

zakneblować *v/p* → **kneblować**

zakochać się *v/p* → **zakochiwać się**

zakochany I *adj* in love; **~ po uszy** head over heels in love, love-struck; **~ w** *L* in love with, *Br* enamoured of, *Am* enamored of; **~ bez wzajemności** lovesick **II** *m* (*-nego*; *-ni*), **-na** *f* (*-nej*; *-ne*) lover; **para ~ch** a couple of lovers

zakochiwać się 〈**-chać**〉 (*-chuję*) fall in love

zakodować *v/p* → **kodować**

zakol|e *n* (*-la*; *-la*) **1.** **~a** (*na głowie*) receding hairline **2.** *rzeki*, *drogi*: curve

zakomunikować *v/p* → **komunikować**

zakon *m* (*-nu*; *-ny*) REL order; **mnisi z ~u cystersów** (**franciszkanów**) monks of the Cistercian (Franciscan) Order; **~ żeński** sisterhood

zakonnic|a *f* (*-cy*; *-ce*) nun; **szkoła prowadzona przez ~e** school run by nuns; **zakonnik** *m* (*-ka*; *-nicy*) monk; **zakonn|y** *adj* monastic; **siostra ~a** nun

zakonserwować *v/p* → **konserwować**; **zakonserwowany** *adj* preserved; **dobrze ~** well-preserved

zakonspirowany *adj* secret

zakończenie *n* (*-nia*; *-nia*) **1.** ending **2.** *rozmowy*, *dyskusji*, *rozdziału*, *wypracowania*: conclusion; **na ~** in conclusion; **zakończony** *adj*: **ostro ~** pointed; **~ szpicem hełm** spiked helmet; **zakończyć** *v/p* → **zakańczać**

zakopać *v/p* → **zakopywać**

zakopcić *v/p* → **kopcić**; **zakopcony** *adj* *knajpa*: smoky

zakopywać 〈**-kopać**〉 (*-puję*) bury

zakorkować *v/p* → **korkować**; **zakorkowany** *adj* **1.** *butelka*: corked **2.** *ulica*: jammed

zakorzeniać się 〈**-nić**〉 (*-niam*) **1.** (*o roślinie*) take root **2.** (*o przekonaniu*, *zwyczaju*) take hold

zakorzenion|y *adj* rooted (**w** *L* in); **~y w tradycji** rooted in tradition; **głęboko ~y** deep-rooted; **głęboko ~e uprzedzenia** deep-rooted prejudices, ingrained prejudices

zakos|y *pl* (*-sów*) twists; **~ami** in zigzags

zakosztować *v/p* → **kosztować**

zakotwiczać 〈**-czyć**〉 (*-czam*) (*cumować*) anchor; **zakotwiczać się** *fig* stay for good; **zakotwiczony** *adj* anchored

zakpić *v/p* → **kpić**

zakradać się 〈**-raść**〉 (*-dam*) steal (up), sneak (up)

zakraplacz *m* (*-cza*; *-cze*) dropper; **zakraplać** 〈**-roplić**〉 (*-lam*): **~ do oczu** apply to the eyes, put in the eyes

zakratowany *adj* barred

zakrawać *v/im*: **to zakrawa na żart** it sounds like a joke

zakres *m* (*-su*; *-sy*) **1.** range, scope; **~ działalności** scope of operation; **~ kompetencji** powers, authority, terms of reference; **we własnym ~ie** on one's own; **wyżywienie we własnym ~ie** board not included **2.** *fal radiowych*: waveband

zakreślać 〈**-lić**〉 (*-lam*) **1.** (*rysując linię wokół*) circle **2.** (*zaznaczając marke-*

rem) highlight **3.** *granice*: mark; **~ łuk** arc

zakręcać ⟨**-cić**⟩ (*-cam*) **1.** *kran*: turn off **2.** *słoik*: screw a lid on **3.** *włosy*: curl: **~ włosy na wałki** put one's hair in curlers **4.** (*o drodze*) curve; **zakręcać się**: **zakręciło jej się w głowie** she felt dizzy; **zakręcić się koło czegoś** *fig* see to s.th.

zakrę|t *m* (*-tu*; *-ty*) bend, turn; **na ~cie** on a bend; **ostry ~t** sharp curve; **~t w lewo** left turn; **brać ~t** take a turn; **wchodzić w ~t** go into a bend

zakrętas *m* (*-sa*; *-sy*) flourish, squiggle

zakrętka *f* (*-ki*; *-ki*) cap, top

zakroplić *v/p* → **zakraplać**

zakrwawić *v/p* (*-wię*) get blood on, stain with blood; **zakrwawiony** *adj* bloody, blood-stained

zakryć *v/p* → **zakrywać**

zakrystia *f* (*-tii*; *-tie*) vestry

zakrywać ⟨**-ryć**⟩ (*-wam*) cover; **~ twarz rękami** bury one's face in one's hands

zakrzątnąć się *v/p* (*-nę*) take care (**koło** *G* of)

zakrzep *m* (*-pu*; *-py*) (blood) clot; **zakrzepły** *adj* **1.** *krew*: clotted **2.** *lawa*: congealed

zakrztusić się *v/p* → **krztusić się**

zakrzywiony *adj* curved, bent

zaksięgować *v/p* → **księgować**

zaktualizować *v/p* → **aktualizować**; **zaktualizowany** *adj* updated

zaktywizować *v/p* → **aktywizować**

zakuć *v/p* → **zakuwać**

zakulisowy *adj* backstage

zakumulować *v/p* → **akumulować**

zakup *m* (*-pu*; *-py*) purchase; **~y** shopping; **robić ~y** do the shopping; **iść na ~y** go shopping

zakupywać ⟨**-pić**⟩ (*-puję*) buy, purchase

zakurzony *adj* dusty

zakurzyć się *v/p* → **kurzyć się**

zakusy *pl* (*-sów*) *lit* designs; **mieć ~ na** *A* have designs on

zakuty *adj*: **~ łeb** *infml* blockhead

zakuwać ⟨**-kuć**⟩ (*-wam*): **~ kogoś w kajdany** chain s.o.

zakwalifikować *v/p* → **kwalifikować**

zakwaszać ⟨**-sić**⟩ (*-szam*) *ogórki, kapustę*: pickle (in brine)

zakwaterowanie *n* (*-nia*) accommodation; **zakwaterowywać** ⟨**-rować**⟩ (*-wuję*) **1.** accommodate **2.** *żołnierzy*: quarter

zakwestionować *v/p* → **kwestionować**

zakwitać ⟨**-tnąć**⟩ (*-tam*) **1.** (*o kwiatach*) bloom, flower **2.** (*o drzewach*) blossom

zalać *v/p* → **zalewać**

zalakować *v/p* → **lakować**

zalakowany *adj* sealed

zalany *adj* **1.** (*wodą*) flooded **2.** (*pijany*) *infml* pissed; **~ w pestkę** totally sloshed

zalatany *adj infml* busy, run off one's feet

zalatywać *v/im* (*-tuję*) smell; **zalatuje od niego piwem** he smells of beer

zalążek *m* (*-żka*; *-żki*) **1.** BIOL ovule **2.** *fig* germ

zalec *v/p* → **zalegać**

zalecać ⟨**-cić**⟩ (*-cam*) (*polecać*) recommend, advise; **zalecać się**: **~ się do** *A* court, woo; **zalecenie** *n* (*-nia*; *-nia*) recommendation

zaledwie I *particle* only (just); **~ przyjechał** he's only just arrived; **sprzedano ~ 200 egzemplarzy książki** the book has sold only 200 copies **II** *conj* as soon as, hardly; **~ usiadłem do obiadu, a zadzwonił telefon** as soon as I sat down to eat, the phone rang

zalegać ⟨**-lec**⟩ (*-gam*) **1.** (*spóźniać się*) fall behind (**z** *I* with), be in arrears (**z** *I* with) **2.** (*leżeć*) lie; **wciąż zalega śnieg** snow is still lying; **~ komuś w żołądku** sit heavily on s.o.'s stomach **3.** (*o milczeniu, ciszy*) fall; **zaległa cisza** silence fell, it got very quiet

zalegalizować *v/p* → **legalizować**

zaległości *pl* (*-ci*): **mieć ~** fall behind (**z** *I* with); **mieć ~ w nauce** fall behind with one's schoolwork; **odrabiać ~** catch up (**z** *I* with); **nadrabiać ~ w nauce** catch up with one's schoolwork; **mieć ~ w pracy** have a backlog of work (to do); **~ płatnicze** arrears

zaległ|y *adj* (*niezapłacony*) outstanding, overdue; **spłacić ~y czynsz** pay off one's rent arrears; **uregulować ~e płatności** settle oustanding payments; **~e pensje** unpaid salaries, overdue salaries

zalepiać ⟨**-pić**⟩ (*-piam*) **1.** *kopertę*: seal **2.** *dziurę*: fill

zalesiać ⟨**-sić**⟩ (*-siam*) afforest; **zalesienie** *n* (*-nia*; *no pl*) afforestation; **zalesiony** *adj* wooded
zaleta *f* (*-ty*; *-ty*) advantage, merit, good point
zalew *m* (*-wu*; *-wy*) **1.** (*zbiornik*) lake, reservoir **2.** (*zatoka*) bay **3.** (*powódź*) flood, flooding **4.** (*napływ*) flood
zalewa *f* (*-wy*; *no pl*) **1.** (*octowa*) pickle **2.** (*z soli*) brine
zalewać ⟨**-lać**⟩ (*-wam*) **1.** (*zatapiać*) flood; ***zalało kilka domów*** a few houses have been flooded; ***rynek zalany towarami pochodzenia zagranicznego*** *fig* the market flooded with foreign products; ***~ robaka*** *infml* drown one's sorrows **2.** (*wypełniać*) fill; ***~ betonem*** fill with concrete **3.** (*polewać*) pour; ***~ coś wodą*** pour water over s.th.; ***~ sosem pomidorowym*** drown with tomato sauce **4.** (*rozlewać*) spill; ***~ obrus kawą*** spill coffee on a tablecloth **5.** (*o świetle*) flood; **zalewać się 1.** (*upijać się*) *infml* get pissed, get wasted **2.** (*oblewać się*) ***zalałem się zupą*** I spilled soup all over myself; ***~ się łzami*** break down in tears
zależeć *v/im* (*-żę*) **1.** (*być uzależnionym*) depend (**od** *G* on); ***~ finansowo od*** *G* be financially dependent on; ***to zależy*** it depends **2.** (*być ważnym*) ***zależy mu na niej*** he cares about her; ***nie zależy mi na tym*** I don't care about it; ***bardzo mi na tym zależy*** it's very important for me
zależnoś|ć *f* (*-ści*; *-ści*) dependence; ***w ~ci od*** *G* depending on; ***wzajemna ~ć*** interdependence; ***~ć polityczna*** political dependence, political subjection
zależn|y *adj* dependent (**od** *G* on); ***mowa ~a*** GRAM reported speech
zalękniony *adj lit* timid, apprehensive
zaliczać ⟨**-czyć**⟩ (*-czam*) **1.** (*uważać, klasyfikować*) regard, count; ***jest zaliczany do najbardziej utalentowanych pisarzy*** he is regarded as one of the most talented authors; ***~ kogoś do najbliższych przyjaciół*** count s.o. among one's closest friends; ***być zalicznym do gadów*** be classed with reptiles **2.** *egzamin*: pass **3.** *zajęcia*: receive a credit for **4.** *rok akademicki*: complete, get credits for **5.** (*uznawać*) recognize **6.** (*odbywać stosunek płciowy*) *infml* score with **7.** (*zwiedzać*) *infml* do; ***zaliczać się*** rank (**do** *G* among), be numbered (**do** *G* among)
zaliczenie *n* (*-nia*; *-nia*) **1.** (*na uczelni*) credit (**z** *G* in), pass (**z** *G* in) **2.** (*na poczcie*) ***za ~m*** cash on delivery
zaliczk|a *f* (*-ki*; *-ki*) advance (payment), down payment; ***tytułem ~i*** as down payment; **zaliczkowo** *adv* in advance
zaliczyć *v/p* → ***zaliczać***
zalogować się *v/p* → ***logować się***
zalotny *adj* flirtatious, *infml* flirty; **zaloty** *pl* (*-tów*) courtship; ***niechciane ~*** unwelcome advances
zaludniać ⟨**-nić**⟩ (*-niam*) people, populate; **zaludniać się** (*o ulicach, barach*) come alive with people
zaludnieni|e *n* (*-nia*; *no pl*) population; ***duża*** (***mała***) ***gęstość ~a*** high (low) population density
zaludniony *adj* populated; ***gęsto ~*** densely populated
załadowywać ⟨**-dować**⟩ (*-dowuję*) load
załadunek *m* (*-nku*; *-nki*) (*ładowanie*) loading; **załadunkowy** *adj* loading
załagodzić *v/p* → ***łagodzić***
załamać *v/p* → ***załamywać***
załamani|e *n* (*-nia*; *-nia*) **1.** *fig* breakdown; ***~e nerwowe*** nervous breakdown **2.** ***~a*** (*zagięcia*) folds
załamany *adj* **1.** (*w depresji*) depressed **2.** (*zagięty*) bent **3.** (*złożony*) folded
załamywać ⟨**-mać**⟩ (*-muję*) **1.** (*psychicznie*) depress; ***~ ręce*** *fig* wring one's hands **2.** (*zaginać*) bend; ***załamywać się*** **1.** (*o lodzie, desce*) break **2.** (*o kładce, moście*) collapse **3.** (*o człowieku*) break down **4.** (*o głosie*) crack **5.** (*o świetle*) be refracted, refract
załapywać ⟨**-pać**⟩ (*-puję*) (*rozumieć*) *infml* cotton on; ***~, jak coś się robi*** twig how to do s.th., get the hang of s.th.; ***załapywać się*** *infml* **1.** luck (**na** *A* into/upon) **2.** ***~ się do pracy*** land oneself a job
załatać *v/p* → ***łatać***
załatwiać ⟨**-wić**⟩ (*-wiam*) **1.** (*organizować, uzyskiwać*) arrange, organize; ***nie wiem, jak to załatwiła*** I don't know how she did it; ***~ komuś miejs-***

Z

ce do spania fix s.o. up with somewhere to sleep; ***~ czyjeś sprawy*** run errands for s.o.; ***to niczego nie załatwia*** this is no solution **2.** (*zdobywać*) get; ***załatw butelkę wódki*** get a bottle of vodka **3.** *sprawy*, *formalności*: take care of, handle; ***pozwól, że ja to załatwię*** let me handle it **4.** *klienta*: deal with **5.** *interesy*: do **6.** (*zabijać*) *infml* do in, dispatch **7.** (*rujnować*) *infml* ruin **8.** (*unieszkodliwiać*) *infml* fix; **załatwiać się** (*wypróżniać się*) relieve oneself; ***muszę się załatwić*** I must go to the toilet

załatwieni|e: ***mieć dużo spraw do ~a*** have a lot of things to do, have a lot of buisness to attend to

załatwion|y *adj*: ***~e!*** (*zgoda*) done!, it's a deal!

załącza|ć ⟨**-czyć**⟩ (*-czam*): ***~ć do*** *G* enclose to; ***~m pozdrowienia*** with kind regards

załączeni|e: ***w ~u*** **a)** (*w liście*) please find enclosed **b)** (*w poczcie elektronicznej*) please find attached

załącznik *m* (*-ka*; *-ki*) **1.** (*do podania*, *umowy*) appendix **2.** (*do listu*) enclosure **3.** (*do poczty elektronicznej*) attachment

załączyć *v/p* → ***załączać***

załog|a *f* (*-gi*; *-gi*) **1.** *statku*, *samolotu*: crew; ***bez ~i*** unmanned **2.** *zakładu*: staff

założeni|e *n* (*-nia*; *-nia*) **1.** (*teza*) assumption; ***wychodzić z ~a, że*** assume that; ***przy ~u, że*** assuming that **2.** (*organizacji*, *miasta*) foundation **3.** (*urządzenia*) installation **4.** (*firmy*) establishment

założyciel *m* (*-la*; *-le*), **~ka** *f* (*-ki*; *-ki*) founder; **założycielski** *adj* founding; **założyć** *v/p* → ***zakładać***

załzawiony *adj* *oczy*: watery

zamach *m* (*-chu*; *-chy*) **1.** (*atak*) attack, assault; ***~ terrorystyczny*** terrorist attack; ***~ bombowy*** bomb attack; ***~ na życie*** assassination attempt; ***~ stanu*** coup; ***~ wojskowy*** military coup **2.** (*zamachnięcie się*) swing; ***z ~em*** with a swing; ***za jednym ~em*** at one go; ***wziąć ~*** take a swing

zamachnąć się *v/p* (*-nę*) swing one's arm, take a swing

zamachowiec *m* (*-wca*; *-wcy*) **1.** (*zabójca*) assassin **2.** (*napastnik*) attacker, assailant **3.** (*podkładający bombę*) bomber; ***~ samobójca*** suicide bomber

zamalowywać ⟨**-lować**⟩ (*-lowuję*) paint over

zamanifestować *v/p* → ***manifestować***

zamarły *adj*: ***~ ze strachu*** petrified by fear

zamartwiać się *v/im* (*-wiam*) worry a lot, be at one's wits' end

zamarynować *v/p* → ***marynować***

zamarzać ⟨**-znąć**⟩ (*-zam*) **1.** freeze **2.** (*o rzece*) freeze (over); **zamarznięty** *adj* frozen

zamaskować *v/p* → ***maskować***

zamaskowany *adj* **1.** *zamachowiec*, *twarz*: masked **2.** *kryjówka*, *wejście*: camouflaged **3.** *agent*: in disguise **4.** *uczucie*: disguised

zamaszysty *adj* **1.** *krok*: vigorous **2.** *ruch*, *gest*, *pismo*: sweeping

zamawiać ⟨**-mówić**⟩ (*-wiam*) **1.** *danie*, *towar*: order **2.** *bilety*, *stolik*: book, reserve **3.** ***~ wizytę u lekarza*** make an appointment with a doctor

zamazany *adj* **1.** *zdjęcie*: blurred **2.** *obraz telewizyjny*: blurred, fuzzy; **zamazywać** ⟨**-zać**⟩ (*-zuję*) **1.** (*zamalowywać*) daub **2.** (*pokrywać*) cover over **3.** (*czynić niewyraźnym*) blur; **zamazywać się** *fig* (*o obrazie*) blur, become blurred

zamącić *v/p* → ***mącić***

zamążpójście *n* (*-cia*; *no pl*) marriage, getting married

zamczysko *n* (*-ka*; *-ka*) castle

zamek[1] *m* (*-mku*; *-mki*) (*budowla*) castle; ***~ z piasku*** sandcastle

zamek[2] *m* (*-mka*; *-mki*) (*zamknięcie*) lock; ***~ szyfrowy*** combination lock; ***~ błyskawiczny*** *Br* zip, *Am* zipper; ***centralny ~*** AUTO central lock; ***zamontować ~*** fit a lock; ***wyposażony w ~*** lockable

zameldować *v/p* → ***meldować***; **zameldowanie** *n* (*-nia*; *no pl*) registration

zamęczać *v/im* (*-czam*) tire out; ***~ kogoś pytaniami*** pester s.o. with questions; **zamęczać się** (*fizycznie*) wear oneself out

zamęczyć *v/p* (*-czę*) torture to death

Z

zamęt *m* (*-tu*; *no pl*) confusion; ***mieć ~ w głowie*** be confused
zamężna *adj* married
zamglenia *pl* (*-leń*) mist *sing*; **zamglony** *adj* misty, hazy
zamian: **w ~** in exchange (**za** *A* for), in return (**za** *A* for)
zamiana *f* (*-ny*; *-ny*) (*wymiana*) exchange; ***~ mieszkania*** flat exchange; ***~ ról*** role reversal
zamiar *m* (*-ru*; *-ry*) intention, plan; ***mieć ~ coś zrobić*** intend to do s.th., plan to do s.th.; ***nosić się z ~em przeprowadzki*** plan to move house; ***mieć dobre ~y*** mean no harm
zamiast **I** *prep* (*G*) instead of; ***~ tego*** instead **II** *conj* instead of, rather than; ***mógłbyś mi pomóc ~ oglądać telewizję*** you could help me instead of watching TV
zamiatacz *m* (*-cza*; *-cze*) sweeper; ***~ ulic*** street sweeper, road sweeper; **zamiatać** ⟨**-mieść**⟩ (*-tam*) sweep (up); **zamiatarka** *f* (*-ki*; *-ki*) sweeper
zamieć *f* (*-ci*; *-cie*) snowstorm, blizzard
zamiejscowy *adj* **1.** *rozmowa*: long-distance **2.** *pracownik*: commuting
zamieniać ⟨**-nić**⟩ (*-niam*) **1.** (*wymieniać*) exchange (**na** *A* for); ***~ kilka słów z*** *I* have a word with **2.** (*przeobrażać*) turn (**w** *A* into); **zamieniać się 1.** (*wymieniać się*) swap, change; ***~ się miejscami*** change places, swap places (**z** *I* with) **2.** (*przeobrażać się*) turn (**w** *A* into); ***zamieniam się w słuch*** I'm all ears
zamienny *adj* **1.** *części*: spare **2.** *lokal*: temporary
zamierać ⟨**-mrzeć**⟩ (*-ram*) **1.** (*o osobie*) freeze; ***~ ze strachu*** be petrified with fear **2.** (*o życiu gospodarczym, kulturalnym*) come to a standstill **3.** (*o rozmowie*) flag
zamierzać *v/im* (*-rzam*) intend, plan, be going; ***co zamierzasz?*** what are you going to do?; **zamierzać się** ⟨**-rzyć**⟩ aim a blow (**na** *A* at)
zamierzchły *adj lit* **1.** ancient; ***w ~ch czasach*** in ancient times **2.** *przeszłość*: distant
zamierzenia *pl* (*-rzeń*) intentions, plans
zamierzony *adj* **1.** *skutek*, *efekt*: intended **2.** *działanie*, *czyn*: deliberate
zamierzyć się *v/p* → ***zamierzać się***
zamieszać *v/p* → ***mieszać***
zamieszanie *n* (*-nia*; *no pl*) confusion, commotion
zamieszany *adj fig* implicated (**w** *A* in), mixed up (**w** *A* in); ***~ w aferę*** implicated in a scandal
zamieszczać ⟨**-mieścić**⟩ (*-czam*) **1.** *artykuł*: run **2.** *ogłoszenie*: put, place
zamieszkać *v/p* (*-kam*) move (**w** *L*/**na** *L* to), take up residence; ***~ na wsi*** move to the country, settle in the country
zamieszkały *adj* **1.** ***~ we Wrocławiu*** resident in Wrocław, living in Wrocław **2.** *dom*, *okolica*: inhabited
zamieszkany *adj teren*, *wyspa*: inhabited
zamieszki *pl* (*-szek*) unrest *sing*, riots
zamieszkiwać *v/im* (*-kuję*) **1.** (*o ludziach*) live, dwell **2.** (*o zwierzętach*) inhabit
zamieścić *v/p* → ***zamieszczać***
zamieść *v/p* → ***zamiatać***
zamilknąć *v/p* → ***milknąć***
zamiłowanie *n* (*-nia*; *-nia*) passion, love (**do** *G* for); ***z ~m*** with passion; **zamiłowany** *adj* keen
zaminować *v/p* → ***minować***; **zaminowany** *adj* mined
zamknąć *v/p* (*-nę*): ***zamknij się!*** shut up!; → ***zamykać***
zamknięci|e *n* (*-cia*; *no pl*) **1.** (*zamek*) lock; ***w ~u*** under lock and key **2.** (*zatrzask*) catch **3.** *fabryki*: closure, shutdown
zamknięt|y *adj* **1.** closed, shut; ***przy drzwiach ~ych*** *fig* in camera; ***obszar ~y*** no-go area, restricted area; ***~y obszar powietrzny*** no-fly zone; ***pokaz ~y*** preview; ***~y w sobie*** withdrawn; ***jest ~a w sobie*** she keeps to herself **2.** (*na klucz*) locked **3.** *system*: self-contained
zamkowy *adj* castle
zamocowywać ⟨**-cować**⟩ (*-cowuję*) fasten, mount, fix
zamoczyć *v/p* (*-czę*) **1.** (*przypadkowo*) wet **2.** (*celowo*) soak; **zamoczyć się** get wet
zamontowywać ⟨**-tować**⟩ (*-towuję*) install
zamordować *v/p* → ***mordować***
zamordowanie *n* (*-nia*; *no pl*) murder; **zamordowany** **I** *adj* murdered **II** *m*

(*-nego*; *-ni*), **-na** *f* (*-nej*; *-ne*) victim of a murder, murdered person
zamordyzm *m* (*-mu*; *no pl*) *infml* despotism, tyranny
zamorski *adj* overseas
zamortyzować *v/p* → ***amortyzować***
zamorzyć *v/p* (*-rzę*): ***~ kogoś głodem*** starve s.o.
zamożny *adj* wealthy, well-off, affluent
zamówić *v/p* → ***zamawiać***
zamówienie *n* (*-nia*; *-nia*) **1.** *na towar, posiłek*: order; ***składać ~ u kogoś na coś*** place an order with s.o. for s.th.; ***zrobić coś na ~*** make s.th. to order **2.** *na obraz, utwór, projekt*: commission
zamrażać ⟨***-rozić***⟩ (*-żam*) freeze
zamrażalnik *m* (*-ka*; *-ki*) freezer compartment; **zamrażarka** *f* (*-ki*; *-ki*) freezer, deep freeze
zamroczeni|e *n* (*-nia*; *no pl*) stupor, daze; ***~e alkoholowe*** drunken stupor; ***stan ~a*** state of stupor; **zamroczony** *adj* dazed; ***~ alkoholem*** dazed by alcohol; **zamroczyć** *v/p* (*-czę*) daze; ***zamroczyło go*** he was dazed
zamrozić *v/p* → ***zamrażać***; **zamrożony** *adj* frozen
zamrzeć *v/p* → ***zamierać***
zamsz *m* (*-szu*; *-sze*) suede
zamurowywać ⟨***-rować***⟩ (*-rowuję*) brick up; ***zamurowało mnie*** *fig* I was speechless
zamykać ⟨***-mknąć***⟩ (*-kam*) **1.** close, shut; ***~ oczy*** close one's eyes; ***~ drzwi*** **a)** shut a door, close a door **b)** (*na klucz*) lock a door; ***~ zebranie*** close a meeting; ***~ coś na cztery spusty*** lock and bolt s.th.; ***~ coś na zasuwę*** bolt s.th. **2.** *fabrykę*: shut down, close down **3.** *prąd, gaz, wodę*: turn off; ***zamykać się*** **1.** close, shut; ***oczy mi się zamykają*** my eyes are closing; ***~ się w sobie*** clam up; ***buzia jej się nie zamyka*** she'a a real chatterbox **2.** *infml* shut up; ***zamknij się!*** shut up!
zamysł *m* (*-łu*; *-ły*) *lit* intention, plan
zamyślać ⟨***-lić***⟩ (*-lam*) *lit* intend, plan; ***zamyślać się*** be lost in thought, become pensive; ***~ się nad*** *I* ponder on
zamyśleni|e *n* (*-nia*; *no pl*) reverie; ***w ~u*** pensively, thoughtfully; ***wyrwać kogoś z ~a*** bring s.o. out of his reverie; **zamyślony** *adj* thoughtful, pensive
zanadrz|e: ***mieć coś w ~u*** *fig* have s.th. up one's sleeve
zanadto *adv* **1.** (*przed czasownikiem*) too much **2.** (*przed przymiotnikiem, przysłówkiem*) too, excessively
zanalizować *v/p* → ***analizować***
zaniechać *v/p* (*-cham*) abandon, give up; **zaniechanie** *n* (*-nia*; *no pl*) JUR nonfeasance
zanieczyszczać ⟨***-czyścić***⟩ (*-czam*) pollute, contaminate; **zanieczyszczeni|e** *n* (*-nia*; *-nia*) **1.** pollution, contamination; ***~e środowiska*** environmental pollution **2.** ***~a*** (*nieczystości*) impurities
zaniedbani|e *n* (*-nia*; *-nia*) **1.** neglect **2.** JUR negligence; ***~a*** negligence; **zaniedbany** *adj* **1.** *budynek, teren*: rundown, neglected **2.** *osoba, wygląd*: scruffy; **zaniedbywać** ⟨***-bać***⟩ (*-buję*) **1.** (*nie dopilnowywać*) neglect; ***~ obowiązki*** neglect one's duties **2.** (*pomijać*) omit; ***zaniedbywać się*** stop looking after oneself
zaniemóc *v/p* (*-mogę*) *lit* fall ill
zaniemówić *v/p* (*-wię*) be speechless, be struck dumb; ***~ z wrażenia*** **a)** (*w podziwie*) be struck dumb with amazement **b)** (*w szoku*) be struck dumb with shock
zaniepokoić *v/p* (*-koję*) worry, alarm; ***zaniepokoić się*** become worried, become alarmed
zaniepokojenie *n* (*-nia*; *no pl*) worry, uneasiness; ***wyrazić swoje ~*** express one's concern; **zaniepokojony** *adj* worried (*I* about), concerned (*I* about)
zanieść *v/p* → ***zanosić***
zanik *m* (*-ku*; *-ki*) **1.** disappearance **2.** (*stopniowy*) decline **3.** MED atrophy; ***~ mięśni*** muscular dystrophy; ***~ pamięci*** memory loss
zanikać ⟨***-knąć***⟩ (*-kam*) **1.** disappear, die out **2.** (*o dźwięku*) die away, fade **3.** (*o mięśniach, organach*) atrophy
zanim *conj* before
zaniżon|y *adj*: ***~a cena*** dumping price
zanosić ⟨***-nieść***⟩ (*-noszę*) take, carry; ***zanosić się***: ***~ się śmiechem*** laugh one's head off; ***~ się płaczem*** sob uncontrollably; ***~ się kaszlem*** cough

violently; ***zanosi się na deszcz*** it's going to rain, it looks like rain; ***zanosi się na zmiany*** it looks as if there are going to be some changes, some changes are in the offing

zanotować *v/p* → ***notować***

zanucić *v/p* → ***nucić***

zanudzać ⟨**-dzić**⟩ (*-dzam*) bore; ***zanudzać się*** get bored

zanurzać ⟨**-rzyć**⟩ (*-rzam*) dip, immerse; ***~ głowę w wodzie*** immerse one's head in water, submerge one's head in water; ***zanurzać się*** **1.** (*o łodzi podwodnej*) submerge **2.** (*o ludziach*) go (**w** *L* into)

zanurzenie *n* (*-nia*; *-nia*) **1.** (*zanurzanie się*) immersion **2.** (*okrętu nawodnego*) draught

zaobserwować *v/p* → ***obserwować***

zaocznie *adv* **1.** *studiować*: part-time, extramurally **2.** *sądzić*, *wybierać*: in absentia

zaoczn|y *adj*: ***studia ~e*** part-time studies, extramural studies; ***kurs ~y*** extramural course

zaoferować *v/p* → ***oferować***

zaofiarować *v/p* (*-ruję*) offer; ***~ pomoc*** volunteer to help

zaogniać ⟨**-nić**⟩ (*-niam*) *sytuację*, *spór*: inflame; ***zaogniać się*** become inflamed

zaokrąglać ⟨**-lić**⟩ (*-lam*) **1.** (*nadawać okrągły kształt*) round **2.** *ceny w górę*: round up **3.** *ceny w dół*: round down; ***zaokrąglać się*** (*o twarzy*, *osobie*) fill out

zaokrętować się *v/p* (*-tuję*) (*o marynarzu*) join a ship

zaopatrywać ⟨**-trzyć**⟩ supply (**w** *A* with), provide (**w** *A* with); ***zaopatrywać się*** get (**w** *A*)

zaopatrzenie *n* (*-nia*; *no pl*) **1.** supply **2.** (*dział*) supplies department, procurement department; ***zaopatrzony*** *adj* **1.** ***dobrze ~ sklep*** well-stocked shop **2.** (*wyposażony*) equipped; ***~ w system alarmowy*** equipped with an alarm system

zaopatrzyć *v/p* → ***zaopatrywać***

zaopiekować się *v/p* → ***opiekować się***

zaopiniować *v/p* → ***opiniować***

zaoponować *v/p* → ***oponować***

zaorywać ⟨**-rać**⟩ (*-ruję*) *Br* plough, *Am* plow

zaostrzać ⟨**-trzyć**⟩ (*-rzam*) **1.** *nóż*: sharpen **2.** *konflikt*, *sytuację*: exacerbate **3.** *przepisy*: toughen **4.** *kontrolę*: tighten **5.** *apetyt*: whet; ***zaostrzać się*** (*o konflikcie*) escalate, intensify

zaoszczędzić *v/p* (*-dzę*) save; ***~ na*** *L* economize on

zaowocować *v/p* → ***owocować***

zapach *m* (*-chu*; *-chy*) **1.** smell; ***przykry ~*** unpleasant smell, *Br* odour, *Am* odor **2.** (*przyjemny*) fragrance, scent

zapaćkać *v/p* (*-kam*) *infml* **1.** (*pobrudzić*) get messy **2.** (*niedbale pomalować*) slap paint on

zapadać ⟨**-paść**⟩ (*-dam*) **1.** (*o ciszy, milczeniu, zmierzchu*) fall; ***zapada zmrok*** dusk is falling **2.** (*zaczynać chorować*) ***~ na zapalenie płuc*** be taken ill with pneumonia: ***ktoś zapada na zdrowiu*** s.o.'s health is declining **3.** (*o decyzji*) be made, be reached **4.** (*o wyroku*) be passed, be reached **5.** ***~ w sen*** go to sleep **6.** ***~ w pamięć*** become embedded in one's memory; ***zapadać się*** **1.** (*o dachu*) cave in, collapse **2.** (*w czymś miękkim*) sink **3.** (*o policzkach*) sink (in) **4.** ***~ się pod ziemię*** *fig* vanish off the face of the earth

zapadł|y *adj* **1.** *policzki*: sunken **2.** ***~y kąt***, ***~a dziura*** *fig* godforsaken hole

zapakować *v/p* (*-kuję*) wrap; ***~ w kolorowy papier*** wrap in colourful paper; ***~ na prezent***, ***~ w ozdobny papier*** gift-wrap

zapalać ⟨**-lić**⟩ (*-lam*) **1.** *świecę*, *papierosa*: light; ***czy można zapalić?*** do you mind if I smoke? **2.** *światło*, *lampę*: turn on, switch on **3.** *samochód*: start; ***zapalać się*** **1.** (*stawać w płomieniach*) catch fire, start burning **2.** (*o świetle*) go on **3.** *fig* become enthusiastic (**do** *G* about)

zapalający *adj* incendiary

zapalarka *f* (*-ki*; *-ki*) (*do zapalania gazu*) (gas) lighter

zapalczywość *f* (*-ści*; *no pl*) impetuosity, vehemence; ***zapalczywy*** *adj* **1.** *osoba*: quick-tempered, impetuous **2.** *dyskusja*: heated

zapalenie *n* (*-nia*; *no pl*) inflammation; ***~ płuc*** pneumonia; ***~ opon mózgowych*** meningitis

zapaleniec *m* (*-leńca*; *-leńcy*) enthusiast
zapalić *v/p* → **zapalać**
zapalniczka *f* (*-ki*; *-ki*) lighter; **zapalnik** *m* (*-ka*; *-ki*) fuse
zapalny *adj* **1.** MED inflammatory; **stan ~** inflammatory condition **2.** (*dający się zapalić*) inflammable **3. punkt ~** POLIT hot spot; **zapalony** *adj* **1. przy ~m świetle** with the lights on **2.** *fig* keen, enthusiastic
zapał *m* (*-łu*; *no pl*) enthusiasm; **~ do pracy** enthusiasm for work; **z ~em** enthusiastically
zapał|ka *f* (*-ki*; *-ki*) match; **pudełko ~ek** box of matches; **pudełko po ~kach** matchbox
zapamiętać *v/p* → **zapamiętywać**
zapamiętale *adv* passionately; **zapamiętały** *adj* **1.** (*zapalony*) passionate, keen **2.** *nienawiść*: passionate, violent **3.** *złość*: furious
zapamiętani|e *n* (*-nia*; *no pl*) **1.** (*nauczenie się*) memorization, remembering; **łatwy do ~a** easy to remember; **godny ~a** worth remembering **2.** (*pasja*) abandon; **z ~em** with abandon
zapamiętywać ⟨**-tać**⟩ (*-tam*) remember; **~ sobie** remember; **zapamiętywać się** become entirely absorbed (**w** *L* in)
zapanować *v/p* (*-nuję*) **1.** (*o ciszy*, *milczeniu*) fall; **nagle zapanowała cisza** a sudden silence fell, all of a sudden everything was quiet **2.** (*o panice*) break out **3.** (*o zwyczaju*) become prevalent **4.** (*obejmować władzę*) take control (**nad** *I* over) **5.** (*powstrzymywać*) control; **~ nad sobą** control oneself
zaparcie *n* (*-cia*; *-cia*) constipation; **mieć ~** be constipated
zaparkować *v/p* → **parkować**
zaparować *v/p* (*-ruję*) (*o szybie*, *okularach*) mist over, fog over
zaparty *adj*: **z ~m tchem** with bated breath
zaparzaczka *f* (*-ki*; *-ki*) tea infuser
zaparzać ⟨**-rzyć**⟩ (*-rzam*) **1.** *herbatę*, *zioła*: brew **2.** *kawę*: make; **zaparzać się** (*o herbacie*, *ziołach*) brew
zapas *m* (*-su*; *-sy*) **1.** supply; **~y** (*żywność*) supplies, provisions; **~y na zimę** winter supplies; **robić ~y** stock up; **mieć w ~ie** have in reserve **2. ~y** ECON stock *sing*
zapaskudzić *v/p* → **paskudzić**
zapasow|y *adj* **1.** *koło*, *części*: spare **2.** *wyjście*: emergency **3. kopia ~a** INF backup copy
zapasy *pl* (*-sów*) wrestling *sing*
zapaść[1] *v/p* → **zapadać**
zapaś|ć[2] *f* (*-ści*; *no pl*) MED collapse; **dostać ~ci** collapse
zapaśniczka *f* (*-ki*; *-ki*) (female) wrestler; **zapaśnicz|y** *adj* wrestling; **walka ~a** wrestling match; **zapaśnik** *m* (*-ka*; *-nicy*) wrestler
zapatrywać się *v/im* (*-ruję*) think (**na** *A* of); **jak się na to zapatrujesz?** what's your opinion of this?
zapatrywania *pl* (*-wań*) view *sing*, opinion *sing*
zapatrzony *adj*: **~ w** *A* with one's eyes fixed on; **być ~m w kogoś** idolize s.o.; **~ w siebie** *Br* self-centred, *Am* self-centered
zapatrzyć się *v/p* (*-rzę*) fix one's eyes (**na** *A*/**w** *A* on)
zapchać *v/p* → **zapychać**
zapchany *adj* blocked, jammed
zapeklować *v/p* → **peklować**
zapełniać ⟨**-nić**⟩ (*-niam*) fill up; **zapełniać się** fill
zaperzać się ⟨**-rzyć**⟩ (*-rzam*) get hot under the collar; **zaperzony** *adj* hot under the collar
zapewne *particle* **1.** (*chyba*) probably **2.** (*niewątpliwie*) surely, certainly
zapewniać ⟨**-nić**⟩ (*-niam*) **1.** (*gwarantować*) ensure; **~ dzieciom przyszłość** secure the future for one's children; **~ sobie zwycięstwo** secure victory **2.** *noclegi*, *wyżywienie*: provide **3.** (*zaręczać*) assure (**kogoś o** *L* s.o. of); **zapewniam was, że** I assure you that; **~ o swojej niewinności** assert one's innocence
zapewnienie *n* (*-nia*; *-nia*) assurance
zapędy *pl* (*-dów*) (*ambicje*) ambitions, aspirations
zapędzać ⟨**-dzić**⟩ (*-dzam*) drive (**do** *G* into); **~ dzieci do odrabiania lekcji** make the children do their homework; **zapędzić kogoś w kozi róg** *fig* drive s.o. into a corner; **zapędzać się** *fig* go too far, get carried away

Z

zapiąć *v/p* → **zapinać**
zapiec *v/p* → **zapiekać**
zapieczętować *v/p* (*-tuję*) seal
zapiekać ⟨**-piec**⟩ (*-kam*) **1.** bake (au gratin) **2.** (*w naczyniu żaroodpornym*) casserole
zapiekanka *f* (*-ki*; *-ki*) **1.** (*kanapka*) toasted sandwich **2.** (*w naczyniu żaroodpornym*) casserole
zapiekany *adj* baked
zapiekły *adj nienawiść*: festering
zapieprzać *v/im* (*-rzam*) *vulg* **1.** (*pracować*) *Br* work one's butt off, *Am* work one's ass off **2.** (*iść lub biec*) tear along
zapieprzyć *v/p* (*-rzę*) *vulg* (*ukraść*) pinch
zapierać[1] ⟨**-prać**⟩ (*-ram*) *plamę*: wash away
zapierać[2] ⟨**-przeć**⟩ (*-ram*): **~ komuś dech** (**w piersiach**) take s.o.'s breath away; **zapierać się 1.** (*zaprzeczać*) deny, renounce **2.** (*opierać się*) brace; **~ się nogami o** *A* brace one's legs against
zapięcie *n* (*-cia*; *-cia*) **1.** fastening **2.** (*klamerka*) clasp **3.** (*sprzączka*) buckle
zapinać ⟨**-piąć**⟩ (*-nam*) **1.** (*na guziki*) button up, do up **2.** (*na zamek*) zip up **3.** *pasy bezpieczeństwa*: fasten; **~ pasy** fasten one's seat belts, *Br infml* belt up, *Am infml* buckle up **4.** *guzik*: do up **5.** *pasek*: buckle **6.** (*na haftkę*) hook up
zapis *m* (*-su*; *-sy*) **1.** (*notacja*) notation **2.** **~y** (*na kurs*) *Br* enrolment *sing*, *Am* enrollment *sing* **3.** (*w księgach rachunkowych*, *rejestrze*) entry **4.** (*rejestrowanie*) recording **5.** (*przepis*) regulation **6.** JUR bequest
zapisać *v/p* → **zapisywać**
zapis|ek *m* (*-sku*; *-ski*) note; **~ki** notes
zapisywać ⟨**-sać**⟩ (*-suję*) **1.** (*notować*) write down, note down **2.** *całą stronę*: write (up) **3.** (*nagrywać*) record **4.** (*do szkoły*) *Br* enrol (**do** *G* on), *Am* enroll (**do** *G* in) **5.** (*w testamencie*) bequeath **6.** *lek*: prescribe; **zapisywać się 1.** (*na kurs*) sign up (**na** *A* for), *Br* enrol (**na** *A* on), *Am* enroll (**na** *A* in) **2.** (*do klubu*, *parti*) join (**do** *G*)
zaplamić *v/p* → **plamić**
zaplanować *v/p* → **planować**; **zaplanowany** *adj* planned; **~ na następny tydzień** scheduled for next week
zaplatać ⟨**-leść**⟩ (*-tam*) *Br* plait, *Am* braid
zaplątywać się ⟨**-tać**⟩ (*-tuję*) tangle up
zaplecze *n* (*-cza*; *-cza*) **1.** (*sklepu*) back **2.** (*pomieszczenie służbowe*) backroom **3.** (*techniczne*, *intelektualne*) base
zapleść *v/p* → **zaplatać**
zapleśniały *adj Br* mouldy, *Am* moldy
zaplombować *v/p* → **plombować**
zapłacić *v/p* → **płacić**
zapładniać ⟨**-łodnić**⟩ (*-niam*) **1.** fertilize **2.** *kobietę*, *samicę*: inseminate
zapłakany *adj* **1.** *osoba*: in tears, weeping **2.** *oczy*: tear-filled
zapłata *f* (*-ty*; *no pl*) payment
zapłodnić *v/p* → **zapładniać**
zapłodnienie *n* (*-nia*; *no pl*) BIOL **1.** fertilization; **~ in vitro** in vitro fertilization **2.** (*kobiety*, *samicy*) insemination; **sztuczne ~** artificial insemination
zapłon *m* (*-nu*; *-ny*) AUTO ignition; **włącznik ~u** ignition switch; **mieć spóźniony ~** *fig* be slow off the mark
zapłonąć *v/p* (*-nę*) **1.** start burning, catch fire **2.** (*o ognisku*, *zniczu*) be lit
zapłonow|y *adj*: **świeca ~a** spark plug
zapobiegać ⟨**-biec**⟩ (*-gam*) prevent
zapobieganie *n* (*-nia*; *no pl*) prevention; **~ ciąży** birth control, contraception
zapobiegawcz|y *adj* preventive; **leczenie ~e** preventive treatment; **środki ~e** preventive measures
zapobiegliwy *adj* far-sighted, *form* provident
zapocony *adj* sweaty
zapoczątkowywać ⟨**-kować**⟩ (*-kowuję*) initiate, start
zapodziewać ⟨**-dziać**⟩ (*-wam*) misplace, lose; **zapodziewać się**: **zapodziały mi się klucze** I've mislaid my keys
zapominać ⟨**-mnieć**⟩ (*-nam*) forget (**o** *L* about); **zapomnijmy o tym!** let's forget about it!; **nie ~** not forget, remember; **~ języka w gębie** forget one's lines, lose one's tongue; **zapominać się** forget oneself

zapominalski **I** *adj* forgetful **II** *m* (*-kiego*; *-scy*), **-ka** *f* (*-kiej*; *-kie*) forgetful person; ***być ~m*** be forgetful
zapomniany *adj* forgotten
zapomnieć *v/p* → ***zapominać***
zapomnienie *n* (*-nia*; *no pl*) (*niepamięć*) oblivion; ***popaść w ~*** sink into oblivion
zapomoga *f* (*-gi*; *-gi*) aid, handout
zapora *f* (*-ry*; *-ry*); ***~ wodna*** water dam; ***~ drogowa*** roadblock; **zaporowy** *adj* **1.** *cło*: protective **2.** *ceny*: prohibitive **3.** ***ogień ~*** barrage
zapotnieć *v/p* → ***potnieć***
zapotrzebowanie *n* (*-nia*; *no pl*) demand (***na*** *A* for)
zapowiadać ⟨**-wiedzieć**⟩ (*-dam*) **1.** (*ogłaszać*) announce **2.** (*wróżyć*) indicate; ***nic nie zapowiada, że*** nothing indicates that **3.** (*mówić*) say; ***zapowiadać się***: ***dobrze się ~*** be promising; ***~ się z wizytą*** announce one's visit; ***zapowiada się ciepły dzień*** it's going to be hot today
zapowie|dź *f* (*-wiedzi*; *-wiedzi*) announcement; ***bez ~dzi*** unannounced
zapoznawać ⟨**-nać**⟩ (*-znaję*) **1.** acquaint (***z*** *I* with) **2.** (*przedstawiać*) introduce (***z*** *I* to); ***zapoznawać się*** **1.** familiarize oneself (***z*** *I* with) **2.** (*z osobą*) become acquainted (***z*** *I* with)
zapożyczać ⟨**-czyć**⟩ (*-czam*) borrow; ***zapożyczać się*** get into debt; ***~ się u*** *G* get into debt with
zapożyczenie *n* (*-nia*; *-nia*) borrowing; **zapożyczony** *adj* borrowed
zapracować *v/p* (*-cuję*) work hard (***na*** *A* for), earn (***na*** *A*)
zapracowany *adj* **1.** *osoba*: busy **2.** (*zarobiony*) earned; ***ciężko ~ pieniądz*** hard-earned money
zapracowywać się *v/im* (*-cowuję*) overwork
zaprać *v/p* → ***zapierać***[1]
zapragnąć *v/p* (*-nę*): ***~ coś zrobić*** feel a desire to do s.th.
zapraszać ⟨**-rosić**⟩ (*-szam*) invite (***na*** *A* to); ***~ na urodziny*** invite to one's birthday party; ***~ na imprezę*** invite to a party; ***~ do stołu*** invite to sit at the table
zaprawa *f* (*-wy*; *no pl*) **1.** BUILD mortar **2.** SPORT training
zaprawiać ⟨**-wić**⟩ (*-wiam*) **1.** (*dodawać przyprawy*) season **2.** (*trenować*) train; ***zaprawiać się*** (*trenować*) train
zapreliminować *v/p* → ***preliminować***
zaprezentować *v/p* → ***prezentować***
zaprocentować *v/p* → ***procentować***
zaprogramować *v/p* → ***programować***
zaprojektować *v/p* → ***projektować***
zaproponować *v/p* → ***proponować***
zaprosić *v/p* → ***zapraszać***
zaproszenie *n* (*-nia*; *-nia*) invitation
zaprotegować *v/p* → ***protegować***
zaprotestować *v/p* → ***protestować***
zaprotokołować *v/p* → ***protokołować***
zaprowadzać ⟨**-dzić**⟩ (*-dzam*) **1.** (*zabierać*) lead, take **2.** *zwyczaj*, *modę*: start, introduce **3.** *porządek*: establish
zaprószy|ć *v/p* (*-szę*): ***~ć ogień*** start a fire; ***~łem sobie oko piaskiem*** I got sand in my eye
zaprząc *v/p* → ***zaprzęgać***
zaprzątać ⟨**-tnąć**⟩ (*-tam*): ***~ kogoś*** absorb s.o.; ***~ sobie głowę*** *I* bother oneself with
zaprzeczać ⟨**-czyć**⟩ (*-czam*) deny; ***~ zarzutom*** deny the accusations; ***~ komuś*** disagree with s.o.; ***~ ruchem głowy*** shake one's head
zaprzeczenie *n* (*-nia*; *-nia*) (*sprostowanie*) denial
zaprzeć *v/p* → ***zapierać***[2]
zaprzedawać ⟨**-dać**⟩ (*-daję*) *lit* sell; ***~ duszę diabłu*** sell one's soul to the devil; ***zaprzedawać się*** sell oneself
zaprzepaszczać ⟨**-paścić**⟩ (*-czam*) *szansę*, *okazję*: waste
zaprzestawać ⟨**-tać**⟩ (*-taję*) cease, stop
zaprzęg *m* (*-gu*; *-gi*) team; ***psi ~*** dog sled team; ***wyścigi psich ~ów*** dog-sled racing
zaprzęgać ⟨**-gnąć**, **-rząc**⟩ (*-gam*) harness (***do*** *G* to); ***zaprzężony w dwa konie*** drawn by two horses
zaprzyjaźniać się ⟨**-nić**⟩ (*-niam*) make friends (***z*** *I* with)
zaprzyjaźni|ony *adj*: ***są ~eni*** they are friends; ***być ~onym z*** *I* be friends with
zaprzysięgać ⟨**-siąc**⟩ (*-gam*) **1.** swear; ***~ zemstę*** swear revenge; ***~ sobie*** promise oneself **2.** *prezydenta*: swear in

zaprzysięgły *adj zwolennik, przeciwnik*: avowed
zaprzysiężenie *n (-nia; -nia) (uroczystość)* swearing-in ceremony
zapuchły, **zapuchnięty** *adj* swollen
zapusty *pl (-tów)* the last days of carnival, Shrovetide *sing*
zapuszczać ⟨**-puścić**⟩ *(-czam)* **1.** *włosy, brodę*: grow **2.** *krople*: *Br* instil, *Am* instill **3.** *silnik*: start **4.** *dom, ogród*: neglect **5.** *korzenie*: put down **6.** **~ żurawia** *infml* peep; **zapuszczać się** **1.** *(docierać)* venture (**do** *G* into) **2.** *(przestawać o siebie dbać) infml* neglect oneself; **zapuszczony** *adj* neglected
zapychać ⟨**-pchać**⟩ *(-cham)* block, jam; **zapychać się** *(o rurze)* block up
zapylać ⟨**-lić**⟩ *(-lam) rośliny*: pollinate; **zapylanie** *n (-nia; no pl)* BIOL pollination; **zapylony** *adj roślina*: pollinated
zapytać *v/p* → **pytać**
zapytanie *n (-nia; -nia)* query, question; **~ poselskie** parliamentary query
zapyziały *adj infml* shabby, sleazy
zarabiać ⟨**-robić**⟩ *(-biam)* **1.** earn; **~ na życie** earn a living; **ile zarabiasz?** how much do you earn?, how much money do you make? **2.** *ciasto*: knead
zaradcz|y *adj*: **środki ~e a)** *(likwidujące skutki)* remedial measures **b)** *(zapobiegające)* preventive measures
zaradny *adj* resourceful
zaradzać ⟨**-dzić**⟩ *(-dzam)* find a remedy for, remedy
zarastać ⟨**-rosnąć**⟩ *(-tam)* **1.** **ogród zarósł chwastami** the garden's overgrown with weeds; **~ brudem** become covered with dirt **2.** *(zabliźniać się)* skin over
zaraz **I** *adv* in a minute, *infml* in a jiffy; **od ~** right now; **kierowca potrzebny od zaraz** driver needed immediately; **~!** I'm on my way!; **~, ~** wait a second; **~ wrócę** I'll be right back **II** *particle* right; **~ po** *L* right after; **~ po powrocie** as soon as s.o. gets back
zaraza *f (-zy; no pl)* plague
zarazki *pl (-ków)* germs
zarazem *adv* at the same time, at once
zaraźliwy *adj* contagious, infectious, catchy; **zarażać** ⟨**-razić**⟩ *(-żam)* infect (*I* with), give (*I*); **zarażać się** become infected, catch; **zarażony** *adj (chorobą)* infected
zardzewiały *adj* rusty; **zardzewieć** *v/p* → **rdzewieć**
zareagować *v/p* → **reagować**
zarejestrować *v/p* → **rejestrować**
zareklamować *v/p* → **reklamować**
zarekomendować *v/p* → **rekomendować**
zarekwirować *v/p* → **rekwirować**
zarepetować *v/p* → **repetować**
zarezerwować *v/p* → **rezerwować**
zaręczać ⟨**-czyć**⟩ *(-czam)* assure, assert, guarantee; **zaręczam, że** I assure you that; **~ za** *A* guarantee for; **zaręczać się** get engaged; **zaręczony** *adj* engaged; **zaręczyny** *pl (-czyn)* engagement
zarob|ek *m (-bku; -bki)* **1.** *(zapłata)* earnings *pl*, pay, income; **dla ~ku** for money; **źródło ~ku** source of income **2.** *(zysk)* profit
zarobić *v/p* → **zarabiać**
zarobkowo *adv*: **pracować ~** be gainfully employed; **atrakcyjny ~** financially rewarding
zarobkow|y *adj*: **praca ~a** gainful employment; **możliwości ~e** earning capacity; **emigracja ~a** emigration for economic reasons
zarod|ek *m (-dka; -dki)* **1.** *(embrion)* embryo; **zdusić coś w ~ku** *fig* nip s.th. in the bud **2.** *(rośliny)* germ; **zarodnik** *m (-ka; -ki)* BIOL spore
zarosnąć *v/p* → **zarastać**
zarost *m (-tu; no pl)* **1.** *(broda)* beard; **trzydniowy ~** three days' stubble **2.** *(na piersiach)* chest hair
zarośla *pl (-li)* shrubbery *sing*, thicket *sing*; **gęste ~** thick brushwood, dense thicket
zarośnięty *adj* **1.** *(pokryty roślinnością)* overgrown (*I* with) **2.** *(nieogolony)* unshaven
zarozumialec *m (-lca; -lcy) infml* bighead, stuck-up twit; **zarozumialstwo** *n (-wa; no pl)* conceit, *infml* big-headedness
zarozumiałość *f (-ści; no pl)* conceit
zarozumiały *adj* conceited, bigheaded
zarówno *conj*: **~..., jak i** both... and
zaróżowiony *adj* rosy, pink

zarumienić się *v/p* → ***rumienić się***; ***zarumieniony*** *adj* **1.** *ciasto*: browned **2.** *policzki*: blushing
zarwać *v/p* → ***zarywać***
zarybiać ⟨*-bić*⟩ (*-biam*) (*narybkiem*) stock with fry
zaryglować *v/p* → ***ryglować***; ***zaryglowany*** *adj* bolted
zarys *m* (*-su*; *-sy*) **1.** (*kontur*) outline; ***w głównych ~ach*** in broad outline **2.** (*szkic*) sketch, draft
zarysowywać ⟨*-sować*⟩ (*-sowuję*) **1.** *arkusz*: cover with drawings **2.** *powierzchnię*: scratch **3.** *fig* outline; ***zarysowywać się*** **1.** (*uszkadzać się*) get scratched **2.** *fig* appear, emerge
zarywać ⟨*-rwać*⟩ (*-wam*): ***~ noc*** *infml* stay up all night, sit up all night
zarząd *m* (*-du*; *-dy*) **1.** (*zespół ludzi*) (executive) board, management board **2.** (*zarządzanie*, *instytucja*) administration, management
zarządzać ⟨*-dzić*⟩ (*-dzam*) **1.** manage **2.** *firmą*: run **3.** (*wydawać polecenie*) order **4.** (*wydawać dekret*) decree
zarządzenie *n* (*-nia*; *-nia*) order, directive
zarządzić *v/p* → ***zarządzać***
zarzekać się *v/im* (*-kam*) swear
zarzewie *n* (*-wia*; *-wia*) *lit* hotbed
zarzucać ⟨*-cić*⟩ (*-cam*) **I** *v/t* **1.** ***~ komuś ręce na szyję*** put one's arms around s.o.'s neck; ***~ coś na ramię*** shoulder s.th.; ***~ płaszcz*** throw on a coat; ***~ kogoś pytaniami*** bombard s.o. with questions **2.** *sieć*, *wędkę*: cast **3.** (*rezygnować*) give up, abandon **4.** (*winić*) ***~ komuś*** *A* blame s.o. for, accuse s.o. of **II** *v/i* ***samochodem zarzuciło*** the car fishtailed
zarzuceni|e: ***co masz mu do ~a?*** what do you have against him?; ***nie mieć komuś nic do ~a*** find no fault with s.o.
zarzucony *adj* (*pokryty*) covered (*I* with)
zarzut *m* (*-tu*; *-ty*) **1.** accusation; ***czynić komuś ~y*** blame s.o.; ***bez ~u*** flawless, faultless **2.** JUR charge; ***aresztować kogoś pod ~em czegoś*** arrest s.o. on a charge of s.th.; ***odpowiadać na ~y*** answer charges
zarzynać ⟨*-rżnąć*⟩ (*-nam*) *bydło*: butcher, slaughter
zasad|a[1] *f* (*-dy*; *-dy*) **1.** (*reguła*) rule; ***~y gry*** rules of the game; ***~y ortografii*** spelling rules; ***przestrzegać ~*** comply with the rules, observe the rules; ***z ~y*** basically, as a rule; ***w ~zie*** actually, as a matter of fact **2.** ***~y*** (*warunki*) conditions **3.** (*reguła*, *podstawa*) principle; ***człowiek bez ~*** unprincipled man **4.** (*podstawa*) basis; ***na tej ~zie*** on that basis; ***na ~zie dobrowolności*** on a voluntary basis
zasada[2] *f* (*-dy*; *-dy*) CHEM base
zasadniczo *adv* basically; **zasadnicz|y** *adj* **1.** (*podstawowy*) basic, elementary, fundamental; ***ustawa ~a*** constitution; ***służba ~a*** mandatory military service; ***pensja ~a*** basic salary; ***odgrywać ~ą rolę*** play a key role **2.** (*z zasadami*) principled
zasadowy *adj* CHEM alkaline
zasadzać ⟨*-dzić*⟩ (*-dzam*) **1.** plant **2.** (*w doniczce*) pot; ***zasadzać się*** (*opierać się*) be based (***na*** *L* on), be grounded (***na*** *L* on/in)
zasadzka *f* (*-ki*; *-ki*) ambush
zasalać ⟨*-solić*⟩ (*-lam*) pickle in brine
zasalutować *v/p* → ***salutować***
zasapać się *v/p* (*-pię*) be out of breath, start panting; ***zasapany*** *adj* breathless, panting for breath
zasądzać ⟨*-dzić*⟩ (*-dzam*) JUR adjudge
zaschły → ***zaschnięty***
zaschnąć *v/p* → ***zasychać***
zaschnięty *adj* **1.** *klej*: set **2.** *błoto*, *krew*: caked
zaserwować *v/p* → ***serwować***
zasępiać się ⟨*-pić*⟩ (*-piam*) *lit* be sad, be distressed; ***zasępiony*** *adj* gloomy, sullen
zasiać *v/p* (*-sieję*): ***~ w kimś wątpliwości*** sow the seeds of doubt in s.o.'s mind; ***było cicho jak makiem zasiał*** you could hear a pin drop; → ***zasiewać***
zasiadać ⟨*-siąść*⟩ (*-dam*) *lit* **1.** (*siadać*) sit down, take one's seat; ***~ do stołu*** sit at the table; ***zasiąść na tronie*** *fig* ascend the throne **2.** (*być*) be; ***~ w komisji*** be on a committee; ***~ na ławie oskarżonych*** be in the dock; ***~ na tronie*** rule
zasiedlać ⟨*-lić*⟩ (*-lam*) settle, populate

Z

zasiedzenie *n* (*-nia*; *no pl*) JUR (positive) prescription; ***przez ~*** by prescription
zasiedzieć się *v/p* (*-dzę*): ***~ u kogoś*** stay too long at s.o.'s place
zasieki *pl* (*-ków*): ***~ z drutu kolczastego*** barbed-wire entanglements, *Am* barbwire entanglements
zasiewać ⟨**-siać**⟩ (*-wam*) sow
zasięg *m* (*-gu*; *-gi*) range, reach; ***w ~u wzroku*** within sight; ***w ~u ręki*** within arm's reach; ***~ wpływów*** sphere of influence; ***pociski dalekiego ~u*** long-range missiles; ***~ nadajnika*** broadcast coverage
zasięgać ⟨**-gnąć**⟩ (*-gam*): ***~ czyjejś rady*** ask s.o.'s advice, consult s.o.; ***~ czyjejś opinii*** consult s.o.; ***~ informacji na temat*** *G* find out about
zasilacz *m* (*-cza*; *-cze*) power supply unit
zasilać ⟨**-lić**⟩ (*-lam*) power, provide, feed; ***~ w energię*** provide energy
zasilanie *n* (*-nia*; *no pl*) power, energy supply
zasiłek *m* (*-łku*; *-łki*) benefit; ***~ dla bezrobotnych*** unemployment benefit, *infml* the dole; ***~ chorobowy*** sickness benefit; ***~ macierzyński*** maternity benefit
zaskakiwać ⟨**-skoczyć**⟩ (*-kuję*) **1.** (*zadziwiać*) surprise, take by surprise **2.** (*rozumieć*) *infml* latch on **3.** (*wprawiać w zakłopotanie*) embarrass; **zaskakujący** *adj* surprising
zaskarżać ⟨**-żyć**⟩ (*-żam*): ***~ kogoś do sądu*** sue s.o.; ***~ wyrok*** appeal against a ruling
zasklepiać się ⟨**-pić**⟩ (*-piam*) (*o ranie*) close up, heal over
zaskoczenie *n* (*-nia*; *-nia*) surprise, astonishment; **zaskoczony** *adj* surprised, astonished; ***mile ~*** pleasently surprised; **zaskoczyć** *v/p* → ***zaskakiwać***
zaskórniaki *pl* (*-ków*) *infml* nest egg *sing*
zaskroniec *m* (*-rońca*; *-rońce*) grass snake
zasłabnąć *v/p* (*-nę*) collapse, faint
zasłać *v/p* → ***zaścielać***
zasłaniać ⟨**-łonić**⟩ (*-niam*) **1.** cover; ***~ od wiatru*** protect from the wind; ***~ usta ręką*** cover one's mouth with one's hand **2.** *widok*, *światło*: block **3.** *twarz*: hide **4.** *zasłonę*, *firankę*: draw **5.** *oczy*: cover up, protect; **zasłaniać się 1.** (*zakrywać się*) cover oneself **2.** (*chronić się*) protect oneself **3.** (*tłumaczyć się*) ***~ się czymś*** use s.th. as an excuse
zasłona *f* (*-ny*; *-ny*) curtain; ***~ dymna*** smoke screen
zasłonić *v/p* → ***zasłaniać***
zasłonki *pl* (*-nek*) curtains
zasłuchać się *v/p* (*-cham*) become engrossed (***w*** *A* in)
zasług|a *f* (*-gi*; *-gi*) service; ***~i*** (*wkład*) contribution; ***to nie jej ~a*** she doesn't deserve the credit
zasługiwać ⟨**-łużyć**⟩ (*-guję*) deserve (***na*** *A*); ***~ na uwagę*** be worthy of notice, be worth paying attention to
zasłużenie *adv* deservedly, justly; **zasłużony** *adj* (well-)deserved; ***~ urlop*** well-earned holiday
zasłużyć się *v/p* (*-żę*): ***~ dla kraju*** render great services to one's country; → ***zasługiwać***
zasłynąć *v/p* (*-nę*) gain fame (***jako*** *N* as), become famous (***z*** *G* for)
zasmakować *v/p* (*-kuję*) acquire a taste (***w*** *L* for)
zasmarkany *adj* snotty
zasmarowywać ⟨**-rować**⟩ (*-rowuję*) **1.** (*bazgrać*) scrawl **2.** (*mazać*) smear
zasmażka *f* (*-ki*; *-ki*) COOK roux
zasmucać ⟨**-cić**⟩ (*-cam*) upset, sadden
zasmucony *adj* sad, unhappy
zasnąć *v/p* (*-nę*): ***~ na wieki*** *fig* pass away; → ***zasypiać***
zasnuwać ⟨**-nuć**⟩ (*-wam*) envelope, cover
zasobny *adj lit* affluent; ***~ w*** *A* abundant in, rich in
zasolenie *n* (*-nia*; *no pl*) salinity; **zasolić** *v/p* → ***zasalać***
zas|ób *m* (*-sobu*; *-soby*) resource; ***~oby naturalne*** natural resources; ***bogaty ~ób słownictwa*** rich vocabulary; ***bogaty ~ób wiedzy*** broad knowledge
zaspa *f* (*-py*; *-py*) snowdrift
zaspać *v/p* (*zaśpię*) (*do szkoły, pracy*) oversleep
zaspany *adj* sleepy
zaspokajać ⟨**-koić**⟩ (*-jam*) **1.** *potrzeby*: meet, *Br* fulfil, *Am* fulfill **2.** *głód*, *cie-*

kawość, *kobietę*: satisfy **3.** *pragnienie*: quench
zaspokojenie *n* (*-nia*; *no pl*) satisfaction, gratification; **~ seksualne** sexual satisfaction
zasrany *adj fig vulg* lousy, crappy
zastać *v/p* → **zastawać**
zastały *adj* **1.** *woda*: stagnant **2.** *powietrze*: stale
zastanawiać ⟨**-nowić**⟩ (*-wiam*): **~ kogoś** puzzle s.o.; **zastanawiać się** think (**nad** *I* about); **zastanawiam się, dlaczego** I wonder why; **zastanowię się** I'll think about it; **zastanów się** (*przemyśl*) think it over
zastanawiający *adj* puzzling
zastanowić *v/p* → **zastanawiać**
zastanowieni|e *n* (*-nia*; *no pl*) reflection; **bez ~a** without thinking; **po długim ~u** after thinking for a long time, after much thought
zastany *adj* existing
zastarzały *adj konflikt*: old-standing
zastaw *m* (*-wu*; *-wy*) pledge, deposit; **oddać coś w ~ a)** put s.th. in pledge, pledge s.th. **b)** (*w lombardzie*) pawn s.th.
zastawa *f* (*-wy*; *-wy*) set; **~ stołowa** tableware set; **~ do kawy** coffee service
zastawać ⟨**-tać**⟩ (*-taję*) find; **nie zastałem jej** (**w domu**) she wasn't at home, she wasn't in; **czy zastałem pana Kowalskiego** is Mr. Kowalski in?
zastawiać ⟨**-wić**⟩ (*-wiam*) **1.** *drzwi*: block **2.** *pułapkę*: lay, set **3.** (*oddawać w zastaw*) pawn
zastawka *f* (*-ki*; *-ki*) valve
zastąpić *v/p* → **zastępować**
zastąpieni|e *n* (*-nia*; *no pl*) replacement; **nie do ~a** irreplaceable
zastęp *m* (*-pu*; *-py*) *harcerzy*: patrol
zastępca *m* (*-cy*; *-cy*), **-czyni** *f* (*-ni*; *-nie*) **1.** (*tymczasowy*) replacement, substitution **2.** (*stały*) deputy, assistant; **~ dyrektora** assistant manager
zastępczo *adv* as a substitute
zastępcz|y *adj* substitute; **mieszkanie ~e** substitute accommodation; **rodzina ~a** foster family; **matka ~a** surrogate mother
zastępować ⟨**-tąpić**⟩ (*-puję*) **1.** substitute for **2. ~ komuś drogę** bar s.o.'s way
zastępstwo *n* (*-wa*; *-wa*) replacement, substitution
zastopować *v/p* → **stopować**
zastosować *v/p* → **stosować**; **zastosowanie** *n* (*-nia*; *-nia*) application, use
zastój *m* (*-toju*; *no pl*) stagnation, standstill
zastraszający *adj* alarming
zastraszyć *v/p* (*-szę*) intimidate
zastrzegać ⟨**-rzec**⟩ (*-gam*): **~ (sobie)** reserve; **~ sobie prawo do** *G* reserve the right to; **zastrzegać się** make it clear (that)
zastrzelić *v/p* (*-lę*) shoot dead
zastrzeże|nie *n* (*-nia*; *-nia*) **1.** reservation; **mieć ~nia co do** *G* have reservations about; **bez ~ń** without reservations; **z ~niem zmian** subject to alteration **2.** (*w umowie*) provision
zastrzeżon|y *adj*: **znak handlowy prawnie ~y** registered trademark; **wszelkie prawa ~e** all rights reserved; **numer ~y** unlisted telephone number
zastrzyk *m* (*-ku*; *-ki*) injection, *infml* shot; **zrobić komuś ~** give s.o. an injection
zastygać ⟨**-gnąć**⟩ (*-gam*) set
zasugerować *v/p* → **sugerować**
zasunąć *v/p* → **zasuwać**
zasuszać ⟨**-szyć**⟩ (*-szam*) *kwiaty*, *zioła*: dry
zasuwa *f* (*-wy*; *-wy*) bolt
zasuwać ⟨**-sunąć**⟩ (*-wam*) **1.** *szufladę*: push shut **2.** *firankę*: draw **3.** *v/im* (*jechać*) *infml* nip along **4.** *v/im* (*pracować*) *infml* beaver away
zasuwka *f* (*-ki*; *-ki*) → **zasuwa**
zasychać ⟨**-schnąć**⟩ (*-cham*) dry (out); **zaschło mi w gardle** my throat is dry
zasygnalizować *v/p* → **sygnalizować**
zasymilować się *v/p* → **asymilować się**
zasypać *v/p* → **zasypywać**
zasypiać ⟨**-snąć**⟩ (*-piam*) (*zapadać w sen*) fall asleep
zasypka *f* (*-ki*; *-ki*) powder; **~ dla niemowląt** baby powder
zasypywać ⟨**-pać**⟩ (*-puję*) **1.** *dół*: fill **2.** *górników*: bury **3.** *fig* flood (*I* with)
zaszaleć *v/p* (*-leję*) go on a spree
zaszczepić *v/p* → **szczepić**
zaszczuć *v/p* (*-czuję*) **1.** bait to death, **2.** *fig* hound

zaszczycać ⟨**-cić**⟩ (*-cam*) *Br* honour, *Am* honor
zaszczycony *adj*: **czuć się ~m** *Br* feel honoured, *Am* feel honored
zaszczyt *m* (*-tu*; *-ty*) *Br* honour, *Am* honor; **mieć ~ coś zrobić** have the honour to do s.th.; **zaszczytn|y** *adj Br* honourable, *Am* honorable; **~e miejsce** place of honour
zaszeregowywać ⟨**-gować**⟩ (*-gowuję*) classify
zaszkodzić *v/p* → **szkodzić**
zasznurować *v/p* → **sznurować**
zaszokować *v/p* → **szokować**
zaszpanować *v/p* → **szpanować**
zasztyletować *v/p* (*-tuję*) stab to death
zaszufladkować *v/p* → **szufladkować**
zaszyć *v/p* → **zaszywać**
zaszyfrować *v/p* → **szyfrować**
zaszywać ⟨**-szyć**⟩ (*-wam*) *dziurę*: sew up, stitch up; **zaszywać się** hole up
zaś *conj* (*przeciwstawienie*) while, on the other hand
zaścianek *m* (*-nka*; *-nki*) **1.** *fig* backwater **2.** *HIST village inhabited by petty gentry*; **zaściankow|y** *fig* parochial; **szlachta ~a** *HIST petty gentry*
zaścielać ⟨**zasłać**⟩ (*-lam*): **~ łóżko** make the bed
zaślepiać ⟨**-pić**⟩ (*-piam*) **1.** (*o miłości, nienawiści*) blind **2.** (*zatykać*) plug (up), close
zaślepienie *n* (*-nia*; *no pl*) *fig* **1.** blindness **2.** (*miłosne*) infatuation; **zaślepiony** *adj fig* blind
zaślubiać ⟨**-bić**⟩ (*-biam*) *lit* wed; **zaślubiny** *pl* (*-bin*) *lit* nuptials
zaśmiecać ⟨**-cić**⟩ (*-cam*) **1.** *ulice*: litter **2.** *pokój*, *pamięć*: clutter up
zaśniedziały *adj* tarnished; **zaśniedzieć** *v/p* → **śniedzieć**
zaśnieżony *adj* snowy, snow-covered
zaśpiewać *v/p* → **śpiewać**
zaświadczać ⟨**-czyć**⟩ (*-czam*) testify, certify; **zaświadczenie** *n* (*-nia*; *-nia*) certificate; **~ lekarskie** medical certificate
zaświat|y *pl* (*-tów*) the spirit world *sing*; **z ~ów** from the beyond
zaświecić *v/p* (*-cę*) *lampę*: turn on, switch on; **zaświecić się 1.** (*o lampie*) go on **2.** (*o oczach*) light up
zaświnić *v/p* → **świnić**
zaświtać *v/p* → **świtać**

zataczać ⟨**-toczyć**⟩ (*-czam*): **~ łuk** describe a curve; **~ koło** describe a circle; **~ coraz szersze kręgi** *fig* spread (wider and wider); **zataczać się** stagger
zatajać ⟨**-taić**⟩ (*-jam*) withhold, conceal
zatamować *v/p* → **tamować**
zatankować *v/p* → **tankować**
zatańczyć *v/p* → **tańczyć**
zatapiać ⟨**-topić**⟩ (*-piam*) **1.** *teren*: flood **2.** *statek*: sink
zatarasować *v/p* → **tarasować**
zatarg *m* (*-gu*; *-gi*) conflict, dispute
zatelefonować *v/p* → **telefonować**
zatem *conj*: (**a**) **~** *lit* so (that), therefore, then
zatemperować *v/p* → **temperować**
zatęchły *adj* musty, *Br* mouldy, *Am* moldy
zatęsknić *v/p* (*-nię*) miss (**za** *I*)
zatkać *v/p* → **zatykać**[1]
zatknąć *v/p* → **zatykać**[2]
zatłoczony *adj* crowded
zatłuc *v/p* (*-łukę*): **~ na śmierć** beat to death, batter to death
zatłuszczony *adj* greasy; **zatłuścić** *v/p* → **tłuścić**
zatoczyć *v/p* → **zataczać**
zatok|a *f* (*-ki*; *-ki*) **1.** (*mała*) bay **2.** (*duża*) gulf **3.** *AUTO* lay-by **4.** *ANAT* sinus; **zapalenie ~** sinusitis **5. ~a niskiego ciśnienia** (*w meteorologii*) (low-pressure) trough: **~a wysokiego ciśnienia** (high-pressure) ridge
zatonąć *v/p* → **tonąć**; **zatonięcie** *n* (*-cia*; *-cia*) sinking
zatopić *v/p* → **zatapiać**
zatopiony *adj* **1.** *statek*: sunken; **~ przez niszczyciel** sunk by a destroyer **2. ~ w myślach** *fig* deep in thought, immersed in thought
zator *m* (*-ru*; *-ry*) **1.** (*w ruchu*) (traffic) hold-up **2.** *MED* embolus; **~ mózgu** cerebral embolism
zatracać ⟨**-cić**⟩ (*-cam*) *lit* lose; **zatracać się** *fig* lose oneself (**w** *L* in)
zatrąbić *v/p* → **trąbić**
zatriumfować *v/p* → **triumfować**
zatroskany *adj lit* worried
zatroszczyć się *v/p* → **troszczyć się**
zatrucie *n* (*-cia*; *-cia*) poisoning; **~ pokarmowe** food poisoning
zatruć *v/p* (*-ruję*) poison; → **zatruwać**; **zatruć się** → **zatruwać się**

zatrudniać ⟨**-nić**⟩ (*-niam*) employ; ***firma zatrudni kierowcę*** lorry driver wanted; ***zatrudnić się*** to get a job
zatrudnienie *n* (*-nia*; *no pl*) employment, work; ***znaleźć ~*** find employment; ***pełne ~*** full employment
zatrudniony **I** *adj* employed (**w** *L* in) **II** *m* (*-nego*; *-dnieni*), **-na** *f* (*-nej*; *-ne*) employee, worker
zatruty *adj* poisoned
zatruwać ⟨**-ruć**⟩ (*-wam*) **1.** *żywność*: poison **2.** *powietrze*: pollute, poison **3**. *glebę*: contaminate **4.** *ząb*: devitalize **5.** *atmosferę*: sour **6.** ***~ komuś życie*** make s.o.'s life unbearable; ***zatruć się*** be poisoned
zatrważać ⟨**-wożyć**⟩ (*-żam*) *Br* appal, *Am* appall; **zatrważający** *adj lit* appalling
zatrzask *m* (*-ku*; *-ki*) (*przy ubraniu*) press stud, snap fastener
zatrzaskiwać ⟨**-snąć**⟩ (*-kuję*) *drzwi*: slam; ***zatrzaskiwać się*** **1.** (*o drzwiach*) slam **2.** (*o osobie*) get stuck (**w** *L* in)
zatrząść *v/p* → **trząść**
zatrzeć *v/p* → **zacierać**
zatrzepotać *v/p* → **trzepotać**
zatrzeszczeć *v/p* → **trzeszczeć**
zatrzęsienie *n* (*-nia*; *no pl*) *infml* heaps of
zatrzymać *v/p* → **zatrzymywać**
zatrzymanie *n* (*-nia*; *-nia*) JUR detention
zatrzymywać ⟨**-mać**⟩ (*-muję*) **1.** stop; ***zatrzymały mnie ważne sprawy*** I had some important business to attend to **2.** *złodzieja*, *podejrzanego*: detain **3.** (*zachowywać*) keep; ***~ coś dla siebie*** keep s.th. to oneself; ***zatrzymywać się*** stop; ***zatrzymaliśmy się w hotelu*** we are staying at a hotel
zatuszować *v/p* → **tuszować**
zatwardzenie *n* (*-nia*; *-nia*) constipation; ***mieć ~*** be constipated
zatwardziały *adj* **1.** *przestępca*: habitual **2.** *kawaler*: confirmed
zatwierdzać ⟨**-dzić**⟩ (*-dzam*) *plan*, *projekt*: approve, sign off
zatyczk|a *f* (*-ki*; *-ki*) plug, stopper; ***~i do uszu*** earplugs; ***~a do długopisu*** ballpen cap; ***wyciągnąć ~ę*** (***z wanny***) pull out a plug
zatykać[1] ⟨**-tkać**⟩ (*-kam*) **1.** block; ***~ sobie uszy*** plug one's ears; ***zatkało mnie*** *infml* I was speechless **2.** *butelkę*: cork; ***zatykać się*** clog up, block up
zatykać[2] ⟨**-tknąć**⟩ (*-kam*) **1.** *flagę*: stick **2.** ***~ za pasek*** put behind one's belt
zatytułować *v/p* → **tytułować**
zaufać *v/p* → **ufać**
zaufani|e *n* (*-nia*; *no pl*) confidence, trust; ***mieć ~e do kogoś*** trust s.o.; ***brak ~a*** lack of trust, distrust; ***godny ~a*** trustworthy; ***w ~u*** in confidence; ***telefon ~a*** helpline
zaufany *adj* trusted
zaułek *m* (*-łku*; *-łki*) backstreet; ***ślepy ~*** blind alley
zautomatyzować *v/p* → **automatyzować**; **zautomatyzowany** *adj* automated
zauważać ⟨**-żyć**⟩ (*-żam*) notice; ***dawać się zauważyć*** be noticeable; ***chciałbym zauważyć, że*** I'd like to point out that
zawada *f* (*-dy*; *-dy*) *fig* hindrance, obstacle
zawadiacki *adj* swashbuckling, daring; **zawadiaka** *m* (*-ki*; *-ki*/*-diacy*) swashbuckler
zawadzać ⟨**-dzić**⟩ (*-dzam*) **1.** (*zahaczać*) catch **2.** (*przeszkadzać*) ***~ komuś*** be in s.o.'s way
zawahać się *v/p* (*-ham*) hesitate; ***nie ~ przed użyciem przemocy*** do not hesitate to use violence
zawalać ⟨**-lić**⟩ (*-lam*) **1.** *mieszkanie*: clutter **2.** *egzamin*: bungle; ***zawalać się*** (*o tunelu*, *dole*) collapse
zawał *m* (*-łu*; *-ły*): ***~ serca*** heart attack
zawarcie *n* (*-cia*; *no pl*) **1.** *umowy*: conclusion **2.** ***~ małżeństwa*** marriage, entering into marriage
zawartość *f* (*-ści*; *no pl*) **1.** *torby*, *szafy*, *kieliszka*: contents **2.** *tłuszczu*, *alkoholu*: content
zaważyć *v/p* (*-żę*) influence (**na** *L*), have impact (**na** *L* on)
zawczasu *adv* beforehand, in advance
zawdzięczać *v/im* (*-czam*) owe; ***wiele komuś ~*** owe a lot to s.o.
zawekować *v/p* → **wekować**
zawędrować *v/p* (*-ruję*) (*zajść*) reach (**do** *G*)
zawiać *v/p* → **zawiewać**
zawiadamiać ⟨**-domić**⟩ (*-miam*) inform (**o** *L* about), notify (**o** *L* about)

zawiadomienie *n* (*-nia*; *-nia*) notification
zawiadowca *m* (*-cy*; *-cy*): **~ stacji** stationmaster
zawiany *adj infml* tipsy
zawias *m* (*-su*; *-sy*) hinge; **wyjąć drzwi z ~ów** unhinge a door
zawiązywać ⟨**-zać**⟩ (*-zuję*) **1.** tie; **~ supeł** tie a knot; **~ komuś oczy** blindfold s.o. **2.** *sznurowadła*: do up; **zawiązywać się 1.** (*o stowarzyszeniu*) be established **2.** (*o owocu*) set
zawiedziony *adj* disappointed
zawieja *f* (*-wiei*; *-je*) blizzard, snowstorm
zawierać ⟨**-wrzeć**⟩ (*-ram*) **1.** (*obejmować*) include **2.** (*mieścić*) contain; **~ sól** contain salt **3.** (*wstępować w*) **~ związek małżeński** enter into marriage; **~ związek małżeński z** *I* marry **4.** *pokój*: make **5.** *umowę*: conclude; **zawierać się** be (a) part (**w** *L* of), be included (**w** *L* in)
zawierucha *f* (*-chy*; *-chy*) gusty weather; **~ śnieżna** snowstorm; **~ wojenna** *fig* the turmoil of war
zawieruszyć *v/p* (*-szę*) mislay; **zawieruszyć się** get mislaid
zawierzać ⟨**-rzyć**⟩ (*-rzam*) *lit* **1.** (*ufać*) trust **2.** (*powierzać*) entrust
zawiesić *v/p* → **zawieszać**
zawiesisty *adj* thick
zawieszać ⟨**-sić**⟩ (*-szam*) **1.** (*wieszać*) hang **2.** (*pokrywać*) cover **3.** (*przerywać*) suspend; **~ karę** suspend a sentence; **~ kogoś w czynnościach urzędowych** suspend s.o.; **zawieszać się** (*o komputerze*) hang up, crash
zawieszeni|e *n* (*-nia*; *no pl*) suspension; **wyrok w ~u** suspended sentence; **dostać dwa lata w ~u** get (a) two years suspended sentence; **~e broni** ceasefire
zawieszony *adj* suspended; **~ w obowiązkach służbowych** suspended in official duties
zawietrzn|y *adj*: **strona ~a** leeward (side)
zawiewać ⟨**zawiać**⟩ (*-wam*) **1.** (*o wietrze*) blow **2.** (*pokrywać*) cover **3. zawiało go** (*przeziębił się*) he got a cold
zawieźć *v/p* → **zawozić**
zawijać ⟨**-winąć**⟩ (*-jam*) **1.** (*owijać*) wrap up **2.** *rękawy*, *nogawki*: roll up **3.** (*do portu*) enter (**do** *G*); **zawijać się** (*o włosach*) curl up
zawijas *m* (*-sa*; *-sy*) flourish
zawikłać *v/p* → **wikłać**; **zawikłany** *adj* complicated, convoluted
zawile *adv* → **zawiły**
zawilec *m* (*-lca*; *-lce*) BIOL anemone
zawilgły *adj* damp
zawilgnąć *v/p* (*-nę*) get damp
zawiły *adj* **1.** complex, complicated **2.** *wzory*, *akcja*: intricate
zawinąć *v/p* → **zawijać**
zawiniątko *n* (*-ka*; *-ka*) bundle
zawinić *v/p*: **to ona zawiniła** *lit* she is to blame; **kto zawinił?** *lit* who's to blame?
zawiniony *adj* culpable
zawisać ⟨**-snąć**⟩ (*-sam*) **1.** hang (**nad** *I* over); **~ w powietrzu** hang in the air **2.** (*o skazańcu*) be hanged
zawistny *adj* envious
zawiść *f* (*-ści*; *no pl*) envy
zawitać *v/p* (*-tam*) *lit* **1.** (*odwiedzić*) visit **2.** (*o wiośnie*) come
zawlec *v/p* (*-lokę*/*-lekę*) draw, drag; **zawlec się** drag oneself, crawl
zawładnąć *v/p* (*-nę*) *krajem*, *wyobraźnią*: capture
zawodnik *m* (*-ka*; *-nicy*), **-niczka** *f* (*-ki*; *-ki*) SPORT competitor
zawodny *adj* unreliable
zawodowiec *m* (*-wca*; *-wcy*) professional, *infml* pro
zawodowo *adv* professionally; **uprawiać sport ~** be a professional player, play sport professionally; **zawodow|y** *adj* professional; **szkoła ~a** vocational school; **choroba ~a** occupational disease; **związek ~y** trade union
zawodówka *f* (*-ki*; *-ki*) *infml* vocational school
zawody *pl* (*-dów*) SPORT competition *sing*; **~ o mistrzostwo Europy** European championship; **iść w ~ z** *I fig* compete with
zawodzić[1] ⟨**-wieść**⟩ (*-dzę*) **I** *v/t* **1.** *oczekiwania*: fall short of **2.** *osobę*: let down **II** *v/i* **1.** (*o pamięci*, *systemie*, *siłach*) fail **2.** (*o planach*) fall through; **zawodzić się** be disappointed (**na** *L* with)
zawodzić[2] *v/im* (*-dzę*) **1.** (*płakać*) wail, lament **2.** (*o wietrze*) moan, wail

Z

zawojować *v/p* (*-juję*) conquer
zawołać *v/p* → **wołać**
zawołanie: ***być na czyjeś każde ~*** be at s.o.'s beck and call
zawozić ⟨**-wieźć**⟩ (*-wożę*) take, deliver
zawód[1] *m* (*-wodu*; *-wody*) (*zajęcie*) profession, trade; ***wolny ~*** freelance occupation; ***był z zawodu mechanikiem*** he was a mechanic by trade; ***kim pan jest z zawodu?*** what's your profession?, what's your trade?
zawód[2] *m* (*-wodu*; *-wody*) (*rozczarowanie*) disappointment; ***spotkał go ~*** he was disappointed; ***sprawić komuś ~*** let s.o. down
zawór *m* (*-woru*; *-wory*) TECH valve; ***~ bezpieczeństwa*** safety valve
zawracać ⟨**-rócić**⟩ (*-cam*) **I** *v/i* turn back **II** *v/t* ***~ sobie głowę*** *I* bother with
zawracanie *n* (*-nia*; *no pl*) **1.** (*nawrót*) U-turn **2.** (*wracanie*) turning back
zawrotny *adj* **1.** *ceny*: exorbitant **2.** *tempo*, *szybkość*: dizzying; ***w ~m tempie*** at dizzying speed **3.** *kariera*: staggering
zawrócić *v/p* (*-cę*): ***~ komuś w głowie*** turn sb's head; → **zawracać**
zawrót *m* (*-rotu*; *-roty*): ***zawroty głowy*** vertigo, dizziness
zawrzeć[1] *v/p* (*-rę*): ***~ swoje myśl*** put one's thoughts (***w*** *L* in); → **zawierać**
zawrzeć[2] *v/p* (*-rę*) (*o wodzie*) boil; ***~ gniewem*** seethe with anger
zawstydzać ⟨**-dzić**⟩ (*-dzam*) shame; ***zawstydzać się*** be ashamed
zawstydzony *adj* ashamed
zawsze I *adv* always; ***na ~*** for ever, for good **II** *particle* still; ***~ to coś*** it's always something
zawyrokować *v/p* → **wyrokować**
zawyżać ⟨**-żyć**⟩ (*-żam*) **1.** *ceny*, *koszty*: inflate **2.** *wartość*: overstate **3.** *poziom*: raise
zawziąć się *v/p* (*-wezmę*): ***~ na kogoś*** be down on s.o., have it in for s.o.; ***zawziął się i chce to skończyć dzisiaj*** he's determined to finish it today
zawzięty *adj* **1.** *osoba*: determined, headstrong **2.** *walka*, *spory*: fierce **3.** *mina*: fierce, determined
zazdrosny *adj* **1.** (*o żonę*, *męża*) jealous **2.** (*o powodzenie*) envious
zazdrościć *v/im* (*-roszczę*) be jealous of, envy; ***~ komuś sukcesu*** envy s.o. their success
zazdrość *f* (*-ści*; *no pl*) **1.** (*o kogoś*) jealousy **2.** (*o coś*) envy
zazdrośnica *f* (*-cy*; *-ce*) jealous woman
zazdrośnie *adv* **1.** *strzec*: jealously **2.** *spoglądać*: enviously
zazdrośnik *m* (*-ka*; *-nicy*) jealous man
zazębiać się ⟨**-bić**⟩ (*-biam*) **1.** (*o zębatkach*) mesh **2.** *fig* be interconnected, be intertwined
zazębiony *adj* meshed
zazieleniać się ⟨**-nić**⟩ (*-niam*) turn green
zaziębiać się ⟨**-bić**⟩ (*-biam*) catch a cold
zaznaczać ⟨**-czyć**⟩ (*-czam*) **1.** (*oznaczać*) mark **2.** (*w tekście*) mark, highlight **3.** (*stwierdzać z naciskiem*) stress; ***zaznaczać się*** be evident
zaznać *v/p* → **zaznawać**
zaznajamiać ⟨**-jomić**⟩ (*-miam*) acquaint (***z*** *I* with); ***zaznajamiać się*** familiarize oneself (***z*** *I* with)
zaznawać ⟨**-nać**⟩ (*-naję*) *lit* experience; ***~ szczęścia*** be happy; ***nie zaznasz spokoju*** you'll never find peace anymore
zazwyczaj *adv* usually
zażalenie *n* (*-nia*; *-nia*) complaint; ***złożyć ~*** file a complaint (***na*** *A* against)
zażarcie *adv* fiercely
zażartować *v/p* (*-tuję*) joke
zażarty *adj* **1.** *spory*, *walka*, *przeciwnik*: fierce **2.** *zwolennik*: keen
zażądać *v/p* (*-dam*) demand; ***~, by ktoś coś zrobił*** demand that s.o. do s.th.
zażegnywać ⟨**-nać**⟩ (*-nuję*) *niebezpieczeństwo*: fend off, avert
zażenować *v/p* → **żenować**
zażenowanie *n* (*-nia*; *no pl*) embarrassment; **zażenowany** *adj* embarrassed
zażyczyć *v/p* (*-czę*): ***~ sobie*** demand, request, want; ***zażyczyła sobie, żeby przyniesiono jej śniadanie do łóżka*** she wanted her breakfast to be served in bed; ***ile sobie zażyczył za naprawę?*** how much did he charge for the repair?; ***daj jej wszystko, czego sobie zażyczy*** give her everything she wants

zażyć *v/p* (*-żyję*) *infml* put on the spot; → **zażywać**

zażyłość *f* (*-ści*; *no pl*) intimacy; **zażyły** *adj* intimate

zażywać ⟨**-żyć**⟩ (*-wam*) **1.** *lek*, *ruchu*: take **2.** *spokoju*, *wolności*, *kąpieli*: enjoy

zażywny *adj lit* portly

ząb *m* (*zęba*; *zęby*) tooth; **zęby** teeth: **~ trzonowy** molar (tooth); **~ mądrości** wisdom tooth; **zęby mleczne** milk teeth; **zęby stałe** permanent teeth; **sztuczne zęby** false teeth; **~ jadowy** venom tooth; **myć zęby** clean one's teeth; **boli mnie ~** I have a toothache; **dać komuś w zęby** punch s.o. on the jaw; **coś na ~** a bite to eat; **(a)ni w ~** not a bit, not at all; **ktoś dzwoni zębami** s.o.'s teeth are chattering; **połamać sobie zęby** *fig* break one's teeth (**na** *L* on); **ostrzyć sobie zęby na** *A* have one's eye on, set one's sights on; **suszyć zęby** grin; **zacisnąć zęby** grit one's teeth; **uzbrojony po zęby** armed to the teeth; **jest nadszarpnięty zębem czasu** it's seen better days; **oko za oko, ~ za ~** an eye for an eye, a tooth for a tooth

ząbek *m* (*-bka*; *-bki*) *dim* **1.** (little) tooth **2.** *czosnku*: clove

ząbkować *v/im* (*-kuję*) teethe

ząbkowany *adj* serrated

zbabieć *v/p* → **babieć**

zbaczać ⟨**-boczyć**⟩ (*-czam*): **~ z drogi** turn aside, take another way; **~ z kursu** veer off course; **~ z tematu** go off the topic

zbadać *v/p* → **badać**

zbagatelizować *v/p* → **bagatelizować**

zbajerować *v/p* → **bajerować**

zbałamucić *v/p* → **bałamucić**

zbankrutować *v/p* → **bankrutować**; **zbankrutowany** *adj* bunkrupt

zbaraniały *adj infml* stupefied; **zbaranieć** *v/p* → **baranieć**

zbawca *m* (*-cy*; *-cy*), **-czyni** *f* (*-ni*; *-nie*) *Br* saviour, *Am* savior

zbawczy → **zbawienny**

zbawiać ⟨**-wić**⟩ (*-wiam*) save, redeem; **jeden dzień mnie nie zbawi** one day won't make any difference

Zbawiciel *m* (*-la*) REL *Br* Saviour, *Am* Savior

zbawić *v/p* → **zbawiać**

zbawienie *n* (*-nia*; *no pl*) salvation; **~ duszy** salvation of the soul; **czekać na coś jak na ~** *fig* be praying for s.th. to happen; **zbawienny** *adj* **1.** *wpływ*, *działanie*: beneficial **2.** *decyzja*: salutary

zbełtać *v/p* → **bełtać**

zbesztać *v/p* → **besztać**

zbezcześcić *v/p* → **bezcześcić**

zbędn|y *adj* **1.** unnecessary; **czuła się ~a** she felt useless **2.** *wysiłek*: unnecessary, useless

zbić *v/p* (*zbiję*) **1.** *osobę*: beat; **~ kogoś do nieprzytomności** beat s.o. unconscious; **~ kogoś na kwaśne jabłko** beat s.o. black and blue **2.** *kieliszek*, *szybę*: break **3.** *kolano*: bruise; **zbić się** (*o kieliszku*, *szybie*) break; → **zbijać**

zbiec *v/p* → **zbiegać**

zbiednieć *v/p* → **biednieć**

zbieg[1] *m* (*-ga*; *-gowie*) (*osoba*) runaway, fugitive

zbieg[2] *m* (*-gu*; *-gi*) **1.** *ulic*: junction **2. ~ okoliczności** coincidence; **szczęśliwy ~ okoliczności** happy coincidence; **nieszczęśliwy ~ okoliczności** unfortunate coincidence

zbiegać ⟨**zbiec**⟩ (*-gam*) **1.** (*uciekać*) run away (**z** *G* from) **2.** (*biec na dół*) **~ po schodach** run down the stairs; **zbiegać się 1.** (*w czasie*) coincide **2.** (*o ulicach*) meet, converge **3.** (*o materiale*) shrink

zbiegowisko *n* (*-ka*; *-ka*) crowd

zbieleć *v/p* → **bieleć**

zbieractwo *n* (*-wa*; *no pl*) **1.** collecting **2.** (*w antropologii*) gathering

zbieracz *m* (*-cza*; *-cze*), **~ka** *f* (*-ki*; *-ki*) **1.** collector; **~ grzybów** mushroom-picker **2.** (*w antropologii*) gatherer

zbierać ⟨**zebrać**, **po-**⟩ (*-ram*) **1.** (*gromadzić*) collect; **~ pieniądze na cele charytatywne** raise money for charity; **~ myśli** collect one's thoughts, gather one's thoughts; **~ siły** build up strength, gather strength **2.** (*oszczędzać*) save up **3.** *zboże*: harvest **4.** *owoce*, *grzyby*: pick **5.** *śmietanę*: take off, skim **6.** (*sprzątać*) clear away **7.** (*zwoływać*) gather, assemble; **zbierać się 1.** (*o osobach*) gather **2.** (*o przedmiotach*, *substancjach*) accumulate, collect **3.** (*mieć zamiar*)

mean; **~ się w sobie** brace up; ***zbierali się do wyjścia*** they were about to leave; ***zbiera mi się na wymioty*** I'm going to be sick; ***zbierało mu się na płacz*** he felt like crying **4.** (*zaczynać się*) ***zbiera się na deszcz*** it's going to rain; ***zbiera się na burzę*** there is going to be a storm; ***zbierają się chmury*** clouds are coming
zbieranina *f* (*-ny*; *no pl*) mixed lot
zbieżność *f* (*-ści*; *no pl*) convergence; ***~ kół*** the toe-in; **zbieżny** *adj* convergent
zbijać ⟨**zbić**⟩ (*-jam*) **1.** *skrzynię*: nail together **2.** *argumenty*: refute **3.** (*gromadzić*) *infml* ***~ majątek na*** *L*, ***~ fortunę na*** *L* make a fortune on **4.** ***~ kogoś z tropu*** confound, confuse s.o.; ***zbijać się*** (*w grudy*) lump
zbilansować *v/p* → ***bilansować***
zbiorczy *adj* collective
zbiornik *m* (*-ka*; *-ki*) container; ***~ paliwa*** fuel tank; ***sztuczny ~ wodny*** artificial water reservoir; **zbiornikowiec** *m* (*-wca*; *-wce*) (oil) tanker
zbiorowisko *n* (*-ka*; *-ka*) gathering; **zbiorowo** *adv* collectively, together
zbiorow|y *adj* **1.** collective; ***odpowiedzialność ~a*** collective responsibility; ***~a mogiła*** mass grave; ***praca ~a*** joint publication **2.** *fotografia*: group **3.** *scena*: crowd **4.** *rezerwacja*, *zamówienie*: group, block
zbi|ór *m* (*zbioru*; *zbiory*) **1.** (*kolekcja*) collection; ***~ory*** (*kolekcja*) collection; ***~ór wierszy*** collection of poems **2.** MATH set **3.** (*żniwa*) harvest **4.** ***~ory*** (*plony*) crop
zbiórka *f* (*-ki*; *-ki*) **1.** (*spotkanie*) meeting, assembly; ***~!*** fall in! **2.** (*zbieranie*) collection
zbir *m* (*-ra*; *-ry*) thug, cut-throat
zbity *adj* **1.** (*pobity*) beaten (up) **2.** *tłum*: tight **3.** *śnieg*: compact **4.** *szkło*: broken
zblaknąć *v/p* → ***blaknąć***
zblazowany *adj* jaded, blasé
zblednąć *v/p* → ***blednąć***
zbliżać ⟨**-żyć**⟩ (*-żam*) *rękę*: move closer; ***zbliżać się*** approach; ***~ się do siebie*** *fig* become close; ***~ się ku końcowi*** be drawing to a close; ***zbliża się północ*** it is approaching midnight, midnight is approaching
zbliżenie *n* (*-nia*; *-nia*) **1.** PHOT FILM close-up **2.** (*stosunek*) intercourse; **zbliżony** *adj* similar (**do** *G* to); ***~ kształtem do*** *G* shaped much like
zbliżyć *v/p* → ***zbliżać***
zbłaźnić się *v/p* → ***błaźnić się***
zbłąkan|y *adj* **1.** *kula*: stray **2.** *osoba*: lost; ***~a owieczka*** *fig* lost lamb
zbocze *f* (*-cza*; *-cza*) slope
zboczenie *n* (*-nia*; *-nia*) deviation, perversion: ***~ seksualne*** sexual perversion, sexual deviation
zboczeniec *m* (*-czeńca*; *-czeńcy*) pervert
zboczyć *v/p* → ***zbaczać***
zbojkotować *v/p* → ***bojkotować***
zbolały *adj mina*: pained
zbombardować *v/p* → ***bombardować***
zborny *adj*: ***punkt ~*** meeting point
zboż|e *n* (*-ża*; *-ża*) cereal, corn; ***~a jare*** spring crops; ***~a ozime*** winter crops
zbożny *adj lit* worthy, godly
zbożow|y *adj* **1.** cereal; ***płatki ~e*** cereal(s); ***rośliny ~e*** cereals, cereal crops; ***otręby ~e*** bran **2.** *elewator*: grain **3.** *kawa*: chicory
zbój *m* (*-ja*; *-je*) highwayman
zbór *m* (*zboru*; *zbory*) **1.** (*świątynia*) (Protestant) church **2.** (*wspólnota*) (Protestant) congregation
zbroczony *adj*: ***~ krwią*** stained with blood
zbrodni|a *f* (*-ni*; *-nie*) crime; ***~e przeciwko ludzkości*** genocide; ***~e wojenne*** war crimes
zbrodniarz *m* (*-rza*; *-rze*), **-rka** *f* (*-ki*; *-ki*) criminal; ***~ wojenny*** war criminal
zbrodniczy *adj* **1.** criminal **2.** (*morderczy*) murderous
zbroić[1] ⟨**u-**⟩ (*-roję*) *teren*: serve with infrastructure, provide with public utilities; ***zbroić się*** arm oneself
zbroić[2] *v/p* → ***broić***
zbroja *f* (*-roi*; *-je*) *Br* armour, *Am* armor
zbroje|nia *pl* (*-jeń*) (*gromadzenie uzbrojenia*) armaments; ***wyścig ~ń*** arms race; **zbrojenie** *n* (*-nia*; *-nia*) BUILD reinforcement; **zbrojeniowy** *adj przemysł*: arms
zbrojnie *adv*: ***interweniować ~*** take military action; **zbrojny** *adj* **1.** *akcja*: military **2.** *konflikt*, *siły*; armed

Z

zbrojony *adj*: **beton ~** reinforced concrete

zbrojownia *f* (*-ni*; *-nie*) HIST *Br* armoury, *Am* armory

zbrukać *v/p* → **brukać**

zbrzydnąć *v/p* → **brzydnąć**

zbudować *v/p* → **budować**

zbuk *m* (*-ka*; *-ki*) addled egg

zbulwersować *v/p* → **bulwersować**; **zbulwersowany** *adj* shocked

zbuntować *v/p* → **buntować**

zburzenie *n* (*-nia*; *no pl*) demolition, pulling down; **zburzyć** *v/p* → **burzyć**

zbutwiały *adj* rotten; **zbutwieć** *v/p* → **butwieć**

zbyci|e *n* (*-cia*; *no pl*): ***mieć coś na ~u*** be able to spare s.th., have s.th. to spare

zbyć *v/p* → **zbywać**

zbyt[1] *adv* too; ***~ twardy*** too hard; ***~ pochopny*** too rash; ***stawiać komuś ~ wysokie wymagania*** ask too much of s.o.

zbyt[2] *m* (*-tu*; *no pl*) ECON market; **cena ~u** selling price; ***rynki ~u*** markets

zbyteczny *adj* unnecessary

zbytek *m* (*-tku*; *-tki*) luxury

zbytni *adj* **1.** excessive; ***nie przywiązywać ~ej wagi do czegoś*** not pay too much attention to something **2.** *zwłoka*, *pośpiech*: undue; **zbytnio** *adv* too much, excessively

zbywać ⟨**zbyć**⟩ (*-wam*) **1.** sell **2.** *osobę*: brush off **3.** ***nie zbywa mu na*** *L lit* he has plenty of, he has enough of

zbzikowany *adj infml* crazy, nuts

z-ca, **zca** *abbr* (= **zastępca**) → **zastępca**

zdać *v/p* (*zdam*): ***~ egzamin*** pass an exam; ***~ do następnej klasy*** be promoted to a higher class; ***~ na studia*** get into college; **zdać się**: ***to się na nic nie zda*** it won't do any good; → **zdawać**

zdalnie *adv* remotely; ***~ sterowany*** remote-controlled; **zdaln|y** *adj* remote; ***~e sterowanie*** remote control

zdanie *n* (*-nia*; *-nia*) **1.** (*opinia*) opinion; ***moim ~m*** in my opinion, I think; ***mieć swoje ~*** have one's own opinion **2.** GRAM sentence, clause; ***~ podrzędne*** subordinate clause; ***~ główne*** main clause

zdany *adj*: ***być ~m na*** *A* be dependent on; ***być ~m na własne siły*** be on one's own, be left to one's own devices; ***być ~m na łaskę losu*** be left to one's fate

zdarci|e: ***nie do ~a*** **a)** *człowiek*: hardy **b)** *przedmiot*: hard-wearing, durable

zdarty *adj* **1.** (*skaleczony*) torn **2.** (*zniszczony*) worn-out

zdarzać się ⟨**-rzyć**⟩ (*-rzam*) happen, occur; ***to zdarzyło się naprawdę*** it really happened; ***zdarzył się wypadek*** there's been an accident; ***rzadko się zdarza, żeby*** it's not often that; ***to się zdarza*** it happens

zdarzeni|e *n* (*-nia*; *-nia*) event, occurrence; ***~a*** events; ***artysta z prawdziwego ~a*** true artist

zdatn|y *adj* fit (**do** *G* for), suitable (**do** *G* for); ***woda ~a do picia*** drinkable water, water fit for drinking; ***~y do spożycia*** fit for human consumption; ***~y do użytku*** usable

zdawać ⟨**zdać**⟩ (*-daję*) **1.** (*egzamin z powodzeniem*) pass **2.** (*podchodzić do egzaminu*) take, sit; ***~ na studia*** take college entrance exams **3.** (*uzyskiwać promocję*) be promoted; ***~ do następnej klasy*** be promoted to a higher class **4.** (*przekazywać*) ***~ relację z*** *G* give an account of; ***~ sobie sprawę z*** *G* be aware of; ***zdała sobie sprawę z grożącego jej niebezpieczeństwa*** she realized she was in danger **5.** *raport*: present **6.** *klucze*: hand over; **zdawać się 1.** (*zawierzać*) count (***na*** *A* on) **2.** (*wydawać się*) seem; ***zdaje mi się, że*** it seems to me that; ***zdaje się, że*** it seems that; ***zdawało się, że śpi*** he seemed to be asleep; ***zdawało ci się*** you must have imagined it

zdawkowo *adv* **1.** cursorily, perfunctorily; ***uśmiechnąć się do kogoś ~*** give s.o. a cursory smile **2.** *odpowiedzieć*: curtly

zdawkowy *adj* **1.** cursory, perfunctory **2.** *odpowiedź*: curt

zdążać *v/im* (*-żam*) **1.** (*iść*) go (**do** *G* to), head (**do** *G* for) **2.** (*dążyć*) strive (**do** *G* for); → **zdążyć**

zdążyć *v/p* (*-żę*) (*być na czas*) be in time, make it; ***nie ~*** be late; ***~ na pociąg*** be in time to catch a train; ***nie ~***

na pociąg miss a train; **~ *w terminie*** meet a deadline; **~ *z oddaniem pracy pisemnej*** manage to hand in one's paper on time
zdecentralizować *v/p* → ***decentralizować***
zdechlak *m* (*-ka*; *-ki*) weakling
zdechły *adj* (*martwy*) dead
zdechnąć *v/p* → ***zdychać***
zdecydować *v/p* → ***decydować***
zdecydowanie[1] *n* (*-nia*; *no pl*) determination, resoluteness; ***brak ~a*** indecision
zdecydowanie[2] *adv* definitely
zdecydowan|y *adj* **1.** (*stanowczy*) resolute, strong-minded **2. *jest ~y na zakup tego domu*** he wants to buy this house, he's decided to buy this house **3.** *kroki*: decisive; ***podjąć ~e kroki*** take decisive steps **4.** *poprawa*: substantial, considerable **5.** *większość*: definite
zdefiniować *v/p* → ***definiować***
zdeformować *v/p* → ***deformować***; **zdeformowany** *adj* deformed, misshapen
zdefraudować *v/p* → ***defraudować***
zdegenerowany *adj lit osoba*: degenerated
zdegradować *v/p* → ***degradować***
zdegustowany *adj lit* disgusted
zdejmować ⟨**zdjąć**⟩ (*-muję*) **1.** take off; **~ *skarpetki*** take off one's socks; **~ *coś z afisza*** *fig* take s.th. off **2.** *skórkę*: remove **3.** (*ogarniać*) *lit* be seized with; ***zdjęło go przerażenie*** he was overcome with terror
zdekompletowany *adj* incomplete
zdekonspirować *v/p* → ***dekonspirować***; **zdekonspirowany** *adj* exposed
zdemaskować *v/p* → ***demaskować***; **zdemaskowany** *adj* unmasked, exposed
zdementować *v/p* → ***dementować***
zdemilitaryzowany *adj* demilitarized
zdemobilizować *v/p* → ***demobilizować***
zdemolować *v/p* → ***demolować***
zdemontować *v/p* → ***demontować***
zdemoralizować *v/p* → ***demoralizować***; **zdemoralizowany** *adj* demoralized, spoilt
zdenerwować *v/p* → ***denerwować***
zdenerwowanie *n* (*-nia*; *no pl*) **1.** (*niepokój*) nervousness **2.** (*irytacja*) annoyance, irritation; **zdenerwowany** *adj* **1.** (*zaniepokojony*) nervous **2.** (*zirytowany*) annoyed, irritated
zdeponować *v/p* → ***deponować***
zdeprawować *v/p* → ***deprawować***; **zdeprawowany** *adj* depraved, corrupt
zdeprymować *v/p* → ***deprymować***; **zdeprymowany** *adj* demoralized, disheartened
zdeptać *v/p* (*-pczę*/*-pcę*) trample, stamp
zderzać się ⟨**-rzyć**⟩ (*-rzam*) crash (**z** *I* with), collide (**z** *I* with)
zderzak (*-ka*; *-ki*) **1.** AUTO bumper **2.** (*wagonu*) buffer
zderzenie *n* (*-nia*; *-nia*) AUTO crash, collision
zderzyć się *v/p* → ***zderzać się***
zdeterminowany *adj* determined
zdetonować *v/p* → ***detonować***
zdetronizować *v/p* → ***detronizować***
zdewastować *v/p* → ***dewastować***; **zdewastowany** *adj* **1.** devastated, destroyed **2.** (*przez wandali*) vandalized
zdezaktualizować *v/p* → ***dezaktualizować***
zdezerterować *v/p* → ***dezerterować***
zdezorganizować *v/p* → ***dezorganizować***
zdezorientować *v/p* → ***dezorientować***
zdezynfekować *v/p* → ***dezynfekować***
zdębieć *v/p* → ***dębieć***
zdiagnozować *v/p* → ***diagnozować***
zdjąć *v/p* → ***zdejmować***
zdjęci|e *n* (*-cia*; *-cia*) photo, photograph; ***~e do paszportu*** passport photo; ***~a z urlopu*** holiday photos; ***robić ~a*** **a)** (*fotografować*) take pictures **b)** (*filmować*) shoot; ***na ~u*** in the picture; ***~e rentgenowskie*** X-ray; ***~a*** **a)** (*filmowanie*) shooting, filming **b)** (*obrazy filmowe*) camerawork
zdławić *v/p* → ***dławić***
zdławiony *adj* **1.** *płacz*: stifled **2.** *powstanie*: suppressed
zdmuchiwać ⟨**-chnąć**⟩ (*-chuję*) **1.** blow off **2.** *ogień, świeczkę*: blow out
zdobić ⟨**o-**⟩ (*-bię*) decorate
zdobnicz|y *adj element*: decorative, ornamental; ***sztuka ~a*** decorative art

zdobyci|e *n* (*-cia*; *no pl*) **1.** (*podbicie*) conquest **2.** (*wspięcie się*) ascent **3.** ***nie do ~a*** **a)** *zamek*, *twierdza*: impregnable **b)** *rzecz*: unavailable

zdobycz *f* (*-czy*; *-cze*) **1.** (*trofeum*) trophy **2.** (*osiągnięcie*) achievement **3.** (*drapieżnika*) prey, kill; **zdobyczny** *adj broń*: captured

zdobywać ⟨**-być**⟩ (*-wam*) **1.** *medal*, *tytuł mistrza*, *zaufanie*, *głosy*: win **2.** *pozycję*, *władzę*, *wiedzę*: gain **3.** *miasto*: capture **4.** *bramkę*, *punkty*: score **5.** *szczyt*: climb, conquer **6.** (*dostawać*) get, acquire; **zdobywać się** summon up (**na** *A*); ***~ się na odwagę i coś zrobić*** pluck up the courage to do s.th., bring oneself to do s.th.

zdobywca *m* (*-cy*; *-cy*), **-czyni** *f* (*-ni*; *-nie*) **1.** *kraju*, *miasta*: conqueror **2.** *nagrody*, *medalu*: winner **3.** *bramki*: scorer

zdolnoś|ć *f* (*-ści*; *-ści*) ability; ***~ci*** talent, ability; ***~ć myślenia*** ability to think; ***~ci organizacyjne*** organizational skills; ***~ci językowe*** linguistic talents; ***~ć produkcyjna*** production capacity

zdolny *adj* **1.** (*utalentowany*) clever, gifted, able **2.** (*potrafiący*) ***~ do zrobienia czegoś*** able to do s.th., capable of doing s.th.

zdołać *v/p* (*-łam*): ***~ coś zrobić*** manage to do s.th., be able to do s.th.

zdołowany *adj*: ***być ~m*** *infml* feel down, be down in the dumps

zdopingować *v/p* → ***dopingować***

zdrada *f* (*-dy*; *-dy*) **1.** POLIT treason; ***~ stanu*** high treason **2.** (*niedochowanie wierności*) unfaithfulness, infidelity; ***~ małżeńska*** marital infidelity

zdradliwy *adj* treacherous

zdradzać ⟨**-dzić**⟩ (*-dzam*) **1.** betray; ***~ czyjeś zaufanie*** betray s.o.'s trust **2.** *męża*, *żonę*: be unfaithful to **3.** (*okazywać*) show, reveal; ***nie ~ zainteresowania*** show no interest

zdradziecki *adj* treacherous; **zdradziecko** *adv* treacherously

zdrajca *m* (*-cy*; *-cy*), **-czyni** (*-ni*; *-nie*) traitor; ***~ ojczyzny*** traitor to one's country

zdrapka *f* (*-ki*; *-ki*) scratchcard

zdrapywać ⟨**-pać**⟩ (*-puję*) scrape off

zdrewnieć *v/p* → ***drewnieć***

zdrętwiały *adj* **1.** *noga*, *ręka*: numb; ***~ z zimna*** numb with cold **2.** *plecy*: stiff; **zdrętwieć** *v/p* → ***drętwieć***

zdrobniały *adj* diminutive

zdrobnienie *n* (*-nia*; *-nia*) diminutive

zdrojow|y *adj*: ***woda ~a*** spa water

zdrowaśka *f* (*-ki*; *-ki*) *infml* Hail Mary

zdrowi|e *n* (*-wia*; *no pl*) health; (***na***) ***~e!*** **a)** (*toast*) cheers! **b)** (*przy kichaniu*) bless you!; ***to jest szkodliwe dla ~a*** it's bad for you, it ruins your health; ***to wyszło mu na ~e*** it was good for him; ***on podupada na ~u*** his health is deteriorating; ***jak ~e?*** how are you?; ***wypiliśmy*** (***za***) ***jego ~e*** we drank to his health; ***mieć końskie ~e*** be (as) healthy as an ox; ***książeczka ~a*** health card; ***ścieżka ~a*** fitness path, fitness trail

zdrowiuteńki, **zdrowiutki** *adj dim* perfectly healthy

zdrowo *adv*: ***~ się odżywiać*** eat healthy

zdrowotn|y *adj*: ***urlop ~y*** sick leave; ***opieka ~a*** health care; ***mieć właściwości ~e*** have medicinal properties

zdrow|y *adj* healthy; ***~a żywność*** healthy food; ***~y jak ryba*** (as) fit as a fiddle; ***~y rozum*** common sense; ***przy ~ych zmysłach*** in one's right mind

zdrożeć *v/p* → ***drożeć***

zdrów *adj*: ***cały i ~*** safe and sound

zdrówko: ***~!*** (*przy kichaniu*) bless you!; ***jak ~?*** how are you?

zdruzgotać *v/p* → ***druzgotać***; **zdruzgotany** *adj* devastated

zdrzemnąć się *v/p* (*-nę*) doze off, take a nap

zdublować *v/p* → ***dublować***

zdumienie *n* (*-nia*; *no pl*) amazement, astonishment; **zdumiewać** ⟨***-mieć***⟩ (*-wam*) amaze, astonish; ***zdumiewać się*** be amazed, be astonished; **zdumiewający** *adj* amazing, astonishing; **zdumiony** *adj* amazed, astonished

zdun *m* (*-na*; *-nowie*/*-ni*) stove maker

zdusić *v/p* → ***dusić***

zduszony *adj* **1.** (*ściśnięty*) squeezed **2.** (*zdławiony*) suppressed, stifled

zdwajać ⟨**-woić**⟩ (*-jam*) double

zdychać ⟨**zdechnąć**⟩ (*-cham*) **1.** die; ***~ z głodu*** be starving; ***zdechnąć z głodu*** starve to death **2.** (*o silniku*) *infml* go dead

zdymisjonować *v/p* → **dymisjonować**
zdyscyplinowany *adj* disciplined
zdyskredytować *v/p* → **dyskredytować**
zdyskwalifikować *v/p* → **dyskwalifikować**; **zdyskwalifikowany** *adj* disqualified
zdystansować *v/p* → **dystansować**
zdyszany *adj* breathless, out of breath
zdziadzieć *v/p* → **dziadzieć**
zdziałać *v/p* (*-łam*) achieve
zdziczały *adj* **1.** *kot, pies*: feral **2.** (*dziki*) wild **3.** (*prymitywny, agresywny*) savage
zdziczeć *v/p* → **dziczeć**
zdziecinniały *adj* childish
zdziecinnienie *n* (*-nia; no pl*): **starcze ~** senility, second childhood
zdzielić *v/p* (*-lę*): **~ kogoś** *infml* fetch s.o. a blow
zdzierać ⟨**zedrzeć**⟩ (*-ram*) **1.** *tapety*: strip off, tear off **2.** *kolano, łokieć*: scrape **3.** *odzież*: wear out **4.** *opony*: wear down **5.** (*rujnować*) **~ sobie zdrowie** ruin one's health; **~ sobie gardło** shout oneself hoarse **6.** (*naciągać*) **~ z kogoś skórę** *infml* rip s.o. off, fleece s.o.
zdzierca *m* (*-cy; -cy*) *infml* rip-off artist; **zdzierstwo** *n* (*-wa; no pl*) *infml* rip-off
zdziesiątkować *v/p* → **dziesiątkować**
zdzira *f* (*-ry; -ry*) *infml* slut
zdziwaczały *adj* eccentric, *Br* cranky; **zdziwaczeć** *v/p* → **dziwaczeć**
zdziwić *v/p* → **dziwić**; **zdziwienie** *n* (*-nia; no pl*) surprise, astonishment; **zdziwiony** *adj* surprised
ze → **z**
zebra *f* (*-ry; -ry*) **1.** (*zwierzę*) zebra **2.** (*na ulicy*) pedestrian crossing, *Br* zebra crossing
zebrać się *v/p* (*zbiorę*): **~ na odwagę** pluck up (the) courage; → **zbierać**
zebranie *n* (*-nia; -nia*) meeting; **zebra|ny** *adj* collected; **dzieła ~e** collected works
zecer *m* (*-ra; -rzy*) type-setter, compositor; **zecernia** (*-ni; -nie*) composing department; **zecerski** *adj błąd*: compositor's
zedrzeć *v/p* → **zdzierać**
zegar *m* (*-ra; -ry*) clock; **~ z kukułką** cuckoo clock; **~ słoneczny** sundial; **~ biologiczny** biological clock; **~ parkingowy** parking meter
zegar|ek *m* (*-rka; -rki*) watch; **wszystko idzie jak w ~ku** everything goes like clockwork, everything goes smoothly; **z ~kiem w ręku** *fig* by the clock; **zegarmistrz** *m* (*-rza; -rze/-rzowie*) watchmaker
zegarow|y *adj* **1.** clock; **mechanizm ~y** clockwork **2. godzina ~a** full hour **3. bomba ~a** time bomb
zegarynka *f* (*-ki; -ki*) TEL speaking clock
zejście *n* (*-cia; -cia*) **1.** (*schodzenie*) descent **2.** (*śmierć*) demise, death
zejść *v/p* → **schodzić**
zekranizować *v/p* → **ekranizować**
zelować ⟨**pod-**⟩ (*-luję*) sole
zelówka *f* (*-ki; -ki*) sole
zelżeć *v/p* (*-żę*) **1.** (*o bólu*) ease off **2.** (*o mrozie*) let up
zelżyć *v/p* → **lżyć**
zemdleć *v/p* → **mdleć**; **zemdlony** *adj* unconscious
zemleć *v/p* → **mleć**
zemrzeć *v/p* (*-rę*) die; **zmarła na raka** she died of cancer; **zmarło mu się** *infml* he passed away
zemst|a *f* (*-ty; -ty*) revenge, vengeance; **dokonać ~y na** *L* take revenge on
zemścić się *v/p* → **mścić się**
zeni|t *m* (*-tu; no pl*) zenith; **słońce w ~cie** the sun at its zenith
zepchnąć *v/p* → **spychać**
zepsuci|e *n* (*-cia; no pl*) **1.** (*demoralizacja*) depravity, corruption; **~e moralne** moral decay **2. ulec ~u** (*o pokarmie*) go bad, go off
zepsuć *v/p* → **psuć**
zepsuty *adj* **1.** *samochód, komputer*: broken, broken-down **2.** *winda*: out of order **3.** *jedzenie*: off, bad **4.** *człowiek*: corrupt, depraved; **~ do szpiku kości** corrupt to the core
zerkać ⟨**-knąć**⟩ (*-kam*) peep, glance
zer|o *n* (*-ra; -ra*) **1.** zero; **cztery stopnie poniżej ~a** four degrees below zero; **cztery stopnie powyżej ~a** four degrees above zero; **siódma ~o ~o** seven o'clock sharp; **zaczynać od ~a** *fig* start from scratch **2.** (*w piłce nożnej*) nil; **przegrać dwa do ~a** be beaten two (goals to) nil **3.** (*w tenisie*) love **4.** (*osoba*) nobody, nonentity

zerow|y *adj* zero; ***ich szanse są ~e*** their chances are zero, their chances are nil; ***miał ~e wiadomości*** he knew absolutely nothing, he was totally ignorant
zerówka *f* (*-ki*; *-ki*) *Br* reception class, *Am* kindergarten
zerwać *v/p* → ***zrywać***
zerżnąć *v/p* (*-nę*) *vulg* fuck, shag; → ***zrzynać***
zeschnąć się *v/p* → ***zsychać się***
zeskakiwać ⟨***-skoczyć***⟩ (*-kuję*) jump down (**z** *G* from), jump (**z** *G* off)
zeskanować *v/p* → ***skanować***
zeskrobywać ⟨***-bać***⟩ (*-buję*) scrape off
zesłać *v/p* → ***zsyłać***
zesłanie *n* (*-nia*; *no pl*) **1.** (*deportacja*) exile, deportation **2.** ***~ Ducha Świętego*** REL **a)** (*wydarzenie*) the descent of the Holy Spirit **b)** (*święto*) Pentecost; **zesłaniec** *m* (*-łańca*; *-łańcy*) exile, deportee
zespalać ⟨***-polić***⟩ (*-lam*) join, unite
zespawać *v/p* → ***spawać***
zespolić *v/p* → ***zespalać***
zespołow|y *adj* team, group, collective; ***gry ~e*** team games; ***praca ~a*** teamwork
zespół *m* (*-połu*; *-poły*) **1.** (*grupa pracowników, graczy*) team; ***~ badawczy*** research team **2.** MUS band, group; ***~ rockowy*** rock group **3.** *teatralny*: group, company **4.** ARCHIT complex **5.** MED syndrome
zesrać się *v/p* (*-ram*) *vulg* shit; ***~ w portki*** shit one's pants
zestarzeć się *v/p* → ***starzeć się***
zestaw *m* (*-wu*; *-wy*) **1.** (*zestawienie*) combination **2.** (*komplet*) set; ***~ mebli*** furniture suite; ***~ narzędzi*** tool kit
zestawiać ⟨***-wić***⟩ (*-wiam*) **1.** (*porównywać*) compare, juxtapose (**z** *I* with) **2.** (*zdejmować*) take down **3.** (*stawiać obok siebie*) put together
zestawieni|e *n* (*-nia*; *-nia*) **1.** (*połączenie*) combination **2.** (*porównanie*) comparison, juxtaposition; ***w ~u z*** *I* in comparison with, compared to **3.** (*spis*) list, specification
zestresować *v/p* → ***stresować***; ***zestresowany*** *adj* stressed (out)
zestrzelić *v/p* (*-lę*) shoot down
zeszczupleć *v/p* → ***szczupleć***
zeszłoroczny *adj* last year's
zeszł|y *adj* last; ***w ~ym roku*** last year; ***~ej nocy*** last night; ***w ~y piątek*** last Friday
zeszpecony *adj* ugly, unsightly
zesztukować *v/p* → ***sztukować***
zesztywnieć *v/p* → ***sztywnieć***
zeszyt *m* (*-tu*; *-ty*) notebook; ***~ ćwiczeń*** exercise book
ześlizgiwać się ⟨***-gnąć***, ***-znąć***⟩ (*-guję*) slip down, slide down
ześrubować *v/p* (*-buję*) screw together
zetknąć *v/p* → ***stykać***
zetrzeć *v/p* → ***ścierać***
zewidencjonować *v/p* → ***ewidencjonować***
zewnątrz: ***na ~*** outside; ***z ~*** from (the) outside; ***temperatura na ~*** the outside temperature
zewnętrzn|y *adj* **1.** *strona*: outside **2.** *wpływy, wygląd*: external; ***do użytku ~ego*** for external use; ***czyjś wygląd ~y*** s.o.'s appearance **3.** *polityka*: foreign
zewrzeć *v/p* → ***zwierać***
zewsząd *pron* from everywhere, from all sides
zez *m* (*-za*; *no pl*) squint, crossed eyes *pl*, *form* strabismus; ***mieć ~a*** have a squint
zeznać *v/p* → ***zeznawać***
zezna|nie *n* (*-nia*; *-nia*) **1.** JUR testimony, evidence; ***złożyć ~nia*** testify, give evidence; ***odmowa ~ń*** refusal to testify **2.** *podatkowe*: statement
zeznawać ⟨***-nać***⟩ (*-znaję*) testify, give evidence
zezować *v/im* (*-zuję*) squint, have a squint
zezowaty *adj* cross-eyed
zezwalać ⟨***-wolić***⟩ (*-lam*) permit (**na** *A*), allow; ***~ komuś na coś*** allow s.o. to do s.th.
zezwierzęcenie *n* (*-nia*; *no pl*) brutality, bestiality
zezwoleni|e *n* (*-nia*; *-nia*) permission, permit; ***bez ~a*** without permission; ***~e na pracę*** work permit; ***~e na broń*** gun permit
zezwolić *v/p* → ***zezwalać***
zeżreć *v/p* → ***zżerać***
zębatka *f* (*-ki*; *-ki*) TECH sprocket, sprocket-wheel
zębat|y *adj*: ***koło ~e***, ***kółko ~e*** cogwheel
zębowy *adj* dental

Z

zęby *pl* → **ząb**
zgadnąć *v/p* → **zgadywać**
zgaduj-zgadula *f* (*-li*; *-le*) quiz, guessing game
zgad|ywać ⟨**-dnąć**⟩ (*-duję*) guess; **~nij!** guess!
zgadywanka *f* (*-ki*; *-ki*) quiz, guessing game
zgadzać się ⟨**zgodzić**⟩ (*-dzam*) **1.** agree (*D* with); ***zgadza się!*** that's right!; ***coś się tu nie zgadza*** there's something wrong with it **2.** (*udzielać zgody*) agree (**na** *A* to), give permission (**na** *A* for); **~ *na propozycję*** agree to a proposal; ***zgadzam się!*** I agree! **3.** (*rozumieć się*) get on well **4.** (*o rachunku*) be correct
zgaga *f* (*-gi*; *no pl*) heartburn
zganiać ⟨**zegnać**⟩ (*-niam*) *bydło*, *owce*: drive (**do** *G* into/to)
zganić *v/p* → **ganić**
zgarbić *v/p* (*-bię*): **~ *plecy*** hunch, stoop; ***zgarbić się*** hunch, stoop; **~ *się pod ciężarem*** *G* bend under the weight of
zgarniać ⟨**-nąć**⟩ (*-niam*) **1.** (*zagarniać*) gather, sweep **2.** *liście*: rake up **3.** (*odgarniać*) brush aside **4.** *nagrody*: take **5.** *złodzieja*, *przestępcę*: *infml* pick up, *Br* nick
zgasić *v/p* → **gasić**
zgasły *adj* **1.** *świeca*, *ognisko*: burned-out **2.** *miłość*: dead
zgasnąć *v/p* → **gasnąć**
zgaszony *adj fig* subdued
zgęstnieć *v/p* → **gęstnieć**
zgiąć *v/p* → **zginać**
zgiełk *m* (*-ku*; *no pl*) tumult; **~ *uliczny*** traffic din
zgięcie *n* (*-cia*; *-cia*) bend; **zgięty** *adj* bent
zginać ⟨**zgiąć**⟩ (*-nam*) bend; ***zginać się*** bend; **~ *się w pół*** bend double
zginąć *v/p* → **ginąć**
zgliszcza *pl* (*-liszcz*) ashes
zgładzić *v/p* (*-dzę*) *lit* **1.** kill **2.** *smoka*, *buntowników*: slay
zgłaszać ⟨**-łosić**⟩ (*-szam*) **1.** report (**coś** *D* s.th. to), notify (**komuś** *A* s.o. of); **~ *kradzież*** (***na policji***) report a theft; **~ *akces*** accede (**do** *G* to); **~ *coś do oclenia*** declare s.th. **2.** *wniosek*, *poprawkę*: put forward, propose **3.** *sprzeciw*, *protest*: voice; ***zgłaszać się*** **1.** (*zgłaszać chęć uczestnictwa*) come forward; **~ *się na ochotnika*** volunteer; **~ *się do odpowiedzi*** raise one's hand **2.** (*do konkursu*) enter (**do** *G*) **3.** (*stawiać się*) report **4.** (*podnosić słuchawkę*) answer
zgłębiać ⟨**-bić**⟩ (*-biam*) explore
zgłodniały *adj* hungry
zgłodnieć *v/p* → **głodnieć**
zgłosić *v/p* → **zgłaszać**
zgłoska *f* (*-ki*; *-ki*) syllable
zgłoszeni|e *n* (*-nia*; *-nia*) **1.** (*zawiadomienie*) notification **2.** (*podanie*) application; ***pisemne ~e*** written application; ***formularz ~a*** application form
zgłupieć *v/p* → **głupieć**
zgnębić *v/p* → **gnębić**
zgniatać ⟨**-nieść**⟩ (*-tam*) **1.** (*miażdżyć*) crush **2.** *papier*, *materiał*: crumple
zgnić *v/p* → **gnić**
zgniecenie *n* (*-nia*; *no pl*) **1.** (*zmiażdżenie*) crushing **2.** *papieru*, *materiału*: crumpling
zgnieść *v/p* → **zgniatać**
zgnilizn|a *f* (*-ny*; *no pl*) rot; ***śmierdzieć ~ą*** reek of decay; ***~a moralna*** moral decay, turpitude
zgniłki *pl* (*-ków*) (half-)rotten fruit *sing*
zgnił|y *adj* rotten; ***~a zieleń*** brownish green
zgnoić *v/p* → **gnoić**
zgnuśniały *adj* **1.** *osoba*: slothful, indolent **2.** *miasteczko*: lethargic, lazy; **zgnuśnieć** *v/p* → **gnuśnieć**
zgo|da *f* (*-dy*; *no pl*) **1.** agreement (**na** *A* to); ***wyrazić ~dę*** agree; ***~da!*** all right!, OK!, done!; ***wyciągnąć rękę na ~dę*** extend one's hand in reconciliation; ***za czyjąś cichą ~dą*** with s.o.'s tacit consent, with s.o.'s tacit approval; ***w ~dzie z obowiązującymi przepisami*** in compliance with applicable regulations **2.** (*harmonia*) harmony; ***w ~dzie z naturą*** in harmony with nature
zgodnie *adv* **1.** **~ *z*** *I* according to; **~ *z tradycją*** according to tradition; **~ *z planem*** according to plan; **~ *z obowiazującymi przepisami*** in compliance with applicable regulations; **~ *z obietnicą*** as promised; ***odpowiedzieć ~ z prawdą*** answer truthfully; **~ *z prawem*** in accordance with the

law, legally **2.** *(bez nieporozumień)* in harmony **3.** *(jednomyślnie)* unanimously
zgodność *f (-ści; no pl)* **1.** *(z przepisami)* compliance **2.** *(z oryginałem)* conformity **3.** *pożycia małżeńskiego*: harmony **4.** *charakterów*: compatibility **5.** *(jednomyślność)* unanimity
zgodn|y *adj* **1.** ***być ~ym z planem*** be as planned, be according to plan; ***być ~ym z prawem*** be legal, be in accordance with the law; ***być ~ym z obowiązującymi przepisami*** be legal, be in compliance with applicable regulations; ***~y z duchem czasu*** in keeping with the times; ***to (nie) jest ~e z prawdą*** this is (not) true **2.** *osoba*: agreeable **3.** *(jednomyślny)* unanimous
zgodzić się *v/p* → ***zgadzać się***
zgolić *v/p (-lę)* shave off
zgoła *adv lit* quite, completely
zgon *m (-nu; -ny)* death, *lit* demise; ***świadectwo ~u*** death certificate
zgonić *v/p* → ***zganiać***
zgorszenie *n (-nia; no pl)* **1.** *(oburzenie)* outrage, indignation; ***wywołać czyjeś ~*** scandalize s.o.; ***ze ~m*** with indignation **2.** *(zepsucie)* corruption; **zgorszony** *adj* scandalized, shocked; **zgorszyć** *v/p* → ***gorszyć***
zgorzkniały *adj osoba, mina*: bitter; **zgorzknieć** *v/p* → ***gorzknieć***; **zgorzknienie** *n (-nia; no pl)* bitterness
zgrabiać ⟨**-bić**⟩ *(-biam)* rake up
zgrabiały *adj*: ***~ z zimna*** numb with cold
zgrabieć *v/p* → ***grabieć***
zgrabn|y *adj* **1.** *nogi, figura, kobieta*: shapely; ***jest bardzo ~a*** she has a great figure **2.** *ruchy*: graceful **3.** *zdanie*: well-turned **4.** *(zręczny)* deft
zgrać *v/p (-ram)* **1.** *(czasowo)* coordinate **2.** *(skopiować)* copy; ***zgrać się***: ***zgrał się doszczętnie*** he lost all his money (gambling)
zgraja *f (-rai; -je)* bunch, pack
zgran|y *adj zespół*: tight, good; ***tworzyć ~ą parę*** make a good couple
zgromadzenie *n (-nia; -nia) (zebranie)* meeting, gathering, assembly
zgromadzić *v/p* → ***gromadzić***
zgroz|a *f (-zy; no pl)* horror; ***patrzeć na coś ze ~ą*** watch s.th. in horror; ***zdjęty ~ą*** horror-stricken; ***o ~o!*** horror of horrors!
zgrubiały *adj naskórek*: thickened
zgrubieć *v/p* → ***grubieć***
zgrubienie *n (-nia; -nia)* **1.** *(na skórze)* callus, callosity **2.** *GRAM* augmentative (form)
zgruchotać *v/p* → ***gruchotać***
zgrupować *v/p* → ***grupować***
zgrupowanie *n (-nia; -nia)* **1.** *(wojsk)* concentration **2.** *SPORT* training camp
zgryw|a: ***dla ~y*** *infml* for a bit of fun, for kicks
zgrywać *v/im (-wam)*: ***~ kogoś*** *infml* play s.o., act s.o.; ***zgrywać się*** *(udawać) infml* show off; ***~ się na kogoś*** play s.o., act s.o.
zgrywus *m (-sa; -sy) infml* prankster
zgryz *m (-zu; no pl)* bite, *form* occlusion; ***mieć krzywy ~*** have a bad bite
zgryzota *f (-ty; -ty)* grief, worry
zgryźliwy *adj* scathing
zgrzać się *v/p (-rzeję)* sweat, get hot; **zgrzany** *adj* sweaty, hot
zgrzebło *n (-ła; -ła) (do czyszczenia konia)* curry comb
zgrzebny *adj* **1.** *płótno*: coarse **2.** *ubranie*: plain
zgrzeszyć *v/p* → ***grzeszyć***
zgrzewać ⟨**-rzać**⟩ *(-wam) TECH* weld
zgrzewarka *f (-ki; -ki) TECH* welder
zgrzybiały *adj* senile, decrepit
zgrzyt *m (-tu; -ty)* **1.** *(o metal, szkło)* scraping **2.** *klucza w zamku*: scrape **3.** *hamulców*: grinding **4.** *drzwi*: creaking **5.** ***~y*** *(nieporozumienia)* friction, misunderstandings **6.** *(dysonans)* clash
zgrzytać ⟨**-tnąć**⟩ *(-tam)* **1.** *(o zawiasach)* grate **2.** *(o hamulcach, częściach maszyn)* grind **3.** ***~ zębami*** **a)** grind one's teeth **b)** *fig* gnash one's teeth
zgub|a *f (-by; no pl)* **1.** *(rzecz)* lost thing, lost item **2.** *(osoba)* lost person **3.** *(nieszczęście)* ***iść na pewną ~ę*** go to certain death; ***doprowadzić do ~y*** *(zrujnować)* bring to ruin; ***ocalić od ~y*** save
zgubić *v/p* → ***gubić***
zgubiony *adj* lost
zgubny *adj* **1.** *decyzja*: fatal **2.** *wpływ*: disastrous, destructive **3.** ***być ~m w skutkach*** have disastrous effects

zgwałcić *v/p* → ***gwałcić***
zhańbić *v/p* → ***hańbić***
zharmonizować *v/p* → ***harmonizować***
ZHP *abbr m/n indecl* (=***Związek Harcerstwa Polskiego***) Polish Scouting and Guiding Association
ziać *v/im* (*zieję*) **1.** (*o przepaści*) yawn **2.** *ogniem*: belch **3.** ~ ***pustką*** be totally empty, be totally deserted; ***w sali ziało pustką*** the hall was totally empty
ziarenko *n* (*-ka*; *-ka*) *dim* **1.** *soli*, *pieprzu*, *piasku*: grain **2.** *kawy*: bean **3.** *słonecznika*: seed **4.** ~ ***prawdy*** *fig* grain of truth
ziarnisty *adj* **1.** *faktura*: grainy **2.** *kawa*: whole bean
ziarnko *n* (*-ka*; *-ka*) → ***ziarenko***
ziarno *n* (*-na*; *-na*) **1.** (*owoc*, *nasiono*) grain; ~ ***fasoli*** bean; ~ ***kawy*** coffee bean; ~ ***kakao*** cocoa bean; ~ ***słonecznika*** sunflower seed; ~ ***prawdy*** *fig* grain of truth **2.** (*do siewu*) grain, seed; ***oddzielać ~ od plewy*** *fig* separate the wheat from the chaff
ziąb *m* (*-bu*; *no pl*) cold, chill
zidentyfikować *v/p* → ***identyfikować***
zidiocieć *v/p* → ***idiocieć***
zielarski *adj* **1.** *wyroby*: herbal **2.** ***sklep*** ~ herb shop, herbalist's
zielarstw|o *n* (*-wa*; *no pl*) **1.** (*leczenie ziołami*) herbal medicine; ***zajmować się ~em*** (*leczyć*) treat people with herbs, practise herbal medicine **2.** (*wiedza*) herbalism **3.** (*uprawa*) herb cultivation
zielarz *m* (*-rza*; *-rze*), **-rka** *f* (*-ki*; *-ki*) herbalist
ziele *n* (*-la*; *zioła*) herb; ***zioła*** herbs; ***pić zioła*** drink herbal teas; ~ ***angielskie*** allspice, pimento
zieleniak *m* (*-ka*; *-ki*) (*sklep*) *Br* greengrocer's, *Am* (fruit and) vegetable shop
zielenić się ⟨**za-**⟩ (*-nię*) **1.** (*stawać się zielonym*) turn green **2.** (*być zielonym*) be green
zielenieć ⟨**z-**⟩ (*-nieję*) **1.** (*stawać się zielonym*) turn green; ~ ***z zazdrości*** turn green with envy **2.** (*stawać się zielonym*) be green
zielenin|a *f* (*-ny*; *no pl*) greens *pl*, green vegetables *pl*; ***sklep z ~ą*** *Br* greengrocer's, *Am* vegetable shop; **zieleń** *f* (*-leni*; *-lenie*) **1.** (*kolor*) green **2.** (*rośliny*) greenery
zielnik *m* (*-ka*; *-ki*) herbarium
zieloniutki *adj dim* bright green
zielonkawy *adj* greenish
zielon|y *adj* green; ***w kolorze ~ym*** green; ***na ~ym*** (***świetle***) on the green light; ***tereny ~e*** (*parki*) parks; ***przejść przez ~ą granicę*** cross the border illegally; ***nie mieć ~ego pojęcia o*** *L* not have the faintest idea of; ***on jest jeszcze ~y*** *infml* he's still green; ***Ze Świątki*** *REL* Pentecost, Whit Sunday; ***Zi*** *POLIT* the Greens, the Green Party
zielsko *n* (*-ka*; *-ka*) **1.** (*rośliny*) weeds *pl* **2.** (*roślina*) weed
ziemi|a *f* (*-mi*; *-mie*) **1.** (*powierzchnia*) ground; ***pod ~ą*** underground; ***upaść na ~ę*** fall to the ground; ***podnieść się z ~*** raise oneself from the ground; ***trzęsienie ~*** earthquake; ***suknia do ~*** full-length dress; ***wyrosnąć jak spod ~*** appear out of nowhere; ***zrównać coś z ~ą*** raze s.th. to the ground; ***~a usuwa mu się spod nóg*** his world is coming crashing around him; ***~a pali mu się pod nogami*** things are getting hot for him; ***ze wstydu najchętniej zapadłbym się pod ~ę*** I wished the earth would open up and swallow me; ***mocno stąpać po ~*** *fig* have one's feet on the ground; ***gryźć ~ę*** *fig* bite the dust **2.** ***Za*** (*planeta*) the earth; ***nie z tej ~*** *fig* unbelievable; ***życie na Z*** life on earth **3.** (*gleba*) soil, earth; ***uprawiać ~ę*** cultivate land **4.** (*obszar*) land; ***~a ojczysta*** motherland; ***Za Święta*** the Holy Land
Ziemianin *m* (*-na*; *-mianie*), **-mianka** *f* (*-ki*; *-ki*) earthling
ziemianin *m* (*-na*; *-mianie*), **-mianka** *f* (*-ki*; *-ki*) *HIST* landowner
ziemianka *f* (*-ki*; *-ki*) (*schronienie*) dugout
ziemiaństwo *n* (*-wa*; *no pl*) (landed) gentry
ziemniaczan|y *adj* potato; ***placki ~e*** potato cakes; ***stonka ~a*** Colorado beetle, (Colorado) potato beetle
ziemniak *m* (*-ka*; *-ki*) potato; ***~i z wody*** boiled potatoes; ***~i w mundurkach*** jacket potatoes

ziemn|y *adj*: ***wał ~y*** earth embankment; ***gaz ~y*** natural gas; ***orzeszki ~e*** peanuts; ***prace ~e*** excavations
ziemsk|i *adj* **1.** (*dotyczący Ziemi*) earth's, terrestrial; ***atmosfera ~a*** the earth's atmosphere; ***~ie formy życia*** terrestrial life forms; ***kula ~a*** the globe; ***przyciąganie ~ie*** gravity **2.** (*doczesny*) earthly, worldly **3.** (*dotyczący gruntu*) landed: ***majątek ~i*** landed estate
ziewać ⟨**-wnąć**⟩ (*-wam*) yawn; **ziewanie** *n* (*-nia*; *no pl*) yawning
zięba *f* (*-by*; *-by*) chaffinch
ziębić *v/im* (*-bię*) chill; ***to mnie ani ziębi, ani grzeje*** it leaves me cold
zięć *m* (*zięcia*; *zięciowie*) son-in-law
zignorować *v/p* → ***ignorować***
zilustrować *v/p* → ***ilustrować***
zim|a *f* (*-my*; *-my*) winter; ***~ą, w ~ie*** in winter
zimnawy *adj* a bit cold, coldish; **zimnica** (*-cy*; *no pl*) *infml* cold; ***ale tu ~!*** it sure is cold here!
zimniejszy *adj comp* → ***zimny*** colder
zimn|o[1] *n* (*-na*; *no pl*) **1.** (*chłód*) cold; ***drżeć z ~a*** shiver with cold; ***siny*** (***zdrętwiały***) ***z ~a*** blue (numb) with cold **2.** (*opryszczka*) cold sore
zimno[2] *adv* cold; ***robi się ~*** it's getting cold; ***~ mi*** I'm cold; ***~ mi w nogi*** my feet are cold; ***w mieszkaniu jest ~*** it's cold in the flat, the flat is cold; ***~ tu jak w psiarni*** *infml* it's freezing in here; ***podawać coś na ~*** serve s.th. cold
zimnokrwisty *adj zwierzę*: cold-blooded
zimn|y *adj* cold; ***~e przekąski*** cold snacks; ***~y jak lód*** ice-cold; ***z ~ą krwią*** in cold blood; ***zachować ~ą krew*** stay cool; ***dmuchać na ~e*** *fig* play it safe; ***~e ognie*** sparklers; ***~a wojna*** *HIST* cold war
zimorodek *m* (*-dka*; *-dki*) kingfisher
zimować ⟨**prze-**⟩ (*-muję*) winter
zimowisko *n* (*-ka*; *-ka*) (*dla młodzieży*) winter camp
zimowy *adj* winter; ***sen ~*** hibernation; ***zapadać w sen ~*** hibernate
zintegrować *v/p* → ***integrować***
zintensyfikować *v/p* → ***intensyfikować***
zinterpretować *v/p* → ***interpretować***
zioła *pl* → ***ziele***
ziołolecznictwo *n* (*-wa*; *no pl*) herbal medicine; **ziołowy** *adj* herbal
ziomek *m* (*-mka*; *-mkowie*) compatriot, countryman
ziomkostwo *n* (*-wa*; *-wa*) territorial association; ***~ Śląskie*** the Territorial Association of Silesia
zionąć *vim/p* (*-nę*): ***~ ogniem*** belch fire; ***~ pustką*** be empty; ***~ nudą*** be boring
ziółk|o *n* (*-ka*; *-ka*) **1.** (*zioło*) herb; ***pić ~a*** drink herbal tea(s) **2.** (*gagatek*) *infml Br* scallywag, *Am* scalawag
zipać *v/im* (*-pię*): ***ledwo ~, ledwie ~*** *infml* be more dead than alive, be on one's last legs
zirytować *v/p* → ***irytować***
zirytowany *adj* annoyed, irritated
ziszczać się ⟨**ziścić**⟩ *lit* come true
zjadacz *m* (*-cza*; *-cze*): (***przeciętny***) ***~ chleba*** the man in the street
zjadać ⟨**zjeść**⟩ (*-dam*) **1.** eat; ***zjadł trochę makaronu*** he had some pasta **2.** *końcówki*: drop; → ***jeść***
zjadliwy *adj* **1.** *krytyka*: scathing **2.** *osoba*: spiteful **3.** *jedzenie*: edible
zjawa *f* (*-wy*; *-wy*) apparition, *Br* spectre, *Am* specter
zjawiać się ⟨**-wić**⟩ (*-wiam*) **1.** (*przybywać*) turn up, show up **2.** (*ukazywać się*) appear
zjawisk|o *n* (*-ka*; *-ka*) phenomenon; ***~a*** phenomena; ***~o przyrody*** natural phenomenon
zjazd *m* (*-du*; *-dy*) **1.** (*zjeżdżanie*) going down, descent **2.** (*fragment terenu*) descent **3.** (*konkurencja narciarska*) downhill (race) **4.** (*zjechanie na nartach*) run **5.** (*z autostrady*) *Br* slip road, *Am* exit ramp **6.** (*partii*) convention **7.** *rodzinny*: reunion; **zjazdowy** *adj bieg*: downhill
zjechać *v/p* (*zjadę*): ***~ kogoś*** *infml* tell s.o. off; → ***zjeżdżać***
zjednać *v/p* → ***zjednywać***
zjednoczeni|e *n* (*-nia*; *-nia*) **1.** (*połączenie*) unification; ***Święto ~a Niemiec*** German Unification Day **2.** (*organizacja*) union, federation
zjednoczon|y *adj* united; ***Stany ~e Ameryki*** the United States of America; ***Organizacja Narodów ~ych*** the United Nations
zjednoczyć *v/p* → ***jednoczyć***

zjednywać ⟨**-nać**⟩ (*-nuję/wam*): **~ sobie** win over
zjełczały *adj* rancid
zjełczeć *v/p* → **jełczeć**
zjeść *v/p* → **zjadać**
zjeździć *v/p* (*zjeżdżę*) *kraj*: travel all over
zjeżdżać ⟨**zjechać**⟩ (*-dżam*) **1.** go down; **~ na nartach** ski downhill; **~ na sankach** ride down on a toboggan; **~ z autostrady** pull off a motorway; **zjeżdżaj stąd!** *infml* get out of here! **2.** (*przybywać*) come **3.** (*zsuwać się*) slip **4.** (*na pobocze*) pull over; **zjeżdżać się** arrive
zjeżdżalnia *f* (*-ni*; *-nie*) slide
zjeżyć *v/p* (*-żę*): **~ sierść** bristle; **zjeżyć się** (*o włosach*, *kocie*) bristle; **włosy zjeżyły mi się na głowie** my hair stood on end
zjonizować *v/p* → **jonizować**
zlać *v/p* (*zleję*) **1.** (*pobić*) *infml* beat up, thrash **2.** (*oblać*) **~ kogoś wodą** pour water on s.o., drench s.o. with water; **zlać się 1.** (*o kolorach*) blur **2.** (*zsiusiać się*) *infml* wet oneself; → **zlewać**
zlany *adj*: **~ potem** bathed in sweat, sweating all over
zlatywać ⟨**-lecieć**⟩ (*-tuję*) **1.** (*o ptaku*, *owadzie*) fly down **2.** (*o osobie*) *infml* run down; **~ po schodach** run down the stairs **3.** (*o czasie*) *infml* go by, pass; **zlatywać się 1.** come running, flock **2.** (*spadać*) fall down
zlecać ⟨**-cić**⟩ (*-cam*) **1. ~ komuś wykonanie czegoś** contract s.th. (out) to s.o. **2.** *obowiązki*: assign **3.** (*polecać*) order
zleceni|e *n* (*-nia*; *-nia*) **1.** (*polecenie*) order, instruction; **~e stałe** FIN standing order **2.** (*umowa*) freelance contract, freelance agreement; **pracować na umowę ~e** do freelance work
zleceniobiorca *m* (*-cy*; *-cy*) contractor;
zleceniodawca *m* (*-cy*; *-cy*) customer
zlecić *v/p* → **zlecać**
zlecieć *v/p* → **zlatywać**
zlecon|y *adj*: **praca ~a** freelance job
zlekceważyć *v/p* → **lekceważyć**
zlepek *m* (*-pku*/*-pka*; *-pki*) **1.** mix **2.** *stylów*, *kultur*: patchwork
zlepiać ⟨**-pić**⟩ (*-piam*) glue together
zlew *m* (*-wu*; *-wy*) sink
zlewać ⟨**zlać**⟩ (*-wam*) **1.** (*odlewać*) pour off **2.** (*do jednego naczynia*) pour; **zlewać się** (*łączyć się*) blur, merge; → **zlać**
zlewki *pl* (*-wek*) slops; **zlewozmywak** *m* (*-ka*; *-ki*) sink
zleźć *v/p* → **złazić**
zlęknąć się *v/p* (*-nę*) be scared (*G* of), take fright (*G* at)
zliberalizować *v/p* → **liberalizować**
zliczać ⟨**-czyć**⟩ (*-czam*) count, sum up
zlikwidować *v/p* → **likwidować**
zlinczować *v/p* → **linczować**
zlitować się *v/p* (*-tuję*) take pity (**nad** *I* on)
zlizywać ⟨**-zać**⟩ (*-zuję*) lick off
zlodowaciały *adj* frozen; **zlodowacieć** *v/p* → **lodowacieć**
zlokalizować *v/p* → **lokalizować**
zlot *m* (*-tu*; *-ty*) **1.** rally; **~ młodzieży** youth rally **2.** *harcerski*: jamboree **3.** *rodzinny*: reunion
zlustrować *v/p* → **lustrować**
zlutować *v/p* → **lutować**
zluzować *v/p* (*-zuję*) **1.** *wartownika*: relieve **2.** *pas*: loosen, slacken
zł *abbr* (= **złoty**) zloty, PLN
złagodnieć *v/p* → **łagodnieć**
złagodzenie *n* (*-nia*; *no pl*) **1.** *bólu*, *cierpień*: alleviation **2.** *wyroku*: commutation **3.** *kary*: mitigation
złagodzić *v/p* → **łagodzić**
złajać *v/p* → **łajać**
złakniony *adj*: **być ~m wiedzy** be hungry for knowledge; **być ~m miłości** crave love
złakomić się *v/p* → **łakomić się**
złamać *v/p* (*-mię*): **~ komuś serce** break s.o.'s heart; → **łamać**
złamanie *n* (*-nia*; *-nia*) MED fracture; **na ~ karku** *infml* at breakneck speed;
złaman|y *adj* broken; **nie dać ~ego grosza** *infml* give nothing
złapać *v/p* (*-pię*): **~ gumę** *infml Br* have a flat tyre, *Am* get a flat; → **łapać**
złazić ⟨**zleźć**⟩ (*złażę*) *infml* **1.** (*chodzić wszędzie*) walk all over **2.** (*schodzić*) come down (**z** *G* from) **3.** (*o farbie*) peel off
złącze *n* (*-cza*; *-cza*) TECH connector
złączyć *v/p* (*-czę*) join; **złączyć się** join (together)
zło *n* (*zła*; *no pl*) evil; **mniejsze ~** lesser evil; **~ konieczne** necessary evil; **na-**

Z

prawić ~ undo the wrong, make amends

złocenie *n* (*-nia*; *-nia*) gilding, gilt

złoci → ***złoty***[1]

złocić ⟨**po-**⟩ (*-cę*) gild; **złocić się** shine like gold

złocisty *adj* golden

złoczyńca *m* (*-cy*; *-cy*) villain

złodziej *m* (*-ja*; *-je*) thief; ***~ kieszonkowy*** pickpocket; ***~ samochodów*** car thief; **złodziejaszek** *m* (*-szka*; *-szki*) *infml* pilferer; **złodziejsk|i** *adj* thief's, thieves', of thieves; ***gwara ~a*** thieves' slang; ***~a nora*** thief's den; **złodziejstwo** *n* (*-wa*; *no pl*) thieving

złoić *v/p* → ***łoić***

złom *m* (*-mu*; *no pl*) scrap; **złomować** *v/im* (*-muję*) scrap

złościć ⟨**ze-**⟩ (*złoszczę*) make angry; **złościć się** get angry (**na** *A* with/at)

złoś|ć *f* (*-ści*; *no pl*) anger, annoyance; ***ze ~cią*** angrily; ***w ~ci*** in anger; ***na ~ć*** out of spite; ***jak na ~ć*** to make matters worse

złośliwie *adv* spitefully, maliciously; **złośliwość** *f* (*-ści*; *no pl*) spite, malice; ***~ rzeczy martwych*** the perversity of inanimate objects; **złośliwy** *adj* **1.** spiteful, nasty, malicious **2.** *nowotwór*: malignant

złośnica *f* (*-cy*; *-ce*) shrew; **złośnik** *m* (*-ka*; *-nicy*) *infml* crosspatch

złotawy *adj* golden; **złotko** *n* (*-ka*; *no pl*) **1.** (*opakowanie*) gold foil **2.** ***~ko!*** *infml* honey!, sugar!

złotnictwo *n* (*-wa*; *no pl*) goldsmithery; **złotnik** *m* (*-ka*; *-nicy*) goldsmith

złot|o[1] *n* (*-ta*; *no pl*) gold; ***kopalnia ~a*** gold mine; ***gorączka ~a*** gold rush; ***wykonany ze ~a*** made of gold; ***coś jest na wagę ~a*** s.th. is worth its weight in gold; ***nie wszystko ~o, co się świeci*** all that glitters is not gold; ***osiemnastokaratowe ~o*** 18-carat gold

złoto[2] *adv* goldenly, *Br* in gold colours, *Am* in gold colors

złotobrunatny *adj* golden brown; **złotodajny** *adj* gold-bearing

złotowłosy *adj lit* golden-haired

złotówka *f* (*-ki*; *-ki*) **1.** (*pieniądz*) zloty **2.** (*moneta*) one-zloty coin

złot|y[1] *adj* **1.** (*ze złota*) gold; ***~y medal*** gold medal; ***mieć ~e serce*** have a heart of gold; ***~a rączka*** *fig* handyman; ***obiecywać ~e góry*** promise the earth; ***~y wiek*** golden age; ***~y środek*** a happy medium, the golden mean **2.** (*o kolorze*) golden

złoty[2] *m* (*-tego*; *-te*) (*waluta*) zloty; ***masz pięć ~ch?*** have you got five zlotys?; ***to kosztuje sto ~ch*** this costs a hundred zlotys

złowić *v/p* → ***łowić***

złowrogi *adj* (*złowieszczy*) ominous

złoża *pl* (*złóż*) deposits; ***~ rudy*** ore deposits; ***~ węgla*** coal deposits

złożenie *n* (*-nia*; *-nia*) GRAM compound

złożony *adj* **1.** (*skomplikowany*) complex **2.** (*składający się*) consisting (**z** *G* of): ***być ~m z*** *G* consist of **3.** *rzeczownik*: compound

złożyć *v/p* → ***składać***

złuda *f* (*-dy*; *no pl*) illusion; **złudny** *adj* illusory

złudze|nie *n* (*-nia*; *-nia*) **1.** (*wrażenie zmysłowe*) illusion; ***~nie wzrokowe*** optical illusion; ***są do ~nia podobni*** they are as like as two peas **2.** (*mrzonka*) illusion, delusion; ***nie mieć ~ń*** have no illusions; ***pozbawić kogoś ~ń*** disillusion s.o.

złupić *v/p* → ***łupić***

zł|y *adj* **1.** bad, evil; ***~y sen*** nightmare; ***~y znak*** bad sign; ***~e maniery*** bad manners; ***~e oceny*** *Br* bad marks, *Am* bad grades; ***~y duch*** evil spirit; ***~a wola*** malice; ***~a wymowa*** mispronunciation; ***być w ~ym humorze*** be in a bad mood; ***w ~ym guście*** in bad taste; ***mieć ~e przeczucia*** have misgivings; ***Uwaga! ~y pies!*** Beware of the dog!; ***nie ma tego ~ego, co by na dobre nie wyszło*** all's well that ends well, every cloud has a silver lining; ***na dobre i na ~e*** for better or for worse **2.** (*rozzłoszczony*) angry, *Am* mad; ***jesteś na mnie ~y?*** are you angry with me?

zm. *abbr* (= **zmarły**) ob., late

zmachać się *v/p* (*-cham*) *infml* run oneself ragged

zmagać się *v/im* (*-gam*) struggle (**z** *I* with), wrestle (**z** *I* with)

zmagania *pl* (*-gań*) struggle *sing*

zmagazynować *v/p* → ***magazynować***

zmajstrować *v/p* → ***majstrować***

zmaleć *v/p* → ***maleć***

zmałpować *v/p* → ***małpować***

zmamić *v/p* → ***mamić***
zmanierowany *adj* **1.** affected, pretentious **2.** *styl*: mannered
zmarkotnieć *v/p* → ***markotnieć***
zmar|ły I *adj* late **II** *m* (*-łego*; *-rli*), **-ła** *f* (*-łej*; *-łe*) the deceased; ***~li*** the dead, the deceased; ***Święto ~łych*** **a)** (*1 listopada*) All Saints' Day **b)** (*2 listopada*) All Souls' Day
zmarnieć *v/p* → ***marnieć***
zmarnotrawić *v/p* → ***marnotrawić***
zmarnować *v/p* → ***marnować***
zmarszczk|i *pl* (*-czek*) wrinkles, lines; ***głębokie ~i*** furrows; ***twarz pokryta ~ami*** wrinkled face; ***przeciw ~om*** anti-wrinkle; **zmarszczony** *adj czoło*: furrowed; **zmarszczyć** *v/p* → ***marszczyć***
zmartwić *v/p* → ***martwić***
zmartwieć *v/p* → ***martwieć***
zmartwienie *n* (*-nia*; *-nia*) worry, trouble, problem; **zmartwiony** *adj* worried
zmartwychwstanie *n* (*-nia*; *no pl*) REL Resurrection; **zmartwychwstawać** ⟨**-tać**⟩ (*-taję*) resurrect, rise from the dead
zmarzluch *m* (*-cha*: *-chy*) *infml* chilly person; **zmarznąć** *v/p* → ***marznąć***; **zmarznięty** *adj* frozen
zmasakrować *v/p* → ***masakrować***
zmasowany *adj atak*: mass, concentrated
zmatowieć *v/p* → ***matowieć***
zmawiać ⟨**-mówić**⟩ (*-wiam*) *modlitwę*: say; ***zmawiać się*** conspire (**przeciw** *D* against)
zmaza *f* (*-zy*; *no pl*) **1.** (*na honorze*) *lit* stain **2.** ***~ nocna*** nocturnal pollution
zmazywać ⟨**-zać**⟩ (*-zuję*) **1.** wipe off; ***~ tablicę*** clean the blackboard **2.** (*gumką*) rub out, erase
zmącić *v/p* → ***mącić***
zmądrzeć *v/p* → ***mądrzeć***
zmechacić się *v/p* → ***mechacić się***
zmechanizować *v/p* → ***mechanizować***
zmęczenie *n* (*-nia*; *no pl*) **1.** tiredness, fatigue **2.** *materiału*: fatigue; **zmęczony** *adj* tired; **zmęczyć** *v/p* → ***męczyć***
zmętnieć *v/p* → ***mętnieć***
zmężnieć *v/p* → ***mężnieć***
zmian|a *f* (*-ny*; *-ny*) **1.** change (*G* of/in); ***~a na lepsze*** change for the better; ***nagła ~a pogody*** sudden change in the weather; ***~a oleju*** change of oil; ***~a pościeli*** change of bed linen; ***na ~ę*** (*po kolei*) in turns; ***ubranie na ~ę*** a change of clothes **2.** (*czas pracy*) shift; ***nocna ~a*** night shift; ***praca na ~y*** shift work; ***pracować na ~y*** work in shifts
zmiatać ⟨**zmieść**⟩ (*-tam*) **1.** (*miotłą*) sweep **2.** (*zjadać*) *infml* gobble up **3.** ***zmiataj!*** *infml* clear off!
zmiażdżyć *v/p* → ***miażdżyć***
zmiąć *v/p* → ***miąć***
zmieniać ⟨**-nić**⟩ (*-niam*) change; ***~ zdanie*** change one's mind; ***~ pracę*** change one's job; ***~ pościel*** change the bedclothes; ***~ pas*** (*na drodze*) change the lane; ***~ bieg*** change gear; ***~ wodę w wino*** turn water into wine; ***zmieniać się*** **1.** change; ***wcale się nie zmieniłeś!*** you haven't changed a bit!; ***~ się na lepsze*** change for the better; ***~ się jak w kalejdoskopie*** change rapidly **2.** (*robić coś na zmianę*) take turns; ***zmieniali się za kierownicą*** they took turns driving
zmienna *f* (*-nej*; *-ne*) MATH variable
zmiennik *m* (*-ka*; *-nicy*), **-niczka** *f* (*-ki*; *-ki*) **1.** (*zastępstwo*) substitute, *Am* alternate **2.** (*kierowca*) relief driver
zmienn|y *adj* **1.** changeable; ***~e koleje losu*** ups and downs **2.** (*w uczuciach*) changeable, fickle **3.** *prąd*: alternating **4.** *oprocentowanie*: variable
zmierzać *v/im* (*-rzam*) **1.** (*kierować się*) head (**do** *G* for) **2.** (*dążyć*) aim (**do** *G* at) **3.** (*chcieć powiedzieć*) get at, drive at; ***do czego zmierzasz?*** what are you getting at?, what are you driving at?
zmierzch *m* (*-chu*; *-chy*) dusk, twilight; **zmierzchać** *v/im*: ***zmierzcha*** it's growing dark
zmierzwić *v/p* → ***mierzwić***; **zmierzwiony** *adj* ruffled
zmierzyć *v/p* → ***mierzyć***
zmieszać *v/p* → ***mieszać***; **zmieszanie** *n* (*-nia*; *no pl*) confusion; **zmieszany** *adj* confused
zmieścić (się) *v/p* → ***mieścić (się)***
zmieść *v/p* → ***zmiatać***
zmiękczać ⟨**-czyć**⟩ (*-czam*) **1.** soften **2.** *głoski*: palatalize
zmięknąć *v/p* → ***mięknąć***

zmiętosić *v/p* → ***miętosić***
zmiksować *v/p* → ***miksować***
zmilitaryzować *v/p* → ***militaryzować***
zmiłować się *v/p* (*-łuję*) have mercy (***nad*** *I* on)
zmiotka *f* (*-ki*; *-ki*) brush
zmistyfikować *v/p* → ***mistyfikować***
zmitygować *v/p* → ***mitygować***
zmizernieć *v/p* → ***mizernieć***
zmizerowany *adj* haggard
zmniejszać ⟨**-szyć**⟩ (*-szam*) **1.** *rozmiar, koszty, niebezpieczeństwo*: reduce **2.** *czcionkę*: make smaller **3.** *karę*: mitigate; ***zmniejszać się*** decrease; ***zmniejszenie*** *n* (*-nia*; *no pl*) **1.** decrease (*G* in/of) **2.** *kary*: mitigation
zmobilizować *v/p* → ***mobilizować***
zmoczyć *v/p* → ***moczyć***
zmodernizować *v/p* → ***modernizować***
zmodyfikować *v/p* → ***modyfikować***
zmokły *adj* wet; ***zmoknąć*** *v/p* → ***moknąć***
zmontować *v/p* → ***montować***
zmor|a *f* (*-ry*; *-ry*) **1.** *fig* curse **2.** (*sen*) nightmare; ***męczyły mnie ~y senne*** I had nightmares
zmordowany *adj infml* weary
zmorzyć *v/p* → ***morzyć***
zmotoryzowany **I** *adj oddziały*: motorized **II** *m* (*-nego*; *-ni*) car owner, motorist
zmow|a *f* (*-wy*; *-wy*) conspiracy; ***~a milczenia*** conspiracy of silence; ***być w ~ie z*** *I* be in league with, *infml* be in cahoots with
zmówić *v/p* → ***zmawiać***
zmrok *m* (*-ku*; *no pl*) dusk, twilight; ***po ~u*** after dusk; ***zapada ~*** it's getting dark
zmrozić *v/p* → ***mrozić***
zmrużyć *v/p* → ***mrużyć***
zmumifikować *v/p* → ***mumifikować***
zmurszały *adj* rotten; ***zmurszeć*** *v/p* → ***murszeć***
zmuszać ⟨**-sić**⟩ (*-szam*) force (***do*** *G* to do), make (***do*** *G* do); ***zmuszać się*** force oneself, make oneself; ***zmuszony*** *adj*: ***czuć się ~m coś zrobić*** feel forced to do s.th.
zmyć *v/p* (*zmyję*): ***~ komuś głowę*** *fig* give s.o. a good dressing down; → ***zmywać***: ***zmyć się*** *infml* clear off
zmykać *v/im* (*-kam*): ***zmykaj!*** *infml* buzz off!, beat it!
zmylić *v/p* → ***mylić***
zmyłk|a *f* (*-ki*; *-ki*) *infml* bluff, trick; ***dla ~i*** to put s.o. off
zmysł *m* (*-łu*; *-ły*) sense; ***~ wzroku*** the sense of sight, seeing; ***~ słuchu*** hearing; ***~ węchu*** the sense of smell; ***~ smaku*** the sense of taste; ***~ organizacyjny*** organizational skills; ***postradać ~y*** lose one's mind; ***przy zdrowych ~ach*** sane, in one's right mind
zmysłowo *adv* sensually; ***świat postrzegany ~*** the world perceived through the senses
zmysłowość *f* (*-ści*; *no pl*) sensuality; ***zmysłow|y*** *adj* **1.** (*erotyczny*) sensual **2.** (*dotyczący zmysłów*) sensory; ***wrażenie ~e*** sensation
zmyślać ⟨**-lić**⟩ (*-lam*) **1.** (*wymyślać*) invent, make up **2.** (*kłamać*) lie
zmyślny *adj* clever
zmyślony *adj* fictitious, made-up, false
zmywacz *m* (*-cza*; *-cze*) remover; ***~ do paznokci*** nail polish remover, *Br* nail varnish remover
zmywać ⟨**zmyć**⟩ (*-wam*) **1.** wash; ***~ naczynia*** wash the dishes, do the dishes; ***zostać zmytym z pokładu*** be washed off the deck **2.** *plamę*: remove **3.** *makijaż*: remove, take off; ***zmywać się*** **1.** (*o plamie*) come off **2.** (*uciekać*) *infml* clear off
zmywak *m* (*-ka*; *-ki*) (*szmatka*) dishcloth; ***zmywalny*** *adj* washable; ***zmywarka*** *f* (*-ki*; *-ki*) dishwasher
znachor *m* (*-ra*; *-rzy*), ***~ka*** *f* (*-ki*; *-ki*) (folk) healer
znacjonalizować *v/p* → ***nacjonalizować***
znaczący *adj* meaningful
znaczek *m* (*-czka*; *-czki*) **1.** (*nalepka*) stamp; ***~ pocztowy*** postage stamp; ***~ skarbowy*** duty stamp **2.** (*odznaka*) badge
znaczeni|e *n* (*-nia*; *-nia*) **1.** meaning **2.** (*waga*) significance; ***mieć ~e dla*** *G* be important for, matter for; ***bez ~a*** not important, unimportant
znaczny *adj* considerable
znaczony *adj karty*: marked
znaczyć *v/im* (*-czę*) **1.** (*mieć znaczenie*) mean; ***co znaczy to słowo?*** what does this word mean?; ***to znaczy, że*** it means that; ***to dla mnie wiele znaczy*** it means a lot to me; ***pienią-***

dze dla niego nic nie znaczą he doesn't care about money; ***co to ma ~?*** what's that supposed to mean? **2.** (*robić znak*) mark

znać[1] *v/im* (*znam*) know; ***~ z widzenia*** know by sight; ***znasz niemiecki?*** can you speak German?; ***on zna dobrze polski*** he can speak Polish very well; ***~ na pamięć*** know by heart; ***znasz drogę?*** do you know the way; ***~ jak własną kieszeń*** know inside out, know like the back of my hand; ***znam ten ból*** *infml* I know the feeling; ***dać komuś ~*** let s.o. know; ***znać się* 1.** (*nawzajem*) know each other; ***~ się jak łyse konie*** know each other inside out **2.** (*mieć wiedzę*) ***~ się na*** *L* know a lot about; ***~ się na ludziach*** be a good judge of character, be a good judge of people; ***ona nie zna się na żartach*** she can't take a joke

znać[2] *v/irreg*: ***~ było po niej zdenerwowanie*** one could see she was nervous, you could see she was nervous

znad *prep* (*G*) from above; ***~ morza*** from the seaside, from the coast; ***~ rzeki*** from the river; ***patrzeć ~ okularów*** look over one's glasses, peer over one's glasses

znajda *f/m* (*-dy*; *-dy*) (*dziecko*) *infml* foundling

znajdować ⟨**znaleźć**⟩ (*-duję*) find; ***~ nocleg*** find accommodation; ***~ uznanie*** find recognition; ***~ spokój*** find peace; ***~ czas dla kogoś*** find time for s.o., make time for s.o.; ***być jak znalazł*** be perfect; ***znajdować się* 1.** (*być*) be, be located; ***w pobliżu znajduje się supermarket*** there's a supermarket nearby **2.** (*o zgubionej rzeczy*) be found

znajomek *m* (*-mka*; *-mki*) *infml* pal

znajomoś|ć *f* (*-ści*; *-ści*) **1.** (*z osobą*) acquaintance; ***~ci*** (*kontakty*) connections **2.** (*wiedza*) knowledge; ***~ć języków obcych*** knowledge of foreign languages

znajomy I *adj* familiar; ***mój ~ weterynarz*** a vet I know, my vet friend **II** *m* (*-mego*; *-mi*), **-ma** *f* (*-mej*; *-me*) friend, acquaintance

znak *m* (*-ku*; *-ki*) sign; ***~ drogowy*** traffic sign, road sign; ***~ zodiaku*** star sign, zodiac sign; ***~ zapytania*** question mark; ***~ interpunkcyjny*** punctuation mark; ***~ fabryczny*** trademark; ***~ wodny*** watermark; ***~i szczególne*** distinguishing marks; ***on jest spod ~u Wagi*** he was born under the sign of Libra, he's a Libra; ***na mój ~*** at my signal; ***zły ~*** ill omen; ***dawać się komuś we ~i*** make oneself felt

znakomicie *adv* superbly; ***~ władał hiszpańskim*** he had an excellent command of Spanish; **znakomitość** *f* (*-ści*; *-ści*) **1.** (*osoba*) celebrity **2.** (*cecha*) distinction; **znakomity** *adj* **1.** (*świetny*) excellent **2.** (*wybitny*) distinguished **3.** *większość*: vast

znakować ⟨**o-**⟩ (*-kuję*) mark

znalazca *m* (*-cy*; *-cy*), **-czyni** *f* (*-ni*; *-nie*) finder

znaleziony *adj* found; ***biuro rzeczy ~ch*** *Br* lost property office, *Am* lost-and-found department

znalezisko *n* (*-ka*; *-ka*) find

znaleźć *v/p* (*znajdę*): ***nie móc sobie ~ miejsca*** *lit* be restless; → ***znajdować***

znaleźne *n* (*-nego*; *no pl*) (finder's) reward

znamienity *adj* outstanding

znamienny *adj* characteristic (***dla*** *G* of)

znamię *n* (*-mienia*; *-miona*) **1.** birthmark **2.** (*cecha*) hallmark

znamionować *v/im* (*-nuję*) characterize, indicate

znany *adj* **1.** (*sławny*) well-known, famous; ***~ z*** *G* (well-)known for **2.** (*znajomy*) familiar; ***ogólnie ~*** generally known

znawc|a *m* (*-cy*; *-cy*), **-czyni** *f* (*-ni*; *-nie*) expert (*G* on/in); ***okiem ~y*** with an expert eye; ***~a przedmiotu*** expert in a subject

znerwicowany *adj* neurotic

zneutralizować *v/p* → ***neutralizować***

znęcać się *v/im* (*-cam*) abuse (***nad*** *I*), maltreat (***nad*** *I*)

znęcić *v/p* → ***nęcić***

znicz *m* (*-cza*; *-cze*) candle; ***~ olimpijski*** the Olympic torch

zniechęcać ⟨**-cić**⟩ (*-cam*) discourage (***kogoś do*** *G* s.o. from); ***zniechęcać się*** become discouraged; **zniechęcający** *adj* discouraging, disheartening

zniechęcenie *n* (*-nia*; *no pl*) discouragement

Z

zniechęcić *v/p* → ***zniechęcać***
zniechęcony *adj* discouraged, disheartened
zniecierpliwić *v/p* → ***niecierpliwić***
zniecierpliwienie *n* (*-nia*; *no pl*) **1.** impatience **2.** (*rozdrażnienie*) irritation, **zniecierpliwiony** *adj* **1.** impatient **2.** (*rozdrażniony*) irritated
znieczulać ⟨**-lić**⟩ (*-lam*) *Br* anaesthetize, *Am* anesthetize
znieczulająco *adv*: **działać ~** *Br* have an anaesthetizing effect, *Am* have an anesthetizing effect; **znieczulający** *adj Br* anaesthetic, *Am* anesthetic
znieczuleni|e *n* (*-nia*; *no pl*) *Br* anaesthesia, *Am* anesthesia; ***w ~u miejscowym*** (***ogólnym***) under local (general) anaesthesia
znieczulica *f* (*-cy*; *no pl*) *infml* callousness
znieczulić *v/p* → ***znieczulać***
zniedołężniały *adj* decrepit, infirm; **zniedołężnieć** *v/p* → ***niedołężnieć***
zniekształcać ⟨**-cić**⟩ (*-cam*) distort; **zniekształcony** *adj* **1.** *twarz*: deformed **2.** *obraz*, *sens*: distorted
znienacka *adv* all of a sudden, unexpectedly
znienawidzić *v/p* (*-dzę*) come to hate; **znienawidzony** *adj* hated
znieruchomiały *adj* motionless; **znieruchomieć** *v/p* → ***nieruchomieć***
zniesieni|e *n* (*-nia*; *no pl*) **1.** ***nie do ~a*** unbearable **2.** (*unieważnienie*) abolition
zniesławiać ⟨**-wić**⟩ (*-wiam*) **1.** (*ustnie*) slander **2.** (*na piśmie*) libel **3.** *lit* defame; **zniesławienie** *n* (*-nia*; *no pl*) **1.** (*ustne*) slander **2.** (*na piśmie*) libel
znieść *v/p* → ***znosić***
zniewaga *f* (*-gi*; *-gi*) insult
zniewalać ⟨**-wolić**⟩ (*-lam*) **1.** *naród*: conquer, subjugate **2.** *fig* put a spell on, captivate; **zniewalający** *adj* captivating
znieważać ⟨**-żyć**⟩ (*-żam*) insult
zniewieściały *adj* effeminate
zniewolić *v/p* → ***zniewalać***
znikać ⟨**-knąć**⟩ (*-kam*) disappear; ***~ bez śladu*** disappear without trace; ***~ z półek*** sell very well
znikąd *pron* from nowhere, out of nowhere; ***człowiek ~*** man from nowhere
zniknąć *v/p* → ***znikać***; **zniknięcie** *n* (*-cia*; *-cia*) disappearance
znikomy *adj* **1.** *ilość*: minute **2.** *szansa*: slim
zniszczeć *v/p* → ***niszczeć***
zniszczeni|e *n* (*-nia*; *-nia*) destruction; ***~a*** damage; ***~a wojenne*** war damage
zniszczony *adj* **1.** destroyed; ***~ wojną*** war-ravaged, destroyed by war; ***~ chorobą*** emaciated **2.** *ubranie*: worn-out **3.** *teren*: devastated **4.** *zdrowie*: ruined
zniszczyć *v/p* → ***niszczyć***
zniweczyć *v/p* → ***niweczyć***
zniwelować *v/p* → ***niwelować***
zniżać ⟨**-żyć**⟩ (*-żam*) lower; ***~ lot*** descend; ***zniżać się*** **1.** (*poniżyć się*) lower oneself, condescend **2.** (*o terenie*) slope, descend
zniżka (*-ki*; *-ki*) **1.** (*obniżka*) reduction **2.** (*niższa opłata*) discount; **zniżkować** *v/im* (*-kuję*) (*o kursie*, *cenach*) be falling; **zniżkow|y** *adj* reduced; ***po cenie ~ej*** at a reduced price
znokautować *v/p* → ***nokautować***
znormalizować *v/p* → ***normalizować***
znosić ⟨**znieść**⟩ (*-szę*) **1.** (*na dół*) carry down; ***~ do piwnicy*** carry down to the cellar **2.** (*wytrzymywać*) stand, put up with; ***nie znoszę go*** I can't stand him; ***nie znoszą się*** they can't stand each other, they hate each other **3.** (*unieważniać*) abolish; ***~ zakaz*** lift a ban **4.** (*gromadzić*) collect **5.** (*o prądzie morskim*) carry away **6.** *jajka*: lay
znoszony *adj ubranie*: worn-out
znośny *adj* bearable, tolerable
znowelizowany *adj ustawa*: amended
znowu, **znów I** *adv* again **II** *particle* **1.** (*przecież*) after all; ***to nie jest ~ tak dużo*** it's not so much after all **2.** ***co znowu?*** what now?; ***skądże znowu!*** nothing of the kind!
znój *m* (*znoju*; *no pl*) *lit* drudgery, toil
znów → ***znowu***
znudzeni|e *n* (*-nia*; *no pl*) boredom; ***do ~a*** endlessly; **znudzić** *v/p* → ***nudzić***; ***znudzić się*** *v/p* (*-dzę*) get bored; → ***nudzić***; **znudzony** *adj* bored
znużenie *n* (*-nia*; *no pl*) weariness; **znużony** *adj* weary, tired; **znużyć** *v/p* → ***nużyć***
zob. *abbr* (=**zobacz**) see

zobaczeni|e: ***coś do ~a*** s.th. to see; ***do ~a!*** see you!
zobaczyć *v/p* (*-czę*) see; ***zobaczymy*** we'll see; ***zobaczymy, czy*** we'll see if; ***zobacz!*** take a look!; ***zobaczyć się* 1.** (*spotkać się*) meet **2.** ***to się jeszcze zobaczy*** we'll see
zobojętniały *adj* indifferent, apathetic; **zobojętnieć** *v/p* → ***obojętnieć***; **zobojętnienie** *n* (*-nia*; *no pl*) indifference, apathy
zobowiązać *v/p* → ***zobowiązywać***
zobowiązanie (*-nia*; *-nia*) obligation, commitment; **zobowiązany** *adj* obliged (**do** *G* to do)
zobowiązujący *adj* binding
zobowiązywać ⟨**-zać**⟩ (*-zuję*) oblige (**do** *G* to do s.th.); ***zobowiązywać się*** oblige oneself, commit oneself
zobrazować *v/p* → ***obrazować***
zodiak (*-ku*; *no pl*) zodiac; ***znak ~u*** sign of the zodiac
zogniskować *v/p* → ***ogniskować***
zołza *f* (*-zy*; *-zy*) *infml* shrew, vixen
zoo *n indecl* zoo; ***iść do ~*** go to the zoo
zoolog *m* (*-ga*; *-gowie*/*-lodzy*) zoologist
zoologiczny *adj* zoological; ***ogród ~*** zoological garden
zoperować *v/p* → ***operować***
zoptymalizować *v/p* → ***optymalizować***
zorganizować *v/p* → ***organizować***
zorganizowan|y *adj* organized; ***przestępczość ~a*** organized crime; ***wyjazd ~y*** package tour
zorientować się *v/p* → ***orientować się***
zorientowany *adj* **1.** (*posiadający wiedzę*) knowledgeable (**w** *L* about); ***być ~m w sytuacji*** know the situation, be aware of the situation **2.** ***~ prawicowo*** right-oriented
zorza *f* (*-rzy*; *-rze*) **1.** ***~ polarna*** **a)** (*na północy*) the northern lights, aurora borealis **b)** (*na południu*) the southern lights, aurora australis **2.** *poranna*: dawn **3.** *wieczorna*: afterglow
zostawać ⟨**-tać**⟩ (*-taję*) **1.** (*nie odchodzić*) stay, remain; ***~ w domu*** stay at home; ***~ w łóżku*** stay in bed; ***~ na noc*** stay overnight, stay the night; ***prawie nic nie zostało*** there's almost nothing left **2.** (*stawać się*) become; ***~ ojcem*** become a father; ***~ nauczycielem*** become a teacher **3.** (*nie nadążać*) ***~ w tyle*** lag behind **4.** (*w określonej sytuacji*) ***~ bez grosza*** be left penniless **5.** (*w stronie biernej*) be; ***~ uszkodzonym*** be damaged; ***~ zaproszonym*** be invited
zostawiać ⟨**-wić**⟩ (*-wiam*) **1.** (*opuszczać*) leave; ***~ wiadomość*** leave a message; ***~ otwarte drzwi*** leave the door open; ***~ dziecko samo*** leave a child alone; ***zostaw mnie*** (***w spokoju***)***!*** leave me alone! **2.** (*zapomnieć*) forget, leave behind; ***~ czapkę w autobusie*** leave a hat behind on a bus **3.** (*osierocać*) orphan **4.** (*w spadku*) bequeath (*D* to)
zracjonalizować *v/p* → ***racjonalizować***
zranić *v/p* → ***ranić***; **zraniony** *adj* **1.** (*na wojnie, polowaniu*) wounded **2.** (*urażony*) hurt
zrastać się ⟨**zrosnąć**⟩ (*-tam*) (*o kościach*) knit (together)
zraszać ⟨**zrosić**⟩ (*-szam*) **1.** *kwiaty doniczkowe*: spray **2.** *trawnik*: sprinkle
zrazić *v/p* → ***zrażać***
zrazy *pl* (*-zów*): ***~ zawijane*** beef roulades
zrażać ⟨**zrazić**⟩ (*-żam*): ***~ kogoś do siebie*** antagonize s.o., put s.o. off; ***zrażać się*** become discouraged, become put off; ***~ się do*** *G* take dislike to
zrąb *m* (*zrębu*; *zręby*) (*podstawa*) foundation
zrąbać *v/p* (*-bię*) *drzewo*: fell, chop
zrealizować *v/p* → ***realizować***
zreasumować *v/p* → ***reasumować***
zrecenzować *v/p* → ***recenzować***
zredagować *v/p* → ***redagować***
zredukować *v/p* → ***redukować***; **zredukowany** *adj* reduced (**do** *G* to)
zreferować *v/p* → ***referować***
zreformować *v/p* → ***reformować***; **zreformowany** *adj* reformed
zregenerować *v/p* → ***regenerować***
zrehabilitować *v/p* → ***rehabilitować***; **zrehabilitowany** *adj* rehabilitated
zrekompensować *v/p* → ***rekompensować***
zrekonstruować *v/p* → ***rekonstruować***
zrelacjonować *v/p* → ***relacjonować***
zrelaksować się *v/p* → ***relaksować się***
zrelatywizować *v/p* → ***relatywizować***
zremisować *v/p* → ***remisować***

zreorganizować *v/p* → **reorganizować**; **zreorganizowany** *adj* reorganized
zreperować *v/p* → **reperować**
zresztą *particle* besides, in any case, anyway
zrewanżować się *v/p* → **rewanżować się**
zrewidować *v/p* → **rewidować**
zrewolucjonizować *v/p* → **rewolucjonizować**
zrezygnować *v/p* → **rezygnować**; **zrezygnowany** *adj* resigned
zręby *pl* → **zrąb**
zręcznościow|y *adj*: **gra ~a** dexterity game
zręczność *f* (*-ści; no pl*) **1.** (*manualna*) dexterity **2.** (*bystrość*) cleverness; **zręczny** *adj* **1.** (*manualnie*) dexterous **2.** (*sprytny*) clever
zrobaczywieć *v/p* → **robaczywieć**
zrobić *v/p* → **robić**
zrodzić *v/p* → **rodzić**
zrogowacenie *n* (*-nia; -nia*) callus, callosity
zrogowaciał|y *adj* callous, horny; **~a skóra** callous skin, horny skin
zrogowacieć *v/p* → **rogowacieć**
zrolować *v/p* → **rolować**
zrosić *v/p* → **zraszać**
zrosnąć się *v/p* → **zrastać się**
zrost *m* (*-tu; -ty*) **1.** (*po operacji*) adhesion **2.** (*złożenie*) compound; **zrośnięty** *adj brwi, bliźnięta*: joined
zroszony *adj*: **~ potem** sweaty, beaded with sweat
zrozpaczony *adj* desperate
zrozumiały *adj* **1.** (*jasny*) clear; **sam przez się ~** self-explanatory **2.** (*uzasadniony*) understandable
zrozumieć *v/p* → **rozumieć**
zrozumieni|e *n* (*-nia; no pl*) **1.** (*pojmowanie*) understanding, comprehension; **trudny do ~a** difficult to understand **2.** (*zdanie sobie sprawy*) realization; **dać do ~a, że** imply that; **dać komuś do ~a, że** make s.o. understand that **3.** (*wyrozumiałość*) understanding
zrównać *v/p* → **zrównywać**
zrównanie *n* (*-nia; no pl*) ASTR equinox; **jesienne ~ dnia z nocą** the autumn(al) equinox; **zrównany** *adj*: **~ z ziemią** razed to the ground
zrównoważony *adj* even-tempered, level-headed
zrównoważyć *v/p* → **równoważyć**
zrównywać ⟨**-nać**⟩ (*-nuję*) *teren*: level; **~ z ziemią** raze to the ground
zróżnicować *v/p* → **różnicować**; **zróżnicowanie** *n* (*-nia; -nia*) diversity; **zróżnicowany** *adj* diverse
zrugać *v/p* → **rugać**
zrujnować *v/p* → **rujnować**; **zrujnowany** *adj* ruined
zryć *v/p* → **ryć**
zryw *m* (*-wu; -wy*): **~ami** by fits and starts; **~ niepodległościowy** bid for independence
zrywać ⟨**zerwać**⟩ (*-wam*) **1.** (*odrywać*) tear off **2.** *kwiaty, owoce*: pick **3.** *stosunki*: break (off); **~ z** *I* break up with **4.** *umowę, zaręczyny*: break **5.** **~ boki** *fig* roll with laughter; **zrywać się 1.** (*o linie*) break **2.** (*wstawać nagle*) spring up; **~ się na równe nogi** jump to one's feet **3.** (*o ptakach*) take wing **4.** (*o wietrze*) start blowing, get up
zrządzenie: **~m losu** by a stroke of fate
zrządzić *v/p*: **przypadek zrządził, że** as fate would have it
zrzednąć *v/p* → **rzednąć**
zrzekać się ⟨**zrzec**⟩ (*-kam*) renounce, waive
zrzeszać się ⟨**-szyć**⟩ (*-szam*) associate; **zrzeszenie** *n* (*-nia; -nia*) association; **zrzeszony** *adj* organized
zrzęda *f/m* (*-dy; -dy*) *infml* grouch; **zrzędzić** *v/im* (*-dzę*) *infml* grumble
zrzucać ⟨**-cić**⟩ (*-cam*) **1.** (*strącać*) knock down; **~ coś ze stołu** knock s.th. off the table **2.** *bomby*: drop **3.** *jeźdźca*: throw **4.** *liście*: shed **5.** *ubranie*: take off **6.** *kilogramy*: lose **7.** (*przypisywać*) **~ winę na** *A* put the blame on; **zrzucać się** *infml* club together
zrzut *m* (*-tu; -ty*) airdrop
zrzynać ⟨**zerżnąć**⟩ (*-nam*) *infml* copy, crib
zsadzać ⟨**-dzić**⟩ (*-dzam*) take down (**z** *G* from)
zsiadać ⟨**zsiąść**⟩ (*-dam*) get off (**z** *G*), dismount (**z** *G*); **~ z roweru** get off a bike
zsiadł|y *adj*: **~e mleko** sour milk
zsiąść *v/p* → **zsiadać**
zsiniały *adj wargi, paznokcie*: blue

Z

zsinieć *v/p* → **sinieć**
zsiusiać się *v/p* (*-siam*) *infml* pee oneself; **~ w majtki** pee one's pants
zsumować *v/p* (*-muję*) sum up
zsuwać ⟨**zsunąć**⟩ (*-wam*) *stoły, krzesła*: push together; **zsuwać się** slip down (**z** *G* from)
zsychać się ⟨**zeschnąć**⟩ (*-cham*) wither
zsyłać ⟨**zesłać**⟩ (*-łam*) exile, banish
zsynchronizować *v/p* → **synchronizować**
zsyp *m* (*-pu*; *-py*): **~ na śmieci** *Br* rubbish chute, *Am* garbage chute
zszarzeć *v/p* → **szarzeć**
zszyć *v/p* → **zszywać**
zszywacz *m* (*-cza*; *-cze*) stapler
zszywać ⟨**zszyć**⟩ (*-wam*) **1.** *materiał, dziurę*: sew up **2.** (*razem*) sew together **3.** *ranę*: stitch up, sew up **4.** *papiery*: staple (together)
zszywka *f* (*-ki*; *-ki*) staple
zubożały *adj* impoverished
zubożeć *v/p* → **ubożeć**
zubożyć *v/p* → **ubożyć**
zuch *m* (*-cha*; *-chy*) **1.** (*członek*) Cub (Scout) **2.** (*członkini*) Brownie
zuchowaty *adj* plucky
zuchwalstwo *n* (*-wa*; *-wa*) (*śmiałość*) impudence
zuchwały *adj* insolent, *infml* cocky
zunifikować *v/p* → **unifikować**
zup|a *f* (*-py*; *-py*) soup; **~a w proszku** powdered soup; **talerz ~y** bowl of soup
zupełnie *adv* completely; **~ sam** all alone; **~ tego nie rozumiem** I don't understand it at all; **zupełnoś|ć**: **w ~ci** absolutely, completely; **zupełny** *adj* complete
ZUS *abbr m* (*ZUS-u*; *no pl*) (= **Zakład Ubezpieczeń Społecznych**) Social Insurance Institution
zużycie *n* (*-cia*; *no pl*) consumption; **~ wody** water consumption; **~ energii elektrycznej** electricity consumption
zużyty *adj* worn-out; **zużywać** ⟨**-żyć**⟩ (*-wam*) **1.** use (up) **2.** (*niszczyć*) wear (out); **zużywać się 1.** (*kończyć się*) run out **2.** (*o urządzeniu*) wear (out)
zwabiać ⟨**-bić**⟩ (*-biam*) entice, lure; **~ w pułapkę** lure into a trap, draw into a trap
zwać *v/im* (*zwę*) *lit* call; **zwać się** be called
zwada *f* (*-dy*; *-dy*) *lit* squabble
zwalać ⟨**-lić**⟩ (*-lam*) **1.** (*zrzucać*) dump; **~ na kupę** heap up **2.** (*przewracać*) knock down **3.** (*przypisywać*) **~ winę na** *A* put the blame on, pin the blame on; **zwalać się** fall down, come down; **~ się komuś na głowę** *infml* descend on s.o.
zwalczać ⟨**-czyć**⟩ (*-czam*) fight, combat
zwalić *v/p* → **zwalać**
zwalisty *adj* stocky, hefty, bulky
zwalniać ⟨**zwolnić**⟩ (*-niam*) **1.** slow down; **~ kroku** slow down **2.** (*wyrzucać*) **~ kogoś z pracy** dismiss s.o. **3.** *zakładnika*: free **4.** *więźnia*: release **5.** *pacjenta*: discharge **6.** *uścisk*: release, relax **7.** *pokój*: vacate **8.** (*od obowiązku, podatku*) exempt (**od** *G*/**z** *G* from); **zwalniać się 1.** (*wyjść za pozwoleniem*) be excused **2.** (*o miejscu*) be vacated **3.** **~ się z pracy** quit
zwany *adj* called; **tak ~** so-called
zwapnieć *v/p* → **wapnieć**; **zwapnienie** *n* (*-nia*; *-nia*) calcification
zwarcie[1] *n* (*-cia*; *-cia*) short-circuit
zwarcie[2] *adv* densely
zwariować *v/p* → **wariować**; **zwariowany** *adj* crazy
zwarty *adj* dense, tight
zwarzony *adj* curdled
zwarzyć się *v/p* (*-rzę*) curdle
zważyć *v/p* (*-żę*): **zważywszy, że** considering that; → **ważyć**
zwąchać *v/p* (*-cham*) nose out
zwątpić *v/p* (*-pię*) **1.** (*stracić wiarę*) lose faith (**w** *A* in), despair (**w** *A* of); **~ w miłość** lose faith in love **2.** (*mieć wątpliwości*) have doubts (**w** *A* about)
zwątpienie *n* (*-nia*; *no pl*) despair
zwerbować *v/p* → **werbować**
zweryfikować *v/p* → **weryfikować**
zwędzić *v/p* (*-dzę*) *infml* swipe, *Br* pinch
zwęglony *adj* carbonized
zwęszyć *v/p* (*-szę*) scent, get wind of
zwężać ⟨**zwęzić**⟩ (*-żam*) **1.** narrow **2.** *suknię*: take in
zwężenie *n* (*-nia*; *-nia*) narrowing
zwiać *v/p* → **zwiewać**

zwiad *m* (*-du*; *-dy*) reconnaissance; **zwiadowca** *m* (*-cy*; *-cy*) scout
zwiastować *v/p* (*-tuję*) herald
zwiastun *m* (*-na*; *-ny*) **1.** (*zapowiedź*) harbinger **2.** *FILM* trailer
związać *v/p* → **związywać**
związany *adj* **1.** (*mający coś wspólnego*) connected (**z** *I* with) **2.** (*emocjonalnie*) ***był ~ z aktorką*** he was (emotionally) involved with an actress, he had a relationship with an actress
związ|ek *m* (*-zku*; *-zki*) **1.** (*partnerski*) relationship **2.** (*zależność*) connection, relation; ***w ~ku z*** *I* in connection with; ***mieć ~ek z*** *I* be connected with **3.** (*organizacja*) union, associaton; ***~ek zawodowy*** trade union **4.** ***~ki*** (*kontakty*) relations **5.** *CHEM* compound
Związek Radziecki *m* (*Związku Radzieckiego*) *HIST* the Soviet Union
związkowiec *m* (*-wca*; *-wcy*) union member, unionist; **związkowy** *adj* union; ***kraj ~wy*** federal state
związywać ⟨**-zać**⟩ (*-zuję*) **1.** tie (up) **2.** *ręce, nogi*: tie; ***związywać się*** (*z osobą*) start a relationship (**z** *I* with); ***~ emocjonalnie*** become emotionally involved
zwichnąć *v/p* (*-nę*): ***~ sobie nogę w kostce*** dislocate one's ankle
zwichnięcie *n* (*-cia*; *-cia*) dislocation; **zwichnięty** *adj* dislocated
zwichrowany *adj drzwi*: warped
zwichrzony *adj* ruffled; **zwichrzyć** *v/p* → **wichrzyć**
zwiedzać ⟨**-dzić**⟩ (*-dzam*) **1.** *zamek, muzeum*: visit **2.** *miasto*: tour; **zwiedzający** *m* (*-cego*; *-cy*), **-ca** *f* (*-cej*; *-ce*) visitor; **zwiedzanie** *n* (*-nia*; *no pl*) sightseeing; ***~ muzeum*** visiting a museum
zwielokrotniać ⟨**-nić**⟩ (*-niam*) multiply
zwieracz *m* (*-cza*; *-cze*) *ANAT* sphincter
zwierać ⟨**zewrzeć**⟩ (*-ram*) *szyki*: close; ***zwierać się*** short-circuit
zwierciadlany *adj* mirror
zwierciadło *n* (*-ła*; *-ła*) *lit* mirror, looking glass
zwierz *m* (*-rza*; *-rze*) *lit* beast; ***gruby ~*** big game
zwierzać się ⟨**-rzyć**⟩ (*-rzam*) confide (*D* in)
zwierzak *m* (*-ka*; *-ki*) **1.** animal **2.** (*trzymany w domu*) pet
zwierzchni *adj* superior; **zwierzchnictwo** *n* (*-wa*; *no pl*) control, authority; **zwierzchnik** *m* (*-ka*; *-nicy*), **-niczka** *f* (*-ki*; *-ki*) superior
zwierzę *n* (*-rzęcia*; *-rzęta*) **1.** animal; ***~ domowe*** domestic animal **2.** (*trzymane w domu*) pet; **zwierzęcy** *adj* animal; **zwierzyna** *f* (*-ny*; *no pl*) game; ***~ gruba*** big game; ***~ płowa*** deer
zwieszać ⟨**-sić**⟩ (*-szam*) hang; ***zwiesić nos na kwintę*** pull a long face
zwieść *v/p* (*zwiodę*) deceive; ***dać się ~*** be deceived; → **zwodzić**
zwietrzały *adj* **1.** *skała*: weathered **2.** *zapach, piwo*: stale
zwietrzeć *v/p* → **wietrzeć**
zwietrzyć *v/p* → **wietrzyć**
zwiewać ⟨**zwiać**⟩ (*-wam*) **1.** (*zdmuchiwać*) blow away **2.** (*uciekać*) *infml* run away
zwiewny *adj* **1.** *tkanina*: airy **2.** *postać*: ethereal
zwieźć *v/p* → **zwozić**
zwiędły *adj* **1.** withered **2.** *kwiat*: wilted; **zwiędnąć** *v/p* → **więdnąć**
zwiększać ⟨**-szyć**⟩ (*-szam*) increase; ***zwiększać się*** increase
zwięzły *adj* succinct, concise
zwijać ⟨**zwinąć**⟩ (*-jam*) **1.** roll (up); ***~ żagle*** *fig* pack it up **2.** *interes*: wind up **3.** *namiot*: take down **4.** *obóz*: break **5.** (*kraść*) *infml* swipe, *Br* nick; ***zwijać się*** **1.** ***~ w kłębek*** curl up **2.** (*śpieszyć się*) *infml* get a move on, hurry up
zwilgotnieć *v/p* → **wilgotnieć**
zwilżać ⟨**-żyć**⟩ (*-żam*) moisten, wet
zwinąć *v/p* → **zwijać**
zwinny *adj* agile, deft
zwiotczały *adj* flabby, limp; **zwiotczeć** *v/p* → **wiotczeć**
zwis *m* (*-su*; *-sy*) *SPORT* hang
zwisać *v/im* (*-sam*) hang down; ***to mu zwisa*** (***i powiewa***) *infml* he doesn't give a shit about it
zwitek *m* (*-tka*; *-tki*) wad; ***~ banknotów*** wad of banknotes
zwlekać ⟨**zwlec**⟩ (*-kam*) delay; ***zwlekać z odpowiedzią*** delay answering a question
zwłaszcza *particle* especially

zwłok|a *f* (*-ki*; *no pl*) delay; ***niecierpiący ~i*** urgent, of utmost urgency; ***bez ~i*** instantly; ***grać na ~ę*** play for time
zwłoki *pl* (*-łok*) dead body *sing*
zwodniczy *adj* deceptive
zwodować *v/p* → ***wodować***
zwodzić ⟨**zwieść**⟩ (*-dzę*) deceive, delude
zwodzony *adj*: ***most ~*** drawbridge
zwolennik *m* (*-ka*; *-nicy*), **-niczka** *f* (*-ki*; *-ki*) advocate, follower
zwolnić *v/p* → ***zwalniać***
zwolnienie *n* (*-nia*; *-nia*) **1.** (*z pracy*) dismissal; ***domagać się zwolnienia kogoś*** call for the dismissal of s.o. **2.** (*od obowiązku*, *podatku*) exemption **3.** (*wolne*) ***~ lekarskie*** sick leave **4.** (*świadectwo*) certificate **5.** ***~ warunkowe*** JUR parole
zwolniony *adj*: ***~ z pracy*** dismissed; ***~ od podatku*** exempt from tax, tax-exempt; ***~ od cła*** duty-free
zwoływać ⟨**-łać**⟩ (*-łuję*) call
zwozić ⟨**zwieźć**⟩ (*zwożę*) bring, gather
zwód *m* (*zwodu*; *zwody*) SPORT dummy, feint; ***zrobić ~*** make a feint
zwój *m* (*zwoju*; *zwoje*) **1.** roll **2.** *drutu*: coil **3.** *papieru*: scroll
zwracać ⟨**-rócić**⟩ (*-cam*) **1.** (*oddawać*) return, give back **2.** (*skupiać*, *przyciągać*) ***~ komuś uwagę na*** *A* draw s.o.'s attention to; ***~ na siebie uwagę*** draw attention to oneself, stand out, ***proszę zwrócić uwagę na*** *A* please pay attention to **3.** (*wymiotować*) vomit, throw up **4.** *koszty*: reimburse; ***zwracać się*** **1.** (*kierować się*, *obracać się*) turn (***do*** *G* to, ***przeciw*** *D* against) **2.** (*o inwestycji*) pay for itself
zwrot *m* (*-tu*; *-ty*) **1.** return **2.** *pieniędzy*: refund **3.** (*skręt*) turn **4.** (*słowa*) phrase; ***~ frazeologiczny*** set phrase
zwrotka *f* (*-ki*; *-ki*) verse, stanza
zwrotnica *f* (*-cy*; *-ce*) (*kolejowa*) *Br* points *pl*, *Am* switch
zwrotnik *m* (*-ka*; *-ki*) GEOGR tropic; ***~ Koziorożca*** (***Raka***) the Tropic of Capricorn (Cancer); **zwrotnikowy** *adj* tropical
zwrotność *f* (*-ści*; *no pl*) *Br* manoeuvrability, *Am* maneuverability; **zwrotny** *adj* **1.** *pojazd*: *Br* manoeuvrable, *Am* maneuvrable **2.** *butelka*: returnable **3.** FIN refundable **4.** *czasownik*, *zaimek*: reflexive **5.** ***punkt ~*** turning point
zwrócić *v/p* → ***zwracać***
zwycięski *adj* victorious
zwycięstwo *n* (*-wa*; *-wa*) victory
zwycięzca *m* (*-cy*; *-cy*) **1.** winner **2.** (*w bitwie*) *lit* victor
zwyciężać ⟨**-żyć**⟩ (*-żam*) win
zwyciężczyni *f* (*-ni*; *-nie*) winner; ***~ w konkursie piękności*** beauty queen
zwyciężony *adj* beaten, defeated; **zwyciężyć** *v/p* → ***zwyciężać***
zwyczaj *m* (*-ju*; *-je*) custom; ***~ ludowy*** folk custom
zwyczajnie *adv* **1.** (*normalnie*) ordinarily **2.** (*po prostu*) just, simply; **zwyczajny** *adj* **1.** (*zwykły*) ordinary, usual **2.** (*normalny*) normal, regular **3.** *profesor*: full; **zwyczajowo** *adv* customarily, according to custom; **zwyczajowy** *adj* customary
zwykle *adv* usually, generally, as a rule; ***jak ~*** as usual; ***wcześniej niż ~*** earlier than usual; **zwykły** *adj* **1.** (*zwyczajny*) ordinary **2.** (*normalny*) normal, regular
zwymiotować *v/p* → ***wymiotować***
zwymyślać *v/p* (*-lam*) *infml* give a dressing-down
zwyrodnialec *m* (*-lca*; *-lcy*) degenerate; **zwyrodniały** *adj przestępca*: degenerate; **zwyrodnieć** *v/p* → ***wyrodnieć***; **zwyrodnienie** *n* (*-nia*; *-nia*) degeneration
zwyżka *f* (*-ki*; *-ki*) rise; **zwyżkować** *v/im* (*-kuję*) rise
zygzak *m* (*-ka*; *-ki*) zigzag; **zygzakowaty** *adj* zigzag
zysk *m* (*-ku*; *-ki*) **1.** FIN profit; ***przynosić ~*** yield a profit, be profitable; ***sprzedawać z ~iem*** sell at a profit; ***spadek ~ów*** fall in profits **2.** (*pożytek*) benefit
zyskiwać ⟨**-kać**⟩ (*-kuję*) **1.** (*zarabiać*) profit (***na*** *L* from) **2.** *przyjaciół*, *zaufanie*: win (over) **3.** *sławę*, *popularność*: gain; ***~ na wartości*** gain in value **4.** ***starać się zyskać na czasie*** play for time
zyskowny *adj* profitable
zza *prep* (*G*) from behind
zziajany *adj* breathless, out of breath
zzielenieć *v/p* → ***zielenieć***

zziębnąć *v/p* → **ziębnąć**; **zziębnięty** *adj* frozen to the bone, very cold
zżerać ⟨**zeżreć**⟩ (*-ram*) **1.** (*zjadać szybko*) devour, *infml* gobble up **2.** (*o rdzy*) eat away at
zżółkły *adj* yellow; **zżółknąć** *v/p* → **żółknąć**
zżyć się *v/p* (*zżyję*) **1.** become intimate (**z** *I* with) **2.** (*przyzwyczaić się*) get accustomed (**z** *I* to)
zżymać się *v/im* (*-mam*) bridle (**na** *A* at), flinch (**na** *A* at)
zżynać ⟨**zżąć**⟩ (*-nam*) (*odpisywać*) *infml* crib
zżyty *adj* close (**z** *I* to), attached (**z** *I* to)
ździebełko, **ździebko** *n* (*-ka*; *-ka*) a bit, a pinch (*G* of)

Ź

ździbło *n* (*-ła*; *-ła*) *trawy*: blade
źle *adv* badly, poorly; ***~ się czuję*** I feel bad; ***jest mi tu ~*** I feel bad here; ***~ wyglądać*** look bad; ***~ płatny*** badly-paid; ***~ odżywiony*** malnourished; ***~ zrozumieć*** misunderstand; ***jest z nim ~*** he's in a serious condition; ***~ wychowany*** ill-mannered; ***~ się zachowywać*** misbehave; ***~, że*** it's bad that
źli → **zły**
źrebak *m* (*-ka*; *-ki*), **źrebię** *n* (*-bięcia*; *-bięta*) **1.** foal **2.** (*samiec*) colt
źrenica *f* (*-cy*; *-ce*) pupil
źródlan|y *adj*: ***woda ~a*** spring water
źródł|o *n* (*-ła*; *-ła*) **1.** (*początek strumienia*) spring; ***~o mineralne*** mineral spring, spa; ***~o lecznicze*** spa, medicinal spring; ***gorące ~a*** hot springs, thermal springs **2.** (*przyczyna*) source; ***~o informacji*** source of information; ***~o dochodów*** source of income

Ż

żaba *f* (*-by*; *-by*) frog
żabi *adj* frog, frog's; ***~ skrzek*** frogspawn
żabk|a *f* (*-ki*; *-ki*) *dim* **1.** (*mała żaba*) little frog **2.** SPORT breaststroke; ***pływać ~ą*** swim breaststroke **3.** (*do firanek*) curtain hook **4.** TECH tongue-and-groove pliers
żachnąć się *v/p* (*-nę*) bridle (**na** *A* at)
żad|en *pron* **1.** (*ani jeden*) no, not any; ***w ~en sposób nie można było tam wejść*** there was no way to get in; ***nie mieli ~nych drobnych*** they had no small change; ***nie mieliśmy ~nych problemów*** we didn't have any problems; ***nie przyszedł ~en list*** there haven't been any letters; ***bez ~nego znaczenia*** of no importance **2.** (*z wielu*) none; ***~en z nas nie był z tego zadowolony*** none of us were happy with it **3.** (*z dwóch*) neither; ***~en z nich mi się nie podoba*** I like neither of them
żagiel *m* (*-gla*; *-gle*) sail; **żaglowiec** *m* (*-wca*; *-wce*) sailing ship; **żaglow|y** *adj*: ***płótno ~e*** sailcloth; ***statek ~y*** sailing ship; **żaglówka** *f* (*-ki*; *-ki*) sailing boat
żakiet *m* (*-tu*; *-ty*) (lady's) jacket
żal *m* (*-lu*; *-le*) **1.** (*smutek*) sorrow; ***~ mi go*** I'm sorry for him; ***było nam jej ~*** we felt sorry for her; ***wyrazić ~ z powodu tego, co się stało*** express one's regret at what had happened **2.** (*po stracie*) grief **3.** (*skrucha*) remorse, regret **4.** (*uraza*) resentment, grudge; ***czuć ~ do*** *G* have a grudge against, feel resentment towards
żalić się *v/im* (*-lę*) complain (**na** *A* about)
żaluzje *pl* (*-ji*) (Venetian) blinds
żałob|a *f* (*-by*; *no pl*) mourning; ***nosić ~ę***, ***chodzić w ~ie*** be in mourning; **żałobnik** *m* (*-ka*; *-nicy*) mourner; **żałobn|y** *adj* mourning; ***msza ~a*** requiem Mass; ***kondukt ~y*** funeral procession
żałosny *adj* **1.** pathetic **2.** (*opłakany*) deplorable, wretched **3.** (*smutny*) doleful, dismal

żałować *v/im* (*-łuję*) **1.** (*odczuwać żal*) regret, be sorry; ***bardzo żałuję*** I'm really sorry; ***będziesz tego ~!*** you'll regret that!; ***żałował, że był taki lekkomyślny*** he wished he hadn't been so reckless; ***niczego nie żałuję*** I have no regrets, I don't regret a thing **2.** (*współczuć*) be sorry for, pity **3.** (*odczuwać skruchę*) repent, regret; ***~ za grzechy*** repent of one's sins **4.** (*skąpić*) stint (*G* on); ***nie ~ pieniędzy*** spare no expense

żandarm *m* (*-ma*; *-mi*) **1.** (*we Francji*) gendarme **2.** (*policjant wojskowy*) military policeman

żar *m* (*-ru*; *no pl*) **1.** embers *pl* **2.** (*zapał*) passion

żarcie *n* (*-cia*; *no pl*) *infml* grub

żargon *m* (*-nu*; *-ny*) jargon

żarliwie *adv* **1.** *kochać*: passionately **2.** *wierzyć*: fervently **3.** *bronić*: vehemently; **żarliwy** *adj* **1.** *modlitwa*, *wyznawca*, *pragnienie*: fervent **2.** *miłość*: passionate

żarłoczność *f* (*-ści*; *no pl*) voracity, gluttony, greediness; **żarłocznie** *adv* voraciously, greedily; **żarłoczny** *adj* voracious, greedy; **żarłok** *m* (*-ka*; *-ki*) glutton

żarna *pl* (*-ren*/*żarn*) HIST quern *sing*

żaroodporny *adj* **1.** heat-resistant **2.** *naczynie*: ovenproof

żarówka *f* (*-ki*; *-ki*) (electric) bulb

żart *m* (*-tu*; *-ty*) joke; ***~em***, ***dla ~u*** as a joke, for fun; ***złośliwy ~*** nasty trick; ***nie znać się na ~ach*** not know how to take a joke; ***robić sobie ~y z kogoś*** pull s.o.'s leg; ***z nim nie ma ~ów*** he isn't to be trifled with; ***~y na bok***, ***~y ~ami*** joking apart; ***to chyba jakiś ~*** it must be a joke, you must be kidding

żartobliwy *adj* humorous, playful, facetious

żartować ⟨**za-**, **po-**⟩ (*-tuję*) joke; ***~ z G*** make fun of, poke fun at; ***on nie żartuje*** he's not joking, he means that; ***nie żartuj!*** you must be kidding!

żartowniś *m* (*-nisia*; *-nisie*), **-nisia** *f* (*-si*; *-sie*) joker

żarzyć się *v/im* (*-rzę*) glow

żądać ⟨**za-**⟩ (*-dam*) demand; ***żądał przeprowadzenia śledztwa*** he demanded that an investigation be carried out

żądanie *n* (*-nia*; *-nia*) demand; ***na ~*** on demand; ***przystanek na ~*** request stop

żądlić ⟨**u-**⟩ (*-lę*) sting

żądło *n* (*-ła*; *-ła*) sting

żądny *adj* greedy (*G* for); ***~ władzy*** greedy for power, power-greedy; ***~ pieniędzy*** greedy for money, money-greedy; ***~ wiedzy*** hungry for knowledge, eager for knowledge; ***~ krwi*** bloodthirsty; ***~ sławy*** fame-seeking; ***~ przygód*** adventurous

żądza *f* (*-dzy*; *-dze*) desire (*G* for), lust (*G* for); ***~ władzy*** lust for power, greed of power; ***~ wiedzy*** eagerness to learn; ***zaspokoić swoją żądzę*** satisfy one's lust, satiate one's lust; ***~ przygód*** adventurousness

żbik *m* (*-ka*; *-ki*) wildcat

że **I** *conj* that; ***wiem, ~ ona tu jest*** I know (that) she's here; ***był tak zajęty, ~ nie zauważył jej*** he was so busy (that) he did not notice her; ***poszedł spać, dlatego ~ był zmęczony*** he went to bed because he was tired; ***chyba ~*** unless; ***nie pozwolę ci wyjść, chyba ~ obiecasz, ~ wrócisz przed ósmą*** I won't let you go out unless you promise to come back before eight **II** *particle* ***mimo ~*** although; ***tyle ~*** only; ***omal ~ nie*** almost; ***~ tak powiem*** so to speak

żeberka *pl* (*-rek*) COOK ribs

żebractwo *n* (*-wa*; *no pl*) begging, beggary; **żebraczka** *f* (*-ki*; *-ki*) (female) beggar; **żebrać** ⟨**wy-**⟩ (*-rzę*) beg; **żebrak** *m* (*-ka*; *-racy*/*-ki*) beggar; **żebranina** *f* (*-ny*; *no pl*) → ***żebractwo***

żebro *n* (*-ra*; *-ra*) rib

żebry: ***chodzić na ~*** go begging

żeby **I** *conj* to, in order to, so as to; ***jest zbyt zmęczony, ~ pracować*** he's too tired to work; ***chciała, ~śmy zaczęli jeść*** she wanted us to start eating; ***nie ~m jej nie lubił*** not that I don't like her **II** *particle* ***~m to wiedział przedtem*** if only I had known that before

żeglarka *f* (*-ki*; *-ki*) (female) sailor

żeglarski *adj* **1.** sailing **2.** SPORT yachting; **żeglarstwo** *n* (*-wa*; *no pl*) **1.** (*po*

Ż

morzu) sailing **2.** SPORT yachting, sailing
żeglarz *m* (*-rza*; *-rze*) sailor, seaman
żeglować *v/im* (*-luję*) sail, navigate
żeglowność *f* (*-ści*; *no pl*) navigability; **żeglowny** *adj* navigable
żegluga *f* (*-gi*; *no pl*) navigation; **~ wielka** ocean sailing
żegnać ⟨**po-**⟩ (*-nam*) say goodbye (*G* to); **żegnać się 1.** (*odchodząc*) say goodbye (**z** *I* to), take one's leave (**z** *I* of); **żegnaj!** farewell!, goodbye! **2.** (*robić znak krzyża*) cross oneself
żel *m* (*-lu*; *-le*) gel; **~ do włosów** hair gel
żelastwo *n* (*-wa*; *no pl*) scrap (metal)
żelatyna *f* (*-ny*; *no pl*) gelatin(e)
żelazisty *adj smak*: metallic
żelazko *n* (*-ka*; *-ka*) iron
żelazn|y *adj* iron; **~a kurtyna** HIST the Iron Curtain; **żelaz|o** *n* (*-za*; *no pl*) iron; **z ~a** iron, (made) of iron; **epoka ~a** the iron age
żelbet (*-tu*; *no pl*), **żelbeton** *m* (*-nu*; *no pl*) reinforced concrete, RC
żeliwny *adj* cast-iron; **żeliwo** *n* (*-wa*; *no pl*) cast iron
żenad|a *f* (*-dy*; *no pl*) **1. bez ~y a)** unceremoniously **b)** *mówić*: openly **2.** (*chłam*) *infml* trash; **to była ~a** it sucked
żeniaczka *f* (*-ki*; *no pl*) marriage
żenić ⟨**o-**⟩ (*-nię*) marry; **żenić się** get married (**z** *I* to), marry (**z** *I*)
żenować ⟨**za-**⟩ (*-nuję*) embarrass
żenujący *adj* **1.** pathetic **2.** *sytuacja*, *cisza*: embarrassing
żeński *adj* **1.** *chór*, *zespół*: women's **2.** *szkoła*: girls' **3.** *narządy*: female; **osobniki ~e** females, female individuals **4.** *rodzaj*: feminine
żeń-szeń *m* (*-szenia*; *-szenie*) ginseng
żer *m* (*-ru*; *no pl*) **1.** feed **2.** (*drapieżnika*) prey; **wychodzić na ~** go hunting
żerdź *f* (*-dzi*; *-dzie*) **1.** pole **2.** (*pozioma*) perch
żerować *v/im* (*-ruję*) **1.** (*o zwierzętach*) feed, prey **2.** (*o ludziach*) prey; **~ na ludzkim nieszczęściu** prey on other people's misfortune
żerowisko *n* (*-ka*; *-ka*) feeding ground
żeton *m* (*-nu*; *-ny*) **1.** (*do automatu*) token **2.** (*w grach*) chip
żleb *m* (*-bu*; *-by*) gully
żłobek *m* (*-bka*; *-bki*), *Br* (day) nursery, *Br* créche, *Am* day care center
żłobić ⟨**wy-**⟩ (*-bię*) carve, furrow
żłopać ⟨**wy-**⟩ (*-pię*) *infml* guzzle
żłób *m* (*żłobu*; *żłoby*) manger, trough; **dostać się do żłobu** *fig* get one's snout in the trough; **żłóbek** *m* (*-bka*; *-bki*) REL manger
żmija *f* (*żmii*; *-je*) viper; **~ zygzakowata** adder
żmudny *adj* arduous, laborious
żniwa *pl* (*żniw*) harvest *sing*
żniwiarka *f* (*-ki*; *-ki*) harvester, reaper
żniwiarz *m* (*-rza*; *-rze*) harvester, reaper
żniwny *adj maszyny*: harvesting
żniwo: **śmierć zebrała krwawe ~** death took its toll
żołąd|ek *m* (*-dka*; *-dki*) stomach; **na pusty ~ek** on an empty stomach; **ból ~ka** stomachache; **przez ~ek do serca** the way to a man's heart is through his stomach
żołądkow|y *adj* stomach, gastric; **zaburzenia ~e** gastric disorders; **soki ~e** gastric juices
żołądź[1] *m* (*-łędzia*; *-łędzie*) **1.** (*owoc*) acorn **2.** (*trefl*) club
żołądź[2] *f* (*-łędzi*; *-łędzie*) ANAT glans
żołd *m* (*-du*; *no pl*) (soldier's) pay; **żołdactwo** *n* (*-wa*; *no pl*) marauding soldiers *pl*; **żołdak** *m* (*-ka*; *-dacy*) marauding soldier
żołnierski *adj* **1.** soldier's, soldier **2.** *piosenki*: war, soldier; **żołnierz** *m* (*-rza*; *-rze*) soldier; **żołnierzyk** *m* (*-ka*; *-ki*): **ołowiany ~** toy soldier
żon|a *f* (*-ny*; *-ny*) wife; **wziął ją za ~ę** he took her as his wife
żonaty I *adj* married **II** *m* (*-tego*; *-naci*) married man
żongler *m* (*-ra*; *-rzy*) juggler; **żonglować** *v/im* (*-luję*) juggle
żonkil *m* (*-la*; *-le*) daffodil
żorżeta *f* (*-ty*; *no pl*) georgette
żółcić się *v/im* (*-cę*) be yellow
żółciow|y *adj* bile; **woreczek ~y** gall bladder; **kamienie ~e** gallstones
żółciutki *adj dim* (deep) yellow
żółć *f* (*-łci*; *no pl*) **1.** ANAT bile **2.** (*kolor*) *lit* yellow
żółknąć ⟨**po-**, **z-**⟩ (*-nę*) turn yellow
żółtaczka *f* (*-ki*; *no pl*) MED jaundice
żółtawy *adj* yellowish

żółtek *m* (*-tka*; *-tki*) *infml* **1.** (*Chińczyk*) Chink **2.** (*Japończyk*) Jap

żółtko *n* (*-ka*; *-ka*) yolk

żółto *adv*: ***malować na ~*** paint yellow; ***ubrany na ~*** (dressed) in yellow; **żółtodziób** *m* (*-dzioba*; *-dzioby*) rookie, greenhorn

żółtozielony *adj* yellow-green

żółt|y *adj* yellow; ***~y ser*** cheese; ***~a kartka*** SPORT yellow card

żółw *m* (*-wia*; *-wie*) **1.** (*wodny*) turtle **2.** (*lądowy*) tortoise; ***jak ~*** at a snail's pace

żółwi *adj* turtle's, tortoise's; ***w ~m tempie*** at a snail's pace

żrący *adj* caustic

żreć ⟨**ze-**⟩ (*żrę*) **1.** *infml* (*zjadać szybko*) guzzle, gobble (up) **2.** (*o zwierzęciu*) feed (*A* on); ***żreć się*** *infml* be at each other's throats

żubr *m* (*-ra*; *-ry*) (European) bison, wisent; **żubrówka** *f* (*-ki*; *-ki*) bison grass vodka

żuchwa *f* (*-wy*; *-wy*) ANAT mandible, lower jaw

żuć *v/im* (*żuję*) chew

żuk *m* (*-ka*; *-ki*) beetle

żur *m* (*-ru*; *-ry*) sour-rye soup, ryemeal soup

żuraw *m* (*-wia*; *-wie*) crane; **żurawi** *adj* crane's

żurawina *f* (*-ny*; *no pl*) cranberry

żurek *m* (*-rku*; *-rki*) → ***żur***

żurnal *m* (*-la*/*-lu*; *-le*) fashion magazine

żużel *m* (*-żla*/*-żlu*; *no pl*) **1.** cinder, clinker **2.** (*wyścigi*) speedway **3.** (*tor*) cinder track; **żużlowy** *adj*: ***tor ~*** cinder track

żwawy *adj* **1.** brisk **2.** *staruszek*: vigorous **3.** *taniec*: lively

żwir *m* (*-ru*; *no pl*) gravel; **żwirować** *v/im* (*-ruję*) gravel; **żwirowy** *adj droga*: gravel

życi|e *n* (*-cia*; *-cia*) **1.** life; ***~e rodzinne*** family life; ***~e prywatne*** private life; ***~e zawodowe*** professional life; ***~e nocne*** night life; ***styl ~a*** lifestyle; ***poziom ~a*** standard of living; ***zarabiać na ~e*** earn a living; ***utrzymać przy ~u*** keep alive; ***bez ~a*** lifeless; ***kochać kogoś nad ~e*** love s.o. more than one's own life; ***~e pozagrobowe*** afterlife, life after death; ***cieszyć się ~em*** enjoy life; ***pełen ~a*** full of life, vigorous; (***nigdy***) ***w ~u!*** never in my life!; ***długość ~a*** life span, longevity; ***oczekiwana długość ~a*** life expectancy **2.** (*koszty utrzymania*) cost of living **3.** ***wejść w ~e*** JUR come into effect

życiodajny *adj* life-giving; **życiorys** *m* (*-su*; *-sy*) CV, curriculum vitae, *Am* resumé

życiowo *adv*: ***zaradny ~*** resourceful; ***doświadczony ~*** experienced in life

życiow|y *adj* **1.** life; ***~a szansa*** chance of a lifetime; ***mądrość ~a*** practical wisdom, common sense; ***stopa ~a*** standard of living; ***rekord ~y*** personal best; ***oferma ~a*** loser **2.** *osoba*: down-to-earth

życzeni|e *n* (*-nia*; *-nia*) wish; ***~a*** wishes; ***~a urodzinowe*** birthday wishes; ***~a imieninowe*** name's day wishes; ***~a świąteczne*** **a)** (*bożonarodzeniowe*) Christmas wishes **b)** (*wielkanocne*) Easter wishes; ***kartka z ~ami świątecznymi*** **a)** (*bożonarodzeniowa*) Christmas card **b)** (*wielkanocna*) Easter card; ***składać komuś najlepsze ~a*** wish s.o. all the best; ***pozostawiać wiele do ~a*** leave a lot to be desired; ***pobożne ~e*** wishful thinking

życzliwość *f* (*-ści*; *no pl*) kindness; **życzliwy** *adj* kind, friendly

życzyć *v/im* (*-czę*) wish; ***~ sobie*** *G* wish for; ***jak pan sobie życzy*** as you wish; ***czego pan sobie życzy?*** how can I help you?; ***~ komuś dobrze*** wish s.o. well; ***~ komuś źle*** wish s.o. ill; ***~ komuś szerokiej drogi*** wish s.o. a safe journey; ***~ komuś powrotu do zdrowia*** wish s.o. a speedy recovery

żyć *v/i* (*żyję*) live (***z*** *I* with); ***~ na wsi*** live in the country; ***~ w zgodzie z naturą*** live in harmony with nature; ***dobrze ~ z*** *I* get on well with; ***źle ~ z*** *I* get on badly with; ***~ z*** *I* (*współżyć*) be with; ***~ własnym życiem*** have a life of one's own; ***nie dawać komuś ~*** plague s.o., make s.o.'s life a misery; ***~ ponad stan*** live beyond one's means; ***~ jak pies z kotem*** fight like cat and dog; ***~ nadzieją, że*** live in the hope that; ***niech żyje król!*** long live the king!

Żyd *m* (*-da*; *-dzi*) Jew; **żydostwo** *n* (*-wa*; *no pl*) Jewry; **żydowski** *adj* Jew-

Ż

ish; **Żydówka** *f* (*-ki*; *-ki*) Jewess, Jewish woman
żyjący **I** *adj* living **II** *m* (*-cego*; *-cy*) the living
żyjątko *n* (*-ka*; *-ka*) (small) creature
żylaki *pl* (*-ków*) varicose veins; **żylasty** *adj* **1.** *mięso*: stringy **2.** *osoba*: wiry, sinewy
żyletka *f* (*-ki*; *-ki*) razor blade
żylny *adj* venous
żył|a *f* (*-ły*; *-ły*) **1.** ANAT GEOL vein; ***podciąć sobie ~y*** slit one's wrists, cut one's wrists; ***~a złota*** *fig* gold mine **2.** (*skąpa osoba*) *infml* skinflint
żyłk|a *f* (*-ki*; *-ki*) *dim* **1.** ANAT vein, veinlet **2.** (*do wędki*) line **3.** *fig* bent; ***mieć ~ę do*** *G* have a bent for
żyrafa *f* (*-fy*; *-fy*) giraffe
żyrandol *m* (*-la*; *-le*) chandelier
żyrant *m* (*-ta*; *-nci*) FIN guarantor; **żyrować** ⟨**pod-**⟩ (*-ruję*) FIN guarantee
żytni *adj* rye; **żytniówka** *f* (*-ki*; *-ki*) rye vodka; **żyto** *n* (*-ta*; *no pl*) rye
żywcem *adv* alive
żywica *f* (*-cy*; *-ce*) resin
żywiciel *m* (*-la*; *-le*), **~ka** *f* (*-ki*; *-ki*) **1.** (*rodziny*) bread-winner **2.** BIOL host
żywiczny *adj* resinous
żywić *v/im* (*-wię*) **1.** (*karmić*) feed **2.** (*odczuwać*): **~ *urazę do*** *G* bear a grudge against; **~ *nadzieję, że*** hope (that); **~ *sympatię do*** *G* like; **~ *przekonanie, że*** be convinced that; ***żywić się*** feed (*I* on)
żywiec *m* (*-wca*; *-wce*) **1.** (*przynęta*) live bait **2.** (*zwierzęta*) livestock
żywienie *n* (*-nia*; *no pl*) nutrition, feeding; **żywieniowy** *adj* **1.** *nawyki*: eating, dietary **2.** *normy*: nutrition, nutritional
żywio|ł *m* (*-łu*; *-ły*) element; ***być w swoim ~le*** be in one's element
żywiołow|y *adj* **1.** *osoba*, *temperament*: impulsive **2.** *reakcja*: spontaneous **3.** ***klęska ~a*** natural disaster
żywnie *adv*: ***możesz robić, co ci się ~ podoba*** you can do whatever you please
żywnościow|y *adj* food; ***artykuły ~e*** foodstuffs
żywnoś|ć *f* (*-ści*; *no pl*) food; ***sklep ze zdrową ~cią*** health food shop
żywo *adv*: ***na ~*** live; → ***żywy***
żywokost *m* (*-tu*; *-ty*) (*roślina*) comfrey
żywopłot *m* (*-tu*; *-ty*) hedge
żyworodny *adj* viviparous
żywot *m* (*-ta*; *-ty*) *lit* life; ***~y świętych*** the lives of the saints; **~ *wieczny*** eternal life
żywotność *f* (*-ści*; *no pl*) vitality; **żywotny** *adj* **1.** *staruszek*: sprightly **2.** *problem*, *pytanie*: vital **3.** *rzeczownik*: animate
żyw|y *adj* **1.** (*żyjący*) living, alive; ***wciąż ~y*** still alive; ***~y język*** living language; ***~a gotówka*** hard cash; ***handel ~ym towarem*** slave trade; ***nie było tam ~ej duszy*** there was nobody there, the place was completely empty **2.** *wspomnienie*, *wyobraźnia*: vivid **3.** *zainteresowanie*: keen **4.** *dyskusja*: heated **5.** *kolor*: bright, vivid
żyzność *f* (*-ści*; *no pl*) fertility; **żyzny** *adj* fertile

Ż

English – Polish

A

A [eɪ] *s* **1.** A *n*; ***from ~ to B*** od punktu A do punktu B **2.** (*najwyższa ocena w systemie szkolnictwa anglosaskiego*) celujący *m*, bardzo dobry *m*; ***an ~ in history*** piątka z historii

a [ə], *strong form* [eɪ] *art przedimek przed wyrazem rozpoczynającym się samogłoską*; **an** [æn] *przedimek przed wyrazem rozpoczynającym się spółgłoską*; ***~ red car*** czerwony samochód; ***an apple*** jabłko

a•back [ə'bæk] *adv*: ***be taken ~*** **a)** być nieprzyjemnie zaskoczonym **b)** być zaszokowanym

a•ban•don [ə'bændən] **I** *v/t* **1.** porzucać ⟨-cić⟩, zostawiać ⟨-wić⟩, opuszczać ⟨opuścić⟩; ***~ ship*** opuścić statek **2.** zaprzestawać ⟨-tać⟩, rezygnować ⟨z-⟩ **II** *s* ***with ~*** bez opamiętania, w uniesieniu

a•bashed [ə'bæʃt] *adj* speszony

a•bate [ə'beɪt] *v/i lit* słabnąć ⟨o-⟩; ***we had to wait until the wind ~d*** musieliśmy poczekać, aż wiatr osłabnie; **abate•ment** [ə'beɪtmənt] *s* słabnięcie *n*, zmniejszenie *n*

ab•bey ['æbɪ] *s* opactwo *n*

ab•bot ['æbət] *s* opat *m*

ab•bre•vi•ate [ə'briːvɪeɪt] *v/t* skracać ⟨-rócić⟩; **ab•bre•vi•a•tion** [əbriːvɪ'eɪʃn] *s* **1.** *of word*: skrót *m* **2.** skracanie *n*

ABC[1] [eɪbiː'siː] *s* **1.** podstawy *pl*, podstawowe zasady *pl*; ***my grandfather taught me the ~ of hunting*** dziadek nauczył mnie najważniejszych rzeczy o polowaniu **2.** abecadło *n*, alfabet *m*; ***she still doesn't know her ~*** ona ciągle nie zna literek

ABC[2] [~] *abbr* (=***American Broadcasting Company***) *Am* sieć *f* telewizyjna ABC

ab•di•cate ['æbdɪkeɪt] *vt* **1.** zrzekać ⟨zrzec⟩ się, wyrzekać ⟨-rzec⟩ się **2.** abdykować; **ab•di•ca•tion** [æbdɪ'keɪʃn] *s* **1.** ***~ of rights*** zrzeczenie się praw, wyrzeczenie się praw **2.** abdykacja *f*

ab•do•men ['æbdəmən] *s* ANAT brzuch *m*; **ab•dom•i•nal** [æb'dɒmɪnl] *adj* brzuszny

ab•duct [əb'dʌkt] *v/t* porywać ⟨-rwać⟩, uprowadzać ⟨-dzić⟩; **ab•duc•tion** [əb'dʌkʃn] *s* porwanie *n*, uprowadzenie *n*

ab•er•ra•tion [æbə'reɪʃn] *s* **1.** aberracja *f*, nienormalność *f*, odchylenie *n* **2.** zachowanie *n* nieakceptowane społecznie **3.** ***mental ~*** zachwianie równowagi umysłowej

a•bet [ə'bet] *v/t* pomagać ⟨-móc⟩ przy popełnieniu przestępstwa; **aiding and abet•ting** *s* pomoc *f* w dokonaniu przestępstwa

a•bey•ance [ə'beɪəns] *s lit*: ***in ~*** w zawieszeniu

ab•hor [əb'hɔːr] *v/t lit* brzydzić się, odczuwać ⟨-czuć⟩ wstręt; **ab•hor•rence** [əb'hɔːrəns] *no pl s* wstręt *m*, obrzydzenie *n*, odraza *f*; **ab•hor•rent** [əb'hɔːrənt] *adj* wstrętny, odrażający, obrzydliwy

a•bide [ə'baɪd] *v/t* **1.** ***he cannot ~ s.th.*** nie znosi czegoś, nie cierpi czegoś **2.** *lit dated* przebywać; ***may the peace of God ~ in us*** niechaj mieszka w nas pokój boży **3.** ***~ by*** przestrzegać *G*, postępować zgodnie z *I*; ***you have to ~ by the rules*** musisz przestrzegać przepisów

a•bid•ing [ə'baɪdɪŋ] *adj* **1.** *feeling, opinion*: długotrwały, zakorzeniony **2.** ***law ~*** przestrzegający prawa

a•bil•i•ty [ə'bɪlətɪ] *s* **1.** umiejętność *f*, zdolność *f* **2.** poziom *m* umiejętności; ***to the best of my ~*** najlepiej jak potrafię

a•blaze [ə'bleɪz] *adj lit* **1.** w płomieniach, płonący; ***the factory was soon ~*** wkrótce fabryka stanęła w płomieniach **2.** *fig* ***~ with colour*** płonący barwami; ***~ with hate*** płonący nienawiścią

a•ble ['eɪbl] *adj* **1.** będący w stanie, posiadający umiejętność; ***be ~ to drive a truck*** umieć prowadzic ciężarówkę **2.** zdolny, inteligentny; ***the ~st***

pupil in the group najzdolniejszy uczeń w grupie

a•ble-bod•ied [eɪbl'bɒdɪd] *adj* cieszący się zdrowiem fizycznym, krzepki, pełen sił; ***all ~ men will defend the country*** wszyscy mężczyźni zdolni do noszenia broni będą bronić kraju

ab•nor•mal [æb'nɔːml] *adj* nienormalny; **ab•nor•mal•ly** [æb'nɔːməlɪ] *adv* nienormalnie

a•board [ə'bɔːd] **I** *prep* ***~ the ship*** na pokładzie statku **II** *adv* ***all ~!*** wszyscy na pokład!

a•bode [ə'boʊd] *no pl s form* (stałe) miejsce *n* zamieszkania; ***persons of no fixed ~*** osoby bez stałego miejsca zamieszkania; ***right of ~*** prawo pobytu

a•bol•ish [ə'bɒlɪʃ] *v/t* **1.** *system*: obalać ⟨-lić⟩ **2.** *right*, *institution*: znosić ⟨znieść⟩; **ab•o•li•tion** [æbə'lɪʃn] *s* **1.** *of system*: obalenie *n* **2.** *of right*, *institution*: zniesienie *n*, abolicja *f*; ***the ~ of the death penalty*** zniesienie kary śmierci

'A-bomb *s* bomba *f* atomowa

a•bom•i•na•ble [ə'bɒmɪnəbl] *adj* wstrętny, obrzydliwy, odrażający; **a•bom•i•na•ble 'snow•man** *s* Yeti *m*; **a•bom•i•na•tion** [əbɒmɪ'neɪʃn] *s* coś *n* wstrętnego, coś *n* obrzydliwego, coś *n* odrażającego

ab•o•rig•i•nal [æbə'rɪdʒənl] **I** *adj* aborygeński **II** *s* Aborygen *m*, rdzenny mieszkaniec *m* Australii; **ab•o•rig•i•ne** [æbə'rɪdʒənɪ] *s* **1.** Aborygen *m*, rdzenny mieszkaniec *m* Australii **2.** tubylec *m*

a•bort [ə'bɔːrt] *v/i* **1.** przerywać ⟨-rwać⟩ ciążę, dokonywać ⟨-nać⟩ aborcji **2.** poronić **3.** zaniechać, przerywać ⟨-rwać⟩; ***are you sure you want to ~ printing?*** czy na pewno chcesz przerwać drukowanie?

a•bor•tion [ə'bɔːrʃn] *s* aborcja *f*, przerwanie *n* ciąży; **a•bor•tion•ist** [ə'bɔːrʃənɪst] *s* aborcjonista *m*

a•bor•tive [ə'bɔːrtɪv] *adj* nieudany, poroniony

a•bound [ə'baʊnd] *v/i lit* **1.** występować ⟨-tąpić⟩ licznie, być w obfitości **2.** ***~ in*** (*a.* ***with***) obfitować w *A*

a•bout [ə'baʊt] **I** *adv* **1.** około; ***~ three dollars*** około trzech dolarów **2.** prawie; ***I am ~ ready*** jestem prawie gotowy **3.** wokoło, dookoła; ***the dogs were running ~*** psy biegały sobie; ***stop leaving your books lying ~!*** przestań wszędzie rozrzucać swoje książki! **4.** *Br* bezczynnie; ***they were just standing ~*** stali nic nie robiąc **5.** TECH *lit zwrócić*: w przeciwną stronę; ***he brought the tank ~*** zawrócił czołg **II** *prep* **1.** (*concerning*) o *L*; ***a book ~ love*** książka o miłości **2.** (*purpose*) o *A*; ***sport is only ~ money these days*** dzisiaj w sporcie chodzi tylko o pieniądze **3.** (*occupation*) ***while you're ~ it*** skoro już to robisz **4.** (*place*) ***wander ~ the town*** *Br* chodzić po mieście **5.** (*some place*) gdzieś; ***somewhere ~ the garden*** *Br* gdzieś w ogrodzie **6.** *lit* wokół *G*; ***a string of pearls ~ the neck*** sznur pereł wokół szyi **7.** ***how*** (*a.* ***what***) ***~ your mother?*** jak się ma twoja matka?; ***how*** (*a.* ***what***) ***~ a glass of wine?*** co powiesz na kieliszek wina? **III** *adj* ***to be ~ to do s.th.*** właśnie zamierzać coś zrobić; ***not to be ~ to do s.th.*** nie zamierzać czegoś robić, nie mieć chęci czegoś robić; ***I am not ~ to start dancing at my age*** nie zamierzam w moim wieku zacząć tańczyć; **a•bout-'face** *s* **1.** wolta *f*, zwrot *m* o 180° **2.** w tył zwrot *m*

a•bove [ə'bʌv] **I** *prep* **1.** nad *I*, ponad *I*, wyżej niż *N*; ***~ all*** zwłaszcza, przede wszystkim; ***~ suspicion*** poza podejrzeniami **2.** powyżej *G*, więcej niż *N* **3.** poprzez *A*; ***shouting ~ the sound of the waterfall*** przekrzykując szum wodospadu **II** *adv* **1.** wyżej, powyżej; ***~ and beyond the call of duty*** wykraczający daleko poza obowiązki służbowe **2.** *lit* w niebie, do nieba **3.** *infml* powyżej zera; **a•bove-'men•tioned** *adj form* wyżej wymieniony, wyżej wspomniany; **a•bove 'board I** *adj* **1.** *transaction*, *deal*: uczciwy, legalny, czysty **2.** jasno postawiony **II** *adv* uczciwie, jasno, bez niedomówień

a•bridge [ə'brɪdʒ] *v/t* **1.** skracać ⟨-rócić⟩, streszczać ⟨-reścić⟩ **2.** redukować ⟨z-⟩, zmniejszać ⟨-szyć⟩

a•broad [ə'brɔːd] *adv* **1.** za granicą; za granicę; ***from ~*** z zagranicy **2.** *rumour*: rozpowszechniony, dyskutowany na forum publicznym
a•brupt [ə'brʌpt] *adj* **1.** nagły, gwałtowny, niespodziewany; ***come to an ~ stop*** zatrzymać się nagle **2.** *behaviour*: szorstki, oschły; **a•brupt•ly** [ə'brʌptlɪ] *adv* **1.** nagle, gwałtownie, niespodziewanie **2.** *behave*: szorstko, obcesowo
ABS [eɪbiː'es] *abbr* (=***anti-lock braking system***) AUTO ABS *m*, system *m* zapobiegający blokowaniu się hamulców
ab•sence ['æbsəns] *s* **1.** nieobecność *f*; ***~ from work*** niestawienie się do pracy **2.** brak *m*; ***in the ~ of evidence*** z braku dowodów
ab•sent ['æbsənt] **I** *adj* **1.** nieobecny; ***an ~ expression*** wyraz roztargnienia **2.** brakujący **II** *v/t*: ***~ oneself*** opuszczać ⟨opuścić⟩ (***from*** *A*), wychodzić ⟨wyjść⟩ (***from*** z *G*)
ab•sen•tee [æbsən'tiː] *s* osoba *f* nieobecna; ***~ ballot*** głosowanie listowne; ***~ landlord*** właściciel wynajmowanej nieruchomości, który rzadko ją odwiedza; ***~ voter*** osoba głosująca listownie; **ab•sen•tee•ism** [æbsən'tɪzəm] *s* absencja *f*, nieobecność *f*
ab•sent-mind•ed [æbsənt'maɪndɪd] *adj* roztargniony; **ab•sent-mind•ed•ly** [æbsənt'maɪndɪdlɪ] *adv* w roztargnieniu; **ab•sent-mind•ed•ness** [æbsənt'maɪndɪdnɪs] *s* roztargnienie *n*
ab•so•lute ['æbsəluːt] *adj* **1.** absolutny, ostateczny, niepodważalny; ***an ~ monarch*** monarcha absolutny **2.** całkowity, zupełny; ***an ~ fool*** skończony głupiec **3.** bezwzględny; ***~ zero*** zero absolutne; ***an ~ majority*** większość bezwzględna; **ab•so•lute•ly** ['æbsəluːtlɪ] *adv* **1.** absolutnie, ostatecznie, niepodważalnie; ***~!*** no właśnie!; ***~ not!*** w żadnym wypadku **2.** całkowicie, zupełnie **3.** bezwzględnie
ab•so•lu•tion [æbsə'luːʃn] *s* REL rozgrzeszenie *n*, odpuszczenie *n* grzechów
ab•solve [əb'zɒlv] *v/t* **1.** REL odpuszczać ⟨-puścić⟩ grzechy, rozgrzeszać ⟨-szyć⟩ **2.** oczyszczać ⟨oczyścić⟩ z zarzutów, uniewinniać ⟨-nić⟩
ab•sorb [əb'sɔːrb] *v/t* **1.** absorbować, pochłaniać ⟨-łonąć⟩, wchłaniać ⟨-łonąć⟩ **2.** *information*: przyswajać ⟨-woić⟩ **3.** łagodzić ⟨z-⟩, osłabiać ⟨-bić⟩, redukować ⟨z-⟩; ***~ the impact of*** osłabić siłę uderzenia *G*; **ab•sorb•en•cy** [əb'zɔːbənsɪ] *s* chłonność *f*; **ab•sorb•ent** [əb'zɔːbənt] *adj* wchłaniający, chłonny; ***~ cotton*** wata; **ab•sorb•ing** [əb'zɔːbɪŋ] *adj* **1.** absorbujący, pochłaniający **2.** wciągający, zajmujący dużo czasu
ab•stain [əb'steɪn] *v/i* powstrzymywać ⟨-mać⟩ się, wstrzymywać ⟨-mać⟩ się (***from*** od *G*); ***they ~ed from voting*** wstrzymali się od głosu; **ab•stain•er** [əb'steɪnə] *s* **1.** abstynent *m* **2.** osoba *f* wstrzymująca się od głosu
ab•ste•mi•ous [əb'stiːmɪəs] *adj* wstrzemięźliwy, powściągliwy
ab•sti•nence ['æbstɪnəns] *s* abstynencja *f*, wstrzemięźliwość *f*, wstrzymywanie *n* się (***from*** od *G*)
ab•stract ['æbstrækt] **I** *adj* abstrakcyjny, oderwany od rzeczywistości **II** *s* **1.** abstrakcja *f*, teoria *f* **2.** streszczenie *n*, podsumowanie *n* **III** *v/t* **1.** rozważać ⟨-żyć⟩ w oderwaniu, wyodrębniać ⟨-nić⟩ **2.** streszczać ⟨-reścić⟩, podsumowywać ⟨-mować⟩; **ab•strac•tion** [æb'strækʃn] *s* abstrakcja *f*, ogólnik *m*, pojęcie *n* oderwane
ab•surd [əb'sɜːrd] *adj* **1.** absuradalny, niedorzeczny, bzdurny **2.** śmieszny; **ab•surd•i•ty** [əb'sɜːrdətɪ] *s* absurd *m*, niedorzeczność *f*, bzdura *f*
a•bun•dance [ə'bʌndəns] *s* **1.** obfitość *f*, dostatek *m*; ***in ~*** pod dostatkiem **2.** nadmiar *m*
a•bun•dant [ə'bʌndənt] *adj* **1.** ***~ in*** obfitujący w *A*, bogaty w *A*, zasobny w *A* **2.** liczny
a•buse **I** [ə'bjuːs] *s* **1.** *of power, alcohol, drugs*: nadużywanie *n* **2.** naruszanie *n* prawa; ***human rights ~*** nieprzestrzeganie praw człowieka **3.** przekleństwo *n*; ***a stream of ~*** stek wyzwisk **II** [ə'bjuːz] *v/t* **1.** molestować seksualnie, znęcać się, wykorzystywać ⟨-tać⟩ **2.** *of power, trust*: nadużywać ⟨-żyć⟩ **3.** *of law*: nie przestrzegać **4.** obrażać ⟨-razić⟩, obrzucać ⟨-cić⟩ obelgami

a•bu•sive [ə'bju:sɪv] *adj* **1.** obraźliwy, obelżywy, wulgarny; **~ *language*** wyzwiska **2. *be ~*** molestować seksualnie; ***an ~ father*** ojciec, który wykorzystuje swoje dziecko
a•bys•mal [ə'bɪʒml] *adj lit* nędzny, beznadziejny, fatalny; ***~ depression*** straszna depresja; **a•byss** [ə'bɪs] *s lit* otchłań *f*, przepaść *f*
AC ['eɪsi:] *abbr* **1.** (=***alternating current***) prąd *m* zmienny **2.** (=***air conditioning***) klimatyzacja *f*
a/c, *A/C* *abbr* (=***account***) konto *n*
a•ca•cia [ə'keɪʃə] *s* akacja *f*
ac•a•de•mi•a [ækə'di:mɪə] *s* **1.** świat *m* nauki **2.** badania *pl* naukowe
ac•a•dem•ic [ækə'demɪk] **I** *adj* **1.** akademicki, dydaktyczny **2.** uniwersytecki, naukowy **3.** formalny, teoretyczny; ***an ~ discussion*** akademicka dyskusja **II** *s* **1.** uczony *m*, naukowiec *m* **2.** wykładowca *m*, nauczyciel *m* akademicki; **ac•a•dem•ic 'free•dom** wolność *f* prowadzenia badań; **ac•a•dem•ic 'year** rok *m* akademicki
a•cad•e•my [ə'kædəmɪ] *s* akademia *f*, uczelnia *f*; ***a police ~*** szkoła policyjna; **A•cad•e•my A'wards (cer•e•mo•ny)** *s* ceremonia *f* przyznania nagród Akademii Filmowej, ceremonia *f* rozdania Oscarów
ac•cel•e•rate [ək'seləreɪt] *v/i* AUTO przyśpieszać ⟨-szyć⟩; **ac•cel•e•ra•tion** [əkselə'reɪʃn] *s* przyśpieszenie *n*; **ac•cel•e•ra•tor** [ək'seləreɪtə] *s* **1.** (*car*) pedał *m* gazu **2.** (*of particles*) akcelerator *m*
ac•cent ['æksənt] *s* **1.** akcent *m* **2.** wymowa *f*, akcent *m*; ***an Edinburgh ~*** akcent edynburski **3.** akcent *m*, znak *m* diakrytyczny **4.** *fig* nacisk *m* (***on*** na *A*)
ac•cen•tu•a•te [ək'sentjuːeɪt] *v/t* **1.** zaznaczać ⟨-czyć⟩ **2.** uwypuklać ⟨-lić⟩ **3.** podkreślać ⟨-lić⟩; **ac•cen•tu•a•tion** [əksentju:'eɪʃn] *s* **1.** podkreślenie *n* **2.** zaznaczenie *n* **3.** uwypuklenie *n*
ac•cept [ək'sept] *v/t* **1.** akceptować ⟨za-⟩, przyjmować ⟨-jąć⟩; ***do you ~ credit cards here?*** czy tu przyjmuje się karty kredytowe? **2.** *cheques*: honorować **3.** zatwierdzać ⟨-dzić⟩, aprobować ⟨za-⟩ **4.** przyjmować ⟨-jąć⟩ do wiadomości **5.** godzić ⟨z-⟩ się na *A* **6. *~ into the university*** przyjąć na uniwersytet
ac•cep•ta•ble [ək'septəbl] *adj* **1.** możliwy, do przyjęcia, zadowalający, dopuszczalny; ***are these figures ~ to you?*** czy te dane cię satysfakcjonują? **2.** *form* mile widziany; **ac•cept•ance** [ək'septəns] *s* akceptacja *f*, zgoda *f*; **ac•cept•ed** [ək'septɪd] *adj* przyjęty, akceptowany, uznawany
ac•cess ['ækses] **I** *s* **1.** dostęp *m*; dostępność *f* **2.** możliwość *f* wglądu (***to*** w *A*) **II** *v/t* **1.** TECH docierać ⟨dotrzeć⟩ do *G* **2.** *file*: otwierać ⟨-worzyć⟩; **'ac•cess code** *s* TECH kod *m* dostępu
ac•ces•si•ble [ək'sesəbl] *adj* **1.** dostępny, łatwo osiągalny **2.** łatwy do zrozumienia **3.** *person*: przystępny; **ac•ces•sion** [ək'seʃn] *s* **1.** *to position*: objęcie *n* **2.** *to throne*: wstąpienie *n* **3. *~ to the EU*** przystąpienie do Unii Europejskiej, akcesja
ac•ces•so•ry [ək'sesərɪ] *s* **1.** dodatek *m*, dodatkowy element *m* wyposażenia, ozdoba *f* **2.** współwinny *m*, współsprawca *m*
'ac•cess road *s* droga *f* dojazdowa; **'ac•cess time** *s* TECH czas *f* uzyskania dostępu do danych
ac•ci•dent ['æksɪdənt] *s* **1.** przypadek *m*, traf *m*; ***it is no ~ that*** nieprzypadkowo **2.** wypadek *m*, nieszczęście *n*, katastrofa *f*; ***be killed in an ~*** zginąć w wypadku; **ac•ci•dent in•'sur•ance** *s* ubezpieczenie *n* przeciwwypadkowe; **ac•ci•dent-prone** ['æksɪdentprəʊn] *adj person*: przyciągający nieszczęścia; ***he is ~*** prawdziwy z niego pechowiec; **ac•ci•den•tal** [æksɪ'dentl] *adj* przypadkowy, nieumyślny, niezamierzony; **ac•ci•den•tal•ly** [æksɪ'dentlɪ] *adv* przypadkowo, przypadkiem, nieumyślnie; ***do s.th. ~ on purpose*** zrobić coś tak, żeby wyglądało na przypadek
ac•claim [ə'kleɪm] **I** *v/t* **1.** wychwalać, witać ⟨przy-⟩, entuzjastycznie oklaskiwać; ***critically ~ed*** przyjęty z uznaniem przez krytyków **2.** okrzyknąć, obwoływać ⟨-łać⟩; ***~ s.o. king*** obwołać kogoś królem **II** *s* aplauz *m*, owacja *f*, uznanie *n*

ac•cla•ma•tion [əklə'meɪʃn] *s* **1.** POLIT aklamacja *f* **2.** aplauz *m*, owacja *f*

ac•cli•ma•tise [ə'klaɪmətaɪz] *Br*, ***ac•cli•ma•tize*** *Am* **I** *v/i* aklimatyzować ⟨za-⟩ się, przyzwyczajać ⟨-czaić⟩ się, zadomawiać ⟨-mowić⟩ się **II** *v/t* ***~ oneself*** zaaklimatyzować się; **ac•cli•ma•ti•za•tion** [əklaɪmətaɪ'zeɪʃn] *s* aklimatyzacja *f*

ac•com•mo•date [ə'kɒmədeɪt] *v/t* **1.** kwaterować ⟨za-⟩, lokować ⟨u-⟩, umieszczać ⟨umieścić⟩ **2.** dbać ⟨za-⟩ o *A*, zaspokajać ⟨-koić⟩ potrzeby *G* **3.** ***~ to*** dostosować się do *G*, dopasować się do *G*

ac•com•mo•da•tion [əkɒmə'deɪʃn] *s* zakwaterowanie *n*, kwatera *f*, lokum *n*, mieszkanie *n*; **ac•com•mo•da•tions** [əkɒmə'deɪʃnz] *s Am* miejsca *pl*, siedzenia *pl*

ac•com•pa•ni•ment [ə'kʌmpənɪmənt] *s* MUS akompaniament *m* **ac•com•pa•nist** [ə'kʌmpənɪst] *s* akompaniator *m*

ac•com•pa•ny [ə'kʌmpənɪ] *v/t* **1.** towarzyszyć, asystować **2.** MUS akompaniować

ac•com•plice [ə'kʌmplɪs] *s* współwinny *m*, współsprawca *m*

ac•com•plish [ə'kʌmplɪʃ] *v/t* **1.** dokonywać ⟨-nać⟩ **2.** osiągać ⟨-gnąć⟩, realizować ⟨z-⟩; **ac•com•plished** [ə'kʌmplɪʃt] *adj* utalentowany, znakomity; ***an ~ fencer*** wytrawny szermierz; **ac•com•plish•ment** [ə'kʌmplɪʃmənt] *s* dokonanie *n*, osiągnięcie *n*, wykonanie *n*

ac•cord [ə'kɔːrd] **I** *v/t* przyznawać ⟨-nać⟩, udzielać ⟨-lić⟩ **II** *v/i* ***~ with*** zgadzać się z *I*, odpowiadać *D* **III** *s* **1.** zgoda *f*, zgodność *f*; ***be in ~ with*** być w zgodzie z *I*; ***with one ~*** jednomyślnie, jak jeden mąż **2.** porozumienie *n*, uzgodnienie *n*; ***of one's own ~*** z własnej woli, bez uzgodnienia; **ac•cord•ance** [ə'kɔːdəns] *s*: ***in ~ with*** zgodnie z *I*, stosownie do *G*, według *G*; **ac•cord•ing** [ə'kɔːdɪŋ] *prep*; ***~ to*** zgodnie z *I*, według *G*; **ac•cord•ing•ly** [ə'kɔːdɪŋlɪ] *adv* odpowiednio, stosownie; ***act ~*** działać odpowiednio do zaistniałej sytuacji

ac•cor•di•on [ə'kɔːdɪən] *s* akordeon *m*; **ac•cor•di•on•ist** [ə'kɔːdɪənɪst] *s* akordeonista *m*

ac•count [ə'kaʊnt] **I** *v/t* uznawać ⟨-nać⟩ (***s.o. s.th.*** kogoś za *A*); ***~ s.o. innocent*** uznawać kogoś za niewinnego; ***he was ~ed as a great artist*** uznano go za wielkiego artystę **II** *s* **1.** konto *n*, rachunek *m*; ***on one's own ~*** *fig* na własną rękę, na własny rachunek; ***settle an ~ with*** wyrównać rachunki z *I*, *fig* porachować się z *I* **2.** sprawozdanie *n*, relacja *f*, opis *m*; ***give an ~ of*** opisać, zrelacjonować; ***by all ~s*** wszystko na to wskazuje **3.** ***on ~ of*** z powodu *G*, ze względu na *A*; ***on no ~, not on any ~*** w żadnym wypadku; ***on my ~*** z mojego powodu; ***leave s.th. out of ~*** nie brać czegoś pod uwagę; ***take s.th. into ~, take ~ of s.th.*** brać coś pod uwagę **4.** ***of no ~, of little ~*** bez znaczenia; ***of great ~*** bardzo ważny **5.** ***put*** (*a.* ***turn***) ***to good ~*** uczynić dobry użytek z *G*, użyć w dobrych celach; **ac•count for** *v/t* **1.** wyjaśniać ⟨-nić⟩, tłumaczyć ⟨wy-⟩ się z *G*; ***there's no accounting for tastes*** są gusta i guściki **2.** stanowić, składać ⟨złożyć⟩ się na *A*; ***paintings ~ the majority of the collection*** kolekcja składa się w większości z obrazów; **ac•count to** *v/t* tłumaczyć się przed *I*, odpowiadać przed *I*, ponosić odpowiedzialność przed *I* (***for*** za *A*)

ac•count•a•bil•i•ty [əkaʊntə'bɪlətɪ] *s* odpowiedzialność *f*; **ac•coun•ta•ble** [ə'kaʊntəbl] *adj* odpowiedzialny (***to*** przed *I*, ***for*** za *A*); ***hold s.o. ~ for*** uznać kogoś odpowiedzialnym za *A*

ac•count•an•cy [ə'kaʊntənsɪ] *s* księgowość *f*; **ac•coun•tant** [ə'kaʊntənt] *s* księgowy *m*; **ac•count•ing** [ə'kaʊntɪŋ] *s* **1.** księgowanie *n*, prowadzenie *n* ewidencji **2.** → ***accountancy***

ac•cred•it [ə'kredɪt] *v/t form* akredytować, uznawać ⟨-nać⟩

ac•crue [ə'kruː] *v/i* narastać ⟨-rosnąć⟩, wzrastać ⟨-rosnąć⟩, zwiększać ⟨-szyć⟩ się; ***~d interest*** odsetki narosłe

ac•cu•mu•late [ə'kjuːmjʊleɪt] **I** *v/i* gromadzić ⟨na-⟩ się, zbierać ⟨zebrać⟩ się, kumulować ⟨s-⟩ się **II** *v/t* gromadzić ⟨z-⟩, zbierać ⟨zebrać⟩;

ac•cu•mu•la•tion [əkjuːmjʊ'leɪʃn] *s* akumulacja *f*, nagromadzenie *n*, zbiór *m*, spiętrzenie *n*; **ac•cu•mu•la•tor** [ə'kjuːmjʊleɪtə] *s TECH* akumulator *m*

ac•cu•ra•cy ['ækjʊrəsɪ] *s* dokładność *f*, precyzja *f*, ścisłość *f*; **ac•cu•rate** ['ækjʊrət] *adj* dokładny, precyzyjny, ścisły, wierny; **ac•cu•rate•ly** ['ækjʊrətlɪ] *adv* dokładnie, precyzyjnie, ściśle, wiernie

ac•cu•sa•tion [ækjuː'zeɪʃn] *s* oskarżenie *n*, zarzut *m*

ac•cu•sa•tive [ə'kjuːzətɪv] **I** *s GRAM* biernik *m* **II** *adj GRAM* biernikowy, w bierniku; ***an ~ noun form*** forma rzeczownika w bierniku

ac•cuse [ə'kjuːz] *v/t* **1.** oskarżać ⟨-żyć⟩, obwiniać ⟨-nić⟩ (***s.o. of*** kogoś o *A*) **2.** zarzucać ⟨-cić⟩ (***s.o. of*** komuś coś); **ac•cused** [ə'kjuːzd] *s*: ***the ~*** **a)** oskarżony **b)** oskarżeni; **ac•cus•ing** [ə'kjuːzɪŋ] *adj* oskarżycielski; **ac•cus•ing•ly** [ə'kjuːzɪŋlɪ] *adv* oskarżycielsko

ac•cus•tom [ə'kʌstəm] *v/t* przyzwyczajać ⟨-czaić⟩ (***s.o. to*** kogoś do *G*); ***~ oneself to*** przyzwyczajać się do *G*; ***be ~ed to*** być przyzwyczajonym do *G*

ace [eɪs] *s* **1.** (*cards*) as *m*; ***an ~ of hearts*** as kier; ***have an ~ up one's sleeve*** mieć asa w rękawie **2.** (*person*) mistrz *m*, as *m*; ***a flying ~*** as lotnictwa **3.** ***come within an ~ of winning*** znaleźć się o włos do zwycięstwa

ache [eɪk] **I** *v/i* **1.** boleć; ***I am aching all over*** wszystko mnie boli **2.** ***~ for*** pragnąć *G*, tęsknić za *I* **II** *s* **1.** ból *m* **2.** smutek *m*

a•chieve [ə'tʃiːv] *v/t* **1.** *aim*: osiągać ⟨-gnąć⟩ **2.** *plan*: realizować ⟨z-⟩; **a•chieve•ment** [ə'tʃiːvmənt] *s* **1.** osiągnięcie *n* **2.** dokonanie *n* **3.** sukces *m*; **a•chiev•er** [ə'tʃiːvə] *s* człowiek *m* sukcesu

A•chil•les heel [əkɪliːz'hiːl] *s* pięta *f* Achillesa, słaby punkt *m*; **A•chil•les heel 'ten•don** *s ANAT* ścięgno *n* Achillesa

ac•id ['æsɪd] **I** *s* **1.** *CHEM* kwas *m* **2.** (*drug*) *infml* kwas *m*, LSD *n* **II** *adj* **1.** *CHEM* kwaśny, kwasowy; ***~ rain*** kwaśny deszcz; ***~ test*** *fig* próba ognia **2.** *taste*: kwaśny, kwaskowaty, cierpki;

a•cid•i•ty [ə'sɪdətɪ] *s* kwaśność *f*, kwasowość *f*, kwaskowatość *f*

ac•knowl•edge [ək'nɔːlɪdʒ] *v/t* **1.** *receipt*: potwierdzać ⟨-dzić⟩ **2.** przyznawać ⟨-nać⟩ rację **3.** uznawać ⟨-nać⟩ (***s.o. as*** kogoś za *A*) **4.** zauważać ⟨-żyć⟩, zwracać ⟨-rócić⟩ uwagę na *A*; ***~ s.o.'s presence*** dać do zrozumienia, że się zauważyło czyjąś obecność; **ac•knowl•edg(e)•ment** [ək'nɔːlɪdʒmənt] *s* **1.** *of receipt*: potwierdzenie *n* **2.** podziękowanie *n*; ***in ~ of*** w dowód uznania za *A*

ac•ne ['æknɪ] *s MED* trądzik *m*

a•cous•tic [ə'kuːstɪk] *adj* akustyczny; ***~ nerve*** nerw słuchowy; **a•cous•tics** [ə'kuːstɪks] *s* akustyka *f*

ac•quaint [ə'kweɪnt] *v/t* zaznajamiać ⟨-jomić⟩, zapoznawać ⟨-nać⟩ (***s.o. with*** kogoś z *I*); ***~ oneself with*** zaznajamiać się z *I*; ***be ~ed with*** znać *A*, być obeznanym z *I*; ***we are ~ed*** znamy się; ***become ~ed with*** nauczyć się *G*; **ac•quaint•ance** [ə'kweɪntəns] *s* **1.** znajomy *m*, znajomek *m* **2.** znajomość *f*; ***make s.o.'s ~*** poznać kogoś **3.** *with subject*: znajomość *f*; ***my ~ with physics*** moja znajomość fizyki

ac•qui•esce [ækwɪ'es] *v/i* przystawać ⟨-tać⟩, przyzwalać ⟨-wolić⟩ (***in*** na *A*); **ac•qui•es•cence** [ækwɪ'esns] *s* zgoda *f*, przyzwolenie *n*

ac•quire [ə'kwaɪə] *v/t* **1.** nabywać ⟨-być⟩, kupować ⟨-pić⟩, wchodzić ⟨wejść⟩ w posiadanie *G* **2.** *knowledge*: zdobywać ⟨-być⟩, przyswajać ⟨-woić⟩; ***~ a language*** nauczyć się języka **3.** *habit*: nabywać ⟨-być⟩; **ac•qui•si•tion** [ækwɪ'zɪʃn] *s* **1.** nabywanie *n*, nabycie *n*, przyswojenie *n* **2.** nabytek *m*, zakup *m*; **ac•quis•i•tive** [æ'kwɪzətɪv] *adj form* zachłanny, żądny zysku; **ac•quis•i•tive•ness** [æ'kwɪzətɪvnɪs] *s* zachłanność *f*

ac•quit [ə'kwɪt] *v/t* **1.** *JUR* uniewinniać ⟨-nić⟩, uwalniać ⟨uwolnić⟩ (od zarzutów) **2.** ***~ oneself well*** (***badly***) *lit* dobrze (źle) się spisać; **ac•quit•tal** [ə'kwɪtl] *s JUR* uniewinnienie *n*, uwolnienie *n* (od zarzutów)

a•cre ['eɪkə] *s* (*4047 m^2*) akr *m*

ac•ro•bat ['ækrəbæt] *s* akrobata *m*; **ac•ro•bat•ic** [ækrə'bætɪk] *adj* akrobatyczny; **ac•ro•bat•ics** [ækrə-

'bætɪks] *s* akrobatyka *f*, akrobacja *f*; ***mental ~*** *fig* kombinowanie, łamańce myślowe
ac•ro•nym ['ækrənɪm] *s* akronim *m*
a•cross [ə'krɔːs] **I** *prep* **1.** przez *A*, w poprzek *G*, na drugą stronę *G*; ***run ~ the road*** przebiec przez ulicę; ***get s.th. ~ to s.o.*** *fig* uświadomić komuś coś; ***go*** (*a.* ***cut***) ***~ the country*** podróżować po bezdrożach **2.** naprzeciwko *G*, po drugiej stronie *G*; ***he lives ~ the road*** mieszka po drugiej stronie ulicy **II** *adv* wszerz; ***a lake three miles ~*** jezioro o szerokości trzech mil; **a•cross-the-'board** *adv* na wszystkich poziomach, w całym zakresie
a•cryl•ic [ə'krɪlɪk] **I** *s* akryl *m*, farba *f* akrylowa **II** *adj* akrylowy
act [ækt] **I** *s* **1.** czyn *m*, uczynek *m*, postępek *m*; ***an ~ of God*** *JUR* siła wyższa; ***catch s.o. in the*** (***very***) ***~*** złapać kogoś na gorącym uczynku; ***in the ~ of doing s.th.*** w trakcie robienia czegoś; ***get one's ~ together*** wziąć się w karby, zmobilizować się **2.** *THEAT* akt *m*, numer *m*, występ *m* sceniczny, punkt *m* programu; ***put on an ~*** udawać **3.** ustawa *f*, akt *m* ustawodawczy, uchwała *f* **4.** ***~s*** sprawozdania, akta, annały **II** *v/i* **1.** działać, zachowywać ⟨-chować⟩ się, postępować ⟨-tąpić⟩; ***~ on s.o.'s behalf*** działać w czyimś imieniu, reprezentować kogoś **2.** ***~ on*** działać na *A*, oddziaływać na *A* **3.** *role*: grać, odgrywać ⟨odegrać⟩; ***~ the fool*** błaznować **4.** ***~ up*** **a)** (*machine*) nawalać, szwankować, *fig* buntować się **b)** (*child*) broić, rozrabiać
act•ing ['æktɪŋ] **I** *adj* pełniący obowiązki, tymczasowy **II** *s* aktorstwo *n*
ac•tion ['ækʃn] *s* **1.** działanie *n*, akcja *f*; ***put into ~*** wprowadzić w czyn, wprowadzać w życie **2.** *FILM* akcja *f*, fabuła *f*; ***~ film*** film akcji; ***~-packed*** o wartkiej akcji; ***~ replay*** powtórka w zwolnionym tempie **3.** czyn *m*, uczynek *m*; ***man of ~*** człowiek czynu; ***~s speak louder than words*** czyny znaczą więcej niż słowa **4.** ruch *m*, gest *m*, czynność *f*, funkcjonowanie *n*; ***the ~ of the heart*** akcja serca **5.** *JUR* powództwo *n*, postępowanie *n* cywilne; ***bring an ~ against s.o.*** pozwać kogoś do sądu **6.** *POLIT* walka *f*, działania *pl* wojskowe; ***be killed in ~*** zginąć w akcji, polec w walce
ac•ti•vate ['æktɪveɪt] *v/t* **1.** *machine*: uruchamiać ⟨-chomić⟩ **2.** *reaction*: przyśpieszać ⟨-szyć⟩ **3.** *alarm*: włączyć
ac•tive ['æktɪv] *adj* **1.** aktywny, czynny, sprawny, działający; ***an ~ volcano*** czynny wulkan; ***~ holiday*** czynny wypoczynek **2.** w stronie czynnej; ***~ voice*** *GRAM* strona czynna; **ac•tiv•ism** ['æktɪvɪzəm] *s* aktywizm *m*, aktywność *f*; **ac•tiv•ist** ['æktɪvɪst] *s* aktywista *m*, działacz *m*; **ac•tiv•i•ty** [æk'tɪvətɪ] *s* **1.** działalność *f*, działanie *n*, aktywność *f* **2.** zajęcia *pl*
ac•tor ['æktə] *s* aktor *m*; **ac•tress** ['æktrɪs] *s* aktorka *f*
ac•tu•al ['æktʃʊəl] *adj* **1.** rzeczywisty, faktyczny; ***in ~ fact*** w rzeczywistości **2.** właściwy, ten sam; **ac•tu•al•ly** ['æktʃʊəlɪ] *adv* **1.** faktycznie, w rzeczywistości, w gruncie rzeczy, naprawdę **2.** właściwie, szczerze mówiąc, prawdę powiedziawszy; ***~, I can't talk to you right now*** szczerze mówiąc, nie mogę z tobą teraz rozmawiać
ac•u•punc•ture ['ækjʊpʌktʃə] *s MED* akupunktura *f*; **ac•u•pres•sure** ['ækjʊpreʃə] *s MED* akupresura *f*
a•cute [ə'kjuːt] *adj* **1.** *pain*: ostry, dotkliwy **2.** silny, poważny, nieprzyjemny **3.** *cold*: przenikliwy **4.** *mind*: wnikliwy **5.** *angle*: ostry; **a•cute•ly** [ə'kjuːtlɪ] *adv* **1.** ostro, dotkliwie **2.** całkowicie, głęboko; ***an ~ embarrassing situation*** niezwykle kłopotliwa sytuacja **3.** przenikliwie, wnikliwie, dogłębnie
ad [æd] *infml* → ***advertisement***
AD [eɪ'diː] *abbr* (=***Anno Domini***) n.e., naszej ery, po Chrystusie
Ad•am ['ædəm] *s*: ***I don't know him from ~*** nie mam pojęcia, kto to jest; ***~'s apple*** *ANAT* jabłko Adama, grdyka
ad•a•mant ['ædəmənt] *adj* niezłomny, nieugięty, niewzruszony; ***~ refusal*** stanowcza odmowa; **ad•a•mant•ly** ['ædəməntlɪ] *adv* nieugięcie, niewzruszenie, stanowczo, twardo

a•dapt [ə'dæpt] **I** *v/i* dostosowywać ⟨-sować⟩ się, przystosowywać ⟨-sować⟩ się (**to** do *G*) **II** *v/t* **1.** dostosowywać ⟨-sować⟩, przystosowywać ⟨-sować⟩ (**to** do *G*); ***~ oneself to*** dostosowywać się do *G* **2.** *text*: adaptować ⟨za-⟩; ***a book ~ed for children*** książka zaadaptowana dla dzieci; **a•dapt•a•bil•i•ty** [ədæptə'bɪlətɪ] *s* umiejętność *f* przystosowywania się; **a•dap•ta•ble** [ə'dæptəbl] *adj* łatwo przystosowujący się, dający się przystosować; **a•dap•ta•tion** [ædæp'ˌteɪʃn] *s* **1.** *of book, for screen*: adaptacja *f* **2.** adaptacja *f*, przystosowanie *n* się

add [æd] *v/t* **1.** dodawać ⟨-dać⟩, dorzucać ⟨-cić⟩, dopowiadać ⟨-wiedzieć⟩ **2.** MATH dodawać ⟨-dać⟩, dołączać ⟨-czyć⟩; **add on** *v/t* doliczać ⟨-czyć⟩, dodawać ⟨-dać⟩ na końcu listy; ***~ 5% to the price*** doliczyć 5% do ceny; **add up I** *v/t* dodawać ⟨-dać⟩, sumować ⟨z-⟩ **II** *v/i* (*facts*) układać się w całość; **add up to** *v/t* sumować się, wynosić

add•ed ['ædɪd] *adj* dodatkowy, dodany; **add•ed 'val•ue** ECON wartość *f* dodana

ad•den•dum [ə'dendəm] *pl -da* [~də] *s form* dodatek *m*, załącznik *m*

ad•der ['ædə] *s* żmija *f*

ad•dict ['ædɪkt] *s* nałogowiec *m*, narkoman *m*, osoba *f* uzależniona; **ad•dic•ted** [ə'dɪktɪd] *adj*: ***be ~ to*** być uzależnionym od *G*; **ad•dic•tion** [ə'dɪkʃn] *s* uzależnienie *n*; ***~ to alcohol*** uzależnienie od alkoholu; **ad•dic•tive** [ə'dɪktɪv] *adj* uzależniający, wciągający; ***computer games can be ~*** gry komputerowe mogą powodować uzależnienie; ***an ~ drug*** środek uzależniający

ad•di•tion [ə'dɪʃn] *s* **1.** MATH dodawanie *n*; ***an ~ sign*** znak dodawania, plus **2.** dodatek *m*, uzupełnienie *n*; ***in ~*** w dodatku, co więcej; ***in ~ to*** oprócz *G*; ***expect an ~ to the family*** oczekiwać powiększenia rodziny **3.** domieszka *f*; **ad•di•tion•al** [ə'dɪʃnl] *adj* dodatkowy; **ad•di•tive** ['ædɪtɪv] *s* **1.** dodatek *m* **2.** środek *m* konserwujący, konserwant *m*

add-on ['ædɒn] *s* TECH dodatek *m*, nakładka *f*

ad•dress [ə'dres] **I** *v/t* **1.** adresować ⟨za-⟩ **2.** przemawiać ⟨-mówić⟩ do *G*, wygłaszać ⟨-łosić⟩ przemowę do *G*; ***the President ~ed Congress*** prezydent wygłosił przemowę w Kongresie **3.** zwracać ⟨-rócić⟩ się do *G*, tytułować; ***he likes to be ~ed with due respect*** lubi, żeby się do niego zwracano z należnym szacunkiem **II** *s* **1.** adres *m* **2.** przemowa *f*; **ad•'dress book** *s* książka *f* adresowa; **ad•dress•ee** [ædre'siː] *s* adresat *m*

ad•ept ['ædept] **I** *adj* biegły, wprawny, sprawny (**at**/**in** w *L*) **II** *s* adept *m*, mistrz *m*; ***an ~ of black magic*** adept czarnej magii

ad•e•qua•cy ['ædɪkwəsɪ] *s* adekwatność *f*, trafność *f*, stosowność *f*; **ad•e•quate** ['ædɪkwət] *adj* **1.** odpowiedni, adekwatny, stosowny **2.** wystarczający, dostateczny, zadowalający **ad•e•quate•ly** ['ædɪkwətlɪ] *adv* **1.** odpowiednio, adekwatnie, stosownie **2.** wystarczająco, zadowalająco, dostatecznie

ad•here [əd'hɪə] *v/t* **1.** przylegać, przywierać ⟨-wrzeć⟩ (**to** do *G*) **2.** **~ to a)** trzymać się *G*, stosować się do *G* **b)** *to terms*: dotrzymywać; **ad•her•ence** [əd'hɪərəns] *s* **1.** przywiązanie *n* (**to** do *G*) **2.** wierność *f* (**to** *D*); **ad•her•ent** [əd'hɪərənt] **I** *adj* **1.** lepiący się, klejący się, przywierający **2.** przywiązany (**to** do *G*) **3.** wierny (**to** *D*) **II** *s* adherent *m*, zwolennik *m*, poplecznik *m*

ad•he•sion [əd'hiːʒn] *s* **1.** → ***adherence*** **2.** PHYS TECH przyczepność *f*, przyleganie *n*, adhezja *f*

ad•he•sive [əd'hiːsɪv] **I** *adj* lepki, klejący, przylepny; ***~ plaster*** *Am* plaster opatrunkowy; ***~ tape*** taśma klejąca **II** *s* klej *m*, spoidło *n*

ad hoc [æd'hɒk] **I** *adj* doraźny, ad hoc **II** *adv* doraźnie, ad hoc

ad in•fi•ni•tum [ædɪnfɪ'naɪtəm] *adv* **1.** ad infinitum, w nieskończoność **2.** *iron* do znudzenia

ad•ja•cent [ə'dʒeɪsnt] *adj form* przyległy, sąsiedni, graniczący (**to** z *I*)

ad•jec•ti•val [ædʒɪk'taɪvl] *adj* GRAM przymiotnikowy; **ad•jec•tive** ['ædʒɪktɪv] *s* GRAM przymiotnik *m*

ad•join [ə'dʒɔɪn] *v/t* przylegać do *G*, stykać się z *I*, sąsiadować z *I*; **ad•join•ing** [ə'dʒɔɪnɪŋ] *adj* przyległy, sąsiedni

ad•journ [ə'dʒɜːn] **I** *v/t form* odraczać ⟨-roczyć⟩, przesuwać ⟨-sunąć⟩, przekładać ⟨przełożyć⟩ **II** *v/i* robić ⟨z-⟩ przerwę; ***shall we ~ for coffee?*** czy zrobimy przerwę na kawę?; **ad•journ•ment** [ə'dʒɜːnmənt] *s JUR* odroczenie *n*, przełożenie *n* na inny termin

ad•junct ['ædʒʌŋkt] *s* **1.** ***~ to*** dodatek do *G* **2.** *GRAM* okolicznik *m*

ad•just [ə'dʒʌst] **I** *v/t* **1.** *mechanism*: regulować ⟨wy-⟩, dostosowywać ⟨-sować⟩, modyfikować ⟨z-⟩ **2.** poprawiać ⟨-wić⟩ **II** *v/i* przystosowywać ⟨sować⟩ się, dostosowywać ⟨-sować⟩ się; **ad•just•a•ble** [ə'dʒʌstəbl] *adj* regulowany; ***~ spanner*** klucz nastawny; **ad•just•ment** [ə'dʒʌstmənt] *s* **1.** regulacja *f*, wyregulowanie *n* **2.** przystosowanie *n* się

ad•ju•tant ['ædʒʊtənt] *s* adiutant *m*

ad•min ['ædmɪn] *abbr* (=***administration***) *infml* **1.** administracja *f*, pracownicy *pl* administracji **2.** *INF* administrator *m*

ad•min•is•ter [əd'mɪnɪstə] *v/t* **1.** administrować, zarządzać, kierować **2.** *medicine*: podawać ⟨-dać⟩, aplikować ⟨za-⟩ **3.** *punishment*: wymierzać ⟨-rzyć⟩, wyznaczać ⟨-czyć⟩; ***~ justice*** wymierzyć sprawiedliwość **4.** ***~ the last rites*** udzielić ostatniego namaszczenia; **ad•min•is•tra•tion** [ədmɪnɪ'streɪʃn] *s* **1.** administracja *f*, zarządzanie *n*, kierowanie *n* **2.** *Am* administracja *f* państwowa, rząd *m* **3.** ***~ of justice*** wymiar sprawiedliwości; **ad•min•is•tra•tive** [ədmɪnɪ'strətɪv] *adj* administracyjny; **ad•min•is•tra•tor** [əd'mɪnɪstreɪtə] *n* administrator *m*, zarządca *m*

ad•mi•ra•ble ['ædmərəbl] *adj* wspaniały, zachwycający, godny podziwu; **ad•mi•ra•bly** ['ædmərəblɪ] *adv* wspaniale, zachwycająco, w sposób godny podziwu

ad•mi•ral ['ædmərəl] *s* admirał *m*; ***reare-~*** kontradmirał; ***vice-~*** wiceadmirał

ad•mi•ra•tion [ædmə'reɪʃn] *s* podziw *m*, zachwyt *m*, uwielbienie *n*; ***she was the ~ of all*** wszyscy ją podziwiali;

ad•mire [əd'maɪə] *v/t* **1.** podziwiać (***s.o. for*** kogoś za *A*) **2.** zachwycać ⟨-cić⟩ się; **ad•mir•er** [əd'maɪərə] *s* **1.** wielbiciel *m*, adorator *m*; ***she has a secret ~*** ma skrytego wielbiciela **2.** zwolennik *m*; **ad•mir•ing** [əd'maɪərɪŋ] *adj* pełen podziwu; **ad•mir•ing•ly** [əd'maɪərɪŋlɪ] *adv* z podziwem, z zachwytem, z uznaniem

ad•mis•si•ble [əd'mɪsəbl] *adj* dopuszczalny, możliwy do przyjęcia; **ad•mis•sion** [əd'mɪʃn] *s* **1.** przyznanie się *n* (***of*** do *G*); ***an ~ of guilt*** przyznanie się do winy; ***by his own ~*** jak sam przyznaje **2.** wstęp *m*; ***~ fee*** opłata za wstęp; ***~ free*** wstęp wolny **3.** przyjęcie *n*; ***~ to a hospital*** przyjęcie do szpitala

ad•mit [əd'mɪt] **I** *v/t* **1.** przyznawać ⟨-nać⟩ się do *G*; ***~ one's mistake*** przyznać się do błędu **2.** wpuszczać ⟨wpuścić⟩ **3.** przyjmować ⟨-jąć⟩ (***to*** do *G*) **4.** ***the amphitheatre ~s 3000 spectators*** amfiteatr mieści 3000 widzów **II** *v/i* uznawać ⟨-nać⟩, przyznawać ⟨-nać⟩; ***~ that*** przyznać, że; **admit of** *v/t* dopuszczać, zostawiać miejsce na *A*, pozwalać na *A*; ***the program does not ~ error*** program nie dopuszcza możliwości błędu

ad•mit•tance [əd'mɪtəns] *s* wejście *n*, wstęp *m*; ***no ~ (except on business)*** wstęp wzbroniony (oprócz interesantów); **ad•mit•ted•ly** [əd'mɪtedlɪ] *adv* co prawda, wprawdzie, trzeba przyznać

ad•mon•ish [əd'mɒnɪʃ] *v/t* karcić ⟨s-⟩, upominać ⟨-mnieć⟩, napominać ⟨-mnieć⟩; ***the teacher ~ed his pupils for the noise*** nauczyciel strofował swoich uczniów za hałas; **ad•mo•ni•tion** [ædmɔ'nɪʃn] *s* upomnienie *n*, napomnienie *n*, przestroga *f*

ad nau•se•am [æd'nɔːzɪæm] *adv lit* do znudzenia

a•do [ə'duː] *s* rwetes *m*, zamieszanie *n*; ***much ~ about nothing*** wiele hałasu o nic; ***without more*** (*a.* ***further***) ***~*** bez dalszych ceregieli

a•do•be [ə'dəʊbeɪ] *no pl s* cegła *f* suszona na słońcu, cegła *f* niewypalana; ***an ~ house*** dom z niewypalanej cegły

ad•o•les•cence [ædə'lesns] *s* wiek *m* dojrzewania, lata *pl* młodzieńcze; **ad•o•les•cent** [ædə'lesnt] **I** *s* nastolatek *m* **II** *adj* **1.** młodzieńczy **2.** młodociany **3.** dorastający, nastoletni **4.** *adult*: niedojrzały, dziecinny, infantylny

a•dopt [ə'dɔpt] *v/t* **1.** *child*: adoptować ⟨za-⟩; ***~ed child*** adoptowane dziecko; ***an ~ed country*** przybrana ojczyzna **2.** *attitude*, *view*: przyjmować ⟨-jąć⟩ **3.** obierać ⟨-obrać⟩ **4.** przyswajać ⟨-woić⟩ sobie; **a•dop•tion** [ə'dɔpʃn] *s* **1.** adopcja *f*; ***give up for ~*** oddać do adopcji; ***country of ~*** ojczyzna z wyboru **2.** *of idea*: przyjęcie *n*; **a•dop•tive** [ədɔptɪv] *adj parent*: przybrany

a•dor•a•ble [ə'dɔːrəbl] *adj* uroczy, śliczny, rozkoszny; ***what an ~ kitten!*** cóż za słodkie kociątko!; **ad•o•ra•tion** [ædə'reɪʃn] *s* **1.** uwielbienie *n* **2.** *REL* adoracja *f*; **a•dore** [ə'dɔː] *v/t* **1.** uwielbiać **2.** adorować, wielbić; **a•dor•ing** [ə'dɔːrɪŋ] *adj* **1.** uwielbiający, wielbiący **2.** kochający, rozkochany

a•dorn [ə'dɔːn] *v/t* ozdabiać ⟨-dobić⟩, zdobić ⟨o-⟩, upiększać ⟨-szyć⟩, stroić ⟨przy-⟩; **a•dorn•ment** [ə'dɔːnmənt] *s* **1.** ozdoba *f*, przybranie *n*, dekoracja *f* **2.** upiększanie *n*, ornamentacja *f*

ad•ren•al•in(e) [ə'drenəlɪn] *s MED* adrenalina *f*

A•dri•at•ic Sea [eɪdrɪætɪk'siː] *s* Morze *n* Adriatyckie, Adriatyk *m*

a•drift [ə'drɪft] *adj* **1.** w dryfie, dryfujący, niezakotwiczony; ***cut*** (*a.* ***set***) ***~*** uwolnić z cumy **2.** *fig* zagubiony, bez celu, zdany na siebie; ***leave s.o. ~*** zostawić kogoś na łasce losu

a•dult ['ædʌlt] **I** *adj* **1.** dorosły, dojrzały; ***~ education*** kształcenie dorosłych; ***~ films*** filmy dla dorosłych **2.** *JUR* pełnoletni **II** *s* **1.** dorosły *m* **2.** pełnoletni *m*

a•dul•ter•y [ə'dʌltərɪ] *s* cudzołóstwo *n*, zdrada *f* małżeńska; **a•dul•ter•er** [ə'dʌltərə] *s* cudzołożnik *m*; **a•dul•ter•ess** [ə'dʌltərəs] *s* cudzołożnica *f*; **a•dul•ter•ous** [ə'dʌltərəs] *adj* pozamałżeński, cudzołożny

ad•vance [əd'væns] **I** *v/i* **1.** posuwać ⟨-sunąć⟩ się (naprzód), nacierać ⟨natrzeć⟩ **2.** robić ⟨z-⟩ postępy **II** *v/t* **1.** promować ⟨wy-⟩; ***~ s.o.'s career*** pomagać komuś w zrobieniu kariery **2.** *theory*: wysuwać ⟨-sunąć⟩ **3.** wypłacać ⟨-cić⟩ tytułem zaliczki **III** *s* **1.** posuwanie się *n*, marsz *m* **2.** ***let me know in ~*** daj mi znać wcześniej, daj mi znać z wyprzedzeniem; ***be in ~ of*** wyprzedzać *A* **3.** postęp *m*, rozwój *m* **4.** zaliczka *f*, zadatek *m* **5.** pożyczka *f* **6.** ***~s*** zaloty, awanse **IV** *adj* wcześniejszy, uprzedni; **ad•vance 'book•ing** *s* wcześniejsza rezerwacja *f*; **ad•vance 'no•tice** *s*: ***we need ~ notice*** proszę nas poinformować wcześniej **ad•vance 'pay•ment** *s* **1.** zaliczka *f* **2.** płatność *f* z góry; **ad•vance•ment** [əd'vansmənt] *s* postęp *m*, rozwój *m*, doskonalenie *n*

ad•vanced [əd'vænst] *adj* zaawansowany, rozwinięty, daleko posunięty; ***an ~ course*** kurs dla zaawansowanych

ad•van•tage [əd'væntɪdʒ] *s* **1.** korzyść *f*; ***to s.o.'s ~*** na czyjąś korzyść, z korzyścią dla kogoś; ***take ~ of*** skorzystać z *G*, wykorzystywać *A* **2.** przewaga *f*; ***have*** (***gain***) ***an ~ over*** mieć (uzyskać) przewagę nad *I* **3.** zaleta *f*; **ad•van•ta•geous** [ædvən'teɪdʒəs] *adj* korzystny, sprzyjający

Ad•vent ['ædvent] *s REL* adwent *m*

ad•vent ['ædvent] *s* nadejście *n*, nastanie *n*

ad•ven•ture [əd'ventʃə] *s* przygoda *f*, przeżycie *n*; ***an ~ playground*** plac zabaw; ***an ~ holiday*** wakacje dla aktywnych; **ad•ven•tur•er** [əd'ventʃərə] *s* **1.** poszukiwacz *m* przygód, awanturnik *m* **2.** ryzykant *m*; **ad•ven•tur•ous** [əd'ventʃərəs] *adj* **1.** odważny, śmiały **2.** pełen przygód; ***an ~ life*** życie pełne przygód

ad•verb ['ædvɜːb] *s GRAM* przysłówek *m*; **ad•ver•bi•al** [əd'vɜːbjəl] *adj GRAM* **1.** przysłówkowy **2.** okolicznikowy

ad•ver•sa•ry ['ædvərserɪ] *s* przeciwnik *m*; **ad•verse** ['ædvɜːs] *adj* niekorzystny, niesprzyjający; ***an ~ balance of trade*** niekorzystny bilans handlowy; **ad•ver•si•ty** [əd'vɜːsətɪ] *s* **1.** trudna sytuacja *f*; ***in times of ~*** w trudnych chwilach **2.** ***adversities*** przeciwności losu

ad•vert ['ædvɜːt] *infml* → ***advertisement 1***

ad•ver•tise ['ædvətaɪz] **I** *v/i* **1.** reklamować ⟨za-⟩ się, ogłaszać ⟨-łosić⟩ się **2.** dawać ⟨dać⟩ ogłoszenie; ***we ~d for a nanny*** daliśmy ogłoszenie, że szukamy niani **II** *v/t* **1.** ogłaszać ⟨-łosić⟩ **2** rozgłaszać ⟨-łosić⟩; ***don't ~ at work the fact that you are divorced*** nie rozgłaszaj w pracy, że jesteś rozwiedziony; **ad•ver•tise•ment** [ədvɜː'tɪsmənt] *s* **1.** reklama *f*, ogłoszenie *n*, anons *m* **2.** → ***advertising***; **ad•ver•tis•er** ['ædvətaɪzə] *s* **1.** reklamodawca *m* **2.** ogłoszeniodawca *m*; **ad•ver•tis•ing** ['ædvərtaɪzɪŋ] **I** *s* reklama *f*; ***~ manager*** kierownik ds. reklamy; ***an ~ medium*** nośnik reklamy; ***~ budget*** budżet na reklamę; ***~ revenue*** przychody z reklamy **II** *adj* reklamowy; ***an ~ agency*** agencja reklamowa

ad•vice [əd'vaɪs] *s* **1.** rada *f*; ***a piece*** (*a.* ***bit***) ***of ~*** rada; ***at*** (*a.* ***on***) ***s.o.'s ~*** za czyjąś radą; ***take my ~*** posłuchaj mojej rady **2.** porada *f*; ***medical*** (***legal***) ***~*** porada lekarska (prawna) **3.** *form* zawiadomienie *n* (urzędowe) **4.** awizo *n*

ad•vis•a•ble [əd'vaɪzəbl] *adj* wskazany

ad•vise [əd'vaɪz] *v/t* **1.** radzić ⟨po-⟩, doradzać ⟨-dzić⟩; ***~ against*** odradzić *A*; ***you would be well ~d to leave the country*** dobrze byś zrobiła, gdybyś wyjechała z kraju **2.** powiadamiać ⟨-domić⟩, informować ⟨po-⟩ (***of*** o *L*)

ad•vis•er [əd'vaɪzə], ***ad•vis•or*** *s* doradca *m*, konsultant *m*; **ad•vi•so•ry** [əd'vaɪzəri] *adj* doradczy

ad•vo•ca•cy ['ædvəkəsɪ] *s* rzecznictwo *n*, obrona *f*; ***~ of minority rights*** obrona praw mniejszości; **ad•vocate** ['ædvəkeɪt] **I** *s* zwolennik *m*, rzecznik *m*, obrońca *m* **II** *v/t* zalecać ⟨-cić⟩, opowiadać ⟨-wiedzieć⟩ się za *I*; ***I ~ extreme caution*** zalecam najwyższą ostrożność

aer•i•al ['eərɪəl] **I** *s* antena *f* **II** *adj* **1.** powietrzny, napowietrzny; ***an ~ view*** widok z lotu ptaka; ***~ combat*** walka powietrzna **2.** lotniczy; ***an ~ photograph*** zdjęcie lotnicze

aer•o•nau•ti•cal [eərə'nɔːtɪkl] *adj* lotniczy; ***~ engineering*** inżynieria lotnicza

aer•o•plane ['eərəpleɪn] *s* samolot *m*; ***an ~ crash*** katastrofa lotnicza

aer•o•space ['eərəspeɪs] **I** *s* przestrzeń *f* powietrzna i kosmiczna **II** *adj* lotniczy i kosmiczny; ***the ~ industry*** przemysł lotniczy

aes•thet•ic [es'θetɪk] *adj* estetyczny; *~ value* wartość estetyczna; ***~ considerations*** względy estetyczne; **aes-thet•ics** [es'θetɪks] *s* estetyka *f*

a•far [ə'fɑː] *adv lit* daleko; ***from ~*** z daleka, z oddali

af•fa•ble ['æfəbl] *adj* życzliwy, przyjacielski

af•fair [ə'feə] *s* **1.** sprawa *f*, kwestia *f*, rzecz *f*, interes *m*; ***it is none of your ~*** to nie twój interes **2.** ***~s*** sprawy; ***current ~s*** sprawy bieżące; ***Ministry of Foreign ~s*** Ministerstwo Spraw Zagranicznych; ***the state of ~*** stan rzeczy, sytuacja **3.** romans *m*; ***she had an ~ with her stepson*** miała romans ze swoim pasierbem **4.** ***on her head she had a little ~ of pink feathers*** na głowie miała coś z różowych piórek

af•fect [ə'fekt] *v/t* **1.** wpływać ⟨-łynąć⟩ na *A*, wywierać ⟨-wrzeć⟩ wpływ na *A* **2.** udawać; ***he ~s an Oxford accent*** udaje oksfordzki akcent **3.** poruszać ⟨-szyć⟩; ***be deeply ~ed*** być głęboko poruszonym

af•fec•tion [ə'fekʃn] *s* **1.** uczucie *n*; ***play on s.o.'s ~s*** grać na czyichś uczuciach **2.** czułość *f*, przywiązanie *n* **3.** ***~s*** względy; ***win s.o.'s ~s*** zdobyć czyjeś względy; **af•fec•tion•ate** [ə'fekʃnət] *adj* czuły, kochający; **af•fec•tion•ate•ly** [ə'fekʃnətlɪ] *adv* czule, z uczuciem; ***yours ~*** Twój kochający

af•fil•i•ated [ə'fɪlɪeɪtɪd] *adj* stowarzyszony; **af•fil•i•a•tion** [əfɪlɪ'eɪʃn] *s* **1.** przynależność *f* **2.** powiązanie *f*

af•fin•i•ty [ə'fɪnətɪ] *s* **1.** podobieństwo *n* **2.** powinowactwo *n* **3.** sympatia *f*, upodobanie *n* (***to*** do *G*)

af•firm [ə'fɜːm] *form* **I** *v/i* **1.** zapewniać ⟨-nić⟩ **2.** twierdzić ⟨s-⟩ **II** *v/t* **1.** zapewniać ⟨-nić⟩ o *L* **2.** potwierdzać ⟨-dzić⟩; **af•fir•ma•tion** [æfər'meɪʃn] *s form* **1.** zapewnienie *n* **2.** potwierdzenie *n*; ***nod one's head in ~*** potwierdzić skinieniem głowy **3.** afirmacja *f*; **af•fir•ma•tive** [ə'fɜːmətɪv] **I** *adj* **1.** twierdzący, potakujący; ***an ~ nod*** potakujące skinienie **2.** *action*: afirmacyjna **II** *s* odpowiedź *f* twierdząca, potwierdzenie *n*; ***answer in the ~*** odpowiedzieć twierdząco

af•fix I [ə'fɪks] *v/t* **1.** przymocowywać ⟨-cować⟩, przytwierdzać ⟨-dzić⟩ **2.** dołączać ⟨-czyć⟩ **3.** *stamp*: naklejać ⟨-leić⟩ **4.** *signature*: składać ⟨złożyć⟩ **5.** *seal*: przykładać ⟨przyłożyć⟩ **II** ['æfɪks] *s* afiks *m*

af•flict [ə'flɪkt] *v/t* (*disease, pain*) dotykać ⟨-tknąć⟩; ***~ed with leprosy*** trędowaty, dotknięty trądem; **af•flic•tion** [ə'flɪkʃn] *s* **1.** dolegliwość *f*, przypadłość *f*; ***~s of the old age*** dolegliwości wieku starczego **2.** nieszczęście *n* **3.** bolączka *f*

af•flu•ence ['æflʊəns] *s* zamożność *f*, dostatek *m*; **af•flu•ent** ['æflʊənt] *adj* zamożny, dostatni

af•ford [ə'fɔːd] *v/t* **1.** pozwalać ⟨-wolić⟩ sobie na *A*; ***we can't ~ it*** nie stać nas na to **2.** *fig* zapewniać ⟨-nić⟩; ***~ shelter from the rain*** dać schronienie przed deszczem; **af•ford•a•ble** [ə'fɔːrdəbl] *adj* **1.** *price*: przystępny **2.** *product*: w przystępnej cenie

af•for•est [ə'fɔrɪst] *v/t* zalesiać ⟨-sić⟩; **af•for•est•a•tion** [əfɔrɪ'steɪʃn] *s* zalesianie *n*

af•front [ə'frʌnt] **I** *s* **1.** obraza *f*; ***an ~ to s.o.'s religious sensibilities*** obraza czyichś uczuć religijnych **2.** afront *m* **II** *v/t* obrażać ⟨-razić⟩

Af•ghan ['æfgæn] **I** *adj* afgański; ***an ~ hound*** chart afgański **II** *s* Afgańczyk *m*, Afganka *f*; **Af•ghan•i•stan** [æf'gænɪstæn] *s* Afganistan *m*

a•field [ə'fiːld] *adv* daleko; ***don't go too far ~*** nie oddalaj się za bardzo

a•fire [ə'faɪə] *lit* **I** *adj* w płomieniach; ***be ~*** płonąć **II** *adv* w płomieniach; ***set s.th. ~*** podpalić coś

a•float [ə'fləʊt] *adv* **1.** ***be ~, remain ~*** unosić się na wodzie; ***I can keep ~, but I can't swim*** potrafię utrzymać się na wodzie, ale nie umiem pływać **2.** ***stay ~*** *fig* utrzymywać się na powierzchni; ***the company barely manages to stay ~*** firma ledwo utrzymuje się na powierzchni

a•foot [ə'fʊt] *adv*: ***be ~*** szykować się

a•fore•men•tioned [əfɔː'menʃənd] *adj*, **a•fore•said** [ə'fɔːsed] *adj* wyżej wymieniony, wcześniej wspomniany

a•fraid [ə'freɪd] *adj* **1.** ***be ~ of*** bać się *G*; ***be ~ to do s.th.*** bać się coś zrobić **2.** (*in expression of regret or politeness*) ***I'm ~*** obawiam się, przykro mi; ***I'm ~ I must go*** niestety muszę już iść

a•fresh [ə'freʃ] *adv* od nowa, od początku

Af•ri•ca ['æfrɪkə] *s* Afryka *f*

Af•ri•kaans [æfrɪ'kɑːns] *s* (*language*) afrikaans *m*

Af•ri•can ['æfrɪkən] **I** *adj* afrykański **II** *s* Afrykańczyk *m*, Afrykanka *f*; **Af•ri•can A•'mer•i•can** *s* Afroamerykanin *m*, Afroamerykanka *f*; **Af•ri•kan•er** [æfrɪ'kɑːnə] *s* Afrykaner *m*, Bur *m*

Af•ro-A•mer•i•can [æfrəʊə'merɪkən] **I** *s* Afroamerykanin *m*, Afroamerykanka *f* **II** *adj* afroamerykański

aft [æft] **I** *adj* rufowy **II** *adv* na rufie, ku rufie; ***fore and ~*** na dziobie i na rufie, z przodu i z tyłu

af•ter ['ɑːftə] **I** *prep* **1.** po *L*; ***~ a week*** po tygodniu; ***he is named ~ his father*** ma imię po ojcu; ***the day ~ tomorrow*** pojutrze **2.** za *I*; ***day ~ day*** dzień za dniem; ***one ~ the other*** jeden za drugim **3.** ***be ~*** gonić za *I*, ścigać *A* **4.** w stylu *G*; ***a painting ~ Watteau*** obraz w stylu Watteau **5.** ***~ all*** przecież, w końcu **II** *conj* po tym, jak, kiedy, gdy **III** *adv* **1.** w tyle, z tyłu **2.** później, potem; ***for months ~*** jeszcze wiele miesięcy później; ***shortly ~*** niedługo potem **IV** *adj lit* późniejszy, następny; ***in ~ years*** w późniejszych latach; **'af•ter•care** *s* **1.** opieka *f* nad rekonwalescentem, leczenie *n* poszpitalne **2.** rehabilitacja *f* **3.** opieka *f* resocjalizacyjna; **'af•ter-ef•fects** *pl* następstwa *pl*; **'af•ter•glow** *s* **1.** poświata *f* **2.** przyjemne wspomnienie *n*; **'af•ter•life** *s* życie *n* pozagrobowe; **'af•ter•math** *s* **1.** następstwo *n*, konsekwencja *f* **2.** *lit* pokłosie *n*

af•ter•noon [ɑːftə'nuːn] **I** *s* popołudnie *n*; ***in the ~*** po południu; ***this afternoon*** dziś po południu **II** *adj* popołudniowy

af•ters ['ɑːftəz] *s* deser *m*; ***for ~*** na deser

af•ter-'sales serv•ice *s* obsługa *f* posprzedażna; **'af•ter•shave** *s* **1.** płyn *m* po goleniu **2.** balsam *m* po goleniu; **'af•ter•shock** *s* **1.** *GEOL* wstrząs *m* następczy **2.** reperkusje *pl*, następstwa *pl*; **'af•ter•sun cream** *s* **1.** krem *m* po opalaniu **2.** balsam *m* po opalaniu; **'af•ter•taste** *s* posmak *m*; ***the affair left a bitter ~*** po romansie pozostał jej niesmak; **'af•ter-thought** *s* namysł *m*; ***as an ~*** po namyśle; ***the roof window was added as an ~*** okno na dachu to późniejsze uzupełnienie

af•ter•wards ['ɑːftəwədz], **af•terward** *adv* potem, później; ***soon ~, shortly ~*** niedługo później

a•gain [ə'geɪn] *adv* **1.** znowu, znów; ***that fool ~!*** znowu ten głupek! **2.** jeszcze raz, ponownie; ***~ and ~*** wielokrotnie

a•gainst [ə'genst] *prep* **1.** przeciw *D*, przeciwko *D*, wbrew *D*; ***I am ~ this proposal*** jestem przeciwny tej propozycji; ***be prejudiced ~*** mieć uprzedzenia do *G*; ***~ my will*** wbrew mojej woli; ***~ the law*** wbrew prawu **2.** przeciwko *D*, na wypadek *G*; ***insurance ~ theft*** ubezpieczenie na wypadek kradzieży; ***vaccination ~ smallpox*** szczepienie przeciw ospie wietrznej **3.** na tle *G*, wobec *G*, w porównaniu z *I*; ***as ~*** w porównaniu z *I*; ***~ the background of*** na tle *G* **4.** przy *L*, obok *G*, ***the table is ~ the wall*** stół stoi pod ścianą

ag•ate ['ægət] *s* agat *m*

age [eɪdʒ] **I** *s* **1.** wiek *m*; ***at the ~ of ten*** w wieku dziesięciu lat; ***when I was your ~*** kiedy byłem w twoim wieku; ***be ten years of ~*** mieć dziesięć lat; ***what ~ is he?*** ile on ma lat?; ***old ~*** starość; ***act your ~!*** zachowuj się, jak na twój wiek przystało!, nie zachowuj się jak dziecko!; ***the ~ of consent*** *granica wieku, od której prawo dopuszcza współżycie seksualne* **2.** pełnoletność *f*; ***come of ~*** osiągnąć pełnoletność; ***under ~*** niepełnoletni **3.** ***s.o. is over ~*** ktoś przekroczył granicę wiekową **4.** epoka *f*, czasy *pl*; ***the ~ of Reason*** epoka rozumu, Oświecenie; ***in our ~*** w naszych czasach **5.** ***~s*** wieki, *infml* kupę czasu; ***I haven't seen him for ~s*** od wieków go nie widziałem **II** *v/i* **1.** starzeć ⟨po-⟩ się **2.** (*cheese*) dojrzewać ⟨-rzeć⟩, (*wine*) leżakować; **'age brack•et** przedział *m* wiekowy; **'age group** *s* grupa *f* wiekowa; **'age lim•it** *s* limit *m* wieku

aged[1] [eɪdʒd] *adj* **1.** stary, w podeszłym wieku **2.** ***~ twenty*** dwudziestoletni, w wieku dwudziestu lat

a•ged[2] ['eɪdʒɪd] *adj*: ***the ~*** ludzie starsi

a•gen•cy ['eɪdʒənsɪ] *s* **1.** agencja *f*, biuro *n*; ***an estate ~*** agencja nieruchomości **2.** pośrednictwo *n*, wstawiennictwo *n*; ***she was admitted through*** (*a.* ***by***) ***the ~ of her uncle*** przyjęto ją dzięki staraniom jej wuja

a•gen•da [ə'dʒendə] *s* **1.** porządek *m* dzienny, porządek *m* obrad; ***this issue is on the ~*** ten problem jest w porządku obrad **2.** ***be high on the ~*** należeć do priorytetów

a•gent ['eɪdʒənt] *s* **1.** agent *m* **2.** przedstawiciel *m* **3.** środek *m* **4.** czynnik *m*; ***a cleaning ~*** środek czyszczący **5.** *lit* sprawca *m*, przyczyna *f*

age-old ['eɪdʒəʊld] *adj* **1.** bardzo stary, wiekowy **2.** *problem*: odwieczny

ag•glom•er•a•tion [əglɒmə'reɪʃn] *s* **1.** aglomeracja *f* **2.** skupisko *n*, zlepek *m*

ag•gra•vate ['ægrəveɪt] **I** *v/t* **1.** pogarszać ⟨-gorszyć⟩; ***the situation was ~d by the arrival of her father*** sytuację pogorszyło przybycie jej ojca **2.** *infml* działać na nerwy, wkurzać ⟨-rzyć⟩ **II** *v/i* pogarszać ⟨-gorszyć⟩ się; **ag•gra•vat•ing** ['ægrəveɪtɪŋ] *adj infml* wkurzający, działający na nerwy; **ag•gra•va•tion** [ægrə'veɪʃn] *s* **1.** pogorszenie *n* **2.** *infml* zdenerwowanie *n* **3.** *infml* kłopot *m*, utrapienie *n*

ag•gre•gate ['ægrɪgət] **I** *adj* łączny, sumaryczny; ***an ~ amount*** suma łączna **II** *v/t* **1.** sumować ⟨z-⟩, dodawać ⟨-dać⟩ **2.** łączyć ⟨po-⟩ **III** *v/i* łączyć ⟨po-⟩ się **IV** *s* **1.** suma *f*; ***in the ~*** w sumie, łącznie **2.** kruszywo *n*

ag•gres•sion [ə'greʃn] *s* agresja *f*, agresywność *f*; **ag•gres•sive** [ə'gresɪv] *adj* agresywny; **ag•gres•sive•ly** [ə'gresɪvlɪ] *adv* agresywnie; **ag•gres•sive•ness** [ə'gresɪvnɪs] *s* agresywność *f*; **ag•gres•sor** [ə'gresə] *s* agresor *m*, napastnik *m*

ag•grieved [ə'griːvd] *adj* **1.** pokrzywdzony; ***the party ~*** strona pokrzywdzona **2.** rozżalony, rozgoryczony

a•ghast [ə'gæst] *adj* przerażony, wstrząśnięty

ag•ile ['ædʒaɪl] *adj* **1.** zwinny, szybki **2.** *mind*: bystry; **a•gil•i•ty** [ə'dʒɪlətɪ] *s* **1.** zwinność *f*, szybkość *f* **2.** *mental*: bystrość *f*

ag•i•tate ['ædʒɪteɪt] **I** *v/t* **1.** mieszać ⟨po-⟩ **2.** wstrząsać ⟨-snąć⟩ **3.** *person*: poruszać ⟨-szyć⟩, niepokoić ⟨za-⟩ **II** *v/i* agitować ⟨za-⟩ (**for** za *I*, **against** przeciw *D*); **ag•i•tat•ed** ['ædʒɪteɪtɪd] *adj person*: poruszony, zaniepokojony; **ag•i•ta•tion** [ædʒɪ'teɪʃn] *s* **1.** poruszenie *n*, niepokój *m* **2.** agitacja *f*; **ag•i•ta•tor** [ædʒɪ'teɪtə] *s* agitator *m*

a•go [ə'gəʊ] *adv* temu; ***a year ~*** rok temu, przed rokiem; ***long ~*** dawno temu; ***not long ~*** niedawno

a•gog [ə'gɔg] **I** *adj* podniecony, przejęty; ***all ~*** bardzo przejęty **II** *adv* z przejęciem

ag•o•nize ['ægənaɪz] *v/i* **1.** zadręczać ⟨-czyć⟩ się **2.** cierpieć; **ag•o•niz•ing** ['ægənaɪzɪŋ] *adj* **1.** *pain*: przejmujący **2.** bolesny, trudny; **ag•o•ny** ['ægənɪ] *s* przejmujący ból *m*, męczarnia *f*, udręka *f*; ***be in ~*** cierpieć męczarnie; '**ag•o•ny aunt/uncle** *s* prowadzący *m* rubrykę porad osobistych; '**ag•o•ny col•umn** *s* rubryka *f* porad osobistych

a•grar•i•an [ə'greriən] *adj* rolny, rolniczy; ***~ reform*** reforma rolna

a•gree [ə'griː] *v/i* **I 1.** zgadzać ⟨zgodzić⟩ się (**with** z *I*); ***~d!*** zgoda!; ***let's ~ to differ*** niech każdy pozostanie przy swoim zdaniu **2.** wyrażać ⟨-razić⟩ zgodę, zgadzać ⟨-zgodzić⟩ się (**to** na *A*) **II** *v/t* **1.** uzgadniać ⟨-godnić⟩; ***~ on a strategy*** uzgodnić strategię **2.** aprobować ⟨za-⟩, akceptować ⟨za-⟩; **agree on** *v/t* zgadzać ⟨zgodzić⟩ się co do *G*; ***we ~ this point, don't we?*** zgadzamy się w tej kwestii, prawda?; **agree to** *v/t* godzić ⟨z-⟩ się na *A*, przystawać ⟨-tać⟩ na *A*; **agree with** *v/i* dobrze robić ⟨z-⟩; ***this food doesn't ~ me*** to jedzenie mi szkodzi

a•greed [ə'griːd] *adj*: ***be ~ on*** zgadzać się co do *G*

a•gree•a•ble [ə'griːəbl] *adj* **1.** miły, sympatyczny **2.** możliwy do przyjęcia **3.** ***she is not ~ to coming*** *form* nie chce przyjść; **a•gree•a•bly** [ə'griːəblɪ] *adv* miło, sympatycznie; ***~ surprised*** mile zaskoczony

a•gree•ment [ə'griːmənt] *s* **1.** zgoda *f*, porozumienie *n*; ***come to an ~*** osiągnąć porozumienie; ***be in ~ on*** (*a.* ***about***) zgadzać się co do *G* **2.** umowa *f*, porozumienie *n*, układ *m* **3.** GRAM związek *m* zgody

ag•ri•cul•tur•al [ægrɪ'kʌltʃərəl] *adj* rolniczy, rolny; ***an ~ country*** kraj rolniczy; ***~ land*** ziemia uprawna; **ag•ri•cul•ture** ['ægrɪkʌltʃə] *s* rolnictwo *n*

a•ground [ə'graʊnd] *adv* **1.** (*of ship*) ***run ~*** osiąść na mieliźnie; ***be ~*** być na mieliźnie **2.** ***our plans have run ~*** *fig* nasze plany legły w gruzach, nasze plany wzięły w łeb

a•head [ə'hed] *adv* **1.** (*in space*) z przodu, do przodu **2.** ***we have lots of work ~*** przed nami wiele pracy **3.** z wyprzedzeniem; ***think ~*** planować z wyprzedzeniem **4.** ***be ~ of time*** być przed czasem; ***be*** (***way***) ***~ of*** (znacznie) wyprzedzać *A*; ***be ~ of one's time*** wyprzedać swoją epokę

AI [eɪ'aɪ] *abbr* **1.** (=***artificial intelligence***) SI, sztuczna inteligencja *f* **2.** (=***artificial insemination***) sztuczne zapłodnienie *n*

aid [eɪd] **I** *s* **1.** pomoc *f*, wsparcie *n*; ***come to s.o.'s ~*** przyjść komuś z pomocą; ***in ~ of*** na rzecz *G* **2.** pomoc *f*; ***a hearing ~*** aparat słuchowy **II** *v/t* **1.** pomagać ⟨-móc⟩; ***he was accused of ~ing and abetting the murderer*** oskarżono go o pomoc mordercy **2.** wspomagać ⟨-móc⟩, wspierać ⟨wesprzeć⟩

aide [eɪd] *s* **1.** doradca *m* **2.** pomocnik *m* **3.** adiutant *m*

AIDS [eɪdz] *abbr* (=***Acquired Immune Deficiency Syndrome***) AIDS *n*

ail•ing ['eɪlɪŋ] *adj* **1.** niedomagający; ***the ~ healthcare system*** niedomagający system opieki zdrowotnej **2.** chory; **ail•ment** ['eɪlmənt] *s* dolegliwość *f*, niedomaganie *n*, choroba *f*

aim [eɪm] **I** *s* cel *m*; ***take ~*** wycelować **II** *v/i* **1.** celować ⟨wy-⟩ (**at** w *A*) **2.** dążyć (**at** do *G*); ***an appeal which ~s to***

raise funds for apel, którego celem jest zebranie środków na *A* **II** *v/t* **1.** *weapon*: mierzyć ⟨wy-⟩ **2.** ***be ~ed*** być skierowanym, być adresowanym; ***this advertising campaign is ~ed at young women*** ta kampania reklamowa jest adresowana do młodych kobiet

aim•less ['eɪmlɪs] *adj* **1.** bezcelowy **2.** bezsensowny

ain't [eɪnt] *infml contracted form* → ***am not***, ***are not***, ***is not***, ***have not***, ***has not***

air[1] [eə] **I** *s* **1.** powietrze *n*; ***by ~*** drogą lotniczą, samolotem; ***in the open ~*** na wolnym powietrzu; ***be in the ~*** lecieć, być w powietrzu **2.** ***on the ~*** RADIO na antenie **3.** ***he had an ~ of sadness about him*** otaczała go aura smutku; ***have an ~ of mystery*** być owianym tajemnicą **4.** ***put on ~s*** (***and graces***) puszyć się **II** *v/t* **1.** wietrzyć ⟨prze-⟩ **2.** głosić, wygłosić ⟨-łaszać⟩, rozgłaszać ⟨-łosić⟩ **3.** *programme*: nadawać ⟨-dać⟩

air[2] [~] *s* melodia *f*; ***he loved to play Scottish ~s*** uwielbiał grać szkockie melodie

'air bag *s* poduszka *f* powietrzna; **'air•base** *s* baza *f* lotnicza; **'airbed** *s* materac *m* nadmuchiwany

'air•borne *adj* **1.** (będący) w powietrzu; ***be ~*** lecieć, być w powietrzu **2.** przenoszony przez wiatr **3.** *troops*: powietrznodesantowy

'air brake *s* hamulec *m* pneumatyczny; **'air•brush** *s* pistolet *m* natryskowy; **'air car•go** *s* **1.** transport *m* lotniczy **2.** ładunek *m* lotniczy

'air-con•di•tioned *adj* klimatyzowany; **'air-con•di•tion•ing** *s* klimatyzacja *f*

air-cooled ['eəkuːld] *adj* chłodzony powietrzem

'air•craft ['eəkræft] *s* **1.** statek *m* powietrzny **2.** samolot *m*; ***an ~ carrier*** lotniskowiec; **'air•drop I** *s* zrzut *m* **II** *v/t* zrzucać ⟨-cić⟩ na spadochronie; **'air•fare** *s* opłata *f* za przelot; **'air•field** *s* lotnisko *n*, lądowisko *n*; **'air•force** *s* **1.** lotnictwo *n* wojskowe, siły *pl* powietrzne; **'air•freight** *s* **1.** transport *m* lotniczy **2.** fracht *m* lotniczy; **'air fresh•en•er** *s* odświeżacz *m* powietrza; **'air•gun** *s* wiatrówka *f*; **'air•head** *s infml* pacan *m*, przygłup *m*; **'air host•ess** *s* stewardesa *f*

air•ing ['eərɪŋ] *s* **1.** wietrzenie *n*; ***give a room an ~*** przewietrzyć pokój; ***the room needs an ~*** pokój trzeba przewietrzyć **2.** ***give s.th. an ~*** przedyskutować coś

'air•lane *s* korytarz *m* powietrzny; **'air•less** *adj* duszny; **'air•let•ter** *s* list *m* lotniczy; **'air•lift** *s* operacja *f* lotnicza; **'air•line** *s* linia *f* lotnicza; **'air•lin•er** *s* samolot *m* pasażerski

'air•mail ['eəmeil] **I** *s* poczta *f* lotnicza **II** *v/t* nadawać ⟨-dać⟩ pocztą lotniczą; **'air•plane** *s* samolot *m*; **'air•pock•et** *s* dziura *f* powietrzna; **'air pol•lu•tion** *s* zanieczyszczenie *n* powietrza

air•port ['eəpɔːt] *s* lotnisko *n*, port *m* lotniczy; **'air•port tax** *s* opłata *f* lotniskowa

'air pres•sure *s* ciśnienie *n* powietrza; **'air pump** *s* pompa *f* próżniowa; **'air raid** *s* nalot *m*; **'air•raid shel•ter** *s* schron *m* przeciwlotniczy; **air•'res•cue serv•ice** *s* ratownictwo *n* powietrzne; **'air•ship** *s* sterowiec *m*; **'air•show** *s* pokaz *m* lotniczy

'air•sick ['eəsɪk] *adj*: ***be ~*** cierpieć na chorobę powietrzną; **'air•sick•ness** *s* choroba *f* powietrzna

'air•space ['eəspeɪs] *s* przestrzeń *f* powietrzna; **'air•speed** *s* prędkość *f* lotu; **'air•strip** *s* **1.** pas *m* startowy, lądowisko *n* **2.** lotnisko *n* polowe; **'air ter•mi•nal** *s* terminal *m* lotniczy; **'air•tight** *adj* **1.** hermetyczny **2.** *alibi*: żelazny; **'air•time** *s* czas *m* antenowy

'air traf•fic *s* ruch *m* powietrzny; **air 'traffic con•'trol** *s* kontrola *f* ruchu powietrznego; **air 'traffic con'trol•ler** *s* kontroler *m* ruchu powietrznego

'air•waves ['eəweɪvz] *pl* fale *pl* radiowe

air•y ['eərɪ] *adj* **1.** przestronny **2.** *manner*: niedbały **3.** *promise*: czczy

air•y-fair•y [eərɪ'ferɪ] *adj* oderwany od rzeczywistości, wydumany

aisle [aɪl] *s* **1.** (*in plane*, *church*) przejście *n*; ***the audience was rolling in the ~s*** widzowie tarzali się ze śmiechu; ***lead s.o. down the ~*** *fig* poprowadzić kogoś do ołtarza **2.** nawa *f* boczna; **'aisle seat** *s* (*in plane*) miejsce *n* przy przejściu

a•jar [ə'dʒɑː] *adj door*: uchylony
aka [eɪkeɪ'eɪ] *abbr* (=**also known as**) alias, zwany; ***Bernardo Belotto ~ Canaletto*** Bernardo Belotto zwany Canaletto
a•kin [ə'kɪn] *adj* **1.** podobny **2.** spokrewniony; ***the Polish language is ~ to Czech*** język polski jest spokrewniony z czeskim
a•larm [ə'lɑːm] **I** *s* **1.** alarm *m*; ***give*** (*a.* ***raise***) ***the ~*** podnieść alarm; ***sound the ~*** bić na alarm; ***a false ~*** fałszywy alarm **2.** niepokój *m*; ***give s.o. cause for ~*** zaniepokoić kogoś **II** *v/t* niepokoić ⟨za-⟩; **a•'larm clock** *s* budzik *m*; **a•larm•ing** [ə'lɑːmɪŋ] *adj* alarmujący, niepokojący; **a•larm•ing•ly** [ə'lɑːmɪŋlɪ] *adv* alarmująco, niepokojąco; **a•larm•ist** [ə'lɑːmɪst] **I** *adj* alarmistyczny, szerzący panikę **II** *s* panikarz *m*
a•las [ə'læs] *interj lit* niestety
Al•ba•ni•a [æl'beɪnɪə] *s* Albania *f*; **Al•ba•ni•an** [æl'beɪnɪən] **I** *adj* albański **II** *s* Albańczyk *m*, Albanka *f*
al•ba•tross ['ælbətrɒs] *s* albatros *m*
al•bi•no [æl'biːnəʊ] *pl -nos* [~nəʊz] **I** *s* albinos *m* **II** *adj* albinotyczny; ***an ~ koala*** koala albinos
al•bum ['ælbəm] *s* **1.** album *m* **2.** klaser *m*
al•co•hol ['ælkəhɒl] *s* alkohol *m*; **al•co•hol•ic** [ælkə'hɒlɪk] **I** *adj* alkoholowy **II** *s* alkoholik *m*; ***≈s Anonymous*** Stowarzyszenie Anonimowych Alkoholików
al•cove ['ælkəʊv] *s* alkowa *f*, wnęka *f*
al•der ['ɔːldə] *s* olcha *f*
ale [eɪl] *s* (*beer*) ale *n*
a•lert [ə'lɜːt] **I** *adj* **1.** czujny, uważny, mający się na baczności **2.** świadomy; ***~ to danger*** świadomy zagrożenia **II** *s* alarm *m*; ***be on the ~*** być w pogotowiu **III** *v/t* alarmować ⟨za-⟩, ostrzegać ⟨-rzec⟩ (***s.o. to*** kogoś o *L*)
A lev•el ['eɪlevl] *abbr* (=**advanced level**) *egzamin końcowy z wybranego przedmiotu zdawany na zakończenie szkoły średniej*
al•ga ['ælgə] *pl -gae* ['~dʒiː] *s* alga *f*, glon *m*; ***algae*** algi, glony
al•ge•bra ['ældʒɪbrə] *s* algebra *f*; **al•ge•bra•ic** [ældʒɪ'breɪɪk] *adj* algebraiczny
Al•ge•ri•a [æl'dʒɪərɪə] *s* Algieria *f*
a•li•as ['eɪlɪəs] **I** *adv* alias, znany też jako **II** *s* pseudonim *m*
al•i•bi ['ælɪbaɪ] *s* **1.** alibi *n*; ***an airtight ~*** żelazne alibi **2.** wymówka *f*, wykręt *m*; ***her illness was just an ~*** jej choroba to był tylko wykręt
al•ien ['eɪlɪən] **I** *adj* obcy, cudzoziemski, innej narodowości **II** *s* **1.** obcokrajowiec *m*, cudzoziemiec *m* **2.** kosmita *m*, przybysz *m* z kosmosu
al•ien•ate ['eɪlɪəneɪt] *v/t* **1.** zrażać ⟨zrazić⟩ **2.** alienować ⟨wy-⟩, wyobcowywać ⟨-cować⟩ **3.** *funds, land*: przenosić ⟨-nieść⟩ prawo własności do G; **al•ien•a•tion** [eɪlɪən'eɪʃn] *s* **1.** alienacja *f*, wyobcowanie *n* **2.** zrażanie *n* **3.** *funds, lands*: przeniesienie *n*
a•light[1] [ə'laɪt] *adj*: ***be ~*** płonąć, palić się, być w ogniu; ***set s.th. ~*** podpalić coś
a•light[2] [~] *v/i lit* **1.** wysiadać ⟨-siąść⟩; ***she ~ed from the carriage*** wysiadła z powozu **2.** lądować ⟨wy-⟩, siadać ⟨usiąść⟩; ***a bird ~ed on her hand*** ptak usiadł jej na ręce
a•lign [ə'laɪn] **I** *v/t* wyrównywać ⟨-nać⟩, ustawiać ⟨-wić⟩ równo; ***~ the wheels*** ustawić zbieżność kół **II** *v/i* zawierać ⟨-wrzeć⟩ sojusz, sprzymierzać ⟨-rzyć⟩ się (***with*** z *I*); **a•lign•ment** [ə'laɪnmənt] *s* **1.** ustawienie *n* w jednej linii, wyrównanie *n* **2.** przymierze *n*, sojusz *m*
a•like [ə'laɪk] **I** *adj* podobny **II** *adv* **1.** podobnie; ***treat both children ~*** traktować oboje dzieci tak samo **2.** zarówno; ***we had great time, young and old ~*** bawiliśmy się świetnie, zarówno młodzi, jak i starzy
al•i•men•ta•ry [ælɪ'mentərɪ] *adj* **1.** pokarmowy; ***~ canal*** przewód pokarmowy **2.** żywieniowy
al•i•mo•ny ['ælɪmənɪ] *s* alimenty *pl*, świadczenia *pl* alimentacyjne
a•live [ə'laɪv] *adj* **1.** żywy; ***be ~*** żyć; ***keep s.o. ~*** utrzymywać kogoś przy życiu; ***be burnt ~*** zostać spalonym żywcem **2.** pełen życia, pełen wigoru; ***be ~ and kicking*** dobrze się mieć; ***come ~*** ożywić się **3.** ***be ~ to*** zdawać sobie sprawę z *G* **4.** ***her hair was ~ with lice*** w jej włosach roiło się od wszy **5.** (*after adjective in superlative*

form) na świecie; ***the best man ~*** najlepszy człowiek pod słońcem

al•ka•li ['ælkəlaɪ] *s* CHEM zasada *f*; **al•ka•line** ['ælkəlaɪn] *adj* zasadowy, alkaliczny

all [ɔːl] **I** *adj* **1.** wszyscy; ***~ the people*** wszyscy ludzie **2.** każdy; ***at ~ hours*** o każdej porze **3.** cały; ***~ day long*** cały dzień; ***~ the time*** cały czas **II** *adv* w pełni; w całości, całkowicie; ***~ the better*** tym lepiej; ***it is ~ over*** już po wszystkim; ***that is John ~ over*** to cały John; ***I'm dirty ~ over*** jestem cały brudny; ***~ right*** w porządku, okej; ***it's ~ right for you to talk!*** łatwo ci mówić!; ***drinks ~ round*** kolejka dla wszystkich; ***~ but*** prawie; ***~ but one of them survived*** nie przeżył tylko jeden z nich **III** *pron* wszystko; ***~ in ~*** ogólnie rzecz biorąc, w sumie; ***~ of five people came*** przyszło zaledwie pięć osób; ***cost ~ of a million dollars*** kosztować co najmniej milion dolarów; ***~ of us*** my wszyscy; ***above ~*** przede wszystkim; ***after ~*** mimo wszystko; ***~ we need*** wszystko, czego nam potrzeba **IV** *s* ***his ~*** wszystko, co posiada

'all-around → ***all-round***

all-A'mer•i•can *adj* **1.** typowo amerykański **2.** ogólnoamerykański; ***an ~ team*** reprezentacja Stanów Zjednoczonych

all-'clear *s* **1.** sygnał *m* odwołania alarmu; ***to give an ~*** odwołać alarm **2.** *fig* zielone światło *n*

al•le•ga•tion [ælɪ'geɪʃn] *s* (niepoparty dowodami) zarzut *m*, twierdzenie *n*; **al•lege** [ə'ledʒ] *v/t* twierdzić ⟨s-⟩, utrzymywać; **al•leged** [ə'ledʒd] *adj* domniemany, rzekomy; **al•leg•ed•ly** [ə'ledʒɪdlɪ] *adv* rzekomo, podobno

al•le•giance [ə'liːdʒəns] *s* **1.** lojalność *f*, wierność *f*, oddanie *n* (***to*** *D*) **2.** posłuszeństwo *n*

al•le•gor•ic [ælɪ'gɔrɪk], ***al•le•gor•i•cal*** [ælɪ'gɔrɪkl] *adj* alegoryczny; **al•le•go•ry** ['æləgərɪ] *s* alegoria *f*

al•ler•gic [ə'lɜːdʒɪk] *adj* alergiczny, uczulony (***to*** na *A*); ***be ~ to*** być uczulonym na *A*, mieć alergię na *A*; **al•ler•gist** ['ælədʒɪst] *s* alergolog *m*; **al•ler•gy** ['ælədʒɪ] *s* alergia *f*, uczulenie *n*

al•ley ['ælɪ] *s* **1.** uliczka *f*, zaułek *m* **2.** przejście *n* między budynkami **3.** alejka *f* **4.** (*in bowling*) tor *m*

al•li•ance [ə'laɪəns] *s* sojusz *m*, przymierze *n*; ***form an ~*** zawrzeć sojusz; **al•lied** ['ælaɪd] *adj* sojuszniczy, sprzymierzony; ***the ~ forces*** siły alianckie; ***the ~ landings in Normandy*** lądowanie aliantów w Normandii

al•li•ga•tor ['ælɪgeɪtə] *s* aligator *m*; ***~ clip*** krokodylek

all-im'por•tant *adj* bardzo ważny, najważniejszy

all-'in *adj price*: za wszystko, łączny; **all-in•'clu•sive 'price** *s* cena *f* za wszystko, cena *f* łączna

al•lit•er•a•tion [əlɪtə'reɪʃn] *s* aliteracja *f*

all-'night *adj* całonocny, czynny całą noc

al•lo•cate ['æləkeɪt] *v/t* przeznaczać ⟨-czyć⟩, przydzielać ⟨-lić⟩, asygnować ⟨wy-⟩; **al•lo•ca•tion** [ælə'keɪʃn] *s* przeznaczenie *n*, przydział *m*, asygnowanie *n*

al•lot [ə'lɔt] *v/t* **1.** przydzielać ⟨-lić⟩ **2.** asygnować ⟨wy-⟩, przyznawać ⟨-nać⟩; **allot•ment** [ə'lɔtmənt] *s* **1.** przydział *m* **2.** ***an ~*** (***garden***) działka

all-'out *adj* **1.** maksymalny **2.** *attack*: zmasowany

al•low [ə'laʊ] *v/t* **1.** pozwalać ⟨-wolić⟩, dopuszczać ⟨-puścić⟩; ***be ~ed to do s.th.*** móc coś robić, mieć pozwolenie, aby coś robić; ***~ me*** proszę mi pozwolić, pan pozwoli **2.** wpuszczać ⟨wpuścić⟩, przepuszczać ⟨-puścić⟩; ***dogs are not ~ed in the shop*** nie wolno wprowadzać psów do sklepu **3.** przyznawać ⟨-nać⟩; ***I ~ed that I might have been wrong*** przyznałem, że mogłem się mylić **4.** ***~ of*** *form* pozwalać na *A*, dopuszczać *A*; ***this rule ~s no exceptions*** od tej zasady nie ma żadnych wyjątków **5.** ***~ for*** brać pod uwagę *A*; ***~ for a possibility that*** wziąć pod uwagę możliwość, że; **al•low•a•ble** [ə'laʊəbl] *adj* **1.** dopuszczalny, dozwolony **2.** podlegający odliczeniu od podatku; **al•low•ance** [ə'laʊəns] *s* **1.** dozwolona ilość *f*; ***duty-free ~*** limit zakupów w strefie bezcłowej **2.** dodatek *m* (do pensji) **3.** kieszonkowe *n*

4. ***make ~s for*** **a)** uwzględniać *A*, brać pod uwagę *A* **b)** traktować pobłażliwie *A*

all-'pow•er•ful *adj* wszechmocny, wszechpotężny

'all-pur•pose *adj* uniwersalny, wielofunkcyjny

'all-round, ***all-around*** *adj* **1.** wszechstronny **2.** *education*: ogólny; **all-'round•er** *s*: ***be an ~*** być wszechstronnym

all-risk in'sur•ance *s* ubezpieczenie *n* od wszelkiego ryzyka

All 'Saints' Day *s REL* Dzień *m* Wszystkich Świętych

All 'Souls' Day *s REL* Zaduszki *pl*; Dzień *m* Zaduszny

all-ter'rain *adj* terenowy; ***~ vehicle*** pojazd terenowy

'all-time *adj* wszechczasów; ***~ low*** najniższy notowany dotychczas poziom, rekordowo niski poziom

al•lure [ə'luːə] *s* atrakcyjność *f*, powab *m*; **al•lur•ing** [ə'luːrɪŋ] *adj* ponętny, kuszący, atrakcyjny

al•lu•sion [ə'luːʒn] *s* aluzja *f*; **al•lude** [ə'luːd] *v/i* ***~ to***: robić ⟨z-⟩ aluzję do *G*

'all-weath•er *adj* na każdą pogodę

all-wheel 'drive *s* napęd *m* na cztery koła

al•ly ['ælaɪ] **I** *s* sprzymierzeniec *m*, sojusznik *m*; ***the Allies*** alianci **II** *v/i* sprzymierzać ⟨-rzyć⟩ się (***with*** z *I*) **III** *v/t* ***~ oneself with*** sprzymierzać się z *I*, zawierać sojusz z *I*

al•might•y [ɔːl'maɪtɪ] *adj* wszechmocny, wszechmogący; ***the ~*** Wszechmogący *m*

al•mond ['ɑːmənd] *s* migdał *m*

al•most ['ɔːlməʊst] *adv* prawie, niemal, o mało nie

alms [ɑːmz] *s* jałmużna *f*

al•oe ['æləʊ] *s* aloes *m*

a•loft [ə'lɒft] *adv* **1.** w górę **2.** w górze

a•lone [ə'ləʊn] **I** *adj* **1.** sam; ***live on rice ~*** jeść tylko ryż **2.** samotny, osamotniony; ***leave me ~*** zostaw mnie w spokoju; ***let ~*** a co dopiero **II** *adv* **1.** samotnie **2.** samodzielnie, w pojedynkę **3.** tylko, jedynie

a•long [ə'lɒŋ] **I** *prep* wzdłuż *G*; ***~ the river*** wzdłuż rzeki; ***go ~ the street*** iść ulicą **II** *adv* **1.** naprzód, do przodu; ***walk ~*** iść przed siebie; ***get ~ well with*** być w dobrych stosunkach z *I*, dobrze żyć z *I* **2.** ze sobą; ***take me ~*** weź mnie ze sobą **3.** ***go ~ to the boss*** iść do szefa; ***I'll be ~ shortly*** niedługo przyjdę

a•long•side [əlɒŋ'saɪd] **I** *adv* obok **II** *prep* obok *G*, przy *L*, wzdłuż *G*

a•loof [ə'luːf] **I** *adj* powściągliwy, zdystansowany, z dystansem **II** *adv* ***keep oneself ~*** zachowywać dystans; ***keep ~ from*** trzymać się z dala od *G*

a•loud [ə'laʊd] *adv* głośno, na głos

al•pha•bet ['ælfəbet] *s* alfabet *m*; **al•pha•bet•i•cal** [ælfə'betɪkl] *adj* alfabetyczny; ***in ~ order*** w kolejności alfabetycznej

al•pine ['ælpaɪn] *adj* **1.** alpejski **2.** górski, wysokogórski; ***the ~ flora*** roślinność górska

Al•pine *adj* alpejski; **Alps** [ælps] *pl*: ***the ~*** Alpy;

al•read•y [ɔːl'redɪ] *adv* **1.** już; ***I have ~ seen this film*** już widziałem ten film **2.** dotychczas, jak dotąd

al•right [ɔːl'raɪt] *infml* → ***all***

Al•sa•tian [æl'seɪʃn] **I** *adj* alzacki **II** *s* owczarek *m* alzacki, wilczur *m*

al•so ['ɔːlsəʊ] *adv* też, także, również

al•tar ['ɔːltə] *s* ołtarz *m*

al•ter ['ɔːltə] **I** *v/i* zmieniać ⟨-nić⟩ się, odmieniać ⟨-nić⟩ się **II** *v/t* **1.** zmieniać ⟨-nić⟩, odmieniać ⟨-nić⟩ **2.** *clothes*: przerabiać ⟨-robić⟩; **al•ter•a•tion** [ɔːltə'reɪʃn] *s* zmiana *f*, przeróbka *f*

al•ter•ca•tion [ɔːltə'keɪʃn] *s* sprzeczka *f*, kłótnia *f*

al•ter•nate I [ɔːl'tɜːnət] *adj* **1.** naprzemienny, występujący na przemian; ***on ~ days*** co drugi dzień **2.** odmienny, inny; ***an ~ point of view*** odmienny punkt widzenia **II** ['ɔːltəneɪt] *v/i* **3.** występować naprzemiennie **4.** wahać się, oscylować **III** *v/t* ['ɔːltəneɪt] przekładać ⟨-łożyć⟩; ***~ meat with slices of red pepper*** przełóż mięso kawałkami czerwonej papryki; **al•ter•nate•ly** [ɔːl'tɜːrnətlɪ] *adv* na przemian; **al•ter•nat•ing** ['ɔːltəneɪtɪŋ] *adj* naprzemienny; ***~ current*** prąd zmienny

al•ter•na•tive [ɔːlt'ɜːnətɪv] **I** *adj* alternatywny, inny; ***~ energy sources*** alternatywne źródła energii **II** *s* alternatywa *f*; ***have no*** (***other***) ***~*** (***but to***)

nie mieć innego wyjścia (tylko); **al•ter•na•tive•ly** [ɔːlt'ɜːnətɪvlɪ] *adv* alternatywnie, zamiast tego
al•though [ɔːl'ðəʊ] *conj* chociaż, mimo że
al•tim•e•ter ['æltɪmiːtə] *s TECH* wysokościomierz *m*
al•ti•tude ['æltɪtjuːd] *s* wysokość *f*; ***at an ~ of*** na wysokości *G*; **'al•ti•tude sick•ness** *s* choroba *f* wysokościowa
al•to•geth•er [ɔːltə'geðə] *adv* **1.** zupełnie, kompletnie, w pełni **2.** w sumie, ogólnie, razem
al•tru•ism ['æltruːɪzm] *s* altruizm *m*; **al•tru•ist** ['æltruːɪst] *s* altruista *m*; **al•tru•is•tic** [æltruː'ɪstɪk] *adj* altruistyczny
al•ways ['ɔːlweɪz] *adv* zawsze; ***as ~*** jak zawsze; ***you are ~ complaining*** zawsze narzekasz, wiecznie narzekasz
Alz•hei•mer's (dis•ease) ['æltshaɪməz] *s MED* choroba *f* Alzheimera
am [æm] → ***be***
a.m. ['eɪem] *adv* rano, przed południem; ***let's meet at 9 ~*** spotkajmy się o 9 rano
a•mass [ə'mæs] *v/t* gromadzić ⟨z-⟩, zbierać ⟨zebrać⟩
am•a•teur ['æmətə] **I** *s* **1.** amator *m* **2.** dyletant *m*, partacz *m* **II** *adj* amatorski; ***an ~ painter*** malarz amator; ***an ~ detective*** detektyw amator; **am•a•teur•ish** ['æmətərɪʃ] *adj* amatorski, dyletancki
a•maze [ə'meɪz] *v/t* zdumiewać ⟨-mieć⟩, zadziwiać ⟨-wić⟩; **a•mazed** [ə'meɪzd] *adj* zdumiony; **a•maze•ment** [ə'meɪzmənt] *s* zdumienie *n*, zadziwienie *n*; ***to my ~*** ku mojemu zdumieniu; **a•maz•ing** [ə'meɪzɪŋ] *adj* zdumiewający, zadziwiający; **a•maz•ing•ly** [ə'meɪzɪŋlɪ] *adv* zdumiewająco, zadziwiająco
Am•a•zon ['æməzən] *s* Amazonka *f*; **Am•a•zo•ni•an** [æmə'zəʊnɪən] *adj* amazoński; ***the ~ jungle*** dżungla amazońska
am•bas•sa•dor [æm'bæsədə] *s* ambasador *m*
am•ber ['æmbə] **I** *s* **1.** bursztyn *m* **2.** bursztynowy kolor *m* **3.** *AUTO* żółte światło *n* **II** *adj* **1.** bursztynowy **2.** *traffic light*: żółty
am•bi•ence ['æmbɪəns], ***am•bi•ance*** *s* (*of place*) atmosfera *f*
am•bi•gu•i•ty [æmbɪ'gjuːətɪ] *s* dwuznaczność *f*; wieloznaczność *f*, niejasność *f*, **am•bi•gu•ous** [æm'bɪgjʊəs] *adj* dwuznaczny, wieloznaczny, niejasny
am•bi•tion [æm'bɪʃn] *s* ambicja *f*; **am•bi•tious** [æm'bɪʃəs] *adj* ambitny
am•bi•va•lence [æm'bɪvələns] *s* **1.** ambiwalencja *f* **2.** mieszane uczucia *pl*; **am•bi•va•lent** [æm'bɪvələnt] *adj* ambiwalentny; ***an ~ attitude***, ***~ feelings*** mieszane uczucia
am•ble ['æmbl] **I** *v/i* spacerować, przechadzać się **II** *s* spacer *m*, przechadzka *f*
am•bu•lance ['æmbjʊləns] *s* karetka *f* pogotowia, ambulans *m*
am•bush ['æmbʊʃ] **I** *s* zasadzka *f* **II** *v/t* wciągać ⟨-gnąć⟩ w zasadzkę
a•mel•io•rate [ə'miːlɪəreɪt] *v/t* doskonalić ⟨u-⟩, ulepszać ⟨-szyć⟩, poprawiać ⟨-wić⟩
a•men [eɪ'men] **I** *interj* amen **II** *s* ***~ to that!*** święta racja!, święte słowa!
a•me•na•ble [ə'miːnəbl] *adj*: ***~ to*** podatny na *A*, skłonny do *G*, nadający się do *G*
a•mend [ə'mend] *v* **1.** poprawiać ⟨-wić⟩ **2.** nowelizować ⟨z-⟩, wnosić ⟨wnieść⟩ poprawki do *G*; **a•mend•ment** [ə'mendmənt] *s* zmiana *f*, poprawka *f*; ***a constitutional ~*** poprawka do konstytucji, poprawka konstytucyjna; **a•mends** [ə'mendz] *pl*: ***make ~ for*** zrekompensować *A*, zadośćuczynić *D*
a•men•i•ty [ə'miːnətɪ] *s* udogodnienie *n*, wygoda *f*; ***a flat with all amenities*** mieszkanie z wszystkimi wygodami
A•mer•i•ca [ə'merɪkə] *s* Ameryka *f*; **A•mer•i•can** [ə'merɪkən] **I** *adj* amerykański; ***the ~ Dream*** amerykański sen **II** *s* Amerykanin *m*, Amerykanka *f*; **A•mer•i•can•ism** [ə'merɪkənɪzm] *s* amerykanizm *m*
A•mer•i•can•iz•a•tion [əmerɪkənaɪ'zeɪʃn] *s* amerykanizacja *f*; **A•mer•i•can•ize** [ə'merɪkənaɪz] *v/t* amerykanizować ⟨z-⟩
a•mi•a•bil•i•ty [eɪmɪə'bɪlətɪ] *s* przyjazność *f*; **a•mi•a•ble** ['eɪmɪəbl] *adj* sympatyczny, miły, przyjazny

a•mi•ca•ble ['æmɪkəbl] *adj* **1.** przyjazny **2.** polubowny, ugodowy; **a•mi•ca•bly** ['æmɪkəblɪ] *adv* **1.** przyjaźnie; ***part ~*** rozstać się w przyjaźni **2.** polubownie, ugodowo

a•mid(st) [ə'mɪd(st)] *prep* wśród *G*, pośród *G*

a•miss [ə'mɪs] **I** *adj* nie w porządku, nie tak; ***s.th. is ~*** coś jest nie tak; ***nothing is ~*** wszystko w porządku **II** *adv* ***take s.th. ~*** poczuć się czymś dotkniętym, obrazić się o coś; ***s.th. would not go ~*** coś przydałoby się

am•mo•ni•a [ə'məʊnɪə] *s* amoniak *m*; ***~ water*** woda amoniakalna

am•mu•ni•tion [æmjʊ'nɪʃn] *s* amunicja *f*

am•ne•sia [æm'niːzɪə] *s* amnezja *f*, zanik *m* pamięci; **am•ne•si•ac** [æm'niːzɪək] **I** *adj* amnezyjny **II** *s* cierpiący *m* na amnezję

am•nes•ty ['æmnəstɪ] *s* amnestia *f*

a•mok [ə'mɒk] *adv*: ***run ~*** wpaść w amok, być w amoku

a•mong(st) [ə'mʌŋst] *prep* wśród *G*, pośród *G*; ***~ others***, ***~ other things*** między innymi

a•mor•al [eɪ'mɒrəl] *adj* amoralny

a•mor•ous ['æmərəs] *adj* miłosny; ***~ advances*** zaloty

a•mor•phous [ə'mɔːfəs] *adj* **1.** bezkształtny, amorficzny **2.** GEOL CHEM bezpostaciowy

a•mount [ə'maʊnt] *s* ilość *f*, kwota *f*, suma *f*; **amount to** *v/i* **1.** wynosić ⟨-nieść⟩; ***his debt ~s to $500*** jego dług wynosi 500 dolarów **2.** równać się

amp [æmp] *abbr infml* **1.** (=***ampere***) amper *m*, A **2.** (=***amplifier***) wzmacniacz *m*

am•pere ['æmpeə] *s* PHYS amper *m*

am•per•sand ['æmpəsænd] *s* znak *m* &

am•phet•a•mine [æm'fetəmiːn] *s* amfetamina *f*

am•phib•i•an [æm'fɪbɪən] *s* BIOL płaz *m*

am•phi•the•a•tre ['æmfɪθɪətə] *Br*, **am•phi•the•a•ter** *Am s* amfiteatr *m*

am•ple ['æmpl] *adj*: ***~ time*** wystarczająco dużo czasu; ***an ~ bosom*** obfity biust

am•pli•fi•ca•tion [æmplɪfɪ'keɪʃn] *s* **1.** wzmocnienie *n* **2.** rozwinięcie *n*; **am•pli•fi•er** ['æmplɪfaɪə] *s* wzmacniacz *m*; **am•pli•fy** ['æmplɪfaɪ] *v/t* **1.** wzmacniać ⟨-mocnić⟩ **2.** rozwijać ⟨-winąć⟩

am•pli•tude ['æmplɪtjuːd] *s* amplituda *f*

am•pu•tate ['æmpjʊteɪt] **I** *v/t* amputować **II** *v/i* przeprowadzać ⟨-dzić⟩ amputację; **am•pu•ta•tion** [æmpjʊ'teɪʃn] *s* amputacja *f*; **am•pu•tee** [æmpjʊ'tiː] *s* osoba *f* po amputacji

a•muck [ə'mʌk] → ***amok***

a•muse [ə'mjuːz] *v/t* **1.** bawić ⟨roz-⟩, śmieszyć ⟨roz-⟩; ***we are not ~d*** to nas nie śmieszy; ***it ~s me to see how*** bawi mnie, kiedy widzę, jak **2.** zabawiać ⟨-wić⟩, rozśmieszać ⟨-szyć⟩; ***keep the children ~d*** zabawiać dzieci; **a•muse•ment** [ə'mjuːzmənt] *s* **1.** wesołość *f*, rozbawienie *n* **2.** rozrywka *f*; ***an ~ arcade*** salon gier; ***an ~ park*** wesołe miasteczko; **a•mus•ing** [ə'mjuːzɪŋ] *adj* zabawny, śmieszny; ***what's so ~?*** co cię tak bawi?; ***I don't find this ~*** nie uważam tego za zabawne; ***I collect stamps because it is ~*** zbieram znaczki, bo to ciekawe

an [æn], *unstressed* [ən] *art* (*before vowel*): ***~ apple*** jabłko; ***~ intelligent person*** inteligenta osoba; → ***a***

a•nach•ro•nism [ə'nækrənɪzəm] *s* anachronizm *m*, przeżytek *m*; **a•nach•ro•nis•tic** [ənækrə'nɪstɪk] *adj* anachroniczny,

a•nae•mi•a [ə'nɪːmiə] *s* anemia *f*, niedokrwistość *f*; **a•nae•mic** [ə'niːmɪk] *adj* anemiczny

an•aes•the•sia [ænəs'θɪːziə] *Br*, **an•es•the•si•a** *Am s* znieczulenie *n*; **an•aes•thet•ic** [ænəs'θetɪk] *Br*, **an•es•thet•ic** *Am* **I** *adj* znieczulający **II** *s* środek *m* znieczulający, anestetyk *m*; **an•aes•thet•ist** [ə'niːsθətɪst] *Br*, **an•es•the•tist** *Am s* anestezjolog *m*; **an•es•thet•ise** [ə'niːsθətaɪz] *Br*, **an•es•thet•ize** *Am v/t* znieczulać ⟨-lić⟩

an•a•l ['eɪnəl] *adj* odbytowy, analny; ***~ sex*** seks analny

a•nal•o•gous [ə'næləgəs] *adj* analogiczny; **an•a•logue** ['ænəlɒg] *s* **1.** odpowiednik *m* **2.** ***an ~ recording***

nagranie analogowe; **a•nal•o•gy** [ə'nælədʒɪ] *s* analogia *f*
an•a•lyse ['ænəlaɪz] *Br*, **an•a•lyze** *Am* *v/t* analizować ⟨z-⟩, przeprowadzać ⟨-dzić⟩ analizę;
an•al•y•sis [ə'næləsɪs] *pl -ses* [~si:z] *s* analiza *f*; **an•a•lyst** ['ænəlɪst] *s* analityk *m*; **an•a•lyt•i•cal** [ænə'lɪtɪkl] *adj* analityczny
an•arch•ist ['ænəkɪst] **I** *adj* anarchistyczny **II** *s* anarchista *m*; **an•arch•y** ['ænəkɪ] *s* anarchia *f*;
a•nath•e•ma [ə'næθəmə] *s* klątwa *f*, anatema *f*, przekleństwo *n*; ***maths is (an) ~ to me*** nienawidzę matematyki
a•nat•o•my [ə'nætəmɪ] *s* **1.** anatomia *f* **2.** *hum* ciało *n*
an•ces•tor ['ænsestə] *s* **1.** przodek *m* **2.** protoplasta *m*; **an•ces•tral** [æn'sestrəl] *adj* rodowy; ***an ~ home*** siedziba rodu; **an•ces•try** ['ænsestrɪ] *s* pochodzenie *n*, rodowód *m*; ***trace one's ~ back to the Vasas*** być potomkiem Wazów
an•chor ['æŋkə] **I** *s* **1.** kotwica *f*; ***drop*** (*a.* ***cast***) *~* rzucić kotwicę; ***lie*** (*a.* ***ride***) ***at ~*** stać na kotwicy **2.** prowadzący *m* (program) **II** *v/i* rzucać ⟨-cić⟩ kotwicę **II** *v/t* **1.** kotwiczyć ⟨za-⟩ **2.** *Am programme*: prowadzić ⟨po-⟩; **an•chor•age** ['æŋkərɪdʒ] *s* kotwicowisko *n*
anchor•man ['æŋkəmæn] *pl -men s Am* prezenter *m*, prowadzący *m*; **anchor•woman** ['æŋkəwʊmən] *pl -men s* prezenterka *f*, prowadząca *f*
an•cho•vy ['æntʃəvɪ] *s* COOK anchois *n*, sardela *f*
an•cient ['eɪnʃənt] **I** *adj* **1.** starożytny; ***~ Greece*** starożytna Grecja; ***~ history*** historia starożytna **2.** bardzo stary, wiekowy **3.** dawny, starodawny **II** *s* ***the ~s*** starożytni
and [ənd], *strong form* [ænd] *conj* i; ***bread ~ butter*** chleb z masłem; ***better ~ better*** coraz lepiej; ***~ so on*** i tak dalej
An•des ['ændi:z] *pl* Andy *pl*
An•dor•ra [æn'dɔ:rə] *s* Andora *f*
an•ec•dot•al [ænek'dəʊtl] *adj* **1.** anegdotyczny **2.** *evidence*: niepotwierdzony; **an•ec•dote** ['ænɪkdəʊt] *s* anegdota *f*
a•ne•mia [ə'ni:mɪə] *Am* → ***anaemia***
a•new [ə'nju:] *adv form* od nowa, ponownie
an•gel ['eɪndʒl] *s* anioł *m*; ***come here, ~*** chodź tu, kochanie; ***you are an ~*** jesteś cudowna; **an•gel•ic** [æn'dʒelɪk] *adj* anielski
an•ger ['æŋgə] **I** *s* złość *f*, gniew *m* **II** *v/t* gniewać ⟨roz-⟩, złościć ⟨roz-⟩
an•gle ['æŋgl] **I** *s* **1.** kąt *m*; ***in ~ brackets*** w nawiasie trójkątnym **2.** narożnik *m* **3.** punkt *m* widzenia, kąt *m*; ***look at it from my ~*** spójrz na to z mojego punktu widzenia; ***from every ~, from all ~s*** z każdej strony **II** *v/t* **1.** kierować ⟨s-⟩ pod kątem **2.** kierować ⟨s-⟩, nastawiać ⟨-wić⟩; ***the programme is ~d towards young viewers*** program jest skierowany do młodych widzów **3.** ***~ for*** przymawiać się o *A* **II** *v/i* łowić ryby na wędkę, wędkować; **an•gled** ['æŋgld] *adj* pod kątem, odchylony, ukośny
an•gler ['æŋglə] *s* wędkarz *m*
An•gli•can ['æŋglɪkən] **I** *adj* anglikański **II** *s* anglikanin *m*, anglikanka *f*; **An•gli•can•ism** ['æŋglɪkənɪzm] *s* anglikanizm *m*
An•gli•cism ['æŋglɪsɪzəm] *s* anglicyzm *m*
An•glo-A•mer•i•can [æŋgləʊə'merɪkən] *adj* angloamerykański
An•glo-Sax•on [æŋgləʊ'sæksən] **I** *adj* anglosaski **II** *s* Anglosas *m*
An•go•la [æŋ'gəʊlə] *s* Angola *f*
an•go•ra [æŋ'gɔ:rə] **I** *s* (*animal*) angora *m* **II** *adj* **1.** angorski; ***~ cat*** kot angorski **2.** z angory
an•gry ['æŋgrɪ] *adj* zły, rozgniewany (***with*** na *A*, ***about/at*** z powodu *G*)
an•guish ['æŋgwɪʃ] *s* cierpienie *n*, ból *m*, udręka *f*; ***be in ~*** cierpieć
an•gu•lar ['æŋgjʊlə] *adj* **1.** kanciasty **2.** kościsty
an•i•mal ['ænɪməl] **I** *s* zwierzę *n*; ***the ~ kingdom*** królestwo zwierząt; ***an ~ lover*** miłośnik zwierząt; ***an ~ shelter*** schronisko dla zwierząt; ***~ welfare*** dobro zwierząt, ochrona zwierząt **II** *adj* zwierzęcy; ***~ magnetism*** zwierzęcy magnetyzm
an•i•mate **I** ['ænɪmeɪt] *v/t* **1.** ożywiać ⟨-wić⟩, pobudzać ⟨-dzić⟩ do życia **2.** animować **II** ['ænɪmət] *adj* **1.** żywy; ***~ beings*** żywe istoty **2.** ożywiony;

an•i•ma•ted ['ænɪmeɪtɪd] *adj* **1.** ożywiony, pobudzony **2.** animowany; ***an ~ cartoon*** kreskówka; ***an ~ film*** film animowany; **an•i•ma•tion** [ænɪ'meɪʃn] *s* **1.** ożywienie *n* **2.** entuzjazm *m* **3.** animacja *f*; **an•i•ma•tor** ['ænɪmeɪtə] *s* animator *m*

an•i•mos•i•ty [ænɪ'mɒsətɪ] *s* **1.** niechęć *f*; ***feel ~ against*** (*a.* ***towards***) czuć niechęć do *G* **2.** wrogość *f*

an•ise ['ænɪs] *s* anyż *m*; **an•i•seed** ['ænɪsiːd] *s* anyż *m*, nasiona *pl* anyżu

an•kle ['æŋkl] *s ANAT* kostka *f* (u nogi); ***~deep*** do kostek; ***~boots*** buty do kostek; **an•klet** ['æŋklət] *s* **1.** bransoletka *f* na nogę **2.** *Am* skarpetka *f* do kostki

an•nals ['ænlz] *pl* annały *pl*, kroniki *pl*; ***go down in the ~as*** przejść do historii jako *N*

an•neal [ə'niːl] *v/t* **1.** wyżarzać ⟨-rzyć⟩, poddawać ⟨-dać⟩ wyżarzaniu **2.** odprężać ⟨-żyć⟩

an•nex [ə'neks] *v/t* **1.** anektować ⟨za-⟩ **2.** przyłączać ⟨-czyć⟩ **3.** załączać ⟨-czyć⟩; **an•nex•a•tion** [ænek'seɪʃn] *s* aneksja *f*, przyłączenie *n*; **an•nexe** ['æneks] *s* **1.** aneks *m* **2.** dodatek *m* **3.** przybudówka *f*

an•ni•hi•late [ə'naɪəleɪt] *v/t* unicestwiać ⟨-wić⟩, niszczyć ⟨z-⟩ doszczętnie; **an•ni•hi•la•tion** [ənaɪə'leɪʃn] *s* unicestwienie *n*, doszczętne zniszczenie *n*

an•ni•ver•sa•ry [ænɪ'vɜːsərɪ] *s* rocznica *f*

An•no Do•mi•ni [ænəʊ'dɔmɪnaɪ] *s form* roku pańskiego

an•no•tate ['ænəteɪt] *v/t* **1.** załączać ⟨-czyć⟩ komentarz do *G* **2.** robić ⟨z-⟩ przypis do *G*; **an•nota•tion** [ænə'teɪʃn] *s* **1.** adnotacja *f* **2.** komentarz *m* **3.** przypis *m* **4.** dopisek *m*

an•nounce [ə'naʊns] *v/t* **1.** ogłaszać ⟨-łosić⟩ **2.** oznajmiać ⟨-mić⟩ **3.** zapowiadać ⟨-wiedzieć⟩; **an•nounce•ment** [ə'naʊnsmənt] *s* **1.** ogłoszenie *n* **2.** obwieszczenie *n* **3.** zawiadomienie *n* **4.** komunikat *m*; **an•nounc•er** [ə'naʊnsə] *s* spiker *m*

an•noy [ə'nɔɪ] *v/t* **1.** irytować ⟨z-⟩, denerwować ⟨z-⟩, drażnić **2.** *infml* działać na nerwy; **an•noy•ance** [ə'nɔɪəns] *s* irytacja *f*, zdenerwowanie *n*, rozdrażnienie *n*; **an•noy•ing** [ə'nɔɪɪŋ] *adj* irytujący, przykry, dokuczliwy

an•nu•al ['ænjuəl] **I** *adj* roczny, coroczny, doroczny; ***~ earnings*** roczne zarobki; ***an ~ general meeting*** walne zgromadzenie; ***~ income*** roczny przychód **II** *s* **1.** (*book*) rocznik *m* **2.** roślina *f* jednoroczna

an•nu•i•ty [ə'njuːətɪ] *s* renta *f* roczna; ***life ~*** renta dożywotnia

an•nul [ə'nʌl] *v/t* anulować, unieważniać ⟨-nić⟩; ***some laws have been ~led*** niektóre przepisy zostały anulowane; **an•nul•ment** [ə'nʌlmənt] *s* anulowanie *n*, unieważnienie *n*

An•nun•ci•a•tion [ənʌnsɪ'eɪʃn] *s REL* Zwiastowanie *n*

an•ode ['ænəʊd] *s* anoda *f*

an•o•dyne ['ænədaɪn] *adj* **1.** neutralny **2.** nieszkodliwy **3.** kojący

a•noint [ə'nɔɪnt] *v/t* namaszczać ⟨-maścić⟩; ***~ing of the sick*** ostatnie namaszczenie; ***an ~ed monarch*** pomazaniec boży

a•nom•a•lous [ə'nɒmələs] *adj* anormalny, nienormalny, nieprawidłowy; **a•nom•a•ly** [ə'nɒməlɪ] *s* anomalia *f*, nieprawidłowość *f*

an•o•nym•i•ty [ænə'nɪmətɪ] *s* anonimowość *f*; **a•non•y•mous** [ə'nɒnɪməs] *adj* anonimowy, nieznany; ***an ~letter*** anonim; ***an ~donor*** anonimowy dawca

an•o•rak ['ænəræk] *s* (*type of jacket*) anorak *m*

anorectic → anorexic

an•o•rex•i•a [ænə'reksɪə] *s* anoreksja *f*, jadłowstręt *m* psychiczny; **an•o•rex•ic** [ænə'reksɪk], **an•o•rec•tic** [ænə'rektɪk] **I** *adj* anorektyczny **II** *s* anorektyk *m*, anorektyczka *f*

an•oth•er [ə'nʌðə] *adj* **1.** następny, jeszcze jeden, kolejny; ***one after ~*** jeden po drugim; ***have ~ slice of cake*** weź jeszcze jeden kawałek ciasta; ***~ ten years*** następne dziesięć lat **2.** inny; ***this is ~ thing altogether*** to całkiem inna rzecz; ***that's ~ story*** to już całkiem inna historia

ans•wer ['aːnsə] **I** *v/t* **1.** odpowiadać ⟨-wiedzieć⟩; ***~ a question*** odpowiedzieć na pytanie **2.** *phone*: odbierać

⟨odebrać⟩ **3.** *door*: otwierać ⟨-worzyć⟩ **4.** *description, demands*: odpowiadać **5.** *expectations*: spełniać ⟨-nić⟩ **II** *s* **1.** odpowiedź *f*; ***in ~ to your letter*** w odpowiedzi na Pana list **2.** rozwiązanie *n*, sposób *m*; ***violence is not an ~*** przemoc nie jest rozwiązaniem; **ans•wer back I** *v/t* pyskować ⟨od-⟩, *infml* odszczekiwać się; ***don't ~ your mother back!*** nie pyskuj matce! **II** *v/i* pyskować ⟨od-⟩, *infml* odszczekiwać się; **ans•wer for** *v/t* być odpowiedzialnym za *A*, ponosić ⟨-nieść⟩ odpowiedzialność za *A*; **ans•wer to** *v/t* być odpowiedzialnym przed *I*, podlegać *D*

an•swer•a•ble ['aːnsərəbl] *adj* odpowiedzialny (***for*** za *A*, ***to*** wobec *G*)

an•swer•ing ma•chine ['aːnsərɪŋ məʃiːn] *s Am* automatyczna sekretarka *f*

ans•wer•phone ['aːnsəfəʊn] *s Br* automatyczna sekretarka *f*

ant [ænt] *s* mrówka *f*

an•tag•on•ism [æn'tægənɪzm] *s* antagonizm *m*, wrogość *f*, konflikt *m*; **an•tag•on•ist** [æn'tægənɪst] *s* **1.** antagonista *m* **2.** strona *f* konfliktu; **an•tag•on•ist•ic** [æntægə'nɪstɪk] *adj* **1.** antagonistyczny **2.** przeciwstawny **3.** pozostający w konflikcie (***to/towards*** z *I*); **an•tag•o•nize** [æn'tægənaɪz] *v/t* zrażać ⟨zrazić⟩, antagonizować ⟨z-⟩

ant•arc•tic [ænt'aːktɪk] **I** *adj* antarktyczny **II** *s* ***the ≈ (zone)*** Antarktyka; ***the ≈ Circle*** koło podbiegunowe południowe; ***the ≈ Ocean*** Ocean Lodowaty Południowy

Ant•arc•ti•ca [ænt'aːktɪkə] *s* Antarktyda *f*

ant•eat•er ['æntiːtə] *s* mrówkojad *m*

an•te•ced•ent [æntɪ'siːdənt] *s* poprzednik *m*, przodek *m*

an•te•di•lu•vi•an [æntɪdɪ'luːvɪən] *adj* przedpotopowy

an•te•lope ['æntɪləʊp] *s* antylopa *f*

an•te•na•tal [æntɪ'neɪtl] *adj Br* prenatalny; ***an ~ examination*** badanie prenatalne; ***~ classes*** szkoła rodzenia

an•ten•na [æn'tenə] *s* **1.** *pl -ne* czułek *m* **2.** *pl -nas Am* antena *f*

an•te•ri•or [æn'tɪərɪə] *adj* przedni

an•te•room ['æntɪrʊm] *s* przedsionek *m*, przedpokój *m*

an•them ['ænθəm] *s* hymn *m*

'ant•hill *s* mrowisko *n*

an•thol•o•gy [æn'θɒlədʒɪ] *s* antologia *f*

an•thra•cite ['ænθrəsaɪt] *s GEOL* antracyt *m*

an•thro•poid ['ænθrəpɪd] **I** *adj* człekokształtny, antropoidalny **II** *s* antropoid *m*

an•thro•po•log•i•cal [ænθrəpə'lɒdʒɪkl] *adj* antropologiczny; **an•thro•pol•o•gist** [ænθrə'pɒlədʒɪst] *s* antropolog *m*; **an•thro•pol•o•gy** [ænθrə'pɒlədʒɪ] *s* antropologia *f*

an•ti- ['æntɪ] (*in combinations*) anty-, przeciw-

an•ti-a'bor•tion•ist I *adj* antyaborcyjny **II** *s* przeciwnik *m* aborcji

an•ti-'air•craft *adj* przeciwlotniczy; ***an ~ gun*** działo przeciwlotnicze

an•ti•bi•ot•ic [æntɪbaɪ'ɒtɪk] *s* antybiotyk *m*

'an•ti•bod•y *s* przeciwciało *n*

an•tic•i•pate [æn'tɪsɪpeɪt] *v/t* **1.** przewidywać ⟨-dzieć⟩ **2.** antycypować **3.** uprzedzać ⟨-dzić⟩; **an•tic•i•pa•tion** [æntɪsɪ'peɪʃn] *s* **1.** przewidywanie *n* **2.** uprzedzenie *n* **3.** antycypacja *f*; ***in ~ of*** w oczekiwaniu na *A*; **an•tic•i•pa•to•ry** [æntɪsɪ'peɪtərɪ] *adj* zapobiegawczy

an•ti•cli•max [æntɪ'klaɪmæks] *s* rozczarowanie *n*

an•ti-clock•wise [æntɪ'klɒkwaɪz] **I** *adv* w kierunku przeciwnym do ruchu wskazówek zegara **II** *adj direction*: przeciwny do ruchu wskazówek zegara

an•tics ['æntɪks] *pl* **1.** wygłupy *pl*, błazenada *f* **2.** figle *pl*, igraszki *pl*

an•ti'cy•clone *s* antycyklon *m*

an•ti•de•pres•sant [æntɪdɪ'presənt] *s* lek *m* przeciwdepresyjny

an•ti•dote ['æntɪdəʊt] *s* antidotum *n*, odtrutka *f*

an•ti'fas•cism *s* antyfaszyzm *m*; **an•ti'fas•cist I** *adj* antyfaszystowski **II** *s* antyfaszysta *m*

'an•ti•freeze *s* płyn *m* do chłodnic

anti-'glare mir•ror *s* lustro *n* z powłoką antyodblaskową

an•ti•his•ta•mine [æntɪ'hɪstəmɪn] *s* antyhistamina *f*

an•ti-lock 'brak•ing sys•tem *s AUTO* system *m* ABS
'an•ti•mat•ter *s PHYS* antymateria *f*
an•tip•a•thy [æn'tɪpəθi] *s* antypatia *f*, niechęć *f* (***to/towards*** do *G*)
an•ti•per•spi•rant [æntɪ'pɜːspərənt] *s* antyperspirant *m*, środek *m* przeciwpotny
An•tip•o•des [æn'tɪpədiːz] *pl*: ***the ~*** antypody
an•ti•quar•i•an [æntɪ'kweəriən] **I** *adj* antykwaryczny; ***an ~ bookstore*** antykwariat **II** *s* (*a.* ***~ bookseller***) antykwariusz *m*, właściciel *m* antykwariatu; **an•ti•quat•ed** ['æntɪkweɪtɪd] *adj* **1.** staroświecki, mający wartość antykwaryczną **2.** przestarzały
an•tique [æn'tiːk] **I** *adj* **1.** zabytkowy; ***an ~ dealer*** handlarz antykami; ***an ~ shop*** sklep z antykami **2.** stylowy **3.** staroświecki, stary **II** *s* antyk *m*
an•tiq•ui•ty [æn'tɪkwəti] *s* **1.** starożytność *f*, świat *m* starożytny **2** zabytkowość *f*, starodawność *f*; ***a book of great ~*** bardzo stara książka **3.** ***antiquities*** antyki, zabytki
an•ti•'rust *adj* przeciw rdzy, przeciwrdzewny
an•ti-Sem•ite [æntɪ'siːmaɪt] *s* antysemita *m*; **an•ti-Se•mit•ic** [æntɪsə'mɪtɪk] *adj* antysemicki; **an•ti-Sem•i•tism** [æntɪ'semɪtɪzəm] *s* antysemityzm *m*
an•ti•sep•tic [æntɪ'septɪk] **I** *adj* antyseptyczny, odkażający, jałowy **II** *s* antyseptyk *m*, środek *m* odkażający
an•ti-'smok•ing *adj* antynikotynowy
an•ti•'so•cial *adj* **1.** aspołeczny **2.** nietowarzyski
an•ti-'theft *adj* przeciwwłamaniowy
an•tith•e•sis [æn'tɪθəsɪs] *pl -ses* [~siːz] *s* **1.** antyteza *f* **2.** przeciwieństwo *n*; **an•tith•e•tic•al** [æntɪ'θetɪkl] *adj* antytetyczny, przeciwstawny
an•ti-'trust laws *pl* przepisy *pl* antymonopolowe
an•ti•'vi•rus pro•gram *s INF* program *m* antywirusowy
ant•lers ['æntlərz] *pl* poroże *n*, rogi *pl*
an•to•nym ['æntənɪm] *s* antonim *m*
a•nus ['eɪnəs] *s* odbyt *m*
an•vil ['ænvɪl] *s* **1.** kowadło *n* **2.** *ANAT* kowadełko *n*
anx•i•e•ty [æŋ'zaɪətɪ] *s* niepokój *m*, obawa *f*, lęk *m*; **anx•ious** ['æŋkʃəs] *adj* **1.** zdenerwowany, zaniepokojony; ***she is ~ about her son*** niepokoi się o swojego syna **2.** ***be ~ to do s.th.*** bardzo chcieć coś zrobić; ***I am ~ to see him*** bardzo mi zależy na spotkaniu z nim
any ['enɪ] **I** *adj* **1.** (*in questions*) jakiś; ***is there ~ wine?*** czy jest wino?; ***she asked if we had ~ questions*** zapytała, czy mamy jakieś pytania **2.** (*with negative*) żaden; ***you can't go out without ~ shoes*** nie możesz wyjść bez butów; ***not ~*** ani trochę, ani jeden **3.** jakikolwiek, którykolwiek, ktokolwiek, cokolwiek, każdy; ***at ~ time*** zawsze **II** *adv* **1.** (*with negative*) w ogóle, ani trochę, wcale; ***I can't run ~ faster*** już szybciej biec nie mogę **2.** (*in questions*) trochę; ***~ more?*** jeszcze trochę? **3.** ***~ old how*** byle jak
any•body ['enɪbɒːdɪ] *pron* **1.** ktokolwiek, każdy; ***~ could do it*** każdy mógłby to zrobić **2.** (*in questions*) ktoś; ***~ for some tea?*** chce ktoś herbaty? **3.** (*with negative*) nikt; ***hardly ~*** prawie nikt, mało kto
any•how ['enɪhaʊ] *adv* **1.** byle jak **2.** → ***anyway***
any•one ['enɪwʌn] → ***anybody***
any•thing ['enɪθɪŋ] *pron* **1.** coś, cokolwiek; ***take ~ you like*** bierz, co chcesz; ***is there ~ I can do?*** czy mogę jakoś pomóc? **2.** (*with negative*) nic; ***for ~*** za nic, za żadne skarby; ***not ~*** nic; ***~ but this*** wszystko, tylko nie to; ***he is ~ but intelligent*** wcale nie jest inteligentny
any•time ['enɪtaɪm] *adv* kiedykolwiek; ***they can arrive ~*** mogą przyjechać w każdej chwili
any•way ['enɪweɪ] *adv* **1.** i tak **2.** w każdym razie **3.** a tak w ogóle **4.** więc
any•where ['enɪweə] *adv* **1.** gdziekolwiek, byle gdzie, gdzieś; ***are you going ~?*** idziesz gdzieś? **2.** (*with negative*) nigdzie; ***I can't find my glasses ~*** nigdzie nie mogę znaleźć okularów; ***hardly ~*** prawie nigdzie
a•or•ta [eɪ'ɔːtə] *s* aorta *f*, tętnica *f* główna
a•part [ə'pɑːt] *adv* **1.** z dala; ***live ~*** mieszkać oddzielnie; ***tell s.th. ~*** od-

różnić coś **2. ~ from** oprócz *G*, poza *I*, z wyjątkiem *G*

a•part•ment [ə'pɑːtmənt] *s* **1.** *Am* mieszkanie *n*; ***an ~ block*** (*a.* ***house***) blok mieszkalny **2.** apartament *m*; ***the Royal ~s*** apartamenty królewskie

ap•a•thet•ic [æpə'θetɪk] *adj* apatyczny, zobojętniały, bierny; **ap•a•thy** ['æpəθi] *s* apatia *f*, zobojętnienie *n*, bierność *f*

ape [eɪp] **I** *s* małpa *f* człekokształtna **II** *v/t* naśladować, małpować

a•pe•ri•tif [əperɪ'tiːf] *s* aperitif *m*

ap•er•ture ['æpərtʃə] *s* **1** otwór *m*, szczelina *f* **2** PHOT przesłona *f* **3.** (*gun*) szczerbina *f*

a•pex ['eɪpeks] *pl apexes* ['eɪpeksɪs], *apices* ['eɪpɪsiːz] *s form* szczyt *m*, wierzchołek *m*

aphid ['eɪfɪd] *s* mszyca *f*

aph•o•rism ['æfərɪzəm] *s* aforyzm *m*

aph•ro•dis•i•ac [æfrə'dɪziæk] **I** *s* afrodyzjak *m* **II** *adj* pobudzający seksualnie

a•piece [ə'piːs] *adv* **1.** *price*: za sztukę **2.** na głowę, na osobę

a•poc•a•lypse [ə'pɒkəlɪps] *s* **1.** apokalipsa *f* **2.** zagłada *f* **3.** katastrofa *f*; **a•poc•a•lyp•tic** [ə'pɒkəlɪptɪk] *adj* **1.** apokaliptyczny **2.** katastroficzny

a•pol•o•get•ic [əpɒlə'dʒetɪk] *adj* przepraszający, skruszony; ***be ~ for*** (*a.* ***about***) przepraszać za *A*; **a•pol•o•get•ic•ally** [əpɒlə'dʒetɪkli] *adv* przepraszająco, ze skruchą; **a•pol•o•gise** [ə'pɒlədʒaɪz] *Br*, ***a•pol•o•gize*** *Am v/t* **1.** przepraszać ⟨-rosić⟩ (***for*** za *A*, ***to*** *A*) **2.** usprawiedliwiać ⟨-wić⟩ się; **a•pol•o•gy** [ə'pɒlədʒɪ] *s* **1.** przeprosiny *pl* **2.** *form* apologia *f*

ap•o•plec•tic [æpə'plektɪk] *adj* **1.** ***~ with rage*** wściekły **2.** apoplektyczny; **ap•o•plex•y** ['æpəpleksɪ] *s* **1.** apopleksja *f*, udar *m* mózgu **2.** wściekłość *f*, furia *f*

a•pos•tle [ə'pɒsl] *s* apostoł *m*

a•pos•tro•phe [ə'pɒstrəfɪ] *s* **1.** (*graphical sign*) apostrof *m* **2.** (*rhetorical figure*) apostrofa *f*

a•poth•e•o•sis [əpɒθɪ'oʊsɪs] *s* **1.** apoteoza *f* **2.** apogeum *n*, szczyt *m*

ap•pal [ə'pɔːl] *Br*, ***ap•pall*** *Am v/t* przerażać ⟨-razić⟩, szokować ⟨za-⟩; **ap•pal•ling** [ə'pɔːlɪŋ] *adj* przerażający, szokujący; ***how ~!*** to okropne!

ap•pa•ra•tus [æpə'reɪtəs] *s* **1.** sprzęt *m* **2.** aparatura *f* **3.** przyrządy *pl* **4.** aparat *m*; ***the state ~*** aparat państwowy

ap•par•el [ə'pærəl] *s form* odzież *f*, strój *m*, szaty *pl*

ap•par•ent [ə'pærənt] *adj* **1.** oczywisty, jasny, wyraźnie widoczny; ***with no ~ reason*** bez wyraźnego powodu **2.** rzekomy; **ap•par•ent•ly** [ə'pærəntlɪ] *adv* widocznie, najwyraźniej, w oczywisty sposób

ap•pa•ri•tion [æpə'rɪʃn] *s* zjawa *f*, duch *m*

ap•peal [ə'piːl] **I** *v/i* **1.** podobać ⟨s-⟩ się, pociągać; ***this doesn't ~ to me*** to do mnie nie przemawia, to mi się nie podoba **2.** wnosić ⟨wnieść⟩ apelację **3.** (*against sentence, decision*) odwoływać ⟨-łać⟩ się (***against*** od *G*) **4.** ***~ to s.o. for*** zwracać się do kogoś z prośbą o *A* **II** *s* **1.** atrakcyjność *f*, urok *m*; ***have popular ~*** cieszyć się dużą popularnością **2.** apelacja *f*; ***file an ~*** wnieść apelację **3.** odwołanie się *n* **4.** apel *m*; **ap•peal•ing** [ə'piːlɪŋ] *adj* miły, sympatyczny; ***an ~ girl*** pociągająca dziewczyna; ***an ~ idea*** kuszący pomysł

ap•pear [ə'pɪə] *v/i* **1.** pojawiać ⟨-wić⟩ się **2.** ukazywać ⟨-zać⟩ się **3.** ***~ to be*** wydawać się, sprawiać wrażenie **4.** (*in film*) występować ⟨-tąpić⟩, grać ⟨za-⟩ **5.** (*in court*) stawiać ⟨-wić⟩ się; **ap•pear•ance** [ə'pɪərəns] *s* **1.** wygląd *m*; ***have an unhealthy ~*** niezdrowo wyglądać **2.** pojawienie *n* się **3.** zjawienie *n* się **4.** wystąpienie *n*; ***make an ~ on television*** wystąpić w telewizji; ***public ~*** wystąpienie publiczne **5.** występ *m*; **ap•pear•ances** [ə'pɪərənsɪz] *pl* pozory *pl*; ***to all ~*** pozornie; ***keep up ~*** zachowywać pozory

ap•pease [ə'piːz] *v/t* **1.** iść ⟨pójść⟩ na ustępstwa wobec *G* **2.** uspokajać ⟨-koić⟩ **3.** ugłaskiwać ⟨-kać⟩; ***a sacrifice was made to ~ the gods*** złożono ofiarę, aby przebłagać bogów; **ap•pease•ment** [ə'piːzmənt] *s*: ***policy of ~*** polityka ustępstw

ap•pend [ə'pend] *v/t* dodawać ⟨-dać⟩, dołączać ⟨-czyć⟩, załączać ⟨-czyć⟩

ap•pend•age [ə'pendɪdʒ] *s* dodatek *m*, wyrostek *m*; ***feel like an ~*** czuć się zbędnym
ap•pen•dec•to•my [æpen'dektəmɪ] *s* wycięcie *n* wyrostka robaczkowego; **ap•pen•di•ci•tis** [əpendɪ'saɪtɪs] *s* zapalenie *n* wyrostka robaczkowego; **ap•pen•dix** [ə'pendɪks] *pl -dixes, -dices s* **1.** ANAT wyrostek *m* robaczkowy **2.** dodatek *m*, załącznik *m*
ap•per•tain [æpə'teɪn] *v/i* **1.** odnosić się (**to** do *G*) **2.** należeć (**to** do *G*)
ap•pe•tite ['æpɪtaɪt] *s* **1.** apetyt *m*; ***spoil s.o.'s ~*** zepsuć komuś apetyt **2.** ochota *f* (***for*** na *A*); ***to give s.o. an ~ for*** narobić komuś ochoty na *A* **3.** żądza *f*; ***~ for power*** żądza władzy; **ap•pe•tiz•er** ['æpɪtaɪzə] *s* zakąska *f*, przystawka *f*; **ap•pe•tiz•ing** ['æpɪtaɪzɪŋ] *adj* kuszący, apetyczny; ***an ~ prospect*** kusząca perspektywa
ap•plaud [ə'plɔːd] *v/t* **1.** bić brawo **2.** *form* przyklaskiwać ⟨-snąć⟩ *D*, zgadzać ⟨zgodzić⟩ się z *I*; ***we ~ your decision*** pochwalamy pańską decyzję; **ap•plause** [ə'plɔːz] *s* aplauz *m*, brawa *pl*; ***a round of ~*** brawa
ap•ple ['æpl] *s* jabłko *n*; ***the ~ of s.o.'s eye*** *fig* czyjeś oczko w głowie
'**ap•ple cart** *s*: ***upset the ~*** wszystko zepsuć; '**ap•ple pie** *s* szarlotka *f*; ***in ~ order*** *fig* w idealnym porządku; '**ap•ple pol•ish•er** *s Am* lizus *m*; **ap•ple 'sauce** *s* **1.** sos *m* jabłkowy **2.** mus *m* jabłkowy; '**ap•ple tree** *s* jabłoń *f*
ap•pli•ance [ə'plaɪəns] *s* urządzenie *n*, przyrząd *m*
ap•plic•a•ble [ə'plɪkəbl] *adj*: ***~ to*** odnoszący się do *G*, stosujący się do *G*; ***not ~ to*** nie mający zastosowania do *G*; ***not ~*** nie dotyczy; **ap•pli•cant** ['æplɪkənt] *s* **1.** kandydat *m* **2.** wnioskodawca *m* **3.** ubiegający się *m*; **ap•pli•ca•tion** [æplɪ'keɪʃn] *s* **1.** podanie *n*, wniosek *m*; ***an ~ form*** formularz podania **2.** zastosowanie *n* **3.** stosowanie *n* **4.** INF aplikacja *f*
ap•plied [ə'plaɪd] *adj* stosowany; ***~ linguistics*** językoznawstwo stosowane
ap•ply [ə'plaɪ] **I** *v/i* **1.** zgłaszać ⟨-łosić⟩ się, składać ⟨złożyć⟩ podanie; ***~ for*** ubiegać się o *A* **2.** ***~ to*** odnosić się do *G*, dotyczyć *G* **II** *v/t* **1.** stosować ⟨za-⟩ **2.** *cream*: nakładać ⟨nałożyć⟩
ap•point [ə'pɔɪnt] *v/t* **1.** mianować **2.** wyznaczać ⟨-czyć⟩ **2.** ustanawiać ⟨-nowić⟩, powoływać ⟨-łać⟩; **ap•point•ee** [əpɔɪn'tiː] *s* mianowana osoba *f*, powołana osoba *f*
ap•point•ment [ə'pɔɪntmənt] *s* **1.** (umówione) spotkanie *n*, wizyta *f*; ***make an ~ with*** wyznaczyć termin spotkania u *G*, umówić się z *I*; ***by ~*** po wcześniejszym ustaleniu terminu; ***an ~s diary*** terminarz **2.** mianowanie *n* **3.** wyznaczenie *n* **4.** powołanie *n*, nominacja *f*; ***s.o.'s ~ as*** wybór kogoś na (stanowisko) *A*
ap•por•tion [ə'pɔːʃn] *v/t* rozdzielać ⟨-lić⟩, przydzielać ⟨-lić⟩
ap•po•site ['æpəzɪt] *adj form* **1.** właściwy **2.** trafny
ap•prais•al [ə'preɪzəl] *s* **1.** ocena *f*; ***employee ~*** ocena pracownika **2.** oszacowanie *n* **3.** wycena *f*; **appraise** [ə'preɪz] *v/t* oceniać ⟨-nić⟩, szacować ⟨o-⟩, wyceniać ⟨-nić⟩
ap•pre•cia•ble [ə'priːʃəbl] *adj* **1.** znaczny **2.** wyraźny; **ap•pre•ci•ate** [ə'priːʃɪeɪt] **I** *v/t* **1.** doceniać ⟨-nić⟩ **2.** wysoko cenić **II** *v/i* (*of object*) podwyższać wartość; **ap•pre•ci•a•tion** [əpriːʃɪ'eɪʃn] *s* **1.** uznanie *n*, docenienie *n* **2.** *of value*: wzrost *m*; **ap•pre•ci•a•tive** [ə'priːʃətɪv] *adj* pełen wdzięczności; ***I am very ~ of your help*** *form* jestem bardzo wdzięczny za pańską pomoc
ap•pre•hend [æprɪ'hend] *v/t form* **1.** aresztować ⟨za-⟩, zatrzymywać ⟨-mać⟩ **2.** rozumieć ⟨z-⟩, pojmować ⟨-jąć⟩; **ap•pre•hen•sion** [æprɪ'henʃn] *s* **1.** aresztowanie *n*, zatrzymanie *n* **2.** obawa *f*, lęk *m* **3.** zrozumienie *n*; **ap•pre•hen•sive** [æprɪ'hensɪv] *adj* zaniepokojony, pełen obaw; ***be ~ that*** obawiać się, że
ap•pren•tice [ə'prentɪs] *s* uczeń *m*, praktykant *m*, czeladnik *m*; **ap•pren•tice•ship** [ə'prentɪsʃɪp] *s* praktyka *f*, nauka *f* zawodu, nauka *f* rzemiosła
ap•proach [ə'prəʊtʃ] **I** *v/i* zbliżać ⟨-żyć⟩ się, nadchodzić ⟨-dejść⟩; ***winter is ~ing*** nadchodzi zima **II** *v/t* **1.** podchodzić ⟨-dejść⟩ do *G* **2.** zwracać ⟨-rócić⟩ się do *G* **3.** zwracać ⟨-rócić⟩ się z prośbą do *G* (***about*** o *G*) **III** *s* **1.** zbliżanie się *n*, nadejście

n; ***~ lights*** światła lądowania (wzdłuż pasa startowego) **2.** podejście *n* **3.** propozycja *f*, oferta *f*; **ap•proach•a•ble** [ə'proʊtʃəbl] *adj* **1.** *place*: dostępny **2.** *person*: bezpośredni, przystępny

ap•pro•ba•tion [æprəʊ'beɪʃn] *s* aprobata *f*, akceptacja *f*

ap•pro•pri•ate [ə'prəʊprɪət] **I** *adj* odpowiedni, właściwy, stosowny (***for*** dla *G*) **II** *v/t* **1.** przywłaszczać ⟨-czyć⟩ sobie, zawłaszczać ⟨-czyć⟩ **2.** *money*: defraudować ⟨z-⟩, sprzeniewierzać ⟨-rzyć⟩ **3.** przeznaczać ⟨-czyć⟩ (***for*** na *A*); **ap•pro•pri•a•tion** [əprəʊprɪ'eɪʃn] *s* **1.** przywłaszczenie *n*, zawłaszczenie *n* **2.** defraudacja *f*, sprzeniewierzenie *n* **3.** przeznaczenie *n*

ap•prov•al [ə'pru:vl] *s* **1.** aprobata *f*, akceptacja *f* **2.** zgoda *f*, zatwierdzenie *n*; **ap•prove** [ə'pru:v] *v/t* **1.** aprobować ⟨za-⟩, akceptować ⟨za-⟩ **2.** popierać ⟨-przeć⟩ **3.** pochwalać (***of*** *A*)

ap•prox•i•mate **I** [ə'prɒksɪmət] *adj* przybliżony, szacunkowy; ***an ~ value*** wartość przybliżona **II** [ə'prɔksɪmeɪt] *v/t* **1.** (*cost*) wynosić ⟨-nieść⟩ w przybliżeniu **2.** być zbliżonym do *G* **III** [ə'prɒksɪmeɪt] *v/i* ***~ to*** być zbliżonym do *G*; **ap•prox•i•mate•ly** [ə'prɒksɪmətlɪ] *adv* około, w przybliżeniu; **ap•prox•i•ma•tion** [əprɒksɪ'meɪʃn] *s* przybliżenie *n*, szacunkowa wartość *f*

APR [eɪpi:'ɑ:] *abbr* (=***Annual Percentage Rate***) roczna stopa *f* oprocentowania

a•pri•cot ['æprɪkɒt] **I** *s* morela *f* **II** *adj* morelowy

A•pril ['eɪprəl] *s* kwiecień *m*; ***~ Fool's Day*** prima aprilis; ***~ Fool!*** prima aprilis!

a•pron ['eɪprən] *s* **1.** fartuch *m*, fartuszek *m*; ***~ strings*** tasiemki od fartucha; ***be tied to s.o.'s ~ strings*** *fig* trzymać się czyjejś spódnicy **2.** (*for planes*) płyta *f* lotniska

apt [æpt] *adj* **1.** trafny, stosowny **2.** zdolny **3.** ***be ~ to do s.th.*** mieć skłonność do robienia czegoś; ***he is ~ to believe it*** jest gotów w to uwierzyć; ***they are ~ to be overlooked*** łatwo je pominąć; **ap•ti•tude** ['æptɪtju:d] *s* **1.** zdolności *pl*, uzdolnienia *pl*; ***an ~ test*** test zdolności **2.** zdolność *f*, uzdolnienie *n*

aq•ua•lung ['ækwəlʌŋ] *s* akwalung *m*

aq•ua•ma•rine [ækwəmə'ri:n] **I** *s* **1.** (*colour*) niebieskozielony *m*, akwamaryna *f* **2.** (*gem*) akwamaryn *m*, akwamaryna *f* **II** *adj* niebieskozielony

a•quar•i•um [ə'kwerɪəm] *s* akwarium *n*

A•quar•i•us [ə'kwerɪəs] *s* ASTR Wodnik *m*; ***be an ~*** być spod znaku Wodnika

a•quat•ic [ə'kwætɪk] *adj* wodny; ***~ plants*** rośliny wodne

aq•ue•duct ['ækwɪdʌkt] *s* akwedukt *m*

Ar•ab ['ærəb] **I** *adj* arabski **II** *s* **1.** Arab *m* **2.** arab *m*, koń *m* arabski; **ar•a•besque** [ærə'besk] *s* arabeska *f*; **A•ra•bi•a** [ə'reɪbɪə] *s* Arabia *f*; **A•ra•bi•an** [ə'reɪbɪən] *adj* **1.** arabski; ***the ~ Nights*** Baśnie z 1001 nocy; **Ar•a•bic** ['ærəbɪk] **I** *adj* arabski; ***an ~ numeral*** cyfra arabska **II** *s* język *m* arabski

ar•a•ble ['ærəbl] *adj* rolny, orny; ***~ land*** grunty orne

ar•bi•ter ['ɑ:bɪtə] *s* arbiter *m*, sędzia *m*; ***the ~ of fashion*** arbiter mody, wyrocznia w sprawach mody

ar•bi•tra•ry ['ɑ:bɪtrerɪ] *adj* **1.** arbitralny **2.** przypadkowy

ar•bi•trate ['ɑ:bɪtreɪt] **I** *v/i* rozsądzać ⟨-dzić⟩, rozstrzygać ⟨-gnąć⟩ **II** *v/t* prowadzić mediacje; **ar•bi•tra•tion** [ɑ:bɪ'treɪʃn] *s* arbitraż *m*; **ar•bi•tra•tor** [ɑ:bɪ'treɪtə] *s* **1.** rozjemca *m* **2.** sędzia *m* polubowny

arbour ['ɑ:bə] *Br*, **ar•bor** *Am s* altana *f*

arc [ɑ:k] **I** *s* 1. łuk *m* **2.** łuk *m* elektryczny **II** *v/i* zakreślać ⟨-lić⟩ łuk

ar•cade [ɑ:'keɪd] *s* **1.** arkada *f* **2.** ***a shopping ~*** pasaż handlowy

arch[1] [ɑ:tʃ] **I** *s* ARCHIT łuk *m*, przęsło *n*, sklepione przejście *n* **II** *v/t* wyginać ⟨-giąć⟩ w łuk; ***~ one's back*** wygiąć grzbiet, zrobić koci grzbiet **III** *v/i* tworzyć ⟨u-⟩ łuk, wyginać ⟨-giąć⟩ się w łuk

arch[2] [~] *adj* łobuzerski

arch- [~] (*in combinations*) arcy-, archi-; ***the ≈-enemy*** szatan

ar•chae•o•log•i•cal [ɑ:kɪə'lɒdʒɪkl] *Br*, ***ar•che•o•log•i•cal*** *Am adj* archeologiczny; **ar•chae•ol•o•gist**

[ɑːkɪ'ɒlədʒɪst] *Br*, ***ar•che•ol•o•gist*** *Am s* archeolog *m*; **ar•chae•ol•o•gy** [ɑːkɪ'ɒlədʒɪ] *Br*, ***ar•che•ol•o•gy*** *Am s* archeologia *f*
ar•cha•ic [ɑː'keɪɪk] *adj* archaiczny
arch•an•gel ['ɑːkeɪndʒəl] *s* archanioł *m*
arch•'bish•op [ɑːtʃ'bɪʃəp] *s* arcybiskup *m*; **arch•'bish•op•ric** [ɑːtʃ'bɪʃərɪk] *s* arcybiskupstwo *n*
arch•duch•ess [ɑːtʃ'dʌtʃɪs] *s* arcyksiężna *f*; **arch•duch•y** [ɑːtʃ'dʌtʃɪ] *s* księstwo *n*; **arch•duke** [ɑːtʃ'djuːk] *s* arcyksiążę *m*
ar•cher ['ɑːtʃə] *s* łucznik *m*; **ar•cher•y** ['ɑːtʃərɪ] **I** *s* łucznictwo *n* **II** *adj* łuczniczy; ***an ~ team*** drużyna łucznicza
ar•che•typ•al [ɑːkɪ'taɪpl] *adj* archetypowy, klasyczny; ***an ~ pop group*** archetyp grupy pop; **ar•che•type** ['ɑːkɪtaɪp] *s* archetyp *m*
ar•chi•pel•a•go [ɑːkɪ'peləgəʊ] *pl -goes, -gos* [~gəʊz] *s* archipelag *m*
ar•chi•tec•t ['ɑːkɪtekt] *s* architekt *m*; **ar•chi•tec•tur•al** [ɑːkɪ'tektʃərəl] *adj* architektoniczny; **ar•chi•tec•ture** ['ɑːkɪtektʃə] *s* **1.** architektura *f* **2.** struktura *f*, budowa *f*
ar•chive ['ɑːkaɪv] *s* archiwum *n*; **ar•chi•vist** ['ɑːkɪvɪst] *s* archiwista *m*
arch•way ['ɑːtʃweɪ] *s* sklepione przejście *n*
Arc•tic ['ɑːktɪk] **I** *adj* arktyczny, polarny **II** *s* ***the ~*** Arktyka; **the Arc•tic 'Cir•cle** *s* koło *n* podbiegunowe północne; **the Arc•tic 'O•cean** *s* Morze *n* Arktyczne
ar•dent ['ɑːdənt] *adj* **1.** żarliwy, gorliwy **2.** namiętny; **ardour** ['ɑːdə] *Br*, **ar•dor** *Am s* **1.** zapał *m*, żarliwość *f*, gorliwość *f* **2.** namiętność *f*
ar•du•ous ['ɑːdjʊəs] *adj* żmudny, mozolny, uciążliwy
are [ɑː] → ***be***
ar•e•a ['eərɪə] *s* **1.** obszar *m*, rejon *m*, region *m*, dzielnica *f*; ***an ~ code*** numer kierunkowy **2.** część *f* **3.** dziedzina *f*, sfera *f* **4.** *MATH* pole *n*, powierzchnia *f*; **ar•e•a 'man•a•ger** *s* szef *m* regionu, kierownik *m* regionu
a•re•na [ə'riːnə] *s* arena *f*
aren't [ɑːnt] *contracted form* → ***are not***
Ar•gen•ti•na [ɑːdʒən'tiːnə] *s* Argentyna *f*; **Ar•gen•tin•i•an** [ɑːdʒən'tɪnɪən] **I** *adj* argentyński **II** *s* Argentyńczyk *m*
ar•gu•a•ble ['ɑːgjʊəbl] *adj* **1.** ***it is ~ that*** można (śmiało) stwierdzić, że **2.** sporny, dyskusyjny; **ar•gu•a•bly** ['ɑːgjʊəblɪ] *adv* zapewne; ***she's ~ the best*** można (śmiało) stwierdzić, że jest najlepsza; **ar•gue** ['ɑːgjuː] **I** *v/i* **1.** kłócić ⟨po-⟩ się, sprzeczać ⟨po-⟩ się (***with*** z *I*, ***about/over*** o *A*); ***don't ~!*** bez dyskusji!, nie kłóć się! **2.** dyskutować **3.** argumentować (***that*** że) **4.** twierdzić ⟨s-⟩, dowodzić ⟨-wieść⟩ (***that*** że) **5.** przytaczać ⟨-toczyć⟩ argumenty (***for*** za *I*, ***against*** przeciwko *D*) **II** *v/t* uzasadniać ⟨-nić⟩; **ar•gu•ment** ['ɑːgjʊmənt] *s* **1.** kłótnia *f*, spór *m* **2.** dyskusja *f* **3.** argument *m*; **ar•gu•men•ta•tion** [ɑːgjʊmen'teɪʃn] *s* argumentacja *f*, uzasadnienie *n*; **ar•gu•ment•a•tive** [ɑːgjʊ'mentətɪv] *adj* **1.** kłótliwy **2.** argumentacyjny
a•ri•a ['ɑːrɪə] *s MUS* aria *f*
ar•id ['ærɪd] *adj* **1.** suchy, bezdeszczowy **2.** *discussion*: jałowy
Ar•i•es ['eəriːz] *s ASTR* Baran *m*; ***be an ~*** być spod znaku Barana
a•rise [ə'raɪz] (*arose*; *arisen*) *v/i* **1.** powstawać ⟨-tać⟩, pojawiać ⟨-wić⟩ się; ***the question ~s*** nasuwa się pytanie **2.** ***~ from*** (*a.* ***out of***) wynikać z *G*, być wynikiem *G* **3.** *form* wstawać ⟨-tać⟩
a•ris•en [ə'rɪzn] *Past Participle* → ***arise***
ar•is•toc•ra•cy [ærɪ'stɒkrəsɪ] *s* arystokracja *f*; **ar•is•to•crat** [ə'rɪstəkræt] arystokrata *m*; **a•ris•to•crat•ic** [ærɪstə'krætɪk] *adj* arystokratyczny
a•rith•me•tic **I** [ə'rɪθmətɪk] *s* arytmetyka *f* **II** [æ'rɪθmetɪk] *adj* → ***arithmetical***; **ar•ith•met•i•cal** [ærɪθ'metɪkl] *adj* arytmetyczny
ark [ɑːk] *s* arka *f*; ***Noah's ~*** arka Noego; ***the ~ of the Covenant*** Arka Przymierza
arm[1] [ɑːm] *s* **1.** ramię *n*, ręka *f*; ***with open ~s*** z otwartymi ramionami; ***within ~'s reach*** w zasięgu ręki; ***keep s.o. at ~'s length*** trzymać kogoś na dystans; ***take s.o. in one's ~*** wziąć kogoś w ramiona **2.** rękaw *m* **3.** (*of chair*) poręcz *f*, podłokietnik *m* **4.** ramię *n*, wysięgnik *m*,

dźwignia *f* **5.** (*of river*) odnoga *f* **6.** cypel *m*

arm[2] [~] **I** *s* **1.** ***~s*** broń; ***under ~s*** pod bronią; ***~s control*** kontrola zbrojeń; ***~s race*** wyścig zbrojeń; ***an ~s dealer*** handlarz bronią; ***lay down ~s*** złożyć broń; ***to ~s!*** do broni!; ***be up in ~s about*** (*a.* ***over***) *infml* być oburzonym na *A*, protestować przeciw *D* **2.** (***coat of***) ***~s*** herb **II** *v/t* ***~ oneself*** zbroić się; ***~ oneself with patience*** uzbroić się w cierpliwość

ar•ma•da [ɑː'mɑːdə] *s* armada *f*, flota *f*; ***the Spanish ~*** Wielka Armada

ar•ma•dil•lo [ɑːmə'dɪləʊ] *s* (*animal*) pancernik *m*

ar•ma•ment ['ɑːməmənt] **I** *s* **1.** uzbrojenie *n* **2.** zbrojenia *pl* **II** *adj* zbrojeniowy

'arm•band *s* **1.** opaska *f* na ramię **2.** ***~s*** rękawki do pływania

arm•chair ['ɑːmtʃe] *s* fotel *m*

armed [ɑːmd] *adj* uzbrojony; ***~ to the teeth*** uzbrojony po zęby; ***an ~ conflict*** konflikt zbrojny; **armed 'forc•es** *pl* siły *pl* zbrojne; ***be in the ~*** być w wojsku; **armed 'rob•ber•y** *s* napad *m* z bronią w ręku

arm•ful ['ɑːmfʊl] *s* naręcze *n*; ***an ~ of flowers*** naręcze kwiatów

ar•mi•stice ['ɑːmɪstɪs] *s* zawieszenie *n* broni, rozejm *m*

ar•mour ['ɑːmə] *Br*, **ar•mor** *Am* **I** *s* **1.** pancerz *m*, opancerzenie *n* **2.** zbroja *f*; ***a suit of ~*** zbroja **II** *v/t* opancerzać ⟨-rzyć⟩; **ar•moured car** [ɑːməd'kɑː] *Br*, **ar•mored car** *Am s* samochód *m* opancerzony; **armoured ve•hi•cle** [ɑːməd'viːəkl] *Br*, **ar•mored ve•hi•cle** *Am s* transporter *m* opancerzony; **ar•mour-plat•ed** [ɑːmə'pleɪtɪd] *Br*, **ar•mor-plat•ed** *Am adj* opancerzony

arm•pit ['ɑːmpɪt] *s* pacha *f*

'arm•rest *s* poręcz *f*, podłokietnik *m*

'arm-twist•ing *s fig* presja *f*

ar•my ['ɑːmɪ] *s* armia *f*, wojsko *n*; ***be in the ~*** być w wojsku; ***join the ~*** wstąpić do wojska

a•ro•ma [ə'rəʊmə] *s* aromat *m*, woń *f*; **a•ro•ma•ther•a•py** [ərəʊmə'θerəpɪ] aromaterapia *f*; **ar•o•mat•ic** [ærə'mætɪk] *adj* aromatyczny, wonny

a•rose [ə'rəʊz] *Past Simple* → ***arise***

a•round [ə'raʊnd] **I** *adv* **1.** około; ***~ 5 o'clock*** około piątej **2.** dookoła, wokół; ***look ~*** rozejrzyj się **3.** w pobliżu, w okolicy; ***I'll be ~*** będę w pobliżu **II** *prep* wokół *G*, dookoła *G*

a•rous•al [ə'raʊzl] *s* pobudzenie *n*; ***sexual ~*** podniecenie seksualne; ***~ from sleep*** przebudzenie; **a•rouse** [ə'raʊz] *v/t* **1.** wzbudzać ⟨-dzić⟩ **2.** wywoływać ⟨-łać⟩ **3.** rozbudzać ⟨-dzić⟩ **4.** podniecać ⟨-cić⟩ **5.** ***~ s.o. from sleep*** obudzić kogoś

ar•range [ə'reɪndʒ] **I** *v/t* **1.** ustawiać ⟨-wić⟩, układać ⟨ułożyć⟩ **2.** organizować ⟨z-⟩ **3.** aranżować ⟨za-⟩ **II** *v/i* **1.** umawiać ⟨umówić⟩ się; ***~ to meet*** umówić się na spotkanie **2.** załatwiać ⟨-wić⟩, uzgadniać ⟨-godnić⟩; ***we have ~d with the neighbours about feeding the cat*** uzgodniliśmy z sąsiadami, że będą karmić kota; **ar•range•ment** [ə'reɪndʒmənt] *s* **1.** przygotowania *pl* **2.** ustalenia *pl* **3.** sprawy *pl* związane z organizacją **4.** ***make ~s*** umówić się **5.** ustawienie *n*, ułożenie *n*, rozmieszczenie *n* **6.** umowa *f*, porozumienie *n* **7.** aranżacja *f*

ar•ray [ə'reɪ] **I** *s* wachlarz *m*, wybór *m*, szereg *m*; ***an ~ of film stars*** plejada gwiazd kina; ***a battle ~*** szyk bitewny **II** *v/t* ustawiać ⟨-wić⟩ (w szeregu)

ar•rears [ə'rɪəz] *s* zaległości *pl* (płatnicze); ***rent ~*** zaległy czynsz, zaległości z tytułu czynszu; ***be in ~ with the rent*** zalegać z zapłatą czynszu

ar•rest [ə'rest] **I** *v/t* **1.** aresztować ⟨za-⟩ **2.** *attention, gaze*: przyciągać ⟨-gnąć⟩ **3.** wstrzymywać ⟨-mać⟩ **II** *s* **1.** aresztowanie *n*; ***s.o. is under ~*** ktoś został aresztowany **2.** wstrzymanie *n*

ar•riv•al [ə'raɪvl] *s* **1.** przybycie *n*, przyjazd *m*, przylot *m*; ***~ time*** godzina przyjazdu, godzina przylotu; ***on ~ at a hotel*** po przybyciu do hotelu **2.** przybyły *m*; ***late ~s*** spóźnieni; ***a new ~*** (nowonarodzone) dziecko

ar•rive [ə'raɪv] *v/i* **1.** przybywać ⟨-być⟩, przyjeżdżać ⟨-jechać⟩; ***~ at the station*** dotrzeć na stację **2.** (*goods*) nadchodzić ⟨-dejść⟩; **arrive at** *v/i*: ***~ a price*** ustalić cenę; ***~ a conclusion*** dojść do wniosku

ar•ro•gance ['ærəgəns] *s* arogancja *f*; **ar•ro•gant** ['ærəgənt] *adj* arogancki; **ar•ro•gant•ly** ['ærəgəntlɪ] *adv* arogancko

ar•row ['ærəʊ] *s* **1.** strzała *f* **2.** strzałka *f*; '**ar•row•head** *s* grot *m* strzały

arse [ɑːs] *Br*, **ass** [æs] *Am s vulg* dupa *f*; ***get off your ~*** rusz dupę; ***s.o. doesn't know his ~ from his elbow*** ktoś nie ma o niczym pojęcia; '**arse-licker** *s vulg* wazeliniarz *m*

ar•se•nal ['ɑːsənl] *s* arsenał *m*, zbrojownia *f*

ar•se•nic ['ɑːsənɪk] *no pl s* arszenik *m*

ar•son ['ɑːsn] *s* podpalenie *n*; **ar•son•ist** ['ɑːsənɪst] *s* podpalacz *m*

art [ɑːt] **I** *s* **1.** sztuka *f*; ***work of ~*** dzieło sztuki; ***the ~ of cooking*** sztuka kulinarna; ***~s and crafts*** rzemiosło artystyczne **2.** dziedzina *f* sztuki **3.** (*at school*) plastyka *f* **4.** **~s** nauki humanistyczne; ***Faculty of ~s*** *Br*, ***~s Department*** *Am* wydział nauk humanistycznych **5.** spryt *m* **II** *adj* artystyczny; '**art crit•ic** *s* krytyk *m* sztuki

ar•te•ri•al [ɑː'tɪərɪəl] *adj* **1.** tętniczy, tętnicowy; ***~ walls*** ściany tętnic **2.** *road*: główny, przelotowy; **ar•te•ri•o•scle•ro•sis** [ɑːtɪərɪəʊsklə'rəʊsɪs] *s* MED miażdżyca *f*; **ar•te•ry** ['ɑːtərɪ] *s* **1.** tętnica *f*; ***the coronary ~*** tętnica wieńcowa **2.** arteria *f*, główna droga *f*

ar•te•sian well [ɑːtiːziən'wel] *s* studnia *f* artezyjska

art•ful ['ɑːtfl] *adj* przebiegły, sprytny, zręczny; ***an ~ politician*** przebiegły polityk

'**art gal•ler•y** *s* galeria *f* sztuki; **art 'his•tory** *s* historia *f* sztuki

ar•thrit•ic [ɑː'θrɪtɪk] *adj* artretyczny; ***~ hands*** dłonie zniekształcone przez artretyzm; **ar•thri•tis** [ɑː'θraɪtɪs] *s* artretyzm *m*, zapalenie *n* stawów

ar•ti•choke ['ɑːtɪtʃəʊk] *s* karczoch *m*

ar•ti•cle ['ɑːtɪkl] *s* **1.** artykuł *m*; ***an ~ of clothing*** część garderoby; ***~s of association*** statut spółki; ***an ~ of faith*** dogmat **2.** przedmiot *m*; ***an ~ of value*** wartościowy przedmiot **3.** *gram* przedimek *m*

ar•tic•u•late **I** [ɑː'tɪkjʊleɪt] *v/t* **1.** wyrażać ⟨-razić⟩ (słowami), formułować ⟨s-⟩; ***~ one's feelings*** wyrazić swoje uczucia **2.** artykułować ⟨wy-⟩, wymawiać ⟨-mówić⟩ **II** [ɑː'tɪkjʊlət] *adj* **1.** *person*: elokwentny **2.** *speech*: wyraźny; **ar•tic•u•lat•ed** [ɑː'tɪkjʊleɪtɪd] *adj* **1.** *bus*: przegubowy **2.** *truck*: z przyczepą; **ar•tic•u•la•tion** [ɑːtɪkjʊ'leɪʃn] *s* **1.** wyrażanie *n*, sformułowanie *n* **2.** artykulacja *f*, wymowa *f*

ar•ti•fice ['ɑːtɪfɪs] *s* **2.** sztuczki *pl* **2.** podstępy *pl*

ar•ti•fi•cial [ɑːtɪ'fɪʃl] *adj* **1.** sztuczny; ***~ fibres*** sztuczne włókna, ***~ sweetener*** słodzik **2.** nieszczery, fałszywy; **ar•ti•fi•cial in•sem•i•'na•tion** *s* sztuczne zapłodnienie *n*; **ar•ti•fi•cial in'tel•li•gence** *s* sztuczna inteligencja *f*; **ar•ti•fi•cial res•pi•'ra•tion** *s* sztuczne oddychanie *n*

ar•til•le•ry [ɑː'tɪlərɪ] *s* artyleria *f*

ar•ti•san ['ɑːtɪzæn] *s* rzemieślnik *m*

ar•tist ['ɑːtɪst] *s* artysta *m*; **ar•tiste** [ɑː'tiːst] *s Br* artysta *m* estradowy; **ar•tis•tic** [ɑː'tɪstɪk] *adj* **1.** artystyczny; ***~ independence*** niezależność twórcza **2.** ***be ~*** mieć zdolności artystyczne

art•less ['ɑːtlɪs] *adj* naturalny, szczery, prostolinijny

'**art school** *s* szkoła *f* sztuk pięknych

'**art stu•dent** *s* student *m* szkoły sztuk pięknych

'**art•work** *s* **1.** szata *f* graficzna **2.** ilustracje *pl* **3.** dzieło *n* sztuki

as [æz] **I** *adv* **1.** (*comparisons*) jak *N*; ***~ tall ~*** tak wysoki jak; ***I have the same dress as you*** mam taką samą sukienkę jak ty; ***I ran ~ fast ~ I could*** biegłam tak szybko, jak tylko potrafiłam; ***just ~ good*** równie dobry; ***twice ~ large*** dwa razy większy; ***~ well*** także, też **II** *adv* **2.** jako *N*; ***she worked ~ a nurse*** pracowała jako pielęgniarka; ***~ a child*** jako dziecko, w dzieciństwie; ***dressed ~*** przebrany za *A* **3.** (taki) jak; ***statesmen ~ Churchill*** mężowie stanu jak Churchill **II** *conj* **1.** ponieważ, bo, jako że; ***~ you are the oldest*** ponieważ jesteś najstarszy **2.** (podczas) gdy; ***as I was getting into the car*** gdy wsiadałem do samochodu; ***~ he gets older*** w miarę jak się starzeje; ***~ of, ~ from*** (począwszy) od **3.** chociaż, mimo że; ***angry ~ he was*** mimo że był zły

4. (tak) jak; **~ *you know*** jak wiesz; **~ *you wish*** jak sobie życzysz; **~ *it turned out*** jak się okazało; ***do ~ I say*** rób, jak mówię, rób, co ci każę; **~ *for*, ~ *to*** jeśli chodzi o *A*; **~ *for me*** jeśli chodzi o mnie; **~ *I was saying*** jak już mówiłem; **~ *and when*** w sytuacji, gdy; **~ *it were*** że tak powiem

asap ['eɪzæp] *abbr* (=***as soon as possible***) jak najszybciej

as•bes•tos [æz'bestəs] *s* azbest *m*

as•cend [ə'send] *v/i* **1.** iść w górę, wspinać ⟨-piąć⟩ się **2.** wznosić ⟨-nieść⟩ się; ***steps ~ing to*** schody prowadzące do *G* **3.** *(fog)* podnosić ⟨-nieść⟩ się **4.** awansować; **~ *to the position of*** awansować na stanowisko *G*; **as•cend•an•cy** [ə'sendənsɪ] *s* wpływy *pl*, władza *f*; **as•cend•ant** [ə'sendənt] *s*: ***be in the ~*** *form* dominować, wieść prym; **as•cend•en•cy** → ***ascendancy***; **as•cend•ent** → ***ascendant***

As•cen•sion [ə'senʃn] *s REL* Wniebowstąpienie *n*

as•cent [ə'sent] *s* **1.** wspinaczka *f* **2.** droga *f* pod górę **3.** *fig* dojście *n* do władzy

as•cer•tain [æsə'teɪn] *v/t* ustalać ⟨-lić⟩; **~ *the facts*** ustalić fakty

as•cet•ic [ə'setɪk] *adj* ascetyczny; **as•cet•i•cism** [ə'setɪsɪzəm] *s* ascetyzm *m*, asceza *f*

ASCII ['æskiː] *abbr* (=***American Standard Code for Information Interchange***) *INF* kodowanie *n* ASCII

a•scor•bic ac•id [ə'skɔːbɪk'æsɪd] *s* kwas *m* askorbinowy

as•cribe [ə'skraɪb] *v/t* przypisywać ⟨-sać⟩ (***s.th. to*** coś *D*)

a•sep•tic [eɪ'septɪk] *adj MED* aseptyczny, jałowy; ***an ~ dressing*** opatrunek jałowy

a•sex•u•al [eɪ'sekʃuəl] *adj* aseksualny, bezpłciowy

ash[1] [æʃ] *s* **1.** popiół *m*; ***~-blond hair*** popielatoblond włosy; ***burn to ~es*** spalić się na popiół **2.** ***~es*** prochy (zmarłych); ***rise from the ~es*** odrodzić się z popiołów

ash[2] [~] *s* jesion *m*

a•shamed [ə'ʃeɪmd] *adj* zawstydzony; ***be*** (*a.* ***feel***) **~ *of s.th.*** wstydzić się czegoś; ***be*** (*a.* ***feel***) **~ *of s.o.*** wstydzić się za kogoś; ***be*** (*a.* ***feel***) **~ *to do s.th.*** wstydzić się coś zrobić

ash•en ['æʃn] *adj* **1** *complexion*: szary, ziemisty **2.** blady; ***he went ~ with fear*** zbladł ze strachu

a•shore [ə'ʃɔː] *adv* do brzegu, na brzegu, na lądzie; ***wade ~*** brodzić w kierunku brzegu; ***go ~*** zejść na ląd

ash•tray ['æʃtreɪ] *s* popielniczka *f*

Ash 'Wednes•day *s* środa *f* popielcowa, Popielec *m*

A•sia ['eɪʃə] Azja *f*; **~ *Minor*** Azja Mniejsza; **A•sian** ['eɪʃən] **I** *adj* azjatycki **II** *s* Azjata *m*, Azjatka *f*; ***an ~ American*** Amerykanin azjatyckiego pochodzenia; **A•si•at•ic** [eɪʃɪ'ætɪk] *adj* azjatycki

a•side [ə'saɪd] **I** *adv* na bok, na stronę, na uboczu; ***stand ~*** stać na boku; ***set ~ some money*** odłożyć trochę pieniędzy **II** *s* **1.** dygresja *f* **2.** uwaga *f* na stronie

as•i•nine ['æsɪnaɪn] *adj* **1.** ośli **2.** idiotyczny

ask [ɑːsk] *v/t* **1.** pytać ⟨za-⟩ (***about*** o *A*) **2.** *question*: zadawać ⟨-dać⟩ **3.** prosić ⟨po-⟩ (***for*** o *A*); **~ *s.o. to do s.th.*** poprosić kogoś, żeby coś zrobił; **~ *s.o. a favour*** poprosić kogoś o przysługę; ***be ~ing for trouble*** prosić się o kłopoty **4.** żądać ⟨za-⟩, wymagać; ***you are ~ing too much of him*** za wiele od niego wymagasz **5.** zapraszać ⟨-rosić⟩; **~ *s.o. to a party*** zaprosić kogoś na imprezę; **ask after** *v/i* pytać ⟨za-⟩ o *G*; **ask around** *v/i* pytać ⟨po-⟩; **ask in** *v/t* zapraszać ⟨-rosić⟩ do środka; **ask out** *v/t* wypraszać ⟨-rosić⟩

a•skance [ə'skæns] *adv*: ***look ~*** popatrzeć z ukosa; spojrzeć spode łba

a•skew [ə'skjuː] *adv* krzywo, nierówno

ask•ing ['ɑːskɪŋ] *s*: ***it's yours for the ~*** wystarczy poprosić; **'ask•ing price** *s* cena *f* wyjściowa, cena *f* ofertowa

a•sleep [ə'sliːp] *adj* **1.** ***be ~*** spać; ***fall ~*** zasnąć; ***be half ~*** być ledwo przytomnym **2.** *limb*: zdrętwiały, sztywny

as•par•a•gus [ə'spærəgəs] *s* szparag *m*, szparagi *pl*

as•pect ['æspekt] *s* **1.** aspekt *m* **2.** punkt *m* widzenia

as•pen ['æspən] *s* osika *f*

as•per•i•ty [æ'sperətɪ] *s* **1.** szorstkość *f* **2.** surowość *f*

as•per•sion [ə'spɜːʃn] *s form* oszczerstwo *n*; ***cast ~s on s.o.*** szkalować kogoś, rzucać na kogoś oszczerstwa

as•phalt ['æsfælt] *s* asfalt *m*

as•phyx•i•a [æs'fɪksɪə] *s MED* uduszenie *n*; **as•phyx•i•ate** [æ'sfɪksɪeɪt] **I** *v/i* dusić ⟨u-⟩ się **II** *v/t* ***be ~d*** udusić się; **as•phyx•i•a•tion** [əsfɪksɪ'eɪʃn] *s* uduszenie *n*

as•pic ['æspɪk] *s COOK* galareta *f*, auszpik *m*

as•pi•rant [ə'spaɪərənt] *s* kandydat *m*

as•pi•ra•tion [æspə'reɪʃn] *s* **1.** aspiracja *f*, dążenie *n* **2.** (*phonetics*) aspiracja *f*, przydech *m*; **as•pire** [ə'spaɪə] *v/i* **1.** dążyć, aspirować (***to*** do *G*) **2.** pragnąć (***to*** *G*)

as•pi•rin ['æsprɪn] *s* aspiryna *f*

as•pir•ing [ə'spaɪərɪŋ] *adj* **1.** ambitny **2.** początkujący

ass[1] [æs] *s Br infml* dureń *m*, osioł *m*; ***make an ~ of oneself*** robić z siebie durnia

ass[2] [~] → ***arse***

as•sail [ə'seɪl] *v/t* napadać ⟨-paść⟩ na *A*, atakować ⟨za-⟩; **as•sai•lant** [ə'seɪlənt] *s* napastnik *m*

as•sas•sin [ə'sæsɪn] *s* **1.** zamachowiec *m* **2.** płatny morderca *m*; **as•sas•sin•ate** [ə'sæsɪneɪt] *v/t* mordować ⟨za-⟩ (w zamachu); ***be ~d*** zginąć w zamachu; **as•sas•sin•a•tion** [əsæsɪ'neɪʃn] *s* **1.** zamach *m* (***of*** na *A*); ***an ~ attempt*** próba zamachu **2.** morderstwo *n*

as•sault [ə'sɔːlt] **I** *v/t* atakować ⟨za-⟩, napadać ⟨-paść⟩ na *A* **II** *s* napaść *f*, atak *m*; ***a charge of sexual ~*** oskarżenie o gwałt; ***launch an ~ on*** przypuścić atak na *A*; ***take by ~*** wziąć szturmem

as•say [ə'seɪ] **I** *v/t* **1.** analizować ⟨z-⟩ **2.** *metal*: oznaczać ⟨-czyć⟩ próbę **II** *s* **1.** *CHEM* analiza *f* **2.** oznaczenie *n* próby

as•sem•ble [ə'sembl] **I** *v/i* gromadzić ⟨z-⟩ się, zbierać ⟨zebrać⟩ się **II** *v/t* **1.** gromadzić ⟨z-⟩, zbierać ⟨zebrać⟩ **2.** składać ⟨złożyć⟩, montować ⟨z-⟩; **as•sem•bler** [ə'semblə] *s* **1.** monter *m* **2.** *INF* asembler *m*; **as•sem•bly** [ə'semblɪ] *s* **1.** zgromadzenie *n*; ***the right of ~*** prawo do zgromadzeń; ***an ~ point*** miejsce zbiórki, punkt zborny **2.** montaż *m*; **as'sem•bly lan•guage** *s INF* asembler *m*; **as'sem•bly line** *s* linia *f* montażowa

as•sent [ə'sent] **I** *v/i* **1.** wyrażać ⟨-razić⟩ zgodę (***to*** na *A*) **2.** akceptować ⟨za-⟩ (***to*** *A*) **II** *s* zgoda *f*, akceptacja *f*; ***give ~ to*** wyrazić zgodę na *A*, zaakceptować *A*; ***by common ~*** za zgodą ogółu

as•sert [ə'sɜːt] **I** *v/t* **1.** zapewniać ⟨-nić⟩ o *L* **2.** *power*, *independence*: zaznaczać ⟨-czyć⟩, zachowywać ⟨-chować⟩ **3.** ***~ oneself*** być pewnym siebie **II** *v/i* zapewniać ⟨-nić⟩, twierdzić ⟨s-⟩ (***that*** że); **as•ser•tion** [ə'sɜːʃn] *s* **1.** zapewnienie *n* **2.** twierdzenie *n*; ***make an ~ that*** stwierdzić, że **3.** zaznaczenie *n*; **as•ser•tive** [ə'sɜːtɪv] *adj* pewny siebie, asertywny; **as•ser•tive•ness** [ə'sɜːtɪvnɪs] *s* pewność *f* siebie, asertywność *f*

as•sess [ə'ses] *v/t* **1.** szacować ⟨o-⟩, wyceniać ⟨-nić⟩; ***~ damage at*** oszacować szkody na *A* **2.** oceniać ⟨-nić⟩; **as•sess•ment** [ə'sesmənt] *s* **1.** oszacowanie *n*, wycena *f* **2.** ocena *f*; ***my ~ of the situation*** moja ocena sytuacji

as•set ['æset] *s* **1.** zaleta *f*, atut *m*; ***be an ~*** być atutem; ***be an ~ to a team*** być wartościowym członkiem zespołu **2.** ***~s*** *ECON* majątek *m*, aktywa *pl*; ***fixed ~s*** środki trwałe; ***~s and liabilities*** aktywa i pasywa

ass•hole ['æshəʊl] *s vulg* dupek *m*

as•sid•u•ous [ə'sɪdjʊəs] *adj* **1.** pilny **2.** sumienny **3.** pracowity; **as•si•du•i•ty** ['æsɪ'djuːətɪ] *s* **1.** pilność *f* **2.** sumienność *f* **3.** pracowitość *f*

as•sign [ə'saɪn] *v/t* **1.** przydzielać ⟨-lić⟩ (***s.o. s.th.*** komuś coś, ***s.th. to*** coś *D*); ***~ s.o. a task*** wyznaczyć komuś zadanie **2.** przypisywać ⟨-sać⟩; ***~ blame to*** przypisywać winę *D*; ***~ great importance to*** przypisywać wielką wagę *D* **3.** *rights*: przenosić ⟨-nieść⟩ (***s.th. to*** coś na *A*); **as•sign•ment** [ə'saɪnmənt] *s* **1.** zadanie *n*; ***reading ~*** zadana lektura **2.** zlecenie *n* **3.** przydział *m* **4.** *blame*: przypisanie *n* **5.** *rights*: przeniesienie *n*

as•sim•i•late [ə'sɪmɪleɪt] **I** *v/t* **1.** asymilować ⟨z-⟩ **2.** wchłaniać ⟨-łonąć⟩, przyswajać ⟨-woić⟩ **3.** przejmować

⟨-jąć⟩ **II** *v/i* asymilować ⟨z-⟩ się; **as·sim·i·la·tion** [əsɪmɪ'leɪʃn] *s* **1.** asymilacja *f* **2.** wchłanianie *n*, przyswajanie *n*

as·sist [ə'sɪst] **I** *v/t* pomagać ⟨-móc⟩, wspierać ⟨wesprzeć⟩; **~ s.o. in doing s.th.** pomóc komuś coś zrobić **II** *v/i* **1.** pomagać ⟨-móc⟩ **2.** asystować; **as·sist·ance** [ə'sɪstəns] *s* pomoc *f*, wsparcie *n*; ***financial ~*** wsparcie finansowe; ***be of ~*** być pomocnym, pomóc; ***come to s.o.'s ~*** przyjść komuś z pomocą; **as·sis·tant** [ə'sɪstənt] *s* asystent *m*, pomocnik *m*; **as·sis·tant di'rec·tor** *s* asystent *m* reżysera; **as·sis·tant 'man·ag·er** *s* **1.** zastępca *m* kierownika **2.** zastępca *m* dyrektora; **as·sis·tant pro'fes·sor** *s* profesor *m* (uczelniany); **as·sis·tant ref·er'ee** *s* sędzia *m* liniowy

as·so·ci·ate [ə'səʊʃɪeɪt] **I** *v/t* kojarzyć ⟨s-⟩, łączyć ⟨po-⟩ (***s.th. with*** coś z *I*); ***I ~ the smell of the perfume with Helen*** zapach tych perfum kojarzy mi się z Helen **II** *v/i* przebywać (***with*** z *I*/w towarzystwie *G*) **III** *s* współpracownik *m*, wspólnik *m* **IV** *adj* stowarzyszony; **as·so·ci·ate 'ed·i·tor** *s* **1.** zastępca *m* redaktora naczelnego **2.** redaktor *m* pomocniczy; **as·so·ci·ate pro'fes·sor** *s* profesor *m* nadzwyczajny; **as·so·ci·a·tion** [əsəʊsɪ'eɪʃn] *s* **1.** stowarzyszenie *n*, związek *m* **2.** współpraca *f*; ***in ~ with*** we współpracy z *I* **3.** skojarzenie *n*, asocjacja *f*

as·sort·ed [ə'sɔːtɪd] *adj* **1.** mieszany, różny; ***~ sweets*** mieszanka słodyczy **2.** ***ill-~ guests*** źle dobrani goście; **as·sort·ment** [ə'sɔːtmənt] *s* **1.** asortyment *m* **2.** zasób *m* **3.** zbieranina *f*

as·sume [ə'sjuːm] *v/t* **1.** zakładać ⟨założyć⟩, przypuszczać ⟨-puścić⟩; ***~ the worst*** zakładać najgorsze; ***let's ~ that*** przyjmijmy, że **2.** *name, expression*: przybierać ⟨-brać⟩; ***an ~d name*** przybrane nazwisko; ***~ a look of indifference*** przybrać obojętny wyraz twarzy **3.** *power*: obejmować ⟨objąć⟩; **as·sump·tion** [ə'sʌmpʃn] *s* **1.** założenie *n*, przypuszczenie *n*; ***on the ~ that*** przy założeniu, że **2.** *of power*: objęcie *n* **3.** °~ *REL* Wniebowzięcie *n*

as·sur·ance [ə'ʃɔːrəns] *s* **1.** zapewnienie *n* **2.** pewność *f* siebie **3.** *Br* ubezpieczenie *n*; ***life ~*** ubezpieczenie na życie **4.** pewność *f*; **as·sure** [ə'ʃɔː] *v/t* **1.** zapewniać ⟨-nić⟩ (***s.o. of*** kogoś o *L*) **2.** gwarantować ⟨za-⟩ **3.** przekonywać ⟨-nać⟩ (***s.o. of*** kogoś o *L*); ***~ oneself*** przekonać się **4.** *Br* ubezpieczać ⟨-czyć⟩; **as·sured** [ə'ʃɔːd] *adj* **1.** pewny (***of*** *G*); ***rest ~ that*** bądź pewny, że **2.** zapewniony **3.** pewny siebie; **as·sur·ed·ly** [ə'ʃɔːrədlɪ] *adv* **1.** na pewno, z pewnością **2.** z pewnością siebie, pewnie

as·ter·isk ['æstərɪsk] **I** *v/t* zaznaczać ⟨-czyć⟩ gwiazdką **II** *s* gwiazdka *f*

a·stern [ə'stɜːn] *adv* na rufie; ***move ~*** (*of ship*) płynąć do tyłu

asth·ma ['æsmə] *s* astma *f*; ***an ~ attack*** atak astmy; **asth·mat·ic** [æs'mætɪk] **I** *s* astmatyk *m* **II** *adj* astmatyczny

a·stig·ma·tism [ə'stɪgmətɪzəm] *s* astygmatyzm *m*

as·ton·ish [ə'stɒnɪʃ] *v/t* dziwić ⟨z-⟩, zaskakiwać ⟨-skoczyć⟩ (***s.o. by*** kogoś *I*); **as·ton·ish·ed** [ə'stɒnɪʃt] *adj* zdumiony, zaskoczony; ***be ~ at*** (*a.* ***by***) być zaskoczonym *I*; **as·ton·ish·ing** [ə'stɒnɪʃɪŋ] *adj* zdumiewający, zaskakujący; **as·ton·ish·ing·ly** [ə'stɒnɪʃɪŋlɪ] *adv* **1.** zdumiewająco, zaskakująco **2.** co zdumiewające, co zaskakujące; **as·ton·ish·ment** [ə'stɒnɪʃmənt] *s* zdumienie *n*, zaskoczenie *n*

as·tound [ə'staʊnd] *v/t* zadziwiać ⟨-wić⟩, zdumiewać ⟨-mieć⟩; **as·tound·ing** [ə'staʊndɪŋ] *adj* zadziwiający, zdumiewający

a·stray [ə'streɪ] *adv*: ***lead s.o. ~*** *fig* sprowadzić kogoś na manowce, zwieść kogoś; ***go ~*** zaginąć

a·stride [ə'straɪd] **I** *adv* okrakiem; ***sit ~ a horse*** siedzieć okrakiem na koniu **II** *prep* po obu stronach *G*; ***the city lies ~ the river*** miasto leży na obu brzegach rzeki

as·trin·gent [ə'strɪndʒənt] **I** *s MED* środek *m* ściągający **II** *adj* **1.** *taste*: cierpki **2.** *remark*: uszczypliwy **3.** *MED* ściągający

as·trol·o·ger [ə'strɒlədʒə] *s* astrolog *m*; **as·tro·log·i·cal** [æstrə'lɒdʒɪkl] *adj* astrologiczny; **as·trol·o·gy** [ə'strɒlədʒɪ] *s* astrologia *f*

as·tro·naut ['æstrənɔːt] *s* astronauta *m*

as•tron•o•mer [əˈstrɒnəmə] *s* astronom *m*; **as•tro•nom•ic** [æstrəˈnɒmɪk], ***as•tro•nom•i•cal*** [æstrəˈnɒmɪkl] *adj* astronomiczny; **as•tron•o•my** [əˈstrɒnəmɪ] *s* astronomia *f*

as•tro•phys•ics [æstrəʊˈfɪzɪks] *s* astrofizyka *f*

as•tute [əˈstjuːt] *adj* **1.** bystry, inteligentny **2.** zręczny, sprytny **2.** przenikliwy; **as•tute•ness** [əˈstjuːtnɪs] *s* **1.** bystrość *f*, inteligencja *f* **2.** zręczność *f*, spryt *m* **3.** przenikliwość *f*

a•sy•lum [əˈsaɪləm] *s* **1.** azyl *m*, schronienie *n* **2.** azyl *m* polityczny **3.** ***a lunatic*** (*a.* ***mental***) ~ szpital psychiatryczny; **aˈsy•lum seek•er** *s* ubiegający *m* się o azyl

a•sym•met•ric [eɪsɪˈmetrɪk], ***a•sym•met•ri•cal*** [eɪsɪˈmetrɪkl] *adj* asymetryczny; **a•sym•me•try** [eɪˈsɪmətrɪ] *s* asymetria *f*

at [ət], *akcentowane* [æt] *prep* **1.** (*denoting place*) w *L*, u *G*, na *L*, pod *I*; ***~ home*** w domu; ***~ the airport*** na lotnisku; ***~ the door*** pod drzwiami, przed drzwiami; ***~ Tom's*** u Toma **2.** (*denoting time, hour*) o *L*; podczas *G*, w porze *G*; ***~ 11 o'clock*** o jedenastej; ***~ the moment*** w tej chwili, obecnie; ***~ the time*** wtedy; ***~ dawn*** o świcie; ***~ night*** w nocy **3.** (*denoting direction*) do *G*, w kierunku *G*, na *A*; ***smile ~*** uśmiechnąć się do *G*; ***shout ~*** krzyknąć na *A*; ***throw s.th. ~*** rzucić czymś w *A* **4.** (*denoting reason*) z *G*, z powodu *G*; ***laugh ~*** śmiać się z *G*; ***~ s.o.'s request*** na czyjąś prośbę **5.** (*denoting state*) w stanie *G*, w trakcie *G*; ***~ war*** w stanie wojny; ***~ play*** w trakcie zabawy **6.** (*denoting speed*) ***drive ~ 100 mph*** jechać 100 mil na godzinę **7.** (*denoting price*) ***sell s.th. ~ 5 dollars*** sprzedawać coś po 5 dolarów **8.** (*denoting age*) ***~*** (***the age of***) ***15*** w wieku 15 lat **9.** *work, study*: w *L*, na *L*; ***study ~ Yale*** studiować w Yale; ***work ~ a bank*** pracować w banku **10.** (*with superlative*) ***~ least*** co najmniej, przynajmniej; ***~ the most*** co najwyżej; ***~ best*** (***worst***) w najlepszym (najgorszym) razie; ***he was ~ his best*** był w szczytowej formie **11.** ***~ all*** wcale, w ogóle

ate [et] *Past Simple* → ***eat***

a•the•ism [ˈeɪθɪɪzəm] *s* ateizm *m*; **a•the•ist** [ˈeɪθɪɪst] *s* ateista *m*; **a•the•is•tic** [eɪθɪˈɪstɪk] *adj* ateistyczny

Ath•ens [ˈæθɪnz] *s* Ateny *pl*

ath•lete [ˈæθliːt] *s* **1.** sportowiec *m* **2.** *Br* lekkoatleta *m* **3.** ***be a good ~*** być wysportowanym; **ath•lete's ˈfoot** *s* MED grzybica *f* stóp; **ath•let•ic** [æθˈletɪk] *adj* **1.** wysportowany **2.** *Br* lekkoatletyczny; **ath•let•ics** [æθˈletɪks] *s* **1.** *Br* lekka atletyka *f* **2.** *Am* sport *m*; ***an ~ field*** boisko sportowe

At•lan•tic [ətˈlæntɪk] **I** *s* ***the ~*** Atlantyk, Ocean Atlantycki **II** *adj* atlantycki

at•las [ˈætləs] *s* atlas *m*; ***a road ~*** atlas drogowy; ***a wine ~*** atlas win

ATM [eɪtiːˈem] *abbr* (=***automated teller machine***) *Am* bankomat *m*

at•mos•phere [ˈætməsfɪə] *s* **1.** atmosfera *f*; ***a friendly ~*** przyjazna atmosfera; ***this place has a lot of atmosphere*** to miejsce ma wspaniałą atmosferę **2.** powietrze *n*; ***the ~ was stuffy*** było duszno **3.** nastrój *m*; **at•mos•pher•ic** [ætməsˈferɪk] *adj* **1.** atmosferyczny; ***~ conditions*** warunki atmosferyczne **2.** nastrojowy; ***~ lighting*** nastrojowe oświetlenie; **at•mos•pher•ic pol•ˈlu•tion** *s* zanieczyszczenie *n* powietrza

at•oll [ˈætɒl] *s* atol *m*; ***the Mururoa ~*** atol Mururoa

at•om [ˈætəm] *s* **1.** atom *m* **2.** *fig* drobina *f*

a•tom•ic [əˈtɒmɪk] *adj* atomowy; ***an ~ bomb*** bomba atomowa *f*; **a•tom•ic ˈen•er•gy** *s* energia *f* atomowa; **a•tom•ic ˈpow•er** *s* energia *f* atomowa; **a•tom•ic-ˈpow•ered** *adj* zasilany energią atomową; **a•tom•ic ˈpow•er plant** *s* elektrownia *f* atomowa; **a•tom•ic ˈwaste** *s* odpady *pl* radioaktywne; **a•tom•ic ˈweight** *s* CHEM masa *f* atomowa

a•tom•ise [ˈætəʊmaɪz] *Br*, **a•tom•ize** *Am v/t* **1.** rozpylać ⟨-lić⟩ **2.** rozdrabniać ⟨-robnić⟩ **3.** rozkładać ⟨-złożyć⟩ na atomy; **a•tom•iz•er** [ˈætəmaɪzə] *s* rozpylacz *m*

a•tone [əˈtəʊn] *v/i form* pokutować ⟨od-⟩ (**for** za *A*) **2.** zadośćuczynić (**for** za *A*); **atonement** [əˈtəʊnmənt] *s* **1.** pokuta *f* **2.** zadośćuczynienie *n*

at•ro•phy ['ætrəfɪ] **I** *v/t* **1.** zanikać ⟨-knąć⟩ **2.** ulegać ⟨ulec⟩ atrofii **II** *s* **1.** atrofia *f* **2.** zanik *m*

'at-sign *s* INF znak *m* @, *infml* małpa *f*

at•tach [ə'tætʃ] **I** *v/t* **1.** załączać ⟨-czyć⟩ (**to** do *G*) **2.** dołączać ⟨-czyć⟩ **3.** *~ great importance to* przywiązywać wielką wagę do *G*; *not ~ any importance to* nie przywiązywać wagi do *G* **4.** *~ oneself* przyłączyć się, przyczepić się **II** *v/i* **1.** być związanym (**to** z *I*) **2.** łączyć się (**to** z *I*)

at•ta•ché [ə'tæʃeɪ] *s* attaché *m*; *a cultural ~* attaché kulturalny; **at'ta•ché case** *s* dyplomatka *f*, aktówka *f*

at•tach•ment [ə'tætʃmənt] *s* **1.** przywiązanie *n*; *form an ~ to* przywiązać się do *G* **2.** więź *f* **3.** załącznik *m* **4.** TECH końcówka *f* **5.** połączenie *n*

at•tack [ə'tæk] **I** *v/t* **1.** atakować ⟨za-⟩; *~ a problem* zmierzyć się z problemem **2.** napadać ⟨-paść⟩ na *A* **II** *s* **1.** atak *m*; *launch an ~* przypuścić atak; *have an ~* dostać ataku, mieć atak **2.** napaść *f*; **at•tack•er** [ə'tækə] *s* napastnik *m*, atakujący *m*

at•tain [ə'teɪn] *v/t* **1.** osiągać ⟨-gnąć⟩; *~ an objective* osiągnąć cel **2.** uzyskiwać ⟨-kać⟩; *~ independence* uzyskać niepodległość; **at•tain•a•ble** [ə'teɪnəbl] *adj* **1.** osiągalny **2.** możliwy do realizacji; **at•tain•ment** [ə'teɪnmənt] *s* **1.** osiągnięcie *n* **2.** dokonanie *n*

at•tempt [ə'tempt] **I** *s* **1.** próba *f*; *make an ~ to do s.th.* spróbować coś zrobić **2.** zamach *m*; *an ~ on s.o's life* zamach na czyjeś życie **II** *v/t* próbować ⟨s-⟩, usiłować; *~ to do s.th.* próbować coś zrobić: **at•temp•ted** [ə'temptɪd] *adj*: *~ murder* usiłowanie morderstwa; *~ suicide* próba samobójstwa

at•tend [ə'tend] *v/t* **1.** uczestniczyć w *L*, brać ⟨wziąć⟩ udział w *L*; *~ a meeting* wziąć udział w zebraniu; *~ a lecture* pójść na wykład; *~ school* chodzić do szkoły **2.** *form* uważać **3.** *form* towarzyszyć, wiązać się z *I*; **attend to** *v/t* **1.** zajmować ⟨-jąć⟩ się *I*; *~ a patient* zajmować się pacjentem **2.** opiekować ⟨za-⟩ się *I* **3.** uważać na *A*, zwracać ⟨-rócić⟩ uwagę na *A* **4.** *client*: obsługiwać ⟨-służyć⟩; **at•tend•ance** [ə'tendəns] *s* **1.** obecność *f*; *a list of ~* lista obecności; *compulsory ~* obecność obowiązkowa; *be in ~ form* być obecnym **2.** frekwencja *f* **3.** opieka *f*; **at•tend•ant** [ə'tendənt] *s* **1.** *a flight ~* stewardesa *f*; *a cloakroom ~* szatniarz; *a parking ~* parkingowy **2.** opiekun *m*; **at•ten•dee** [əten'diː] *s* uczestnik *m*; *a meeting ~* uczestnik zebrania

at•ten•tion [ə'tenʃn] *s* **1.** uwaga *f*; *pay ~ to* zwracać uwagę na *A*, uważać na *A*; *draw ~* zwracać uwagę; *attract ~* budzić zainteresowanie; *be the centre of ~* być w centrum zainteresowania; *give full ~ to* poświęcić całą uwagę *D*; *for the ~ of* do wiadomości *G* **2.** koncentracja *f* **3.** opieka *f*, pomoc *f*; *medical ~* opieka lekarska, pomoc lekarska **4.** *stand to ~* stanąć na baczność; **at'ten•tion span** *s* długość *f* koncentracji; *have a short ~* nie potrafić się dłużej skoncentrować; **at•ten•tive** [ə'tentɪv] *adj* **1.** opiekuńczy, troskliwy; *be ~ to* troszczyć się o *A* **2.** uważny; *an ~ listener* uważny słuchacz

at•test [ə'test] **I** *v/i* świadczyć (**to** o *L*) **II** *v/t* **1.** potwierdzać ⟨-dzić⟩ **2.** poświadczać ⟨-czyć⟩

at•tic ['ætɪk] *s* **1.** strych *m* **2.** poddasze *n*

at•ti•tude ['ætɪtjuːd] *s* **1.** nastawienie *n*, stosunek *m*; *a friendly ~* przyjazne nastawienie; *have an ~ problem* być trudnym we współżyciu **2.** *fig* charakter *m* **3.** *form* pozycja *f*

attn *abbr* (=**for the attention of**) *form* do wiadomości

at•tor•ney [ə'tɜːnɪ] *s* **1.** *Am* adwokat *m*; *a defence ~* adwokat obrony **2.** *Am* prawnik *m* **3.** pełnomocnik *m*; *power of ~* pełnomocnictwo; **At•tor•ney 'Gen•e•ral** *s* minister *m* sprawiedliwości

at•tract [ə'trækt] *v/t* **1.** przyciągać ⟨-gnąć⟩; *~ attention* zwracać uwagę, przyciągać uwagę **2.** pociągać; *be ~ed by* (*a.* **to**) odczuwać pociąg do *G* **3.** wabić ⟨z-⟩ **4.** *support*: zdobywać ⟨-być⟩; **at•trac•tion** [ə'trækʃn] *s* **1.** atrakcyjność *f*; *hold ~* być atrakcyjnym; *hold little ~ for* być mało interesującym dla *G* **2.** urok *m* **3.** przyciąganie *n* **4.** atrakcja *f*; *the main ~* główna atrakcja; *a tourist ~* atrakcja turystyczna **5.** pociąg *m*; **at•trac•tive** [ə'træktɪv] *adj* **1.** atrakcyjny **2.** pociągający; ***an ~ prospect*** pociągająca perspektywa **3.** ***~ force*** *PHYS* siła przyciągania; **at•trac•tive•ness** [ə'træktɪvnɪs] *s* atrakcyjność *f*

at•trib•ute[1] [ə'trɪbjuːt] *v/t* przypisywać ⟨-sać⟩ (***s.th. to*** coś *D*); ***~ a painting to*** przypisywać autorstwo obrazu *D*

at•trib•ute[2] ['ætrɪbjuːt] *s* **1.** cecha *f* **2.** atrybut *m* **3.** właściwość *f*

at•trib•u•tive [ə'trɪbjʊtɪv] *adj* *GRAM* atrybutywny, występujący przed rzeczownikiem

a•typ•i•cal [eɪ'tɪpɪkl] *adj* nietypowy

au•burn ['ɔːbən] *adj* kasztanowy, rudobrązowy; ***~ hair*** kasztanowe włosy

auc•tion ['ɔːkʃn] **I** *s* aukcja *f*, licytacja *f*; ***hold an ~*** zorganizować aukcję; ***be put up for an ~*** zostać wystawionym na licytację; ***sell by ~*** sprzedawać na licytacji **II** *v/t* licytować ⟨z-⟩, sprzedawać ⟨-dać⟩ na aukcji; **auction off** *v/t* sprzedawać ⟨-dać⟩ na licytacji; **auc•tio•neer** [ɔːkʃə'nɪə] *s* licytator *m*, prowadzący *m* aukcję

au•da•cious [ɔː'deɪʃəs] *adj* **1.** śmiały; ***an ~ offer*** śmiała propozycja **2.** zuchwały; **au•dac•i•ty** [ɔː'dæsətɪ] *s* **1.** śmiałość *f*, zuchwałość *f* **2.** tupet *m*

au•di•ble ['ɔːdəbl] *adj* **1.** słyszalny; ***scarcely ~*** ledwie słyszalny **2.** wyraźny

au•di•ence ['ɔːdɪəns] *s* **1.** publiczność *f*, widownia *f* **2.** audiencja *f*; ***a private ~*** prywatna audiencja

au•di•o ['ɔːdɪəʊ] *adj* dźwiękowy; ***an ~ cassette*** kaseta audio; **au•di•o•vi•su•al** [ɔːdɪəʊ'vɪʒʊəl] *adj* audiowizualny; ***~ aids*** pomoce audiowizualne

au•dit ['ɔːdɪt] **I** *s* audyt *m*; ***an internal ~*** audyt wewnętrzny; ***carry out an ~*** przeprowadzać audyt **II** *v/t* przeprowadzać ⟨-dzić⟩ audyt; **au•di•tor** ['ɔːdɪtə] *s* **1.** audytor *m* **2.** rewident *m*

au•di•tion [ɔː'dɪʃn] **I** *s actor*: przesłuchanie *n* **II** *v/t actor*: przesłuchiwać ⟨-chać⟩ **III** *v/t* (*actor*) brać ⟨wziąć⟩ udział w przesłuchaniu

au•di•to•ri•um [ɔːdɪ'tɔːrɪəm] *pl -riums, -ria s* **1.** widownia *f* **2.** audytorium *n*

Au•gust ['ɔːgəst] *s* sierpień *m*; ***in ~*** w sierpniu

aunt [ɑːnt] *s* ciotka *f*

aunt•ie, ***aunt•y*** ['ɑːntɪ] *s dim* ciocia *f*, cioteczka *f*

au pair [əʊ'peə] *s* au pair *f*

au•ra ['ɔːrə] *s* **1.** aura *f*; ***s.o. has an ~ of sadness*** (***about him***) kogoś otacza aura smutku; ***have an ~ of confidence*** emanować pewnością siebie **2.** atmosfera *f* **3.** nastrój *m*

aus•pic•es ['ɔːspɪsɪz] *pl* auspicje *pl*, patronat *m*; ***under the ~ of*** pod auspicjami *G*, pod patronatem *G*

Aus•sie ['ɒzɪ] **I** *s infml* Australijczyk *m*, Australijka *f* **II** *adj infml* australijski

Aus•tra•la•sia [ɒstrəl'eɪʒə] *s* Australia i Oceania *f*

Aus•tra•li•a [ɒ'streɪljə] *s* Australia *f*; **Aus•tra•li•an** [ɒ'streɪljən] **I** *adj* australijski **II** *s* Australijczyk *m*, Australijka *f*

Aus•tri•a ['ɒstrɪə] *s* Austria *f*; **Aus•tri•an** ['ɒstrɪən] **I** *adj* austriacki **II** *s* Austriak *m*, Austriaczka *f*

au•then•tic [ɔː'θentɪk] *adj* **1.** autentyczny **2.** prawdziwy **3.** oryginalny; ***an ~ painting*** oryginalny obraz, oryginał **4.** wiarygodny

au•then•ti•cate [ɔː'θentɪkeɪt] *v/t* poświadczać ⟨-czyć⟩, uwierzytelniać ⟨-nić⟩; **au•then•ti•ca•tion** [ɔː'θentɪkeɪʃn] *no pl s* poświadczenie *n*, uwierzytelnienie *n*

au•then•tic•i•ty [ɔːθen'tɪsətɪ] *s* autentyczność *f*, prawdziwość *f*

au•thor ['ɔːθə] **I** *s* **1.** autor *m* **2.** literat *m* **3.** pisarz *m* **4.** twórca *m* **II** *v/t* **1.** *book*: pisać ⟨na-⟩ **2.** *scheme*: opracowywać ⟨-cować⟩ **3.** *report*: sporządzać ⟨-dzić⟩, przygotowywać ⟨-tować⟩

au•thor•i•tar•i•an [ɔːθɒrɪ'teərɪən] *adj* autorytarny, despotyczny

au•thor•i•ta•tive [ɔː'θɒrɪtətɪv] *adj* **1.** apodyktyczny **2.** autorytatywny **3.** miarodajny; **au•thor•i•ty** [ɔː'θɒrətɪ] *s* **1.** władza *f*; ***exercise ~*** sprawować władzę; ***people in ~*** sprawujący władzę; ***local authorities*** lokalne władze **2.** kontrola *f* **3.** upoważnienie *n*; ***give s.o. ~ to do s.th.*** upoważnić kogoś do zrobienia czegoś **4.** autorytet *m*; ***be an ~ on*** być autorytetem w dziedzinie *G* **5.** ***have s.th. on good***

~ dowiedzieć się czegoś z wiarygodnego źródła
au•thor•i•sa•tion [ɔːθəraɪ'zeɪʃn] *Br*, ***au•thor•i•za•tion*** *Am s* **1.** upoważnienie *n*; ***an ~ to do s.th.*** upoważnienie do zrobienia czegoś **2.** zezwolenie *n* **3.** autoryzacja *f*; **au•thor•ise** ['ɔːθəraɪz] *Br*, ***au•thor•ize*** *Am v/t* **1.** upoważniać ⟨-nić⟩; ***~ s.o. to do s.th.*** upoważnić kogoś do zrobienia czegoś **2.** zezwalać ⟨-wolić⟩ na *A*; ***~ an attack*** zezwolić na atak **3.** autoryzować
au•thor•ship ['ɔːθəʃɪp] *s* autorstwo *n*; ***of unknown ~*** nieznanego autorstwa; ***ascribe ~ to*** przypisywać autorstwo *D*
au•tism ['ɔːtɪzm] *no pl s* MED autyzm *m*; **au•tis•tic** [ɔː'tɪstɪk] *adj* autystyczny; ***an ~ child*** autystyczne dziecko, dziecko z autyzmem
au•to- ['ɔːtəʊ] (*in combinations*) auto-, samo-; ***~focus*** autofocus, automatyczne nastawianie ostrości
au•to•bi•o•graph•i•cal [ɔːtəbaɪə'græfɪkl] *adj* autobiograficzny; ***~ novel*** powieść autobiograficzna; **au•to•bi•og•ra•phy** ['ɔːtəbaɪ'ɒgrəfɪ] *s* autobiografia *f*; ***Churchill's ~*** autobiografia Churchilla
au•toc•ra•cy [ɔː'tɒkrəsɪ] *s* autokracja *f*; **au•to•crat** ['ɔːtəkræt] *s* autokrata *m*; **au•to•crat•ic** ['ɔːtə'krætɪk] *adj* autokratyczny
au•to•graph ['ɔːtəgrɑːf] *s* autograf *m*; ***~ collection*** kolekcja autografów
au•to•mate ['ɔːtəmeɪt] *v/t* automatyzować ⟨z-⟩
au•to•ma•ted 'tel•ler ma•chine *s* bankomat *m*
au•to•mat•ic [ɔtə'mætɪk] **I** *adj* **1.** automatyczny, zautomatyzowany, samoczynny; ***an ~ washing machine*** pralka automatyczna; ***~ gear change*** automatyczna skrzynia biegów **2.** mechaniczny, machinalny, nieświadomy **II** *s* **1.** automat *m* **2.** samochód *m* z automatyczną skrzynią biegów; **au•to•mat•i•cal•ly** [ɔːtə'mætɪklɪ] *adv* automatycznie
au•to•ma•tion [ɔːtə'meɪʃn] *s* automatyzacja *f*
au•tom•a•ton [ɔː'tɒmətən] *pl -ta* [~tə], *-tons s t fig* automat *m*
au•to•mo•bile ['ɔːtəməbiːl] *s Am* samochód *m*; **'au•to•mo•bile in•dus•try** *s Am* przemysł *m* samochodowy
au•to•mo•tive [ɔːtə'məʊtɪv] *adj* samochodowy; ***the ~ industry*** przemysł motoryzacyjny
au•ton•o•mous [ɔː'tɒnəməs] *adj* autonomiczny, niezależny; ***an ~ province*** autonomiczna prowincja; ***be ~ of*** być niezależnym od *G*
au•ton•o•my [ɔː'tɒnəmɪ] *s* autonomia *f*, niezależność *f*; ***demand ~ for*** domagać się autonomii dla *G*; ***preserve one's ~*** zachować niezależność
au•to•pi•lot ['ɔːtəʊpaɪlət] *s* (*plane*) autopilot *m*, pilot *m* automatyczny; ***be on ~*** lecieć na autopilocie; ***do s.th. on ~*** *fig* robić coś mechanicznie
au•top•sy ['ɔːtɒpsɪ] MED *s* **1.** autopsja *f* **2.** sekcja *f* zwłok
au•to-sug•ges•tion [ɔːtəʊsə'dʒestʃn] *no pl s* autosugestia *f*
au•tumn ['ɔːtəm] *s* jesień *f*; ***in ~*** jesienią; ***this ~*** tej jesieni; ***~ colours*** barwy jesieni; ***~ years*** jesień życia; **au•tum•nal** [ɔː'tʌmnəl] *adj* jesienny
a•vail•a•bil•i•ty [əveɪlə'bɪlətɪ] *s* dostępność *f*, osiągalność *f*, łatwy dostęp *m*; ***~ of guns*** łatwy dostęp do broni; ***~ of medical services*** dostępność usług medycznych; **a•vai•la•ble** [ə'veɪləbl] *adj* **1.** dostępny, osiągalny (***to*** dla *G*); ***make s.th. ~*** udostępnić coś **2.** ***be ~*** mieć czas, być wolnym
av•a•lanche ['ævəlɑːnʃ] *s* lawina *f*; ***risk of ~s*** zagrożenie lawinowe
a•vant-garde [ævɔːŋ'gɑːd] **I** *s* awangarda *f* **II** *adj* awangardowy
av•a•rice ['ævərɪs] *s* chciwość *f*, skąpstwo *n*; **av•a•ri•cious** ['ævərɪʃəs] *adj* chciwy, skąpy
a•venge [ə'vendʒ] *v/t* **1.** mścić ⟨po-⟩ **2.** ***~ oneself on s.o. for*** zemścić się na kimś za *A*
av•e•nue ['ævənjuː] *s* **1.** aleja *f* **2.** możliwość *f*; ***the only open ~*** jedyna możliwość **3.** sposób *m*
av•e•rage ['ævərɪdʒ] **I** *adj* **1.** średni, przeciętny; ***~ income*** średni dochód; ***~ earnings*** średnie zarobki; ***an ~ person*** przeciętna osoba; ***~ abilities*** przeciętne zdolności **2.** typowy **II** *s* średnia *f*, przeciętna *f*; ***above*** (***below***) ***~*** powyżej (poniżej) średniej; ***on***

~ średnio, przeciętnie **III** *v/t* **1.** wynosić ⟨-nieść⟩ średnio **2.** pracować średnio; **~ *35 hours per week*** pracować średnio 35 godzin w tygodniu **3.** osiągać ⟨-gnąć⟩ średnią prędkość; **average out I** *v/i* **1.** wyrównywać ⟨-nać⟩ się; ***pros and cons ~*** plusy i minusy wzajemnie się znoszą **2.** wynosić ⟨-nieść⟩; ***costs ~ at $6 per person*** koszty wynoszą 6 dolarów na osobę **II** *v/t* obliczać ⟨-czyć⟩ średnią

a•verse [ə'vɜːs] *adj* **1.** przeciwny; ***I wouldn't be ~ to it*** nie miałbym nic przeciwko temu **2.** niechętny; **a•ver•sion** [ə'vɜːʃn] *s* **1.** niechęć *f*; ***~ to do s.th.*** niechęć do zrobienia czegoś **2.** awersja *f* **3.** odraza *f*

a•vert [ə'vɜːt] *v/t* **1.** unikać ⟨-knąć⟩; ***~ a confrontation*** uniknąć konfrontacji **2.** zapobiegać ⟨-biec⟩; ***~ a conflict*** zapobiec konfliktowi **3.** *danger*: zażegnywać ⟨-gnać⟩ **4.** *gaze*, *attention*: odwracać ⟨-rócić⟩; ***~ one's eyes from*** odwrócić wzrok od *G*

a•vi•a•tion [eɪvɪ'əɪʃn] *s* lotnictwo *n*; ***~ fuel*** paliwo lotnicze; **a•vi•a•tor** ['eɪvɪeɪtə] *s* lotnik *m*

av•id ['ævɪd] *adj* **1.** zagorzały; ***an ~ supporter*** zagorzały zwolennik; ***be ~ for*** gorąco popierać *A* **2.** zapalony, namiętny; ***an ~ collector*** zapalony kolekcjoner; ***an ~ reader*** namiętny czytelnik

av•o•ca•do [ævə'kɑːdəʊ] *s* awokado *n*

a•void [ə'vɔɪd] *v/t* **1.** unikać ⟨-knąć⟩; ***~ s.th. like the plague*** unikać czegoś jak ognia; **2.** stronić od *G* **3.** omijać ⟨ominąć⟩; **a•void•a•ble** [ə'vɔɪdəbl] *adj* możliwy do uniknięcia; ***an ~ mistake*** błąd, którego można uniknąć; **a•void•ance** [ə'vɔɪdəns] *no pl s* unikanie *n*

a•wait [ə'weɪt] *v/t form* oczekiwać *G*, czekać na *A*; ***~ the results*** czekać na wyniki; ***long ~ed*** długo oczekiwany; ***eagerly ~ed*** niecierpliwie oczekiwany

a•wake [ə'weɪk] **I** *adj* ***be ~*** nie spać; ***be wide ~*** być całkowicie przytomnym; ***keep s.o. ~*** nie pozwalać komuś zasnąć; ***be ~ to*** być świadomym *G* **II** (*awoke/awaked*; *awoken/awaked*) *v/t* **1.** budzić ⟨o-⟩ **2.** uświadamiać ⟨-domić⟩ sobie (***to*** *A*) **3.** wzbudzać ⟨-dzić⟩ **III** (*awoke/awaked*; *awoken/awaked*) *v/i* budzić ⟨o-⟩ się

a•wak•en [ə'weɪkn] **I** *v/t* **1.** budzić ⟨o-⟩ **2.** uświadamiać ⟨-domić⟩ (***s.o. to*** komuś *A*) **3.** rozbudzać ⟨-dzić⟩, wzbudzać ⟨-dzić⟩; ***~ interest*** wzbudzić zainteresowanie **II** *v/i* budzić ⟨o-⟩ się; **a•wak•en•ing** [ə'weɪkənɪŋ] *s t fig* **1.** przebudzenie *n*; ***a rude ~*** przykra niespodzianka **2.** obudzenie *n* **3.** budzenie się *n*

a•ward [ə'wɔːd] **I** *s* **1.** nagroda *f* (***for*** za *A*) **2.** odszkodowanie *n* **II** *v/t* przyznawać ⟨-nać⟩; ***~ s.o. a scholarship*** przyznać komuś stypendium; **a'wards cer•e•mo•ny** *s* ceremonia *f* wręczenia nagród; **a'ward-win•ning** *adj* nagrodzony

a•ware [ə'weə] *adj* **1.** świadomy (***of*** *G*); ***are you ~ that*** czy wiesz, że; ***as far as I'm ~*** o ile wiem **2.** zorientowany (***of*** w *L*); **a•ware•ness** [ə'weənəs] *s* **1.** świadomość *f* **2.** znajomość *f* **3.** orientacja *f* **4.** rozeznanie *n*

a•wash [ə'wɒʃ] *adj* **1.** zalany; ***the floor is ~*** podłoga jest zalana **2.** *fig* zasypany, pełen; ***be ~ with rumours*** huczeć od plotek; ***the office is ~ with computers*** biuro jest zastawione komputerami

a•way [ə'weɪ] *adv* **1.** (*distance*) ***the shop is 2 kilometres ~*** do sklepu są dwa kilometry; ***she's ~ on holidays*** wyjechała na wakacje; ***stay ~ from*** trzymać się z daleka od *G*; ***go away!*** idź stąd!; ***move ~*** wyprowadzić się; ***give s.th. ~*** oddać coś; ***to take ~*** na wynos **2.** (*time*) ***a week ~*** za tydzień; ***dance the night ~*** przetańczyć całą noc **3.** (*process*) ***rust ~*** zardzewieć; ***boil ~*** wygotować się; ***be chattering ~*** gadać sobie w najlepsze **4.** (*aside*) ***put s.th. ~*** odłożyć coś; ***hidden ~*** schowany; **a'way game** *s* mecz *m* na wyjeździe; ***play an ~*** grać mecz na wyjeździe; **a'way team** *s* drużyna *f* gości; **a'way win** *s* zwycięstwo *n* na wyjeździe

awe [ɔː] **I** *no pl s* podziw *m* (połączony z lękiem); ***be in ~ of*** podziwiać *A* **II** *v/t* **~** *s.o.* wzbudzać ⟨-dzić⟩ w kimś podziw (połączony z lękiem); ***be ~d into silence*** zaniemówić z podziwu; **'awe-in•spir•ing** *adj* budzący podziw (połączony z lękiem); ***an ~ sight*** imponujący widok; **awe•some** ['ɔːsəm] *adj* niesamowity; ***look ~*** *infml* wyglądać odlotowo; **'awe-struck** *adj* **1.** pełen podziwu (połączonego z lękiem) **2.** pod wrażeniem

aw•ful ['ɔːfəl] *adj* **1.** okropny; ***you look ~*** fatalnie wyglądasz; ***an ~ headache*** okropny ból głowy **2.** potworny **3.** paskudny; ***~ weather*** paskudna pogoda; ***feel ~*** czuć się paskudnie **4.** straszny; ***~ risk*** straszne ryzyko; ***~ beating*** straszne lanie; ***know an ~ lot*** strasznie dużo wiedzieć; **aw•ful•ly** ['ɔːfəlɪ] *adv* strasznie, okropnie, bardzo; ***it's an ~ long time since I saw you*** strasznie dawno cię nie widziałem; ***I'm ~ sorry*** strasznie mi przykro; ***be ~ good at*** być bardzo dobrym w *L*

awk•ward ['ɔːkwəd] *adj* **1.** niezdarny **2.** niezręczny; ***an ~ situation*** niezręczna sytuacja **3.** kłopotliwy; ***an ~ customer*** kłopotliwy klient **4.** trudny; ***an ~ ascent*** trudna wspinaczka; ***make things ~ for*** utrudnić zdot;ycie *D*

a•woke [ə'wəʊk] *Past Simple* → ***awake***; **awok•en** [ə'wəʊkən] *Past Participle* → ***awake***

a•wry [ə'raɪ] *adv* **1.** ***go ~*** (*plan*) nie powieść się, *infml* wziąć w łeb **2.** w nieładzie **3.** krzywo

ax [æks] *Am* → ***axe***

axe [æks] **I** *s* **1.** siekiera *f*, topór *m*; ***have one's own ~ to grind*** *fig* działać interesownie **2.** ***get the ~*** *infml* **a)** stracić pracę, *infml* zostać wylanym (z pracy) **b)** zostać zlikwidowanym **II** *v/t* **1.** *expenses*: redukować ⟨z-⟩, obcinać ⟨-ciąć⟩ **2.** likwidować ⟨z-⟩ **3.** *infml* wylać (z pracy) **4.** usuwać ⟨usunąć⟩ **5.** zabijać ⟨-bić⟩ siekierą

ax•is ['æksɪs] *pl axes* ['æksiːz] *s* oś *f*; ***the ~ of the Earth*** oś Ziemi; ***the X-~*** oś odciętych; ***the Y-~*** oś rzędnych; ***the ≈ Powers*** HIST państwa Osi

ax•le ['æksl] *s* oś *f*, ośka *f*; ***an ~ of a wheel*** oś koła

ay(e) [aɪ] **I** *interj* (*denoting approval*) tak; ***~ ~, Captain*** tak jest, panie kapitanie **II** *s* ***the ~s*** głosujący za, głosujący na „tak"

Az•er•bai•jan [æzəbaɪ'dʒɑːn] *s* Azerbejdżan *m*

az•ure ['æʒə] **I** *adj* lazurowy **II** *s* lazur *m*

B

B & B *abbr* (=***bed and breakfast***) pensjonat *m* (oferujący pokoje ze śniadaniem)

BA [biː'eɪ] *abbr* (=***Bachelor of Arts***) *s* licencjat *m*; ***~ in history*** licencjat z historii

baa [bɑː] **I** *v/i* (*sheep*) beczeć ⟨za-⟩ **II** *s* bek *m*, beczenie *n*

bab•ble ['bæbl] **I** *v/i* **1.** bełkotać **2.** paplać; **3.** (*water*) szumieć, szemrać; ***a babbling brook*** szemrzący potok **II** *s* **1.** bełkot *m* **2.** paplanina *f* **3.** (*of baby*) gaworzenie *n* **4.** *loud voices*: gwar *m*

babe [beɪb] **I** *s* **1.** *infml* laska *f*; ***what a ~!*** ale laska! **2.** *dated* (małe) dziecko *n*, niemowlę *n*; ***a newborn ~*** niemowlę **II** *interj* kochanie, skarbie

ba•boon [bə'buːn] *s* pawian *m*

ba•by ['beɪbɪ] **1.** *s* niemowlę *n*; ***a six-week-old ~*** sześciotygodniowe niemowlę; ***~ clothes*** ubranka dla niemowląt **2.** dziecko *n*; ***a ~ boy*** chłopczyk; ***expect a ~*** spodziewać się dziecka; ***the ~ of the family*** najmłodszy członek rodziny, beniaminek **3.** (*animal*) młode *n*; ***a ~ elephant*** słoniątko **4.** ***~ carrots*** małe marchewki; **'ba•by boom** *s* wyż *m* demograficzny; **'ba•by bug•gy** *s Am* wózek *m* spacerowy; **'ba•by car•riage** *s* wózek *m* dziecięcy; **'ba•by-faced** *adj* o dziecinnej twarzy, mający dziecinną twarz

ba•by•hood ['beɪbɪhʊd] *s* niemowlęctwo *n*

ba•by•ish ['beɪbɪɪʃ] *adj* dziecinny; ***find s.th. too ~*** uważać coś za zbyt dziecinne

ba•by-mind•er ['beɪbɪmaɪndə] *s* opiekunka *f* do dziecka

ba•by-sit ['beɪbɪsɪt] **I** *v/i* opiekować ⟨za-⟩ się dzieckiem **II** *v/t* opiekować ⟨za-⟩ się; **ba•by-sit•ter** ['beɪbɪsɪtə] *s* opiekunka *f* do dziecka; **ba•by sit•ting** *s* opiekowanie *n* się dzieckiem

B

ba•by talk *s* język *m* dziecięcy
bach•e•lor ['bætʃələ] *s* **1.** kawaler *m*; ***a confirmed bachelor*** zatwardziały kawaler; ***a ~ apartment, a ~ pad*** kawalerka **2.** → ***BA***; **bach•e•lor•hood** ['bætʃələhʊd] *s* kawalerstwo *n*
ba•cil•lus [bə'sɪləs] *pl bacilli* [bə'sɪlaɪ] (*of bacteria*) laseczka *f*
back [bæk] **I** *adv* **1.** do tyłu, z powrotem; ***~ and forth*** tam i z powrotem; ***move ~*** cofnąć się; ***be ~*** wrócić **2.** przed; ***20 years ~*** przed dwudziestu laty; ***~ in 1920*** w roku 1920 **II** *s* **1.** tył *m*; ***the ~ of the head*** tył głowy; ***in the ~ of the car*** **a)** na tylnym siedzeniu **b)** w bagażniku; ***put s.th. on ~ to front*** założyć coś tył na przód **2.** plecy *pl*; ***at the ~ of*** z tyłu *G*, za *I*; ***break s.o.'s ~*** złamać komuś kręgosłup; ***behind s.o.'s ~*** *fig* za czyimiś plecami; ***be on s.o.'s ~*** *fig* wiercić komuś dziurę w brzuchu; ***have one's ~ to the wall*** być przypartym do muru; ***turn one's ~ on*** **a)** odwrócić się plecami do *G* **b)** *fig* odwrócić się od *G*, zignorować *A* **3.** *of book, hand*: grzbiet *m* **4.** *of chair*: oparcie *n* **5.** *of fabric*: lewa strona *f* **6.** SPORT obrońca *m* **III** *v/t* **1.** popierać ⟨-przeć⟩; ***~ s.o.'s choice*** poprzeć czyjś wybór; **2.** cofać ⟨-fnąć⟩; ***~ the car*** cofnąć samochód **3.** osłaniać ⟨-łonić⟩, ochraniać ⟨-ronić⟩ **4.** stawiać ⟨postawić⟩ na *A* **IV** *v/i* cofać ⟨-fnąć⟩ się **V** *adj* **1.** tylny; ***a ~ entrance*** tylne wejście **2.** zaległy; ***~ payments*** zaległe płatności **3.** stary, zalegający; ***~ papers*** stare gazety; **back away** *v/i* wycofywać ⟨-fać⟩ się; **back down** *v/i* wycofywać ⟨-fać⟩ się (***on/from*** z *G*); **back off** *v/i* **1.** odsuwać ⟨-sunąć⟩ się **2.** wycofywać ⟨-fać⟩ się (***from*** z *G*) **3.** ***~!*** daj mi spokój!; **back onto** *v/t* wychodzić na *A*; **back out** *v/i* wycofywać ⟨-fać⟩ się; ***~ of a promise*** wycofać się z obietnicy; **back up** *v/t* **1.** popierać ⟨-przeć⟩; udzielać ⟨-lić⟩ poparcia **2.** INF robić ⟨z-⟩ kopię zapasową
'back•ache *s* ból *m* pleców
back 'al•ley *s* boczna uliczka *f*
back•bench•er [bæk'bentʃə] *s członek parlamentu niepełniący ważnych funkcji państwowych ani partyjnych*
'back•bit•ing *s* obgadywanie *n*
'back•board *s* (*in basketball*) tablica *f*
'back•bone *s* **1.** kręgosłup *m*; ***to the ~*** na wskroś; ***be the ~ of*** być podporą *G* **2.** *fig* siła *f* charakteru; ***have the ~ to do sth*** mieć odwagę coś zrobić
'back-break•ing *adj* **1.** wyczerpujący **2.** morderczy
back 'burn•er *s*: ***be put on the ~*** *fig* zostać odłożonym na później
'back•chat *s* pyskowanie *n*
'back•cloth *s* THEAT prospekt *m*
'back•comb *v/t hair*: tapirować ⟨wy-⟩
'back cop•y *s magazine*: stary numer *m*
back•'date *v/t* antydatować, wpisywać ⟨-sać⟩ wcześniejszą datę na *L*; ***~ a cheque*** antydatować czek
back•door **I** *s* **1.** tylne drzwi *pl* **2.** tylne wejście *n* **II** *adj* **1.** tajemny **2.** dla wtajemniczonych
'back•drop *s* **1.** THEAT prospekt *m* **2.** *fig* tło *n*
back•er ['bækə] *s* **1.** stronnik *m*, zwolennik *m* **2.** sponsor *m*; ***a financial ~*** sponsor
back'fire *v/i* **1.** *fig* przynosić ⟨-nieść⟩ rezultat odwrotny do zamierzonego **2.** strzelać (w gaźniku)
'back for•ma•tion *s* GRAM derywacja *f* wsteczna
back•ground *s* **1.** tło *n*; ***against the ~ of*** na tle *G*; ***~ music*** tło muzyczne; ***keep in the ~*** trzymać się na uboczu **2.** ***educational ~*** wykształcenie **3.** ***social ~*** pochodzenie społeczne **4.** doświadczenie *n*; ***have a ~ in*** mieć doświadczenie w *L* **5.** kontekst *m*; ***~ information*** informacje wprowadzające
back•hand ['bækhænd] *s* SPORT bekhend *m*, backhand *m*; **back•hand•ed** [bæk'hændɪd] *adj* **1.** SPORT bekhendowy **2.** zakamuflowany **3.** *compliment*: pozorny; **back•hand•er** ['bækhændə] *s* łapówka *f*
back•ing ['bækɪŋ] *s* **1.** poparcie *n* **2.** wsparcie *n*; ***financial ~*** wsparcie finansowe; **'back•ing group** *Br*, **'back-up group** *Am s* **1.** grupa *f* akompaniująca **2.** chórek *m*
'back•lash *s* **1.** (ostry) sprzeciw *m*; ***provoke a ~*** wywołać (ostry) sprzeciw **2.** negatywna reakcja *f* (***against*** na *A*)
'back•pack *s Am* plecak *m*; **'back•pack•er** *s* podróżujący *m* z pleca-

kiem; '**back•pack•ing** *s* podróżowanie *n* z plecakiem

back•'ped•al *v/i* **1.** (*bicycle*) pedałować do tyłu **2.** wycofywać ⟨-fać⟩ się (***on*** z *G*); **~ *on a promise*** wycofać się z obietnicy

back 'seat *s* tylne siedzenie *n*; ***take a ~*** *fig* usunąć się w cień; **'back-seat 'driv•er** *s*: *pasażer pouczający kierowcę, jak powinien prowadzić samochód*

'back•side *s infml* tyłek *m*; ***sit on one's ~*** siedzieć na tyłku, zbijać bąki

'back•slash *s* INF lewy ukośnik *m*, odwrotny ukośnik *m*

back•slid•ing ['bækslaɪdɪŋ] *s* **1.** niedotrzymanie *n* obietnicy **2.** powrót *m* do złych zwyczajów

'back•space (key) *s* INF klawisz *m* Backspace, klawisz *m* kasowania poprzedniego znaku

'back•spin *s* SPORT rotacja *f* wsteczna

back•'stage I *adj* zakulisowy; **~ *negotiations*** zakulisowe negocjacje **II** *adv* za kulisami; ***go ~*** pójść za kulisy

'back•stairs *pl* tylne schody *pl*

'back street I *s* **1.** boczna uliczka *f* **2.** zaułek *m* **II** *adj* **1.** potajemny **2.** nielegalny; **~ *abortion*** pokątnie wykonany zabieg aborcji

'back•stroke *s* SPORT styl *m* grzbietowy

'back talk *s* pyskowanie *n*

'back•track *v/i* **1.** wracać ⟨wrócić⟩ tą samą drogą **2.** wycofywać ⟨-fać⟩ się (***from*** z *G*)

'back•up I *s* **1.** wsparcie *n* **2.** INF kopia *f* zapasowa **II** *adj* **1.** wspierający, wspomagający **2.** *copy*: zapasowy **3.** rezerwowy **4.** *system*: awaryjny

back•ward ['bækwəd] **I** *adj* **1.** do tyłu, w tył, wstecz; **~ *glance*** spojrzenie wstecz **2.** opóźniony (w rozwoju) **3.** zaległy **II** *adv* wstecz; **~ *and forward*** w przód i w tył

'back•wash *s fig* następstwa *pl*, reperkusje *pl*

'back•wa•ter *s* **1.** *fig* dziura *f*, prowincja *f* **2.** stojąca woda *f*

back•woods ['bækwʊdz] *pl* **1.** *fig* dziura *f*, prowincja *f* **2.** puszcza *f*

back'yard *s* **1.** *Br* podwórko *n* **2.** *Am* ogród *m* za domem

ba•con ['beɪkən] *s* bekon *m*; ***bring home the ~*** utrzymywać rodzinę, zarabiać na chleb

bac•te•ri•a [bæk'tɪərɪə] *pl* → ***bacterium***; **bac•te•ri•al** [bæk'tɪərɪəl] *adj* bakteryjny

bac•te•ri•o•log•i•cal [bæktɪərɪɒ'lɒdʒɪkl] *adj* bakteriologiczny; **bac•te•ri•ol•o•gist** [bæktɪərɪ'ɒlədʒɪst] *s* bakteriolog *m*

bac•te•ri•um [bæk'tɪərɪəm] *pl bacteria* [bæk'tɪərɪə] *s* bakteria *f*

bad [bæd] **I** (*worse*; *worst*) *adj* **1.** zły; **~ *news*** zła wiadomość **2.** kiepski; ***be ~ at*** być kiepskim w *L* **3.** szkodliwy; ***it's ~ for your health*** to niezdrowe **4.** *food*: zepsuty; ***go ~*** zepsuć się **5.** słaby; **~ *health*** słabe zdrowie **6.** *smell*: paskudny **7.** *cold*: ciężki **8.** *boy*: niegrzeczny **9.** *cheque*: bez pokrycia **II** (*worse*; *worst*) *adv* źle; ***look ~*** źle wyglądać; ***feel ~*** źle się czuć; ***feel ~ about*** czuć się nie w porządku z powodu *G*; ***not ~!*** nieźle!; ***that's too ~*** to niedobrze **III** *s* **1.** ***the ~*** zło; ***the good and the ~*** dobro i zło; ***go from ~ to worse*** pogarszać się; ***go to the ~*** zejść na złą drogę **2.** ***be 50 dollars to the ~*** mieć 50 dolarów straty

bad•die ['bædɪ], ***bad•dy*** *Br infml s* czarny charakter *m*

badge [bædʒ] *s* **1.** odznaka *f* **2.** plakietka *f* **3.** znaczek *m* **4.** identyfikator *m* **5.** naszywka *f* **6.** oznaka *f* **7.** symbol *m*

bad•ger ['bædʒə] **I** *s* borsuk *m* **II** *v/t* **1.** namawiać ⟨-mówić⟩ (***s.o. into*** kogoś na *A*) **2.** nagabywać (***about*** o *A*)

bad 'lan•guage *no pl s* wulgarny język *m*, *infml* brzydkie słowa *pl*; ***use ~*** wyrażać się wulgarnie

bad•ly ['bædlɪ] (*worse*; *worst*) *adv* **1.** źle; ***s.o. is ~ off*** komuś źle się powodzi; ***do ~ in*** nie radzić sobie w *L* **2.** *wanted*: bardzo **3.** *injured*: ciężko

bad-man•nered [bæd'mænəd] *adj* źle wychowany

bad-mouth ['bædmaʊθ] *v/i infml* **1.** krytykować ⟨s-⟩ **2.** czepiać się **3.** obgadywać ⟨-dać⟩

bad-tem•pered [bæd'tempəd] *adj*: ***be ~*** **a)** mieć zły humor **b)** mieć trudny charakter

baf•fle ['bæfl] *v/t* zbijać ⟨-bić⟩ z tropu; ***I'm ~d why*** zupełnie nie rozumiem, dlaczego

baf•fling ['bæflɪŋ] *adj* **1.** zagadkowy **2.** zbijający z tropu

bag [bæg] **I** *s* **1.** torba *f*; ***a shopping ~*** torba na zakupy; ***a ~ of bones*** *fig* skóra i kości **2.** siatka *f* **3.** torebka *f* **4.** worek *m*; ***~s under the eyes*** worki pod oczami **II** *v/t* **1.** (*a.* ***~ up***) wkładać ⟨włożyć⟩ do torby, pakować ⟨s-⟩ **2.** *infml fish, animals*: łapać ⟨z-⟩ **3.** *infml goal*: strzelać ⟨-lić⟩

ba•gel ['beɪgəl] *s* bajgel *m*

bag•gage ['bægɪdʒ] *no pl s* bagaż *m*; **'bag•gage al•low•ance** *s* dopuszczalna ilość *f* bagażu, limit *m* bagażu; **'bag•gage car** *s Am* wagon *m* bagażowy; **bag•gage check** *s* kwit *m* bagażowy; **'bag•gage claim** *s Am* odbiór *m* bagażu; **'bag•gage lock•er** *s* skrytka *f* bagażowa; **'bag-gage re•claim** *s Br* odbiór *m* bagażu; **'bag•gage room** *s* przechowalnia *f* bagażu

bag•gy ['bægɪ] *adj* **1.** *trousers*: workowaty, luźny **2.** *jumper*: luźny, rozciągnięty

bag•pip•er ['bægpaɪpə] *s* dudziarz *m*; **bag•pipes** ['bægpaɪps] *pl* dudy *pl*

bag•snatch•er ['bægsnætʃə] *s* złodziej *m* torebek

baguette [bæ'get] *s* bagietka *f*

Ba•ha•mas [bə'hɑːməz] *pl*: ***the ~*** Wyspy Bahama, Bahamy

Bah•rain [bɑː'reɪn] *s* Bahrajn *m*

bail [beɪl] **I** *s* **1.** kaucja *f*; ***be released on ~*** zostać zwolnionym za kaucją; ***go*** (*a.* ***stand***) ***~ for*** wpłacić kaucję za *A* **2.** zwolnienie *n* za kaucją **II** *v/t* zwalniać ⟨zwolnić⟩ za kaucją; **bail out I** *v/t* **1.** wyciągać ⟨-gnąć⟩ z kłopotów **2.** wpłacać ⟨-cić⟩ kaucję za *A* **3.** *water*: wybierać ⟨-brać⟩ **II** *v/i* **1.** wyskakiwać ⟨-skoczyć⟩ z samolotu (ze spadochronem) **2.** (*in emergency*) katapultować się

bail•iff ['beɪlɪf] *s Br* **1.** komornik *m* **2.** zarządca *m* majątku

bait [beɪt] **I** *s* **1.** przynęta *f*; ***take the ~*** *a. fig* połknąć przynętę **2.** wabik *m* **II** *v/t* **1.** zakładać ⟨założyć⟩ przynętę na *A* **2.** umieszczać ⟨umieścić⟩ przynętę w *L* **3.** drażnić

bake [beɪk] **I** *v/t* **1.** piec ⟨u-⟩; ***~ a cake*** upiec ciasto **2.** *clay*: wypalać ⟨-lić⟩ **II** *v/i* **1.** piec ⟨u-⟩ się **2.** *fig* smażyć się; ***~ in the sun*** smażyć się na słońcu

baked 'beans *pl* fasola *f* w sosie pomidorowym; **baked po•'ta•to** *s* pieczony ziemniak *m*

bak•er ['beɪkə] *s* piekarz *m*; ***at the ~'s*** u piekarza, w piekarni; ***a ~'s dozen*** trzynaście; **bak•er•y** ['beɪkərɪ] *s* piekarnia *f*

bak•ing hot ['beɪkɪŋhɒt] *adj* bardzo gorący

'bak•ing pow•der *s* proszek *m* do pieczenia; **'bak•ing sheet**, **'bak•ing tray** *s* blacha *f* do pieczenia

bal•ance ['bæləns] **I** *s* **1.** równowaga *f*; ***the ~ of power*** równowaga sił; ***the ~ of s.o.'s mind*** równowaga umysłowa; ***keep one's ~*** zachowywać równowagę; ***lose one's ~*** stracić równowagę; ***strike a ~ between*** zachowywać właściwie proporcje pomiędzy *I* **2.** waga *f* **3.** *fig* szala *f* **4.** ECON saldo *n* **5.** ECON bilans *m* **6.** balans *m* **II** *v/i* **1.** utrzymywać ⟨-mać⟩ równowagę; ***~ on*** balansować na *L* **2.** bilansować ⟨z⟩ się, wyrównywać ⟨-nać⟩ się **III** *v/t* **1.** balansować *I* **2.** utrzymywać ⟨-mać⟩ w równowadze **3.** ECON bilansować ⟨z-⟩; ***~ the books*** zbilansować stan ksiąg rachunkowych **4.** *fig* zachowywać ⟨-chować⟩ równowagę (***between*** między *I*)

bal•anced ['bælənst] *adj* **1.** zrównoważony **2.** w stanie równowagi

bal•ance of 'pay•ments *s* bilans *m* płatniczy; **bal•ance of 'trade** *s* bilans *m* handlowy; **'bal•ance sheet** *s* bilans *m*, zestawienie *n* bilansowe

bal•co•ny ['bælkənɪ] *s* balkon *m*

bald [bɔːld] *adj* łysy; ***go ~*** wyłysieć; **bald 'ea•gle** *s* bielik *m* amerykański

bal•der•dash ['bɔːldədæʃ] *s* brednie *pl*, bzdury *pl*

bald-head•ed [bɔːld'hedɪd] *adj* łysy; **bald•ing** ['bɔːldɪŋ] *adj* łysiejący; **bald-y** ['bɔːldɪ] *s infml* łysy

bale [beɪl] **I** *s* bela *f*; ***in ~s*** w belach **II** *v/t* **1.** *hay*: belować **2.** → *Br* ***bail out I.3.***

Bal•e•ar•ics [bælɪ'ærɪks] *pl* Baleary *pl*, Wyspy *pl* Balearskie

balk [bɔːk] *v/i* **1.** wzdragać ⟨-rygnąć⟩ się; ***~ at the prospect of*** wzdragać się na myśl o *L* **2.** zapierać ⟨-przeć⟩ się

Bal•kan ['bɔːlkən] *adj* bałkański; **the Bal•kans** ['bɔːlkənz] *pl* Bałkany *pl*

ball[1] [bɔːl] *s* **1.** piłka *f*; ***the ~ is in your court*** *fig* twoja kolej, twój ruch; ***be on the ~*** *fig* znać się na rzeczy; ***play ~*** *fig* współdziałać; ***set*** (*a.* ***start***) ***the ~ rolling*** *fig* wykazać inicjatywę **2.** kula *f* **3.** kłębek *m*; → ***balls***

ball[2] [~] *s* bal; ***have a ~*** *infml* świetnie się bawić

bal•lad ['bæləd] *s* ballada

ball-and-'sock•et joint *s ANAT* staw *m* panewkowy

bal•last ['bæləst] *s* balast *m*

bal•let [bæ'leɪ] *s* balet *m*; ***modern ~*** balet nowoczesny; ***~ shoes*** baletki; **'bal•let danc•er** *s* **1.** tancerz *m* baletowy **2.** tancerka *f* baletowa, baletnica *f*

ball game *s Am* mecz *m* baseballa; ***it's a*** (***whole***) ***different ~*** to zupełnie inna sytuacja

bal•lis•tic mis•sile [bəlɪstɪk'mɪsaɪl] *s* pocisk *m* balistyczny; **bal•lis•tics** [bə'lɪstɪks] *s* balistyka *f*

bal•loon [bə'luːn] **I** *s* **1.** balon *m*; ***fly in a ~*** latać balonem **2.** (*in cartoon*) dymek *m* **II** *v/i* **1.** wydymać ⟨-dąć⟩ się (jak balon) **2.** ***go ~ing*** latać balonem; **bal•loon•ist** [bə'luːnɪst] *s* baloniarz *m*

bal•lot ['bælət] **I** *s* **1.** głosowanie *n*; ***secret ~*** głosowanie tajne **2.** karta *f* do głosowania **3.** ***the ~*** (oddane) głosy **II** *v/i* głosować ⟨za-⟩ (***for*** na *A*); **'bal•lot box** *s* urna *f* wyborcza; **'bal•lot pa•per** *s* karta *f* do głosowania; **'bal•lot rig•ging** *s* fałszowanie *n* wyników głosowania

'ball•park *s Am* boisko *n* do gry w baseball; **'ball•park fig•ure** *s Am* wartość *f* orientacyjna; **'ball•point** (**pen**) *s* długopis *m* kulkowy; **'ball•room** *s* sala *f* balowa; **ball•room 'danc•ing** *s* taniec *m* towarzyski

balls [bɔːlz] *pl vulg* (*testicles*) jaja *pl*; ***have ~s*** *infml* mieć jaja, mieć odwagę; ***it takes a lot of ~*** to wymaga odwagi; **'balls-up** *s infml* klapa *f*, klęska *f*

balm [bɑːm] *s* balsam *m*; **balm•y** ['bɑːmɪ] *adj* **1.** balsamiczny **2.** *evening*: ciepły, przyjemny **3.** *Br infml* szurnięty

Bal•tic ['bɔːltɪk] **I** *s* ***the ~*** Bałtyk *m* **II** *adj* bałtycki; ***the ~ Sea*** Morze Bałtyckie

bal•us•trade [bælə'streɪd] *s* balustrada *f*

bam•boo [bæm'buː] *s* bambus *m*

bam•boo•zle [bæm'buːzl] *v/t infml* **1.** wykiwać, wrabiać ⟨wrobić⟩ **2.** wprowadzać ⟨-dzić⟩ w błąd

ban [bæn] **I** *v/t* zakazywać ⟨-zać⟩; ***~ s.o. from doing s.th.*** zabronić komuś coś robić **II** *s* zakaz *m* (***on*** *G*); ***an import ~*** zakaz importu

ba•nal [bə'ɑːl] *adj* banalny; **ba•nal•i•ty** [bə'nɑːlɪtɪ] *s* **1.** banalność *f* **2.** banał *m*

ba•na•na [bə'nɑːnə] *s* **1.** banan *m* **2.** ***be ~s*** *infml* być stukniętym; ***go ~s*** *infml* ześwirować; **ba•'na•na re•pub•lic** *s* republika *f* bananowa; **ba•'na•na tree** *s* bananowiec *m*

band[1] [bænd] **I** *s* **1.** grupa *f* **2.** banda *f* **3.** *MUS* zespół *m*; ***a rock ~*** zespół rockowy **II** *v/i* ***~ together*** jednoczyć siły

band[2] [~] *s* **1.** opaska *f* **2.** pasek *m* **3.** obręcz *f* **4.** pasmo *n*; ***radio ~*** pasmo radiowe **5.** przedział *m*; ***an age ~*** przedział wiekowy **6.** zakres *m*

ban•dage ['bændɪdʒ] **I** *s* bandaż *m* **II** *v/t* bandażować ⟨za-, o-⟩

Band-Aid® *s Am* plaster *m* opatrunkowy

ban•dan•a [bæn'dænə] *s* (*scarf*) bandanka *f*

ban•dit ['bændɪt] *s* bandyta *m*

'band•lead•er *s MUS* lider *m* zespołu; **band•mas•ter** *s MUS* kapelmistrz *m*; **'band•stand** *s* estrada *f*; **band•wag•on** *s*: ***climb on the ~*** *fig* przyłączyć się, wykorzystać koniunkturę; **'band•width** *s* **1.** szerokość *f* pasma **2.** *INF* przepustowość *f* łącza

ban•dy[1] ['bændɪ] *v/t* **1.** ***~ words with*** *dated* kłócić się z *I* **2.** ***be bandied about*** (*a.* ***around***) (*of rumours*) krążyć

ban•dy[2] [~] *adj* krzywy, wygięty na zewnątrz; ***~ legs*** krzywe nogi; **ban•dy-leg•ged** ['bændɪlegd] *adj*: ***be ~*** mieć krzywe nogi

bane [beɪn] *s* zmora *f*, nieszczęście *n*

bang [bæŋ] **I** *v/t* **1.** walić ⟨-lnąć⟩; ***~ one's fist on the table*** walnąć pięścią w stół **2.** uderzać ⟨-rzyć⟩;

B

~ **the table with a spoon** uderzać łyżką w stół **3.** zatrzaskiwać ⟨-snąć⟩; ~ **the door** trzasnąć drzwiami **4.** uderzać ⟨-rzyć⟩; ~ **one's hand against** (*a.* **on**) uderzyć się głową o *A* **5.** rzucać ⟨-cić⟩; ~ **the money down on the table** rzucić pieniądze na stół **6.** *vulg* pieprzyć się z *I* **II** *v/i* **1.** walić ⟨-lnąć⟩; ~ **on the door** walić w drzwi **2.** trzaskać ⟨-snąć⟩ **3.** ~ **into** wpaść na *A* **III** *s* **1.** huk *m*; **shut a door with a ~** zamknąć drzwi z hukiem **2.** trzask *m* **3.** łomot *m* **4.** hałas *m* **5.** uderzenie *n*, cios *m* (**on** w *A*) **IV** *adv* **1.** dokładnie, prosto; ~ **in the eye** prosto w oko **2.** **go** ~ *infml* wybuchnąć **V** *interj* bum!

Ban•gla•desh [bæŋglə'deʃ] *s* Bangladesz *m*

ban•gle ['bæŋgl] *s* bransoleta *f*

bangs [bæŋz] *pl Am* grzywka *f*

ban•ish ['bænɪʃ] *v/t* **1.** wygnać **2.** zsyłać ⟨zesłać⟩ **3.** pozbywać ⟨-być⟩ się **4.** odpędzać ⟨-dzić⟩; ~ **gloomy thoughts** odpędzić ponure myśli; **ban•ish•ment** ['bænɪʃmənt] *s* **1.** wygnanie *n* **2.** banicja *f*

ban•is•ter ['bænɪstə] *s* poręcz *f* (schodów)

bank[1] [bæŋk] **I** *s* bank *m*; **break** (**keep**) **the** ~ rozbić (trzymać) bank; **a blood** ~ bank krwi **II** *v/t* wpłacać ⟨-cić⟩ do banku, deponować ⟨z-⟩ w banku **III** *v/i* **1.** ~ **with** mieć konto w *L* **2.** liczyć (**on** na *A*)

bank[2] [~] **I** *s* **1.** *of river*: brzeg *m* **2.** skarpa *f* **3.** nasyp *m* **4.** łacha *f* **5.** *of clouds*: wał *m*, kłęby *pl* **6.** **a ~ of snow** zaspa, zwał śniegu **II** *v/t* obwałowywać ⟨-łować⟩ **III** *v/i* **1.** (*of plane*) kłaść ⟨położyć⟩ się na skrzydło **2.** ~ **up** piętrzyć ⟨s-⟩ się, gromadzić ⟨z-⟩ się

bank•a•ble ['bæŋkəbl] *adj film star*: kasowy

'**bank ac•count** *s* konto *n* bankowe, rachunek *m* bankowy; '**bank balance** *s* saldo *n* rachunku; '**bank bill** *Am* → **banknote**; '**bank card** *s* karta *f* bankowa; '**bank charg•es** *pl* opłaty *pl* bankowe; '**bank clerk** *s* urzędnik *m* bankowy; '**bank de•tails** *pl* dane *pl* rachunku; '**bank draft** *s* przekaz *m* bankowy

bank•er ['bæŋkə] *s* **1.** bankier *m* **2.** bankowiec *m*; '**bank•er's card** *s* karta *f* czekowa

bank 'hol•i•day *s Br dzień ustawowo wolny od pracy*

bank•ing ['bæŋkɪŋ] *s* bankowość *f*; '**bank loan** *s* kredyt *m*; '**bank•note** *s Br* banknot *m*; '**bank raid** *s* napad *m* na bank; '**bank rate** *s* stopa *f* procentowa kredytu; '**bank rob•ber** *s* bandyta *m* napadający na banki; '**bank rob•ber•y** *s* napad *m* na bank; '**bank•roll** *s* fundusze *pl*

bank•rupt ['bæŋkrʌpt] **I** *s* bankrut *m*; **the ~'s estate** (*a.* **property**) masa upadłościowa **II** *adj* zbankrutowany; **go** ~ zbankrutować; **declare a company** ~ ogłaszać upadłość firmy; **bank•rupt•cy** ['bæŋkrʌpsɪ] *s* bankructwo *n*

ban•ner ['bænə] *s* **1.** sztandar *m* **2.** transparent *m*; **ban•ner 'headline** *s* tytuł *m* na całą stronę

ban•quet ['bæŋkwɪt] **I** *s* **1.** bankiet *m* **2.** uczta *f* **II** *v/i* **1.** bankietować **2.** ucztować; '**ban•quet•ing hall** sala *f* bankietowa

ban•ter ['bæntə] **I** *v/i* żartować, przekomarzać się **II** *s* żarty *pl*, przekomarzanie *n* się

bap•tism ['bæptɪzm] *s* chrzest *m*; **bap•tis•mal font** [bæp'tɪzmlfɔnt] *s* chrzcielnica *f*

Bap•tist ['bæptɪst] *s* baptysta *m*

bap•tise [bæp'taɪz] *Br*, **bap•tize** *Am* *v/t* chrzcić ⟨o-⟩

bar[1] [bɑ:] **I** *s* **1.** pręt *m*; **~s** kraty; **behind ~s** za kratkami **2.** drążek *m* **3.** poprzeczka *f* **4.** sztaba *f* **5.** rygiel *m*, zasuwa *f* **6.** *of soap*: kostka *f* **7.** **a chocolate ~** **a)** tabliczka czekolady **b)** baton **8.** *of gold*: sztabka *f* **9.** pasek *m* **10.** bar *m* **11.** bufet *m* **12.** *MUS* takt *m* **13.** **the** ≈ *Br* adwokatura, palestra **II** *v/t* **1.** zagradzać ⟨-grodzić⟩ **2.** ryglować ⟨za-⟩ **3.** zabraniać ⟨-ronić⟩; ~ **s.o. from doing s.th.** zabronić komuś robić coś **4.** uniemożliwiać ⟨-wić⟩ (**s.o. from** komuś *A*)

bar[2] [~] *prep* z wyjątkiem *G*, oprócz *G*, wyjąwszy *A*; ~ **none** bez wyjątku

barb [bɑ:b] *s* **1.** zadzior *m*, wąs *m* **2.** (*on fence*) kolec *m* **3.** *fig* docinek *m*

bar•bar•i•an [bɑː'beərɪən] *s* barbarzyńca *m*; **bar•ba•ric** [bɑː'bærɪk] *adj* barbarzyński; **bar•bar•ism** ['bɑːbərɪzm] *s* barbarzyństwo *n*: **bar•bar•i•ty** [bɑː'bærɪtɪ] *s* barbarzyństwo *n*; **bar•ba•rous** ['bɑːbərəs] *adj* barbarzyński

bar•be•cue ['bɑːbɪkjuː] **I** *s* grill *m* **II** *v/t* grillować, piec ⟨u-⟩ na grillu

barbed [bɑːbd] *adj* **1.** z zadziorem, z wąsem; **~ wire** drut kolczasty **2.** kąśliwy

bar•bell ['bɑːbel] *s* sztanga *f*

bar•ber ['bɑːbə] *s* fryzjer *m* męski; ***the ~'s, a ~ shop*** zakład fryzjerski, *infml* fryzjer

'**bar chart** *s* wykres *m* słupkowy, histogram *m*; '**bar code** *s* kod *m* kreskowy, kod *m* paskowy; **bar-code 'reader** *s* czytnik *m* kodów kreskowych

bare [beə] **I** *adj* **1.** nagi; ***on one's ~ feet*** bosy; ***in one's ~ skin*** nagi; ***~ facts*** *fig* nagie fakty **2.** goły **3.** obnażony **4.** odkryty; ***lay s.th. ~*** ujawnić coś, wyjawić coś **5.** zaledwie, jedynie; ***earn a ~ living*** ledwie wiązać koniec z końcem **6.** ***the ~ thought*** sama myśl **II** *v/t* **1.** obnażać ⟨-żyć⟩; ***~ one's teeth*** wyszczerzyć kły, obnażyć kły **2.** odkrywać ⟨-ryć⟩ **3.** *fig* odsłaniać ⟨-łonić⟩; '**bare•back** *adv* na oklep; '**bare•faced** *adj* **1.** bezczelny **2.** bezwstydny; '**bare•foot I** *adj* bosy **II** *adv* boso; **bare•head•ed** [beə'hedɪd] **I** *adj* z gołą głową **II** *adv* z gołą głową

bare•ly ['beəlɪ] *adv* ledwie, ledwo

barf [bɑːf] *Am infml* **I** *v/i* rzygać **II** *s* rzygi *pl*

bar•gain ['bɑːgɪn] **I** *s* **1.** okazja *f*; ***it's a ~*** to okazja **2.** umowa *f*; ***strike a ~*** zawierać umowę, dobić targu **3.** ***into the ~*** *Br*, ***in the ~*** *Am* na dodatek, w dodatku **II** *v/i* **1.** negocjować ⟨wy-⟩ (***over/about*** *A*) **2.** targować się (***for*** o *A*) **3.** oczekiwać, spodziewać się (***for*** *G*); **bar•gain 'base•ment** *s* dział *m* z towarami przecenionymi; '**bar•gain hunt•er** *s* łowca *m* okazji; **bar•gain 'of•fer** *s* okazja *f*; '**bar•gain price** *s* okazyjna cena *f*; **bar•gain•ing** ['bɑːgɪnɪŋ] *s* negocjacje *pl*, targi *pl*

barge [bɑːdʒ] *s* barka *f*; ***I wouldn't touch it with a ~pole*** *fig* nie chcę mieć z tym nic wspólnego; **barge in** *v/i* **1.** wtrącać ⟨-cić⟩ się **2.** wtargnąć

bar•i•tone ['bærɪtəʊn] *s* baryton *m*

bark[1] [bɑːk] **I** *s* kora *f* **II** *v/t* **1.** korować, odzierać ⟨odrzeć⟩ z kory **2.** ***~ one's knee*** zedrzeć sobie skórę z kolana

bark[2] [~] **I** *v/i* szczekać ⟨-knąć⟩ (***at*** na *A*); ***be ~ing up the wrong tree*** *fig* mylić się, być w błędzie **II** *s* szczekanie *n*; ***his ~ is worse than his bite*** nie jest taki groźny, jak się wydaje

bar•ley ['bɑːlɪ] *s* jęczmień *m*; '**bar•ley sug•ar** *s* twardy cukierek *m*

'**barmaid** *s* barmanka *f*

'**barman** *s* barman *m*

bar mitz•vah [bɑː'mɪtzvə] *s* bar micwa *f*

barm•y ['bɑːmɪ] *adj Br infml* stuknięty; ***go ~*** ześwirować

barn [bɑːn] *s* stodoła *f*

'**barn dance** *s* zabawa *f* z tańcami ludowymi; '**barn owl** *s* sowa *f* płomykówka

ba•rom•e•ter [bə'rɒmɪtə] *s* barometr *m*

bar•on ['bærən] *s* **1.** baron *m* **2.** magnat *m*; **bar•on•ess** ['bærənes] *s* baronowa *f*

Ba•roque [bə'rɒk] **I** *s* barok *m* **II** *adj* barokowy

bar•racks ['bærəks] *pl* koszary *pl*

bar•rel ['bærəl] **I** *s* **1.** beczka *f* **2.** baryłka *f* **3.** lufa *f* **II** *v/t* beczkować ⟨za-⟩; ***~led beer*** piwo z beczki; '**bar•rel or•gan** *s* katarynka *f*

bar•ri•cade [bærɪ'keɪd] **I** *s* barykada *f*; ***go to the ~s*** *fig* iść na barykady **II** *v/t* barykadować ⟨za-⟩

bar•ri•er ['bærɪə] *s* **1.** bariera *f*; ***sound ~*** bariera dźwieku **2.** barierka *f* **3.** szlaban *m* **4.** bramka *f* **5.** przeszkoda *f*; **bar•ri•er 'cream** *s* krem *m* ochronny

bar•ring ['bɑːrɪŋ] *prep* wyjąwszy *A*; ***~ a miracle*** jeśli nie zdarzy się cud

bar•ris•ter ['bærɪstə] *s Br* adwokat *m*, obrońca *m*

'**bar staff** *s* obsługa *f* baru; '**bar ten•der** *s Am* barman *m*

ba•salt ['bæsɔːlt] *s* bazalt *m*

base [beɪs] **I** *s* **1.** podstawa *f* **2.** podkład *m* **3.** baza *f* **4.** *fig* punkt *m* wyjścia **II** *v/t* opierać (***on*** na *L*); ***the***

film is ~d on a novel film oparty jest na powieści **III** *adj* **1.** podły **2.** nikczemny **3.** pośledni **4.** *metal*: nieszlachetny

'base•ball *s* baseball *m*, bejsbol *m*; ***a ~ bat*** kij bejsbolowy; ***a ~ cap*** czapka bejsbolówka; ***a ~ player*** bejsbolista; **'base•board** *s* listwa *f* przypodłogowa; **base•less** ['beɪslɪs] *adj* bezpodstawny, nieuzasadniony; **'base•line** *s* **1.** (*in tennis*) linia *f* końcowa **2.** punkt *m* odniesienia, podstawa *f*; **base•ment** ['beɪsmənt] *s* suterena *f*; **'base rate** *s* stopa *f* bazowa

bash [bæʃ] *infml* **I** *v/t* **1.** walić ⟨-lnąć⟩ **2.** wyrżnąć **3.** trzasnąć **4.** *infml* zjechać **II** *s* **1.** walnięcie *n*; ***give s.o. a ~ on the nose*** walnąć kogoś w nos **2.** balanga *f* **3.** ***have a ~*** spróbować (***at*** *G*); **bash•ful** ['bæʃfʊl] *adj* nieśmiały, wstydliwy

ba•sic ['beɪsɪk] *adj* podstawowy, zasadniczy; ***~ fee*** opłata podstawowa; ***~ salary*** wynagrodzenie zasadnicze; **ba•sics** ['beɪsɪks] *pl* podstawy *pl*; **ba•sic•al•ly** ['beɪsɪklɪ] *adv* w zasadzie, zasadniczo

bas•il ['bæzɪl] *s* bazylia *f*

ba•sin ['beɪsn] *s* **1.** *Br* umywalka *f* **2.** miednica *f* **3.** miska *f*, misa *f* **4.** dorzecze *n* **5.** kotlina *f*

ba•sis ['beɪsɪs] *pl -ses* ['beɪsiːz] *s* podstawa *f*; ***on the ~ of*** na podstawie *G*; ***a ~ of discussion*** punkt wyjścia do dyskusji; ***on a voluntary ~*** na zasadzie dobrowolności; ***on a regular ~*** regularnie

bask [bɑːsk] *v/i*: ***~ in the sun*** wygrzewać się na słońcu

bas•ket ['bɑːskɪt] *s* **1.** kosz *m* **2.** koszyk *m*; **'bas•ket•ball** *s* koszykówka *f*; ***a ~ player*** koszykarz

Basque [bæsk] **I** *adj* baskijski **II** *s* Bask *m*; **'Basque Coun•try** *s* Kraj *m* Basków

bass[1] [beɪs] **I** *s* **1.** bas *m* **2.** kontrabas *m* **3.** niskie tony *pl*, basy *pl* **II** *adj* basowy

bass[2] [bæs] *s* okoń *m*; ***sea ~*** strzępiel

bas•set hound ['bæsɪthaʊnd] *s* (*dog*) basset *m*

bass 'gui•tar *s* gitara *f* basowa; **bass 'gui•tar•ist** *s* gitarzysta *m* basowy

bassist ['beɪsɪst] *s* basista *m*

bas•tard ['bɑːstəd] **I** *s* **1.** bękart *m* **2.** *vulg* sukinsyn *m*; ***a ~ of a headache*** cholerny ból głowy **II** *adj child*: nieślubny

bat[1] [bæt] *s* nietoperz *m*; (***as***) ***blind as a ~*** ślepy jak kret; ***have ~s in the belfry*** mieć nie po kolei w głowie

bat[2] [~] **I** *s* (*in cricket, baseball*) kij *m*; ***off one's own ~*** *fig* z własnej inicjatywy **II** *v/i* odbijać ⟨-bić⟩ (piłkę)

bat[3] [~] *v/t*: ***without ~ting an eyelid*** bez mrugnięcia okiem

batch [bæθ] **I** *s* **1.** grupa *f* **2.** porcja *f* **3.** *of goods*: partia *f* **4.** seria *f* **5.** plik *m* **II** *v/t* dzielić ⟨po-⟩ na partie; **'batch pro•cess•ing** *s* INF przetwarzanie *n* wsadowe

bath [bæθ] **I** *s* **1.** kąpiel *f*; ***have*** (*a.* ***take***) ***a ~*** wziąć kąpiel **2.** wanna *f*; ***run a ~*** napuścić wodę do wanny **3.** *Am* łazienka *f* **4.** łaźnia *f* **II** *v/i Br* kąpać ⟨wy-⟩ się, brać ⟨wziąć⟩ kąpiel **III** *v/t Br* kąpać ⟨wy-⟩

bathe [beɪð] **I** *v/i* **1.** brać ⟨wziąć⟩ kąpiel, kąpać ⟨wy-⟩ się **2.** *dated* pływać ⟨po-⟩ **II** *v/t* **1.** kąpać ⟨wy-⟩; ***~d in sunlight*** skąpany w słońcu **2.** przemywać ⟨-myć⟩ **III** *s* ***have*** (*a.* ***take***) ***a ~*** popływać

'bath•ing cap *s* czepek *m* kąpielowy; **'bath•ing suit** *s* kostium *m* kąpielowy; **'bath•ing trunks** *pl* kąpielówki *pl*; **'bath•mat** *s* mata *f* łazienkowa; **'bath•robe** *s* szlafrok *m* kąpielowy; **'bath•room** *s* łazienka *f*; **'bath•sheet,** ***'bath•towel*** *s* ręcznik *m* kąpielowy; **'bath•tub** *s* wanna *f*

bat•on [bæ'tɒn] *s* **1.** pałka *f* (policyjna) **2.** MUS batuta *f* **3.** pałeczka *f* (sztafetowa) **4.** buława *f*

bat•tal•i•on [bə'tælɪən] *s* batalion *m*

bat•ter[1] ['bætə] **I** *v/t* **1.** bić ⟨po-⟩ **2.** maltretować **3.** walić w *A* **4.** niszczyć ⟨z-⟩ **II** *v/i* **1.** walić; ***~ at the door*** walić do drzwi, dobijać się do drzwi **2.** tłuc **3.** ***~ down*** *door*: wyważyć

bat•ter[2] [~] *s* (*in cricket, baseball*) pałkarz *m*

bat•ter[3] [~] *s* rzadkie ciasto *n*; ***fish in ~*** ryba w cieście

bat•tered ['bætəd] *adj* **1.** maltretowany **2.** zniszczony

battering ram ['bætərɪŋræm] *s* taran *m*

B

bat•ter•y ['bætərɪ] *s* **1.** bateria *f* **2.** AUTO akumulator *m* '**bat•ter•y charg•er** *s* ładowarka *f* do akumulatorów; '**bat•ter•y life** *s* żywotność *f* baterii; **bat•ter•y-'op•e•rat•ed** *adj* na baterie

bat•tle ['bætl] **I** *s* **1.** bitwa *f* **2.** walka *f* (***against*** z *I*, ***for*** o *A*) **II** *adj* **1.** bitewny; ***a ~ field***, ***a ~ ground*** pole bitwy **2.** bojowy **3.** wojenny **III** *v/i* walczyć (***with*** z *I*, ***against*** przeciw *D*); '**bat•tle•axe** *Br*, **bat•tle•ax** *Am s* topór *m*; '**bat•tle•ship** *s* okręt *m* wojenny, pancernik *m*

bat•ty ['bætɪ] *adj infml* stuknięty

bawl [bɔːl] *v/i* **1.** drzeć się, wydzierać się (***at*** na *A*); ***~ for help*** wołać o pomoc; **bawl out** *v/t* wymyślać ⟨z-⟩

bay[1] [beɪ] *s* zatoka *f*

bay[2] [~] *s* wykusz *m*; ***a ~ window*** okno wykuszowe

bay[3] [~] *s* laur *m*; ***a ~ leaf*** listek laurowy; ***a ~ tree*** drzewo laurowe, wawrzyn

bay[4] [~] **I** *v/i* wyć **II** *s* wycie *n*; ***be*** (*a.* ***stand***) ***at ~*** być osaczonym, znaleźć się w matni; ***hold*** (*a.* ***keep***) ***s.o. at ~*** trzymać kogoś na dystans

bay•o•net ['beɪənɪt] *s* bagnet *m*

ba•zaar [bə'zɑː] *s* **1.** bazar *m* **2.** kiermasz *m* dobroczynny

BC [biː'siː] *abbr* (=***before Christ***) p.n.e.

be [biː] **I** (*was*; *been*) *v/i* **1.** być; ***it's me*** to ja; ***to be or not to be*** być albo nie być; ***have you ever been to London?*** czy byłeś kiedyś w Londynie?; ***this book is mine*** ta książka jest moja; ***I'll be an engineer*** będę inżynierem, zostanę inżynierem **2.** być, pochodzić (***from*** z *G*) **3.** kosztować; ***how much are these gloves?*** ile kosztują te rękawiczki? **4.** ***she is in for a surprise*** czeka ją niespodzianka; ***you're in for it*** *infml* oberwie ci się **II** (*was*; *been*) *v aux* **1.** (*continuous tenses*) ***he is reading*** on czyta **2.** (*passive voice*) ***I was cheated*** zostałem oszukany **3.** (*duty*) ***you are to tell him*** masz mu powiedzieć **4.** (*future*) ***I am leaving tomorrow*** jutro wyjeżdżam

beach [biːtʃ] **I** *s* plaża *f* **II** *adj* plażowy; ***~ ball*** piłka plażowa; ***~ wear*** strój plażowy **III** *v/t* wyciągać ⟨-gnąć⟩ na brzeg; '**beach buggy** *s pojazd terenowy do jazdy po piasku*

bea•con ['biːkən] *s* światło *n* nawigacyjne

bead [biːd] **I** *s* **1.** koralik *m* **2.** paciorek *m* **3.** kropla *f* **II** *v/t* obszywać ⟨-szyć⟩ koralikami; **bead•ing** ['biːdɪŋ] *s* koraliki *pl*, paciorki *pl*; **beads** [biːdz] *pl* **1.** korale *pl* **2.** różaniec *m*; ***say*** (*a.* ***tell***) ***one's ~s*** odmawiać różaniec; **bead•y** ['biːdɪ] *adj*: ***~ eyes*** przenikliwe spojrzenie; ***keep a ~ eye on*** *Br* mieć oko na *A*, uważnie się przyglądać *D*

beak [biːk] *s* **1.** dziób *m* **2.** dzióbek *m*

beam [biːm] **I** *s* **1.** belka *f* **2.** dźwigar *m* **3.** *of light*: snop *m*; ***a ~ of hope*** promyk nadziei **4.** *of rays*: wiązka *f* **5.** równoważnia *f* **6.** promienny uśmiech *m* **7.** ***be off ~*** **a)** być błędnym **b)** (*ship*) zejść z kursu **II** *v/t* nadawać ⟨-dać⟩, przesyłać ⟨-słać⟩ **III** *v/i* rozpromieniać ⟨-nić⟩ się; ***~ing with joy*** promieniejąc z radości

bean [biːn] *s* fasola *f*, fasolka *f*; ***be full of ~s*** *fig* tryskać energią; ***spill the ~s*** *infml* wygadać się; **coffee bean** ziarno *n* kawy; '**bean•bag** *s* **1.** (*for throwing*) woreczek *m* (wypełniony ziarnkami grochu) **2.** (*seat*) poducha *f* do siedzenia; '**bean curd** *s* COOK tofu *n*; '**bean•pole** *s* (*person*) *infml* tyczka *f*; '**bean•sprouts** *pl* COOK kiełki *pl*

bear[1] [beə] **I** *s* **1.** niedźwiedź *m*; ***a ~ hug*** niedźwiedzi uścisk; ***be like a ~ with a sore head*** być złym jak osa **2.** (*stock exchange*) gracz *m* na zniżkę **II** *v/i* (*stock exchange*) grać na zniżkę

bear[2] [~] **I** (*bore*; *borne*) *v/t* **1.** nieść **2.** *name*: nosić **3.** *responsibility*: ponosić ⟨-nieść⟩ **4.** (*tolerate*) znosić ⟨znieść⟩ **5.** wytrzymywać ⟨-mać⟩; ***not ~ comparison with*** nie wytrzymywać porównania z *I* **6.** rodzić ⟨u-⟩ **7.** *grudge*: żywić **8.** *company*: dotrzymywać ⟨-mać⟩ **9.** ***~ resemblance to*** być podobnym do *G* **10.** ***~ oneself*** nosić się, zachowywać się **II** (*bore*; *borne*) *v/i* ***~*** (***to the***) ***left*** skręcić w lewo; **bear down on** *v/i* **1.** *Br* ruszać ⟨-szyć⟩ ku *D* **2.** *Am* przyciskać ⟨-snąć⟩ **3.** *Am* opierać ⟨oprzeć⟩ się o *A*; **bear out** *v/i* **1.** potwierdzać ⟨-dzić⟩ **2.** popierać ⟨-przeć⟩

bear•a•ble ['beərəbl] *adj* znośny, do zniesienia
beard [bɪəd] **I** *s* **1.** broda *f* **2.** zarost *m* **II** *v/t* **~ *the lion in his den*** *fig* wejść do jaskini lwa, urągać niebezpieczeństwu; **beard•ed** ['bɪədɪd] *adj* brodaty
bear•er ['beərə] *s* **1.** doręczyciel *m* **2.** właściciel *m*, posiadacz *m* **3.** okaziciel *m*
bear•ing ['beərɪŋ] *s* **1.** wpływ *m* (***on*** na *A*) **2.** związek *m* (***on*** z *I*) **3.** postawa *f* **4.** zachowanie *n* **5.** pozycja *f*, położenie *n*; ***take one's ~s*** *fig* zorientować się w sytuacji; ***lose one's ~s*** *fig* stracić orientację **6.** *TECH* łożysko *n*
beast [biːst] *s* **1.** zwierzę *n*; ***a ~ of burden*** zwierzę juczne; ***a ~ of prey*** zwierzę drapieżne **2.** *fig* bestia *f*, potwór *m*; **beastly** [biːstlɪ] *adj* **1.** wredny **2.** wstrętny **3.** paskudny
beat [biːt] **I** (*beat*; *beaten*) *v/t* **1.** bić ⟨z-⟩ **2.** wygrywać ⟨-rać⟩ z *I* **3.** pobić, pokonywać ⟨-nać⟩; ***that ~s everything!*** to szczyt wszystkiego! **4.** *carpet*: trzepać ⟨wy-⟩ **5.** *metal*: kuć ⟨wy-⟩ **6.** *eggs*: ubijać ⟨-bić⟩ **7.** ***that ~s me*** nie mogę tego zrozumieć, nie pojmuję **8.** ***~ it!*** spływaj! **9.** ***he beat me to it*** ubiegł mnie **II** (*beat*; *beaten*) *v/i* **1.** bić, uderzać ⟨-rzyć⟩; ***~ at the door*** dobijać się do drzwi; ***her heart is still ~ing*** jej serce wciąż bije **2.** bębnić **3.** ***not ~ about*** (*a.* ***around***) ***the bush*** nie owijać w bawełnę **III** *s* **1.** *heart*: bicie *n* **2.** *MUS* rytm *m*; ***off the ~*** nie w rytm **3.** rewir *m* **4.** obchód *m*; ***be on one's ~*** robić obchód **IV** *adj infml* wykończony, zmordowany; **beat out** *v/t* **1.** *rhythm*: wybijać **2.** *fire*: tłumić ⟨s-⟩; **beat up** *v/t* **1.** bić ⟨po-⟩ **2.** ubijać ⟨-bić⟩
beat•en ['biːtən] **I** *v Past Participle* → **beat II** *adj* **1.** *earth*: ubity; ***off the ~ track*** z dala od cywilizacji **2.** wyklepany; ***~ gold*** złota folia; **beater** ['biːtə] *s* trzepaczka *f*
be•a•ti•fi•ca•tion [bɪætɪfɪ'keɪʃn] *s* beatyfikacja *f*; **be•a•ti•fy** [bɪ'ætɪfaɪ] *v/t* beatyfikować
beat•ing ['biːtɪŋ] *s* **1.** lanie *n*; ***give s.o. a ~*** pobić kogoś, sprawić komuś lanie **2.** *heart*: bicie *n* **3.** *fig* (sromotna) porażka *f*
'**beat-up** *adj* poobijany
beau•ti•cian [bjuː'tɪʃn] *s* kosmetyczka *f*
beau•ti•ful ['bjuːtəfl] *adj* piękny; **beau•ti•ful•ly** ['bjuːtɪflɪ] *adv* **1.** pięknie **2.** doskonale
beau•ti•fy ['bjuːtɪfaɪ] *v/t* upiększać ⟨-szyć⟩
beaut•y ['bjuːtɪ] *s* **1.** piękno *n* **2.** uroda *f* **3.** piękność *f* **4.** cudo *n*; '**beaut•y com•pe•ti•tion**, '***beaut•y con•test*** *s* konkurs *m* piękności; '**beaut•y parlour** *Br*, '***beaut•y par•lor*** *Am s* salon *m* piękności; '**beaut•y queen** *s* królowa *f* piękności; '**beaut•y salon**, '***beaut•y shop*** *Am* → ***beauty parlour***; '**beaut•y sleep** *s*: ***get one's ~*** wyspać się; '**beaut•y spot** *s* **1.** (*on skin*) pieprzyk *m* **2.** (*fake*) muszka *f* **3.** (*landscape*) atrakcja *f* krajobrazowa
bea•ver ['biːvə] *s* bóbr *m*; **beaver away** *v/i infml* pracować pilnie (***at*** nad *I*)
be•came [bɪ'keɪm] *Past Simple* → **become**
be•cause [bɪ'kɒz] *conj* ponieważ, dlatego, że; ***~ of*** z powodu *G*
beck [bek] *s*: ***be at s.o.'s ~ and call*** być na czyjeś każde zawołanie
beck•on ['bekən] **I** *v/i* skinąć (***to*** na *A*) **II** *v/t* skinąć na *A*
be•come [bɪ'kʌm] **I** (*became*; *become*) *v/i* stawać ⟨stać⟩ się; ***~ more difficult*** stawać się trudniejszym; ***~ angry*** zezłościć się; ***what has ~ of him?*** co się z nim stało? **II** (*became*; *become*) *v/t* **1.** zostawać ⟨-tać⟩; ***~ queen*** zostać królową **2.** pasować; ***this colour ~s you*** w tym kolorze ci do twarzy; **be•com•ing** [bɪ'kʌmɪŋ] *adj* **1.** stosowny **2.** właściwy **3.** twarzowy
bed [bed] *s* **1.** łóżko *n*; ***go to ~*** iść do łóżka; ***go to ~ with*** pójść do łóżka z *I*; ***make the ~*** posłać łóżko; ***put s.o. to ~*** położyć kogoś do łóżka, ułożyć kogoś do snu **2.** nocleg *m* **3.** grządka *f* **4.** rabata *f* **5.** klomb *m* **6.** *GEOL* złoże *n*, pokład *m* **7.** dno *n*; ***ocean ~*** dno oceanu; **bed and 'breakfast** *s* **1.** nocleg *m* ze śniadaniem **2.** pensjonat *m* oferujący pokoje ze śniadaniem
'**bed•bug** *s* pluskwa *f*; '**bed•clothes** *pl* pościel *f*; '**bed•cov•er** *s* **1.** narzuta *f* **2.** kołdra *f*

bed•ding ['bedɪŋ] *s* **1.** posłanie *n* **2.** pościel *f*
be•deck [bɪ'dek] *v/t* **1.** ozdabiać ⟨-dobić⟩ **2.** dekorować ⟨u-⟩
be•dev•il [bɪ'devl] *v/t* nękać
'**bed•lin•en** *s* pościel *f*; '**bed•pan** *s MED* basen *m*; '**bed•post** *s* kolumna *m* łóżka
'**bed rest** *s* leżenie *n* w łóżku; '**bed•rid•den** *adj* przykuty do łóżka; '**bed•room** *s* sypialnia *f*; '**bed•side** *s* brzeg *m* łóżka; ***sit at s.o.'s ~*** siedzieć przy czyimś łóżku; ***a ~ lamp*** lampka nocna; ***a ~ table*** stolik przy łóżku; ***~ manner*** podejście do pacjenta; '**bed-sit**, ***bed-'sit•ter***, ***bed-'sit•ting room*** *s Br* kawalerka *f*; '**bed•spread** *s* narzuta *f*, kapa *f*; '**bed•stead** *s* rama *f* łóżka; '**bed•time** *s*: ***it's ~*** pora spać; ***at ~*** przed zaśnięciem; ***a ~ story*** bajka na dobranoc; ***~ reading*** lektura do poduszki
bee [biː] *s* pszczoła *f*; **(*as*) *busy as a ~*** bardzo zajęty, zabiegany
beech [biːtʃ] *s* buk *m*; '**beech•nuts** *pl* bukiew *f*, buczyna *f*; '**beech•wood** *s* (*wood*) buczyna *f*
beef [biːf] **I** *s* wołowina *f* **II** *v/i infml* gderać, jęczeć; **beef up** *v/t infml* **1.** poprawiać ⟨-wić⟩ **2.** wzmacniać ⟨-mocnić⟩ **3.** uatrakcyjniać ⟨-nić⟩; '**beef•bur•ger** *s* hamburger *m* z wołowiny; **beef•eater** *s Br* strażnik *m* londyńskiej twierdzy Tower; '**beef•steak** *s* befsztyk *m*; **beef•y** ['biːfɪ] *adj infml* **1.** muskularny **2.** potężny
'**bee•hive** *s* ul *m*; '**bee•line** *s*: ***to make a ~ for*** ruszyć prosto do *G*
been [bɪn] *Past Participle* → **be**
beep [biːp] **I** *v/i* pikać ⟨-knąć⟩ **II** *s* (*sound*) piknięcie *n*; **beep•er** ['biːpə] *s* biper *m*
beer [bɪə] *s* piwo *n*; ***a ~ garden*** ogródek piwny; '**beer•mat** *s* podstawka *f* pod kufel; **beer•y** ['bɪərɪ] *adj* piwny
'**bees•wax** *s* wosk *m* pszczeli
beet [biːt] *s* **1.** burak *m*; ***sugar ~*** burak cukrowy **2.** burak *m* pastewny **3.** *Am* burak *m* ćwikłowy
bee•tle ['biːtl] *s* chrząszcz *m*, żuk *m*
beet•root ['biːtruːt] *s Br* burak *m* ćwikłowy
befall [bɪ'fɔːl] (*befell; befallen*) *v/t lit* przytrafiać ⟨-fić⟩ się, spotykać ⟨-tkać⟩
be•fore [bɪ'fɔː] **I** *prep* przed *I*; ***~ my eyes*** na moich oczach; ***~ witnesses*** przy świadkach; ***the week ~ last*** dwa tygodnie temu; ***~ long*** wkrótce, niedługo; ***go ~*** poprzedzać **II** *adv* wcześniej; ***the year ~*** rok wcześniej, w poprzednim roku **III** *conj* zanim; ***do it ~ you forget*** zrób to, zanim zapomnisz
be•fore•hand [bɪ'fɔːhænd] *adv* wcześniej, z wyprzedzeniem
be•friend [bɪ'frend] *v/t* zaprzyjaźniać ⟨-nić⟩ się z *I*
beg [beg] **I** *v/t* **1.** błagać ⟨wy-⟩ **2.** prosić ⟨po-⟩; ***~ s.o.'s pardon*** prosić kogoś o wybaczenie; ***I ~ your pardon*** przepraszam **II** *v/i* **1.** błagać (***for*** o *A*) **2.** żebrać (***for*** o *A*); ***go ~ging*** iść na żebry, żebrać
began [bɪ'gæn] *Past Simple* → **begin**
beg•gar ['begə] *s* żebrak *m*; ***a lucky ~*** *infml* farciarz; **beggarly** ['begəlɪ] *adj* **1.** żebraczy **2.** nędzny; **beggary** ['begərɪ] *s* żebractwo *n*
be•gin [bɪ'gɪn] **I** (*began*; *begun*) *v/t* **1.** zaczynać ⟨-cząć⟩ **2.** rozpoczynać ⟨-cząć⟩ **II** (*began*; *begun*) *v/i* **1.** zaczynać ⟨-cząć⟩ się; ***~ with a vowel*** zaczynać się od samogłoski; ***I ~ to feel dizzy*** zaczyna mi się kręcić w głowie; ***to ~ with*** na początek, po pierwsze **2.** rozpoczynać ⟨-cząć⟩ się
be•gin•ner [bɪ'gɪnə] *s* **1.** początkujący *m* **2.** nowicjusz *m*; **be•gin•ning** [bɪ'gɪnɪŋ] *s* początek *m*; ***from the*** (***very***) ***~*** od (samego) początku
be•grudge [bɪ'grʌdʒ] *v/t* **1.** żałować ⟨po-⟩ **2.** zazdrościć ⟨po-⟩
be•gun [bɪ'gʌn] *Past Participle* → **begin**
be•half [bɪ'hɑːf] *s*: ***on ~ of*** w imieniu *G*; ***in ~ of*** *Am* na rzecz *G*
be•have [bɪ'heɪv] **I** *v/i* **1.** zachowywać ⟨-chować⟩ się **2.** postępować ⟨-tąpić⟩ **3.** (*machine*) działać, funkcjonować **II** *v/t* ***~ oneself*** być grzecznym; ***~ yourself!*** zachowuj się!
be•hav•iour [bɪ'heɪvɪə] *Br*, ***be•hav•ior*** *Am s* **1.** zachowanie *n* **2.** postępowanie *n*; **be•'hav•iour•al** [bɪ'heɪvɪərəl] *Br*, ***be•'hav•ior•al*** *Am adj* **1.** beha-

B

wioralny **2.** *~ disorders* zaburzenia zachowania; **be•'hav•iour•ism** [bɪ'heɪvɪərɪzm] *Br*, ***be•'hav•ior•ism*** *Am* *s* behawioryzm *m*; **be•'hav•iour•ist** [bɪ'heɪvɪərɪst] *Br*, ***be•'hav•ior•ist*** *Am* **I** *s* behawiorysta *m* **II** *adj* behawiorystyczny

be•head [bɪ'hed] *v/t* ścinać ⟨ściąć⟩ głowę

be•hind [bɪ'haɪnd] **I** *prep* za *I* **II** *adv* **1.** z tyłu **2.** do tyłu; ***look ~*** spojrzeć za siebie **III** *adj* ***be ~*** być spóźnionym; ***be ~ with one's rent*** zalegać z czynszem **IV** *s infml* tyłek *m*, pupa *f*

be•'hind•hand *adj*: ***be ~ with*** zalegać z *I*, mieć zaległości w *L*

be•hold [bɪ'həʊld] (*beheld*; *beheld*) *v/t lit* ujrzeć; ***~!*** spójrz!; **be•hold•er** [bɪ'həʊldə] *s lit* obserwator *m*; ***beauty is in the eye of the ~*** nie to ładne, co ładne, ale co się komu podoba

beige [beɪʒ] **I** *adj* beżowy **II** *s* beż *m*

Bei•jing [beɪ'ʒɪŋ] *s* Pekin *m*

be•ing ['biːɪŋ] *s* **1.** istnienie *n*, byt *m*; ***call into ~*** powołać do życia; ***come into ~*** powstać **2.** istota *f*, stworzenie *n*; ***a human ~*** człowiek; → ***be***

be•lat•ed [bɪ'leɪtɪd] *adj* spóźniony

belch [beltʃ] **I** *v/i* **1.** czkać ⟨-knąć⟩ **2.** odbijać ⟨-bić⟩ się **II** *v/t* (*a.* ***~ out***, ***~ forth***) buchać **III** *s* **1.** czknięcie *n* **2.** *of smoke, flames*: kłąb *m*

Bel•gian ['beldʒən] **I** *adj* bejgijski **II** *s* Belg *m*, Belgijka *f*; **Bel•gium** ['beldʒəm] *s* Belgia *f*

be•lie [bɪ'laɪ] *v/t* **1.** przeczyć ⟨za-⟩ **2.** zadawać ⟨-dać⟩ kłam

be•lief [bɪ'liːf] *s* **1.** wiara *f*; ***beyond ~*** nie do wiary **2.** przekonanie *n*, opinia *f*; ***contrary to popular ~*** wbrew obiegowej opinii **3.** przeświadczenie *n*; **be•liev•a•ble** [bɪ'liːvəbl] *adj* wiarygodny; **be•lieve** [bɪ'liːv] **I** *v/t* wierzyć ⟨u-⟩; ***I don't ~ you*** nie wierzę ci; ***I don't ~ it's possible*** nie wierzę, że to możliwe **II** *v/i* **1.** wierzyć ⟨u-⟩; ***~ in ghosts*** wierzyć w duchy **2.** uważać, sądzić; ***I ~ so*** tak sądzę; ***would you ~ it!*** wyobrażasz to sobie?; ***he is ~d to be rich*** podobno jest bogaty; **be•liev•er** [bɪ'liːvə] *s* **1.** wyznawca *m*, wierzący *m* **2.** zwolennik *m*; ***be a great ~ in*** być wielkim zwolennikiem *G*

be•lit•tle [bɪ'lɪtl] *v/t* umniejszać ⟨-szyć⟩

Be•lize [be'liːz] *s* Belize *n*

bell [bel] *s* **1.** dzwon *m*; ***that rings a ~*** coś mi to przypomina **2.** dzwonek *m* **3.** dzwon *m* nurkowy; **'bell•boy**, ***'bell•hop*** *s Am* goniec *m* hotelowy; **'bell cap•tain** *s Am* portier *m* hotelowy

bel•low ['beləʊ] **I** *v/i* **1.** ryczeć ⟨ryknąć⟩ **2.** *fig* grzmieć ⟨za-⟩ **II** *v/t orders*: wykrzykiwać ⟨-rzyczeć⟩; **bel•lows** ['beləʊz] *pl* miech *m*, miechy *pl*

bel•ly ['belɪ] **I** *s* **1.** brzuch *m* **2.** żołądek *m* **II** (*a.* ***~ out***) *v/i* wydymać ⟨-dąć⟩ się; **'bel•ly•ache I** *s* ból *m* brzucha **II** *v/i* kwękać, stękać; **'bel•ly but•ton** *s* pępek *m*; **'bel•ly danc•er** *s* tancerka *f* brzucha

be•long [bɪ'lɒŋ] *v/i* należeć (***to*** do *G*); **be•long•ings** [bɪ'lɒŋɪŋz] *pl* rzeczy *pl*, dobytek *m*

be•loved [bɪ'lʌvɪd] **I** *adj* ukochany **II** *s* ukochany *m*, ukochana *f*

be•low [bɪ'ləʊ] **I** *prep* pod *I*, poniżej *G* **II** *adv* poniżej, pod spodem

belt [belt] **I** *s* **1.** pas *m*; ***fasten one's ~*** zapiąć pasy; ***a hit below the ~*** cios poniżej pasa **2.** pasek *m* **3.** strefa *f* **II** *v/t* **1.** przewiązywać ⟨-zać⟩ paskiem **2.** walić ⟨-lnąć⟩; **belt up** *v/i* **1.** *Br* zapinać ⟨-piąć⟩ pas **2.** *infml* zamykać ⟨-mknąć⟩ się; ***~!*** zamknij się!

'belt•way *s* obwodnica *f*

be•mused [bɪ'mjuːzd] *adj* zdezorientowany

bench [bentʃ] *s* **1.** ławka *f* **2.** ława *f* **3.** warsztat *m*, stół *m* do pracy **4.** ***the ~*** sąd, sędzia; **'bench•mark** *s fig* punkt *m* odniesienia

bend [bend] **I** *s* **1.** zakręt *m*; ***drive s.o. round the ~*** *fig* doprowadzać kogoś do szału **2.** zagięcie *n* **II** (*bent*; *bent*) *v/t* **1.** zginać ⟨zgiąć⟩ **2.** wyginać ⟨-giąć⟩ **3.** *head*: schylać ⟨-lić⟩ **4.** *rules*: naginać ⟨-giąć⟩ **III** (*bent*; *bent*) *v/i* **1.** zginać ⟨zgiąć⟩ się **2.** schylać ⟨-lić⟩ się **3.** pochylać ⟨-lić⟩ się **4.** uginać ⟨ugiąć⟩ się (***to*** przed *I*) **5.** (*road*) zakręcać ⟨-cić⟩; **bend down** *v/i* **1.** schylać ⟨-lić⟩ się **2.** kłaniać ⟨ukłonić⟩ się

be•neath [bɪ'niːθ] **I** *adv* poniżej, pod spodem **II** *prep* pod *I*, poniżej *G*; ***it's ~ me*** to poniżej mojej godności

ben•e•dic•tion [benɪ'dɪkʃn] *s* błogosławieństwo *n*
ben•e•fac•tor ['benɪfæktə] *s* **1.** dobroczyńca *m* **2.** ofiarodawca *m*
be•nef•i•cence [bɪ'nefɪsns] *s* dobroczynność *f*, wspaniałomyślność *f*; **be•nef•i•cent** [bɪ'nefɪsənt] *adj* **1.** dobroczynny **2.** szczodry
ben•e•fi•cial [benɪ'fɪʃl] *adj* **1.** korzystny **2.** dobroczynny
ben•e•fi•ci•a•ry [benɪ'fɪʃərɪ] *s* beneficjent *m*
ben•e•fit ['benɪfɪt] **I** *s* **1.** korzyść *f*, pożytek *m*; ***be of ~ to*** być korzystnym dla *G*; ***for the ~ of*** na korzyść *G* **2.** zasiłek *m* **3.** ***a ~ concert*** koncert na cele dobroczynne **II** *v/t* **1.** być korzystnym dla *G* **2.** przynosić ⟨-nieść⟩ korzyść **III** *v/i* korzystać ⟨s-⟩ (***from/by*** z *G*)
Be•ne•lux coun•tries ['benɪlʌkskʌntrɪəs] *pl* kraje *pl* Beneluksu
be•nev•o•lence [bɪ'nevələns] *s* **1.** życzliwość *f* **2.** dobrotliwość *f*, dobroć *f* **3.** hojność *f*; **be•nev•o•lent** [bɪ'nevələnt] *adj* **1.** życzliwy **2.** dobrotliwy, dobry **3.** hojny
be•nign [bɪ'naɪn] *adj* **1.** dobroduszny **2.** *climate*, *tumour*: łagodny
bent [bent] **I** *v Past Simple and Past Participle* → ***bend*** **II** *adj* **1.** zgięty, wygięty **2.** ***he's ~ on getting it done*** zawziął się, że to zrobi **III** *s fig* żyłka *f*
ben•zene ['benziːn] *s* benzen *m*
ben•zine ['benziːn] *s* (*oil fraction*) benzyna *f*
berate [bɪ'reɪt] *v/t* łajać ⟨z-⟩, zwymyślać
Ber•mu•da [bə'mjuːdə] *s* Bermudy *pl*; ***the ~ triangle*** trójkąt bermudzki; **Ber•'mu•da shorts** *pl* bermudy *pl*
ber•ry ['berɪ] *s* jagoda *f*
ber•serk [bɜːs'zɜːk] *adj*: ***go ~*** wpaść w szał, wariować
berth [bɜːθ] **I** *s* **1.** koja *f* **2.** miejsce *n* do spania **3.** kuszetka *f* **4.** miejsce *n* postoju statku **5.** ***give s.o. a wide ~*** *fig* omijać kogoś szerokim łukiem **II** *v/i* cumować ⟨za-⟩
be•seech [bɪ'siːtʃ] (*beseeched*/*besought*) *v/t* błagać ⟨u-⟩; **be•seech•ing** [bɪ'siːtʃɪŋ] *adj* błagalny; **be•seech•ing•ly** [bɪ'siːtʃɪŋlɪ] *adv* błagalnie
be•side [bɪ'saɪd] *prep* **1.** obok *G* **2.** w porównaniu z *I* **3.** ***be ~ oneself with rage*** nie posiadać się ze złości
be•sides [bɪ'saɪdz] **I** *adv* poza tym, oprócz tego **II** *prep* poza *I*, oprócz *G*
be•siege [bɪ'siːdʒ] *v/t* **1.** *city*: oblegać **2.** otaczać ⟨otoczyć⟩ **3.** *with letters*, *questions*: zasypywać ⟨-pać⟩
be•sought [bɪ'sɔːt] *Past Simple and Past Participle* → ***beseech***
best [best] **I** *adj superl* → ***good*** najlepszy; ***the ~ part of*** większa część *G* **II** *adv superl* → ***well***[2] najlepiej; ***you had ~ go*** najlepiej już idź; ***as ~ they could*** najlepiej, jak potrafili **III** *s* ***the ~*** to, co najlepsze; ***I'll do my ~*** zrobię, co w mojej mocy; ***make the ~ of*** jak najlepiej wykorzystać *A*; ***all the ~*** wszystkiego najlepszego!; ***be at one's ~*** (*of sportsman*) być w szczytowej formie; **best be'fore date** *s* data *f* przydatności do spożycia
bes•tial ['bestiəl] *adj* bestialski; **bes•ti•al•i•ty** [bestɪ'ælətɪ] *s* **1.** sodomia *f* **2.** bestialstwo *n*
best 'man *s* drużba *m*
be•stow [bɪ'stəʊ] *v/t* **1.** *title*: nadawać ⟨-dać⟩ (***on*** *D*) **2.** *friendship*, *smile*: obdarzać ⟨-rzyć⟩ (***on*** *D*)
best 'sell•er *s* bestseller *m*; **'best-sell•ing** *adj* bestsellerowy
bet [bet] **I** (*bet*; *bet*) *v/i* **1.** zakładać ⟨założyć⟩ się **2.** ***you ~!*** żebyś wiedział!; ***I ~!*** **a)** nie dziwię się **b)** akurat! **II** (*bet*; *bet*) *v/t* **1.** zakładać ⟨założyć⟩ się z *I*; ***I'll ~ you $10 that*** założę się o 10 dolarów, że; ***you can ~ your bottom dollar that*** możesz być pewien, że **2.** stawiać ⟨postawić⟩ (***on*** na *A*) **III** *s* **1.** zakład *m*; ***have*** (*a.* ***make***) ***a ~*** zakładać się; ***my ~ is that*** założę się, że; ***it's a safe ~ that*** to pewne jak w banku, że **2.** ***your best ~ is to take the car*** najlepiej weź samochód
be•tray [bɪ'treɪ] *v/t* **1.** zdradzać ⟨-dzić⟩ **2.** *trust*: zawodzić ⟨-wieść⟩; **be•tray•al** [bɪ'treɪəl] *s* zdrada *f*
be•trothed [bɪ'trəʊðd] *adj lit* zaręczony
bet•ter ['betə] **I** *adj comp* → ***good*** lepszy; ***I am ~*** czuję się lepiej; ***get ~*** poprawić się; ***the patient was getting better*** pacjent czuł się coraz lepiej **II** *adv comp* → ***well*** lepiej; ***think ~***

B

of it! przemyśl to jeszcze!; *you'd ~ go!* lepiej już idź **III** *s* **for ~ or for worse** na dobre i złe; ***get the ~ of*** wziąć górę nad *I* **I** *v/t* **1.** poprawiać ⟨-wić⟩ **2.** przebijać ⟨-bić⟩; **bet•ter•ment** ['betəmənt] *s* **1.** poprawa *f* **2.** wzrost *m* wartości; **bet•ter 'off** *adj* **1.** lepiej sytuowany **2.** zamożniejszy

bet•ting ['betɪŋ] *s* zakłady *pl*; **'bet•ting shop** *s Br* punkt *m* przyjmowania zakładów, kolektura *f*

be•tween [bɪ'twiːn] **I** *prep* między *I*, pomiędzy *I*; ***~ you and me*** tak między nami; ***we had only $5 ~ us*** mieliśmy razem tylko 5 dolarów **II** *adv* ***in ~*** pośrodku

bev•er•age ['bevərɪdʒ] *s* napój *m*

be•ware [bɪ'weə] *v/i* strzec się, wystrzegać się; ***~ of the dog!*** uwaga, zły pies!; ***~ of pickpockets!*** uwaga na kieszonkowców!

be•wil•der [bɪ'wɪldə] *v/t* dezorientować ⟨z-⟩; **be•wil•der•ing** [bɪ'wɪldərɪŋ] *adj* **1.** dezorientujący **2.** zbijający z tropu; **be•wil•der•ment** [bɪ'wɪldərmənt] *s* konsternacja *f*

be•witch [bɪ'wɪtʃ] *v/t* **1.** oczarowywać ⟨-rować⟩ **2.** urzekać ⟨urzec⟩ **3.** zaczarowywać ⟨-rować⟩; **bewitching** *adj* [bɪ'wɪtʃɪŋ] **1.** czarujący **2.** urzekający

be•yond [bɪ'jɒnd] **I** *prep* poza *L*, za *L*, po *L*; ***that is ~ me*** to mnie przerasta; ***it's ~ repair*** tego nie da się naprawić **II** *adv* dalej

bi•an•nu•al [baɪ'ænjʊəl] *adj* odbywający się dwa razy do roku; **bi•an•nu•al•ly** [baɪ'ænjʊəlɪ] *adv* dwa razy do roku

bi•as ['baɪəs] **I** *s* **1.** uprzedzenia *pl*; ***free from ~*** nieuprzedzony, bez uprzedzeń **2.** stronniczość *f*, tendencyjność *f* **3.** nastawienie *n* **II** *v/t* **1.** uprzedzać ⟨-dzić⟩ (***against*** do *G*) **2.** nastawiać ⟨-wić⟩; ***~ in favour of*** nastawiać pozytywnie do *G*; ***~ against*** nastawiać negatywnie do *G*; **bi•as(s)ed** ['baɪəst] *adj* **1.** stronniczy, tendencyjny **2.** uprzedzony (***against*** do *G*)

Bi•ble ['baɪbl] *s* Biblia *f*; **bib•li•cal** ['bɪblɪkl] *adj* biblijny

bib•li•o•graph•i•cal [bɪblɪəʊ'græfɪkl] *adj* bibliograficzny; **bib•li•og•ra•phy** [bɪblɪ'ɒgrəfɪ] *s* bibliografia *f*

bib•li•o•phile ['bɪblɪəfaɪl] *s* bibliofil *m*

bick•er ['bɪkə] *v/i* **1.** sprzeczać ⟨po-⟩ się; **bick•er•ing** ['bɪkərɪŋ] *s* sprzeczki *pl*

bi•cy•cle ['baɪsɪkl] **I** *s* rower *m*; ***a ~ path*** ścieżka rowerowa; ***a ~ pump*** pompka rowerowa **II** *v/i* jeździć na rowerze, jechać ⟨po-⟩ na rowerze

bid[1] [bɪd] (*bade*/*bid*; *bidden*) *v/t*: ***~ s.o. good morning*** (***farewell***) witać (żegnać) się z kimś

bid[2] [~] **I** *s* **1.** oferta *f*; ***the highest ~*** najwyższa oferowana cena **2.** próba *f*; ***a ~ for power*** próba przejęcia władzy; ***make a ~ for power*** podjąć próbę przejęcia władzy **II** (*bid*; *bid*) *v/t* oferować ⟨za-⟩ **III** (*bid*; *bid*) *v/i* **1.** licytować **2.** stawać ⟨stanąć⟩ do przetargu **3.** ubiegać się (***for*** o *A*) **4.** starać się; ***~ for power*** próbować przejąć władzę; **bid•der** ['bɪdə] *s* oferent *m*; ***the highest ~*** osoba oferująca najwyższą stawkę; **bid•ding** ['bɪdɪŋ] *s* **1.** licytacja *f* **2.** przetarg *m*

bide [baɪd] *v/t*: ***~ one's time*** czekać na właściwy moment

big [bɪg] **I** *adj* **1.** duży; ***the ~gest house*** największy dom; ***earn ~ money*** zarabiać duże pieniądze; ***a ~ eater*** żarłok; ***be too ~ for one's boots*** zadzierać nosa **2.** *moment*, *decision*, *fan*: wielki **3.** *plans*: wielki, ambitny **4.** starszy; ***the ~ sister*** starsza siostra **5.** znaczny, ważny **6.** obfity; ***a ~ meal*** obfity posiłek **7.** zarozumiały **8.** ***that's very ~ of you*** *iron* to bardzo szlachetne z twojej strony **9.** *infml* popularny **II** *adv* ***talk ~*** mądrzyć się; ***think ~*** snuć ambitne plany

big•a•mist ['bɪgəmɪst] *s* bigamista *m*; **big•a•mous** ['bɪgəməs] *adj* bigamiczny; **big•a•my** ['bɪgəmɪ] *s* bigamia *f*

big 'bang *s* ASTR Wielki Wybuch *m*; **big 'dip•per** *s* (*in funfair*) *Br* kolejka *f* górska; ***the Big Dipper*** ASTR *Am* Wielki Wóz; **'big•head** *s* bufon *m*, zarozumialec *m*; **big-'head•ed** *adj* przemądrzały; **big-'heart•ed** *adj* wielkoduszny; **'big mouth** *s*: ***he has***

a ~ *infml* wszystko wypaple, nie umie trzymać gęby na kłódkę; **big 'name** *s* **1.** (*person*) sława *f* **2.** znane nazwisko *n*

big•ot ['bɪgət] *s* **1.** bigot *m* **2.** fanatyk *m*; **big•ot•ed** ['bɪgətɪd] *adj* **1.** bigoteryjny **2.** fanatyczny **3.** nietolerancyjny; **big•ot•ry** ['bɪgətrɪ] *s* **1.** bigoteria *f* **2.** fanatyzm *m*

big 'screen *s* (*movie*) duży ekran *m*; **'big shot** *s infml* gruba ryba *f*; **'big time** *infml* **I** *s* ***the ~*** sława *f*, szczyty *pl* sławy **II** *adj* **1.** u szczytu sławy **2.** na wielką skalę **big 'toe** *s* ANAT paluch *m*, duży palec *m* u nogi; **big 'top** *s* namiot *m* cyrkowy; **'big•wig** *s infml* gruba ryba *f*; **big 'words** *pl* **1.** trudne słowa *pl*, uczone słowa *pl* **2.** wielkie słowa *pl*

bike [baɪk] **I** *s* **1.** rower *m* **2.** motor *m* **II** *v/i* **1.** jeździć na rowerze, jechać ⟨po-⟩ na rowerze **2.** jeździć na motorze, jechać ⟨po-⟩ na motorze

bik•er ['baɪkə] *s* **1.** rowerzysta *m* **2.** motocyklista *m*

bi•lat•er•al [baɪ'lætərəl] *adj* dwustronny, bilateralny

bil•ber•ry ['bɪlbərɪ] *s* czarna borówka *f*, czarna jagoda *f*

bile [baɪl] *s* **1.** MED żółć *f* **2.** *fig* gorycz *f*

bi•lin•gual [baɪ'lɪŋgwəl] *adj* dwujęzyczny, bilingwalny

bill [bɪl] **I** *s* **1.** rachunek *m* **2.** *Am* banknot *m* **3.** dziób *m* **4.** projekt *m* ustawy **5.** ***~ of exchange*** weksel **6.** THEAT program *m*; ***be on the ~*** być w programie, występować **7.** plakat *m*, afisz *m* **8.** ***fit the ~*** być odpowiednim, nadawać się **II** *v/t* **1.** wystawiać ⟨-wić⟩ rachunek (***for*** za *A*) **2.** ogłaszać ⟨-łosić⟩ **3.** reklamować ⟨za-⟩; **'bill•board** *s* billboard *m*, tablica *f* reklamowa

bil•let ['bɪlɪt] **I** *s* kwatera *f* (wojskowa) **II** *v/t* kwaterować ⟨za-⟩

billiard ['bɪljəd] *adj* bilardowy; ***a ~ ball*** bila; ***a ~ cue*** kij bilardowy; **bil•liards** ['bɪljədz] *s* bilard *m*

bil•ling ['bɪlɪŋ] *s* **1.** miejsce *n* na afiszu **2.** fakturowanie *n*

bil•lion ['bɪljən] *s* **1** miliard *m* **2.** *Br dated* bilion *m*

bim•bo ['bɪmbəʊ] *s infml* lalka

bi•month•ly [baɪ'mʌnθlɪ] **I** *adj* odbywający się co dwa miesiące **II** *adv* co dwa miesiące

bin [bɪn] *s* **1.** pojemnik *m* **2.** *Br* pojemnik *m* na śmieci

bi•na•ry ['baɪnərɪ] *adj* dwójkowy, binarny

bind [baɪnd] **I** (*bound*; *bound*) *v/t* **1.** wiązać ⟨z-, przy-⟩; ***~ s.th. together*** związać coś **2.** *wound*: przewiązywać ⟨-zać⟩ **3.** *book*: oprawiać ⟨-wić⟩ **4.** zobowiązywać ⟨-zać⟩ **II** (*bound*; *bound*) *v/i* związywać ⟨-zać⟩, twardnieć ⟨s-⟩; **bind•er** ['baɪndə] *s* **1.** segregator *m* **2.** introligator *m*; **bind•ing** ['baɪndɪŋ] **I** *adj* **1.** wiążący; ***legally ~*** prawnie wiążący **2.** obowiązujący **II** *s* **1.** oprawa *f* **2.** (*on ski*) wiązanie *n*

bi•noc•u•lars [bɪ'nɒkjʊləz] *pl*: (***a pair of***) ***~*** lornetka

bi•o•chem•i•cal [baɪəʊ'kemɪkl] *adj* biochemiczny; **bi•o•chem•ist** [baɪəʊ'kemɪst] *s* biochemik *m*; **bi•o•chem•is•try** [baɪəʊ'kemɪstrɪ] *s* biochemia *f*

bi•o•en•gi•neer•ing [baɪəʊendʒɪ'nɪərɪŋ] *s* bioinżynieria *f*

bi•og•ra•pher [baɪ'ɒgrəfə] *s* biograf *m*; **bi•o•graph•i•cal** [baɪə'græfɪkl] *adj* biograficzny; **bi•og•ra•phy** [baɪ'ɒgrəfɪ] *s* biografia *f*

bi•o•haz•ard ['baɪəʊhæzərd] *s* zagrożenie *n* biologiczne

bi•o•log•i•cal [baɪə'lɒdʒɪkl] *adj* biologiczny; **bi•ol•o•gist** [baɪə'ɒlədʒɪst] *s* biolog *m*; **bi•ol•o•gy** [baɪə'ɒlədʒɪ] *s* biologia *f*

bi•o•pic ['baɪəʊpɪk] *s infml* film *m* biograficzny

bi•op•sy ['baɪɒpsɪ] *s* biopsja *f*

bi•o•rhythm ['baɪəʊrɪðm] *s* biorytm *m*

bi•o•sphere ['baɪəsfɪə] *s* biosfera *f*

bi•o•tech•nol•o•gy [baɪəʊtek'nɒlədʒɪ] *s* biotechnologia *f*

birch [bɜːtʃ] *s* brzoza *f*

bird [bɜːd] *s* **1.** ptak *m*; ***a ~ in the hand is worth two in the bush*** lepszy wróbel w garści niż gołąb na dachu; ***tell a child about the ~s and the bees*** uświadomić dziecko; ***give s.o. the ~*** **a)** *Br* wygwizdać kogoś **b)** *Am* pokazać komuś środkowy palec **2.** (*person*) gość *m*; ***a queer ~*** dziwny gość **3.** (*girl*) *Br infml* kociak *m*; **'bird•brain** *s* (*person*) ptasi móżdżek *m*;

B

'bird•cage *s* klatka *f* dla ptaków; **bird of 'passage** *s* ptak *m* wędrowny; **bird of 'prey** *s* ptak *m* drapieżny

bird•ie ['bɜːdɪ] *s* **1.** ptaszek *m* **2.** (*in badminton*) lotka *f*

'bird sanc•tu•a•ry *s* **1.** ostoja *f* ptactwa **2.** rezerwat *m* ptactwa; **'bird•seed** *s* karma *f* dla ptaków; **bird's eye 'view** *s* widok *m* z lotu ptaka; **'bird's nest** *s* ptasie gniazdo *n*; **'bird watch•ing** *s* obserwowanie *n* ptaków

birth [bɜːθ] *s* **1.** narodziny *pl*; ***at ~*** po urodzeniu, przy urodzeniu; ***from*** (*a.* ***since***) **~** od urodzenia; ***give ~ to*** **a)** urodzić *A* **b)** *fig* dać początek *D* **2.** urodzenie *n*, pochodzenie *n*; ***she's French by ~*** jest z pochodzenia Francuzką; **'birth cer•tif•i•cate** *s* świadectwo *n* urodzenia, metryka *f* urodzenia; **'birth con•trol** *s* **1.** kontrola *f* urodzeń **2.** planowanie *n* rodziny; **'birth•day I** *s* urodziny *pl*; ***happy ~!*** wszystkiego najlepszego z okazji urodzin! **II** *adj* urodzinowy; ***in one's ~ suit*** *hum* **a)** w stroju Ewy **b)** w stroju Adama; **'birth•day cake** *s* tort *m* urodzinowy; **'birth•mark** *s* znamię *n*; **'birth•place** *s* **1.** miejsce *n* urodzenia **2.** *fig* kolebka *f*; **'birth•rate** *s* wskaźnik *m* urodzeń

bis•cuit ['bɪskɪt] *s* **1.** *Br* herbatnik *m*, kruche ciasteczko *n* **2.** *Am* bułeczka *f*

bi•sex•u•al [baɪ'sekʃʊəl] *adj* biseksualny

bish•op ['bɪʃəp] *s* **1.** biskup *m* **2.** (*in chess*) goniec *m*; **bish•opric** ['bɪʃəprɪk] *s* biskupstwo *n*

bi•son ['baɪsən] *s* bizon *m*; ***European ~*** żubr europejski

bit[1] [bɪt] *s* **1.** kawałek *m*; ***~ by ~*** po trochu, pomału; ***do one's ~*** zrobić swoje **2.** ***a ~*** trochę; ***not a ~*** ani trochę; ***he's a ~ of a coward*** jest trochę tchórzliwy **3.** kęs *m*, kąsek *m* **4.** INF bit *m* **5.** wiertło *n* **6.** wędzidło *n*

bit[2] [~] *Past Simple* → **bite**

bitch [bɪtʃ] *s* suka *f*; **bitch•y** ['bɪtʃɪ] *adj* złośliwy

bite [baɪt] **I** (*bit*; *bitten*) *v/t* **1.** gryźć ⟨u-⟩; ***~ s.th. off*** odgryźć coś; ***~ one's nails*** obgryzać paznokcie; ***he's bitten off more that he can chew*** *fig* sytuacja go przerosła; ***~ the dust*** *infml* **a)** (*person*) kopnąć w kalendarz **b)** (*plan*) wziąć w łeb **c)** (*firm*) paść **2.** kąsać ⟨ukąsić⟩ **3.** żądlić ⟨u-⟩ **II** (*bit*; *bitten*) *v/i* **1.** gryźć, kąsać **2.** (*smoke*, *smell*) gryźć **3.** (*fish*) brać ⟨wziąć⟩ **4.** dawać ⟨dać⟩ się we znaki **III** *s* **1.** ugryzienie *n*; ***give s.o. a ~*** ugryźć kogoś **2.** ukąszenie *n* **3.** kęs *m*, kąsek *m*; ***let's have a ~*** przekąśmy coś; **bit•ing** ['baɪtɪŋ] *adj* **1.** gryzący **2.** *of cold*: przenikliwy **3.** kąśliwy, uszczypliwy

bit-map ['bɪtmæp] *s* INF bitmapa *f*

bit•ten ['bɪtn] **I** *v Past Participle* → **bite** **II** *adj* ***once ~ twice shy*** kto się na gorącym sparzył, ten na zimne dmucha

bit•ter ['bɪtə] **I** *adj* **1.** gorzki; ***to the ~ end*** do samego końca, do upadłego **2.** zgorzkniały **3.** *of cold*: przejmujący, przenikliwy **II** *s Br* piwo *n* typu bitter; **bit•ter•ly** ['bɪtəlɪ] *adv* **1.** gorzko **2.** zawzięcie **3.** *of cold*: przejmująco, przenikliwie; **bit•ter•ness** ['bɪtənɪs] *s* **1.** gorycz *f* **2.** rozgoryczenie *n*

biv•ou•ac ['bɪvʊæk] *s* biwak *m*

biz [bɪz] *abbr* (=**business**) biznes *m*, interesy *pl*

bi•zarre [bɪ'zɑː] *adj* dziwaczny

blab [blæb] *infml* **I** *v/t* wygadać **II** *v/t* wygadać się

black [blæk] **I** *adj* **1.** czarny; ***~ humour*** czarny humor; ***~ and blue*** *fig* posiniaczony; ***beat s.o. ~ and blue*** *infml* zbić kogoś na kwaśne jabłko; ***he's not so ~ as he's painted*** nie taki diabeł straszny jak go malują **2.** czarnoskóry **3.** murzyński **4.** ponury **II** *s* **1.** czerń *f*, czarny *m*; ***in ~*** w czerni, ubrany na czarno **2.** czarnoskóry *m*, Murzyn *m* **3.** ***be in the ~*** ECON być na plusie **III** *v/t* bojkotować ⟨z-⟩; **black out I** *v/i* **1.** tracić ⟨s-⟩ przytomność **2.** ***he ~ed out*** *infml* urwał mu się film **II** *v/t* ***the town was ~ed out*** miasto było pozbawione prądu; **black-and-'white** *adj*: ***in ~*** czarno na białym; ***~ television*** czarnobiała telewizja; **'black•ber•ry** *s* jeżyna *f*; **'black•bird** *s* **1.** kos *m* **2.** (*in USA*) kacyk *m*; **'black•board** *s* tablica *f*; **black•'box** *s* (*plane*) czarna skrzynka *f*; **black•'cof•fee** *s* czarna kawa *f*; **black•'cur•rant** *s* czarna porzeczka *f*; **black e'con•o•my** *s* szara strefa *f*

B

black•en ['blækn] **I** *v/t* **1.** czernić ⟨po-⟩ **2.** kopcić ⟨o-⟩ **3.** *~ s.o.'s name* oczerniać kogoś **II** *v/i* czernieć ⟨s-⟩
black 'eye *s*, podbite oko *n*: *give s.o. a ~* podbić komuś oko; **black-eyed 'pea** *s* fasolnik *m* chiński; **'blackhead** *s* wągier *m*, zaskórnik *m*; **black 'hole** *s* ASTR czarna dziura *f*; **black 'ice** *s* gołoledź *f*; **black•ish** ['blækɪʃ] *adj* czarniawy; **'black•list** *s* czarna lista *f*; **black 'mag•ic** *s* czarna magia *f*: **'black•mail I** *s* szantaż *m* **II** *v/t* szantażować ⟨za-⟩; **'black•mail•er** *s* szantażysta *m*; **black 'mar•ket** *s* czarny rynek *m*; **black mar•ket•'eer** *s* czarnorynkowy handlarz *m*; **black•ness** ['blæknɪs] *s* czerń *f*; **'black•out** *s* **1.** (*in wartime*) zaciemnienie *n* **2.** przerwa *f* w dostawie prądu **3.** blokada *f* (informacyjna) **4.** utrata *f* przytomności; **black 'pud•ding** *s* COOK kaszanka *f*; **Black 'Sea** *s* Morze *n* Czarne; **black 'sheep** *s fig* czarna owca *f*; **'black•smith** *s* kowal *m*; **'black spot** *s* (*on road*) czarny punkt *m*; **black 'tie** *s* czarna muszka *f*; '~' (*on invitation*) „smoking"
blad•der ['blædə] *s* **1.** pęcherz *m* **2.** dętka *f*
blade [bleɪd] *s* **1.** ostrze *n* **2.** klinga *f* **3.** ANAT łopatka *f* **4.** źdźbło *n*; *a ~ of grass* źdźbło trawy
blame [bleɪm] **I** *v/t* winić, obwiniać ⟨-nić⟩ (*s.o. for* kogoś o *A*); *he is to ~ for it* on jest temu winien; *he has only himself to ~* sam jest sobie winien; *the police are blaming the accident on dangerous driving* policja uważa, że przyczyną wypadku była niebezpieczna jazda **II** *s* wina *f*; *put the ~ on* obwiniać *A*, zrzucać winę na *A*; *bear* (*a. take*) *the ~* brać winę na siebie; **blameless** ['bleɪmlɪs] *adj* niewinny
blanch [blɑːntʃ] **I** *v/i* blednąć ⟨z-⟩ **II** *v/t* parzyć ⟨s-⟩, blanszować ⟨z-⟩
bland [blænd] *adj* mdły, nijaki
blank [blæŋk] **I** *adj* **1.** czysty, niezapisany; *leave this field ~* nie wypełniaj tego pola **2.** pusty; *a ~ cartridge* ślepy nabój **3.** *cheque*: in blanco **4.** bez wyrazu, obojętny **II** *s* **1.** puste miejsce *n* **2.** puste pole *n* **3.** pusty los *m* **4.** ślepy nabój *m* **5.** *my mind was a ~* miałem pustkę w głowie; **blank 'cheque** *Br*, **blank 'check** *Am s* czek *m* in blanco
blan•ket ['blæŋkɪt] **I** *s* **1.** koc *m* **2.** kołdra *f* **3.** *a ~ of snow* pokrywa śnieżna **II** *v/t* przykrywać ⟨-ryć⟩; *~ed in* (*a. with*) *fog* spowity we mgle **III** *adj ban*: całkowity
blare [bleə] **I** *v/i* **1.** (*horn*) wyć ⟨za-⟩ **2.** (*radio*) ryczeć ⟨za-⟩ **II** *s* **1.** wycie *n* **2.** ryk *m*; **blare out** *v/t* (*radio*) ryczeć ⟨za-⟩
bla•sé ['blɑːzeɪ] *adj* zblazowany
blas•pheme [blæs'fiːm] *v/i* bluźnić; **blas•phe•mous** ['blæsfəməs] *adj* bluźnierczy; **blas•phe•my** ['blæsfəmɪ] *s* bluźnierstwo *n*
blast [blæst] **I** *s* **1.** wybuch *m* **2.** podmuch *m* **3.** *of wind*: poryw *m* **4.** *at full ~* **a)** pełną parą **b)** na cały regulator **II** *v/t* **1.** wysadzać ⟨-dzić⟩ **2.** rozsadzać ⟨-dzić⟩ **3.** *fig* nie zostawić suchej nitki na *L* **4.** *infml ~ it* (*all*)! a niech to szlag!; *~ him!* do diabła z nim!; **'blast fur•nace** *s* wielki piec *m*; **'blast-off** *s of rocket*: odpalenie *n*, start *m*; **'blast wave** *s* fala *f* uderzeniowa; **blast•ed** ['blæstɪd] *adj infml* cholerny, przeklęty
bla•tant ['bleɪtənt] *adj* **1.** rażący **2.** *lie*: w żywe oczy, bezczelny
blaze [bleɪz] **I** *s* **1.** pożar *m* **2.** płomienie *pl* **3.** blask *m*; *a ~ of colours* feeria barw **4.** *of emotion*: wybuch *m* **II** *v/i* **1.** płonąć ⟨za-⟩ **2.** buchać ⟨-chnąć⟩ płomieniami; **blaze up** *v/i* **1.** buchać ⟨-chnąć⟩ płomieniem **2.** rozgorzeć
blaz•er ['bleɪzə] *s* marynarka *f*
blaz•ing ['bleɪzɪŋ] *adj infml* **1.** *heat*: piekielny; *a ~ hot day* piekielnie upalny dzień **2.** *argument*: gwałtowny
bleach [bliːtʃ] **I** *v/t* **1.** wybielać ⟨-lić⟩ **2.** *hair*: rozjaśniać ⟨-nić⟩, utleniać ⟨-nić⟩ **II** *s* **1.** wybielacz *m* **2.** (*for hair*) rozjaśniacz *m*, utleniacz *m*; **bleachers** ['bliːtʃəz] *pl Am* odkryta trybuna *f*
bleat [bliːt] **I** *v/i* (*sheep, goat*) beczeć ⟨za-⟩ **II** *s* beczenie *n*, bek *m*
bled [bled] *Past Simple and Past Participle* → **bleed**
bleed [bliːd] **I** (*bled*; *bled*) *v/i* **1.** krwawić **2.** wykrwawiać ⟨-wić⟩ się; *~ to death* wykrwawić się na śmierć **II** (*bled*; *bled*) *v/t* **1.** puszczać ⟨puścić⟩ krew **2.** *fig* wyciągać ⟨-gnąć⟩

B

ostatni grosz od *G*; **~ s.o. *for*** oskubać kogoś z *G* **5.** odpowietrzać ⟨-rzyć⟩; **bleed•ing** ['bli:dɪŋ] **I** *s* krwawienie *n* **II** *adj* **1.** krwawiący **2.** zakrwawiony **3.** *Br infml* cholerny

blend [blend] **I** *v/t* **1.** mieszać ⟨wy-⟩ **2.** miksować ⟨z-⟩ **3.** łączyć ⟨po-⟩ **II** *v/i* **1.** mieszać ⟨z-⟩ się, zlewać ⟨-lać⟩ się **2.** wtapiać ⟨wtopić⟩ się (***into*** w *A*) **3. *~ well with*** pasować do *G* **III** *s* mieszanina *f*, mieszanka *f*; **blend in** *v/i* harmonizować (***with*** z *I*); **blend•er** ['blendə] *s* mikser *m*, blender *m*

bless [bles] *v/t* (*a. blest*; *blest*) **1.** błogosławić ⟨po-⟩, ***be ~ed with*** *fig* być obdarzonym *I*; (***God***) ***~ you*** (*after sneeze*) na zdrowie! **2. *~ oneself*** przeżegnać się; **bless•ed** ['blesɪd] *adj* **1.** błogosławiony **2.** święty; ***the ~ Virgin*** Najświętsza Maria Panna; **bless•ing** ['blesɪŋ] *s* **1.** *a. fig* błogosławieństwo *n* **2.** szczęście *n*; ***a ~ in disguise*** błogosławione w skutkach nieszczęście

blest [blest] *Past Simple and Past Participle* → **bless**

blew [blu:] *Past Simple* → **blow**[1]

blight [blaɪt] **I** *s* **1.** *fig* plaga *f* **2.** *fig* cień *m* **3. *potato ~*** zaraza ziemniaczana **4.** choroba *f* (zboża) **II** *v/t* **1.** rujnować ⟨z-⟩ **2.** rzucać ⟨-cić⟩ cień na *A*

bli•mey ['blaɪmɪ] *interj Br infml dated* a niech to!

blind [blaɪnd] **I** *adj* **1.** niewidomy **2.** *a. fig* ślepy; ***~ to*** ślepy na *A*; ***be ~ in one eye*** nie widzieć na jedno oko; ***turn a ~ eye to*** przymykać oko na *A* **3.** *turning*: z ograniczoną widocznością **II** *adv* ***~ drunk*** *infml* zalany w trupa **III** *v/t* **1.** (*sun*) oślepiać ⟨-pić⟩ **2.** powodować ⟨s-⟩ utratę wzroku u *G* **IV** *s* **1.** żaluzja *f* **2.** roleta *f*; **blind 'al•ley** *s* ślepa uliczka *f*; **blind 'date** *s* randka *f* w ciemno; **blind•ers** ['blaɪndərz] *pl Am* końskie okulary *pl*; **'blind•fold** ['blaɪndfəʊld] **I** *adv* z zawiązanymi oczami **II** *v/t* zawiązywać ⟨-zać⟩ oczy **III** *s* przepaska *f* na oczy; **blind•folded** → ***blindfold I***; **blind•ing** ['blaɪndɪŋ] *adj* **1.** oślepiający **2.** *pain*: nieznośny; **blind•ly** ['blaɪndlɪ] *adv* po omacku; **blind-man's 'buff** *s* ciuciubabka *f*

blind•ness ['blaɪndnɪs] *s* ślepota *f*

blink [blɪŋk] **I** *v/i* **1.** mrugać ⟨-gnąć, za-⟩ (***at*** do *G*) **2.** migotać ⟨za-⟩ **II** *v/t* ***~ one's eyes*** mrugać **III** *s* mrugnięcie *n*; ***in the ~ of an eye*** w mgnieniu oka

bliss [blɪs] *s* **1.** szczęście *n* **2.** błogość *f*; **bliss•ful** ['blɪsfʊl] *adj* **1.** błogi **2.** rozkoszny

blis•ter ['blɪstə] **I** *s* **1.** pęcherz *m* **2.** bąbel *m* **II** *v/i* ***her skin was beginning to ~*** na skórze zaczynały jej się robić pęcherze; **'blis•ter pack** *s* (*container*) blister *m*

blithe•ly ['blaɪðlɪ] *adv* beztrosko, niefrasobliwie

bliz•zard ['blɪzəd] *s* zamieć *f*, śnieżyca *f*

bloat•ed ['bləʊtɪd] *adj* **1.** wzdęty **2.** nadęty **3.** *face*: nalany **4.** *bureaucracy*: nadmiernie rozbudowany **5.** przesadzony

blob [blɒb] *s* **1.** plama *f* **2.** kleks *m*

block [blɒk] **I** *v/t* **1.** blokować ⟨za-⟩ **2.** zapychać ⟨-pchać⟩ **3.** tarasować ⟨za-⟩ **II** *s* **1.** bryła *f* **2.** blok *m*; ***a ~ of flats*** *Br* blok mieszkalny **3.** kawał *m* **4.** kloc *m* **5.** kostka *f* **6.** (*toy*) klocek *m* **7.** kwartał *m* (uliczny); **block in** *v/t car*: blokować ⟨za-⟩; **block out** *v/t* **1.** zasłaniać ⟨-łonić⟩ **2.** zapominać ⟨-mnieć⟩; **block up** *v/t* **1.** zatykać ⟨-tkać⟩ **2.** zapychać ⟨-pchać⟩ **3.** blokować ⟨za-⟩

block•ade [blɒ'keɪd] **I** *s* blokada *f* **II** *v/t* blokować ⟨za-⟩

block•age ['blɒkɪdʒ] **1.** zator *m* **2.** niedrożność *f*

block 'book•ing *s* grupowa rezerwacja *f*; **block•bust•er** ['blɒkbʌstə] *s* hit *m*; **'block•buster mov•ie** *s* przebój *m* kinowy; **block 'cap•i•tal** *s* wielka litera *f*, drukowana litera *f*; **'block•head** *s infml* tępak *m*; **block 'let•ters** *pl* wielkie litery *pl*, pismo *n* drukowane; ***in ~*** wielkimi literami

bloke [bləʊk] *s Br infml* gość *m*, facet *m*

blond [blɒnd] **I** *adj* **1.** blond **2.** *wood*: jasny **II** *s* blondyn *m*; **blonde** [blɔnd] **I** *s* blondynka *f* **II** *adj* blond

blood [blʌd] *s* krew *f*; ***make s.o.'s ~ freeze*** zmrozić komuś krew w żyłach; **'blood bank** *s* bank *m* krwi; **'blood•bath** *s* masakra *f*, rzeź *f*;

'**blood clot** *s* skrzep *m*; '**blood curdling** *adj* mrożący krew w żyłach; '**blood donor** *s* krwiodawca *m*; '**blood group** *s* grupa *f* krwi; '**blood•hound** *s* posokowiec *m*

blood•less ['blʌdlɪs] *adj* **1.** bezkrwawy **2.** blady; '**blood or•ange** *s* czerwona pomarańcza *f*; '**blood poi•son•ing** *s* MED posocznica *f*, *infml* zakażenie *n* krwi; '**blood pres•sure** *s* ciśnienie *n* krwi; '**blood re•la•tion**, '***blood relative*** *s* krewny *m*; '**blood sam•ple** *s* próbka *f* krwi; ***take a ~*** pobrać krew; '**blood•shed** *s* **1.** rozlew *m* krwi **2.** rzeź *f*; '**blood•shot** *adj* nabiegły krwią; '**blood•stain** *s* plama *f* krwi; '**blood•stain•ed** *adj* poplamiony krwią; '**blood•stream** *s* krwiobieg *m*; **blood** '**sug•ar lev•el** *s* poziom *m* cukru we krwi; '**blood test** *s* badanie *n* krwi; '**blood•thirst•y** *adj* krwiożerczy; '**blood trans•fusion** *s* transfuzja *f* krwi; '**blood type** *s* grupa *f* krwi; '**blood ves•sel** *s* naczynie *n* krwionośne

blood•y ['blʌdɪ] **I** *adj* **1.** krwawy; ***2 Mary*** (*cocktail*) krwawa Mary **2.** *Br infml* cholerny **II** *adv Br infml* cholernie; **bloody-mind•ed** [blʌdɪ'maɪndɪd] *adj Br infml* złośliwy

bloom [blu:m] **I** *v/i* kwitnąć **II** *s* kwitnienie *n*; ***be in ~*** kwitnąć; **blooming** ['blu:mɪŋ] *adj* **1.** kwitnący **2.** *Br infml* cholerny

blos•som ['blɔsəm] **I** *v/i* **1.** kwitnąć ⟨za-⟩ **2.** rozkwitać ⟨-tnąć⟩ **II** *s lit* kwiaty *pl*, kwiecie *n*; ***be in ~*** kwitnąć

blot [blɒt] **I** *s* **1.** plama *f* **2.** kleks *m* **3.** *fig* wada *f*; ***be a ~ on the face of humanity*** być zakałą ludzkości **II** *v/t* **1.** plamić ⟨po-⟩ **2.** osuszać ⟨-szyć⟩; **blot out** *v/t* wymazywać ⟨-zać⟩ z pamięci; '**blot•ting pa•per** *s* bibuła *f*

blouse [blaʊz] *s* **1.** bluzka *f* **2.** bluza *f*

blow[1] [bləʊ] **I** (*blew*; *blown*) *v/i* **1.** (*wind*) wiać ⟨po-⟩, dąć ⟨za-⟩ **2.** dmuchać ⟨-chnąć⟩ **3.** gwizdać ⟨za-⟩ **4.** (*tyre*) pękać ⟨-knąć⟩ **5.** (*fuse*) przepalać ⟨-lić⟩ się **II** (*blew*; *blown*) *v/t* **1.** wydmuchiwać ⟨-chać⟩; ***~ one's nose*** wydmuchać nos; ***~ glass*** wydmuchiwać szkło; ***~ bubbles*** puszczać bańki **2.** dmuchać w *A* **3.** grać ⟨za-⟩ na *L*; ***~ the trumpet*** grać na trąbce **4.** *money*: przepuszczać ⟨-puścić⟩ **5.** *chance*: marnować ⟨z-⟩ **6.** ***~ one's top*** *Br*, ***~ one's stack*** *Am infml* wściec się **III** *s* **1.** dmuchnięcie *n*; ***give one's nose a ~*** wydmuchać nos **2.** podmuch *m*; **blow away** *v/t* (*wind*) porywać ⟨-rwać⟩, zdmuchiwać ⟨-chnąć⟩; **blow in** *v/i infml* wpadać ⟨-paść⟩ (z wizytą); **blow off** → ***blow away***; **blow out** *v/t* **1.** *light*: gasić ⟨z-⟩ **2.** ***blow s.o's brains out*** *infml* wpakować komuś kulę w łeb; **blow over** *v/i* mijać ⟨minąć⟩; **blow up** **I** *v/t* **1.** wysadzać ⟨-dzić⟩ (w powietrze) **2.** pompować ⟨na-⟩ **3.** *photo*: powiększać ⟨-szyć⟩ **4.** wyolbrzymiać ⟨-mić⟩ **II** *v/i* **1.** wybuchać ⟨-chnąć⟩, wylatywać ⟨-lecieć⟩ w powietrze **2.** naskakiwać ⟨-skoczyć⟩ (***at*** na *A*) **3.** (*storm*) rozpętywać ⟨-tać⟩ się

blow[2] [~] *s* cios *m*, uderzenie *n*: ***at one ~***, ***at a single ~*** jednym ciosem; ***come to ~s*** przejść do rękoczynów

blow-dry ['bləʊdraɪ] *v/i* **1.** modelować ⟨wy-⟩ **2.** suszyć ⟨wy-⟩; '**blow dryer** *s* suszarka *f* do włosów

blow•er ['bləʊə] *s* **1.** wentylator *m* **2.** dmuchawa *f*

blown [bləʊn] *Past Participle* → ***blow***[1]

'**blow•out** *s* **1.** pęknięcie *n* opony; ***have a ~*** *infml* złapać gumę **2.** *infml* wyżerka *f*

'**blow•torch** *s Am* lampa *f* lutownicza

'**blow-up** *s* **1.** *infml* wybuch *m* (złości) **2.** powiększenie *n*

blue [blu:] **I** *adj* **1.** niebieski **2.** siny **3.** *infml* przybity, zdołowany **4.** *joke*: pieprzny **5.** *film*: erotyczny **II** *s* niebieski *m*; ***dressed in ~*** ubrany na niebiesko; ***out of the ~*** *fig* ni z tego, ni z owego; '**blue•bell** *s* **1.** dzwonek *m* okrągłolistny **2.** edymion *m* zwisły; '**blue•ber•ry** *s* czarna jagoda *f*; '**blue•bird** *s* drozd *m* północnoamerykański; '**blue-blood•ed** *adj*: ***be ~*** mieć błękitną krew; **blue** '**chip** *adj stocks*: pierwszorzędny; **blue-**'**col•lar work•er** *s* **1.** pracownik *m* fizyczny **2.** robotnik *m*; '**blue•jay** *s* sójka *f* błękitna; '**blue jeans** *pl* (niebieskie) dżinsy *pl*; **blue** '**mov•ie** *s infml* film *m* erotyczny; '**blue•print** *s* **1.** plan *m* **2.** projekt *m* **3.** światłokopia *f* planu

B

blues [blu:z] *s* **1.** blues *m* **2.** *infml* chandra *f*; ***have the ~s*** mieć chandrę: '**blues mu•si•cian** *s* muzyk *m* bluesowy

bluff [blʌf] **I** *s* blef *m* **II** *v/i* blefować

blu•ish ['blu:ɪʃ] *adj* niebieskawy

blun•der ['blʌndə] **I** *s* **1.** (głupi) błąd *m* **2.** gafa *f* **II** *v/i* popełniać ⟨-nić⟩ (głupi) błąd; **blun•der into** *v/t* wpadać ⟨wpaść⟩ na *A*

blunt [blʌnt] **I** *adj* **1.** tępy **2.** otwarty, szczery **3.** (*of refusal*) kategoryczny **II** *v/t* **1.** tępić ⟨s-⟩ **2.** *fig* osłabiać ⟨-bić⟩; **blunt•ly** ['blʌntlɪ] *adv* **1.** otwarcie, szczerze; ***to put it ~*** mówiąc szczerze

blur [blɜ:] **I** *v/i* **1.** rozmazywać ⟨-zać⟩ się **2.** (*memories*, *differences*) zacierać ⟨zatrzeć⟩ się **II** *v/t* **1.** rozmazywać ⟨-zać⟩ **2.** *difference*: zacierać ⟨zatrzeć⟩

blurred [blɜ:d] *adj* **1.** zamazany **2.** rozmazany **3.** niewyraźny **4.** *photo*: nieostry

blush [blʌʃ] **I** *v/i* rumienić ⟨za-⟩ się, czerwienić ⟨za-⟩ się; ***~ with shame*** zarumienić się ze wstydu **II** *s* rumieniec *m*; **blush•er** ['blʌʃə] *s* (*cosmetic*) róż *m*

BMI *abbr* (=***Body Mass Index***) wskaźnik *m* masy ciała

'**B-mov•ie** *s* film *m* klasy B

bo•a con•strict•or [bəʊəkən'strɪktə] *s* boa *m* dusiciel

boar [bɔ:] *s* **1.** dzik *m* **2.** knur *m*

board [bɔ:d] **I** *s* **1.** deska *f* **2.** płyta *f* **3.** ***a skirting ~*** listwa przypodłogowa **4.** ***~s*** parkiet **5.** tablica *f* **6.** plansza *f* **7.** ***~s*** scena, deski (teatru) **8.** wyżywienie *n*; ***~ and lodging*** wyżywienie i nocleg **9.** zarząd *m* **10.** rada *f* **11.** komisja *f*; ***a ~ of examiners*** komisja egzaminacyjna **12.** ***the ~ of Trade*** **a)** *Br* Ministerstwo Handlu **b)** *Am* Izba Handlowa **13.** ***on ~*** na pokładzie; ***on ~ a bus*** w autobusie; ***go on ~*** **a)** wejść na pokład **b)** wsiąść **II** *v/i* **1.** *ship*, *plane*: wejść na pokład *G* **2.** *bus*: wsiadać ⟨wsiąść⟩ do *G* **III** *v/i* mieszkać (***with*** u *G*); **board up** *v/t* zabijać ⟨-bić⟩ deskami; **board•er** ['bɔ:də] *s* **1.** lokator *m* **2.** pensjonariusz *m* **3.** uczeń *m* mieszkający w internacie

'**board game** *s* gra *f* planszowa

'**board•ing card** *s Br* karta *f* pokładowa; '**board•ing house** *s* pensjonat *m*; '**board•ing pass** *s* karta *f* pokładowa; '**board meet•ing** *s* spotkanie *n* zarządu; '**board•ing school** *s* szkoła *f* z internatem; '**board•room** *s* sala *f* posiedzeń zarządu

boast [bəʊst] **I** *v/i* chwalić ⟨po-⟩ się (***of/about*** *I*) **II** *v/t* szczycić się posiadaniem *G*; ***the hotel ~s a swimming pool*** w hotelu znajduje się basen **III** *s* przechwałka *f*; **boast•er** ['bəʊstə] *s* chwalipięta *m*; **boast•ful** ['bəʊstfʊl] *adj* chełpliwy

boat [bəʊt] **I** *s* **1.** łódź *f*; ***be in the same ~*** *fig* jechać na tym samym wózku; ***burn one's ~s*** (***behind one***) palić za sobą mosty **2.** łódka *f* **3.** statek *m*; ***take to the ~s*** ewakuować się **II** *v/i* ***go ~ing*** pływać łódką

bob[1] [bɒb] *s* fryzura *f* na pazia; ***have one's hair cut in a ~*** mieć włosy ostrzyżone na pazia

bob[2] [~] **I** *v/t head*: kiwać ⟨-wnąć⟩, skinąć **II** *v/i* **1.** (*boat*) podskakiwać ⟨-skoczyć⟩, poruszać się w górę i w dół **2.** dygać ⟨-gnąć⟩; **bob up** *v/i* **1.** wynurzać ⟨-rzyć⟩ się **2.** pojawiać ⟨-wić⟩ się niespodziewanie

bob•by ['bɒbɪ] *s infml dated* policjant *m*; '**bob•by pin** *s Am* szpilka *f* do włosów

bode[1] [bəʊd] *v/i*: ***~ well*** (***ill***) dobrze (źle) wróżyć

bode[2] [~] *Past Simple and Past Participle* → ***bide***

bod•i•ly ['bɒdɪlɪ] **I** *adj* **1.** fizjologiczny; ***~ needs*** potrzeby fizjologiczne **2.** cielesny **3.** fizyczny; ***~ harm*** obrażenia fizyczne **II** *adv* w całości

bod•y ['bɒdɪ] *s* **1.** ciało *n* **2.** organizm *m* **3.** (*a.* **dead ~**) zwłoki *pl* **4.** tułów *m* **5.** ADM organ *m* **6.** grupa *f* **7.** gremium *n* **8.** część *f*; ***the main ~*** główna część **9.** ilość *f*; ***a vast ~ of information*** ogromna ilość informacji **10.** zbiór *m*; ***the ~ of laws*** ustawodawstwo **11.** karoseria *f*, nadwozie *n* **12.** kadłub *m* **13.** pudło *n* rezonansowe

'**body bag** *s* worek *m* na zwłoki; '**bodybuild•er** *s* kulturysta *m*; '**body build•ing** *s* kulturystyka *f*; '**body•guard** *s* **1.** ochroniarz *m* **2.** ochrona

B

f osobista; '**body lan•guage** *s* mowa *f* ciała; '**body o•dour** *s* **1.** zapach *m* ciała **2.** zapach *m* potu; '**body piercing** *s* piercing *m*, kolczykowanie *n*; '**body search** *s* rewizja *f* osobista; '**body•shop** *s* warsztat *m* blacharski; '**body stock•ing**, '***body suit*** *s* trykot *m*; '**body•work** *s* nadwozie *n*, karoseria *f*

bog [bɒg] **I** *s* **1.** bagno *n* **2.** *Br infml* kibel *m* **II** *v/i* **3.** ugrzęznąć **4.** znaleźć się w martwym punkcie **III** *v/t* ***get ~ged down*** **a)** ugrzęznąć **b)** znaleźć się w martwym punkcie

bo•gey → ***bogy***

bog•gle ['bɒgl] *v/i*: ***the mind ~s*** to nie mieści się w głowie

bog•gy ['bɒgɪ] *adj* bagnisty, grząski

bo•gie → ***bogy***

bo•gus ['bəʊgəs] *adj* **1.** udawany **2.** fikcyjny **3.** podrabiany

bo•gy ['bəʊgɪ] *s* postrach *m*

boil[1] [bɔɪl] *s* czyrak *m*

boil[2] [~] **I** *v/i* **1.** gotować ⟨za-⟩ się; ***~ with anger*** gotować się ze złości **2.** wrzeć ⟨za-⟩ **II** *v/t* gotować ⟨u-⟩ **III** *s* wrzenie *n*; ***bring s.th. to the ~*** *Br*, ***bring s.th. to a ~*** *Am* doprowadzić coś do wrzenia, zagotować coś; **boil down to** *v/t fig* sprowadzać się do *G*; **boil over** *v/i* **1.** kipieć ⟨wy-⟩ **2.** (*situation*) wymykać ⟨-mknąć⟩ się spod kontroli **3.** przeradzać ⟨-rodzić⟩ się (***into*** w *A*)

boil•er ['bɔɪlə] *s* **1.** kocioł *m* **2.** bojler; '**boil•er suit** *s Br* kombinezon *m* roboczy

boil•ing point ['bɔɪlɪŋpɔɪnt] *s a. fig* temperatura *f* wrzenia

bois•ter•ous ['bɔɪstərəs] *adj* **1.** hałaśliwy, głośny **2.** żywy **3.** *sea*: wzburzony

bold [bəʊld] *adj* **1.** śmiały, odważny; ***if I may be so ~ as to suggest that*** ośmielę się zasugerować, że **2.** zuchwały **3.** *print*: tłusty; ***in ~*** (***type***) tłustym drukiem **4.** *font*: pogrubiony

Bo•liv•i•a [bɒ'lɪvɪə] *s* Boliwia *f*

bol•locks ['bɒləks] *pl Br vulg* pierdoły *pl*

bol•ster ['bəʊlstə] **I** *v/t* **1.** ***~ s.o.'s confidence*** (***courage***) dodać komuś pewności siebie (odwagi) **2.** *morale*: podnosić ⟨-nieść⟩ **3.** ***~*** (***up***) ***the economy*** poprawić sytuację gospodarczą, wzmocnić gospodarkę **II** *s* podgłówek *m*, wałek *m*

bolt [bəʊlt] **I** *s* **1.** zasuwa *f* **2.** śruba *f* **3.** sworzeń *m* **4.** bolec *m* **5.** (*crossbow*) bełt *m* **6.** piorun *m*; ***a ~ from the blue*** *fig* grom z jasnego nieba **7.** ***a ~ of lightning*** błyskawica **8.** sus *m*, skok *m*; ***he made a ~ for the door*** rzucił się w stronę drzwi **II** *v/t* ryglować ⟨za-⟩, zamykać ⟨-knąć⟩ na zasuwę **III** *v/i* **1.** rzucać ⟨-cić⟩ się do ucieczki **2.** zwiewać ⟨zwiać⟩ **3.** (*horse*) ponosić ⟨-nieść⟩ **IV** *adv* ***~ upright*** prosty jak strzała

bomb [bɒm] **I** *s* bomba *f* **II** *v/t* bombardować ⟨z-⟩; '**bomb alert** *s* alarm *m* bombowy

bom•bard [bɒm'bɑːd] *v/t t fig* bombardować ⟨z-⟩; ***~ s.o. with questions*** zasypać kogoś pytaniami; **bom•bard•ment** [bɒm'bɑːdmənt] *s* bombardowanie *n*

bom•bast ['bɒmbæst] *s form* **1.** górnolotne słowa *pl* **2.** patos *m*; **bom•bas•tic** [bɒm'bæstɪk] *adj* **1.** górnolotny **2.** napuszony

'**bomb attack** *s* atak *m* bombowy; '**bomb dis•pos•al u•nit** *s* oddział *m* saperski

bombed [bɒmbd] *adj infml* **1.** nawalony, narąbany **2.** naćpany

bomb•er ['bɒmə] *s* **1.** bombowiec *m* **2.** terrorysta *m* podkładający bomby, zamachowiec *m*; '**bomb•er jack•et** *s* (krótka) kurtka *f*

bomb•ing ['bɒmɪŋ] *s* **1.** bombardowanie *n* **2.** zamach *m* bombowy

'**bomb•proof** *adj* przeciwbombowy; '**bomb shelter** *s* schron *m* przeciwbombowy; '**bomb scare** *s* alarm *m* bombowy; '**bomb•shell** *s* (*news*) bomba *f*, sensacja *f*

bo•na fi•de [bəʊnə'faɪdɪ] *adj* **1.** prawdziwy **2.** realny **3.** szczery **4.** rzetelny

bo•nan•za [bə'nænzə] **I** *s fig* żyła *f* złota, bonanza *f* **II** *adj year*: bardzo dobry

bond [bɒnd] **I** *s* **1.** więź *f*, więzi *pl*; ***emotional ~s*** więzi emocjonalne **2.** wiązanie *n* **3.** obligacja *f* **4.** kaucja *f* **II** *v/t* **1.** spajać ⟨spoić⟩ **2.** wiązać ⟨z-⟩

bond•age ['bɒndɪdʒ] *s* **1.** niewola *f* **2.** niewolnictwo *n* **3.** poddaństwo *n*

bond•ed 'ware•house *s* magazyn *m* celny
'bond•hold•er *s* posiadacz *m* obligacji
bond•ing ['bɒndɪŋ] *s* **1.** tworzenie *n* więzi **2.** *CHEM* wiązanie *n*
bone [bəʊn] **I** *s* **1.** kość *f*; ***make no ~s about*** (*a.* ***of***) nie ukrywać *G*, nie robić ceregieli z *G*; ***feel s.th. in one's ~s*** przeczuwać coś; ***have a ~ to pick with*** mieć na pieńku z *I*; ***chilled*** (*a.* ***frozen***) ***to the ~*** zmarznięty na kość **2.** ość *f* **II** *v/t* filetować **II** *v/i* ***~ up on*** *infml* poduczyć się; **bone-'dry** *adj* wyschnięty na kość, suchuteńki; **'bonehead** *s infml* tępak *m*; **'bone-idle** *adj*: ***be ~*** być patentowanym leniem
bon•fire ['bɒnfaɪə] *s* ognisko *n*; **'Bonfire Night** *s Br* (*rocznica spisku prochowego z 1605 roku*) noc *f* 5 listopada
bonk [bɒŋk] *infml* **I** *v/i* **1.** stukać ⟨-knąć⟩ **2.** bzykać ⟨-knąć⟩ się (***with*** z *I*) **II** *v/t* bzykać ⟨-knąć⟩
bon•net ['bɒnɪt] *s* **1.** czapeczka *f* **2.** czepek *m*
bo•nus ['bəʊnəs] *s* **1.** premia *f* **2.** dodatek *m* **3.** bonus *m* **4.** (dodatkowa) zaleta *f*
bon•y ['bəʊnɪ] *adj* **1.** kościsty **2.** *fish*: ościsty **3.** kostny
boo [buː] **I** *s* okrzyk *m* niezadowolenia **II** *v/t* wygwizdywać ⟨-dać⟩ **III** *interj* u!
boob [buːb] *s infml* cycek *m*
boo•by prize ['buːbɪpraɪz] *s* nagroda *f* pocieszenia; **'boo•by trap** *s* **1.** bomba pułapka *f* **2.** psikus *m*
book [bʊk] **I** *s* **1.** książka *f*; ***a closed ~*** *fig* czarna magia (***to*** dla *G*); ***an open ~*** *fig* otwarta księga *f* (***to*** dla *G*) **2.** zeszyt *m*, notes *m*; ***be in s.o.'s good*** (***bad***) ***~s*** *infml* być u kogoś dobrze (źle) notowanym **3.** księga *f* rachunkowa **4.** rejestr *m* **5.** lista *f*, spis *m*; ***be in the ~s*** figurować na liście **6.** książeczka *f* czekowa **7.** *of tickets, stamps*: bloczek *m* **II** *v/t* **1.** *room, ticket*: rezerwować ⟨za-⟩; ***the hotel is fully ~ed*** w hotelu nie ma już wolnych pokoi **2.** zamawiać ⟨-mówić⟩ **3.** *infml* (*policeman*) spisywać ⟨-sać⟩ **4.** *infml* (*in football*) ukarać żółtą kartką; **book in** *v/i Br* (*in hotel*) meldować ⟨za-⟩ się
'book•case *s* (*cabinet*) biblioteczka *f*; **'book club** *s* klub *m* książki
book•ie ['bʊkɪ] *s infml* bukmacher *m*
book•ing ['bʊkɪŋ] *s Br* **1.** rezerwacja *f*; ***make a ~*** dokonać rezerwacji **2.** *SPORT Br* żółta kartka *n*; **'book•ing clerk** *s Br* kasjer *m*; **'book•ing fee** *s* opłata *f* rezerwacyjna; **'book•ing office** *s Br* kasa *f* biletowa
book•ish ['bʊkɪʃ] *adj* **1.** oczytany **2.** *style*: książkowy
'book•keep•er *s* księgowy *m*; **'book-keep•ing** *s* księgowość *f*; **'book•let** ['bʊklɪt] *s* broszura *f*; **'book•mak•er** *s* bukmacher *m*; **'book•mark** *s* zakładka *f*
'book•sell•er *s* księgarz *m*; **'bookshelf** *pl -shelves s* **1.** regał *m* na książki **2.** półka *f* na książki: **'book•shop** *s* księgarnia *f*; **'book•stall** *s* **1.** stoisko *n* z książkami **2.** *Br* kiosk *m* (z gazetami i książkami); **'book•store** *s Am* księgarnia *f*; **'book to•ken** *s Br* talon *m* na książki; **'book val•ue** *s* wartość *f* księgowa; **'book•worm** *s* mól *m* książkowy
boom¹ [buːm] **I** *s* **1.** boom *m*, ożywienie *n* gospodarcze **2.** (*of stock exchange*) hossa *f*, (gwałtowny) wzrost *m* **II** *v/i* przeżywać boom
boom² [~] **I** *v/i* **1.** grzmieć ⟨za-⟩ **2.** huczeć ⟨huknąć⟩ **II** *s* **1.** grzmot *m* **2.** huk *m*
boom³ [~] *s* **1.** bom *m* **2.** wysięgnik *m*, ramię *n* **3.** tyczka *f* mikrofonowa
boom•er•ang ['buːməræŋ] **I** *s* bumerang *m* **II** *v/i* ***~ on*** obrócić się przeciwko *D*
boost [buːst] **I** *v/t* **1.** zwiększać ⟨-szyć⟩ **2.** *growth*: pobudzać ⟨-dzić⟩ **3.** ***~ s.o.'s confidence*** dodać komuś pewności siebie **4.** *morale*: podnosić ⟨-nieść⟩ **II** *s* **1.** ***give a ~ to the economy*** pobudzić gospodarkę **2.** ***give a ~ to s.o.'s confidence*** dodać komuś odwagi **3.** zachęta *f*
boost•er ['buːstə] *s* **1.** rakieta *f* nośna **2.** dawka *f* przypominająca **3.** wzmacniacz *m* **4.** ***be a confidence ~ to s.o.*** dodać komuś odwagi; **'boost•er rock•et** *s* rakieta *f* nośna; **'boost•er seat** *s* (*in car*) fotelik *m* dziecięcy; **'boost•er shot** dawka *f* przypominająca

B

boot [buːt] **I** *s* **1.** but *m* **2.** kozak *m* **3.** *infml* kop *m*, kopniak *m*; ***give s.o. a ~*** kopnąć *A*; ***get the ~*** *fig* zostać wylanym (z pracy) **4.** *Br* bagażnik *m* **II** *v/t* **1.** *infml* kopać ⟨-pnąć⟩ **2.** *system*: inicjować ⟨za-⟩; **boot out** *v/t infml* **1.** wylać (z pracy) **2.** wykopywać ⟨-pać⟩; **boot up** *v/t system*: inicjować ⟨za-⟩
'boot•camp *s* obóz *m* dla rekrutów
'boot disk *s INF* dysk *m* startowy
boot•ee ['buːtiː] *s* **1.** bucik *m* (dla niemowlęcia) **2.** bucik *m* do kostki
booth [buːð] *s* **1.** kabina *f*; ***a voting ~*** kabina wyborcza **2.** budka *f*; ***a phone ~*** budka telefoniczna **3.** stoisko *n*
boot•ie ['buːtiː] → ***bootee***
'boot•lace *s* sznurowadło *n*; **'boot•leg** **I** *adj* **1.** *record, tape*: piracki **2.** *liquor*: nielegalnie pędzony **II** *v/t* **1.** nielegalnie handlować **2.** nielegalnie pędzić; **'boot•lick•er** *s infml* wazeliniarz *m*; **'boot•strap** *s* (*on boot*) ucho; ***to pull oneself up by one's own ~*** samemu dać sobie radę
boo•ty ['buːtɪ] *s* łup *m*, łupy *pl*
booze [buːz] *infml* **I** *s* alkohol *m* **II** *v/i* chlać
bor•dello [bɔː'deləʊ] *pl -los s Am* burdel *m*
bor•der ['bɔːdə] **I** *s* **1.** granica *f*; ***a ~ incident*** incydent na granicy **2.** brzeg *m* **3.** skraj *m* **4.** obwódka *f* **5.** lamówka *f* **6.** szlaczek *m* **II** *v/i* **1.** graniczyć (***on*** z *I*) **2.** przylegać (***on*** do *G*) **III** *v/t* **1.** graniczyć z *I* **2.** okalać
'border cros•sing *s* przejście *n* graniczne; **'border guard** *s* żołnierz *m* wojsk ochrony pogranicza, *infml* pogranicznik *m*; **'border•land** *s* rejon *m* przygraniczny; **'border•line** **I** *s* **1.** granica *f* **2.** linia *f* graniczna **II** *adj* **1.** wątpliwy **2.** graniczny
bore[1] [bɔː] **I** *v/t* nudzić ⟨za-⟩; ***be ~d*** nudzić się; ***I was ~d stiff*** *infml* myślałem, że się zanudzę na śmierć **II** *s* **1.** nudziarz *m* **2.** nuda *f*
bore[2] [~] **I** *v/t* **1.** wiercić ⟨wy-⟩ **2.** drążyć ⟨wy-⟩ **II** *v/i* **1.** wwiercać ⟨-cić⟩ się (***into*** w *A*) **2.** przewiercać ⟨-cić⟩ się (***through*** przez *A*) **III** *s* **1.** otwór *m* wiertniczy, odwiert *m* **2.** kaliber *m* **3.** średnica *f*
bore[3] [~] *Past Simple* → ***bear***[2]
bored [bɔːd] *adj* znudzony; **bore•dom** ['bɔːdəm] *s* **1.** nuda *f* **2.** znudzenie *n*; **bor•ing** ['bɔːrɪŋ] *adj* nudny
born [bɔːn] **I** *v Past Participle* → ***bear***[2] **II** *adj* urodzony; ***a ~ poet*** urodzony poeta; **'born-a•gain** *adj* nawrócony
borne [bɔːn] *Past Participle* → ***bear***[2]
bor•ough ['bʌrə] *s* **1.** miasto *n* **2.** dzielnica *f* **3.** gmina *f*
bor•row ['bɒrəʊ] **I** *v/t* **1.** pożyczać ⟨-czyć⟩ (***from*** od *G*); ***a ~ed word*** zapożyczenie **2.** wypożyczać ⟨-czyć⟩ **II** *v/i* zapożyczać ⟨-czyć⟩ się
bor•row•er ['bɒrəʊə] *s* **1.** wypożyczający *m* **2.** kredytobiorca *m* **3.** pożyczkobiorca *m*
Bos•ni•a ['bɒznɪə] *s* Bośnia *f*; **Bos•ni•a-Her•ze•go•vi•na** [bɒznɪəhɜːtsə'gəʊvɪnə] *s* Bośnia i Hercegowina *f*; **Bos•ni•an** ['bɒznɪən] **I** *adj* bośniacki **II** *s* Bośniak *m*, Bośniaczka *f*
bos•om ['bʊzəm] *s* **1.** biust *m*, piersi *pl* **2.** *fig* łono *n*; ***in the ~ of one's family*** na łonie rodziny; **'bos•om friend** *s* serdeczny przyjaciel *m*, przyjaciel *m* od serca
boss [bɒs] *infml* **I** *s* szef *m* **II** *v/t* ***~ around*** (*a.* ***about***) dyrygować, rządzić; **boss•y** ['bɒsɪ] *adj* apodyktyczny
bo•tan•i•cal [bə'tænɪkl] *adj* botaniczny; **bo'tan•ic(•al) gar•den** *s* ogród *m* botaniczny; **bot•a•nist** ['bɒtənɪst] *s* botanik *m*; **bot•a•ny** ['bɒtənɪ] *s* botanika *f*
both [bəʊθ] **I** *pron* obaj, obydwaj; ***both of them*** oni dwaj **II** *conj* ***both... and*** zarówno..., jak i
both•er ['bɒðə] **I** *v/i* **1.** robić sobie kłopot **2.** przejmować się (***about*** *I*) **II** *v/t* **1.** przeszkadzać; ***don't ~ me!*** nie przeszkadzaj mi!; ***I can't be ~ed to do homework*** nie chce mi się odrabiać lekcji **2.** niepokoić **III** *s* kłopot *m*, problem *m*; **both•er•some** ['bɒðəsəm] *adj* kłopotliwy, uciążliwy
bot•tle ['bɒtl] **I** *s* butelka *f* **II** *v/t* butelkować ⟨za-⟩; ***~d beer*** piwo butelkowe; **bottle up** *v/t anger, grief*: dusić ⟨z-⟩ w sobie, tłumić ⟨s-⟩; **bottled-up** *adj* nagromadzony
'bot•tle bank *s* pojemnik *m* na szkło; **'bot•tled wa•ter** *s* woda *f* mineralna; **'bot•tle•neck** *s* **1.** szyjka *f* (butelki)

B

2. zwężenie *n* (jezdni) **3.** *fig* wąskie gardło *n*; '**bot•tle-o•pen•er** *s* otwieracz *m* do butelek

bot•tom ['bɒtəm] **I** *s* **1.** dół *m*; ***at the ~ of the street*** na końcu ulicy; ***from the ~ of one's heart*** z głębi serca **2.** *of glass, sea*: dno *n*; ***~s up!*** *infml* do dna! **3.** *of hill*: podnóże *n* **4.** podłoże *n* **5.** ***be at the ~ of*** być przyczyną *G*, kryć się za *I*; ***get to the ~ of*** odkryć przyczynę *G* **6.** *infml* tyłek *m*, siedzenie *n* **II** *adj* **1.** najniższy **2.** dolny **3.** *line*: ostatni; **bot•tom out** *v/i* (*recession*) osiągać ⟨-gnąć⟩ najniższy poziom; **bot•tom 'gear** *s* jedynka *f*, pierwszy bieg *m*; **bot•tom•less** ['bɒtəmlɪs] *adj* **1.** bezdenny **2.** niewyczerpany; **bot•tom 'line** *s* **1.** konkluzja *f* **2.** wynik *m* końcowy

bought [bɔːt] *Past Simple and Past Participle* → ***buy***

boul•e•vard ['buːlvɑːd] *s* bulwar *m*

bounce [baʊns] **I** *v/i* **1.** odbijać ⟨-bić⟩ się (***off/against*** od *G*) **2.** podskakiwać ⟨-skoczyć⟩ **3.** ***~ into a room*** wpaść do pokoju **4.** (*cheque*) nie mieć pokrycia **II** *v/t* **1.** *ball*: odbijać ⟨-bić⟩ **2.** *cheque*: odmawiać ⟨-mówić⟩ realizacji **III** *s* **1.** odbicie *n* (się) **2.** podskok *m* **3.** sprężystość *f* **4.** wigor *m*, werwa *f*; **bounc•er** ['baʊnsə] *s* *infml* bramkarz *m*; **bounc•ing** ['baʊnsɪŋ] *adj* tryskający zdrowiem; **bounc•y** ['baʊnsɪ] *adj* **1.** sprężysty **2.** pełen wigoru

bound[1] [baʊnd] **I** *v Past Simple and Past Participle* → ***bind*** **II** *adj* **1.** ***he is ~ to be late*** na pewno się spóźni **2.** ***be ~ to do s.th.*** być zobowiązanym coś zrobić

bound[2] [~] *adj*: ***~ for*** **a)** jadący do *G* **b)** (*plane*) lecący do *G* **c)** (*ship*) płynący do *G*

bound[3] [~] **I** *v/t* ***be ~ed by*** **a)** graniczyć z *I* **b)** być okolonym *I* **II** *s* ***~s*** **a)** granice **b)** strefa; ***within reasonable ~s*** w granicach rozsądku; ***it's not beyond the ~s of possibility that*** nie jest wykluczone, że

bound[4] [~] **I** *s* **1.** skok *m* **2.** podskok *m* **3.** sus *m* **II** *v/i* → ***bounce I.3, II.1***

bound•a•ry ['baʊndərɪ] *s* granica *f*

bound•less ['baʊndlɪs] *adj* **1.** *sea*: bezkresny **2.** *confidence*: bezgraniczny

boun•ti•ful ['baʊntɪfʊl] *adj* **1.** obfity **2.** szczodry

boun•ty ['baʊntɪ] *s* **1.** szczodrość *f* **2.** nagroda *f*; '**boun•ty hunt•er** *s* łowca *m* nagród

bou•quet [bəʊ'keɪ] *s* **1.** *of flowers*: bukiet *m*, wiązanka *f* **2.** *of wine*: bukiet *m*

bour•geois ['bʊəʒwɑː] *adj* **1.** mieszczański **2.** burżuazyjny **3.** drobnomieszczański

bour•geoi•sie [bʊəʒwɑː'ziː] *s* **1.** mieszczaństwo *n* **2** burżuazja *f* **3.** drobnomieszczaństwo *n*

bout [baʊt] *s* **1.** *SPORT* walka *f* **2.** okres *m* **3.** *MED* atak *m*, napad *m*; ***a ~ of rheumatism*** atak reumatyzmu

bow[1] [baʊ] **I** *v/i* kłaniać ⟨ukłonić⟩ się (***to*** przed *I*) **II** *v/t* *head*: pochylać ⟨-lić⟩ **III** *s* ukłon *m*; **bow out** *v/i* wycofywać ⟨-fać⟩ się (***of*** z *G*)

bow[2] [baʊ] *s* *of ship*: dziób *m*

bow[3] [bəʊ] *s* **1.** łuk *m* **2.** *MUS* smyczek *m* **3.** kokarda *f*, kokardka *f*

bow•el ['baʊəl] *s* *ANAT* jelito *n*; '**bow•el cancer** *s* *MED* rak *m* jelita

bowl[1] [bəʊl] *s* **1.** misa *f* **2.** miska *f*; ***a salad ~*** salaterka **3.** miednica *f* **4.** muszla *f* (klozetowa) **5.** amfiteatr *m* **6.** stadion *m*

bowl[2] [~] *s* **1.** (*in bowling*) kula *f*; **bowl over** *v/t* **1.** przewracać ⟨-rócić⟩ **2.** *fig* zwalać ⟨-lić⟩ z nóg

bowl•er[1] ['bəʊlə] *s* (*in cricket*) serwujący *m*

bowl•er[2] [~] (*a.* ***~ hat***) melonik *m*

bowl•ing ['bəʊlɪŋ] *s* (*game*) kręgle *pl*: '**bowl•ing al•ley** *s* **1.** kręgielnia *f* **2.** tor *m* kręglarski

bowtie ['bəʊ'taɪ] *s* muszka *f*, mucha *f*

box[1] [bɒks] **I** *s* **1.** pudełko *n*; ***a ~ of chocolates*** bombonierka **2.** pudło *n*; ***a cardboard ~*** karton **3.** skrzynia *f* **4.** skrzynka *f*; ***a mail ~*** skrzynka pocztowa **5.** (*on page*) pole *n* **6.** futerał *m* **7.** pojemnik *m* **8.** *Br* budka *f* (telefoniczna) **9.** kabina *f* **10.** urna *f* (wyborcza) **11.** *THEAT* loża *f* **12.** (*in stable*) boks *m* **13.** skrytka *f* pocztowa **14.** ***the ~*** *infml* telewizor *m* **II** (*a.* ***~ up***) *v/t* pakować ⟨za-⟩ (do pudeł)

box[2] [~] **I** *v/i* **1.** boksować się **2.** uprawiać boks **II** *v/t* **1.** (*boxer*) walczyć z *I*

B

2. ~ *s.o.'s ears* trzepnąć kogoś w ucho **III** *s* trzepnięcie *n*

'box car *s Am* wagon *m* towarowy

box•er ['bɒksə] *s* bokser *m*; **'box•er shorts** *pl*: (***a pair of***) ~ bokserki

box•ing ['bɒksɪŋ] *s* SPORT boks *m*, pięściarstwo *n*; **'Box•ing Day** *s Br* drugi dzień *m* świąt Bożego Narodzenia; **'boxing glove** *s* rękawica *f* bokserska; **'boxing match** *s* walka *f* bokserska; **'boxing ring** *s* ring *m* (bokserski)

'box lunch *s Am* drugie śniadanie *n*; **'box num•ber** *s* numer *m* skrytki pocztowej; **'box of•fice I** *s* **1.** kasa *f* biletowa **2. *be a good*** ~ być przebojem kasowym **II** *adj* kasowy; ***a ~ success***, ***a ~ hit*** przebój kasowy

boy [bɔɪ] *s* chłopiec *m*, chłopak *m*

boy•cott ['bɔɪkɔt] **I** *v/t* bojkotować ⟨z-⟩ **II** *s* bojkot *m*

'boy•friend *s* (*partner*) chłopak *m*

boy•ish ['bɔɪɪʃ] *adj* chłopięcy; ***~ games*** chłopięce zabawy

boy 'scout *s* **1.** skaut *m* **2.** harcerz *m*

bra [brɑː] *s* biustonosz *m*, stanik *m*

brace [breɪs] **I** *v/i* ***~ oneself for*** *fig* przygotowywać się na *A* **II** *v/t* **1.** podpierać ⟨-deprzeć⟩ **2.** *muscles*: napinać ⟨-piąć⟩ **III** *s* **1.** (*for teeth*) aparat *m* korekcyjny **2.** aparat *m* ortopedyczny; ***a neck ~*** kołnierz ortopedyczny **3.** nawias *m* klamrowy **4. ~s** *Br* szelki

brace•let ['breɪslɪt] *s* bransoleta *f*, bransoletka *f*

brac•ing ['breɪsɪŋ] *adj climate, air*: rześki

brack•et ['brækɪt] **I** *s* **1.** nawias *m*; ***in ~s*** w nawiasie; ***round*** (***square***) ***~s*** nawiasy okrągłe (kwadratowe) **2.** *of age*: przedział *m*, kategoria *f* **3.** wspornik *m* **II** *v/t* **1.** ujmować ⟨ująć⟩ w nawias **2. *~ together*** zaliczać ⟨-czyć⟩ do jednej grupy

brag [bræg] *v/i* **1.** chwalić się (***about/of*** *I*) **2.** przechwalać się (***about/of*** *I*); **brag•gart** ['brægət] *s* chwalipięta *m*

braid [breɪd] *s* **1.** *Am* warkocz *m* **2.** galon *m*, szamerunek *m* **II** *v/t hair*: *Am* splatać ⟨-leść⟩ w warkocz

brain [breɪn] *s* **1.** mózg *m* **2. ~s** rozum, umysł; ***rack one's ~s*** łamać sobie głowę; **'brain•child** *s infml* pomysł *m*; **'brain dam•age** *s* uszkodzenie *n* mózgu; **'brain dead** *adj* **1.** w stanie śmierci mózgowej **2.** *infml* beznadziejnie głupi; **'brain death** *s* śmierć *f* mózgowa; **'brain drain** *s* drenaż *m* mózgów

brain•less ['breɪnlɪs] *adj* **1.** bezmózgi **2.** idiotyczny

brains [breɪnz] → ***brain 2***

'brain•storm *s infml* **1. *have a ~*** *Br* mieć zaćmienie umysłu **2.** *Am* olśnienie *n*; **'brain•storm•ing** *s* burza *f* mózgów; **'brain sur•geon** *s* neurochirurg *m*; **'brain sur•ger•y** *s* **1.** neurochirurgia *f* **2.** operacja *f* mózgu; **'brain teas•er** *s infml* łamigłówka *f*; **'brain tu•mor** *s* guz *m* mózgu; **'brain-wash** *v/t* robić ⟨z-⟩ pranie mózgu; **'brain•wash•ing** *s* pranie *n* mózgu; **'brain•wave** *s infml* **1.** olśnienie *n* **2. ~s** fale mózgowe; **'brain•worker** *s* pracownik *m* umysłowy

brain•y ['breɪnɪ] *adj infml* łebski, bystry

braise [breɪz] *v/t meat, vegetables*: dusić ⟨u-⟩

brake [breɪk] **I** *s* hamulec *m* **II** *v/i* hamować ⟨za-⟩; **'brake flu•id** *s* płyn *m* hamulcowy; **'brake light** *s* światło *n* stopu; **'brake lin•ing** *s* okładzina *f* ścierna tarczy hamulcowej; **'brake ped•al** *s* pedał *m* hamulca; **'brake shoe** *s* szczęka *f* hamulcowa

branch [bræntʃ] **I** *s* **1.** gałąź *f* **2.** konar *m* **3.** oddział *m* **4.** filia *f* **5.** wydział *m* **6.** *of river*: odnoga *f* **II** *v/i* (*road*) rozwidlać ⟨-lić⟩ się; **branch off** *v/i* (*road*) odchodzić ⟨odejść⟩; **branch out** *v/i* **1.** rozszerzać ⟨-rzyć⟩ działalność **2.** rozwijać ⟨-winąć⟩ zainteresowania

'branch man•ag•er *s* (*in bank*) dyrektor *m* oddziału; **'branch of•fice** *s* oddział *m*, filia *f*

brand [brænd] **I** *s* **1.** marka *f* **2.** rodzaj *m* **3.** piętno *n* **II** *v/t* **1.** znakować ⟨o-⟩ **2.** przyczepiać ⟨-pić⟩ etykietkę; **brand a•'ware•ness** *s* popularność *f* marki; **brand•ed** ['brændɪd] *adj goods*: markowy; **brand 'im•age** *s* wizerunek *m* marki

'brand name *s* nazwa *f* firmowa; **brand-'new** *adj* nowiusieńki, fabrycznie nowy

bran•dy ['brændɪ] *s* **1.** brandy *f* **2.** koniak *m*; **'bran•dy glass** *s* kieliszek *m* do koniaku, koniakówka *f*

B

brass [brɑːs] *s* **1.** mosiądz *m* **2.** ***the ~ instruments*** instrumenty dęte blaszane **3.** *fig* grube ryby *pl*; **brass 'band** *s* orkiestra *f* dęta

bras•siere ['bræzɪə] *s form* biustonosz *m*

brass 'tacks *pl*: ***get down to ~*** *infml* przejść do sedna sprawy, przejść do konkretów

brat [bræt] *infml* **1.** bachor *m* **2.** łobuz *m*

bra•va•do [brə'vɑːdəʊ] *s* brawura *f*

brave [breɪv] **I** *adj* dzielny, odważny **II** *v/t* stawiać ⟨-wić⟩ czoła; ***~ it out*** być dzielnym; **brave•ly** ['breɪvlɪ] *adv* dzielnie; **brav•er•y** ['breɪvərɪ] *s* odwaga *f*

brawl [brɔːl] **I** *s* burda *f*, bójka *f* **II** *v/i* awanturować się

Bra•zil [brə'zɪl] *s* Brazylia *f*; **Bra•zil•ian** [brə'zɪlɪən] **I** *adj* brazylijski **II** *s* Brazylijczyk *m*, Brazylijka *f*; **Bra'zil nut** *s* orzech *m* brazylijski

breach [briːtʃ] **I** *s* **1.** naruszenie *n* **2.** pogwałcenie *n* **3.** wyłom *m* **4.** *trust*: nadużycie *n* **II** *v/t* **1.** *law, terms*: naruszać ⟨-szyć⟩ **2.** (*wall*) robić ⟨z-⟩ wyłom w *L* **3.** *defence line*: przełamywać ⟨-mać⟩; **breach of 'con•tract** *s* naruszenie *n* warunków umowy; **breach of 'trust** *s* nadużycie *n* zaufania

bread [bred] **I** *s* **1.** chleb *m*; ***~ and butter*** chleb z masłem; ***earn*** (*a.* ***make***) ***one's ~*** zarabiać na chleb; ***she knows which side her ~ is buttered*** (***on***) *infml* wie, co się jej opłaca **2.** pieczywo *n* **II** *v/t* panierować; **'bread•bas•ket** *s* **1.** koszyk *m* na chleb **2.** *fig* spichlerz *m*; **'bread bin** *s Br* pojemnik *m* na chleb; **'bread board** *s* deska *f* do krojenia chleba; **'bread box** *s Am* pojemnik *m* na chleb; **'bread•crumbs** *pl* bułka *f* tarta; **'bread knife** *s* nóż *m* do chleba; **'bread•line** *s*: ***live on the ~*** *Br* żyć na granicy ubóstwa; **'bread roll** *s* bułka *f*

breadth [bredθ] *s* szerokość *f*; ***be ten feet in ~*** mieć 10 stóp szerokości; ***what ~ is it?*** jaką to ma szerokość?

break [breɪk] **I** (*broke*; *broken*) *v/t* **1.** łamać ⟨z-, po-⟩; ***~ one's arm*** złamać sobie rękę; ***~ s.o.'s resistance*** złamać czyjś opór **2.** rozbijać ⟨-bić⟩ **3.** psuć ⟨ze-⟩ **4.** *record*: bić ⟨po-⟩ **5.** przerywać ⟨-rwać⟩; ***~ a journey*** zrobić przerwę w podróży **6.** *news*: przekazywać ⟨-zać⟩ **7.** *sound barrier*: przekraczać ⟨-roczyć⟩ **8.** ***~ the habit of*** odzwyczaić się od *G* **9.** *money*: rozmieniać ⟨-nić⟩ **10.** ***break s.o.'s serve*** SPORT przełamać czyjś serwis **II** (*broke*; *broken*) *v/i* **1.** łamać ⟨z-⟩ się **2.** psuć ⟨ze-⟩ się **3.** tłuc ⟨s-, po-⟩ się **4.** zrywać ⟨zerwać⟩; ***~ with*** zerwać z *I* **5.** załamywać ⟨-mać⟩ się **6.** (*day*) nastawać ⟨-tać⟩ **7.** (*storm*) rozpętywać ⟨-tać⟩ się **8.** (*scandal*) wybuchać ⟨-chnąć⟩ **9.** ***~ into tears*** wybuchnąć płaczem **III** *s* **1.** przerwa *f*; ***take a ~ for a cigarette*** zrobić przerwę na papierosa **2.** wolne *n* **3.** zerwanie *n* (***from/with*** z *I*); ***make a ~ from*** zerwać z *I* **4.** złamanie *n* **5.** pęknięcie *n* **6.** rozłam *m* **7.** (nagła) zmiana *f*; ***~ in the weather*** zmiana pogody **8.** ***at the ~ of day*** o świcie **9.** (*in tennis*) przełamanie *n* (serwisu); **break away I** *v/i* **1.** odrywać ⟨oderwać⟩ się (***from*** od *G*) **2.** zrywać ⟨zerwać⟩ się z *I* **3.** uciekać ⟨uciec⟩ **II** *v/t* odrywać ⟨oderwać⟩ (***from*** od *G*); **break down I** *v/i* **1.** psuć ⟨po-⟩ się **2.** załamywać ⟨-mać⟩ się **3.** (*marriage*) rozpadać ⟨-paść⟩ się **II** *v/t* **1.** dzielić ⟨po-⟩ **2.** rozbijać ⟨-bić⟩ **3.** *door*: wyważać ⟨-żyć⟩ **4.** *blockade*: przełamywać ⟨-mać⟩ **5.** (*bacteria*) rozkładać ⟨-złożyć⟩; **break even** *v/i* wychodzić ⟨wyjść⟩ na czysto; **break in I** *v/i* **1.** włamywać ⟨-mać⟩ się **2.** wtargnąć **3.** wtrącać ⟨-cić⟩ się (***on*** do *G*) **II** *v/t* **1.** *car*: docierać ⟨dotrzeć⟩ **2.** *shoes*: rozchodzić ⟨-zejść⟩ **3.** wdrażać ⟨-rożyć⟩ do pracy; **break into** *v/t* **1.** włamywać ⟨-mać⟩ się do *G* **2.** ***~ a run*** zacząć biec; ***~ song*** zacząć śpiewać; **break off I** *v/t* **1.** → ***break away II* 2.** *negotiations, engagement*: zrywać ⟨zerwać⟩ **II** *v/i* → ***break away I.1***; **break out** *v/i* wybuchać ⟨-chnąć⟩; ***~ in laughter*** (***tears***) wybuchnąć śmiechem (płaczem); ***he broke out in a cold sweat*** oblał się zimnym potem; **break up I** *v/i* **1.** zrywać ⟨zerwać⟩ (***with*** z *I*) **2.** rozstawać ⟨-tać⟩ się **3.** rozpadać ⟨-paść⟩ się **4.** ***the meeting broke up*** uczestnicy spotkania rozeszli się **II** *v/t* **1.** łamać ⟨po-⟩

B

2. rozbijać ⟨-bić⟩ 3. przełamywać ⟨-mać⟩ 4. dzielić ⟨po-⟩
break•a•ble ['breɪkəbl] *adj* kruchy, łatwo tłukący się
break•age ['breɪkɪdʒ] *s* 1. stłuczenie *n* 2. stłuczony przedmiot *m*, stłuczka *f*
break•a•way ['breɪkəweɪ] *s* 1. zerwanie *n* (***from*** z *I*) 2. oderwanie się *n* (***from*** od *G*) 3. rozłam *m*
break•down *s* ['breɪkdaʊn] 1. awaria *f*, uszkodzenie *n* 2. załamanie *n* (się); ***nervous ~*** załamanie nerwowe 3. *marriage*: rozpad *m* 4. wykaz *m*; **'break•down ser•vice** *s Br* pomoc *f* drogowa; **'break•down truck** *s Br* samochód *m* pomocy drogowej
break•er ['breɪkə] *s* (*wave*) bałwan *m*, grzywacz *m*
break-'e•ven point *s* granica *f* opłacalności
break•fast ['brekfəst] I *s* śniadanie *n*; ***have ~*** jeść śniadanie II *v/i* jeść ⟨z-⟩ śniadanie; **break•fast 'tel•e•vi•sion** *s* telewizja *f* śniadaniowa
'break-in *s* włamanie *n*
break•ing and 'en•ter•ing *s* włamanie *n*
'break•ing point *s* 1. granica *f* wytrzymałości 2. punkt *m* krytyczny
'break•neck *adj speed*: zawrotny; **'break•out** *s* grupowa ucieczka *f* (z więzienia); **'break•through** *s* 1. przełom *m* 2. przełomowe osiągnięcie *n* 3. przełamanie *n* linii frontu; **'break•up** *s* 1. rozpad *m* 2. podział *m*; **'break•wat•er** *s* falochron *m*
breast [brest] I *s* pierś *f*; ***make a clean ~ of*** wyznać *A* II *v/t* wspinać ⟨-piąć⟩ się na szczyt; **'breast•bone** *s* ANAT mostek *m*; **'breast•feed** (*breastfed*; *breastfed*) *v/t* karmić ⟨na-⟩ piersią; **'breast pock•et** *s* górna kieszeń *f*; **'breast•stroke** *s* SPORT styl *m* klasyczny, żabka *f*
breath [breθ] *s* 1. oddech *m*; ***bad ~*** nieświeży oddech; ***be out of ~*** mieć zadyszkę; ***get one's ~ back*** złapać oddech; ***under one's ~*** pod nosem, cicho; ***waste one's ~*** strzępić sobie język; ***in the same ~*** za jednym zamachem 2. wdech *m* 3. wydech *m*; ***in one ~*** jednym tchem 4. (*a.* ***~ of air***) powiew *m*, tchnienie *n*
breathe [bri:ð] I *v/i* 1. oddychać ⟨odetchnąć⟩ 2. dmuchać ⟨-chnąć⟩ 3. chuchać ⟨-chnąć⟩ II *v/t* 1. zionąć 2. szeptać ⟨wy-⟩; **breathe in** I *v/i* robić ⟨z-⟩ wdech II *v/t* wdychać; **breathe out** I *v/i* robić ⟨z-⟩ wydech II *v/t* wydychać
breath•er ['bri:ðə] *s infml* krótka przerwa *f*, chwila *f* wytchnienia, odpoczynek *m*; ***have*** (*a.* ***take***) ***a ~*** zrobić sobie krótką przerwę; ***I need a ~*** muszę odsapnąć
breath•ing ['bri:ðɪŋ] *s* 1. oddychanie *n*; ***~ exercises*** ćwiczenia oddechowe 2. oddech *m*
breath•less ['breθlɪs] *adj* 1. zdyszany, zasapany 2. *pace*: zawrotny; **breath-less•ness** ['breθlɪsnɪs] *s* zadyszka *f*
breath•tak•ing ['breθteɪkɪŋ] *adj* 1. zapierający dech (w piersiach) 2. *speed*: zawrotny 3. oszałamiający; **'breath test** *s Br* test *m* na zawartość alkoholu w organizmie
bred [bred] *Past Simple and Past Participle* → ***breed***
breed [bri:d] I (*bred*; *bred*) *v/t* 1. hodować ⟨wy-⟩ 2. *problems*: rodzić ⟨z-⟩, wywoływać ⟨-łać⟩ II (*bred*; *bred*) *v/i* rozmnażać ⟨-nożyć⟩ się III *s* 1. rasa *f* 2. typ *m*, rodzaj *m*; ***be a rare ~*** należeć do rzadkości; **breed•er** ['bri:də] *s* hodowca *m*; **breed•ing** ['bri:dɪŋ] *s* 1. hodowla *f* 2. rozmnażanie *n* 3. wychowanie *n*; ***good ~*** dobre wychowanie, dobre maniery; **breed-ing ground** *s* lęgowisko *n*
breeze [bri:z] I *s* 1. wiaterek *f* 2. bryza *f* II *v/i* ***~ through the exams*** z łatwością zdać egzaminy
'breeze block *s Br* 1. bloczek *m* żużlobetonowy 2. pustak *m* żużlobetonowy
breez•i•ly ['bri:zɪlɪ] *adv* pogodnie; **breez•y** ['bri:zɪ] *adj* 1. wietrzny 2. *person*: pogodny
brev•i•ty ['brevətɪ] *s* zwięzłość *f*
brew [bru:] I *v/t* 1. *beer*: warzyć ⟨u-⟩ 2. *tea*: parzyć ⟨za-⟩ II *v/i* 1. (*tea*) parzyć się 2. ***s.th. is brewing*** zanosi się na coś III *s* 1. piwo *n* 2. herbata *f* 3. napar *m*; **brew•er** ['bru:ə] *s* piwowar *m*; **brew•er•y** ['bru:ərɪ] *s* browar *m*
bribe [braɪb] I *s* łapówka *f* II *v/t* dawać ⟨dać⟩ łapówkę, przekupywać ⟨-pić⟩; **brib•er•y** ['braɪbərɪ] *s* łapówkar-

B

stwo *n*, przekupstwo *n*; ***open to ~*** przekupny

bric-a-brac ['brɪkəbræk] *no pl s* bibeloty *pl*

brick [brɪk] *s* **1.** cegła *f*; ***drop a ~*** *Br infml* popełnić gafę **2.** (*toy*) klocek *m*; **brick in**, ***brick up*** *v/t* zamurowywać ⟨-rować⟩

'**brick•bat** *s fig* atak *m*; '**brick•lay•er** *s* murarz *m*; **brick** '**wall** *s* mur *m*; '**brick•work** *s* murarka *f*

bride [braɪd] *s* panna *f* młoda; ***give away a ~*** prowadzić pannę młodą do ołtarza; '**bride•groom** *s* pan *m* młody; '**brides•maid** *s* druhna *f*

bridge[1] [brɪdʒ] **I** *s* **1.** most *m*; ***burn one's ~s*** (***behind one***) palić za sobą mosty **2.** mostek *m* **3.** ***the ~*** mostek kapitański **4.** ***the ~ of the nose*** grzbiet nosa **II** *v/t* **1.** przerzucać ⟨-cić⟩ most przez *A* **2.** ***~ the gap between*** **a)** zbliżyć *A* **b)** łączyć w sobie elementy *G*

bridge[2] [~] *s* (*card-game*) brydż *m*

bri•dle [braɪdl] **I** *s* uzda *f* **II** (*a.* ***~ up***) *v/i* obruszać ⟨-szyć⟩ się **III** *v/t* zakładać ⟨założyć⟩ uzdę

brief [bri:f] **I** *adj* **1.** krótki; ***be ~!*** *infml* streszczaj się! **2.** zwięzły **3.** *bikini*: skąpy **II** *v/t* **1.** informować ⟨po-⟩ **2.** instruować ⟨po-⟩ **III** *s* **1.** ***in ~*** pokrótce, w skrócie **2.** zadanie *n* **3.** → ***briefs***; '**brief•case** *s* **1.** teczka *f* **2.** aktówka *f*

brief•ing ['bri:fɪŋ] *s* **1.** briefing *m*, konferencja *f* prasowa **2.** wytyczne *pl*, informacje *pl*

brief•ly ['bri:flɪ] *adv* **1.** krótko **2.** zwięźle **3.** przelotnie **4.** krótko mówiąc; **brief•ness** ['bri:fnɪs] → ***brevity***

briefs [bri:fs] *pl*: (***a pair of***) ~ slipy *pl*

bri•gade [brɪ'geɪd] *s* brygada *f*; ***fire ~*** straż pożarna; **brig•a•dier** [brɪgə'dɪə] *s Br* brygadier *m*

bright [braɪt] *adj* **1.** *light*, *room*: jasny **2.** *colour*: żywy, jaskrawy; ***a ~ green logo*** jaskrawozielone logo **3.** *eyes*: błyszczący **4.** *day*: słoneczny, pogodny **5.** bystry, inteligentny **6.** optymistyczny **7.** radosny **8.** *future*: wspaniały, świetlany; **bright•en up** ['braɪtnʌp] *v/i* **1.** rozpogadzać ⟨-godzić⟩ się **2.** (*situation*) poprawiać ⟨-wić⟩ się; **bright•ly** ['braɪtlɪ] *adv* **1.** jasno **2.** ***~ coloured*** jaskrawy **3.** pogodnie **4.** radośnie; **bright•ness** ['braɪtnɪs] *s* **1.** jasność *f* **2.** (*of colour*) żywość *f*, jaskrawość *f* **3.** blask *m* **4.** pogoda *f* **5.** radość *f* **6.** bystrość *f*, inteligencja *f*; '**bright•ness con•trol** *s* regulacja *f* jasności

bril•liance ['brɪljəns] *s* **1.** błyskotliwość *f* **2.** jaskrawość *f* **3.** blask *m*; **bril•liant** ['brɪljənt] **I** *adj* **1.** błyskotliwy **2.** olśniewający **3.** błyszczący **II** *interj* świetnie!, super!

brim [brɪm] **I** *s* **1.** brzeg *m*; ***filled to the ~*** wypełniony po brzegi **2.** (*of hat*) rondo *n* **II** *v/i* być pełnym; **brim over** *v/i* **1.** być przepełnionym (***with*** *I*) **2.** *happiness*: nie posiadać się (***with*** z *I*)

brim•ful ['brɪmfʊl] *adj* pełen (**of** *G*)

bring [brɪŋ] (*brought*; *brought*) *v/t* **1.** przynosić ⟨-nieść⟩; ***what ~s you here?*** co cię tu sprowadza? **2.** przyprowadzać ⟨-dzić⟩ **3.** *benefits*: przynosić ⟨-nieść⟩ **4.** ***I can't ~ myself to do it*** nie mogę się zmusić, żeby to zrobić **4.** ***~ s.th. to an end*** zakończyć coś, doprowadzić coś do końca **5.** ***~ a legal action against*** wnieść powództwo przeciwko *D*; **bring about** *v/t* **1.** powodować ⟨s-⟩ **2.** doprowadzać ⟨-dzić⟩ do *G* **3.** wywoływać ⟨-łać⟩; **bring around** *v/t* **1.** cucić ⟨o-⟩ **2.** przekonywać ⟨-nać⟩ (**to** do *G*); **bring back** *v/t* **1.** *book*: zwracać ⟨-rócić⟩ **2.** odwozić ⟨-wieźć⟩ **3.** *memories*: przywoływać ⟨-łać⟩ **4.** *death penalty*: przywracać ⟨-rócić⟩ **5.** przywozić ⟨-wieźć⟩; **bring down** *v/t* **1.** *government*: obalać ⟨-lić⟩ **2.** *prices*: obniżać ⟨-żyć⟩ **3.** zestrzeliwać ⟨-lić⟩ **4.** przynosić ⟨-nieść⟩ z góry; **bring forward** *v/t* **1.** przyspieszać ⟨-szyć⟩ termin **2.** przedstawiać ⟨-wić⟩ **3.** przedkładać ⟨-dłożyć⟩ **4.** *total balance*: przenosić ⟨-nieść⟩; **bring in** *v/t* **1.** wprowadzać ⟨-dzić⟩ **2.** *income*: przynosić ⟨-nieść⟩ **3.** *verdict*: wydawać ⟨-dać⟩ **4.** *capital*: wnosić ⟨-nieść⟩; **bring off** *v/t*: ***we brought it off*** udało nam się; **bring on** *v/t* **1.** powodować ⟨s-⟩ **2.** doprowadzać ⟨-dzić⟩ do *G*; **bring out** *v/t* **1.** *record*, *book*: wydawać ⟨-dać⟩ **2.** *play*: wystawiać ⟨-wić⟩ **3.** podkreślać ⟨-lić⟩, uwydatniać ⟨-nić⟩ **4.** wydobywać ⟨-być⟩; **bring round,** ***bring to*** *v/t* cucić ⟨o-⟩; **bring up** *v/t*

B

1. wychowywać ⟨-chować⟩ 2. *subject*: poruszać ⟨-szyć⟩ 3. *Br* wymiotować ⟨z-⟩
brink [brɪŋk] *s* krawędź *f*; ***on the ~ of war*** na krawędzi wojny; ***bring s.o. to the ~ of ruin*** doprowadzić kogoś na skraj ruiny
brin•y ['braɪnɪ] *adj* słony
brisk [brɪsk] *adj* 1. energiczny 2. szybki 3. żwawy 4. ożywiony 5. *air, wind*: rześki
bris•tle ['brɪsl] I *s* szczecina *f* II *v/i* 1. (*a.* ***~ up***) jeżyć ⟨na-, z-⟩ się 2. być najeżonym (***with*** *I*), być pełnym (***with*** *G*); **bris•tly** ['brɪslɪ] *adj* 1. szczeciniasty; ***~ beard*** kilkudniowy zarost 2. zarośnięty
Brit [brɪt] *s infml* Brytyjczyk *m*
Brit•ain ['brɪtn] *s* Wielka Brytania *f*; **Brit•ish** ['brɪtɪʃ] I *adj* brytyjski; ***he's ~*** jest Brytyjczykiem II *s* ***the ~*** Brytyjczycy; **Brit•ish•er** ['brɪtɪʃə] *s Am* Brytyjczyk *m*; **Brit•ish 'Isles** *pl* Wyspy *pl* Brytyjskie
Brit•on ['brɪtn] *s* 1. Brytyjczyk *m* 2. HIST Bryt *m*
broad [brɔːd] I *adj* 1. szeroki; ***be 5 metres ~*** mieć pięć metrów szerokości 2. ogólny; ***in ~ outline*** w ogólnym zarysie 3. *hint, wink*: wyraźny 4. *variety*: wielki 5. rozległy II *s Am infml dated* babka *f*, kobietka *f*
'broad•cast I *v/t* (*broadcast/broadcasted; broadcast/broadcasted*) 1. nadawać ⟨-dać⟩, transmitować 2. rozgłaszać ⟨-łosić⟩, rozpowiadać ⟨-wiedzieć⟩ II *v/i* (*a. broadcast/broadcasted; broadcast/broadcasted*) nadawać ⟨-dać⟩ III *s* 1. program *m* 2. audycja *f* 3. transmisja *f*; **'broad•cast•er** *s* 1. prezenter *m* 2. stacja *f* telewizyjna 3. stacja *f* radiowa; **'broad•cast•ing** I *s* 1. radio *n* i telewizja *f* 2. nadawanie *n* 3. programy *pl* II *adj* 1. radiowo-telewizyjny 2. nadawczy; **'broadcasting station** *s* stacja *f* nadawcza; **'broad•casting rights** *pl* prawa *pl* do transmisji
broad•en ['brɔːdn] I *v/t* 1. rozszerzać ⟨-rzyć⟩ 2. poszerzać ⟨-rzyć⟩; ***~ s.o.'s horizons*** poszerzać czyjeś horyzonty; ***travel ~s the mind*** podróże kształcą II *v/i* 1. (*a.* ***~ out***) rozszerzać ⟨-rzyć⟩ się 2. poszerzać ⟨-rzyć⟩ się
'broad•jump *s Am* skok *m* w dal
broad•ly ['brɔːdlɪ] *adv* 1. szeroko 2. zasadniczo; ***~ speaking*** ogólnie rzecz biorąc
broad•'mind•ed *adj* 1. tolerancyjny 2. ***be ~*** mieć otwarty umysł; **broad-'mind•ed•ness** *s* 1. tolerancja *f*, tolerancyjność *f* 2. otwartość *f* umysłu; **'broad•sheet (news•pap•er)** *s* gazeta *f* dużego formatu; **'broad•side** *s* burta *f*
bro•cade [brə'keɪd] *s* brokat *m*
broc•co•li ['brɒkəlɪ] *pl* brokuł *m*, brokuły *pl*
bro•chure ['brəʊʃə] *s* broszura *f*
broil [brɔɪl] I *v/t* 1. grillować 2. piec ⟨u-⟩ II *v/i* smażyć ⟨wy-⟩ się; ***be ~ing in the sun*** smażyć się na słońcu; **broil•er** ['brɔɪlə] *s* brojler *m*
broke [brəʊk] I *v Past Simple* → ***break*** II *adj infml* 1. spłukany, bez grosza
2. ***go ~*** zbankrutować 3. ***go for ~*** iść va banque, postawić wszystko na jedną kartę
bro•ken ['brəʊkən] I *v Past Participle* → ***break*** II *adj* 1. zepsuty 2. złamany; ***a ~ leg*** złamana noga; ***a ~ promise*** złamana obietnica 3. rozbity; ***a ~ marriage*** rozbite małżeństwo 4. przerwany, urwany 5. *person*: załamany 6. łamany; ***speak ~ English*** mówić łamaną angielszczyzną; **bro•ken-'heart•ed** *adj* zrozpaczony; ***be ~*** mieć złamane serce
bro•ker ['brəʊkə] *s* 1. makler *m* 2. broker *m* 3. pośrednik *m* handlowy; **bro•ker•age** ['brəʊkərədʒ] *s* 1. maklerstwo *n*; ***a ~ house*** dom maklerski 2. prowizja *f* maklerska
bron•chi•tis [brɒŋ'kaɪtɪs] *s* zapalenie *n* oskrzeli
bronze [brɒnz] I *s* brąz *m* II *adj* 1. brązowy 2. z brązu; **'Bronze Age** epoka *f* brązu; **'bronze med•al** *s* brązowy medal *m*; **'bronze med•al•(l)ist** *s* brązowy medalista *m*
brooch [brəʊtʃ] *s* broszka *f*
brood[1] [bruːd] *v/t* 1. dumać, rozmyślać (***about/on/over*** o *L*) 2. rozpamiętywać (***about/on/over*** *A*)
brood[2] [~] I *v/t eggs*: wysiadywać ⟨-siedzieć⟩ II *s* potomstwo *n*, młode *pl*

B

brood•y ['bruːdɪ] *adj* **1.** ponury **2.** *hen*: niosący się **3.** ***feel ~*** (*woman*) pragnąć mieć dziecko
brook [brʊk] *s* strumyk *m*
broom [bruːm] *s* miotła *f*; **'broom•stick** *s* kij *m* od miotły; ***a witch on a ~*** czarownica na miotle
broth [brɒθ] *s* bulion *m*
broth•el ['brɒθl] *s* burdel *m*
broth•er ['brʌðə] *s* **1.** brat *m*; ***~s and sisters*** rodzeństwo, bracia i siostry **2.** ***~s, brethren*** *REL* bracia zakonni; **broth•er•hood** ['brʌðəhʊd] *s* **1.** braterstwo *n* **2.** bractwo *n* **3.** stowarzyszenie *n* **4.** związek *m*; **'broth•er-in-law** *pl brothers-in-law s* szwagier *m*; **broth•er•ly** ['brʌðərlɪ] *adj* braterski
brought [brɔːt] *Past Simple and Past Participle* → **bring**
brow [braʊ] *s* **1.** czoło *n* **2.** brew *f*
'brow•beat (*browbeat; browbeaten*) *v/t* zastraszać ⟨-szyć⟩
brown [braʊn] **I** *adj* **1.** brązowy **2.** opalony (na brąz); ***go ~*** opalić się **II** *s* brąz *m*, brązowy *m* **III** *v/t* rumienić ⟨za-⟩ **IV** *v/i* rumienić ⟨za-⟩ się; **brown•ie** ['braʊnɪ] *s* ciastko *n* czekoladowe; **Brown•ie** *s* (*girl*) zuch *m*; **'brown•ie points** *pl*: ***do s.th. to get ~*** robić coś, żeby dostać pochwałę **brown•ish** ['braʊnɪʃ] *adj* brązowawy; **'brown-nos•ing** *s* podlizywanie *n* się; **brown 'pa•per** *s* szary papier *m*, papier *m* pakowy; **brown 'sug•ar** *s* brązowy cukier *m* (z trzciny cukrowej)
browse [braʊz] *v/i* **1.** przeglądać ⟨przejrzeć⟩ (***through*** *A*); ***~ through a book*** przeglądać książkę **2.** rozglądać ⟨przejrzeć⟩ się **3.** szperać ⟨po-⟩ **4.** paść się; **brows•er** ['braʊzə] *s INF* przeglądarka *f*
bruise [bruːz] **I** *v/t* **1.** siniaczyć ⟨po-⟩; ***~ one's knee*** stłuc sobie kolano **2.** *fruit*: obijać ⟨obić⟩ **II** *s* **1.** siniak *m* **2.** ***with a ~*** (*fruit*) obity
bruis•ing ['bruːzɪŋ] *adj* **1.** przykry **2.** bolesny
brunch [brʌntʃ] *s późne śniadanie połączone z lunchem*
bru•nette [bruː'net] *s* brunetka *f*
brush [brʌʃ] **I** *s* **1.** szczotka *f* **2.** szczoteczka *f* **3.** pędzel *m* **4.** pędzelek *m* **5.** ***give one's teeth a ~*** umyć zęby **6.** ***give one's hair a ~*** uczesać się **7.** otarcie *n* się, muśnięcie *n* **8.** spięcie *n*, utarczka *f* **II** *v/t* **1.** szczotkować ⟨wy-⟩ **2.** czyścić ⟨wy-⟩ **3.** myć ⟨u-⟩; ***~ one's teeth*** umyć zęby **4.** ocierać ⟨otrzeć⟩ się o *A*, muskać ⟨-snąć⟩; **brush against** *v/i* ocierać ⟨otrzeć⟩ się o *A*, muskać ⟨-snąć⟩; **brush aside** *v/t* **1.** ignorować ⟨z-⟩ **2.** odrzucać ⟨-cić⟩ **3.** odsuwać ⟨-sunąć⟩; **brush off** *v/t* **1.** *dust, crumbs*: strzepywać ⟨-pać⟩ **2.** odrzucać ⟨-cić⟩ **3.** odtrącać ⟨-cić⟩; **brush up on** *v/i* **1.** *language*: podszlifować **2.** doskonalić ⟨u-⟩
'brush-off *s*: ***give s.o. a ~*** *infml* spławić kogoś; **'brush•work** *s ART* faktura *f*
Brus•sels ['brʌslz] *s* Bruksela *f*
brus•sels 'sprouts *pl* brukselka *f*
bru•tal ['bruːtl] *adj* **1.** brutalny **2.** okrutny; **bru•tal•i•ty** [bruː'tælətɪ] *s* **1.** brutalność *f* **2.** okrucieństwo *n*; **bru•tal•ize** ['bruːtəlaɪz] *v/t* **1.** odczłowieczać ⟨-czyć⟩ **2.** traktować ⟨po-⟩ brutalnie; **bru•tal•ly** ['bruːtəlɪ] *adv* brutalnie; **brute** [bruːt] **I** *adj* brutalny; ***by ~ force*** siłą **II** *s* **1.** (*person*) brutal *m* **2.** (*animal*) bestia *f*
B.S. [biː'es] *abbr* **1.** (=***British Standard***) brytyjska norma *f* **2.** (=***Bachelor of Science***) *Am* licencjat *m* z nauk ścisłych **3.** → ***bull shit***
B.Sc. [biːes'siː] *abbr* (=***Bachelor of Science***) *Br* licencjat *m* z nauk ścisłych
BSE [biːes'iː] *abbr* (=***Bovine Spongiform Encephalopathy***) *MED* BSE *n*, gąbczaste zapalenie *n* mózgu
'B-side *s* strona *f* B
bub•ble ['bʌbl] **I** *s* **1.** bąbelek *m* **2.** pęcherzyk *m* **3.** bańka *f* **II** *v/i* **1.** pienić się **2.** bulgotać; **bubble over with** *v/i joy, ideas*: tryskać
'bub•ble bath *s* **1.** kąpiel *f* w pianie **2.** płyn *m* do kąpieli; **'bub•ble gum** guma *f* balonowa; **bub•bly** ['bʌblɪ] **I** *adj* **1.** *person*: pełen życia **2.** pieniący się **II** *s infml* szampan *m*
buck[1] [bʌk] *s Am infml* dolec *m*; ***ten ~s*** dziesięć dolców; ***make a fast ~*** zrobić szybką kasę
buck[2] [~] **I** *s* **1.** samiec *m* **2.** kozioł *m* **3.** (*young man*) *infml* byczek *m* **II** *v/i* **1.** wierzgać ⟨-gnąć⟩ **2.** przeciw-

stawiać ⟨-wić⟩ się (**at/against** *D*); **buck up I** *v/i* rozchmurzać ⟨-rzyć⟩ się **II** *v/t* rozchmurzać ⟨-rzyć⟩, rozweselać ⟨-lić⟩

buck[3] [~] *s* odpowiedzialność *f*; ***pass the ~*** zrzucić odpowiedzialność na innych

buck•et ['bʌkɪt] **I** *s* **1.** wiadro *n* **2.** kubeł *m* **3.** ***~s of*** *infml* fura *G*, kupa *G*; ***cry ~s*** zalewać się łzami **II** *v/i* ***it's ~ing down*** leje jak z cebra; **buck•et•ful** ['bʌkɪtfʊl] *s* (pełne) wiadro *n* (**of** *G*); **'buck•et seat** *s* fotel *m* kubełkowy, fotel *m* anatomiczny

buck•le ['bʌkl] **I** *s* klamra *f*, sprzączka *f* **II** *v/t* zapinać ⟨-piąć⟩ na klamrę, zapinać ⟨-piąć⟩ na sprzączkę; **buckle down** *v/i* zabierać ⟨-brać⟩ się (**to** za *A*); **buck•le up** *v/i Am* zapinać ⟨-piąć⟩ pasy

'buck•skin *s* koźla skóra *f*; **'buck teeth** *pl* wystające zęby *pl*; **'buck•wheat** *s* **1.** gryka *f* **2.** ***roasted ~*** kasza gryczana

bud[1] [bʌd] **I** *s* pąk *m* **II** *v/i* wypuszczać ⟨-puścić⟩ pąki, pączkować

bud[2] [~] *s Am infml* koleś *m*

Bud•dhism ['bʊdɪzəm] *s* buddyzm *m*; **Bud•dhist** ['bʊdɪst] **I** *s* buddysta *m* **II** *adj* buddyjski

bud•ding ['bʌdɪŋ] *adj* **1.** dobrze się zapowiadający, obiecujący **2.** *beauty*: rozkwitający

bud•dy ['bʌdɪ] *s Am* **1.** kumpel *m* **2.** koleś *m*

budge [bʌdʒ] *v/i* **1.** drgać ⟨-gnąć⟩ **2.** poruszać ⟨-szyć⟩ się

bud•ger•i•gar ['bʌdʒərɪgɑː] *s* papużka *f* falista

budg•et ['bʌdʒɪt] **I** *s* budżet *m* **II** *adj* **1.** tani **2.** bużetowy **III** *v/t* **1.** (rozsądnie) gospodarować pieniędzmi **2.** przeznaczać ⟨-czyć⟩; **budget for** *v/i* uwzględniać ⟨-nić⟩ w budżecie

budg•et•ar•y ['bʌdʒɪtərɪ] *adj* budżetowy; **'budg•et def•i•cit** *s* deficyt *m* budżetowy; **'budg•et ho•tel** *s* tani hotel *m*; **budg•et•ing** ['bʌdʒɪtɪŋ] *s* planowanie *n* wydatków; **'budg•et sur•plus** *s* nadwyżka *f* budżetowa

bud•gie ['bʌdʒɪ] *infml* → ***budgerigar***

buff[1] [bʌf] *s* **1.** *infml* entuzjasta *m*; ***be a film ~*** być zapalonym kinomanem **2.** (*colour*) płowożółty *m* **3.** skóra *f* bawola **4.** ***in the ~*** *infml* na golasa

buff[2] [~] *v/t* polerować ⟨wy-⟩

buf•fa•lo ['bʌfələʊ] *s pl -los, -loes* **1.** bawół *m* **2.** *Am* bizon *m*

buff•er ['bʌfə] **I** *s* **1.** bufor *m*; ***~ memory*** pamięć buforowa **2.** *fig* ochrona *f*, zabezpieczenie *n* **II** *v/t* **1.** ochraniać ⟨-ronić⟩, zabezpieczać ⟨-czyć⟩ (**against** przed *I*) **2.** *effects*: łagodzić ⟨z-⟩

buf•foon [bə'fuːn] *s dated* **1.** błazen *m* **2.** pajac *m*

bug [bʌg] **I** *s* **1.** *Am* robak *m* **2.** pluskwa *f* **3.** *infml* wirus *m* **4.** ***be bitten by the ~*** *fig* złapać bakcyla **II** *v/t* zakładać ⟨założyć⟩ podsłuch; **bug off** *v/i*: ***~!*** *Am infml* spadaj!

bug•ger ['bʌgə] **I** *s* **1.** *infml* gnojek *m* **2.** ***poor ~!*** biedaczysko **3.** *vulg* pedał *m*, ciota *f* **II** *interj* ***~!*** *infml* szlag by trafił!; ***~ that!*** pieprzyć to!; **bugger off** *v/i infml* ulotnić się; ***~!*** spieprzaj!; **bugger up** *v/t infml* spieprzyć

bug•gy ['bʌgɪ] *s* **1.** mały samochód *m* terenowy **2.** wózek *m* (spacerowy)

build [bɪld] **I** (*built*; *built*) *v/t* **1.** budować ⟨z-⟩ **2.** tworzyć ⟨s-⟩ **II** (*built*; *built*) *v/i* (*tension*) narastać **III** *s* budowa *f* (ciała); **build on** *v/t* dobudowywać ⟨-dować⟩; **build up I** *v/t* **1.** wzmacniać ⟨-mocnić⟩ **2.** tworzyć ⟨s-⟩ **II** *v/i* **1.** (*clouds*, *crowd*) gromadzić ⟨z-⟩ się **2.** (*tension*) narastać

build•er ['bɪldə] *s* **1.** przedsiębiorca *m* budowlany **2.** robotnik *m* budowlany; **build•ing** ['bɪldɪŋ] *s* **1.** budynek *m* **2.** budowa *f* **3.** budownictwo *n*; **'build•ing blocks** *pl* (*toy*) klocki *pl*; **'build•ing site** *s* plac *m* budowy; **'build•ing so•ci•e•ty** *s Br* kasa *f* mieszkaniowa; **'build•ing trade** *s* budownictwo *n*; **'build-up** *s* **1.** wzrost *m* **2.** *of troops*: koncentracja *f* **3.** nasilanie *n* się

built [bɪlt] *Past Simple and Past Participle* → ***build***

built-in [bɪlt'ɪn] *adj* wbudowany

built-up 'ar•e•a *s* teren *m* zabudowany

bulb [bʌlb] *s* **1.** żarówka *f* **2.** cebulka *f*; **bul•bous** ['bʌlbəs] *adj nose*: kartoflowaty

Bul•gar•i•a [bʌl'geərɪə] *s* Bułgaria *f*; **Bul•gar•i•an** [bʌl'gerɪən] **I** *adj* bułgarski **II** *s* **1.** Bułgar *m*, Bułgarka *f* **2.** język *m* bułgarski

B

B

bulge [bʌldʒ] **I** *v/i* **1.** wybrzuszać ⟨-szyć⟩ się **2.** ***be bulging with*** być wypchanym *I*; ***the bus was ~ing with passengers*** *infml* autobus był zapchany **3.** ***bulging eyes*** wybałuszone oczy **II** *s* **1.** wybrzuszenie *n* **2.** wypukłość *f* **3.** nagły wzrost *m*

bu•lim•i•a [buːˈlɪmɪə] *s MED* bulimia *f*; **bu•lim•ic** [buːˈlɪmɪk] *adj* bulimiczny

bulk [bʌlk] *s* **1.** większość *f* **2.** wielkość *f*, pokaźny rozmiar *m* **3.** cielsko *n* **4.** ***in ~*** hurtowo **II** *v/i* wybrzuszać ⟨-szyć⟩ się; ***the bus was ~ing with passengers*** *infml* autobus był zapchany; **ˈbulk buy•ing** *s* zakup *m* hurtowy; **ˈbulk•head** *s* przegroda *f*; **ˈbulk or•der** *s* zamówienie *n* hurtowe; **bulk•y** [ˈbʌlkɪ] *adj* **1.** pokaźnych rozmiarów **2.** nieporęczny

bull [bʊl] *s* **1.** byk *m* **2.** samiec *m* **3.** *FIN* grający *m* na zwyżkę

ˈbull•dog *s* buldog *m*; **bulldog clip** *s* spinacz *m* do papieru

bull•doze [ˈbʊldəʊz] *v/t* **1.** wyburzać ⟨-rzyć⟩ za pomocą spycharki **2.** ***~ s.o. into doing s.th.*** zmusić kogoś do zrobienia czegoś; **bull•doz•er** [ˈbʊldəʊzə] *s* spycharka *f*, buldożer *m*

bul•let [ˈbʊlɪt] *s* **1.** kula *f* **2.** pocisk *m*; **ˈbul•let-proof** *adj* kuloodporny

bul•le•tin [ˈbʊlətɪn] *s* biuletyn *m*; **ˈbul•le•tin board** *s* tablica *f* informacyjna

ˈbull fight *s* walka *f* byków; **ˈbull fight•er** *s* torreador *m*; **ˈbull fight•ing** *s* walka *f* byków, corrida *f*; **ˈbull•horn** *s Am* megafon *m*

bul•lion [ˈbʊljən] *s*: ***gold ~*** złoto w sztabach

bull•ish [ˈbʊlɪʃ] *adj* **1.** *trend, market*: wzrostowy **2.** optymistyczny; **ˈbull mar•ket** *s* **1.** rynek *m* wzrostowy **2.** hossa *f*

bull•ock [ˈbʊlək] *s* młody wół *m*, *infml* wołek *m*

ˈbull ring *s* arena *f* (walki byków); **ˈbull's-eye** *s* środek *m* tarczy, dziesiątka *f*; ***hit the ~*** trafić w dziesiątkę; **ˈbull•shit I** *s infml* bzdury *pl*; ***talk ~*** pieprzyć bzdury **II** *v/t* wciskać ⟨-snąć⟩ kit

bul•ly [ˈbʊlɪ] **I** *v/t* **1.** znęcać się nad *I* **2.** zastraszać ⟨-szyć⟩ **II** *s* łobuz *m* (znęcający się nad słabszymi); **bul•ly•ing** [ˈbʊlɪɪŋ] *s* **1.** znęcanie *n* się nad słabszymi **2.** zastraszanie *n*

bum¹ [bʌm] *s Br infml* tyłek *m*, pupa *f*

bum² [~] **I** *s* **1.** *Am* włóczęga *m* **2.** *Am* menel *m* **3.** obibok *m* **II** *v/t infml* wyciągać ⟨-gnąć⟩, wyżebrać; ***can I ~ a fag off you?*** kopsniesz szluga?; **bum around** *v/i* **1.** obijać się **2.** włóczyć się

bum•ble•bee [ˈbʌmblbiː] *s* trzmiel *m*, *infml* bąk *m*

bum•mer [ˈbʌmə] *s*: ***what a ~!*** *infml* co za beznadzieja!; ***I had a ~ of a day*** *infml* miałem okropny dzień

bump [bʌmp] **I** *s* **1.** guz *m* **2.** wybój *m* **3.** ***a speed ~*** próg zwalniający, *infml* śpiący policjant **4.** uderzenie *n* **5.** stłuczka *f* **II** *v/t* uderzać ⟨-rzyć⟩; ***~ one's elbow against*** uderzyć łokciem o *A* **III** *v/i* uderzać ⟨-rzyć⟩ (***against*** o *A*); **bump into** *v/i infml* wpadać ⟨wpaść⟩ na *A*; **bump off** *v/t* (*kill*) *infml* sprzątnąć; **bump up** *v/t infml price*: podnosić ⟨-nieść⟩

bump•er [ˈbʌmpə] *s* zderzak *m*; **ˈbump•er car** *s infml* samochodzik *m* w wesołym miasteczku; **ˈbump•er stick•er** *s* nalepka *f* na zderzak

bump•y [ˈbʌmpɪ] *adj road*: wyboisty

bun [bʌn] *s* **1.** bułka *f* **2.** słodka bułka *f*, drożdżówka *f* **3.** (*hair*) kok *m*

bunch [bʌntʃ] **I** *s* **1.** bukiet *m* **2.** pęk *m* **3.** pęczek *m* **4.** kiść *f* **5.** *infml* grupa *f*; ***they're a nice ~*** to fajni goście **6.** *infml* masa *f*, kupa *f*; ***thanks a ~*** wielkie dzięki **7.** (*hair*) *Br* kucyk *m* **II** *v/t* (*fabric*) marszczyć ⟨z-⟩ się

bun•dle [ˈbʌndl] **I** *s* **1.** paczka *f* **2.** zawiniątko *n* **3.** tobołek *m* **4.** pakiet *m* **5.** plik *m* **6.** szereg *m* **7.** dziecko *n*, maleństwo *n* **II** *v/i* ***~ into a car*** *infml* władować się do samochodu **III** *v/t* ***s.th. is ~d with*** do czegoś dołączony jest *N*, coś zawiera *A*; **bundle up** *v/t* **1.** zwijać ⟨zwinąć⟩ **2.** zbierać ⟨zebrać⟩ w plik **3.** ***~ oneself up*** opatulić się

bung [bʌŋ] **I** *v/t* **1.** *Br infml* rzucać ⟨-cić⟩ **2.** szpuntować ⟨za-⟩ **II** *s* **1.** szpunt *m* **2.** zatyczka *f*; **bung up** *v/t* zatykać ⟨-tkać⟩

bun•gle [ˈbʌŋgl] **I** *v/t infml* partaczyć ⟨s-⟩, knocić ⟨s-⟩ **II** *s* fuszerka *f*; **bun•gler** [ˈbʌŋglə] *s* partacz *m*; **bun•gling** [ˈbʌŋglɪŋ] *adj* nieudolny

bunk•er ['bʌŋkə] *s* **1.** bunkier *m* **2.** komórka *f* na węgiel
bun•ny ['bʌnɪ] *s* króliczek *m*
bunt [bʌnt] *v/i* (*in baseball*) *Am odbicie piłki na niewielką odległość*
buoy [bɔɪ] **I** *s* **1.** boja *f* **2.** koło *n* ratunkowe **II** (*a.* **~ up**) *v/t* **1.** podnosić ⟨-nieść⟩ na duchu, podnosić ⟨-nieść⟩ morale **2.** utrzymywać ⟨-mać⟩ na powierzchni; **buoy•an•cy** ['bɔɪənsɪ] *s* **1.** pływalność *f* **2.** pogoda *f* ducha **3.** optymizm *m* **4.** ***~ of the economy*** prężna gospodarka; **buoy•ant** ['bɔɪənt] *adj* **1.** *mood*: świetny **2.** *economy*: prężny **3.** utrzymujący się na powierzchni **4.** ***sea water is more ~ than fresh water*** woda morska ma większą wyporność niż zwykła woda
bur•ble ['bɜːbəl] *v/i* **1.** bełkotać **2.** (*water*) szemrać
bur•den ['bɜːdn] **I** *s* **1.** obowiązek *m*; ***the ~ of proof is on the prosecution*** to oskarżenie musi udowodnić winę **2.** ciężar *m* **3.** brzemię *n*; ***the ~ of responsibility*** brzemię odpowiedzialności **II** *v/t* **1.** obarczać ⟨-czyć⟩ **2.** obciążać ⟨-żyć⟩ **3.** obładowywać ⟨-dować⟩ (***s.o. with*** kogoś *I*)
bur•den•some ['bɜːdnsəm] *adj* uciążliwy
bu•reau ['bjʊrəʊ] *pl bureaux, bureaus* *s* **1.** biuro *n*; ***the Federal ≈ of Investigation*** Federalne Biuro Śledcze **2.** agencja *f* **3.** urząd *m* **4.** *Br* biurko *n* **5.** *Am* komoda *f*
bu•reauc•ra•cy [bjʊə'rɒkrəsɪ] *s* **1.** urzędy *pl* **2.** biurokracja *f*; **bu•reau•crat** ['bjʊərəkræt] *s* **1.** urzędnik *m* **2.** biurokrata *m*; **bu•reau•crat•ic** [bjʊərə'krætɪk] *adj* biurokratyczny; **bu•reau de change** [bjʊərəʊ də'ʃɑːnʒ] *pl bureaux de change, bureaus de change s* kantor *m* wymiany walut
bur•geon ['bɜːrdʒən] *v/i* **1.** *fig* rozkwitać ⟨-tnąć⟩ **2.** *fig* rosnąć ⟨u-⟩ **3.** wypuszczać ⟨-puścić⟩ pędy **4.** wypuszczać ⟨-puścić⟩ pąki; **bur•geon•ing** ['bʌrdʒənɪŋ] *adj fig* **1.** rozkwitający **2.** rosnący
bur•ger ['bɜːgə] *s* hamburger *m*
bur•glar ['bɜːglə] *s* włamywacz *m*; '**bur•glar a•larm** *s* alarm *m* antywłamaniowy; **bur•glar•ize** ['bɜːgləraɪz] *v/t Am* włamywać ⟨-mać⟩ się do *G*; ***their house was ~d*** włamano się do ich domu; '**bur•glar•proof** *adj* **1.** *house*: zabezpieczony przed włamaniem **2.** *door*: antywłamaniowy; **bur•glar•y** ['bɜːglərɪ] *s* włamanie *n*; **bur•gle** ['bɜːgl] *v/t* włamywać ⟨-mać⟩ się do *G*
bur•i•al ['berɪəl] *s* **1.** pogrzeb *m* **2.** pochówek *m* **3.** pogrzebanie *n*
bur•lesque [bɜː'lesk] *s* **1.** burleska *f* **2.** parodia *f*
bur•ly ['bɜːlɪ] *adj* tęgi, przysadzisty
Bur•ma ['bɜːmə] *s* Birma *f*
burn [bɜːn] **I** (*burnt*; *burnt*) *v/t* **1.** palić ⟨s-⟩; ***be ~ed to the ground*** zostać doszczętnie spalonym, doszczętnie się spalić **2.** parzyć ⟨o-⟩; ***~ one's finger*** oparzyć sobie palec **3.** sparzać ⟨-rzyć⟩ **4.** *food*: przypalać ⟨-lić⟩ **5.** *CD, DVD*: nagrywać ⟨-rać⟩, wypalać ⟨-lić⟩ **II** (*burnt*; *burnt*) *v/i* **1.** palić ⟨s-⟩ się **2.** płonąć ⟨s-⟩ **3.** (*wound*) piec **III** *s* **1.** oparzenie *n*; ***a third degree ~*** oparzenie trzeciego stopnia **2.** wypalona dziura *f*; **burn down** *v/i* **1.** spalać ⟨-lić⟩ się, płonąć ⟨s-⟩ **2.** wypalać ⟨-lić⟩ się; **burn out I** *v/i* wypalać ⟨-lić⟩ się **II** *v/t* ***burn oneself out*** wypalić się; **burn up I** *v/i* spalać ⟨-lić⟩ się **II** *v/t* spalać ⟨-lić⟩
'**burn•out** *s* wypalenie *n*; ***the ~ syndrome*** zespół wypalenia zawodowego; **burnt** [bɜːnt] **I** *Past Simple i Past Participle* → **burn II** *adj* **1.** przypalony **2.** spalony **3.** oparzony
burn•er ['bɜːnə] *s* palnik *m*
burn•ing ['bɜːnɪŋ] *adj* **1.** palący się **2.** płonący **3.** zapalony **4.** *desire, problem*: palący **5.** rozpalony
bur•nish ['bɜːnɪʃ] *v/t* polerować ⟨wy-⟩
burp [bɜːp] **I** *v/i* bekać ⟨-knąć⟩ **II** *s* beknięcie *n*; ***give a ~*** beknąć
bur•row ['bʌrəʊ] **I** *s* **1.** jama *f* **2.** nora *f* **II** *v/i* **1.** kopać ⟨wy-⟩ jamę (**into** w *L*) **2.** zakopywać ⟨-pać⟩ się (**into** w *L*)
burst [bɜːst] **I** (*burst*; *burst*) *v/i* **1.** pękać ⟨-knąć⟩ **2.** wybuchać ⟨-chnąć⟩ **3.** ***~ open*** otworzyć się gwałtownie **II** (*burst*; *burst*) *v/t* **1.** *baloon*: przekłuwać ⟨-łuć⟩ **2.** *dam*: zrywać ⟨zerwać⟩ **III** *s* **1.** wybuch *m*, eksplozja *f* **2.** ***a ~ of applause*** burza oklasków

B

3. ***in ~s*** zrywami; **burst into** *v/t* **1.** ***~ tears*** zalać się łzami; ***~ flames*** zapalić się **2.** wpadać ⟨-paść⟩ do *G*

bur•y ['berɪ] *v/t* **1.** chować ⟨po-⟩, grzebać ⟨po-⟩ **2.** zakopywać ⟨-pać⟩; ***~ the hatchet*** zakopać topór wojenny **3.** zasypywać ⟨-pać⟩ **4.** chować ⟨s-⟩; ***~ one's head in the sand*** chować głowę w piasek **5.** ***~ oneself in work*** oddać się pracy

bus [bʌs] *s* autobus *m*; ***by ~*** autobusem; '**bus•boy** *s Am* pomocnik *m* kelnera; '**bus driv•er** *s* kierowca *m* autobusu; '**bus lane** *s* pas *m* dla autobusów; '**bus•man's hol•i•day** *s Br urlop połączony z pracą zarobkową*; '**bus shel•ter** *s* wiata *f* (przystanku autobusowego); '**bus sta•tion** *s* dworzec *m* autobusowy; '**bus stop** *s* przystanek *m* autobusowy; '**bus tick•et** *s* bilet *m* autobusowy

bush [bʊʃ] *s* **1.** krzak *m* **2.** krzew *m* **3.** busz *m*; **bush•y** ['bʊʃɪ] *adj* **1.** *area*: porośnięty krzakami **2.** *eyebrows*: krzaczasty

bushed [bʊʃt] *adj infml* wykończony, skonany

busi•ness ['bɪznɪs] *s* **1.** interesy *pl*; ***do ~ with*** prowadzić interesy z *I*; ***how's ~?*** jak idą interesy?; ***we are doing much more ~ this year*** nasze obroty w tym roku są znacznie większe **2.** biznes *m* **3.** działalność *f* gospodarcza; ***the firm is no longer in ~*** firma już nie istnieje **4.** firma *f* **5.** przedsiębiorstwo *n* **6.** zakład *m* **7.** branża *f*; ***what's your line of ~?*** czym się pan zajmuje? **8.** sprawy *pl* do załatwienia, obowiązki *pl* **9.** sprawa *f*, rzecz *f*; ***it's none of your ~!*** to nie twoja sprawa!; ***mind your own ~!*** pilnuj swoich spraw!; '**busi•ness ad•dress** *s* **1.** adres *m* służbowy **2.** adres *m* firmy; '**busi•ness card** *s* wizytówka *f*; '**busi•ness class** *s* (*plane*) pierwsza klasa *f*; '**busi•ness hours** *pl* **1.** godziny *pl* urzędowania **2.** godziny *pl* pracy; '**busi•ness let•ter** *s* list *m* handlowy; **busi•ness•like** ['bɪznɪslaɪk] *adj* rzeczowy; '**busi•ness lunch** *s* służbowy lunch *m*; '**busi•ness•man** *pl -men s* **1.** biznesmen *m* **2.** przedsiębiorca *m*; '**busi•ness meet•ing** *s* spotkanie *n* służbowe; '**busi•ness peo•ple** *pl* **1.** biznesmeni *pl* **2.** przedsiębiorcy *pl*; '**busi•ness plan** *s* biznesplan *m*; '**busi•ness relations** *pl* stosunki *pl* handlowe; '**busi•ness school** *s* szkoła *f* biznesu; '**busi•ness stud•ies** *s* zarządzanie *n*; '**busi•ness suit** *s* garnitur *m*; '**busi•ness trip** *s* **1.** podróż *f* służbowa **2.** delegacja *f*; '**busi•ness•wom•an** *pl -men s* **1.** businesswoman *f* **2.** kobieta *f* interesu

bust[1] [bʌst] *s* **1.** biust *m* **2.** popiersie *n*

bust[2] [~] **I** (*bust*; *bust*) *v/t* **1.** psuć ⟨po-⟩ **2.** (*police*) robić ⟨z-⟩ nalot na *A* **3.** *infml* przymykać ⟨-mknąć⟩, zapuszkować **II** *adj* **1.** zepsuty **2.** ***go ~*** splajtować; '**bust up** *v/i* (*couple*) *infml* zrywać ⟨zerwać⟩

bus•tle *v/i* ***~ around*** krzątać się, uwijać się

bust•y ['bʌsti] *adj infml* piersiasty

bus•y ['bɪzɪ] *adj* **1.** zajęty (***with*** *I*) **2.** zapracowany **3.** *day*: pracowity **4.** *street*: ruchliwy **5.** *line*: zajęty **6.** *shop*: pełen klientów; '**bus•y•bod•y** *s* **1.** ciekawski *m* **2.** intrygant *m*; '**bus•y sig•nal** *s* sygnał *m* zajętości

but [bət] *strong form* [bʌt] **I** *conj* ale, lecz; ***I agree ~ I may be wrong*** zgadzam się, ale mogę się mylić; ***it wasn't Eva ~ Mark who told me that*** to nie Ewa, lecz Marek mi to powiedział **II** *prep* **1.** tylko nie *N*; ***anybody ~ him*** wszyscy, tylko nie on **2.** ***~ for*** gdyby nie; ***~ for you I would have died*** gdyby nie ty, umarłbym **III** *adv* tylko

butch [bʊtʃ] *s infml* **1.** babochłop *m* **2.** macho *m*

butch•er ['bʊtʃə] **I** *s* rzeźnik *m* **II** *v/t* **1.** zarzynać ⟨-rżnąć⟩ **2.** (*kill*) masakrować ⟨z-⟩; **butch•er•y** ['bʊtʃərɪ] *s* **1.** masakra *f* **2.** rzeźnictwo *n*

but•ler ['bʌtlə] *s* kamerdyner *m*

butt [bʌt] *s* **1.** ***a cigarette ~*** niedopałek **2.** (*of gun*) kolba *f* **3.** *Am infml* tyłek *m*; **butt in** *v/i* wtrącać ⟨-cić⟩ się; ***sorry to ~*** przepraszam, że się wtrącam; **butt out** *v/i*: ***~!*** *Am infml* odczep się!

but•ter ['bʌtə] **I** *s* masło *n* **II** *v/t* smarować ⟨po-⟩ masłem; **butter up** *v/i infml* podlizywać ⟨-zać⟩ się

'but•ter dish *s* maselniczka *f*; **'but•ter-fin•gers** *s* niezdara *f*; **'but•ter•milk** *s* maślanka *f*; **'but•ter•cup** *s* jaskier *m*; **'but•ter•fly** *s* **1.** motyl *m* **2.** SPORT styl *m* motylkowy, motylek *m*

but•tocks ['bʌtəks] *pl* pośladki *pl*

but•ton ['bʌtn] **I** *s* **1.** guzik *m* **2.** przycisk *m* **II** *v/i* zapinać ⟨-piąć⟩ się (na guziki); **~ *at the back*** mieć zapięcie z tyłu; **button up** *v/t* zapinać ⟨-piąć⟩ (na guziki)

'but•ton-down col•lar *s* kołnierzyk *m* z przypinanymi rogami; **but•toned-'down** *adj* **1.** zapinany na guziki **2.** zapięty na guziki; **'but•ton•hole** *s* dziurka *f* od guzika; **'but•ton mush-room** *s* młoda pieczarka *f*

buy [baɪ] **I** (*bought*; *bought*) *v/t* **1.** kupować ⟨-pić⟩ (***from/off*** od *G*) **2.** przekupywać ⟨-pić⟩ **3.** stawiać ⟨postawić⟩; ***~ s.o. a drink*** postawić komuś drinka **II** *s* zakup *m*; ***a good ~*** dobry zakup; **buy off** *v/t* przekupywać ⟨-pić⟩; **buy out** *v/t* ECON **1.** wykupywać ⟨-pić⟩ **2.** wykupywać ⟨-pić⟩ udziały; **buy up** *v/t* wykupywać ⟨-pić⟩; **'buy•back** *s* odkupienie *n*; **buy•er** [baɪə] *s* nabywca *m*, kupujący *m*; **'buyers mar•ket** *s* rynek *m* nabywcy; **'buy•out** *s* wykup *m* (akcji)

buzz [bʌz] **I** *s* **1.** bzyczenie *n*, brzęczenie *n* **2.** gwar *m* **3.** ***give s.o. a ~*** *infml* przedzwonić do kogoś, przekręcić do kogoś **II** *v/i* **1.** bzyczeć **2.** ***the town ~ed with rumours*** *fig* w mieście huczało od plotek; **buzz off** *v/i*: ***~!*** *Br infml* spadaj!; **buzz•er** ['bʌzə] *s* **1.** brzęczyk *m* **2.** dzwonek *m*; **'buzz•word** *s infml* modne słowo *n*

by [baɪ] **I** *prep* **1.** przez *A*, ***~ mistake*** przez pomyłkę; ***divide ten ~ two*** podziel dziesięć przez dwa; ***he was bitten by a snake*** ugryzł go wąż; ***we entered ~ the back door*** weszliśmy tylnymi drzwiami; ***he's an architect ~ profession*** z zawodu jest architektem **2.** (*indicating method*) ***made ~ hand*** wykonany ręcznie; ***~ train*** pociągiem; ***pay ~ credit card*** zapłacić kartą kedytową **3.** po *L*; ***judging ~ what he says*** sądząc po tym, co mówi; ***I knew him ~ his voice*** rozpoznałem go po głosie **4.** według *G*, przez *A*; ***forbidden ~ law*** zakazany przez prawo **5.** koło *G*, obok *G*; ***~ the window*** koło okna; ***come and sit ~ me*** podejdź i usiądź obok mnie **6.** (*indicating time*) do *L*, przed *I*; ***it must be done ~ two o'clock*** trzeba to zrobić do drugiej **7.** w czasie *G*; ***Warsaw ~ night*** Warszawa nocą **8.** (*extent of difference*) o *A*; ***rise ~ 10%*** wzrosnąć o 10% **9.** (*measurement*) ***a room five metres ~ six metres*** pokój 5 metrów na 6 **10.** (*quantity*) ***sell s.th. ~ metre*** (***kilo***) sprzedawać coś na metry (kilogramy) **II** *adv* obok; ***walk ~*** przejść obok; ***close ~*** w pobliżu

bye(-bye) [baɪ] *interj infml* na razie!, pa pa!

'by-e•lec•tion *s Br* wybory *pl* uzupełniające

Bye•lo•rus•sian [bɪeləʊ'rʌʃn] **I** *adj* białoruski **II** *s* Białorusin, *m* Białorusinka *f*

by•gones ['baɪgɔnz] *s*: ***let ~ be ~*** co było to było, zapomnijmy o przeszłości

'by•law *s* **1.** *Br* rozporządzenie *n* władz lokalnych **2.** *Am* przepis *m* wewnętrzny

'by-line *s* nazwisko *n* autora

'by•pass *s* **1.** obwodnica *f* **2.** MED bajpas *m*, pomost *m* naczyniowy

'by-prod•uct *s* **1.** produkt *m* uboczny **2.** *fig* efekt *m* uboczny

'by•road, **'by•way** *s* boczna droga *f*

by•stand•er ['baɪstændə] *s* **1.** naoczny świadek *m* **2.** bierny widz *m*

byte [baɪt] *s* INF bajt *m*

'by•word *s fig* synonim *m* (**for** *G*)

C

c&f, **c&fr** *abbr* (=***cost and freight***) koszt i fracht

cab [kæb] *s* **1.** taksówka *f* **2.** szoferka f; **'cab driv•er** *s* taksówkarz *m*; **'cab rank**, **'*cab stand*** *s* postój *m* taksówek

cab•a•ret ['kæbəreɪ] *s* kabaret *m*

cab•bage ['kæbɪdʒ] *s* kapusta *f*

C

cab•in ['kæbɪn] *s* **1.** (*in ship*) kajuta *f*, kabina *f* **2.** (*in plane*) kabina *f* **3.** chata *f* **4.** domek *m*; '**cab•in baggage** *s* bagaż *m* podręczny; '**cab•in crew**, '***cab•in staff*** *s* personel *m* pokładowy; '**cab•in cruis•er** *s* łódź *f* motorowa z kabiną
cab•i•net ['kæbɪnɪt] *s* **1.** szafka *f* **2.** gablotka *f* **3.** *POLIT* gabinet *m*; '**cab•i•net-mak•er** *s* stolarz *m* zajmujący się wyrobem mebli artystycznych
ca•ble ['keɪbl] **I** *s* **1.** lina *f* **2.** kabel *m* **3.** przewód *m*; ***a fibre-optic cable*** światłowód **4.** telegram *m* **II** *v/t* przesyłać ⟨-słać⟩ telegraficznie; '**ca•ble car** *s* wagonik *m* kolejki linowej; '**ca•ble net•work** *s* sieć *f* telewizji kablowej; '**ca•ble tel•e•vi•sion** *s* telewizja *f* kablowa
cack•le ['kækl] **I** *v/i* (*laugh*) rechotać ⟨za-⟩ **II** *s* gdakanie *n*
cac•tus ['kæktəs] *pl -tuses, -ti s* kaktus *m*
ca•dav•er [kə'dævə] *s* zwłoki *pl*; **ca•dav•er•ous** [kə'dævərəs] *adj* wynędzniały, o trupim wyglądzie
ca•det [kə'det] *s* **1.** kadet *m* **2.** podchorąży *m*
Cae•sar•e•an [sɪ'zerɪən] *adj*: ***a ~ (section)*** *MED* cesarskie cięcie
caf•é ['kæfeɪ] *s* **1.** (tania) restauracja *f* **2.** kawiarnia *f*
caf•e•te•ri•a [kæfɪ'tɪrɪə] *s* bar *m* szybkiej obsługi
caf•feine ['kæfiːn] *s* kofeina *f*
cage [keɪdʒ] **I** *s* klatka *f* **II** *v/t* **1.** zamykać ⟨-mknąć⟩ w klatce **2.** trzymać w klatce
ca•jole [kə'dʒəʊl] *v/t* przymilać ⟨-lić⟩ się do *G*; ***~ s.o. into doing s.th.*** nakłonić kogoś do zrobienia czegoś
cake [keɪk] **I** *s* **1.** ciasto *n* **2.** ciastko *n* **3.** tort *m* **4.** ***it's a piece of ~*** *fig* to łatwizna, to bułka z masłem **5.** ***you can't have your ~ and eat it*** *infml* nie można mieć dwóch rzeczy naraz **II** *v/i* zasychać ⟨-schnąć⟩
CAL [kæl] *abbr* (=***computer aided learning***) nauka *f* wspomagana komputerowo
ca•lam•i•tous [kə'læmɪtəs] *adj* **1.** katastrofalny **2.** zgubny; **ca•lam•i•ty** [kə'læmətɪ] *s* **1.** klęska *f* **2.** katastrofa *f*
cal•ci•fy ['kælsɪfaɪ] **I** *v/i* wapnieć ⟨z-⟩ **II** *v/t* powodować ⟨s-⟩ wapnienie; **cal•ci•um** ['kælsɪəm] *s* wapń *m*
cal•cu•la•ble ['kælkjʊləbl] *adj* dający się obliczyć, obliczalny: **cal•cu•late** ['kælkjʊleɪt] *v/t* **1.** obliczać ⟨-czyć⟩ **2.** oceniać ⟨-nić⟩ **3.** szacować ⟨o-⟩; **cal•cu•lat•ed** ['kælkjʊleɪtɪd] *adj* **1.** umyślny **2.** z premedytacją **3.** *risk*: wkalkulowany; **cal•cu•lat•ing** ['kælkjʊleɪtɪŋ] *adj* wyrachowany; **cal•cu•la•tion** [kælkjʊ'leɪʃn] *s* **1.** obliczenie *n* **2.** wyliczenie *n* **3.** wyrachowanie *n*; **cal•cu•la•tor** ['kælkjʊleɪtə] *s* kalkulator *m*
cal•en•dar ['kælɪndə] *s* kalendarz *m*; '**cal•en•dar year** *s* rok *m* kalendarzowy
calf[1] [kɑːf] *pl calves* [kævz] *s* *ANAT* łydka *f*
calf[2] [~] *pl calves* [kævz] *s* **1.** cielę *n* **2.** słoniątko *n* **3.** młody wieloryb *m*; '**calf•skin** *s* cielęca skóra *f*
cal•i•bre ['kælɪbə] *Br*, ***cal•i•ber*** *Am s* kaliber *m*
Cal•i•for•ni•an [kælɪ'fɔːnɪən] **I** *adj* kalifornijski **II** *s* Kalifornijczyk *m*
call [kɔːl] **I** *v/t* **1.** nazywać ⟨-zwać⟩; ***~ s.o. a liar*** nazwać kogoś kłamcą; ***they ~ her Chloe*** mówią na nią Chloe; ***I wouldn't ~ this house big*** nie powiedziałbym, że ten dom jest duży **2.** wołać ⟨za-⟩ **3.** dzwonić ⟨za-⟩ do *G*; ***~ s.o. on his mobile*** zadzwonić do kogoś na telefon komórkowy **4.** nadawać ⟨-dać⟩ imię **5.** wzywać ⟨wezwać⟩; ***~ the next witness*** proszę wezwać następnego świadka **6.** wywoływać ⟨-łać⟩; ***~ the register*** sprawdzać listę obecności **7.** przywoływać ⟨-łać⟩ **8.** *meeting*: zwoływać ⟨-łać⟩ **9.** *strike*: ogłaszać ⟨-łosić⟩ **10.** wywoływać ⟨-łać⟩; ***the line judge ~ed the ball out*** sędzia liniowy wywołał out **II** *v/i* **1.** wołać ⟨za-⟩ **2.** dzwonić ⟨za-⟩; ***I'm ~ing about your advertisement*** dzwonię w sprawie ogłoszenia **3.** wpadać ⟨-paść⟩ (***at*** do *G*) **4.** ***~ oneself*** nazywać siebie *I*, uważać siebie za *A* **III** *s* **1.** rozmowa *f* (telefoniczna); ***give s.o. a ~*** zadzwonić do kogoś, ***I have a ~ for you*** telefon do ciebie; ***receive*** (*a.* ***take***) ***a ~*** odebrać telefon **2.** wołanie *n*; ***a ~ for help*** wołanie

o pomoc **3.** wezwanie *n*; ***this is the last ~ for passengers travelling to Sydney*** kończymy odprawę pasażerów odlatujących do Sydney **4.** wizyta *f*; ***make*** (*a.* ***pay***) ***a ~ on s.o.*** złożyć komuś wizytę **5.** ***make a ~ for*** zaapelować o *A* **6.** żądanie *n* **7.** ***there was no ~ for him to say that*** niepotrzebnie to mówił **8.** *SPORT* decyzja *f* sędziego **9.** *FIN* wezwanie *n* do zapłaty **10.** ***be on ~*** (*doctor*) dyżurować pod telefonem **11.** powołanie *n* **12.** zew *m*; **call at** *v/i* **1.** (*train*) zatrzymywać ⟨-mać⟩ się w *L* **2.** (*ship*) zawijać ⟨-winąć⟩ do *G*; **call away** *v/t* wywoływać ⟨-łać⟩; ***we had to ~ him away from the concert*** musieliśmy wywołać go z koncertu; **call back** *v/t* oddzwaniać ⟨-wonić⟩ do *G*; **call for** *v/i* **1.** wymagać; ***this calls for a celebration*** to trzeba uczcić **2.** domagać się **3.** apelować ⟨za-⟩ o *A* **4.** przychodzić ⟨przyjść⟩ po *G* **5.** przyjeżdżać ⟨-jechać⟩ po *A*; **call in** *v/i* **1.** wzywać ⟨wezwać⟩ **2.** wstępować ⟨-tąpić⟩ (z wizytą) **3.** ***she called in sick*** zadzwoniła i powiedziała, że nie może przyjść do pracy, bo jest chora; **call off** *v/t* **1.** odwoływać ⟨-łać⟩ **2.** *engagement*: zrywać ⟨zerwać⟩ **3.** powstrzymywać ⟨-mać⟩; **call on** *v/i* **1.** wzywać ⟨wezwać⟩; ***~ the president to resign*** wezwać prezydenta do ustąpienia **2.** ***~ s.o.*** wstąpić do kogoś; **call out** *v/t* **1.** wołać ⟨za-⟩ **2.** wzywać ⟨wezwać⟩ **3.** wywoływać ⟨-łać⟩; ***the teacher ~ed me out to the front of the class*** nauczyciel wywołał mnie na środek klasy; **call up** *v/t* **1.** dzwonić ⟨za-⟩ do *G* **2.** przywoływać ⟨-łać⟩ **3.** powoływać ⟨-łać⟩ do wojska

'call box *s* budka *f* telefoniczna; **'call cen•tre** *Br*, ***'call cen•ter*** *Am s* centrum *n* telefonicznego kontaktu z klientami; **'call charg•es** *pl* opłaty *pl* telefoniczne; **call•er** ['kɔlə] *s* dzwoniący *m*; **call for 'ten•ders** *s* zaproszenie *f* do przetargu; **call 'for•ward•ing** *s* przenoszenie *n* rozmów; **'call girl** *s* call-girl *f*; **'call hold•ing** *s* zawieszenie *n* połączenia; **call•ing** ['kɔːlɪŋ] *s* **1.** powołanie *n* **2.** *form* zawód *m*; **'call•ing card** *s* karta *f* telefoniczna

cal•lous ['kæləs] *adj* **1.** bezduszny **2.** bezwzględny; **cal•lous•ly** ['kæləslɪ] *adv* **1.** bezdusznie **2.** bezwzględnie; **cal•lous•ness** ['kæləsnɪs] *s* **1.** bezduszność *f* **2.** bezwzględność *f*; **call 'trans•fer** *s* przenoszenie *n* rozmów; **'call-up** *s* pobór *m*

cal•lus ['kæləs] *s* **1.** odcisk *m* **2.** stwardnienie *n*, zgrubienie *n*

calm [kɑːm] **I** *adj* **1.** spokojny; ***keep ~*** zachować spokój **2.** cichy **II** *s* **1.** spokój *m* **2.** cisza *f* **III** *v/t* uspokajać ⟨-koić⟩; **calm down I** *v/i* uspokajać ⟨-koić⟩ się **II** *v/t* uspokajać ⟨-koić⟩

calm•ly ['kɑːmlɪ] *adv* spokojnie

cal•o•rie ['kælərɪ] *s* kaloria *f*

calve [kɑːv] *v/i* (*cow*) cielić ⟨o-⟩ się

calves [kɑːvz] *pl* → ***calf***

Cam•bo•di•a [kæm'bəʊdɪə] *s* Kambodża *f*

cam•cor•der ['kæmkɔːdə] *s* kamera *f* wideo

came [keɪm] *Past Simple* → ***come***

cam•el ['kæml] *s* wielbłąd *m*; **'cam•el-hair** *s* wełna *f* wielbłądzia

cam•e•ra ['kæmərə] *s* **1.** aparat *m* (fotograficzny) **2.** kamera *f*; **'cam•e•ra crew** *s* ekipa *f* telewizyjna; **'cam•e•ra•man** *pl -men s* kamerzysta *m*; **'cam•er•a-shy** *adj*: ***he's ~*** on nie lubi się fotografować

cam•o•mile ['kæməmaɪl] *s* rumianek *m*; ***~ tea*** herbata rumiankowa

cam•ou•flage ['kæməflɑːʒ] **I** *s* **1.** kamuflaż *m* **2.** maskowanie *n* **II** *v/t* maskować ⟨za-⟩ (***with*** *I*); ***~ oneself*** maskować się

camp [kæmp] **I** *s* **1.** obóz *m*; ***make*** (*a.* ***pitch***) ***~*** rozbić obóz **2.** obozowisko *n* **II** *v/i* **1.** obozować; ***go ~ing*** pojechać pod namiot **2.** rozbijać ⟨-bić⟩ obóz; **camp out** *v/i* **1.** spać w namiocie **2.** biwakować

'camp cot, ***'camp bed*** *s* łóżko *n* polowe; **camp•er** ['kæmpə] *s* **1.** biwakowicz *m* **2.** *Br* samochód *m* z częścią mieszkalną **3.** *Am* przyczepa *f* kempingowa; **'camp•fire** *s* ognisko *n*; **camp•ing** ['kæmpɪŋ] *s* biwakowanie *n*, wypoczynek *m* pod namiotem; ***go ~*** **a)** pojechać pod namioty **b)** podróżować z przyczepą kempingową; **'camp•site** *s* pole *n* namiotowe

C

C

cam•paign [kæm'peɪn] *s* kampania *f*; ***launch a ~ for*** (***against***) rozpocząć kampanię na rzecz *G* (przeciwko *D*); **cam•paign•er** [kæm'peɪnə] *s* **1.** uczestnik *m* kampanii **2.** prowadzący *m* kampanię

cam•phor ['kæmfə] *s* kamfora *f*

cam•pus ['kæmpəs] *s* campus *m*, miasteczko *n* uniwersyteckie

can[1] [kæn] *unstressed form* [kən] *v aux* (*could*) **1.** móc; ***we ~ rent a house*** możemy wynająć dom; ***how ~ you do it?*** jak można to zrobić?; ***they ~'t afford to fly*** nie stać ich na podróż samolotem; ***you ~ turn right here*** tu można skręcić w prawo; ***we ~not allow dogs in the shop*** nie możemy wpuszczać psów do sklepu; ***~ you do me a favour?*** możesz coś dla mnie zrobić?; ***~ I speak to Adam?*** czy mogę rozmawiać z Adamem?; ***~ I give you a hand?*** mogę ci pomóc?; ***what ~ I do for you?*** czym mogę panu służyć?; ***you ~ always change it*** zawsze możesz to zmienić; ***~ you see it?*** widzisz to?; ***I ~'t hear anything*** nic nie słyszę; ***I ~ not give up work*** nie mogę rzucić pracy; ***how could you!*** jak mogłeś! **2.** umieć, potrafić; ***he ~'t drive yet*** on jeszcze nie umie prowadzić; ***she ~ speak French*** ona mówi po francusku

can[2] [~] **I** *s* **1.** puszka *f*; ***a ~ of worms*** *infml* puszka Pandory; ***carry the ~*** *fig* wziąć na siebie odpowiedzialność **2.** pojemnik *m*; ***a watering ~*** konewka **3.** kanister *m* **4.** ***the ~*** *Am infml* pudło *n*, paka *f* **II** *v/t* puszkować ⟨za-⟩; '**can o•pen•er** *s* otwieracz *m* do konserw

Can•a•da ['kænədə] *s* Kanada *f*; **Ca•na•di•an** [kə'neɪdɪən] **I** *adj* kanadyjski **II** *s* Kanadyjczyk *m*, Kanadyjka *f*

ca•nal [kə'næl] *s* **1.** kanał *m* **2.** przewód *m*; ***the alimentary ~*** *ANAT* przewód pokarmowy; **ca•nal•ize** ['kænəlaɪz] *v/t* kanalizować ⟨s-⟩

ca•nar•y [kə'neərɪ] *s* kanarek *m*

Ca'na•ry Is•lands, ***Ca•na•ries*** [kə'neərɪz] *pl* Wyspy *pl* Kanaryjskie

can•cel ['kænsl] *v/t* **1.** odwoływać ⟨-łać⟩ **2.** anulować **3.** *contract*: unieważniać ⟨-nić⟩; **cancel out** *v/t* **1.** znosić się ⟨znieść⟩; **2.** wykluczać ⟨-czyć⟩ się (wzajemnie); **can•cel•la•tion** [kænsə'leɪʃn] *s* **1.** odwołanie *n* **2.** anulowanie *n* **3.** *of contract*: unieważnienie *n*; **can•cel•'la•tion fee** *s* kara *f* za anulowanie rezerwacji

Can•cer ['kænsə] *s* **1.** *ASTR* Rak *m* **2.** ***the Tropic of ~*** zwrotnik Raka; **can•cer** ['kænsə] *s MED* nowotwór *m*, rak *m*; ***have a lung ~*** mieć raka płuc; **can•cer•ous** ['kænsərəs] *adj* nowotworowy

can•did ['kændɪd] *adj* **1.** szczery **2.** *photograph*: nieupozowany, zrobiony z zaskoczenia; '**can•did camera** *s* ukryta kamera *f*; **can•did•ly** ['kændɪdlɪ] *adv* szczerze, otwarcie

can•dle ['kændl] *s* świeca *f*, świeczka *f*; '**can•dle•light** *s* blask *m* świec; ***by ~*** przy świecach; '**can•dle•lit** *adj* przy świecach, oświetlony świecami; '**can•dle•stick** *s* **1.** świecznik *m* **2.** lichtarz *m*

can•dy ['kændɪ] *s* **1.** słodycze *pl* **2.** cukierek *m* **3.** czekoladka *f*; '**can•dy bar** *s* baton *m*, batonik *m*; '**can•dy-floss** *s* wata *f* cukrowa

cane [keɪn] *s* **1.** (*material*) trzcina *f*; ***a ~ backed chair*** krzesło z wyplatanym oparciem **2.** ***sugar ~*** trzcina (cukrowa) **3.** laska *f*; '**cane sug•ar** *s* cukier *m* trzcinowy

ca•nine ['keɪnaɪn] **I** *s* **1.** kieł *m* **2.** *form* pies *m* **II** *adj* **1.** psi; ***~ diseases*** choroby psów **2.** z rodziny psowatych

can•is•ter ['kænɪstə] *s* **1.** puszka *f* **2.** pojemnik *m*

can•na•bis ['kænəbɪs] *pl* marihuana *f*, konopie *pl* indyjskie

canned [kænd] *adj* **1.** *food*: puszkowany, w puszce **2.** *music*, *laughter*: z taśmy

can•ni•bal ['kænɪbl] *s* kanibal *m*; **can•ni•bal•ism** ['kænɪbəlɪzəm] *s* kanibalizm *m*

can•ni•bal•ize ['kænɪbəlaɪz] *v/t*: ***~ s.th.*** (***for parts***) rozebrać coś na części

can•non ['kænən] *pl cannon*, *cannons* *s* armata *f*, działo *n*; '**can•non•ball** *s* kula *f* armatnia; '**can•non fod•der** *s* mięso *n* armatnie

can•not ['kænɔt] → ***can***[1]

can•ny ['kænɪ] *adj* **1.** sprytny **2.** *infml* obrotny

ca•noe [kə'nuː] *s* **1.** kanadyjka *f* **2.** *Br* kajak *m* **3.** kanoe *n*; **ca•noe•ing** [kə'nuːɪŋ] *s* **1.** kanadyjkarstwo *n* **2.** *Br* kajakarstwo *n*; ***go ~*** pójść popływać kajakiem
can•on ['kænən] *s* **1.** kanon *m* **2.** norma *f* **3.** kanonik *m*; **can•on•ize** ['kænənaɪz] *v/t* kanonizować; **'can•on law** *s* prawo *n* kanoniczne
can't [kænt] *contracted form* → ***cannot***
can•teen [kæn'tiːn] *s* **1.** stołówka *f* **2.** menażka *f*
can•vas ['kænvəs] *s* **1.** (grube) płótno *n* **2.** płótno *n* (malarskie)
can•vass ['kænvəs] **I** *v/i* ***~ for votes*** zabiegać o głosy wyborców **II** *v/t* **1.** ***~s.o. for their vote/support*** zabiegać o czyjeś głosy/poparcie **2.** ***~ opinion*** przeprowadzać sondaż; **can•vass•er** ['kænvəsə] *s* **1.** agitator *m* **2.** ankieter *m*
can•yon ['kænjən] *s* kanion *m*
cap [kæp] **I** *s* **1.** czapka *f*; ***go to s.o. ~ in hand*** *fig* zwrócić się do kogoś z pokorną prośba **2.** czepek *m* **3.** zakrętka *f* **4.** kapsel *m* **5.** nasadka *f* **6.** pokrywa *f* **7.** kapiszon *m* **8.** kapturek *m* dopochwowy **9.** limit *m* **II** *v/t* **1.** ograniczać ⟨-czyć⟩ **2.** ***snow~ped peaks*** ośnieżone szczyty gór **3.** wieńczyć ⟨z-⟩, koronować ⟨u-⟩; ***to ~ it all*** na domiar złego
ca•pa•bil•i•ty [keɪpə'bɪlətɪ] *s* **1.** zdolność *f* **2.** zdolności *pl* **3.** potencjał *m* **4.** możliwości *pl*; ***be within s.o.'s ~*** być w zasięgu czyichś możliwości **5.** wydajność *f*; **ca•pa•ble** ['keɪpəbl] *adj* **1.** ***be ~ of doing s.th.*** potrafić coś zrobić, być zdolnym do czegoś **2.** kompetentny **3.** dobry
ca•pa•cious [kə'peɪʃəs] *adj* **1.** pojemny **2.** przestronny **3.** obszerny; **capac•i•tor** [kə'pæsətə] *s* kondensator *m*; **ca•pac•i•ty** [kə'pæsətɪ] *s* **1.** pojemność *f*; ***storage ~*** powierzchnia magazynowa; ***seating ~*** liczba miejsc siedzących **2.** ładowność *f* **3.** zdolność *f* produkcyjna **4.** wydajność *f* **5.** kompetencje *pl*; ***in s.o.'s ~ as a doctor*** jako lekarz
cape[1] [keɪp] *s* peleryna *f*
cape[2] [~] *s* przylądek *m*
ca•per ['keɪpə] **I** *v/i* ***~ about***, ***~ around*** radośnie skakać, hasać **II** *s* ***~s*** wygłupy
cap•il•lar•y [kə'pɪlərɪ] *s* ANAT kapilara *f*, naczynie *n* włosowate
cap•i•tal ['kæpɪtl] **I** *s* **1.** kapitał *m* **2.** stolica *f* **3.** wielka litera *f*, wersalik *m* **II** *adj* **1.** *letter*: wielki; ***~ A*** duże A **2.** *crime*: zagrożony karą śmierci, karany śmiercią **cap•i•tal 'cit•y** *s* stolica *f*; **cap•i•tal con•tri•'bu•tion** *s* ECON wkład *m* kapitałowy; **cap•i•tal ex•'pend•i•ture** *s* nakłady *pl* kapitałowe; **cap•i•tal 'gains tax** *s* podatek *m* od zysków kapitałowych; **cap•i•tal 'goods** *pl* środki *pl* produkcji; **cap•i•tal 'growth** *s* wzrost *m* kapitału; **cap•i•tal-in•'ten•sive** *adj* kapitałochłonny, wymagający dużych nakładów finansowych; **capital intensity** *s* kapitałochłonność *f*; **cap•i•tal in•'vest•ment** *s* inwestycje *pl* kapitałowe
cap•i•tal•ism ['kæpɪtəlɪzm] *s* kapitalizm *m*; **cap•i•tal•ist** ['kæpɪtəlɪst] **I** *s* kapitalista *m* **II** *adj* kapitalistyczny; **cap•i•tal•ize** ['kæpɪtəlaɪz] *v/t* zmieniać ⟨-nić⟩ pierwszą literę na wielką; **cap•i•tal•ize on** *v/t* wykorzystywać ⟨-tać⟩
cap•i•tal 'let•ter *s* wielka litera *f*, wersalik *m*; **cap•i•tal 'pun•ish•ment** *s* kara *f* śmierci
Cap•i•tol ['kæpɪtl] *s* (*seat of Congress*) Kapitol *m*
ca•pit•u•late [kə'pɪʃʊleɪt] *v/i* kapitulować ⟨s-⟩; **ca•pit•u•la•tion** [kæpɪʃʊ'leɪʃn] *s* kapitulacja *f*
ca•pri•cious [kə'prɪʃəs] *adj* kapryśny
Cap•ri•corn ['kæprɪkɔːn] *s* **1.** ASTR Koziorożec *m* **2.** ***the Tropic of ~*** zwrotnik Koziorożca
cap•sule ['kæpsjuːl] *s* **1.** kapsułka *f* **2.** kapsuła *f* **3.** BIOL torebka *f*
cap•tain ['kæptɪn] kapitan *m*
cap•tion ['kæpʃn] **I** *s* (*photograph*) podpis *m* **II** *v/t* podpisywać ⟨-sać⟩
cap•ti•vate ['kæptɪveɪt] *v/t* fascynować ⟨za-⟩; **cap•ti•vat•ing** ['kæptɪveɪtɪŋ] *adj* fascynujący; **cap•tive** ['kæptɪv] **I** *s* **1.** jeniec *m*; ***take s.o. ~*** wziąć kogoś do niewoli **2.** więzień *m* **II** *adj* więziony; **cap•tive 'au•di•ence** *s* **1.** widzowie *pl* mimo woli

C

2. słuchacze *pl* mimo woli; **cap•tiv•i•ty** [kæp'tɪvətɪ] *s* niewola *f*

cap•ture ['kæpʃə] **I** *v/t* **1.** chwytać ⟨s-⟩, pojmać **2.** brać ⟨wziąć⟩ do niewoli **3.** *hostages*: brać ⟨wziąć⟩ **4.** *stronghold*: zdobywać ⟨-być⟩ **5.** *market*: opanowywać ⟨-nować⟩ **6.** *~ s.th. on film* utrwalić coś na taśmie filmowej **II** *s* **1.** zdobycie *n* **2.** pojmanie *n*, schwytanie *n*

car [kɑː] **I** *s* **1.** samochód *m* **2.** *Am* wagon *m* **II** *adj* **1.** samochodowy **2.** motoryzacjny; **'car bomb** *s* samochód-pułapka *m*; **'car chase** *s* pościg *m* samochodowy

car•a•mel ['kærəmel] *s* **1.** karmel *m* **2.** (*toffee*) krówka *f*

car•at ['kærət] *s* karat *m*; ***18-~ gold*** osiemnastokaratowe złoto

car•a•van ['kærəvæn] **1.** *Br* przyczepa *f* kempingowa **2.** wóz *m* **3.** karawana *f*

car•a•way ['kærəweɪ] *s* kminek *m*

car•bine ['kɑːbaɪn] *s* karabinek *m*

car•bo•hy•drate [kɑːbəʊ'haɪdreɪt] *s* węglowodan *m*

car•bon ['kɑːbən] *s* CHEM węgiel *m*; **car•bon•ate** ['kɑːbənɪt] *s* węglan *m*; **car•bon•at•ed** ['kɑːbəneɪtɪd] *adj drink*: gazowany; **car•bon 'co•py** *s* **1.** kopia *f* (wykonana przez kalkę) **2.** *fig* wierna kopia *f*; **car•bon di•ox•ide** [kɑːbəndaɪ'ɔksaɪd] *s* dwutlenek *m* węgla; **car•bon mon•ox•ide** [kɑːbənmən'ɒksaɪd] *s* tlenek *m* węgla; **'carbon paper** *s* kalka *f*

car•cass ['kɑːkəs] *s* **1.** padlina *f*; ***the ~ of a dead whale*** martwy wieloryb **2.** *meat*: tusza *f*

car•cin•o•gen [kɑː'sɪnədʒen] *s* czynnik *m* rakotwórczy; **car•cin•o•genic** [kɑːsɪnəʊ'dʒenɪk] *adj* MED rakotwórczy; **car•ci•no•ma** [kɑːsɪ'nəʊmə] *s* nowotwór *m* złośliwy

card [kɑːd] *s* **1.** kartka *f*; ***a birthday ~*** kartka urodzinowa **2.** karta *f*; ***play ~s*** grać w karty; ***have a ~ up one's sleeve*** *fig* mieć asa w rękawie **3.** fiszka *f*

'card•board *s* tektura *f*; **card•board 'box** *s* karton *m*, pudło *n* tekturowe; **'card game** *s* gra *f* karciana; **'card•hold•er** *s* FIN posiadacz *m* karty

car•di•ac ['kɑːdɪæk] *adj* MED **1.** ***~ diseases*** choroby serca **2.** *medicine*: nasercowy, na serce; **car•di•ac ar'rest** *s* MED zatrzymanie *n* akcji serca

car•di•gan ['kɑːdɪgən] *s* rozpinany sweter *m*

car•di•nal ['kɑːdɪnl] **I** *s* **1.** kardynał *m* **2.** liczebnik *m* **II** *adj* **1.** kardynalny **2.** główny, zasadniczy **3.** ***a ~ number*** liczebnik główny

'card in•dex *s* **1.** kartoteka *f* **2.** katalog m; **'card key** *s* karta *f* magnetyczna (do otwierania drzwi); **'card phone** *s* automat *m* telefoniczny na kartę; **'card•sharp** *s* szuler *m*; **'card trick** *s* sztuczka *f* karciana

care [keə] **I** *s* **1.** opieka *f* (**for**/**of** nad *I*); ***take ~ of*** **a)** zajmować się *I* **b)** opiekować się *I*; ***put*** (*a.* ***leave***) ***s.o. in s.o.'s ~*** zostawić kogoś pod czyjąś opieką **2.** troska *f* (**for**/**of** o *A*); ***be without a ~ in the world*** być wolnym od wszelkich trosk **3.** ostrożność *f* **4.** uwaga *f*; ***take ~ when doing s.th.*** robić coś uważnie; ***'Glass. Handle with ~'*** „Ostrożnie. Szkło!" **II** *v/i* **1.** przejmować ⟨-jąć⟩ się (**about** *I*) **2.** troszczyć ⟨za-⟩ się (**about** o *A*) **3.** ***she ~s about you*** zależy jej na tobie; ***I don't ~*** nie zależy mi **4.** ***I don't ~ about it*** nie obchodzi mnie to; ***I don't care what she thinks*** nie obchodzi mnie, co ona myśli; **care for** *v/i* **1.** opiekować ⟨za-⟩ się *I* **2.** ***she cared for him*** zależało jej na nim **3.** ***would you ~ for another drink?*** napijesz się jeszcze?

'care•free *adj* beztroski

care•ful ['keəfəl] *adj* **1.** ostrożny; ***this matter needs ~ handling*** to delikatna sprawa **2.** ***be ~ of*** uważać na *A*; ***be ~ not to do s.th.*** uważać, żeby czegoś nie zrobić; ***be ~!*** uważaj! **3.** staranny; **care•ful•ly** ['keəfəlɪ] *adv* **1.** ostrożnie **2.** uważnie **3.** starannie; **care•ful•ness** ['keəfəlnɪs] *s* **1.** ostrożność *f* **2.** staranność *f*

care•less ['keələs] *adj* **1.** nieostrożny; ***~ driving*** nieostrożna jazda **2.** nieprzemyślany **3.** nieuważny **4.** niedbały **5.** niestaranny; **care•less•ly** ['keələslɪ] *adv* **1.** nieostrożnie **2.** niedbale **3.** nierozważnie; **care•less•ness** ['keələsnɪs] *s* **1.** nieostrożność *f*

C

2. niedbalstwo *n* **3.** beztroska *f* **4.** niestaranność *f*

ca•reer[1] [kəˈrɪə] *s* **1.** praca *f* zawodowa; ***a teaching ~*** kariera nauczycielska, praca w zawodzie nauczyciela **2.** przebieg *m* pracy zawodowej **3.** kariera *f*; **caˈreers ad•viser** *Br*, ***caˈreers of•fi•cer*** *Br s* doradca *m* zawodu

ca•reer[2] [~] *v/i* mknąć ⟨prze-⟩; ***~ in*** (***out***) *infml* wjechać (wyjechać) na pełnym gazie

car•er [ˈkeərə] *s* opiekun *m*

ca•ress [kəˈres] **I** *v/t* pieścić **II** *s* pieszczota *f*

care•tak•er [ˈkeəteɪkə] **I** *s* **1.** *Br* dozorca *m* **2.** opiekun *m* **II** *adj* ***a ~ government*** rząd tymczasowy

ˈcare•worn *adj* zatroskany; ***look ~*** mieć zatroskaną minę

ˈcar fer•ry *s* prom *m* samochodowy

car•go [ˈkɑːgəʊ] *s* ładunek *m*; **ˈcar•go plane** *s* samolot *m* transportowy; **ˈcar•go ship** *s* statek *m* towarowy

ˈcar hire *s* wynajem *m* samochodów

car•i•ca•ture [ˈkærɪkətʃʊə] **I** *s* karykatura *f* **II** *v/t* karykaturować ⟨s-⟩; **car•i•ca•tur•ist** [ˈkærɪkətʃʊərɪst] *s* karykaturzysta *m*

car•i•es [ˈkeəriːz] *s* MED próchnica *f*

car•ing [ˈkeərɪŋ] *adj* opiekuńczy, troskliwy

ˈcar in•sur•ance *s* ubezpieczenie *n* samochodu

ˈcar me•chan•ic *s* mechanik *m* samochodowy

car•nage [ˈkɑːnɪdʒ] *s* rzeź *f*, masakra *f*

car•nal [ˈkɑːnl] *adj* **1.** cielesny **2.** zmysłowy

car•ni•val [ˈkɑːnɪvl] *s* **1.** karnawał *m* **2.** święto *n* **3.** *Am* wesołe miasteczko *n*

car•ni•vore [ˈkɑːnɪvɔː] *s* mięsożerca *m*; **car•niv•o•rous** [kɑːˈnɪvərəs] *adj* mięsożerny

car•ol [ˈkærəl] **I** *s* kolęda *f* **II** *v/i* kolędować

car•ou•sel [kærəˈsel] *s* **1.** karuzela *f* **2.** (*airport*) taśma *f* bagażowa

ˈcar own•er *s* właściciel *m* samochodu

carp[1] [kɑːp] *s* karp *m*

carp[2] [~] *v/i* **1.** zrzędzić **2.** narzekać (***about*** na *A*)

ˈcar park *s Br* parking *m*

car•pen•ter [ˈkɑːpəntə] *s* **1.** stolarz *m* **2.** cieśla *m*; **car•pen•try** [ˈkɑːpəntrɪ] *s* **1.** stolarstwo *n* **2.** ciesielstwo *n*

car•pet [ˈkɑːpɪt] **I** *s* **1.** dywan *m* **2.** (*a.* **fitted ~**) wykładzina *f* **II** *v/t* **1.** wykładać ⟨wyłożyć⟩ dywanem; ***the room was ~ed*** w pokoju był dywan **2.** wykładać ⟨wyłożyć⟩ wykładziną **3.** *infml* brać ⟨wziąć⟩ na dywanik; **car•pet•ing** [ˈkɑːpɪtɪŋ] *s* **1.** wykładzina *f* (dywanowa) **2.** dywany *pl*; **ˈcar•pet sweep•er** *s* szczotka *f* do dywanów

ˈcar phone *s* telefon *m* samochodowy; **ˈcar•pool** *s* **1.** ***be in a ~*** **a)** podwozić się wzajemnie do pracy **b)** na zmianę wozić dzieci do szkoły **2.** *Br* flota *f* samochodowa; **ˈcar port** *s* wiata *f* samochodowa; **ˈcar ra•di•o** *s* radio *n* samochodowe; **ˈcar ren•tal** *s* wynajem *m* samochodów

car•riage [ˈkærɪdʒ] *s* **1.** wagon *m* (pasażerski) **2.** powóz *m*, kareta *f* **3.** przewóz *m*, transport *m*; ***~ free*** (***forward***) koszty transportu ponosi sprzedawca (kupujący)

car•ri•er [ˈkærɪə] *s* **1.** (*airline*) przewoźnik *m* **2.** MED nosiciel *m* **3.** transporter *m* **4.** transportowiec *m* **5.** ***an aircraft ~*** lotniskowiec **6.** ***a ~ bag*** torba (na zakupy); **car•ri•er pigeon** *s* gołąb *m* pocztowy

car•ri•on [ˈkærɪən] *s* padlina *f*; **car•ri•on crow** *s* czarnowron *m*, wrona *f* czarna

car•rot [ˈkærət] *s* **1.** marchewka *f* **2.** *infml* zachęta *f*, bodziec *m*; ***the ~ and the stick method*** metoda kija i marchewki

car•ry [ˈkærɪ] **I** *v/t* **1.** nosić, nieść **2.** przenosić ⟨-nieść⟩ **3.** mieć przy sobie, nosić (przy sobie); ***~ a gun*** nosić broń **4.** *label*: być opatrzonym **5.** *information*: zawierać **6.** *guarantee*: posiadać **7.** utrzymywać ⟨-mać⟩, dźwigać **8.** *disease*: przenosić ⟨-nieść⟩; ***~ the HIV virus*** być nosicielem wirusa HIV **9.** (*newspaper*) publikować ⟨o-⟩ **10.** (*shop*) sprzedawać, prowadzić sprzedaż **11.** *risk*: nieść, pociągać ⟨-gnąć⟩ za sobą **12.** *penalty*: być zagrożonym **13.** *support*: zdobywać ⟨-być⟩; ***~ weight with s.o.*** przekonywać kogoś **14.** ***~ s.th.***

C

too far *fig* przesadzać z czymś **15.** być w ciąży z *I*, spodziewać się *G* **II** *v/i* (*sound*) nieść się; **car•ry about** *v/t* nosić ⟨nieść⟩ ze sobą; **car•ry away** *v/t* **1.** zabierać ⟨-brać⟩ **2.** unosić ⟨unieść⟩ **3.** ***s.o. got carried away*** kogoś poniosło; **car•ry forward** *v/t amount, sum*: przenosić ⟨-nieść⟩; **car•ry off** *v/t* **1.** wynosić ⟨-nieść⟩ **2.** poradzić sobie z *I* **3.** *prize*: zdobywać ⟨-być⟩; **car•ry on** *v/t* **1.** ***~ with*** kontynuować, robić dalej **2.** *infml* robić ⟨z-⟩ aferę, wykłócać ⟨-cić⟩ się **3.** *infml* mieć romans z *I*; **car•ry out** *v/t* **1.** *research, experiment*: przeprowadzać ⟨-dzić⟩ **2.** *plan, idea*: realizować ⟨z-⟩ **3.** *promise, duty*: spełniać ⟨-nić⟩; **car•ry over** *v/t* **1.** przenosić ⟨-nieść⟩ **2.** mieć wpływ na *A*; **car•ry through** *v/t* **1.** pomagać ⟨-móc⟩ przetrwać **2.** przeprowadzać ⟨-dzić⟩ **3.** realizować ⟨z-⟩

'car•ry-on *s* **1.** *infml* afera *f*, zamieszanie *n* **2.** torba *f* podręczna; **'car•ry-on bag•gage** *s* bagaż *m* podręczny

'car•ry•out *Am* → ***takeaway***

'car seat *s* **1.** siedzenie *n* samochodowe **2.** (*for child*) fotelik *m* samochodowy

'car•sick *adj*: ***be ~*** mieć nudności; ***do you get ~?*** czy cierpisz na chorobę lokomocyjną; **'car sick•ness** *s* choroba *f* lokomocyjna

cart [kɑːt] *s* **1.** wóz *m*, furmanka *f*; ***put the ~ before the horse*** *fig* stawiać sprawę na głowie **2.** wózek *m*

car•tel [kɑː'tel] *s* *ECON* kartel *m*

car•tog•ra•pher [kɑː'tɒgrəfə] *s* kartograf *m*; **cartog•ra•phy** [kɑː'tɒgrəfɪ] *s* kartografia *f*

car•ton ['kɑːtən] *s* karton *m*, pudełko *n* kartonowe

car•toon [kɑː'tuːn] *s* **1.** film *m* rysunkowy, kreskówka *f* **2.** komiks *m* **3.** dowcip *m* rysunkowy **4.** *ART* szkic *m*, karton *m*; **car•toon•ist** [kɑː'tuːnɪst] *s* rysownik *m*; **car•'toon strip** *s* komiks *m*

car•tridge ['kɑːtrɪdʒ] *s* **1.** nabój *m* **2.** wkład *m* **3.** kaseta *f*

'cart•wheel *s* **1.** koło *n* wozu

carve [kɑːv] *v/t* **1.** rzeźbić ⟨wy-⟩ (***from/out of*** z *G*) **2.** *inscription*: wycinać ⟨-ciąć⟩ **3.** *meat*: kroić ⟨po-⟩; **carv•ing** ['kɑːvɪŋ] *s* **1.** rzeźba *f* **2.** rzeźbiarstwo *n*, rzeźba *f*; ***wood ~*** rzeźba w drewnie, snycerstwo

'car wash *s* myjnia *f* samochodowa

cas•cade [kæ'skeɪd] *s* **1.** kaskada *f* **2.** wodospad *m*

case[1] [keɪs] *s* **1.** futerał *m* **2.** walizka *f* **3.** gablotka *f* **4.** skrzynia *f* **5.** (*for pillow*) poszewka *f*

case[2] [~] *s* **1.** przypadek *m*, wypadek *m*; ***in any ~*** w każdym razie; ***in no ~*** w żadnym wypadku; ***in ~ of fire*** w razie pożaru **2.** sytuacja *f* **3.** *JUR* sprawa *f* **4.** przykład *m*; ***a ~ in point*** dobry przykład **5.** ***in upper*** (***lower***) ***~*** dużymi (małymi) literami; **'case his•to•ry** *s* *MED* historia *f* choroby (pacjenta); **'case stud•y** *s* studium *n* przypadku, analiza *f* przypadku

'case•load *s*: ***have a heavy ~*** (*doctor*) mieć wielu pacjentów

cash [kæʃ] *s* **1.** gotówka *f*; ***payment in ~*** płatność gotówką; ***~ up front, ~ down*** *Br* gotówką, za gotówkę; ***~ on delivery*** płatność przy odbiorze **2.** *infml* forsa *f*, kasa *f*; ***be short of ~*** nie mieć forsy; **cash in I** *v/t* **1.** *cheque*: realizować ⟨z-⟩ **2.** spieniężać ⟨-żyć⟩ **II** *v/i* ***~ in on*** **a)** zarabiać na *L* **b)** czerpać korzyści z *G*; **cash and 'car•ry** *s* hurtownia *f* cash and carry; **'cash bal•ance** *s* saldo *n* gotówkowe; **'cash card** *s* *Br* karta *f* bankomatowa; **'cash desk** *s* *Br* kasa *f*, okienko *n* kasowe; **cash 'dis•count** *s* *ECON* rabat *m*, zniżka *f*; **'cash de•pos•it** *s* kaucja *f* gotówkowa; **'cash dis•pens•er** *s* *Br* bankomat *m*; **'cash flow** *s* przepływ *m* gotówki

cash•ier [kæ'ʃɪə] *s* kasjer *m*; **cash'ier's check** *s* czek *m* bankierski

'cash in hand *s* *FIN* środki *pl* pieniężne w kasie

cash•less ['kæʃlɪs] *adj* bezgotówkowy

'cash ma•chine *s* *Br* bankomat *m*

cash•mere ['kæʃmɪə] *s* kaszmir *m*

'cash pay•ment *s* płatność *f* gotówką; **'cash•point** *s* *Br* bankomat *m*; **'cash price** *s* cena *f* gotówkowa, cena *f* przy płatności gotówką; **'cash pur•chase** *s* kupno *n* za gotówkę; **'cash re•gis•ter** *s* kasa *f* (sklepowa)

cas•ing ['keɪsɪŋ] *s* **1.** obudowa *f* **2.** łuska *f* **3.** futryna *f* **4.** *cable*: osłona *f* **5.** *sausage*: osłonka *f*

ca•si•no [kə'siːnəʊ] *s* kasyno *n*
cask [kɑːsk] *s* beczka *f*, beczułka *f*
cas•ket ['kɑːskɪt] *s* **1.** szkatuła *f*, szkatułka *f* **2.** *Am* trumna *f*
cas•se•role ['kæsərəʊl] *s* **1.** zapiekanka *f* **2.** naczynie *n* żaroodporne
cas•sette [kə'set] *s* kaseta *f*; **cas'sette deck** *s* (*stereo*) magnetofon *m*; **cas•'sette play•er** *s* odtwarzacz *m* kasetowy; **cas•'sette re•cord•er** *s* magnetofon *m*
cast [kɑːst] **I** *s* **1.** (*film, play*) obsada *f* **2.** TECH odlew *m* **3.** TECH forma *f* **4.** MED gips *m*, opatrunek *m* gipsowy **5.** rzut *m* **6.** *fishing rod, net*: zarzucenie *n* **II** *v/t* (*cast*; *cast*) **1.** rzucać ⟨-cić⟩; ***~ a glance at*** spojrzeć na *A* **2.** *actor*: obsadzać ⟨-dzić⟩; ***she was ~ as a taxi driver*** została obsadzona w roli taksówkarza **3.** *voice*: oddawać ⟨-dać⟩ **4.** *sculpture*: odlewać ⟨-lać⟩ **5.** *skin*: zrzucać ⟨-cić⟩ **6.** *fishing rod, net*: zarzucać ⟨-cić⟩; **cast about for**, **cast around for** *v/i* **1.** szukać *G* **2.** rozglądać się za *I*; **cast aside** *v/t* **1.** pozbywać ⟨-być⟩ się **2.** usuwać ⟨usunąć⟩ **3.** zarzucać ⟨-cić⟩; **cast down** *v/t*: ***~ one's eyes*** opuszczać ⟨opuścić⟩ oczy; **cast off** *v/t* *yoke*: zrzucać ⟨-cić⟩
'cast•a•way *s* rozbitek *m*
caste [kɑːst] *s* kasta *f*
Castile [kæ'stiːl] *s* Kastylia *f*
cast•ing ['kæstɪŋ] *s* **1.** (*film, play*) obsada *f*, casting *m* **2.** TECH odlew *m*; **cast•ing 'vote** *s* decydujący głos *m*; **'cast•ing di•rec•tor** *s* kierownik *m* obsady
cast 'i•ron **I** *s* żeliwo *n* **II** *adj* żeliwny
cas•tle ['kæsl] **I** *s* **1.** zamek *m* **2.** (*chess*) wieża *f* **II** *v/i* (*chess*) dokonywać ⟨-nać⟩ roszady
'cast-off **I** *s* **1.** używane ubranie *n* **2.** niepotrzebne ubranie *n* **3.** rupieć *m* **II** *adj* **1.** używany **2.** niepotrzebny
cas•trate [kæ'streɪt] *v/t* kastrować ⟨wy-⟩; **cas•tra•tion** [kæ'streɪʃn] *s* kastracja *f*
cas•u•al ['kæʒʊəl] *adj* **1.** nonszalancki, luźny, swobodny; ***be ~ about s.th.*** nie przejmować się czymś zbytnio **2.** *gesture*: niedbały **3.** *remark*: rzucony mimochodem **4.** *onlooker, sex*: przypadkowy **5.** *clothes*: zwykły, codzienny **6.** *glance*: przelotny, pobieżny **7.** *work*: dorywczy **8.** nieformalny, nieoficjalny; **cas•u•al•ly** ['kæʒʊəlɪ] *adv* **1.** swobodnie, nonszalancko **2.** mimochodem **3.** niedbale **4.** *dressed*: w zwykłe ubranie **5.** przelotnie, pobieżnie **6.** doraźnie **7.** nieformalnie, nieoficjalnie
cas•u•al•ty ['kæʒʊəltɪ] *s* **1.** ofiara *f* **2.** *Br* oddział *m* urazowy **3.** *Br* ostry dyżur *m*; **'cas•u•al•ty department** *s* *Br* **1.** oddział *m* urazowy **2.** ostry dyżur *m*
cat [kæt] *s* **1.** kot *m*; ***let the ~ out of the bag*** nie dochować tajemnicy, *infml* wszystko wypaplać; ***play ~ and mouse*** bawić się w kotka i myszkę; ***it is raining ~s and dogs*** leje jak z cebra; ***look like something the ~ dragged in*** **a)** wyglądać jak strach na wróble **b)** wyglądać jak siedem nieszczęść **2.** ***old ~*** *fig* stara jędza
cat•a•combs ['kætəkuːmz] *pl* katakumby *pl*
cat•a•logue ['kætəlɒg] *Br*, **cat•a•log** *Am* **I** *s* **1.** katalog *m* **2.** spis *m* **3.** *fig* seria *f* **II** *v/t* katalogować ⟨s-⟩
Cat•a•lon•i•a [kætə'ləʊnɪə] *s* Katalonia *f*
cat•a•lyst ['kætəlɪst] *s* CHEM katalizator *m*
cat-and-'dog *adj*: ***lead a ~ life*** żyć jak pies z kotem, drzeć koty
cat•a•pult ['kætəpʌlt] **I** *s* **1.** proca *f* **2.** katapulta *f* **II** *v/t* wyrzucać ⟨-cić⟩; ***she was ~ed to fame*** *fig* z dnia na dzień stała się sławna
cat•a•ract ['kætərækt] *s* **1.** katarakta *f* **2.** MED zaćma *f*, katarakta *f*
ca•tarrh [kə'tɑː] *s* MED katar *m*
ca•tas•tro•phe [kə'tæstrəfɪ] *s* katastrofa *f*; **cat•a•stroph•ic** [kætə'strɒfɪk] *adj* **1.** katastrofalny **2.** *vision*: katastroficzny
'cat bur•glar *s* włamywacz *m* (wspinający się po rynnach lub gzymsach)
cat•call *v/i* wygwizdywać ⟨-dać⟩; **'cat•calls** *pl* gwizdy *pl*, okrzyki *pl* niezadowolenia
catch [kætʃ] **I** (*caught*; *caught*) *v/t* **1.** łapać ⟨z-⟩, chwytać ⟨chwycić⟩ **2.** zdążać ⟨-żyć⟩ na *A*, *infml* łapać ⟨z-⟩ **3.** zarazić się, *infml* złapać; ***~ a cold*** przeziębić się **4.** przyłapywać ⟨-pać⟩ (***s.o. at***

C

kogoś na *L*) **5. ~ *fire*** zapalić się **6. ~ *one's fingers*** przytrzasnąć sobie palce **7. ~ *a glimpse of*** dostrzec *A* **8.** dosłyszeć **II** *v/i* (*engine*) zapalić **III** *s* **1.** zapięcie *n* **2.** zatrzask *m* **3.** połów *m* **4.** *fig* haczyk *m* **5. *make a ~*** chwycić piłkę **6.** *infml* dobra partia *f*; **catch at** *v/i* chwytać ⟨chwycić⟩; **catch on** *v/i* **1.** przyjmować ⟨-jąć⟩ się, zyskiwać ⟨-kać⟩ popularność **2.** *infml* załapać; **catch out** *v/t* **1.** przyłapywać ⟨-pać⟩ **2.** zaskakiwać ⟨-skoczyć⟩; **catch up** *v/t* doganiać ⟨-gonić⟩; **catch up on** *v/i* nadrabiać ⟨-robić⟩ zaległości w *L*; **catch up with** *v/i* **1.** doganiać ⟨-gonić⟩ **2.** dorównywać ⟨-nać⟩ **3.** nadrabiać ⟨-robić⟩ zaległości w *L*

catch-22 [kætʃtwentɪ'tuː] *s* błędne koło *n*, sytuacja *f* bez wyjścia

catch•er ['kætʃə] *s* (*baseball*) łapacz *m*

catch•ing ['kætʃɪŋ] *adj* **1.** zakaźny **2.** *fig* zaraźliwy

'catch•phrase *s* **1.** slogan *m* **2.** powiedzenie *n*

catch•y ['kætʃɪ] *adj* **1.** chwytliwy **2.** *tune*: wpadający w ucho

cat•e•chism ['kætəkɪzəm] *s* REL katechizm *m*

cat•e•go•ric [kætə'gɒrɪk], ***cat•e•gor•i•cal*** [kætə'gɒrɪkl] *adj* kategoryczny, stanowczy; **cat•e•gor•i•cal•ly** [kætə'gɒrɪklɪ] *adv* kategorycznie, stanowczo

cat•e•go•rize ['kætəgəraɪz] *v/t* **1.** klasyfikować ⟨s-⟩ **2.** dzielić ⟨po-⟩ (na grupy); **cat•e•go•ry** ['kætəgərɪ] *s* kategoria *f*

ca•ter ['keɪtə] *v/i* **1. ~ *for parties*** zapewniać obsługę gastronomiczną przyjęć, obsługiwać przyjęcia **2. ~ *for*** *fig* kierować swoją ofertę do *G*; ***~ for the needs of*** zaspokajać potrzeby *G*; ***~ to*** *needs*: zaspokajać; **ca•ter•er** ['keɪtərə] *s* (*firm*) firma *f* cateringowa; **ca•ter•ing** ['keɪtərɪŋ] *s* catering *m*, obsługa *f* gastronomiczna; **'ca•ter•ing com•pa•ny** *s* firma *f* kateringowa

ca•ter•pil•lar ['kætəpɪlə] *s* **1.** BIOL gąsienica *f* **2.** ® TECH pojazd *m* gąsienicowy

ca•the•dral [kə'θiːdrəl] **I** *s* katedra *f* **II** *adj* katedralny; ***a ~ town*** stolica diecezji

cath•ode ['kæθəʊd] *s* katoda *f*

Cath•o•lic ['kæθəlɪk] REL **I** *adj* katolicki **II** *s* katolik *m*; **Ca•thol•i•cism** [kə'θɒlɪsɪzm] *s* REL katolicyzm *m*

'cat lit•ter *s* żwirek *m* dla kotów; **'cat•nap** *s* drzemka *f*; **'cat's eye** *s* odblask *m* najezdniowy; **'cat tray** *s* kuweta *f* dla kota

'cat•suit *s* obcisły kombinezon *m*

cat•tle ['kætl] *s* bydło *n*; **'cat•tle breed•ing** *s* hodowla *f* bydła

'cat•walk *s* **1.** pomost *m*, kładka *f* **2.** (*between buildings*) łącznik *m* **3.** (*for models*) *Br* wybieg *m*

caught [kɔːt] *Past Simple and Past Participle* → **catch**

caul•dron ['kɔːldrən] *s* kocioł *m*

cau•li•flow•er ['kɒlɪflaʊə] *s* BIOL kalafior *m*

caus•al ['kɔːzl] *adj* przyczynowy; **cau•sal•i•ty** [kɔː'zælətɪ] *s* **1.** związek *m* przyczynowy **2.** przyczynowość *f*

cause [kɔːz] **I** *s* **1.** przyczyna *f* **2.** powód *m* **3.** sprawa *f*; ***a lost ~*** przegrana sprawa; ***for a good ~*** na szlachetny cel **4.** JUR sprawa *f* sądowa **II** *v/t* **1.** powodować ⟨s-⟩ **2.** wywoływać ⟨-łać⟩ **3.** *problems*: stwarzać ⟨-worzyć⟩

cau•tion ['kɔːʃn] **I** *s* **1.** ostrożność *f*, rozwaga *f* **2.** rezerwa *f* **3.** pouczenie *n* **4. *a word of ~*** ostrzeżenie *n*; *~!* Uwaga! **II** *v/t* **1.** ostrzegać ⟨-rzec⟩, przestrzegać ⟨-rzec⟩ (***against*** przed *I*) **2.** pouczać ⟨-czyć⟩, udzielać ⟨-lić⟩ upomnienia; **cau•tious** ['kɔːʃəs] *adj* **1.** ostrożny **2.** rozważny **3.** przezorny **4.** *optimism*: umiarkowany; **cau•tious•ly** ['kɔːʃəslɪ] *adv* **1.** ostrożnie **2.** rozważnie **3.** przezornie **4.** *optimistic*: umiarkowanie

cav•a•lier [kævə'lɪə] *adj* nonszalancki, niefrasobliwy

cav•al•ry ['kævəlrɪ] *s* **1.** kawaleria *f* **2.** oddziały *pl* pancerne i zmechanizowane

cave [keɪv] *s* **1.** jaskinia *f*, grota *f*; **cave in** *v/i* **1.** zawalać ⟨-lić⟩ się **2.** (*ground*) zapadać ⟨-paść⟩ się **3.** ustępować ⟨-tąpić⟩, uginać ⟨ugiąć⟩ się; **'cave•man** *s* jaskiniowiec *m*

cav•ern ['kævən] *s* grota *f*, pieczara *f*, jaskinia *f*

cav•i•ar(e) ['kævɪɑː] *s* kawior *m*

cav•i•ty ['kævətɪ] *s* **1.** zagłębienie *n,* jama *f* **2.** otwór *m* **3.** (*tooth*) ubytek *m, infml* dziura *f*
CB ra•di•o [siːbiː'reɪdɪəʊ] *abbr* (=***Citizens' Band radio***) CB radio *n*
cc[1] [siː'siː] *abbr* (=***cubic centimetre***) cm³, centymetr *m* sześcienny
cc[2] [~] *abbr* (=***carbon copy***) do wiadomości
CCTV [siːsiːtiː'**viː**] *abbr* (=***closed-circuit television***) telewizja *f* przemysłowa
CD [siː'diː] *abbr* (=***compact disc***) płyta *f* kompaktowa, *infml* kompakt *m;* **CD 'play•er** *s* odtwarzacz *m* CD, odtwarzacz *m* płyt kompaktowych
CD-ROM [siːdiː'rɒm] *abbr* (=***compact disc read-only memory***) CD-ROM *m,* płyta *f* CD-ROM; **CD-ROM 'drive** *s* INF napęd *m* CD-ROM
cease [siːs] *v/i form* **1.** przestawać ⟨-tać⟩ **2.** kończyć ⟨s-⟩ **3.** *fire*: wstrzymywać ⟨-mać⟩; **'cease-fire** *s* zawieszenie *n* broni
cedar [siːdə] *s* cedr *m*
cei•ling ['siːlɪŋ] *s* **1.** sufit *m* **2.** ECON pułap *m,* limit *m*
cel•e•brate ['selɪbreɪt] *v/t* **1.** świętować, czcić ⟨u-⟩ **2.** *birthday*: obchodzić **3.** sławić **4.** REL celebrować, odprawiać ⟨-wić⟩; **cel•e•brat•ed** ['selɪbreɪtɪd] *adj* sławny, słynny; **cel•e•bra•tion** [selɪ'breɪʃn] *s* **1.** obchody *pl* **2.** uroczystość *f* **3.** feta *f;* **ce•leb•ri•t y** [sɪ'lebrətɪ] *s* **1.** (*person*) znakomitość *f* **2.** sława *f,* popularność *f*
cel•e•ry ['selərɪ] *s* BOT seler *m* (naciowy)
ce•les•tial [sɪ'lestiəl] *adj* **1.** ASTR niebieski **2.** niebiański
cel•i•ba•cy ['selɪbəsɪ] *s* celibat *m;* **cel•i•bate** ['selɪbət] **I** *adj* żyjący w celibacie **II** *s* żyjący *m* w celibacie
cell [sel] *s* **1.** cela *f* **2.** BIOL komórka *f* **3.** ogniwo *n*
cel•lar ['selə] *s* **1.** piwnica *f* **2. *salt*** ~ *Br* solniczka *f*
cel•list ['tʃelɪst] *s* MUS wiolonczelista *m*
cel•lo ['tʃeləʊ] *s* MUS wiolonczela *f*
cel•lo•phane ['seləʊfeɪn] *s* celofan *m*
'cell•phone ['selfəʊn] *s* telefon *m* komórkowy
cel•lu•lar ['seljʊlə] *adj* komórkowy; **cel•lu•lar 'phone** → ***cellphone***
cel•lu•lite ['seljʊlaɪt] *s* cellulit *m*
cel•lu•loid ['seljʊlɔɪd] *s* **1.** celuloid *m* **2.** taśma *f* filmowa
cel•lu•lose ['seljʊləʊs] *s* celuloza *f*
Cel•si•us ['selsɪəs] *adv*: ***20 degrees*** ~ 20 stopni (w skali) Celsjusza; ***the*** ~ ***scale*** skala *f* Celsjusza
Celt [kelt] *s* Celt *m;* **Celt•ic** ['keltɪk] *adj* celtycki
ce•ment [sɪ'ment] **I** *s* cement *m;* ***a*** ~ ***mixer*** betoniarka **II** *v/t* **1.** *fig* cementować ⟨s-⟩ **2.** cementować ⟨za-⟩ **3.** kleić ⟨s-⟩
cem•e•tery ['semɪtrɪ] *s* cmentarz *m*
cen•sor ['sensə] **I** *s* cenzor *m* **II** *v/t* cenzurować ⟨o-⟩; ***some data was*** ~***ed from the report*** niektóre dane usunięto z raportu; **cen•so•ri•ous** [sen'sɔːrɪəs] *adj* bardzo surowy, bardzo krytyczny; **cen•sor•ship** ['sensəʃɪp] *s* cenzura *f*
cen•sus ['sensəs] *s* spis *m* ludności
cent [sent] *s* cent *m*
cen•te•nar•i•an [sentɪ'neərɪən] *s* stulatek *m;* **cen•ten•ni•al** [sen'teniəl], ***cen•te•na•ry*** [sen'tiːnərɪ] *Br* **I** *adj* stuletni **II** *s* stulecie *n,* setna rocznica *f*
cen•ter *Am* → ***centre***
cen•ti•grade ['sentɪgreɪd] *adj* (w skali) Celsjusza
cen•ti•gram(me) ['sentɪgræm] *s* centygram *m*
cen•ti•me•tre ['sentɪmiːtə], ***cen•ti•me•ter*** *Am s* centymetr *m*
cen•tral ['sentrəl] *adj* **1.** centralny; ***a*** ~ ***bank*** bank centralny **2.** główny, kluczowy; ***be*** ~ ***to*** mieć kluczowe znaczenie dla *G* **3.** (znajdujący się) w centrum
Cen•tral A•'mer•i•ca *s* GEOGR Ameryka *f* Środkowa; **Cen•tral A•'mer•i•can** *adj* GEOGR środkowoamerykański
cen•tral 'heat•ing *s* centralne ogrzewanie *n;* **cen•tral 'lock•ing** *s* AUTO centralny zamek *m;* **cen•tral 'nerv•ous sys•tem** *s* ANAT ośrodkowy układ *m* nerwowy; **cen•tral 'pro•ces•sing u•nit** *s* INF jednostka *f* centralna, procesor *m* główny; **Cen•tral 'Eu•ro•pe•an Time** *s* czas *m* środkowoeuropejski

C

C

cen•tral•iz•a•tion [sentrəlaɪz'eɪʃn] *s* centralizacja *f*; **cen•tral•ize** ['sentrəlaɪz] *v/t* centralizować ⟨s-⟩

cen•tre ['sentə] *Br,* **cen•ter** *Am* **I** *s* **1.** środek *m* **2.** centrum *n*; ***at the ~ of attention*** w centrum uwagi **3.** centrum *n,* ośrodek *m* **4.** SPORT środkowy *m* **5.** nadzienie *n* **II** *v/t* **1.** umieszczać ⟨umieścić⟩ na środku **2.** SPORT dośrodkowywać ⟨-kować⟩; **cen•tre on** *v/i*: ***be centred on*** koncentrować się na *L,* skupiać się na *L*; **cen•tre round** *v/i*: ***be centred round*** koncentrować się wokół *G,* skupiać się wokół *G*

cen•tu•ry ['sentʃərɪ] *s* wiek *m,* stulecie *n*

CEO [siːiː'əʊ] *abbr* (=***chief executive officer***) dyrektor *m* wykonawczy, prezes *m* (zarządu)

ce•ram•ic [sɪ'ræmɪk] *adj* ceramiczny; **ce•ram•ics** [sɪ'ræmɪks] *s* ceramika *f*

ce•re•al ['sɪərɪəl] **I** *s* **1.** zboże *n* **2.** płatki *pl* zbożowe, płatki *pl* śniadaniowe **II** *adj* zbożowy

cer•e•mo•ni•al [serɪ'məʊnɪəl] **I** *adj* **1.** uroczysty, ceremonialny **2.** rytualny **3.** *function*: reprezentacyjny **II** *adj* **1.** ceremoniał *m* **2.** rytuał *m*; **cer•e•mo•ni•ous** [serɪ'məʊnɪəs] *adj* ceremonialny; **cer•e•mo•ny** ['serɪmənɪ] *s* **1.** ceremonia *f,* uroczystość *f* **2.** ceremoniał *m* **3.** ceregiele *pl,* ceremonie *pl*; ***without ~*** bezceremonialnie

cer•tain ['sɜːtn] *adj* **1.** pewny, pewien (***about/of*** *G*); ***for ~*** na pewno; ***make ~ that*** upewnić się, że **2.** (*definite*) pewien; ***for ~ reasons*** z pewnych powodów **3.** pewien, niejaki; ***a ~ Mr Brown*** niejaki pan Brown **4.** *medicine*: niezawodny **5.** *fact*: niewątpliwy; **certain•ly** ['sɜːtnlɪ] *adv* **1.** z pewnością **2.** (*answer*) oczywiście, rzecz jasna; **cer•tain•ty** ['sɜːtntɪ] *s* **1.** pewność *f* **2.** rzecz *f* pewna, pewnik *m*; ***s.th. seems to be a ~*** coś wydaje się pewne

cer•tif•i•cate [sər'tɪfɪkət] **I** *s* **1.** świadectwo *n,* certyfikat *m*; ***a quality ~*** certyfikat jakości, atest **2.** zaświadczenie *f* **3.** *of marriage, death*: akt *m* **4.** *birth*: metryka *f* **II** *v/t* zaświadczać ⟨-czyć⟩; **cer•tif•i•cate of 'or•i•gin** *s* świadectwo *n* pochodzenia

cer•ti•fy ['sɜːtɪfaɪ] *v/t* **1.** zaświadczać ⟨-czyć⟩, poświadczać ⟨-czyć⟩; ***this is to ~ that*** niniejszym zaświadcza się, że **2.** ***~ a document as a true copy*** uwierzytelniać dokument **3.** uznawać ⟨-nać⟩ (**as** za *A*) **4.** uznawać ⟨-nać⟩ za psychicznie chorego

Ce•sar•e•an *adj* MED → **Caesarean**

ces•sa•tion [se'seɪʃn] *s* **1.** wstrzymanie *n,* zaprzestanie *n* **2.** ustanie *n*

cess•pit ['sespɪt], **cess•pool** ['sespuːl] *s* szambo *n*

chain [tʃeɪn] **I** *s* **1.** łańcuch *m*; ***a mountain ~*** łańcuch górski **2.** *shops*: sieć *f* **3.** *events*: seria *f,* ciąg *m* **4.** *fig* okowy *pl,* pęta *pl* **II** (*a.* ***~ up***) *v/t* **1.** przykuwać ⟨-kuć⟩ (łańcuchem) **2.** przymocowywać ⟨-cować⟩ **3.** skuwać ⟨skuć⟩; **chain re•'ac•tion** *s* PHYS reakcja *f* łańcuchowa; **'chain•saw** *s* piła *f* łańcuchowa; **'chain-smoke** *v/i* palić jednego papierosa za drugim; **'chain store** *s* **1.** sklep *m* należący do sieci handlowej **2.** sieć *f* handlowa

chair [tʃeə] **I** *s* **1.** krzesło *n*; ***take a ~ please*** proszę usiąść **2.** fotel *m* **3.** ***the ~*** przewodniczący **4.** ***hold the ~ of physics*** kierować katedrą fizyki **5.** ***the ~*** krzesło (elektryczne) **II** *v/t meeting*: przewodniczyć; ***the meeting was ~ed by*** zebraniu przewodniczył; **'chairlift** *s* wyciąg *m* krzesełkowy

'chair•man *pl -men s* **1.** przewodniczący *m* **2.** prezes *m*; **'chair•man•ship** *s* **1.** przewodniczenie *n,* przewodnictwo *n* **2.** prezesura *f* **3.** kadencja *f*; **chair•per•son** *s* **1.** przewodniczący *m* **2.** prezes *m*

chal•ice ['tʃælɪs] *s* REL kielich *m* mszalny

chalk [tʃɔːk] **I** *s* kreda *f*; ***be as different as ~ and cheese*** różnić się jak noc i dzień, różnić się diametralnie **II** *v/t* **1.** pisać ⟨na-⟩ (kredą) **2.** rysować ⟨na-⟩ (kredą); **chalk up** *v/t* **1.** zapisywać ⟨-pisać⟩ (kredą) **2.** *victory*: odnosić ⟨-nieść⟩

chal•lenge ['tʃælɪndʒ] **I** *s* **1.** wyzwanie *n*; ***accept a ~*** przyjąć wyzwanie; ***meet the ~ of s.th.*** sprostać czemuś; ***rise to the ~*** stanąć na wysokości zadania **2.** zadanie *n* **3.** podważenie *n,* zakwestionowanie *n* **4.** sprzeciw *m*

II *v/t* **1.** podważać ⟨-żyć⟩, podawać ⟨-dać⟩ w wątpliwość **2.** rzucać ⟨-cić⟩ wyzywanie; **~ s.o.** ***to a game of chess*** wyzwać kogoś na szachowy pojedynek, zaproponować komuś partię szachów **3.** być wyzwaniem dla *G*; **chal•len•ger** ['tʃælɪndʒə] *s* **1.** rywal *m* **2.** kandydat *m*; ***a ~ for the world championship*** kandydat do tytułu mistrza świata; **chal•len•ging** ['tʃælɪndʒɪŋ] *adj plan, project*: ambitny, stanowiący wyzwanie

cham•ber ['tʃeɪmbə] *s* **1.** sala *f* **2.** *dated* komnata *f*; '**cham•ber•maid** *s* pokojówka *f*; '**Cham•ber of 'Com•merce** *s* Izba *f* Handlowa; '**cham•ber pot** *s* nocnik *m*

cha•me•le•on [kə'miːljən] *s* BIOL kameleon *m*

champ[1] [tʃæmp], ***chomp*** [tʃɒmp] *v/i* głośno przeżuwać, chrupać (***on/through*** *A*); ***~ at the bit*** *fig* niecierpliwić się, rwać się do czynu; ***he was ~ing at the bit to tell her about it*** nie mógł się doczekać, kiedy będzie mógł jej o tym powiedzieć

champ[2] [~] *s infml* czempion *m*, mistrz *m*

cham•pagne [ʃæm'peɪn] *s* szampan *m*

cham•pi•on ['tʃæmpɪən] **I** *s* **1.** SPORT mistrz *m*; ***the defending ~*** obrońca tytułu; ***a ~ boxer*** mistrz bokserski **2.** obrońca *f*, orędownik *m* **II** *v/t* **1.** walczyć o *A* **2.** bronić **3.** wspierać; **cham•pi•on•ship** ['tʃæmpɪənʃɪp] *s* SPORT **1.** mistrzostwo *n*, mistrzostwa *pl* **2.** tytuł *m* mistrzowski

chance [tʃæns] **I** *s* **1.** szansa *f*; ***~s are that*** możliwe, że; ***you don't stand a ~*** nie masz szans; ***there's no ~*** nie ma szans **2.** okazja *f*; ***a ~ of a lifetime*** życiowa szansa **3.** przypadek *m*, zrządzenie *n* losu; ***by ~*** przypadkiem; ***a game of ~*** gra losowa **4.** ryzyko *n*; ***let's take a ~*** zaryzykujmy; ***take no ~s*** nie ryzykować **II** *v/i* ***~ on*** spotykać przypadkiem, natknąć się przypadkiem na *A* **III** *v/t* ryzykować ⟨za-⟩; ***they ~d to be staying at the same hotel*** przypadek sprawił, że zatrzymali się w tym samym hotelu **IV** *adj* przypadkowy; ***a ~ meeting*** przypadkowe spotkanie

chan•cel•lor ['tʃɑːnsələ] *s* **1.** kanclerz *m*; ***~ of the Exchequer*** *Br* minister skarbu **2.** *Am* rektor *m* (uniwersytetu)

chanc•y ['tʃænsɪ] *adj infml* niepewny, ryzykowny

chan•de•lier [ʃændə'lɪə] *s* żyrandol *m*

change [tʃeɪndʒ] **I** *v/t* **1.** zmieniać ⟨-nić⟩ (***for*** na *A*); ***~ trains*** przesiąść się (do innego pociągu); ***~ clothes*** przebrać się **2.** wymieniać ⟨-nić⟩ (***for*** na *A*) **3.** (*currency*) wymieniać ⟨-nić⟩ (***into*** na *A*) **4.** rozmieniać ⟨-nić⟩ (***into*** na *A*) **5.** zamieniać ⟨-nić⟩ się *I*; ***~ places*** zamienić się miejscami **6.** *baby*: przewijać ⟨-winąć⟩ **II** *v/i* **1.** zmieniać ⟨-nić⟩ się (***into*** w *A*) **2.** przebierać ⟨-brać⟩ się (***into*** w *A*) **3.** przesiadać ⟨-siąść⟩ się

change•a•ble ['tʃeɪndʒəbl] *adj* zmienny, niestały

'**change•o•ver** *s* **1.** zmiana *f*, przejście *n* (***to*** na *A*); ***a ~ period*** okres przejściowy

'**chang•ing room** *s* **1.** SPORT szatnia *f* **2.** przebieralnia *f*

chan•nel ['tʃænl] *s* **1.** *television*: program *m*, kanał *m*; ***~ hopping*** *Br*, ***~ surfing*** *Am infml* skakanie po kanałach (telewizyjnych) **2.** *radio*: pasmo *n*, kanał *m* **3.** kanał *m*; ***through official ~s*** drogą oficjalną **4.** możliwość *f*, sposób *m* **5.** kanał *m*, przesmyk *m*; ***the (English) ~*** Kanał La Manche; ***the ~ Tunnel*** tunel pod Kanałem La Manche

chant [tʃænt] **I** *s* **1.** (monotonny) śpiew *m* **2.** okrzyki *pl*, skandowanie *n* **3.** REL chorał *m* **II** *v/t* **1.** (monotonnie) śpiewać **2.** skandować

cha•os ['keɪɒs] *s* **1.** chaos *m* **2.** zamęt *m*; **cha•ot•ic** [keɪ'ɒtɪk] *adj* **1.** chaotyczny **2.** bezładny, nieuporządkowany

chap[1] [tʃæp] *v/t* (*skin*) pierzchnąć ⟨s-⟩, pękać ⟨po-⟩; ***a ~ping stick*** szminka ochronna

chap[2] [~] *s infml* facet *m*, gość *m*

chap•el ['tʃæpl] *s* kaplica *f*

chap•er•on(e) ['ʃæpərəʊn] **I** *s* **1.** przyzwoitka *f* **2.** opiekun *m* **II** *v/t* **1.** towarzyszyć w roli przyzwoitki **2.** opiekować się

chap•lain ['tʃæplɪn] *s* kapelan *m*

C

chapped [tʃæpt] *adj hands*: popękany, spierzchnięty
chap•ter [ˈtʃæptə] *s a. fig* rozdział *m*
char•ac•ter [ˈkærəktə] *s* **1.** charakter *m*; ***in ~*** typowy; ***out of ~*** nietypowy **2.** postać *f*; ***the main ~*** główny bohater **3.** *infml* oryginał *m* **4.** znak *m*; **ˈchar•ac•ter actor** *s* aktor *m* charakterystyczny
char•ac•ter•is•tic [kærɪktəˈrɪstɪk] **I** *adj* charakterystyczny, typowy (**of** dla *G*); ***she spoke with ~ enthusiasm*** mówiła z typowym dla siebie entuzjazmem **II** *s* cecha *f* (charakterystyczna); **char•ac•ter•is•ti•cal•ly** [kærɪktəˈrɪstɪklɪ] *adv* charakterystycznie, typowo; **char•ac•ter•ize** [ˈkærɪktəraɪz] *v/t* **1.** charakteryzować, cechować **2.** opisywać ⟨-sać⟩, charakteryzować ⟨s-⟩
cha•rade [ʃəˈrɑːd] *s fig* **1.** gra *f* pozorów **2.** fasada *f*
charge [tʃɑːdʒ] **I** *v/t* **1.** liczyć ⟨po-⟩, pobierać ⟨-brać⟩ opłatę; ***~ low prices*** mieć niskie ceny; ***he ~s 40 pounds a day*** bierze 40 funtów dziennie **2.** ***~ s.th. to s.o.'s account*** doliczyć coś komuś do rachunku, obciążyć za coś czyjś rachunek **3.** *interest*: naliczać ⟨-czyć⟩ **4.** *battery*: ładować ⟨na-⟩ **5.** ***~ s.o. with s.th.*** JUR zarzucać komuś coś, oskarżać kogoś o coś **II** *v/i* **1.** pobierać ⟨-brać⟩ opłatę (**for** za *A*) **2.** nacierać ⟨natrzeć⟩, atakować ⟨za-⟩; ***~!*** do ataku! **3.** ładować ⟨na-⟩ się **III** *s* **1.** opłata *f*, koszt *m*; ***free of ~*** bezpłatny **2.** JUR zarzut *m* **3.** ***be in ~ of, have ~ of*** **a)** kierować *I* **b)** być odpowiedzialnym za *A*; ***take ~ of*** **a)** objąć kierownictwo *G* **b)** zająć się *I*; ***a person in ~*** osoba odpowiedzialna **4.** ładunek *m* **5.** atak *m*, natarcie *n*
charg•er [ˈtʃɑːdʒə] *s* **1.** ładowarka *f* **2.** rumak *m*
cha•ris•ma [kəˈrɪzmə] *s* charyzma *f*; **char•is•ma•tic** [kærɪzˈmætɪk] *adj* charyzmatyczny
char•i•ta•ble [ˈtʃærətəbl] *adj* **1.** charytatywny, dobroczynny **2.** *donation*: na cele charytatywne **3.** wyrozumiały; **char•i•ty** [ˈtʃærətɪ] *s* **1.** organizacja *f* charytatywna **2.** działalność *f* charytatywna; ***for ~*** na cele charytatywne **3.** wyrozumiałość *f*
char•la•tan [ˈʃɑːlətən] *s* szarlatan *m*
charm [tʃɑːm] **I** *s* **1.** urok *m*, wdzięk *m* **2.** zaklęcie *n*, czar *m* **3.** talizman *m*, amulet *m* **II** *v/t* **1.** oczarowywać ⟨-rować⟩, zauroczyć **2.** czarować ⟨za-⟩; **charm•er** [ˈtʃɑːmə] *s* **1.** ***he's a ~*** jest czarujący, potrafi każdego oczarować; ***a snake ~*** zaklinacz węży **2.** *infml* czaruś *m*, bajerant *m*; **charm•ing** [ˈtʃɑːmɪŋ] *adj* uroczy, czarujący
charred [tʃɑːd] *adj* **1.** przypalony **2.** zwęglony
chart [tʃɑːt] **I** *s* **1.** wykres *m*, diagram *m* **2.** schemat *m* **3.** tabela *f* **4.** mapa *f* **5.** ***the ~s*** lista przebojów **II** *v/t* **1.** wykreślać ⟨-lić⟩ **2.** sporządzać ⟨-dzić⟩ mapę **3.** przedstawiać ⟨-wić⟩ (na wykresie)
char•ter [ˈtʃɑːtə] **I** *s* **1.** karta *f* **2.** statut *m* **3.** prawa *pl* miejskie **4.** czarter *m* **5.** wynajem *m* **II** *v/t* **1.** *institution*: powoływać ⟨-łać⟩, ustanawiać ⟨-nowić⟩ **2.** czarterować ⟨wy-⟩ **3.** wynajmować ⟨-jąć⟩; **ˈchar•ter flight** *s* lot *m* czarterowy; **ˈchar•ter plane** *s* samolot *m* czarterowy
char•tered [tʃɑːtərd] *adj* **1.** dyplomowany, licencjonowany **2.** czarterowy
chase [tʃeɪs] **I** *v/t* **1.** gonić **2.** ścigać **3.** uganiać się za *I* **4.** polować na *A* **II** *s* **1.** pościg *m*, pogoń *f* **2.** polowanie *n*; **chase after** *v/i* **1.** gonić **2.** uganiać się za *I*; **chase away** *v/t* **1.** przeganiać ⟨-gonić⟩, wyganiać ⟨-gonić⟩ **2.** odpędzać ⟨-dzić⟩; **chase up** *v/t* popędzać ⟨-dzić⟩, ponaglać ⟨-lić⟩
chas•er [ˈtʃeɪsə] *s infml* **1.** utrwalacz *m* **2.** popitka *f*
cha•sm [ˈkæzəm] *s* **1.** przepaść *f* **2.** (głęboka) szczelina *f*, rozpadlina *f* **3.** *fig* przepaść *f*, rozziew *m*
chaste [tʃeɪst] *adj* **1.** czysty, cnotliwy **2.** niewinny
chas•ten [ˈtʃeɪsn] *v/t* zawstydzać ⟨-dzić⟩; **chas•ten•ed** [ˈtʃeɪsnd] *adj* skruszony
chas•tise [tʃæˈstaɪz] *v/t* **1.** ostro krytykować ⟨s-⟩, potępiać ⟨-pić⟩ **2.** karać ⟨u-⟩
chas•ti•ty [ˈtʃæstətɪ] *s* czystość *f*, niewinność *f*
chat [tʃæt] **I** *v/i* gadać ⟨po-⟩, gawędzić ⟨po-⟩ **II** *s* **1.** rozmowa *f*, pogawędka *f*; ***have a ~ with*** pogadać z *I* **2.** INF

czat *m*; **'chat show** *s Br* talk show *m*
chat•ter ['tʃætə] **I** *v/i* **1.** paplać, trajkotać **2.** świergotać, ćwierkać **3.** (*teeth*) szczękać **II** *s* **1.** paplanie *n* **2.** ćwierkanie *n*; **'chat•ter•box** *s infml* gaduła *f*, papla *f*
chat•ty ['tʃætɪ] *adj infml* **1.** gadatliwy, towarzyski **2.** gawędziarski
chauf•feur ['ʃəʊfə] *s* szofer *m*, kierowca *m*; **'chauf•feur-driv•en** *adj car*: z kierowcą, z szoferem
chau•vin•ism ['ʃəʊvɪnɪzəm] *s* szowinizm *m*; **chau•vin•ist** ['ʃəʊvɪnɪst] **I** *s* szowinista *m* **II** *adj* szowinistyczny; ***a male ~ pig*** męska szowinistyczna świnia; **chau•vin•ist•ic** [ʃəʊvɪ'nɪstɪk] *adj* szowinistyczny
cheap [tʃiːp] **I** *adj* **1.** tani, niedrogi; ***not come ~*** nie być tanim **2.** *price*: niski **3.** tani, tandetny **4.** *Am* skąpy **II** *adv* tanio, niedrogo; **cheap•en** ['tʃiːpən] *v/t* **1.** obniżać ⟨-żyć⟩ cenę **2.** umniejszać ⟨-szyć⟩ wartość **3.** ***~ oneself*** poniżyć się; **cheap•ness** ['tʃiːpnɪs] *s* **1.** taniość *f* **2.** niska cena *f*
'cheap•skate *s infml* kutwa *m*, sknera *m*
cheat [tʃiːt] **I** *v/t* **1.** oszukiwać ⟨-kać⟩ **2.** w oszukańczy sposób pozbawiać ⟨-wić⟩ (***out of*** *G*) **II** *v/i* **1.** oszukiwać ⟨-kać⟩ **2.** (*on test*) ściągać **3.** zdradzać ⟨-dzić⟩ (***on*** *A*) **III** *s* **1.** oszust *m* **2.** oszustwo *n*, szwindel *m*
Chech•ni•a ['tʃetʃnɪə] *s* Czeczenia *f*
check[1] [tʃek] **I** *v/t* **1.** sprawdzać ⟨-dzić⟩, kontrolować ⟨s-⟩ **2.** powstrzymywać ⟨-mać⟩; ***~ oneself*** powstrzymać się **3.** ograniczać ⟨-czyć⟩ **4.** *luggage*: nadawać ⟨-dać⟩ **5.** szachować ⟨za-⟩ **6.** *Am* zaznaczać ⟨-czyć⟩, *infml* odfajkowywać ⟨-kować⟩ **II** *s* **1.** kontrola *f*, przegląd *m*; ***keep s.th. in ~*** kontrolować coś **2.** (*chess*) szach *m*; ***the king is in ~ from*** król jest szachowany przez *A* **3.** *Am* czek *m*; ***pay by ~*** zapłacić czekiem **4.** *Am* rachunek *m* **5.** *Am* numerek *m* (z szatni) **6.** *Am* szatnia *f* **7.** *Am infml* ptaszek *m*, fajka *f*; **check in** *v/i* **1.** (*airport*) zgłaszać ⟨-łosić⟩ się do odprawy **2.** (*hotel*) meldować ⟨za-⟩ się; **check off** *v/t* sprawdzać ⟨-dzić⟩ na liście; **check on** *v/i* sprawdzać ⟨-dzić⟩; **check out I** *v/t* sprawdzać ⟨-dzić⟩ **II** *v/i* wymeldowywać ⟨-dować⟩ się (z hotelu); **check up on** *v/i* **1.** sprawdzać ⟨-dzić⟩ **2.** kontrolować ⟨s-⟩; ***Mom's always checking up on me*** mama mnie bez przerwy pilnuje **3.** zasięgać ⟨-gnąć⟩ informacji na temat *G*; **check with** *v/i*: ***~ s.o. that*** pytać kogoś, czy, dowiadywać się od kogoś, czy
check[2] [~] **I** *s* (*pattern*) krata *f* **II** *adj* w kratkę, w kratkę, kraciasty; **'check•book** *s Am* książeczka *f* czekowa
checked [tʃekt] *adj* kraciasty, w krat(k)ę
check•er ['tʃekə] *s* **1.** *Am* kasjer *m* **2.** kontroler *m* **3.** ***a virus ~*** INF program antywirusowy; ***a spelling ~*** moduł sprawdzania pisowni
check•er•board ['tʃekərbɔːd] *s Am* plansza *f* do gry w warcaby
check•ered ['tʃekəd] *adj* w kratkę
check•ers ['tʃekəz] *s Am* warcaby *pl*
'check-in *s* **1.** (*airport*) stanowisko *n* odpraw **2.** odprawa *f*; **'check-in desk** *s* (*airport*) stanowisko *n* odpraw
'check•ing ac•count *s* rachunek *m* bieżący, rachunek *m* oszczędnościowo-rozliczeniowy
'check•list *s* **1.** lista *f* (kontrolna) **2.** wykaz *m*
'check mark *s infml* ptaszek *m*, fajka *f*
'check•mate I *s* szach-mat *m* **II** *v/t* dawać ⟨dać⟩ mata, matować ⟨za-⟩ **III** *interj* ***~!*** szach-mat!
'check•out *s* **1.** (*supermarket*) kasa *f* **2.** (*hotel*) wymeldowanie *n*; **'check•out time** *s* godzina *f*, przed którą należy zwolnić pokój (hotelowy)
'check•point *s* **1.** punkt *m* kontrolny **2.** posterunek *m*
'check•room *s Am* **1.** szatnia *f* **2.** przechowalnia *f* bagażu
'check•up *s* MED **1.** (okresowe) badanie *n* **2.** (okresowe) badania *pl* **3.** (*dentist*) przegląd *m*
cheek [tʃiːk] *s* **1.** policzek *m*; ***turn the other ~*** nadstawić drugi policzek **2.** *infml* pośladek *m* **3.** bezczelność *f*, tupet *m*; **'cheek•bone** *s* kość *f* policzkowa
cheer [tʃɪə] **I** *s* **1.** okrzyk *m* (radości) **2.** wiwat *m* **3.** radość *f* **II** *v/t* **1.** dopingować ⟨z-⟩, zagrzewać ⟨-rzać⟩ do

C

walki **2.** wiwatować **3.** pocieszać ⟨-szyć⟩, dodawać ⟨-dać⟩ otuchy; ***a ~ing thought*** pocieszająca myśl; **cheer on** *v/t* dopingować ⟨z-⟩, zagrzewać ⟨-rzać⟩ do walki; **cheer up I** *v/t* pocieszać ⟨-szyć⟩, dodawać ⟨-dać⟩ otuchy **II** *v/i* rozchmurzać ⟨-rzyć⟩ się

cheer•ful ['tʃɪərfəl] *adj* **1.** radosny, wesoły **2.** pogodny

cheer•i•o [tʃɪərɪ'əʊ] *interj Br infml* cześć, trzymaj się

'cheer•lead•er *s SPORT* czirliderka *f*

cheer•less ['tʃɪəlɪs] *adj* smętny, ponury

cheers ['tʃɪəz] *interj* **1.** na zdrowie! **2.** *Br infml* cześć!, trzymaj się! **3.** *Br infml* dzięki!

cheer•y ['tʃɪərɪ] *adj* **1.** radosny **2.** *smile*: promienny

cheese [tʃiːz] *s* ser *m*; ***say ~!*** uśmiech (proszę)!; **'cheese•burg•er** *s* cheeseburger *m*; **'cheese•cake** *s* sernik *m*, ciasto *n* z serem; **'cheese•par•ing** *s* skąpstwo *n*; **'cheese spread** *s* **1.** ser *m* topiony **2.** serek *m* twarogowy

chees•y ['tʃiːzɪ] *adj* **1.** *infml* tandetny, tani **2.** serowy **3.** o smaku sera

chee•tah ['tʃiːtə] *s BIOL* gepard *m*

chef [ʃef] *s* **1.** szef *m* kuchni **2.** kucharz *m*

chem•i•cal ['kemɪkl] **I** *adj* **1.** chemiczny **2.** *fertilizer*: sztuczny **II** *s* substancja *f* chemiczna; **chem•i•cal 'war•fare** *s* wojna *f* chemiczna

chem•ist ['kemɪst] *s* **1.** chemik *m* **2.** *Br* aptekarz *m* **3.** ***the ~'s*** *Br* apteka

chem•is•try ['kemɪstrɪ] *s* chemia *f*

chem•o•ther•a•py [kiːməʊ'θerəpɪ] *s* chemioterapia *f*

cheque [tʃek] *s Br* czek *m*; ***pay by ~*** zapłacić czekiem; **'cheque card** *s Br* karta *f* czekowa

cheq•uered ['tʃekərd] *Br* w kratkę

cher•ish ['tʃerɪʃ] *v/t* **1.** hołubić, otaczać ⟨otoczyć⟩ miłością i opieką **2.** *hope*: żywić **3.** *memories*: pielęgnować **4.** *ambitions*: mieć

cher•ry ['tʃerɪ] **I** *s* **1.** wiśnia *f* **2.** czereśnia *f* **II** *adj* **1.** wiśniowy **2.** czereśniowy; **cher•ry 'bran•dy** *s* likier *m* wiśniowy, wiśniówka *f*

cher•ry to'ma•to *pl -toes s* **1.** pomidor *m* drobnoowocowy **2.** pomidor *m* malinowy

cher•ub ['tʃerəb] *s* cherubin *m*, aniołek *m*

chess [tʃes] *s* szachy *pl*; **'chess•board** *s* szachownica *f*; **'chess•man**, **'chess•piece** *s* (*pawn or piece*) bierka *f*

chest [tʃest] *s* **1.** *ANAT* klatka *f* piersiowa, pierś *f*; ***get s.th. off one's ~*** *fig* wyrzucić coś z siebie **2.** skrzynia *f*, kufer *m*; **chest of 'draw•ers** *s* komoda *f*

chest•nut ['tʃesnʌt] **I** *s* **1.** kasztan *m* (jadalny) **2.** (*a.* **horse ~**) kasztanowiec *m*, *infml* kasztan *m* **3.** kasztan *m* **4.** (*colour*) kasztanowy *m*, kasztan *m* **5.** ***an old ~*** kawał z brodą **II** *adj* kasztanowy

chew [tʃuː] **I** *v/t* żuć, przeżuwać **II** *v/i* **1.** *bone*: gryźć (**on** *A*) **2.** *lip*: przygryzać ⟨-gryźć⟩ (**on** *A*) **3.** *nails*: obgryzać ⟨-gryźć⟩ (**on** *A*); **chew over** *v/t* przemyśliwać ⟨-leć⟩, zastanawiać ⟨-nowić⟩ się nad *I*; **'chew•ing gum** *s* guma *f* do żucia

chic [ʃiːk] **I** *adj* szykowny, elegancki **II** *s* szyk *m*, styl *m*

chick [tʃɪk] *s* **1.** pisklę *n* **2.** kurczę *n*, kurczak *m* **3.** (*woman*) *infml* laska *f*, cizia *f*

chick•en ['tʃɪkɪn] **I** *s* **1.** kurczak *m* **2.** kura *f* **3.** *infml* cykor *m* **II** *adj* **1.** kurczaka **2.** z kurczaka **3.** z kurczakiem **4.** tchórzliwy; **chick•en out** *v/i* tchórzyć ⟨s-⟩; **'chick•en broth** *s* rosół *m* z kury **'chick•en farm** *s* kurza ferma *f*; **'chick•en farm•er** *s* hodowca *m* drobiu; **'chick•en•feed** *s* **1.** karma *f* dla drobiu **2.** *infml* marne grosze *pl*; **'chick•en pox** *s MED* ospa *f* wietrzna

chic•o•ry ['tʃɪkərɪ] *s BIOL* cykoria *f*

chief [tʃiːf] **I** *s* **1.** szef *m* **2.** wódz *m* (plemienia) **II** *adj* **1.** główny **2.** *editor*: naczelny; **chief ex•ec•u•tive 'of•fi•cer** *s* dyrektor *m* wykonawczy, prezes *m* (zarządu); **chief•ly** ['tʃiːflɪ] *adv* **1.** głównie **2.** przede wszystkim

chif•fon ['ʃɪfɒn] *s* szyfon *m*

child [tʃaɪld] *pl children* ['tʃɪldrən] *s* **1.** dziecko *n*; ***an only ~*** jedynak; ***it's ~s play!*** *infml* to łatwizna! **2.** potomek *m*; **'child a•buse** *s* **1.** molestowanie *n* seksualne nieletnich **2.** maltretowanie *n* nieletnich; **'child a•bus•er** *s*: ***he was a ~*** molestował seksualnie

nieletnich; 'child•birth *s* poród *m*; *die in ~* umrzeć przy porodzie
child•hood ['tʃaɪldhʊd] **I** *s* dzieciństwo *n*; ***from ~*** od dziecka **II** *adj* **1.** dziecięcy **2.** dzieciństwa **3.** z dzieciństwa **4.** *illness*: wieku dziecięcego
child•ish ['tʃaɪldɪʃ] *adj* **1.** dziecięcy **2.** dziecinny, infantylny; **child•ish•ly** ['tʃaɪldɪʃlɪ] *adv* dziecinnie, infantylnie; **child•ish•ness** ['tʃaɪldɪʃnɪs] *s* dziecinność *f*, infantylność *f*
child•less ['tʃaɪldlɪs] *adj* **1.** bezdzietny **2.** bezpotomny; **child•like** ['tʃaɪldlaɪk] *adj* dziecięcy; '**child•mind•er** *s* opiekun *m* do dzieci, opiekunka *f* do dzieci; '**child•mind•ing** *s* opiekowanie *n* się dziećmi; **child 'prod•i•gy** *s* cudowne dziecko *n*; '**child-proof** *adj* bezpieczny dla dziecka
child•ren ['tʃɪldrən] *pl* → ***child***
Chil•e ['tʃɪlɪ] *s* GEOGR Chile *n*; **Chil•e•an** ['θɪlɪən] **I** *s* Chilijczyk *m* **II** *adj* chilijski
chill [tʃil] **I** *s* **1.** chłód *f* **2.** ziąb *m* **3.** (lekkie) przeziębienie *n* **4.** *fig* dreszcz *m* **II** *v/t* **1.** chłodzić ⟨s-⟩ **2.** studzić ⟨o-⟩ **3.** ***be ~ed*** marznąć; ***be ~ed to the bone*** przemarznąć do szpiku kości **4.** oziębiać ⟨-bić⟩ **5.** przerażać ⟨-razić⟩, przejmować ⟨-jąć⟩ lękiem; **chill out** *v/i infml* wyluzować się
chilled [tʃild] *adj* schłodzony
chilli ['tʃɪlɪ] *Br*, **chili** *Am s* COOK chili *n*
chill•y ['tʃɪlɪ] *adj* chłodny; ***it's ~*** jest chłodno
chime [tʃaɪm] **I** *s* **1.** dzwonienie *n* **2.** bicie *n* dzwonu **3.** kurant *m* **4.** ***~s*** dzwonki (poruszane podmuchami wiatru) **II** *v/i* **1.** dzwonić **2.** bić, wybijać godziny **III** *v/t* wybijać ⟨-bić⟩ godzinę; **chime in with** *v/i* współgrać z *I*, pokrywać ⟨-ryć⟩ się z *I*
chim•ney ['tʃimnɪ] *s* komin *m*; '**chimney sweep** *s* kominiarz *m*
chim•pan•zee [tʃɪmpæn'ziː] *s* szympans *m*
chin [tʃɪn] *s* broda *f*, podbródek *m*; ***~ up!*** głowa do góry!
Chi•na ['tʃaɪnə] *s* Chiny *pl*; '**Chi•na•man** *pl -men s* **1.** Chińczyk, *m* Chinka *f* **2.** *infml* żółtek *m*, chinol *m*
chi•na ['tʃaɪnə] *s* porcelana *f*
'**Chi•na•town** *s* dzielnica *f* chińska
Chi•nese [tʃaɪ'niːz] **I** *s* Chińczyk *m*; ***he's ~*** jest Chińczykiem; ***a ~ woman*** Chinka; ***the ~*** Chińczycy **II** *adj* chiński
chink[1] [tʃɪŋk] *s* **1.** szpara *f* **2.** szczelina *f*; ***a ~ in one's armour*** *fig* czyjś słaby punkt, czyjaś pięta achillesowa
chink[2] [~] **I** *v/i* **1.** brzęczeć ⟨za-⟩, pobrzękiwać **2.** dzwonić ⟨za-⟩ **II** *v/t* **1.** brzęczeć ⟨za-⟩ **2.** *glasses*: stukać ⟨-knąć⟩ się
'**chin•wag** *s Br infml* pogawędka *f*
chip[1] [tʃɪp] *s* **1.** *Br* frytka *f* **2.** *Am* chips *m* **3.** INF układ *m* scalony, chip *m* **4.** odłamek *m*; ***a ~ off the old block*** *fig* **a)** nieodrodny syn **b)** nieodrodna córka **5.** odprysk *m* **6.** wiór *m*; ***have a ~ on one's shoulder about*** *fig* być przewrażliwionym na punkcie *G* **7.** żeton *m*
chip[2] [~] **I** *s* wyszczerbienie *n*, szczerba *f* **II** *v/t* wyszczerbiać ⟨-bić⟩ **III** *v/i* **1.** wyszczerbiać ⟨-bić⟩ się **2.** odpryskiwać ⟨-snąć⟩
chip in I *v/i* **1.** (*give money*) składać ⟨złożyć⟩ się **2.** wtrącać ⟨-cić⟩ się **II** *v/t* dokładać ⟨dołożyć⟩
chirp [tʃɜːp] **I** *v/i* **1.** ćwierkać, świergotać **2.** szczebiotać **II** *s* **1.** ćwierkanie *n*, świergotanie *n* **2.** szczebiotanie *n*; **chirp•y** ['tʃɜːpɪ] *adj infml* wesolutki, radosny
chir•rup ['tʃɪrəp] → ***chirp***
chis•el ['tʃɪzl] **I** *s* dłuto *n* **II** *v/t* rzeźbić ⟨wy-⟩, dłutować ⟨wy-⟩
chit[1] [tʃɪt] *s Br* **1.** notatka *f* **2.** pokwitowanie *n*
chit[2] [~] *s Br* smarkula *f*
chit•chat ['tʃɪtʃæt] *s* pogaduszki *pl*, plotki *pl*
chiv•al•rous ['ʃɪvəlrəs] *adj* **1.** szarmancki **2.** rycerski **3.** szlachetny
chiv•al•ry ['ʃɪvəlrɪ] *s* **1.** szarmanckość *f* **2.** rycerskość *f*
chives [tʃaɪvz] *pl* BIOL szczypiorek *m*
chlo•ric ['klɔːrɪk] *adj* CHEM chlorowy; **chlor•ide** ['klɔːraɪd] *s* CHEM chlorek *m*; **chlo•ri•nate** ['klɔːrɪneɪt] *v/t* chlorować; **chlo•rine** ['klɔːriːn] *s* CHEM chlor *m*
chlor•o•form ['klɒrəfɔːm] *s* CHEM chloroform *m*
chlo•ro•phyll ['klɔːrəfɪl] *s* BIOL chlorofil *m*

C

C

chock [tʃɒk] *s* **1.** klocek *m* **2.** klin *m*
chock-a-block [tʃɒkə'blɒk], ***chock-full*** [tʃɒk'fʊl] *adj Br infml* nabity, zapchany; ***~ with traffic*** zakorkowany
choc•o•late ['tʃɒklət] **I** *s* **1.** czekolada *f*; ***dark ~, plain ~*** czekolada gorzka **2.** czekoladka *f*, pralinka *f*; ***a box of ~s*** pudełko czekoladek **II** *adj* czekoladowy; **'choc•o•late bar** *s* tabliczka *f* czekolady; **'choc•o•late cake** *s* tort *m* czekoladowy
choice [tʃɔɪs] **I** *s* **1.** wybór *m*; ***a wide ~ of*** szeroki wybór *G*; ***of ~*** z wyboru, z własnej woli; ***of your ~*** dowolny **2.** wybór *m*, możliwość *f* **3.** typ *m*, wybór *m*; ***she's a bad choice for the job*** ona nie nadaje się na to stanowisko; ***this is a perfect ~ for a summer holiday*** to idealne miejsce na letnie wakacje **II** *adj* w najlepszym gatunku, wyborowy
choir [kwaɪə] *s* MUS ARCHIT chór *m*; **'choir•boy** *s* chłopiec *m* śpiewający w chórze kościelnym; ***he was a ~*** śpiewał w chórze kościelnym
choke [tʃəʊk] **I** *s* AUTO ssanie *n* **II** *v/t* **1.** dusić ⟨u-⟩ **2.** dławić ⟨z-⟩ **3.** zatykać ⟨-tkać⟩ **III** *v/i* **1.** dusić ⟨u-⟩ się **2.** dławić ⟨u-⟩ się, ksztusić ⟨za-⟩ się (**on** *I*); ***~ to death*** udławić się; **choke back** *v/t* powstrzymywać ⟨-mać⟩; **choke up** *v/i* zaniemówić (ze wzruszenia)
chol•er•a ['kɒlərə] *s* MED cholera *f*; **chol•er•ic** ['kɒlərɪk] *adj* wybuchowy, choleryczny
cho•les•te•rol [kə'lestərɒl] *s* cholesterol *m*
choose [tʃuːz] **I** *v/t* wybierać ⟨-brać⟩ (**as/for** na *A*); ***there are three versions to ~ from*** są trzy wersje do wyboru; ***she chose her words carefully*** starannie dobierała słowa **II** *v/i* **1.** ***~ to do s.th.*** postanowić coś zrobić, zdecydować się coś zrobić **2.** woleć, chcieć; **choos•(e)y** ['tʃuːzɪ] *adj* wybredny, grymaśny
chop [tʃɒp] **I** *s* **1.** uderzenie *n* **2.** cios *m* **3.** kotlet *m* **II** *v/t* **1.** rąbać ⟨po-⟩ **2.** kroić ⟨po-⟩, siekać ⟨po-⟩ **3.** *budget*: ciąć ⟨ob-⟩, ograniczać ⟨-czyć⟩; **chop down** *v/t* **1.** rąbać ⟨z-⟩, ścinać ⟨ściąć⟩ **2.** wycinać ⟨-ciąć⟩; **chop off** *v/t* **1.** odcinać ⟨-ciąć⟩, odrąbywać ⟨-bać⟩ **2.** *head*: ścinać ⟨ściąć⟩; **chop up** *v/t* kroić ⟨po-⟩, siekać ⟨po-⟩
chop•per ['tʃɒpə] *s* **1.** tasak *m* **2.** *infml* helikopter *m*
chop•py ['tʃɒpɪ] *adj sea*: (lekko) wzburzony
'chop•sticks *pl* COOK pałeczki *pl*
cho•ral ['kɔːrəl] *adj* chóralny
chord [kɔːd] *s* **1.** MUS akord *m*; ***strike a ~ with s.o.*** **a)** trafić komuś do przekonania **b)** trafić komuś do serca
chore [tʃɔː] *s* **1.** (przykry) obowiązek *m*; ***household ~s*** prace domowe **2.** udręka *f*
chor•e•o•graph ['kɒrɪəgrɑːf] *v/i* opracowywać ⟨-cować⟩ choreografię; **chor•e•og•ra•pher** [kɒrɪ'ɒgrəfə] *s* choreograf *m*; **chor•e•og•ra•phy** [kɒrɪ'ɒgrəfɪ] *s* choreografia *f*
chor•is•ter ['kɒrɪstə] *s* chórzysta *m*
cho•rus ['kɔːrəs] **I** *s* **1.** refren *m* **2.** chór *m*; ***in ~*** chórem **3.** chórek *m* **II** *v* mówić ⟨powiedzieć⟩ chórem; **'cho•rus girl** *s* tancerka *f* rewiowa
chose [tʃəʊz] *Past Simple* → ***choose***
cho•sen [tʃəʊzn] *Past Participle* → ***choose***
chow [tʃaʊ] *s* **1.** *infml* żarcie *n* **2.** (*dog*) chow-chow *m*
Christ [kraɪst] *s* Chrystus *m*
chris•ten ['krɪsn] *v/t* **1.** chrzcić ⟨o-⟩ **2.** nazywać ⟨-zwać⟩; **chris•ten•ing** ['krɪsnɪŋ] *s* chrzciny *pl*, chrzest *m*
Chris•tian ['krɪstʃən] **I** *s* chrześcijanin *m* chrześcijanka *f* **II** *adj* chrześcijański; **'Chris•tian name** *s* imię *n* (nadane na chrzcie)
Chris•ti•an•i•ty [krɪstɪ'ænətɪ] *s* chrześcijaństwo *n*; **Chris•tian•ize** ['krɪsjənaɪz] *v/t* chrystianizować ⟨s-⟩
Christ•mas ['krɪsməs] *s* Boże Narodzenie *n*; **Christ•mas 'bo•nus** *s* premia *f* świąteczna; **'Christ•mas card** *s* kartka *f* bożonarodzeniowa; **'Christ•mas car•ol** *s* kolęda; **Christ•mas 'Day** *s* pierwszy dzień świąt Bożego Narodzenia *n*; **Christ•mas 'Eve** *s* Wigilia *f*; **'Christ•mas present** *s* prezent *m* pod choinkę; **Christ•mas 'pud•ding** *s* pudding *m* bożonarodzeniowy; **'Christ•mas•time** *s* okres *m* bożonarodzeniowy; **'Christ•mas tree** *s* choinka *f* (bożonarodzeniowa)

chrome [krəʊm], ***chro•mi•um*** ['krəʊmɪəm] *s* CHEM chrom *m*
chro•mo•some ['krəʊməsəʊm] *s* BIOL chromosom *m*
chron•ic ['krɒnɪk] *adj* **1.** chroniczny, przewlekły **2.** stały, ustawiczny **3.** nałogowy **4.** *infml* fatalny
chron•i•cle ['krɒnɪkl] **I** *s* kronika *f* **II** *v/t* przedstawiać ⟨-wić⟩; **chron•i•cler** ['krɒnɪklə] *s* kronikarz *m*
chron•o•log•i•cal [krɒnə'lɒdʒɪkl] *adj* chronologiczny; **chron•o•log•i•cal•ly** [krɒnə'lɒdʒɪklɪ] *adv* chronologicznie; **chro•nol•o•gy** [krə'nɒlədʒɪ] *s* chronologia *f*
chrys•an•the•mum [krɪ'sænθəməm] *s* chryzantema *f*
chub•by ['tʃʌbɪ] *adj* **1.** pucołowaty, pyzaty **2.** pulchny
chuck [tʃʌk] *v/t* **1.** *infml* rzucać ⟨-cić⟩; ***~ it all!*** rzuć to wszystko!, daj sobie z tym wszystkim spokój! **2.** ***~ s.o. under the chin*** pogłaskać kogoś pod brodą; **chuck away** *v/t* **1.** wywalać ⟨-lić⟩, wyrzucać ⟨-cić⟩ **2.** *chance*: marnować ⟨z-⟩; **chuck out** *v/t* **1.** wywalać ⟨-lić⟩, wyrzucać ⟨-cić⟩ **2.** (*of work*) wylewać ⟨-lać⟩; **chuck up** *v/t* rzucać ⟨-cić⟩
chuck•le ['tʃʌkl] **I** *s* chichot *m*, stłumiony śmiech *m* **II** *v/i* chichotać ⟨za-⟩
chuffed [tʃʌft] *adj Br infml* zachwycony, uradowany
chum [tʃʌm] *s infml* kumpel *m*; **chum up with** *v/i* kolegować ⟨za-⟩ się z *I*, skumać się z *I*; **chum•my** ['tʃʌmɪ] *adj*: ***be ~ with*** *infml* kumplować się z *I*
chump [tʃʌmp] *s infml* matoł *m*
chunk [tʃʌŋk] *s* **1.** kawał *m* **2.** kawałek *m* **3.** kloc *m*; **chunk•y** ['tʃʌŋkɪ] *adj* **1.** *person*: krępy, przysadzisty **2.** masywny **3.** *book*: opasły, gruby **4.** *marmalade*: z dużymi kawałkami owoców
church [tʃɜːtʃ] **I** *s* **1.** kościół *m* **2.** nabożeństwo *n*, msza *f*; ***go to ~*** chodzić do kościoła **II** *adj* **1.** kościelny **2.** parafialny; **church•go•er** ['tʃɜːtʃgəʊə] *s*: ***be a ~*** chodzić do kościoła; **church 'hall** *s* **1.** sala *f* parafialna **2.** kościół *m*; **church 'serv•ice** *s* nabożeństwo *n*, msza *f*; **'church wed•ding** *s* ślub *m* kościelny; **'church•yard** *s* cmentarz *m* przykościelny
churl•ish ['tʃɜːlɪʃ] *adj* gburowaty, chamski
churn [tʃɜːn] **I** *s* **1.** (*for butter*) maselnica *f* **2.** (*for milk*) bańka *f* **II** *v/t* **1.** *butter*: ubijać ⟨-bić⟩ **2.** wzburzać ⟨-rzyć⟩ **III** *v/i* **1.** kotłować się **2.** kłębić się; ***her stomach ~ed*** *fig* żołądek podszedł jej do gardła; **churn out** *v/i* produkować masowo, *infml* tłuc, *infml* trzaskać; **churn up** *v/i* wzburzać ⟨-rzyć⟩
chute [ʃuːt] *s* **1.** zsyp *m* **2.** zjeżdżalnia *f* **3.** (*emergency exit*) rękaw *m* **4.** *infml* spadochron *m*
CIA [siːaɪ'eɪ] *abbr* (=***Central Intelligence Agency***) CIA *f*, Centalna Agencja *f* Wywiadowcza
CID [siːaɪ'diː] *abbr* (=***Criminal Investigation Department***) *Br* Wydział *m* Kryminalny
ci•der ['saɪdə] *s* cydr *m*, jabłecznik *m*
CIF [siːaɪ'ef] *abbr* (=***cost, insurance and freight***) CIF, koszt, ubezpieczenie i fracht
ci•gar [sɪ'gɑːr] *s* cygaro *n*; **ci•'gar cutter** *s* gilotynka *f* do cygar
cig•a•rette [sɪgə'ret] *s* papieros *m*; **cig•a•'rette case** *s* papierośnica *f*; **cig•a•'rette end**, **cig•a•'rette butt** *s* niedopałek *m* papierosa; **cig•a•'rette hold•er** *s* cygarniczka *f*, fifka *f*; **cig•a•'rette light•er** *s* zapalniczka *f*; **cig•a•'rette pa•per** *s* bibułka *f* papierosowa; **cig•a•'rette ma•chine** *s* automat *m* z papierosami
ci'gar light•er *s* zapalniczka *f* (do cygar)
cinch [sɪntʃ] *s infml* **1.** pestka *f*, łatwizna *f* **2.** pewniak *m*
cin•der ['sɪndə] *s* **1.** węgielek *m*; ***burn s.th. to a ~*** spalić coś na węgiel **2.** ***~s*** popiół **3.** żużel *m*, szlaka *f*
Cin•der•el•la [sɪndə'relə] *s* Kopciuszek *m*
'cin•der track *s* SPORT tor *m* żużlowy
cin•e-cam•er•a ['sɪnɪkæmərə] *s Br* kamera *f* filmowa
cin•e-film ['sɪnɪfɪlm] *s Br* taśma *f* filmowa
cin•e•ma ['sɪnɪmə] *s* **1.** kino *n*; ***go to the ~*** *Br* iść do kina, chodzić do kina **2.** (*art*) film *m*, kino *n* **3.** kinematografia *f*; **cin•e•ma•go•er** ['sɪnɪmə-

gəʊə] *s* kinoman *m*; **cin•e•mat•ic** [sɪnɪ'mætɪk] *adj* kinematograficzny, filmowy

C

cin•na•mon ['sɪnəmən] **I** *s* **1.** cynamon *m* **2.** cynamonowiec *m* **II** *adj* cynamonowy, z cynamonem

ci•pher ['saɪfə] **I** *s* **1.** szyfr *m*; ***in ~*** zaszyfrowany **2.** *fig* zero *n*, nikt *m* **3.** *fig* pionek *m*, marionetka *f* **4.** inicjał *m* **5.** cyfra *f* (arabska) **II** *v/t* szyfrować ⟨za-⟩

cir•cle ['sɜːkl] **I** *s* **1.** koło *n*, kółko *n*; ***go round in ~s*** zataczać kręgi, *fig* kręcić się w kółko **2.** okrąg *m* **3.** krąg *m* **4.** *THEAT Br* balkon *m* **II** *v/t* **1.** okrążać ⟨-żyć⟩ **2.** krążyć wokół *G* **3.** obchodzić ⟨obejść⟩ (dookoła) **4.** objeżdżać ⟨-jechać⟩ (dookoła) **5.** zakreślać ⟨-lić⟩, brać ⟨wziąć⟩ w kółko **III** *v/i* **1.** krążyć **2.** kołować

cir•cuit ['sɜːkɪt] *s* **1.** okrążenie *n*; ***make a ~*** zrobić okrążenie **2.** *TECH* obwód *m*; ***a short ~*** zwarcie, *infml* spięcie **3.** tor *m* **4.** bieżnia *f* **5.** cykl *m*; ***a tennis ~*** cykl turniejów tenisowych, rozgrywki tenisowe

cir•cu•i•tous [sɜː'kjuːɪtəs] *adj* **1.** *route*: okrężny **2.** *explanation*: pokrętny, zawiły **3.** pośredni

cir•cu•lar ['sɜːkjʊlə] **I** *adj* **1.** kolisty, okrągły; ***a ~ argument*** tautologia **2.** okrężny **3.** pokrętny **II** *s* okólnik *m*; **cir•cu•late** ['sɜːkjʊleɪt] **I** *v/i* **1.** krążyć **2.** cyrkulować **3.** (*money*) być w obiegu **II** *v/t* **1.** rozsyłać ⟨-zesłać⟩ **2.** rozpowszechniać ⟨-nić⟩ **3.** puszczać ⟨puścić⟩ w obieg

cir•cu•la•tion [sɜːkjʊ'leɪʃn] *s* **1.** *blood*: krążenie *n* **2.** obieg *m*; ***put s.th. into ~*** wprowadzić coś do obiegu, puścić coś w obieg; ***withdraw s.th. from ~*** wycofać coś z obiegu **3.** cyrkulacja *f* **4.** *newspaper*: nakład *m*

cir•cum•fer•ence [sə'kʌmfərəns] *s* obwód *m*

cir•cum•spect ['sɜːkəmspekt] *adj* ostrożny, rozważny

cir•cum•stances ['sɜːkəmstənsɪs] *pl* **1.** okoliczności *pl*, sytuacja *f*; ***in the ~, under the ~*** w tych okolicznościach; ***under no ~*** w żadnym wypadku; ***due to ~ beyond our control*** z powodów od nas niezależnych **2.** sytuacja *f* materialna; ***live in poor ~*** być źle sytuowanym

cir•cum•stan•tial ev•i•dence [sɜːkəmstænʃl'evɪdəns] *s JUR* poszlaki *pl*

cir•cus ['sɜːkəs] **I** *s* **1.** cyrk *m* **2.** (*in place names*) *Br* plac *m* **II** *adj* cyrkowy

cis•tern ['sɪstɜːn] *s* **1.** spłuczka *f*, rezerwuar *m* **2.** rezerwuar *m*, zbiornik *m* (na wodę)

cit•a•del ['sɪtədəl] *s* cytadela *f*

ci•ta•tion [saɪ'teɪʃn] *s* **1.** cytat *m* **2.** cytowanie *n* **3.** pochwała *f*; **cite** [saɪt] *v/t* **1.** podawać ⟨-dać⟩ (**as** jako *N*) **2.** cytować ⟨za-⟩

cit•i•zen ['sɪtɪzn] *s* obywatel *m*; **cit•i•zen•ship** ['sɪtɪznʃɪp] *s* obywatelstwo *n*

cit•ric ac•id [sɪtrɪk'æsɪd] *s* kwas *m* cytrynowy

citr•us ['sɪtrəs] *s* cytrus *m*; **'citr•us fruit** *s* **1.** owoc *m* cytrusowy **2.** cytrusy *pl*, owoce *pl* cytrusowe

cit•y ['sɪtɪ] *s* miasto *n*; ***the ~*** *Br* (londyńskie) City; **city 'centre** *Br*, **city 'cen•ter** *Am s* centrum *n* (miasta), śródmieście *n*; **city 'fa•thers** *pl* ojcowie *pl* miasta; **city 'hall** *s* **1.** ratusz *m* **2.** władze *pl* miasta; **city 'plan•ning** *s* urbanistyka *f*; **city 'state** *s* miasto-państwo *n*

civ•ic ['sɪvɪk] *adj* **1.** miejski **2.** obywatelski; **civ•ics** ['sɪvɪks] *s* (*at school*) wiedza *f* o społeczeństwie

civ•il ['ʃɪvl] *adj* **1.** cywilny **2.** obywatelski **3.** społeczny **4.** świecki **5.** uprzejmy

Civ•il Aer•o'nau•tics Board *s* Główny Inspektorat *m* Lotnictwa Cywilnego

civ•il avi•'a•tion *s* lotnictwo *n* cywilne; **civ•il en•gi•'neer** *s* specjalista *m* w dziedzinie inżynierii lądowej i wodnej; **civ•il en•gi•'neer•ing** *s* inżynieria *f* lądowa i wodna; **civ•il 'law** *s* prawo *n* cywilne; **civ•il 'rights I** *pl* prawa *pl* obywatelskie **II** *adj* **1.** *movement*: ochrony praw obywatelskich **2.** *activist*: (ruchu) na rzecz praw obywatelskich; **civ•il 'ser•vant** *s* urzędnik *m* służby cywilnej, urzędnik *m* państwowy; **civ•il 'ser•vice** *s* służba *f* cywilna, administracja *f* państwowa; **civ•il 'war** *s* wojna *f* domowa

ci•vil•i•an [sɪ'vɪljən] **I** *s* cywil *m* **II** *adj* cywilny

ci•vil•i•ty [sɪ'vɪlɪtɪ] *s* uprzejmość *f*

civ•i•li•za•tion [sɪvəlaɪ'zeɪʃn] *s* cywilizacja *f*; **civ•i•lize** ['sɪvəlaɪz] *v/t* cywilizować ⟨u-⟩; **civ•i•lized** ['sɪvəlaɪzd] *adj* **1.** cywilizowany; **~ nations** kraje cywilizowane **2.** kulturalny

CJD [siːdʒeɪ'diː] *abbr* (=**Creutzfeldt-Jakob disease**) *s* choroba *f* Creutzfeldta-Jakoba

clad [klæd] *adj lit* ubrany, odziany (**in** w *A*); **scantily ~** skąpo odziany

claim [kleɪm] **I** *v/t* **1.** twierdzić, utrzymywać (**that** że) **2.** ubiegać się o *A*, występować ⟨-tąpić⟩ o *A* **3.** żądać ⟨za-⟩, domagać się **4.** występować ⟨-tąpić⟩ o zwrot **5. ~ credit for a)** przypisywać sobie autorstwo *G* **b)** przypisywać sobie zasługę za *A*; **she ~s innocence** twierdzi, że jest niewinna; **~ responsibility for** przyznać się do *G* **6.** *title*: sięgnąć po *A*, zdobywać ⟨-być⟩ **7. the crash ~ed two lives** w wypadku zginęły dwie osoby **II** *v/i* **1. he ~s to be a prophet** twierdzi, że jest prorokiem **2. ~ for damages** wystąpić o odszkodowanie **III** *s* **1.** twierdzenie *n*; **I make no ~ to understand it** nie twierdzę, że to rozumiem; **~s of innocence** zapewnienia o niewinności **2.** roszczenie *n*; **a ~ for damages** roszczenie odszkodowawcze; **make an insurance ~** złożyć wniosek o wypłatę odszkodowania **3.** żądanie *n*; **pay ~s** żądania płacowe **4.** prawo *n*, tytuł *m* **5. lay ~ to** rościć sobie prawo do *G*; **claim back** *v/t* **1.** występować ⟨-tąpić⟩ o zwrot **2.** żądać ⟨za-⟩ zwrotu; **claim•ant** ['kleɪmənt] *s* **1.** poszkodowany *m* **2.** *Br* beneficjent *m*; **benefit ~s** beneficjenci świadczeń **3.** petent *m* **4.** pretendent *m*

clam [klæm] **I** *s* małż *m* jadalny **II** *adj soup*: z małży; **clam up** *v/i* milknąć ⟨za-⟩, przestawać ⟨-tać⟩ się odzywać

clam•ber ['klæmbə] *v/i* wdrapywać ⟨-pać⟩ się, *infml* gramolić ⟨w-⟩ się

clam•my ['klæmɪ] *adj* **1.** lepki **2.** oślizgły **3.** spocony **4.** przepocony

clam•our ['klæmə] *Br*, **clam•or** *Am* **I** *s* **1.** hałas *m*, zgiełk *m* **2.** (głośne) żądania *pl* (**for** *G*) **II** *v/i* **1.** wrzeszczeć, *infml* drzeć się **2.** podnosić ⟨-nieść⟩ krzyk **3.** (głośno) żądać (**for** *G*);

clam•or•ous ['klæmərəs] *adj* **1.** hałaśliwy **2.** donośny **3.** *protest*: głośny

clan [klæn] *s* **1.** klan *m* **2.** grupa *f*, klika *f*

clang [klæŋ] **I** *s* **1.** brzęk *m* **2.** dzwonienie *n* **II** *v/i* **1.** dźwięczeć ⟨za-⟩ **2.** dzwonić ⟨za-⟩ **III** *v/t door*: zatrzaskiwać ⟨-snąć⟩

clank [klæŋk] **I** *s* **1.** brzęk *m* **2.** szczęk *m* **II** *v/i* **1.** brzęczeć ⟨brzęknąć⟩ **2.** szczękać ⟨-knąć⟩ **III** *v/t* pobrzękiwać

clap [klæp] **I** *v/t* **1. ~ one's hands** klaskać **2.** oklaskiwać **3.** klepać ⟨-pnąć⟩ **II** *v/i* **1.** klaskać ⟨-snąć⟩ **2.** bić brawo **III** *s* **1.** klaśnięcie *n* **2. give s.o. a ~** bić komuś brawo **3.** klepnięcie *n* **4. a ~ of thunder** grzmot

clar•et ['klærɪt] **I** *s* **1.** (*wine*) bordo *n*, klaret *m* **2.** (*colour*) bordo *n* **II** *adj* bordo, bordowy

clar•i•fi•ca•tion [klærɪfɪ'keɪʃn] *s* **1.** wyjaśnienie *n* **2.** *wine, butter*: klarowanie *n*; **clar•i•fy** ['klærɪfaɪ] *v/t* **1.** wyjaśniać ⟨-nić⟩ **2.** *wine, butter*: klarować ⟨s-⟩

clar•i•net [klærɪ'net] *s* MUS klarnet *m*

clar•i•net•(t)ist [klærɪ'netɪst] *s* klarnecista *m*

clar•i•ty ['klærətɪ] *s* **1.** jasność *f* **2.** wyrazistość *f* **3.** klarowność *f* **4.** przejrzystość *f*

clash [klæʃ] **I** *s* **1.** starcie *n* **2.** utarczka *f* **3.** zderzenie *n* **4.** sprzeczność *f*, konflikt *f*; **a ~ of interests** sprzeczność interesów **5. there's a ~ between the meetings** terminy spotkań kolidują ze sobą **6.** brzęk *m* **II** *v/i* **1.** ścierać ⟨zetrzeć⟩ się **2.** SPORT zmierzyć się (ze sobą) **3.** być sprzecznym (ze sobą) **4.** (*of colours*) gryźć się (ze sobą), nie pasować (do siebie)

clasp [klæsp] **I** *v/t* **1.** ściskać ⟨-snąć⟩, trzymać **2.** chwytać ⟨-wycić⟩; **~ s.o.'s hand** chwycić kogoś za rękę **3. ~ one's hands** spleść dłonie **4.** zapinać ⟨-piąć⟩ **II** *s* **1.** zapięcie *n* **2.** zatrzask *m* **3.** uścisk *m*; '**clasp knife** *s* scyzoryk *m*

class [klæs] **I** *s* **1.** klasa *f*; **the ~ system** system klasowy; **have ~** mieć klasę; **be in a ~ of one's own** stanowić klasę samą dla siebie, być bezkonkurencyjnym **2.** lekcja *f*, zajęcia *pl*; **in ~** na lekcji, na zajęciach **3.** (*students*) grupa *f*

C

4. rocznik *m* **5.** (*botany*) klasa *f* **6.** (*zoology*) gromada **7.** kategoria *f* **II** *v/t* klasyfikować ⟨za-⟩ (***with*** do *G*); **ˈclass-con•scious** *adj* świadomy różnic klasowych

clas•sic [ˈklæsɪk] **I** *adj* **1.** klasyczny **2.** klasyczny, typowy; ***a ~ example*** klasyczny przykład **3.** tradycyjny **II** *s* **1.** klasyczne dzieło *n*; ***be a ~*** należeć do klasyki; ***read the ~s*** czytać klasykę **3.** ***~s*** filologia klasyczna

clas•si•cal [ˈklæsɪkl] *adj* **1.** klasyczny; ***the ~ languages*** języki klasyczne; ***~ studies*** filologia klasyczna **2.** klasyczny, antyczny

clas•si•fi•ca•tion [klæsɪfɪˈkeɪʃn] *s* **1.** klasyfikacja *f* **2.** kategoryzacja *f*; **clas•si•fied** [ˈklæsɪfaɪd] *adj* **1.** tajny **2.** sklasyfikowany; ***a ~ directory*** branżowy katalog firm; **ˈclas•si•fied ad(ver•tise•ment)** *s* ogłoszenie *n* drobne; **clas•si•fy** [ˈklæsɪfaɪ] *v/t* **1.** klasyfikować ⟨s-⟩ **2.** utajniać ⟨-nić⟩

class•less [ˈklɑːslɪs] *adj* bezklasowy

ˈclass•mate *s* kolega *m* z klasy; **class re•ˈun•ion** *s* zjazd *m* absolwentów; **ˈclass•room** *s* klasa *f*, sala *f* lekcyjna; **class ˈstrug•gle** *s* walka *f* klasowa

class•y [ˈklɑːsɪ] *adj infml* **1.** z klasą **2.** wielkiej klasy **3.** szykowny, luksusowy

clat•ter [ˈklætə] **I** *v/i* **1.** brzęczeć ⟨za-⟩ **2.** stukać ⟨za-⟩ **3.** klekotać ⟨za-⟩ **II** *v/t* **1.** brzęczeć ⟨za-⟩ **2.** stukać ⟨za-⟩ **III** *s* **1.** brzęk *m* **2.** stukot *m*

clause [klɔːz] *s* **1.** zdanie *n* (składowe) **2.** klauzula *f*

claus•tro•pho•bi•a [klɔːstrəˈfəʊbɪə] *s* klaustrofobia *f*; **claus•tro•pho•bic** [klɔːstrəˈfəʊbɪk] **I** *adj* **1.** klaustrofobiczny **2.** cierpiący na klaustrofobię **II** *s* klaustrofobik *m*

claw [klɔː] **I** *s* **1.** pazur *m* **2.** szpon *m* **3.** ***~s*** szczypce, kleszcze **II** *v/t* **1.** drapać ⟨po-⟩ **2.** rozszarpywać ⟨-pać⟩ **III** *v/i* **1.** drapać ⟨po-⟩ (***at*** *A*) **2.** rozszarpywać ⟨-pać⟩ (***at*** *A*) **3.** ***~ at s.o.*** *fig* rzucić się na kogoś z pazurami

clay [kleɪ] **I** *s* **1.** glina *f* **2.** ił *m* **II** *adj* gliniany; **ˈclay court** *s* kort *m* ziemny; **clay•ey** [ˈkleɪɪ] *adj* gliniasty

clean [kliːn] **I** *adj* **1.** czysty; ***keep one's room ~*** utrzymywać porządek w pokoju, mieć w pokoju porządek; ***make a ~ copy of s.th.*** przepisać coś na czysto; ***he has a ~ police record*** nie był notowany; ***have a ~ driving licence*** nie mieć punktów karnych **2.** przyzwoity **3.** gładki **4.** *reputation*: nieposzlakowany **5.** bezpieczny dla środowiska **II** *adv* zupełnie **III** *v/t* **1.** myć ⟨u-⟩ **2.** czyścić ⟨wy-⟩ **3.** sprzątać ⟨po-⟩ **IV** *v/i* **1.** sprzątać ⟨po-⟩ **2.** czyścić się, prać się; **clean out** *v/t* **1.** sprzątać ⟨wy-⟩ **2.** szorować ⟨wy-⟩ **3.** *infml* obrabiać ⟨-robić⟩; **clean up I** *v/t* sprzątać ⟨-tnąć⟩ **II** *v/i infml* myć ⟨u-⟩ się

clean-ˈcut *adj* **1.** wyraźny **2.** schludny

clean•er [ˈkliːnə] *s* **1.** sprzątacz *m*, sprzątaczka *f* **2.** środek *m* czyszczący **3.** (*a.* **~'s**) pralnia *f* chemiczna

clean•ing [ˈkliːnɪŋ] *s* sprzątanie *n*; ***do the ~*** sprzątać; **ˈclean•ing cloth** *s* szmata *f*, ścierka *f*; **ˈclean•ing woman**, ***clean•ing lady*** *s* sprzątaczka *f*

clean•li•ness [ˈklenlɪnɪs] *s* **1.** czystość *f* **2.** schludność *f*; **clean•ly** [ˈkliːnlɪ] **I** *adj* **1.** czysty **2.** schludny **II** *adv* **1.** równo **2.** czysto

clean•ness [ˈkliːnnɪs] *s* **1.** czystość *f* **2.** schludność *f*

cleanse [klenz] *v/t* **1.** oczyszczać ⟨oczyścić⟩ **2.** przemywać ⟨-myć⟩; **cleans•er** [ˈklenzə] *s* **1.** środek *m* do demakijażu **2.** środek *m* czyszczący; **ˈcleans•ing cream** *s* krem *m* oczyszczający

clean-ˈshav•en *adj* gładko ogolony

clear [klɪə] **I** *adj* **1.** jasny; ***do I make myself ~?*** czy wyrażam się jasno? **2.** przezroczysty **3.** czysty, przejrzysty **4.** *photograph*: wyraźny, ostry **5.** czysty; ***a ~ conscience*** czyste sumienie **6.** klarowny; ***a ~ soup*** bulion **7.** *skin*: gładki **8.** oczywisty; ***for no ~ reason*** bez wyraźnej przyczyny **9.** *victory, majority*: zdecydowany **10.** bezchmurny **11.** wolny; ***~ of debt*** niezadłużony, wolny od długów **12.** *profit*: czysty, netto **II** *adv* ***stand ~ of*** odsunąć się od *G*; ***steer ~ of*** trzymać się z dala od *G* **III** *v/t* **1.** sprzątać ⟨-tnąć⟩, uprzątać ⟨-tnąć⟩; ***~ a space for*** zrobić miejsce na *A* **2.** usuwać ⟨-nąć⟩ **3.** *dishes*: zbierać ⟨zebrać⟩ **4.** *snow*: odgarniać ⟨-nąć⟩ **5.** ***~ one's throat*** odchrząknąć **6.** *of blame*: oczyszczać ⟨oczyścić⟩ (**of** z *G*) **7.** *forests*: wycinać ⟨-ciąć⟩ **8.** *cheque*: rozliczać ⟨-czyć⟩ **IV** *v/i* **1.** przejaśniać ⟨-nić⟩ się **2.** oczyszczać ⟨oczyścić⟩ się **3.** (*fog*) rozwiewać ⟨-zwiać⟩ się; **clear away I** *v/t* **1.** usuwać ⟨usunąć⟩ **2.** uprzątać ⟨-tnąć⟩ **II** *v/i* **1.** sprzątać ⟨po-⟩ **2.** (*fog*) rozwiewać ⟨-wiać⟩ się; **clear off** *v/i infml* zwiewać ⟨-wiać⟩, zmywać ⟨-myć⟩ się; *~!* zjeżdżaj!; **clear out I** *v/t* **1.** sprzątać ⟨-tnąć⟩ **2.** opróżniać ⟨-nić⟩ **3.** wyrzucać ⟨-cić⟩ **II** *v/i* **1.** sprzątać ⟨-tnąć⟩ **2.** *infml* zjeżdżać; *~!* zjeżdżaj!; **clear up I** *v/t* **1.** sprzątać ⟨-tnąć⟩ **2.** uprzątać ⟨-tnąć⟩ **II** *v/i* **1.** robić ⟨z-⟩ porządek **2.** przejaśniać ⟨-nić⟩ się

clear•ance ['klıərəns] *s* **1.** oczyszczanie *n*; *~ of forests* wyrąb lasów **2.** odstęp *m*, miejsce *n* **3.** pozwolenie *n*, zezwolenie *n* **4.** odprawa *f* celna **5.** całkowita wyprzedaż *f*

'clear•ance sale *s* wyprzedaż *f*

clear-'cut *adj* **1.** wyraźny **2.** jednoznaczny

clear-'head•ed *adj* trzeźwo myślący

clear•ing ['klıərıŋ] *s* **1.** polana *f* **2.** *of forests*: wyrąb *m*, wycinka *f* **3.** wyburzanie *n*

clear•ly ['klıəlı] *adv* **1.** wyraźnie **2.** jasno **3.** najwyraźniej

clear•ness ['klıənıs] *s* **1.** jasność *f* **2.** wyrazistość *f* **3.** przejrzystość *f* **4.** czystość *f* **5.** bezchmurność *f* **6.** *photograph*: ostrość *f*

cleav•age ['kli:vıdʒ] *s* **1.** rowek *m* między piersiami; ***show*** (***off***) ***one's ~*** **a)** odsłaniać dekolt **b)** być wydekoltowanym **2.** *fig* przepaść *f* **3.** *fig* podział *m*, rozłam *m*

cleave [kli:v] *v/t* (*clove/cleft/cleaved; cloven/cleft/cleaved*) rozłupywać ⟨-pać⟩; **cleav•er** ['kli:və] *s* tasak *m* (rzeźniczy)

cleft [kleft] **I** *Past Simple and Past Participle* → ***cleave*** **II** *s* rozpadlina *f*, szczelina *f*; **cleft 'stick** *s*: ***to be in a ~*** znaleźć się między młotem a kowadłem

clem•en•cy ['klemənsı] *s* **1.** łaska *f*, łaskawość *f* **2.** łagodność *f*; **clem•ent** ['klemənt] *adj* **1.** *weather*: przyjemny **2.** łagodny

clem•en•tine ['kleməntaın] *s* BIOL klementynka *f*

clench [klentʃ] *v/t* zaciskać ⟨-snąć⟩, ściskać ⟨-snąć⟩; ***~ one's fists*** zacisnąć pięści; ***~ one's teeth*** zacisnąć zęby

cler•gy ['klɜ:dʒı] *s* duchowieństwo *n*, kler *m*; **cler•gy•man** ['klɜ:dʒımæn] *pl -men s* **1.** duchowny *m* **2.** pastor *m* **3.** ksiądz *m*

cler•i•cal ['klerıkl] *adj* **1.** biurowy; ***~ work*** praca biurowa; ***a ~ error*** pomyłka urzędnika **2.** klerykalny **3.** *power*: sprawowany przez duchowieństwo

clerk [klɑ:k] *s* **1.** urzędnik *m* **2.** *Am* sprzedawca *m*, ekspedient *m* **3.** *Am* recepcjonista *m*

clev•er ['klevə] *adj* **1.** zdolny, bystry, inteligentny **2.** pomysłowy **3.** *idea*: świetny **4.** zręczny, sprytny; **clev•er•ly** ['klevəlı] *adv* **1.** inteligentnie **2.** pomysłowo **3.** sprytnie; **clev•er•ness** ['klevərnıs] *s* **1.** inteligencja *f* **2.** pomysłowość *f* **3.** spryt *m*

cli•ché ['kli:ʃeı] *s* **1.** banał *m*, frazes *m* **2.** wyświechtany zwrot *m*; **cli•chéd** ['kli:ʃeıd] *adj* **1.** wyświechtany, oklepany **2.** banalny **3.** oparty na stereotypach

click [klık] **I** *s* **1.** INF kliknięcie *n* **2.** trzask *m* **3.** mlaśnięcie *n* **II** *v/t* **1.** INF klikać ⟨-knąć⟩ **2.** ***~ one's fingers*** pstryknąć palcami; ***~ one's tongue*** mlasnąć językiem **III** *v/i* **1.** INF klikać ⟨-knąć⟩ **2.** ***~ shut*** zamykać ⟨-mknąć⟩ się z trzaskiem **3.** *infml* przypadać ⟨-paść⟩ sobie do gustu; **click on** *v/i* INF klikać ⟨-knąć⟩ na *A*

cli•ent ['klaıənt] *s* klient *m*; **cli•en•tele** [kli:ən'tel] *s* klientela *f*

cliff [klıf] *s* klif *m*; urwisko *n*; **'cliff-hang•er** *s* chwila *f* napięcia

cli•mac•ter•ic [klaı'mæktərık] *s* klimakterium *n*

cli•mate ['klaımət] *s* **1.** klimat *m* **2.** *fig* atmosfera *f*, klimat *m*; **'cli•mate change** *s* zmiana *f* klimatu; **cli•mat•ic** [klaı'mætık] *adj* klimatyczny

cli•max ['klaımæks] **I** *s* **1.** punkt *m* kulminacyjny **2.** szczytowanie *n*, orgazm *m* **II** *v/i* **1.** osiągać ⟨-gnąć⟩ moment kulminacyjny **2.** osiągać ⟨-gnąć⟩ orgazm **III** *v/t* stanowić moment kulminacyjny *G*

C

climb [klaɪm] **I** *s* **1.** wspinaczka *f,* wejście *n* na szczyt **2.** podejście *n* **3.** *fig* droga *f* na szczyty (**to** *G*) **II** *v/i* **1.** wspinać ⟨-piąć⟩ się; **~ *up a tree*** wejść na drzewo; **~ *down a tree*** zejść z drzewa **2.** (*road*) wznosić ⟨-nieść⟩ się, piąć ⟨ws-⟩ się **III** *v/t* **1.** wchodzić ⟨wejść⟩ na *A,* wspinać ⟨-piąć⟩ się na *A* **2.** wchodzić ⟨wejść⟩ po *L,* wspinać ⟨-piąć⟩ się po *L* **3.** **~ *over a wall*** przejść przez płot; **climb down** *v/i* **1.** ustępować ⟨-tąpić⟩ **2.** wycofywać ⟨-fać⟩ się

climb•er ['klaɪmə] *s* wspinacz *m,* alpinista *m*

climb•ing ['klaɪmɪŋ] **I** *s* wspinaczka *f,* alpinistyka *f* **II** *adj plant*: pnący; **'climb•ing boots** *pl* **1.** buty *pl* górskie **2.** buty *pl* trekingowe; **'climb•ing frame** *s* (*playground*) *Br* drabinki *pl*; **'climb•ing wall** *s* ściana *f* wspinaczkowa

clinch [klɪntʃ] **I** *v/t* **1.** zawierać ⟨-wrzeć⟩; **~ *a deal*** ubić interes **2.** rozstrzygać ⟨-gnąć⟩; ***that ~ed it*** to przesądziło sprawę **3.** **~ *a victory*** SPORT wygrać **II** *s* uścisk *m*

cling [klɪŋ] (*clung*; *clung*) *v/i* **1.** trzymać się kurczowo, uczepić się (**to** *G*) **2.** przylegać ⟨-lgnąć⟩ (**to** do *G*) **3.** *fig* przylgnąć (**to** do *G*); **cling to** *v/i* **1.** uparcie trzymać się *G* **2.** *hope*: uchwycić się; **cling together** *v/i* **1.** przywierać ⟨-wrzeć⟩ do siebie **2.** przylgnąć do siebie

cling•y ['klɪŋɪ] *adj* **1.** *child*: *infml* przylepny **2.** przesadnie zależny

clin•ic ['klɪnɪk] *s* **1.** przychodnia *f,* poradnia *f* **2.** klinika *f*; **clin•i•cal** ['klɪnɪkl] *adj* kliniczny; ***a ~ thermometer*** termometr lekarski

clink[1] [klɪŋk] **I** *v/i* **1.** brzęczeć ⟨za-⟩ **2.** pobrzękiwać **II** *v/t* **~ *one's glasses*** stuknąć się kieliszkami **III** *s* **1.** brzęk *m* **2.** pobrzękiwanie *n*

clink[2] [~] *s infml* ciupa *f,* paka *f*

clip[1] [klɪp] **I** *v/t* przypinać ⟨-piąć⟩, przyczepiać ⟨-pić⟩ (**to** do *G*); **~ *together*** spiąć razem **II** *s* **1.** spinka *f* **2.** klips *m* **3.** zacisk *m* **4.** klamerka *f*

clip[2] [~] **I** *v/t* **1.** przycinać ⟨-ciąć⟩, strzyc ⟨przy-⟩ **2.** odcinać ⟨-ciąć⟩ **3.** wycinać ⟨-ciąć⟩ (***from/out of*** z *G*) **4.** skracać ⟨-rócić⟩ **II** *s* **1.** urywek *m* **2.** wycinek *m* **3.** ***give s.th. a ~*** przycinać coś **4.** ***give s.o. a ~ round the ear*** strzelić kogoś w ucho

'clip•board *s* **1.** podkładka *f* do pisania **2.** INF schowek *m*

clip•pers ['klɪpəz] *pl* **1.** cążki *pl* do paznokci **2.** sekator *m* **3.** maszynka *f* do strzyżenia włosów

clip•ping ['klɪpɪŋ] *s Am* wycinek *m* (z gazety)

clip•pings ['klɪpɪŋz] *pl* **1.** ścinki *pl* **2.** ścięte włosy *pl* **3.** ścięte gałęzie *pl*

clique [kliːk] *s* klika *f*

clit [klɪt] *s infml* łechtaczka *f*

clit•o•ris ['klɪtərɪs] *s* łechtaczka *f*

cloak ['kləʊk] **I** *s* peleryna *f,* płaszcz *m*; ***under the ~ of darkness*** *fig* pod osłoną ciemności **II** *v/t* okrywać ⟨-ryć⟩; ***~ed in mist*** zasnuty mgłą; ***~ed in mystery*** owiany tajemnicą

'cloak•room *s* szatnia *f*

clock [klɒk] **I** *s* **1.** zegar *m*; ***around the ~*** całą dobę; ***put the ~s forward*** (***back***) ***1 hour*** przestawić zegary o godzinę do przodu (do tyłu) **2.** licznik *m* **3.** taksometr *m* **4.** stoper *m* **II** *v/t* SPORT uzyskać czas; **clock in** *v/i Br* podbijać ⟨-bić⟩ kartę zegarową (przychodząc do pracy); **clock out** *v/i Br* podbijać ⟨-bić⟩ kartę zegarową (wychodząc z pracy); **clock up** *v/t* **1.** przejechać **2.** przepracować

'clock•face *s* tarcza *f* zegara, cyferblat *m*; **'clock ra•di•o** *s* radio *n* z budzikiem; **'clock•wise I** *adj* zgodny z ruchem wskazówek zegara **II** *adv* zgodnie z ruchem wskazówek zegara; **'clock•work** *s* mechanizm *m* zegarowy

clod [klɒd] *s* **1.** gruda *f* (ziemi) **2.** matoł *m*

clog (up) [klɒg] *v/i* zatykać ⟨-tkać⟩ się, zapychać ⟨-pchać⟩ się

clois•ter ['klɔɪstə] *s* krużganek *m*

clone [kləʊn] **I** *s* klon *m* **II** *v/t* klonować ⟨s-⟩; **clon•ing** ['kləʊnɪŋ] *s* klonowanie *n*

close[1] [kləʊs] **I** *adj* **1.** (*space*) bliski (**to** *G*); ***be ~ together*** być blisko siebie; ***a ~ combat*** walka wręcz **2.** (*time*) bliski; ***~ to tears*** bliski łez **3.** *friend*: bliski **4.** drobiazgowy, gruntowny **5.** *attention*: baczny **6.** wyrównany **7.** zbliżony, podobny **8.** zwarty **II**

adv blisko; ***get ~*** zbliżyć się; ***~ by*** blisko, w pobliżu; ***~ at hand*** pod ręką, w zasięgu ręki; ***hold s.o. close*** mocno kogoś obejmować **III** *s* zaułek *m*, ślepa uliczka *f*

close[2] [kləuz] **I** *s* koniec *m*, zakończenie *n*; ***draw to a ~*** zbliżać się do końca **II** *v/t* **1.** zamykać ⟨-mknąć⟩ **2.** kończyć ⟨za-⟩; **close down** *v/i* **1.** zostać zamkniętym **2.** ulegać ⟨ulec⟩ likwidacji; **close in** *v/i* **1.** zbliżać ⟨-żyć⟩ się, nadchodzić ⟨-dejść⟩ **2.** (*days*) stawać się krótszym; **close in on** *v/t* otaczać ⟨otoczyć⟩, zacieśniać ⟨-nić⟩ krąg wokół *G*; **close up I** *v/i* **1.** zamykać ⟨-mknąć⟩ się **2.** zasklepiać ⟨-pić⟩ się **3.** milknąć ⟨za-⟩ **II** *v/t* zamykać ⟨-mknąć⟩

closed [kləuzd] *adj* zamknięty; ***behind ~ doors*** za zamkniętymi drzwiami

'close-down *s* **1.** zamknięcie *n* **2.** likwidacja *f* **3.** *RADIO TEL* zakończenie *n* programu

close•'fist•ed *adj* skąpy; **close-'fit•ting** *adj* dopasowany, obcisły; **close-'knit** *adj* **1.** *community*: zwarty **2.** *group*: zżyty

close•ly ['kləuslɪ] *adv* **1.** blisko; ***work ~*** ściśle współpracować **2.** bacznie, uważnie **3.** bardzo **4.** dokładnie

'close sea•son *s Br* okres *m* ochronny

clos•et ['klɒzɪt] *s* szafa *f* ścienna; ***a ~ gay*** ukryty homoseksualista

'close-up *s* zbliżenie *n*

'clos•ing date *s* ostateczny termin *m*

'clos•ing time *s* godzina *f* zamknięcia

clo•sure ['kləuʒə] *s* zamknięcie *n*

clot [klɒt] **I** *s* **1.** zakrzep *m* **2.** *Br infml* baran *m*, pacan *m* **II** *v/i* krzepnąć ⟨s-⟩

cloth [klɒθ] *s* **1.** tkanina *f*, materiał *m* **2.** szmatka *f*, ściereczka *f* **3.** obrus *f*

clothe [kləuð] *v/t* ubierać ⟨ubrać⟩

clothes [kləuðz] *pl* **1.** ubranie *n*, rzeczy *pl*; ***change one's ~*** przebrać się **2.** pościel *f* **3.** pranie *n*; **'clothes bas•ket** *s* kosz *m* na bieliznę; **'clothes brush** *s* szczotka *f* do ubrań; **'clothes hang•er** *s* wieszak *m*; **'clothes•horse** *s* suszarka *f* do bielizny; **'clothes•line** *s* sznur *m* do bielizny; **'clothes peg**, **'clothes•pin** *s* klamerka *f* (do bielizny)

cloth•ing ['kləuðɪŋ] *s* odzież *f*; ***the ~ industry*** przemysł odzieżowy

cloud [klaud] **I** *s* **1.** chmura *f*; ***a ~ of dust*** chmura pyłu; ***have one's head in the ~s*** bujać w obłokach; ***be on ~ nine*** *infml* być w siódmym niebie **2.** *fig* cień *m*; ***cast a ~ on*** rzucać cień na *A* **II** *v/t* **1.** przesłaniać ⟨-łonić⟩ **2.** mącić ⟨z-⟩ **III** *v/i* **1.** chmurzyć ⟨za-⟩ się **2.** mętnieć ⟨z-⟩; **cloud over** *v/i* chmurzyć ⟨za-⟩ się

'cloud•burst *s* oberwanie *n* chmury

cloud•less ['klaudlɪs] *adj* bezchmurny; **cloud•y** ['klaudɪ] *adj* **1.** pochmurny **2.** mętny

clout [klaut] **I** *s* **1.** *POLIT* znaczenie *n*, wpływy *pl*; ***carry considerable ~ with*** mieć znaczne wpływy wśród *G* **2.** *infml* walnięcie *n*; ***give s.o. a ~*** walnąć kogoś **II** *v/t infml* walić ⟨-lnąć⟩

clove[1] [kləuv] *s* **1.** goździk *m* **2.** *garlic*: ząbek *m*

clove[2] [~] *Past Simple* → ***cleave***

clo•ven [kləuvn] *Past Participle* → ***cleave***

clo•ver ['kləuvə] *s* koniczyna *f*

clown [klaun] *s* **1.** klaun *m*, błazen *m* **2.** *fig* błazen *m*; **clown around** *v/i* błaznować; **clown•ish** ['klaunɪʃ] *adj* błazeński

club [klʌb] **I** *s* **1.** klub *m*; ***a night ~*** klub nocny; ***join the ~!*** *fig* witaj w klubie! **2.** pałka *f* **3.** maczuga *f* **4.** *SPORT* kij *m* **5.** trefl *m* **II** *adj* klubowy **III** *v/t* bić ⟨z-⟩; ***~ s.o. to death*** zatłuc kogoś na śmierć **IV** *v/i* ***go ~bing*** chodzić po klubach, uprawiać clubbing; **club together** *v/i Br* składać ⟨złożyć⟩ się, zrzucać ⟨-cić⟩ się

club 'chair *s* fotel *m* klubowy

club'foot *s MED* **1.** wrodzone zniekształcenie *n* stopy

'club•house *s* budynek *m* klubu

cluck [klʌk] **I** *v/i* gdakać **II** *s* gdakanie *n*

clue [kluː] *s* **1.** wskazówka *f*, trop *m*; ***I haven't a ~*** *infml* nie mam pojęcia; ***give s.o. a ~*** naprowadzić kogoś na ślad, podpowiedzieć komuś **2.** (*crossword*) hasło *n* **3.** (*investigation*) klucz *m*; ***hold the ~ to the mystery*** stanowić klucz do rozwiązania zagadki; **clue in** *v/i* informować ⟨po-⟩ (***on*** o *L*)

clued-up [kluːd'ʌp] *adj Br infml* oblatany (***on*** w *L*)

clump [klʌmp] **I** *s* **1.** kępa *f*, kępka *f* **2.** grupa *f*, grupka *f* **3.** gruda *f* **4.** cięż-

C

kie stapanie *n*, tupanie *n* **II** *v/i* ciężko stąpać, tupać
clum•si•ness ['klʌmzɪnɪs] *s* **1.** niezdarność *f*, niezgrabność *f* **2.** nieporadność *f*, toporność *f*; **clum•sy** ['klʌmzɪ] *adj* **1.** niezdarny, niezręczny **2.** niezgrabny **3.** nieudolny **4.** nieporęczny **5.** *style*: toporny
clung [klʌŋ] *Past Simple and Past Participle* → **cling**
clus•ter ['klʌstə] **I** *s* **1.** kiść *f* **2.** grono *n* **3.** grupa *f*, gromada *f* **4.** skupisko *n* **II** *v/i* skupiać ⟨-pić⟩ się, gromadzić ⟨z-⟩ się
clutch [klʌtʃ] **I** *v/t* **1.** trzymać kurczowo, ściskać ⟨-snąć⟩ **2.** chwytać ⟨-wycić⟩ się **II** *s* **~es** *fig* szpony, sidła; ***fall into s.o.'s ~es*** wpaść w czyjeś szpony, wpaść w czyjeś sidła; **clutch at** *v/i* chwytać ⟨-wycić⟩ się; ***be ~ing at straws*** *fig* chwytać się brzytwy
clut•ter ['klʌtə] **I** (*a.* **~ up**) *v/t* **1.** zagracać ⟨-cić⟩ **2.** zaśmiecać ⟨-cić⟩ **II** *s* **1.** bałagan *m*; ***in a ~*** w nieładzie **2.** rupiecie *pl*
CNN [siːen'en] *abbr* (=**Cable News Network**) CNN *f*
Co. *abbr* (=**company**) spółka *f*
c/o *abbr* (=**care of**) na adres
coach [kəʊtʃ] **I** *s* **1.** *Br* autobus *m* (dalekobieżny), autokar *m* **2.** *Br* wagon *m* **3.** trener *m* **4.** korepetytor *m* **5.** powóz *m*, kareta *f* **II** *v/t* **~ s.o. in s.th.** **a)** udzielać komuś korepetycji z *G* **b)** trenować kogoś w *L*
coach•ing ['kəʊtʃɪŋ] *s* **1.** trening *m* **2.** korepetycje *pl*
'**coach•man** *pl -men s* woźnica *m*, stangret *m*; '**coach station** *s Br* dworzec *m* autobusowy; '**coach trip** *s* wycieczka *f* autokarowa
coal [kəʊl] *s* **1.** węgiel *m* **2.** węgielek *m*; ***carry ~s to Newcastle*** *Br* wozić drzewo do lasu; ***haul s.o. over the ~s*** *fig* dać komuś reprymendę, *infml* dać komuś burę
co•a•li•tion [kəʊə'lɪʃn] **I** *s* **1.** POLIT koalicja *f*; ***form a ~*** utworzyć koalicję **2.** sojusz *m* **II** *adj* koalicyjny
'**coal•mine** *s* kopalnia *f* węgla; '**coal min•er** *s* górnik *m* (węglowy)
coarse [kɔːs] *adj* **1.** szorstki, chropowaty **2.** ordynarny **3.** gruboziarnisty;
coarse•ly ['kɔːslɪ] *adv* **1.** ordynarnie **2.** grubo
coast [kəʊst] **I** *s* wybrzeże *n*; ***the ~ is clear*** *fig* droga wolna **II** *v/i* płynąć wzdłuż wybrzeża; **coast•al** ['kəʊstl] *adj* przybrzeżny, nadbrzeżny, nadmorski
coast•er ['kəʊstə] *s* **1.** podkładka *f* **2.** kabotażowiec *m*
'**coast•guard** *s* straż *f* przybrzeżna
'**coast•line** *s* linia *f* brzegowa, brzeg *m*
coat [kəʊt] **I** *s* **1.** płaszcz *m* **2.** kurtka *f* **3.** sierść *f*, futro *n* **4.** warstwa *f*, powłoka *f* **II** *v/t* **1.** powlekać ⟨-lec⟩ **2.** *paint*: pokrywać ⟨-ryć⟩; '**coat-hang•er** *s* wieszak *m* na ubrania
coat•ing ['kəʊtɪŋ] *s* **1.** polewa *f* **2.** panierka *f* **3.** TECH powłoka *f*
coat of 'arms *s* **1.** herb *m* **2.** tarcza *f* herbowa
co-au•thor ['kəʊɔːθə] *s* współautor *m*
coax [kəʊks] *v/t* **1.** namawiać ⟨-mówić⟩, nakłaniać ⟨-łonić⟩ (***to do s.th./into doing s.th.*** do zrobienia *G*) **2.** wyprosić (***out of*** u *G*) **3.** odwodzić ⟨-wieść⟩ (***out of doing*** od *G*)
cob [kɒb] *s corn*: kolba *f*
co•balt ['kəʊbɔːlt] *s* kobalt *m*; ***~ blue*** kobaltowy
cob•ble[1] ['kɒbl] **I** *s* kostka *f* brukowa; **~s** kocie łby, bruk **II** *v/t* brukować ⟨wy-⟩
cob•ble[2] [~] *v/t* **1.** *shoes*: szyć ⟨u-⟩ **2.** *shoes*: naprawiać ⟨-wić⟩; **cob•ble together** *v/t infml* **1.** klecić ⟨s-⟩ (naprędce) **2.** pisać ⟨na-⟩ na kolanie
cob•bled [kɒbəld] *adj street*: brukowany
cob•bler ['kɒblə] *s* **1.** szewc *m* **2.** **~s** *Br infml* bzdury
'**cob•ble•stone** *s* kamień *m* brukowy; **~s** bruk
co•bra ['kəʊbrə] *s* BIOL kobra *f*
cob•web ['kɒbweb] *s* pajęczyna *f*
co•caine [kə'keɪn] *s* kokaina *f*
cock [kɒk] **I** *s* **1.** *Br* kogut *m* **2.** samiec *m*; ***a ~ pheasant*** samiec bażanta, kogut **3.** *vulg* kutas *m* **4.** (*valve*) kurek *m* **II** *v/t* **1.** unosić ⟨unieść⟩; ***~ one's ears*** nastawić uszu **2.** przekrzywiać ⟨-wić⟩; ***~ one's hat*** przekrzywić kapelusz **3.** *gun*: odbezpieczać ⟨-czyć⟩; **cock up** *infml v/t* spieprzyć

cock-and-'bull sto•ry *s* bajeczka *f*, bujda *f*
cock•eyed [kɒk'aɪd] *adj infml* **1.** *infml* zwariowany, absurdalny **2.** przekrzywiony
'cock•fight *s* walka *f* kogutów; **'cock•fight•ing** *s* walki *pl* kogutów
'cock•pit *s* **1.** *plane, yacht*: kokpit *m* **2.** arena *f* walk kogutów
cock•roach ['kɒkrəʊtʃ] *s* karaluch *m*
cock'sure *adj* **1.** pewny siebie **2.** zadufany w sobie, pyszny
cock•tail ['kɒkteɪl] *s* **1.** koktajl *m* **2.** mieszanka *f*; **'cock•tail bar** *s* koktajlbar *m*: **'cock•tail par•ty** *s* koktajl *m*; **'cock•tail shak•er** *s* shaker *m*
'cock-up *s Br infml* obsuwa *f*; ***make a ~ of*** spieprzyć *A*
cock•y ['kɒkɪ] *adj* pewny siebie
co•coa ['kəʊkəʊ] **I** *s* kakao *n* **II** *adj* kakaowy
co•co•nut ['kəʊkənʌt] *s* kokos *m*, orzech *m* kokosowy; **'co•co•nut palm** *s* palma *f* kokosowa
co•coon [kə'kuːn] **I** *s* BIOL kokon *m* **II** *v/t* **1.** opatulać ⟨-lić⟩ **2.** otaczać ⟨otoczyć⟩ **3.** osłaniać ⟨-łonić⟩
COD [siːəʊ'diː] *abbr* (=***cash on delivery, collect on delivery***) płatne gotówką przy odbiorze
cod [kɒd] *s* dorsz *m*
cod•dle ['kɒdl] *v/t* rozpieszczać ⟨-pieścić⟩
code [kəʊd] **I** *s* **1.** szyfr *m*, kod *m* **2.** kodeks *m*; ***~ of practice*** **a)** kodeks postępowania **b)** MED kodeks etyki lekarskiej; ***the penal ~*** kodeks karny **3.** regulamin *m* **4.** zasady *pl* **5.** (*a.* ***~ number***) numer *m* kierunkowy **6.** INF kod **II** *v/t* **1.** szyfrować ⟨za-⟩, kodować ⟨za-⟩ **2.** programować ⟨za-⟩; **'code•word** *s* **1.** kryptonim *m* **2.** hasło *n* **3.** eufemizm *m*
cod•i•fy ['kəʊdɪfaɪ] *v/t* kodyfikować ⟨s-⟩
cod•ing ['kəʊdɪŋ] *s* kodowanie *n*
co•ed [kəʊ'ed] **I** *s Am dated* studentka *f* **II** *abbr* (=***coeducational***) koedukacyjny
co•ed•u•ca•tion•al [kəʊedjʊ'keɪʃnl] *adj* koedukacyjny; ***~ teaching*** koedukacja
co•ef•fi•cient [kəʊɪ'fɪʃnt] *s* współczynnik *m*
co•ex•ist [kəʊɪg'zɪst] *v/i* współistnieć, koegzystować; **co•ex•ist•ence** [kəʊɪg'zɪstəns] *s* współistnienie *n*, koegzystencja *f*
cof•fee ['kɒfɪ] *s* kawa *f*; **'cof•fee bar** *s* kawiarnia *f*, bar *m* kawowy; **'cof•fee bean** *s* ziarno *n* kawy, ziarenko *n* kawy; **'cof•fee break** *s* przerwa *f* na kawę; **'cof•fee cup** *s* filiżanka *f* do kawy; **'cof•fee grind•er** *s* młynek *m* do kawy; **'cof•fee grounds** *pl* fusy *pl*; **'cof•fee ma•chine** *s* **1.** ekspres *m* do kawy **2.** automat *m* z kawą; **'cof•fee mak•er** *s* **1.** ekspres *m* do kawy **2.** maszynka *f* do kawy; **'cof•fee mill** *s* młynek *m* do kawy; **'cof•fee pot** *s* dzbanek *m* do kawy; **'cof•fee shop** *s* **1.** sklep *m* z kawą **2.** kawiarnia *f*, bar *m* kawowy; **'cof•fee ta•ble** *s* (niski) stolik *m*, ława *f*; **'cof•fee-ta•ble book** *s* (*book*) album *m*
cof•fin ['kɒfɪn] *s* trumna *f*
cog•i•tate ['kɒdʒɪteɪt] *v/i* rozmyślać (***about***/***on*** nad *I*)
co•gnac ['kɒnjæk] *s* koniak *m*
cog•ni•tion [kɒg'nɪʃn] *s* **1.** PHIL poznanie *n* **2.** pojęcie *n*, zrozumienie *n*; **cog•ni•tive** ['kɒgnətɪv] *adj* **1.** poznawczy **2.** kognitywny
co•hab•it [kəʊ'hæbɪt] *v/i* mieszkać razem, żyć w konkubinacie; **co•hab•i•ta•tion** [kəʊhæbɪ'teɪʃn] wolny związek *m*, konkubinat *m*
co•here [kəʊ'hɪə] *v/i* być spójnym: **co•her•ence** [kəʊ'hɪərəns], **co•her•en•cy** [kəʊ'hɪərənsɪ] **1.** spójność *f* **2.** koherencja *f*; **co•her•ent** [kəʊ'hɪrənt] *adj* **1.** spójny, koherentny **2.** zrozumiały; **co•he•sion** [kəʊ'hiːʒn] *s* **1.** spójność *f* **2.** kohezja *f*; **co•he•sive** [kəʊ'hiːsɪv] *adj* **1.** spójny, zwarty **2.** spajający
coil [kɔɪl] **I** *s* **1.** zwój *m*; ***a ~ of hair*** lok **2.** rolka *f*, szpula *f* **II** *v/t* owijać ⟨owinąć⟩; **coil up** **I** *v/t* zwijać ⟨zwinąć⟩ **II** *v/i* (*snake*) zwijać ⟨zwinąć⟩ się
coin [kɔɪn] **I** *s* moneta *f*; ***pay s.o. back in the same ~*** *fig* odpłacić komuś tą samą monetą; ***but the other side of the ~ is that*** *fig* ale z drugiej strony **II** *v/t* **1.** *phrase*: ukuwać ⟨ukuć⟩ **2.** ***~ money*** bić monety ***be ~ing it*** *infml* zbijać kokosy, robić grubą forsę; **coin•age** ['kɔɪnɪdʒ] *s* **1.** monety

pl, bilon *m* **2.** system *m* monetarny **3.** bicie *n* monet **4.** neologizm *m*

co•in•cide [kəʊɪn'saɪd] *v/i* **1.** (*in time*) zbiegać ⟨zbiec⟩ się **2.** pokrywać ⟨-ryć⟩ się **3.** być zbieżnym; **co•in•ci•dence** [kəʊ'ɪnsɪdəns] *s* **1.** zbieg *m* okoliczności; ***by mere ~*** czystym zbiegiem okoliczności **2.** zbieżność *f*; **co•in•ci•den•tal** *adj* przypadkowy

'coin-op•er•at•ed *adj machine*: na monety

coke [kəʊk] *s* **1.** koks *m* **2.** *infml* koka *f*

cold [kəʊld] **I** *adj* **1.** zimny; ***I feel ~*** zimno mi; ***in ~ blood*** z zimną krwią; ***~ snap*** nagłe (przejściowe) ochłodzenie; ***get ~ feet*** *fig* stchórzyć; ***it left me ~*** *fig* nie zrobiło to na mnie wrażenia **2.** *expression*: chłodny **3.** *fact*: suchy **4.** spokojny, opanowany **II** *s* **1.** zimno *n*, chłód *m*; ***be left out in the ~*** *fig* zostać na lodzie **2.** (*a.* ***common ~***) *MED* **a)** przeziębienie *n* **b)** katar *m*

cold-'blood•ed *adj* **1.** dokonany z zimną krwią **2.** bezwzględny **3.** *BIOL* zimnokrwisty, zmiennocieplny

'cold cuts *pl* **1.** zimne mięsa *pl* **2.** wędliny *pl*; **'cold drink** *s* zimny napój *m*; **cold-'heart•ed** *adj* nieczuły, zimny

'cold•ish ['kəʊldɪʃ] *adj* zimnawy, dość zimny; **cold•ly** ['kəʊldlɪ] *adv* chłodno, ozięble; **cold•ness** ['kəʊldnɪs] *s* chłód *m*

'cold room *s* komora *f* chłodnicza; **cold 'shoul•der** *s*: ***give s.o. the ~*** potraktować kogoś chłodno; **'cold sore** *s* opryszczka *f*; **cold 'stor•age** *s* przechowywanie *n* w warunkach chłodniczych; ***keep in ~*** przechowywać w warunkach chłodniczych; ***put s.th. into ~*** *fig* odłożyć coś na półkę; **'cold store** *s* chłodnia *f*; **cold 'tur•key** *s infml* głód *m* narkotykowy; ***go ~ on*** nagle odstawić *A*; **cold 'war** *s* zimna wojna *f*

col•lab•or•ate [kə'læbəreɪt] *v/i* **1.** współpracować **2.** kolaborować; **col•lab•or•ation** [kəlæbə'reɪʃn] *s* **1.** współpraca *f*; ***in ~ with*** we współpracy z *I* **2.** kolaboracja *f*; **col•lab•or•ator** [kə'læbəreɪtə] *s* **1.** współpracownik *m* **2.** kolaborant *m*

col•lage [kɒ'lɑːʒ] *s ART* kolaż *m*

col•lapse [kə'læps] **I** *v/i* **1.** walić ⟨za-⟩ się, runąć **2.** upadać ⟨upaść⟩ **3.** mdleć ⟨ze-⟩, słabnąć ⟨za-⟩ **4.** upadać ⟨upaść⟩, bankrutować ⟨z-⟩ **5.** załamywać ⟨-mać⟩ się **6.** składać ⟨złożyć⟩ się **II** *v/t chair, bike*: składać ⟨złożyć⟩ **III** *s* **1.** zawalenie się *n* **2.** upadek *m* **3.** załamanie *n* się **4.** *MED* zapaść *f*; ***nervous ~*** załamanie nerwowe; **col•lap•si•ble** [kə'læpsəbl] *adj chair*: składany

col•lar ['kɒlə] *s* **1.** kołnierz *m*, kołnierzyk *m*; ***a clerical ~*** koloratka **2.** obroża *f* **3.** kolia *f*, naszyjnik *m*

col•lat•er•al [kə'lætərəl] **I** *adj* **1.** dodatkowy **2.** poboczny, uboczny **3.** drugorzędny, podrzędny **II** *s FIN* zabezpieczenie *n*; **col•lat•er•al 'dam•age** *s* (*war*) straty *pl* wśród ludności cywilnej

col•league ['kɒliːg] *s* kolega *m* z pracy, współpracownik *m*

col•lect [kə'lekt] **I** *v/t* **1.** zbierać ⟨zebrać⟩, kolekcjonować **2.** zbierać ⟨zebrać⟩, gromadzić ⟨z-⟩ **3.** ściągać ⟨-gnąć⟩, pobierać ⟨-brać⟩ **4.** *rubbish*: wywozić ⟨-wieźć⟩ **5.** ***~ s.o.*** wziąć się w garść **6.** *children from school*: odbierać ⟨odebrać⟩ **II** *v/i* **1.** zbierać ⟨zebrać⟩ się, gromadzić ⟨z-⟩ się **2.** kwestować (***for*** na rzecz *G*); **col•lect 'call** *s* rozmowa *f* na koszt odbierającego; **col•lect•ed** [kə'lektɪd] *adj* **1.** spokojny, opanowany **2.** zebrany; ***~ works*** dzieła zebrane

col•lec•tion [kə'lekʃn] *s* **1.** zbiór *m*, kolekcja *f* **2.** zbieranie *n*, kolekcjonowanie *n* **3.** zbiórka *f* pieniężna, kwesta *f* **5.** odbiór *m* **6.** *fig* opanowanie *n*; **col•lec•tive** [kə'lektɪv] **I** *adj* **1.** wspólny **2.** zbiorowy; ***a ~ agreement*** umowa zbiorowa; ***~ bargaining*** negocjacje w sprawie zawarcia umowy zbiorowej; ***a ~ noun*** rzeczownik zbiorowy **II** *s* spółdzielnia *f*; **col•lec•tive•ly** [kə'lektɪvlɪ] *adv* wspólnie, razem; **col•lec•tor** [kə'lektə] *s* **1.** kolekcjoner *m*; ***~'s item*** rzadki okaz, rarytas **2.** poborca *m*

col•lege ['kɒlɪdʒ] *s* **1.** szkoła *f* wyższa, college *m*; ***go to ~*** iść na studia **2.** szkoła *f* pomaturalna **3.** kolegium *n* **4.** (*institution*) stowarzyszenie *n*; **col•le•gi•ate** [kə'liːdʒɪət] *adj* **1.** uczelniany, akademicki **2.** ***a ~ church*** *REL* kolegiata

col•lide [kə'laɪd] *v/i* **1.** zderzać ⟨-rzyć⟩ się **2.** ścierać ⟨zetrzeć⟩ się **3.** kolidować (ze sobą); **col•li•sion** [kə'lɪʒn] *s* **1.** zderzenie *n,* kolizja *f*; ***come into ~ with*** zderzyć się z *I*; ***on a ~ course*** na kursie kolizyjnym **2.** konflikt *m,* sprzeczność *f*

col•lo•qui•al [kə'ləʊkwɪəl] *adj* potoczny, kolokwialny; ***~ English*** potoczna angielszczyzna; **col•lo•qui•al•ism** [kə'ləʊkwɪəlɪzəm] kolokwializm *m*

Co•lom•bi•a [kə'lʌmbɪə] *s* Kolumbia *f*

co•lon ['kəʊlən] *s* dwukropek *m*

colo•nel ['kɜːnl] *s* pułkownik *m*

co•lo•ni•al [kə'ləʊnɪəl] *adj* kolonialny; **co•lo•ni•al•ism** [kə'ləʊnɪəlɪzəm] *s* kolonializm *m*; **col•o•nist** ['kɒlənɪst] *s* **1.** kolonista *m* **2.** osadnik *m*; **col•o•ni•za•tion** [kɒlənaɪ'zeɪʃn] *s* kolonizacja *f*; **col•o•nize** ['kɒlənaɪz] *v/t* **1.** kolonizować ⟨s-⟩ **2.** zasiedlać ⟨-lić⟩

col•on•nade [kɒlə'neɪd] *s* ARCHIT kolumnada *f*

co•lo•ny ['kɒlənɪ] *s* kolonia *f*

col•or *Am* → ***colour***

co•los•sal [kə'lɒsl] *adj* ogromny, kolosalny; **co•los•sus** [kə'lɒsəs] *pl -si* [~saɪ], *-suses* [~səsɪs] *s* kolos *m,* olbrzym *m*

col•our ['kʌlə] *Br,* ***col•or*** *Am* **I** *s* **1.** kolor *m,* barwa *f*; ***what ~ is her bike?*** jakiego koloru jest jej rower?; ***paint s.th. in bright*** (***gloomy***) ***~s*** *fig* malować coś w jasnych (ciemnych) barwach **2.** barwnik *m*; ***hair ~*** farba do włosów **3.** kolor *m* skóry, rumieniec *m*; ***lose ~*** blednąć **4.** kolor *m* skóry; ***people of ~*** kolorowi **5.** barwność *f,* koloryt *m*; ***local ~*** koloryt lokalny **6.** ***~s*** barwy *pl* **7.** ***~s*** sztandar *m,* bandera *f*; ***pass an exam with flying ~s*** *fig* zdać egzamin śpiewająco; ***sail under false ~s*** *fig* stroić się w cudze piórka; ***show one's true ~s*** *fig* pokazać swoje prawdziwe oblicze **II** *v/t* **1.** kolorować ⟨po-⟩ **2.** malować ⟨po-⟩ **3.** farbować ⟨u-⟩ **4.** rzutować na *A* **5.** barwić ⟨u-⟩ **III** *v/i* **1.** zmieniać ⟨-nić⟩ kolor **2.** rumienić ⟨za-⟩ się, czerwienić ⟨za-⟩ się; **col•our bar** *Br,* ***col•or bar*** *Am s* dyskryminacja *f* rasowa; **'col•our-blind** *Br,* ***col•or-blind*** *Am adj*: ***be ~*** być daltonistą; **'col•our-blind•ness** *Br,* ***color-blind•ness*** *Am s* daltonizm *m*; **'col•our chart** *Br,* ***'col•or chart*** *Am s* paleta *f* kolorów; **'col•our-cod•ed** *Br,* ***'col•or cod•ed*** *Am adj* oznaczony kolorami; **'col•our cod•ing** *Br,* ***'col•or cod•ing*** *Am s* klasyfikacja *f* za pomocą kolorów

col•oured ['kʌləd] *Br,* ***col•ored*** *Am adj* kolorowy; ***a ~ pencil*** kredka

'col•our fast *Br,* ***col•or fast*** *Am adj* o trwałych kolorach; **'col•our 'film** *Br,* ***col•or 'film*** *Am* film *m* kolorowy

col•our•ful ['kʌləfəl] *Br,* ***col•or•ful*** *Am adj* **1.** kolorowy, barwny **2.** *fig* barwny; **col•our•ing** ['kʌlərɪŋ] *Br,* ***col•or•ing*** *Am s* **1.** ubarwienie *n* **2.** kolorystyka *f* **3.** karnacja *f* **4.** barwnik *m* **5.** kolorowanie *n*; ***a ~ book*** kolorowanka

col•our•less ['kʌləlɪs] *Br,* ***col•or•less*** *Am adj* **1.** *a. fig* bezbarwny **2.** blady

'col•our pho•to•graph *Br,* ***'col•or pho•to•graph*** *Am s* zdjęcie *n* kolorowe; **'col•our print•er** *Br,* ***'col•or print•er*** *Am s* drukarka *f* kolorowa; **'col•our print•ing** *Br,* ***'col•or printing*** *Am s* drukowanie *n* w kolorze; **'col•our scheme** *Br,* ***'col•or scheme*** *Am s* tonacja *f* kolorystyczna; **col•our 'sup•ple•ment** *Br,* ***col•or supple•ment*** *Am* dodatek *m* ilustrowany; **col•our T'V** *Br,* ***col•or T'V*** *Am s* kolorowa telewizja *f*

Co•lum•bus [kə'lʌmbəs] *s* (Krzysztof) Kolumb *m*

col•umn ['kɒləm] *s* **1.** kolumna *f* **2.** filar *m* **3.** kolumna *f* **4.** rubryka *f,* dział *m* **5.** felieton *m*; **col•umn•ist** ['kɒləmnɪst] *s* felietonista *m*

co•ma ['kəʊmə] *s* MED śpiączka *f*; ***be in a ~*** być w śpiączce

comb [kəʊm] **I** *s* **1.** grzebień *m*; ***your hair needs a ~*** powinnaś się uczesać **2.** zgrzebło *n* **3.** plaster *m* miodu **II** *v/t* **1.** ***~ one's hair, ~ oneself*** czesać ⟨-u⟩ się **2.** *fig* przeczesywać ⟨-sać⟩; **comb out** *v/t* rozczesywać ⟨-sać⟩; **comb through** *v/t* przeglądać ⟨przejrzeć⟩

com•bat ['kɒmbæt] **I** *s* walka *f,* bój *m* **II** *v/t* **1.** walczyć z *I* **2.** zwalczać ⟨-czyć⟩; ***how to ~ stress*** jak pokonać stres

com•bi•na•tion [kɒmbɪ'neɪʃn] *s* **1.** połączenie *n,* kombinacja *f*; ***in ~ with***

C

C

a) w połączeniu z *I* **b)** we współpracy z *I* **2.** *circumstances, events*: splot *m*, zbieg *m* **3.** *factors*: szereg *m* **4.** szyfr *m*; **com•bi•'na•tion lock** *s* zamek *m* szyfrowy

com•bine **I** [kəm'baın] *v/t* **1.** łączyć ⟨po-⟩; **~ *business with pleasure*** łączyć przyjemne z pożytecznym **2.** wiązać ⟨po-⟩ **3.** mieszać ⟨z-, wy-⟩ **II** [kəm'baın] *v/i* **1.** łączyć ⟨po-⟩ się **2.** jednoczyć ⟨z-⟩ się; ***everything ~d against him*** wszystko sprzysięgło się przeciwko niemu **III** [kɒmbaın] *s* **1.** kombajn *m* **2.** kartel *m*, syndykat *m*; **com•bined** [kəm'baınd] *adj* **1.** łączny; ***they scored a ~ total of 530*** uzyskali łączny wynik 530 punktów **2.** połączony **3.** wspólny

come [kʌm] **I** (*came*; *come*) *v/i* **1.** przychodzić ⟨przyjść⟩; ***he came to see us*** odwiedził nas; **~ *and go*** **a)** przychodzić i odchodzić **b)** pojawiać się i znikać **2.** przyjeżdżać ⟨-jechać⟩ **3.** nadchodzić ⟨-dejść⟩ **4. ~ *to*** sięgać *G*, dochodzić do *G* **5. ~ *true*** urzeczywistnić się; **~ *what may*** bez względu na to, co się stanie; ***how ~ that*** jak to jest, że **6. *it ~s expensive*** *infml* jest drogi **7. ~ *to know s.o.*** poznać kogoś; **~ *to know s.th.*** nauczyć się czegoś; **~ *to like*** polubić; ***I have ~ to believe that*** przekonałem się, że **8. *in the week* (*month*) *to ~*** w przyszłym tygodniu (miesiącu); ***in the years to ~*** w nadchodzących latach; ***for all time to ~*** (na) zawsze **9.** mieć orgazm **II** (*came*; *come*) *v/t* **1.** przebywać ⟨-być⟩ **2.** zgrywać się na *A*, udawać **III** *interj* **~ *now!*** już, już!, już dobrze!; **~, ~! a)** no, no! **b)** no, dosyć tego!; **come again** *v/i*: **~?** proszę?, słucham?; **come about** *v/i* mieć miejsce, zdarzać ⟨-rzyć⟩ się; **come across** *v/i* **1.** być jasnym, być zrozumiałym **2.** wypadać ⟨-paść⟩; **~ *well*** dobrze wypaść, sprawić dobre wrażenie **3.** natykać ⟨-tknąć⟩ się na *A* **4.** wpadać ⟨wpaść⟩ na *A*; **come across with** *v/i* **1.** przekazywać ⟨-zać⟩ **2.** wyjawiać ⟨-wić⟩; **come along** *v/i* **1.** pojawiać ⟨-wić⟩ się, zjawiać ⟨-wić⟩ się **2.** przychodzić ⟨przyjść⟩; **~!** chodź już! **3.** robić ⟨z-⟩ postępy, posuwać ⟨-sunąć⟩ się; **come apart** *v/i* rozpadać ⟨-paść⟩ się (na kawałki); **come around** → ***come round***; **come at** *v/i* **1.** rzucać ⟨-cić⟩ się na *A*, atakować ⟨za-⟩; **come away** *v/i* **1.** odpadać ⟨-paść⟩ **2.** odchodzić ⟨odejść⟩; **come back** *v/i* **1.** wracać ⟨wrócić⟩ (***to*** do *G*) **2.** przypominać ⟨-mnieć⟩ się; ***it's all coming back to me now*** teraz już sobie wszystko przypominam **3.** wracać ⟨wrócić⟩, znowu być w modzie; **come between** *v/i* **1.** rozdzielać ⟨-lić⟩ **2.** interweniować ⟨za-⟩ **3.** *fig* stawać ⟨stanąć⟩ pomiędzy *I*; **come by** *v/i* **1.** wpadać ⟨wpaść⟩ **2.** zdobywać ⟨-być⟩; **come down** *v/i* **1.** zmiejszać ⟨-szyć⟩ się; **~ *in s.o.'s opinion*** stracić w czyichś oczach **2.** (*prices*) spadać ⟨-paść⟩ **3.** schodzić ⟨zejść⟩ **4.** zjeżdżać ⟨zjechać⟩ **5.** (*snow*) padać ⟨spaść⟩ **6.** runąć **7.** lądować ⟨wy-⟩; **come down on** *v/i* **1.** rugać ⟨z-⟩ **2.** *infml* zjechać; **come down to** *v/i* sprowadzać się do *G*; **come down with** *v/i* zachorować na *A*; ***I think I'm coming down with a flu*** chyba łapie mnie grypa; **come for** *v/i* **1.** przychodzić ⟨przyjść⟩ po *A* **2.** odbierać ⟨odebrać⟩; **come forward** *v/i* zgłaszać ⟨-łosić⟩ się; **come from** *v/i* pochodzić z *G*; **come in** *v/i* **1.** wchodzić ⟨wejść⟩; **~!** proszę! **2.** nadchodzić ⟨-dejść⟩ **3.** przyjeżdżać ⟨-jechać⟩ **4.** stawać ⟨stać⟩ się modnym **5. ~ *first* (*second*)** zająć pierwsze (drugie) miejsce **6.** dochodzić ⟨dojść⟩ do władzy **7. *where do I ~?*** jaka jest w tym moja rola?; **come in for** *v/i*: **~ *criticism*** spotkać się z krytyką; **come in on** *v/i* przyłączać ⟨-czyć⟩ się do *G*; **come into** *v/i* **1.** wchodzić ⟨wejść⟩ do *G* **2.** dziedziczyć ⟨o-⟩ **3. ~ *fashion*** stawać się modnym; **come off** *v/i* **1.** odpadać ⟨-paść⟩ **2.** urywać ⟨urwać⟩ się **3.** spadać ⟨spaść⟩ **4.** dochodzić ⟨dojść⟩ do skutku, powieść się, *infml* wypalać ⟨-lić⟩ **5.** THEAT schodzić ⟨zejść⟩ z afisza **6.** *pills, drugs*: przestawać ⟨-tać⟩ brać; **come on** *v/i* **1.** nadchodzić ⟨-dejść⟩ **2.** zaczynać ⟨-cząć⟩ się **3. ~! a)** no już!, dalej! **b)** akurat! **4.** (*actor*) wychodzić ⟨wyjść⟩ na scenę **5.** (*play*) wchodzić ⟨wejść⟩ na afisz; **come on to** *v/i infml* podrywać ⟨-derwać⟩; **come out** *v/i* **1.** wychodzić ⟨wyjść⟩ **2.** (*book*) ukazywać ⟨-zać⟩ się **3.** (*hair*) wypadać ⟨-paść⟩ **4.** (*stain*) schodzić ⟨zejść⟩ **5.** *~ well* udawać ⟨udać⟩ się **6.** blaknąć ⟨z-⟩ **7.** *~ of* wynikać z *G*, wyrastać z *G* **8.** wychodzić ⟨wyjść⟩ na jaw **9.** *~ in a rash* dostać wysypki **10.** *~ on strike* strajkować ⟨za-⟩ **11.** *~ in favour of* (*against*) opowiadać się za *I* (przeciwko *D*); **come out with** *v/i infml* **1.** wymyślać ⟨-lić⟩ **2.** wyskoczyć z *I*; **come over** *v/i* **1.** podchodzić ⟨-dejść⟩ **2.** (*drop in*) przychodzić ⟨przyjść⟩, *infml* wpadać ⟨wpaść⟩ **3.** przyjeżdżać ⟨-jechać⟩ **4.** przylatywać ⟨-lecieć⟩ **5.** wypadać ⟨-paść⟩, zostać odebranym **6.** (*feeling*) ogarniać ⟨-nąć⟩ **7.** *what has ~ you?* co cię napadło?; **come round** *v/i* **1.** (*visit*) przychodzić ⟨przyjść⟩, *infml* wpadać ⟨wpaść⟩ **2.** dochodzić ⟨dojść⟩ do siebie, ocknąć się **3.** objeżdżać ⟨-jechać⟩ dookoła, obchodzić ⟨obejść⟩; **come through** *v/i* **1.** przetrwać **2.** przenikać ⟨-knąć⟩, przedostawać ⟨-tać⟩ się przez *A*; **come to** *v/i* **1.** dochodzić ⟨dojść⟩ do siebie, ocknąć się **2.** wynosić ⟨-nieść⟩, kosztować **3.** dochodzić ⟨dojść⟩ do *G*; *it came to nothing* nic z tego nie wyszło **4.** *when it comes to paying* jeśli idzie o zapłatę; **come together** *v/i* **1.** zbierać ⟨zebrać⟩ się **2.** łączyć ⟨po-⟩ się **3.** tworzyć ⟨u-⟩ całość; **come under** *v/i* **1.** być zaliczonym do *G* **2.** podlegać **3.** *criticism*: zostać poddanym; **come up** *v/i* **1.** podchodzić ⟨-dejść⟩ do *G* **2.** (*sun*) wschodzić ⟨wzejść⟩ **3.** (*problem*) pojawiać ⟨-wić⟩ się, wyłaniać ⟨-łonić⟩ się **4.** (*subject*) zostać poruszonym **5.** wypadać ⟨-paść⟩; *She can't go with us. Something has ~.* Nie może jechać z nami – coś jej wypadło; **come up against** *v/i* stawać ⟨stanąć⟩ wobec *G*, napotykać ⟨-tkać⟩; **come up for** *v/i* podlegać; **come upon** *v/i* natykać ⟨-tknąć⟩ się na *A*; **come up to** *v/i* (*nearly*) zbliżać ⟨-żyć⟩ się, dochodzić; **come up with** *v/i* **1.** *answer*; znajdować ⟨znaleźć⟩ **2.** wymyślać ⟨-lić⟩ **3.** (*proposal*) występować ⟨-tąpić⟩ z *I*

'come•back *s* comeback *m*; *make a ~* **a)** (*musician*) wznawiać działalność **b)** (*politician*) wracać na scenę polityczną

co•me•di•an [kə'miːdıən] *s* **1.** artysta *m* komediowy **2.** wesołek *m*

'come•down *s* **1.** degradacja *f*, upadek *m* **2.** rozczarowanie *n*, zawód *m*

com•e•dy ['kɒmədı] *s* **1.** komedia *f* **2.** komizm *m*

come•ly ['kʌmlı] *adj lit* urodziwy, nadobny

com•er ['kʌmə] *s* przybysz *m*

com•et ['kɒmıt] *s* ASTR kometa *f*

come•up•pance [kʌm'ʌpəns] *s*: *to get one's ~* dostać za swoje

com•fort ['kʌmfət] **I** *v/t* pocieszać ⟨-szyć⟩, dodawać ⟨-dać⟩ otuchy **II** *s* **1.** pociecha *f*, pocieszenie *n*, *cold ~* niewielkie pocieszenie **2.** ulga *f* **3.** wygoda *f*, komfort *m*; *live in ~* mieszkać wygodnie **4.** udogodnienie *n*, wygoda *f*; *all modern ~s* wszelkie nowoczesne udogodnienia

com•for•ta•ble ['kʌmfətəbl] *adj* **1.** wygodny; *are you ~?* wygodnie ci?; *make oneself* usadowić się wygodnie **2.** komfortowy **3.** odprężony; *feel ~* czuć się swobodnie **4.** dobrze sytuowany **5.** znaczny **6.** *he's ~ with computers* dobrze sobie radzi z komputerami, zna się na komputerach

com•for•ta•bly ['kʌmfətəblı] *adv* **1.** wygodnie **2.** swobodnie **3.** dostatnio; *be ~ off* być dobrze sytuowanym; **com•fort•er** ['kʌmfətə] *s* **1.** pocieszyciel *m* **2.** *Am* kołdra *f* **3.** *Br* smoczek *m*; **com•fort•ing** ['kʌmfətıŋ] *adj* pocieszający, podnoszący na duchu; **com•fort•less** ['kʌmfətlıs] **1.** niewygodny **2.** niepocieszony

com•fy ['kʌmfı] *infml* → ***comfortable***

com•ic ['kɒmık] **I 1.** *adj* komiczny, zabawny **2.** komediowy; *~ tragedy* tragikomedia **II** *s* **1.** komik *m* **2.** komiks *m*; **com•i•cal** ['kɒmıkl] *adj* komiczny; **'com•ic book** *s* komiks *m*; **com•ic 'op•er•a** *s* opera *f* komiczna; **'com•ic strip** *s* historyjka *f* obrazkowa, komiks *m*

com•ing ['kʌmıŋ] **I** *adj* nadchodzący, najbliższy; *the ~ week* w przyszłym tygodniu **II** *s* **1.** przybycie *n*; *~s and go-*

C

ings ruch, krzątanina **2.** nadejście *n* **3.** nastanie *n*; **com•ing of 'age** *s* osiągnięcie *n* pełnoletności

com•ma ['kɒmə] *s* przecinek *m*

com•mand [kə'mɑːnd] **I** *v/t* **1.** rozkazywać ⟨-zać⟩; **~ s.o. to do s.th.** rozkazać komuś coś zrobić **2.** nakazywać ⟨-zać⟩ **3.** dowodzić **4.** *respect*: cieszyć się **5.** *admiration*: wzbudzać ⟨-dzić⟩ **6.** górować nad *I* **7.** dysponować **II** *v/i* sprawować dowództwo **III** *s* **1.** rozkaz *m*, komenda *f* **2.** *INF* polecenie *n* **3.** dowodzenie *n*; **be in ~** sprawować dowództwo, dowodzić **4.** dowództwo *n* **5.** **be at s.o.'s ~** być do czyjejś dyspozycji; **have s.th. at one's ~** mieć coś do dyspozycji **6.** **a good ~ of English** dobra znajomość języka angielskiego; **com•man•dant** ['kɒməndænt] *s* komendant *m*

com•mand•er [kə'mændə] *s* **1.** dowódca *m* **2.** komandor porucznik *m*; **com•mand•er-in-'chief** *s* głównodowodzący *m*

com•'mand•ing of•fi•cer *s* dowódca *m*

com•mand•ment [kə'mɑːndmənt] *s* przykazanie *n*, nakaz *m*; **the Ten ≈s** dziesięcioro przykazań

comman•do [kə'mɑːndəʊ] *pl -dos, -does* [~dəʊz] *s* **1.** jednostka *f* do zadań specjalnych **2.** komandos *m*

com•mem•o•rate [kə'meməreɪt] *v/t* upamiętniać ⟨-nić⟩, czcić ⟨u-⟩ pamięć; **com•mem•o•ra•tion** [kəmemə'reɪʃn] *s* obchody *pl*; **in ~ of a)** ku czci *G* **b)** dla upamiętnienia *G*; **com•mem•o•ra•tive** [kə'memərətɪv] *adj* **1.** pamiątkowy; **a ~ plaque** tablica pamiątkowa **2.** *edition*: okolicznościowy

com•mence [kə'mens] **I** *v/t* **1.** rozpoczynać ⟨-cząć⟩ **2.** wszczynać ⟨-cząć⟩ **II** *v/i* **1.** rozpoczynać ⟨-cząć⟩ się **2.** rozpoczynać ⟨-cząć⟩ (**to do s.th.** robienie czegoś); **com•mence•ment** [kə'mensmənt] *s* **1.** rozpoczęcie *n* **2.** wszczęcie *n* **3.** *Am* rozdanie *n* dyplomów

com•mend [kə'mend] *v/t* **1.** chwalić ⟨po-⟩ **2.** polecać ⟨-cić⟩ **3.** powierzać ⟨-rzyć⟩; **com•mend•able** [kə'mendəbl] *adj* **1.** chwalebny, godny pochwały **2.** godny polecenia; **com•men•da•tion** [kəmen'deɪʃn] *s* **1.** pochwała *f* **2.** wyróżnienie *n* **3.** rekomendacja *f*

com•ment ['kɒment] **I** *s* komentarz *m*, uwaga *f*; **no ~!** bez komentarza! **II** *v/i* komentować ⟨s-⟩, wypowiadać ⟨-wiedzieć⟩ się (**on** na temat *G*) **III** *v/t* **~ that** zauważyć, że

com•men•ta•ry ['kɒməntərɪ] *s* **1.** komentarz *m* **2.** sprawozdanie *n*, relacja *f*; **com•men•tate** ['kɒmənteɪt] *v/t SPORT* komentować (**on** *A*); **com•men•ta•tor** ['kɒmənteɪtə] *s* komentator *m*, sprawozdawca *m*

com•merce ['kɒmɜːs] *s* handel *m*; **com•mer•cial** [kə'mɜːʃl] **I** *s RADIO TEL* reklama *f* **II** *adj* **1.** handlowy; **~ correspondence** korespondencja handlowa **2.** komercyjny; **~ broadcasting** radio komercyjne **3.** rynkowy, na skalę przemysłową; **com•mer•cial 'bank** *s* bank *m* handlowy; **com•mer•cial 'break** *s* przerwa *f* na reklamy; **com•mer•cial•ize** [kə'mɜːʃlaɪz] *v/t* komercjalizować ⟨s-⟩

com•mie ['kɒmɪ] *infml* **I** *s* komuch *m* **II** *adj* komuchowaty

com•mis•sion [kə'mɪʃn] **I** *s* **1.** prowizja *f*; **on a ~ basis** na zasadzie prowizji **2.** zamówienie *n*, zlecenie *n* **3.** komisja *f*; **be on the ~** być w komisji **4.** *of crime*: popełnienie *n* **II** *v/t* **1.** zamawiać ⟨-mówić⟩ **2.** zlecać ⟨-cić⟩; **~ed work** praca zlecona

com•mis•sion•er [kə'mɪʃənə] *s* **1.** członek *m* komisji **2.** komisarz *m*

com•mis•sion•ing [kə'mɪʃənɪŋ] *adj*: **a ~ editor** redaktor prowadzący

com•mit [kə'mɪt] *v/t* **1.** popełniać ⟨-nić⟩; **~ suicide** popełnić samobójstwo; **~ a theft** dokonać kradzieży **2.** zobowiązywać ⟨-zać⟩ **3.** angażować ⟨za-⟩ **4.** przeznaczać ⟨-czyć⟩ (**to** na *A*) **5.** powierzać ⟨-rzyć⟩; **~ s.th. to s.o.'s care** powierzyć coś czyjejś opiece; **~ s.th. to paper** przelać coś na papier

com•mit•ment [kə'mɪtmənt] *s* **1.** zobowiązanie *n* **2.** oddanie *n*, zaangażowanie *n*; **com•mit•ted** [kə'mɪtɪd] *adj* **1.** zaangażowany, oddany **2.** zobowiązany

com•mit•tee [kə'mɪtɪ] *s* **1.** komitet *m* **2.** komisja *f*; **com•mit•tee 'meet•ing** *s* **1.** posiedzenie *n* komitetu **2.** posiedzenie *n* komisji; **com•mit•tee 'mem•ber** *s* **1.** członek *m* komitetu **2.** członek *m* komisji

com•mode [kə'məʊd] *s* **1.** komoda *f* **2.** sedes *m* pokojowy; **com•mo•di•ous** [kə'məʊdiəs] *adj* przestronny

com•mod•i•ty [kə'mɒdətɪ] *s* **1.** towar *m* **2.** artykuł *m*; **com•'mod•i•ty ex•change** *s* **1.** giełda *f* towarowa **2.** wymiana *f* towarowa

com•mon ['kɒmən] **I** *adj* **1.** wspólny **2.** ogólny; ***by ~ consent*** za ogólnym przyzwoleniem; ***it is ~ knowledge that*** powszechnie wiadomo, że **3.** zwykły; ***~ people*** prości ludzie; ***~ or garden*** *Br* zwykły, typowy **4.** pospolity **5.** *name*: popularny **6.** *view*: często spotykany **7.** *soldier*: szeregowy, zwykły **II** *s* **1.** ***they have a lot in ~*** mają ze sobą wiele wspólnego, wiele ich łączy **2.** ***out of the ~*** niezwykły **3.** błonie *n*, błonia *pl*

com•mon•er ['kɒmənə] *s* plebejusz *m*

com•mon•ly ['kɒmənlɪ] *adv* **1.** powszechnie **2.** popularnie

Com•mon 'Mar•ket *s* Wspólny Rynek *m*

'com•mon•place I *adj* **1.** powszechny **2.** pospolity **II** *s* banał *m*; **'com•mon room** *s* świetlica *f*; **com•mon 'sense** *s* zdrowy rozsądek *m*

Com•mons ['kɒmənz] *pl*: ***the House of ~*** *Br* Izba Gmin

Com•mon•wealth ['kɒmənwelθ] *s* Wspólnota *f* Narodów, Commonwealth *m*

com•mo•tion [kə'məʊʃn] *s* **1.** zgiełk *m*, tumult *m* **2.** zamieszki *pl*, rozruchy *pl*

com•mu•nal [kə'mjuːnl] *adj* **1.** wspólny; ***a ~ aerial*** antena zbiorcza **2.** społeczny; **com•mu•nal•ly** [kəm'juːnəlɪ] *adv* wspólnie

com•mune[1] ['kɒmjuːn] *s* **1.** komuna *f* **2.** gmina *f*

com•mune[2] [kə'mjuːn] *v/i*: ***~ with nature*** obcować z naturą; ***~ with s.o.*** rozmawiać z kimś od serca

com•mu•ni•ca•ble [kə'mjuːnɪkəbl] *adj* **1.** zrozumiały, łatwy do pojęcia **2.** zaraźliwy; **com•mu•ni•cate** [kə'mjuːnɪkeɪt] **I** *v/t* **1.** przekazywać ⟨-zać⟩ **2.** wyrażać ⟨-razić⟩ **3.** ***be ~d*** *MED* rozprzestrzeniać się **II** *v/i* **1.** porozumiewać ⟨-mieć⟩ się, komunikować się **2.** kontaktować ⟨s-⟩ się **3.** łączyć ⟨po-⟩ się; ***a communicating door*** drzwi łączące; **com•mu•ni•ca•tion** [kəmjuːnɪ'keɪʃn] *s* **1.** komunikacja *f*, porozumiewanie się *n* **2.** łączność *f*, kontakt *m*; ***be in ~ with*** być w kontakcie z *I* **3.** przekazywanie *n* **4.** wyrażanie *n* **5.** ***a ~ cord*** hamulec bezpieczeństwa; **com•mu•nica•tions** [kə'mjuːnɪ'kaɪʃns] *pl* **1.** łączność *f*, komunikacja *f*; ***a ~ system*** system łączności; ***a ~ satellite*** satelita komunikacyjny **2.** połączenia *pl*; **com•mu•ni•ca•tive** [kə'mjuːnɪkətɪv] *adj* rozmowny, komunikatywny

Com•mu•nion [kə'mjuːnjən] *s* *REL* komunia *f*

com•mu•ni•qué [kə'mjuːnɪkeɪ] *s* komunikat *m*

Com•mu•nism ['kɒmjʊnɪzəm] *s* komunizm *m*; **Com•mu•nist** ['kɒmjʊnɪst] **I** *s* **1.** komunista *m*, komunistka *f* **II** *adj* **2.** komunistyczny

com•mu•ni•ty [kə'mjuːnətɪ] *s* **1.** społeczność *f* **2.** społeczeństwo *n* **3.** wspólnota *f*; ***~ singing*** wspólny śpiew; ***~ spirit*** poczucie wspólnoty; ***a ~ home*** dom poprawczy; **com•mu•ni•ty 'cen•tre** *s* dom *m* kultury; **com•mu•ni•ty 'serv•ice** *s* praca *f* na rzecz społeczności lokalnej

com•mu•ta•tion [kɒmjuː'teɪʃn] *Am* dojeżdżanie *n* do pracy

com•mute [kə'mjuːt] *v/t* dojeżdżać do pracy; **com•mut•er** [kə'mjuːtə] *s* dojeżdżający *m* (do pracy); **com•'muter 'air•line** *s* regionalne linie *pl* lotnicze; **com•'muter belt** *s* obszar *m* podmiejski; **com•'muter plane** *s* samolot *m* regionalnych linii lotniczych; **com•'muter town** *s* miasto-sypialnia *n*, miasto-satelita *n*; **com•'muter traf•fic** *s* ruch *m* podmiejski; **com•'muter train** *s* pociąg *m* podmiejski

com•pact I [kəm'pækt] *adj* **1.** kompaktowy; ***a ~ camera*** kompakt, aparat kompaktowy **2.** niewielki (lecz funkcjonalny) **3.** zbity, ubity **4.** zwięzły **5.** ***of ~ built*** krępy **II** ['kɒmpækt] *s* **1.** *AUTO* kompakt *m* **2.** puderniczka *f* **III** [kəm'pækt] *v/t* **3.** ubijać ⟨ubić⟩; **com•pact 'disc** *s* płyta *f* kompaktowa; **com•pact 'disc play-**

C

er *s* odtwarzacz *m* płyt kompaktowych

com•pan•ion [kəm'pænjən] *s* **1.** towarzysz *m* **2.** opiekun *m* **3.** (*item*) para *f* **4.** poradnik *m*, przewodnik *m*; **com•pan•ion•a•ble** [kəm'pænjənəbl] *adj* towarzyski, przyjacielski, sympatyczny; **com•pan•ion•ship** [kəm'pænjənʃɪp] *s* towarzystwo *n*

C

com•pa•ny ['kʌmpənɪ] *s* **1.** firma *f*, przedsiębiorstwo *n* **2.** spółka *f* **3.** towarzystwo *n*; ***keep s.o. ~*** dotrzymywać komuś towarzystwa; ***keep good*** (***bad***) ***~*** obracać się w dobrym (złym) towarzystwie; ***be fond of ~*** być towarzyskim; ***present ~ excepted*** z wyjątkiem tu obecnych; ***part ~ with*** rozstać się z *I* **4.** kompania *f* **5.** *form* goście *pl*; **com•pa•ny 'car** *s* samochód *m* firmowy; **com•pa•ny 'law** *s* JUR prawo *n* o spółkach; **com•pa•ny 'name** *s* nazwa *f* spółki, firma *f*; **com•pa•ny 'pen•sion scheme** *s* system *m* emerytalny przedsiębiorstwa; **com•pa•ny 'pro•file** *s* charakterystyka *f* firmy

com•pa•ra•ble ['kɒmpərəbl] *adj* porównywalny

com•par•a•tive [kəm'pærətɪv] **I** *s* stopień *m* wyższy **II** *adj* **1.** porównawczy **2.** względny **3.** *form*: wyższy; **com•par•a•tive•ly** [kəm'pærətɪvlɪ] *adv* **1.** stosunkowo **2.** porównawczo; **com•pare** [kəm'pe] **I** *v/t* porównywać ⟨-nać⟩ (***with***/***to***/***and*** z *I*); ***~d with*** w porównaniu z *I* **II** *v/i* dorównywać ⟨-nać⟩; ***~ favourably with*** korzystnie wypadać w porównaniu z *I* **III** *s* ***beyond ~, without ~*** niezrównany; **com•pa•ri•son** [kəm'pærɪsn] *s* **1.** porównanie *n*; ***in ~ with*** w porównaniu z *I*; ***make a ~ with*** porówywać z *I*; ***stand ~ with*** dorównywać *D* **2.** stopniowanie *n*

com•part•ment [kəm'pɑːtmənt] *s* **1.** przedział *m* **2.** przegródka *f* **3.** schowek *m*

com•pass ['kʌmpəs] *s* **1.** kompas *m* **2.** zasięg *m*, ramy *pl* **3.** *voice*: skala *f*

com•pas•sion [kəm'pæʃn] *s* współczucie *n* (***for*** dla *G*); ***have ~ for*** współczuć *D*; **com•pas•sion•ate** [kəm'pæʃənət] *adj* pełen współczucia

com•pat•i•bil•i•ty [kəmpætə'bɪlɪtɪ] *s* zgodność *f*, kompatybilność *f*; **com•pat•i•ble** [kəm'pætəbl] *adj* **1.** zgodny (***with*** *I*) **2.** kompatybilny

com•pa•tri•ot [kəm'peɪtrɪət] *s* rodak *m*

com•pel [kəm'pel] *v/t form* **1.** zmuszać ⟨-sić⟩ (***to do s.th.*** do zrobienia czegoś); ***he was ~led to quit*** musiał odejść, został zmuszony do odejścia **2.** wymuszać ⟨-sić⟩ **3.** *respect, admiration*: wzbudzać ⟨-dzić⟩ **4.** *attention*: przykuwać ⟨-kuć⟩; **com•pel•ling** [kəm'pelɪŋ] *adj* **1.** wciągający, frapujący **2.** *reason*: istotny **3.** *argument*: przekonujący **4.** *need*: pilny, palący **5.** *answer*: narzucający się **6.** nieodparty

com•pen•di•um [kəm'pendɪəm] *pl* *-diums, -dia* [~ə] *s* **1.** poradnik *m* **2.** kompendium *n*

com•pen•sate ['kɒmpənseɪt] *v/t* **1.** rekompensować ⟨z-⟩, wynagradzać ⟨-grodzić⟩ **2.** wypłacać ⟨-cić⟩ odszkodowanie (***for*** za *A*); ***be ~d*** otrzymać odszkodowanie **3.** równoważyć ⟨z-⟩; **com•pen•sa•tion** [kɒmpən'seɪʃn] *s* **1.** rekompensata *f* **2.** odszkodowanie *n* **3.** PSYCH kompensacja *f*

com•pete [kəm'piːt] *v/i* **1.** konkurować **2.** rywalizować **3.** brać ⟨wziąć⟩ udział w zawodach

com•pe•tence ['kɒmpɪtəns] *s* **1.** kwalifikacje *pl* **2.** umiejętności *pl* **4.** kompetencja *f* językowa; **com•pe•tent** ['kɒmpɪtənt] *adj* **1.** kompetentny; ***be ~ at one's work*** dobrze wykonywać swoją pracę **2.** fachowo wykonany **3.** wykwalifikowany; **com•pe•tent•ly** ['kɒmpɪtəntlɪ] *adv* **1.** kompetentnie **2.** fachowo

com•pe•ti•tion [kɒmpə'tɪʃn] *s* **1.** konkurencja *f*; ***unfair ~*** nieuczciwa konkurencja **2.** rywalizacja *f*, współzawodnictwo *n* **3.** konkurs *m*, zawody *pl*; **com•pet•i•tive** [kəm'petətɪv] *adj* **1.** ambitny **2.** konkurencyjny; ***a ~ advantage*** przewaga konkurencyjna; ***~ spirit*** duch współzawodnictwa, wola walki **3.** *sport*: wyczynowy **4.** konkursowy; **com•pet•i•tive 'edge** *s* przewaga *f* konkurencyjna, konkurencyjność *f*; **com•pet•i•tive•ly** [kəm'petətɪvlɪ] *adv* **1.** ambitnie **2.** konkurencyjnie; **com•pet•i•tive•ness** [kəm'petɪtɪvnɪs] *s* **1.** konkurencyjność *f* **2.** duch *m* współzawodnictwa; **com•pet•i•tor** [kəm'petɪtə] *s* **1.** konkurent *m* **2.** zawodnik *m* **3.** uczestnik *m* **4.** rywal *m*

com•pi•la•tion [kɒmpɪ'leɪʃn] *s* **1.** składanka *f* **2.** kompilacja *f* **3.** wybór *m*; **com•pile** [kəm'paɪl] *v/t* **1.** sporządzać ⟨-dzić⟩, opracowywać ⟨-cować⟩ **2.** kompilować ⟨s-⟩

com•plain [kəm'pleɪn] *v/i* **1.** narzekać, skarżyć ⟨po-⟩ się (***of/about*** na *A*) **2.** składać ⟨złożyć⟩ skargę **3.** reklamować ⟨za-⟩; **com•plaint** [kəm'pleɪnt] *s* **1.** skarga *f*, zażalenie *n*; ***make a ~*** złożyć skargę; ***a ~ book*** książka skarg i zażaleń **2.** reklamacja *f* **3.** MED choroba *f*, dolegliwość *f*

com•ple•ment ['kɒmplɪmənt] **I** *s* **1.** uzupełnienie *n* **2.** dopełnienie *n* **3.** zestaw *m* **II** *v/t* uzupełniać ⟨-nić⟩; **com•ple•men•ta•ry** [kɒmplɪ'mentərɪ] *adj* uzupełniający, dopełniający

com•plete [kəm'pliːt] **I** *adj* **1.** kompletny, całkowity, zupełny **2.** ukończony **II** *v/t* **1.** kończyć ⟨u-⟩ **2.** uzupełniać ⟨-nić⟩, kompletować ⟨s-⟩; **com•plete•ly** [kəm'pliːtlɪ] *adv* całkowicie, zupełnie, kompletnie; **com•plete•ness** [kəm'pliːtnɪs] *s* całość *f*, kompletność *f*; **com•ple•tion** [kəm'pliːʃn] *s* **1.** ukończenie *n*, zakończenie *n*; ***bring s.th. to ~*** ukończyć coś

com•plex ['kɒmpleks] **I** *adj* złożony, skomplikowany **II** *s* kompleks *m*; **com•plex•ion** [kəm'plekʃn] *s* **1.** cera *f*, karnacja *f* **2.** charakter *m*, oblicze *n*

com•plex•i•ty [kəm'pleksɪtɪ] *s* złożoność *f*, zawiłość *f*

com•pli•ance [kəm'plaɪəns] *s* **1.** zgodność *f*; ***in ~ with*** zgodnie z *I* **2.** zastosowanie *n* się, podporządkowanie *n* się **3.** uległość *f*; **com•pli•ant** [kəm'plaɪənt] *adj* uległy

com•pli•cate ['kɒmplɪkeɪt] *v/t* komplikować ⟨s-⟩; **com•pli•cat•ed** ['kɒmplɪkeɪtɪd] *adj* skomplikowany; **com•pli•ca•tion** [kɒmplɪ'keɪʃn] *s* **1.** komplikacja *f* **2.** problem *m* **3.** MED powikłanie *n*, komplikacja *f*

com•pli•ment ['kɒmplɪmənt] **I** *s* **1.** komplement *m*; ***pay s.o. a ~*** powiedzieć komuś komplement; ***fish for ~s*** dopraszać się komplementów **2.** pozdrowienie *n*; ***with the ~s of the season*** (*card*) pozdrowienia z okazji świąt **3.** wyrazy *pl* uznania **II** *v/t* chwalić ⟨po-⟩; **com•pli•men•ta•ry** [kɒmplɪ'mentərɪ] *adj* **1.** pochlebny; ***be ~ about*** wyrażać się pochlebnie o *L*, chwalić *A* **2.** bezpłatny, gratisowy; ***a ~ ticket*** bilet bezpłatny; **'com•pli•ment slip** *s* bilet *m* grzecznościowy

com•ply [kəm'plaɪ] *v/i* stosować ⟨za-⟩ się (***with*** do *G*); ***~ with the law*** zastosować się do przepisów prawa

com•po•nent [kəm'pəʊnənt] *s* **1.** część *f* (składowa), komponent *m* **2.** składnik *m*, element *m*

com•pose [kəm'pəʊz] **I** *v/t* **1.** stanowić, tworzyć; ***be ~ed of*** składać się z *G* **2.** układać ⟨ułożyć⟩ **3.** pisać ⟨na-⟩ **4.** MUS ART komponować ⟨s-⟩ **5.** (*print*) składać ⟨złożyć⟩ **6.** ***~ oneself*** uspokajać się **7.** *thoughts*: zbierać ⟨zebrać⟩, porządkować ⟨u-⟩ **II** *v/i* MUS komponować

com•posed [kəm'pəʊzd] *adj* opanowany, spokojny

com•pos•er [kəm'pəʊzə] *s* kompozytor *m*

com•pos•ite ['kɒmpəzɪt] **I** *adj* **1.** złożony **2.** niejednorodny **3.** kompozytowy **II** *s* kompozyt *m*

com•po•si•tion [kɒmpə'zɪʃn] *s* **1.** skład *m*, struktura *f* **2.** kompozycja *f*, utwór *m* **3.** wypracowanie *n* **4.** budowa *f*, struktura *f* **5.** (*print*) skład *m*

com•pos•i•tor [kəm'pɒzɪtə] *s* zecer *m*

com•post ['kɒmpəst] **I** *s* kompost *m* **II** *v/t* kompostować; **'com•post heap** *s* góra *f* kompostu, składowisko *n* kompostu

com•po•sure [kəm'pəʊʒə] *s* opanowanie *n*, spokój *m*

com•pote ['kɒmpɒt] *s* kompot *m*

com•pound[1] **I** [kəm'paʊnd] *v/t* **1.** potęgować ⟨s-⟩ **2.** łączyć ⟨po-⟩ **3.** ***be ~ed of*** składać się z *G* **II** ['kɒmpaʊnd] *adj* złożony; ***~ interest*** odsetki składane **III** ['kɒmpaʊnd] *s* **1.** złożenie *n*, wyraz *m* złożony **2.** połączenie *n*

com•pound[2] ['kɒmpaʊnd] *s* **1.** teren *m* zamknięty; ***a prison ~*** zakład karny; ***a military ~*** jednostka wojskowa **2.** kompleks *m*

com•pre•hend [kɒmprɪ'hend] *v/t* **1.** pojmować ⟨-jąć⟩, rozumieć ⟨z-⟩

C

2. obejmować ⟨objąć⟩, zawierać; **com•pre•hen•si•ble** [kəmprɪ'hensɪbl] *adj* zrozumiały

com•pre•hen•sion [kɒmprɪ'henʃn] *s* zrozumienie *n*, zdolność *f* pojmowania; ***past ~*** niepojęty; **com•pre•hen•sive** [kɒmprɪ'hensɪv] **I** *adj* **1.** wszechstronny **2.** wyczerpujący **3.** gruntowny **4.** ogólnodostępny, publiczny; ***a ~ school*** państwowa szkoła średnia **II** *s* państwowa szkoła *f* średnia; **com•pre•hen•sive in'sur•ance** *s* ubezpieczenie *n* pełne; **com•pre•hen•sive•ly** [kɒmprɪ'hensɪvlɪ] *adv* **1.** wszechstronnie **2.** wyczerpująco **3.** gruntownie

com•press **I** [kəm'pres] *v/t* **1.** sprężać ⟨-żyć⟩; ***~ed air*** sprężone powietrze **2.** INF kompresować ⟨s-⟩, *infml* pakować ⟨s-⟩ **3.** kondensować ⟨s-⟩, skracać ⟨-rócić⟩ **4.** sprasowywać ⟨-sować⟩, zgniatać ⟨-nieść⟩, ubijać ⟨ubić⟩ **II** ['kɒmpres] *s* kompres *m*, okład *m*; **com•pres•sion** [kəm'preʃn] *s* **1.** sprężanie *n*, kompresja *f* **2.** INF kompresja *f* **3.** skracanie *n*, kondensacja *f*; **com•pres•sor** [kəm'presə] *s* sprężarka *f*, kompresor *m*

com•prise [kəm'praɪz] *v/t* **1.** zawierać, obejmować, składać się z *G* **2.** tworzyć, składać się na *A*

com•pro•mise ['kɒmprəmaɪz] **I** *s* kompromis *m*; ***reach a ~*** osiągnąć kompromis; ***a ~ solution*** rozwiązanie kompromisowe **II** *v/t* **1.** postępować ⟨-tąpić⟩ niezgodnie z *I* **2.** kompromitować ⟨s-⟩ **III** *v/i* iść ⟨pójść⟩ na kompromis

com•pu•ta•tion [kɒmpjuː'teɪʃn] *s* obliczenie *n*, wyliczenie *n*; **com•pu•ta•tion•al** [kɒmpjuː'teɪʃnl] *adj* **1.** obliczeniowy **2.** komputerowy, informatyczny; **com•pute** [kəm'pjuːt] *v/t* obliczać ⟨-czyć⟩, wyliczać ⟨-czyć⟩; **com•put•er** [kəm'pjuːtə] **I** *s* komputer *m* **II** *adj* komputerowy; ***~ tomography*** MED tomografia komputerowa; **com'put•er age** *s* era *f* komputerów

com•put•er-'aid•ed *adj* wspomagany komputerowo; **com•put•er-aid•ed de'sign** *s* projektowanie *n* wspomagane komputerowo; **com•put•er-aid•ed man•u'fac•ture** *s* wytwarzanie *n* wspomagane komputerowo; **com•put•er-aid•ed 'learn•ing** *s* nauka *f* wspomagana komputerowo

com•put•er an•i•'ma•tion *s* animacja *f* komputerowa; **com•put•er-as•'sist•ed** *adj* wspomagany komputerowo; **com•put•er-con•'trolled** *adj* sterowany komputerowo; **com•'put•er game** *s* gra *f* komputerowa; **com•'put•er ex•pert** *s* **1.** informatyk *m* **2.** ekspert *m* od komputerów; **com•put•er 'graph•ics** *s* grafika *f* komputerowa; **com•put•er 'hard•ware** *s* sprzęt *m* komputerowy

com•put•er•i•za•tion [kəmpjuːtəraɪz'eɪʃn] *s* komputeryzacja *f*; **com•put•er•ize** [kəm'pjuːtəraɪz] *v/t* komputeryzować ⟨s-⟩

com'put•er lan•guage *s* język *m* programowania; **com•put•er 'lit•er•a•cy** *s* znajomość *f* obsługi komputera; **com•put•er 'lit•er•ate** *adj* biegły w obsłudze komputera; **com•put•er 'net•work** *s* sieć *f* komputerowa; **com•put•er 'op•er•a•tor** *s* operator *m* komputera; **com•put•er 'print•out** *s* wydruk *m* komputerowy; **com•put•er 'pro•gram** *s* program *m* komputerowy; **com•put•er 'program•mer** *s* programista *m* (komputerowy); **com•put•er 'sci•ence** *s* informatyka *f*; **com•put•er 'sci•en•tist** *s* informatyk *m*; **com•put•er 'sys•tem** *s* system *m* komputerowy; **com•put•er 'ter•min•al** *s* terminal *m* komputerowy; **com•put•er 'vi•rus** *s* wirus *m* komputerowy

com•put•ing [kəm'pjuːtɪŋ] *s* informatyka *f*; ***work in ~*** pracować w branży komputerowej, być informatykiem; ***a ~ system*** system komputerowy, system obliczeniowy; ***~ power*** moc obliczeniowa

com•rade ['kɒmreɪd] *s* towarzysz *m*; **com•rade•ship** ['kɒmreɪdʃɪp] *s* braterstwo *n*

con[1] [kɒn] **I** *s* argument *m* przeciw **II** *adv* przeciw

con[2] [~] **I** *s infml* kant *m*, szwindel *m* **II** *v/t* kantować ⟨o-⟩, oszukiwać ⟨-kać⟩

con•ceal [kən'siːl] *v/t* **1.** ukrywać ⟨-ryć⟩, skrywać ⟨-ryć⟩ (***from*** przed *I*) **2.** przemilczać ⟨-czeć⟩

con•ceal•ment [kən'siːlmənt] *s* ukrywanie *n,* skrywanie *n*
con•ceit [kən'siːt] *s* zarozumiałość *f*; ***full of ~*** zarozumiały **2.** pycha *f*; **con•ceit•ed** [kən'siːtɪd] *adj* zarozumiały, przemądrzały
con•cei•va•ble [kən'siːvəbl] *adj* wyobrażalny; ***the best plan ~*** najlepszy możliwy plan; **con•ceive** [kən'siːv] **I** *v/t* **1.** tworzyć ⟨s-⟩, wymyślać ⟨-lić⟩ **2.** pojmować ⟨-jąć⟩ **3.** *child*: począć **II** *v/i* **1.** zachodzić ⟨zajść⟩ w ciążę **2.** *~* ***of*** wyobrazić sobie *A*
con•cen•trate ['kɒnsəntreɪt] **I** *v/t* **1.** koncentrować ⟨s-⟩, skupiać ⟨-pić⟩ **2.** *CHEM* zagęszczać ⟨-gęścić⟩, stężać **II** *v/i* koncentrować ⟨s-⟩ się **III** *s* koncentrat *m*; **con•cen•trat•ed** ['kɒnsəntreɪtɪd] *s* **1.** skoncentrowany **2.** zagęszczony, stężony; **con•cen•tra•tion** [kɒnsən'treɪʃn] *s* **1.** koncentracja *f,* skupienie *n* **2.** stężenie *n*; **con•cen•'tra•tion camp** *s* obóz *m* koncentracyjny
con•cept ['kɒnsept] *s* pojęcie *n*
con•cep•tion [kən'sepʃn] *s* **1.** *MED* poczęcie *n,* zapłodnienie *n* **2.** początek *m* **3.** koncepcja *f,* pojęcie *n*
con•cep•tu•al [kən'septʃʊəl] *adj* pojęciowy, konceptualny
con•cern [kən'sɜːn] **I** *v/t* **1.** dotyczyć **2.** martwić ⟨z-⟩, niepokoić ⟨za-⟩ **3.** *~* ***oneself with*** zajmować się *I* **II** *s* **1.** sprawa *f,* interes *m*; ***that is no ~ of mine*** to nie mój interes **2.** *ECON* przedsiębiorstwo *n,* firma *f* **3.** niepokój *m,* obawa *f,* troska *f* (***at***/***about***/***over*** z powodu *G*/o *A*) **4.** zainteresowanie *n* **5.** znaczenie *n*; ***a matter of national ~*** sprawa wagi państwowej; **con•cerned** [kən'sɜːnd] *adj* **1.** zaniepokojony **2.** zainteresowany; **con•cern•ing** [kən'sɜːnɪŋ] *prep* **1.** odnośnie *G* **2.** związany z *I*
con•cert ['kɒnsət] *s* **1.** *MUS* koncert *m* **2.** ***in ~ with*** wspólnie z *I*; **con•cert•ed** [kən'sɜːtɪd] *adj* wspólny
'con•cert hall *s* sala *f* koncertowa; **'con•cert•mas•ter** *s Am* koncertmistrz *m*; **con•cert 'pi•an•ist** *s* pianista *m* koncertowy
con•cer•to [kən'tʃɜːtəʊ] *s* koncert *m*
con•ces•sion [kən'seʃn] *s* **1.** ustępstwo *n* **2.** koncesja *f* **3.** zniżka *f,* ulga *f*

con•cil•i•a•tion [kənsɪlɪ'eɪʃn] *s* **1.** pojednanie *n* **2.** mediacja *f* **3.** *JUR* postępowanie *n* rozjemcze; **con•cil•i•a•to•ry** [kən'sɪlɪətərɪ] *adj* pojednawczy
con•cise [kən'saɪs] *adj* zwięzły, krótki
con•cise•ness [kən'saɪsnɪs], ***con•ci•sion*** [kən'sɪʒn] *s* zwięzłość *f*
con•clude [kən'kluːd] **I** *v/i* **1.** wnioskować ⟨wy-⟩, dochodzić ⟨dojść⟩ do wniosku (***that*** że) **2.** kończyć ⟨za-⟩ się **II** *v/t* **1.** kończyć ⟨za-⟩ **2.** *deal*: zawierać ⟨-wrzeć⟩; **con•clud•ing** [kən'kluːdɪŋ] *adj* końcowy; **con•clu•sion** [kən'kluːʒn] *s* **1.** wniosek *m*; ***come to the ~ that*** dojść do wniosku, że; ***draw a ~*** wyciągnąć wniosek; ***jump to ~s, rush to ~s*** wyciągać pochopne wnioski **2.** zakończenie *n*; ***bring s.th. to a ~*** doprowadzić coś do końca; ***in ~*** na zakończenie, na koniec **3.** *deal*: zawarcie *n,* finalizacja *f*; **con•clu•sive** [kən'kluːsɪv] *adj* ostateczny, rozstrzygający
con•coct [kən'kɒkt] *v/t* **1.** przyrządzać ⟨-dzić⟩, *infml* pichcić ⟨u-⟩ **2.** wymyślać ⟨-lić⟩; **con•coc•tion** [kən'kɒkʃn] *s* **1.** mieszanka *f* **2.** mikstura *f*
con•cord ['kɒŋkɔːd] *s* **1.** zgoda *f,* harmonia *f* **2.** ugoda *f*
con•crete **I** ['kɒŋkriːt] *s* beton *m* **II** *adj* **1.** betonowy; ***a ~ jungle*** betonowa dżungla **2.** konkretny **III** *v/t* betonować ⟨wy-⟩, wylewać ⟨-lać⟩ betonem; **'con•crete mix•er** *s* betoniarka *f*
con•cur [kən'kɜː] *v/i* **1.** zgadzać ⟨zgodzić⟩ się (***with*** z *I*) **2.** współuczestniczyć **3.** zbiegać ⟨zbiec⟩ się; **con•cur•rent** [kən'kʌrənt] *adj* **1.** jednoczesny, równoczesny **2.** zbieżny
con•demn [kən'demn] *v/t* **1.** potępiać ⟨-pić⟩ **2.** skazywać ⟨-zać⟩ **3.** przeznaczać ⟨-czyć⟩ do rozbiórki; ***~ed property*** budynek przeznaczony do rozbiórki **4.** uznawać ⟨-nać⟩ za niezdatny do spożycia; **con•dem•na•tion** [kɒndəm'neɪʃn] *s* **1.** potępienie *n* **2.** *JUR* skazanie *n*; **con•'demned cell** *s* cela *f* śmierci
con•den•sa•tion [kɒnden'seɪʃn] *s* **1.** skroplona para *f* **2.** skraplanie *n,* kondensacja *f* **3.** skrót *m*; **con•dense** [kən'dens] **I** *v/i* skraplać ⟨-roplić⟩ się **II** *v/t* **1.** skraplać ⟨-roplić⟩ **2.** kondensować ⟨s-⟩, zagęszczać ⟨-gęścić⟩

C

3. skracać ⟨-rócić⟩; **con•densed 'milk** *s* mleko *n* zagęszczone, mleko *n* skondensowane; **con•dens•er** [kən'densə] *s* **1.** skraplacz *m* **2.** kondensator *m*

con•de•scend [kɒndɪ'send] *v/i* **1.** traktować ⟨po-⟩ protekcjonalnie **2.** *~ to do s.th.* zniżać się do czegoś, raczyć coś zrobić; **con•de•scend•ing** [kɒndɪ'sendɪŋ] *s* protekcjonalny

con•di•tion [kən'dɪʃn] **I** *s* **1.** warunek *m*; ***on ~ that*** pod warunkiem, że; ***on no ~*** pod żadnym warunkiem; ***living ~s*** warunki życia; ***weather ~s*** warunki pogodowe **2.** stan *m*, kondycja *f*; ***the ~ of her health*** jej stan zdrowia **3.** forma *f*; ***out of ~*** bez formy **4.** choroba *f* **II** *v/t* **1.** warunkować ⟨u-⟩ **2.** wpajać ⟨wpoić⟩ **3.** odżywiać ⟨-wić⟩; **con•di•tion•al** [kən'dɪʃnl] **I** *adj* **1.** warunkowy **2.** zależny (***on*** od *G*); ***make s.th. ~ on*** uzależniać coś od *G* **II** *s* ***the ~*** tryb warunkowy; **con•di•tion•al 'clause** *s* zdanie *n* warunkowe; **con•di•tioned res•'ponse, con•di•tioned 're•flex** *s* odruch *m* warunkowy; **con•di•tion•er** [kən'dɪʃnə] *s* **1.** (*hair*) odżywka *f* **2.** płyn *m* do płukania (tkanin); **con•di•tion•ing** [kən'dɪʃnɪŋ] **I** *s* **1.** warunkowanie *n* **2.** pielęgnacja *f* **II** *adj* **1.** z odżywką **2.** pielęgnacyjny

con•do ['kɒndəʊ] *Am infml* mieszkanie *n* własnościowe

con•do•lences [kən'dəʊlənsɪz] *pl* kondolencje *pl*

con•dom ['kɒndəm] *s* prezerwatywa *f*, kondom *m*

con•do•min•i•um [kɒndə'mɪnɪəm] *s* **1.** POLIT kondominium *n* **2.** *Am* mieszkanie *n* własnościowe **3.** *Am* budynek *m* z mieszkaniami własnościowymi

con•done [kən'dəʊn] *v/t* akceptować ⟨za-⟩, zgadzać ⟨zgodzić⟩ się na *A*

con•dor ['kɒndɔː] *s* kondor *m*

con•du•cive [kən'djuːsɪv] *adj* sprzyjający (***to*** *D*)

con•duct **I** [kən'dʌkt] *v/t* **1.** przeprowadzać ⟨-dzić⟩ **2.** MUS dyrygować **3.** oprowadzać ⟨-dzić⟩ **4.** *business*: prowadzić **5.** *electricity*: przewodzić **6.** ***~ oneself*** zachowywać się **II** ['kɒndʌkt] *s* **1.** zachowanie *n* **2.** prowadzenie *n*; **con•duct•ed 'tour** *s* wycieczka *f* z przewodnikiem; **con•duc•tion** [kən'dʌkʃn] *s* przewodnictwo *n*; **con•duc•tor** [kən'dʌktə] *s* **1.** MUS dyrygent *m* **2.** konduktor *m* **3.** PHYS przewodnik *m*

cone [kəʊn] **I** *s* **1.** stożek *m* **2.** szyszka *f* **3.** (*ice-cream*) rożek *m* **4.** (*traffic*) pachołek *m* **II** *v/t* ***~ off*** odgradzać pachołkami

con•fec•tion [kən'fekʃn] *s* **1.** ciastko *n* **2.** wyrób *m* cukierniczy; **con•fec•tion•er** [kən'fekʃənə] *s* cukiernik *m*; **con•'fec•tion•ers' sug•ar** *s Am* cukier puder *m*

con•fed•er•a•cy [kən'fedərəsɪ] *s* **1.** konfederacja *f* **2.** związek *m*; **con•fed•er•ate** [kən'fedərət] **I** *adj* sprzymierzony, konfederacki **II** *s* wspólnik *m*; **con•fed•e•ra•tion** [kənfedə'reɪʃn] *s* konfederacja *f*

con•fer [kən'fɜː] **I** *v/t title*: nadawać ⟨-dać⟩, przyznawać ⟨-nać⟩ **II** *v/i* naradzać ⟨-dzić⟩ się, konferować; **con•fe•rence** ['kɒnfərəns] *s* **1.** konferencja *f* **2.** zjazd *m* **3.** narada *f*; ***be in ~ with*** naradzać się z *I*; **'con•fe•rence room** *s* sala *f* konferencyjna

con•fess [kən'fes] **I** *v/t* **1.** przyznawać ⟨-nać⟩ się do *G* **2.** wyznawać ⟨-nać⟩ **3.** spowiadać ⟨wy-⟩ się z *G* **II** *v/i* **1.** przyznawać ⟨-nać⟩ się (***to*** do *G*); ***she ~ed to having an affair*** przyznała się, że miała romans **2.** przyznawać ⟨-nać⟩ (***that*** że) **3.** JUR przyznawać ⟨-nać⟩ się do winy **4.** spowiadać ⟨wy-⟩ się; **con•fes•sion** [kən'feʃn] *s* **1.** przyznanie *n* się; ***he made a full ~*** przyznał się do wszystkiego, przyznał się do popełnienia wszystkich zarzucanych mu czynów; ***I have a ~ to make*** muszę coś wyznać **2.** REL spowiedź *f*; ***go to ~*** przystąpić do spowiedzi **3.** wyznanie *n*; ***the ~ of faith*** wyznanie wiary; **con•fes•sion•al** [kən'feʃnl] *s* konfesjonał *m*; **con•fes•sor** [kən'fesə] *s* spowiednik *m*

con•fi•dant [kɒnfɪ'dænt] *s* powiernik *m*; **con•fi•dante** [kɒnfɪ'dænt] *s* powierniczka *f*, powiernica *f*; **con•fide** [kən'faɪd] **I** *v/i* zwierzać ⟨-rzyć⟩ się (***in*** *D*) **II** *v/t* powierzać ⟨-rzyć⟩ (***to*** *D*)

con•fi•dence ['kɒnfɪdəns] *s* **1.** zaufanie *n*; ***have ~ in*** mieć zaufanie do

G; ***take s.o. into one's ~*** zwierzać się komuś; ***in ~*** w zaufaniu **2.** pewność *f* siebie **3.** pewność *f* **4.** zwierzenie *n*, sekret *m*; **'con•fi•dence man** *pl -men s Br* oszust *m*; **'con•fi•dence trick** *s* oszustwo *n*; **'con•fi•dence trick•ster** *s* oszust *m*; **con•fi•dent** ['kɒnfɪdənt] *adj* **1.** pewny (***of*** *G*), przekonany (***of*** o *L*) **2.** pewny siebie; **con•fi•den•tial** [kɒnfɪ'denʃl] *adj* **1.** poufny; ***strictly ~*** ściśle tajny **2.** konfidencjonalny; **con•fi•den•tial•ly** [kɒnfɪ'denʃlɪ] *adv* w zaufaniu; **con•fi•dent•ly** ['kɒnfɪdəntlɪ] *adv* **1.** pewnie **2.** śmiało

con•fig•u•ra•tion [kənfɪgjʊ'reɪʃn] *s* konfiguracja *f*; **con•fig•ure** [kən'fɪgə] *v/t* konfigurować ⟨s-⟩

con•fine [kən'faɪn] **I** *v/t* **1.** ograniczać ⟨-czyć⟩; ***~d to bed*** przykuty do łóżka **2.** zamykać ⟨-mknąć⟩ **II** *s* **~s** ograniczenia, ramy; **con•fined** [kən'faɪnd] *adj* **1.** ograniczony **2.** zamknięty; **con•fine•ment** [kən'faɪnmənt] *s* **1.** zamknięcie *n*; ***be held in ~*** być uwięzionym; ***be in solitary ~*** przebywać w (więziennej) izolatce

con•firm [kən'fɜːm] **I** *v/t* **1.** potwierdzać ⟨-dzić⟩ **2.** *REL* konfirmować, bierzmować **II** *v/i* potwierdzać ⟨-dzić⟩; **con•fir•ma•tion** [kɒnfə'meɪʃn] *s* **1.** potwierdzenie *n*; **confirmed** [kən'fɜːmd] *adj* **1.** zatwardziały; ***a ~ bachelor*** zatwardziały stary kawaler **2.** *opinion*: niewzruszony

con•fis•cate ['kɒnfɪskeɪt] *v/t* konfiskować ⟨s-⟩; **con•fis•ca•tion** [kɒnfɪs'keɪʃn] *s* konfiskata *f*, zajęcie *n*

con•flict **I** ['kɒnflɪkt] *s* **1.** konflikt *m*; ***an armed ~*** konflikt zbrojny; ***come into ~ with*** wejść w konflikt z *I* **2.** sprzeczność *f*; ***~ of interests*** konflikt interesów **II** [kən'flɪkt] *v/i* **1.** być sprzecznym, kolidować (***with*** z *I*) **2.** kolidować ze sobą; **con•flict•ing** [kən'flɪktɪŋ] *adj* sprzeczny

con•form [kən'fɔːm] *v/i* **1.** dostosowywać ⟨-sować⟩ się (***to*** do *G*) **2.** spełniać ⟨-nić⟩ wymagania (***to/with*** *G*) **3.** być zgodnym (***to/with*** z *I*) **4.** pasować (***to*** do *G*); **con•form•ist** [kən'fɔːmɪst] **I** *s* konformista *m* **II** *adj* konformistyczny; **con•form•i•ty** [kən'fɔːmətɪ] *s* **1.** zgodność *f*; ***be in ~ with*** **a)** zgadzać się z *I* **b)** spełniać wymagania *G*; ***in ~ with*** w zgodzie z *I* **2.** konformizm *m*

con•front [kən'frʌnt] *v/t* **1.** stawać ⟨stanąć⟩ przed *I*; ***be ~ed with danger*** stanąć w obliczu niebezpieczeństwa **2.** stawać ⟨stanąć⟩ twarzą w twarz z *I* **3.** konfrontować ⟨s-⟩ (***with*** z *I*); **con•fron•ta•tion** [kɒnfrən'teɪʃn] *s* **1.** starcie *n* **2.** konfrontacja *f*; **con•front•a•tion•al** [kɒnfrən'teɪʃnl] *adj* konfrontacyjny

con•fuse [kən'fjuːz] *v/t* **1.** mylić ⟨po-⟩ **2.** zbijać ⟨zbić⟩ z tropu, dezorientować ⟨z-⟩ **3.** gmatwać ⟨za-⟩; **con•fused** [kən'fjuːzd] *adj* **1.** zdezorientowany; ***I'm ~*** nie rozumiem, o co chodzi; ***he was totally ~*** zupełnie nie rozumiał, o co chodzi, *infml* miał zupełny mętlik w głowie **2.** zmieszany, speszony **3.** bezładny, chaotyczny; **con•fus•ing** [kən'fjuːzɪŋ] *adj* **1.** dezorientujący **2.** zawiły **3.** zagmatwany; **con•fu•sion** [kən'fjuːʒn] *s* **1.** zamieszanie *n*, zamęt *m*, chaos *m*; ***cause ~*** wywołać zamieszanie **2.** zmieszanie *n*, konsternacja *f* **3.** mylenie *n*

con•gen•ial [kən'dʒiːnɪəl] *adj* **1.** przyjemny **2.** sympatyczny, miły **2.** *form* sprzyjający, odpowiedni

con•gest•ed [kən'dʒestɪd] *adj* **1.** zatłoczony; ***~ streets*** zatłoczone ulice **2.** przeludniony; **con•ges•tion** [kən'dʒestʃn] *s* **1.** zator *m*; ***traffic ~*** korki **2.** przeludnienie *n*

con•glom•er•ate [kən'glɒmərət] **I** *s* konglomerat *m* **II** *adj* **1.** zbity **2.** zlepiony; **con•glom•er•a•tion** [kənglɒmə'reɪʃn] *s* **1.** konglomerat *m* **2.** konglomeracja *f*

con•grats [kən'græts] *pl infml* gratulacje *pl*

con•grat•u•late [kən'grætʃuleɪt] *v/t* gratulować ⟨po-⟩

con•grat•u•la•tions [kəngrætʃʊ'leɪʃnz] *pl* gratulacje *pl*

con•grat•u•la•to•ry [kəngrætʃʊ'leɪtərɪ] *adj* gratulacyjny

con•gre•gate ['kɒŋgrɪgeɪt] *v/i* zbierać ⟨zebrać⟩ się, gromadzić ⟨z-⟩ się; **con•gre•ga•tion** [kɒŋgrɪ'geɪʃn] *s* **1.** zgromadzenie *n* **2.** parafianie *pl* **3.** kongregacja *f*

con•gress ['kɒŋgres] *s* **1.** kongres *m* **2.** zjazd *m*; **Con•gres•sion•al** [kən-

C

'greʃnl] *adj* **1.** *elections, candidate*: do Kongresu **2.** *decision, committee*: Kongresu; **Con•gress•man** ['kɒŋgresmən] *pl -men s* kongresman *m*, członek *m* Kongresu; **Con•gress•wo•man** ['kɒŋgreswʊmən] *pl -men s* członkini *f* Kongresu

con•i•cal ['kɒnɪkl] *adj* **1.** stożkowy **2.** stożkowaty

con•junc•tion [kən'dʒʌŋkʃn] *s* **1.** *form* połączenie; ***in ~ with*** wraz z *I*; ***work in ~ with*** *I* współpracować z *I* **2.** spójnik *m*

con•jure ['kʌndʒə] **I** *v/t* **1.** wyczarowywać ⟨-rować⟩; ***~ s.th. away*** spowodować zniknięcie czegoś **2.** przywoływać ⟨-łać⟩ **II** *v/i* robić sztuczki (magiczne); **con•jure up** *v/t* **1.** przywoływać ⟨-łać⟩ **2.** wyczarowywać ⟨-rować⟩ **3.** *spirits*: wywoływać ⟨-łać⟩; **con•jur•er**, ***con•jur•or*** ['kʌndʒərə] *s* **1.** sztukmistrz *m* **2.** prestidigitator *m* **3.** iluzjonista *m*; **'con•jur•ing trick** *s* sztuczka *f* magiczna

con man ['kɒnmæn] *pl -men s infml* kanciarz *m*, oszust *m*

con•nect [kə'nekt] **I** *v/t* **1.** łączyć ⟨po-⟩ **2.** podłączać ⟨-czyć⟩, przyłączać ⟨-czyć⟩ **II** *v/i* **1.** łączyć ⟨po-⟩ się **2.** przylegać ⟨-lgnąć⟩ **3.** (*bus, train*) zapewniać ⟨-nić⟩ połączenie; **con•nect•ed** [kə'nektɪd] *adj* **1.** połączony **2.** podłączony **3.** związany, powiązany (***with*** z *I*) **4.** pokrewny **5.** spokrewniony; ***~ by marriage*** spowinowacony **6.** ***be well ~*** (*person*) być ustosunkowanym, mieć koneksje; **con•nect•ing** [kə'nektɪŋ] *adj* **1.** łączący **2.** *room*: przejściowy; **con•nect•ing 'door** *s* drzwi *pl* łączące; **con•nect•ing 'flight** *s* połączenie *n*; **con•nec•tion** [kə'nekʃn] *s* **1.** związek *m*; ***in ~ with*** w związku z *I*; ***in this ~*** w związku z tym **2.** połączenie *n* **3.** podłączenie *n* **4.** ***~s*** znajomości, koneksje; **con•nec•tive tissue** [kənektɪv'tɪʃuː] *s* ANAT tkanka *f* łączna; **con•nec•tor** [kə'nektə] *s* TECH **1.** wtyczka *f* **2.** złącze *n*; **con•'nex•ion** → ***connection***

con•nois•seur [kɒnə'sɜː] *s* **1.** koneser *m* **2.** znawca *m*

con•no•ta•tion [kɒnəʊ'teɪʃn] *s* konotacja *f*; **con•note** [kə'nəʊt] *v/t* **1.** przywodzić na myśl, kojarzyć się z *I* **2.** konotować

con•quer ['kɒŋkə] *v/t* **1.** podbijać ⟨-bić⟩ **2.** pokonywać ⟨-nać⟩ **3.** zdobywać ⟨-być⟩; **con•quer•or** ['kɒŋkərə] *s* **1.** zdobywca *m* **2.** zwycięzca *m*

con•quest ['kɒŋkwest] *s* **1.** podbój *m* **2.** pokonanie *n* **3.** zdobycie *n* **4.** zdobycz *f*

con•science ['kɒnʃəns] *s* **1.** sumienie *n*; ***a clear*** (***guilty***) ***~*** czyste (nieczyste) sumienie; ***have s.th on one's ~*** mieć coś na sumieniu; ***for ~'s sake*** dla spokoju sumienia **2.** przekonania *pl* **3.** wyrzuty *pl* sumienia

con•sci•en•tious [kɒnʃɪ'enʃəs] *adj* **1.** sumienny **2.** skrupulatny; **con•sci•en•tious•ness** [kɒnʃɪ'enʃəsnəs] *s* **1.** sumienność *f* **2.** skrupulatność *f*

con•scious ['kɒnʃəs] *adj* **1.** świadomy (***of*** *G*); ***be fashion ~*** podążać za modą, modnie się ubierać **2.** przytomny; **con•scious•ly** ['kɒnʃəslɪ] *adv* **1.** świadomie **2.** umyślnie; **con•scious•ness** ['kɒnʃəsnɪs] *s* **1.** świadomość *f* **2.** MED przytomność *f*; ***lose*** (***regain***) ***~*** stracić (odzyskać) przytomność

con•script I ['kɒnskrɪpt] *s* **1.** poborowy *m* **2.** powołany *m* **II** [kən'skrɪpt] *v/t* **1.** powoływać ⟨-łać⟩ do wojska **2.** werbować ⟨z-⟩; **con•scrip•tion** [kən'skrɪpʃn] *s* pobór *m*, werbunek *m* (***into*** do *G*)

con•se•crate ['kɒnsɪkreɪt] *v/t* **1.** REL poświęcać ⟨-cić⟩, konsekrować **2.** *fig* poświęcać ⟨-cić⟩ (***to*** *D*); **con•se•cra•tion** [kɒnsɪ'kreɪʃn] *s* poświęcenie *n*, konsekracja *f*

con•sec•u•tive [kən'sekjʊtɪv] *s* **1.** kolejny; ***for two ~ days*** przez dwa kolejne dni **2.** następujący po sobie; **con•sec•u•tive•ly** [kən'sekjʊtɪvlɪ] *adv* kolejno

con•sen•sus [kən'sensəs] *s* konsensus *m*; ***a ~ of opinion*** zgodne przekonanie, konsensus

con•sent [kən'sent] **I** *v/i* zgadzać ⟨zgodzić⟩ się **II** *s* **1.** zgoda *f*; ***with the ~ of*** za zgodą *G*; ***by common ~*** jednomyślnie **2.** pozwolenie *n* **3.** aprobata *f*

con•se•quence ['kɒnsɪkwəns] *s* **1.** skutek *m*, konsekwencja *f*, następstwo *n*; ***in ~*** w konsekwencji; ***as a ~ of*** wskutek *G*, w następstwie *G*; ***take the ~s, suffer the ~s*** ponieść konsekwencje **2.** znaczenie *n*, waga *f*; ***of ~*** ważny; ***of no ~*** nieważny; ***a person of ~*** ważna osobistość; **con•se•quent** ['kɒnsɪkwənt] *adj* wynikły, spowodowany przez to; **con•se•quent•ly** ['kɒnsɪkwəntlɪ] *adv* wskutek tego, w rezultacie

con•ser•va•tion [kənsə'veɪʃn] *s* **1.** ochrona *f* **2.** konserwacja *f* **3.** zachowanie *n*; **con•ser•'va•tion a•re•a** *s* zespół *m* zabytkowy objęty ochroną; **con•ser•va•tion•ist** [kənsər'veɪʃnɪst] *s* działacz *m* (ruchu) na rzecz ochrony przyrody, ekolog *m*

con•ser•va•tive [kən'sɜːvətɪv] **I** *s* konserwatysta *m* **II** *adj* konserwatywny

con•ser•va•toire [kən'sɜːvətwɑː] *s Br* konserwatorium *n*

con•ser•va•to•ry [kən'sɜːvətərɪ] *s* **1.** *Br* oranżeria *f* **2.** *Am* konserwatorium *m*

con•serve **I** ['kənsɜːv] *v/t* **1.** *energy*: oszczędzać ⟨zaoszczędzić⟩ **2.** chronić **3.** konserwować **4.** zachowywać ⟨-chować⟩ **II** [kɒn'sɜːv] *s* konfitura *f*

con•sid•er [kən'sɪdər] **I** *v/t* **1.** rozważać ⟨-żyć⟩, zastanawiać ⟨-nowić⟩ się nad *I* **2.** brać ⟨wziąć⟩ pod uwagę; ***all things ~ed*** w sumie **3.** uważać za *A*, uznawać za *A*; ***he is ~ed (to be) a genius*** uważa się go za geniusza **II** *v/i* zastanawiać ⟨-nowić⟩ się

con•sid•e•ra•ble [kən'sɪdrəbl] *adj* znaczny; **con•sid•e•ra•bly** [kən'sɪdrəblɪ] *adv* znacznie

con•sid•er•ate [kən'sɪdərət] *adj* **1.** liczący się z innymi; ***it was ~ of her to wait*** to miło z jej strony, że poczekała **2.** taktowny (***to/towards*** wobec *G*) **3.** ***be ~ of s.th.*** brać coś pod uwagę; **con•sid•er•ate•ly** [kən'sɪdərətlɪ] *adv* **1.** uprzejmie **2.** taktownie; **con•sid•e•ra•tion** [kənsɪdə'reɪʃn] *s* **1.** namysł *m*, rozwaga *f*; ***give s.th. ~*** rozważyć coś, przemyśleć coś; ***take s.th. into ~*** wziąć coś pod uwagę; ***leave s.th. out of ~*** nie brać czegoś pod uwagę **2.** wzgląd *m*; ***in ~ of*** zważywszy na *A*, przez wzgląd na *A*; ***have no ~ for*** nie liczyć się z *I* **3.** czynnik *m* **4.** wynagrodzenie *n*, opłata *f*; **con•sid•er•ing** [kən'sɪdərɪŋ] **I** *prep* zważywszy na *A* **II** *adv* mimo wszystko

con•sist [kən'sɪst] *v/i* **1.** ***~ of*** składać się z *G* **2.** ***~ in*** polegać na *L*

con•sis•ten•cy [kən'sɪstənsɪ] *s* **1.** konsekwencja *f*; ***play with ~*** utrzymywać równy poziom gry **2.** spójność *f* **3.** konsystencja *f* **4.** zgodność *f*; **con•sis•tent** [kən'sɪstənt] *adj* **1.** stały; ***his game is ~*** SPORT gra równo, utrzymuje równy poziom gry **2.** konsekwentny **3.** uporczywy **4.** spójny, logiczny **5.** zgodny (***with*** z *I*); **con•sis•tent•ly** [kən'sɪstəntlɪ] *adv* **1.** konsekwentnie **2.** równo **3.** spójnie, logicznie

con•so•la•tion [kɒnsə'leɪʃn] *s* pociecha *f*, pocieszenie *n*; ***a ~ goal*** honorowa bramka; **con•so•'la•tion prize** *s* nagroda *f* pocieszenia; **con•sol•a•to•ry** [kən'sɒlətərɪ] *adj* pocieszający

con•sole[1] ['kənsəʊl] *v/t* pocieszać ⟨-szyć⟩

con•sole[2] [kɒn'səʊl] *s* **1.** konsola *f* **2.** konsoleta *f* **3.** pulpit *m* sterowniczy

con•sol•i•date [kən'sɒlɪdeɪt] **I** *v/t* **1.** umacniać ⟨umocnić⟩ **2.** konsolidować ⟨s-⟩ **3.** łączyć ⟨po-⟩ **II** *v/i* **1.** umacniać ⟨umocnić⟩ się **2.** łączyć ⟨po-⟩ się; **con•sol•id•a•tion** [kənsɒlɪ'deɪʃn] *s* **1.** umocnienie *n* **2.** konsolidacja *f* **3.** połączenie *n*

con•so•nant ['kɒnsənənt] **I** *s* spółgłoska *f* **II** *adj* zgodny (***with*** z *I*)

con•sor•ti•um [kən'sɔːtɪəm] *s* FIN konsorcjum *m*

con•spic•u•ous [kən'spɪkjʊəs] *adj* **1.** widoczny **2.** zwracający uwagę, rzucający się w oczy; ***be ~*** zwracać uwagę, rzucać się w oczy; ***he was ~ by his absence*** jego nieobecność rzucała się w oczy **3.** wyjątkowy

con•spi•ra•cy [kən'spɪrəsɪ] *s* spisek *m*; **con•spi•ra•tor** [kən'spɪrətə] *s* konspirator *m*, spiskowiec *m*; **con•spire** [kən'spaɪə] *v/i* **1.** spiskować **2.** sprzysięgać ⟨-siąc⟩ się

con•sta•ble ['kʌnstəbl] *s Br* posterunkowy *m*; **con•stab•u•lar•y** [kən'stæbjʊlərɪ] *s Br* policja *f*

con•stan•cy ['kɒnstənsɪ] *s* stałość *f*; **con•stant** ['kɒnstənt] **I** *adj* **1.** stały **2.** ciągły, nieustanny **II** *s* stała *f*; **con-**

C

C

stant•ly ['kɒnstəntlɪ] *adv* ciągle, stale, nieustannie
con•stel•la•tion [kɒnstə'leɪʃn] *s* konstelacja *f*, gwiazdozbiór *m*
con•ster•na•tion [kɒnstə'neɪʃn] *s* konsternacja *f*; ***in ~*** skonsternowany; ***to my ~*** ku memu zakłopotaniu
con•sti•tute ['kɒnstɪtjuːt] *v/t* **1.** stanowić **2.** tworzyć ⟨u-⟩, powoływać ⟨-łać⟩; **con•sti•tu•tion** [kənstɪ'tjuːʃn] *s* **1.** konstytucja *f* **2.** stan *m* zdrowia; ***have a healthy ~*** cieszyć się dobrym zdrowiem; ***have a weak ~*** być słabego zdrowia **3.** budowa *f* **4.** utworzenie *n*, powołanie *n*; **con•sti•tu•tion•al** [kɒnstɪ'tuːʃənl] **I** *adj* **1.** konstytucyjny; ***a ~ amendment*** poprawka do konstytucji **2.** zgodny z konstytucją **II** *s* przechadzka *f*; **con•sti•tu•tion•al 'mon•arch•y** *s* monarchia *f* konstytucyjna
con•strain [kən'streɪn] *v/t* **1.** zmuszać ⟨-sić⟩ **2.** ograniczać ⟨-czyć⟩ **3.** hamować ⟨za-⟩; **con•straint** [kən'streɪnt] *s* **1.** ograniczenie *n* **2.** wymóg *m* **3.** powściągliwość *f*; ***without ~*** **a)** bez skrępowania **b)** bez ogródek
con•struct **I** [kən'strʌkt] *v/t* **1.** budować ⟨z-⟩ **2.** konstruować ⟨s-⟩ **II** [kɒstrʌkt] *s* **1.** konstrukcja *f* **2.** konstrukt *m*; **con•struc•tion** [kən'strʌkʃn] *s* **1.** budowa *f*; ***under ~*** w budowie **2.** konstrukcja *f*; ***a steel ~*** konstrukcja stalowa **3.** struktura *f*; **con•struc•tion•al** [kən'strʌkʃnl] *adj* **1.** budowlany **2.** konstrukcyjny
con'struc•tion in•dus•try *s* budownictwo *n*, branża *f* budowlana; **con•'struc•tion site** *s* plac *m* budowy; **con•'struc•tion work•er** *s* robotnik *m* budowlany
con•struc•tive [kən'strʌktɪv] *adj* konstruktywny
con•struc•tor [kən'strʌktə] *s* konstruktor *m*
con•sul ['kɒnsl] *s* konsul *m*; **con•sul•ar** ['kɒnsjʊlə] *adj* konsularny; **con•su•late** ['kɒnsjʊlət] *s* konsulat *m*; **con•su•late 'gen•er•al** *s* konsulat *m* generalny; **con•sul 'gen•er•al** *s* konsul *m* generalny
con•sult [kən'sʌlt] **I** *v/t* **1.** radzić ⟨po-⟩ się; ***~ a doctor*** zasięgnąć rady lekarza; ***~ a dictionary*** zajrzeć do słownika, sprawdzić w słowniku; ***~ one's watch*** spojrzeć na zegarek, sprawdzić, która godzina **2.** konsultować ⟨s-⟩ się z *I* **II** *v/i* konsultować ⟨s-⟩ się; **con•sul•tan•cy** [kən'sʌltənsɪ] *s* **1.** doradztwo *n*, konsulting *m* **2.** firma *f* konsultingowa; **con•sul•tant** [kən'sʌltənt] *s* **1.** doradca *m*, konsultant *m* **2.** *Br* lekarz *m* specjalista; **con•sul•ta•tion** [kənsəl'teɪʃn] *s* **1.** konsultacja *f*; ***on ~ with*** po konsultacji z *I*; ***~ hours*** konsultacje, godziny przyjęć **2.** narada *f* **3.** porada *f*; **con•sult•ing en•gi'neer** [kən'sʌltɪŋ] *s* doradca *m* techniczny; **con•'sult•ing room** *s* MED gabinet *m* lekarski
con•sume [kən'sjuːm] *v/t* **1.** pochłaniać ⟨-łonąć⟩, zużywać ⟨-żyć⟩ **2.** zjadać ⟨zjeść⟩ **3.** wypijać ⟨-pić⟩ **4.** trawić ⟨s-⟩; ***the house was ~d by fire*** budynek strawił ogień **5.** (*envy*) zżerać
con•sum•er [kən'suːmə] *s* **1.** konsument *m* **2.** odbiorca *m*; **con•sum•er ad'vice cen•tre** *s* urząd *m* ochrony konsumenta; **con•sum•er 'con•fi•dence index** *s*: ***~ index*** wskaźnik optymizmu konsumentów; **con•'sum•er goods** *pl* towary *pl* konsumpcyjne; **con•sum•er 'price in•dex** *s* wskaźnik *m* cen towarów konsumpcyjnych; **con•sum•er pro•'tec•tion** *s* ochrona *f* konsumenta; **con•sum•er re•search** *s* badania *pl* zachowań konsumentów, badania *pl* rynku; **con•sum•er so•'ci•e•ty** *s* społeczeństwo *n* konsumpcyjne
con•sump•tion [kən'sʌmpʃn] *s* **1.** zużycie *n* **2.** spożycie *n*, konsumpcja *f*
con•tact ['kɒntækt] **I** *s* **1.** kontakt *m*; ***business ~s*** kontakty służbowe; ***make ~ with*** kontaktować się z *I*; ***make ~s*** nawiązywać kontakty **2.** styczność *f*, kontakt *m*; ***come into ~ with*** dotykać *G* **3.** zetknięcie się *n* **4.** łączność *f* **II** *v/t* kontaktować ⟨s-⟩ się (***with*** z *I*) **III** *adj* kontaktowy; ***a ~ man*** kontakt; **'con•tact lens** *s* soczewka *f* kontaktowa; ***~es*** szkła kontaktowe; **'con•tact num•ber** *s* numer *m* kontaktowy
con•ta•gion [kən'teɪdʒən] *s* **1.** MED zarażenie *n* **2.** *fig* zaraza *f*; **con•ta•gious** [kən'teɪdʒəs] *adj* MED zaraźliwy

con•tain [kən'teɪn] *v/t* **1.** zawierać ⟨-wrzeć⟩ **2.** powstrzymywać ⟨-mać⟩; ~ ***oneself*** opanować się

con•tain•er [kən'teɪnə] *s* **1.** pojemnik *m* **2.** kontener *m*; **con•tain•er•ize** [kən'teɪnəraIz] *v/t* ładować ⟨za-⟩ w kontenery; **con•'tain•er ship** *s* kontenerowiec *m*, statek *m* kontenerowy

con•tam•i•nate [kən'tæmɪneɪt] *v/t* **1.** zanieczyszczać ⟨-czyścić⟩, skażać ⟨skazić⟩ **2.** zatruwać ⟨-ruć⟩; **contaminated** [kən'tæmɪneɪtɪd] *adj* skażony; **con•tam•i•na•tion** [kəntæmɪ'neɪʃn] *s* **1.** skażenie *n*, zanieczyszczenie *n* **2.** zatrucie *n*

con•tem•plate ['kɒntəmpleɪt] **I** *v/t* **1.** rozważać ⟨-żyć⟩, zastanawiać ⟨-nowić⟩ się nad *I*; ~ ***suicide*** myśleć o samobójstwie **2.** kontemplować **3.** przyglądać ⟨przyjrzeć⟩ się **II** *v/i* **1.** kontemplować **2.** rozmyślać; **contem•pla•tion** [kəntəm'pleɪʃn] *s* **1.** kontemplacja *f* **2.** rozmyślania *pl*; **con•tem•pla•tive** [kən'templətɪv] *adj* refleksyjny

con•tem•po•ra•ry [kən'tempərerɪ] **I** *adj* **1.** współczesny **2.** nowoczesny **3.** z tego (samego) okresu **4.** w tym samym wieku **II** *s* **1.** współczesny *m* **2.** rówieśnik *m*

con•tempt [kən'tempt] *s* **1.** pogarda *f*; ***feel ~ for s.o., hold s.o. in ~*** gardzić kimś; ***feel nothing but ~ for s.o.*** żywić dla kogoś tylko pogardę; ***beneath ~*** zasługujący na najgłębszą pogardę, poniżej wszelkiej krytyki **2.** lekceważenie *n*; ~ ***of court*** **a)** lekceważenie sądu **b)** obraza sądu; **con•temp•ti•ble** [kən'temptəbl] *adj* godny pogardy; **con•temp•tu•ous** [kən'temptʃʊəs] *adj* **1.** pogardliwy **2.** pełen pogardy; ***be ~ of*** gardzić *I*

con•tend [kən'tend] **I** *v/i* **1.** walczyć (***for*** o *A*) **2.** rywalizować, ubiegać się (***for*** o *A*) **II** *v/t* twierdzić, utrzymywać; **con•tend•er** [kən'tendə] *s* **1.** zawodnik *m* **2.** kandydat *m* **3.** pretendent *m*

con•tent[1] ['kɒntent] *s* **1.** treść *f*; ***a table of ~s*** spis treści; ***~s page*** strona ze spisem treści **2.** ***~s*** zawartość; ***gold ~s*** zawartość złota **3.** *course*: program *m*

con•tent[2] [kən'tent] **I** *adj* zadowolony, rad; ***have to be ~ with*** musieć się zadowolić *I* **II** *v/t* zadowalać ⟨-wolić⟩; ***~ oneself with*** zadowolić się *I* **III** *s* zadowolenie *n*

con•tent•ed [kən'tentɪd] *adj* zadowolony

con•tent•ment [kən'tentmənt] *s* zadowolenie *n*

con•test[1] [kən'test] *v/t* **1.** kwestionować ⟨za-⟩ **2.** *law*: podważać ⟨-żyć⟩

con•test[2] ['kɒntest] **I** *s* **1.** konkurs *m* **2.** zawody *pl* **II** *v/t* rywalizować; **contes•tant** [kən'testənt] *s* **1.** zawodnik *m* **2.** rywal *m*, przeciwnik *m*

con•text ['kɒntekst] *s* kontekst *m*; ***in this ~*** w tym kontekście; ***out of ~*** bez kontekstu

con•ti•nent ['kɒntɪnənt] *s* kontynent *m*, stały ląd *m*; ***the*** **2** kontynent europejski; **con•ti•nen•tal** [kɒntɪ'nentl] **I** *adj* kontynentalny **II** *s* Europejczyk *m* z kontynentu; **con•ti•nen•tal 'break•fast** *s* śniadanie *n* kontynentalne

con•tin•gent [kən'tɪndʒənt] **I** *adj* **1.** zależny (***on/upon*** od *G*), uwarunkowany (***on/upon*** *I*) **2.** możliwy, ewentualny **II** *s* **1.** kontyngent *m* **2.** grupa *f*

con•tin•u•al [kən'tɪnjʊəl] *adj* ciągły, nieustanny; **con•tin•u•al•ly** [kən'tɪnjʊəlɪ] *adv* ciągle, nieustannie; **contin•u•ance** [kən'tɪnjʊəns] *form* → ***continuation***; **con•tin•u•a•tion** [kəntɪnjʊ'eɪʃn] *s* **1.** kontynuacja *f* **2.** ciąg *m* dalszy **3.** ciągłość *f*; **con•tinue** [kən'tɪnjuː] **I** *v/i* **1.** trwać; ***~ in office*** pozostać na stanowisku **2.** utrzymywać ⟨-mać⟩ się **3.** iść ⟨pójść⟩ dalej **4.** jechać ⟨po-⟩ dalej **5.** mówić dalej, ciągnąć **II** *v/t* **1.** kontynuować; ***to be ~ed*** ciąg dalszy nastąpi **2.** podtrzymywać ⟨-mać⟩, kultywować; **con•ti•nu•i•ty** [kɒntɪ'njuːətɪ] *s* ciągłość *f*; **con•tin•u•ous** [kən'tɪnjʊəs] *adj* **1.** ciągły, ustawiczny; ***present ~*** czas teraźniejszy ciągły **2.** stały **3.** nieprzemijający; **con•tin•u•ous•ly** [kən'tɪnjʊəslɪ] *adv* **1.** ciągle, bez przerwy **2.** stale

con•tort [kən'tɔːt] **I** *v/t* **1.** wykrzywiać ⟨-wić⟩; ***~ed with pain*** wykrzywiony bólem **2.** wykręcać ⟨-cić⟩ **3.** wypaczać ⟨-czyć⟩ **4.** przeinaczać ⟨-czyć⟩ **II** *v/i*

C

C

(*face*) wykrzywiać ⟨-wić⟩ się; **con•tor•tion** [kən'tɔːʃn] *s* **1.** grymas *m* **2.** wygibas *m*; **con•tor•tion•ist** [kən'tɔːʃnɪst] *s* człowiek-guma *m*

con•tour ['kɒntʊə] *s* kontur *m,* zarys *m*

con•tra•band ['kɒntrəbænd] *s* kontrabanda *f*

con•tra•cep•tion [kɒntrə'sepʃn] *s* antykoncepcja *f,* zapobieganie *n* ciąży; **con•tra•cep•tive** [kɒntrə'septɪv] **I** *s* środek *m* antykoncepcyjny **II** *adj* antykoncepcyjny

con•tract ['kɒntrækt] **I** *s* kontrakt *m,* umowa *f*; ***a ~ of employment*** umowa o pracę; ***a ~ of sale*** umowa sprzedaży; ***enter into a ~, make a ~*** zawrzeć umowę; ***be under ~ to*** pracować dla *G*; ***a ~ killer*** płatny morderca **II** [kən'trækt] *v/t* **1.** zawierać ⟨-wrzeć⟩ **2.** zlecać ⟨-cić⟩ **3.** zatrudniać ⟨-nić⟩ **III** [kən'trækt] *v/i* zawierać ⟨-wrzeć⟩ umowę

con•trac•tor [kən'træktə] *s* **1.** wykonawca *m* **2.** dostawca *m* **3.** przedsiębiorca *m*; ***a building ~*** przedsiębiorca budowlany **4.** kontrahent *m*; **con•trac•tu•al** [kən'træktʊəl] *adj* **1.** kontraktowy, umowny **2.** wynikający z umowy

con•tra•dict [kɒntrə'dɪkt] *v/t* przeczyć, zaprzeczać ⟨-czyć⟩; ***~ each other*** przeczyć sobie wzajemnie; **con•tra•dic•tion** [kɒntrə'dɪkʃn] *s* **1.** sprzeczność *f*; ***be in ~ to*** stać w sprzeczności z *I*; ***~ in terms*** sprzeczność sama w sobie **2.** zaprzeczenie *n*; **con•tra•dic•to•ry** [kɒntrə'dɪktərɪ] *adj* sprzeczny

con•tral•to [kən'træltəʊ] *pl -tos* [~əʊz] *s* MUS kontralt *m*

con•trar•y ['kɒntrərɪ] **I** *prep* ***~ to*** wbrew *D*; ***~ to expectations*** wbrew oczekiwaniom **II** *s* ***the ~*** przeciwieństwo *n*; ***on the ~, to the ~*** (wręcz) przeciwnie; ***be the ~ to*** być przeciwieństwem *G*; ***a proof to the ~*** dowód przeciwny **III** *adj* **1.** przeciwny **2.** sprzeczny **3.** przeciwstawny

con•trast **I** ['kɒntræst] *s* kontrast *m,* przeciwieństwo *n*; ***~ control*** regulacja kontrastu; ***form a ~ to*** stanowić kontrast z *I*; ***by ~ with*** w porównaniu z *I*; ***in ~ to*** **a)** w przeciwieństwie do *G* **b)** w porównaniu z *I* **II** [kan'traːst] *v/t* **1.** zestawiać ⟨-wić⟩ **2.** porównywać ⟨-nać⟩ **III** [kən'træst] *v/i* **1.** różnić się **2.** kontrastować; **con•trast•ing** [kən'traːstɪŋ] *adj* kontrastowy, kontrastujący

con•trib•ute [kən'trɪbjuːt] **I** *v/t* **1.** wnosić ⟨wnieść⟩ **2.** wpłacać ⟨-cić⟩ **3.** ofiarowywać ⟨-rować⟩ **4.** *article*: pisać ⟨na-⟩ **II** *v/i* **1.** przyczyniać ⟨-nić⟩ się (***to*** do *G*) **2.** wpłacać ⟨-cić⟩ pieniądze (***to*** na *A*); ***~ to the expenses*** brać udział w kosztach **3.** ofiarowywać ⟨-rować⟩ pieniądze (***to*** na *A*), wspierać ⟨wesprzeć⟩ finansowo (***to*** *A*) **4.** współpracować (***to*** z *I*); **con•tri•bu•tion** [kɒntrɪ'bjuːʃn] *s* **1.** wkład *m* **2.** udział *m*; ***~ to the expenses*** udział w kosztach **3.** składka *f* **4.** wpłata *f* **5.** datek *m* **6.** artykuł *m*; **con•trib•u•tor** [kən'trɪbjʊtə] *s* **1.** uczestnik *m* **2.** ofiarodawca *m* **3.** współpracownik *m* **4.** ***be a ~ to*** przyczyniać się do *G*

con•trol [kən'trəʊl] **I** *v/t* **1.** kontrolować; ***~ a parliament*** mieć większość w parlamencie; ***~ a company*** mieć udział większościowy w spółce **2.** kierować **3.** rządzić; ***~ a country*** sprawować rządy w państwie **4.** opanowywać ⟨-nować⟩; ***~ oneself*** opanować się **5.** zwalczać ⟨-czyć⟩ **6.** ograniczać ⟨-czyć⟩ **7.** *market, prices*: regulować, kontrolować **8.** TECH sterować **II** *s* **1.** kontrola *f*; ***bring s.th. under ~*** opanować coś, zapanować nad czymś; ***get out of ~*** wymknąć się spod kontroli; ***lose ~ of*** stracić panowanie nad *I* **2.** władza *f,* panowanie *n*; ***in ~*** u władzy; ***under s.o.'s ~*** w czyichś rękach **3.** nadzór *m,* kontrola *f*; ***be in ~ of*** kierować, mieć kontrolę nad *I* **4.** zarządzanie *n* **5.** TECH przełącznik *m* **6.** TECH regulator *m,* pokrętło *n* **7.** ***~s*** TECH układ sterowania *m*; ***be at the ~s*** **a)** siedzieć za sterami **b)** *fig* mieć głos decydujący

con•'trol cen•tre *s* **1.** centrum *n* kontroli **2.** centrum *n* sterowania; **con•'trol desk** *s* pulpit *m* sterowniczy; **con•'trol group** *s* grupa *f* kontrolna; **con•'trol key** *s* INF **1.** klawisz *m* Ctrl **2.** klawisz *m* sterujący

con•trolled [kən'trəʊld] *adj* **1.** kontrolowany **2.** sterowany; ***computer-~***

sterowany komputerowo **3.** opanowany

con•'trol pan•el *s* **1.** *AUTO* deska *f* rozdzielcza **2.** (*plane*) tablica *f* przyrządów **3.** panel *m* sterowania, pulpit *m* sterowniczy; **con•'trol room** *s* **1.** *RADIO TEL* reżyserka *f* **2.** sterownia *f*; **con•'trol tow•er** *s* wieża *f* kontroli lotów; **con•'trol u•nit** *s* jednostka *f* sterująca

con•tro•ver•sial [kɒntrə'vɜːʃl] *adj* kontrowersyjny; **con•tro•ver•sy** ['kɒntrəvɜːsɪ] *s* kontrowersja *f*; ***be the subject of much ~*** wzbudzać wiele kontrowersji

con•tu•sion [kən'tjuːʒn] *s MED* stłuczenie (**to** *G*)

co•nun•drum [kə'nʌndrəm] *s* zagadka *f*

con•ur•ba•tion [kɒnɜː'beɪʃn] *s* konurbacja *f*, aglomeracja *f* (miejska)

con•va•lesce [kɒnvə'les] *v/i* wracać do zdrowia; **con•va•les•cence** [kɒnvə'lesns] *s* rekonwalescencja *f*; **con•vales•cent** [kɒnvə'lesnt] **I** *s* rekonwalescent *m* **II** *adj* powracający do zdrowia

con•vect•or (heat•er) [kən'vektə (hiːtə)] *s* konwektor *m*, grzejnik *m* konwektorowy

con•vene [kən'viːn] **I** *v/t meeting*: zwoływać ⟨-łać⟩ **II** *v/i* zbierać ⟨zebrać⟩ się

con•ve•ni•ence [kən'viːnɪəns] *s* **1.** wygoda *f*; ***at s.o.'s ~*** w dogodnym dla kogoś terminie; ***at your earliest ~*** jak najszybciej **2.** zaleta *f*, dogodność *f* **3.** udogodnienie *n* **4.** *Br* toaleta *f*; **con•'ve•ni•ence food** *s* dania *pl* gotowe; **con•'ve•ni•ence store** *s* (całodobowy) sklep *m* ogólnospożywczy; **con•ve•ni•ent** [kən'viːnɪənt] *adj* **1.** wygodny **2.** dogodny **3.** praktyczny **4.** blisko położony; **con•ve•ni•ent•ly** [kən'viːnɪəntlɪ] *adv* **1.** dobrze; ***~ situated*** dogodnie położony **2.** na dogodnych warunkach

con•vent ['kɒnvənt] *s* klasztor *m* (żeński)

con•ven•tion [kən'venʃn] **1.** konwencja *f* **2.** konwenanse *pl* **3.** konferencja *f* **4.** zjazd *m* **5.** konwencja *f* wyborcza; **con•ven•tion•al** [kən'venʃnl] *adj* konwecjonalny; **con•ven•tion•eer** [kən'venʃnɪə] *s* **1.** uczestnik *m* konferencji **2.** uczestnik *m* zjazdu

con•verge [kən'vɜːdʒ] *v/i* **1.** zbiegać ⟨zbiec⟩ się, schodzić ⟨zejść⟩ się **2.** zbliżać ⟨-żyć⟩ się do siebie; **converge on** *v/i* przybywać ⟨-być⟩ do *G*; **con•ver•gence** [kən'vɜːdʒəns] *s* **1.** zbieżność *f* **2.** *BIOL* konwergencja *f*

con•ver•sa•tion [kɒnvə'seɪʃn] *s* rozmowa *f*, konwersacja *f*; ***to have a ~ with*** rozmawiać z *I*, odbyć rozmowę z *I*; **con•ver•sa•tion•al** [kɒnvə'seɪʃnl] *adj* **1.** potoczny **2.** gawędziarski **3.** konwersacyjny

con•verse[1] [kən'vɜːs] *v/i form* rozmawiać ⟨po-⟩

con•verse[2] ['kɒnvɜːs] *form* **I** *s* ***the ~*** odwrotność **II** *adj* **1.** przeciwny **2.** odwrotny; **con•verse•ly** [kən'vɜːslɪ] *adv* odwrotnie

con•ver•sion [kən'vɜːʃn] *s* **1.** *ARCHIT* adaptacja *f* **2.** przebudowa *f* **3.** przejście *n* (**into**/**to** na *A*); ***~ to the metric system*** przejście na system metryczny **4.** przetwarzanie *n* (**into**/**to** na *A*) **5.** *REL* nawrócenie *n* **6.** *MATH* przeliczenie *n*; **con•ver•sion 'ta•ble** *s* tabela *f* przeliczeniowa

con•vert **I** [kən'vɜːt] *v/t* **1.** przerabiać ⟨-robić⟩ (**into**/**to** na *A*) **2.** przetwarzać ⟨-worzyć⟩ (**into**/**to** na *A*) **3.** *MATH* przeliczać ⟨-czyć⟩ (**into**/**to** na *A*) **4.** *ARCHIT* adaptować ⟨za-⟩ (**into**/**to** na *A*) **5.** nawracać ⟨wrócić⟩ się (**to** na *A*) **II** [kən'vɜːt] *v/i* **1.** przechodzić ⟨przejść⟩ (**into**/**to** na *A*) **2.** nawracać ⟨-rócić⟩ **3.** (*sofa*) rozkładać się **III** ['kɒnvɜːt] *s* nawrócony *m*, neofita *m*

con•vey [kən'veɪ] *v/t* **1.** przekazywać ⟨-zać⟩ **2.** oddawać ⟨-dać⟩, wyrażać ⟨-razić⟩ **3.** przewozić ⟨-wieźć⟩; **conveyancing** [kən'veɪənsɪŋ] przeniesienie *n* własności; **con•'vey•or belt** *s* przenośnik *m* taśmowy, taśmociąg *m*

con•vict **I** ['kɒnvɪkt] *s* **1.** więzień *m* **2.** skazany *m* **II** [kən'vɪkt] *v/t* **1.** uznawać ⟨-nać⟩ za winnego (**of doing** popełnienia *G*), skazywać ⟨-zać⟩ **2.** (*evidence*) obciążać ⟨-żyć⟩; **con•vic•tion** [kən'vɪkʃn] *s* **1.** *JUR* skazanie *n* (**for** za *A*) **2.** przekonanie *n*

con•vince [kən'vɪns] *v/t* **1.** przekonywać ⟨-nać⟩ (**of** o *L*) **2.** namawiać ⟨-mówić⟩; ***I tried to ~ her to stay***

C

próbowałam namówić ją, żeby została; **con•vinc•ing** [kən'vınsıŋ] *adj* przekonujący
con•viv•i•al [kən'vıvıəl] *adj* **1.** wesoły **2.** towarzyski
con•voy ['kɒnvɔı] **I** *s* konwój *m*; ***under ~*** pod eskortą **II** *v/t* eskortować, konwojować
con•vulse [kən'vʌls] **I** *v/t* wstrząsać ⟨-snąć⟩; ***be ~d with pain*** zwijać się z bólu; ***be ~d with laughter*** pokładać się ze śmiechu **II** *v/i* mieć drgawki; **con•vul•sions** [kən'vʌlʃnz] *pl* **1.** drgawki *pl*, konwulsje *pl* **2.** rozruchy *pl*; **convul•sive** [kən'vʌlsıv] *adj* **1.** konwulsyjny **2.** burzliwy **3.** gwałtowny
coo [kuː] *v/i* **1.** gruchać **2.** gaworzyć
cook [kʊk] **I** *s* kucharz *m* **II** *v/t* gotować ⟨u-⟩ **III** *v/i* **1.** (*person*) gotować **2.** (*vegetables*) gotować się **3.** ***there's something ~ing*** *infml* coś się święci; **cook up** *v/t infml* wymyślać ⟨-lić⟩
'cook•book *s* książka *f* kucharska; **cook•er** ['kʊkə] *s* kuchenka *f*; **cook•e•ry** ['kʊkərı] *s* kuchnia *f*; ***Italian ~*** kuchnia włoska; **cook•ie** ['kʊkı] *s* **1.** ciastko *n* **2.** herbatnik *m*; **cook•ing** ['kʊkıŋ] *s* gotowanie *n*; ***home ~*** kuchnia domowa; ***French ~*** kuchnia francuska
cool [kuːl] **I** *adj* **1.** chłodny; ***it was ~*** było chłodno **2.** lekki, przewiewny **3.** *colour*: zimny **3.** spokojny, opanowany **4.** *infml* super, odjazdowy, cool; ***~, man!*** spoko!, luz! **II** *s* **1.** chłód *m* **2.** spokój *m*; ***keep your ~!*** *infml* spokojnie!; ***keep one's ~*** *infml* nie tracić głowy, zachować spokój **III** *v/i* **1.** chłodzić ⟨o-⟩ się **2.** stygnąć ⟨o-⟩ **IV** *v/t* **1.** chłodzić ⟨s-⟩ **2.** studzić ⟨o-⟩; **cool down 1.** stygnąć ⟨o-⟩ **2.** ochłonąć, uspokajać ⟨-koić⟩ się
'cool bag *n Br* torba *f* termiczna; **'cool box** *s* lodówka *f* turystyczna; **cool-'head•ed** *adj* opanowany; **cool•ing** ['kuːlıŋ] **I** *s* chłodzenie *n* **II** *adj* **1.** chłodzący **2.** orzeźwiający; **'cooling system** *s* układ *m* chłodzenia; **cool•ness** ['kuːlnıs] *s* **1.** chłód *m* **2.** oziębłość *f* **3.** opanowanie *n*
coop [kuːp] *v/t*: ***~up*** zamykać ⟨-mknąć⟩; ***keep s.o. cooped up*** trzymać kogoś w zamknięciu
co-op ['kəʊɒp] *s infml* spółdzielnia *f*; **co•op•e•rate** [kəʊ'ɒpəreıt] *v/i* **1.** współpracować **2.** współdziałać; **co•op•e•ra•tion** [kəʊ'ɒpə'reıʃn] *s* współpraca *f*; **co•op•e•ra•tive** [kəʊɒpərətıv] **I** *adj* **1.** wspólny **2.** skłonny do współpracy **3.** spółdzielczy **II** *s* spółdzielnia *f*
co•or•di•nate [kəʊ'ɔːdıneıt] **I** *v/t* **1.** koordynować ⟨s-⟩ **2.** uzgadniać ⟨-godnić⟩ **II** *v/i* ***~ with*** harmonizować z *I*, pasować do *G* **III** *s* ***~s*** dopasowane elementy (stroju) **IV** *adj* koordynujący; **co•or•di•na•tion** [kəʊ'ɔːdı'neıʃn] *s* koordynacja *f*; **co•or•di•na•tor** [kəʊ'ɔːdıneıtə] *s* koordynator *m*
co-own•er [kəʊ'əʊnə] *s* współwłaściciel *m*; **co-own•er•ship** [kəʊ'əʊnəʃıp] *s* współwłasność *f*
cop [kɒp] *infml* **I** *s* gliniarz *m*, glina *m* **II** *v/t* ***s.o. copped it*** *Br* komuś się dostało, ktoś oberwał; **cop out** *v/i* tchórzyć ⟨s-⟩
cope [kəʊp] *v/i* radzić sobie ⟨po-⟩, dawać ⟨dać⟩ sobie radę (***with*** z *I*)
cop•i•er ['kɒpıə] *s* (ksero)kopiarka *f*
co•pi•lot ['kəʊpaılət] *s* drugi pilot *m*
co•pi•ous ['kəʊpıəs] *adj* **1.** obfity **2.** obszerny
cop•per ['kɒpə] **I** *s* **1.** miedź *f* **2.** *infml* gliniarz *m*, glina *m* **3.** (*colour*) miedziany *m* **II** *adj* miedziany
co•pro•duc•er [kəʊprəd'juːsə] *s* koproducent *m*; **co•pro•duc•tion** [kəʊprə'dʌkʃn] *s* koprodukcja *f*
cop•u•late ['kɒpjʊleıt] *v/i* kopulować; **cop•ula•tion** [kɒpjʊ'leıʃn] *s* kopulacja *f*
cop•y ['kɒpı] **I** *s* **1.** kopia *f* **2.** egzemplarz *m* **3.** imitacja *f* **4.** odpis *m* **II** *v/t* **1.** kopiować ⟨s-⟩ **2.** przegrywać ⟨-rać⟩ **3.** nagrywać ⟨-rać⟩ (***onto*** na *A*) **4.** przepisywać ⟨-sać⟩; ***they copied the exercise into their books*** przepisali ćwiczenie do zeszytów **III** *v/i* ściągać ⟨-gnąć⟩; **'cop•y cat** *s infml* papuga *f*; **'cop•y•cat crime** *s* przestępstwo *n* wzorowane na innym; **'cop•y ed•i•tor** *s* adiustator *m*; **'cop•y reader** *s Am* adiustator *m*; **'cop•y•right** **I** *s* prawo *n* autorskie **II** *adj* chroniony prawem autorskim; **'cop•y•writ•er** *s* autor *m* tekstów reklamowych, copywriter *m*

cor•al ['kɒrəl] **I** *s* *BIOL* koral *m*, koralowiec *m* **II** *adj* koralowy
cord [kɔːd] *s* **1.** sznur *m*, sznurek *m* **2.** przewód *m* (elektryczny) **3.** ***vocal ~s*** *ANAT* struny głosowe **4.** sztruks *m*; **cord•less 'phone** ['kɔːdlɪsfəʊn] *s* telefon *m* bezprzewodowy
cor•di•al ['kɔːdɪəl] **I** *s* **1.** *Br* syrop *m* owocowy **2.** *Am* likier *m* **II** *adj* **1.** serdeczny **2.** przyjacielski **3.** szczery; **cor•di•al•i•ty** [ˌkɔːdɪ'ælətɪ] *s* serdeczność *f*
cor•don ['kɔːdn] *s* kordon *m*; **cor•don off** *v/t* otaczać ⟨otoczyć⟩ kordonem; zamykać ⟨-mknąć⟩ kordonem
cords [kɔːdz] *pl* sztruksy *pl*
core [kɔː] *s* **1.** gniazdo *n* nasienne **2.** ogryzek *m* **3.** *reactor, magnet*: rdzeń *m* **4.** *planet*: jądro *n* **5.** *fig* istota *f*, sedno *n*
cork [kɔːk] **I** *s* korek *m* **II** *v/t* korkować ⟨za-⟩; **'cork•screw** *s* korkociąg *m*
corn [kɔːn] *s* **1.** *Br* zboże *n* **2.** *Br* ziarno *n* **3.** *Am* kukurydza *f*; **'corn bread** *s* *Am* chleb *m* z mąki kukurydzianej; **'corn cob** *s* kolba *f* kukurydzy
cor•ner ['kɔːnə] **I** *s* **1.** róg *m*; ***the house on the ~*** dom na rogu **2.** kąt *m*; ***watch s.o. out of the ~ of one's eye*** obserwować kogoś kątem oka **3.** zakręt *m* **4.** zakątek *m*; ***in a remote ~ of India*** w dalekim zakątku Indii **5.** *SPORT* rzut *m* rożny **II** *v/t* **1.** osaczać ⟨-czyć⟩ **2.** przypierać ⟨-przeć⟩ do muru **3.** *AUTO* brać ⟨wziąć⟩ zakręt, skręcać ⟨-cić⟩; **'cor•ner kick** *s* rzut *m* rożny
'corn•field *s* **1.** *Br* pole *n* uprawne **2.** *Am* pole *n* kukurydzy; **'corn•flakes** *pl* płatki *pl* kukurydziane; **cornflour** *s* *Br* mąka *f* kukurydziana
'corn pop•py *s* mak *m* polny; **'corn•starch** *s* *Am* mąka *f* kukurydziana
corn•y ['kɔːnɪ] *adj* **1.** oklepany **2.** kiepski **3.** *joke*: z brodą
cor•o•na•tion [kɒrə'neɪʃn] *s* koronacja *f*
cor•o•ner ['kɒrənə] *s* koroner *m*
cor•po•ral ['kɔːpərəl] **I** *s* kapral *m* **II** *adj* cielesny; **cor•po•ral 'pun•ish•ment** *s* kara *f* cielesna
cor•po•rate ['kɔːpərət] *adj* **1.** *image, culture*: spółki **2.** *tax*: od osób prawnych **3.** korporacyjny; **'cor•po•rate body** *s* osoba *f* prawna; **'cor•po•rate i•dent•i•ty** *s* identyfikacja *f* wizualna, tożsamość *f* firmy; **cor•po•ra•tion** [kɔːpə'reɪʃn] *s* *COMM* korporacja *f*
corps [kɔː] *s* korpus *m*; ***an intelligence ~*** służby wywiadowcze
corpse [kɔːps] *s* zwłoki *pl*
cor•pu•lence ['kɔːpjʊləns] *s form* otyłość *f*; **cor•pu•lent** ['kɔːpjʊlənt] *adj* korpulentny
cor•pus ['kɔːpəs] *s* korpus *m* (językowy)
Cor•pus Chris•ti [kɔːpəs'krɪstɪ] *s* Boże Ciało *n*
cor•ral [kə'rɑːl] *s* korral *m*
cor•rect [kə'rekt] **I** *adj* **1.** poprawny; ***that's ~*** dobrze, zgadza się; ***he's ~*** on ma rację **2.** właściwy, odpowiedni **II** *v/t* **1.** poprawiać ⟨-wić⟩; ***~ me if I'm wrong*** mogę się mylić; ***I stand ~ed*** przyznaję się do błędu **2.** naprawić ⟨-wiać⟩ **3.** prostować ⟨s-⟩; **cor•rec•tion** [kə'rekʃn] *s* **1.** poprawienie *n* **2.** poprawka *f* **3.** korekta *f* **4.** sprostowanie *n*; **cor•'rec•tion fluid** *s* korektor *m* w płynie; **cor•rec•tive** [kə'rektɪv] *adj* **1.** korekcyjny **2.** korygujący; **cor•rect•ly** [kə'rektlɪ] *adv* **1.** poprawnie **2.** właściwie; **correct•ness** [kə'rektnɪs] poprawność *f*; ***political ~*** polityczna poprawność
cor•re•late ['kɒrəleɪt] **I** *v/t* **1.** wiązać ⟨po-⟩ (***with*** z *I*) **2.** korelować ⟨s-⟩ (***with*** z *I*) **II** *v/i* ***be ~d with*** być powiązanym z *I*, korelować z *I*; **cor•rela•tion** [kɒrə'leɪʃn] *s* **1.** korelacja *f* **2.** współzależność *f*
cor•re•spond [kɒrɪ'spɒnd] *v/i* **1.** zgadzać ⟨-dzić⟩ się (***to/with*** z *I*), być zgodnym (***to/with*** z *I*) **2.** odpowiadać (***to/with*** z *D*) **3.** korespondować (***with*** z *I*); **cor•re•spon•dence** [kɒrɪ'spɒndəns] *s* **1.** związek *m* **2.** podobieństwo *f* **3.** zgodność *f* **4.** korespondencja *f*; ***enter into ~*** nawiązać korespondencję; **cor•re•'spon•dence course** *s* kurs *m* korespondencyjny; **cor•re•'spon•dence school** *s* szkoła *f* oferująca kursy korespondencyjne; **cor•re•spon•dent** [kərɪ'spɒndənt] *s* korespondent *m*; **cor•re•spon•ding** [kərɪ'spɒndɪŋ] *adj* **1.** odpowiedni; ***~ to*** odpowiadający *D* **2.** analogiczny

C

cor•ri•dor ['kɒrɪdər] *s* korytarz *m*
cor•rode [kə'rəʊd] **I** *v/i* korodować ⟨s-⟩ **II** *v/t* powodować ⟨s-⟩ korozję; **cor•ro•sion** [kə'rəʊʒn] *s* **1.** korozja *f* **2.** rdza *f*
cor•rupt [kə'rʌpt] **I** *adj* **1.** skorumpowany **2.** zdeprawowany, zepsuty **3.** *INF* uszkodzony **II** *v/t* **1.** korumpować ⟨s-⟩ **2.** demoralizować ⟨z-⟩ **3.** *INF* uszkadzać ⟨-kodzić⟩ **III** *v/i* demoralizować ⟨z-⟩; ***power ~s*** władza demoralizuje; **cor•rup•tion** [kə'rʌpʃn] *s* **1.** korupcja *f* **2.** demoralizacja *f*, zepsucie *n* **3.** *INF* uszkodzenie *n*
cor•set ['kɔːsɪt] *s* gorset *m*
'cos [kɒz] *infml* → ***because***
co•si•ness ['kəʊzɪnɪs] *s Br* **1.** przytulność *f* **2.** wygoda *f*
cos•met•ic [kɒz'metɪk] **I** *s* kosmetyk *m* II *adj* kosmetyczny; **cos•met•ics** [kɒz'metɪks] *s* kosmetyka *f*; **cos•met•ic 'sur•geon** *s* chirurg *m* plastyczny; **cos•met•ic 'sur•ger•y** *s* chirurgia *f* plastyczna
cos•mic ['kɒzmɪk] *adj* kosmiczny
cos•mo•naut ['kɒzmənɒːt] *s* kosmonauta *m*
cos•mo•pol•i•tan [kɒzmə'pɒlɪtən] **I** *s* kosmopolita *m* **II** *adj* kosmopolityczny
cos•mos ['kɒzməs] *s* kosmos *m*
cost [kɒst] **I** *s* **1.** koszt *m*; ***transport ~s*** koszty transportu; ***the total ~ came to $500*** łączny koszt wyniósł 500 dolarów **2.** cena *f*; ***at a ~ of $100*** w cenie 100 dolarów **3.** *fig* koszt *m*, cena *f*; ***at all ~*** za wszelką cenę **4.** procesowe *n* **II** (*cost*; *cost*) *v/t* kosztować; ***how much does it ~?*** ile to kosztuje?; ***it ~ me a lot of time and effort*** kosztowało mnie to wiele czasu i wysiłku; **'cost an•al•y•sis** *s* analiza *f* kosztów; **cost and 'freight** *s* koszt *m* i fracht; **'cost, in•sur•ance, freight** *s* koszt *m*, ubezpieczenie i fracht
co-star ['kəʊstɑː] **I** *v/i* ***to ~ with*** grać u boku *G* **II** *v/t* ***a movie ~ing X and Y*** film z udziałem X i Y **III** *s* **3.** ***her ~ is X*** obok niej w roli głównej występuje X
Cos•ta Ri•ca ['kəstə'riːkə] *s GEOGR* Kostaryka *f*
cost•ing ['kɒstɪŋ] *s* kalkulacja *f* kosztów
cost•ly ['kɒstlɪ] *adj* **1.** kosztowny **2.** drogocenny
cost of 'liv•ing *s* koszty *pl* utrzymania; **cost-of-'liv•ing al•low•ance** *s* dodatek *m* drożyźniany; **cost 'price** *s*: ***at ~*** *COMM* po cenie kosztów własnych; ***below ~*** poniżej kosztów własnych
cos•tume ['kɒstjuːm] *s* **1.** strój *m*; ***a national ~*** strój narodowy **2.** kostium *m*; **'cos•tume de•sign•er** *s* projektant *m* kostiumów; **'cos•tume dra•ma** *s* **1.** film *m* kostiumowy **2.** sztuka *f* kostiumowa; **cos•tume 'jew•el•lery** *s* sztuczna biżuteria *f*
co•sy ['kəʊzɪ] *adj Br*, **co•zy** *Am* **1.** przytulny **2.** *chair*: wygodny **3.** *atmosphere*: miły, kameralny
cot [kɒt] *s* **1.** *Br* łóżeczko *n* dziecięce **2.** *Am* łóżko *n* polowe; **'cot death** *s MED* śmierć *f* łóżeczkowa
cott•age ['kɒtɪdʒ] *s* **1.** domek *m* (wiejski); ***a summer ~*** domek letniskowy **2.** chata *f*; **cott•age 'cheese** *s* serek *m* wiejski, twarożek *m*; **cott•age 'in•dus•try** *s* chałupnictwo *n*
cot•ton ['kɒtn] **I** *s* bawełna *f* **II** *adj* bawełniany; **cot•ton on** *v/i Br infml* załapywać ⟨-pać⟩, zaskakiwać ⟨-skoczyć⟩
'cot•ton bud *s Br* patyczek *m* higieniczny; **cot•ton 'can•dy** *s Am* wata *f* cukrowa; **'cot•ton•seed oil** *s* olej *m* bawełniany; **cot•ton 'wool** *s* wata *f* (bawełniana)
couch [kaʊtʃ] *s* **1.** kanapa *f* **2.** kozetka *f* **3.** leżanka *f*; **'couch po•ta•to** *s*: ***he's a ~*** *infml* cały dzień leży na kanapie i ogląda telewizję
cough [kɒf] **I** *s* kaszel *m*: ***to have a ~*** kasłać, kaszleć **II** *v/i* kasłać, kaszleć; **cough up** *v/t* **1.** *infml* wybulić **2.** *infml* wykrztusić, wydusić z siebie **3.** kasłać; ***~ blood*** kasłać krwią
'cough drop *s* cukierek *m* na kaszel; **'cough•ing bout** *s* napad *m* kaszlu; **'cough loz•enge** → ***cough drop***; **'cough med•i•cine**, ***'cough syr•up*** *s* syrop *m* na kaszel
could [kəd, kʊd] *Past Simple* → ***can***
coun•cil ['kaʊnsl] *s* **1.** rada *f*; ***a city ~*** rada miejska; ***the ≈ of Europe*** Rada Europy **2.** *form* narada *f*; **'coun•cil es•tate** *s Br* osiedle *n* komunalne; **'coun•cil flat** *s Br* mieszkanie *n* komunalne; **'coun•cil house** *s Br* komunalny dom *m* mieszkalny

C

coun•cil•lor ['kaʊnsələ] *s* radny *m*; **'coun•cil•man** ['kaʊnslmən] *s* radny *m*

coun•sel ['kaʊnsl] **I** *s* **1.** *form* rada *f*, porada *f* **2.** adwokat *m* **3.** adwokaci *pl* **II** *v/t* **1.** doradzać ⟨-dzić⟩ **2.** *form* zalecać ⟨-cić⟩; **coun•sel•ling** ['kaʊnslɪŋ] *Br*, ***coun•sel•ing*** *Am s* **1.** doradztwo *n*; ***careers ~*** doradztwo zawodowe **2.** poradnictwo *n* **3.** pomoc *f* psychologa; **coun•sel•lor** ['kaʊnslə] *s* **1.** doradca *m* **2.** *Am* adwokat *m* **3.** (*camp*) *Am* opiekun *m* **4.** *Am* psycholog *m* szkolny

count[1] [kaʊnt] **I** *s* **1.** liczenie *n*; ***do a ~ of*** liczyć *A* **2.** liczba *f*; ***the body ~*** liczba ofiar **3.** przeliczenie *n* (głosów) **5.** ***cholesterol ~*** MED poziom cholesterolu; ***calorie ~*** wartość kaloryczna; ***blood ~*** analiza krwi **II** *v/t* **1.** liczyć ⟨po-⟩ **2.** przeliczać ⟨-czyć⟩ **3.** wyliczać ⟨-czyć⟩ **III** *v/i* **1.** liczyć ⟨po-⟩; ***~ to 100*** policzyć do stu **2.** liczyć się; ***that doesn't ~*** to się nie liczy **3.** liczyć się, znaczyć; **count against** *v/i* działać na niekorzyść; **count down** *v/i* odliczać ⟨-czyć⟩; ***they are counting down to vacation*** *fig* odliczają dni do wakacji; **count in** *v/t* uwzględniać ⟨-nić⟩; ***if you're organizing a trip, count me in!*** jeśli organizujecie wycieczkę, jadę z wami!; **count on** *v/i* liczyć na *A*; **count out** *v/t* odliczać ⟨-czyć⟩; ***she counted out $10 in coins*** odliczyła 10 dolarów w bilonie; **count up** *v/i* **1.** liczyć ⟨po-⟩ **2.** podliczać ⟨-czyć⟩; **count•a•ble** ['kaʊntəbl] *adv* policzalny

count[2] [~] *s* hrabia *m*

coun•te•nance ['kaʊntənəns] **I** *s* **1.** *form* oblicze *n* **2.** wyraz *m* twarzy **II** *v/t* **1.** przyzwalać ⟨-wolić⟩ na *A* **2.** akceptować ⟨za-⟩

coun•ter[1] ['kaʊntə] *s* **1.** lada *f*; ***the man behind the ~*** sprzedawca; ***over the ~*** *medicine*: bez recepty; ***under the ~*** spod lady **2.** okienko *n* **3.** blat *m* (kuchenny) **4.** stoisko *n* **5.** żeton *m* **6.** pionek *m*

coun•ter[2] [~] *s* licznik *m*

coun•ter•'act *v/t* **1.** przeciwdziałać **2.** neutralizować ⟨z-⟩ **3.** równoważyć ⟨z-⟩

'coun•ter-ar•gu•ment *s* kontrargument *m*; **'coun•ter-at•tack** *s* kontratak *m*; **coun•ter•'bal•ance** **I** *s* przeciwwaga *f* **II** *v/t* stanowić przeciwwagę dla *G*; **'coun•ter•blast** *s* ostra replika *f*, riposta *f*; **'coun•ter•charge** *s* **1.** JUR kontroskarżenie *n* **2.** kontratak *m*; **'coun•ter•claim** *s* **1.** odpowiedź *f*, replika *f* **2.** JUR roszczenie *n* wzajemne

coun•ter clerk *s* **1.** kasjer *m* **2.** sprzedawca *m*

coun•ter•'clock•wise **I** *adv* przeciwnie do ruchu wskazówek zegara **II** *adj* przeciwny do ruchu wskazówek zegara; **coun•ter•dem•on•'stra•tion** *s* kontrdemonstracja *f*; **'coun•ter-'es•pi•o•nage** *s* kontrwywiad *m*

coun•ter•feit ['kaʊntəfɪt] **I** *s* **1.** falsyfikat *m* **2.** podróbka *f* **II** *adj* **1.** sfałszowany **2.** podrobiony **III** *v/t* **1.** fałszować ⟨s-⟩ **2.** podrabiać ⟨-robić⟩; **counterfeiter** ['kaʊntəfɪtə] *s* fałszerz *m*

coun•ter-in'tel•li•gence *s* kontrwywiad *m*

'coun•ter•meas•ure *s* środek *m* zaradczy; **'coun•ter•move** *s* kontrakcja *f*; **coun•ter•of•'fen•sive** *s* kontrofensywa *f*; **'coun•ter-of•fer** *s* kontroferta *f*

'coun•ter•part *s* **1.** (*person*) odpowiednik *m* **2.** (*document*) kopia *f*; **'counter•point** *s* kontrapunkt *m*; **counter•pro•'duc•tive** *adj*: ***be ~*** przynieść efekt odwrotny od zamierzonego; **counter•pro•'pos•al** *s* kontrpropozycja *f*; **coun•ter-rev•o•'lu•tion** *s* kontrrewolucja *f*; **'coun•ter•sign** *v/t* kontrasygnować; **coun•ter-'ter•ror•ism** **I** *adj* antyterrorystyczny **II** *s* antyterroryzm *m*; **'coun•ter•weight** *s* przeciwwaga *f* (***to*** dla *G*)

coun•tess ['kaʊntɪs] *s* hrabina *f*

count•less ['kaʊntlɪs] *adj* niezliczony

coun•try ['kʌntrɪ] **I** *s* **1.** kraj *m* **2.** państwo *n* **3.** ojczyzna *f* **4.** wieś *f*; ***in the ~*** na wsi **5.** kraina *f*, region *m*; ***fishing ~*** atrakcyjne tereny wędkarskie **II** *adj* wiejski; **coun•try and 'west•ern** *s* muzyka *f* country; **coun•try 'house** *s* wiejska rezydencja *f*; **'coun•try•man** *pl -men s* **1.** rodak *m* **2.** mieszkaniec *m* wsi; **'coun•try mu•sic** *s* muzyka *f* country; **'coun•try•side** *s* **1.** wieś *f*, wiejska okolica *f* **2.** krajobraz *m* (wiejski); **coun•try-'wide** **I** *adj* ogólnokrajowy **II** *adv* w całym kraju;

C

'coun•try•wom•an *s* **1.** rodaczka *f* **2.** mieszkanka *f* wsi

coun•ty ['kaʊntɪ] **I** *s* hrabstwo *n* **II** *adj* **1.** *council, capital*: hrabstwa **2.** *court*: okręgowy

coup [kuː] **1.** *s* zamach *m* stanu **2.** wyczyn *m*

cou•ple ['kʌpl] **I** *s* **1.** (*pair*) para *f*; ***a married ~*** małżeństwo; ***I saw a ~ of children*** widziałem dwoje dzieci **2.** (*few*) ***a ~ of people*** kilka osób, parę osób **II** *v/t* **1.** łączyć ⟨po-⟩ **2.** doczepiać ⟨-pić⟩ **III** *v/i* parzyć się, kopulować

cou•pon ['kuːpɒn] *s* **1.** bon *m*, talon *m* **2.** kupon *m*

cour•age ['kʌrɪdʒ] *s* odwaga *f*; ***to lack ~ to do s.th.*** nie mieć odwagi czegoś zrobić; **cou•ra•geous** [kə'reɪdʒəs] *adj* **1.** odważny **2.** dzielny; **cou•ra•geous•ly** [kə'reɪdʒəslɪ] *adv* odważnie

cou•ri•er ['kʊrɪə] *s* **1.** kurier *m* **2.** goniec *m* **3.** *Br* pilot *m* wycieczki

course [kɔːs] **I** *s* **1.** kurs *m*; ***an advanced ~*** kurs dla zaawansowanych **2.** studia *pl*; ***a three year ~*** trzyletnie studia **3.** przebieg *m*, bieg *m*; ***in the ~ of*** w trakcie *G*; ***in the ~ of time*** z biegiem czasu; ***an unexpected ~ of events*** niespodziewany bieg zdarzeń **4.** (*ship*) kurs *m*; ***to be on ~*** trzymać się kursu; ***to go off ~*** zboczyć z kursu **5.** (*river*) bieg *m* **6.** tor *m* **7.** *SPORT* pole *n* golfowe **8.** danie *n*; ***a fish ~*** danie rybne **9.** *MED* terapia *f* **II** *v/i* ***~ down*** (*tears*) spływać strumieniem po *L* **III** *adv* ***of ~!*** oczywiście!

court [kɔːt] **I** *s* **1.** sąd *m*; ***to bring a case to ~*** wnieść sprawę do sądu; ***to take s.o. to ~*** pozwać kogoś do sądu **2.** kort *m* **3.** boisko *n* **4.** dwór *m* **5.** dziedziniec *m* **6.** podwórze *n* **II** *v/i* **1.** zalecać się do *G* **2.** zabiegać o względy *G*; ***~ publicity*** szukać rozgłosu; **'court case** *s* sprawa *f* sądowa

cour•te•ous ['kɜːtjəs] *adj* uprzejmy

cour•te•sy ['kɜːtəsɪ] *s* uprzejmość *f*, grzeczność *f*; ***by ~ of*** za zgodą *G*; **'cour•te•sy car** *s* **1.** samochód *m* zastępczy **2.** samochód *m* (oddany komuś do dyspozycji); **'cour•te•sy light** *s* *AUTO* oświetlenie *n* włączające się przy otwieraniu drzwi

'court•house *s* gmach *m* sądu; **court 'mar•tial** *s* **1.** sąd *m* wojskowy **2.** sąd *m* wojenny; **'court or•der** *s* *JUR* nakaz *m* sądowy; **'court•room** *s* sala *f* sądowa; **court•ship** ['kɔːtʃɪp] *s* **1.** zaloty *pl* **2.** gody *pl*; **court•yard** ['kɔtjaːd] *s* **1.** dziedziniec *m* **2.** podwórze *n*

cous•in ['kʌzn] *s* kuzyn *m*

cove [kəʊv] *s* zatoczka *f*

cov•er ['kʌvə] **I** *s* **1.** pokrowiec *m*; ***a cushion ~*** poszewka **2.** pokrywka *f* **3.** okładka *f*; ***on the ~*** na okładce **4.** oprawa *f* **5.** narzuta *f* **6.** ***the ~s*** pościel *f* **7.** schronienie *n*; ***to provide ~ for*** dawać schronienie *D*; ***take ~*** chronić się; ***under ~ of darkness*** pod osłoną nocy **8.** (*fire*) osłona *f* **9.** *fig* przykrywka *f* **10.** *Br* ubezpieczenie *n*, ochrona *f* ubezpieczeniowa; ***medical ~*** ubezpieczenie zdrowotne **11.** *MUS* cover *m*, nowa wersja *f* **II** *v/t* **1.** przykrywać ⟨-ryć⟩ (***with*** *I*) **2.** nakrywać ⟨-ryć⟩; ***you must ~ your head*** musisz założyć coś na głowę **3.** pokrywać ⟨-ryć⟩; ***fish are ~ed with scales*** ciało ryb jest pokryte łuskami **4.** pokrywać ⟨-ryć⟩ koszty; ***£ 20 should ~ it*** 20 funtów powinno wystarczyć **5.** *distance*: pokonywać ⟨-nać⟩ **6.** obejmować; ***the price ~s everything*** cena obejmuje wszystko **7.** (*regulations*) dotyczyć **8.** relacjonować ⟨z-⟩; ***the game will be ~ed live on BBC*** mecz będzie transmitowany na żywo przez BBC **9.** ubezpieczać ⟨-czyć⟩ **10.** *SPORT* kryć **11.** osłaniać ⟨-łonić⟩; ***I'll ~ you*** będę cię osłaniać **12.** *emotion*: ukrywać ⟨-ryć⟩ **13.** *smell*: zabijać ⟨-bić⟩ **14.** *MUS* nagrywać ⟨-rać⟩ cover, nagrywać ⟨-rać⟩ nową wersję; **cov•er up** **I** *v/t* **1.** przykrywać ⟨-ryć⟩ **2.** ukrywać ⟨-ryć⟩ **3.** tuszować ⟨za-⟩ **4.** ***cover oneself up with*** **a)** okryć się *I* **b)** założyć *A* **II** *v/i* ***~ for s.o.*** kryć kogoś

cov•er•age ['kʌvərɪdʒ] *s* **1.** doniesienia *pl*; ***it received wide media coverage*** było o tym głośno w mediach **2.** relacja *f*, transmisja *f*; ***live ~*** relacja na żywo, transmisja na żywo **3.** miejsce *n*; ***provide extensive ~ of*** poświęcić wiele miejsca *D* **4.** *Am* ubezpieczenie *n*, ochrona *f* ubezpieczeniowa

'cov•er girl *s* dziewczyna *f* z okładki

C

'cov•er story *s* artykuł *m* główny (anonsowany na okładce)
cov•ert [kʌvət] *adj* tajny, potajemny
'cov•er-up *s* próba *f* zatuszowania faktów
cov•et ['kʌvɪt] *v/t form* **1.** pragnąć; ***she ~ed that job*** pragnęła dostać tę pracę **2.** być żądnym; **cov•et•ous** ['kʌvɪtəs] *adj* **1.** chciwy **2.** pożądliwy
cow [kaʊ] *s* krowa *f*
cow•ard ['kaʊəd] *s* tchórz *m*; **cow•ard•ice** ['kaʊədɪs] *s* tchórzostwo *n*; **cow•ard•ly** ['kaʊədlɪ] *adj* tchórzliwy
'cow•boy *s* kowboj *m*
cow•er ['kaʊə] *v/i* kulić ⟨s-⟩ się (ze strachu)
'cow•girl *s* kowbojka *f*
cowl [kaʊl] *s* kaptur *m*
co-work•er [kəʊ'wɜːkə] *s* współpracownik *m*
'cow•pat *s Br* krowi placek *m*; **'cow•shed** *s* obora *f*; **'cow•skin** *s* skóra *f* wołowa
cox [kɒks] **I** *s* sternik *m* **II** *v/t* sterować **III** *v/i* być sternikiem
coy [kɔɪ] *adj* **1.** wstydliwy **2.** nieskory
co•zi•ness *s Am* → ***cosiness***
co•zy *Am* → ***cosy***
CPU [siːpiː'juː] (=***central processing unit***) *s* INF jednostka *f* centralna, procesor *m* centralny
crab[1] [kræb] *s* **1.** BIOL krab *m* **2.** ***the ~*** ASTR Rak
crab[2] [~] *infml* **I** *v/t* paprać ⟨s-⟩ **II** *v/i* marudzić
crab•bed ['kræbɪd] *adj* **1.** *handwriting*: drobny **2.** nieprzyjemny **3.** zrzędliwy
crab•by ['kræbɪ] *adj infml* **1.** nieprzyjemny **2.** zrzędliwy
crack [kræk] **I** *s* **1.** pęknięcie *n* **2.** rysa *f* **3.** szpara *f*, szczelina *f*; ***to open the door a ~*** lekko uchylić drzwi **4.** (*cocaine*) *infml* crack *m* **5.** trzask *m* **6.** huk *m* **7.** grzmot *m* **8.** ***to have a ~ at s.th.*** *infml* spróbować coś zrobić **9.** *infml* kawał *m* **10.** docinek *m* **11.** ***at the ~ of dawn*** bladym świtem **II** *adj* **1.** wyborowy **2.** pierwszorzędny **III** *v/i* **1.** pękać ⟨-knąć⟩ **2.** popękać **3.** (*person, voice*) załamywać ⟨-mać⟩ się; ***her voice ~ed with emotion*** głos jej się łamał ze wzruszenia **4.** (*twig*) trzaskać ⟨-snąć⟩ **IV** *v/t* **1.** rozbijać ⟨-bić⟩ **2.** rozłupywać ⟨-pać⟩; ***I ~ed a glass*** pękła mi szklanka **3.** *problem*: rozgryzać ⟨-ryźć⟩ **4.** *code*: łamać ⟨z-⟩ **5.** trzaskać ⟨-snąć⟩ **6.** łamać ⟨z-⟩ z trzaskiem **7.** ***to ~ a joke*** *infml* **a)** opowiedzieć kawał **b)** zażartować; **crack down on** *v/t* rozprawiać ⟨-wić⟩ się z *I*; **crack up** *v/i infml* **1.** fiksować ⟨s-⟩ **2.** wybuchać ⟨-chnąć⟩ śmiechem
'crack•down *s* **1.** zdecydowane kroki *pl* (**on** przeciw *D*) **2.** rozprawienie *n* się (**on** z *I*) **3.** interwencja *f*
cracked [krækt] *adj* **1.** pęknięty **2.** popękany **3.** spękany **4.** *voice*: łamiący się **5.** *infml* stuknięty
crack•er ['krækə] *s* **1.** krakers *m* **2.** petarda *f* **3.** *papierowa tuba z niespodzianką, strzelająca przy otwarciu* **4.** włamywacz *m* komputerowy
crack•ers ['krækəz] *adj infml* stuknięty
crack•le ['krækl] **I** *s* **1.** trzaski *pl* **2.** szelest *m* **3.** skwierczenie *n* **II** *v/i* **1.** trzeszczeć ⟨za-⟩ **2.** trzaskać **3.** szeleścić ⟨za-⟩ **4.** skwierczeć ⟨za-⟩
crack•ling ['kræklɪŋ] *s* **1.** trzaski *pl*, trzeszczenie *n* **2.** szelest *m* **3.** skwierczenie *n* **4.** COOK chrupiąca skórka *f* (wieprzowa)
'crack•pot *infml* **I** *s* świr *m* **II** *adj* stuknięty
cra•dle ['kreɪdl] **I** *s* **1.** kołyska *f*; ***from the ~*** od kołyski **2.** kolebka *f* **3.** (*telephone*) widełki *pl* **II** *v/t* **1.** kołysać ⟨u-⟩ **2.** ***~ s.th. in one's arms*** tulić coś w ramionach
craft [krɑːft] *s* **1.** rzemiosło *n*; ***the potter's ~*** garncarstwo **2.** rękodzieło; ***arts and ~s*** rękodzieło artystyczne **3.** spryt *m*, przebiegłość *f* **4.** samolot *m* **5.** samoloty *pl* **6.** statek *m* **7.** statki *pl*
craft•i•ness ['kræftɪnɪs] *s* spryt *m*, przebiegłość *f*
crafts•man ['krɑːftsmən] *pl -men s* rzemieślnik *m*, rękodzielnik *m*; **crafts•man•ship** ['krɑːftsmənʃɪp] *s* kunszt *m*, mistrzostwo *n*; **crafts•wom•an** ['krɑːftswʊmən] *pl -men s* rzemieślniczka *f*, rękodzielniczka *f*
craft•y ['krɑːftɪ] *adj* chytry, przebiegły
cram [kræm] **I** *v/t* **1.** wepchnąć ⟨wpychać⟩; ***I ~med all my things into one case*** upchnąłem wszystkie rzeczy do

C

jednej walizki **2.** wypełniać ⟨-nić⟩ (*with I*); ***the attic is ~med with junk*** strych zapchany jest rupieciami **II** *v/i* **1.** ***we all ~med into one car*** wszyscy wcisnęliśmy się do jednego samochodu **2.** *infml* kuć, wkuwać

cramp [kræmp] **I** *s* skurcz *m*; ***I have (a) ~ in my leg*** chwycił mnie skurcz w nodze **II** *v/t development*: hamować ⟨za-⟩

cramped [kræmpt] *adj* **1.** *room*: ciasny **2.** *handwriting*: ścisły

cran•ber•ry ['krænberɪ] *s* BIOL żurawina *f*

crane [kreɪn] *s* **1.** BIOL żuraw *m* **2.** dźwig *m*, żuraw *m*; **crane forward** *v/i* wyciągać ⟨-gnąć⟩ szyję

'crane driv•er *s* operator *m* dźwigu

crank [kræŋk] *s* **1.** *infml* maniak *m*, fanatyk *m* **2.** zrzęda *m*; **crank•y** ['kræŋkɪ] *adj* **1.** stuknięty, zbzikowany **2.** marudny

cran•ny ['krænɪ] → ***nook***

crap [kræp] **I** *s* **1.** *infml* pierdoły *pl*; ***to talk ~*** pieprzyć, gadać pierdoły **2.** (*book, film*) *infml* gniot *m*, *vulg* gówno *n* **3.** ***to have a ~*** *vulg* wysrać się **II** *adj vulg* gówniany **III** *v/t Am infml* wciskać ⟨-snąć⟩ komuś kit; **crap•py** ['kræpɪ] *adj vulg* do dupy

crash [kræʃ] **I** *s* **1.** wypadek *m*, katastrofa *f* **2.** trzask *m*, łomot *m* **3.** (*stock exchange*) krach *m* **II** *v/t* rozbijać ⟨-bić⟩; ***she ~ed the car*** rozbiła samochód **III** *v/i* **1.** roztrzaskiwać ⟨-kać⟩ się, rozbijać ⟨-bić⟩ się, zderzać ⟨-rzyć⟩ się **2.** FIN upadać ⟨upaść⟩, bankutować ⟨z-⟩; ***the stock market ~ed*** nastąpił krach na giełdzie **3.** (*person*) tłuc się; ***I could hear him ~ing around downstairs*** słyszałem jak tłukł się na dole **4.** ***~ to the ground*** spaść na ziemię z hałasem **5.** (*tree*) runąć **6.** (*computer*) *infml* padać ⟨paść⟩, siadać ⟨siąść⟩; **crash out** *v/i infml* **1.** kimnąć się, uderzyć w kimono **2.** przekimać się, przenocować

'crash bar•ri•er *s Br* bariera *f* bezpieczeństwa na autostradzie; **'crash course** *s* intensywny kurs *m*; **'crash di•et** *s* intensywna dieta *f* odchudzająca; **'crash hel•met** *s* kask *m* ochronny; **'crash-land** *v/i* lądować ⟨wy-⟩ awaryjnie; **crash 'land•ing** *s* lądowanie *n* awaryjne; **'crash-test** *s* AUTO test *m* zderzeniowy

crate [kreɪt] *s* (*fruit, bottles*) skrzynka *f*

crave [kreɪv] *v/t* mieć ogromną ochotę na *A*, bardzo pragnąć *G*; **crav•ing** ['kreɪvɪŋ] *s* ogromna ochota *f* (***for*** na *A*)

crawl [krɔːl] **I** *s* **1.** SPORT kraul *m*; ***swim the ~*** pływać kraulem **2.** ***at a ~*** noga za nogą, w żółwim tempie **II** *v/i* **1.** pełzać ⟨-znąć⟩, czołgać się **2.** (*child*) raczkować **3.** (*car, time*) wlec się **4.** *infml* podlizywać się; **crawl with** *v/i*: ***to be crawling with*** *infml* roić się od *G*

cray•on ['kreɪən] **I** *s* **1.** kredka *f*, kolorowy ołówek *m* **2.** rysunek *m* kredką **II** *v/i* rysować ⟨na-⟩ kredką

craze [kreɪz] *s* szaleństwo *n*, (chwilowa) moda *f*; ***the latest ~*** ostatni krzyk mody; **cra•zi•ness** ['kreɪzɪnɪs] *s* szaleństwo *n*; **cra•zy** ['kreɪzɪ] *adj* **1.** szalony; ***are you ~?*** zwariowałaś?; ***go ~*** wariować **2.** zwariowany; ***be ~ about*** szaleć za *I*

creak [kriːk] *v/i* skrzypieć; **creak•y** ['kriːkɪ] *adj* skrzypiący

cream [kriːm] **I** *s* **1.** śmietana *f*; ***coffee ~*** śmietanka do kawy; ***sour ~*** kwaśna śmietana; ***whipped ~*** bita śmietana **2.** krem *m*; ***hand ~*** krem do rąk **II** *v/t* **1.** smarować ⟨po-⟩ kremem **2.** *milk*: odciągać ⟨-gnąć⟩ śmietankę z *G* **3.** dodawać ⟨-dać⟩ śmietanki do *G* **III** *adj* **1.** śmietankowy **2.** kremowy; **cream off** *v/t fig* odławiać ⟨-łowić⟩

cream 'cheese *s* serek *m* kremowy; **'cream-col•oured** *Br*, **'cream-col•ored** *Am adj colour*: kremowy; **cream•er** ['kriːmə] *s* (*coffee*) śmietanka *f* w proszku; **cream•y** ['kriːmɪ] *adj* **1.** śmietankowy **2.** *coffee*: ze śmietanką **3.** *milk*: tłusty **4.** o konsystencji kremu **5.** kremowy

crease [kriːs] **I** *s* **1.** zagięcie *n* **2.** kant *m*; ***iron a ~ into*** zaprasować kant na *L* **II** *v/i* marszczyć ⟨z-⟩ się, miąć ⟨z-⟩ się **III** *v/t* **1.** marszczyć ⟨z-⟩, miąć ⟨z-⟩ **2.** prasować ⟨za-⟩ w kant; **'crease-proof** *adj* niemnący się; **'crease-re•sist•ant** *adj* niemnący się

cre•ate [kriː'eɪt] *v/t* **1.** tworzyć ⟨s-⟩, kreować ⟨wy-⟩ **2.** *interest, scandal*: wywoływać ⟨-łać⟩ **3.** *crisis*: powodować ⟨s-⟩ **4.** *problems*: stwarzać ⟨-wo-rzyć⟩; **cre•a•tion** [kriː'eɪʃn] *s* **1.** tworzenie *n* **2.** stworzenie *n*, akt *m* twórczy **3.** ***the*** ≈ *REL* stworzenie *n* świata **4.** (*outfit*) kreacja *f*; **cre•a-tive** [kriː'eɪtɪv] *adj* twórczy, kreatywny; **cre•ativ•i•ty** [kriːeɪ'tɪvɪtɪ] *s* kreatywność *f*, talent *m* twórczy; **cre•a-tor** [kriː'eɪtə] *s* **1.** twórca *m* **2.** ***the*** ≈ *REL* Stwórca

crea•ture ['kriːtʃə] *s* **1.** istota *f* żywa, stworzenie *n*, żyjątko *n*; ***sea ~s*** zwierzęta morskie **2.** (*person*) istota *f*, stworzenie *n*; ***a charming ~*** czarująca istota; ***a ~ of habit*** niewolnik własnych przyzwyczajeń; **crea•ture 'com-forts** *pl* wygody *pl*

cre•dence ['kriːdəns] *s form* wiara *f*, wiarygodność *f*; ***give ~ to s.th.*** dawać czemuś wiarę; ***gain ~*** zyskać wiarygodność

cre•den•tials [krɪ'denʃlz] *pl* **1.** kwalifikacje *pl* **2.** referencje *pl*

cred•i•bil•i•ty [kredə'bɪlətɪ] *s* wiarygodność *f*; **cred•i•ble** ['kredəbl] *adj* wiarygodny

cred•it ['kredɪt] **I** *s* **1.** uznanie *n*; ***get the ~ for*** zdobyć uznanie za *A*; ***she gets all the ~ for the success*** uważa się, że sukces był wyłącznie jej zasługą; ***give s.o. ~ for*** **a)** chwalić kogoś za *A* **b)** docenić kogoś za *A*; ***I can't take any of the ~*** nie mnie należą się wyrazy uznania **2.** wiara *f* **3.** *FIN* kredyt *m*; ***to buy s.th. on ~*** kupować coś na kredyt; ***live on ~*** żyć na kredyt **4.** *FIN* saldo *n* dodatnie **5.** (*at school*) *Am* zaliczenie *n* **II** *v/t* **1.** ***~ s.o. with s.th.*** przypisywać coś komuś; ***~ s.o. with honesty*** uważać, że ktoś jest uczciwy **2.** *bill*: uznawać ⟨-nać⟩; ***~ s.th. to s.o.'s account*** zapisać coś na dobro czyjegoś rachunku; **cred•i•ta•ble** ['kredɪtəbl] *adj* **1.** godziwy, przyzwoity **2.** godny uznania

'cred•it bal•ance *s* saldo *n* kredytowe (dodatnie); **'cred•it card** *s* karta *f* kredytowa; **'cred•it con•trol** *s* kontrola *f* kredytów; **'cred•it lim•it** *s* limit *m* kredytu; **'cred•it note** *s Br* nota *f* kredytowa; **cred•i•tor** ['kredɪtə] *s* wierzyciel *m*; **'cred•it rat•ing** *FIN* rating *m* kredytowy

cred•its ['kredɪts] *pl FILM* **1.** napisy *pl* **2.** czołówka *f*

cre•du•li•ty [krɪ'djuːlətɪ] *s* łatwowierność *f*; **cred•u•lous** ['kredʊləs] *adj* łatwowierny

creed [kriːd] *s* **1.** wyznanie *n* **2.** kredo *n* **3.** ***the*** ≈ *REL* wyznanie *n* wiary

creek [kriːk] *s* **1.** *Br* zatoka *f* **2.** *Am* strumień *m*

creep [kriːp] **I** *s infml* **1.** wazeliniarz *m*, wazelina *f* **2.** kreatura *f*, menda *f* **3.** ***it gives me the ~s*** dostaję od tego gęsiej skórki; **II** (*crept; crept*) *v/i* **1.** skradać się; ***to ~ behind*** zakraść się od tyłu **2.** ***to ~ forward*** (***along***) wlec się **3.** (*inflation, prices*) rosnąć, wzrastać ⟨-rosnąć⟩ powoli **4.** (*insect*) pełznąć ⟨po-⟩ **5.** (*cat*) skradać się; **creep in** *v/i* (*error, bitterness*) wkradać ⟨-raść⟩ się; **creep up on** *v/t* **1.** podkradać ⟨-raść⟩ się niepostrzeżenie (***on s.o.*** do *G*) **2.** zaskakiwać ⟨-skoczyć⟩

creep•er ['kriːpə] *s* **1.** liana *f* **2.** roślina *f* pnąca **3.** roślina *f* płożąca; **creep-ing** ['kriːpɪŋ] *adj* **1.** *inflation*: pełzający **2.** *change*: postępujący **3.** pnący **4.** płożący się

creep•y ['kriːpɪ] *adj* **1.** *feeling*: przyprawiający o gęsią skórkę **2.** *person*: odrażający

cre•mate [krɪ'meɪt] *v/t* poddawać ⟨-dać⟩ kremacji; **cre•ma•tion** [krɪ'meɪʃn] *s* kremacja *f*; **cre•ma•to•ri-um** [kremə'tɔːrɪəm] *pl -ria, -riums s* krematorium *n*

crept [krept] *Past Simple and Past Participle* → **creep**

cres•cent ['kresnt] *s* półksiężyc *m*

crest [krest] *s* **1.** grzebień *m* **2.** (*feather*) czubek *m* **3.** *wave*: grzebień *m*, grzbiet *m*; ***be on the ~ of a wave*** *fig* przeżywać dobry okres, *infml* być na fali **4.** *mountain*: grań *m* **5.** kita *f*, czub *m* **6.** herb *m*

crest•fal•len ['krestfɔːln] *adj* zawiedziony, przybity

crew [kruː] *s* **1.** załoga *f* **2.** (*rowing*) osada *f* **3.** *FILM* ekipa *f* **4.** *infml* banda *f*, zgraja *f*; **'crew cut** *s* fryzura *f* na jeża; **'crew neck** *s* wycięcie *n* pod szyją

crib [krɪb] **I** *s* **1.** łóżeczko *n* dziecinne **2.** szopka *f*, żłóbek *m* **3.** (*for animals*) żłób *m* **4.** *infml* ściągawka *f* **II** *v/t*

C

C

infml ściągać ⟨-gnąć⟩ **III** *v/i infml* ściągać ⟨-gnąć⟩ (***from*** od *G*)
crick [krɪk] *s* bolesny kurcz *m*
crick•et[1] ['krɪkɪt] *s BIOL* świerszcz *m*
crick•et[2] [~] *s SPORT* krykiet *m*; **crick•et•er** ['krɪkɪtə] *s* gracz *m* w krykieta
crime [kraɪm] *s* **1.** przestępstwo *n*; ***commit a ~*** popełnić przestępstwo; ***a ~ of violence*** akt przemocy **2.** przestępczość *n* **3.** *fig* zbrodnia *f*; ***it's a ~ to waste such a talent*** to zbrodnia marnować taki talent; **'crime•wave** *s* fala *f* przestępstw
crim•i•nal ['krɪmɪnl] **I** *s* przestępca *m* **II** *adj* przestępczy; ***~ history*** przeszłość kryminalna; **crim•i•nal 'law** *s* prawo *n* karne; **crim•i•nal pro'ceedings** *pl* postępowanie *n* karne; **crim•i•nal 're•cord** *s* karalność *f* uprzednia; ***she has no ~*** nie była karana
crimp [krɪmp] *v/t* **1.** *hair*: karbować **2.** *fabric*: przymarszczać ⟨-czyć⟩
crim•son ['krɪmzn] **I** *s* szkarłat *m* **II** *adj* szkarłatny, pąsowy
cringe [krɪndʒ] *v/i* **1.** kulić ⟨s-⟩ się **2.** czuć ⟨po-⟩ zażenowanie **3.** wzdrygać ⟨-gnąć⟩ się; ***I ~ at the thought of it*** wzdrygam się na myśl o tym **4.** ***~ before s.o.*** płaszczyć się przed kimś
crin•kle ['krɪŋkl] **I** *s* **1.** (*fabric*) fałda *f* **2.** (*skin*) zmarszczka *f* **II** *v/i* marszczyć ⟨z-⟩ się **III** *v/t* **1.** *fabric*: marszczyć ⟨z-⟩, przymarszczać ⟨-czyć⟩ **2.** *eyes*: mrużyć ⟨z-⟩
crip•ple ['krɪpl] **I** *s* kaleka *m* **II** *v/t* **1.** czynić ⟨u-⟩ kaleką **2.** *fig* powodować ⟨s-⟩ uraz psychiczny **3.** *industry, economy*: paraliżować ⟨s-⟩
cri•sis ['kraɪsɪs] *pl -ses* ['kraɪsiːz] *s* kryzys *m*; ***an economic ~*** kryzys ekonomiczny; ***reach ~ point*** osiągnąć punkt krytyczny
crisp [krɪsp] **I** *s Br* chips *m* **II** *adj* **1.** kruchy, chrupiący **2.** *clothing*: świeżo wyprasowany **3.** *paper*: szeleszczący **4.** *air*: rześki; **'crisp•bread** *s Br* pieczywo *n* chrupkie
criss•cross ['krɪskrɒs] **I** *s* (*pattern*) siatka *f* **II** *adj* **1.** kratkowany **2.** krzyżujący się
cri•te•ri•on [kraɪ'tɪrɪən] *pl -ria s* kryterium *n*; ***meet a ~*** spełniać kryterium
crit•ic ['krɪtɪk] *s* krytyk *m*
crit•i•cal ['krɪtɪkl] *adj* **1.** krytyczny (***of*** wobec *G*) **2.** *stage*: decydujący **3.** *moment*: krytyczny; **crit•i•cal•ly** ['krɪtɪklɪ] *adv* krytycznie; **crit•i•cism** ['krɪtɪsɪzəm] *s* **1.** krytyka *f*; ***literary ~*** krytyka literacka **2.** krytyczna ocena *f*; **crit•i•cize** ['krɪtɪsaɪz] *v/t* **1.** krytykować ⟨s-⟩ **2.** poddawać ⟨-dać⟩ krytycznej ocenie
cri•tique [krɪ'tiːk] *s* **1.** krytyka *f* **2.** opracowanie *n* krytyczne
croak [krəʊk] **I** *s* **1.** *frog*: rechot *m* **2.** krakanie *n* **3.** chrapliwy głos *m* **II** *v/i* **1.** (*frog*) rechotać ⟨za-⟩ **2.** chrypieć, mówić chrapliwym głosem
Cro•at ['krəʊæt] *s* Chorwat *m*, Chorwatka *f*; **Cro•a•tia** [krəʊ'eɪʃə] *s* Chorwacja *f*; **Cro•a•tian** [krəʊ'eɪʃən] *adj* chorwacki
crock [krɒk] *s Br infml* **1.** gruchot *m*, grat *m* **2.** ramol *m*
crock•e•ry ['krɒkərɪ] *s* naczynia *pl* stołowe
croc•o•dile ['krɒkədaɪl] *s BIOL* krokodyl *m*; ***shed ~ tears*** płakać krokodylimi łzami
crook [krʊk] **I** *s* **1.** *infml* oszust *m*, kanciarz *m* **2.** zakręt *m*; ***the ~ of one's arm*** zgięcie łokciowe **II** *v/t* zginać ⟨zgiąć⟩; **crook•ed** ['krʊkɪd] *adj* **1.** krzywy, zakrzywiony, **2.** *path*: kręty **3.** *infml* nieuczciwy
crop [krɒp] **I** *s* **1.** uprawa *f*; uprawy *pl*; ***cereal ~*** uprawy zbóż **2.** plon *m*, zbiory *pl* **3.** krótka fryzura *f* **II** *v/t* **1.** obcinać ⟨-ciąć⟩ **2.** uprawiać; **crop up** *v/i* (*problem, opportunity*) pojawiać ⟨-wić⟩ się
cross [krɒs] **I** *s* **1.** krzyż *m*; ***make the sign of the ~*** uczynić znak krzyża; ***bear one's ~*** *fig* dźwigać swój krzyż **2.** krzyżyk *m*; ***put a ~ against*** postawić krzyżyk przy *L* **3.** *BIOL* krzyżówka *f* **4.** skos *m*, ukos *m* **II** *adj* **1.** zły (***with*** na *A*); ***we've never had a ~ word*** nigdy się nie pokłóciliśmy **2.** *wave, wind*: boczny **III** *v/t* **1.** przekraczać ⟨-roczyć⟩ **2.** przejeżdżać ⟨-jechać⟩ przez *A* **3.** przepływać ⟨-łynąć⟩ przez *A* **4.** przelatywać ⟨-lecieć⟩ nad *I* **5.** (*path, road*) przecinać ⟨-ciąć⟩, krzyżować się z *I*; ***~ each other*** krzyżować się, przecinać się **6.** ***~ oneself*** *REL* przeżegnać się **IV** *v/i* **1.** (*lines,*

roads) przecinać ⟨-ciąć⟩ się **2.** (*cars*) mijać ⟨minąć⟩ się **3.** przechodzić ⟨przejść⟩ (na drugą stronę) **4.** przejeżdżać ⟨-jechać⟩ (na drugą stronę); **cross off**, **cross out** skreślać ⟨-lić⟩; ***~ s.o.'s name off a list*** skreślić kogoś z listy; **cross over** *v/i* **1.** → ***cross III*** **2.** ***~ into France*** przekroczyć granicę Francji **3.** ***~ to*** *fig* przejść na stronę *G*

'cross•bar *s* SPORT poprzeczka *f*; **'cross•beam** *s* poprzecznica *f*; **'cross•breed I** *s* (*animal*) mieszaniec *m* **II** (*crossbred*; *crossbred*) *v/t* krzyżować ⟨s-⟩ (***with*** z *I*); **cross-'check I** *s* weryfikacja *f* **II** *v/t* sprawdzać ⟨-dzić⟩ ponownie, weryfikować ⟨z-⟩; **cross-'coun•try** *adj* **1.** *race*: przełajowy, krosowy **2.** *route*: prowadzący przez tereny wiejskie; **cross-coun•try 'ski•ing** *s* narciarstwo *n* biegowe; **'cross•cur•rent** *s fig* prąd *m* przeciwny, tendencja *f* przeciwna; **cross-'dress•ing** *s* transwestytyzm *m*

cross-ex•am•i'na•tion *s* **1.** JUR pytania *pl* strony przeciwnej **2.** krzyżowy ogień *m* pytań; **cross-ex•'am•ine** *v/t* **1.** JUR zadawać ⟨-dać⟩ pytania stronie przeciwnej **2.** brać ⟨wziąć⟩ w krzyżowy ogień pytań; **cross-'eyed** *adj* zezowaty; **'cross-fire** *s* krzyżowy ogień *m*

cross•ing ['krɒsɪŋ] *s* **1.** przejście *n* dla pieszych **2.** ***a border ~*** przejście graniczne **3.** przeprawa *f* **4.** przelot *m*

cross-'leg•ged *adj*: ***sit ~*** siedzieć po turecku; **cross-'pur•pos•es** *pl*: ***we are at ~*** nie możemy dojść do porozumienia; ***talk at ~*** mówić o dwóch różnych rzeczach; **cross-'ref•er•ence** *s* odnośnik *m*, odsyłacz *m*; **'cross•roads** *pl* skrzyżowanie *n*, rozdroże *n*; **'cross-sec•tion** *s* **1.** przekrój *m* poprzeczny **2.** *fig* przekrój *m*; **'cross•walk** *s Am* przejście *n* dla pieszych; **'cross•ways**, **'cross•wise** *adv* ukośnie, poprzecznie; **'cross•word (puz•zle)** *s* krzyżówka *f*; ***do a ~*** rozwiązywać krzyżówkę

crotch [krɒtʃ] *s* **1.** ANAT krocze *n* **2.** (*trousers*) krok *m*

crouch [krautʃ] *s* **1.** przysiad *m* **2.** kucki *pl*; **crouch down** *v/i* **1.** przykucać ⟨-cnąć⟩ **2.** (*animal*) przyczajać ⟨-czaić⟩ się

crow[1] [krəʊ] *s* BIOL wrona *f*: ***as the ~ flies*** w linii prostej

crow[2] [~] **I** *s cock*: pianie *n* **II** *v/i* piać (z zachwytu) (***over***/***about*** nad *I*)

crow•bar [krəʊbaː] *s* łom *m*

crowd [kraʊd] **I** *s* **1.** tłum *m*; ***~s of people*** tłumy ludzi; ***draw ~s*** przyciągać tłumy; ***we ski in Norway to avoid the ~s*** jeździmy na narty do Norwegii, żeby uniknąć tłoku **2.** publiczność *f*, widownia *f* **3.** *infml* paczka *f*; ***the ~ from the office*** kumple z biura **II** *v/t* **1.** tłoczyć ⟨s-⟩ się; ***the roads were ~ed with cars*** drogi były zatłoczone; ***tourists ~ed the trains*** pociągi pełne były turystów **2.** wtłaczać ⟨-łoczyć⟩; ***they have ~ed a lot of information into this brochure*** w tej broszurze zawarto ogromną ilość informacji **3.** *room, house*: zastawiać ⟨-wić⟩, zagracać ⟨-cić⟩; ***the house was ~ed with paintings*** w domu było mnóstwo obrazów **III** *v/i* tłoczyć ⟨s-⟩ się; ***~ into*** wepchnąć się do *G*; **crowd around** *v/i* gromadzić ⟨z-⟩ się wokół *G*; otaczać ⟨otoczyć⟩; ***don't ~ the entrance*** proszę nie tłoczyć się przy wejściu; **crowd in** *v/i* wciskać ⟨-snąć⟩ się do środka

crowd•ed ['kraʊdɪd] *adj* **1.** zatłoczony, przepełniony; ***a ~ bus*** zatłoczony autobus **2.** pełen (***with*** *G*) **3.** zastawiony, zagracony **4.** przeładowany

crown [kraʊn] **I** *s* **1.** korona *f*; ***a ~ of flowers*** wianek **2.** SPORT mistrzostwo *n* **3.** FIN korona *f* **II** *v/t* **1.** *king*: koronować ⟨u-⟩ **2.** dekorować ⟨u-⟩, wręczać ⟨-czyć⟩ trofeum **3.** wieńczyć ⟨u-⟩, koronować ⟨u-⟩; ***her efforts were ~ed by success*** jej starania zostały uwieńczone sukcesem **4.** ***to ~ it all*** na domiar wszystkiego

crown•ing ['kraʊnɪŋ] **I** *s* koronacja *f* **II** *adj achievement*: szczytowy

crown 'jew•els *pl* klejnoty *pl* koronne; **crown 'prince** *s* następca *m* tronu; **crown prin'cess** *s* następczyni *f* tronu

'crow's feet *s* (*face*) kurze łapki *pl*; **'crow's nest** *s* (*ship*) bocianie gniazdo *n*

cru•cial ['kruːʃl] *adj* **1.** kluczowy, zasadniczy **2.** decydujacy **3.** rozstrzygający

C

cru•ci•fix ['kruːsɪfɪks] *s* krucyfiks *m*; **cru•ci•fix•ion** [kruːsɪ'fɪkʃn] *s* ukrzyżowanie *n*; **cru•ci•fy** ['kruːsɪfaɪ] *v/t* krzyżować ⟨u-⟩
crude [kruːd] *adj* **1.** surowy; *~ **oil*** ropa naftowa **2.** *method*: prymitywny **3.** niedopracowany **4.** prostacki, ordynarny; **crude•ly** ['kruːdlɪ] *adv* **1.** prosto **2.** prymitywnie **3.** prostacko, ordynarnie; **crude•ness** ['kruːdnɪs], ***cru•di•ty*** ['kruːdɪtɪ] *s* **1.** grubiaństwo *n*, ordynarność *f* **2.** prymitywność *f*
cru•el ['kruːəl] *adj* okrutny (**to** wobec *G*); **cru•el•ty** ['kruːəltɪ] *s* okrucieństwo *n*
cruise [kruːz] **I** *s* rejs *m* wycieczkowy; ***go on a ~*** wyruszyć w rejs **II** *v/t* ***~ a sea*** (***river***) pływać po morzu (rzece) **III** *v/i* **1.** odbywać ⟨-być⟩ rejs wycieczkowy **2.** lecieć (ze stałą prędkością); ***~ at 10,000 m*** lecieć na wysokości 10.000 metrów **3.** jechać (ze stałą prędkością); '**cruise lin•er** *s* statek *m* wycieczkowy; **cruise 'mis•sile** *s* pocisk *m* samosterujący dalekiego zasięgu; **cruis•er** ['kruːzə] *s* **1.** krążownik *m* **2.** łódź *f* motorowa (z kabiną); '**cruis•ing speed** *s* stała prędkość *f* (jazdy)
crumb [krʌm] *s* **1.** okruch *m*, okruszyna *f* **2.** odrobina *f*; ***a ~ of hope*** iskierka nadziei
crum•ble ['krʌmbl] **I** *s* ***apple ~*** szarlotka z kruszonką **II** (*a.* ***~ up***) *v/t* kruszyć ⟨po-⟩ **III** *v/i* **1.** kruszyć ⟨po-⟩ się **2.** rozpadać ⟨-paść⟩ się **3.** (*economy*) popadać ⟨-paść⟩ w ruinę; **crum•bly** ['krʌmblɪ] *adj* **1.** *bread*: kruszący się **2.** *pastry*: kruchy
crum•ple ['krʌmpl] **I** *v/t* zgniatać ⟨zgnieść⟩ **II** *v/i* **1.** (*clothes, paper*) gnieść ⟨po-⟩ się **2.** (*metal*) zgniatać ⟨zgnieść⟩ się **3.** (*face*) marszczyć ⟨z-⟩ się; **crumple up** *v/t* zgniatać ⟨zgnieść⟩
crunch [krʌntʃ] **I** *v/i* **1.** chrzęścić ⟨za-⟩; ***his shoes ~ed on the gravel*** żwir chrzęścił mu pod stopami **2.** skrzypieć ⟨za-⟩ **3.** zgrzytać ⟨za-⟩ **II** *v/t* **1.** *apple*: chrupać ⟨s-⟩ **2.** *nuts*: rozłupywać ⟨-pać⟩ **III** *s* **1.** chrzęst *m* **2.** zgrzyt *m* **3.** skrzypienie *n*; **crunch•y** ['krʌntʃɪ] *adj* **1.** chrupki, chrupiący **2.** *snow*: skrzypiący
cru•sade [kruː'seɪd] *s* wyprawa *f* krzyżowa, krucjata *f*; **cru•sad•er** [kruː'seɪdə] *s* **1.** krzyżowiec *m* **2.** *fig* bojownik *m*
crush [krʌʃ] **I** *s* **1.** ścisk *m*, tłok *m*; ***in the ~*** w tłoku **2.** zadurzenie *n*; ***have a ~ on*** być zadurzonym w *L* **3.** *Br* napój *m* ze świeżych owoców **II** *v/t* **1.** *can*: zgniatać ⟨zgnieść⟩ **2.** miażdżyć ⟨z-⟩ **3.** *ice*: rozkruszać ⟨-szyć⟩ **4.** *garment*: gnieść ⟨po-⟩, miąć ⟨z-⟩ **5.** *protest, insurrection*: dławić ⟨z-⟩ **III** *v/i* **1.** ***~ together*** stłoczyć się **2.** ***~ forward*** przeć do przodu **3.** ***~ into*** wciskać się do *G*; '**crush bar•ri•er** *s* bariera *f* zabezpieczająca; **crush•ing** ['krʌʃɪŋ] *adj* **1.** przygniatający **2.** miażdżący **3.** druzgocący; '**crush-re•sist•ant** *adj* **1.** *fabric*: niemnący się **2.** *packing*: sztywny
crust [krʌst] *s* **1.** *bread*: skórka *f* **2.** *ice*: skorupa *f* **3.** *snow*: pokrywa *f* **4.** MED strup *m*; **crust•y** ['krʌstɪ] *adj* chrupiący
crutch [krʌtʃ] *s* **1.** MED kula inwalidzka *f*; ***walk on ~es*** chodzić o kulach **2.** *fig* oparcie *n*, podpora *f*
cry [kraɪ] **I** *s* **1.** krzyk *m*, okrzyk *m*; ***a ~ for help*** wołanie o pomoc; ***a ~ for mercy*** błaganie o litość **2.** płacz *m* **3.** *wolf*: wycie *n* **4.** zawołanie *n* **II** *v/i* **1.** płakać ⟨za-⟩ (**about** z powodu *G*); ***I laughed till I cried*** uśmiałem się do łez **2.** krzyczeć ⟨krzyknąć⟩ **III** *v/t* wykrzykiwać ⟨-knąć⟩ (**to** do *G*); **cry off** *v/i Br* odwoływać ⟨-łać⟩ spotkanie; **cry out** *v/i* **1.** krzyczeć ⟨krzyknąć⟩; ***~ in pain*** krzyczeć z bólu **2.** wołać ⟨za-⟩; ***~ against*** głośno protestować przeciwko *D*; **cry out for** *v/t* **1.** błagać o *A* **2.** domagać się *G* **3.** pilnie potrzebować *G*
'**cry•ba•by** *s infml* beksa *f*
cry•ing ['kraɪɪŋ] *adj* **1.** zapłakany **2.** *injustice*: krzyczący **3.** *need*: palący
crypt [krɪpt] *s* krypta *f*
cryp•tic ['krɪptɪk] *adj* tajemniczy, zagadkowy
crys•tal ['krɪstl] *s* **1.** kryształ *m*; ***as clear as ~*** jasny jak słońce **3.** szkło *n* kryształowe **4.** (*watch*) szkiełko *n*; **crys•tal-'clear** *adj* **1.** *water, sound*:

C

krystalicznie czysty **2.** *explanation*: jasny; **crys•tal•li•za•tion** [krɪstəlaɪ'zeɪʃn] *s* krystalizacja *f*; **crys•tal•lize** ['krɪstəlaɪz] **I** *v/t* **1.** krystalizować ⟨s-⟩ **2.** precyzować ⟨s-⟩ **II** *v/i* **1.** krystalizować ⟨s-⟩ się **2.** konkretyzować ⟨s-⟩ się

CST *abbr* (=***Central Standard Time***) *Am* urzędowy czas *m* środkowoamerykański

Cu•ba ['kju:bə] *s* Kuba *f*

cube [kju:b] **I** *s* **1.** sześcian *m* **2.** kostka *f*; ***ice*** ~ kostka lodu **3.** *MATH* trzecia potęga *f* **II** *v/t* **1.** podnosić ⟨-nieść⟩ do trzeciej potęgi **2.** kroić ⟨po-⟩ w kostkę; **cu•bic** ['kju:bɪk] *adj* sześcienny; ***two ~ metres*** dwa metry sześcienne; **cu•bic ca'pac•i•ty** *s* pojemność *f*

cuck•old ['kʌkəld] *s dated* rogacz *m*

cuck•oo ['kʊku:] **I** *s BIOL* kukułka *f* **II** *adj infml* stuknięty; **'cuck•oo clock** *s* zegar *m* z kukułką

cu•cum•ber ['kju:kʌmbə] *s* ogórek *m*

cud•dle ['kʌdl] **I** *s* ***give s.o. a*** ~ przytulić kogoś; ***have a*** ~ tulić się **II** *v/t* przytulać ⟨-lić⟩ **III** *v/i* tulić się, przytulać ⟨-lić⟩ się; **cud•dle up** *v/i* przytulać ⟨-lić⟩ się, tulić się (***against*** do *G*); **cud•dly** ['kʌdlɪ] *adj* milusieńki, mięciutki; ***he's very*** ~ aż chce się go przytulić

cue[1] [kju:] **I** *s* **1.** znak *m*, sygnał *m* dla aktora **2.** wskazówka *f*; ***take one's ~ from*** brać przykład z *G* **3.** sygnał *m* **4.** *MUS* znak *m* rozpoczęcia partii **II** *v/t* dawać ⟨dać⟩ sygnał

cue[2] [~] *s* kij *m* (bilardowy)

'cue ball *s* kula *f* bilardowa, bila *f*; **'cue card** *s TEL* teleprompter *m*

cuff [kʌf] *s* **1.** mankiet *m* **2.** ***~s*** *infml* kajdanki *pl*; **'cuff link** *s* spinka *f* do mankietu

cui•sine [kwɪ'zi:n] *s* kuchnia *f*; ***Italian*** ~ włoska kuchnia

cu•li•nar•y ['kʌlɪnərɪ] *adj* kulinarny

cul•mi•nate ['kʌlmɪneɪt] *v/i*: ~ ***in*** **a)** zakończyć się *I* **b)** *in success*: zostać uwieńczonym *I*; **cul•mi•na•tion** [kʌlmɪ'neɪʃn] *s* **1.** punkt *m* kulminacyjny **2.** rezultat *m*, wynik *m* **3.** *of work*: ukoronowanie *n*

cul•pa•ble ['kʌlpəbl] *adj* **1.** *person*: winny **2.** *behaviour*: karygodny

cult [kʌlt] *s* **1.** sekta *f* **2.** kult *m*; ***personality*** ~ kult jednostki

cul•ti•vate ['kʌltɪveɪt] *v/t* **1.** *soil*: uprawiać **2.** *flowers*: hodować **3.** *mind*: doskonalić **4.** *friendship*: kultywować **5.** *sense of responsibility*: rozwijać ⟨-winąć⟩ w sobie; **cul•ti•vat•ed** ['kʌltɪveɪtɪd] *adj* **1.** *land*: uprawiany **2.** hodowany; **cul•ti•va•tion** [kʌltɪ'veɪʃn] *s* **1.** uprawa *f* **2.** hodowla *f* **3.** doskonalenie *n* **4.** rozwijanie *n* **5.** ogłada *f*; **cul•ti•va•tor** ['kʌltɪveɪtə] *s* **1.** kultywator *m* **2.** hodowca *m*

cul•tu•ral ['kʌltʃərəl] *adj* **1.** kulturalny **2.** *traditions*, *influences*: kulturowy; **cul•tu•ral 'her•i•tage** *s* dziedzictwo *n* kulturowe

cul•ture ['kʌltʃə] *s* **1.** kultura *f*; ***high*** (***popular***) ~ kultura wysoka (popularna); ***minority ~s*** kultura mniejszości etnicznych; ***street*** ~ kultura ulicy **2.** uprawa *f* **3.** hodowla *f* **4.** *of bacteria*: kultura *f*; **cul•tured** ['kʌltʃəd] *adj* **1.** kulturalny **2.** *taste*: wyrobiony; **'cul•ture shock** *s* szok *m* kulturowy

cum•ber•some ['kʌmbəsəm] *adj* **1.** *luggage*: nieporęczny **2.** *furniture*: nieustawny **3.** *method*: kłopotliwy

cu•mu•la•tive ['kju:mjʊlətɪv] *adj* **1.** *process*: narastający **2.** *effect*: kumulacyjny

cun•ning ['kʌnɪŋ] **I** *s* przebiegłość *f* **II** *adj* **1.** przebiegły **2.** sprytny

cunt [kʌnt] *s vulg* cipa *f*, pizda *f*

cup [kʌp] **I** *s* **1.** filiżanka *f*; ***two ~s of flour*** dwie szklanki mąki **2.** *SPORT* puchar *m* **3.** (*bra*) miseczka *f* **4.** *flower*: kielich *m* **II** *v/t* ~ ***s.th. in one's hands*** trzymać coś w złączonych dłoniach; ~ ***one's hands around*** otoczyć dłońmi, osłonić dłońmi

cup•board ['kʌbəd] *s* kredens *m*, szafka *f*; ***a kitchen*** ~ szafka kuchenna

'cup fi•nal *s SPORT* finał *m* rozgrywek pucharowych

cup•ful ['kʌpfʊl] *s* (*measure*) szklanka *f*

cu•ra•ble ['kjʊrəbl] *adj* uleczalny

cu•ra•tor [kjʊ'reɪtə] *s* **1.** *exhibition*: kurator *m* **2.** *museum*: kustosz *m*

curb [kɜ:b] **I** *s* **1.** ograniczenie *n*; ***put a ~ on*** ograniczyć *A* **2.** *Am* krawężnik *m* **II** *v/t* **1.** ograniczać ⟨-czyć⟩ **2.** powściągać ⟨-gnąć⟩ **3.** *anger*: hamować

C

⟨po-⟩ **4.** *horse*: okiełznywać ⟨-nać⟩; **'curb•stone** *s Am* krawężnik *m*

cur•dle ['kɜːdl] **I** *v/i* **1.** (*milk*) zsiadać ⟨zsiąść⟩ się **2.** (*sauce*) warzyć ⟨z-⟩ się **II** *v/t* **1.** *milk, eggs*: ścinać ⟨ściąć⟩ **2.** *~ s.o.'s blood* *fig* mrozić komuś krew w żyłach

cure [kjʊə] **I** *s* **1.** lekarstwo *n* **2.** metoda *f* leczenia **3.** środek *m* zaradczy **4.** wyzdrowienie *n* **5.** *fig* lekarstwo *n*, recepta *f*; ***the best ~ for boredom is hard work*** najlepszym lekarstwem na nudę jest ciężka praca **II** *v/t* **1.** leczyć ⟨wy-⟩ (**of** z *G*) **2.** *bad habit*: wykorzeniać; **'cure-all** *s* panaceum *n*, złoty środek *m*

cu•ri•os•i•ty [kjʊrɪ'ɒsətɪ] *s* **1.** ciekawość *f* (***about*** *G*) **2.** osobliwość *f*, kuriozum *n*; **cu•ri•ous** ['kjʊərɪəs] *adj* **1.** ciekawy; ***~ to know why*** ciekaw dlaczego; ***I'm just ~!*** jestem po prostu ciekawy! **2.** ciekawski **3.** osobliwy, dziwny; **cu•ri•ous•ly** ['kjʊərɪəslɪ] *adv* **1.** z zaciekawieniem **2.** dziwnie **3.** co ciekawe

curl [kɜːl] **I** *s* **1.** lok *m* **2.** zawijas *m* **3.** *smoke*: kłąb *m* **4.** wiór *m* **5.** obierka *f* **II** *v/i* **1.** (*hair*) kręcić się **2.** (*leaf, paper*) zwijać ⟨zwinąć⟩ się **III** *v/t* **1.** ***~ oneself around*** owinąć się wokół *G* **2.** ***~ one's fingers around*** zacisnąć palce wokół *G* **3.** *hair*: zakręcać ⟨-cić⟩ **4.** zwijać ⟨zwinąć⟩; **curl up** *v/i* **1.** (*person, animal*) zwijać ⟨zwinąć⟩ się w kłębek **2.** (*smoke*) kłębić się **3.** (*corners*) wywijać ⟨-winąć⟩ się; **curl•er** ['kɜːlə] *s* lokówka *f*, wałek *m* (do włosów); **curl•ing** ['kɜːlɪŋ] *s* SPORT curling *m*; **curl•y** ['kɜːlɪ] *adj* **1.** *hair*: kręcony **2.** *moustache*: zakręcony **3.** *eyelashes*: podwinięty do góry

cur•rant ['kʌrənt] *s* **1.** koryntka *f* **2.** porzeczka *f*

cur•ren•cy ['kʌrənsɪ] *s* **1.** FIN waluta *f*, środek *m* płatniczy **2.** *words*: częstotliwość *f* użycia **3.** popularność *f* **4.** ***give ~ to a rumour*** potwierdzić pogłoskę

cur•rent ['kʌrənt] **I** *s* **1.** *electricity, water*: prąd *m*; ***go with*** (***against***) ***the ~*** płynąć z prądem (pod prąd) **2.** *history*: bieg *m* **3.** *thought*: tok *m* **4.** tendencja *f*, prąd *m* **II** *adj* **1.** bieżący **2.** obecny **3.** aktualny; **'cur•rent account** *s* ECON rachunek *m* bieżący; **cur•rent af'fairs, *cur•rent e'vents*** *pl* aktualności *pl*, aktualne wydarzenia *pl*; **cur•rent af'fairs pro•gram** *s* program *m* publicystyczny; **cur•rent•ly** ['kʌrəntlɪ] *adv* obecnie

cur•ric•u•lum [kə'rɪkjələm] *pl -la, -lums s* program *m* nauczania; **cur•ric•u•lum vi•tae** [kərɪkjələm'viːtaɪ] *s pl curricula vitae, curriculums vitae Br* życiorys *m*, CV *n*, curriculum vitae *n*

cur•ry[1] ['kʌrɪ] **I** *s* curry *n*; ***chicken ~*** curry z kurczaka **II** *v/t* ***~ favour with s.o.*** zabiegać o czyjeś względy

cur•ry[2] [~] *v/t horse*: szczotkować ⟨wy-⟩

curse [kɜːs] **I** *s* **1.** przekleństwo *n*; ***that car is a ~!*** ten samochód to przekleństwo! **2.** klątwa *f*, przekleństwo *n*; ***put a ~ on*** przekląć *A*, rzucić klątwę na *A* **II** *v/t* przeklinać ⟨-ląć⟩; ***~d be the day that*** niech będzie przeklęty dzień, w którym **III** *v/i* kląć, przeklinać

cur•so•ry ['kɜːsərɪ] *adj glance, inspection*: pobieżny

cur•tain ['kɜːtn] *s* **1.** zasłona *f* **2.** firanka *f* **3.** kotara *f* **4.** THEAT kurtyna *f*; **cur•tain off** *v/t* **1.** oddzielać ⟨-lić⟩ kurtyną **2.** przesłaniać ⟨-łonić⟩

'cur•tain call *s* THEAT wywołanie *n* aktora przed kurtynę; **'cur•tain rais•er** *s* THEAT jednoaktówka *f* poprzedzająca właściwe przedstawienie

curt•sey ['kɜːtsɪ] **I** *s* **1.** dygnięcie *n*, dyg *m* **2.** głęboki ukłon *m* **II** *v/i* **1.** dygać ⟨-gnąć⟩ **2.** składać ⟨złożyć⟩ głęboki ukłon (***to*** przed *I*)

curve [kɜːv] **I** *s* **1.** (*graph*) krzywa *f* **2.** łuk *m* **3.** ugięcie *n* **4.** (łagodny) zakręt *m* **5.** ***~s*** (*woman*) krągłości *pl* **II** *v/t* **1.** zakrzywiać ⟨-wić⟩ **2.** wyginać ⟨-giąć⟩ **III** *v/i* **1.** (*line*) wyginać ⟨-giąć⟩ się **2.** (*wall*) zaokrąglać ⟨-lić⟩ się **3.** (*road*) zakręcać ⟨-cić⟩ łukiem

cush•ion ['kʊʃn] **I** *s* **1.** poduszka *f* **2.** zabezpieczenie *n* (***against*** przed *I*) **II** *v/t* **1.** *fall*: amortyzować ⟨z-⟩ **2.** osłabiać ⟨-bić⟩; **cush•y** ['kʊʃɪ] *adj infml* cichy, spokojny

cus•to•di•al [kʌ'stəʊdjəl] *adj* **1.** ***~ sentence*** JUR kara pozbawienia wolności

C

2. *be put in ~ care* zostać oddanym do domu dziecka; **cus•to•di•an** [kʌ'stəʊdɪən] *s* **1.** dozorca *m* **2.** strażnik *m* **3.** kustosz *m*; **cus•to•dy** ['kʌstədɪ] *s* **1.** areszt *m*; ***in ~*** w areszcie **2.** opieka *f*; ***grant s.o. ~ of a child*** przyznać komuś opiekę nad dzieckiem

cus•tom ['kʌstəm] **I** *s* **1.** zwyczaj *m*, obyczaj *m*; ***~ requires that*** obyczaj nakazuje, żeby **2.** nawyk *m*, przyzwyczajenie *n* **3.** zwyczaj *m* **4.** JUR prawo *n* zwyczajowe **II** *adj article*: na zamówienie; **cus•tom•a•ry** ['kʌstəmərɪ] *adj* tradycyjny, zwyczajowy; **cus•tom-'built 1.** *car*: wykonany na zamówienie **2.** *house*: zbudowany według indywidualnego projektu

cus•tom•er ['kʌstəmə] *s* klient *m*; ***~ loyalty*** przywiązanie klienta do marki; **cus•tom•er re'la•tions** *pl* łączność *f* z klientami; **cus•tom•er 'serv•ice** *s* obsługa *f* klienta

cus•tom•ize ['kʌstəmaɪz] *v/t* **1.** wykonywać ⟨-nać⟩ na zamówienie **2.** przerabiać ⟨-robić⟩ zgodnie z zamówieniem klienta; **cus•tom-'made** *adj* wykonany na zamówienie

cus•toms ['kʌstəmz] *pl* **1.** urząd *m* celny **2.** odprawa *f* celna; ***go through ~*** przejść odprawę celną **3.** cło *n*; **'cus•toms clear•ance** *s* odprawa *f* celna; **'cus•toms dec•la•ra•tion** *s* deklaracja *f* celna; **'cus•toms du•ties** *pl* opłaty *pl* celne; **'cus•toms ex•am•i•nation** *s* kontrola *f* celna; **'cus•toms in•spec•tion** *s* kontrola *f* celna; **'cus•toms of•fi•cer** *s* celnik *m*

cut [kʌt] **I** *s* **1.** cięcie *n* **2.** *fabric*: rozcięcie *n* **3.** *wood*: nacięcie *n* **4.** (*wound*) skaleczenie *n*, rozcięcie *n*, rana *f* cięta **5.** fryzura *f* **6.** *infml* część *f*, udział *m*, działka *f*; ***she takes a 25% ~ of the total sum*** ona bierze 25% całej sumy **7.** cięcie *n*, obniżka *f*; ***a ~ in interest rates*** obniżka stóp procentowych **8. *give s.th. a ~*** ostrzyć coś, ściąć coś **9.** COOK kawałek *m*, część *f*; ***fillet is the most tender ~*** polędwica to najdelikatniejsza część (mięsa) **10.** krój *m*, fason *m* **11.** FILM cięcie *n* **II** (*cut*; *cut*) *v/t* **1.** *bread*, *fruit*: kroić ⟨po-⟩ **2.** *metal*, *paper*: ciąć ⟨po-⟩ **3.** *slice*, *piece*: kroić ⟨u-⟩; ***~ s.th. in half*** przekroić coś na pół **4.** *rope*: przecinać ⟨-ciąć⟩ **5.** *flower*: ucinać ⟨uciąć⟩, ścinać ⟨ściąć⟩ **6.** *grass*: kosić ⟨s-⟩ **7.** *tunnel*: drążyć ⟨wy-⟩ **8.** MED otwierać ⟨-worzyć⟩ **9.** kaleczyć ⟨s-, po-⟩; ***~ one's finger*** skaleczyć się w palec **10.** *fig* ranić ⟨z-⟩ **11.** *hair*: ścinać ⟨ściąć⟩, strzyc ⟨o-⟩ **12.** *hedge*, *grass*: przycinać ⟨-ciąć⟩ **13.** *gem*: szlifować ⟨o-⟩ **14.** *wood*: ociosywać ⟨-sać⟩ **15.** *suit*: kroić ⟨s-⟩ **16. *~ s.o. from*** *wreckage*: wydobyć kogoś z *G* **17.** *article*, *film*: skracać ⟨-rócić⟩ **18.** *price*: obniżać ⟨-żyć⟩; ***we've ~ prices by 10%*** obniżyliśmy ceny o 10% **19.** *spending*: zmniejszać ⟨-szyć⟩ **20.** *album*, *track*: nagrywać ⟨-rać⟩ **21.** traktować ⟨po-⟩ jak powietrze; ***she ~ me dead*** udała, że mnie nie widzi **III** (*cut*; *cut*) *v/i* **1.** ciąć, kroić; ***this knife ~s well*** tym nożem dobrze się kroi; ***metal doesn't ~ very easily*** trudno jest przeciąć metal **2. *~ across the park*** pójść na przełaj przez park **3.** *fig remark*, *criticism*: ranić ⟨z-⟩ **4.** (*cards*) przekładać ⟨przełożyć⟩ **IV** *adj* **1.** pocięty **2.** *gem*: oszlifowany **3.** *stone*: ociosany **4.** *wound*: cięty; **cut back 1.** *spending*, *production*: ograniczać ⟨-czyć⟩ **2.** *bush*: przycinać ⟨-ciąć⟩; **cut back on** *v/t* **1.** oszczędzać ⟨-dzić⟩ na *L* **2.** *spending*, *size*: redukować ⟨z-⟩, zmniejszać ⟨-szyć⟩ **3.** *consumption*: ograniczać ⟨-czyć⟩; **cut in** *v/i* **1.** (*in conversation*) wtrącać ⟨-cić⟩ się; ***~ on*** przerywać *A* **2. *the taxi ~ in infront of me*** taksówka zajechała mi drogę; **cut off** *v/t* **1.** *tip*, *power*: odcinać ⟨-ciąć⟩ **2.** *slice*: odkrawać ⟨-roić⟩ **3. *~ s.o.'s head*** ściąć komuś głowę **4. *cut 1% off inflation*** obniżyć inflację o 1%; ***she cut 10 seconds off the world record*** poprawiła rekord świata o 10 sekund **5.** *financial aid*: wstrzymywać ⟨-mać⟩ **6.** (*army*) odcinać ⟨-ciąć⟩ **7.** (*telephone*) rozłączać ⟨-czyć⟩; ***we were ~*** coś nam przerwało **8.** wydziedziczać ⟨-czyć⟩; **cut out I** *v/i* **1.** (*engine*) gasnąć ⟨z-⟩ **2.** (*machine*) wyłączać ⟨-czyć⟩ się **3.** wycinać ⟨-ciąć⟩ (***from*** z *G*) **II** *v/t* **1.** usuwać ⟨usunąć⟩ **2.** *skirt*: kroić ⟨s-⟩ **3.** *view*: przesła-

C

niać ⟨-łonić⟩ **4.** wyłączać ⟨-czyć⟩, eliminować ⟨wy-⟩ (***of*** z *G*); ***~ s.o. out of one's will*** pominąć kogoś w testamencie **5.** ***be ~ for teaching*** być urodzonym nauczycielem; **cut up** *v/t* **1.** *victim*: ranić ⟨po-⟩, haratać ⟨po-⟩ **2.** ***be very ~*** nie móc się pozbierać (***about*** po *L*)

'cutback *s* ECON redukcja *f*; ***~s in*** cięcia wydatków na *A*

cute [kjuːt] *adj* **1.** słodki, milutki, uroczy **2.** *infml* sprytny

cut•ler•y ['kʌtlərɪ] *s* sztućce *pl*

cut•let ['kʌtlət] *s* **1.** kotlet *m* **2.** filet *m*

'cut-off date *s* termin *m* ostateczny; **'cut•out** *s* **1.** (wycięta) sylwetka *f* **2.** wycinanka *f*; **cut-'price, cut-'rate** *Am adj* przeceniony, po obniżonej cenie

cut•ter ['kʌtə] *s* **1.** nóż *m* **2.** szczypce *pl* **3.** kuter *m*

'cut-throat I *s* rzezimieszek *m* **II** *adj* **1.** *battle*: zaciekły **2.** *world*: okrutny

cut•ting ['kʌtɪŋ] **I** *s* **1.** (*newspaper*) wycinek *m* **2.** wykop *m* **3.** *tunnel*: drążenie *n* **4.** *cake*, *meat*: krojenie *n* **II** *adj* **1.** *tool*: tnący **2.** *pain*, *wind*: przenikliwy, przejmujący

CV [siː'viː] → ***curriculum vitae***

cy•a•nide ['saɪənaɪd] *s* cyjanek *m*

cy•ber•net•ics [saɪbə'netɪks] *s* cybernetyka *f*; **cy•ber•space** ['saɪbərspeɪs] *s* cyberprzestrzeń *m*

cy•cle ['saɪkl] **I** *s* **1.** cykl *m* **2.** rower *m* **3.** motocykl *m* **II** *v/i* jeździć na rowerze; **'cy•cle lane, 'cy•cle path** *s* ścieżka *f* rowerowa; **cy•cler** ['saɪklə] *Am* → ***cyclist***; **'cy•cle•way** → ***cycle path***

cy•clic ['saɪklɪk], ***cy•cli•cal*** ['saɪklɪkl] *adj* cykliczny

cy•cling ['saɪklɪŋ] *s* **1.** jazda *f* na rowerze **2.** SPORT kolarstwo *n*; **cy•clist** ['saɪklɪst] *s* **1.** rowerzysta *m* **2.** SPORT kolarz *m*

cy•clone ['saɪkləʊn] *s* cyklon *m*

cyn•ic ['sɪnɪk] *s* **1.** cynik *m* **2.** sceptyk *m*; **cyn•i•cal** ['sɪnɪkl] *adj* **1.** cyniczny **2.** sceptyczny; **cyn•i•cal•ly** ['sɪnɪklɪ] *adv* **1.** cynicznie **2.** sceptycznie; **cyn•i•cism** ['sɪnɪsɪzm] *s* **1.** cynizm *m* **2.** sarkastyczna uwaga *f*

Cyp•ri•ot ['sɪprɪət] **I** *s* Cypryjczyk *m* **II** *adj* cypryjski; **Cy•prus** ['saɪprəs] *s* Cypr *m*

cyst [sɪst] *s* MED torbiel *m*, cysta *f*; **cys•ti•tis** [sɪ'staɪtɪs] *s* MED zapalenie *n* pęcherza moczowego

czar [zɑː] *s* car *m*

Czech [tʃek] **I** *s* **1.** Czech *m*, Czeszka *f*; ***the ~ Republic*** Czechy *pl* **2.** (*language*) czeski *m* **II** *adj* czeski

D

DA (=***District Attorney***) *s Am* prokurator *m* okręgowy

dab•ble ['dæbl] *v/i* bawić się (***in/with*** w *A*), zajmować się amatorsko (***in/with*** *I*)

dachs•hund ['dækshʊnd] *s* jamnik *m*

dad [dæd] *s infml* tata *m*, tato *m*

dad•dy ['dædɪ] *s infml* tatuś *m*

dad•dy 'long•legs *s* **1.** *Br* komarnica *f* **2.** *Am* kosarz *m*

daf•fo•dil ['dæfədɪl] *s* BIOL żonkil *m*

daft [dɑːft] *adj* **1.** głupi, durny **2.** zwariowany

dag•ger ['dægə] *s* sztylet *m*

dai•ly ['deɪlɪ] **I** *s* dziennik *m*, gazeta *f* codzienna **II** *adj* codzienny, dzienny, powszechny; ***on a ~ basis*** codziennie **III** *adv* codziennie; ***be taken twice ~*** zażywać dwa razy dziennie

dain•ty ['deɪntɪ] **I** *s* przysmak *m* **II** *adj* **1.** delikatny, maleńki, filigranowy **2.** *dish:* delikatny, wykwintny **3.** wybredny

dair•y ['deərɪ] *s* **1.** mleczarnia *f* **2.** sklep *m* nabiałowy; **'dair•y cat•tle** *s* bydło *n* mleczne; ***'dair•y pro•d•uce*** *s*, ***dai•ry pro•d•ucts*** *pl* produkty *pl* mleczne

dai•sy ['deɪzɪ] *s* BIOL stokrotka *f*; **'dai•sy wheel** *s* głowica *f* wirująca

dam [dæm] **I** *s* **1.** zapora *f* (wodna) **2.** zbiornik *m*, sztuczne jezioro *n* **II** *v/t river*: budować ⟨z-⟩ tamę na; **dam up** *v/t anger*, *tears*: tłumić, powstrzymywać ⟨-mać⟩

dam•age ['dæmɪdʒ] **I** *s* **1.** uszkodzenia *pl* (**to** *G*), szkoda *f*; ***cause ~*** wyrządzić szkodę **2.** uszkodzenie *n*; ***irreversible brain ~*** nieodwracalne uszkodzenie mózgu **II** *v/t* **1.** *machine*: uszkadzać ⟨-kodzić⟩ **2.** *reputation*: szkodzić ⟨za-⟩, wyrządzać ⟨-dzić⟩ szkodę; **dam•ages** ['dæmɪdʒɪz] *pl* JUR odszkodowanie *n*, suma *f* odszkodowania; ***a claim for ~*** roszczenie o odszkodowanie; **dam•ag•ing** ['dæmɪdʒɪŋ] *adj* przynoszący szkodę, szkodliwy, szkodzący

dame [deɪm] *s* **1.** ⁂ *Br tytuł przysługujący kobietom uhonorowanym najwyższymi odznaczeniami Imperium Brytyjskiego* **2.** *Am infml* kobitka *f*

damn [dæm] **I** *s* ***I don't give a ~ about it*** *infml* mam to gdzieś **II** *adj infml* cholerny, przeklęty; ***I can't see a ~ thing*** cholera, nic nie widzę **III** *adv inflm* cholernie; **dam•na•tion** [dæm'neɪʃn] *s* REL potępienie *n*; **damned** [dæmd] *adj* **I** *s* ***the ~*** potępieńcy **II** *adj* **1.** REL potępiony **2.** → ***damn II III*** *adv inflm* cholernie; **damn•ing** ['dæmɪŋ] *adj* **1.** *evidence*: obciążający **2.** *criticism*: potępiający

damp [dæmp] **I** *s* wilgoć *f* **II** *adj* wilgotny; **damp•en** ['dæmpən] *v/t* **1.** zwilżać ⟨-żyć⟩; ***~ s.o.'s spirits*** zepsuć komuś humor **2.** *enthusiasm*: studzić ⟨o-⟩

damp•er ['dæmpə] *s* **1.** szyber *m* **2.** MUS tłumik *m*

damp•ness ['dæmpnɪs] *s* **1.** wilgoć *f* **2.** wilgotność *f*

dance [dɑːns] **I** *s* **1.** taniec *m*; ***to ask s.o. for a ~*** poprosić kogoś do tańca **2.** zabawa *f*, tańce *pl* **II** *v/t* tańczyć ⟨za-⟩ **III** *v/i* tańczyć ⟨za-⟩ (**with** z *I*); **'dance class** *s* lekcja *f* tańca; **'dance floor** *s* parkiet *m*; **danc•er** ['dɑːnsə] *s* tancerz *m*; **'dance school** *s* szkoła *f* tańca; **danc•ing** ['dɑːnsɪŋ] **I** *s* tańce *pl* **II** *adj* tańczący

dan•druff ['dændrʌf] *s* łupież *m*; **dandruff sham'poo** *s* szampon *m* przeciwłupieżowy

dan•dy ['dændɪ] **I** *s* elegant *m*, dandys *m* **II** *adj* wspaniały

Dane [deɪn] *s* Duńczyk *m*, Dunka *f*; ***great ~*** dog

dang [dæŋ] *Am* → ***darn²***

dan•ger ['deɪndʒə] *s* **1.** niebezpieczeństwo *n* (**of** *G*), zagrożenie *n* (**to** dla *G*); ***put s.o. in ~*** narazić kogoś na niebezpieczeństwo **2.** niebezpieczeństwo *n*, ryzyko *n*; ***there is a ~ that*** istnieje ryzyko, że; **'dan•ger mon•ey** *s* dodatek *m* za pracę w niebezpiecznych warunkach; **dan•ger•ous** ['deɪndʒərəs] *adj* niebezpieczny; **dan•ger•ous 'driv•ing** *s* ryzykowna jazda *f*; **dan•ger•ous•ly** ['deɪndʒərəslɪ] *adv* niebezpiecznie; **'dan•ger pay** *s* dodatek *m* za pracę w niebezpiecznych warunkach; **'dan•ger zone** *s* strefa *f* zagrożenia

dan•gle ['dæŋgl] **I** *v/i* dyndać, zwisać **II** *v/t* ***~ s.th. in front of s.o.*** *fig* nęcić kogoś czymś

Da•nish ['deɪnɪʃ] **I** *s* (*language*) duński *m* **II** *adj* duński

dare [deə] **I** *s* wyzwanie *n* **II** *v aux* **1.** odważać ⟨-żyć⟩ się, ośmielać ⟨-lić⟩ się; ***nobody ~d ask*** nikt nie odważył się zapytać **2.** ważyć się, ośmielać ⟨-lić⟩ się (**do s.th.** zrobić coś); ***he wouldn't ~ show his face here!*** nie ośmieliłby się tu pokazać! **III** *v/t* ***~ s.o. to do s.th.*** rzucić komuś wyzwanie do zrobienia czegoś; **dare•dev•il** ['deədevɪl] *s* śmiałek *m*, szaleniec *m*; **dar•ing** ['deərɪŋ] **I** *s* odwaga *f*, śmiałość *f* **II** *adj* **1.** odważny, śmiały **2.** szokujący, śmiały

dark [dɑːk] **I** *adj* **1.** ciemny; ***it's getting ~*** zapada zmrok; ***~ forces, ~ powers*** ciemne moce **2.** *complexion*: śniady **3.** *mood*: ponury **II** *s* ***the ~*** ciemność *f*, ciemności *pl*; **'Dark Ag•es** *pl*: ***the ~*** wczesne średniowiecze

dark•en ['dɑːkn] **I** *v/i* **1.** *sky*: ciemnieć ⟨po-⟩ **2.** robić ⟨z-⟩ się coraz ciemniejszym **3.** (*face*) pochmurnieć ⟨s-⟩ **II** *v/t* **1.** przesłaniać ⟨-łonić⟩ **2.** przyćmiewać ⟨-mić⟩ **3.** zaciemniać ⟨-nić⟩ **4.** przyciemniać ⟨-nić⟩ **5.** *fig* rzucać ⟨-cić⟩ cień na *A*

dark 'glass•es *pl* okulary *pl* słoneczne; **dark 'horse** *s* **1.** *Br* tajemnicza postać *f* **2.** (*sports*) czarny koń *m*

dark•ness ['dɑːknɪs] *s* ciemność *f*

'dark•room *s* ciemnia *f*; **'dark•skinned** *adj* ciemnoskóry

dar•ling ['dɑːlɪŋ] **I** *s* **1.** kochanie *n* **2.** (*affectedly*) mój drogi *m* **II** *adj* kochany

D

D

darn[1] [dɑːn] **I** *v/t* cerować ⟨za-⟩ **II** *s* cera *f* (*in* w *L*)
darn[2] [~], ***darned*** [dɑːnd] **I** *adj infml* cholerny, przeklęty **II** *adv infml* cholernie **III** *interj infml* cholera!
dart [dɑːt] **I** *s* **1.** SPORT strzałka *f* **2.** strzała *f*; ***poisoned ~*** zatruta strzała **3.** gwałtowny ruch *m* **II** *v/t* rzucać ⟨-cić⟩ **III** *v/i* rzucać ⟨-cić⟩ się; ***~ away*** rzucić się do ucieczki
darts [dɑːts] *pl* SPORT gra *f* w strzałki; **'dart(s)•board** *s* tarcza *f* do gry w strzałki
dash [dæʃ] **I** *s* **1.** ***make a ~ for*** rzucić się do *G* **2.** SPORT sprint *m* **3.** myślnik *m* **4.** odrobina *f*, szczypta *f*, kropla *f* **II** *v/t* **1.** *boat, glass*: roztrzaskiwać ⟨-kać⟩ **2.** *fig* niweczyć ⟨z-⟩, burzyć ⟨z-⟩ **III** *v/i* **1.** pędzić ⟨po-⟩, mknąć ⟨po-⟩, śmigać ⟨-gnąć⟩ **2.** roztrzaskiwać ⟨-kać⟩ się; **dash off** *v/i* oddalać ⟨-lić⟩ się pędem
'dash•board s tablica *f* rozdzielcza
dash•ing ['dæʃɪŋ] *adj* dziarski, żwawy
da•ta ['deɪtə] *pl* dane *pl*; **'da•ta bank** *s* bank *m* danych; **'da•ta•base** *s* baza *f* danych; **da•ta•base 'man•age•ment** *s* INF system *m* zarządzania bazą danych; **da•ta 'cap•ture** *s* INF gromadzenie *n* danych; **'da•ta car•ri•er** *s* INF nośnik *m* danych; **da•ta 'pro•cess•ing** *s* INF przetwarzanie *n* danych; **da•ta pro•'tec•tion** *s* JUR ochrona *f* danych; **da•ta 'stor•age** *s* przechowywanie *n* danych; **da•ta trans•'mis•sion** *s* transmisja *f* danych
date[1] [deɪt] *s* daktyl *m*
date[2] [~] **I** *s* **1.** data *f*; ***~ of expiry*** data ważności; ***what's the ~ today?*** jaki dzień dziś mamy? **2.** (umówione) spotkanie *n* **3.** randka *f*; ***he has a ~ with Anna tonight*** idzie dziś wieczorem na randkę z Anną **4.** ***John is her ~ for the party*** idzie na przyjęcie z Johnem **II** *v/t* **1.** pisać ⟨na-⟩ datę na *L*; ***a letter ~d May 13*** list opatrzony datą 13 maja **2.** *skeleton*: datować **3.** spotykać się z *I*, *infml* chodzić z *I*; **date back to, *date from*** *v/t* pochodzić z *G*, datować się na *A*
dat•ed [deɪtɪd] *adj* **1.** datowany **2.** przestarzały **3.** niemodny
'date line *s* GEOGR linia *f* zmiany daty; **date of 'birth** *s* data *f* urodzenia; **'date rape** *s* gwałt *m* na randce; **'date stamp** *s* **1.** datownik *m* **2.** data *f* na stemplu; **'dat•ing a•gen•cy** *s* agencja *f* kojarząca pary
daugh•ter [dɔːtə] *s* **1.** córka *f* **2.** ***~ company*** ECON spółka córka; **'daugh•ter•board** *s* INF płyta *f* rozszerzania; **'daugh•ter-in-law** *pl daughers-in-law* *s* synowa *f*
daunt [dɔːnt] *v/t* zniechęcać ⟨-cić⟩, onieśmielać ⟨-lić⟩; **daunt•less** [dɔːntlɪs] *adj* nieustraszony
dawn [dɔːn] **I** *s* **1.** świt *m*, brzask *m*; ***at ~*** o świcie **2.** *fig* zaranie *n*, początek *m* **II** *v/i* **1.** świtać, dnieć **2.** *lit* rozpoczynać ⟨-cząć⟩ się
day [deɪ] *s* **1.** dzień *m*; ***what is the ~ today?*** jaki dziś dzień?; ***~ after ~*** dzień w dzień; ***every ~*** codziennie; ***every other ~*** co drugi dzień; ***from ~ to ~*** z dnia na dzień; ***one fine ~*** *fig* pewnego pięknego dnia; ***any ~ now*** lada dzień; ***the ~ before yesterday*** przedwczoraj; ***the ~ after tomorrow*** pojutrze; ***a working ~*** dzień pracy; ***during the ~*** w ciągu dnia; ***spend the ~ doing s.th.*** spędzić dzień robiąc coś; ***what a ~!*** co za dzień!; ***as soon as ~ breaks*** jak tylko wstanie dzień; ***Independence ~*** Dzień Niepodległości; ***Tuesday is my shopping ~*** zakupy robię we wtorek **2.** doba *f* **3.** czas *m*, czasy *pl*; ***in those ~s*** w tamtych czasach; ***in his ~s*** za jego czasów; ***in her early ~s*** za czasów jej młodości; ***those were the ~s!*** to były czasy!; ***it's one of those ~s!*** to jeden tych (okropnych) dni!; ***let's call it a ~!*** na dziś koniec!; **'day•break** *s* świt *m*, brzask *m*; **'day care** *s* opieka *f* dzienna; **'day•dream I** *s* marzenie *n* **II** *v/i* marzyć, fantazjować; **'day dream•er** *s* marzyciel *m*; **'day•light** *s* **1.** światło *n* dzienne; ***in broad ~*** w biały dzień **2.** świt *m*, brzask *m*; ***knock the ~s out of s.o.*** *fig* stłuc kogoś na kwaśne jabłko; ***see ~*** *fig* zaczynać rozumieć; **day•light 'sav•ing time** *s Am* czas *m* letni; **'day nurs•er•y** *s* **1.** przedszkole *n* **2.** żłobek *m*; **'day pu•pil** *s Br* eksternista *m*, uczeń *m* dochodzący; **'day shift** *s* dzienna zmiana *f*; **'day•time** *s* dzień *m*; ***in the ~*** w dzień,

za dnia; **'day trip** *s* wycieczka *f* jednodniowa; **day-to-'day** *adj* codzienny

daze [deɪz] **I** *s* oszołomienie *n* **II** *v/t* oszałamiać ⟨-łomić⟩; **dazed** [deɪzd] *adj* oszołomiony

daz•zle [dæzl] **I** *v/t* **1.** oślepiać ⟨-pić⟩ **2.** *fig* olśniewać ⟨-nić⟩ **II** *s* oślepiające światło *n*

DC [diː'siː] *abbr* (=***District of Columbia***) Dystrykt *m* Kolumbii

dea•con [diːkən] *s* REL **1.** (*Catholic*) diakon *m* **2.** (*Protestant*) urzędnik *m* świecki

dead [ded] **I** *adj* **1.** martwy; ***he's ~*** on nie żyje **2.** zmarły, nieżywy **3.** obumarły, zwiędnięty **4.** *town*: wymarły **5.** zdrętwiały; ***go ~*** zdrętwieć **6.** nieczuły, głuchy, obojętny **7.** *engine*: zepsuty **8.** *phone*: głuchy **9.** *battery*: wyładowany **10.** *feeling, emotion*: wygasły **11.** (*tired*) *infml* skonany, nieżywy **12.** całkowity, absolutny; ***~ silence*** głucha cisza; ***come to a ~ stop*** stanąć w miejscu **II** *s* **1.** ***the ~*** zmarli **2.** ***the ~ of night*** środek nocy **III** *adv* **1.** zupełnie, całkowicie; ***~ tired*** wykończony **2.** nagle, momentalnie **3.** dokładnie, prosto: ***~ ahead*** prosto przed siebie

dead•en [dedn] *v/t pain*: tłumić ⟨s-⟩, łagodzić ⟨z-⟩

dead 'end *s* ślepa uliczka *f*, ślepy zaułek *m*; **dead-end 'job** *s* praca *f* bez perspektyw; **dead 'heat** *s* SPORT nierozstrzygnięty bieg *m*; ***be in a ~*** *fig* iść łeb w łeb; **'dead•line** *s* ostateczny termin *m*; ***meet the ~*** dotrzymać terminu; **'dead•lock I** *s* impas *m* **II** *v/t* doprowadzać ⟨-dzić⟩ do impasu; **'dead•locked** *adj*: ***be ~*** być w impasie

dead•ly [dedlɪ] **I** *adj* **1.** *poison, disease*: śmiertelny **2.** *weapon*: śmiercionośny **3.** ***in ~ earnest*** ze śmiertelną powagą **4.** *Br infml* śmiertelnie nudny **II** *adv* śmiertelnie, potwornie: ***~ serious*** śmiertelnie poważny

'deadpan I *adj* śmiertelnie poważny **II** *adv* śmiertelnie poważnie

dead 'tired *adj* wykończony; **'dead weight** *s* wielki ciężar *m*; **'dead wood** *s* **1.** uschnięte drzewo *n* **2.** *fig* balast *m*

deaf [def] **I** *adj* głuchy; ***go ~*** ogłuchnąć; ***be ~ to*** *fig* pozostawać głuchym na *A* **II** *s* ***the ~*** głusi

deaf-and-'dumb I *adj* głuchoniemy **II** *s* ***the ~s*** głuchoniemi

deaf•en ['defn] *v/t* **1.** ogłuszać ⟨-szyć⟩ **2.** zagłuszać ⟨-szyć⟩; **deaf•en•ing** ['defnɪŋ] *adj* ogłuszający

deaf-'mute I *adj* głuchoniemy **II** *s* głuchoniemy *m*

deaf•ness ['defnɪs] *s* głuchota *f*

deal [diːl] **I** *s* **1.** umowa *f*; ***make a ~ with, strike a ~ with*** zawrzeć umowę z *I*, dojść do porozumienia z *I*, *infml* ubić interes z *I*; ***a good ~*** dobry interes **2.** transkacja *f*; ***property ~*** transakcja na rynku nieruchomości **3.** dobra oferta *f*; ***I got a good ~ on a used Toyota*** kupiłem używaną Toyotę po korzystnej cenie **4.** ***a great ~ of, a good ~ of*** dużo *G*; ***he travels a great ~*** on dużo podróżuje **5.** *cards*: rozdanie *n* **II** (*dealt*; *dealt*) *v/t cards*: rozdawać ⟨-dać⟩ **III** (*dealt*; *dealt*) *v/i* handlować, prowadzić interesy; **deal in** *v/t* handlować, sprzedawać; ***~ software*** zajmować się sprzedażą oprogramowania; **deal out** *v/t money, profits*: rozdzielać ⟨-lić⟩ **2.** *punishment*: wymierzać ⟨-rzyć⟩; **deal with** *v/t* **1.** uporać się z *I*, radzić ⟨po-⟩ sobie z *I* **2.** *matter*, *topic*: zajmować ⟨-jąć⟩ się *I* **3.** utrzymywać stosunki handlowe z *I*

deal•er ['diːlə] *s* **1.** handlowiec *m* **2.** dealer *m* **3.** handlarz *m*; ***an arms ~*** handlarz bronią **4.** *infml* dealer *m* (narkotykowy); **deal•er•ship** ['diːləʃɪp] *s* przedstawicielstwo *n* handlowe

deal•ing ['diːlɪŋ] *s* **1.** prowadzenie *n* działalności handlowej **2.** obrót *m* akcjami **3.** *cards*: rozdawanie *n* **4.** ***arms*** (***drugs***) ***~*** handel bronią (narkotykami); **deal•ings** ['diːlɪŋz] *pl* stosunki *pl*, kontakty *pl* (***with*** z *I*)

dealt [delt] *Past Simple and Past Participle* → ***deal***

dean [diːn] *s* dziekan *m*

dear [dɪə] **I** *s* kochany *m*, mój drogi *m* **II** *adj* **1.** kochany, drogi **2.** (*letters*) drogi; ***~ Sir*** (***Madam***) Szanowny Panie (Szanowna Pani); ***~ Sirs*** Szanowni Państwo; ***~ Patricia*** Droga

D

Patrycjo, Kochana Patrycjo **3.** *shop, article*: drogi **III** *adv* drogo **IV** *interj* ***oh ~!*** o Boże!, o jejku!; **dear•ly** ['dɪəlɪ] *adv* **1.** bardzo; ***love s.o. ~*** bardzo kogoś kochać **2.** *pay*: drogo

D

death [deθ] *s* **1.** śmierć *f*; ***come close to ~*** otrzeć się o śmierć; ***frightened to ~*** śmiertelnie przerażony **2.** zgon *m*; '**death•bed** *s* łoże *n* śmierci; '**death-blow** *s* śmietelny cios *m*; '**death cell** *s* cela *f* śmierci; '**death cer•tif•i•cate** *s* akt *m* zgonu; '**death knell** *s* dzwony *pl* pogrzebowe

death•less ['deθlɪs] *adj* nieśmiertelny, nieprzemijający

death•ly ['deθlɪ] **I** *adj* trupi, grobowy **II** *adv* ***~ pale*** blady jak śmierć

'**death mask** *s* maska *f* pośmiertna; '**death pen•al•ty** *s* kara *f* śmierci; '**death rate** *s* śmiertelność *f*; **death** '**row** *s* cele *pl* skazańców; ***be on ~*** przebywać w celi śmierci; '**death sen•tence** *s* wyrok *m* śmierci; '**death's head** *s* trupia czaszka *f*; '**death squad** *s* pluton *m* egzekucyjny; '**death throes** *s* agonia *f*; '**death toll** *s* liczba *f* ofiar śmiertelnych; '**death trap** *s* śmiertelna pułapka *f*; '**death war•rant** *s* (pisemny) rozkaz *m* wykonania wyroku śmierci; '**death wish** *s* pragnienie *n* śmierci

de•base [dɪ'beɪs] *v/t* **1.** *currency*: deprecjonować ⟨z-⟩, dewaluować ⟨z-⟩ **2.** poniżać ⟨-żyć⟩

de•ba•ta•ble [dɪ'beɪtəbl] *adj* dyskusyjny; **de•bate** [dɪ'beɪt] **I** *s* debata *f* (***on*** nad *I*), dyskusja *f* (***about*** na temat *G*) **II** *v/t* **1.** debatować nad *I* **2.** zastanawiać się nad *I*

deb•it ['debɪt] **I** *s* debet *m* **II** *v/t account*: obciążać ⟨-żyć⟩; '**deb•it card** *s* karta *f* debetowa

de•brief [diː'briːf] *v/t* wysłuchiwać ⟨-chać⟩ sprawozdania

deb•ris ['debriː] *s* **1.** szczątki *pl*, ruiny *pl* **2.** GEOGR rumowisko *n* skalne **3.** gruz *m*

debt [det] *s* **1.** dług *m* (***to*** wobec *G*); ***bad ~*** dług nieściągalny; ***honorary ~*** dług honorowy; '**debt col•lec•tion** *s* windykacja *f* należności; **debt col-lec•tion a•'gen•cy** *s* firma *f* windykacji należności; **debt•or** ['detə] *s* dłużnik *m*; '**debt ser•vic•ing** *s* obsługa *f* długu

de•bug [diː'bʌg] *v/t* **1.** INF usuwać ⟨usunąć⟩ usterki **2.** usuwać ⟨usunąć⟩ podsłuch w *L*

dé•but ['deɪbjuː] *s* debiut *m*; ***make one's screen ~*** zadebiutować na ekranie; **deb•u•tant** ['deɪbjuːtɑːnt] *s* debiutant *m*

Dec. *abbr* → ***December***

dec•ade ['dekeɪd] *s* dekada *f*, dziesięciolecie *n*

dec•a•dence ['dekədəns] *s* dekadencja *f*; **dec•a•dent** ['dekədənt] *adj* dekadencki

de•caf ['diːkæf] *s infml* kawa *f* bezkofeinowa; **de•caf•fein•at•ed** [dɪ'kæfɪneɪtɪd] *adj* bezkofeinowy

de•cap•i•tate [dɪ'kæpɪteɪt] *v/t* ścinać ⟨ściąć⟩ głowę

de•cath•lete [dɪ'kæθliːt] *s* dziesięcioboista *m*; **de•cath•lon** [dɪ'kæθlɒn] *s* dziesięciobój *m*

de•cay [dɪ'keɪ] **I** *s* **1.** rozkład *m* **2.** gnicie *n* **3.** butwienie *n* **4.** próchnienie *n* **5.** niszczenie *n* **6.** upadek *m* **7.** ***tooth ~*** próchnica **II** *v/i* **1.** rozkładać ⟨-złożyć⟩ się **2.** gnić ⟨z-⟩ **3.** próchnieć ⟨s-⟩ **4.** niszczeć **5.** podupadać ⟨-paść⟩

de•ceased [dɪ'siːst] **I** *s* ***the ~*** **a)** zmarły **b)** zmarli **II** *adj* zmarły

de•ceit [dɪ'siːt] *s* **1.** oszukiwanie *n* **2.** oszustwo *n*; **de•ceit•ful** [dɪ'siːtfəl] *adj* **1.** oszukańczy **2.** kłamliwy; **de-ceive** [dɪ'siːv] **I** *v/t* **1.** oszukiwać ⟨-kać⟩; ***~ s.o. into doing s.th.*** podstępem skłonić kogoś do zrobienia czegoś **2.** *wife, husband*: zdradzać ⟨-dzić⟩ **II** *v/i* oszukiwać ⟨-kać⟩

de•cel•er•ate [diː'seləreɪt] *v/i* zwalniać ⟨zwolnić⟩, zmniejszać ⟨-szyć⟩ prędkość

De•cem•ber [dɪ'sembə] *s* grudzień *m*

de•cen•cy ['diːsənsɪ] *s* przyzwoitość *f*; ***for the sake of ~*** dla przywoitości; **de-cent** ['diːsənt] *adj person*: przyzwoity, porządny **2.** *thing*: przyzwoity, całkiem dobry

de•cep•tion [dɪ'sepʃn] *s* **1.** oszukiwanie *n* **2.** oszustwo *n*; **de•cep•tive** [dɪ'septɪv] *adj* zwodniczy; ***appearances can be ~*** pozory mylą; **de•cep•tive•ly** [dɪ'septɪvlɪ] *adv*: ***it's ~ easy*** to tylko wydaje się proste

de•cide [dɪ'saɪd] **I** *v/t* **1.** postanawiać ⟨-nowić⟩, decydować ⟨z-⟩ (***to do s.th.*** coś zrobić) **2.** przekonywać ⟨-nać⟩ **3.** decydować ⟨z-⟩ o *L* **II** *v/i* decydować ⟨z-⟩; ***it's up to him to ~*** decyzja należy do niego; ***~ in favour of (against)*** rozstrzygnąć na korzyść (niekorzyść) *G* **4.** decydować ⟨z-⟩ się; **de•cide on** *v/t* decydować ⟨z-⟩ się na *A*

de•cid•ed [dɪ'saɪdɪd] *adj* **1.** zdecydowany **2.** *person*: zdecydowany, stanowczy; **de•cid•er** [dɪ'saɪdə] *s* **1.** decydujący punkt *m* **2.** decydująca bramka *f*; **de•cid•ing** [dɪ'saɪdɪŋ] *adj* decydujący

dec•i•mal ['desɪml] *adj* dziesiętny; **dec•i•mal 'frac•tion** *s* ułamek *m* dziesiętny; **dec•i•mal 'point** *s* MATH przecinek *m*; **'dec•i•mal sys•tem** *s* system *m* dziesiętny

dec•i•mate ['desɪmeɪt] *v/t* dziesiątkować ⟨z-⟩

de•ci•pher [dɪ'saɪfə] *v/t* rozszyfrowywać ⟨-rować⟩, odszyfrowywać ⟨-rować⟩

de•ci•sion [dɪ'sɪʒn] *s* **1.** decyzja *f* (***on/about*** dotycząca *G*); ***make a ~*** podjąć decyzję **2.** postanowienie *n* **3.** zdecydowanie *n*, stanowczość *n*; **de•'ci•sion-mak•er** *s* decydent *m*; **de•'ci•sion-mak•ing** *s* podejmowanie *n* decyzji; **de•ci•sive** [dɪ'saɪsɪv] *adj* **1.** decydujący **2.** stanowczy **3.** zdecydowany

deck [dek] **I** *s* **1.** pokład *m*; ***be on ~*** być na pokładzie **2.** *Am* taras *m* **3.** (*bus*) piętro *n* **II** *v/t* dekorować ⟨u-⟩, przyozdabiać ⟨-dobić⟩; **deck out** *v/t* **1.** dekorować ⟨u-⟩ (***with*** *I*) **2.** stroić ⟨wy-⟩ kogoś (***in*** w *A*)

'deck•chair *s* leżak *m*

dec•la•ra•tion [deklə'reɪʃn] *s* **1.** oświadczenie *n* **2.** deklaracja *f*; ***a customs ~*** deklaracja celna **3.** ogłoszenie *n* **4.** *of war*: wypowiedzenie *n*; **de•clare** [dɪ'kleə] **I** *v/t* **1.** ogłaszać ⟨-łosić⟩ **2.** *war*: wypowiadać ⟨-wiedzieć⟩ **3.** zgłaszać ⟨-łosić⟩ do oclenia; ***have you got anything to ~?*** czy ma pan coś do oclenia? **II** *v/i* **1.** oświadczać ⟨-czyć⟩ **2.** opowiadać ⟨-wiedzieć⟩ się (***for*** za *I*); **declared** [dɪ'kleərd] *adj* **1.** zdeklarowany **2.** jawny

de•cline [dɪ'klaɪn] **I** *s* **1.** spadek *m*; ***a ~ in sales*** spadek sprzedaży **2.** upadek *m*, kryzys *m*; ***be in ~*** **a)** chylić się ku upadkowi, podupadać **b)** przeżywać kryzys **3.** pogarszanie się *n* **II** *v/t* **1.** *offer, invitation*: odrzucać ⟨-cić⟩ **III** *v/i* **1.** spadać ⟨spaść⟩ **2.** chylić się ku upadkowi, podupadać ⟨-paść⟩ **3.** przeżywać kryzys **4.** odmawiać ⟨-mówić⟩

de•code [diː'kəʊd] *v/t* **1.** dekodować **2.** rozszyfrowywać ⟨-rować⟩, odszyfrowywać ⟨-rować⟩

de•cod•ing [diː'koədɪŋ] *s* **1.** dekodowanie *n* **2.** rozszyfrowanie *n*

de•com•pose [diːkəm'pəʊz] **I** *v/i* rozkładać ⟨-złożyć⟩ się **II** *v/t* powodować ⟨s-⟩ rozkład; **de•com•po•si•tion** [diːkɒmpə'zɪʃn] *s* **1.** rozkład *m* **2.** rozpad *m*; **de•com•pres•sion chamber** [diːkəm'preʃntʃeɪmbə] *s* komora *f* dekompresyjna

de•con•tam•i•nate [diːkən'tæmɪneɪt] *v/t* odkażać ⟨-kazić⟩; **de•con•tam•i•na•tion** [diːkəntæmɪ'neɪʃn] *s* odkażanie *n*

dé•cor ['deɪkɔː] *s* **1.** wystrój *m* **2.** dekoracja *f*

dec•o•rate ['dekəreɪt] *v/t* **1.** dekorować ⟨u-⟩ **2.** *Christmas tree*: ubierać ⟨-brać⟩ **3.** odnawiać ⟨-nowić⟩, remontować ⟨wy-⟩; **dec•o•ra•tion** [dekə'reɪʃn] *s* **1.** dekoracja *f* **2.** ozdoba *f* **3.** wzór *m* **4.** wystrój *m* **5.** *Br* odnawianie *n*, remont *m*; **dec•o•ra•tive** ['dekərətɪv] *adj* ozdobny, dekoracyjny; **dec•o•ra•tor** ['dekəreɪtə] *s* **1.** malarz *m* pokojowy **2.** tapeciarz *m*

de•co•rum [dɪ'kɔːrəm] *s*: ***with ~*** godnie, obyczajnie; ***a breach of ~*** naruszenie zasad przyzwoitości

de•crease **I** ['diːkriːs] *s* spadek *m*, redukcja *f* **II** [diː'kriːs] *v/t* zmniejszać ⟨-szyć⟩, obniżać ⟨-żyć⟩ **III** [diː'kriːs] *v/i* spadać ⟨spaść⟩, obniżać ⟨-żyć⟩ się

de•crim•in•al•ize [diː'krɪmɪnəlaɪz] *v/t* legalizować ⟨za-⟩

de•cry [dɪ'kraɪ] *v/t* potępiać ⟨-pić⟩

ded•i•cate ['dedɪkeɪt] *v/t* **1.** poświęcać ⟨-cić⟩; ***she ~d her life to helping the poor*** poświęciła życie pomocy biednym **2.** *book, film*: dedykować ⟨za-⟩

D

ded•i•ca•ted ['dedɪkeɪtɪd] *adj* **1.** oddany **2.** gorliwy **3.** *opponent*: zagorzały **4.** *church*: pod wezwaniem (**to** *G*)

ded•i•ca•tion [dedɪ'keɪʃn] *s* **1.** poświęcenie *n*, oddanie *n* (**to** *D*) **2.** zaangażowanie *n* **3.** dedykacja *f*

de•duce [dɪ'djuːs] *v/t* wnioskować ⟨wy-⟩, dedukować ⟨wy-⟩

de•duct [dɪ'dʌkt] *v/t* **1.** *cost*: odliczać ⟨-czyć⟩ **2.** odejmować ⟨odjąć⟩ **2.** *tax*: potrącać ⟨-cić⟩

de•duct•i•ble [dɪ'dʌktəbl] *adj* FIN **1.** podlegający odliczeniu **2.** potrącany; **de•duc•tion** [dɪ'dʌkʃn] *s* **1.** FIN potrącenie *n* **2.** FIN odliczenie *n* **3.** wniosek *m*, konkluzja *f*

deed [diːd] *s* **1.** czyn *m* **2.** uczynek *m* **3.** JUR akt *m* notarialny; **deed of 'sale** *s* akt *m* sprzedaży

deem [diːm] *v/t* uznawać ⟨-nać⟩; ***it was ~ed necessary*** uznano to za konieczne

deep [diːp] **I** *adj* **1.** głęboki; ***the lake is 13 m ~*** jezioro ma 13 m głębokości **2.** *grass*: wysoki **3.** *book*: mądry **4.** *discussion*: wnikliwy **5.** *voice*: niski **II** *adv* **1.** głęboko **2.** w głąb; ***go ~ into the woods*** wejść w głąb lasu; ***~ down she was frightened*** *fig* w głębi duszy bała się **III** *s* ***the ~*** *lit* morze, głębiny morskie

deep•en ['diːpn] **I** *v/t* pogłębiać ⟨-bić⟩ **II** *v/i* **1.** pogłębiać ⟨-bić⟩ się **2.** (*admiration*, *interest*) wzmagać ⟨-móc⟩ się

'deep end *s* najgłębsza część *f* (basenu); **'dep-felt** *adj* **1.** szczery **2.** głęboki; **deep 'freeze I** *s Br* zamrażarka *f* **II** (*deepfroze*; *deepfrozen*) *v/t* zamrażać ⟨-rozić⟩; **deep 'freez•er** *s Am* zamrażarka *f*; **'deep-froz•en food** *s* mrożonki *pl*; **'deep-fried** *adj* smażony w głębokim tłuszczu; **deep 'fry•er** *s* frytkownica *f*

deep•ly ['diːplɪ] *adv* **1.** głęboko **2.** mocno **3.** *in love*: bardzo

deep-'root•ed *adj* głęboko zakorzeniony; **deep-sea 'div•er** *s* nurek *m* głębinowy; **deep-sea 'div•ing** *s* nurkowanie *n* głębokowodne; **deep-sea 'fish•ing** *s* rybołówstwo *n* dalekomorskie; **deep-'seat•ed** → ***deep-rooted***; **deep-'set** *adj eyes*: głęboko osadzony

Deep 'South *s* głębokie Południe *n* (Stanów Zjednoczonych)

deer [dɪə] *s* **1.** jeleń *m* **2.** łania *f*

de-es•ca•late [diː'eskəleɪt] **I** *v/t* **1.** *war*, *violence*: powstrzymywać ⟨-mać⟩ **2.** *conflict*: łagodzić ⟨za-⟩ **II** *v/t* **1.** słabnąć **2.** zostać zahamowanym

de•face [dɪ'feɪs] *v/t* **1.** niszczyć ⟨z-⟩ **2.** zamazywać ⟨-zać⟩

de fac•to [deɪ'fæktəʊ] **I** *adj* faktyczny **II** *adv* faktycznie, de facto

de•fame [dɪ'feɪm] *v/t* zniesławiać ⟨-wić⟩

de•fault [dɪː'fɒlt] **I** *s* **1.** FIN nieuiszczenie *n* należności, niewywiązanie się *n* z płatności **2.** JUR niestawiennictwo *n* **3.** SPORT walkower *m* **4.** brak *m*; ***elected by ~*** wybrany z braku kandydatów **5.** INF wartość *f* domyślna **II** *v/i* **1.** FIN nie uiszczać ⟨uiścić⟩ należności **2.** JUR nie stawiać ⟨-wić⟩ się w sądzie; **de•'fault drive** *s* dysk *m* domyślny; **de•'fault set•tings** *pl* **1.** ustawienia *pl* domyślne **2.** wartość *f* domyślna

de•feat [dɪ'fiːt] **I** *s* **1.** porażka *f*; ***suffer a ~*** doznać porażki **2.** klęska *f* **3.** pokonanie *n* (**of** *G*) **II** *v/t* **1.** zwyciężać ⟨-żyć⟩, pokonywać ⟨-nać⟩ **2.** *proposal*, *amendment*: odrzucać ⟨-cić⟩ **3.** *attempt*: udaremniać ⟨-nić⟩

def•e•cate ['defəkeɪt] *v/i* wypróżniać ⟨-nić⟩ się, oddawać ⟨-dać⟩ stolec

de•fect I ['diːfekt] *s* **1.** wada *f*; ***sight ~*** wada wzroku **2.** defekt *m* **3.** usterka *f* **4.** upośledzenie *n* **II** [dɪ'fekt] *v/i* **1.** zbiegać ⟨zbiec⟩ (**from** z *G*) **2.** uciekać ⟨uciec⟩ (za granicę) (**from** z *G*) **3.** występować ⟨-tąpić⟩ (**from** z *G*) **4.** dezerterować ⟨z-⟩ (**from** z *G*) **5.** przechodzić ⟨przejść⟩ na stronę wroga; **de•fec•tion** [dɪ'fekʃn] *s* **1.** ucieczka *f* (za granicę) **2.** wystąpienie *n* (z partii) **3.** wyparcie *n* się **4.** dezercja *f* **5.** zdrada *f*

de•fec•tive [dɪ'fektɪv] **I** *adj* **1.** wadliwy **2.** błędny **3.** ułomny **II** *s* niedorozwinięty *m* umysłowo

de•'fence [dɪ'fens] *Br*, **de•fense** *Am s* **1.** obrona *f* (**against** przed *I*); ***in the ~ of freedom*** w obronie wolności; ***I have nothing to say in his ~*** nie mogę nic powiedzieć na jego obronę; ***give evidence for the ~*** JUR zeznawać jako świadek obrony **2.** broń *f*; **de-**

'fence coun•sel *s* JUR obrońca *m*; **de•'fence law•yer** *s* JUR adwokat *m* obrony
de•fence•less [dɪ'fenslɪs] *adj* **1.** bezbronny **2.** pozbawiony obrony
de•'fence play•er *s* SPORT obrońca *m*; **de•'fence wit•ness** *s* świadek *m* obrony
de•fend [dɪ'fend] *v/t* bronić ⟨o-⟩ (***against*** przed *I*); ***you must ~ your interests*** musisz bronić swoich interesów; ***~ a thesis*** obronić pracę; ***~ oneself*** bronić się; **de•fend•ant** [dɪ'fendənt] *s* JUR oskarżony *m*, pozwany *m*; **de•fend•er** [dɪ'fendə] *s* obrońca *m*
de•fense [dɪ'fens] *Am* → ***defence***; **De•'fense Se•cre•ta•ry** *s Am* sekretarz *m* obrony
de•fen•sive [dɪ'fensɪv] **I** *adj* **1.** obronny **2.** defensywny; ***a ~ player*** obrońca **II** *s* ***on the ~*** w defensywie
de•fen•sive•ly [dɪ'fensɪvlɪ] *adv* defensywnie, obronnie, ostrożnie
de•fer[1] [dɪ'fɜː] *v/t* odraczać ⟨-roczyć⟩; ***~ judgment*** wstrzymać się z wydaniem wyroku
de•fer[2] [~] *v/i*: ***~ to*** zdać się na *A*
de•fer•ence ['defərəns] *s* szacunek *m*, poważanie *n*; ***in ~ to*** przez wzgląd na *A*, przez szacunek dla *G*; **def•er•en•tial** [defə'renʃl] *adj* pełen szacunku (***to*** dla *G*)
de•fer•ment [dɪ'fɜːmənt] *s* odłożenie *n*, odroczenie *n*
de•fi•ance [dɪ'faɪəns] *s* **1.** nieposłuszeństwo *n*, niepodporządkowanie *n* się (***of*** *D*) **2.** opór *m*, sprzeciw *m* **3.** wyzwanie *n*; ***in ~*** bezczelnie; **de•fi•ant** [dɪ'faɪənt] *adj* buntowniczy, wyzywający, arogancki
de•fi•cien•cy [dɪ'fɪʃənsɪ] *s* **1.** niedostatek *m* (***of*** *G*) **2.** MED niedobór *m* **3.** niedoskonałość *f* **4.** ułomność *f*; **de•fi•cient** [dɪ'fɪʃənt] *adj* niedostateczny; ***be ~ in*** wykazywać brak *G*
def•i•cit ['defɪsɪt] *s* **1.** deficyt *m* **2.** niedobór *m*
de•fine [dɪ'faɪn] *v/t* **1.** definiować ⟨z-⟩ (***as*** jako *N*) **2.** określać ⟨-lić⟩ **3.** precyzować ⟨s-⟩; **def•i•nite** ['defɪnɪt] *adj* **1.** ostateczny **2.** pewny **3.** określony **4.** *contract, decision*: wiążący **5.** zdecydowany, stanowczy; **def•i•nite 'ar•ti•cle** *s* rodzajnik *m* określony; **def•i•nite•ly** ['defɪnɪtlɪ] *adv* **1.** z pewnością, na pewno; ***he's ~ not coming*** na pewno nie przyjdzie **2.** zdecydowanie; ***it's ~ colder today*** dzisiaj jest zdecydowanie chłodniej; **def•i•ni•tion** [defɪ'nɪʃn] *s* **1.** definicja *f* **2.** określenie *n*; **def•i•ni•tive** [dɪ'fɪnətɪv] *adj* ostateczny, definitywny
de•form [dɪ'fɔːm] *s* **1.** deformować ⟨z-⟩ **2.** zniekształcać ⟨-cić⟩ **3.** odkształcać ⟨-cić⟩; **de•for•ma•tion** [diːfɔː'meɪʃn] *s* **1.** deformacja *f* **2.** zniekształcenie *n*; **de•for•mi•ty** [dɪ'fɔːmɪtɪ] *s* **1.** deformacja *f* **2.** zniekształcenie *n* **3.** ułomność *f*, kalectwo *n*
de•frost [diː'frɒst] **I** *v/t* rozmrażać ⟨-rozić⟩ **II** *v/i* rozmrażać ⟨-rozić⟩ się, odmrażać ⟨-rozić⟩ się
de•funct [dɪ'fʌŋkt] *adj* nieistniejący, zlikwidowany
de•fuse [diː'fjuːz] *v/t bomb*: rozbrajać ⟨-roić⟩
de•fy [dɪ'faɪ] *v/t* **1.** przeciwstawiać ⟨-wić⟩ się **2.** *order*: ignorować ⟨z-⟩ **3.** igrać z *I* **4.** prowokować ⟨s-⟩
de•gen•e•rate [dɪ'dʒenəreɪt] **I** *adj* zdegenerowany, zwyrodniały **II** *v/i* degenerować ⟨z-⟩ się, pogarszać ⟨-gorszyć⟩ się; **de•gen•er•a•tion** [dɪdʒenə'reɪʃn] *s* **1.** pogorszenie *n* się **2.** degeneracja *f*
deg•ra•da•tion [degrə'deɪʃn] *s* **1.** poniżenie *n*, upokorzenie *n* **2.** nędza *f*; **de•grade** [dɪ'greɪd] *v/t* **1.** poniżać ⟨-żyć⟩, upokarzać ⟨-korzyć⟩ **2.** *officer*: degradować ⟨z-⟩; **de•grad•ing** [dɪ'greɪdɪŋ] *adj* poniżający, upokarzający
de•gree [dɪ'griː] *s* stopień *m*; ***to some ~*** do pewnego stopnia; ***an alarming ~ of ignorance*** zatrważający stopień niewiedzy; ***ten ~s of latitude*** dziesięć stopni szerokości geograficznej; ***at the angle of 40 ~s*** pod kątem 40 stopni; ***30 ~s Celsius*** 30 stopni Celsjusza; ***murder in the first ~*** JUR *Am* morderstwo pierwszego stopnia; ***the bachelor's ~*** licencjat
de•hy•drate [diː'haɪdreɪt] **I** *v/t* **1.** odwadniać ⟨-wodnić⟩ **2.** *food*: liofilizować **II** *v/i* odwadniać ⟨-wodnić⟩ się; **de•hy•drat•ed** [diːhaɪ'dreɪtɪd] *adj*

D

D

1. *food*: liofilizowany **2.** *body*: odwodniony
de•i•fy ['diːfaɪ] *v/t* ubóstwiać, deifikować
deign [deɪn] *v/i* raczyć (***to do s.th.*** zrobić coś)
de•i•ty ['diːɪtɪ] *s* bóg *m*, bóstwo *n*, bożek *m*; ***the*** ⁓ *form* Bóg
de•lay [dɪ'leɪ] **I** *s* **1.** opóźnienie *n* **2.** zwłoka *f*; ***without*** ⁓ bezzwłocznie **3.** zator *m*, korek *m* **II** *v/t* **1.** opóźnić ⟨-niać⟩; ***the flight was ⁓ed 2 hours*** samolot był opóźniony o 2 godziny **2.** odkładać ⟨odłożyć⟩, odwlekać ⟨-lec⟩ **3.** zatrzymywać ⟨-mać⟩ **4.** wstrzymywać ⟨-mać⟩ **III** *v/i* zwlekać; **de•'lay•ing tac•tics** *s* gra *f* na zwłokę
del•e•gate I ['delɪgət] *s* delegat *m* **II** ['delɪgeɪt] *v/t* **1.** *power*, *duty*: przekazywać ⟨-zać⟩ **2.** *work*: zlecać ⟨-cić⟩ **3.** oddelegowywać ⟨-gować⟩, wyznaczać ⟨-czyć⟩ **III** ['delɪgeɪt] *v/i* **1.** dzielić ⟨po-⟩ się obowiązkami **2.** dzielić ⟨po-⟩ się władzą; **del•e•ga•tion** [delɪ'geɪʃn] *s* **1.** delegacja *f* **2.** delegowanie *n* **3.** udzielanie *n* pełnomocnictw
de•lete [dɪ'liːt] *v/t* **1.** INF usuwać ⟨usunąć⟩, kasować ⟨s-, wy-⟩ **2.** wykreślać ⟨-lić⟩ **3.** wymazywać ⟨-zać⟩; **de•'lete key** *s* klawisz *m* „Delete", klawisz *m* kasowania; **de•le•tion** [dɪ'liːʃn] *s* **1.** INF usunięcie *n*, skasowanie *n* **2.** wykreślenie *n*
del•i ['delɪ] *infml* → ***delicatessen***
de•lib•e•rate [dɪ'lɪbərət] **I** *adj* **1.** umyślny, zamierzony **2.** *gesture*: powolny **3.** *step*: miarowy **4.** *decision*: przemyślany **II** *v/t* **1.** rozważać ⟨-żyć⟩ **2.** zastanawiać ⟨-nowić⟩ się nad *I*; **de•lib•e•rate•ly** [dɪ'lɪbərətlɪ] *adv* **1.** umyślnie **2.** z rozwagą; **de•lib•era•tion** [dɪlɪbə'reɪʃn] *s* **1.** namysł *m* **2.** ⁓**s** narada *f* dyskusja *f* **3.** rozwaga *f*
del•i•ca•cy ['delɪkəsɪ] *s* **1.** delikatność *f* **2.** przysmak *m*
del•i•cate ['delɪkət] *adj* delikatny
del•i•ca•tes•sen [delɪkə'tesn] *s* delikatesy *pl*
del•i•cious [dɪ'lɪʃəs] *adj* pyszny
de•light [dɪ'laɪt] **I** *s* **1.** (wielka) przyjemność *f*, rozkosz *f*; ***take*** ⁓ ***in doing s.th.*** robić coś z wielką przyjemnością **2.** (wielka) radość *f*; ***to my*** ⁓ ku mojej wielkiej radości **3.** zachwyt *m* **II** *v/t* bardzo cieszyć ⟨u-⟩, zachwycać ⟨-cić⟩ **III** *v/i* ⁓ ***in s.th.*** robić coś z wielką przyjemnością, czerpać wielką radość z czegoś; **de•light•ed** [dɪ'laɪtɪd] *adj* zachwycony; ***I'm*** ⁓ ***to hear that*** miło mi słyszeć, że; **de•light•ful** [dɪ'laɪtfəl] *adj* **1.** zachwycający **2.** uroczy
de•lim•it [diː'lɪmɪt] *v/t form* określać ⟨-lić⟩
de•lin•quen•cy [dɪ'lɪŋkwənsɪ] *s* **1.** przestępczość *f* (nieletnich) **2.** przestępstwo *n*, wykroczenie *n*; **de•lin•quent** [dɪ'lɪŋkwənt] **I** *s* przestępca *m* **II** *adj* przestępczy; ***a*** ⁓ ***child*** nieletni przestępca **3.** *payment*: zaległy
de•lir•i•ous [dɪ'lɪːrɪəs] *adj* **1.** majaczący; ***be*** ⁓ majaczyć **2.** ***be*** ⁓ ***with joy*** *fig* szaleć z radości
de•lir•i•ous•ly [dɪ'lɪːrɪəslɪ] *adv* **1.** w delirium **2.** *fig* szaleńczo; **de•lir•i•um** [dɪ'lɪrɪəm] *pl -riums* [⁓ɪəmz], *-ria* [⁓ɪə] *s* delirium *n*, majaczenie *n*
de•liv•er [dɪ'lɪvə] *v/t* **1.** *goods*: dostarczać ⟨-czyć⟩ **2.** przywozić ⟨-wieźć⟩ (***to*** do *G*) **3.** *newspapers*: roznosić ⟨-nieść⟩ **4.** *post*: doręczać ⟨-czyć⟩ **5.** odbierać ⟨odebrać⟩ poród **6.** *speech*, *sermon*: wygłaszać ⟨-łosić⟩ **7.** przekazywać ⟨-zać⟩, oddawać ⟨-dać⟩ (***over to*** *D*) **8.** ratować ⟨u-⟩, wybawiać ⟨-wić⟩ (***from*** z *G*); **de•liv•er•y** [dɪ'lɪvərɪ] *s* **1.** dostawa *f*; ***pay on*** ⁓ zapłacić przy odbiorze **2.** doręczenie *n* **3.** poród *m* **4.** sposób *m* wygłaszania; ***his*** ⁓ ***is poor*** jest słabym mówcą; **de•'liv•er•y charge** *s* opłata *f* za dostawę; **de•'liv•er•y date** *s* data *f* doręczenia, data *f* dostawy; **de•'liv•er•y man** *pl -men s* roznosiciel *m*, doręczyciel *m*; **de•'liv•er•y room** *s Am* sala *f* porodowa; **de•'liv•er•y serv•ice** *s* dostawa *f*; **de•'liv•er•y van** *s* samochód *m* dostawczy
dell [del] *s lit* (zadrzewiona) dolina *f*
de•lude [dɪ'luːd] *v/t* zwodzić ⟨zwieść⟩ (***with*** *I*)
de•luge ['deljuːdʒ] *s* **1.** potop *m* **2.** *fig* zalew *m*
de•lu•sion [dɪ'luːʒn] *s* iluzja *f*, urojenie *n*, złudzenie *n*; ***be under*** ⁓ ***that*** wyobrażać sobie, że
de luxe [də'lʌks] *adj* luksusowy

delve [delv] *v/i* **1.** sięgać ⟨-gnąć⟩ (***into*** do *G*) **2.** *past*: badać ⟨z-⟩ (***into*** *A*) **3.** zagłębiać ⟨-bić⟩ się (***into*** w *A*)

dem•a•gog•ic [demə'gɒgɪk] *adj* demagogiczny; **dem•a•gogue** ['deməgɒg] *s* demagog *m*; **dem•a•gog•y** ['deməgɒgɪ] *s* demagogia *f*

de•mand [dɪ'mɑːnd] **I** *s* **1.** żądanie *n*; ***on ~*** na żądanie **2.** wymóg *m* **3.** ECON popyt *m*, zapotrzebowanie *n* (***for*** na *A*) **II** *v/t* **1.** żądać ⟨za-⟩, domagać się **2.** *patience*, *punctuality*: wymagać; ***we ~ of our employees that they be punctual*** od naszych pracowników wymagamy punktualności; **de•mand•ing** [dɪ'mɑːndɪŋ] *adj* **1.** *person*: wymagający **2.** *work*: trudny **3.** *schedule*: napięty

de•mar•cate ['diːmɑːkeɪt] *v/t* **1.** *boundary*: wytyczać ⟨-czyć⟩ **2.** *territory*: wytyczać ⟨-czyć⟩ granicę *G* **3.** *scope*, *pace*: wyznaczać ⟨-czyć⟩; **de•mar•ca•tion** [diːmɑː'keɪʃn] *s* **1.** podział *m* **2.** rozgraniczenie *n* **3.** wytyczenie *n* granic; **de•mar•'ca•tion line** *s* POLIT linia *f* demarkacyjna

de•mean•our [dɪ'miːnə] *Br*, **de•mean•or** *Am s form* zachowanie *n*, postawa *f*

de•men•ted [dɪ'mentɪd] *adj* **1.** obłąkany **2.** *fig* bliski obłędu; **de•men•tia** [dɪ'menʃə] *s* demencja *f*, otępienie *n* umysłowe

dem•i•god *s* ['demigɒd] półbóg *m*

de•mil•i•ta•rize [diː'mɪlɪtəraɪz] *v/t* demilitaryzować ⟨z-⟩

de•mise [dɪ'maɪz] *s form* **1.** upadek *m* **2.** koniec *m* **3.** zgon *m*

de•mist [diː'mɪst] *v/t* usuwać ⟨usunąć⟩ zamglenie

dem•o ['deməʊ] *s infml* **1.** → ***demonstration*** **2.** demo *n*; ***a ~ tape*** kaseta demo

de•mo•bil•ize [dɪ'məʊbəlaɪz] *v/t* demobilizować ⟨z-⟩

de•moc•ra•cy [dɪ'mɒkrəsɪ] *s* demokracja *f*; **dem•o•crat** ['deməkræt] *s* demokrata *m*; **dem•o•crat•ic** [demə'krætɪk] *adj* demokratyczny; **dem•o•crat•ic•al•ly** [demə'krætɪklɪ] *adv* demokratycznie

de•mo•graph•ic [deməʊ'græfɪk] *adj* demograficzny; **de•mog•ra•phy** [dɪ'mɒgrəfɪ] *s* demografia *f*

de•mol•ish [dɪ'mɒlɪʃ] *v/t* **1.** *building*: wyburzać ⟨-rzyć⟩, rozbierać ⟨-zebrać⟩ **2.** *theory*: obalać ⟨-lić⟩ **3.** *infml* rozgramiać ⟨-romić⟩; **dem•o•li•tion** [demə'lɪʃn] *s* **1.** *building*: rozbiórka *f* **2.** *theory*: obalenie *n* **3.** *town*: zburzenie *n*

de•mon ['diːmən] *s* demon *m*; ***the ~ drink*** szatański napój; **de•mon•iac** [dɪ'mɒnɪək] *adj* **1.** diaboliczny **2.** koszmarny; **de•mon•ic** [dɪ'mɒnɪk] *adj* demoniczny, szatański

de•mon•stra•ble [dɪ'mɒnstrəbl] *adj*: ***be ~*** dać się udowodnić; **de•mon•stra•bly** [dɪ'mɒnstrəblɪ] *adv* w sposób oczywisty; **dem•on•strate** ['demənstreɪt] *v/t* **1.** dowodzić ⟨-wieść⟩ **2.** prezentować ⟨za-⟩ **3.** demonstrować ⟨za-⟩ **4.** *concern*: okazywać ⟨-zać⟩; **dem•on•stra•tion** [demən'streɪʃn] *s* **1.** demonstracja *f*, manifestacja *f* (***against*** przeciw *D*, ***for*** za *I*) **2.** demonstracja *f*, pokaz *m* **3.** *feelings*: manifestacja *f*, okazanie *n* **4.** dowiedzenie *n*; **de•mon•stra•tive** [dɪ'mɒnstrətɪv] *adj* **1.** *person*: wylewny **2.** ***be ~ of*** świadczyć o *L*; **de•mon•stra•tive 'pro•noun** *s* zaimek *m* wskazujący; **de•mon•stra•tor** ['demənstreɪtə] *s* **1.** demonstrant *m* **2.** demonstrator *m* **3.** samochód *m* do jazd próbnych

de•mor•al•ize [dɪ'mɒrəlaɪz] *v/t* zniechęcać ⟨-cić⟩; **de•mor•al•ized** [dɪ'mɔːrəlaɪzd] *adj* zniechęcony; **de•mor•al•iz•ing** [dɪ'mɒrəlaɪzɪŋ] zniechęcający

de•mote [dɪ'məʊt] *v/t* degradować ⟨z-⟩

de•mo•ti•vate [diː'məʊtɪveɪt] *v/t* zniechęcać ⟨-cić⟩

de•mur [dɪ'mɜː] *v/t* **1.** sprzeciwiać ⟨-wić⟩ się (***at*** *D*) **2.** odnosić ⟨-nieść⟩ się niechętnie (***at*** do *G*)

de•mure [dɪ'mjʊə] *adj* skromny

de•myst•i•fy [diː'mɪstɪfaɪ] *v/t story*: wyjaśniać ⟨-nić⟩, tłumaczyć ⟨wy-⟩

de•na•tion•al•ize [diː'næʃnəlaɪz] *v/t* prywatyzować ⟨s-⟩

de•ni•al [dɪ'naɪəl] *s* **1.** zaprzeczenie *n* **2.** odmowa *f* **3.** *guilt*: wyparcie *n* się **4.** *visa*: odmowa *f* wydania **5.** PSYCH wyparcie *n*

Den•mark ['denmɑːk] *s* Dania *f*

D

de•nom•i•nate [dɪ'nɒmɪneɪt] *v/t* nazywać ⟨-zwać⟩; **de•nom•i•na•tion** [dɪnɒmɪ'neɪʃn] *s* **1.** *REL* wyznanie *n* **2.** *FIN* wartość *f* nominalna, nominał *m* **3.** nazwa *f*; **de•nom•ina•tion•al** [dɪnɒmɪ'neɪʃənl] *adj* wyznaniowy

D

denom•i•na•tor [dɪ'nɒmɪneɪtə] *s MATH* mianownik *m*

de•note [dɪ'nəʊt] *v/t* **1.** oznaczać **2.** wskazywać na *A*

dé•noue•ment [deɪ'nuːmɒŋ] *s* rozwiązanie *n*

de•nounce [dɪ'naʊns] *v/t* **1.** potępiać ⟨-pić⟩, ostro krytykować ⟨s-⟩ (***for*** za *A*) **2.** denuncjonować ⟨za-⟩, donosić ⟨-nieść⟩ na *A*

dense [dens] *adj* **1.** gęsty **2.** *housing*: zwarty **3.** *infml* tępy; **dense•ly** ['densli] *adv* gęsto; **den•si•ty** ['densɪtɪ] *s* **1.** gęstość *f* **2.** *housing*: zwartość *f*

den•tal ['dentl] *adj* dentystyczny, stomatologiczny; **den•tal 'floss** *s* nić *f* stomatologiczna; **den•tal 'hy•giene** *s* higiena *f* jamy ustnej; **den•tal 'hy•gien•ist** *s* asystent *m* dentysty; **'den•tal nurse** *s* pomoc *f* dentystyczna; **den•tal 'sur•geon** *s* dentysta *m*, stomatolog *m*

den•tist ['dentɪst] *s* stomatolog *m*, dentysta *m*; **den•tist•ry** ['dentɪstrɪ] *s* stomatologia *f*

den•tures ['denʃəz] *pl* proteza *f* zębowa

denude [dɪ'njuːd] *v/t form* ogałacać ⟨ogołocić⟩ (***of*** z *G*)

de•nun•ci•a•tion [dɪnʌnsɪ'eɪʃn] *s* potępienie *n*

de•ny [dɪ'naɪ] *v/t* **1.** zaprzeczać ⟨-czyć⟩; ***~ the rumour that*** zaprzeczyć pogłoskom, jakoby **2.** odmawiać ⟨-mówić⟩ **3.** *guilt*: wypierać ⟨-przeć⟩ się *G*

de•o•do•rant [diː'əʊdərənt] **I** *s* dezodorant *m* **II** *adj* dezodorujący; **de•o•dor•ize** [diː'əʊdəraɪz] *v/t* usuwać ⟨usunąć⟩ brzydki zapach

de•part [dɪ'pɑːt] *v/t* **1.** wyruszać ⟨-szyć⟩ **2.** (*train*) odjeżdżać ⟨-jechać⟩ **3.** (*plane*) odlatywać ⟨-lecieć⟩ **4.** *from road, subject*: odchodzić ⟨odejść⟩ (***from*** od *G*); ***~ from the truth*** rozminąć się z prawdą; **de•part•ed** [dɪ'pɑːtɪd] **I** *s **the ~*** nieboszczyk *m* **II** *adj* zmarły

de•part•ment [dɪ'pɑːtmənt] *s* **1.** dział *m*, wydział *m* **2.** departament *m* **3.** ministerstwo *n* **4.** (*shop*) stoisko *n*, dział *m* **5.** (*hospital*) oddział *m* **6.** (*university*) wydział *m*; **de•part•ment•al** [diːpət'mentl] *adj* **1.** *manager*: działu, wydziału, departamentu **2.** ministerialny; **De•part•ment of 'De•fense** *s Am* Departament *m* Obrony; **De•part•ment of the In•'te•ri•or** *s Am* Departament *m* Spraw Wewnętrznych; **De•part•ment of 'State** *s Am* Departament *m* Stanu; **de'part•ment store** *s* dom *m* towarowy

de•par•ture [dɪ'pɑːtʃə] *s* **1.** wyjazd *m* **2.** *train*: odjazd *m* **3.** *plane*: odlot *m* **4.** *from position*: odejście *n* **5.** odstępstwo *n* (***from*** od *G*); **de•'par•ture date** *s* data *f* wyjazdu; **de•'par•ture lounge** *s* hala *f* odlotów; **de•'par•ture time** *s* **1.** godzina *f* odjazdu **2.** godzina *f* odlotu

de•pend [dɪ'pend] *v/i* **1.** polegać, liczyć (***on*** na *L*); ***you can always ~ on him*** zawsze można na niego liczyć **2.** zależeć (***on*** od *G*); ***the temperature varies ~ing on the season*** temperatura zależy od pory roku **3.** (*financially*) być zależnym (***on*** od *G*); **de•pen•da•ble** [dɪ'pendəbl] *adj* godny zaufania, niezawodny; **de•pen•dant** [dɪ'pendənt] *s*: ***be s.o.'s ~*** być na czyimś utrzymaniu; ***have 3 ~s*** mieć trzy osoby na utrzymaniu

de•pen•dence [dɪ'pendəns], ***de•pen•den•cy*** [dɪ'pendənsɪ] *s* **1.** zależność *f* (***on*** od *G*) **2.** uzależnienie *n* (***on*** od *G*); **de•pen•dent** [dɪ'pendənt] *adj* **1.** zależny (***on*** od *G*) **2.** uzależniony (***on*** od *G*) **3.** uwarunkowany (***on*** *I*)

de•pict [dɪ'pɪkt] *v/t* **1.** przedstawiać ⟨-wić⟩ **2.** malować ⟨na-⟩; **de•pic•tion** [dɪ'pɪkʃn] *s* **1.** obraz *m* **2.** przedstawienie *n*

de•plane ['diːpleɪn] *v/i Am* wysiadać ⟨-siąść⟩ z samolotu

de•plete [dɪ'pliːt] *v/t* **1.** *reserves*: uszczuplać ⟨-lić⟩ **2.** *number*: zmniejszać ⟨-szyć⟩ **3.** *energy*: wyczerpywać ⟨-pać⟩

de•plor•a•ble [dɪ'plɔːrəbl] *adj* godny ubolewania, żałosny; **de•plore** [dɪ'plɔː] *v/t* ubolewać nad *I*, boleć nad *I*

de•ploy [dɪ'plɔɪ] *v/t* **1.** *soldiers*: rozmieszczać ⟨-mieścić⟩ **2.** wykorzystywać ⟨-stać⟩, stosować ⟨za-⟩; **de•ploy•ment** [dɪ'plɔɪmənt] *s* **1.** *soldiers*: rozmieszczenie *n* **2.** wykorzystanie *n*, zastosowanie *n*

de•pop•u•la•tion [diːpɒpjə'leɪʃn] *s* wyludnienie *n*

de•port [dɪ'pɔːt] *v/t* **1.** *immigrant*: deportować **2.** *prisoner*: zsyłać ⟨zesłać⟩; **de•por•ta•tion** [diːpɔː'teɪʃn] *s* **1.** deportacja *f* **2.** zesłanie *n*; **de•por'ta•tion or•der** *s* nakaz *m* deportacji

de•port•ment [dɪ'pɔːtmənt] *s Br form* postawa *f*, sposób *m* poruszania się

de•pose [dɪ'pəʊz] *v/t* **1.** *king*: detronizować ⟨z-⟩ **2.** *dictator*: obalać ⟨-lić⟩ **3.** *minister*: dymisjonować ⟨z-⟩

de•pos•it [dɪ'pɒzɪt] **I** *v/t* **1.** wpłacać ⟨-cić⟩ **2.** umieszczać ⟨umieścić⟩ **3.** deponować ⟨z-⟩ **II** *v/t* osadzać ⟨-dzić⟩ się **III** *s* **1.** wpłata *f* **2.** lokata *f* **3.** depozyt *m* **4.** kaucja *f*, zastaw *m* **5.** zaliczka *f* **6.** *CHEM* osad *m* **7.** *GEOL* złoże *n*, pokład *m*; **de•'pos•it ac•count** *s FIN Br* rachunek *m* depozytowy

de•prave [dɪ'preɪv] *v/t* deprawować ⟨z-⟩; **de•praved** [dɪ'preɪvd] *adj* zdeprawowany, niemoralny; **de•prav•i•ty** [dɪ'prævətɪ] *s* deprawacja *f*

dep•re•cate ['deprɪkeɪt] *v/t* **1.** potępiać ⟨-pić⟩ **2.** deprecjonować ⟨z-⟩; **dep•reca•tion** [deprɪ'keɪʃn] *s* **1.** potępienie *n* **2.** deprecjacja *f*; **dep•re•ca•to•ry** [deprɪ'keɪtərɪ] *adj* potępiający

de•pre•ci•ate [dɪ'priːʃɪeɪt] **I** *v/t* **1.** *form* deprecjonować ⟨z-⟩, lekceważyć ⟨z-⟩ **2.** *ECON* amortyzować ⟨z-⟩ **3.** obniżać ⟨-żyć⟩ wartość **II** *v/i* tracić ⟨s-⟩ na wartości; **de•pre•ci•a•tion** [dɪpriːʃɪ'eɪʃn] *s* **1.** deprecjonowanie *n*, lekceważenie *n* **2.** spadek *m* wartości, deprecjacja *f* **3.** amortyzacja *f*; ***a ~ period*** okres amortyzacji; ***a ~ rate*** stopa amortyzacji

dep•re•da•tion [deprɪ'deɪʃn] *s* rabunek *m*, grabież *f*

de•press [dɪ'pres] *v/t* **1.** przygnębiać ⟨-bić⟩ **2.** *prices, salaries*: obniżać ⟨-żyć⟩ **3.** naciskać ⟨-snąć⟩ **4.** *market*: osłabiać ⟨-bić⟩; **de•pres•sant** [dɪ'presənt] *s MED* środek *m* uspokajający; **de•pressed** [dɪ'prest] *adj* **1.** przygnębiony **2.** w depresji **3.** *market*: dotknięty kryzysem, osłabiony **4.** ***~ area*** **a)** obszar dotknięty bezrobociem **b)** obszar dotknięty kryzysem **5.** obniżony; **de•press•ing** [dɪ'presɪŋ] *adj* **1.** przygnębiający **2.** depresyjny; **de•pres•sion** [dɪ'preʃn] *s* **1.** *PSYCH* depresja *f* **2.** przygnębienie *n* **3.** obniżenie *n* terenu **4.** *ECON* kryzys *m* **5.** niż *m*

dep•ri•va•tion [deprɪ'veɪʃn] *s* **1.** nędza *f*, ubóstwo *n* **2.** pozbawienie *n*, utrata *f*; **de•prive** [dɪ'praɪv] *v/t* pozbawiać ⟨-wić⟩ (**of** *G*); **de•prived** [dɪ'praɪvd] *adj* **1.** ubogi **2.** pozbawiony (**of** *G*)

depth [depθ] *s* **1.** głębokość *f*; ***at a ~ of 100 m*** na głębokości 100 m; ***five feet in ~*** głęboki na pięć stóp; ***in ~*** dogłębnie, dokładnie; ***in the ~s of winter*** w samym środku zimy; ***be out of one's ~*** **a)** nie sięgać dna **b)** *fig* gubić się; ***he's out of his ~ as a manager*** praca na stanowisku kierowniczym go przerasta **2.** głębia *f*; ***~ of field, ~ of focus*** *PHOT* głębia ostrości **3.** otchłań *f*, czeluści *pl*; **'depth charge** *s* bomba *f* głębinowa

dep•u•ta•tion [depjʊ'teɪʃn] *s* delegacja *f*; **dep•u•tize** ['depjʊtaɪz] *v/i* zastępować ⟨-tąpić⟩ (***for*** *A*)

dep•u•ty ['depjʊtɪ] **I** *s* **1.** zastępca *m* **2.** deputowany *m*, poseł *m* **3.** (*a.* ***~ sheriff***) zastępca *m* szeryfa **II** *adj* wice-; **dep•u•ty 'head** *s* (*school*) *Br* wicedyrektor *m*; **'dep•u•ty lead•er** *s* wiceprzewodniczący *m*

de•rail [dɪ'reɪl] **I** *v/t* **1.** *fig* niweczyć ⟨z-⟩, powodować ⟨s-⟩ fiasko **2.** ***be ~ed*** wykoleić się **II** *v/i* wykolejać ⟨-leić⟩ się

de•ranged [dɪ'reɪndʒd] *adj* (*a.* ***mentally ~***) obłąkany, niepoczytalny; **de•range•ment** [dɪ'reɪndʒmənt] *s* obłęd *m*, niepoczytalność *f*

der•by ['dɑːbɪ] *s* **1.** *SPORT* derby *pl* **2.** (*a.* ***~ hat***) melonik *m*

de•reg•u•late [diː'regjʊleɪt] *v/t ECON* **1.** *prices, market*: uwalniać ⟨uwolnić⟩ **2.** wyjmować ⟨-jąć⟩ spod kontroli; **de•reg•u•la•tion** [diːregjʊ'leɪʃn] *s ECON* **1.** uwolnienie *n* **2.** zniesienie *n* kontroli

D

D

der•e•lict ['derəlɪkt] **I** *adj* **1.** zrujnowany **2.** zaniedbany **3.** opuszczony **II** *s* bezdomny *m*, włóczęga *m*

der•i•va•tion [derɪ'veɪʃn] *s* **1.** (*word*) derywacja *f* **2.** pochodzenie *n*; **de•riv•a•tive** [dɪ'rɪvətɪv] **I** *s* **1.** CHEM MATH pochodna *f* **2.** (*word*) derywat *m*, wyraz *m* pochodny **II** *adj* **1.** wtórny, nieoryginalny **2.** pochodny; **de•rive** [dɪ'raɪv] **I** *v/t* **1.** ***be ~d from*** **a)** (*word*) pochodzić od *G* **b)** (*substance*) być otrzymywanym z *G* **2.** *profit, pleasure*: czerpać; ***she ~s great pleasure from painting*** malowanie sprawia jej wielką przyjemność **3.** derywować **II** *v/i* pochodzić (***from*** od *G*)

de•scend [dɪ'send] **I** *v/i* **1.** schodzić ⟨zejść⟩ **2.** (*plane, parachute*) obniżać ⟨-żyć⟩ lot **3.** (*terrain*) opadać ⟨opaść⟩, obniżać ⟨-żyć⟩ się **4.** ***~ from*** pochodzić od *G*, być potomkiem *G* **5.** (*night*) zapadać ⟨-paść⟩ **6.** (*sun*) zniżać ⟨-żyć⟩ się **7.** przybywać ⟨-być⟩ (***on*** do *G*) **8.** ***the country ~ed into chaos*** w kraju zapanował chaos **9.** zjeżdżać ⟨zjechać⟩ **10.** spadać ⟨spaść⟩ **II** *v/t* (*stairs*) schodzić ⟨zejść⟩ po *L*

de•scen•dant [dɪ'sendənt] *s* potomek *m*

de•scent [dɪ'sent] *s* **1.** zejście *n* **2.** zjazd *m* **3.** schodzenie *n*; ***the plane began its ~*** samolot zaczął zniżać lot **4.** pochyłość *f* **5.** pochodzenie *n*; ***she's of French ~*** jest z pochodzenia Francuzką **6.** *fig* najazd *m*

de•scribe [dɪ'skraɪb] *v/t* **1.** opisywać ⟨-sać⟩ (***to*** *D*) **2.** określać ⟨-lić⟩ (***as*** jako *N*); **de•scrip•tion** [dɪ'skrɪpʃn] *s* **1.** opis *m*; ***give a ~ of*** opisać *A* **2.** rodzaj *m*; ***of all ~s*** wszelkiego rodzaju; **de•scrip•tive** [dɪ'skrɪptɪv] *adj* opisowy

des•e•crate ['desɪkreɪt] *v/t* profanować ⟨s-⟩, bezcześcić ⟨z-⟩; **des•e•cra•tion** [desɪ'kreɪʃn] *s* profanacja *f*, zbezczeszczenie *n*

de•seg•re•gate [diː'segrəgeɪt] *v/t* znosić ⟨znieść⟩ sergegację rasową w *L*; **de•seg•re•ga•tion** [diːsegrə'geɪʃn] *s* desegregacja *f* (rasowa)

de•sen•si•tize [diː'sensətaɪz] *v/t* **1.** ***~ s.o. to*** stępić czyjąś wrażliwość na *A* **2.** odczulać ⟨-lić⟩

des•ert[1] ['dezərt] **I** *s* pustynia *f* **II** *adj* pustynny

des•ert[2] [dɪ'zɜːt] **I** *v/t* opuszczać ⟨opuścić⟩, porzucać ⟨-cić⟩ **II** *v/i army*: dezerterować ⟨z-⟩

des•ert•ed [dɪ'zɜːtɪd] *adj* **1.** *place*: opustoszały, wyludniony **2.** *person*: opuszczony, porzucony

de•sert•er [dɪ'zɜːtə] *s* dezerter *m*

de•ser•tion [dɪ'zɜːʃn] *s* **1.** dezercja *f* **2.** JUR porzucenie *n*

des•ert 'is•land *s* bezludna wyspa *f*

de•serts [dɪ'zɜːts] *pl* ***he got his (just) ~*** dostał to, na co sobie zasłużył

de•serve [dɪ'zɜːv] *v/t* zasługiwać ⟨-łużyć⟩; **de•serv•ed•ly** [dɪ'zɜːvɪdlɪ] *adv* zasłużenie; ***~ so*** słusznie; **de•serv•ing** [dɪ'zɜːvɪŋ] *adj* **1.** zasłużony **2.** *cause*: słuszny

de•sign [dɪ'zaɪn] **I** *v/t* **1.** projektować ⟨za-⟩ **2.** konstruować ⟨s-⟩ **3.** przeznaczać ⟨-czyć⟩ **4.** opracowywać ⟨-cować⟩, tworzyć ⟨s-⟩ **II** *s* **1.** projekt *m*; ***have a good ~*** być dobrze zaprojektowanym **2.** wzór *m* **3.** projektowanie *n* **4.** zamiar *m*, zamysł *m*; ***by ~*** celowo, umyślnie; ***have ~s on*** mieć zakusy na *A*; ***have ~s on s.o.*** mieć kogoś na oku

des•ig•nate ['dezɪgneɪt] **I** *v/t* **1.** określać ⟨-lić⟩ **2.** uznawać ⟨-nać⟩ (***as*** za *N*) **3.** wyznaczać ⟨-czyć⟩ **4.** desygnować **II** *adj* **1.** nowo mianowany **2.** desygnowany

de•sign•er [dɪ'zaɪnə] **I** *s* **1.** projektant *m* **2.** konstruktor *m* **3.** autor *m* **II** *adj* **1.** (od) znanego projektanta **2.** (ze) znanego domu mody **3.** markowy; **de•'sign•er clothes** *pl* **1.** ubrania *pl* (od) znanego projektanta **2.** ubrania *pl* (ze) znanego domu mody; **de•'sign•er la•bel** *s* metka *f* domu mody; **de•'sign•er fault** *s* wada *f* konstrukcyjna; **de•'sign school** *s* szkoła *f* wzornictwa

de•sir•a•ble [dɪ'zaɪərəbl] *adj* **1.** pożądany **2.** wskazany **3.** upragniony **4.** atrakcyjny **5.** pociągający; **de•sire** [dɪ'zaɪə] **I** *s* **1.** ochota *f*, chęć *f*, pragnienie *n*; ***~ for knowledge*** głód wiedzy; ***~ for power*** żądza władzy **2.** życzenie *n* **3.** pożądanie *n* (seksualne) **II** *v/t* **1.** pragnąć ⟨za-⟩ **2.** mieć ochotę na *A* **3.** życzyć ⟨za-⟩ sobie, ***if ~d***

na życzenie; ***leave much to be ~d*** pozostawiać wiele do życzenia **4.** pożądać, pragnąć; **de•sir•ous** [dɪ'zaɪərəs] *adj*: ***be ~ to know s.th.*** chcieć się czegoś dowiedzieć

desk [desk] **I** *s* **1.** biurko *n* **2.** (*school*) ławka *f* **3.** (*a.* **cash ~**) kasa *f* **4.** (*a.* ***reception ~***) recepcja *f* **5.** (*a.* ***information ~***) informacja *f*, punkt *m* informacyjny **II** *adj work*: biurowy; **'desk clerk** *s* recepcjonista *m*; **'desk di•a•ry** *s* terminarz *m* biurowy

'desk•top *s* **I** *s* blat *m* **II** *adj computer*: biurkowy; **desk•top 'cal•cu•la•tor** *s* kalkulator *m* biurkowy; **desk•top 'pub•lish•ing** *s* mała poligrafia *f* komputerowa

des•o•late ['desələt] *adj* **1.** opustoszały **2.** wymarły **3.** bardzo przygnębiony; **des•o•la•tion** [desə'leɪʃn] *s* **1.** ogromny żal *m* **2.** beznadziejny smutek *m* **3.** spustoszenie *n*

de•spair [dɪ'speə] **I** *s* **1.** rozpacz *f* **2.** desperacja *f*; ***a look of ~*** rozpaczliwe spojrzenie; ***drive s.o. to ~, be the ~ of s.o.*** doprowadzać kogoś do rozpaczy **II** *v/i* **1.** rozpaczać **2.** tracić ⟨s-⟩ nadzieję; **des•pair•ing** [dɪ'speərɪŋ] *adj* **1.** zrozpaczony **2.** rozpaczliwy

de•spatch [dɪ'spætʃ] *Br* → ***dispatch***

des•per•ate ['despərət] *adj* **1.** zrozpaczony **2.** rozpaczliwy, desperacki **3.** zdesperowany; ***be ~ for*** **a)** rozpaczliwie potrzebować *G* **b)** bardzo pragnąć *G*; ***I'm ~ for a cigarette*** *infml* muszę sobie zapalić **3.** straszliwy, beznadziejny; **des•per•ate•ly** ['despərətlɪ] *adv* rozpaczliwie, desperacko; **des•per•a•tion** [despə'reɪʃn] *s* **1.** rozpacz *f*; ***in ~*** w rozpaczy, ***drive s.o. to ~*** doprowadzać kogoś do rozpaczy **2.** desperacja *f*

des•pic•a•ble [dɪ'spɪkəbl] *adj* podły, nikczemny

de•spise [dɪ'spaɪz] *v/t* gardzić, pogardzać; ***not to be ~d*** nie do pogardzenia

de•spite [dɪ'spaɪt] *prep* mimo *G*, pomimo *G*

de•spon•dent [dɪ'spɒndənt] *adj* przygnębiony, zniechęcony

des•pot ['despɒt] *s* despota *m*; **des•pot•ic** [de'spɒtɪk] *adj* despotyczny

des•sert [dɪ'zɜːt] **I** *s* COOK deser *m* **II** *adj* deserowy; **des•'sert•spoon** *s* łyżeczka *f* deserowa; **des•'sertwine** *s* wino *n* deserowe

de•sta•bi•lize [diː'steɪbəlaɪz] *v/t* **1.** destabilizować ⟨z-⟩ **2.** podważać ⟨-żyć⟩ pozycję

des•ti•na•tion [destɪ'neɪʃn] *s* **1.** cel *m* podróży; ***the country of ~*** kraj docelowy **2.** miejsce *n* przeznaczenia **3.** stacja *f* docelowa; **des•tined** ['destɪnd] *adj* **1.** przeznaczony; ***he was ~ to become a scientist*** przeznaczona mu była kariera naukowca; ***it was ~ to happen*** to musiało się stać **2.** ***the parcel is ~ for Italy*** miejscem przeznaczenia tej paczki są Włochy

des•ti•ny ['destɪnɪ] *s* los *m*, przeznaczenie *n*

de•stroy [dɪ'strɔɪ] *v/t* **1.** niszczyć ⟨z-⟩ **2.** *health, reputation*: rujnować ⟨z-⟩ **3.** niweczyć ⟨z-⟩ **4.** tępić ⟨wy-⟩ **5.** *animal*: zabijać ⟨-bić⟩; **de•stroy•er** [dɪ'strɔɪə] *s* **1.** niszczyciel *m* **2.** zabójca *m*

de•struc•tion [dɪ'strʌkʃn] *s* **1.** zniszczenie *n* **2.** zagłada *f* **3.** unicestwienie *n*; **de•struc•tive** [dɪ'strʌktɪv] *adj* **1.** niszczący **2.** niszczycielski, destrukcyjny **3.** destruktywny; **de•struc•tive•ness** [dɪ'strʌktɪvnɪs] *s* **1.** niszczące działanie *n* **2.** niszczycielska siła *f* **3.** destrukcyjny charakter *m*

de•tach [dɪ'tætʃ] *v/t* **1.** odłączać ⟨-czyć⟩ **2.** oddzielać ⟨-lić⟩ **3.** odrywać ⟨oderwać⟩ **4.** odpinać ⟨-piąć⟩; **de•tach•a•ble** [dɪ'tætʃəbl] *adj* **1.** odpinany **2.** zdejmowany **3.** do oderwania

de•tached [dɪ'tætʃt] *adj* **1.** oddzielny, osobny; ***become ~*** oddzielić się; ***a ~ house*** dom wolno stojący **2.** obojętny **3.** bezstronny; **de•tach•ment** [dɪ'tætʃmənt] *s* **1.** oddzielenie *n* (się), oderwanie *n* (się) **2.** obojętność *f* **3.** bezstronność *f*

de•tail ['diːteɪl] **I** *s* **1.** szczegół *m*; ***down to the smallest ~*** w najdrobniejszych szczegółach; ***in ~*** dokładnie, szczegółowo; ***go into ~s*** zagłębiać się w szczegóły **2.** ***~s*** informacje; ***personal ~s*** dane personalne **II** *v/t* **1.** wyszczególniać ⟨-nić⟩ **2.** opisywać ⟨-sać⟩ szczegółowo **3.** (*army*) odkomenderowywać ⟨-rować⟩; **de•tailed** ['diːteɪld] *adj* **1.** szczegółowy **2.** wymagający precyzji

D

D

de•tain [dɪ'teɪn] *v/t* zatrzymywać ⟨-mać⟩; ~ ***in custody*** zatrzymać w areszcie; **de•tain•ee** [diːteɪ'niː] *s* zatrzymany *m*
de•tect [dɪ'tekt] *v/t* **1.** wykrywać ⟨-ryć⟩ **2.** wyczuwać ⟨-czuć⟩; **de•tec•tion** [dɪ'tekʃn] *s* wykrycie *n*; ***crime ~ rate*** wykrywalność przestępstw
de•tec•tive [dɪ'tektɪv] **I** *s* **1.** oficer *m* z wydziału dochodzeniowo-śledczego **2.** detektyw *m* **II** *adj* detektywistyczny; **de'tec•tive mov•ie** *s* film *m* kryminalny; **de'tec•tive nov•el** *s* powieść *f* detektywistyczna, powieść *f* kryminalna
de•tec•tor [dɪ'tektə] *s* wykrywacz *m*, detektor *m*
de•ten•tion [dɪ'tenʃn] *s* **1.** pozbawienie *n* wolności **2.** zatrzymanie *n*; ***in ~*** w areszcie; ***~ pending trial*** areszt tymczasowy **3.** (*school*) ***be kept in ~*** za karę zostać po lekcjach
de•ter [dɪ'tɜː] *v/t* **1.** powstrzymywać ⟨-mać⟩ **2.** zniechęcać ⟨-cić⟩ **3.** odstraszać ⟨-szyć⟩
de•te•ri•o•rate [dɪ'tɪrɪəreɪt] *v/i* **1.** pogarszać ⟨-gorszyć⟩ się **2.** psuć ⟨po-⟩ się **3.** podupadać ⟨-paść⟩; **de•te•ri•o•ra•tion** [dɪtɪrɪə'reɪʃn] *s* **1.** pogorszenie *n* (się) **2.** spadek *m* jakości
de•ter•mi•na•tion [dɪtɜːmɪ'neɪʃn] *s* **1.** determinacja *f*, zdecydowanie *n* **2.** określenie *n* **3.** ustalenie *n*; **de•ter•mine** [dɪ'tɜːmɪn] *v/t* **1.** określać ⟨-lić⟩ **2.** ustalać ⟨-lić⟩ **3.** decydować ⟨z-⟩ o *L*; **de•ter•mined** [dɪ'tɜːmɪnd] *adj* **1.** zdecydowany **2.** zdeterminowany
de•test [dɪ'test] *v/t* nie cierpieć *G*, nie znosić *G*; **de•test•a•ble** [dɪ'testəbl] *adj* wstrętny, obrzydliwy; **de•tes•ta•tion** [diːte'steɪʃn] *s* wstręt *m* (***of*** do *G*)
de•throne [dɪ'θrəʊn] *v/t* detronizować ⟨z-⟩
de•to•nate ['detəneɪt] **I** *v/t* detonować ⟨z-⟩ **II** *v/i* wybuchać ⟨-chnąć⟩; **de•to•na•tion** [detə'neɪʃn] *s* **1.** detonacja *f* **2.** wybuch *m*; **de•to•na•tor** ['detəneɪtə] *s* detonator *m*
de•tour ['diːtʊə] **I** *s* objazd *m*, okrężna droga *f*; ***make a ~*** pojechać okrężną drogą **II** *v/i Am* jechać ⟨po-⟩ okrężną drogą
de•tract [dɪ'trækt] *v/t*: ***~ from*** umniejszać *A*; **de•tract•or** [dɪ'træktə] *s* krytyk *m*
de•tri•ment ['detrɪmənt] *s* szkoda *f*; ***to the ~ of*** ze szkodą dla *G*; **de•tri•men•tal** [detrɪ'mentl] *adj* **1.** szkodliwy (***to*** dla *G*) **2.** krzywdzący
deuce [djuːs] *s* **1.** (*tennis*) równowaga *f* **2.** (*cards*) *Am* dwójka **3.** licho *n*; ***what the ~?*** co u licha?
de•val•u•a•tion [diːvæljʊ'eɪʃn] *s* **1.** *currency*: dewaluacja *f* **2.** obniżenie *n* wartości; **de•val•ue** [diː'væljuː] *v/t* **1.** dewaluować ⟨z-⟩ **2.** deprecjonować ⟨z-⟩, nie doceniać ⟨-nić⟩
dev•a•state ['devəsteɪt] *v/t* **1.** pustoszyć ⟨s-⟩ **2.** obracać ⟨-rócić⟩ w perzynę **3.** ***be ~d*** *person*: być zdruzgotanym, zupełnie się załamać; **dev•a•stat•ing** ['devəsteɪtɪŋ] *adj* **1.** *criticism*: miażdżący, druzgocący **2.** destruktywny **3.** *news*: szokujący **4.** *beauty*: olśniewający; **dev•as•ta•tion** [devə'steɪʃn] *s* **1.** spustoszenie *n* **2.** zniszczenie *n* **3.** dewastacja *f*
de•vel•op [dɪ'veləp] **I** *v/i* rozwijać ⟨-winąć⟩ się **II** *v/t* **1.** rozwijać ⟨-winąć⟩ **2.** zachorować na *A* **3.** zagospodarowywać ⟨-rować⟩ **4.** zabudowywać ⟨-dować⟩ **5.** *PHOT* wywoływać ⟨-łać⟩; **de'vel•oped coun•try** *s* kraj *m* rozwinięty; **de•vel•op•er** [dɪ'veləpə] *s* **1.** *BUILD* developer *m*, firma *f* deweloperska **2.** ***a software ~*** *INF* **a)** programista komputerowy **b)** producent oprogramowania **3.** ***be a late ~*** być (lekko) opóźnionym w rozwoju **4.** *PHOT* wywoływacz *m*; **de•vel•op•ing 'coun•try** *s* kraj *m* rozwijający się; **de•vel•op•ment** [dɪ'veləpmənt] *s* **1.** rozwój *m* **2.** ***a new ~*** nowość **3.** *BUILD* obiekt *f* **4.** osiedle *n* **5.** zagospodarowanie *n* **6.** wydarzenie *n*; ***latest ~s*** ostatnie wydarzenia
de•vi•ant ['diːvɪənt] **I** *s* dewiant *m* **II** *adj* dewiacyjny
de•vi•ate ['diːvɪeɪt] *v/i* **1.** odbiegać ⟨-biec⟩ (***from*** od *G*) **2.** odstępować ⟨-tąpić⟩ (***from*** od *G*); **de•vi•a•tion** [diːvɪ'eɪʃn] *s* **1.** odstępstwo *n* **2.** dewiacja *f* **3.** odchylenie *n*
de•vice [dɪ'vaɪs] *s* **1.** urządzenie *n* **2.** przyrząd *m* **3.** sposób *m*, meto-

da *f*; ***a marketing ~*** chwyt reklamowy; ***leave s.o. to their own ~s*** pozostawić kogoś samemu sobie **4.** wybieg *m*, sztuczka *f*
dev•il ['devl] *s* **1.** szatan *m*, diabeł *m*, demon *m*; ***be between the ~ and the deep blue sea*** znaleźć się między młotem a kowadłem; ***go to the ~!*** idź do diabła!; ***like the ~*** jak szalony; ***speak of the ~, talk of the ~*** o wilku mowa; ***what the ~?*** co u diabła? **2.** ***poor ~*** biedaczysko; ***lucky ~*** szczęściarz; **dev•il•ish** ['devlɪʃ] *adj* **1.** diabelski **2.** potworny, ohydny **3.** *smile*: diaboliczny; **dev•il-may-'care I** *adj* lekkomyślny, niefrasobliwy **II** *s* lekkoduch *m*; **dev•il•ry** ['devlrɪ] *s lit* **1.** złośliwość *f* **2.** łobuzeria *f* **3.** nikczemność *f*
de•vi•ous ['diːvɪəs] *adj* **1.** kręty **2.** okrężny; ***a ~ route*** okrężna droga **3.** krętacki, pokrętny; ***by ~ means*** nieuczciwie
de•vise [dɪ'vaɪz] *v/t* **1.** tworzyć ⟨s-⟩ **2.** wymyślać ⟨-lić⟩ **3.** opracowywać ⟨-cować⟩
de•void [dɪ'vɔɪd] *adj* pozbawiony (***of*** *G*)
dev•o•lu•tion [diːvə'luːʃn] *s* **1.** *POLIT* przekazanie *n* władzy **2.** *JUR* przejście *n*; **de•volve** [dɪ'vɒlv] **I** *v/t* **1.** *duty*: przekazywać ⟨-zać⟩ (***to***/***on*** *D*) **2.** *right*: przenosić ⟨-nieść⟩ **II** *v/i* przechodzić ⟨przejść⟩ (***on*** na *A*), przypadać ⟨-paść⟩ w udziale (***on*** *D*)
de•vote [dɪ'vəʊt] **I** *v/t* poświęcać ⟨-cić⟩ **II** *v/i* ***~ oneself to*** oddawać się *D*, poświęcać się *D*; **de•vot•ed** [dɪ'vəʊtɪd] *adj* **1.** oddany **2.** wierny **3.** przywiązany; **dev•o•tee** [dɪvə'tiː] *s* **1.** miłośnik *m* **2.** wielbiciel *m* **3.** zwolennik *m* **4.** *REL* wyznawca *m*; **de•vo•tion** [dɪ'vəʊʃn] *s* **1.** oddanie *n*, przywiązanie *n* **2.** poświęcenie *n* **3.** pobożność *f* **4.** ***~s*** *REL* modlitwy
de•vour [dɪ'vaʊə] *v/t* **1.** pożerać ⟨-żreć⟩ **2.** *fig* pochłaniać ⟨-łonąć⟩ **3.** *fig* zżerać; ***she's ~ed by jealousy*** zżera ją zazdrość
de•vout [dɪ'vaʊt] *adj* **1.** pobożny **2.** nabożny **3.** żarliwy **4.** szczery, gorący
dew [djuː] *s* rosa *f*; **'dew•drop** *s* kropla *f* rosy
dex•ter•i•ty [dek'sterətɪ] *s* zręczność *f*, sprawność *f*; **dex•ter•ous** ['dekstərəs] *adj* zręczny, wprawny
dex•trous ['dekstrəs] → ***dexterous***
di•a•be•tes [daɪə'biːtiːz] *s MED* cukrzyca *f*; **di•a•bet•ic** [daɪə'betɪk] *s* diabetyk *m*, cukrzyk *m*; ***a ~ chocolate*** czekolada dla diabetyków
di•a•bol•i•cal [daɪə'bɒlɪkl] *adj* **1.** potworny, okropny **2.** diaboliczny
di•ag•nose ['daɪəgnəʊz] *MED* diagnozować ⟨z-⟩, rozpoznawać ⟨-nać⟩; ***he was ~d with asthma*** rozpoznano u niego astmę; **di•ag•no•sis** [daɪəg'nəʊsɪs] *pl -ses* [daɪəg'nəʊsiːz] *s* rozpoznanie *n*, diagnoza *f*; ***make a ~, give a ~*** postawić diagnozę; **di•ag•nos•tic** [daɪəg'nɒstɪk] *adj* diagnostyczny
di•ag•o•nal [daɪ'ægənl] **I** *adj* ukośny **II** *s* **1.** ukośna linia *f* **2.** *MATH* przekątna *f*; **di•ag•o•nal•ly** [daɪ'ægənlɪ] *adv* ukośnie, na skos, na ukos
di•a•gram ['daɪəgræm] *s* wykres *m*, schemat *m*, diagram *m*
di•al ['daɪl] **I** *s* **1.** tarcza *f* **2.** pokrętło *n* (regulatora) **II** *v/t* **1.** wykręcać ⟨-cić⟩ **2.** wybierać ⟨-brać⟩ **3.** dzwonić ⟨za-⟩ do *G*; ***~ direct*** dzwonić bezpośrednio
di•a•lect ['daɪəlekt] **I** *s* **1.** dialekt *m* **2.** gwara *f* **II** *adj* **1.** dialektalny **2.** w dialekcie
'di•al•ling code *s TEL Br* numer *m* kierunkowy; **'di•al•ling tone** *s TEL Br* sygnał *m* zgłoszenia
di•a•logue ['daɪəlɒg] *Br*, **'di•a•log** *Am* **I** *s* **1.** dialog *m* **2.** rozmowa *f* **II** *v/i* rozmawiać; **'di•a•logue box** *s INF* okno *n* dialogowe
'di•al tone *Am* → ***dialling tone***
di•am•e•ter [daɪ'æmɪtə] *s MATH* średnica *f*; ***be 10 inches in ~*** mieć 10 cali średnicy; **di•a•met•ri•cal•ly** [daɪə'metrɪkəlɪ] *adv* diametralnie
di•a•mond ['daɪmənd] **I** *s* **1.** diament *m* **2.** brylant *m* **3.** *MATH* romb *m* **3.** (*cards*) ***~s*** karo *n*, *infml* dzwonek *m* **II** *adj* **1.** diamentowy; ***a ~ cutter*** szlifierz diamentów **2.** brylantowy; ***a ~ ring*** pierścionek z brylantem
di•a•per ['daɪpə] *s Am* pieluszka *f*, pielucha *f*
di•a•phragm ['daɪəfræm] *s* **1.** *BIOL* przepona *f* **2.** *TEL* membrana *f* **3.** *PHOT*

D

przesłona *f* **4.** *MED* krążek *m* dopochwowy
di•ar•rhoe•a [daɪə'rɪə] *Br*, ***di•ar•rhe•a*** *Am s* biegunka *f*, rozwolnienie *n*
di•a•ry ['daɪrɪ] *s* **1.** terminarz *m*, kalendarz *m* **3.** agenda *f* **2.** dziennik *m* **4.** pamiętnik *m*

D

dice [daɪs] **I** *pl dice s* **1.** kostka *f* (do gry) **2.** kości *pl* (do gry) **II** *v/t* kroić ⟨po-⟩ w kostkę **III** *v/i* grać w kości; ***~ with death*** *fig* igrać ze śmiercią, igrać z ogniem
di•chot•o•my [daɪ'kɒtəmɪ] *s* dychotomia *f*
dick [dɪk] *s vulg* kutas *m*, fiut *m*
dic•ta•te **I** [dɪk'teɪt] *v/t* **1.** dyktować ⟨po-⟩ **2.** dyktować, narzucać ⟨-cić⟩ **II** [dɪk'teɪt] *v/i* dyrygować, rządzić (***to*** *I*) **III** ['dɪkteɪt] *s* dyktat *m*, nakaz *m*; ***follow the ~s of fashion*** *fig* podążać za modą; **dic•ta•tion** [dɪk'teɪʃn] *s* **1.** dyktowanie *n* **2.** dyktando *n*
dic•ta•tor [dɪk'teɪtə] *s* **1.** dyktator *m* **2.** despota *m*; **dic•ta•tor•i•al** [dɪktə'tɔːrɪəl] *adj* **1.** dyktatorski **2.** despotyczny; **dic•ta•tor•ship** [dɪk'teɪtərʃɪp] *s* **1.** dyktatura *f* **2.** tyrania *f*
dic•tion ['dɪkʃn] *s* dykcja *f*
dic•tion•a•ry ['dɪkʃənerɪ] **I** *s* słownik *m* **II** *adj* słownikowy
did [dɪd] *Past Simple* → ***do***[1]
di•dac•tic [daɪ'dæktɪk] *adj* dydaktyczny
did•n't *contracted form* → ***did not***
die[1] [daɪ] **I** *v/i* **1.** umierać ⟨umrzeć⟩; ***~ of hunger*** umrzeć z głodu; ***never say ~!*** nie opuszczaj rąk! **2.** (*animal*) zdychać ⟨zdechnąć⟩ **3.** (*plant*) usychać ⟨uschnąć⟩ **4.** ***be dying to do s.th.*** nie móc się doczekać, żeby coś zrobić, palić się do zrobienia czegoś **II** *v/t* umierać ⟨umrzeć⟩; ***~ a natural death*** umrzeć śmiercią naturalną; **die away** *v/i* **1.** cichnąć ⟨u-⟩ **2.** ustawać ⟨-tać⟩; **die down** *v/i* (*wind*) uspokajać ⟨-koić⟩ się, przycichać ⟨-chnąć⟩; **die out** *v/i* wymierać ⟨-mrzeć⟩
die[2] [~] *pl dice* [daɪs] *s* kość *f* do gry; ***the ~ is cast*** kości zostały rzucone
di•et ['daɪət] **I** *s* dieta *f*, sposób *m* odżywiania; ***be on a ~*** być na diecie **II** *adj* dietetyczny **III** *v/i* **1.** stosować ⟨za-⟩ dietę **2.** odchudzać ⟨-dzić⟩ się; **di•e•ti•tian** [daɪə'tɪʃn] *s* dietetyk *m*
dif•fer ['dɪfə] *v/i* **1.** różnić się; ***opinions ~*** zdania są podzielone **2.** nie zgadzać się (***on/about/over*** co do *G*); **dif•fe•rence** ['dɪfrəns] *s* **1.** różnica *f*; ***make no ~*** nie mieć znaczenia; ***a ~ in price, a price ~*** różnica w cenie **2.** różnica *f* zdań; **dif•fe•rent** ['dɪfrənt] *adj* **1.** inny **2.** różny **3.** odmienny **4.** szczególny, wyjątkowy
dif•fer•en•tial [dɪfə'renʃl] **I** *adj* **1.** zróżnicowany **2.** *MATH* różniczkowy **II** *s* **1.** *MATH* różniczka *f* **2.** (*a.* ***~ gear***) *TECH* dyferencjał *m*, mechanizm *m* różnicowy; **dif•fer•en•tial 'cal•cu•lus** *s MATH* rachunek *m* różniczkowy; **dif•fe•ren•ti•ate** [dɪfə'renʃɪeɪt] **I** *v/t* **1.** odróżniać ⟨-nić⟩, rozróżniać ⟨-nić⟩; ***it's difficult to ~ between the two*** trudno je od siebie odróżnić, trudno je rozróżnić **2.** odmiennie traktować ⟨po-⟩ (***between*** *A*) **II** *v/i* **1.** różnić się, odróżniać ⟨-nić⟩ się **2.** *MATH* różniczkować; **di•fer•en•ti•a•tion** [dɪfərenʃɪ'eɪʃn] *s* **1.** rozróżnienie *n*, odróżnienie *n* **2.** *MATH* różniczkowanie *n*
dif•fe•rent•ly ['dɪfrəntlɪ] *adv* inaczej, odmiennie
dif•fi•cult ['dɪfɪkəlt] *adj* trudny; ***it was ~ for me to do it*** miałem z tym kłopot, to było dla mnie trudne; **dif•fi•cul•ty** ['dɪfɪkəltɪ] *s* **1.** trudność *f*; ***with ~*** z trudem; ***have ~ (in) doing s.th.*** mieć trudności ze zrobieniem czegoś; ***make difficulties*** robić trudności **2.** kłopot *m*
dif•fuse **I** [dɪ'fjuːz] *adj* **1.** rozproszony; ***~ light*** światło rozproszone **2.** rozmyty **3.** przegadany **II** [dɪ'fjuːs] *v/t* **1.** rozpraszać ⟨-roszyć⟩ **2.** rozpowszechniać ⟨-nić⟩ **III** [dɪ'fjuːs] *v/i* **1.** dyfundować **2.** rozprzestrzeniać ⟨-nić⟩ się
dig [dɪg] **I** *s* **1.** szturchaniec *m*, kuksaniec *m* **2.** → ***digs*** **II** (*dug*; *dug*) *v/t* **1.** kopać, wykopywać ⟨-pać⟩ **2.** dawać ⟨dać⟩ kuksańca **3.** *infml* kapować ⟨s-⟩ **4.** ***I ~ it*** *infml* to mi się podoba **III** (*dug*; *dug*) *v/i* **1.** kopać, prowadzić wykopaliska **2.** ***~ in*** przeszukiwać; **dig in** *v/i* **1.** okopywać ⟨-pać⟩ się **2.** umacniać ⟨umocnić⟩ się; **dig into** *v/i* **1.** grzebać ⟨po-⟩ w *L* **2.** przekopywać

⟨-pać⟩; **dig out** *v/t* **1.** wykopywać ⟨-pać⟩ **2.** wygrzebywać ⟨-bać⟩, wyszperać; **dig up** *v/t* **1.** odkopywać ⟨-pać⟩ **2.** odgrzebywać ⟨-bać⟩ **3.** przekopywać ⟨-pać⟩

di•gest [daɪ'dʒest] **I** *v/t* trawić ⟨s-⟩ **II** *s* **1.** skrót *m*, streszczenie *n* **2.** przegląd *m*

di•gest•i•ble [daɪ'dʒestəbl] *adj* strawny; **di•ges•tion** [daɪ'dʒestʃn] *s* trawienie *n*; **di•ges•tive** [daɪ'dʒestɪv] *adj* trawienny; **di•'ges•tive sys•tem** *s* system *m* trawienny, układ *m* pokarmowy; **di•ges•tive 'tract** *s* przewód *m* pokarmowy

dig•ger ['dɪgə] *s* **1.** koparka *f* **2.** kopacz *m*

di•git ['dɪdʒɪt] *s* **1.** *MATH* cyfra *f* **2.** *ANAT* palec *m*; **di•gi•tal** ['dɪdʒɪtl] *adj TECH INF* cyfrowy; **di•gi•tal 'clock** *s* zegar *m* elektroniczny; **di•gi•tal di•'splay** *s* **1.** wyświetlacz *m* cyfrowy **2.** monitor *m* cyfrowy; **di•gi•tal 'read•out** *s* odczyt *m* cyfrowy; **di•gi•tal 'tel•e•vi•sion** *s* telewizja *f* cyfrowa; **di•gi•tal 'watch** *s* zegarek *m* elektroniczny;

dig•i•tize ['dɪdʒɪtaɪz] *v/t data*: dyskretyzować ⟨z-⟩, zapisywać ⟨-sać⟩ w formie cyfrowej

dig•ni•fied ['dɪgnɪfaɪd] *adj* **1.** dostojny **2.** pełen godności; **dig•ni•fy** ['dɪgnɪfaɪ] *v/t* **1.** dodawać ⟨-dać⟩ powagi **2.** nobilitować

dig•ni•ta•ry ['dɪgnɪtərɪ] *s* dygnitarz *m*, dostojnik *m*

dig•ni•ty ['dɪgnɪtɪ] *s* **1.** godność *f* **2.** powaga *f* **3.** tytuł *m*, godność *f*

di•gress [daɪ'gres] *v/i* robić ⟨z-⟩ dygresję; **di•gres•sion** [daɪ'greʃn] *s* dygresja *f*

digs [dɪgz] *pl Br* **1.** wynajęty pokój *m* **2.** wynajęte mieszkanie *n* **3.** stancja *f*

dike [daik] *s* **1.** grobla *f*, wał *m* **2.** rów *m* odwadniający **3.** *vulg* lezba *f*

di•lap•i•dat•ed [dɪ'læpɪdeɪtɪd] *adj* **1.** *building*: rozpadający się, zniszczony **2.** *machine, car*: zdezelowany

di•late [daɪ'leɪt] *v/i* rozszerzać ⟨-rzyć⟩ się; **di•late on** *v/i* rozwodzić się nad *I*;

dil•a•to•ry ['dɪlətərɪ] *adj* opieszały; ***be ~ in*** zwlekać z *I*; ***~ tactics*** gra na zwłokę

di•lem•ma [dɪ'lemə] *s* rozterka *f*, dylemat *m*; ***be in a ~*** być w rozterce, mieć dylemat

dil•et•tante [dɪle'tæntɪ] **I** *s* dyletant *m* **II** *adj* dyletancki

dil•i•gence ['dɪlɪdʒəns] *s* **1.** pilność *f* **2.** staranność *f*, skrupulatność *f* **3.** pracowitość *f*; **dil•i•gent** ['dɪlɪdʒənt] *adj* **1.** pilny **2.** staranny, skrupulatny **3.** pracowity

di•lute [daɪ'luːt] **I** *v/t* **1.** rozcieńczać ⟨-czyć⟩, rozrzedzać ⟨-dzić⟩ **2.** osłabiać ⟨-bić⟩ **II** *adj* rozcieńczony; **di•lu•tion** [daɪ'luːʃn] *s* **1.** rozcieńczenie *n* **2.** osłabienie *n* **3.** *quality*: obniżenie *n*

dim [dɪm] **I** *adj* **1.** *light*: słaby, przyćmiony **2.** ciemny, przyciemniony **3.** niewyraźny, mglisty **4.** *colour*: wyblakły **5.** *fig infml* ciemny, tępy **II** *v/t* **1.** ściemniać ⟨-nić⟩, przygaszać ⟨-sić⟩; ***~ the headlights*** *AUTO* przygaszać reflektory **2.** zacierać ⟨zatrzeć⟩, zamazywać ⟨-zać⟩ **III** *v/i* **1.** przygasać ⟨-snąć⟩ **2.** zacierać ⟨zatrzeć⟩ się

dime [daɪm] *s* **1.** dziesięciocentówka *f*; ***a ~ novel*** powieść popularna **2.** *fig* grosz *m*

di•men•sion [daɪ'menʃn] *s* wymiar *m*; **dimensional** [daɪ'menʃnl] *adj*: ***two-~*** dwuwymiarowy; ***three-~*** trójwymiarowy

di•min•ish [dɪ'mɪnɪʃ] **I** *v/i* **1.** zmniejszać ⟨-szyć⟩ się, maleć ⟨z-⟩; ***~ in value*** tracić na wartości **2.** słabnąć ⟨o-⟩ **3.** wyczerpywać ⟨-pać⟩ się **II** *v/t* **1.** zmniejszać ⟨-szyć⟩ **2.** obniżać ⟨-żyć⟩ **3.** umniejszać ⟨-szyć⟩

dim•i•nu•tion [dɪmɪ'njuːʃn] *s* **1.** zmniejszenie *n* (się) **2.** spadek *m* **3.** ograniczenie *n* **4.** uszczuplenie *n*; **di•min•u•tive** [dɪ'mɪnjʊtɪv] **I** *adj* **1.** drobny, malutki **2.** zdrobniały **II** *s* zdrobnienie *n*

dim•ly ['dɪmlɪ] *adj* **1.** słabo; ***~ lit*** słabo oświetlony **2.** niewyraźnie **3.** blado; **dim•mer** ['dɪmə] *s* **1.** regulator *m* oświetlania, ściemniacz *m* **2.** *Am* światło *n* postojowe

dim•ple ['dɪmpl] *s* **1.** dołeczek *m* (w policzku) **2.** (*glass*) wgłębienie *n*

dim•wit•ted [dɪm'wɪtɪd] *adj infml* tępy, ograniczony

D

din [dɪn] **I** *s* hałas *m*, zgiełk *m*, harmider *m*; ***kick up a ~, make a ~*** hałasować **II** *v/i* hałasować **III** *v/t* **~ *s.th. into s.o.*** *infml* wbijać coś komuś do głowy
dine [daɪn] **I** *v/i* **1.** jeść ⟨z-⟩ obiad **2.** jeść ⟨z-⟩ kolację **II** *v/t* **1.** podejmować ⟨-djąć⟩ obiadem **2.** podejmować ⟨-djąć⟩ kolacją; **dine in** *v/i* **1.** jeść ⟨z-⟩ obiad w domu **2.** jeść ⟨z-⟩ kolację w domu; **dine on** *v/i* **1.** jeść ⟨z-⟩ na obiad **2.** jeść ⟨z-⟩ na kolację; **dine out** *v/i* **1.** jeść ⟨z-⟩ obiad poza domem **2.** jeść ⟨z-⟩ kolację poza domem
din•er ['daɪnə] *s* **1.** gość *m* **2.** *Am* (tania) restauracja *f* **3.** *Am* wagon *m* restauracyjny
'din•ing car *s* wagon *m* restauracyjny; **'din•ing room** *s* pokój *m* stołowy, jadalnia *f*; **'din•ing ta•ble** *s* stół *m* w jadalni
dink•y ['dɪŋkɪ] *adj* **1.** *Br* słodki, śliczny **2.** *Am* tandetny, byle jaki
din•ner ['dɪnə] *s* **1.** obiad *m*; ***at ~*** przy obiedzie **2.** kolacja *f* **3.** przyjęcie *n*, uroczysta kolacja *f*; **'din•ner coat** *Am* → ***dinner jacket***; **'din•ner guest** *s* **1.** gość *m* na obiedzie **2.** gość *m* na przyjęciu; **'din•ner jack•et** *s* smoking *m*; **'din•ner par•ty** *s* przyjęcie *n*, uroczysta kolacja *f*; **'din•ner service** *s* serwis *m* obiadowy; **'din•ner table** *s* stół *m* w jadalni; **'din•ner time** *s* **1.** pora *f* obiadowa **2.** pora *f* kolacji
di•no•saur ['daɪnəsɔː] *s* dinozaur *m*
dint [dɪnt] *s*: ***by ~ of*** dzięki *D*
di•ode ['daɪəʊd] *s* dioda *f*
di•ox•ide [daɪ'ɒksaɪd] *s* dwutlenek *m*
dip [dɪp] **I** *v/t* **1.** zanurzać ⟨-rzyć⟩ **2.** **~ *one's headlights*** *Br* przełączyć światła z długich na światła mijania **II** *v/i* nurkować ⟨za-⟩ **III** *s* **1.** (krótka) kąpiel *f*; ***go for a ~*** wskoczyć na chwilę do wody **2.** spadek *m* **3.** (*sauce*) dip *m*; **dip into** *v/t* **1.** zaglądać ⟨zajrzeć⟩ do *G* **2.** rzucać ⟨-cić⟩ okiem na *A* **3.** **~ *into one's pocket*** *fig* sięgnąć do kieszeni
di•plo•ma [dɪ'pləʊmə] *s* dyplom *m*
di•plo•ma•cy [dɪ'pləʊməsɪ] *s a. fig* dyplomacja *f*; **di•plo•mat** ['dɪpləmæt] *s* dyplomata *m*; **di•plo•mat•ic** [dɪplə'mætɪk] *adj* dyplomatyczny; **~ *relations*** stosunki dyplomatyczne; **dip•lo•mat•i•cal•ly** [dɪplə'mætɪklɪ] *adv* dyplomatycznie
di•plo•mat•ic 'bag *s Br* poczta *f* dyplomatyczna; **di•plo•'mat•ic corps** *s* korpus *m* dyplomatyczny; **di•plo•mat•ic im•'mu•ni•ty** *s* immunitet *m* dyplomatyczny
dip•py ['dɪpɪ] *adj infml* pomylony, stuknięty
dip•so•man•i•ac [dɪpsə'meɪnɪæk] *s* MED alkoholik *m*
dire [daɪə] *adj* **1.** poważny; ***be in ~ need of*** pilnie potrzebować *G* **2.** *poverty*: skrajny **3.** *Br infml* beznadziejny
di•rect [dɪ'rekt] **I** *v/t* **1.** kierować ⟨s-⟩ (***to*** do *G*); **~ *away from*** odciągać od *G* **2.** *company*: kierować **3.** reżyserować ⟨wy-⟩ **4.** mierzyć ⟨wy-⟩ w *A* **5.** polecać ⟨-cić⟩ (***to do s.th.*** zrobić coś); **~ *s.th. to be done*** polecić, żeby coś zrobiono **II** *adj* bezpośredni; ***a ~ flight*** lot bezpośredni **III** *adv* bezpośrednio; **di•rect 'cur•rent** *s* PHYS prąd *m* stały
di•rec•tion [dɪ'rekʃn] *s* **1.** kierunek *m*; ***in the ~ of*** w kierunku *G*; ***from all ~s*** ze wszystkich stron; ***the sense of ~*** zmysł orientacji **2.** kierowanie *n* **3.** reżyseria *f* **4.** **~s** instrukcje, wskazówki; **di•rec•tion 'in•di•ca•tor** *s* kierunkowskaz *m*
di•rec•tive [dɪ'rektɪv] *s* **1.** dyrektywa *f* **2.** wytyczna *f*
di•rect•ly [dɪ'rektlɪ] *adv* **1.** bezpośrednio **2.** zupełnie, całkowicie
di•rect 'ob•ject *s* dopełnienie *n* bliższe
di•rec•tor [dɪ'rektə] *s* **1.** dyrektor *m* **2.** reżyser *m* **3.** członek *m* zarządu; ***a board of ~s*** zarząd; **di•rec•tor-'gen•e•ral** *s* dyrektor *m* naczelny; **di•rec•tor•ship** [dɪ'rektərʃɪp] *s* kierownictwo *n*
di•rec•to•ry [daɪ'rektərɪ] *s* **1.** książka *f* telefoniczna **2.** branżowy katalog *m* firm; **di•rec•to•ry en'qui•ries** *pl Br* informacja *f* telefoniczna
di•rect 'speech *s* mowa *f* niezależna
dirt [dɜːt] *s* **1.** brud *m*; ***treat s.o. like ~*** pomiatać kimś, mieć kogoś za nic **2.** ziemia *f*, błoto *n*; **dirt 'cheap I** *adj infml* tani jak barszcz **II** *adv infml* za psie pieniądze; **dirt 'poor** *adj Am* w skrajnej nędzy; **'dirt road,**

'**dirt track** *s* droga *f* gruntowa; **dirt•y** ['dɜːtɪ] **I** *adj* **1.** brudny; **~ *work*** *fig* brudna robota **2.** sprośny; ***a ~ word*** brzydkie słowo, przekleństwo; ***have a ~ mind*** być zbereźnikiem, *infml* mieć kosmate myśli **3.** *weather*: paskudny **II** *v/t* brudzić ⟨za-⟩; **~ *one's hands*** ubrudzić sobie ręce; **dirt•y 'trick** *s* chwyt *m* poniżej pasa, świństwo *n*

dis•a•bil•i•ty [dɪsə'bɪlətɪ] *s* **1.** inwalidztwo *n*, kalectwo *n*; **~ *benefit*** renta inwalidzka **2.** upośledzenie *n*; **dis•a•ble** [dɪs'eɪbl] *v/t* **1.** ***she was ~d in an accident*** została kaleką w wyniku wypadku **2.** unieruchamiać ⟨-chomić⟩ **3.** blokować ⟨za-⟩; **dis•a•bled** [dɪs'eɪbld] *adj* **1.** niepełnosprawny **2.** upośledzony

dis•ad•van•tage [dɪsəd'ɑːntɪdʒ] **I** *s* **1.** wada *f*, ujemna strona *f* **2.** niekorzyść *f*; ***to s.o.'s ~*** na czyjąś niekorzyść; ***be at a ~*** być w niekorzystnej sytuacji **II** *v/t* **1.** krzywdzić ⟨s-⟩ **2.** szkodzić ⟨za-⟩; **dis•ad•van•taged** [dɪsəd'vɑːntɪdʒd] *adj* pokrzywdzony przez los; **dis•ad•van•ta•geous** [dɪsædvən'teɪdʒəs] *adj* niekorzystny (***to*** dla *G*)

dis•a•gree [dɪsə'griː] *v/i* **1.** nie zgadzać ⟨zgodzić⟩ się **2.** być sprzecznym **3.** sprzeczać ⟨po-⟩ się; **dis•a•gree with** *v/i* (*food, climate*) nie służyć; **dis•a•gree•a•ble** [dɪsə'griːəbl] *adj* **1.** niemiły **2.** nieprzyjemny **3.** przykry; **dis•a•gree•ment** [dɪsə'griːmənt] *s* **1.** niezgoda *f* **2.** różnica *f* zdań; ***be in ~ with*** nie zgadzać się z *I* **3.** rozbieżność *f*

dis•al•low [dɪsə'laʊ] *v/t* **1.** odrzucać ⟨-cić⟩ **2.** SPORT nie uznawać ⟨-nać⟩

dis•ap•pear [dɪsə'pɪə] *v/i* **1.** znikać ⟨-knąć⟩ **2.** ginąć ⟨z-⟩ **3.** zaginąć **4.** wyginąć; **dis•ap•pear•ance** [dɪsə'pɪrəns] *s* **1.** zniknięcie *n* **2.** zaginięcie *n*

dis•ap•point [dɪsə'pɔɪnt] *v/t* **1.** rozczarowywać ⟨-rować⟩; ***be ~ed*** być rozczarowanym, być zawiedzionym **2.** *hopes*: zawodzić ⟨-wieść⟩; **dis•ap•point•ed** [dɪsə'pɔɪntɪd] *adj* rozczarowany, zawiedziony (***with***/***in***/***at***/***about*** *I*); **dis•ap•point•ing** [dɪsə'pɔɪntɪŋ] *adj* rozczarowujący; ***be ~ for s.o.*** rozczarować kogoś, nie spełnić czyichś oczekiwań; **dis•ap•point•ment** [dɪsə'pɔɪntmənt] *s* rozczarowanie *n*, zawód *m*

dis•ap•prov•al [dɪsə'pruːvl] *s* dezaprobata *f*; ***in ~*** z dezaprobatą; **dis•ap•prove** [dɪsə'pruːv] *v/i* **1.** być przeciwnym **2.** nie pochwalać ⟨-lić⟩; ***my father ~s of my boyfriend*** mojemu ojcu nie podoba się mój chłopak; **dis•ap•prov•ing** [dɪsə'pruːvɪŋ] *adj* pełen dezaprobaty, ganiący; **dis•ap•prov•ing•ly** [dɪsə'pruːvɪŋlɪ] *adv* z dezaprobatą

dis•arm [dɪs'ɑːm] **I** *v/t* **1.** rozbrajać ⟨-roić⟩ **2.** demilitaryzować ⟨z-⟩ **II** *v/i* rozbrajać ⟨-roić⟩ się; **dis•ar•ma•ment** [dɪs'ɑːməmənt] *s* rozbrojenie *n*; **dis•arm•ing** [dɪs'ɑːmɪŋ] **I** *s* rozbrojenie *n* **II** *adj* **1.** rozbrojeniowy **2.** *smile*: rozbrajający

dis•ar•range [dɪsə'reɪndʒ] *v/t* **1.** robić ⟨z-⟩ bałagan w *L* **2.** *hair*: targać ⟨po-⟩

dis•as•sem•ble [dɪsə'sembl] *v/t* **1.** demontować ⟨z-⟩ **2.** rozkładać ⟨-złożyć⟩; **dis•as•sem•bly** [dɪsə'semblɪ] *s* **1.** demontaż *m* **2.** rozłożenie *n*

dis•as•ter [dɪ'zɑːstə] *s* **1.** katastrofa *f* **2.** klęska *f* żywiołowa **3.** nieszczęście *n*; **dis•'as•ter ar•e•a** *s* rejon *m* klęski żywiołowej; **di•sas•trous** [dɪ'zɑːstrəs] *adj* **1.** katastrofalny **2.** fatalny **3.** tragiczny

dis•be•lief [dɪsbə'liːf] *s* niedowierzanie *n*; ***in ~*** z niedowierzaniem; **dis•be•lieve** [dɪsbə'liːv] *v/t* *form* nie wierzyć ⟨u-⟩

disc [dɪsk] → ***disk***

dis•card [dɪ'skɑːd] **I** *v/t* **1.** wyrzucać ⟨-cić⟩ **2.** pozbywać ⟨-być⟩ się *G* **3.** zarzucać ⟨-cić⟩ **4.** *cards, clothes*: zrzucać ⟨-cić⟩ **II** *s* **1.** (*cards*) zrzutka *f* **2.** rupieć *m* **3.** łach *m*

di•scern [dɪ'sɜːn] *v/t* *form* dostrzegać ⟨-rzec⟩, zauważać ⟨-żyć⟩; **di•scern•i•ble** [dɪ'sɜːnəbl] *adj* zauważalny, dostrzegalny; **di•scern•ing** [dɪ'sɜːnɪŋ] *adj* **1.** wymagający **2.** wytrawny; **dis•cern•ment** [dɪ'sɜːnmənt] *s* **1.** wnikliwość *f* **2.** znawstwo *n*

dis•charge **I** [dɪs'tʃɑːdʒ] *v/t* **1.** *hospital*: wypisywać ⟨-sać⟩ **2.** *work*: zwalniać ⟨zwolnić⟩ **3.** emitować ⟨wy-⟩, wypuszczać ⟨-puścić⟩ **4.** MED wydzielać ⟨-lić⟩; **~ *pus*** ropieć; **~ *blood*** krwawić

5. *duty*: spełniać ⟨-nić⟩, wywiązywać ⟨-zać⟩ się z *G* 6. wyładowywać ⟨-dować⟩, rozładowywać ⟨-dować⟩ 7. strzelać ⟨-lić⟩ z *G* 8. zwalniać ⟨zwolnić⟩ (**from** z *G*) **II** [dɪst'ʃɑːdʒ] *v/i* 1. MED ropieć, jątrzyć się 2. PHYS wyładowywać ⟨-dować⟩ się **III** ['dɪstʃɑːdʒ] *s* 1. MED wydzielina *f* 2. MED sączenie się *n* 3. *hospital*: wypisanie *n* 4. *work*: zwolnienie *n* 5. emisja *f* 6. wystrzał *m* 7. wykonywanie *n*, wywiązywanie *n* się

di•sci•ple [dɪ'saɪpl] *s* 1. uczeń *m* 2. REL apostoł *m*

dis•ci•pli•nar•y [dɪsɪ'plɪnərɪ] *adj* dyscyplinarny; **dis•ci•pline** ['dɪsɪplɪn] **I** *s* dyscyplina *f*; **keep ~** utrzymywać dyscyplinę **II** *v/t* dyscyplinować ⟨z-⟩; **dis•ci•plined** ['dɪsɪplɪnd] *adj* 1. zdyscyplinowany 2. metodyczny

'disc jock•ey *s* disc jockey *m*, didżej *m*

dis•claim [dɪs'kleɪm] *v/t* 1. wypierać ⟨-przeć⟩ się 2. zaprzeczać ⟨-czyć⟩ 3. zrzekać ⟨-rzec⟩ się; **dis•claim•er** [dɪs'kleɪmə] *s* 1. wyłączenie *n* odpowiedzialności 2. sprostowanie *n*, dementi *n* 3. zrzeczenie *n* się

dis•close [dɪs'kləʊs] *v/t* 1. ujawniać ⟨-nić⟩ 2. ukazywać ⟨-zać⟩; **dis•clo•sure** [dɪs'kləʊʒə] *s* 1. ujawnienie *n* 2. (ujawniona) informacja *f*

dis•co ['dɪskəʊ] *s* dyskoteka *f*, disco *n*

dis•col•our [dɪs'kʌlə] *Br*, **dis•col•or** *Am* **I** *v/i* odbarwiać ⟨-wić⟩ się **II** *v/t* odbarwiać ⟨-wić⟩

dis•com•fort [dɪs'kʌmfərt] *s* 1. niewygoda *f* 2. dolegliwość *f* 3. dyskomfort *m*

dis•con•cert [dɪskən'sɜːt] *v/t* 1. wprawiać ⟨-wić⟩ w zakłopotanie 2. niepokoić ⟨za-⟩; **dis•con•cert•ed** [dɪskən'sɜːtɪd] *adj* 1. zakłopotany 2. zaniepokojony; **dis•con•cert•ing** [dɪskən'sɜːtɪŋ] *adj* 1. niepokojący 2. irytujący

dis•con•nect [dɪskə'nekt] *v/t* 1. *gas, power*: odłączać ⟨-czyć⟩; **we have been ~ed** odłączyli nam prąd 2. wyłączać ⟨-czyć⟩ 3. rozłączać ⟨-czyć⟩

dis•con•so•late [dɪs'kɒnsələt] *adj* 1. niepocieszony 2. przygnębiony (**about/at** *I*)

dis•con•tent [dɪskən'tent] **I** *s* niezadowolenie *n* **II** *adj* niezadowolony; **dis•con•tent•ed** [dɪskən'tentɪd] *adj* niezadowolony

dis•con•tin•ue [dɪskən'tɪnjuː] *v/t* 1. przerywać ⟨-rwać⟩ 2. wycofywać ⟨-fać⟩ z produkcji, zaprzestawać ⟨-tać⟩ produkcji 3. zawieszać ⟨-sić⟩ wypłatę; **dis•con•tin•u•ous** [dɪskən'tɪnjʊəs] *adj* 1. przerywany 2. niespójny

dis•cord ['dɪskɔːd] *s* 1. niezgoda *f*; **the apple of ~** kość niezgody 2. rozdźwięk *m* 3. MUS dysonans *m*; **dis•cord•ant** [dɪs'kɔːdənt] *adj* 1. niezgodny, sprzeczny 2. MUS fałszywie brzmiący

dis•count I ['dɪskaʊnt] *s* 1. zniżka *f*, rabat *m*; **at a ~** ze zniżką, z rabatem 2. upust *m* **II** [dɪs'kaʊnt] *v/t* 1. *price*: obniżać ⟨-żyć⟩ 2. udzielać ⟨-lić⟩ zniżki na *A* 3. FIN dyskontować 4. nie brać ⟨wziąć⟩ pod uwagę; **'dis•count rate** *s* stopa *f* dyskontowa; **'dis•count store** *s* (*shop*) dyskont *m*

dis•cour•age [dɪs'kʌrɪdʒ] *v/t* 1. zniechęcać ⟨-cić⟩ 2. odwodzić ⟨-wieść⟩ (**from** od *G*); **dis•cour•age•ment** [dɪs'kʌrɪdʒmənt] *s* zniechęcenie *n*; **dis•cour•ag•ing** [dɪs'kʌrɪdʒɪŋ] *adj* zniechęcający

dis•course I ['dɪskɔːs] *s* 1. dialog *m* 2. wykład *m* 3. omówienie *n* 4. dyskusja *f* 5. dyskurs *m* **II** [dɪ'skɔːs] *v/i* rozprawiać (**about** o *L*)

dis•cour•te•ous [dɪs'kɜːtjəs] *adj* nieuprzejmy; **dis•cour•te•sy** [dɪs'kɜːtɪsɪ] *s* nieuprzejmość *f*

dis•cov•er [dɪs'kʌvə] **I** *v/t* 1. odkrywać ⟨-ryć⟩ (**that** że) 2. odnajdować ⟨-naleźć⟩ 3. znajdować ⟨znaleźć⟩ 4. dowiadywać ⟨-wiedzieć⟩ się (**that** że); **dis•cov•er•er** [dɪs'kʌvərə] *s* odkrywca *m*; **dis•cov•e•ry** [dɪs'kʌvərɪ] *s* odkrycie *n*

dis•cred•it [dɪs'kredɪt] **I** *v/t* 1. kompromitować ⟨s-⟩ 2. dyskredytować ⟨z-⟩ 3. podważać ⟨-żyć⟩ **II** *s* ujma *f*; **bring ~ on s.o.** kompromitować kogoś, przynosić komuś ujmę

di•screet [dɪ'skriːt] *adj* 1. dyskretny 2. stonowany; **di•screet•ly** [dɪ'skriːtlɪ] *adv* dyskretnie

di•screp•an•cy [dɪ'skrepənsɪ] *s* rozbieżność *f*

di•scre•tion [dɪ'skreʃn] *s* **1.** dyskrecja *f* **2.** uznanie *n*; ***at*** (***s.o.'s***) ~ według (czyjegoś) uznania; ***it is at your*** ~ zrób, jak uważasz; ***leave s.th. to s.o.'s*** ~ pozostawić coś do czyjegoś uznania **3.** uprawnienia *pl*
di•scrim•i•nate [dɪ'skrɪmɪneɪt] *v/i* **1.** odróżniać ⟨-nić⟩; ~ ***between males and females*** odróżniać samce od samic **2.** rozróżniać ⟨-nić⟩ **3.** dyskryminować (***against*** *A*); **di•scrim•i•nat•ing** [dɪskrɪmɪ'neɪtɪŋ] *adj* **1.** wyrobiony **2.** wytrawny **3.** wybredny; **di•scrim•i•na•tion** [dɪ'skrɪmɪneɪʃn] *s* **1.** dyskryminacja *f* (***against*** *A*) **2.** rozeznanie *n* **3.** wyczucie *n*; **dis•crim•i•na•to•ry** [dɪ'skrɪmɪnətərɪ] *adj* dyskryminacyjny
dis•cur•sive [dɪ'skɜːsɪv] *adj* **1.** dygresyjny **2.** dyskursywny
dis•cus ['dɪskəs] *s* SPORT dysk *m*; ***the*** ~ rzut dyskiem; ***a*** ~ ***thrower*** dyskobol
di•scuss [dɪ'skʌs] *v/t* **1.** omawiać ⟨omówić⟩; dyskutować ⟨prze-⟩ **2.** rozmawiać o *L*; **di•scus•sion** [dɪ'skʌʃn] *s* **1.** dyskusja *f*; ***be under*** ~ być dyskutowanym, być omawianym **2.** omówienie *n* **3.** rozmowa *f*
dis•dain [dɪs'deɪn] **I** *v/t* gardzić ⟨wz-⟩ **II** *s* pogarda *f*; **dis•dain•ful** [dɪs'deɪnfəl] *adj* pogardliwy; ***be*** ~ ***of s.th.*** gardzić czymś, traktować coś z pogardą
dis•ease [dɪ'ziːz] *s* choroba *f*; ***a sexually transmitted*** ~ choroba weneryczna
dis•em•bark [dɪsəm'bɑːk] **I** *v/i* (*passengers*) wysiadać ⟨-siąść⟩ **II** *v/t passengers*: wysadzać ⟨-dzić⟩ **3.** *goods*: wyładowywać ⟨-dować⟩
dis•en•chant•ed [dɪsən'tʃæntɪd] *adj* rozczarowany
dis•en•gage [dɪsən'geɪdʒ] **I** *v/t* **1.** zwalniać ⟨zwolnić⟩; ~ ***the clutch*** zwolnić sprzęgło **2.** rozłączać ⟨-czyć⟩ **II** *v/i* **1.** uwalniać ⟨uwolnić⟩ się **2.** odrywać ⟨oderwać⟩ się
dis•en•tan•gle [dɪsən'tæŋgl] *v/t* **1.** rozplątywać ⟨-tać⟩ **2.** wyplątywać ⟨-tać⟩ **3.** *fig* rozwikływać ⟨-łać⟩
dis•fa•vour [dɪs'feɪvə] *Br*, ***dis•fa•vor*** *Am s* **1.** dezaprobata *f* **2.** niełaska *f*; ***in*** ~ w niełasce; ***fall in*** ~ popaść w niełaskę
dis•fig•ure [dɪs'fɪgə] *v/t* oszpecać ⟨-cić⟩
dis•grace [dɪs'greɪs] **I** *s* **1.** wstyd *m*; ***bring*** ~ ***on s.o.*** przynieść komuś wstyd **2.** hańba *f* **II** *v/t* **1.** przynosić ⟨-nieść⟩ wstyd **2.** kompromitować ⟨s-⟩; **dis•grace•ful** [dɪs'greɪsfəl] *adj* **1.** skandaliczny **2.** kompromitujący **3.** haniebny
dis•guise [dɪs'gaɪz] **I** *v/t* **1.** przebierać ⟨-brać⟩ (**as** za *A*) **2.** ukrywać ⟨-ryć⟩ **II** *v/i* ~ ***oneself as*** przebierać się za *A* **III** *s* **1.** przebranie *n*; ***in*** ~ w przebraniu **2.** kamuflaż *m*
dis•gust [dɪs'gʌst] **I** *v/t* **1.** wzbudzać ⟨-dzić⟩ odrazę w *L*, napawać obrzydzeniem **2.** ~***ed with*** **a)** zniesmaczony *I* **b)** oburzony na *A* **II** *s* wstręt *m*, obrzydzenie *n*, odraza *f*; **dis•gust•ing** [dɪs'gʌstɪŋ] *adj* obrzydliwy, wstrętny, odrażający
dish [dɪʃ] **I** *s* **1.** talerz *m*, półmisek *m* **2.** potrawa *f* **3.** danie *n* **4.** ~***es*** naczynia; ***wash the*** ~***es, do the*** ~***es*** zmywać naczynia **II** *v/t infml* niweczyć ⟨z-⟩; **dish out** *v/t* **1.** rozdawać ⟨-dać⟩ **2.** nakładać ⟨nałożyć⟩; **dish up** *v/t* **1.** podawać ⟨-dać⟩ **2.** nakładać ⟨nałożyć⟩
dis•har•mo•ny [dɪs'hɑːmənɪ] *s* **1.** niezgoda *f* **2.** dysonans *m*
'dish•cloth *s* ściereczka *f* do naczyń
dis•heart•en [dɪs'hɑːtn] *v/t* zniechęcać ⟨-cić⟩; **dis•heart•en•ed** [dɪs'hɑːtnd] *adj* **1.** zniechęcony **2.** przygnębiony; **dis•heart•en•ing** [dɪs'hɑːtnɪŋ] *adj* **1.** zniechęcający **2.** przygnębiający
dis•hon•est [dɪs'ɒnɪst] *adj* nieuczciwy; **dis•hon•est•y** [dɪs'ɒnɪstɪ] *s* nieuczciwość *f*
dis•hon•our [dɪs'ɒnə] *Br*, ***dis•hon•or*** *Am* **I** *s* **1.** hańba *f* **2.** ujma *f* **II** *v/t* **1.** hańbić ⟨z-⟩ **2.** przynosić ⟨-nieść⟩ ujmę **3.** *cheque*: nie honorować **4.** *promises*: nie dotrzymywać ⟨-mać⟩; **dis•hon•our•ab•le** [dɪs'ɒnərəbl] *Br*, ***dis•hon•or•ab•le*** *Am adj* **1.** haniebny **2.** niegodny, niegodziwy
'dish tow•el *s* ścierka *f* do naczyń; **'dish•wash•er** *s* **1.** zmywarka *f* do naczyń **2.** pomywacz *m*; **'dish•wash•ing liq•uid** *s* płyn *m* do mycia naczyń; **'dish•wa•ter** *s* **1.** pomyje *pl* **2.** *fig* lura *f*
dish•y ['dɪʃɪ] *adj Br infml* seksowny
dis•il•lu•sion [dɪsɪ'luːʒn] **I** *s* rozczarowanie *n* **II** *v/t* rozczarowywać ⟨-ro-

wać〉; **dis•il•lu•sioned** [dɪsɪ'luːʒnd] *adj* **1.** rozczarowany **2.** pozbawiony złudzeń; **dis•il•lu•sion•ment** [dɪsɪ'luːʒnmənt] *s* rozczarowanie *n*

dis•in•cli•na•tion [dɪsɪnklɪ'neɪʃn] *s form* niechęć *f*; **dis•in•clined** [dɪsɪn'klaɪnd] *adj form* niechętny

D

dis•in•fect [dɪsɪn'fekt] *v/t* dezynfekować 〈z-〉, odkażać 〈-kazić〉; **dis•in•fec•tant** [dɪsɪn'fektənt] *s* środek *m* dezynfekujący, środek *m* odkażający; **dis•in•fec•tion** [dɪsɪn'fekʃn] *s* dezynfekcja *f*, odkażanie *n*

dis•in•gen•u•ous [dɪsɪn'dʒenjʊəs] *adj* nieszczery

dis•in•her•it [dɪsɪn'herɪt] *v/t* wydziedziczać 〈-czyć〉

dis•in•te•grate [dɪs'ɪntəgreɪt] *v/i* rozpadać 〈-paść〉 się; **dis•in•te•gra•tion** [dɪsɪntə'greɪʃn] *s* **1.** rozpad *m* **2.** rozkład *m*

dis•in•ter•est•ed [dɪs'ɪntərestɪd] *adj* **1.** bezstronny **2.** niezainteresowany

dis•joint•ed [dɪs'dʒɔɪntɪd] *adj* chaotyczny

disk [dɪsk] *s* **1.** INF dysk *m*; ***a hard ~*** dysk twardy **2.** INF dyskietka *f* **3.** MUS płyta *f* **4.** tarcza *f*, krążek *m*; ***a ~ brake*** hamulec tarczowy; **'disk drive** *s* INF napęd *m* dysku

disk•ette [dɪs'ket] *s* INF dyskietka *f*

dis•like [dɪs'laɪk] **I** *v/t* nie lubić **II** *s* niechęć *f*, awersja *f* (***of/for*** do *G*); ***take a ~ to*** poczuć niechęć do *G*

dis•lo•cate ['dɪsləkeɪt] *v/t* **1.** zwichnąć, wywichnąć **2.** przemieszczać 〈-mieścić〉 **2.** zakłócać 〈-cić〉, zaburzać 〈-rzyć〉; **dis•lo•ca•tion** [dɪslə'keɪʃn] *s* **1.** zwichnięcie *n*, wywichnięcie *n* **2.** zakłócenie *n*, zaburzenie *n*

dis•lodge [dɪs'lɒdʒ] *v/t* **1.** zrywać 〈zerwać〉 **2.** obalać 〈-lić〉, odsuwać 〈-sunąć〉 od władzy **3.** powodować 〈s-〉 obsunięcie się

dis•loy•al [dɪs'lɔɪəl] *adj* nielojalny; **dis•loy•al•ty** [dɪs'lɔɪəltɪ] *s* nielojalność *f*

dis•mal ['dɪzməl] *adj* **1.** ponury, posępny **2.** *news*: fatalny **3.** *infml* beznadziejny

dis•man•tle [dɪs'mæntl] *v/t* **1.** rozmontowywać 〈-tować〉, rozbierać 〈-zebrać〉 **2.** likwidować 〈z-〉 **3.** rozwiązywać 〈-zać〉

dis•may [dɪs'meɪ] **I** *v/t* **1.** wprawiać 〈-wić〉 w konsternację **2.** przerażać 〈-razić〉 **II** *s* konsternacja *f*; ***in ~*** skonsternowany; ***to s.o.'s ~*** ku czyjejś konsternacji **4.** przerażenie *n*

dis•miss [dɪs'mɪs] *v/t* **1.** zwalniać 〈zwolnić〉 **2.** odprawiać 〈-wić〉 **3.** dymisjonować 〈z-〉 **4.** odrzucać 〈-cić〉 **5.** lekceważyć 〈z-〉 **6.** JUR oddalać 〈-lić〉; **dis•miss•al** [dɪs'mɪsl] *s* **1.** zwolnienie *n* **2.** odprawienie *n* **3.** JUR oddalenie *n*; **dis•mis•sive** [dɪs'mɪsɪv] *adj* lekceważący

dis•mount [dɪs'maʊnt] **I** *v/i* zsiadać 〈zsiąść〉 (***from*** z *G*) **II** *v/t* **1.** demontować 〈z-〉 **2.** *rider*: zrzucać 〈-cić〉

dis•o•be•di•ence [dɪsə'biːdɪəns] *s* nieposłuszeństwo *n*; **dis•o•be•di•ent** [dɪsə'biːdɪənt] *adj* nieposłuszny

dis•o•bey [dɪsə'beɪ] *v/t* **1.** nie słuchać 〈po-〉 **2.** nie przestrzagać **3.** łamać 〈z-〉

dis•ob•lig•ing [dɪsə'blaɪdʒɪŋ] *adj* **1.** nieuprzejmy **2.** nieuczynny

dis•or•der [dɪs'ɔːdə] **I** *s* **1.** nieład *m*, bałagan *m*; ***in ~*** w nieładzie **2.** rozruchy *pl*, zamieszki *pl* **3.** MED zaburzenie *n*; ***a mental ~*** zaburzenie psychiczne **II** MED choroba *f*; **dis•or•dered** [dɪs'ɔːdərd] *adj* **1.** w nieładzie **2.** nieuporządkowany **3.** MED zaburzony; ***be mentally ~*** cierpieć na zaburzenia psychiczne; **dis•or•der•ly** [dɪs'ɔːdərlɪ] *adj* **1.** nieporządny, niechlujny **2.** bezładny **3.** hałaśliwy **4.** awanturniczy

dis•or•gan•ize [dɪs'ɔːgənaɪz] *v/t* dezorganizować 〈z-〉; **dis•or•gan•ized** [dɪs'ɔːgənaɪzd] *adj* zdezorganizowany, źle zorganizowany

dis•o•ri•en•tate [dɪs'ɔːrɪənteɪt] *v/t* dezorientować 〈z-〉; **dis•o•ri•ent•ed** [dɪs'ɔːrɪəntɪd] *adj* zdezorientowany

dis•own [dɪs'əʊn] *v/t* wyrzekać 〈-rzec〉 się, wypierać 〈-przeć〉 się

dis•par•age [dɪ'spærɪdʒ] *v/t form* dyskredytować 〈z-〉; **dis•par•age•ment** [dɪ'spærɪdʒmənt] *s* zdyskredytowanie *n*; **di•spar•ag•ing** [dɪ'spærɪdʒɪŋ] *adj* **1.** lekceważący **2.** pogardliwy

dis•pa•rate ['dɪspərət] *adj* **1.** odmienny **2.** niejednorodny **3.** nieporównywalny; **di•spar•i•ty** [dɪ'spærətɪ] *s* **1.** (duża) różnica *f*; ***a ~ in age*** (duża) różnica wieku **2.** dysproporcja *f*

dis•pas•sion•ate [dɪs'pæʃənət] *adj* **1.** bezstronny **2.** beznamiętny, obojętny

di•spatch [dɪ'spætʃ] **I** *v/t* **1.** wysyłać ⟨-słać⟩ **2.** ekspediować ⟨wy-⟩ **3.** szybko załatwiać ⟨-wić⟩ **4.** likwidować ⟨z-⟩, wysyłać ⟨-słać⟩ na tamten świat **II** *s* **1.** wysyłka *f* **2.** meldunek *m* **3.** komunikat *m* **4.** ***with ~*** szybko, bez zwłoki; **di•spatch•er** [dɪ'spætʃə] *s Am* dyspozytor *m*

dis•pel [dɪ'spel] *v/t* **1.** rozpraszać ⟨-roszyć⟩ **2.** rozpędzać ⟨-dzić⟩ **3.** rozwiewać ⟨-wiać⟩

dis•pen•sa•ble [dɪ'spensəbl] *adj* **1.** zbędny **2.** niekonieczny

di•spen•sa•ry [dɪ'spensərɪ] *adj* apteka *f*

dis•pen•sa•tion [dɪspen'seɪʃn] *s* **1.** REL dyspensa *f* **2.** pozwolenie *n* **3.** *justice*: wymierzanie *n*; **dis•pense** [dɪ'spens] *v/t* **1.** wydawać ⟨-dać⟩ **2.** udzielać ⟨-lić⟩ **3.** *justice*: wymierzać ⟨-rzyć⟩ **4.** *medicines*: sporządzać ⟨-dzić⟩; **dis•pense with** *v/i* **1.** obywać ⟨obyć⟩ się bez *G* **2.** pomijać ⟨-minąć⟩

dis•pens•er [dɪ'spensə] *s* **1.** dozownik *m* **2.** automat *m*; ***a cash ~*** bankomat; **dis•'pens•ing chem•ist** *s Br* farmaceuta *m*

dis•per•sal [dɪ'spɜːsl] *s* **1.** rozproszenie *n* się **2.** rozpowszechnianie *n* **3.** rozsiewanie *n* się; **di•sperse** [dɪ'spɜːs] **I** *v/t* **1.** rozpraszać ⟨-roszyć⟩ **2.** rozpędzać ⟨-dzić⟩ **3.** ropowszechniać ⟨-nić⟩ **4.** rozsiewać ⟨-siać⟩ **II** *v/i* rozpraszać ⟨-roszyć⟩ się

di•spir•it•ed [dɪs'pɪrɪtɪd] *adj* **1.** zniechęcony **2.** przygnębiony

dis•place [dɪs'pleɪs] *v/t* **1.** wypierać ⟨-przeć⟩ **2.** zastępować ⟨-tąpić⟩ **3.** wysiedlać ⟨-lić⟩ **4.** *employee*: zwalniać ⟨zwolnić⟩; **dis•placed 'per•son** *s* wysiedleniec *m*; **dis•place•ment** [dɪs'pleɪsmənt] *s* **1.** wysiedlenie *n* **2.** zastąpienie *n* **3.** *employee*: zwolnienie *n* **4.** *ship*: wyporność *f*

di•splay [dɪ'spleɪ] **I** *v/t* **1.** ART wystawiać ⟨-wić⟩, prezentować ⟨za-⟩ **2.** *goods*: wykładać ⟨wyłożyć⟩ **3.** wywieszać ⟨-sić⟩; ***a notice will be ~ed*** wywieszona zostanie informacja **4.** okazywać ⟨-zać⟩ **5.** przejawiać ⟨-wić⟩ **6.** zdradzać ⟨-dzić⟩ **II** *s* **1.** wystawa *f*, ekspozycja *f*; ***on ~*** wystawiony; ***her works are on ~ in our gallery*** jej prace można oglądać w naszej galerii **2.** monitor *m*, wyświetlacz *m* **3.** pokaz *m* **4.** przejaw *m* **III** *adj* wystawowy; **di•splay 'cab•i•net**, ***di•splay 'case*** *s* **1.** oszklona szafka *f* **2.** gablota *f*; **di•splay 'stand** *s* **1.** gablota *f* **2.** stelaż *m* do wystawiania towarów; **di•splay 'unit** *s* **1.** monitor *m* **2.** stelaż *m* do wystawiania towarów

dis•please [dɪs'pliːz] *v/t* **1.** wywoływać ⟨-łać⟩ niezadowolenie; ***be ~d at*** być niezadowolonym z *G* **2.** denerwować ⟨z-⟩; **dis•pleas•ing** [dɪs'pliːzɪŋ] *adj* nieprzyjemny; **dis•plea•sure** [dɪs'pleʒə] *s* niezadowolenie *n*

dis•po•sa•ble [dɪ'spəʊzəbl] *adj* **1.** jednorazowy, jednorazowego użytku **2.** do dyspozycji **3.** *income*: netto; **dis•pos•al** [dɪ'spəʊzl] *s* **1.** wywóz *m*, wywózka *f* **2.** usunięcie *n* **3.** pozbycie *n* się **4.** sprzedaż *f*, zbycie *n* **5.** ***be at s.o.'s ~*** być do czyjejś dyspozycji; ***put s.th. at s.o.'s ~*** oddać coś do czyjejś dyspozycji; ***have the ~ of*** **a)** rozporządzać *I* **b)** dysponować *I*

dis•pose [dɪ'spəʊz] *v/t* układać ⟨ułożyć⟩; **dis•pose of** *v/i* **1.** pozbywać ⟨-być⟩ się *G* **2.** usuwać ⟨usunąć⟩ **3.** rozprawiać ⟨-wić⟩ się z *I*, uporać się z *I*; **dis•posed** [dɪ'spəʊzd] *adj* skłonny, chętny; ***be well ~ towards*** mieć pozytywny stosunek do *G*; ***feel ~ to do s.th.*** mieć ochotę coś zrobić

dis•po•si•tion [dɪspə'zɪʃn] *s* **1.** usposobienie *n* **2.** skłonność *f*, tendencja *f*; ***have a ~ to*** mieć skłonność do *G* **3.** JUR dyspozycja *f*

dis•pos•sess [dɪspə'zes] *v/t* wywłaszczać ⟨-czyć⟩

dis•pro•por•tion•ate [dɪsprə'pɔːʃənət] *adj* nieproporcjonalny; ***be ~ to*** być niewspółmiernym do *G*

dis•prove [dɪs'pruːv] *v/t* **1.** obalać ⟨-lić⟩ **2.** zadawać ⟨-dać⟩ kłam *D*

dis•put•a•ble [dɪ'spjuːtəbl] *adj* dyskusyjny, sporny; **dis•pu•ta•tion** [dɪspjuː'teɪʃn] *s* dysputa *f*, spór *m*; **dis•pu•ta•tious** [dɪspjuː'teɪʃəs] *adj form* kłótliwy, swarliwy; **di•spute** [dɪ'spjuːt] **I** *v/t* **1.** kwestionować ⟨za-⟩, podawać ⟨-dać⟩ w wątpliwość **2.** zgłaszać ⟨-łosić⟩ pretensje do *G* **3.** spierać się o *A* **II** *v/i* spierać się **III** *s* **1.** spór *m* **2.** kontrowersja *f*; ***under ~*** kontrowersyjny, sporny; ***beyond ~*** bezdyskusyjny

D

dis•qual•i•fi•ca•tion [dɪskwɒlɪfɪ'keɪʃn] *s* **1.** dyskwalifikacja *f* **2.** wykluczenie *n*; **dis•qual•i•fy** [dɪs'kwɒlɪfaɪ] *v/t* **1.** dyskwalifikować ⟨z-⟩ **2.** wykluczać ⟨-czyć⟩

dis•qui•et [dɪs'kwaɪət] **I** *v/t* niepokoić ⟨za-⟩ **II** *s* niepokój *m*, zaniepokojenie *n*; **dis•qui•et•ing** [dɪs'kwaɪətɪŋ] *adj* niepokojący

dis•re•gard [dɪsrɪ'gɑːd] **I** *v/t* **1.** ignorować ⟨z-⟩ **2.** lekceważyć ⟨z-⟩, nie zważać na *A* **3.** okazywać ⟨-zać⟩ brak szacunku *D* **II** *s* **1.** lekceważenie *n* **2.** brak *m* szacunku

dis•re•pair [dɪsrɪ'peə] *s*: ***in (a state of) ~*** w złym stanie; ***fall into ~*** popaść w ruinę

dis•re•spect [dɪsrɪ'spekt] *s* brak *m* szacunku; **dis•re•spect•ful** [dɪsrə'spektfəl] *adj* lekceważący; ***be ~ to s.o.*** nie okazywać komuś szacunku, lekceważyć kogoś

dis•rupt [dɪs'rʌpt] **1.** zakłócać ⟨-cić⟩ **2.** przerywać ⟨-rwać⟩; **dis•rup•tion** [dɪs'rʌpʃn] *s* **1.** zakłócenie *n* **2.** przerwanie *n* **3.** niewygoda *f* **4.** zamęt *m*; **dis•rup•tive** [dɪs'rʌptɪv] *adj* **1.** ***be ~ in class*** przeszkadzać na lekcji **2.** *influence*: zły

dis•sat•is•fac•tion [dɪsætɪs'fækʃn] *s* niezadowolenie *n*; **dis•sat•is•fac•to•ry** [dɪsætɪs'fæktərɪ] *adj* niezadowalający; **dis•sat•is•fied** [dɪ'sætɪsfaɪd] *adj* niezadowolony

dis•sect [dɪ'sekt] *v/t* **1.** MED przeprowadzać ⟨-dzić⟩ sekcję **2.** *organ*: preparować ⟨s-⟩ **3.** *fig* rozprawiać ⟨-wić⟩ się z *I*; **dis•sec•tion** [dɪ'sekʃn] *s* **1.** MED sekcja *f* (zwłok) **2.** wnikliwa analiza *f*

dis•sem•ble [dɪ'sembl] *v/i* **1.** ukrywać ⟨-ryć⟩ **2.** przemilczać ⟨-czeć⟩

dis•sent [dɪ'sent] **I** *v/i* **1.** mieć odmienne zdanie (***from*** od *G*) **2.** odcinać ⟨-ciąć⟩ się (***from*** od *G*) **II** *s* **1.** różnica *f* zdań **2.** sprzeciw *m*; **dis•sent•er** [dɪ'sentə] *s* **1.** człowiek *m* myślący inaczej **2.** dysydent *m*

dis•ser•ta•tion [dɪsər'teɪʃn] *s* **1.** rozprawa *f* doktorska **2.** praca *f* magisterska **3.** dysertacja *f*

dis•serv•ice [dɪ'sɜːvɪs] *s* szkoda *f*, niedźwiedzia przysługa *f*; ***do s.o. a ~*** źle się komuś przysłużyć

dis•si•dent ['dɪsɪdənt] **I** *s* POLIT dysydent *m* **II** *adj* dysydencki

dis•sim•i•lar [dɪ'sɪmɪlə] *adj* **1.** niepodobny (***to/from*** do *G*); ***not ~*** podobny **2.** odmienny, różny (***to/from*** od *G*); **dis•sim•i•lar•i•ty** [dɪsɪmɪ'lærətɪ] *s* **1.** różnica *f* **2.** odmienność *f*

dis•si•pate ['dɪsɪpeɪt] **I** *v/t* **1.** rozpraszać ⟨-roszyć⟩ **2.** rozwiewać ⟨-wiać⟩ **3.** trwonić ⟨roz-⟩, marnować ⟨z-⟩ **II** *v/i* **1.** rozpraszać ⟨-roszyć⟩ się **2.** (*energy*) wyczerpywać ⟨-pać⟩ się; **dis•si•pat•ed** ['dɪsɪpeɪtɪd] *adj*: ***lead a ~ life*** prowadzić hulaszcze życie; **dis•si•pa•tion** [dɪsɪ'peɪʃn] *s* **1.** rozpraszanie *n* **2.** trwonienie *n* **3.** ***a life of ~*** hulaszcze życie

dis•so•ci•ate [dɪ'səʊʃɪeɪt] **I** *v/t* **1.** oddzielać ⟨-lić⟩ **2.** rozdzielać ⟨-lić⟩ **II** *v/i* **1.** ***~ oneself from*** odcinać się od *G* **2.** CHEM dysocjować; **dis•so•ci•a•tion** [dɪsəʊsɪ'eɪʃn] *s* **1.** oddzielenie *n* **2.** rozdzielenie *n* **3.** CHEM dysocjacja *f*

dis•so•lute ['dɪsəluːt] *adj* rozwiązły, rozpustny; **dis•so•lu•tion** [dɪsə'luːʃn] *s* **1.** rozwiązanie *n*; ***a ~ of marriage*** rozwód **2.** zamknięcie *n* **3.** rozpad *m* **4.** rozwiązłość *f*; **dis•solve** [dɪ'zɒlv] **I** *v/t* **1.** rozpuszczać ⟨-puścić⟩; ***~d in tears*** zalany łzami **2.** *parliament*: rozwiązywać ⟨-zać⟩ **II** *v/i* rozpuszczać ⟨-puścić⟩ się

dis•so•nance ['dɪsənəns] *s* **1.** MUS dysonans *m* **2.** dysharmonia *f* **3.** rozdźwięk *m*; **dis•so•nant** ['dɪsənənt] *adj* **1.** MUS dysonansowy **2.** sprzeczny **3.** rozbieżny

dis•suade [dɪ'sweɪd] *v/t* odwodzić ⟨-wieść⟩ (***from*** od *G*), perswadować ⟨wy-⟩ (***from*** *A*)

dis•tance ['dɪstəns] **I** *s* **1.** odległość *f*; ***at a ~, from a ~*** **a)** na odległość **b)** z daleka; ***go the (full) ~*** wytrwać do końca; ***keep one's ~ from s.o.*** **a)** trzymać kogoś na dystans **a)** trzymać się od kogoś z daleka **2.** SPORT dystans *m* **3.** perspektywa *f*; ***at this***

~ ***in time*** z tej perspektywy czasowej **II** *v/t* ~ ***oneself from*** dystansować się od *G*; '**dis•tance run•ner** *s* długodystansowiec *m*; **dis•tant** ['dɪstənt] *adj* **1.** daleki, odległy **2.** oddalony **3.** *face expression, glance*: nieobecny

dis•taste [dɪs'teɪst] *s* **1.** niesmak *m* **2.** wstręt *m*, obrzydzenie *n*; **dis•taste•ful** [dɪs'teɪstfəl] *adj* **1.** niesmaczny **2.** wstrętny, obrzydliwy

dis•tend [dɪ'stend] *v/t* **1.** wzdymać ⟨-dąć⟩ **2.** rozdymać ⟨-dąć⟩

dis•til(l) [dɪ'stɪl] *v/t* **1.** destylować **2.** rektyfikować; **dis•til•la•tion** [dɪstɪ'leɪʃn] *s* **1.** destylacja *f* **2.** rektyfikacja *f* **3.** destylat *m*; **dis•till•er•y** [dɪ'stɪlərɪ] *s* gorzelnia *f*

dis•tinct [dɪ'stɪŋkt] *adj* **1.** wyraźny, wyraźnie widoczny **2.** różny, odmienny; ***as*** ~ ***from*** w odróżnieniu od *G*; **dis•tinc•tion** [dɪ'stɪŋkʃn] *s* **1.** rozróżnienie *n* **2.** różnica *f*; ***in*** ~ ***from*** w odróżnieniu od *G*; ***make a*** ~ ***between*** rozróżniać pomiędzy *I* **3.** wyróżnienie *n* **4.** dystynkcja *f*; ***of*** ~ dystyngowany; **dis•tinc•tive** [dɪ'stɪŋktɪv] *adj* charakterystyczny; **dis•tinct•ly** [dɪ'stɪŋktlɪ] *adv* **1.** wyraźnie **2.** dokładnie

dis•tin•guish [dɪ'stɪŋgwɪʃ] **I** *v/t* **1.** odróżniać ⟨-nić⟩ (***from*** od *G*) **2.** rozróżniać ⟨-nić⟩ **3.** *words*: rozumieć ⟨z-⟩ **II** *v/i* **1.** odróżniać ⟨-nić⟩; ~ ***between right and wrong*** odróżniać dobro od zła **2.** ~ ***oneself*** wyróżnić się; **dis•tin•guished** [dɪ'stɪŋgwɪʃt] *adj* **1.** wybitny **2.** dystyngowany, wytworny; **dis•tin•guish•ing** '**mark** *s* znak *m* szczególny

dis•tort [dɪ'stɔːt] *v/t* **1.** zniekształcać ⟨-cić⟩, deformować ⟨z-⟩; ~***ed with pain*** wykrzywiony bólem **2.** wypaczać ⟨-czyć⟩ **3.** przeinaczać ⟨-czyć⟩; **dis•tor•tion** [dɪ'stɔːʃn] *s* **1.** zniekształcenie *n*, deformacja *f* **2.** wypaczenie *n* **3.** przeinaczenie *n*

dis•tract [dɪ'strækt] *v/t* **1.** rozpraszać ⟨-roszyć⟩ **2.** *attention*: odwracać ⟨-rócić⟩; **dis•tract•ed** [dɪ'stræktɪd] *adj* **1.** roztargniony **2.** nieobecny myślami; **dis•trac•tion** [dɪ'strækʃn] *s* **1.** rozrywka *f* **2.** odskocznia *f* **3.** ***I can't work here! There are too many*** ~***s.*** Nie mogę tu pracować – zbyt dużo rzeczy mnie rozprasza.

dis•tress [dɪ'stres] **I** *s* **1.** ból *m*, cierpienie *n*, udręka *f*; ***be in*** ~ cierpieć **2.** problemy *pl*; ***financial*** ~ problemy finansowe **3.** niebezpieczeństwo *n*; ***in*** ~ w niebezpieczeństwie **II** *v/t* **1.** przygnębiać ⟨-bić⟩ **2.** martwić ⟨z-⟩; **dis'tress call** *s* wezwanie *n* o pomoc; **dis•tressed** [dɪ'stresd] *adj* **1.** przygnębiony **2.** ***be*** ~ cierpieć; **dis•tress•ing** [dɪ'stresɪŋ] *adj* **1.** przygnębiający, smutny **2.** przy kry; **dis•'tress sig•nal** *s* sygnał *m* SOS

dis•trib•ute [dɪ'strɪbjuːt] *v/t* **1.** rozdzielać ⟨-lić⟩ **2.** rozdawać ⟨-dać⟩ **3.** *goods*: dystrybuować, prowadzić dystrybucję **4.** rozprowadzać ⟨-dzić⟩ **5.** rozpowszechniać ⟨-nić⟩; **dis•tri•'bu•tion** [dɪstrɪ'bjuːʃn] *s* **1.** rozdział *m*; ***a*** ~ ***of seats*** (*parliament*) podział miejsc **2.** rozkład *m* **3.** rozmieszczenie *n* **4.** ECON dystrybucja *f* **5.** rozpowszechnianie *n*; **dis•tri•'bu•tion ar•range•ment** *s* umowa *f* dystrybucyjna; **dis•tri•'bu•tion net•work** *s* sieć *f* dystrybucji; **dis•trib•u•tor** [dɪ'strɪbjuːtə] *s* **1.** dystrybutor *m* **2.** TECH rozdzielacz *m*

dis•trict ['dɪstrɪkt] *s* **1.** dzielnica *f* **2.** rejon *m* **3.** region *m* **4.** okręg *m*; **dis•trict at•'tor•ney** *s Am* prokurator *m* okręgowy; **dis•trict 'man•ag•er** *s* dyrektor *m* oddziału

dis•trust [dɪs'trʌst] **I** *s* nieufność *f*, brak *m* zaufania **II** *v/t* nie ufać, nie mieć zaufania do *G*; **dis•trust•ful** [dɪs'trʌstfʊl] *adj* nieufny

dis•turb [dɪ'stɜːb] *v/t* **1.** przeszkadzać ⟨-kodzić⟩ **2.** zakłócać ⟨-cić⟩ **3.** martwić ⟨z-⟩; **dis•turb•ance** [dɪ'stɜːbəns] *s* **1.** zakłócenie *n* **2.** niepokoje *pl*; ***cause a*** ~ JUR zakłócić porządek publiczny; **dis•turbed** [dɪ'stɜːbd] *adj* **1.** zaniepokojony **2.** poruszony **3.** niezrównoważony; **dis•turb•ing** [dɪ'stɜːbɪŋ] *adj* niepokojący

dis•u•nite [dɪsjuː'naɪt] *v/t* dzielić ⟨po-⟩, poróżniać ⟨-nić⟩; **disunited** [dɪsjuː'naɪtɪd] *adj* podzielony, poróżniony; **dis•u•ni•ty** [dɪs'juːnətɪ] *s* rozłam *m*

dis•use [dɪs'juːs] *s*: ***fall into*** ~ **a)** przestać być używanym **b)** wyjść z użycia; **dis•used** [dɪs'juːzd] *adj* **1.** opuszczony **2.** nieużywany

D

ditch [dɪtʃ] **I** *s* rów *m* **II** *v/t* **1.** *infml* rzucać ⟨-cić⟩ **2.** *infml* zarzucać ⟨-cić⟩ **3.** **~ *a plane*** wylądować awaryjnie (na wodzie)

dive [daɪv] **I** (*dive/dove; dived*) *v/i* **1.** skakać ⟨skoczyć⟩ na główkę **2.** nurkować ⟨za-⟩ **3.** zanurzać ⟨-rzyć⟩ się **4.** gwałtownie spadać ⟨spaść⟩ **5.** gwałtownie tracić ⟨s-⟩ na wartości **6.** *infml* skakać ⟨skoczyć⟩ **II** *s* **1.** skok *m* na główkę **2.** zejście *n* (pod wodę); ***make a ~*** zanurkować **3.** lot *m* nurkowy, pikowanie *n* **4.** *infml* speluna *f*; **div•er** ['daɪvə] *s* **1.** nurek *m* **2.** skoczek *m* do wody

di•verge [daɪ'vɜːdʒ] *v/i* **1.** rozchodzić ⟨-zejść⟩ się **2.** odchodzić (***from*** od *G*) **3.** odbiegać (***from*** od *G*) **4.** odróżniać ⟨-nić⟩ się; **di•verg•ence** [daɪ'vɜːdʒəns] *s* **1.** rozbieżność *f* **2.** BIOL dywergencja *f*; **di•ver•gent** [daɪ'vɜːdʒənt] *adj* **1.** rozbieżny **2.** rozchodzący się

di•verse [daɪ'vɜːs] *adj* **1.** różnorodny **2.** wieloraki **3.** różny; **di•ver•si•fi•ca•tion** [daɪvəsɪfɪ'keɪʃn] *s* **1.** zróżnicowanie *n* **2.** różnorodność *f* **3.** ECON dywersyfikacja *f*; **di•ver•si•fy** [daɪ'vɜːsɪfaɪ] **I** *v/i* **1.** różnicować ⟨z-⟩ się **2.** stawać ⟨stać⟩ się bardziej różnorodnym **II** *v/t* **1.** urozmaicać ⟨-cić⟩ **2.** *offer*: poszerzać ⟨-rzyć⟩

di•ver•sion [daɪ'vɜːʃn] *s* **1.** *Br* objazd *m* **2.** zmiana *f* kierunku **3.** odwrócenie *n* biegu **4.** rozrywka *f* **5.** ***create a ~*** odwrócić (czyjąś) uwagę

di•ver•si•ty [daɪ'vɜːsətɪ] *s* **1.** różnorodność *f*; ***a ~ of opinion*** zróżnicowane opinie, bardzo różne zdania **2.** rozmaitość *f*

di•vert [daɪ'vɜːt] *v/t* **1.** zmieniać ⟨-nić⟩ kierunek **2.** odwracać ⟨-rócić⟩ **3.** obracać ⟨-rócić⟩ **4.** *form* zabawiać ⟨-wić⟩

di•vide [dɪ'vaɪd] **I** *v/t* **1.** dzielić ⟨po-⟩ (***into*** na *A*); ***opinion is ~d*** zdania są podzielone; ***six ~d by three is two*** sześć (po)dzielone przez trzy równa się dwa **2.** rozdzielać ⟨-lić⟩ **II** *v/i* **1.** MATH dzielić się, być podzielnym **2.** rozwidlać ⟨-lić⟩ się **3.** rozdzielać ⟨-lić⟩ się; ***a ~d highway*** *Am* droga dwujezdniowa

div•i•dend ['dɪvɪdend] *s* **1.** FIN dywidenda *f*; ***pay ~s*** *fig* procentować **2.** MATH dzielna *f*

di•'vid•ing line *s* granica *f*

div•i•na•tion [dɪvɪ'neɪʃn] *s* wróżenie *n*, przepowiadanie *n* przyszłości

di•vine [dɪ'vaɪn] **I** *adj* boski **II** *v/t* **1.** odgadywać ⟨-dnąć⟩ **2.** *future*: przepowiadać ⟨-wiedzieć⟩ **3.** szukać (za pomocą różdżki); **diviner** [dɪ'vaɪnə] *s* **1.** różdżkarz *m* **2.** wróżbita *m*

div•ing ['daɪvɪŋ] *s* **1.** nurkowanie *n* **2.** skoki *pl* do wody; **'div•ing bell** *s* keson *m*, dzwon *m* nurkowy; **'div•ing board** *s* trampolina *f*; **'div•ing helmet** *s* hełm *m* nurkowy; **'div•ing mask** *s* maska *f* do nurkowania; **'diving suit** *s* skafander *m* nurka

di•vin•i•ty [dɪ'vɪnətɪ] *s* **1.** boskość *f* **2.** bóstwo *n* **3.** teologia *f*

di•vis•i•ble [dɪ'vɪzəbl] *adj* MATH podzielny; **di•vi•sion** [dɪ'vɪʒn] *s* **1.** podział *m*; ***the ~ of labour*** podział pracy **2.** rozłam *m* **3.** MATH dzielenie *n*; ***a ~ sign*** znak dzielenia **4.** (*parliament*) *Br* głosowanie *n* **5.** oddział *m* **6.** dywizja *f* **7.** SPORT liga *f*

di•vorce [dɪ'vɔːs] **I** *s* **1.** rozwód *m*; ***get a ~*** rozwieść się **2.** *fig* rozdział *m* **II** *v/t* **3.** rozwodzić ⟨-wieść⟩ się z *I* **2.** udzielać ⟨-lić⟩ rozwodu **III** *v/i* rozwodzić ⟨-wieść⟩ się; **di•vorced** [dɪ'vɔːst] *adj* rozwiedziony; ***get ~*** rozwieść się; **di•vor•cee** [dɪvɔː'siː] *s* **1.** rozwodnik *m* **2.** rozwódka *f*

di•vulge [daɪ'vʌldʒ] *v/t* ujawniać ⟨-nić⟩

DIY [diːaɪ'waɪ] *abbr* (=***do-it-yourself***) majsterkowanie *n*; **~ *store*** sklep dla majsterkowiczów

diz•zi•ness ['dɪzɪnɪs] *s* zawroty *pl* głowy; **diz•zy** ['dɪzɪ] *adj* **1.** ***be ~*** mieć zawroty głowy **2.** przyprawiający o zawrót głowy, zawrotny

DJ [diː'dʒeɪ] *s* **1.** → ***disc jockey*** **2.** → ***dinner jacket***

DNA [diːen'eɪ] *abbr* (=***deoxyribonucleic acid***) DNA *n*; ***a ~ fingerprint*** genetyczny odcisk palca

do[1] [duː] **I** (*did; done*) *v/t* **1.** robić ⟨z-⟩ **2.** wykonywać ⟨-nać⟩ **3.** *favour*: oddawać ⟨-dać⟩ **4.** sprzątać ⟨po-⟩ **5.** *room*: urządzać ⟨-dzić⟩ **6.** ***~ one's face ~*** umalować się; ***~ one's hair***

uczesać się **7.** jechać z prędkością; ***the car was ~ing 100 m.p.h.*** samochód jechał z prędkością 160 km/h **8.** kończyć ⟨s-⟩ **9.** odbywać ⟨-być⟩ **10.** przerabiać ⟨-robić⟩ **11.** *drugs*: *infml* brać **II** (*did*; *done*) *v/i* **1.** robić ⟨z-⟩ **2.** wykonywać ⟨-nać⟩ **3.** wypadać ⟨-paść⟩ **4.** radzić ⟨po-⟩ sobie; ***he's ~ing well*** dobrze sobie radzi **5.** ***be ~ing well*** czuć się dobrze **6.** wystarczać ⟨-czyć⟩ **7.** ***how are you ~ing?*** **a)** jak leci? *inflm* **b)** jak się masz? **8.** nadawać ⟨-dać⟩ się, spełniać ⟨-nić⟩ swoją rolę **III** *v aux* **1.** ***~ you know him?*** znasz go?; ***I don't believe you*** nie wierzę ci **2.** (*emphatic*) ***I did like it*** naprawdę mi się podobało **3.** ***you know it as well as I ~*** wiesz o tym tak dobrze jak ja; ***so ~ I*** ja też; ***he works hard, doesn't he?*** ciężko pracuje, nieprawdaż?; ***– 'Did he buy it?' – 'He did.'*** – „Kupił to?" – „Tak, kupił."; ***– 'He sold his car.' – 'Did he?'*** – „Sprzedał samochód." – „Naprawdę?" **IV** *s* **1.** *infml* impreza *f* **2.** ***~s and don'ts*** reguły, nakazy i zakazy; **do about** *v/t*: ***do something about it!*** zrób coś z tym!; **do away with** *v/i* **1.** pozbywać ⟨-być⟩ się **2.** *infml* likwidować ⟨z-⟩; **do down** *v/t Br infml* kantować ⟨o-⟩; **do in** *v/t infml* załatwiać ⟨-wić⟩, wykańczać ⟨-kończyć⟩; ***I'm done in*** jestem załatwiony; **do out of** *v/t* **1.** oszukiwać ⟨-kać⟩ na *A* **2.** pozbawiać ⟨-wić⟩; **do over** *v/t* **1.** robić ⟨z-⟩ jeszcze raz **2.** *infml* spuścić manto; **do up** *v/t* **1.** zawiązywać ⟨-zać⟩ **2.** zapinać ⟨-piąć⟩; **do with** *v/t* **1.** ***I won't have anything to ~ it*** nie chcę mieć z tym nic wspólnego; ***it has nothing to ~ you*** to nie ma z tobą nic wspólnego **2.** ***he could ~ the money*** te pieniądze by mu się przydały; ***I could ~ a glass of beer*** mam ochotę na piwo; **do without** *v/t* obywać ⟨obyć⟩ się bez *G*

doc [dɒk] → ***doctor***

do•cile ['dəʊsaɪl] *adj* potulny, uległy; **do•cil•i•ty** [dəʊ'sɪlətɪ] *s* potulność *f*, uległość *f*

dock[1] [dɒk] **I** *s* **1.** dok *m* (portowy) **2.** nabrzeże *n* **3.** ***~s*** port **II** *v/t* **1.** wprowadzać ⟨-dzić⟩ do portu, dokować **2.** łączyć ⟨po-⟩ **III** *v/i* **1.** przybijać ⟨-bić⟩ do portu **2.** łączyć ⟨po-⟩ się

dock[2] [~] *v/t* **1.** *tail, ears*: przycinać ⟨-ciąć⟩, obcinać ⟨-ciąć⟩ **2.** *salary*: obcinać ⟨-ciąć⟩; ***~ £50 off s.o.'s pay*** potrącić komuś 50 funtów z pensji

dock[3] [~] *s Br* JUR ława *f* oskarżonych; ***be in the ~*** zasiadać na ławie oskarżonych

dock•er ['dɒkə] *s* doker *m*, robotnik *m* portowy; **'dock•yard** *s* stocznia *f*

doc•tor ['dɒktə] **I** *s* **1.** lekarz *m*; ***a ~'s certificate*** dyplom lekarski **2.** doktor *m*; ***~ of Laws*** (***Divinity***) doktor nauk prawnych (teologicznych); ***~'s degree*** stopień doktorski; ***take one's ~'s degree*** doktoryzować się **II** *v/t* fałszować ⟨s-⟩; ***she ~ed his beer with vodka*** dodała mu do piwa wódki; **doc•tor•al the•sis** [dɒktərəl'θiːsɪs] *pl* ***~ theses*** *s* praca *f* doktorska; **doc•tor•ate** ['dɒktərət] *s* doktorat *m*

doc•trine ['dɒktrɪn] *s* doktryna *f*; ***a party ~*** program partyjny

doc•u•dra•ma ['dɒkjʊdrɑːmə] *s* dokument *m* fabularyzowany

doc•u•ment ['dɒkjʊmənt] **I** *s* dokument *m* **II** *v/t* dokumentować ⟨u-⟩; **doc•u•men•ta•ry** [dəkjʊ'mentərɪ] **I** *s* dokument *m*, film *m* dokumentalny **II** *adj* dokumentalny; ***~ novel*** powieść oparta na faktach; **doc•u•men•ta•tion** [dəkjʊmen'teɪʃn] *s* dokumentacja *f*

dod•der•er ['dɒdərə] *s infml* ramol *m*; **dod•der•ing** ['dɒdərɪŋ] *adj* **1.** trzęsący się (ze starości) **2.** *infml* zramolały

dodge [dɒdʒ] **I** *v/i* robić ⟨z-⟩ unik **II** *v/t* **1.** uchylać ⟨-lić⟩ się przed *I* **2.** unikać ⟨-knąć⟩ **III** *s* **1.** unik *m* **2.** sztuczka *f*, trik *m*

doe [dəʊ] *s* **1.** łania *f* **2.** królica *f* **3.** zajęczyca *f*

do•er ['duːə] *s* **1.** wykonawca *m* czynności **2.** człowiek *m* czynu

does [dəz, dʌz] → ***do***[1]

'doe•skin *s* ircha *f*

does•n't *contracted form* → ***does not***

dog [dɒg] **I** *s* **1.** pies *m*; ***a ~ in the manger*** pies ogrodnika; ***go to the ~s*** *fig* zejść na psy; ***lead a ~'s life*** wieść pieskie życie; ***let sleeping ~s lie*** nie wywołuj wilka z lasu **2.** *infml* pies *m*; ***a lazy ~*** leniuch; ***a lucky ~*** szczęściarz

D

3. ***the ~s*** wyścigi psów **II** *v/t* chodzić krok w krok za *I*, nie odstępować *G* **'dog bis•cuit** *s* ciasteczko *n* dla psa; **'dog catch•er** *s* rakarz *m*, hycel *m*; **'dog col•lar** *s* **1.** obroża *f* **2.** *infml* koloratka *f*; **'dog•eared** *adj*: ***be ~*** mieć ośle uszy; **dog-eat-'dog** *adj* **1.** bezwzględny **2.** (idący) po trupach; **'dogfight** *s* **1.** walka *f* psów **2.** *fig* bójka *f*, szarpanina *f*; **'dog•fish** *s* *BIOL COOK* rekinek *m*

dog•gy ['dɒgɪ] **I** *s* piesek *m* **II** *adj* psi; **doggy bag** *s* torba *f* na resztki

'dog•house *s* psia buda *f*

dog•ma ['dɒgmə] *s* dogmat *m*; **dogmat•ic** [dɒg'mætɪk] *adj* dogmatyczny

do-good•er [duː'gʊdə] *s*: ***be a ~*** uszczęśliwiać innych na siłę

dog 'tag *s Am infml* identyfikator *m*

dog-'tired *adj infml* skonany, wykończony

do•ing ['duːɪŋ] *s* **1.** ***it was your ~*** to była twoja sprawka **2.** ***~s*** poczynania *pl*, wypadki *pl*

do-it-your•self [duːɪtjər'self] **I** *s* majsterkowanie *n* **II** *adj* dla majsterkowiczów

dole [dəʊl] *s Br infml* zasiłek *m* (dla bezrobotnych); ***go on the ~*** iść na zasiłek; **dole out** *v/t* rozdzielać ⟨-lić⟩

doll [dɒl] *s* **1.** lalka *f*; ***a ~'s house*** domek dla lalek; ***a ~'s pram*** wózek dla lalek **2.** *infml* lala *f*, laleczka *f*; **doll up** *v/i infml*: ***get dolled up*** wystroić się, wyelegantować się

dol•lar ['dɒlə] *s* dolar *m*; **'dol•lar ar•e•a** *s* strefa *f* dolarowa; **'dol•lar di•plo•ma•cy** *s* dyplomacja *f* dolarowa; **'dollar sign** *s* symbol *m* dolara

'dollhouse *s Am* domek *m* dla lalek

dol•ly ['dɒlɪ] *s* **1.** laleczka *f* **2.** (*girl*) *infml* kociak *m* **3.** dolka *f*

dol•phin ['dɒlfɪn] *s* delfin *m*

do•main [də'meɪn] *s* **1.** dziedzina *f* **2.** sfera *f* **3.** domena *f*

dome [dəʊm] *s ARCHIT* kopuła *f*

do•mes•tic [də'mestɪk] **I** *adj* **1.** domowy; ***~ science*** zajęcia praktyczno-techniczne; ***a ~ animal*** zwierzę domowe **2.** rodzinny **3.** krajowy; ***~ products*** produkty krajowe **4.** wewnętrzny; ***~ trade*** handel wewnętrzny; ***~ policy*** polityka wewnętrzna **II** *s* (*a.* ***~ servant***) służący *m*; **do•mestic a'p•pli•ance** *s* sprzęt *m* gospodarstwa domowego; **do•mes•ti•cate** [də'mestɪkeɪt] *v/t* **1.** udomawiać ⟨-mowić⟩ **2.** oswajać ⟨-woić⟩

dom•i•nance ['dɒmɪnəns] *s* **1.** dominacja *f* **2.** przewaga *f*; **dom•i•nant** ['dɒmɪnənt] **I** *adj* **1.** dominujący **2.** główny **3.** górujący **4.** widoczny **II** *s* **1.** *MUS* dominanta *f* **2.** *BIOL* gen *m* dominujący; **dom•i•nate** ['dɒmɪneɪt] **I** *v/t* dominować ⟨z-⟩ **II** *v/i* dominować (***over*** nad *I*); **dom•i•na•tion** [dɒmɪ'neɪʃn] *s* dominacja *f*; **dom•i•neer•ing** [dəmɪ'nɪərɪŋ] *adj* despotyczny, apodyktyczny

do•min•ion [də'mɪnjən] *s* **1.** władza *f*, zwierzchnictwo *n* **2.** dominium *n*

do•nate [dəʊ'neɪt] *v/t* ofiarowywać ⟨-rować⟩; **do•na•tion** [dəʊ'neɪʃn] *s* **1.** datek *m* **2.** ofiarowanie *n*

done [dʌn] **I** *v Past Participle* → ***do*** **II** *adj* **1.** zrobiony; ***it isn't ~*** tak się nie robi; ***get s.th. ~*** zrobić coś **2.** załatwiony **3.** ugotowany, upieczony; ***well ~*** dobrze wysmażony **4.** gotowy; ***have ~ with*** skończyć z *I*

don•key ['dɒŋkɪ] *s a. fig* osioł *m*; ***~'s years*** *infml* całe wieki, kopę lat; ***~ work*** *s Br infml* czarna robota *f*

do•nor ['dəʊnə] *s* **1.** dawca *m*; ***a ~'s card*** karta dawcy **2.** ofiarodawca *m*

do•nut ['dəʊnʌt] → ***doughnut***

doo•dle ['duːdl] **I** *s* bazgroły *pl*, gryzmoły *pl* **II** *v/i* gryzmolić ⟨na-⟩, bazgrać ⟨na-⟩

doom [duːm] **I** *s* **1.** zguba *f*, śmierć *f* **2.** klęska *f*, nieszczęście *n*; ***a sense of impending ~*** przeczucie nadchodzącego nieszczęścia **3.** przeznaczenie *n* **4.** ***be full of ~ and gloom*** widzieć przyszłość w czarnych barwach **II** *v/t* skazywać ⟨-zać⟩; **doomed** [duːmd] *adj* skazany; ***~ to failure, ~ to fail*** skazany na porażkę; **dooms•day** ['duːmzdeɪ] *s* **1.** sądny dzień *m* **2.** *REL* dzień *m* Sądu Ostatecznego

door [dɔː] *s* **1.** drzwi *pl*; ***from ~ to ~*** od drzwi do drzwi; ***out of ~s*** na dworze; ***two ~s down the street*** dwa domy dalej; ***close the ~ on*** *fig* zamknąć drogę do *G*; ***lay s.th. at s.o.'s door*** obarczyć kogoś czymś; ***show s.o. the ~*** wyprosić kogoś za drzwi **2.** wejście *n*; ***a ~***

chain łańcuch do drzwi; **~ *frame*** futryna drzwiowa; ***a ~ plate*** tabliczka na drzwiach
'**door•bell** *s* dzwonek *m* u drzwi; ***ring the ~*** zadzwonić do drzwi; '**door-bel-ling** *s* akwizycja *f*; '**doorhan•dle** *s* klamka *f*; '**door•knob** *s* gałka *f* u drzwi; '**door•knock•er** *s* kołatka *f*; **door•man** ['dɔːmən] *pl -men s* **1.** odźwierny *m*, portier *m* **2.** bileter *m*; '**door•mat** *s* wycieraczka *f*; '**door•post** *s* słupek *m* (framugi); '**door•step** *s* próg *m*; **door-to-door** '**sales•man** *pl -men s* domokrążca *m*, akwizytor *m*; **door-to-door** '**sel•ling** *s* handel *m* bezpośredni, handel *m* obwoźny po domach; '**door•way** *s* otwór *m* drzwiowy; ***in the ~*** w drzwiach
dope [dəʊp] **I** *s* **1.** *infml* prochy *pl*, dragi *pl*; ***a ~ addict*** ćpun **2.** *Br infml* trawka *f* **3.** *Am infml* hera *f* **4.** środek *m* dopingujący **5.** *infml* palant *m* **6.** ***the ~, the inside ~*** *infml* informacje, info **II** *v/t* **1.** podawać ⟨-dać⟩ środek dopingujący **2.** podawać ⟨-dać⟩ środek odurzający, odurzać ⟨-rzyć⟩ **3.** dodawać ⟨-dać⟩ środek odurzający do *G*; '**dope test** *s* test *m* antydopingowy; **dop•ey** ['dəʊpɪ] *adj* **1.** *infml* głupkowaty **2.** półprzytomny, otumaniony
dork [dɔːk] *s infml* głąb *m*, tępak *m*
dorm [dɔːm] → ***dormitory***
dor•mer win•dow [dɔːmə'wɪndəʊ] *s* okno *n* mansardowe, lukarna *f*
dor•mi•to•ry ['dɔːmɪtərɪ] *s* **1.** sala *f* sypialna **2.** *Am* akademik *m* **3.** *fig* sypialnia *f*; '**dor•mi•to•ry sub•urb** *s* dzielnica-sypialnia *f*
dos•age ['dəʊsɪdʒ] *s* dawka *f*; **dose** [dəʊs] **I** *s* **1.** dawka *f* **2.** doza *f* **II** *v/t* **1.** dozować **2.** aplikować ⟨za-⟩
dot [dɒt] **I** *s* **1.** kropka *f*; ***at 5 on the ~*** punkt piąta **2.** MATH przecinek *m* **3.** punkt *m* **II** *v/t* **1.** stawiać ⟨postawić⟩ kropkę nad *I* **2.** kropkować ⟨wy-⟩
dot•age ['dəʊtɪdʒ] *s* zdziecinnienie *n*
dot.com (***com•pany***) [dɒt'kɒm('kʌmpənɪ)] *s* firma *f* internetowa, *infml* dotcom *m*
dote [dəʊt] *v/i* **1.** hołubić (***on*** *A*) **2.** mieć bzika (***on*** na punkcie *G*); **dot•ing** ['dəʊtɪŋ] *adj* **1.** kochający **2.** czuły
dot•ted line [dɒtɪdlaɪn] *s* linia *f* kropkowana; ***sign on the ~*** złożyć swój podpis
dot•ty ['dɒtɪ] *adj infml* zbzikowany
doub•le ['dʌbl] **I** *adj* **1.** podwójny; ***a ~ bottom*** podwójne dno; ***a ~ bend*** podwójny zakręt; ***a ~ density disk*** dyskietka o podwójnej gęstości zapisu; ***~ Dutch*** niezrozumiały szwargot, chińszczyzna; ***~ faced*** obłudny, nieszczery; ***a ~ life*** podwójne życie **2.** dwuosobowy **3.** dwuznaczny **II** *adv* podwójnie, dwukrotnie; ***~ as long*** dwa razy dłużej **III** *s* **1.** podwójna ilość *f*; ***at the ~, on the ~*** migiem, na jednej nodze **2.** dubler *m* **3.** sobowtór *m* **4.** **~s** SPORT debel *m* **IV** *v/t* **1.** podwajać ⟨-woić⟩ **2.** składać ⟨złożyć⟩ na pół **V** *v/i* **1.** podwajać ⟨-woić⟩ się **2.** składać ⟨złożyć⟩ się (wpół); **double back** *v/i* zawracać ⟨-rócić⟩; **double up** *v/i* **1.** zginać ⟨zgiąć⟩ się wpół **2.** ***~ on*** dzielić *A*; **doub•le up with** *v/t pain, laughter*: skręcać się z *G*
doub•le 'a•gent *s* podwójny agent *m*; **doub•le -bar•relled 'name** *s* nazwisko *n* dwuczłonowe; **doub•le-bar•relled 'shot•gun** *s* dubeltówka *f*, dwururka *f*; **doub•le 'bass I** *s* kontrabas *m* **II** *adj* kontrabasowy; **doub•le 'bed** *s* podwójne łóżko *n*; **doub•le-'book** *v/t* robić ⟨z-⟩ podwójną rezerwację na *A*; **doub•le-'breast•ed** *adj jacket*: dwurzędowy; **doub•le-'check** *v/t* **1.** ponownie sprawdzać ⟨-dzić⟩ **2.** dokładnie sprawdzać ⟨-dzić⟩; **doub•le 'chin** *s* podwójny podbródek *m*; **doub•le-'click I** *s* podwójne kliknięcie *n* **II** *v/i* klikać ⟨-knąć⟩ dwa razy; **double-'cross I** *s* podstęp *m* **II** *v/t* wystawiać ⟨-wić⟩ kogoś do wiatru; **doub•le-'deal•ing I** *s* dwulicowość *f* **II** *adj* dwulicowy; **doub•le-'deck•er** *s Br* autobus *m* piętrowy, *infml* piętrus *m*; **doub•le-'edged** *adj* obosieczny, dwusieczny; **doub•le en•try 'book-keep•ing** *s* podwójna księgowość *f*; **doub•le-'glaz•ing** *s* podwójne szyby *f*; **doub•le-'park** *v/i* parkować ⟨za-⟩ na drugiego; **doub•le-'quick I** *adj **in ~ time*** *infml* migiem, piorunem **II** *adv infml* w mig, piorunem; **doub•le 'room** *s* pokój *m* dwuosobowy

D

D

doub•le 'take *s* opóźniona reakcja *f*; ***do a ~*** zareagować z opóźnieniem; **doub•le 'time** *s* podwójna stawka *f*; **doub•le 'vi•sion** *s* podwójne widzenie *n*; ***have ~*** widzieć podwójnie

doubt [daʊt] **I** *v/i* wątpić **II** *v/t* **1.** wątpić w *A* **2.** mieć wątpliwości co do *G* **3.** nie wierzyć ⟨u-⟩ **III** *s* wątpliwość *f*; ***no ~*** bez wątpienia, niewątpliwie; ***be in ~*** mieć wątpliwości; ***cast ~ on s.th.*** podawać coś w wątpliwość; ***if in ~, when in ~*** w razie wątpliwości; ***leave no ~ about*** nie pozostawić najmniejszych wątpliwości co do *G*; **doubt•er** ['daʊtə] *s* niedowiarek *m*; **doubt•ful** ['daʊtfəl] *adj* **1.** niepewny; ***be ~ of*** mieć wątpliwości co do *G*, wahać się co do *G* **2.** wątpliwy; **doubt•ful•ly** ['daʊtfəlɪ] *adv* **1.** niepewnie, z wahaniem **2.** powątpiewająco **3.** nieprzekonująco; **doubt•less** ['daʊtlɪs] *adv* bez wątpienia, niewątpliwie

dough•nut [dəʊnʌt] *s* pączek *m*

dove[1] [dʌv] *s* **1.** gołąb *m*; ***a ~ of peace*** gołąbek pokoju **2.** gołębica *f*

dove[2] [dəʊv] *Past Simple* → ***dive***

down[1] [daʊn] **I** *adv* **1.** w dół, na dół; ***come ~*** zejść; ***go ~ by 10 degrees*** spaść o 10 stopni; ***~ with*** precz z *I*; ***he's ~ with the flu*** ma grypę **2.** ***go ~ to the country*** wyjechać na wieś **3.** ***they were 2 points ~*** przegrywali o 2 punkty; ***the price is ~*** cena spadła **II** *adj* **1.** na dół, w dół **2.** ***a ~ trend*** ECON tendencja spadkowa **3.** ***be ~*** nie działać **III** *prep* ***~ the river*** w dół rzeki **IV** *s* ***have a ~ on s.o.*** *Br infml* nie trawić kogoś **V** *v/t* **1.** wypijać ⟨-pić⟩ do dna **2.** powalać ⟨-lić⟩ na ziemię **3.** *plane*: zestrzeliwać ⟨-lić⟩ **4.** odkładać ⟨odłożyć⟩; ***~ tools*** *Br fig* rozpocząć strajk

down[2] [~] *s* **1.** puch *m*; ***a ~ quilt*** kołdra puchowa **2.** meszek *m*

down-and-'out **I** *adj* **1.** podupadły **2.** zaniedbany **II** *s* kloszard *m*; **down-at-'heel** *adj* **1.** nędzny **2.** obskórny **3.** zabiedzony; **'down•beat** *adj* **1.** struty, przygaszony **2.** minorowy; **'down•cast** *adj* **1.** przybity **2.** *eyes*: spuszczony

'down•fall *s* **1.** *fig* upadek *m* **2.** (intensywne) opady *pl*; **'down•grade** *v/t* **1.** degradować ⟨z-⟩ **2.** umniejszać ⟨-szyć⟩ **3.** dyskredytować ⟨z-⟩; **down•'heart•ed** *adj* przygnębiony; **down•'hill** **I** *adj* **1.** w dół **2.** z góry, z górki **3.** zjazdowy; ***a ~ race*** bieg zjazdowy **II** *adv* z góry, z górki; ***the rest was ~ (all the way)*** *infml* dalej było już z górki; ***go ~*** *fig* **a)** podupadać **b)** psuć się; **down•hill 'ski•ing** *s* narciarstwo *n* zjazdowe; **down•'load** *v/t* pobierać ⟨-brać⟩, *infml* ściągać ⟨-gnąć⟩; **down•'mark•et** *adj* **1.** niskiej jakości **2.** tani **3.** tandetny; **down 'pay•ment** *s* **1.** zaliczka *f* **2.** przedpłata *f*; **down•'play** *v/t* bagatelizować ⟨z-⟩; **'down•pour** *s* ulewa *f*; **'down•right** **I** *adj* **1.** jawny **2.** kategoryczny **3.** skończony **4.** wierutny **II** *adv* wręcz; **'down•side** *s* minus *m*, minusy *pl*; **'down•size** *v/i* redukować ⟨z-⟩ zatrudnienie; ***downsizing*** redukcja zatrudnienia

down•'stairs **I** *adv* **1.** na dole **2.** na dół **3.** piętro niżej **4.** na parterze **II** *adj* **1.** na dole **2.** piętro niżej **3.** na parterze **III** *s* **1.** parter *m* **2.** dół *m*; **down'stream** **I** *adj* **1.** w dół rzeki, z prądem **2.** w dole rzeki **II** *adv* z prądem, w dół rzeki; **'down•time** *s* **1.** przestój *m* **2.** czas *m* przestoju; **down-to-'earth** *adj* praktyczny; **down•'town** *s* **I** *adj shops*: w centrum; ***in ~ Los Angeles*** w centrum Los Angeles **II** *adv* w centrum, w mieście; **'down•trod•den** *adj* **1.** uciskany **2.** poniewierany; **'down•turn** *s* spadek *m*; ***a ~ in the economy*** spadek koniunktury; **down 'un•der** *s infml* **1.** Australia *f* **2.** Nowa Zelandia *f* **3.** antypody *pl*

down•ward ['daʊnwəd] *adj* **1.** w dół **2.** spadkowy **3.** pochyły

down•wards ['daʊnwədz] *adv* **1.** w dół; ***face ~*** twarzą w dół; ***inflation is moving ~*** inflacja spada

doze [dəʊz] **I** *s* drzemka *f* **II** *v/i* zdrzemnąć się, drzemać; **doze off** *v/i* przysypiać ⟨-snąć⟩, zasypiać ⟨-snąć⟩

doz•en ['dʌzn] *s* tuzin *m*; ***~s of times*** dziesiątki razy; ***talk nineteen to the ~*** gadać jak najęty

draft [drɑːft] **I** *s* **1.** szkic *m* **2.** brudnopis *m* **3.** projekt *m*; ***the final ~*** ostateczna wersja **4.** *Am* przeciąg *m* **5.** FIN polecenie *n* wypłaty **6.** FIN trata *f*, weksel *m* **7.** *Am army*: pobór *m* **8.** → ***draught*** **II** *v/t* **1.** szkicować

⟨na-⟩ **2.** pisać ⟨na-⟩ na brudno **3.** sporządzać ⟨-dzić⟩ projekt **4.** *Am* powoływać ⟨-łać⟩ (do wojska); **'draft dodg•er** *s Am* dekownik *m*; **draft•ee** [dræft'iː] *s Am* rekrut *m*

drafts•man ['dræftsmən] *Am* → ***draughtsman***

draft•y ['dræftɪ] *Am* → ***draughty***

drag [dræg] **I** *s* **1.** *infml* nuda *f*; ***be a ~*** być nudnym **2.** *infml* nudziarz *m* **3.** PHYS opór *m* **4.** przeszkoda *f* **5.** *infml* sztach *m*; ***give me a ~*** daj się sztachnąć **6.** kobiecy strój *m* **II** *v/t* **1.** ciągnąć, wlec; ***~ one's feet*** powłóczyć nogami; ***~ one's heels*** *fig* ociągać się **2.** wciągać ⟨-gnąć⟩ (***into*** do *G*) **III** *v/i* **1.** wlec się **2.** trzeć **3.** zaciągać ⟨-gnąć⟩ się (***at/on*** *I*); **drag along** *v/t* **1.** ciągnąć, wlec **2.** *fig* ciągnąć ⟨za-⟩, wlec ⟨za-⟩; **drag away** *v/t* **1.** odciągać ⟨-gnąć⟩ (***from*** z *G*) **2.** wyciągać ⟨-gnąć⟩ (***from*** z *G*); **drag in** *v/t* wspominać ⟨-mnieć⟩ o *L*; **drag on** *v/i* *fig* ciągnąć się; **drag out** *v/t* przeciągać ⟨-gnąć⟩; **drag up** *v/t* wyciągać ⟨-gnąć⟩, wywlekać ⟨-lec⟩ (na światło dzienne)

drag•on ['drægn] *s* smok *m*

'drag•on•fly *s* BIOL ważka *f*

'drag queen *s* **1.** drag queen *f* **2.** THEAT aktor *m* grający rolę kobiecą

drain [dreɪn] **I** *v/t* **1.** osuszać ⟨-szyć⟩ **2.** spuszczać ⟨spuścić⟩ wodę z *G* **3.** drenować **4.** opróżniać ⟨-nić⟩, wypijać ⟨-pić⟩ do dna **5.** wyczerpywać ⟨-pać⟩ **II** *v/i* **1.** wypływać ⟨-łynąć⟩, wyciekać ⟨-ciec⟩ **2.** obciekać ⟨-ciec⟩ **III** *s* **1.** rura *f* kanalizacyjna **2.** studzienka *f* (kanalizacyjna) **3.** kanał *m* **4.** ***~s*** kanalizacja *f* **5.** odpływ *m* **6.** MED dren *m*; **drain away** *v/i* **1.** spływać ⟨-łynąć⟩ **2.** wygasać ⟨-snąć⟩ **3.** wyczerpywać ⟨-pać⟩ się; **drain off I** *v/t* odlewać ⟨-lać⟩ **II** *v/i* spływać ⟨-łynąć⟩

drain•age ['dreɪnɪdʒ] *s* **1.** system *m* kanalizacyjny **2.** *soil*: drenaż *m* **3.** osuszanie *n*, drenowanie *n*; **'drain•ing board** *s* ociekacz *m*; **'drain•pipe** *s* **1.** rynna *f* **2.** rura *f* kanalizacyjna

dram [dræm] *s* kieliszek *f*; ***be fond of a ~*** lubić sobie wypić

dra•ma ['drɑːmə] *s* **1.** THEAT sztuka *f* **2.** dramat *m*; ***a ~ class*** zajęcia teatralne; **'dra•ma school** *s* szkoła *f* teatralna; **'dra•ma se•ries** *s* serial *m* telewizyjny; **dra•mat•ic** [drə'mætɪk] *adj* **1.** teatralny; ***a ~ critic*** krytyk teatralny **2.** dramatyczny **3.** → ***dramatics***; **dra•mat•i•cal•ly** [drə'mætɪklɪ] *adv* **1.** radykalnie, drastycznie **2.** THEAT dramatycznie; **dra•mat•ics** [drə'mætɪks] *pl* **1.** teatr *m* **2.** *fig* egzaltacja *f* **3.** *fig* przedstawienie *n*; **dram•a•tist** ['dræmətɪst] *s* dramaturg *m*, dramatopisarz *m*; **dram•a•ti•za•tion** [dræmətaɪ'zeɪʃn] *s* **1.** adaptacja *f* (sceniczna) **2.** ekranizacja *f*; **dram•a•tize** ['dræmətaɪz] *v/t* **1.** dokonywać ⟨-nać⟩ adaptacji scenicznej **2.** ekranizować ⟨z-⟩ **3.** *fig* dramatyzować ⟨u-⟩

drank [dræŋk] *Past Simple* → ***drink***

dras•tic ['dræstɪk] *adj* **1.** radykalny **2.** daleko idący **3.** drastyczny

drat [dræt] *interj*: ***~ (it)!*** *infml* a niech to!

draught [drɑːft] *Br*, ***draft*** *Am s* **1.** przeciąg *m* **2.** łyk *m*; ***at a ~*** jednym haustem **3.** ***beer on ~, ~ beer*** piwo z beczki **4.** ***~s*** *Br* warcaby **5.** *Br* pionek *m* (warcabowy); ***a ~ board*** plansza (do gry w warcaby); **'draughts•man** *pl -men s* **1.** pionek *m* (do gry) **2.** rysownik *m* **3.** kreślarz *m*; **draugh•ty** [drɑːftɪ] *adj* pełen przeciągów

draw [drɔː] **I** *s* **1.** losowanie *n* **2.** SPORT remis *m*; ***end in a ~*** zakończyć się remisem **3.** atrakcja *f* **4.** loteria *f* **5.** ***take a ~*** zaciągnąć się **II** (*drew*; *drawn*) *v/t* **1.** rysować ⟨na-⟩ **2.** szkicować ⟨na-⟩ **3.** ciągnąć ⟨po-⟩; ***~ s.o. into*** wciągnąć kogoś w *A* **4.** czerpać; ***~ inspiration from*** czerpać inspirację z *G* **5.** *attention*: przyciągać ⟨-gnąć⟩ **6.** *interest*: wzbudzać ⟨-dzić⟩; ***feel drawn to*** **a)** czuć pociąg do *G* **b)** być zainteresowanym *I* **7.** *cheque*: wystawiać ⟨-wić⟩ **8.** *money*: wypłacać ⟨-cić⟩, podejmować ⟨-djąć⟩ **9.** wyciągać ⟨-gnąć⟩ (***from*** od *G*) **III** (*drew*; *drawn*) *v/i* **1.** (*tea*) naciągać ⟨-gnąć⟩ **2.** rysować **3.** ***be ~ing near*** zbliżać się; ***be ~ing to a close*** zbliżać się do końca **4.** ciągnąć, ssać **5.** SPORT remisować ⟨z-⟩ **6.** ciągnąć losy; **draw apart** *v/i* oddzielać ⟨-lić⟩ się (***from*** od *G*); **draw aside** *v/t* **1.** rozsuwać ⟨-sunąć⟩ **2.** odsuwać ⟨-sunąć⟩; **draw**

D

D

away *v/i* **1.** oddalać ⟨-lić⟩ się **2.** odsuwać ⟨-sunąć⟩ się; **draw back** *v/i* odsuwać ⟨-sunąć⟩ się, cofać ⟨-fnąć⟩ się; **draw down** *v/t curtains*: opuszczać ⟨opuścić⟩; **draw in** *v/i* **1.** (*day, night*) stawać się (coraz) krótszym **2.** wciągać ⟨-gnąć⟩; **draw on** *v/i* **1.** (*date, anniversary*) nadchodzić ⟨-dejść⟩ **2.** upływać ⟨-łynąć⟩, mijać ⟨minąć⟩; **draw out I** *v/i* wydłużać ⟨-żyć⟩ się **II** *v/t* **1.** przeciągać ⟨-gnąć⟩ **2.** wyjmować ⟨-jąć⟩ **3.** *fig* rozruszać; **draw up I** *v/t* **1.** sporządzać ⟨-dzić⟩ **2.** przysuwać ⟨-sunąć⟩ **II** *v/i* **1.** zatrzymywać ⟨-mać⟩ się **2.** podjeżdżać ⟨-jechać⟩

'draw•back *s* wada *f*, minus *m*; **'draw•bridge** *s* most *m* zwodzony

draw•ing ['drɔːɪŋ] *s* **1.** rysunek *m* **2.** rysowanie *n*; ***a ~ block*** blok rysunkowy; **'draw•ing board** *s* deska *f* kreślarska; **'draw•ing pin** *s* pinezka *f*; **'draw•ing room** *s* salon *m*

drawn [drɔːn] **I** *Past Participle* → ***draw*** **II** *adj* **1.** remisowy; ***a ~ game*** remis **2.** wymizerowany

dread [dred] **I** *v/t* bać się, lękać się (***to do s.th.***/***doing s.th.*** zrobić coś) **II** *s* strach *m*, lęk *m*; **dread•ed** ['dredɪd] *adj* budzący postrach; **dread•ful** ['dredfəl] *adj* okropny, straszny; **dread•ful•ly** ['dredfəlɪ] *adv* okropnie, strasznie

dread•locks ['dredlɒks] *pl* dredy *pl*

dream [driːm] **I** *s* **1.** sen *m*; ***have a ~ about*** śnić o *L*; ***sweet ~s!*** kolorowych snów! **2.** marzenie *n*; ***that was beyond my wildest ~s*** to przeszło moje najśmielsze oczekiwania; ***a ~ of a hat*** *fig* kapelusz jak marzenie; ***an absolute ~*** ideał, spełnienie marzeń **II** *v/i* (*dreamt*/*dreamed*; *dreamt*/*dreamed*) **1.** śnić (***of***/***about*** o *L*) **2.** marzyć; ***~ of doing s.th.*** marzyć, żeby coś zrobić **III** *v/t* (*dreamt*/*dreamed*; *dreamt*/*dreamed*) śnić, mieć sny (***of***/***about*** o *L*); **dream away** *v/t* spędzać ⟨-dzić⟩ na marzeniach; **dream up** *v/t infml* **1.** wymyślać ⟨-lić⟩ **2.** wykombinować; **dream•er** ['driːmə] *s* marzyciel *m*; **dream•like** ['driːmlaɪk] *adj* **1.** jak ze snu **2.** oniryczny **3.** odrealniony

dreamt [dremt] *Past Simple and Past Participle* → ***dream***

dream•y ['driːmɪ] *adj* **1.** marzycielski **2.** rozmarzony **3.** jak ze snu **4.** kojący

drear•y ['drɪərɪ] *adj* **1.** ponury, posępny **2.** monotonny **3.** szary **4.** nudny

dregs [dregz] *pl* **1.** fusy *pl*; ***drain s.th. to the ~*** wypić coś do dna **2.** resztki *pl* **3.** *fig* męty *pl*, szumowiny *pl*

drench [drentʃ] *v/t* przemaczać ⟨-moczyć⟩

dress [dres] **I** *s* **1.** sukienka *f* **2.** ubranie *n* **3.** strój *m*; ***battle ~*** mundur polowy **II** *v/t* **1.** ubierać ⟨ubrać⟩; ***get ~ed*** ubrać się **2.** ozdabiać ⟨-dobić⟩, dekorować ⟨u-⟩ **3.** COOK przyprawiać ⟨-wić⟩ sosem **4.** *chicken*: oporządzać ⟨-dzić⟩ **5.** opatrywać ⟨-trzeć⟩ **III** *v/i* **1.** ubierać ⟨ubrać⟩ się **2.** przebierać ⟨ubrać⟩ się (**as** za *A*); **dress down I** *v/i* ubierać ⟨ubrać⟩ się mniej oficjalnie **II** *v/t* besztać ⟨z-⟩, *fig* zmyć głowę; **dress up** *v/i* **1.** stroić ⟨wy-⟩ się **2.** przebierać ⟨-brać⟩ się (**as** za *A*) **3.** ozdabiać ⟨-dobić⟩

'dress cir•cle *s* THEAT pierwszy balkon *m*

dress•ing ['dresɪŋ] *s* **1.** MED opatrunek *m* **2.** COOK sos *m* **3.** COOK nadzienie *n*, farsz *m*; **dress•ing-'down** *s* reprymenda *f*; ***give s.o. a ~*** zrugać kogoś; ***get a ~*** dostać burę; **'dress•ing gown** *s Br* szlafrok *m*; **'dress•ing room** *s* **1.** garderoba *f* **2.** *Br* szatnia *f* **3.** przebieralnia *f*; **'dress•ing ta•ble** *s* toaletka *f*

'dress•mak•er *s* **1.** krawiec *m* damski **2.** krawcowa *f* damska

'dress re•hears•al *s* próba *f* generalna

dress•y ['dresɪ] *adj* **1.** elegancki **2.** szykowny

drew [druː] *Past Simple* → ***draw***

dried [draɪd] *adj* **1.** suszony; ***~ fruit*** suszone owoce **2.** w proszku

dri•er [draɪə] *s* suszarka *f*

drift [drɪft] **I** *s* **1.** dryf *m* **2.** prąd *m* **3.** ruch *m*; ***the ~ towards the cities*** napływ ludności do miast **4.** tendencja *f* **5.** zaspa *f* **6.** ***catch s.o.'s ~*** rozumieć, o co komuś chodzi **II** *v/i* **1.** dryfować, płynąć z prądem **2.** *fig* dać się unosić prądowi; ***let things ~*** zostawić sprawy ich biegowi; **drift apart** *v/i* (*person*) oddalać ⟨-lić⟩ się od siebie, odsuwać ⟨-sunąć⟩ się; **drift•er** ['drɪftə] *s*: ***he***

was a ~ nigdzie nie mógł zagrzać miejsca

'drift ice *s* kra *f*, lód *m* dryfujący; **'drift net** *s* pławnica *f*, sieć *f* dryfująca; **'drift•wood** *s* **1.** dryfujące drewno *n* **2.** drewno *n* wyrzucone na brzeg

drill [drɪl] **I** *s* **1.** wiertarka *f* **2.** wiertło *n* **3.** musztra *f* **4.** dryl *m* **II** *v/t* **1.** wywiercać ⟨-cić⟩ **2.** przewiercać ⟨-cić⟩ **3.** musztrować **4.** ***~ s.th. into s.o.*** wbijać coś komuś do głowy

dri•ly ['draɪlɪ] *adv* **1.** sucho **2.** oschle

drink [drɪŋk] **I** *s* **1.** napój *m*; ***let's have a ~*** napijmy się czegoś **2.** drink *m* **3.** napój *m* alkoholowy; ***take to ~*** zacząć pić **4.** łyk *m* **II** (*drank*; *drunk*) *v/t* **1.** pić ⟨wy-⟩; ***~ and drive*** prowadzić po pijanemu; ***~ a toast to*** wznieść toast za *A*; ***~ down*** wypijać do dna; ***~ off*** dopijać **2.** napić się; **drink in** *v/t* wchłaniać ⟨-łonąć⟩; **drink up** *v/t* dopijać ⟨-pić⟩ do końca

drink•a•ble ['drɪŋkəbl] *adj* zdatny do picia

drink-'driv•er *s Br* nietrzeźwy kierowca *m*, pijany kierowca *m*; **drink 'driv•ing** *s Br* jazda *f* w stanie nietrzeźwym, jazda *f* po pijanemu

drink•er ['drɪŋkə] *s* **1.** pijak *m*; ***he's not much of a ~*** on niewiele pije **2.** pijący *m* **3.** (*bar*) klient *m*

drink•ing ['drɪŋkɪŋ] **I** *s* **1.** picie *n* **2.** picie *n* alkoholu **II** *adj* **1.** *song*: pijacki **2.** *straw*: do napojów; **'drink•ing wa•ter** *s* woda *f* pitna

drip [drɪp] **I** *v/i* **1.** kapać; ***the tap was ~ping*** z kranu kapała woda **2.** ściekać ⟨-ciec⟩, ciec **II** *v/t* **1.** wylewać ⟨-lać⟩ **2.** ociekać; ***he was ~ping sweat*** lał się z niego pot **III** *s* **1.** kropla *f* **2.** kapanie *n* **3.** MED kroplówka *f*; ***be on the ~*** mieć podłączoną kroplówkę, być pod kroplówką; **drip•'dry** *v/i* suszyć bez wyżymania; **drip•ping** ['drɪpɪŋ] **I** *s* tłuszcz *m* z pieczonego mięsa **II** *adj* cieknący, kapiący; ***~ wet*** przemoknięty

drive [draɪv] **I** *s* **1.** jazda *f*; ***an hour's ~ from here*** godzina drogi stąd **2.** przejażdżka *f*; ***go for a ~*** przejechać się **3.** droga *f* dojazdowa **4.** podjazd *m* **5.** dążenie *n*; ***in a ~ to improve quality*** w celu podwyższenia jakości **6.** próba *f* **7.** popęd *m* **8.** TECH INF napęd *m*; ***a disk ~*** stacja dysków **II** (*drove*; *driven*) *v/t* **1.** prowadzić, kierować **2.** wieźć ⟨za-⟩ **3.** napędzać **4.** wbijać ⟨-bić⟩; ***~ s.th. into s.o.*** *fig* wbijać coś komuś do głowy **5.** powodować ⟨s-⟩; ***driven by hunger*** powodowany głodem **6.** doprowadzać ⟨-dzić⟩; ***~ s.o. insane*** doprowadzać kogoś do szału **7.** powozić **III** (*drove*; *driven*) *v/i* **1.** prowadzić ⟨po-⟩ samochód, jechać ⟨po-⟩ samochodem; ***~ into a wall*** wjechać na mur **2.** (*rain*) zacinać; **drive at** *v/i*: ***what are you driving at?*** do czego zmierzasz?; **drive away I** *v/i* odjeżdżać ⟨-jechać⟩ **II** *v/t* **1.** odpędzać ⟨-dzić⟩ **2.** odstraszać ⟨-szyć⟩; **drive back I** *v/i* przyjeżdżać ⟨-jechać⟩ z powrotem **II** *v/t* **1.** przywozić ⟨-wieźć⟩ z powrotem **2.** odpierać ⟨odeprzeć⟩ **3.** przyganiać ⟨-gonić⟩ z powrotem; **drive off** *v/i* **1.** odjeżdżać ⟨-jechać⟩ **2.** ruszać ⟨-szyć⟩; **drive out I** *v/i* wyjeżdżać ⟨-jechać⟩ (**of** z *G*) **II** *v/t* **1.** odpędzać ⟨-dzić⟩ **2.** wypędzać ⟨-dzić⟩

'drive-in I *s* **1.** kino *n* samochodowe **2.** restauracja *f* drive-in **II** *adj* dla zmotoryzowanych

driv•en [drɪvn] *Past Participle* → **drive**

driv•er ['draɪvə] *s* **1.** kierowca *m*; ***a ~'s cab*** kabina kierowcy **2.** maszynista *m* **3.** motorniczy *m* **4.** INF sterownik *m*; **'driv•er's li•cense** *s Am* prawo *n* jazdy

drive•thru ['draɪvθruː] *s Am* **1.** sklep *m* dla zmotoryzowanych **2.** restauracja *f* dla zmotoryzowanych

'drive•way *s* podjazd *m*

driv•ing ['draɪvɪŋ] **I** *s* **1.** jazda *f* **2.** prowadzenie *n* (samochodu) **II** *adj* **1.** napędowy **2.** *lessons*: jazdy; ***take ~ lessons*** brać lekcje jazdy; **driv•ing 'force** *s fig* siła *f* napędowa, motor *m*; **'driv•ing in•struct•or** *s* instruktor *m* nauki jazdy; **'driv•ing les•son** *s* lekcja *f* jazdy; **'driv•ing li•cence** *s Br* prawo *n* jazdy; **'driv•ing school** *s* szkoła *f* jazdy; **'driv•ing test** *s* egzamin *m* na prawo jazdy

driz•zle ['drɪzl] **I** *s* mżawka *f* **II** *v/i* mżyć **III** *v/t* kropić ⟨po-, s-⟩

droll [drəʊl] *adj dated* zabawny, śmieszny

D

D

drool [druːl] *v/i* **1.** ślinić ⟨za-⟩ się **2.** *~ over infml* pożerać wzrokiem

droop [druːp] *v/i* **1.** opadać ⟨opaść⟩ **2.** słabnąć ⟨o-⟩ **3.** więdnąć ⟨z-⟩

drop [drɒp] **I** *s* **1.** kropla *f*; ***a ~ in the ocean*** kropla w morzu; ***empty s.th. to the last ~*** wypić coś do ostatniej kropli; ***he has had a ~ too much*** wypił o jednego za dużo **2.** drażetka *f*, drops *m*; ***a fruit ~*** drażetka owocowa **3.** spadek *m*, obniżenie *n*; ***a ~ in prices*** spadek cen; ***a ~ in temperature*** spadek temperatury **4.** wysokość *f* **5.** zrzut *m* **II** *v/i* **1.** kapać **2.** spadać ⟨spaść⟩; ***let s.th. ~*** upuścić coś **3.** opadać ⟨opaść⟩; ***~ into a chair*** opaść na krzesło **4.** (*prices*) spadać ⟨spaść⟩ **5.** upadać ⟨upaść⟩; ***be fit to ~*** (***with fatigue***) padać ze zmęczenia; ***~ dead*** nagle umrzeć, paść martwym; ***~ dead!*** *infml* idź do diabła! **6.** przycichać ⟨-chnąć⟩, uspokajać ⟨-koić⟩ się **III** *v/t* **1.** upuszczać ⟨upuścić⟩ **2.** rzucać ⟨-cić⟩; ***~ everything*** rzucić wszystko **3.** *bombs*: zrzucać ⟨-cić⟩ **4.** ***~ s.o. a line*** napisać do kogoś **5.** opuszczać ⟨opuścić⟩, pomijać ⟨-minąć⟩ **6.** zarzucać ⟨-cić⟩; ***~ it!*** daj temu spokój! **7.** *passengers*: wysadzać ⟨-dzić⟩ **8.** *goods*: wyładowywać ⟨-dować⟩ **9.** *point*: tracić ⟨s-⟩, oddawać ⟨-dać⟩ **10.** ***his voice ~ped to a whisper*** zniżył głos do szeptu; **drop away** *v/i* (*interest*) spadać ⟨spaść⟩, zmniejszać ⟨-szyć⟩ się; **drop back** *v/i* zostawać ⟨-tać⟩ w tyle; **drop behind** *v/i* zostawać ⟨-tać⟩ w tyle; **drop in** *v/i* (*visit*) zachodzić ⟨zajść⟩, wpadać ⟨wpaść⟩; **drop off** *v/i* **1.** odpadać ⟨-paść⟩ **2.** opadać ⟨opaść⟩ **3.** *Br infml* zasypiać ⟨-snąć⟩, przysypiać ⟨-snąć⟩ **4.** zmniejszać ⟨-szyć⟩ się, spadać ⟨spaść⟩; **drop out** *v/i* **1.** rezygnować ⟨z-⟩ (***of*** z *G*) **2.** rzucać ⟨-cić⟩ (***of*** *A*) **3.** wycofywać ⟨-fać⟩ się (***of*** z *G*)

drop•let [ˈdrɒplɪt] *s* kropelka *f*

ˈ**drop•out** *s* **1.** ***she's a college ~*** rzuciła studia, nie skończyła studiów **2.** wyrzutek *m*

drop•per [ˈdrɒpə] *s* **1.** kroplomierz *m* **2.** zakraplacz *m*

drop•pings [ˈdrɒpɪŋz] *pl* bobki *pl*, odchody *pl*

drops [drɒps] *pl* MED krople *pl* (do oczu)

drought [draʊt] *s* susza *f*

drove[1] [drəʊv] *Past Simple* → **drive**

drove[2] [~] *s* **1.** stado *n* **2.** tłum *m*; ***in ~s*** tłumnie

drown [draʊn] **I** *v/i* tonąć ⟨u-⟩, topić ⟨u-⟩ się **II** *v/t* **1.** topić ⟨u-⟩; ***be ~ed*** utonąć; ***~ one's sorrows*** *infml* zalewać robaka, topić smutki w alkoholu **2.** zalewać ⟨-lać⟩; ***be ~ed in tears*** zalewać się łzami; **drown out** *v/t* zagłuszać ⟨-szyć⟩

drowse [draʊz] **I** *v/i* drzemać; ***~ off*** przysnąć **II** *v/t* usypiać ⟨uśpić⟩ **III** *s* drzemka *f*; **drow•sy** [ˈdraʊzɪ] *adj* senny, śpiący

drudge [drʌdʒ] **I** *s fig* wół *m* roboczy **II** *v/i infml* harować, tyrać; **drudg•e•ry** [ˈdrʌdʒərɪ] *s* mozół *m*, harówka *f*

drug [drʌg] **I** *s* **1.** lek *m*, lekarstwo *n*; ***be on ~s*** brać leki **2.** narkotyk *m*; ***do ~s*** *infml* ćpać **3.** środek *m* usypiający **II** *v/t* **1.** podawać ⟨-dać⟩ środki usypiające **2.** podawać ⟨-dać⟩ środki dopingujące **3.** dosypywać ⟨-pać⟩ środków usypiających do *G* **4.** usypiać ⟨uśpić⟩; ˈ**drug a•buse** *s* **1.** narkomania *f* **2.** lekomania *f*; ˈ**drug ad•dict** *s* narkoman *m*, osoba *f* uzależniona od narkotyków; ˈ**drug ad•dic•tion** *s* narkomania *f*, uzależnienie *n* od narkotyków; ˈ**drug clin•ic** *s* klinika *f* odwykowa; ˈ**drug deal•er** *s* diler *m* narkotykowy; ˈ**drug de•pend•ency** *s* uzależnienie *n* od narkotyków

drug•gist [ˈdrʌgɪst] *s Am* aptekarz *m*

ˈ**drug•push•er** *s* diler *m* narkotykowy; ˈ**drug scene** *s* świat *m* narkotyków; ˈ**drug squad** *s Br* wydział *m* do spraw narkotyków

ˈ**drug•store** *s Am* **1.** drogeria *f* **2.** apteka *f*

ˈ**drug test** *s* SPORT test *m* antydopingowy, kontrola *f* antydopingowa; ˈ**drug traf•fick•ing** *s* handel *m* narkotykami

drum [drʌm] **I** *s* **1.** bęben *m*; ***~s*** perkusja **2.** ANAT bębenek *m* **3.** beczka *f* **II** *v/t* bębnić; ***~ one's fingers*** bębnić palcami **III** *v/i* **1.** grać na bębnie **2.** (*rain*) bębnić; **drum into** *v/t*: ***drum s.th. into s.o.*** wbijać coś komuś do głowy; **drum up** *v/t* **1.** *business*: nakręcać ⟨-cić⟩ **2.** *support*: uzyskiwać

⟨-kać⟩; '**drum•beat** *s MUS* rytm *m* wybijany na perkusji; '**drum•kit** *s MUS* zestaw *m* perkusyjny, perkusja *f*; **drum•mer** ['drʌmə] *s* **1.** dobosz *m* **2.** perkusista *m*

drunk [drʌŋk] **I** *Past Participle* → ***drink*** **II** *adj* pijany; ***get ~*** upić się; **(*as*)** ***~ as a lord*** *Br,* **(*as*)** ***~ as a skunk*** *Am* pijany jak bela; ***~ with joy*** *fig* pijany ze szczęścia **III** *s* pijak *m*

drunk•ard ['drʌŋkəd] *s* pijak *m*

drunk-'driv•ing *s* jazda *f* w stanie nietrzeźwym, jazda *f* po pijanemu

drunk•en [drʌŋkn] *adj* **1.** pijany **2.** pijacki; ***a ~ party*** popijawa; ***~ driving*** jazda w stanie nietrzeźwym, jazda po pijanemu; **drunk•en•ness** ['drʌŋkənnɪs] *s* nietrzeźwość *f*

dry [draɪ] **I** *adj* **1.** *a. fig* suchy; **(*as*) *dry as a bone*** suchy jak pieprz **2.** wyschnięty; ***rub s.th. ~*** wytrzeć coś do sucha **3.** *infml* spragniony **4.** bezdeszczowy **5.** nudny, nieciekawy **6.** *wine*: wytrawny **7.** bezalkoholowy; ***a ~ bar*** bar, w którym nie podaje się alkoholu **II** *v/t* **1.** suszyć ⟨wy-⟩ **2.** wycierać ⟨wytrzeć⟩ (do sucha); ***~ one's hands*** wytrzeć ręce **III** *v/i* **1.** suszyć ⟨wy-⟩ się, schnąć ⟨wy-⟩ **2.** zapominać ⟨-mnieć⟩ tekstu; **dry off** *v/i* wysychać ⟨-schnąć⟩; **dry out** *v/i* **1.** wysychać ⟨-schnąć⟩ **2.** *infml* być na odwyku; **dry up** *v/i* **1.** wysychać ⟨-schnąć⟩ **2.** wycierać ⟨wytrzeć⟩ **3.** zaniemówić

dry 'cell *s* ogniwo *n* suche; **dry•'clean** *v/t* prać ⟨wy-⟩ chemicznie, prać ⟨wy-⟩ na sucho; **dry 'clean•er's** *s* pralnia *f* chemiczna; **dry•'clean•ing** *s* pranie *n* chemiczne, pranie *n* na sucho; '**dry dock** *s* suchy dok *m*

dry•er [draɪə] → ***drier***

du•al ['du:əl] *adj* **1.** podwójny; ***~ citizenship*** podwójne obywatelstwo **2.** dwoisty; **du•al 'car•riage•way** *s Br* droga *f* dwujezdniowa

du•bi•ous ['dju:bɪəs] *adj* **1.** powątpiewający; ***be ~ about*** mieć wątpliwości co do *G* **2.** wątpliwy; ***~ pleasure*** wątpliwa przyjemność **3.** dyskusyjny **4.** niepewny

duch•ess ['dʌtʃɪs] *s* księżna; **duch•y** ['dʌtʃɪ] *s* księstwo *n*

duck [dʌk] **I** *s* **1.** kaczka *f* **2.** *Br infml* złotko *n*, skarb *m* **II** *v/i* robić ⟨z-⟩ unik **III** *v/t* uchylać ⟨-lić⟩ się przed *I*; **duck out** *v/i* wymykać ⟨-mknąć⟩ się

duck•ling ['dʌklɪŋ] *s* kaczątko *n*

duct [dʌkt] *s* **1.** *TECH* kanał *m* **2.** *ANAT* przewód *m*; ***tear ~s*** kanaliki łzowe

dude [dju:d] *s Am infml* gość *m*, facet *m*

due [dju:] **I** *adj* **1.** ***~ to*** **a)** z powodu *G* **b)** dzięki *D*; ***it is ~ to him*** to dzięki niemu **2.** planowy; ***the train is ~ to leave at 8 p.m.*** pociąg odjeżdża o godz. 20.00; ***her new book is ~ out in May*** jej nowa książka ma się ukazać w maju; ***he is ~ to start work next week*** zacznie pracę w przyszłym tygodniu; ***the payment becomes ~ on*** termin zapłaty upływa w dniu **3.** należny; ***be ~ to s.o.*** należeć się komuś; ***I'm ~ 30-day's leave*** mam prawo do 30-dniowego urlopu **4.** należyty, właściwy; ***when ~*** w odpowiednim terminie; ***in ~ course, in ~ time*** we właściwym czasie **II** *s* należność *f*; ***give them their ~*** oddaj im, co im się należy; **due 'date** *s* **1.** termin *m* płatności **2.** termin *m* zwrotu

du•el ['dju:əl] **I** *v/i* pojedynkować się **II** *s* pojedynek *m*

dues [dju:z] *pl* składka *f* (członkowska)

dug [dʌg] *Past Simple and Past Participle* → ***dig***

'**dug•out** *s* **1.** ziemianka *f* **2.** ławka *f* rezerwowych **3.** dłubanka *f*, czółno *n*

duke [dju:k] *s* **1.** książę *m* **2.** diuk *m*

dull [dʌl] **I** *adj* **1.** nudny **2.** bezbarwny, mdły **3.** matowy **4.** przyćmiony **5.** zmętniały **6.** pochmurny **7.** *ECON* w zastoju **8.** *infml* tępy **9.** *sound*: głuchy **10.** *blade*: tępy **II** *v/t* **1.** tępić ⟨s-⟩ **2.** matowić ⟨z-⟩ **3.** *pain*: uśmierzać ⟨-rzyć⟩ **4.** przytępiać ⟨-pić⟩, osłabiać ⟨-bić⟩

dullard ['dʌləd] *s infml* tępak *m*

dull•ness ['dʌlnɪs] *s* **1.** nuda *f* **2.** szarzyzna *f*, szarość *f* **3.** *infml* tępota *f* **4.** *ECON* zastój *m*

du•ly ['dju:lɪ] *adv* **1.** należycie, odpowiednio **2.** zgodnie z planem **3.** punktualnie

dumb [dʌm] *adj* **1.** niemy; ***a ~ show*** pantomima **2.** oniemiały; ***struck ~*** oniemiały **3.** *Am infml* tępy; **dumb down** *v/t* upraszczać ⟨-rościć⟩

D

dumbfound [dʌm'faʊnd] *v/t* wprawiać ⟨-wić⟩ w osłupienie; **dumb•found•ed** [dʌm'faʊndɪd] *adj* oniemiały

dumb 'wait•er *s* winda *f* kuchenna

dum•my ['dʌmɪ] **I** *s* **1.** manekin *m* **2.** atrapa *f* **3.** *Am infml* głąb *m*, młotek *m* **4.** *Br* smoczek *m* **II** *adj* **1.** ***a ~ bomb*** (***weapon***) atrapa bomby (broni) **2.** fikcyjny

dump [dʌmp] **I** *v/t* **1.** wyrzucać ⟨-cić⟩ **2.** porzucać ⟨-cić⟩ **3.** pozbywać ⟨-być⟩ się **4.** rzucać ⟨-cić⟩; ***he ~ed her*** rzucił ją **5.** sprzedawać ⟨-dać⟩ po cenach dumpingowych **II** *s* **1.** wysypisko *n* **2.** *infml* nora *f*, śmietnik *m*; **dump on** *v/i Am infml* przypieprzać ⟨-rzyć⟩ się do *G*

dump•ing ['dʌmpɪŋ] *s* **1.** wyrzucanie *n* **2.** ECON dumping *m*; **'dump•ing ground** *s* wysypisko *n*; **'dump•ing price** *s* cena *f* dumpingowa

dump•ling ['dʌmplɪŋ] *s* **1.** kluska *f* **2.** knedel *m* **3.** pierożek *m* **4.** *infml* klucha *f*, pulpet *m*

dumps [dʌmps] *pl*: ***down in the ~*** *infml* przybity

dunce [dʌns] *s dated infml* matoł *m*

dune [djuːn] *s* wydma *f*; **'dune bug•gy** *s Am* lekki samochód *m* terenowy (do jazdy po piasku)

dung [dʌŋ] *s* **1.** łajno *n* **2.** obornik *m*, gnój *m* **3.** *fig infml* gówno *n*

dun•geon ['dʌndʒən] *s* loch *m*

dunk [dʌŋk] *v/t* **1.** moczyć ⟨za-⟩ **2.** zanurzać ⟨-rzyć⟩

dun•no ['dʌnəʊ] *infml* → ***don't know***

du•pli•cate **I** ['djuːplɪkət] *s* **1.** kopia *f*, duplikat *m* **2.** powtórka *f* **II** ['djuːplɪkeɪt] *v/t* **1.** sporządzać ⟨-dzić⟩ kopię, sporządzać ⟨-dzić⟩ odpis **2.** ponownie wykonywać ⟨-nać⟩, powtarzać ⟨-tórzyć⟩ **III** ['djuːplɪkət] *adj* z kopią, w dwóch egzemplarzach; **duplicate 'key** *s* **1.** zapasowy klucz *m* **2.** duplikat *m* klucza; **duplicator** ['djuːplɪkeɪtə] *s* powielacz *m*

du•ra•bil•i•ty [djʊərə'bɪlətɪ] *s* **1.** trwałość *f* **2.** wytrzymałość *f*, **du•ra•ble** ['djʊərəbl] **I** *adj* **1.** trwały **2.** wytrzymały **II** *s* **~s** artykuły trwałego użytku

du•ra•tion [djʊ'reɪʃn] *s* czas *m* trwania, okres *m*; ***of three years' ~*** trzyletni; ***for the ~ of*** na czas trwania *G*, na okres *G*

du•ress [djʊ'res] *s* przymus *m*

dur•ing ['djʊrɪŋ] *prep* podczas *G*; ***~ the night*** w nocy; ***~ the 1960s*** w latach sześćdziesiątych; ***~ my stay in Paris*** gdy byłam w Paryżu

dusk [dʌsk] *s* zmierzch *m*, zmrok *m*; ***at ~*** o zmroku; **dusky** ['dʌskɪ] *adj* **1.** ciemny **2.** przyćmiony **3.** stonowany **4.** śniady, smagły

dust [dʌst] **I** *s* **1.** kurz *m*; ***the ~ has settled*** *fig* sytuacja się uspokoiła; ***a ~ cart*** *Br* śmieciarka **2.** pył *m* **II** *v/t* **1.** odkurzać ⟨-rzyć⟩ **2.** posypywać ⟨-pać⟩ **III** *v/i* ścierać ⟨zetrzeć⟩ kurze; **'dust•bin** *s Br* pojemnik *m* na śmieci; **'dust cov•er** *s* obwoluta *f*

dust•y ['dʌstɪ] *adj* zakurzony

Dutch [dʌtʃ] **I** *adj* holenderski **II** *adv* ***go ~*** płacić każdy za siebie **III** *s* **1.** (*language*) holenderski *m* **2.** ***the ~*** Holendrzy; **Dutch 'cour•age** *s* pijacka odwaga *f*; **'Dutch•man** *pl -men s* Holender *m*; ***the Flying ~*** Latający Holender; **'Dutch•wom•an** *pl -men s* Holenderka *f*

du•ti•ful ['djuːtɪfʊl] *adj* **1.** posłuszny **2.** obowiązkowy, sumienny

du•ty ['djuːtɪ] *s* **I** *s* **1.** obowiązek *m*; ***do one's ~*** wykonywać swój obowiązek; ***a breach of ~*** niedopełnienie obowiązku **2.** służba *f*; ***be on ~*** **a)** być na służbie **b)** mieć dyżur; ***be off ~*** **a)** nie być na służbie **b)** nie mieć dyżuru; ***do one's ~ for*** pełnić służbę dla *G*, służyć dla *G* **3.** ECON cło *n* **II** *adj* **1.** pełniący służbę **2.** dyżurny; **du•ty-'free** **I** *adj* wolnocłowy, bezcłowy **II** *adv* bez cła; **du•ty-'free shop** *s* sklep *m* wolnocłowy

'du•ty of•fi•cer *s* oficer *m* dyżurny; **'du•ty ros•ter** *s* grafik *m* dyżurów

du•vet ['duːveɪ] *s Br* kołdra *f*

DVD [diːviː'diː] *abbr* (=***Digital Video Disc***, ***Digital Versatile Disc***) **1.** DVD *n* **2.** płyta *f* DVD

dwarf [dwɔːf] **I** *s* karzeł *m* **II** *adj* karłowaty, skarłowaciały **III** *v/t* przyćmiewać ⟨-mić⟩; **dwarf•ish** [dwɔːfɪʃ] *adj* karzełkowaty

dwarves [dwɔːvz] *pl* → ***dwarf***

dwell [dwel] *v/i* (*dwelt*/*dwelled*; *dwelt*/*dwelled*) mieszkać, zamieszkiwać; **dwell on** *v/i* **1.** rozpamiętywać **2.** rozwodzić się nad *I*

dwell•er ['dwelə] *s* mieszkaniec *m*; **dwell•ing** ['dwelɪŋ] *s* **1.** mieszkanie *n* **2.** dom *m* (mieszkalny)
dwelt [dwelt] *Past Simple and Past Participle* → **dwell**
dye [daɪ] **I** *v/t* farbować ⟨u-⟩ **II** *s* **1.** farba *f* **2.** barwnik *m*; '**dyeworks** *s* farbiarnia *f*; **dyed-in-the-'wool** *adj* zatwardziały
dy•ing ['daɪɪŋ] *adj* umierający; ***be ~*** umierać, być umierającym; ***a ~ wish*** ostatnie życzenie; ***a ~ hour*** godzina śmierci
dyke → ***dike***
dy•nam•ic [daɪ'næmɪk] *adj* **1.** dynamiczny **2.** żywy; **dy•na•mics** [daɪ'næmɪks] *s* **~s** dynamika *f*; **dy•na•mism** ['daɪnəmɪzm] *s* dynamizm *m*
dy•na•mite ['daɪnəmaɪt] **I** *s* dynamit *m* **II** *v/t* wysadzać ⟨-dzić⟩ w powietrze
dy•nas•ty ['dɪnəstɪ] *s* dynastia *f*
dys•func•tional [dɪs'fʌŋkʃnl] *adj family*: patologiczny
dys•lex•i•a [dɪs'leksɪə] *s* dysleksja *f*; **dys•lex•ic** [dɪs'leksɪk] **I** *s* dyslektyk *m* **II** *adj* dyslektyczny

E

each [iːtʃ] **I** *adj* każdy; ***~ one*** każdy; ***~ month*** co miesiąc **II** *pron* ***~ of us*** każdy z nas; ***know ~ other*** znać się; ***look at ~ other*** patrzeć na siebie; ***give ~ other a gift*** wręczyć sobie po prezencie **III** *adv* każdy; ***we got two cakes ~*** dostaliśmy po dwa ciastka, każdy z nas dostał dwa ciastka
ea•ger ['iːgə] *adj* **1.** ochoczy **2.** spragniony, żądny; ***she's ~ to start the new job*** nie może się doczekać, kiedy zacznie nową pracę **3.** przejęty, podekscytowany; **ea•ger 'bea•ver** *s infml* gorliwiec *m*; **ea•ger•ly** ['iːgəlɪ] *adv* **1.** z zapałem, gorliwie **2.** niecierpliwie; **ea•ger•ness** ['iːgənɪs] *s* **1.** zapał *m*, ochota *f* **2.** przejęcie *n*, podniecenie *n*
ea•gle ['iːgl] *s* orzeł *m*; **ea•gle-'eyed** *adj* o sokolim wzroku
ear[1] [ɪə] *s* **1.** ucho *n*; ***be all ~s*** zamienić się w słuch; ***be up to one's ~s in debt*** siedzieć po uszy w długach; ***keep one's ~ to the ground***, ***keep one's ~s open*** trzymać rękę na pulsie; ***turn a deaf ~ to s.th.*** puszczać coś mimo uszu **2.** *fig* ucho *n*, słuch *m*; ***play s.th. by ~*** grać coś ze słuchu; ***play it by ~*** improwizować
ear[2] [~] *s* **1.** kłos *m* **2.** kolba *f*
'**ear•ache** *s* ból *m* ucha; ***I've got an ~***, ***I have an ~*** boli mnie ucho; '**eardrum** *s* błona *f* bębenkowa; '**earlobe** *s* płatek *m* ucha
earl ['ɜːl] *s Br* hrabia *m*
ear•ly ['ɜːlɪ] **I** *adv* **1.** wcześnie; ***as ~ as possible*** jak najszybciej; ***as ~ as May*** już w maju **2.** zbyt wcześnie, przed czasem; ***be ~*** być przed czasem, przyjść przed czasem **II** *adj* **1.** wczesny; ***~ riser*** ranny ptaszek; ***the ~ bird catches the worm*** kto rano wstaje, temu Pan Bóg daje; ***Thursday is ~ closing*** w czwartki zamykają wcześniej sklepy; ***at an ~ hour*** wcześnie; ***at the earliest*** najwcześniej **2.** przedwczesny; ***his ~ death*** jego przedwczesna śmierć **3.** wczesny, pierwszy; ***~ Christian*** wczesnochrześcijański; '**ear•ly bird** *s* ranny ptaszek *m*; **ear•ly re•'tire•ment** *s* wcześniejsza emerytura *f*; **ear•ly 'warn•ing sys•tem** *s* system *m* wczesnego ostrzegania
ear•mark ['ɪəmɑːk] *v/t* **1.** *money*: przeznaczać ⟨-czyć⟩ (**for** na *A*) **2.** znakować ⟨o-⟩, znaczyć ⟨o-⟩
'**ear•muff** *s* nausznik *m*
earn [ɜːn] *v/t* **1.** zarabiać ⟨-robić⟩ **2.** przynosić ⟨-nieść⟩ zysk **3.** *fig* zdobywać ⟨-być⟩
ear•nest ['ɜnɪst] **I** *adj* **1.** poważny **2.** szczery **3.** sumienny, rzetelny **II** *s* ***in ~*** na poważnie; ***are you in ~?*** mówisz poważnie?; ***I'm in ~*** nie żartuję, mówię poważnie; **ear•nest•ness** ['ɜnɪstnɪs] *s* **1.** powaga *f* **2.** szczerość *f* **3.** rzetelność *f*, sumienność *f*
earn•ings ['ɜːnɪŋz] *pl* zarobki *pl*, dochody *pl*
'**ear•phones** *pl* słuchawki *pl*; '**earpiece** *s* słuchawka *f*; '**ear-pierc•ing**

I *s* przekłuwanie *n* uszu **II** *adj* przeraźliwy, rozdzierający; **'ear•plug** *s* zatyczka *f* do uszu; **'ear•ring** *s* **1.** kolczyk *m* **2.** klips *m*; **'ear•shot** *s*: ***within ~*** **a)** w zasięgu głosu **b)** w zasięgu słuchu; ***out of ~*** **a)** poza zasięgiem głosu **b)** poza zasięgiem słuchu; **'ear•splitting** *adj dźwięk*: przeraźliwy, ogłuszający

E

earth [ɜːθ] **I** *s* **1.** ***the*** **≈** Ziemia *f* **2.** ziemia *f*; ***on ~*** na ziemi; ***what on ~?*** co u licha?; ***come back to ~, come down to ~*** *fig* zejść na ziemię **3.** nora *f*, jama *f* **4.** TECH uziemienie *n*; ***~ cable*** kabel uziemiający **II** *v/t* uziemiać ⟨-mić⟩; **earth•en** [ɜːθən] *adj* ziemny; **earth•en•ware** ['ɜːθənweə] *s* wyroby *pl* ceramiczne, ceramika *f*

earth•ly ['ɜːθlɪ] *adj* ziemski; ***there's no ~ reason*** nie ma najmniejszego powodu

earth•quake ['ɜːθkweɪk] *s* trzęsienie *n* ziemi; **'earth•quake-proof** *adj* odporny na wstrząsy tektoniczne

'earth sci•en•ces *pl* nauki *pl* o Ziemi; **'earth-shat•ter•ing** *adj* epokowy; **'earth trem•or** *s* wstrząs *m*, (słabe) trzęsienie *n* ziemi; **'earth•worm** *s* dżdżownica *f*

earth•y ['ɜːθɪ] *adj* **1.** dosadny **2.** ziemisty

ease [iːz] **I** *s* **1.** łatwość *f*; ***with ~*** z łatwością **2.** ***~ of mind*** spokój, opanowanie; ***at (one's) ~*** spokojny, odprężony; ***be at ~, feel at ~*** czuć się swobodnie; ***feel ill at ~*** czuć się nieswojo, być skrępowanym **3.** wygoda *f*; ***live a life of ~*** wieść beztroskie życie; ***at ~!*** spocznij! **II** *v/t* **1.** ułatwiać ⟨-wić⟩ **2.** uspokajać ⟨-koić⟩; ***~ s.o. mind*** uspokajać kogoś **3.** *pain*: łagodzić ⟨z-⟩ **III** *v/i* **1.** ustępować ⟨-tąpić⟩ **2.** zelżeć **3.** słabnąć ⟨o-⟩; **ease off** *v/i* **1.** zmniejszać ⟨-szyć⟩ się **2.** zelżeć **3.** ustępować ⟨-tąpić⟩

ea•sel ['iːzl] *s* sztaluga *f*

eas•i•ly ['iːzɪlɪ] *adv* **1.** łatwo, bez trudu **2.** swobodnie **3.** spokojnie **4.** niewątpliwie, z pewnością

east [iːst] **I** *s* **1.** wschód *m*; ***in the ~*** na wschodzie (***of*** *G*); ***to the ~ of*** na wschód od *G* **2.** ***the*** **≈** Wschód *m* **II** *adj* wschodni **III** *adv* na wschód; **'east•bound** *adj* **1.** prowadzący na wschód **2.** w kierunku wschodnim **3.** jadący na wschód

Eas•ter ['iːstə] **I** *s* Wielkanoc *f*; ***at ~*** na Wielkanoc; ***happy ~!*** Wesołego Alleluja!, Wesołych Świąt Wielkanocnych! **II** *adj* wielkanocny; **Eas•ter 'Day** *s* niedziela *f* wielkanocna; **'Eas•ter egg** *s* **1.** pisanka *f* **2.** kraszanka *f*; **Eas•ter 'Mon•day** *s* poniedziałek *m* wielkanocny; **Eas•ter 'Sun•day** *s* niedziela *f* wielkanocna

eas•ter•ly ['iːstəlɪ] *adj* **1.** wschodni **2.** ze wschodu

east•ern ['iːstən] *adj* wschodni; **east•er•ner** ['iːstənə] *s* mieszkaniec *m* wschodniego wybrzeża USA; **'east•ern•most** *adj* położony najdalej na wschód

East•ern 'Stand•ard Time *s* czas *m* urzędowy wschodnioamerykański

east•ward ['iːstwəd] **I** *adj* **1.** wschodni; ***in an ~ direction*** w kierunku wschodnim **2.** na wschód **II** *adv* (*a.* **~s**) na wschód

eas•y ['iːzɪ] **I** *adj* **1.** łatwy, prosty; ***it's ~ for him to talk*** łatwo mu mówić; ***~ money*** łatwy pieniądz; ***be on ~ street*** *infml* mieć forsy jak lodu **2.** *pace*: spokojny, nieśpieszny **3.** *punishment*: lekki **4.** *terms*: dogodny **5.** niewymuszony **II** *adv* spokojnie; ***go ~, take it ~*** nie przemęczać się; ***take it ~!*** tylko spokojnie!; ***go ~ on s.o.*** traktować kogoś łagodnie; ***easier said than done*** łatwiej powiedzieć niż zrobić; ***~ come, ~ go*** łatwo przyszło, łatwo poszło; **'eas•y chair** *s* (głęboki) fotel *m*; **'eas•y•go•ing** *adj* **1.** wyrozumiały, niewymagający **2.** spokojny **3.** niefrasobliwy; **eas•y-peas•y** [iːzɪ'piːzɪ] *adj infml* łatwiutki; ***it's ~*** to łatwizna, to bułka z masłem

eat [iːt] **I** *s* **~s** *Br infml* jedzenie *n*, jedzonko *n* **II** (*ate*; *eaten*) *v/t* **1.** jeść ⟨z-⟩, jadać ⟨z-⟩; ***~ one's words*** odwołać, co się powiedziało, *infml* odszczekać wszystko; ***what's ~ing him?*** co go gryzie?; ***he's eaten up with jealousy*** zżera go zazdrość **2.** żreć ⟨ze-⟩, zżerać **III** (*ate*; *eaten*) *v/i* **1.** jeść ⟨z-⟩ **2.** żreć ⟨ze-⟩; **eat away** *v/t* **1.** *bank*: podmywać ⟨-myć⟩ **2.** trawić; **eat away at** *v/i* **1.** (*rust*) zżerać ⟨zeżreć⟩ **2.** *profits*: uszczuplać

⟨-lić⟩; **eat into** *v/i* **1.** wżerać ⟨weżreć⟩ się w *A* **2.** *savings*: nadszarpywać ⟨-pnąć⟩, uszczuplać ⟨-lić⟩; **eat out** *v/i* jeść ⟨z-⟩ poza domem, jeść ⟨z-⟩ w restauracji; **eat up** *v/t* zjadać ⟨zjeść⟩ do końca, dojadać ⟨-jeść⟩

eat•a•ble ['iːtəbl] **I** *adj* **1.** jadalny **2.** *infml* zjadliwy **II** *s* **~s** jedzenie *n*; **'eat-by date** *s Br* data *f* przydatności do spożycia; **eat•en** ['iːtn] *Past Participle* → **eat**; **eat•ing** ['iːtɪŋ] *s* jedzenie *n*

eaves•drop ['iːvzdrɒp] *v/i* podsłuchiwać ⟨-chać⟩ (**on** *A*); **eaves•drop•per** ['iːvzdrɒpə] *s infml* podsłuchiwacz *m*

ebb [eb] **I** *s* odpływ *m*; **be at a low ~** *fig* przechodzić kryzys **II** *v/i* ustępować ⟨-tąpić⟩; **ebb away** *v/i* **1.** (*funds*) topnieć ⟨s-⟩ **2.** (*enthusiasm*) gasnąć ⟨z-⟩; **'ebb tide** *s* odpływ *m*

eb•on•y ['ebənɪ] **I** *s* heban *m* **II** *adj* hebanowy

ec•cen•tric [ɪk'sentrɪk] **I** *s* ekscentryk *m* **II** *adj* **1.** ekscentryczny, dziwaczny **2.** *TECH* mimośrodowy; **ec•cen•tric•i•ty** [ɪksen'trɪsɪtɪ] *s* ekscentryczność *f*, dziwaczność *f*

ECG [iːsiː'dʒiː] *abbr* (=**electrocardiogram**, **electrocardiograph**) EKG *n*

ech•o ['ekəʊ] **I** *s* echo *n*, odgłos *m* **II** *v/i* odbijać ⟨-bić⟩ się echem, rozbrzmiewać ⟨-mieć⟩ echem **III** *v/t* **1.** rozbrzmiewać echem **2.** powtarzać ⟨-tórzyć⟩; **'ech•o sound•er** *s* echosonda *f*

e•clair [ɪ'kleə] *s COOK* ekler *m*, eklerka *f*

e•clipse [ɪ'klɪps] **I** *s* **1.** *ASTR* zaćmienie *n* **2.** *fig* kryzys *m*; **be in ~ a)** przeżywać kryzys **b)** pozostawać w cieniu **3.** *fig* upadek *m* **II** *v/t* **1.** *ASTR* zasłaniać ⟨-łonić⟩, przysłaniać ⟨-łonić⟩ **2.** *fig* przyćmiewać ⟨-mić⟩, spychać ⟨zepchnąć⟩ na drugi plan

e•co•lo•gi•cal [iːkə'lɒdʒɪkl] *adj* ekologiczny; **~ balance** równowaga ekologiczna; **e•co•lo•gi•cal•ly** [iːkə'lɒdʒɪklɪ] *adv* ekologicznie; **~ harmful** szkodliwy dla środowiska; **~ friendly** przyjazny środowisku; **e•col•o•gist** [iː'kɒlədʒɪst] *s* ekolog *m*; **e•col•o•gy** [iː'kɒlədʒɪ] *s* ekologia *f*

ec•o•nom•ic [iːkə'nɒmɪk] *adj* **1.** gospodarczy, ekonomiczny; **~ aid** pomoc gospodarcza; **~ refugee** emigrant ekonomiczny **2.** opłacalny, rentowny; **ec•o•nom•i•cal** [iːkə'nɒmɪkl] *adj* **1.** oszczędny; **be ~ with the truth** nie mówić całej prawdy **2.** gospodarny; **ec•o•nom•i•cal•ly** [iːkə'nɒmɪklɪ] *adv* **1.** gospodarczo, ekonomicznie **2.** oszczędnie **3.** zwięźle, lakonicznie; **ec•o•nom•ics** [iːkə'nɒmɪks] *s* **1.** ekonomia *f* **2.** ekonomika *f*; **e•con•o•mist** [ɪ'kɒnəmɪst] *s* ekonomista *m*; **e•con•o•mize** [ɪ'kɒnəmaɪz] *v/i* oszczędzać ⟨-dzić⟩, zaoszczędzić (**on** na *L*)

e•con•o•my [ɪ'kɒnəmɪ] *s* **1.** gospodarka *f* **2.** oszczędność *f* **3.** gospodarność *f* **4.** zwięzłość *f*; **e'con•o•my class** *s* (*plane*) klasa *f* turystyczna; **e'con•o•my drive** *s*: **be on an ~** *Br* oszczędzać; **e'con•o•my price** *s* niska cena *f*; **e'con•o•my sized** *s package*: duży

e•co•sys•tem ['iːkəʊsɪstm] *s* ekosystem *m*, **e•co•tour•ism** ['iːkəʊtʊrɪzm] *s* ekoturystyka *f*, turystyka *f* ekologiczna

ec•sta•sy ['ekstəsɪ] *s* **1.** ekstaza *f*, uniesienie *n*; **in ~** w ekstazie; **go into ecstasies over** zachwycać się *I* **2.** **Ȣ** (*drug*) ecstasy *f*; **ec•sta•tic** [ɪk'stætɪk] *adj* **1. be ~** szaleć z radości **2.** zachwycony (**about** *I*) **3.** ekstatyczny **4.** entuzjastyczny

Ec•ua•dor ['ekwədɔː] *s* Ekwador *m*; **Ec•ua•dor•ean** [ekwə'dɔːrɪən] **I** *adj* ekwadorski **II** *s* Ekwadorczyk *m*

edge [edʒ] **I** *s* **1.** ostrze *n*; **take the ~ off s.o.'s appetite** odebrać komuś apetyt; **take the ~ off s.o.'s anger** złagodzić czyjś gniew **2.** krawędź *f*, skraj *m*; **on the ~ of bankruptcy** na krawędzi bankructwa; **on the ~ of despair** na granicy załamania; **on ~** *fig* podenerwowany; **set s.o.'s teeth on ~** irytować kogoś **3.** kant *m* **4.** brzeg *m* **5.** przewaga *f*; **have the ~ on** mieć przewagę nad *I* **II** *v/i* **1.** przesuwać ⟨-sunąć⟩ się **2.** nieznacznie wzrastać ⟨-rosnąć⟩ **III** *v/t* **1.** przesuwać ⟨-sunąć⟩ **2.** obszywać ⟨-szyć⟩, oblamowywać ⟨-mować⟩; **edge away** *v/i*: **~ from** odsuwać się od *G*

edg•i•ness ['edʒɪnɪs] *s infml* podenerwowanie *n*, zdenerwowanie *n*; **edg•y** ['edʒɪ] *adj infml* podenerwowany, zdenerwowany

E

ed•i•ble ['edɪbl] *adj* **1.** jadalny, zdatny do spożycia **2.** znośny

ed•it ['edɪt] *v/t* **1.** redagować ⟨z-⟩ **2.** INF edytować **3.** *film*: montować ⟨z-⟩ **4.** *newspaper*: wydawać **5.** opracowywać ⟨-cować⟩ **6.** skracać ⟨-rócić⟩; **e•di•tion** [ɪ'dɪʃn] *s* **1.** wydanie *n*; ***first ~*** wydanie pierwsze; ***morning ~*** wydanie poranne **2.** edycja *f* **3.** nakład *m*; **ed•i•tor** ['edɪtə] *s* **1.** redaktor *m*; ***~ in chief*** redaktor naczelny **2.** INF edytor *m* **3.** montażysta *m*; **ed•i•to•ri•al** [edɪ'tɔːrɪəl] **I** *s* artykuł *m* wstępny, *infml* wstępniak *m* **II** *adj* **1.** redakcyjny **2.** wydawniczy

E

ed•u•cate ['edʒəkeɪt] *v/t* **1.** kształcić ⟨wy-⟩; ***he was ~d at Cambridge*** studiował w Cambridge **2.** rozwijać ⟨-winąć⟩; **ed•u•cat•ed** ['edʒəkeɪtɪd] *adj* **1.** wykształcony **2.** kulturalny, wyrobiony **3.** ***~ guess*** domysł (oparty na racjonalnych przesłankach) **ed•u•ca•tion** [edʒə'keɪʃn] *s* **1.** szkolnictwo *n*, oświata *f* **2.** edukacja *f* **3.** kształcenie *n*, nauczanie *n* **4.** pedagogika *f*; **ed•u•ca•tion•al** [edʒə'keɪʃnl] *adj* **1.** oświatowy; ***~ level*** poziom nauczania **2.** edukacyjny, dydaktyczny; ***~ film*** film edukacyjny; ***~ television*** telewizja edukacyjna **3.** pedagogiczny

EEG [iːiː'dʒiː] *abbr* (=***electroencephalogram***, ***electroencephalograph***) EEG *m*

eel [iːl] *s* węgorz *m*

ee•rie ['ɪərɪ] *adj* **1.** niesamowity **2.** przejmujący grozą **3.** upiorny; **ee•ri•ness** ['ɪərɪnɪs] *s* **1.** niesamowitość *f* **2.** nastrój *m* grozy **3.** upiorność *f*

ef•fect [ɪ'fekt] **I** *s* **1.** skutek *m*, rezultat *m* **2.** efekt *m*; ***special ~s*** efekty specjalne **3.** wpływ *m*; ***have an ~ on*** mieć wpływ na *A* **4.** ***a letter to the ~ that*** list, z którego wynika, że; ***or words to that ~*** lub coś w tym sensie **5.** ***be in ~*** obowiązywać; ***take ~***, ***come into ~*** wejść w życie; ***with ~ from*** obowiązujący od *G* **6.** ***in ~*** faktycznie, w rzeczywistości **7.** ***~s*** *form* rzeczy **II** *v/t reforms*: wprowadzać ⟨-dzić⟩; **ef•fec•tive** [ɪ'fektɪv] *adj* **1.** skuteczny, efektywny **2.** obowiązujący; ***be ~*** obowiązywać; ***become ~*** wejść w życie; ***~ from***, ***~ as of*** obowiązujący od *G* **3.** faktyczny, rzeczywisty; ***~ salary*** płaca realna; **ef•fec•tive•ly** [ɪ'fektɪvlɪ] *adv* **1.** skutecznie, efektywnie **2.** faktycznie, w rzeczywistości **ef•fec•tive•ness** [ɪ'fektɪvnɪs] *s* skuteczność *f*, efektywność *f*

ef•fem•i•nate [ɪ'femɪnət] *adj* zniewieściały

ef•fi•cien•cy [ɪ'fɪʃənsɪ] *s* **1.** wydajność *f*; ***~ expert*** specjalista ds. wydajności pracy **2.** skuteczność *f*, efektywność *f* **3.** sprawność *f*; **ef•fi•cient** [ɪ'fɪʃənt] *adj* **1.** wydajny **2.** skuteczny, efektywny **3.** sprawny; **ef•fi•cient•ly** [ɪ'fɪʃəntlɪ] *adv* **1.** wydajnie **2.** sprawnie, efektywnie **3.** skutecznie

ef•fort ['efət] *s* wysiłek *m*, trud *m*; ***make an ~*** starać się, próbować; ***make every ~*** dokładać wszelkich starań; ***spare no ~*** nie żałować sił; ***without ~*** bez wysiłku; ***in an ~ to save time*** żeby zaoszczędzić czas; ***worth the ~*** wart zachodu; **ef•fort•less** ['efərtlɪs] *adj* łatwy, nie wymagający wysiłku; **ef•fort•less•ly** ['efətlɪslɪ] *adv* łatwo, bez wysiłku, bez trudu

EFL [iːef'el] *abbr* (=***English as a Foreign Language***) angielski *m* jako język obcy

e.g. [iː'dʒiː] *abbr* (=***for example***) np.

e•gal•i•tar•i•an [ɪgælɪ'terɪən] **I** *adj* **1.** egalitarny **2.** egalitarystyczny **II** *s* egalitarysta *m*

egg[1] [eg] *s* **1.** jajko *n*, jajo *n*; ***be left with ~ on one's face*** *infml* wyjść na durnia; ***don't put all your ~s in one basket*** *fig* nie stawiaj wszystkiego na jedną kartę **2.** BIOL komórka *f* jajowa, jajeczko *n*

egg[2] [~] *v/t*: ***~ on*** namawiać

'egg•cup *s* kieliszek *m* do jajek; **'egg•head** *s infml* jajogłowy *m*; **'egg•plant** *s Am* bakłażan *m*, oberżyna *f*; **'egg•shell** *s* skorupka *f* jajka; **'egg tim•er** *s* minutnik *m*; **'egg whisk** *s* trzepaczka *f*; **'egg white** *s* białko *n* (jajka); **'egg yolk** *s* żółtko *n* (jajka)

e•go ['iːgəʊ] *s* ego *n*, ja *n*; ***boost s.o.'s ~***, ***give s.o. an ~ boost*** dodać komuś pewności siebie, dowartościować kogoś; ***be on an ~ trip*** zaspokajać własną próżność

e•go•cen•tric [iːgəʊ'sentrɪk] **I** *s* egocentryk *m* **II** *adj* egocentryczny;

e•go•ism ['i:gəʊɪzm] *s* egoizm *m*; **e•go•ist** ['i:gəʊɪst] *s* egoista *m*; **e•go•is•tic** [i:gəʊ'ɪstɪk] *adj* egoistyczny; **e•go•tism** ['i:gəʊtɪzəm] *s* egotyzm *m*; **e•go•tist** ['i:gəʊtɪst] *s* egotysta *m*; **e•go•tis•tic** [i:gəʊ'tɪstɪk] *adj* egotystyczny

E•gypt ['i:dʒɪpt] *s* Egipt *m*; **E•gyp•tian** [ɪ'dʒɪpʃn] **I** *s* Egipcjanin *m*, Egipcjanka *f* **II** *adj* egipski

eight [eɪt] **I** *num* osiem, ośmiu, ośmioro; ***~-hour working day*** ośmiogodzinny dzień pracy **II** *s* ósemka *f*; ***an ~ of hearts*** ósemka kier

eigh•teen [eɪ'ti:n] *num* osiemnaście; **eigh•teenth** [eɪ'ti:nθ] *adj* osiemnasty

eighth [eɪtθ] *adj* ósmy; ***the ~ of May*** ósmy maja

eigh•ti•eth ['eɪtɪɪθ] *adj* osiemdziesiąty

eigh•t|y ['eɪtɪ] **I** *num* osiemdziesiąt **II** *s* osiemdziesiątka *f*; ***be in one's ~ies*** mieć osiemdziesiąt kilka lat, być po osiemdziesiątce; ***in the ~ies*** w latach osiemdziesiątych

Eir•e ['eərə] Irlandia *f*, Republika *f* Irlandii

ei•ther ['aɪðə] **I** *pron* **1.** którykolwiek, albo jeden, albo drugi; ***~ of us*** jeden z nas **2.** żaden, ani jeden, ani drugi; ***I haven't seen ~*** nie widziałam ani jednego, ani drugiego, nie widziałam żadnego (z nich) **3.** każdy **4.** obydwa, obaj, obie, oboje; ***on ~ side*** po obu stronach; ***~ way*** tak czy owak, i tak, i tak **II** *conj* ***~... or*** **a)** albo..., albo **b)** ani..., ani; ***it isn't enough ~ for you or for me*** nie wystarczy ani dla ciebie, ani dla mnie **III** *adv* ***not ~*** też nie

e•ject [ɪ'dʒekt] **I** *v/t* **1.** wyrzucać ⟨-cić⟩ **2.** usuwać ⟨usunąć⟩ **3.** wypuszczać ⟨-puścić⟩ **II** *v/i* katapultować się; **e•jec•tor seat** [ɪ'dʒektərsi:t] *s* fotel *m* wyrzucany, fotel *m* katapultowy

e•lab•o•rate I [ɪ'læbərət] *adj* **1.** złożony, skomplikowany **2.** misterny **3.** wymyślny **4.** drobiazgowy, staranny **II** [ɪ'læbəreɪt] *v/t* **1.** opracowywać ⟨-cować⟩ w szczegółach **2.** rozwijać ⟨-winąć⟩ **III** [ɪ'læbəreɪt] *v/i* **1.** rozwijać ⟨-winąć⟩ (***on*** *A*), podawać ⟨-dać⟩ szczegóły (***on*** *G*) **2.** omawiać ⟨omówić⟩ szczegółowo (***on*** A) **3.** rozwodzić się (***on*** nad *I*); **e•lab•o•rate•ly** [ɪ'læbəreɪtlɪ] *adv* **1.** szczegółowo, drobiazgowo **2.** misternie **3.** wymyślnie

e•lapse [ɪ'læps] *v/i* upływać ⟨-łynąć⟩, mijać ⟨minąć⟩

e•las•tic [ɪ'læstɪk] **I** *adj* elastyczny; ***an ~ band*** gumka; ***an ~ stocking*** pończocha elastyczna **II** *s* gumka *f*; **e•las•ti•ca•ted** [ɪ'læstɪkeɪtɪd] *adj* elastyczny; ***with an ~ waist*** ze ściągaczem, na gumkę; **e•las•ti•ci•ty** [ɪlæs'tɪsətɪ] *s* elastyczność *f*; **e•las•ti•cized** [ɪ'læstɪsaɪzd] *adj* elastyczny; ***with an ~ waist*** ze ściągaczem, na gumkę

e•lat•ed [ɪ'leɪtɪd] *adj* **1.** zachwycony **2.** uszczęśliwiony; **el•at•ion** [ɪ'leɪʃn] *s* (wielka) radość *f*, euforia *f*

el•bow ['elbəʊ] **I** *s* **1.** łokieć *m* **2.** *pipe*: kolanko *n* **3.** ostry zakręt *m* **II** *v/t* przepychać ⟨-pchnąć⟩ się; ***~ out*** wypychać; ***~ one's way through the crowd*** (łokciami) torować sobie drogę w tłumie; **'el•bow grease** *s infml* wysiłek *m*; **'el•bow•room** *s* **1.** (wolna) przestrzeń *f* **2.** pole *n* manewru, swoboda *f* działania

el•der ['eldə] **I** *comp* → ***old*** *adj brother*, *son*: starszy **II** *s* osoba *f* starsza; ***~s*** starsi

el•der•ly ['eldərlɪ] *adj* starszy, w podeszłym wieku; **el•der 'states•man** *s* **1.** nestor *m* **2.** wybitny mąż *m* stanu

el•dest ['eldəst] *superl* → ***old*** *adj brother*, *son*: najstarszy

e•lect [ɪ'lekt] **I** *v/t* **1.** wybierać ⟨obrać⟩ **2.** obierać ⟨obrać⟩ **II** *adj* nowo wybrany, elekt; ***the president ~*** prezydent elekt; **e•lect•ed** [ɪ'lektɪd] *adj* **1.** obieralny, wybieralny **2.** elekcyjny

e•lec•tion [ɪ'lekʃn] **I** *s* wybory *pl* **II** *adj* **1.** wyborczy **2.** przedwyborczy; **e•lec•tion cam•'paign** *s* kampania *f* wyborcza; **e•lec•tion 'day** *s* dzień *m* wyborów; **e•lec•tion•eer** [ɪlekʃə'nɪə] *v/i* agitować, prowadzić kampanię wyborczą; ***~ for*** agitować za *I*; **e•lec•tion•eer•ing** [ɪlekʃə'nɪərɪŋ] *s* agitacja *f* przedwyborcza; **e•lec•tive** [ɪ'lektɪv] **I** *adj* **1.** obieralny, wybieralny **2.** fakultatywny, opcjonalny **II** *s* przedmiot *m* fakultatywny; **e•lec•tor** [ɪ'lektə] *s* **1.** wyborca *m* **2.** elektor *m* **3.** *Am* elektor *m*, członek *m* kolegium elektorów; **e•lec•tor•al** [ɪ'lektərəl] *adj*

E

wyborczy; **e•lec•to•rate** [ɪ'lektərət] *s* elektorat *m*, wyborcy *pl*

e•lec•tric [ɪ'lektrɪk] *adj* **1.** elektryczny; ***an ~ guitar*** gitara elektryczna; ***an ~ chair*** krzesło elektryczne; ***an ~ kettle*** czajnik elektryczny; ***an ~ razor*** golarka elektryczna; ***an ~ torch*** latarka **2.** *atmosphere*: naelektryzowany, pełen napięcia **3.** *news*: elektryzujący; **e•lec•tric 'shock** *s* **1.** wstrząs *m* elektryczny, porażenie *n* prądem **2.** MED elektrowstrząs *m*

e•lec•tri•cal [ɪ'lektrɪkl] *adj* elektryczny; **e•lec•tri•cal en•gi•'neer** *s* **1.** elektrotechnik *m* **2.** inżynier elektryk *m*; **e•lec•tri•cal en•gi•'neer•ing** *s* **1.** elektrotechnika *f* **2.** inżynieria *f* elektryczna

e•lec•tri•cian [ɪlek'trɪʃn] *s* elektryk *m*

e•lec•tri•ci•ty [ɪlek'trɪsətɪ] *s* elektryczność *f*, energia *f* elektryczna, prąd *m* (elektryczny)

e•lec•tri•fy [ɪ'lektrɪfaɪ] *v/t* **1.** elektryfikować ⟨z-⟩ **2.** PHYS elektryzować ⟨na-⟩ **3.** *audience*: elektryzować ⟨z-⟩; **e•lec•tri•fy•ing** [ɪ'lektrɪfaɪɪŋ] *adj fig* elektryzujący

e•lec•tro•cute [ɪ'lektrəkjuːt] *v/t* **1.** ***be ~d*** zostać straconym na krześle elektrycznym **2.** porażać ⟨-razić⟩ prądem; **e•lec•tro•cu•tion** [ɪlektrə'kjuːʃn] *s* **1.** egzekucja *f* na krześle elektrycznym **2.** śmiertelne porażenie *n* prądem elektrycznym

e•lec•trode [ɪ'lektrəʊd] *s* elektroda *f*

e•lec•tro•lyte [ɪ'lektrəlaɪt] *s* elektrolit *m*

e•lec•tron [ɪ'lektrɒn] *s* elektron *m*

e•lec•tron•ic [ɪlek'trɒnɪk] *adj* elektroniczny; ***~ banking*** bankowość elektroniczna; ***~ cash*** elektroniczny pieniądz; ***~ flash*** elektroniczna lampa błyskowa; **e•lec•tron•ic da•ta 'pro•ces•sing** *s* elektroniczne przetwarzanie *n* danych; **e•lec•tron•ic 'mail** *s* poczta *f* elektroniczna; **e•lectronic 'mail•box** *s* skrzynka *f* pocztowa

e•lec•tron•ics [ɪlek'trɒnɪks] *s* elektronika *f*

e•lec•tro•ther•a•py [ɪlektrəʊ'θerəpɪ] *s* elektroterapia *f*

el•e•gance ['elɪgəns] *s* elegancja *f*, szyk *m*; **el•e•gant** ['elɪgənt] *adj* **1.** elegancki, wytworny **2.** zgrabny, zgrabnie wykonany; **el•e•gant•ly** ['elɪgəntlɪ] *adv* **1.** elegancko, wytwornie **2.** zgrabnie

el•e•ment ['elɪmənt] *s* **1.** element *m*; ***an ~ of uncertainty*** element niepewności; ***an ~ of surprise*** element zaskoczenia **2.** składnik *m*, część *f* składowa **3.** czynnik *m* **4.** pierwiastek *m* **5.** odrobina *f* **6.** żywioł *m*; ***be in one's ~*** być w swoim żywiole; ***be out of one's ~*** czuć się nieswojo

el•e•men•ta•ry [elɪ'mentərɪ] *adj* podstawowy, zasadniczy; **el•e•men•ta•ry 'school** *s Am* szkoła *f* podstawowa

el•e•phant ['elɪfənt] *s* słoń *m*

el•e•vate ['elɪveɪt] *v/t* **1.** podnosić ⟨-nieść⟩ **2.** awansować; ***she was ~d to a higher position*** otrzymała wyższe stanowisko; ***~ s.o. to the peerage*** nadać komuś tytuł szlachecki **3.** podnosić ⟨-nieść⟩ rangę; **el•e•vated 'rail•road** *s Am* (miejska) kolej *f* nadziemna; **el•e•va•tion** [elɪ'veɪʃn] *s* **1.** podniesienie *n* **2.** podniesienie *n* rangi **3.** wysokość *f* (nad poziomem morza) **4.** ARCHIT elewacja *f*; **el•e•va•tor** ['elɪveɪtə] *s* (*building*) *Am* winda *f*, dźwig *m*; ***an ~ shaft*** szyb windy

el•e•ven [ɪ'levn] **I** *num* jedenaście, jedenastu, jedenaścioro **II** *s* jedenaście *n*, jedenastka *f*; ***~ses*** *Br infml* drugie śniadanie

el•e•venth [ɪ'levnθ] *adj* jedenasty; ***at the ~ hour*** *fig* w ostatniej chwili, za pięć dwunasta

elf [elf] *pl elves* [elvz] *s* elf *m*, chochlik *m*

el•i•gi•bil•i•ty [elɪdʒə'bɪlətɪ] *s* **1.** prawo *n* **2.** uprawnienia *pl* **3.** (odpowiednie) kwalifikacje *pl*; **el•i•gi•ble** ['elɪdʒəbl] *adj* **1.** ***be ~ for*** mieć prawo ubiegać się o *A*, kwalifikować się do *G*; ***be ~ to vote*** mieć czynne prawo wyborcze **2.** wolny, do wzięcia; **el•i•gi•ble 'bach•e•lor** *s* kawaler *m* do wzięcia

e•lim•i•nate [ɪ'lɪmɪneɪt] *v/t* **1.** eliminować ⟨wy-⟩; ***be ~d*** SPORT odpaść, zostać wyeliminowanym **2.** wykluczać ⟨-czyć⟩ **3.** likwidować ⟨z-⟩; **e•lim•i•na•tion** [ɪ'lɪmɪneɪʃn] *s* **1.** eliminacja *f* **2.** wyeliminowanie *n* **3.** odrzucenie *n*

e•lite [eɪ'liːt] **I** *adj* elitarny **II** *s* elita *f*; **e•lit•ism** [eɪ'liːtɪzəm] *s* **1.** elitaryzm *m* **2.** *POLIT* elityzm *m*; **e•lit•ist** [eɪ'liːtɪst] *adj* **1.** elitarny **2.** elitarystyczny

elk [elk] *s* łoś *m*

el•lipse [ɪ'lɪps] *s* **1.** *MATH* elipsa *f* **2.** elipsa *f*, wyrzutnia *f*

elm [elm] *s BIOL* wiąz *m*

e•lon•gate ['iːlɒŋgeɪt] **I** *v/i* wydłużać ⟨-żyć⟩ się **II** *v/t* wydłużać ⟨-żyć⟩

e•lope [ɪ'ləʊp] *v/i* (*lovers*) uciekać ⟨uciec⟩ (żeby się potajemnie pobrać)

el•o•quence ['eləkwəns] *s* elokwencja *f*, wymowność *f*; **el•o•quent** ['eləkwənt] *adj* elokwentny, wymowny; **el•o•quent•ly** ['eləkwəntlɪ] *adv* **1.** elokwentnie, wymownie **2.** ze swadą

El Sal•va•dor [el'sælvədɔː] *s* Salwador *m*

else [els] *adv* **1.** jeszcze; ***anything ~?*** coś jeszcze?; ***what ~ can we do?*** co jeszcze możemy zrobić?; ***no one ~*** nikt więcej **2.** inny; ***someone ~*** ktoś inny; ***that's something ~*** to co innego; ***everybody ~*** wszyscy inni, (cała) reszta **3.** ***or ~*** w przeciwnym razie, albo; **else•where** [els'weə] *adv* gdzie indziej

ELT [iːel'tiː] *abbr* (=***English Language Teaching***) nauczanie *n* języka angielskiego

e•lude [ɪ'luːd] *v/t* **1.** wymykać ⟨-mknąć⟩ się, umykać ⟨umknąć⟩ **2.** *responsibility*: unikać ⟨-knąć⟩, uchylać ⟨-lić⟩ się od *G*; **e•lu•sive** [ɪ'luːsɪv] *adj* **1.** nieuchwytny **2.** trudno osiągalny **3.** niedający się określić, trudny do zdefiniowania **4.** ulotny **5.** *answer*: wymijający

elves [elvz] *pl* → ***elf***

e-mail ['iːmeɪl] **I** *s* e-mail *m* **II** *v/t* **1.** przesyłać ⟨-słać⟩ e-mail **2.** mailować **III** *adj* e-mailowy, mailowy; **'e-mail ad•dress** *s* adres *m* e-mailowy, adres *m* poczty elektronicznej

em•a•nate ['eməneɪt] **I** *v/t* **1.** emanować **2.** wydzielać ⟨-lić⟩ **II** *v/i* **1.** emanować **2.** wydzielać ⟨-lić⟩ się

e•man•ci•pat•ed [ɪ'mænsɪpeɪtɪd] *adj* wyzwolony, wyemancypowany

e•man•ci•pa•tion [ɪmænsɪ'peɪʃn] *s* emancypacja *f*, wyzwolenie *n*

em•balm [ɪm'bɑːm] *v/t* balsamować ⟨za-⟩

em•bank•ment [ɪm'bæŋkmənt] *s* **1.** wał *m* **2.** *for railway*: nasyp *m* **3.** skarpa *f*

em•bar•go [em'bɑːgəʊ] **I** *s* embargo *n*; ***impose an ~ on*** nałożyć embargo na *A* **II** *v/t* wprowadzać ⟨-dzić⟩ embargo na *A*

em•bark [ɪm'bɑːk] **I** *v/i* wchodzić ⟨wejść⟩ na pokład **II** *v/t* **1.** wprowadzać ⟨-dzić⟩ na pokład **2.** ładować ⟨za-⟩; **em•bark on** *v/i* **1.** wyruszać ⟨-szyć⟩ w *A* **2.** podejmować ⟨-djąć⟩ **3.** zabierać ⟨-brać⟩ się do *G*

em•bar•ka•tion [embɑː'keɪʃn] *s* **1.** wejście *n* na pokład **2.** załadunek *m*

em•bar•rass [ɪm'bærəs] *v/t* **1.** wprawiać ⟨-wić⟩ w zakłopotanie **2.** peszyć ⟨s-⟩; **em•bar•rassed** [ɪm'bærəst] *adj* **1.** zażenowany **2.** zakłopotany; ***be financially ~*** *infml* mieć problemy finansowe **3.** speszony; **em•bar•rass•ing** [ɪm'bærəsɪŋ] *adj* **1.** żenujący **2.** kłopotliwy **3.** wprawiający w zakłopotanie; **em•bar•rass•ment** [ɪm'bærəsmənt] *s* **1.** zażenowanie *n*; ***be an ~ to s.o.*** przynosić komuś wstyd **2.** zakłopotanie *n* **3.** skrępowanie *n*

em•bas•sy ['embəsɪ] *s* ambasada *f*

em•bed [ɪm'bed] *v/t* **1.** osadzać ⟨-dzić⟩ (***in*** w *L*); ***~ded in concrete*** zabetonowany, zatopiony w betonie; ***a bullet ~ded in his leg*** pocisk, który utkwił w jego nodze **2.** ***deeply ~ded beliefs*** *fig* głęboko zakorzenione przekonania

em•bel•lish [ɪm'belɪʃ] *v/t* **1.** ozdabiać ⟨-dobić⟩ **2.** upiększać ⟨-szyć⟩ **3.** *fig* podkolorowywać ⟨-rować⟩, ubarwiać ⟨-wić⟩; ***~ one's story*** koloryzować; **em•bel•lish•ment** [ɪm'belɪʃmənt] *s* **1.** ozdoba *f*, upiększenie *n* **2.** (*story*) upiększenie *n*

em•ber ['embə] *s* rozżarzony węgielek *m*; ***~s*** żar

em•bez•zle [ɪm'bezl] *v/t* defraudować ⟨z-⟩, sprzeniewierzać ⟨-rzyć⟩; **em•bez•zle•ment** [ɪm'bezlmənt] *s* defraudacja *f*, sprzeniewierzenie *n*; **em•bez•zler** [ɪm'bezlə] *s* defraudant *m*, malwersant *m*

em•bit•ter [ɪm'bɪtə] *v/t* **1.** rozgoryczać ⟨-czyć⟩, wprawiać ⟨-wić⟩ w rozgoryczenie **2.** *relations*: zatruwać ⟨-ruć⟩
em•blem ['embləm] *s* **1.** godło *n*; ***national ~*** godło państwowe **2.** emblemat *m* **3.** symbol *m*
em•bod•i•ment [ɪm'bɒdɪmənt] *s* ucieleśnienie *n*, uosobienie *n*; **em•bod•y** [ɪm'bɒdɪ] *v/t* **1.** ucieleśniać ⟨-nić⟩, uosabiać ⟨-sobić⟩ **2.** wyrażać ⟨-razić⟩ **3.** urzeczywistniać ⟨-nić⟩ **4.** *form* zawierać ⟨-wrzeć⟩
em•brace [ɪm'breɪs] **I** *v/t* **1.** obejmować ⟨objąć⟩, brać ⟨wziąć⟩ w objęcia **2.** (*subject area*) obejmować ⟨objąć⟩ **3.** korzystać ⟨s-⟩ z *G* **4.** stawać ⟨-tać⟩ się zwolennikiem **5.** przyjmować ⟨-jąć⟩ **II** *v/i* obejmować ⟨objąć⟩ się **III** *s* **1.** uścisk *m* **2.** objęcia *pl*
em•broi•der [ɪm'brɔɪdə] **I** *v/t* **1.** haftować ⟨wy-⟩, wyszywać ⟨-szyć⟩ **2.** *story*: ubarwiać ⟨-wić⟩ **II** *v/i* haftować, wyszywać; **em•broi•der•y** [ɪm'brɔɪdərɪ] *s* **1.** haft *m*, haftowanie *n*; **2.** *fig* upiększenia *pl*
em•bry•o ['embrɪəʊ] *s* BIOL embrion *n*, zarodek *m*; ***in ~*** *fig* w stanie zarodkowym, w stanie embrionalnym; **em•bry•on•ic** [embrɪ'ɒnɪk] *adj* **1.** embrionalny, zarodkowy **2.** *plan*: rodzący się
em•cee [em'siː] **I** *s* prowadzący *m*, konferansjer *m* **II** *v/t* prowadzić ⟨po-⟩
em•e•rald ['emərəld] **I** *s* **1.** szmaragd *m* **2.** (kolor) szmaragdowy *m* **II** *adj* szmaragdowy
e•merge [ɪ'mɜːdʒ] *v/i* **1.** pojawiać ⟨-wić⟩ się **2.** wynurzać ⟨-rzyć⟩ się **3.** wyłaniać ⟨-łonić⟩ się **4.** wychodzić ⟨wyjść⟩ na jaw; **e•mer•gence** [ɪ'mɜːdʒəns] *s* **1.** pojawienie się *n* **2.** wyjście *n* na jaw
e•mer•gen•cy [ɪ'mɜːdʒənsɪ] *s* nagły wypadek *m*; ***in an ~, in case of ~*** **a)** w nagłym przypadku **b)** w razie niebezpieczeństwa; ***state of ~*** POLIT stan wyjątkowy; **e•'mer•gen•cy call** *s* nagłe wezwanie *n*; **e•mer•gen•cy 'ex•it** *s* wyjście *n* ewakuacyjne, wyjście *n* awaryjne; **e•'mer•gen•cy land•ing** *s* lądowanie *n* awaryjne; **e•mer•gen•cy 'meet•ing** *s* posiedzenie *n* nadzwyczajne, zebranie *n* nadzwyczajne; **e•mer•gen•cy 'num•ber** *s* numer *m* alarmowy; **e•mer•gen•cy op•er'a•tion** *s* MED nagła operacja *f*; **e•'mer•gen•cy serv•i•ces** *pl Br* służby *pl* pomocnicze, służby *pl* publiczne; **e•mer•gen•cy 'stop** *s* nagłe hamowanie *n*; ***make an ~*** nagle zahamować
e•mer•gent [iː'mɜːdʒənt] *adj* **1.** powstający **2.** nowo powstały **3.** *market*: wschodzący, rozwijający się **4.** kształtujący się
em•i•grant ['emɪgrənt] **I** *s* emigrant *m* **II** *adj* emigrancki; **em•i•grate** ['emɪgreɪt] *v/i* emigrować ⟨wy-⟩; **em•i•gra•tion** [emɪ'greɪʃn] *s* emigracja *f*
em•i•nence ['emɪnəns] *s* **1.** sława *f*; ***achieve ~*** zyskać sławę **2.** renoma *f* **3.** ***Eminence*** REL Eminencja; **em•i•nent** ['emɪnənt] *adj* **1.** wybitny **2.** znakomity **3.** niezwykły; **em•i•nent•ly** ['emɪnəntlɪ] *adv* nadzwyczaj, wyjątkowo, wysoce
e•mis•sion [ɪ'mɪʃn] *s* emisja *f*; **e•mis•sion-'free** *adj* niezanieczyszczający środowiska
e•mit [ɪ'mɪt] *v/t* **1.** emitować ⟨wy-⟩ **2.** *sound*: wydawać ⟨-dać⟩ **3.** wydzielać ⟨-lić⟩ **4.** wyrzucać ⟨-cić⟩
e•mo•ti•con [ɪ'məʊtɪkɒn] *s* INF TEL emotikon *m*
e•mo•tion [ɪ'məʊʃn] *s* **1.** uczucie *n*, emocja *f* **2.** emocje *pl* **3.** wzruszenie *n*; **e•mo•tion•al** [ɪ'məʊʃənl] *adj* **1.** emocjonalny, uczuciowy; ***~ balance*** równowaga emocjonalna; ***get ~*** dawać się ponieść emocjom **2.** budzący emocje **3.** wzruszający; **e•mo•tion•al•ly** [ɪ'məʊʃənlɪ] *adv* **1.** emocjonalnie **2.** uczuciowo, z uczuciem, z przejęciem
e•mo•tive [ɪ'məʊtɪv] *adj* **1.** budzący emocje **2.** *word*: silnie zabarwiony emocjonalnie
em•pa•thize ['empəθaɪz] *v/i*: ***~ with s.o.*** identyfikować się z kimś, wczuwać się w czyjąś sytuację
em•pa•thy ['empəθɪ] *s* empatia *f*, współodczuwanie *n*, zrozumienie *n*; ***feel ~ for s.b.*** wczuwać się w czyjąś sytuację
em•pe•ror ['empərə] *s* cesarz *m*, imperator *m*
em•pha•sis ['emfəsɪs] *pl emphases* ['emfəsiːz] *s* **1.** nacisk *m*; ***put ~ on,***

place ~ on kłaść nacisk na *A*; ***with ~*** z naciskiem **2.** emfaza *f*
em•pha•size ['emfəsaɪz] *v/t* **1.** podkreślać ⟨-lić⟩, kłaść ⟨położyć⟩ nacisk na *A* **2.** uwydatniać ⟨-nić⟩; **em•phat•ic** [ɪm'fætɪk] *adj* **1.** wymowny **2.** dobitny **3.** stanowczy
em•pire ['empaɪə] *s* **1.** imperium *n* **2.** cesarstwo *n* **3.** *fig* królestwo *n*
em•pir•i•cal [em'pɪrɪkl] *adj* empiryczny, doświadczalny
em•ploy [ɪm'plɔɪ] **I** *v/t* **1.** zatrudniać ⟨-nić⟩ **2.** stosować ⟨za-⟩, wykorzystywać ⟨-tać⟩ **3.** *energy, time*: poświęcać ⟨-cić⟩ **4.** ***be ~ed in doing s.th.*** zajmować się robieniem czegoś **II** *s* zatrudnienie *n*, usługi *pl*; ***in the ~ of*** zatrudniony przez *G*, na usługach *G*; **em•ploy•ee** [emplɔɪ'iː] *s* pracownik *m*, zatrudniony *m*; ***the ~s*** pracownicy; **em•ploy•er** [em'plɔɪə] *s* pracodawca *m*; **em•ploy•ment** [em'plɔɪmənt] *s* **1.** zatrudnienie *n*, praca *f*; ***~ contract*** umowa o pracę; ***~ market*** rynek pracy; ***~ office*** urząd pracy; ***~ permit*** pozwolenie na pracę **2.** zastosowanie *n*, wykorzystanie *n*; **em•'ploy•ment a•gen•cy** *s* biuro *n* pośrednictwa pracy
em•pow•er [ɪm'paʊə] *v/t* **1.** upoważniać ⟨-nić⟩ **2.** dawać ⟨dać⟩ prawo do *G*
em•press ['emprɪs] *s* cesarzowa *f*
emp•ti•ness ['emptɪnɪs] *s* pustka *f*
emp•ty ['emptɪ] **I** *adj* **1.** pusty; ***feel ~*** odczuwać pustkę; ***the house is standing ~*** dom jest niezamieszkany; ***be ~ of meaning*** być pozbawionym sensu, nie mieć znaczenia **2.** opustoszały, wyludniony **3.** *promises*: pusty, czczy **II** *v/t* **1.** opróżniać ⟨-nić⟩ **2.** wylewać ⟨-lać⟩ **3.** wysypywać ⟨-pać⟩ **III** *v/i* **1.** opróżniać ⟨-nić⟩ się **2.** pustoszeć ⟨o-⟩ **3.** (*river*) uchodzić ⟨ujść⟩, wpadać ⟨wpaść⟩ (***do*** *G* into); **emp•ty-'hand•ed** *adj* z pustymi rękami, z niczym; **emp•ty-'head•ed** *adj* głupkowaty, niemądry
em•u•late ['emjʊleɪt] *v/t* **1.** naśladować **2.** dorównać **3.** INF emulować
e•mul•sion [ɪ'mʌlʃn] *s* emulsja *f*
en•a•ble [ɪ'neɪbl] *v/t* umożliwiać ⟨-wić⟩; ***~ s.o. to do s.th.*** umożliwiać komuś zrobienie czegoś, pozwalać komuś coś zrobić; ***~ s.th. to be done*** umożliwiać zrobienie czegoś
en•act [ɪ'nækt] *v/t* **1.** uchwalać ⟨-lić⟩ **2.** *scene*: odgrywać ⟨odegrać⟩ **3.** *role*: grać ⟨za-⟩; **en•act•ment** [ɪ'nɑːktmənt] *s* **1.** uchwalenie *n* **2.** akt *m* prawny, ustawa *f* **3.** *scene*: odegranie *n*
en•am•our [ɪ'næmə] *Br*, **en•am•or** *Am v/t*: ***be ~ed of s.o.*** uwielbiać kogoś, być zachwyconym kimś
en•case [ɪn'keɪs] *v/t*: ***~d in*** **a)** pokryty *I*, powleczony *I* **b)** zamknięty w *L*
en•chant [ɪn'tʃɑːnt] *v/t* **1.** oczarowywać ⟨-rować⟩, zauroczyć, zachwycać ⟨-cić⟩ **2.** zaczarować, rzucać ⟨-cić⟩ zaklęcie na *A*; **en•chant•ed** [ɪn'tʃɑːntɪd] *adj* **1.** oczarowany, zauroczony, zachwycony **2.** zaczarowany, zaklęty; **en•chant•ing** [ɪn'tʃɑːntɪŋ] *adj* czarujący, uroczy
en•cir•cle [ɪn'sɜːkl] *v/t* **1.** okrążać ⟨-żyć⟩ **2.** otaczać ⟨otoczyć⟩; ***~d with*** otoczony *I*; **en•cir•cle•ment** [ɪn'sɜːklmənt] *s* (*army*) okrążenie *n*
encl *abbr* **1.** (=***enclosure***) zał. **2.** (=***enclosed***) w załączeniu
en•close [ɪn'kləʊz] *v/t* **1.** otaczać ⟨otoczyć⟩ **2.** ogradzać ⟨-rodzić⟩ **3.** zamykać ⟨-mknąć⟩ **4.** (*letter*) załączać ⟨-czyć⟩; ***~d please find*** w załączeniu, w załączniku; **en•clo•sure** [ɪn'kləʊʒə] *s* **1.** zagroda *f* **2.** miejsce *n* ogrodzone **3.** załącznik *m*
en•code [ɪn'kəʊd] *v/t* kodować ⟨za-⟩, szyfrować ⟨za-⟩
en•com•pass [ɪn'kʌmpəs] *v/t* **1.** (*take in*) obejmować ⟨objąć⟩ **2.** ogarniać ⟨-rnąć⟩ **3.** zajmować ⟨-jąć⟩ **4.** otaczać ⟨otoczyć⟩
en•core ['ɒŋkɔː] **I** *interj* bis! **II** *s* bis *m*; ***as an ~*** na bis
en•coun•ter [ɪn'kaʊntə] **I** *v/t* **1.** napotykać ⟨-tkać⟩ **2.** spotykać ⟨-tkać⟩ **3.** natykać ⟨-tknąć⟩ się na *A* **4.** natrafiać ⟨-fić⟩ na *A* **II** *s* **1.** spotkanie *n* **2.** kontakt *m*, zetknięcie *n* się **3.** potyczka *f*
en•cour•age [ɪn'kʌrɪdʒ] *v/t* **1.** zachęcać ⟨-cić⟩, ośmielać ⟨-lić⟩ **2.** dodawać ⟨-dać⟩ otuchy, wspierać ⟨wesprzeć⟩ **3.** sprzyjać **4.** pobudzać ⟨-dzić⟩; **en•cour•age•ment** [ɪn'kʌrɪdʒmənt] *s* **1.** zachęta *f* **2.** otucha *f*; **en•cour•ag•ing** [ɪn'kʌrɪdʒɪŋ] *adj* **1.** zachęcający **2.** obiecujący **3.** krzepiący, pokrzepiający

E

en•croach [ɪn'krəʊtʃ] *v/i*: ***~ on* a)** *law, privacy*: naruszać **b)** naruszać granicę *G*; ***~ on s.o.'s time*** zajmować komuś czas

en•crypt [ɪn'krɪpt] *v/t* kodować ⟨za-⟩, szyfrować ⟨za-⟩; **en•cryp•tion** [ɪn'krɪpʃn] *s* TEL INF kodowanie *n*

en•cy•clo•p(a)e•di•a [ɪnsaɪklə'piːdɪə] *s* encyklopedia *f*; **en•cy•clo•p(a)e•dic** [ɪnsaɪklə'piːdɪk] *adj* encyklopedyczny

end [end] **I** *s* **1.** koniec *m*; ***in the ~*** w końcu; ***at the ~ of May*** pod koniec maja; ***without ~*** bez końca; ***come to an ~, draw to an ~*** zbliżać się do końca, kończyć się; ***put an ~ to s.th., bring s.th. to an ~*** położyć czemuś kres; ***struggle to make ~s meet*** *fig* ledwo wiązać koniec z końcem **2.** zakończenie *n* **3.** kres *m* **4.** kraniec *m* **5.** końcówka *f* **6.** cel *m*; ***the ~ justifies the means*** cel uświęca środki; ***to this ~*** w tym celu **II** *v/t* **1.** kończyć ⟨s-, za-⟩ **2.** kłaść ⟨położyć⟩ kres **III** *v/i* **1.** kończyć ⟨s-, za-⟩ się **2.** wygasać ⟨-snąć⟩; **end up I** *v/t* kończyć ⟨s-⟩ **II** *v/i* **1.** kończyć ⟨s-⟩ się; ***~ happily*** skończyć się szczęśliwie; ***~ in disaster*** *fig* zakończyć się fiaskiem **2.** kończyć ⟨s-⟩ (**as** jako *N*); ***~ in jail*** skończyć w więzieniu, wylądować w więzieniu

en•dan•ger [ɪn'deɪndʒə] *v/t* **1.** zagrażać ⟨-rozić⟩ **2.** narażać ⟨-zić⟩ na niebezpieczeństwo; **en•dan•gered 'spe•cies** *s* zagrożony gatunek *m*

en•dear•ing [ɪn'dɪərɪŋ] *adj* ujmujący, uroczy; **en•dear•ment** [ɪn'dɪərmənt] *s*: (***term of***) ***~*** **a)** czułe słowo, czułe słówko **b)** pieszczotliwe określenie

en•deav•our [ɪn'devə] *Br*, **en•deav•or** *Am* **I** *v/t* usiłować, starać się, próbować **II** *s* staranie *n*, wysiłek *m*, próba *f*; ***make every ~*** dokładać wszelkich starań

end•ing ['endɪŋ] *s* **1.** zakończenie *n*, koniec *m*; ***happy ~*** szczęśliwe zakończenie **2.** *verb*: końcówka *f*

end•less ['endlɪs] *adj* **1.** niekończący się **2.** nieskończony **3.** niezliczony **4.** niewyczerpany

en•dorse [ɪn'dɔːs] *v/t* **1.** zatwierdzać ⟨-dzić⟩ **2.** popierać ⟨-przeć⟩, udzielać ⟨-lić⟩ poparcia **3.** *cheque*: indosować **4.** *product*: promować; **en•dorse•ment** [ɪn'dɔːsmənt] *s* **1.** zatwierdzenie *n* **2.** poparcie *n* **3.** *cheque*: indos *m*

en•dow [ɪn'daʊ] *v/t* **1.** wspomagać ⟨-móc⟩ finansowo **2.** obdarzać ⟨-rzyć⟩; ***be ~ed with s.th.*** być obdarzonym czymś, posiadać coś; **en•dow•ment** [ɪn'daʊmənt] *s* **1.** dofinansowanie *n* **2.** darowizna *f* **3.** uzdolnienie *n*, (przyrodzony) dar *m*

'end prod•uct *s* **1.** produkt *m* końcowy **2.** wynik *m* końcowy

end re'sult *s* wynik *m* końcowy

en•dur•a•ble [ɪn'djʊərəbl] *adj* (możliwy) do zniesienia, znośny; **en•dur•ance** [ɪn'djʊərəns] *s* **1.** wytrzymałość *f*; ***beyond ~*** nie do wytrzymania; ***an ~ test*** **a)** test wytrzymałościowy **b)** TECH próba zmęczeniowa **2.** odporność *f*

en•dure [ɪn'djʊə] **I** *v/t* **1.** znosić ⟨znieść⟩ **2.** przetrzymywać ⟨-mać⟩ **II** *v/i* przetrwać; **en•dur•ing** [ɪn'djʊərɪŋ] *adj* **1.** trwały **2.** długotrwały **3.** uporczywy

'end us•er *s* użytkownik *m* końcowy

en•e•my ['enəmɪ] **I** *s* **1.** wróg *m* **2.** przeciwnik *m*; ***make an ~ of s.o.*** zrobić sobie z kogoś wroga; ***an ~ of reform*** przeciwnik reform **II** *adj* wrogi, nieprzyjacielski

en•er•get•ic [enə'dʒetɪk] *adj* **1.** energiczny **2.** żwawy **3.** dynamiczny; **en•er•get•ic•al•ly** [enə'dʒetɪklɪ] *adv* energicznie, z energią, z werwą; **en•er•gy** ['enədʒɪ] *s* **1.** energia *f* **2.** siła *f*

'en•er•gy-sav•ing *adj* energooszczędny; **'en•er•gy sup•ply** *s* dostawy *pl* energii

en•force [ɪn'fɔːs] *v/t* **1.** egzekwować ⟨wy-⟩ **2.** wprowadzać ⟨-dzić⟩ w życie **3.** narzucać ⟨-cić⟩ **4.** wymuszać ⟨-sić⟩; **en•force•ment** [ɪn'fɔːsmənt] *s* **1.** egzekwowanie *n* **2.** wprowadzanie *n* w życie **3.** zmuszanie *n*; **en•force•ment 'a•gen•cies** *pl Am* organy *pl* ścigania

en•gage [ɪn'geɪdʒ] **I** *v/t* **1.** zajmować ⟨-jąć⟩ **2.** zatrudniać ⟨-nić⟩, angażować ⟨za-⟩ **3.** *clutch*: naciskać ⟨-snąć⟩ **4.** ***become ~d*** zaręczyć się **II** *v/i* **1.** ***~ in*** zajmować ⟨-jąć⟩ się **2.** (*cog-wheel*) zazębiać ⟨-bić⟩ się

en•gaged [ɪn'geɪdʒd] *adj* **1.** **~ (*to be married*)** zaręczony (***to*** z *I*) **2.** zajęty; ***be ~ in doing s.th.*** być czymś zajętym, zajmować się czymś **3.** TEL zajęty; ***an ~ tone*** sygnał zajęty **4.** **~!** (*toilet*) zajęte!; **en•gage•ment** [ɪn'geɪdʒmənt] *s* **1.** umówione spotkanie *n*; ***have an ~*** być umówionym **2.** zaręczyny *pl* **3.** THEAT występ *m*; **en'gage•ment ring** *s* pierścionek *m* zaręczynowy; **en•gag•ing** [ɪn'geɪdʒɪŋ] *adj* **1.** ciekawy, zajmujący **2.** ujmujący, sympatyczny

en•gine ['endʒɪn] *s* **1.** silnik *m*, motor *m* **2.** lokomotywa *f*; **'en•gine driv•er** *s* maszynista *m*

en•gi•neer [endʒɪ'nɪə] **I** *s* **1.** inżynier *m* **2.** mechanik *m* **3.** technik *m* **4.** *Am* maszynista *m* **II** *v/t* doprowadzać ⟨-dzić⟩ do *G*; **en•gi•neer•ing** [endʒɪ'nɪrɪŋ] *s* inżynieria *f*

En•gland ['ɪŋglənd] *s* Anglia *f*

En•glish ['ɪŋglɪʃ] **I** *adj* angielski **II** *s* **1.** ***he's ~*** jest Anglikiem; ***the ~*** Anglicy **2.** angielski *m*; ***in ~*** po angielsku; ***in plain ~*** jasno; ***Queen's ~, King's ~*** wzorcowa angielszczyzna

Eng•lish 'Chan•nel *s* kanał *m* La Manche **'En•glish•man** ['ɪŋglɪʃmən] *pl -men s* Anglik *m* **'En•glish•wom•an** *pl -men s* Angielka *f*

en•grave [ɪn'greɪv] *v/t* **1.** grawerować ⟨wy-⟩ **2.** ryć ⟨wy-⟩; ***~d in stone*** wyryty w kamieniu; ***it's ~d in his memory*** to wryło mu się w pamięć **3.** ozdabiać ⟨-dobić⟩; **en•grav•ing** [ɪn'greɪvɪŋ] *s* **1.** grafika *f* **2.** sztych *m* **3.** rycina *f* **4.** grawerowanie *n*

en•grossed [ɪn'grəʊst] *adj* pochłonięty, zaabsorbowany (***in*** *I*); **en•gross•ing** [ɪn'grəʊsɪŋ] *adj* wciągający, zajmujący, absorbujący

en•gulf [ɪn'gʌlf] *v/t* **1.** otaczać ⟨otoczyć⟩ **2.** ogarniać ⟨-rnąć⟩ **3.** pochłaniać ⟨-łonąć⟩

en•hance [ɪn'hæns] *v/t* **1.** poprawiać ⟨-wić⟩, udoskonalać ⟨-lić⟩ **2.** zwiększać ⟨-szyć⟩ **3.** *value*: podnosić ⟨-nieść⟩

e•nig•ma [ɪ'nɪgmə] *s* zagadka *f*; **e•nig•mat•ic** [enɪg'mætɪk] *adj* zagadkowy, enigmatyczny, tajemniczy

en•joy [ɪn'dʒɔɪ] *v/t* **1.** lubić; ***~ doing s.th.*** lubić coś robić; ***did you ~ the play?*** czy podobała ci się sztuka?; ***~ oneself*** dobrze się bawić; ***~ yourself!*** baw się dobrze! **2.** cieszyć się, korzystać z *G*; ***~ good health*** cieszyć się dobrym zdrowiem; **en•joy•a•ble** [ɪn'dʒɔɪəbl] *adj* przyjemny, miły; **en•joy•ment** [ɪn'dʒɔɪmənt] *s* przyjemność *f*, radość *f*

en•large [ɪn'lɑːdʒ] **I** *v/t* **1.** powiększać ⟨-szyć⟩ **2.** rozszerzać ⟨-rzyć⟩ **3.** rozwijać ⟨-winąć⟩ **II** *v/i* **1.** powiększać ⟨-szyć⟩ się **2.** wzrastać ⟨-rosnąć⟩ **3.** **~ *on*** *form* rozwijać; **en•large•ment** [ɪn'lɑːdʒmənt] *s* **1.** powiększenie *n* **2.** rozszerzenie *n* **3.** MED przerost *m*

en•light•en [ɪn'laɪtn] *v/t* oświecać ⟨-cić⟩

en•list [ɪn'lɪst] **I** *v/t* **1.** werbować ⟨z-⟩ do wojska **2.** *fig* pozyskiwać ⟨-skać⟩ **II** *v/i* zaciągać ⟨-gnąć⟩ się do wojska

en•liv•en [ɪn'laɪvn] *v/t* ożywiać ⟨-wić⟩

en•mi•ty ['enmətɪ] *s* wrogość *f*

e•nor•mi•ty [ɪ'nɔːmətɪ] *s* **1.** ogrom *m* **2.** potworność *f*; **e•nor•mous** [ɪ'nɔːməs] *adj* ogromny, olbrzymi; **e•nor•mous•ly** [ɪ'nɔːməslɪ] *adv* ogromnie, niezmiernie, niezwykle

e•nough [ɪ'nʌf] **I** *adj* dość, dosyć, wystarczająco dużo; ***there's ~ room*** jest wystarczająco dużo miejsca **II** *pron* dość, dosyć, wystarczająco dużo; ***I have had ~, thank you!*** dziękuję, najadłam się; ***~ of that!*** dość tego! **III** *adv* dość, dostatecznie, wystarczająco; ***be kind ~ to do this for me*** bądź tak miły i zrób to dla mnie; ***curiously ~*** co ciekawe

en•quire [ɪn'kwaɪə] → ***inquire***

en•raged [ɪn'reɪdʒd] *adj* **1.** wściekły **2.** rozjuszony

en•rich [ɪn'rɪtʃ] *v/t* **1.** wzbogacać ⟨-cić⟩ **2.** użyźniać ⟨-nić⟩

en•rol [ɪn'rəʊl] *Br*, **en•roll** *Am* **I** *v/i* zapisywać ⟨-sać⟩ się (***on/in*** na *A*) **II** *v/t* **1.** przyjmować ⟨-jąć⟩ **2.** zapisywać ⟨-sać⟩; **en•roll•ment** [ɪn'rəʊlmənt] *s* **1.** zapisy *pl* **2.** zapisanie *n* się **3.** liczba *f* przyjętych

en•snare [ɪn'sneə] *v/t* **1.** łapać ⟨z-⟩ w sidła **2.** *fig* usidlać ⟨-lić⟩, omotywać ⟨-tać⟩

en•sue ['ɪnsjuː] *v/i* **1.** wywiązać ⟨-zać⟩ się **2.** następować ⟨-tąpić⟩; ***the ensuing years*** kolejne lata

E

en suite [ɒn'swiːt] *adj bathroom, room*: przyległy

en•sure [ɪn'ʃʊə] *v/t* **1.** upewniać ⟨-nić⟩ się (***that*** że) **2.** zapewniać ⟨-nić⟩ **3.** gwarantować ⟨za-⟩

ENT [iːen'tiː] *abbr* (=***Ear, Nose and Throat***) otorynolaryngologia *f*, laryngologia *f*

en•tail [ɪn'teɪl] *v/t* **1.** pociągać ⟨-gnąć⟩ za sobą **2.** wiązać się z *I* **3.** wymagać

en•tan•gle [ɪn'tæŋgl] *v/t*: ***become ~d in*** **a)** zaplątać się w *A* **b)** *fig* uwikłać się w *A*

en•ter ['entə] **I** *v/t* **1.** wchodzić ⟨wejść⟩ do *G*; ***it never ~ed my mind*** nigdy mi to nie przyszło do głowy **2.** wkraczać ⟨-roczyć⟩ do *G* **3.** przystępować ⟨-tąpić⟩ do *G* **4.** wstępować ⟨-tąpić⟩ do *G* **5.** wpisywać ⟨-sać⟩ **6.** *data*: wprowadzać ⟨-dzić⟩ **7.** zgłaszać ⟨-łosić⟩ się do *G* **II** *v/i* **1.** wchodzić ⟨wejść⟩; ***~ Hamlet*** (*stage*) wchodzi Hamlet **2.** zgłaszać ⟨-łosić⟩ się (***do*** *G* for); **en•ter into** *v/i* nawiązywać ⟨-zać⟩, podejmować ⟨-djąć⟩ ***~ correspondence with*** nawiązać korespondencję z *I*

'en•ter key *s* klawisz *m* Enter

en•ter•prise ['entəpraɪz] *s* **1.** przedsięwzięcie *n*, projekt *m* **2.** przedsiębiorstwo *n* **3.** przedsiębiorczość *f*, inicjatywa *f*; **en•ter•pris•ing** ['entəpraɪzɪŋ] *adj* przedsiębiorczy, rzutki

en•ter•tain [entə'teɪn] *v/t* **1.** zabawiać ⟨-wić⟩ **2.** zajmować ⟨-jąć⟩ **3.** podejmować ⟨-djąć⟩ **4.** żywić **5.** rozważać, brać pod uwagę; ***~ an idea*** nosić się z myślą; **en•ter•tain•er** [entə'teɪnə] *s* artysta *m* estradowy; **en•ter•tain•ing** [entə'teɪnɪŋ] *adj* **1.** zabawny **2.** zajmujący **3.** przyjemny; **en•ter•tain•ment** [entə'teɪnmənt] *s* **1.** rozrywka *f*; ***much to his ~*** ku jego (wielkiej) uciesze; ***the ~ industry*** przemysł rozrywkowy **2.** *guests*: zabawianie *n*, podejmowanie *n*

en•thral(l) [ɪn'θrɔːl] *v/t* fascynować ⟨za-⟩, urzekać ⟨urzec⟩, zauroczyć; **en•thrall•ing** [ɪn'θrɔːlɪŋ] *adj* fascynujący, urzekający

en•thuse [ɪn'θjuːz] *v/i* **1.** zachwycać ⟨-cić⟩ się (***about/over*** *I*) **2.** opowiadać ⟨-wiedzieć⟩ z entuzjazmem (***about/over*** o *L*)

en•thu•si•asm [ɪn'θjuːzɪæzm] *s* entuzjazm *m*; **en•thu•si•ast** [ɪn'θjuːzɪ'æst] *s* entuzjasta *m*, miłośnik *m*

en•thu•si•as•tic [ɪnθjuːzɪ'æstɪk] *adj* **1.** entuzjastyczny **2.** rozentuzjazmowany **3.** gorliwy **4.** zapalony; **en•thu•si•as•tic•al•ly** [ɪnθjuːzɪ'æstɪklɪ] *adv* entuzjastycznie, z entuzjazmem, ochoczo

en•tice [ɪn'taɪs] *v/t* kusić ⟨s-⟩, nęcić ⟨z-⟩, wabić ⟨z-⟩; **en•tice away** *v/t* odciągać ⟨-gnąć⟩; ***entice s.o.'s girlfriend away*** poderwać komuś dziewczynę

en•tice•ment [ɪn'taɪsmənt] *s* **1.** pokusa *f* **2.** kusząca obietnica *f* **3.** kuszenie *n*, nęcenie *n*; **en•tic•ing** [ɪn'taɪsɪŋ] *adj* **1.** kuszący, nęcący **2.** ponętny, powabny

en•tire [ɪn'taɪə] *adj* **1.** cały **2.** całkowity, kompletny; ***be in ~ agreement with*** całkowicie się zgadzać z *I* **3.** pełny; **en•tire•ly** [ɪn'taɪəlɪ] *adv* całkowicie, zupełnie; **en•tire•ty** [ɪn'taɪrətɪ] *s* całość *f*

en•ti•tle [ɪn'taɪtl] *v/t* **1.** tytułować ⟨za-⟩ **2.** upoważniać ⟨-nić⟩; **en•ti•tled** [ɪn'taɪtld] *adj* **1.** zatytułowany **2.** upoważniony (***to*** do *G*); ***be ~ to*** mieć prawo do *G*; ***be ~ to vote*** mieć prawo głosu

en•ti•ty ['entətɪ] *s* **1.** ECON JUR jednostka *f*; ***a legal ~*** osoba prawna **2.** (*being*) istota *f*

en•tou•rage ['ɒntʊrɑːʒ] *s* **1.** osoby *pl* towarzyszące **2.** świta *f*

en•trance¹ ['entrəns] *s* **1.** wejście *n*; ***~ hall*** hol (wejściowy), przedpokój **2.** wjazd *m* **3.** wejście *n*, wchodzenie *n*; ***make an ~*** THEAT zrobić wejście **4.** wstęp *m*; ***no ~!*** wstęp wzbroniony!

en•trance² [ɪn'træns] *v/t* urzekać ⟨urzec⟩; **en•tranced** [ɪn'trænst] *adj* urzeczony

'en•trance ex•am(•i•na•tion) *s* egzamin *m* wstępny; **'en•trance fee** *s* **1.** opłata *f* za wstęp **2.** wpisowe *n*

en•treat [ɪn'triːt] *v/t form* błagać, usilnie prosić; **en•treat•y** [ɪn'triːtɪ] *s form* błaganie *n*, usilna prośba *f*

en•trée ['ɒntreɪ] *s* **1.** COOK danie *n* główne **2.** COOK przystawka *f* **3.** prawo *n* wstępu, wstęp *m*

en•tre•pre•neur [ɒntrəprəˈnɜː] *s* przedsiębiorca *m*; **en•tre•pre•neur•i•al** [ɒntrəprəˈnɜːrɪəl] *adj* **1.** przedsiębiorczy **2.** gotowy podejmować ryzyko
en•trust [ɪnˈtrʌst] *v/t*: ~ ***s.o. with s.th***, ~ ***s.th. to s.o.*** powierzyć komuś coś
en•try [ˈentrɪ] *s* **1.** wejście *n* **2.** wjazd *m*; ***no*** ~ zakaz wjazdu **3.** wstęp *m*; ***no*** ~ zakaz wstępu **4.** (*competition*) zgłoszenie *n* **5.** wpis *m* **6.** (*dictionary*) hasło *n*, artykuł *m* hasłowy **7.** (*diary*) notatka *f* **8.** wstąpienie *n* **9.** przystąpienie *n* **10.** ilość *f* zgłoszeń; **ˈen•try form** *s* formularz *m* zgłoszeniowy; **ˈen•try•phone** *s* domofon *m*; **ˈen•try vi•sa** *s* wiza *f* wjazdowa
en•twine [ɪnˈtwaɪn] *v/t* **1.** splatać ⟨-leść⟩ **2.** oplatać ⟨-leść⟩
e•nu•me•rate [ɪˈnjuːməreɪt] *v/t* wyliczać ⟨-czyć⟩, wymieniać ⟨-nić⟩
en•vel•op [ɪnˈveləp] *v/t* **1.** okrywać ⟨-ryć⟩ **2.** otulać ⟨-lić⟩, spowijać ⟨-wić⟩
en•ve•lope [ˈenvələʊp] *s* koperta *f*
en•vi•a•ble [ˈenvɪəbl] *adj* godny pozazdroszczenia
en•vi•ous [ˈenvɪəs] *adj* **1.** zazdrosny **2.** zawistny
en•vi•ron•ment [ɪnˈvaɪrənmənt] *s* **1.** środowisko *n* naturalne **2.** otoczenie *n*, środowisko *n*, warunki *pl*; **en•vi•ron•men•tal** [ɪnvaɪrənˈmentl] *adj* **1.** środowiskowy; ***an*** ~ ***impact*** wpływ na środowisko naturalne **2.** związany z ochroną środowiska **3.** ekologiczny; **en•vi•ron•men•tal•ist** [ɪnvaɪrənˈmentəlɪst] *s* **1.** ekolog *m* **2.** specjalista *m* w zakresie ochrony środowiska **3.** działacz *m* na rzecz ochrony środowiska
en•vi•ron•men•tal•ly ˈfriend•ly *adj* przyjazny dla środowiska, ekologiczny; **en•vi•ron•men•tal polˈlu•tion** *s* zanieczyszczenie *n* środowiska naturalnego; **en•vi•ron•men•tal proˈtec•tion** *s* ochrona *f* środowiska (naturalnego)
en•vi•rons [ɪnˈvaɪrənz] *pl* okolice *pl*
en•voy [ˈenvɔɪ] *s* **1.** poseł *m* **2.** wysłannik *m*
en•vy [ˈenvɪ] **I** *s* **1.** zazdrość *f* **2.** zawiść *f* **3.** przedmiot *m* zazdrości; ***his car is the*** ~ ***of everybody*** wszyscy zazdroszczą mu samochodu **II** *v/t* zazdrościć ⟨po-⟩; ***I don't*** ~ ***you that responsibility*** nie zazdroszczę ci tego obowiązku
en•zyme [ˈenzaɪm] *s* enzym *m*
e•phem•er•al [ɪˈfemərəl] *adj* **1.** efemeryczny **2.** ulotny
ep•ic [ˈepɪk] **I** *adj* **1.** epicki **2.** heroiczny **3.** homerycki **II** *s* epos *m*, epopeja *f*
ep•i•cen•tre [ˈepɪsentə] *Br*, ***ep•i•center*** *Am s* epicentrum *f*
ep•i•dem•ic [epɪˈdemɪk] **I** *adj* epidemiczny **II** *s* **1.** epidemia *f* **2.** plaga *f*
ep•i•lep•sy [ˈepɪlepsɪ] *s* padaczka *f*, epilepsja *f*; **ep•i•lep•tic** [epɪˈleptɪk] **I** *s* epileptyk *m* **II** *adj* epileptyczny, padaczkowy; **ep•i•lep•tic ˈfit** *s* atak *m* epileptyczny, atak *m* padaczki
ep•i•logue [ˈepɪlɒg] *Br*, ***ep•i•log*** *Am s* epilog *m*
E•piph•a•ny [ɪˈpɪfənɪ] *s* REL święto *n* Trzech Króli
e•pis•co•pal [ɪˈpɪskəpl] *adj* **1.** episkopalny **2.** biskupi
ep•i•sode [ˈepɪsəʊd] *s* **1.** zdarzenie *n* **2.** epizod *m* **3.** (*series*) odcinek *m*
e•pis•tle [ɪˈpɪsl] *s lit* list *m*
ep•i•taph [ˈepɪtɑːf] *s* epitafium *n*
ep•i•thet [ˈepɪθet] *s* **1.** epitet *m* **2.** określenie *n* **3.** miano *n*
e•poch [ˈiːpɒk] *s* epoka *f*; **ˈe•poch-mak•ing** *adj* epokowy, przełomowy
e•qual [ˈiːkwl] **I** *adj* **1.** równy; ~ ***to s.th.*** równy czemuś; ***on*** ~ ***terms*** na równych prawach; ~ ***opportunities*** równe szanse; ~ ***rights for women*** równouprawnienie kobiet **2.** jednakowy, taki sam; ~ ***in size***, ***of*** ~ ***size*** w tym samym rozmiarze **3.** ***prove*** ~ ***to s.th.*** *form* sprostać czemuś **4.** równorzędny **II** *s* równy *m*; ***your*** ~***s*** tacy jak ty, równi tobie; ***he has no*** ~, ***he is without*** ~ nikt mu nie dorównuje, nikt nie może się z nim równać **III** *v/t* **1.** równać się **2.** dorównywać ⟨-nać⟩ **3.** *record*: wyrównywać ⟨-nać⟩; **e•qual•i•ty** [ɪˈkwɒlətɪ] *s* równość *f*; ~ ***of rights*** równouprawnienie; ~ ***of opportunity*** równe szanse; **e•qual•ize** [ˈiːkwəlaɪz] **I** *v/t* **1.** zrównywać ⟨-nać⟩ **2.** wyrównywać ⟨-nać⟩ **II** *v/i* SPORT wyrównywać ⟨-nać⟩; **e•qual•iz•er** [ˈiːkwəlaɪzə] *s* SPORT **1.** bramka *f* wyrównująca **2.** punkt *m* wyrównujący; **e•qual•ly** [ˈiːkwəlɪ] *adv* **1.** równo **2.** tak samo,

jednakowo **3.** równie, tak samo; **e•qual 'rights** *pl* równe prawa *pl*; **'e•quals sign** znak *m* równości
e•quate [ɪ'kweɪt] *v/t* **1.** utożsamiać ⟨-mić⟩ **2.** porównywać ⟨-nać⟩, przyrównywać ⟨-nać⟩; **e•qua•tion** [ɪ'kweɪʒn] *s* **1.** MATH równanie *n* **2.** utożsamianie *n* **3.** porównanie *n*, przyrównanie *n*
E
e•qua•tor [ɪ'kweɪtə] *s*: ***the ~*** równik *m*; **e•qua•to•ri•al** [ekwə'tɔːrɪəl] *adj* równikowy
e•qui•lib•ri•um [iːkwɪ'lɪbrɪəm] *s* równowaga *f*
e•qui•nox ['iːkwɪnɒks] *s* równonoc *f*, zrównanie *n*
e•quip [ɪ'kwɪp] *v/t* **1.** wyposażać ⟨-żyć⟩ **2.** zaopatrywać ⟨-trzyć⟩ **3.** *fig* przygotowywać ⟨-tować⟩; ***be well ~ped for*** być dobrze przygotowanym do *G*; **e•quip•ment** [ɪ'kwɪpmənt] *s* **1.** wyposażenie *n* **2.** sprzęt *m* **3.** urządzenia *pl* **4.** aparatura *f*
e•quiv•a•lence [ɪ'kwɪvələns] *s* **1.** równoważność *f* **2.** ekwiwalencja *f*; **e•quiv•a•lent** [ɪ'kwɪvələnt] **I** *s* **1.** odpowiednik *m* **2.** ekwiwalent *m* **II** *adj* **1.** taki sam, jednakowy **2.** ***be ~ to*** odpowiadać *D* **3.** równorzędny
e•ra ['ɪrə] *s* **1.** era *f* **2.** epoka *f*
e•rad•i•cate [ɪ'rædɪkeɪt] *v/t* **1.** wykorzeniać ⟨-nić⟩ **2.** wypleniać ⟨-nić⟩ **3.** zwalczać ⟨-czyć⟩; **e•rad•i•ca•tion** [ɪrædɪ'keɪʃn] *s* **1.** wykorzenienie *n* **2.** wyplenienie *n* **3.** zwalczenie *n*
e•rase [ɪ'reɪz] *v/t* **1.** ścierać ⟨zetrzeć⟩ **2.** *a. fig* wymazywać ⟨-zać⟩ **3.** zwalczać ⟨-czyć⟩, likwidować ⟨z-⟩ **4.** kasować ⟨s-⟩; **e•ras•er** [ɪ'reɪzə] *s* **1.** gumka *f* do ścierania **2.** gąbka *f* do tablicy; **e•ras•ure** [ɪ'reɪʒə] *s* **1.** likwidacja *f* **2.** zmazanie *n* **3.** skasowanie *n*
e•rect [ɪ'rekt] **I** *adj* **1.** podniesiony; ***with*** (***one's***) ***head ~*** z podniesioną głową **2.** wyprostowany **3.** *penis*: w stanie wzwodu **4.** *nipple*: stwardniałe **II** *v/t* **1.** wznosić ⟨-nieść⟩ **2.** stawiać ⟨postawić⟩ **3.** budować ⟨z-⟩; **e•rec•tion** [ɪ'rekʃn] *s* **1.** wzwód *m*, erekcja *f* **2.** wzniesienie *n* **3.** budowa *f* **4.** gmach *m*, budowla *f*
e•rode [ɪ'rəʊd] **I** *v/t* **1.** powodować ⟨s-⟩ erozję **2.** wżerać ⟨weżreć⟩ się w *A* **3.** *fig* podkopywać ⟨-pać⟩ **II** *v/i* **1.** ulegać ⟨ulec⟩ erozji **2.** *fig* spadać ⟨spaść⟩
e•ro•sion [ɪ'rəʊʒn] *s* **1.** GEOL erozja *f* **2.** pogorszenie *n* stanu **3.** *right*: ograniczenie *n*
e•rot•ic [ɪ'rɒtɪk] *adj* erotyczny; **e•rot•i•cism** [ɪ'rɒtɪsɪzm] *s* erotyka *f*, erotyczność *f*
err [ɜː] *v/i* **1.** mylić ⟨po-⟩ się; ***it's better to ~ on the side of caution*** lepiej dmuchać na zimne; ***to ~ is human*** błądzić jest rzeczą ludzką **2.** robić ⟨z-⟩ błąd
er•rand ['erənd] *s* polecenie *n*, sprawa *f* do załatwienia; ***go on an ~, run an ~*** załatwiać sprawę; **'er•rand boy** *s* chłopiec *m* na posyłki
er•ra•ta [e'rɑːtə] *s* errata *f*, arkusz *m* poprawek
er•rat•ic [ɪ'rætɪk] *adj* **1.** nieobliczalny **2.** SPORT nierówny; ***he's ~*** **a)** jego gra jest nierówna **b)** popełnia sporo błędów **3.** niekonsekwentny **4.** nierównomierny
er•ro•ne•ous [ɪ'rəʊnɪəs] *adj* błędny, mylny; **er•ro•ne•ous•ly** [ɪ'rəʊnɪəslɪ] *adv* błędnie, mylnie
er•ror ['erə] *s* błąd *m*, pomyłka *f*; ***in ~*** omyłkowo; ***an ~ of judgement*** błędna ocena *f* sytuacji, błąd *m* w ocenie sytuacji; **'er•ror mes•sage** *s* INF komunikat *m* o błędzie
er•u•dite ['erʊdaɪt] *adj* uczony, erudycyjny; **er•u•di•tion** [erʊ'dɪʃn] *s* erudycja *f*
e•rupt [ɪ'rʌpt] *v/i* (*volcano, war*) wybuchać ⟨-chnąć⟩; **e•rup•tion** [ɪ'rʌpʃn] *s* **1.** wybuch *m*, erupcja *f* **2.** *fig* wybuch *m*; ***an angry ~*** wybuch złości **3.** MED wykwit *m* skórny
es•ca•late ['eskəleɪt] **I** *v/i* **1.** nasilać ⟨-lić⟩ się **2.** wzrastać ⟨-rosnąć⟩ **3.** potęgować ⟨s-⟩ się **II** *v/t* **1.** potęgować ⟨s-⟩ **2.** zwiększać ⟨-szyć⟩; **es•ca•la•tion** [eskə'leɪʃn] *s* **1.** eskalacja *f* **2.** wzrost *m*; **es•ca•la•tor** ['eskəleɪtə] *s* ruchome schody *pl*
es•ca•pade ['eskəpeɪd] *s* **1.** eskapada *f* **2.** wyskok *m*
es•cape [ɪ'skeɪp] **I** *v/i* **1.** uciekać ⟨uciec⟩ **2.** ratować ⟨u-⟩ się **3.** uchodzić ⟨ujść⟩; ***~ with one's life*** ujść z życiem **II** *v/t* **1.** unikać ⟨-knąć⟩ **2.** umykać ⟨umknąć⟩ **3.** ***his name ~s me*** je-

go imię wyleciało mi z głowy **7.** (*curse*) wymykać ⟨-mknąć⟩ się **III** *s* **1.** ucieczka *f*; ***have a narrow ~*** o włos uniknąć nieszczęścia, cudem ujść cało; ***that was a narrow ~!*** było blisko! **2.** wyciek *m*; **'es•cape chute** *s* rynna *f* ratunkowa; **'es•cape key** *s* klawisz *m* Escape

es•cort **I** ['eskɔːt] *s* **1.** eskorta *f*; ***the President and his motorcycle ~*** prezydent i jego eskorta motocyklowa **2.** osoba *f* towarzysząca **3.** partner *m* **II** [ɪ'skɔːt] *v/t* **1.** eskortować **2.** konwojować **3.** towarzyszyć **4.** odprowadzać ⟨-dzić⟩; **'es•cort a•gen•cy** *s* agencja *f* towarzyska

Es•ki•mo ['eskɪməʊ] *pl -mos* [‿məʊz] **I** *s* Eskimos *m* **II** *adj* eskimoski

ESL [iːes'el] *abbr* (=***English as a Second Language***) język *m* angielski jako drugi język, język *m* angielski jako pierwszy język obcy

es•o•ter•ic [esəʊ'terɪk] *adj* **1.** ezoteryczny **2.** tajemny

es•pe•cial [ɪ'speʃl] *adj Br form* szczególny; **es•pe•cial•ly** [ɪ'speʃlɪ] *adv* **1.** zwłaszcza **2.** szczególnie **3.** specjalnie

es•pi•o•nage ['espɪənɑːʒ] *s* **1.** wywiad *m* **2.** szpiegostwo *n*

es•say ['eseɪ] *s* **1.** esej *m* **2.** wypracowanie *n*

es•sence ['esns] *s* **1.** istota *f*, sedno *n*; ***in ~*** w gruncie rzeczy, zasadniczo **2.** COOK esencja *f*, wyciąg *m*; **es•sen•tial** [ɪ'senʃl] **I** *adj* **1.** niezbędny; ***~ to life*** niezbędny do życia **2.** podstawowy **3.** zasadniczy, istotny **4.** eteryczny; ***~ oil*** olejek eteryczny **II** *s* **1.** rzecz *f* niezbędna **2.** podstawa *f*; **es•sen•tial•ly** [ɪ'senʃlɪ] *adv* zasadniczo, w gruncie rzeczy, w zasadzie

es•tab•lish [ɪ'stæblɪʃ] *v/t* **1.** *firm*: zakładać ⟨założyć⟩ **2.** *government*, *department*: tworzyć ⟨u-⟩ **3.** ustalać ⟨-lić⟩ **4.** ustanawiać ⟨-nowić⟩ **5.** wprowadzać ⟨-dzić⟩ **6.** *reputation*: wyrobić sobie; **es•tab•lished** [ɪ'stæblɪʃt] *adj* **1.** uznany **2.** przyjęty **3.** *church*: państwowy; **es•tab•lish•ment** [ɪ'stæblɪʃmənt] *s* **1.** organizacja *f* **2.** firma *f* **3.** założenie *n* **4.** utworzenie *n* **5.** ustanowienie *n* **6.** ***the ~*** establishment *m*

es•tate [ɪ'steɪt] *s* **1.** posiadłość *f*, majątek *m* ziemski **2.** majątek *m* **3.** *Br* osiedle *n*; **es•'tate a•gen•cy** *s Br* agencja *f* nieruchomości; **es•'tate a•gent** *s Br* pośrednik *m* w handlu nieruchomościami; **es•'tate car** *s Br* (samochód) kombi *n*

es•teem [ɪ'stiːm] **I** *s* szacunek *m*, poważanie *n*; ***hold s.o. in (high) ~*** darzyć kogoś (wielkim) szacunkiem **II** *v/t* **1.** poważać, szanować **2.** cenić **3.** *form* uznawać za *G*

es•thet•ic [es'θetɪk] *Am* → ***aesthetic***

es•ti•mate **I** ['estɪmeɪt] *v/t* **1.** szacować ⟨o-⟩; ***an ~d value*** wartość szacunkowa; ***an ~d 200 people*** około 200 osób **2.** oceniać ⟨-nić⟩ **3.** określać ⟨-lić⟩, ustalać ⟨-lić⟩ **II** ['estɪmət] *s* **1.** ocena *f*; ***at a rough ~*** w przybliżeniu, z grubsza **2.** szacunek *m* **3.** wycena *f* (szacunkowa) **4.** kosztorys *m*

es•ti•ma•tion [estɪ'meɪʃn] *s* **1.** zdanie *f*; ***in my ~*** w moim odczuciu, moim zdaniem; ***go down in s.o.'s ~*** stracić w czyichś oczach **2.** szacunek *m*, ocena *f* szacunkowa

ETA [iːtiː'eɪ] *abbr* (=***estimated time of arrival***) przewidywany czas *m* przybycia

etc [et'setrə] *abbr* (=***et cetera***) **1.** itd. **2.** itp.

et cet•er•a [et'setrə] *adv* **1.** i tak dalej **2.** i tym podobne

e•ter•nal [ɪ'tɜːnl] *adj* **1.** wieczny **2.** ciągły, nieustanny **3.** *truth*: uniwersalny; **e•ter•nal•ly** [ɪ'tɜːnəlɪ] *adv* **1.** wiecznie **2.** dozgonnie; **e•ter•ni•ty** [ɪ'tɜːnətɪ] *s* wieczność *f*; **e•ter•nal 'tri•angle** *s* trójkąt *m* małżeński

e•ther ['iːθə] *s CHEM* eter *m*; **e•the•re•al** [ɪ'θɪrɪəl] *adj* eteryczny

eth•i•cal ['eθɪkl] *adj* etyczny; **eth•ics** ['eθɪks] *s* etyka *f*

E•thi•o•pi•a [iːθɪ'əʊpɪə] *s* Etiopia *f*

eth•nic ['eθnɪk] *adj* **1.** etniczny **2.** rodowity; ***~ Germans*** rodowici Niemcy **3.** rdzenny; **eth•nic 'cleans•ing** *s* czystka *f* etniczna; **eth•nic 'group** *s* grupa *f* etniczna; **eth•nic mi•'nor•i•ty** *s* mniejszość *f* etniczna

e•thos ['iːθɒs] *s* etos *m*

et•i•quette ['etɪket] *s* **1.** (*social*) etykieta *f* **2.** normy *pl* postępowania

EU [iː'juː] *abbr* (=***European Union***) UE *f*

eu•ca•lyp•tus [juːkə'lɪptəs] **I** *s* eukaliptus *m* **II** *adj* eukaliptusowy

eu•phe•mism ['juːfəmɪzm] *s* eufemizm *m*; **eu•phe•mis•tic** [juːfə'mɪstɪk] *adj* eufemistyczny

eu•pho•ri•a [juː'fɔːrɪə] *s* euforia *f*; **eu•phor•ic** [juː'fɒrɪk] *adj* **1.** euforyczny **2.** w stanie euforii

E

eu•ro ['jʊərəʊ] *s FIN* euro *n*

Eu•rope ['jʊrəp] *s* Europa *f*

Eu•ro•pe•an [jʊrə'piːən] **I** *adj* europejski; ***a ~ champion*** mistrz Europy; ***the ~ championship*** mistrzostwo Europy; ***the ~ Cup*** Puchar Europy; ***~ Monetary System*** Europejski System Monetarny **II** *s* Europejczyk *m*, Europejka *f*; **Eu•ro•pe•an Com•'mis•sion** *s* Komisja *f* Europejska; **Eu•ro•pe•an 'Par•lia•ment** *s* Parlament *m* Europejski; **Eu•ro•pe•an 'Un•ion** *s* Unia *f* Europejska

eu•tha•na•si•a [jʊθə'neɪzɪə] *s* eutanazja *f*

e•vac•u•ate [ɪ'vækjʊeɪt] *v/t* **1.** ewakuować **2.** opróżniać ⟨-nić⟩; **e•vac•u•a•tion** [ɪvækjʊ'eɪʃn] *s* **1.** ewakuacja *f* **2.** opróżnienie *n*; **e•vac•u•ee** [ɪvækjuː'iː] *s* osoba *f* ewakuowana, ewakuant *m*

e•vade [ɪ'veɪd] *v/t* **1.** uchylać ⟨-lić⟩ się od *G*, ***~ answering a question*** unikać odpowiedzi na pytanie, wykręcać się od odpowiedzi na pytanie **2.** uchylać ⟨-lić⟩ się przed *G*

e•val•u•ate [ɪ'væljʊeɪt] *v/t* **1.** oceniać ⟨-nić⟩ **2.** wyceniać ⟨-nić⟩ **3.** oszacowywać ⟨-cować⟩; **e•val•u•a•tion** [ɪvæljʊ'eɪʃn] *s* **1.** ocena *f* **2.** wycena *f* **3.** oszacowanie *n*

e•van•gel•i•cal [iːvæn'dʒelɪkl] *REL* **I** *adj* **1.** ewangeliczny, ewangelijny **2.** ewangelicki **II** *s* ewangelik *m*; **e•van•ge•lism** [ɪ'vændʒəlɪzəm] *s* ewangelizacja *f*; **e•van•gel•ist** [ɪ'vændʒəlɪst] *s* **1.** kaznodzieja *m* **2.** ewangelista *m*; **e•van•ge•lize** [ɪ'vændʒəlaɪz] *v/t* ewangelizować

e•vap•o•rate [ɪ'væpəreɪt] **I** *v/i* **1.** wyparowywać ⟨-rować⟩ **2.** *fig* rozwiewać ⟨-wiać⟩ się **3.** mijać ⟨minąć⟩ **II** *v/t* odparowywać ⟨-rować⟩; **e•vap•o•rated 'milk** *s* mleko *n* skondensowane; **e•vap•o•ra•tion** [ɪvæpə'reɪʃn] *s PHYS* parowanie *n*

e•va•sion [ɪ'veɪʒn] *s* **1.** uchylanie *n* się; ***tax ~*** uchylanie się od płacenia podatków **2.** wykręt *m*; **e•va•sive** [ɪ'veɪsɪv] *adj* wymijający; ***be ~*** mówić mało konkretnie; ***take ~ action*** zrobić unik; **e•va•sive•ness** [ɪ'veɪsɪvnɪs] *s* pokrętność *f*

eve [iːv] *s* wigilia *f*; ***on the ~ of*** w przeddzień *G*

e•ven[1] ['iːvn] *adv* **1.** nawet; ***not ~*** nawet nie; ***~ if*** nawet jeśli, nawet gdyby; ***~ though*** chociaż, mimo że; ***~ as a child he was serious*** nawet jako dziecko był poważny **2.** nawet, jeszcze; ***~ better*** jeszcze lepiej

even[2] [~] *adj* **1.** równy **2.** gładki **3.** równomierny, jednolity **4.** spokojny; ***of an ~ temper*** zrównoważony; ***an ~ voice*** spokojny głos **5.** ***be ~ with*** mieć równe szanse z *I*, iść łeb w łeb z *I* **6.** *MATH* parzysty; **even out** *v/t* **1.** wyrównywać ⟨-nać⟩ **2.** wygładzać ⟨-dzić⟩; **even up** *v/t* **1.** wyrównywać ⟨-nać⟩ **2.** równoważyć ⟨z-⟩; ***~ things up*** zrewanżować się

eve•ning ['iːvnɪŋ] *s* wieczór *m*; ***in the ~*** wieczorem; ***on the ~ of the 16th of May*** szesnastego maja wieczorem; ***yesterday ~, last ~*** wczoraj wieczorem; ***this ~*** dziś wieczorem; **'eve•ning class** *s* kurs *m* wieczorowy; **'eve•ning dress** *s* **1.** suknia *f* wieczorowa **2.** strój *m* wieczorowy; **eve•ning 'pa•per** *s* popołudniówka *f*; **eve•ning 'star** *s* gwiazda *f* wieczorna

e•ven•ly ['iːvnlɪ] *adv* **1.** równo **2.** równomiernie; **e•ven•ness** ['iːvnnɪs] *s* **1.** równość *f* **2.** równomierność *f* **3.** zrównoważenie *n*

e•vent [ɪ'vent] *s* **1.** wydarzenie *n*, zdarzenie *n*; ***after the ~*** po fakcie **2.** wypadek *m*, przypadek *m*; ***at all ~s, in any ~*** w każdym razie; ***in the ~ of*** w razie *G* **3.** *SPORT* konkurencja *f*

e•ven-'tem•pered *adj* zrównoważony

e•vent•ful [ɪ'ventfəl] *adj* **1.** ciekawy **2.** bogaty w wydarzenia **3.** barwny **4.** burzliwy

e•ven•tu•al [ɪ'ventʃʊəl] *adj* ostateczny, końcowy; **e•ven•tu•al•i•ty** [ɪventʃʊ'ælətɪ] *s* ewentualność *f*; **e•ven•tu-**

al•ly [ɪ'ventʃʊəlɪ] *adv* **1.** ostatecznie **2.** w końcu
ev•er ['evə] *adv* **1.** zawsze; **~ *since*** od tego czasu, odtąd **2.** (*comparison*) coraz; **~ *larger*** coraz większy **3.** kiedykolwiek, kiedyś; ***have you ~ been to London?*** byłeś kiedyś w Londynie; ***hardly ~*** prawie nigdy **4.** **~ *so*** *infml* naprawdę, bardzo; ***thank you ~ so much*** naprawdę bardzo ci dziękuję **5.** ***what ~ does he want?*** czegóż on chce?
ev•er•green ['evərgriːn] **I** *s* **1.** drzewo *n* wiecznie zielone **2.** niestarzejący się przebój *m* **II** *adj* **1.** *plant*: wiecznie zielony **2.** *song*: niestarzejący się
ev•er•last•ing [evər'lɑːstɪŋ] *adj* **1.** wieczny **2.** *fig* nieustanny
ev•er•y ['evrɪ] *adv* **1.** każdy; **~ *day*** codziennie; **~ *other day*** co drugi dzień; **~ *bit as much*** równie dużo; ***have ~ reason*** mieć wszelkie powody
ev•er•y•bod•y ['evrɪbɒdɪ] → ***everyone***
ev•er•y•day ['evrɪdeɪ] *adj* **1.** codzienny **2.** powszedni **3.** zwykły
ev•er•y•one ['evrɪwʌn] *pron* **1.** każdy **2.** wszyscy; ***to ~'s amazement*** ku zdumieniu wszystkich
ev•er•y•place ['evrɪpleɪs] *Am* → ***everywhere***
ev•er•y•thing ['evrɪθɪŋ] *pron* wszystko; ***and ~*** *infml* i cała reszta
ev•er•y•where ['evrɪweə] *adv* wszędzie; **~ *he goes*** gdziekowiek pójdzie
e•vict [ɪ'vɪkt] *v/t* eksmitować ⟨wy-⟩; **e•vic•tion** [ɪ'vɪkʃn] *s* eksmisja *f*
ev•i•dence ['evɪdəns] *s* **1.** dowody *pl*; ***for lack of ~*** z braku dowodów **2.** JUR zeznania *pl*; ***give ~ for*** (***against***) składać zeznania na korzyść (niekorzyść) *G*; ***turn Queen's ~*** *Br*, ***turn King's ~*** *Br*, ***turn State's ~*** *Am* wystąpić jako świadek koronny **3.** oznaki *pl*
ev•i•dent ['evɪdənt] *adj* **1.** widoczny **2.** ewidentny **3.** wyraźny **4.** oczywisty; **ev•i•dent•ly** ['evɪdəntlɪ] *adv* **1.** widocznie **2.** wyraźnie **3.** najwyraźniej
e•vil ['iːvl] **I** *adj* **1.** zły; **~ *eye*** zły urok **2.** nikczemny, niegodziwy **II** *s* **1.** zło *n*; ***the lesser of two ~s*** mniejsze zło **2.** nikczemność *f*, niegodziwość *f*; **e•vil-'mind•ed** *adj* **1.** zły **2.** złośliwy
e•voc•a•tive [ɪ'vɒkətɪv] *adj* **1.** ***be ~ of*** przywodzić na myśl *A* **2.** sugestywny; **e•voke** [ɪ'vəʊk] *v/t* **1.** przywoływać ⟨-łać⟩ **2.** *smile*, *spirits*: wywoływać ⟨-łać⟩
ev•o•lu•tion [iːvə'luːʃn] *s* **1.** BIOL ewolucja *f* **2.** rozwój *m*; ***the ~ of events*** rozwój wypadków; **e•volve** [ɪ'vɒlv] **I** *v/i* **1.** rozwijać ⟨-winąć⟩ się **2.** ewoluować **II** *v/t* opracowywać ⟨-cować⟩
ewe [juː] *s* owca *f*
ex- [eks] *adj* były
ex•act [ɪg'zækt] **I** *adj* **1.** dokładny **2.** ścisły **3.** precyzyjny **II** *v/t* **1.** egzekwować ⟨wy-⟩ **2.** *taxes*: ściągać ⟨-gnąć⟩ **3.** wymagać; **ex•act•ing** [ɪg'zæktɪŋ] *adj* **1.** wymagający **2.** rygorystyczny **3.** wymagający wysiłku; **ex•ac•ti•tude** [ɪg'zæktɪtjuːd] *s* **1.** dokładność *f* **2.** ścisłość *f*; **ex•act•ly** [ɪg'zæktlɪ] *adv* **1.** dokładnie; ***not ~*** niezupełnie **2.** ściśle; **ex•act•ness** [ɪg'zæktnɪs] *s* **1.** dokładność *f* **2.** ścisłość *f* **3.** precyzja *f*
ex•ag•ge•rate [ɪg'zædʒəreɪt] **I** *v/i* przesadzać ⟨-dzić⟩ **II** *v/t* wyolbrzymiać ⟨-mić⟩; **ex•ag•ge•ra•tion** [ɪgzædʒə'reɪʃn] *s* przesada *f*
ex•am [ɪg'zæm] *infml* → ***examination***
ex•am•i•na•tion [ɪgzæmɪ'neɪʃn] *s* **1.** egzamin *m*; ***an ~ paper*** test egzaminacyjny **2.** badanie *n*; ***on ~*** po zbadaniu **3.** analiza *f* **4.** ***the proposals are currently under ~*** propozycje są obecnie rozpatrywane **5.** JUR przesłuchanie *n* **6.** MED badanie *n* (lekarskie); **ex•am•ine** [ɪg'zæmɪn] *v/t* **1.** badać ⟨z-⟩ **2.** sprawdzać ⟨-dzić⟩ **3.** kontrolować ⟨s-⟩ **4.** rozpatrywać ⟨-trzeć⟩ **5.** przyglądać ⟨przyjrzeć⟩ się (dokładnie) **6.** poddawać ⟨-dać⟩ oględzinom **7.** egzaminować ⟨prze-⟩ **8.** przesłuchiwać ⟨-chać⟩; **ex•am•i•nee** [ɪgzæmɪ'niː] *s* **1.** egzaminowany *m* **2.** kandydat *m*; **ex•am•in•er** [ɪg'zæmɪnə] *s* egzaminator *m*
ex•am•ple [ɪg'zæmpl] *s* **1.** przykład *m*; ***for ~*** na przykład **2.** przykład *m*, wzór *m*; ***set a good ~*** dawać dobry przykład **3.** przykład *m*, nauczka *f*; ***make an ~ of s.o.*** przykładnie kogoś ukarać; ***let this be an ~ to you*** niech to będzie dla was nauczką

E

E

ex•as•per•ate [ɪg'zæspəreɪt] *v/t* irytować ⟨z-⟩ drażnić ⟨roz-⟩; **ex•as•per•at•ed** [ɪg'zæspəreɪtɪd] *adj* zirytowany, rozdrażniony; **ex•as•pe•rat•ing** [ɪg'zæspəreɪtɪŋ] *adj* irytujący, nieznośny; **ex•as•per•at•ing•ly** [ɪg'zæspəreɪtɪŋlɪ] *adv* irytująco; **ex•as•per•a•tion** [ɪgzæspə'reɪʃn] *s* irytacja *f*, złość *f*

ex•ca•vate ['ekskəveɪt] *v/t* **1.** *site*: badać ⟨prze-⟩ **2.** wykopywać ⟨-pać⟩ **3.** *ruins*: odkopywać ⟨-pać⟩; **ex•ca•va•tion** [ekskə'veɪʃn] *s* **1.** wykopalisko *n* **2.** **~s** prace wykopaliskowe **3.** kopanie *n* **4.** wykop *m*, rozkop *m*

ex•ceed [ɪk'siːd] *v/t* **1.** przekraczać ⟨-roczyć⟩ **2.** przewyższać ⟨-szyć⟩ **3.** prześcigać ⟨-gnąć⟩

ex•ceed•ing•ly [ɪk'siːdɪŋlɪ] *adv* niezmiernie, nadzwyczaj; ***~ kind*** niezmiernie miły

ex•cel [ɪk'sel] **I** *v/i* celować, wyróżniać się (***in***/***at*** w *L*) **II** *v/t* ***~ oneself*** *Br* przejść samego siebie; **ex•cel•lence** ['eksələns] *s* **1.** perfekcja *f*, doskonałość *f* **2.** wysoki poziom *m*; **Ex•cel•lency** ['eksələnsɪ] *s* (*title*) Ekscelencja; **ex•cel•lent** ['eksələnt] *adj* znakomity, doskonały, świetny; **ex•cel•lent•ly** ['eksələntlɪ] *adv* znakomicie, doskonale, świetnie

ex•cept [ɪk'sept] **I** *prep* (*a.* ***~ for***) oprócz *G*, z wyjątkiem *G*, poza *I* **II** *v/t* **1.** wyłączać ⟨-czyć⟩; ***present company ~ed*** z wyjątkiem tu obecnych **2.** wykluczać ⟨-czyć⟩ **3.** zastrzegać ⟨-rzec⟩ sobie **III** *conj* ***~ that*** chyba że; **ex•cept•ing** [ɪk'septɪŋ] *prep* z wyjątkiem *G*; **ex•cep•tion** [ɪk'sepʃn] *s* **1.** wyjątek *m*; ***~ to the rule*** wyjątek od reguły; ***by way of ~*** wyjątkowo; ***with the ~ of*** z wyjątkiem; ***without ~*** bez wyjątku; ***make an ~*** (***in s.o.'s case***) zrobić wyjątek (w przypadku kogoś) **2.** ***take ~ to s.th.*** protestować przeciwko czemuś, czuć się urażonym czymś; **ex•cep•tion•al** [ɪk'sepʃnl] *adj* wyjątkowy; **ex•cep•tion•al•ly** [ɪk'sepʃnlɪ] *adv* wyjątkowo

ex•cerpt ['eksɜːpt] *s* wyjątek *m*, fragment *m*, wyimek *m*, urywek *m*

ex•cess **I** [ɪk'ses] *s* **1.** nadmiar *m*; ***in ~ of*** ponad *I*, powyżej *G* **2.** przesada *f*, brak *m* umiaru; ***to ~*** do przesady **3.** **~s** ekscesy *pl*, wybryki *pl* **II** ['ekses] *adj* **1.** nadmierny **2.** dodatkowy; **ex•cess 'bag•gage** *s* dodatkowy bagaż *m*; **ex•cess 'fare** *s* dopłata *f* (do biletu); **ex•ces•sive** [ɪk'sesɪv] *adj* **1.** nadmierny **2.** wygórowany

ex•change [ɪks'tʃeɪndʒ] **I** *v/t* **1.** wymieniać ⟨-nić⟩ się **2.** wymieniać ⟨-nić⟩ **3.** zamieniać ⟨-nić⟩; ***~ a few words*** zamienić kilka słów **4.** ***~ blows*** pobić się **II** *s* **1.** wymiana *f*; ***an ~ of views*** wymiana poglądów **2.** zamiana *f*; ***in ~*** w zamian **3.** *currency*: wymiana *f*; ***a rate of ~*** kurs wymiany (walut) **4.** ECON giełda *f*; ***a stock ~*** giełda papierów wartościowych **5.** TEL centrala *f*

ex•change•a•ble [ɪks'tʃeɪndʒəbl] *adj* **1.** wymienny **2.** podlegający wymianie

ex'change rate *s* kurs *f* wymiany

ex•ci•ta•ble [ɪk'saɪtəbl] *adj* pobudliwy; **ex•cite** [ɪk'saɪt] *v/t* **1.** ekscytować ⟨pod-⟩, podniecać ⟨-cić⟩; ***get ~d*** ekscytować się, podniecać się **2.** emocjonować ⟨roz-⟩ **3.** *interest*: wzbudzać ⟨-dzić⟩ **4.** pobudzać ⟨-dzić⟩ **5.** rozbudzać ⟨-dzić⟩; **ex•cit•ed** [ɪk'saɪtɪd] *adj* **1.** podniecony, podekscytowany **2.** rozentuzjazmowany **3.** przejęty; **ex•cite•ment** [ɪk'saɪtmənt] *s* **1.** radosne podniecenie *n*, ekscytacja *f* **2.** rozemocjonowanie *n*; **ex•cit•ing** [ɪk'saɪtɪŋ] *adj* **1.** ekscytujący **2.** pasjonujący; **ex•cit•ing•ly** [ɪk'saɪtɪŋlɪ] *adv* **1.** ekscytująco **2.** pasjonująco

ex•claim [ɪk'skleɪm] **I** *v/i* **1.** wołać ⟨za-⟩ **2.** krzyczeć ⟨krzyknąć⟩ **II** *v/t* **1.** wołać ⟨za-⟩ **2.** wykrzykiwać ⟨-knąć⟩

ex•cla•ma•tion [ekskləˈmeɪʃn] *s* okrzyk *m*; ***an ~ of pain*** okrzyk bólu; ***an ~ mark*** *Br*, ***an ~ point*** *Am* wykrzyknik

ex•clude [ɪk'skluːd] *v/t* **1.** wyłączać ⟨-czyć⟩ **2.** wykluczać ⟨-czyć⟩ **3.** (*from school*) usuwać ⟨usunąć⟩; **ex•clud•ing** [ɪk'skluːdɪŋ] *prep* wyłączając *A*, nie licząc *G*; **ex•clu•sion** [ɪk'skluːʒn] *s* **1.** wykluczenie *n* **2.** pominięcie *n*; ***to the ~ of*** z pominięciem *G* **3.** *from school*: usunięcie *n*; **ex•clu•sive** [ɪk'skluːsɪv] **I** *adj* **1.** wyłączny **2.** *interview*: publikowany na prawach wyłączności **3.** ekskluzywny **4.** ***~ of*** nie licząc *G* **5.** ***be mutually ~***

wykluczać się wzajemnie **II** *s* materiał *m* publikowany na prawach wyłączności; **ex•clu•sive•ly** [ɪk'skluːsɪvlɪ] *adv* wyłącznie, jedynie

ex•com•mu•ni•cate [ekskə'mjuːnɪkeɪt] *v/t* ekskomunikować, nakładać ⟨nałożyć⟩ ekskomunikę na *A*; **ex•com•mu•ni•ca•tion** [ekskəmjuːnɪ'keɪʃn] *s* ekskomunika *f*, klątwa *f*

ex•cru•ci•a•ting [ɪk'skruːʃɪeɪtɪŋ] *adj pain, noise*: koszmarny, potworny, nie do zniesienia; **ex•cru•ci•a•ting•ly** [ɪk'skruːʃɪeɪtɪŋlɪ] *adv* koszmarnie, potwornie, nieznośnie

ex•cur•sion [ɪk'skɜːʃn] *s* **1.** wycieczka *f*, *infml* wypad *m*; ***go on an ~*** jechać na wycieczkę **2.** dygresja *f*; ***an ~ into politics*** dygresja na temat polityki

ex•cus•a•ble [ɪk'skjuːzəbl] *adj* wybaczalny; **ex•cuse** [ɪk'skjuːs] **I** *v/t* **1.** wybaczać ⟨-czyć⟩; ***~ me*** przepraszam!; ***~ me for being late***, ***~ my being late*** przepraszam za spóźnienie **2.** usprawiedliwiać ⟨-wić⟩, tłumaczyć ⟨wy-⟩; ***~ oneself*** usprawiedliwić się, tłumaczyć się; ***I cannot ~ his conduct*** nie mogę usprawiedliwić jego zachowania **3.** ***~ s.o. from*** zwolnić kogoś z *G* **II** *s* **1.** usprawiedliwienie *n*, wytłumaczenie *n*; ***offer an ~***, ***make an ~*** usprawiedliwiać się; ***in ~ of*** jako usprawiedliwienie *G*; ***without ~*** bez usprawiedliwienia **2.** pretekst *m* **3.** wymówka *f* **4.** wykręt *m*

ex•e•cute ['eksɪkjuːt] *v/t* **1.** tracić ⟨s-⟩, dokonywać ⟨-nać⟩ egzekucji **2.** wykonywać ⟨-nać⟩ **3.** przeprowadzać ⟨-dzić⟩; **ex•e•cu•tion** [eksɪ'kjuːʃn] *s* **1.** stracenie *n*, egzekucja *f* **2.** wykonanie *n* **3.** przeprowadzenie *n* **4.** realizacja *f*; **ex•e•cu•tion•er** [eksɪ'kjuːʃnə] *s* kat *m*

ex•ec•u•tive [ɪg'zekjʊtɪv] *adj* **1.** kierowniczy; ***an ~ board*** zarząd; ***an ~ position*** stanowisko kierownicze **2.** wykonawczy; ***~ power*** władza wykonawcza

ex•ec•u•tor [ɪg'zekjʊtə] *s* JUR wykonawca *m* testamentu

ex•em•pla•ry [ɪg'zemplərɪ] *adj* **1.** przykładny **2.** wzorowy

ex•em•pli•fy [ɪg'zemplɪfaɪ] *v/t* **1.** stanowić przykład **2.** ilustrować ⟨z-⟩ za pomocą przykładu

ex•er•cise ['eksəsaɪz] **I** *s* **1.** gimnastyka *f*, ćwiczenia *pl* fizyczne; ***do one's ~s*** ćwiczyć; ***an ~ ball*** piłka do ćwiczeń; ***an ~ machine*** maszyna treningowa, atlas **2.** ruch *m*; ***take more ~***, ***get more ~*** zażywać więcej ruchu **3.** ćwiczenie *n* **4.** zadanie *n* **5.** *power*: sprawowanie *n* **6.** wykonywanie *n* **7.** korzystanie *n* (**of** z *G*) **II** *v/i* ćwiczyć, gimnastykować się **III** *v/t* **1.** *authority*: sprawować **2.** *influence*: wywierać **3.** ćwiczyć, gimnastykować; **'ex•er•cise bike** *s* rower *m* treningowy; **'ex•er•cise book** *s* zeszyt *m*

ex•hale [eks'heɪl] *v/t* **1.** wydychać **2.** wydmuchiwać ⟨-chać⟩ **3.** wydzielać ⟨-lić⟩ **4.** emitować ⟨wy-⟩

ex•haust [ɪg'zɔːst] *v/t* **1.** wyczerpywać ⟨-pać⟩, męczyć ⟨z-⟩ **2.** *topic*: wyczerpywać ⟨-pać⟩; ***~ all possibilities*** wyczerpać wszystkie możliwości **3.** eksploatować ⟨wy-⟩; **ex•haust•ed** [ɪg'zɔːstɪd] *adj* **1.** *person*: wyczerpany **2.** *resources*: wyczerpany, wyeksploatowany; **ex•haust•ing** [ɪg'zɔːstɪŋ] *adj* wyczerpujący; **ex•haus•tion** [ɪg'zɔːstʃən] *s* **1.** wyczerpanie *n*, przemęczenie *n* **2.** wyczerpanie *n*; ***an ~ of supplies*** wyczerpanie zapasów; **ex•haus•tive** [ɪg'zɔːstɪv] *adj* **1.** wyczerpujący **2.** dogłębny **3.** drobiazgowy

ex•hib•it [ɪg'zɪbɪt] **I** *v/t* **1.** wystawiać ⟨-wić⟩ (na pokaz) **2.** okazywać ⟨-zać⟩ **3.** wykazywać ⟨-zać⟩ **II** *v/i* wystawiać ⟨-wić⟩ **III** *s* **1.** eksponat *m* **2.** JUR dowód *m* rzeczowy **3.** załącznik *m*; **ex•hi•bi•tion** [eksɪ'bɪʃn] *s* **1.** wystawa *f*; ***on ~*** wystawiony (na pokaz) **2.** ekspozycja *f* **3.** ***make an ~ of oneself*** *fig* zrobić z siebie widowisko **4.** *fig* popis *m*, pokaz *m*; **ex•hi•'bi•tion cen•tre** *s* centrum *n* wystawiennicze, centrum *n* wystawowe

ex•hi•bi•tion•ist [eksɪ'bɪʃnɪst] **I** *s* ekshibicjonista *m* **II** *adj* ekshibicjonistyczny

ex•hib•i•tor [ɪg'zɪbɪtə] *s* wystawca *m*

ex•hil•a•rat•ed [ɪg'zɪləreɪtɪd] *adj* szczęśliwy, bardzo uradowany; **ex•hil•a•rat•ing** [ɪg'zɪləreɪtɪŋ] *adj* **1.** ożywczy **2.** porywający **3.** emocjonujący; **ex•hil•a•ra•tion** [ɪgzɪlə'reɪʃn] *s* **1.** wielka radość *f* **2.** radosne podniecenie *n*

E

ex•hu•ma•tion [ekshjʊ'meɪʃn] *s* ekshumacja *f*; **ex•hume** [eg'zjuːm] *v/t* ekshumować

ex•ile ['eksaɪl] **I** *s* **1.** wygnanie *n*, emigracja *f*; ***go into*** **~** wyemigrować; ***live in*** **~** żyć na wygnaniu, żyć na emigracji; ***government in*** **~** rząd na emigracji, rząd emigracyjny **2.** wygnaniec *m*, emigrant *m* **II** *v/t* wygnać

E

ex•ist [ɪg'zɪst] *v/i* **1.** istnieć; ***do such things ~?*** czy takie rzeczy istnieją?; ***the right to*** **~** prawo do życia **2.** egzystować, żyć; **ex•ist•ence** [ɪg'zɪstəns] *s* **1.** istnienie *n*; ***come into*** **~** powstać; ***remain in*** **~** wciąż istnieć **2.** egzystencja *f*, życie *n*; **ex•is•ten•tial** [egzɪ'stenʃəl] *adj* egzystencjalny; **ex•is•ten•tial•ism** [egzɪ'stenʃəlɪzəm] *s* egzystencjalizm *m*; **ex•is•ten•tial•ist** [egzɪ'stenʃəlɪst] **I** *adj* egzystencjalistyczny **II** *s* egzystencjalista *m*; **ex•ist•ing** [ɪg'zɪstɪŋ] *adj* **1.** istniejący **2.** obecny **3.** dotychczasowy

ex•it ['egzɪt] **I** *s* **1.** wyjście *n* **2.** wyjazd *m*; ***an ~ visa*** wiza wyjazdowa **3.** THEAT zejście *n* (ze sceny) **II** *v/i* **1.** wychodzić ⟨wyjść⟩ **2.** THEAT schodzić ⟨zejść⟩ ze sceny; **~ *Hamlet*** Hamlet wychodzi **3.** INF wychodzić ⟨wyjść⟩ z *G*

ex•or•cism ['eksɔːsɪzəm] *s* egzorcyzm *m*; **ex•or•cist** ['eksɔːsɪst] *s* egzorcysta *m*; **ex•or•cize** ['eksɔːsaɪz] *v/t* **1.** egzorcyzmować **2.** *fig* uwalniać ⟨uwolnić⟩ się od *G*

ex•ot•ic [ɪg'zɒtɪk] *adj* egzotyczny

ex•pand [ɪk'spænd] **I** *v/i* **1.** rozszerzać ⟨-rzyć⟩ się **2.** (*firm*) rozszerzać ⟨-rzyć⟩ działalność **3.** rozwijać ⟨-winąć⟩ się **II** *v/t* **1.** rozszerzać ⟨-rzyć⟩; ***~ed memory*** INF pamięć rozszerzona **2.** rozwijać ⟨-winąć⟩; ***could you ~ on this?*** czy mógłbyś rozwinąć temat? **3.** powiększać ⟨-szyć⟩ **4.** rozbudowywać ⟨-dować⟩

ex•panse [ɪk'spæns] *s* **1.** przestrzeń *f* **2.** przestwór *m* **3.** przestworze *n*; **ex•pan•sion** [ɪk'spænʃn] *s* **1.** rozwój *m*, wzrost *m* **3.** rozwinięcie *n* **4.** rozbudowa *f* **5.** ekspansja *f* **6.** PHYS rozszerzenie *n*; **ex•pan•sive** [ɪk'spænsɪv] *adj* **1.** szeroki **2.** rozległy **3.** ekspansywny **4.** rozmowny

ex•pat•ri•ate [eks'pætrɪət] **I** *s* ekspatriant *m*, osoba *f* żyjąca na obczyźnie **II** *adj* żyjący na obczyźnie **II** *v/t* skazywać ⟨-zać⟩ na wygnanie, ekspatriować

ex•pect [ɪk'spekt] **I** *v/t* **1.** oczekiwać, spodziewać się; ***~ s.o. to do s.th.*** oczekiwać, że ktoś coś zrobi; **~ *s.th. of*** oczekiwać czegoś od *G* **2.** *Br* przypuszczać, sądzić; ***I ~ so*** sądzę, że tak **II** *v/i* ***be ~ing*** spodziewać się dziecka, być przy nadziei

ex•pect•an•cy [ɪk'spektənsɪ] *s* **1.** wyczekiwanie *n*, nadzieja *f* **2.** ***life ~*** średnia długość życia; **ex•pec•tant** [ɪk'spektənt] *adj* wyczekujący, pełen wyczekiwania; ***an ~ mother*** przyszła matka, kobieta w ciąży; **ex•pec•ta•tion** [ekspek'teɪʃn] *s* **1.** oczekiwanie *n*; ***in ~ of*** spodziewając się *G*; ***against all ~s, contrary to all ~s*** wbrew wszelkim oczekiwaniom, niespodziewanie; ***come up to s.o.'s ~s*** spełniać czyjeś oczekiwania; ***fall short of s.o.'s ~s*** nie spełniać czyichś oczekiwań **2.** przewidywanie *n* **3.** ***~ of life*** przeciętna długość życia

ex•pe•di•tion [ekspɪ'dɪʃn] *s* ekspedycja *f*, wyprawa *f*; ***go on an ~*** wyruszyć na wyprawę

ex•pel [ɪk'spel] *v/t* **1.** wydalać ⟨-lić⟩ **2.** usuwać ⟨usunąć⟩ **3.** wykluczać ⟨-czyć⟩ **4.** *smoke*, *air*: wypuszczać ⟨-puścić⟩

ex•pend [ɪk'spend] *v/t* **1.** *time*: poświęcać ⟨-cić⟩ **2.** *effort*: wkładać ⟨włożyć⟩ **3.** zużywać ⟨-żyć⟩, wyczerpywać ⟨-pać⟩; **ex•pend•a•ble** [ɪk'spendəbl] *adj* zbyteczny, zbędny

ex•pen•di•ture [ɪk'spendɪtʃə] *s* **1.** wydatki *pl* **2.** nakłady *pl* **3.** FIN rozchód *m* **4.** nakład *m* **5.** wykorzystanie *n*

ex•pense [ɪk'spens] *s* **1.** koszt *m*; ***at s.o.'s ~*** czyimś kosztem **2.** wydatek *m* **3.** nakład *m*; **ex•'pense ac•count** *s* fundusz *m* reprezentacyjny; **ex•pen•ses** [ɪk'spensɪz] *pl* **1.** koszty *pl*; ***travelling ~*** koszty podróży **2.** wydatki *pl*; **ex•pen•sive** [ɪk'spensɪv] *adj* **1.** drogi **2.** kosztowny

ex•pe•ri•ence [ɪk'spɪərɪəns] **I** *s* **1.** doświadczenie *n*; ***from ~*** z doświadczenia; ***in my ~*** wiem z doświadczenia, że **2.** przeżycie *n* **3.** doznanie *n* **II** *v/t* **1.** przeżywać ⟨-żyć⟩ **2.** doświadczać ⟨-czyć⟩, doznawać ⟨-nać⟩; **ex•pe•ri-**

enced [ɪk'spɪərɪənst] *adj* doświadczony, wytrawny
ex•per•i•ment [ɪk'sperɪmənt] **I** *s* eksperyment *m*, doświadczenie *n*; ***~s on animals*** eksperymenty na zwierzętach **II** *v/i* eksperymentować, robić doświadczenia; **ex•per•i•men•tal** [ɪksperɪ'mentl] *adj* **1.** doświadczalny **2.** eksperymentalny **3.** próbny; **ex•per•i•men•ta•tion** [ɪksperɪmen'teɪʃn] *s* eksperymentowanie *n*
ex•pert ['ekspɜːt] **I** *s* **1.** ekspert *m*, specjalista *m* **2.** fachowiec *m* **3.** biegły *m* **II** *adj* **1.** specjalistyczny **2.** fachowy; ***be ~ at doing s.th.*** świetnie coś robić; ***~ knowledge*** wiedza fachowa; ***~ opinion*** opinia fachowca **3.** biegły
ex•pert•ise [ekspɜː'tiːz] *s* **1.** wiedza *f* (fachowa) **2.** znajomość *f* (przedmiotu)
ex•pi•ra•tion [ekspɪ'reɪʃn] *s* **1.** wygaśnięcie *n* **2.** upływ *m* **3.** zakończenie *n*; **ex•pi•'ra•tion date** *Am s* data *f* ważności; **ex•pire** [ɪk'spaɪə] *v/i* **1.** tracić ⟨s-⟩ ważność **2.** wygasać ⟨-snąć⟩ **3.** upływać ⟨-łynąć⟩ **4.** umierać ⟨umrzeć⟩, wyzionąć ducha; **ex•piry date** [ɪk'spaɪərɪdeɪt] *Br s* data *f* ważności
ex•plain [ɪk'spleɪn] *v/t* **1.** wyjaśniać ⟨-nić⟩ **2.** tłumaczyć ⟨wy-⟩; ***~ oneself*** tłumaczyć się; **ex•pla•na•tion** [eksplə'neɪʃn] *s* **1.** wyjaśnienie *n* **2.** wytłumaczenie *n*; **ex•plan•a•tor•y** [ɪk'splænətərɪ] *adj* **1.** objaśniający **2.** wyjaśniający
ex•pli•ca•ble [ek'splɪkəbl] *adj* wytłumaczalny
ex•plic•it [ɪk'splɪsɪt] *adj* **1.** jasny **2.** wyraźny **3.** jednoznaczny **4.** jawny; ***be sexually ~*** zawierać treści o tematyce erotycznej **5.** otwarty; **ex•plic•it•ly** [ɪk'splɪsɪtlɪ] *adv* **1.** jasno **2.** wyraźnie **3.** otwarcie
ex•plode [ɪk'spləʊd] **I** *v/i* **1.** *a. fig* wybuchać ⟨-chnąć⟩ **2.** eksplodować **3.** *fig* gwałtownie wzrastać ⟨-rosnąć⟩ **II** *v/t* **1.** odpalać ⟨-lić⟩ **2.** *fig* obalać ⟨-lić⟩
ex•ploit ['eksplɔɪt] *v/t* **1.** wykorzystywać ⟨-tać⟩ **2.** eksploatować ⟨wy-⟩ **3.** wyzyskiwać ⟨-kać⟩
ex•ploi•ta•tion [eksplɔɪ'teɪʃn] *s* **1.** wykorzystywanie *n* **2.** wyzysk *m* **3.** eksploatacja *f*
ex•plo•ra•tion [eksplə'reɪʃn] *s* **1.** badanie *n* **2.** eksploracja *f* **3.** poszukiwanie *n*; **ex•plor•a•to•ry** [ɪk'splɒrətərɪ] *adj* **1.** badawczy **2.** eksploracyjny **3.** wstępny; ***~ talks*** rozmowy wstępne **4.** przygotowawczy
ex•plore [ɪk'splɔː] *v/t* **1.** badać ⟨z-⟩ **2.** zgłębiać ⟨-bić⟩ **3.** penetrować ⟨s-⟩ **4.** zwiedzać ⟨-dzić⟩; **ex•plo•rer** [ɪk'splɔːrə] *s* **1.** badacz *m* **2.** eksplorator *m*
ex•plo•sion [ɪk'spləʊʒn] *s* **1.** *a. fig* wybuch *m*; ***an ~ of laughter*** wybuch śmiechu **2.** *a. fig* eksplozja *f* **3.** gwałtowny wzrost *m* **4.** szybki rozkwit *m*; **ex•plo•sive** [ɪk'spləʊsɪv] **I** *s* materiał *m* wybuchowy **II** *adj* **1.** *a. fig* wybuchowy **2.** *situation*: zaogniony, zapalny
ex•port **I** ['ekspɔːt] *s* **1.** eksport *m*, wywóz *m* **2.** towar *m* eksportowy **II** [ɪk'spɔːt] *v/t* eksportować **III** [ɪk'spɔːt] *v/i* eksportować **IV** [ɪk'spɔːt] *adj* eksportowy; **'ex•port com•pa•ny** *s* firma *f* eksportowa; **ex•port•er** ['ekspɔːtə] *s* eksporter *m*; **'ex•port trade** *s* eksport *m*
ex•pose [ɪk'spəʊz] *v/t* **1.** wystawiać ⟨-wić⟩, narażać ⟨-razić⟩ (**to** na *A*); ***~ oneself to ridicule*** narażać się na śmieszność **2.** ujawniać ⟨-nić⟩, demaskować ⟨z-⟩ **3.** odsłaniać ⟨-łonić⟩, obnażać ⟨-żyć⟩; ***~ oneself*** obnażać się **4.** PHOT naświetlać ⟨-lić⟩
ex•po•sé [ek'spəʊzeɪ] *s* **1.** publikacja *f* demaskatorska **2.** omówienie *n*
ex•posed [ɪk'spəʊzd] *adj* **1.** odkryty **2.** obnażony **3.** eksponowany; **ex•po•si•tion** [ekspə'zɪʃn] *s* **1.** przedstawienie *n*, prezentacja *f* **2.** wystawa *f*; **ex•po•sure** [ɪk'spəʊʒə] *s* **1.** ujawnienie *n*, zdemaskowanie *n* **2.** *light, sun, radiation*: wystawienie *n* na działanie **3.** (*media*) nagłośnienie *n*; ***it had a lot of ~ in the media*** było o tym głośno w mediach **5.** obnażenie *n* **6.** PHOT naświetlenie *n*, ekspozycja *f*; **ex•'po•sure me•ter** *s* PHOT światłomierz *m*
ex•pound [ɪk'spaʊnd] **I** *v/t* objaśniać ⟨-nić⟩, wyjaśniać ⟨-nić⟩, wykładać ⟨wyłożyć⟩ **II** *v/i* wyjaśniać ⟨-nić⟩ (**on** *A*)
ex•press[1] [ɪk'spres] *v/t* wyrażać ⟨-razić⟩, dawać ⟨dać⟩ wyraz; ***~ the hope***

that wyrazić nadzieję, że; ~ ***oneself*** wyrażać się, wysławiać się
ex•press[2] [~] *adj* **1.** ekspresowy **2.** wyraźny **3.** jawny
ex•press[3] [~] *s* **1.** ekspres *m* **2.** pociąg *m* ekspresowy **3.** autobus *m* ekspresowy
ex•pres•sion [ɪk'spreʃn] *s* **1.** wyrażenie *n* **2.** zwrot *m* **3.** wyraz *m*; ***find ~ in*** znaleźć wyraz w *L*, być wyrażonym w *L*; ***give ~ to s.th.*** dać wyraz czemuś **4.** ekspresja *f* **5.** wyraz *m* twarzy, mina *f*
ex•pres•sion•ism [ɪk'spreʃnɪzəm] *s* ekspresjonizm *m*; **ex•pres•sion•ist** [ɪk'spreʃnɪst] **I** *s* ekspresjonista *m* **II** *adj* ekspresjonistyczny
ex•pres•sion•less [ɪk'spreʃnləs] *adj* bez wyrazu
ex•pres•sive [ɪk'spresɪv] *adj* **1.** pełen wyrazu; ***be ~ of*** wyrażać *A* **2.** ekspresyjny, ekspresywny
ex•press•ly [ɪk'spreslɪ] *adv* **1.** wyraźnie **2.** stanowczo, kategorycznie **3.** specjalnie
ex•press•way [ɪk'spresweɪ] *s Am* autostrada *f*
ex•pul•sion [ɪk'spʌlʃn] *s* **1.** *country*: wydalenie *n* **2.** *school*: wydalenie *n*, usunięcie *n* **3.** *group*: wykluczenie *n* **4.** *gas*: wypuszczenie *n*; ***~ of breath*** wydech *m*
ex•qui•site [ek'skwɪzɪt] *adj* **1.** piękny **2.** znakomity **3.** wyszukany, wyrafinowany **4.** *pain*: dotkliwy, przejmujący
ex•tend [ɪk'stend] **I** *v/t* **1.** powiększać ⟨-szyć⟩ **2.** rozbudowywać ⟨-dować⟩ **3.** przedłużać ⟨-żyć⟩ **4.** *hand*: wyciągać ⟨-gnąć⟩ **5.** *influence*: rozszerzać ⟨-rzyć⟩, zwiększać ⟨-szyć⟩ **6.** *congratulations*: składać ⟨złożyć⟩ **7.** *credit*: udzielać ⟨-lić⟩ **8.** ***~ oneself*** wysilać ⟨-lić⟩ się **II** *v/i* **1.** rozciągać ⟨-gnąć⟩ się **2.** rozpościerać się **3.** ciągnąć się **4.** trwać; **ex•ten•sion** [ɪk'stenʃn] *s* **1.** rozszerzenie *n* **2.** przedłużenie *n* **3.** poszerzenie *n*; **ex•ten•sive** [ɪk'stensɪv] *adj* **1.** rozległy **2.** szeroki **3.** obszerny **4.** znaczny, **ex•ten•sive•ly** [ɪk'stensɪvlɪ] *adv* **1.** szeroko **2.** *use*: powszechnie **3.** *travel*: wiele **4.** obszernie **5.** w znacznym stopniu
ex•tent [ɪk'stent] *s* **1.** zakres *m*, stopień *m*; ***to a large ~*** w znacznym stopniu; ***to some ~, to a certain ~*** do pewnego stopnia; ***to such an ~ that*** do tego stopnia, że **2.** rozmiary *pl*
ex•te•ri•or [ɪk'stɪrɪə] **I** *s* **1.** zewnętrzna strona *f*; ***the ~ of the house needs painting*** dom trzeba pomalować (z zewnątrz) **2.** powierzchowność *f* **II** *adj* **1.** zewnętrzny **2.** pozorny
ex•ter•mi•nate [ɪk'stɜːmɪneɪt] *v/t* **1.** tępić ⟨wy-⟩ **2.** dokonywać ⟨-nać⟩ eksterminacji, dokonywać ⟨-nać⟩ zagłady; **ex•ter•mi•na•tion** [ɪkstɜːmɪ'neɪʃn] *s* **1.** wytępienie *n* **2.** tępienie *n* **3.** eksterminacja *f*, zagłada *f*
ex•ter•nal [ɪk'stɜːnl] *adj* **1.** zewnętrzny; ***for ~ use*** MED do użytku zewnętrznego **2.** *debt*, *affairs*: zagraniczny; **ex•ter•nal•ly** [ɪk'stɜːnəlɪ] *adv* **1.** z zewnątrz **2.** zewnętrznie **3.** pozornie
ex•tinct [ɪk'stɪŋkt] *adj* **1.** *species*: wymarły **2.** *language*: martwy **3.** *volcano*, *feeling*: wygasły; **ex•tinc•tion** [ɪk'stɪŋkʃn] *s* **1.** wymarcie *n* **2.** wytępienie *n* **3.** wygaśnięcie *n*
ex•tin•guish [ɪk'stɪŋgwɪʃ] *v/t* **1.** *fire*: gasić ⟨u-⟩ **2.** *light*: gasić ⟨z-⟩ **3.** *hope*: rozwiewać ⟨-wiać⟩; **ex•tin•guish•er** [ɪk'stɪŋgwɪʃə] *s* gaśnica *f*
ex•tra ['ekstrə] **I** *adj* dodatkowy; ***an ~ pay*** wynagrodzenie dodatkowe; ***if you pay an ~ two pounds*** za dopłatą dwóch funtów; ***at no ~ charge*** bez dodatkowej opłaty **II** *adv* **1.** dodatkowo; ***charge ~ for*** żądać dopłaty za *A* **2.** szczególnie; ***you'll have to be ~ careful*** musisz szczególnie uważać **III** *s* **1.** dopłata *f*, dodatkowa opłata *f* **2.** dodatek *m* **3.** statysta *m*; **ex•tra 'charge** *s* dodatkowa opłata *f*, dopłata *f*
ex•tract **I** ['ekstrækt] *s* **1.** urywek *m*, wyjątek *m* **2.** wyciąg *m*, ekstrakt *m* **II** [ɪk'strækt] *v/t* **1.** *tooth*: wyrywać ⟨-rwać⟩, usuwać ⟨usunąć⟩ **2.** wyciągać ⟨-gnąć⟩ **3.** wydobywać ⟨-być⟩ **4.** czerpać **5.** uzyskiwać ⟨-kać⟩
ex•trac•tion [ɪk'strækʃn] *s* **1.** uzyskiwanie *n* **2.** *tooth*: usunięcie *n* **3.** pochodzenie *n*; ***an American of Polish ~*** Amerykanin polskiego pochodzenia; **'ex•trac•tion fan** *s* wyciąg *m*
ex•tra•cur•ric•u•lar [ekstrəkə'rɪkjələ] *adj* **1.** dodatkowy **2.** ponadprogramowy

ex•tra•dite ['ekstrədaɪt] *v/t* dokonywać ⟨-nać⟩ ekstradycji; **ex•tra•di•tion** [ekstrə'dɪʃn] **I** *s* ekstradycja *f* **II** *adj* ekstradycyjny

ex•tra•mar•i•tal [ekstrə'mærɪtl] *adj* pozamałżeński

ex•tra•ne•ous [ɪk'streɪnɪəs] *adj form* nieistotny; ***be ~ to*** nie mieć związku z *I*, być nieistotnym dla *G*

ex•tra•or•di•nar•i•ly [ɪk'strɔːdɪnerɪlɪ] *adv* **1.** niezwykle, nadzwyczaj **2.** wyjątkowo; **ex•tra•or•di•na•ry** [ɪk'strɔːdɪnerɪ] *adj* **1.** niezwykły **2.** wyjątkowy **3.** zadziwiający, niesłychany

ex•tra•sen•so•ry [ekstrə'sensərɪ] *adj* pozazmysłowy

ex•tra•ter•res•tri•al [ekstrətə'restrɪəl] **I** *adj* pozaziemski **II** *s* istota *f* pozaziemska, kosmita *m*

ex•trav•a•gance [ɪk'strævəgəns] *s* **1.** rozrzutność *f* **2.** luksus *m* **3.** ekstrawagancja *f*; **ex•trav•a•gant** [ɪk'strævəgənt] *adj* **1.** rozrzutny **2.** przesadny, przesadzony **3.** ekstrawagancki

ex•treme [ɪk'striːm] **I** *adj* **1.** ogromny, wielki **2.** wyjątkowy **3.** najdalszy **4.** najwyższy **5.** ekstremalny **6.** skrajny **7.** radykalny **II** *s* **1.** koniec *m*; ***at the other ~*** na drugim końcu **2.** kraniec *m* **3.** skrajność *f*; ***in the ~*** skrajnie; ***go to ~s*** popadać w skrajność; **ex•treme•ly** [ɪk'striːmlɪ] *adv* **1.** niezmiernie, niezwykle **2.** w najwyższym stopniu; **ex•trem•ism** [ɪk'striːmɪzəm] *s* ekstremizm *m*; **ex•trem•ist** [ɪk'striːmɪst] **I** *s* ekstremista *m* **II** *adj* ekstremistyczny; **ex•trem•i•ty** [ɪk'stremətɪ] *s* **1.** koniec *m* **2.** kraniec *m* **3.** skrajność *f*

ex•tro•vert ['ekstrəvɜːt] **I** *s* ekstrawertyk *m* **II** *adj* ekstrawertyczny

ex•ult [ɪg'zʌlt] *v/i* nie posiadać się z radości, radować się; **ex•ult•ant** [ɪg'zʌltənt] *adj* **1.** (bardzo) uradowany **2.** triumfalny

eye [aɪ] **I** *s* **1.** oko *n*; ***before s.o.'s very ~s*** na czyichś oczach; ***be up to one's ~s in work*** mieć po uszy roboty; ***cry one's ~s out*** wypłakiwać sobie oczy; ***in my ~s*** *fig* według mnie **2.** *fig* spojrzenie *n*, wzrok *m*; ***have an ~ for*** **a)** mieć wyczucie *G* **b)** potrafić dostrzec *A* **3.** *needle*: ucho *n* **4.** *cyclone*: centrum *n*, oko *n* **5.** (*potato*) oczko *n* **II** *v/t* przyglądać ⟨przyjrzeć⟩ się, przypatrywać ⟨-trzeć⟩ się; **'eye•ball** *s* ANAT gałka *f* oczna; **'eye•brow** *s* brew *f*; ***raise one's ~s*** unieść brwi; **eye-brow 'pen•cil** *s* ołówek *m* do brwi; **'eye-catch•ing** *adj* **1.** efektowny **2.** przyciągający uwagę; **'eye contact** *s* kontakt *m* wzrokowy; **eye•ful** ['aɪfʊl] *s*: ***have an ~ of*** *Br infml* przypatrywać się *D*; **'eye•glass-es** *pl Am* okulary *pl*; **'eye•lash** *s* rzęsa *f*; **'eye lev•el** *s*: ***at ~*** na wysokości oczu

'eye•lid *s* powieka *f*; **'eye•lin•er** *s* **1.** kredka *f* do oczu **2.** tusz *m* do kresek; **'eye-o•pen•er** *s* rewelacja *f*; **'eye-pen•cil** *s* kredka *f* do oczu; **'eye-sha•dow** *s* cień *m* do powiek; **'eye-sight** *s* wzrok *m*; ***lose one's ~*** stracić wzrok, oślepnąć; **'eye•sore** *s* brzydactwo *n*, szkaradzieństwo *n*; **'eye strain** *s* przemęczenie *n* wzroku; **'eye-wit•ness** *s* naoczny świadek *m*

F

fab [fæb] *adj Br infml* super

fa•ble ['feɪbl] *s* **1.** *a. fig* bajka *f* **2.** baśń *f*

fab•ric ['fæbrɪk] *s* **1.** materiał *m*, tkanina *f* **2.** konstrukcja *f*, struktura *f* **3.** *fig* tkanka *f*

fab•ri•cate ['fæbrɪkeɪt] *v/t* **1.** zmyślać ⟨-lić⟩, fabrykować ⟨s-⟩ **2.** wytwarzać ⟨-worzyć⟩; **fab•ri•ca•tion** [fæbrɪ'keɪʃn] *s* **1.** zmyślenie *n* **2.** wytwarzanie *n*

fab•u•lous ['fæbjʊləs] *adj* **1.** *infml* fantastyczny, rewelacyjny **2.** bajeczny; **fab•u•lous•ly** ['fæbjʊləslɪ] *adv* **1.** *infml* fantastycznie, rewelacyjnie **2.** bajecznie

fa•çade [fə'sɑːd] *s* ARCHIT fasada *f*

face [feɪs] **I** *s* **1.** twarz *f*; ***in the ~ of*** w obliczu *G*; ***~ to ~ with*** twarzą w twarz z *I*; ***do one's ~*** malować się; ***say s.th. to s.o.'s ~*** powiedzieć coś komuś (prosto) w twarz; ***save one's ~*** *fig* zachować twarz; ***lose ~*** *fig* stracić twarz **2.** mina *f*; ***make a ~, pull a ~*** zrobić minę **3.** oblicze *n*; ***on the ~ of it*** na pierwszy rzut oka **4.** wierzch *m* **5.** (*clock*) tarcza *f* **II** *v/t* **1.** (*window*) wychodzić na *A* **2.** stawać ⟨stanąć⟩ w obliczu *G*, stawać ⟨stanąć⟩ naprzeciw *G* **3.** ***be ~d with*** mieć przed sobą *A*, stać w obliczu *G* **III** *v/i* ***~ towards*** stać przodem do *G*; **face up to** *v/i* **1.** godzić ⟨po-⟩ się z *I* **2.** sprostać *D* **3.** stawiać czoła *D*

F

'face card *s* (*cards*) *Am* figura *f*; **'face-cloth** *s Br* myjka *f* do twarzy; **'face cream** *s* krem *m* do twarzy; **face•less** ['feɪslɪs] *adj fig* anonimowy, bezimienny; **'face•lift** *s* **1.** lifting *m* **2.** *fig* zmiany *pl*; **'face pack** *s* maseczka *f* kosmetyczna

fa•cial ['feɪʃl] *adj* **1.** ***~ expression*** wyraz twarzy **2.** na twarzy **3.** do twarzy

fa•cil•i•tate [fə'sɪlɪteɪt] *v/t* ułatwiać ⟨-wić⟩; **fa•cil•i•ties** [fə'sɪlətɪz] *pl* **1.** infrastruktura *f* **2.** udogodnienia *pl* **3.** obiekty *pl* **4.** usługi *pl* **5.** urządzenia *pl*; **fa•cil•i•ty** [fə'sɪlətɪ] *s* **1.** obiekt *m* **2.** udogodnienie *n* **3.** urządzenie *n* **4.** talent *m* **5.** możliwość *f* **6.** funkcja *f* **7.** opcja *f*

fact [fækt] *s* fakt *m*; ***know s.th. for a ~*** wiedzieć coś na pewno; ***tell s.o. the ~s of life*** uświadomić kogoś, powiedzieć komuś, skąd się biorą dzieci; **fact-find•ing** ['fæktfaɪndɪŋ] *adj* **1.** rozpoznawczy **2.** badawczy

fac•tion ['fækʃn] *s* POLIT frakcja *f*, odłam *m*

fac•tor ['fæktə] *s* czynnik *m*

fac•to•ry ['fæktərɪ] **I** *s* **1.** fabryka *f* **2.** wytwórnia *f* **II** *adj* fabryczny **'fac•to•ry farm•ing** *s* chów *m* przemysłowy; **'fac•to•ry work•er** *s* robotnik *m*; **'fac•to•ry out•let** *s* sklep *m* fabryczny; **'fac•to•ry ship** *s* statek *m* przetwórnia

'fact sheet *s* **1.** arkusz *m* informacyjny **2.** informacje *pl*

fac•tu•al ['fæktʃʊəl] *adj* oparty na faktach

fac•ul•ty ['fækəltɪ] *s* **1.** zdolność *f*; ***mental ~ies*** zdolności umysłowe, władze umysłowe; ***be in possession of all one's ~ies*** być w pełni władz fizycznych i umysłowych **2.** (*university*) wydział *m*

fade [feɪd] *v/i* **1.** blaknąć ⟨wy-⟩, płowieć ⟨s-⟩ **2.** przemijać ⟨-minąć⟩ **3.** zanikać ⟨-knąć⟩ **4.** przygasać ⟨-snąć⟩ **5.** zacierać ⟨zatrzeć⟩ się; **fade away** *v/i* **1.** cichnąć ⟨u-⟩ **2.** gasnąć ⟨z-⟩ **3.** zacierać ⟨zatrzeć⟩ się; **fade in** *v/i* **1.** pojawiać ⟨-wić⟩ się **2.** rozjaśniać ⟨-nić⟩ się **3.** nasilać ⟨-lić⟩ się; **fade out** *v/i* **1.** znikać ⟨-knąć⟩ **2.** ściemniać ⟨-nić⟩ się **3.** cichnąć ⟨u-⟩; **fad•ed** ['feɪdɪd] *adj* **1.** wyblakły **2.** spłowiały **3.** sprany

faeces [fiːsiːz] *pl* kał *m*

fag [fæg] *s infml* fajka *f*, szlug *m*

fagged [fægd] *adj Br infml* wykończony

fag•got ['fægət] *s* **1.** COOK *Br* pulpet *m* **2.** *Am vulg* pedał *m*, ciota *f*

Fahr•en•heit ['færənhaɪt] *adj*: ***10 degrees ~*** 10 stopni w skali Fahrenheita

fail [feɪl] **I** *v/i* **1.** ***she ~ed*** nie udało jej się; ***he ~ed to do it*** nie udało mu się tego zrobić, nie zdołał tego zrobić; ***he ~ed in his attempt*** jego próba się nie powiodła **2.** nie powieść się, nie udawać ⟨udać⟩ się **3.** ***~ to do s.th.*** nie zrobić czegoś; ***I ~ to see*** nie pojmuję **4.** (*student*) nie zdać **5.** zawodzić ⟨-wieść⟩; ***if all else ~s*** jeśli wszystko inne zawiedzie; ***the song can't ~ to be a hit*** ta piosenka to murowany przebój, ta piosenka na pewno będzie przebojem **6.** słabnąć ⟨o-⟩ **7.** pogarszać ⟨-gorszyć⟩ się **8.** psuć ⟨ze-⟩ się **9.** bankrutować ⟨z-⟩ **II** *v/t* **1.** zawodzić ⟨-wieść⟩; ***his memory ~ed him*** zawiodła go pamięć; ***words ~ me*** brakuje mi słów **2.** *student*: *infml* oblewać ⟨-lać⟩ **III** *s* ***without ~*** **a)** niezawodnie **b)** z całą pewnością

fail•ing ['feɪlɪŋ] **I** *s* słabość *f*, słabostka *f*, wada *f* **II** *adj sight, health*: pogarszający się **III** *prep* przy braku *G*, w razie nieobecności *G*; ***~ that*** a jeśli to się nie uda, to

'fail-safe *adj* TECH bezpieczny w razie uszkodzenia

fail•ure ['feɪljə] *s* **1.** niepowodzenie *n*, porażka *f* **2.** ***~ to pay*** niezapłacenie, nieuiszczenie; ***~ to comply with the regulations*** niezastosowanie się do przepisów **3.** awaria *f* **4.** MED niewydolność *f* **5.** bankructwo *n*, plajta *f* **6.** ***crop ~***, ***harvest ~*** nieurodzaj **7.** nieudacznik *m*; ***he was a ~ as an actor*** nie sprawdził się jako aktor

faint [feɪnt] **I** *adj* **1.** słaby **2.** lekki **3.** niewyraźny **4.** blady; ***I haven't the ~est idea*** *fig* nie mam bladego pojęcia **5.** nikły **6.** nieśmiały **II** *s* omdlenie *n*; ***in a ~*** nieprzytomny **III** *v/i* mdleć ⟨ze-⟩, zasłabnąć, tracić ⟨s-⟩ przytomność; **faint•'heart•ed I** *adj* bojaźliwy, tchórzliwy **II** *s* ***the ~*** tchórzliwi *pl*; ***not for the ~*** nie dla osób o słabych nerwach; **faint•ly** ['feɪntlɪ] *adv* **1.** słabo **2.** lekko **3.** trochę

fair[1] [feə] **I** *adj* **1.** sprawiedliwy **2.** uczciwy **3.** ***~ play*** fair play **4.** niezły, spory **5.** *weather*: ładny, sprzyjający **6.** *forecast*: dobry **7.** jasny, blond **8.** *lit* piękny **II** *adv* uczciwie, fair; ***play ~*** grać uczciwie, grać fair

fair[2] [~] *s* **1.** jarmark *m*, targ *m* **2.** wesołe miasteczko *n* **3.** targi *pl*; **'fair•ground** *s* **1.** plac *m* targowy **2.** wesołe miasteczko *n*

fair-'haired *adj* jasnowłosy

fair•ly ['feəlɪ] *adj* **1.** dość, dosyć **2.** uczciwie **3.** sprawiedliwie; **fair•ly-'mind•ed** *adj* **1.** bezstronny **2.** sprawiedliwy; **fair•ness** ['feənɪs] *s* sprawiedliwość *f*, uczciwość *f*; ***in ~ to him*** oddając mu sprawiedliwość

'fair-weath•er *adj friend*: tylko na dobre czasy

fair•y ['fərɪ] *s* **1.** duszek *m* **2.** wróżka *f* **3.** *vulg* ciota *m*; **fair•y 'god•moth•er** *s fig* dobra wróżka *f*; **'fair•y sto•ry**, **'*fair•y tale*** *s* **1.** bajka *f* **2.** baśń *f*

faith [feɪθ] *s* **1.** wiara *f*, zaufanie *n*; ***have ~ in*** ufać *D*, wierzyć w *A*; ***in good ~*** w dobrej wierze **2** *REL* wiara *f*; **faith•ful** ['feɪθfəl] **I** *adj* wierny **II** *s REL* wierny *m*; **faith•ful•ly** ['feɪθfəlɪ] *adv* **1.** wiernie **2.** dokładnie **3.** solennie **4.** ***yours ~*** z wyrazami szacunku

'faith heal•er *s* uzdrowiciel *m*; **'faith heal•ing** *s* uzdrawianie *n*

fake [feɪk] **I** *v/t* **1.** fałszować ⟨s-⟩ **2.** udawać ⟨-dać⟩ **3.** symulować **4.** pozorować ⟨u-⟩ **II** *s* **1.** imitacja *f* **2.** *infml* podróbka *f* **3.** *infml* fałszywka *f* **4.** oszust *m*

fal•con ['fɔːlkən] *s* sokół *m*

Falk•lands ['fɔːkləndz] *pl* Falklandy *pl*, Wyspy *pl* Falklandzkie

fall [fɔːl] **I** *s* **1.** upadek *m*; ***have a ~*** upaść, przewrócić się **2.** *fig* spadek *m*; ***a ~ in temperature*** spadek temperatury; ***a ~ in demand*** spadek popytu **3.** *government*, *monarchy*: upadek *m* **4.** *snow*, *rain*: opad *m* **5.** *Am* jesień *f*; ***in*** (***the***) ***~*** na jesieni **6.** ***~s*** wodospad *m* **II** (*fell*; *fallen*) *v/i* **1.** spadać ⟨spaść⟩ **2.** upadać ⟨upaść⟩, przewracać ⟨-rócić⟩ się **3.** ***~ apart*** rozpadać ⟨-paść⟩, się **4.** (*town*, *regime*) upadać ⟨upaść⟩, padać ⟨paść⟩ **5.** padać ⟨paść⟩, polec **6.** (*night*) zapadać ⟨-paść⟩ **7.** przypadać ⟨-paść⟩ w udziale; **fall about** *v/i*: ***~ laughing***, ***~ with laughter*** tarzać ze śmiechu; **fall away** → ***fall off***; **fall back** *v/i* cofać ⟨-fnąć⟩ się; **fall back on** *v/i* uciekać ⟨uciec⟩ się do *G*; **fall behind** *v/i* **1.** zostawać ⟨-tać⟩ w tyle **2.** opóźniać ⟨-nić⟩ się **3.** ***~ with*** mieć zaległości w *L*; **fall down** *v/i* **1.** spadać ⟨spaść⟩ **2.** przewracać ⟨-rócić⟩ się **3.** zawodzić ⟨-wieść⟩; **fall for** *v/i* **1.** dawać ⟨dać⟩ się nabrać na *A* **2.** zakochiwać ⟨-chać⟩ się w *L*; **fall in** *v/i* zapadać ⟨-paść⟩ się; **fall into** *v/i* wpadać ⟨wpaść⟩ w *A*; ***~ difficulties*** wpaść w kłopoty; ***~ a habit*** nabrać zwyczaju; **fall in with** *v/i* **1.** zgadzać ⟨zgodzić⟩ się z *I* **2.** przystawać ⟨-tać⟩ na *A* **3.** dołączać ⟨-czyć⟩ do *G*; **fall off** *v/i* **1.** spadać ⟨spaść⟩ **2.** opadać ⟨opaść⟩ **3.** odpadać ⟨-paść⟩; **fall on** *v/i* **1.** rzucać ⟨-cić⟩ się na *A*, napadać ⟨-paść⟩ na *A* **2.** przypadać ⟨-paść⟩; ***the festival falls on Monday this year*** to święto przypada w tym roku w poniedziałek; **fall out** *v/i* **1.** wypadać ⟨-paść⟩ **2.** *infml* kłócić ⟨po-⟩ się; **fall over** *v/i* **1.** przewracać ⟨-rócić⟩ się **2.** potykać ⟨-tknąć⟩ się; ***~ oneself to do s.th.*** *infml* wyłazić ze skóry, żeby coś zrobić; **fall through** *v/i* nie dochodzić ⟨dojść⟩ do skutku, nie udawać ⟨udać⟩ się; **fall to** *v/i* **1.** przypadać ⟨-paść⟩ w udziale *D* **2.** zabierać ⟨-brać⟩ się do *G*; **fall under** *v/i* podpadać ⟨-paść⟩ pod *A*

fal•len ['fɔːlən] *adj* **1.** *tree*: powalony **2.** poległy **3.** upadły **4.** opadły

'fall guy *s Am* kozioł *m* ofiarny

F

fall•ing'star *s* spadająca gwiazda *f*
'fall•out *s* **1.** opad *m* radioaktywny **2.** *fig* (przykre) następstwa *pl*; **'fall-out shel•ter** *s* schron *m* przeciwatomowy
false [fɔːls] *adj* **1.** błędny **2.** nieprawdziwy **3.** fałszywy **4.** sztuczny; **false a•'larm** *s* fałszywy alarm *m*; **false-hood** ['fɔːlshʊd] *s* fałsz *m*, nieprawda *f*, kłamstwo *n*
false•ly ['fɔːlslɪ] *adv* **1.** fałszywie **2.** sztucznie **3.** *accused*: niesłusznie
false 'mod•es•ty *s* fałszywa skromność *f*; **false•ness** ['fɔːlsnəs] *s* fałszywość *f*, fałsz *m*; **false 'start** *s* SPORT falstart *m*; **false 'teeth** *s* sztuczna szczęka *f*
fal•si•fi•ca•tion [fɔːlsɪfɪ'keɪʃn] **1.** fałszowanie *n* **2.** zafałszowanie *n*; **fal•si-fy** ['fɔːlsɪfaɪ] *v/t* fałszować ⟨s-, za-⟩
fa•mil•i•ar [fə'mɪlɪə] *adj* **1.** znajomy; ***a ~ sight*** znajomy widok; ***be ~ with*** znać *A*; ***make o.s. ~ with*** zaznajomić się z *I*, zapoznać się z *I* **2.** dobrze znany **3.** serdeczny, zażyły; ***be on ~ terms with*** być w zażyłych stosunkach z *I*; **fa•mil•i•ar•i•ty** [fəmɪlɪ'ærɪtɪ] *s* **1.** znajomość *f* **2.** serdeczność *f* **3.** poufałość *f*; **fa•mil•i•ar•ize** [fə'mɪlɪəraɪz] *v/t*: ***~ oneself with*** zaznajamiać się z *I*, zapoznawać się z *I*; **fa•mil•i•ar•ly** [fə'mɪlɪəlɪ] *adv* poufale
fam•i•ly ['fæməlɪ] **I** *s* **1.** rodzina *f*; ***a ~ of four*** czteroosobowa rodzina; ***of good ~*** z dobrej rodziny **2.** ród *m* **II** *adj* rodzinny; ***a ~ allowance*** zasiłek rodzinny; ***a ~ man*** dobry mąż i ojciec; **fam-i•ly 'doc•tor** *s* lekarz *m* rodzinny; **'fam•i•ly name** *s* nazwisko *n*; **fam•i•ly 'plan•ning** *s* planowanie *n* rodziny; **fam•i•ly 'tree** *s* drzewo *n* genealogiczne
fam•ine ['fæmɪn] *s* głód *m*
fam•ished ['fæmɪʃt] *adj infml* zgłodniały
fa•mous ['feɪməs] *adj* słynny, sławny, znany; **fa•mous•ly** ['feɪməslɪ] *adv* **1.** ***he is ~ arrogant*** powszechnie znana jest jego arogancja; ***she ~ said*** wyrzekła słynne słowa **2.** doskonale
fan[1] [fæn] **I** *s* **1.** wentylator *m* **2.** wiatrak *m* **3.** wachlarz *m* **II** *v/t* **1.** wachlować ⟨po-⟩ **2.** podsycać ⟨-cić⟩; **fan out** *v/i* rozchodzić ⟨-zejść⟩ się promieniście
fan[2] [~] *s* **1.** fan *m* **2.** kibic *m* **3.** wielbiciel *m*
fa•nat•ic [fə'nætɪk] *s* fanatyk *m*; **fa-nat•i•cal** [fə'nætɪkl] *adj* fanatyczny; **fa•nat•i•cal•ly** [fə'nætɪklɪ] *adv* fanatycznie; **fa•nat•i•cism** [fə'nætɪsɪzm] *s* fanatyzm *m*
fan•ci•ful ['fænsɪfʊl] *adj* **1.** zmyślony, urojony **2.** wymyślny, fantazyjny
fan•cy ['fænsɪ] **I** *s* **1.** zamiłowanie *n*, ochota *f* **2.** zachcianka *f* **2.** *lit* imaginacja *f*, mrzonka *f* **II** *adj* **1.** luksusowy **2.** kunsztowny, wymyślny, skomplikowany **3.** wyimaginowany **III** *v/t* **1.** mieć ochotę na *A*; ***would you ~ a walk?*** miałabyś ochotę na spacer?; ***she ~s you*** podobasz jej się **2.** wyobrażać ⟨-razić⟩ sobie; ***~ that!*** coś podobnego!; ***he fancies himself a great driver*** wydaje mu się, że jest świetnym kierowcą, uważa się za świetnego kierowcę
fan•cy 'dress *s* przebranie *n*, kostium *m*; **fan•cy-'dress par•ty** *s* bal *m* przebierańców
fan•fare ['fænfeə] *s* MUS fanfara *f*; ***a ~ of publicity*** *fig* rozgłos
fang [fæŋ] *s* **1.** kieł *m* **2.** ząb *m* jadowy
'fan mail *s* listy *pl* od wielbicieli
fan•ta•size ['fæntəsaɪz] **I** *v/i* fantazjować, marzyć (**about** o *L*) **II** *v/t* wyobrażać ⟨-razić⟩ sobie; **fan•tas•tic** [fæn'tæstɪk] *adj* **1.** fantastyczny **2.** niesamowity, nieprawdopodobny; **fan•tas•tic•al•ly** [fæn'tæstɪklɪ] *adv* **1.** niesamowicie **2.** fantastycznie; **fan•ta•sy** ['fæntəsɪ] *s* **1.** fantazja *f* **2.** urojenie *n*, wymysł *m* **3.** (*genre*) fantasy *f*
fan•zine ['fænziːn] *s* fanzin *m*, magazyn *m* fanów
far [fɑː] **I** *adj* **1.** daleki, odległy **2.** ***at the ~ end*** na drugim końcu **II** *adv* **1.** daleko; ***go as ~ as Paris*** pojechać aż do Paryża **2.** ***so ~ so good*** jak dotąd w porządku; ***~ from completed*** wcale nie ukończony; ***he worked ~ into the night*** pracował do późna **3.** ***by ~*** zdecydowanie
far•a•way ['fɑːrəweɪ] *adj a. fig* odległy
farce [fɑːs] *s a. fig* farsa *f*; **far•ci•cal** ['fɑːsɪkl] *adj* **1.** farsowy **2.** absurdalny
fare [feə] **I** *s* **1.** opłata *f* za przejazd; ***what's the ~?*** ile kosztuje przejazd?;

a ~ dodger gapowicz **2.** *taxi driver*: pasażer *m*, klient *m* **3.** *form* dania *pl*, kuchnia *f* **II** *v/i* ***how did you ~?*** jak ci poszło?

Far 'East *s*: ***the ~*** Daleki Wschód *m*

fare•well [feə'wel] **I** *interj* żegnaj! **II** *s* pożegnanie *n*; ***make one's ~s*** pożegnać się **III** *adj* pożegnalny; **fare•'well par•ty** *s* przyjęcie *n* pożegnalne

far•fetched [fɑː'fetʃt] *adj* naciągany

far-flung [fɑː'flʌŋ] *adj* **1.** odległy **2.** rozległy **3.** rozrzucony

farm [fɑːm] **I** *s* gospodarstwo *n* (rolne), farma *f* **II** *adj* gospodarski **III** *v/t* uprawiać **IV** *v/i* gospodarować; **farm out** *v/t* **1.** *work*: zlecać ⟨-cić⟩ (**to** *D*) **2.** oddawać ⟨-dać⟩ pod opiekę (**to** *D*); **farm•er** ['fɑːmə] *s* **1.** rolnik *m* **2.** farmer *m*

'farm•hand → ***farm worker***; **'farm•house** *s* wiejski dom *m*; **farm•ing** ['fɑːmɪŋ] *s* **1.** rolnictwo *n* **2.** uprawa *f* **3.** hodowla *f*; **'farm•land** *s* ziemia *f* uprawna; **'farm work•er** *s* robotnik *m* rolny; **'farm•yard** *s* wiejskie podwórze *n*

far-'off *adj* daleki, odległy

far-'out *adj* **1.** awangardowy **2.** *infml* odlotowy

far-'reach•ing *adj* **1.** dalekosiężny **2.** dogłębny **3.** daleko idący

far'see•ing *adj fig* dalekowzroczny

far•sight•ed [fɑː'saɪtɪd] *adj* dalekowzroczny

fart [fɑːt] *vulg* **I** *s* **1.** pierdnięcie *n* **2.** pierdoła *m* **II** *v/i* pierdzieć ⟨-dnąć⟩

far•ther ['fɑːðə] *comp* → ***far***

far•thest ['fɑːðəst] *superl* → ***far***

fas•ci•nate ['fæsɪneɪt] *v/t* fascynować ⟨za-⟩; **fas•ci•nat•ing** ['fæsɪneɪtɪŋ] *adj* fascynujący, pasjonujący; **fas•ci•na•tion** [fæsɪ'neɪʃn] *s* fascynacja *f*, zafascynowanie *n*

fas•cism ['fæʃɪzm] *s* faszyzm *m*; **fas•cist** ['fæʃɪst] **I** *s* faszysta *m* **II** *adj* faszystowski

fash•ion ['fæʃn] **I** *s* **1.** moda *f*; ***come into ~*** stawać się modnym; ***go out of ~*** wychodzić z mody **2.** styl *m*, sposób *m*; ***after a ~*** jako tako **II** *v/t* **1.** modelować ⟨wy-⟩ **2.** robić ⟨z-⟩; **fash•ion•a•ble** ['fæʃnəbl] *adj* modny, w modzie; **fash•ion•a•bly** ['fæʃnəblɪ] *adv* modnie

'fash•ion-con•scious *adj* modny, podążający za modą; **'fash•ion de•sign•er** *s* projektant *m* mody; **'fash•ion mag•a•zine** *s* magazyn *m* mody; **'fash•ion mod•el** *s* **1.** model *m* **2.** modelka *f*; **'fash•ion show** *s* pokaz *m* mody; **'fash•ion vic•tim** *s* niewolnik *m* mody

fast[1] [fɑːst] **I** *adj* **1.** szybki; ***my watch is 10 minutes ~*** mój zegarek śpieszy się o 10 minut **2.** *film*: czuły **II** *adv* szybko

fast[2] [~] **I** *adj* **1.** *colour*: trwały **2.** ***make s.th. ~*** umocować coś; ***make a boat ~*** przycumować łódź **II** *adv* mocno; ***be ~ asleep*** spać głęboko;

fast[3] [~] **I** *s* post *m* **II** *v/i* pościć

'fast•back *s* AUTO *Br* fastback *m*

fas•ten ['fɑːsn] **I** *v/t* **1.** zapinać ⟨-piąć⟩; ***~ (up) one's coat*** zapiąć kurtkę **2.** przymocowywać ⟨-cować⟩ **3.** zawiązywać ⟨-zać⟩ **4.** ***~ one's eyes on*** utkwić wzrok w *L* **II** *v/i* **1.** zamykać ⟨-mknąć⟩ się **2.** zapinać ⟨-piąć⟩ się **3.** zaciskać ⟨-snąć⟩ się; **fas•ten•er** ['fɑːsnə] *s* **1.** zapięcie *n* **2.** zamek *m* **3.** zamknięcie *n*

'fast food I *s* fast food *m* **II** *adj* fast food; **fast food 'res•tau•rant** *s* restauracja *f* typu fast food, fast food *m*

fast 'for•ward *s* przewijanie *n* do przodu

'fast lane *s* pas *m* szybkiego ruchu

'fast train *s* pociąg *m* pośpieszny

fat [fæt] **I** *adj* **1.** gruby **2.** tłusty **3.** *wallet*: gruby, wypchany **II** *s* tłuszcz *m*; ***the ~ is in the fire*** *infml* będzie awantura; ***chew the ~*** *infml* gadać, gawędzić; ***live off the ~ of the land*** opływać w dostatki

fa•tal ['feɪtl] *adj* **1.** śmiertelny **2.** fatalny, zgubny; **fa•tal•ism** ['feɪtəlɪzəm] *s* fatalizm *m*; **fa•ta•list** ['feɪtəlɪst] *s* fatalista *m*; **fa•tal•is•tic** [feɪtə'lɪstɪk] *adj* fatalistyczny; **fa•tal•i•ty** [fə'tælətɪ] *s* **1.** ofiara *f* śmiertelna **2.** śmiertelne skutki *pl*; **fa•tal•ly** ['feɪtəlɪ] *adv* **1.** śmiertelnie **2.** nieodwracalnie

fate [feɪt] *s* **1.** los *m*; (**as**) ***sure as ~*** pewny **2.** przeznaczenie *n* **3.** fatum *n*; **fat•ed** ['feɪtɪd] *adj*: ***they were ~ to meet*** było im pisane się spotkać; **fate•ful** ['feɪtfʊl] *adj* brzemienny w skutki

fat-'free *adj* beztłuszczowy

fa•ther ['fɑːðə] *s* **1.** ojciec *m*; ***like ~, like son*** jaki ojciec, taki syn **2.** ~ (Bóg) Ojciec *m*; ***the Holy ~*** Ojciec Święty; **Father 'Christ•mas** *s* Święty Mikołaj *m*
'fa•ther fig•ure *s* (*person*) autorytet *m*
fa•ther•hood ['fɑːðəhʊd] *s* ojcostwo *n*
'fa•ther-in-law *pl -fathers-in-law s* teść *m*; **'fa•ther•land** *s* ojczyzna *f*; **fa•ther•less** ['fɑːðəlɪs] *adj* bez ojca; **fa•ther•ly** ['fɑːðəlɪ] *adj* ojcowski; **'Fa•ther's Day** *s* Dzień *m* Ojca

F

fa•tigue [fə'tiːg] *s* znużenie *n*, zmęczenie *n*; **fa•tigued** [fə'tiːgd] *adj* znużony, zmęczony
fat•ten ['fætn] *v/t*: ~ (***up***) tuczyć ⟨u-⟩, paść ⟨pod-⟩; **fat•ten•ing** ['fætnɪŋ] **I** *adj* tuczący **II** *s* tuczenie *n*, tucz *m*; **fat•ty** ['fætɪ] **I** *adj* **1.** tłusty **2.** tłuszczowy **II** *s infml* grubas *m*, tłuścioch *m*
fau•cet ['fɔːsɪt] *s Am* **1.** kran *m* **2.** kurek *m*
fault [fɔːlt] *s* **1.** wina *f*; ***it's my ~*** to moja wina; ***be at ~*** być winnym **2.** wada *f*; ***find ~ with*** **a)** krytykować *A* **b)** podważać *A* **3.** usterka *f* **4.** (*tennis*) błąd *m* serwisowy; **'fault•find•er** *s* **1.** krytykant *m* **2.** szukający *m* dziury w całym; **'fault•find•ing I** *s* **1.** krytykanctwo *n* **2.** szukanie *n* dziury w całym **II** *adj* **1.** krytykancki **2.** szukający dziury w całym; **fault•less** ['fɔːltlɪs] *adj* **1.** bezbłędny **2.** nienaganny; **fault•y** ['fɔːltɪ] *adj* **1.** wadliwy **2.** błędny
fa•vour ['feɪvə] *Br*, ***fa•vor*** *Am* **I** *s* **1.** przysługa *f*; ***do s.o. a ~*** wyświadczyć komuś przysługę; ***ask s.o. a ~*** poprosić kogoś o przysługę **2.** (*approval*) ***be in ~ of*** być za *I* **3.** (*advantage*) ***in his ~*** na jego korzyść **4.** przychylność *f*; ***look with ~ upon*** patrzeć przychylnie na *A*; ***be out of ~ with s.o.*** być u kogoś w niełasce **II** *v/t* **1.** woleć **2.** opowiadać się za *I* **3.** sprzyjać **4.** faworyzować; **fa•vour•a•ble** ['feɪvərəbl] *Br*, ***fa•vor•a•ble*** *Am adj* **1.** sprzyjający **2.** przychylny; **fa•vour•a•bly** ['feɪvərəblɪ] *Br*, ***fa•vor•a•bly*** *Am adv* **1.** przychylnie **2.** korzystnie; **fa•vourite** ['feɪvərɪt] *Br*, ***fa•vo•rite*** *Am* **I** *adj* ulubiony **II** *s* **1.** ulubieniec *m* **2.** SPORT faworyt *m*; **fa•vour•it•ism** ['feɪvrɪtɪzm] *Br*, ***fa•vor•it•ism*** *Am s* faworyzowanie *n*
fax [fæks] **I** *s* faks *m* **II** *v/t* **1.** faksować ⟨prze-⟩ **2.** wysyłać ⟨-słać⟩ faks do *G*; **'fax ma•chine** *s* faks *m*; **'fax num•ber** *s* numer *m* faksu
faze [feɪz] *v/t infml* peszyć ⟨s-⟩
FBI [efbiː'aɪ] *abbr* (=***Federal Bureau of Investigation***) FBI *n*
fear [fɪə] **I** *s* **1.** strach *m*, lęk *m* **2.** obawa *f*; ***for ~ that*** z obawy, że; ***for ~ of hurting him*** z obawy, że go skrzywdzi **3.** bojaźń *f*; ***the ~ of God*** bojaźń Boża **II** *v/t* **1.** bać się **2.** obawiać się; **fear for** *v/i* bać się o *A*
fear•ful ['fɪəfʊl] *adj* **1.** przestraszony; ***be ~ of*** bać się *G* **2.** przerażający; **fear•less** ['fɪəlɪs] *adj* nieustraszony; **fear•less•ly** ['fɪəlɪslɪ] *adv* nieustraszenie
feast [fiːst] **I** *s* **1.** *a. fig* uczta *f* **2.** bankiet *m* **3.** REL święto *n* **II** *v/t* ***~ one's eyes on*** napawać wzrok widokiem *G* **III** *v/i* **1.** ucztować **2.** zajadać się (***on*** *I*); **'feast day** *s* REL święto *n*
feat [fiːt] wyczyn *m*
fea•ther ['feðə] **I** *s* pióro *n*; ***birds of a ~ flock together*** *fig* ciągnie swój do swego; ***a ~ in s.o.'s cap*** *fig* czyjś sukces **II** *v/t* ***~ one's nest*** mościć sobie gniazdko **III** *adj* **1.** pierzasty **2.** z pierza; **'fea•ther•brained** *adj*: ***be ~*** *infml* mieć ptasi móżdżek; **fea•ther 'dust•er** *s* miotełka *f* z piór
'feath•er•weight I *s* waga *f* piórkowa **II** *adj* wagi piórkowej
fea•ture ['fiːtʃə] **I** *s* **1.** cecha *f* **2.** rys *m* (twarzy) **3.** element *m* **4.** (obszerny) artykuł *m* **II** *v/t* **1.** zamieszczać ⟨-mieścić⟩ **2.** zawierać ⟨-wrzeć⟩ **3.** przedstawiać ⟨-wić⟩ **4.** ukazywać ⟨-zać⟩ **5.** ***a film featuring X*** film z X w roli głównej
Feb•ru•a•ry ['februərɪ] *s* luty *m*; ***in ~*** w lutym
fe•ces ['fiːsiːz] *pl Am* → ***faeces***
feck•less ['feklɪs] *adj* **1.** nieodpowiedzialny **2.** nieudolny
fed[1] [fed] *Past Simple and Past Participle* → **feed**
fed[2] [~] *s Am infml* agent *m* federalny
fed•e•ral ['fedərəl] *adj* **1.** federalny; ***~ Bureau of Investigation*** *Am* Federalny Urząd Śledczy; ***~ Republic of Germany*** Republika Federalna Niemiec **2.** federacyjny

fed•er•al•ism ['fedərəlɪzəm] *s* federalizm *m*; **fed•er•al•ist** ['fedərəlɪst] **I** *s* federalista *m* **II** *adj* federalistyczny; **fed•e•ra•tion** [fedə'reɪʃn] *s* federacja *f*

fed 'up *adj*: ***be ~ with*** *infml* mieć dosyć *G*

fee [fiː] *s* **1.** honorarium *n* **2.** opłata *f*; ***entrance ~*** opłata *f* za wstęp **3.** wpisowe *n*

fee•ble ['fiːbl] *adj* **1.** słaby **2.** nikły **3.** marny; **fee•ble-'minded** *adj* ograniczony umysłowo; **fee•ble•ness** ['fiːblnɪs] *s* słabość *f*; **fee•bly** ['fiːblɪ] *adv* słabo

feed [fiːd] **I** (*fed*; *fed*) *v/t* **1.** karmić ⟨na-⟩ **2.** żywić ⟨wy-⟩ **3.** *TECH* dostarczać ⟨-czyć⟩ **4.** *TECH* zasilać ⟨-lić⟩ **5.** *INF* wprowadzać ⟨-dzić⟩ (***into*** do *G*) **6.** *fig* podsycać ⟨-cić⟩ **II** (*fed*; *fed*) *v/i* ***~ on*** żywić się *I* **III** *s* **1.** pasza *f* **2.** *baby*: karmienie *n* **3.** *paper*: podawanie *n*; **feed into** *v/t paper, materials*: podawać ⟨-dać⟩

'feed•back *s* **1.** *TECH* sprzężenie *n* (zwrotne) **2.** reakcje *pl*, opinie *pl*

'feed•ing bot•tle *s Br* butelka *f* do karmienia niemowląt

feel [fiːl] **I** (*felt*; *felt*) *v/i* **1.** czuć ⟨po-⟩ się **2.** ***~ like*** (***doing***) ***s.th.*** mieć ochotę coś zrobić, mieć na coś ochotę **3.** ***~ in one's pockets*** grzebać w kieszeniach; ***~ around*** macać **II** (*felt*; *felt*) *v/t* **1.** czuć ⟨po-⟩, odczuwać ⟨-czuć⟩ **2.** macać ⟨po-⟩; ***~ one's way*** iść po omacku, *fig* badać grunt **3.** dotykać ⟨-tknąć⟩ **4.** *pulse*: badać ⟨z-⟩ **5.** wyczuwać ⟨-czuć⟩ **III** *s* nastrój *m*, atmosfera *f*; **feel up to** *v/i* czuć się na siłach (***doing s.th.*** coś zrobić)

feel•er ['fiːlə] *s* czułek *m*; ***put out ~s*** *infml* zbadać grunt

feel•ing ['fiːlɪŋ] *s* **1.** uczucie *n* **2.** odczucie *n* **3.** wrażenie *n*; ***have a ~ that*** mieć wrażenie, że **4.** ***~s of guilt*** poczucie winy **3.** wrażliwość *f*; ***have a ~ for*** być wrażliwym na *A*

'fee-pay•ing **I** *s* opłacanie *n* czesnego **II** *adj* **1.** *school, course*: płatny **2.** *student*: płacący czesne

feet [fiːt] *pl* → ***foot***

feign [feɪn] *v/t* udawać ⟨udać⟩; ***~ death*** udać nieżywego

feint [feɪnt] *s SPORT* finta *f*, zwód *m*

feist•y ['faɪstɪ] *adj Am infml* zadziorny

fe•line ['fiːlaɪn] **I** *adj* koci **II** *s* kot *m*

fell[1] [fel] *Past Simple* → ***fall***

fell[2] [~] *v/t* **1.** *trees*: ścinać ⟨ściąć⟩ **2.** *person*: powalać ⟨-lić⟩

fel•low ['feləʊ] **I** *s* **1.** *infml* facet *m*, gość *m* **2.** kolega *m* **3.** *society*: członek *m* **II** *adj* ***a ~ citizen*** współobywatel; ***a ~ countryman*** rodak, krajan; ***a ~ man*** bliźni

felt[1] [felt] *Past Simple and Past Participle* → **feel**

felt[2] [~] *s* **1.** filc *m* **2.** pilśń *f* **III** *adj* **1.** filcowy **2.** pilśniowy

felt 'tip, ***felt-tip 'pen*** *s* flamaster *m*, mazak *m*

fe•male ['fiːmeɪl] **I** *adj* **1.** żeński; ***a ~ student*** studentka; ***~ screw*** gwint żeński **2.** kobiecy **II** *s* **1.** samica *f* **2.** kobieta *f*

fem•i•nine ['femɪnɪn] *adj* **1.** kobiecy; ***look very ~*** wyglądać bardzo kobieco **2.** rodzaju żeńskiego **3.** żeński; **fem•i•nin•i•ty** [femɪ'nɪnɪtɪ] *s* kobiecość *f*

fem•i•nism ['femɪnɪzm] *s* feminizm *m*; **fem•i•nist** ['femɪnɪst] **I** *s* feministka *f* **II** *adj* feministyczny

fence [fens] **I** *s* **1.** ogrodzenie *n* **2.** płot *m* **3.** *infml* paser *m* **II** *v/t* ogradzać ⟨-rodzić⟩; ***~ s.th. in*** ogrodzić coś, zagrodzić coś; ***~ s.th. off*** odgrodzić coś **III** *v/i SPORT* uprawiać szermierkę; **fenc•er** ['fensə] *s SPORT* szermierz *m*; **fenc•ing** ['fensɪŋ] **I** *s* **1.** *SPORT* szermierka *f* **2.** ogrodzenie *n* **II** *adj* szermierczy; ***a ~ master*** mistrz szermierki

fend [fend] *v/i*: ***~ for oneself*** radzić sobie samemu, samemu dbać o siebie; **fend off** *v/t attack*: odpierać ⟨odeprzeć⟩

fer•ment[1] **I** [fɜːment] *s a. fig* ferment *m* **II** ['fə'ment] *v/i* fermentować ⟨s-⟩

fer•men•ta•tion [fɜːmen'teɪʃn] *s* fermentacja *f*

fe•ro•cious [fə'rəʊʃəs] *adj* **1.** *animal*: dziki **2.** *dog*: zły **3.** brutalny **4.** zażarty **5.** srogi; **fe•roc•i•ty** [fə'rɒsɪtɪ] *s* **1.** brutalność *f* **2.** dzikość *f* **3.** ostrość *f* **4.** srogość *f*

fer•ret ['ferɪt] *s BIOL* fretka *f*; **fer•ret around** *v/i* myszkować; **fer•ret out** *v/t* **1.** wyszperać **2.** wywęszyć **3.** wytropić

F

fer•ry ['ferɪ] **I** *s* prom *m* **II** *v/t* przewozić ⟨-wieźć⟩ (promem); **'fer•ry•boat** *s* prom *m*; **'fer•ry•man** *pl -men s* przewoźnik *m*; **'fer•ry serv•ice** *s* połączenia *pl* promowe

fer•tile ['fɜːtaɪl] *adj* **1.** płodny **2.** żyzny; **fer•til•i•ty** [fɜː'tɪlətɪ] *s* **1.** płodność *f* **2.** żyzność *f*; **fer'til•i•ty drug** *s* lek *m* na bezpłodność; **fer•til•i•za•tion** [fɜːtɪlaɪ'zeɪʃn] *s* **1.** zapłodnienie *n* **2.** nawożenie *n* **3.** użyźnianie *n*; **fer•ti•lize** ['fɜːtəlaɪz] *v/t* **1.** zapładniać ⟨-łodnić⟩ **2.** nawozić ⟨-wieźć⟩ **3.** użyźniać ⟨-nić⟩; **fer•ti•liz•er** ['fɜːtəlaɪzə] *s* nawóz *m*

fer•vent ['fɜːvənt] *adj* **1.** zagorzały **2.** gorący **3.** żarliwy **4.** płomienny; **fer•vent•ly** ['fɜːvəntlɪ] *adv* **1.** zagorzale **2.** gorąco **3.** żarliwie **4.** z zapałem; **fer•vour** ['fɜːvə] *Br*, **fer•vor** *Am* **1.** zapał *m* **2.** ferwor *m*

fes•ti•val ['festɪvl] *s* **1.** święto *n* **2.** festiwal *m*; **fes•tive** ['festɪv] *adj* **1.** świąteczny **2.** odświętny; **fes•tiv•i•ties** [fe'stɪvətɪz] *pl* **1.** zabawa *f* **2.** uroczystości *pl*

fes•toon [fe'stuːn] **I** *s* girlanda *f* **II** *v/t* przystrajać ⟨-roić⟩, ubierać ⟨ubrać⟩

fe•tal ['fiːtl] → ***foetal***

fetch [fetʃ] *v/t* **1.** przynosić ⟨-nieść⟩ **2.** przyprowadzać ⟨-dzić⟩; (***go and***) **~ *a doctor*** (iść) sprowadzić lekarza **3.** przywozić ⟨-wieźć⟩ **4. *~ s.o. one*** *infml* przyłożyć komuś

fetch•ing ['fetʃɪŋ] *adj infml* **1.** atrakcyjny **2.** uroczy

fet•id ['fetɪd] *adj* cuchnący

fet•ish ['fetɪʃ] *s* **1.** fetysz *m* **2.** obsesja *f*; **fet•ish•ism** ['fetɪʃɪzəm] *s* fetyszyzm *m*; **fet•ish•ist** ['fetɪʃɪst] *adj* fetyszysta *m*; **fet•ish•ist•ic** [fetɪ'ʃɪstɪk] *adj* fetyszystyczny

fet•ter ['fetər] **I *~s*** *pl* **1.** kajdany *pl* **2.** *fig* pęta *pl* **II** *v/t* **1.** zakuwać ⟨-kuć⟩ w kajdany **2.** *fig* pętać, wiązać

fe•tus ['fiːtəs] *s* → ***foetus***

feud [fjuːd] **I** *s* zatarg *m*, spór *m*; ***have a ~ with*** toczyć spór z *I* **II** *v/i* toczyć spór

feu•dal ['fjuːdl] *adj* feudalny; **feu•dal•ism** ['fjuːdəlɪzəm] *s* feudalizm *m*

fe•ver ['fiːvə] *s* **1.** gorączka *f*; ***have a ~*** mieć gorączkę **2.** rozgorączkowanie *n*; ***in a ~ of excitement*** rozgorączkowany, podekscytowany; **fe•ver•ish** ['fiːvərɪʃ] *adj* **1.** w gorączce; ***be ~*** mieć gorączkę; ***a ~ cold*** przeziębienie z gorączką **2.** gorączkowy

few [fjuː] **I** *adj* mało, niewiele; ***no ~er than 40 people*** nie mniej niż 40 osób **II** *pron* niewiele; ***~ of his friends*** niewielu z jego przyjaciół **3. *a ~*** kilka, parę; ***a good ~, quite a ~*** sporo; ***every ~ days*** co kilka dni; **fewer** ['fjuːə] **I** *comp* → ***few*** *adj* mniej **II** *pron* mniej

fi•an•cé [fɪ'ɒnseɪ] *s* narzeczony *m*; **fi•an•cée** [fɪ'ɒnseɪ] *s* narzeczona *f*

fi•as•co [fɪ'æskəʊ] *s* fiasko *n*, *infml* klapa *f*

fib [fɪb] *infml* **I** *s* kłamstwo *n*, kłamstewko *n* **II** *v/i* bujać, zmyślać

fibre ['faɪbə] *Br*, **fi•ber** *Am* **1.** włókno *n* **2.** błonnik *m* **3.** *fig* charakter *m*

fick•le ['fɪkl] *adj* **1.** zmienny **2.** kapryśny **3.** nieprzewidywalny

fic•tion ['fɪkʃn] *s* **1.** fikcja *f* **2.** beletrystyka *f*, literatura *f* piękna; **fic•tion•al** ['fɪkʃnl] *adj* **1.** fikcyjny **2.** literacki; **fic•ti•tious** [fɪk'tɪʃəs] *adj* **1.** zmyślony **2.** fikcyjny

fid•dle ['fɪdl] **I** *s* MUS skrzypce *pl*; ***play second ~ to*** *fig* pozostawać w cieniu *G*; (***as***) ***fit as a ~*** zdrów jak ryba **II** *v/i* **1. *~ about***, ***~ around*** *infml* obijać się **2. *~ about with***, ***~ around with*** majstrować przy *I*, bawić się *I* **III** *v/t figures*: fałszować ⟨s-⟩; **fid•dler** ['fɪdlə] *s* skrzypek *m*; **fid•dly** ['fɪdlɪ] *adj*: ***a ~ job*** *infml* dłubanina

fi•del•i•ty [fɪ'delətɪ] *s* wierność *f*

fid•get ['fɪdʒɪt] **I** *v/i* wiercić się **II** *s* wiercipięta *m/f*; ***have the ~s*** nie móc usiedzieć w miejscu; **fid•get•y** ['fɪdʒɪtɪ] *adj* **1.** ruchliwy **2.** niespokojny

field [fiːld] **I** *s* **1.** pole *n*; ***in the ~*** w polu; ***in the ~ of vision*** w polu widzenia **2.** dziedzina *f*; ***in my ~*** w mojej dziedzinie; ***the ~ of application*** zakres zastosowania **3.** SPORT boisko *n* **II** *v/t* **1.** *candidates*: wystawiać ⟨-wić⟩ **2.** *ball*: podawać ⟨-dać⟩; **'field day** *s*: ***have a ~*** *infml* mieć używanie

'field e•vents *pl* SPORT konkurencje *pl* techniczne; **'field hock•ey** *s* SPORT *Am* hokej *m* na trawie; **'field mar•shal** *s* **1.** marszałek *m* **2.** feldmarszałek *m*; **'field test** *s* próba *f* terenowa; **'field tri•als** *pl* próby *pl* terenowe;

ˈ**field trip** *s* **1.** wycieczka *f* (edukacyjna) **2.** zajęcia *pl* w terenie; ˈ**fieldwork** *s* praca *f* w terenie
fieldwork [fiːnd] *s* **1.** demon *m* **2.** szatan *m* **3.** maniak *m* **4.** fanatyk *m*
fiend•ish [ˈfiːndɪʃ] *adj* **1.** nieludzki **2.** diabelski, szatański, piekielny
fierce [fɪəs] *adj* **1.** agresywny **2.** *dog*: groźny, ostry **3.** zażarty **4.** zacięty **5.** zagorzały **6.** *expression*, *look*: dziki, wściekły; **fierce•ly** [ˈfɪəslɪ] *adv* **1.** gwałtownie **2.** zaciekle **3.** zażarcie **4.** strasznie **5.** bezwzględnie
fi•er•y [ˈfaɪərɪ] *adj* **1.** ognisty **2.** wybuchowy **3.** wściekły **4.** bardzo ostry **5.** płomienny
fif•teen [fɪfˈtiːn] **I** *num* piętnaście **II** *s* piętnastka *f*
fif•teenth [fɪfˈtiːnθ] *adj* piętnasty
fifth [fɪfθ] *adj* piąty; ***the ~ column*** piąta kolumna; ***the ~ wheel*** piąte koło u wozu; ***the ~ of May***, ***May ~*** *Am* piąty maja
fif•ti•eth [ˈfɪftɪɪθ] *adj* pięćdziesiąty
fif•ty [ˈfɪftɪ] **I** *num* pięćdziesiąt **II** *s* pięćdziesiątka *f*; ***be in one's fifties*** być po pięćdziesiątce; ***in the fifties*** w latach pięćdziesiątych
fif•ty-ˈfif•ty **I** *adj* ***a ~ chance*** pięćdziesiąt procent szans **II** *adv* **1.** pół na pół **2.** po połowie, po równo; ***go ~*** podzielić się po połowie, podzielić się po równo
fig [fɪg] *s* figa *f*; ***I don't care a ~*** jest mi wszystko jedno
fight [faɪt] **I** *s* **1.** walka *f* (**for** o *A*, ***against*** z *I*); ***put up a good ~*** walczyć dzielnie **2.** bójka *f*; ***have a ~ with*** wdać się w bójkę z *I* **II** (*fought*; *fought*) *v/t* walczyć z *I* **III** (*fought*; *fought*) *v/i* walczyć (**for** o *A*, ***against*** z *I*); **fight back** **I** *v/t tears*: tłumić ⟨s-⟩, powstrzymywać ⟨-mać⟩ **II** *v/i* **1.** stawiać opór, bronić się **2.** kłócić ⟨po-⟩ się; **fight off** *v/t* **1.** *attack*: odpierać ⟨odeprzeć⟩ **2.** *weakness*: przemóc, zwalczać ⟨-czyć⟩
fight•er [ˈfaɪtə] *s* **1.** SPORT bokser *m* **2.** ***he's a ~*** on się łatwo nie poddaje **3.** ***a ~ plane*** myśliwiec, samolot myśliwski
fight•ing [ˈfaɪtɪŋ] **I** *s* walki *pl*; ***heavy ~*** ciężkie walki **II** bojowy; ***~ spirit*** wola walki, duch walki; **fight•ing** ˈ**chance** *adj* pewna szansa *f*; **fight•ing** ˈ**fit** *adj* w pełni sił
ˈ**fig tree** *s* figowiec *m*
fig•u•ra•tive [ˈfɪgjərətɪv] *adj meaning*: przenośny
fig•ure [ˈfɪgə] **I** *s* **1.** cyfra *f*; ***run into three ~s*** iść w setki; ***a six-~ income*** dochody wyrażone liczbą sześciocyfrową **2.** liczba *f* **3.** suma *f*, kwota *f* **4.** figura *f* **5.** sylwetka *f* **6.** postać *f*; ***a ~ of fun*** zabawna postać; ***cut a poor ~*** *fig* wyglądać marnie; ***cut a striking ~*** *fig* rzucać się w oczy **7.** ***a ~ of speech*** figura retoryczna **II** *v/t* ***~ s.th. to oneself*** pomyśleć coś, wyobrazić sobie coś **III** *v/i* występować, figurować; **figure on** *v/i infml* liczyć na *A*; **figure out** *v/t* **1.** *solution*: znajdować ⟨znaleźć⟩ **2.** *problem*: rozgryzać ⟨-ryźć⟩, rozwiązywać ⟨-zać⟩
ˈ**fig•ure•head** *s* **1.** figurant *m* **2.** nominalny przywódca *m*; ˈ**fig•ure skat•er** *s* łyżwiarz *m* figurowy; ˈ**fig•ure skat•ing** *s* łyżwiarstwo *n* figurowe
filch [fɪltʃ] *v/t infml* podwędzać ⟨-dzić⟩
file [faɪl] **I** *s* **1.** segregator *m* **2.** teczka *f* **3.** akta *pl*; ***keep a ~ on s.o.*** przechowywać czyjeś akta; ***a ~ number*** numer katalogowy; ***on ~*** w aktach **4.** kartoteka *f* **5.** INF plik *m*; ***open a ~*** otworzyć plik **6.** rząd *m*; ***in Indian ~***, ***in single ~*** gęsiego **II** *v/t* **1.** włączać ⟨-yć⟩ do dokumentacji **2.** *complaint*: wnosić ⟨wnieść⟩, składać ⟨złożyć⟩; **file away** *v/t* odkładać ⟨odłożyć⟩ do akt
ˈ**file cab•i•net** *Am* → ***filing cabinet***; ˈ**file clerk** *s* pracownik *m* biurowy; ˈ**file man•ag•er** *s* INF menedżer *m* plików
fi•li•al [ˈfɪlɪəl] *adj*: ***~ duties*** obowiązki dzieci (wobec rodziców)
fil•i•gree [ˈfɪlɪgriː] **I** *s* filigran *m* **II** *adj* filigranowy
ˈ**fil•ing cab•i•net** *s Br* **1.** szafka *f* na dokumenty **2.** szafa *f* na dokumenty
fill [fɪl] **II** *v/t* **1.** napełniać ⟨-nić⟩; ***~ed with*** pełny *G*; ***~ed with envy*** *fig* pełen zawiści **2.** wypełniać ⟨-nić⟩ **3.** ***~ a post*** **a)** obsadzić stanowisko **b)** objąć stanowisko **c)** zajmować stanowisko **4.** *order*, *prescription*: realizować ⟨z-⟩ **5.** *tooth*: plombować ⟨za-⟩ **II** *s* **7.** ***eat one's ~*** najeść się do syta; ***I've had my ~ of*** mam już dość *G*; **fill**

F

in *v/t* **1.** *Br form*: wypełniać ⟨-nić⟩ **2.** wpisywać ⟨-sać⟩ **3.** uzupełniać ⟨-nić⟩ **4.** informować ⟨po-⟩ (***on*** o *L*); **fill in for** *v/i* zastępować ⟨-tąpić⟩; **fill out I** *v/t Am form*: wypełniać ⟨-nić⟩ **II** *v/i* zaokrąglać ⟨-lić⟩ się; **fill up** *v/i* **1.** wypełniać ⟨-nić⟩ się **2.** zapełniać ⟨-nić⟩ się

fil•let ['fɪlɪt] *s COOK* filet *m*; *~ **steak*** polędwica wołowa

fill•ing ['fɪlɪŋ] **I** *s* **1.** *COOK* nadzienie *n* **2.** plomba *f*, wypełnienie *n* **II** *adj* sycący; **'fill•ing sta•tion** *s* stacja *f* benzynowa

F

film [fɪlm] **I** *s* **1.** film *m* **2.** *PHOT* klisza *f* **3.** warstewka *f* **II** *adj* filmowy **III** *v/t* filmować ⟨s-⟩; **'film di•rec•tor** *s* reżyser *s* filmowy; **'film fes•ti•val** *s* festiwal *m* filmowy; **'film-mak•er** *s* filmowiec *m*; **'film star** *s* gwiazda *f* filmowa; **'film stu•di•o** *s* studio *n* filmowe

fil•ter ['fɪltə] **I** *s* filtr *m* **II** *v/t* filtrować ⟨prze-⟩ **III** *v/i* **1.** przenikać ⟨-knąć⟩ **2.** *~ **out*** (*news*) wydostawać ⟨-tać⟩ się, przeciekać ⟨-ciec⟩ na zewnątrz **3.** *Br* zjeżdżać ⟨zjechać⟩; *~ **to the left*** skręcić w lewo; **fil•ter through** *v/i* **1.** wychodzić ⟨wyjść⟩ **2.** (*news*) wydostawać ⟨-tać⟩ się, przeciekać ⟨-ciec⟩ na zewnątrz

'fil•ter pa•per *s COOK* bibuła *f* filtracyjna; **'fil•ter tip** *s* **1.** filtr *m* **2.** papieros *m* z filtrem

filth [fɪlθ] *s* **1.** brud *m* **2.** świństwa *pl*; **filth•y** ['fɪlθɪ] *adj* **1.** obrzydliwie brudny **2.** ordynarny **3.** rynsztokowy **4.** *weather*: paskudny, okropny

fin [fɪn] *s* **1.** *BIOL* płetwa *f* **2.** *yacht*: miecz *m* **3.** *plane*: statecznik *m*

fi•nal ['faɪnl] **I** *adj* **1.** ostatni **2.** końcowy; ***the ~ examination*** egzamin końcowy; ***the ~ score*** wynik końcowy; ***the ~ whistle*** *SPORT* gwizdek końcowy **II** *s* **1.** *SPORT* finał *m* **2.** egzamin *m* końcowy; **fi•na•le** [fɪ'nɑːlɪ] *s MUS THEAT* finał *m*; **fi•nal•ist** ['faɪnəlɪst] *s* finalista *m*; **fi•nal•i•ty** [faɪ'næləti] *s* **1.** ostateczność *f* **2.** nieodwracalność *f*; **fi•nal•ize** ['faɪnəlaɪz] *v/t* **1.** finalizować ⟨s-⟩ **2.** kończyć ⟨za-⟩; **fi•nal•ly** ['faɪnəlɪ] *adv* **1.** w końcu, wreszcie **2.** na koniec **3.** ostatecznie

fi•nance ['faɪnæns] **I** *s* **1.** finanse *pl*; ***a ~ company*** spółka finansująca sprzedaż ratalną **2.** fundusze *pl* **II** *v/t* finansować ⟨s-⟩; **fi•nan•ces** ['faɪnænsɪz] *pl* finanse *pl*; **fi•nan•cial** [faɪ'nænʃl] *adj* finansowy; **fi•nan•cial•ly** [faɪ'nænʃəlɪ] *adv* finansowo; **fi•nan•cial 'year** *s FIN Br* rok *m* obrotowy; **fi•nan•cier** [faɪ'nænsɪə] *s* finansista *m*

find [faɪnd] **I** (*found*; *found*) *v/t* **1.** znajdować ⟨znaleźć⟩, odnajdywać ⟨-naleźć⟩ **2.** odkrywać ⟨-ryć⟩, zastawać ⟨-tać⟩ **3.** spotykać ⟨-tkać⟩, natrafiać ⟨-fić⟩ na *A*, widywać ⟨-dzieć⟩ **4.** dowiadywać ⟨-wiedzieć⟩ się, odkrywać ⟨-ryć⟩, wykrywać ⟨-ryć⟩ **5.** uznawać ⟨-nać⟩ za *A*, uważać za *A*; *~ **s.th. impossible*** uważać coś za niemożliwe **6.** stwierdzać ⟨-dzić⟩, przekonywać ⟨-nać⟩ się; ***she found it hard to accept this loss*** było jej trudno pogodzić się z tą stratą **II** (*found*; *found*) *v/i ~ **for** (**against**) **the defendant** JUR* orzec na korzyść (niekorzyść) oskarżonego **III** *s* **1.** odkrycie *n* **2.** znalezisko *n*; **find out** *v/t* **1.** dowiadywać ⟨-wiedzieć⟩ się **2.** *answer*: znajdować ⟨znaleźć⟩; **find out about** *v/i* dowiadywać ⟨-wiedzieć⟩ się o *L*

find•ings ['faɪndɪŋs] *s* **1.** ustalenia *pl* **2.** wnioski *pl*, konkluzje *pl* **3.** *research*, *experiment*: wyniki *pl* **4.** *JUR* orzeczenie *n*

fine[1] [faɪn] **I** *adj* **1.** świetny **2.** dobry; ***I'm ~*** mam się dobrze **3.** udany **4.** *standard*: wysoki **5.** *fabric*: delikatny, cienki **II** *adv* świetnie; ***that will suit me ~*** to mi odpowiada, to mi pasuje

fine[2] [~] **I** *s* **1.** grzywna *f* **2.** mandat *m* **II** *v/t* **1.** karać ⟨u-⟩ grzywną **2.** karać ⟨u-⟩ mandatem; ***he was ~d £50*** dostał mandat w wysokości 50 funtów

fine 'arts *pl* sztuki *pl* piękne

fine•ly ['faɪnlɪ] *adv* **1.** drobno **2.** cienko **3.** precyzyjnie, starannie **4.** świetnie

fine 'print *s* drobny druk *m*

fi•nesse [fɪ'nes] *s* **1.** finezja *f* **2.** misterność *f*

fine-'tooth comb *s* gęsty grzebień *m*; **fine-'tune** *v/t* **1.** udoskonalać ⟨-lić⟩ **2.** *fig* szlifować ⟨do-⟩ **3.** dostrajać ⟨-roić⟩

fin•ger ['fɪŋgə] **I** *s* palec *m* (u ręki); ***the first ~*** palec wskazujący; ***the second ~***

palec środkowy; ***the third ~*** palec serdeczny; ***the fourth ~, the little ~*** mały palec; ***he has a ~ in every pie*** zajmuje się wszystkim, wtrąca się do wszystkiego; ***keep one's ~s crossed for s.o.*** trzymać za kogoś kciuki; ***not to lift a ~*** nawet nie ruszyć palcem **II** *v/t* **1.** dotykać ⟨-tknąć⟩ **2.** macać ⟨po-⟩; **'fin•ger•mark** *s* ślad *m* palca; **'fin•ger•nail** *s* paznokieć *m*; **'fin•ger•print** *s* odcisk *m* palca; ***take s.o.'s ~s*** zdjąć komuś odciski palców; **'finger•tip** *s* koniuszek *m* palca; ***have s.th. at one's ~s*** *fig* mieć coś w małym palcu

fin•ish ['fɪnɪʃ] **I** *v/t* **1.** kończyć ⟨s-⟩; ***~ reading*** skończyć czytać **2.** zakończyć **3.** dopijać ⟨-pić⟩ **4.** TECH wykańczać ⟨-kończyć⟩ **II** *v/i* **1.** kończyć ⟨s-⟩; ***have you ~ed?*** skończyłeś? **2.** kończyć ⟨s-⟩ się **3.** ***~ third*** SPORT zająć trzecie miejsce **III** *s* **1.** koniec *m* **2.** SPORT końcówka *f*, finisz *m* **3.** wykończenie *n*; **fin•ish off** *v/t* **1.** kończyć ⟨s-⟩ **2.** wykańczać ⟨-kończyć⟩ **3.** *career*: niszczyć ⟨z-⟩; **fin•ish up I** *v/t* **1.** kończyć ⟨s-⟩ **2.** zużywać ⟨-żyć⟩ do końca **II** *v/i* **1.** *Br* kończyć ⟨s-⟩ **2.** *Br infml* lądować ⟨wy-⟩; **fin•ish with** *v/i* **1.** kończyć ⟨s-⟩ z *I* **2.** zrywać ⟨zerwać⟩ z *I*

fin•ished ['fɪnɪʃt] *adj* **1.** skończony; ***I'm not ~ yet*** jeszcze nie skończyłem **2.** gotowy **3.** *interior*: wykończony; **'fin•ished goods** *pl* wyroby *pl* gotowe

fin•ish•ing ['fɪnɪʃɪŋ] *adj* **1.** końcowy **2.** ostatni **3.** wykończeniowy; **'fin•ish•ing line** *s Br* linia *f* mety

fi•nite ['faɪnaɪt] *adj* **1.** ograniczony **2.** MATH skończony

Fin•land ['fɪnlənd] *s* Finlandia *f*; **Finn** [fɪn] *s* Fin *m*, Finka *f*; **Finn•ish** ['fɪnɪʃ] **I** *s* (*language*) fiński *m* **II** *adj* fiński

fir [fɜː] *s* jodła *f*; **'fir cone** *s* szyszka *f* jodłowa

fire [faɪə] **I** *s* **1.** ogień *m*; ***be on ~*** płonąć; ***catch ~*** zapalić się; ***set s.th. on ~, set ~ to s.th.*** podpalić coś; ***play with ~*** *fig* igrać z ogniem; ***come under ~*** znaleźć się pod obstrzałem; ***be in the line of ~*** znajdować się na linii ognia **2.** pożar *m* **3.** ognisko *n* **II** *v/i* **1.** strzelać ⟨-lić⟩, wystrzelić (***at/on*** do *G*) **2.** otwierać ⟨-worzyć⟩ ogień **3.** (*engine*) zapalać ⟨-lić⟩, odpalać ⟨-lić⟩ **III** *v/t* **1.** strzelać ⟨-lić⟩ z *G*, wystrzelić z *G* **2.** wypalać ⟨-lić⟩ **3.** (*work*) *infml* wylewać ⟨-lać⟩ **4.** *imagination*: rozpalać ⟨-lić⟩; **'fire a•larm** *s* alarm *m* pożarowy; **'fire•arms** *pl* broń *f* palna; **fire brigade** *s Br* straż *f* pożarna; **'fire•crack•er** *s* petarda *f*; **'fire de•part•ment** *s Am* straż *f* pożarna; **'fire door** *s* drzwi *pl* przeciwpożarowe; **'fire drill** *s* ćwiczenia *pl* przeciwpożarowe; **'fire en•gine** *s* wóz *m* strażacki; **'fire es•cape** *s* **1.** schody *pl* pożarowe **2.** drabinka *f* pożarowa; **'fire ex•tin•guish•er** *s* gaśnica *f*; **'fire fight•er** *s* strażak *m*; **'fire•guard** *s* ekran *m* kominkowy; **'fire•house** *s Am* remiza *f* strażacka; **'fire hy•drant** *s* hydrant *m* przeciwpożarowy; **'fire•light** *s* blask *m* ognia; **'fire•man** *pl -men s* strażak *m*; **'fire•place** *s* kominek *m*; **'fire•plug** *s Am* hydrant *m* przeciwpożarowy; **'fire pre•ven•tion** *s* ochrona *f* przeciwpożarowa; **'fire•proof** *adj* ognioodporny; **'fire•side** *s*: ***by the ~*** przy kominku; **'fire sta•tion** *s* remiza *f* strażacka; **'fire truck** *s Am* wóz *m* strażacki; **'fire•wood** *s* drewno *n* na opał; **'fire•works** *pl* sztuczne ognie *pl*, fajerwerki *pl*; **'fire•works dis•play** *s* pokaz *m* sztucznych ogni

fir•ing ['faɪərɪŋ] *s ceramics*: wypalanie *n*; **'fir•ing range** *s* zasięg *m* ognia; **fir•ing squad** *s* pluton *m* egzekucyjny

firm[1] [fɜːm] **I** *adj* **1.** twardy **2.** mocny **3.** *base*: stabilny **4.** solidny **5.** *fruit*: jędrny **6.** ubity **7.** *evidence*: niezbity **8.** *offer*: wiążący **9.** stanowczy **10.** ostateczny **II** *adv* ***stand ~*** trwać przy swoim, nie ustępować

firm[2] [~] *s* firma *f*, przedsiębiorstwo *n*

firm•ness ['fɜːmnɪs] *s* **1.** twardość *f* **2.** stabilność *f* **3.** stanowczość *f*

first [fɜːst] **I** *adj* **1.** pierwszy; ***it was the ~ time they met*** to było ich pierwsze spotkanie **2.** *duty*: podstawowy **II** *adv* **1.** pierwszy; ***when did you ~ meet her?*** kiedy po raz pierwszy ją spotkałeś?; ***~ come, ~ served*** kto pierwszy, ten lepszy; ***his family always comes ~*** jego rodzina jest zawsze na pierwszym miejscu; ***~ of all*** przede wszystkim **2.** najpierw; ***at ~*** najpierw **III** *s* **1.** ***the ~*** pierwszy; ***the ~ of May*** pierwszy mają; ***from the very ~*** od samego początku **2.** *AUTO* jedynka *f*; **first 'aid** *s* pierwsza pomoc *f*; ***give s.o. ~*** udzielić komuś pierwszej pomocy; **first 'aid•er** *s infml* ratownik *m* (udzielający pierwszej pomocy); **first-'aid kit** *s* apteczka *f*; **'first•born I** *s* pierworodny *m* **II** *adj* pierworodny; **'first class I** *s* pierwsza klasa *f* **II** *adj* **1.** pierwszej klasy **2.** w pierwszej klasie **3.** o najwyższym standardzie **4.** pierwszorzędny; **first 'cous•in** *s* kuzyn *m*; **first-de'gree** *adj burn*: pierwszego stopnia; **first 'floor** *s* **1.** *Br* pierwsze piętro *n* **2.** *Am* parter *m*; **first 'hand** *adv* **1.** bezpośrednio **2.** z pierwszej ręki; **First 'La•dy** *s* pierwsza dama *f*

first•ly ['fɜːstlɪ] *adv* po pierwsze

'first name *s* imię *n*; ***what is his ~?*** jak on ma na imię?; **first 'night** *s* premiera *f*; **first of•'fend•er** *s* przestępca *m* dotychczas niekarany; ***she's a ~*** nie była dotychczas karana; **first of•'fence** *s* pierwsze wykroczenie *n*; **first-'rate** *adj* pierwszorzędny

fish [fɪʃ] **I** *s* ryba *f*; ***have bigger ~ to fry*** *fig* mieć ważniejsze sprawy na głowie **II** *v/t* łowić ⟨z-⟩ **III** *v/i* łowić, wędkować; ***~ for herring*** łowić śledzie; **fish out** *v/t* **1.** wyławiać ⟨-łowić⟩ **2.** wydobywać ⟨-być⟩

fish and 'chips *s* (smażona) ryba *f* z frytkami; **'fish•bone** *s* ość *f*; **'fish bowl** *s* (kuliste) akwarium *n*; **'fish cake** *s* kotlecik *m* rybny; **'fish•er•man** *pl -men s* **1.** rybak *m* **2.** wędkarz *m*; **fish 'fin•ger** *s COOK Br* paluszek *m* rybny

fish•ing ['fɪʃɪŋ] *s* **1.** rybołówstwo *n* **2.** wędkowanie *n*; ***go ~*** iść na ryby; **'fish•ing boat** *s* łódź *f* rybacka; **'fish•ing grounds** *s* łowisko *n*; **'fish•ing line** *s* żyłka *f* wędkarska; **'fish•ing net** *s* sieć *f* rybacka; **'fish•ing rod** *s* wędka *f*; **'fish•ing tack•le** *s* sprzęt *m* wędkarski; **'fish•ing vil•lage** *s* wioska *f* rybacka

'fish stick *s COOK Am* paluszek *m* rybny; **'fish•mon•ger** *s Br* **1.** handlarz *m* ryb **2.** właściciel *m* sklepu rybnego; **'fish tank** *s* akwarium *n*

fish•y ['fɪʃɪ] *adj* **1.** rybi **2.** *business*: śmierdzący, mętny

fist [fɪst] *s* pięść *f*, piąstka *f*

fit[1] [fɪt] **I** *v/i* **1.** pasować **2.** dobrze leżeć **3.** mieścić ⟨z-⟩ się **II** *v/t* **1.** pasować do *G* **2.** ~ (*up*) zaopatrzyć (***with*** w *A*) **3.** (*garment*) dobrze leżeć na *L* **4.** zmieścić, pomieścić **5.** zakładać ⟨założyć⟩ **6.** montować ⟨za-⟩ **III** *adj* **1.** odpowiedni, właściwy; ***be ~ to drink*** (***eat***) nadawać się do picia (jedzenia); ***be ~ to drive*** móc prowadzić; ***see fit to do s.th.*** uznać za stosowne coś zrobić **2.** w dobrej formie, wysportowany; ***keep ~*** utrzymywać formę, utrzymywać kondycję **IV** *s* **1.** ***be a perfect ~*** (*garment*) doskonale pasować, świetnie leżeć; ***be a tight ~*** być ciasnym; **fit in I** *v/i* **1.** pasować **2.** wchodzić ⟨wejść⟩, mieścić ⟨z-⟩ się **II** *v/t* **1.** pasować do *G* **2.** mieścić ⟨z-⟩ **3.** zgadzać się z *I* **4.** znajdować ⟨znaleźć⟩ czas na *A* **5.** znajdować ⟨znaleźć⟩ czas dla *G*

fit[2] [~] *s* **1.** *MED* atak *m*, napad *m*; ***a ~ of coughing*** atak kaszlu **2.** *fig* napad *m*, przypływ *m*; ***a ~ of anger*** napad gniewu; ***a ~ of laughter*** atak śmiechu; ***by ~s and starts***, ***in ~s and starts*** zrywami

fit•ful ['fɪtfəl] *adj* **1.** niespokojny **2.** zmienny **3.** *light*: przerywany

fit•ness ['fɪtnɪs] *s* **1.** sprawność *f* fizyczna; ***a ~ test*** test sprawnościowy **2.** zdatność *f*, przydatność *f*; ***~ to drive*** zdolność prowadzenia pojazdów; **'fit•ness cen•tre** *Br*, **fit•ness cen•ter** *Am s* centrum *n* fitness

fit•ted ['fɪtɪd] *adj* **1.** dopasowany **2.** obcisły **3.** wbudowany; **fit•ted 'carpet** *s* wykładzina *f* dywanowa; **fit•ted 'kitch•en** *s* wyposażona kuchnia *f*

fit•ting ['fɪtɪŋ] **I** *adj* **1.** odpowiedni, stosowny **2.** trafny **II** *s* **1.** element *m* instalacji **2.** przymiarka *f*; **'fit•ting room** *s* przymierzalnia *f*; **fit•tings** ['fɪtɪŋz] *pl* **1.** wyposażenie *n* **2.** armatura *f*

five [faɪv] **I** *num* pięć, pięciu, pięcioro; ***a ~-day week*** pięciodniowy tydzień pracy **II** *s* piątka *f*; ***the ~ of hearts*** piątka kier

fix [fɪks] **I** *v/t* **1.** umocowywać ⟨-cować⟩ **2.** przymocowywać ⟨-cować⟩ **3.** ustalać ⟨-lić⟩ **4.** naprawiać ⟨-wić⟩, reperować ⟨z-⟩ **5.** *attention*: skupiać ⟨-pić⟩ **6.** organizować ⟨z-⟩, przygotowywać ⟨-tować⟩; ***~ one's face*** umalować się; **~ one's hair** zrobić sobie fryzurę, uczesać się **7.** *Am drink, meal*: robić ⟨z-⟩ **8.** *match*: ustawiać ⟨-wić⟩ **II** *v/i infml* szprycować się **III** *s* **1.** *infml* rozwiązanie *n* **2. be in a ~** być w kropce **3. s.th. is a ~** *infml* coś zostało ukartowane, coś zostało ustawione **4.** *infml* dawka *f*, działka *f*; **give oneself a ~** dać sobie w żyłę; **fix on** *v/i* **1.** decydować ⟨z-⟩ się na *A* **2.** ustalać ⟨-lić⟩; **fix up** *v/t* **1.** *meeting*: organizować ⟨z-⟩, ustalać ⟨-lić⟩ **2.** *flat*: odnawiać ⟨-nowić⟩ **3.** naprawiać ⟨-wić⟩, reperować ⟨z-⟩

fix•ated [fɪk'seɪtɪd] *adj*: **be ~d on** mieć bzika na punkcie *G*; **fix•a•tion** [fɪk'seɪʃn] *s* **1.** fiksacja *f* **2.** *infml* bzik *m*

fixed [fɪkst] *adj* **1.** stały; **~ costs** koszty stałe **2.** ustalony **3.** sztywny **4.** niezmienny **5.** nieruchomy **6. ~ assets** *FIN* środki trwałe; **'fixed in•ter•est** *s* stałe oprocentowanie

fix•ed•ly ['fɪksɪdlɪ] *adv look*: nieruchomo; **fix•er** ['fɪksə] *s* **1.** *PHOT* utrwalacz *m* **2.** kombinator *m*; **fix•ings** ['fɪksɪŋz] *pl COOK Am* dodatki *pl*; **fix•ture** ['fɪkstʃə] *s* **1.** stały element *m* wyposażenia; **~s** wyposażenie; **lighting ~s** oświetlenie **2.** *SPORT Br* impreza *f* sportowa **3.** *SPORT Br* mecz *m*

fizz [fɪz] **I** *v/i* **1.** musować **2.** syczeć ⟨za-⟩ **II** *s* **1.** gaz *m*, bąbelki *pl* **2.** syk *m* **3.** *Br infml* szampan *m*

fiz•zle out ['fɪzlaʊt] *v/i* **1.** (*enthusiasm*) wygasać ⟨-snąć⟩ **2.** wypalać ⟨-lić⟩ się **3.** kończyć ⟨za-⟩ się rozczarowaniem

fizz•y ['fɪzɪ] *adj Br* gazowany

flab•ber•gast ['flæbərgæst] *v/t* wprawiać ⟨-wić⟩ w osłupienie; **be ~ed** osłupieć

flag [flæg] **I** *s* **1.** flaga *f*; **be like a red ~ to a bull to s.o.** działać na kogoś jak płachta na byka; **keep the ~ flying** *fig* godnie reprezentować kraj **2.** bandera *f* **3.** sztandar *m* **4.** chorągiewka *f* **II** *v/t* zaznaczać ⟨-czyć⟩ **III** *v/i* **1.** słabnąć ⟨o-⟩ **2.** opadać ⟨opaść⟩ z sił **3.** tracić ⟨s-⟩ zapał; **flag down** *v/t taxi*: zatrzymywać ⟨-mać⟩

fla•grant ['fleɪgrənt] *adj* rażący

'flag•ship *s* statek *m* flagowy; **'flag•stone** *s* płyta *f* kamienna

flail [fleɪl] **I** *v/t* **1.** młócić ⟨wy-⟩ **2. ~ one's arms** wymachiwać rękami **II** *v/i* młócić powietrze; **her arms were ~ing** wymachiwała rękami **III** *s* cep *m*

flair [fleə] *s* **1.** talent *m*, dar *m*; **have a ~ for art** być uzdolnionym artystycznie **2.** polot *m*

flake [fleɪk] **I** *s snow, dandruff*: płatek *m* **II** *v/i* **1.** łuszczyć ⟨z-⟩ się **2.** odpadać ⟨-paść⟩; **flake off** *v/i* **1.** łuszczyć ⟨z-⟩ się **2.** odpadać ⟨-paść⟩; **flak•y** ['fleɪkɪ] *adj* **1.** łuszczący się **2.** odpadający **3.** *snow*: puszysty

flam•boy•ance [flæm'bɔɪəns] *s* **1.** ekstrawagancja *f* **2.** krzykliwość *f*; **flam•boy•ant** [flæm'bɔɪənt] *adj* **1.** ekstrawagancki **2.** krzykliwy; **flam•boy•ant•ly** [flæm'bɔɪəntlɪ] *adv* **1.** ekstrawagancko **2.** krzykliwie

flame [fleɪm] **I** *s* **1.** płomień *m*; **be in ~s** stać w płomieniach **2. an old ~ of mine** *infml* moja dawna miłość **3.** *fig* płomień *m*, żar *m* **II** *v/i* płonąć ⟨za-⟩

flam•ma•ble ['flæməbl] *adj* palny

flank [flæŋk] **I** *s* **1.** bok *m* **2.** flanka *f* **3.** *SPORT* skrzydło *n* **II** *v/t* **1.** otaczać ⟨otoczyć⟩ **2.** oskrzydlać ⟨-lić⟩

flap [flæp] **I** *s* **1.** klapa *f* **2.** klapka *f* **3.** wieczko *n* **4.** nausznik *m* **5.** trzepot *m* **6.** łopot *m* **7. be in a ~ over** *infml* przejmować się *I* **II** *v/t* **1.** machać ⟨za-⟩ **2.** łopotać ⟨za-⟩ **III** *v/i* **1.** trzepotać ⟨za-⟩ **2.** łopotać ⟨za-⟩ **3.** *infml* panikować ⟨s-⟩

flare [fleə] **I** *s* **1.** błysk *m*, rozbłysk *m* **2.** raca *f* **3. a skirt with a ~** rozszerzana spódnica, rozkloszowana spódnica **4. ~s** (*trousers*) dzwony *pl* **II** *v/i* rozbłyskiwać ⟨-snąć⟩; **flare up** *v/i* **1.** zapłonąć jaśniej **2.** buchać ⟨-chnąć⟩ płomieniem **3.** wybuchać ⟨-chnąć⟩ (gniewem) **4.** *fig* nasilać ⟨-lić⟩ się

flash [flæʃ] **I** *s* **1.** błysk *m*; **a ~ of lightning** błyskawica; **a ~ of wit** przebłysk humoru; **a ~ in the pan** *fig* chwilowy sukces; **in a ~** *fig* w okamgnieniu **2.** *anger, inspiration*: przypływ *m* **3.** *PHOT* lampa *f* błyskowa **4.** *Br* wiadomość *f* z ostatniej chwili **II** *v/t* błyskać ⟨-snąć⟩ **III** *v/i* **6.** błyskać ⟨-snąć⟩ **2.** płonąć ⟨za-⟩ **3.** pojawiać ⟨-wić⟩ się; **it ~ed across my mind that** przemknęło mi przez myśl, że; **flash back** *v/i*: **his mind flashed back to** przypomniał sobie o *L*, wrócił myślami do *G*; '**flash•back** *n* **1.** wspomnienie *n* **2.** (*film*) retrospekcja *f*; '**flash bulb** *s* żarówka *f* błyskowa

flash•er ['flæʃə] *s infml* ekshibicjonista *m*

'**flash•light** *s* latarka *f*

flash•y ['flæʃɪ] *adj infml* **1.** krzykliwy **2.** efekciarski **3.** szpanerski

flask [flæsk] *s* **1.** butelka *f*, flaszka *f* **2.** termos *m*

flat[1] [flæt] **I** *adj* **1.** płaski **2.** *tyre*: przebity **3.** kategoryczny; ***and that's ~!*** *infml* i już!, i koniec! **4.** *water*: bez gazu **5.** *battery*: rozładowany; ***go ~*** rozładować się **6.** *voice*: bezbarwny, beznamiętny **7.** nudny **8.** *MUS* obniżony o pół tonu, z bemolem **II** *s* **1.** płaszczyzna *f* **2.** płaska strona *f*; ***the ~ of the hand*** otwarta dłoń **3.** równina *f* **4.** *infml* flak *m* **III** *adv* **1.** płasko **2.** ***fall ~*** **a)** upaść jak długi **b)** nie wypalić **c)** nie udać się **d)** zrobić klapę **3.** *sing*: za nisko **4.** *infml* wprost **5.** *infml* zaledwie; ***in 5 minutes ~*** w zaledwie 5 minut

flat[2] [~] *s Br* mieszkanie *n*

flat-'chest•ed *adj woman*: płaski jak deska; '**flat•foot** *s* płaskostopie *n*; ***be ~ed*** mieć płaskostopie; **flat•ly** ['flætlɪ] *adv* **1.** kategorycznie **2.** beznamiętnie

'**flat•mate** *s* współlokator *m*

flat•ness ['flætnəs] *s* płaskość *f*

'**flat-rate** *adj* **1.** *tax*: liniowy **2.** *fee*: jednolity, zryczałtowany

flat•ten ['flætn] **I** *v/t* **1.** spłaszczać ⟨-czyć⟩ **2.** wyrównywać ⟨-nać⟩ **3.** miażdżyć ⟨z-⟩ **II** (*a.* ***~ out***) *v/i* **1.** wyrównywać ⟨-nać⟩ się **2.** spłaszczać ⟨-czyć⟩ się

flat•ter ['flætə] *v/t* pochlebiać ⟨-bić⟩; ***I'm ~ed*** to mi pochlebia; **flat•ter•er** ['flætərə] *s* pochlebca *m*; **flat•ter•ing** ['flætərɪŋ] *adj* **1.** pochlebny **2.** korzystny; **flat•ter•y** ['flætərɪ] *s* pochlebstwo *n*

'**flat•ware** *s* **1.** *Am* sztućce *pl* **2.** naczynia *pl*

flaunt [flɔːnt] *v/t* **1.** obnosić się z *I* **2.** afiszować się z *I* **3.** popisywać się

flau•tist ['flɔːtɪst] *adj Br* flecista *m*

fla•vor *Am* → ***flavour***; **fla•vor•ing** *Am* → ***flavouring***

fla•vour ['fleɪvə] *Br*, ***fla•vor*** *Am* **I** *s* **1.** smak *m* **2.** *fig* posmak *m* **II** *v/t* **1.** przyprawiać ⟨-wić⟩ **2.** nadawać ⟨-dać⟩ smak **3.** *fig* zaprawiać ⟨-wić⟩; **fla•vour•ing** ['fleɪvərɪŋ] *Br*, ***fla•vor•ing*** *Am s* **1.** dodatek *m* smakowy **2.** aromat *m* **3.** przyprawa *f*

flaw [flɔː] *s* **1.** błąd *m* **2.** wada *f* **3.** skaza *f* **4.** usterka *f*; **flawed** [flɔːd] *adj* **1.** błędny **2.** wadliwy **3.** ze skazą; ***be ~*** mieć skazę; **flaw•less** ['flɔːlɪs] *adj* **1.** bezbłędny **2.** nieskazitelny **3.** bez skazy

flax•en ['flæksən] *adj* lniany

flay [fleɪ] *v/t* obdzierać ⟨obedrzeć⟩ ze skóry; ***~ s.o. alive*** *fig* nie zostawić na kimś suchej nitki

flea [fliː] *s* pchła *f*; ***a ~ bite*** *fig* łatwizna, pestka; '**flea mar•ket** *s* pchli targ *m*

fleck [flek] *s* **1.** drobinka *f* **2.** plamka *f* **3.** ciapka *f* **4.** cętka *f*

fled [fled] *Past Simple and Past Participle* → ***flee***

flee [fliː] **I** (*fled*; *fled*) *v/i* **1.** uciekać ⟨uciec⟩ **2.** umykać ⟨umknąć⟩ **II** (*fled*; *fled*) *v/t* **1.** uciekać ⟨uciec⟩ z *G* **2.** uciekać ⟨uciec⟩ przed *I*

fleece [fliːs] *v/t infml* oskubywać ⟨-bać⟩

fleet [fliːt] *s* **1.** flota *f* **2.** ***a ~ of cars*** park samochodowy

fleet•ing ['fliːtɪŋ] *adj* **1.** chwilowy **2.** przelotny **3.** krótki

flesh [fleʃ] *s* **1.** ciało *n*; ***my own ~ and blood*** krew z krwi, kość z kości; ***in the ~*** we własnej osobie **2.** mięso *n* **3.** miąższ *m*; **flesh-col•oured** ['fleʃkʌləd] *Br*, ***flesh-col•ored*** *Am adj* cielisty; '**flesh wound** *s* rana *f* powierzchowna

flew [fluː] *Past Simple* → ***fly***

flex [fleks] **I** *v/t* **1.** *muscles*: napinać ⟨-piąć⟩; ***~ one's muscles*** *fig* prężyć muskuły **2.** rozciągać ⟨-gnąć⟩ **3.** zginać ⟨zgiąć⟩ **4.** poruszać ⟨-szyć⟩ **II** *s Br* kabel *m*, przewód *m*

flex•i•bil•i•ty [fleksə'bɪlətɪ] *s* **1.** giętkość *f*, elastyczność *f* **2.** gibkość *f*; **flex•i•ble** ['fleksəbl] *adj* **1.** giętki, elastyczny **2.** gibki; '**flexi•time** ['fleksɪtaɪm] *Br*, ***flex•time*** *Am s* ruchomy czas *m* pracy; ***be on ~*** mieć ruchomy czas pracy

flick [flɪk] **I** *s* **1.** szybki ruch *m* **2.** prztyczek *m* **3.** pstryknięcie *n* **4.** ***a ~ of one's tongue*** mlaśnięcie **5.** *Am infml* film *m* **II** *v/t* **1.** machać ⟨-chnąć⟩ **2.** *fingers*: pstrykać ⟨-knąć⟩ **3.** trzepać ⟨-pnąć⟩ **4.** ***~ s.th. on*** (***off***) włączyć (wyłączyć) coś; **flick through** *v/i* **1.** kartkować ⟨prze-⟩ **2.** *channels*: przerzucać ⟨-cić⟩, skakać po *L*

flick•er ['flɪkə] **I** *v/i* **1.** migotać ⟨za-⟩ **2.** błyskać ⟨-snąć⟩ **3.** drgać ⟨-gnąć⟩ **II** *s* **1.** migotanie *n* **2.** błysk *m* **3.** drganie *n* **4.** *hope*: iskierka *f*; **flick•er-'free** *adj screen*: niemigoczący

fli•er [flaɪə] *s* **1.** ulotka *f* **2.** *infml* lotnik *m* **3.** pasażer *m* (samolotu) **4.** ***be a good ~*** dobrze latać

flies [flaɪz] *pl Br* rozporek *m*

flight [flaɪt] *s* **1.** lot *m*; ***in ~*** w locie **2.** loty *pl* **3.** latanie *n* **4.** ***a ~ of stairs*** **a)** bieg schodowy **b)** schody **5.** ucieczka *f*; ***be in ~ from*** uciekać przed *I*; ***put s.o. to ~*** zmusić kogoś do ucieczki; ***take ~*** salwować się ucieczką; ***the ~ of capital*** *ECON* ucieczka kapitału **6.** *birds*: stado *n* **7.** (*aircraft*) eskadra *f*; **'flight at•tend•ant** *s* **1.** stewardesa *f* **2.** steward *m*; **'flight bag** *s* torba *f* na ramię; **'flight con•trol•ler** *s* kontroler *m* lotu; **'flight crew** *s* personel *m* latający; **'flight deck** *s* **1.** kabina *f* pilotów **2.** pokład *m* startowy (lotniskowca); **flight 'en•gi•neer** *s* mechanik *m* pokładowy; **'flight num•ber** *s* numer *m* lotu; **'flight path** *s* tor *m* lotu; **flight 're•cord•er** *s* rejestrator *m* parametrów lotu, czarna skrzynka *f*; **'flight time** *s* czas *m* (prze)lotu

flight•y ['flaɪtɪ] *adj infml* **1.** niestały **2.** zmienny

flim•sy ['flɪmzɪ] *adj* **1.** cienki **2.** delikatny **3.** lichy, marny **4.** *evidence*: słaby

flinch [flɪntʃ] *v/i* wzdrygać ⟨-gnąć⟩ się; ***without ~ing*** z kamienną twarzą

fling [flɪŋ] **I** (*flung*; *flung*) *v/t* **1.** rzucać ⟨-cić⟩; ***~ s.th. away*** odrzucić coś; ***~ oneself into the preparations for*** rzucić się w wir przygotowań do *G* **2.** ***~ the door open*** gwałtownie otworzyć drzwi **II** *s* **1.** rzut *m* **2.** próba *f*; ***have a ~ at*** spróbować *G* **3.** ***have a ~*** *infml* zaszaleć **4.** *infml* romans *m*

flint [flɪnt] *s* **1.** krzemień *m* **2.** kamień *m* do zapalniczki

flip [flɪp] **I** *v/t* **1.** *fingers*, *switch*: pstrykać ⟨-knąć⟩ **2.** przewracać ⟨-rócić⟩, przerzucać ⟨-cić⟩ **3.** *coin*: rzucać ⟨-cić⟩ **4.** koziołkować ⟨prze-⟩ **II** *s* **1.** *SPORT* salto *n*, koziołek *m* **2.** rzut *m*; **flip on** *v/t engine*, *light*: włączać ⟨-czyć⟩; **flip over** *v/t pages*: przewracać ⟨-rócić⟩; **flip through** *v/t newspaper*: kartkować ⟨prze-⟩

'flip•chart *s Br* tablica *f* flipchart

'flip-flop *s* (*sandal*) japonka *f*

flip•pan•cy ['flɪpənsɪ] *s* nonszalancja *f*; **flip•pant** ['flɪpənt] *adj* nonszalancki

flip•per ['flɪpə] *s* płetwa *f*

'flip side *s* **1.** *record*: strona *f* B **2.** *fig* druga strona *f*

flirt [flɜːt] **I** *v/i* **1.** flirtować; ***~ with death*** *fig* igrać ze śmiercią **2.** rozważać (***with*** *A*) **II** *s* **3.** flirt *m* **2.** flirciarz *m*; ***she's a ~*** jest flirciarą, ona lubi flirtować; **flir•ta•tion** [flɜː'teɪʃn] *s* flirt *m*; **flir•ta•tious** [flɜː'teɪʃəs] *adj* kokieteryjny, zalotny

flit [flɪt] *v/i* **1.** śmigać ⟨-gnąć⟩ **2.** przemykać ⟨-mknąć⟩

float [fləʊt] **I** *v/i* **1.** pływać, unosić się na wodzie **2.** lecieć, unosić się w powietrzu **II** *v/t* **1.** wprowadzać ⟨-dzić⟩ na giełdę **2.** uwalniać ⟨uwolnić⟩ kurs **III** *s* **1.** spławik *m* **2.** pływak *m* **3.** platforma *f* (na kołach); **float•ing 'vot•er** *s POLIT* niezdecydowany wyborca *m*

flock [flɒk] **I** *s* **1.** stado *n* **2.** grupa *f* **3.** gromada *f* **4.** *REL* parafianie *pl*; *fig* trzódka *f* **II** *v/i* gromadzić ⟨z-⟩ się

flog [flɒg] *v/t* **1.** chłostać ⟨wy-⟩; ***it's ~ging a dead horse*** *fig* to strata czasu **2.** *Br infml* opychać ⟨opchnąć⟩

flood [flʌd] **I** *s* **1.** powódź *f*; ***the river is in ~*** rzeka wylała **2.** *fig* zalew *m*; ***in ~s of tears*** zalany łzami **II** *v/t* **1.** zalewać ⟨-lać⟩ **2.** *requests*: zasypywać ⟨-pać⟩ **III** *v/i* **1.** (*river*) wylewać ⟨-lać⟩, występować ⟨-tąpić⟩ z brzegów **2.** zostać zalanym, być zalewanym; **flood in** *v/i* **1.** wdzierać ⟨wedrzeć⟩ się **2.** *fig* napływać

flood•ing ['flʌdɪŋ] *s* **1.** powodzie *pl* **2.** powódź *f* **3.** zalewanie *n* **2.** wylew *m* (rzeki); **'flood•light I** *s* **1.** reflektor *m* **2.** światło *n* reflektorów; ***under ~s*** przy sztucznym świetle **II** *v/t* **3.** oświetlać ⟨-lić⟩; **'flood•lit** *adj* oświetlony; **'flood plain** *s* obszar *m* zalewowy; '**flood wa•ters** *pl* wody *pl* powodziowe

floor [flɔː] **I** *s* **1.** podłoga *f*; ***take the ~*** *fig* zabrać głos **2.** posadzka *f* **3.** piętro *n* **4.** parkiet *m*; ***take to the ~*** (*dancers*) wyjść na parkiet **5.** *FIN* parkiet *m* **6.** (*parliament*) sala *f* obrad **7.** dno *n* **II** *v/t* **1.** kłaść ⟨położyć⟩ podłogę; ***~ed with*** wyłożony *I* **2.** powalać ⟨-lić⟩ (na ziemię) **3.** *fig* zbijać ⟨-bić⟩ z tropu; '**floor•board** *s* **1.** deska *f* podłogowa **2.** deska *f* parkietowa; '**floor cloth** *s* ścierka *f* do podłogi; '**floor ex•er•cis•es** *pl* **1.** *SPORT* ćwiczenia *pl* wolne **2.** ćwiczenia *pl* na podłodze; **floor•ing** ['flɔːrɪŋ] *s* **1.** podłoga *f* **2.** parkiet *m* **3.** wykładzina *f*; '**floor lamp** *s Am* lampa *f* stojąca; '**floor lead•er** *s Am* przewodniczący *m* klubu parlamentarnego; '**floor plan** *s* plan *m* piętra; '**floor show** *s* (*restaurant*) program *m* rozrywkowy; '**floor wait•er** *s* kelner *m* hotelowy

F

floo•zy ['fluːzɪ] *s infml* zdzira *f*

flop [flɒp] **I** *v/i* **1.** opadać ⟨opaść⟩ **2.** *infml* klapnąć **3.** *infml* zrobić klapę **II** *infml s* klapa *f*

flop•py ['flɒpɪ] **I** *adj* **1.** opadający **2.** zwisający **3.** oklapły **4.** obwisły **II** *s* dyskietka *f*; **flop•py 'disk** *s* dyskietka *f*; **flop•py-'disk drive** *s* stacja *f* dyskietek

flo•ra ['flɔːrə] *s* flora *f*; **flo•ral** ['flɔːrəl] *adj* **1.** *pattern*: w kwiaty **2.** kwiecisty **3.** ***a ~ arrangement*** wiązanka, kompozycja kwiatowa

flor•id ['flɒrɪd] *adj* **1.** *face*: rumiany **2.** *style*: kwiecisty

flor•ist ['flɒrɪst] *s* **1.** kwiaciarz *m* **2.** ***~'s*** kwiaciarnia

floss [flɒs] *s* **1.** nić *f* dentystyczna **2.** puszek *m* **3.** jedwab *m* **4.** mulina *f*

floun•der ['flaʊndə] *v/i* **1.** brnąć **2.** (*speaker*) plątać się

flour [flaʊə] **I** *s* mąka *f* **II** *v/t* **1.** posypywać ⟨-pać⟩ mąką **2.** obtaczać ⟨-toczyć⟩ w mące

flour•ish ['flʌrɪʃ] **I** *v/i* **1.** *a. fig* kwitnąć **2.** rozkwitać ⟨-tnąć⟩ **3.** prosperować **II** *v/t* wymachiwać **III** *s* **1.** *MUS* fanfary *pl* **2.** ozdobnik *m* **3.** zawijas *m*; **flour•ish•ing** ['flʌrɪʃɪŋ] *adj* **1.** w rozkwicie **2.** kwitnący **3.** dobrze prosperujący

flout [flaʊt] *v/t* lekceważyć ⟨z-⟩

flow [fləʊ] **I** *v/i* **1.** płynąć; ***~ freely*** (*champaigne*) płynąć strumieniami **2.** wpływać ⟨-łynąć⟩ **3.** (*dress, hair*) spływać **II** *s* **1.** przepływ *m*; ***information ~*** przepływ informacji **2.** ruch *m*; ***traffic ~*** ruch uliczny **3.** napływ *m* **4.** strumień *m*

flow•er [flaʊə] **I** *s* kwiat *m*; ***be in ~*** kwitnąć **II** *v/i* **1.** *a. fig* kwitnąć **2.** zakwitać ⟨-tnąć⟩ **3.** (*talent*) rozkwitać ⟨-tnąć⟩; '**flow•er ar•range•ment** *s* **1.** kompozycja *f* kwiatowa **2.** wiązanka *f*; '**flow•er•bed** *s* **1.** kwietnik *m* **2.** klomb *m*; '**flow•er girl** *s* **1.** kwiaciarka *f* **2.** dziewczynka *f* sypiąca kwiaty (na weselu); '**flow•er•pot** *s* **1.** doniczka *f* **2.** donica *f*; '**flow•er show** *s* wystawa *f* kwiatów

flow•er•y ['flaʊərɪ] *adj* **1.** kwiatowy **2.** w kwiaty **3.** ukwiecony **4.** kwiecisty

flown [fləʊn] *Past Participle* → **fly**

flu [fluː] *s* grypa *f*; ***he's got (the) ~*** ma grypę, zachorował na grypę

flu•en•cy ['fluːənsɪ] *s* **1.** biegła znajomość *f* **2.** płynność *f*; **flu•ent** ['fluːənt] *adj* **1.** biegły; ***speak ~ Polish***, ***be ~ in Polish*** biegle mówić po polsku; ***in ~ English*** płynną angielszczyzną **2.** elokwentny **3.** potoczysty; **flu•ent•ly** ['fluːəntlɪ] *adv* **1.** biegle **2.** płynnie

fluff [flʌf] **I** *s* **1.** kłaczki *pl* **2.** puszek *m* **3.** *infml* gafa *f*, potknięcie *n* **II** *v/t* *infml* schrzanić; ***~ one's lines*** sypnąć się; **fluff•y** ['flʌfɪ] *adj* **1.** puszysty **2.** puchaty **3.** mechaty

fluid ['fluːɪd] **I** *s* **1.** płyn *m* **2.** ciecz *f* **II** *adj* **1.** płynny **2.** ciekły

flung [flʌŋ] *Past Simple and Past Participle* → **fling**

flunk [flʌŋk] *Am* **I** *v/t exam, student*: oblewać ⟨-lać⟩ **II** *v/i* oblewać ⟨-lać⟩

flu•o•res•cent [flʊə'resnt] *adj* **1.** fluorescencyjny **2.** odblaskowy

flu•o•ride ['flʊəraɪd] **I** *s* fluorek *m* **II** *adj* fluoryzowany; **flu•o•ride 'tooth•paste** *s* pasta *f* do zębów z fluorem

flur•ry ['flʌrɪ] *s* **1.** ***a ~ of activity*** (***excitement***) nagłe ożywienie (podniecenie) **2.** ***snow flurries*** przelotne opady śniegu **3.** podmuch *m* wiatru

flush [flʌʃ] **I** *s* **1.** rumieńce *pl*, wypieki *pl* **2.** *fig* przypływ *m* **3.** ***give the toilet a ~*** spuścić wodę **4.** spłuczka *f*

II *v/t* płukać, przepłukiwać ⟨-kać⟩; *~ **the toilet*** spuścić wodę **III** *v/i* **1.** czerwienić ⟨za-⟩ się, rumienić ⟨za-⟩ się **2.** spuszczać ⟨spuścić⟩ wodę **IV** *adj* **1.** ***be ~*** *infml* być przy forsie **2.** ***~ with*** w jednej linii z *I* **3.** ***~ left, ~ right*** bez wcięcia; **flush out** *v/t* **1.** wypłaszać ⟨-łoszyć⟩ **2.** wykurzać ⟨-rzyć⟩

flus•ter ['flʌstə] **I** *v/t* wytrącać ⟨-cić⟩ z równowagi **II** *s* podenerwowanie *n*; ***get in a ~*** tracić głowę; ***all in a ~*** zdenerwowany, podenerwowany

flute [fluːt] *s* flet *m*; **flut•ist** ['fluːtɪst] *s Am* flecista *m*

flut•ter ['flʌtə] **I** *v/i* trzepotać ⟨za-⟩ **II** *v/t* **1.** trzepotać ⟨za-⟩ **2.** (*heart*) bić nierówno **III** *s* **1.** trzepot *m*, trzepotanie *n* **2.** zamieszanie *n*

fly[1] [flaɪ] *s* mucha *f*; ***he wouldn't hurt a ~*** nie skrzywdziłby nawet muchy; ***a ~ in the ointment*** *fig* łyżka dziegciu w beczce miodu

fly[2] [~] **I** (*flew; flown*) *v/i* **1.** latać, fruwać **2.** lecieć ⟨po-⟩; ***the bird has flown*** *fig* ptaszek się ulotnił **3.** (*time*) lecieć; ***~ flies!*** czas leci! **4.** (*holidays, time*) zlatywać ⟨zlecieć⟩ **5.** powiewać **6.** rzucać ⟨-ić⟩ się (***at*** na *A*) **II** (*flew; flown*) *v/t* **1.** latać, pilotować **2.** *kite*: puszczać ⟨puścić⟩ **III** *s* rozporek *m*; **fly away** *v/i* odlatywać ⟨-lecieć⟩; **fly back** *v/i* lecieć ⟨po-⟩ z powrotem, przylatywać ⟨-lecieć⟩ z powrotem; **fly in** *v/i* wlatywać ⟨wlecieć⟩; **fly off** *v/i* odlatywać ⟨-lecieć⟩; ***~ the handle*** *infml* stracić panowanie nad sobą; **fly out** *v/i* wylatywać ⟨-lecieć⟩; **fly past** *v/i* **1.** przelatywać ⟨-lecieć⟩ (obok) **2.** (*time*) zlatywać ⟨zlecieć⟩

fly•ing ['flaɪɪŋ] **I** *adj* **1.** latający **2.** lecący **3.** lotniczy **II** *s* latanie *n*; ***a fear of ~*** strach przed lataniem; ***have a fear of ~*** bać się latać; **fly•ing 'sau•cer** *s* latający talerz *m*, latający spodek *m*

'fly•o•ver *s Br* wiadukt *m*

'fly spray *s* spray *m* na muchy; **'fly•swat•ter** *s* packa *f* na muchy; **'fly•weight** *s* SPORT waga *f* musza

FM [ef'em] *abbr* (=***frequency modulation***) modulacja *f* częstotliwości

FO [ef'əʊ] *abbr* (=***Foreign Office***) *Br* Ministerstwo *n* Spraw Zagranicznych

foal [fəʊl] *s* źrebak *m*, źrebię *n*; ***in ~*** źrebny

foam [fəʊm] **I** *s* **1.** piana *f* **2.** pianka *f* **II** *v/i* pienić ⟨s-⟩ się; **'foam bath** *s* **1.** kąpiel *f* z pianą **2.** płyn *m* do kąpieli

FOB [efəʊ'biː] *abbr* (=***free on board***) z dostawą na pokład

fo•cal ['fəʊkl] *adj* **1.** ogniskowy **2.** *fig* centralny; **'fo•cal point** *s* **1.** centralny punkt *m* **2.** TECH ognisko *n*

fo•cus ['fəʊkəs] **I** *s* **1.** TECH ognisko *n*; ***in ~*** ostry; ***out of ~*** nieostry **2.** centrum *n*; ***be the ~ of attention*** być w centrum uwagi; ***bring s.th. into ~*** zwrócić uwagę na *A* **II** *v/t* **1.** *attention*: skupiać ⟨-pić⟩ **2.** ogniskować ⟨z-⟩ **3.** kierować ⟨s-⟩; **fo•cus on** *v/t* skupiać ⟨-pić⟩ się na *L*, koncentrować ⟨s-⟩ się na *L*

fo•cus•ed ['fəʊkəst] *adj* **1.** dążący do celu **2.** zdecydowany

fod•der ['fɒdə] *s* **1.** pasza *f* **2.** *fig* pożywka *f*; ***cannon ~*** mięso armatnie

foe•tal ['fiːtl] *adj* płodowy; ***a ~ position*** pozycja embrionalna; **foe•tus** ['fiːtəs] *s* płód *m*

fog [fɒg] **I** *s* mgła *f* **II** *v/i* zaparowywać ⟨-rować⟩ **III** *v/t* ***~ the issue*** *fig* zaciemniać sprawę; ***~ s.o.'s brain*** otumanić kogoś; **fog up I** *v/i* zaparowywać ⟨-rować⟩ **II** *v/t* ***be fogged up*** zaparowywać ⟨-rować⟩; **'fog•bound** *adj* **1.** sparaliżowany przez mgłę **2.** unieruchomiony przez mgłę

fog•gy ['fɒgɪ] *adj* mglisty; ***a ~ day*** mglisty dzień; ***I haven't got the foggiest idea*** *infml* nie mam zielonego pojęcia; **'fog•horn** *s* syrena *f* mgłowa; **'fog lamp, 'fog light** *s* światło *n* przeciwmgielne

foil[1] [fɔɪl] *s* **1.** folia *f* (aluminiowa) **2.** tło *n*

foil[2] [~] *v/t* **1.** udaremniać ⟨-nić⟩ **2.** krzyżować ⟨po-⟩ **3.** powstrzymywać ⟨-mać⟩

fold [fəʊld] **I** *v/t* **1.** składać ⟨złożyć⟩; ***~ s.th. in half, ~ s.th. in two*** złożyć coś wpół **2.** zginać ⟨-giąć⟩ **3.** zawijać ⟨-winąć⟩ **4.** ***~ s.o. in one's arms*** wziąć kogoś w ramiona **II** *v/i* **1.** składać ⟨złożyć⟩ się **2.** uginać ⟨ugiąć⟩ się **3.** (*firm*) upadać ⟨upaść⟩ **III** *s* fałda

F

f, fałd *m*; **fold up I** *v/i* składać ⟨złożyć⟩ **II** *v/t* składać ⟨złożyć⟩ się

fold•a•way ['fəʊldəweɪ] *s* **1.** składany **2.** rozkładany; **fold•er** ['fəʊldə] *s* **1.** teczka *f* **2.** folder *m*, broszura *f* **3.** *INF* katalog *m*, folder *m*; **fold•ing** ['fəʊldɪŋ] *adj* **1.** składany; ***a ~ bicycle*** składak **2.** rozkładany

fo•li•age ['fəʊlɪɪdʒ] *s* liście *pl*, listowie *n*

folk [fəʊk] **I** *s* **1.** (*a.* **~s**) *infml* ludzie *pl* **2.** lud *m* **3. ~s** *infml* rodzice *pl*, starzy *pl* **4.** *MUS* folk *m* **II** *adj* ludowy; '**folk dance** *s* taniec *m* ludowy; '**folk•lore** [fəʊklɔː] *s* **1.** folklor *m* **2.** tradycja *f* ludowa; '**folk mu•sic** *s* **1.** muzyka *f* ludowa **2.** muzyka *f* folk; '**folk sing•er** *s* piosenkarz *m* folkowy; '**folk song** *s* **1.** piosenka *f* ludowa **2.** piosenka *f* folk

fol•low ['fɒləʊ] **I** *v/t* **1.** iść ⟨pójść⟩ za *I* **2.** podążać ⟨-żyć⟩ za *I* **3.** śledzić **4.** następować ⟨-tąpić⟩ po *L* **4.** *map*: iść według *G*, jechać według *G* **5.** kierować się *I* **6.** trzymać się *G* **7.** wyznawać **8.** postępować ⟨-tąpić⟩ zgodnie z *I* **9.** śledzić, interesować się *I* **10.** *profession*: wykonywać **II** *v/i* **1.** następować ⟨-tąpić⟩; ***as ~s*** następujący **2.** wynikać ⟨-knąć⟩; **fol•low through I** *v/i SPORT* wykańczać ⟨-kończyć⟩ uderzenie **II** *v/t* doprowadzać ⟨-dzić⟩ do końca; **fol•low up** *v/t* **1.** iść ⟨pójść⟩ śladem *G* **2.** *complaint*: rozpatrywać ⟨-trzyć⟩

fol•low•er ['fɒləʊə] *s* **1.** zwolennik *m* **2.** wyznawca *m* **3.** kibic *m*; **fol•low•ing** ['fɒləʊɪŋ] **I** *adj* **1.** następny **2.** następujący **II** *s* **1.** zwolennicy *pl* **2.** wyznawcy *pl* **3.** fani *pl* **4.** co następuje, następujące (rzeczy) **III** *prep* **1.** po *L* **2.** w następstwie *G*

'**fol•low-up** *s* **1.** dalszy ciąg *m* **2.** kontynuacja *f*; ***a ~ meeting to the workshops*** spotkanie będące kontynuacją warsztatów; '**fol•low-up vis•it** *s MED* wizyta *f* kontrolna

fol•ly ['fɒlɪ] *s* **1.** głupota *f* **2.** szaleństwo *n*

fond [fɒnd] *adj* **1.** ***be ~ of*** lubić *A*; ***be ~ of doing s.th.*** lubić coś robić **2.** czuły **3.** miły **4.** *hope*: naiwny

fon•dle ['fɒndl] *v/t* **1.** głaskać ⟨po-⟩ **2.** pieścić ⟨po-⟩

fond•ly ['fɒndlɪ] *adv* **1.** czule; ***remember s.th. ~*** wspominać coś z czułością **2.** naiwnie

fond•ness ['fɒndnɪs] *s* **1.** ***have a ~ for*** lubić *A* **2.** czułość *f* **3.** sympatia *f* **4.** ***a ~ for*** słabość do *G*

font [fɒnt] *s* **1.** czcionka *f* **2.** *REL* chrzcielnica *f*

food [fuːd] *s* **1.** jedzenie *n*; ***he's off his ~*** nie chce nic jeść **2.** żywność *f*; ***~ additives*** dodatki do żywności; ***the ~ industry*** branża spożywcza **3.** pożywienie *n*, pokarm *m* **4.** *fig* pożywka *f*; ***be ~ for thought*** dawać do myślenia **5.** kuchnia *f*, jedzenie *n*; '**food chain** *s* łańcuch *m* pokarmowy

food•ie ['fuːdɪ] *s infml* łakomczuch *m*

'**food poi•son•ing** *s* zatrucie *n* pokarmowe; '**food pro•cess•or** *s* robot *m* kuchenny; '**food•stuff** *s* artykuł *m* spożywczy

fool [fuːl] **I** *s* **1.** idiota *m*, dureń *m*; ***make a ~ of oneself*** zbłaźnić się, zrobić z siebie idiotę; ***make a ~ of s.o.*** zrobić z kogoś durnia **2.** głupiec *m* **II** *v/t* **1.** nabierać ⟨-brać⟩ **2.** oszukiwać ⟨-kać⟩; ***don't be ~ed into thinking that*** nie łudź się, że; **fool around** *v/i Br infml* **1.** obijać się **2.** wygłupiać się; **fool around with** *v/i Br infml* **1.** bawić się z *I* **2.** kręcić z *I*

'**fool•har•dy** *adj* **1.** ryzykancki **2.** brawurowy **3.** lekkomyślny

fool•ish ['fuːlɪʃ] *adj* niemądry, głupi; **fool•ish•ly** ['fuːlɪʃlɪ] *adv* niemądrze, głupio

'**fool•proof** *adj* **1.** niezawodny **2.** łatwy w obsłudze

foot [fʊt] **I** *pl feet* [fiːt] *s* **1.** stopa *f*; ***on ~*** pieszo; ***in bare feet*** boso; ***be on one's feet again*** *fig* stanąć na nogi; ***put one's ~ in it*** *fig* popełnić gafę **2.** ***at the ~ of*** u dołu *G* **3.** *of mountain*: podnóże *n*; ***at the ~ of a mountain*** u stóp góry **4.** ***at the ~ of a bed*** w nogach łóżka **II** *v/t* **1.** ***~ the bill*** zapłacić rachunek **2.** ***~ it*** iść pieszo

foot•age ['fʊtɪdʒ] *s* materiał *m* (filmowy)

foot-and-'mouth dis•ease *s* pryszczyca *f*

'**foot•ball I** *s* **1.** *Br* piłka *f* nożna **2.** *Am* futbol *m* amerykański **3.** piłka *f* futbolowa, *infml* futbolówka *f* **II** *adj*

1. piłkarski **2.** futbolowy; **'foot•ball boots** *pl* buty *pl* piłkarskie; **'foot•ball coach** *s* trener *m* piłkarski; **'foot•ball-cra•zy** *adj* zwariowany na punkcie piłki nożnej; **'foot•baller** *s* piłkarz *m*; **'foot•ball pitch** *s* boisko *n* piłkarskie; **'foot•ball play•er** *s* piłkarz *m*; **'foot•ball sta•di•um** *s* stadion *m* piłkarski

'foot•bridge *s* kładka *f* dla pieszych; **foot•er** ['fʊtə] *s* **1.** (*print*) stopka *f* **2.** (*football*) *Br infml* noga *f*; **'foot•fall** *s* krok *m*, odgłos *m* kroków; **'foot-hills** *pl* pogórze *n*; **'foot•hold** *s* **1.** oparcie *n* dla nóg **2.** *fig* punkt *m* zaczepienia

foot•ing ['fʊtɪŋ] *s* **1.** podstawa *f*; ***on an equal ~, on the same ~*** na równej stopie; ***be on a friendly ~ with*** być na dobrej stopie z *I* **2.** równowaga *f*; ***lose one's ~*** stracić równowagę

'foot•loose *adj* niczym nieskrępowany; ***~ and fancy free*** wolny jak ptak; **'foot•mark** *s* ślad *m* stopy; **'foot•note** *s* przypis *m*; **'foot pas•sen•ger** *s* (*ferry*) pasażer *m* bez samochodu; **'foot-path** *s* **1.** ścieżka *f*, dróżka *f* **2.** chodnik *m*; **'foot•print** *s* ślad *m* stopy; **'foot-rest** *s* podnóżek *m*; **foot•sie** ['fʊtsɪ] *s*: ***play ~*** *infml* dotykać się stopami pod stołem; **'foot•sore** *adj* z obolałymi nogami; **'foot•step** *s* krok *m*, odgłos *m* kroków; ***to follow in s.o.'s ~s*** *fig* pójść w czyjeś ślady; **'foot-stool** *s* podnóżek *m*; **'foot•wear** *s* obuwie *n*; **'foot•work** *s* SPORT praca *f* nóg

for [fə, fɔː] **I** *prep* **1.** dla *G*; ***flowers ~ Agata*** kwiaty dla Agaty; ***work ~ a big company*** pracować w dużej firmie **2.** do *G*; ***what is it ~?*** do czego to służy? **3.** po *A*; ***I'll go ~ the paper*** pójdę po gazetę; ***what ~?*** po co? **4.** (*reason*) z *G*; ***famous ~ his oddities*** znany ze swoich dziwactw; ***there is no reason ~*** nie ma powodu do *G* **5.** jak na *A*; ***be mature ~ one's age*** być dojrzałym jak na swój wiek **6.** za *G*; ***~ £5*** za 5 funtów **7.** za *I*; ***be ~*** być za *I*, popierać *A* **8.** na *A*; ***~ Monday*** na poniedziałek **9.** przez *A*; ***~ two weeks*** przez dwa tygodnie **10.** od *G*; ***I've lived here ~ 2 years*** mieszkam tu od dwóch lat **11.** ***~ miles*** kilometrami **II** *conj form* ponieważ, gdyż

for•bade [fə'bæd] *Past Simple* → ***forbid***

for•bear•ance [fɔː'beərəns] *s form* wyrozumiałość *f*; **for•bear•ing** [fɔː'beərɪŋ] *adj form* wyrozumiały

for•bid [fər'bɪd] **I** (*forbade*; *forbidden*) *v/t* **1.** zakazywać ⟨-zać⟩, zabraniać ⟨-ronić⟩; ***~ s.o. the sugar*** zabronić komuś jeść cukier **2.** nie pozwalać ⟨-wolić⟩ **3.** uniemożliwiać ⟨-wić⟩ **II** (*forbade*; *forbidden*) *v/i* ***God ~!, heaven ~!*** nie daj Boże!; **for•bid•den** [fə'bɪdn] **I** *Past Participle* → ***forbid*** **II** *adj* zakazany, zabroniony; **for•bid-ding** [fər'bɪdɪŋ] *adj* **1.** złowrogi **2.** nieprzystępny

force [fɔːs] **I** *s* **1.** siła *f*; ***by ~*** siłą; ***the ~ of gravity*** siła grawitacji; ***the ~s of nature*** siły natury; ***the ~ of habit*** siła przyzwyczajenia; ***armed ~s*** siły zbrojne; ***join ~s*** połączyć siły; ***by ~ of arms*** przy pomocy wojska **2.** ***come into ~*** JUR wejść w życie; ***put s.th. into ~*** wprowadzić coś w życie **II** *v/t* **1.** zmuszać ⟨-sić⟩ **2.** wymuszać ⟨-sić⟩ **3.** ***~ one's way through*** przedzierać się przez *A* **4.** ***~ s.th. on s.o.*** narzucać coś komuś; ***~ oneself on s.o.*** narzucać się komuś **5.** forsować ⟨s-⟩; ***~ the door open*** wyważyć drzwi; **force back** *v/t* **1.** *attack, enemy*: odpierać ⟨odeprzeć⟩ **2.** *tears*: powstrzymywać ⟨-mać⟩

forced [fɔːst] *adj* **1.** wymuszony **2.** przymusowy; **forced 'land•ing** *s* przymusowe lądowanie *n*

'force-feed *adj* karmić na siłę

force•ful ['fɔːsfəl] *adj* **1.** silny **2.** przekonujący **3.** dokonany siłą; **force•ful-ly** ['fɔːsfəlɪ] *adv* **1.** przekonująco **2.** silnie

for•ci•ble ['fɔːsəbl] *adj* **1.** siłowy; ***a ~ entry*** włamanie **2.** przekonujący **3.** stanowczy **4.** przymusowy; **for•ci-bly** ['fɔːsəblɪ] *adv* **1.** siłą **2.** na siłę **3.** z zastosowaniem siły **4.** przekonująco **5.** przymusowo

ford [fɔːd] **I** *s* bród *m* **II** *v/t* przeprawiać ⟨-wić⟩ się w bród przez *A*

fore [fɔː] **I** *adj* przedni **II** *s* ***come to the ~*** *fig* wysunąć się na pierwszy plan; **'fore•arm** *s* przedramię *n*; **fore•bears** ['fɔːberz] *pl form* przodkowie *pl*;

F

fore•bod•ing [fər'bəudɪŋ] *s* złe przeczucie *n*; **'fore•cast I** *s* prognoza *f*; ***a weather ~*** prognoza pogody **II** (*forecast*; *forecast*) *v/t* **1.** przepowiadać ⟨-wiedzieć⟩ **2.** prognozować; **'forecourt** *s* **1.** parking *m* **2.** podjazd *m*; **fore•fa•thers** ['fɔːfɑːðəz] *pl* przodkowie *pl*; **'fore•fin•ger** *s* palec *m* wskazujący; **'fore•front** *s* **1.** pierwsza linia *f* **2.** pierwszy plan *m*; **'fore•gone** *adj*: ***be a ~ conclusion*** być z góry przesądzonym, być z góry wiadomym; **'fore•ground** *s* pierwszy plan *m*; **'fore•hand I** *s* forhend *m* **II** *adj volley*: z forhendu; **'fore•head** *s* czoło *n*

for•eign ['fɒrən] *adj* **1.** obcy; ***a ~ language*** język obcy; ***a ~ word*** wyraz obcy; ***this is ~ to his nature*** to jest obce jego naturze **2.** zagraniczny; ***~ trade, ~ commerce*** handel zagraniczny; ***a ~ visit*** wizyta zagraniczna; ***a ~ correspondent*** korespondent zagraniczny; ***≗ Office*** *Br* Ministerstwo Spraw Zagranicznych; ***~ policy*** polityka zagraniczna; ***≗ Secretary*** *Br* minister spraw zagranicznych; **for•eign af•'fairs** *pl* sprawy *pl* zagraniczne; **for•eign 'aid** *s* pomoc *f* zagraniczna; **for•eign 'bod•y** *s* MED ciało *n* obce; **for•eign 'cur•ren•cy** *s* waluta *f* obca

for•eign•er ['fɒrənə] *s* cudzoziemiec *m*

for•eign ex'change *s* **1.** wymiana *f* walut **2.** waluty *pl* obce, dewizy *pl*; **for•eign 'lan•guage** *s* język *m* obcy

'fore•most I *adj* **1.** czołowy **2.** główny **3.** najważniejszy **II** *adv* ***first and ~*** przede wszystkim

'fore•play *s* gra *f* wstępna; **'fore•run•ner** *s* **1.** prekursor *m* **2.** zapowiedź *f* **3.** zwiastun *m*; **fore•saw** [fɔː'sɔː] *Past Simple* → **foresee**

fore•see [fɔː'siː] (*foresaw*; *foreseen*) *v/t* przewidywać ⟨-dzieć⟩; **fore•see•a•ble** [fɔː'siːəbl] *adj* przewidywalny; ***in the ~ future*** w niedalekiej przyszłości; **fore•seen** [fɔː'siːn] *Past Participle* → **foresee**

fore'shad•ow *v/t lit* **1.** zapowiadać ⟨-wiedzieć⟩ **2.** zwiastować; **'fore•sight** *s* dalekowzroczność *f*; **'fore•skin** *s* napletek *m*

for•est ['fɒrɪst] *s* **1.** las *m* **2.** bór *m* **3.** puszcza *f*

fore'stall *v/t* **1.** zapobiegać ⟨-biec⟩ **2.** uprzedzać ⟨-dzić⟩, ubiegać ⟨ubiec⟩

for•est•er ['fɒrɪstə] *s* **1.** leśnik *m* **2.** leśniczy *m*; **for•est•ry** ['fɒrɪstrɪ] *s* leśnictwo *n*

'fore•taste *s* przedsmak *m*; **fore'tell** (*foretold*; *foretold*) *v/t* przepowiadać ⟨-dzieć⟩; ***~ the future*** przepowiadać przyszłość; **'fore•thought** *s* **1.** przezorność *f* **2.** przewidywanie *n*

for•ev•er [fər'evə] *adv* **1.** na zawsze **2.** zawsze **3.** wiecznie **4.** bez przerwy, ciągle

fore'warn *v/t* ostrzegać ⟨-rzec⟩ zawczasu

fore•word ['fɔːwɜːd] *s* przedmowa *f*, słowo *n* wstępne

for•feit ['fɔːfət] **I** *v/t* **1.** tracić ⟨s-⟩ **2.** zrzekać ⟨zrzec⟩ się

for•gave [fə'geɪv] *Past Simple* → ***forgive***

forge [fɔːdʒ] **I** *v/t* **1.** *contacts*: nawiązywać ⟨-zać⟩ **2.** podrabiać ⟨-robić⟩ **3.** kuć, wykuwać ⟨-kuć⟩ **II** *s* kuźnia *f*; **forge ahead** *v/i* **1.** posuwać ⟨-sunąć⟩ się naprzód **2.** rozwijać ⟨-winąć⟩ się

forg•er ['fɔːdʒə] *s* fałszerz *m*; **forg•er•y** ['fɔːdʒərɪ] *s* **1.** fałszerstwo *n* **2.** falsyfikat *m*

for•get [fər'get] **I** (*forgot*; *forgotten*) *v/t* zapominać ⟨-mnieć⟩; ***I've forgotten his name*** nie pamiętam jego imienia; ***~ oneself*** zapominać się **II** (*forgot*; *forgotten*) *v/i* zapominać ⟨-mnieć⟩ (***about*** o *L*); **for•get•ful** [fər'getfəl] *adj* **1.** zapominalski **2.** roztargniony; **for'get-me-not** *s* niezapominajka *f*; **for•get•ta•ble** [fər'getəbl] *adj* **1.** niewart zapamiętania **2.** przeciętny

for•give [fər'gɪv] (*forgave*; *forgiven*) *v/t* **1.** wybaczać ⟨-czyć⟩ **2.** przebaczać ⟨-czyć⟩ **3.** darować; **for•gi•ven** [fə'gɪvn] *Past Participle* → ***forgive***; **for•give•ness** [fər'gɪvnɪs] *s* **1.** przebaczenie *n* **2.** darowanie *n* win; **for•giv•ing** [fər'gɪvɪŋ] *adj* **1.** wielkoduszny **2.** łagodny

for•go [fɔː'gəʊ] (*forwent*; *forgone*) *v/t form* **1.** rezygnować ⟨z-⟩ z *G* **2.** odmawiać ⟨-mówić⟩ sobie

for•got [fə'gɒt] *Past Simple* → ***forget***; **for•got•ten** [fə'gɒtn] **I** *Past Participle* → ***forget*** **II** *adj* zapomniany

fork [fɔːk] **I** *s* **1.** widelec *m* **2.** widły *pl* **3.** rozwidlenie *n* **II** *v/i* **1.** rozwidlać ⟨-lić⟩ się **2.** skręcać ⟨-cić⟩; **fork out** *v/i infml* bulić ⟨za-, wy-⟩; **forked** [fɔːkt] *adj* rozwidlony

for•lorn [fə'lɔːn] *adj* **1.** opuszczony **2.** wymarły **3.** opustoszały **4.** rozpaczliwy **5.** *hope*: płonny

form [fɔːm] **I** *s* **1.** forma *f*; ***the ~ of government*** forma rządów; ***in*** (***out of***) *~ Br* w formie (bez formy) **2.** postać *f*; ***in the ~ of*** w postaci *G*; ***in tablet ~*** w tabletkach **3.** kształt *m*; ***take ~*** (*plan*, *idea*) nabierać kształtu **4.** formularz *m*; ***a printed ~*** formularz; ***a ~ letter*** szablon listu **5.** formy *pl*; ***it's good*** (***bad***) *~* to w dobrym (złym) tonie **6.** procedura *f* **7.** (*school*) *Br* klasa *f*, ***a ~ master*** (***mistress***) wychowawca (wychowawczyni) **II** *v/t* **1.** tworzyć ⟨u-⟩ **2.** formować ⟨u-⟩ **3.** zakładać ⟨założyć⟩ **4.** *character*: kształtować ⟨u-⟩ **5.** *opinion*: wyrabiać ⟨-robić⟩ sobie **6.** *friendship*: zawierać ⟨-wrzeć⟩ **III** *v/i* **1.** tworzyć ⟨u-⟩ się **2.** rodzić ⟨na-⟩ się

form•al ['fɔːml] *adj* **1.** oficjalny **2.** formalny; ***~ dress*** strój wizytowy, strój wieczorowy **2.** formalny; **for•mal•ism** ['fɔːməlɪzəm] *s* formalizm *m*; **for•mal•i•ty** [fə'mælətɪ] *s* **1.** formalność *f* **2.** oficjalność *f*; **for•mal•ize** ['fɔːməlaɪz] *v/t* **1.** nadawać ⟨-dać⟩ formalny charakter **2.** formalizować ⟨s-⟩; **for•mal•ly** ['fɔːməlɪ] *adj* **1.** formalnie **2.** oficjalnie

for•mat ['fɔːmæt] **I** *s* **1.** kształt *m* **2.** (*group*) skład *m* **3.** *book*, *paper*: format *m* **4.** formuła *f* **II** *v/t* INF formatować ⟨s-⟩

for•ma•tion [fɔː'meɪʃn] *s* **1.** formowanie *n* **2.** sformowanie *n* **3.** tworzenie *n* **4.** stworzenie *n* **5.** formacja *f*; **for•ma•tive** ['fɔːmətɪv] *adj*: ***have a ~ influence on s.o.*** ukształtować kogoś, ukształtować czyjeś poglądy; ***one's ~ years*** okres dojrzewania, okres rozwoju osobowości

for•mer ['fɔːmə] **I** *adj* **1.** były; ***in the ~ Soviet Union*** w byłym Związku Radzieckim **2.** dawny; ***in ~ times*** w dawnych czasach **3.** ***the ~*** poprzedni **4.** ***the ~*** pierwszy **II** *pron* ***the ~*** to pierwsze; **for•mer•ly** ['fɔːməlɪ] *adv* **1.** niegdyś, dawniej **2.** poprzednio

for•mu•la ['fɔːmjʊlə] *s* **1.** formuła *f* **2.** formułka *f* **3.** MATH PHYS wzór *m* **4.** *fig* recepta *f*; **for•mu•late** ['fɔːmjʊleɪt] *v/t* **1.** formułować ⟨s-⟩ **2.** opracowywać ⟨-cować⟩; **for•mu•la•tion** [fɔːmjʊ'leɪʃn] *s* **1.** sformułowanie *n* **2.** opracowanie *n*

for•ni•cate ['fɔːnɪkeɪt] *v/i form* cudzołożyć, mieć stosunki pozamałżeńskie; **for•ni•ca•tion** [fɔːnɪ'keɪʃn] *s* cudzołóstwo *n*

for•sake [fər'seɪk] (*forsook*; *forsaken*) *v/t* **1.** opuszczać ⟨opuścić⟩ **2.** *custom*: zarzucać ⟨-cić⟩

fort [fɔːt] *s* fort *m*; ***hold the ~ for s.o.*** *fig* dopilnować czyichś spraw

forth [fɔːθ] *adv* dalej; ***and so ~*** i tak dalej; **forth•com•ing** ['fɔːθkʌmɪŋ] *adj* nadchodzący, zbliżający się; **'forth-right** *adj* **1.** prostolinijny **2.** bezpośredni **3.** szczery; **forth•'with** *adv form* niezwłocznie

for•ti•eth ['fɔːtɪəθ] *adj* czterdziesty

for•ti•fi•ca•tion [fɔːtɪfɪ'keɪʃn] *s* **1.** fortyfikacja *f* **2.** umocnienie *n* **3.** fortyfikowanie *n* **4.** umacnianie *n*

for•ti•fy ['fɔːtɪfaɪ] *v/t* **1.** umacniać ⟨umocnić⟩ **2.** fortyfikować ⟨u-⟩ **3.** wzmacniać ⟨-mocnić⟩; ***~ied with*** z dodatkiem *G* **4.** wzbogacać ⟨-cić⟩

for•ti•tude ['fɔːtɪtjuːd] *s* hart *m* ducha

fort•night ['fɔːtnaɪt] *s Br* dwa tygodnie *pl*

for•tress ['fɔːtrɪs] *s* twierdza *f*, forteca *f*

for•tu•nate ['fɔːtʃnət] *adj* **1.** szczęśliwy; ***be ~*** mieć szczęście; ***be ~ in having s.th.*** mieć szczęście coś posiadać, mieć szczęście coś mieć; ***it was ~ for him that*** miał szczęście, że **2.** pomyślny **3.** sprzyjający

for•tu•nate•ly ['fɔːtʃnətlɪ] *adv* na szczęście; ***~ for me*** na szczęście dla mnie

for•tune ['fɔːtʃən] *s* **1.** fortuna *f*, majątek *m*; ***come into a ~*** odziedziczyć fortunę, odziedziczyć majątek; ***make a ~*** zbić fortunę, zbić majątek **2.** szczęście *n*; ***good ~*** szczęście **3.** los *m*; ***tell s.o.'s ~*** powróżyć komuś; **'for•tune hunt•er** *s* łowca *m* po-

F

sagów; **'for•tune-tell•er** *s* **1.** wróżbiarz *m* **2.** wróżka *f*

for•t|y ['fɔːtɪ] **I** *num* czterdzieści; ***have ~y winks*** *fig* uciąć sobie drzemkę **II** *s* czterdziestka *f*; ***be in one's ~ies*** być po czterdziestce; ***in the ~ies*** w latach czterdziestych

for•ward ['fɔːwəd] **I** *adv* **1.** do przodu **2.** w przód, naprzód **II** *adj* **1.** do przodu; ***~ planning*** planowanie perspektywiczne **2.** z przodu **3.** przedni **4.** postępowy **5.** bezpośredni **6.** poufały **III** *s* SPORT napastnik *m* **IV** *v/t* **1.** wysyłać ⟨-słać⟩ **2.** przesyłać ⟨-słać⟩ dalej; **'for•ward•ing ad•dress** *s* (nowy) adres *m* korespondencyjny; **'for•ward•ing a•gent** *s* spedytor *m*; **'for•ward-look•ing** *adj* **1.** postępowy **2.** przewidujący **3.** myślący przyszłościowo; **for•wards** ['fɔːwədz] *adv* do przodu

fos•ter ['fɒstə] **I** *v/t* **1.** sprzyjać **2.** rozwijać **3.** promować **4.** brać ⟨wziąć⟩ na wychowanie, wychowywać ⟨-chować⟩ **II** *adj child*: przybrany; **'fos•ter child** *s* przybrane dziecko *n*; **'fos•ter home** *s* rodzina *f* zastępcza; **'fos•ter par•ents** *s* rodzice *pl* zastępczy

fought [fɔːt] *Past Simple and Past Participle* → ***fight***

foul [faʊl] **I** *adj* **1.** obrzydliwy **2.** cuchnący **3.** *weather*: paskudny **4.** nikczemny **5.** rynsztokowy **6.** SPORT nieczysty, nieprzepisowy, niedozwolony **II** *adv* ***fall ~ of*** zadrzeć z *I*; ***fall ~ of the law*** wejść w konflikt z prawem **III** *s* SPORT faul *m*; ***commit a ~ on*** sfaulować *A* **IV** *v/t* **1.** zanieczyszczać ⟨-czyścić⟩; ***~ one's own nest*** kalać własne gniazdo **2.** SPORT faulować ⟨s-⟩ **3.** ***~ up*** *infml* knocić ⟨s-⟩; **foul-'mouthed** *adj* ordynarny; **'foul-smelling** *adj* cuchnący

found[1] [faʊnd] *Past Simple and Past Participle* → ***find***

found[2] [~] *v/t* **1.** zakładać ⟨założyć⟩ **2.** fundować ⟨u-⟩ **3.** opierać ⟨oprzeć⟩; ***be ~ed on*** opierać się na *L*

foun•da•tion [faʊn'deɪʃn] *s* **1.** fundament *m* **2.** podstawa *f* **3.** fundacja *f* **4.** założenie *n* **5.** ufundowanie *n*; **foun•da•tions** [faʊn'deɪʃnz] *pl* fundamenty *pl*; ***lay the ~s for*** kłaść fundamenty pod *A*; **foun•'da•tion stone** *s* kamień *m* węgielny

found•er ['faʊndə] *s* **1.** założyciel *m*; ***a ~ member*** *Br* członek założyciel **2.** twórca *m* **3.** fundator *m*; **founding** ['faʊndɪŋ] *s* założenie *n*

foun•tain ['faʊntɪn] *s* fontanna *f*, wodotrysk *m*; **'foun•tain pen** *s* wieczne pióro *n*

four [fɔː] **I** *num* cztery, czterech, czworo **II** *s* czwórka *f*; ***the ~ of hearts*** czwórka kier; ***on all ~s*** na czworakach; **four•fold** ['fɔːfəʊld] **I** *adj* **1.** czterokrotny **2.** poczwórny **II** *adv* czterokrotnie; **four-leaf 'clo•ver** *s* czterolistna koniczyna *f*; **'four-leg•ged** *adj* czworonożny; **four-let•ter 'word** *s* niecenzuralne słowo *n*; **four-post•er 'bed** *s* łóżko *n* z baldachimem; **'four-star** *adj* czterogwiazdkowy

four•teen [fɔː'tiːn] **I** *num* czternaście **II** *s* czternastka *f*

four•teenth [fɔː'tiːnθ] *adj* czternasty

fourth [fɔːθ] *adj* czwarty

fox [fɒks] **I** *s* lis *m*; ***an old ~*** *fig* szczwany lis **II** *v/t infml* zbijać ⟨-bić⟩ z tropu; **'fox cub** *s* lisek *m*; **'fox•glove** *s* BIOL naparstnica *f* purpurowa; **'fox•hole** *s* lisia nora *f*; **fox 'ter•ri•er** *s* foksterier *m*

fox•y ['fɒksɪ] *adj* **1.** lisi **2.** przebiegły

foy•er ['fɔɪəɪ] *s* **1.** foyer *n* **2.** hol *m*

fra•cas ['frækɑː] *s* **1.** awantura *f* **2.** burda *f*

frac•tion ['frækʃn] *s* **1.** MATH ułamek *m* **2.** niewielka część *f*; **frac•tion•al** ['frækʃnəl] *adj* **1.** nieznaczny **2.** ułamkowy; **frac•tion•al•ly** ['frækʃnəlɪ] *adv* nieznacznie, odrobinę

frac•ture ['fræktʃə] **I** *s* **1.** złamanie *n* **2.** pęknięcie *n* **II** *v/t* łamać ⟨z-⟩; ***~ one's arm*** złamać rękę; ***a ~d skull*** pęknięcie czaszki **III** *v/i* **1.** łamać ⟨z-⟩ się **2.** pękać ⟨-knąć⟩

fra•gile ['frædʒaɪl] *adj* **1.** kruchy **2.** delikatny **3.** słaby, wątły; **fra•gil•i•ty** [frə'dʒɪlətɪ] *s* **1.** kruchość *f* **2.** delikatność *f* **3.** słabość *f*, wątłość *f*

frag•ment ['frægmənt] *s* **1.** fragment *m* **2.** urywek *m* **3.** kawałek *m* **4.** odłamek *m*; **frag•men•tar•y** [fræg'məntərɪ] *adj* fragmentaryczny

fra•grance ['freɪgrəns] *s* zapach *m*; **fra•grant** ['freɪgrənt] *adj* pachnący, aromatyczny

frail [freɪl] *adj* **1.** słaby **2.** słabowity **3.** wątły **4.** delikatny; **frail•ty** ['freɪltɪ] *s* **1.** słabość *f* **2.** słabowitość *f* **3.** wątłość *f* **4.** delikatność *f*

frame [freɪm] **I** *s* **1.** rama *f* **2.** ramka *f* **3.** framuga *f* **4.** szkielet *m* **5.** *film*: klatka *f* **6.** ***the ~ of mind*** nastrój *m*, humor *m* **II** *v/t* **1.** oprawiać ⟨-wić⟩ **2.** formułować ⟨s-⟩ **3.** opracowywać ⟨-cować⟩ **4.** *infml* wrabiać ⟨wrobić⟩; **'frame house** *s* dom *m* o drewnianej konstrukcji; **'frame-up** *s*: ***he was the victim of a ~*** *infml* został wrobiony, wrobiono go; **'frame•work** *s* **1.** konstrukcja *f* **2.** szkielet *m* **3.** *fig* podstawa *f*, ramy *pl*; ***within the ~ of*** w ramach *G*

France [fræns] *s* Francja *f*

frank [fræŋk] **I** *adj* **1.** szczery; ***to be ~*** szczerze mówiąc **2.** nieskrywany **II** *v/t* frankować ⟨o-⟩; ***a ~ing machine*** frankownica; **frank•ly** ['fræŋklɪ] *adv* **1.** szczerze; ***~ speaking*** szczerze mówiąc **2.** otwarcie; **frank•ness** ['fræŋknɪs] *s* szczerość *f*

fran•tic ['fræntɪk] *adj* **1.** gorączkowy **2.** wariacki **3.** oszalały; ***drive s.o. ~*** doprowadzać kogoś do szału; **fran•tic•al•ly** ['fræntɪklɪ] *adv* **1.** gorączkowo **2.** jak szalony

fra•ter•nal [frə'tɜːnl] *adj* braterski; **fra•ter•ni•ty** [frə'tɜːnətɪ] *s* braterstwo *n*; **frat•er•ni•za•tion** [frætənaɪ'zeɪʃn] *s* fraternizacja *f*, bratanie *n* się; **frat•er•nize** ['frætənaɪz] *v/i* bratać się (***with*** z *I*)

fraud [frɔːd] *s* **1.** oszustwo *n*; ***by ~*** nieuczciwie **2.** *infml* oszust *m*

fraud•u•lence ['frɔːdjʊləns] *s* nieuczciwość *f*; **fraud•u•lent** ['frɔːdjʊlənt] *adj* **1.** nieuczciwy **2.** fałszywy **3.** nielegalny; **fraud•u•lent•ly** ['frɔːdjʊləntlɪ] *adv* **1.** nieuczciwie **2.** fałszywie

frayed [freɪd] *adj* **1.** postrzępiony **2.** *nerves*: stargany

freak [friːk] **I** *s* **1.** *infml* maniak *m* **2.** dziwoląg *m* **3.** dziwak *m* **4.** anomalia *f*; ***a ~ of nature*** wybryk natury **II** **freak out** *v/i infml* **1.** wpadać ⟨wpaść⟩ w szał **2.** doznawać ⟨-nać⟩ szoku **3.** przerazić się

freak•y ['friːkɪ] *adj* **1.** wynaturzony **2.** dziwaczny

freck•le ['frekl] *s* pieg *m*; **freckled** ['frekld] *adj* piegowaty

free [friː] **I** *adj* **1.** wolny; ***he's ~ to go*** może iść; ***set s.o. ~*** uwolnić kogoś; ***~ translation*** wolne tłumaczenie; ***give s.o. a ~ hand*** *fig* dać komuś wolną rękę **2.** (*a.* ***~ of charge***) bezpłatny, darmowy; ***a ~ copy*** egzemplarz bezpłatny; ***for ~*** za darmo **3.** swobodny **4.** dowolny; ***~ skating*** program dowolny **5.** ***~ of***, ***~ from*** bez *G*; ***~ from error*** bezbłędny; ***~ from debt*** bez długów, niezadłużony **6.** ***be ~ with*** nie skąpić *G*, nie żałować *G* **II** *adv* **1.** bezpłatnie, za darmo **2.** swobodnie; ***break ~*** uwolnić się **III** *v/t* **1.** uwalniać ⟨uwolnić⟩ **2.** wyzwalać ⟨-wolić⟩ **3.** wypuszczać ⟨puścić⟩ na wolność

free•bie ['friːbɪː] *infml* **I** *s* upominek *m* **II** *adj* darmowy

free•dom ['friːdəm] *s* **1.** wolność *f* **2.** swoboda *f*; **'free•dom fight•er** *s* bojownik *m* o wolność; **free•dom of 'speech** *s* wolność *f* słowa; **free•dom of the 'press** *s* wolność *f* prasy

free 'en•ter•prise *s* wolna przedsiębiorczość *f*

free 'kick *s* SPORT rzut *m* wolny; **free-lance** ['friːlæns] **I** *s* wolny strzelec *m* **II** *adj journalist*: niezależny; ***do ~ work*** pracować jako wolny strzelec, pracować na umowy zlecenia **III** *adv work*: jako wolny strzelec, na umowy zlecenia; **free•lanc•er** ['friːlænsə] *s* wolny strzelec *m*; **free-load•er** ['friːləʊdə] *s* pasożyt *m*, darmozjad *m*; **free•ly** ['friːlɪ] *adv* **1.** swobodnie **2.** bez ograniczeń **3.** łatwo **4.** otwarcie **5.** *elected*: w wolnych wyborach; **free 'mar•ket** *s* wolny rynek *m*; **free mar•ket e•'con•o•my** *s* gospodarka *f* wolnorynkowa; **free 'port** *s* port *m* wolnocłowy; **free 'sam•ple** *s* darmowa próbka *f*; **'free•style** SPORT **I** *s* **1.** styl *m* wolny **2.** (*snowboarding*) freestyle *m* **II** *adj* w stylu wolnym; **free 'trade** *s* wolny handel *m*; **free-'trade ar•e•a** *s* strefa *f* wolnego handlu; **'free•way** *s Am* autostrada *f*; **free 'will** *s* wolna wola *f*

freeze [friːz] **I** (*froze*; *frozen*) *v/i* **1.** zamarzać ⟨-znąć⟩; ***it's ~ing hard*** jest

F

duży mróz **2.** przemarzać ⟨-znąć⟩ **3.** marznąć ⟨z-⟩; **~ to death** zamarznąć; **I am ~ing** bardzo mi zimno **4.** przymarzać ⟨-znąć⟩ (**to** do *G*) **5.** *fig* zastygać ⟨-gnąć⟩ w bezruchu; **~!** stój! **II** (*froze*; *frozen*) *v/t* **1.** zamrażać ⟨-rozić⟩ **2.** *account*: blokować ⟨za-⟩ **III** *s* **1.** mróz *m* **2.** *wages, prices*: zamrożenie *n*; **a ~ on wages** zamrożenie płac; **freeze out** *v/t Am* bojkotować ⟨z-⟩; **freeze over** *v/i* (*lake*) zamarzać ⟨-znąć⟩

F

freez•er ['fri:zə] *s* **1.** zamrażarka *f* **2.** chłodnia *f* **3. a ~ bag** torba termoizolacyjna

'freeze-frame *s* stop-klatka *f*

freez•ing ['fri:zɪŋ] *adj* **1.** mroźny **2.** poniżej zera **3.** przemarznięty; **'freez•ing com•part•ment** *s* zamrażalnik *m*; **'freez•ing point** *s* temperatura *f* zamarzania

freight [freɪt] **I** *s* **1.** ładunek *m* **2.** towary *pl* **3.** przewóz *m* towarów, fracht *m* **II** *v/t* **1.** przewozić ⟨-wieźć⟩ **2.** wysyłać ⟨-słać⟩; **'freight car** *s* wagon *m* towarowy; **freight•er** ['freɪtə] *s* **1.** frachtowiec *m* **2.** transportowiec *m*; **'freight for•ward•er** *s* spedytor *m*; **'freight train** *s* pociąg *m* towarowy

French [frentʃ] **I** *adj* **1.** francuski; **a ~ kiss** pocałunek z języczkiem **2.** Francuz *m*; **he's ~** jest Francuzem; **the ~** Francuzi **II** *s* (*language*) francuski *m*; **French beans** *pl* fasola *f* (zwykła); **French 'bread** *s* bagietka *f*; **French 'doors** *pl Am* drzwi *pl* balkonowe; **French 'fries** *pl* frytki *pl*; **'French•man** *pl -men s* Francuz *m*; **'French•wom•an** *pl -men s* Francuzka *f*

fre•net•ic [frə'netɪk] *adj* **1.** szaleńczy **2.** gorączkowy

fren•zied ['frenzɪd] *adj* **1.** szalony **2.** gorączkowy **3.** desperacki; **fren•zy** ['frenzɪ] *s* **1.** *fig* gorączka *f* **2.** wrzawa *f*

fre•quen•cy ['fri:kwənsɪ] *s* częstotliwość *f*

fre•quent ['fri:kwənt] **I** *adj* częsty **II** [frɪ'kwent] *v/t* bywać w *L*; **fre•quent•ly** ['fri:kwentlɪ] *adv* często

fres•co ['freskəʊ] *s* fresk *m*

fresh [freʃ] **I** *adj* **1.** świeży; **~ meat** świeże mięso; **a ~ shirt** świeża koszula, czysta koszula **2.** nowy **3.** niedoświadczony **4.** rześki **5. she's ~ from school** dopiero co ukończyła szkołę **6.** *Am infml* bezczelny; **don't get ~ with me!** nie pozwalaj sobie za dużo! **II** *adv* świeżo; **~ from the oven** prosto z pieca; **~-laid eggs** świeże jajka; **fresh 'air** *s* świeże powietrze *n*

fresh•en ['freʃn] **I** *v/t* odświeżać ⟨-żyć⟩ **II** *v/i* ochładzać ⟨-łodzić⟩ się; **freshen up** *v/i* odświeżać ⟨-żyć⟩ się

fresh•ly ['freʃlɪ] *adv* **1.** świeżo **2.** dopiero co; **'fresh•man** *pl -men s* **1.** student *m* pierwszego roku **2.** pierwszoklasista *m*; **fresh•ness** ['freʃnɪs] *s* świeżość *f*; **a ~ date** data przydatności do spożycia, data przydatności do użycia; **'fresh•wa•ter** *adj* słodkowodny *f*

fret [fret] *v/i* **1.** przejmować się (**about**/**over** *I*) **2.** martwić się, niepokoić się (**about**/**over** *I*) **3.** (*child*) złościć się, marudzić; **fret•ful** ['fretfəl] *adj* **1.** niespokojny **2.** rozdrażniony **3.** marudny

Freud•i•an ['frɔɪdɪən] *adj* freudowski; **a ~ slip** freudowska pomyłka

FRG [efɑ:'dʒi:] *abbr* (=**Federal Republic of Germany**) RFN *f*

Fri•day ['fraɪdɪ] *s* piątek *m*; **on ~** w piątek; **on ~s** w piątki

fridge [frɪdʒ] *s* lodówka *f*; **a ~-freezer** *Br* lodówko-zamrażarka *f*

fried [fraɪd] *adj* smażony; **fried 'egg** *s* jajko *n* sadzone; **fried po•'ta•toes** *pl* frytki *pl*

friend [frend] *s* **1.** znajomy *m*; **a circle of ~s** grono znajomych **2.** przyjaciel *m*; **be ~s with** przyjaźnić się z *I*; **make ~s with** zaprzyjaźnić się z *I*; **be ~s again** pogodzić się **3.** kolega *m*; **friend•li•ness** ['frendlɪnɪs] *s* **1.** życzliwość *f* **2.** przyjacielska atmosfera *f*; **friend•ly** ['frendlɪ] **I** *adj* **1.** życzliwy **2.** przyjazny **3.** przyjacielski **4.** miły **5.** *match*: towarzyski **6.** zaprzyjaźniony **II** *s* SPORT mecz *m* towarzyski; **friend•ship** ['frendʃɪp] *s* przyjaźń *f*

fries [fraɪz] *pl Am* frytki *pl*

frig•ate ['frɪgət] *s* fregata *f*

frig•ging ['frɪgɪŋ] *adj infml* pieprzony

fright [fraɪt] *s* **1.** strach *m*; **give s.o. a ~** przestraszyć kogoś; **get a ~, have a ~** przestraszyć się; **stage ~** trema **2. look a ~** wyglądać jak straszydło

fright•en ['fraɪtn] **I** *v/t* przestraszyć; ***be ~ed by*** bać się *G*; ***~ s.o. to death*** śmiertelnie kogoś wystraszyć **II** *v/i* ***he ~s easily*** łatwo go wystraszyć; **fright•en away** *v/t* **1.** odstraszać ⟨-szyć⟩ **2.** odganiać ⟨-gonić⟩ **3.** przeganiać ⟨-gonić⟩

fright•en•ing ['fraɪtnɪŋ] *adj* **1.** napawający lękiem **2.** przerażający; **fright•en•ing•ly** ['fraɪtnɪŋlɪ] *adv* **1.** przerażająco **2.** potwornie

fright•ful ['fraɪtfəl] *adj* potworny, okropny; **fright•ful•ly** ['fraɪtfəlɪ] *adv* potwornie, okropnie

fri•gid ['frɪdʒɪd] *adj* **1.** oziębły **2.** lodowaty **3.** oschły; **fri•gid•i•ty** [frɪ'dʒɪdətɪ] *s* oziębłość *f*

frill [frɪl] *s* **1.** falbana *f* **2.** żabot *m* **3.** ***~s*** dodatki *pl*, *infml* bajery *pl*; **frill•y** ['frɪlɪ] *adj* z falbankami

fringe [frɪndʒ] **I** *s* **1.** grzywka *f* **2.** frędzle *pl* **3.** skraj *m* **4.** obrzeża *pl* **5.** awangarda *f* **II** *v/t* otaczać ⟨otoczyć⟩ **III** *adj theater*: awangardowy; '**fringe ben•e•fits** *pl* dodatkowe korzyści *pl*; '**fringe group** *s* odłam *m* (partii)

frisk [frɪsk] **I** *v/i* brykać **II** *v/t* przeszukiwać ⟨-kać⟩, rewidować ⟨z-⟩; **frisk•y** ['frɪskɪ] *adj* **1.** rozbrykany **2.** pełen wigoru

fri•vol•i•ty [frɪ'vɒlətɪ] *s* **1.** brak *m* powagi **2.** wygłup *m*; **friv•o•lous** ['frɪvələs] *adj* **1.** niepoważny **2.** lekkomyślny **3.** błahy

frizz•y ['frɪzɪ] *adj* mocno kręcony, kędzierzawy

fro [frəʊ] → ***to***

frog [frɒg] *s* żaba *f*; ***have a ~ in one's throat*** *fig* mieć chrypkę; '**frog•man** *pl -men s* płetwonurek *m*

frol•ic ['frɒlɪk] *v/i* figlować

from [frəm, frɒm] *prep* **1.** (*place of origin*) z *G*, ze *G*; ***come ~*** pochodzić z *G*; ***~ what he said*** z tego, co mówił; ***a letter ~ his son*** list od jego syna **2.** (*time span*) od *G*; ***~ 2 to 4 o'clock*** od drugiej do czwartej; ***~ day to day*** z dnia na dzień **3.** (*scope*) od *G*; ***~ A to B*** od A do B **4.** (*distinction*) od *G*; ***he doesn't know right ~ wrong*** on nie odróżnia dobra od zła **5.** (*cause*) z *G*; ***he died ~ exhaustion*** zmarł z wyczerpania

front [frʌnt] **I** *s* **1.** przód *m*; ***at the ~*** z przodu; ***in ~ of*** przed *I*; ***to the ~*** z przodu; ***be in ~*** **a)** być na przedzie **b)** być na czele **2.** front *m*, fasada *f*; ***keep up a ~*** *fig* zachować pozory **3.** (*war*) front *m*; ***go to the ~*** iść na front; ***on all ~s*** na wszystkich frontach **4.** *fig* pole *n*, dziedzina *f*; ***on the educational ~*** w dziedzinie edukacji **5.** front *m* (pogodowy) **II** *adj* **1.** przedni; ***a ~ tooth*** przedni ząb **2.** frontowy; ***the ~ entrance*** główne wejście, wejście frontowe **III** *v/t* wychodzić na *A*; ***the windows ~ the street*** okna wychodzą na ulicę

front 'cov•er *s* okładka *f*; **front 'door** *s* drzwi *pl* główne; **front 'en•trance** *s* główne wejście *n*, wejście *n* frontowe

fron•tier ['frʌntɪə] **I** *s* granica *f* **II** *adj* graniczny

front 'line *s* **1.** linia *f* frontu **2.** *fig* pierwsza linia *f*; ***be in the ~*** być na pierwszej linii; **front 'page** *s* (*newspaper*) pierwsza strona *f*; ***hit the ~s*** trafić na pierwsze strony gazet; **front 'row** *s* pierwszy rząd *m*; **front-'run•ner** *s* faworyt *m*; **front-seat 'pas•sen•ger** *s* pasażer *m* na siedzeniu obok kierowcy; **front-wheel 'drive** *s* napęd *m* na przednie koła

frost [frɒst] **I** *s* **1.** mróz *m* **2.** szron *m* **3.** przymrozek *m*; ***ground ~*** przygruntowe przymrozki **II** *v/t* **1.** pokrywać ⟨-ryć⟩ się szronem **2.** lukrować ⟨po-⟩ **3.** ***~ed glass*** szkło matowe, szkło mrożone; '**frost•bite** *s* odmrożenie *n*; '**frost•bit•ten** *adj* **1.** odmrożony **2.** *vegetable*: zmarznięty; **frost•ing** ['frɒstɪŋ] *adj* lukier *m*; **frost•y** ['frɒstɪ] *adj* **1.** mroźny **2.** oszroniony **3.** *fig* lodowaty

froth [frɒθ] **I** *s* piana *f* **II** *v/i* pienić ⟨s-⟩ się; **froth•y** ['frɒθɪ] *adj* **1.** z pianką **2.** spieniony **3.** zwiewny

frown [fraʊn] **I** *v/i* **1.** marszczyć ⟨z-⟩ brwi **2.** *fig* krzywo patrzeć (**on** na *A*) **II** *s* zmarszczenie *n* brwi; ***with a ~*** marszcząc brwi

froze [frəʊz] *Past Simple* → ***freeze***

fro•zen ['frəʊzn] **I** *Past Participle* → ***freeze*** **II** *adj* **1.** zamarznięty **2.** mrożony; **fro•zen 'food** *s* mrożonki *pl*

fruit [fruːt] *s a. fig* owoc *m*, owoce *pl*; ***bear ~*** owocować; '**fruit•bowl** *s* salaterka *f*, miseczka *f*; **'fruit cake** *s* COOK keks *m*; **fruit•ful** ['fru:tfəl] *adj* **1.** owocny **2.** *lit* urodzajny; **'fruit juice** *s* sok *m* owocowy; **fruit•less** ['fru:tlɪs] *adj* bezowocny; **'fruit ma•chine** *s* jednoręki bandyta *m*; **fruit 'sal•ad** *s* sałatka *f* owocowa; **'fruit tree** *s* drzewo *n* owocowe

fruit•y ['fru:tɪ] *adj* **1.** owocowy **2.** *a. fig* soczysty

frus•trate [frʌ'streɪt] *v/t* **1.** frustrować ⟨s-⟩ **2.** denerwować ⟨z-⟩ **3.** udaremniać ⟨-nić⟩ **4.** *plans*: krzyżować ⟨po-⟩; **frus•trat•ed** [frʌ'streɪtɪd] *adj* **1.** sfrustrowany **2.** zdenerwowany **3.** niespełniony **4.** niezaspokojony; **frus•trat•ing** [frʌ'streɪtɪŋ] *adj* **1.** frustrujący **2.** zniechęcający **3.** denerwujący; **frus•trat•ing•ly** [frʌ'streɪtɪŋlɪ] *adv* zniechęcająco; **frus•tra•tion** [frʌ'streɪʃn] *s* **1.** frustracja *f* **2.** fiasko *n* **3.** niespełnienie *n*

fry [fraɪ] **I** *v/t* smażyć ⟨u-⟩ **II** *v/i* smażyć ⟨u-⟩ się

'frying•pan *s* patelnia *f*; ***jump out of the ~ into the fire*** wpaść z deszczu pod rynnę

fuck [fʌk] *vulg* **I** *v/i* pieprzyć się, pierdolić się (**z** *I*) **II** *v/t* pieprzyć, pierdolić; ***~ you!*** pierdol się! **III** *interj* kurwa (mać)!; **fuck off** *v/i* spierdalać, odpierdolić się; **fuck up** *v/t* pieprzyć ⟨s-⟩, pierdolić ⟨s-⟩; **fuck•ing** ['fʌkɪŋ] *adj vulg* pieprzony, pierdolony

fu•el ['fju:əl] *s* **1.** paliwo *n*; ***add ~ to the fire*** dolewać oliwy do ognia **2.** opał *m*; **'fu•el cell** *s* ogniwo *n* paliwowe; **'fu•el in•jec•tion** *s* wtrysk *m* paliwa; **'fu•el tank** *s* bak *m*, zbiornik *m* paliwa

fug [fʌg] *s Br infml* zaduch *m*

fu•gi•tive ['fju:dʒətɪv] **I** *s* zbieg *m*, uciekinier *m* **II** *adj* zbiegły

ful•fil [fʊl'fɪl] *Br*, ***ful•fill*** *Am v/t* **1.** spełniać ⟨-nić⟩; ***~ oneself*** spełniać się **2.** realizować ⟨z-⟩ **3.** zaspokajać ⟨-koić⟩ **4.** *conditions*: wypełniać ⟨-nić⟩; **ful•fill•ing** [fʊl'fɪlɪŋ] *adj* **1.** dający satysfakcję **2.** udany; **ful•fil•ment** [fʊl'fɪlmənt] *Br*, ***ful•fill•ment*** *Am s* **1.** satysfakcja *f* **2.** spełnienie *n*

full [fʊl] **I** *adj* **1.** pełny (**of** *G*); ***in ~ bloom*** w pełnym rozkwicie; ***take ~ advantage of s.th.*** w pełni coś wykorzystać; ***a ~ hour*** pełna godzina; ***at ~ speed*** z maksymalną prędkością; ***~ power*** pełnia władzy; ***have ~ power to do s.th.*** być upoważnionym do zrobienia czegoś **2.** wypełniony **3.** ***~ of oneself*** zarozumiały **4.** *member*: pełnoprawny **5.** ~ (***up***) syty, najedzony **II** *adv* ***know ~ well*** wiedzieć doskonale **III** *s* ***in ~*** w całości; ***to the ~est*** w pełni; ***live one's life to the ~est*** żyć pełnią życia

full-'blood•ed *adj* **1.** czystej krwi **2.** zaciekły **3.** zagorzały; **'full-blown** *adj* **1.** *flower*: rozwinięty **2.** MED pełnoobjawowy **3.** na wielką skalę; **full-'bod•ied** *adj wine*: pełny, treściwy; **full-'fledged** → ***fully-fledged***; **full-'front•al** *adj picture*: ukazujący nagą postać z przodu; **full-'grown** *adj* **1.** w pełni wyrośnięty **2.** dorosły; **full-'length** *adj* **1.** *dress*: długi **2.** *film*: pełnometrażowy; **full 'moon** *s* pełnia *f*

full•ness ['fʊlnɪs] *s* **1.** pełność *f* **2.** pełnia *f* **3.** ***the feeling of ~*** uczucie sytości

full-'page *adj* całostronnicowy; **full-'scale** *adj* **1.** naturalnej wielkości **2.** na szeroką skalę **3.** *attack*: zmasowany; **full 'stop** *s* (*punctuation*) *Br* kropka *f*; **full 'time I** *adj* **1.** na pełen etat **2.** pełnoetatowy **3.** *student*: stacjonarny, studiów stacjonarnych **II** *adv* na pełnym etacie

ful•ly ['fʊlɪ] *adv* **1.** w pełni; ***~ automatic*** w pełni automatyczny; ***~ two hours*** pełne dwie godziny **2.** całkowicie; **fully-fledged** [fʊlɪ'fledʒd] *adj* **1.** opierzony **2.** pełnoprawny **3.** rozwinięty

fum•ble ['fʌmbl] *v/i* szukać po omacku (***for*** *G*); ***~ for words*** szukać odpowiednich słów; ***~ in one's pockets*** grzebać w kieszeniach; **fum•ble around** *v/i*: ***~ looking for s.th.*** szukać czegoś po omacku

fume [fju:m] *v/i* **1.** dymić **2.** wydzielać opary **3.** złościć się, kipieć ze złości; **fumes** [fju:mz] *pl* **1.** spaliny *pl* **2.** wyziewy *pl* **3.** opary *pl* **4.** dym *m*

fun [fʌn] *s* zabawa *f*; ***for ~*** dla zabawy; ***make ~ of*** nabijać się z *G*; ***have ~!*** dobrej zabawy!

func•tion ['fʌŋkʃn] **I** *s* funkcja *f*; ***a ~ key*** INF klawisz funkcyjny **II** *v/i* **1.** funkcjonować **2.** działać **3.** ***~ as*** pełnić funkcję *G*, służyć jako *N*; **func•tion•al** ['fʌŋkʃnl] *adj* **1.** funkcjonalny **2.** dzia-

łający **3.** *disorder*: czynnościowy; **func•tion•ar•y** ['fʌŋkʃnrɪ] *s* funkcjonariusz *m*
fund [fʌnd] **I** *s* **1.** fundusz *m* **2.** **~s** środki *pl* **II** *v/t* finansować ⟨s-⟩
fun•da•men•tal [fʌndə'mentl] **I** *adj* **1.** fundamentalny **2.** zasadniczy **II** *s* **~s** podstawy *pl*; **fun•da•men•tal•ism** [fʌndə'mentlɪzəm] *s* fundamentalizm *m*; **fun•da•men•tal•ist** [fʌndə'mentlɪst] **I** *s* fundamentalista *m* **II** *adj* fundamentalistyczny; **fun•da•men•tal•ly** [fʌndə'mentlɪ] *adv* **1.** zasadniczo **2.** z gruntu
fund•ing ['fʌndɪŋ] *s* ECON finansowanie *n*
fu•ne•ral ['fjuːnərəl] **I** *s* pogrzeb *m*; ***it's your ~!*** *infml* rób jak chcesz, to twój problem! **II** *adj* pogrzebowy; ***a ~ parlour*** *Br*, ***a ~ home*** *Am* zakład pogrzebowy **3.** żałobny; ***a ~ march*** marsz żałobny; ***a ~ service*** nabożeństwo żałobne; **'fu•ne•ral di•rec•tor** *s* przedsiębiorca *m* pogrzebowy
'fun•fair *s* wesołe miasteczko *n*
fun•nies ['fʌnɪz] *pl infml* dowcipy *pl* rysunkowe; **fun•ni•ly** ['fʌnɪlɪ] *adv* **1.** śmiesznie **2.** dziwnie; **fun•ny** ['fʌnɪ] *adj* **1.** śmieszny, zabawny **2.** dziwny; **'fun•ny bone** *s infml* czułe miejsce w łokciu
fur [fɜː] *s* futro *n*, futerko *n*; ***set the ~ flying*** wywołać awanturę
fu•ri•ous ['fjʊərɪəs] *adj* **1.** wściekły (***with/at*** na *A*) **2.** zażarty **3.** szalony
fur•nace ['fɜːnɪs] *s* piec *m* (hutniczy)
fur•nish ['fɜːnɪʃ] *v/t* **1.** meblować ⟨u-⟩; ***a ~ed room*** umeblowany pokój **2.** dostarczać ⟨-czyć⟩; ***~ proof*** dostarczyć dowodów **3.** wyposażać ⟨-żyć⟩ **4.** zaopatrywać ⟨-trzyć⟩ (***with*** w *A*)
fur•nish•ings ['fɜːnɪʃɪŋz] *pl* **1.** umeblowanie *n* **2.** meble *pl* **3.** wyposażenie *n*; **fur•ni•ture** ['fɜːnɪtʃə] *s* meble *pl*; ***a piece of ~*** mebel
fur•row ['fʌrəʊ] **I** *s* bruzda *f* **II** *v/t brow*: marszczyć ⟨z-⟩; **fur•row•ed** ['fʌrəʊd] *adj brow*: zmarszczony
fur•ry ['fɜːrɪ] *adj* **1.** futerkowy **2.** puszysty
fur•ther ['fɜːðə] **I** *comp* → ***far*** *adv* **1.** dalej **2.** ponadto **II** *comp* → ***far*** *adj* **1.** dalszy **2.** następny **3.** kolejny **III** *v/t* **1.** przyczyniać ⟨-nić⟩ się do rozwoju **2.** wspomagać ⟨-móc⟩ **3.** posuwać ⟨-sunąć⟩ naprzód; **fur•ther edu'cation** *s Br* doskonalenie *n* zawodowe; **fur•thermore** [fɜːðə'mɔː] *adv* ponadto; **fur•ther•most** ['fɜːðəməʊst] *adj* **1.** najdalszy **2.** najodleglejszy
fur•thest ['fɜːðɪst] **I** *superl* → ***far*** *adj* najdalszy **II** *superl* → ***far*** *adv* najdalej
fu•ry ['fjʊərɪ] *s* wściekłość *f*, furia *f*; ***fly into a ~*** wściec się
fu•sion ['fjuːʒn] *s* **1.** *a. fig* połączenie *n* **2.** ***nuclear ~*** PHYS fuzja jądrowa, synteza termojądrowa **3.** ECON fuzja *f* **4.** MUS fusion *n*
fuss [fʌs] **I** *s* **1.** zamieszanie *n*; ***make a ~*** robić zamieszanie; ***a lot of ~ about nothing*** wiele hałasu o nic **2.** *infml* afera *f* **3.** fochy *pl* **II** *v/i* **1.** przejmować się **2.** robić zamieszanie (***about*** z powodu *G*) **3.** wydziwiać (***about*** z *I*); **fuss•pot** *Br*, **'fuss•budg•et** *Am s infml* grymaśnik *m*; **fuss•y** ['fʌsɪ] *adj* **1.** wybredny **2.** grymaśny **3.** pedantyczny
fu•ture ['fjuːtʃə] **I** *s* przyszłość *f*; ***in (the) ~*** w przyszłości **II** *adj* przyszły; ***~ perfect*** GRAM czas przyszły względny, czas przyszły uprzedni; **futures** ['fjuːtʃərz] *pl* FIN transakcje *pl* terminowe; ***the ~ market*** rynek transakcji terminowych; **fu•tur•is•tic** [fjuːtʃə'rɪstɪk] *adj* futurystyczny; **fu•tur•ol•o•gy** [fjuːtʃər'ɒlədʒɪ] *s* futurologia *f*
fuzz [fʌz] *s* **1.** (*downy hair*) meszek *m* **2.** ***the ~*** *infml* gliny; **fuzz•y** ['fʌzɪ] *adj* **1.** puszysty **2.** *hair*: mocno kręcony, kędzierzawy **3.** niewyraźny, zamazany

G

gad•get ['gædʒɪt] *s* gadżet *m*; **gadg•et•ry** ['gædʒɪtrɪ] *s* gadżety *pl*
Gael•ic ['geɪlɪk] **I** *s* (język) gaelicki *m* **II** *adj* gaelicki
gaff [gæf] *s*: ***blow the ~*** *Br infml* wygadać się
gaffe [gæf] *s* gafa *f*, nietakt *m*
gaf•fer ['gæfə] *s Br infml* szef *m*

gag [gæg] **I** *s* **1.** knebel *m* **2.** gag *m* **II** *v/t* **1.** kneblować ⟨za-⟩ **2.** *fig* zamykać ⟨-mknąć⟩ usta
ga•ga ['gɑːgɑː] *adj infml* zdziecinniały
gage [geɪdʒ] *Am* → ***gauge***
gag•gle ['gægl] *s* **1.** stado *n* **2.** (hałaśliwa) grupa *f*
gai•e•ty ['geɪətɪ] *s* wesołość *f*; **gail•y** ['geɪlɪ] *adv* radośnie, wesoło
gain [geɪn] **I** *v/t* **1.** zyskiwać ⟨-kać⟩ **2.** zdobywać ⟨-być⟩ **3.** nabierać ⟨-brać⟩; ***~ speed*** nabrać prędkości; ***he ~ed 10 kilos*** przytył 10 kilo; ***~ weight*** przytyć **II** *v/i* (*watch*) śpieszyć się **III** *s* **1.** korzyść *f* **2.** zysk *m* **3.** przyrost *m*; **gain on** *v/i* **1.** doganiać ⟨-gonić⟩ **2.** zbliżać ⟨-żyć⟩ się do *G*
gain•ful ['geɪnful] *adj* ***~ employment*** zatrudnienie przynoszące dochód; **gain•ful•ly** ['geɪnfʊlɪ] *adv* korzystnie, zyskownie, z pożytkiem
gal [gæl] *s infml* dziewczyna *f*
ga•la ['gɑːlə] **I** *s* gala *f* **II** *adj* galowy
ga•lac•tic [gə'læktɪk] *adj* galaktyczny; **gal•ax•y** ['gæləksɪ] *s* galaktyka *f*
gale [geɪl] **1.** wichura *f* **2.** *laughter*: salwa *f*
gall [gɔːl] **I** *s* **1.** czelność *f*, tupet *m* **2.** *fig* żółć *f* **3.** MED żółć *f* **II** *v/t* irytować ⟨z-⟩
gal•lant ['gælənt] *adj* **1.** waleczny **2.** odważny **3.** szarmancki; **gal•lan•try** ['gæləntrɪ] *s* **1.** waleczność *f* **2.** męstwo *n* **3.** szarmanckość *f*
gal•le•ry ['gælərɪ] *s* **1.** galeria *f*; ***play to the ~*** grać pod publiczkę **2.** krużganek *m* **3.** empora *f*, balkon *m*
Gal•lic ['gælɪk] *adj* francuski
gall•ing ['gɔːlɪŋ] *adj* irytujący
gal•lon ['gælən] *s* (*Br* =3,5 l, *Am* = 3,7 l) galon *m*
gal•lop ['gæləp] **I** *v/i* **1.** cwałować **2.** galopować; ***~ing inflation*** galopująca inflacja **II** *s* **1.** cwał *m*; ***at a ~*** cwałem **2.** galop *m*
gal•lows ['gæləʊz] *s* szubienica *f*
ga•lore [gə'lɔː] *adv* w bród; ***have money ~*** mieć pieniędzy w bród
gam•bit ['gæmbɪt] *s* **1.** gambit *m* **2.** *fig* manewr *m*
gam•ble ['gæmbl] **I** *v/i* **1.** uprawiać hazard **2.** grać na pieniądze **3.** ryzykować ⟨za-⟩; ***~ with s.th.*** ryzykować coś **II** *v/t* stawiać ⟨postawić⟩ **III** *s* zakład *m*; **gam•ble away** *v/t* przegrywać ⟨-rać⟩
gam•bler ['gæmblə] *s* hazardzista *m*;
gam•bling ['gæmblɪŋ] **I** *s* hazard *m* **II** *adj* hazardowy; ***a ~ den*** jaskinia hazardu
game [geɪm] *s* **I** *s* **1.** gra *f*; ***play the ~*** *fig* grać fair; ***beat s.o. at his own ~*** pokonać kogoś jego własną bronią **2.** zabawa *f* **3.** mecz *m* **4.** partia *f* ***a ~ of chess*** partia szachów **5.** ***be in the advertising ~*** *infml* siedzieć w branży reklamowej **6.** zwierzyna *f* (łowna) **7.** ***what's her ~?*** co ona knuje? **II** *adj* gotowy, skory; ***be ~ to do s.th.*** gotowy coś zrobić
game•keep•er ['geɪmkiːpə] *s* leśniczy *m*; '**game park** → ***game reserve***; '**game plan** *s* **1.** strategia *f* gry **2.** strategia *f* działania; '**game re•serve** *s* rezerwat *m* dzikich zwierząt; '**game show** *s* teleturniej *m*
gam•ma rays ['gæməreɪz] *pl* promienie *pl* gamma
gang [gæŋ] *s* **1.** banda *f* **2.** gang *m* **3.** paczka *f* **4.** ekipa *f*; **gang up on** *v/i* zmawiać ⟨zmówić⟩ się przeciw *D*
'**gang rape** *s* gwałt *m* zbiorowy
gang•ling ['gæŋglɪŋ] *adj* tyczkowaty
gan•grene ['gæŋgriːn] *s* gangrena *f*, zgorzel *m*
gang•ster ['gæŋstə] *s* **1.** gangster *m* **2.** bandyta *m*
'**gang war•fare** *s* wojna *f* gangów
'**gang•way** *s* **1.** przejście *n* **2.** trap *m*
gap [gæp] *s* **1.** przerwa *f* **2.** odstęp *m* **3.** luka *f* **4.** puste miejsce *n* **5.** prześwit *m* **6.** dziura *f* **7.** *fig* przepaść *f*; ***the generation ~*** konflikt pokoleń, różnica pokoleń
gape [geɪp] *v/i* **1.** wpatrywać się (***at*** w *A*) **2.** gapić się (***at*** na *A*) **3.** rozdziawiać ⟨-wić⟩ się; **gap•ing** ['geɪpɪŋ] *adj* **1.** wpatrujący się **2.** rozdziawiony **3.** *wound*: ziejący
gar•age ['gærɑːʒ] **I** *s* **1.** garaż *m* **2.** warsztat *m* samochodowy **3.** parking *m* **4.** *Br* stacja *f* benzynowa **II** *v/t* **1.** wprowadzać ⟨-dzić⟩ do garażu **2.** trzymać w garażu **3.** parkować ⟨za-⟩
gar•bage ['gɑːbɪdʒ] *s* **1.** *Am* śmieci *pl* **2.** bzdury *pl*, głupoty *pl*; '**gar•bage bag** *s Am* worek *m* na śmieci; '**gar•bage can** *s Am* pojemnik *m* na śmie-

ci; **'gar•bage chute** *s Am* zsyp *m*; **'gar•bage col•lec•tion** *s Am* wywóz *m* śmieci; **'gar•bage col•lec•tor, garbage man** *pl -men s Am* śmieciarz *m*; **'gar•bage truck** *s Am* śmieciarka *f*

gar•den ['gɑːdn] **I** *s* **1.** ogród *m* **2.** ogródek *m* **II** *adj* **1.** ogrodowy; ***a ~ city*** *Br* miasto-ogród; ***a ~ party*** przyjęcie w ogrodzie **2.** ogrodniczy; ***lead s.o. up the ~ path*** *infml* wyprowadzić kogoś w pole **III** *v/i* uprawiać ogródek; **'gar•den cen•tre** *Br*, **gar•den cen•ter** *Am s* centrum *n* ogrodnicze; **gar•den•er** ['gɑːdnə] *s* ogrodnik *m*; **gar•den•ing** ['gɑːdnɪŋ] *s* ogrodnictwo *n*

gar•goyle ['gɑːgɔɪl] *s* gargulec *m*

gar•ish ['geərɪʃ] *adj* jaskrawy, krzykliwy

gar•land ['gɑːlənd] **I** *s* **1.** wianek *m* **2.** wieniec *m* **3.** girlanda *f* **II** *v/t* dekorować ⟨u-⟩ girlandami

gar•lic ['gɑːlɪk] *s* czosnek *m*; **garl•ic 'bread** *s* pieczywo *n* czosnkowe

gar•ment ['gɑːmənt] *s* **1.** ubranie *n* **2.** część *f* garderoby

gar•ner ['gɑːnə] *v/t* **1.** gromadzić ⟨z-⟩ **2.** zdobywać ⟨-być⟩

gar•ri•son ['gærɪsn] **I** *s* garnizon *m* **II** *v/i* (*army*) stacjonować

gar•ter ['gɑːtə] *s* podwiązka *f*; **'gar•ter belt** *s* pas *m* do pończoch

gas [gæs] **I** *s* **1.** gaz *m* **2.** *Am* benzyna *f* **3.** pedał *m* gazu; ***step on the ~*** nacisnąć na gaz, dodać gazu **4.** *Am infml* ubaw *m* **II** *v/t* **1.** truć ⟨za-⟩ gazem; ***be ~ed*** otruć się gazem **2.** gazować ⟨za-⟩; **'gas•bag** *s infml* gaduła *m/f*; **'gas cham•ber** *s* komora *f* gazowa; **gas 'cook•er** *s* kuchenka *f* gazowa

gas•e•ous ['gæsɪəs] *adj* gazowy

gas-fired cen•tral 'heat•ing *s* gazowe centralne ogrzewanie *n*; **'gas-guz•zler** *s*: ***the car is a ~*** *infml* ten samochód dużo pali

gash [gæʃ] **I** *s* **1.** rozcięcie *n* **2.** rana *f* cięta **II** *v/t* rozcinać ⟨-ciąć⟩

'gas•man *pl -men s* **1.** inkasent *m* z gazowni **2.** gazownik *m*; **'gas mask** *s* maska *f* przeciwgazowa; **'gas me•ter** *s* licznik *m* gazu, gazomierz *m*

gas•o•line ['gæsəliːn] *s Am* benzyna *f*

'gas ov•en *s* piekarnik *m* gazowy

gasp [gɑːsp] **I** *v/i* **1.** dyszeć; ***~ for breath*** z trudem łapać powietrze, sapać **2.** ***make s.o. ~*** zapierać komuś dech w piersiach **II** *v/t* **1.** dyszeć ⟨wy-⟩ **2.** sapać ⟨wy-⟩ **III** *s* ***she gave a ~ of surprise*** zaparło jej dech z wrażenia; ***be at one's last ~*** ledwie dyszeć; ***to the last ~*** do ostatniego tchu

'gas ped•al *s Am* pedał *m* gazu; **'gas pipe•line** *s* gazociąg *m*; **'gas pump** *s Am* dystrybutor *m*; **'gas sta•tion** *s Am* stacja *f* benzynowa; **'gas stove** *s* kuchenka *f* gazowa

gas•sy ['gæsɪ] *adj Br* gazowany

'gas tank *s Am* zbiornik *m* paliwa, bak *m*

gas•tro•nom•ic [gæstrə'nɒmɪk] *adj* kulinarny; **gas•tron•o•my** [gæ'strɒnəmɪ] *s* sztuka *f* kulinarna

'gas•works *s* gazownia *f*

gate [geɪt] *s* **1.** brama *f*; **~s** brama **2.** bramka *f* **3.** furtka *f* **4.** wyjście *n* **5.** *fig* wrota *pl*, brama *f* **6.** barierka *f*, szlaban *m* **7.** *Br* SPORT wpływy *pl* z biletów

'gate•crash *v/i infml* **1.** wchodzić ⟨wejść⟩ bez zaproszenia **2.** wchodzić ⟨wejść⟩ bez biletu; **'gate•crash•er** *s* **1.** osoba *f*, która przyszła bez zaproszenia **2.** osoba *f*, która przyszła bez biletu

'gate•house *s* stróżówka *f*; **'gate•keep•er** *s* portier *m*; **'gate mon•ey** *s* SPORT wpływy *pl* z biletów; **'gate•post** *s* słupek *m* (bramy); **'gate•way** *s* **1.** wejście *n* **2.** wjazd *m*

gath•er ['gæðə] **I** *v/t* **1.** zbierać ⟨zebrać⟩; ***~ dust*** *fig* kurzyć się, stać bezużytecznie **2.** nabierać ⟨-brać⟩; ***~ speed*** nabierać prędkości **3.** wnioskować ⟨wy-⟩ **II** *v/i* zbierać ⟨zebrać⟩ się, gromadzić ⟨z-⟩ się; **gather up** *v/t* zbierać ⟨po-, zebrać⟩; **gather•ing** ['gæðərɪŋ] *s* **1.** spotkanie *n* **2.** zebranie *n* **3.** zgromadzenie *n* **4.** gromadzenie *n*

gauge [geɪdʒ] **I** *s* **1.** miernik *m* **2.** wskaźnik *m* **3.** grubość *f* **4.** przekrój *m* **5.** rozstaw *m* torów (kolejowych) **II** *v/t* **1.** mierzyć ⟨z-⟩ **2.** badać ⟨wy-⟩ **3.** oceniać ⟨-nić⟩ **4.** stwierdzać ⟨-dzić⟩

gaunt [gɔːnt] *adj* **1.** wychudły **2.** wyniszczony

gaunt•let ['gɔːntlɪt] *s* rękawica *f*; ***throw down the ~*** rzucić wyzwanie; ***take up***

G

the ~ podjąć wyzwanie, podnieść rękawicę; ***run the ~ of*** narażać się na ataki ze strony *G*

gauze [gɔːz] *s* **1.** gaza *f* **2.** bandaż *m* **3.** (druciana) siatka *f*

gave [geɪv] *Past Simple* → ***give***

gawk [gɔːk] *v/i infml* gapić się; **gaw•ky** ['gɔːkɪ] *adj* niezdarny

gawp [gɔːp] → ***gawk***

gay [geɪ] **I** *adj* **1.** homoseksualny; ***he's ~*** on jest homoseksualistą, on jest gejem; ***is she ~?*** czy ona jest lesbijką?; ***~ men*** homoseksualiści, geje; ***a ~ marriage*** małżeństwo homoseksualne; ***~ liberation movement*** ruch wyzwolenia gejów, ruch emancypacyjny gejów **2.** gejowski **3.** dla gejów **4.** *dated* wesoły **5.** *colour*: *dated* żywy **II** *s* **1.** homoseksualista *m*, gej *m* **2.** lesbijka *f*

gaze [geɪz] **I** *v/i* wpatrywać się (***at*** w *A*) **II** *s* spojrzenie *n*

ga•zelle [gə'zel] *s* gazela *f*

ga•zette [gə'zet] *s* **1.** (*journal*) monitor *m* **2.** dziennik *m*

GB [dʒiː'biː] *abbr* (=***Great Britain***) Wielka Brytania *f*

GDP [dʒiːdiː'piː] *abbr* (=***gross domestic product***) PKB *n*

gear [gɪə] **I** *s* **1.** *AUTO* bieg *m*; ***change ~, shift ~*** zmieniać biegi; ***change into second ~*** wrzucić dwójkę; ***bottom ~, low ~*** jedynka **2.** sprzęt *m* **3.** strój *m* **II** *v/t* **1.** przygotowywać ⟨-tować⟩ (***to*** do *G*) **2.** przystosowywać ⟨-sować⟩ (***to*** do *G*); **gear up** *v/i* przygotowywać ⟨-tować⟩ się (***for*** do *G*)

'gear•box *s* skrzynia *f* biegów; **'gear lever**, **'gear shift** *Am s* dźwignia *f* zmiany biegów

gee [dʒiː] *interj Am infml* o kurczę! o rany!

geek [giːk] *s Am infml* **1.** frajer *m* **2.** maniak *m* komputerowy

geese [giːs] *pl* → ***goose***

gee•zer ['giːzə] *s infml* **1.** *Am* staruch *m*, ramol *m* **2.** *Br* gość *m*

Gei•ger count•er ['gaɪgəkaʊntə] *s* licznik *m* Geigera

gel [dʒel] *s* żel *m*

gel•a•tine ['dʒelətiːn] *s* żelatyna *f*; **gelatinous** [dʒə'lætɪnəs] *adj* galaretowaty

gem [dʒem] *s* **1.** klejnot *m* **2.** kamień *m* szlachetny **3.** *fig* perła *f* **4.** *fig* skarb *m*

Gem•i•ni ['dʒemɪnaɪ] *s pl ASTR* Bliźnięta *pl*; **be (a) ~** być spod znaku Bliźniąt, *infml* być Bliźniakiem

gen•der ['dʒendə] *s* **1.** rodzaj *m* (gramatyczny); ***what ~ is it?*** jakiego rodzaju to jest?; **2.** płeć *f*; **'gen•der bend•er** *s infml* transwestyta *m*; **'gen•der gap** *s* **1.** różnice *pl* między płciami **2.** nierówność *f* w traktowaniu płci

gene [dʒiːn] *s BIOL* gen *m*; **'gene pool** *s* pula *f* genowa

ge•ne•a•log•i•cal [dʒiːnɪə'lɒdʒɪkl] *adj* genealogiczny; **ge•ne•al•o•gist** [dʒiːnɪ'ælədʒɪst] *s* genealog *m*; **ge•ne•al•o•gy** [dʒiːnɪ'ælədʒɪ] *s* genealogia *f*

gen•e•ral ['dʒenrəl] *adj* **1.** ogólny; ***in ~*** ogólnie, na ogół; ***as a ~ rule*** z reguły; ***the ~ public*** ogół społeczeństwa; ***a ~ term*** termin ogólny; ***a ~ idea*** ogólne pojęcie **2.** generalny **3.** powszechny **4.** przeciętny; ***the ~ reader*** przeciętny czytelnik; **gen•e•ral an•(a)es•'thet•ic** *s* środek *m* znieczulenia ogólnego; **gen•e•ral e•'lec•tion** *s* wybory *pl* powszechne; **gen•er•al•i•za•tion** [dʒenrəlaɪ'zeɪʃn] *s* **1.** uogólnienie *n* **2.** uogólnianie *n*, generalizowanie *n*; **gen•e•ral•ize** ['dʒenrəlaɪz] *v/i* uogólniać ⟨-nić⟩, generalizować

gen•er•al•ly ['dʒenrəlɪ] *adv* **1.** ogólnie; ***~ speaking*** ogólnie mówiąc **2.** powszechnie **3.** zwykle

gen•er•al prac'ti•tion•er *s* lekarz *m* ogólny, lekarz *m* pierwszego kontaktu; **gen•e•ral 'staff** *s* sztab *m* generalny; **'gen•e•ral store** *s* sklep *m* wielobranżowy; **gen•e•ral 'strike** *s* strajk *m* generalny

gen•e•ra•tion [dʒenə'reɪʃn] *s* **1.** pokolenie *n* **2.** generacja *f* **3.** wytwarzanie *n* **4.** generowanie *n*

gen•er•a•tive ['dʒenərətɪv] *adj* **1.** wytwórczy **2.** twórczy

gen•e•ros•i•ty [dʒenə'rɒsətɪ] *s* **1.** hojność *f*, szczodrość *f* **2.** wspaniałomyślność *f*; **gen•e•rous** ['dʒenərəs] *adj* **1.** hojny, szczodry **2.** wspaniałomyślny, wielkoduszny

gen•e•sis ['dʒenəsɪs] *s* **1.** geneza *f* **2.** ~ *REL* Księga Rodzaju

'gene ther•a•py *s* terapia *f* genowa

ge•net•ic [dʒɪ'netɪk] *adj* genetyczny; **ge•net•i•cal•ly** [dʒɪ'netɪklɪ] *adv* genetycznie
ge•net•ic 'code *s* kod *m* genetyczny; **ge•net•ic en•gi•'neer•ing** *s* inżynieria *f* genetyczna; **ge•net•ic 'fin•ger•print** *s* genetyczny odcisk *m* palca; **ge•net•i•cist** [dʒɪ'netɪsɪst] *s* genetyk *m*; **ge•net•ics** [dʒɪ'netɪks] *s* genetyka *f*
ge•nie ['dʒiːnɪ] *s* dżin *m*, dżinn *m*
gen•i•tals ['dʒenɪtlz] *pl* genitalia *pl*
gen•i•tive ['dʒenətɪv] *s* (*a.* **~ case**) *GRAM* dopełniacz *m*
ge•ni•us ['dʒiːnɪəs] *s* geniusz *m*; ***have a ~ for languages*** być wybitnie uzdolnionym językowo; ***be a ~ at*** być mistrzem w *L*
gen•teel [dʒen'tiːl] *adj* **1.** dystyngowany, wytworny **2.** szacowny, nobliwy
gen•tle ['dʒentl] *adj* **1.** delikatny; ***a ~ hint*** delikatna aluzja **2.** łagodny
gen•tle•man ['dʒentlmən] *pl -men s* **1.** pan *m*; ***ladies and gentlemen!*** panie i panowie! **2.** dżentelmen *m*; ***a ~'s agreement*** dżentelmeńska umowa; **gen•tle•man•ly** ['dʒentlmənlɪ] *adj* dżentelmeński
gen•tle•ness ['dʒentlnɪs] *s* **1.** delikatność *f* **2.** łagodność *f*; **gen•tly** ['dʒentlɪ] *adv* **1.** delikatnie **2.** łagodnie
gen•u•ine ['dʒenjʊɪn] *adj* **1.** prawdziwy **2.** autentyczny **3.** oryginalny **4.** szczery **5.** uczciwy; **gen•u•ine•ly** ['dʒenjʊɪnlɪ] *adv* **1.** autentycznie **2.** rzeczywiście, naprawdę **3.** szczerze
ge•og•ra•pher [dʒɪ'ɒgrəfə] *s* geograf *m*; **ge•o•graph•i•cal** [dʒɪə'græfɪkl] *adj* geograficzny; **ge•og•ra•phy** [dʒɪ'ɒgrəfɪ] *s* geografia *f*
ge•o•log•i•cal [dʒɪə'lɒdʒɪkl] *adj* geologiczny; **ge•ol•o•gist** [dʒɪ'ɒlədʒɪst] *s* geolog *m*; **ge•ol•o•gy** [dʒɪ'ɒlədʒɪ] *s* geologia *f*
ge•o•met•ric, ***ge•o•met•ri•cal*** [dʒɪə'metrɪk(l)] *adj* geometryczny; **ge•om•e•try** [dʒɪ'ɒmətrɪ] *s* geometria *f*
ge•o•phys•i•cist [dʒɪəʊ'fɪzɪsɪst] *s* geofizyk *m*; **ge•o•phys•ics** [dʒɪəʊ'fɪzɪks] *s* geofizyka *f*
germ [dʒɜːm] *s* **1.** drobnoustrój *m*, zarazek *m* **2.** *BIOL* zarodek *m*
Ger•man ['dʒɜːmən] **I** *adj* niemiecki **II** *s* **1.** Niemiec *m*, Niemka *f* **2.** (*language*) niemiecki *m*; ***in ~*** po niemiecku; **Ger•man•ic** [dʒɜː'mænɪk] *adj* germański; **Ger•man 'shep•herd** *s* owczarek *m* niemiecki
Ger•man•y ['dʒɜːmənɪ] *s* Niemcy *pl*
ger•und ['dʒerənd] *s* rzeczownik *m* odczasownikowy, gerundium *n*
ges•tic•u•late [dʒe'stɪkjʊleɪt] *v/i* gestykulować; **ges•tic•u•la•tion** [dʒestɪkjʊ'leɪʃn] *s* gestykulacja *f*
ges•ture ['dʒestʃə] *s* gest *m*
get [get] **I** (*get; got/Am gotten*) *v/t* **1.** dostawać ⟨-tać⟩ **2.** kupować ⟨-pić⟩ (**for** *D*) **3. *have got*** mieć; ***have got to*** musieć **4.** zdobywać ⟨-być⟩ **5.** znajdować ⟨znaleźć⟩ **6.** zyskiwać ⟨-kać⟩ **7.** zarabiać ⟨-robić⟩ **8.** dodzwaniać ⟨-wonić⟩ się do *G* **9.** przynosić ⟨-nieść⟩ **10.** dziedziczyć ⟨o-⟩ **11. *~ s.th. ready*** przygotować coś **12. *~ one's hair cut*** (*hairdresser*) obciąć włosy **13. *~ s.th. going*** **a)** uruchomić coś **b)** ruszyć z czymś, wystartować z czymś **14.** rozumieć ⟨z-⟩; ***don't ~ me wrong*** nie zrozum mnie źle **II** (*get; got/Am gotten*) *v/i* **1.** dostawać ⟨-tać⟩ się **2.** docierać ⟨dotrzeć⟩; ***~ home*** wrócić do domu, dotrzeć do domu **3. *~ to know*** dowiedzieć się **4.** stawać ⟨-tać⟩ się; ***~ tired*** zmęczyć się; ***~ dressed*** ubrać się **5. *~ going*** ruszyć, zabrać się do roboty; ***let's ~ going!*** zaczynajmy! **6. *~ together*** **a)** zebrać się, zgromadzić się **b)** spotykać ⟨-tkać⟩ się; ***get about*** → ***get around***; **get across** *v/t* tłumaczyć ⟨wy-⟩, przekazywać ⟨-zać⟩; **get behind** *v/i* spóźniać ⟨-nić⟩ się; **get along** *v/i* **1.** posuwać ⟨-sunąć⟩ się **2.** radzić ⟨po-⟩ sobie, dawać ⟨dać⟩ sobie radę **3.** być w dobrych stosunkach (**with** z *I*); **get around** *v/i* **1.** poruszać się **2.** podróżować **3.** rozchodzić ⟨rozejść⟩ się **4.** zabierać ⟨-brać⟩ się (**to** do *G*); **get at** *v/i* **1.** dostawać ⟨-tać⟩ się do *G* **2.** naskakiwać ⟨-koczyć⟩ na *A* **3. *what are you getting at?*** co chcesz przez to powiedzieć?, do czego zmierzasz?; **get away** *v/i* **1.** wyrywać ⟨-rwać⟩ się **2.** uciekać ⟨uciec⟩; **get away with** *v/i* **1.** unikać ⟨-knąć⟩ kary za *A*; ***you won't ~ away with it!*** nie ujdzie ci to na sucho! **2.** kraść ⟨u-⟩; ***the thieves got away with 3 computers*** łupem złodziei

padły trzy komputery; **get back** **I** *v/t* **1.** odzyskiwać ⟨-kać⟩ **2.** dostawać ⟨-tać⟩ z powrotem **3.** ***get one's own back on*** zemścić się na *L* **II** *v/i* **1.** wracać ⟨wrócić⟩ **2.** mścić ⟨ze-⟩ się (***at*** na *L); **get by** v/i* **1.** przechodzić ⟨przejść⟩ **2.** dawać ⟨dać⟩ sobie radę, radzić ⟨po-⟩ sobie; **get down** **I** *v/i* schodzić ⟨zejść⟩ **II** *v/t* **1.** notować ⟨za-⟩ **2.** połykać ⟨-łknąć⟩; **get down to** *v/i* zabierać ⟨-brać⟩ się do *G*; **get in** **I** *v/i* **1.** wchodzić ⟨wejść⟩ **2.** wsiadać ⟨wsiąść⟩ **3.** przyjeżdżać ⟨-jechać⟩ **II** *v/t* **1.** kupować ⟨-pić⟩ **2.** wzywać ⟨wezwać⟩; **get into** *v/i* **1.** wchodzić ⟨wejść⟩ **2.** dostawać ⟨-tać⟩ się do *G* **3.** wciskać ⟨-snąć⟩ się w *A*; **get off** *v/i* **1.** wyruszać ⟨-szyć⟩ **2.** wyjeżdżać ⟨-jechać⟩ **3.** wysiadać ⟨-siąść⟩ z *G* **4.** zsiadać ⟨zsiąść⟩ z *G* **5.** wywijać ⟨-winąć⟩ się; **get off with** *v/i* **1.** *Br infml* podrywać ⟨-derwać⟩ **2.** ***she got off with it*** uszło jej to na sucho; **get on** *v/i* **1.** wsiadać ⟨wsiąść⟩ do *G* **2.** posuwać ⟨-sunąć⟩ się; ***he is getting on for sixty*** dobiega sześćdziesiątki; ***it is getting on for 5 o'clock*** dochodzi piąta **3.** *Br* być w dobrych stosunkach; **get out** **I** *v/i* **1.** wychodzić ⟨wyjść⟩ **2.** wysiadać ⟨-siąść⟩ **II** *v/t* **1.** wyjmować ⟨-jąć⟩ **2.** wyciągać ⟨-gnąć⟩; **get over** *v/i* **1.** przechodzić ⟨przejść⟩ **2.** dochodzić ⟨dojść⟩ do siebie po *L* **3.** przezwyciężać ⟨-żyć⟩; **get over with** *v/i* **1.** przejść przez *A* **2.** mieć za sobą; **get through** *v/i* **1.** przedostawać ⟨-tać⟩ się **2.** przeciskać ⟨-snąć⟩ się **3.** dodzwaniać ⟨-wonić⟩ się **4.** robić ⟨z-⟩; **get up** *v/i* **1.** wstawać ⟨-tać⟩ **2.** podnosić ⟨-nieść⟩ się **3.** wsiadać ⟨wsiąść⟩

'get•a•way *s* ucieczka *f*; ***make a ~*** uciec

'get-to•geth•er *s* spotkanie *n*; ***have a ~*** spotkać się

'get-up *s infml* dziwaczny strój *m*

gey•ser ['giːzə] *s* **1.** *GEOL* gejzer *m* **2.** *Br* piecyk *m*, terma *f*

ghast•ly ['gɑːstlɪ] *adj* **1.** koszmarny, potworny **2.** upiorny

ghet•to ['getəʊ] *s* getto *n*; ***a ~ blaster*** przenośny magnetofon

ghost [gəʊst] *s* **1.** duch *m*; ***give up the ~*** wyzionąć ducha **2.** widmo *n* **3.** upiór *m* **4.** *fig* cień *m*; **ghost•ly** ['gəʊstlɪ] *adj* upiorny

'ghost sto•ry *s* historia *f* o duchach; **'ghost town** *s* wymarłe miasto *n*; **'ghost train** *s* (*amusement park*) pociąg *m* duchów; **'ghost writ•er** *s* autor *m* piszący za kogoś innego, piszący *m* na zamówienie

ghoul [guːl] *s* **1.** (*Arabic myths*) gul *m*, zły duch *m* **2.** *fig* osoba *f* gustująca w makabrze; **ghoul•ish** ['guːlɪʃ] *adj* **1.** upiorny **2.** makabryczny

gi•ant ['dʒaɪənt] **I** *s* olbrzym *m*, gigant *m* **II** *adj* olbrzymi, gigantyczny; ***~ slalom*** *SPORT* slalom gigant

gib•ber ['dʒɪbə] *v/i* bełkotać; **gib•ber•ish** ['dʒɪbərɪʃ] *s* **1.** bełkot *m* **2.** bzdury *pl*

gib•bon ['gɪbən] *s BIOL* gibon *m*

gid•di•ness ['gɪdɪnɪs] *s* zawroty *pl* głowy; **gid•dy** ['gɪdɪ] *adj* **1.** ***I am ~, I feel ~*** kręci mi się w głowie **2.** zawrotny

gift [gɪft] *s* **1.** prezent *m*; ***don't look a ~ horse in the mouth*** darowanemu koniowi nie zagląda się w zęby **2.** upominek *m*; ***a ~ token, a ~ voucher*** bon towarowy **3.** dar *m*, talent *m*; ***a ~ for languages*** talent do języków, zdolności językowe; **'gift cer•ti•fi•cate** *s* bon *m* towarowy; **gift•ed** ['gɪftɪd] *adj* uzdolniony, utalentowany; **'gift shop** *s* sklep *m* z upominkami; **'gift-wrap** *s* ozdobny papier *m* do pakowania

gig [gɪg] *s infml* koncert *m*

gi•ga•byte ['gɪgəbaɪt] *s* gigabajt *m*

gi•gan•tic [dʒaɪ'gæntɪk] *adj* gigantyczny

gig•gle ['gɪgl] **I** *v/i* chichotać ⟨za-⟩ **II** *s* chichot *m*; **gig•gly** ['gɪglɪ] *adj* rozchichotany, chichoczący

gild [gɪld] *v/t* pozłacać ⟨-łocić⟩, złocić; ***~ the lily*** *fig* przedobrzyć

gill [gɪl] *s* skrzele *n*

gilt [gɪlt] **I** *s* **1.** złocenie *n* **2.** pozłota *f* **II** *adj* złocony, pozłacany; **gilt-edged se•'cur•i•ties** *pl* obligacje *pl* państwowe

gim•crack ['dʒɪmkræk] **I** *s* tandeta *f*, *infml* chłam *m* **II** *adj* tandetny

gim•mick ['gɪmɪk] *s* **1.** gadżet *m* **2.** chwyt *m*; **gim•mick•y** ['gɪmɪkɪ] *adj* **1.** efekciarski **2.** *infml* bajerancki **3.** wymyślny

G

gin [dʒɪn] *s* gin *m*, dżin *m*
gin•ger ['dʒɪndʒə] **I** *s* **1.** imbir *m* **2.** rudy *m* **II** *adj* **1.** imbirowy; ***~ beer*** piwo imbirowe **2.** rudy; **gin•ger 'ale** *s* (gazowany) napój *m* imbirowy; **'gin-ger•bread** *s* **1.** piernik *m* **2.** pierniczek *m*
gin•ger•ly ['dʒɪndʒərlɪ] *adv* ostrożnie
gip•sy ['dʒɪpsɪ] → ***gypsy***
gi•raffe [dʒɪ'rɑːf] *s* żyrafa *f*
girl [gɜːl] *s* **1.** dziewczyna *f* **2.** dziewczynka *f*; **'girl•friend** *s* dziewczyna *f*, sympatia *f*; **girl•hood** ['gɜːlhʊd] *s* dzieciństwo *n*; **girl•ie** ['gɜːlɪ] *adj magazine, calendar*: z nagimi panienkami; **girl•ish** [***'gó:lIS]*** *adj* **1.** dziewczęcy **2.** dziecinny; **girl 'scout** *s Am* skautka *f*
girth [gɜːθ] *s* **1.** obwód *m* **2.** popręg *m*
gist [dʒɪst] *s* sedno *n*; ***get the ~*** zrozumieć, o co chodzi, zrozumieć sedno sprawy
give [gɪv] **I** (*gave*; *given*) *v/t* **1.** dawać ⟨dać⟩; ***~ s.o. a kiss*** pocałować kogoś; ***~ me a break!*** daj spokój!; ***I was given to understand that*** dano mi do zrozumienia, że **2.** darować ⟨po-⟩ **3.** ofiarowywać ⟨-rować⟩ **4.** podawać ⟨-dać⟩; ***~ s.o. one's hand*** podać komuś rękę **5.** *advice*: udzielać ⟨-lić⟩ **6.** poświęcać ⟨-cić⟩ **7.** przyznawać ⟨-nać⟩ **8.** nadawać ⟨-dać⟩ **9.** *order*: wydawać ⟨-dać⟩ **10.** przekazywać ⟨-zać⟩; ***~ him my love*** pozdrów go ode mnie, przekaż mu pozdrowienia **11.** *punishment*: wymierzać ⟨-rzyć⟩ **12.** *blow*: zadawać ⟨-dać⟩ **13.** *sound*: wydawać ⟨-dać⟩; ***~ a cry*** krzyknąć; ***~ a laugh*** zaśmiać się **14.** *medicine, reason*: podawać ⟨-dać⟩ **15.** *party*: wydawać ⟨-dać⟩, urządzać ⟨-dzić⟩ **II** (*gave*; *given*) *v/i* **1.** dawać ⟨dać⟩ **2.** ustępować ⟨-tąpić⟩ **3.** ***what ~s?*** *infml* co słychać?, co nowego?; **give away** *v/t* **1.** oddawać ⟨-dać⟩ **2.** rozdawać ⟨-dać⟩ **3.** *secret*: zdradzać ⟨-dzić⟩; **give back** *v/t* **1.** oddawać ⟨-dać⟩, zwracać ⟨-rócić⟩ **2.** *sound*: odbijać ⟨-bić⟩; **give in I** *v/i* **1.** ulegać ⟨-lec⟩ (*to D*) **2.** poddawać ⟨-dać⟩ się **II** *v/t homework*: oddawać ⟨-dać⟩; **give off** *v/i* **1.** wydzielać ⟨-lić⟩ **2.** wysyłać ⟨-słać⟩ **3.** ***~ light*** świecić, emitować światło; **give on(to)** *v/i* (*window*) wychodzić na *A*; **give out I** *v/t* **1.** rozdawać ⟨-dać⟩ **2.** (*from storage*) wydawać ⟨-dać⟩ **3.** wydzielać ⟨-lić⟩ **II** *v/i* wyczerpywać ⟨-pać⟩ się; **give up I** *v/i* poddawać ⟨-dać⟩ się **II** *v/t* **1.** rezygnować ⟨z-⟩ z *G* **2.** rozstawać ⟨-stać⟩ się z *G* **3.** *smoking*: rzucać ⟨-cić⟩ **4.** porzucać ⟨-cić⟩ **5.** oddawać ⟨-dać⟩ **6.** ustępować ⟨-tąpić⟩ **7.** wydawać ⟨-dać⟩ **8.** ***give oneself up*** poddać się; ***give oneself up to s.o.*** oddać się w czyjeś ręce; **give way** *v/i* **1.** (*chair, ice*) załamywać ⟨-mać⟩ się **2.** walić ⟨za-⟩ się **3.** (*legs*) uginać ⟨ugiąć⟩ się **4.** *Br* ustępować ⟨-tąpić⟩ pierwszeństwa **5.** ustępować ⟨-tąpić⟩
give and 'take *s* kompromis *m*, wzajemne ustępstwa *pl*
'give•a•way *s* **I** *s* **1.** darmowy upominek *m* **2.** ***be a ~ that*** zdradzać, że **II** *adj price*: bardzo niski; ***for a ~ price*** bardzo tanio, za bezcen
giv•en ['gɪvn] **I** *Past Participle* → ***give*** **II** *adj* **1.** dany **2.** określony; ***meet at a ~ time*** spotkać się o określonej godzinie; ***within a ~ time*** w określonym czasie **3.** ***be ~ to (doing) s.th.*** mieć skłonność do (robienia) czegoś **4.** ***~ that*** **a)** biorąc pod uwagę, że **b)** przyjmując, że; **'giv•en name** *s* imię *n*
giv•er ['gɪvə] *s* darczyńca *m*
giz•mo ['gɪzməʊ] *s infml* **1.** ustrojstwo *n* **2.** gadżet *m*
gla•cial ['gleɪʃəl] *adj* **1.** lodowcowy, glacjalny **2.** polodowcowy **3.** lodowaty; **gla•ci•er** ['gleɪsɪə] *s* lodowiec *m*
glad [glæd] *adj* **1.** zadowolony; ***I am ~ to hear that*** miło mi słyszeć, że; ***I am ~ to be leaving*** cieszę się, że wyjeżdżam **2.** dobry; **glad•den** ['glædn] *v/t* cieszyć ⟨u-⟩, radować ⟨u-⟩
glad•ly ['glædlɪ] *adv* **1.** chętnie, z ochotą **2.** z przyjemnością
glad•ness ['glædnɪs] *s* radość *f*
glam•or•ize ['glæməraɪz] *v/t* **1.** upiększać ⟨-szyć⟩ **2.** gloryfikować; **glam•or•ous** ['glæmərəs] *adj* **1.** efektowny **2.** atrakcyjny **3.** prestiżowy **4.** uroczysty
glam•o(u)r ['glæmə] *s* **1.** *Br*, ***glamor*** *Am* powab *m*, urok *m* **2.** atrakcyjność *f* **3.** splendor *m* **4.** prestiż *m* **5.** efektowność *f*

G

glance [glɑːns] **I** *v/i* **1.** rzucać ⟨-cić⟩ okiem **2.** zerkać ⟨-knąć⟩ **3.** *~ through a report* przejrzeć raport **4.** *~ off* odbijać się **II** *s* **1.** rzut *m* oka; *at a ~, at first ~* na pierwszy rzut oka **2.** zerknięcie *n*

glare [gleə] **I** *v/i* **1.** piorunować ⟨s-⟩ wzrokiem, gniewnie spoglądać ⟨spojrzeć⟩ **2.** świecić oślepiającym blaskiem **3.** razić **II** *s* **1.** piorunujące spojrzenie *n*, gniewne spojrzenie *n* **2.** oślepiające światło *n*; **glare at** *v/t* piorunować ⟨s-⟩ wzrokiem, gniewnie spoglądać ⟨spojrzeć⟩ na *A*; **glar•ing** ['gleərɪŋ] *adj* **1.** rażący **2.** oczywisty **3.** oślepiający **4.** gniewny; **glar•ing•ly** ['gleərɪŋlɪ] *adv* **1.** rażąco **2.** zupełnie

G

glass [glɑːs] **I** *s* **1.** szkło *n* **2.** kieliszek *m* **3.** szklanka *f* **4.** lustro *n* **5.** (*a pair of*) *~es* okulary **6.** (*field*) *~es* lornetka **II** *adj* szklany, ze szkła; *a ~ eye* szklane oko; **'glass•blow•er** *s* dmuchacz *m* szkła; **glass 'case** *s* gablota *f*; **glass 'ceil•ing** *s fig* szklany sufit *m*

glass•es [glæsɪz] *pl* **1.** okulary *pl* **2.** lornetka *f*

glass•ful ['glɑːsfʊl] *s* **1.** kieliszek *m* **2.** szklanka *f*

'glass•house *s* szklarnia *f*

glass•ware ['glɑːsweə] *s* (*goods*) szkło *n*

glass•y ['glɑːsɪ] *adj* **1.** szklisty **2.** jak ze szkła **3.** oblodzony **4.** gładki **5.** przejrzysty

glaze [gleɪz] **I** *v/t* **1.** szklić ⟨o-⟩ **2.** glazurować **3.** szkliwić **4.** polewać ⟨-lać⟩ polewą **II** *s* **1.** glazura *f* **2.** szkliwo *n* (ceramiczne) **3.** polewa *f*; **glaze over** *v/i* szklić ⟨za-⟩ się; **glazed** [gleɪzd] *adj* **1.** oszklony **2.** w polewie **3.** szklisty **4.** glazurowany **5.** szkliwiony **6.** oblodzony; **gla•zi•er** ['gleɪzɪə] *s* szklarz *m*; **glaz•ing** ['gleɪzɪŋ] *s* **1.** szyby *pl* **2.** szklenie *n*

gleam [gliːm] **I** *v/i* **1.** świecić (się) **2.** jaśnieć **3.** błyszczeć się **II** *s* **1.** poświata *f* **2.** poblask *m* **3.** *fig* błysk *m* **4.** *hope*: promyk *m*

glean [gliːn] *v/t information*: zbierać ⟨zebrać⟩

glee [gliː] *s* **1.** radość *f* **2.** złośliwa satysfakcja *f*; **glee•ful** ['gliːfəl] *adj* radosny

glide [glaɪd] **I** *v/i* **1.** sunąć **2.** szybować ⟨po-⟩ **II** *s* **1.** ślizg *m* **2.** szybowanie *n* **3.** lot *m* ślizgowy; **glid•er** ['glaɪdə] *s* **1.** szybowiec *m* **2.** *Am* huśtawka *f*; **glid•ing** ['glaɪdɪŋ] *s* SPORT szybownictwo *n*

glim•mer ['glɪmə] **I** *v/i* migotać ⟨za-⟩ **II** *s* **1.** migotanie *n* **2.** *fig* iskra *f*, iskierka *f*

glimpse [glɪmps] **I** *s* **1.** mignięcie *n*; *he caught a ~ of her face* mignęła mu jej twarz **2.** spojrzenie *n* **II** *v/t he ~d her figure* mignęła mu jej postać

glint [glɪnt] **I** *s* błysk *m* **II** *v/i* błyskać ⟨-snąć⟩

glis•ten ['glɪsn] *v/i* lśnić ⟨za-⟩

glitch [glɪtʃ] *s infml* **1.** usterka *f* **2.** zakłócenie *n* **3.** drobny problem *m*

glit•ter ['glɪtə] **I** *v/i* **1.** mienić się **2.** błyszczeć; *all that ~s is not gold* nie wszystko złoto, co się świeci **II** *s* **1.** blask *m* **2.** migotanie *n* **3.** skrzenie *n* się **4.** brokat *m* **5.** *fig* powab *m* **6.** *fig* blichtr *m*; **glit•ter•ing** ['glɪtərɪŋ] *adj* **1.** skrzący się **2.** mieniący się **3.** błyskotliwy

glitz [glɪts] *s infml* blichtr *m*; **glitz•y** ['glɪtsɪ] *adj* efekciarski

gloat [gləʊt] *v/i* **1.** chełpić się (*about/over I*) **2.** napawać się (*about/over I*)

glo•bal ['gləʊbl] *adj* **1.** globalny **2.** ogólnoświatowy **3.** całościowy; **glo•bal e•'con•o•my** *s* gospodarka *f* światowa; **glob•al•i•za•tion** [gləʊbəlaɪ'zeɪʃn] *s* globalizacja *f*; **glob•al•ly** ['gləʊbəlɪ] *adv* **1.** globalnie **2.** całościowo; **glo•bal 'mar•ket** *s* światowy rynek *m*; **glo•bal 'war•ming** *s* globalne ocieplenie *n*

globe [gləʊb] *s* **1.** kula *f* ziemska, glob *m* **2.** globus *m* **3.** kula *f*

globe•trot•ter ['gləʊbtrɒtə] *s* globtroter *m*, obieżyświat *m*

glob•ule ['glɒbjuːl] *s* **1.** kropla *f* **2.** kulka *f* **3.** MED globulka *f*

gloom [gluːm] *s* **1.** mrok *m* **2.** przygnębienie *n*; *cast a ~ over* rzucać cień na *A*; **gloom•i•ly** ['gluːmɪlɪ] *adv* ponuro, posępnie; **gloom•y** ['gluːmɪ] *adj* **1.** ciemny, mroczny **2.** ponury, posępny

glo•ri•fi•ca•tion [glɔːrɪfɪ'keɪʃn] *s* **1.** wysławianie *n* **2.** gloryfikacja *f*; **glo•ri•fied** ['glɔːrɪfaɪd] *adj* zachwalany; **glo-**

ri•fy ['glɔːrɪfaɪ] *v/t* **1.** wysławiać, sławić **2.** wychwalać **3.** gloryfikować; **glo•ri•ous** ['glɔːrɪəs] *adj* **1.** wspaniały **2.** *day, holidays*: cudowny **3.** chwalebny; **glo•ry** ['glɔːrɪ] **I** *s* **1.** chwała *f* **2.** wspaniałość *f* **3.** świetność *f* **4.** duma *f*, chluba *f* **II** *v/i* ~ ***in*** upajać się *I*

gloss[1] [glɒs] *s* **1.** połysk *m* **2.** blask *m* **3.** blichtr *m* **4.** farba *f* z połyskiem **5.** emalia *f* **6.** ***lip*** ~ błyszczyk do ust; **gloss over** *v/i* tuszować ⟨za-⟩

gloss[2] [~] *s* **1.** przypis *m* **2.** glosa *f*

glos•sa•ry ['glɒsərɪ] *s* słowniczek *m*, glosariusz *m*

'gloss paint *s* **1.** farba *f* z połyskiem **2.** emalia *f*; **gloss•y** ['glɒsɪ] **I** *adj* **1.** błyszczący **2.** lśniący **3.** *magazine*: ilustrowany **II** *s infml* magazyn *m* ilustrowany

glove [glʌv] *s* rękawiczka *f*, rękawica *f*; ***fit like a*** ~ pasować jak ulał; **'glove com•part•ment** *s* (*car*) schowek *m*; **'glove pup•pet** *s* pacynka *f*

glow [gləʊ] **I** *v/i* **1.** jarzyć się **2.** żarzyć się **3.** świecić **II** *s* **1.** blask *m* **2.** poświata *f*

glow•er [glaʊə] *v/i* patrzeć ⟨po-⟩ groźnie (**at** na *A*), piorunować ⟨s-⟩ wzrokiem (**at** *A*)

glow•ing ['gləʊɪŋ] *adj* **1.** jarzący się **2.** żarzący się, rozżarzony **3.** entuzjastyczny; **glow•ing•ly** ['gləʊɪŋlɪ] *adv* entuzjastycznie

glu•cose ['gluːkəʊs] *s* glukoza *f*

glue [gluː] **I** *s* klej *m* **II** *v/t* kleić ⟨przy-, za-⟩; ***be*** ~***ed to the screen*** *fig* wlepiać oczy w telewizor; **'glue-sniff•ing** *s* wąchanie *n* kleju; **glu•ey** ['gluːɪ] *adj* **1.** kleisty **2.** lepki

glum [glʌm] *adj* ponury, posępny, przygnębiony; **glum•ly** ['glʌmlɪ] *adv* ponuro, posępnie

glut [glʌt] **I** *v/t market*: zalewać ⟨-lać⟩ **II** *s* **1.** zalew *m* **2.** nadmiar *m*

glut•ton ['glʌtən] *s* **1.** żarłok *m*, obżartuch *m* **2.** ***a*** ~ ***for work*** pracuś; ***a*** ~ ***for punishment*** cierpiętnik, *fig* masochista; **glut•ton•ous** ['glʌtənəs] *adj* żarłoczny; **glut•ton•y** ['glʌtənɪ] *s* obżarstwo *n*

glyc•er•in(e) ['glɪsərɪn] *s* gliceryna *f*

GMT [dʒiːem'tiː] *abbr* (=**Greenwich Mean Time**) czas *m* uniwersalny, czas *m* Greenwich

gnarled [nɑːld] *adj* **1.** sękaty **2.** powykręcany

gnash [næʃ] *v/t*: ~ ***one's teeth*** zgrzytać zębami

gnat [næt] *s Br* komar *m*

gnaw [nɔː] *v/i* **1.** obgryzać ⟨-ryźć⟩ (**at** *A*) **2.** gryźć (**at** *A*) **3.** przegryzać ⟨-ryźć⟩ (**through** *A*) **4.** *fig* dręczyć (**at** *A*)

gnome [nəʊm] *s* gnom *m* , krasnal *m*

GNP [dʒiːen'piː] *abbr* (=**gross national product**) PNB *n*

go [gəʊ] **I** (*went*; *gone*) *v/i* **1.** iść ⟨pójść⟩; ~ ***on foot*** iść pieszo; ~ ***swimming*** iść popływać; ***I must be*** ~***ing*** muszę już iść; ***how is it*** ~***ing?*** jak leci?, co słychać?; ***he went to find her*** poszedł jej szukać; ***she went to see him*** poszła się z nim spotkać **2.** chodzić **3.** jechać ⟨po-⟩ **4.** lecieć ⟨po-⟩; ~ ***by plane***, ~ ***by air*** lecieć samolotem **5.** (*street*) prowadzić **6.** (*bus*) kursować **7.** (*die*) odchodzić ⟨odejść⟩ **8.** (*machine*) działać; ***set s.th.*** ~***ing*** uruchomić coś **9.** ~ ***green*** zazielenić się; ~ ***bad*** zepsuć się; ~ ***unnoticed*** nie zostać zauważonym **10.** kierować się; ~***ing by her clothes*** sądząc po jej ubraniu **11.** mijać ⟨minąć⟩; ***one minute to*** ~ jeszcze minuta **12.** pasować (**with** do *G*) **13.** *infml* mówić ⟨powiedzieć⟩ **14.** zostać sprzedanym, *infml* pójść **15.** służyć: ***it*** ~***es to show that*** to dowodzi, że **16.** ~***!*** *SPORT* start! **17.** ***it*** ~***es without saying*** to się rozumie samo przez się **18.** ***the story*** ~***es that*** mówi się, że, fama głosi, że **19.** ***it is*** ~***ing to rain*** będzie padać; ***she is*** ~***ing to have a baby*** będzie miała dziecko; ***I am*** ~***ing to tell him*** powiem mu **II** (*went*; *gone*) *v/t* **1.** *distance*: przebywać ⟨-być⟩ **2.** ~ ***it alone*** zrobić to samemu **III** *s* **1.** próba *f*, podejście *n*; ***have a*** ~ ***at*** spróbować *G*; ***at one*** ~ od razu, za jednym zamachem **2.** ***we made a*** ~ ***of it*** *infml* udało nam się **3.** ***have a*** ~ ***at*** dogadywać *D*, krytykować *A*; **go ahead** *v/i* **1.** iść ⟨pójść⟩ przodem **2.** ~***!*** no dalej!; **go ahead with** *v/i* rozpoczynać ⟨-cząć⟩ realizację *G*; **go along with** *v/i* zgadzać ⟨zgodzić⟩ się z *I*; **go at** *v/i* rzucać ⟨-cić⟩ się na *A*, atakować ⟨za-⟩; **go away** *v/i* **1.** wyjeżdżać ⟨-jechać⟩ **2.** odchodzić

⟨odejść⟩ **3.** (*pain*) ustępować ⟨-tąpić⟩; **go back** *v/i* **1.** wracać ⟨wrócić⟩ **2.** zawracać ⟨-rócić⟩ **3.** *promise*: cofać ⟨-fnąć⟩ (**on** *A*); **go by** *v/i* **1.** (*time*) mijać ⟨minąć⟩ **2.** przechodzić ⟨przejść⟩ obok **3.** przejeżdżać ⟨-jechać⟩ obok; **go down** *v/i* **1.** schodzić ⟨zejść⟩ **2.** zjeżdżać ⟨zjechać⟩ **3.** spadać ⟨spaść⟩ **4.** iść ⟨pójść⟩ na dno **5.** (*sun*) zachodzić ⟨zajść⟩ **6.** *well, badly*: zostać przyjętym **7.** obniżać ⟨-żyć⟩ się **8.** *~ in history* przejść do historii; **go for** *v/i* **1.** lubić **2.** decydować ⟨z-⟩ się na *A*; *~ plan B* zdecydować się na plan B; **go in** *v/i* **1.** wchodzić ⟨wejść⟩ **2.** *fig* wkraczać ⟨-roczyć⟩; **go in for** *v/i* **1.** lubić **2.** zajmować ⟨-jąć⟩ się; **go off** *v/i* **1.** wychodzić ⟨wyjść⟩ **2.** odchodzić ⟨odejść⟩ **3.** odjeżdżać ⟨-jechać⟩ **4.** wyłączać ⟨-czyć⟩ się **5.** (*light*) gasnąć ⟨z-⟩ **6.** wybuchać ⟨-chnąć⟩ **7.** (*alarm clock*) włączać ⟨-czyć⟩ się **8.** (*food*) psuć ⟨ze-⟩ się **9.** ***I have gone off it*** zbrzydło mi to; **go on** *v/i* **1.** kontynuować; *~ talking* mówić dalej; ***he went on to say*** następnie powiedział; *~!* dalej! **2.** dziać się **3.** iść ⟨pójść⟩ dalej **4.** jechać ⟨po-⟩ dalej **5.** dobiegać; ***he is going on for 60*** dobiega sześćdziesiątki; ***it is going on for 5 o'clock*** dochodzi piąta **6.** (*lights*) zapalać ⟨-lić⟩ się; **go on at** *v/i* krytykować, czepiać się; **go out** *v/i* **1.** wychodzić ⟨wyjść⟩ **2.** (*lights*) gasnąć ⟨z-⟩ **3.** wyłączać ⟨-czyć⟩ się **4.** wychodzić ⟨wyjść⟩ z mody; **go out with** *v/i* chodzić z *I*; **go over** *v/i* **1.** podchodzić ⟨-dejść⟩ **2.** podjeżdżać ⟨-jechać⟩ **3.** sprawdzać ⟨-dzić⟩ **4.** *material*: powtarzać ⟨-tórzyć⟩ sobie; **go through** *v/i* **1.** przechodzić ⟨przejść⟩ przez *A* **2.** *fig* przechodzić ⟨przejść⟩, przeżywać ⟨-żyć⟩ **3.** sprawdzać ⟨-dzić⟩ **4.** zostawać ⟨-tać⟩ przyjętym; **go under** *v/i* **1.** tonąć ⟨za-⟩ **2.** *fig* uginać ⟨ugiąć⟩ się; **go up** *v/i* **1.** wchodzić ⟨wejść⟩ **2.** (*prices*) wzrastać ⟨-rosnąć⟩ **3.** *~ in flames* spłonąć; *~ in smoke* pójść z dymem; **go without** *v/i* obywać ⟨-być⟩ się bez *G*

goad [gəʊd] *v/t* **1.** prowokować ⟨s-⟩ (***into*** do *G*, ***to do s.th.*** do zrobienia czegoś) **2.** nakłaniać ⟨-łonić⟩ (***into*** do *G*, ***to do s.th.*** do zrobienia czegoś)

'go-a•head *s*: ***get the ~*** dostać zielone światło, dostać zgodę

goal [gəʊl] *s* **1.** cel *m* **2.** SPORT bramka *f*, gol *m*; ***score a ~*** strzelić gola; ***keep ~*** stać na bramce; ***the ~ area*** pole bramkowe; **goal•ie** ['gəʊlɪ] *s* SPORT *infml* bramkarz *m*

'goal•keep•er *s* SPORT bramkarz *m*

goat [gəʊt] *s* **1.** koza *f*; ***get s.o.'s ~*** wkurzać kogoś **2.** kozioł *m*

goa•tee [gəʊ'tiː] *s* kozia bródka *f*

gob•ble ['gɒbl] *v/t*: ***~ s.th.*** (**up**) pożerać coś, pochłaniać coś

'go-be•tween *s* pośrednik *m*

gob•let ['gɒblət] *s* kielich *m*

gob•lin ['gɒblɪn] *s* skrzat *m*, chochlik *m*

'go-cart *s* SPORT gokart *m*

god [gɒd] *s* **1.** bóg *m* **2.** bóstwo *n* **3.** bożek *m* **4.** *2* Bóg; ***so help me 2!*** tak mi dopomóż Bóg!; ***thank 2!*** Bogu dzięki!; **god-'aw•ful** *adj infml* okropny; **'god•child** *s* chrześniak *m*; **god-'dam•mit** *interj Am infml* a niech to szlag!; **'god•damned** *adj infml* cholernie; **'god•daugh•ter** *s* chrześniaczka *f*, córka *f* chrzestna

god•dess ['gɒdɪs] *s* bogini *f*

'god•fa•ther *s* chrzestny *m*, ojciec *m* chrzestny; **'god-fear•ing** *adj* bogobojny; **'god•for•sak•en** *adj* zapadły, zapomniany przez Boga i ludzi; **god•less** ['gɒdlɪs] *adj* bezbożny; **god•like** ['gɒdlaɪk] *adj* boski

god•ly ['gɒdlɪ] *adj* pobożny

'god•moth•er *s* chrzestna *f*, matka *f* chrzestna; **'god•pa•rent** *s* rodzic *m* chrzestny *m*, chrzestny *m*; **'god•send** *s* dar *m* niebios; ***to have come as a ~ for s.o.*** spaść komuś z nieba; **'god•son** *s* chrześniak *m*, syn *m* chrzestny

go-'get•ter *s*: ***be a ~*** być przebojowym

gog•gle ['gɒgl] *v/i infml* **1.** wybałuszać ⟨-szyć⟩ oczy **2.** gapić się z wybałuszonymi oczami (**at** na *A*); **gog•le-'eyed** *adj* z wybałuszonymi oczami; **gog•gles** ['gɒglz] *pl* **1.** gogle *pl* **2.** okularki *pl* pływackie **3.** okulary *pl* ochronne

'go-go danc•er *s* tancerka *f* go-go

go•ing ['gəʊɪŋ] **I** *s* **1.** wyjście *n* **2.** odejście *n* **3.** odjazd *m* **4.** tempo *n* **5.** ***when the ~ is good*** póki jest okazja, póki to jeszcze możliwe **II** *adj* **1.** aktualny **2.** ***a ~ concern*** prosperująca firma; **go-**

ings-on [gəʊɪŋz'ɒn] *pl infml* sprawy *pl*; ***there were some strange ~ there*** działy się tam dziwne rzeczy

gold [gəʊld] **I** *s* złoto *n* **II** *adj* złoty; **'gold dig•ger** *s* **1.** poszukiwacz *m* złota **2.** naciągaczka *f*; **'gold dust** *s* złoty pył *m*

gold•en ['gəʊldn] *adj* **1.** złoty; ***a ~ opportunity*** *fig* wspaniała okazja, wyjątkowa okazja **2.** złocisty; **gold•en 'hand•shake** *s* hojna odprawa *f*; **gold•en 'wed•ding (an•ni•ver•sa•ry)** *s* złote gody *pl*

'gold•field *s* pole *n* złotonośne; **'gold-fish** *s* **1.** złota rybka *f* **2.** karaś *m* złocisty; **'gold med•al** *s* złoty medal *m*; **'gold mine** *s* **1.** kopalnia *f* złota **2.** *fig* żyła *f* złota; **gold-'plat•ed** *adj* pozłacany; **'gold•smith** *s* złotnik *m*

golf [gɒlf] *SPORT* **I** *s* golf *m* **II** *adj* golfowy; **'golf ball** *s* piłka *f* golfowa; **'golf club** *s* **1.** klub *m* golfowy **2.** kij *m* golfowy; **'golf course** *s* pole *n* golfowe; **golf•er** ['gɒlfə] *s* golfista *m*

golf•ing ['gɒlfɪŋ] *s* gra *f* w golfa

'golf links *pl* pole *n* golfowe

Go•li•ath [gə'laɪəθ] *s* Goliat *m*

gone [gɒn] **I** *Past Participle* → **go II** *adj* **1.** ***he's ~*** **a)** wyjechał **b)** odszedł **2.** ***she's six months ~*** *Br infml* jest w szóstym miesiącu ciąży; **go•ner** ['gɒnə] *s*: ***be a ~*** *infml* nie nadawać się do niczego; ***he's a ~*** *infml* długo już nie pożyje

gon•na ['gɒnə] *infml contracted form* → ***going to***

goo [guː] *s* **1.** breja *f* **2.** *fig* sentymentalna szmira *f*

good [gʊd] **I** *adj* **1.** dobry; ***as ~ as*** równie dobry jak; ***have a ~ time*** dobrze się bawić; ***~ for colds*** dobry na przeziębienie; ***~ for one's health*** zdrowy; ***be so ~ as to fetch it*** bądź tak dobry i mi to przynieś; ***a ~ hour*** dobrą godzinę **2.** odpowiedni; ***in ~ time*** we właściwym czasie; ***all in ~ time*** wszystko w swoim czasie **3.** porządny **4.** ***a ~ many*** całkiem sporo; ***a ~ while*** dużo czasu **5.** ***~ and*** *infml* całkiem **6.** dokładny, wierny **7.** łagodny **II** *s* dobro *n*; ***for one's own ~*** dla własnego dobra; ***what ~ is it?*** co to da?; ***be no ~*** do niczego się nie nadawać; ***it is no ~ trying*** nie mo co próbować; ***be up to no ~*** **a)** kombinować **b)** rozrabiać

good•bye [gʊd'baɪ] **I** *s* pożegnanie *n*; ***say ~ to*** pożegnać się z *I* **II** *adj* pożegnalny; ***a ~ kiss*** pocałunek na do widzenia **III** *interj* **1.** do widzenia! **2.** do usłyszenia!

'good-for-no•thing I *s* **1.** nierób *m* **2.** nicpoń *m* **II** *adj* bezużyteczny

Good 'Fri•day *s REL* Wielki Piątek *m*

good-'heart•ed *adj* o dobrym sercu; ***be ~*** mieć dobre serce; **good-'hu-mo(u)red** *adj* **1.** wesoły **2.** przyjazny; **good-'look•ing** *adj* **1.** przystojny **2.** atrakcyjny **3.** ładny; **good-'na-tured** *adj* **1.** dobroduszny **2.** pogodny **3.** przyjacielski

G

good•ness ['gʊdnɪs] *s* **1.** dobroć *f* **2.** (***my***) ***~!***, ***~ gracious!*** mój Boże!, Boże drogi!; ***thank ~!*** dzięki Bogu!

goods [gʊdz] *pl* **1.** towary *pl*; ***a ~ lift*** winda towarowa; ***a ~ train*** pociąg towarowy **2.** dobytek *m*; ***~ and chattels*** majątek ruchomy, ruchomości

good-'tem•pered *adj* **1.** łagodny **2.** spokojny

good•'will *s* **1.** życzliwość *f* **2.** *ECON* renoma *f* firmy, dobre imię *n* **3.** *ECON* wartość *f* firmy

good•y-good•y ['gʊdɪgʊdɪ] **I** *s* świętoszek *m* **II** *adj* świętoszkowaty

goo•ey ['guːɪ] *adj infml* **1.** brejowaty, maziowaty **2.** ckliwy

goof [guːf] *infml* **I** *s* **1.** głupi błąd *m* **2.** palant *m*, matoł *m* **II** *v/i* dać plamę

goose [guːs] *pl geese* [giːs] *s* **1.** gęś *f*; ***cook s.o.'s ~*** *infml* załatwić kogoś **2.** *fig* głuptas *m*; **goose•ber•ry** ['gʊzbərɪ] *s* agrest *m*; **'goose bumps** *Am*, **'*goose pim•ples*** *pl* gęsia skórka *f*; **'goose step** *s* krok *m* defiladowy

Gor•di•an knot [gɔːdɪə'nɒt]: ***cut the ~*** przeciąć węzeł gordyjski

gore [gɔː] *s* krew *f*

gorge [gɔːdʒ] **I** *s* **1.** (*river*) przełom *m* **2.** wąwóz *m* **II** *v/i* obżerać ⟨obeżreć⟩ się (***on*** *I*) **III** *v/t* **~ o.s.** obżerać ⟨obeżreć⟩ się (***on*** *I*)

gor•geous ['gɔːdʒəs] *adj infml* **1.** cudowny, wspaniały **2.** zachwycający

go•ril•la [gə'rɪlə] *s* **1.** goryl *m* **2.** *fig* goryl *m*, osiłek *m*

gor•y ['gɔːrɪ] *adj* **1.** krwawy **2.** pełen przemocy

gosh [gɒʃ] *interj infml* o rety!
gos•pel ['gɒspl] *s* **1.** ewangelia *f*, dobra nowina *f*; ***the ~ truth*** *fig* szczera prawda, święta prawda **2.** MUS gospel *m*
gos•sip ['gɒsɪp] **I** *s* **1.** plotki *pl*; ***have a ~*** plotkować **2.** plotkarz *m* **II** *v/i* plotkować; '**gos•sip col•umn** *s* rubryka *f* towarzyska; '**gos•sip col•um•nist** *s* redaktor *m* rubryki towarzyskiej; **gos•sip•y** ['gɒsɪpɪ] *adj* **1.** plotkarski **2.** lubiący plotkować
got [gɒt] *Past Simple and Past Participle* → ***get***
Goth•ic ['gɒθɪk] **I** *adj* gotycki; ***a ~ novel*** powieść gotycka **II** *s* ARCHIT gotyk *m*
got•ta ['gɒtə] *infml contracted form* → **got to**, **got a**
got•ten ['gɒtn] *Am Past Participle* → ***get***
gou•lash ['guːlæʃ] *s* COOK gulasz *m*
gov•ern ['gʌvən] **I** *v/t* **1.** rządzić **2.** regulować **3.** kierować **4.** ***be ~ed by*** zależeć od *G* **II** *v/i* rządzić, sprawować władzę
gov•ern•ing ['gʌvənɪŋ] *adj* **1.** rządzący **2.** *body*: zarządzający **3.** *factor*: decydujący; **gov•ern•ment** ['gʌvəmənt] *s* **1.** rząd *m*; ***a ~ spokesman*** rzecznik rządu **2.** rządy *pl* **3.** rządzenie *n*, sprawowanie *n* władzy **4.** państwo *n*; ***~ monopoly*** monopol rządowy, monopol państwowy; **gov•ernment•al** ['gʌvən'mentl] *adj* rządowy; **gov•er•nor** ['gʌvənə] *s* **1.** gubernator *m* **2.** członek *m* zarządu **3.** prezes *m* **4.** naczelnik *m*
gown [gaʊn] *s* **1.** suknia *f* **2.** toga *f* **3.** fartuch *m* **4.** ***a dressing ~*** szlafrok *m*
grab [græb] **I** *v/t* **1.** łapać ⟨z-⟩, chwytać ⟨-wycić⟩ **2.** *opportunity*: korzystać ⟨s-⟩ z *G* **3.** *attention*: przyciągać ⟨-gnąć⟩ **II** *v/i* rzucać ⟨-cić⟩ się (***at*** na *A*) **III** *s* **1.** ***make a ~ at s.th.*** próbować coś chwycić **2.** ***be up for ~s*** *infml* być do wzięcia
grace [greɪs] **I** *s* **1.** wdzięk *m* **2.** gracja *f* **3.** łaska *f*, względy *pl* **4.** ***a month's ~*** dodatkowy miesiąc **5.** ***say ~*** odmówić modlitwę (przed posiłkiem) **II** *v/t* **1.** ozdabiać ⟨-dobić⟩ **2.** zaszczycać ⟨-cić⟩ **3.** uświetniać ⟨-nić⟩; **grace•ful** ['greɪsfəl] *adj* **1.** pełen wdzięku **2.** pełen gracji **3.** elegancki; **grace•ful•ly** ['greɪsfəlɪ] *adv* **1.** z wdziękiem **2.** z gracją **3.** elegancko
gra•cious ['greɪʃəs] **I** *adj* **1.** uprzejmy **2.** łaskawy **II** *interj* ***good ~!***, ***~ me!*** Boże jedyny!
gra•da•tion [grə'deɪʃn] *s* **1.** gradacja *f* **2.** stopniowanie *n*
grade [greɪd] **I** *s* **1.** stopień *m* **2.** klasa *f* **3.** gatunek *m* **4.** (*hierarchy*) szczebel *m* **5.** poziom *m* **6.** ***make the ~*** sprostać wymaganiom **II** *v/t* **1.** oceniać ⟨-nić⟩ **2.** dzielić ⟨po-⟩; '**grade crossing** *s Am* przejazd *m* kolejowy; '**grade school** *s Am infml* szkoła *f* podstawowa
grad•u•al ['grædʒʊəl] *adj* **1.** stopniowy **2.** łagodny; **grad•u•al•ly** ['grædʒʊəlɪ] *adv* stopniowo
grad•u•ate I ['grædʒʊət] *s* absolwent *m* **II** ['grædʒʊət] *adj* **1.** magisterski **2.** podyplomowy **III** ['grædʒʊeɪt] *v/i* **1.** kończyć ⟨u-⟩ studia, otrzymywać ⟨-mać⟩ dyplom **2.** kończyć ⟨u-⟩ (***from*** *A*); '**grad•u•ate school** *s* **1.** (uzupełniające) studia *pl* magisterskie **2.** studia *pl* doktoranckie
grad•u•a•tion [grædʒʊ'eɪʃn] *s* **1.** ukończenie *n* studiów **2.** uroczystość *f* wręczenia dyplomów; **grad•u•a•tion** '**cer•e•mon•y** *s* uroczystość *f* wręczenia dyplomów
grain [greɪn] *s* **1.** zboże *n* **2.** zboża *pl* **3.** ziarno *n* **4.** ziarnko *n* **5.** *sugar*: kryształek *m* **6.** *fig* odrobina *f*; ***there's not a ~ of truth in it*** nie ma w tym krzty prawdy
gram [græm] *s* gram *m*
gram•mar ['græmə] *s* gramatyka *f*; ***bad ~*** błędy gramatyczne; ***a ~ book*** podręcznik do gramatyki; **gram•mat•i•cal** [grə'mætɪkl] *adj* gramatyczny; **gram•mat•i•cal•ly** [grə'mætɪklɪ] *adv* **1.** gramatycznie **2.** pod względem gramatycznym
grand [grænd] **I** *adj* **1.** wielki **2.** okazały **3.** doniosły **4.** wytworny **5.** główny **6.** ***the ~ total*** łączna suma, końcowa suma **II** *s* **1.** MUS fortepian *m* **2.** *Am infml* tysiąc *m*, tysiak *m*, patyk *m*
gran•dad *s* dziadek *m*
'**grand•child** *s* **1.** wnuk *m* **2.** wnuczka *f*; '**grand•dad** *s* dziadek *m*; '**grand•daugh•ter** *s* wnuczka *f*

gran•deur ['grændʒə] *s* **1.** wspaniałość *f*; ***delusions of ~*** mania wielkości **2.** okazałość *f* **3.** majestatyczność *f*
'**grand•fa•ther** *s* dziadek *m*; '**grand•fa•ther clock** *s* zegar *m* szafkowy
gran•di•ose ['grændɪəʊs] *adj* **1.** wielki **2.** ambitny **3.** górnolotny **4.** okazały
grand 'jur•y *s* JUR wielka ława *f* przysięgłych; '**grand•ma** *s* babcia *f*, babunia *f*; '**grand•moth•er** *s* babcia *f*, babka *f*; '**grand•pa** *s* dziadziuś *m*; '**grand•par•ents** *pl* dziadkowie *pl*; **grand pi•'an•o** *s* fortepian *m*; '**grand•son** *s* wnuk *m*; '**grand•stand** *s* SPORT trybuna *f* główna
gran•ite ['grænɪt] *s* GEOL granit *m*
gran•ny ['grænɪ] *s* babcia *f*, babunia *f*
grant [grænt] **I** *v/t* **1.** przyznawać ⟨-nać⟩ **2.** dawać ⟨dać⟩; ***be ~ed a divorce*** otrzymać rozwód; ***be ~ed permission*** uzyskać zgodę **3.** spełniać ⟨-nić⟩ **4.** udzielać ⟨-lić⟩ zgody na *A* **5.** ***I ~ you that*** przyznaję, że **6.** ***take s.th. for ~ed*** uważać coś za oczywiste **II** *s* **1.** stypendium *n* **2.** grant *m* **3.** dotacja *f* **4.** subwencja *f*
gran•u•lar ['grænjʊlə] *adj* **1.** ziarnisty **2.** granulowany
gran•ule ['grænju:l] *s* **1.** granulka *f* **2.** kryształek *m*
grape [greɪp] *s* winogrono *n*
'**grape•fruit** *s* grejpfrut *m*; '**grape•fruit juice** *s* sok *m* grejpfrutowy
grape•vine ['greɪpvaɪn] *s* **1.** winorośl *f* **2.** poczta *f* pantoflowa; ***I heard on the ~ that*** słyszałem, że
graph [græf] **I** *s* **1.** MATH graf *m* **2.** wykres *m* **II** *v/t* przedstawiać ⟨-wić⟩ na wykresie
graph•ic ['græfɪk] *adj* **1.** graficzny **2.** *fig* obrazowy, plastyczny **3.** ***a ~ artist*** artysta grafik; ***~ arts*** grafika; **graph•ic•al•ly** ['græfɪklɪ] *adv* **1.** graficznie **2.** *fig* obrazowo, plastycznie
graph•ic de'sign *s* grafika *f*; **graph•ic de•'sign•er** *s* grafik *m*
'**graph•ics card** *s* INF karta *f* graficzna
graph•ite ['græfaɪt] *s* grafit *m*
graph•ol•o•gy [græ'fɒlədʒɪ] *s* grafologia *f*
grap•ple ['græpl] *v/i* **1.** zmagać się, borykać się (***with*** z *I*) **2.** mocować się (***with*** z *I*)
grasp [græsp] **I** *v/t* **1.** chwytać ⟨-wycić⟩ **2.** *opportunity*: korzystać ⟨s-⟩ z *G* **3.** pojmować ⟨-jąć⟩ **II** *v/i* łapać ⟨z-⟩ (***at*** *A*), chwytać ⟨-wycić⟩ (***at*** za *A*) **III** *s* **1.** chwyt *m* **2.** uścisk *m* **3.** ***have a good ~ of*** dobrze znać *A*; ***be beyond s.o.'s ~*** być niepojętym dla kogoś, być poza zasięgiem czyichś możliwości **8.** zasięg *m*; **grasp•ing** ['græspɪŋ] *adj* pazerny
grass [græs] **I** *s* **1.** trawa *f*; ***not let the ~ grow under one's feet*** *fig* nie zasypiać gruszek w popiele **2.** trawnik *m*; ***keep off the ~!*** nie deptać trawników! **3.** *infml* trawka *f* **4.** *Br infml* kapuś *m* **II** *v/i Br infml* sypać ⟨-pnąć⟩ (***on*** *A*); **grass 'wid•ow** *s* słomiana wdowa *f*; **grass 'wid•ow•er** *s* słomiany wdowiec *m*
gras•sy ['græsɪ] *adj* trawiasty
grate[1] [greɪt] **I** *s* **1.** krata *f* **2.** ruszt *m* **II** *v/t* kratować ⟨za-⟩
grate[2] [~] **I** *v/t* **1.** trzeć ⟨ze-⟩ **2.** ucierać ⟨utrzeć⟩ **II** *v/i* **1.** skrzypieć ⟨za-⟩ **2.** zgrzytać ⟨za-⟩ **3.** *fig* drażnić; ***~ on s.o.'s nerves*** działać komuś na nerwy
grate•ful ['greɪtfəl] *adj* wdzięczny; (***to s.o. for*** komuś za *A*); **grate•ful•ly** ['greɪtfəlɪ] *adv* z wdzięcznością
grat•i•fi•ca•tion [grætɪfɪ'keɪʃn] *s* **1.** zaspokojenie *n* **2.** satysfakcja *f* **3.** zadowolenie *n* **2.** **grat•i•fy** ['grætɪfaɪ] *v/t* **1.** cieszyć ⟨u-⟩, radować ⟨u-⟩; ***I am gratified to hear that*** miło mi słyszeć, że **2.** spełniać ⟨-nić⟩, zaspokajać ⟨-koić⟩; **grat•i•fy•ing** ['grætɪfaɪɪŋ] *adj* **1.** przyjemny, sprawiający przyjemność **2.** dający satysfakcję
grat•ing ['greɪtɪŋ] *s* **1.** krata *f* **2.** okratowanie *n*
grat•i•tude ['grætɪtju:d] *s* wdzięczność *f*; ***in ~ for*** z wdzięczności za *A*
gra•tu•i•tous [grə'tju:ɪtəs] *adj* **1.** bezpłatny, nieodpłatny **2.** nieuzasadniony; **gra•tu•i•ty** [grə'tju:ətɪ] *s* **1.** napiwek *m* **2.** *Br* odprawa *f* (emerytalna)
grave[1] [greɪv] *adj* poważny
grave[2] [~] *s* **1.** grób *m*; ***dig one's own ~*** *fig* kopać sobie grób; ***turn in one's ~*** *fig* przewracać się w grobie **2.** mogiła *f*; '**grave•dig•ger** *s* grabarz *m*
grav•el ['grævl] **I** *s* żwir *m* **II** *v/t* żwirować, wysypywać ⟨-pać⟩ żwirem;

G

a ~(l)led path droga żwirowa; ***a ~ pit*** żwirownia
grave•ly ['greɪvlɪ] *adv* **1.** poważnie **2.** ogromnie
'grave•stone *s* **1.** nagrobek *m* **2.** płyta *f* nagrobna; **'grave•yard** *s* cmentarz *m*
grav•i•tate ['grævɪteɪt] *v/i* skłaniać ⟨-łonić⟩ się (***toward/to*** ku *D*); **grav•i•ta•tion** [grævɪ'teɪʃn] *s PHYS* grawitacja *f*, ciążenie *n*; **grav•i•ta•tion•al** [grævɪ'teɪʃnl] *adj PHYS* grawitacyjny; ***~ force, ~ pull*** siła ciążenia; **grav•i•ta•tion•al 'field** *s PHYS* pole *n* grawitacyjne; **grav•i•ty** ['grævətɪ] *s* **1.** powaga *f* **2.** *PHYS* ciążenie *n*

G

gray [greɪ] *Am* → ***grey***
graze[1] [greɪz] *v/i* paść się
graze[2] [~] **I** *v/t* **1.** *knee*: obcierać ⟨obetrzeć⟩ **2.** muskać ⟨-snąć⟩ **II** *s* obtarcie *n*
grease [gri:s] **I** *s* **1.** *COOK* tłuszcz *m* **2.** *TECH* smar *m* **II** *v/t* smarować ⟨na-⟩; **greas•y** ['gri:sɪ] *adj* **1.** tłusty **2.** przetłuszczający się; **greasy 'spoon** *s infml* garkuchnia *f*
great [greɪt] *adj* **1.** wielki; ***a ~ many*** bardzo wiele **2.** świetny; ***be ~ at*** *infml* być świetnym w *L* **3.** znakomity **4.** wybitny **5.** ogromny **6.** potężny **7.** ważny; **great-'aunt** *s* **1.** cioteczna babka *f* **2.** stryjeczna babka *f*; **Great 'Brit•ain** *s* Wielka Brytania *f*; **great-'grand•child** *s* prawnuk *m*; **great-'grand•daugh•ter** *s* prawnuczka *f*; **great-'grand•fa•ther** *s* **1.** pradziadek *m* **2.** *lit* pradziad *m*; **great-'grand•moth•er** *s* prababka *f*, prababcia *f*; **great-'grand•par•ents** *pl* pradziadkowie *pl*; **great-'grand•son** *s* prawnuk *m*; **great•ly** ['greɪtlɪ] *adv* **1.** bardzo **2.** wielce **3.** znacznie **4.** niezwykle
great•ness ['greɪtnɪs] *s* wielkość *f*
great-'un•cle *s* **1.** cioteczny dziadek *m* **2.** stryjeczny dziadek *m*
Greece [gri:s] *s* Grecja *f*
greed [gri:d] *s* **1.** chciwość *f*, zachłanność *f*; ***~ for power*** żądza władzy **2.** łakomstwo *n*; **greed•i•ly** ['gri:dɪlɪ] *adv* **1.** łakomie **2.** chciwie, zachłannie; **greed•i•ness** ['gri:dɪnɪs] → ***greed***; **greed•y** ['gri:dɪ] *adj* **1.** chciwy, zachłanny; ***~ for power*** żądny władzy **2.** łakomy
Greek [gri:k] **I** *adj* grecki **II** *s* **1.** Grek *m*, Greczynka *f* **2.** (*language*) grecki *m*; ***it's all ~ to me*** to dla mnie chińszczyzna
green [gri:n] **I** *adj* **1.** zielony; ***have ~ fingers, have a ~ thumb*** *Am* mieć dobrą rękę do roślin; ***the lights are ~*** jest zielone światło; ***give s.o. the ~ light*** *fig* dać komuś zielone światło; ***~ with envy*** zielony z zazdrości **2.** *infml* zielony, niedoświadczony **II** *s* **1.** zieleń *f*, zielony *m*; ***dressed in ~*** ubrany na zielono; ***the lights are at ~*** jest zielone światło **2.** ***~s*** *Br* warzywa zielone, zielenina; **'green•back** *s* (*dollar*) *Am infml* zielony *m*; **green 'beans** *pl* fasolka *f* szparagowa; **'green belt** *s* pas *m* zieleni; **green 'card** *s* zielona karta *f*
green•er•y ['gri:nərɪ] *s* zieleń *f*
'green•field site *s* teren *m* niezabudowany; **'green•fly** *s* mszyca *f*; **'green•gro•cer's** *s* **1.** warzywniak *m* **2.** sklep *m* owocowo-warzywny; **'green•horn** *s infml* żółtodziób *m*; **'green•house** *s* **1.** szklarnia *f* **2.** cieplarnia *f*; **'green•house ef•fect** *s* efekt *m* cieplarniany; **'green•house gas** *s* gaz *m* cieplarniany; **green•ish** ['gri:nɪʃ] *adj* zielonkawy
Green•land ['gri:nlənd] *s* Grenlandia *f*
'green light *s* zielone światło *n*; **green 'pep•per** *s* zielona papryka *f*
Green•wich Mean Time [grenɪtʃ'mi:ntaɪm] *s* czas *m* uniwersalny, czas *m* Greenwich
greet [gri:t] *v/t* **1.** witać ⟨przy-⟩ się z *I* **2.** witać ⟨po-⟩ **3.** pozdrawiać ⟨-rowić⟩ **4.** przyjmować ⟨-jąć⟩
greet•ing ['gri:tɪŋ] *s* **1.** powitanie *n* **2.** przywitanie *n*; ***exchange ~s*** przywitać się **3.** ***~s*** pozdrowienia **4.** ***~s*** życzenia; **'greet•ings card** *s* kartka *f* z życzeniami
grem•lin ['gremlɪn] *s* chochlik *m*
gre•nade [grɪ'neɪd] *s* (*weapon*) granat *m*
grew [gru:] *Past Simple* → ***grow***
grey [greɪ] **I** *adj* **1.** szary; ***be a ~ area*** *fig* **a)** być niezbadanym **b)** być niejasnym; **2.** siwy **3.** *fig* bezbarwny **II** *s* (*colour*) szary *m*, szarość *f*; ***dressed in ~*** ubrany na szaro **III** *v/i* siwieć ⟨po-⟩; ***~ing*** siwiejący; **grey-'haired** [greɪ'-

hed] *adj* siwy, siwowłosy; '**grey-hound** *s* chart *m*; **grey•ish** ['greɪɪʃ] *adj* szarawy
grid [grɪd] *s* **1.** krata *f* **2.** GEOGR siatka *f* **3.** *streets*: sieć *f* **4.** TECH sieć *f* **5.** ruszt *m*
grief [griːf] *s* **1.** smutek *m* **2.** żal *m* **3.** zmartwienia *pl* **4.** ***come to ~*** zakończyć się niepowodzeniem, lec w gruzach; '**grief-strick•en** *adj* pogrążony w smutku
griev•ance ['griːvəns] *s* **1.** żal *m*, uraza *f*; ***nurse a ~ against*** mieć żal do *G*, chować urazę do *G* **2.** skarga *f*; **grieve** [griːv] **I** *v/t* smucić ⟨za-⟩; ***it ~s me that*** bardzo mi przykro, że **II** *v/i* rozpaczać; ***~ for*** rozpaczać po stracie *G*, opłakiwać *A*; **griev•ous** ['griːvəs] *adj* **1.** poważny **2.** *injustice*: wielki, bolesny
grill [grɪl] **I** *s* **1.** grill *m* **2.** *Br* opiekacz *m* **3.** potrawa *f* z grilla **II** *v/t* **1.** grillować, piec ⟨u-⟩ na grillu **2.** (*interrogate*) maglować (***about*** o *A*) **III** *v/i* piec się na grillu
grille [grɪl] *s* krata *f*
gril•ling ['grɪlɪŋ] *s*: ***give s.o. a ~ about*** wypytywać kogoś (***about*** o *A*)
'**grill•room** *s* bar *m* z grillem
grim [grɪm] *adj* **1.** ponury **2.** smętny **3.** zacięty **4.** *Br infml* nędzny
gri•mace [grɪ'meɪs] **I** *s* grymas *m* **II** *v/i* krzywić ⟨s-⟩ się
grime [graɪm] **I** *s* brud *m* **II** *v/t* brudzić ⟨u-⟩
grim•ly ['grɪmlɪ] *adv* ponuro
grim•y ['graɪmɪ] *adj* brudny
grin [grɪn] **I** *v/i* **1.** uśmiechać ⟨-chnąć⟩ się (szeroko) (***at*** do *G*); ***~ and bear it*** robić dobrą minę do złej gry **2.** szczerzyć ⟨wy-⟩ zęby w uśmiechu **II** *s* (szeroki) uśmiech *m*
grind [graɪnd] **I** (*ground*; *ground*) *v/t* **1.** mielić ⟨z-⟩ **2.** kruszyć ⟨roz-⟩ **3.** rozdrabniać ⟨-robnić⟩ **4.** tłuc ⟨u-⟩ **5.** ostrzyć ⟨na-⟩, szlifować ⟨wy-⟩ **6.** ***~ one's teeth*** zgrzytać zębami **II** *s* **1.** zgrzyt *m* **2.** *infml* harówka *f*, mordęga *f*; **grind•er** ['graɪndə] *s* **1.** młynek *m* **2.** ostrzałka *f* **3.** ząb *m* trzonowy; '**grind•stone** *s* kamień *m* szlifierski; ***keep one's nose to the ~*** *infml* harować jak wół; **grind•ing** ['graɪndɪŋ] **I** *s* zgrzytanie *n* **II** *adj* zgrzytliwy
grip [grɪp] **I** *s* **1.** chwyt *m*; ***get to ~s with*** uporać się z *I*, dać sobie radę z *I* **2.** uścisk *m* **3.** kontrola *f*; ***have a ~ on s.th.*** trzymać coś w garści **4.** uchwyt *m*, rączka *f* **II** *v/t* **1.** chwytać ⟨-wycić⟩, łapać ⟨z-⟩ **2.** *audience*: porywać ⟨-rwać⟩ **3.** (*book*) wciągać ⟨-gnąć⟩
gripe [graɪp] *infml* **I** *v/i* biadolić; ***~ at*** skarżyć się na *A*, użalać się na *A* **II** *s* powód *m* do narzekań
grip•ping ['grɪpɪŋ] *adj* **1.** porywający **2.** wciągający
gris•ly ['grɪzlɪ] *adj* makabryczny
grit [grɪt] **I** *s* **1.** piasek *m* **2.** GEOL gruboziarnisty piaskowiec *m* **3.** *fig* wytrwałość *f*, determinacja *f* **II** *v/t* **1.** posypywać ⟨-pać⟩ piaskiem **2.** ***~ one's teeth*** zacisnąć zęby; **grit•ty** ['grɪtɪ] *adj* **1.** piaszczysty **2.** zapiaszczony **3.** *fig* twardy **4.** naturalistyczny
griz•zle ['grɪzl] *v/i Br infml* **1.** mazać się **2.** marudzić
groan [grəʊn] **I** *v/i* **1.** jęczeć ⟨jęknąć, za-⟩ **2.** *fig* jęczeć **II** *s* jęk *m*
gro•cer ['grəʊsə] *s* właściciel *m* sklepu spożywczego, sklepikarz *m*; **gro•cer•ies** ['grəʊsərɪz] *pl* artykuły *pl* spożywcze; '**gro•cer•y store** *s* sklep *m* spożywczy
grog•gy ['grɒgɪ] *adj infml* półprzytomny, *infml* przymulony
groin [grɔɪn] *s* pachwina *f*
groom [gruːm] **I** *s* **1.** stajenny *m* **2.** pan *m* młody **II** *v/t* **1.** *horses*: oporządzać ⟨-dzić⟩ **2.** pielęgnować **3.** przygotowywać ⟨-tować⟩
groove [gruːv] **I** *s* **1.** rowek *m*, wyżłobienie *n* **2.** rutyna *f* **II** *v/t* żłobić ⟨wy-⟩; **groov•y** ['gruːvɪ] *adj infml* **1.** fajny **2.** trendy
grope [grəʊp] **I** *v/i* **1.** szukać po omacku (***for*** *G*) **2.** iść po omacku **II** *v/t* ***~ one's way*** iść po omacku
gross [grəʊs] **I** *adj* **1.** brutto **2.** rażący; ***~ negligence*** rażące zaniedbanie **3.** ***~!*** *infml* ohyda! **4.** ordynarny, grubiański **5.** spasiony, gruby **II** *s* (*12 dozens*) gros *m* **III** *v/t* **1.** zarabiać ⟨-robić⟩ brutto **2.** przynosić ⟨-nieść⟩ dochód brutto; **gross out** *v/t Am infml* przyprawiać ⟨-wić⟩ o mdłości
gross do•mes•tic 'prod•uct *s* ECON produkt *m* krajowy brutto; **gross•ly** ['grəʊslɪ] *adv* **1.** grubo **2.** rażąco

G

3. okropnie 4. wielce; **gross na•tion•al 'prod•uct** *s ECON* produkt *m* narodowy brutto
gro•tesque [grəʊ'tesk] *adj* groteskowy
grot•to ['grɒtəʊ] *pl -toes, -tos* [~təʊz] *s* 1. grota *f* 2. pieczara *f*
grot•ty ['grɒtɪ] *adj Br infml* 1. paskudny 2. podły
grouch [graʊtʃ] *infml* I *v/i* zrzędzić II *s* zrzęda *m*; **grouch•y** ['graʊtʃɪ] *adj infml* zrzędliwy
ground[1] [graʊnd] I *s* 1. ziemia *f*; ***above ~*** nad ziemią; ***below ~*** pod ziemią; ***fall to the ~*** spaść na ziemię; ***break new ~*** otworzyć nowe horyzonty; ***~ forces*** siły lądowe 2. teren *m*; ***gain ~*** (*product*) stawać się coraz popularniejszy 3. obszar *m* 4. *SPORT* boisko *n* 5. podstawa *f*; ***on the ~ of*** ze względu na *A*; ***on the ~ that there was no evidence*** z braku dowodów; ***on health ~s*** z przyczyn zdrowotnych 6. ***hold one's ~, stand one's ~*** nie ustępować 7. *Am* uziemienie *n* II *v/t* 1. ***be ~ed*** (*plane*) nie móc wystartować 2. *infml* dawać ⟨dać⟩ szlaban 3. *Am* uziemiać ⟨-mić⟩ III *v/i* osiadać ⟨osiąść⟩ na mieliźnie
ground[2] [~] I *Past Simple and Past Participle* → **grind** II *adj meat*: mielony
'ground•break•ing *adj* nowatorski, pionierski; **'ground con•trol** *s* kontrola *f* naziemna; **'ground crew** *s* obsługa *f* naziemna; **'ground for•ces** *pl* siły *pl* lądowe; **'ground frost** *s* przygruntowy przymrozek *m*; **'ground•hog** *s* świstak *m* amerykański
ground•ing ['graʊndɪŋ] *s* znajomość *m* podstaw (**in** *G*)
ground•less ['graʊndlɪs] *adj* 1. bezpodstawny 2. nieuzasadniony
'ground•nut *s* orzeszek *m* ziemny; **'ground plan** *s* 1. plan *m* parteru 2. *fig* ogólny plan *m* (działania); **'ground rules** *pl* ogólne zasady *pl*; **'ground staff** *s* personel *m* naziemny; **'ground wa•ter** *s GEOL* wody *pl* gruntowe; **'ground•work** *s* prace *pl* przygotowawcze
group [gruːp] I *s* 1. grupa *f* 2. *ECON* grupa *f* kapitałowa II *v/t* grupować ⟨z-, po-⟩ III *v/i* grupować ⟨z-⟩ się, zbierać ⟨zebrać⟩ się IV *adj* grupowy; ***~ dynamics*** dynamika grupy; ***~ sex*** seks grupowy
group•ie ['gruːpɪ] *s* (*girl*) *infml* groupie *f*; **group•ing** ['gruːpɪŋ] *s* 1. ugrupowanie *n* 2. grupa *f*
group 'ther•a•py *s* terapia *f* grupowa
grove [grəʊv] *s* zagajnik *m*, gaj *m*
grov•el ['grɒvl] *v/i fig* płaszczyć się; **grov•el•(l)er** ['grɒvələ] *s* lizus *m*; **grov•el•(l)ing** ['grɒvəlɪŋ] *adj* uniżony
grow [grəʊ] I (*grew*; *grown*) *v/i* 1. rosnąć ⟨u-⟩ (**out of** z *G*) 2. rozwijać ⟨-winąć⟩ się 3. wzrastać ⟨-rosnąć⟩, narastać ⟨-rosnąć⟩ 4. stawać ⟨stać⟩ się; ***~ less popular*** tracić na popularności; ***~ old*** starzeć się; ***~ to like s.o.*** polubić kogoś II (*grew*; *grown*) *v/t* 1. hodować ⟨wy-⟩ 2. uprawiać 3. *beard*: zapuszczać ⟨-puścić⟩; **grow up** *v/i* 1. rosnąć ⟨u-⟩ 2. dorastać ⟨-rosnąć⟩ 3. rozwijać ⟨-winąć⟩ się
grow•er ['grəʊə] *s* hodowca *m*
growl [graʊl] I *v/i* 1. warczeć ⟨-rknąć⟩ 2. (*thunder*) rozlegać ⟨-lec⟩ się II *v/t* 1. warczeć ⟨-rknąć⟩ 2. *insult*: rzucać ⟨-cić⟩ III *s* 1. warknięcie *n* 2. pomruk *m*
grown [grəʊn] I *Past Participle* → **grow** II *adj* 1. dorosły 2. dla dorosłych; **grown-up** ['grəʊnʌp] I *s* dorosły *m* II *adj* dorosły
growth [grəʊθ] *s* 1. wzrost *m* 2. *MED* narośl *f* 3. *MED* guz *m* 4. *BIOL* odrost *m*; **growth 'in•dus•try** *s* dynamicznie rozwijająca się branża *f*; **'growth rate** *s* tempo *n* wzrostu
grudge [grʌdʒ] I *s* uraza *f*; ***bear s.o. a ~*** mieć coś komuś za złe, żywić do kogoś urazę; ***he has a ~ against the whole world*** ma pretensje do całego świata II *v/t* 1. żałować ⟨po-⟩; ***~ s.o. s.th.*** pożałować komuś czegoś 2. ***~ doing s.th.*** robić coś niechętnie; **grudg•ing** ['grʌdʒɪŋ] *adj* niechętny; **grudg•ing•ly** ['grʌdʒɪŋlɪ] *adv* niechętnie
grue•some ['gruːsəm] *adj* 1. makabryczny 2. straszliwy 3. przerażający
gruff [grʌf] *adj* szorstki
grum•ble ['grʌmbl] I *v/i* 1. narzekać 2. zrzędzić 3. (*thunder*) rozlegać ⟨-lec⟩ się II *s* powód *m* do narzekań; **grum•bler** ['grʌmblə] *s infml* zrzęda *m*
grump•y ['grʌmpɪ] *adj* 1. zrzędliwy 2. gderliwy 3. opryskliwy

grunt [grʌnt] **I** *v/i* **1.** chrząkać ⟨-knąć⟩ **2.** stękać ⟨-knąć⟩ **3.** burczeć ⟨-rknąć⟩ **II** *v/t* burknąć **III** *s* **1.** chrząknięcie *n* **2.** stęknięcie *n* **3.** burknięcie *n*

guar•an•tee [gærən'tiː] **I** *s* **1.** gwarancja *f*; ***the watch is still under ~*** zegarek jest wciąż na gwarancji; ***a ~ card*** karta gwarancyjna **2.** poręczenie *n* **3.** kaucja *f* **4.** zabezpieczenie *n* **II** *v/t* **1.** udzielać ⟨-lić⟩ gwarancji na *A* **2.** gwarantować ⟨za-⟩ **3.** zapewniać ⟨-nić⟩

guard [gɑːd] **I** *v/t* **1.** chronić (***against*** przed *I*) **2.** strzec (***against*** przed *I*); ***a closely ~ed secret*** pilnie strzeżona tajemnica **3.** pilnować **II** *s* **1.** strażnik *m* **2.** wartownik *m* **3.** straż *f* **4.** warta *f*; ***be on ~*** stać na warcie **5.** *Br* kierownik *m* pociągu **6.** gwardia *f*; ***the ~ of honour*** gwardia honorowa **7.** czujność *f*; ***be on (off) one's ~*** być (nie być) czujnym **8.** *SPORT* garda *f*; **guard against** *v/i* **1.** wystrzegać się **2.** chronić się przed *I*; **'guard dog** *s* pies *m* stróżujący; **'guard du•ty** *s* warta *f*; ***be on ~*** stać na warcie; **guard•ed** ['gɑːdɪd] *adj* **1.** strzeżony **2.** ostrożny **3.** powściągliwy; **'guard•house** *s* **1.** wartownia *f* **2.** strażnica *f*

guard•i•an ['gɑːdɪən] *s* **1.** strażnik *m* **2.** *JUR* opiekun *m*; **guard•i•an 'an•gel** *s* anioł *m* stróż; **guard•i•an•ship** ['gɑːdɪənʃɪp] *s JUR* opieka *f*

'guard•rail *s* **1.** barierka *f* **2.** bariera *f* **3.** poręcz *f*

'guards•man *pl -men s Br* gwardzista *m*

Gua•te•ma•la [gwɑːtə'mɑːlə] *s* Gwatemala *f*

guer•ril•la [gə'rɪlə] *s* partyzant *m*; **guer•ril•la 'war•fare** *s* wojna *f* partyzancka

guess [ges] **I** *v/t* **1.** zgadywać ⟨-dnąć⟩, odgadywać ⟨-dnąć⟩ **2.** przewidywać ⟨-dzieć⟩ **3.** *Am infml* myśleć **II** *v/i* **1.** zgadywać ⟨-dnąć⟩; ***a ~ing game*** zgadywanka **2.** domyślać ⟨-lić⟩ się **III** *s* **1.** ***have a ~!*** zgadnij!; ***I'll give you three ~es*** zgaduj, do trzech razy sztuka; ***at a ~*** na oko **2.** przypuszczenie *n* **3.** domysł *m*; **guess•ti•mate** ['gestɪmət] *s infml* **1.** szacunkowa ocena *f* **2.** przypuszczenia *pl*; **'guess•work** *s* przypuszczenia *pl*, domysły *pl*

guest [gest] **I** *s* gość *m* **II** *adj* gościnny; ***a ~ list*** lista gości; ***a ~ speaker*** zaproszony mówca; **'guest•house** *s Br* pensjonat *m*; **'guest•room** *s* pokój *m* dla gości

guf•faw [gə'fɔː] **I** *s* głośny śmiech *m* **II** *v/i* głośno śmiać ⟨za-⟩ się

guid•ance ['gaɪdəns] *s* **1.** wskazówki *pl* **2.** pomoc *f*; ***under the ~ of*** pod opieką *G*, pod okiem *G* **3.** poradnictwo *n* **4.** *TECH* naprowadzanie *n*

guide [gaɪd] **I** *v/t* **1.** prowadzić ⟨po-⟩ **2.** kierować ⟨po-⟩; ***be ~ed by*** kierować się *I* **3.** oprowadzać ⟨-dzić⟩ **4.** *missile*: naprowadzać ⟨-dzić⟩ **II** *s* **1.** przewodnik *m* **2.** poradnik *m* **3.** wskazówka *f*; **'guide•book** *s* **1.** przewodnik *m* **2.** poradnik *m*; **guid•ed 'mis•sile** *s* pocisk *m* kierowany; **'guide dog** *s* pies *m* przewodnik; **guid•ed 'tour** *s* zwiedzanie *n* z przewodnikiem; **guide•lines** ['gaɪdlaɪnz] *pl* **1.** wskazówki *pl* **2.** wytyczne *pl*; **guid•ing** ['gaɪdɪŋ] *adj principle*: przewodni

guild [gɪld] *s* **1.** stowarzyszenie *n* **2.** cech *m* **3.** gildia *f*

guile [gaɪl] *s* przebiegłość *f*; **guile•less** ['gaɪlləs] *adj* prostolinijny

guil•lo•tine ['gɪlətiːn] **I** *s* gilotyna *f* **II** *v/t* gilotynować ⟨z-⟩

guilt [gɪlt] *s* wina *f*; ***a ~ complex*** kompleks winy; **guilt•i•ly** ['gɪltɪlɪ] *adv say*: z miną winowajcy; **guilt•y** ['gɪltɪ] *s* **1.** winny **2.** pełen skruchy

guin•ea pig ['gɪnɪpɪg] *s* **1.** świnka *f* morska **2.** *fig* królik *m* doświadczalny

guise [gaɪz] *s* **1.** pozór *m*; ***under the ~ of*** pod pozorem *G*, pod pretekstem *G* **2.** postać *f*, wersja *f*; ***in different ~s*** pod różnymi postaciami

gui•tar [gɪ'tɑː] *s* gitara *f*; **gui•tar•ist** [gɪ'tɑːrɪst] *s* gitarzysta *m*; **gui'tar play•er** *s* gitarzysta *m*

gulf [gʌlf] *s* **1.** *GEOGR* zatoka *f*; ***the* ≈ *States*** *Br* państwa Zatoki Perskiej; ≈ ***of* 'Mex•i•co** *s* Zatoka *f* Meksykańska **2.** *fig* przepaść *f*, rozłam *m*

gull [gʌl] *s* mewa *f*

gulp [gʌlp] **I** *v/t* **1.** łykać, połykać ⟨-łknąć⟩ **2.** przełykać ⟨-łknąć⟩; **gulp down** *v/i* **1.** przełykać ⟨-łknąć⟩ **2.** wypijać ⟨-pić⟩ szybko **II** *s* **1.** łyk *m*, haust *m*; ***at one ~*** jednym haustem, na raz **2.** kęs *m*

G

gum[1] [gʌm] **I** *s* **1.** (*chewing*) guma *f* **2.** guma *f* (naturalna) **3.** klej *m* **II** *v/t* przyklejać ⟨-leić⟩
gum[2] [~] *s* dziąsło *n*
gun [gʌn] *s* **1.** broń *f* (palna); ***stick to one's ~s*** *infml* upierać się przy swoim **2.** pistolet *m* **3.** karabin *m* **4.** strzelba *f* **5.** SPORT strzał *m* startera **6.** TECH pistolet *m*; **gun down** *v/t* zastrzelić; **'gun•boat** *s* kanonierka *f*; **'gun•fight** *s* strzelanina *f*; **'gun•fire** *s* **1.** strzelanina *f* **2.** strzały *pl* **3.** ogień *m* artyleryjski
gung-ho [gʌŋ'həʊ] *adj infml* **1.** bojowy **2.** *infml* napalony
'gun li•cense *s* pozwolenie *n* na broń; **'gun•man** *pl -men s* uzbrojony bandyta *f*; **'gun•point** *s* celownik *m*; ***at ~*** na muszce; **'gun•pow•der** *s* proch *m* (strzelniczy); **'gun-run•ner** *s* przemytnik *m* broni; **'gun-run•ning** *s* przemyt *m* broni; **'gun•shot** *s* **1.** wystrzał *m* **2.** zasięg *m* strzału; ***within ~*** w zasięgu strzału; ***out of ~*** poza zasięgiem strzału; **'gun•shot wound** *s* rana *f* postrzałowa; **'gun•smith** *s* rusznikarz *m*
gur•gle ['gɜːgl] *v/i* **1.** bulgotać ⟨za-⟩ **2.** gaworzyć
gush [gʌʃ] **I** *v/i* **1.** tryskać ⟨-snąć⟩, wytryskiwać ⟨-snąć⟩ **2.** *fig* rozpływać się **II** *s* **1.** tryśnięcie *n*, wytryśnięcie *n* **2.** *fig* wybuch *m*; **gush•y** ['gʌʃɪ] *adj* egzaltowany
gust [gʌst] *s* **1.** podmuch *m* **2.** *a. fig* poryw *m* **3.** *fig* wybuch *m*
gus•to ['gʌstəʊ] *s* entuzjazm *m*
gust•y ['gʌstɪ] *adj* **1.** porywisty **2.** wietrzny
gut [gʌt] **I** *s* **1.** jelito *n* **2.** *infml* bebech *m* **3.** **~s a)** *animal*: wnętrzności **b)** *infml* flaki, bebechy **c)** *infml* odwaga; ***hate s.o.'s ~s*** szczerze kogoś nienawidzić **II** *v/t* COOK patroszyć ⟨wy-⟩; **gut•less** ['gʌtlɪs] *adj* tchórzliwy; **guts•y** ['gʌtsɪ] *adj* waleczny, odważny
gut•ter[1] ['gʌtə] *v/i* (*flame*) migotać ⟨za-⟩
gut•ter[2] [~] *s* **1.** rynna *f* **2.** rynsztok *m*, ściek *m*; **gut•ter•ing** ['gʌtərɪŋ] *s* orynnowanie *n*; **gut•ter 'press** *s* prasa *f* brukowa
gut•tur•al ['gʌtərəl] **I** *adj* gardłowy **II** *s* spółgłoska *f* gardłowa
guy [gaɪ] *s infml* facet *m*, gość *m*; ***he's a nice ~*** to miły facet; ***are you ~s going?*** idziecie?
guz•zle ['gʌzl] *v/t* **1.** *infml* żreć ⟨ze-⟩ **2.** *infml* żłopać ⟨wy-⟩ **3.** *fig* pożerać ⟨-żreć⟩
gym [dʒɪm] *s* **1.** sala *f* gimnastyczna **2.** siłownia *f* **3.** gimnastyka *f*, WF *m*; ***a ~ teacher*** nauczyciel wuefu; **gym•na•si•um** [dʒɪm'neɪzɪəm] *s* **1.** sala *f* gimnastyczna **2.** siłownia *f*; **gym•nast** ['dʒɪmnæst] *s* gimnastyk *m*; **gym•nas•tics** [dʒɪm'næstɪks] *pl* gimnastyka *f*; ***mental ~*** *fig* gimnastyka umysłowa; **'gym shoes** *pl* tenisówki *pl*
gy•nae•col•o•gy [gaɪnɪ'kɒlədʒɪ] *Br*, ***gy•ne•col•o•gy*** *Am s* ginekologia *f*; **gy•nae•col•ogist** [gaɪnɪ'kɒlədʒɪst] *Br*, ***gy•ne•col•ogist*** *Am s* ginekolog *m*
gyp•sum ['dʒɪpsəm] *s* gips *m*
gyp•sy ['dʒɪpsɪ] **I** *s* Cygan *m*, Cyganka *f* **II** *adj* cygański

H

hab•it ['hæbɪt] *s* **1.** zwyczaj *m*, nawyk *m*; ***out of ~*** z przyzwyczajenia; ***be in the ~ of doing s.th.*** mieć zwyczaj coś robić; ***get into a ~*** nabrać nawyku **2.** nałóg *m*
hab•it•a•ble ['hæbɪtəbl] *adj* nadający się do zamieszkania
hab•i•tat ['hæbɪtæt] *s* siedlisko *n*
habitation [hæbɪ'teɪʃn] *s* **1.** zamieszkanie *n*; ***unfit for ~*** nienadający się do zamieszkania **2.** domostwo *n* **3.** miejsce *n* zamieszkania
'hab•it-form•ing *adj* uzależniający, powodujący uzależnienie
ha•bit•u•al [hə'bɪtʃʊəl] *adj* **1.** charakterystyczny **2.** notoryczny; ***a ~ criminal*** notoryczny przestępca **3.** nałogowy; **ha•bit•u•al•ly** [hə'bɪtʃʊəlɪ] *adv* **1.** jak zwykle; ***be ~ late*** spóźniać się jak zwykle **2.** notorycznie **3.** nałogowo; **ha•bit•u•at•ed** [hə'bɪtʃʊeɪtɪd] *adj* przyzwyczajony, wdrożony

hack[1] [hæk] *s* **1.** *infml* pismak *m* **2.** *Am infml* taryfa *f*, taksówka *f* **3.** koń *m* pod siodło

hack[2] [~] **I** *v/t* rąbać ⟨po-⟩; **~ s.th. to pieces** porąbać coś na kawałki **II** *v/i* **1.** **~ away** rąbać, ciąć (**at** *A*) **2.** INF włamywać ⟨-mać⟩ się (**into** do *G*) **III** *s* cięcie *n*; **hack into** *v/i* INF włamywać ⟨-mać⟩ się do *G*

hack•er ['hækə] *s* INF haker *m*

hack•le ['hækl] *s*: ***get one's ~s up*** *fig* zjeżyć się, najeżyć się

had [hæd] *Past Simple and Past Participle* → ***have***

had•n't ['hædnt] *contracted form* → ***had not***

hae•mo•glo•bin [hiːmə'gləʊbɪn] *Br*, ***he•mo•glo•bin*** *Am s* ANAT hemoglobina *f*; **hae•mo•phil•i•a** [hiːmə'fɪlɪə] *Br*, ***he•mo•phil•i•a*** *Am s* MED hemofilia *f*; **hae•mor•rhage** ['hemərɪdʒ] *Br*, ***hem•or•rhage*** *Am s* MED krwotok *m*; **haem•or•rhoids** ['hemərɔɪdz] *Br*, ***hem•or•rhoids*** *Am pl* MED hemoroidy *pl*

hag [hæg] *s* wiedźma *f*

hag•gard ['hægəd] *adj* wymizerowany, wynędzniały

hag•gle ['hægl] *v/i* targować się

Hague ['heɪg] *s*: ***the ~*** Haga

hail[1] [heɪl] **I** *s* grad *m* **II** *v/i* ***it's hailing*** pada grad

hail[2] [~] *v/t* **1.** okrzyknąć, obwoływać ⟨-łać⟩ **2.** *taxi*: zatrzymywać ⟨-mać⟩ **3.** *lit* wołać ⟨za-⟩ do *G*; **hail from** *v/i form* pochodzić z *G*

'hail•stone *s* ziarnko *n* gradu; **'hail•storm** *s* burza *f* gradowa, gradobicie *n*

hair [heə] *s* **1.** włosy *pl*; ***do one's ~*** czesać się; ***keep your ~ on!*** *Br infml* uspokój się!; ***let one's ~ down*** *infml* wyluzować się; ***tear one's ~ (out)*** rwać włosy z głowy **2.** sierść *f* **3.** włos *m*; ***split ~s*** *fig* dzielić włos na czworo; **'hair•band** *s* opaska *f* na włosy; **'hair•brush** *s* szczotka *f* do włosów; **'hair•cut** *s* **1.** strzyżenie *n* **2.** fryzura *f*, uczesanie *n*; **'hair•do** *s infml* fryzura *f*, uczesanie *n*; **'hair•dress•er** *s* fryzjer *m*; **'hair•dress•ing** *s* fryzjerstwo *n*; **'hair•dress•ing sal•on** *s* salon *m* fryzjerski

'hair•dri•er, ***'hair•dry•er*** *s* suszarka *f* do włosów; **'hair gel** *s* żel *m* do włosów; **'hair•grip** *s Br* wsuwka *f* (do włosów); **'hair•less** ['heəlɪs] *adj* **1.** łysy **2.** bez zarostu, nieowłosiony **3.** pozbawiony sierści; **'hair•line** *s* linia *f* włosów; ***receding ~*** zakola; **'hair•net** *s* siatka *f* na włosy; **'hair•piece** *s* treska *f*, tupecik *m*; **'hair•pin** *s* szpilka *f* do włosów; **hair•pin 'bend** *s* ostry zakręt *m*; **'hair-rais•ing** *adj* jeżący włosy na głowie; **hair re•'mov•er** *s* **1.** depilator *m* **2.** krem *m* do depilacji; **'hair's breadth** *s*: ***by a ~*** o (mały) włos; **'hair slide** *s Br* wsuwka *f* (do włosów); **'hair-split•ting** *s fig* dzielenie *n* włosa na czworo; **'hair spray** *s* lakier *m* do włosów; **'hair•style** *s* fryzura *f*, uczesanie *n*; **'hair styl•ist** *s* fryzjer *m*

hair•y ['heərɪ] *adj* **1.** owłosiony **2.** włochaty **3.** kosmaty **4.** jeżący włosy na głowie, mrożący krew w żyłach

hake [heɪk] *s* morszczuk *m*

hale [heɪl] *adj* czerstwy, krzepki; ***~ and hearty*** w świetnej formie

half [hɑːf] *pl halves* [hɑːvz] **I** *adj* pół; ***~ a mile*** pół mili; ***two and a ~ pounds*** dwa i pół funta **II** *adv* **1.** do połowy **2.** o połowę; ***~ as long*** o połowę krótszy **3.** wpół; ***~ past two*** wpół do trzeciej **4.** nie całkiem, na wpół; ***~ dead*** na wpół żywy, na wpół martwy; ***not ~ bad*** całkiem niezły **III** *s* **1.** połowa *f*; ***by ~*** o połowę; ***in ~*** na pół; ***go halves with s.o. on s.th.*** podzielić się czymś z kimś po połowie **2.** połówka *f*; **half-and-'half** **I** *adj* pół na pół **II** *adv* pół na pół

half 'arsed [hɑːf'ɑːst] *Br*, ***half-'assed*** *Am adj infml* **1.** do chrzanu **2.** tępy; **half-'baked** *adj infml* niedopracowany; **half 'board** *s* nocleg *m* z niepełnym wyżywieniem; **'half-breed** **I** *s* mieszaniec *m* **II** *adj* półkrwi; **'half broth•er** *s* przyrodni brat *m*; **'half-caste** **I** *s* mieszaniec *m* **II** *adj* półkrwi; **half 'dol•lar** *s* półdolarówka *f*, pół *n* dolara; **half-'heart•ed** *adj* mało entuzjastyczny; ***make a ~ effort to do s.th.*** bez przekonania próbować coś zrobić

half-'hour *s* pół *n* godziny; **'half light** *s* półmrok *m*; **half-'mast** *s*: ***be flying at ~*** być opuszczonym do połowy ma-

H

sztu; **half 'meas•ure** *s* półśrodek *m*; **'half-moon** *s* półksiężyc *m*; **'half note** *s Am* półnuta *f*; **half-'price** *adj* za pół ceny; **'half sis•ter** *s* przyrodnia siostra *f*; **half 'term I** *s* przerwa *f* międzysemestralna **II** *adj* w połowie semestru

half 'time I *adj* **1.** na pół etatu **2.** w połowie (meczu) **3.** *score*: do przerwy **II** *adv* na pół etatu **III** *s SPORT* przerwa *f*; ***the score at ~*** wynik do przerwy

'half-truth *s* półprawda *f*, część *f* prawdy; **half•'way I** *adj* w połowie drogi **II** *adv* **1.** w połowie drogi; ***meet s.o. ~*** *fig* wyjść komuś naprzeciw **2.** połowicznie; **half•way 'house** *s fig* kompromis *m*; **'half-wit** *s infml* półgłówek *m*; **'half-wit•ted** *adj infml* durny, głupi; **half-'year•ly I** *adj* półroczny **II** *adv* co pół roku

H

hall [hɔːl] *s* **1.** przedpokój *m* **2.** korytarz *m* **3.** hol *m* **4.** sala *f* **5.** **~** ***(of residence)*** *Br* akademik *m*

hal•le•lu•jah [hælɪ'luːjə] *interj* alleluja!

hall•mark ['hɔːlmɑːk] **I** *s* **1.** cecha *f* charakterystyczna; ***have all the ~s of*** mieć wszystkie cechy *G* **2.** cecha *f* probiercza **II** *v/t gold*: cechować

hal•lo [hə'ləʊ], ***hel•lo*** *interj* **1.** cześć! **2.** halo! **3.** dzień dobry!

'hall por•ter *s* portier *m*

hal•lu•ci•nate [hə'luːsɪneɪt] *v/i* mieć halucynacje; **hal•lu•ci•na•tion** [həluːsɪ'neɪʃn] *s* **1.** halucynacja *f* **2.** halucynacje *pl*, przywidzenia *pl*; **hal•lu•ci•no•gen•ic** [həluːsɪnə'dʒenɪk] *adj* halucynogenny

'hall•way *s* **1.** przedpokój *m* **2.** korytarz *m*

ha•lo ['heɪləʊ] *s* **1.** aureola *f*, nimb *m* **2.** halo *n*

halt [hɔːlt] **I** *s* ***come to a ~*** zatrzymać się; ***bring s.th. to a ~*** zatrzymać coś **II** *v/t* zatrzymywać ⟨-mać⟩ **III** *v/i* zatrzymywać ⟨-mać⟩ się; **hal•ter** ['hɔːltə] *s* kantar *m*; **'halter top** *s* top *m* z odkrytymi plecami; **halt•ing** ['hɔːltɪŋ] *adj* **1.** niepewny, niezdecydowany **2.** *fig* kulawy

halve [hɑːv] *v/t* **1.** dzielić ⟨po-⟩ na pół **2.** przepoławiać ⟨-łowić⟩

ham [hæm] *s* **1.** *COOK* szynka *f*; ***~ and eggs*** *Am* jajka na szynce

ham•let ['hæmlɪt] *s* wioska *f*, osada *f*

ham•mer ['hæmə] **I** *s* **1.** młotek *m*; ***come under the ~, go under the ~*** iść pod młotek; ***go at it ~ and tongs*** **a)** kłócić się zawzięcie **b)** zacięcie walczyć **2.** młot *m*; ***the ~*** *SPORT* rzut młotem; ***a ~ thrower*** *SPORT* miotacz, lekkoatleta rzucający młotem **II** *v/t* walić (młotkiem) w *A*, uderzać (młotkiem) w *A*; ***~ s.th. in*** wbić coś; ***~ s.th. into s.o.'s head*** *fig* wbić coś komuś do głowy **III** *v/i* walić młotkiem, uderzać młotkiem; ***~ at*** walić w *A*, uderzać w *A*

ham•mock ['hæmək] *s* hamak *m*

ham•per[1] ['hæmpə] *v/t* **1.** przeszkadzać ⟨-kodzić⟩ **2.** utrudniać ⟨-nić⟩ **3.** hamować

ham•per[2] [~] *s* **1.** kosz *m* **2.** *Am* kosz *m* na brudną bieliznę

ham•ster ['hæmstə] *s* chomik *m*

hand [hænd] **I** *s* **1.** ręka *f*; ***at ~*** pod ręką; ***by ~*** ręcznie; ***~s down*** z łatwością, bez wysiłku; ***~s off!*** ręce precz!; ***~s up!*** ręce do góry!; ***be ~ in glove with*** mieć konszachty z *I*; ***change ~s*** zmienić właściciela; ***give s.o. a ~*** pomóc komuś; ***lend a ~*** wyciągnąć pomocną dłoń; ***have a ~ in*** przyłożyć rękę do *G*, mieć udział w *L*; ***hold ~s*** trzymać się za ręce; ***live from ~ to mouth*** żyć z dnia na dzień; ***shake ~s with s.o.*** podać komuś rękę; ***be entirely in s.o.'s ~s*** być całkowicie w czyichś rękach; ***fall into s.o.'s ~*** wpaść w czyjeś ręce; ***in good ~s*** w dobrych rękach; ***on the one ~..., on the other ~*** z jednej strony..., z drugiej strony; ***he's an old ~ at photography*** od dawna zajmuje się fotografią; ***be a dab ~ at*** mieć złote ręce do *G*; ***at first ~*** z pierwszej ręki **2.** robotnik *m* **3.** ***get a big ~*** dostać duże brawa **4.** marynarz *m* **5.** *clock*: wskazówka *f* **6.** karty *pl*; ***show one's ~*** odkryć karty **7.** rozdanie *n* **II** *v/t* **1.** podawać ⟨-dać⟩ **2.** wręczać ⟨-czyć⟩; **hand around** *v/t* **1.** rozdawać ⟨-dać⟩ **2.** częstować ⟨po-⟩; **hand back** *v/t* zwracać ⟨-rócić⟩; **hand down** *v/t* **1.** przekazywać ⟨-zać⟩ **2.** podawać ⟨-dać⟩; **hand in** *v/t* **1.** *notice*: składać ⟨złożyć⟩ **2.** *homework*: oddawać ⟨-dać⟩; **hand on** *v/t* **1.** przekazywać ⟨-zać⟩ **2.** podawać ⟨-dać⟩ dalej; **hand out** *v/t* **1.** rozdawać

⟨-dać⟩ **2.** *punishment*: wymierzać ⟨-rzyć⟩; **hand over** *v/i* **1.** *power*: przekazywać ⟨-zać⟩ **2.** oddawać głos ⟨-dać⟩; **hand round** → ***hand around***

'hand•bag *s* torebka *f*; **'hand baggage** *s* bagaż *m* podręczny; **'handball** *s* piłka *f* ręczna; **'hand•book** *s* **1.** podręcznik *m* **2.** przewodnik *m* **3.** informator *m* **4.** poradnik *m*; **'hand•brake** *s* *AUTO* hamulec *m* ręczny; **'hand cream** *s* krem *m* do rąk

hand•cuff ['hændkʌf] *v/t* zakuwać ⟨-kuć⟩ w kajdanki; **hand•cuffs** ['hæn(d)kʌfs] *pl* kajdanki *pl*

hand•ful ['hændfʊl] *s* **1.** garść *f* **2.** *fig* garstka *f* **3.** *infml* urwis *m*

'hand gre•nade *s* granat *m* ręczny; **'hand•gun** *s* **1.** krótka broń *f* palna **2.** pistolet *m*

hand-'held *adj* **1.** ręczny; ***a ~ computer*** palmtop, komputer naręczny **2.** podręczny **3.** kieszonkowy

hand•i•cap ['hændɪkæp] **I** *s* **1.** ułomność *f* **2.** upośledzenie *n* **3.** przeszkoda *f* **4.** utrudnienie *n* **5.** handicap *m* **II** *v/t* **1.** utrudniać ⟨-nić⟩ **2.** hamować; **hand•i•capped** ['hændɪkæpt] *adj* **1.** upośledzony **2.** z handicapem

hand•i•craft ['hændɪkræft] *s* **1.** rękodzieło *n* **2.** rzemiosło *n* artystyczne

hand•i•work ['hændɪwɜːk] *s* **1.** rękodzieło *n* **2.** własne dzieło *n*

hand•ker•chief ['hæŋkətʃɪf] *s* chustka *f*, chusteczka *f* (do nosa)

han•dle ['hændl] **I** *s* **1.** klamka *f*; ***fly off the ~*** *infml* wpaść w szał, wyjść z siebie **2.** rączka *f* **3.** uchwyt *m* **4.** uszko *n* **II** *v/t* **1.** zajmować ⟨-jąć⟩ się **2.** obsługiwać ⟨-łużyć⟩ **3.** radzić ⟨po-⟩ sobie z *I* **4.** znosić ⟨znieść⟩; ***I can't ~ it anymore*** dłużej tego nie zniosę **5.** *transaction*: przeprowadzić ⟨-dzić⟩ **6.** przenosić ⟨-nieść⟩ **7.** dotykać ⟨-tknąć⟩ **III** *v/i* **1.** ***glass – ~ with care!*** ostrożnie, szkło! **2.** ***the car ~s well*** ten samochód dobrze się prowadzi

'hand lug•gage *s* bagaż *m* podręczny

hand•'made *adj* wykonany ręcznie; **hand-'o•per•at•ed** *adj* **1.** obsługiwany ręcznie **2.** sterowany ręcznie; **'handout** *s* **1.** datek *m* **2.** jałmużna *f* **3.** ulotka *f* **4.** materiały *pl*; **'hand•o•ver** *s* przekazanie *n*; **hand•'picked** *adj* starannie wyselekcjonowany; **'hand•rail** *s* **1.** poręcz *f* **2.** balustrada *f*; **'hand•set** *s* słuchawka *f*; **'handshake** *s* uścisk *m* dłoni; ***give s.o. a firm ~*** mocno uścisnąć komuś rękę; **hands-'off** *adj* dający wolną rękę

hand•some ['hænsəm] *adj* **1.** przystojny **2.** ładny **3.** pokaźny **4.** znaczny

hands-on ['hændzɒn] *adj* **1.** praktyczny **2.** bezpośredni

'hand•stand *s* stójka *f* na rękach; ***do a ~*** zrobić stójkę; **hand-to-'hand** *adj* *fight*: wręcz; **hand-to-'mouth** *adj* **1.** marny; ***lead a ~ existence*** żyć z dnia na dzień **2.** nędznie płatny; **'hand tow•el** *s* ręcznik *m* do rąk; **'hand•writ•ing** *s* charakter *m* pisma, pismo *n*; **hand•'writ•ten** *adj* odręcznie napisany

hand•y ['hændɪ] *adj* **1.** przydatny; ***come in ~*** przydać się **2.** praktyczny **3.** użyteczny **4.** poręczny; ***keep s.th. ~*** trzymać coś pod ręką **5.** dogodnie położony **6.** *infml person*: zręczny; **'handy•man** *pl -men s* złota rączka *f*

hang [hæŋ] **I** (*hung*; *hung*) *v/i* **1.** wisieć; ***~ by a thread*** wisieć na włosku; ***~ over s.o.*** *fig* wisieć nad kimś **2.** zwisać **II** (*hung*; *hung*) *v/t* **1.** wieszać ⟨powiesić⟩, zawieszać ⟨-sić⟩ **2.** *head*: zwieszać ⟨-sić⟩ **3.** *wallpaper*: naklejać ⟨-leić⟩ **4.** (*hanged*; *hanged*) *criminal*: wieszać ⟨powiesić⟩; ***~ oneself*** powiesić się **III** *s* ***get the ~ of s.th.*** *infml* chwycić coś, załapać coś; **hand around** *v/i* **1.** pałętać się **2.** być w pobliżu **3.** trzymać się (***with*** z *I*); **hang back** *v/i* ociągać się; **hang down** *v/i* zwisać; **hang on** *v/i* **1.** czekać ⟨po-⟩ **2.** wytrzymywać ⟨-mać⟩; **hang on to** *v/i* trzymać się kurczowo *G*; **hang out** *v/i* *infml* **1.** spędzać czas **2.** zadawać się (***with*** z *I*) **3.** przesiadywać **4.** wystawać; **hang over** *v/i*: ***be hung over*** mieć kaca; **hang together** *v/i* trzymać się razem; **hang up** *v/i* odkładać ⟨odłożyć⟩ słuchawkę; ***be hung up on*** mieć kompleks z powodu *G*

hang•er ['hæŋə] *s* wieszak *m*

hang•ing ['hæŋɪŋ] *s* **1.** powieszenie *n*; ***by ~*** przez powieszenie **2.** egzekucja *f* przez powieszenie **3.** tkanina *f* dekoracyjna **4.** zawieszanie *n*

'hang•out *s* *infml* miejsce *n* spotkań; **'hang•o•ver** *s* **1.** kac *m* **2.** pozosta-

H

łość *f*; **'hang-up** *s infml* kompleks *m* (***about*** na punkcie *G)*

han•ker ['hæŋkə] *v/i* **1.** pragnąć (***after/ for*** *G*) **2.** tęsknić (***after/for*** za *I*) **3.** ***~ to do s.th.*** marzyć o tym, żeby coś zrobić; **han•ker•ing** ['hæŋkərɪŋ] *s* pragnienie *n*

han•kie, ***han•ky*** ['hæŋkɪ] *s infml* chusteczka *f* (do nosa)

han•ky-pan•ky [hæŋkɪ'pæŋkɪ] *s infml* **1.** bara-bara *n* **2.** machlojki *pl*

hap•haz•ard [hæp'hæzəd] *adj* **1.** chaotyczny **2.** przypadkowy

hap•less ['hæplɪs] *adj lit* nieszczęsny

hap•pen ['hæpn] *v/i* **1.** zdarzać ⟨-rzyć⟩ się, stać się; ***it will not ~ again*** to się już nie powtórzy **2.** dziać się **3.** przydarzać ⟨-rzyć⟩ się, przytrafiać ⟨-fić⟩ się **4.** ***if you*** (***should***) ***~ to see it*** jeśli przypadkiem to zobaczysz; ***it ~ed to be cold*** tak się złożyło, że było zimno; **hap•pen across** *v/i* natykać ⟨-tknąć⟩ się na *A*; **hap•pen on** *v/i* natrafiać ⟨-fić⟩ na *A*

hap•pen•ing ['hæpnɪŋ] *s* **1.** wydarzenie *n* **2.** zdarzenie *n* **3.** ART happening *m*

hap•pi•ly ['hæpɪlɪ] *adv* **1.** radośnie, wesoło **2.** szczęśliwie **3.** na szczęście **4.** ochoczo; **hap•pi•ness** ['hæpɪnɪs] *s* szczęście *n*; **hap•py** ['hæpɪ] *adj* **1.** szczęśliwy; ***~ birthday!*** wszystkiego najlepszego z okazji urodzin! **2.** zadowolony; ***I am ~ to see you*** cieszę się, że cię widzę **3.** udany **4.** trafny; **hap•py-go-'luck•y** *adj* niefrasobliwy, beztroski; **'hap•py hour** *s pora, kiedy w lokalu alkohol sprzedawany jest po niższych cenach*

har•ass ['hærəs] *v/t* **1.** nękać **2.** dręczyć **3.** *sexually*: molestować; **har•assed** ['hærəst] *adj* **1.** udręczony **2.** *sexually*: molestowany; **har•ass•ment** ['hærəsmənt] *s* **1.** nękanie *n* **2.** *sexual*: molestowanie *n* **3.** ***~ at work*** mobbing

har•bour ['hɑːbə] *Br*, ***har•bor*** *Am* **I** *s* **1.** port *m* **2.** przystań *f* **3.** schronienie *n* **II** *v/t* **1.** *suspicion*: żywić **2.** *criminal*: ukrywać ⟨-ryć⟩

hard [hɑːd] **I** *adj* **1.** twardy; ***go ~*** stwardnieć **2.** trudny; ***it's ~ to believe*** trudno w to uwierzyć; ***she's ~ to please*** trudno ją zadowolić; ***give s.o. a ~ time*** dać się komuś we znaki **3.** ciężki; ***~ work*** ciężka praca; ***~ times*** ciężkie czasy; ***it is ~ on him*** ciężko mu, trudno mu **4.** silny **5.** *fig blow*: poważny **6.** surowy; ***be too ~ on s.o.*** być dla kogoś zbyt surowym **7.** niezbity, niepodważalny **8.** *liquor*: mocny **9.** ***~ of hearing*** niedosłyszący **II** *adv* **1.** mocno; ***frozen ~*** zamarznięty na kamień **2.** *work*: ciężko **3.** z całych sił; ***brake ~*** hamować z całych sił; ***think ~*** dobrze się zastanowić; ***try ~*** bardzo się starać **4.** tuż

'hard•back *s* książka *f* w twardej oprawie; **'hard•ball** *s* SPORT baseball *m*; **'hard•board** *s* płyta *f* pilśniowa twarda; **hard-'boiled** *adj* **1.** *egg*: na twardo **2.** *infml* twardy; **'hard cop•y** *s* wydruk *m* (komputerowy); **'hardcore** *s* **I 1.** MUS hardcore *m* **2.** tłuczeń *m* **3.** *fig* trzon *n* **II** *adj* **1.** zagorzały, twardogłowy **2.** *pornography*: twardy **3.** MUS hardcorowy; **'hard-cov•er** *s* **1.** twarda okładka *f* **2.** → ***hardback***; **hard 'cur•ren•cy** *s* twarda waluta *f*; **hard 'disk** *s* twardy dysk *m*; **'hard drug** *s* twardy narkotyk *m*; **hard-'earned** *adj* **1.** ciężko zarobiony **2.** z trudem zdobyty

hard•en ['hɑːdn] **I** *v/i* **1.** twardnieć ⟨s-⟩ **2.** tężeć ⟨s-⟩ **3.** umacniać ⟨umocnić⟩ się **4.** wzmacniać ⟨-mocnić⟩ się **II** *v/t* **1.** utwardzać ⟨-dzić⟩ **2.** hartować ⟨za-⟩ **3.** umacniać ⟨umocnić⟩; **hard-ened** ['hɑːdnd] *adj* **1.** stwardniały **2.** utwardzony **3.** hartowany **4.** zatwardziały

hard 'hat *s* kask *m*; **hard•'head•ed** *adj* trzeźwo myślący; **hard•'heart•ed** *adj* **1.** nieczuły **2.** bezlitosny **3.** bezwzględny; **hard-'hit•ting** *adj* demaskatorski; **hard-'line** *adj* **1.** bezkompromisowy **2.** twardogłowy; **hard-'lin•er** *s* twardogłowy *m*; **hard 'liq•uor** *s Am* alkohol *m* wysokoprocentowy

hard•ly ['hɑːdlɪ] *adv* **1.** ledwie, ledwo **2.** prawie nie; ***~ ever*** prawie nigdy

hard•ness ['hɑːdnɪs] *s* **1.** twardość *m* **2.** trudność *f* **3.** surowość *f*

hard-'nosed *adj* praktyczny; **hard-'pressed** ; *adj*: ***be ~*** mieć trudności finansowe

hard•ship ['hɑːdʃɪp] *s* **1.** trudności *pl* **2.** ubóstwo *n*, bieda *f* **3.** ciężkie doświadczenie *n*

hard 'up *adj infml* spłukany; **'hard•ware** *s* **1.** sprzęt *m* komputerowy, hardware *m* **2.** artykuły *pl* żelazne; **'hard•ware store** *s* sklep *m* żelazny; **'hard•wood** *s* twarde drewno *n*; **hard-'work•ing** *adj* **1.** pracowity **2.** ciężko pracujący

har•dy ['hɑːdɪ] *adj* **1.** śmiały, odważny **2.** odporny, wytrzymały

hare [heə] *s* zając *m*; ***as mad as a March ~*** kompletnie zbzikowany; **'hare•bell** *s* (*flower*) dzwonek *m* (okrągłolistny); **'hare•brained** *adj* idiotyczny

hare•'lip *s* zajęcza warga *f*

hark [hɑːk] *v/i*: ***~ back to*** **a)** powracać do *G* **b)** nawiązywać do *G*

harm [hɑːm] **I** *s* **1.** krzywda *f*; ***do s.o. ~*** zrobić komuś krzywdę; ***s.o. came to ~*** komuś stała się krzywda; ***bodily ~*** uszkodzenie ciała **2.** szkoda; ***there is no ~ in doing s.th.*** nie zaszkodzi coś zrobić; ***there is no ~ in trying*** nie zaszkodzi spróbować **II** *v/t* **1.** krzywdzić ⟨s-⟩, wyrządzać ⟨-dzić⟩ krzywdę *D* **2.** szkodzić ⟨za-, u-⟩; **harm•ful** ['hɑːmfəl] *adj* **1.** szkodliwy **2.** krzywdzący; **harm•less** ['hɑːmlɪs] *adj* **1.** niegroźny **2.** nieszkodliwy

har•mon•ic [hɑː'mɒnɪk] *adj* harmoniczny; **har•mon•i•ca** [hɑː'mɒnɪkə] *s* harmonijka *f* ustna, organki *pl*; **har•mo•ni•ous** [hɑː'məʊnɪəs] *adj* **1.** harmonijny **2.** zgodny; **har•mo•ni•za•tion** [hɑːmənaɪ'zeɪʃn] *s* harmonizacja *f*; **har•mo•nize** ['hɑːmənaɪz] *s* harmonizować ⟨z-⟩; **har•mo•ny** ['hɑːmənɪ] *s* harmonia *f*; ***in ~ with*** w harmonii z *I*

har•ness ['hɑːnɪs] **I** *s* uprząż *f*; ***in ~*** *fig* w pracy **II** *v/t* **1.** zaprzęgać ⟨-rząc⟩ **2.** przypinać ⟨-piąć⟩ **3.** *fig* poskramiać ⟨-romić⟩

harp [hɑːp] *s* harfa *f*; **harp on about** *v/i infml* nudzić o *L*, ciągle gadać o *L*

harp•ist ['hɑːpɪst] *s* harfista *m*

har•poon [hɑː'puːn] **I** *s* harpun *m* **II** *v/t* trafiać ⟨-fić⟩ harpunem

har•ry ['hærɪ] *v/t* **1.** nękać **2.** zadręczać ⟨-czyć⟩

harsh [hɑːʃ] *adj* **1.** surowy **2.** twardy **3.** ostry **4.** trudny **5.** szorstki; **harsh•ly** ['hɑːʃlɪ] *adv* **1.** surowo **2.** ostro **3.** szorstko; **harsh•ness** ['hɑːʃnɪs] *s* **1.** surowość *f* **2.** ostrość *f* **3.** szorstkość *f*

har•vest ['hɑːvɪst] **I** *s* **1.** żniwa *pl* **2.** zbiór *m* **3.** plon *m* **II** *v/t* zbierać ⟨zebrać⟩; ***a ~ festival*** dożynki

has [hæz] → ***have***

has-been ['hæzbiːn] *s* człowiek *m* skończony

hash [hæʃ] *s* **1.** *COOK* siekane mięso *n* smażone z ziemniakami i cebulą **2.** *infml* haszysz *m* **3.** ***make a ~ of*** *infml* sknocić *A*; **hash 'browns** *pl Am COOK* pokrojone ziemniaki *pl* smażone z cebulą

hash•ish ['hæʃiːʃ] *s* haszysz *m*

has•n't ['hæznt] *contracted form* → ***has not***

has•sle ['hæsl] *infml* **I** *s* **1.** kłopot *m*; ***it was quite a ~*** było z tym sporo kłopotu **2.** zawracanie *n* głowy **3.** sprzeczka *f*, utarczka *f* **II** *v/i* handryczyć się

haste [heɪst] *s* pośpiech *m*; ***make ~*** śpieszyć się; ***more ~, less speed*** śpiesz się powoli; **has•ten** ['heɪsn] **I** *v/t* przyśpieszać ⟨-szyć⟩ **II** *v/i* śpieszyć się **3.** ***s.o. ~s to do s.th.*** komuś śpieszno, żeby coś zrobić; **hast•i•ly** ['heɪstɪlɪ] *adv* **1.** pośpiesznie, w pośpiechu **2.** pochopnie; **hast•y** ['heɪstɪ] *adj* **1.** pośpieszny **2.** pochopny

hat [hæt] *s* **1.** kapelusz *m*; ***I'll eat my ~ if*** *fig* kaktus mi na dłoni wyrośnie, jeśli; ***talk through one's ~*** pleść bzdury **2.** czapka *f*; ***~s off!*** czapki z głów!

hatch[1] [hætʃ] *s* **1.** właz *m* **2.** luk *m* **3.** okienko *n* (między kuchnią a jadalnią) **4.** wyłaz *m*

hatch[2] [~] **I** *v/i* wykluwać ⟨-luć⟩ się **II** *v/t* obmyślać ⟨-lić⟩, knuć ⟨u-⟩ **III** *s* ląg *m*, lęg *m*; **hatch out** *v/i* wykluwać ⟨-luć⟩ się

hatch•et ['hætʃɪt] *s* **1.** topór *m*; ***bury the ~*** *fig* zakopać topór wojenny **2.** siekiera *f*

hate [heɪt] **I** *v/t* **1.** nienawidzić **2.** nie znosić, nie cierpieć (***doing s.th.***/***to do s.th.*** robienia czegoś) **II** *s* **1.** nienawiść *f*; ***full of ~*** pełen nienawiści **2.** ***s.th. is s.o.'s pet ~*** coś kogoś mierzi; **hated** ['heɪtɪd] *adj* znienawidzony; **hateful** ['heɪtfʊl] *adj* **1.** nienawistny **2.** pełny nienawiści; **'hate mail** *s* listy *pl* z inwektywami

ha•tred ['heɪtrɪd] *s* nienawiść *f*
'hat stand *s Br* stojący wieszak *m* na kapelusze
haugh•ty ['hɔːtɪ] *adj* wyniosły
haul [hɔːl] **I** *s* **1.** łup *m* **2.** połów *m* **3.** droga *f* **II** *v/t* **1.** ciągnąć **2.** przewozić ⟨-wieźć⟩ **III** *v/i* ciągnąć
haunch [hɔːntʃ] *s* **1.** pośladek *m* **2.** zad *m* **3.** *COOK* udziec *m*
haunt [hɔːnt] **I** *v/t* **1.** nawiedzać ⟨-dzić⟩; ***a ~ed castle*** nawiedzony zamek **2.** straszyć w *L*; ***this room is ~ed*** w tym pokoju straszy **3.** dręczyć, prześladować; ***have a ~ed look*** wyglądać na zaszczutego **4.** być bywalcem *G*, często bywać w *L* **II** *s* ulubione miejsce *n* spotkań; **haunt•ing** ['hɔːntɪŋ] *adj* **1.** dręczący, niedający spokoju **2.** zapadający w pamięć
have [hæv] **I** (*had*; *had*) *v/t* **1.** mieć **2.** posiadać **3.** jeść ⟨z-⟩; ***~ breakfast*** jeść śniadanie **4.** pić ⟨wy-⟩ **5.** przyjmować ⟨-jąć⟩ **6.** dostawać ⟨-tać⟩, otrzymywać ⟨-mać⟩; ***may I have it?*** czy mogę to wziąć? **7.** *party*: wydawać ⟨-dać⟩, urządzać ⟨-dzić⟩ **8.** rodzić ⟨u-⟩; ***she had a baby*** urodziła dziecko **9.** ***~ a look*** spojrzeć; ***~ a try*** spróbować; ***~ a walk*** pójść na spacer **10.** ***~ to*** musieć; ***I ~ to go now*** muszę już iść **11.** ***I've had my hair cut*** byłem u fryzjera; ***she's having her car repaired*** jej samochód jest w naprawie; ***he had his camera stolen*** skradziono mu aparat **12.** *Am* ***I had him sit down*** powiedziałem mu, żeby usiadł **13.** ***I'd rather go than stay*** wolałbym iść niż zostać; ***you'd better go*** lepiej już idź **II** *v aux* ***I have come*** przyszedłem **III** *s* ***the ~s and the ~-nots*** bogaci i biedni; **have back** *v/t* **1.** odzyskiwać ⟨-kać⟩ **2.** dostawać ⟨-tać⟩ z powrotem; **have on** *v/t clothes*: mieć na sobie
ha•ven ['heɪvn] *s* **1.** *fig* przystań *f* **2.** schronienie *n*
have-nots [hæv'nɒts] → ***have III***
haven't ['hævnt] *contracted form* → ***have not***
hav•oc ['hævək] *s* **1.** spustoszenie *n* **2.** zniszczenie *n*; ***wreak ~ on, play ~ with*** **a)** niszczyć **b)** zaszkodzić **3.** zamęt *m*, zamieszanie *n*
hawk [hɔːk] *s* jastrząb *m*
hay [heɪ] *s* siano *n*; ***make ~ while the sun shines*** *fig* kuć żelazo póki gorące; ***hit the ~*** *infml* uderzyć w kimono; **'hay fe•ver** *s MED* katar *m* sienny; **'hay•stack** *s* stóg *m* siana; **'hay•wire** *adj*: ***go ~*** *infml* **a)** (*device*) szwankować **b)** (*plan*) wziąć w łeb **c)** (*person*) fiksować
haz•ard ['hæzəd] **I** *s* niebezpieczeństwo *n*, ryzyko *n*; ***a ~ to health*** zagrożenie zdrowia **II** *v/t* **1.** ryzykować ⟨za-⟩ **2.** narażać ⟨-zić⟩ na szwank; **'haz•ard lights** *pl AUTO* światła *pl* awaryjne; **haz•ard•ous** ['hæzədəs] *adj* **1.** niebezpieczny **2.** ryzykowny
haze [heɪz] *s* **1.** mgiełka *f* **2.** opary *pl* **3.** *fig* otumanienie *n*
ha•zel ['heɪzl] *s* leszczyna *f*; **'ha-zel•nut** *s* orzech *m* laskowy
haz•y ['heɪzɪ] *adj* **1.** mglisty; ***be rather ~ about*** *fig* mieć raczej mgliste pojęcie o *L* **2.** zamglony **3.** niewyraźny **4.** zamazany
H-bomb ['eɪtʃbɒm] *abbr* (=***hydrogen bomb***) bomba *f* wodorowa
he [hiː] *pron* on; ***~ who*** ten, kto
head [hed] **I** *s* **1.** głowa *f*; ***from ~ to foot*** od stóp do głów; ***be ~ over heels in love*** być zakochanym po uszy; ***go to s.o.'s ~*** (*alcohol*, *success*) uderzyć komuś do głowy; ***keep one's ~ above water*** utrzymywać się na powierzchni; ***lose one's ~*** stracić głowę; ***I can't make ~ nor tail of it*** nie mogę się w tym połapać **2.** *coin*: awers *m*; reszka *f*; ***~s or tails?*** orzeł czy reszka?; **3.** *lettuce*, *hammer*: główka *f* **4.** *nail*: łeb *m* **5.** *TECH* głowica *f* **6.** czoło *n*; ***at the ~ of the group*** na czele grupy **7.** góra *f*; ***at the ~ of the page*** u góry strony **8.** *table*: szczyt *m* **9.** wezgłowie *n* **10.** osoba *f*, głowa *f*; ***one pound a ~*** funt na głowę **11.** szef *m*; ***the ~ of government*** szef rządu **12.** przywódca *m* **13.** (*beer*) piana *f* **II** *adj* główny; ***the ~ nurse*** siostra przełożona **III** *v/t* **1.** być na czele **2.** kierować; ***~ed by*** pod kierownictwem *G* **3.** stać na czele **4.** prowadzić ⟨po-⟩ **5.** (*on list*) być na początku **6.** *ball*: uderzać ⟨-rzyć⟩ głową **IV** *v/i* **1.** kierować ⟨s-⟩ się; ***let's ~ back home*** wracajmy do domu **2.** zmierzać; **head for** *v/i* **1.** kierować

się do *G* **2.** zmierzać do *G* **3.** *fig* zmierzać ku *D*

'head•ache *s* ból *m* głowy; ***be a bit of a ~ for s.o.***, ***give s.o. a ~*** być dla kogoś utrapieniem, przyprawiać kogoś o ból głowy

'head•band *s* opaska *f* na czoło; **'head•butt** *v/t* uderzać ⟨-rzyć⟩ głową, *infml* przypakować z główki; **'head•case** *s*: ***be a ~*** *Br infml* mieć nie po kolei w głowie; **'head•dress** *s* **1.** pióropusz *m* **2.** stroik *m* **3.** uczesanie *n*

head•er ['hedə] *s* **1.** *SPORT* główka *f* **2.** nagłówek *m*

head-'first *adv* **1.** *fall*: na główkę **2.** bez zastanowienia

'head•hunt *v/t* zatrudniać ⟨-nić⟩; **'head•hunt•er** *s a. fig* łowca *m* głów

head•ing ['hedɪŋ] *s* **1.** tytuł *m* **2.** nagłówek *m* **3.** ***see below under the ~ of Archives*** patrz niżej w punkcie „Archiwa"

'head•lamp → ***headlight***; **'head•land** *s* **1.** cypel *m* **2.** przylądek *m*; **'head•light** *s AUTO* (przedni) reflektor *m*; ***~s*** przednie światła

'head•line *s* nagłówek *m*; ***hit the ~s*** trafić na pierwsze strony gazet

'head•long **I** *adv* **1.** głową naprzód **2.** na łeb, na szyję **3.** bez zastanowienia **II** *adj* **1.** *fall*: na główkę **2.** *dash*: na oślep, szalony

head•'mas•ter *s* dyrektor *m* szkoły; **head•'mis•tress** *s* dyrektorka *f* szkoły

head 'of•fice *s* **1.** centrala *f* **2.** główna siedziba *f*; **head of 'state** *s* głowa *f* państwa; **head-'on** *adj* **1.** czołowy **2.** bezpośredni; **'head•phones** *pl* słuchawki *pl*; **'head•quar•ters** *pl* **1.** centrala *f* **2.** główna siedziba *f* **3.** kwatera *f* główna; **'head•rest** *s* **1.** podgłówek *m* **2.** *AUTO* zagłówek *m*; **'head•room** *s* **1.** prześwit *m* **2.** ***in vans there's more ~*** w vanach jest więcej miejsca nad głową; **'head•scarf** *pl -scarves s* chustka *f* (na głowę); **'head•set** *s* słuchawki *pl*; **'head start** *s*: ***have a ~*** mieć przewagę (na starcie); **'head•stone** *s* **1.** kamień *m* nagrobny **2.** nagrobek *m*; **'head•strong** *adj* uparty; **head 'teach•er** *s Br* dyrektor *m* szkoły; **head 'wait•er** *s* **1.** kierownik *m* sali **2.** maître d'hôtel *m*; **'head•way** *s* postęp *m*; ***make ~ with*** robić postępy w *L*; **'head•wind** *s* wiatr *m* przeciwny; **'head•word** *s* hasło *n*

head•y ['hedɪ] *adj* **1.** uderzający do głowy **2.** mocny

heal [hi:l] **I** *v/t* leczyć ⟨wy-⟩ (**of** z *G*) **II** (*a.* ***~ up***) *v/i* goić ⟨za-⟩ się; **heal•ing** ['hi:lɪŋ] **I** *s* **1.** leczenie *n* **2.** gojenie *n* się **II** *adj* **1.** leczniczy **2.** gojący

health [helθ] *s* zdrowie *n*; ***on ~ grounds*** z przyczyn zdrowotnych; ***a ~ hazard*** zagrożenie zdrowia; ***the ~ service*** służba zdrowia; ***in good ~*** zdrowy; ***be in poor ~*** mieć problemy zdrowotne, być schorowanym; ***drink to s.o.'s ~*** *Br* wypić czyjeś zdrowie; ***your*** (***very good***) ***~!*** twoje zdrowie!; **'health care** *s* **1.** opieka *f* zdrowotna **2.** służba *f* zdrowia; **'health club** *s* klub *m* fitness; **'health-con•scious** *adj* dbający o zdrowie; **'health farm** *s* ośrodek *m* odnowy biologicznej; **'health food** *s* zdrowa żywność *f*; **'health food store** *s* sklep *m* ze zdrową żywnością; **'health in•su•rance** *s* ubezpieczenie *n* zdrowotne; **'health re•sort** *s* uzdrowisko *n*

health•y ['helθɪ] *adj* **1.** zdrowy **2.** *profit*: znaczny

heap [hi:p] **I** *s* **1.** sterta *f* **2.** ***~s of*** *infml* kupa *G*, mnóstwo *G*; ***~s of time*** *infml* kupa czasu; ***~s of times*** *infml* mnóstwo razy; ***~s better*** *infml* dużo lepiej **II** *v/t* **1.** → ***heap up*** **2.** ***~ praise on s.o.*** obsypać kogoś pochwałami; **heap up** *v/t* **1.** zgarniać ⟨-nąć⟩ na stertę **2.** układać ⟨ułożyć⟩ górę *G* **3.** nakładać ⟨nałożyć⟩ mnóstwo *G*; ***he ~ed his plate with rice*** nałożył sobie na talerz mnóstwo ryżu **4.** układać ⟨ułożyć⟩ jedno na drugim

hear [hɪə] **I** (*heard*; *heard*) *v/t* **1.** słyszeć ⟨u-⟩; ***I heard him laughing*** słyszałem, jak się śmieje **2.** wysłuchiwać ⟨-chać⟩ **II** (*heard*; *heard*) *v/i* słyszeć (**of/about** o *L*); ***he would not ~ of it*** nie chciał nawet o tym słyszeć; **hear from** *v/i* dostawać ⟨-tać⟩ wiadomość od *G*; ***I haven't heard from him for 2 weeks*** nie odzywa się od dwóch tygodni, nie daje znaku życia od dwóch tygodni; **hear out** *v/t* wysłuchiwać ⟨-chać⟩

hear•ing ['hɪərɪŋ] *s* słuch *m*; **'hear•ing aid** *s* aparat *m* słuchowy

H

'**hear•say** *s* pogłoski *pl*

heart [hɑːt] *s* **1.** serce *n*; ***by ~*** na pamięć; ***to one's ~'s content*** do woli; ***with all one's ~*** z całego serca, całym sercem; ***break s.o.'s ~*** złamać komuś serce; ***cry one's ~ out*** wypłakiwać sobie oczy; ***have no ~*** nie mieć serca; ***my ~ sank*** załamałem się; ***take s.th. to ~*** wziąć coś sobie do serca **2.** kier *m*; '**heart•ache** *s fig* **1.** cierpienie *n* **2.** zmartwienie *n*; '**heart at•tack** *s* atak *m* serca, zawał *m* serca; '**heart-beat** *s* bicie *n* serca; '**heart•break•ing** *adj* rozdzierający serce; '**heart•brok-en** *adj* **1.** zrozpaczony **2.** załamany; '**heart•burn** *s MED* zgaga *f*; '**heart con-di•tion**, ***heart dis•ease*** *s MED* choroba *f* serca

H

heart•en ['hɑːtn] *v/t* dodawać ⟨-dać⟩ otuchy; **hear•en•ing** ['hɑːtnɪŋ] *adj* **1.** pokrzepiający **2.** dodający otuchy

'**heart fail•ure** *s MED* **1.** niewydolność *f* serca **2.** zatrzymanie *n* akcji serca; '**heart•felt** *adj* **1.** szczery **2.** serdeczny **3.** gorący

hearth [hɑːθ] *s* **1.** palenisko *n* **2.** ~ (***and home***) ognisko domowe

heart•i•ly ['hɑːtɪlɪ] *adv* **1.** serdecznie **2.** z całego serca **3.** z apetytem **4.** na cały głos **5.** z zapałem

heart•less ['hɑːtlɪs] *adj* bez serca, nieczuły, bezduszny; '**heart•rend•ing** *adj* rozdzierający serce; '**heart throb** *s* obiekt *m* (kobiecych) westchnień; **heart-to-'heart** *s* rozmowa *f* od serca; '**heart trans•plant** *s* **1.** przeszczep *m* serca **2.** transplantacja *f* serca

heart•y ['hɑːtɪ] *adj* **1.** serdeczny **2.** *meal*: solidny **3.** *appetite*: wilczy

heat [hiːt] **I** *s* **1.** gorąco *n*, upał *m* **2.** ciepło *n* **3.** ferwor *m*; ***in the ~ of the moment*** pod wpływem chwili; ***in the ~ of passion*** *JUR* w afekcie **4.** ***the ~s*** *SPORT* eliminacje; ***a*** (***qualifying***) ~ wyścig eliminacyjny **5.** (*animal*) ***on ~***, ***in ~*** w okresie rui **II** *v/t* **1.** ogrzewać ⟨-rzać⟩ **2.** podgrzewać ⟨-rzać⟩ **3.** rozgrzewać ⟨-rzać⟩ **III** *v/i* **1.** ogrzewać ⟨-rzać⟩ się **2.** podgrzewać ⟨-rzać⟩ się; **heat up** *v/t* **1.** podgrzewać ⟨-rzać⟩, ogrzewać ⟨-rzać⟩, zagrzewać ⟨-rzać⟩ **2.** *atmosphere*, *discussion*: podgrzewać ⟨-rzać⟩

heat•ed ['hiːtɪd] *adj* **1.** podgrzewany **2.** ogrzewany **3.** *fig* zaciekły, zajadły, gorący, gwałtowny; **heat•er** ['hiːtə] *s* grzejnik *m*

hea•th ['hiːθ] *s* wrzosowisko *m*

heat•ing ['hiːtɪŋ] *s* ogrzewanie *n*

'**heat•proof** *adj* żaroodporny; '**heat rash** *s MED* potówki *pl*; '**heat-re•sis-tant** *adj* **1.** żaroodporny **2.** termoodporny; '**heat•stroke** *s* udar *m* cieplny; '**heat•wave** *s* fala *f* upałów

heave [hiːv] **I** (*heaved*/*hove*; *heaved*/*hove*) *v/t* **1.** dźwigać ⟨-gnąć⟩ **2.** podźwignąć **3.** przeciągać ⟨-gnąć⟩ **4.** ciskać ⟨-snąć⟩ **II** (*heaved*/*hove*; *heaved*/*hove*) *v/i* **1.** falować **2.** podnosić się i opadać **3.** ciągnąć ⟨po-⟩ z całych sił (***on*** *A*) **4.** mieć nudności **5.** ***~ to*** (*yacht*) zatrzymać się **III** *s* **1.** przeciągnięcie *n* **2.** pchnięcie *n* **3.** dźwignięcie *n*

heav•en ['hevn] *s* **1.** niebo *n*; ***move ~ and earth*** poruszyć niebo i ziemię; ***in seventh ~*** w siódmym niebie; ***thank ~!*** dzięki Bogu! **2.** *fig* raj *m*; **heav-en•ly** ['hevənlɪ] *adj* niebiański, boski

heav•y ['hevɪ] *adj* **1.** ciężki; ***lie ~ on s.o.*** ciążyć komuś **2.** *fabric*: gruby **3.** *blow*, *smell*: mocny **4.** *fine*: wysoki **5.** *rain*: ulewny **6.** *snow*: gęsty **7.** ciężkostrawny **8.** solidny **9.** ociężały **10.** niezgrabny **11.** ***~ with meaning*** *words*: głęboki **12.** ***~ with sleep*** śpiący; **heav-y-'du•ty** *adj* **1.** trwały **2.** wytrzymały **3.** przemysłowy; **heav•y 'goods ve-hi•cle** *s* ciężarówka *f*; **heav•y-'hand-ed** *adj* **1.** niedelikatny **2.** nieokrzesany **3.** *methods*: brutalny **4.** ***don't be too ~ with the salt*** nie przesadzaj z solą; **heav•y 'met•al** *MUS* **I** *s* heavy metal *m* **II** *adj* heavy metalowy; '**heav•y•weight** *SPORT* **I** *s* waga *f* ciężka **II** *adj* wagi ciężkiej

Hebrew ['hiːbruː] **I** *s* **1.** Hebrajczyk *m* **2.** język *m* hebrajski **II** *adj* hebrajski

heck [hek] *s*: ***what the ~?*** *infml* co u licha?

hec•tic ['hektɪk] *adj* gorączkowy, nerwowy

he'd [hiːd] *contracted form* → ***he would, he had***

hedge [hedʒ] **I** *s* **1.** żywopłot *m* **2.** *FIN* zabezpieczenie *n* (***against*** przed *I*) **II** *v/t* **1.** ***~ s.th. in***, ***~ s.th. round*** otoczyć coś żywopłotem; ~ ***s.th. off*** odgrodzić coś żywopłotem **2.** *FIN* zabezpieczać ⟨-czyć⟩ (***against*** przed *I*) **III** *v/i* wykręcać ⟨-cić⟩ się, kluczyć

hedge•hog ['hedʒhɒg] *s* jeż *m*

hedonism ['hiːdənɪzm] *s* hedonizm *m*; **hedonist** ['hiːdənɪst] *s* hedonista *m*; **hedonistic** ['hiːdənɪstk] *adj* hedonistyczny

heed [hiːd] **I** *v/t* zważać ⟨-żyć⟩ na *A* **II** *s* ***pay ~ to***, ***take ~ of*** *form* **a)** zważać na *A* **b)** zwracać uwagę na *A*; **heed•less** ['hiːdlɪs] *adj*: ***be ~ of*** nie zważać na *A*

heel [hiːl] **I** *s* **1.** pięta *f m*; ***follow at s.o.'s ~s*** deptać komuś po piętach; (***hard***) ***on the ~s of*** bezpośrednio po *L*; ***take to one's ~*** wziąć nogi za pas, dać nogę **2.** obcas *m* **II** *v/t* **1.** *ball*: kopać ⟨-pnąć⟩ piętą **2.** reperować ⟨z-⟩ obcas

hef•ty ['heftɪ] *adj* masywny, zwalisty, ciężki, ogromny

he•gem•o•ny [hi'dʒemənɪ] *s* hegemonia *f*

height [haɪt] *s* **1.** wysokość *f*; ***be 10 feet in ~*** mieć 10 stóp wysokości **2.** wzrost *m*; ***what ~ are you?*** ile masz wzrostu? **3.** szczyt *m*; ***at the ~ of one's fame*** u szczytu sławy **4.** pełnia *f*; ***at the ~ of summer*** w pełni lata; **height•en** ['haɪtn] **I** *v/t* zwiększać ⟨-szyć⟩, wzmagać ⟨-móc⟩, potęgować ⟨s-⟩ **II** *v/i* wzrastać ⟨-rosnąć⟩, potęgować ⟨s-⟩ się, wzmagać ⟨-móc⟩ się

heir [eə] *s* spadkobierca *m*, następca *m*; ***an ~ to the throne*** następca tronu; **heir•ess** ['eərɪs] *s* spadkobierczyni *f*, następczyni *f*; **heir•loom** ['eərluːm] *s* pamiątka *f* rodzinna

held [held] *Past Simple and Past Participle* → ***hold***

hel•i•cop•ter ['helɪkɒptə] *s* helikopter *m*, śmigłowiec *m*; **hel•i•port** ['helɪpɔːt] heliport *m*

he•li•um ['hiːlɪəm] *s* *CHEM* hel *m*

hell [hel] *s* **1.** piekło *n*; ***hurt like ~*** boleć jak diabli; ***a ~ of a noise*** straszny hałas; ***what the ~?*** co do diabła?; ***give s.o. ~*** **a)** zrobić komuś piekielną awanturę **b)** dać się komuś we znaki; ***go to ~!*** idź do diabła! **2.** ***oh ~!*** o cholera!

he'll [hiːl] *contracted form* → ***he will***

hell-'bent *adj*: ***be ~ on doing s.th.*** chcieć coś zrobić (nie bacząc na konsekwencje); ***he's ~ on finding her*** *infml* uparł się, że ją znajdzie; ***be ~ on revenge*** być zaślepionym żądzą zemsty; '**hell•hole** *s* **1.** *fig* piekło *n* **2.** nora *f*; **hell•ish** ['helɪʃ] *adj* potworny, piekielny, okropny

hel•lo [hə'ləʊ] **I** *interj* cześć!, halo! **II** *s* ***say ~*** przywitać się (***to*** z *I*)

helm [helm] *s* ster *m*; ***be at the ~*** być u steru, być przy sterze; ***take the ~*** przejąć ster

hel•met ['helmɪt] *s* **1.** kask *m* **2.** hełm *m*

help [help] **I** *v/t* **1.** pomagać ⟨-móc⟩ (***s.o. in/with*** komuś przy *L*); ***~ s.o.*** (***to***) ***do s.th.*** pomóc komuś coś zrobić **2.** ***~ s.o. to*** poczęstować kogoś *I*; ***~ oneself*** poczęstować się **3.** ***I can't ~ it*** nic na to nie poradzę; ***it cannot be ~ed*** nie ma na to rady; ***I could not ~ laughing*** nie mogłem się powstrzymać od śmiechu **II** *v/i* pomagać ⟨-móc⟩ **III** *s* **1.** pomoc *f*; ***come to s.o.'s ~*** przyjść komuś z pomocą **2.** pomoc *f* domowa **3.** służba *f*; **help out** *v/t* pomagać ⟨-móc⟩

help•er ['helpə] *s* pomocnik *m*; **help•ful** ['helpfəl] *adj* **1.** pomocny, użyteczny, przydatny **2.** uczynny; **help•ing** ['helpɪŋ] *s* porcja *f*; ***have a second ~*** zjeść dokładkę; **help•less** ['helplɪs] *adj* bezradny, bezsilny **2.** bezbronny; **help•less•ly** ['helplɪslɪ] *adv* bezradnie, bezsilnie; **help•less•ness** ['helplɪsnɪs] *s* bezradność *f*, bezsilność *f*, bezbronność *f*; '**help line** *s* telefon *m* zaufania

hel•ter-skel•ter [heltə'skeltə] **I** *adj* **1.** bezładny **2.** *rush*: szalony **II** *adv* *run*: na łeb, na szyję

hem [hem] **I** *s* **1.** rąbek *m* **2.** brzeg *m* **II** *v/t* **1.** obszywać ⟨-szyć⟩ **2.** obrębiać ⟨-bić⟩ **3.** ***be ~med in by*** być otoczonym przez *A* **4.** ***~ and haw*** *Am* **a)** długo się zastanawiać **b)** zwlekać z decyzją

he-man ['hiːmæn] *s* *infml* **1.** mięśniak *m* **2.** macho *m*

hem•i•sphere ['hemɪsfɪə] *s* półkula *f*

he•mo•glo•bin *Am* → ***haemoglobin***

he•mo•phil•i•a *Am* → ***haemophilia***

hem•or•rhage *Am* → ***haemorrhage***

hem•or•rhoids *Am* → ***haemorrhoids***

H

hemp [hemp] *s* **1.** konopie *pl* (indyjskie) **2.** haszysz *m*
hen [hen] *s* kura *f*
hence [hens] *adv form* **1.** stąd, a więc; *~ **it follows that*** z tego wynika, że **2.** za *A*; ***eight months** ~* za osiem miesięcy
hence•forth [hens'fɔːθ] ***hence•forward(s)*** [hens'fɔːwəd(z)] *adv lit* **1.** odtąd **2.** od tamtego czasu
'hen par•ty *s* **1.** wieczór *m* panieński **2.** babski wieczór *m*
hen•pecked ['henpekt] *adj*: ***a ~ husband*** pantoflarz *m*
hep•a•ti•tis [hepə'taɪtɪs] *s MED* zapalenie *n* wątroby
heptagon ['heptəgən] *s* siedmiokąt *m*
heptagonal [hep'tʌgənl] *adj* siedmiokątny
her [hɜː] **I** *pron* **1.** ***I gave ~ the book*** dałem jej tę książkę; ***I know ~*** znam ją; ***he's younger than ~*** on jest młodszy od niej; → ***she*** **2.** ***it's ~*** to ona **3.** (*reflexive*) ***she looked about ~*** rozejrzała się **II** *poss* jej, swój; ***she likes her job*** lubi swoją pracę; ***I like her dress*** podoba mi się jej sukienka
herald ['herəld] **I** *s* **1.** herold *m* **2.** *fig* zwiastun *m* **II** *v/t* zwiastować, zapowiadać
herb [hɜːb] *s* zioło *n*, ziele *n*, przyprawa *f* ziołowa; **herb•al** ['hɜːbl] *adj* ziołowy; **herb(al) 'tea** *s* herbata *f* ziołowa; **her•bi•cide** ['hɜːbɪsaɪd] *s* herbicyd *m*; **her•bi•vore** ['hɜːbɪvɔː] *s* zwierzę *n* roślinożerne; **her•biv•o•rous** [hɜː'bɪvərəs] *adj* roślinożerny
herd [hɜːd] **I** *s* **1.** stado *n* **2.** tłum *m*; ***follow the ~*** płynąć z falą, płynąć z prądem **II** *v/t* **1.** zaganiać ⟨-gonić⟩ **2.** pędzić ⟨za-, prze-⟩ **3.** *people*: gromadzić ⟨z-⟩, tłoczyć ⟨s-⟩ **III** *v/i* ***~ together*** **a)** gromadzić się **b)** żyć w stadzie; **'herd in•stinct** *s* instynkt *m* stadny; **'herds•man** *pl -men s* pasterz *m*
here [hɪə] *adv* tutaj, tu; ***come ~*** chodź tu; ***~ and there*** tu i tam; ***~'s to you!*** twoje zdrowie!; ***~ you are*** (*handing in*) proszę; **here•abouts** [hɪərə'baʊts] *adv* **1.** w okolicy **2.** w pobliżu **3.** tutaj; **hereaf•ter** [hɪər'ɑːftə] *adv* **1.** dalej **2.** odtąd, od tej chwili **3.** *life*: po śmierci; **here•by** [hiə'baɪ] *adv JUR* niniejszym
he•red•i•ta•ry [hə'redɪterɪ] *adj* dziedziczny; ***a ~ disease*** choroba dziedziczna; **he•red•i•ty** [hə'redɪtɪ] *s* dziedziczność *f*
here•in [hiər'ɪn] *adv JUR* **1.** tu, tutaj **2.** w niniejszej umowie **3.** w niniejszym piśmie; **here•of** [hiər'ɒv] *adv*: ***from the date ~*** *form* **a)** od daty zawarcia niniejszej umowy **b)** od daty niniejszego pisma
her•e•sy ['herəsɪ] *s* herezja *f*; **her•e•tic** ['herətɪk] *s* heretyk *m*; **he•ret•i•cal** [hɪ'retɪkl] *adj* heretycki
here•with [hiə'wɪð] *adv form* w załączeniu; ***I enclose ~*** załączam
her•it•a•ble ['herɪtəbl] *adj JUR* dziedziczny; **her•i•tage** ['herɪtɪdʒ] *s* **1.** spadek *m* **2.** dziedzictwo *n* **3.** spuścizna *f*
her•maph•ro•dite [hɜː'mæfrədaɪt] **I** *s* hermafrodyta *m* **II** *adj* hermafrodytyczny
her•met•ic [hɜː'metɪk] *adj* hermetyczny; **her•met•i•cal•ly** [hɜː'metɪklɪ] *adv* hermetycznie
her•mit ['hɜːmɪt] *s* pustelnik *m*; **her•mit•age** ['hɜːmɪtɪdʒ] *s* pustelnia *f*
her•ni•a ['hɜːnjə] *s* przepuklina *f*
he•ro ['hɪərəʊ] *s* **1.** bohater *m*, heros *m* **2.** idol *m*, bożyszcze *n*; **he•ro•ic** [hɪ'rəʊɪk] *adj* bohaterski, heroiczny; **he•ro•ic•ally** [hi'rəʊɪklɪ] *adv* bohatersko, heroicznie
her•o•in ['herəʊɪn] *s* heroina *f*; **'her•o•in ad•dict** *s* heroinista *m*
her•o•ine ['herəʊɪn] *s* **1.** bohaterka *f* **2.** heroina *f* **3.** idolka *f*, bożyszcze *n*
her•o•ism ['herəʊɪzm] *s* bohaterstwo *n*, heroizm *m*
her•ring ['herɪŋ] *s* śledź *m*; **'her•ring•bone** *s* jodełka *f*; ***a ~ design*** jodełka, wzór w jodełkę
hers [hɜːrz] *poss* jej; ***it's ~*** to jej, to jest jej; ***a friend of ~*** jej przyjaciel
her•self [hɜːr'self] *pron* **1.** sama; ***she did it ~*** zrobiła to sama **2.** się; ***she killed ~*** zabiła się **3.** siebie; ***she wants it for ~*** chce tego dla siebie
he's [hiːz] *contracted form* → **he is, he has**
hes•i•tant ['hezɪtənt] *adj* niepewny, niezdecydowany, wahający się; ***be ~ about doing s.th.*** wahać się, czy coś zrobić; **hes•i•tant•ly** ['hezɪtəntlɪ]

H

adv niepewnie, z wahaniem; **hes•i•tate** ['hezɪteɪt] *v/i* wahać ⟨za-⟩ się; **~ *about doing s.th.*** wahać się, czy coś zrobić; ***not ~ to do s.th.*** nie wahać się czegoś zrobić; **hes•i•ta•tion** [hezɪ'teɪʃn] *s* wahanie *n*, niezdecydowanie *n*, niepewność *f*

het•er•o•ge•ne•ous [hetərəʊ'dʒiːnɪəs] *adj* heterogeniczny

het•er•o•sex•u•al [hetərəʊ'sekʃʊəl] **I** *s* heteroseksualista *m* **II** *adj* heteroseksualny

hew [hjuː] (*hewed*; *hewn*) *v/t* **1.** rąbać; **~ *s.th. down*** porąbać coś; **~ *s.th. off*** odrąbać coś **2.** ociosywać ⟨-sać⟩

hewn [hjuːn] *Past Participle* → **hew**

hex•a•gon ['heksəgən] *s* sześciobok *m*, sześciokąt *m*; **hex•ag•o•nal** [hek'sægənl] *adj* sześciokątny

hey [heɪ] *interj* **1.** hej! **2.** ejże! **3. *~ presto!*** hokus-pokus!

hey•day ['heɪdeɪ] *s* **1.** okres *m* rozkwitu **2.** złoty okres *m* **3.** najlepsze czasy *pl*; ***in its ~*** za swoich najlepszych czasów **4.** najlepsze lata *pl*; ***be in one's ~*** przeżywać najlepsze lata

hi [haɪ] *interj infml* cześć!

hi•ber•nate ['haɪbəneɪt] *v/i* zapadać ⟨-paść⟩ w sen zimowy

hi•bis•cus [hɪ'bɪskəs] *s* hibiskus *m*, ketmia *f*

hic•cough ['hɪkʌp], ***hic•cup*** **I** *s* **1.** czkawka *f*; ***have the ~s*** mieć czkawkę **2.** drobny problem *m*, drobna przeszkoda *f* **II** *v/i* mieć czkawkę, czkać ⟨-knąć⟩

hick [hɪk] *Am infml* **I** *s* kmiot *m*, prostak *m* **II** *adj* prostacki; **'hick town** *s Am infml* prowincjonalna dziura *f*

hid [hɪd] *Past Simple* → **hide**[1]

hid•den ['hɪdn] **I** *Past Participle* → **hide**[1] **II** *adj* ukryty; **hid•den a'gen•da** *s* ukryte motywy *pl*

hide[1] [haɪd] **I** (*hid*; *hidden*) *v/t* ukrywać ⟨-ryć⟩, chować ⟨s-⟩ (***from*** przed *I*) **II** (*hid*; *hidden*) *v/i* **1.** ukrywać ⟨-ryć⟩ się **2.** chować ⟨s-⟩ się

hide[2] [~] *s* skóra *f*; ***save one's own ~*** ratować (własną) skórę; ***tan s.o.'s ~*** wygarbować komuś skórę

hide-and-'seek *s Br* zabawa *f* w chowanego; ***play ~*** bawić się w chowanego; **'hide•a•way**, **'*hide out*** *s* kryjówka *f*

'hide•bound *adj* skostniały, konserwatywny

hid•e•ous ['hɪdɪəs] *adj* szkaradny, ohydny, okropny

hid•ing ['haɪdɪŋ] *s* ***be in ~*** ukrywać się; ***he had to go into ~*** musiał się ukrywać; **'hid•ing place** *s* kryjówka *f*

hierarchical [haɪə'rɑːkɪkl] *adj* hierarchiczny; **hi•er•ar•chy** ['haɪərɑːkɪ] *s* hierarchia *f*

hi•er•oglyph•ic [haɪərə'glɪfɪk] **I** *s* hieroglif *m* **II** *adj* hieroglificzny; **hi•er•oglyph•ics** [haɪərə'glɪfɪks] *pl* pismo *n* hieroglificzne

hi-fi ['haɪfaɪ] **I** *s* **1.** → ***high fidelity*** **2.** zestaw *m* hi-fi **II** *adj* hi-fi

high [haɪ] **I** *adj* **1.** wysoki; ***be 10 feet ~*** mieć 10 stóp wysokości; ***it's ~ time*** najwyższy czas **2. *be ~ in fat*** zawierać dużo tłuszczu **3.** *tension*: wielki **4. *in ~ season*** w sezonie **5.** *infml* na haju, naćpany **6.** *principle*: szlachetny **7.** *food*: niezbyt świeży **II** *adv* wysoko; ***aim ~*** mierzyć wysoko; ***search ~ and low*** szukać wszędzie **III** *s* **1.** wysokość *f*; ***from on ~*** **a)** z góry **b)** z niebios **2.** obszar *m* wysokiego ciśnienia **3.** (wysoki) poziom *m*; ***the company profits reached an all-time ~*** firma zanotowała najwyższe zyski w swojej historii **4.** *Am infml* → ***high school***

high 'al•tar *s* ołtarz *m* główny; **high-'al•ti•tude** *s* duża wysokość *f*; **high and 'might•y** *adj* napuszony, arogancki; **high 'beam** *s AUTO Am* światła *pl* długie; **'high•brow I** *s* intelektualista *m* **II** *adj* intelektualny, trudny w odbiorze; **high•'chair** *s* wysokie krzesełko *n* (dziecięce); **high-'class** *adj* luksusowy, wysokiej klasy; **high 'div•ing** *s SPORT* skoki *pl* z wieży

high•er ed•u•ca•tion [haɪəedjʊ'keɪʃn] *s* **1.** szkolnictwo *n* wyższe **2.** wyższe wykształcenie *n*

high ex'plo•sive *s* materiał *m* wybuchowy kruszący; **high-fi'del•i•ty** *s MUS* wysoka wierność *f* odtwarzania dźwieku, hi-fi *n*; **high-'fli•er** *s*: ***be a ~*** *infml* mierzyć wysoko, być ambitnym; **high-'flown** *adj* górnolotny; **high 'fre•quen•cy** *s* wysoka częstotliwość *f*; **high-'grade** *adj* **1.** wysokogatunkowy **2.** *ore*: wysokoprocentowy; **high-'hand•ed** *adj* **1.** arbitralny

H

2. arogancki; **high-ˈheeled** *adj* na wysokim obcasie; **ˈhigh jump** *s SPORT* skok *m* wzwyż; **ˈhigh jump•er** *s SPORT* skoczek *m* wzwyż; **ˈhigh•lands** *pl* obszar *m* górski; ***the*** ***~*** *góry i wyżyny w północnej Szkocji*; **high-ˈlev•el** *adj* **1.** *talks*: na wysokim szczeblu **2.** *official*: wysoki; **ˈhigh life** *s* światowe życie *n*; **ˈhigh•light I** *s* **1.** główna atrakcja *f* **2.** punkt *m* kulminacyjny; ***the ~s of a match*** najciekawsze momenty meczu **3.** **~s** pasemka **II** *v/t* **1.** podkreślać ⟨-lić⟩, uwydatniać ⟨-nić⟩ **2.** zwracać ⟨-rócić⟩ uwagę na *A* **3.** rozjaśniać ⟨-nić⟩ **4.** zakreślać ⟨-lić⟩, zaznaczać ⟨-czyć⟩; **ˈhigh•light•er** *s* marker *m*, mazak *m* fluorescencyjny

H

high•ly [ˈhaɪlɪ] *adv* **1.** bardzo; ***~ interesting*** bardzo interesujący **2.** wysoce; ***be ~ regarded*** być wysoce cenionym **3.** wielce; ***~ gifted*** wielce utalentowany **4.** wysoko; ***~ paid*** wysoko opłacony **5.** bardzo dobrze; ***think ~ of s.o.*** mieć o kimś wysokie mniemanie

high-necked [haɪˈnekt] *adj* pod szyję

High•ness [ˈhaɪnɪs] *s*: ***Your ~*** Wasza Wysokość

high-perˈform•ance *s* **1.** bardzo wydajny, wysokowydajny **2.** *car*: o wysokich parametrach silnika; **high-ˈpitched** *adj* **1.** *voice*: cienki, piskliwy **2.** *sound*: wysoki; **ˈhigh point** *s fig* apogeum *n*; **high-ˈpow•ered** *adj* **1.** o dużej mocy **2.** o dużym zasięgu **3.** *person*: dynamiczny; **high ˈpres•sure** *s* wysokie ciśnienie *n*; **high-ˈpres•sure** *adj* **1.** *area*: wysokiego ciśnienia **2.** wysokociśnieniowy **3.** *job*: stresujący; **high ˈpriest** *s REL* arcykapłan *m*; **high-ˈqual•i•ty** *adj* wysokiej jakości; **high-ˈrank•ing** *adj* **1.** wysoki, wysoki rangą **2.** ważny; **high-res•oˈlu•tion** *s* wysoka rozdzielczość *f*; **ˈhigh-rise** *s* wieżowiec *m*, wysokościowiec *m*; **high ˈseas** *pl* wody *pl* eksterytorialne; **ˈhigh school** *s Am* liceum *n*; **high soˈci•e•ty** *s* wytworne towarzystwo *n*, socjeta *f*; **high-speed ˈtrain** *s* superszybki pociąg *m*; **high-ˈspir•it•ed** *adj* pełen życia; **ˈhigh street** *s* główna ulica *f*; **high-ˈstrung** *adj Am* bardzo nerwowy; **high ˈtech** *adj* nowoczesny, zaawansowany technologicznie; **high techˈnol•o•gy** *s* **1.** nowoczesna technika *f* **2.** zaawansowana technologia *f*; **high-ˈten•sion** *adj*: ***~ cables*** przewody wysokiego napięcia; **high ˈtide** *s* przypływ *m*; **high ˈtrea•son** *s* zdrada *f* stanu; **high ˈwa•ter** *s* przypływ *m*, wysoka woda *f*; **ˈhigh•way** *s* **1.** *Br* droga *f* (publiczna); ***the ~ code*** kodeks drogowy **2.** *Am* autostrada *f*; **ˈhigh wire** *s* lina *f* do balansowania

hi•jack [ˈhaɪdʒæk] **I** *v/t* **1.** porywać ⟨-rwać⟩ **2.** uprowadzać ⟨-dzić⟩ **II** *s* **1.** porwanie *n* **2.** uprowadzenie *n*; **hi•jack•er** [ˈhaɪdʒækə] *s* porywacz *m*

hike[1] [haɪk] *v/t*: ***~ up*** *trousers*: podciągać ⟨-gnąć⟩

hike[2] [~] **I** *v/i* wędrować **II** *s* **1.** piesza wycieczka *f*; ***go on a ~*** iść na wycieczkę **2.** wędrówka *f*; **hik•er** [ˈhaɪkə] *s* turysta *m* (pieszy); **hik•ing** [ˈhaɪkɪŋ] *s* **1.** turystyka *f* piesza **2.** piesze wycieczki *pl*; ***go ~*** pójść na wycieczkę pieszą; **ˈhik•ing boots** *pl* buty *pl* turystyczne

hi•lar•i•ous [hɪˈleərɪəs] *adj* bardzo zabawny, komiczny; **hi•lar•i•ty** [hɪˈlærətɪ] *s* (wielka) radość *f*

hill [hɪl] *s* wzgórze *n*, pagórek *m*, wzniesienie *n*; (***as***) ***old as the ~s*** stary jak świat; ***be over the ~*** mieć (już) z górki

hill•bil•ly [ˈhɪlbɪlɪ] *s Am infml* prostak *m*, wieśniak *m*

ˈhill•side *s* zbocze *n*, stok *m*; **ˈhill•top** *s* szczyt *m* (wzgórza); **ˈhill walk•er** *s* turysta *m* górski; **ˈhill walk•ing** *s* turystyka *f* górska

hill•y [ˈhɪlɪ] *adj* pagórkowaty

him [hɪm] *pron* **1.** ***I know ~*** znam go; ***she's younger than ~*** jest od niego młodsza; ***I gave ~ a book*** dałem mu książkę; → ***he*** **2.** ***it's ~*** to on **3.** ***he looked about ~*** rozejrzał się

him•self [hɪmˈself] *pron* **1.** sam; ***he did it ~*** zrobił to sam **2.** się; ***he killed ~*** zabił się **3.** siebie; ***he wants it for ~*** chce tego dla siebie

hin•der [ˈhɪndə] *v/t* **1.** przeszkadzać ⟨-kodzić⟩ (***s.o. from*** komuś w *L*) **2.** utrudniać ⟨-nić⟩ (***s.o. from*** komuś *A*) **3.** opóźniać ⟨-nić⟩

Hindi [ˈhɪndɪ] *s* hindi *n*, język *m* hindi

hin•drance ['hɪndrəns] *s* **1.** przeszkoda *f*; ***be a ~ to*** przeszkadzać *D*, być przeszkodą dla *G* **2.** zawada *f*
hind•sight ['haɪndsaɪt] *s* ***with ~*** z perspektywy czasu
Hin•du [hɪn'duː] **I** *s* **1.** Hindus *m* **2.** *REL* hinduista *m* **II** *adj* **1.** hinduski **2.** *REL* hinduistyczny; **Hin•du•ism** ['hɪnduɪzəm] *s* hinduizm *m*
hinge [hɪndʒ] **I** *s* zawias *m* **II** *v/t* zawieszać ⟨-sić⟩ na zawiasach; **hinge on** *v/i* **1.** obracać ⟨rócić⟩ się na *L* **2.** *fig* zależeć od *G*
hinged ['hɪndʒd] *adj* na zawiasach
hint [hɪnt] **I** *s* **1.** aluzja *f*; ***drop a ~ that*** napomknąć, że; ***a broad ~*** wyraźna aluzja **2.** wskazówka *f*, rada *f* (**on** na temat *G*, co do *G*), **3.** odrobina *f*, cień *m* (**of** *G*) **II** *v/i* **1.** ***~ that*** dać do zrozumienia, że **2.** robić ⟨z-⟩ aluzję; ***what are you ~ing at?*** co chcesz przez to powiedzieć?
hin•ter•land ['hɪntəlænd] *s*: ***in the ~*** w głębi lądu
hip[1] [hɪp] *s* **1.** biodro *n* **2.** staw *m* biodrowy
hip[2] [~] *s* owoc *m* dzikiej róży
hip[3] [~] *adj*: ***be ~*** *infml* być na czasie, być trendy
'**hip•bone** *s* kość *f* biodrowa; '**hip flask** *s* piersiówka *f*; '**hip joint** *s* staw *m* biodrowy
hip•pie ['hɪpɪ] **I** *s* hipis *m* **II** *adj* hipisowski
hippo ['hɪpəʊ] *s infml* hipopotam *m*
hip 'pock•et *s* tylna kieszeń *f* (spodni)
hip•po•pot•a•mus [hɪpə'pɒtəməs] *s* hipopotam *m*
hip•py → ***hippie***
hire [haɪə] **I** *v/t* **1.** wynajmować ⟨-jąć⟩; ***a ~d killer*** wynajęty zabójca **2.** wypożyczać ⟨-czyć⟩ **3.** zatrudniać ⟨-nić⟩ **II** *s* wynajem *m*, wypożyczanie *n*; ***a ~ company*** **a)** wypożyczalnia **b)** firma zajmująca się wynajmem samochodów; ***s.th. is on ~*** **a)** coś można wynająć **b)** coś można wypożyczyć; ***for ~*** **a)** do wynajęcia **b)** do wypożyczenia; **hire out** *v/t* **1.** wynajmować ⟨-jąć⟩ **2.** wypożyczać ⟨-czyć⟩; **hire 'pur•chase** *s* sprzedaż *f* ratalna
his [hɪz] *poss* jego, swój; ***it's ~*** to jego, to jest jego; ***he likes ~ job*** lubi swoją pracę; ***a friend of ~*** jego przyjaciel

His•pan•ic [hɪ'spænɪk] **I** *s* Latynos *m* **II** *adj* **1.** latynoski **2.** iberyjski
hiss [hɪs] **I** *v/i* syczeć ⟨za-⟩ (**at** na *A*), syknąć (**at** na *A*) **II** *v/t* **1.** wysyczeć **2.** *performance*, *speech*: wygwizdywać ⟨-dać⟩ **III** *s* **4.** syk *m*, syknięcie *n*, syczenie *n*
his•to•ri•an [hɪ'stɔːrɪən] *s* historyk *m*; **his•tor•ic** [hɪ'stɒrɪk] *adj* historyczny, o znaczeniu historycznym; **his•tor•i•cal** [hɪ'stɒrɪkl] *adj* historyczny; ***a ~ novel*** powieść historyczna
his•to•ry ['hɪstərɪ] *s* **1.** historia *f*; ***contemporary ~*** historia najnowsza; ***~ of art*** historia sztuki; ***go down in ~ as*** przejść do historii jako; ***make ~*** przejść do historii **2.** tradycja *f*
hit [hɪt] **I** *s* **1.** cios *m*, uderzenie *n* **2.** *SPORT* trafienie *n*; ***make a ~, score a ~*** zdobyć punkt **3.** przebój *m*, hit *m*; ***it was a big ~*** to był wielki przebój **4.** *drug*: działka *f*, szpryca *f*, sztach *m* **5.** *Am infml* mokra robota *f* **II** (*hit*; *hit*) *v/t* **1.** uderzać ⟨-rzyć⟩; ***~ one's head against*** uderzyć głową w *A* **2.** trafiać ⟨-fić⟩; ***~ the nail on the head*** *fig* trafić w sedno; ***he hit the bottle*** *fig* zaczął pić, zaczął zaglądać do kieliszka **3.** uderzać ⟨-rzyć⟩ w *A*; ***the car ~ a tree*** samochód uderzył w drzewo **4.** napotykać ⟨-tkać⟩ **5.** dojeżdżać ⟨-jechać⟩ do *G* **6.** *level*: osiągać ⟨-gnąć⟩ **7.** (*kill*) *infml* załatwiać ⟨-wić⟩, sprzątnąć; **hit back** *v/i* **1.** oddawać ⟨-dać⟩ (cios), odpowiadać ⟨-wiedzieć⟩ na cios **2.** odgrywać ⟨odegrać⟩ się; ***~ at the critics*** odpowiedzieć na zarzuty krytyków; **hit on** *v/i* wpadać ⟨wpaść⟩ na *A*, odkrywać ⟨-ryć⟩, napotykać ⟨-tkać⟩; **hit out** *v/i fig* atakować ⟨za-⟩ (**at** *A*), krytykować ⟨s-⟩ (**at** *A*)
hit-and-'run *adj*: ***a ~ accident*** wypadek, którego sprawca zbiegł; ***a ~ driver*** kierowca, który zbiegł z miejsca wypadku
hitch [hɪtʃ] **I** *s* **1.** szarpnięcie *n* **2.** (drobny) problem *m*; ***without a ~*** bez problemów, gładko **II** *v/t* **1.** uwiązywać ⟨-zać⟩, doczepiać ⟨-pić⟩ **2.** ***get ~ed*** *infml* hajtnąć się **3.** ***~ a ride, ~ a lift*** złapać okazję **III** *v/i* **1.** → ***hitch up 1, 2*** **2.** → ***hitchhike***; **hitch up** *v/t*

H

1. podciągać ⟨-gnąć⟩ **2.** podkasywać ⟨-sać⟩ **3.** zaprzęgać ⟨-rząc⟩

'hitch•hike *v/i* jeździć autostopem, jechać ⟨po-⟩ autostopem; **'hitch•hik•er** *s* autostopowicz *m*; **'hitch•hik•ing** *s* autostop *m*

hi-'tech → ***high tech***

hith•er ['hɪðə] *adv* tutaj; **hith•er•to** [hɪðə'tuː] *adv* **1.** dotychczas, do tej pory **2.** do tamtej pory

'hit•list *s* czarna lista *f*; ***be on the ~*** *fig* być do odstrzału; **'hit•man** *pl -men s* płatny zabójca *m*; **hit-or-'miss** *adj* nieprzewidywalny; **'hit squad** *s* oddział *m* specjalny

HIV [eɪtʃaɪ'viː] *abbr* (=***human immunodeficiency virus***) wirus *m* HIV

hive [haɪv] *s* **1.** ul *m* **2.** rój *m*; **hive off** *v/t* **1.** sprzedawać ⟨-dać⟩ **2.** odłączać ⟨-czyć⟩

hoard [hɔːd] **I** *v/t* **1.** gromadzić ⟨z-⟩ **2.** ciułać ⟨u-⟩ **II** *s* **1.** zapas *m* **2.** skarb *m*; **hoard•er** ['hɔːdə] *s* **1.** *fig* chomik *m* **2.** ciułacz *m*

hoar•frost [hɔː'frɒst] *s* szron *m*

hoarse [hɔːs] *adj* zachrypnięty, ochrypły; **hoarse•ness** ['hɔːsnɪs] *s* chrypka *f*

hoar•y ['hɔːrɪ] *adj* **1.** ***a ~ old joke*** dowcip z brodą **2.** siwy

hoax [həʊks] **I** *s* **1.** kawał *m*; ***play a ~ on s.o.*** nabrać kogoś, zrobić komuś kawał **2.** ***a bomb ~*** fałszywy alarm o podłożeniu bomby **II** *v/t* **1.** nabierać ⟨-brać⟩; **hoax•er** ['həʊksə] *s* kawalarz *m*

hob•by ['hɒbɪ] *s* konik *m*, hobby *n*

hob•gob•lin ['hɒbgɒblɪn] *s* chochlik *m*, gnom *m*

hob•nob ['hɒbnɒb] *v/i*: ***~ with*** *infml* kręcić się koło *G*

hock[1] [hɒk] *s* białe wino *n* reńskie

hock[2] [~] **I** *s* zastaw *m*; ***in ~*** **a)** zadłużony **b)** zastawiony; ***put s.th. into ~*** zastawiać coś **II** *v/t* zastawiać ⟨-wić⟩

hock•ey ['hɒkɪ] *s* SPORT **1.** *Br* hokej *m* na trawie **2.** *Am* hokej *m* na lodzie

ho•cus-po•cus [həʊkəs'pəʊkəs] *s* **1.** bzdury *pl* **2.** sztuczki *pl* **3.** hokus-pokus *m*

hodge•podge ['hɒdʒpɒdʒ] *Am* → ***hotchpotch***

hoe [həʊ] **I** *s* motyka *f* **II** *v/t* **1.** *plants*: okopywać ⟨-pać⟩ **2.** *ground*: spulchniać ⟨-nić⟩

hog [hɒg] **I** *s* **1.** *Am* świnia *f*, tucznik *m*; ***go the whole ~*** *fig* pójść na całego **2.** *Br* wieprz *m* **II** *v/t infml bathroom*: okupować; ***~ the road*** jechać środkiem (jezdni)

'hog•wash *s* **1.** *infml* bzdury *pl*, bzdety *pl* **2.** pomyje *pl*

hoist [hɔɪst] **I** *v/t* wciągać ⟨-gnąć⟩, dźwigać ⟨-gnąć⟩ **II** *s* dźwig *m*, winda *f*

hold [həʊld] **I** (*held*; *held*) *v/t* **1.** trzymać; ***~ o.s. erect*** trzymać się prosto **2.** trzymać się za *A*, trzymać się za *G*; ~ hands trzymać się za ręce; ***~ one's nose*** zatykać nos **3.** *party*, *meeting*, *conference*: organizować ⟨z-⟩; ***the meeting will be held on Monday*** spotkanie odbędzie się w poniedziałek **4.** *shares*, *licence*: posiadać **5.** *opinion*: mieć **6.** ***s.o. ~s a record*** rekord należy do kogoś **7.** *weight*: utrzymywać ⟨-mać⟩ **8.** ***~ oneself ready*** być gotowym **9.** powstrzymywać ⟨-mać⟩; ***there was no ~ing him*** nie dało się go powstrzymać **10.** *election*: przeprowadzać ⟨-dzić⟩ **11.** *army*: utrzymywać ⟨-mać⟩ **12.** ***~ one's own*** nie poddawać się **13.** przechowywać ⟨-chować⟩ **14.** wyznawać ⟨-nać⟩, uważać **15.** ***s.o. will be held responsible for*** ktoś zostanie pociągnięty do odpowiedzialności za *A* **16.** *seat*: zajmować ⟨-jąć⟩ **17.** *hostages*: przetrzymywać **18.** zawierać **19.** mieścić **II** (*held*; *held*) *v/i* **1.** wytrzymywać ⟨-mać⟩ **2.** (*glue*) trzymać **3.** (*a.* ***~ good***) obowiązywać, pozostawać ⟨-tać⟩ w mocy **4.** (*weather*) utrzymywać ⟨-mać⟩ się **5.** czekać; ***please ~*** proszę poczekać **III** *s* **1.** chwyt *m*, uścisk *m*; ***catch ~ of***, ***get ~ of*** chwycić *A*, złapać *A*; ***get ~ of s.o.*** *fig* złapać kogoś, skontaktować się z kimś; ***keep ~ of*** trzymać się *G*; ***let go one's ~ of*** puścić *A*; ***no ~s barred*** wszyskie chwyty dozwolone **2.** kontrola *f*; ***lose one's ~*** stracić kontrolę nad sobą; ***have a (firm) ~ over s.o.*** mieć kogoś w garści; **hold against** *v/t*: ***hold s.th. against s.o.*** mieć coś komuś za złe; **hold back I** *v/t* **1.** powstrzymywać

⟨-mać⟩ **2.** hamować ⟨po-, za-⟩ **3.** ukrywać ⟨-ryć⟩ **4.** utrzymywać ⟨-mać⟩ w tajemnicy **II** *v/i* **1.** powstrzymywać ⟨-mać⟩ się **2.** wahać się ⟨za-⟩; **hold on I** *v/i* **1.** poczekać **2.** nie odkładać słuchawki **3.** trzymać się **4.** wytrwać, wytrzymywać ⟨-mać⟩ **II** *v/t* **1.** podtrzymywać ⟨-mać⟩ **2.** utrzymywać ⟨-mać⟩; **hold on to** *v/i* **1.** trzymać się *G* **2.** nie puszczać ⟨puścić⟩ *G* **3.** nie pozbywać ⟨-być⟩ się *G*; **hold out I** *v/i* **1.** wytrzymywać ⟨-mać⟩ **2.** wystarczać ⟨-czyć⟩ **II** *v/t* **1.** podawać ⟨-dać⟩; ***hold s.th. out to s.o.*** podać coś komuś **2.** *hands*: wyciągać ⟨-gnąć⟩; **hold up I** *v/t* **1.** unosić ⟨unieść⟩, podnosić ⟨-nieść⟩ **2.** podtrzymywać ⟨-mać⟩, podpierać ⟨-deprzeć⟩ **3.** zatrzymywać ⟨-mać⟩, opóźniać ⟨-nić⟩ **4.** napadać ⟨-paść⟩ na *A* **5.** ***~ s.o. as an example*** stawiać kogoś za przykład **II** *v/i* **1.** wytrzymywać ⟨-mać⟩ **2.** radzić ⟨po-⟩ sobie **3.** być nadal aktualnym, utrzymywać się; **hold with** *v/i*: ***not ~*** nie popierać *G*, być przeciwnikiem *G*

hold•er ['həʊldə] *s* **1.** posiadacz *m* **2.** pojemnik *m* **3.** stojak *m* **4.** ***a cigarette ~*** cygarniczka, *infml* fifka

hold•ing ['həʊldɪŋ] *s* **1.** *FIN* udział *m* **2.** dzierżawa *f*; **'hold•ing com•pa•ny** *s* holding *m*

'hold-up *s* napad *m* z bronią w ręku

hole [həʊl] **I** *s* **1.** dziura *f*; ***be in a ~*** *fig* być w tarapatach; ***make a ~ in s.o.'s savings*** poważnie uszczuplić czyjeś oszczędności; ***pick ~s in*** szukać słabych punktów w *L* **2.** wyłom *m*, wyrwa *f* **3.** norka *f*, nora *f*, jama *f* **II** *v/t* **1.** dziurawić ⟨po-⟩ **2.** robić ⟨z-⟩ dziurę w *L* **II** *v/i* (*golf*) trafiać ⟨-fić⟩ do dołka

hol•i•day ['hɒlədeɪ] **I** *s* **1.** dzień *m* wolny, święto *n*; ***take a three days' ~*** wziąć trzy dni wolnego **2.** wakacje *pl*; ***be on ~*** być na wakacjach **3.** urlop *m* **II** *adj* **1.** *season*: urlopowy **2.** *region*: letniskowy **III** *v/i* spędzać ⟨-dzić⟩ wakacje; **'hol•i•day home** *s* letni dom *m*, domek *m* letniskowy; **'hol•i•day•mak•er** *s* wczasowicz *m*, letnik *m*

ho•li•ness ['həʊlɪnɪs] *s* świętość *f*; ***Your ≈*** (*addressing pope*) Wasza Świątobliwość

Hol•land ['hɒlənd] *s* Holandia *f*

hol•ler ['hɒlə] *infml* **I** *v/i* wrzeszczeć ⟨wrzasnąć⟩ **II** *v/t* wykrzykiwać ⟨-knąć⟩

hol•low ['hɒləʊ] **I** *s* **1.** wgłębienie *n* **2.** zagłębienie *n* **3.** wklęsłość *f* **4.** dziupla *f* **II** *adj* **1.** pusty, wydrążony **2.** *sound*: głuchy **3.** czczy, pusty **4.** *eyes, cheeks*: zapadnięty **III** *adv* ***ring ~*** brzmieć nieszczerze; **hol•low out** *v/t* wydrążać ⟨-żyć⟩

hol•o•caust ['hɒləkɔːst] *s* **1.** *fig* holokaust *m*; ***a nuclear ~*** nuklearna zagłada **2.** ***the ≈*** Holocaust

ho•ly ['həʊlɪ] *adj* święty; **Ho•ly 'Ghost** → ***Holy Spirit***; **Ho•ly 'Scrip•ture** *s REL* Pismo *n* Święte; **Ho•ly 'Spir•it** *s*: ***the ~*** *REL* Duch *m* Święty; **ho•ly 'war** *s* święta wojna *f*; **ho•ly 'wa•ter** *s REL* woda *f* święcona; **'Ho•ly Week** *s REL* Wielki Tydzień *m*

hom•age ['hɒmɪdʒ] *s* hołd *m*; ***pay ~ to s.o.*** złożyć komuś hołd

home [həʊm] **I** *s* **1.** dom *m*; ***at ~*** w domu; ***feel at ~*** *fig* czuć się jak w domu; ***make oneself at ~*** rozgościć się; ***play at ~*** *SPORT* grać na własnym boisku, grać u siebie **2.** mieszkanie *n* **3.** ojczyzna *f*; ***at ~ and abroad*** w kraju i za granicą **II** *adj* **1.** domowy; ***~ life*** życie prywatne **2.** krajowy; ***the ~ market*** rynek krajowy **3.** wewnętrzny; ***~ affairs*** sprawy wewnętrzne **4.** rodzinny **5.** *team*: miejscowy **III** *adv* **1.** do domu; ***go ~*** pójść do domu; ***that's nothing to write ~ about*** *fig* to nic nadzwyczajnego **2.** w domu **3.** ***bring s.th. ~ to s.o.*** *fig* uświadomić komuś coś; ***the thrust went ~*** *fig* cios sięgnął celu

'home ad•dress *s* adres *m* stałego zamieszkania, adres *m* prywatny; **home 'bank•ing** *s* home banking *m*; **'home•com•ing** *s* powrót *m* do domu; **home com'put•er** *s* komputer *m* osobisty; **home ec•o•'nom•ics** *s* (*school*) zajęcia *pl* z gospodarstwa domowego; **home-'grown** *adj vegetables, fruit*: z własnego ogródka; **home 'help** *s Br* opiekun *m* domowy, opiekunka *f* domowa; **'home•land** *s* rodzinny kraj *m*, ojczyzna *f*

home•less ['həʊmlɪs] *adj* bezdomny, bez dachu nad głową; ***be left ~*** znaleźć się bez dachu nad głową; **home•ly** ['həʊmlɪ] *adj* **1.** przytulny **2.** prosty,

H

niewyszukany; **home•'made** *adj* domowy, domowej roboty; **'home-mak•er** *s* gospodyni *f* domowa, osoba *f* prowadząca dom; **'home match** *s* mecz *m* na własnym boisku **home 'mov•ie** *s* film *m* amatorski; **'Home Office** *s Br* Ministerstwo *n* Spraw Wewnętrznych

ho•me•o•path ['həʊmɪəpæθ] *s* homeopata *m*; **ho•me•o•path•ic** [həʊmɪə'pæθɪk] *adj* homeopatyczny; **ho-me•op•a•thy** [həʊmɪ'ɒpəθɪ] *s* homeopatia *f*

'home•own•er *s* **1.** właściciel *m* domu **2.** właściciel *m* mieszkania

'home page *s* INF strona *f* startowa

home 'run *s* (*baseball*) *uderzenie, pozwalające zawodnikowi zaliczyć wszystkie bazy i zdobyć punkt*

H

'home•sick *adj*: ***be ~*** tęsknić za domem, tęsknić za krajem; **'home-sick•ness** ['həʊmsɪknɪs] *s* tęsknota *f* za domem, nostalgia *f*

home 'town *s* rodzinne miasto *n*; **home 'truth** *s*: ***tell s.o. a few ~s*** wygarnąć komuś; **home•ward** ['həʊmwəd] **I** *adj* powrotny **II** *adv* do domu; **'home-work** *s* (*school*) praca *f* domowa, zadanie *n* domowe; ***do one's ~*** odrobić lekcje; **'home•work•er** *s* pracujący *m* w domu; **'home•work•ing** *s* praca *f* w domu

hom•i•cide ['hɒmɪsaɪd] *s Am* JUR zabójstwo *n*

ho•mo•ge•ne•ous [həʊmə'dʒiːnɪəs] *adj* jednorodny, homogeniczny

ho•mog•e•nize [hə'mɒdʒənaɪz] *v/t* homogenizować

hom•o•phobe ['hɒməfəʊb] *s* homofob *m*; **hom•o•pho•bi•a** [hɒmə'fəʊbɪə] *s* homofobia; **hom•o•pho•bic** [hɒmə-'fəʊbɪk] *adj* homofobiczny

ho•mo•sex•u•al [hɒmə'sekʃʊəl] **I** *s* homoseksualista *m* **II** *adj* homoseksualny; **ho•mo•sex•ual•i•ty** [hɒməsekʃʊ'ælətɪ] *s* homoseksualizm *m*

hom•y ['həʊmɪ] *adj* przytulny

hone [həʊn] *v/t* **1.** *skills*: doskonalić ⟨u-⟩ **2.** *knife*: ostrzyć ⟨na-⟩

hon•est ['ɒnɪst] *adj* **1.** uczciwy, rzetelny **2.** szczery; **hon•est•ly** ['ɒnɪstlɪ] *adv* **1.** uczciwie **2.** szczerze **3.** ***~!*** **a)** naprawdę!, serio!; **b)** no nie!; **hon-es•ty** ['ɒnɪstɪ] *s* **1.** uczciwość *f* **2.** szczerość *f*

hon•ey ['hʌnɪ] *s* **1.** miód *m*; **(*as*) *sweet as ~*** słodki jak miód **2.** *Am infml* kochanie *n*; **'hon•ey•bee** *s* pszczoła *f* miodna; **'hon•ey•comb** *s* plaster *m* miodu; **hon•ey•dew 'mel•on** *s* melon *m* miodowy

'hon•ey•moon I *s* miesiąc *m* miodowy, podróż *f* poślubna **II** *v/i* spędzać ⟨-dzić⟩ miesiąc miodowy; **'hon-ey•moon•ers** *pl* nowożeńcy *pl*

honk [hɒŋk] **I** *s* **1.** ***give a ~*** zatrąbić **II** *v/i* **2.** trąbić ⟨za-⟩ **III** *v/t* ***~ one's horn*** zatrąbić

hon•ky ['hɒŋkɪ] *s Am infml* biały *m*

hon•or•ar•y ['ɒnərərɪ] *adj* **1.** honorowy **2.** honoris causa

hon•our ['ɒnə] *Br*, ***hon•or*** *Am* **I** *v/t* **1.** honorować ⟨u-⟩ (***with*** *I*), oddawać ⟨-dać⟩ honory **2.** *cheque*: honorować **II** *s* **1.** honor *m*; ***a guest of ~*** gość honorowy; ***do s.o. ~*** czynić komuś zaszczyt **2.** ***in s.o.'s ~*** na cześć kogoś **3.** ***Your ~*** JUR Wysoki Sądzie; **hon-our•a•ble** ['ɒnrəbl] *Br*, ***honorable*** *Am adj* **1.** honorowy **2.** z honorem **3.** zaszczytny **4.** szanowny

hood [hʊd] *s* **1.** kaptur *m* **2.** AUTO *Am* maska *f* **3.** AUTO *Br* buda *f* **4.** okap *m*

hood•lum ['huːdləm] *s infml* **1.** chuligan *m*, żul *m* **2.** *Am* oszust *m*

'hood•wink ['hʊdwɪŋk] *v/t* naciągać ⟨-gnąć⟩, oszukiwać ⟨-kać⟩

hoo•ey ['huːɪ] *s Am infml* bzdury *pl*, bzdety *pl*

hoof [huːf] *s* kopyto *n*, racica *f*

hook [hʊk] **I** *s* **1.** hak *m*; ***by ~ or by crook*** takim czy innym sposobem **2.** haczyk *m*; ***~, line and sinker*** *fig* w całości **3.** (*boxing*) sierpowy *m* **II** *v/t* **1.** przyczepiać ⟨-pić⟩ **2.** zahaczać ⟨-czyć⟩ **3.** wieszać ⟨powiesić⟩ **4.** *fish*: łapać ⟨z-⟩ **III** *v/i* **1.** zahaczać ⟨-czyć⟩ się **2.** zapinać ⟨-piąć⟩ się na haftki; **hook up** *v/t* **1.** podłączać ⟨-czyć⟩ **2.** zapinać ⟨-piąć⟩

hooked [hʊkt] *adj* **1.** haczykowaty, zakrzywiony **2.** ***~ on*** *infml* uzależniony od *G*; **hook•er** ['hʊkə] *s Am infml* dziwka *f*; **hook•ey** ['hʊkɪ] *adj*: ***play ~*** *Am infml* chodzić na wagary

hoo•li•gan ['huːlɪgən] *s* chuligan *m*; **hoo•li•gan•ism** ['huːlɪgənɪzm] *s* chuligaństwo *n*
hoop [huːp] *s* obręcz *f*, pierścień *m*
hoot [huːt] **I** *v/i* **1.** (*driver*) *Br* trąbić ⟨za-⟩ **2.** (*siren*) wyć ⟨za-⟩ **3.** pohukiwać **4.** ~ ***with laughter*** ryknąć śmiechem **II** *v/t* ~ ***the horn*** (*driver*) zatrąbić **III** *s* **1.** klakson *m*; ***give a*** ~ zatrąbić **2.** ***I don't care*** (*a.* ***give***) ***a*** ~ *infml* mam to w nosie; **hoot•er** ['huːtə] *s* **1.** klakson *m* **2.** syrena *f* **3.** *Br infml* nochal *m*
Hoo•ver® ['huːvə] *s Br* odkurzacz *m*
hoover I *v/t* odkurzać ⟨-rzyć⟩ **II** *v/i* odkurzać ⟨-rzyć⟩
hooves [huːvz] *pl* → ***hoof***
hop¹ [hɒp] **I** *v/i* **1.** skakać ⟨skoczyć⟩; ~ ***in*** wskoczyć do *G*; ~ ***out of*** wyskoczyć z *G*; ~ ***off s.th.*** zeskoczyć z czegoś; ~ ***off*** *infml* zwiać, prysnąć **2.** podskakiwać ⟨-skoczyć⟩ **II** *v/t* **1.** przeskakiwać ⟨-skoczyć⟩ **2.** ~ ***it*** *Br infml* zmyć się **III** *s* **1.** podskok *m*; ***keep s.o. on the*** ~ *Br infml* nie dać komuś się lenić **2.** skok *m* **3.** *infml* tańce *pl*
hop² [~] **I** *s* **1.** chmiel *m* **II** *adj* **2.** chmielowy
hope [həʊp] **I** *s* nadzieja *f* (***of*** na *A*); ***be past all*** ~, ***be beyond all*** ~ nie rokować żadnych nadziei; ***in the*** ~ ***of doing s.th.*** mając nadzieję coś zrobić; ***with no*** ~ ***of success*** bez szans powodzenia; ~***s of victory*** nadzieje na zwycięstwo **II** *v/i* mieć nadzieję (***for*** na *A*); ~ ***that*** mieć nadzieję, że; ~ ***for the best*** być dobrej myśli; ***I*** ~ ***so*** mam nadzieję, że tak; ***I*** ~ ***not*** mam nadzieję, że nie; **hope•ful** ['həʊpfəl] *adj* optymistyczny, pełen nadziei; ***be*** ~ ***that*** mieć nadzieję, że; **hope•ful•ly** ['həʊpfəlɪ] *adv* **1.** przy odrobinie szczęścia **2.** miejmy nadzieję **3.** z nadzieją
hope•less ['həʊplɪs] *adj* beznadziejny
hop•ping ['hɒpɪŋ] *adj*: ***be*** ~ ***mad*** *infml* być wściekłym jak wszyscy diabli
ho•ri•zon [hə'raɪzn] *s* horyzont *m*; ***appear on the*** ~ pojawić się na horyzoncie; **hor•i•zon•tal** [hɒrɪ'zɒntl] **I** *adj* poziomy **II** *s MATH* pozioma *f*; **hor•i•zon•tal 'bar** *s* **1.** (*gymnastics*) drążek *m* **2.** (*high jump*) poprzeczka *f*
hor•mone ['hɔːməʊn] *s* hormon *m*; **hor•mone re'place•ment ther•a•py** *s MED* hormonalna terapia *f* zastępcza
horn [hɔːn] *s* **1.** róg *m*; ***the*** ~ ***of plenty*** róg obfitości; ~***-rimmed spectacles*** okulary w rogowej oprawce **2.** *AUTO* klakson *m*; ***honk one's car*** ~ zatrąbić
hor•net ['hɔːnɪt] *s* szerszeń *m*; ***stir up a*** ~***'s nest*** *fig* wsadzić kij w mrowisko
horn•y ['hɔːnɪ] *adj* **1.** zrogowaciały, stwardniały, rogowaty **2.** *infml* napalony
hor•o•scope ['hɒrəskəʊp] *s* horoskop *m*
hor•ren•dous [hɒ'rendəs] *adj* horrendalny, potworny, straszny, okropny
hor•ri•ble ['hɒrɪbl] *adj* **1.** straszny **2.** okropny **3.** obrzydliwy **4.** makabryczny
hor•rid ['hɒrɪd] → ***horrible***; **hor•rif•ic** [hɒ'rɪfɪk] *adj* przerażający; **hor•ri•fy** ['hɒrɪfaɪ] *v/t* przerażać ⟨-razić⟩, wstrząsać ⟨-snąć⟩; **hor•ri•fy•ing** ['hɒrɪfaɪɪŋ] *adj* przerażający, wstrząsający, okropny
hor•ror ['hɒrə] *s* **1.** przerażenie *n* **2.** ***have a*** ~ ***of*** panicznie bać się *G* **3.** okropieństwo *n*; **'hor•ror mov•ie** *s* film *m* grozy, horror *m*; **'hor•ror sto•ry** *s* opowieść *f* z dreszczykiem; **'hor•ror-strick•en** ['~strɪkən], ***hor•ror-struck*** *adj* przerażony, zdjęty przerażeniem
horse [hɔːs] *s* koń *m*; ***back the wrong*** ~ postawić na złego konia; ***eat like a*** ~ jeść za trzech; ***it's a*** ~ ***of a different colour*** to (już) inna para kaloszy; ***straight from the*** ~***'s mouth*** z pierwszej ręki; **'horse•back I** *adv* konno, wierzchem **II** *s* ***on*** ~ konno, wierzchem; **horse 'chest•nut** *s* kasztan *m*, kasztanowiec *m*; **'horse•fly** *s* giez *m*, mucha *f* końska; **'horse•man** *pl* *-men s* jeździec *m*; **'horse•pow•er** *s TECH* koń *m* mechaniczny; ***a 100*** ~ ***engine*** silnik o mocy stu koni mechanicznych; **'horse race** *s* gonitwa *f*; **'horse•rad•ish** *s* chrzan *m*; **'horse riding** *s* jazda *f* konna, jeździectwo *n*; **'horse•shoe** *s* podkowa *f*; **'horse trad•ing** *s* **1.** handel *m* końmi **2.** *fig* przetargi *pl*; **'horse•wom•an** *s pl* *-men* amazonka *f*
hose [həʊz] **I** *s* wąż *m*, szlauch *m* **II** *v/t* polewać ⟨-lać⟩

H

hos•pice ['hɒspɪs] *s* hospicjum *n*
hos•pi•ta•ble ['hɒspɪtəbl] gościnny, serdeczny, przyjazny
hos•pi•tal ['hɒspɪtl] *s* szpital *m*; ***in ~, in the ~ Am*** w szpitalu
hos•pi•tal•i•ty [hɒspɪ'tælətɪ] *s* gościnność *f*
hos•pi•tal•ize ['hɒspɪtlaɪz] *v/t* hospitalizować
Host [həʊst] *s* REL Hostia *f*
host[1] [həʊst] **I** *s* **1.** gospodarz *m* **2.** BIOL żywiciel *m* **3.** (*TV, radio*) gospodarz *m* programu **II** *v/t* **1.** gościć **2.** *programme*: prowadzić ⟨po-⟩
host[2] [~] *s* chmara *f*, mnóstwo *n*; ***a ~ of questions*** mnóstwo pytań
hos•tage ['hɒstɪdʒ] *s* zakładnik *m*; '**hos•tage tak•er** *s* porywacz *m*
hos•tel ['hɒstl] *s* **1.** akademik *m*, dom *m* studencki **2.** ***a*** (***youth***) ~ schronisko młodzieżowe
hos•tess ['həʊstɪs] *s* **1.** gospodyni *f*, pani *f* domu **2.** (*TV, radio*) gospodyni *f* programu **3.** stewardesa *f* **4.** hostessa *f* **5.** panienka *f* do towarzystwa
hos•tile ['hɒstaɪl] *adj* nieprzyjazny, wrogi; ***a ~ takeover*** ECON wrogie przejęcie; **hos•til•i•ty** [hɒ'stɪlətɪ] *s* **1.** niechęć *f*, wrogość *f* **2.** ***hostilities*** walki, działania wojenne
hot [hɒt] *adj* **1.** gorący; ***I am ~*** gorąco mi; ***a ~ favourite*** zdecydowany faworyt; ***be in ~ water*** *infml* mieć kłopoty, być w tarapatach **2.** ciepły **3.** pikantny **4.** ***be ~ on s.th.*** **a)** mieć bzika na punkcie czegoś **b)** mieć coś w jednym palcu **5.** ***~ from the press*** prosto z drukarni **6.** na topie **7.** podniecający **8.** trefny **9** *infml* napalony (***for*** na *A*); **hot up** *v/i* rozkręcać ⟨-cić⟩ się
hot 'air *s infml* pustosłowie *n*; '**hot•bed** *s* **1.** inspekt *m* **2.** *criminals*: gniazdo *n*; **hot•'blood•ed** *adj* porywczy, gorącej krwi; **hot 'chocolate** *s* czekolada *f* na gorąco
hotch•potch ['hɒtʃpɒtʃ] *s Br* miszmasz *m*, (bezładna) mieszanina *f*
ho•tel [həʊ'tel] **I** *s* hotel *m* **II** *adj* hotelowy; **ho•tel•ier** [həʊ'telɪeɪ] *Br s* hotelarz *m*
'**hot•foot** *v/t*: ***~ it*** *infml* gnać; '**hot•head** *s fig* gorąca głowa *f*; ***be a ~*** być w gorącej wodzie kąpanym; **hot•'head•ed** *adj* w gorącej wodzie kąpany, porywczy; '**hot•house** *s* cieplarnia *f*, szklarnia *f*; '**hot line** *s* **1.** linia *f* specjalna **2.** POLIT gorąca linia *f*
hot•ly ['hɒtlɪ] *adv* gorąco, zawzięcie, żarliwie; ***be ~ debated*** **a)** być żywo dyskutowanym **b)** wzbudzać wiele kontrowersji
'**hot•plate** *s* płyta *f* grzejna; **hot po•'tato** *s infml* śliska sprawa *f*; '**hot spot** *s* **1.** POLIT punkt *m* zapalny **2.** (popularny) klub *m* **3.** modne miejsce *n*; **hot-'wa•ter bottle** *s* termofor *m*
hound [haʊnd] **I** *s* pies *m* gończy, ogar *m* **II** *v/t* nękać, prześladować
hour [aʊə] *s* **1.** godzina *f*; ***for ~s*** (***and hours***) godzinami; ***be paid by the ~*** otrzymywać wynagrodzenie godzinowe; ***on the ~*** o pełnej godzinie; ***24 ~s a day*** 24 godziny na dobę, całą dobę; ***at all ~s*** o każdej porze
hour•ly ['aʊəlɪ] **I** *adj* **1.** cogodzinny **2.** *rate*: od godziny **II** *adv* co godzinę
house [haʊs] **I** *s* **1.** dom *m*; ***keep ~*** prowadzić dom; ***put*** (*a.* ***set***) ***one's ~ in order*** zająć się własnymi sprawami **2.** dynastia *f*; ***the ≈ of Hannover*** dynastia hanowerska **3.** ród *m* **II** *v/t* **1.** mieścić; ***be ~d*** mieścić się **2.** zapewniać ⟨-nić⟩ dach nad głową **3.** kwaterować ⟨za-⟩ '**house ar•rest** *s* areszt *m* domowy; '**house•boat** *s* barka *f*, łódź *f* mieszkalna; '**house•bound** *adj* **1.** ***be ~*** nie opuszczać domu **2.** *fig* uwiązany w domu; '**house•break•ing** *s* JUR włamanie *n*; '**house•fly** *s* mucha *f* domowa
'**house•hold I** *s* **1.** rodzina *f*, domownicy *pl* **2.** gospodarstwo *n* domowe **II** *adj* domowy; **house 'name** *s* **1.** powszechnie znane nazwisko *n* **2.** powszechnie znana nazwa *f*
'**house-hunt•ing** *s*: ***go ~*** szukać domu, szukać mieszkania; '**house hus•band** *s* mąż *m* zajmujący się domem; '**house•keep•er** *s* **1.** gosposia *f*, gospodyni *f* **2.** administrator *m*; '**house•keep•ing** *s* **1.** prowadzenie *n* domu **2.** administracja *f*; '**house mar•tin** *s* jaskółka *f* oknówka; **House of 'Commons** *s Br* Izba *f* Gmin; **House of 'Lords** *s Br* Izba *f* Lordów; **House of Rep•re'sent•a•tives** *s Am* Izba *f* Reprezentantów; '**house•plant** *s* roślina *f* domowa; '**house•proud** *adj*

H

dbający o porządek; **house-to-house 'search** *s*: ***carry out a ~*** przeszukać wszystkie domy w okolicy; **'house-trained** *Br*, ***'house•bro•ken*** *Am adj*: ***be ~*** **a)** (umieć) załatwiać się na dworze **b)** (umieć) załatwiać się do kuwety; **'house•warm•ing (party)** *s* parapetówka *f*; **'house•wife** *s* (niepracująca zawodowo) gospodyni *f* domowa; **'house•work** *s* prace *pl* domowe

hous•ing ['haʊzɪŋ] *s* **1.** domy *pl* mieszkalne, mieszkania *pl* **2.** gospodarka *f* mieszkaniowa; ***the ~ market*** rynek mieszkaniowy; ***a ~ shortage*** brak mieszkań; ***~ benefit*** zasiłek mieszkaniowy; **'hous•ing de•vel•op•ment**, ***'hous•ing es•tate*** *s* osiedle *n* mieszkaniowe; **'hous•ing con•di•tions** *pl* warunki *pl* mieszkaniowe

hove [həʊv] *Past Simple and Past Participle* → ***heave***

hov•er ['hɒvə] *v/i* **1.** unosić się w powietrzu, wisieć w powietrzu **2.** wahać się; ***~ between life and death*** balansować na krawędzi życia i śmierci **3.** (*linger*) kręcić się; **'hov•er•craft** *s* poduszkowiec *m*

how [haʊ] *adv* jak; ***~ are you?*** jak się masz?; ***~ is your toothache?*** jak tam twój ból zęba?; ***~ about...?*** a co powiesz na...?; ***~ do you know?*** skąd wiesz?; ***~ much?***, ***~ many?*** ile?; ***~ old are you?*** ile masz lat?; ***~ come?*** **a)** jak to? **b)** dlaczego?; ***~ absurd!*** co za absurd!; ***know ~ to party*** potrafić się bawić; ***I know ~ to do it*** wiem, jak to zrobić

how•ev•er [haʊ'evə] **I** *conj* **1.** jednak **2.** jednakże **II** *adv* **1.** jakkolwiek; ***~ you look at it*** jakkolwiek by na to nie patrzeć **2.** ***~ much it costs*** bez względu na cenę

howl [haʊl] **I** *v/i* wyć ⟨za-⟩; ***~ with laughter*** ryczeć ze śmiechu **II** *v/t* wykrzykiwać ⟨-knąć⟩ **III** *s* **1.** wycie *n* **2.** *laughter*: salwa *f* **3.** *pain*: skowyt *m*; **howl down** *v/t* zakrzykiwać ⟨-rzyczeć⟩

howl•er ['haʊlə] *s infml* **1.** gafa *f* **2.** (*spelling mistake*) byk *m*

howl•ing ['haʊlɪŋ] *adj* **1.** *storm*: gwałtowny **2.** *infml* niesamowity; ***a ~ success*** niesamowity sukces

HP [eɪtʃ'piː] → ***hire purchase***

HQ [eɪtʃ'kjuː] → ***headquarters***

HRT [eɪtʃɑː'tiː] *abbr* (=***hormone replacement therapy***) HTZ *f*, hormonalna terapia *f* zastępcza

hubbub ['hʌbbʌb] *s* gwar *m*, wrzawa *f*, zgiełk *m*

hud•dle ['hʌdl] *v/i* **1.** ***~ (together)*** przytulać ⟨-ić⟩ się do siebie **2.** kulić ⟨s-⟩ się

hue[1] [hjuː] *s* **1.** barwa *f* **2.** odcień *m* **3.** ***politicians of every ~*** *fig* politycy wszelkiej maści; ***vices of every ~*** *fig* wszelkiego rodzaju występki

hue[2] [~] *s*: ***to raise a ~ and cry against*** podnieść wrzawę w związku z *I*

huff [hʌf] **I** *v/i* ***~ and puff*** sapać i dyszeć **II** *s* ***be in a ~*** *infml* być nabzdyczonym; ***go into a ~*** *infml* nabzdyczyć się; **huff•y** ['hʌfɪ] *adj infml* nabzdyczony

hug [hʌg] **I** *v/t* **1.** uścisnąć, uściskać **2.** obejmować ⟨objąć⟩ **3.** przytulać ⟨-lić⟩ **4.** (*road*) biec wzdłuż *G* **II** *v/i* przytulać ⟨-lić⟩ się **III** *s* uścisk *m*; ***give s.o. a ~*** uścisnąć kogoś, przytulić kogoś

huge [hjuːdʒ] *adj* **1.** ogromny **2.** olbrzymi **3.** potężny **4.** wielki; **huge•ly** ['hjuːdʒlɪ] *adv* **1.** bardzo **2.** niezwykle **3.** ogromnie; ***her novel was ~ successful*** jej powieść odniosła ogromny sukces

hulk [hʌlk] *s* **1.** kadłub *m* **2.** hulk *m* **3.** ***a ~ of a man*** zwalisty mężczyzna; **hulk•ing** ['hʌlkɪŋ] *adj* **1.** wielki **2.** zwalisty

hull[1] [hʌl] *s* kadłub *m*

hull[2] [~] *v/t* **1.** obierać ⟨obrać⟩ **2.** łuskać

hul•la•ba•loo [hʌləbə'luː] *s* rwetes *m*, rejwach *m*, zgiełk *m*

hum [hʌm] **I** *v/i* **1.** nucić **2.** brzęczeć **3.** buczeć **4.** rozbrzmiewać gwarem; ***~ with life*** tętnić życiem **II** *v/t* nucić ⟨za-⟩ **III** *s* **1.** brzęczenie *n* **2.** szum *m* **3.** gwar *m*

hu•man ['hjuːmən] **I** *adj* ludzki; ***~ rights*** prawa człowieka **II** *s* człowiek *m*; **hu•man 'be•ing** *s* istota *f* ludzka

hu•mane [hjuː'meɪn] *adj* **1.** ludzki **2.** humanitarny; **hu•man•ism** ['hjuːmənɪzəm] *s* humanizm *m*; **hu•man•ist** [hjuːmənɪst] **I** *s* humanista **II** *adj* humanistyczny; **hu•manis•tic** *adj* [hjuːme'nɪstɪk] humanistyczny;

H

hu•man•i•tar•i•an [hjuːmænɪ'teəriən] *adj* humanitarny; **hu•man•i•ty** [hjuː'mænəti] **1.** ludzkość *f* **2.** człowieczeństwo *n* **3.** ***humanities*** nauki humanistyczne; **hu•man•kind** [hjuː'mən'kaɪnd] *s* ludzkość *f*, rodzaj *m* ludzki; **hu•man•ly** ['hjuːmənlɪ] *adv*: ***do everything ~ possible*** zrobić wszystko, co w ludzkiej mocy; **human 'race** *s* rasa *f* ludzka; **hu•man re•'sourc•es** *pl* **1.** zasoby *pl* ludzkie **2.** dział *m* personalny, kadry *pl*

hum•ble ['hʌmbl] **I** *adj* skromny; ***in my ~ opinion*** moim skromnym zdaniem; ***eat ~ pie*** uderzyć się w pierś; ***of ~ birth*** z prostej rodziny **II** *v/t* **1.** upokarzać ⟨-korzyć⟩, poniżać ⟨-żyć⟩ **2.** uczyć ⟨na-⟩ pokory

H

hu•mid ['hjuːmɪd] *adj* wilgotny; **hu•mid•i•fi•er** [hjuː'mɪdɪfaɪə] *s* nawilżacz *m* powietrza; **humid•i•fy** ['hjuː'mɪdɪfaɪ] *v/t* nawilżać ⟨-żyć⟩; **hu•mid•i•ty** ['hjuːmɪdɪtɪ] *s* wilgoć *f*, wilgotność *f*

hu•mil•i•ate [hjuː'mɪlɪeɪt] *v/t* upokarzać ⟨-korzyć⟩, poniżać ⟨-żyć⟩; **hu•mil•i•at•ing** ['hjuː'mɪlɪeɪtɪŋ] *adj* upokarzający, poniżający; **hu•mil•i•a•tion** ['hjuː'mɪlɪ'eɪʃn] *s* upokorzenie *n*, poniżenie *n*

hu•mil•i•ty [hjuː'mɪlətɪ] *s* pokora *f*

hum•ming bird ['hʌmɪŋbɜːd] *s* koliber *m*

hu•mor *Am* → ***humour***

hu•mor•ist ['hjuːmərɪst] *s* **1.** satyryk *m* **2.** humorysta *m*

hu•mor•ous ['hjuːmərəs] *adj* **1.** zabawny **2.** żartobliwy **3.** satyryczny

hu•mour ['hjuːmə] *Br*, **hu•mor** *Am* **I** *s* **1.** humor *m*; ***a sense of ~*** poczucie humoru; ***out of ~*** nie w humorze **2.** komizm *m* **3.** nastrój *m*; ***in a good (bad) ~*** w dobrym (złym) nastroju **II** *v/t* **~ s.o.** ustąpić komuś; **hu•mour•less** ['hjuːmələs] *Br*, ***hu•mor•less*** *Am adj* bez poczucia humoru, pozbawiony humoru

hump [hʌmp] **I** *s* **1.** garb *m* **2.** ***be over the ~*** mieć już z górki **II** *v/t Br* dźwigać na plecach; **'hump•back** *s* **1.** garb *m* **2.** *infml* garbus *m*; **'hump•backed** *adj* zgarbiony **hump•back 'whale** *s* (*whale*) humbak *m*

hunch [hʌntʃ] **I** *s* **1.** → ***hump I.1*** **2.** przeczucie *n*; ***have a ~ that*** mieć przeczucie, że **II** *v/i* garbić ⟨z-⟩ się **III** *v/t* ***~ one's shoulders*** przygarbić się; **'hunch•back** → ***humpback***; **'hunch-backed** → ***humpbacked***

hun•dred ['hʌndrəd] **I** *num* sto; ***a ~, one ~*** sto **II** *s* setka *f*; ***~s of times*** setki razy; ***~s of thousands*** setki tysięcy; **hun•dred•fold** ['hʌndrədfəʊld] **I** *adj* stokrotny **II** *adv* stokrotnie; **hundredth** ['hʌndrədθ] **I** *adj* setny **II** *s* **1.** setny *m* **2.** setna część *f*; ***a ~ of a second*** jedna setna sekundy; **'hun-dred•weight** *s* cetnar *m*

hung [hʌŋ] *Past Simple and Past Participle* → ***hang***

Hun•gar•i•an [hʌŋ'geərɪən] **I** *adj* węgierski **II** *s* **1.** Węgier *m*, Węgierka *f* **2.** język *m* węgierski; **Hun•ga•ry** ['hʌŋgərɪ] *s* Węgry *pl*

hun•ger ['hʌŋgə] **I** *s* głód *m*; ***a ~ for knowledge*** głód wiedzy **II** *v/i* ***~ for*** *fig* być spragnionym *G*, pragnąć *G*; **'hun•ger strike** *s* strajk *m* głodowy, głodówka *f*

hung•'o•ver *adj* skacowany

hun•gry ['hʌŋgrɪ] *adj* **1.** głodny; ***be ~, feel ~*** być głodnym; ***go ~*** cierpieć głód, nie mieć co jeść; ***~ for knowledge*** żądny wiedzy **2.** wygłodniały

hunk [hʌŋk] *s* kawał *m*, duży kawałek *m*

hunt [hʌnt] **I** *s* **1.** polowanie *n*, łowy *pl* **2.** poszukiwania *pl*; ***be on the ~ for*** poszukiwać *G* **II** *v/t* **1.** szukać **2.** poszukiwać **3.** polować na *A*, tropić **III** *v/i* ***go hunting*** jechać na polowanie; **hunt down** *v/t* **1.** szukać ⟨od-⟩ **2.** tropić ⟨wy-⟩; **hunt for** *v/i* **1.** poszukiwać, szukać **2.** ścigać; **hunt out** *v/t* odszukać

hunt•er ['hʌntə] *s* myśliwy *m*, łowca *m*; **hunt•ing** ['hʌntɪŋ] **I** *s* **1.** polowanie *n* **2.** myślistwo *n* **II** *adj* ***the ~ season*** sezon łowiecki; **'hunt•ing ground** *s* **1.** teren *m* łowiecki **2.** *fig* raj *m* (*for* dla *G*)

hur•dle ['hɜːdl] *s* **1.** *SPORT* płotek *m* **2.** *fig* przeszkoda *f*; **hur•dler** ['hɜːdlə] *s SPORT* płotkarz *m*; **hurdles** ['hɜːdls] *pl SPORT* bieg *m* przez płotki

hurl [hɜːl] *v/t* rzucać ⟨-cić⟩, ciskać ⟨-snąć⟩; ***~ oneself at*** rzucić się na *A*; ***~ abuse at s.o.*** obrzucić kogoś obelgami

hur•ri•cane ['hʌrɪkən] *s* huragan *m*
hur•ried ['hʌrɪd] *adj* pośpieszny, szybki
hur•ry ['hʌrɪ] **I** *s* pośpiech *m*; ***be in a ~*** śpieszyć się; ***be in no ~*** nie śpieszyć się; ***do s.th. in a ~*** robić coś w pośpiechu; ***there is no ~*** nie ma pośpiechu **II** *v/i* **1.** śpieszyć ⟨po-⟩ się **2.** biec ⟨po-⟩ **3.** śpieszyć ⟨po-⟩ **III** *v/t* poganiać ⟨-gonić⟩; **hur•ry up I** *v/i* śpieszyć ⟨po-⟩ się; ***~!*** pośpiesz się! **II** *v/t* **1.** popędzać ⟨-dzić⟩ **2.** przyśpieszać ⟨-szyć⟩
hurt [hɜːt] **I** (*hurt*; *hurt*) *v/i* boleć **II** (*hurt*; *hurt*) *v/t* **1.** ranić ⟨z-⟩; ***no one was ~*** nikomu nic się nie stało, nikt nie doznał obrażeń **2.** kaleczyć ⟨s-⟩ się w *A*; ***~ one's knee*** skaleczyć się w kolano **3.** krzywdzić ⟨s-⟩ **4.** urazić **5.** sprawiać ⟨-wić⟩ przykrość **6.** szkodzić ⟨za-⟩; **hurt•ful** ['hɜːtfʊl] *adj* przykry, bolesny; ***be ~ to*** zranić *A*, urazić *A*
hus•band ['hʌzbənd] **I** *s* mąż *m*, małżonek *m* **II** *v/t form* oszczędnie gospodarować
hush [hʌʃ] **I** *interj* cicho!, sza!, ćśśś! **II** *v/t* uciszać ⟨-szyć⟩, uspokajać ⟨-koić⟩ **III** *v/i* uciszać ⟨-szyć⟩ się **IV** *s* cisza *f*; **hush up** *v/t* tuszować ⟨za-⟩
'**hush mon•ey** *s* pieniądze *pl* za milczenie; **hush-'hush** *adj infml* poufny
husk [hʌsk] **I** *s* **1.** *grain*: łuska *f* **2.** *nut*: łupina *f* **II** *v/t* łuskać
hus•ky ['hʌskɪ] *adj* **1.** chropowaty, chropawy **2.** *Am* silny, krzepki
hus•tle ['hʌsl] **I** *v/t* **1.** popychać ⟨-pchnąć⟩ **2.** ponaglać ⟨-lić⟩; ***~ s.o. into doing s.th.*** ponaglać kogoś, żeby coś zrobił **3.** przyśpieszać ⟨-szyć⟩ **4.** *Am infml* sprzedawać ⟨-dać⟩ na lewo **5.** *infml* skombinować **II** *v/i Am infml* uprawiać nierząd **III** *s* krzątanina *f*; ***the ~ and bustle of a city*** zgiełk wielkiego miasta; **hus•tler** ['hʌslə] *s Am infml* **1.** kanciarz *m* **2.** dziwka *f*
hut [hʌt] *s* **1.** buda *f* **2.** chata *f* **3.** szałas *m* **4.** barak *m*
hutch [hʌtʃ] *s* klatka *f*
hy•a•cinth ['haɪəsɪnθ] *s* hiacynt *m*
hy•ae•na → ***hyena***
hy•brid ['haɪbrɪd] *s* BIOL hybryda *f*, mieszaniec *m*
hy•drant ['haɪdrənt] *s* hydrant *m*
hy•draul•ic [haɪ'drɒlɪk] **I** *adj* hydrauliczny **II** *s* **~s** PHYS hydraulika
hy•dro•car•bon [haɪdrə'kɑːbən] *s* węglowodór *m*; **hy•dro•chlo•ric acid** [haɪdrəklɒrɪk'æsɪd] *s* kwas *m* chlorowodorowy, kwas *m* solny; **hy•dro•elec•tric** [haidrəʊɪ'lektrɪk] *adj* hydroelektryczny; **hy•dro•foil** ['hæɪdrəfɔɪl] *s* wodolot *m*
hy•dro•gen ['haɪdrədʒən] *s* wodór *m*; '**hy•drogen bomb** *s* bomba *f* wodorowa
hy•dro•pho•bi•a [haɪdrə'fəʊbɪə] *s* wodowstręt *m*, wścieklizna *f*
hy•e•na [haɪ'iːnə] *s* hiena *f*
hy•giene ['haɪdʒiːn] *s* higiena *f*; **hy•gien•ic** [haɪ'dʒiːnɪk] *adj* higieniczny
hymn [hɪm] *s* **1.** REL hymn *m* **2.** *fig* apoteoza *f*; '**hymn•book** *s* śpiewnik *m* kościelny, zbiór *m* hymnów
hype [haɪp] **I** *s* **1.** rozgłos *m* **2.** reklama *f* **II** *v/t* **1.** reklamować ⟨roz-⟩ **2.** robić ⟨z-⟩ dużo szumu wokół *G*
hy•per ['haɪpə] *adj infml* podekscytowany; **hy•per•ac•tive** [haɪpə'æktɪv] *adj* nadpobudliwy
hyperbole [haɪ'pɜːbəlɪ] *s* hiperbola *f*
hy•per•crit•i•cal [haɪpə'krɪtɪkl] *adj* przesadnie krytyczny; **hy•per•infla•tion** [haɪpərɪn'fleɪʃn] *s* hiperinflacja *f*; **hy•per•link** ['haɪpəlɪŋk] *s* INF hiperłącze *n*; **hy•per•mar•ket** ['haɪpəmɑːkɪt] *s* hipermarket *m*; **hy•per•sen•si•tive** [haɪpə'sensɪtɪv] *adj* nadwrażliwy; **hy•per•ten•sion** [haɪpə'tenʃn] *s* nadciśnienie *n*; **hy•per•text** [haɪpətekst] *s* hipertekst *m*; **hy•per•ven•ti•la•tion** ['haɪpəventɪ'leɪʃn] *s* **1.** hiperwentylacja *f* **2.** szok *m* tlenowy
hy•phen ['haɪfn] *s* łącznik *m*, dywiz *m*; **hy•phen•ate** ['haɪfəneɪt] *v/t* pisać ⟨na-⟩ z łącznikiem, pisać ⟨na-⟩ z dywizem
hyp•no•sis [hɪp'nəʊsɪs] *pl -ses* [~sɪːz] *s* hipnoza *f*; **hyp•not•ic** [hɪp'nɒtɪk] *adj* hipnotyczny; **hyp•no•tize** ['hɪpnətaɪz] *v/t* hipnotyzować ⟨za-⟩
hy•po•chon•dri•a [haɪpə'kɒndrɪə] *s* hipochondria *f*

hy•poc•ri•sy [hɪ'pɒkrəsɪ] *s* hipokryzja *f*; **hyp•o•crite** ['hɪpəkrɪt] *s* hipokryta *m*; **hyp•o•crit•i•cal** [hɪpə'krɪtɪkl] *adj* obłudny

hy•po•der•mic [haɪpə'dɜːmɪk] **I** *adj* podskórny **II** *s* **1.** strzykawka *f* (do zastrzyków podskórnych) **2.** zastrzyk *m* podskórny

hy•poth•e•sis [haɪ'pɒθəsɪs] *pl* *-ses* [~siːz] *s* hipoteza *f*; **hy•po•thet•i•cal** [haɪpə'θetɪkl] *adj* hipotetyczny

hys•te•ri•a [hɪ'stɪəɪrɪə] *s* histeria *f*; **hys•ter•i•cal** [hɪ'stərɪkl] *adj* **1.** histeryczny, rozhisteryzowany **2.** *MED* cierpiący na histerię; **hys•ter•ics** [hɪ'sterɪks] *s* atak *m* histerii; ***go (off) into ~*** mieć napad histerii

I

I [aɪ] *pron* ja

ice [aɪs] **I** *s* **1.** lód *m*; ***be (skating) on thin ~*** *fig* stąpać po cienkim lodzie; ***break the ~*** *fig* przełamać lody; ***cut no ~ with*** nie zrobić wrażenia na *L* **2.** *Am* → **ice-cream II** *v/t* lukrować ⟨po-⟩; **ice up** *v/i* **1.** zamarzać ⟨-znąć⟩ **2.** obladzać ⟨-lodzić⟩ się; **'Ice Age** *s* epoka *f* lodowcowa; **'ice ax(e)** *s* czekan *m*; **'ice bag** *s* woreczek *m* z lodem; **'ice•berg** *s* góra *f* lodowa; ***the tip of the ~*** wierzchołek góry lodowej; ***~ lettuce*** sałata lodowa; **'ice-bound** *adj* skuty lodem; **'ice•box** *s* **1.** zamrażalnik *m* **2.** *Am* lodówka *f*; **'ice•break•er** *s* lodołamacz *m*; **'ice buck•et** *s* wiaderko *n* na lód, kubełek *m* na lód; **ice-'cold** *adj* **1.** lodowaty, zimny jak lód **2.** dobrze schłodzony

ice 'cream *s* lody *pl*; **'ice-cream par•lor** *s* *Am* lodziarnia *f*

'ice cube *s* kostka *f* lodu

iced [aɪst] *adj* **1.** mrożony; ***~ coffee (tea)*** mrożona kawa (herbata) **2.** lukrowany

'ice danc•er *s* *SPORT* tancerz *m* na lodzie; **'ice danc•ing** *s* *SPORT* tańce *pl* na lodzie; **'ice floe** *s* kra *f*; **'ice hock•ey** *s* hokej *m* na lodzie

Ice•land ['aɪslənd] *s* Islandia *f*; **Ice•land•er** ['aɪsləndə] *s* Islandczyk *m*, Islandka *f*; **Ice•lan•dic** [aɪs'lændɪk] **I** *adj* islandzki **II** *s* język *m* islandzki

'ice lol•ly *s* *Br* lody *pl* na patyku; **'ice pack** *s* worek *m* z lodem; **'ice rink** *s* lodowisko *n*, ślizgawka *f*; **'ice skate** *s* łyżwa *f*; **'ice-skate** *v/i* jeździć na łyżwach; **ice-skat•er** *s* łyżwiarz *m*; **'ice-skat•ing** *s* łyżwiarstwo *n*, jazda *f* na łyżwach; **'ice wa•ter** *s* woda *f* z lodem

i•ci•cle ['aɪsɪkl] *s* sopel *m*

i•ci•ly ['aɪsɪlɪ] *adv* lodowato, lodowatym tonem; **i•ci•ness** ['aɪsɪnɪs] *s* lodowate zimno *n*

ic•ing ['aɪsɪŋ] *s* lukier *m*; ***~ sugar*** *Br* cukier puder

i•con ['aɪkɒn] *s* **1.** ikona *f* **2.** *INF* ikona *f*, ikonka *f* **3.** *fig* symbol *m*

ICU [aɪsiː'juː] *abbr* (=***intensive care unit***) OIOM *m*, oddział *m* intensywnej opieki medycznej

icy ['aɪsɪ] *adj* lodowaty, oblodzony

ID [aɪ'diː] *abbr* (=***identification, identity***) dowód *m* tożsamości

I'd [aɪd] *contracted form* → ***I had, I would***

idea [aɪ'diːə] *s* **1.** pomysł *m* **2.** myśl *f* **3.** pojęcie *n*; ***I have no ~*** nie mam pojęcia **4.** wyobrażenie *n* **5.** cel *m*; ***the ~ is*** chodzi o to, żeby

i•deal [aɪ'diːəl] **I** *adj* idealny, doskonały **II** *s* ideał *m*; **i•deal•ism** [aɪ'dɪəlɪzəm] *s* idealizm *m*; **i•deal•ist** [aɪ'dɪəlɪst] *s* idealista *m*; **i•deal•is•tic** [aɪ'dɪəlɪstɪk] *adj* idealistyczny; **i•deal•ize** [aɪ'dɪəlaɪz] *v/t* idealizować ⟨wy-⟩; **i•deal•ly** [aɪ'dɪəli] *adv* idealnie

i•den•ti•cal [aɪ'dentɪkl] *adj* identyczny

i•den•ti•fi•ca•tion [aɪdentɪfɪ'keɪʃn] *s* **1.** identyfikacja *f* **2.** tożsamość *f*; ***an ~ card*** dowód tożsamości; ***~ papers*** dokumenty **3.** ***an ~ parade*** → **identity parade**; **i•den•ti•fy** [aɪ'dentɪfaɪ] *v/t* **1.** identyfikować ⟨z-⟩ **2.** rozpoznawać ⟨-nać⟩ **3.** ***~ oneself*** przedstawiać ⟨-wić⟩ się; **i•den•ti•fy with** *v/t* **1.** identyfikować z *I*; ***~ oneself with*** identyfikować się z *I* **2.** utożsamiać ⟨-mić⟩ z *I*

i•den•ti•ty [aɪ'dentətɪ] *s* tożsamość *f*; ***prove one's ~*** potwierdzić swoją tożsamość; ***an ~ card*** **a)** dowód tożsamości **b)** identyfikator; **i•den•ti•ty 'cri•sis** *s* kryzys *m* tożsamości; **i•den•ti•ty pa•'rade** *s* JUR *Br* okazanie *n*

i•de•o•log•i•cal [aɪdɪə'lɒdʒɪkl] *adj* ideologiczny; **i•de•ol•o•gy** [aɪdɪ'ɒlədʒɪ] *s* ideologia *f*

id•i•o•cy ['ɪdɪəsɪ] *s* głupota *f*, idiotyzm *m*

id•i•om ['ɪdɪəm] *s* idiom *m*; **id•i•o•mat•ic** [ɪdɪə'mætɪk] *adj* idiomatyczny

id•i•ot ['ɪdɪət] *s* idiota *m*; **id•i•ot•ic** [ɪdɪ'ɒtɪk] *adj* idiotyczny

i•dle ['aɪdl] **I** *adj* **1.** leniwy **2.** jałowy, czczy, pusty; ***~ gossip*** czcze gadanie **3.** bezczynny, bierny **4.** bezrobotny **5.** TECH nieczynny **6.** leżący odłogiem; ***run ~*** leżeć odłogiem **II** *v/i* **1.** próżnować **2.** (*engine*) pracować na biegu jałowym; **i•dle away** *v/t time*: trwonić

i•dler ['aɪdlə] *s* próżniak *m*; **i•dly** ['aɪdlɪ] *adv* **1.** leniwie **2.** bezczynnie; ***stand ~ by*** *fig* stać z założonymi rękami

i•dol ['aɪdl] *s* **1.** idol *m*, bożek *m* **2.** bożyszcze *n*; **idol•a•try** [aɪ'dɒlətrɪ] *s* bałwochwalstwo *n*, idolatria *f*; **i•dol•ize** ['aɪdəlaɪz] *v/t* wielbić, ubóstwiać

i•dyll ['ɪdɪl] *s* idylla *f*, sielanka *f*; **i•dyl•lic** [ɪ'dɪlɪk] *adj* idylliczny, sielankowy

i.e. [aɪ'iː] *abbr* (=***that is***) tj.

if [ɪf] **I** *conj* **1.** jeśli, jeżeli; ***~ I were you*** na twoim miejscu; ***as ~*** tak jakby; ***~ so*** jeśli tak **2.** gdy tylko **3.** czy; ***ask him ~ he can come*** zapytaj go, czy może przyjść **II** *s* ***without any ~s or buts*** bez żadnych wątpliwości ani zastrzeżeń

ig•nite [ɪg'naɪt] **I** *v/i* **1.** zapalać ⟨-lić⟩ się **2.** zająć się ogniem **II** *v/t* **1.** zapalać ⟨-lić⟩ **2.** *explosion of rioting*: wywoływać ⟨-łać⟩ **3.** *interest*: zapoczątkowywać ⟨-kować⟩; **ig•ni•tion** [ɪg'nɪʃn] **I** *s* **1.** zapłon *m* **2.** stacyjka *f* **3.** zapalenie *n* **II** *adj* **1.** *coil*: zapłonowy **2.** ***an ~ key*** kluczyk do stacyjki

ig•no•rant ['ɪgnərənt] *adj* **1.** nieświadomy; ***be ~ of*** **a)** nie znać *G* **b)** nie wiedzieć o *L* **2.** niedouczony; ***be ~ about*** nie znać się na *L* **3.** prymitywny

ig•nore [ɪg'nɔː] *v/t* ignorować ⟨z-⟩, nie reagować ⟨za-⟩ na *A*, lekceważyć ⟨z-⟩

I'll [aɪl] *contracted form* → ***I will***

ill [ɪl] **I** *adj* chory; ***fall ~*** zachorować, rozchorować się **II** *adv* źle; ***speak ~ of*** mówić źle o *L* **III** *s* **1.** zło *n* **2.** dolegliwość *f*; **ill-ad'vised** *adj* nierozważny, nierozsądny; **ill-'bred** *adj* źle wychowany, niewychowany; **ill-con'ceived** *adj* nieprzemyślany; **ill-de'fined** *adj* niejasno sformułowany, niewyraźny; **ill-dis'posed** *adj* źle nastawiony, nieprzychylnie nastawiony

il•le•gal [ɪ'liːgl] *adj* **1.** nielegalny **2.** niezgodny z prawem **3.** niedozwolony **4.** *parking*: nieprzepisowy; **il•le•gal•i•ty** [ɪlɪ'gælətɪ] *s* nielegalność *f*, bezprawność *f*, niezgodność *f* z przepisami

il•le•gi•ble [ɪ'ledʒəbl] *adj* nieczytelny

il•le•git•i•mate [ɪlɪ'dʒɪtɪmət] *adj* **1.** nielegalny, bezprawny, nieprawny **2.** nieślubny, z nieprawego łoża

ill-e'quipped *adj* **1.** nieodpowiednio wyposażony **2.** nieprzygotowany; **ill-'fat•ed** *adj* niefortunny

il•li•cit [ɪ'lɪsɪt] *adj* niedozwolony, zakazany

il•lit•er•a•cy [ɪ'lɪtərəsɪ] *s* analfabetyzm *m*; **il•lit•e•rate** [ɪ'lɪtərət] **I** *adj* **1.** niepiśmienny **2.** niedouczony **3.** ***be computer ~*** nie potrafić obsługiwać komputera **II** *s* analfabeta *m*

ill-'judged *adj* nierozsądny; **ill-'man•nered** *adj* niekulturalny, prostacki; **ill-'matched** *adj* niedopasowany; **ill-'na•tured** *adj* nieprzyjemny, złośliwy

ill•ness ['ɪlnɪs] *s* choroba *f*

il•log•i•cal [ɪ'lɒdʒɪkl] *adj* nielogiczny, bezsensowny

ill-'suit•ed *adj* nieodpowiedni, niepasujący; **ill-'tem•pered** *adj* zrzędliwy, łatwo wpadający w gniew; **ill-'timed** *adj* nie w porę; **ill-'treat** *v/t* **1.** źle traktować **2.** znęcać się nad

il•lu•mi•nate [ɪ'luːmɪneɪt] *v/t* **1.** oświetlać ⟨-lić⟩, rozświetlać ⟨-lić⟩ **2.** wyjaśniać ⟨-nić⟩, rzucać ⟨-cić⟩ światło na *A* **3.** *manuscript*: iluminować; **il•lu•mi•nat•ing** [ɪ'luːmɪneɪtɪŋ] *adj* pouczający, kształcący; **il•lu•mina•tion** [ɪluːmɪ'neɪʃn] *s* **1.** światło *n* **2.** oświetlenie *n* **3.** iluminacja *f*

I

il•lu•sion [ɪ'luːʒn] *s* złudzenie *n*, iluzja *f*; ***be under the ~ that*** łudzić się, że; ***have no ~s about*** nie mieć złudzeń co do *G*; **il•lu•so•ry** [ɪ'luːsərɪ] *adj* złudny, zwodniczy, iluzoryczny
il•lus•trate ['ɪləstreɪt] *v/t* ilustrować ⟨z-⟩; **il•lus•tra•tion** [ɪlə'streɪʃn] *s* **1.** ilustracja *f* **2.** przykład *m*; ***by way of ~*** dla przykładu; **il•lus•tra•tive** ['ɪləstrətɪv] *adj* **1.** ilustrujący **2.** ilustracyjny; **il•lus•tra•tor** ['ɪləstreɪtə] *s* ilustrator *m*
il•lus•tri•ous [ɪ'lʌstrɪəs] *adj* znamienity, znakomity, prześwietny
ill 'will *s* **1.** wrogość *f* **2.** uraza *f*
I'm [aɪm] *contracted form* → ***I am***
im•age ['ɪmɪdʒ] *s* **1.** wizerunek *m* **2.** image *m* **3.** obraz *m* **4.** podobizna *f* **5.** wyobrażenie *n*; **'im•age-con•scious** *adj* **be ~** dbać o swój wizerunek
i•ma•gi•na•ble [ɪ'mædʒɪnəbl] *adj* wyobrażalny; ***the greatest stupidity ~*** największa głupota, jaką można sobie wyobrazić; **i•ma•gi•na•ry** [ɪ'mædʒɪnərɪ] *adj* zmyślony, wymyślony, wyimaginowany; **i•ma•gi•na•tion** [ɪmædʒɪ'neɪʃn] *s* **1.** wyobraźnia *f* **2.** fantazja *f*; ***it's pure ~*** to czysta fantazja **3.** wytwór *m* wyobraźni **4.** urojenie *n*; **i•ma•gi•na•tive** [ɪ'mædʒɪnətɪv] *adj* **1.** obdarzony wyobraźnią, pełen polotu **2.** pomysłowy; **i•ma•gine** [ɪ'mædʒɪn] **I** *v/t* wyobrażać ⟨-razić⟩ sobie; ***I ~d him as a tall man*** wyobrażałem go sobie jako wysokiego mężczyznę; ***can you ~ him becoming famous?*** możesz sobie wyobrazić, żeby został sławny?; ***don't ~ that*** nie wyobrażaj sobie, że **II** *v/i* ***just ~!*** pomyśl tylko!
im•bal•ance [ɪm'bæləns] *s* brak *m* równowagi
im•be•cile ['ɪmbəsiːl] **I** *adj* idiotyczny **II** *s* imbecyl *m*
IMF [aɪem'ef] *abbr* (=***International Monetary Fund***) MFW *m*
im•i•tate ['ɪmɪteɪt] *v/t* **1.** naśladować, imitować **2.** podrabiać ⟨-robić⟩; **im•i•ta•tion** [ɪmɪ'teɪʃn] **I** *s* **1.** imitacja *f* **2.** naśladowanie *n*; ***in ~ of*** na wzór *G* **3.** naśladownictwo *n* **II** *adj* sztuczny; **im•i•ta•tor** ['ɪmɪteɪtə] *s* naśladowca *m*, imitator *m*
im•mac•u•late [ɪ'mækjʊlət] *adj* **1.** nieskazitelnie czysty **2.** nieskazitelny **3.** *condition*: idealny **4.** nienaganny **5.** bezbłędny
im•ma•te•ri•al [ɪmə'tɪərɪəl] *adj* **1.** nieistotny, bez znaczenia **2.** niematerialny
im•ma•ture [ɪmə'tʃʊə] *adj* niedojrzały; **im•ma•tu•ri•ty** [ɪmə'tʃʊərətɪ] *s* niedojrzałość *f*
im•meas•ur•a•ble [ɪ'meʒərəbl] *adj* niezmierny, niezmierzony, ogromny
im•me•di•ate [ɪ'miːdɪət] *adj* **1.** najbliższy; ***in the ~ vicinity*** w najbliższej okolicy **2.** natychmiastowy **3.** najpilniejszy **4.** bezpośredni; **im•me•di•ate•ly** [ɪ'miːdɪətlɪ] *adv* natychmiast, od razu, bezpośrednio
im•me•mo•ri•al [ɪmə'mɔːrɪəl] *adj* odwieczny; ***since/from time ~*** od niepamiętnych czasów
im•mense [ɪ'mens] *adj* ogromny; **im•men•si•ty** [ɪ'mensɪtɪ] *s* ogrom *m*, bezmiar *m*
im•merse [ɪ'mɜːs] *v/t* zanurzać ⟨-rzyć⟩; ***~d in thought*** zatopiony w myślach; ***~d in conversation*** pochłonięty rozmową; ***he ~d himself in work*** rzucił się w wir pracy
im•mi•grant ['ɪmɪgrənt] *s* imigrant *m*; **im•mi•grate** ['ɪmɪgreɪt] *v/i* imigrować, migrować; **im•mi•gra•tion** [ɪmɪ'greɪʃn] *s* imigracja *f*
im•mi•nent ['ɪmɪnənt] *adj* **1.** nadciągający **2.** bliski **3.** rychły
im•mo•bile [ɪ'məʊbaɪl] *adj* nieruchomy, unieruchomiony; **im•mo•bil•ity** [ɪmə'bɪlətɪ] *s* nieruchomość *f*, bezruch *m*; **im•mo•bi•lize** [ɪ'məʊbɪlaɪz] *v/t* unieruchamiać ⟨-chomić⟩, paraliżować ⟨s-⟩
im•mod•est [ɪ'mɒdɪst] *adj* nieskromny
im•mor•al [ɪ'mɒrəl] *adj* niemoralny; **im•mor•al•i•ty** [ɪmə'rælɪtɪ] *s* **1.** niemoralność *f* **2.** niemoralny czyn *m*
im•mor•tal [ɪ'mɔːtl] *adj* nieśmiertelny; **im•mor•tal•i•ty** [ɪmɔː'tælɪtɪ] *s* nieśmiertelność *f*; **im•mor•tal•ize** [ɪ'mɔːtəlaɪz] *v/t* uwieczniać ⟨-nić⟩, unieśmiertelniać ⟨-nić⟩
im•mov•a•ble [ɪ'muːvəbl] *adj* **1.** nieruchomy **2.** nie do ruszenia **3.** niezłomny, niezachwiany, niewzruszony

I

im•mune [ɪ'mjuːn] *adj* **1.** odporny (***to*** na *A*) **2.** nieczuły (***to*** na *A*) **3. ~ *deficiency*** obniżona odporność **4.** chroniony (***from*** przed *I*); ***be ~ from prosecution*** nie podlegać ściganiu; **im'mune sys•tem** *s* układ *m* odpornościowy; **im•mu•ni•ty** [ɪ'mjuːnətɪ] *s* **1.** odporność *f* **2.** *fig* nieczułość *f* **3.** *JUR* immunitet *m* **4.** *JUR* nietykalność *f*; **im•mu•nize** ['ɪmjʊnaɪz] *v/t* uodparniać ⟨-pornić⟩; **im•mu•no•de•fi•cien•cy** [ɪmjuːnəʊdɪ'fɪʃənsɪ] *s* niedobór *m* odpornościowy; **im•mu•nol•o•gist** [ɪmjʊ'nɒlədʒɪst] *s* immunolog *m*; **im•mu•nol•o•gy** [ɪmjʊ'nɒlədʒɪ] *s* immunologia *f*

im•pact ['ɪmpækt] **I** *s* **1.** wpływ *m* **2.** uderzenie *n* **3.** siła *f* (uderzenia) **4.** zderzenie *n* **II** *adj* mieć (duży) wpływ na *A*

im•pair [ɪm'peə] *v/t* **1.** szkodzić ⟨za-⟩, niekorzystnie wpływać ⟨-łynąć⟩ na *A* **2.** osłabiać ⟨-bić⟩, nadwerężać ⟨-żyć⟩ **im•paired** [ɪm'peəd] *adj* **1.** osłabiony **2.** ograniczony **3.** nadwątlony **4. *visually ~*** niedowidzący

im•pale [ɪm'peɪl] *v/t* **1.** nabijać ⟨-bić⟩ (***on*** na *A*) **2.** nadziewać ⟨-dziać⟩ (***on*** na *A*) **3.** wbijać ⟨wbić⟩ na pal

im•part [ɪm'pɑːt] *v/t* **1.** przekazywać ⟨-zać⟩ **2.** dodawać ⟨-dać⟩ **3.** przydawać ⟨-dać⟩

im•par•tial [ɪm'pɑːʃl] *adj* bezstronny; **impar•tial•i•ty** [ɪmpɑːʃɪ'ælətɪ] *s* bezstronność *f*

im•pass•a•ble [ɪm'pɑːsəbl] *adj* **1.** nieprzejezdny **2.** nieżeglowny **3.** nie do przebycia, nie do pokonania

im•passe ['ɪmpɑːs] *s* impas *m*; ***reach an ~*** znaleźć się w impasie

im•pas•sioned [ɪm'pæʃnd] *adj* **1.** *plea*, *appeal*: gorący **2.** żarliwy **3.** płomienny **4.** namiętny

im•pa•tience [ɪm'peɪʃəns] *s* **1.** niecierpliwość *f* **2.** zniecierpliwienie *n*; **im•pa•tient** [ɪm'peɪʃənt] *adj* **1.** niecierpliwy; ***be ~ to do s.th.*** nie móc się doczekać, żeby coś zrobić; ***be ~ for*** czekać z niecierpliwością na *A* **2.** zniecierpliwiony; ***be ~ with*** nie mieć cierpliwości do *G*; **im•pa•tient•ly** [ɪm'peɪʃəntlɪ] *adv* **1.** niecierpliwie **2.** ze zniecierpliwieniem

im•pec•ca•ble [ɪm'pekəbl] *adj* nienaganny, wzorowy, znakomity; **im•pec•ca•bly** [ɪm'pekəblɪ] *adv* **1.** nienagannie **2.** *clean*: nieskazitelnie **3.** wzorowo

im•pede [ɪm'piːd] *v/t* zakłócać ⟨-cić⟩, przeszkadzać ⟨-kodzić⟩, utrudniać ⟨-nić⟩; **im•ped•i•ment** [ɪm'pedɪmənt] *s* **1.** przeszkoda *f* **2.** utrudnienie *n* **3.** *MED* wada *f*

im•pend•ing [ɪm'pendɪŋ] *adj* **1.** zbliżający się **2.** nadciągający

im•pen•e•tra•ble [ɪm'penɪtrəbl] *adj* **1.** nieprzenikniony **2.** *jungle*, *forest*: nieprzebyty **3.** *fortress*: nie do zdobycia **4.** nieprzepuszczalny **5.** niezrozumiały **6.** *fig* hermetyczny **7.** *secret*: niezgłębiony

im•per•a•tive [ɪm'perətɪv] **I** *adj* **1.** pilny, palący, konieczny **2.** władczy, rozkazujący **3. *the ~ mood*** *GRAM* tryb rozkazujący **II** *s* ***the ~*** *GRAM* tryb rozkazujący

im•per•cep•ti•ble [ɪmpə'septɪbl] *adj* niezauważalny, niedostrzegalny, nieuchwytny

im•per•fect [ɪm'pɜːfekt] **I** *adj* **1.** niedoskonały **2.** uszkodzony, wadliwy **3.** błędny **4. *the ~ tense*** *GRAM* czas przeszły niedokonany **II** *s* ***the ~*** *GRAM* czas przeszły niedokonany; **im•per•fec•tion** [ɪmpə'fekʃn] *s* **1.** niedoskonałość *f* **2.** wada *f*

im•pe•ri•al [ɪm'pɪərɪəl] *adj* **1.** imperialny **2.** cesarski **3.** carski **4. *the ~ system*** angielski system miar i wag; **im•pe•ri•al•ism** [ɪm'pɪərɪəlɪzəm] *s* imperializm *m*; **im•pe•ri•al•ist** [ɪm'pɪərɪəlɪst] **I** *s* imperialista *m* **II** *adj* imperialistyczny

im•per•ma•nent [ɪm'pɜːmənənt] *adj* chwilowy, nietrwały, przejściowy

im•per•son•al [ɪm'pɜːsənl] *adj* **1.** bezosobowy **2.** beznamiętny **3.** *statistics*: anonimowy

im•per•so•nate [ɪm'pɜːsəneɪt] *v/t* **1.** naśladować **2.** parodiować ⟨s-⟩ **3.** podawać ⟨-dać⟩ się za *A*; **im•per•sona•tion** [ɪmpɜːsə'neɪʃn] *s* naśladowanie *n*; ***do an ~ of s.o.*** naśladować kogoś

im•per•ti•nence [ɪm'pɜːtɪnəns] *s* impertynencja *f*, zuchwałość *f*; **im•per•ti•nent** [ɪm'pɜːtɪnənt] *adj* **1.** impertynencki, bezczelny **2.** bez związku

im•per•tur•ba•ble [ɪmpə'tɜːbəbl] *adj* niewzruszony

im•per•vi•ous [ɪm'pɜːvɪəs] *adj* **1.** nieprzepuszczalny **2.** nieczuły (***to*** na *A*) **3.** obojętny (***to*** na *A*)

im•pe•tu•ous [ɪm'petʃʊəs] *adj* **1.** porywczy, impulsywny **2.** pochopny

im•pe•tus ['ɪmpɪtəs] *s* **1.** *PHYS* pęd *m* **2.** bodziec *m*, impuls *m*; ***give an ~ to*** stać się bodźcem do *G*

im•plant [ɪm'plɑːnt] *v/t* wszczepiać ⟨-pić⟩; *fig* zaszczepiać ⟨-pić⟩

im•plau•si•ble [ɪm'plɔːzəbl] *adj* **1.** nieprzekonujący **2.** niewiarygodny

im•ple•ment I ['ɪmplɪmənt] *s* narzędzie *n* **II** ['ɪmplɪment] *v/t* wprowadzać ⟨-dzić⟩ (w życie), realizować ⟨z-⟩, wdrażać ⟨-rożyć⟩; **im•ple•men•ta•tion** [ɪmplɪmən'teɪʃn] *s* wprowadzenie *n* (w życie), realizacja *f*, wdrożenie *n*

im•pli•cate ['ɪmplɪkeɪt] *v/t* **1.** ***be ~d in*** być zamieszanym w *A* **2.** ***~ s.o. in s.th.*** wskazywać na czyjś udział w czymś; **im•pli•ca•tion** [ɪmplɪ'keɪʃn] *s* **1.** konsekwencja *f*; ***by ~*** tym samym **2.** sugestia *f*; ***the ~ of his statement is that*** z jego wypowiedzi wynika, że **3.** implikacja *f* **4.** wniosek *m* **5.** uwikłanie *n* (***in*** w *A*)

im•pli•cit [ɪm'plɪsɪt] *adj* **1.** ***~ in her suggestion was that*** z jej propozycji wynikało, że **2.** ukryty **3.** *form* implicytny **4.** bezgraniczny **5.** *faith*, *obedience*: bezwarunkowy; **im•pli•cit•ly** [ɪm'plɪsɪtlɪ] *adv* **1.** nie wprost **2.** bezgranicznie **3.** bezwarunkowo

im•plied [ɪm'plaɪd] *adj* ukryty, pośredni, nie wprost

im•plode [ɪm'pləʊd] *v/i* implodować

im•plore [ɪm'plɔː] *v/t* błagać

im•ply [ɪm'plaɪ] **I** *v/t* **1.** sugerować ⟨za-⟩ **2.** oznaczać **3.** (*logic*) implikować **II** *v/i* sugerować ⟨za-⟩ (***that*** że), dawać ⟨dać⟩ do zrozumienia (***that*** że)

im•po•lite [ɪmpə'laɪt] *adj* nieuprzejmy, niegrzeczny

im•pon•der•a•ble [ɪm'pɒndərəbl] *s* niewiadoma *f*

im•port I [ɪm'pɔːt] *v/t* **1.** importować, sprowadzać ⟨-dzić⟩ **II** ['ɪmpɔːt] *s* **1.** import *m* **2.** towar *m* importowany **3.** waga *f*; ***of great ~*** wielkiej wagi **III** ['ɪmpɔːt] *adj* **1.** importowy **2.** ***an ~ country***, ***an ~ company*** importer

im•por•tance [ɪm'pɔːtəns] *s* znaczenie *n*; ***attach ~ to*** przykładać wagę do *G*; ***be of no ~ to*** być bez znaczenia dla *G*; ***a matter of some ~*** dość istotna sprawa; **im•por•tant** [ɪm'pɔːtənt] *adj* ważny, istotny; **im•por•tant•ly** [ɪm'pɔːtəntlɪ] *adv* w istotny sposób; ***more ~*** co ważniejsze

im•por•tune [ɪmpə'tjuːn] *v/t* naprzykrzać się, narzucać się

im•pose [ɪm'pəʊz] **I** *v/t* **1.** nakładać ⟨nałożyć⟩ (***on*** na *A*) **2.** narzucać ⟨-cić⟩; ***~ oneself on*** narzucać się *D*; ***~ one's presence on*** narzucać swoje towarzystwo *D*; ***~ one's will on*** narzucać swoją wolę *D* **3.** *pressure*: wywierać ⟨-wrzeć⟩ **II** *v/i* ***~ on*** narzucać się *D*; **im•pos•ing** [ɪm'pəʊzɪŋ] *adj* imponujący **im•po•si•tion** [ɪmpə'zɪʃn] *s* **1.** *duty*: nałożenie *n* **2.** *ban*, *tax*: wprowadzenie *n* **3.** ***I know this is an ~, but please help me*** wiem, że się narzucam, ale pomóż mi, proszę

im•pos•si•bil•i•ty [ɪmpɒsɪ'bɪlɪtɪ] *s* niemożliwość *f*, niemożność *f*; **im•pos•sible** [ɪm'pɒsɪbəl] *adj* **1.** niemożliwy; ***it's ~ for me to come*** nie mogę przyjść **2.** niewykonalny; **im•pos•si•bly** [ɪm'pɒsɪblɪ] *adv* niemożliwie, niesamowicie

im•pos•tor [ɪm'pɒstə] *s* (*a person who pretends to be s.o. else*) oszust *m*

im•po•tence ['ɪmpətəns] *s* **1.** bezsilność *f* **2.** impotencja *f*, niemoc *f* płciowa; **im•po•tent** ['ɪmpətənt] *adj* **1.** bezsilny **2.** cierpiący na impotencję

im•pov•e•rished [ɪm'pɒvərɪʃt] *adj* zubożały

im•prac•ti•ca•ble [ɪm'præktɪkəbl] *adj* nierealny, niewykonalny

im•prac•ti•cal [ɪm'præktɪkəl] *adj* **1.** niepraktyczny **2.** nierealny

im•preg•nate ['ɪmpregneɪt] *v/t* **1.** zapładniać ⟨-łodnić⟩ **2.** impregnować ⟨za-⟩ **3.** nasączać ⟨-czyć⟩, nasycać ⟨-cić⟩

im•pre•sa•ri•o [ɪmprɪ'sɑːrɪəʊ] *pl -os* [~əʊz] *s* impresario *m*

I

im•press [ɪm'pres] *v/t* **1.** robić ⟨z-⟩ wrażenie na *L*, wywierać ⟨-wrzeć⟩ wrażenie na *L* **2.** imponować ⟨za-⟩ **3.** wzbudzać ⟨-dzić⟩ podziw **4.** odciskać ⟨-snąć⟩, robić ⟨z-⟩ wycisk; **im•pres•sion** [ɪm'preʃn] *s* **1.** wrażenie *n*; ***make a good (bad) ~ on*** zrobić dobre (złe) wrażenie na *L*; ***I have the ~ that*** mam wrażenie, że; ***I was under the ~ that*** sądziłem, że **2.** impresja *f* **3.** odcisk *m*, wycisk *m*, ślad *m* **4.** nakład *m* **5.** przedruk *m*; **im•pres•sion•a•ble** [ɪm'preʃənəbl] *adj* podatny na wpływy; **im•pres•sion•ism** [ɪm'preʃənɪzəm] *s* impresjonizm *m*; **impres•sion•ist** [ɪm'preʃənɪst] **I** *s* impresjonista *m* **II** *adj* impresjonistyczny; **im•pres•sion•is•tic** [ɪmpreʃə'nɪstɪk] *adj* impresjonistyczny, impresyjny; **im•pres•sive** [ɪm'presɪv] *adj* imponujący, robiący wrażenie

im•print **I** ['ɪmprɪnt] *s* **1.** odcisk *m* **2.** piętno *n*, znamię *n* **3.** znak *m* wydawcy **II** [ɪm'prɪnt] *v/t* **1.** odciskać ⟨-snąć⟩ **2.** ***s.th. is ~ed in s.o.'s memory*** *fig* coś wryło się komuś w pamięć

im•pris•on [ɪm'prɪzn] *v/t* zamykać ⟨-mknąć⟩ w więzieniu, więzić ⟨u-⟩; **im•pris•on•ment** [ɪm'prɪznmənt] *s* **1.** kara *f* więzienia **2.** uwięzienie *n*

im•prob•a•bil•i•ty [ɪmprɒbə'bɪlətɪ] *s* małe prawdopodobieństwo *n*, nieprawdopodobieństwo *n*; **im•prob•a•ble** [ɪm'prɒbəbl] *adj* **1.** mało prawdopodobny **2.** nieprawdopodobny **3.** dziwny

im•promp•tu [ɪm'prɒmptjuː] **I** *adj* improwizowany **II** *adv* bez przygotowania

im•prop•er [ɪm'prɒpə] *adj* **1.** niestosowny **2.** niewłaściwy **3.** nieprzyzwoity **4.** niedozwolony **5.** mylny; **im•pro•pri•e•ty** [ɪmprə'praɪətɪ] *s* **1.** nieprawidłowość *f* **2.** nieprzyzwoitość *f*, niestosowność *f*

im•prove [ɪm'pruːv] **I** *v/t* **1.** poprawiać ⟨-wić⟩ **2.** polepszać ⟨-szyć⟩ **3.** zwiększać ⟨-szyć⟩ **4.** podnosić ⟨-nieść⟩ **II** *v/i* **1.** poprawiać ⟨-wić⟩ się **2.** polepszać ⟨-szyć⟩ się **3.** ***he's improving*** jego stan zdrowia poprawia się; **im•prove•ment** [ɪm'pruːvmənt] *s* **1.** poprawa *f*; ***~ in the weather*** poprawa pogody **2.** udoskonalenie *n* **3.** postęp *m*

im•prov•i•sa•tion [ɪmprəvaɪ'zeɪʃn] *s* improwizacja *f*; **im•pro•vise** ['ɪmprəvaɪz] *v/i* improwizować ⟨za-⟩

im•pru•dence [ɪm'pruːdəns] *s* brak *m* rozwagi, brak *m* rozsądku; **im•pru•dent** [ɪm'pruːdənt] *adj* nierozważny, nierozsądny

im•pu•dence ['ɪmpjʊdəns] *s* zuchwalstwo *n*, bezczelność *f*; **im•pu•dent** ['ɪmpjʊdənt] *adj* zuchwały, bezczelny

im•pulse ['ɪmpʌls] *s* **1.** impuls *m*; ***act on ~*** działać pod wpływem impulsu **2.** bodziec *m* **3.** nagła chęć *f*; **'impulse buy** *s* zakup *m* dokonany pod wpływem impulsu; **im•pul•sive** [ɪm'pʌlsɪv] *adj* impulsywny, porywczy

im•pu•ni•ty [ɪm'pjuːnətɪ] *s* bezkarność *f*; ***with ~*** bezkarnie

im•pure [ɪm'pjʊə] *adj* **1.** zanieczyszczony **2.** nieczysty; **impu•ri•ty** [ɪm'pjʊərətɪ] *s* **1.** zanieczyszczenie *n* **2.** domieszka *f* **3.** nieczystość *f*

im•pute [ɪm'pjuːt] *v/t* **1.** zarzucać ⟨-cić⟩ (***s.th. to*** coś *D*) **2.** imputować (***s.th. to*** coś *D*)

in [ɪn] **I** *prep* **1.** w *L*; ***~ London*** w Londynie; ***~ April*** w kwietniu; ***~ 2001*** w 2001 roku; ***be injured ~ an accident*** zostać rannym w wypadku **2.** na *L*, na *A*; ***~ the sky*** na niebie; ***~ the beginning*** na początku; ***~ honour of*** na cześć *G*; ***one ~ ten Americans*** jeden na dziesięciu Amerykanów; ***cut s.th. ~ two*** przeciąć coś na dwie części **3.** do *G*; ***put it ~ your pocket*** włóż to do kieszeni **4.** za *A*; ***~ two hours*** za dwie godziny **5.** po *L*; ***~ English*** po angielsku **6.** ***~ the evening*** wieczorem; ***~ cash*** gotówką; ***~ my opinion*** moim zdaniem **7.** u *G*; ***~ Shakespeare*** u Szekspira **8.** ***~ brief*** krótko mówiąc **9.** ***equal ~ length*** tej samej długości **II** *adv* **1.** w domu; ***she's not ~*** nie ma jej **2.** do środka; ***come ~*** wejść (do środka) **3.** ***with milk ~*** z mlekiem **4.** ***he's ~ for a surprise*** czeka go niespodzianka **5.** ***be ~ on*** być wtajemniczonym w *A* **III** *adj* modny **IV** *s* ***know the ~s and outs of s.th.*** znać coś na wylot

in•a•bil•i•ty [ɪnə'bɪlɪtɪ] *s* **1.** niezdolność *f* **2.** niemożność *f*

in•ac•ces•si•ble [ɪnək'sesɪbl] *adj* niedostępny (***to*** dla *G*)

in•ac•cu•ra•cy [ɪn'ækjʊrəsɪ] *s* niedokładność *f*, nieścisłość *f*; **in•ac•cu•rate** [ɪn'ækjʊrət] *adj* niedokładny, nieprecyzyjny, nieścisły

in•ac•tion [ɪn'ækʃn] *s* **1.** bezczynność *f* **2.** bierność *f* **3.** zaniechanie *n*; **in•ac•tive** [ɪn'æktɪv] *adj* **1.** bezczynny **2.** nieczynny **3.** bierny **4.** nieaktywny **5.** *market*: ospały; **in•activ•i•ty** [ɪnæk'tɪvɪtɪ] *s* bezczynność *f*, brak *m* aktywności

in•ad•e•quate [ɪn'ædɪkwət] *adj* **1.** niedostateczny, niewystarczający; ***be ~ to meet the needs of*** nie spełniać potrzeb *G* **2.** nieodpowiedni, nieadekwatny; ***I felt ~ as a leader*** czułem, że rola lidera mnie przerasta

in•ad•mis•si•ble [ɪnəd'mɪsəbl] *adj* niedopuszczalny, nie do przyjęcia

in•ad•vis•a•ble [ɪnəd'vaɪzəbl] *adj* niewskazany

in•al•ien•a•ble [ɪn'eɪlɪənəbl] *adj rights*: niezbywalny

in•ane [ɪ'neɪn] *adj* **1.** idiotyczny **2.** niedorzeczny

in•an•i•mate [ɪn'ænɪmət] *adj* nieożywiony, martwy

in•ap•pli•ca•ble [ɪnə'plɪkəbl] *adj* **1.** ***be ~ to*** **a)** nie mieć zastosowania do *G*, nie stosować się do *G* **b)** nie obejmować *G* **2.** nieodpowiedni

in•ap•pro•pri•ate [ɪnə'prəʊprɪət] *adj* niestosowny, nieodpowiedni, niewłaściwy

in•ar•tic•u•late [ɪnɑː'tɪkjʊlət] *adj* **1.** ***be ~*** mieć trudności z wysławianiem się **2.** nieartykułowany **3.** niewyraźny; ***her speech was ~*** mówiła niewyraźnie **2.** niejasny

in•as•much as [ɪnəz'mʌtʃæz] *conj* jako że

in•at•ten•tion [ɪnə'tenʃn] *s* nieuwaga *f*, niedbałość *f*; **in•atten•tive** [ɪnə'tentɪv] *adj* nieuważny, niedbały

in•au•di•ble [ɪn'ɔːdəbl] *adj* niesłyszalny

in•au•gu•ral [ɪ'nɔːgjʊrəl] *adj* inauguracyjny; ***an ~ speech*** przemówienie inauguracyjne; **in•au•gu•rate** [ɪ'nɔːgjʊreɪt] *v/t* **1.** inaugurować ⟨za-⟩ **2.** otwierać ⟨-worzyć⟩ **3.** zapoczątkowywać ⟨-kować⟩ **4.** zaprzysięgać ⟨-siąc⟩; ***be ~d as president*** zostać zaprzysiężonym na (urząd) prezydenta **5.** konsekrować; **inau•gura•tion** [ɪnɔːgjʊ'reɪʃn] *s* **1.** inauguracja *f* **2.** otwarcie *n* **3.** zapoczątkowanie *n* **4.** zaprzysiężenie *n* (na urząd)

in•born ['ɪnbɔːn] *adj* wrodzony

in•bred [ɪn'bred] *adj* **1.** wrodzony **2.** endogamiczny **3.** wsobny; **in-breed•ing** ['ɪnbriːdɪŋ] *adj* **1.** chów *m* wsobny **2.** endogamia *f*

inc. → ***incorporated***

incalculable [ɪn'kælkjʊləbl] *adj* **1.** nieoceniony **2.** *loss*: nieoszacowany **3.** nieobliczalny

in•ca•pa•bil•i•ty [ɪnkeɪpə'bɪlətɪ] *s* niezdolność *f*; **in•ca•pa•ble** [ɪn'keɪpəbl] *adj* **1.** ***be ~ of doing s.th.*** nie potrafić czegoś zrobić; ***be ~ of speech*** **a)** nie potrafić mówić **b)** być niemową **2.** ***~ of proof*** nie do udowodnienia **3.** nieudolny

in•ca•pac•i•tate [ɪnkə'pæsɪteɪt] *v/t* **1.** ***a stroke left him partially ~d*** po udarze wystąpił u niego częściowy paraliż ciała **2.** obezwładniać ⟨-nić⟩ **3.** pozbawiać ⟨-wić⟩ zdolności prawnej; **in•ca•pac•i•tat•ed** [ɪnkə'pæsɪteɪtɪd] *adj* **1.** niesprawny **2.** ***~ for work*** niezdolny do pracy **3.** ***legally ~*** pozbawiony zdolności prawnej; **incapac•i•ty** [ɪnkə'pæsətɪ] *s* **1.** niesprawność *f* **2.** ***~ for work*** niezdolność do pracy **3.** ***legal ~*** brak zdolności prawnej

in•car•nate [ɪn'kɑːnət] *adj* wcielony; **in•carna•tion** [ɪnkɑː'neɪʃn] *s* wcielenie *n*, ucieleśnienie *n*

in•cen•tive [ɪn'sentɪv] *s* **1.** bodziec *m* **2.** motywacja *f* **3.** zachęta *f*; ***an ~ to buy*** zachęta do kupna

in•ces•sant [ɪn'sesnt] *adj* nieustanny, bezustanny; **in•ces•sant•ly** [ɪn'sesntlɪ] *adv* nieustannie

in•cest ['ɪnsest] *s* kazirodztwo *n*; **in-ces•tu•ous** [ɪn'sestʃʊəs] *adj* kazirodczy

inch [ɪntʃ] **I** *s* cal *m*; ***by ~es, ~ by ~*** cal po calu, centymetr po centymetrze; ***come within an ~ of death*** otrzeć się o śmierć **II** *v/i* posuwać się powoli

in•ci•dence ['ɪnsɪdəns] *s* częstość *f* występowania; ***regions with a high ~ of unemployment*** regiony, w których występuje wysokie bezrobocie; **in•ci•dent** ['ɪnsɪdənt] *s* **1.** wydarzenie *n* **2.** wypadek *m*; ***an isolated ~*** odosobniony wypadek **3.** incydent *m*; **in•ci•den•tal** [ɪnsɪ'dentl] *adj* **1.** uboczny **2.** *earning*: dodatkowy **3.** ***~ music*** podkład muzyczny **4.** ***be ~ to s.th.*** *form* towarzyszyć czemuś; **in•ci•den•tal•ly** [ɪnsɪ'dentlɪ] *adv* nawiasem mówiąc, à propos

in•cite [ɪn'saɪt] *v/t* **1.** podburzać ⟨-rzyć⟩ **2.** *mutiny*: wzniecać ⟨-cić⟩; **in•cite•ment** [ɪn'saɪtmənt] *s* podburzanie *n* (***to*** do *G*)

in•clem•ent [ɪn'klemənt] *adj* **1.** ***~ weather*** niepogoda, złe warunki pogodowe **2.** *climate*: surowy

in•cli•na•tion [ɪnklɪ'neɪʃn] *s* **1.** skłonność *f*, inklinacja *f* **2.** chęć *f*, ochota *f* **3.** nachylenie *n*, pochyłość *f*; **in•cline I** [ɪn'klaɪn] *v/i* **1.** skłaniać się (***to/towards*** ku *D*) **2.** mieć skłonność (***to/towards*** do *G*) **II** [ɪn'klaɪn] *v/t* **1.** *head*: pochylać ⟨-lić⟩ **2.** (*terrain*) opadać ⟨opaść⟩ **III** ['ɪnklaɪn] *s* pochyłość *f*; **inclined** [ɪn'klaɪnd] *adj* **1.** ***feel ~ to do s.th.*** mieć ochotę coś zrobić **2.** skłonny; ***I'm ~ to agree with you*** jestem skłonny się z panem zgodzić; ***be ~ to be lazy*** mieć skłonność do lenistwa

in•close → ***enclose***; **in•clos•ure** → ***enclosure***

in•clude [ɪn'klu:d] *v/t* **1.** zawierać ⟨-wrzeć⟩; ***VAT ~d*** cena zawiera podatek VAT **2.** obejmować ⟨objąć⟩ **3.** włączać ⟨-czyć⟩; ***be ~d on a list*** znajdować się na liście **4.** załączać ⟨-czyć⟩; **in•clud•ing** [ɪn'klu:dɪŋ] *prep* w tym, wliczając w to; **in•clu•sion** [ɪn'klu:ʒn] *s* włączenie *n*; **in•clu•sive** [ɪn'klu:sɪv] *adj* **1.** łączny **2.** ***be ~ of*** zawierać *A*

in•co•her•ence [ɪnkəʊ'hɪərəns] *s* niespójność *f* **in•co•her•ent** [ɪnkəʊ'hɪərənt] *adj* **1.** ***be ~*** (*person*) mówić bez ładu i składu **2.** niespójny **3.** nieskładny **4.** chaotyczny

in•come ['ɪnkʌm] *s* **1.** dochód *m*, dochody *pl* **2.** przychód *m*; **'in•come brack•et**, ***'in•come group*** *s* grupa *f* dochodu; **in•come sup'port** *s Br* dodatek *m* socjalny; **'in•come tax** *s* podatek *m* dochodowy

in•com•ing ['ɪnkʌmɪŋ] *adj* **1.** *calls, mail:* przychodzący **2.** ***an ~ flight*** przylot **3.** nadchodzący **4.** *government:* nowy

in•com•pa•ra•ble [ɪn'kɒmpərəbl] *adj* **1.** niezrównany **2.** nieporównywalny (***with/to*** z *I*)

in•com•pat•i•bil•i•ty [ɪnkəmpætɪ'bɪlɪtɪ] *s* niezgodność *f*, rozbieżność *f*, niedopasowanie *n*; **in•com•pat•i•ble** [ɪnkəm'pætɪbl] *adj* **1.** niezgodny, rozbieżny, niedobrany **2.** *INF* niekompatybilny

in•com•pe•tence [ɪn'kɒmpɪtəns] *s* **1.** niekompetencja *f* **2.** nieudolność *f*; **in•com•pe•tent** [ɪn'kɒmpɪtənt] *adj* **1.** niekompetentny **2.** nieudolny

in•com•plete [ɪnkəm'pli:t] *adj* **1.** niekompletny **2.** niepełny **3.** niezupełny **4.** niedokończony

in•com•pre•hen•si•ble [ɪnkɒmprɪ'hensəbl] *adj* niezrozumiały; ***I find it ~ that*** nie mogę zrozumieć, że; **in•com•pre•hen•si•bly** [ɪnkɒmprɪ'hensəblɪ] *adv* niezrozumiale, niejasno; **in•com•pre•hen•sion** [ɪnkɒmprɪ'henʃn] *s* niezrozumienie *n*, brak *m* zrozumienia

in•con•cei•va•ble [ɪnkən'si:vəbl] *adj* niewyobrażalny; ***it's ~ to me that*** nie mogę pojąć, że

in•con•clu•sive [ɪnkən'klu:sɪv] *adj* bezowocny

in•con•gru•i•ty [ɪnkəŋ'gru:ətɪ] *s* **1.** niestosowność *f* **2.** niedopasowanie *n* **3.** sprzeczność *f*; **in•con•gru•ous** [ɪn'kɒŋgruəs] *adj* **1.** nie na miejscu **2.** niestosowny **3.** dziwny

in•con•se•quen•tial [ɪnkɒnsɪ'kwənʃəl] *adj* **1.** nieistotny **2.** błahy

in•con•sid•er•a•ble [ɪnkən'sɪdərəbl] *adj* nieznaczny, niewielki

in•con•sid•er•ate [ɪnkən'sɪdərət] *adj* **1.** nieliczący się z innymi **2.** nietaktowny **3.** niedelikatny

in•con•sis•ten•cy [ɪnkən'sɪstənsɪ] *s* **1.** niespójność *f* **2.** niekonsekwencja *f* **3.** *of work*: nierówny poziom *m*; **in•con•sis•tent** [ɪnkən'sɪstənt] *adj* **1.** niekonsekwentny **2.** nie-

I

spójny **3.** sprzeczny **4.** *player*: nierówny

in•con•so•la•ble [ɪnkən'səʊləbl] *adj lit* nieukojony w żalu

in•con•spic•u•ous [ɪnkən'spɪkjʊəs] *adj* niepozorny, nierzucający się w oczy

in•con•ve•ni•ence [ɪnkən'viːnɪəns] **I** *s* **1.** niedogodność *f* **2.** kłopot *m*; ***put s.o. to ~, be an ~ to s.o.*** sprawić komuś kłopot **3.** niewygoda *f* **II** *v/t* sprawiać ⟨-wić⟩ kłopot; **in•con•ve•ni•ent** [ɪnkən'viːnɪənt] *adj* **1.** niedogodny (***to*** dla *G*); ***at an ~ time*** o nieodpowiedniej porze **2.** niewygodny; **in•con•ven•ient•ly** [ɪnkən'viːnɪəntlɪ] *adv* niedogodnie

in•cor•po•rate [ɪn'kɔːpəreɪt] *v/t* **1.** włączać ⟨-czyć⟩ (***to*** do *G*) **2.** zawierać ⟨-wrzeć⟩ (w sobie) **3.** łączyć ⟨po-⟩ (***to*** z *I*); **in•cor•po•rat•ed** [ɪn'kɔːpəreɪtɪd] *adj*; ***Bowles Services ~*** spółka Bowles Services; **in•cor•pora•tion** [ɪnkɔːpə'reɪʃn] *s* **1.** włączenie *n* **2.** przyłączenie *n* **3.** ECON rejestracja *f* (spółki)

in•cor•rect [ɪnkə'rekt] *adj* niepoprawny, błędny, niewłaściwy; **in•cor•rect•ly** [ɪnkə'rektlɪ] *adv* niepoprawnie, błędnie, niewłaściwie

in•cor•ri•gi•ble [ɪn'kɒrɪdʒəbl] *adj* niepoprawny

in•cor•rupt•i•ble [ɪnkə'rʌptəbl] *adj* **1.** nieprzekupny **2.** niezniszczalny **3.** nieniszczejący

in•crease I [ɪn'kriːs] *v/i* rosnąć, wzrastać ⟨-rosnąć⟩, zwiększać ⟨-szyć⟩ się; ***~ in price*** podrożeć **II** [ɪn'kriːs] *v/t* zwiększać ⟨-szyć⟩, podnosić ⟨-nieść⟩, podwyższać ⟨-szyć⟩ **III** ['ɪnkriːs] *s* wzrost *m*; ***an ~ in value*** wzrost wartości; ***an ~ in population*** wzrost liczby ludności; ***be on the ~*** **a)** rosnąć **b)** zwiększać się; **in•creas•ing** [ɪn'kriːsɪŋ] *adj* **1.** rosnący **2.** zwiększający się; **in•creas•ing•ly** [ɪn'kriːsɪŋlɪ] *adv* coraz bardziej; ***~ clear*** coraz wyraźniejszy

in•cred•i•ble [ɪn'kredɪbl] *adj* **1.** niewiarygodny **2.** niesamowity

in•cred•u•lous [ɪn'kredjʊləs] *adj* pełen niedowierzania; ***be ~ that*** nie wierzyć, że

in•crim•i•nate [ɪn'krɪmɪneɪt] *v/t* obciążać ⟨-żyć⟩; **in•crim•i•nat•ing** [ɪn'krɪmɪneɪtɪŋ] *adj* obciążający

in•cu•bate ['ɪŋkjʊbeɪt] **I** *v/t* **1.** wysiadywać ⟨-siedzieć⟩ **2.** inkubować **II** *v/i* **1.** ***the disease ~s for 7 days*** okres wylęgania choroby wynosi 7 dni **2.** przechodzić inkubację; **in•cu•ba•tion** [ɪŋkjʊ'beɪʃn] *s* inkubacja *f*; **in•cu•'ba•tion pe•ri•od** *s* okres *m* inkubacji; **in•cu•ba•tor** ['ɪŋkjʊbeɪtə] *s* inkubator *m*

in•cul•cate ['ɪnkʌlkeɪt] *v/t* **1.** wpajać ⟨wpoić⟩ (***s.th. in/into*** coś *D*, ***s.o. with*** komuś *A*) **2.** wszczepiać ⟨-pić⟩ (***s.th. in/into*** coś *D*, ***s.o. with*** komuś *A*)

in•cur [ɪn'kɜː] *v/t* **1.** *debts*: zaciągać ⟨-gnąć⟩ **2.** *loss*: ponosić ⟨-nieść⟩

in•cu•ra•ble [ɪn'kjʊərəbl] *adj* **1.** nieuleczalny **2.** nieuleczalnie chory

in•cur•sion [ɪn'kɜːʃn] *s* wtargnięcie *n*; ***make an ~*** wtargnąć

in•debt•ed [ɪn'detɪd] *adj* **1.** zobowiązany; ***be greatly ~ to s.o.*** być komuś wielce zobowiązanym **2.** zadłużony

in•de•cen•cy [ɪn'diːsnsɪ] *s* **1.** nieprzyzwoitość *f* **2.** obraza *f* moralności; **in•de•cent** [ɪn'diːsnt] *adj* **1.** nieprzyzwoity **2.** skandaliczny **3.** nadmierny; **in•de•cent as•'sault** *s* czyn *m* lubieżny

in•de•ci•pher•a•ble [ɪndɪ'saɪfərəbl] *adj* nie do odcyfrowania, nie do rozszyfrowania

in•de•ci•sion [ɪndɪ'sɪʒn] *s* niezdecydowanie *n*; **in•de•ci•sive** [ɪndɪ'saɪsɪv] *adj* niezdecydowany; **in•de•ci•sive•ness** [ɪndɪ'saɪsɪvnɪs] *s* niezdecydowanie *n*

in•deed [ɪn'diːd] *adv* **1.** rzeczywiście, istotnie; ***thank you very much ~*** naprawdę bardzo dziękuję **2.** naprawdę?; ***– 'I saw him yesterday.' – 'Did you ~?'*** – „Widziałem go wczoraj." – „Naprawdę?"

in•de•fen•si•ble [ɪndɪ'fensəbl] *adj* **1.** nie do obrony **2.** niedający się usprawiedliwić

in•de•fi•na•ble [ɪndɪ'faɪnəbl] *adj* nieuchwytny, nieokreślony

in•def•i•nite [ɪn'defɪnɪt] *adj* **1.** nieokreślony; ***for an ~ period*** na czas nieokreślony **2.** niejasny; **in•def•i•nite 'ar•ticle** *s* przedimek *m* nieokreślony; **in-**

def•i•nite•ly [ɪn'defɪnɪtlɪ] *adv* **1.** na czas nieokreślony **2.** bez końca
in•del•i•cate [ɪn'delɪkət] *adj* **1.** niedelikatny **2.** grubiański
in•dem•ni•fy [ɪn'demnɪfaɪ] *v/t* **1.** ubezpieczać ⟨-czyć⟩ (***against*** od *G*) **2.** wypłacać ⟨-cić⟩ odszkodowanie (***for*** za *A*); **in•dem•ni•ty** [ɪn'demnɪtɪ] *s* **1.** ubezpieczenie *n* **2.** odszkodowanie *n*
in•de•pen•dence [ɪndɪ'pendəns] *s* **1.** niezależność *f* (***from*** od *G*) **2.** niepodległość *f*; **In•de•'pen•dence Day** *s* Dzień *m* Niepodległości; **in•de•pen•dent** [ɪndɪ'pendənt] *adj* **1.** niezależny **2.** niepodległy **3.** samodzielny **4.** oddzielny; **in•de•pen•dent•ly** [ɪndɪ'pendəntlɪ] *adv* **1.** niezależnie **2.** samodzielnie **3.** oddzielnie
'in-depth *adj* dogłębny, szczegółowy, wyczerpujący
in•de•scri•ba•ble [ɪndɪs'kraɪbəbl] *adj* nieopisany; **in•de•scrib•a•bly** [ɪndɪs'kraɪbəblɪ] *adv* **1.** nieopisanie **2.** *boring*: nieprawdopodobnie
in•de•struc•ti•ble [ɪndɪ'strʌktəbl] *adj* niezniszczalny, trwały
in•de•ter•mi•nate [ɪndɪ'tɜːmɪnət] *adj* nieokreślony; ***his eyes were an ~ colour*** miał oczy nieokreślonego koloru
in•dex ['ɪndeks] *pl -dexes, -dices* ['ɪndɪsiːz] **I** *s* **1.** indeks *m* **2.** spis *m* **3.** *Br* katalog *m* **4.** wskaźnik *m* **5.** współczynnik *m* **6.** oznaka *f*, ***be an ~ of*** być oznaką *G* **II** *v/t* **1.** katalogować ⟨s-⟩ **2.** opracowywać ⟨-cować⟩ indeks do *G* **3.** *ECON* indeksować; **in-dexed** → ***index-linked***; **'in•dex card** *s* karta *f* katalogowa, fiszka *f*; **'in•dex fin•ger** *s* palec *m* wskazujący; **in•dex-'linked** *adj Br* indeksowany
In•di•a ['ɪndɪə] *s* Indie *pl*
In•di•an ['ɪndɪən] **I** *adj* **1.** indyjski **2.** indiański **II** *s* **1.** Hindus *m*, Hinduska *f* **2.** Indianin *m*, Indianka *f*; ***in ~ file*** gęsiego; **In•di•an 'corn** *s* kukurydza *f*; **'In•di•an Ocean** *s* Ocean *m* Indyjski; **In•di•an 'sum•mer** *s* babie lato *n*
in•di•cate ['ɪndɪkeɪt] **I** *v/t* **1.** wskazywać ⟨-zać⟩ na *A* **2.** świadczyć o *L* **3.** oznaczać **II** *v/i* **1.** wskazywać ⟨-zać⟩ **2.** *Br* włączać ⟨-czyć⟩ kierunkowskaz ***~ right*** *Br* zasygnalizować skręt w prawo; **in•di•ca•tion** [ɪndɪ'keɪʃn] *s* **1.** oznaka *f* (***of*** *G*); ***there is every ~ that*** wszystko wskazuje na to, że **2.** *MED* zalecenie *n*; **in•dic•a•tive** [ɪn'dɪkətɪv] **I** *adj* **1.** ***be ~ of*** wskazywać na *A*, świadczyć o *L* **2.** ***the ~ mood*** tryb oznajmujący, tryb orzekający **II** *s* ***the ~*** tryb *m* oznajmujący, tryb *m* orzekający; **in•di•ca•tor** ['ɪndɪkeɪtə] *s* **1.** wskaźnik *m* **2.** oznaka *f* **3.** *Br* kierunkowskaz *m*
in•dict [ɪn'daɪt] *v/t* **1.** stawiać ⟨postawić⟩ w stan oskarżenia (***for*** pod zarzutem *G*) **2.** oskarżać ⟨-żyć⟩ (***for*** o *A*); **indict•ment** [ɪn'daɪtmənt] *s* **1.** akt *m* oskarżenia **2.** oskarżenie *n* **3.** potępienie *n*
in•dif•fer•ence [ɪn'dɪfrəns] *s* obojętność *f*; **in•dif•fer•ent** [ɪn'dɪfrənt] *adj* **1.** obojętny; ***he is ~ to it*** jest mu to obojętne **2.** przeciętny
in•dig•e•nous [ɪn'dɪdʒənəs] *adj* **1.** tubylczy; ***~ people*** autochtoni, tubylcy **2.** lokalny, miejscowy
in•di•ges•ti•ble [ɪndɪ'dʒestɪbl] *adj* niestrawny; **in•di•ges•tion** [ɪndɪ'dʒestʃn] *s MED* niestrawność *f*
in•dig•nant [ɪn'dɪgnənt] *adj* oburzony (***at/with*** na *A*); ***become ~*** oburzyć się; **in•dig•na•tion** [ɪndɪg'neɪʃn] *s* oburzenie *n*; ***fill s.o. with ~*** oburzyć kogoś
in•dig•ni•ty [ɪn'dɪgnɪtɪ] *s* **1.** zniewaga *f* **2.** upokorzenie *n*
in•di•rect [ɪndɪ'rekt] *adj* **1.** pośredni **2.** okrężny; ***by ~ means*** okrężną drogą **3.** ***~ object*** dopełnienie dalsze; ***~ speech*** mowa zależna; **in•di•rect•ly** [ɪndɪ'rektlɪ] *adv* pośrednio, nie wprost
in•dis•cern•i•ble [ɪndɪ'sɜːnəbl] *adj* niezauważalny, niedostrzegalny
in•dis•creet [ɪndɪ'skriːt] *adj* **1.** niedyskretny **2.** nieostrożny; **in•dis•cre•tion** [ɪndɪ'skreʃn] *s* **1.** niedyskrecja *f* **2.** nieostrożność *f*
in•dis•crim•i•nate [ɪndɪ'skrɪmɪnət] *adj* niewybredny, niewymagający, bezkrytyczny
in•dis•pen•sa•ble [ɪndɪ'spensəbl] *adj* niezbędny
in•dis•posed [ɪndɪ'spəʊzd] *adj form* **1.** niedysponowany **2.** niechętny; ***be ~ to do s.th.*** nie być skłonnym czegoś zrobić

I

in•dis•pu•ta•ble [ɪndɪ'spjuːtəbl] *adj* niekwestionowany, bezdyskusyjny; **in•dis•pu•ta•bly** [ɪndɪ'spjuːtəbli] *adv* bezspornie, bezdyskusyjnie

in•dis•tinct [ɪndɪ'stɪŋkt] *adj* niewyraźny, nieostry, mglisty

in•dis•tin•guish•a•ble [ɪndɪ'stɪŋgwɪʃəbl] *adj* **1.** nie do odróżnienia **2.** niewyraźny

in•di•vid•u•al [ɪndɪ'vɪdʒʊəl] **I** *adj* **1.** indywidualny **2.** osobisty **3.** pojedynczy; ***an ~ case*** pojedynczy przypadek **4.** poszczególny **II** *s* **1.** osoba *f* **2.** jednostka *f* **3.** oryginał *m* **4.** indywiduum *n*; **5.** osobnik *m* **in•di•vid•u•al•ism** [ɪndɪ'vɪdʒʊəlɪzəm] *s* indywidualizm *m*; **in•di•vid•u•a•list** [ɪndɪ'vɪdʒʊəlɪst] *s* indywidualista *m*; **in•di•vid•u•al•is•tic** [ɪndɪvɪdʒʊəl'ɪstɪk] *adj* **1.** indywidualistyczny **2.** oryginalny; **in•di•vid•u•al•i•ty** [ɪndɪvɪdʒʊ'æləti] *s* indywidualność *f*, oryginalność *f*; **in•di•vid•u•al•ize** [ɪndɪ'vɪdʒʊəlaɪz] *v/t* indywidualizować ⟨z-⟩, nadawać ⟨-dać⟩ indywidualny charakter; **in•di•vid•u•al•ly** [ɪndɪ'vɪdʒʊəlɪ] *adv* **1.** indywidualnie, pojedynczo, oddzielnie **2.** osobiście

in•di•vis•i•ble [ɪndɪ'vɪzɪbl] *adj* niepodzielny

In•do•ne•sia [ɪndə'niːzjə] *s* Indonezja

in•door ['ɪndɔː] *adj* **1.** kryty **2.** halowy **3.** ***an ~ market*** hala targowa **4.** domowy **5.** pokojowy

in•doors [ɪn'dɔːz] *adv* **1.** wewnątrz, w środku **2.** do środka

in•dorse → ***endorse***

in•du•bi•ta•ble [ɪn'djuːbɪtəbl] *adj* niewątpliwy, niekwestionowany

in•duce [ɪn'djuːs] *v/t* **1.** skłaniać ⟨-łonić⟩, nakłaniać ⟨-łonić⟩ **2.** wywoływać ⟨-łać⟩; ***~ labour*** wywołać poród **3.** indukować; ***~d current*** prąd indukcyjny; **in•duce•ment** [ɪn'djuːsmənt] *s* **1.** zachęta *f*; ***an ~ to buy*** zachęta do kupna **2.** motywacja *f*

in•dulge [ɪn'dʌldʒ] **I** *v/t* **1.** dogadzać ⟨-godzić⟩ **2.** ***~ oneself in*** pozwalać sobie na *A* **3.** *fantasy*: zaspokajać ⟨-koić⟩ **II** *v/i* **1.** pozwalać ⟨-wolić⟩ sobie (***in*** na *A*) **2.** oddawać ⟨-dać⟩ się (***in*** *D*); **in•dul•gence** [ɪn'dʌldʒəns] *s* **1.** pobłażliwość *f* **2.** przyjemność *f* **3.** słabość *f* **4.** REL odpust *m*; **in•dul•gent** [ɪn'dʌldʒənt] *adj* pobłażliwy

in•dus•tri•al [ɪn'dʌstrɪəl] *adj* przemysłowy; ***~ espionage*** szpiegostwo przemysłowe; ***an ~ tribunal*** sąd pracy; ***an ~ estate***, ***an ~ park*** strefa przemysłowa; ***~ action*** akcja protestacyjna, strajk; **in•dus•tri•al•ist** [ɪn'dʌstrɪəlɪst] *s* przemysłowiec *m*; **in•dus•tri•al•i•za•tion** [ɪndʌstrɪəlaɪz'eɪʃn] *s* uprzemysłowienie *n*, industrializacja *f*; **in•dus•tri•al•ize** [ɪn'dʌstrɪəlaɪz] *v/t* uprzemysławiać ⟨-łowić⟩, industrializować ⟨z-⟩

in•dus•tri•ous [ɪn'dʌstrɪəs] *adj* pracowity, pilny

in•dus•try ['ɪndəstrɪ] *s* **1.** przemysł *m*; ***the steel ~*** przemysł stalowy **2.** *form* pracowitość *f*

in•e•bri•at•ed [ɪ'niːbrɪeɪtɪd] *adj form* nietrzeźwy, w stanie nietrzeźwym

in•ed•i•ble [ɪn'edəbl] *adj* niejadalny

in•ef•fec•tive [ɪnɪ'fektɪv] *adj* nieskuteczny, nieudolny

in•ef•fec•tu•al [ɪnɪ'fektʃʊəl] *adj* **1.** nieudolny **2.** bezowocny, bezskuteczny

in•ef•fi•cient [ɪnɪ'fɪʃənt] *adj* nieskuteczny, niewydajny, nieudolny

in•el•e•gant [ɪn'elɪgənt] *adj* nieelegancki, niegustowny

in•eli•gi•ble [ɪn'elɪdʒɪbl] *adj*: ***s.o. is ~ for*** **a)** komuś nie przysługuje prawo do *G* **b)** ktoś nie spełnia wymaganych warunków do *G*; ***s.o. is ~ to vote*** komuś nie przysługuje prawo głosu

in•e•qual•i•ty [ɪnɪ'kwɒlɪtɪ] *s* nierówność *f*

in•ert [ɪ'nɜːt] *adj* bezwładny; **in•er•ti•a** [ɪ'nɜːʃə] *s* PHYS bezwładność *f*, inercja *f*

in•es•ca•pa•ble [ɪnɪ'skeɪpəbl] *adj* nieunikniony, nieodparty

in•es•sen•tial [ɪnɪ'senʃl] *adj* zbędny, nieistotny

in•es•ti•ma•ble [ɪn'estɪməbl] *adj* nieoceniony

in•ev•i•ta•bil•i•ty [ɪnevɪtə'bɪlɪtɪ] *s* nieuchronność *f*; **in•ev•i•ta•ble** [ɪn'evɪtəbl] **I** *adj* nieunikniony, nieuchronny **II** *s* ***the ~*** to, co nieuniknione; **in•ev•i•ta•bly** [ɪn'evɪtəblɪ] *adv* nieuchronnie

in•ex•act [ɪnɪg'zækt] *adj* niedokładny

in•ex•cu•sa•ble [ɪnɪk'skjuːzəbl] *adj* niewybaczalny

in•ex•haus•ti•ble [ɪnɪg'zɔːstəbl] *adj* niewyczerpany

in•ex•pen•sive [ɪnɪk'spensɪv] *adj* niedrogi

in•ex•pe•ri•ence [ɪnɪk'spɪərɪəns] *s* brak *m* doświadczenia; **in•ex•pe•ri•enced** [ɪnɪk'spɪrɪənst] *adj* niedoświadczony

in•ex•pert [ɪn'ekspɜːt] *adj* niewprawny, niefachowy

in•ex•plic•a•ble [ɪnɪk'splɪkəbl] *adj* niewytłumaczalny

in•ex•pres•si•ble [ɪnɪk'spresɪbl] *adj* niewysłowiony

in•fa•mous ['ɪnfəməs] *adj* niesławny, niechlubny, haniebny; **in•fa•my** ['ɪnfəmɪ] *s* **1.** niesława *f*, zła sława *f* **2.** niegodziwość *f*

in•fan•cy ['ɪnfənsɪ] *s* wczesne dzieciństwo *n*, niemowlęctwo *n*; ***be in its ~ fig*** być w powijakach; **in•fant** ['ɪnfənt] **I** *s* niemowlę *n*, małe dziecko *n* **II** *adj* dziecięcy; ***~ mortality*** umieralność noworodków; ***an ~ prodigy*** cudowne dziecko; **in•fan•ti•cide** [ɪn'fæntɪsaɪd] *s* **1.** dzieciobójstwo *n* **2.** dzieciobójca *m*; **in•fan•tile** ['ɪnfəntaɪl] *adj* **1.** infantylny **2.** dziecięcy

in•fan•try ['ɪnfəntrɪ] *s* (*army*) piechota *f*; **in•fan•try•man** *pl -men*, ***in•fan•try sol•dier*** *s* żołnierz *m* piechoty, piechur *m*

'in•fant school *s* (*for children 4-7 years old*) zerówka *f*

in•fat•u•at•ed [ɪn'fætʃʊeɪtɪd] *adj* zauroczony (***with*** *I*), zadurzony (***with*** w *L*); **in•fat•ua•tion** [ɪnfætʃʊ'eɪʃn] *s* zauroczenie *n*, zadurzenie *n*

in•fect [ɪn'fekt] *v/t* **1.** *a. fig* zarażać ⟨-razić⟩; ***become ~ed*** zarazić się **2.** zakażać ⟨-kazić⟩ **3.** *air*, *water*: skażać ⟨skazić⟩; **in•fec•tion** [ɪn'fekʃn] *s* **1.** zakażenie *n* **2.** infekcja *f*; **in•fec•tious** [ɪn'fekʃəs] *adj* **1.** zakaźny; ***an ~ disease*** choroba zakaźna **2.** infekcyjny **3.** ***I'm still ~*** wciąż można się ode mnie zarazić **4.** *laughter*: zaraźliwy

in•fer [ɪn'fɜː] *v/t* wnioskować ⟨wy-⟩ (***from*** z *G*); **in•fer•ence** ['ɪnfərəns] *s* **1.** wniosek *m* **2.** wnioskowanie *n*

in•fe•ri•or [ɪn'fɪərɪə] **I** *adj* **1.** gorszy (***to*** od *G*); **2.** niskiej jakości **3.** niższy rangą **4.** ***be ~ to s.o.*** podlegać komuś **II** *s* podwładny *m*; **in•fe•ri•or•i•ty** [ɪnfɪərɪ'ɒrətɪ] *s* **1.** niższość *f* **2.** gorsza jakość *f* **3.** podrzędność *f*; **in•fe•ri•'or•i•ty complex** *s* kompleks *m* niższości

in•fer•nal [ɪn'fɜːnl] *adj* **1.** piekielny **2.** diabelski; **infer•no** [ɪn'fɜːnəʊ] *pl -nos s* piekło *n*

in•fer•tile [ɪn'fɜːtaɪl] *adj* **1.** bezpłodny **2.** jałowy; **in•fer•til•i•ty** [ɪnfə'tɪlɪtɪ] *s* **1.** bezpłodność *f* **2.** jałowość *f*

in•fi•del ['ɪnfɪdəl] *adj* HIST REL niewierny *m*; **in•fi•del•i•ty** [ɪnfɪ'delɪtɪ] *s* niewierność *f*

in•fight•ing ['ɪnfaɪtɪŋ] *s* konflikt *m* wewnętrzny

in•fil•trate ['ɪnfɪltreɪt] **I** *v/t* infiltrować **II** *v/i* **1.** przesączać ⟨-czyć⟩ się **2.** przenikać ⟨-knąć⟩; **in•fil•tra•tion** [ɪnfɪl'treɪʃn] *s* **1.** infiltracja *f* **2.** przenikanie *n*

in•fi•nite ['ɪnfɪnət] *adj* **1.** nieskończony **2.** *patience*: bezgraniczny **3.** niezmierny **4.** niezliczony; **in•fi•nite•ly** ['ɪnfɪnətlɪ] *adv* **1.** nieskończenie **2.** niezmiernie; **in•fin•i•tes•i•mal** [ɪnfɪnɪ'tesɪml] *adj* **1.** znikomy **2.** śladowy **3.** bardzo mały **4.** bardzo krótki; **in•fin•i•tive** [ɪn'fɪnətɪv] *s* bezokolicznik *m*; **in•fin•i•ty** [ɪn'fɪnətɪ] *s* nieskończoność *f*

I

in•firm [ɪn'fɜːrm] *adj* **1.** chory **2.** niedołężny; **in•fir•ma•ry** [ɪn'fɜːmərɪ] *s* **1.** szpital *m* **2.** izba *f* chorych; **in•fir•mi•ty** [ɪn'fɜːmətɪ] *s* **1.** choroba *f* **2.** niemoc *f*

in•flame [ɪn'fleɪm] *v/t* **1.** rozpalać ⟨-lić⟩; ***be ~d with rage*** płonąć z wściekłości **2.** zaogniać ⟨-nić⟩ **3.** oburzać ⟨-rzyć⟩

in•flam•ma•ble [ɪn'flæməbl] *adj* **1.** palny, łatwopalny **2.** *situation*: wybuchowy; **in•flam•ma•tion** [ɪnflə'meɪʃn] *s* MED zapalenie *n*

in•flat•a•ble [ɪn'fleɪtəbl] *adj* nadmuchiwany, pneumatyczny; **inflate** [ɪn'fleɪt] *v/t* pompować ⟨na-⟩, nadmuchiwać ⟨-chać⟩; ***be ~d with pride*** pękać z dumy

in•fla•tion [ɪn'fleɪʃən] *s* ECON inflacja *f*; ***the rate of ~*** stopa inflacji; **in•fla•tion•a•ry** [ɪn'fleɪʃənərɪ] *adj* **1.** inflacyjny;

an ~ spiral spirala inflacji **2.** inflacjogenny

in•flec•tion [ɪn'flekʃn] *s* **1.** *GRAM* odmiana *f*, fleksja *f* **2.** modulacja *n* **3.** intonacja *f*

in•flex•i•ble [ɪn'fleksɪbl] *adj* **1.** nieelastyczny **2.** nieugięty

in•flict [ɪn'flɪkt] *v/t* **1.** wymierzać ⟨-rzyć⟩ (***on*** *D*) **2.** zadawać ⟨-dać⟩ (***on*** *D*) **3.** wyrządzać ⟨-dzić⟩ (***on*** *D*) **4.** ***~ oneself on*** narzucać się *D*; **in•flic•tion** [ɪn'flɪkʃn] *s* zadawanie *n*, wymierzanie *n*, narzucanie *n*

'in-flight *adj*: ***~ meals*** posiłki (serwowane) podczas lotu

in•flu•ence ['ɪnflʊəns] *s* wpływ *m* (***on***/***over*** na *A*); ***be under s.o.'s ~*** być pod czyimś wpływem; ***under the ~ of alcohol*** pod wpływem alkoholu; **in•flu•en•tial** [ɪnflʊ'enʃl] *adj* wpływowy, znaczący, istotny

in•flu•en•za [ɪnflʊ'enzə] *s* grypa *f*

in•flux ['ɪnflʌks] *s* napływ *m*

in•form [ɪn'fɔːm] **I** *v/t* powiadamiać ⟨-domić⟩ (***s.o. of***/***about*** kogoś o *L*), informować ⟨po-⟩ (***s.o. of***/***about*** kogoś o *L*); ***keep s.o. ~ed*** informować kogoś na bieżąco **II** *v/i* donosić ⟨-nieść⟩ (***against***/***on*** na *A*)

in•for•mal [ɪn'fɔːməl] *adj* **1.** swobodny **2.** potoczny **3.** nieformalny **4.** nieoficjalny **5.** prywatny; **in•for•mal•i•ty** [ɪnfə'mælɪtɪ] *s* **1.** swobodny styl *m* **2.** nieoficjalny charakter *m* **3.** potoczność *f*; **in•for•mal•ly** [ɪn'fɔːməlɪ] *adv* **1.** swobodnie **2.** na gruncie towarzyskim **3.** nieformalnie **4.** nieoficjalnie

in•form•ant [ɪn'fɔːmənt] *s* informator *m*

in•for•ma•tion [ɪnfə'meɪʃn] *s* informacja *f*, informacje *pl*; ***a piece of ~*** informacja *f*, wiadomość *f*; **in•for•'ma•tion desk** *s* informacja *f*, punkt *m* informacyjny; **in•for•ma•tion 'sci•ence** *s* informatyka *f*; **in•for•ma•tion 'sci•en•tist** *s* informatyk *m*; **in•for•ma•tion tech•'nol•o•gy** *s* technologia *f* informacyjna, informatyka *f*

in•for•ma•tive [ɪn'fɔːmətɪv] *adj* bogaty w informacje, pouczający; **in•formed** [ɪn'fɔːmd] *adj* **1.** poinformowany; ***keep s.o. ~ of*** informować kogoś na bieżąco o *L* **2.** kompetentny **3.** *decision*: przemyślany; **in•form•er** [ɪn'fɔːmə] *s* informator *m*, donosiciel *m*

infra-red [ɪnfrə'red] *adj* podczerwony

in•fra•struc•ture ['ɪnfrəstrʌktʃə] *s* infrastruktura *f*

in•fre•quent [ɪn'friːkwənt] *adj* rzadki, nieczęsty

in•fu•ri•ate [ɪn'fjʊərɪeɪt] *v/t* rozwścieczać ⟨-czyć⟩, doprowadzać ⟨-dzić⟩ do szału; **in•fu•ri•at•ing** [ɪn'fjʊərɪeɪtɪŋ] *adj* doprowadzający do szału

in•fuse [ɪn'fjuːz] *v/t* **1.** *tea*: zaparzać ⟨-rzyć⟩ **2.** *fig* przepełniać; ***~d with sadness*** przepełniony smutkiem; **in•fu•sion** [ɪn'fjuːʒn] *s* **1.** *fig* zastrzyk *m* **2.** napar *m*

in•ge•ni•ous [ɪn'dʒiːnɪəs] *adj* pomysłowy; **in•ge•nu•i•ty** [ɪndʒɪ'njuːətɪ] *s* pomysłowość *f*

in•gen•u•ous [ɪn'dʒenjʊəs] *adj* prostoduszny, naiwny

in•grained [ɪn'greɪnd] *adj* (głęboko) zakorzeniony

in•gra•ti•ate [ɪn'greɪʃɪeɪt] *v/t*: ***~ oneself with s.o.*** przypochlebiać się komuś; **in•gra•ti•at•ing** [ɪn'greɪʃɪeɪtɪŋ] *adj* przymilny, przypochlebny

in•grat•i•tude [ɪn'grætɪtjuːd] *s* niewdzięczność *f*

in•gre•di•ent [ɪn'griːdɪənt] *s* **1.** składnik *m* **2.** *fig* element *m*

in•grown ['ɪngrəʊn] *adj* wrastający; ***an ~ toenail*** wrastający paznokieć u nogi

in•hab•it [ɪn'hæbɪt] *v/t* zamieszkiwać; **in•hab•it•a•ble** [ɪn'hæbɪtəbl] *adj* nadający się do zamieszkania; **in•hab•i•tant** [ɪn'hæbɪtənt] *s* mieszkaniec *m*; **in•hab•it•ed** [ɪn'hæbɪtɪd] *adj* zamieszkany

in•hale [ɪn'heɪl] **I** *v/t* **1.** wdychać **2.** zaciągać ⟨-gnąć⟩ się *I* **II** *v/t* robić ⟨z-⟩ wdech, wciągać ⟨-gnąć⟩ powietrze; **in•ha•ler** [ɪn'heɪlə] *s* inhalator *m*

in•her•ent [ɪn'hɪərənt] *adj* nieodłączny; **in•her•ent•ly** [ɪn'hɪərəntlɪ] *adv* z natury

in•her•it [ɪn'herɪt] *v/t* dziedziczyć ⟨o-⟩, otrzymywać ⟨-mać⟩ w spadku; **in•her•i•tance** [ɪn'herɪtəns] *s* spadek *m*, dziedzictwo *n*, spuścizna *f*

in•hib•it [ɪn'hɪbɪt] *v/t* **1.** hamować ⟨po-⟩ **2.** spowalniać ⟨-wolnić⟩ **3.** blokować ⟨za-⟩ **4.** powstrzymywać ⟨-mać⟩ (***s.o. from*** kogoś przed *I*)

5. utrudniać ⟨-nić⟩; **in•hib•it•ed** [ɪn'hɪbɪtɪd] *adj* **1.** skrępowany **2.** pełen zahamowań; ***be ~ about doing s.th.*** mieć opory przed zrobieniem czegoś; **in•hi•bi•tion** [ɪnhɪ'bɪʃn] *s* zahamowanie *n*

in•hos•pi•ta•ble [ɪnhɒ'spɪtəbl] *adj* **1.** niegościnny **2.** *climate*: surowy

in•hu•man [ɪn'hjuːmən] *adj* nieludzki; **in•hu•mane** [ɪnhjuː'meɪn] *adj* niehumanitarny, nieludzki; **in•hu•man•i•ty** [ɪnhjuː'mænətɪ] *s* bestialstwo *n*, nieludzkość *f*

i•ni•tial [ɪ'nɪʃl] **I** *adj* początkowy **II** *s* inicjał *m*, pierwsza litera *f* **III** *v/t* parafować; **i•ni•tial•ly** [ɪ'nɪʃlɪ] *adv* początkowo, pierwotnie

i•ni•ti•ate [ɪ'nɪʃɪeɪt] **I** *v/t* **1.** zapoczątkowywać ⟨-kować⟩, inicjować ⟨za-⟩ **2.** wprowadzać ⟨-dzić⟩ **3.** przyjmować ⟨-jąć⟩ (***s.o. into*** kogoś do *G*) **II** *s* **1.** nowoprzyjęty *m* **2.** wtajemniczony *m*; ***the ~*** wtajemniczeni; **i•ni•ti•a•tion** [ɪnɪʃɪ'eɪʃn] *s* **1.** inicjacja *f* **2.** wszczęcie *n* **3.** wprowadzenie *n* **4.** wtajemniczenie *n*

i•ni•ti•a•tive [ɪ'nɪʃətɪv] *s* inicjatywa *f*; ***on one's own ~*** z własnej inicjatywy; **i•ni•ti•a•tor** [ɪ'nɪʃɪeɪtə] *s* inicjator *m*

in•ject [ɪn'dʒekt] *v/t* wstrzykiwać ⟨-knąć⟩ (***s.o. with*** komuś *A*); **in•jec•tion** [ɪn'dʒekʃn] *s* **1.** *a. fig* zastrzyk *m* **2.** *TECH* wtrysk *m*

'in-joke *s* (*shared by a small group of people*) prywatny dowcip *m*

in•junc•tion [ɪn'dʒʌŋkʃn] *s* **1.** nakaz *m* sądowy **2.** zakaz *m* sądowy (***against*** *G*) **3.** napomnienie *n*

in•jure ['ɪndʒə] *v/t* **1.** ranić ⟨z-⟩; ***~ one's leg*** zranić się w nogę **2.** ***~ one's foot*** *SPORT* nabawić się kontuzji stopy **3.** szkodzić ⟨za-⟩; **in•jured** ['ɪndʒəd] *adj* **1.** ranny, zraniony **2.** kontuzjowany; **in•ju•ry** ['ɪndʒərɪ] *s* **1.** uraz *m*; ***an ~ to the head*** uraz głowy **2.** kontuzja *f* **3.** *JUR* szkoda *f*; **'in•ju•ry time** *s SPORT* czas *m* doliczony (za przerwy w grze)

in•jus•tice [ɪn'dʒʌstɪs] *s* niesprawiedliwość *f*

ink [ɪŋk] *s* **1.** atrament *m* **2.** tusz *m*; **'ink•jet (prin•ter)** *s* drukarka *f* atramentowa

ink•ling ['ɪŋklɪŋ] *s* **1.** pojęcie *n*; ***I had no ~ that*** nie miałem pojęcia, że **2.** ***he had an ~ that*** podejrzewał, że; domyślał się, że

in•land ['ɪnlənd] **I** *adj* **1.** śródlądowy **2.** leżący w głębi lądu **II** *adv* **1.** w głąb lądu **2.** w głębi lądu; **In•land 'Rev•e•nue** *s Br* urząd *m* skarbowy

in-laws ['ɪnlɔːz] *pl infml* **1.** teściowie *pl* **2.** powinowaci *pl*

in•lay I [ɪn'leɪ] *v/t* **1.** inkrustować (***with*** *I*) **2.** *wood*: intarsjować **II** ['ɪnleɪ] *s* **1.** inkrustacja *f* **2.** intarsja *f*

in•let ['ɪnlet] *s* **1.** zatoczka *f* **2.** odnoga *f* **3.** przesmyk *m* **4.** *TECH* wlot *m*

in•line skates ['ɪnlaɪnskeɪts] *pl* łyżworolki *pl*

in•mate ['ɪnmeɪt] *s* **1.** więzień *m* **2.** pacjent *m*

in•most ['ɪnməʊst] → ***innermost***

inn [ɪn] *s* gospoda *f*, zajazd *m*, pub *m*

in•nate [ɪ'neɪt] *adj* wrodzony

in•ner ['ɪnə] *adj* wewnętrzny; ***an ~ door*** drzwi wewnętrzne; ***the ~ man*** wnętrze człowieka; **in•ner 'cit•y** *s zaniedbana część śródmieścia*; **'in•ner•most** *adj* najskrytszy, najgłębszy; **'in•ner tube** *s* dętka *f*

in•no•cence ['ɪnəsəns] *s* **1.** niewinność *f*; ***lose one's ~*** stracić cnotę **2.** naiwność *f*; **in•no•cent** ['ɪnəsənt] *adj* niewinny; (**as**) ***~ as a newborn baby*** niewinny jak dziecko; ***an ~ air*** mina niewiniątka

in•no•vate ['ɪnəveɪt] *v/i* wprowadzać ⟨-dzić⟩ innowacje; **in•no•va•tion** [ɪnə'veɪʃn] *s* innowacja *f*; **in•no•va•tive** ['ɪnəveɪtɪv] *adj* innowacyjny, nowatorski; **in•no•va•tor** ['ɪnəveɪtə] *s* innowator *m*

in•nu•en•do [ɪnjuː'endəʊ] *pl -dos, -does s* insynuacja *f*, osobista wycieczka *f*

in•nu•me•ra•ble [ɪ'njuːmərəbl] *adj* niezliczony

i•noc•u•late [ɪ'nɒkjʊleɪt] *v/t* szczepić ⟨za-⟩ (***against*** przeciwko *D*); ***~ s.o. with s.th.*** *fig* zaszczepić komuś coś; **i•noc•u•la•tion** [ɪnɒkjʊ'leɪʃn] *s MED* szczepienie *n*

in•of•fen•sive [ɪnə'fensɪv] *adj* **1.** nieszkodliwy **2.** niewadzący nikomu

in•op•er•a•ble [ɪn'ɒpərəbl] *adj* **1.** *cancer*: nieoperacyjny **2.** bezużyteczny

in•op•er•a•tive [ɪn'ɒpərətɪv] *adj* **1.** nieobowiązujący **2.** niedziałający

I

in•op•por•tune [ɪn'ɒpətjuːn] *adj moment*: nieodpowiedni

in•or•di•nate [ɪn'ɔːdɪnət] *adj* nadmierny, niezmierny

in•or•gan•ic [ɪnɔː'gænɪk] *adj* nieorganiczny

in•put ['ɪnpʊt] *s* **1.** wkład *m* **2.** materiały *pl* **3.** ECON nakłady *pl* **4.** INF dane *pl* wejściowe **5.** TECH wejście *n*

inquest [ɪŋkwest] *s* dochodzenie *n*; ***to hold an ~*** prowadzić dochodzenie

in•quire [ɪn'kwaɪə] **I** *v/i* **1.** pytać ⟨za-⟩ (***about/of*** o *A*); ***~ within*** wiadomość na miejscu **2.** badać ⟨z-⟩ (***into*** *A*) **II** *v/t* pytać ⟨za-⟩ (***s.th.*** o *A*); **in•quir•y** [ɪn'kwaɪərɪ] *s* **1.** pytanie *n*; ***make inquiries about s.o.*** pytać o kogoś **2.** zapytanie *n* **3.** ***on ~*** na żądanie **4.** dochodzenie *n*, śledztwo *n* **5.** ***inquiries*** informacja, punkt informacji

in•qui•si•tion [ɪnkwɪ'zɪʃn] *s* **1.** ***the ~*** HIST Inkwizycja **2.** *fig* przesłuchanie *n*; **in•quis•i•tive** [ɪn'kwɪzətɪv] *adj* dociekliwy, wścibski; **in•quis•i•tive•ness** [ɪn'kwɪzətɪvnɪs] *s* dociekliwość *f*, wścibstwo *n*; **in•quis•i•tor** [ɪn'kwɪzɪtə] *s* **1.** dociekliwy rozmówca *m* **2.** HIST inkwizytor *m*

in•roads ['ɪnrəʊdz] *pl*: ***make ~ into*** **a)** *market*: wkraczać na *A* **b)** *rights*: naruszać *A*; ***make significant ~ into a problem*** poczynić znaczne postępy na drodze do rozwiązania problemu

in•sane [ɪn'seɪn] *adj* **1.** obłąkany, szalony **2.** JUR niepoczytalny; **in•sane•ly** [ɪn'seɪnlɪ] *adv* **1.** szaleńczo **2.** jak obłąkany

in•san•i•ta•ry [ɪn'sænɪterɪ] *adj* niehigieniczny, niezdrowy

in•san•i•ty [ɪn'sænɪtɪ] *s* **1.** obłęd *m*, szaleństwo *n* **2.** JUR niepoczytalność *f*

in•sa•ti•a•ble [ɪn'seɪʃəbl] *adj* nienasycony

in•scribe [ɪn'skraɪb] *v/t* **1.** pisać ⟨na-⟩; ***a plaque ~d with s.o.'s name*** tablica, na której widnieje czyjeś nazwisko **2.** ryć ⟨wy-⟩ **3.** grawerować ⟨wy-⟩ **4.** umieszczać ⟨-mieścić⟩ dedykację na *L*; **in•scrip•tion** [ɪn'skrɪpʃn] *s* **1.** napis *m*, inskrypcja *f* **2.** dedykacja *f*

in•scru•ta•ble [ɪn'skruːtəbl] *adj* nieprzenikniony, zagadkowy

in•sect ['ɪnsekt] *s* owad *m*; **in•sec•ti•cide** [ɪn'sektɪsaɪd] *s* środek *m* owadobójczy; **'in•sect re•pel•lent** *s* środek *m* odstraszający owady

in•se•cure [ɪnsɪ'kjʊə] *adj* **1.** niepewny, niestabilny **2.** niespokojny, bez wiary w siebie; **in•se•cu•ri•ty** [ɪnsɪ'kjʊərɪtɪ] *s* niepewność *f*, brak *m* pewności siebie, poczucie *n* zagrożenia

in•sem•i•nate [ɪn'semɪneɪt] *v/t* **1.** zapładniać ⟨-łodnić⟩ **2.** dokonywać ⟨-nać⟩ sztucznego zapłodnienia; **in•sem•ina•tion** [ɪnsemɪ'neɪʃn] *s* zapłodnienie *n*, inseminacja *f*

in•sen•si•tive [ɪn'sensɪtɪv] *adj* **1.** niewrażliwy (***to*** na *A*) **2.** obojętny (***to*** na *A*) **3.** niedelikatny **4.** gruboskórny **5.** bezduszny; **in•sen•si•tiv•i•ty** [ɪnsensɪ'tɪvɪtɪ] *s* brak *m* wrażliwości, niewrażliwość *f*

in•sep•a•ra•ble [ɪn'sepərəbl] *adj* **1.** nierozłączny **2.** ***be ~ from*** być nierozłącznie związanym z *I*

in•sert I ['ɪnsɜːt] *s* **1.** (*magazine*, *shoe*) wkładka *f* **2.** (*dress*) wstawka *f* **3.** ***an ~ key*** INF klawisz Insert **II** [ɪn'sɜːt] *v/t* **1.** wstawiać ⟨-wić⟩ **2.** wkładać ⟨włożyć⟩ **3.** wrzucać ⟨-cić⟩; **in•ser•tion** [ɪn'sɜːrʃn] *s* **1.** wstawienie *n* **2.** włożenie *n* **3.** wrzucenie *n* **4.** (*magazine*) wkładka *f*

in•side I [ɪn'saɪd] *prep* **1.** w *L*; ***~ the house*** w domu; ***~ of a year*** w przeciągu roku **2.** wewnątrz **3.** w środku *G* **II** [ɪn'saɪd] *adv* **1.** wewnątrz **2.** do środka **III** ['ɪnsaɪd] *adj* **1.** wewnętrzny; ***an ~ lane*** SPORT tor wewnętrzny **2.** środkowy **3.** *information*: poufny **IV** ['ɪnsaɪd] *s* ***the ~*** wnętrze; ***on the ~*** **a)** w środku **b)** od środka; ***from the ~*** od środka; ***turn s.th. ~ out*** wywrócić coś na lewą stronę; ***know s.th. ~ out*** znać coś od podszewki, znać coś na wylot; ***overtake s.o. on the ~*** **a)** (*England, Australia*) wyprzedzić kogoś z lewej strony **b)** (*USA, Poland*) wyprzedzić kogoś z prawej strony; **in•sid•er** [ɪn'saɪdə] *s* osoba *f* dobrze poinformowana; **in•sid•er 'trad•ing** *s* FIN *wykorzystywanie informacji poufnych w obrocie giełdowym*

in•sight ['ɪnsaɪt] *s* **1.** przenikliwość *f* **2.** zrozumienie *n*; ***give s.o. ~s into*** pozwolić komuś zrozumieć *A*, dać komuś jasny obraz *G* **3.** wgląd *m* **4.** spostrzeżenie *n*

I

in•sig•nif•i•cant [ɪnsɪɡ'nɪfɪkənt] *adj* nieznaczny, niewielki, mało znaczący
in•sin•cere [ɪnsɪn'sɪə] *adj* nieszczery, obłudny; **in•sin•cer•i•ty** [ɪnsɪn'serɪtɪ] *s* nieszczerość *f*, obłuda *f*, hipokryzja *f*
in•sin•u•ate [ɪn'sɪnjʊeɪt] *v/i* insynuować, dawać ⟨dać⟩ do zrozumienia; **in•sin•ua•tion** [ɪnsɪnjʊ'eɪʃn] *s* insynuacja *f*
in•sist [ɪn'sɪst] *v/i* **1.** nalegać; ***she ~ed that he should come*** nalegała, żeby przyszedł **2.** upierać się; **in•sist on** *v/i* **1.** ***he ~ed on her going with him*** nalegał, żeby z nim poszła **2.** upierać się przy *I*; ***~ doing s.th.*** upierać się, żeby coś zrobić **3.** zapewniać o *L*; ***she ~ed on her innocence*** zapewniała o swojej niewinności; **in•sist•ence** [ɪn'sɪstəns] *s* **1.** naleganie *n*; ***at s.o.'s ~*** na skutek czyichś nalegań **2.** zapewnienia *pl* **3.** nacisk *m*; **in•sis•tent** [ɪn'sɪstənt] *adj* **1.** ***be ~ that*** nalegać, żeby **2.** uparty **3.** uporczywy
in•sofar [ɪnsə'fɑː] *adv*: ***~ as*** o tyle, o ile
in•so•lence ['ɪnsələns] *s* bezczelność *f*; **in•so•lent** ['ɪnsələnt] *adj* bezczelny
in•sol•u•ble [ɪn'sɒljʊbl] *adj* **1.** nie do rozwiązania **2.** niemożliwy do rozstrzygnięcia **3.** nierozpuszczalny
in•sol•ven•cy [ɪn'sɒlvənsɪ] *s* niewypłacalność *f*; **in•sol•vent** [ɪn'sɒlvənt] *adj* niewypłacalny
in•som•ni•a [ɪn'sɒmnɪə] *s* bezsenność *f*; **in•som•ni•ac** [ɪn'sɒmnɪæk] *s* osoba *f* cierpiąca na bezsenność
in•spect [ɪn'spekt] *v/t* **1.** sprawdzać ⟨-dzić⟩ **2.** kontrolować ⟨s-⟩ **3.** przeprowadzać ⟨-dzić⟩ inspekcję, **in•spec•tion** [ɪn'spekʃn] *s* **1.** kontrola *f* **2.** inspekcja *f* **3.** wizytacja *f* **4.** badanie *n*; ***on closer ~*** po bliższym zbadaniu **5.** *army*: przegląd *m*; **in•spec•tor** [ɪn'spektə] *s* **1.** inspektor *m*; ***a police ~*** inspektor policji **2.** kontroler *m*
in•spi•ra•tion [ɪnspə'reɪʃn] *s* **1.** inspiracja *f* **2.** natchnienie *n* **3.** źródło *n* inspiracji (***to*** dla *G*); **in•spire** [ɪn'spaɪə] *v/t* **1.** inspirować ⟨za-⟩ **2.** wpływać ⟨-łynąć⟩ na *A* **3.** wzbudzać ⟨-dzić⟩ **4.** pobudzać ⟨-dzić⟩; ***~ s.o. to act*** pobudzić kogoś do działania
in•sta•bil•i•ty [ɪnstə'bɪlɪtɪ] *s* **1.** niestabilność *f* **2.** chwiejność *f* **3.** nietrwałość *f*
in•stal(l) [ɪn'stɔːl] *v/t* **1.** instalować ⟨za-⟩ **2.** zakładać ⟨założyć⟩ **3.** wprowadzać ⟨-dzić⟩ na urząd **4.** ***~ oneself*** **a)** zamieszkać **b)** zasiąść; **in•stal•la•tion** [ɪnstə'leɪʃn] *s* **1.** instalacja *f* **2.** założenie *n* **3.** wprowadzenie *n* na urząd
in•stal•ment [ɪn'stɔːlmənt], ***in•stall•ment*** *Am s* **1.** *ECON* rata *f*; ***by ~s, in ~s*** w ratach, ratalnie; ***a monthly ~*** rata miesięczna **2.** odcinek *m* **3.** wydanie *n*; **in'stall•ment plan** *s Am* system *m* sprzedaży ratalnej; ***purchases on the ~*** zakupy w systemie ratalnym
in•stance ['ɪnstəns] *s* **1.** przypadek *m*; ***in this ~*** w tym przypadku **2.** przykład *m*; ***for ~*** na przykład; ***as an ~ of*** jako przykład *G* **3.** ***in the first ~*** po pierwsze
in•stant ['ɪnstənt] **I** *s* chwila *f*; ***in an ~*** w jednej chwili **II** *adj* **1.** natychmiastowy; ***an ~ camera*** polaroid; ***~ replay*** *SPORT Br* powtórka **2.** *meal*: błyskawiczny **3.** *coffee*: rozpuszczalny, instant
in•stan•ta•ne•ous [ɪnstən'teɪnɪəs] *adj* natychmiastowy; ***his death was ~*** zmarł na miejscu, śmierć nastąpiła natychmiast; **in•stan•ta•ne•ous•ly** [ɪnstən'teɪnɪəslɪ] *adv* natychmiast
in•stant•ly ['ɪnstəntlɪ] *adv* natychmiast, od razu
in•stead [ɪn'sted] *adv* **1.** ***~ of*** zamiast *G*; ***~ of me*** zamiast mnie; ***~ of going*** zamiast pójść **2.** natomiast, za to
in•sti•gate ['ɪnstɪɡeɪt] *v/t* **1.** wszczynać ⟨-cząć⟩ **2.** inicjować ⟨za-⟩ **3.** przystępować ⟨-tąpić⟩ do *G* **4.** podżegać do *G*; **in•stiga•tion** [ɪnstɪ'ɡeɪʃn] *s*: ***at s.o.'s ~*** **a)** z czyjejś inicjatywy **b)** za czyjąś namową
in•stinct ['ɪnstɪŋkt] *s* **1.** instynkt *m*; ***by ~*** instynktownie; ***the ~ for self-preservation*** instynkt samozachowawczy **2.** odruch *m*; **in•stinc•tive** [ɪn'stɪŋktɪv] *adj* instynktowny; **in•stinc•tive•ly** [ɪn'stɪŋktɪvlɪ] *adv* instynktownie
in•sti•tute ['ɪnstɪtjuːt] **I** *s* instytut *m* **II** *v/t* **1.** *proceedings*: wszczynać ⟨-cząć⟩ **2.** *scheme*: wprowadzać ⟨-dzić⟩ **3.** *therapy*: stosować ⟨za-⟩ **4.** tworzyć ⟨u-⟩; **in•sti•tu•tion** [ɪnstɪ'tjuːʃn] *s* **1.** instytucja *f* **2.** zakład *m*; ***a mental ~*** zakład dla umysłowo chorych **3.** *proceedings*: wszczęcie *n*

I

4. *scheme*: wprowadzenie *n*; **in•sti•tu•tion•al** [ɪnstɪ'tjuːʃənl] *adj* instytucjonalny; **in•sti•tu•tion•al•ize** [ɪnstɪ'tjuːʃənəlaɪz] *v/t* **1.** umieszczać ⟨umieścić⟩ w zakładzie **2.** instytucjonalizować ⟨z-⟩

in•struct [ɪn'strʌkt] *v/t* **1.** instruować ⟨po-⟩ **2.** zalecać ⟨-cić⟩ **3.** nakazywać ⟨-zać⟩ **4.** uczyć; **in•struc•tion** [ɪn'strʌkʃn] *s* **1.** ***~s for use*** instrukcja obsługi; ***an ~ manual*** instrukcja obsługi **2.** polecenie *n* **3.** wskazówka *f* **4.** instruktaż *m* **5.** nauczanie *n*; **in•struc•tive** [ɪn'strʌktɪv] *adj* pouczający; **in•struc•tor** [ɪn'strʌktə] *s* **1.** instruktor *m* **2.** *Am* nauczyciel *m*

in•stru•ment ['ɪnstrʊmənt] *s* **1.** instrument *m* **2.** przyrząd *m*; ***an ~ panel*** tablica przyrządów **3.** narzędzie *n*; ***~s of torture*** narzędzia tortur **4.** środek *m*; **in•stru•men•tal** [ɪnstrʊ'mentl] *adj* **1.** instrumentalny **2.** ***be ~ in*** walnie przyczynić się do *G*

in•sub•or•di•nate [ɪnsə'bɔːdɪnət] *adj* niesubordynowany, niezdyscyplinowany; **in•sub•or•di•na•tion** [ɪnsəbɔːdɪ'neɪʃn] *s* niesubordynacja *f*

in•sub•stan•tial [ɪnsəb'stænʃl] *adj* **1.** niematerialny **2.** słaby **3.** bezpodstawny

in•suf•fer•a•ble [ɪn'sʌfərəbl] *adj* nieznośny

in•suf•fi•cien•cy [ɪnsə'fɪʃnsɪ] *s* **1.** niewystarczająca ilość *f* **2.** niedostatek *m* **3.** *MED* niewydolność *f*; **in•suf•fi•cient** [ɪnsə'fɪʃnt] *adj* niewystarczający

in•su•late ['ɪnsjʊleɪt] *v/t* izolować ⟨za-⟩; ***an insulating tape*** taśma izolacyjna; **in•su•la•tion** [ɪnsjʊ'leɪʃn] *s* izolacja *f*

in•sult **I** [ɪn'sʌlt] *v/t* obrażać ⟨-razić⟩, znieważać ⟨-żyć⟩ **II** ['ɪnsʌlt] *s* zniewaga *f*, obelga *f*

in•sur•ance [ɪn'ʃʊərəns] *s* **1.** ubezpieczenie *n* **2.** suma *f* ubezpieczenia **3.** składka *f* ubezpieczeniowa **4.** odszkodowanie *n* **5.** *fig* zabezpieczenie *n*; **in•'sur•ance a•gent** *s* agent *m* ubezpieczeniowy; **in•'sur•ance bro•ker** *s* broker *m* (ubezpieczeniowy); **in•'sur•ance claim** *s* roszczenie *n* ubezpieczeniowe; **in•'sur•ance com•pa•ny** *s* towarzystwo *n* ubezpieczeniowe; **in•'sur•ance pol•i•cy** *s* polisa *f* ubezpieczeniowa; **in•'sur•ance pre•mi•um** *s* składka *f* ubezpieczeniowa

in•sure [ɪn'ʃɔː] *v/t* ubezpieczać ⟨-czyć⟩ (***against*** od *G*); ***my bike was ~d for £500*** mój rower był ubezpieczony na 500 funtów; **in•sured** [ɪn'ʃɔːd] *adj* ubezpieczony; **insur•er** [ɪn'ʃɔːrə] *s* ubezpieczyciel *m*

in•sur•moun•ta•ble [ɪnsə'maʊntəbl] *adj* nie do pokonania

in•sur•rec•tion [ɪnsə'rekʃn] *s* powstanie *n*, insurekcja *f*

in•tact [ɪn'tækt] *adj* nietknięty, nienaruszony

in•take ['ɪnteɪk] *s* **1.** spożycie *n* **2.** nabór *m* **3.** *immigrants*: napływ *m* **4.** *TECH* wlot *m* **5.** *oxygen*: zużycie *n*

in•tan•gi•ble [ɪn'tændʒəbl] *adj* **1.** nieuchwytny **2.** niematerialny

in•te•gral ['ɪntɪgrəl] *adj* integralny; ***be ~ to*** być nieodłączną częścią *G*

in•te•grate ['ɪntɪgreɪt] **I** *v/t* **1.** integrować ⟨z-⟩ **2.** łączyć ⟨po-⟩ **3.** włączać ⟨-czyć⟩ (***into*** do *G*) **II** *v/i* integrować ⟨z-⟩ się; **in•te•grated 'cir•cuit** *s* układ *m* scalony; **in•tegra•tion** [ɪntɪ'greɪʃn] *s* integracja *f*

in•teg•ri•ty [ɪn'tegrətɪ] *s* **1.** prawość *f*, uczciwość *f* **2.** integralność *f*

in•tel•lect ['ɪntəlekt] *s* intelekt *m*; **in•tel•lec•tual** [ɪntə'lektʃʊəl] **I** *adj* **1.** intelektualny **2.** o wysokiej kulturze umysłowej **II** *s* intelektualista *m*

in•tel•li•gence [ɪn'telɪdʒəns] *s* **1.** inteligencja *f* **2.** wywiad *m*; **in•'tel•li•gence quo•tient** *s* iloraz *m* inteligencji, IQ *n*; **in•'tel•li•gence test** *s* test *m* na inteligencję; **in•'tel•li•gence of•fi•cer** *s* oficer *m* wywiadu; **in•'tel•li•gence ser•vice** *s* służby *pl* wywiadowcze

in•tel•li•gent [ɪn'telɪdʒənt] *adj* inteligentny; **in•tel•li•gent•si•a** [ɪntelɪ'dʒentsɪə] *s*: ***the ~*** (*social group*) inteligencja

in•tel•li•gi•ble [ɪn'telɪdʒəbl] *adj* zrozumiały

in•tem•per•ate [ɪn'tempərət] *adj* **1.** przesadny **2.** dosadny **3.** niekontrolowany **4.** ***~ drinking*** nadużywanie alkoholu

in•tend [ɪn'tend] *v/t* **1.** zamierzać; ***~ doing s.th.***, ***~ to do s.th.*** zamierzać coś

I

zrobić; ***was this ~ed?*** czy to było zamierzone?; ***it was ~ed as a compliment*** to miał być komplement **2.** planować ⟨za-⟩ **3.** mieć na myśli; **intend·ed** [ɪn'tendɪd] *adj* **1.** zamierzony; ***originally, it was ~ to be a hotel*** początkowo miał to być hotel **2.** planowany **3.** zakładany **4.** przeznaczony; ***the book is ~ for beginners*** książka jest przeznaczona dla początkujących

in•tense [ɪn'tens] *adj* **1.** wielki **2.** ogromny **3.** intensywny **4.** *pain*: silny **5.** *cold*: dotkliwy **6.** *fight*: zacięty **7. be ~** *(person)* reagować emocjonalnie

in•ten•si•fi•ca•tion [ɪntensɪfɪ'keɪʃn] *s* **1.** nasilenie *n* **2.** *crisis*: zaostrzenie *n* **3.** intensyfikacja *f* **4.** wzrost *m*; **in•ten•si•fy** [ɪn'tensɪfaɪ] **I** *v/t* **1.** nasilać ⟨-lić⟩ **2.** *crisis*: zaostrzać ⟨-rzyć⟩ **3.** intensyfikować ⟨z-⟩ **II** *v/i* **1.** nasilać ⟨-lić⟩ się **2.** *(crisis)* zaostrzać ⟨-rzyć⟩ się; **in•ten•si•ty** [ɪn'tensətɪ] *s* intensywność *f*, nasilenie *n*; **in•ten•sive** [ɪn'tensɪv] *adj* intensywny; **in•ten•sive 'care (u•nit)** *s* oddział *m* intensywnej opieki medycznej; **in•ten•sive 'course** *s* intensywny kurs *m*

in•tent [ɪn'tent] **I** *s* zamiar *m*; ***with ~*** celowo; ***to all ~s and purposes*** praktycznie rzecz biorąc **II** *adj* **1. *be ~ on doing s.th.*** być zdecydowanym coś zrobić **2.** skupiony

in•ten•tion [ɪn'tenʃn] *s* zamiar *m* (***of doing s.th./to do s.th.*** zrobienia czegoś); ***I have no ~ to pay*** nie mam zamiaru płacić; **in•ten•tion•al** [ɪn'tenʃənl] *adj* zamierzony, celowy, umyślny; **in•ten•tion•al•ly** [ɪn'tenʃnlɪ] *adv* celowo

in•ter•act [ɪntə'ækt] *v/i* **1.** oddziaływać na siebie **2.** reagować (***with*** z *I*) **3.** komunikować się **4.** wchodzić w interakcję; **in•ter•ac•tion** [ɪntə'ækʃn] *s* interakcja *f*; **in•ter•ac•tive** [ɪntə'æktɪv] *adj* **1.** interaktywny **2.** wchodzący w reakcję

in•ter•breed [ɪntə'briːd] **I** *(interbred; interbred) v/t* krzyżować ⟨s-⟩ **II** *(interbred; interbred) v/i* krzyżować ⟨s-⟩ się

in•ter•cept [ɪntə'sept] *v/t* przechwytywać ⟨-wycić⟩, przejmować ⟨-jąć⟩; **in•ter•cep•tion** [ɪntə'sepʃn] *s* przechwycenie *n*, przejęcie *n*

in•ter•ces•sion [ɪntə'seʃn] *s* **1.** interwencja *f* **2.** wstawiennictwo *n*

in•ter•change [ɪntə'tʃeɪndʒ] **I** *v/t* **1.** wymieniać ⟨-nić⟩ **2.** zamieniać ⟨-nić⟩ (miejscami) **II** *s* wymiana *f*; ***an ~ of ideas*** wymiana poglądów; **in•ter•change•a•ble** [ɪntə'tʃeɪndʒəbl] *adj* wymienny

in•ter•com•mu•ni•cate [ɪntəkə'mjuːnɪkeɪt] *v/i* **1.** porozumiewać ⟨-mieć⟩ się **2.** *(rooms)* być połączonym

in•ter•con•ti•nen•tal [ɪntəkɒntɪ'nentl] *adj* międzykontynentalny; ***an ~ ballistic missile*** międzykontynentalny pocisk balistyczny

in•ter•course ['ɪntəkɔːs] *s* **1.** stosunek *m*; ***sexual ~*** stosunek płciowy **2.** kontakty *pl*

in•ter•de•part•men•tal [ɪntədiːpɑːt'mentl] *adj* **1.** międzywydziałowy **2.** międzyresortowy

in•ter•de•pen•dence [ɪntədɪ'pendəns] *s* współzależność *f*; **in•ter•de•pen•dent** [ɪntədɪ'pendənt] *adj* współzależny

in•ter•dis•ci•plin•ar•y [ɪntədɪsə'plɪnerɪ] *adj* interdyscyplinarny

in•ter•est ['ɪntrəst] **I** *s* **1.** zainteresowanie *n*; ***take an ~ in, have an ~ in*** interesować się *I*; ***be of ~*** być ciekawym **2.** FIN udział *m* **3.** interes *m*; ***be in s.o.'s ~*** być w czyimś interesie **4.** odsetki *pl*; ***bear ~ at 4%*** być oprocentowanym na 4%; ***an ~ rate*** stopa procentowa **II** *v/t* interesować ⟨za-⟩; **'in•ter•est-bear•ing** *adj* procentujący, oprocentowany; **in•ter•est-'free loan** *s* pożyczka *f* nieoprocentowana

in•ter•est•ed ['ɪntrəstɪd] *adj* zainteresowany; ***be ~ in*** interesować się *I*; **in•ter•est•ing** ['ɪntrəstɪŋ] *adj* interesujący, ciekawy; **in•ter•est•ing•ly** ['ɪntrestɪŋlɪ] *adv* **1.** co ciekawe **2.** interesująco

in•ter•fere [ɪntə'fɪə] *v/i* wtrącać ⟨-cić⟩ się, mieszać ⟨w-⟩ się, ingerować; **in•ter•fere with** *v/i* **1.** przeszkadzać w *L*, zakłócać **2.** kolidować z *I* **3.** ruszać

in•ter•fer•ence [ɪntə'fɪərəns] *s* **1.** ingerencja *f* **2.** interferencja *f*, zakłócenia *pl*

in•ter•im ['ɪntərɪm] **I** *adj* **1.** tymczasowy; ***an ~ government*** rząd tymczasowy

I

2. doraźny; *~ aid* pomoc doraźna **II** *s in the ~* w międzyczasie, tymczasem
in•te•ri•or [ɪn'tɪərɪə] **I** *s* **1.** wnętrze *n* **2.** interior *m*, głąb *f* kraju **II** *adj* **1.** wewnętrzny **2.** krajowy; **in•te•ri•or 'dec•o•ra•tor** *s* dekorator *m* wnętrz; **in•te•ri•or de•'sign 1.** projektowanie *n* wnętrz **2.** architektura *f* wnętrz; **in•te•ri•or de•'sign•er** *s* projektant *m* wnętrz
in•ter•ject [ɪntə'dʒekt] *v/t* wtrącać ⟨-cić⟩; **in•ter•jec•tion** [ɪntə'dʒekʃn] *s* **1.** wykrzyknik *m* **2.** wtrącenie *n*
in•ter•lace [ɪntə'leɪs] *v/t* **1.** przeplatać ⟨-leść⟩ **2.** splatać ⟨-leść⟩
in•ter•lude ['ɪntəluːd] *s* **1.** przerwa *f*; *a brief ~* krótka przerwa **2.** okres *m* **3.** *THEAT* antrakt *m* **4.** *MUS* interludium *n*
in•ter•mar•riage [ɪntə'mærɪdʒ] *s* **1.** małżeństwo *n* mieszane **2.** małżeństwo *n* w obrębie rodziny; **in•ter•mar•ry** [ɪntə'mærɪ] *v/i* **1.** zawierać ⟨-wrzeć⟩ małżeństwo mieszane **2.** zawierać ⟨-wrzeć⟩ małżeństwo w obrębie rodziny
in•ter•me•di•ar•y [ɪntə'miːdɪərɪ] *s* **1.** mediator *m*, rozjemca *m* **2.** pośrednik *m*; **in•ter•me•di•ate** [ɪntə'miːdɪət] *adj* **1.** pośredni **2.** średnio zaawansowany
in•ter•mi•na•ble [ɪn'tɜːmɪnəbl] niekończący się
in•ter•min•gle [ɪntə'mɪŋgl] **I** *v* mieszać ⟨wy-⟩ się **II** *v/t* mieszać ⟨wy-⟩
in•ter•mis•sion [ɪntə'mɪʃn] *s* przerwa *f*
in•ter•mit•tent [ɪntə'mɪtənt] *adj* **1.** sporadyczny **2.** przerywany; *there was ~ rain* deszcz to padał, to przestawał
in•tern [ɪn'tɜːn] *v/t* internować
in•ter•nal [ɪn'tɜːnl] *adj* wewnętrzny; *~ injuries* obrażenia wewnętrzne
in•ter•nal com'bus•tion en•gine *s* silnik *m* spalinowy (wewnętrznego spalania)
in•ter•nal•ize [ɪn'tɜːnəlaɪz] *v/t* przyswajać ⟨-woić⟩ (sobie)
in•ter•nal•ly [ɪn'tɜːnəlɪ] *adv* wewnętrznie, wewnątrz
in•ter•na•tion•al [ɪntə'næʃnl] **I** *adj* międzynarodowy; *~ law* prawo międzynarodowe; *the ~ Date Line* linia zmiany daty **II** *s SPORT Br* zawodnik *m* kadry narodowej; **In•ter•na•tion•al Court of 'Jus•tice** *s* Międzynarodowy Trybunał *m* Sprawiedliwości; **in•ter•na•tion•al•ize** [ɪntə'næʃnəlaɪz] *v/t* umiędzynarodawiać ⟨-dowić⟩; **in•ter•na•tion•al•ly** [ɪntə'næʃnəlɪ] *adv* **1.** na świecie **2.** w wielu krajach **3.** *nationally and ~* w kraju i za granicą; **In•ter•na•tion•al 'Mon•e•tar•y Fund** *s* Międzynarodowy Fundusz *m* Walutowy
in•ter•nist [ɪn'tɜːnɪst] *s Am* internista *m*
in•ter•per•son•al [ɪntə'pɜːsənl] *adj* międzyludzki, interpersonalny
in•ter•pret [ɪn'tɜːprɪt] **I** *v/t* **1.** interpretować ⟨z-⟩, objaśniać ⟨-nić⟩ **2.** tłumaczyć ⟨prze-⟩ (ustnie) **II** *v/i* tłumaczyć ⟨prze-⟩ (ustnie); **in•ter•pre•ta•tion** [ɪn'tɜːprɪ'teɪʃn] *s* **1.** interpretacja *f* **2.** tłumaczenie *n* ustne; **in•ter•pret•er** [ɪn'tɜːprɪtə] *s* tłumacz *m* ustny
in•ter•ra•cial [ɪntə'reɪʃl] *adj marriage*: mieszany
in•ter•re•lat•ed [ɪntərɪ'leɪtɪd] *adj* powiązany, współzależny; **in•ter•re•la•tion•ship** [ɪntərɪ'leɪʃnʃɪp] *s* **1.** związek *m* **2.** (wzajemne) powiązania *pl*
in•ter•ro•gate [ɪn'terəgeɪt] *v/t* przesłuchiwać ⟨-chać⟩; **in•ter•ro•ga•tion** [ɪnterə'geɪʃn] *s* **1.** przesłuchanie *n* **2.** *an ~ mark* znak zapytania; **in•ter•rog•a•tive** [ɪntə'rɒgətɪv] *adj* pytający; **in•ter•ro•ga•tor** [ɪnterə'geɪtə] *s* przesłuchujący *m*; **in•ter•rog•a•to•ry** [ɪnte'rɒgətrɪ] *adj* dociekliwy
in•ter•rupt [ɪntə'rʌpt] **I** *v/t* przerywać ⟨-rwać⟩ **II** *v/i don't ~!* nie przerywaj!; **in•ter•rup•tion** [ɪntə'rʌpʃn] *s* **1.** przerwa *f*; *without ~* bez przerwy **2.** przerwanie *n*
in•ter•sect [ɪntə'sekt] **I** *v/i* przecinać ⟨-ciąć⟩ się, krzyżować się **II** *v/t* przecinać ⟨-ciąć⟩; **in•ter•sec•tion** [ɪntə'sekʃn] *s* **1.** skrzyżowanie *n* **2.** przecięcie *n*, punkt *m* przecięcia
in•ter•state ['ɪntəsteɪt] **I.** *adj Am* międzystanowy **II.** *s* autostrada *f* międzystanowa
in•ter•twine [ɪntə'twaɪn] **I** *v/i* splatać ⟨-leść⟩ się **II** *v/t* splatać ⟨-leść⟩
in•ter•val ['ɪntəvl] *s* **1.** odstęp *m*; *at regular ~s* w regularnych odstępach **2.** przerwa *f* **3.** *MUS* interwał *m*
in•ter•vene [ɪntə'viːn] *v/i* **1.** interweniować **2.** wtrącać ⟨-cić⟩ się **3.** stawać

⟨stanąć⟩ na przeszkodzie **4.** (*time*) upływać ⟨-łynąć⟩; **in•ter•ven•tion** [ɪntəˈvenʃn] *s* interwencja *f*

in•ter•view [ˈɪntəvjuː] **I** *s* **1.** wywiad *m*; ***give s.o. an ~*** udzielić komuś wywiadu **2.** rozmowa *f* kwalifikacyjna **II** *v/t* **1.** przeprowadzać ⟨-dzić⟩ wywiad z *I* **2.** przeprowadzać ⟨-dzić⟩ rozmowę kwalifikacyjną z *I* **3.** przesłuchiwać ⟨-chać⟩; **in•ter•view•ee** [ɪntəvjuːˈiː] *s* **1.** osoba *f* udzielająca wywiadu **2.** osoba *f* ankietowana **3.** kandydat *m*; **in•ter•view•er** [ˈɪntəvjuːə] *s* **1.** osoba *f* przeprowadzająca rozmowę kwalifikacyjną **2.** osoba *f* przeprowadzająca wywiad **3.** ankieter *m*

in•ter•weave [ɪntəˈwiːv] **I** (*interwove; interwoven*) *v/t* **1.** splatać ⟨-leść⟩ **2.** przeplatać ⟨-leść⟩ **3.** łączyć ⟨po-⟩; ***the problems are closely interwoven*** te problemy są ze sobą ściśle związane **II** (*interwove; interwoven*) *v/i* **1.** splatać ⟨-leść⟩ się **2.** przeplatać ⟨-leść⟩ się

in•ti•ma•cy [ˈɪntɪməsɪ] *s* **1.** zażyłość *f* **2.** intymność *f*

in•ti•mate **I** [ˈɪntɪmət] *adj* **1.** bliski **2.** zażyły; ***be on ~ terms with*** być w zażyłych stosunkach z *I* **3.** intymny **4.** osobisty **5.** kameralny **II** [ˈɪntɪmeɪt] *v/t*: ***~ to s.o. that*** dać komuś do zrozumienia, że; **in•ti•mate•ly** [ˈɪntɪmətlɪ] *adv* **1.** blisko **2.** *connected*: ściśle **3.** *know*: dobrze **4.** *talk*: na tematy osobiste **5.** w sposób erotyczny

in•tim•i•date [ɪnˈtɪmɪdeɪt] *v/t* **1.** zastraszać ⟨-szyć⟩ **2.** ***~ s.o. into doing s.th.*** wymusić na kimś zrobienie czegoś; **in•tim•i•da•tion** [ɪntɪmɪˈdeɪʃn] *s* zastraszanie *n*

in•to [ˈɪntə] *prep* **1.** do *G* **2.** w *A*; ***turn s.th. ~ a desert*** zmienić coś w pustynię **3.** przez *A*; **4.** na *A*; ***divide s.th. ~*** podzielić coś na *A* **5.** ***be ~*** interesować się *I*

in•tol•e•ra•ble [ɪnˈtɒlərəbl] *adj* **1.** nieznośny **2.** niedopuszczalny, nie do przyjęcia; **in•tol•er•ance** [ɪnˈtɒlərəns] *s* **1.** nietolerancja *f* **2.** brak *m* tolerancji; **in•tol•e•rant** [ɪnˈtɒlərənt] *adj* nietolerancyjny

in•tox•i•cant [ɪnˈtɒksɪkənt] *s* środek *m* odurzający; **in•tox•i•cat•ed** [ɪnˈtɒksɪkeɪtɪd] *adj* **1.** odurzony **2.** w stanie upojenia alkoholowego; **in•tox•ica•tion** [ɪntɒksɪˈkeɪʃn] *s* **1.** upojenie *n* alkoholowe **2.** odurzenie *n* **3.** upojenie *n*

in•tran•si•tive [ɪnˈtrænsɪtɪv] *adj verb*: nieprzechodni

in•tra•ve•nous [ɪntrəˈviːnəs] *adj* dożylny

in•tri•ca•cy [ˈɪntrɪkəsɪ] *s* **1.** zawiłość *f*, złożoność *f* **2.** misterność *f*; **in•tri•cate** [ˈɪntrɪkət] *adj* **1.** zawiły, złożony, skomplikowany **2.** misterny

in•trigue **I** [ɪnˈtriːg] *v/t* intrygować ⟨za-⟩, fascynować ⟨za-⟩ **II** [ɪnˈtriːg] *v/i* snuć intrygi **III** [ˈɪntriːg] *s* intryga *f*, knowanie *n*; **in•trigu•ing** [ɪnˈtriːgɪŋ] *adj* intrygujący

in•tro•duce [ɪntrəˈdjuːs] *v/t* **1.** *law, change*: wprowadzać ⟨-dzić⟩ **2.** *person*: przedstawiać ⟨-wić⟩ (**to** *D*) **3.** zaznajamiać ⟨-jomić⟩ (**to** z *I*) **4.** zapowiadać ⟨-wiedzieć⟩; **in•tro•duc•tion** [ɪntrəˈdʌkʃn] *s* **1.** wprowadzenie *n* **2.** wstęp *m* **3.** prezentacja *f* **4.** pierwszy kontakt *m*; **in•tro•duc•to•ry** [ɪntrəˈdʌktərɪ] *adj* wstępny, wprowadzający

in•tro•spec•tion [ɪntrəˈspekʃn] *s* introspekcja *f*; **in•tro•spec•tive** [ɪntrəˈspektɪv] *adj* introspekcyjny, introspektywny

in•tro•vert [ˈɪntrəvɜːt] **I** *s* introwertyk *m* **II** *adj* → ***introverted***; **in•tro•vert•ed** [ˈɪntrəvɜːtɪd] *adj* introwertyczny, zamknięty w sobie

in•trude [ɪnˈtruːd] *v/i* **1.** przeszkadzać ⟨-kodzić⟩ **2.** *privacy*: naruszać ⟨-szyć⟩ (**on** *A*) **3.** zakłócać ⟨-cić⟩ (**on** *A*); **in•trud•er** [ɪnˈtruːdə] *s* intruz *m*; **in•tru•sion** [ɪnˈtruːʒn] *s* **1.** najście *n* **2.** wtrącenie się *n* **3.** *privacy*: naruszenie *n*; **in•tru•sive** [ɪnˈtruːsɪv] *adj* wścibski, natrętny, nachalny

in•tu•i•tion [ɪntjuːˈɪʃn] *s* **1.** intuicja *f* **2.** przeczucie *n*; **in•tu•i•tive** [ɪnˈtjuːɪtɪv] *adj* intuicyjny

in•un•date [ˈɪnʌndeɪt] *v/t* **1.** zalewać ⟨-lać⟩ **2.** *fig* zasypywać ⟨-pać⟩ (***with*** *I*)

in•vade [ɪnˈveɪd] *v/t* **1.** najeżdżać ⟨-jechać⟩, atakować ⟨za-⟩ **2.** opanowywać ⟨-nować⟩ **3.** zakłócać ⟨-cić⟩; **invad•er** [ɪnˈveɪdə] *s* najeźdźca *m*

in•va•lid[1] [ɪnˈvælɪd] *adj* **1.** nieważny **2.** nieprawomocny **3.** bezpodstawny

I

in•val•id² ['ɪnvəlɪ:d] **I** *s* **1.** (obłożnie) chory *m* **2.** inwalida *m* **II** *v/t Br* zwalniać ⟨zwolnić⟩ z przyczyn zdrowotnych

in•val•i•date [ɪn'vælɪdeɪt] *v/t* **1.** unieważniać ⟨-nić⟩ **2.** obalać ⟨-lić⟩; **in•val•ida•tion** [ɪnvælɪ'deɪʃn] *s JUR* unieważnienie *n*

in•va•lid•i•ty pen•sion [ɪnvə'lɪdətɪpenʃn] *s* renta *f* inwalidzka

in•val•u•a•ble [ɪn'væljʊəbl] *adj* nieoceniony, bezcenny

in•var•i•a•ble [ɪn'veərɪəbl] *adj* niezmienny; **in•var•i•a•bly** [ɪn'veərɪəblɪ] *adv* niezmiennie

in•va•sion [ɪn'veɪʒn] *s* najazd *m*

in•vec•tive [ɪn'vektɪv] *s* inwektywy *pl*, obelgi *pl*

in•vei•gle [ɪn'veɪgl] *v/t*: ***~ s.o. into doing s.th.*** podstępnie nakłonić kogoś do zrobienia czegoś

I

in•vent [ɪn'vent] *v/t* **1.** wynaleźć **2.** wymyślać ⟨-lić⟩ **3.** zmyślać ⟨-lić⟩; **in•ven•tion** [ɪn'venʃn] *s* **1.** wynalazek *m* **2.** wynalezienie *n* **3.** zmyślenie *n*, wymysł *m*; **in•ven•tive** [ɪn'ventɪv] *adj* **1.** pomysłowy **2.** wynalazczy; **in•ven•tive•ness** [ɪn'ventɪvnɪs] *s* inwencja *f*, pomysłowość *f*; **in•ven•tor** [ɪn'ventə] *s* wynalazca *m*

in•ven•tory ['ɪnvəntrɪ] **I** *s* **1.** spis *m* (inwentarza); ***take an ~ of*** inwentaryzować *A* **2.** *Am* zapas *m* **II** *v/t* inwentaryzować ⟨z-⟩

in•verse [ɪn'vɜ:s] *adj* odwrotny; **inver•sion** [ɪn'vɜ:ʃn] *s* inwersja *f*; **in•vert** [ɪn'vɜ:t] *v/t* **1.** odwracać ⟨-rócić⟩ **2.** wywracać ⟨-rócić⟩ (na lewą stronę); **in•vert•ed 'com•mas** *pl Br* cudzysłów *m*

invest [ɪn'vest] **I** *v/t* **1.** inwestować ⟨za-⟩ (***in*** w *A*) **2.** *time*: poświęcać ⟨-cić⟩ (***in*** *D*) **3.** *effort*: wkładać ⟨włożyć⟩ (***in*** w *A*) **4.** nadawać ⟨-dać⟩ (***s.o. with*** komuś *A*) **II** *v/i* inwestować ⟨za-⟩ (***in*** w *A*)

in•ves•ti•gate [ɪn'vestɪgeɪt] **I** *v/t* **1.** prowadzić ⟨prze-⟩ dochodzenie w sprawie *G* **2.** badać ⟨z-⟩ **II** *v/i* prowadzić ⟨prze-⟩ dochodzenie; **in•ves•ti•ga•tion** [ɪnvestɪ'geɪʃn] *s* **1.** śledztwo *n*, dochodzenie *n* **2.** badanie *n*; **in•ves•ti•ga•tive 'jour•nal•ism** [ɪn'vestɪgətɪv'dʒɜ:nəlɪzəm] *s* dziennikarstwo *n* śledcze; **inves•ti•ga•tor** [ɪn'vestɪgeɪtə] *s* **1.** śledczy *m* **2.** badacz *m*

in•vest•ment [ɪn'vestmənt] *s* **1.** inwestycja *f* **2.** inwestowanie *n* **3.** inwestycje *pl* **4.** *time*: poświęcenie *n*; **in'vest•ment bank** *s Am* bank *m* inwestycyjny; **in•'vest•ment in•come** *s* dochód *m* z inwestycji kapitałowych; **in'vest•ment trust** *s* fundusz *m* inwestycyjny; **in•ves•tor** [ɪn'vestə] *s* inwestor *m*

in•vig•i•late [ɪn'vɪdʒɪleɪt] *v/i exam*: nadzorować przebieg

in•vig•or•ate [ɪn'vɪgəreɪt] *v/t* **1.** ożywiać ⟨-wić⟩ **2.** pobudzać ⟨-dzić⟩ **3.** orzeźwiać ⟨-wić⟩; **in•vig•or•at•ing** [ɪn'vɪgəreɪtɪŋ] *adj* **1.** ożywczy **2.** inspirujący **3.** orzeźwiający

in•vin•ci•ble [ɪn'vɪnsəbl] *adj* **1.** niezwyciężony **2.** niezachwiany

in•vis•i•ble [ɪn'vɪzɪbl] *adj* niewidoczny, niewidzialny

in•vi•ta•tion [ɪnvɪ'teɪʃn] *s* **1.** zaproszenie *n*; ***at the ~ of*** na zaproszenie *G* **2.** *fig* zachęta *f*

in•vite [ɪn'vaɪt] **I** *v/t* **1.** zapraszać ⟨-rosić⟩; ***~ s.o. to dinner*** zaprosić kogoś na obiad; ***~ trouble*** kusić los, prosić się o kłopoty **2.** prosić ⟨po-⟩ o *A* **3.** zachęcać ⟨-cić⟩ do *G* **II** *s infml* zaproszenie *n*; **in•vite in** *v/t* zapraszać ⟨-rosić⟩ do środka; **in•vit•ing** [ɪn'vaɪtɪŋ] *adj* kuszący, zachęcający

in•voke [ɪn'vəʊk] *v/t* **1.** odwoływać ⟨-łać⟩ się do *G* **2.** powoływać ⟨-łać⟩ się na *A* **3.** wzywać ⟨wezwać⟩ **4.** przywoływać ⟨-łać⟩

in•vol•un•ta•ry [ɪn'vɒlənterɪ] *adj* mimowolny

in•volve [ɪn'vɒlv] *v/t* **1.** wiązać się z *I* **2.** *risk*: nieść ze sobą *A* **3.** polegać na *L* **4.** *form* wymagać **5.** obejmować ⟨objąć⟩; ***an accident involving three cars*** wypadek, w którym wzięły udział trzy samochody; ***the persons ~d*** osoby zainteresowane, zainteresowani **6.** dotyczyć **7.** włączać ⟨-czyć⟩ **8.** wciągać ⟨-gnąć⟩ **9.** skłaniać ⟨skłonić⟩ do współuczestnictwa; **in•volved** [ɪn'vɒlvd] *adj* **1.** związany (***with*** z *I*) **2.** *person*: zainteresowany **3.** zamieszany **4.** zaangażowany **5.** zawiły; **in•volve•ment** [ɪn'vɒlvmənt] *s*

1. uczestnictwo *n*, udział *m*, zaangażowanie *n* **2.** powiązania *pl*
in•vul•ne•ra•ble [ɪn'vʌlnərəbl] *adj* **1.** ***be ~ to*** nie być zagrożonym *I* **2.** niewrażliwy (***to*** na *A*) **3.** niepodatny (***to*** na *A*) **4.** bezpieczny
in•ward ['ɪnwəd] **I** *adj* **1.** wewnętrzny **2.** skryty **3.** (skierowany) do wewnątrz; ***an ~ breath*** wdech **II** *adv* do wewnątrz; **in•ward•ly** ['ɪnwədlɪ] *adv* **1.** w duchu **2.** wewnątrz; **in•wards** ['ɪnwədz] *adv* **1.** do wewnątrz **2.** do środka
IOU [aɪəʊ'juː] *abbr* (=***I owe you***) *infml* skrypt *m* dłużny
IQ [aɪ'kjuː] *abbr* (=***intelligence quotient***) IQ *n*
I•ran [ɪ'rɑːn] *s* Iran *m*
I•raq [ɪ'ræːk] *s* Irak *m*
i•rate [aɪ'reɪt] *adj* oburzony
Ire•land ['aɪərlənd] *s* Irlandia *f*
i•ris ['aɪərɪs] *s* **1.** tęczówka *f* **2.** irys *m*
I•rish ['aɪərɪʃ] **I** *adj* irlandzki; ***~ coffee*** kawa po irlandzku **II** *s* **1.** ***he's ~*** jest Irlandczykiem; ***the ~*** Irlandczycy **2.** język *m* irlandzki; **'I•rish•man** *pl -men s* Irlandczyk *m*; **'I•rish•wom•an** *pl -men s* Irlandka *f*
irk [ɜːk] *v/t form* irytować; **irk•some** ['ɜːksəm] *adj form* irytujący
i•ron ['aɪən] **I** *s* **1.** żelazo *n*; ***a will of ~*** żelazna wola; ***have several ~s in the fire*** *fig* łapać kilka srok za ogon; ***strike while the ~ is hot*** *fig* kuć żelazo póki gorące **2.** żelazko *n* **II** *adj* żelazny; ***~ ore*** ruda żelaza **III** *v/t* prasować ⟨wy-⟩; **i•ron out** *v/t* **1.** rozprasowywać ⟨-sować⟩ **2.** *problem*: rozwiązywać ⟨-zać⟩ **3.** ***~ out differences*** dojść do porozumienia; **I•ron 'Cur•tain** *s* HIST żelazna kurtyna *f*
i•ron•ic(al) [aɪ'rɒnɪk(l)] *adj* ironiczny
i•ron•ing ['aɪənɪŋ] *s* prasowanie *n*; ***do the ~*** prasować; **'i•ron•ing board** *s* deska *f* do prasowania
i•ron•y ['aɪrənɪ] *s* ironia *f*; ***an ~ of fate*** ironia losu
ir•ra•tion•al [ɪ'ræʃənl] *adj* **1.** irracjonalny **2.** nierozsądny
ir•rec•on•ci•la•ble [ɪrekən'saɪləbl] *adj* nie do pogodzenia, nierozwiązywalny
ir•re•cov•e•ra•ble [ɪrɪ'kʌvərəbl] *adj* **1.** bezpowrotnie stracony **2.** nie do odzyskania **3.** niepowetowany
ir•re•deem•a•ble [ɪrɪ'diːməbl] *adj* **1.** zatwardziały **2.** niereformowalny **3.** FIN niepodlegający wykupowi
ir•re•gu•lar [ɪ'regjʊlə] *adj* **1.** nieregularny **2.** nierówny **3.** nietypowy; **ir•reg•u•lar•i•ty** [ɪregjʊ'lærətɪ] *s* **1.** nieregularność *f* **2.** nierówność *f* **3.** nieprawidłowość *f*
ir•rel•e•vance, **ir•rel•e•van•cy** [ɪ'reləvəns(ɪ)] *s* **1.** brak *m* związku **2.** rzecz *m* nieistotna; **ir•rel•e•vant** [ɪ'reləvənt] *adj* niezwiązany z tematem, nieistotny
ir•rep•a•ra•ble [ɪ'repərəbl] *adj* **1.** nieodwracalny **2.** nie do naprawienia **3.** niepowetowany
ir•re•place•a•ble [ɪrɪ'pleɪsəbl] *adj* niezastąpiony
ir•re•pres•si•ble [ɪrɪ'presəbl] *adj* **1.** żywiołowy **2.** pełen niespożytej energii **3.** *confidence*: niezachwiany **4.** niepohamowany
ir•re•proach•a•ble [ɪrɪ'prəʊtʃəbl] *adj* nienaganny, bez zarzutu, nieskazitelny
ir•re•sis•ti•ble [ɪrɪ'zɪstəbl] *adj* nieodparty, przemożny
ir•res•o•lute [ɪ'rezəluːt] *adj* niezdecydowany
ir•re•spec•tive [ɪrɪ'spektɪv] *adv* ***~ of*** bez względu na *A*
ir•re•spon•si•ble [ɪrɪ'spɒnsəbl] *adj* nieodpowiedzialny
ir•re•trie•va•ble [ɪrɪ'triːvəbl] *adj* **1.** niepowetowany **2.** nie do odzyskania **3.** nie do naprawienia
ir•re•vers•i•ble [ɪrɪ'vɜːsəbl] *adj* **1.** nieodwracalny, nieodwołalny **2.** nieuleczalny
ir•ri•gate ['ɪrɪgeɪt] *v/t* **1.** nawadniać ⟨-wodnić⟩, irygować **2.** *wound*: przepłukiwać ⟨-kać⟩; **ir•ri•ga•tion** [ɪrɪ'geɪʃn] *s* **1.** nawadnianie *n*, irygacja *f*; ***an ~ ditch*** rów irygacyjny, rów nawadniający **2.** MED irygacja *f*
ir•ri•ta•bil•i•ty [ɪrɪtə'bɪlɪtɪ] *s* **1.** drażliwość *f* **2.** skłonność *f* do irytacji; **ir•ri•ta•ble** ['ɪrɪtəbl] *adj* **1.** drażliwy **2.** rozdrażniony
ir•ri•tate ['ɪrɪteɪt] *v/t* **1.** drażnić ⟨roz-⟩, irytować ⟨z-⟩ **2.** podrażniać ⟨-nić⟩; **ir•ri•tat•ing** ['ɪrɪteɪtɪŋ] *adj* **1.** drażniący **2.** irytujący; **ir•ri•ta•tion** [ɪrɪ'teɪʃn] *s* **1.** rozdrażnienie *n* **2.** irytacja *f* **3.** podrażnienie *n*

is [ɪz] → ***be***

Is•lam ['ɪzlɑːm] *s* islam *m*; **Is•lam•ic** [ɪz'læmɪk] *adj* islamski

is•land ['aɪlənd] *s* wyspa; **is•land•er** ['aɪləndə] *s* wyspiarz *m*, mieszkaniec *m* wyspy

i•so•late ['aɪsəleɪt] *v/t* **1.** izolować ⟨od-, wy-⟩ **2.** odseparowywać ⟨-rować⟩ **3.** wyodrębniać ⟨-nić⟩; **i•so•lat•ed** ['aɪsəleɪtɪd] *adj* **1.** samotny **2.** *case*: odosobniony; **i•so•la•tion** [aɪsə'leɪʃn] *s* **1.** izolacja *f*; ***an ~ ward*** *Br* izolatka **2.** izolowanie *n* **3.** wyodrębnienie *n* **4.** ***consider s.th. in ~ from*** rozpatrywać coś w oderwaniu od *G*

Is•rael ['ɪzreɪl] *s* Izrael *m*; **Is•rae•li** [ɪz'reɪlɪ] **I** *adj* izraelski **II** *s* Izraelczyk *m* Izraelka *f*

is•sue ['ɪʃuː] **I** *s* **1.** kwestia *f*; ***your honesty is not at ~*** tu nie chodzi o twoją uczciwość; ***a point at ~*** rozważana kwestia **2.** wystawienie *n* **3.** wydanie *n* **4.** *stocks*: emisja *f* **5.** (*magazine*) numer *m* **6.** JUR potomstwo *n*; ***die without ~*** umrzeć bezpotomnie **II** *v/t* **1.** wydawać ⟨-dać⟩ **2.** (*warning*) udzielać ⟨-lić⟩ **3.** (*ultimatum*) stawiać ⟨postawić⟩ **4.** emitować ⟨wy-⟩ **5.** ***be ~d with*** otrzymać *A* **III** *v/i form* **1.** wydobywać ⟨-być⟩ się **2.** dobywać ⟨-być⟩ się

IT [aɪ'tiː] *abbr* (=***information technology***) technologia *f* informacyjna, IT *n*

it [ɪt] *pron* **1.** to; ***~ was a surprise*** to była niespodzianka **2.** ***~ is to him that you should turn*** to do niego powinieneś się zwrócić **3.** ono **4.** ***~'s raining*** pada (deszcz)

I•tal•ian [ɪ'tælɪən] **I** *adj* włoski **II** *s* **1.** Włoch *m*, Włoszka *f* **2.** język *m* włoski

i•tal•ic [ɪ'tælɪk] *adj* drukowany kursywą; **i•tal•i•cize** [ɪ'tælɪsaɪz] *v/t* drukować ⟨wy-⟩ kursywą; **i•tal•ics** [ɪ'tælɪks] *pl* kursywa *f*, italiki *pl*; ***in ~s*** kursywą

I•ta•ly ['ɪtəlɪ] *s* Włochy *pl*

itch [ɪtʃ] **I** *s* **1.** swędzenie *n* **2.** MED świąd *m*, świerzb *m* **3.** chętka *f*; ***I had an ~ to do it*** *infml* miałem wielką ochotę to zrobić, korciło mnie, żeby to zrobić **II** *v/i* **1.** swędzieć **2.** ***be ~ing for*** palić się do *G*; ***he's ~ing to do it*** pali się, żeby to zrobić, nie może się doczekać, żeby to zrobić; **itch•y** ['ɪtʃɪ] *adj* **1.** swędzący **2.** drapiący

i•tem ['aɪtəm] *s* **1.** rzecz *m* **2.** artykuł *m* **3.** pozycja *f* **4.** punkt *m* **5.** ***a news ~*** wiadomość; **i•tem•ize** ['aɪtəmaɪz] *v/t* wyszczególniać ⟨-nić⟩, rozpisywać ⟨-sać⟩ na pozycje

i•tin•e•ra•ry [aɪ'tɪnərerɪ] *s* **1.** plan *m* podróży **2.** trasa *f*

its [ɪts] *poss* **1.** jego **2.** swój

it•self [ɪt'self] *pron* **1.** się **2.** sam; ***by ~*** sam, samodzielnie

i•vo•ry ['aɪvərɪ] **I** *s* kość *f* słoniowa; ***ivories*** wyroby z kości słoniowej **II** *adj* z kości słoniowej; ***live in an ~ tower*** żyć w wieży z kości słoniowej; **I•vo•ry 'Coast** *s*: ***the ~*** Wybrzeże Kości Słoniowej

i•vy ['aɪvɪ] *s* bluszcz *m*

J

jab [dʒæb] **I** *v/t* **1.** dźgać ⟨-gnąć⟩ (***into*** *A*) **2.** uderzać ⟨-rzyć⟩ prostym **II** *s* **1.** dźgnięcie *n* **2.** *blow*: prosty *m* **3.** *infml* zastrzyk *m*

jab•ber ['dʒæbə] **I** *v/i* **~** (***away***) paplać **II** *v/t* paplać ⟨wy-⟩ **III** *s* paplanina *f*

jack [dʒæk] *s* **1.** (*cards*) walet *m*; ***the ~ of hearts*** walet kier **2.** podnośnik *m*, lewarek *m* **3.** wtyczka *f* typu „jack"

jack up *v/t* **1.** podnosić ⟨-nieść⟩ lewarkiem **2.** *prices*: *infml* windować

jack•ass ['dʒækæs] *s infml* osioł *m*

jack•et ['dʒækɪt] *s* **1.** marynarka *f* **2.** kurtka *f* **3.** żakiet *m* **4.** TECH osłona *f* **5.** obwoluta *f* **6.** koperta *f* **7.** koszulka *f* **8.** łupina *f*

'jack-knife *s* składany nóż *m*; **jack-of-all-trades** [dʒækəv'ɔːltreɪdz] *s* majster *m* do wszystkiego; **'jack plug** *s* wtyczka *f* typu „jack"

jack•pot ['dʒækpɒt] *s* **1.** pula *f* **2.** główna wygrana *f*; ***hit the ~*** **a)** zgarnąć główną wygraną **b)** *fig* odnieść wielki sukces

jad•ed ['dʒeɪdɪd] *adj* **1.** znużony **2.** zblazowany
jag•ged ['dʒægɪd] *adj* **1.** postrzępiony **2.** poszarpany **3.** wyszczerbiony
jail [dʒeɪl] **I** *s* **1.** więzienie *n*; ***in ~*** w więzieniu; ***put s.o. in ~*** zamknąć kogoś w więzieniu **2.** areszt *m* **II** *v/t* osadzać ⟨-dzić⟩ w więzieniu; **'jail•bird** *s infml* kryminalista *m*; **'jail•break** *s* ucieczka *f* z więzienia
jam[1] [dʒæm] *s* dżem *m*
jam[2] [~] **I** *v/t* **1.** wciskać ⟨-snąć⟩; ***he ~med his finger in the door, he got his finger ~med in the door*** przyciął sobie palec drzwiami; ***be ~med in*** zaklinować się w *L* **2.** upychać ⟨upchać⟩ **3.** wpychać ⟨wepchnąć⟩ **4.** ściskać ⟨-snąć⟩ **5.** ~ (***up***) blokować ⟨za-⟩ **6.** *transmission*: zagłuszać ⟨-szyć⟩ **7.** ***~ on the brakes*** gwałtownie wcisnąć hamulec **II** *v/i* **1.** zacinać ⟨-ciąć⟩ się **2.** wciskać ⟨-snąć⟩ się **III** *s* **1.** korek *m* (uliczny) **2.** ścisk *m* **3.** ***be in a ~*** *infml* być w tarapatach
Ja•mai•ca [dʒə'meɪkə] *s* Jamajka *f*
jam•bo•ree [dʒæmbə'riː] *s* **1.** zlot *m* **2.** zjazd *m*
jan•i•tor ['dʒænɪtə] *s Am* dozorca *m*, woźny *m*
Jan•u•a•ry ['dʒænjʊərɪ] *s* styczeń *m*; ***in ~*** w styczniu
Ja•pan [dʒə'pæn] *s* Japonia *f*; **Jap•a•nese** [dʒæpə'niːz] **I** *adj* japoński **II** *s* Japończyk *m*, Japonka *f*
jar[1] [dʒɑː] *s* **1.** słoik *m* **2.** słój *m* **3.** dzban *m* **4.** *Br infml* kufel *m*
jar[2] [~] **I** *v/t* **1.** wstrząsać ⟨-snąć⟩ **2.** uderzać ⟨-rzyć⟩ **II** *v/i* **1.** denerwować ⟨z-⟩ (***on*** *A*) **2.** ***~ on s.o.'s nerves*** działać komuś na nerwy **3.** (*colours*) gryźć się **4.** ***a ~ring tone*** fałszywy ton **III** *s* wstrząs *m*
jar•gon ['dʒɑːgən] *s* żargon *m*
jas•min(e) ['dʒæzmɪn] *s* jaśmin *m*
jaw [dʒɔː] **I** *s* **1.** szczęka *f*; ***the lower*** (***upper***) ~ dolna (górna) szczęka **2.** ***~s*** paszcza **3.** TECH zacisk *m* **4.** ***have a ~*** *infml* pogadać (sobie) **II** *v/i infml* gadać ⟨po-⟩; **'jaw•bone** *s* żuchwa *f*, kość *f* szczękowa (dolna)
jay [dʒeɪ] *s* sójka *f*; **'jay•walk•ing** *s* przechodzenie *n* przez jezdnię w niedozwolonym miejscu
jazz [dʒæz] **I** *s* **1.** jazz *m* **2.** ***and all that ~*** *infml* i tak dalej **II** *adj* jazzowy; **jazz up** *v/t infml* **1.** ożywiać ⟨-wić⟩ **2.** ubarwiać ⟨-wić⟩ **3.** unowocześniać ⟨-nić⟩
jazz•y ['dʒæzɪ] *adj* **1.** jazzowy **2.** krzykliwy
jeal•ous ['dʒeləs] *adj* zazdrosny; ***be ~ of s.o.'s success*** zazdrościć komuś sukcesu; **jeal•ous•ly** ['dʒeləsi] *adv* zazdrośnie; **jeal•ous•y** ['dʒeləslɪ] *s* zazdrość *f*
jeer [dʒɪə] **I** *v/i* **1.** szydzić (***at*** z *G*) **2.** drwić (***at*** z *G*) **3.** wyśmiewać się (***at*** z *G*) **II** *v/t* **1.** wyszydzać ⟨-dzić⟩ **2.** wyśmiewać ⟨-miać⟩ **III** *s* szyderstwo *n*; **jeer•ing** ['dʒɪərɪŋ] *adj* szyderczy; ***~ laughter*** szyderczy śmiech
jel•ly ['dʒelɪ] *s* **1.** galareta *f* **2.** galaretka *f*; ***a ~ roll*** (*cake*) rolada **3.** *Am* dżem *m*; **'jel•ly bean** *s* cukierek w kształcie ziarna fasoli; **'jel•ly•fish** *s* meduza *f*
jem•my ['dʒemɪ] *s Br* (krótki) łom *m*
jeop•ar•dize ['dʒepədaɪz] *v/t* zagrażać ⟨-rozić⟩, narażać ⟨-razić⟩ na szwank; **jeop•ar•dy** ['dʒepədɪ] *s* niebezpieczeństwo *n*; ***put s.o. in ~*** narazić kogoś na niebezpieczeństwo
jerk [dʒɜːk] **I** *s* **1.** szarpnięcie *n*; ***give a ~*** szarpnąć **2.** drgnięcie *n* **3.** ruch *m*; ***indicate s.th. with a ~ of one's head*** wskazać coś ruchem głowy **4.** *Am* palant *m* **II** *v/i* **1.** szarpać ⟨-pnąć⟩ (***at*** *A*); ***~ to a stop*** gwałtownie zahamować **2.** drgać ⟨-gnąć⟩ **III** *v/t* szarpać ⟨-pnąć⟩; **jerk off** *v/i vulg* walić konia; **jerk out** *v/t* **1.** bełkotać ⟨wy-⟩ **2.** wyszarpywać ⟨-pnąć⟩
jerk•y ['dʒɜːkɪ] *adj* nerwowy
jer•ry-built ['dʒərɪbɪlt] *adj* **1.** tandetny **2.** sklecony naprędce
jest [dʒest] **I** *s* żart *m*; ***in ~*** żartem **II** *v/i* żartować ⟨za-⟩; **jest•er** ['dʒəstə] *s* błazen *m*
Jes•u•it ['dʒezjʊɪt] **I** *s* jezuita **II** *adj* jezuicki
jet [dʒet] **I** *s* **1.** odrzutowiec *m*, samolot *m* odrzutowy **2.** *water*, *air*: strumień *m* **II** *v/i* **1.** tryskać ⟨-snąć⟩ **2.** strzelić ⟨wy-⟩ **3.** *infml* lecieć ⟨po-⟩ samolotem; **jet-'black** *adj* kruczoczarny, czarny jak węgiel; **jet 'en•gine** *s* silnik *m* odrzutowy; **jet 'fight•er** *s* myśliwiec *m* odrzutowy; **'jet•lag** *s* zespół *m* długu czasowego; **'jet plane** *s* samolot *m*

J

odrzutowy, odrzutowiec *m*; **jet-'propelled** *adj* odrzutowy, o napędzie odrzutowym
'jet set *s*: ***the ~*** znani i bogaci
jet•ty ['dʒetɪ] *s* molo *n*
Jew [dʒuː] *s* Żyd *m*
jew•el ['dʒuːəl] **I** *s* **1.** klejnot *m*; ***a ~ box*** szkatułka **2.** *TECH* kamień *m* **3.** *fig* skarb *m*, perła *f* **II** *v/t* **~led** wysadzany kamieniami; **jew•el•ler** ['dʒuːələ] *Br*, ***jew•el•er*** *Am s* jubiler *m*; **jew•ellery** ['dʒuːəlrɪ] *Br*, ***jew•el•ry*** *Am s* biżuteria *f*, klejnoty *pl*, kosztowności *pl*
Jew•ish ['dʒuːɪʃ] *adj* żydowski
jig•gle ['dʒɪgl] **I** *v/t* potrząsać, szarpać **II** *v/i* podrygiwać, wiercić się
jig•saw (puz•zle) ['dʒɪgsɔː(pʌzəl)] *s* układanka *f*, puzzle *pl*
jilt [dʒɪlt] *v/t girlfriend*, *lover*: porzucać ⟨-cić⟩
jim•my ['dʒɪmɪ] *Am* → ***jemmy***
jin•gle ['dʒɪŋgl] **I** *v/i* **1.** dzwonić ⟨za-⟩ **2.** pobrzękiwać **II** *v/t* **1.** dzwonić ⟨za-⟩ **2.** pobrzękiwać **III** *s* **1.** dzwonienie *n* **2.** brzęk *m* **3.** melodyjka *f* reklamowa, dżingiel *m*
jin•go•ism ['dʒɪŋgəʊɪzm] *s* szowinizm *m*; **jin•go•is•tic** [dʒɪŋgəʊ'ɪstɪk] *adj* szowinistyczny
jinks [dʒɪŋks] *pl*: ***high ~*** *dated* zabawa w najlepsze, szaleństwo
jinx [dʒɪŋks] *s* przekleństwo *n*, fatum *n*; ***put a ~ on s.o.*** rzucić na kogoś zły urok
jit•ters ['dʒɪtəz] *pl infml* drżączka *f*; **jitter•y** ['dʒɪtərɪ] *adj infml* cały w nerwach, stremowany
job [dʒɒb] **I** *s* **1.** praca *f*, robota *f*; ***make a good*** (***bad***) ***~ of s.th.*** zrobić coś dobrze (źle); ***a ~ centre*** *Br* biuro pośrednictwa pracy; ***~ creation*** tworzenie nowych miejsc pracy; ***a ~ interview*** rozmowa o pracę; ***on the ~*** podczas pracy; ***out of a ~*** bezrobotny **2.** posada *f* **3.** stanowisko *n* **4.** rola *f* **5.** obowiązek *m* **6.** zadanie *n* **7.** zlecenie *n* **8.** ***make the best of a bad ~*** robić dobrą minę do złej gry **9.** *infml* skok *m*; ***pull a ~*** (***off***) zrobić skok **II** *v/i* pracować na zlecenie
Job [dʒəʊb] *s* Hiob *m*; ***have the patience of ~***, ***be*** (***as***) ***patient as ~*** mieć anielską cierpliwość
'job de•scrip•tion *s* zakres *m* obowiązków; **'job hunt** *v/i* poszukiwać pracy; **job•less** ['dʒɒblɪs] *adj* bezrobotny; **'job of•fer** *s* oferta *f* pracy; **job satis•'fac•tion** *s* zadowolenie *n* z pracy; **'job se•cu•ri•ty** *s* pewność *f* stałego zatrudnienia; **'job seek•er** *s* osoba *f* poszukująca pracy; **'job-shar•ing** *s* dzielenie *n* etatu
jock•ey ['dʒɒkɪ] *s* dżokej *m*; **jock•ey for** *v/i* zaciekle walczyć o *A*
joc•u•lar ['dʒɒkjʊlə] *adj* **1.** żartobliwy **2.** pełen humoru
jog ['dʒɒg] **I** *v/t* **1.** potrącać ⟨-cić⟩, trącać ⟨-cić⟩ **2.** ***~ s.o.'s memory*** odświeżyć komuś pamięć **II** *v/i* uprawiać jogging **III** *s* **1.** trącenie *n*, szturchnięcie *n* **2.** trucht *m*; **jog along** *v/i fig* powoli posuwać ⟨-sunąć⟩ się naprzód
jog•ging ['dʒɒgɪŋ] *s* jogging *m*
jog•gle ['dʒɒgl] *v/t* potrząsać ⟨-snąć⟩, kołysać ⟨za-⟩
john [dʒɒn] *s* **1.** *Am infml* kibel *m* **2.** **~** ***Bull*** przeciętny Anglik
join [dʒɔɪn] **I** *v/t* **1.** łączyć ⟨po-⟩; ***~ hands*** wziąć się za ręce **2.** dołączać ⟨-czyć⟩ do *G*; ***I'll ~ you later*** dołączę do was później **3.** przyłączać ⟨-czyć⟩ się do *G* **4.** zatrudniać ⟨-nić⟩ się w *A* **5.** zapisywać ⟨-sać⟩ się na *A* **6.** zapisywać ⟨-sać⟩ się do *G* **7.** ***~ the army*** wstąpić do wojska **8.** (*road*) łączyć się z *I* **9.** (*river*) wpadać do *G* **II** *v/i* łączyć się ⟨po-⟩; **join in** *v/i* przyłączać ⟨-czyć⟩ się do *G*; **join up** *v/i Br* wstępować ⟨-tąpić⟩ do wojska
join•er ['dʒɔɪnə] *s* stolarz *m* **join•er•y** ['dʒɔɪnərɪ] *s* stolarka *f* (drzwiowa i okienna)
joint [dʒɔɪnt] **I** *s* **1.** *ANAT* staw *m*; ***out of ~*** zwichnięty **2.** *COOK* mięso *n* na pieczeń, pieczeń *f* **3.** *infml* speluna *f* **4.** *infml* skręt *m*, joint *m* **II** *adj* **1.** wspólny; ***take ~ action*** podjąć wspólne działania **2.** połączony **3.** łączny; **joint ac'count** *s* wspólny rachunek *m*, wspólne konto *n*; **joint 'ven•ture** *s* **1.** spółka *f* typu joint venture **2.** wspólne przedsięwzięcie *n*
joke [dʒəʊk] **I** *s* **1.** dowcip *m* **2.** kawał *m*; ***crack ~s*** opowiadać kawały; ***play a ~ on s.o.*** zrobić komuś kawał **3.** żart *m*; ***for a ~*** dla żartu; ***that's going beyond a ~*** to przestaje być śmieszne;

he can't take a ~ on się nie zna na żartach; ***a practical ~*** psikus, figiel **II** *v/i* żartować ⟨za-⟩; ***I'm not joking*** nie żartuję; ***you must be joking*** chyba żartujesz; **jok•er** ['dʒəʊkə] *s* **1.** żartowniś *m*, kawalarz *m* **2.** (*cards*) dżoker *m*; **jok•ey** ['dʒəʊkɪ] *adj infml* żartobliwy; **jok•ing** ['dʒəʊkɪŋ] **I** *adj* żartobliwy **II** *s* żartowanie *n*, żarty *pl*; **jok•ing•ly** ['dʒəʊkɪŋlɪ] *adv* żartem, żartobliwie

jol•ly ['dʒɒlɪ] **I** *adj* **1.** wesoły **2.** *dated infml* udany **II** *adv dated infml* bardzo; ***a ~ good idea*** świetny pomysł; **Jol•ly 'Rog•er** *s* wesoły Roger *m* (*bandera piracka*)

jolt [dʒəʊlt] **I** *v/t* **1.** rzucać ⟨-cić⟩ **2.** wstrząsać ⟨-snąć⟩; ***~ s.o. into action*** skłonić kogoś do działania **II** *v/i* **1.** trząść się **2.** szarpać ⟨-pnąć⟩; ***~ to a halt*** gwałtownie zahamować **3.** podskakiwać ⟨-skoczyć⟩ **4.** telepać się **III** *s* **1.** szarpnięcie *n* **2.** wstrząs *m*; ***give s.o. a ~*** wstrząsnąć kimś

Jor•dan ['dʒɔːdn] *s* Jordania *f*

jos•tle ['dʒɒsl] **I** *v/t* **1.** popychać ⟨-pchnąć⟩ **2.** potrącać ⟨-cić⟩ **3.** ***~ one's way through*** przedzierać się przez *A* **II** *v/i* **1.** rywalizować (***against*** z *I*) **2.** rozpychać się **3.** przepychać się

jot [dʒɒt] *s*: ***there is not a ~ of truth in s.th.*** w czymś nie ma ani krzty prawdy; **jot down** *v/t* notować ⟨za-⟩; **jot•ter** ['dʒɒtə] *s Br* notatnik *m*

joule [dʒuːl] *s* PHYS dżul *m*

jour•nal ['dʒɜːnl] *s* **1.** czasopismo *n* **2.** dziennik *m*; **jour•nal•ism** ['dʒɜːnəlɪzm] *s* dziennikarstwo *n*; **jour•nal•ist** ['dʒɜːnəlɪst] *s* dziennikarz *m*

jour•ney ['dʒɜːnɪ] *s* **1.** podróż *f*; ***go on a ~*** wyjechać w podróż, wybrać się w podróż **2.** droga *f*; ***it's a one-day ~ from*** to o dzień drogi z *G*

jo•vi•al ['dʒəʊvɪəl] *adj* **1.** wesoły **2.** jowialny

joy [dʒɔɪ] *s* **1.** radość *f*; ***jump for ~*** skakać z radości; ***tears of ~*** łzy szczęścia **2.** ***I didn't have any ~*** nie miałem szczęścia, nie udało mi się; **joy•ful** ['dʒɔɪfʊl] *adj* radosny, szczęśliwy, uradowany; **joy•less** ['dʒɔɪlɪs] *adj* smutny, ponury, nieszczęśliwy; **joy•ous** ['dʒɔɪəs] *adj lit* radosny, pełen radości

'joy•rid•er *s* amator jazdy kradzionym samochodem; **'joy-rid•ing** *s* jazda *f* kradzionym samochodem; **'joy•stick** *s* **1.** joystick *m* **2.** drążek *m* sterowy

ju•bi•lant ['dʒuːbɪlənt] *adj* **1.** radosny; ***~ shouts*** okrzyki radości **2.** rozradowany **3.** rozentuzjazmowany; **ju•bi•la•tion** [dʒuːbɪ'leɪʃn] *s* radość *f*

ju•bi•lee ['dʒuːbɪliː] *s* jubileusz *m*

judge [dʒʌdʒ] **I** *s* **1.** sędzia *m* **2.** juror *m* **3.** *fig* znawca *m*; ***a (good) ~ of wine*** znawca win **II** *v/t* **1.** oceniać ⟨-nić⟩ **2.** osądzać ⟨-dzić⟩ **3.** sędziować w *L* **4.** uznawać ⟨-nać⟩ (**as** za *A*) **III** *v/i* **1.** sędziować **2.** sądzić; ***judging by his words*** (sądząc) z tego, co powiedział

judg(e)•ment ['dʒʌdʒmənt] *s* **1.** zdanie *n*, pogląd *m*; ***form a ~ on*** wyrobić sobie zdanie na temat *G*; ***in my ~*** moim zdaniem **2.** umiejętność *f* trafnej oceny sytuacji; ***an error in ~*** błąd, błędna ocena sytuacji; ***he did it against his better ~*** zrobił to, choć wiedział, że nie jest to najlepsze rozwiązanie **3.** wyrok *m* **4.** orzeczenie *n* **5.** ***the Last ~*** REL Sąd Ostateczny; **judg•men•tal** [dʒʌdʒ'mentl] *adj* krytyczny; **Judg•ment Day** *s* Dzień *m* Sądu Ostatecznego

ju•di•cial [dʒuː'dɪʃl] *adj* sądowy; ***a ~ error*** pomyłka sądowa; ***a ~ system*** system sądownictwa; ***a ~ battle*** batalia sądowa

ju•di•ci•ar•y [dʒuː'dɪʃərɪ] *s* **1.** sędziowie *pl* **2.** sądownictwo *n*

ju•di•cious [dʒuː'dɪʃəs] *adj* rozsądny, roztropny

jug [dʒʌg] *s* **1.** dzbanek *m* **2.** dzban *m*

juice [dʒuːs] *s* **1.** sok *m* **2.** *Br infml* paliwo *n* **3.** *Am infml* prąd *m*

juic•er ['dʒuːsə] *s* sokowirówka *f*

juic•y ['dʒuːsɪ] *adj* **1.** soczysty **2.** *infml* pikantny

juke•box ['dʒuːkbɒks] *s* szafa *f* grająca

Ju•ly [dʒʊ'laɪ] *s* lipiec *m*; ***in ~*** w lipcu

jum•ble ['dʒʌmbl] **I** *s* **1.** mieszanina *f* **2.** miszmasz *m* **3.** *Br* rzeczy *pl* używane **II** *v/t* mieszać ⟨po-⟩; **jum•ble together** *v/i* mieszać ⟨po-⟩ się; **jumble up** *v/t* mieszać ⟨po-⟩

'jum•ble sale *s Br* wyprzedaż *m* rzeczy używanych, kiermasz *m* dobroczynny

jum•bo [dʒʌmbəʊ] *pl -bos s fig* wielkolud *m*; **'jum•bo jet** *s* jumbo jet *m*; **'jum•bo(-sized)** *adj infml* wielki, olbrzymi

jump [dʒʌmp] **I** *s* **1.** skok *m*; ***take a ~*** wykonać skok; ***give a ~*** podskoczyć **2.** skokowy wzrost *m* **II** *v/i* **1.** skakać ⟨skoczyć⟩; ***~ for joy*** skakać z radości; ***~ off s.th.*** zeskoczyć z czegoś; ***~ up*** (***to one's feet***) zerwać się (na równe nogi) **2.** podskakiwać ⟨-skoczyć⟩ **3.** wzrastać ⟨-rosnąć⟩ gwałtownie **III** *v/t* **1.** przeskakiwać ⟨-skoczyć⟩ **2.** omijać ⟨ominąć⟩ **3.** ***~ the gun*** zbytnio się pośpieszyć **4.** ***~ the queue*** wepchać się bez kolejki; **jump at** *v/i* **1.** (skwapliwie) skorzystać z *G* **2.** entuzjastycznie przyjąć **3.** *conclusion*: pochopnie wyciągać ⟨-gnąć⟩; **jump up** *v/i* podskakiwać ⟨-skoczyć⟩

jumped-'up *adj* napuszony

jump•er[1] ['dʒʌmpə] *s SPORT* skoczek *m*

jump•er[2] [~] *s* **1.** *Br* sweter *m*, pulower *m* **2.** *Am* fartuszek *m*

'jump-rope *s Am* skakanka *f*; **jump-'start** *v/t* **1.** odpalać ⟨-lić⟩ z innego akumulatora **2.** uruchamiać ⟨-chomić⟩ przez zwarcie przewodów **3.** *career*: zapoczątkować; **'jump suit** *s* kombinezon *m* jednoczęściowy

jump•y ['dʒʌmpɪ] *adj* nerwowy, niestabilny

junc•tion ['dʒʌŋkʃn] *s* **1.** skrzyżowanie *n* **2.** połączenie *n* **3.** węzeł *m* kolejowy

junc•ture ['dʒʌŋktʃə] *s*: ***at this ~*** w tym momencie

June [dʒuːn] *s* czerwiec *m*; ***in ~*** w czerwcu

jun•gle ['dʒʌŋgl] *s* dżungla *f*

ju•ni•or ['dʒuːnɪə] **I** *adj* **1.** młodszy; ***a ~ partner*** młodszy wspólnik **2.** ***~ school*** (*for children 7–11 years old*) *Br* szkoła podstawowa **3.** juniorski; ***the world ~ championships*** mistrzostwa świat juniorów **II** *s* **1.** *SPORT* junior *m* **2.** ***he is two years my ~*** jest ode mnie młodszy o 2 lata; **ju•ni•or 'high school** *s* (*for children 12–14 years old*) *Am* szkoła *f* średnia

junk [dʒʌŋk] **I** *s* **1.** graty *pl*, rupiecie *pl* **2.** tandeta *f* **3.** starzyzna *f* **4.** *infml* hera *f* **II** *v/t infml* **1.** wyrzucać ⟨-cić⟩ na śmietnik **2.** oddawać ⟨-dać⟩ na złom

'junk bond *s* obligacja *f* śmieciowa; **'junk food** *s* tanie, niezdrowe jedzenie *n*

junk•ie ['dʒʌŋkɪ] *s infml* ćpun *m*

'junk mail *s* **1.** niezamówione przesyłki *pl* reklamowe **2.** *INF* spam *m*; **'junk shop** *s* sklep *m* ze starzyzną; **'junk-yard** *s* złomowisko *n*, *infml* szrot *m*

jur•is•dic•tion [dʒʊərɪs'dɪkʃn] *s* **1.** *JUR* jurysdykcja *f* **2.** kompetencje *pl*

ju•ris•pru•dence [dʒʊərɪs'pruːdəns] *s JUR* prawoznawstwo *n*

ju•ror ['dʒʊərə] *s* **1.** przysięgły *m* **2.** juror *m*

ju•ry ['dʒʊərɪ] *s* **1.** *JUR* ława *f* przysięgłych **2.** jury *n*; **ju•ry•man** *pl -men s* **1.** członek *m* ławy przysięgłych **2.** juror *m*; **ju•ry•wo•man** *pl -men s* **1.** członkini *f* ławy przysięgłych **2.** jurorka *f*

just[1] [dʒʌst] *adv* **1.** właśnie; ***~ now*** **a)** teraz **b)** przed chwilą **2.** dopiero co **3.** dokładnie **4.** ***~ before*** (***after***) tuż przed (po); ***~ as important as*** równie ważny jak **5.** ***that is ~ like you*** to do ciebie podobne **6.** ***~ for fun*** dla zabawy **7.** ***~ about*** około **8.** ***~ a minute!*** *infml* chwileczkę!

just[2] [~] *adj* **1.** sprawiedliwy **2.** słuszny **3.** usprawiedliwiony **4.** uzasadniony

jus•tice ['dʒʌstɪs] *s* **1.** sprawiedliwość *f*; ***do ~ to*** wymierzyć sprawiedliwość *D*; ***bring s.o. to ~*** postawić kogoś przed sądem, oddać kogoś w ręce sprawiedliwości **2.** *Br* sędzia *m*; ***a ~ of the peace*** sędzia pokoju

jus•ti•fi•a•ble [dʒʌstɪ'faɪəbl] *adj* uzasadniony, dający się uzasadnić, słuszny; **jus•ti•fi•a•bly** [dʒʌstɪ'faɪəblɪ] *adv* słusznie, nie bez powodu; **jus•ti•fi•ca•tion** [dʒʌstɪfɪ'keɪʃn] *s* **1.** usprawiedliwienie *n*; ***there's no ~ for it*** nic tego nie usprawiedliwia **2.** uzasadnienie *n*; ***in ~ of*** w uzasadnieniu *G*; **jus•ti•fy** ['dʒʌstɪfaɪ] *v/t* **1.** usprawiedliwiać ⟨-wić⟩; ***be justified in doing s.th.*** mieć prawo coś zrobić **2.** uzasadniać ⟨-nić⟩ **3.** tłumaczyć ⟨wy-⟩ **4.** *text*: justować ⟨wy-⟩, wyrównywać ⟨-nać⟩; ***left*** (***right***) ***justified*** wyrównany do lewej (prawej)

just•ly ['dʒʌstlɪ] *adv* sprawiedliwie, słusznie

jut (out) [dʒʌt(aʊt)] *v/i* wystawać, sterczeć

J

ju•ve•nile ['dʒuːvənaɪl] **I** *s* nieletni *m* **II** *adj* **1.** młodociany **2.** *~ crime* przestępczość nieletnich; *a ~ court* sąd dla nieletnich **3.** dziecinny; **ju•ve•nile de•'lin•quen•cy** *s* przestępczość *f* nieletnich; **ju•ve•nile de'lin•quent** *s* młodociany przestępca *m*

jux•ta•pose [dʒʌkstə'pəuz] *v/t* zestawiać ⟨-wić⟩; **jux•ta•po•si•tion** [dʒʌkstəpə'zɪʃn] *s* zestawienie *n*

K

ka•lei•do•scope [kə'laɪdəskəup] *s* kalejdoskop *m*

kan•ga•roo [kæŋgə'ruː] *s* kangur *m*

KB [keɪ'biː] *abbr* (=***kilobyte***) kB, kilobajt *m*

keel [kiːl] *s* kil *m*, stępka *f*; **keel over** *v/i* **1.** przewracać ⟨-rócić⟩ się **2.** wywracać ⟨-rócić⟩ się do góry dnem

keen [kiːn] *adj* **1.** *be ~ on doing s.th.* **a)** uwielbiać coś robić **b)** mieć wielką ochotę coś zrobić **2.** chętny; *be ~ to do s.th.* bardzo chcieć coś zrobić **3.** *mind*: bystry, przenikliwy **4.** *senses*: wyostrzony **5.** *interest*: żywy **6.** ostry **7.** *competition*: bardzo duży **8.** zapalony, zagorzały; **keen•ness** ['kiːnnɪs] *s* **1.** zapał *m* **2.** przenikliwość *f*

keep [kiːp] **I** (*kept*; *kept*) *v/t* **1.** trzymać; *~ s.o. waiting* kazać komuś czekać **2.** zatrzymywać ⟨-mać⟩; *~ the change!* reszty nie trzeba!; *don't let me ~ you* nie chcę cię zatrzymywać **3.** przechowywać ⟨-chować⟩ **4.** utrzymywać ⟨-mać⟩; *~ s.th. a secret* utrzymywać coś w tajemnicy; *have a family to ~* mieć rodzinę na utrzymaniu **5.** zachowywać ⟨-chować⟩ **6.** *~ walking* nie zatrzymywać się; *~ crying* nie przestawać płakać; *~ forgetting* wciąż zapominać, nigdy nie pamiętać; *~ smiling!* głowa do góry! **7.** dotrzymywać ⟨-mać⟩; *~ one's word* dotrzymać słowa **8.** *~ s.th. dry* chronić coś przed wilgocią **9.** dochowywać ⟨-chować⟩; *can you ~ a secret?* czy potrafisz dochować tajemnicy? **10.** *diary*: prowadzić **II** (*kept*; *kept*) *v/i* **1.** *~ still* być cicho **2.** trzymać się **3.** *~ on trying* nie dawać za wygraną **III** *s* **1.** utrzymanie *n* **2.** *for ~s* na zawsze; *it's yours for ~s* możesz to zatrzymać; **keep at** *v/i*: *~ it* **a)** nie poddawać się **b)** być wytrwałym; **keep away** *v/i* trzymać się z daleka (*from* od *G*); **keep back** *v/t* **1.** nie pozwalać ⟨-wolić⟩ się zbliżyć, nie dopuszczać ⟨-puścić⟩ **2.** *keep s.o. back from doing s.th.* powstrzymywać kogoś przed zrobieniem czegoś; **keep down I** *v/t* **1.** utrzymywać ⟨-mać⟩ na niskim poziomie **2.** ograniczać ⟨-czyć⟩ **3.** uciskać **4.** nie zwymiotować **5.** *keep your voice down* mów cicho **II** *v/i* nie podnosić ⟨-nieść⟩ się; **keep from I** *v/i* powstrzymywać ⟨-mać⟩ (*s.o. from* kogoś od *G*) **II** *v/i* *keep oneself from* powstrzymać się od *G*; *I could hardly keep myself from laughing* ledwie mogłem powstrzymać się od śmiechu; **keep in** *v/t* **1.** zatrzymywać ⟨-mać⟩ **2.** powstrzymywać ⟨-mać⟩; **keep in with** *v/i* być w dobrych stosunkach z *I*; **keep off** *v/t* **1.** unikać **2.** nie zbliżać się (do *G*) **3.** trzymać się z daleka od *G* **4.** *~ the grass!* nie deptać trawników! **5.** *keep your hands off me!* *infml* łapy przy sobie!; **keep on I** *v/i* **1.** nie przestawać ⟨-tać⟩; *~ trying!* nie poddawaj się! **2.** nie przerywać ⟨-rwać⟩ **II** *v/t* nie zdejmować ⟨zdjąć⟩; **keep on at** *v/i* molestować (*s.o. about* kogoś o *A*); **keep out I** *v/i* **1.** nie wchodzić ⟨wejść⟩ (*of* do *G*) **2.** unikać (*of G*) **3.** nie narażać ⟨-razić⟩ się (*of* na *A*) **4.** nie mieszać ⟨w-⟩ się (*of* w *A*) **II** *v/t* **1.** nie wpuszczać ⟨wpuścić⟩ **2.** chronić ⟨o-⟩ (*of* przed *I*); **keep to** *v/i* **1.** trzymać się; *~ the left* trzymać się lewej strony **2.** dotrzymywać ⟨-mać⟩ **3.** przestrzegać **4.** *keep s.th. to a minimum* ograniczyć coś do minimum **5.** *keep s.th. to oneself* zachować coś dla siebie; **keep together** *v/i* trzymać się razem; **keep up** *v/i* **1.** dotrzymywać ⟨-mać⟩ kroku (*with D*) **2.** nadążać ⟨-żyć⟩ (*with* z *I*) **3.** być na bieżąco (*with* z *I*)

keep•er ['ki:pə] *s* **1.** dozorca *m* **2.** *SPORT infml* bramkarz *m* **3.** strażnik *m* **4.** właściciel *m* **5.** kustosz *m*
keep-'fit *adj* gimnastyczny
keep•ing ['ki:pɪŋ] *s* **1.** opieka *f*; ***in s.o.'s ~*** pod czyjąś opieką **2.** nadzór *m* **3.** ***be in*** (***out of***) ***~ with*** **a)** (nie) być zgodnym z *I* **b)** (nie) pasować do *G*
'keep•sake *s* pamiątka *f*; ***as a ~*** na pamiątkę, jako pamiątkę
ken•nel ['kenl] *s Br* **1.** buda *f* (dla psa) **2.** psiarnia *f*
Ken•ya ['kenjə] *s* Kenia *f*
kept [kept] *Past Simple and Past Participle* → **keep**
kerb [kɜ:b] *s Br* krawężnik *m*
ker•nel ['kɜ:nl] *s* **1.** (*nut*) jądro *n*, ziarno *n* **2.** sedno *n*, istota *f*
ket•tle ['ketl] *s* czajnik *m*; ***an electric ~*** czajnik elektryczny; ***put the ~ on*** nastawić wodę w czajniku, ***that's a different ~ of fish*** to inna para kaloszy; **'ket•tle•drum** *s MUS* kocioł *m*
key [ki:] **I** *s* **1.** klucz *m* **2.** kluczyk *m* **3.** klawisz *m* **4.** *MUS* tonacja *f*; ***a major*** (***minor***) ***~*** tonacja durowa (molowa); ***sing off ~*** fałszować **II** *adj* **1.** kluczowy **2.** najważniejszy **III** *v/t* dostosowywać ⟨-sować⟩; **key in** *v/t data*: wprowadzać ⟨-dzić⟩
'key•board *s* **1.** klawiatura *f*; ***a ~ instrument*** instrument klawiszowy **2.** ***~s*** syntezator; **keyed-'up** *adj* **1.** podekscytowany **2.** podenerwowany; **'key-hole** *s* dziurka *f* od klucza; ***~ surgery*** *MED* chirurgia endoskopowa; **key-note 'speech** *s POLIT* przemówienie *n* programowe; **'key•pad** *s* **1.** blok *m* klawiszy **2.** klawiatura *f* pomocnicza **3.** klawiatura *f* numeryczna; **'key-ring** *s* kółko *n* na klucze; **'key•stone** *s* **1.** *ARCHIT* zwornik *m* **2.** *fig* filar *m*, podstawa *f*
kha•ki ['kɑ:kɪ] **I** *s* khaki **II** *adj* khaki
kick [kɪk] **I** *s* **1.** kopnięcie *n*; ***give s.o. a ~*** kopnąć kogoś **2.** *infml* kopniak *m* **3.** *infml* kop *m* **4.** ***a penalty*** (***free***) ***~*** rzut karny (wolny) **5.** odrzut *m* **6.** ***for ~s*** *infml* dla zabawy; ***he gets a ~ out of it*** *infml* to mu sprawia wielką frajdę, to go kręci **II** *v/t* **1.** kopać ⟨-pnąć⟩ **2.** *bad habit*: rzucać ⟨-cić⟩ **III** *v/i* **1.** kopać ⟨-pnąć⟩ **2.** wierzgać ⟨-gnąć⟩ **3.** buntować ⟨z-⟩ się; **kick around** *v/t* poniewierać, pomiatać; **kick in** *v/i infml* **1.** włączać ⟨-czyć⟩ się **2.** zaczynać ⟨-cząć⟩ działać **3.** *Am* dorzucać ⟨-cić⟩ się; **kick off I** *v/i* **1.** zaczynać ⟨-cząć⟩ się, startować ⟨wy-⟩ **2.** zaczynać ⟨-cząć⟩ **3.** (*football*) rozpoczynać ⟨-cząć⟩ mecz **4.** (*performance*) wchodzić ⟨wejść⟩ na afisz **II** *v/t* **1.** rozpoczynać ⟨-cząć⟩ **2.** zrzucać ⟨-cić⟩; **kick out** *v/t infml* **1.** wykopać **2.** wyrzucać ⟨-cić⟩; **kick over** *v/t* przewracać ⟨-rócić⟩ (kopnięciem); **kick up** *v/t* **1.** *dust*: wzbijać ⟨-bić⟩ **2.** ***~ a fuss*** zrobić aferę
'kick•off *s* **1.** *SPORT* rozpoczęcie *n* meczu **2.** *infml* rozpoczęcie *n*
kid [kɪd] **I** *s* **1.** dziecko *n*; ***my ~ brother*** mój młodszy brat, mój braciszek **2.** dzieciak *m* **3.** koźlę *n*; ***~ leather*** skóra koźlęca, giemza **II** *v/t* nabierać ⟨-brać⟩, stroić sobie żarty z *G* **III** *v/i* żartować, wygłupiać się; ***he was only ~ding*** on tylko żartował, on nie mówił poważnie; ***no ~ding?*** naprawdę?, poważnie?
kid•nap ['kɪdnæp] *v/t* uprowadzać ⟨-dzić⟩, porywać ⟨-rwać⟩ **kid•nap(p)er** ['kɪdnæpə] *s* porywacz *m*; **'kid-nap•(p)ing** ['kɪdnæpɪŋ] *s* uprowadzenie *n*, porwanie *n*
kid•ney ['kɪdnɪ] *s* **1.** nerka *f* **2.** *COOK* cynaderka *f*; **'kid•ney bean** *s* czerwona fasola *f*; **'kid•ney ma•chine** *s MED* sztuczna nerka *f*; ***put s.o. on a ~*** podłączyć kogoś do sztucznej nerki; **'kid-ney stone** *s MED* kamień *m* nerkowy; **'kid•ney trans•plant** *s* przeszczep *m* nerki
kill [kɪl] **I** *v/t* **1.** zabijać ⟨-bić⟩; ***~ two birds with one stone*** *fig* upiec dwie pieczenie przy jednym ogniu; ***be ~ed*** zginąć, zostać zabitym **2.** ***my feet are ~ing me*** *infml* strasznie bolą mnie nogi **3.** tłumić ⟨s-⟩ **4.** uśmierzać ⟨-rzyć⟩ **II** *v/i* **1.** zabijać ⟨-bić⟩ **2.** ***dressed to ~*** *infml* wystrzałowo ubrany; **kill off** *v/t* **1.** wymordowywać ⟨-dować⟩ **2.** zabijać ⟨-bić⟩ **3.** tępić ⟨wy-⟩ **4.** wypleniać
kil•ler ['kɪlə] **I** *s* **1.** zabójca *m* **2.** przyczyna *f* śmierci **II** *adj* zabójczy, śmiertelny; **'kil•ler whale** *s* orka *f*; **kil•ling** ['kɪlɪŋ] **I** *s* **1.** zabójstwo *n* **2.** zabijanie *n* **II** *adj* **1.** *fig* morderczy **2.** zabójczy

'kill•joy *s*: ***don't be a ~!*** nie psuj zabawy!
kiln [kɪln] *s* piec *m*
ki•lo•gram ['kɪləgræm] *s* kilogram *m*
ki•lo•me•tre ['kɪləmɪtə] *Br*, ***ki•lo•meter*** *Am s* kilometr *m*
ki•lo•watt ['kɪləwɒt] *s* kilowat *m*
kilt [kɪlt] *s* kilt *m*, szkocka spódnica *f*
kin [kɪn] *s* rodzina *f*, krewni *pl*
kind[1] [kaɪnd] *s* **1.** rodzaj *m*; ***all ~s of books*** wszelkiego rodzaju książki; ***nothing of the ~*** nic z tych rzeczy; ***one of a ~*** jedyny w swoim rodzaju **2.** typ *m* **3. *~ of* a)** trochę **b)** jakby; ***–'Did you miss me?' – 'Yeah, ~ of'*** *infml* –„Tęskniłeś za mną?" – „No, trochę" **4. *in ~*** w naturze
kind[2] [~] *adj* **1.** dobry; ***~ to animals*** dobry dla zwierząt **2.** życzliwy **3.** miły; ***would you be so ~ as to do this for me?*** czy byłbyś tak miły i zrobił to dla mnie?
kin•der•gar•ten ['kɪndəgɑːrtn] *s* **1.** *Br* przedszkole *n*; ***a ~ teacher*** nauczyciel wychowania przedszkolnego **2.** *Am* zerówka *f*, klasa *f* zerowa
kind-'heart•ed *adj* dobry, życzliwy
kin•dle ['kɪndl] *v/t* **1.** roznieciać ⟨-cić⟩ **2.** rozpalać ⟨-lić⟩ **3.** rozbudzać ⟨-dzić⟩; **kin•dling** ['kɪndlɪŋ] *s* podpałka *f*
kind•ly ['kaɪndlɪ] **I** *adv* **1.** życzliwie, z życzliwością; ***could you ~ tell me*** czy mógłby mi pan łaskawie powiedzieć **2.** z sympatią **II** *adj lit* dobry; **kind•ness** ['kaɪndnɪs] *s* **1.** dobroć *f* **2.** życzliwość *f* **3.** dobry uczynek *m* **4.** przysługa *f*
kin•dred ['kɪndrəd] *adj* pokrewny; ***a ~ spirit*** bratnia dusza
ki•net•ic [kɪ'netɪk] **I** *adj* kinetyczny **II** *s* ***~s*** kinetyka
king [kɪŋ] *s* **1.** król *m*; ***the ~ of hearts*** król kier **2.** (*draughts*) damka *f*; **kingdom** ['kɪŋdəm] *s* królestwo *n*; ***the animal (plant) ~*** królestwo zwierząt (roślin); ***the ~ of God*** REL królestwo niebieskie
kin•ship ['kɪnʃɪp] *s* **1.** pokrewieństwo *n* **2.** więź *f*
kiosk ['kiːɒsk] **1.** *s* kiosk *m*, budka *f* **2.** budka *f* telefoniczna
kip•per ['kɪpə] *s Br* wędzony śledź *m*
kiss [kɪs] **I** *s* **1.** pocałunek *m* **2.** *infml* całus *m* **II** *v/t* całować ⟨po-, u-⟩; ***~ s.o. good night*** pocałować kogoś na dobranoc **III** *v/i* **1.** całować ⟨po-⟩ się **2.** (*blanche*) muskać ⟨-snąć⟩ kulę; **kiss•er** ['kɪsə] *s infml* pysk *m*, morda *f*; **kiss of 'life** *s* sztuczne oddychanie *n* metodą usta-usta
kit [kɪt] *s* **1.** komplet *m* **2.** zestaw *m*; ***a first-aid ~*** zestaw pierwszej pomocy **3.** SPORT *Br* strój i sprzęt *m*; **kit out** *v/t* **1.** wyposażać ⟨-żyć⟩ (***with*** w *A*) **2.** zaopatrywać ⟨-trzeć⟩ (***with*** w *A*)
'kit bag *s Br* **1.** worek *m* żeglarski **2.** torba *f* (podróżna)
kitch•en ['kɪtʃɪn] **I** *s* kuchnia *f* **II** *adj* kuchenny; ***a ~ knife*** nóż kuchenny; ***~ foil*** folia spożywcza; ***a ~ garden*** ogródek warzywny; **kitch•en•ette** [kɪtʃɪ'net] *s* **1.** mała kuchnia *f* **2.** aneks *m* kuchenny, wnęka *f* kuchenna; **kitch•en 'sink** *s* zlewozmywak *m*, zlew *m* (kuchenny); ***everything but the ~*** wszystko, co się da
kite [kaɪt] *s* latawiec *m*; ***fly a ~*** puszczać latawca; ***go fly a ~!*** *infml* spadaj!
kit•ten ['kɪtn] *s* kocię *n*, kociak *m*; ***have ~s*** *infml* być całym w nerwach
kit•ty ['kɪtɪ] *s infml* kicia *f*, kiciuś *m*
ki•wi ['kiːwiː] *s* **1.** (*animal*) kiwi *m* (*fruit*) kiwi *n*
Klee•nex® ['kliːneks] *s* chusteczka *f* (higieniczna)
klep•to•ma•ni•a [kleptə'meɪnɪə] *s* kleptomania *f*; **klep•to•ma•ni•ac** [kleptə'meɪnɪæk] *s* kleptoman *m*
knack [næk] *s infml* **1.** talent *m*, dryg *m*; ***have the ~ for*** mieć dryg do *G* **2.** wprawa *f*; ***get the ~ of*** nabrać wprawy w *L*
knack•ered ['nækəd] *adj infml* wykończony
knap•sack ['næpsæk] *s* **1.** plecaczek *m* **2.** (mały) plecak *m*
knave [neɪv] *s* **1.** (*cards*) walet *m* **2.** *dated* niegodziwiec *m*
knead [niːd] *v/t* **1.** *dough*: zagniatać ⟨-nieść⟩ **2.** masować ⟨wy-⟩
knee [niː] *s* kolano *n*; ***on one's ~s*** na kolanach, klęcząc; ***bring s.o. to their ~s*** *fig* zmusić kogoś do uległości; ***go down on one's ~s*** paść na kolana; **'knee•cap** *s* rzepka *f*; **knee-'deep** *adj* po kolana; ***be ~*** sięgać po kolana;

K

knee-jerk re•'ac•tion *s* odruchowa reakcja *f*
kneel [ni:l] (*knelt/kneeled*; *knelt/kneeled*) *v/i* **1.** klęczeć **2.** klęknąć ⟨u-⟩
'knee-length *adj skirt*: do kolan
knelt [nelt] *Past Simple and Past Participle* → **kneel**
knew [nju:] *Past Simple* → ***know***
knick•ers ['nɪkəz] *pl* majtki *pl*, figi *pl*; ***get one's ~ in a twist*** *Br infml* wkurzyć się
knife [naɪf] **I** *pl knives s* **1.** nóż *m*; ***have one's ~ into s.o.*** *infml* zawziąć się na kogoś; ***go under the ~*** *infml* pójść pod nóż, poddać się operacji **2.** ostrze *n* **II** *v/t* **1.** sztyletować ⟨za-⟩ **2.** pchnąć nożem; **'knife-edge** *s*: ***on a ~*** *fig* **a)** na krawędzi **b)** niepewny; **'knife point** *s* czubek *m* noża; ***at ~*** z nożem na gardle
knight [naɪt] **I** *s* **1.** rycerz *m* **2.** (*chess*) koń *m*, skoczek *m* **II** *v/t Br* **1.** pasować na rycerza **2.** nadawać ⟨-dać⟩ tytuł szlachecki
knit [nɪt] (*knitted/knit*; *knitted/knit*) **I** *v/t* robić ⟨z-⟩ na drutach **II** *v/i* robić na drutach; **knit together I** *v/t* łączyć ⟨po-, z-⟩ **II** *v/i* zrastać ⟨zrosnąć⟩ się
knit•ting ['nɪtɪŋ] *s* **1.** robótka *f* **2.** robienie *n* na drutach; ***~ needles*** druty (do robótek)
knives [naɪvz] *pl* → ***knife***
knob [nɒb] *s* **1.** gałka *f* **2.** pokrętło *n*
knob•bly ['nɒblɪ] *adj knees*: kościsty
knock [nɒk] **I** *v/i* **1.** pukać ⟨za-⟩, stukać ⟨za-⟩ (***at/on*** do *G*); ***~ at the door*** pukać do drzwi; ***~ on wood*** *Am fig* odpukać w niemalowane drewno **2.** uderzać ⟨-rzyć⟩ (***against/into/on*** w *A*) **II** *v/t* uderzać ⟨-rzyć⟩; ***~ one's head against*** uderzyć głową o *A*; ***~ one's head against a brick wall*** walić głową w mur **III** *s* **1.** uderzenie *n* **2.** pukanie *n*; ***there was a ~ at*** (*a.* ***on***) ***the door*** rozległo się pukanie do drzwi; **knock around I** *v/i* **1.** poniewierać się, walać się **2.** zadawać się (***with*** z *I*) **3.** włóczyć się **II** *v/t infml* lać ⟨z-⟩, tłuc ⟨s-⟩; **knock down** *v/t* **1.** przewracać ⟨-rócić⟩ **2.** powalać ⟨-lić⟩ **3.** potrącać ⟨-cić⟩ **4.** *door*: wyważać ⟨-żyć⟩ **5.** burzyć ⟨z-⟩ **6.** *price*: zbijać ⟨-bić⟩; **knock off** *v/t* **1.** przewracać ⟨-rócić⟩ **2.** zrzucać ⟨-cić⟩ **3.** kończyć ⟨s-⟩; ***knock it off!*** przestań! **4.** obniżać ⟨-żyć⟩ cenę o *A*, spuszczać ⟨spuścić⟩ **5.** *infml* zwędzić, podprowadzić ⟨-dzić⟩; **knock out** *v/t* **1.** *tooth*: wybijać ⟨-bić⟩ **2.** nokautować ⟨z-⟩ **3.** ***the blow knocked her out*** uderzenie było tak silne, że straciła przytomność **4.** eliminować ⟨wy-⟩; ***he was knocked out in the first round*** odpadł w pierwszej rundzie **5.** *infml* zwalać ⟨-lić⟩ z nóg; **knock over** *v/t* **1.** przewracać ⟨-rócić⟩ **2.** potrącać ⟨-cić⟩; **knock together** *v/t* **1.** klecić ⟨s-⟩ **2.** pichcić ⟨u-⟩ **3.** zbijać ⟨-bić⟩ **4.** *Br* łączyć ⟨po-⟩; **knock up I** *v/t* **1.** klecić ⟨s-⟩ **2.** robić ⟨z-⟩ (naprędce) **3.** *Br infml* budzić ⟨o-⟩ (pukaniem do drzwi) **4.** ***knock s.o. up*** *infml* zrobić komuś dziecko **II** *v/i* (*tennis*) robić ⟨z-⟩ rozgrzewkę
knock•er ['nɒkə] *s* **1.** kołatka *f* **2.** ***~s*** *infml* cycki, balony
knock-kneed [nɒk'ni:d] *adj*: ***be ~*** mieć iksowate nogi; **knock-'knees** *pl* iksowate nogi *pl*; **'knock•out** *s* **1.** SPORT nokaut *m*; ***win by a ~*** wygrać przez nokaut **2.** ***be a ~*** *infml* być super, zwalać z nóg
knot [nɒt] **I** *s* **1.** węzeł *m*; ***tie a ~*** zawiązać węzeł; ***a ~ of hair*** (*hairstyle*) włosy upięte w węzeł **2.** supeł *m* **3.** sęk *m* **4.** *people*: grupka *f* **5.** problem *m* **II** *v/t* **1.** związywać ⟨-zać⟩ **2.** zawiązywać ⟨-zać⟩ **III** *v/i* napinać ⟨-piąć⟩ się; **knot•ty** ['nɒtɪ] *adj* **1.** *problem*: trudny, zawiły **2.** sękaty
know [nəʊ] **I** (*knew*; *known*) *v/t* **1.** wiedzieć; ***~ how to do s.th.*** wiedzieć, jak coś zrobić, umieć coś zrobić; – ***'Was anyone else there?'*** – ***'Not that I ~ of.'*** – „Czy był tam ktoś jeszcze?" – „O ile wiem, nie." **2.** znać **3.** umieć **4.** znać się na *L* **5.** zaznawać ⟨-nać⟩ **6.** rozpoznawać ⟨-nać⟩ **II** (*knew*; *known*) *v/i* wiedzieć; ***you never ~*** nigdy (nic) nie wiadomo; ***~ better than to do s.th.*** wiedzieć, że nie należy czegoś robić **III** *s* ***be in the ~*** być wtajemniczonym, wiedzieć; **'know-all** *s Br infml* mądrala *m*; **'know•how** *s infml* wiedza *f* specjalistyczna, know-how *m/n*
know•ing ['nəʊɪŋ] *adj* **1.** porozumiewawczy **2.** znaczący; **know•ing•ly** ['nəʊ-

ɪŋlɪ] *adv* **1.** porozumiewawczo **2.** znacząco **3.** świadomie **4.** rozmyślnie
'know-it-all *Am* → ***know-all***
knowl•edge ['nɒlɪdʒ] *s* **1.** wiedza *f*; ***it has come to my ~ that*** dowiedziałem się, że; doszło do mojej wiadomości, że; ***not to my ~*** o ile mi wiadomo, nie **2.** znajomość *f*; ***have a good ~ of*** dobrze znać *A*, posiadać dobrą znajomość *G*; **knowl•edge•a•ble** ['nɒlɪdʒəbl] *adj* **1.** znający się na rzeczy **2.** mądry **3.** wnikliwy
known [nəʊn] **I** *Past Participle* → **know** **II** *adj* znany; ***~ to the police*** znany policji; ***one of the best ~*** jeden z najbardziej znanych
knuck•le ['nʌkl] *s* **1.** knykieć *m* **2.** *infml* kostka *f* **3.** *COOK* nóżka *f* **4.** *COOK* golonka *f* **5.** ***near the ~*** *Br joke*: ciężki; **knuck•le down** *v/i infml* przysiąść fałdów; ***~ to work*** zabrać się na serio do pracy; **knuck•le under** *v/i infml* ustępować ⟨-tąpić⟩ (***to*** *D*), poddawać ⟨-dać⟩ się (***to*** *D*)
'kuck•le-dust•er *s* kastet *m*
KO [keɪ'əʊ] *abbr* (=***knock-out***) k.o., nokaut *m*
ko•a•la (bear) [kəʊ'ɑːlə(beə)] *s* koala *m*, niedźwiadek *m* koala
kohl [kəʊl] *s* (*make-up*) kohl *m*, proszek *m* antymonowy
kook [kuːk] *s Am infml* czub *m*, czubek *m*
Ko•ran [kɔː'rɑːn] *s* Koran *m*
Ko•re•a [kə'riːə] *s* Korea *f*; **Ko•re•an** [kə'riːən] **I** *adj* koreański **II** *s* Koreańczyk *m*, Koreanka *f*
kph [keɪpiː'eɪtʃ] *abbr* (=***kilometres per hour***) km/godz.
Krem•lin ['kremlɪn] *s* Kreml *m*
Ku•wait [kʊ'weɪt] *s* Kuwejt *m*

L

lab [læb] *s infml* laboratorium *n*
la•bel ['leɪbl] **I** *s* **1.** *a. fig* etykieta *f* **2.** nalepka *f* **3.** metka *f* **II** *v/t* **1.** opatrywać ⟨-rzyć⟩ etykietą **2.** etykietować **3.** oznakowywać ⟨-kować⟩ **4.** szufladkować ⟨za-⟩ **5.** nazywać ⟨-zwać⟩; ***he was ~led a criminal*** nazwano go przestępcą
la•bi•al ['leɪbɪəl] *s* głoska *f* wargowa
la•bor *Am* → ***labour***; **'La•bor Day** *s Am* święto *n* pracy (*pierwszy poniedziałek września*); **'la•bor un•ion** *s Am* związek *m* zawodowy
la•bor•a•to•ry [lə'bɒrətərɪ] **I** *s* laboratorium *n* **II** *adj* laboratoryjny; ***a ~ assistant*** laborant; **la•bor•a•to•ry tech'ni•cian** *s* technik-laborant *m*
la•bo•ri•ous [lə'bɔːrɪəs] *adj* **1.** ***be a ~ task*** wymagać dużego nakładu pracy **2.** mozolny **3.** ciężki
la•bo•ri•ous•ly [lə'bɔːrɪəslɪ] *adv* **1.** pracowicie **2.** z mozołem **3.** skrzętnie
la•bour ['leɪbə] *Br*, ***lab•or*** *Am* **I** *s* **1.** (ciężka) praca *f*; ***~s*** wysiłki **2.** robota *f* **3.** siła *f* robocza **4.** robocizna *f* **5.** ***L*** *Br POLIT* Partia Pracy **6.** *MED* poród *m*; ***be in ~*** rodzić **II** *v/i* **1.** (ciężko) pracować **2.** wysilać ⟨-lić⟩ się **3.** mozolić się **4.** przedzierać ⟨-drzeć⟩ się (***through*** przez *A*) **III** *v/t* ***~ the point*** wałkować temat **IV** *adj* **1.** pracowniczy **2.** związkowy **3.** ***the L Party*** *Br* Partia Pracy; **'la•bour camp** *Br*, ***'la•bor camp*** *Am s* obóz *m* pracy; **'la•bour mar•ket** *Br*, ***'la•bor mar•ket*** *Am s* rynek *m* pracy; **'la•bour ward** *Br*, ***'la•bor ward*** *Am s MED* sala *f* porodowa, *infml* porodówka *f*
la•bour•er ['leɪbərə] *s* pracownik *m* fizyczny, robotnik *m*
la•boured ['leɪbəd] *adj* **1.** ciężki **2.** mozolny **3.** *infml* wymęczony
lab•y•rinth ['læbərɪnθ] *s* labirynt *m*; **lab•y•rin•thine** [læbə'rɪnθaɪn] *adj* zawiły, pogmatwany
lace [leɪs] *s* **1.** koronka *f* **2.** sznurowadło *n*; **lace up** *v/t* sznurować ⟨za-⟩; **'lace-up** *adj*: *shoes*: sznurowany
lack [læk] **I** *s* **1.** brak *m*; ***~ of sleep*** brak snu; ***for ~ of time, through ~ of time*** z braku czasu **2.** niedostatek *m* **II** *v/t* nie mieć, cierpieć na brak; ***we ~ confidence*** brakuje nam pewności siebie **III** *v/i* brakować; ***he is ~ing in courage*** brakuje mu odwagi; ***he ~s for nothing*** niczego mu nie brak

L

lack•ing ['lækɪŋ] *adj*: ***be ~*** brakować; ***she is ~ in experience*** brakuje jej doświadczenia
lack•lus•tre ['læklʌstə] *Br*, ***lack•lus•ter*** *Am adj* nijaki, bez wyrazu
lad [læd] *s infml* **1.** chłopak *m* **2.** *Br* ***he's a bit of a ~*** niezły z niego numer
lad•der ['lædə] **I 1.** *s* drabina *f* **2.** (*stocking*) *Br* oczko *n* **II** *v/i* ***my stocking has ~ed*** poszło mi oczko w pończosze
la•den ['leɪdn] *adj* **1.** obładowany (***with*** *I*) **2.** załadowany (***with*** *I*) **3.** uginający się pod ciężarem (***with*** *G*) **4.** ***~ with guilt*** dręczony poczuciem winy
'la•dies' man *pl -men s* bawidamek *m*; **'la•dies' room** *s Am* damska toaleta *f*
la•dy ['leɪdɪ] **I** *s* **1.** pani; ***ladies and gentlemen!*** panie i panowie! **2.** (*noble title*) *Br* lady *f* **3.** ***Our ~*** *REL* Matka Boska **4.** ***the Ladies*** *Br* toaleta damska **II** *adj* ***a ~ doctor*** lekarka; **'la•dy•bird** *Br*, ***'la•dy•bug*** *Am s* biedronka *f*, boża krówka *f*; **la•dy-in-'wait•ing** *s* dama *f* dworu; **'la•dy-kill•er** *s infml* podrywacz *m*, pożeracz *m* niewieścich serc; **'la•dy•like** *adj* **1.** dystyngowany **2.** wytworny
lag [læg] **I** *v/i* **1.** (*a.* ***~ behind***) **1.** zostawać ⟨-tać⟩ w tyle (***za*** *I*) **2.** nie nadążać ⟨-żyć⟩ (***za*** *I*) **II** *s* **1.** odstęp *m* czasu **2.** opóźnienie *n*
la•ger ['lɑːgə] *s* piwo *n* jasne pełne
la•goon [lə'guːn] *s* laguna *f*
laid [leɪd] *Past Simple and Past Participle* → **lay**[1]
laid•'back *adj infml* **1.** wyluzowany **2.** niefrasobliwy
lain [leɪn] *Past Participle* → **lie**[2]
lair [leə] *s* **1.** legowisko *n* **2.** nora *f* **3.** gawra *f* **4.** *infml* kryjówka *f*
lake [leɪk] *s* jezioro *n*; ***~ Constance*** Jezioro Bodeńskie
lam [læm] *s*: ***be on the ~*** *infml Am* ukrywać się przed policją
lamb [læm] **I** *s* **1.** jagnię *n* **2.** baranek *m*; (***as***) ***meek as a ~*** łagodny jak baranek **3.** *COOK* jagnięcina *f* **II** *v/i* jagnić się; **lamb 'chop** *s* kotlet *m* jagnięcy; **'lamb•skin** *s* jagnięca skórka *f*; **'lambs•wool** *s* miękka owcza wełna *f*
lame [leɪm] *adj* **1.** *a. fig* kulejący **2.** utykający **3.** kulawy **4.** słaby; **lame 'duck** *s* nieudacznik *m*
la•ment [lə'ment] **I** *v/i* lamentować (***for***/***over*** nad *I*) **II** *v/t* **1.** opłakiwać **2.** lamentować nad *I* **III** *s* **1.** lamenty *pl* **2.** *MUS* pieśń *f* żałobna, lamentacja *f*; **lam•ent•a•ble** ['læməntəbl] *adj* opłakany, godny pożałowania; **lam•en•ta•tion** [læmen'teɪʃn] *s* lament *m*
lam•i•nate ['læmɪneɪt] **I** *s* laminat *m* **II** *v/t* laminować **lam•i•nat•ed** ['læmɪneɪtɪd] *adj* wielowarstwowy, laminowany; **lam•i•nat•ed 'glass** *s* szkło *n* warstwowe
lamp [læmp] *s* **1.** lampa *f* **2.** światło *n* **3.** światełko *n* **4.** latarnia *f*; **'lamp•light** *s* światło *n* lampy, światło *n* latarni; **'lamp•post** *s* słup *m* latarni; **'lamp•shade** *s* abażur *m*, klosz *m*
LAN [læn] *abbr* (=***local area network***) *INF* lokalna sieć *f* komputerowa
lance [lɑːns] **I** *s* kopia *f*, lanca *f* **II** *v/t* nacinać ⟨-ciąć⟩
land [lænd] **I** *s* **1.** ląd *m*; ***by ~*** lądem, drogą lądową; ***see how the ~ lies*** *fig* wybadać, co w trawie piszczy, wybadać sytuację **2.** ziemia *f* **3.** kraj *m* **4.** kraina *f* **5.** rola *f* **6.** teren *m* **II** *v/i* lądować ⟨wy-⟩ **III** *v/t* **1.** ***~ a plane*** wylądować, sprowadzić samolot na ziemię **2.** *passengers*: wysadzać ⟨-dzić⟩ **3.** ***~ oneself in trouble*** wpakować się w tarapaty **4.** ***he ~ed him one*** *infml* walnął go **5.** *infml job, role*: dostawać ⟨-tać⟩, załapywać ⟨-pać⟩; **land up in** *v/i infml* lądować ⟨wy-⟩ w *L* trafiać ⟨-fić⟩ do *G*; ***~ prison*** wylądować w więzieniu
land•ed ['lændɪd] *adj*: ***~ property*** własność ziemska
'land forc•es *pl* siły *pl* lądowe, wojska *pl* lądowe
land•ing ['lændɪŋ] *s* **1.** lądowanie *n* **2.** podest *m* (schodów); **'land•ing field** *s* lądowisko *n*; **'land•ing gear** *s* podwozie *n*; **'land•ing strip** *s* (prowizoryczny) pas *m* do lądowania
'land•la•dy *s* **1.** właścicielka *f* **2.** gospodyni *f*; **'land•locked** *adj* **1.** *country*: bez dostępu do morza **2.** *sea*: śródlądowy; **'land•lord** *s* **1.** właściciel *m* **2.** gospodarz *m*; **'land•lub•ber** *s dated* szczur *m* lądowy; **'land•mark** *s* **1.** charakterystyczny obiekt *m* **2.** punkt *m* orientacyjny **3.** *fig* kamień *m* milowy; **'land•mine** *s* mina *f* przeciwpie-

chotna; 'land own•er s właściciel m ziemski; land•scape s krajobraz m, pejzaż m; land•scape 'arch•i•tect s architekt m krajobrazu; land•scape 'gar•den•er s projektant m ogrodów; 'land•slide s 1. osuwisko n 2. a ~ victory walne zwycięstwo

lane [leın] s 1. (wąska) droga f 2. dróżka f 3. uliczka f 4. pas m (ruchu); change ~s zmieniać pasy 5. SPORT tor m 6. tor m wodny 7. korytarz m powietrzny

lan•guage ['læŋgwıdʒ] s język m; bad ~ wulgarne słownictwo, brzydkie słowa; 'lan•guage bar•ri•er s bariera f językowa; 'lan•guage course s kurs m językowy; 'lan•guage lab•o•ra•to•ry, 'lan•guage lab s laboratorium n językowe; 'lan•guage school s szkoła f języków obcych

lan•guish ['læŋgwıʃ] v/i 1. marnieć ⟨z-⟩ 2. fig gnić ⟨z-⟩ 3. podupadać ⟨-paść⟩ 4. usychać ⟨uschnąć⟩ z tęsknoty

lank [læŋk] adj: ~ hair cienkie, proste włosy; lank•y ['læŋkı] adj chudy, tyczkowaty

lan•tern ['læntən] s latarnia f

La•os ['lɑːɒs, 'laʊs] s Laos m

lap[1] [læp] s kolana pl; sit on s.o.'s ~ siedzieć u kogoś na kolanach; drop s.th. into s.o.'s ~ infml zwalić coś na czyjeś barki

lap[2] [~] I v/t 1. zachodzić na A 2. (runner) dublować ⟨z-⟩ II v/i zachodzić (over na A) III s SPORT okrążenie n; a ~ of honour runda honorowa

lap[3] [~] I v/t chłeptać ⟨wy-⟩ II v/i pluskać; lap up v/t 1. infml kupować ⟨-pić⟩, brać ⟨wziąć⟩ za dobrą monetę 2. chłeptać ⟨wy-⟩

lapse [læps] I s 1. chwila f słabości; a ~ in concentration chwila dekoncentracji, chwilowy brak koncentracji; a ~ in memory chwilowy zanik pamięci 2. potknięcie n 3. gafa f 4. upływ m; after a ~ of 2 years po dwóch latach, po upływie dwóch lat 5. okres m II v/i 1. (time) upływać ⟨-łynąć⟩, mijać ⟨minąć⟩ 2. ~ into silence zamilknąć 3. (contract) wygasać ⟨-snąć⟩

large [lɑːdʒ] I adj 1. duży; (as) ~ as life we własnej osobie; ~r than life a) nietuzinkowy b) przejaskrawiony 2. scope: szeroki II s 1. at ~ na wolności; set an animal at ~ wypuścić zwierzę na wolność 2. the nation at ~ cały naród; by and ~ infml ogólnie rzecz biorąc

large•ly ['lɑːdʒlı] adv w znacznym stopniu, w dużej mierze, wyraźnie; large•ness ['lɑːdʒnıs] s duże rozmiary pl, wielkość f

large-'scale adj 1. (zakrojony) na szeroką skalę; a ~ experiment zakrojony na szeroką skalę eksperyment 2. duży 3. w dużej skali

lark[1] [lɑːk] s skowronek m

lark[2] [~] s infml wygłup m; for a ~ dla hecy; lark about, lark around v/i Br infml wygłupiać się

la•ser ['leızə] s laser m; 'la•ser beam s promień m lasera, wiązka f laserowa; 'la•ser print•er s drukarka f laserowa; 'la•ser sur•ger•y s chirurgia f laserowa

lash [læʃ] I s 1. rzęsa f 2. bat m 3. smagnięcie n 4. (part of lash) rzemień m II v/t 1. chłostać ⟨wy-⟩ 2. smagać ⟨wy-⟩ 3. fig ostro atakować ⟨za-⟩ 4. chlastać ⟨-snąć⟩; ~ its tail chlastać ogonem 5. (mocno) przywiązywać ⟨-zać⟩ III v/i uderzać ⟨-rzyć⟩ (against o A); lash down v/i (rain) lać; lash out v/i 1. atakować ⟨za-⟩ (at A) 2. rzucać ⟨-cić⟩ się (at na A) 3. fig ostro atakować ⟨za-⟩ (at A)

last[1] [lɑːst] I adj 1. ostatni; ~ but one przedostatni; ~ night wczoraj w nocy, wczoraj wieczorem 2. zeszły, ubiegły; ~ Monday w zeszły poniedziałek II adv 1. ostatni; he came ~ on przyszedł ostatni; ~ but not least co nie mniej ważne, i wreszcie 2. na końcu 3. po raz ostatni 4. ~-mentioned ostatni z wymienionych III s 1. at ~ w końcu 2. ostatni m; she was the ~ to arrive ona przyjechała ostatnia 3. to the ~ do końca

last[2] [~] I v/i 1. trwać 2. utrzymywać ⟨-mać⟩ się 3. (a. ~ out) wystarczać ⟨-czyć⟩ 4. (a. ~ out) wytrzymywać ⟨-mać⟩ II v/t (a. ~ out) przetrzymywać ⟨-mać⟩, przetrwać

last•ing ['lɑːstıŋ] adj 1. trwały; ~ peace trwały pokój 2. impression, memory: niezatarty

L

last•ly ['lɑːstlɪ] *adv* na koniec, wreszcie

last-'min•ute *adj* **1.** *news*: z ostatniej chwili **2.** (zrobiony) w ostatniej chwili **3.** ostatni; **last 'name** *s* nazwisko *n*; **last 'rites** *pl* REL namaszczenie *n* chorych, ostatnie namaszczenie *n*; **last 'straw** *s* kropla, która przepełniła czarę (goryczy); ***that's the ~!*** tego już za wiele!

latch [lætʃ] **I** *s* **1.** zasuwa *f* **2.** zasuwka *f* **3.** zatrzask *m* **II** *v/t* zamykać ⟨-mknąć⟩ na zatrzask **III** *v/i* **~ *on*** *infml* załapać, skapować; **latch onto** *v/t* **1.** przyczepić się do *G* **2.** uczepić się *G* **3.** dorywać ⟨-rwać⟩ się do *G*

'latch key *s* klucz *m* (od drzwi wejściowych); ***a ~ child*** dziecko „z kluczem na szyi"

late [leɪt] **I** *adj* **1.** późny; ***~ summer*** późne lato; **2.** spóźniony; ***be ~*** spóźnić się **3.** opóźniony **4.** zmarły **II** *adv* **1.** późno; ***it's getting ~*** robi się późno; ***before it's too ~*** zanim będzie za późno; ***see you ~r*** na razie; ***as ~ as last year*** jeszcze w zeszłym roku **2.** z opóźnieniem; **late•com•er** ['leɪtkʌmə] *s* spóźniony *m*, *infml* spóźnialski *m*

L

late•ly ['leɪtlɪ] *adv* ostatnio; **late•ness** ['leɪtnɪs] *s* **1.** późna pora *f*; ***despite the ~ of the hour*** pomimo późnej pory **2.** spóźnienie *n* **3.** opóźnienie *n*

la•tent ['leɪtənt] *adj* ukryty

lat•er ['leɪtə] **I** *adv* później **II** *adj* późniejszy

lat•er•al ['lætərəl] *adj* **1.** boczny **2.** lateralny

lat•est ['leɪtɪst] **I** *adj* **1.** ostatni **2.** najnowszy; ***the ~ trends*** najnowsze trendy; ***the ~ fashion*** ostatni krzyk mody **3.** najświeższy **II** *s* ***at the ~*** najpóźniej

Lat•in ['lætɪn] **I** *adj* łaciński **II** *s* łacina *f*

Lat•in A•'mer•i•ca *s* Ameryka *f* Łacińska; **La•tin A•'mer•i•can I** *adj* latynoamerykański, latynoski **II** *s* Latynos *m*; **La•ti•no** [læ'tiːnəʊ] *s Am* Latynos *m*, Latynoska *f*

lat•i•tude ['lætɪtjuːd] *s* szerokość *f* geograficzna

lat•ter ['lætə] *adj form* **1.** drugi **2.** późniejszy; ***in the ~ half of June*** w drugiej połowa czerwca

Lat•vi•a ['lætvɪə] *s* Łotwa *f*; **Lat•vi•an** ['lætvɪən] **I** *adj* łotewski **II** *s* Łotysz *m*, Łotyszka *f*

laugh [lɑːf] **I** *s* śmiech *m*; ***have a good ~*** uśmiać się; ***have the last ~*** triumfować **II** *v/i* śmiać się; ***~ out loud*** roześmiać się głośno; **laugh at** *v/i* śmiać się z *G*, wyśmiewać *A*; **laugh off** *v/t* zbywać ⟨zbyć⟩ śmiechem

laugh•a•ble ['lɑːfəbl] *adj* śmieszny, śmiechu wart

'laugh•ing gas *s* gaz *m* rozweselający; **'laugh•ing stock** *s* pośmiewisko *n*

laugh•ter ['lɑːftə] *s* śmiech *m*

launch [lɔːntʃ] **I** *v/t* **1.** wystrzeliwać ⟨-lić⟩ **2.** wodować ⟨z-⟩ **3.** rozpoczynać ⟨-cząć⟩ **4.** wprowadzać ⟨-dzić⟩ na rynek **II** *v/i* ***~ into*** **a)** zacząć **b)** podjąć **III** *s* **1.** wodowanie *n* **2.** wystrzelenie *n* **3.** wprowadzenie *n* na rynek

'launch pad, ***'launch•ing pad*** *s* **1.** płyta *f* wyrzutni rakietowej **2.** *fig* odskocznia *f*; **'launch site** *s* baza *f* kosmiczna

laun•der ['lɔːndə] **I** *v/t* prać ⟨wy-, u-⟩; ***~ money*** prać brudne pieniądze **II** *v/i* prać ⟨wy-, u-⟩ się; **laun•der•ette** [lɔːn'dret] *s Br* pralnia *f* samoobsługowa; **laun•dro•mat** ['lɔːndrəmæt] *s Am* pralnia *f* samoobsługowa

laun•dry ['lɔːndrɪ] *s* **1.** pranie *n* **2.** (*a.* ***dirty ~***) brudne rzeczy *pl*, rzeczy *pl* do prania **3.** pralnia *f*; **'laun•dry bas•ket** *s* kosz *m* na brudną bieliznę

lau•rel ['lɒrəl] *s* **1.** wawrzyn *m*, drzewo *n* laurowe **2.** wieniec *m* laurowy **3.** ***rest on one's ~s*** spocząć na laurach

lav•a•to•ry ['lævətərɪ] *s* toaleta *f*, ubikacja *f*; **'lav•a•to•ry attendant** *s* osoba *f* obsługująca toaletę, *infml* babcia *f* klozetowa; **'lav•a•to•ry paper** *s* papier *m* toaletowy

lav•en•der ['lævəndə] *s* lawenda *f*

lav•ish ['lævɪʃ] **I** *adj* **1.** *party*, *lifestyle*: wystawny **2.** imponujący **3.** pełen przepychu **4.** ekstrawagancki **5.** ***be ~ in one's praise for* s.o.** nie szczędzić komuś pochwał **II** *v/t* ***~ praise on* s.o.** nie szczędzić komuś pochwał; ***~* s.o. *with gifts*** obsypać kogoś prezentami

law [lɔː] *s* **1.** prawo *n*; ***be against the ~*** być niezgodnym z prawem; ***under Polish ~*** zgodnie z polskim prawem; ***~ and order*** prawo i porządek; ***study***

~, *read* ~ studiować prawo **2.** przepis *m* **3.** ustawa *f*, prawo *n* **4.** wymiar *m* sprawiedliwości; ***go to*** ~ pójść do sądu **5.** ***the*** ~ policja *f* **6.** zasada *f*; **'law-a•bid•ing** *adj* przestrzegający prawa, praworządny; **'law•break•er** *s* osoba *f* łamiąca prawo; **'law court** *s* sąd *m*

law•ful ['lɔːfəl] *adj* **1.** legalny, zgodny z prawem **2.** prawowity; **law•less** ['lɔːlɪs] *adj* **1.** bezprawny **2.** nieprzestrzegający prawa **3.** awanturniczy

lawn [lɔːn] *s* trawnik *m*; **'lawn chair** *s* krzesło *n* ogrodowe; **'lawn mow•er** *s* kosiarka *f* do trawy

'law•suit *s* JUR proces *m*, sprawa *f*

law•yer ['lɔːjə] *s* **1.** prawnik *m* **2.** adwokat *m*

lay¹ [leɪ] **I** (*laid*; *laid*) *v/t* **1.** kłaść ⟨położyć⟩ **2.** *eggs*: znosić ⟨znieść⟩ **3.** ~ ***the table*** nakryć stół **4.** rozkładać ⟨-złożyć⟩ **5.** układać ⟨ułożyć⟩ **6.** ustawiać ⟨-wić⟩ **7.** *complaint*, *guilt*: składać ⟨złożyć⟩ **8.** *money*: stawiać ⟨postawić⟩ **9.** *plans*: snuć **II** (*laid*; *laid*) *v/i* (*hen*) znosić ⟨znieść⟩ jajka, nieść się; **lay into** *v/i infml* zjechać; **lay off I** *v/t* **1.** *employee*: zwalniać ⟨zwolnić⟩ **2.** ~ ***fatty foods*** przestać jeść tłuste potrawy **II** *v/i* przestawać ⟨-tać⟩; **lay on** *v/t* zapewniać ⟨-nić⟩; **lay out** *v/t* **1.** wykładać ⟨wyłożyć⟩ **2.** rozkładać ⟨-złożyć⟩ **3.** rozplanowywać ⟨-nować⟩ **4.** projektować ⟨za-⟩ **5.** przedstawiać ⟨-wić⟩ **6.** *infml fortune*: wydawać ⟨-dać⟩ **7.** powalać ⟨-lić⟩

lay² [~] *Past Simple* → **lie²**

lay³ [~] *adj* świecki

'lay•a•bout *s Br infml* nierób *m*, obibok *m*

lay•er ['leɪə] **I** *s* **1.** warstwa *f*; ***in*** ~***s*** warstwami **2.** nioska *f* **II** *v/t* układać ⟨ułożyć⟩ warstwami

lay•ette [leɪ'et] *s* wyprawka *f* (dla noworodka)

'lay•man *s* **1.** laik *m* **2.** REL świecki *m*

'lay-off *s* **1.** zwolnienie *n* z pracy **2.** przymusowy urlop *m* bezpłatny

'lay•out *s* **1.** plan *m* **2.** rozkład *m* **3.** rozmieszczenie *n* **4.** układ *m* (strony) **5.** opracowanie *n* graficzne

'lay•o•ver *s Am* przerwa *f* w podróży

laze [leɪz] *v/i* leniuchować; **laze around** *v/i* leniuchować; **laze away** *v/t* przeleniuchować; **la•zi•ness** ['leɪzɪnɪs] *s* lenistwo *n*; **la•zy** ['leɪzɪ] *adj* **1.** leniwy **2.** senny **3.** niedbały; **'la•zy•bones** *s infml* leniuch *m*

lb *abbr* (=***pound***) funt *m* (*jednostka masy*)

lead¹ [led] **I** *s* **1.** ołów *m* **2.** grafit *m* **3.** ***pump s.o. full of*** ~ *infml* podziurawić kogoś jak sito **II** *adj* ołowiany

lead² [liːd] **I** (*led*; *led*) *v/t* **1.** prowadzić ⟨za-, po-, do-⟩ **2.** ~ ***the way*** **a)** wskazywać drogę **b)** *fig* przodować, wieść prym **3.** kierować ⟨po-⟩ **4.** iść na czele **II** (*led*; *led*) *v/i* **1.** prowadzić **2.** wieść ⟨za-⟩ **3.** być na czele **III** *s* **1.** prowadzenie *n*; ***be in the*** ~ prowadzić; ***take the*** ~ objąć prowadzenie; ***under s.o.'s*** ~ pod czyimś kierownictwem **2.** przewaga *f* (***over*** nad *I*) **3.** ***follow s.o.'s*** ~ iść za czyimś przykładem **3.** trop *m* **4.** wskazówka *f* **5.** główna rola *f* **6.** odtwórca *m* głównej roli **7.** smycz *f*; ***keep a dog on a*** ~ trzymać psa na smyczy **IV** *adj* **1.** wiodący **2.** *role*: główny **3.** prowadzący; ~ ***guitar*** gitara prowadząca; **lead on** *v/t* **1.** zwodzić ⟨zwieść⟩ **2.** podpuszczać ⟨-puścić⟩ **3.** mamić ⟨o-⟩; **lead up to** *v/i* **1.** poprzedzać ⟨-dzić⟩ **2.** doprowadzać ⟨-dzić⟩ do *G* **3.** zmierzać do *G*

lead•ed ['ledɪd] *adj* ołowiowy; **lead•en** ['ledn] *adj* **1.** *sky*: ołowiany **2.** *steps*: ciężki

lead•er ['liːdə] *s* **1.** lider *m* **2.** przywódca *m* **3.** szef *m* **4.** SPORT lider *m*, prowadzący *m* **5.** MUS *Br* pierwszy skrzypek *m* **6.** *Br* artykuł *m* wstępny, *infml* wstępniak *m*

lead•er•ship ['liːdəʃɪp] *s* **1.** kierownictwo *n* **2.** przywództwo *n*; ~ ***qualities*** zdolności przywódcze **3.** władze *pl*; **'lead•er•ship con•test** *s* wybory *pl* do władz partyjnych

lead-free ['ledfriː] *adj* bezołowiowy

lead•ing ['liːdɪŋ] *adj* **1.** czołowy **2.** wybitny **3.** główny **4.** (*race*) prowadzący; **lead•ing 'ar•ti•cle** *s* artykuł *m* wstępny; **lead•ing 'edge** *s*: ***at the*** ~ ***of world science*** w czołówce światowej nauki; **lead•ing-'edge** *adj technology*: najnowszy; **lead•ing 'la•dy** *s* odtwórczyni *f* głównej roli; **'lead•ing light** *s fig* czołowa postać *f*; **'lead•ing man** *pl -men s* odtwórca *m* głównej roli; **lead•ing 'ques•tion** *s* pytanie *n* sugerujące odpowiedź

leaf [li:f] *pl leaves* [li:vz] *s* **1.** liść *m*; ***come into ~*** wypuszczać liście **2.** kartka *f*; ***take a ~ out of s.o.'s book*** wziąć przykład z kogoś, pójść w czyjeś ślady; ***turn over a new ~*** poprawić się **3.** (*door*) skrzydło *n* **4. *pull out the leaves*** rozsunąć stół; **leaf through** *v/i* kartkować ⟨prze-⟩

leaf•let ['li:flət] *s* ulotka *f*; **leaf•y** ['li:fɪ] *adj* **1.** *tree*: bujny **2.** *suburb*: pełen zieleni **3.** *vegetables*: liściasty

league [li:g] *s* **1.** liga *f*; ***a ~ game*** mecz ligowy; ***she's out of my ~*** nie mam u niej szans; ***he's not in the same ~ as me*** nie może się ze mną równać **2. *be in ~ with*** być w zmowie z *I*, mieć konszachty z *I*

leak [li:k] **I** *s* **1.** szczelina *f* **2.** dziura *f* **3.** wyciek *m* **4.** przeciek *m* **II** *v/i* **1.** przeciekać ⟨-ciec⟩ **2.** być nieszczelnym **3.** wyciekać ⟨-ciec⟩ **4.** ulatniać ⟨ulotnić⟩ się **III** *v/t* ujawniać ⟨-nić⟩; **leak out** *v/i* wychodzić ⟨wyjść⟩ na jaw

leak•age ['li:kɪdʒ] *s* **1.** wyciek *m* **2.** przeciek *m* **3.** ulatnianie *n* się **4.** *information*: przeciek *m*, przecieki *pl*; **leak•y** ['li:kɪ] *adj* **1.** przeciekający **2.** cieknący **3.** nieszczelny

lean[1] [li:n] **I** *v/i* (*leaned/leant*; *leaned/leant*) **1.** przechylać ⟨-lić⟩ się **2.** opierać ⟨oprzeć⟩ się (***on/against*** o *A*) **3.** nachylać ⟨-lić⟩ się (***over*** nad *I*); ***~ back*** odchylić się; ***~ forward*** pochylić się do przodu; ***~ over backwards*** *fig* stawać na głowie **4. *~ to(wards)*** *fig* skłaniać się ku *D* **II** *v/t* (*leaned/leant*; *leaned/leant*) opierać ⟨oprzeć⟩ (***s.th. on/against*** coś o *A*) **III** *s* nachylenie *n*

lean[2] [~] **I** *adj* **1.** szczupły **2.** smukły **3.** *years*: chudy **II** *s* chude mięso *n*

lean•ing ['li:nɪŋ] **I** *adj* pochyły **II** *s* skłonność *f*, tendencja *f*

leant [lent] *Past Simple and Past Participle* → ***lean***

leap [li:p] **I** *v/i* (*leaped/leapt*; *leaped/leapt*) **1.** skakać ⟨skoczyć⟩; ***~ up*** podskoczyć; ***~ for joy*** podskoczyć z radości **2. *~ at a chance*** skwapliwie skorzystać z okazji; ***~ out at s.o.*** *fig* rzucić się komuś w oczy **II** *v/t* (*leaped/leapt*; *leaped/leapt*) przeskakiwać ⟨-skoczyć⟩ **III** *s* **1.** skok *m* **2.** sus *m*; ***take a ~*** dać susa; ***by/in ~s and bounds*** **a)** w szybkim tempie **b)** gwałtownie; **'leap•frog I** *s* skakanie *n* przez plecy **II** *v/i fig* przeskakiwać ⟨-skoczyć⟩ (***over*** przez *A*)

leapt [lept] *Past Simple and Past Participle* → ***leap***

'leap year *s* rok *m* przestępny

learn [lɜ:n] **I** *v/t* (*learned/learnt*; *learned/learnt*) **1.** uczyć ⟨na-⟩ się; ***~ (how) to swim*** nauczyć się pływać **2.** dowiadywać ⟨-wiedzieć⟩ się (***about/of*** o *L*); ***how did she react when she ~ed the news?*** jak zareagowała, gdy się o tym dowiedziała? **II** *v/i* (*learned/learnt*; *learned/learnt*) **1.** uczyć ⟨na-⟩ się **2.** dowiadywać ⟨-wiedzieć⟩ się; **learn•ed** ['lɜ:nɪd] *adj* **1.** uczony **2.** wyuczony; **learn•er** ['lɜ:nə] *s* uczący się *m*; ***be a fast (slow) ~*** uczyć się szybko (wolno)

learn•ing ['lɜ:nɪŋ] *s* **1.** nauka *f* **2.** uczenie *n* się **3.** wiedza *f*; **'learn•ing curve** *s* krzywa *f* uczenia się; **'learn•ing dif•fi•cul•ties** *pl* trudności *pl* w nauce

lease [li:s] **I** *s* **1.** najem *m*; ***take a ~ on*** wynająć *A* **2.** dzierżawa *f* **3.** okres *m* najmu **4.** okres *m* dzierżawy **II** *v/t* **1.** wynajmować ⟨-jąć⟩ **2.** dzierżawić ⟨wy-⟩; **lease out** *v/t* **1.** wynajmować ⟨-jąć⟩ **2.** dzierżawić ⟨wy-⟩

'lease•hold•er *s* **1.** najemca *f* **2.** dzierżawca *m*

leash [li:ʃ] *s* smycz *f*; ***keep a dog on a ~*** trzymać psa na smyczy

least [li:st] **I** *s* ***at (the) ~*** co najmniej; ***she wasn't worried in the ~*** wcale się nie martwiła; ***to say the ~*** delikatnie mówiąc **II** *adv* ***the ~*** najmniej; ***~ of all*** najmniej (ze wszystkich) **III** *adj* najmniejszy; ***the ~ amount*** najmniejsza ilość; ***have the ~ experience*** mieć najmniejsze doświadczenie

leath•er ['leðə] *s* skóra *f*; ***a ~ jacket*** skórzana kurtka; **leath•er•y** ['leðərɪ] *adj* **1.** twardy i szorstki **2.** łykowaty

leave [li:v] **I** (*left*; *left*) *v/t* **1.** wychodzić ⟨wyjść⟩ z *G* **2.** wyjeżdżać ⟨-jechać⟩ z *G* **3.** zostawiać ⟨-wić⟩; ***~ s.o. alone*** zostawić kogoś w spokoju; ***~ s.o. to himself*** zostawić kogoś samemu sobie; ***be left*** zostać **4.** porzucać

L

⟨-cić⟩; ***she left him for another man*** porzuciła go dla innego mężczyzny **5.** opuszczać ⟨opuścić⟩ **6.** odkładać ⟨odłożyć⟩ **7.** zostawiać ⟨-wić⟩ w spadku **8.** (*after death*) pozostawiać ⟨-wić⟩ **II** (*left*; *left*) *v/i* **1.** wychodzić ⟨wyjść⟩ **2.** wyjeżdżać ⟨-jechać⟩ **3.** wyruszać ⟨-szyć⟩ **4.** odchodzić ⟨odejść⟩; **leave behind** *v/t* **1.** zostawiać ⟨-wić⟩ w tyle **2.** porzucać ⟨-cić⟩ **3.** zostawiać ⟨-wić⟩ za sobą **4.** zostawiać ⟨-wić⟩, nie brać ⟨wziąć⟩; **leave on** *v/t* **1.** zostawiać ⟨-wić⟩ włączony **2.** nie zdejmować ⟨zdjąć⟩ **3.** zostawiać ⟨-wić⟩; **leave out** *v/t* **1.** pomijać ⟨-minąć⟩ **2.** opuszczać ⟨opuścić⟩ **3.** nie dodawać ⟨-dać⟩ **4.** ***leave me out of this!*** nie mieszaj mnie w to!

leaves [liːvz] *pl* → ***leaf***

'leav•ing par•ty *s* pożegnalne przyjęcie *n*

Leb•a•non ['lebənən] *s* Liban *m*

lech•er ['letʃə] *s* rozpustnik *m*, *infml* zbereźnik *m*; **lech•er•ous** ['letʃərəs] *adj* lubieżny

lec•tern ['lektən] *s* **1.** katedra *f* **2.** pulpit *m* **2.** mównica *f*

lec•ture ['lektʃə] **I** *s* **1.** wykład *m*; ***give a ~*** wygłosić wykład; ***give s.o. a ~*** *fig* zrobić komuś wykład **2.** odczyt *m* **II** *v/i* wykładać (***in*** *A*) **III** *v/t* pouczać ⟨-czyć⟩; **'lec•ture hall** *s* sala *f* wykładowa, aula *f*; **'lec•tur•er** ['lektʃərə] *s* **1.** wykładowca *m* **2.** prelegent *m*

led [led] *Past Simple and Past Participle* → ***lead***[2]

leech [liːtʃ] *s a. fig* pijawka *f*

leek [liːk] *s* por *m*

leer [lɪə] **I** *s* **1.** lubieżne spojrzenie *n*; ***look at s.o. with a ~*** spojrzeć na kogoś lubieżnym wzrokiem **2.** lubieżny uśmieszek *m* **II** *v/i* **1.** spoglądać ⟨spojrzeć⟩ lubieżnym wzrokiem (**at** na *A*) **2.** lubieżnie się uśmiechać ⟨-chnąć⟩ (**at** do *G*)

left[1] [left] *Past Simple and Past Participle* → ***leave***

left[2] [~] **I** *adj* lewy **II** *s* **1.** ***the ~*** lewa strona; ***on the ~*** po lewej (stronie); ***to the ~ of*** na lewo od *G*, po lewej stronie *G*; ***twist one's body to the ~*** wykonać skręt w lewo; ***take the second turn on the ~*** skręcić w drugą przecznicę w lewo; ***on our ~*** po naszej lewej stronie; ***keep to the ~*** trzymać się lewej strony **2.** ***the ~*** lewica **III** *adv* **1.** w lewo; ***turn ~*** skręcić w lewo **2.** na lewo; **'left-hand** *adj* **1.** lewy **2.** leworęczny; **left-hand 'drive** *s* lewostronny układ *n* kierowniczy; **left-'hand•ed** *adj* **1.** leworęczny **2.** dla leworęcznych

left•ist ['leftɪst] *adj* lewicowy

left 'lug•gage (of•fice) *s Br* przechowalnia *f* bagażu

'left-o•vers *pl* resztki *pl*

'left-wing *adj* lewicowy; **left-'wing•er** *s* **1.** działacz *m* lewicy **2.** lewicowiec *m* **3.** SPORT lewoskrzydłowy *m*

leg [leg] **I** *s* **1.** noga *f*; ***stretch one's ~s*** rozprostować nogi; ***pull s.o.'s ~*** *fig* nabierać kogoś; ***be on one's last ~s*** **a)** być jedną nogą w grobie **b)** być na ostatnich nogach; ***give s.o. a ~ up*** **a)** podsadzić kogoś **b)** pomóc komuś **2.** łapa *f* **3.** nogawka *f* **4.** udziec *m*; ***a ~ of mutton*** udziec barani **5.** udko *n* **6.** nóżka *f* **7.** etap *m* **8.** mecz *m* **II** *v/i* ***~ it*** *infml* zwiać, dać nogę

leg•a•cy ['legəsɪ] *s* **1.** JUR spadek *m* **2.** dziedzictwo *n* **3.** spuścizna *f*

le•gal ['liːgl] *adj* **1.** prawny; ***~ aid*** pomoc prawna **2.** legalny **3.** prawniczy **4.** sądowy; ***~ proceedings*** postępowanie sądowe; ***take ~ action against s.o.*** wystąpić na drogę sądową przeciwko komuś **5.** ustawowy; ***a ~ holiday*** dzień ustawowo wolny od pracy; **le•gal ad•'vis•er** *s* doradca *m* prawny; **le•gal•i•ty** [lɪ'gælətɪ] *s* **1.** zgodność *f* z prawem **2.** legalność *f*; **le•gal•i•za•tion** [liːgəlaɪ'zeɪʃn] *s* legalizacja *f*; **le•gal•ize** ['liːgəlaɪz] *v/t* legalizować ⟨za-⟩; **le•gal•ly** ['liːgəlɪ] *adv* **1.** zgodnie z prawem **2.** legalnie

le•ga•tion [lɪ'geɪʃn] *s* poselstwo *n*

le•gend ['ledʒənd] *s* legenda *f*; **le•gen•da•ry** ['ledʒəndərɪ] *adj* legendarny

leg•gy ['legɪ] *adj* długonogi

le•gi•ble ['ledʒəbl] *adj* czytelny

le•gion ['liːdʒən] *s* legion *m*; **le•gion•ar•y** ['liːdʒənərɪ] *s* legionista *m*

le•gis•late ['ledʒɪsleɪt] *v/i* ***~ on*** (***aginst***) ***s.th.*** **a)** wprowadzać ⟨-dzić⟩ przepisy dotyczące (zakazujące) czegoś **b)** uchwalać ⟨-lić⟩ ustawę dotyczącą (zakazującą) czegoś; **le•gis•la•tion** [ledʒɪs'leɪʃn] *s* ustawodawstwo *n*; **le•gis•la•tive** ['ledʒɪslətɪv] *adj* ustawo-

L

dawczy; ***a ~ body*** ciało ustawodawcze; ***~ power*** władza ustawodawcza; **leg•is•la•tor** ['ledʒɪsleɪtə] *s* ustawodawca *m*; **le•gis•la•ture** ['ledʒɪslətʃə] *s* zgromadzenie *n* ustawodawcze
le•git•i•ma•cy [lɪ'dʒɪtɪməsɪ] *s* **1.** zgodność *f* z prawem **2.** legalność *f* **3.** prawowitość *f* **4.** zasadność *f*; **le•git•i•mate** [lɪ'dʒɪtɪmət] *adj* **1.** legalny **2.** uzasadniony **3.** zasadny **4.** prawowity; **le•git•i•mize** [lɪ'dʒɪtəmaɪz] *v/t* **1.** legalizować ⟨za-⟩ **2.** sankcjonować ⟨u-⟩ **3.** usprawiedliwiać ⟨-wić⟩ **4.** zatwierdzać ⟨-dzić⟩ **5.** uznawać ⟨-nać⟩
'leg room *s* miejsce *n* na nogi
'leg warm•ers *pl* getry *pl*
lei•sure ['leʒə] **I** *s* **1.** czas *m* wolny; ***at your ~*** *form* **a)** w wolnej chwili **b)** kiedy panu pasuje; ***at ~*** bez pośpiechu **2.** wypoczynek *m* **II** *adj* **1.** wolny; ***~ hours*** godziny wolne od pracy **2.** rekreacyjny; ***~ activities*** sport i rozrywki; ***a ~ centre*** centrum sportu i rozrywki; ***~ facilities*** baza rekreacyjna; ***a ~ occupation*** hobby; **lei•sure•ly** ['leʒəlɪ] **I** *adj* nieśpieszny **II** *adv* bez pośpiechu; **'lei•sure time** *s* czas *m* wolny
le•mon ['lemən] **I** *s* **1.** cytryna *f* **2.** *Br* głupek *m* **II** *adj* cytrynowy; **le•mon•ade** [lemə'neɪd] *s* lemoniada *f*; **'le•mon juice** *s* sok *m* cytrynowy, sok *m* z cytryny; **le•mon 'tea** *s* **1.** herbata *f* cytrynowa **2.** herbata *f* z cytryną
lend [lend] (*lent*; *lent*) *v/t* **1.** pożyczać ⟨-czyć⟩ **2.** nadawać ⟨-dać⟩; ***~ itself to*** nadawać się do *G* **3.** przydawać ⟨-dać⟩ **4.** *support*: udzielać ⟨-lić⟩; **lend•er** ['lendə] *s* **1.** kredytodawca *m* **2.** pożyczkodawca *m*; **'lend•ing li•bra•ry** *s* wypożyczalnia *f* książek
length [leŋθ] *s* **1.** długość *f*; ***be two feet in ~*** mieć dwie stopy długości; ***what ~ is the trailer?*** jakiej długości jest przyczepa?; ***go to great ~s*** zadać sobie wiele trudu; ***at ~*** **a)** obszernie **b)** długo **c)** szczegółowo **2.** kawałek *m* **3.** odcinek *m*
length•en ['leŋθən] **I** *v/t* **1.** wydłużać ⟨-żyć⟩ **2.** przedłużać ⟨-żyć⟩ **II** *v/i* **1.** wydłużać ⟨-żyć⟩ się **2.** przedłużać ⟨-żyć⟩ się; **length•ways** ['leŋθweɪz], ***length•wise*** ['leŋθwaɪz] *adv Br* wzdłuż; **length•y** ['leŋθɪ] *adj* **1.** przydługi **2.** bardzo długi **3.** rozwlekły
lens [lenz] *s* **1.** soczewka *f* **2.** (*glasses*) szkło *n* **3.** obiektyw *m*
lent [lent] *Past Simple and Past Participle* → ***lend***
Lent [lent] *s* Wielki Post *m*
len•til ['lentl] *s* soczewica *f*; **len•til 'soup** *s* zupa *f* z soczewicy
Le•o ['liːəʊ] *s* ASTR Lew *m*
leop•ard ['lepəd] *s* lampart *m*, pantera *f*
lep•er ['lepə] *s* trędowaty *m*; **lep•ro•sy** ['leprəsɪ] *s* trąd *m*
les•bi•an ['lezbɪən] **I** *s* lesbijka *f* **II** *adj* lesbijski
le•sion ['liːʒn] *s* **1.** uszkodzenie *n* **2.** rana *f* **3.** zmiana *f* patologiczna
less [les] **I** *adv* mniej; ***~ and ~*** coraz mniej; ***~ often*** rzadziej **II** *adj* ***in ~ time*** szybciej, w krótszym czasie **III** *pron* ***no ~ than*** aż; ***it was nothing ~ than a miracle*** to był po prostu cud **IV** *prep* minus
les•see [le'siː] *s* JUR najemca *m*
les•sen ['lesn] **I** *v/i* **1.** zmniejszać ⟨-szyć⟩ się **2.** cichnąć ⟨przy-⟩ **3.** słabnąć ⟨o-⟩ **II** *v/t* **1.** zmniejszać ⟨-szyć⟩ **2.** osłabiać ⟨-bić⟩ **3.** łagodzić ⟨z-⟩
less•er ['lesə] *adj* **1.** mniejszy; ***of ~ importance*** mniej ważny **2.** pomniejszy; **less•er-'known** *adj* mniej znany
les•son ['lesn] *s* **1.** lekcja *f*; ***give piano ~s*** udzielać lekcji gry na fortepianie **2.** *fig* nauczka *f*; ***this was a ~ to me*** to była dla mnie nauczka
les•sor [le'sɔː] *s* JUR wynajmujący *m*
lest [lest] *conj form* **1.** żeby nie; ***he ran away ~ he should be seen*** uciekł, aby nikt go nie zobaczył **2.** na wypadek, gdyby
let[1] [let] *s* SPORT net *m*
let[2] [~] **I** (*let*; *let*) *v/t* **1.** pozwalać ⟨-wolić⟩; ***~ s.o. go*** puścić kogoś; ***~ oneself go*** **a)** rozluźnić się, *infml* wyluzować się **b)** przestać o siebie dbać; ***~ s.o. know*** dać komuś znać **2.** ***~'s go*** chodźmy **3.** ***~ s.o. alone*** zostawić kogoś w spokoju **4.** *Br* wynajmować ⟨-jąć⟩; ***'to ~'*** „do wynajęcia" **II** (*let*; *let*) *v/i* ***~ go of*** puścić *A*; **let down** *v/t* zawodzić ⟨-wieść⟩; **let in** *v/t* **1.** wpuszczać ⟨wpuścić⟩ **2.** *infml* wtajemniczać ⟨-czyć⟩ (***on*** w *A*); ***let s.o. in***

L

on a secret zdradzić komuś sekret **3.** ***let oneself in for*** *infml* wpakować się w *A*; **let into** *v/i infml* wtajemniczać ⟨-czyć⟩ w *A*; ***let s.o. into a secret*** zdradzić komuś sekret; **let off** *v/t* **1.** *fireworks*: puszczać ⟨puścić⟩, odpalać ⟨-lić⟩ **2.** ***let s.o. off*** (***lightly***) potraktować kogoś łagodnie **3.** zwalniać ⟨zwolnić⟩ z *G*; **let out** *v/t* **1.** wypuszczać ⟨-puścić⟩ **2.** spuszczać ⟨spuścić⟩; ***let the air out of*** spuścić powietrze z *G* **3.** *scream*: wydawać ⟨-dać⟩ **4.** *skirt*: poszerzać ⟨-rzyć⟩ **5.** *Br* wynajmować ⟨-jąć⟩; **let up** *v/i* **1.** ustawać ⟨-tać⟩ **2.** słabnąć ⟨o-⟩ **3.** milknąć ⟨u-, za-⟩

'let•down *s* rozczarowanie *n*, zawód *m*

le•thal ['li:θl] *adj* śmiertelny, śmiercionośny

leth•ar•gic [lɪ'θɑ:dʒɪk] *adj* **1.** apatyczny **2.** ospały; **leth•ar•gy** ['leθədʒɪ] *s* letarg *m*

let's [lets] *contracted form* → ***let us***

let•ter ['letə] **I** *s* **1.** litera *f*; ***to the ~*** co do joty **2.** list *m*; ***by ~*** listownie; ***a ~ of application*** podanie; ***a ~ of complaint*** pisemna skarga; ***a ~ to the editor*** list do redakcji **II** *v/t* ***~ed in green*** z zielonymi literami; **'let•ter bomb** *s* przesyłka *f* z materiałem wybuchowym; **'let•ter•box** *s* skrzynka *f* na listy; **let•ter 'car•ri•er** *s* listonosz *m*; **'let•ter•head** *s* nagłówek *m* (na papierze firmowym); **let•ter of 'cred•it** *s* FIN akredytywa *f*; **let•ter 'o•pen•er** *s* nóż *m* do papieru

let•tuce ['letɪs] *s* sałata *f*

'let•up *s*: ***there was no sign of a ~ in attacks*** ataki nie ustawały

leu•k(a)e•mi•a [lu:'ki:mɪə] *s* białaczka *f*

leu•ko•cyte ['lu:kəsaɪt] *s* leukocyt *m*

lev•el ['levl] **I** *s* **1.** poziom *m*; ***below ground ~*** pod ziemią **2.** szczebel *m*; ***at government ~*** na szczeblu rządowym **3.** wysokość *f*; ***be on a ~*** **a)** być tej samej wysokości **b)** być na tej samej wysokości **4.** *fig* płaszczyzna *f* **5.** TECH poziomica *f* **II** *adj* **1.** poziomy **2.** równy; ***draw ~ with*** zrównać się z *I*, dogonić *A*; ***our team drew ~*** nasza drużyna wyrównała **3.** płaski; ***a ~ teaspoon*** płaska łyżeczka **4.** ***a ~ crossing*** przejazd kolejowy **5.** ***do one's ~ best*** dokładać wszelkich starań **6.** ***keep a ~ head*** nie tracić głowy **III** *v/t* **1.** wyrównywać ⟨-nać⟩ **2.** ***~ s.th.*** (***to the ground***) zrównać coś z ziemią

lev•el-'head•ed *adj* rozsądny, trzeźwo myślący

le•ver ['li:və] **I** *s* **1.** dźwignia *f* **2.** *fig* środek *m* nacisku **II** *v/t* **1.** podważać ⟨-żyć⟩ **2.** ***~ a door open with a crowbar*** wyważyć drzwi łomem; **lev•er•age** ['li:vrɪdʒ] *s* **1.** wpływy *pl* **2.** FIN dźwignia *f* finansowa

lev•y ['levɪ] **I** *s* podatek *m* **II** *v/t* **1.** *tax, payment*: nakładać ⟨nałożyć⟩ **2.** *payment*: pobierać ⟨-brać⟩

lex•i•cog•ra•pher [leksɪ'kɒgrəfə] *s* leksykograf *m*; **lex•i•cog•ra•phy** [leksɪ'kɒgrəfɪ] *s* leksykografia *f*, słownikarstwo *n*

li•a•bil•i•ty [laɪə'bɪlətɪ] *s* **1.** odpowiedzialność *f* **2.** ***liabilities*** FIN zobowiązania, pasywa; **li•a•bil•i•ty in•'sur•ance** *s* ubezpieczenie *n* od odpowiedzialności cywilnej

li•a•ble ['laɪəbl] *adj* **1.** odpowiedzialny; ***be ~ for*** ponosić odpowiedzialność za *A*; ***s.o. cannot be held ~ for*** ktoś nie może zostać pociągnięty do odpowiedzialności za *A*, ktoś nie ponosi odpowiedzialności za *A* **2.** ***be ~ to a fine*** podlegać karze grzywny; ***be ~ to taxation*** podlegać opodatkowaniu **3.** ***the roof is ~ to collapse at any moment*** dach może w każdej chwili runąć **4.** ***be ~ to injury*** być narażonym na kontuzje **5.** ***that is ~ to happen*** tak się pewnie stanie

li•aise [lɪ'eɪz] *v/i* współpracować (***with*** z *I*); **li•ai•son** [lɪ'eɪzən] *s* **1.** współpraca *f* **2.** łączność *f* **3.** romans *m*

li•ar [laɪə] *s* **1.** kłamca *m* **2.** *infml* kłamczuch *m*

lib•e•ral ['lɪbərəl] **I** *adj* **1.** liberalny **2.** tolerancyjny **3.** ***be ~ with*** nie szczędzić *G*; ***be ~ with praise*** nie szczędzić pochwał **II** *s* liberał *m*; **lib•er•al•ism** ['lɪbərəlɪzəm] *s* liberalizm *m*; **lib•er•al•i•ty** [lɪbə'rælətɪ] *s* **1.** liberalność *f* **2.** tolerancyjność *f* **3.** hojność *f*; **lib•er•al•ize** ['lɪbərəlaɪz] *v/t* liberalizować ⟨z-⟩

lib•e•rate ['lɪbəreɪt] *v/t* **1.** wyzwalać ⟨-wolić⟩ **2.** uwalniać ⟨uwolnić⟩; **lib-**

L

e•rat•ed ['lıbəreıtıd] *adj* wyzwolony, wyemancypowany; **lib•e•ra•tion** [lıbə'reıʃn] *s* **1.** wyzwolenie *n*; ***the war of ~*** wojna wyzwoleńcza **2.** uwolnienie *n*

Li•ber•i•a [laı'bırıə] *s* Liberia *f*

lib•er•ty ['lıbətı] *s* **1.** wolność *f*; ***at ~*** *form* na wolności; ***be at ~ to do s.th.*** móc coś zrobić, mieć prawo coś zrobić **2.** swoboda *f* **3.** prawo *n* **4.** ***take liberties with s.o.*** za dużo sobie pozwalać w stosunku do kogoś

li•bi•do [lı'bi:dəʊ] *s* libido *n*, popęd *m* płciowy

Li•bra ['li:brə] *s* ASTR Waga *f*

li•brar•i•an [laı'brerıən] *s* bibliotekarz *m*; **li•bra•ry** ['laıbrerı] *s* **1.** biblioteka *f*; ***a ~ ticket*** karta biblioteczna **2.** archiwum *n*

Lib•y•a ['lıbıə] *s* Libia *f*

lice [laıs] *pl* → ***louse***

li•cence ['laısns] *s* **1.** licencja *f* **2.** pozwolenie *n* **3.** zezwolenie *n* **4.** koncesja *f* **5.** ***a driving ~*** *Br*, ***a driver's ~*** *Am* prawo jazdy **6.** swoboda *f*

li•cense ['laısns] **I** *s Am* → ***licence*** **II** *v/t* **1.** udzielać ⟨-lić⟩ zezwolenia; ***~ a company to produce a drug*** udzielić firmie zezwolenia na produkcję leku **2.** wydawać ⟨-dać⟩ pozwolenie na *A*; ***~ guns*** wydawać pozwolenia na broń **3.** przyznawać ⟨-nać⟩ koncesję **4.** udzielać ⟨-lić⟩ licencji **5.** licencjonować; **li•censed** ['laısnst] *adj* **1.** ***be ~ to do s.th.*** mieć pozwolenie na robienie czegoś; ***be ~ to carry a gun*** mieć pozwolenie na posiadanie boni **2.** licencjonowany **3.** koncesjonowany **4.** zarejestrowany **5.** ***be ~*** (***to sell alcohol***) mieć koncesję na sprzedaż alkoholu; **'li•cense num•ber** *s Am* numer *m* rejestracyjny; **'li•cense plate** *s Am* tablica *f* rejestracyjna

lick [lık] **I** *v/t* **1.** lizać ⟨po-, -znąć⟩; ***~ s.th. off*** zlizać coś z *G*; ***~ s.o.'s boots*** *infml* podlizywać się komuś **2.** oblizywać ⟨-zać⟩; ***~ one's lips*** oblizać wargi **3.** *infml* spuszczać ⟨spuścić⟩ manto **II** *v/i* lizać **III** *s* **1.** liźnięcie *n*; ***give s.th. a ~*** polizać coś; ***at full ~*** *infml* na pełnym gazie, pełnym gazem **2.** odrobina *f*; **lick•ing** ['lıkıŋ] *s infml* baty *pl*, manto *n*

lid [lıd] *s* **1.** pokrywka *f*; ***put a ~ on*** przykryć pokrywką **2.** pokrywa *f* **3.** wieczko *n* **4.** wieko *n* **5.** powieka *f*

lie[1] [laı] **I** *s* kłamstwo *n*; ***tell ~s*** kłamać; ***tell a ~*** skłamać; ***give the ~ to*** zadawać kłam *D*; **II** *v/i* **1.** kłamać ⟨s-⟩ **2.** okłamywać ⟨-mać⟩ (***to*** *A*)

lie[2] [~] **I** (*lay*; *lain*) *v/i* **1.** leżeć; ***the town ~s on a river*** miasto leży nad rzeką; ***~ heavy on s.o.'s stomach*** leżeć komuś na żołądku **2.** znajdować się; ***~ second*** SPORT być na drugim miejscu **3.** ***~ ahead*** nadchodzić; ***what ~s ahead of us?*** co nam przyniesie przyszłość? **4.** ***~ low*** przyczaić się **II** *s* ***the ~ of the land*** ukształtowanie terenu; **lie about**, **lie around** *v/i* **1.** poniewierać się **2.** wylegiwać się; **lie back** *v/i* **1.** kłaść ⟨położyć⟩ się na plecach **2.** wyciągać ⟨-gnąć⟩ się; **lie down** *v/i* kłaść ⟨położyć⟩ się; **lie in** *v/i* zostawać ⟨-tać⟩ w łóżku dłużej niż zwykle, wylegiwać się

'lie down *s*: ***have a ~*** *Br infml* położyć się na chwilę; **'lie-in** *s*: ***have a ~*** zostać w łóżku dłużej niż zwykle

lieu [lju:] *s*: ***in ~ of*** zamiast *G*, w miejsce *G*

lieu•ten•ant [lef'tenənt] *s* **1.** porucznik *m* **2.** kapitan *m* (marynarki); **lieu•ten•ant 'colo•nel** *s* podpułkownik *m*

life [laıf] *pl lives* [laıvz] *s* życie *n*; ***they lost their lives*** stracili życie; ***a matter of ~ and death*** sprawa życia i śmierci; ***early in ~*** bardzo wcześnie; ***late in ~*** w późnym wieku; ***all his ~*** (przez) całe życie; ***for ~*** na całe życie; ***full of ~*** pełen życia **2.** *contract*: okres *m* ważności **3.** dożywocie *n*; ***he is doing ~*** odsiaduje dożywocie; ***he got ~*** dostał dożywocie; **life an'nu•i•ty** *s* dożywotnia renta *f*; **life as•'sur•ance** *s Br* ubezpieczenie *n* na życie; **'life belt** *s* koło *n* ratunkowe; **'life•boat** *s* łódź *f* ratunkowa, szalupa *f*; **'life cy•cle** *s* **1.** BIOL cykl *m* życiowy **2.** *product*: cykl *m* życia; **life ex•'pect•an•cy** *s* średnia długość *f* życia; **'life guard** *s* ratownik *m*; **life im•'pris•on•ment** *s* dożywotnie więzienie *n*, dożywocie *n*; **life in•'sur•ance** *s* ubezpieczenie *n* na życie; **'life jack•et** *s* kamizelka *f* ratunkowa

life•less ['laɪflɪs] *adj* **1.** martwy **2.** bez życia **3.** nieożywiony **4.** przywiędły
life•like ['laɪflaɪk] *adj* realistyczny; **'life•line** *s* lina *f* ratownicza; **'life•long** *adj* **1.** trwający całe życie **2.** dozgonny; **life 'mem•ber** *s* dożywotni członek *m*; **life 'peer** *s Br* dożywotni członek *m* Izby Lordów; **'life pre•serv•er** *s Am* **1.** → ***life jacket*** **2.** → ***life belt***
lif•er ['laɪfə] *s infml* skazany *m* na dożywocie
'life raft *s* tratwa *f* ratunkowa; **'life-sav•er** *s* **1.** ratownik *m* **2.** ***the drug is a ~*** ten lek ratuje ludziom życie; **'life-sav•ing** *adj* **1.** ratujący życie **2.** ratowniczy **3.** ratunkowy; **life 'sen•tence** *s* wyrok *m* dożywotniego więzienia, dożywocie *n*; **'life-sized** *adj* naturalnej wielkości, naturalnych rozmiarów; **'life•style** *s* styl *m* życia; **life sup•port ma•'chine** *s* respirator *m*; **'life-threat•en•ing** *adj* zagrażający życiu, grożący śmiercią; **'life•time** *s* życie *n*; ***once in a ~*** raz w życiu; ***during s.o.'s ~*** w ciągu swego życia
lift [lɪft] **I** *s* **1.** winda *f*; ***take a ~*** pojechać windą **2.** dźwig *m* **3.** ***give s.o. a ~*** podwieźć kogoś; ***hitch a ~*** złapać okazję **4.** wyciąg *m*; ***a ski ~*** wyciąg narciarski **5.** siła *f* nośna **6.** ***give s.o. a ~*** dodać komuś pewności siebie **II** *v/t* **1.** (*a.* **~ up**) podnosić ⟨-nieść⟩; ***~ one's eyes*** podnieść wzrok **2.** *ban*: znosić ⟨znieść⟩ **3.** *infml* podwędzać ⟨-dzić⟩ **III** *v/i* **4.** podnosić ⟨-nieść⟩ się; **lift off** *v/i* startować ⟨wy-⟩
'lift-off *s rocket*: start *m*
light[1] [laɪt] **I** *s* **1.** światło *n*, ***stand in s.o.'s ~*** zasłaniać komuś światło; ***by the ~ of a candle*** przy świetle świecy; ***jump the ~*** przejechać na czerwonym świetle; ***come to ~*** wyjść na światło dzienne; ***bring s.th. to ~*** wydobyć coś na światło dzienne; ***see the ~*** (***of day***) ujrzeć światło dzienne; ***in the ~ of*** w świetle *G*; ***cast ~ on, shed ~ on*** rzucić światło na *A*; ***he has finally seen the ~*** wreszcie zrozumiał, wreszcie doznał olśnienia **2.** oświetlenie *n* **3.** reflektor *m* **4.** ogień *m*; ***have you got a ~?*** masz ogień? **II** *adj* **1.** jasny; ***it's ~*** jest jasno; ***it's getting ~*** robi się jasno; ***~ blue*** jasnoniebieski **2.** widny **III** (*lit/lighted*; *lit/lighted*) *v/t* **1.** zapalać ⟨-lić⟩; ***~ a cigarette*** zapalić papierosa **2.** oświetlać ⟨-lić⟩ **3.** rozjaśniać ⟨-nić⟩; **light up I** *v/t* → ***light*** **II** *v/i* **1.** zapalać ⟨-lić⟩ papierosa **2.** zapalać ⟨-lić⟩ się **3.** rozbłyskiwać ⟨-snąć⟩ **4.** ożywiać ⟨-wić⟩ się
light[2] [~] *adj* **1.** lekki; (**as**) ***~ as a feather*** lekki jak piórko; ***it's no ~ matter*** to nie przelewki, to poważna sprawa; ***~ reading*** coś lekkiego do czytania; ***make ~ of*** lekceważyć *A*; ***make ~ work of s.th.*** łatwo sobie z czymś poradzić **2.** delikatny **3.** *traffic*: mały **4.** *sentence*: łagodny **5.** pogodny **6.** ***a ~-heavyweight boxer*** bokser wagi półciężkiej
'light bulb *s* żarówka *f*; **light-e'mit•ting di•ode** *s* dioda *f* świecąca, dioda *f* elektroluminescencyjna, LED
light•en[1] ['laɪtn] **I** *v/t* rozjaśniać ⟨-nić⟩ **II** *v/i* jaśnieć ⟨po-⟩
light•en[2] [~] *v/t* **1.** zmniejszać ciężar ⟨-szyć⟩ **2.** *atmosphere*: rozładowywać ⟨-dować⟩
light•er ['laɪtə] *s* zapalniczka *f*, zapalarka *f*
light-'fin•gered *adj*: ***be ~ fig*** mieć lepkie ręce; **light-'head•ed** *adj* **1.** beztroski **2.** ***she felt ~*** kręciło jej się w głowie; **light-'heart•ed** *adj* **1.** lekki **2.** wesoły **3.** beztroski
'light•house *s* latarnia *f* morska
light•ing ['laɪtɪŋ] *s* oświetlenie *n*, światło *n*
light•ly ['laɪtlɪ] *adv* **1.** lekko; ***sleep ~*** mieć lekki sen; ***eat ~*** jeść lekkostrawne potrawy **2.** cicho **3.** niefrasobliwie **4.** pochopnie
light•ness[1] ['laɪtnɪs] *s* jasność *f*
light•ness[2] [~] *s* **1.** lekkość *f* **2.** niefrasobliwość *f* **3.** lekkostrawność *f*
light•ning ['laɪtnɪŋ] **I** *s* **1.** błyskawice *pl*; ***a flash of ~*** błyskawica; (**as**) ***quick as ~*** szybki jak błyskawica **2.** piorun *m*; ***she was struck by ~*** trafił ją piorun **II** *adj* błyskawiczny; **'light•ning con•duc•tor** *Br*, **'light•ning rod** *Am s* piorunochron *m*
like[1] [laɪk] **I** *prep* **1.** jak; ***what is he ~?*** jaki on jest?; ***what does it look ~?*** jak to wygląda? **2.** taki jak **3.** ***that is just ~ him*** to do niego podobne, to cały on **4.** na przykład **II** *adj* podobny; ***in ~ manner*** w podobny sposób **III** *s* ***the***

L

~ temu podobne; ***burglaries, car thefts and the ~*** włamania, kradzieże samochodów i podobne przestępstwa; ***the ~s of her*** *infml* tacy jak ona, ludzie jej pokroju

like² [~] **I** *v/t* lubić; ***I ~ it*** to mi się podoba; ***I ~ him*** lubię go; ***~ doing s.th., ~ to do s.th.*** lubić coś robić; ***how do you ~ it?*** jak ci się podoba?; ***which one do you ~ better?*** który podoba ci się bardziej? **II** *v/i* chcieć; ***I'd ~ to know*** chciałbym wiedzieć; **(*just*) *as you ~*** jak chcesz; ***do as you ~*** rób, jak chcesz; ***if you ~*** jeśli chcesz **III** *s* ***~s*** upodobania

like•a•ble ['laɪkəbl] *adj* sympatyczny, miły, przyjemny

like•li•hood ['laɪklɪhʊd] *s* prawdopodobieństwo *n*; ***in all ~*** najprawdopodobniej; **like•ly** ['laɪklɪ] **I** *adj* prawdopodobny; ***she's ~ to agree*** prawdopodobnie się zgodzi; ***he is not ~ to come*** prawdopodobnie nie przyjdzie; ***a ~ story!*** *infml* akurat! **II** *adv* prawdopodobnie; ***most ~*** najprawdopodobniej; **(*as*) *~ as not*** pewnie; ***not ~!*** *Br* na pewno nie!, w żadnym razie!

like-'mind•ed *adj* podobnie myślący

lik•en ['laɪkən] *v/t* porównywać ⟨-nać⟩, przyrównywać ⟨-nać⟩

like•ness ['laɪknɪs] *s* **1.** podobieństwo *n* **2.** podobizna *f* **3.** wizerunek *m*

'like•wise ['laɪkwaɪz] *adv* podobnie

lik•ing ['laɪkɪŋ] *s*: ***have a ~ for s.th.*** lubić coś; ***have a ~ for s.o.*** darzyć kogoś sympatią; ***take a ~ to*** polubić *A*; ***for my ~*** jak na mój gust; ***be to s.o.'s ~*** odpowiadać komuś

limb [lɪm] *s* **1.** kończyna *f*; ***be out on a ~*** nie mieć w nikim oparcia **2.** konar *m*

lim•ber up [lɪmbər'ʌp] *v/i* rozgrzewać ⟨-rzać⟩ się

lime¹ [laɪm] **I** *s* wapno *n* **II** *v/t* wapnować

lime² [~] *s* **1.** lipa *f* **2.** limeta *f*, limetka *f*; **lime 'green** *adj* żółtozielony

'lime•stone *s* wapień *m*

'lime•wash **I** *s* wapno *n* **II** *v/t* bielić ⟨po-⟩

lim•it ['lɪmɪt] **I** *s* **1.** granica *f*; ***within ~s*** w pewnych granicach; ***off ~s*** *Am* zamknięty; ***that's the ~!*** to szczyt wszystkiego! **2.** granice *pl*; ***there is a ~ to everything*** wszystko ma swoje granice **3.** ograniczenie *n*; ***a speed ~*** ograniczenie prędkości **4.** limit *m* **II** *v/t* ograniczać ⟨-czyć⟩; **lim•i•ta•tion** [lɪmɪ'teɪʃn] *s* **1.** ograniczenie *n*; ***~ of liability*** ograniczenie odpowiedzialności **2.** niedoskonałość *f*; ***know one's*** (***own***) ***~*** znać swoje możliwości; **lim•it•ed 'com•pa•ny** *s* spółka *f* z ograniczoną odpowiedzialnością

li•mo ['lɪməʊ] *s* *infml* limuzyna *f*

lim•ou•sine ['lɪməziːn] *s* **1.** limuzyna *f* **2.** *Am* mikrobus *m*

limp¹ [lɪmp] **I** *v/i* utykać, kuleć **II** *s* ***walk with a ~*** utykać, kuleć

limp² [~] *adj* **1.** wiotki **2.** zwiotczały; ***go ~*** zwiotczeć **3.** słaby

line¹ [laɪn] **I** *s* **1.** linia *f*; ***a dividing ~*** granica; ***the front ~*** linia frontu; ***be in ~ with*** **a)** być w jednej linii z *I* **b)** zgadzać się z *I*; ***the ~ is busy*** linia jest zajęta; ***please hold the ~*** proszę nie odkładać słuchawki, proszę poczekać **2.** kreska *f* **3.** zmarszczka *f* **4.** bruzda *f* **5.** linijka *f*, wiersz *m*; ***read between the ~s*** czytać między wierszami **6.** wers *m* **7.** ***~s*** tekst *m*, rola *f* **8.** rząd *m* **9.** szereg *m* **10.** kolejka *f*; ***stand in ~*** stać w kolejce **11.** lina *f* **12.** sznurek *m* **13.** trasa *f*; ***the end of the ~*** koniec trasy **14.** przewód *m* **15.** pozycja *f*; ***behind enemy ~s*** na tyłach wroga **16.** granica *f*; ***draw the ~*** określić granicę **17.** ***along these ~s*** **a)** w ten sposób, według tych zasad **b)** w tym guście **18.** ***a ~ of thought***, ***a ~ of reasoning*** tok rozumowania **19.** ***take a strong ~ with*** zająć twarde stanowisko wobec *G* **20.** ***bring s.o. into ~*** przywołać kogoś do porządku; ***fall into ~*** podporządkować się **21.** ***a ~ of business*** branża *f* **II** *v/t* **1.** ***thousands of people ~d the streets*** tysiące ludzi stało wzdłuż ulic **2.** ***a road ~d with trees*** droga wysadzana drzewami; **line up** **I** *v/i* **1.** ustawiać ⟨-wić⟩ się w szeregu **2.** ustawiać ⟨-wić⟩ się w kolejce **II** *v/t* **1.** ustawiać ⟨-wić⟩ w rzędzie **2.** organizować ⟨z-⟩

line² [~] *v/t* **1.** wykładać ⟨wyłożyć⟩ (***with*** *I*) **2.** wyściełać ⟨wysłać⟩; ***cells that ~ the intestines*** komórki wyściełające jelita **3.** podszywać ⟨-szyć⟩; ***~ one's pockets*** *fig* nabijać sobie kabzę

L

lin•e•age ['lɪnɪɪdʒ] *s* rodowód *m*
lin•e•al ['lɪnɪəl] *adj* w prostej linii
lin•e•a•ment ['lɪnɪəmənt] *s form* charakterystyczna cecha *f*
lin•e•ar ['lɪnɪə] *adj* liniowy, linearny
lin•en ['lɪnɪn] **I** *s* **1.** płótno *n* (lniane) **2.** bielizna *f* (pościelowa); ***wash one's dirty ~ in public*** *fig* publicznie prać brudy **II** *adj* lniany; ***a ~ basket*** kosz na brudną bieliznę
lin•er ['laɪnə] *s* **1.** (*ship*) liniowiec *m* **2.** → ***eyeliner***
lines•man ['laɪnzmən] *s* SPORT sędzia *m* liniowy
'line•up *s* **1.** SPORT skład *m* **2.** (*suspect*) okazanie *n*
lin•ger ['lɪŋgə] *v/i* **1.** (*smell*) utrzymywać ⟨-mać⟩ się **2.** (*taste*, *sensation*) pozostawać ⟨-tać⟩ **3.** zostawać ⟨-tać⟩ **4.** zwlekać; **lin•ger on** *v/i* **1.** zostawać ⟨-tać⟩ **2.** nie ustępować ⟨-tąpić⟩
lin•ge•rie ['lænʒəriː] *s* bielizna *f* damska
lin•ger•ing ['lɪŋgərɪŋ] *adj* **1.** *smell*: utrzymujący się **2.** *taste*: pozostający w ustach **3.** *death*: powolny **4.** *pain*: długotrwały, uporczywy **5.** *kiss*: namiętny **6.** *memory*: powracający
lin•go ['lɪŋgəʊ] *s infml* **1.** żargon *m* **2.** język *m*
lin•guist ['lɪŋgwɪst] *s* językoznawca *m*, lingwista *m*; **lin•guis•tic** [lɪŋ'gwɪstɪk] *adj* **1.** językowy **2.** językoznawczy, lingwistyczny
lin•ing ['laɪnɪŋ] *s* **1.** podszewka *f* **2.** podbicie *n* **3.** ***brake ~*** okładzina hamulcowa **4.** ANAT wyściółka *f*
link [lɪŋk] **I** *s* **1.** związek *m* **2.** połączenie *n* **3.** ogniwo *n*; ***the missing ~*** brakujące ogniwo **4.** ***trade ~s*** kontakty handlowe **5.** spinka *f* do mankietu **II** *v/t* **1.** łączyć ⟨po-⟩ **2.** ***~ arms*** wziąć się pod ręce **III** *v/i* → ***link up***; **link up** *v/i* łączyć ⟨po-⟩ się
links [lɪŋks] *pl* pole *n* golfowe
'link•up *s* **1.** połączenie *n* **2.** powiązania *pl*
li•on ['laɪən] *s* lew *m*; ***venture into the ~'s den*** wejść do jaskini lwa; ***the ~'s share*** *Br* lwia część; **'li•on cub** *s* lwiątko *n*, lwie szczenię *n*; **li•on•ess** ['laɪənes] *s* lwica *f*

lip [lɪp] *s* **1.** warga *f*; ***the lower*** (***upper***) ***~*** dolna (górna) warga; ***lick one's ~s*** oblizać się; ***be on everyone's lips*** być na ustach wszystkich; ***keep a stiff upper ~*** trzymać fason **2.** ***none of your ~!*** *infml* uważaj, co mówisz!, nie pyskuj! **3.** brzeg *m*, krawędź *f*; **'lip gloss** *s* błyszczyk *m* do ust
lip•o•suc•tion ['lɪpəʊsʌkʃn] *s* odsysanie *n* tłuszczu, liposukcja *f*
'lip-read *v/i* czytać z ruchu warg; **'lip serv•ice** *s*: ***pay ~ to*** składać gołosłowne deklaracje poparcia *G*; **'lip•stick** *s* szminka *f*, pomadka *f*
li•queur [lɪ'kjʊə] *s* likier *m*
liq•uid ['lɪkwɪd] **I** *s* płyn *m*, ciecz *f* **II** *adj* **1.** płynny **2.** ciekły; ***a ~ crystal display*** wyświetlacz ciekłokrystaliczny **3.** w płynie **4.** ***~ assets*** środki obrotowe
liq•ui•date ['lɪkwɪdeɪt] *v/t* **1.** likwidować ⟨z-⟩ **2.** upłynniać ⟨-nić⟩; **liq•ui•da•tion** [lɪkwɪ'deɪʃn] *s* **1.** FIN likwidacja *f* **2.** FIN upłynnienie *n* **3.** (*murder*) zlikwidowanie *n*; **liq•ui•di•ty** [lɪ'kwɪdɪtɪ] *s* płynność *f*
liq•uid•ize ['lɪkwɪdaɪz] *v/t Br* miksować ⟨z-⟩, przecierać ⟨przetrzeć⟩; **liq•uid•iz•er** ['lɪkwɪdaɪzə] *s Br* COOK mikser *m*
liq•uor ['lɪkə] *s Am* alkohol *m* wysokoprocentowy; ***hard ~*** mocny trunek; ***a ~ store*** sklep monopolowy
lisp [lɪsp] **I** *v/i* seplenić **II** *s* ***speak with a ~*** seplenić
list[1] [lɪst] **I** *s* **1.** lista *f*; ***be on the ~*** być na liście; ***the ~ price*** cena katalogowa **2.** spis *m* **3.** wykaz *m* **II** *v/t* **1.** sporządzać ⟨-dzić⟩ listę **2.** ***be ~ed in alphabetical order*** być podanym w kolejności alfabetycznej **3.** umieszczać ⟨umieścić⟩ w spisie
list[2] [~] **I** *s* przechył *m*, pochylenie *n* się **II** *v/i* **1.** (*ship*, *boat*) mieć przechył, przechylać ⟨-lić⟩ się **2.** (*building*) pochylać ⟨-lić⟩ się
list•ed 'build•ing *s* zabytek *m*, obiekt *m* pod ochroną
lis•ten ['lɪsn] *v/i* słuchać ⟨wy-, po-⟩ (***to*** *G*); ***~!*** słuchaj!, posłuchaj!; **lis•ten in** *v/i* podsłuchiwać ⟨-chać⟩ (***on*** *A*); **lis•ten•er** ['lɪsnə] *s* słuchacz *m*; ***be a good ~*** być dobrym słuchaczem, umieć słuchać

L

'list•ings mag•a•zine *s* informator *m* kulturalny
list•less ['lɪstlɪs] *adj* apatyczny, ospały
lit [lɪt] *Past Simple and Past Participle* → ***light***[1]
lit•a•ny ['lɪtənɪ] *s* litania *f*
li•ter *Am* → ***litre***
lit•er•a•cy ['lɪtərəsɪ] *s* umiejętność *f* czytania i pisania; ***computer ~*** umiejętność obsługi komputera
lit•e•ral ['lɪtərəl] *adj* **1.** dosłowny **2.** bez polotu; **lit•e•ral•ly** ['lɪtərəlɪ] *adv* **1.** dosłownie; ***he did ~ nothing*** nie zrobił dosłownie nic **2.** słowo w słowo
lit•e•ra•ry ['lɪtərerɪ] *adj* literacki; ***a ~ critic*** krytyk literacki; ***~ history*** historia literatury; **lit•e•rate** ['lɪtərət] *adj* piśmienny; ***be ~*** umieć czytać i pisać; **lit•e•ra•ture** ['lɪtrətʃə] *s* **1.** literatura *f* **2.** materiały *pl* informacyjne
lithe [laɪð] *adj* **1.** gibki **2.** giętki **3.** *walk*: sprężysty
Lith•u•a•ni•a [lɪθuː'eɪnɪə] *s* Litwa *f*; **Lith•u•a•ni•an** [lɪθuː'eɪnɪən] **I** *adj* litewski **II** *s* **1.** Litwin *m*, Litwinka *f* **2.** (*language*) litewski *m*
li•tre ['liːtə] *Br*, ***li•ter*** *Am s* litr *m*
lit•ter ['lɪtə] **I** *s* **1.** śmieci(e) *pl* **2.** ***a litter of papers*** rozrzucone papiery **3.** miot *m* **4.** ***cat ~*** żwirek dla kota **5.** (pod)ściółka *f* **6.** lektyka *f* **II** *v/t* **1.** być rozrzuconym na *L*; ***broken glass ~ed the streets*** na ulicach pełno było rozbitego szkła; ***the floor was ~ed with papers*** na podłodze leżały porozrzucane papiery **2.** ***be ~ed with mistakes*** być najeżonym błędami **III** *v/i* **1.** śmiecić; **'lit•ter bas•ket** *s* kosz *m* na śmieci; **'lit•ter bin** *s* pojemnik *m* na śmieci; **'lit•ter bug** *s infml* osoba *f* śmiecąca w miejscach publicznych
lit•tle ['lɪtl] **I** *adj* **1.** mały; ***the ~ ones*** maluchy **2.** *while*, *way*: krótki **3.** niewielki **4.** ***a ~ jam*** trochę dżemu **5.** drobny **6.** nieznaczny **7.** słaby **II** *adv* **1.** ***a ~*** trochę; ***a ~ smaller*** trochę mniejszy **2.** mało, niewiele; ***~ known*** mało znany; ***as ~ as possible*** jak najmniej; ***for as ~ as 10 pounds*** za jedyne 10 funtów **3.** ***I see ~ of him*** rzadko go widuję **III** *pron* ***~ by ~*** pomału, stopniowo
live[1] [lɪv] *v/i* **1.** żyć; ***~ through the night*** przeżyć noc; ***you ~ and learn*** człowiek uczy się całe życie; ***~ and let ~*** żyj i daj żyć innym **2.** mieszkać **3.** zamieszkiwać; **live on** *v/i* **1.** żyć nadal **2.** przeżyć **3.** żyć z *G*; **live off** *v/i* **1.** być na utrzymaniu *G* **2.** żyć na koszt *G*; **live up to** *v/i expectations*: spełniać ⟨-nić⟩; ***the team didn't ~ its promise*** drużyna nie spełniła pokładanych w niej nadziei; **live with** *v/i* **1.** mieszkać z *I* **2.** pogodzić się z *I*
live[2] [laɪv] **I** *adj* **1.** żywy **2.** aktualny **3.** *ammunition*: ostry **4.** ***a ~ wire*** kabel pod napięciem **5.** ***a ~ broadcast*** transmisja na żywo **II** *adv* na żywo
live•li•hood ['laɪvlɪhʊd] *s* utrzymanie *n*; ***earn one's ~*** zarabiać na życie; ***means of ~*** środki utrzymania
live•li•ness ['laɪvlɪnɪs] *s* żywość *f*, ożywienie *n*; **live•ly** ['laɪvlɪ] *adj* **1.** żwawy **2.** żywy **3.** pełen życia **4.** tętniący życiem **5.** *discussion*: ożywiony **6.** energiczny; **liv•en up** [laɪvn'ʌp] **I** *v/t* ożywiać ⟨-wić⟩ **II** *v/i* ożywiać ⟨-wić⟩ się
liv•er ['lɪvə] *s* **1.** wątroba *f* **2.** COOK wątróbka *f*; **'liv•er sau•sage** *s Br* kiszka *f* pasztetowa, *infml* pasztetówka *f*; **'liv•er spot** *s* plama *f* wątrobowa; **liv•er•wurst** ['lɪvəwɜːst] *Am* → ***liver sausage***
liv•er•y ['lɪvərɪ] *s* liberia *f*; ***in ~*** w liberii
lives [laɪvz] *pl* → ***life***
live•stock ['laɪvstɒk] *s* inwentarz *m* żywy
liv•ing ['lɪvɪŋ] **I** *adj* **1.** żywy **2.** życiowy; ***~ conditions*** warunki życia **II** *s* **1.** życie *n*; ***earn a ~, make a ~*** zarabiać na życie **2.** ***the ~*** żywi; **'liv•ing room** *s* pokój *m* dzienny; **liv•ing 'will** *s Am* testament *m* życia
liz•ard ['lɪzəd] *s* jaszczurka *f*
load [ləʊd] **I** *s* **1.** ładunek *m*; ***get a ~ of his hat!*** *infml* popatrz na jego czapkę! **2.** ciężar *m*; ***knowing that she's safe took a ~ off my mind*** gdy dowiedziałem się, że jest bezpieczna, spadł mi kamień z serca **3.** ***~s of*** *infml* mnóstwo *G*, kupa *G*; ***there was ~s to eat*** było mnóstwo jedzenia **4.** obciążenie *n* **II** *v/t* **1.** (*a.* ***~ up***) ładować ⟨za-, na-⟩ (***s.th. into*** coś do *G*, ***s.th. onto*** coś na *A*); ***~ a camera*** włożyć film do aparatu **2.** obciążać ⟨-żyć⟩; **'load-bearing** *adj wall*: nośny

L

load•ed ['ləʊdɪd] *adj* **1.** załadowany **2.** wyładowany **3.** naładowany **4.** pełny **5.** *infml* nadziany **6.** ***a ~ question*** pytanie z podtekstem **7.** *word*: emocjonalnie nacechowany
loaf [ləʊf] *pl loaves* [ləʊvz] *s* **1.** bochenek *m* **2.** ***a meat ~*** klops **3.** ***use one's ~*** *infml* ruszyć makówką; **loaf around** *v/i* **1.** obijać się **2.** włóczyć się; ***~ the streets*** włóczyć się po ulicach
loam [ləʊm] *s* (*soil*) glina *f*; ***sandy ~*** glina piaszczysta
loan [ləʊn] **I** *s* **1.** kredyt *m*, pożyczka *f*; ***take out a ~*** wziąć kredyt **2.** ***on ~*** wypożyczony; ***a book on ~*** wypożyczona książka **II** *v/t* **1.** pożyczać ⟨-czyć⟩ **2.** wypożyczać ⟨-czyć⟩; '**loan shark** *s* lichwiarz *m*; '**loan•word** *s* zapożyczenie *n*
loath [ləʊθ] *adj* ***be ~ to do s.th.*** *form* nie chcieć czegoś zrobić, nie mieć ochoty czegoś zrobić
loathe [ləʊð] *v/t* nie cierpieć, nie znosić; **loath•ing** ['ləʊðɪŋ] *s* wstręt *m*, odraza *f*; **loath•some** ['ləʊðsəm] *adj* wstrętny, obrzydliwy
loaves [ləʊvz] *pl* → ***loaf***
lob [lɒb] **I** *s* SPORT lob *m* **II** *v/t* **1.** lobować **2.** rzucać ⟨-cić⟩ (wysokim łukiem)
lob•by ['lɒbɪ] **I** *s* **1.** hol *m* **2.** foyer *n* **3.** POLIT lobby *n* **II** *v/i* **1.** lobbować **2.** wywierać ⟨-wrzeć⟩ nacisk
lobe [ləʊb] *s* **1.** ***an ear ~*** płatek ucha **2.** płat *m*
lob•ster ['lɒbstə] *s* homar *m*
lo•cal ['ləʊkl] **I** *adj* **1.** miejscowy; ***a ~ derby*** derby piłkarskie **2.** lokalny; ***~ news*** wiadomości lokalne **3.** tutejszy **II** *s* **1.** lokalny mieszkaniec *m* **2.** *Br* pobliski pub *m*; **lo•cal anes'thet•ic** *s* MED znieczulenie *n* miejscowe; '**lo•cal call** *s* TEL połączenie *n* miejscowe; **lo•cal e'lec•tions** *pl* wybory *pl* lokalne, wybory *pl* do władz lokalnych; **lo•cal 'gov•ern•ment** *s* **1.** władze *pl* lokalne **2.** samorząd *m* lokalny
lo•cal•i•ty [ləʊ'kælətɪ] *s* **1.** okolica *f* **2.** miejsce *n*
lo•cal•ize ['ləʊkəlaɪz] *v/t* **1.** lokalizować ⟨z-⟩ **2.** ograniczać ⟨-czyć⟩; **lo•cal•ly** ['ləʊkəlɪ] *adv* **1.** w okolicy **2.** w pobliżu **3.** lokalnie; '**lo•cal time** *s* czas *m* lokalny
lo•cate [ləʊ'keɪt] **I** *v/t* **1.** ***be ~d*** znajdować się **2.** lokalizować ⟨z-⟩ **3.** znajdować ⟨znaleźć⟩ **4.** lokować ⟨u-⟩ **II** *v/i* lokować ⟨u-⟩ się; **lo•ca•tion** [ləʊ'keɪʃn] *s* **1.** lokalizacja *f* **2.** położenie *n* **3.** FILM plener *m*
lock[1] [lɒk] **I** *s* **1.** zamek *m*; ***under ~ and key*** pod kluczem; ***~, stock and barrel*** *fig* cały **2.** *bike*: zapięcie *n*, zamknięcie *n* **3.** INF blokada *f* **II** *v/t* **1.** zamykać ⟨-mknąć⟩ na klucz **2.** blokować ⟨za-⟩ **III** *v/i* **1.** zamykać ⟨-mknąć⟩ się na klucz **2.** blokować ⟨za-⟩ się; **lock away** *v/t* **1.** zamykać ⟨-mknąć⟩ **2.** trzymać pod kluczem; **lock in** *v/t* **1.** zamykać ⟨-mknąć⟩ **2.** zatrzaskiwać ⟨-snąć⟩ w środku; **lock out** *v/t* **1.** nie wpuszczać ⟨wpuścić⟩ do środka; ***he's locked me out*** nie wpuszcza mnie do domu **2.** ***I locked myself out of my apartment*** zatrzasnęły mi się drzwi do mieszkania; **lock up** *v/t* **1.** zamykać ⟨-mknąć⟩ **2.** trzymać pod kluczem **3.** zamykać ⟨-mknąć⟩ w więzieniu
lock[2] [~] *s* **1.** kosmyk *m* **2.** lok *m*
lock•er ['lɒkə] *s* **1.** szafka *f* **2.** schowek *m* na bagaż; '**lock•er room** *s* szatnia *f*
lock•et ['lɒkɪt] *s* medalion *m*
lo•co•mo•tion [ləʊkə'məʊʃn] *s* *form* ruch *m*; **lo•co•mo•tive** [ləʊkə'məʊtɪv] **I** *s* lokomotywa *f* **II** *adj form* motoryczny
lo•cum ['ləʊkəm] *s Br* zastępca *m*
lo•cu•tion [ləʊ'kjuːʃn] *s* **1.** sposób *m* wyrażania się, lokucja *f* **2.** wyrażenie *n*
lodge [lɒdʒ] **I** *s* **1.** domek *m* **2.** portiernia *f* **3.** żeremie *n* **4.** *masonic*: loża *f* **II** *v/t* **1.** *complaint*: wnosić ⟨wnieść⟩, składać ⟨złożyć⟩ **2.** dawać ⟨dać⟩ zakwaterowanie, nocować ⟨prze-⟩ **III** *v/i* **1.** *dated* mieszkać **2.** tkwić ⟨u-⟩; **lodg•er** ['lɒdʒə] *s Br* lokator *m*; ***take in ~s*** wynajmować pokoje; **lodg•ing** ['lɒdʒɪŋ] *s* kwatera *f*; ***night's ~, ~ for the night*** nocleg; ***live in ~*** wynajmować pokój
loft [lɒft] *s* **1.** strych *m*; ***in the ~*** na strychu **2.** poddasze *n*; **loft•y** ['lɒftɪ] *adj* **1.** wzniosły **2.** wysoki **3.** strzelisty **4.** wyniosły

log [lɒg] **I** *s* dziennik *m* pokładowy **II** *v/t* notować ⟨za-⟩; **log off** *v/i* wylogowywać ⟨-gować⟩ się; **log on** *v/i* logować ⟨za-⟩ się; **log on to** *v/i* logować ⟨za-⟩ się do *G*

lo•gic ['lɒdʒɪk] *s* logika *f*; **lo•gic•al** ['lɒdʒɪkl] *adj* logiczny; **lo•gic•al•ly** ['lɒdʒɪklɪ] *adv* logicznie

loin [lɔɪn] *s* **1.** schab *m* **2.** polędwica *f*

loll [lɒl] *v/i* **1.** wylegiwać się; ***she ~ed on the sofa*** wylegiwała się na kanapie **2.** zwisać ⟨-snąć⟩; **loll about**, ***loll around*** *v/i* leniuchować

lol•li•pop ['lɒlɪpɒp] *s* lizak *m*; **'lol•li•pop man** *pl -men*, ***'lol•li•pop lady*** *s* osoba przeprowadzająca przez jezdnię dzieci idące do lub ze szkoły

Lon•don ['lʌndən] *s* Londyn *m*; **Lon•don•er** ['lʌndənə] *s* londyńczyk *m*

lone [ləʊn] *adj* **1.** samotny **2.** pojedynczy; **lone•li•ness** ['ləʊnlɪnɪs] *s* samotność *f*; **lone•ly** ['ləʊnlɪ] *adj* samotny; **lon•er** ['ləʊnə] *s* samotnik *m*; **lone•some** ['ləʊnsəm] *adj* samotny

L

long[1] [lɒŋ] **I** *adj* **1.** długi; ***be two feet ~*** mieć dwie stopy długości; ***be 20 pages ~*** mieć dwadzieścia stron; ***how ~ is the course?*** ile trwa kurs?; ***for a ~ time*** długo; ***it's a ~ way from here*** to daleko stąd; ***in the ~ run*** na dłuższą metę **2.** *memory*: dobry **3.** długoletni **II** *adv* długo; ***he is ~ dead*** od dawna nie żyje; ***for as ~ as possible*** tak długo, jak to tylko możliwe; ***as ~ as you keep quiet*** pod warunkiem, że będziesz cicho; ***~ after he left*** długo po jego wyjeździe; ***~ ago*** dawno temu; ***as ~ ago as 1900*** już w 1900 roku; ***so ~!*** do zobaczenia!

long[2] [~] *v/i*: ***~ for* a)** tęsknić za *I* **b)** marzyć o *L*; ***~ to do s.th.*** marzyć o zrobieniu czegoś

long-a•'wait•ed *adj* długo oczekiwany; **long-'dis•tance** *adj* **1.** ***a ~ phone call*** **a)** rozmowa międzymiastowa **b)** rozmowa międzynarodowa **2.** daleki **3.** długodystansowy **4.** dalekobieżny; **long-dis•tance 'run•ner** *s* długodystansowiec *m*

lon•gev•i•ty [lɒn'dʒevɪtɪ] *s* **1.** długowieczność *f* **2.** trwałość *f* **3.** długość *f*

long•'haired *adj* długowłosy

long•ing ['lɒŋɪŋ] **I** *s* **1.** tęsknota *f* **2.** ochota *f* **3.** pożądanie *n* **II** *adj* **1.** tęskny **2.** pożądliwy

long•ish ['lɒŋɪʃ] *adj* długawy, przydługi

lon•gi•tude ['lɒndʒɪtjuːd] *s* długość *f* geograficzna

'long johns *pl infml* kalesony *pl*; **'long jump** *s Br* skok *m* w dal; **'long jumper** *s* skoczek *m* w dal; **long-life 'milk** *s* mleko *n* o przedłużonej trwałości; **long-'lived** *adj* **1.** długowieczny **2.** długotrwały **3.** wieloletni **long-play•ing 're•cord** *s* płyta *f* długogrająca, longplay *m*; **long-'range** *adj* **1.** dalekiego zasięgu **2.** długoterminowy **3.** długofalowy; **'long•shore•man** *pl -men s Am* doker *m*, robotnik *m* portowy; **'long shot** *s*: ***not by a ~*** bynajmniej, wcale nie; **long•'sight•ed** *adj Br* dalekowzroczny; **long-'sleeved** *adj* z długim rękawem; **long-'stand•ing** *adj* **1.** długoletni **2.** długi **3.** wieloletni **4.** stary; **long-'term** *adj* **1.** długoterminowy **2.** długofalowy **3.** *memory*: długotrwały; **long 'wave I** *s* fale *pl* długie; ***on ~*** na falach długich **II** *adj* **1.** na falach długich **2.** odbierający fale długie; **long•'wind•ed** *adj* **1.** rozwlekły **2.** długi **3.** gadatliwy

loo [luː] *s infml* ubikacja *f*

look [lʊk] **I** *v/i* **1.** patrzeć ⟨po-⟩ (**at** na *A*); ***don't ~!*** nie patrz!; ***~ who is coming!*** patrz, kto idzie! **2.** spoglądać ⟨spojrzeć⟩ (**at** na *A*); ***~ in the mirror*** spojrzeć w lustro **3.** wyglądać; ***~ good*** dobrze wyglądać **4.** przyglądać ⟨przyjrzeć⟩ się **5.** ***it ~s like rain*** wygląda na to, że będzie padać, zanosi się na deszcz **4.** ***my room ~s north*** okna mojego pokoju wychodzą na północ **6.** rozważać ⟨-żyć⟩ (**at** *A*) **II** *v/t* **1.** spoglądać ⟨spojrzeć⟩; ***~ s.o. in the eye*** spojrzeć komuś w oczy **2.** wyglądać na *A*; ***she does not ~ her age*** nie wygląda na swój wiek; ***~ an idiot*** wyjść na idiotę **III** *s* **1.** spojrzenie *n*; ***give s.o. an angry ~*** popatrzeć na kogoś ze złością; ***have a ~ at s.th.*** przyjrzeć się czemuś, obejrzeć coś; ***have a ~ around*** rozejrzeć się **2.** wygląd *m*; ***have the ~ of*** wyglądać jak *N* **3.** ***~s*** wygląd, uroda **4.** mina *f*, wyraz *m* twarzy; ***the ~ on his face*** wyraz jego twarzy; **look after 1.** opiekować ⟨za-⟩ się **2.** zajmować ⟨-jąć⟩ się **3.** pilnować ⟨po-⟩; **look ahead** *v/i* **1.** patrzeć ⟨po-⟩ przed siebie **2.** patrzeć w przyszłość; **look around** *v/i* **1.** oglądać ⟨obejrzeć⟩ się **2.** rozglądać ⟨-zejrzeć⟩ się; **look back** *v/i* **1.** oglądać ⟨obejrzeć⟩ się (za siebie) **2.** wracać myślami (***to*** do *G*); **look down on** *v/i* **1.** patrzeć z góry na *A* **2.** gardzić *I*; **look for** *v/i* szukać ⟨po-⟩, poszukiwać; **look forward to** *v/i* **1.** cieszyć się na *A*; ***I ~ working with you*** cieszę się, żę będziemy razem pracować **2.** oczekiwać; ***I ~ hearing from you*** czekam na odpowiedź; **look in on** *v/i* zaglądać ⟨zajrzeć⟩ do *G*; **look into** *v/i* **1.** badać ⟨z-⟩ **2.** zajmować ⟨-jąć⟩ się **3.** ***~ s.o.'s eyes*** spojrzeć komuś w oczy; **look on** *v/i* **1.** przyglądać się **2.** uznawać (***as*** za *A*); **look onto** *v/i* wychodzić na *A*; ***the window looks onto the garden*** okno wychodzi na ogród; **look out I** *v/i* **1.** wyglądać ⟨wyjrzeć⟩ **2.** uważać; ***~!*** uważaj!, uwaga! **3.** ***~ on*** wychodzić na *A* **II** *v/t* przeszukiwać ⟨-ać⟩; **look out for** *v/i* **1.** rozglądać ⟨-zejrzeć⟩ się za *I* **2.** uważać na *A* **3.** ***~ oneself*** troszczyć się o własne interesy; ***~ s.o.*** troszczyć się o czyjeś interesy **4.** *Br* szukać ⟨po-⟩; **look out of** *v/i* wyglądać ⟨wyjrzeć⟩ przez *A*; ***~ the window*** wyjrzeć przez okno; **look over** *v/i* **1.** oglądać ⟨obejrzeć⟩ **2.** *notes*: przeglądać ⟨przejrzeć⟩; **look through** *v/i* **1.** *notes*: przeglądać ⟨przejrzeć⟩ **2.** przeszukiwać ⟨-kać⟩ **3.** traktować ⟨po-⟩ jak powietrze; **look to** *v/i form* **1.** liczyć na *A*; ***~ s.o. for help*** liczyć na czyjąś pomoc **2.** próbować ⟨s-⟩ znaleźć **3.** ***~ it that*** dopilnować, żeby; **look up I** *v/i* **1.** patrzeć ⟨po-⟩ w górę **2.** podnosić ⟨-nieść⟩ wzrok **3.** ***things are looking up*** *infml* jest coraz lepiej, sytuacja się poprawia **II** *v/t* **1.** znajdować ⟨znaleźć⟩ **2.** *word*: sprawdzać ⟨-dzić⟩ **3.** ***look s.o. up and down*** zmierzyć kogoś wzrokiem; **look up to** *v/i* podziwiać

'look-a•like *s* sobowtór *m*

look•ers-'on *pl* gapie *pl*

'look-in *s*: ***he's such a good player that I didn't even get a ~*** *infml* jest tak dobry, że nie miałem z nim żadnych szans

'look•ing glass *s lit* zwierciadło *n*, lustro *n*

loom [luːm] *v/i* **1.** wyłaniać ⟨-łonić⟩ się **2.** majaczyć ⟨za-⟩; ***~ on the horizon*** majaczyć na horyzoncie **3.** wisieć w powietrzu

loon•y ['luːnɪ] *infml* **I** *adj* pomylony, zbzikowany **II** *s* świr *m*

loop [luːp] **I** *s* **1.** pętla *f* **2.** pętelka *f* **3.** szlufka *f* **4.** (*knitting*) oczko *n* **5.** MED spirala *f* **II** *v/t* **1.** owijać ⟨owinąć⟩; ***~ a rope over*** owinąć linę wokół *G* **2.** robić ⟨z-⟩ pętlę na *L* **III** *v/i* **1.** (*road*) zakręcać ⟨-cić⟩ **2.** (*plane*) robić ⟨z-⟩ pętlę; **'loop•hole** *s fig* **1.** luka *f*; ***a legal ~*** luka w prawie **2.** furtka *f*

loose [luːs] **I** *adj* **1.** luźny; ***come ~*** **a)** obluzować się **b)** rozwiązać się **c)** odpaść **2.** obluzowany **3.** ***break ~*** **a)** wydostać na wolność **b)** zerwać się (z uwięzi); ***let a dog ~*** wypuścić psa, spuścić psa ze smyczy **4.** *hair*: rozpuszczony; ***let one's hair ~*** rozpuścić włosy **5.** ***~ change*** drobne **6.** sypki **7.** *translation*: wolny **8.** ***~ bowels*** biegunka **9.** rozwiązły **II** *s* ***be on the ~*** być na wolności; ***go on the ~*** wydostać się na wolność; **loose-'leaf** *adj*: ***a ~ binder*** skoroszyt, segregator; **loose•ly** ['luːslɪ] *adv* **1.** luźno **2.** nieprecyzyjnie **3.** ***~ translated*** w wolnym tłumaczeniu **4.** ***the movie is ~ based on John Updike's novel*** film jest swobodną adaptacją powieści Johna Updike'a

loos•en ['luːsn] **I** *v/t* **1.** luzować ⟨po-⟩; ***he ~ed his grip and let her go*** puścił ją i pozwolił jej odejść; ***~ s.o.'s tongue*** rozwiązać komuś język **2.** poluźniać ⟨-nić⟩ **3.** rozluźniać ⟨-nić⟩ **II** *v/i* **1.** rozluźniać ⟨-nić⟩ się **2.** obluzowywać ⟨-zować⟩ się; **loos•en up I** *v/i* rozluźniać ⟨-nić⟩ się **II** *v/t muscles*: rozgrzewać ⟨-rzać⟩

lord [lɔːd] **I** *s* **1.** *Br* lord *m*; ***the ≈s*** Izba Lordów **2.** pan *m* **3.** ***the ≈*** Pan, Pan Bóg; ***≈ (only) knows where*** Bóg (jeden) wie gdzie; ***≈'s Prayer*** Modlitwa Pańska; ***≈'s Supper*** Ostatnia Wieczerza **II** *v/t* **4.** ***~ it over s.o.*** *infml* tyranizować kogoś

lor•ry ['lɒrɪ] *s Br* ciężarówka *f*, samochód *m* ciężarowy

L

lose [luːz] **I** (*lost*; *lost*) *v/t* **1.** tracić ⟨s-, u-⟩; **~ *10 pounds* a)** stracić 10 funtów, **b)** schudnąć 10 funtów; ***you have nothing to ~*** nie masz nic do stracenia; ***her company is losing money*** jej firma przynosi straty **2.** przegrywać ⟨-rać⟩ **3.** gubić ⟨z-⟩ **4.** *opportunity*: tracić ⟨s-⟩, przegapiać ⟨-pić⟩ **5.** ***his arrogance lost him the job*** przez swoją arogancję stracił pracę **6.** spóźniać ⟨-nić⟩ się na *A* **7.** (*watch*) późnić się o *A* **II** (*lost*; *lost*) *v/i* przegrywać ⟨-rać⟩; **lose out** *v/i* **1.** tracić ⟨s-⟩ **2.** przegrywać ⟨-rać⟩ **3.** przegrywać ⟨-rać⟩ konkurencję (***to*** z *I*); **los•er** [ˈluːzə] *s* **1.** przegrany *m*; ***be a good*** (***bad***) **~** umieć (nie umieć) przegrywać **2.** nieudacznik *m*, ofiara *f* losu; **los•ing** [ˈluːzɪŋ] *adj* **1.** przegrywający; ***fight a ~ battle*** toczyć z góry przegraną walkę **2.** przynoszący straty **3.** deficytowy

loss [lɒs] *s* **1.** strata *f*; **~ *of time*** strata czasu; ***sell s.th. at a ~*** sprzedać coś ze stratą **2.** utrata *f*; **~ *of memory*** utrata pamięci **3.** straty *pl* **4.** ***I was a dead ~*** *infml* byłem beznadziejny **5.** ***be at a ~*** być w rozterce; ***be at a ~ for words*** nie wiedzieć, co powiedzieć

L

lost [lɒst] **I** *Past Simple and Past Participle* → **lose II** *adj* **1.** zgubiony; ***I'm ~*** zgubiłem się; ***get ~*** zgubić się; ***get ~!*** *infml* spadaj! **2.** zaginiony; ***give s.o. up for ~*** uznać kogoś za zaginionego **3.** zagubiony, zdezorientowany **4.** stracony; ***all is not ~*** nie wszystko stracone **5.** przegrany **6.** ***be ~ on*** nie zostać zrozumianym przez *G*; ***the joke was ~ on her*** nie zrozumiała dowcipu **7.** **~ *in thought*** zatopiony w myślach, zamyślony **8.** ***be ~ for words*** nie wiedzieć, co powiedzieć; **lost-and-ˈfound** *s Am* biuro *n* rzeczy znalezionych; **lost ˈprop•er•ty** *s Br* **1.** rzeczy znalezione **2.** biuro *n* rzeczy znalezionych; **lost ˈprop•er•ty of•fice** *s Br* biuro *n* rzeczy znalezionych

lot[1] [lɒt] **I** *pron* ***a ~ of*** dużo *G*, wiele *G*; **~*s of*** *infml* dużo *G*, mnóstwo *G*; ***he's a ~ better*** czuje się dużo lepiej **II** *s* ***the*** (***whole***) **~** wszystko

lot[2] [~] *s* **1.** los *m*; ***draw ~s*** ciągnąć losy **2.** działka *f* **3.** parcela *f* **4.** ***a parking ~*** parking **5.** pozycja *f* **6.** ***a bad ~*** *Br dated* paskudny typ

lo•tion [ˈləʊʃn] *s* płyn *m*

lot•te•ry [ˈlɒtərɪ] *s* loteria *f*; **ˈlot•te•ry tick•et** *s* los *m*, kupon *m*

lo•tus [ˈləʊtəs] *s* lotos *m*

loud [laʊd] *adj* **1.** głośny **2.** hałaśliwy **3.** krzykliwy; **loud•ˈhail•er** *s Br* megafon *m*; **ˈloud•mouth** *s* krzykacz *m*; **loud•ˈspeak•er** *s* głośnik *m*

lounge [laʊndʒ] **I** *s* **1.** *Br* salon *m* **2.** hol *m* **3.** poczekalnia *f* **II** *v/i* → **loll 1**; **ˈlounge bar** *s Br* bar *f* wyższej kategorii; **lounge around** *v/i* **1.** leniuchować **2.** wylegiwać się

louse [laʊs] *pl lice s* **1.** wesz *f* **2.** *infml* gnida *f*; **louse up** *v/t infml* pieprzyć ⟨s-⟩

lous•y [ˈlaʊzɪ] *adj infml* **1.** podły; ***feel ~*** czuć się podle **2.** nędzny **3.** beznadziejny

lov•a•ble [ˈlʌvəbl] *adj* rozkoszny, uroczy

love [lʌv] **I** *s* **1.** miłość *f*; ***be in ~*** być zakochanym; ***fall in ~ with*** zakochać się w *L*; ***make ~ to*** kochać się z *I*, uprawiać miłość z *I*; ***not for ~ or money*** za nic na świecie; ***there is no ~ lost between them*** serdecznie się nienawidzą; **~ *of one's country*** miłość do ojczyzny; ***give one's ~ to*** pozdrowić *A*; ***he's a real ~*** jest naprawdę kochany; **~** (*letter ending*) serdeczne pozdrowienia **2.** umiłowanie *n* **3.** **~!** kochanie!, skarbie! **4.** (*tennis*) zero *n* **II** *v/t* **1.** kochać **2.** uwielbiać; **~ *doing s.th.***, **~ *to do s.th.*** uwielbiać coś robić; **ˈlove af•fair** *s* romans *m*; **ˈlove bite** *s* (*after kissing*) *Br* malinka *f*; **love-ˈhate re•la•tion•ship** *s Br* miłość *f* połączona z nienawiścią

love•less [ˈlʌvlɪs] *adj* **1.** bez miłości **2.** niekochany

ˈlove let•ter *s* list *m* miłosny; **ˈlove life** *s* życie *n* intymne, życie *n* erotyczne

love•ly [ˈlʌvlɪ] *adj* **1.** śliczny **2.** uroczy **3.** rozkoszny **4.** czarujący

ˈlove•mak•ing *s* współżycie *n*; **love match** *s* małżeństwo *n* z miłości; **ˈlove po•em** *s* wiersz *m* miłosny

lov•er [ˈlʌvə] *s* **1.** kochanek *m* **2.** miłośnik *m*; ***a music ~*** miłośnik muzyki, meloman **3.** zakochany *m*

lov•ing [ˈlʌvɪŋ] *adj* **1.** kochający; ***your ~ father*** (*letter ending*) twój kochający ojciec **2.** czuły **3.** pełen miłości;

lov•ing•ly ['lʌvɪŋlɪ] *adv* **1.** czule **2.** z miłością **3.** pieczołowicie

low [ləʊ] **I** *adj* **1.** niski; ***a ~ bow*** niski ukłon; ***the sun is ~ in the sky*** słońce jest nisko na niebie **2.** nisko położony **3.** ***be ~ in fat*** zawierać mało tłuszczu; ***be ~ on funds*** mieć niewielkie fundusze **4.** na wyczerpaniu; ***run ~, get ~*** kończyć się, wyczerpywać się; ***we are running ~ on sugar*** kończy się nam cukier **5.** przybity; ***feel ~*** być przybitym, mieć chandrę; ***in ~ spirits*** w złym nastroju **6.** nienajlepszy; ***have a ~ opinion of*** mieć nienajlepsze zdanie na temat *G* **7.** podły **8.** cichy; ***in a ~ voice*** cicho, ściszonym głosem **II** *adv* nisko; ***sink ~er*** zniżyć się; ***he sunk so ~*** *fig* tak nisko upadł; ***please turn the music ~er*** proszę, przycisz muzykę **III** *s* **1.** ***be at record ~*** być na rekordowo niskim poziomie **2.** niż *m*

'low•brow *adj* **1.** niewysokich lotów **2.** niewyszukany; **low-'cal•o•rie** *adj* niskokaloryczny; **'low-cost** *adj* tani, niskonakładowy; **'low-cut** *adj* z głębokim dekoltem, wydekoltowany; **'low•down I** *s* ***give s.o. the ~ on*** zdać komuś sprawę z *G* **II** *adj* podły, nikczemny; **low-e•'mis•sion** *adj* o obniżonej emisji spalin

low•er ['ləʊə] **I** *comp* → **low** *adj* **1.** niższy; ***in ~ case*** małymi literami; ***the ~ court*** sąd niższej instancji; ***the ~ classes*** młodsze klasy **2.** dolny; ***the ~ deck*** dolny pokład **II** *v/t* **1.** obniżać ⟨-żyć⟩ **2.** spuszczać ⟨spuścić⟩ **3.** opuszczać ⟨opuścić⟩ **4.** ***~ oneself*** zniżyć się **III** *v/i* obniżać ⟨-żyć⟩ się

'low-fat *adj* niskotłuszczowy, o obniżonej zawartości tłuszczu; **low-'fly•ing** *adj* nisko latający; **low-'in•come** *adj* o niskich dochodach; **low•'key** *adj* **1.** kameralny **2.** dyskretny; **'low-lands** *pl* niziny *pl*, nizina *f*; **low-'pres-sure ar•e•a** *s* obszar *m* niskiego ciśnienia; **'low sea•son** *s Br* martwy sezon *m*; **low-'ly•ing** *adj* nisko położony; **low-'spir•it•ed** [ləʊ'spɪrɪtɪd] *adj* przygnębiony; **low 'tide** *s* odpływ *m*

loy•al ['lɔɪəl] *adj* lojalny (***to*** wobec *G*); **loy•al•ist** ['lɔɪəlɪst] *s* lojalista *m*; **loy•al•ly** ['lɔɪəlɪ] *adv* lojalnie; **loy•al•ty** ['lɔɪəltɪ] *s* lojalność *f* (***to*** wobec *G*)

Ltd *abbr* (=***limited liability***) z o.o.

lu•bri•cant ['luːbrɪkənt] *s* **1.** smar *m* **2.** środek *m* nawilżający; **lu•bri•cate** ['luːbrɪkeɪt] *v/t* **1.** smarować ⟨po-⟩ **2.** nawilżać ⟨-żyć⟩; **lu•bri•ca•tion** [luːbrɪ'keɪʃn] *s* **1.** smarowanie *n* **2.** nawilżanie *n*

lu•cid ['luːsɪd] *adj* **1.** jasny **2.** przejrzysty **3.** przytomny; ***a ~ moment*** przebłysk świadomości

luck [lʌk] *s* **1.** szczęście *n*; ***good ~*** szczęście, *infml* fart; ***bad ~, hard ~*** pech, *infml* niefart; ***be in ~*** mieć szczęście; ***be out of ~*** nie mieć szczęścia; ***try one's ~*** spróbować szczęścia; ***good ~!*** powodzenia! **2.** traf *m*; ***as ~ would have it*** traf chciał, że; **luck out** *v Am infml* mieć szczęście, *infml* mieć fart

luck•i•ly ['lʌkɪlɪ] *adv* **1.** na szczęście **2.** szczęśliwie; ***~ for me*** szczęśliwie dla mnie; **luck•less** ['lʌklɪs] *adj* nieszczęśliwy, niefortunny; **luck•y** ['lʌkɪ] *adj* **1.** szczęśliwy; ***be ~*** mieć szczęście; ***a ~ day*** szczęśliwy dzień; ***a ~ guy*** szczęściarz **2.** przynoszący szczęście; ***be ~*** przynosić szczęście

lug•gage ['lʌgɪdʒ] *s* bagaż *m*; **'lug-gage al•low•ance** *s* dopuszczalna waga *f* bagażu; **'lug•gage lock•er** *s* schowek *m* na bagaż; **'lug•gage trol•ley** *s* wózek *m* bagażowy

luke•warm [luːk'wɔːm] *adj* **1.** letni **2.** ciepławy **3.** ***he was ~ about it*** przyjął to bez entuzjazmu; ***receive a ~ response*** zostać przyjętym bez entuzjazmu

lull [lʌl] **I** *v/t* **1.** usypiać ⟨uśpić⟩; ***~ s.o. to sleep*** uśpić kogoś **2.** *fig* uśpić; ***~ s.o. into a false sense of security*** uśpić czyjąś czujność **II** *v/i* (*storm*) uspokajać ⟨-koić⟩ się **III** *s* **1.** chwila *f* ciszy; ***the ~ before the storm*** cisza przed burzą **2.** przerwa *f*

lul•la•by ['lʌləbaɪ] *s* kołysanka *f*

'lum•ber•jack ['lʌmbədʒæk] *s* drwal *m*

lu•mi•nous ['luːmɪnəs] *adj* **1.** świecący **2.** błyszczący **3.** *paint*: fosforyzujący **4.** jaskrawy

lump [lʌmp] *s* **1.** kawałek *m* **2.** grudka *f* **3.** gruda *f* **4.** bryła *f* **5.** guz *m* **6.** guzek *m* **7.** *sugar*: kostka *f* **8.** ***have a ~ in one's throat*** mieć ściśnięte gardło;

L

lump together *v/t* wrzucać ⟨-cić⟩ do jednego worka
lump 'sum *s* **1.** wypłacana jednorazowo kwota *f* **2.** jednorazowa wypłata *f*; **lump•y** ['lʌmpɪ] *adj* **1.** pełen grudek **2.** grudkowaty **3.** nierówny
lu•na•cy ['lu:nəsɪ] *s* **1.** *fig* szaleństwo *n* **1.** *dated* obłęd *m*
lu•nar ['lu:nə] *adj* księżycowy; ***a ~ eclipse*** zaćmienie Księżyca; ***a ~ landing*** lądowanie na Księżycu
lu•na•tic ['lu:nətɪk] **I** *s* **1.** *fig* szaleniec *m* **2.** *dated* obłąkany *m* **II** *adj* **1.** *fig* szalony **2.** *dated* obłąkany; ***a ~ asylum*** zakład dla umysłowo chorych
lunch [lʌntʃ] **I** *s* lunch *m*; **have s.th. for ~** zjeść coś na lunch **II** *v/i* jeść ⟨z-⟩ lunch; **'lunch hour** *s* przerwa *f* na lunch; **'lunch•time** *s* pora *f* lunchu
lung [lʌŋ] *s* płuco *n*
lure [lʊə] **I** *s* **1.** pokusa *f* **2.** wabik *m* **3.** przynęta *f* **4.** urok *m* **II** *v/t* **1.** wabić ⟨z-⟩ (***to/into*** do *G*); ***~ s.o. into a trap*** zwabić kogoś w pułapkę; ***~ s.o. away from*** odciągnąć kogoś od *G* **2.** nęcić ⟨z-⟩
lu•rid ['lʊərɪd] *adj* **1.** drastyczny **2.** krzykliwy **3.** jaskrawy
lurk [lɜ:k] *v/i* czaić się; **lurk about, *lurk around*** *v/i* czaić się, kręcić się w pobliżu
lush [lʌʃ] *adj* **1.** bujny **2.** porośnięty bujną roślinnością **3.** luksusowy
lust [lʌst] *s* **1.** pożądanie *n* **2.** żądza *f*; ***~ for power*** żądza władzy; **lust after** *v/i* **1.** pożądać **2.** pragnąć
lus•ter *Am* → ***lustre***
lust•ful ['lʌstfəl] *adj* pożądliwy, lubieżny
lus•tre ['lʌstə] *Br*, ***lus•ter*** *Am s* **1.** *a. fig* blask *m*; ***add ~ to an occassion*** uświetnić okazję; ***lose one's ~*** *fig* tracić na atrakcyjności **2.** połysk *m*
lus•trous ['lʌstrəs] *adj lit* lśniący
Lux•em•bourg ['lʌksəmbɜ:g] *s* Luksemburg *m*
lux•u•ri•ous [lʌg'ʒjʊərɪəs] *adj* luksusowy, komfortowy; **lux•u•ri•ous•ly** [lʌg'ʒjʊərɪəslɪ] *adv* luksusowo, komfortowo, w luksusie; **lux•u•ry** ['lʌkʃərɪ] **I** *s* **1.** luksus *m*; ***a life of ~*** życie w luksusie **2.** *lit* zbytek *m* **II** *adj* **1.** luksusowy **2.** luksusowo urządzony **3.** *lit* zbytkowny
ly•ing ['laɪɪŋ] *adj* kłamliwy
lynx [lɪŋks] *s* ryś *m*
lyr•ic ['lɪrɪk] **I** *adj* liryczny **II** *s* **1.** liryk *m*, utwór *m* liryczny **2.** **~s** słowa piosenki, tekst; **lyr•i•cal** ['lɪrɪkl] *adj* **1.** liryczny **2.** ***wax ~ about*** rozpływać się nad *I*

M

MA [em'eɪ] *abbr* (=***Master of Arts***) magister *m* (nauk humanistycznych), mgr *m*
ma'am [mæm] *s* pani *f*; ***yes, ~*** tak, proszę pani
mac [mæk] → ***mackintosh***
ma•ca•bre mə'kɑ:brə] *adj* makabryczny
mac•a•ro•ni [mækə'roʊnɪ] *s* makaron *m* rurki; **mac•a•ro•ni 'cheese** *Br*, ***mac•a•ro•ni and* 'cheese** *Am s* makaron *m* z sosem serowym
mace[1] [meɪs] *s* **1.** buława *f* **2.** maczuga *f*
mace[2] [~] *s* COOK gałka *f* muszkatołowa
Mace® [~] *s* gaz *m* łzawiący (w aerozolu)
ma•che•te [mə'ʃetɪ] *s* maczeta *f*
ma•chine [mə'ʃi:n] *s* **1.** maszyna *f*, urządzenie *n*; ***washing ~*** pralka **2.** automat *m* **3.** POLIT *fig* aparat *m*, maszyna *f*; ***propaganda ~*** aparat propagandowy; **ma'chine gun** *s* karabin *m* maszynowy; **ma•chine-'read•a•ble** *adj passport*: elektroniczny; **ma•chin•e•ry** [mə'ʃi:nərɪ] *no pl s* **1.** maszyny *pl*; ***~ and equipment*** maszyny i urządzenia **2.** park *m* maszynowy **3.** mechanizm *m* **4.** *fig* aparat *m*, machina *f*; ***the state ~*** aparat państwowy; **ma'chine tool** *s* TECH obrabiarka *f*; **ma•'chine transla•tion** *s* tłumaczenie *n* komputerowe; **ma•chine 'wash•a•ble** *adj* nadający się do prania w pralce

mack•er•el ['mækrəl] *pl mackerel s* BIOL makrela *f*
mack•in•tosh ['mækıntɒʃ] *s Br* płaszcz *m* przeciwdeszczowy
mac•ro ['mækroʊ] *s* INF makro *n*
mac•ro•bi•ot•ic [mækroʊbaı'ɒtık] *adj* makrobiotyczny
mac•ro•cosm ['mækroʊkɒzəm] *s* makrokosmos *m*
macro•eco•nom•ics [mækroʊiːkə'nɒmıks] *s* ECON makroekonomia *f*
mad [mæd] *adj* **1.** *a. fig* szalony, obłąkany; ***go ~*** oszaleć; ***like ~*** jak szalony **2.** *Am infml* wściekły, zły (***with***/***at*** na *A*); ***drive s.o. ~*** doprowadzać kogoś do szału **3.** ***be ~*** *infml* szaleć, mieć bzika (***about***/***on*** na punkcie *G*)
mad•am ['mædəm] *s* pani *f*; ***are you being served, ~?*** czy ktoś panią obsługuje?
'mad•cap *adj infml* zwariowany; **mad 'cow dis•ease** *s infml* choroba *f* szalonych krów; **mad•den** ['mædn] *v/t* doprowadzać ⟨-dzić⟩ do szału; **mad•den•ing** ['mædnıŋ] *adj* doprowadzający do szału, denerwujący; **mad•den•ing•ly** ['mædnıŋlı] *adv* nieznośnie, denerwująco
made [meıd] **I** *Past Simple and Past Participle* → ***make*** **II** *adj*: ***be ~ for each other*** być dla siebie stworzonym; ***he is ~ for this job*** jest do tej pracy stworzony; **made-to-'meas•ure** *adj suit* (uszyty) na miarę; **made-to-'or•der** *adj Am* (wykonany) na zamówienie; **made-'up** *adj* **1.** zmyślony **2.** wymyślony **3.** umalowany
'mad•house *s infml* dom *m* wariatów; **mad•ly** ['mædlı] *adv* **1.** jak szalony **2.** *infml* szaleńczo, bardzo; ***he is ~ in love with her*** jest w niej szaleńczo zakochany; **'mad•man** *pl -men s* szaleniec *m*; **mad•ness** ['mædnıs] *s* szaleństwo *n*; ***sheer ~*** czyste szaleństwo
Ma•don•na [mə'dɒnə] *s* **1.** ***the ~*** Madonna, Matka Boska **2.** ART Madonna *f*
'mad•wom•an *pl -men s* wariatka *f*, szalona *f*
Ma•fi•a ['mɑːfıə] *s* mafia *f*; **ma•fi•o•so** [mɑːfı'əʊsəʊ] *pl -si* [~sI] *s* mafioso *m*
mag•a•zine [mægə'ziːn] *s* **1.** magazyn *m*, czasopismo *n* **2.** RADIO TEL magazyn *m* **3.** magazynek *m* **4.** skład *m* broni (i amunicji); **mag•a•'zine rack** *s* stojak *m* na czasopisma
ma•gen•ta [mə'dʒentə] **I** *adj* purpurowy **II** *s* **1.** purpurowy *m*, purpura *f* **2.** INF magenta *f*
mag•got ['mægət] *s* **1.** BIOL czerw *m* **2.** (*fishing*) robak *m*
Ma•gi ['meıdʒaı] *pl*: ***the ~*** REL Trzej Królowie
mag•ic ['mædʒık] **I** *s* **1.** magia *f*, czary *pl*; ***black ~*** czarna magia; ***as if by ~***, ***like ~*** jak za dotknięciem czarodziejskiej różdżki **2.** sztuczki *pl* magiczne **II** *adj* magiczny, czarodziejski; ***~ carpet*** latający dywan; **mag•i•cal** ['mædʒıkl] *adj* **1.** magiczny **2.** cudowny; **mag•i•cal•ly** ['mædʒıklı] *adv* **1.** w magiczny sposób **2.** w cudowny sposób; **ma•gi•cian** [mə'dʒıʃn] *s* **1.** magik *m*, sztukmistrz *m* **2.** czarodziej *m*, czarownik *m*; **ma•gic 'spell** *s* czarodziejskie zaklęcie *n*; **ma•gic 'trick** *s* magiczna sztuczka *f*; **mag•ic 'wand** *s* czarodziejska różdżka *f*
mag•is•trate ['mædʒıstreıt] *s* JUR sędzia *m* (w sądzie pierwszej instancji), sędzia *m* pokoju; **'magistrates' court** *s* JUR sąd *m* (pierwszej instancji)
mag•na•nim•i•ty [mægnə'nımətı] *s* wielkoduszność *f*, wspaniałomyślność *f*; **mag•nan•i•mous** [mæg'nænıməs] *adj* wielkoduszny, wspaniałomyślny
mag•nate ['mægneıt] *s* magnat *m*, potentat *m*
mag•ne•sia [mæg'niːʃə] *s* CHEM magnezja *f*
mag•ne•si•um [mæg'niːzıəm] *s* CHEM magnez *m*
mag•net ['mægnət] *s a. fig* magnes *m*; **mag•net•ic** [mæg'netık] *adj* magnetyczny; ***~ field*** pole magnetyczne; ***~ pole*** biegun magnetyczny; **mag•net•ic 'stripe** *s* pasek *m* magnetyczny; **mag•net•ism** ['mægnətızəm] *s* magnetyzm *m*; ***personal ~*** *fig* urok osobisty; **mag•net•ize** ['mægnətaız] *v/t* PHYS magnesować ⟨na-⟩
mag•ni•fi•ca•tion [mægnıfı'keıʃn] *s* powiększenie *n*; ***under ~*** **a)** w powiększeniu **b)** pod mikroskopem
mag•nif•i•cence [mæg'nıfısəns] *s* wspaniałość *f*; **mag•nif•i•cent** [mæg'nıfısənt] *adj* **1.** wspaniały **2.** doskonały;

M

mag•nif•i•cent•ly [mæg'nɪfɪsəntlɪ] *adv* **1.** wspaniale **2.** doskonale
mag•ni•fy ['mægnɪfaɪ] *v/t* powiększać ⟨-szyć⟩; '**mag•ni•fy•ing glass** *s* szkło *n* powiększające
mag•ni•tude ['mægnɪtjuːd] *s* **1.** rozmiar *m* **2.** waga *f*; ***of great ~*** wielkiej wagi **3.** *earthquake*: siła *f*
mag•no•li•a [mæg'nəʊlɪə] *s* magnolia *f*
mag•num ['mægnəm] *s butelka o pojemności 1,5 litra*
mag•num o•pus [mægnəm'əʊpəs] *no pl s* opus *n* magnum
mag•pie ['mægpaɪ] *s* sroka *f*
ma•hog•a•ny [mə'hɒgənɪ] *s* mahoń *m*
maid [meɪd] *s* **1.** pokojówka *f* **2.** służąca *f* **3.** *dated* panna; '**maid•en name** ['meɪdnneɪm] *s* nazwisko *n* panieńskie *f*; **maid•en** '**voy•age** *s* dziewiczy rejs *m*; **maid of** '**hon•our** *Br*, ***maid of*** '***ho•nor*** *Am s* pierwsza druhna *f*
mail [meɪl] **I** *s* **1.** poczta *f*; ***by ~*** pocztą **2.** poczta *f*, korespondencja *f*; ***check one's ~*** sprawdzić pocztę; ***incoming*** (***outgoing***) ~ poczta przychodząca (wychodząca) **II** *v/t Am letter*: wysyłać ⟨-słać⟩; '**mail•box** *s Am* **1.** skrzynka *f* na listy **2.** skrzynka *f* pocztowa; '**mail car•ri•er** *s Am* listonosz *m*; '**mail•ing list** *s* lista *f* dyskusyjna, lista *f* mailingowa; '**mail•man** *pl -men s Am* listonosz *m*; **mail-'or•der firm** *s* firma *f* wysyłkowa; **mail-'or•der cat•a•logue** *s* katalog *m* wysyłkowy; '**mail•shot** *s Am* **1.** druki *pl* reklamowe **2.** *INF* mailing *m* list *m* reklamowy
maim [meɪm] *v/t* okaleczać ⟨-czyć⟩
main [meɪn] *adj* główny; '**main course** *s* danie *n* główne; **main** '**en•trance** *s* wejście *n* główne; '**main•frame (computer)** *s INF* komputer *m* typu mainframe; '**main•land I** *s* stały ląd *m* **II** *adj Europe*, *Greece*: kontynentalny; **main•ly** ['meɪnlɪ] *adv* głównie; **main** '**road** *s* droga *f* główna
mains [meɪnz] *pl*: ***the ~*** **a)** *Br* sieć (elektryczna) **b)** sieć wodociągowa **c)** sieć kanalizacyjna **d)** sieć gazowa
'**main•spring** *s fig* sprężyna *f*, siła *f* napędowa
'**main•stay** *s fig* filar *m*, podstawa *f*
'**main•stream I** *s* główny nurt *m* **II** *adj* **1.** *writer*: należący do głównego nurtu; ***~ jazz*** mainstream; ***~ politics*** główny nurt polityki **2.** *production*: masowy **3.** *opinion*: powszechnie panujący
'**main street** *s* główna ulica *f*
main•tain [meɪn'teɪn] *v/t* **1.** utrzymywać ⟨-mać⟩; ***~ standards*** spełniać wymagania **2.** *silence*: zachowywać ⟨-chować⟩ **3.** konserwować ⟨za-⟩, utrzymywać ⟨-mać⟩ w dobrym stanie **4.** twierdzić, utrzymywać (***that*** że);
main•te•nance ['meɪntənəns] *s* **1.** konserwacja *f*, utrzymanie *n* (w dobrym stanie); ***~-free*** niewymagający konserwacji **2.** *Br* alimenty *pl*; '**main•te•nance costs** *pl* koszty *pl* konserwacji; '**main•te•nance staff** *s* personel *m* techniczny
mai•son•ette [meɪzə'net] *s Br* mieszkanie *f* dwupoziomowe
maize [meɪz] *s Br* kukurydza *f*
ma•jes•tic [mə'dʒestɪk] *adj* majestatyczny; **ma•'jes•ti•cal•ly** [mə'dʒestɪklɪ] *adv* majestatycznie; **maj•es•ty** ['mædʒəstɪ] *s* majestat *m*; ***His*** (***Her***) ~ Jego (Jej) Wysokość
ma•jor ['meɪdʒər] **I** *s* **1.** major *m* **2.** *MUS* tonacja *f* durowa, dur *m* **3.** *Am* przedmiot *m* główny **II** *adj* **1.** *role*: ważny, znaczący **2.** *city*, *firm*: duży, wielki **3.** *contribution*: znaczny **4.** *road*: główny **5.** *problem*: poważny **6.** *MUS* durowy; ***in C ~*** C-dur **III** *v/t **~ in*** *Am* specjalizować się w *L*, studiować
Ma•jor•ca [mə'jɔːrkə] *s* Majorka *f*
ma•jor•ette [meɪdʒə'ret] *s* mażoretka *f*, majorette *f*
ma•jor•i•ty [mə'dʒɒrətɪ] *s* **1.** większość *f*; ***by a large ~*** znaczną większością; ***in the ~ of cases*** w większości przypadków **2.** *JUR* pełnoletność *f*; **ma•'jor•i•ty hold•ing** *s ECON* kontrolny pakiet *m* akcji
'**ma•jor-league** *adj a. fig* pierwszoligowy
make [meɪk] **I** *s* **1.** marka *f* **2.** model *m* **II** (*made*; *made*) *v/t* **1.** robić ⟨z-⟩ **2.** robić ⟨z-⟩, produkować ⟨wy-⟩, wytwarzać ⟨-worzyć⟩ (***from***/***of***/***out of*** z *G*) **3.** *decision*, *effort*: podejmować ⟨-djąć⟩ **4.** *bed*: słać ⟨po-⟩ **5.** *mistake*: robić ⟨z-⟩, popełniać ⟨-nić⟩ **6.** *offer*: składać ⟨złożyć⟩ **7.** *speech*: wygłaszać ⟨-łosić⟩ **8.** powodować ⟨s-⟩ **9.** *money*:

M

zarabiać ⟨-robić⟩ **10.** *profit, loss*: przynosić ⟨-nieść⟩ **11.** *fortune*: zbijać ⟨zbić⟩ **12.** (*with adjectives*) ***~ s.o. angry*** złościć kogoś; ***~ s.th. secure*** zabezpieczać coś **13.** mianować; ***~ s.o. (a) director*** mianować kogoś dyrektorem **14.** (*be suitable*) ***he would ~ a good teacher*** byłby z niego dobry nauczyciel **15.** ***~ s.o. wait*** kazać komuś czekać; ***~ s.o. talk*** zmuszać kogoś do mówienia; ***~ s.o. cry*** doprowadzić kogoś do płaczu **16.** docierać ⟨dotrzeć⟩ do *G*; ***I couldn't ~ your party*** nie mogłem przyjść na twoją imprezę **17.** wynosić ⟨-nieść⟩, dawać ⟨dać⟩; ***two and two ~ four*** dwa plus dwa daje cztery **III** (*made*; *made*) *v/i* ***she made as if to turn away*** zrobiła ruch, jakby chciała się odwrócić; ***~ believe that*** udawać, że; **make for** *v/i* **1.** ruszać ⟨-szyć⟩ ku *D*, kierować ⟨s-⟩ się do *G*; ***~ the exit*** skierować się do wyjścia **2.** sprzyjać; **make off** *v/i* uciekać ⟨-ciec⟩ (**with** z *I*); **make off with** *v/t infml* zwinąć, zwiać z *I*; **make out I** *v/t* **1.** *cheque, bill, prescription*: wypisywać ⟨-sać⟩ **2.** rozumieć ⟨z-⟩; ***I can't make him out*** nie mogę go rozgryźć **3.** twierdzić ⟨s-⟩; ***make s.o. out to be a liar*** twierdzić, że ktoś jest kłamcą; ***make oneself out to be important*** udawać ważniaka **II** *v/i* **1.** *infml* dawać ⟨dać⟩ radę **2.** *Am infml* całować się, obściskiwać się; **make over** *v/t* **1.** przekazywać ⟨-zać⟩ **2.** *skirt*: przerabiać ⟨-robić⟩; **make up I** *v/t* **1.** wymyślać ⟨-lić⟩ **2.** zmyślać ⟨-lić⟩ **3.** *report*: sporządzać ⟨-dzić⟩ **4.** stanowić; ***be made up of*** składać się z *G* **5.** godzić ⟨po-⟩ się (**with** z *I*) **6.** ***~ one's mind*** zdecydować się **II** *v/i* malować ⟨u-⟩ się; **make up for** *v/t* **1.** nadrabiać ⟨-robić⟩ **2.** rekompensować ⟨z-⟩; **make up to** *v/t Br* podlizywać ⟨-zać⟩ się *D*

'make-be•lieve *s* **1.** fantazja *f*, fikcja *f* **2.** udawanie *n*; **'make•o•ver** *s* **1.** (całkowita) metamorfoza *f* **2.** przebudowa *f*; **mak•er** ['meɪkər] *s* **1.** twórca *m* **2.** producent *m* **3.** ***the ~*** Stwórca *m*; **'make•shift** *adj* prowizoryczny; **'make-up** *s* **1.** makijaż *m* **2.** charakteryzacja *f* **3.** kosmetyki *pl* **4.** skład *m* **5.** skład *m* tekstu **6.** natura *f*; ***it's not part of her ~*** to nie leży w jej naturze **7.** *Am* egzamin *m* poprawkowy; **'make-up bag** *s* kosmetyczka *f*; **'make-up re•mo•ver** *s* preparat *m* do demakijażu; **mak•ing** ['meɪkɪŋ] *s* **1.** tworzenie *n* **2.** produkcja *f*; ***this model was three years in the ~*** prace nad tym modelem trwały trzy lata **3.** ***have the ~s of*** mieć zadatki na *A*

mal•ad•just•ed [mælə'dʒʌstɪd] *adj* nieprzystosowany (społecznie)

mal•ad•min•is•tra•tion [mælədmɪnɪ'streɪʃən] *s* ECON złe zarządzanie *n*

mal•a•droit [mælə'drɔɪt] *adj* niezręczny, nietaktowny

ma•laise [mæ'leɪz] *no pl s* **1.** złe samopoczucie *n* **2.** trudności *pl*

mal•a•prop•ism ['mæləprɒpɪzəm] *s* przejęzyczenie *n*

ma•lar•i•a [mə'lerɪə] *s* MED malaria *f*

mal•con•tent ['mælkəntent] *s* malkontent *m*

Mal•dives ['mɔːldiːvz] *pl* Malediwy *pl*

male [meɪl] **I** *adj* **1.** męski; ***~ bonding*** męska przyjaźń **2.** *child*: płci męskiej **3.** samczy; ***a ~ bird*** samiec ptaka **II** *s* **1.** mężczyzna *m* **2.** BIOL samiec *m*; **male 'chau•vin•ism** *s* męski szowinizm *m*; **male chau•vin•ist 'pig** *s infml* męska szowinistyczna świnia *f*; **male 'mod•el** *s* model *m*; **male 'nur•se** *s* pielęgniarz *m*; **male 'pros•ti•tute** *s* męska prostytutka *f*

ma•lev•o•lence [mə'levələns] *s* wrogość *f*, zła wola *f*; **ma•lev•o•lent** [mə'levələnt] *adj* **1.** wrogi **2.** złośliwy

mal•for•ma•tion [mælfɔː'meɪʃn] *s* deformacja *f*; **mal•formed** [mæl'fɔːmd] *adj* zdeformowany

mal•func•tion [mæl'fʌŋkʃn] **I** *s* **1.** zaburzenia *pl* (funkcjonowania) **2.** awaria *f* **II** *v/i* źle funkcjonować

mal•ice ['mælɪs] *s* **1.** złośliwość *f*; ***bear s.o. no ~*** nie życzyć komuś źle **2.** ***with ~ aforethought*** JUR umyślnie; **ma•li•cious** [mə'lɪʃəs] *adj* złośliwy

ma•lig•nan•cy [mə'lɪgnənsɪ] *s* MED nowotwór *m* złośliwy; **ma•lig•nant** [mə'lɪgnənt] *adj* złośliwy

ma•lin•ger [mə'lɪŋgər] *v/i* symulować (chorobę); **ma•lin•ger•er** [mə'lɪŋgərə] *s* symulant *m*

mall [mɔːl] *s Am* **1.** centrum *n* handlowe **2.** pasaż *m* handlowy

M

mal•lard ['mælɑːrd] *s* kaczka *f* krzyżówka
mal•le•a•ble ['mælɪəbl] *adj* **1.** podatny na wpływy **2.** *substance*: plastyczny **3.** *metal*: kowalny
mal•let ['mælɪt] *s* **1.** drewniany młotek *m* **2.** (*croquet*) młotek *m* **3.** (*polo*) kij *m*
mal•low ['mæləʊ] *s* malwa *f*, ślaz *m*
mal•nour•ished [mæl'nʌrɪʃt] *adj* niedożywiony
mal•nu•tri•tion [mælnjʊ'trɪʃn] *s* niedożywienie *n*
mal•prac•tice [mæl'præktɪs] *s* JUR **1.** błąd *m* w sztuce (lekarskiej) **2.** zaniedbanie *n* obowiązków służbowych
malt [mɔːlt] *s* słód *m*; **malt 'whis•ky** *Br*, ***malt 'whis•key*** *Am s* whisky *f* słodowa
Mal•ta ['mɔːltə] *s* Malta *f*
mal•treat [mæl'triːt] *v/t* **1.** źle traktować ⟨po-⟩ **2.** maltretować; **mal•treat•ment** [mæl'triːtmənt] *s* **1.** złe traktowanie *n* **2.** maltretowanie *n*
mam•mal ['mæml] *s* ssak *m*
mam•moth ['mæməθ] **I** *s* mamut *m* **II** *adj* ogromny, gigantyczny
man [mæn] **I** *pl* ***men*** [men] *s* **1.** mężczyzna *m*; ***be one's own ~*** być panem samego siebie; ***a blind ~*** niewidomy **2.** człowiek *m* **3.** mąż *m* **4.** osoba *f*; ***every ~*** każdy; ***no ~*** nikt **5.** *infml* facet *m* **6.** (*chess*, *draughts*) bierka *f* **II** *v/t switchboard*: obsługiwać; ***the line is ~ned 24 hours a day*** linia telefoniczna jest czynna 24 godziny na dobę; ***a ~ned space flight*** załogowy lot kosmiczny; ***officers and men*** oficerowie i żołnierze
man•age ['mænɪdʒ] **I** *v/t* **1.** *firm*, *time*, *money*: zarządzać **2.** zdołać (***to do s.th.*** zrobić coś) **3.** obchodzić się z *I* **II** *v/i* radzić ⟨po-⟩ sobie, dawać ⟨dać⟩ sobie radę (***with*** z *I*; ***without*** bez *G*); **man•age•a•ble** ['mænɪdʒəbl] *adj* **1.** możliwy do opanowania **2.** *level*, *size*: rozsądny **3.** *hair*: łatwo układający się; **man•age•ment** ['mænɪdʒmənt] *s* **1.** *firm*, *time*, *money*: zarządzanie *n* **2.** zarząd *m*, kierownictwo *n*; ***under new ~*** pod nowym kierownictwem; **man•age•ment 'buy•out** *s* ECON wykup *m* menedżerski; **man•age•ment con•'sult•an•cy** *s* ECON doradztwo *m* w zakresie zarządzania; **man•age•ment con•'sult•ant** *s* ECON konsultant *m* w zakresie zarządzania; **'man•age•ment fee** *s* opłata *f* za zarządzanie, opłata *f* manipulacyjna; **'man•age•ment stud•ies** *pl* zarządzanie *n*; **'man•age•ment team** *s* zespół *m* zarządzający
man•ag•er ['mænɪdʒə] *s* **1.** menedżer *m* **2.** kierownik *m* **3.** dyrektor *m*; **man•ag•er•ess** [mænɪdʒə'res] *s dated* kierowniczka *f*; **man•a•ge•ri•al** [mænɪ'dʒɪərɪəl] *adj* menedżerski, kierowniczy; ***~ position*** stanowisko kierownicze; **man•ag•ing di•'rec•tor** *s Br* dyrektor *m* (naczelny); **man•ag•ing 'ed•i•tor** *s* redaktor *m* naczelny
man•da•rin [mændərɪn] *s* mandarynka *f*
man•date ['mændeɪt] *s* **1.** JUR upoważnienie *n*, pełnomocnictwo *n* **2.** POLIT mandat *m*
man•da•to•ry ['mændətərɪ] *adj* obowiązkowy, przymusowy
man•di•ble ['mændɪbl] *s* ANAT żuchwa *f*, szczęka *f* dolna
man•do•lin ['mændəlɪn] *s* MUS mandolina *f*
mane [meɪn] *s* **1.** *horse*, *lion*: grzywa *f* **2.** *fig* czupryna *f*
man-eat•er ['mæniːtə] *s* **1.** ludojad *m* **2.** *fig* modliszka *f*
ma•neu•ver [mə'nuːvər] → ***manoeuvre***
man•ful•ly ['mænfəlɪ] *adv* mężnie, dzielnie
man•ga•nese ['mæŋgəniːz] *s* CHEM mangan *m*
mange [meɪndʒ] *s* BIOL parch *m*, świerzb *m*
man•ger ['meɪndʒər] *s* żłób *m*
mange•tout [mɒnʒ'tuː] *Br s* groch *m* cukrowy
man•gle[1] ['mæŋgl] *s* wyżymaczka *f*
man•gle[2] [~] *v/t* **1.** miażdżyć ⟨z-⟩ **2.** psuć ⟨ze-⟩, *infml* knocić ⟨s-⟩
man•go ['mæŋgəʊ] *pl -gos*, *-goes s* BIOL mango *n*
man•grove ['mæŋgrəʊv] *s* BIOL mangrowiec *m*; ***~s*** namorzyny
man•gy ['meɪndʒɪ] *adj* **1.** parchaty **2.** *infml coat*: wyświechtany
man•han•dle ['mænhændl] *v/t* **1.** poniewierać ⟨s-⟩ **2.** przenosić ⟨-nieść⟩

M

'man•hole *s* **1.** właz *m* **2.** studzienka *f* włazowa

man•hood ['mænhʊd] *s* **1.** wiek *m* męski **2.** męskość *f*

man-'hour *s* roboczogodzina *f*

'man•hunt *s* pościg *m*

ma•ni•a ['meɪnɪə] *s* **1.** *PSYCH* mania *f* **2.** mania *f*, szaleństwo *n*, obsesja *f* (**for** na punkcie *G*); **ma•ni•ac** ['meɪnɪæk] **I** *s* **1.** *PSYCH* maniak *m*; ***a homicidal ~*** maniakalny zabójca **2.** maniak *m*, fanatyk *m* **II** *adj PSYCH* maniakalny; **man•ic-de•pres•sive** [mænɪkdɪ'presɪv] **I** *adj PSYCH* maniakalno-depresyjny **II** *s* cierpiący *m* na psychozę maniakalno-depresyjną

man•i•cure ['mænɪkjʊə] **I** *s* manicure *m*; ***have a ~*** zrobić (sobie) manicure **II** *v/t* robić ⟨z-⟩ manicure

man•i•fest ['mænɪfest] **I** *adj* widoczny, rzucający się w oczy **II** *v/t* **1.** okazywać ⟨-zać⟩, demonstrować ⟨za-⟩ **2.** ***~ itself*** pojawiać ⟨-wić⟩ się, ujawniać ⟨-nić⟩ się **III** *s* **1.** *passengers*: lista *f* **2.** manifest *m* ładunkowy; **man•i•fes•ta•tion** [mænɪfe'steɪʃn] *s* **1.** *beliefs, feelings*: wyraz *m*, manifestacja *f*; **2.** *MED* objaw *m*; **man•i•fest•ly** ['mænɪfestlɪ] *adv* wyraźnie, jawnie; **man•i•fes•to** [mænɪ'festəʊ] *pl -tos, -toes s* manifest *m*

man•i•fold ['mænɪfəʊld] **I** *adj* różnorodny, różnoraki **II** *s* ***exhaust ~*** *AUTO* kolektor wydechowy

ma•nip•u•late [mə'nɪpjəleɪt] *v/t* **1.** manipulować **2.** obsługiwać ⟨-łużyć⟩ **3.** *data*: przetwarzać ⟨-worzyć⟩ **4.** *data, figures*: zafałszowywać ⟨-szować⟩ **5.** *broken leg*: nastawiać ⟨-wić⟩; **ma•nip•u•la•tion** [mənɪpjə'leɪʃn] *s* **1.** manipulowanie *n*, manipulacja *f* **2.** obsługa *f* **3.** *data*: przetwarzanie *n* **4.** *data, figures*: zafałszowywanie *n*; **ma•nip•u•la•tive** [mə'nɪpjələtɪv] *adj* **1.** manipulacyjny; ***he's ~*** jest manipulantem **2.** *talent*: manualny

man'kind *s* ludzkość *f*; **man•ly** ['mænlɪ] *adj* męski; **man-'made** *adj* sztuczny, stworzony przez człowieka; ***~ lake*** sztuczne jezioro

man•ne•quin ['mænɪkɪn] *s* manekin *m*

man•ner ['mænə] *s* **1.** sposób *m*; ***in this ~*** w ten sposób; ***in such a ~ that*** w taki sposób, że; ***in a ~ of speaking*** w pewnym sensie **2.** zachowanie *n*, sposób *m* zachowania; ***an aggressive ~*** agresywne zachowanie; **man•ner•ism** ['mænərizm] *s* **1.** maniera *f* **2.** zwyczaj *m* **3.** ***≗*** *ART* manieryzm *m*; **man•ners** ['mænəz] *pl* **1.** maniery *pl*; ***it is bad ~*** nie wypada (***to do s.th.*** robić czegoś) **3.** zwyczaje *pl*

ma•noeu•vre [mə'nuːvə] *Br*, **ma•neu•ver** *Am* **I** *s* manewr *m*; ***be on ~s*** być na manewrach; ***this leaves us no room for ~*** to nie daje nam pola manewru **II** *v/i a. fig* manewrować **III** *v/t a. fig* manewrować

man•or ['mænə] *s Br* **1.** (*a.* ***~ house***) rezydencja *f* **2.** majątek *m* ziemski

'man•pow•er *s* siła *f* robocza; ***skilled ~*** wykwalifikowana siła robocza

man•sion ['mænʃn] *s* rezydencja *f*, pałac *m*

'man•slaugh•ter *s JUR* nieumyślne spowodowanie *n* śmierci

man•tel•piece ['mæntlpiːs] *s Br* gzyms *m* kominka; ***on the ~*** na kominku

man•tle ['mæntl] **I** *s* **1.** obowiązki *pl* **2.** *snow*: całun *m* **3.** *GEOL* płaszcz *m* Ziemi **II** *v/t* okrywać ⟨-ryć⟩

man-to-'man **I** *adj* szczery, otwarty **II** *adv* szczerze, otwarcie

man•u•al ['mænjʊəl] **I** *adj* **1.** *work, worker*: fizyczny **2.** *gearbox*: ręczny **3.** *skills*: manualny **II** *s* **1.** podręcznik *m* **2.** instrukcja *f* obsługi; **man•u•al•ly** ['mænjʊəlɪ] *adv* ręcznie

man•u•fac•ture [mænjʊ'fæktʃə] **I** *v/t* **1.** produkować ⟨wy-⟩, wytwarzać ⟨-worzyć⟩ **2.** *excuse*: wymyślać ⟨-lić⟩ **3.** *story*: zmyślać ⟨-lić⟩ **II** *s* **1.** produkcja *f*, wytwarzanie *n* **2.** ***~s*** produkty, wyroby; **man•u•fac•tur•er** [mænjʊ'fæktʃərə] *s* producent *m*, wytwórca *m*; **man•u•fac•tur•ing** [mænjʊ'fæktʃərɪŋ] **I** *adj* produkcyjny **II** *s* **1.** produkcja *f* **2.** przemysł *m* (wytwórczy)

ma•nure [mə'njʊə] **I** *s* nawóz *m* naturalny **II** *v/t* nawozić ⟨-wieźć⟩

man•u•script ['mænjʊskrɪpt] *s* rękopis *m*, manuskrypt *m*

Manx [mæŋks] *adj* **1.** *landscape*: wyspy Man **2.** *language*: manx

man•y ['menɪ] (*more*; *most*) *pron* wiele, dużo; ***~ times*** wiele razy; ***~ people*** wielu ludzi; ***a great ~*** bardzo dużo;

M

twice as ~ dwa razy więcej; ***one too ~*** o jeden za dużo; ***as ~ as*** aż; ***~ a man*** *form* wielu ludzi
man-'year *s* osoborok *m*
man•y-'sid•ed [menɪ'saɪdɪd] *adj* **1.** *a. fig* wielostronny **2.** *problem*: złożony
map [mæp] **I** *s* **1.** *world*: mapa; ***on the ~*** na mapie; ***put on the ~*** rozsławiać, nadawać rozgłos **2.** *city*: mapa *f*, plan *m* **II** *v/t* **1.** sporządzać ⟨-dzić⟩ mapę **2.** odwzorowywać ⟨-rować⟩, mapować; **map out** *v/t* wytyczać ⟨-czyć⟩, planować ⟨za-⟩
ma•ple ['meɪpl] *s* klon *m*; **ma•ple 'syr-up** *s* COOK syrop *m* klonowy
mar [mɑːr] *v/t* **1.** zakłócać ⟨-cić⟩ **2.** psuć ⟨ze-⟩
mar•a•thon ['mærəθən] *s* maraton *m*
ma•raud•er [mə'rɔːdə] *s* rabuś *m*
mar•ble ['mɑːbl] **I** *s* **1.** marmur *m* **2.** szklana kulka *f*; ***~s*** gra w kulki **II** *adj* marmurowy
March [mɑːtʃ] *s* marzec *m*
march [mɑːtʃ] **I** *v/i* **1.** maszerować ⟨prze-⟩; ***time ~es on*** czas ucieka **2.** demonstrować, maszerować **II** *v/t* prowadzić ⟨za-⟩; ***~ s.o. off to*** zaprowadzić (siłą) do *G* **III** *s* marsz *m*; ***a day's ~*** dzień marszu; ***a protest ~*** marsz protestacyjny; ***steal a ~ on s.o.*** *fig* ubiec kogoś; ***the ~ of time*** upływ czasu; **march•er** ['mɑːtʃə] *s* demonstrant *m*, uczestnik *m* marszu (protestacyjnego); **'march•ing orders** *pl* rozkaz *m* wymarszu; ***get one's ~*** *Br infml* **a)** *work*: wylecieć **b)** SPORT zostać usuniętym z boiska
Mardi Gras [mɑːdɪ'grɑː] *s* ostatki *pl*, Mardi gras *m*
mare [meə] *s* klacz *f*, kobyła *f*
mar•ga•rine [mɑːdʒə'riːn], ***marge*** [mɑːdʒ] *Br infml s* margaryna *f*
mar•gin ['mɑːdʒɪn] *s* **1.** *a. fig* margines *m*; ***in the ~*** na marginesie; ***leave a ~ for*** zostawiać margines swobody na *A*; ***a ~ of error*** margines błędu; ***on the ~s of society*** na marginesie społeczeństwa **2.** przewaga *f*; ***win by a narrow ~*** wygrać niewielką przewagą **3.** ECON marża *f* (zysku), zysk *m*; **mar•gin•al** ['mɑːdʒɪnl] *adj* **1.** *improvement*, *interest*: znikomy, minimalny **2.** marginalny **3.** marginesowy;
mar•gin•al•ize ['mɑːdʒɪnəlaɪz] *v/t* spychać ⟨zepchnąć⟩ na margines; **mar•gin•al•ly** ['mɑːdʒɪnlɪ] *adv* minimalnie, niewiele
mar•i•hua•na, ***mar•i•jua•na*** [mærɪ'wɑːnə] *s* marihuana *f*
ma•ri•na [mə'riːnə] *s* przystań *f*
mar•i•nade [mærɪ'neɪd] *s* COOK marynata *f*; **mar•i•nate** ['mærɪneɪt] *v/t* COOK marynować ⟨za-⟩
ma•rine [mə'riːn] **I** *adj* morski **II** *s* żołnierz *m* piechoty morskiej; ***the ~s*** *Am* piechota morska
mar•i•o•nette [mærɪə'net] *s* marionetka *f*
mar•i•tal ['mærɪtl] *adj* małżeński; ***~ status*** stan cywilny
mar•i•time ['mærɪtaɪm] *adj* morski; ***~ museum*** muzeum morskie; ***~ blockade*** blokada morska
mar•jo•ram ['mɑːdʒərəm] *s* COOK majeranek *m*
mark[1] [mɑːk] *s* ECON marka *f* (niemiecka)
mark[2] [~] **I** *s* **1.** ślad *m*; ***a dirty ~*** plama **2.** znak *m*, symbol *m*; ***a question ~*** znak zapytania; ***an exclamation ~*** wykrzyknik **3.** znamię *n*; ***distinguishing ~s*** znaki szczególne; ***leave its ~ on*** odcisnąć swoje piętno na *L* **4.** *fig* dowód *m*; ***a ~ of confidence*** dowód zaufania **5.** ocena *f* **6.** *a. fig* cel *m*; ***hit the ~*** **a)** trafić w cel **b)** *fig* trafić w sedno, trafić w dziesiątkę; ***miss the ~*** chybić celu; ***be wide of the ~*** *fig* **a)** grubo się mylić **b)** być błędnym **7.** ***on your ~s, get set, go!*** SPORT na miejsca, gotowi, start!; ***be quick off the ~*** *fig* mieć (dobry) refleks; ***be slow off the ~*** *fig* mieć spóźniony refleks, wolno myśleć **II** *v/t* **1.** zaznaczać ⟨-czyć⟩, oznaczać ⟨-czyć⟩, znakować ⟨o-⟩ **2.** zostawiać ⟨-wić⟩ ślad na *L*, szpecić ⟨o-⟩ **3.** upamiętniać ⟨-nić⟩, czcić ⟨u-⟩ **4.** oceniać ⟨-nić⟩ **5.** zapamiętywać ⟨-tać⟩; ***~ my words*** zapamiętaj moje słowa **6.** SPORT kryć **III** *v/i* plamić ⟨za-⟩ się, brudzić ⟨za-⟩ się; **mark down** *v/t* **1.** *price*: obniżać ⟨-żyć⟩ **2.** przeznaczać ⟨-czyć⟩ (***for*** do *G*); **mark off** *v/t* **1.** wyznaczać ⟨-czyć⟩ granicę, oddzielać ⟨-lić⟩ **2.** odróżniać ⟨-nić⟩ (***from*** od *G*); **mark out** *v/t* **1.** wyznaczać ⟨-czyć⟩,

M

wytyczać ⟨-czyć⟩ **2.** wyróżniać ⟨-nić⟩; **mark up** *v/t price*: podwyższać ⟨-szyć⟩

'mark•down *s ECON* obniżka *f* (ceny)

marked [mɑːkt] *adj* wyraźny, widoczny; ***a ~ difference*** wyraźna różnica; **mark•ed•ly** ['mɑːkədlɪ] *adv* wyraźnie

mark•er ['mɑːkə] *s* **1.** wskaźnik *m* **2.** marker *m* **3.** *Br* oceniający *m* **4.** *INF SPORT* znacznik *m*

mar•ket ['mɑːkɪt] **I** *s* **1.** *ECON* rynek *m*; ***on the ~*** (dostępny) na rynku; ***put a house on the ~*** wystawić dom na sprzedaż; ***a share of the ~*** udział w rynku; ***play the ~*** grać na giełdzie **2.** rynek *m*, targ *m*; ***at the ~*** na targu **3.** sklep *m*, market *m* **II** *v/t* **1.** sprzedawać ⟨-dać⟩ **2.** promować ⟨wy-⟩, reklamować ⟨za-⟩ (**as** jako *A*); **mar•ket•a•ble** ['mɑːkɪtəbl] *adj* **1.** *product*: atrakcyjny, chodliwy **2.** *skills*: poszukiwany; **market 'analyst** *s* analityk *m* rynku; **'mar•ket day** *s* dzień *m* targowy; **mar•ket e•'con•o•my** *s* gospodarka *f* rynkowa; **mar•ket 'for•ces** *pl* siły *pl* rynku

mar•ket•ing ['mɑːkɪtɪŋ] *s ECON* marketing *m*; **'mar•ket•ing cam•paign** *s* kampania *f* marketingowa; **'mar•ket•ing de•part•ment** *s* dział *m* marketingu; **'mar•ket•ing strat•e•gy** *s* strategia *f* marketingowa

mar•ket 'lead•er *s ECON* (*company*) lider *m* (na) rynku; **'mar•ket mak•er** *s ECON* animator *m* rynku; **'marketplace** *s* **1.** rynek *m* **2.** plac *m* targowy; **mar•ket re•'search** *s* badania *pl* rynku; **mar•ket 'share** *s* udział *m* w rynku; **'mar•ket town** *s* miasto *n* targowe; **mar•ket 'val•ue** *s* wartość *f* rynkowa

mark•ing ['mɑːkɪŋ] *s* **1.** *Br* ocenianie *n* (prac) **2.** *SPORT* krycie *n*; **mark•ings** ['mɑːkɪŋz] *pl* **1.** (*skin*) deseń *m*, wzór *m* **2. *road ~*** *AUTO* znaki drogowe poziome

marks•man ['mɑːksmən] *pl -men s* **1.** snajper *m* **2.** *SPORT* strzelec *m*

'mark-up *s ECON* marża *f*

mar•lin ['mɑːlɪn] *pl marlin s BIOL* marlin *m*

mar•ma•lade ['mɑːməleɪd] *s* dżem *m* (z owoców cytrusowych)

ma•roon [mə'ruːn] **I** *adj* **1.** bordowy **2.** kasztanowy **II** *s* **1.** (*colour*) bordo *n* **2.** (*colour*) kasztan *m* **3.** *Br* raca *f*

ma•rooned [mə'ruːnd] *adj*: ***~ on a desert island*** wyrzucony na bezludną wyspę; ***a ~ sailor*** rozbitek

mar•quee [mɑː'kiː] *s* **1.** (duży) namiot *m* **2.** *Am* markiza *f*

mar•riage ['mærɪdʒ] *s* **1.** małżeństwo *n*; ***related by ~*** spowinowacony **2.** (*ceremony*) ślub *m*; **'mar•riage cer•tif•i•cate** *Br*, ***'mar•riage li•cense*** *Am s* akt *m* ślubu; **mar•riage 'guid•ance cen•tre** *Br s* poradnia *f* małżeńska; **'mar•riage vows** *pl* przysięga *f* małżeńska; **mar•ried** ['mærɪd] *adj* **1.** *woman*: zamężna; ***she's ~ to him*** jest jego żoną **2.** *man*: żonaty **3.** małżeński; **mar•ried 'cou•ple** *s* para *f* małżeńska; **mar•ried 'name** *s* nazwisko *n* po mężu

mar•row ['mærəʊ] *s* **1.** *ANAT* szpik *m* kostny; ***be frozen to the ~*** przemarznąć do szpiku kości **2.** *Br* kabaczek *m*

mar•ry ['mærɪ] **I** *v/t* **1.** (*woman*) wychodzić ⟨wyjść⟩ za mąż, (*man*) żenić ⟨o-⟩ się; ***get married to*** **a)** wyjść za mąż za *A* **b)** ożenić się z *I*; ***~ me*** **a)** wyjdź za mnie **b)** ożeń się ze mną; ***they got married*** pobrali się **2.** udzielać ⟨-lić⟩ ślubu **II** *v/i* brać ⟨wziąć⟩ ślub; **marry into** *v/i* wżenić się w *A*; **marry off** *v/t* **1.** *daughter*: wydawać ⟨-dać⟩ za mąż **2.** *son*: żenić ⟨o-⟩

Mars [mɑːz] *s ASTR* Mars *m*

marsh [mɑːʃ] *s* bagno *n*

mar•shal ['mɑːʃl] **I** *s* **1.** marszałek *m* **2.** (*police*, *fire service*) *Am* komendant *m* **II** *v/t* zbierać ⟨zebrać⟩, organizować ⟨z-⟩, aranżować ⟨za-⟩

marsh•land ['mɑːʃlænd] *s* bagno *n*, teren *m* bagnisty

marsh•mal•low [mɑːʃ'mæləʊ] *s* (*sweet*) pianka *f* żelowa

marsh•y ['mɑːʃɪ] *adj* bagnisty

mar•su•pi•al [mɑː'suːpɪəl] *s BIOL* torbacz *m*

mar•ten ['mɑːtɪn] *s BIOL* kuna *f*

mar•tial ['mɑːʃl] *adj* **1.** wojskowy **2.** wojenny; **mar•tial arts** *pl* sztuki *pl* walki; **mar•tial 'law** *s* stan *m* wyjątkowy

Mar•tian ['mɑːʃn] *s* Marsjanin *m*

mar•ti•ni [mɑːˈtiːnɪ] *s* martini *n*
mar•tyr [ˈmɑːtə] **I** *s a. fig* męczennik *m* **II** *v/t* męczyć ⟨za-⟩, katować ⟨za-⟩; **mar•tyr•dom** [ˈmɑːtədəm] *s* męczeństwo *n*; **mar•tyred** [ˈmɑːtərd] *adj* **1.** *fig* cierpiętniczy **2.** męczeński
mar•vel [ˈmɑːvl] **I** *s* cud *m* **II** *v/i* zdumiewać ⟨-mieć⟩ się (**at** *I*); **mar•vel•lous** [ˈmɑːvələs] *Br*, ***mar•ve•lous*** *Am adj* wspaniały, cudowny
Marx•ism [ˈmɑːksɪzm] *s* marksizm *m*; **Marx•ist** [ˈmɑːksɪst] **I** *s* marksista *m* **II** *adj* marksistowski
mar•zi•pan [ˈmɑːzɪpæn] *s* marcepan *m*
mas•ca•ra [mæˈskɑːrə] *s* maskara *f*, tusz *m* do rzęs
mas•cot [ˈmæskət] *s* maskotka *f*
mas•cu•line [ˈmæskjʊlɪn] *adj* męski; **mas•cu•lin•i•ty** [mæskjʊˈlɪnətɪ] *s* męskość *f*
mash [mæʃ] **I** *s* COOK pureé *n* **II** *v/t* **1.** rozgniatać ⟨-nieść⟩ **2.** *potatoes*: tłuc ⟨u-⟩; *vegetables*: robić ⟨z-⟩ puree z *G*; **mashed po•ˈta•toes** *pl* ziemniaki *pl* pureé, pureé *n* z ziemniaków
mask [mɑːsk] **I** *s* **1.** *a. fig* maska *f* **2.** maseczka *f* (kosmetyczna) **II** *v/t* maskować ⟨za-⟩, ukrywać ⟨-ryć⟩; **mask•ed ˈball** *s* bal *m* maskowy; **ˈmask•ing tape** *s* taśma *f* malarska
mas•o•chism [ˈmæsəkɪzm] *s* PSYCH masochizm *m*; **mas•o•chist** [ˈmæsəkɪst] *s* PSYCH masochista *m*; **mas•o•chis•tic** [mæsəˈkɪstɪk] *adj* masochistyczny
ma•son [ˈmeɪsn] *s* **1.** kamieniarz *m* **2.** mason *m*, wolnomularz *m*; **Ma•son•ic** [məˈsɒnɪk] *adj* masoński; **ma•son•ry** [ˈmeɪsnrɪ] *s* **1.** kamieniarstwo *n* **2.** kamieniarka *f*
mas•que•rade [mæskəˈreɪd] **I** *s* maskarada *f* **II** *v/i* udawać ⟨-dać⟩ (**as** *A*)
mass[1] [mæs] *s* msza *f*; ***go to ~*** iść na mszę; ***say ~*** odprawiać mszę
mass[2] [~] **I** *s* masa *f*; ***a ~ of errors*** masa błędów; ***a ~ of people*** masa ludzi; ***the ~es*** (*people*) masy **II** *adj* masowy; ***~ unemployment*** masowe bezrobocie; ***weapons of ~ destruction*** broń masowej zagłady **III** *v/t* gromadzić ⟨z-⟩ **IV** *v/i* gromadzić ⟨z-⟩ się
mas•sa•cre [ˈmæsəkər] **I** *s a. fig* masakra *f* **II** *v/t a. fig* masakrować ⟨z-⟩
mas•sage [ˈmæsɑːʒ] **I** *s* masaż *m*; ***give s.o. a ~*** zrobić komuś masaż **II** *v/t* **1.** masować ⟨wy-⟩ **2.** wmasowywać ⟨-sować⟩ (***into*** w *A*) **3.** ***~ s.o.'s ego*** połechtać czyjąś próżność; **ˈmas•sage par•lour** *Br*, ***ˈmas•sage par•lor*** *Am s* salon *m* masażu; **mas•seur** [mæˈsɜːr] *s* masażysta *m*; **mas•seuse** [mæˈsɜːz] *s* masażystka *f*
mas•sive [ˈmæsɪv] *adj* **1.** masywny **2.** ogromny; ***on a ~ scale*** na ogromną skalę; **mas•sive•ly** [ˈmæsɪvlɪ] *adv* **1.** masywnie **2.** ogromnie **3.** znacznie
mass-ˈmar•ket *adj product*: dla masowego odbiorcy; **mass ˈme•di•a** *pl*: ***the ~*** mass media, środki masowego przekazu; **mass ˈmur•der** *s* masowy mord *m*; **mass ˈmur•der•er** *s* seryjny morderca *m*; **mass-pro•ˈduce** *v/t* masowo produkować; **mass pro•ˈduc•tion** *s* masowa produkcja *f*
mast [mɑːst] *s* maszt *m*
mas•ter [ˈmɑːstər] **I** *s* **1.** *a. fig* mistrz *m*; ***a ~ of disguise*** mistrz kamuflażu; ***an old ~*** ART stary mistrz **2.** pan *m*; ***be ~ of the situation*** być panem sytuacji; ***be one's own ~*** być panem samego siebie **3.** *Br* nauczyciel *m*, profesor *m* **4.** magister *m*; ***≈ of Arts*** magister nauk humanistycznych; ***≈ of Science*** magister nauk ścisłych **II** *v/t* **1.** *language, skill*: opanowywać ⟨-nować⟩ **2.** panować ⟨za-⟩ nad *I*, kontrolować; ***~ one's temper*** opanować się **III** *adj* **1.** doskonały **2.** główny; **ˈmas•ter bed•room** *s* główna sypialnia *f*; **ˈmas•ter cop•y** *s* oryginał *m*; **mas•ter•ful** [ˈmɑːstərfʊl] *adj* **1.** pewny siebie **2.** mistrzowski, doskonały; **ˈmas•ter fuse** *s* bezpiecznik *m* główny; **ˈmas•ter key** *s* klucz *m* uniwersalny; **mas•ter•ly** [ˈmɑːstərlɪ] → ***masterful***
ˈmas•ter•mind **I** *s* (*person*) mózg *m* **II** *v/t* planować ⟨za-⟩, być mózgiem *G*
mas•ter of ˈcer•e•mo•nies *s* mistrz *m* ceremonii
ˈmas•ter•piece *s* arcydzieło *n*
ˈmas•ter's de•gree, master's *s* stopień *m* magistra
ˈmas•terstroke *s* mistrzowskie posunięcie *n*
ˈmas•ter•switch *s* TECH wyłącznik *m* główny

M

mas•ter•y ['mɑːstərɪ] *s* **1.** mistrzostwo *n*, biegłe opanowanie *n* **2.** władza *f* (***of***/***over*** nad *I*)

mas•ti•cate ['mæstɪkeɪt] *v/i* przeżuwać ⟨-żuć⟩; **mas•ti•ca•tion** [mæstɪ'keɪʃn] *s* przeżuwanie *n*

mas•tur•bate ['mæstəbeɪt] *v/i* masturbować się; **mas•tur•ba•tion** [mæstə'beɪʃn] *s* masturbacja *f*

mat [mæt] *s* **1.** mata *f* **2.** dywanik *m* **3.** wycieraczka *f* **4.** podstawka *f*

match[1] [mætʃ] *s* zapałka *f*

match[2] [~] **I** *s* **1.** mecz *m* **2.** partner *m*; ***be no ~ for*** nie móc się równać z *I*; ***meet one's ~*** trafić na godnego siebie przeciwnika **3.** ***be a good ~*** pasować do siebie; ***they are a perfect ~*** (*partners*) tworzą doskonałą parę **4.** (*marriage*) *dated* partia *f* **II** *v/t* **1.** pasować do *G* **2.** odpowiadać **3.** dorównywać ⟨-nać⟩; ***no one can ~ her cooking*** nikt nie gotuje tak dobrze jak ona **4.** dopasowywać ⟨-sować⟩ (***to***/***with*** do *G*) **5.** porównywać ⟨-nać⟩ (***against*** z *I*) **III** *v/i* pasować do siebie; **match up to** *v/t* dorównywać ⟨-nać⟩

'match•box *s* **1.** (*full*) pudełko *n* zapałek **2.** (*empty*) pudełko *n* od zapałek

match•ing ['mætʃɪŋ] *adj* pasujący, do kompletu; **match•less** ['mætʃlɪs] *adj* niezrównany

match•mak•er ['mætʃmeɪkər] *s* swat *m*, swatka *f*; **match 'point** *s* (*tennis*) piłka *f* meczowa, meczbol *m*; **'match-stick** *s* zapałka *f*

mate[1] [meɪt] → ***checkmate***

mate[2] [~] **I** *s* **1.** *Br infml* kumpel *m*, kolega *m*; ***work~*** kolega z pracy; ***class~*** kolega z klasy; ***all right, ~?*** jak leci, stary? **3.** BIOL partner *m* **4.** *infml* partner *m* **5.** (*navy*) oficer *m* **II** *v/t animals*: łączyć ⟨po-⟩ w pary **III** *v/i* (*animals*) łączyć ⟨po-⟩ się w pary

ma•te•ri•al [mə'tɪərɪəl] **I** *adj* **1.** materialny; ***~ goods*** dobra materialne **2.** *form* istotny; ***~ damage*** poważne szkody **II** *s a. fig* materiał *m*; ***building ~s*** materiały budowlane; **ma•te•ri•al•ism** [mə'tɪərɪəlɪzm] *s* materializm *m*; **ma•te•ri•al•ist** [mətɪərɪəlɪst] *s* materialista *m*; **ma•te•ri•al•is•tic** [mətɪərɪə'lɪstɪk] *adj* materialistyczny; **ma•te•ri•al•ize** [mə'tɪərɪəlaɪz] *v/i* materializować ⟨z-⟩ się

ma•ter•nal [mə'tɜːrnl] *adj* **1.** *instinct*: macierzyński **2.** *love*: matczyny **3.** *grandpa*, *grandma*: ze strony matki; **ma•ter•ni•ty** [mə'tɜːrnətɪ] *s* macierzyństwo *n*; **ma•'ter•ni•ty clothes** *pl* ubrania *pl* ciążowe; **ma•'ter•ni•ty dress** *s* sukienka *f* ciążowa; **ma•'ter•ni•ty leave** *s* urlop *m* macierzyński; **ma•'ter•ni•ty ward** *s* oddział *m* położniczy

mat•ey ['meɪtɪ] *adj Br infml*: ***be ~ with*** bratać się z *I*, kumplować się z *I*

math [mæθ] *s Am infml* matma *f*

math•e•mat•i•cal [mæθə'mætɪkl] *adj* matematyczny; **math•e•ma•ti•cian** [mæθəmə'tɪʃn] *s* matematyk *m*; **math•e•mat•ics** [mæθə'mætɪks] *s* **1.** matematyka *f* **2.** obliczenia *pl*

maths [mæθs] *s Br infml* **1.** matma *f* **2.** (*counting*) ***if my ~ is right*** jeśli się nie pomyliłem; **'maths teach•er** *s Br infml* matematyk *m*

mat•i•née ['mætɪneɪ] *s* **1.** seans *m* popołudniowy **2.** THEAT *infml* popołudniówka *f*

mat•ing ['meɪtɪŋ] *s* BIOL **1.** gody *pl* **2.** łączenie *n* się w pary; **'mat•ing rit•u•al** *s* rytuał *m* godowy; **'mat•ing sea•son** *s* sezon *m* godowy

ma•tri•arch ['meɪtrɪɑːk] *s* (*woman*) głowa *f* rodziny; **ma•tri•arch•al** [meɪtrɪ'ɑːkəl] *adj* matriarchalny; **ma•tri•arch•y** ['meɪtrɪɑːkɪ] *s* matriarchat *m*

ma•tri•ces ['meɪtrɪsiːz] *pl* → ***matrix***

ma•tric•u•late [mə'trɪkjʊleɪt] *v/i form* rozpoczynać ⟨-cząć⟩ studia, immatrykulować się; **ma•tric•u•la•tion** [mətrɪkjʊ'leɪʃn] *s* immatrykulacja *f*

mat•ri•mo•ni•al [mætrə'məʊnɪəl] *adj* małżeński; **mat•ri•mo•ny** ['mætrəmənɪ] *s* związek *m* małżeński, małżeństwo *n*

ma•trix ['meɪtrɪks] *pl -rices* ['meɪtrɪsiːz], *-rixes* ['meɪtrɪksəz] *s* **1.** MATH macierz *f* **2.** TECH INF matryca *f*

ma•tron ['meɪtrən] *s* **1.** *dated* matrona *f* **2.** (szkolna) pielęgniarka *f* **3.** *Br dated* przełożona *f* pielęgniarek; **ma•tron of 'hon•our** *Br*, ***ma•tron of 'hon•or*** *Am s* (*married woman*) pierwsza druhna *f*

M

matt, matte [mæt] *adj* matowy
mat•ter ['mætə] **I** *s* **1.** sprawa *f*; ***a private ~*** sprawa prywatna; ***to make ~s worse*** na domiar złego; ***take ~s into one's own hands*** wziąć sprawy w swoje ręce **2.** kwestia *f*; ***a ~ of taste*** kwestia smaku; ***a ~ of time*** kwestia czasu; ***it's a ~ of life and death*** to kwestia życia i śmierci; ***as a ~ of course*** rutynowo; ***as a ~ of fact*** właściwie, prawdę mówiąc; ***that's a ~ of opinion*** to kwestia dyskusyjna **3.** ***what's the ~ with you?*** co się z tobą dzieje?; ***no ~ how hard I try*** bez względu na to, jak bardzo się staram; ***no matter what happens*** choćby nie wiem, co się stało **4.** *PHYS BIOL* materia *f*, substancja *f* **II** *v/i* mieć znaczenie, liczyć się (***to*** dla *G*); ***it doesn't ~*** (to) nieważne; ***it does not really ~ to me*** niewiele mnie to obchodzi; ***it's all that ~s*** tylko to się liczy; **mat•ter-of-'fact** *adj* rzeczowy
mat•tress ['mætrɪs] *s* materac *m*
ma•ture [mə'tʃʊr] **I** *adj* **1.** dojrzały **2.** dorosły **3.** *bill*, *loan*: przypadający do zapłaty, płatny **II** *v/i* **1.** *a. fig* dojrzewać ⟨-rzeć⟩ **2.** dorośleć ⟨wy-⟩ **3.** (*bill*, *loan*) przypadać do zapłaty; **ma•tu•ri•ty** [mə'tʃʊərətɪ] *s* **1.** dojrzałość *f* **2.** *FIN* termin *m* płatności
maud•lin ['mɔːdlɪn] *adj* **1.** rzewny **2.** *story*: ckliwy
maul [mɒːl] *v/t* **1.** ranić ⟨z-⟩ **2.** rozszarpywać ⟨-pać⟩ **3.** obłapiać **4.** (*criticize*) zjechać
mau•so•le•um [mɔːsə'lɪəm] *s* mauzoleum *n*
mauve [məʊv] *adj* fioletoworóżowy, fiołkowy
mav•er•ick ['mævərɪk] *s* indywidualista *m*
mawk•ish ['mɔːkɪʃ] *adj fig* przesłodzony, czułostkowy
max•im ['mæksɪm] *s* maksyma *f*, sentencja *f*
max•i•mi•za•tion [mæksɪmaɪ'zeɪʃn] *s* maksymalizacja *f*; **max•i•mize** ['mæksɪmaɪz] *v/t* **1.** maksymalizować ⟨z-⟩ **2.** *opportunity*, *potential*: wykorzystywać ⟨-tać⟩ w sposób maksymalny; **max•i•mum** ['mæksɪməm] **I** *adj* maksymalny; ***~ (permissible) speed*** maksymalna (dopuszczalna) prędkość **II** *s* maksimum *n*
May [meɪ] *s* maj *m*; ***in May*** w maju
may [meɪ] (*might*) *v aux* **1.** (*possibility*) móc; ***that ~ be true*** to może być prawda; ***he ~ have missed the train*** możliwe, że spóźnił się na pociąg; ***you ~ be right, but*** może i masz rację, ale **2.** (*permission*) móc; ***~ I come in?*** czy mogę wejść?; ***if I ~ say so*** jeśli można zauważyć, jeśli wolno tak powiedzieć **3.** ***~ he rest in peace*** niech spoczywa w pokoju; ***come what ~*** cokolwiek się zdarzy; ***be that as it ~*** *form* niemniej jednak, mimo to
may•be ['meɪbiː] *adv* (być) może; ***– 'Try some.' – 'Yes, ~ I will.'*** – „Spróbuj." – „Dobrze, może spróbuję."
'May Day *s* 1 maja; **'may•day** *interj* mayday; **may•fly** *s BIOL* jętka *f*
may•hem ['meɪhem] *s* chaos *m*, zamęt *m*
may•o ['meɪəʊ] *infml* → ***mayonnaise***
may•on•naise [meɪə'neɪz] *s* majonez *m*
may•or [meə] *s* burmistrz *m*; ***the Lord ~ of London*** burmistrz Londynu
maze [meɪz] *s a. fig* labirynt *m*; ***a ~ of streets*** labirynt ulic; ***a ~ of regulations*** gąszcz przepisów
MB [em'biː] *abbr* **1.** (=***Bachelor of Medicine***) licencjat *m* medycyny **2.** (=***megabyte***) *INF* MB
MBA [embiː'eɪ] *abbr* (=***Master of Business Administration***) magister *m* nauk ekonomicznych
MBO [embiː'əʊ] *abbr* (=***management buyout***) MBO *m*, wykup *m* menedżerski
MC [em'siː] *abbr* **1.** (=***master of ceremonies***) mistrz *m* ceremonii **2.** (=***Member of Congress***) kongresman *m*
Mc•Coy [mə'kɔɪ] *s infml*: ***this is an American flying jacket, the real ~*** to najprawdziwsza amerykańska kurtka lotnicza
MD [em'diː] *abbr* (=***Doctor of Medicine***) lek. med.
me [miː] *pron* **1.** mnie, mi; ***he knows ~*** on mnie zna; ***he gave ~ the book*** dał mi tę książkę; → ***I*** **2.** ja; ***hello, it's me*** cześć, to ja;
mead•ow ['medəʊ] *s* łąka *f*

mea•gre ['miːgə] *Br*, ***mea•ger*** *Am adj* marny, mizerny
meal[1] [miːl] *s* posiłek *m*; ***the main ~ of the day*** główny posiłek dnia; ***a three-course ~*** trzydaniowy posiłek; ***enjoy your ~!*** smacznego!
meal[2] [~] *s* mączka *f*
'meal•time *s* pora *f* posiłku
meal•y ['miːli] *adj* **1.** *taste*: mączny **2.** *apple*: mączysty; **meal•y-'mouth-ed** *adj* nieszczery,
mean[1] [miːn] *adj* **1.** *Br* skąpy **2.** niedobry, wredny **3.** złośliwy **4.** podły; ***feel ~*** czuć się podle (***about*** z powodu *G*) **5.** ***he's no ~ tennis player*** świetnie gra w tenisa
mean[2] [~] **I** *adj* średni **II** *s* **1.** MATH średnia *f*; ***arithmetic ~*** średnia arytmetyczna **2.** ***the golden ~*** złoty środek
mean[3] [~] **I** (*meant*; *meant*) *v/t* **1.** znaczyć; ***what does this word ~*** co znaczy to słowo?; ***does this ~ anything to you?*** czy to ci coś mówi? **2.** mieć na myśli; ***what do you ~ by this?*** co chcesz przez to powiedzieć?; ***if you know what I ~*** jeżeli wiesz, co mam na myśli **3.** zamierzać (***to do s.th.*** zrobić coś); ***I'm sorry, I didn't ~ to*** przepraszam, nie chciałem; ***I ~ it*** poważnie, nie żartuję; ***I meant him no harm*** nie chciałem go skrzywdzić **4.** ***be meant*** być przeznaczonym (***for*** dla *G*); ***they were meant for each other*** byli sobie przeznaczeni; ***it was meant to be*** tak było pisane **5.** oznaczać; ***it ~s working overtime*** to oznacza pracę po godzinach **6.** znaczyć, liczyć się; ***money ~s nothing to him*** pieniądze nie mają dla niego znaczenia **II** (*meant*; *meant*) *v/i* ***~ well*** mieć dobre intencje
me•an•der [mɪ'ændə] *v/i* **1.** wić się **2.** włóczyć się, chodzić bez celu
mean•ing ['miːnɪŋ] *s* **1.** znaczenie *n*; ***do you get my ~?*** rozumiesz, o co mi chodzi?; ***what's the ~ of this?*** co to ma znaczyć? **2.** *life*: sens *m*; **mean-ing•ful** ['miːnɪŋfəl] *adj* **1.** ważny **2.** znaczący **3.** sensowny **4.** *look*: wymowny, wiele mówiący; **mean-ing•ful•ness** ['miːnɪŋfəlnɪs] *s* znaczenie *n*, sens *m*, sensowność *f*; **mean-ing•less** ['miːnɪŋlɪs] *adj* **1.** bezsensowny, bez sensu **2.** nic nieznaczący **3.** niezrozumiały; **mean•ing-less•ness** ['miːnɪŋlɪsnɪs] *s* bezsens *m*, bezsensowność *f*
means [miːnz] *pl means s* **1.** środek *m*, sposób *m*, metoda *f*; ***a ~ of transport*** środek transportu; ***is there any ~ of contacting him?*** czy jest jakiś spoób, żeby się z nim skontaktować?; ***by ~ of*** za pomocą *G*; ***by all ~*** jak najbardziej, ależ oczywiście; ***by no ~*** **a)** w żadnym wypadku **b)** wcale nie; ***a ~ to an end*** środek (prowadzący) do celu **2.** środki *pl*; ***financial ~*** środki finansowe
meant [ment] *Past Simple and Past Participle* → ***mean***
mean•time ['miːntaɪm] **I** *adv* w międzyczasie, tymczasem **II** *adj* ***in the ~*** w międzyczasie; **mean•while** ['miːnwaɪl] → ***meantime***
mea•sles ['miːzlz] *no pl s* MED odra *f*
meas•ly ['miːzlɪ] *adj infml* marny, nędzny
meas•ur•a•ble ['meʒərəbl] *adj* **1.** wymierny **2.** *progress*: wyraźny, widoczny; **meas•ur•a•bly** ['meʒərəblɪ] *adv* znacznie, wyraźnie
mea•sure ['meʒə] **I** *v/t* **1.** mierzyć ⟨z-⟩ **2.** mieć, mierzyć; ***it ~s 7 inches*** ma siedem cali **3.** oceniać ⟨-nić⟩ **4.** porównywać ⟨-nać⟩ (***against*** z *I*) **II** *s* **1.** środek *m*, krok *m*; ***take ~s*** podjąć kroki; ***precautionary ~s*** środki ostrożności; ***preventive ~s*** środki zapobiegawcze **2.** miara *f*, stopień *m*; ***in some ~, in a*** (***certain***) ***~*** w pewnej mierze; ***beyond ~*** niezmiernie **3.** miara *f*, kryterium *n*; ***a ~ of length*** miara długości **4.** miara *f*, miarka *f* **5.** MUS *Am* takt *m*; **measure out** *v/t* odmierzać ⟨-rzyć⟩; **measure up I** *v/t* mierzyć ⟨z-⟩ **II** *v/i* **~** (***to s.o.'s expectations***) spełniać (czyjeś) oczekiwania; **mea•sure•ment** ['meʒəmənt] *s* **1.** pomiar *m* **2.** wymiar *m* **3.** miara *f*; ***take s.o.'s ~s*** wziąć z kogoś miarę (***for*** na *A*); **'meas•ur•ing jug** *Br*, ***'meas-ur•ing cup*** *Am s* miarka *f* (kuchenna); **'meas•ur•ing tape** *s* **1.** taśma *f* miernicza **2.** centymetr *m*
meat [miːt] *s* **1.** mięso *n* **2.** *fig* sedno *n*; **'meat•ball** *s* klopsik *m*, pulpet *m*; **'meat•loaf** *s* pieczeń *f* rzymska

M

Mec•ca ['mekə] *s* Mekka *f*; **mec•ca** ['mekə] *s* mekka *f*
me•chan•ic [mɪ'kænɪk] *s* **1.** mechanik *m* **2.** ***mechanics*** mechanika **3.** ***the mechanics*** mechanizm; **mechan•i•cal** [mɪ'kænɪkl] *adj* **1.** mechaniczny; ***a ~ device*** urządzenie mechaniczne **2.** *fig* machinalny, mechaniczny; **me•chan•i•cal en•gi'neer** *s* inżynier *m* mechanik; **me•chan•i•cal•ly** [mɪ'kænɪklɪ] *adv* **1.** mechanicznie **2.** *fig* machinalnie, mechanicznie; **me•chan•i•cal 'pen•cil** *s Am* ołówek *m* automatyczny
mech•a•nism ['mekənɪzm] *s a. fig* mechanizm *m*; ***a natural defence ~*** naturalny mechanizm obronny
mech•a•ni•za•tion [mekənaɪ'zeɪʃn] *s* mechanizacja *f*; **mech•a•nize** ['mekənaɪz] *v/t* mechanizować ⟨z-⟩
med•al ['medl] *s* **1.** medal *m* **2.** order *m*; **me•dal•lion** [mɪ'dælɪən] *s* medalion *m*; **med•al•list** *Br*, ***med•a•list*** *Am* ['medəlɪst] *s* medalista *m*
med•dle ['medl] *v/i* **1.** mieszać ⟨w-⟩ się, wtrącać ⟨-cić⟩ się (***in/with*** w *A*) **2.** *s.o.'s things*: ruszać ⟨-szyć⟩ (***with*** *A*); **med•dle•some** ['medlsəm] *adj* wścibski
me•di•a ['miːdɪə] *pl* **1.** ***the ~*** media, środki przekazu; **'me•di•a cov•er•age** *s*: ***it received wide ~*** dużo o tym mówiono i pisano w mediach **2.** → ***medium II.1***
me•di•ae•val → ***medieval***
'me•di•a e•vent *s* wydarzenie *n* medialne; **me•di•a 'hype** *s infml* szum *m* medialny;
me•di•an strip [miːdɪən'strɪp] *s* (*highway*) pas *m* rozdzielczy, pas *m* dzielący
'me•d•ia stud•ies *pl* dziennikarstwo *n*
me•di•ate ['miːdɪeɪt] **I** *v/i* **1.** prowadzić mediacje (***between*** między *I*) **2.** pośredniczyć (***in*** w *L*) **II** *v/t* **1.** negocjować ⟨wy-⟩ **2.** wpływać ⟨-łynąć⟩ (na *A*); **me•di•a•tion** [miːdɪ'eɪʃn] *s* mediacja *f*; **me•di•a•tor** ['miːdɪeɪtə] *s* mediator *m*
med•ic ['medɪk] *s* **1.** *Br infml* student *m* medycyny **2.** *infml* lekarz *m*; **med•i•cal** ['medɪkl] **I** *adj* **1.** medyczny; ***a ~ student*** student medycyny **2.** zdrowotny **3.** lekarski **II** *s infml* badania *pl*; **'med•i•cal cer•tif•i•cate** *s* zaświadczenie *n* lekarskie; **'med•i•cal ex•am•i•na•tion** *s* **1.** badania *pl* lekarskie **2.** badanie *n* lekarskie; **'med•i•cal ex•am•in•er** *s Am* patolog *m*; **'med•i•cal his•to•ry** *s* **1.** karta *f* pacjenta **2.** historia *f* choroby; **'med•i•cal in•sur•ance** *s* ubezpieczenie *n* zdrowotne; **'med•i•cal rec•ords** *pl* dokumentacja *f* medyczna
Med•i•care ['medɪker] *s system opieki zdrowotnej w Stanach Zjednoczonych*
med•i•cat•ed ['medɪkeɪtɪd] *adj* leczniczy; ***~ shampoo*** szampon leczniczy; **med•i•ca•tion** [medɪ'keɪʃn] *s* kuracja *f* lekami
me•di•ci•nal [mɪ'dɪsɪnl] *adj* leczniczy; ***~ herbs*** zioła lecznicze
med•i•cine ['medsən] *s* **1.** medycyna *f*; ***conventional*** (***alternative***) **~** medycyna konwencjonalna (alternatywna) **2.** lekarstwo *n*, lek *m*; ***give s.o. a taste of their own ~*** odpłacić komuś pięknym za nadobne; **'med•i•cine ball** *s* piłka *f* lekarska; **'med•i•cine cab•i•net** *s* (*cupboard*) apteczka *f*; **'med•i•cine man** *s* szaman *m*, czarownik *m*
med•i•co ['medɪkəʊ] *pl -cos s infml* lekarz *m*
med•i•e•val [medɪ'iːvl] *adj* średniowieczny
me•di•o•cre [miːdɪ'əʊkə] *adj* przeciętny; **me•di•oc•ri•ty** [miːdɪ'ɒkrətɪ] *s* przeciętność *f*
med•i•tate ['medɪteɪt] **I** *v/i* **1.** medytować **2.** rozmyślać (***on/upon*** nad *I*) **II** *v/t* rozważać ⟨-żyć⟩, planować ⟨za-⟩; ***~ revenge*** planować zemstę; **med•i•ta•tion** [medɪ'teɪʃn] *s* **1.** medytacja *f* **2.** rozmyślanie *n* (***on*** nad *I*); ***deep in ~*** pogrążony w rozmyślaniach
Med•i•ter•ra•ne•an [medɪtə'reɪnɪən] *adj* śródziemnomorski; ***the ~*** (***Sea***) Morze Śródziemne
me•di•um ['miːdɪəm] **I** *adj* średni; ***of ~ height*** średniego wzrostu; ***cook over a ~ heat*** gotować na średnim ogniu **II** *s* **1.** *pl -diums, -dia* środek *m* przekazu, medium *n* **2.** *pl -diums, -dia* medium *n*, nośnik *m*; ***English is the ~ of instruction*** wykłady odbywają się w języku angielskim **3.** *pl -dia* ART środek *m* wyrazu, medium *n*;

watercolour is her favourite ~ akwarela to jej ulubiona technika **4.** *pl -diums* *BIOL* podłoże *n*, pożywka *f* **5.** *pl -diums* (*person*) medium *n*; **me•di•um-'range** *adj rocket*: średniego zasięgu; **me•di•um-'rare** *adj steak*: średnio wysmażony; **me•di•um-'sized** *adj* średniej wielkości; **'me•di•um-term** *adj* średnioterminowy; **'me•di•um wave** *s RADIO* fale *pl* średnie; ***on (the) ~*** na falach średnich

med•ley ['medlɪ] *s* **1.** mieszanina *f*, mieszanka *f* **2.** (*music*) składanka *f* **3.** ***a 4 x 100 m ~ relay*** *SPORT* sztafeta 4 x 100 m stylem zmiennym

meek [mi:k] *adj* potulny, uległy

meet [mi:t] **I** (*met*; *met*) *v/t* **1.** spotykać ⟨-tkać⟩ **2.** poznawać ⟨-nać⟩; ***pleased to ~ you*** bardzo mi miło **3.** odbierać ⟨odebrać⟩; ***will you ~ me at the airport?*** przyjedziesz po mnie na lotnisko? **4.** stykać ⟨zetknąć⟩ się z *I* **5.** *SPORT* spotykać ⟨-tkać⟩ się z *I*, zmierzyć się z *I* **6.** natrafiać ⟨-fić⟩ na *A*, napotykać ⟨-tkać⟩; ***~ problems*** napotkać problemy; ***there is more to s.th. than ~s the eye*** w czymś kryje się coś wiecej, niż się (na pierwszy rzut oka) wydaje **7.** *needs*: zaspokajać ⟨-koić⟩ **8.** *condition*: spełniać ⟨-nić⟩ **9.** *deadline*: dotrzymywać ⟨-mać⟩ **10.** ***~ s.o. halfway*** *fig* iść na ustępstwa, ustąpić (częściowo) **II** (*met*; *met*) *v/i* **1.** spotykać ⟨-tkać⟩ się **2.** poznawać ⟨-nać⟩ się; **meet up** *v/i* spotykać ⟨-tkać⟩ się (***with*** z *I*); **meet with** *v/i* spotykać ⟨-tkać⟩ się z *I*; ***~ success*** **a)** odnieść sukces **b)** być udanym; ***~ failure*** **a)** ponieść porażkę **b)** nie udać się

meet•ing ['mi:tɪŋ] *s* **1.** spotkanie *n* **2.** zebranie *n*, posiedzenie *n*; ***be at a ~*** być na zebraniu **3.** *SPORT* mityng *m*, zawody *pl*; **'meet•ing place** *s* miejsce *n* spotkań

meg•a ['megə] *adj infml* mega-, wielki; ***a ~ hit*** megahit; **meg•a•byte** ['megəbaɪt] *s INF* megabajt *m*

meg•a•lo•ma•ni•a [megələʊ'meɪnɪə] *s* megalomania *f*; **meg•a•lo•ma•ni•ac** [megələʊ'meɪnɪæk] **I** *s* megaloman *m* **II** *adj* megalomański

meg•a•phone ['megəfəʊn] *s* megafon *m*

mel•an•chol•y ['melənkəlɪ] **I** *s* melancholia *f* **II** *adj* melancholijny

mel•a•no•ma [melə'nəʊmə] *s MED* czerniak *m*

me•lee ['meleɪ] *s* przepychanka *f*, zamieszanie *n*

mel•low ['meləʊ] **I** *adj* **1.** dojrzały **2.** *colour*, *voice*: ciepły, głęboki **3.** *taste*: pełny **4.** *sound*: miękki, aksamitny **5.** *infml* na rauszu **II** *v/t* łagodzić ⟨z-⟩ **III** *v/i* **1.** łagodnieć ⟨z-⟩ **2.** (*wine*) dojrzewać ⟨-rzeć⟩

me•lod•ic [mə'lɒdɪk] *adj* **1.** *MUS* melodyczny; ***a ~ line*** linia melodyczna **2.** melodyjny; **me•lo•di•ous** [mə'ləʊdɪəs] *adj* melodyjny

mel•o•dra•ma ['meləʊdrɑ:mə] *s a. fig* melodramat *m*; **mel•o•dra•mat•ic** [melədrə'mætɪk] *adj a. fig* melodramatyczny

mel•o•dy ['melədɪ] *s* melodia *f*

mel•on ['melən] *s BIOL* melon *m*

melt [melt] **I** *v/i* **1.** topić ⟨s-⟩ się, roztapiać ⟨-topić⟩ się, topnieć ⟨s-⟩; ***~ in the mouth*** rozpływać się w ustach **2.** *fig* topnieć ⟨s-⟩ **II** *v/t* **1.** topić ⟨s-⟩, roztapiać ⟨-topić⟩ **2.** *fig* zmiękczać ⟨-czyć⟩; **melt away** *v/i* (*people*) rozchodzić ⟨-zejść⟩ się (powoli); **melt down I** *v/t* rozpuszczać ⟨-puścić⟩ **II** *v/i* rozpuszczać ⟨-puścić⟩ się; **melt into** *v/i* **1.** *crowd*: wtapiać ⟨w-⟩ się w *A* **2.** (*colours*) przechodzić ⟨przejść⟩ w *A*

'melt•ing point *s* temperatura *f* topnienia; **'melt•ing pot** *s fig* tygiel *m*

mem•ber ['membər] *s* **1.** członek *m*; ***a ~ of the family*** członek rodziny; ***a ~ country*** państwo członkowskie **2.** *infml* członek *m*, penis *m*; **Mem•ber of 'Con•gress** *s Am* kongresman *m*; **Mem•ber of 'Par•lia•ment** *s Br* poseł *m*, deputowany *m*; **mem•ber•ship** ['membəʃɪp] *s* członkostwo *n* (***of/in*** w *L*); **'mem•ber•ship card** *s* karta *f* członkowska; **'mem•ber•ship fee** *s* składka *f* członkowska

mem•brane ['membreɪn] *s* **1.** *BIOL* błona *f* **2.** membrana *f*

me•men•to [me'mentəʊ] *pl -toes*, *-tos* *s* pamiątka *f*

mem•o ['meməʊ] *s* notatka *f* służbowa

mem•oirs ['memwɑ:rz] *pl* wspomnienia *pl*, pamiętniki *pl*

M

'mem•o pad *s* **1.** notatnik *m* **2.** bloczek *m* na notatki
mem•o•ra•bil•i•a [memərə'bɪlɪə] *pl* pamiątki *pl*
mem•o•ra•ble ['memərəbl] *adj* pamiętny, niezapomniany
mem•o•ran•dum [memə'rændəm] *pl* *-da* [~də], *-dums* *s* **1.** → ***memo*** **2.** *form* memorandum *n*
me•mo•ri•al [mɪ'mɔːrɪəl] **I** *s* **1.** pomnik *m* (**to** *G*) **II** *adj* pamiątkowy; **Me•'mo•ri•al Day** *s Am* dzień *m* pamięci narodowej (*ostatni poniedziałek maja*); **me•'mo•ri•al ser•vice** *s* nabożeństwo *n* żałobne
mem•o•rize ['meməraɪz] *v/t* zapamiętywać ⟨-tać⟩, uczyć ⟨na-⟩ się na pamięć
mem•o•ry ['memərɪ] *s* **1.** pamięć *f*; ***~ for names*** pamięć do nazwisk; ***recite from ~*** recytować z pamięci; ***have a good*** (***bad***) ***~*** mieć dobrą (złą) pamięć; ***8 megabytes of ~*** *INF* 8 megabajtów pamięci **2.** wspomnienie *n*; ***childhood memories*** wspomnienia z dzieciństwa; ***have vivid memories of s.th.*** doskonale coś pamiętać, mieć coś żywo w pamięci; ***bring back memories*** ożywiać wspomnienia; ***bring back memories of s.th.*** przypominać coś; **'mem•o•ry ca•pac•i•ty** *s INF* pojemność *f* pamięci; **'mem•o•ry chip** *s INF* układ *m* pamięciowy; **mem•o•ry ex•'pan•sion card** *s INF* karta *f* rozszerzenia pamięci
men [men] *pl*: ***~'s room*** *Am* toaleta męska; → ***man***
men•ace ['menɪs] **I** *s* **1.** groźba *f* **2.** zagrożenie *n* (**to** dla *G*) **3.** *infml* zmora *f*, utrapienie *n* **4.** **~s** *Br JUR* pogróżki **II** *v/t* **1.** zagrażać ⟨-rozić⟩; **men•ac•ing** ['menɪsɪŋ] *adj* groźny, niebezpieczny
mend [mend] **I** *v/t* **1.** naprawiać ⟨-wić⟩ **2.** cerować ⟨za-⟩, reperować ⟨z-⟩ **3.** ***~ one's differences*** pogodzić się **II** *v/i* **1.** wracać ⟨wrócić⟩ do zdrowia, zdrowieć ⟨wy-⟩; ***~ one's ways*** *fig* poprawić się **2.** (*bone*) zrastać ⟨zrosnąć⟩ się **III** *s* **3.** ***be on the ~*** *infml* wracać do zdrowia
men•da•cious [men'deɪʃəs] *adj* **1.** zakłamany **2.** kłamliwy
men•folk ['menfəʊk] *pl dated* mężczyźni *pl*
me•ni•al ['miːnɪəl] *adj work*: podrzędny, niewymagający kwalifikacji
men•in•gi•tis [menɪn'dʒaɪtɪs] *s MED* zapalenie *n* opon mózgowych
men•o•pause ['menəpɒːz] *s MED* menopauza *f*; ***go through the ~*** przechodzić menopauzę
men•stru•ate ['menstrueɪt] *v/i* miesiączkować, mieć miesiączkę; **men•stru•a•tion** [menstru'eɪʃn] *s* miesiączka *f*, menstruacja *f*
men•tal ['mentl] *adj* **1.** umysłowy; ***a ~ process*** proces umysłowy; ***make a ~ note of s.th.*** zapamiętać coś; ***form a ~ picture of s.th.*** wyobrazić sobie coś **2.** psychiczny; ***~ health*** zdrowie psychiczne; ***a ~ disorder*** zaburzenie psychiczne **3.** *infml* psychiczny; ***he's ~*** jest psychiczny, to świr; **men•tal a•'rith•me•tic** *s* liczenie *n* w pamięci; **men•tal 'cru•el•ty** *s* psychiczne znęcanie *n* się ; **men•tal 'hand•i•cap** *s* upośledzenie *n* umysłowe; **'men•tal hos•pi•tal** *s* szpital *m* psychiatryczny; **men•tal 'ill•ness** *s* choroba *f* psychiczna; **men•tal•i•ty** [men'tælətɪ] *s* mentalność *f*; **men•tal•ly** ['mentəlɪ] *adv* **1.** umysłowo **2.** psychicznie; **men•tal•ly 'hand•i•capped** *adj* upośledzony umysłowo; **men•tal•ly 'ill** *adj* chory umysłowo
men•thol ['menθɒl] *s* mentol *m*
men•tion ['menʃn] **I** *v/t* wspominać ⟨-mnieć⟩; ***nobody mentioned anything to me about it*** nikt mi o tym nic nie wspominał; ***now that you ~ it*** skoro już o tym mowa; ***don't ~ it!*** nie ma o czym mówić!; ***not to ~*** nie mówiąc (już) o *L*, nie wspominając o *L* **II** *s* wzmianka *f*; ***make no ~ of*** nic nie wspomnieć o *L*; ***get a ~*** zostać wspomnianym
men•tor ['mentɔː] *s* mentor *m*
men•u ['menjuː] *s* **1.** menu *n*, jadłospis *m*, karta *f* (dań) **2.** *INF* menu *n*; **'menu bar** *s INF* pasek *m* menu
MEP [emiː'piː] *abbr* (=***Member of the European Parliament***) poseł *m* do Parlamentu Europejskiego
mer•can•tile ['mɜːkəntaɪl] *adj form* handlowy; ***~ law*** prawo handlowe
mer•ce•na•ry ['mɜːsɪnərɪ] **I** *s* najemnik *m* **II** *adj* merkantylny; ***for ~ reasons*** dla pieniędzy

M

mer•chan•dise ['mɜːtʃəndaɪz] **I** *s* **1.** towar *m*, towary *pl* **2.** artykuły *pl* promocyjne **II** *v/t* **1.** sprzedawać ⟨-dać⟩ **2.** promować ⟨wy-⟩; **mer•chan•dis•ing** ['mɜːtʃəndaɪzɪŋ] *s* merchandising *m*, promocja *f* w miejscach sprzedaży; **mer•chant** ['mɜːtʃənt] **I** *s* handlowiec *m*, kupiec *m* **II** *adj* handlowy; ***a ~ ship*** statek handlowy; **mer•chant 'bank** *s* bank *m* handlowy

mer•ci•ful ['mɜːsɪfəl] *adj* **1.** litościwy **2.** miłosierny; **mer•ci•ful•ly** ['mɜːsɪfəlɪ] *adv* **1.** na szczęście **2.** litościwie, miłosiernie; **mer•ci•less** ['mɜːsɪlɪs] *adj* bezlitosny; **mer•ci•less•ly** ['mɜːsɪlɪslɪ] *adv* bezlitośnie

mer•cu•ri•al [mɜː'kjʊərɪəl] *adj* **1.** *temper*: żywy **2.** *CHEM* rtęciowy; ***~ poisoning*** zatrucie rtęcią; **Mer•cu•ry** ['mɜːkjʊrɪ] *s ASTR* Merkury *m*; **mer•cu•ry** ['mɜːkjʊrɪ] *s CHEM* rtęć *f*

mer•cy ['mɜːsɪ] *s* **1.** litość *f*, miłosierdzie *n*; ***ask for ~*** prosić o litość; ***show no ~ to*** być bezlitosnym wobec *G*; ***God have ~ on us*** Boże, zmiłuj się nad nami; ***be at the ~ of*** być zdanym na łaskę *G* **2.** ***it's a ~*** (***that***) na szczęście; **'mer•cy kill•ing** *s* eutanazja *f*

mere [mɪə] *adj* **1.** zwykły; ***a ~ 20 minutes*** tylko 20 minut **2.** *formality, coincidence*: czysty **3.** sam; ***the ~ thought of eating made him feel sick*** na samą myśl o jedzeniu robiło mu się niedobrze; ***the ~st*** nawet najmniejszy; **mere•ly** ['mɪəlɪ] *adv* **1.** tylko, jedynie; ***it's not ~ a job, but*** to nie tylko praca, lecz także; ***he ~ smiled*** tylko się uśmiechał **2.** zaledwie

merge [mɜːdʒ] **I** *v/t* łączyć ⟨po-⟩ **II** *v/i* **1.** łączyć ⟨po-⟩ się (***with*** z *I*) **2.** przechodzić ⟨przejść⟩ (***into*** w *A*), zlewać ⟨zlać⟩ się (***into*** z *I*); ***~ into the background*** wtapiać się w tło; **merg•er** ['mɜːdʒə] *s ECON* fuzja *f*

me•rid•i•an [mə'rɪdɪən] *s GEOGR* południk *m*

mer•it ['merɪt] **I** *s* **1.** wartość *f*; ***of artistic ~*** o wartości artystycznej; ***without ~*** bezwartościowy, bez wartości **2.** zaleta *f* **3.** zasługa *f* **II** *v/t* zasługiwać ⟨-łużyć⟩ na *A*; ***~ attention*** zasługiwać na uwagę; **mer•i•toc•ra•cy** [merɪ'tɒkrəsɪ] *s* merytokracja *f*

mer•maid ['mɜːmeɪd] *s* syrena *f*

mer•ri•ment ['merɪmənt] *s* wesołość *f*, radość *f*, zabawa *f*

mer•ry ['merɪ] *adj* **1.** wesoły, radosny; ***~ Christmas*** Wesołych Świąt **2.** *infml* wstawiony, podchmielony; **'mer•ry-go-round** *pl merry-go-rounds s a. fig* karuzela *f*

mesh [meʃ] **I** *s* siatka *f*, sieć *f* **II** *v/t* łączyć ⟨po-⟩ **III** *v/i* **1.** pasować (do siebie); ***~ with*** pasować do *G* **2.** *TECH* zazębiać ⟨-bić⟩ się

mess [mes] **I** *s* **1.** bałagan *m*, nieporządek *m*, nieład *m*; ***the room was in a ~*** w pokoju był bałagan; ***make a ~*** nabałaganić, narobić bałaganu; ***the economy is in a ~*** gospodarka jest w fatalnym stanie; ***make a ~ of s.th.*** *infml* spartaczyć coś **2.** kłopoty *pl*, tarapaty *pl*; ***get into a ~*** wpaść w tarapaty **3.** kantyna *f*; ***officers' ~*** kantyna oficerska **II** *v/t infml* brudzić ⟨po-⟩ **III** *v/i* **1.** zadawać się (***with*** z *I*) **2.** zadzierać ⟨-drzeć⟩ (***with*** z *I*); **mess about**, ***mess around*** *v/i* **1.** wygłupiać się **2.** obijać się **3.** romansować (***with*** z *I*); **mess around with** *v/i* **1.** ruszać, grzebać w *L* **2.** grzebać przy *L*, dłubać przy *L*; **mess up** *v/t* **1.** bałaganić ⟨na-⟩ w *L* **2.** psuć ⟨ze-⟩, partaczyć ⟨s-⟩ **3.** brudzić ⟨po-⟩ **4.** *Am* wlać

mes•sage ['mesɪdʒ] *s* **1.** wiadomość *f*; ***leave a ~*** zostawić wiadomość; ***can I take a ~ for him?*** czy mam mu coś przekazać? **2.** przesłanie *n*; ***he finally got the ~*** wreszcie do niego dotarło; ***get the ~ across to*** zostać zrozumianym przez *G*; **mes•sen•ger** ['mesɪndʒə] *s* posłaniec *m*, goniec *m*; ***by ~*** przez posłańca; **'mes•sen•ger boy** *s* chłopiec *m* na posyłki

Mes•si•ah [mə'saɪə] *s* Mesjasz *m*

'mess-up *s infml* **1.** zamieszanie *n*, bałagan *m* **2.** ***make a ~ of s.th.*** *infml* schrzanić coś, spieprzyć coś; ***what a ~!*** *infml* ale kicha!

mess•y ['mesɪ] *adj* **1.** ***the room was messy*** w pokoju był bałagan **2.** *hair*: rozczochrany **3.** brudny **4.** *situation*: nieprzyjemny

met [met] *Past Simple and Past Participle* → ***meet***

met•a•bol•ic [metə'bɒlɪk] *adj* metaboliczny; **me•tab•o•lism** [mə'tæbəlɪzm]

M

s przemiana *f* materii, metabolizm *m*
met•al ['metl] **I** *s* metal *m*; ***precious ~*** metal szlachetny **II** *adj* metalowy; **'met•al de•tec•tor** *s* wykrywacz *m* metali; **me•tal•lic** [mɪ'tælɪk] *adj* **1.** *sound, colour, taste*: metaliczny **2.** metalowy; **me•tal•lic 'paint** *s* lakier *m* o metalicznym połysku, *infml* metalik *m*; **met•al•lur•gy** [me'tælədʒɪ] *s* metalurgia *f*; **'met•al•work** *s* **1.** ART metaloplastyka *f* **2.** TECH części *pl* metalowe, wyroby *pl* metalowe
met•a•mor•pho•sis [metə'mɔːfəsɪs] *pl* *-ses* [metə'mɔːfəsiːz] *s* metamorfoza *f*
met•a•phor ['metəfə] *s* metafora *f*, przenośnia *f*; **met•a•phor•i•cal** [metə'fɒrɪkl] *adj* metaforyczny, przenośny; **met•a•phor•i•cal•ly** [metə'fɒrɪklɪ] *adv* metaforycznie, przenośnie
met•a•phys•i•cal [metə'fɪzɪkl] *adj* metafizyczny; **met•a•phys•i•cian** [metə'fɪzɪʃn] *s* metafizyk *m*; **met•a•phys•ics** [metə'fɪzɪks] *s* metafizyka *f*
me•tas•ta•sis [mə'tæstəsɪs] *pl* *-ses* [~siːz] *s* MED przerzut *m*
me•te•or ['miːtɪə] *s* ASTR meteor *m*; ***a ~ shower*** deszcz meteorów; **me•te•or•ic** [miːtɪ'ɒrɪk] *adj* **1.** meteorowy **2.** *fig* błyskawiczny, nagły; **me•te•or•ite** ['miːtɪəraɪt] *s* ASTR meteoryt *m*
me•te•or•o•log•i•cal [miːtɪərə'lɒdʒɪkl] *adj* meteorologiczny; **me•te•or•ol•o•gist** [miːtɪə'rɒlədʒɪst] *s* meteorolog *m*; **me•te•o•rol•o•gy** [miːtɪə'rɒlədʒɪ] *s* meteorologia *f*
me•ter[1] ['miːtə] **I** *s* **1.** licznik *m*; ***a taxi ~*** taksometr **2.** parkometr *m* **II** *v/t* mierzyć ⟨z-⟩ (zużycie); **'met•er read•er** *s* odczytujący *m* wskazania liczników
me•ter[2] *Am* → ***metre***
meth•a•done ['meθədəʊn] *s* MED metadon *m*
meth•ane ['miːθeɪn] *s* CHEM metan *m*
meth•od ['meθəd] *s* **1.** metoda *f*, sposób *m*; ***a ~ of data analysis*** metoda analizy danych; ***there's ~ in this madness*** w tym szaleństwie jest metoda **2.** *payment*: forma *f*; **me•thod•i•cal** [mɪ'θɒdɪkl] *adj* metodyczny, uporządkowany, systematyczny; **me•thod•i•cal•ly** [mɪ'θɒdɪklɪ] *adv* metodycznie
Meth•od•ist ['meθədɪst] **I** *s* metodysta *m* **II** *adj* metodystyczny; ***the ≈ Church*** Kościół metodystów

meth•yl ['meθɪl] *s* CHEM metyl *m*; ***~ alcohol*** alkohol metylowy; **meth•yl•a•ted 'spir•its** *pl* CHEM denaturat *m*
me•tic•u•lous [mə'tɪkjʊləs] *adj* **1.** drobiazgowy, bardzo dokładny **2.** skrupulatny; **me•tic•u•lous•ly** [mə'tɪkjʊləslɪ] *adv* **1.** drobiazgowo, bardzo dokładnie **2.** skrupulatnie
me•tre ['miːtə] *Br*, ***me•ter*** *Am* *s* **1.** metr *m* **2.** *poem*: metrum *n*; **met•ric** ['metrɪk] *adj* metryczny; ***the ~ system*** system metryczny
me•trop•olis [mɪ'trɒpəlɪs] *s* metropolia *f*; **met•ro•pol•i•tan** [metrə'pɒlɪtən] *adj* **1.** metropolitalny **2.** stołeczny
mew [mjuː] **I** *v/i* miauczeć ⟨miauknąć⟩ **II** *interj* miau
Mex•i•can ['meksɪkən] *adj* meksykański; ***a ~ wave*** fala meksykańska; **Mex•i•co** ['meksɪkəʊ] *s* Meksyk *m*; **Mex•i•co 'Cit•y** *s* (miasto) Meksyk *m*
mez•za•nine ['mezəniːn] *s* antresola *f*
MIA [emaɪ'eɪ] *abbr* (=***missing in action***) *soldier*: zaginiony
mi•aow [mɪaʊ] *interj* miau
mice [maɪs] *pl* → ***mouse***
mick•ey ['mɪkɪ] *s*: ***take the ~ out of s.o.*** *Br infml* **a)** nabierać kogoś **b)** przedrzeźniać kogoś
Mick•ey Mouse [mɪkɪ'maʊs] **I** *n* myszka *f* Miki **II** *adj* **1.** śmieszny **2.** dziecinnie prosty
mi•cro- ['maɪkrəʊ] *adj* (*in combinations*) mikro-
mi•crobe ['maɪkrəʊb] *s* BIOL drobnoustrój *m*, mikrob *m*; **mi•cro•bi•ol•o•gy** [maɪkrəʊbaɪ'ɒlədʒɪ] *s* mikrobiologia *f*
'mi•cro•chip *s* INF mikroukład *m*, (mikro)chip *m*; **'mi•cro•cli•mate** *s* mikroklimat *m*; **'mi•cro•com•put•er** *s* INF mikrokomputer *m*; **mi•cro•cosm** ['maɪkrəʊkɒzm] *s* mikrokosmos *m*; ***in ~*** w miniaturze, w skali mikro; **mi•cro•eco•'nom•ics** *s* ECON mikroekonomia *f*; **mi•cro•'e•lec•tron•ics** *s* mikroelektronika *f*; **mi•cro•fiche** ['maɪkrəʊfiːʃ] *s* mikrofilm *m*, mikrofiszka *f*; **'mi•cro•film** *s* mikrofilm *m*; **'mi•cro•light** *s* samolot *m* klasy microlight; **mi•cro•'or•gan•ism** *s* mikroorganizm *m*, drobnoustrój *m*, **'mi•cro•phone** *s* mikrofon *m*, **mi•cro•'pro•ces•sor** *s* mikroprocesor *m*;

'mi•cro•scope *s* mikroskop *m*; ***under the ~*** pod mikroskopem; **mi•cro'scop•ic** *adj* **1.** mikroskopowy **2.** mikroskopijny; **'mi•cro•sur•ger•y** *s MED* mikrochirurgia *f*; **'mi•cro•wave** *s* **1.** (*a.* ***~ oven***) kuchenka *f* mikrofalowa, *infml* mikrofalówka *f* **2.** *PHYS* mikrofala *f*

mid- [mɪd] (*in combinations*) ***in the mid-19th century*** w połowie XIX wieku; ***he stopped in mid-sentence*** przerwał w połowie zdania; ***she's in her mid-thirties*** ma około 35 lat; ***in mid-April*** w połowie kwietnia

mid•air [mɪd'eə] **I** *s* ***in ~*** w powietrzu **II** *adj* **1.** powietrzny **2.** w powietrzu; **mid•day** [mɪd'deɪ] *s* (*time*) południe *n*; ***at ~*** w południe

mid•dle ['mɪdl] **I** *s* **1.** środek *m*; ***in the ~ of*** **a)** w środku *G* **b)** w połowie *G*; ***we were in the ~ of dinner*** jedliśmy właśnie obiad; ***in the ~ of nowhere*** *infml* na odludziu, na końcu świata **2.** pas *m*, talia *f* **II** *adj* środkowy; ***in the ~ drawer*** w środkowej szufladzie; ***the ~ ear*** ucho środkowe; **'mid•dle-aged** *adj* w średnim wieku; **Mid•dle 'Ages** *pl* Średniowiecze *n*; **mid•dle-age 'spread** *s infml* brzuszek *m*; **Mid•dle A'merica** *s* **1.** stany *pl* środkowozachodnie **2.** klasa *f* średnia; **mid•dle 'class** *s* klasa *f* średnia; **mid•dle 'distance run•ner** *s* średniodystansowiec *m*; **Mid•dle 'East** *s* Bliski Wschód *m*, Środkowy Wschód *m*; **mid•dle 'finger** *s* palec *m* środkowy; **'mid•dle•man** *pl -men s* pośrednik *m*; **mid•dle 'man•age•ment** *s ECON* kadra *f* menedżerska średniego szczebla; **middle 'manager** *s ECON* menedżer *m* średniego szczebla; **mid•dle 'name** *s* drugie imię *n*; **mid•dle-of-the-'road** *adj opinions, policy*: umiarkowany; ***~ music*** muzyka środka; **'mid•dle•weight** *s SPORT* waga *f* średnia

mid•dling ['mɪdlɪŋ] *adj* średni, przeciętny; – ***'How are you feeling?'*** – ***'Fair to ~.'*** – „Jak się czujesz?" – „Tak sobie."

'midfield *s*: ***in ~*** *SPORT* na środku boiska, w pomocy; ***~ player*** *SPORT* (środkowy) pomocnik; **'mid•field•er** *s SPORT* środkowy *m*

midge [mɪdʒ] *s BIOL* muszka *f*

midg•et ['mɪdʒɪt] **I** *s* karzeł *m* **II** *adj* **1.** karłowaty **2.** miniaturowy

Mid•lands ['mɪdləndz] *s*: ***the ~*** środkowa Anglia

mid•life 'cri•sis *s* kryzys *m* wieku średniego

'mid•night ['mɪdnaɪt] *s* (*time*) północ *f*; ***at ~*** o północy; ***at the stroke of ~*** z wybiciem północy; ***the ~ sun*** słońce polarne, polarne słońce; **'mid•point** *s* środek *m*, połowa *f*; **mid•'sum•mer** *s* **1.** środek *m* lata **2.** przesilenie *n* letnie; **mid•'way** *adv* **1.** w połowie **2.** w połowie drogi; **mid•'week** *s*: ***in ~*** w połowie tygodnia; **Mid•'west**, ***Middle West*** *s*: ***the ~*** środkowy zachód (Stanów Zjednoczonych); **'mid•wife** *pl -wives s* położna *f*, akuszerka *f*; **mid'win•ter** *s* **1.** środek *m* zimy **2.** przesilenie *n* zimowe

might[1] [maɪt] *s lit* potęga *f*, moc *f*, siła *f*; ***with all one's ~*** z całej siły

might[2] [~] *Past Simple* → ***may***

might•y ['maɪtɪ] **I** *adj lit* **1.** potężny **2.** ogromny **II** *adv infml* bardzo; ***~ difficult*** niesamowicie trudny; ***~ easy*** dziecinnie łatwy

mi•graine ['miːgreɪn] *s* migrena *f*

mi•grant ['maɪgrənt] *s* **1.** migrant *m* **2.** zwierzę *n* wędrowne **3.** ptak *m* wędrowny; **mi•grant 'work•er** *s* **1.** pracownik *m* przemieszczający się **2.** gastarbeiter *m*; **mi•grate** [maɪ'greɪt] *v/i* **1.** (*people*) migrować przemieszczać ⟨-mieścić⟩ się **2.** (*animals*) migrować; **mi•gra•tion** [maɪ'greɪʃn] *s* **1.** migracja *f* **2.** przemieszczanie *n* się **3.** wędrówka *f*; **mi•gra•to•ry** ['maɪgrətərɪ] *adj* **1.** migracyjny **2.** wędrowny

mike [maɪk] *s infml* mikrofon *m*

mild [maɪld] *adj* **1.** łagodny **2.** *fever, irritation*: lekki

mil•dew ['mɪldjuː] *s BIOL* pleśń *f*

mild•ly ['maɪldlɪ] *adv* **1.** łagodnie; ***~ surprised*** lekko zdziwiony; ***to put it ~*** łagodnie mówiąc **2.** lekko; **'mild-man•nered** *adj* łagodny, o łagodnym usposobieniu; **mild•ness** ['maɪldnɪs] *s* łagodność *f*

mile [maɪl] *s* (*1609 metres*) mila *f*; ***it's ~s away*** to kawał drogi stąd; ***he was ~s ahead of the others*** znacznie wyprzedzał pozostałych; ***feel ~s***

M

better *infml* czuć się o niebo lepiej; ***be ~s away*** *infml* być daleko myślami; ***it sticks out a ~*** *fig* nawet ślepy by (to) zauważył; **mile•age** ['maılıdʒ] *s* przebieg *m* (w milach); **'mile•age al•low•ance** *s* dodatek *m* na pokrycie kosztów podróży (samochodem); **mile•om•e•ter** [maı'lɒmıtə] *s* licznik *m* mil; **'mile•stone** *s a. fig* kamień *m* milowy

mil•i•tant ['mılıtənt] *adj* **1.** walczący **2.** bojowy **3.** agresywny; **mil•i•ta•rism** ['mılıtərızəm] *s* militaryzm *m*; **mil•i•ta•rist** ['mılıtərıst] *s* militarysta *m*; **mil•i•ta•ris•tic** [mılıtə'rıstık] *adj* militarystyczny

mil•i•ta•ry ['mılıterı] **I** *adj* wojskowy, militarny **II** *s* ***the ~*** wojsko; **mil•i•ta•ry a'cad•e•my** *s* akademia *f* wojskowa; **mil•i•ta•ry 'cem•e•ter•y** *s* cmentarz *m* wojskowy; **mil•i•ta•ry dic•'ta•tor•ship** *s* dyktatura *f* wojskowa; **mil•i•ta•ry po•'lice** *s* żandarmeria *f* wojskowa; **mil•i•tar•y 'serv•ice** *s* służba *f* wojskowa; ***do one's ~*** odbywać służbę wojskową

mi•li•tia [mı'lıʃə] *s* **1.** milicja *f* **2.** rezerwa *f*; **mi•li•tia•man** [mı'lıʃəmən] *pl -men s* **1.** milicjant *m* **2.** rezerwista *m*

milk [mılk] **I** *s* **1.** mleko *n*; ***a bottle of ~*** butelka mleka; ***do you take ~ in your tea?*** pijesz herbatę z mlekiem?; ***a land of ~ and honey*** kraj mlekiem i miodem płynący; ***it's no use crying over spilt ~*** nie ma co płakać nad rozlanym mlekiem **2.** mleczko *n*; ***coconut ~*** mleczko kokosowe; ***cleansing ~*** mleczko *n* kosmetyczne **II** *v/t* **1.** doić ⟨wy-⟩ **2.** *fig* wykorzystywać ⟨-tać⟩, doić ⟨wy-⟩; **'milk bar** *s* bar *m* mleczny; **milk 'choc•o•late** *s* czekolada *f* mleczna; **'milk jug** *s* dzbanek *m* na mleko; **'milk•man** *pl -men s* mleczarz *m*; **milk pow•der** *s* mleko *n* w proszku; **'milk•shake** *s* koktajl *m* mleczny; **'milk tooth** *pl* ***~ teeth*** *s Br* ząb *m* mleczny; **milk•y** ['mılkı] *adj* **1.** *drink*, *colour*: mleczny **2.** *coffee*: z mlekiem; **Milk•y 'Way** *s*: ***the ~*** *ASTR* Droga Mleczna

mill [mıl] **I** *s* **1.** młyn *m*; ***put s.o. through the ~*** *fig* przemaglować kogoś **2.** fabryka *f*; ***paper ~*** papiernia, fabryka papieru; ***saw~*** tartak **3.** młynek *m*; ***pepper ~*** młynek do pieprzu **II** *v/t* mielić ⟨z-⟩; **mill around**, ***mill about*** *Br v/i* kręcić się

mil•len•ni•um [mı'lenıəm] *pl -niums, -nia s* tysiąclecie *n*, milenium *n*; ***at the turn of the ~*** na przełomie tysiącleci; ***~ bug*** *INF* pluskwa milenijna

mil•le•pede ['mılıpi:d] *s BIOL* krocionóg *m*

mill•er ['mılə] *s* młynarz *m*

mil•let ['mılıt] *s BIOL* proso *n*

mil•li•gram ['mılıgræm], ***mil•i•gramme*** *Br s* miligram *m*

mil•li•me•tre ['mılımi:tə] *Br*, ***mil•li•meter*** *Am s* milimetr *m*

mil•lion ['mıljən] *s* milion *m*; ***one in a ~*** jeden na milion; ***he's one in a ~*** drugiego takiego nie znajdziesz; ***thanks a ~*** stokrotne dzięki; ***feel like a ~ dollars*** *infml* czuć się bosko; ***never in a ~ years*** nigdy w życiu; **mil•lion•aire** [mıljə'neə] *s* milioner *m*

'mill•pond *s* staw *n* młyński; **'mill•stone** *s* kamień *m* młyński; **'mill wheel** *s* koło *n* młyńskie

mime [maım] **I** *s* pantomima *f*; ***a ~ artist*** mim **II** *v/t* **1.** odgrywać ⟨odegrać⟩, przedstawiać ⟨-wić⟩ **2.** pokazywać ⟨-zać⟩ na migi **III** *v/i* **1.** śpiewać ⟨za-⟩ z playbacku **2.** grać ⟨za-⟩ z playbacku

mim•ic ['mımık] **I** *v/t* **1.** naśladować **2.** imitować **II** *s* **1.** naśladowca *m* **2.** imitator *m*

mim•ic•ry ['mımıkrı] *s* **1.** naśladowanie *n* **2.** *BIOL* mimikra *f*

mi•mo•sa [mı'moʊzə] *s BIOL* mimoza *f*

min•a•ret [mınə'ret] *s ARCHIT* minaret *m*

mince [mıns] **I** *v/t* **1.** *meat*: mielić ⟨z-⟩; ***~d meat*** mięso mielone; ***not ~ one's words*** nie owijać w bawełnę **2.** rozdrabniać ⟨-robnić⟩ **II** *v/i* drobić kroki, dreptać **III** *s* mięso *n* mielone; **'mince•meat** *s* nadzienie bakaliowe *n* (z przyprawami korzennymi); ***make ~ of*** *infml* zrobić miazgę z *G*; **mince 'pie** *s* bożonarodzeniowe ciasto *n* z bakaliowym nadzieniem; **minc•er** ['mınsə] *s* maszynka *f* do (mielenia) mięsa; **mincing** ['mınsıŋ] *adj* afektowany, sztuczny

mind [maınd] **I** *s* **1.** umysł *m*; ***a brilliant ~*** błyskotliwy umysł; **see s.th. in one's**

M

~'s eye widzieć coś oczyma duszy; **2.** rozum *m*, głowa *f*; ***she's out of her ~*** zwariowała; ***lose one's ~*** stracić głowę; ***put s.th. out of one's ~*** wybić sobie coś z głowy; ***my ~ went blank*** miałem w głowie pustkę **3.** myśl *f*, myśli *pl*; ***have s.th. in ~*** mieć coś na myśli; ***you are on my ~*** myślę o tobie; ***read s.o.'s ~*** czytać w czyichś myślach; ***come to*** (***s.o.'s***) ***~*** przychodzić (komuś) na myśl; ***keep s.th. in ~, bear s.th. in ~*** pamiętać o czymś **4.** (*person*) umysł *m*, mózg *m* **5.** zdanie *n*, pogląd *m*; ***make up one's ~*** zdecydować się; ***change one's ~*** zmienić zdanie, rozmyślić się; ***to my ~*** *infml* moim zdaniem; ***I've half a ~ to go*** chyba pójdę, ale nie jestem jeszcze do końca zdecydowany **II** *v/t* **1.** uważać na *A*; ***~ the step!*** uwaga na stopień!; ***~ your head!*** uwaga na głowę! **2.** pilnować ⟨przy-⟩, zajmować ⟨-jąć⟩ się *I*; ***who's ~ing the children?*** kto opiekuje się dziećmi?; ***~ your own business!*** zajmij się swoimi sprawami! **3.** mieć coś przeciwko *D*; ***do you ~ me smoking, do you ~ if I smoke?*** czy można zapalić?; ***would you ~ coming?*** czy mógłbyś przyjść?; ***I don't ~ the noise*** nie przeszkadza mi ten hałas; ***if you don't ~ me asking*** jeśli wolno spytać **III** *v/i* ***I don't ~*** wszystko mi jedno; ***never ~*** **a)** (już) nieważne **b)** nie szkodzi

'mind-bog•gling *adj* zadziwiający, niewyobrażalny; **mind•ed** ['maɪndɪd] *adj* ***independently ~*** niezależny; ***be politically ~*** interesować się polityką; **'mind•er** ['maɪndə] *s* **1.** (*bodyguard*) goryl *m* **2.** opiekun *m*; **'mind-ex-pand•ing** *adj* **1.** psychodeliczny **2.** otwierający oczy; **mind•ful** ['maɪndfʊl] *adj* świadomy (***of*** *G*, ***that*** że); **mind-less** ['maɪndlɪs] *adj* **1.** bezmyślny **2.** niewymagający myślenia **3.** ***~ of*** nieświadomy *G*; **'mind read•er** *s*: ***I'm not a ~*** nie umiem czytać w myślach

mine[1] [maɪn] *poss* mój; ***it's ~*** to moje; ***a friend of ~*** mój przyjaciel; ***his mother and ~*** jego i moja matka

mine[2] [~] **I** *s* kopalnia *f*; ***a coal ~*** kopalnia węgla; ***be a ~ of information about*** *fig* być kopalnią informacji o *L* **II** *v/t* *coal, gold*: wydobywać ⟨-być⟩

mine[3] [~] **I** *s* (*explosive*) mina *f* **II** *v/t* zaminowywać ⟨-nować⟩; **mine clear-ance** *s* rozminowywanie *n*; **'mine de•tec•tor** *s* wykrywacz *m* min; **'mine•field** *s* pole *n* minowe

min•er ['maɪnər] *s* górnik *m*

min•e•ral ['mɪnərəl] *s* **1.** GEOL minerał *m* **2.** *Br* napój *m* gazowany; **min•er-al•og•i•cal** [mɪnərə'lɒdʒɪkl] *adj* GEOL mineralogiczny; **min•er•al•o•gist** [mɪnə'rælədʒɪst] *s* GEOL mineralog *m*; **min•er•al•o•gy** [mɪnə'rælədʒɪ] *s* GEOL mineralogia *f*; **'min•e•ral wa•ter** *s* woda *f* mineralna

'mine•sweep•er *s* trałowiec *m*

min•gle ['mɪŋgl] **I** *v/i* **1.** (*sounds, tastes*) mieszać ⟨z-⟩ się (***with*** z *I*) **2.** ***~ with guests*** rozmawiać z gośćmi **II** *v/t* mieszać ⟨z-⟩

min•i- ['mɪnɪ] *adj* (*in combinations*) mini-

min•i•a•ture ['mɪnɪtʃə] **I** *s* miniatura *f*; ***in ~*** w miniaturze **II** *adj* miniaturowy; **min•i•a•tur•i•za•tion** [mɪnɪtʃəraɪ'zeɪʃn] *s* miniaturyzacja *f*; **min•i•a-tur•ize** ['mɪnɪtʃəraɪz] *v/t* miniaturyzować ⟨z-⟩

'min•i•bar *s* minibar *m*; **'min•i•bus** *s Br* minibus *m*, mikrobus *m*

min•im ['mɪnɪm] *s* MUS *Br* półnuta *f*

min•i•mal ['mɪnɪməl] *adj* minimalny; **min•i•mal•ism** ['mɪnɪməlɪzm] *s* minimalizm *m*; **min•i•mize** ['mɪnɪmaɪz] *v/t* **1.** minimalizować ⟨z-⟩ **2.** pomniejszać ⟨-szyć⟩

min•i•mum ['mɪnɪməm] **I** *pl minima* *s* minimum *n*; ***keep s.th. to a ~*** ograniczać coś do mimimum **II** *adj* minimum, minimalny; **min•i•mum 'wage** *s* płaca *f* minimalna

min•ing ['maɪnɪŋ] *s* górnictwo *n*; **'min-ing en•gi•neer** *s* inżynier *m* górnictwa

min•ion ['mɪnɪən] *s* **1.** popychadło *n* **2.** *infml* murzyn *m*

'min•i•se•ries *pl miniseries s* (krótki) serial *m* telewizyjny; **'min•i•skirt** *s* minispódniczka *f*, mini *f*

min•is•ter ['mɪnɪstər] **I** *s* **1.** *Br* minister *m*; ***Prime ~*** premier **2.** REL pastor *m*, duchowny *m* **II** *v/t form* opiekować ⟨za-⟩ się (***to*** *I*); **min•is•te•ri•al** [mɪnɪ'stɪrɪəl] *adj* ministerialny; ***hold ~ office*** sprawować urząd ministra; **min•is•tra•tions** [mɪnɪ'streɪʃnz] *pl* opieka *f*; **min•is•try** ['mɪnɪstrɪ] *s* **1.** ministerstwo *n* **2.** *REL* urząd *m* duchownego, posługa *f* duszpasterska

'min•i•van *s Am* minivan *m*

mink [mɪŋk] *pl mink, minks s* **1.** *BIOL* norka *f* **2.** (*fur*) norki *pl*

mi•nor ['maɪnə] **I** *s* **1.** *JUR* niepełnoletni *m* **2.** *MUS* moll *m*, tonacja *f* molowa **3.** *Am* przedmiot *m* dodatkowy **II** *adj* **1.** niewielki **2.** drobny **3.** nieznaczny **4.** *injury*: niegroźny **5.** *MUS* molowy; ***in A ~*** A-moll **III** *v/t* ***~ in*** *Am* studiować jako przedmiot dodatkowy

Mi•nor•ca [mɪ'nɔːrkə] *s* Minorka *f*

mi•nor•i•ty [maɪ'nɒrətɪ] *s* **1.** mniejszość *f*; ***ethnic minorities*** mniejszości etniczne; ***be in the ~*** być w mniejszości; ***a ~ government*** rząd mniejszościowy **2.** *JUR* niepełnoletność *f*

'mi•nor-league *adj* drugoligowy

mint[1] [mɪnt] *s* **1.** *BIOL* mięta *f*; ***~ sauce*** sos miętowy **2.** (*sweet*) miętówka *f*, cukierek *m* miętowy

mint[2] [~] **I** *s* **1.** mennica *f*; ***in ~ condition*** w idealnym stanie **2.** ***a ~*** (***of money***) *infml* kupa forsy **II** *v/t coins*: bić ⟨wy-⟩

mi•nus ['maɪnəs] **I** *prep* **1.** minus; ***seven ~ three is four*** siedem odjąć trzy równa się cztery; ***it was ~ 10 degrees*** było minus 10 stopni **2.** bez *G* **II** *s* minus *m*; ***consider the pluses and ~es*** wziąć pod uwagę plusy i minusy **III** *adj* **1.** *MATH* ujemny **2.** ***a ~ point*** minus **3.** (*school*) ***A ~*** piątka z minusem

mi•nus•cule ['mɪnəskjuːl] *adj* malutki; ***have ~ handwriting*** pisać maczkiem

min•ute[1] ['mɪnɪt] **I** *s* **1.** minuta *f*; ***to the ~*** co do minuty; ***ten-~*** dziesięciominutowy **2.** chwila *f*, moment *m*; ***hang on a ~*** zaczekaj chwilę; ***I'll be with you in a ~*** zaraz się tobą zajmę; ***just a ~!*** chwileczkę!; ***at the very ~*** dokładnie w tej chwili **3.** *MATH GEOGR* minuta *f* **4.** ***the ~s*** protokółł (z zebrania); ***take the ~s*** protokołować **II** *v/t* protokołować ⟨za-⟩

mi•nute[2] [maɪ'njuːt] *adj* **1.** maleńki, drobny **2.** śladowy **3.** szczegółowy, drobiazgowy; ***in ~ detail*** w najdrobniejszych szczegółach

'min•ute hand *s* wskazówka *f* minutowa

mi•nute•ly [maɪ'nuːtlɪ] *adv* **1.** szczegółowo **2.** minimalnie

'min•ute steak *s COOK* krwisty befsztyk *m*

mir•a•cle ['mɪrəkl] **I** *s* cud *m*; ***by some ~*** jakimś cudem; ***it's a ~ that*** to cud, że; ***work ~s*** czynić cuda, zdziałać cuda; ***a ~ of engineering*** cud techniki **II** *adj* cudowny; **mi•rac•u•lous** [mɪ'rækjʊləs] *adj* cudowny; **mi•rac•u•lous•ly** [mɪ'rækjʊləslɪ] *adv* **1.** cudem **2.** cudownie

mi•rage ['mɪrɑːʒ] *s* **1.** fatamorgana *f*, miraż *m* **2.** iluzja *f*

mire ['maɪə] *s* **1.** bagno *n*, błota *pl* **2.** *a. fig* błoto *n*; ***sink into the ~*** grzęznąć w błocie; ***drag s.o.'s name through the ~*** oczernić kogoś

mir•ror ['mɪrə] **I** *s* lustro *n*, lusterko *n*; ***in the ~*** w lustrze; ***a wing ~*** lusterko boczne; ***the face is the ~ of the soul*** twarz jest zwierciadłem duszy **II** *v/t* **1.** *fig* odzwierciedlać ⟨-lić⟩ **2.** (*mirror*) odbijać ⟨-bić⟩; **'mir•ror im•age** *s* lustrzane odbicie *n*; **'mir•ror writ•ing** *s* pismo *n* lustrzane

mirth [mɜːθ] *s lit* wesołość *f*, radość *f*; **mirth•ful** ['mɜːfʊl] *adj lit* **1.** wesoły **2.** radosny; **mirth•less** ['mɜːθlɪs] *adj lit* **1.** niewesoły **2.** *laughter*: wymuszony

mis•ad•ven•ture [mɪsəd'ventʃə] *s* nieszczęśliwy wypadek *m*; ***death by ~*** śmierć wskutek nieszczęśliwego wypadku

mis•an•thrope ['mɪsənθrəʊp] *s* mizantrop *m*, odludek *m*; **mis•an•throp•ic** [mɪsən'θrɒpɪk] *adj* **1.** niechętny ludziom **2.** unikający ludzi; **mis•an•thro•pist** [mɪsænθrəpɪst] *s* → ***misanthrope***; **mis•an•thro•py** [mɪs'ænθrəpɪ] *s* mizantropia *f*

mis•ap'ply [mɪsə'plaɪ] *v/t* źle stosować ⟨za-⟩, błędnie stosować ⟨za-⟩

mis•ap•pre•hen•sion [mɪsæprɪ'henʃn] *s* **1.** niezrozumienie *n* **2.** błędne mniemanie *n*; ***be under the ~ that*** mylić się, sądząc, że; ***a common ~ is that*** częstym błędem jest mniemanie, że

mis•ap•pro•pri•ate [mɪsə'prəʊprɪeɪt] *v/t* sprzeniewierzać ⟨-rzyć⟩; **mis•ap•pro•pri•a•tion** [mɪsəprəʊprɪ'eɪʃn] *s* sprzeniewierzenie *n*

M

mis•be•have [mɪsbə'heɪv] *v/i* źle się zachowywać ⟨-chować⟩, niewłaściwie się zachowywać ⟨-chować⟩, być niegrzecznym; **mis•be•hav•iour** [mɪsbə'heɪvɪə] *Br*, ***mis•be•hav•ior*** *Am s* niewłaściwe zachowanie *n*, złe sprawowanie *n*

mis•cal•cu•late [mɪs'kælkjʊleɪt] **I** *v/t* **1.** błędnie obliczać ⟨-czyć⟩, błędnie szacować ⟨o-⟩ **2.** *situation*: źle oceniać ⟨-nić⟩ **II** *v/i* mylić ⟨po-⟩ się (w obliczeniach); **mis•cal•cu•la•tion** [mɪskælkjʊ'leɪʃn] *s* **1.** błąd *m* w obliczeniach **2.** błędna ocena *f*

mis•car•riage [mɪs'kærɪdʒ] *s MED* poronienie *n*; ***have a ~*** poronić; ***a ~ of justice*** pomyłka sądowa; **mis•car•ry** [mɪs'kærɪ] *v/i* **1.** *MED* ronić ⟨po-⟩ **2.** (*plan*) nie powieść się

mis•cel•la•ne•ous [mɪsə'leɪnɪəs] *adj* różnorodny

mis•chance [mɪs'tʃaːns] *s lit* nieszczęśliwy traf *m*, pech *m*; ***by ~*** fatalnym zrządzeniem losu

mis•chief ['mɪstʃɪf] *s* **1.** złe zachowanie *n* **2.** psoty *pl*, figle *pl*; ***be up to (some) ~*** napsocić **3.** figlarność *f* **4.** *form* szkoda *f*; ***make ~*** powodować szkodę **5.** ***do oneself a ~*** zrobić sobie krzywdę; **mis•chie•vous** ['mɪstʃɪvəs] *adj* **1.** psotny, figlarny **2.** złośliwy **3.** *lie*: oszczerczy; **mis•chie•vous•ly** ['mɪstʃɪvəslɪ] *adv* **1.** psotnie, figlarnie **2.** złośliwie **3.** oszczerczo

mis•con•ceived [mɪskən'siːvd] *adj* **1.** chybiony **2.** błędny; **mis•con•cep•tion** [mɪskən'sepʃn] *s* nieporozumienie *n*, błędne przekonanie *n*

mis•con•duct [mɪs'kɒndʌkt] *s* **1.** niewłaściwe zachowanie *n*; ***professional ~*** postępowanie niezgodne z etyką zawodową **2.** niewłaściwe zarządzanie *n*

mis•con•strue [mɪskən'struː] *v/t* błędnie interpretować ⟨z-⟩ (***as*** jako *A*)

mis•deed [mɪs'diːd] *s lit* **1.** występek *m* **2.** czyn *m* karygodny; ***financial ~s*** nadużycia finansowe

mis•de•mea•nour [mɪsdə'miːnə] *Br*, ***mis•de•mea•nor*** *Am s* **1.** *JUR* wykroczenie *n* **2.** czyn *m* karygodny; ***financial ~s*** nadużycia finansowe

mis•di•ag•nose [mɪsdaɪəg'nəʊs] *s MED* **1.** błędnie diagnozować ⟨z-⟩ (***as*** jako *A*) **2.** stawiać ⟨postawić⟩ błędną diagnozę

mis•di•rect [mɪsdɪ'rekt] *v/t* **1.** niewłaściwie wykorzystywać ⟨-tać⟩ **2.** *people*: kierować ⟨s-⟩ w złą stronę **3.** wprowadzać ⟨-dzić⟩ w błąd

mi•ser ['maɪzə] *s* skąpiec *m*, sknera *m*

mis•e•ra•ble ['mɪzrəbl] *adj* **1.** nieszczęśliwy; ***make life ~ for s.o.*** dać się komuś we znaki **2.** ponury **3.** żałosny, nędzny **4.** opłakany; **mis•er•a•bly** ['mɪzrəblɪ] *adv* żałośnie; ***fail ~*** zawieść na całej linii

mi•ser•ly ['maɪzəlɪ] *adj* **1.** skąpy **2.** nędzny, mizerny

mis•e•ry ['mɪzərɪ] *s* **1.** cierpienie *n*, ból *m* **2.** nędza *f*, bieda *f*

mis•fire [mɪs'faɪə] *v/i* **1.** (*plan*) nie powieść się, *infml* nie wypalić **2.** (*gun*) nie wypalić **3.** (*engine*) nie zapalić, gasnąć ⟨z-⟩

mis•fit ['mɪsfɪt] *s* outsider *m*

mis•for•tune [mɪs'fɔːrtʃən] *s* **1.** nieszczęście *n*, pech *m* **2.** trudny los *m*

mis•giv•ings [mɪs'gɪvɪŋz] *pl* złe przeczucia *pl*, obawy *pl*

mis•gov•ern [mɪs'gʌvən] *v/t* źle rządzić

mis•guid•ed [mɪs'gaɪdɪd] *adj* **1.** chybiony **2.** błędny

mis•han•dle [mɪs'hændl] *v/t* **1.** źle przeprowadzać ⟨-dzić⟩ **2.** źle obchodzić ⟨obejść⟩ się z *I*

mis•hap ['mɪshæp] *s* niefortunny wypadek *m*; ***without ~*** bez problemu

mis•hear [mɪs'hɪə] **I** (*misheard*; *misheard*) *v/t* źle usłyszeć **II** (*misheard*; *misheard*) *v/i* przesłyszeć się

mis•hit **I** [mɪs'hɪt] (*mishit*; *mishit*) *v/t* (*golf*, *cricket*) źle uderzać ⟨-rzyć⟩ **II** ['mɪshɪt] *s* złe uderzenie *n*

mish•mash ['mɪʃmæʃ] *s infml* misz-masz *m*

mis•in•form [mɪsɪn'fɔːm] *v/t*: ***~ s.o. about*** wprowadzać kogoś w błąd co do *G*; **mis•in•for•ma•tion** [mɪsɪnfər'meɪʃn] *s* **1.** dezinformacja *f* **2.** wprowadzenie *n* w błąd

mis•in•ter•pret [mɪsɪn'tɜːprɪt] *v/t* błędnie interpretować ⟨z-⟩, źle rozumieć ⟨z-⟩; **mis•in•ter•pre•ta•tion** [mɪsɪntɜːprɪ'teɪʃn] *s* błędna interpretacja *f*; ***s.th. could be open to ~*** coś może zostać źle zrozumiane

M

mis•judge [mɪs'dʒʌdʒ] *v/t* **1.** źle oceniać ⟨-nić⟩ **2.** *person*: nie doceniać ⟨-nić⟩
mis•lay [mɪs'leɪ] (*mislaid*; *mislaid*) *v/t* zapodziewać ⟨-dziać⟩, zawieruszać ⟨-szyć⟩
mis•lead [mɪs'liːd] (*misled*; *misled*) *v/t* wprowadzać ⟨-dzić⟩ w błąd; **mis•lead•ing** [mɪs'liːdɪŋ] *adj* mylący, zwodniczy
mis•man•age [mɪs'mænɪdʒ] *v/t* **1.** źle zarządzać **2.** źle przeprowadzać ⟨-dzić⟩; **mis•man•age•ment** [mɪs'mænɪdʒmənt] *s* **1.** złe zarządzanie *n* **2.** złe przeprowadzenie *n* **3.** niegospodarność *f*
mis•match I ['mɪsmætʃ] *s* rozziew *m*, rozdźwięk *m* (**between** między *I*) **II** [mɪs'mætʃ] *v/t* źle dopasowywać ⟨-sować⟩; ***a ~ed couple*** źle dobrana para
mis•no•mer [mɪs'nəʊmə] *s* niewłaściwe określenie *n*
mi•sog•y•nist [mɪ'sɒdʒɪnɪst] *s* mizogin *m*; **mi•sog•y•ny** [mɪ'sɒdʒɪnɪ] *s* mizoginia *f*, mizoginizm *m*
mis•place [mɪs'pleɪs] *v/t* zapodziewać ⟨-dziać⟩, zawieruszać ⟨-szyć⟩; **mis•placed** ['mɪspleɪst] *adj* **1.** nie na miejscu **2.** *love*: źle ulokowany
mis•print ['mɪsprɪnt] *s* błąd *m* w druku, literówka *f*
mis•pro•nounce [mɪsprə'naʊns] *v/t* źle wymawiać ⟨-mówić⟩; **mis•pro•nun•ci•a•tion** [mɪsprənʌnsɪ'eɪʃn] *s* **1.** niepoprawna wymowa *f* **2.** błąd *m* w wymowie
mis•quo•ta•tion [mɪskwəʊ'teɪʃn] *s* **1.** błędny cytat *m* **2.** błędne (za)cytowanie *n*; **mis•quote** [mɪs'kwəʊt] *v/t* błędnie cytować ⟨za-⟩
mis•read [mɪs'riːd] (*misread*; *misread*) *v/t* **1.** błędnie interpretować ⟨z-⟩, źle rozumieć ⟨z-⟩ **2.** źle przeczytać
mis•rep•re•sent [mɪsreprɪ'zent] *v/t* **1.** fałszywie przedstawiać ⟨-wić⟩ **2.** przeinaczać ⟨-czyć⟩; **mis•rep•re•sen•ta•tion** [mɪsreprɪzen'teɪʃn] *s* **1.** fałszywe przedstawienie *n*, fałszywy obraz *m* **2.** przeinaczenie *n*
mis•rule [mɪs'ruːl] *s* złe rządy *pl*
Miss [mɪs] *s* **1.** (*woman's title*) panna *f*, pani *f*; ***thank you, ~ Lipman*** dziękuję, panno Lipman; ***will that be all, ~?*** czy to wszystko, proszę pani?; ***good morning, ~*** (*to teacher*) dzień dobry pani **2.** miss *f*; ***~ America*** Miss Ameryki
miss [mɪs] **I** *v/t* **1.** nie trafiać ⟨-fić⟩ w *A*, chybiać ⟨-bić⟩; ***the bullet ~ed her*** kula jej nie trafiła **2.** przeoczać ⟨-czyć⟩, przegapiać ⟨-pić⟩, tracić ⟨s-⟩; ***you can't ~ the meals*** nie możesz opuszczać posiłków; ***it was an opportunity not to be ~ed*** takiej okazji nie można było przepuścić **3.** tęsknić za *I*; ***I ~ you*** tęsknię za tobą **4.** spóźniać ⟨-nić⟩ się na *A*; ***~ the plane*** spóźnić się na samolot **5.** nie dosłyszeć; ***I ~ed her name*** nie dosłyszałem jej nazwiska **6.** nie zauważać ⟨-żyć⟩ **7.** nie rozumieć ⟨z-⟩; ***he ~ed the joke*** nie zrozumiał dowcipu; ***you're ~ing the point*** nie rozumiesz, o co chodzi, nie rozumiesz sedna sprawy **8.** unikać ⟨-knąć⟩; ***if you go now you should ~ the crowds*** jeżeli wyjdziesz teraz, powinieneś uniknąć tłumów **9.** brakować; ***I ~ some students*** brakuje mi kilku uczniów **II** *v/i* **1.** nie trafiać ⟨-fić⟩ **2.** brakować; ***some students are ~ing*** brakuje kilku uczniów **III** *s* niecelny strzał *m*, niecelny rzut *m*, *infml* pudło *n*; **give s.th. a ~** *infml* darować sobie coś; **miss out** *v/t* **1.** ***~ on an opportunity*** przegapiać okazję, przepuszczać okazję; ***you missed out on a good time*** ominęła cię dobra zabawa **2.** *Br* pomijać ⟨-minąć⟩; ***I'm sure I haven't missed anything out*** jestem pewien, że niczego nie pominąłem
mis•shap•en [mɪs'ʃeɪpən] *adj* zniekształcony, zdeformowany
mis•sile ['mɪsaɪ] **I** *s* **1.** pocisk *m* **2.** rakieta *f* **II** *adj* rakietowy; **'mis•sile launch•er** *s* wyrzutnia *f* pocisków rakietowych
miss•ing ['mɪsɪŋ] *adj* **1.** brakujący; ***~ pages*** brakujące strony **2.** zgubiony; ***go ~*** zgubić się **3.** *soldier*: zaginiony; ***he was reported ~*** został uznany za zaginionego; **miss•ing 'link** *s* brakujące ogniwo *n*; **miss•ing 'per•son** *s* zaginiony *m*
mis•sion ['mɪʃn] *s* **1.** misja *f*, zadanie *n*; ***~ accomplished*** zadanie wykonane **2.** REL misja *f* **3.** lot *m* (kosmiczny), misja *f* (kosmiczna); ***~ control*** kon-

trola lotu **4.** misja *f* (dyplomatyczna) **5.** misja *f*, posłannictwo *n*; **mis•sion•a•ry** ['mɪʃənerɪ] *s* misjonarz *m*; '**mis•sion•a•ry po•si•tion** *s* pozycja *f* klasyczna, *infml* pozycja *f* misjonarska; '**mis•sion state•ment** *s* misja *f* (firmy)

mis•spell [mɪs'spel] *v/t* (*misspelled/misspelt; misspelled/misspelt*) **1.** robić ⟨z-⟩ błąd (ortograficzny) w *L* **2.** błędnie pisać ⟨na-⟩; **mis•spell•ing** [mɪs'spelɪŋ] *s* błąd *m* (ortograficzny)

mis•spent [mɪs'spent] *adj time, money, youth*: zmarnowany

mis•state [mɪs'steɪt] *v/t* **1.** fałszywie przedstawiać ⟨-wić⟩ **2.** *facts*: przeinaczać ⟨-czyć⟩; **mis•state•ment** [mɪs'steɪtmənt] *s* **1.** nieprawdziwa informacja *f* (**of** o *L*) **2.** fałszywe oświadczenie *n* (**of** na temat *G*) **3.** *facts*: przeinaczenie *n*

mist [mɪst] **I** *s* **1.** mgła *f*; ***be lost in the ~s of time*** ginąć w mroku dziejów **2.** mgiełka *f*, obłoczek *m* **II** *v/i* (*a.* ***~ over***, ***~ up***) **1.** zaparowywać ⟨-rować⟩ **2.** (*eyes*) zachodzić ⟨zajść⟩ łzami **III** *v/t* pryskać ⟨s-⟩ (wodą)

mis•take [mɪ'steɪk] **I** *s* **1.** błąd *m*, pomyłka *f*; ***make a ~*** pomylić się, popełnić błąd, zrobić błąd; ***learn from one's ~s*** uczyć się na własnych błędach; ***spelling ~s*** błędy ortograficzne; ***by ~*** przez pomyłkę; ***they shot him in ~ for a terrorist*** postrzelili go, biorąc go omyłkowo za terrorystę **II** (*mistook*; *mistaken*) *v/t* **1.** mylić ⟨po-⟩ (***s.o. for*** kogoś z *I*); ***he mistook me for someone else*** wziął mnie za kogoś innego **2.** źle rozumieć ⟨z-⟩; ***I mistook her offer as a joke*** pomyliłem się, uznając jej propozycję za żart; **mis•tak•en** [mɪ'steɪkən] **I** *Past Participle* → ***mistake II*** **II** *adj* **1.** ***be ~*** mylić się, nie mieć racji; ***unless I am ~*** o ile się nie mylę **2.** błędny; ***in the ~ belief*** w błędnym przekonaniu; ***it was a case of ~ identity*** wzięto go za kogoś innego, wzięto mnie za kogoś innego; **mis•tak•en•ly** [mɪ'steɪkənlɪ] *adv* błędnie, mylnie; ***he ~ believed that*** mylił się, sądząc, że

Mis•ter ['mɪstə] *s* pan *m*

mis•time [mɪs'taɪm] *v/t* wybierać ⟨-brać⟩ zły moment na *A*

mis•tle•toe ['mɪsltəʊ] *s* jemioła *f*

mis•took [mɪ'stʊk] *Past Simple* → ***mistake***

mis•trans•late [mɪstrænz'leɪt] *v/t* błędnie tłumaczyć ⟨prze-⟩; **mis•trans•la•tion** [mɪstrænz'leɪʃn] *s* błędne tłumaczenie *n*

mis•treat [mɪs'triːt] *v/t* maltretować ⟨z-⟩, znęcać się nad *I*; **mis•treat•ment** [mɪs'triːtmənt] *s* maltretowanie *n*, znęcanie *n* się

mis•tress ['mɪstrɪs] *s* **1.** kochanka *f* **2.** *Br* nauczycielka *f* **3.** pani *f*

mis•tri•al [mɪs'traɪəl] *s* JUR nieważne postępowanie *n* sądowe, nieważny proces *m*; ***declare a ~*** uznać proces za nieważny

mis•trust [mɪs'trʌst] **I** *v/t* nie ufać *D* **II** *s* brak *m* zaufania, nieufność *f*, podejrzliwość *f*; **mis•trust•ful** [mɪs'trʌstfʊl] *adj* nieufny, podejrzliwy (**of** wobec *G*)

mist•y ['mɪstɪ] *adj* **1.** *a. fig* mglisty; ***~ memories*** mgliste wspomnienia **2.** zamglony **3.** ***her eyes grew ~*** jej oczy zaszły łzami

mis•un•der•stand [mɪsʌndə'stænd] (*misunderstood*; *misunderstood*) *v/t* źle rozumieć ⟨z-⟩; ***don't ~ me*** nie zrozum mnie źle; **mis•un•der•stand•ing** [mɪsʌndə'stændɪŋ] *s* **1.** nieporozumienie *n* **2.** sprzeczka *f*

mis•use **I** [mɪs'juːs] *s* **1.** nadużywanie *n*; ***alcohol ~*** nadużywanie alkoholu **2.** nadużycie *n*, ***a ~ of power*** nadużycie władzy **3.** niewłaściwe wykorzystanie *n* **II** [mɪs'juːz] *v/t* **1.** nadużywać ⟨-żyć⟩ **2.** niewłaściwie wykorzystywać ⟨-tać⟩, używać ⟨użyć⟩ niezgodnie z przeznaczeniem **3.** *word*: błędnie używać ⟨użyć⟩

mite[1] [maɪt] *s* BIOL roztocz *m*

mite[2] [~] *s* (*animal*, *child*) maleństwo *n*, kruszynka *f*; ***poor little ~!*** biedne maleństwo!

mit•i•gate ['mɪtɪgeɪt] *v/t* **1.** zmniejszać ⟨-szyć⟩ **2.** *anger*, *punishment*: łagodzić ⟨z-⟩ **3.** *risk*: minimalizować ⟨z-⟩; **mit•i•ga•tion** [mɪtɪ'geɪʃn] *s* **1.** zmniejszenie *n* **2.** *risk*: minimalizacja *f* **3.** *punishment*: złagodzenie *n*; ***say s.th. in ~ of*** podać coś jako okoliczność łagodzącą; **miti•ga•ting** '**cir•cum•stan•ces** *pl* JUR okoliczności *pl* łagodzące

M

mitt [mɪt] *s* **1.** → ***mitten*** **2.** *SPORT* rękawica *f* baseballowa **3.** (*hand*) *Br infml* łapa *f*
mit•ten ['mɪtən] *s* rękawiczka *f* z jednym palcem
mix [mɪks] **I** *v/t* **1.** mieszać ⟨wy-⟩; ***~ the cream with the sauce*** wymieszać śmietanę z sosem; ***~ s.th. into a smooth dough*** wyrobić coś na gładką masę **2.** łączyć ⟨po-⟩; ***~ business with pleasure*** łączyć przyjemne z pożytecznym **3.** *drinks*: mieszać **4.** *MUS* miksować ⟨z-⟩ **II** *v/i* **1.** mieszać się; ***oil and water don't ~*** woda i olej nie mieszają się ze sobą **2.** pasować do siebie **3.** udzielać się towarzysko; utrzymywać kontakty towarzyskie (***with*** z *I*) **III** *s* **1.** połączenie *n*, mieszanka *f*; ***an interesting ~ of personalities*** interesująca mieszanka osobowości **2.** ***cake ~*** ciasto w proszku; ***cement ~*** mieszanka cementowa; **mix up** *v/t* **1.** mieszać ⟨po-⟩ **2.** mylić ⟨po-⟩ (***with*** z *I*) **3.** ***mixed up in*** wplątany w *A*; ***get mixed up in*** wplątać się w *A* **4.** ***get mixed up with*** zadawać się z *I*
mixed [mɪkst] *adj* **1.** *feelings, marriage*: mieszany **2.** *weather*: zmienny **3.** *school*: koedukacyjny; **mixed 'bag** *s infml* mieszanina *f*, mieszanka *f*; **mixed 'bless•ing** *s*: ***be a ~*** mieć swoje dobre i złe strony; **mixed 'dou•bles** *pl s* mikst *m*, gra *f* mieszana; **mixed e•'con•o•my** *s ECON* gospodarka *f* mieszana; **mixed 'mar•riage** *s* małżeństwo *n* mieszane **mix•er** ['mɪksə] *s* **1.** *COOK MUS* mikser *m* **2.** napój *m* bezalkoholowy (dodawany do drinków) **3.** ***be a good ~*** być towarzyskim; ***be a bad ~*** nie być towarzyskim, być mało towarzyskim; **'mix•ing bowl** *s* miska *f* (do mieszania składników); **mix•ture** ['mɪkstʃə] *s* **1.** mieszanka *f*, mieszanina *f*; ***with a ~ of surprise and horror*** z mieszaniną zdziwienia i przerażenia **2.** *CHEM* mieszanina *f* **3.** (*medicine*) mikstura *f*; **'mix-up** *s infml* **1.** zamieszanie *n* **2.** pomyłka *m*
mne•mon•ic [niː'mɒnɪk] **I** *adj* mnemotechniczny **II** *s* pomoc *f* mnemotechniczna
MO [em'əʊ] *abbr* (=***medical officer***) **1.** lekarz *m* (zatrudniony w firmie lub instytucji) **2.** lekarz *m* wojskowy
mo [məʊ] *s Br infml* chwilka *f*, moment *m*; ***just a ~!*** chwileczkę!
moan [məʊn] **I** *v/i* **1.** *a. fig* jęczeć ⟨jęknąć⟩ **2.** (*wind*) zawodzić **II** *s* **1.** jęczenie *n*, jęk *m* **2.** zawodzenie *n*
moat [məʊt] *s* fosa *f*
mob [mɒb] **I** *s* **1.** tłum *m* **2.** motłoch *m* **3.** ***the ~*** mafia **4.** *infml* banda *f*, gang *m* **5.** *infml* ludzie *pl* **II** *v/t* ***be ~bed*** (***by a crowd of people***) zostać otoczonym (przez tłum ludzi)
mo•bile ['məʊbəl] **I** *adj* **1.** mobilny; ***be ~*** **a)** (*an elderly person*) móc się poruszać o własnych siłach **b)** (*driver*) mieć samochód **2.** ruchomy **II** *s Br* telefon *m* komórkowy, *infml* komórka *f*; **mo•bile 'home** *s Br* przyczepa *f* kempingowa; **mo•bile 'phone** *s Br* telefon *m* komórkowy; **mo•bil•i•ty** [mə'bɪlətɪ] *s* **1.** mobilność *f* **2.** zdolność *f* poruszania się
mo•bi•li•za•tion [məʊbɪlaɪ'zeɪʃn] *s* mobilizacja *f*; **mo•bi•lize** ['məʊbɪlaɪz] **I** *v/t* **1.** mobilizować ⟨z-⟩ **2.** *support*: pozyskiwać ⟨-kać⟩ **3.** *resources*: gromadzić ⟨z-⟩ **II** *v/i* mobilizować ⟨z-⟩ się
mob•ster ['mɒbstə] *s* gangster *m*, mafioso *m*
moc•ca•sin ['mɒkəsɪn] *s* mokasyn *m*
mo•cha ['mɒkə] *s* mokka *f*
mock [mɒk] **I** *v/t* **1.** przedrzeźniać **2.** drwić z *G*, wydrwić **II** *adj* **1.** udawany; ***~ leather*** imitacja skóry **2.** *exam*: próbny **III** *s Br infml* egzamin *m* próbny; **mock•er•y** ['mɒkərɪ] *s* **1.** drwiny *pl*, kpiny *pl* **2.** parodia *f*; **mock•ing** ['mɒkɪŋ] *adj* drwiący, szyderczy; **mock•ing•bird** ['mɒkɪŋbɜːd] *s* (*bird*) przedrzeźniacz *m*; **mock•ing•ly** ['mɒkɪŋlɪ] *adv* drwiąco, szyderczo; **'mock-up** *s* **1.** model *m*, makieta *f* **2.** atrapa *f*
mod•al ['məʊdl] **I** *s* czasownik *m* modalny **II** *adj* modalny; ***~ verb***, ***~ auxiliary*** (***verb***) czasownik modalny, czasownik posiłkowy; **mo•dal•i•ty** [məʊ'dælətɪ] *s* modalność *f*
mod cons [mɒd'kɒnz] *abbr* (=***modern conveniences***) *pl infml* wygody *pl*
mode [məʊd] *s* **1.** sposób *m*; ***a ~ of behaviour*** sposób zachowania; ***a ~ of***

M

transport środek transportu; ***a ~ of life*** styl życia **2.** tryb *m*; ***switch the camera into the automatic ~*** przełącz aparat na tryb automatyczny **3.** ***I'm in holiday ~*** *infml* jestem w nastroju wakacyjnym; ***I'm in music ~*** *infml* mam ochotę na muzykę

mod•el ['mɒdl] **I** *s* **1.** model *m*; ***the latest ~*** najnowszy model; ***a mathematical ~*** model matematyczny; ***a scale ~*** makieta **2.** wzór *m*; ***he's a ~ of self-control*** jest wzorem opanowania **3.** model *m*, modelka *f* **II** *adj* **1.** wzorowy; ***a ~ student*** wzorowy student **2.** wzorcowy, modelowy **3.** ***a ~ ship (plane)*** model statku (samolotu) **III** *v/t* **1.** ***be ~led on*** być wzorowanym na *L*; ***~ oneself on*** wzorować się na *L* **2.** tworzyć ⟨s-⟩ model **3.** *clothes*: prezentować ⟨za-⟩ **4.** kształtować ⟨u-⟩, modelować ⟨wy-⟩ **IV** *v/i* **1.** pracować jako model, pracować jako modelka **2.** pozować; **mod•el•ling** ['mɒdəlɪŋ] *Br*, **mod•el•ing** *Am s* **1.** praca *f* modela, praca *f* modelki; ***a ~ agency*** agencja modelek **2.** modelowanie *n*; ***computer ~*** modelowanie komputerowe

mo•dem ['məʊdem] *s INF* modem *m*

mod•e•rate I ['mɒdərət] *adj* **1.** umiarkowany; ***~ success*** umiarkowany sukces; ***a ~ climate*** klimat umiarkowany; ***~ views*** umiarkowane poglądy **2.** średni; ***cook over a ~ heat*** gotować na średnim ogniu **3.** *punishment*: łagodny **4.** *demands*: rozsądny **II** ['mɒdərət] *s* osoba *f* o umiarkowanych poglądach **III** ['mɒdəreɪt] *v/t* **1.** łagodzić ⟨z-⟩ **2.** obniżać ⟨-żyć⟩ **3.** *demands*: ograniczać ⟨-czyć⟩ **IV** ['mɒdəreɪt] *v/i* (*wind*) zelżeć, osłabnąć; **mod•e•rate•ly** ['mɒdərətlɪ] *adv* **1.** dość, całkiem, w miarę **2.** *drink*: z umiarem **3.** umiarkowanie **4.** *fall*: nieznacznie; **mod•e•ra•tion** [mɒdə'reɪʃn] *s* umiarkowanie *n*; ***in ~*** z umiarem; **mod•er•a•tor** ['mɑːdəreɪtə] *s* (*in debates*) moderator *m*

mod•ern ['mɒdən] *adj* **1.** współczesny; ***in ~ times*** w dzisiejszych czasach **2.** *equipment, technology*: nowoczesny **3.** *era, languages*: nowożytny **4.** *beliefs*: nowoczesny '**mod•ern-day** *adj* współczesny; **mod•ern•ism** ['mɒdənɪzəm] *s ART* modernizm *m*; **mod•ern•is•tic** [mɒdən'ɪstɪk] *adj* **1.** modernistyczny **2.** nowoczesny; **mo•der•ni•ty** [mɒ'dɜːnɪtɪ] *s* nowoczesność *f*; **mod•ern•i•za•tion** [mɒdənaɪ'zeɪʃn] *s* modernizacja *f*, unowocześnianie *n*; **mod•ern•ize** ['mɒdənaɪz] *v/t* modernizować ⟨z-⟩, unowocześniać ⟨-nić⟩;

mod•est ['mɒdɪst] *adj* **1.** skromny **2.** *changes, improvement*: niewielki; **mod•es•ty** ['mɒdɪstɪ] *s* skromność *f*

mod•i•cum ['mɒdɪkəm] *s*: ***a ~ of luck*** łut szczęścia; ***a ~ truth*** ziarno prawdy

mod•i•fi•a•ble ['mɒdɪfaɪəbl] *adj* modyfikowalny; **mod•i•fi•ca•tion** [mɒdɪfɪ'keɪʃn] *s* modyfikacja *f*, zmiana *f* (***of/to*** *G*); **mod•i•fy** ['mɒdɪfaɪ] *v/t* **1.** modyfikować ⟨z-⟩, wprowadzać ⟨-dzić⟩ (drobne) zmiany w *L* **2.** ulepszać ⟨-szyć⟩ **3.** *verb*: określać

mod•u•lar ['mɒdjʊlə] *adj* modułowy; **mod•u•late** ['mɒdjʊleɪt] *v/t* **1.** modulować **2.** regulować; **mod•u•la•tion** [mɒdjʊ'leɪʃn] *s* modulacja *f*

mod•ule ['mɒdʒʊl] *s* moduł *m*

mo•dus o•pe•ran•di [məʊdəsɒpə'rændɪ] *s* sposób *m* działania

mog•gy ['mɒgɪ] *s Br infml* kot *m*

mo•gul ['məʊgəl] *s* magnat *m*, potentat *m*

mo•hair ['məʊheə] *s* moher *m*

Mo•hi•can [məʊ'hiːkən] *s* (*hairstyle*) irokez *m*

moist [mɔɪst] *adj* wilgotny; ***~ with tears*** wilgotny od łez; **moist•en** ['mɔɪsn] **I** *v/t* zwilżać ⟨-żyć⟩ **II** *v/i* wilgotnieć ⟨z-⟩; **mois•ture** ['mɔɪstʃə] *s* **1.** wilgoć *f* **2.** *skin*: wilgotność *f*; **mois•tur•iz•er** ['mɔɪstʃəraɪzə] *s* **1.** krem *m* nawilżający **2.** środek *m* nawilżający

mo•lar ['məʊlər] *s ANAT* ząb *m* trzonowy

mo•las•ses [mə'læsɪz] *s Am* melasa *f*

mold *Am* → ***mould***; **mold•er** *Am* → ***moulder***; **mold•y** *Am* → ***mouldy***

mole[1] [məʊl] *s* **1.** kret *m* **2.** (*spy*) wtyczka *f*

mole[2] [~] *s* **1.** znamię *n* **2.** pieprzyk *m*

mole[3] [~] *s CHEM* mol *m*

mo•lec•u•lar [mə'lekjʊlə] *adj CHEM* molekularny, cząsteczkowy; **mol•e•cule** ['mɒlɪkjuːl] *s* cząsteczka *f*, molekuła *f*

'**mole•hill** *s* kretowisko *n*; ***make a mountain out of a ~*** robić z igły widły

M

mo•lest [mə'lest] *v/t* molestować; **mo-les•ta•tion** [le'steɪʃn] *s* molestowanie *n*

mol•li•fy ['mɒlɪfaɪ] *v/t* uspokajać ⟨-koić⟩, udobruchać

mol•lusc ['mɒləsk], ***mol•lusk*** *Am s* BIOL mięczak *m*

mol•ly•cod•dle ['mɒlɪkɒdl] *v/t infml* **1.** rozpieszczać **2.** trzymać pod kloszem

Mol•o•tov cock•tail [mɒlətɒf'kɒkteɪl] *s* koktajl *m* Mołotowa

molt *Am* → ***moult***

mol•ten ['moʊltən] *Present Perfect* → ***melt***

mom [mɑːm] *s Am infml* mama *f*; **mom-and-'pop store** *s* mały rodzinny sklepik *m*

mo•ment ['məʊmənt] *s* **1.** chwila *f*, moment *m*; ***at the ~*** w tej chwili; ***at the last ~*** w ostatniej chwili; ***at that very ~ the phone rang*** w tej samej chwili zadzwonił telefon; ***for a ~*** na chwilę; ***just a ~!*** chwileczkę!; ***hold on a ~*** proszę chwilę zaczekać; ***in a ~ of weakness*** w chwili słabości; ***not a ~ too soon*** w ostatniej chwili; ***I'm waiting for the right ~*** czekam na odpowiednią okazję; ***for the ~*** na razie; ***of ~*** wielkiej wagi **2.** PHYS moment *m*; ***~ of inertia*** moment bezwładności; **mo•men•tar•i•ly** [məʊmən'terɪlɪ] *adv* **1.** na (krótką) chwilę **2.** *Am infml* za chwilę; **mo•men•ta•ry** ['məʊmənterɪ] *adj* chwilowy; **mo•men•tous** [məʊ'mentəs] *adj* doniosły, brzemienny w skutki

mo•men•tum [məʊ'mentəm] *s* **1.** rozpęd *m*, impet *m*; ***gather ~*** nabierać rozpędu, nabierać impetu; ***lose ~*** tracić impet **2.** PHYS pęd *m*

Mo•na•co ['mɒnəkəʊ] *s* Monako *n*

mon•arch ['mɒnək] *s* monarcha *m*; **mo-nar•chical** [mə'nɑːkɪkl] *adj power, system*: monarchiczny; **mon•ar•chist** ['mɒnəkɪst] *s* monarchista *m*; **mon-ar•chy** ['mɒnəkɪ] *s* monarchia *f*; ***a constitutional ~*** monarchia konstytucyjna

mon•as•tery ['mɒnəstrɪ] *s* klasztor *m* (męski); **mo•nas•tic** [mə'næstɪk] *adj* **1.** klasztorny **2.** zakonny **3.** *life*: surowy, klasztorny

Mon•day ['mʌndeɪ] *s* poniedziałek *m*; ***on ~*** w poniedziałek

mon•e•tar•ism ['mʌnɪtərɪzəm] *s* monetaryzm *m*; **mon•e•tar•ist** ['mʌnɪtərɪst] monetarysta *m*; **mon•e•ta•ry** ['mʌnɪterɪ] *adj* monetarny; ***a ~ union*** unia monetarna

mon•ey ['mʌnɪ] **I** *s* pieniądze *pl*; ***earn ~*** zarabiać pieniądze; ***make ~*** **a)** zarabiać, *infml* robić pieniądze **b)** przynosić zysk; ***change ~*** **a)** wymieniać pieniądze **b)** rozmieniać pieniądze; ***put ~ into*** zainwestować w *A*; ***be in the ~*** *infml* być przy forsie; ***be out of ~*** nie mieć pieniędzy; ***have ~ to burn*** *fig* mieć forsy jak lodu; ***get one's ~'s worth*** dobrze wydać swoje pieniądze; ***~ talks*** pieniądz rządzi światem; ***throw one's ~ around*** szastać pieniędzmi **II** *adj* **1.** *problems, matters*: finansowy **2.** *market*: pieniężny; **'mon-ey•bags** *pl moneybags s infml*: ***be a ~*** być nadzianym; **'mon•ey belt** *s* saszetka *f* na pieniądze, pas *m* na pieniądze; **'mon•ey box** *s Br* skarbonka *f*; **'mon•ey-chang•er** *s* **1.** właściciel *m* kantoru **2.** *infml* cinkciarz *m*; **mon•eyed** ['mʌnɪd] *adj* bogaty, majętny; **'mon•ey•lend•er** *s dated* lichwiarz *m*; **'mon•ey•mak•er, *mon-ey-spin•ner*** *Br s* dobry interes *m*; **'mon•ey mar•ket** *s* FIN rynek *m* pieniężny; **'mon•ey or•der** *s* przekaz *m* pieniężny; **'mon•ey-spin•ner** → ***moneymaker***

mon•ger ['mʌŋgə] → ***scandalmonger***, ***scaremonger***

mon•gol•ism ['mɒŋgəlɪzəm] *s dated* mongolizm *m*

mon•grel ['mʌŋgrəl] *s* kundel *m*

mon•i•tor ['mɑːnɪtə] **I** *s* **1.** monitor *m* **2.** ***a heart ~*** MED kardiomonitor **3.** obserwator *m*; ***UN ~s*** obserwatorzy ONZ **II** *v/t* monitorować

monk [mʌŋk] *s* mnich *m*

mon•key ['mʌŋkɪ] *s* **1.** małpa *f*; ***don't make a ~ out of me*** *infml* nie rób ze mnie idioty **2.** *infml* łobuziak *m*, gagatek *m*; **monkey about with, *monkey around with*** *v/i* majstrować przy *L*; **'mon•key busi•ness** *s infml* **1.** machlojki *pl*, kombinacje *pl* **2.** wygłupy *pl*; **'mon•key wrench** *s* TECH klucz *m* francuski

M

monk•fish ['mʌŋkfɪʃ] *pl s BIOL* **1.** żabnica *f*, diabeł *m* morski **2.** raszpla *f*, anioł *m* morski
mon•o ['mɒnəʊ] **I** *s* mono *n*, monofonia *f* **II** *adj* mono, monofoniczny
mon•o- [~] *adj* (*in combinations*) mono-
mon•o•chrome ['mɒnəkrəʊm] *adj* **1.** monochromatyczny, jednobarwny **2.** *fig* bezbarwny
mon•o•cle ['mɒnəkl] *s* monokl *m*
mo•nog•a•mous [mə'nɒgəməs] *adj* monogamiczny; **mo•nog•a•my** [mə'nɒgəmɪ] *s* monogamia *f*
mon•o•gram ['mɒnəgræm] *s* monogram *m*; **mon•o•grammed** ['mɒnəgræmd] *adj* z monogramem
mon•o•lith ['mɒnəlɪθ] *s* monolit *m*; **mon•o•lith•ic** [mɒnə'lɪθɪk] *adj* monolityczny
mon•o•logue ['mɒnəlɒg] *Br*, ***mon•o•log*** *Am s* monolog *m*
mon•o•nu•cle•o•sis [mɒnəʊnju:klɪ'əʊsɪs] *s MED* mononukleoza *f*
mo•nop•o•lis•tic [mənɒpə'lɪstɪk] *adj* monopolistyczny; **mo•nop•o•lize** [mə'nɒpəlaɪz] *v/t* **1.** monopolizować ⟨z-⟩ **2.** *conversation*: dominować ⟨z-⟩; **mo•nop•o•ly** [mə'nɒpəlɪ] *s a. fig* monopol *m*, wyłączność *f* (***on*** na *A*)
mon•o•rail ['mɒnəʊreɪl] *s* kolejka *f* jednoszynowa
mon•o•so•di•um glu•ta•mate [mɒnəʊsəʊdɪəm'glutəmeɪt] *s CHEM* glutaminian *m* sodu
mon•o•syl•lab•ic [mɒnəʊsɪ'læbɪk] *adj* jednosylabowy
mon•o•the•is•tic [mɒnəʊθeɪ'ɪstɪk] *adj* monoteistyczny; **mon•o•the•ism** ['mɒnəʊθeɪzəm] *s* monoteizm *m*
mo•not•o•nous [mə'nɒtənəs] *adj* monotonny; **mo•not•o•ny** [mə'nɒtənɪ] *s* monotonia *f*
mon•ox•ide [mə'nɒksaɪd] *s CHEM* tlenek *m*
mon•soon [mɒn'su:n] *s* **1.** monsun *m* **2.** pora *f* monsunowa
mon•ster ['mɒnstə] **I** *s a. fig* potwór *m* **II** *adj* gigantyczny, monstrualny
mon•strance ['mɒnstrəns] *s REL* monstrancja *f*
mon•stros•i•ty [mɒn'strɒsətɪ] *s* **1.** okropieństwo *n*, monstrum *n* **2.** potworność *f*; **mon•strous** ['mɒnstrəs] *adj* **1.** monstrualny, potworny **2.** gigantyczny, monstrualnie wielki; **mon•strous•ly** ['mɒnstrəslɪ] *adv* potwornie
mon•tage [mɒn'tɑ:ʒ] *s* montaż *m*; ***a photographic ~*** fotomontaż
month [mʌnθ] *s* miesiąc *m*; ***in a ~*** **a)** za miesiąc **b)** w miesiąc, w ciągu miesiąca; ***~ by ~*** z miesiąca na miesiąc; ***not in a ~ of Sundays*** nigdy w życiu; **month•ly** ['mʌnθlɪ] **I** *adj* **1.** comiesięczny; ***a ~ magazine*** miesięcznik **2.** *ticket*, *salary*: miesięczny **II** *adv* **1.** co miesiąc **2.** miesięcznie **III** *s* miesięcznik *m*
mon•u•ment ['mɒnjʊmənt] *s* **1.** pomnik *m* (***to*** *G*) **2.** zabytek *m* **3.** świadectwo *n*; **mon•u•ment•al** [mɒnjʊ'mentl] *adj* **1.** monumentalny; ***of ~ significance*** ogromnej wagi, o kolosalnym znaczeniu **2.** *task*: gigantyczne
moo [mu:] **I** *interj* (*cow*) mu **II** *v/i* ryczeć ⟨za-⟩
mood[1] [mu:d] *s* (*grammar*) tryb *m*
mood[2] [~] *s* **1.** humor *m*, nastrój *m*; ***be in a good*** (***bad***) ***~*** być w dobrym (złym) humorze; ***be in the ~ for*** mieć ochotę na *A*; ***he was in no ~ to laugh*** nie było mu do śmiechu **2.** ***be in a ~*** być w złym humorze; ***he was in one of his ~s*** był nie w humorze **3.** nastrój *m*, atmosfera *f*; **mood•i•ly** ['mu:dɪlɪ] *adv* **1.** markotnie **2.** melancholijnie **3.** kapryśnie; '**mood music** *s* nastrojowa muzyka *f*; **mood•y** ['mu:dɪ] *adj* **1.** humorzasty, kapryśny **2.** markotny, nie w humorze **3.** *music*: melancholijny
moon [mu:n] *s* księżyc *m*; ***full ~*** pełnia; ***new ~*** nów; ***by the light of the ~*** przy świetle księżyca; ***be over the ~*** nie posiadać się ze szczęścia; ***cry for the ~*** pragnąć gwiazdki z nieba; ***once in a blue ~*** od święta, bardzo rzadko; ***promise s.o. the ~*** obiecywać komuś gruszki na wierzbie; **moon about**, ***moon around*** *v/i* snuć się z kąta w kąt, snuć się bez celu; '**moon•beam** *s* promień *m* księżyca; '**moon landing** *s* lądowanie *n* na księżycu; '**moon•light** **I** *s* światło *n* księżyca **II** *v/i infml* dorabiać na boku; '**moon•light•er** *s* dorabiający *m* na boku; '**moon•lit** *adj* **1.** *night*: księżycowy

M

2. *sky*, *sea*: rozświetlony księżycową poświatą; **'moon•shine** *s* **1.** *Am dated* bimber *m*, księżycówka *f* **2.** *infml* bzdury *pl*
moor¹ [muə] *s* wrzosowisko *n*
moor² [~] *v/t boat*: cumować ⟨przy-⟩ (**to** do *G*) **III** *v/i* cumować ⟨za-⟩; **moor•ing** ['muərıŋ] *s* **1. ~s** cumy, liny cumownicze **2.** miejsce *n* cumowania
moose [mu:s] *s* łoś *m*
moot [mu:t] *v/t* poddawać ⟨-dać⟩ pod dyskusję; **'moot point** *s* kwestia *f* sporna, punkt *m* sporny
mop [mɒp] **I** *s* **1.** mop *m* **2.** *infml* czupryna *f* **II** *v/t* **1.** myć ⟨u-⟩ (mopem) **2.** *brow*: ocierać ⟨otrzeć⟩; **mop up** *v/t* **1.** ścierać ⟨zetrzeć⟩ **2.** *resistance*: likwidować ⟨z-⟩ **3.** *savings*: pochłaniać ⟨-łonąć⟩
mope [məup] *v/i* (*a.* ***~ about***, ***~ around***) snuć się z kąta w kąt, snuć się bez celu
mo•ped ['məuped] *s* motorower *m*
mo•raine [mə'reın] *s* GEOL morena *f*
mor•al ['mɒrəl] **I** *adj* **1.** moralny; ***~ standards*** normy moralne; ***a ~ obligation*** moralny obowiązek; ***take the ~ high ground*** przyjąć postawę moralizatorską **2.** moralny, etyczny **II** *s* **1. ~s** moralność; ***public ~s*** dobre obyczaje; ***a code of ~s*** kodeks moralny; ***have no ~s*** być pozbawionym zasad (moralnych); ***a woman of loose ~s*** kobieta lekkich obyczajów **2.** morał *m*; ***draw the ~ from*** wyciągnąć morał z *G*
mo•rale [mə'ra:l] *s* morale *n*; ***raise ~*** podnosić morale
mor•al•ist ['mɒrəlıst] *s* moralista *m*; **mor•al•is•tic** [mɒrə'lıstık] *adj* **1.** *tone*: moralizatorski **2.** *person*: moralizujący; **mo•ral•i•ty** [mə'rælətı] *s* moralność *f*; **mor•al•ize** ['mɒrəlaız] *v/i* moralizować; **mor•al•ly** ['mɒrəlı] *adv* moralnie; ***~ wrong*** moralnie naganny
mor•a•to•ri•um [mɒrə'tɔ:rıəm] *pl -ria s* [~rıə], *-riums* [~rıəmz] POLIT moratorium *n*
mor•bid ['mɔ:bıd] *adj* **1.** *interest*: chorobliwy, niezdrowy **2.** *scene*: makabryczny **3.** MED chorobowy; **mor•bid•i•ty** [mɔ:'bıdıtı] *s* **1.** MED zapadalność *f* **2.** chorobliwość *f* **3.** makabryczność *f*
mor•dant ['mɔ:rdənt] *adj humour*, *criticism*: zjadliwy
more [mɔ:] **I** *comp* → **much**, **many** *pron* więcej; ***~ money*** więcej pieniędzy; ***there's no ~ money*** nie ma już pieniędzy; ***are there any ~ questions?*** czy są jeszcze jakieś pytania?; ***no ~ than three cars*** nie więcej niż trzy samochody; ***~ and ~ work*** coraz więcej pracy **II** *comp* → **much**, **many** *adv* **1.** (*comparative*) bardziej; ***~ intelligent*** bardziej inteligentny, inteligentniejszy; ***~ carefully*** ostrożniej **2.** bardziej; ***I like this movie ~*** ten film podoba mi się bardziej; ***~ and ~ dangerous*** coraz bardziej niebezpieczny; ***it had ~ the appearance of a deliberate crime*** to wyglądało raczej na morderstwo z premedytacją; ***be ~ than happy*** nie posiadać się z radości, być wniebowziętym; ***it's little ~ than formality*** to jedynie formalność **3.** więcej; ***once ~*** jeszcze raz; ***no ~*** nigdy więcej; ***~ or less*** **a)** mniej więcej **b)** prawie; ***what's ~*** co więcej; ***~ than ten people*** ponad dziesięć osób
more•ish ['mɔ:rıʃ] *adj infml Br* pyszny
mo•rel•lo (cherry) [mə'reləutʃerı] *pl -los s* wiśnia *f*
more•o•ver [mɔ:r'əuvər] *adv* ponadto, poza tym
morgue [mɔ:g] *s* kostnica *f*
Mor•mon ['mɔ:mən] **I** *s* Mormon *m* **II** *adj* mormoński
morn•ing ['mɔ:nıŋ] **I** *s* ranek *m*, poranek *m*; ***this ~*** dzisiaj rano; ***tomorrow ~*** jutro rano; ***early in the ~*** wczesnym rankiem; ***two in the ~*** druga nad ranem; ***good ~*** dzień dobry **II** *adj* ranny, poranny; **morn•ing-'af•ter pill** *s* tabletka *f* wczesnoporonna; **'morning sick•ness** *s* poranne nudności *pl*
Marokańczyk *m* **II** *adj* marokański; **Mo•roc•co** [mə'rɒkə] *s* Maroko *n*
mo•ron ['mɔ:rɒn] *s infml* kretyn *m*; **mo•ron•ic** [mə'rɒnık] *adj* kretyński
mo•rose [mə'rəus] *adj* ponury; **mo•rose•ly** [mə'rəuslı] *adv* ponuro
mor•pheme ['mɔ:rfi:m] *s* morfem *m*
mor•phine ['mɔ:rfi:n] *s* morfina *f*
mor•phing ['mɔ:fıŋ] *s* INF morfing *m*, morphing *m*

M

mor•pho•log•i•cal [mɔːfəˈlɒdʒɪkl] *adj* BIOL morfologiczny; **mor•phol•o•gy** [mɔːˈfɒlədʒɪ] *s* morfologia *f*
mor•ris dance [ˈmɒrɪsdɑːnsɪŋ] *s tradycyjny taniec angielski*
Morse code [mɔːrsˈkəʊd] *s* alfabet *m* Morse'a
mor•sel [ˈmɔːrsl] *s* kęs *m*; ***a tasty ~*** smaczny kąsek *m*; ***a ~ of information*** (drobna) informacja
mor•tal [ˈmɔːtl] **I** *adj* **1.** śmiertelny; ***we are all ~*** wszyscy jesteśmy śmiertelni **2.** *combat*: na śmierć i życie **II** *s* śmiertelnik *m*; ***an ordinary ~*** zwykły śmiertelnik; **mor•tal ˈdan•ger** *s* śmiertelne niebezpieczeństwo *n*; **mor•tal ˈen•e•my** *s* śmiertelny wróg *m*; **mor•tal•i•ty** [mɔːˈtælətɪ] *s* śmiertelność *f*; ***infant ~ rate*** śmiertelność niemowląt; ***~ from lung cancer*** śmiertelność z powodu raka płuc; **mor•tal•ly** [ˈmɔːtəlɪ] *adj* śmiertelnie; ***~ wounded*** śmiertelnie raniony; ***~ offended*** śmiertelnie obrażony; ***he's ~ afraid of her*** panicznie się jej boi; **mor•tal ˈsin** *s* grzech *m* śmiertelny
mor•tar[1] [ˈmɔːtə] *s* zaprawa *f* murarska
mor•tar[2] [***~***] *s* **1.** (*cannon*) moździerz *m* **2.** COOK moździerz *m*
mort•gage [ˈmɔːgɪdʒ] **I** *s* **1.** hipoteka *f* **2.** kredyt *m* hipoteczny; ***take out a ~*** wziąć kredyt hipoteczny **II** *adj credit*: hipoteczny **III** *v/t* obciążać ⟨-żyć⟩ hipotekę
mor•ti•cian [mɔːˈtɪʃn] *s Am* przedsiębiorca *m* pogrzebowy
mor•ti•fi•ca•tion [mɔːtɪfɪˈkeɪʃn] *s* **1.** wielki wstyd *m* **2.** ogromne zażenowanie *n*; **mor•ti•fy** [ˈmɔːtɪfaɪ] *v/t* **1.** (wielce) zawstydzać ⟨-dzić⟩ **2.** (ogromnie) żenować ⟨za-⟩
mor•tu•a•ry [ˈmɔːtʃuerɪ] *s Am* **1.** kostnica *f* **2.** dom *m* pogrzebowy
mo•sa•ic [məʊˈzeɪɪk] *s* mozaika *f*
Mos•cow [ˈmɒskəʊ] *s* Moskwa *f*
Mos•lem [ˈmʊzlɪm] → ***Muslim***
mosque [mɒsk] *s* meczet *m*
mos•qui•to [məˈskɪːtəʊ] *pl -toes, -tos s* **1.** komar *m* **2.** moskit *m*; **moˈsqui•to net** *s* moskitiera *f*
moss [mɒs] *s* mech *m*; **moss•y** [ˈmɑːsɪ] *adj* omszały, porośnięty mchem
most [məʊst] **I** *superl* → ***much***, ***many*** *pron* **1.** najwięcej; ***~ time*** najwięcej czasu; ***who ate the ~?*** kto zjadł najwięcej?; ***have the ~ to lose*** mieć najwięcej do stracenia **2.** większość *f*; ***I like ~ vegetables*** lubię większość warzyw; ***as ~ of you know*** jak większość z was wie; ***~ of the people*** większość ludzi; ***at*** (***the***) ***~*** (co) najwyżej **II** *superl* → ***much***, ***many*** *adv* **1.** (*superlative*) najbardziej; ***the ~ beautiful part*** najpiękniejsza część; ***~ frequently*** najczęściej **2.** niezmiernie, bardzo; ***it was what she wanted ~ of all*** właśnie tego chciała najbardziej; ***it was ~ kind of you*** to bardzo miło z twojej strony; **most•ly** [ˈməʊstlɪ] *adv* **1.** głównie **2.** w większości **3.** przeważnie
MOT [eməʊˈtiː] *abbr* (=***Ministry of Transport***) *Br* (*a.* ***~ test***) *s* przegląd *m* techniczny (pojazdu)
mo•tel [məʊˈtel] *s* motel *m*
moth [mɒθ] *s* **1.** ćma *f* **2.** mól *m*; **ˈmoth•ball I** *s* kulka *f* naftalinowa **II** *v/t idea*, *plan*: odkładać ⟨odłożyć⟩ na półkę; **ˈmoth-eat•en** *adj* **1.** zjedzony przez mole **2.** *furniture*: wysłużony **3.** *phrase*: wyświechtany
moth•er [ˈmʌðə] **I** *s* **1.** matka *f*; ***at one's ~'s knee*** *fig* jako małe dziecko, we wczesnym dzieciństwie **2.** mama *f*; ***I'm here, ~*** jestem tutaj, mamo **II** *v/t* **1.** *family*: mieć, wychowywać ⟨-chować⟩ **2.** matkować; **ˈmoth•er•board** *s* INF płyta *f* główna; **ˈmoth•er•hood** [ˈmʌðəhʊd] *s* macierzyństwo *n*; **ˈmoth•er-in-law** *pl mothers-in-law s* teściowa *f*; **ˈmoth•er•land** *s* ojczyzna *f*; **moth•er•less** [ˈmʌðəlɪs] *adj* pozbawiony matki, bez matki; **moth•er•ly** [ˈmʌðərlɪ] *adj* **1.** *love*: matczyny **2.** *instinct*: macierzyński; **Moth•er ˈNa•ture** *s* matka *f* natura; **moth•er-of-ˈpearl** *s* macica *f* perłowa; **ˈMoth•er's Day** *s* Dzień *m* Matki; **moth•er-to-ˈbe** *pl mothers-to-be s* przyszła matka *f*; **moth•er ˈtongue** *s* język *m* ojczysty
mo•tif [məʊˈtiːf] *s* ART MUS motyw *m*
mo•tion [ˈməʊʃn] **I** *s* **1.** ruch *m*; ***be in ~*** być w ruchu, poruszać się; ***put s.th. in ~***, ***set s.th. in ~*** *a. fig* wprawić coś w ruch; ***go through the ~s of doing s.th.*** robić coś mechanicznie **2.** ruch *m*, gest *m*; ***make a ~ with one's hand***

M

wykonać gest ręką **3.** wniosek *m*; ***put forward a ~*** wysunąć wniosek **II** *v/i* skinąć (***to*** na *A*); ***~ s.o. in*** zaprosić kogoś ruchem ręki do środka; **mo•tion•less** ['məʊʃnlɪs] *adj* nieruchomy; ***stand ~*** stać nieruchomo, stać bez ruchu; **mo•tion 'pic•ture** *s Am* film *m*; **'mo•tion sick•ness** *s MED* choroba *f* lokomocyjna

mo•ti•vate ['məʊtɪveɪt] *v/t* **1.** motywować ⟨z-⟩; ***he is ~d entirely by self-interest*** szuka tylko własnej korzyści **2.** skłaniać ⟨-łonić⟩ (***to do s.th.*** do *G*); **mo•ti•va•tion** [məʊtɪ'veɪʃn] *s* **1.** motywacja *f* **2.** motywy *pl*

mo•tive ['məʊtɪv] **I** *s* **1.** *JUR* motyw *m*, pobudka *f* **2.** powód *m*; ***ulterior ~s*** ukryte powody **II** *adj TECH* napędowy; ***~ power*** siła napędowa; **mo•tive•less** ['məʊtɪvlɪs] *adj JUR* bez motywu

mot•ley ['mɒtlɪ] *adj*: ***a ~ collection*** zbieranina, ***a ~ crew*** mieszanka

mo•tor ['məʊtə] **I** *s* **1.** *TECH* silnik *m*, motor *m* **2.** *Br infml* wóz *m*, maszyna *f* **II** *adj* **1.** *industry*: motoryzacyjny **4.** *accident*: drogowy **3.** *fuel*: silnikowy **4.** *activity*: motoryczny; **'mo•tor•bike** *s* motocykl *m*, motor *m*; **'mo•tor•boat** *s* łódź *f* motorowa, motorówka *f*; **mo•tor•cade** ['məʊtəkeɪd] *s* kawalkada *f*; **'mo•tor•cy•cle** *s* motor *m*, motocykl *m*; **'mo•tor•cy•clist** *s* motocyklista *m*; **'mo•tor home** *s* samochód *m* kempingowy; **'mo•tor in•dus•try** *s* przemysł *m* motoryzacyjny; **mo•tor•ing** ['məʊtərɪŋ] *adj offence*: drogowy; **'mo•tor in•sur•ance** *s* ubezpieczenie *n* pojazdów mechanicznych; **mo•tor•ist** ['məʊtərɪst] *s* kierowca *m*; **mo•tor•i•za•tion** [məʊtəraɪ'zeɪʃn] *s* motoryzacja *f*; **'mo•tor•ize** [məʊtəraɪz] *v/t* motoryzować ⟨z-⟩; **mo•tor•ized** [məʊtəraɪzd] *adj* **1.** zmotoryzowany **2.** *vehicle*: mechaniczny; **'mo•tor me•chan•ic** *s* mechanik *m* samochodowy; **'mo•tor•mouth** *s infml* gaduła *m*; **mo•tor 'neu•rone dis•ease** *s MED* choroba *f* neuronu ruchowego; **'mo•tor rac•ing** *s* wyścigi *pl* samochodowe (i motocyklowe); **'mo•tor ve•hi•cle** *s* pojazd *m* mechaniczny; **'mo•tor•way** *s* autostrada *f*

mot•tled ['mɑːtld] *adj* nakrapiany, cętkowany

mot•to ['mɒtəʊ] *pl -toes, -tos s* dewiza *f*, motto *n*

mould[1] [məʊld] *Br*, ***mold*** *Am* **I** *s* **1.** *TECH COOK* forma *f* **2.** pokrój *m*, typ *m*, styl *m*; ***a hero in the Superman ~*** bohater w stylu Supermana; ***she doesn't fit the ~ of a typical poet*** nie jest typową poetką; ***cast in the same ~*** *fig* ulepiony z tej samej gliny **II** *v/t* **1.** formować ⟨u-⟩; ***~ the clay into the desired shape*** nadać glinie pożądany kształt **2.** *character*, *opinion*: kształtować ⟨u-⟩

mould[2] [~] *Br*, ***mold*** *Am s BIOL* pleśń *f*; **mould•er** ['məʊldə] *Br*, ***mold•er*** *Am v/t* **1.** rozpadać ⟨-paść⟩ się **2.** butwieć ⟨z-⟩ **3.** rozkładać ⟨-złożyć⟩ się; **mouldy** ['məʊldɪ] *Br*, ***moldy*** *Am adj* spleśniały; ***go ~*** pleśnieć; ***a ~ smell*** zapach stęchlizny

moult [məʊlt] *Br*, ***moult*** *Am v/i* **1.** gubić ⟨z-⟩ pióra **2.** linieć ⟨wy-⟩

mound [maʊnd] *s* **1.** kopiec *m* **2.** wzgórek *m* **3.** stos *m*, sterta *f* **4.** ***a ~ of*** *infml* całe mnóstwo *G*

mount [maʊnt] **I** *v/t* **1.** *protest*, *campaign*: organizować ⟨z-⟩ **2.** *climber*: wchodzić ⟨wejść⟩ na *A* **3.** *stairs*: wchodzić ⟨wejść⟩ po *L* **4.** *bike*: wsiadać ⟨wsiąść⟩ na *A* **5.** *horse*: dosiadać ⟨-siąść⟩ **6.** *gem*, *painting*: oprawiać ⟨-wić⟩ **7.** (*male*) pokrywać ⟨-ryć⟩ **II** *v/i* **1.** rosnąć, wzrastać ⟨-rosnąć⟩ **2.** (*problems*) narastać ⟨-rosnąć⟩, piętrzyć ⟨s-⟩ się **III** *s* **1.** (*mountain*) góra *f*; ***≈ Everest*** Mount Everest; ***≈ Sinai*** góra Synaj **2.** *lit* wierzchowiec *m* **3.** *gem*: oprawa *f* **4.** *photograph*: ramka *f*, passe-partout *n* **5.** podstawa *f*, stojak *m*; **mount up** *v/i* **1.** rosnąć, wzrastać ⟨-rosnąć⟩ **2.** (*problems*) narastać ⟨-rosnąć⟩, piętrzyć ⟨s-⟩ się

moun•tain ['maʊntɪn] *s a. fig* góra *f*; ***in the ~s*** w górach; ***we made ~s of sandwiches*** *infml* zrobiliśmy góry kanapek; **'moun•tain bike** *s* rower *m* górski; **'moun•tain chain** *s GEOGR* łańcuch *m* górski; **moun•tain•eer** [maʊntɪ'nɪ] *s* alpinista *m*, wspinacz *m*; **moun•tain•eer•ing** [maʊntɪ'nɪrɪŋ] *s* alpinizm *m*, wspinaczka *f* górska; **'moun•tain goat** *s BIOL* kozioł *m*

M

śnieżny; ˈ**moun•tain li•on** *s* BIOL puma *f*; **moun•tain•ous** [ˈmaʊntɪnəs] *adj* **1.** górzysty **2.** ogromny; **moun•tain ˈrange** *s* pasmo *n* górskie; ˈ**mountain•side** *s* zbocze *n* (górskie)

mount•ed [ˈmaʊntɪd] *adj* **1.** *policeman, soldier*: konny, na koniu **2.** *painting*: oprawiony; **mount•ed po•ˈlice** *s* policja *f* konna

Moun•tie [ˈmaʊntɪ] *s infml* członek *m* kanadyjskiej policji konnej

mount•ing [ˈmaʊntɪŋ] *adj tension, interest*: rosnący, wzrastający

mourn [mɔːn] *v/t* **1.** opłakiwać ⟨-kać⟩; ***she ~ed for her lost childhood*** opłakiwała swoje utracone dzieciństwo **2.** być w żałobie po *L*; ***he is ~ing his brother's death*** jest w żałobie po śmierci brata; **mourn•er** [ˈmɔːrnə] *s* żałobnik *m*; **mourn•ful** [ˈmɔːnfəl] *adj* **1.** smętny, przygnębiony **2.** *sound, cry*: żałosny, smętny **3.** *eyes*: pełen smutku; **mourn•ing** [ˈmɔːnɪŋ] *s* żałoba *f*: ***be in ~ for*** być w żałobie po *L*

mouse [maʊs] *pl mice* [maɪs] *s* **1.** mysz *f*; ***sit quiet as a ~*** siedzieć cicho jak mysz pod miotłą; ***she's quiet as a ~*** jest cicha jak myszka **2.** *pl mouses, mice* INF mysz *f*, myszka *f*; ***click the left ~ button*** kliknij lewym przyciskiem myszy ˈ**mouse•hole** *s* mysia dziura *f*; ˈ**mouse mat** *Br*, **mouse pad** *Am s* INF podkładka *f* pod mysz; ˈ**mouse•trap** *s* pułapka *f* na myszy

mousse [muːs] *s* **1.** COOK mus *m* **2.** pianka *f* (do włosów)

mous•tache [məˈstaːʃ] *Br*, **mus•tache** *Am s* wąsy *pl*

mous•y [ˈmaʊsɪ] *adj* **1.** *colour*: mysi **2.** *person*: cichy, nieśmiały

mouth [maʊθ] **I.** *s* **1.** usta *pl*; ***talk with one's ~ full*** mówić z pełnymi ustami; ***keep your ~ shut!*** zamknij się!; ***you took the words out of my ~*** *fig* wyjąłeś mi to z ust **2.** pysk *m*, morda *f* **3.** otwór *n* gębowy **4.** *river*: ujście *n* **5.** *bottle*: otwór *m* **6.** *tunnel, cave*: wylot *m* **7.** *port*: wejście *n* **II.** [maʊð] *v/t* **1.** *words*: wymawiać ⟨-mówić⟩ bezgłośnie; **mouth•ful** [ˈmaʊθfəl] *s* **1.** kęs *m* **2.** łyk *m* **3.** (*word, phrase*) ***s.th. is quite a ~*** coś jest trudne do wymówienia

ˈ**mouth•or•gan** *s* MUS harmonijka *f* ustna, organki *pl*; ˈ**mouth•piece** *s* **1.** MUS ustnik *m* **2.** słuchawka *f* (telefonu); **mouth-to-mouth re•sus•ciˈtation** *s* sztuczne oddychanie *n* metodą usta-usta; ˈ**mouth•wash** *s* płyn *m* do płukania ust; ˈ**mouth•wa•ter•ing** *adj* apetyczny

mov•able [ˈmuːvəbəl] **I** *adj* ruchomy **II** *s* **~s** JUR ruchomości

move [muːv] **I** *v/i* **1.** ruszać ⟨-szyć⟩ się, poruszać ⟨-szyć⟩ się; ***don't ~!*** nie ruszaj się!; ***~ with the times*** iść z duchem czasu **2.** jechać; ***the train began to ~*** pociąg ruszył **3.** (*a.* ***~ ahead***) (*talks*) posuwać ⟨-sunąć⟩ się naprzód **4.** (*time*) mijać ⟨minąć⟩ **5.** przeprowadzać ⟨-dzić⟩ się, przenosić ⟨-nieść⟩ się (***from*** z *G*, ***to*** do *G*) **6.** (*game*) wykonywać ⟨-nać⟩ ruch **II** *v/t* **1.** ruszać ⟨-szyć⟩, poruszać ⟨-szyć⟩; ***I can't ~ my fingers*** nie mogę poruszyć palcami; ***~ heaven and earth*** poruszyć niebo i ziemię **2.** *meeting*: przenosić ⟨-nieść⟩ **3.** (*change place*) przenosić ⟨-nieść⟩ (***to*** do *G*); ***~ house*** *Br* przeprowadzić się; ***~ jobs*** zmieniać pracę **4.** *chessman*: wykonywać ⟨-nać⟩ ruch **5.** wzruszać ⟨-szyć⟩, poruszać ⟨-szyć⟩; ***she was ~d to tears*** była wzruszona do łez **6.** skłaniać ⟨-łonić⟩ (***to do s.th.*** do zrobienia *G*) **7.** stawiać ⟨postawić⟩, wysuwać ⟨-sunąć⟩ wniosek **8.** działać ⟨za-⟩, podejmować ⟨-djąć⟩ działania **III** *s* ruch *m*; ***don't make a ~!*** nie ruszaj się!; ***on the ~*** w ruchu; ***get a ~ on!*** *infml* ruszaj się!; ***make the first ~*** uczynić pierwszy krok; ***watch s.o.'s every ~*** obserwować czyjś każdy krok; ***a clever ~*** sprytne posunięcie; ***it's your ~*** twój ruch; **move along** *v/i* **1.** przesuwać ⟨-sunąć⟩ się; ***they were ordered to ~*** kazano im się rozejść **2.** (*talks*) posuwać ⟨-sunąć⟩ się naprzód; **move around** *v/i* poruszać ⟨-szyć⟩ się, przemieszczać ⟨-mieścić⟩ się; **move away** *v/i* wyprowadzać ⟨-dzić⟩ się; **move in** *v/i* **1.** wprowadzać ⟨-dzić⟩ się **2.** (*company*) obracać się w *L*; **move in on** *v/t* otaczać ⟨otoczyć⟩; **move on** *v/i* **1.** iść ⟨pójść⟩ naprzód **2.** (*discussion*) posuwać ⟨-sunąć⟩ się naprzód **3.** (*time*) mijać ⟨minąć⟩ **4.** ***~ to*** przechodzić do *G*; **move out** *v/i* wyprowadzać ⟨-dzić⟩ się; **move over** *v/i* posuwać ⟨-sunąć⟩ się; **move up** → ***move over***

move•ment ['mu:vmənt] *s* **1.** ruch *m*; ***the ~ towards democracy*** postępująca demokratyzacja **2.** gest *m* **3.** *goods*: przepływ *m* **4.** *MUS* część *f* (utworu)

mov•er ['mu:və] *s* **1.** pracownik *m* firmy spedycyjnej **2.** ***~s and shakers*** *fig* grube ryby

mov•ie ['mu:vɪ] *Am s* **1.** film *m* **2.** ***the ~s*** **a)** kino **b)** przemysł filmowy; '**mov•ie cam•er•a** *s* kamera *f* filmowa; '**mov•ie•go•er** *s* kinoman *m*; '**mov•ie star** *s* gwiazda *f* filmowa; '**mov•ie thea•ter** *s* kino *n*

mov•ing ['mu:vɪŋ] *adj* **1.** wzruszający, poruszający **2.** ruchomy; ***a ~ target*** ruchomy cel; ***a ~ staircase*** *dated* ruchome schody

mow [məʊ] *v/t* (*mowed*; *mowed/mown*) *lawn*: kosić ⟨s-⟩; **mow down** *v/t* **1.** kłaść ⟨położyć⟩ trupem **2.** rozjeżdżać ⟨-jechać⟩; **mow•er** ['məʊər] *s* kosiarka *f*

MP [em'pi:] *abbr* **1.** (=***Member of Parliament***) poseł *m*, deputowany *m* **2.** (=***Military Police***) funkcjonariusz *m* żandarmerii wojskowej

M

mpg [empi:'dʒi:] *abbr* (=***miles per gallon***) mile na galon

mph [empi:'eɪtʃ] *abbr* (=***miles per hour***) mile na godzinę

Mr ['mɪstə] *abbr* (=***mister***) pan *m*

Mrs ['mɪsɪz] *abbr* (*married woman*) pani *f*

Ms [mɪz] *abbr* (*married or unmarried woman*) pani *f*

MS [em'es] *abbr* (=***multiple sclerosis***) stwardnienie *n* rozsiane

much [mʌtʃ] **I** (*more*; *most*) *pron* (*with uncountable nouns*) dużo, wiele; ***how ~ is it?*** ile to kosztuje?; ***take as ~ as you want*** weź tyle, ile chcesz; ***it can cost as ~ as 50 pounds*** to może kosztować aż 50 funtów; ***think ~ of*** *fig* mieć dobre zdanie o *L*; ***he's not ~ of a tennis player*** nie jest zbyt dobrym tenisistą **II** (*more*; *most*) *adv* bardzo; ***thank you very ~*** bardzo dziękuję; ***too ~*** zbytnio, za bardzo; ***~ more*** (***better***) o wiele więcej (lepiej); ***I thought as ~*** tak (właśnie) myślałem; ***~ to my surprise*** ku mojemu wielkiemu zaskoczeniu; ***they are ~ the same*** są bardzo do siebie podobni

muck [mʌk] *s* **1.** (*fertilizer*) gnój *m* **2.** *infml* brud *m*, błoto *n* **3.** *infml* świństwo *n*; **muck about**, ***muck around*** *v/i Br infml* **1.** pajacować **2.** obijać się; **muck about with**, ***muck around with*** *v/t Br infml* grzebać przy *L*; **muck up** *v/t infml* **1.** pieprzyć ⟨s-⟩ **2.** *exam*: zawalać ⟨-lić⟩ **3.** uświnić; '**muck•raking** *s infml* pogoń *f* za sensacją; **muck•y** ['mʌkɪ] *adj infml* **1.** uświniony, upaprany **2.** sprośny

mu•cous ['mju:kəs] *adj ANAT* śluzowy; ***a ~ membrane*** błona śluzowa; **mucus** ['mju:kəs] *s ANAT* śluz *m*

mud [mʌd] *s* błoto *n*; ***drag s.o. through the ~*** *fig* obrzucić kogoś błotem; '**mud•bath** *s* kąpiel *f* błotna, kąpiel *f* borowinowa

mud•dle ['mʌdl] **I** *v/t* (*a.* ***~ up***) **1.** robić ⟨z-⟩ bałagan w *L* **2.** mylić ⟨po-⟩, mieszać ⟨po-⟩ (***with*** z *I*) **II** *s* **1.** bałagan *m* **2.** mętlik *m*; ***my thoughts are all in a ~*** mam zupełny mętlik w głowie **3.** zamieszanie *n*; **muddle through** *v/i*: ***we'll ~ somehow*** damy radę, jakoś to będzie

mud•dy ['mʌdɪ] *adj* **1.** zabłocony **2.** *water*: mętny, błotnisty **3.** *pond*: błotnisty '**mud•flap** *s Br AUTO* chlapacz *m*; '**mud•flat** *s* równina *f* błotna; '**mud•guard** *s Br* błotnik *m* (rowerowy); '**mud•pack** *s* maseczka *f* błotna; '**mud•sling•ing** *s fig* obrzucanie *n* błotem

mues•li ['mju:zlɪ] *s* musli *n*

muff [mʌf] *s* mufka *f*

muf•fin ['mʌfɪn] *s* **1.** *Am* babeczka *f* (z owocami) **2.** *Br* bułeczka *f*

muf•fle ['mʌfl] *v/t* **1.** *sound*: tłumić ⟨s-⟩ **2.** (*a.* ***~ up***) owijać ⟨owinąć⟩; **muf•fler** ['mʌflə] *s* **1.** *Am AUTO* tłumik *m* **2.** *dated* (ciepły) szal *m*

muf•ti ['mʌftɪ] *s*: ***in ~*** *dated* po cywilnemu

mug [mʌg] **I** *s* **1.** kubek *m* **2.** *infml* frajer *m* **3.** *vulg* gęba *f*, japa *f* **II.** *v/t* napadać ⟨-paść⟩ **III** *v/i* **1.** *infml* robić głupie miny **2.** wygłupiać się; **mug up** *v/t* (*learn*) *Br infml* wkuwać; **mug•ger** ['mʌgə] *s* bandyta *f*, napastnik *m*;

mug•ging ['mʌgɪŋ] *s* napad *m* rabunkowy, rozbój *m*
mug•gins ['mʌgɪnz] *s*: ***and ~ here believed him*** *Br infml* a ja, głupi, mu uwierzyłem
mug•gy ['mʌgɪ] *adj day*: parny, duszny
'mug•shot *s infml* zdjęcie *m* policyjne
mule [mjuːl] *s* **1.** *BIOL* muł *m*; ***as stubborn as a ~*** uparty jak osioł **2.** (*smuggler*) kurier *m* narkotykowy
mull over [mʌləʊvə] *v/t* przemyśleć
mulled [mʌld] *adj wine*: grzane
mul•ti- ['mʌltɪ] *adj* (*in combinations*) multi-, wielo-
mul•ti•col•oured ['mʌltɪkʌləd] *Br*, ***mul•ti•col•ored*** *Am adj* różnokolorowy, wielokolorowy
mul•ti'cul•tur•al *adj* wielokulturowy
mul•ti•fac•et•ed [mʌltɪ'fæsɪtɪd] *adj* **1.** *problem*: złożony **2.** wieloaspektowy
mul•ti•far•i•ous [mʌltɪ'ferɪəs] *adj form* różnorodny, różnoraki; ***the reasons are ~*** powodów jest wiele
mul•ti'func•tion•al *adj* wielofunkcyjny
mul•ti•lat•e•ral [mʌltɪ'lætərəl] *adj talks*: wielostronny
mul•ti•lin•gual [mʌltɪ'lɪŋgwəl] *adj* wielojęzyczny
mul•ti•me•di•a [mʌltɪ'miːdɪə] *adj* multimedialny
mul•ti•mil•lion'aire *s* multimilioner *m*
mul•ti•na•tion•al [mʌltɪ'næʃnl] **I** *adj* **1.** wielonarodowy **2.** *company*: międzynarodowy **II** *s* międzynarodowa korporacja *f*
mul•ti•ple ['mʌltɪpl] **I** *adj* **1.** liczny **2.** wieloraki **3.** *birth*: mnogi **II** *s MATH* wielokrotność *f*; **mul•ti•ple 'choice test** *s* test *m* wielokrotnego wyboru; **mul•ti•ple col•'li•sion** *s* karambol *m*; **mul•ti•ple 'entry visa** *s* wiza *f* wielokrotna; **mul•ti•ple scle•'ro•sis** *s MED* stwardnienie *n* rozsiane
mul•ti•plex ['mʌltɪpleks] *s* multipleks *m*
mul•ti•pli•ca•tion [mʌltɪplɪ'keɪʃn] *s* **1.** *MATH* mnożenie *n*; ***the ~ table*** tabliczka mnożenia **2.** *BIOL* rozmnażanie *n* (się); **mul•ti•pli•'ca•tion sign** *s MATH* znak *m* mnożenia; **mul•ti•plic•i•ty** [mʌltɪ'plɪsətɪ] *s form* **1.** różnorodność *f*, ***a ~ of cultures*** wiele różnych kultur **2.** mnogość *f*; **mul•ti•pli•er** ['mʌltɪplaɪə] *s MATH* mnożnik *m*; **mul•ti•ply** ['mʌltɪplaɪ] *v/t* **1.** mnożyć ⟨po-⟩ (***by*** przez *A*); ***two multiplied by four equals eight*** dwa razy cztery równa się osiem **2.** *risk*: wielokrotnie zwiększać ⟨-szyć⟩ **II** *v/i* **3.** *BIOL* rozmnażać ⟨-nożyć⟩ się
mul•ti'pur•pose *adj tool*: wielofunkcyjny
mul•ti'ra•cial *adj* wielorasowy
multi-'screen *adj cinema*: wielosalowy
mul•ti-'sto•rey *adj carpark*: wielopoziomowy
'mul•ti-task•ing *s INF* wielozadaniowość *f*
mul•ti•tude ['mʌltɪtjuːd] *s* **1.** ogromna ilość *f*; ***for a ~ of reasons*** z bardzo wielu powodów **2.** ***the ~(s)*** masy *pl*
mum[1] [mʌm] *s* mama *f*
mum[2] [~] *adj*: ***keep ~*** *infml* nie puścić pary z ust
mum•ble ['mʌmbl] **I** *v/t* mamrotać ⟨wy-⟩ **II** *s* mamrotanie *n*
mum•bo jum•bo [mʌmbəʊ'dʒʌmbəʊ] *s infml* bzdury *pl*
mum•mi•fy ['mʌmɪfaɪ] *v/t* mumifikować ⟨z-⟩
mum•my ['mʌmɪ] *s* **1.** *Br* mama *f* **2.** mumia *f*
mumps [mʌmps] *s MED* świnka *f*
munch [mʌntʃ] *v/t* żuć
mun•dane [mʌn'deɪn] *adj* **1.** nieciekawy **2.** prozaiczny, przyziemny
mu•ni•ci•pal [mjuː'nɪsɪpl] *adj* miejski; ***a ~ council*** rada miejska; ***~ elections*** wybory do rady miejskiej; **mu•ni•ci•pal•i•ty** [mjuːnɪsɪ'pælətɪ] *s* **1.** miasto *n* **2.** gmina *f* **3.** władze *pl* miasta **4.** władze *pl* gminy
mu•ni•tions [mjuː'nɪʃənz] *pl* uzbrojenie *n*, broń i amunicja *f*; **mu'ni•tions factory** *s* fabryka *f* broni, zakład *m* zbrojeniowy
mu•ral ['mjʊərəl] **I** *s* malowidło *n* ścienne **II** *adj* ścienny
mur•der ['mɜːdə] **I** *s* morderstwo *n*, zabójstwo *n*; ***an attempted ~*** próba morderstwa; ***mass ~*** masowy mord; ***he gets away with ~*** *infml* wszystko mu uchodzi na sucho; ***scream blue ~*** **a)** drzeć się wniebogłosy **b)** *fig* narobić krzyku; ***the traffic was ~*** *infml* były straszne korki **II** *v/t* **1.** mordować ⟨za-⟩ **2.** *fig* zarzynać ⟨-rżnąć⟩; **mur•der•er** ['mɜːdərə] *s* morderca *m*, zabójca *m*; **mur•der-**

ess ['mɜːdəres] *s* morderczyni *f*; **mur•der•ous** ['mɜːdrəs] *adj* **1.** morderczy **2.** *regime*: zbrodniczy; '**mur•der weap•on** *s* narzędzie *n* zbrodni

murk•y ['mɜːkɪ] *adj* **1.** ciemny, mroczny **2.** *past*: mętny

mur•mur ['mɜːmər] **I** *v/i* **1.** mruczeć, szeptać **2.** (*wind*) szumieć **3.** (*stream*) szemrać **4.** *fig* szemrać (***against*** przeciw *D*) **II** *v/t* szeptać ⟨wy-⟩, mamrotać ⟨wy-⟩ **III** *s* **1.** mamrotanie *n*, szept *m*; ***without a ~*** *fig* bez szemrania **2.** *wind*: szum *m* **3.** *stream*: szemranie *n* **4.** MED szmery *pl*

mus•cle ['mʌsl] *s* **1.** ANAT mięsień *m* **2.** *fig* siła *f*; **muscle in** *v/i* pakować ⟨w-⟩ się, wdzierać ⟨wedrzeć⟩ się (***on*** do *G*); '**mus•cle•man** *pl -men s infml* mięśniak *m*

mus•cu•lar ['mʌskjʊlə] *adj* **1.** mięśniowy **2.** umięśniony, muskularny; **mus•cu•lar** '**dys•troph•y** *s* MED zanik *m* mięśni

muse [mjuːz] **I** *s* **1.** muza *f* **2.** wena *f*, natchnienie *n* **II** *v/i* rozmyślać (***about***/***on***/***over*** nad *I*)

mu•se•um [mjuː'zɪːəm] *s* muzeum *n*

mush [mʌʃ] *no pl s* papka *f*, breja *f*, maź *f*

mush•room ['mʌʃruːm] **I** *s* **1.** grzyb *m* **2.** pieczarka *f* **II** *v/i* **1.** zbierać ⟨zebrać⟩ grzyby; ***go ~ing*** iść na grzyby **2.** *fig* (szybko) rozrastać ⟨-rosnąć⟩ się **3.** *fig* wyrastać ⟨-rosnąć⟩ jak grzyby po deszczu; '**mush•room cloud** *s* grzyb *m* atomowy

mush•y ['mʌʃɪ] *adj* **1.** papkowaty, brejowaty, rozgotowany **2.** ckliwy, sentymentalny

mu•sic ['mjuːzɪk] *s* **1.** muzyka *f*; ***a piece of ~*** utwór muzyczny; ***make ~*** **a)** grać, muzykować **b)** tworzyć muzykę; ***set s.th. to ~*** napisać muzykę do *G*; ***that's ~ to my ears*** (*information*) miło mi to słyszeć **2.** nuty *pl*; ***read ~*** czytać nuty; **mu•sic•al** ['mjuːzɪkl] **I** *adj* **1.** muzyczny **2.** muzykalny **II** *s* musical *m*; '**mu•sic book** *s* (*book*) nuty *pl*; '**mu•sic•al box** *s Br* pozytywka *f*; **mu•sic•al** '**in•stru•ment** *s* instrument *m* muzyczny; '**mu•sic box** *s Am* → ***musical box***; **mu•sic hall** *s* music-hall *m*

mu•si•cian [mjuː'zɪʃn] *s* muzyk *m*

mu•si•col•o•gy [mjuːzɪ'kɒlədʒɪ] *s* muzykologia *f*

'**mu•sic stand** *s* stojak *m* na nuty; '**mu•sic stool** *s* taboret *m* do fortepianu

musk [mʌsk] *s* piżmo *n*

Mus•lim ['mʊzlɪm] **I** *s* Muzułmanin *m* **II** *adj* muzułmański

mus•sel ['mʌsl] *s* małż *m*

must [mʌst] **I** *v aux* musieć; ***I ~ go to the bank*** muszę iść do banku; ***I ~ admit*** muszę przyznać; ***you ~ not smoke here*** tu nie wolno palić; ***you ~ be hungry*** musisz być głodny; ***you ~ read this book*** musisz przeczytać tę książkę **II** *s infml* **this book is a ~** tę książkę trzeba (koniecznie) przeczytać

mus•tache → ***moustache***

mus•tard ['mʌstəd] *s* **1.** COOK musztarda *f* **2.** BIOL gorczyca *f*; '**mus•tard gas** *s* gaz *m* musztardowy

mus•ter ['mʌstə] **I** *v/t* (*a.* ***~ up***) **1.** *energy, troops*: zbierać ⟨zebrać⟩ **2.** *courage*: zdobywać ⟨-być⟩ się na *A* **3.** *enthusiasm*: wykrzesywać ⟨-sać⟩ z siebie **4.** *support*: zdobywać ⟨-być⟩ **II** *v/i* zbierać ⟨zebrać⟩ się

must•n't ['mʌsnt] *contracted form* → ***must not***

must•y ['mʌstɪ] *adj* stęchły, zatęchły

mu•tant [mjuː'tənt] **I** *s* BIOL mutant *m* **II** *adj* BIOL zmutowany; **mu•tate** [mjuː'teɪt] **I** *v/t* BIOL mutować ⟨z-⟩; ***~d genes*** zmutowane geny **II** *v/i* BIOL ulegać ⟨ulec⟩ mutacji; **mu•ta•tion** [mjuː'teɪʃn] *s* BIOL mutacja *f*

mute [mjuːt] **I** *adj* **1.** niemy **2.** milczący **II** *s* **1.** MUS tłumik *m* **2.** *dated* niemowa *m* **III** *v/t* tłumić ⟨s-⟩; **mut•ed** ['mjuːtɪd] *adj* **1.** przytłumiony, stłumiony **2.** *colours*: stonowany, łagodny

mu•ti•late ['mjuːtɪleɪt] *v/t* okaleczać ⟨-czyć⟩; **mu•ti•la•tion** [mjuːtɪ'leɪʃn] *s* okaleczenie *n*

mu•ti•neer [mjuːtɪ'nɪə] *s* buntownik *m*; **mu•ti•nous** ['mjuːtɪnəs] *adj* buntowniczy; **mu•ti•ny** ['mjuːtɪnɪ] *s* bunt *m*

mut•ter ['mʌtə] **I** *v/t* **1.** mamrotać ⟨wy-⟩, mruczeć ⟨mruknąć⟩ **II** *v/i* mamrotać ⟨wy-⟩; ***~ to oneself*** mamrotać do siebie **III** *s* mamrotanie *n*

mut•ton ['mʌtn] *s* baranina *f*; ***a ~ chop*** kotlet barani

mu•tu•al ['mjuːtʃuəl] *adj* **1.** wzajemny; ***he loves her, and the feeling is ~*** on ją

M

kocha, a ona odwzajemnia jego uczucie **2.** obopólny; ***by ~ consent*** za obopólną zgodą **3.** wspólny; ***our ~ friend*** nasz wspólny znajomy; **mu•tu•al•ly** ['mjuːtʃuəlɪ] *adv* **1.** wzajemnie; ***be ~ exclusive*** wzajemnie się wykluczać **2.** obopólnie

mu•zak ['mjuːzæk] *s* (*muzyka odtwarzana w miejscach publicznych*) muzak *m*

muz•zle ['mʌzl] **I** *s* **1.** pysk *m* **2.** kaganiec *m* **3.** wylot *m* lufy **II** *v/t* **1.** nakładać ⟨nałożyć⟩ kaganiec **2.** *fig* zamykać ⟨-mknąć⟩ usta

my [maɪ] *poss* mój

my•o•pi•a [maɪ'əʊpɪə] *s a. fig* krótkowzroczność *f*; **my•op•ic** [maɪ'ɒpɪk] *adj a. fig* krótkowzroczny

myr•i•ad ['mɪrɪəd] *s lit* multum *n*, miriady *pl*; ***available in a ~ of colours*** dostępny w szerokiej palecie kolorów

myrrh [mɜː] *s* BIOL mir(r)a *f*

myr•tle ['mɜːtl] *s* BIOL mirt *m*

my•self [maɪ'self] *pron* **1.** (*emphatic*) sam; ***I did it ~*** zrobiłam to sama; ***I ~ do not agree*** ja się z tym nie zgadzam; ***like ~*** jak ja **2.** się, siebie; ***I cut ~*** skaleczyłem się; ***I do it for ~*** robię to dla siebie; ***I haven't been feeling ~ recently*** *fig* ostatnio nie czuję się najlepiej

mys•te•ri•ous [mɪ'stɪərɪəs] *adj* tajemniczy, zagadkowy; **mys•te•ri•ous•ly** [mɪ'stɪərɪəslɪ] *adv* **1.** tajemniczo **2.** *disappear*: w tajemniczy sposób; **mys•te•ry** ['mɪstərɪ] *s* **1.** tajemnica *f*, zagadka *f*; ***it's a complete ~ to me*** zupełnie tego nie rozumiem; ***make a ~ of s.th.*** ukrywać coś, utrzymywać coś w tajemnicy; ***shrouded in ~*** owiany tajemnicą **2.** (*book*, *film*) kryminał *m* **3.** ***mysteries*** tajniki

mys•tic ['mɪstɪk] *s* mistyk *m*; **mys•tic•al** ['mɪstɪkl] *adj* mistyczny; **mys•ti•cism** ['mɪstɪsɪzəm] *s* mistycyzm *m*

mys•ti•fy ['mɪstɪfaɪ] *v/t* zbijać ⟨zbić⟩ z tropu; **mys•ti•fy•ing** ['mɪstɪfaɪɪŋ] *adj* zagadkowy, niezrozumiały

mys•tique [mɪ'stiːk] *s* aura *f* tajemnicy

myth [mɪθ] *s* mit *m*; ***Greek ~s*** mity greckie; ***debunk ~s*** obalać mity; **myth•i•cal** ['mɪθɪkl] *adj* mityczny

myth•o•log•i•cal [mɪθə'lɒdʒɪkl] *adj* mitologiczny; **my•thol•o•gy** [mɪ'θɒlədʒɪ] *s* mitologia; ***Greek ~*** mitologia grecka

N

N

n/a [en'eɪ] *abbr* (=***not applicable***) nie dotyczy

nab [næb] *v/t infml* **1.** łapać ⟨z-⟩, przyłapywać ⟨-pać⟩ **2.** zabierać ⟨-brać⟩

na•dir ['neɪdɪə] *s* **1.** ASTR nadir *m* **2.** *fig* zero *n*, dno *n*; ***reach its ~*** sięgnąć dna

naff [næf] *adj Br infml* niegustowny, w złym guście

nag [næg] **I** *v/t* **1.** zamęczać ⟨-czyć⟩ prośbami **2.** (*doubts*, *conscience*) dręczyć **II** *v/i* zrzędzić, gderać; **nag•ger** ['nægə] *s* zrzęda *m*, maruda *m*; **nag•ging** ['nægɪŋ] **I** *s* zrzędzenie *n*, gderanie *n* **II** *adj* **1.** gderliwy, zrzędliwy, marudny **2.** *pain*: dokuczliwy

nail [neɪl] **I** *s* **1.** paznokieć *m* **2.** TECH gwóźdź *m*; ***as hard as ~s*** twardy jak skała; ***a ~ in s.th.'s coffin*** gwóźdź do trumny **II** *v/t* **1.** przybijać ⟨-bić⟩ gwoździami **2.** *lie*: udowadniać ⟨-wodnić⟩ **3.** *fig* przygważdżać ⟨-woździć⟩; **nail down** *v/t* **1.** przybijać ⟨-bić⟩ gwoździami **2.** *deal*: osiągać ⟨-gnąć⟩ **3.** zobowiązywać ⟨-zać⟩ (***s.o. to*** kogoś do *G*)

'nail-bit•ing **I** *s* obgryzanie *n* paznokci **II** *adj* **1.** ekscytujący **2.** *wait*: nerwowy; **'nail brush** *s* szczoteczka *f* do paznokci; **'nail clip•pers** *pl* cążki *pl* do paznokci; **'nail file** *s* pilnik *m* do paznokci; **'nail pol•ish** *s* lakier *m* do paznokci; **'nail pol•ish re•mov•er** *s* zmywacz *m* do paznokci; **'nail scis•sors** *pl* nożyczki *pl* do paznokci; **'nail var•nish** *s Br* lakier *m* do paznokci

na•ive [naɪ'iːv] *adj* **1.** naiwny **2.** prostoduszny; **na•ive•ty** [naɪ'iːvtɪ] *s* naiwność *f*

na•ked ['neɪkɪd] *adj a. fig* nagi; *~ truth* naga prawda; *with the ~ eye* gołym okiem
name [neɪm] **I** *s* **1.** imię *n* nazwisko *n*; *what's your ~?* jak się nazywasz?; *by ~* **a)** po nazwisku **b)** po imieniu; *in the ~ of* w imieniu *G*; *put one's ~ down for* zgłosić się do *G* **2.** nazwa *f* **3.** reputacja *f*, opinia *f*; *make a ~ for oneself* wyrobić sobie nazwisko; *have a good* (*bad*) *~* cieszyć się dobrą (złą) opinią **4.** wyzwisko *n*; *call s.o. ~s* wyzywać kogoś, wymyślać komuś **II** *v/t* **1.** nazywać ⟨-zwać⟩ (*after/for* po *L*) **2.** identyfikować ⟨z-⟩ (*as* jako *A*) **3.** podawać ⟨-dać⟩ nazwę **4.** *date, price*: określać ⟨-lić⟩, podawać ⟨-dać⟩, wymieniać ⟨-nić⟩; *to ~ but a few* by wymienić choć kilka **5.** mianować, nominować (*s.o.* (*as*) kogoś na *A*); '**name day** *s* imieniny *pl*; '**name-drop•per** *s osoba próbująca zaimponować znajomością ze sławnymi osobami*
name•less ['neɪmlɪs] *adj* **1.** bezimienny, nieznany **2.** anonimowy **3.** nieopisany
name•ly ['neɪmlɪ] *adv* (a) mianowicie
'**name plate** *s* tabliczka *f* z nazwiskiem; '**name•sake** *s* imiennik *m*; '**name•tag** *s* (*badge*) identyfikator *m*
nan•ny ['nænɪ] *s* **1.** niania *f* **2.** *Br infml* babcia *f*; '**nan•ny goat** *s* koza *f*; **nanny state** *s Br* państwo *n* opiekuńcze
nap [næp] **I** *s* drzemka *f*; *have* (*a. take*) *a ~* zdrzemnąć się **II** *v/i* zdrzemnąć się
na•palm ['neɪpɑːm] *s* napalm *m*; *~ bomb* bomba napalmowa
nape [neɪp] *s*: *~* (*of s.o.'s neck*) kark
nap•kin ['næpkɪn] *s* **1.** serwetka *f* **2.** *Am* podpaska *f* **3.** *Br dated* pielucha *f*
Na•ples ['neɪplz] *s* Neapol *m*
nap•py ['næpɪ] *s Br* pielucha *f*
nar•cis•si [nɑː'sɪsaɪ] → *narcissus*; **nar•cis•sism** ['nɑːsɪsɪzəm] *s* narcyzm *m*; '**nar•cis•sist** ['nɑːsɪsɪst] *s* narcyz *m*; **nar•cis•'sis•tic** [nɑːsɪ'sɪstɪk] *adj* narcystyczny
nar•cis•sus [nɑː'sɪsəs] *pl -ses* [~'sɪsəsəs], *-si* [~'sɪsaɪ] *s* BIOL narcyz *m*
nar•co•sis [nɑː'kəʊsɪs] *pl -ses* [~siːz] *s* MED narkoza *f*
nar•cot•ic [nɑː'kɒtɪk] **I** *s* **1.** narkotyk *m* **2.** MED środek *m* znieczulający **II** *adj* **1.** narkotyczny **2.** znieczulający

nark [nɑːk] *s* (*informant*) *Br infml* wtyczka *f*
nar•rate [nə'reɪt] *v/t* **1.** opowiadać ⟨-wiedzieć⟩ **2.** komentować ⟨s-⟩, relacjonować ⟨z-⟩; **nar•ra•tion** [nə'reɪʃn] *s* narracja *f*; **nar•ra•tive** ['nærətɪv] **I** *s* **1.** opowiadanie *n* **2.** narracja *f* **3.** relacja *f*, opis *m* **II** *adj* narracyjny; **nar•ra•tor** [nə'reɪtə] *s* narrator *m*
nar•row ['nærəʊ] **I** *adj* **1.** wąski **2.** wąski, ograniczony; *in the ~est sense* w najwęższym znaczeniu; *a ~ circle of friends* wąskie grono przyjaciół; *~ interests* ograniczone zainteresowania **3.** niewielki; *a ~ majority of votes* niewielka większość głosów; *he had a ~ escape* ledwo uszedł z życiem; *he lost by a ~ margin* przegrał o włos **II** *v/i* zwężać ⟨zwęzić⟩ się **III** *v/t* zwężać ⟨zwęzić⟩; **narrow down** *v/t choice*: zawężać ⟨-węzić⟩, ograniczać ⟨-czyć⟩
'**nar•row gauge** *adj railway*: wąskotorowy; **nar•row•ly** ['nærəʊlɪ] *adv* **1.** w ograniczony sposób **2.** ledwo, ledwie; *the car ~ missed a cyclist* samochód ledwo ominął rowerzystę; **nar•row-'mind•ed** *adj* ograniczony, bez wyobraźni
NASA ['næsə] *abbr* (=*National Aeronautics and Space Administration*) NASA *f*
na•sal ['neɪzl] *adj* **1.** nosowy; *~ consonant* spółgłoska nosowa; *~ passages* drogi nosowe **2.** *~ spray* spray do nosa
nas•ty ['nɑːstɪ] *adj* **1.** okropny, obrzydliwy **2.** przykry, niemiły **3.** niebezpieczny **4.** niesmaczny, budzący niesmak
na•tion ['neɪʃn] *s* naród *m*; **na•tion•al** ['næʃənl] **I** *adj* **1.** narodowy; *~ heritage* dziedzictwo narodowe; *~ currency* waluta narodowa **2.** państwowy; *the ~ Health Service Br* publiczna służba zdrowia **3.** krajowy **II** *s* obywatel *m*; **na•tion•al 'an•them** *s* hymn *m* narodowy; **na•tion•al 'debt** *s* ECON dług *m* publiczny; **Na•tion•al 'Guard** *s Am* Gwardia *f* Narodowa; **na•tion•al•ism** ['næʃənəlɪzm] *s* nacjonalizm *m*; **na•tion•al•is•tic** [næʃənə'lɪstɪk] *adj* nacjonalistyczny; **na•tion•al•i•ty** [næʃə'nælətɪ] *s* **1.** narodowość *f*

N

2. obywatelstwo *n*; ***dual ~*** podwójne obywatelstwo; **na•tion•al•i•za•tion** [næʃənəlaɪ'zeɪʃn] *s* nacjonalizacja *f*, upaństwowienie *n*; **na•tion•al•ize** ['næʃənəlaɪz] *v/t* nacjonalizować ⟨z-⟩, upaństwawiać ⟨-twowić⟩; **na•tion•al 'park** *s* park *m* narodowy; **na•tion•'wide I** *adj* ogólnonarodowy **II** *adv* w całym kraju

na•tive ['neɪtɪv] **I** *adj* **1.** ojczysty, rodzimy; ***~ language*** język ojczysty; ***~ land*** kraj ojczysty **2.** krajowy, miejscowy, wewnętrzny; ***go ~*** przystosować się do miejscowych zwyczajów; ***≈ American*** Indianin (północnoamerykański) **3.** ludowy; ***~ dance*** taniec ludowy **4.** wrodzony; ***~ intelligence*** wrodzona inteligencja **II** *s* miejscowy *m*; ***a ~ of London*** Londyńczyk; **na•tive 'coun•try** *s* ojczyzna *f*; **na•tive 'speak•er** *s* rodzimy użytkownik *m* języka

Na•tiv•i•ty [nə'tɪvətɪ] *s* **1.** Narodziny *pl* Jezusa **2.** szopka *f* bożonarodzeniowa

NATO ['neɪtəʊ] *abbr* (=***North Atlantic Treaty Organization***) NATO *n*

nat•ter ['nætə] (*a.* ***~ away***) *v/i Br infml* gadać, plotkować (**about** o *L*)

nat•ty ['nætɪ] *adj dated* elegancki

nat•u•ral ['nætʃrəl] **I** *adj* **1.** naturalny; ***~ disaster*** klęska żywiołowa **2.** naturalny, normalny; ***die a ~ death*** umrzeć śmiercią naturalną; ***~ law*** prawo naturalne **3.** wrodzony, urodzony; ***he's a ~ leader*** jest urodzonym przywódcą **4.** MUS nialterowany **II** *s* **1.** ***be a ~ for*** być stworzonym do *G* **2.** MUS kasownik *m*; **nat•u•ral 'gas** *s* gaz *m* ziemny; **nat•u•ral 'his•to•ry** *s* przyrodoznawstwo *n*, historia *f* naturalna; **nat•u•ral•ism** ['nætʃrəlɪsm] *s* ART naturalizm *m*; **nat•u•ral•ist** ['nætʃrəlɪst] *s* przyrodnik *m*; **nat•u•ral•is•tic** [nætʃrə'lɪstɪk] *adj* naturalistyczny; **nat•u•ral•i•za•tion** [nætʃrəlaɪ'zeɪʃn] *s* naturalizacja *f*; **nat•u•ral•ize** ['nætʃrəlaɪz] *v/t* **1.** naturalizować ⟨z-⟩ **2.** BIOL aklimatyzować ⟨za-⟩; **nat•u•ral•ly** ['nætʃərəlɪ] *adv* **1.** naturalnie, oczywiście **2.** naturalnie, w naturalny sposób; ***substances which occur ~*** substancje występujące w naturze; ***learning comes ~ to him*** nauka idzie mu bez trudu; **nat•u•ral re•'sour•ces** *pl* bogactwa *pl* naturalne; **nat•u•ral 'sci•ence** *s* nauka *f* przyrodnicza; **nat•u•ral 'sci•en•tist** *s* przyrodnik *m*

na•ture ['neɪtʃə] *s* **1.** przyroda *f*, natura *f*; ***laws of ~*** prawa przyrody; ***Mother ≈*** Matka Natura; ***against ~*** wbrew naturze **2.** natura *f*, charakter *m*, usposobienie *n*; ***it's not in her ~*** to nie leży w jej naturze; ***human ~*** natura ludzka; ***by ~*** z natury **3.** natura *f*, istota *f*, charakter *m*; ***the ~ of the problem*** istota problemu; **'na•ture re•ser•ve** *s* rezerwat *m* przyrody; **'na•ture trail** *s* szlak *m* przyrodniczy

na•tur•ism ['neɪtʃərɪzm] *s* naturyzm *m*, nudyzm *m*; **na•tur•ist** ['neɪtʃərɪst] *s* naturysta *m*, nudysta *m*

naugh•ty ['nɒːtɪ] *adj* **1.** *child*: niegrzeczny **2.** *joke, word*: nieprzyzwoity

nau•se•a ['nɔːzɪə] *s* nudności *pl*, mdłości *pl*; **nau•se•ate** ['nɔːzɪeɪt] *v/t a. fig* mdlić ⟨ze-⟩, przyprawiać ⟨-wić⟩ o mdłości; **nau•se•at•ing** ['nɔːzɪeɪtɪŋ] *adj* przyprawiający o mdłości; **nau•seous** ['nɔːzɪəs] *adj* mdlący; ***I feel ~*** jest mi niedobrze

nau•ti•cal ['nɔːtɪkl] *adj* morski; **nau•ti•cal 'mile** *s* mila *f* morska

na•val ['neɪvl] *adj* **1.** morski; ***~ battle*** bitwa morska **2.** *officer, base*: marynarki; **'na•val base** *s* baza *f* marynarki

nave [neɪv] *s* ARCHIT nawa *f* główna

na•vel ['neɪvl] *s* ANAT pępek *m*

nav•i•ga•ble ['nævɪgəbl] *adj river*: żeglowny, spławny; **nav•i•gate** ['nævɪgeɪt] *v/t* **1.** *ship, plane*: nawigować **2.** *fig* kierować ⟨po-⟩; **nav•i•ga•tion** [nævɪ'geɪʃn] *s* **1.** nawigacja *f* **2.** żegluga *f* **3.** przelot *m*; **nav•i•ga•tor** ['nævɪgeɪtə] *s* nawigator *m*

nav•vy ['nævɪ] *s Br* robotnik *m*

na•vy ['neɪvɪ] *s*: ***the ~*** marynarka wojenna; **na•vy 'blue** *adj* granatowy

nay [neɪ] *adv dated* nie

Na•zi ['nɑːtsɪ] **I** *s* nazista *m* **II** *adj* nazistowski; **Na•zism** ['nɑːtsɪzəm] *s* nazizm *m*

near [nɪə] **I** *adj* bliski; ***where is the ~est bank?*** gdzie jest najbliższy bank?; ***in the ~ future*** w najbliższej przyszłości;

~ relative bliski krewny; **that was a ~ thing!** o mały włos! **II** *adv* **1.** blisko, w pobliżu; **draw ~** zbliżać się; **somewhere ~** gdzieś blisko **2.** niemal, prawie; **~ impossible** prawie niemożliwe **III** *prep* **1.** niedaleko, w pobliżu; **do you live ~ here?** mieszkasz niedaleko stąd?; **be ~ to tears** być bliskim łez **2.** około; **~ 8 million** około 8 milionów **IV** *v/t* zbliżać ⟨-żyć⟩ się; **be ~ing completion** być na ukończeniu; **near•by** ['nɪəbaɪ] **I** *adj* pobliski **II** *adv* w pobliżu; **near•ly** ['nɪəlɪ] *adv* niemal, prawie; **not ~** wcale nie; **near'sight•ed** *adj Am a. fig* krótkowzroczny; **near•'sight•ed•ness** *s Am a. fig* krótkowzroczność *f*

neat [niːt] *adj* **1.** czysty, uporządkowany **2.** *person*: lubiący porządek, zadbany, schludny **3.** *row*: równy **4.** *explanation*: zgrabny **5.** *Br alcohol*: czysty

ne•ces•sar•i•ly ['nesəserəlɪ] *adv* koniecznie, z konieczności; **not ~** niekoniecznie; **ne•ces•sa•ry** ['nesəserɪ] *adj* **1.** konieczny, niezbędny; **it is ~ for us to meet** musimy się spotkać; **if ~** jeśli to konieczne; **a ~ evil** zło konieczne **2.** nieunikniony

ne•ces•si•tate [nɪ'sesɪteɪt] *v/t* wymuszać ⟨-music⟩, czynić ⟨u-⟩ niezbędnym; **ne•ces•si•ty** [nɪ'sesɪtɪ] *s* **1.** konieczność *f* (**for**/**of** *G*); **of ~** z konieczności; **air-conditioning is a ~ in this climate** klimatyzacja to konieczność w tym klimacie **2.** potrzeba *f*; **basic necessities** podstawowe potrzeby; **~ is the mother of invention** potrzeba jest matką wynalazków

neck [nek] **I** *s* **1.** szyja *f*; **be up to one's ~ in** tkwić po uszy w *L*; **get it in the ~** *infml* oberwać; **risk one's ~** ryzykować głową; **save one's ~** ocalić głowę **2.** kark *m*; **break one's ~** skręcić kark **3.** *bottle*: szyjka *f* **4.** GEOGR przesmyk *m* **II** *v/i infml* całować się; **neck and 'neck** *adj* łeb w łeb; **'neck•lace** *s* naszyjnik *m*; **'neck•let** *s* łańcuszek *m*; **'neck•line** *s* dekolt *m*, wycięcie *n*; **with a low ~** z dużym dekoltem; **'neck•tie** *s Am* krawat *m*

nec•tar ['nektə] *s* BIOL nektar *m*; **nec•tar•ine** ['nektəriːn] *s* nektarynka *f*

née [neɪ] *adj* z domu; **Jane Smith, ~ Brown** Jane Smith, z domu Brown

need [niːd] **I** *v/t* **1.** potrzebować; **do you ~ any help?** potrzebujesz pomocy? **2.** musieć; **I ~ to get some sleep** muszę się przespać; **you don't ~ to go yet** nie musisz jeszcze iść; **this shirt ~s washing** tę koszulę trzeba wyprać; **all you ~ to do** wszystko, co musisz zrobić **II** *v aux* musieć; **you ~ not hurry** nie musisz się spieszyć; **you ~ not have hurried** niepotrzebnie się spieszyłeś; **I hardly ~ tell you** chyba nie muszę ci mówić **III** *s* **1.** potrzeba *f*; **satisfy a ~** zaspokoić potrzebę; **financial ~s** potrzeby finansowe; **people in ~** ludzie w potrzebie **2.** potrzeba *f*, konieczność *f*; **there is no ~ for you to get up** nie musisz wstawać; **be in ~ of** potrzebować *G*; **if ~ be** w razie potrzeby

nee•dle ['niːdl] **I** *s* **1.** igła *f*; **a ~ and thread** igła z nitką; **look for a ~ in a haystack** szukać igły w stogu siana **2.** (*knitting*) drut *m* **3.** (*leaf*) igła *f*, szpilka *f* **II** *v/t* drażnić ⟨roz-⟩, złościć ⟨roz-⟩

need•less ['niːdlɪs] *adj* niepotrzebny; **~ to say** oczywiście, naturalnie; **need•less•ly** ['niːdlɪslɪ] *adv* niepotrzebnie

'nee•dle•work *s* robótka *f* ręczna

need•y ['niːdɪ] *adj* w potrzebie; **the ~** potrzebujący, osoby w potrzebie

neg [neg] *s* PHOT negatyw *m*

ne•gate [nɪ'geɪt] *v/t* **1.** znosić ⟨znieść⟩ działanie, neutralizować ⟨z-⟩ **2.** przeczyć ⟨za-⟩, negować ⟨za-⟩; **ne•ga•tion** [nɪ'geɪʃn] *s* **1.** przeczenie *n*; **she shook her head in ~** potrząsnęła przecząco głową **2.** zaprzeczenie *n*; **this system is the ~ of democracy** ten system jest zaprzeczeniem demokracji

neg•a•tive ['negətɪv] **I** *adj* **1.** negatywny **2.** *sentence*: przeczący **3.** *number*: ujemny **II** *s* **1.** zaprzeczenie *n*, odmowa *f*; **answer in the ~** zaprzeczyć, odmówić **2.** PHOT negatyw *m*

ne•glect [nɪ'glekt] **I** *v/t* **1.** zaniedbywać ⟨-bać⟩, nie troszczyć ⟨za-⟩ się o *A* **2. ~ to do s.th.** nie robić ⟨z-⟩ czegoś **II** *s* zaniedbywanie *n*; **~ of children** zaniedbywanie dzieci; **~ of duties** zaniedbywanie obowiązków; **ne•glect-**

N

ed [nɪ'glektɪd] *adj* zaniedbany; **ne·glect·ful** [nɪ'glektfʊl] → ***negligent 1***
neg·li·gee ['neglɪʒeɪ] *s* peniuar *m*
neg·li·gence ['neglɪdʒəns] *s* JUR niedbalstwo *n*, niedbałość *f*; **neg·li·gent** ['neglɪdʒənt] *adj* **1.** JUR niedbały; ***be ~ in*** zaniedbać *A* **2.** nonszalancki
neg·li·gi·ble ['neglɪdʒəbl] *adj* **1.** nieistotny, nieważny **2.** *amount*: znikomy
ne·go·ti·a·ble [nɪ'gəʊʃəbl] *adj* **1.** podlegający negocjacji **2.** zbywalny; **negotiable paper** *s* ECON instrument *m* zbywalny; **ne·go·ti·ate** [nɪ'gəʊʃieɪt] **I** *v/i* negocjować (***with*** z *I*, ***for/about*** *A*) **II** *v/t* **1.** negocjować ⟨wy-⟩ **2.** *obstacle*: pokonywać ⟨-nać⟩; **ne·go·ti·a·tion** [nɪgoʊʃɪ'eɪʃn] *s* negocjacja *f*; ***by way of negotiations*** na drodze negocjacji; ***the price is open to ~*** cenę można negocjować; ***it is still under ~*** wciąż trwają negocjacje; **ne·go·ti·a·tor** [nɪ'gəʊʃieɪtə] *s* negocjator *m*
Ne·gress ['niːgrɪs] *s* (*offensive*) Murzynka *f*; **Ne·gro** ['niːgrəʊ] *pl -groes s* (*offensive*) Murzyn *m*
neigh [neɪ] **I** *v/i* rżeć **II** *s* rżenie *n*
neigh·bour ['neɪbə] *Br*, ***neigh·bor*** *Am s* sąsiad *m*; **neigh·bour·hood** ['neɪbəhʊd] *Br*, ***neigh·bor·hood*** *Am s* **1.** sąsiedztwo *n*; ***in the ~*** w sąsiedztwie **2.** okolica *f*; **neigh·bour·ing** ['neɪbərɪŋ] *Br*, ***neigh·bor·ing*** *Am adj* sąsiedni, sąsiadujący; **neigh·bour·ly** ['neɪbəlɪ] *Br*, ***neigh·bor·ly*** *Am adj* **1.** sąsiedzki **2.** pomocny, przyjazny
nei·ther ['naɪðə, 'niːðər] **I** *pron* żaden; ***~ answer is correct*** żadna odpowiedź nie jest prawidłowa; ***~ of them*** żaden z nich **II** *adv* **1.** też nie; ***he does not know and ~ do I*** on tego nie wie i ja też nie **2.** ani; ***the house is ~ big nor small*** dom nie jest ani duży, ani mały
ne·o·clas·si·cal [niːəʊ'klæsɪkəl] *adj* ART neoklasyczny
ne·o·lith·ic [niːə'lɪθɪk] *adj* neolityczny
ne·ol·o·gism [niː'ɒlədʒɪzəm] *s* neologizm *m*
ne·on ['niːɒn] *s* CHEM neon *m*; ***~ lamp*** lampa neonowa; ***~ sign*** (*advert*) neon
ne·o-na·zi [niːəʊ'nɑːtsɪ] **I** *s* neonazista *m* **II** *adj* neonazistowski
ne·on 'light *s* neon *m*
Ne·pal [nə'pɔːl] *s* Nepal *m*
neph·ew ['nefjuː] *s* **1.** siostrzeniec *m* **2.** bratanek *m*
nerd [nɜːrd] *s infml* **1.** głupek *m* **2.** maniak *m* komputerowy
nerve [nɜːrv] **I** *s* **1.** nerw *m*; ***get on s.o.'s ~s*** grać komuś na nerwach; ***have ~s of steel*** mieć nerwy ze stali; ***hit*** (*a.* ***touch***) ***a ~*** trafić w czuły punkt; ***be a bag*** (*a.* ***bundle***) ***of ~s*** być kłębkiem nerwów **2.** odwaga *f*; ***have the ~ to do s.th.*** mieć odwagę coś zrobić **3.** czelność *f*, tupet *m*; ***he's got a ~ asking us for money!*** ma czelność prosić nas o pieniądze!; ***what a ~!*** co za tupet! **II** *v/i* ***~ oneself*** ośmielić się (***to do s.th.*** zrobić coś); **'nerve cell** *s* komórka *f* nerwowa; **'nerve cen·tre** *Br*, ***nerve cen·ter*** *s Am fig* centrum *n*; **'nerve gas** *s* gaz *m* paraliżujący; **'nerve-rack·ing** *adj atmosphere*: nerwowy
ner·vous ['nɜːrvəs] *adj* nerwowy; **nervous 'break·down** *s* załamanie *n* nerwowe; **nerv·ous·ly** ['nɜːrvəslɪ] *adv* nerwowo; **ner·vous·ness** ['nɜːrvəsnɪs] *s* nerwowość *f*; **ner·vous 'wreck** *s* kłębek *m* nerwów
nerv·y ['nɜːrvɪ] *adj infml* **1.** *Br* zdenerwowany **2.** *Am* zuchwały
nest [nest] **I** *s* **1.** *a. fig* gniazdo *n* **2.** zestaw *m* **II** *v/i* gnieździć ⟨za-⟩ się; **'nest egg** *s infml* oszczędności *pl*
nes·tle ['nesl] **I** *v/i* **1.** mościć ⟨u-⟩ się, układać ⟨ułożyć⟩ się wygodnie; ***a village nestling at the foot of the hill*** wioska położona u stóp góry **2.** przytulać ⟨-lić⟩ się (***against*** do *G*) **II** *v/t* przytulać ⟨-lić⟩ (***against*** do *G*); **nestle up to** *v/t* przytulać ⟨-lić⟩ się do *G*
net[1] [net] **I** *s* **1.** sieć *f*, siatka *f* **2.** ***the ~*** (*a.* ~̣) *infml* sieć, Internet, net; ***on the ~*** w sieci, na necie **II** *v/t* **1.** łowić ⟨z-⟩ w sieć **2.** *fig* chwytać ⟨s-⟩, łapać ⟨z-⟩ **3.** *goal*: strzelać ⟨-lić⟩ **4.** przykrywać ⟨-ryć⟩ siatką
net[2] [~] **I** *adj* netto; ***~ profit*** zysk netto; ***~ weight*** waga netto **II** *v/t* **1.** przynosić ⟨-nieść⟩ zysk netto **2.** zarabiać ⟨-robić⟩ netto; **net 'as·sets** *pl* ECON aktywa *pl* netto; **net re·'turn** *s* ECON zysk *m* netto; **net 'worth** *s* ECON wartość *f* netto

net•ball ['netbɔːl] *s SPORT* netball *m* (*gra podobna do koszykówki*); **net 'cur•tain** *s* firanka *f*

Neth•er•lands ['neðələndz] *pl*: ***the ~*** Holandia

'Net surf•er *s* internauta *m*

net•tle ['netl] **I** *s* pokrzywa *f*; ***grasp the ~*** *Br* chwycić byka za rogi **II** *v/t* denerwować ⟨z-⟩; **'net•tle rash** *s MED* pokrzywka *f*

'net•work I *s* sieć *f* **II** *v/t INF TEL* łączyć ⟨po-⟩ w sieć **III** *v/i* budować ⟨z-⟩ sieć kontaktów; **net•work 'driv•er** *s INF* sterownik *m* sieci; **'net•work•ing** *s* **1.** nawiązywanie *n* kontaktów **2.** praca *f* w sieci, networking *m*

neu•ral ['nʊrəl] *adj* nerwowy; **neu•ral•gi•a** [njʊə'rældʒə] *s MED* neuralgia *f*, nerwoból *m*; **neu•ral•gic** [njʊr'ældʒɪk] *adj* neuralgiczny

neu•ri•tis [njʊə'raɪtɪs] *s MED* zapalenie *n* nerwu

neu•ro•log•i•cal [njʊrə'lɒdʒɪkl] *adj MED* neurologiczny; **neu•rol•o•gist** [njʊə'rɒlədʒɪst] *s MED* neurolog *m*; **neu•rol•o•gy** [njʊə'rɒlədʒɪ] *s MED* neurologia *f*

neu•ron ['njʊərɒn] *s ANAT* neuron *m*, komórka *f* nerwowa; **neu•ro•sis** [njʊ'rəʊsɪs] *pl -ses s MED* nerwica *f*; **neu•ro•sur•geon** ['njʊərəʊsɜːrdʒən] *s MED* neurochirurg *m*; **neu•rot•ic** [njʊə'rɒtɪk] **I** *adj* neurotyczny **II** *s* neurotyk *m*

neu•ter ['njuːtə] *adj* **1.** *gender*: nijaki; ***be ~*** być rodzaju nijakiego **2.** *v/t* kastrować ⟨wy-⟩

neu•tral ['njuːtrl] **I** *adj* **1.** neutralny **2.** *tone, expression*: obojętny **3.** *colour*: neutralny, stonowany **II** *s* **1.** *AUTO* luz *m*; ***leave the car in ~*** zostawić samochód na luzie **2.** (*in war*) strona *f* neutralna; **neu•tral•i•ty** [njuː'trælətɪ] *s* neutralność *f*, bezstronność *f*; **neu•tral•ize** ['njuːtrəlaɪz] *v/t* **1.** neutralizować ⟨z-⟩ **2.** *CHEM* zobojętniać ⟨-nić⟩

neu•tron ['njuːtrɒn] *s PHYS* neutron *m*

nev•er ['nevə] *adv* nigdy; ***~ ever*** nigdy w życiu; ***no, I ~!*** ależ skąd!; ***she ~ so much as smiled*** ani razu się nie uśmiechnęła; **nev•er-'end•ing** *adj* niekończący się; **nev•er-'nev•er** *s*: ***to buy on the ~*** *infml* kupić na raty

nev•er•the•less [nevəðə'les] *adv* (niemniej) jednak, mimo wszystko

new [njuː] *adj* nowy; ***be ~ to s.o.*** być dla kogoś nowością; ***be ~ to s.th.*** nie znać się na czymś; ***as good as ~***, ***like ~*** jak nowy; ***what's ~?*** co nowego?; ***feel*** (***like***) ***a ~ man*** czuć się jak nowo narodzony; **'new•born** *adj*: ***~ baby*** noworodek; **'new•com•er** *s* **1.** nowo przybyły *m* **2.** nowicjusz *m* (***to*** w dziedzinie *G*); **new•'fan•gled** *adj* nowomodny; **new•'found** *adj* nowo odkryty

New•'found•land *s GEOGR* Nowa Fundlandia *f*; **New 'Guin•ea** *s GEOGR* Nowa Gwinea *f*

new•ly ['njuːlɪ] *adv* **1.** nowo **2.** *created*: niedawno **3.** *independent*: od niedawna; **'new•ly-weds** *pl* nowożeńcy *pl*

new 'moon *s* nów *m*

news [nuːz] *no pl s* wiadomość *f*, nowina *f*; ***this is good*** (***bad***) ***~*** to dobra (zła) wiadomość; ***I haven't had any ~ from her*** nie miałem od niej żadnych wiadomości; ***I heard it on the ~*** słyszałem o tym w wiadomościach; ***~ in brief*** wiadomości w skrócie; **'news a•gen•cy** *s* agencja *f* informacyjna; **'news•a•gent** *Br*, **'news•deal•er** *Am s* **1.** kioskarz *m* **2.** ***~'s*** kiosk; **'news black•out** *s* blokada *f* informacyjna; **'news•cast** *s TEL Am* wiadomości *pl*; **'news•cast•er** *s TEL* spiker *m*; **'news channel** *s TEL* kanał *m* informacyjny; **'news•deal•er** → ***newsagent***; **'news•flash** *s Br* wiadomość *f* z ostatniej chwili; **'news•let•ter** *s* biuletyn *m*; **'news•paper** *s* gazeta *f*; **'news•read•er** → ***newscaster***; **'news re•lease** *s* oświadczenie *n* prasowe, oświadczenie *n* dla mediów; **'news re•port** *s* doniesienie *n* prasowe; **'news•sheet** *s* biuletyn *m*; **'news•stand** *s* kiosk *m* z gazetami, stoisko *n* z gazetami; **'news•ven•dor** *s* gazeciarz *m*; **'news•wor•thy** *adj information*: wart opublikowania

newt [njuːt] *s BIOL* traszka *f*

New 'Tes•ta•ment *s REL* Nowy Testament *m*

New 'World *s* Nowy Świat *m*

'New Year *s* Nowy Rok *m*; ***Happy ~*** Szczęśliwego Nowego Roku; **New Year's 'Day** *s* (*1 January*) Nowy

Rok *m*; **New Year's 'Eve** *s* Sylwester *m*

New 'York *s* Nowy Jork *m*; **New 'York City** *s* (*city*) Nowy Jork *m*; **New 'Yorker** *s* Nowojorczyk *m*

New Zea•land [nju:'zi:lənd] *s* Nowa Zelandia *f*; **New Zea•land•er** *s* Nowozelandczyk *m*

next [nekst] **I** *adj* następny, najbliższy; ***who's ~?*** kto następny?; ***~ Monday*** w najbliższy poniedziałek; ***~ time*** następnym razem; ***~ to*** **a)** obok *G* **b)** prawie **c)** po *L* **II** *adv* **1.** następnie, potem, później **2.** ***~ biggest*** drugi pod względem wielkości; ***~ most important*** drugi najważniejszy (***to/after*** po *L*) **III** *s* następny *m*; **next 'door I** *adj* **1.** *house*: sąsiedni, obok **2.** *neighbour*: mieszkający obok, najbliższy **3.** *girl*: z sąsiedztwa **II** *adv* **1.** w domu obok **2.** w pokoju obok **III** *s* sąsiedzi *pl*; **next of 'kin** *s* najbliższy krewny *m*

NGO [endʒi:'əʊ] *abbr* (=***non-governmental organization***) organizacja *f* pozarządowa

NHS [eneɪtʃ'es] *abbr* (=***National Health Service***) *Br* publiczna służba *f* zdrowia

nib•ble ['nɪbl] **I** *v/t food*: skubać ⟨-bnąć⟩ **II** *v/i* **1.** *food*: skubać ⟨-bnąć⟩ (***at*** *A*) **2.** okazywać ⟨-zać⟩ nikłe zainteresowanie (***at*** *I*) **III** *s* kęs *m*; ***~s*** przekąski

Nic•a•ra•gua [nɪkə'rægjuə] *s* Nikaragua *f*

nice [naɪs] *adj* **1.** miły, przyjemny; ***have a ~ time*** dobrze się bawić; ***have a ~ day!*** miłego dnia!; ***~ to meet you*** miło cię poznać; ***a ~ long walk*** długi, przyjemny spacer; ***~ work!*** dobra robota! **2.** miły, uprzejmy **3.** *difference*: subtelny

nice•ly ['naɪslɪ] *adv* **1.** dobrze, ładnie; ***she is doing ~*** dobrze jej idzie; ***tomorrow will do ~*** jutro mi pasuje; ***~ furnished*** ładnie umeblowany **2.** grzecznie, uprzejmie; ***if you ask her ~*** jeśli ją grzecznie poprosisz **3.** dokładnie, drobiazgowo

ni•ce•ty ['naɪsətɪ] *s* **1.** subtelność *f*, niuans *m* **2.** dokładność *f*, drobiazgowość *f*; ***analyzed to a ~*** drobiazgowo przeanalizowany; **ni•ce•ties** ['naɪsətɪz] *pl* grzeczności *pl*

niche [ni:ʃ] *s* nisza *f*; ***he has finally found his ~ in life*** znalazł w końcu swoje miejsce w życiu; ***a ~ in the market*** nisza na rynku; **'niche market** *s* ECON rynek *m* niszowy; **'niche marketing** *s* ECON marketing *m* niszowy; **'niche product** *s* ECON produkt *m* niszowy

nick[1] [nɪk] **I** *s* **1.** (*jail*) ***the ~*** *Br infml* ciupa *f*, paka *f* **2.** nacięcie *n* **3.** ***in the ~ of time*** w ostatniej chwili; ***in good ~*** w dobrym stanie **II** *v/t* **1.** nacinać ⟨-ciąć⟩, zacinać ⟨-ciąć⟩; ***~ oneself while shaving*** zaciąć się przy goleniu **2.** (*steal*) *Br infml* podwędzić, zwinąć **3.** *Br infml* aresztować ⟨za-⟩

nick[2] [~] *s internet*: nick *m*

nick•el ['nɪkl] *s* **1.** CHEM nikiel *m* **2.** *Am* pięciocentówka *f*; **nick•el-'plate** *v/t* niklować

nick•name ['nɪkneɪm] **I** *s* przezwisko *n*, przydomek *m* **II** *v/t* przezywać ⟨-zwać⟩, nadawać ⟨-dać⟩ przezwisko

nic•o•tine ['nɪkəti:n] *s* nikotyna *f*; **'nic•o•tine poi•son•ing** *s* zatrucie *n* nikotynowe

niece [ni:s] *s* **1.** siostrzenica *f* **2.** bratanica *f*

niff [nɪf] *s Br infml* smród *m*; **'niff•y** *adj Br infml* śmierdzący

nif•ty ['nɪftɪ] *adj infml* **1.** zmyślny, sprytny **2.** zręczny

Ni•ger•i•a [naɪ'dʒɪrɪə] *s* Nigeria *f*

nig•gard•ly ['nɪgədlɪ] *adj lit* skąpy

nigger ['nɪgə] *s* (*offensive*) czarnuch *m*

nig•gle ['nɪgl] **I** *s* **1.** lekki ból *m* **2.** *fig* ukłucie *n*; ***a ~ of jealousy*** ukłucie zazdrości **II** *v/t* zadręczać ⟨-czyć⟩, martwić ⟨z-⟩ **III** *v/i*, spierać ⟨po-⟩ się (***about/over*** o *A*); **nig•gling** ['nɪglɪŋ] *adj* **1.** *pain, doubt*: dręczący **2.** *detail*: nieważny

night [naɪt] *s* **1.** noc *f*; ***at*** (*a.* ***in the***) ***~*** w nocy; ***by ~*** nocą; ***~ and day*** dniem i nocą; ***have a good*** (***bad***) ***~*** dobrze (źle) spać w nocy; ***good ~*** dobranoc; ***stay the ~*** przenocować **2.** wieczór *m*; ***on Saturday ~*** w sobotę wieczorem; ***last ~*** wczoraj wieczorem; ***on the ~ of May 5th*** wieczorem 5. maja; ***late at ~*** późno wieczorem; ***let's have a ~ out*** wyjdźmy gdzieś wieczorem; **'night bird** *s* **1.** ptak *m* nocny **2.** *fig* nocny marek *m*; **'night blind•ness** *s*

N

MED kurza ślepota *f*; '**night•cap** *s*: ***have a ~*** wypić drinka przed snem; '**night•club** *s* klub *m* nocny; '**night-dress** *Br s* koszula *f* nocna; '**night•fall** *s* zmierzch *m*; '**night flight** *s* nocny lot *m*; '**night•gown** *Am* → ***nightdress***

night•ie ['naɪtɪ] *s infml* koszula *f* nocna

nigh•tin•gale ['naɪtɪŋgeɪl] *s* słowik *m*

'**night•life** *s* nocne życie *n*

night•ly ['naɪtlɪ] **I** *adj* wieczorny, nocny **II** *adv* co wieczór, co noc

night•mare ['naɪtmeə] *s a. fig* koszmar *m*, zły sen *m*; **night•mar•ish** ['naɪtmeərɪʃ] *adj* koszmarny

'**night nurse** *s* nocna pielęgniarka *f*; '**night owl** *s* nocny marek *m*; '**night por•ter** *s* portier *m* nocny; '**night school** *s* szkoła *f* wieczorowa; '**night shift** *s* nocna zmiana *f*; '**night•shirt** *s* koszula *f* nocna; '**night•spot** *s infml* nocny lokal *m*; '**night•stick** *s Am* pałka *f* policyjna; '**night•time** *s* noc *f*; **night** '**watch•man** *pl -men s* stróż *m* nocny

ni•hil•ism ['naɪlɪzəm] *s* nihilizm *m*; **ni•hil•ist** ['naɪlɪst] *s* nihilista *m*; **ni•hil•is•tic** [naɪ'lɪstɪk] *adj* nihilistyczny

nil [nɪl] *s* **1.** *Br* zero *n*; ***our team won four ~*** nasza drużyna wygrała cztery do zera **2.** nic *n*; ***doctors rated her chances as ~*** lekarze nie dawali jej żadnych szans na przeżycie

N

Nile [naɪl] *s* Nil *m*

nim•ble ['nɪmbl] *adj* **1.** *fingers*: zręczny **2.** *mind*: sprawny

nim•by ['nɪmbɪ] (***=not in my backyard***) *s osoba sprzeciwiająca się inwestycji w pobliżu miejsca jej zamieszkania*

nin•com•poop ['nɪŋkəmpuːp] *s infml* głupek *m*

nine [naɪn] **I** *num* dziewięć, dziewięciu, dziewięcioro; ***~ times out of ten*** w dziewięciu przypadkach na dziesięć; ***a ~ days' wonder*** gwiazda jednego sezonu **II** *s* **2.** dziewiątka *f*; ***dressed up to the ~s*** *infml* wystrojony, *infml* odszykowany; **nine•fold** ['naɪnfəʊld] **I** *adj* **1.** dziewięciokrotny **II** *adv* dziewięciokrotnie; **nine•teen** [naɪn'tiːn] **I** *num* dziewiętnaście **II** *s* dziewiętnastka *f*; **nine•teenth** [naɪn'tiːnθ] *num* dziewiętnasty; **nine•ti•eth** ['naɪntɪɪθ] *num* dziewięćdziesiąty; '**nine-time** *adj* dziewięciokrotny; **nine-to-'five** *adj work*: na etat, od ósmej do czwartej; **nine•ty** ['naɪntɪ] *num* dziewięćdziesiąt

nin•ny ['nɪnɪ] *s infml* półgłówek *m*

ninth [naɪnθ] *num* dziewiąty

nip[1] [nɪp] **I** *v/t* szczypać ⟨-pnąć⟩; ***~ s.th. in the bud*** zdusić coś w zarodku **II** *v/i* **1.** szczypać (**at** w *A*); ***the wind ~ped at our faces*** wiatr szczypał nas w twarz **2.** (*go*) *infml* wyskakiwać ⟨-skoczyć⟩ **3.** (*car*) ***~ in*** zajechać drogę **III** *s* szczypanie *n*; ***there is a ~ in the air*** jest chłodno; **nip off** *v/t* odrywać ⟨oderwać⟩

nip[2] [~] *s infml alcohol*: łyk *m*

nipper ['nɪpə] *s infml* dzieciak *m*

nip•pers ['nɪpəz] *pl* szczypce *pl*

nip•ple ['nɪpl] *s* **1.** ANAT brodawka *f* (sutkowa), sutek *m* **2.** (*bottle*) *Am* smoczek *m* **3.** (**grease**) ~ TECH smarowniczka

nip•py ['nɪpɪ] *adj* **1.** *Br* zwinny **2.** ***it's ~*** *infml* jest chłodno

nit [nɪt] *s* **1.** BIOL gnida *f* **2.** *infml* pacan *m*, głąb *m*

ni•ter *Am* → ***nitre***

nit•pick•er ['nɪtpɪkə] *s infml* szukający *m* dziury w całym; **nit•pick•ing** ['nɪtpɪkɪŋ] *s infml* czepianie się *n*, szukanie *n* dziury w całym

ni•trate ['naɪtreɪt] *s* CHEM azotan *m*

ni•tre ['naɪtə] *Br*, **ni•ter** *Am s* CHEM azotan *m* potasu, saletra *f* potasowa

ni•tric ac•id [naɪtrɪk'æsɪd] *s* CHEM kwas *m* azotowy

ni•tro•gen ['naɪtrədʒn] *s* CHEM azot *m*; **ni•trog•e•nous** [naɪ'trədʒɪnɪs] *adj* CHEM azotowy

ni•tro•glyc•er•in(e) [naɪtrəʊ'glɪsəriːn] *s* CHEM nitrogliceryna *f*

nit•ty-grit•ty [nɪtɪ'grɪtɪ] *s infml* konkrety *pl*; ***get down to the ~*** przejść do konkretów

nit•wit ['nɪtwɪt] *s infml* półgłówek *m*

no [nəʊ] **I** *interj* nie **II** *adj* żaden; ***there were ~ letters*** nie było żadnych listów; ***she is ~ fool*** nie jest głupia; ***~ one*** nikt; ***in ~ time*** natychmiast **III** *adv* nie; ***she's feeling ~ better*** nie czuje się lepiej; ***they ~ longer live here*** już tu nie mieszkają **IV** *pl -es s* nie; ***the ~es*** głosy przeciw; ***the ~es have it*** przeważyły głosy przeciw

No•bel peace prize [nəʊbel'pi:spraɪz] *s* pokojowa nagroda *f* Nobla; **No•bel prize** ['nəʊbelpraɪz] *s* nagroda *f* Nobla; **No•bel prize win•ner** [nəʊbel'praɪzwɪnə] *s* laureat *m* nagrody Nobla, noblista *m*
no•bil•i•ty [nəʊ'bɪlətɪ] *s* **1.** ***the ~*** **a)** arystokracja **b)** szlachta **2.** szlachetność *f*
no•ble ['nəʊbl] *adj* **1.** szlachetny **2.** *act*: szczytny **3.** wspaniały, okazały **4.** szlachecki, arystokratyczny
no•bod•y ['nəʊbədɪ] *pron* nikt
no-claims bo•nus [nəʊ'kleɪmzbəʊnəs] *s Br* zniżka *f* za bezszkodowość
noc•tur•nal [nɒk'tɜ:rnl] *adj* nocny
nod [nɒd] **I** *v/i* skinąć głową; ***~ at*** (*a.* ***to***) ***s.o.*** skinąć komuś głową; ***have a ~ding acquaintance with s.o.*** znać kogoś z widzenia **II** *v/t* ***~ one's head*** skinąć głową **III** *s* skinienie *n* głową; ***give s.o. the ~*** *infml* dać komuś zielone światło; **nod off** *v/i* przysypiać ⟨-snąć⟩
node [nəʊd] *s* węzeł *m*
nod•ule ['nɒdju:l] *s* **1.** guzek *m* **2.** (*plant*) brodawka *f*
no-'go ar•e•a *s Br* niebezpieczna dzielnica *f*
no-hop•er [noəʊ'həʊpə] *s infml* nieudacznik *m*
noise [nɔɪz] *s* **1.** hałas *m*; ***~ level*** poziom hałasu; ***what's this ~?*** co to za hałas?; ***not to make any ~*** nie robić hałasu; ***make a lot of ~ about*** robić wiele hałasu o *A* **2.** TECH szum *m*; **noise•less** ['nɔɪzlɪs] *adj* bezgłośny, bezszelestny
nois•y ['nɔɪzɪ] *adj* hałaśliwy, głośny
no•mad ['nəʊmæd] *s* koczownik *m*, nomada *m*; **no•mad•ic** [nəʊ'mædɪk] *adj* koczowniczy, nomadyczny
no-man's land ['nəʊmænzlænd] *s* ziemia *f* niczyja
no•men•cla•ture [nə'menklətʃə] *s* nomenklatura *f*, nazewnictwo *n*
nom•i•nal ['nɒmɪnl] *adj* **1.** nominalny **2.** nominalny, formalny **3.** *sum*: symboliczny **4.** rzeczownikowy
nom•i•nate ['nɒmɪneɪt] *v/t* **1.** nominować, wysuwać ⟨-sunąć⟩ kandydaturę (***for*** do *G*, ***as*** na *A*); ***he was ~d for the presidency*** wysunięto jego kandydaturę na prezydenta **2.** nominować, mianować (***to*** do *G*, ***as*** na *A*); **nom•i•na•tion** [nɒmɪ'neɪʃn] *s* **1.** nominacja *f*, mianowanie *n* **2.** kandydatura *f*
nom•i•na•tive ['nɒmɪnətɪv] *s* GRAM mianownik *m*
nom•i•nee [nɒmɪ'ni:] *s* kandydat *m*, nominowany *m*
non- [nɒn] (*in combinations*) bez-, nie-
non•ac'cept•ance *s* **1.** brak *m* akceptacji, niezaakceptowanie *n* **2.** *order, goods*: odmowa *f* przyjęcia
non•ag'gres•sion pact *s* pakt *m* o nieagresji
non•al•co'hol•ic *adj* bezalkoholowy
non•a'ligned *adj country*: niezaangażowany
non•ap'pear•ance *s* niestawiennictwo *n*
non•at'tend•ance *s* **1.** nieobecność *f* **2.** nieobecności *pl*
non•be'liev•er *s* niewierzący *m*, osoba *f* niewierząca
non•cha•lance ['nɒnʃələns] *s* nonszalancja *f*; **non•cha•lant** ['nɒnʃəlɑ:nt] *adj* nonszalancki
non•com•mis•sioned 'of•fi•cer *s* podoficer *m*
non•com'mit•tal *adj answer*: wymijający
non•com'pli•ance *s* nieprzestrzeganie *n* (***with*** *G*), brak *m* zgodności (***with*** z *I*)
non com•pos men•tis [nɒn'kɒmpəs'mentɪs] *adj* JUR niepoczytalny, nie w pełni władz umysłowych
non•con'form•ist **I** *s* nonkonformista *m* **II** *adj* nonkonformistyczny
non•co•op•er'a•tion *s* odmowa *f* współpracy
non•de•script ['nɒndɪskrɪpt] *adj* **1.** nijaki **2.** nieokreślony
none [nʌn] **I** *pron* żaden; ***~ of them is*** (*a.* ***are***) ***here*** żadnego z nich tu nie ma; ***~ but he*** tylko on; ***~ other than*** nie kto inny jak **II** *adv* wcale nie, ani trochę; ***~ the worse*** wcale nie gorszy; ***~ too wiser*** wcale nie mądrzejszy
non•'en•ti•ty *s* (*person*) nikt *m*, zero *n*
non•es'sen•tial *adj* nieistotny, niekonieczny
none•the•less [nʌnðə'les] *adv* (niemniej) jednak, mimo wszystko
non•e'vent *s* rozczarowanie *n*, *inflm* niewypał *m*

N

non•ex'ist•ence *s* **1.** nieistnienie *n*, niebyt *m* **2.** brak *m*; **non•ex'ist•ent** *adj* nieistniejący; ***his social life is ~*** nie ma żadnego życia towarzyskiego

non'fic•tion *s* literatura *f* faktu

non(•in)'flam•ma•ble *adj* niepalny

non•ful•'fil•ment *Br*, ***non•ful•'fill•ment*** *Am s* niespełnienie *n*

non•in•ter•'fer•ence, ***non•in•ter•'ven•tion*** *s* POLIT nieinterwencja *f*; ***a policy of ~*** polityka nieinterwencji

non-'i•ron *adj* non-iron, niewymagający prasowania

'non•mem•ber *s* niebędący *m* członkiem

'no-no *s*: ***it's a ~*** *infml* tak się nie robi

non•ob'serv•ance *s* nieprzestrzeganie *n*

no-'non•sense *adj* konkretny, rzeczowy

non•par•ti'san *adj* **1.** bezpartyjny, bezstronny **2.** ponadpartyjny

non-'payment *s* niezapłacenie *n*, niepłacenie *n*

non•plussed [nɒn'plʌst], ***non•plused*** *Am adj* skonsternowany, zszokowany

non•pol•'lut•ing *adj* przyjazny dla środowiska

non•'prof•it ***non•'prof•it-mak•ing*** *Br adj organization*: non-profit

non•pro•lif•e'ra•tion *s*: ***~ treaty*** układ o nierozprzestrzenianiu broni jądrowej

non-res•i•dent **I** *s* **1.** nierezydent *m*, zamieszkały *m* na stałe za granicą **2.** niezameldowany *m*; **non-res•i•den•tial** *adj* **1.** niezameldowany **2.** dojeżdżający **3.** mający stałą siedzibę za granicą

non•re•'turn•a•ble *adj* **1.** *goods*, *fee*: niepodlegający zwrotowi **2.** *bottle*: bezzwrotny

non•sense ['nɒnsəns] *s* nonsens *m*, bezsens *m*, absurd *m*; ***talk ~*** mówić głupstwa; ***make (a) ~ of s.th.*** sprowadzać coś do absurdu; **non•sen•si•cal** [nɒn'sensɪkl] *adj* nonsensowny, absurdalny, niedorzeczny

non•'skid *adj* AUTO antypoślizgowy

non•'slip *adj* antypoślizgowy, przeciwpoślizgowy; ***~ mat*** mata antypoślizgowa

non-'smok•er *s* niepalący *m*; **non-'smok•ing** *adj* **1.** dla niepalących **2.** niepalący

non•'stand•ard *adj* **1.** niestandardowy **2.** niepoprawny

non•'start•er *adj*: ***be a ~*** nie mieć szans (na sukces)

non•'stick *adj pan*: pokryta nieprzywierającą powłoką

non•'stop **I** *adj* **1.** non stop, bez przerwy, nieprzerwany **2.** *flight*: bezpośredni **3.** *train*: niezatrzymujący się na stacjach pośrednich **II** *adv* non stop, bez przerwy, nieprzerwanie

non•'tox•ic *adj* nietoksyczny

non•'u•nion *adj person*: nienależący do związków zawodowych

non-'vi•o•lence *adj* niestosowanie *n* przemocy; **non-'vi•o•lent** *adj* bez użycia przemocy

noo•dles ['nuːdlz] *pl* makaron *m* (nitki)

nook [nʊk] *s* kącik *m*, zakątek *m*; ***every ~ and cranny*** każdy kąt

noo•kie ['nʊkɪ], ***nooky*** *s infml* seks *m*, *infml* bara bara *n*

noon [nuːn] *s* (*hour*) południe *n*; ***at ~*** w południe

'no one → ***nobody***

noose [nuːs] *s* pętla *f*

nope [nəʊp] *interj* nie

nor [nɔː] **I** *conj* ani; ***she seemed neither surprised ~ worried*** nie wydawała się ani zaskoczona, ani zmartwiona **II** *adv* też nie; ***– 'I'm not going.' – '~ am I.'*** – „Ja nie idę." – „Ja też nie."

norm [nɔːm] *s* norma *f*

nor•mal ['nɔːml] **I** *adj* normalny **II** *s* normalność *f*; ***return to ~*** wrócić do normy; ***above*** (***below***) ***~*** powyżej (poniżej) normy; **nor•mal•i•ty** [nɔː'mælətɪ] *s* normalność *f*; **nor•mal•ize** ['nɔːrməlaɪz] **I** *v/t* normalizować ⟨z-⟩ **II** *v/i* normalizować ⟨z-⟩ się; **nor•mal•ly** ['nɔːməlɪ] *adv* **1.** zazwyczaj **2.** normalnie, prawidłowo

Nor•man ['nɔːmən] **I** *s* Norman *m* **II** *adj* normański

north [nɔːθ] **I** *s* (*direction*) północ *f*; ***in the ~ of*** na północy *G*; ***to the ~ of*** na północ od *G* **II** *adj* północny; ***~ wind*** wiatr północny **III** *adv* na północ; **North A•'mer•i•ca** *s* Ameryka *f* Pół-

N

nocna; **North A•'mer•i•can** *adj* północnoamerykański; **'north•bound** *adj* **1.** w kierunku północnym **2.** *bus*: jadący na północ; **north-'east** **I** *s* północny wschód *m* **II** *adj* północno-wschodni **III** *adv* na północny wschód

nor•ther•ly ['nɔːðəlɪ] **I** *adj* **1.** północny **2.** w kierunku północnym **II** *s* wiatr *m* północny

nor•thern ['nɔːðən] *adj* północny; ***the ~ lights*** zorza polarna; **North•ern 'Ire•land** *s* Irlandia *f* Północna; **nor•thern•er** ['nɔːðərnə] *s* mieszkaniec *m* północy (kraju); **north•ern•most** ['nɔːðənməʊst] *adj* najbardziej wysunięty na północ; **North Ko•'re•a** *s* Korea *f* Północna; **North 'Pole** *s*: ***the ~*** biegun północny; **North 'Sea** *s*: ***the ~*** Morze Północne; **North 'Star** *s*: ***the ~*** ASTR Gwiazda Polarna

north•ward ['nɔːðwəd] **I** *adj direction*: północny **II** *adv* w kierunku północnym, na północ; **north•west** [nɔːð'west] **I** *s* północny zachód *m* **II** *adj* północno-zachodni **III** *adv* na północny zachód

Nor•way ['nɔːweɪ] *s* Norwegia *f*; **Nor•we•gian** [nɔː'wiːdʒn] **I** *s* **1.** Norweg *m*, Norweżka *f* **2.** język *m* norweski **II** *adj* **3.** norweski

nose [nəʊz] **I** *s* **1.** *a. fig* nos *m*; ***blow one's ~*** wydmuchać nos, *infml* wysmarkać się; ***pick one's ~*** dłubać w nosie; ***to cut off one's ~ to spike one's face*** *infml* postępować w myśl zasady „na złość mamie odmrożę sobie uszy"; ***follow one's ~*** *fig* robić coś na nosa; ***lead s.o. by the ~*** wodzić kogoś za nos; ***look down one's ~ at*** *infml* patrzeć z góry na *A*; ***poke*** (*a.* ***stick***) ***one's ~ into*** *infml* wtykać swój nos w *A*; ***keep one's ~ out of*** trzymać się z dala od *G*; ***under s.o.'s ~*** *infml* pod czyimś nosem; ***have a ~ for*** mieć nosa do *G* **2.** węch *m* **3.** *plane*, *ship*: dziób *m* **II** *v/i* **1.** (*vehicle*) poruszać się wolno **2.** węszyć ⟨wy-⟩; **nose around** (*a.* **~ about**) *v/i* węszyć, niuchać (**for** za *I*); **nose out** *v/t* wywęszyć, wyniuchać

'nose•bleed *s* krwawienie *n* z nosa; **'nose dive** *s* **1.** *prices*, *course*: gwałtowny spadek *m* **2.** lot *m* nurkowy; **'nose-dive** *v/i* **1.** (*prices*, *course*) gwałtownie spadać ⟨spaść⟩ **2.** (*plane*) nurkować ⟨za-⟩; **'nose drops** *pl* krople *pl* do nosa

nosh [nɒʃ] **I** *s infml* **1.** *Br* żarcie *n* **2.** *Am* przekąska *f* **II** *v/t* przegryzać ⟨-ryźć⟩

no-'smok•ing → ***non-smoking***

nos•tal•gia [nɒ'stældʒə] *s* tęsknota *f*, nostalgia *f* (**for** za *I*); **nos•tal•gic** [nɒ'stældʒɪk] *adj* przepełniony tęsknotą, nostalgiczny

nos•tril ['nəstrəl] *s* ANAT nozdrze *n*

nos•y ['nəʊzɪ] *adj infml* ciekawski; **nos•y 'par•ker** *s Br* ciekawski *m*

not [nɒt] *adv* nie; ***it is ~ raining*** nie pada; ***I hope ~*** mam nadzieję, że nie; ***she didn't say a word*** nie powiedziała ani słowa; ***~ at all*** **a)** wcale nie **b)** nie ma za co; ***~ only... but also*** nie tylko..., lecz również

no•ta•ble ['nəʊtəbl] **I** *adj* **1.** godny uwagi, warty wzmianki **2.** wybitny **II** *s* notabl *m*, znakomitość *f*; **no•ta•bly** ['nəʊtəblɪ] *adv* szczególnie, przede wszystkim

no•ta•ry (**public**) ['nəʊtərɪ('pʌblɪk)] *s* notariusz *m*

notch [nɒθ] **I** *s* **1.** (*degree*) *infml* stopień *m*; ***be a ~ above*** być lepszym od *G* **2.** nacięcie *n* **II** *v/t* nacinać ⟨-ciąć⟩

note [nəʊt] **I** *s* **1.** notatka *f*, uwaga *f*; ***make ~s*** robić notatki; ***make a ~ of*** zapisać *A*; ***take ~ of*** zwrócić uwagę na *A*; ***of ~*** wybitny **2.** liścik *m* **3.** przypis *m* **4.** banknot *m* **5.** MUS nuta *f*; ***there was a ~ of amusement in his voice*** *fig* w jego głosie słychać było rozbawienie; ***hit*** (*a.* ***strike***) ***the right ~*** *fig* uderzyć we właściwy ton **6.** ***sick ~*** zwolnienie lekarskie; ***promissory ~*** weksel własny **7.** *diplomatic*: nota *f* **II** *v/t* **1.** zwracać ⟨-rócić⟩ uwagę na *A* **2.** zauważać ⟨-żyć⟩; **note down** *v/t* notować ⟨za-⟩; **'note•book** *s* **1.** notes *m*, notatnik *m* **2.** notebook *m*, komputer *m* przenośny

not•ed ['nəʊtɪd] *adj* znany, sławny (**for** z *G*)

'note•pad *s* notes *m*, blok *m*; **'note•pa•per** *s* papier *m* listowy; **'note•wor•thy** *adj* godny uwagi

not-for-'pro•fit *adj organization*: nonprofit

N

noth•ing ['nʌθɪŋ] *pron* nic; ***as if ~ had happened*** jak gdyby nic się nie stało; ***~ else*** nic innego; ***she's ~ to me*** ona nic dla mnie znaczy; ***have ~ to do with*** nie mieć nic wspólnego z *I*; ***to say ~ of*** nie mówiąc (już) o *L*; ***for ~*** **a)** za darmo **b)** na darmo; ***~ but*** tylko; ***~ much*** niewiele; ***there is ~ to it*** to nic trudnego; ***there is ~ else for it but*** nie pozostaje nic innego jak (tylko); ***there is ~ like*** nie ma jak *N*; **noth•ing•ness** ['nʌθɪŋnɪs] *s* nicość *f*

no•tice ['nəʊtɪs] **I** *s* **1.** uwaga *f*; ***take no ~ of*** nie zwracać uwagi na *A*; ***bring s.th. to s.o.'s ~*** zwrócić czyjąś uwagę na coś; ***escape s.o.'s ~*** ujść czyjejś uwadze **2.** informacja *f*, ogłoszenie *n* **3.** napis *m* **4.** zawiadomienie *n*, powiadomienie *n*; ***give s.o. ~ of*** zawiadomić kogoś o *L*; ***at short ~*** w krótkim czasie; ***until further ~*** do odwołania; ***without ~*** bez uprzedzenia **5.** wypowiedzenie *n*; ***give s.o. two weeks' ~*** zwolnić kogoś z dwutygodniowym wypowiedzeniem; ***hand in one's ~*** złożyć wypowiedzenie **II** *v/t* **1.** zauważać ⟨-żyć⟩ **2.** zwracać ⟨-rócić⟩ uwagę na *A*; **no•tice•a•ble** ['nəʊtɪsəbl] *adj* widoczny, zauważalny; **no•tice•a•bly** ['nəʊtɪsəblɪ] *adv* widocznie, zauważalnie; **'no•tice board** *s Br* tablica *f* ogłoszeń

no•ti•fi•a•ble ['nəʊtɪfaɪəbl] *adj crime*: podlegający obowiązkowi zgłoszenia

no•ti•fi•ca•tion [nəʊtɪfɪ'keɪʃn] *s* zawiadomienie *n*, powiadomienie *n*; **no•ti•fy** ['nəʊtɪfaɪ] *v/t* zawiadamiać ⟨-domić⟩, powiadamiać ⟨-domić⟩ (***s.o. of*** kogoś o *L*)

no•tion ['nəʊʃn] *s* **1.** pojęcie *n*; ***not to have the faintest*** (*a.* ***vaguest***) ***~ of*** nie mieć bladego pojęcia o *L* **2.** pomysł *m*, idea *f*; **no•tion•al** ['nəʊʃənl] *adj* hipotetyczny

no•tions ['nəʊʃnz] *pl Am* pasmanteria *f*

no•to•ri•e•ty [nəʊtə'raɪətɪ] *no pl s* zła sława *f*; **no•to•ri•ous** [nəʊ'tɔːrɪəs] *adj* cieszący się złą sławą (***for*** z powodu *G*), notoryczny; **no•to•ri•ous•ly** [nəʊ'tɔːrɪəslɪ] *adv* notorycznie

not•with•stand•ing [nɒtwɪθ'stændɪŋ] **I** *prep* pomimo *G* **II** *adv* jednakże, mimo to

nou•gat ['nuːgət] *s* nugat *m*

nought [nɔːt] *s Br* zero *n*; ***come to ~*** spełznąć na niczym; **noughts and 'cross•es** *s Br* gra *f* w kółko i krzyżyk

noun [naʊn] *s GRAM* rzeczownik *m*

nour•ish ['nʌrɪʃ] *v/t* **1.** odżywiać, żywić **2.** *feelings*: żywić, pielęgnować; **nour•ish•ing** ['nʌrɪʃɪŋ] *adj* pożywny; **nour•ish•ment** ['nʌrɪʃmənt] *s* **1.** pożywienie *n*, pokarm *m*; ***spiritual ~*** *fig* strawa duchowa **2.** odżywianie *n*

nous [naʊs] *s Br infml* rozum *m*, zdrowy rozsądek *m*

nou•veau riche [nuːvəʊ'riːʃ] *pl nouveaux riches* [nuːvəʊ'riːʃ] *s* nowobogacki *m*, nuworysz *m*

nov•el ['nɒvl] **I** *s* powieść *f* **II** *adj* nowatorski; **nov•el•ist** ['nɒvlɪst] *s* powieściopisarz *m*; **no•vel•la** [nəʊ'velə] *pl -las, -le* [~liː] *s* nowela *f*; **no•vel•ty** ['nɒvəltɪ] **I** *s* **1.** nowość *f*, nowinka *f* **2.** tani drobiazg *m* **II** *adj* śmieszny, niezwykły

No•vem•ber [nəʊ'vembə] *s* listopad *m*; ***in ~*** w listopadzie

nov•ice ['nɒvɪs] *s* **1.** nowicjusz *m*, początkujący *m* **2.** *REL* nowicjusz *m*

no•vi•ti•ate [nəʊ'vɪʃɪət] *s* nowicjat *m*

now [naʊ] **I** *adv* **1.** teraz; ***from ~ on*** od teraz; ***for ~*** póki co; ***~ and again***, ***~ and then*** od czasu do czasu; ***it's ~ or never*** teraz albo nigdy **2.** natychmiast; ***I must go ~*** muszę już iść **II** *conj* (*a.* ***~ that***) teraz, gdy, skoro już

now•a•days ['naʊədeɪz] *adv* teraz, w dzisiejszych czasach

no•where ['nəʊwe] *adv* nigdzie; ***have ~ to live*** nie mieć gdzie mieszkać; ***this will get you ~*** to ci nic nie da

no-'win sit•ua•tion *s* sytuacja *f* bez wyjścia

nox•ious ['nɒkʃəs] *adj* szkodliwy, trujący

noz•zle ['nɒzl] *s hose*: końcówka *f*

nu•ance ['njuːɑːns] *s* niuans *m*

nu•bile ['njuːbaɪl] *adj girl*: apetyczny

nu•cle•ar ['njuːklɪə] *adj* jądrowy, nuklearny; **nu•cle•ar 'en•er•gy** *s* energia *f* jądrowa; **nu•cle•ar 'fis•sion** *s* rozszczepienie *n* jądra atomowego; **nu•cle•ar-'free** *adj area*: bezatomowy; **nu•cle•ar 'phys•ics** *s* fizyka *f* jądrowa; **nu•cle•ar 'pow•er** *s* **1.** → ***nuclear energy*** **2.** mocarstwo *n* atomowe;

'**nu•cle•ar-pow•ered** *adj* zasilany energią jądrową; **nu•cle•ar 'pow•er sta•tion** *s* elektrownia *f* atomowa; **nu•cle•ar re•'ac•tor** *s* reaktor *m* jądrowy; **nu•cle•ar 'sci•en•tist** *s* fizyk *m* jądrowy; **nu•cle•ar 'shelter** *s* schron *m* przeciwatomowy; **nu•cle•ar 'sub•ma•rine** *s* atomowa łódź *f* podwodna; **nu•cle•ar 'test** *s* próba *f* jądrowa; **nu•cle•ar 'war•(fare)** *s* wojna *f* atomowa; **nu•cle•ar 'war•head** *s* głowica *f* jądrowa; **nu•cle•ar 'waste** *s* odpady *pl* radioaktywne; **nu•cle•ar 'weap•on** *s* broń *f* jądrowa; **nu•cle•ar 'win•ter** *s* zima *f* atomowa

nu•cle•us ['nju:klɪəs] *pl -clei* ['nju:klɪaɪ] *s* **1.** BIOL PHYS jądro *n* **2.** *fig* rdzeń *m*

nude [nju:d] **I** *adj* nagi; **~ beach** plaża dla nudystów **II** *s* ART akt *m*; ***in the ~*** nago

nudge [nʌdʒ] **I** *v/t* szturchać ⟨-chnąć⟩ **II** *s* szturchaniec *m*

nud•ism ['nu:dɪzəm] *s* nudyzm *m*, naturyzm *m*; **nud•ist** ['nu:dɪst] *s* nudysta *m*, naturysta *m*

nu•di•ty ['nju:dɪtɪ] *s* nagość *f*

nui•sance ['nju:sns] *s* **1.** uciążliwość *f*, niedogodność *f* **2.** utrapienie *n*; ***I don't want to be a ~*** nie chcę się naprzykrzać; ***make a ~ of o.s.*** naprzykrzać się **3.** ***public ~*** JUR zakłócenie porządku publicznego

nuke [nju:k] **I** *v/t infml* zrzucać ⟨-cić⟩ atomówkę **II** *s infml* atomówka *f*

null and 'void [nʌlən'vɔɪd] *adj* JUR nieważny

nul•li•fy ['nʌlɪfaɪ] *v/t* **1.** JUR unieważniać ⟨-nić⟩ **2.** *effects*: niweczyć ⟨z-⟩

numb [nʌm] **I** *adj* **1.** zdrętwiały, zesztywniały; ***~ with cold*** zdrętwiały z zimna **2.** *fig* otępiały, odrętwiały **II** *v/t* **1.** ***be ~ed*** zdrętwiały, sztywny **2.** *fig* paraliżować ⟨s-⟩

num•ber ['nʌmbə/ɸoʊθđr] **I** *s* **1.** liczba *f*; ***be good at ~s*** umieć dobrze liczyć, być dobrym z matematyki; ***an even ~*** liczba parzysta; ***an odd ~*** liczba nieparzysta **2.** cyfra *f* **3.** *house, phone*: numer *m*; ***they live at ~ 6*** mieszkają pod szóstką; ***be ~ one*** być numerem jeden; ***have s.o.'s ~*** *infml* przejrzeć kogoś; ***your ~ is up!*** *infml* koniec z tobą! **4.** ilość *f*; ***a great ~ of people*** ogromna ilość ludzi, bardzo wiele osób; ***a ~ of times*** kilka razy; ***in large ~*** w dużych ilościach, licznie **5.** *magazine*: numer *m*, wydanie *n* **II** *v/t* **1.** numerować ⟨po-⟩; ***his days are ~ed*** jego dni są policzone **2.** **~ s.o. among** zaliczać kogoś do *G* **3.** liczyć; ***the crowd ~ed more than a thousand*** tłum liczył ponad tysiąc osób; **num•ber•ing** ['nʌmbərɪŋ] *s* numerowanie *n*; '**num•ber•less** ['nʌmbərləs] *adj* niezliczony, nieprzebrany; '**num•ber•plate** *s Br* AUTO tablica *f* rejestracyjna

numb•ness ['nʌmnɪs] *s* **1.** zdrętwienie *n*, zesztywnienie *n* **2.** *fig* odrętwienie *n*

numb•skull ['nʌmskʌl] *s infml* głąb *m*, matoł *m*

nu•mer•a•cy ['nju:mərəsɪ] *s* umiejętność *f* liczenia

nu•mer•al ['nju:mərəl] *s* **1.** cyfra *f*; ***Arabic ~s*** cyfry arabskie **2.** liczebnik *m*

nu•me•rate ['nju:mərət] *adj*: ***be ~*** umieć liczyć

numeric [nju:'merɪk] *adj* numeryczny; **numeric keypad** *s* INF klawiatura *f* numeryczna

nu•mer•i•cal [nju:'merɪkl] *adj* numeryczny, liczbowy

nu•me•rous ['nju:mərəs] *adj* wiele; ***there are ~ reasons*** jest wiele powodów

nun [nʌn] *s* zakonnica *f*

nup•tial ['nʌpʃl] **I** *adj* ślubny **II** *s* **~s** *dated* ślub

nurse [nɜ:rs] **I** *s* **1.** pielęgniarka *f*; ***male ~*** pielęgniarz **2.** *dated* opiekunka *f* do dzieci **II** *v/t* **1.** *patient*: opiekować się **2.** *baby*: karmić ⟨na-⟩ piersią **3.** *illness*: leczyć ⟨wy-⟩ **4.** *grudge*: żywić

nur•se•ry ['nɜ:rsərɪ] **I** *s* **1.** *Br* żłobek *m* **2.** → ***nursery school*** **3.** szkółka *f* leśna **II** *adj* przedszkolny; '**nur•se•ry rhyme** *s* wierszyk *m* dla dzieci; '**nur•se•ry school** *s Br* przedszkole *n*; '**nur•se•ry school teach•er** *Br s* przedszkolanka *f*

nurs•ing ['nɜ:rsɪŋ] *s* (*job*) pielęgniarstwo *n*; '**nurs•ing bot•tle** *s Am* butelka *f* ze smoczkiem; '**nurs•ing home** *s* **1.** dom *m* spokojnej starości **2.** *Br* prywatna klinika *f*

N

nut [nʌt] *s* **1.** orzech *m*; ***a hard*** (*a.* ***tough***) ***~ to crack*** twardy orzech do zgryzienia **2.** *TECH* nakrętka *f* **3.** *infml* świr *m* **4.** *infml* maniak *m*; ***he's a football ~*** ma bzika na punkcie piłki nożnej **5.** *infml* łeb *m* **6.** ***~s*** (*testicles*) *infml* jaja; **'nut•crack•er** *s* dziadek *m* do orzechów; **nut•meg** ['nʌtmeg] *s* gałka *f* muszkatołowa

nu•tri•ent ['nju:triənt] *s* składnik *m* odżywczy

nu•tri•tion [nju:'trɪʃn] *s* żywienie *n*, odżywianie *n*; **nu•tri•tion•al** [nju:'trɪʃnl] *adj* odżywczy; ***~ value*** wartość odżywcza; **nu•tri•tion•ist** [nju:'trɪʃnɪst] *s* dietetyk *m*; **nu•tri•tious** [nju:'trɪʃəs] *adj* pożywny, zdrowy

nuts [nʌts] *adj infml* stuknięty; ***go ~*** sfiksować; ***drive s.o. ~*** doprowadzać kogoś do szału; ***be ~ about*** mieć bzika na punkcie *G*

'nut•shell *s* łupina *f* (orzecha); ***to put it in a ~*** krótko mówiąc

nut•ter ['nʌtə] *s infml* świr *m*

nut•ty ['nʌtɪ] *adj* **1.** orzechowy **2.** *infml* zwariowany, stuknięty

ny•lon ['naɪlɒn] *s* nylon *m*

nymph [nɪmf] *s* nimfa *f*

nym•pho•ma•ni•ac [nɪmfə'meɪnɪæk] *s* nimfomanka *f*

O

oaf [əʊf] *s* niezdara *m*; **oaf•ish** ['əʊfɪʃ] *adj* niezdarny

oak [ɛəʊk] *s BIOL* dąb *m*; **oak•en** ['əʊkən] *adj* dębowy

OAP [əʊeɪ'pi:] *abbr* (=***old age pensioner***) *Br* emeryt *m*

oar [ɔ:] *s* wiosło *n*; ***put*** (*a.* ***stick***) ***one's ~ in*** wtrącić swoje trzy grosze w *A*; **oars•man** *pl -men s* wioślarz *m*; **'oars•wom•an** *pl -men s* wioślarka *f*

o•a•sis [əʊ'eɪsɪs] *pl -ses* [əʊ'eɪsi:z] *s a. fig* oaza *f*; ***~ of calm*** oaza spokoju

oat [əʊt] *adj* owsiany; ***~ cakes*** ciasteczka owsiane

oath [əʊθ] *pl oaths* [əʊθz] *s* **1.** przysięga *f*; ***swear*** (*a.* ***take***) ***an ~*** złożyć przysięgę; ***on*** (*a.* ***under***) ***~*** pod przysięgą **2.** *dated* przekleństwo *n*

'oat•meal *s Am COOK* owsianka *f*

oats [əʊts] *pl BIOL* owies *m*; ***sow one's wild ~*** wyszumieć się

ob•du•ra•cy ['ɒbdərəsɪ] *s* upór *m*; **ob•du•rate** ['ɒbdərət] *adj* **1.** uparty **2.** *sinner*: zatwardziały

o•be•di•ence [ə'bi:dɪəns] *s* posłuszeństwo *n*; **o•be•di•ent** [ə'bi:dɪənt] *adj* posłuszny; **o•be•di•ent•ly** [ə'bi:dɪəntlɪ] *adv* posłusznie

ob•e•lisk ['ɒbəlɪsk] *s* obelisk *m*

o•bese [əʊ'bi:s] *adj* otyły; **o•bes•i•ty** [əʊ'bi:sɪtɪ] *s* otyłość *f*

o•bey [əʊ'beɪ] *v/t* **1.** słuchać ⟨po-⟩, być posłusznym **2.** *law*: przestrzegać **3.** *rule*: stosować ⟨za-⟩ się do *G*

o•bit•u•a•ry [ə'bɪtʊerɪ] *s* nekrolog *m*

ob•ject[1] ['ɑ:bdʒɪkt] *s* **1.** przedmiot *m*, rzecz *f*; ***everyday ~s*** przedmioty codziennego użytku **2.** przedmiot *m*, obiekt *m*; ***~ of desire*** przedmiot pożądania; ***~ of study*** przedmiot studiów; ***money is no ~*** pieniądze nie grają roli **3.** cel *m*; ***the ~ of the exercise*** cel ćwiczenia **4.** *GRAM* dopełnienie *n*

ob•ject[2] [əb'dʒekt] **I** *v/i* sprzeciwiać ⟨-wić⟩ się (**to** *D*), wnosić ⟨wnieść⟩ sprzeciw (**to** wobec *D*); ***many people ~ to the building of a new airport*** wiele osób sprzeciwia się budowie nowego lotniska; ***if you don't ~*** jeżeli nie masz nic przeciwko temu **II** *v/t* protestować ⟨za-⟩

ob•jec•tion [əb'dʒekʃn] *s* zastrzeżenie *n*, sprzeciw *m* (**to** wobec *G*); ***raise an ~*** wnieść sprzeciw; ***if you have no ~s*** jeżeli nie masz nic przeciwko temu **2.** zarzut *m*; **ob•jec•tion•a•ble** [əb'dʒekʃnəbl] *adj* **1.** budzący sprzeciw **2.** nieprzyjemny, niemiły

ob•jec•tive [əb'dʒektɪv] **I** *s* **1.** cel *m*; ***reach one's ~s*** osiągnąć swoje cele **2.** *PHOT* obiektyw *m* **II** *adj* obiektywny; **ob•jec•tiv•i•ty** [əb'dʒektɪvətɪ] *s* obiektywność *f*; **ob•jec•tive•ly** [əb'dʒektɪvlɪ] *adv* obiektywnie

'ob•ject les•son *s* **1.** lekcja *f* poglądowa **2.** przykład *m*

ob•jec•tor [əb'dʒektə] *s* przeciwnik *m*

ob•li•gated ['ɒblɪgeɪtɪd] *adj*: ***feel ~d to do s.th.*** czuć się zobowiązanym do zrobienia czegoś; **ob•li•ga•tion** [ɒblɪ'geɪʃn] *s* zobowiązanie *n*; ***under an ~ to do s.th.*** zobowiązany do zrobienia czegoś; ***financial ~s*** zobowiązania finansowe; **ob•lig•a•to•ry** [ə'blɪgətɒrɪ] *adj* obowiązkowy, przymusowy; ***attendance is ~*** obecność obowiązkowa

o•blige [ə'blaɪdʒ] *v/t* **1.** zobowiązywać ⟨-zać⟩; ***feel ~d to do s.th.*** czuć się zobowiązanym do zrobienia czegoś; ***I am much ~d to you*** jestem ci bardzo zobowiązany **2.** pomagać ⟨-móc⟩, być pomocnym; ***I'd be happy to ~*** z przyjemnością pomogę; **o•blig•ing** [ə'blaɪdʒɪŋ] *adj* uczynny

o•blique [ə'bliːk] *adj* **1.** niebezpośredni **2.** *line*: ukośny; **o•'blique angle** *s* kąt *m* wypukły

o•blit•er•ate [ə'blɪtəreɪt] *v/t* **1.** niszczyć ⟨z-⟩, równać ⟨z-⟩ z ziemią **2.** zasłaniać ⟨-łonić⟩ **3.** *memory*: wymazywać ⟨-zać⟩; **ob•lit•er•a•tion** [əblɪtər'eɪʃn] *s* **1.** zniszczenie *n*, zrównanie *n* z ziemią **2.** zasłonięcie *n*

o•bliv•i•on [ə'blɪvɪən] *s* **1.** zapomnienie *n*; ***fall*** (*a.* ***sink***) ***into ~*** popaść w zapomnienie, pójść w niepamięć **2.** nieprzytomność *f*; ***he often drinks himself into ~*** często upija się do nieprzytomności; **o•bliv•i•ous** [ə'blɪvɪəs] *adj* nieświadomy (**to**/**of** *G*)

ob•long ['ɒblɒːŋ] **I** *adj* **1.** *Br* prostokątny **2.** *Am* podłużny **II** *s* prostokąt *m*

ob•nox•ious [əb'nɒkʃəs] *adj* odrażający, wstrętny

o•boe ['əʊbəʊ] *s* *MUS* obój *m*; **o•bo•ist** ['əʊbəʊɪst] *s* *MUS* oboista *m*

ob•scene [əb'siːn] *adj* obsceniczny, nieprzyzwoity; **ob•scen•i•ty** [əb'senətɪ] *s* obsceniczność *f*, nieprzyzwoitość *f*

ob•scure [əb'skjʊə] **I** *adj* **1.** niejasny, trudny do zrozumienia; ***for some ~ reason*** z jakiegoś niejasnego powodu **2.** mało znany **II** *v/t* zaciemniać ⟨-nić⟩, zasłaniać ⟨-łonić⟩; **ob•scu•ri•ty** [əb'skjʊərətɪ] *s* **1.** niejasność *f* **2.** anonimowość *f*

ob•se•qui•ous [əb'siːkwɪəs] *adj* służalczy; **ob•se•qui•ous•ness** [əb'siːkwɪəsnɪs] *s* służalczość *f*

ob•serv•a•ble [əb'zɜːvəbl] *adj* zauważalny, widoczny; **ob•ser•vance** [əb'zɜːvns] *s* **1.** *law*: przestrzeganie *n* **2.** *Christmas*: obchodzenie **3.** ***religious ~s*** *REL* praktyki religijne; **ob•ser•vant** [əb'zɜːvnt] *adj* **1.** spostrzegawczy **2.** *form* religijny; **ob•ser•va•tion** [ɒbzə'veɪʃn] *s* **1.** obserwacja *f*; ***keep s.o. under ~*** obserwować kogoś; ***powers of ~*** spostrzegawczość *f* **2.** komentarz *m*, uwaga *f* (**about**/**on** na temat *G*); **ob•ser•va•to•ry** [əb'zɜːvətərɪ] *s* obserwatorium *m*; **observe** [əb'zɜːv] *v/t* **1.** zauważać ⟨-żyć⟩, spostrzegać ⟨-rzec⟩; ***they ~d a man enter the building*** widzieli, jak do budynku wszedł mężczyzna **2.** obserwować ⟨za-⟩ **3.** (*say*) zauważać ⟨-żyć⟩ **4.** *law*: przestrzegać **5.** *Christmas*: obchodzić; **ob•serv•er** [əb'zɜːvə] *s* obserwator *m*

ob•sess [əb'ses] *v/t*: ***be ~ed with*** (*a.* ***by***) mieć obsesję na punkcie *G*; **ob•session** [əb'seʃn] *s* **1.** obsesja *f* (**with** na punkcie *G*) **2.** natręctwo *n*; **obsession•al** [əb'seʃnl] *adj* obsesyjny; ***~ neurosis*** nerwica natręctw; **ob•sessive** [əb'sesɪv] *adj* obsesyjny

ob•so•les•cence [ɒbsə'lesəns] *s* **1.** przestarzałość *f*; ***built-in ~*** zakładana żywotność **2.** wychodzenie *n* z użycia; **ob•so•les•cent** [ɒbsə'lesnt] *adj* wychodzący z użycia; **'ob•so•lete** ['ɒbsəliːt] *adj* przestarzały

ob•sta•cle ['ɒbstəkl] *s* przeszkoda *f*; ***overcome all ~s*** pokonać wszystkie przeszkody; ***be an ~ to*** być przeszkodą na drodze do *G*; **'ob•sta•cle course** *s* tor *m* przeszkód; **ob•sta•cle race** *s* *SPORT* bieg *m* z przeszkodami

ob•ste•tri•cian [ɒbstə'trɪʃn] *s* *MED* położnik *m*; **ob•stet•rics** [əb'stetrɪks] *s* *MED* położnictwo *n*

ob•sti•na•cy ['ɒbstɪnəsɪ] *s* upór *m*; **ob•sti•nate** ['ɒbstɪnət] *adj* uparty; **ob•sti•nate•ly** ['ɒbstɪnətlɪ] *adv* uparcie

ob•strep•er•ous [əb'strepərəs] *adj* **1.** krnąbrny **2.** krzykliwy, hałaśliwy

ob•struct [əb'strʌkt] *v/t* **1.** blokować ⟨za-⟩ **2.** *view*: zasłaniać ⟨-łonić⟩ **3.** *work*: utrudniać ⟨-nić⟩ **4.** *MED* zatykać ⟨-tkać⟩, czopować ⟨za-⟩; **ob•struc•tion** [əb'strʌkʃn] *s* **1.** przeszkoda *f* **2.** *AUTO* zator *m*, ***cause an ~*** blokować przejazd, tamować ruch uliczny **3.** utrudnianie *n*; ***~ of justice*** utrudnianie pracy sądowi **4.** zator *n* **5.** zasłonięcie *n* **6.** *MED* niedrożność *f* **7.** *SPORT* faul *m*, (niedozwolone) zatrzymanie *n*; **ob•struc•tion•ism** [əb'strʌkʃənɪzəm] *s POL* obstrukcjonizm *m*, stosowanie *n* obstrukcji (parlamentarnej); **ob•struc•tive** [əb'strʌktɪv] *adj*: ***be ~*** *(person)* stwarzać trudności

ob•tain [əb'teɪn] **I** *v/t* otrzymywać ⟨-mać⟩, uzyskiwać ⟨-kać⟩ **II** *v/i* **1.** obowiązywać, być ważnym; **ob•tain•a•ble** [əb'teɪnəbl] *adj* **1.** możliwy do uzyskania, osiągalny; ***full details are ~ from any post office*** szczegółowe informacje można uzyskać w każdym urzędzie pocztowym **2.** do kupienia, dostępny

ob•trude [əb'tru:d] **I** *v/t* narzucać ⟨-cić⟩ (***s.th. on*** coś *D*, ***oneself on*** się *D*) **II** *v/i* narzucać ⟨-cić⟩ się (***on*** *D*); ***~ upon s.o.'s privacy*** naruszać czyjąś prywatność; **ob•tru•sive** [əb'tru:sɪv] *adj* **1.** natrętny, uciążliwy **2.** rzucający się w oczy

ob•tuse [əb'tju:s] *adj* **1.** nierozgarnięty; ***be deliberately ~*** udawać głupiego **2.** *angle*: rozwarty

ob•vi•ate ['ɒbvɪeɪt] *v/t*: ***~ the need for*** sprawiać, że coś staje się niepotrzebne

O

ob•vi•ous ['ɒbvɪəs] *adj* oczywisty, jasny; ***for ~ reasons*** z oczywistych względów; ***state the ~*** stwierdzić oczywisty fakt; **ob•vi•ous•ly** ['ɒbvɪəslɪ] *adv* oczywiście

oc•ca•sion [ə'keɪʒn] **I** *s* **1.** okazja *f*, sytuacja *f*; ***on one ~*** (jeden) raz; ***on several ~s*** kilka razy, kilkakrotnie; ***on ~(s)*** okazjonalnie, sporadycznie; ***take the ~ to do s.th.*** wykorzystać okazję, aby coś zrobić; ***rise to the ~*** stanąć na wysokości zadania **2.** okazja *f*, wydarzenie *n*; ***on this ~*** przy tej okazji; ***on the ~ of*** z okazji *G* **3.** powód *m* (***for***/***of*** do *G*) **II** *v/t* powodować ⟨s-⟩, wywoływać ⟨-łać⟩; **oc•ca•sion•al** [ə'keɪʒənl] *adj* okazjonalny, sporadyczny; ***she drinks an ~ glass of wine*** od czasu do czasu wypija kieliszek wina; **oc•ca•sion•al•ly** [ə'keɪʒnlɪ] *adv* czasami, okazjonalnie, sporadycznie

oc•ci•den•tal [ɒksɪ'dentl] *adj* zachodni, okcydentalny

oc•cult ['ɒkʌlt] **I** *adj* **1.** okultystyczny **2.** *powers*: nadprzyrodzony **II** *s* ***the ~*** okultyzm; **oc•cult•ism** ['ɒkəltɪzəm] *s* okultyzm *m*

oc•cu•pant ['ɒkjʊpənt] *s* **1.** *house, building*: mieszkaniec *m*, lokator *m* **2.** *car*: pasażer *m*

oc•cu•pa•tion [ɒkjʊ'peɪʃn] *s* **1.** zawód *m*, zajęcie *n*; ***state your name, age and ~*** proszę podać nazwisko, wiek i zawód; ***by ~*** z zawodu **2.** zajęcie *n*; ***her main ~ seems to be shopping*** jej głównym zajęciem jest robienie zakupów **3.** okupacja *f*; ***under ~*** pod okupacją; ***~ troops*** wojska okupacyjne **4.** (*house, building*) ***ready for ~*** gotowy do zamieszkania; ***be in ~ of a flat*** zajmować mieszkanie; **oc•cu•pa•tion•al** [ɒkjʊ'peɪʃənl] *adj* zawodowy; **oc•cu•'pa•tion•al ac•ci•dent** *s* wypadek *m* przy pracy; **oc•cu•pa•tion•al dis•'ease** *s* choroba *f* zawodowa; **oc•cu•pa•tion•al 'haz•ard** *s* ryzyko *n* zawodowe; **oc•cu•pa•tion•al health and 'safe•ty** *s* bezpieczeństwo *n* i higiena *f* pracy; **oc•cu•pa•tion•al 'ther•a•pist** *s* terapeuta *m* zajęciowy; **oc•cu•pa•tion•al 'ther•a•py** *s* terapia *f* zajęciowa; **oc•cu•pi•er** ['ɒkjʊpaɪə] **1.** mieszkaniec *m*, lokator *m* **2.** najemca *m* **3.** okupant *m*

oc•cu•py ['ɒkjʊpaɪ] *v/t* **1.** zajmować ⟨-jąć⟩; ***~ oneself with*** zajmować się *I*; ***is the seat occupied?*** czy to miejsce jest zajęte?; ***~ s.o.'s mind*** zaprzątać czyjeś myśli **2.** okupować

oc•cur [ə'kɜ:] *v/i* **1.** zdarzać ⟨-rzyć⟩ się, mieć miejsce **2.** (*mistake*) występować ⟨-pić⟩ **3.** (*death*) następować ⟨-pić⟩ **4.** występować ⟨-pić⟩; ***sugar ~s in fruit*** cukier występuje w owocach **5.** przychodzić ⟨przyjść⟩ do głowy (***to*** *D*, ***that*** że); ***it didn't ~ to her to ask for help*** nie przyszło jej na myśl, żeby poprosić o pomoc; **oc•cur•rence** [ə'kʌrəns] *s* **1.** zjawisko *n*; ***be a frequent ~*** zdarzać się często **2.** zdarzenie *n*, wydarzenie *n* **3.** wystąpienie *n* **4.** występowanie *n*

o•cean ['əʊʃn] *s* ocean *m*; ***an ~** (a. **~s**) **of*** mnóstwo *G*; **o•cean 'floor** *s* dno *n* oceanu; **o•cean•go•ing** ['əʊʃngəʊɪŋ] *adj ship*: oceaniczny; **o•cean 'lin•er** *s* liniowiec *m* oceaniczny

o•ce•an•og•ra•phy [əʊʃn'ɒgrəfɪ] *s* oceanografia *f*

o•chre ['əʊkə] *Br*, ***o•cher*** *Am s* ochra *f*

o'clock [ə'klɒk] *adv*: ***at 5 ~*** o godzinie piątej; ***before 11 ~*** przed godziną jedenastą

oc•ta•gon ['ɒktəgən] *s* MATH ośmiokąt *m*, ośmiobok *m*; **oc•tag•o•nal** [ɒk'tægənl] *adj* ośmiokątny, ośmioboczny

oc•tane ['ɒkteɪn] *s* CHEM oktan *m*; ***~ number*** liczba oktanowa; ***high-~ fuel*** paliwo wysokooktanowe

oc•tave ['ɒktɪv] *s* MUS oktawa *f*

Oc•to•ber [ɒk'təʊbər] *s* październik *m*; ***in ~*** w październiku

oc•to•ge•nar•i•an [ɒktəʊdʒə'nerɪən] *s*: ***be an ~*** być po osiemdziesiątce

oc•to•pus ['ɒktəpəs] *pl -puses s* BIOL ośmiornica *f*

oc•u•lar ['ɒkjʊlə] *adj muscle*: oczny; **oc•u•list** ['ɒkjʊlɪst] *s dated* okulista *m*

OCR *abbr* (=***optical character recognition***) INF OCR *n*, komputerowe rozpoznawanie *n* pisma

OD [əʊ'diː] *abbr* (=***overdose***) *infml* przedawkowywać ⟨-kować⟩

odd [ɒd] *adj* **1.** dziwny, osobliwy **2.** ***we can all make the ~ mistake*** każdemu z nas zdarza się czasem popełnić błąd **3.** różny, rozmaity **4.** *shoe, sock*: nie do pary **5.** *number*: nieparzysty **6.** jakiś; ***he has worked here for twenty-odd years*** pracuje tu jakieś dwadzieścia lat **7.** ***be the ~ one out*** nie pasować, odstawać od reszty; **'odd•ball** *s infml* dziwak *m*

odd•i•ty ['ɒdɪtɪ] *s* **1.** dziwność *f*, osobliwość *f* **2.** dziwadło *n*, dziwoląg *m*

odd•ly ['ɒdlɪ] *adv* dziwnie, osobliwie; ***~ enough*** to dziwne, ale

odd-'job man *pl* **~men** *s*: ***be an ~ Br*** wykonywać różne drobne prace; **odd 'jobs** *pl* (różne) drobne prace *pl*

odds [ɒdz] *pl* **1.** szanse *pl* (powodzenia), prawdopodobieństwo *n*; ***~ 10 to 1*** szanse (jak) 10 do 1; ***the ~ are that he will come*** jest bardzo prawdopodobne, że przyjdzie; ***the ~ are in our favour*** mamy duże szanse; ***the ~ are against us*** mamy małe szanse **2.** ***against all the ~*** wbrew wszelkim oczekiwaniom **3.** ***be at ~ with*** nie pasować do *G*, stać w sprzeczności z *I*; ***be at ~ with s.o. over*** nie zgadzać się z kimś w kwestii *G*; ***it makes no ~ Br** infml* wszystko jedno **4.** (*betting*) notowania *pl*; **odds and 'ends**, ***odds and 'sods** Br pl* drobiazgi *pl*; **odds-'on** *adj*: ***it is ~ that*** jest prawie pewne, że; ***~ favourite*** pewniak

o•di•ous ['əʊdɪəs] *adj* okropny, odrażający

o•dom•e•ter [əʊ'dɒmətə] *s* AUTO *Am* licznik *m* (mil)

o•dor *Am* → ***odour***

o•dour ['əʊdə] *Br*, ***o•dor*** *Am s* zapach *m*, smród *m*; **o•dour•less** ['əʊdələs] *Br*, ***o•dor•less*** *Am adj* bez zapachu, bezwonny

od•ys•sey ['ɒdɪsɪ] *s* odyseja *f*

Oed•i•pus com•plex ['iːdɪpəs kɒmpleks] *s* PSYCH kompleks *m* Edypa

oe•soph•a•gus [ɪ'sɒfəgəs] *Br*, ***eso•phagus*** *Am pl -gi* [~gaɪ], *-guses* [~gəsɪs] *s* ANAT przełyk *m*

oes•tro•gen ['iːstrədʒən] *Br*, **es•tro•gen** *Am s* estrogen *m*

of [əv], *strong form* [ɒv] *prep* **1.** (*belonging or connection*) ***the paintings ~ Monet*** obrazy Moneta; ***the director ~ the company*** dyrektor firmy; ***a member ~ the team*** członek drużyny; ***some ~ his friends*** niektórzy z jego przyjaciół; ***a few ~ the problems*** kilka problemów **2.** (*origin*) z *G*; ***Mr Brown ~ London*** pan Brown z Londynu; ***a woman ~ Italian descent*** kobieta włoskiego pochodzenia; ***people ~ Wales*** mieszkańcy Walii **3.** (*identity*) ***a map ~ India*** mapa Indii; ***a photo ~ my dog*** zdjęcie mojego psa **4.** (*topic*) o *L*; ***he told us ~ his travels*** opowiedział nam o swoich podróżach; ***she dreams ~ a new life*** marzy o nowym życiu **5.** (*contents*) ***a crowd ~ people*** tłum ludzi; ***a glass ~ milk*** szklanka mleka **6.** (*material*) z *G*; ***a dress ~ silk*** sukienka z jedwabiu, jedwabna sukienka; ***made ~ steel*** ze stali **7.** (*quantity*) ***2 kilos ~ potatoes*** 2 kilo ziemniaków; ***an increase ~ 2%*** wzrost o 2%; ***a girl***

~ 12 dziewczynka w wieku 12 lat **8.** (*place*) **north ~ London** na północ od Londynu; **the battle ~ Hastings** bitwa pod Hastings **9.** (*time*) **the fourth ~ July** czwarty lipca; **your letter ~ March 3rd** Pański list z trzeciego marca; **at the time ~ the revolution** w czasie rewolucji

off [ɑf] **I** *adv* **1.** (*space, time*) **I must be ~ soon** muszę niedługo wyjść; **three miles ~** trzy mile stąd; **a solution is still some way ~** do rozwiązania jest jeszcze daleko; **they are ~!** SPORT ruszyli! **2.** (*remove*) **he's had his beard shaved ~** zgolił brodę; **take your coat ~** zdejmij płaszcz **3.** odwołany; **the wedding is ~** ślub został odwołany **4.** wyłączony, zakręcony; **the water is ~** woda jest zakręcona; **make sure the TV is ~** sprawdź, czy telewizor jest wyłączony **5.** (*free*) **a day ~** dzień wolny; **I've got three days ~ this week** w tym tygodniu mam trzy dni wolne; **she's ~ today** ma dziś wolne; **how many days did you take ~?** ile wziąłeś wolnego? **6.** (*discount*) **5% ~** pięcioprocentowa obniżka; **all shirts 10% ~** wszystkie koszule 10% taniej **7. s.o. is better ~** komuś się lepiej powodzi, ktoś jest lepiej sytuowany; **we would have been better ~ staying at home** lepiej by było, gdybyśmy zostali w domu; **~ and on, on and ~** od czasu do czasu **II** *prep* **1.** (*leaving*) od *G*, z *G*; **fall ~ a ladder** spaść z drabiny; **he jumped ~ the bus** wyskoczył z autobusu; **keep ~ the grass!** nie deptać trawników! **2.** (*distance*) od *G*; **100 metres ~ the summit** 100 metrów od szczytu **3.** (*sea*) u *G*, od *G*; **an island ~ the coast of Spain** wyspa u wybrzeży Hiszpanii; **six miles ~ Portsmouth** sześć mil od Portsmouth **4.** (*remove*) z *G*, od *G*; **cut a piece ~** odkroić kawałek *G*; **a button came ~ my shirt** odpadł mi guzik od koszuli **5.** (*direction, subject*) z *G*, od *G*; **we're going ~ the subject** odchodzimy od tematu; **the ship was blown ~ course** statek zszedł z kursu; **a street ~ the High Street** ulica odchodząca od High Street **6.** (*free*) od *G*; **he had 10 days ~ school** miał 10 dni wolnego od szkoły **7.** (*discount*) od *G*; **knock $500 ~ the price** opuścić cenę o 500 dolarów **8.** (*stop being interested in*) **he's finally ~ drugs** nareszcie przestał brać narkotyki; **I'm ~ alcohol for a week** przez tydzień nie piję alkoholu **III** *adj* **1.** zepsuty, nieświeży; **the fish has gone ~** ryba się zepsuła **2.** *period, day*: gorszy; **this is one of his ~ days** to jeden z jego gorszych dni **3.** *Br infml* niemiły, nieuprzejmy; **he was a bit ~ with me this morning** był dla mnie niezbyt uprzejmy dziś rano **4.** *Br infml* nie do zaakceptowania

off•'beat *adj infml* nieszablonowy, niekonwencjonalny

off-'cen•tre *Br*, **off-'cen•ter** *Am adj*: **be ~** nie być na samym środku

off-'col•our *Br*, **off-'col•or** *Am adj* **1. feel** (*a.* **be**) **~** nie czuć się najlepiej **2.** *joke*: pikantny

of•fence [ə'fens] *Br*, **of•fense** *Am s* **1.** przestępstwo *n*, wykroczenie *n*; **commit an ~** popełnić przestępstwo; **an ~ against humanity** zbrodnia przeciwko ludzkości **2.** obraza *f*, zniewaga *f*; **he meant no ~** nie miał zamiaru nikogo obrazić; **cause ~ to s.o.** obrazić kogoś; **take ~** obrazić się; **no ~** bez urazy

of•fend [ə'fend] **I** *v/t* obrażać ⟨-razić⟩; **they will be ~ed if** obrażą się, jeśli; **he didn't mean to ~ anybody** nie chciał nikogo obrazić; **she looked ~ed** wyglądała na obrażoną **II** *v/i* **1.** obrażać ⟨-razić⟩ (**against** *A*); **~ against s.o.'s religious beliefs** obrażać czyjeś uczucia religijne **2.** *form* łamać ⟨z-⟩ prawo; **of•fend•er** [ə'fendə] *s* **1.** przestępca *m* **2.** sprawca *m* wykroczenia; **he's a first ~** nie był wcześniej karany; **of•fend•ing** [ə'fendɪŋ] *adj* **1.** problematyczny, kontrowersyjny **2.** JUR winny; **an ~ driver** kierowca, który złamał przepisy

of•fense *s* **1.** *Am* → **offence 2.** *Am* SPORT (**the**) **~** atak

of•fen•sive [ə'fensɪv] **I** *adj* **1.** obraźliwy; **~ behaviour** obraźliwe zachowanie **2.** *smell*: odpychający **3.** *war*: ofensywny **4.** *Am* SPORT ofensywny, w ataku **II** *s* **1.** (*war*) ofensywa *f*; **take** (*a.* **go on**) **the ~** przejść do ofensywy **2.** SPORT atak *m* **3.** kampania *f*; **of-**

fen•sive•ness [ə'fensɪvnɪs] *s behaviour, style*: obraźliwość *f*

of•fer ['ɒfə] **I** *v/t* oferować ⟨za-⟩, proponować ⟨za-⟩; ***they ~ed her a job*** zaoferowali jej pracę; ***the kids ~ed to do the dishes*** dzieci zaproponowały, że pozmywają naczynia; ***have s.th. to ~*** mieć coś do zaoferowania **II** *s* **1.** oferta *f*; ***a job ~*** oferta pracy; ***make an ~*** złożyć ofertę; ***on ~*** **a)** w ofercie **b)** na sprzedaż **2.** propozycja *f*; ***an ~ of marriage*** propozycja małżeństwa; ***accept*** (***decline***) ***an ~*** przyjąć (odrzucić) propozycję **3.** (***special***) **~** promocja, oferta specjalna; ***on*** (***special***) **~** w promocji

off'hand I *adj* niedbały, lekceważący; ***be ~ about*** lekceważyć *A* **II** *adv* na poczekaniu, bez zastanowienia

of•fice ['ɒfɪs] *s* **1.** biuro *n*; ***are you going to the ~ today?*** idziesz dziś do biura?; ***tourist ~*** biuro informacji turystycznej; ***~ block***, ***~ building*** biurowiec **2.** *Am* gabinet *m* **3.** *Br* ministerstwo *n*; ***the Foreign ~*** Ministerstwo Spraw Zagranicznych; ***the Home ~*** Ministerstwo Spraw Wewnętrznych **4.** urząd *m*, funkcja *f*; ***hold ~***, ***be in ~*** sprawować urząd **5.** władza *f*; ***be out of ~*** nie być przy władzy; ***take ~*** przejąć władzę; **'of•fice boy** *s dated* pomocnik *m* biurowy; **'of•fice girl** *s dated* pomocnica *f* biurowa; **'of•fice•hold•er** *s* urzędnik *m* (wysokiego szczebla); **'of•fice hours** *pl* godziny *pl* urzędowania; **of•fice 'jun•ior** *s* pracownik *m* biurowy

of•fi•cer ['ɒfɪsə] *s* **1.** oficer *m*; ***naval ~*** oficer marynarki **2.** urzędnik *m* (wysokiego szczebla) **3.** (***police***) **~** policjant *m*, funkcjonariusz *m* policji

'of•fice sup•plies *pl* artykuły *pl* biurowe; **'of•fice work•er** *s* pracownik *m* biurowy

of•fi•cial [ə'fɪʃl] **I** *adj* **1.** oficjalny; ***~ version of the events*** oficjalna wersja wydarzeń **2.** służbowy; ***~ responsibilities*** obowiązki służbowe **3.** urzędowy; ***~ language*** język urzędowy **II** *s* urzędnik *m*; **of•fi•cial•dom** [ə'fɪʃldəm] *s*, urzędnicy *pl*, aparat *pl* urzędniczy; **of•fi•cial•ese** [əfɪʃə'liːz] *s* język *m* urzędniczy; **of•fi•cial•ly** [ə'fɪʃlɪ] *adv* oficjalnie

of•fi•ci•ate [ə'fɪʃɪeɪt] *v/t* **1.** przewodniczyć (***at*** *D*) **2.** *mass*: celebrować (***at*** *A*)

of•fi•cious [ə'fɪʃəs] *adj* **1.** gorliwy **2.** ***be ~*** lubić rozkazywać

off•ing ['ɒfɪŋ] *s*: ***be in the ~*** *infml* szykować się; ***I hear there are some changes in the ~*** *infml* podobno szykują się jakieś zmiany

'off-li•cence *s Br* sklep *m* monopolowy, sklep *m* z alkoholem

'off-line *adj* INF offline, odłączony

off-'peak *adj* **1.** poza godzinami szczytu **2.** poza sezonem

'off-put•ting *adj Br* odpychający

'off•ramp *s Am* zjazd *m* z autostrady

off-road 've•hi•cle *s* **1.** samochód *m* terenowy **2.** pojazd *m* terenowy

off-'sea•son I *s* ***in the ~*** poza sezonem **II** *adj* pozasezonowy

'off•set I *v/t* **1.** równoważyć ⟨z-⟩ **2.** *Br* odliczać ⟨-czyć⟩ (***against*** od *G*) **II** *adj print*: offsetowy

'off•shoot *s* **1.** pęd *m* boczny, odrost *m* **2.** *fig* odgałęzienie *n*

off•'shore *adj* **1.** przybrzeżny **2.** *wind*: od lądu **3.** *company*: zarejestrowany w raju podatkowym, offshore

'off•side I *adj* **1.** SPORT spalony; ***be ~*** być na spalonym **2.** AUTO po stronie kierowcy **II** *s* **1.** SPORT spalony *m*, ofsajd *m* **2.** AUTO strona *f* kierowcy

'off•spring *pl offspring s* **1.** potomek *m* **2.** (*children*) potomstwo *n* **3.** (*animal*) młode *n*

off•'stage I *adv* poza sceną, za kulisami **II** *adj voice*: (dochodzący) spoza sceny

off-street 'park•ing *s* (prywatne) miejsca parkingowe *pl*

off-the-'cuff I *adj remark*: spontaniczny **II** *adv* **1.** *speak*: bez przygotowania **2.** *answer*: bez namysłu

off-the-'rec•ord I *adj* nieoficjalny **II** *adv* nieoficjalnie

off-the-'wall *adj infml* zwariowany

off-'white *adj* w kolorze złamanej bieli

of•ten ['ɒfn] *adv* często; ***more ~*** częściej; ***how ~*** jak często; ***it's not ~ that*** nieczęsto; ***all too ~*** (aż) nazbyt często; ***as ~ as possible*** tak często, jak to tylko możliwe; ***every so ~*** od czasu do czasu; ***as ~ as not***, ***more ~ than not*** zazwyczaj, bardzo często

O

o•gle ['əʊgl] *v/t* patrzeć ⟨po-⟩ pożądliwie na *A*, pożerać wzrokiem *A*
o•gre ['əʊg] *s* ogr *m*
oh [əʊ] *interj* och!; *~ no!* o, nie!; *~ dear!* o mój Boże!
OHP [əʊeɪtʃ'piː] *abbr* (=***overhead projector***) rzutnik *m*
oil [ɔɪl] **I** *s* **1.** ropa *f* naftowa **2.** olej *m*; ***engine ~*** olej silnikowy; ***vegetable ~*** olej roślinny; ***olive ~*** oliwa z oliwek **3.** olejek *m*; ***suntan ~*** olejek do opalania **4.** ***~s*** farby olejne; ***a painting in ~*** obraz olejny **5.** obraz *m* olejny **II** *v/t* TECH oliwić ⟨na-⟩; **'oil can** *s* TECH olejarka *f*; **'oil change** *s* wymiana *f* oleju; **'oil com•pa•ny** *s* spółka *f* naftowa; **'oil•field** *s* pole *n* naftowe; **'oil-fired** *adj heating*: olejowy; **'oil lamp** *s* lampa *f* naftowa; **'oil lev•el** *s* AUTO poziom *m* oleju; **'oil paint** *s* farba *f* olejna; **'oil paint•ing** *s* obraz *m* olejny; **'oil pipe•line** *s* rurociąg *m* naftowy, naftociąg *m*; **'oil re•fin•e•ry** *s* rafineria *f* naftowa; **'oil rig**, ***oil plat•form*** *Am s* **1.** platforma *f* naftowa **2.** szyb *m* naftowy; **oil•seed 'rape** *s* rzepak *m*; **'oil•skins** *pl* sztormiak *m*; **'oil slick** *s* (*sea surface*) plama *f* ropy; **'oil sump** AUTO miska *f* olejowa; **'oil tank•er** *s* (*ship*) tankowiec *m*; **'oil well** *s* szyb *m* naftowy
oil•y ['ɔɪlɪ] *adj* **1.** tłusty, zatłuszczony **2.** oleisty **3.** *fig* wazeliniarski
oint•ment ['ɔɪntmənt] *s* MED maść *f*
ok [əʊ'keɪ] *infml* **I** *interj* OK, dobrze **II** *adv* dobrze, w porządku, OK; ***are you ~?*** nic ci nie jest?, wszystko w porządku?; ***is it ~ if I go now?*** czy mogę już iść? **III** *adj* OK, niezły **IV** *s infml* zgoda *f*, akceptacja *f* **V** *v/t* akceptować ⟨za-⟩
old [əʊld] *adj* stary; ***he is 18 years ~*** on ma osiemnaście lat; ***how ~ are you?*** ile masz lat?; ***a ten-year-~ boy*** dziesięcioletni chłopiec; ***grow*** (*a.* ***get***) ***~*** starzeć się; ***~ habits*** stare nawyki; ***in the ~ days*** dawniej; ***she's an ~ friend of mine*** jest moją starą przyjaciółką; ***the ~*** starsi ludzie; ***as ~ as the hills*** stary jak świat; ***the good ~ days*** stare, dobre czasy; ***the ~ World*** Stary Świat; ***have a fine ~ time*** świetnie się bawić; ***come any ~ time*** *infml* przyjdź, kiedy ci pasuje
old 'age *s* starość *f*; ***die of ~*** umrzeć ze starości; **old-age 'pen•sion** *s Br* emerytura *f*; **old-age 'pen•sion•er** *s Br* emeryt *m*
'old boy *s* były uczeń *m*, absolwent *m*; **old-'fash•ioned** *adj* **1.** *clothes*: niemodny **2.** *opinions*: staromodny, staroświecki; **'old girl** *s Br* była uczennica, absolwentka *f*; **old 'guard** *s*: ***the ~*** stara gwardia; **old 'hand** *s* stary wyjadacz *m*; ***be an ~ at*** mieć duże doświadczenie w *L*; **old•ie** ['əʊldɪ] *s infml* **1.** (*person*) staruszek *m* **2.** (*song*) przebój *m* sprzed lat; **old 'maid** *s* stara panna *f*; **Old 'Test•a•ment** *s*: ***the ~*** Stary Testament *m*; **old 'wives' tale** *s* bajka *f*, bajeczka *f*
ol•fac•to•ry [ɒl'fæktərɪ] *adj* **1.** *nerve*: węchowy **2.** *sense*: węchu
ol•i•gar•chy ['ɒlɪgɑːkɪ] *s* oligarchia *f*
ol•ive ['ɒlɪv] **I** *s* oliwka *f* **II** *adj* **1.** *colour, tree*: oliwkowy **2.** *grove*: oliwny; **olive 'oil** *s* oliwa *m* z oliwek
O•lym•pi•ad [ə'lɪmpɪæd] *s* olimpiada *f*; **O•lym•pic** [ə'lɪmpɪk] *adj* olimpijski; ***~ medallist*** medalista olimpijski; ***~ athlete*** olimpijczyk; **O•lym•pic 'Games** *pl*: ***the ~*** igrzyska olimpijskie; **O•lym•pics** [ə'lɪmpɪks] *s pl*: ***the ~*** olimpiada
om•buds•man ['ɒmbʊdzmən] *pl -men s* rzecznik *m* praw obywatelskich, ombudsman *m*
om•e•lette ['ɒmlɪt], ***om•e•let*** *Am s* omlet *m*
om•i•nous ['ɒmɪnəs] *adj* złowieszczy, złowrogi; **om•i•nous•ly** ['ɒmɪnəslɪ] *adv* złowieszczo, złowrogo
o•mis•sion [əʊ'mɪʃn] *s* **1.** pominięcie *n* **2.** przeoczenie *n* **3.** zaniedbanie *n*
o•mit [əʊ'mɪt] *v/t* **1.** pomijać ⟨-minąć⟩ **2.** nie uwzględniać ⟨-nić⟩ (***from*** w *L*); ***he was ~ted from the list*** nie został umieszczony na liście **3.** ***~ to do s.th.*** nie zrobić czegoś; ***she ~ted to mention that*** nie wspomniała, że
om•ni•bus ['ɒmnɪbəs] *s* **1.** antologia *f*, zbiór *m* (dzieł) **2.** *dated* autobus *m*
om•nip•o•tence [ɒmnɪpətəns] *s* wszechmoc *f*; **om•nip•o•tent** [ɒm'nɪpətənt] *adj* wszechmocny, wszechmogący
om•nis•ci•ence [ɒm'nɪsɪəns] *s* wszechwiedza *f*; **om•nis•ci•ent** [ɒm'nɪsɪənt] *adj* wszechwiedzący

O

on [ɒn] **I** *prep* **1.** (*position*) na *L*, (*direction*) na *A*; ***a picture ~ a wall*** obraz na ścianie; ***the diagram ~ page 5*** wykres na stronie 5; ***put it down ~ the table*** połóż to na stole; ***a town ~ the Thames*** miasto nad Tamizą; ***a house ~ the coast*** dom na wybrzeżu; ***drop s.th. ~ the floor*** upuścić coś na podłogę; ***hang s.th. ~ a peg*** powiesić coś na wieszaku **2.** (*transport*) ***~ a plane*** (***train***) w samolocie (pociągu); ***travel ~ the bus*** (***tram***) jechać autobusem (tramwajem); ***I came ~ my bike*** przyjechałem rowerem **3.** (*day, date*) w *A*; ***~ Sunday*** w niedzielę; ***~ May the first*** pierwszego maja; ***~ your birthday*** w dniu twoich urodzin **4.** (*time*) zaraz po *L*; ***~ his return*** zaraz po jego powrocie; ***~ arriving home*** zaraz po przyjściu do domu **5.** (*topic*) o *L*, na temat *G*; ***book ~ Africa*** książka o Afryce; ***test ~ irregular verbs*** test z czasowników nieregularnych **6.** (*with*) przy *L*; ***have you got any money ~ you?*** masz przy sobie (jakieś) pieniądze? **7.** (*belonging*) w *L*; ***be ~ the jury*** być w jury; ***whose side are you ~?*** po czyjej jesteś stronie? **8.** (*state*) na *L*; ***be ~ a diet*** być na diecie; ***be ~ antibiotics*** brać antybiotyki; ***be ~ holiday*** być na wakacjach **9.** (*direction*) ***~ the left*** po lewej stronie; ***he turned his back ~ us*** odwrócił się do nas plecami **10.** (*reason, implication*) ***~ their advice*** za ich radą; ***story based ~ facts*** historia oparta na faktach **11.** (*support*) z *G*; ***live ~ pension*** żyć z renty **12.** (*media*) ***~ the Internet*** w Internecie; ***~ TV*** w telewizji; ***~ Channel 4*** na kanale 4; ***speak ~ the phone*** rozmawiać przez telefon **II** *adv* **1.** *work, go*: dalej, przed siebie; ***he worked ~ without a break*** pracował dalej bez przerwy; ***read ~*** czytaj dalej; ***go straight ~*** idź prosto; ***from then ~*** od tego czasu; ***~ and ~*** bez przerwy, stale **2.** *have*: na sobie; *put*: na siebie; ***put your coat ~!*** nałóż płaszcz!; ***what did she have ~?*** co ona miała na sobie? **3.** *light, TV*: włączony; ***switch ~ the light!*** włącz światło! **4.** (*event*) ***be ~*** **a)** trwać **b)** być w planach; ***what's ~ at the cinema?*** co grają w kinie?; ***there was a war ~ at the time*** wówczas trwała wojna; ***we don't have anything ~ this weekend*** na ten weekend niczego nie zaplanowaliśmy

once [wʌns] **I** *adv* **1.** raz; ***~ a week*** raz w tygodniu; ***~ or twice*** raz czy dwa (razy); ***~ in a while*** raz na jakiś czas, od czasu do czasu; ***~ and for all*** raz na zawsze; ***not ~*** ani razu; ***all at ~*** **a)** nagle **b)** na raz, za jednym razem; ***at ~*** **a)** natychmiast **b)** na raz **2.** kiedyś; ***I ~ met your mother*** kiedyś poznałem twoją matkę; ***~ upon a time*** dawno, dawno temu **II** *conj* jak tylko, kiedy już; ***we didn't know what to do ~ the money had gone*** nie wiedzieliśmy, co robić, kiedy skończyły się pieniądze

on•com•ing ['ɒnkʌmɪŋ] *adj* **1.** nadchodzący, zbliżający się **2.** *car*: nadjeżdżający; ***the ~ traffic*** pojazdy nadjeżdżające z przeciwka

one [wʌn] **I** *num* jeden; ***there is only ~ room*** jest tylko jeden pokój; ***~ hundred*** sto; ***~ thousand*** tysiąc **II** *adj* **1.** jedyny; ***he's the ~ person I can trust*** jest jedyną osobą, której mogę zaufać; ***my ~ and only hope*** moja jedyna nadzieja **2.** pewien; ***~ day*** pewnego dnia **3.** niejaki, jakiś; ***assistant to ~ Mr Ming*** asystentka niejakiego pana Minga **4.** ten sam; ***they all went off in ~ direction*** wszyscy poszli w tym samym kierunku **III** *pron* **1.** (*replacing*) ***a red pencil and a blue ~*** czerwony ołówek i niebieski; ***our car is always breaking down, but we are getting a new ~ soon*** nasz samochód ciągle się psuje, ale niedługo kupujemy nowy **2.** (*pointing*) ten; ***our house is the ~ next to the school*** nasz dom to ten obok szkoły; ***the ~ who*** ten, który **3.** (*impersonal*) ***~ gets the impression*** odnosi się wrażenie; ***~ cannot be sure*** nie można być pewnym; ***break ~'s leg*** złamać (sobie) nogę

one-armed: ***~ bandit*** jednoręki bandyta *m*; **one-'eyed** *adj* jednooki; **one-'hand•ed** *adj* jednoręki; **one-horse 'town** *s infml* (*village*) dziura *f*; **one-'leg•ged** *adj* jednonogi; **'one-man** *adj* jednoosobowy; **one-man 'band** *s* człowiek *m* orkiestra; **one-man 'show** *s* **1.** monodram *m*

O

2. wystawa *f* indywidualna; **one•ness** ['wʌnnɪs] *s* jedność *f*; **one-night 'stand** *s* **1.** romans *m* na jedną noc **2.** dziewczyna *f* na jedną noc **3.** chłopak *m* na jedną noc; **one-'off** *Br* **I** *adj* jednorazowy **II** *s* ***it was a ~*** to się już nie powtórzy; **one-on-'one** *adj Am* **1.** *meeting*: w cztery oczy **2.** *tuition*: indywidualny; **one-par•ent 'fam•i•ly** *s* niepełna rodzina *f*; **'one-piece** *adj swimsuit*: jednoczęściowy

on•er•ous ['ɒnərəs] *adj task, responsibility*: uciążliwy

oneself [wʌn'self] *pron* **1.** się; ***cut ~*** skaleczyć się **2.** siebie; ***for ~*** dla siebie; ***be ~*** być sobą **3.** sam(emu); (***all***) ***by ~*** (zupełnie) sam; → ***one***

one-'sid•ed *adj* jednostronny; **'one-time** *adj* **1.** były; ***a ~ best friend*** były najlepszy przyjaciel **2.** jednorazowy; **one-to-'one** *adj Br* **1.** *discuss*: w cztery oczy **2.** *correspondence*: jeden do jednego; **one-track 'mind** *s*: ***have a ~*** myśleć tylko o jednym; **'one-way street** *s* ulica *f* jednokierunkowa; **'one-way tick•et** *s* bilet *m* w jedną stronę

on•go•ing ['ɒngəʊɪŋ] *adj* **1.** trwający **2.** *investigation*: w toku

on•ion ['ʌnjən] *s BIOL* cebula *f*

'on-line *adj INF* online, podłączony; **'online serv•ice** *s* usługa *f* on-line

on•look•er ['ɒnlʊkə] *s* **1.** gap *m* **2.** obserwator *m* **3.** naoczny świadek *m*

on•ly ['əʊnlɪ] **I** *adv* **1.** tylko, jedynie; ***for members ~*** tylko dla członków; ***you ~ have to look at her*** wystarczy na nią spojrzeć; ***~ because*** tylko dlatego, że; ***if ~ he would stop drinking!*** gdyby tylko przestał pić!; ***it is ~ a suggestion*** to tylko propozycja **2.** dopiero; ***we ~ got here yesterday*** przyjechaliśmy dopiero wczoraj; ***~ just*** **a)** dopiero co **b)** ledwo; ***~ too well*** aż za dobrze **II** *adj* jedyny; ***an ~ child*** jedynak; ***we were the ~ people there*** tylko my tam byliśmy **III** *conj* tylko; ***not ~, ... but also*** nie tylko,... lecz również

'on-ramp *s Am* wjazd *m* na autostradę

'on•rush *no pl s* **1.** napływ *m* **2.** *emotion*: przypływ *m* **3.** *new technologies*: gwałtowny rozwój *m*; **'on•set** *no pl s* początek *m*, nadejście *n*; **on•'shore** *adj* **1.** lądowy, na lądzie **2.** *wind*: od morza; **on•'side** *adj SPORT*: ***be ~*** nie być na spalonym

on•slaught ['ɒnslɔːt] *s a. fig* **1.** (gwałtowny) atak *m* (***on*** na *A*) **2.** najazd *m*; ***an ~ of tourists*** najazd turystów

on-the-job 'train•ing *s* szkolenie *n* w miejscu pracy

on•to ['ɒntuː] *prep* na *A*; ***move the books ~ another shelf*** przenieś książki na inną półkę; ***be ~ s.o.*** **a)** *infml* przejrzeć kogoś **b)** nie dawać komuś spokoju; ***be ~ s.th.*** *fig* być na tropie czegoś

o•nus ['əʊnəs] *s* obowiązek *f*; ***the ~ is on the employer to do s.th.*** na pracodawcy spoczywa obowiązek zrobienia czegoś

on•ward ['ɒnwəd] *adv* **1.** do przodu **2.** od; ***from May ~*** od maja **3.** *flight, journey*: dalszy

oo•dles ['uːdlz] *pl infml*: ***~ of s.th.*** mnóstwo czegoś, cała masa czegoś

oomph [ʊmf] *s infml* **1.** wigor *m*, ikra *f* **2.** para *f*

ooze [uːz] **I** *v/i* **1.** sączyć się (***from/out of*** z *G*); ***blood ~ed out of the wound*** krew sączyła się z rany; ***~ out*** sączyć się, wypływać **2.** ***~ with confidence*** *fig* emanować pewnością siebie **II** *v/t* **1.** wydzielać; ***s.th. was oozing blood*** z czegoś sączyła się krew; ***~ butter*** ociekać tłuszczem **2.** *fig* ***~ confidence*** emanować pewnością siebie; ***~ charm*** roztaczać wokół siebie urok

o•pal ['əʊpəl] *s* opal *m*

o•paque [əʊ'peɪk] *adj* **1.** nieprzezroczysty, nieprzejrzysty **2.** matowy **3.** *tights*: kryjący **4.** *text, speech*: niejasny, mętny

OPEC ['əʊpek] *abbr* (=***Organization of Petroleum Exporting Countries***) OPEC

o•pen ['əʊpən] **I** *adj* **1.** otwarty; ***leave the door ~*** nie zamykaj drzwi; ***keep one's eyes ~*** *fig* mieć oczy szeroko otwarte; ***with ~ arms*** z otwartymi ramionami **2.** *office, shop*: czynny, otwarty **3.** *space, sea, wound*: otwarty; ***in the ~ air*** na wolnym powietrzu, pod gołym niebem **4.** *discussion, competition*: otwarty; ***the competition is ~ to*** w konkursie mogą wziąć udział **5.** *disagreement*: jawny **6.** dostępny; otwarty (***to*** dla *G*); ***what op-***

O

tions are ~ to us? jaki mamy wybór?; jakie mamy możliwości wyboru?; ***is the offer still ~?*** czy ta oferta jest nadal aktualna? **7.** podatny; ***the system is ~ to abuse*** system jest podatny na nadużycia **8.** szczery **9.** ***be ~ to new suggestions*** (***new ideas***) być otwartym na propozycje (nowe pomysły) **10.** *question*: otwarty; ***the price is ~ to negotiations*** cenę można negocjować; ***it is an ~ question whether*** (jak na razie) nie wiadomo, czy **11.** *flower*: rozwinięty **12.** *jacket*: rozpięty **13.** *vowel*: otwarty **II** *v/t* **1.** otwierać ⟨-worzyć⟩; ***~ your eyes*** otwórz oczy; ***~ a bank account*** otworzyć konto w banku **2.** rozpoczynać ⟨-cząć⟩, otwierać ⟨-worzyć⟩; ***~ an investigation*** rozpocząć dochodzenie; ***~ the new season*** rozpocząć sezon; ***~ fire on*** otworzyć ogień do *G* **III** *v/i* **1.** otwierać ⟨-worzyć⟩ się; ***the new hospital ~s in July*** nowy szpital zostanie otwarty w lipcu **2.** zaczynać ⟨-cząć⟩ się, rozpoczynać ⟨-cząć⟩ się; ***the story ~s with a murder*** historia rozpoczyna się od morderstwa; **open out** *v/i* **1.** rozszerzać ⟨-rzyć⟩ się **2.** przechodzić ⟨przejść⟩ (***into*** w *A*); ***the street opens out into a square*** ulica przechodzi w plac **2.** otwierać ⟨-worzyć⟩ się, zwierzać ⟨-rzyć⟩ się; **open up I** *v/i* **1.** otwierać ⟨-worzyć⟩ się **2.** rozpoczynać ⟨-cząć⟩ działalność **3.** (*gap, crack*) powstawać ⟨-tać⟩ **II** *v/t* otwierać ⟨-worzyć⟩

o•pen-'air *adj* **1.** na wolnym powietrzu, pod gołym niebiem **2.** *swimming pool*: odkryty; **'o•pen•cast** *adj mine*: odkrywkowy; **'o•pen day** *Br s* dzień *m* otwarty; **o•pen-'end•ed** *adj* **1.** otwarty **2.** *contract*: na czas nieokreślony

o•pen•er ['əʊpnə] *s* otwieracz *m*

o•pen-'eyed *adj*: ***in ~ wonder*** z szeroko otwartymi ze zdziwienia oczami; **o•pen•'hand•ed** *adj* **1.** hojny, szczodry **2.** *blow*: otwartą dłonią; **o•pen-heart 'sur•ger•y** *s MED* operacja *f* na otwartym sercu; **o•pen 'house** *Am* → ***open day***

o•pen•ing ['əʊpənɪŋ] **I** *s* **1.** otwór *m*, szpara *f* **2.** początek *m* **3.** otwarcie *n* **4.** *film*: premiera *f* **5.** *exhibition*: otwarcie *n*, wernisaż *m* **6.** otwieranie *n* **II** *adj* początkowy, pierwszy; **'o•pen•ing hours** *pl* godziny *pl* otwarcia

o•pen 'let•ter *s* list *m* otwarty

o•pen•ly ['əʊpənlɪ] *adv* **1.** otwarcie **2.** jawnie

o•pen-'mind•ed *adj* otwarty; ***be ~*** mieć otwarty umysł; **o•pen-'mouthed** *adj* z otwartymi (ze zdziwienia) ustami; **o•pen-'necked** *adj shirt*: rozpięty pod szyją; **o•pen•ness** ['əʊpənnɪs] *s* otwartość *f*; **o•pen-'plan** *adj* bez ścian działowych; **'o•pen sea•son** *s* sezon *m* (łowiecki) (***for*** na *A*); **o•pen 'se•cret** *s* tajemnica *f* poliszynela; **'o•pen tick•et** *s* bilet *m* otwarty; **'o•pen tour•na•ment** *s* turniej *m* otwarty; **O•pen U•ni•'ver•si•ty** *s Br* uniwersytet *m* otwarty

op•e•ra ['ɒpərə] *s MUS* opera *f*; ***go to the ~*** iść do opery

op•er•a•ble ['ɒpərəbl] *adj*: ***be ~*** **a)** obowiązywać **b)** działać, funkcjonować **c)** *MED* kwalifikować się do operacji; ***manually ~*** obsługiwany ręcznie

'op•e•ra glass•es *pl* lornetka *f* teatralna; **'op•e•ra house** *s* opera *f*, budynek *m* opery; **'op•e•ra sing•er** *s* śpiewak *m* operowy

op•e•rate ['ɒpəreɪt] **I** *v/i* **1.** działać, funkcjonować **2.** działać, prowadzić działalność **3.** operować ⟨z-⟩ (***on s.o. for*** kogoś na *A*) **4.** obowiązywać **II** *v/t* **1.** *machine*: obsługiwać **2.** *button*: naciskać ⟨-snąć⟩ **3.** *company*: prowadzić

op•e•rat•ic [ɒpə'rætɪk] *adj MUS* operowy

op•e•rat•ing ['ɒpəreɪtɪŋ] *adj* **1.** działający, funkcjonujący **2.** *system*: operacyjny **3.** *manual*: obsługi **4.** *MED* operacyjny; **'op•e•rat•ing costs** *pl ECON* koszty *pl* operacyjne; **'op•e•rat•ing in•struc•tions** *pl* instrukcja *f* obsługi; **'op•e•rat•ing mar•gin** *s ECON* marża *f* zysku (operacyjnego); **'op•e•rat•ing pro•fit** *s ECON* zysk *m* operacyjny; **'op•e•rat•ing ta•ble** *s MED* stół *m* operacyjny; **'op•e•rat•ing room** *Am* → ***operating theatre***; **'op•e•rat•ing the•a•tre** *Br s MED* sala *f* operacyjna; **'op•e•rat•ing sys•tem** *s INF* system *m* operacyjny

O

op•e•ra•tion [ɒpəˈreɪʃn] *s* **1.** działanie *n*, funkcjonowanie *n*; ***be in ~*** działać; ***put into ~*** **a)** (*line*) uruchomić **b)** *scheme*: wdrożyć **c)** *plan*: wcielić w życie **2.** *law*: obowiązywanie *n*; ***be in ~*** obowiązywać; ***come into ~*** wejść w życie **3.** *MED* operacja *f*; ***he underwent a heart ~*** przeszedł operację serca **4.** operacja *f*, działanie *n*; ***UN peacekeeping ~s*** działania pokojowe ONZ **5.** *ECON* transakcja *f*, operacja *f* **6.** *TECH* obsługa *f*; **op•e•ra•tion•al** [ɒpərˈeɪʃənl] *adj* **1.** operacyjny; ***~ activities*** działalność, działania **2.** sprawny, gotowy do eksploatacji **3.** *manual*: obsługi; **op•e•ra•tive** [ˈɒpərətɪv] *adj* **1.** *MED* operacyjny; ***~ mortality*** śmiertelność okołooperacyjna **2.** działający, sprawny; ***be ~*** działać, być sprawnym; **3.** obowiązujący; ***become ~*** wejść w życie **4.** ***'was' being the ~ word*** z akcentem na słowo „była"

op•e•ra•tor [ˈɒpəreɪtə] *s* **1.** *TECH* operator *m* **2.** telefonista *m* **3.** organizator *m*; ***a bus ~*** przewoźnik (autobusowy); ***a tour ~*** organizator wycieczek **4.** ***a smooth ~*** *infml* spryciarz, kombinator

op•er•et•ta [ɒpəˈretə] *s MUS* operetka *f*

oph•thal•mic [ɒfˈθælmɪk] *adj* **1.** okulistyczny **2.** *operation*: oczu **3.** *nerve*: oczny; **oph•thal•mol•o•gist** [ɒfθælˈmɒlədʒɪst] *s MED* okulista *m*

O

o•pi•ate [ˈoʊpɪət] *s MED* **1.** opiat *m*, opioid *m* **2.** *fig* narkotyk *m*

o•pin•ion [əˈpɪnjən] *s* **1.** opinia *f*, pogląd *m* (**about**/**on**/**of** o *L*/na temat *G*); ***in my ~*** moim zdaniem; ***be of the ~ that*** być zdania, że; ***that is a matter of ~*** to kwestia subiektywna; ***have a good ~ of*** mieć dobre zdanie o *L*, wysoko cenić *A*; ***public ~*** opinia publiczna; ***~ is divided on the issue*** zdania na ten temat są podzielone **2.** opinia *f*, ekspertyza *f* **3.** *MED* porada *f*, opinia *f*; ***get a second ~*** poprosić o opinię innego lekarza; **o'pin•ion poll** *s* badanie *n* opinii publicznej; **o•pin•ion•at•ed** [əˈpɪnjəneɪtɪd] *adj* zadufany w sobie, zarozumiały

o•pi•um [ˈəʊpjəm] *s* opium *n*

o•pos•sum [əˈpɒsəm] *s BIOL* opos *m*

op•po•nent [əˈpəʊnənt] *s* przeciwnik *m*; ***a political ~*** przeciwnik polityczny; ***~s of abortion*** przeciwnicy aborcji

op•por•tune [ˈɒpətjuːn] *adj* **1.** *time*, *moment*: właściwy, odpowiedni; ***at the most ~ moment*** w najwłaściwszym momencie **2.** *action*: podjęty we właściwym momencie

op•por•tun•ism [ɒpəˈtjuːnɪzəm] *s* oportunizm *m*; **op•por•tun•ist** [ɒpəˈtjuːnɪst] **I** *s* oportunista *m* **II** *adj* oportunistyczny; **op•por•tun•is•tic** [ɒpətjuːnˈɪstɪk] *adj* oportunistyczny

op•por•tu•ni•ty [ɒpərˈtjuːnətɪ] *s* **1.** okazja *f* (**for** do *G*), szansa *f* (**for** na *A*); ***the ~ to ask questions*** okazja do zadania pytań; ***take the ~ to congratulate s.o.*** skorzystać z okazji, by komuś pogratulować; ***I took the ~ to visit her*** skorzystałem z okazji i ją odwiedziłem; ***at the earliest ~*** przy pierwszej nadarzającej się okazji **2.** możliwość *f*; ***a job ~*** **a)** oferta pracy **b)** miejsce pracy; ***equal opportunities for women*** równe szanse dla kobiet

op•pose [əˈpəʊz] *v/t* sprzeciwiać ⟨-wić⟩ się; ***~ the death penalty*** sprzeciwiać się karze śmierci; **opposed** *adj* przeciwny (**to** *D*); ***as ~ to*** w przeciwieństwie do *G* **2.** różny; **op•pos•ing** [əˈpəʊzɪŋ] *adj* przeciwny

op•po•site [ˈɒpəzɪt] **I** *adj* **1.** przeciwny; ***in the ~ direction*** w przeciwnym kierunku; ***the ~ sex*** płeć przeciwna; ***we live on the ~ side of the road*** mieszkamy po drugiej stronie drogi **2.** *effect*: odwrotny **II** *adv* naprzeciw(ko); ***there is a newly married couple living ~*** naprzeciwko mieszka para nowożeńców **III** *s* przeciwieństwo *n*; ***quite the ~*** wręcz przeciwnie; ***what is the ~ of 'heavy'*** co jest przeciwieństwem słowa „ciężki"?, jaki jest antonim słowa „ciężki"?; ***~es attract*** przeciwieństwa się przyciągają **IV** *prep* naprzeciw(ko) *G*; ***I sat ~ him*** usiadłem naprzeciw niego; ***the bank is ~ the supermarket*** bank jest naprzeciwko supermarketu; **op•po•site 'num•ber** *s* kolega *m* po fachu

op•po•si•tion [ɒpəˈzɪʃn] *s* **1.** sprzeciw *m* (**to** wobec *G*) **2.** opór *m*; ***the army met with fierce ~*** armia napotkała silny opór; ***a march held in ~ to*** marsz zorganizowany na znak protestu wobec *G* **3.** ***the ~*** *POLIT* opozycja **4.** ***the ~*** *ECON* konkurencja **5.** ***the ~*** *SPORT* przeciwnik **4.** przeciwstawność *f*, opozycja *f*; **op•po•'si•tion par•ty** *s POLIT* partia *f* opozycyjna

op•press [ə'pres] *v/t* **1.** uciskać, ciemiężyć **2.** przytłaczać ⟨-łoczyć⟩; ***the atmosphere ~ed her*** atmosfera ją przygnębiała; **op•pres•sion** [ə'preʃn] *s* ucisk *m*; **op•pres•sive** [ə'presɪv] *adj* **1.** *regime*, *law*: okrutny, oparty na ucisku **2.** *heat*: uciążliwy **3.** *atmosphere*: przytłaczający, przygnębiający; **op•pres•sor** [ə'presə] *s* ciemiężca *m*

opt [ɒpt] *v/i*: ***~ to do s.th.*** decydować się coś zrobić; ***~ for*** wybierać *A*, decydować się na *A*; ***~ against*** odrzucać *A*, nie zdecydować się na *A*; ***many workers ~ed to leave their jobs*** wielu pracowników postanowiło zrezygnować z pracy; ***~ in to*** przystąpić do *G*; ***~ out of*** zdecydować się nie przystępować do *G*

op•tic ['ɒptɪk] *adj nerve*: wzrokowy; **op•ti•cal** ['ɒptɪkl] *adj* optyczny; **op•ti•cal 'char•ac•ter re•cog•ni•tion** *s INF* optyczne rozpoznawanie *n* pisma; **op•ti•cal 'fi•bre** *Br*, ***op•ti•cal fi•ber*** *Am s TECH* włókno *n* światłowodowe, światłowód *m*; **op•ti•cal fi•bre cable** *Br*, ***op•ti•cal fi•ber cable*** *Am s TECH* kabel *m* światłowodowy; **op•ti•cal il'lu•sion** *s* złudzenie *n* optyczne

op•ti•cian [ɒp'tɪʃn] *s Br* optyk *m*; **op•tics** ['ɒptɪks] *s PHYS* optyka *f*

op•ti•ma ['ɒptɪmə] *pl* → ***optimum II***; **op•ti•mal** ['ɒptɪml] *adj* optymalny

op•ti•mism ['ɒptɪmɪzm] *s* optymizm *m*; **op•ti•mist** ['ɒptɪmɪst] *s* optymista *m*; **op•ti•mist•ic** [ɒːptɪ'mɪstɪk] *adj* optymistyczny; **op•ti•mist•ic•ally** [ɒptɪ'mɪstɪklɪ] *adv* optymistycznie

op•ti•mize ['ɒptɪmaɪz] *v/t* optymalizować ⟨z-⟩

op•ti•mum ['ɒptɪməm] **I** *adj* optymalny **II** *pl optima s* optimum *n*

op•tion ['ɒpʃn] *s* **1.** możliwość *f* (wyboru), opcja *f*; ***have no ~*** nie mieć wyboru; ***have no ~ but to do s.th.*** nie mieć innego wyjścia, jak tylko coś zrobić; ***leave one's ~s open*** wstrzymywać się z decyzją **2.** *ECON INF* opcja *f*; ***share ~s*** opcje na akcje; ***choose the Cut ~ from the Edit menu*** wybierz opcję Wytnij z menu Edycja; **op•tion•al** ['ɒpʃnl] *adj* **1.** opcjonalny, nieobowiązkowy **2.** *course*: nieobowiązkowy, dodatkowy; **op•tion•al 'ex•tras** *pl* wyposażenie *n* dodatkowe; **'op•tions mar•ket** *s ECON* rynek *m* opcji

op•u•lence ['ɒpjʊləns] *s* **1.** bogactwo *n* **2.** luksus *m* **3.** wystawność *f* **4.** bujność *f*; **op•u•lent** ['ɒpjʊlənt] *adj* **1.** bogaty **2.** *hotel*: luksusowy **3.** *lifestyle*: wystawny **4.** *palace*: okazały **5.** *greenery*: bujny

o•pus ['əʊpəs] *pl s MUS* opus *n*

or [ɔːə] *conj* **1.** lub, albo; ***we can go to the cinema ~ to the theatre*** możemy iść do kina albo do teatru; ***in a day ~ two*** za dzień lub dwa **2.** czy; ***are you coming ~ not?*** idziesz czy nie? **3.** ani; ***he can't read ~ write*** nie umie czytać ani pisać **4.** (*a.* ***~ else***) bo (inaczej); ***turn the heat down ~ it will burn*** zmniejsz ogień, bo się przypali; ***he must like her ~ he wouldn't keep calling her*** musi ją lubić, bo inaczej by do niej nie dzwonił

or•a•cle ['ɒrəkl] *s a. fig* wyrocznia *f*; ***the ~ on fashion*** wyrocznia w sprawach mody; **o•rac•u•lar** [ə'rækjʊlə] *adj* **1.** proroczy **2.** enigmatyczny, dwuznaczny

o•ral ['ɔːrəl] **I** *adj* **1.** *language*: mówiony **2.** ustny; ***~ cavity*** jama ustna **3.** *hygiene*: jamy ustnej **4.** *sex*: oralny **5.** *medicine*: doustny **II** *s* egzamin *m* ustny; **o•ral•ly** ['ɔːrəlɪ] *adv* **1.** ustnie **2.** *administer*: doustnie

or•ange ['ɒrɪndʒ] **I** *s* **1.** *BIOL* pomarańcza *f* **2.** kolor *m* pomarańczowy **3.** *Br* sok *m* pomarańczowy; ***vodka and ~, please*** poproszę wódkę z sokiem pomarańczowym **II** *adj colour*: pomarańczowy; **or•ange•ade** ['ɒrɪndʒeɪd] *s* oranżada *f*; **'or•ange juice** *s* sok *m* pomarańczowy

o•rang-u•tan [ɔːræŋuː'tæn] *s BIOL* orangutan *m*

o•ra•tion [ɔː'reɪʃn] *s* mowa *f*, oracja *f*; **or•a•tor** ['ɒrətə] *s* mówca *m*, orator *m*; **or•a•tor•i•cal** [ɒrə'tɒrɪkl] *adj* oratorski

or•a•to•ri•o [ɒrə'tɔːrɪəʊ] *pl -rios s* MUS oratorium *n*

or•bit ['ɔːbɪt] **I** *s* **1.** ASTR orbita *f*; ***put into ~*** umieścić na orbicie **2.** *fig* orbita *f* (wpływów), sfera *f* wpływów **II** *v/t* ASTR okrążać ⟨-żyć⟩; ***the earth takes a year to ~ the sun*** obieg Ziemi dokoła Słońca trwa rok

or•chard ['ɔːtʃəd] *s* sad *m*

or•ches•tra ['ɔːkɪstrə] *s* MUS orkiestra *f*; **or•ches•tral** [ɔː'kestrəl] *adj* orkiestralny; **'or•ches•tra pit** *s* kanał *m* orkiestrowy; **or•ches•trate** ['ɔːkɪstreɪt] *v/t* **1.** MUS rozpisywać ⟨-sać⟩ na orkiestrę **2.** organizować ⟨z-⟩

or•chid ['ɔːkɪd] *s* BIOL storczyk *m*, orchidea *f*

or•dain [ɔː'deɪn] *v/t* REL wyświęcać ⟨-cić⟩; ***~ s.o. (as) a priest*** wyświęcić kogoś na księdza

or•deal [ɔː'diːl] *s a. fig* tortura *f*, udręka *f*; ***the interview was a real ~*** rozmowa była prawdziwą udręką

or•der ['ɔːdər] **I** *s* **1.** porządek *m*; ***in alphabetical ~*** w kolejności alfabetycznej; ***in ~ of priority*** według ważności; ***put s.th. in ~*** uporządkować coś, doprowadzić coś do porządku; ***restore public ~*** przywrócić porządek publiczny; ***call s.o. to ~*** przywołać kogoś do porządku; ***be the ~ of the day*** być na porządku dziennym; ***in ~*** **a)** na miejscu **b)** w porządku **c)** ważny, aktualny; ***be in perfect working ~*** działać bez zarzutu; ***be out of ~*** **a)** nie działać, być zepsutym **b)** (*behaviour*) być nie na miejscu **2.** rozkaz *m*, polecenie *n*; ***the general gave the ~ to advance*** generał dał rozkaz do ataku; ***by ~ of*** na polecenie *G*; ***I'm under ~s not to let anyone in*** polecono mi nikogo nie wpuszczać **3.** zalecenie *n*; ***doctor's ~s*** zalecenie lekarza **4.** zamówienie *n*; ***place an ~ for*** złożyć zamówienie na *A*; ***made to ~*** wykonany na zamówienie; ***may I take your ~?*** czy mogę przyjąć państwa zamówienie? **5.** FIN przekaz *m*; ***a money ~*** przekaz pieniężny; ***a postal ~*** przekaz pocztowy **6.** REL zakon *m*; ***the Benedictine ~*** zakon Benedyktynów **7.** ***in ~ to, in ~ that*** aby, żeby; ***she arrived early in ~ to get a good seat*** przyszła wcześnie, aby zająć dobre miejsce **II** *v/t* **1.** zamawiać ⟨-mówić⟩; ***shall I ~ a taxi?*** czy mam zamówić taksówkę? **2.** porządkować ⟨u-⟩; ***I need time to ~ my thoughts*** potrzebuję czasu, żeby uporządkować myśli **3.** zalecać ⟨-cić⟩; ***~ s.o. to stay in bed*** zalecić komuś leżenie w łóżku **4.** rozkazywać ⟨-zać⟩, polecać ⟨-cić⟩; ***the officer ~ed them to fire*** oficer rozkazał im strzelać; ***the government ~ed an investigation*** rząd polecił wszcząć śledztwo; **order about, *order around*** *v/t infml* rozstawiać po kątach; **order in** *v/t* prosić ⟨po-⟩ do środka, kazać wejść; **order out** *v/t* wypraszać ⟨-rosić⟩, kazać wyjść

'or•der book *s* ECON **1.** rejestr *m* zamówień **2.** portfel *m* zamówień; **'or•der form** *s* formularz *m* zamówienia; **or•der•ly** ['ɔːdəlɪ] **I** *adj* **1.** uporządkowany **2.** *demonstration*: spokojny **II** *s* **1.** MED sanitariusz *m* **2.** ordynans *m*

or•di•nal num•ber ['ɔːdɪnlnʌmbə] *s* GRAM liczebnik *m* porządkowy

or•di•nar•i•ly [ɔːdɪ'nerɪlɪ] *adv* **1.** zwyczajnie, normalnie **2.** zwykle

or•di•nary ['ɔːdɪnerɪ] **I** *adj* **1.** zwykły, zwyczajny; ***~ people like you and me*** zwyczajni ludzie jak ty i ja; ***it was no ~ meeting*** to nie było zwykłe zebranie; ***in the ~ way*** normalnie, zwykle **2.** normalny **3.** zwykły, przeciętny **II** *s* ***out of the ~*** niezwykły

ore [ɔː] *s* GEOL ruda *f*; ***iron ~*** ruda żelaza

or•gan ['ɔːgən] *s* **1.** ANAT narząd *m*, organ *m*; ***internal ~s*** narządy wewnętrzne; ***an ~ transplant*** przeszczep narządu **2.** *fig* organ *m*; ***government ~s*** organy rządowe; ***this paper is the official ~ of the Socialist party*** ta gazeta jest oficjalnym organem partii socjalistycznej **3.** MUS organy *pl*; ***~ music*** muzyka organowa; ***a mouth ~*** MUS *Br* organki; **'or•gan grind•er** *s* kataryniarz *m*

or•gan•ic [ɔː'gænɪk] *adj a. fig* organiczny; ***~ chemistry*** chemia organiczna; **or•gan•i•cal•ly** [ɔː'gænɪklɪ] *adv a. fig* organicznie; **or•gan•ism** ['ɔːgənɪzm] *s* BIOL organizm *m*

or•gan•ist ['ɔːgənɪst] *s* MUS organista *m*

or•gan•i•za•tion [ɔːgənaɪ'zeɪʃn] *s* **1.** organizacja *f*; ***a political ~*** organizacja polityczna; ~ ***of labour*** organizacja pracy **2.** przygotowania *pl*; **organization chart** *s* struktura *f* organizacyjna; **or•gan•ize** ['ɔːgənaɪz] **I** *v/t* **1.** organizować ⟨z-⟩ **2.** przygotowywać ⟨-tować⟩ **II** *v/i* organizować ⟨z-⟩ się; **or•gan•ized 'crime** *s* przestępczość *f* zorganizowana; **or•gan•iz•er** ['ɔːgənaɪzə] *s* **1.** organizator *m* **2.** notes *m*, organizer *m*

or•gas•m ['ɔːgæzm] *s* orgazm *m*

or•gy ['ɔːdʒɪ] *s a. fig* orgia *f*

o•ri•ent ['ɔːrɪənt] *v/t* nastawiać ⟨-wić⟩ (***s.o./s.th. to/towards*** kogoś/coś na *A*); ***a profit ~ed organization*** organizacja nastawiona na zysk; ~ ***oneself*** orientować się (w terenie); ~ ***oneself in a new situation*** odnaleźć się w nowej sytuacji; **O•ri•ent** ['ɔːrɪənt] *s*: ***the*** ~ Orient, Wschód; **o•ri•en•tal** [ɔːrɪ'entl] *adj* orientalny, wschodni; **o•ri•en•tate** ['ɔːrɪenteɪt] *Br* → ***orient***; **o•ri•en•ta•tion** [ɔːrɪen'teɪʃn] *s* **1.** orientacja *f*, nastawienie *n*; ***a political*** ~ orientacja polityczna **2.** szkolenie *n*

or•i•fice ['ɒrɪfɪs] *s ANAT* otwór *m*

or•i•gin ['ɒrɪdʒɪn] *s* **1.** początek *m*; ***the ~s of life on earth*** początki życia na ziemi; ***the ~s of the world*** powstanie świata **2.** pochodzenie *n*; ***a country of ~*** kraj pochodzenia; ***be of German ~*** być Niemcem z pochodzenia; ***viral in ~*** pochodzenia wirusowego

o•rig•i•nal [ə'rɪdʒənl] **I** *adj* **1.** pierwotny, początkowy; ***go back to your ~ plan*** wróć do swojego pierwotnego planu **2.** oryginalny; ***an ~ writer*** oryginalny pisarz; ~ ***documents*** oryginalne dokumenty, oryginały **II** *s* oryginał *m*; ***in the ~*** w oryginale; **o•rig•i•nal•i•ty** [ərɪdʒə'nælətɪ] *s* oryginalność *f*; **o•rig•i•nal•ly** [ə'rɪdʒənəlɪ] *adv* **1.** początkowo, pierwotnie; ***she comes ~ from France*** pochodzi z Francji **2.** *published*: po raz pierwszy **o•rig•i•nal 'sin** *s REL* grzech *m* pierworodny

o•rig•i•nate [ə'rɪdʒɪneɪt] **I** *v/i* powstawać ⟨-tać⟩, rodzić ⟨z-⟩ się (***in*** w *L*), pochodzić (***in*** z *I*); ***this disease is thought to have ~d in the tropics*** uważa się, że ta choroba pochodzi z tropików **II** *v/t* tworzyć ⟨s-⟩, zapoczątkowywać ⟨-kować⟩; **o•rig•i•na•tor** [ə'rɪdʒɪneɪtə] *s* twórca *m*

Ork•neys ['ɔːknɪz] *pl GEOGR* Orkady *pl*

or•na•ment ['ɔːnəmənt] **I** *s* **1.** dekoracja *f*, ozdoba *f*; ***for ~*** dla dekoracji **2.** ornament *m* **II** *v/t* dekorować ⟨u-⟩, ozdabiać ⟨-dobić⟩; **or•na•men•tal** [ɔːnə'mentl] *adj* dekoracyjny, ozdobny; **or•na•men•ta•tion** [ɔːnəmen'teɪʃn] *s* **1.** ornamentacja *f* **2.** dekoracje *pl*

or•nate [ɔː'neɪt] *adj* bogato zdobiony, zdobny

or•ni•thol•o•gist [ɔːnɪ'θɒlədʒɪst] *s* ornitolog *m*; **or•ni•thol•o•gy** [ɔːnɪ'θɒlədʒɪ] *s* ornitologia *f*

or•phan ['ɔːfn] **I** *s* sierota *f* **II** *v/t* osierocać ⟨-cić⟩; **or•phan•age** ['ɔːfənɪdʒ] *s* sierociniec *m*, dom *m* dziecka

or•tho•don•tist [ɔːθə'dɒntɪst] *s* ortodonta *m*

or•tho•dox ['ɔːθədɒks] *adj* **1.** ortodoksyjny **2.** *REL* ortodoksyjny, prawosławny; ***the Russian ~ Church*** Rosyjski Kościół Prawosławny

or•tho•graph•ic [ɔːθə'græfɪk] *adj* ortograficzny; **or•thog•ra•phy** [ɔː'θɒgrəfɪ] *s* ortografia *f*

or•tho•pae•dic [ɔːθə'piːdɪk] *Br*, ***or•tho•pe•dic*** *Am adj* ortopedyczny; **or•tho•pae•dics** [ɔːθə'piːdɪks] *Br*, ***or•tho•pe•dics*** *Am s* ortopedia *f*; ***or•tho•pae•dist*** [ɔːθə'piːdɪst] *Br*, ***or•tho•pe•dist*** *Am s* ortopeda *m*

os•cil•late ['ɒsɪleɪt] *v/i* **1.** wahać się, oscylować **2.** drgać; **os•cil•la•tion** [ɒsɪ'leɪʃn] *s* **1.** wahanie *n* **2.** oscylacja *f* **3.** drganie *n*

os•mo•sis [ɒz'məʊsɪs] *s BIOL CHEM* osmoza *f*

os•si•fy ['ɒsɪfaɪ] *v/t* kostnieć ⟨s-⟩; ***ossified political system*** skostniały system polityczny

os•ten•si•ble [ɒ'stensəbl] *adj* rzekomy, pozorny; **os•ten•si•bly** [ɒ'stensəblɪ] *adv* rzekomo, pozornie

os•ten•ta•tion [ɒsten'teɪʃn] *s* ostentacja *f*, pretensjonalność *f*; **os•ten•ta•tious** [ɒsten'teɪʃəs] *adj* ostentacyjny, pretensjonalny; **os•ten•ta•tious•ly** [ɒsten'teɪʃəslɪ] *adv* ostentacyjnie, pretensjonalnie

os•te•o•ar•thri•tis [ɒstɪəʊɑːr'θraɪtɪs] *s MED* choroba *f* zwyrodnieniowa stawów

O

os•te•o•path ['ɒstɪəpæθ] *s MED* osteopata *m*; **os•te•op•a•thy** [ɒstɪ'ɒpəθɪ] *s MED* osteopatia *f*

os•te•o•po•ro•sis [ɒstɪəʊpə'rəʊsɪs] *s MED* osteoporoza *f*

os•tra•cism ['ɒstrəsɪzəm] *s* ostracyzm *m*; **os•tra•cize** ['ɒstrəsaɪz] *v/t* **1.** bojkotować ⟨z-⟩ **2.** wykluczać ⟨-czyć⟩ (***from*** z *G*)

os•trich ['ɒstrɪtʃ] *s BIOL* struś *m*

oth•er ['ʌðə] **I** *adj* **1.** inny; ***some ~ time*** innym razem; ***the ~ day*** ostatnio, niedawno **2.** (*with pl nouns*) inny, pozostały; ***are there any ~ questions?*** czy są jeszcze jakieś inne pytania?; ***the ~ guests*** pozostali goście; ***what about the ~ ones?*** co z pozostałymi? **3.** drugi; ***my ~ sister*** moja druga siostra; ***one son went to Australia, the ~ one to America*** jeden syn wyjechał do Australii, drugi do Ameryki; ***every ~ day*** co drugi dzień **4.** ***the ~*** przeciwny; ***on the ~ side of town*** po drugiej stronie miasta; ***a car coming the ~ way*** samochód nadjeżdżający z naprzeciwka; ***the ~ way round*** odwrotnie **II** *pron* inny; ***some designs are better that ~s*** niektóre projekty są lepsze niż inne **III** *adv* ***~ than*** **a)** oprócz *G*, z wyjątkiem *G* **b)** inaczej niż *N*

oth•er•wise ['ʌðəwaɪz] **I** *adv* **1.** w przeciwnym razie; ***~ I couldn't have afforded the trip*** w przeciwnym razie nie byłoby mnie stać na wycieczkę **2.** poza tym; ***~ the house was silent*** poza tym w domu panowała cisza **3.** inaczej, w inny sposób; ***~ known as*** znany także jako; ***he was ~ engaged*** był zajęty czymś innym, miał inne zobowiązania; ***why pretend ~?*** dlaczego udajesz, że jest inaczej?; ***accidental or ~*** przypadkowy lub umyślny; ***genuine or ~*** prawdziwy lub nie **II** *conj* bo (inaczej); ***don't take drugs, ~ you'll end up like me*** nie bierz narkotyków, bo skończysz jak ja

ot•ter ['ɒtə] *s BIOL* wydra *f*

ought [ɔːt] *v aux*: ***he ~ to do it*** powinien to zrobić; ***they ~ to have apologized*** powinni byli przeprosić; ***he ~ to have arrived by now*** powinien już tu być

ounce [aʊns] *s* **1.** uncja *f* **2.** *fig* odrobina *f*, krzta *f*; ***there is not an ~ of truth in her story*** w jej opowiadaniu nie ma za grosz prawdy

our [aʊə] *poss* nasz; ***≈ Father*** Ojcze Nasz

ours [aʊəz] *poss* nasz; ***their house is very similar to ~*** ich dom jest bardzo podobny do naszego; ***he's a friend of ~*** jest naszym przyjacielem

our•selves [aʊə'selvz] *pron* **1.** (my) sami; ***we thought of going there ~*** sami myśleliśmy, żeby tam pojechać **2.** się; ***we shouldn't blame ~ for what happened*** nie powinniśmy obwiniać się o to, co się stało; ***let's enjoy ~*** bawmy się; ***we want it for ~*** chcemy to dla siebie; → ***we***

oust [aʊst] *v/t* **1.** usuwać ⟨usunąć⟩ (***from*** z *G*); ***~ s.o. from power*** odsunąć kogoś od władzy **2.** wypierać ⟨-przeć⟩

out [aʊt] *adv* **1.** na zewnątrz; ***a way ~*** wyjście; ***run ~*** wybiec; ***some coins fell ~*** wypadło kilka monet; ***be ~ for*** próbować coś osiągnąć; ***be ~ for revenge*** szukać zemsty, chcieć się zemścić; ***he was just ~ for money*** chodziło mu tylko o pieniądze **2.** poza, poza domem; ***let's go ~ this evening*** chodźmy gdzieś dziś wieczorem; ***he is ~ of town*** nie ma go w mieście; ***she's not at home, she's ~*** nie ma jej w domu, wyszła **3.** (*distance*) ***she's working ~ in Australia*** pracuje w Australii; ***the ship sank ten miles ~ of Stockholm*** statek zatonął dziesięć mil od Sztokholmu **4.** (*remove*) ***get stains ~*** wywabiać plamy; ***the book is ~*** ta książka jest wypożyczona; ***they want the government ~*** chcą ustąpienia rządu **5.** (*finish*) ***this was an awful job and I'm glad to be ~ of it*** to była okropna praca i cieszę się, że już tam nie pracuję **6.** zabroniony, niemożliwy **7.** niemodny; ***go ~*** wychodzić z mody **8.** (*light*) zgaszony; ***the lights went ~*** światła zgasły **9.** dostępny; ***when does her new book come ~?*** kiedy ukaże się jej najnowsza książka?; ***the secret is ~*** tajemnica wyszła na jaw; ***~ with it!*** wyduś to z siebie! **10.** (*over*) ***it was summer and school was ~*** było lato i szkoła się już skończyła; ***before the week is ~*** przed końcem tygodnia **11.** nieprzytomny

O

12. do końca; ***hear me ~ please*** wysłuchaj mnie, proszę **13.** ***the ball was ~*** *SPORT* piłka wyszła na aut; **out of I** *prep* **1.** z *G*; ***drink beer ~ the bottle*** pić piwo z butelki; ***a statue made ~ bronze*** pomnik z brązu; ***I paid for the damage ~ my savings*** zapłaciłem za szkodę ze swoich oszczędności; ***a frog jumped ~ the box*** z pudełka wyskoczyła żaba; ***lean ~ the window*** wychylać się z okna **2.** z *G*, z powodu *G*; ***~ curiosity*** z ciekawości **3.** (*ratio*) na *A*; ***he scored six ~ ten*** zdobył sześć punktów na dziesięć możliwych; ***two ~ three people think the president should resign*** dwie osoby na trzy uważają, że prezydent powinien ustąpić **II** *adv* (*lacking*) ***we're ~ milk*** nie mamy (już) mleka, skończyło nam się mleko; ***you're ~ luck*** masz pecha; ***stay ~ trouble*** nie wpakuj się w kłopoty; ***I watched her car until it was ~ sight*** obserwowałem jej samochód, dopóki nie zniknął mi z oczu

out•age ['aʊtɪdʒ] *s Am*: ***a power ~*** przerwa w dostawie prądu, brak prądu; **out-and-'out** *adj* **1.** zupełny **2.** *lie*: wierutny **2.** *success*: pełny **4.** co się zowie, *infml* pełną gębą; **out•'bid** (*outbid*; *outbid*) *v/t* przelicytowywać ⟨-tować⟩; **out•board 'mo•tor** *s TECH* silnik *m* przyczepny; **'out•break** *s* **1.** wybuch *m* **2.** *disease*: wybuch *m* epidemii; **'out•build•ing** *s* budynek *m* gospodarczy; **~s** zabudowania gospodarcze; **'out•burst** *s* wybuch *m*; **'out•cast** *s* **1.** (***social***) **~** wyrzutek (społeczny) **2.** wygnaniec *m*; **out-'class** *v/t SPORT* deklasować ⟨z-⟩; **'out•come** *s* wynik *m*, rezultat *m*; **'out•cry** *s* głosy *pl* protestu (***at/over/against*** przeciw *D*); ***the new law provoked a public ~*** nowa ustawa wywołała publiczny sprzeciw; **out•'dat•ed** *adj* **1.** przestarzały **2.** nieaktualny; **out•'dis•tance** *v/t* dystansować ⟨z-⟩; **out•'do** (*outdid*; *outdone*) *v/t* **1.** prześcigać ⟨-gnąć⟩ **2.** pokonywać ⟨-nać⟩

out•'door *adj* **1.** na zewnątrz, pod gołym niebem **2.** *swimming pool*: odkryty; ***be the ~ type*** lubić spędzać czas na świeżym powietrzu; **out-'doors I** *adv* na zewnątrz, pod gołym niebem; ***eat ~*** jeść na dworze **II** *s* ***in the ~*** pod gołym niebem; ***the great ~*** (dzika) przyroda

out•er ['aʊtə] *adj* **1.** zewnętrzny **2.** skrajny, najdalszy; **out•er 'space** *s* kosmos *m*

'out•field *s SPORT* zapole *n*

'out•fit I *s* **1.** strój *m*, kostium *m*; ***a skiing ~*** kombinezon narciarski **2.** ubranie *n* **3.** zespół *m*, ekipa *f* **4.** zestaw *m* (narzędzi) **II** *v/t* wyposażać ⟨-żyć⟩ (***with*** w *A*); **'out•fit•ter** *s* **1.** *Br* sklep *m* z odzieżą męską **2.** *Am* sklep *m* turystyczny

'out•flow *s money*, *people*: odpływ *m*; **out•'fox** *v/t* przechytrzać ⟨-rzyć⟩; **out-'go•ing** *adj* **1.** *person*: towarzyski **2.** *mail*, *call*: wychodzący **3.** *government*, *president*: ustępujący; **out-'grow** (*outgrew*; *outgrown*) *v/t* **1.** wyrastać ⟨-rosnąć⟩ z *G*; ***~ one's school uniform*** wyrosnąć ze swojego szkolnego mundurka **2.** przerastać ⟨-rosnąć⟩; ***he's outgrown his older brother*** przerósł swojego starszego brata; **'out•house** *s* **1.** *Br* budynek *m* gospodarczy **2.** *Am infml* wychodek *m*

out•ing ['aʊtɪŋ] *s* wycieczka *f*; ***we went on an ~ to London*** pojechaliśmy na wycieczkę do Londynu

out•land•ish [aʊt'lændɪʃ] *adj* dziwaczny; **out•'last** *v/t* **1.** przeżywać ⟨-żyć⟩ **2.** przetrzymywać ⟨-mać⟩; ***he can ~ anyone on the dance floor*** może wytrzymać dłużej na parkiecie niż ktokolwiek inny

'out•law I *v/t* **1.** delegalizować ⟨z-⟩ **2.** *dated* wyjmować ⟨-jąć⟩ spod prawa **II** *s dated* wyjęty *m* spod prawa

'out•lay *s* nakład *m*, wydatek *m*; ***capital ~s*** nakłady inwestycyjne; ***the ~ on advertising was quickly repaid*** wydatki poniesione na reklamę szybko się zwróciły

'out•let *s* **1.** *a. fig* ujście *n*; ***~ for s.o.'s aggression*** ujście dla czyjejś agresji **2.** *ECON* punkt *m* sprzedaży **3.** odpływ *m* **4.** *Am* gniazdko *n*;

'out•line I *v/t* **1.** przedstawiać ⟨-wić⟩ w zarysie, nakreślać ⟨-lić⟩ **2.** ***be ~d against the sky*** rysować się na tle nieba **II** *s* **1.** zarys *m*, szkic *m*; ***in ~*** w zarysie; ***give an ~ of*** przedstawić coś w zarysie **2.** kontur *m*

O

out•'live *v/i* przeżyć; ***he ~d his wife by three years*** przeżył swoją żonę o trzy lata; ***s.th. has ~d its usefulness*** coś nie jest już potrzebne, coś jest już zbędne

'out•look *s* **1.** pogląd *m*, spojrzenie *n* (**on** na *A*); ***a positive ~ on life*** pozytywne podejście do życia **2.** perspektywy *pl*, widoki *pl* (**for** na *A*); ***the ~ for jobs*** widoki na pracę **3.** widok *m*; ***a pleasant ~ over the valley*** ładny widok na dolinę

'out•ly•ing *adj* odległy, oddalony; **out-ma•'noeu•vre** *Br*, ***out•ma•'neu•ver*** *Am v/t* wymanewrowywać ⟨-rować⟩, przechytrzać ⟨-rzyć⟩; **out•'mod•ed** *adj* **1.** przestarzały **2.** niemodny; **out•'num•ber** *v/t* przewyższać ⟨-szyć⟩ liczebnie; **out-of-'date** *adj* przestarzały, nieaktualny, nieważny; **out-of-the-'way** *adj* **1.** odległy, oddalony **2.** dziwny, osobliwy, nieznany; **'out-pa•tient** *s* pacjent *m* ambulatoryjny; ***~ clinic*** klinika ambulatoryjna; ***~ treatment*** leczenie ambulatoryjne; **out•per•'form** *v/t* osiągać ⟨-gnąć⟩ lepsze wyniki od *G*; **out•'play** *v/t* SPORT ogrywać ⟨-rać⟩; **'out•post** *s* wysunięty posterunek *m*, wysunięta placówka *f*; **'out•pour•ing** *s* **1.** *emotion*, *love*: wybuch *m*, (nagły) poryw *m* **2.** *aid*: napływ *m*

'out•put **I** *s* **1.** produkcja *f*, wielkość *f* produkcji **2.** wydajność *f* **3.** twórczość *f*, dorobek *m* **4.** TECH wyjście *n* **5.** INF dane *pl* wyjściowe **II** *v/t* INF przetwarzać ⟨-worzyć⟩; **out•put de•'vice** *s* INF urządzenie *n* wyjściowe

'out•rage **I** *s* **1.** oburzenie *n*; ***cause public ~*** wywołać oburzenie opinii publicznej **2.** akt *m* przemocy; ***a bomb ~*** zamach bombowy **3.** skandal *m* **II** *v/t* oburzać ⟨-rzyć⟩; **out•ra-geous** [aʊtˈreɪdʒəs] *adj* **1.** oburzający **2.** szokujący

out•'rank *v/t* być wyższym rangą od *G*

'out•right **I** *adj* **1.** całkowity **2.** *winner*: bezdyskusyjny **3.** *majority*: bezwzględny **4.** *refusal*: kategoryczny, zdecydowany **5.** *rejection*: otwarty **II** *adv* **1.** wprost; ***ask him ~*** zapytaj go wprost **2.** całkowicie **3.** *win*, *refuse*: zdecydowanie **4.** na miejscu; ***most of the crash victims were killed ~*** większość ofiar wypadku zginęła na miejscu **5.** natychmiast, od ręki

out•'run (*outran*; *outrun*) *v/t* **1.** (*run faster*) prześcigać ⟨-gnąć⟩, wyprzedzać ⟨-dzić⟩ **2.** uciekać ⟨-ciec⟩ **3.** *fig* przewyższać ⟨-szyć⟩; ***demand is ~ning supply*** popyt przewyższa podaż; **out•'sell** (*outsold*; *outsold*) *v/t* mieć większą sprzedaż od; **'out•set** *s* początek *m*; ***at the ~*** na początku *G*; ***from the ~ of*** od początku *G*; **out•'-shine** (*outshone*; *outshone*) *v/t fig* przyćmiewać ⟨-mić⟩

out•side [ˈaʊtˈsaɪd] **I** *adv* na zewnątrz; ***please wait ~*** proszę poczekać na zewnątrz; ***eat ~*** jeść na dworze **II** *adj* **1.** zewnętrzny, (znajdujący się) na zewnątrz; ***~ walls*** ściany zewnętrzne; ***~ calls*** rozmowy zewnętrzne; ***be cut off from the ~ world*** być odciętym od świata zewnętrznego **2.** *chance*: znikomy **III** *prep* **1.** poza *I*; ***the biggest theme park ~ Europe*** największy park tematyczny poza Europą; ***this is ~ my area of responsibility*** to wykracza poza moje kompetencje **2.** ***~ of*** poza *I*, za wyjątkiem *G*; ***there was nothing they could do, ~ of hoping that*** nie mogli zrobić nic innego, jak tylko mieć nadzieję, że **IV** *s* **1.** strona *f* zewnętrzna; ***from the ~*** z zewnątrz; ***the ~ of the house needs painting*** dom trzeba pomalować; ***at the ~*** (co) najwyżej, maksymalnie; ***on the ~*** **a)** *seem*: na pozór **b)** na wolności **2.** ***overtake on the ~*** **a)** (*Europe*, *USA*) wyprzedzać lewą stroną **b)** (*England*, *Australia*) wyprzedzać prawą stroną; **out•side 'broad•cast** *s* TEL *Br* **1.** nagranie *n* poza studiem **2.** transmisja *f*

out•sid•er [aʊtˈsaɪdə] *s* **1.** obcy *m*, outsider *m* **2.** osoba *f* z zewnątrz

'out•size *adj* **1.** wielki **2.** *clothing*: w nietypowych rozmiarach; **'out•skirts** *s pl* peryferie *pl*, obrzeża *pl*; ***they live on the ~ of the city*** mieszkają na obrzeżach miasta; **out•'smart** *v/t* przechytrzać ⟨-rzyć⟩; **out•'source** *v/t* ECON zlecać ⟨-cić⟩ na zewnątrz; **'out-sourc•ing** *s* ECON outsourcing *m*, obsługa *f* zewnętrzna; **out•'spo•ken** *adj* szczery; ***be ~*** mówić bez ogródek;

O

out•'stand•ing *adj* **1.** wybitny **2.** znakomity, doskonały **3.** *beauty*: niezwykły **4.** charakterystyczny **5.** *debt, work*: zaległy; **out•'stay** *v/t*: **~ *one's welcome*** nadużywać czyjejś gościnności; **out•'stretched** *adj arms*: rozpostarty; **out•'strip** *v/t* **1.** przewyższać ⟨-szyć⟩ **2.** prześcigać ⟨-gnąć⟩; **'out•tray** *s* tacka *f* na dokumenty (wychodzące); **out•'vote** *v/t* przegłosowywać ⟨-sować⟩

out•ward ['aʊtwəd] *adj* **1.** zewnętrzny, pozorny; **~ *cheerfulness*** pozorna wesołość; ***to all ~ appearances they were happy*** wyglądało na to, że są szczęśliwi **2.** na zewnątrz; **~ *investment*** zagraniczne inwestycje; **~*-looking*** otwarty na nowe pomysły; **out•ward•ly** ['aʊtwədlɪ] *adv* **1.** na pozór **2.** na zewnątrz

out•'weigh *v/t* przeważać ⟨-żyć⟩ nad *I*; ***the advantages ~ the disadvantages*** zalety przeważają nad wadami; **out•'wit** *v/t* przechytrzać ⟨-rzyć⟩; **'out•work•er** *s* ECON telepracownik *m*

o•va ['əʊvə] *pl* → ***ovum***

o•val ['əʊvl] **I** *s* owal *m* **II** *adj* owalny

o•var•i•an [oʊ'verɪən] *adj* ANAT : jajnikowy

o•va•ry ['əʊvərɪ] *s* **1.** ANAT jajnik *m* **2.** BIOL zalążnia *f*

o•va•tion [əʊ'veɪʃn] *s* owacja *f*; ***standing ~*** owacja na stojąco

ov•en ['ʌvn] *s* piekarnik *m*; ***a microwave ~*** kuchenka mikrofalowa; **'ov•en glove**, **'ov•en mitt** *s* rękawica *f* kuchenna; **'ov•en•proof** *adj pot*: żaroodporny; **ov•en-'read•y** *adj* gotowy (do podgrzania w piekarniku lub kuchence mikrofalowej)

o•ver ['əʊvə] **I** *prep* **1.** (*place*) nad *I*; **~ *the table*** nad stołem; ***she put a blanket ~ the child*** przykryła dziecko kocem; ***she put her hand ~ her mouth*** zakryła usta dłonią **2.** (*direction*) przez *A*; ***a bridge ~ the river*** most przez rzekę; ***jump ~ the fence*** przeskoczyć przez płot; ***run ~ the grass*** biec po trawie **3.** po przeciwnej stronie *G*; ***she lives ~ the road*** mieszka po drugiej stronie drogi **4.** (*from*) z *G*; ***fall down ~ the cliff*** spaść z urwiska; ***look ~ the edge*** spojrzeć w dół znad krawędzi **5.** (*quantity*) ponad *N*; **~ *3 million*** ponad 3 miliony; ***for ~ a month*** przez ponad miesiąc **6.** (*control*) nad *I*; ***rule ~ an empire*** rządzić imperium; ***she has only the director ~ her*** ma nad sobą tylko dyrektora **7.** (*time*) przez *A*, podczas *G*; ***we'll discuss it ~ lunch*** omówimy to podczas lunchu; **~ *the next few days*** przez następnych kilka dni **8.** (*because of*) o *A*, z powodu *G*; ***an argument ~ money*** kłótnia o pieniądze **9.** przez *A*; ***hear s.th. ~ the radio*** usłyszeć coś w radiu; ***say s.th. ~ the phone*** powiedzieć coś przez telefon **10.** ***all ~ the world*** na całym świecie; ***all ~ the country*** w całym kraju **11.** ***be*** (*a.* ***get***) **~ *s.th.*** **a)** radzić sobie z *I*, uporać się z *I* **b)** przezwyciężyć *A*; ***she'll get ~ it*** dojdzie do siebie **12.** **~ *and above*** poza *I*, oprócz *G* **II** *adv* **1.** ***try not to knock the vase ~*** postaraj się nie przewrócić tego wazonu; ***the wind must have blown the tree ~*** wiatr musiał przewrócić to drzewo **2.** na drugą stronę; ***he stopped and crossed ~*** zatrzymał się i przeszedł na drugą stronę **3.** (*place*) **~ *here*** tutaj; **~ *there*** tam; ***let's ask some friends ~*** zaprośmy (do nas) paru znajomych **4.** ***the lake was frozen ~*** jezioro było zupełnie zamarznięte; ***cover her ~*** przykryj ją **5.** więcej; ***children of 14 and ~*** dzieci w wieku od 14 lat **6.** ***if there is any food left ~*** jeżeli zostało jeszcze coś do jedzenia **7.** ponownie, jeszcze raz; ***you'll have to do it ~*** będziesz musiał to zrobić jeszcze raz **8.** (*finished*) ***the meeting is ~*** zebranie się skończyło **9.** (*change*) ***go ~ to the enemy*** przejść na stronę wroga; ***hand ~ the money*** przekazać pieniądze **10.** (*radio*) **~*!*** odbiór!; **~ *and out!*** bez odbioru! **11.** ***all ~ again*** **a)** od nowa **b)** znowu; **~ *and ~ again*** wielokrotnie, ciągle; ***I've told you ~ and ~ again not to do that*** mówiłem ci setki razy, żebyś tego nie robił

o•ver•'act *v/t* THEAT popadać ⟨-paść⟩ w przesadę; **o•ver•'age** *adj*: ***he is ~*** przekroczył limit wiekowy

o•ver•all ['əʊvərɔːl] **I** *adj* **1.** całkowity; **~ *length*** długość całkowita; ***she has ~ responsibility for the project*** odpo-

O

wiada za całość projektu **2.** *effect*: ogólny **II** *adv* **1.** w sumie; ***the company will invest 2 million ~*** firma zainwestuje w sumie dwa miliony; ***~, this is a good book*** w sumie jest to dobra książka **2.** ogólnie **III** *s Br* → ***overalls***; **o•ver•alls** ['əʊvərɔːlz] *pl* **1.** *Br* kombinezon *m* roboczy **2.** *Br* fartuch *m* roboczy **3.** (*trousers*) *Am* ogrodniczki *pl*

o•ver•'anx•ious *adj*: ***be ~*** za bardzo się przejmować; **o•ver•'awe** *v/t* onieśmielać ⟨-lić⟩; **o•ver•'bal•ance** *v/i* tracić ⟨s-⟩ równowagę; **o•ver•'bear•ing** *adj* apodyktyczny; ***in an ~ manner*** apodyktycznie; **o•ver•'bid** (*overbid*; *overbid*) *v/t* **1.** przebijać ⟨-bić⟩; ***they were ~ by another company*** ich oferta została przebita przez ofertę innej firmy **2.** przelicytowywać ⟨-tować⟩; **'o•ver•board** *adv jump*, *fall*: za burtę; ***throw s.th. ~*** *fig* pozbyć się czegoś; ***go ~ on*** *infml* przesadzać z *I*; **o•ver•'book** *v/t*: ***the flight was ~ed*** sprzedano więcej biletów na ten lot niż było miejsc; ***the hotel is ~ed*** hotel przyjął zbyt wiele rezerwacji

'o•ver•cast *adj* **1.** *sky*: zachmurzony **2.** *day*: pochmurny; **o•ver•'charge** *v/t* liczyć ⟨po-⟩ za dużo; ***we were ~d by £5*** policzyli nam o 5 funtów za dużo; **'o•ver•coat** *s* płaszcz *m*

o•ver'come (*overcame*; *overcome*) *v/t* **1.** *difficulties*, *enemy*, *fear*: przezwyciężać ⟨-żyć⟩, pokonywać ⟨-nać⟩; ***be ~ with smoke*** dusić się (od dymu) **2.** (*emotion*) ogarniać ⟨-nąć⟩; ***they were ~ with grief*** ogarnął ich przejmujący smutek; ***be ~ with joy*** nie posiadać się z radości; ***he was ~ with fear*** zdjął go strach

o•ver•'cook *v/t* rozgotowywać ⟨-tować⟩, **o•ver•'crowd•ed** *adj* zatłoczony, przepełniony; **o•ver•'do** (*overdid*; *overdone*) *v/t* **1.** przesadzać ⟨-dzić⟩ z *I*; ***she overdid the sympathy*** przesadziła ze współczuciem; ***~ it***, ***~ things*** przesadzić, przedobrzyć **2.** rozgotowywać ⟨-tować⟩ **3.** przesmażać ⟨-żyć⟩; **o•ver•'done** *adj* **1.** rozgotowany **2.** przesmażony

'o•ver•dose **I** *s* przedawkowanie *n*; ***take an ~ of*** przedawkować **II** *v/t* przedawkowywać ⟨-kować⟩ (**on** *A*); ***he has ~d on heroin*** przedawkował heroinę; **'o•ver•draft** *s FIN* debet *m*, przekroczenie *n* stanu konta; **overdraft fa'cility** *s FIN* debet *m*; **o•ver•'draw** (*overdrew*; *overdrawn*) *v/t*: ***~ one's account*** *FIN* przekraczać stan konta; ***be overdrawn by £100*** mieć 100 funtów debetu; **o•ver•'dress** *v/i* ubierać ⟨-brać⟩ się zbyt elegancko, wystroić się; **o•ver•'dressed** *adj* zbyt elegancko ubrany, (przesadnie) wystrojony; **'o•ver•drive** *s AUTO* nadbieg *m*; ***go into ~*** ruszać pełną parą; **o•ver•'due** *adj* **1.** opóźniony; ***the reforms are long ~*** te reformy należało wprowadzić już dawno **2.** *payment*: zaległy **3.** *cheque*: przeterminowany; **o•ver•'eat** (*overate*; *overeaten*) *v/i* przejadać ⟨-jeść⟩ się; **o•ver•'es•ti•mate** *v/t* **1.** przeceniać ⟨-nić⟩ **2.** szacować ⟨o-⟩ za wysoko; **o•ver•ex'cit•ed** *adj*: ***be ~*** zbyt się podniecać ⟨-cić⟩; **o•ver•'ex•pose** *v/t PHOT* prześwietlać ⟨-lić⟩; **o•ver•'fish•ing** *s* nadmierne połowy *pl* (ryb)

o•ver•flow **I** [əʊvə'fləʊ] *v/i* **1.** przelewać ⟨-lać⟩ się; ***the bath is ~ing*** z wanny wylewa się woda; ***her heart ~ed with love*** jej serce przepełniała miłość **2.** (*river*) wylewać ⟨-lać⟩ **3.** być przepełnionym; ***the streets were ~ing with crowds*** tłumy przepełniały ulice; ***the hospitals are filled to ~ing*** szpitale są przepełnione **II** [əʊvə'fləʊ] *v/t* ***the river overflowed its banks*** rzeka wystąpiła z brzegów **III** ['əʊvəfləʊ] *s* **1.** przepełnienie *n* **2.** nadmiar *m* **3.** przelewanie *n* się, przelew *m* **4.** wylewanie *n* się, wylew *m* **5.** ~ (**pipe**) *TECH* przelew *m* **6.** *INF* przekroczenie *n* zakresu, nadmiar *m*

o•ver•'grown *adj* **1.** *path*, *garden*: zarośnięty (**with** *I*) **2.** przerośnięty; ***they behave like ~ children*** zachowują się jak duże dzieci

'o•ver•hang **I** [əʊvə'hæŋ] (*overhung*; *overhung*) *v/i* zwisać, zwieszać się **II** [əʊvə'hæŋ] (*overhung*; *overhung*) *v/t* zwisać nad *I*, zwieszać się nad *I* **III** [əʊvəhæŋ] *s* **1.** nawis *m*, zwis *m* **2.** okap *m*

o•verhaul **I** [əʊvəhɔːl] *v/t* **1.** *TECH* robić ⟨z-⟩ przegląd **2.** *SPORT* wyprzedzać ⟨-dzić⟩ **II** [əʊvəhɔːl] *s* TECH przegląd *m*

'o•ver•head **I** [əʊvə'hed] *adv* nad głową, w górze **II** [əʊvə'hed] *adj* **1.** nad głową, w górze **2.** *cable*: napowietrzny **III** *s Am* → ***overheads***; **o•ver•'head kick** *s* SPORT przewrotka *f*; **over•'head pro•jec•tor** *s* rzutnik *m*; **o•ver•heads** ['əʊvəheds] *Br pl* ECON koszty *pl* ogólne, koszty *pl* stałe

o•ver•'hear (*overheard*; *overheard*) *v/t* słyszeć ⟨u-⟩ przypadkiem; **o•ver•'heat** **I** *v/i* (*engine*, *economy*) przegrzewać ⟨-rzać⟩ się **II** *v/t engine*, *economy*: przegrzewać ⟨-rzać⟩; **o•ver•'heat•ed** *adj* **1.** przegrzany, zbyt ciepły; ***the room was ~*** w pokoju było zbyt ciepło **2.** *imagination*: rozpalony; **o•ver•in'dulge** **I** *v/t children*: rozpuszczać ⟨-puścić⟩, pozwalać ⟨-wolić⟩ na zbyt wiele **II** *v/i* **1.** przesadzać ⟨-dzić⟩ (**in** z *I*); ***~ in chocolate*** przesadzić z czekoladą **2.** objadać ⟨-jeść⟩ się **3.** za dużo wypijać ⟨-pić⟩; **o•ver•'joyed** *adj* wielce uradowany, bardzo szczęśliwy (**at** z powodu *G*); ***she was ~ at his success*** jego sukces ogromniej ją ucieszył; ***be absolutely ~*** nie posiadać się z radości; **'o•ver•kill** *s* **1.** nadmiar *m*, przesada *f* **2.** możność *f* wielokrotnego zniszczenia przeciwnika

o•ver•'land **I** *adj route*: lądowy **II** *adv travel*: lądem

o•ver•'lap **I** *v/i* **1.** nakładać ⟨nałożyć⟩ się (na siebie), zachodzić ⟨zajść⟩ na siebie **2.** (*events*) pokrywać ⟨-ryć⟩ się (częściowo), kolidować; **II** *s* **1.** ***there is an ~ between the two subjects*** zakresy tych przedmiotów częściowo się pokrywają **2.** ***there is an ~ of 5 cm on each roof tile*** dachówki zachodzą na siebie na 5 cm **3.** ***there was an ~ between the two events*** terminy tych dwóch wydarzeń kolidowały ze sobą; **o•ver•'leaf** *adv* na odwrocie

o•ver•'load **I** *v/t* **1.** przeciążać ⟨-żyć⟩ (**with** *I*); ***~ed with work*** przeciążony **2.** *lorry*: przeładowywać ⟨-dować⟩ **II** *s* **1.** nadmiar *m*; ***information ~*** nadmiar informacji **2.** przeciążenie *n*; **o•ver•'look** *v/t* **1.** przeoczać ⟨-czyć⟩, nie zauważać ⟨-żyć⟩ **2.** ignorować ⟨z-⟩ **3.** *window*: wychodzić na *A*; ***a room ~ing the sea*** pokój z widokiem na morze

o•ver•ly ['əʊvəlɪ] *adv* (na)zbyt; ***I'm not ~ fond of pizza*** niezbyt lubię pizzę, nie przepadam za pizzą

o•ver•'manned *adj*: ***the office was ~*** w biurze było zbyt wielu pracowników; ***the company is ~*** w firmie występuje przerost zatrudnienia; **o•ver•'man•ning** *s* przerost *m* zatrudnienia; **o•ver•'much** *Br* **I** *adv* zbyt, zbytnio; ***she didn't worry ~ about it*** niezbyt się tym martwiła **II** *adj* zbytni

'o•ver•night **I** [əʊvə'nait] *adv* **1.** na noc; ***stay ~ in London*** zatrzymać się na noc w Londynie **2.** z dnia na dzień, nagle; ***improve ~*** polepszyć się z dnia na dzień **II** [əʊvənait] *adj* **1.** nocny; ***~ flight*** nocny lot; ***~ accommodation*** nocleg(i) **2.** z dnia na dzień, nagły; **o•ver•night 'bag** *s* **1.** niewielka torba *f* (podróżna) **2.** kosmetyczka *f*

o•ver•'paid *adj person*: zbyt dobrze opłacany; ***be ~*** otrzymywać zbyt wysokie wynagrodzenie; **'o•ver•pass** *s Am* estakada *f*, wiadukt *m*; **o•ver•'pay** (*overpaid*; *overpaid*) *v/t* **1.** *tax*: płacić ⟨za-⟩ zbyt wysoki **2.** *employee*: płacić ⟨za-⟩ zbyt wysokie wynagrodzenie; **o•ver•'play** *v/t* przeceniać ⟨-nić⟩; ***his role was ~ed*** przeceniono jego rolę; ***~ one's hand*** *fig* przeliczyć się (ze swoimi możliwościami); **o•ver•pop•u•lat•ed** *adj country*, *town*: przeludniony; **'o•ver•pop•u•'la•tion** *s* przeludnienie *n*; **o•ver•'pow•er** *v/t* **1.** obezwładniać ⟨-nić⟩ **2.** rozgramiać ⟨-romić⟩, pokonywać ⟨-nać⟩; **o•ver•'pow•ering** *adj* **1.** *heat*: nieznośny, obezwładniający **2.** *desire*: przemożny **3.** *smell*: bardzo intensywny **4.** *personality*: bardzo silny, dominujący

o•ver•'priced *adj* zbyt drogi; **o•ver•pro•'duc•tion** *s* ECON nadprodukcja *f*; **o•ver•'rate** *v/t* **1.** przeceniać ⟨-nić⟩ **2.** przereklamowywać ⟨-mować⟩; **o•ver•rat•ed** *adj* **1.** przeceniony **2.** przereklamowany; **o•ver•'reach** *v/t*: ***~ oneself*** przecenić własne możliwości, przeliczyć się ze swoimi siłami; **o•ver•re'act** *v/i* reagować ⟨za-⟩ nerwowo, reagować ⟨za-⟩ przesad-

O

nie (*to* na *A*); ***the financial markets ~ed to the news*** rynki finansowe zareagowały na tę wiadomość nerwowo; **o•ver•re•'ac•tion** *s* nerwowa reakcja *f*, przesadna reakcja *f* (*to* na *A*); **o•ver•'ride** (*overrode*; *overridden*) *v/t* **1.** unieważniać ⟨-nić⟩ **2.** *objection*: odrzucać ⟨-cić⟩ **3.** być ważniejszym od *G* **4.** *law*: znosić ⟨znieść⟩, uchylać ⟨-lić⟩; **o•ver•'rid•ing** *adj* **1.** nadrzędny **2.** główny **3.** najważniejszy; ***his ~ concern was to meet the deadline*** najbardziej zależało mu na tym, by skończyć w terminie; **o•ver•'rule** *v/t* **1.** unieważniać ⟨-nić⟩ **2.** *objection*: odrzucać ⟨-cić⟩; **o•ver•'run** (*overran*; *overrun*) *v/t* **1.** opanowywać ⟨-nować⟩; ***enemy soldiers overran the island*** żołnierze wroga opanowali wyspę **2.** *time, costs*: przekraczać ⟨-roczyć⟩; ***you've ~ your time by 10 minutes*** przekroczyłeś wyznaczony czas o 10 minut

o•ver•'seas I ['əʊvəsiːz] *adj* zagraniczny; ***~ students*** zagraniczni studenci **II** ['əʊvə'siːz] *adv* **1.** za granicą; ***the product is sold both at home and ~*** produkt jest sprzedawany zarówno w kraju, jak i za granicą **2.** za granicę **3.** na kontynencie

o•ver•'see (*oversaw*; *overseen*) *v/t* **1.** nadzorować **2.** *elections*: obserwować; **o•ver•'sexed** *adj infml* niewyżyty seksualnie; ***be ~*** mieć obsesję na punkcie seksu; **o•ver•'shad•ow** *v/t* **1.** usuwać ⟨usunąć⟩ w cień; ***he had always been ~ed by his elder sister*** zawsze stał w cieniu swojej starszej siostry **2.** *fig* kłaść ⟨położyć⟩ się cieniem na *L* **3.** zacieniać ⟨-nić⟩; **o•ver•'shoot** (*overshot*; *overshot*) *v/t* **1.** mijać ⟨minąć⟩ **2.** *limit*: przekraczać ⟨-roczyć⟩; **'o•ver•sight** *s* **1.** przeoczenie *n*, niedopatrzenie *n*; ***by ~*** przez niedopatrzenie **2.** nadzór *m*

o•ver•sim•pli•fi'ca•tion zbytnie uproszczenie *n*; **o•ver•'sim•pli•fy** *v/t* zbytnio upraszczać ⟨-rościć⟩; **'o•ver•size(d)** *adj* **1.** wielki, olbrzymi **2.** zbyt duży; **o•ver•'sleep** (*overslept*; *overslept*) *v/i* zasypiać ⟨-spać⟩; **o•ver•'spend I** (*overspent*; *overspent*) *v/i* **1.** wydawać ⟨-dać⟩ za dużo **2.** przekraczać ⟨-roczyć⟩ budżet **II** (*overspent*; *overspent*) *v/t budget*: przekraczać ⟨-roczyć⟩; **o•ver•'staffed** *adj*: ***the office was ~*** w biurze było zbyt wielu pracowników; ***the company is ~*** w firmie występuje przerost zatrudnienia; **o•ver•'state** *v/t* przeceniać ⟨-nić⟩; ***~ one's case*** przesadzać; ***s.th. cannot be ~d*** coś jest nie do przecenienia, czegoś nie można przecenić; **o•ver•'state•ment** *s* przesada *f*; **o•ver•'stay** *v/t*: ***~ one's visa*** pozostać po upływie ważności wizy ***~ one's welcome*** nadużyć czyjejś gościnności; **o•ver•'step** *v/t limits*: przekraczać ⟨-roczyć⟩; ***~ one's authority*** przekroczyć swoje kompetencje

o•vert ['əʊvɜːt] *adj* **1.** jawny **2.** otwarty **3.** wyraźny

o•ver•'take (*overtook*; *overtaken*) *v/t* **1.** *a. fig* wyprzedzać ⟨-dzić⟩; ***it's dangerous to ~ on a bend*** wyprzedzanie na zakręcie jest niebezpieczne **2.** (*emotion*) ogarniać ⟨-nąć⟩; ***a sudden panic overtook her*** nagle ogarnęła ją panika **3.** (*weather*) zaskakiwać ⟨-skoczyć⟩; ***the climbers were overtaken by bad weather*** alpinistów zaskoczyła zła pogoda; **o•ver•'tax** *v/t* **1.** *person, company*: obciążać ⟨-żyć⟩ zbyt wysokim podatkiem **2.** nakładać ⟨nałożyć⟩ zbyt wysoki podatek na *A* **3.** przemęczać ⟨-czyć⟩, nadwerężać ⟨-żyć⟩; ***~ oneself*** przeforsować się

o•ver•throw I [əʊvə'θrəʊ] (*overthrew*; *overthrown*) *v/t government*: obalać ⟨-lić⟩ **II** ['əʊvə'θrəʊ] *s* obalenie *n*

'o•ver•time *s* **1.** nadgodziny *pl*; ***work ~*** pracować w nadgodzinach; ***they pay £60 a day plus ~*** płacą 60 funtów dziennie plus nadgodziny **2.** SPORT *Am* dogrywka *f*

o•vert•ly ['əʊvɜːtlɪ] *adv* **1.** jawnie **2.** otwarcie **3.** wyraźnie

o•ver•ture ['əʊvətʃʊə] *s* MUS uwertura *f*; **o•ver•tures** *pl* zabiegi *pl*; ***make ~ to*** zwrócić się do *G*; ***make sexual ~ to*** *infml* przystawiać się do *G*

o•ver•'turn I *v/t* **1.** wywracać ⟨-rócić⟩ **2.** *decision*: unieważniać ⟨-nić⟩ **3.** *sentence*: uchylać ⟨-lić⟩ **II** *v/i* **1.** wywracać ⟨-rócić⟩ się **2.** (*car*) wywracać ⟨-rócić⟩ się na dach **3.** (*boat*) wywracać ⟨-rócić⟩ się do góry dnem; **o•ver-**

O

use I *v/t* **1.** nadużywać ⟨-żyć⟩ **2.** zbyt intensywnie użytkować **II** [əʊvə'juːs] *s* **1.** nadużywanie *n* **2.** zbyt intensywnie użytkownie *n*; **'o•ver•view** *s* **1.** przegląd *m* **2.** zarys *m*; **o•ver'weight** *adj*: ***be ~*** mieć nadwagę; ***~ people*** ludzie z nadwagą; **o•ver'whelm** [əʊvə'welm] *v/t* **1.** przytłaczać ⟨-łoczyć⟩ **2.** ogarniać ⟨-nąć⟩; ***she was ~ed with grief*** ogarnął ją przejmujący smutek **3.** głęboko poruszać ⟨-szyć⟩; ***he felt ~ed by their kindness*** był głęboko poruszony ich dobrocią **4.** *opponent*: rozgramiać ⟨-romić⟩, miażdżyć ⟨z-⟩ **5.** *fig* zarzucać ⟨-cić⟩, zasypywać ⟨-pać⟩; ***we were ~ed by requests of information*** zostaliśmy zasypani prośbami o informacje; **o•ver'whelm•ing** [əʊvə'welmɪŋ] *adj* **1.** przytłaczający **2.** *defeat*: druzgocący **3.** *desire*: przemożny **4.** *sorrow*: przejmujący, wszechogarniający **5.** *relief*: ogromny; **o•ver•'work I** *v/i* przepracowywać ⟨-cować⟩ się; ***you have been ~ing*** za dużo pracujesz **II** *s* przepracowanie *n*; **o•ver•'work•ed** *adj* przepracowany; **o•ver•'write** (*overwrote*; *overwritten*) *v/t* INF nadpisywać ⟨-sać⟩

o•vi•duct ['əʊvɪdʌkt] *s* ANAT jajowód *m*

o•vip•a•rous [əʊ'vɪpərəs] *adj* BIOL jajorodny

ov•u•late ['ɒvjʊleɪt] *v/i* BIOL jajeczkować, mieć owulację; **ov•u•la•tion** [ɒvjʊ'leɪʃn] *s* BIOL owulacja *f*, jajeczkowanie *n*

o•vum ['əʊvəm] *pl ova* ['əʊvə] *s* BIOL komórka *f* jajowa, jajo *n*

owe [əʊ] *v/t* **1.** *a. fig* być winnym (**s.th. to** coś *D*); ***she still ~s her father £300*** ciągle jest winna swojemu ojcu 300 funtów; ***how much do I ~ you?*** **a)** ile ci jestem winien? **b)** ile płacę? ***you ~ me a favour*** jesteś mi winien przysługę; ***you ~ us an apology*** jesteś nam winien przeprosiny **2.** mieć dług (**to** wobec *G*); ***I ~ a debt of gratitude to all my family*** mam dług wdzięczności wobec całej mojej rodziny **3.** zawdzięczać (**s.th. to** coś *D*); ***he ~s his success to hard work*** swój sukces zawdzięcza ciężkiej pracy; **ow•ing** ['oʊɪŋ] *adj* **1.** *money*: należny; ***be still ~*** pozostawać do zapłaty **2. ~ to** **a)** z powodu *G* **b)** dzięki *D*

owl [aʊl] *s* BIOL sowa *f*

own [əʊn] **I** *adj* własny; ***I saw it with my ~ eyes*** widziałem to na własne oczy; ***I need a room of my ~*** potrzebuję własnego pokoju; ***she makes all her ~ clothes*** sama szyje sobie wszystkie ubrania; ***for reasons of his ~*** z sobie tylko znanych powodów; ***come into one's ~*** okazywać się bardzo przydatnym; ***on one's ~*** sam; ***she's all on her ~*** jest zupełnie sama **II** *v/t* posiadać, mieć; ***who ~s that car?*** kto jest właścicielem tego samochodu?; ***do you ~ the house or do you rent it?*** to twój dom czy go wynajmujesz?; ***an American ~ed company*** amerykańska firma **III** *v/i dated* przyznawać ⟨-nać⟩ (**that** że); **own up** *v/i* przyznawać ⟨-nać⟩ się (**to** do *G*); **own 'brand** *s* ECON *Br* marka *f* własna; **own•er** ['əʊnə] *s* właściciel *m*; ***rightful ~*** prawowity właściciel; **own•er-'oc•cu•pied** *adj* zajmowany przez właściciela; **own•er-'oc•cu•pi•er** *s* **1.** właściciel *m* zajmowanego (przez siebie) lokalu **2.** właściciel *m* zajmowanej (przez siebie) nieruchomości; **own•er•ship** ['əʊnəʃɪp] *s* własność *f*; ***be in s.o.'s ~*** należeć do kogoś, być w czyimś posiadaniu; **own 'goal** *s* SPORT bramka *f* samobójcza

ox [ɒks] *pl oxen* ['ɒksn] *s* BIOL wół *m*

Ox•bridge ['ɒksbrɪdʒ] *s* uniwersytety *pl* Oksford i Cambridge; ***~ graduates*** absolwenci Oksfordu lub Cambridge

ox•en ['ɒksn] *pl* → **ox**

ox•ide ['ɒksaɪd] *s* CHEM tlenek *m*; **ox•i•dize** ['ɒksɪdaɪz] **I** *v/t* CHEM utleniać ⟨-nić⟩ **II** *v/i* utleniać ⟨-nić⟩ się

'ox•tail *s* COOK ogon *m* wołowy; ***~ soup*** zupa ogonowa

ox•y•gen ['ɒksɪdʒən] *s* CHEM tlen *m*; **'ox•y•gen mask** *s* maska *f* tlenowa; **'ox•y•gen tent** *s* namiot *m* tlenowy

oy•ster ['ɔɪstə] *s* BIOL ostryga *f*; **'oys•ter bed** *s* ławica *f* ostryg

oz *abbr* (=**ounce**) → **ounce**

o•zone ['əʊzəʊn] *s* CHEM ozon *m*; **o•zone 'friend•ly** *adj* nieszkodliwy dla warstwy ozonowej; **'o•zone hole** *s* dziura *f* ozonowa; **'o•zone lay•er** *s* warstwa *f* ozonowa

O

P

p. *abbr* **1.** (= ***page***) s. **2.** (= ***penny*** lub ***pence***) pens

PA [piː'eɪ] **1.** (=***public address system***) system *m* nagłaśniający **2.** (=***personal assistant***) asystent *m*

pace [peɪs] **I** *s* **1.** tempo *n*; ***at a slow ~*** w wolnym tempie, wolno; ***at one's own ~*** własnym rytmem; ***set the ~*** dyktować tempo **2.** krok *m*; ***quicken one's ~*** przyśpieszyć kroku; ***keep ~ with*** dotrzymywać kroku *D*; ***keep ~ with the time*** iść z duchem czasu; ***put s.o. through his ~s*** poddać kogoś próbie **II** *v/i* **~** (***up and down***) chodzić tam i z powrotem **III** *v/t* **1.** chodzić tam i z powrotem po *L* **2.** ***~ oneself*** wyznaczyć sobie odpowiednie tempo; **pace off**, ***pace out*** odmierzać ⟨-rzyć⟩ krokami

'pace•mak•er *s* **1.** MED rozrusznik *m* **2.** (*runner*) *infml* zając *m* **3.** lider *m*

Pa•cif•ic [pə'sɪfɪk] *s*: ***the ~*** (*Ocean*) Ocean Spokojny, Pacyfik

pac•ifi•er ['pæsɪfaɪə] *s Am* smoczek *m*

pac•i•fism ['pæsɪfɪzm] *s* pacyfizm *m*; **pac•i•fist** ['pæsɪfɪst] **I** *s* pacyfista *m* **II** *adj* pacyfistyczny

pac•i•fy ['pæsɪfaɪ] *v/t* **1.** uspokajać ⟨-koić⟩ **2.** *critics*: uciszać ⟨-szyć⟩ **3.** zaprowadzać ⟨-dzić⟩ pokój w *L*

pack [pæk] **I** *s* **1.** paczka *f*; ***a ~ of cigarettes*** paczka papierosów **2.** opakowanie *n* **3.** pakiet *m*; ***an information ~*** pakiet informacyjny **4.** plecak *m* **5.** grupa *f* **6.** *wolves*: wataha *f* **7.** *dogs*: sfora *f* **8.** banda *f*; ***a ~ of thieves*** banda złodziei **9.** peleton *m* **10.** *cards*: talia *f* **11.** maseczka *m* **12.** okład *m* **13.** ***a ~ of lies*** stek kłamstw **II** *v/t* **1.** pakować ⟨za-⟩; ***did you ~ the camera?*** zapakowałeś aparat?; ***~ one's bags*** *fig* pakować manatki **2.** (*a.* ***~ up***) pakować ⟨o-⟩; ***the paintings were carefully ~ed*** obrazy zostały dokładnie opakowane **3.** wypełniać ⟨-nić⟩ **4.** ubijać ⟨ubić⟩; ***~ the earth down around the plant*** ubij ziemię wokół rośliny **III** *v/i* **1.** pakować ⟨s-⟩ się; ***I haven't ~ed yet*** jeszcze się nie spakowałem **2.** (*a.* ***~ together***) mieścić ⟨z-⟩ się, wciskać ⟨-snąć⟩ się; ***we ~ed together into one car*** wcisnęliśmy się do jednego samochodu; **pack in** *v/t infml* **1.** *work*: rzucać ⟨-cić⟩ **2.** ***pack it in!*** przestań!; **pack into** *v/t* **1.** mieścić ⟨z-⟩ **2.** pakować ⟨u-⟩ **3.** wypełniać ⟨-nić⟩; **pack off** *v/t infml* wysyłać ⟨-słać⟩; ***my parents always packed me off to bed early*** moi rodzice zawsze wcześnie wysyłali mnie do łóżka; **pack up I** *v/t* **1.** pakować ⟨za-⟩ **2.** *Br infml work*: rzucać ⟨-cić⟩ **II** *v/i* **1.** pakować ⟨s-⟩ się **2.** (*machine*) *Br infml* nawalać ⟨-lić⟩

pack•age ['pækɪdʒ] **I** *s* **1.** paczka *f*; ***a ~ arrived for you*** przyszła do ciebie paczka **2.** opakowanie *n* **3.** pakiet *m* **II** *v/t* (*a.* ***~ up***) pakować ⟨za-⟩; **'pack•age deal** *s* pakiet *m*; **'pack•age hol•i•day** *s* wakacje *pl* zorganizowane; **'pack•age tour** *s* wycieczka *f* zorganizowana; **pack•ag•ing** ['pækɪdʒɪŋ] *s* **1.** opakowanie *n* **2.** pakowanie *n*

'pack an•i•mal *s* zwierzę *n* juczne

packed [pækt] *adj* **1.** pełny; ***the play ran to ~ houses*** przedstawienia odbywały się przy kompletach widzów; ***a book ~ with information*** książka zawierająca wielką ilość informacji **2.** zatłoczony **3.** *infml* spakowany; **packed 'lunch** *s* drugie śniadanie *n*

pack•et ['pækɪt] *s* **1.** paczka *f*; ***a ~ of biscuits*** paczka ciastek **2.** opakowanie *n* **3.** *Am* saszetka *f* **4.** *data*: pakiet *m* **5.** ***it must have cost a ~*** *infml* to musiało kosztować kupę forsy

'pack horse *s* koń *m* juczny

'pack ice *s* (*ice*) pak *m*

pack•ing ['pækɪŋ] *s* **1.** pakowanie *n*; ***do one's ~*** spakować się **2.** opakowanie *n*; **'pack•ing case** *s* skrzynia *f*

pact [pækt] *s* pakt *m*; ***a non-aggression ~*** pakt o nieagresji; ***make a ~ with*** zawrzeć umowę z *I*

pad[1] [pæd] *v/i* cicho chodzić

pad[2] [~] **I** *s* **1.** wacik *m* **2.** (*a.* ***sanitary ~***) podpaska *f* **3.** (*a.* ***writing ~***) notatnik *m*, bloczek *m* **4.** INF podkładka *f* pod mysz **5.** lądowisko *n* **6.** SPORT ochraniacz *m*; ***an elbow ~*** nałokietnik **7.** *foot*: poduszka *f* **8.** *infml* mieszkanie *n* **II** *v/t* **1.** → ***pad out*** **1**, **2**, **3** **2.** *bill*: zawyżać ⟨-żyć⟩; **pad out** *v/t* **1.** wypychać ⟨-pchać⟩ **2.** wyściełać ⟨-cielić⟩

3. wykładać ⟨wyłożyć⟩ 4. *text*: wydłużać ⟨-żyć⟩; **be padded out with** być pełnym *G*; **pad•ded shoulders** *pl* watowane ramiona *pl*; **pad•ding** ['pædıŋ] *s* 1. wyściółka *f* 2. obicie *n* 3. *infml* lanie *n* wody

pad•dle ['pædəl] I *s* 1. wiosło *n* 2. *mixer*: łopatka *f* 3. *Am* rakietka *f* (do ping-ponga) 4. ***we went for a ~*** brodziliśmy po wodzie, chodziliśmy (przy brzegu) po wodzie II *v/i* 1. wiosłować 2. brodzić III *v/t* ***~ a boat*** wiosłować; **'pad•dle steam•er** *Br*, **'pad•dle boat** *Am s* parowiec *m* kołowy

pad•dling pool ['pædlıŋpu:l] *s* brodzik *m*

pad•dock ['pædək] *s* 1. padok *m* 2. wybieg *m*

pad•dy[1] ['pædı] *s* (*a.* ***~ field***) pole *n* ryżowe

pad•dy[2] [~] *s*: ***he was in a ~*** *Br infml* był wściekły

Pad•dy ['pædı] *s* (*offensive*) *infml* Irlandczyk *m*

'pad•dy wag•on *s Am infml* samochód *m* więźniarka *f*

pad•lock ['pædlɒk] I *s* kłódka *f* II *v/t* zamykać ⟨-mknąć⟩ na kłódkę

pae•di•at•ric [pi:dı'ætrık] *Br*, **pe•di•at•ric** *Am adj* 1. pediatryczny 2. dziecięcy

pae•di•a•tri•cian [pi:dıə'trıʃn] *Br*, **pe•di•at•ri•cian** *Am s* pediatra *m*; **pae•di•at•rics** [pi:dı'ætrıks] *Br*, **pe•di•at•rics** *Am s* pediatria *f*

pae•do•phile ['pi:dəfaıl] *Br*, **pe•do•phile** *Am s* pedofil *m*

pa•gan ['peıgən] I *adj* pogański II *s* poganin *m*; **pa•gan•ism** ['peıgənızəm] *s* pogaństwo *n*

page[1] [peıdʒ] *s* 1. strona *f*; ***on ~ 10*** na stronie 10; ***turn to ~ 64*** przejdź na stronę 64; ***four-~*** czterostronicowy; ***a home ~*** INF strona główna 2. kartka *f* 3. karta *f*; ***a glorious ~ in the history of Australia*** chlubna karta w historii Australii

page[2] [~] I *s* 1. giermek *m* 2. paź *m* 3. *Br* boy *m* (hotelowy) II *v/t* 1. wzywać ⟨wezwać⟩ (przez głośnik) 2. wysyłać ⟨-słać⟩ wiadomość na pager do *G*

pa•geant ['peıdʒənt] *s* 1. *Am* konkurs *m* piękności 2. widowisko *n* 3. parada *f*

'page•boy *s* 1. *Br* boy *m* hotelowy 2. (*hairstyle*) paź *m*

pag•er ['peıdʒə] *s* pager *m*

pag•i•nate ['pædʒıneıt] *v/t* paginować; **pag•i•na•tion** [pædʒı'neıʃn] *s* paginacja *f*

pa•go•da [pə'gəʊdə] *s* pagoda *f*

paid [peıd] I *Past Simple and Past Participle* → **pay** II *adj* płatny; ***a well-~ job*** dobrze płatna praca; **paid em'ploy•ment** *s* zatrudnienie *n* za wynagrodzeniem; **paid-'up cap•it•al** *s* ECON kapitał *m* wpłacony

pail [peıl] *s dated* wiadro *n*, kubeł *m*

pain [peın] I *s* 1. ból *m*; ***be in ~*** cierpieć, odczuwać ból; ***I have a ~ in my back*** boli mnie kręgosłup; ***be a ~ in the neck*** *infml* być denerwującym, być nieznośnym 2. cierpienie *n* 3. ***on*** (*a.* ***under***) ***~ of*** *form* pod groźbą *G* II *v/t* 1. *fig* ranić ⟨z-⟩ 2. boleć 3. sprawiać ⟨-wić⟩ ból; ***he was deeply ~ed by her words*** jej słowa bardzo go zraniły; **pain•ful** ['peınfəl] *adj* 1. bolesny; ***be ~*** boleć; ***is your back still ~?*** ciągle boli cię kręgosłup?; ***a ~ memory*** bolesne wspomnienie 2. obolały 3. przykry; **pain•ful•ly** ['peınfəlı] *adv* 1. boleśnie 2. bardzo; ***~ slow*** bardzo powolny; **pain•kill•er** ['peınkılə] *s* środek *m* przeciwbólowy; **pain•less** ['peınlıs] *adj* 1. bezbolesny 2. łatwy 3. prosty

pains•tak•ing ['peınzteıkıŋ] *adj* dokładny, drobiazgowy; **pains•tak•ing•ly** ['peınzteıkıŋlı] *adv* dokładnie, drobiazgowo

paint [peınt] I *s* 1. farba *f*; ***wet ~!*** świeżo malowane!; ***the ~ is starting to peel off*** farba zaczyna odchodzić 2. ***~s*** farby, farbki; ***oil ~s*** farby olejne II *v/t* 1. malować ⟨po-, na-⟩; ***the walls were ~ed yellow*** ściany zostały pomalowane na żółto; ***~ nails*** malować paznokcie; ***~ the town red*** *infml* zaszaleć 2. *fig* przedstawiać ⟨-wić⟩; ***she was ~ed in a bad light*** przedstawiono ją w niekorzystnym świetle; ***~ a gloomy picture of s.th.*** odmalować coś w czarnym barwach; **paint out, paint over** *v/t* zamalowywać ⟨-lować⟩

'paint•box *s* pudełko *n* farb; **'paint•brush** *s* pędzel *m*; **paint•er** ['peıntə] *s* malarz *m*

P

'pain thresh•old *s* próg *m* bólu
paint•ing ['peɪntɪŋ] *s* **1.** obraz *m* **2.** malowidło *n* **3.** malowanie *n* **4.** malarstwo *n*; **'paint strip•per** *s* rozpuszczalnik *m* do farb; **'paint•work** *s* farba *f*
pair [peə] **I** *s* para *f*; ***a ~ of shoes*** para butów; ***a ~ of scissors*** nożyczki; ***a ~ of children*** dwoje dzieci; ***in ~s*** w parach, parami; ***we need an extra ~ of hands*** potrzebujemy jeszcze jednej pary rąk **II** *v/t* **1.** (*a.* ***~ up***) łączyć ⟨po-⟩ w pary **2.** dopasowywać ⟨-sować⟩ **III** *v/i* (*a.* ***~ up***) łączyć ⟨po-⟩ się w pary; **pair off I** *v/t* kojarzyć ⟨s-⟩ (w parę) **II** *v/t* tworzyć ⟨s-⟩ parę
pa•ja•mas *Am* → ***pyjamas***
Pa•ki•stan [pɑːkɪ'stɑːn] *s* Pakistan *m*; **Pa•ki•sta•ni** [pɑːkɪ'stɑːnɪ] **I** *adj* pakistański **II** *s* Pakistańczyk *m*, Pakistanka *f*
pal [pæl] **I** *s infml* kumpel *m*; ***if I were you, pal*** na twoim miejscu, stary **II** *v/i* ***~ up with*** *infml* kumplować się z *I*
pal•ace ['pælɪs] *s* pałac *m*
pal•ae•o•lith•ic [pælɪəʊ'lɪθɪk] *Br*, ***pal•e•o•lith•ic*** *Am adj* paleolityczny; **pal•ae•on•tol•o•gy** [pælɪɒn'tɒlədʒɪ] *Br*, ***pa•le•on•tol•o•gy*** *Am s* paleontologia *f*
pal•at•a•ble ['pælətəbl] *adj* smaczny; ***make s.th. ~ to s.o.*** *fig* dopasować coś do czyichś gustów
pal•ate ['pælət] *s* podniebienie *n*; ***have a jaded ~*** być wybrednym
pa•la•tial [pə'leɪʃl] *adj* okazały, wspaniały
pa•lav•er [pə'lɑːvər] *s infml* **1.** zamieszanie *n* **2.** bzdury *pl*
pale[1] [peɪl] **I** *adj* **1.** blady; ***turn ~*** zblednąć; ***~ with fear*** blady ze strachu **2.** jasny; ***a ~ complexion*** jasna cera; ***~ blue eyes*** jasnoniebieskie oczy **3.** *light*: blady, słaby **II** *v/i* blednąć ⟨z-⟩; ***~ in comparison with*** blednąć przy *L*
pale[2] [~] *s*: ***beyond the ~*** nie do przyjęcia
pale•ness ['peɪlnɪs] *s* bladość *f*
Pal•e•stine ['pæləstaɪn] *s* Palestyna *f*; **Pal•e•stin•i•an** [pælə'stɪnɪən] **I** *adj* palestyński **II** *s* Palestyńczyk *m*, Palestynka *f*

pall[1] [pɔːl] *s* **1.** kir *m* **2.** (gęsta) chmura *f*; ***a ~ of smoke*** gęsta chmura dymu; ***cast a ~ over*** kłaść się cieniem na *L*
pall[2] [~] *v/i* **1.** nudzić ⟨z-⟩ się (***on*** *A*) **2.** blednąć ⟨przy-⟩
pal•let ['pælɪt] *s TECH* paleta *f*; **'pal•let truck** *s TECH* wózek *m* widłowy
pal•li•a•tive ['pælɪətɪv] **I** *adj* paliatywny **II** *s* **1.** *MED* paliatyw *m* **2.** *fig* półśrodek *m*
pal•lid ['pælɪd] *adj* blady, jasny; **pal•lor** ['pælə] *s* bladość *f*
pal•ly ['pælɪ] *adj*: ***she's ~ with him*** *infml* kumpluje się z nim
palm [pɑːm] **I** *s* **1.** dłoń *f*; ***read s.o.'s ~*** wróżyć komuś z ręki; ***have s.o. in the ~ of one's hand*** trzymać kogoś w garści; ***grease s.o.'s ~*** *infml* dać komuś w łapę **2.** (*a.* ***~ tree***) palma *f*; ***a coconut ~*** palma kokosowa **II** *v/t* ukrywać ⟨-ryć⟩ w dłoni; **palm off** *v/t* **1.** ***palm s.o. off with s.th.*** zbyć kogoś czymś **2.** ***palm s.th. off on s.o.*** wcisnąć komuś coś
palm•ist ['pɑːmɪst] *s* chiromanta *m*; **palm•is•try** ['pɑːmɪstrɪ] *s* chiromancja *f*
Palm 'Sun•day *s REL* Niedziela *f* Palmowa
palm•top ['pɑːmtɔp] *s INF* palmtop *m*
'palm tree *s* palma *f*, drzewo *n* palmowe
pa•lo•mi•no [pælə'miːnəʊ] *pl -nos s* koń *m* palomino
pal•pa•ble ['pælpəbl] *adj* **1.** wyczuwalny **2.** namacalny **3.** wyraźny; **pal•pa•bly** ['pælpəblɪ] *adv* wyraźnie
pal•pi•tate ['pælpɪteɪt] *v/i* (*heart*) kołatać; **pal•pi•ta•tions** [pælpɪ'teɪʃnz] *pl MED* palpitacje *pl*, kołatanie *n* serca
pal•sy ['pɔːlzɪ] *s MED* porażenie *n*
pal•try ['pɔːltrɪ] *adj* **1.** mizerny; ***a ~ sum*** mizerna suma **2.** marny; ***a ~ excuse*** marna wymówka
pam•pas ['pæmpəz] *s* pampa *f*, pampasy *pl*; **'pam•pas grass** *s* trawa *f* pampasowa
pam•per ['pæmpə] *v/t* rozpieszczać ⟨-pieścić⟩
pam•phlet ['pæmflɪt] *s* broszura *f*
pan[1] [pæn] **I** *s* **1.** ***a frying ~*** patelnia **2.** rondel *m* **3.** *scales*: szala *f* **4.** *Br*

muszla *f* klozetowa **II** *v/t infml* zjechać **III** *v/i gold*: wypłukiwać ⟨-kać⟩, płukać (**for** *A*); **pan out** *v/i infml* **1.** toczyć ⟨po-⟩ się **2.** iść ⟨pójść⟩; ***things have panned out well*** wszystko poszło dobrze

pan² [~] *v/i* (*camera*) przesuwać ⟨-sunąć⟩ się, panoramować

pan•a•ce•a [pænəˈsɪə] *s* panaceum *n* (**for** na *A*)

pa•nache [pəˈnæʃ] *s* polot *m*

Pan•a•ma [ˈpænəmɑː] *s* Panama *f*; **Pan•a•ma Ca•ˈnal** *s* Kanał *m* Panamski

pan•a•ma [ˈpænəmɑː] *s* (*hat*) panama *f*

Pan-A•ˈmer•i•can *adj* panamerykański

pan•cake [ˈpænkeɪk] *s* **1.** naleśnik *m* **2.** ~ ***rolls*** sajgonki

pan•cre•as [ˈpæŋkrɪəs] *s* ANAT trzustka *f*

pan•da [ˈpændə] *s* **1.** panda *f* **2.** ***a ~ car*** *Br infml* (mały) radiowóz

pan•dem•ic [pænˈdemɪk] *s* pandemia *f*

pan•de•mo•ni•um [pændɪˈməʊnɪəm] *s* pandemonium *n*, chaos *m*

pan•der [ˈpændə] *v/i*: ***~ to s.o.'s wishes*** spełniać czyjeś zachcianki

pane [peɪn] *s* szyba *f*, tafla *f* (szkła)

pan•el [ˈpænl] **I** *s* **1.** panel *m*; ***a ~ discussion*** dyskusja panelowa **2.** płyta *f* **3.** płytka *f* **4.** płycina *f* **5.** uczestnicy *pl* dyskusji **6.** *Am* ława *f* przysięgłych **7.** panel *m* sterowania **8.** deska *f* rozdzielcza **II** *v/t* **1.** wykładać ⟨wyłożyć⟩ (**in** *I*) **2.** wykładać ⟨wyłożyć⟩ panelami **pan•el•ling** [ˈpænəlɪŋ] *Br*, ***pan•el•ing*** *Am s* boazeria *f*; **pan•el•list** [ˈpænəlɪst] *Br*, ***pan•el•ist*** *Am s* uczestnik *m* dyskusji

pang [pæŋ] *s* **1.** ból *m*; ***he felt ~s of hunger*** skręcało go z głodu **2.** ukłucie *n*; ***a sudden ~ of jealousy*** nagłe ukłucie zazdrości; ***~s of conscience*** wyrzuty sumienia

ˈpan•han•dle *v/i Am infml* żebrać

pan•ic [ˈpænɪk] **I** *s* panika *f*; ***in ~*** w panice; ***get into a ~*** wpaść w panikę; ***cause ~*** wywołać panikę **II** *v/i* panikować ⟨s-⟩, wpadać ⟨wpaść⟩ w panikę **III** *v/t* przestraszyć; **ˈpan•ic buy•ing** *s* masowe wykupywanie *n* towarów; **ˈpan•ic sel•ling** *s* masowa wyprzedaż *f* towarów; **pan•ic•ky** [ˈpænɪkɪ] *adj* spanikowany, przestraszony; **ˈpan•ic-strick•en** *adj* spanikowany, przejęty panicznym strachem

pan•ni•er [ˈpænɪə] *s* **1.** sakwa *f* **2.** kufer *m* (boczny) **3.** kosz *m*

pan•o•ply [ˈpænəplɪ] *s fig* wachlarz *m*, zbiór *m*

pan•o•ra•ma [pænəˈrɑːmə] *s* **1.** panorama *f* **2.** przegląd *m*; **pa•no•ra•mic** [pænəˈræmɪk] *adj* panoramiczny; ***a ~ view*** widok panoramiczny

pan•sy [ˈpænzɪ] *s* **1.** (*flower*) bratek *m* **2.** *infml* ciota *f*

pant [pænt] *v/i* dyszeć, oddychać z trudem; ***~ for breath*** nie móc złapać tchu

pan•the•ism [ˈpænθiɪzəm] *s* panteizm *m*; **pan•the•is•tic** [pænθɪˈɪstɪk] *adj* panteistyczny

pan•ther [ˈpænθə] *s* **1.** pantera *f* **2.** *Am* puma *f*

pan•ti•hose → ***pantyhose***

pan•ties [ˈpæntɪz] *pl Am* majtki *pl*

pan•to•mime [ˈpæntəmaɪm] *s* przedstawienie *n* gwiazdkowe

pan•try [ˈpæntrɪ] *s* spiżarnia *f*

pants [pænts] *pl* **1.** *Br* majtki *pl* **2.** *Am* spodnie *pl*; ***catch s.o. with his ~ down*** nieprzyjemnie kogoś zaskoczyć; ***scare the ~ off s.o.*** śmiertelnie kogoś wystraszyć; ***bore the ~ off s.o.*** zanudzać kogoś na śmierć

pant•suit [ˈpæntsuːt] *s Am* spodnium *m*

pan•ty•hose [ˈpæntɪhəʊz] *pl Am* rajstopy *pl*

ˈpant•y lin•er *s* wkładka *f* higieniczna

pap [pæp] *s a. fig* papka *f*

pa•pa•cy [ˈpeɪpəsɪ] *s* **1.** papiestwo *n* **2.** pontyfikat *m*; ***the ~ of John Paul II*** pontyfikat Jana Pawła II

pa•pal [ˈpeɪpəl] *adj* papieski

pa•pa•ya [pəˈpaɪə] *s* papaja *f*

pa•per [ˈpeɪpə] **I** *s* **1.** papier *m*; ***a piece of ~*** kartka papieru **2.** gazeta *f* **3.** ***~s*** papiery, dokumenty; ***his desk was covered with ~s*** jego biurko było zarzucone papierami; ***divorce ~s*** dokumenty rozwodowe **4.** tapeta *f* **5.** artykuł *m* **6.** referat *m*; ***give a ~ on*** wygłosić referat na temat *G* **7.** *Am* praca *f* (pisemna) **8.** *Br* egzamin *m* (pisemny) **II** *v/t* tapetować ⟨wy-⟩; **paper over** *v/t fig* tuszować ⟨za-⟩, ukrywać ⟨-ryć⟩

ˈpa•per•back *s* książka *f* w miękkiej okładce; **pa•per ˈbag** *s* torebka *f* papierowa; **ˈpa•per boy** *s* gazeciarz *m*;

P

'pa•per•clip *s* spinacz *m* do papieru; **'pa•per cup** *s* papierowy kubek *m*; **'pa•per feed** *s* podajnik *m* (papieru); **'pa•per girl** *s* gazeciarka *f*; **pa•per 'hand•ker•chief** *s* chusteczka *f* higieniczna; **'pa•per knife** *s* nóż *m* do papieru; **'pa•per mon•ey** *s* banknoty *pl*; **pa•per 'plate** *s* papierowa tacka *f*; **'pa•per round** *s* roznoszenie *n* gazet; **'pa•per-thin** *adj* cieniutki, cienki jak papier; **'pa•per ti•ger** *s fig* papierowy tygrys *m*; **pa•per 'tis•sue** *s* chusteczka *f* higieniczna; **'pa•per•weight** *s* przycisk *m* do papieru; **'pa•per•work** *s* **1.** papierkowa *f* robota **2.** papiery *pl*, dokumenty *pl*

pa•pier-mâ•ché [pæpɪeɪ'mæʃeɪ] *s* masa *f* papierowa

pap•ri•ka ['pæprɪkə] *s* (*seasoning*) papryka *f*

pa•py•rus [pə'paɪərəs] *pl* *-ri* [~raɪ], *-ruses* *s* papirus *m*

par [pɑː] *s* **1.** ***be on a ~ with*** dorównywać *D*, być na równi z *I* **2.** norma *f*; ***the teaching is below ~*** poziom nauczania jest zbyt niski; ***feel below ~, feel under ~*** nie czuć się najlepiej, nie być w formie **3.** (*a.* ***~ value***) *ECON* wartość *f* nominalna (akcji) **4.** (*golf*) norma *f* (uderzeń); ***to be ~ for the course*** *fig* być na porządku dziennym, być normalnym

par•a•ble ['pærəbl] *s* przypowieść *f*

pa•rab•o•la [pə'ræbələ] *s MATH* parabola *f*; **par•a•bol•ic** [pærə'bɒlɪk] *adj* paraboliczny

par•a•chute ['pærəʃuːt] **I** *s* spadochron *m*; ***a ~ jump*** skok ze spadochronem **II** *v/i* skakać ⟨skoczyć⟩ ze spadochronem **III** *v/t* zrzucać ⟨-cić⟩ na spadochronie; **par•a•chut•ist** ['pærəʃuːtɪst] *s* spadochroniarz *m*

pa•rade [pə'reɪd] **I** *s* **1.** parada *f*; ***St Patrick's Day ~*** parada w dniu św. Patryka **2.** pochód *m* **3.** defilada *f*; ***a military ~*** defilada, parada wojskowa **4.** *fashion*: pokaz *m* **5.** ***a shopping ~*** *Br* galeria sklepów **II** *v/i* **1.** maszerować ⟨prze-⟩ **2.** defilować ⟨prze-⟩ **3.** paradować **III** *v/t* afiszować się obnosić się z *I*; **pa•rade ground** *s* plac *m* apelowy

par•a•digm ['pærədaɪm] *s* **1.** paradygmat *m* **2.** *form* przykład *m* **3.** wzór *m*

par•a•dise ['pærədaɪs] *s* raj *m*

par•a•dox ['pærədɒks] *s* paradoks *m*; **par•a•dox•i•cal** [pærə'dɒksɪkl] *adj* paradoksalny; **par•a•dox•i•cal•ly** [pærə'dɒksɪklɪ] *adv* paradoksalnie

par•af•fin ['pærəfɪn] *s* **1.** (*a.* ***~ oil***) *Br* nafta *f* **2.** (*a.* ***~ wax***) parafina *f*

pa•ra•glid•er ['pærəglaɪdə] *s* **1.** paralotnia *f* **2.** paralotniarz *m*; **pa•ra•glid•ing** ['pærəglaɪdɪŋ] *s* paralotniarstwo *n*

par•a•gon ['pærəgən] *s* (*person*) wzór *m*; ***a ~ of virtue*** wzór cnót

par•a•graph ['pærəgræf] *s* akapit *m*

Par•a•guay ['pærəgwaɪ] *s* Paragwaj *m*

par•a•keet ['pærəkiːt] *s* papużka *f*

par•al•lel ['pærəlel] **I** *adj* **1.** równoległy (***to/with*** do *G*); ***a ~ port*** *INF* port równoległy **2.** paralelny **3.** podobny **4.** analogiczny **II** *adv* równolegle (***to*** do *G*) **III** *s* **1.** *GEOGR* równoleżnik *m* **2.** *MATH* równoległa *f* **3.** odpowiednik *m*; ***this tradition has no ~ in our culture*** ta tradycja nie ma odpowiednika w naszej kulturze; ***without ~*** bez precedensu **4.** paralela *f*; ***draw a ~ between*** przeprowadzić paralelę między *I* **IV** *v/t* **1.** być podobnym do *G*; ***their legal system ~s our own*** ich system prawny jest podobny do naszego **2.** ***s.th. is ~led by*** czemuś towarzyszy *A* **3.** dorównywać ⟨-nać⟩; **par•al•lel 'bars** *pl SPORT* poręcze *pl*; **par•al•lel•ism** ['pærəlelɪzəm] *s* podobieństwo *n*, paralelizm *m*; **par•al•lel•o•gram** [pærə'leləgræm] *s MATH* równoległobok *m*

Par•a•lym•pics [pærə'lɪmpɪks] *pl SPORT* paraolimpiada *f*

par•a•lyse ['pærəlaɪz] *Br*, **par•a•lyze** *Am v/t* paraliżować ⟨s-⟩; ***an accident left him ~d from the waist down*** na skutek wypadku jest sparaliżowany od pasa w dół; ***the airport is ~d by a strike*** lotnisko jest sparaliżowane przez strajk; ***~d with fear*** sparaliżowany ze strachu; **pa•ral•y•sis** [pə'ræləsɪs] *s* paraliż *m*; **par•a•lyt•ic** [pærə'lɪtɪk] *adj* **1.** sparaliżowany **2.** *fear*: paraliżujący **3.** *Br infml* zalany w trupa

par•a•med•ic [pærə'medɪk] *s* ratownik *m* medyczny

P

pa•ram•e•ter [pəˈræmɪtə] *s* **1.** parametr *m* **2.** kryterium *n* **3.** granica *f*; ***within the ~ of*** w granicach *G*

par•a•mil•i•tar•y [pærəˈmɪlɪterɪ] *adj* paramilitarny

par•a•mount [ˈpærəmaʊnt] *adj* najważniejszy; ***this matter is of ~ importance*** to sprawa najwyższej wagi

par•a•noi•a [pærəˈnɔɪə] *s* paranoja *f*; **par•a•noid** [ˈpærənɔɪd], ***par•a•noi•ac*** [pærəˈnɔɪæk] **I** *adj* **1.** paranoiczny; ***be ~ about*** *infml* mieć paranoję na punkcie *G* **2.** paranoidalny **II** *s* paranoik *m*

par•a•nor•mal [pærəˈnɔːməl] *adj* paranormalny

par•a•pet [ˈpærəpet] *s* balustrada *f*; ***put one's head above the ~*** *fig inflm* wychylać się

par•a•pher•na•li•a [pærəfəˈneɪlɪə] *pl* **1.** wyposażenie *n* **2.** akcesoria *pl* **3.** *infml* zawracanie *n* głowy

par•a•phrase [ˈpærəfreɪz] **I** *s* parafraza *f* **II** *v/t* parafrazować ⟨s-⟩

par•a•ple•gia [pærəˈpliːdʒɪə] *s* MED paraplegia *f*, porażenie *n* poprzeczne; **par•a•ple•gic** [pærəˈpliːdʒɪk] *adj*: ***be ~*** cierpieć na paraliż kończyn dolnych, być paraplegikiem

par•a•psy•chol•o•gy [pærəsaɪˈkɒlədʒɪ] *s* parapsychologia *f*

par•as•cend•ing [ˈpærəsendɪŋ] *s* SPORT *latanie na spadochronie wyniesionym w powietrze przez samochód lub motorówkę*

par•a•site [ˈpærəsaɪt] *s a. fig* pasożyt *m*; **par•a•sit•ic** [pærəˈsɪtɪk] *adj* pasożytniczy

par•a•sol [ˈpærəsɒl] *s* **1.** parasolka *f* (przeciwsłoneczna) **2.** parasol *m* (plażowy)

par•a•troop•er [ˈpærətruːpə] *s* (*soldier*) spadochroniarz *m*; **par•a•troops** [ˈpærətruːps] *pl* oddział *m* spadochronowy

par•boil [ˈpɑːbɔɪl] *v/t* **1.** gotować ⟨u-⟩ na półtwardo, podgotowywać ⟨-tować⟩ **2.** *rice*: preparować termicznie

par•cel [ˈpɑːsl] **I** *s* **1.** paczka *f* **2.** działka *f* **II** *v/t* (*a.* ***~ up***) pakować ⟨za-⟩; **par•cel out** *v/t* dzielić ⟨po-⟩ (***into*** na *A*); **ˈpar•cel bomb** *s* przesyłka *f* z materiałem wybuchowym; **ˈpar•cel post** *s Am* wysyłka *f* paczek

parch [pɑːtʃ] *v/t* suszyć ⟨wy-⟩

parch•ment [ˈpɑːtʃmənt] *s* pergamin *m*

par•don [ˈpɑːdn] **I** *s* **1.** ~, ***~ me*** *Am* **a)** słucham? **b)** przepraszam **2.** JUR ułaskawienie *n*, akt *m* łaski **3.** wybaczenie *n* (***for*** *A*); ***he asked her ~*** poprosił ją o wybaczenie **II** *v/t* **1.** ułaskawiać ⟨-wić⟩ **2.** wybaczać ⟨-czyć⟩ (***s.o. for*** komuś *A*); ***~ my ignorance, but*** proszę wybaczyć moją ignorancję, ale; ***if you'll ~ the expression*** przepraszam za wyrażenie; ***~ me for interrupting you*** przepraszam, że przeszkadzam; **par•don•a•ble** [ˈpɑːdnəbl] *adj mistake*: wybaczalny

pare [peə] *v/t* **1.** (*a.* ***~ off***, ***~ away***) usuwać ⟨usunąć⟩ **2.** (*a.* ***~ off***, ***~ away***) obierać ⟨obrać⟩ **3.** (*a.* ***~ back***, ***~ down***) *quantity*: ograniczać ⟨-czyć⟩, redukować ⟨z-⟩ **4.** *Br nails*: obcinać ⟨-ciąć⟩

par•ent [ˈpeərənt] **I** *s* rodzic *m*; ***he's still living with his ~s*** nadal mieszka z rodzicami **II** *adj* ***a ~ company*** ECON spółka matka; **par•ent•age** [ˈpeərəntɪdʒ] *s* pochodzenie *n*; ***an American of French ~*** Amerykanin francuskiego pochodzenia; **pa•ren•tal** [pəˈrentl] *adj* rodzicielski; ***~ rights*** prawa rodzicielskie; ***~ leave*** urlop wychowawczy

pa•ren•the•sis [pəˈrenθəsɪs] *pl* *-ses* [~siːz] *s* **1.** nawias *m*; ***in ~*** w nawiasie **2.** wtrącenie *n*

par•ent•hood [ˈpeərənthʊd] *s* rodzicielstwo *n*; **par•ent•ing** [ˈpeərəntɪŋ] *s* opieka *f* rodzicielska; **par•ent•less** [ˈpeərəntlɪs] *adj* osierocony; **ˈpar•ents-in-law** *pl* teściowie *pl*; **par•ent-ˈteach•er as•so•ci•a•tion** *s* komitet *m* rodzicielski

Par•is [ˈpærɪs] *s* Paryż *m*

par•ish [ˈpærɪʃ] *s* **1.** parafia *f*; ***a ~ church*** kościół parafialny; ***a ~ register*** księga parafialna **2.** *Br* gmina *f*; ***a ~ council*** rada gminy; **pa•rish•ion•er** [pəˈrɪʃənə] *s* parafianin *m*

par•i•ty [ˈpærətɪ] *s* **1.** równość *f* (***with*** z *I*) **2.** ECON parytet *m*

park [pɑːk] **I** *s* park *m*; ***a national ~*** park narodowy; ***an amusement ~*** park rozrywki **II** *v/t* parkować ⟨za-⟩; ***a ~ed car*** zaparkowany samochód; ***he ~ed badly*** źle zaparkował; ***a place to ~*** miejsce do zaparkowania

P

par•ka ['pɑːkə] *s* (*jacket*) parka *f*
park-and-'ride *s system parkowania na obrzeżach miasta i dojazdu do centrum autobusem*
park•ing ['pɑːkɪŋ] *s* **1.** parkowanie *n*; ***no ~*** zakaz parkowania **2.** miejsca *pl* parkingowe; ***~ is limited*** liczba miejsc parkingowych jest ograniczona; **'park•ing brake** *s* hamulec *m* ręczny; **'park•ing fee** *s* opłata *f* parkingowa; **'park•ing ga•rage** *s Am* parking *m* wielopoziomowy; **'park•ing lot** *s Am* parking *m*; **'park•ing me•ter** *s* parkometr *m*; **park•ing of•'fence** *Br*, ***park•ing of•fense*** *Am s* nieprawidłowe parkowanie *n*; **'park•ing place, *park•ing space*** *s* miejsce *n* parkingowe; **'park•ing tick•et** *s* mandat *m* za nieprawidłowe parkowanie
Par•kin•son's dis•ease ['pɑːkɪnsnzdɪziːz] *s MED* choroba *f* Parkinsona
'park keep•er *s Br* dozorca *m* parku
par•lance ['pɑːləns] *s* żargon *m*; ***legal ~*** żargon prawniczy; ***in common ~*** w języku potocznym, potocznie
par•lia•ment ['pɑːləmənt] *s* parlament *m*; **par•lia•men•tar•i•an** [pɑːləmen'teərɪən] *s* parlamentarzysta *m*; **par•lia•men•ta•ry** [pɑːlə'mentrɪ] *adj* parlamentarny
par•lour ['pɑːlə] *Br*, ***par•lor*** *Am s* **1.** salon *m*; ***a beauty ~*** salon piękności; ***a massage ~*** salon masażu; ***a funeral ~*** zakład pogrzebowy **2.** *dated* bawialnia *f*; **'par•lour game** *Br*, ***par•lor game*** *Am s* gra *f* towarzyska
pa•ro•chi•al [pə'rəʊkɪəl] *adj* **1.** zaściankowy **2.** parafialny
par•o•dist ['pærədɪst] *s* parodysta *m*; **par•o•dy** ['pærədɪ] **I** *s a. fig* parodia *f* **II** *v/t* parodiować ⟨s-⟩
pa•role [pə'roʊl] **I** *s JUR* zwolnienie *n* warunkowe; ***on ~*** na zwolnieniu warunkowym **II** *v/t* zwalniać ⟨zwolnić⟩ warunkowo
par•quet ['pɑːkeɪ] *s* parkiet *m*; **parquet 'floor** *s* (*floor*) parkiet *m*
par•rot ['pærət] **I** *s* papuga *f* **II** *v/t* bezmyślnie powtarzać ⟨-tórzyć⟩; **'par•rot-fash•ion** *adv*: ***repeat s.th. ~*** *Br* powtarzać coś jak papuga
par•ry ['pærɪ] **I** *v/t* **1.** *blow*: parować ⟨s-⟩ **2.** ***~ a shot*** (*goal keeper*) wybić piłkę **3.** *argument*: odpierać ⟨odeprzeć⟩ **II** *s* (*sport*) parada *f*, zasłona *f*
par•si•mo•ni•ous [pɑːsɪ'məʊnɪəs] *adj lit* skąpy; **par•si•mo•ny** ['pɑːsɪmənɪ] *s lit* skąpstwo *n*
pars•ing ['pɑːsɪŋ] *s* **1.** *GRAM* analiza *f* składniowa **2.** *INF* parsing *m*
pars•ley ['pɑːslɪ] *s* pietruszka *f*
pars•nip ['pɑːsnɪp] *s* pasternak *m*
par•son ['pɑːsn] *s dated* pastor *m*; **'par•son•age** ['pɑːsənɪdʒ] *s* plebania *f*; **par•son's 'nose** *s* kuper *m* (drobiowy)
part [pɑːt] **I** *s* **1.** część *f*; ***in ~*** po części, częściowo; ***which ~ of London are you from?*** z której części Londynu pochodzisz?; ***a ~ of speech*** część mowy; ***for the most ~*** w większości, przeważnie; ***for my ~*** jeżeli o mnie chodzi; ***~ and parcel of*** nieodłączna część *G*; ***take s.o.'s ~*** wziąć czyjąś stronę; ***we spent ~ of the time in a museum*** trochę czasu spędziliśmy w muzeum; ***work as ~ of a team*** pracować jako członek zespołu; ***spare ~s*** części zamienne **2.** rola *f*; ***he plays the ~ of Hamlet*** gra rolę Hamleta **3.** *MUS* głos *m* **4.** partia *f*; ***the clarinet ~*** partia klarnetu **5.** *Am* przedziałek *m* **6.** ***take ~ in s.th.*** wziąć udział w *L*, uczestniczyć w *L* **II** *v/i* **1.** rozstawać ⟨-tać⟩ się (***from*** z *I*); ***he has recently ~ed from his wife*** niedawno rozstał się z żoną; ***~ as friends*** rozstać się w przyjaźni; ***~ company with***, ***~ company from*** **a)** rozstać się z *I* **b)** nie zgadzać się z *I* **2.** rozdzielać ⟨-lić⟩ się **3.** (*door*) rozsuwać ⟨-sunąć⟩ się **III** *v/t* **1.** rozdzielać ⟨-lić⟩ **2.** oddzielać ⟨-lić⟩; ***the puppies were ~ed from their mother*** szczeniaki zostały zabrane od matki **3.** *curtains*: rozsuwać ⟨-sunąć⟩ **IV** *adv* częściowo; ***she's ~ Russian, ~ French*** jest w połowie Rosjanką a w połowie Francuzką; **part with** *v/i* rozstawać ⟨-tać⟩ się z *I*; **'part ex•change** *s*: ***take s.o.'s car in ~*** *Br* przyjąć czyjś samochód w rozliczeniu; **'part own•er** *s* współwłaściciel *m*
par•tial ['pɑːʃl] *adj* **1.** częściowy; ***~ success*** częściowy sukces **2.** ***be ~ to*** *dated* mieć słabość do *G*, lubić *A* **3.** stronniczy; **par•ti•al•i•ty** [pɑːʃɪ'ælətɪ] *s* **1.** stronniczość *f* **2.** słabość *f* (***for*** do *G*) **3.** zamiłowanie *n* (***for***

do *G*); **par•tial•ly** ['pɑːʃəlɪ] *adv* częściowo, po części; ***be ~ to blame for*** być współwinnym *D*; ***~ sighted*** niedowidzący

par•ti•ci•pant [pɑː'tɪsɪpənt] *s* uczestnik *m*; **par•ti•ci•pate** [pɑː'tɪsɪpeɪt] *v/i* uczestniczyć, brać ⟨wziąć⟩ udział (***in*** w *L*); **par•ti•ci•pa•tion** [pɑːtɪsɪ'peɪʃn] *s* udział *m*, uczestnictwo *n*

par•ti•ci•ple ['pɑːtɪsɪpl] *s GRAM* imiesłów *m*; ***past ~*** *GRAM* imiesłów czasu przeszłego

par•ti•cle ['pɑːtɪkl] *s* **1.** cząsteczka *f*, drobina *f*; **2.** *PHYS* cząstka *f*; ***elementary ~*** cząstka elementarna **3.** *GRAM* partykuła *f*

par•tic•u•lar [pə'tɪkjələ] **I** *adj* **1.** szczególny; ***pay ~ attention to*** zwrócić szczególną uwagę na *A*; ***of ~ interest*** szczególnie interesujący; ***this ~ case*** ten szczególny przypadek; ***for no ~ reason*** bez żadnego konkretnego powodu; ***in ~*** szczególnie, zwłaszcza **2.** specjalny; ***of no ~ importance*** niespecjalnie ważny **3.** ***be very ~ about*** przywiązywać dużą wagę do *G* **II** *s* **1.** szczegół *m*; ***in every ~*** w każdym szczególe; ***enter into ~s*** wchodzić w szczegóły **2.** ***~s*** **a)** (szczegółowe) informacje **b)** dane (osobowe); **par•tic•u•lar•ize** [pə'tɪkjələraɪz] *v/i* **1.** wyszczególniać ⟨-nić⟩ **2.** określać ⟨-lić⟩ bliżej; **par•tic•u•lar•ly** [pə'tɪkjələlɪ] *adv* szczególnie; ***not ~ interesting*** niezbyt interesujący

par•tic•u•late e•mis•sions [pə'tɪkjəlɪtɪmɪʃns] *pl* emisja *f* pyłów

part•ing ['pɑːtɪŋ] **I** *s* **1.** rozstanie *n*; ***the pain of ~*** ból rozstania **2.** *Br* przedziałek *m* **3.** rozdzielenie się *n* **II** *adj* pożegnalny; ***a ~ kiss*** pożegnalny pocałunek; '**part•ing shot** *s* uwaga *f* rzucona na odchodnym

par•ti•san [pɑːtɪ'zæn] **I** *adj* stronniczy **II** *s* **1.** partyzant *m* **2.** zwolennik *m*

par•ti•tion [pɑː'tɪʃn] **I** *s* **1.** podział *m*; ***the ~ of Poland*** rozbiór Polski **2.** ścianka *f*; ***a ~ wall*** ścianka działowa **3.** parawan *m* **II** *v/t* dzielić ⟨po-⟩; ***the room is ~ed into two parts*** pokój podzielony jest na dwie części; **partition off** *v/t* oddzielać ⟨-lić⟩ (***s.th. from*** coś od *G*)

part•ly ['pɑːtlɪ] *adv* częściowo, po części

part•ner ['pɑːtnə] **I** *s* **1.** partner *m*; ***a dancing ~*** partner do tańca; ***a marriage ~*** małżonek; ***a life ~*** partner życiowy; ***a trading ~*** partner handlowy **2.** wspólnik *m* **II** *v/t* być partnerem; **part•ner•ship** ['pɑːtnəʃɪp] *s* **1.** współpraca *f*; ***in ~ with*** we współpracy z *I* **2.** wspólnictwo *n*; ***be in ~ with s.o.*** być czyimś wspólnikiem **3.** *ECON* spółka *f* osobowa; ***a limited ~*** spółka komandytowa; ***a general ~*** spółka jawna **4.** partnerstwo *n* **5.** para *f*

par•tridge ['pɑːtrɪdʒ] *pl s* kuropatwa *f*

part-'time **I** *adj job*: w niepełnym wymiarze godzin **II** *adv work*: w niepełnym wymiarze godzin; **part-'tim•er** *s* osoba *f* zatrudniona w niepełnym wymiarze godzin

par•ty ['pɑːtɪ] **I** *s* **1.** partia *f*; ***the Labour ~*** Patria Pracy **2.** przyjęcie *n*; ***a birthday ~*** przyjęcie urodzinowe; ***give a ~*** urządzić przyjęcie, wydać przyjęcie **3.** impreza *f* **4.** zabawa *f* **5.** grupa *f*; ***a ~ of 10 children*** grupa dziesięciorga dzieci; ***a 10% discount for parties*** zniżka 10% dla grup (zorganizowanych) **6.** *JUR* strona *f*; ***the contract can be terminated by either ~*** każda ze stron ma prawo odstąpić od umowy; ***a third ~*** osoba trzecia; **be (a) ~ to** wziąć udział w *L* **II** *v/i infml* imprezować; '**par•ty line** *s POLIT* linia *f* partii; **par•ty poop•er** ['pɑːtɪpuːpə] *s*: ***be a ~*** *infml* psuć zabawę

par•venu ['pɑːvənjuː] *pl -nus s* parweniusz *m*

pass [pɑːs] **I** *v/i* **1.** przechodzić ⟨przejść⟩; ***let s.o. ~*** pozwolić komuś przejść; ***let s.th. ~*** nie sprzeciwiać się czemuś; ***his remark ~ed unnoticed*** jego uwaga przeszła niezauważona **2.** przejeżdżać ⟨-jechać⟩ **3.** przelatywać ⟨-lecieć⟩ **4.** (*title*, *inheritance*) przechodzić ⟨przejść⟩ (***to*** na *A*) **5.** (*a.* ***~ away***) (*time*) mijać ⟨minąć⟩; ***six months ~ed*** minęło sześć miesięcy **6.** wydarzyć się; ***after what has ~ed between them*** po tym, co zaszło między nimi **7.** kończyć ⟨s-⟩ się; ***they waited for the storm to ~*** czekali, aż burza się skończy **8.** rezygnować ⟨z-⟩ (***on*** z *G*); ***~ on the dessert*** zrezygnować z deseru **9.** (*cards*) pasować ⟨s-⟩ **II** *v/t* **1.** mijać ⟨minąć⟩;

P

she ~ed me in the street minęła mnie na ulicy **2.** podawać 〈-dać〉 (***s.o. s.th.*** komuś coś); ***he ~ed the ball to Owen*** *SPORT* podał piłkę do Owena **3.** przekraczać 〈-roczyć〉; ***unemployment has ~ed three million*** bezrobocie przekroczyło trzy miliony **4.** *time, evening*: spędzać 〈-dzić〉; ***how did you ~ the evening?*** jak spędziłeś wieczór? **5.** *exam*: zdać **6.** *bill*: przyjmować 〈-jąć〉 **7.** *sentence*: wydawać 〈-dać〉 **8.** *fig* przekraczać 〈-roczyć〉; ***it ~es belief that*** trudno uwierzyć, że **III** *s* **1.** przełęcz *f* **2.** bilet *m*; ***a bus ~*** bilet autobusowy **3.** karta *f*; ***a free ~*** karta wolnego wstępu; ***a boarding ~*** karta pokładowa **4.** *SPORT* podanie *n* **5.** etap *m*; ***in the first ~*** na pierwszym etapie **6.** pozytywna ocena *f*; ***get a ~ in physics*** zdać egzamin z fizyki **7.** ***make a ~ at*** **a)** podrywać *A* **b)** przystawiać się do *G* **8.** ***things have come to such a pretty ~*** *dated infml* sprawy wyglądają kiepsko; **pass as** → **pass for**; **pass away,** **pass on** *v/i* **1.** (*die*) odchodzić 〈odejść〉 **2.** przestawać 〈-tać〉 istnieć; **pass by** *v/t* **1.** mijać 〈minąć〉 **2.** przechodzić 〈przejść〉 obok; ***life is passing him by*** życie przechodzi obok niego; **pass down** *v/t tradition*: przekazywać 〈-zać〉 (***to*** *D*); **pass for** *v/t* uchodzić 〈ujść〉 za *A*; ***she speaks Russian so well she could easily ~ a Russian*** tak dobrze mówi po rosyjsku, że mogłaby uchodzić za Rosjankę; **pass into** *v/i* przechodzić 〈przejść〉 do *G*; ***many foreign words have passed into English*** wiele obcych słów przeszło do języka angielskiego; **pass off I** *v/i* (*demonstration*) *Br* przebiegać 〈-biec〉 **II** *v/t* ***pass oneself off as*** podawać się za *A*; **pass on** *v/t* przekazywać 〈-zać〉; ***I passed your message on to my mother*** przekazałem twoją wiadomość mojej matce; **pass out** *v/i* mdleć 〈ze-〉; **pass over** *v/t* **1.** pomijać 〈-minąć〉 przy awansie **2.** ignorować 〈z-〉; ***she passed over his rude remarks*** puściła jego nieuprzejme uwagi mimo uszu; **pass through** *v/i* **1.** przejeżdżać 〈-jechać〉 **2.** przechodzić 〈przejść〉; **pass up** *v/t opportunity*: *infml* przepuszczać 〈-puścić〉

pass•a•ble ['pæsəbl] *adj* **1.** *road*: przejezdny **2.** zadowalający; ***he speaks ~ Spanish*** mówi jako tako po hiszpańsku

pas•sage ['pæsɪdʒ] *s* **1.** przejście *n* **2.** korytarz *m* **3.** *ANAT* droga *f*; ***nasal ~es*** drogi nosowe **4.** *book*: fragment *m*, ustęp *m* **5.** ***force one's ~ through the crowd*** przepchać się przez tłum **6.** *time*: upływ *m*; ***with the ~ of time*** z upływem czasu **7.** *bill*: przyjęcie *n*; **pas•sage•way** ['pæsɪdʒweɪ] *s* **1.** przejście *n* **2.** korytarz *m*

'pass•book *s* książeczka *f* oszczędnościowa

pas•sen•ger ['pæsɪndʒə] *s* pasażer *m*; **'pas•sen•ger seat** *s* siedzenie *n* dla pasażera; **'pas•sen•ger train** *s* pociąg *m* osobowy

pas•ser-by [pɑːsə'baɪ] *pl passers-by s* przechodzień *m*

pass•ing ['pɑːsɪŋ] **I** *s* **1.** upływ *m*; ***with the ~ of the years*** z upływem lat; ***mention s.th. in ~*** wspomnieć o czymś mimochodem **2.** odejście *n* **3.** *bill*: przyjęcie *n* **II** *adj* **1.** przelotny **2.** krótkotrwały **3.** *time, days*: upływający

pas•sion ['pæʃn] *s* **1.** namiętność *f* **2.** pasja *f* **3.** zamiłowanie *n*; ***the English have a ~ for gardening*** Anglicy mają zamiłowanie do ogrodnictwa **4.** ***a crime of ~*** zabójstwo w afekcie **5.** furia *f*; ***fly into ~*** wpaść w furię **6.** ***the ~*** *REL* Pasja; **pas•sion•ate** ['pæʃənət] *adj* namiętny; **pas•sion•ate•ly** ['pæʃənətlɪ] *adv* namiętnie; **'pas•sion fruit** *s* passiflora *f*, marakuja *f*

pas•sive ['pæsɪv] **I** *adj* **1.** bierny; ***a ~ observer*** bierny obserwator; ***~ resistance*** bierny opór; ***~ smoking*** bierne palenie; ***the ~ voice*** *GRAM* strona bierna **2.** pasywny **II** *s* ***the ~*** *GRAM* strona *f* bierna; **pas•siv•i•ty** [pæ'sɪvətɪ] *s* bierność *f*

'pass•key *s* klucz *m* uniwersalny

Pass•o•ver ['pæsəʊvə] *s* Pascha *f*

pass•port ['pɑːspɔːt] *s* **1.** paszport *m*; ***hold a British ~*** mieć brytyjski paszport; ***a ~ picture*** zdjęcie paszportowe **2.** *fig* droga *f*; ***the ~ to success*** droga do sukcesu; **'pass•port con•trol** *s* kontrola *f* paszportowa

pass•word ['pɑːswɜːd] *s* hasło *n*
past [pɑːst] **I** *s* ***the ~*** przeszłość *f*; ***in the ~*** w przeszłości, dawniej **2.** ***the ~*** *GRAM* czas przeszły **II** *adj* **1.** miniony **2.** zeszły **3.** ostatni; ***in the ~ two weeks*** w ciągu ostatnich dwóch tygodni; ***for some time ~*** od jakiegoś czasu **4.** dawny; ***in times ~*** w dawnych czasach **5.** były; ***I know from ~ experience that*** wiem z doświadczenia, że; ***~ and present students*** byli i obecni studenci **6.** ***the ~ tense*** *GRAM* czas przeszły **III** *prep* **1.** po *L*; ***it's twenty ~ six*** jest dwadzieścia po szóstej; ***it was ~ midnight*** było po północy **2.** obok *G*; ***~ the church*** obok kościoła; ***he walked ~ them*** przeszedł obok nich **3.** ponad *A*, powyżej *G*; ***unemployment is ~ 3 million*** bezrobocie przekroczyło trzy miliony **IV** *adv run, go*: obok
pas•ta ['pæstə] *s* makaron *m*
paste [peɪst] **I** *s* **1.** masa *f*; ***a smooth ~*** jednolita masa **2.** pasta *f*; ***fish ~*** pasta rybna **3.** klej *m*; ***wallpaper ~*** klej do tapet **II** *v/t* **1.** przyklejać ⟨-leić⟩ **2.** wklejać ⟨-leić⟩; ***cut and ~*** *INF* wytnij i wklej; '**paste•board** *s* tektura *f*
pas•tel ['pæstl] **I** *s* pastel *m* **II** *adj* pastelowy
pas•teur•ize ['pɑːstʃəraɪz] *v/t* pasteryzować; ***~d milk*** pasteryzowane mleko
pas•tille ['pæstəl] *s Br* pastylka *f*, cukierek *m*; ***a throat ~*** cukierek na kaszel
pas•time ['pɑːstaɪm] *s* hobby *n*
pas•tor ['pɑːstə] *s* pastor *m*; **pas•to•ral** ['pɑːstərəl] *adj* **1.** duszpasterski **2.** sielankowy
past 'par•ti•ci•ple *s GRAM* imiesłów *m* czasu przeszłego
pas•try ['peɪstrɪ] *s* **1.** ciasto *n* **2.** słodka bułka *f*
pas•ture ['pɑːstʃə] **I** *s* pastwisko *n*; ***move on to ~s new*** rozpocząć nowy etap życia **II** *v/t* wypasać
past•y[1] ['peɪstɪ] *adj complexion*: blady, niezdrowy
past•y[2] ['pæstɪ] *s Br* pasztecik *m*
pat [pæt] **I** *v/t* **1.** klepać ⟨po-⟩; ***~ s.o. on the back*** **a)** poklepać kogoś po plecach **b)** *fig* pochwalić kogoś **2.** głaskać ⟨po-⟩ **II** *s* **1.** klepnięcie *n*; ***give s.o. a ~*** poklepać kogoś; ***a ~ on the back*** *fig* pochwała **2.** *butter*: porcja *f* **III** *adj* **1.** (zbyt) prosty **2.** (zbyt) gładki **IV** *adv*: ***he knows his answers off ~*** *Br*, ***he knows his answers down ~*** *Am* potrafi odpowiedzieć bez zastanowienia, ma przygotowane odpowiedzi
patch [pætʃ] **I** *s* **1.** łata *f*; ***a black dog with a white ~*** czarny pies z białą łatą; ***be not a ~ on*** *Br infml* nie umywać się do *G* **2.** łatka *f* **3.** plama *f* **4.** ***a bald ~*** łysina **5.** ***go through a difficult ~*** przechodzić trudny okres **6.** grządka *f* **7.** kępka *f* **II** *v/t* łatać ⟨za-⟩; ***~ed jeans*** połatane dżinsy; **patch up** *v/t* **1.** naprawiać ⟨-wić⟩ **2.** ***~ up one's differences with***, ***~ things up with*** pogodzić się z *I* **3.** łatać ⟨za-⟩ **4.** *wound*: opatrywać ⟨-rzyć⟩ **5.** ***~ up a deal*** osiągnąć porozumienie; '**patch•work** *s* **1.** patchwork *m* **2.** *fig* mieszanka *f*, zlepek *m*
patch•y ['pætʃɪ] *adj* **1.** *knowledge*: fragmentaryczny, niepełny **2.** *fog*: zalegający miejscami **3.** *colour*: niejednolity **4.** *performance*: nierówny
pâ•té ['pæteɪ] *s* pasztet *m*
pa•tent ['peɪtnt] **I** *s* patent *m*; ***obtain a ~*** uzyskać patent; ***be protected by ~*** być pod ochroną patentową **II** *adj* **1.** patentowy; ***the ~ office*** urząd patentowy; ***a ~ lawyer*** rzecznik patentowy **2.** opatentowany **3.** *lie*: wierutny **4.** oczywisty **III** *v/t* patentować ⟨o-⟩; **pa•tent 'leath•er** *s* skóra *f* lakierowana; **pa•tent•ly** ['peɪtntlɪ] *adv* zupełnie; ***it's ~ obvious that*** jest zupełnie oczywiste, że; ***he was ~ lying*** było oczywiste, że kłamie
pa•ter•nal [pə'tɜːnl] *adj* **1.** ojcowski **2.** ze strony ojca; ***my ~ grandmother*** babcia ze strony ojca; **pa•ter•nal•is•tic** [pətɜːnəl'ɪstɪk] *adj* paternalistyczny; **pa•ter•nal•ism** [pə'tɜːnəlɪzəm] *s* paternalizm *m*; **pa•ter•ni•ty** [pə'tɜːnɪtɪ] *s* ojcostwo *n*; ***~ leave*** urlop ojcowski; ***a ~ suit*** *JUR* sprawa o ojcostwo
path [pɑːθ] *s* **1.** ścieżka *f*; ***walk along a ~*** iść ścieżką **2.** droga *f*; ***stand in s.o.'s ~*** stać komuś na drodze; ***a ~ to success*** droga do sukcesu **3.** tor *m*
pa•thet•ic [pə'θetɪk] *adj* **1.** żałosny; ***you're ~!*** jesteś żałosny!; ***a ~ excuse*** żałosna wymówka **2.** budzący litość **3.** *view*: smutny

P

path•o•gen ['pæθədʒən] *s MED* patogen *m*
path•o•log•i•cal [pæθə'lɒdʒɪkl] *adj* **1.** patologiczny **2.** chorobliwy; **pa•thol•o•gist** [pə'θɒlədʒɪst] *s* patolog *m*; **pa•thol•o•gy** [pə'θɒlədʒɪ] *s* patologia *f*
path•way ['pɑːθweɪ] *s* **1.** ścieżka *f* **2.** droga *f*; ***a ~ to success*** droga do sukcesu
pa•tience ['peɪʃns] *s* **1.** cierpliwość *f*; ***lose one's ~ with*** stracić cierpliwość do *G*; ***I've run out of ~*** skończyła się moja cierpliwość **2.** *Br* pasjans *m*; ***play ~*** układać pasjansa
pa•tient ['peɪʃnt] **I** *s* pacjent *m* **II** *adj* cierpliwy; ***she's ~ with young children*** ma cierpliwość do małych dzieci; **pa•tient•ly** ['peɪʃntlɪ] *adv* cierpliwie
pat•i•na ['pætɪnə] *s* patyna *f*
pat•i•o ['pætɪəʊ] *pl -tios s* **1.** taras *m* **2.** patio *n*
pa•tri•arch ['peɪtrɪɑːk] *s* patriarcha *f*; **pa•tri•ar•chal** [peɪtrɪ'ɑːkl] *adj* patriarchalny
pat•ri•ot ['pætrɪət] *s* patriota *m*; **pat•ri•ot•ic** [pætrɪ'ɒtɪk] *adj* patriotyczny; **pa•tri•ot•ism** ['pætrɪətɪzəm] *s* patriotyzm *m*
pa•trol [pə'trəʊl] **I** *s* **1.** patrol *m*; ***a police ~*** patrol policyjny; ***make ~s*** patrolować **2.** *scouts*: zastęp *m* **II** *v/t* patrolować; **pa'trol car** *s* samochód *m* patrolowy, wóz *m* patrolowy; **pa'trol•man** *pl -men s Am* (*policeman*) patrolowy *m*; **pa'trol wag•on** *s Am* samochód *m* więźniarka

P

pa•tron ['peɪtrən] *s* **1.** patron *m* **2.** mecenas *m* **3.** stały klient *m*; **pa•tron•age** ['pætrənɪdʒ] *s* **1.** patronat *m*; ***under the ~ of*** pod patronatem *G* **2.** mecenat *m*, sponsoring *m*; **pa•tron•ize** ['pætrənaɪz] *v/t* **1.** traktować ⟨po-⟩ protekcjonalnie **2.** być stałym klientem **3.** często bywać w *L* **4.** wspierać ⟨wesprzeć⟩; **pa•tron•iz•ing** ['pætrənaɪzɪŋ] *adj* protekcjonalny
pa•tron 'saint *s* (*saint*) patron *m*
pat•ter ['pætə] **I** *s* **1.** tupot *m*; ***the ~ of feet*** tupot nóg **2.** stukot *m* **3.** *rain*: stuk *n* **4.** *infml* gadka *f* **II** *v/i* **1.** stukać **2.** tupać **3.** dreptać
pat•tern ['pætn] **I** *s* **1.** wzór *m*; ***follow a ~*** przebiegać według wzoru; ***a floral ~*** wzór kwiatowy; ***set the ~ to follow*** stanowić wzór do naśladowania **2.** wzorzec *m*; ***changing ~s of behaviour*** zmieniające się wzorce postępowania **3.** próbka *f* **4.** wykrój *m* **II** *v/t* **1.** kształtować ⟨u-⟩ **2.** wzorować (***s.th. on/after*** coś na *L*) **3.** tworzyć ⟨s-⟩ wzór na *L*; **pat•terned** ['pætənd] *adj* wzorzysty; ***~ with flowers*** w kwiaty, w kwiatki
pat•ty ['pætɪ] *s Am* **1.** kotlet *m* **2.** hamburger *m*
paunch [pɔːntʃ] *s* (tłusty) brzuch *m*
pau•per ['pɔːpə] *s dated* biedak *m*, nędzarz *m*
pause [pɔːz] **I** *s* **1.** przerwa *f*; ***without ~*** bez przerwy **2.** pauza *f* **3.** *MUS* fermata *f* **II** *v/i* **1.** przerywać ⟨-rwać⟩, robić ⟨z-⟩ przerwę **2.** zatrzymywać ⟨-mać⟩ się
pave [peɪv] *v/t* brukować ⟨wy-⟩; ***~ the way for s.th.*** *fig* utorować czemuś drogę; **pave•ment** ['peɪvmənt] *s* **1.** *Br* chodnik *m*; ***a ~ artist*** uliczny artysta **2.** *Am* jezdnia *f* **3.** *Am* nawierzchnia *f*; **'pav•ing stone** *s* płyta *f* chodnikowa
paw [pɔː] **I** *s a. infml* łapa *f*; ***take your ~s off me!*** weź te łapska!, łapy przy sobie! **II** *v/t* **1.** drapać (łapą) **2.** ***~ the ground*** (*horse*) grzebać kopytem w ziemi **3.** *infml* obmacywać
pawn[1] [pɔːn] *s a. fig* pionek *m*
pawn[2] [~] **I** *v/t* zastawiać ⟨-wić⟩ w lombardzie **II** *s* ***in ~*** zastawniony (w lombardzie); **'pawn•bro•ker** *s* właściciel *m* lombardu; **'pawn•shop** *s* lombard *m*
pay [peɪ] **I** (*paid*; *paid*) *v/i* **1.** płacić ⟨za-⟩ (***for*** za *A*); ***~ in cash*** zapłacić gotówką; ***~ by credit card*** zapłacić kartą kredytową; ***you'll ~ for it!*** zapłacisz za to!; ***~ with one's life for s.th.*** zapłacić za coś życiem; ***the project will ~ for itself*** koszty projektu się zwrócą **2.** przynosić ⟨-nieść⟩ zysk, opłacać ⟨-cić⟩ się; ***crime doesn't ~*** przestępstwo nie popłaca **II** (*paid*; *paid*) *v/t* **1.** płacić ⟨za-⟩; ***~ a bill*** zapłacić rachunek, uregulować rachunek **2.** spłacać ⟨-cić⟩; ***~ a debt*** spłacić dług **3.** oddawać ⟨-dać⟩; ***he still hasn't paid me the money he owes me*** nie oddał mi jeszcze pieniędzy, które jest mi winien **4.** opłacać ⟨-cić⟩ się; ***it would***

~ you to hire an accountant opłaciłoby ci się zatrudnić księgowego **5.** ***~ attention*** uważać, zwracać uwagę (***to*** na *A*) **6.** ***~ s.o. a compliment*** powiedzieć komuś komplement **7.** ***~ s.o. a visit*** odwiedzić kogoś **III** *s* płaca *f*; ***~ claims*** żądania płacowe; **pay back** *v/t* **1.** *credit*: spłacać ⟨-cić⟩ **2.** *money*: oddawać ⟨-dać⟩ **3.** odpłacać ⟨-cić⟩; **pay in** *v/t* wpłacać ⟨-cić⟩; **pay off I** *v/i* opłacać ⟨-cić⟩ się **II** *v/t* **1.** spłacać ⟨-cić⟩ **2.** przekupić **3.** wypłacać ⟨-cić⟩ odprawę; **pay out** *v/t* wypłacać ⟨-cić⟩; **pay up** *v/i* **1.** oddawać ⟨-dać⟩ pieniądze **2.** spłacać ⟨-cić⟩ wszystkie długi

pay•a•ble ['peɪəbl] *adj* **1.** płatny **2.** wystawiony; ***a cheque ~ to*** czek wystawiony na *A*

'pay cheque *Br*, ***pay check*** *Am s* pensja *f*

'pay day *s* dzień *m* wypłaty

pay•ee [peɪ'iː] *s* **1.** beneficjent *m* **2.** odbiorca *m*

pay•er ['peɪə] *s* płatnik *m*

pay•ing 'guest *s* sublokator *m*

paying-'in slip *s* blankiet *m* wpłaty

pay•load ['peɪləʊd] *s* **1.** ładunek *m* użyteczny **2.** ładunek *m* wybuchowy

pay•ment ['peɪmənt] *s* **1.** płatność *f*; ***~ in advance*** płatność z góry **2.** opłata *f*; ***monthly ~s of £50*** miesięczne opłaty w wysokości 50 funtów **3.** zapłata *f* **4.** spłata *f* **5.** *fig* podziękowanie *n*; ***in ~ for*** w podziękowaniu za *A*

'pay•off *s* **1.** korzyść *f* **2.** *infml* łapówka *f* **3.** odprawa *f* **4.** nagroda *f*; ***it's a ~ for my efforts*** to nagroda za moje wysiłki; **'pay•out** *s* wypłata *f*; **'pay pack•et** *s* koperta *f* z wypłatą; **'pay phone** *s* automat *m* telefoniczny; **'pay rise** *s* podwyżka *f* płac; **'pay•roll** *s* lista *f* płac; **'pay•slip** *s* pasek *m* wypłaty; **'pay TV** *s* płatna telewizja *f*

PC [piː'siː] *abbr* **1.** (=***personal computer***) PC *m*, komputer *m* osobisty **2.** (=***Police Constable***) posterunkowy *m* **3.** (=***political correctness***) poprawność *f* polityczna

PE [piː'iː] *abbr* (=***physical education***) WF *m*, wychowanie *n* fizyczne

pea [piː] *s* groszek *m*; ***they are like two ~s in a pod*** są do siebie podobni jak dwie krople wody

peace [piːs] **I** *s* **1.** pokój *m*; ***war and ~*** wojna i pokój; ***make ~ with*** pogodzić się z *I*; ***live in ~*** żyć w pokoju; ***the two countries are at ~*** między tymi dwoma krajami panuje pokój **2.** spokój *m*; ***in ~ and quiet*** w spokoju; ***leave me in ~*** zostaw mnie w spokoju; ***~ of mind*** spokój **II** *adj* pokojowy; ***~ negotiations*** negocjacje pokojowe; ***a ~ treaty*** traktat pokojowy; ***a ~ movement*** ruch na rzecz pokoju; ***a ~ pipe*** fajka pokoju; **peace•a•ble** ['piːsəbl] *adj* **1.** pokojowy **2.** nastawiony pokojowo **3.** *person*: spokojny; **'Peace Corps** *s* Korpus *m* Pokoju; **peace•ful** ['piːsfəl] *adj* **1.** pokojowy **2.** *sleep*, *life*: spokojny **3.** pokojowo nastawiony; **peace•ful•ly** ['piːsfəlɪ] *adv* **1.** pokojowo **2.** spokojnie

peace•keep•ing ['piːskiːpɪŋ] *adj forces*: pokojowy

peace-lov•ing ['piːslʌvɪŋ] *adj* **1.** pokojowy **2.** miłujący pokój

'peace•time *s* pokój *m*, czas *m* pokoju

peach [piːtʃ] **I** *s* **1.** brzoskwinia *f* **2.** kolor *m* brzoskwiniowy **II** *adj* brzoskwiniowy

pea•cock ['piːkɒk] *s* paw *m*; (***as***) ***proud as a ~*** dumny jak paw

peak [piːk] **I** *s* **1.** *a. fig* szczyt *m*; ***a mountain ~*** górski szczyt; ***reach one's ~*** osiągnąć szczyt; ***she's at the ~ of her career*** jest u szczytu kariery; ***the ~s and troughs*** wzloty i upadki **2.** *hat*: daszek *m* **II** *v/i* **1.** osiągać ⟨-gnąć⟩ szczyt **2.** osiągać ⟨-gnąć⟩ najwyższą wartość **III** *adj* **1.** szczytowy; ***~ hours*** godziny szczytu; ***~ viewing time*** godziny największej oglądalności; ***a ~ season*** szczyt sezonu **2.** maksymalny **3.** najlepszy; **peaked** [piːkt] *adj* **1.** *hat*: z daszkiem **2.** *Am* → ***peaky***; **peak•y** ['piːkɪ] *adj Br infml* mizerny

peal [piːl] **I** *v/i* **1.** (*a.* ***~ out***) rozbrzmiewać, dzwonić **2.** ***~ with laughter*** wybuchnąć śmiechem **II** *s* **1.** dzwonienie *n* **2.** ***he burst into ~s of laughter*** zaczął się zanosić śmiechem; ***~s of laughter*** salwy śmiechu

pea•nut ['piːnʌt] *s* **1.** orzech *m* ziemny, orzech *m* arachidowy **2.** ***~s*** *infml* marne pieniądze; **pea•nut 'but•ter** *s* masło *n* orzechowe

P

pear [peə] *s* gruszka *f*; ***a ~ tree*** grusza

pearl [pɜːl] **I** *s* **1.** perła *f*; ***cast ~s before swine*** rzucać perły przed wieprze **2.** macica *f* perłowa **II** *adj* **1.** perłowy **2.** z pereł **3.** z macicy perłowej; **pearl 'bar•ley** *s* kasza *f* perłowa; **'pearl div•er** *s* poławiacz *m* pereł

pearl•y ['pɜːlɪ] *adj* perłowy; ***~ white*** perłowobiały; ***the ~ gates*** *infml* wrota raju

peas•ant ['peznt] *s* **1.** chłop *m* **2.** *a. infml* wieśniak *m*

pea•shoot•er ['piːʃuːtə] *s* (*toy weapon*) dmuchawka *f*

peat [piːt] *s* torf *m*

peb•ble ['pebl] *s* kamyk *m*, kamyczek *m*; ***you are not the only ~ on the beach*** świat się na tobie nie kończy; **peb•bly** ['peblɪ] *adj* kamienisty

pe•can ['piːkən] *s* orzech *m* pekan

pec•ca•dil•lo [pekə'dɪləʊ] *pl -loes, -los s lit* drobny grzeszek *m*

peck [pek] **I** *v/i* **1.** dziobać (**at** *A*) **2.** skubać ⟨-bnąć⟩ (**at** *A*) **II** *v/t* **1.** dziobać ⟨wy-⟩; ***~ing order*** *fig* porządek dziobania **2.** dawać ⟨dać⟩ całusa; ***he ~ed her on the cheek*** cmoknął ją w policzek **III** *s* **1.** całus *m*, cmoknięcie *n* **2.** dziobnięcie *n*

pec•to•ral ['pektərəl] *adj* piersiowy

pe•cu•li•ar [pɪ'kjuːljə] *adj* **1.** dziwny **2.** specyficzny **3.** charakterystyczny, typowy (**to** dla *G*); **pe•cu•li•ar•i•ty** [pɪkjuːlɪ'ærətɪ] *s* **1.** charakterystyczna cecha *f* **2.** osobliwość *f*; **pe•cu•li•ar•ly** [pɪ'kjuːlɪəlɪ] *adv* **1.** szczególnie **2.** typowo; ***a ~ British feature*** typowo brytyjska cecha **3.** dziwnie **4.** osobliwie

P

pe•cu•ni•ar•y [pɪ'kjuːnɪərɪ] *adj form* pieniężny

ped•a•go•gi•c [pedə'gɒdʒɪk], ***ped•a•go•gi•cal*** [pedə'gɒdʒɪkl] *adj* pedagogiczny; **ped•a•gogue** ['pedəgɒg] *s dated* nauczyciel *m*; **ped•a•go•gy** ['pedəgɒdʒɪ] *s* pedagogika *f*

ped•al ['pedl] **I** *s* pedał *m* **II** *v/i* **1.** pedałować **2.** jechać na rowerze; ***he ~led up the hill*** jechał pod górkę **III** *v/t* ***~ a bicycle*** jechać na rowerze; **'ped•al bin** *s* pojemnik *m* na śmieci (otwierany pedałem); **'ped•al boat** *s* rower *m* wodny

ped•ant ['pedənt] *s* pedant *m*; **pe•dan•tic** [pɪ'dæntɪk] *adj* pedantyczny; **ped•ant•ry** ['pedəntrɪ] *s* pedanteria *f*

ped•dle ['pedl] *v/t* **1.** sprzedawać ⟨-dać⟩ (w sprzedaży bezpośredniej) **2.** *drugs*: rozprowadzać ⟨-dzić⟩ **3.** rozpowszechniać ⟨-nić⟩; **'ped•dler** → ***pedlar***

ped•e•rast ['pedəræst] *s* pederasta *m*; **ped•e•rasty** ['pedərəstɪ] *s* pederastia *f*

ped•es•tal ['pedəstl] *s* piedestał *m*; ***put s.o. on a ~, place s.o. on a ~*** stawiać kogoś na piedestale

pe•des•tri•an [pɪ'destrɪən] **I** *s* pieszy *m* **II** *adj* **1.** dla pieszych; ***a ~ zone*** strefa dla pieszych; ***~ accidents*** wypadki z udziałem pieszych **2.** bezbarwny, nudny; **pe•des•tri•an 'cros•sing** *s Br* przejście *n* dla pieszych; **pe•des•tri•an 'pre•cinct** *s Br* strefa *f* zamknięta dla ruchu kołowego; **pe•des•tri•a•nize** [pɪ'destrɪənaɪz] *v/t* zamykać ⟨-mknąć⟩ dla ruchu kołowego

pe•di•at•ric *Am* → ***paediatric***; **pe•di•a•tri•cian** *Am* → ***paediatrician***; **pe•di•at•rics** *Am* → ***paediatrics***

ped•i•cure ['pedɪkjʊə] *s* pedikiur *m*, pedicure *m*

ped•i•gree ['pedɪgriː] **I** *s* **1.** rodowód *m*; ***a dog with a ~*** pies z rodowodem **2.** pochodzenie *n* **II** *adj dog*: z rodowodem, rasowy

ped•lar ['pedlə] *Br*, ***ped•dler*** *Am s dated* komiwojażer *m*, domokrążca *m*

pe•do•phile *Am* → ***paedophile***

pee [piː] *infml* **I** *v/i* siusiać, wysiusiać się **II** *s* siki *pl*; ***go for a ~*** iść siku

peek [piːk] **I** *v/i* **1.** zerkać ⟨-knąć⟩ (**at** na *A*) **2.** podglądać ⟨-dnąć⟩ (**at** *A*); ***no ~ing!*** nie podglądaj! **3.** wystawać, być widocznym; ***her feet ~ed out from under the blanket*** jej nogi wystawały spod koca **II** *s* ***have a ~ at, take a ~ at*** zerknąć na *A*

peel [piːl] **I** *v/t* **1.** obierać ⟨obrać⟩ (ze skórki) **2.** *wallpaper*: zrywać ⟨zerwać⟩ **II** (*a.* ***~ off***) *v/i* **1.** (*wallpaper*) odchodzić ⟨odejść⟩ **2.** (*skin*) schodzić ⟨zejść⟩ **3.** (*paint*) łuszczyć ⟨z-⟩ się **III** *s* **1.** skórka *f* **2.** ***~s*** obierki; ***peel•er*** ['piːlə] *s* nożyk *m* do obierania warzyw; **peel•ings** ['piːlɪŋz] *pl* obierki *pl*

peep[1] [piːp] **I** *v/i* piszczeć **II** *s* pisk *m*
peep[2] [~] **I** *v/i* **1.** → ***peek I.1, I.2*** **2.** *lit* wychylać ⟨-lić⟩ się **3.** wystawać **4.** wyglądać ⟨wyjrzeć⟩; ***the sun ~ed out from behind the clouds*** słońce wyjrzało zza chmur **II** *s* → ***peek II***; **peepers** ['piːpəz] *pl infml* gały *pl*; '**peep•hole** *s* **1.** dziurka *f* **2.** (*door*) judasz *m*; **Peep•ing 'Tom** *s* podglądacz *m*; '**peep•show** *s* peep show *m*
peer[1] [pɪə] *v/i* **1.** spoglądać ⟨spojrzeć⟩ **2.** wpatrywać się (***at*** w *A*)
peer[2] [~] *s* **1.** rówieśnik *m* **2.** osoba *f* o tym samym statusie społecznym **3.** *Br* par *m*; **peer•age** ['pɪərɪdʒ] *s Br* parostwo *n*; ***raise s.o. to the ~*** podnieść kogoś do godności para; '**peer•ess** ['pɪərɪs] *s* (*holder of title*) *Br* arystokratka *f*; '**peer group** *s* grupa *f* rówieśnicza; **peer•less** ['pɪərlɪs] *adj lit* **1.** niezrównany **2.** niemający sobie równych; '**peer pres•sure** *s* presja *f* grupy rówieśniczej
peeved [piːvd] *adj infml* wkurzony (***about*** z powodu *G*/na *A*)
peev•ish ['piːvɪʃ] *adj* drażliwy
peg [peg] **I** *s* **1.** kołek *m*; ***be a square ~ (in a round hole)*** *Br* nie pasować; ***take s.o. down a ~ (or two)*** sprowadzić kogoś na ziemię **2.** wieszak *m*; ***hang your coat on the ~*** powieś płaszcz na wieszaku; ***buy one's clothes off the ~*** kupować gotowe ubrania **3.** hak *m* **4.** haczyk *m* **5.** (*tent*) śledź *m* **6.** (*clothes*) klamerka *f* **II** *v/t* **1.** *washing*: przypinać ⟨-piąć⟩ klamerkami **2.** przymocowywać ⟨-cować⟩ **3.** *prices*: zamrażać ⟨-rozić⟩; **peg out** *v/i Br infml* wykorkować
pe•jo•ra•tive [pɪ'dʒɒrətɪv] *adj* pejoratywny
pe•kin•ese [piːkɪ'niːz] *pl pekinese s* (*dog*) pekińczyk *m*
pel•i•can ['pelɪkən] *s* pelikan *m*; **pel•i•can 'cross•ing** *s Br* przejście *n* dla pieszych (*z sygnalizacją sterowaną przyciskami*)
pel•let ['pelɪt] *s* **1.** granulka *f* **2.** grudka *f* **3.** śrucina *f*
pelt[1] [pelt] *s* skóra *f* (zwierzęca)
pelt[2] [~] **I** *v/t a. fig* obrzucać ⟨-cić⟩ (***s.o. with*** kogoś *I*) **II** *v/i* **1.** ***it's ~ing (down)*** leje jak z cebra **2.** *infml* gnać ⟨po-⟩ **III** *s* ***at full ~*** **a)** pędem **b)** *infml* na pełnym gazie
pel•vic ['pelvɪk] *adj* miedniczny; ***~ bones*** kości miednicy
pel•vis ['pelvɪs] *s* ANAT miednica *f*
pen[1] [pen] **I** *s* **1.** pióro *n* **2.** długopis *m* **II** *v/t* pisać ⟨na-⟩
pen[2] [~] **I** *s* zagroda *f* **II** *v/t* **1.** zamykać ⟨-knąć⟩ **2.** zamykać ⟨-knąć⟩ w zagrodzie
pe•nal ['piːnl] *adj* **1.** karny; ***the ~ code*** kodeks karny; ***a ~ colony*** kolonia karna; ***~ reform*** reforma systemu karnego **2.** karalny **3.** *infml per cent*: złodziejski; **pe•nal•ize** ['piːnəlaɪz] *v/t* **1.** karać ⟨u-⟩ (***s.o. for*** kogoś za *A*) **2.** krzywdzić ⟨s-⟩ **3.** traktować ⟨po-⟩ gorzej; **pen•al•ty** ['penəltɪ] *s* **1.** kara *f* (***for*** za *A*); ***a death ~*** kara śmierci **2.** *fig* cena *f* **3.** (*football*) rzut *m* karny; '**pen•al•ty ar•e•a** *s* SPORT pole *n* karne; '**pen•al•ty clause** *s* JUR klauzula *f* kar umownych; '**pen•al•ty kick** *s* (*football*) rzut *m* karny; **pen•al•ty 'shoot-out** *s* (*football*) rzuty *pl* karne
pen•ance ['penəns] *s* REL pokuta *f*; ***do ~ for one's sins*** odpokutować za grzechy
pence [pens] *pl* → ***penny***
pen•chant ['pɒnʃɒn] *s* zamiłowanie *n*, upodobanie *n* (***for*** do *G*)
pen•cil ['pensɪl] **I** *s* **1.** ołówek *m* **2.** kredka *f*; ***coloured ~s*** kredki **II** *v/t* **1.** rysować ⟨na-⟩ ołówkiem **2.** pisać ⟨na-⟩ ołówkiem; **pen•cil in** *v/t* **1.** wstępnie wyznaczać ⟨-czyć⟩ termin; ***we have pencilled the meeting in for Monday*** wstępnie wyznaczyliśmy termin spotkania na poniedziałek **2.** wstępnie umawiać ⟨umówić⟩
'**pen•cil case** *s* piórnik *m*; '**pen•cil sharp•en•er** *s* temperówka *f*
pen•dant ['pendənt] *s* wisiorek *m*
pend•ing ['pendɪŋ] **I** *prep* **1.** do (czasu) *G* **2.** w oczekiwaniu na *A* **II** *adj* **1.** w toku; ***the case is ~*** sprawa jest w toku **2.** zbliżający się; ***an election is ~*** zbliżają się wybory **3.** do załatwienia
pen•du•lum ['pendjʊləm] *s a. fig* wahadło *n*
pen•e•trate ['penɪtreɪt] *v/t* **1.** przenikać ⟨-knąć⟩ **2.** penetrować ⟨s-⟩ **3.** przebijać ⟨-bić⟩ **4.** przenikać ⟨-knąć⟩ do *G*

P

5. przenikać ⟨-knąć⟩ przez *A* **6.** wtargnąć na *A*; **pen•e•trat•ing** ['penıtreıtıŋ] *adj* wnikliwy, przenikliwy; **pen•e•tra•tion** [penı'treıʃn] *s* **1.** penetracja *f* **2.** przenikanie *n* **3.** infiltracja *f* **4.** przenikliwość *f*

'pen friend *s Br* przyjaciel *m* korespondencyjny

pen•guin ['peŋgwın] *s* pingwin *m*

pen•i•cil•lin [penı'sılın] *s MED* penicylina *f*

pe•nin•su•la [pə'nınsjʊlə] *s* półwysep *m*; **pe•nin•su•lar** [pə'nınsjʊlə] *adj* półwyspowy

pe•nis ['pi:nıs] *s* penis *m*, członek *m*

pen•i•tence ['penıtəns] *s REL* skrucha *f*; **pen•i•tent** ['penıtənt] *adj* skruszony; **pen•i•ten•tial** [penı'tənʃl] *adj* pokutny; **pen•i•ten•tia•ry** [penı'tenʃərı] *s Am* zakład *m* karny

'pen•knife *pl -knives s* scyzoryk *m*; **'pen name** *s* pseudonim *m* literacki

pen•nant ['penənt] *s* **1.** proporczyk *m* **2.** chorągiewka *f* **3.** flaga *f*

pen•ni•less ['penılıs] *adj* bez grosza

pen•ny ['penı] *pl pennies, pence s* **1.** *Br* pens *m*; ***it didn't cost me a ~*** to mnie nic nie kosztowało; ***the ~ dropped for me in the end*** w końcu zrozumiałem; ***in for a ~, in for a pound*** *Br* jak się powiedziało A, trzeba powiedzieć B; ***a ~ for your thoughts*** o czym myślisz?, o czym tak rozmyślasz? **2.** *Am* cent *m*; **'pen•ny pinch•er** *s* dusigrosz *m*, skąpiradło *n*; **'pen•ny-pinch•ing** *adj* skąpy

'pen pal *Am* → ***pen friend***; **'pen pusher** *Br*, *s infml* gryzipiórek *m*

pen•sion¹ ['penʃn] *s* **1.** emerytura *f* **2.** renta *f*; **pen•sion off** *v/t* przenosić ⟨-nieść⟩ na emeryturę; **'pen•sion fund** *s* fundusz *m* emerytalny; **'pension scheme** *Br*, **'pen•sion plan** *Am* system *m* emerytalny; **pen•sion•a•ble** ['penʃənəbl] *adj age*: emerytalny; **pen•sion•er** ['penʃənə] *s* emeryt *m*

pen•sion² [~] *s* pensjonat *m*

pen•sive ['pensıv] *adj* **1.** zatopiony w myślach, pogrążony w zadumie **2.** melancholijny

pen•ta•gon ['pentəgən] *s* pięciokąt *m*; ***the*** ≈ Pentagon; **pen•tag•o•nal** [pen'tægənl] *adj* pięciokątny

pen•tath•lete [pen'tæθli:t] *s SPORT* pięcioboista *m*; **pen•tath•lon** [pen'tæθlən] *s SPORT* pięciobój *m*

Pen•te•cost ['pentıkɔɒst] *s REL* Zielone Świątki *pl*

pent•house ['penthaʊs] *s apartament na najwyższym piętrze*

pent-up [pentʌp] *adj feelings*: tłumiony

pe•nul•ti•mate [pe'nʌltımət] *adj* przedostatni

pe•o•ny ['pi:ənı] *s* piwonia *f*, peonia *f*

peo•ple ['pi:pl] **I** *pl* **1.** ludzie *pl*; ***he doesn't care what ~ think of him*** nie obchodzi go, co ludzie o nim myślą; ***young ~*** młodzi ludzie, młodzież; ***business ~*** ludzie biznesu, biznesmeni; ***our ~ are highly trained*** nasi pracownicy są bardzo dobrze wyszkoleni **2.** osoby *pl*; ***three ~ were killed in the accident*** w wypadku zginęły trzy osoby **3.** naród *m*; ***a ~'s republic*** republika ludowa; ***the French ~*** Francuzi, naród francuski; ***the native ~ of Siberia*** mieszkańcy Syberii **II** *v/t* **1.** zamieszkiwać ⟨-kać⟩; ***the town was ~d by workers from the car factory*** w mieście mieszkali pracownicy fabryki samochodów **2.** wypełniać ⟨-nić⟩

pep [pep] **I** *s* **1.** animusz *m*; **pep up** *v/t infml* **1.** uatrakcyjniać ⟨-nić⟩ **2.** dodawać ⟨-dać⟩ energii

pep•per ['pepə] **I** *s* **1.** pieprz *m* (mielony) **2.** papryka *f* **II** *v/t* **1.** pieprzyć ⟨po-⟩, przyprawiać ⟨-wić⟩ pieprzem **2.** ***be ~ed with*** roić się od *G*; **'pep•per box** *s Am* pieprzniczka *f*; **'pep•per•corn** *s* pieprz *m* (w ziarenkach); **pep•per•corn 'rent** *s Br* niski czynsz *m*; **'pep•per mill** *s* młynek *m* do pieprzu; **'pep•per•mint** *s* **1.** mięta *f* pieprzowa **2.** cukierek *m* miętowy, miętówka *f*; **'pep•per pot** *s Br* pieprzniczka *f*

pep•per•y ['pepərı] *adj* **1.** *dish*: pieprzny **2.** *person*: porywczy

'pep pill *s infml tabletka zawierająca środek pobudzający*; **'pep talk** *s infml* słowa *pl* otuchy

pep•tic ['peptık] *adj*: ***~ ulcers*** wrzody żołądka

per [pɜ:] *prep* **1.** na *A*; ***60 miles ~ hour*** 60 mil na godzinę; ***rooms cost £50***

P

per person, per night pokoje kosztują 50 funtów na osobę za noc; **~ *annum*** na rok **2.** za *A* **~ *kilo*** za kilogram **3. *as* ~** zgodnie z *I*; ***as* ~ *usual*** jak zwykle; **per cap•i•ta** [pəˈkæpɪtə] **I** *adj* na osobę; **~ *income*** dochód na osobę **II** *adv* na osobę

per•ceive [pəˈsiːv] *v/t* **1.** zauważać ⟨-żyć⟩, spostrzegać ⟨-rzec⟩ ***I ~d a change in his behaviour*** zauważyłem zmianę w jego zachowaniu **2.** uznawać ⟨-nać⟩ (***s.th. as*** coś jako *A*) **3.** postrzegać (***s.th. as*** coś jako *A*)

per cent [pəˈsent] *Br*, ***per•cent*** *Am* **I** *s* procent *m* **II** *adj* procentowy; ***a 10 ~ rise in price*** dziesięcioprocentowy wzrost ceny; **per•cen•tage** [pəˈsentɪdʒ] *s* **1.** procent *m*; ***what ~ of Americans are overweight?*** jaki procent Amerykanów ma nadwagę?; ***one ~ point*** jeden punkt procentowy; ***in ~ terms*** procentowo; ***he gets a ~ for every car sold*** dostaje procent od każdego sprzedanego samochodu **2.** udział *m* (procentowy)

per•cep•ti•ble [pəˈseptəbl] *adj* zauważalny, dostrzegalny; **per•cep•ti•bly** [pəˈseptəblɪ] *adv* zauważalnie, dostrzegalnie; **per•cep•tion** [pəˈsepʃn] *s* **1.** percepcja *f* **2.** postrzeganie *n* **3.** rozumienie *n*; **per•cep•tive** [pəˈseptɪv] *adj* **1.** wnikliwy **2.** *remark*: trafny **3.** spostrzegawczy **4.** percepcyjny

perch[1] [pɜːtʃ] *pl perch s* okoń *m*

perch[2] [~] **I** *s* **1.** grzęda *f* **2.** żerdź *f* **3.** stanowisko *n* (obserwacyjne) **II** *v/i* **1.** (*birds*) siadać ⟨usiąść⟩ (***on*** na *L*) **2.** przycupnąć (***on*** na *L*) **III** *v/t* sadzać ⟨posadzić⟩

per•co•late [ˈpɜːkəleɪt] **I** *v/t coffee*: zaparzać ⟨-rzyć⟩ (w ekspresie) **II** *v/i* **1.** (*coffee*) zaparzać ⟨-rzyć⟩ się (w ekspresie) **2.** przesączać ⟨-czyć⟩ się **3.** przesiąkać ⟨-knąć⟩ **4.** rozchodzić ⟨-zejść⟩ się; ***it has ~d through to us that*** doszły nas słuchy, że **5.** (*changes*) dokonywać ⟨-nać⟩ się; **per•co•la•tor** [ˈpɜːkəleɪtə] *s* ekspres *m* do kawy

per•cus•sion [pəˈkʌʃn] *s* perkusja *f*; **perˈcus•sion in•stru•ment** *s* instrument *m* perkusyjny; **per•cus•sion•ist** [pəˈkʌʃnɪst] *s* muzyk *m* grający na perkusji

pe•re•grine fal•con [perəgrɪnˈfɔːlkən] *s* sokół *m* wędrowny

pe•remp•to•ry [pəˈremptərɪ] *adj* **1.** kategoryczny **2.** władczy

pe•ren•ni•al [pəˈrenɪəl] *adj* **1.** stały **2.** powracający **3.** *plant*: wieloletni

per•e•stroi•ka [pereˈstrɔɪkə] *s* POLIT pierestrojka *f*

per•fect **I** [ˈpɜːfɪkt] *adj* **1.** doskonały; ***nobody's ~*** nikt nie jest doskonały; ***a ~ crime*** przestępstwo doskonałe **2.** idealny; ***~ weather for a picnic*** idealna pogoda na piknik **3.** perfekcyjny **4.** znakomity **5.** świetny; ***she speaks ~ English*** świetnie mówi po angielsku **6.** zupełny; ***she is a ~ stranger to me*** w ogóle jej nie znam **7. *the present ~ tense*** GRAM czas teraźniejszy dokonany; ***the past ~ tense*** GRAM czas przeszły uprzedni, czas zaprzeszły **II** [pəˈfekt] *v/t* doskonalić ⟨u-⟩; **per•fec•tion** [pəˈfekʃn] *s* **1.** doskonałość *f* **2.** perfekcja *f*; ***bring s.th. to ~*** doprowadzić coś do perfekcji **3.** doskonalenie *n*; **per•fec•tion•ism** [pəˈfekʃnɪzəm] *s* perfekcjonizm *m*; **per•fec•tion•ist** [pəˈfekʃnɪst] *s* perfekcjonista *m*; **per•fect•ly** [ˈpɜːfɪktlɪ] *adv* **1.** doskonale **2.** idealnie **3.** perfekcyjnie **4.** znakomicie **5.** świetnie

per•fid•i•ous [pəˈfɪdɪəs] *adj* **1.** zdradliwy **2.** perfidny; **per•fi•dy** [ˈpɜːfɪdɪ] *s* **1.** zdradliwość *f* **2.** perfidia *f*

per•fo•rate [ˈpɜːfəreɪt] *v/t* dziurawić ⟨prze-⟩, perforować; **per•fo•rat•ed** [ˈpɜːfəreɪtɪd] *adj* przedziurawiony, perforowany; **per•fo•ra•tions** [pɜːfəˈreɪʃnz] *pl* perforacja *f*

per•form [pəˈfɔːm] **I** *v/t* **1.** wykonywać ⟨-nać⟩ **2.** przeprowadzać ⟨-dzić⟩ **3.** *music, play, role*: grać ⟨za-⟩ **4.** *role*: pełnić ⟨s-⟩; ***~ an important role in*** pełnić ważną rolę w *L* **5.** *concert*: dawać ⟨dać⟩, grać ⟨za-⟩ **6.** *song*: śpiewać ⟨za-⟩, grać ⟨za-⟩ **II** *v/i* **1.** występować ⟨-tąpić⟩ **2. *~ well*** (***poorly***) **a)** dobrze (słabo) wypaść **b)** uzyskać dobry (słaby) wynik **c)** dobrze (źle) się spisać **d)** mieć dobre (złe) wyniki **3.** funkcjonować **4.** działać; **per•form•ance** [pəˈfɔːməns] *s* **1.** występ *m*; ***a live ~*** występ na żywo **2.** wykonanie *n* **3.** rola *f*; ***an Oscar-winning ~*** rola nagrodzona Oskarem **4.** wyniki *pl*; ***poor***

P

~ of the company słabe wyniki firmy **5.** wydajność *f* **6.** efektywność *f*; ***a ~-related pay*** zarobki uzależnione od efektywności pracy **7.** przeprowadzenie *n* **8.** funkcjonowanie *n*; **per'form•ance car** *s* samochód *m* sportowy; **per•form•er** [pə'fɔːmə] *s* **1.** wykonawca *m* **2.** artysta *m*; **per•'form•ing** [pə'fɔːmɪŋ] *adj animal*: tresowany; **per•form•ing 'arts** *pl* sztuka *f* widowiskowa

per•fume ['pɜːfjuːm] **I** *s* **1.** perfumy *pl* **2.** zapach *m* **II** *v/t* perfumować ⟨po-⟩

per•func•to•ry [pə'fʌŋktərɪ] *adj* **1.** przelotny **2.** powierzchowny **3.** zdawkowy

per•haps [pə'hæps] *adv* **1.** może **2.** być może

per•il ['perəl] *s* **1.** niebezpieczeństwo *n*; ***be in ~*** być w niebezpieczeństwie; ***the ~s of drug abuse*** niebezpieczeństwa związanie z zażywaniem narkotyków **2.** ryzyko *n*; ***at one's ~*** na własne ryzyko; **per•il•ous** ['perələs] *adj* niebezpieczny, ryzykowny

pe•rim•e•ter [pə'rɪmɪtə] *s* **1.** MATH obwód *m* **2.** obrzeża *pl*; **pe•'rim•e•ter fence** *s* ogrodzenie *n*

pe•ri•od ['pɪərɪəd] **I** *s* **1.** okres *m*; ***over a ~ of four years*** przez okres czterech lat; ***a six-month trial ~*** sześciomiesięczny okres próbny **2.** czas *m*; ***the ~ of mourning*** czas żałoby **3.** epoka *f*; ***Jurassic ~*** jura, epoka jurajska **4.** miesiączka *f* **5.** lekcja *f* **6.** (*punctuation*) *Am* kropka *f* **II** *adj* **1.** z epoki **2.** stylowy **3.** historyczny **4.** zabytkowy; **pe•ri•od•ic** [pɪərɪ'ɒdɪk] *adj* **1.** okresowy **2.** periodyczny; **pe•ri•od•i•cal** [pɪərɪ'ɒdɪkl] **I** *adj* → ***periodic*** **II** *s* czasopismo *n*, periodyk *m*; **pe•ri•od•i•cal•ly** [pɪərɪ'ɒdɪklɪ] *adv* **1.** okresowo **2.** periodycznie

pe•riph•e•ral [pə'rɪfərəl] **I** *adj* **1.** poboczny **2.** mający drugorzędne znaczenie **3.** peryferyjny; ***~ devices*** urządzenia peryferyjne **II** *s* INF urządzenie *n* peryferyjne; **pe•riph•e•ry** [pə'rɪfərɪ] *s* **1.** peryferie *pl*; ***on the ~ of the town*** na peryferiach miasta **2.** obrzeża *pl* **3.** skraj *m*

per•i•scope ['perɪskəʊp] *s* peryskop *m*

per•ish ['perɪʃ] **I** *v/i* **1.** ginąć ⟨z-⟩ **2.** niszczyć ⟨z-⟩ się **II** *v/t* niszczyć ⟨z-⟩;

per•ish•a•ble ['perɪʃəbl] *adj food*: łatwo psujący się; '**per•ish•ing** ['perɪʃɪŋ] *adj Br infml* **1.** ***I'm ~*** umieram z zimna **2.** *dated* sakramencki

per•i•to•ni•tis [perɪtə'naɪtɪs] *s* MED zapalenie *n* otrzewnej

per•jure ['pɜːdʒə] *v/t*: ***~ oneself*** krzywoprzysięgać; **per•ju•ry** ['pɜːdʒərɪ] *s* krzywoprzysięstwo *n*

perk[1] [pɜːk] → ***percolate I***

perk[2] [~] *s* **1.** dodatek *m* (do pensji) **2.** dodatkowa korzyść *f*; **perk up** *infml* **I** *v/i* **1.** wzrastać ⟨-rosnąć⟩ **2.** (*person*) rozchmurzać ⟨-rzyć⟩ się **II** *v/t* **1.** rozweselać ⟨-lić⟩, poprawiać ⟨-wić⟩ humor **2.** uatrakcyjniać ⟨-nić⟩; **perk•y** ['pɜːkɪ] *adj* **1.** radosny **2.** dziarski

perm [pɜːm] **I** *s* (*hairstyle*) trwała *f* **II** *v/t* robić ⟨z-⟩ trwałą; ***I had my hair ~ed*** zrobiłam trwałą; ***shampoo for ~ed hair*** szampon do włosów po trwałej

per•ma•nence ['pɜːmənəns] *s* trwałość *f*; **per•ma•nent** ['pɜːmənənt] *adj* **1.** trwały **2.** stały; ***~ address*** stały adres; **per•ma•nent•ly** ['pɜːmənəntlɪ] *adv* trwale, stale

per•me•a•ble ['pɜːmɪəbl] *adj* przepuszczalny (***to*** dla *G*); **per•me•ate** ['pɜːmɪeɪt] **I** *v/t a. fig* przenikać ⟨-knąć⟩; ***the air was ~d with the odour of burning rubber*** w powietrzu roznosił się smród palonej gumy **II** *v/i* przenikać ⟨-knąć⟩ (***through*** przez *A*, ***to*** do *G*)

per•mis•si•ble [pə'mɪsəbl] *adj* dozwolony, dopuszczalny; **per•mis•sion** [pə'mɪʃn] *s* **1.** pozwolenie *n*; ***ask (for) ~*** poprosić o pozwolenie; ***give ~*** udzielić pozwolenia **2.** zezwolenie *n*; **per•mis•sive** [pə'mɪsɪv] *adj* **1.** liberalny **2.** pobłażliwy **3.** *society*: permisywny

per•mit I [pə'mɪt] *v/t* **1.** pozwalać ⟨-wolić⟩; ***~ s.o. to do s.th.*** pozwolić komuś coś zrobić; ***s.th. is not ~ted*** coś jest zabronione; ***if time ~s*** jeżeli czas pozwoli; ***weather ~ting*** jeżeli będzie ładna pogoda **2.** zezwalać ⟨-wolić⟩ **3.** umożliwiać ⟨-wić⟩ **4.** pozwalać ⟨-wolić⟩ na *A*; ***cash machines ~ you to withdraw money at any time*** bankomaty umożliwiają wypłatę pieniędzy przez całą dobę **II** ['pɜːmɪt] *s*

P

pozwolenie, zezwolenie *n*; ***a work ~*** pozwolenie na pracę

per•ni•cious [pəˈnɪʃəs] *adj lit* szkodliwy

per•nick•e•ty [pəˈnɪkətɪ] *adj Br infml* drobiazgowy

per•pen•dic•u•lar [pɜːpənˈdɪkjʊlə] **I** *adj* prostopadły **II** *s* prostopadła *f*

per•pe•trate [ˈpɜːpətreɪt] *v/t crime*: popełniać ⟨-nić⟩; **per•pe•tra•tor** [ˈpɜːpətreɪtə] *s* sprawca *m*

per•pet•u•al [pəˈpətʃʊəl] *adj* **1.** ciągły **2.** wieczny; **per•pet•u•al•ly** [pəˈpetʃʊəlɪ] *adv* **1.** ciągle **2.** wiecznie; **per•pet•u•ate** [pəˈpetʃʊeɪt] *v/t* **1.** *stereotype*: utrwalać ⟨-lić⟩ **2.** *hostility*: podsycać ⟨-cić⟩; **per•pe•tu•i•ty** [pɜːpəˈtjuːətɪ] *s*: ***in ~*** **a)** w wieczyste użytkowanie **b)** na zawsze

per•plex [pəˈpleks] *v/t* **1.** zbijać ⟨zbić⟩ z tropu **2.** konsternować ⟨s-⟩; **per•plexed** [pəˈplekst] *adj* **1.** zmieszany **2.** skonsternowany; **per•plex•i•ty** [pəˈpleksɪtɪ] *s* **1.** zmieszanie *n* **2.** konsternacja *f*

per•qui•site [ˈpɜːkwɪzɪt] → ***perk***[2]

per•se•cute [ˈpɜːsɪkjuːt] *v/t* **1.** prześladować (***s.o. for*** kogoś za *A*) **2.** dręczyć; **per•se•cu•tion** [pɜːsɪˈkjuːʃn] *s* **1.** prześladowanie *n*; ***~ mania*** mania prześladowcza; ***the victims of religious ~*** ofiary prześladowań religijnych **2.** dręczenie *n*; **per•se•cu•tor** [ˈpɜːsɪkjuːtə] *s* prześladowca *m*

per•se•ver•ance [pɜːsɪˈvɪərəns] *s* wytrwałość *f*; **per•se•vere** [pɜːsɪˈvɪə] *v/i* wytrwale kontynuować (***in/with*** *A*); ***~ in one's attempts*** wytrwale ponawiać próby; **per•se•ˈver•ing** [pɜːsɪˈvɪərɪŋ] *adj* wytrwały

Per•sian [ˈpɜːʃn] **I** *adj* perski; ***a ~ carpet*** perski dywan **II** *s* **1.** Pers *m* **2.** język *m* perski **3.** (*a.* ***~ cat***) kot *m* perski, pers *m*; **Per•sian ˈGulf** *s* Zatoka *f* Perska

per•sist [pəˈsɪst] *v/i* **1.** wytrwale kontynuować (***in/with*** *A*); ***why do you ~ in blaming yourself for what happened?*** dlaczego uparcie obwiniasz się o to, co zaszło? **2.** nie ustawać (***in/with*** w *L*) **3.** utrzymywać ⟨-mać⟩ się; ***if the symptoms ~*** jeżeli objawy nie ustapią; **per•sis•tence** [pəˈsɪstəns] *s* **1.** wytrwałość *f* **2.** upór *m* **3.** utrzymywanie *n* się; **per•sis•tent** [pəˈsɪstənt] *adj* **1.** wytrwały **2.** uparty **3.** ciągły **4.** nieustający **5.** utrzymujący się **6.** ***a ~ offender*** recydywista; **per•sis•tent•ly** [pəˈsɪstəntlɪ] *adv* **1.** wytrwale **2.** uparcie **3.** ciągle

per•snick•e•ty [pəˈsnɪkətɪ] *Am* → ***pernickety***

per•son [ˈpɜːsn] *pl people*, *persons s* **1.** osoba *f*; ***the price is £40 per ~*** cena wynosi 40 funtów za osobę; ***in ~*** osobiście **2.** człowiek *m*; ***he's a fascinating ~*** jest fascynującym człowiekiem; **per•son•a•ble** [ˈpɜːsənəbl] *adj* **1.** sympatyczny **2.** o miłej aparycji; **per•sonage** [ˈpɜːsənɪdʒ] *s* **1.** osobistość *f* **2.** postać *f*

per•son•al [ˈpɜːsənl] *adj* **1.** osobisty; ***a ~ question*** pytanie osobiste **2.** osobowy; ***~ details*** dane osobowe **3.** prywatny; ***~ life*** życie prywatne **4.** własny; ***from ~ experience*** z własnego doświadczenia **5.** indywidualny; ***a ~ account*** rachunek indywidualny; **person•al as•ˈsist•ant** *s* asystent *m*; **ˈperson•al col•umn** *s* ogłoszenia *pl* drobne; **per•son•al com•ˈput•er** *s* komputer *m* osobisty; **ˈper•son•al file** *s* akta *pl* personalne; **per•son•al ˈhy•giene** *s* higiena *f* osobista

per•son•al•i•ty [pɜːsəˈnælətɪ] *s* **1.** osobowość *f*; ***a TV ~*** osobowość telewizyjna **2.** charakter *m*; ***have a strong ~*** mieć silny charakter **3.** osobistość *f* **4.** postać *f*

per•son•al•ize [ˈpɜːsənəlaɪz] *v/t* **1.** dostosowywać ⟨-sować⟩ do indywidualnych potrzeb **2.** nadawać ⟨-dać⟩ indywidualny charakter

per•son•al ˈloan *s* kredyt *f* indywidualny

per•son•al•ly [ˈpɜːsənəlɪ] *adv* **1.** osobiście; ***take s.th. ~*** wziąć coś do siebie, obrazić się; ***I'll deal with the matter ~*** zajmę się tym osobiście **2.** jeżeli o mnie chodzi

per•son•al ˈor•gan•iz•er *s* organizer *m*; **per•son•al ˈpro•noun** *s GRAM* zaimek *m* osobowy; **per•son•al ˈster•e•o** *s* walkman *m*, odtwarzacz *m* osobisty

per•son•i•fi•ca•tion [pəsɒnɪfɪˈkeɪʃn] *s* **1.** personifikacja *f* **2.** uosobienie *n*; ***she was the ~ of elegance*** była uosobieniem elegancji; **per•son•i•fy** [pɜːˈsɒnɪfaɪ] *v/t* uosabiać ⟨-sobić⟩;

P

he is kindness personified jest uosobieniem dobroci

per•son•nel [pɜːsəˈnel] *s* **1.** personel *m* **2.** dział *m* kadr, *infml* kadry *pl*

per•spec•tive [pəˈspektɪv] *s* **1.** perspektywa *f*; ***try to see it from a different ~*** spróbuj na to spojrzeć z innej perspektywy **2.** punkt *m* widzenia

per•spex® [ˈpɜːspeks] *s Br* pleksiglas *m*

per•spi•ra•tion [pɜːspɪˈreɪʃn] *s* **1.** pot *m* **2.** pocenie się *n*; **per•spire** [pəˈspaɪə] *v/i* pocić ⟨s-⟩ się

per•suade [pəˈsweɪd] *v/t* **1.** przekonywać ⟨-nać⟩; ***I'm still not ~d of the plan's merits*** nadal nie jestem przekonany o zaletach tego planu **2.** namawiać ⟨-mówić⟩ (***s.o. into*** kogoś na *A*); ***~ s.o. out of*** wyperswadować komuś *A*; ***try to ~ him to come*** namów go, żeby przyszedł; **per•sua•sion** [pəˈsweɪʒn] *s* **1.** przekonywanie *n* **2.** namowy *pl*; ***after much ~*** po długich namowach **3.** perswazja *f* **4.** przekonania *pl*; ***of liberal ~*** o przekonaniach liberalnych **per•sua•sive** [pəˈsweɪsɪv] *adj* przekonujący

pert [pɜːt] *adj* **1.** zadziorny **2.** ***a ~ nose*** mały, zgrabny nos

per•tain [pəˈteɪn] *v/i* **1.** obowiązywać; ***those laws no longer ~*** te przepisy już nie obowiązują **2.** (*conditions*) panować, istnieć; **per•tain to** *v/i* **1.** dotyczyć **2.** odnosić się do *G*

per•ti•na•cious [pɜːtɪˈneɪʃəs] *adj* wytrwały

per•ti•nent [ˈpɜːtɪnənt] *adj* **1.** na temat **2.** ***be ~ to*** mieć związek z *I*

P

per•turb [pəˈtɜːrb] *v/t* niepokoić ⟨za-⟩; ***I was ~ed by his lack of interest*** niepokoił mnie jego brak zainteresowania; **per•turb•ing** [pəˈtɜːbɪŋ] *adj* niepokojący

Pe•ru [pəˈruː] *s* Peru *n*

pe•ruse [pəˈruːz] *v/t* **1.** studiować ⟨prze-⟩ **2.** dokładnie czytać ⟨prze-⟩

per•vade [pəˈveɪd] *v/t* **1.** przenikać ⟨-knąć⟩ **2.** wypełniać ⟨-nić⟩

per•va•sive [pəˈveɪsɪv] *adj* wszechobecny

per•verse [pəˈvɜːs] *adj* **1.** przekorny **2.** złośliwy **3.** perwersyjny; **per•ver•sion** [pəˈvɜːʃn] *s* **1.** perwersja *f* **2.** zboczenie *n* **3.** wypaczenie *n*; ***the ~ of justice*** parodia wymiaru sprawiedliwości; **per•ˈver•si•ty** [pəˈvɜːsɪtɪ] *s* przekora *f*, złośliwość *f*; ***out of ~*** z przekory, ze złośliwości

per•vert **I** [ˈpɜːvɜːt] *s* zboczeniec *m*, dewiant *m* **II** [pəˈvɜːt] *v/t* **1.** wykorzystywać ⟨-tać⟩ w złym celu **2.** wywierać ⟨-wrzeć⟩ zły wpływ na *A*

pes•ky [ˈpeskɪ] *adj Am infml* wkurzający

pes•sa•ry [ˈpesərɪ] *s* **1.** krążek *m* domaciczny **2.** czopek *m*

pes•si•mism [ˈpesɪmɪzm] *s* pesymizm *m*; **pes•si•mist** [ˈpesɪmɪst] *s* pesymista *m*; **pes•si•mis•tic** [pesɪˈmɪstɪk] *adj* pesymistyczny

pest [pest] *s* **1.** szkodnik *m* **2.** *infml* urwis *m*, nieznośny dzieciak *m*

pes•ter [ˈpestə] *v/t* **1.** dręczyć, zadręczać (***s.o. with*** kogoś *I*); ***he has been ~ing her with phone calls*** zadręczał ją telefonami; ***journalists ~ed neighbours for information*** dziennikarze nagabywali sąsiadów o informacje **2.** zamęczać (***s.o. with*** kogoś *I*) **3.** nie dawać spokoju

pes•ti•cide [ˈpestɪsaɪd] *s* pestycyd *m*

pes•tle [ˈpesəl] *s* (*mortar*) tłuczek *m*

pet [pet] **I** *s* **1.** zwierzę *n* domowe; ***~ food*** pokarm dla zwierząt; ***~ shop*** sklep zoologiczny; ***s.th. is s.o.'s ~ hate*** coś kogoś szczególnie mierzi **2.** pupil *m*, ulubieniec *m*; ***she's the teacher's ~*** jest pupilką nauczyciela **3.** ***what's wrong, ~?*** coś nie tak, kochanie? **II** *v/t* głaskać ⟨po-⟩ **III** *v/i infml* pieścić się, *infml* obściskiwać się

pet•al [ˈpetl] *s* płatek *m*

pe•ter out [piːtəˈaʊt] *v/i* **1.** stopniowo zanikać ⟨-knąć⟩ **2.** umierać ⟨umrzeć⟩ naturalną śmiercią

pe•tite [pəˈtiːt] *adj* drobny; ***a ~ blonde*** drobna blondynka

pe•ti•tion [pəˈtɪʃn] **I** *s* **1.** petycja *f* (***for/against*** za *I*/przeciw *D*) **2.** prośba *f* (***for*** o *A*) **3.** JUR pozew *m*, wniosek *m*; ***a ~ for divorce*** pozew o rozwód **II** *v/i* **1.** składać ⟨złożyć⟩ petycję **2.** wystosowywać ⟨-sować⟩ prośbę **3.** składać ⟨złożyć⟩ pozew (***for*** o *A*) **III** *v/t* wystosowywać ⟨-sować⟩ petycję do *G*; **petition in ˈbankruptcy** *s* wniosek *m* o upadłość; **pe•ti•tion•er** [pəˈtɪʃnə] *s* **1.** wnioskodawca *m* **2.** JUR powód *m*

'pet name *s* zdrobnienie *n*, spieszczenie *n*

pet•ri•fied ['petrɪfaɪd] *adj* **1.** przerażony; ***I'm ~ of snakes*** panicznie boję się węży; ***be ~ with fear*** być sparaliżowanym ze strachu **2.** skamieniały; **pet•ri•fy** ['petrɪfaɪ] **I** *v/t* **1.** *fig* paraliżować ⟨s-⟩ **2.** wprawiać ⟨-wić⟩ w osłupienie **II** *v/t* ulegać ⟨ulec⟩ skamienieniu

pet•rol ['petrəl] *s Br* benzyna *f*; ***fill a car up with ~*** zatankować samochód; **'pet•rol bomb** *Br s* koktajl *m* Mołotowa; **'pet•rol sta•tion** *Br s* stacja *f* benzynowa

pe•tro•le•um [pɪ'trəʊlɪəm] *s* ropa *f* naftowa; **pet•ro•chem•i•cal** [petrəʊ'kemɪkl] *s CHEM* produkt *m* petrochemiczny; ***the ~ industry*** przemysł petrochemiczny

pet•ti•coat ['petɪkəʊt] *s Br* halka *f*

pet•ti•fog•ging ['petɪfɒgɪŋ] *adj Br dated* **1.** drobiazgowy **2.** błahy

pet•ting ['petɪŋ] *s* petting *m*, pieszczoty *pl*

pet•ty ['petɪ] *adj* **1.** drobny; ***~ theft*** drobna kradzież; ***a ~ criminal*** drobny przestępca **2.** nieistotny **3.** małostkowy; **pet•ty 'cash** *s* (*money*) drobne *pl*

pet•u•lant ['petjʊlənt] *adj* **1.** rozkapryszony **2.** nadąsany

pe•tu•ni•a [pə'tjuːnɪə] *s* petunia *f*

pew [pjuː] *s* (*church*) ławka *f*; ***take a ~*** *infml* usiądź

pew•ter ['pjuːtə] *s* (*alloy*) cyna *f*

pH-bal•anced [piːeɪtʃ'bælənsd] *adj* o neutralnym pH; **pH fac•tor** [piːeɪtʃ'fæktə] *s* współczynnik *m* pH

pha•lanx ['fælæŋks] *pl -lanxes* ['fælæŋksɪs], *-langes* [fæ'lændʒiːz] *s* **1.** falanga *f* **2.** *ANAT* paliczek *m*

phal•li ['fælaɪ] *pl* → ***phallus***

phal•lic ['fælɪk] *adj* falliczny; **phal•lus** ['fæləs] *pl -li* ['~laɪ] *s* fallus *m*

phan•tom ['fæntəm] **I** *s* **1.** duch *m* **2.** fantom *m* **II** *adj* **1.** urojony **2.** *leg, pain*: fantomowy

Phar•i•see ['færɪsiː] *s* faryzeusz *m*

phar•ma•ceu•ti•cal [fɑːmə'sjuːtɪkl] **I** *adj* farmaceutyczny; ***the ~ industry*** przemysł farmaceutyczny **II** *s* lekarstwo *n*, lek *m*; **phar•ma•cist** ['fɑːməsɪst] *s* **1.** farmaceuta *m* **2.** aptekarz *m*; ***the ~'s*** *Br* apteka; **phar•ma•cy** ['fɑːrməsɪ] *s* **1.** farmacja *f* **2.** *Am* apteka *f*

phar•yn•gi•tis [færɪn'dʒaɪtɪs] *s* zapalenie *n* gardła

phase [feɪz] **I** *s* **1.** faza *f*; ***the ~s of the moon*** fazy księżyca **2.** etap *m* **II** *v/t* dzielić ⟨po-⟩ na etapy; ***a ~d withdrawal of*** stopniowe wycofywanie *G*; **phase in** *v/t* stopniowo wprowadzać ⟨-dzić⟩; **phase out** *v/t* stopniowo wycofywać ⟨-fać⟩

PhD [piːeɪtʃ'diː] *abbr* (=***doctor of philosophy***) (*academic degree*) dr

pheas•ant ['feznt] *s* bażant *m*

phe•nom•e•na [fɪ'nɒmɪnə] *pl* → ***phenomenon***; **phe•nom•e•nal** [fɪ'nɒmɪnl] *adj* fenomenalny, fantastyczny; **phe•nom•e•nal•ly** [fɪ'nɒmɪnlɪ] *adv* fenomenalnie, fantastycznie; **phe•nom•e•non** [fɪ'nɒmɪnən] *pl -na s* zjawisko *n*; ***a natural ~*** zjawisko naturalne

phew [fjuː] *interj* uf!

phi•al ['faɪəl] *s* fiolka *f*

Phi Be•ta Kap•pa [faɪbiːtə'kæpə] *s stowarzyszenie zrzeszające wybitnie uzdolnionych studentów*

phi•lan•derer [fɪ'lændərə] *s dated* kobieciarz *m*

phil•an•throp•ic [fɪlən'θrɒpɪk] *adj* **1.** filantropijny **2.** dobroczynny; ***a ~ organization*** organizacja dobroczynna; **phi•lan•thro•pist** [fɪ'lænθrəpɪst] *s* filantrop *m*; **phi•lan•thro•py** [fɪ'lænθrəpɪ] *s* filantropia *f*, dobroczynność *f*

phil•a•tel•ic [fɪlə'telɪk] *adj* filatelistyczny; **phi•lat•e•list** [fɪ'lætəlɪst] *s* filatelista *m*; **phi•lat•e•ly** [fɪ'lætəlɪ] *s* filatelistyka *f*

phil•har•mon•ic [fɪlɑː'mɒnɪk] *adj* filharmoniczny; ***a ~ orchestra*** orkiestra filharmoniczna

Phil•ip•pines ['fɪlɪpiːnz] *pl* Filipiny *pl*

Phil•lips screw [fɪlɪp'skruː] *s* wkręt *f* z gniazdem krzyżowym; **Phil•lips 'screw•driv•er** *s* wkrętak *m* krzyżowy

phil•is•tine ['fɪlɪstaɪn] **I** *s* filister *m* **II** *adj* filisterski

phil•o•log•i•cal [fɪlə'lɒdʒɪkl] *adj* filologiczny; **phi•lol•o•gist** [fɪ'lɒlədʒɪst] *s* filolog *m*; **phi•lol•o•gy** [fɪ'lɒlədʒɪ] *s* filologia *f*

phi•los•o•pher [fɪ'lɒsəfə] *s* filozof *m*; **phil•o•soph•i•cal** [fɪlə'sɒfɪkl] *adj* filo-

P

zoficzny; **phi•los•o•phize** [fɪ'lɒsəfaɪz] *v/i* filozofować (*on*/*about* o *L*); **phi•los•o•phy** [fɪ'lɒsəfɪ] *s* filozofia *f*

phlegm [flem] *s a. fig* flegma *f*; **phleg•mat•ic** [fleg'mætɪk] *adj* flegmatyczny

pho•bi•a ['fəʊbɪə] *s* fobia *f*; ***have a ~ about darkness*** panicznie bać się ciemności

phone [fəʊn] **I** *s* **1.** telefon *m*; ***make a ~ call*** zadzwonić; ***by*** (*a.* ***over the***) ~ telefonicznie, przez telefon **2.** słuchawka *f* (telefoniczna); ***pick up the ~*** odebrać telefon, podnieść słuchawkę **II** *v/i* dzwonić ⟨za-⟩; ***he ~d to invite me for dinner*** zadzwonił zaprosić mnie na kolację; ***someone ~ for an ambulance!*** niech ktoś zadzwoni po karetkę!; ***~ back*** oddzwonić **III** *v/t* (*a.* ***~ up***) dzwonić ⟨za-⟩; ***~ them up and ask when they are coming*** zadzwoń do nich i zapytaj, kiedy przyjdą; '**phone book** *s* książka *f* telefoniczna; '**phone booth** *s* budka *f* telefoniczna; '**phone call** *s* rozmowa *f* telefoniczna; '**phone card** *s* karta *f* telefoniczna; '**phone-in** *s Br* **1.** program *m* z telefonicznym udziałem słuchaczy **2.** program *m* z telefonicznym udziałem widzów

'**phone num•ber** *s* numer *m* telefonu

pho•net•ic [fə'netɪk] *adj* fonetyczny; ***~ transcription*** transkrypcja fonetyczna; **pho•net•ics** [fə'netɪks] *s* fonetyka *f*

pho•ney ['fəʊnɪ] *Br*, **pho•ny** *Am infml* **I** *adj* **1.** udawany; ***a ~ British accent*** udawany brytyjski akcent **2.** fałszywy **3.** podrobiony **4.** wymyślony **II** *s* **1.** pozer *m* **2.** oszust *m*

P

phos•phate ['fɒsfeɪt] *s CHEM* fosforan *m*; **phos•phate-'free** *adj* bez fosforanów, niezawierający fosforanów

phos•pho•res•cent [fɒsfə'resnt] *adj* fosforyzujący

phos•pho•rus ['fɒsfərəs] *s CHEM* fosfor *m*

pho•to ['fəʊtəʊ] *s* zdjęcie *n*, fotografia *f*; ***take a ~*** zrobić zdjęcie; ***in the ~*** na zdjęciu; '**pho•to al•bum** *s* album *m* fotograficzny; '**pho•to•cell** *s TECH* fotokomórka *f*; '**pho•to•cop•i•er** *s* kserokopiarka *f*; '**pho•to•cop•y** *s* kserokopia *f*; **pho•to 'fin•ish** *s*: ***a race with a ~*** *SPORT* wyścig, którego wynik ustalany jest za pomocą fotokomórki; '**Pho•to-fit**® *s Br* portret *m* pamięciowy

pho•to•gen•ic [fəʊtəʊ'dʒenɪk] *adj* fotogeniczny

pho•to•graph ['fəʊtəgrɑːf] **I** *s* fotografia *f* **II** *v/t* fotografować ⟨s-⟩ **III** *v/i* wychodzić ⟨wyjść⟩ na fotografii; **pho•tog•ra•pher** [fə'tɒgrəfə] *s* fotograf *m*; **pho•to•graph•ic** [fəʊtə'græfɪk] *adj* fotograficzny; ***a ~ memory*** fotograficzna pamięć; **pho•tog•ra•phy** [fə'tɒgrəfɪ] *s* fotografia *f*

pho•to'jour•nal•ist *s* fotoreporter *m*; **pho•to•mon'tage** *s* fotomontaż *m*

pho•ton ['fəʊtɒn] *s PHYS* foton *m*

pho•to'sen•si•tive *adj* światłoczuły; '**pho•to ses•sion**, '***pho•to shoot*** *s* sesja *f* fotograficzna; **pho•to•'syn•the•sis** *s BIOL* fotosynteza *f*

phras•al ['freɪzl] *adj* frazowy; ***~ verbs*** *GRAM* czasowniki złożone

phrase [freɪz] **I** *s* **1.** fraza *f* **2.** określenie *n* **3.** słowa *pl*; ***empty ~s*** puste słowa **II** *v/t* **1.** formułować ⟨s-⟩ **2.** wyrażać ⟨-razić⟩; '**phrase•book** *s* rozmówki *pl*

phra•se•ol•o•gy [freɪzɪ'ɒlədʒɪ] *s* frazeologia *f*

phys•i•cal ['fɪzɪkl] **I** *adj* **1.** fizyczny; ***~ education*** wychowanie fizyczne; ***~ strength*** siła fizyczna; ***~ examination*** badanie lekarskie; ***~ properties*** właściwości fizyczne; ***~ chemistry*** chemia fizyczna **2.** cielesny **II** *s* badanie *n* lekarskie; **phys•i•cal 'hand•i•cap** *s* upośledzenie *n* fizyczne; **phys•i•cal•ly** ['fɪzɪklɪ] *adv* fizycznie; ***it's ~ impossible*** to fizycznie niemożliwe; **phys•i•cal•ly 'hand•i•cap•ped** *adj* upośledzony fizycznie; **phy•si•cian** [fɪ'zɪʃn] *s Am form* lekarz *m*; **phys•i•cist** ['fɪzɪsɪst] *s* fizyk *m*

phys•ics ['fɪzɪks] *s* fizyka *f*

phys•i•og•no•my [fɪzɪ'ɒnəmɪ] *s lit* fizjonomia *f*

phys•i•o•log•i•cal [fɪzɪə'lɒdʒɪkl] *adj* fizjologiczny; **phys•i•ol•o•gy** [fɪzɪ'ɒlədʒɪ] *s* fizjologia *f*

phys•i•o•ther•a•pist [fɪzɪəʊ'θerəpɪst] *s* fizjoterapeuta *m*; **phys•i•o•ther•a•py** [fɪzɪəʊ'θerəpɪ] *s* fizjoterapia *f*

phy•sique [fɪ'ziːk] *s* **1.** budowa *f* ciała **2.** postura *f*

pi•a•nist ['pɪənɪst] *s* pianista *m*

pi•an•o [pɪ'ænəʊ] *pl -nos s* fortepian *m*; ***an upright ~*** pianino; ***play the ~*** grać na fortepianie, grać na pianinie; **pi•an•o ac•'cor•de•on** *s Br* akordeon *m*; **pi•'an•o play•er** *s* pianista *m*

pick [pɪk] **I** *v/t* **1.** wybierać ⟨-brać⟩; ***~ a number from one to twenty*** wybierz numer od jednego do dwudziestu; ***he ~ed his words carefully*** starannie dobierał słowa; ***~ and choose*** przebierać; ***~ a winner*** **a)** *infml* dokonać dobrego wyboru **b)** wytypować zwycięzcę **2.** *flowers*: zrywać ⟨zerwać⟩ **3.** *berries*: zbierać ⟨zebrać⟩ **4.** wydłubywać ⟨-bać⟩ **5.** *bones*: obgryzać ⟨-ryźć⟩ **6.** *hen*: skubać ⟨o-⟩ **7.** dłubać ⟨wy-⟩; ***~ one's nose*** dłubać w nosie; ***~ one's teeth*** dłubać w zębach; ***~ holes in*** wytknąć słabe punkty *G* **8.** ***~ a lock*** otworzyć wytrychem zamek **9.** ***~ a fight with*** prowokować *A* **10.** ***~ one's way*** stąpać ostrożnie **II** *s* **1.** wybór *m*; ***take one's ~*** dokonać wyboru, wybrać; ***Owen was their ~ for the best player*** uznali Owena za najlepszego zawodnika; ***he can have his ~ of any girl*** może mieć każdą dziewczynę; ***the ~ of the bunch*** najlepszy z najlepszych **2.** → **pickax**; **pick at** *v/i* **1.** dłubać w *L* **2.** skubać ⟨-bnąć⟩ **3.** majstrować przy *I*; **pick on** *v/i* **1.** *infml* czepiać ⟨-pić⟩ się *G* **2.** wybierać ⟨-brać⟩; **pick out** *v/t* **1.** wybierać ⟨-brać⟩; ***he was picked out from hundreds of applicants*** został wybrany spośród setek kandydatów **2.** rozpoznawać ⟨-nać⟩; ***can you pick me out in this photo?*** rozpoznajesz mnie na tym zdjęciu? **3.** wydobywać ⟨-być⟩, wyróżniać ⟨-nić⟩; ***the car lights picked out a cat*** w świetle reflektorów pojawił się kot; **pick up I** *v/t* **1.** podnosić ⟨-nieść⟩; ***~ the phone*** podnieść słuchawkę, odebrać telefon **2.** brać ⟨wziąć⟩ **3.** *child*: brać ⟨wziąć⟩ na ręce **4.** *passenger*: zabierać ⟨-brać⟩; ***I'll pick you up at 2*** przyjadę po ciebie o drugiej **5.** *habit*: nabierać ⟨-brać⟩ **6.** *girl*: podrywać ⟨-derwać⟩ **7.** *signal*: odbierać ⟨odebrać⟩, *infml* łapać ⟨z-⟩ **8.** *language*: uczyć ⟨na-⟩ się **9.** *illness*: *infml* łapać ⟨z-⟩ **10.** *subject*: podejmować ⟨-djąć⟩ **11.** ***~ speed*** przyśpieszać **12.** stawiać ⟨postawić⟩ na nogi, pomagać ⟨-móc⟩; ***try this, it will pick you up*** weź to, to cię postawi na nogi **13.** (*police*) *infml* zatrzymywać ⟨-mać⟩ **II** *v/i* **1.** poprawiać ⟨-wić⟩ się **2.** polepszać ⟨-szyć⟩ się **3.** rosnąć ⟨wz-⟩ **4.** podnosić ⟨-nieść⟩ się **5.** ***the wind is picking up*** wiatr się wzmaga; **pick up on** *v/i* **1.** reagować ⟨za-⟩ na *A* **2.** wracać ⟨wrócić⟩ do *G*

'pick•ax(e) *s* **1.** kilof *m* **2.** oskard *m*

pick•er ['pɪkə] *s* zbieracz *m*

pick•et ['pɪkɪt] **I** *s* **1.** sztacheta *f* **2.** uczestnik *m* pikiety **3.** straż *f* **II** *v/t* pikietować; **'pick•et fence** *s* płot *m* ze sztachet; **'pick•et line** *s* pikieta *f*

pick•ings ['pɪkɪŋz] *pl infml* zysk *m*; ***there are easy ~ in this job*** w tej pracy można się łatwo dorobić

pick•le ['pɪkl] **I** *s* **1.** *Br* **~s** pikle **2.** *Br* marynata *f*; ***in a ~*** *infml* w tarapatach, w opałach **3.** *Am* korniszon *m*, ogórek *m* konserwowy **II** *v/t* marynować ⟨za-⟩; **pick•led** ['pɪkld] *adj* **1.** marynowany **2.** (*drunk*) *dated infml* zalany

'pick•lock *s* włamywacz *m*; **'pick-me-up** *s infml* **1.** coś *m* na wzmocnienie **2.** *fig* lekarstwo *n*; **'pick•pocket** *s* kieszonkowiec *m*; **'pick•up** *s* **1.** (*a.* ***~ truck***) furgonetka *f*, pickup *m* **2.** ***casual ~s*** przypadkowe znajomości **3.** poprawa *f*; ***a ~ in the housing market*** poprawa na rynku mieszkaniowym **4.** odbiór *m* **5.** przetwornik *m* **6.** AUTO *Am* przyśpieszenie *n*

pick•y ['pɪkɪ] *adj infml* wybredny

pic•nic ['pɪknɪk] **I** *s* piknik *m*; ***go for a ~*** wybrać się na piknik; ***it's no ~*** *infml* to nie przelewki **II** *v/i* urządzać ⟨-dzić⟩ piknik

pic•to•gram ['pɪktəgræm] *s* piktogram *m*

pic•to•ri•al [pɪk'tɔːrɪəl] *adj* **1.** ilustrowany **2.** graficzny **3.** obrazowy

pic•ture ['pɪktʃə] **I** *s* **1.** obrazek *m*; ***draw ~s*** rysować obrazki; ***look a ~*** wyglądać jak z obrazka; ***be the ~ of health*** być okazem zdrowia **2.** obraz *m*; ***paint a ~*** namalować obraz; ***paint a gloomy ~ of s.th.*** przedstawić coś w ciemnych barwach; ***I've got a vivid ~ of my grandfather*** bardzo dobrze pamiętam mojego dziadka **3.** rysu-

P

nek *m* **4.** zdjęcie *n*; ***in the ~*** na zdjęciu **5.** ***the ~*** sytuacja; ***just a few years ago the ~ was different*** jeszcze kilka lat temu sytuacja była inna; ***get the ~?*** *infml* kapujesz?; ***put s.o. in the ~*** przedstawić komuś sytuację **6.** film *m*; ***the ~s*** *dated* kino **II** *v/t* **1.** wyobrażać ⟨-razić⟩ sobie (***s.o. as*** kogoś jako *A*) **2.** przedstawiać ⟨-wić⟩ (***s.o. as*** kogoś jako *A*); **'pic•ture book** *s* książka *f* z obrazkami; **'pic•ture frame** *s* **1.** rama *f* obrazu **2.** ramka *f* (na zdjęcia)

pic•tur•esque [pɪktʃə'resk] *adj* malowniczy

'pic•ture win•dow *s* okno *n* panoramiczne

pid•dle ['pɪdl] *v/i infml* robić ⟨z-⟩ siku; **pid•dling** ['pɪdlɪŋ] *adj infml* bzdurny

pidg•in ['pɪdʒɪn] *s* pidgin *m*, pidżyn *m*; ***~ English*** łamana angielszczyzna

pie [paɪ] *s* **1.** placek *m*; ***an apple ~*** szarlotka, ciasto z jabłkami; ***a piece*** (*a.* ***share***) ***of the ~*** *infml* udział **2.** pasztecik *m*; ***a pork ~*** pasztecik z nadzieniem z wieprzowiny **3.** pieróg *m*

piece [piːs] *s* **1.** kawałek *m*; ***a ~ of cheese*** kawałek sera; ***a ~ of cake*** **a)** kawałek ciasta **b)** *fig* bułka z masłem; ***a ~ of paper*** kartka papieru; ***a ~ of bread*** kromka chleba; ***a ~ of furniture*** mebel; ***a ~ of advice*** rada; ***a ~ of information*** informacja; ***in ~s*** w kawałkach, rozbity; ***fall to ~s*** rozpaść się; ***in one ~*** **a)** w jednym kawałku, **b)** bezpiecznie; ***~ by ~*** kawałek po kawałku; ***go to ~s*** *fig* załamać się **2.** część *f*; ***take s.th. to ~s*** rozłożyć coś na części; ***a 28-~ dinner service*** 28-częściowy serwis obiadowy **3.** fragment *m* **4.** element *m* **5.** utwór *m*; ***a ~ by Bach*** utwór Bacha **6.** dzieło *n* **7.** (*newspaper*) artykuł *m* **8.** moneta *f*; ***a five-cent ~*** pięciocentówka **9.** pionek *m*; **piece together** *v/t* **1.** składać ⟨po-⟩ **2.** układać ⟨ułożyć⟩ (w całość); ***~ together a jigsaw*** ułożyć puzzle; ***the police are trying to ~ the last hours of her life*** policja próbuje odtworzyć ostatnie godziny jej życia

piece•meal ['piːsmiːl] **I** *adj* **1.** niesystematyczny **2.** fragmentaryczny **II** *adv* **1.** niesystematycznie **2.** po trochu; **piece•work** ['piːswɜːrk] *s* praca *f* na akord

P

'pie chart *s* wykres *m* kołowy

pie-'eyed *adj dated infml* zalany

pier [pɪə] *s* **1.** molo *n* **2.** pomost *m* **3.** pirs *m* **4.** filar *m*

pierce [pɪəs] *v/t* **1.** przebijać ⟨-bić⟩; ***the arrow ~d his shoulder*** strzała przebiła mu ramię **2.** dziurawić ⟨prze-⟩ **3.** *hole*: robić ⟨z-⟩ **4.** *fig* rozdzierać ⟨-zedrzeć⟩; ***sirens ~d the silence*** wycie syren rozdarło ciszę **5.** *fig* przedzierać ⟨-drzeć⟩; ***sunlight ~d the mist*** przez mgłę przedzierało się słońce; **pierc•ing** ['pɪəsɪŋ] *adj* **1.** *eyes*, *look*: przeszywający **2.** *sound*, *cold*: przenikliwy **3.** ostry

pi•e•ty ['paɪətɪ] *s* pobożność *f*

pif•fle ['pɪfl] *s dated* bzdury *pl*; **'pif•fling** ['pɪflɪŋ] *adj dated* bzdurny

pig [pɪg] **I** *s* **1.** świnia *f*; ***buy a ~ in a poke*** kupować kota w worku; ***make a ~'s ear*** (***out***) ***of s.th.*** *Br infml* schrzanić coś **2.** *infml* (*policeman*) pies *m* **II** *v/t* ***~ oneself*** *Br infml* obżerać ⟨obeżreć⟩ się; **pig out** *v/t* nażreć się (***on*** *G*)

pi•geon ['pɪdʒɪn] *s* gołąb *m*; **'pi•geon-hole I** *s* **1.** przegródka *f* **2.** szufladka *f* **II** *v/t* **1.** szufladkować ⟨za-⟩ (***as*** *A*) **2.** odkładać ⟨odłożyć⟩ na później

pig•gish ['pɪgɪʃ] *adj* **1.** żarłoczny **2.** zachłanny

pig•gy•back ['pɪgɪbæk] **I** *s* (*a.* ***~ ride***) ***give s.o. a ~*** wziąć kogoś na barana **II** *v/i* ***~ on*** oprzeć się na *L*; **pig•gy•bank** ['pɪgɪbæŋk] *s* (*money box*) świnka *f*

pig•'head•ed *adj* uparty

'pig i•ron *s* (*iron industry*) surówka *f*

pig•let ['pɪglɪt] *s* prosiaczek *m*

pig•ment ['pɪgmənt] *s* pigment *m*

pig•my → ***pygmy***

'pig•pen *s* zagroda *f* dla świń; **'pig•skin** *s* świńska skóra *f*; **'pig•sty** *s a. fig* chlew *m*; **'pig•swill** *s* pomyje *pl*; **'pig•tail** *s Br* **1.** warkoczyk *m* **2.** warkocz *m*

pike[1] [paɪk] *pl pike s* szczupak *m*

pike[2] [~] *s* **1.** pika *f* **2.** *Am* → ***turnpike***; **'pike•staff** *s*: (***as***) ***plain as a ~*** jasne jak słońce

pil•chard ['pɪltʃəd] *s* sardynka *f*

pile[1] [paɪl] *s* pal *m*

pile[2] [~] **I** *s* **1.** stos *m* **2.** sterta *f* **3.** góra *f* **4.** *fig* kupa *f*; ***I have ~s of work*** mam kupę roboty; ***make a ~ of money*** zarabiać grube pieniądze **5.** gmach *m*

II *v/t* **1.** (*a.* **~ up**) układać ⟨ułożyć⟩ w stos **2.** ładować ⟨za-⟩ (***s.th. on*** coś na *A*, ***s.th. with*** coś *I*) **3.** nakładać ⟨nałożyć⟩; ***he ~d as much food as he could on his plate*** nałożył sobie na talerz tyle jedzenia, ile się tylko zmieściło **III** *v/i* **~ *into*** wcisnąć się do *G*, wepchnąć się do *G*; **pile on I** *v/t* **1.** zwiększać ⟨-szyć⟩ **2.** **~ *the pounds*** tyć **3.** ***pile it on*** przesadzać **II** *v/i* (*weight*) podskakiwać ⟨-skoczyć⟩ **pile up** *v/i* **1.** piętrzyć ⟨s-⟩ się **2.** gromadzić ⟨na-⟩ się

'pile driv•er *s* **1.** *Br infml* kopniak *m* **2.** *Br infml* fanga *f* **3.** kafar *m*

piles [paɪlz] *s MED* hemoroidy *pl*

pile-up ['paɪlʌp] *s* karambol *m*

pil•fer ['pɪlfə] *v/t infml* podwędzić; **pil•fer•er** ['pɪlfərə] *s infml* złodziejaszek *m*; **pil•fer•ing** ['pɪlfərɪŋ] *s infml* drobna kradzież *f*

pil•grim ['pɪlgrɪm] *s* pielgrzym *m*; **pil•grim•age** ['pɪlgrɪmɪdʒ] *s* pielgrzymka *f*; ***go on*** (*a.* ***make***) ***a ~*** udać się na pielgrzymkę

pill[1] [pɪl] *s* **1.** pigułka *f*; ***it was a bitter ~ for them to swallow*** musieli przełknąć gorzką pigułkę; ***sugar*** (*a.* ***sweeten***) ***the ~ by doing s.th.*** zrobić coś na pocieszenie **2.** tabletka *f* **3.** ***the ~*** pigułka antykoncepcyjna; ***be on the ~*** *infml* brać pigułki

pill[2] [~] *v/i* (*sweater*) mechacić ⟨z-⟩ się

pil•lage ['pɪlɪdʒ] **I** *v/t* **1.** plądrować ⟨s-⟩ **2.** łupić ⟨z-⟩ **II** *s* plądrowanie *n*

pil•lar ['pɪlə] *s* **1.** *a. fig* filar *m*; ***be driven from ~ to post*** być odsyłanym od Annasza do Kajfasza; ***the ~ of the Church*** filar Kościoła **2.** kolumna *f* **3.** słup *m*; ***a ~ of smoke*** słup dymu

pil•lion ['pɪljən] **I** *s* tylne siodełko *n* (motocykla) **II** *adv* na tylnym siodełku

pil•lo•ry ['pɪlərɪ] **I** *s* dyby *pl* **II** *v/t fig* stawiać ⟨postawić⟩ pod pręgierzem

pil•low ['pɪləʊ] *s* poduszka *f*; **'pil•low-case** *s* poszewka *f* na poduszkę; **'pil-low fight** *s* bitwa *f* na poduszki; **'pil-low•slip** → ***pillowcase***; **'pil•low talk** *s* rozmowa *f* kochanków

pi•lot ['paɪlət] **I** *s* pilot *m*; ***an automatic ~*** autopilot; ***a ~'s licence*** licencja pilota **II** *v/t* **1.** pilotować **2.** prowadzić ⟨po-⟩ **III** *adj* pilotażowy; **'pi•lot light** *s* płomyk *m*; **'pi•lot scheme** *s* projekt *m* pilotażowy; **'pi•lot stud•y** *s* badanie *n* pilotażowe

pi•men•to [pɪ'mentəʊ] *pl* *-tos* *s COOK* ziele *n* angielskie

pimp [pɪmp] **I** *s* sutener *m*, *infml* alfons *m* **II** *v/i* **1.** uprawiać sutenerstwo **2.** **~ *for s.o.*** być czyimś alfonsem

pim•ple ['pɪmpl] *s* pryszcz *m*; **pim•ply** ['pɪmplɪ] *adj* pryszczaty

PIN [pɪn] *abbr* (=***personal identification number***) PIN *m*

pin [pɪn] **I** *s* **1.** szpilka *f* **2.** *Am* broszka *f* **3.** *MED* gwóźdź *m* **4.** bolec *m* **5.** wtyk *m* **6.** zawleczka *f* **7.** kręgiel *m* **8.** odznaka *f* **9.** **~*s*** *infml* giry **II** *v/t* **1.** (*a.* **~ up**) przypinać ⟨-piąć⟩ (***to*** do *G*) **2.** spinać ⟨-piąć⟩ (***s.th. together*** coś ze sobą) **3.** upinać ⟨upiąć⟩ **4.** przytrzymywać ⟨-mać⟩ **5.** unieruchamiać ⟨-chomić⟩ **6.** *blame*: zrzucać ⟨-cić⟩ (***on*** na *A*) **7.** **~ *one's hopes on s.th.*** pokładać w czymś nadzieję

pin down *v/t* **1.** ustalać ⟨-lić⟩ **2.** przytrzymywać ⟨-mać⟩ **3.** zastać, złapać; ***I can't pin him down at the office*** nie mogę go zastać w biurze **4.** zmuszać ⟨zmusić⟩; **~ *s.o. to fixing a date for a meeting*** zmusić kogoś do ustalenia terminu spotkania

pin•a•fore ['pɪnəfɔː] *s* **1.** fartuch *m* **2.** (*a.* **~ *dress***) sukienka *f* na szelkach, *infml* bezrękawnik *m*

'pin•ball *s* (*game*) pinball *m*; **pin•ball ma•'chine** *s infml* fliper *m*

pin•cer move•ment ['pɪnsəmuːvmənt] *s* kleszcze *pl*

pin•cers ['pɪnsəz] *pl* **1.** obcęgi *pl* **2.** obcążki *pl* **3.** *BIOL* szczypce *pl*

pinch [pɪntʃ] **I** *v/i* **1.** szczypać ⟨uszczypnąć⟩; **~ *s.o. on the arm*** uszczypnąć kogoś w ramię; ***she had to ~ herself to make sure she was not dreaming*** musiała się uszczypnąć, żeby upewnić się, że nie śni **2.** *nose*: zatykać ⟨-tkać⟩ **3.** *Br infml* buchnąć, podwędzić **II** *v/i* (*shoes*) obcierać ⟨obetrzeć⟩ **III** *s* **1.** szczypta *f*; ***a ~ of salt*** szczypta soli; ***take s.th. with a ~ of salt*** *fig* potraktować coś z rezerwą; ***at a ~*** *Br*, ***in a ~*** *Am* w razie potrzeby **2.** uszczypnięcie *n*; ***give s.o. a ~*** uszczypnąć kogoś

'pin•cush•ion *s* poduszeczka *f* do szpilek

P

pine[1] [paɪn] *s* **1.** (*a.* **~tree**) sosna *f* **2.** (*a.* **~ wood**) sosna *f*, drewno *n* sosnowe
pine[2] [~] *v/i* **1.** być pogrążonym w smutku **2.** tęsknić (**for** za *I*); **~ away** *v/i* **1.** usychać z tęsknoty **2.** rozpaczać
pine•ap•ple ['paɪnæpl] *s* ananas *m*
'pine mar•ten *s* kuna *f* leśna
'pine nee•dle *s* igła *f* sosnowa
ping [pɪŋ] **I** *s* brzęk *m* **II** *v/i* brzęknąć
ping-pong ['pɪŋpɒŋ] *s infml* ping--pong *m*
pin•ion ['pɪnjən] *v/t* **1.** przyciskać ⟨-snąć⟩ **2.** wiązać ⟨przy-⟩
pink [pɪŋk] **I** *adj* **1.** różowy; ***she went ~ with embarrassment*** zarumieniła się ze wstydu **2.** lewicujący **II** *s* **1.** róż *m*, kolor *m* różowy; ***she was dressed in ~*** była ubrana na różowo; ***be in the ~*** *dated* cieszyć się dobrym zdrowiem **2.** goździk *m*
pin•kie ['pɪŋkɪ] *s Am* mały palec *m*; **'pin•kie ring** *s Am* pierścionek *m* na mały palec
'pin mon•ey *s* pieniądze *pl* na drobne wydatki
pin•na•cle ['pɪnəkl] *s* **1.** *fig* szczyt *m*; ***the ~ of his career*** szczyt jego kariery **2.** szczyt *m*, wierzchołek *m* **3.** *ARCHIT* pinakiel *m*
'pin•point I *v/t* **1.** wskazywać ⟨-zać⟩; ***~ the exact position on the map*** wskazać na mapie dokładną pozycję **2.** określać ⟨-lić⟩ **II** *adj* ***with ~ accuracy*** z wielką dokładnością **III** *s* punkt *m*; ***a ~ of light*** punkt światła
'pin•prick *s* **1.** punkcik *m* **2.** dziurka *f* (po szpilce)
pins and 'nee•dles *s* mrowienie *n*; ***have ~*** czuć mrowienie; ***be on ~*** *Am* siedzieć jak na szpilkach
'pin•stripe *s* (wąski) prążek *m*; **'pin-striped** *adj* w (wąskie) prążki
pint [paɪnt] *s* **1.** (*Br = 0,57 litre, Am = 0,47 litre*) pinta *f* **2.** *Br* piwo *n*; ***go for a ~*** pójść na piwo
'pin-up *s* plakat *m*; ***a ~ girl*** pinup girl
pi•o•neer [paɪə'nɪə] **I** *s* pionier *m*; ***a ~ in the field of microsurgery*** pionier mikrochirurgii **II** *v/t* **1.** być jednym z pionierów *G* **2.** zapoczątkowywać ⟨-kować⟩ **3.** po raz pierwszy zastosowywać ⟨-sować⟩; ***a new method ~ed by our scientists*** nowa metoda po raz pierwszy zastosowana przez naszych naukowców **III** *adj* pionierski; ***~ aviators*** pionierzy awiacji; **pi•o•neer•ing** [paɪə'nɪəɪŋ] *adj* pionierski
pi•ous ['paɪəs] *adj* pobożny; ***~ hopes*** pobożne życzenia
pip[1] [pɪp] *s* **1.** *Br* pestka *f*; ***apple ~s*** pestki jabłek **2.** (*dice, cards*) oczko *n*
pip[2] [~] *v/t Br infml* minimalnie pokonywać ⟨-nać⟩; ***~ s.o. at the post*** *fig* wyprzedzić kogoś na ostatniej prostej
pipe [paɪp] **I** *s* **1.** rura *f*; ***hot and cold water ~s*** rury z ciepłą i zimną wodą **2.** fajka *f*; ***smoke a ~*** palić fajkę **3.** fujarka *f*, piszczałka *f* **4. *~s*** dudy **II** *v/t* **1.** doprowadzać ⟨-dzić⟩ rurami **2.** przesyłać ⟨-słać⟩ rurociągiem **3.** nadawać (przez głośniki); ***be ~d*** (*music*) płynąć z głośników **4.** *cake*: dekorować ⟨u-⟩ (napisem) **5.** obszywać ⟨-szyć⟩ **III** *v/i* **1.** grać ⟨za-⟩ na fujarce **2.** grać ⟨za-⟩ na kobzie; **pipe down** *v/i*: ***~!*** *infml* cicho!; **pipe up** *v/i infml* **1.** odzywać ⟨odezwać⟩ się **2.** rozlegać ⟨-lec⟩ się; **'pipe clean•er** *s* wycior *m* (do fajki); **piped 'mu-sic** *s* (*shops, restaurants*) muzyka *f* z głośników; **'pipe dream** *s* mrzonki *pl*, *infml* marzenie *n* ściętej głowy; **'pipe•line** *s* rurociąg *m*; ***in the ~*** *fig* **a)** w przygotowaniu **b)** w toku
pip•er ['paɪpə] *s* **1.** dudziarz *m* **2.** grający *m* na fujarce
'pipe smok•er *s* palacz *m* fajki; ***he's a ~*** pali fajkę
pip•ing [paɪpɪŋ] **I** *s* **1.** rury *pl* **2.** orurowanie *n* **3.** rura *f* **4.** lamówka *f* **5.** (*cake*) dekoracja *f* **II** *adj voice*: piskliwy; **pip•ing 'hot** *adj* (bardzo) gorący
pi•quant ['piːkənt] *adj* pikantny
pique [piːk] **I** *s* ***in a fit of ~*** w przypływie złości **II** *v/t pride*: ranić ⟨z-⟩
pi•ra•cy ['paɪrəsɪ] *s* piractwo *n*; ***computer ~*** piractwo komputerowe; **pi•rate** ['paɪrət] **I** *s* pirat *m* **II** *v/t* wykonywać ⟨-konać⟩ piracką kopię; ***a ~d copy, a ~ copy*** piracka kopia; **pi•rate 'ra-di•o sta•tion** *s* nielegalna rozgłośnia *f* radiowa; **'pi•rate ship** *s* statek *m* piracki
pir•ou•ette [pɪrʊ'et] *s* piruet *m*
Pis•ces ['paɪsiːz] *s ASTR* Ryby *pl*

P

piss [pɪs] *infml* **I** *v/i* sikać, *infml* lać; **~ oneself laughing** posikać się ze śmiechu; **it's ~ing down** strasznie leje **II** *s* **1.** siki *pl*; **take the ~ out of** nabijać się z *G* **2. go for a ~** iść się wysikać, iść się odlać; **piss off** *infml* **I** *v/i* odpieprzać ⟨-rzyć⟩ się **II** *v/t* wkurzać ⟨-rzyć⟩, *vulg* wkurwiać ⟨-wić⟩; **his attitude really pisses me off** jego podejście naprawdę mnie wkurza; **s.o. is pissed off with s.th.** coś kogoś wkurza; **pissed** [pɪst] *adj* **1.** *Br infml* schlany, urżnięty **2.** *Am infml* wkurzony, *vulg* wkurwiony

'piss-up *s infml* chlanie *n*

pis•tach•i•o [pɪ'stɑːʃɪəʊ] *pl -chios* **1.** pistacja *f* **2.** orzech *m* pistacjowy **3.** (*colour*) pistacjowy *m*

piste [piːst] *s* trasa *f* narciarska

pis•til ['pɪstl] *s* (*flower*) słupek *m*

pis•tol ['pɪstl] *s* pistolet *m*; **'pis•tol-whip** *v/t* bić ⟨o-⟩ kolbą pistoletu

pis•ton ['pɪstən] *s* TECH tłok *m*; **a ~ engine** silnik tłokowy; **'pis•ton ring** *s* TECH pierścień *m* tłokowy

pit [pɪt] **I** *s* **1.** dół *m*; **dig a deep ~** wykopać głęboki dół **2.** jama *f* **3.** kopalnia *f*; **a gravel ~** kopalnia żwiru **4.** szyb *m*; **a ~ closure** zamknięcie szybu **5.** blizna *f* po ospie, *infml* dziób *m* **6.** THEAT kanał *m* (dla orkiestry) **7.** *Am* pestka *f* **8.** (*car racing*) **the ~s** *Br* boks *m*; **a ~ stop** przerwa serwisowa **II** *v/t* **1. the surface of the moon is ~ted with craters** powierzchnia Księżyca jest usiana kraterami; **~ted with smallpox** poznaczony bliznami po ospie **2. ~ one's strength against** zmierzyć się z *I*

pit•bull 'ter•ri•er *s* pitbulterier *m*

pitch [pɪtʃ] **I** *s* **1.** *Br* boisko *n* **2.** MUS wysokość *f* tonu **3.** poziom *m* **4.** szczyt *m* **5.** treść *f*, przekaz *m* **6. a sales ~** prezentacja towaru **7.** smoła *f* **8.** *roof*: nachylenie *n*, spadek *m* **9.** *ship*: kołysanie *n* **10. have perfect ~** mieć słuch doskonały **II** *v/t* **1.** rzucać ⟨-cić⟩ **2.** *prices*: ustalać ⟨-lić⟩ **3.** *offer*: kierować ⟨s-⟩ **4.** *product*: sprzedawać ⟨-dać⟩ **5.** *tent*: rozbijać ⟨-bić⟩ **III** *v/i* (*ship*) kołysać się; **pitch in I** *v/i* **1.** pomagać ⟨-móc⟩; **~ with the work** pomóc w pracy **2.** wspomagać ⟨-móc⟩ (**with** *I*) **3.** dokładać ⟨dołożyć⟩ się **II** *v/t* **1.** dokładać ⟨dołożyć⟩ **2. we pitched in $20 to buy them a gift** zrzuciliśmy się po 20 dolarów, żeby kupić im prezent

'pitch-black, **'pitch-dark** *adj* czarny jak smoła; **pitched 'bat•tle** *s* bitwa *f* pozycyjna

pitch•er[1] ['pɪtʃə] *s Am* dzban *m*

pitch•er[2] [~] *s* (*baseball*) miotacz *m*

pitch•fork ['pɪtʃfɔːk] *s* widły *pl*

pit•e•ous ['pɪtɪəs] *adj lit* żałosny, budzący litość

pit•fall ['pɪtfɔːl] *s fig* pułapka *f*

pith [pɪθ] *s* **1.** *orange*: biała skórka *f* **2.** *fig* sedno *n*; **pith•y** ['pɪθɪ] *adj* **1.** zwięzły **2.** trafny

pit•i•a•ble ['pɪtɪəbl], **pit•i•ful** ['pɪtɪfəl] *adj* **1.** żałosny **2.** budzący litość; **pit•i•ful•ly** ['pɪtɪfəlɪ] *adv* żałośnie; **pit•i•less** ['pɪtɪləs] *adj* **1.** bezlitosny **2.** okrutny; **pit•i•less•ly** ['pɪtɪləslɪ] *adv* **1.** bezlitośnie **2.** okrutnie

pit•ta bread ['pɪtəbred] *s* chleb *m* pita

pit•tance ['pɪtns] *s* marne pieniądze *pl*, nędzne grosze *pl*

pi•tu•i•tar•y (gland) [pɪ'tjuːɪtərɪ (glænd)] *s* ANAT przysadka *f* mózgowa

pit•y ['pɪtɪ] **I** *s* **1. it's a ~ that** szkoda, że; **what a ~** jaka szkoda **2.** litość *f*; **out of ~** z litości **3.** współczucie *n* **4.** żal *m*; **I feel ~ for him** jest mi go żal; **I took ~ on her** zrobiło mi się jej żal **II** *v/t* **1.** współczuć **2. I ~ her** żal mi jej; **pit•y•ing** ['pɪtɪɪŋ] *adj* **1.** litościwy **2.** pełen litości

piv•ot ['pɪvət] **I** *s* **1.** *a. fig* oś *f* **2.** sworzeń *m* **3.** sedno *n* **4.** główna część *f* **5.** centralna postać *f* **II** *v/i* **1.** obracać ⟨-rócić⟩ się (**on/around** na *L*) **2.** odwracać ⟨-rócić⟩ się; **piv•ot around**, **piv•ot on** *v/i* **1.** zasadzać się na *L* **2.** zależeć od *G*; **piv•ot•al** ['pɪvətl] *adj role*: kluczowy

pix•el ['pɪksl] *s* piksel *m*

pix•ie ['pɪksɪ], **pix•y** *s* **1.** chochlik *m* **2.** wróżka *f* **3.** skrzat *m*

piz•za ['piːtsə] *s* pizza *f*; **piz•ze•ri•a** [piːtsə'riːə] *s* pizzeria *f*

plac•ard ['plækɑːd] *s* **1.** transparent *m* **2.** plakat *m*

pla•cate [plə'keɪt] *v/t* **1.** łagodzić ⟨u-⟩ **2.** ugłaskiwać ⟨-kać⟩

place [pleɪs] **I** *s* **1.** miejsce *n*; **~ of birth** miejsce urodzenia; **a meeting ~**

a) miejsce spotkania **b)** miejsce spotkań; ***I can't be in two ~s at once*** nie mogę być w dwóch miejscach jednocześnie; ***we're looking for a ~ to eat*** szukamy miejsca, gdzie można coś zjeść; ***there are a few ~s left on the course*** na kursie jest jeszcze kilka wolnych miejsc; ***in some ~*** gdzieś; ***in ~*** na (swoim) miejscu; ***out of ~*** nie na miejscu, na niewłaściwym miejscu; ***from ~ to ~*** z miejsca na miejsce; ***if I were in your ~*** (gdybym był) na twoim miejscu; ***in ~ of*** zamiast *G*; ***put oneself in s.o.'s ~*** postawić się na czyimś miejscu; ***take s.o.'s ~*** zająć czyjeś miejsce; ***in the first ~*** po pierwsze, przede wszystkim **2.** mieszkanie *n*; ***at my ~*** u mnie; ***I'm looking for a ~ of my own*** szukam własnego mieszkania **3.** dom *m* **4.** miejscowość *f* **II** *v/t* **1.** kłaść ⟨położyć⟩; ***great emphasis is ~d on education*** duży nacisk kładzie się na edukację **2.** umieszczać ⟨umieścić⟩ **3.** *advert*: zamieszczać ⟨-mieścić⟩ **4.** ***I've seen him before but I can't ~ him*** gdzieś już go widziałem, ale nie mogę sobie przypomnieć gdzie **5.** znajdować ⟨znaleźć⟩ pracę dla *G* **6.** ***be ~d fifth*** zająć piąte miejsce, uplasować się na piątej pozycji

pla•ce•bo [plə'siːbəʊ] *pl -bos* [~bəʊz] *s* MED placebo *n*; ***the ~ effect*** efekt placebo

'place card *s* karteczka *f* z nazwiskiem; **'place mat** *s* podkładka *f* pod talerz; **place•ment** ['pleɪsmənt] *s* **1.** ***job ~*** pośrednictwo pracy **2.** *Br* praktyka *f* (studencka) **3.** umieszczenie *n* **4.** rozmieszczenie *n*; **'place name** *s* nazwa *f* miejscowości

pla•cen•ta [plə'sentə] *s* ANAT łożysko *n*

'place set•ting *s* nakrycie *n* (stołowe)

plac•id ['plæsɪd] *adj* spokojny

pla•gia•rism ['pleɪdʒərɪzm] *s* plagiat *m*; **pla•gia•rist** ['pleɪdʒərɪst] *s* plagiator *m*; **pla•gia•rize** ['pleɪdʒəraɪz] *v/t* **1.** przepisywać ⟨-sać⟩ **2.** przywłaszczać ⟨-czyć⟩ sobie **3.** ***be ~d from*** być plagiatem *G*

plague [pleɪg] **I** *s* **1.** epidemia *f* **2.** plaga *f*; ***a ~ of rats*** plaga szczurów **3.** dżuma *f* **II** *v/t* nękać; ***financial problems are plaguing the company*** firma ma problemy finansowe

plaice [pleɪs] *pl plaice s* (*fish*) gładzica *f*

plaid [plæd] *s* **1.** tartan *m* **2.** pled *m* w szkocką kratę

plain [pleɪn] **I** *s* równina *f* **II** *adj* **1.** prosty **2.** zwykły **3.** *fabric*: bez wzorów, gładki **4.** *paper*: gładki **5.** niewyszukany **6.** *yoghurt*: naturalny **7.** *chocolate*: gorzki **8.** ***she's rather ~*** nie jest zbyt ładna **9.** jasny; ***make s.th. ~*** nie ukrywać czegoś; ***as ~ as the nose on your face*** oczywisty, jasny jak słońce **10.** szczery; ***be ~ with s.o.*** być z kimś szczerym **III** *adv* po prostu, wprost; ***it's ~ obvious*** to oczywiste

plain 'clothes *pl*: ***in ~*** (ubrany) po cywilnemu **plain-'clothes** *adj* (ubrany) po cywilnemu; **plain 'flour** *s* zwykła mąka *f*; **plain•ly** ['pleɪnlɪ] *adv* **1.** jasno **2.** wyraźnie **3.** wprost, bez ogródek; ***to put it ~*** mówiąc wprost **4.** najwyraźniej; ***she was ~ angry*** widać było, że jest zła **5.** bez wątpienia **6.** prosto **7.** skromnie; ***~ dressed*** skromnie ubrany; **plain•ness** ['pleɪnnɪs] *s* **1.** prostota *f* **2.** skromność *f* **3.** jasność *f* **4.** szczerość *f* **5.** pospolitość *f*; **plain 'spo•ken** *adj* szczery

plain•tiff ['pleɪntɪf] *s* JUR powód *m*

plain•tive ['pleɪntɪv] *adj* pełen smutku, smutny

plait [plæt] **I** *s* warkocz *m* **II** *v/t* **1.** zaplatać ⟨-leść⟩ **2.** splatać ⟨-leść⟩

plan [plæn] **I** *s* **1.** plan *m*; ***according to ~*** zgodnie z planem; ***make ~s for the future*** snuć plany na przyszłość **2.** zamiar *m* **3.** ARCHIT projekt *m* **II** *v/t* **1.** planować ⟨za-⟩; ***~ a meeting*** zaplanować spotkanie; ***a ~ned economy*** gospodarka planowa **2.** zamierzać; ***we're ~ning to go to France*** zamierzamy pojechać do Francji **3.** projektować ⟨za-⟩ **III** *v/i* **1.** planować ⟨za-⟩ (**for** *A*) **2.** zamierzać (**on** *A*)

plane[1] [pleɪn] *s* samolot *m*; ***travel by ~*** podróżować samolotem

plane[2] [~] **I** *s* **1.** płaszczyzna *f* **2.** TECH strug *m*, hebel *m* **3.** poziom *m* **II** *adj* **1.** płaski **2.** równy **III** *v/t* TECH strugać ⟨o-⟩, heblować ⟨o-⟩

plan•et ['plænɪt] *s* planeta *f*; **plan•e•tar•i•um** [plænɪ'teərɪəm] *pl -riums s* pla-

P

netarium *n*; **plan•e•tar•y** ['plænətrı] *adj* planetarny

plank [plæŋk] *s* **1.** deska *f* **2.** klepka *f* **3.** *fig* (główny) punkt *m*; **plank•ing** ['plæŋkıŋ] *s* **1.** deski *pl* **2.** klepki *pl*

plank•ton ['plæŋktən] *s* plankton *m*

plan•ner ['plænə] *s* **1.** planista *m* **2.** urbanista *m* **3.** (*calendar*) planer *m*; **plan•ning** ['plænıŋ] *s* planowanie *n*; ***family ~*** planowanie rodziny; **'plan•ning per•mis•sion** *s* zezwolenie *n* na budowę

plant [plɑːnt] **I** *s* **1.** roślina *f*; ***garden ~s*** rośliny ogrodowe **2.** fabryka *f*; ***car ~*** fabryka samochodów **3.** zakład *m* produkcyjny **4.** maszyny *pl*; ***~ and equipment*** maszyny i urządzenia **5.** instalacje *pl* **6.** informator *m*, *infml* wtyczka *f* **II** *v/t* **1.** sadzić ⟨za-⟩; ***he ~ed the seeds of doubts in my mind*** *fig* zasiał we mnie wątpliwości **2.** *field*, *garden*: obsadzać ⟨-dzić⟩ **3.** *bomb*: podkładać ⟨-dłożyć⟩ **4.** podrzucać ⟨-cić⟩ (***s.th. on s.o.*** komuś coś) **5.** umieszczać ⟨umieścić⟩ **6.** stawiać ⟨postawić⟩ **7.** *informer*: podstawiać ⟨-wić⟩ **8.** ***~ a kiss on s.o.'s lips*** pocałować kogoś w usta; **plan•ta•tion** [plæn'teıʃn] *s* plantacja *f*; ***a banana ~*** plantacja bananów; **plant•er** ['plɑːntə] *s* **1.** plantator *m* **2.** donica *f* **3.** siewnik *m* **4.** sadzarka *f*

plaque [plɑːk] *s* **1.** tablica *f* (pamiątkowa) **2.** *MED* płytka *f* nazębna

plas•ma ['plæzmə] *s* **1.** *ANAT* osocze *n* **2.** *PHYS* plazma *f*

plas•ter ['plɑːstə] **I** *s* **1.** tynk *m* **2.** gips *m*; ***have one's leg in ~*** mieć nogę w gipsie **3.** plaster *m* **II** *v/t* **1.** *wall*: tynkować ⟨o-⟩ **2.** smarować ⟨wy-⟩; ***we were ~ed from head to foot with mud*** byliśmy wysmarowani błotem od stóp do głów **3.** oklejać ⟨-leić⟩; **plas•ter over** *v/t* **1.** tynkować ⟨za-⟩ **2.** gipsować ⟨za-⟩

plas•ter 'cast *s* **1.** gips *m* **2.** odlew *m* gipsowy; **plas•tered** ['plɑːstəd] *infml* zalany; ***get ~*** zalać się

plas•tic ['plæstık] **I** *s* **1.** plastik *m* **2.** tworzywo *n* sztuczne **II** *adj* **1.** plastikowy **2.** z tworzywa sztucznego **3.** plastyczny **4.** *fig* sztuczny; **plas•tic 'bag** *s* **1.** plastikowa torba *f* **2.** plastikowa torebka *f*; **plas•tic 'bul•let** *s* plastikowa kula *f*; **plas•tic ex•'plo•sive** *s* (*explosive*) plastik *m*; **plas•tic 'film** *s* folia *f* (plastikowa); **plas•tic 'mon•ey** *s* *infml* plastikowe pieniądze *pl*; **'plas•tics in•dus•try** *s* przemysł *m* tworzyw sztucznych; **plas•tic 'sur•geon** *s* chirurg *m* plastyczny; **plas•tic 'sur•ge•ry** *s* chirurgia *f* plastyczna

plate [pleıt] **I** *s* **1.** talerz *m*; ***have a lot on one's ~*** *fig* mieć dużo spraw na głowie **2.** danie *n*; ***try the seafood ~*** spróbuj owoców morza **3.** płytka *f* **4.** płyta *f*; ***tectonic ~s*** płyty tektoniczne **5.** tabliczka *f* **6.** tablica *f* rejestracyjna *f* **7.** (*book*) tablica *f*, ilustracja *f* **8.** ***the cutlery is ~, not silver*** sztućce są platerowane, nie srebrne **9.** srebra *pl* **II** *v/t* **1.** pokrywać ⟨-ryć⟩ (***with*** *I*) **2.** platerować

pla•teau ['plætəʊ] *pl -teaux*, *-teaus* *s* *GEOGR* płaskowyż *m*

'plate rack *s* suszarka *f* do naczyń

plat•form ['plætfɔːm] *s* **1.** peron *m*; ***what ~ does the train leave from?*** z którego peronu odjeżdża pociąg? **2.** platforma *f*; ***an oil ~*** platforma wiertnicza; ***a viewing ~*** taras widokowy **3.** scena *f* **4.** podium *n* **5.** trybuna *f* **6.** pomost *m* **7.** koturn *m*; ***~ shoes*** buty na koturnach, *infml* koturny **8.** *POLIT* program *m* platforma *f*

plat•i•num ['plætınəm] *s* platyna *f*; **plat•i•num 'blonde** *s* platynowa blondynka *f*

plat•i•tude ['plætıtjuːd] *s* banał *m*

pla•ton•ic [plə'tɒnık] *adj* *love*: platoniczny

pla•toon [plə'tuːn] *s* pluton *m*

plat•ter ['plætə] *s* półmisek *m*

plau•si•bil•i•ty [plɔːzə'bılətı] *s* **1.** wiarygodność *f* **2.** prawdopodobieństwo *n*; **plau•si•ble** ['plɔːzəbl] *adj* **1.** wiarygodny **2.** przekonujący

play [pleı] **I** *v/i* **1.** bawić ⟨po-⟩ się; ***~ with s.o.*** bawić się z kimś; ***~ with a doll*** bawić się lalką; ***I have no one to ~ with*** nie mam się z kim bawić **2.** grać ⟨za-⟩; ***~ for money*** grać na pieniądze; ***~ for time*** grać na czas; ***~ safe*** nie narażać się, nie ryzykować **II** *v/t* **1.** bawić ⟨po-⟩ się w *A*; ***let's ~ pirates*** pobawmy się w piratów **2.** grać ⟨za-⟩ w *A*; **~ *tennis*** grać w tenisa **3.** grać ⟨za-⟩ na *L*; **~ *the violin*** grać na skrzypcach **4.** *role*: grać ⟨za-⟩, odgrywać ⟨odegrać⟩ **5. ~ *a trick on s.o.*** zrobić komuś kawał **6.** *situation*: rozgrywać ⟨-zegrać⟩ **III** *s* **1.** zabawa *f*; ***children at ~*** bawiące się dzieci **2.** gra *f*; ***a ~ on words*** gra słów; ***come into ~*** wchodzić w grę; ***the ball is out of ~*** piłka jest poza boiskiem; ***the ball went out of ~*** piłka wyszła na out; ***make great ~ for s.th.*** robić z czegoś wielkie halo **3.** THEAT sztuka *f* **4.** TECH luz *m*; **play about**, ***play around*** *v/i* **1.** *fig* bawić się; ***don't ~ with my computer*** nie baw się moim komputerem **2.** *infml* romansować; **play at** *v/t* bawić się w *A*; **play back** *v/t* odtwarzać ⟨-worzyć⟩, *infml* puszczać ⟨puścić⟩; **play down** *v/t* bagatelizować ⟨z-⟩; **play off** *v/i* pudburzać ⟨-rzyć⟩; ***play s.o. off against*** podburzać kogoś przeciw *D*, napuszczać kogoś na *A*; **play up I** *v/t* **1.** wyolbrzymiać ⟨-mić⟩ **2.** dawać ⟨dać⟩ się we znaki **3.** dokuczać ⟨-czyć⟩ **II** *v/i* **1.** dawać ⟨dać⟩ się we znaki **2.** *fig* wariować ⟨z-⟩

play•a•ble ['pleɪəbl] *adj* **1.** *passage*: łatwy do zagrania **2. *be ~*** (*field*) nadawać się do gry

'play•act *v/i* udawać ⟨udać⟩; **'play-back** *s* playback *m*; **play•boy** ['pleɪbɔɪ] *s* playboy *m*

play•er ['pleɪə] *s* **1.** *a. fig* gracz *m*; ***a chess ~*** szachista; ***a trumpet ~*** trębacz **2.** odtwarzacz *m*; ***a CD ~*** odtwarzacz płyt CD; **play•ful** ['pleɪfəl] *adj* **1.** rozbrykany **2.** rozochocony **3.** żartobliwy

play•ground ['pleɪgraʊnd] *s* **1.** plac *m* zabaw **2.** boisko *n*; **'play•group** *s Br* przedszkole *n*; **'play•house** *s* **1.** teatr *m* **2.** (*toy*) domek *m*; **'play•ing card** *s* karta *f* do gry; **'play•ing field** *s* boisko *n*

play•mate ['pleɪmeɪt] *s* towarzysz *m* zabaw; **'play•off** *s* spotkanie *n* barażowe; **'play•pen** *s* kojec *m* dziecięcy; **'play•room** *s* pokój *m* zabaw; **'play-school** → ***playgroup***; **'play•thing** *s* *a. fig* zabawka *f*; **'play•time** *Br s* **1.** przerwa *f* (między lekcjami) **2.** czas *m* wolny; **play•wright** ['pleɪraɪt] *s* dramatopisarz *m*

pla•za ['plɑːzə] *s Am* **1.** plac *m* **2. *a shopping ~*** centrum handlowe

plc [piːel'siː] *abbr* (=***public limited company***) *Br* SA

plea [pliː] *s* **1.** apel *m* (**for** o *A*); ***make a ~ for*** zaapelować o *A* **2.** prośba *f* (**for** o *A*) **3.** błaganie *n* (**for** o *A*) **4. *enter a ~ of*** (***not***) ***guilty*** (nie) przyznać się do winy

plead [pliːd] **I** (*pleaded*/*Am pled*; *pleaded*/*Am pled*) *v/i* **1.** błagać (**for** o *A*); ***she ~ed with him not to go*** błagała go, aby nie odchodził **2. ~** (***not***) ***guilty*** (nie) przyznać się do winy **3.** apelować (**for** o *A*) **4.** twierdzić ⟨s-⟩ (**that** że) **II** (*pleaded*/*Am pled*; *pleaded*/*Am pled*) *v/t* **1.** tłumaczyć się **2.** opowiadać ⟨-wiedzieć⟩ się za *I*

pleas•ant ['pleznt] *adj* **1.** przyjemny **2.** miły; ***what a ~ surprise*** co za miła niespodzianka

please [pliːz] **I** *interj* proszę; ***two coffees, ~*** (po)proszę dwie kawy; ***~ sit down*** proszę usiąść; ***~ don't leave me alone*** proszę, nie zostawiaj mnie samej; – ***'Would you like a tea?'*** – ***'Yes, ~.'*** – „Napijesz się herbaty?" – „Tak, proszę." **II** *v/t* zadowalać ⟨-wolić⟩; ***you cannot ~ everyone*** nie można zadowolić wszystkich; ***~ the eye*** cieszyć oko; ***~ yourself*** twoja sprawa, rób, jak uważasz **III** *v/i* chcieć; ***do as you ~*** rób, jak chcesz; ***as long as you ~*** tak długo, jak zechcesz; ***if you ~*** *dated* **a)** bądź łaskaw **b)** wyobraź sobie

pleased [pliːzd] *adj* **1.** zadowolony (***with*** z *G*); ***I'm ~ to hear that*** miło mi słyszeć, że; ***I'm ~ to inform you*** miło mi Pana poinformować; ***aren't you ~ to see me?*** nie cieszysz się, że mnie widzisz?; ***~ to meet you*** miło mi panią poznać

pleas•ing ['pliːzɪŋ] *adj* **1.** przyjemny **2.** miły **3.** ładny; ***be ~ to the eye*** być ładnym, cieszyć oko

plea•sur•a•ble ['pleʒərəbl] *adj* przyjemny

plea•sure ['pleʒə] *s* przyjemność *f*; ***with ~*** z przyjemnością; ***give s.o. ~*** sprawiać komuś przyjemność; ***have the ~ of doing s.th.*** mieć przyjemność coś zrobić; ***he takes no ~ in it*** nie sprawia mu to przyjemności; ***the simple***

P

~s of the countryside proste przyjemności życia na wsi; ***– 'Thank you.' – 'It's a ~.'*** – „Dziękuję." – „Nie ma za co."; ***at s.o.'s ~*** według czyjegoś uznania; **'pleas•ure boat** *s* statek *m* wycieczkowy

pleat [pliːt] *s* **1.** plisa *f* **2.** fałda *f*; **'pleat-ed skirt** *s* plisowana spódnica *f*

plebs [plebz] *s*: ***the ~*** *infml* plebs

ple•be•ian [plə'biːən] **I** *adj* plebejski **II** *s* plebejusz *m*

pleb•i•scite ['plebɪsɪt] *s* POLIT plebiscyt *m*

plec•trum ['plektrəm] *pl -trums, -tra s* MUS piórko *n*, plektron *m*

pled [pled] *Past Simple and Past Participle* → ***plead***

pledge [pledʒ] **I** *s* **1.** obietnica *f*; ***give s.o. a ~*** złożyć komuś obietnicę **2.** zobowiązanie *n* **3.** zastaw *m* **II** *v/t* **1.** przyrzekać ⟨-rzec⟩ **2.** zobowiązywać ⟨-zać⟩ się; ***the government ~d their support for the plan*** rząd zobowiązał się poprzeć plan; ***~ oneself to do s.th.*** zobowiązać się do zrobienia czegoś **3.** dawać ⟨dać⟩ w zastaw

ple•na•ry ['pliːnərɪ] **I** *adj* **1.** plenarny; ***a ~ session*** sesja plenarna **2.** *authority*: nieograniczony **II** *s* sesja *f* plenarna

plen•i•po•ten•ti•ar•y [plenɪpə'tenʃərɪ] *s* pełnomocnik *m*

plen•ti•ful ['plentɪfəl] *adj*: ***a ~ supply of*** **a)** mnóstwo *G* **b)** dość *G*; ***vineyards are ~ in the area*** w okolicy jest wiele winnic; ***jobs were ~ in Glasgow*** w Glasgow łatwo było znaleźć pracę

plen•ty ['plentɪ] **I** *pron* ***~ of*** **a)** mnóstwo *G* **b)** dość *G*; ***~ of time*** mnóstwo czasu; ***we have ~ to talk about*** mamy wiele spraw do omówienia **II** *adv* **1.** o wiele; ***there is ~ more*** jest o wiele więcej **2.** *Am infml* dużo **III** *s* dostatek *m*, dobrobyt *m*; ***in times of ~*** w czasach dostatku, w okresie dobrobytu; ***have s.th. in ~*** mieć czegoś pod dostatkiem

ple•o•nasm ['plɪːənæzəm] *s* pleonazm *m*

pleth•o•ra ['pleθərə] *s* nadmiar *m*

pleu•ri•sy ['plʊərəsɪ] *s* MED zapalenie *n* opłucnej

pli•a•ble ['plaɪəbl], ***pli•ant*** ['plaɪənt] *adj* **1.** *twig*: giętki **2.** *person*: podatny na wpływy

pli•ers ['plaɪəz] *pl* szczypce *pl*

plight [plaɪt] *s* **1.** trudna sytuacja *f* **2.** ciężkie położenie *n*

plim•soll ['plɪmsəl] *s Br* tenisówka *f*

plod [plɒd] *v/i* wlec się; **plod on** *v/i fig* wlec się; **plod•der** ['plɒdə] *s*: ***be a ~*** pracować powoli, *infml* guzdrać się

plonk[1] [plɒŋk] *infml v/t* **1.** rzucać ⟨-cić⟩; ***he ~ed the shoes down on the floor*** rzucił buty na podłogę **2.** ***he ~ed himself down on the sofa*** *infml* klapnął na kanapę

plonk[2] [~] *s infml* bełt *m*, sikacz *m*

plop [plɒp] **I** *s* plusk *m* **II** *v/i* **1.** wpadać ⟨wpaść⟩ z pluskiem **2.** wskakiwać ⟨-koczyć⟩ z pluskiem **III** *v/t* **1.** wrzucać ⟨-cić⟩ **2.** ***~ down on a chair*** *infml* klapnąć na fotel

plot[1] [plɒt] **I** *s* **1.** akcja *f* **2.** fabuła *f*; ***lose the ~*** *Br infml* stracić wątek; ***the ~ thickens*** sytuacja się komplikuje **3.** spisek *m* **4.** intryga *f* **II** *v/t* **1.** przygotowywać ⟨-tować⟩; ***~ a coup*** przygotowywać przewrót **2.** knuć ⟨u-⟩ **3.** (*map*) nanosić ⟨-nieść⟩ (**on** na *A*) **4.** (*graph*) zaznaczać ⟨-czyć⟩ (**on** na *L*) **5.** wyznaczać ⟨-czyć⟩ **III** *v/i* spiskować (***with s.o. against*** z kimś przeciw *D*)

plot[2] [~] *s* działka *f*

plot•ter ['plɒtə] *s* **1.** INF ploter *m* **2.** spiskowiec *m*

plough [plaʊ] *Br*, ***plow*** *Am* **I** *s* pług *m* **II** *v/t* orać ⟨za-⟩; **plough back** *v/t profit*: inwestować ⟨za-⟩ ponownie (**into** w *A*); **plough into I** *v/i* rąbnąć w *A* **II** *v/t* wykładać ⟨wyłożyć⟩ (**into** na *A*); ***the government ~ed $10 million into building new schools*** rząd wyłożył 10 milionów dolarów na budowę nowych szkół; **plough through** *v/i* **1.** brnąć ⟨prze-⟩ przez *A* **2.** przedzierać ⟨-drzeć⟩ się przez *A*

ploy [plɔɪ] *s* sztuczka *f*

pluck [plʌk] **I** *v/t* **1.** *eyebrows*: skubać ⟨wy-⟩ **2.** wyrywać ⟨-rwać⟩ **3.** *fruit, flowers*: zrywać ⟨zerwać⟩ **4.** *chicken*: skubać ⟨o-⟩ **5.** *strings*: szarpać ⟨-pnąć⟩ **6.** wydobywać ⟨-być⟩ **7.** ***~ up the courage to do s.th.*** zdobyć się na odwagę, żeby coś zrobić, ze-

P

brać się na odwagę, żeby coś zrobić **II** *s dated* odwaga *f*; **pluck at** *v/i* szarpać ⟨-pnąć⟩; ***~ someone's sleeve*** szarpać kogoś za rękaw; **pluck•y** ['plʌkɪ] *adj infml* dzielny

plug [plʌg] **I** *s* **1.** wtyczka *f* **2.** *Br infml* gniazdko *n* **3.** korek *m* **4.** zatyczka *f* **5.** TECH kołek *m* rozporowy **6.** TECH świeca *f* (zapłonowa) **7.** reklama *f* **II** *v/t* **1.** zatykać ⟨-tkać⟩; ***~ the gap*** wypełnić lukę **2.** korkować ⟨za-⟩ **3.** reklamować ⟨za-⟩; **plug away** *v/i* **1.** ślęczeć (***at*** nad *I*) **2.** męczyć się (***at*** z *I*); **plug in** *v/t* podłączać ⟨-czyć⟩ do sieci; '**plug•hole** *s* odpływ *m*

plum [plʌm] **I** *s* **1.** śliwka *f*; ***a ~ tree*** śliwa *f* **2.** kolor *m* śliwkowy, śliwka *f* **II** *adj Br work*: świetny

plum•age ['plu:mɪdʒ] *s* upierzenie *n*

plumb [plʌm] **I** *v/t* zgłębiać ⟨-bić⟩ **II** *adv* ***~ in the middle of the room*** na samym środku pokoju; **plumb in** *v/t Br* podłączać ⟨-czyć⟩

plumb•er ['plʌmə] *s* hydraulik *m*; **plumb•ing** ['plʌmɪŋ] *s* **1.** instalacja *f* wodno-kanalizacyjna **2.** rury *pl* **3.** prace *pl* instalacyjne; '**plumb line** *s* (*device*) pion *m*

plume [plu:m] *s* **1.** pióro *n*; ***an ostrich ~*** strusie pióro **2.** pióropusz *m* **3.** *smoke*: pióropusz *m*, smuga *f*

plum•met ['plʌmɪt] *v/i* gwałtownie spadać ⟨-paść⟩; ***share prices ~ed to an all-time low*** ceny akcji gwałtownie spadły, osiągając najniższy w historii poziom

plum•my ['plʌmɪ] *adj* **1.** śliwkowy **2.** *Br accent*: afektowany

plump [plʌmp] **I** *adj* **1.** *person*: pulchny **2.** *face*: okrągły **3.** *fruit*: dorodny **II** *v/t* (*a.* **~ up**) *pillow*: poprawiać ⟨-wić⟩; **plump for** *v/i* decydować ⟨z-⟩ się na *A*

plum 'pud•ding *s Br* pudding *m* bożonarodzeniowy; '**plum to•ma•to** *pl -toes s* pomidor *m* podłużny

plun•der ['plʌndə] **I** *v/t* **1.** plądrować ⟨s-⟩ **2.** grabić ⟨o-, za-⟩ **3.** łupić ⟨z-⟩ **II** *s* **1.** plądrowanie *n* **2.** grabież *f* **3.** rabunek *m* **4.** łup *m*; **plun•der•er** ['plʌndərə] *s* grabieżca *f*

plunge [plʌndʒ] **I** *v/i* **1.** runąć; ***she lost her balance and ~d down*** straciła równowagę i runęła w dół **2.** gwałtownie spadać ⟨spaść⟩; ***share prices ~d*** ceny akcji gwałtownie spadły **3.** nurkować ⟨za-⟩ **4.** ***she ~d into the room*** wpadła do pokoju jak burza **5.** (*road*) opadać **II** *v/t* strącać ⟨-cić⟩ **III** *s* **1.** *prices*: gwałtowny spadek *m* **2.** nur *m*; ***take the ~*** *fig* podjąć decyzję, zaryzykować **3.** skok *m* do wody; **plung•er** ['plʌndʒə] *s* przepychacz *m* do rur; **plung•ing** ['plʌndʒɪŋ] *adj blouse*: z dekoltem; ***with a ~ neckline*** głęboko wycięty

plu•per•fect [plu:'pɜ:fɪkt] *s* czas *m* zaprzeszły

plu•ral ['plʊərəl] **I** *adj* w liczbie mnogiej; ***the ~ form*** forma liczby mnogiej **II** *s* ***the ~*** GRAM liczba mnoga; **plu•ral•ism** ['plʊərəlɪzəm] *s* pluralizm *m*; **plu•ral•is•tic** [plʊərə'lɪstɪk] *adj* pluralistyczny

plus [plʌs] **I** *prep* plus, dodać; ***7 ~ 5 is 12*** siedem plus pięć równa się dwanaście **II** *adj* **1.** dodatni **2.** ponad; ***$100 ~*** ponad 100 dolarów **3.** (*temperature*) plus, powyżej zera **III** *s* **1.** plus *m*; ***a ~ sign*** znak plus **2.** zaleta *f*

plush [plʌʃ] **I** *s* plusz *m* **II** *adj* **1.** pluszowy **2.** *infml* luksusowy

plu•to•ni•um [plu:'təʊnɪəm] *s* CHEM pluton *m*

ply [plaɪ] **I** *v/i* kursować; ***the bus plies every hour*** autobus kursuje co godzinę **II** *v/t* **1.** *tool*: posługiwać ⟨-łużyć⟩ się **2.** ***~ s.o. with questions*** zasypywać kogoś pytaniami **III** *s* nić *f*

ply•wood ['plaɪwʊd] *s* sklejka *f*

PM [pi:'em] *abbr* (=***Prime Minister***) *Br* premier *m*

p.m. [pi:'em] *adv* po południu; ***at 5 p.m.*** o piątej po południu, o siedemnastej

pneu•mat•ic [nju:'mætɪk] *adj* pneumatyczny; **pneu•mat•ic 'drill** *s* **1.** młot *m* pneumatyczny **2.** wiertarka *f* pneumatyczna

pneu•mo•ni•a [nju:'məʊnɪə] *s* MED zapalenie *n* płuc

poach[1] [pəʊtʃ] **I** *v/i* **1.** kłusować **2.** nielegalnie polować (***for*** na *A*) **II** *v/t* nielegalnie polować na *A*

poach[2] [~] *v/t* **1.** *fish*: gotować ⟨u-⟩ **2.** *eggs*: gotować ⟨u-⟩ w koszulkach

poach•er ['pəʊtʃə] *s* kłusownik *m*

poached 'eggs *pl* jajka *pl* w koszulkach

P

PO Box [piːəʊ'bɒks] *s* skrytka *f* pocztowa

pock•et ['pɒkɪt] **I** *s* **1.** kieszeń *f*; ***take your hands out of your ~s*** wyjmij ręce z kieszeni; ***to suit every ~*** na każdą kieszeń; ***pay out of one's own ~*** zapłacić z własnej kieszeni; ***have s.o. in one's ~*** mieć kogoś w kieszeni **2.** (*billiards*) łuza *f* **3.** *opposition*: ognisko *n* **4.** ***an air ~*** (*pipe*) korek powietrzny **II** *v/t* **1.** chować ⟨s-⟩ do kieszeni **2.** *money*: zatrzymywać ⟨-mać⟩ **3.** (*billiards*) wbijać ⟨wbić⟩ do łuzy; **'pock•et•book** *s* **1.** *Am* portfel *m*; ***too expensive for my ~*** *dated* nie na moją kieszeń **2.** *Br* notes *m*; **pock•et 'cal•cu•la•tor** *s* kieszonkowy kalkulator *m*; **pock•et e•'di•tion** *s* kieszonkowe wydanie *n*; **'pock•et•knife** *pl -knives s Am* scyzoryk *m*; **'pock•et money** *s* kieszonkowe *pl*

pock•mark ['pɒkmɑːk] *s* blizna *f* po ospie; **~s** *infml* dzioby; **pock•marked** ['pɒkmɑːkd] *adj* pokryty bliznami (po ospie), *infml* dziobaty

pod [pɒd] *s* **1.** strąk *m*; ***a vanilla ~*** **a)** strąk wanilii **b)** COOK laska wanilii **2.** strączek *m* **3.** gondola *f* (silnikowa) **4.** podwieszany zbiornik *m*

po•di•um ['pəʊdɪəm] *s* podium *n*

po•em ['pəʊɪm] *s* wiersz *m*

po•et ['pəʊɪt] *s* poeta *m*; **po•et•ess** [pəʊɪ'təs] *s dated* poetka *f*; **po•et•ic** [pəʊ'etɪk] *adj* poetyczny, poetycki; **po•et•ic 'jus•tice** *s*: ***it's ~*** *infml* sprawiedliwości stało się zadość; **po•et•ic 'li•cence** *s* licentia *f* poetica; **po•'et•i•cal** [pəʊ'etɪkl] → ***poetic***; **po•et•ry** ['pəʊɪtrɪ] *s* poezja *f*

poign•ant ['pɔɪnjənt] *adj* wzruszający, poruszający

poin•set•ti•a [pɔɪn'setɪə] *s* poinsecja *f*, gwiazda *f* betlejemska

point [pɔɪnt] **I** *s* **1.** punkt *m*; ***lose a ~*** stracić punkt; ***ten percentage ~s*** dziesięć punktów procentowych; ***from ~ A to ~ B*** z punktu A do punktu B; ***a ~ of contact*** punkt styku; ***up to a ~*** do pewnego stopnia **2.** miejsce *n*; ***a meeting ~*** miejsce spotkania **3.** opinia *f*; ***she made several interesting ~s*** poruszyła kilka interesujących kwestii; ***I take your ~*** zgadzam się z tobą **4.** stwierdzenie *n* **5.** punkt *m* widzenia **6.** sedno *n* (sprawy); ***the ~ is that*** chodzi o to, że; ***that's not the ~*** nie o to chodzi; ***get to the ~*** mów na temat; ***I'll come straight to the ~*** przejdę od razu do rzeczy; ***I miss the ~*** nie rozumiem **7.** moment *m*; ***at this ~*** w tym momencie; ***at some ~*** w pewnym momencie; ***be on the ~ of doing s.th.*** mieć właśnie coś zrobić **8.** powód *m*; ***there is no ~ in getting angry*** nie ma co się złościć; ***I don't see the ~ of doing it again*** nie widzę powodu, żeby robić to jeszcze raz **9.** cel *m* **10.** strona *f*; ***her strong ~s*** jej mocne strony; ***it has its good ~s*** ma to swoje dobre strony **11.** (*decimal*) przecinek *m*; ***four ~ three*** cztery przecinek trzy, cztery i trzy dziesiąte **12.** (*punctuation*) kropka *f* **13.** *knife*: czubek *m* **14.** GEOGR cypel *m* **15.** *Br* gniazdko *n* (elektryczne) **16.** (*railway*) **~s** zwrotnica *f* **17.** (*font*) punkt *m* **II** *v/t* **1.** celować ⟨wy-⟩ z *G* (**at** w *A*) **2.** ***~ one's finger at*** wskazać palcem *A* **III** *v/i* **1.** wskazywać ⟨-zać⟩ (**at**/**to** na *A*); ***the compass needle ~s north*** igła kompasu wskazuje północ; ***a series of arrows ~ed the way to*** strzałki wskazywały drogę do *G* **2.** pokazywać ⟨-zać⟩ palcem (**at**/**to** na *A*); **point out I** *v/t* **1.** wskazywać ⟨-zać⟩ **2.** zwracać ⟨-rócić⟩ uwagę na *A* **II** *v/t* zauważać ⟨-żyć⟩ (**that** że); **point to** *v/i* **1.** zwracać ⟨-rócić⟩ uwagę na *A* **2.** wskazywać ⟨-zać⟩ na *A*; ***all the signs point to a successful year ahead*** wszystko wskazuje na to, że będzie do dobry rok

point-'blank *adv* **1.** *refuse*: kategorycznie **2.** *ask*: wprost, *infml* prosto z mostu

point•ed ['pɔɪntɪd] *adj* **1.** szpiczasty, spiczasty **2.** z czubkami **3.** ostro zakończony **4.** ostry

point•er ['pɔɪntə] *s* **1.** *infml* wskazówka *f* **2.** oznaka *f*; ***a ~ to an improvement in the economy*** oznaka ożywienia gospodarki **3.** wskaźnik *m* **4.** strzałka *f*

point•less ['pɔɪntləs] *adj* bezcelowy

'point of sale *s* punkt *m* sprzedaży; **point-of-sale pro'motion** *s* promocja *f* w miejscu sprzedaży; **point of 'view** *s* punkt *m* widzenia; ***from my ~*** z mojego punktu widzenia

P

poise [pɔɪz] **I** *s* **1.** opanowanie *n* **2.** (pełna gracji) postawa *f* i sposób poruszania się **II** *v/t* **1.** *~ oneself to s.th.* przygotowywać się do *G* **2.** (pewnie) trzymać **III** *v/i* przyjmować ⟨-jąć⟩ pozycję; **poised** [pɔɪzd] *adj* **1.** nieruchomy **2.** opanowany **3.** *be ~ to do s.th.* być gotowym coś zrobić

poi•son ['pɔɪzn] **I** *s* trucizna *f* **II** *v/t* **1.** truć ⟨o-⟩ **2.** zatruwać ⟨-ruć⟩; **poi•son 'gas** *s* trujący gaz *m*; **poi•son•ing** ['pɔɪzənɪŋ] *s MED* zatrucie *n*; **poi•son 'i•vy** *s* trujący bluszcz *m*; **poi•son•ous** ['pɔɪznəs] *adj* **1.** trujący **2.** *snake*: jadowity; **poi•son 'pill** *s ECON* *środki podjęte w celu obrony przed wrogim przejęciem*

poke [pəʊk] **I** *v/t* **1.** dźgać ⟨-gnąć⟩ (*s.o. in* kogoś w *A*) **2.** szturchać ⟨-chnąć⟩; *~ s.o. in the ribs* dać komuś kuksańca w żebra **3.** wkładać ⟨włożyć⟩ (*s.th. into* coś do *G*) **4.** wtykać ⟨wetknąć⟩ (*s.th. into* coś do *G*) **5.** *~ one's head* wychylić głowę, wychylić się **6.** *~ s.o.'s eyes out* wydłubać komuś oczy **7.** *~ fun at* wyśmiewać się z *G* **8.** *hole*: robić ⟨z-⟩ **II** *v/i ~ out of* wystawać z *G* **III** *s* szturchnięcie *n*, kuksaniec *m*; *give s.o. a ~ in the ribs* szturchnąć kogoś w żebra, dać komuś kuksańca w żebra; **poke around** *v/i infml* **1.** szperać **2.** grzebać **3.** przeszukiwać ⟨-kać⟩ (*in A*)

pok•er[1] ['pəʊkə] *s* pogrzebacz *m*

pok•er[2] [~] *s* (*cards game*) poker *m*; **pok•er-faced** [pəʊkə'feɪst] *adj* z pokerową twarzą

P

pok•y ['pəʊkɪ] *adj infml* ciasny

Po•land ['pəʊlənd] *s* Polska *f*

po•lar ['pəʊlə] *adj* **1.** polarny **2.** *circle*: podbiegunowy **3.** *PHYS* biegunowy **4.** *opposite*: całkowity; **po•lar 'bear** *s* niedźwiedź *m* polarny; **po•lar•i•ty** [pə'lærɪtɪ] *s* **1.** *PHYS* biegunowość *f* **2.** *fig* opozycja *f*; **po•lar•ize** ['pəʊləraɪz] *v/t* **1.** *a. fig* polaryzować ⟨s-⟩ **2.** dzielić ⟨po-⟩ na dwa skrajne obozy; **po•lar•i•za•tion** [pəʊləraɪ'zeɪʃn] *s a. fig* polaryzacja *f*

Pole [pəʊl] *s* Polak *m*, Polka *f*

pole[1] [pəʊl] *s* biegun *m*; *the North ~* Biegun Północny; *be ~s apart fig* skrajnie się różnić

pole[2] [~] *s* **1.** słup *m* **2.** kij *m* **3.** kijek *m*; *a ski ~* kijek narciarski **4.** słupek *m* **5.** *tent*: maszt *m*

'pole•cat *s* (*animal*) **1.** tchórz *m* **2.** *Am* skunks *m*

po•lem•ic [pə'lemɪk] **I** *s* polemika *f* **II** *adj* polemiczny; **po'lem•i•cal** [pə'lemɪkl] → *polemic II*

'Pole Star *s*: *the ~* Gwiazda *f* Polarna; **'pole•vault** *s* skok *m* o tyczce; **'pole-vault•er** *s SPORT* tyczkarz *m*

po•lice [pə'liːs] **I** *s* **1.** policja *f*; *call the ~* wezwać policję **2.** policjanci *pl* **II** *v/t* **1.** *frontier*: patrolować **2.** nadzorować; **po'lice car** *s* samochód *m* policyjny; **po'lice dog** *s* pies *m* policyjny; **po'lice force** *s* policja *f*; **po'lice•man** *pl -men s* policjant *m*; **po'lice of•fi•cer** *s* policjant *m*, funkcjonariusz *m* policji; **po•lice pro'tec•tion** *s* ochrona *f* policyjna; **po'lice rec•ord** *s* kartoteka *f* policyjna; **po'lice state** *s* państwo *n* policyjne; **po'lice sta•tion** *s* komisariat *m* policji; **po'lice•wo•man** *pl -men s* policjantka *f*

pol•i•cy[1] ['pɒlɪsɪ] *s* **1.** polityka *f*; *foreign ~* polityka zagraniczna; *government's ~ on education* polityka rządu w zakresie edukacji **2.** strategia *f*; *adopt a ~* przyjąć strategię **3.** zasada *f*

pol•i•cy[2] [~] *s* polisa *f*; **'pol•i•cy hold•er** *s* ubezpieczony *m*, posiadacz *m* polisy

po•li•o ['pəʊlɪəʊ] *s MED* polio *n*; **po•li•o•my•e•li•tis** [pəʊlɪəʊmaɪə'laɪtɪs] *s MED* choroba *f* Heinego-Medina, polio *n*

Pol•ish ['pəʊlɪʃ] **I** *adj* **1.** polski **2.** *he's ~* jest Polakiem **II** *s* **1.** język *m* polski **2.** *the ~ pl* Polacy

pol•ish ['pɒlɪʃ] **I** *v/t* **1.** polerować ⟨wy-⟩ **2.** pastować ⟨wy-⟩ **3.** *infml* glansować ⟨wy-⟩ **4.** (*a. ~ up*) *fig* szlifować ⟨wy-⟩ **II** *s* **1.** pasta *f*, środek *m* do polerowania **2.** *give s.th. a ~* **a)** wypolerować coś **b)** wypastować coś **3.** ogłada *f* **4.** połysk *m*; **polish off** *v/t* **1.** *Am infml* sprzątnąć **2.** *infml* spałaszować

pol•ished ['pɒlɪʃt] *adj* **1.** wyczyszczony do połysku **2.** *infml* wyglansowany **3.** wypolerowany **4.** *manners*: wytworny **5.** *performance*: świetny, doskonały

po•lite [pə'laɪt] *adj* **1.** uprzejmy **2.** grzeczny **3.** kulturalny; **po•lite•ly**

[pəˈlaɪtlɪ] *adv* **1.** uprzejmie **2.** grzecznie; **po•lite•ness** [pəˈlaɪtnɪs] *s* **1.** uprzejmość *f* **2.** grzeczność *f*

po•lit•i•cal [pəˈlɪtɪkl] *adj* polityczny; ***for ~ reasons*** z powodów politycznych; **po•lit•i•cal a•ˈsy•lum** *s* azyl *m* polityczny; **po•lit•i•cal e•ˈcon•o•my** *s* ekonomia *f* polityczna

po•lit•i•cal•ly cor•ˈrect *adj* politycznie poprawny

po•lit•i•cal ˈpris•on•er *s* więzień *m* polityczny; **po•lit•i•cal ˈsci•ence** *s* politologia *f*, nauki *pl* polityczne; **po•lit•i•cal ˈsci•en•tist** *s* politolog *m*

pol•i•ti•cian [pɒlɪˈtɪʃn] *s* polityk *m*

po•li•ti•cize [pəˈlɪtɪsaɪz] *v/t* **1.** upolityczniać ⟨-nić⟩ **2.** ***become more ~d*** bardziej angażować się w politykę

po•lit•i•co [pəˈlɪtɪkəʊ] *pl -cos s infml* politykier *m*

pol•i•tics [ˈpɒlətɪks] *s* **1.** polityka *f*; ***local ~*** polityka lokalna; ***go into ~*** zająć się polityką; ***talk ~*** rozmawiać o polityce **2.** poglądy *pl* polityczne **3.** politologia *f*

pol•ka [ˈpɒlkə] *s* MUS polka *f*; **ˈpol•ka-dot** *adj* **1.** w groszki **2.** w kropki; **ˈpol•ka-dots** *pl* **1.** groszki *pl* **2.** kropki *pl*

poll [pəʊl] **I** *s* **1.** (*a.* **opinion ~**) badanie *n* opinii publicznej, sondaż *m* **2.** (*a.* **the ~s**) wybory *pl*; ***the day when Americans go to the ~s*** dzień, w którym Amerykanie udają się do urn wyborczych **3.** liczba *f* głosów, głosy *pl*; ***gain 45% of the ~*** uzyskać 45% głosów **II** *v/t* **1.** *votes*: uzyskiwać ⟨-kać⟩ **2.** przeprowadzać ⟨-dzić⟩ sondaż wśród *G*; ***over 50% of the ~ed*** ponad 50% respondentów

pol•len [ˈpɒlən] *s* pyłek *m* (kwiatowy); **ˈpol•len count** *s* stężenie *n* pyłków; **ˈpol•len fil•ter** *s* filtr *m* zatrzymujący pyłki

pol•li•nate [ˈpɒləneɪt] *v/t flowers*: zapylać ⟨-lić⟩

ˈpoll•ing booth *s Br* kabina *f* do głosowania; **ˈpoll•ing day** *s Br* dzień *m* wyborów; **ˈpoll•ing sta•tion** *s Br* lokal *m* wyborczy

poll•ster [ˈpəʊlstə] *s* **1.** ankieter *m* **2.** badacz *m* opinii publicznej

pol•lu•tant [pəˈluːtənt] *s* substancja *f* zanieczyszczająca środowisko

pol•lute [pəˈluːt] *v/t* zanieczyszczać ⟨-czyścić⟩ (***with*** *I*); **pol•lut•er** [pəˈluːtə] *s* truciciel *m* (środowiska)

pol•lu•tion [pəˈluːʃn] *s* **1.** zanieczyszczenie *n*; ***a ~ level*** poziom zanieczyszczenia **2.** zanieczyszczenia *pl*; ***~ control*** kontrola zanieczyszczeń **3.** ***noise ~*** hałas

po•lo [ˈpəʊləʊ] *s* SPORT polo *n*; **ˈpo•lo neck** *s Br* golf *m*; ***a ~ sweater*** sweter z golfem; **ˈpo•lo shirt** *s* koszulka *f* polo

pol•y•es•ter [pɒlɪˈestə] **I** *s* poliester *m* **II** *adj* poliestrowy

pol•y•eth•yl•ene [pɒlɪˈeθəliːn] *s* **I** *s* polietylen *m* **II** *adj* polietylenowy

po•lyg•a•mous [pəˈlɪgəməs] *adj* poligamiczny; **po•lyg•a•my** [pəˈlɪgəmɪ] *s* poligamia *f*

pol•y•glot [ˈpɒlɪglɒt] *s* poliglota *m*

pol•y•gon [ˈpɒlɪgən] *s* wielokąt *m*

pol•y•mer [ˈpɒlɪmə] *s* polimer *m*

Pol•y•ne•sia [pɒlɪˈniːʒə] *s* Polinezja *f*

pol•yp [ˈpɒlɪp] *s* polip *m*

pol•y•sty•rene [pɒlɪˈstaɪriːn] *s* **1.** styropian *m* **2.** polistyren *m*

pol•y•syl•lab•ic [pɒlɪsɪˈlæbɪk] *adj* wielosylabowy

pol•y•tech•nic [pɒlɪˈteknɪk] *s Br* wyższa szkoła *f* zawodowa

pol•y•thene [ˈpɒlɪθiːn] → ***polyethylene***

pol•y•un•sat•u•rat•ed [pɒlɪʌnˈsætʃəreɪtɪd] *adj* wielonienasycony kwas tłuszczowy

pol•y•u•re•thane [pɒlɪˈjʊərəθeɪn] **I** *s* poliuretan *m* **II** *adj* poliuretanowy

pol•y•va•lent [pɒlɪˈveɪlənt] *adj* wielowartościowy

po•made [pəˈmeɪd] *s* pomada *f*

po•me•gran•ate [ˈpɒmɪgrænɪt] *s* (*fruit*) granat *m*

pomp [pɒmp] *s* (*splendour*) pompa *f*; **pom•pous** [ˈpɒmpəs] *adj* napuszony

ponce [pɒns] *s Br infml* **1.** alfons *m* **2.** ciota *f*

pond [pɒnd] *s* **1.** staw *m* **2.** sadzawka *f* **3.** oczko *n* wodne

pon•der [ˈpɒndə] **I** *v/i* rozmyślać (**about**/**on**/**over** nad *I*) **II** *v/t* rozważać ⟨-żyć⟩; **pon•der•ous** [ˈpɒndərəs] *adj* **1.** powolny **2.** ociężały **3.** *tone*: poważny

pone [pəʊn] *s Am* placek *m* kukurydziany

P

pong [pɒŋ] *Br infml* **I** *v/i* śmierdzieć ⟨za-⟩ **II** *s* smród *m*
pon•tiff ['pɒntɪf] *s form* papież *m*
pon•toon [pɒn'tuːn] *s* ponton *m*; **pon'toon bridge** *s* most *m* pontonowy
pon•y ['pəʊnɪ] *s* kucyk *m*, kuc *m*; **'pon•y•tail** *s* (*hairstyle*) **1.** koński ogon *m* **2.** *infml* kucyk *m*; **'po•ny trek•king** *s* rajd *m* konny
poo•dle ['puːdl] *s* **1.** pudel *m* **2.** *fig* piesek *m*
poof [pʊf], ***poof•ter*** [pʊftə] *s Br vulg* ciota *f*
pooh [puː] *s* **1.** (*disgust*) fuj! **2.** (*indifference*) phi!; **pooh-'pooh** *v/t suggestion*: odrzucać ⟨-cić⟩
pool[1] [puːl] *s* **1.** basen *m* **2.** staw *m* **3.** *blood*: kałuża *f* **4.** *light*: krąg *m*
pool[2] [~] **I** *s* **1.** pula *f* **2.** zasoby *pl*, rezerwy *pl*; ***a ~ of cheap labour*** zasoby taniej siły roboczej **3.** ***a ~ of cars*** park samochodowy **4.** (*billiards*) bilard *m*, pool-bilard *m* **5.** ***the ~s*** totalizator *m* piłkarski **II** *v/t* **1.** łączyć ⟨po-⟩ **2.** zbierać ⟨zebrać⟩ **3.** mobilizować ⟨z-⟩ **4.** dzielić ⟨po-⟩ się; **'pool hall** *s* sala *f* do gry w bilard; **'pool table** *s* stół *m* bilardowy
poop [puːp] **I** *s* **1.** rufa *f* **2.** *Am infml* kupa *f*; ***dog ~*** psia kupa **II** *v/i Am infml* robić ⟨z-⟩ kupę **III** *v/t* (*a.* ***~ out***) wykańczać ⟨-kończyć⟩; **poop•ed** [puːpt] *adj Am infml* wykończony; **poop•er-scoop•er** ['puːpəskuːpə] *s infml* łopatka *f* do sprzątania psich odchodów
poor [pɔː] **I** *adj* **1.** biedny; ***~ thing*** biedactwo, biedak **2.** ubogi (***in*** w *A*) **3.** słaby; ***~ health*** słabe zdrowie; ***she's ~ at biology*** jest słaba z biologii; ***the visibility was ~*** widoczność była słaba **4.** marny **5.** *quality*: niski **6.** ***have a ~ opinion of s.o.*** nie mieć dobrego zdania o *L* **II** *s* ***the ~*** ubodzy; **poor•ly** ['pʊəlɪ] **I** *adv* **1.** słabo; ***a ~ paid job*** słabo płatna praca; ***the meeting was ~ attended*** frekwencja na spotkaniu była niska **2.** marnie **3.** źle **4.** biednie **II** *adj* ***feel ~*** *Br infml* czuć się kiepsko
pop[1] [pɒp] MUS **I** *s* pop *m* **II** *adj* popowy pop; ***a ~ concert*** koncert muzyki pop
pop[2] [~] *s Am infml* tato *m*
pop[3] [~] **I** *s* **1.** huk *m* **2.** *cork*: wystrzał *m* **3.** trzask *m* **4.** napój *m* gazowany **II** *v/i* **1.** strzelać, wystrzelić; ***the sound of champagne corks ~ping*** odgłos strzelających korków od szampana **2.** pękać ⟨-knąć⟩ (z hukiem); ***balloon ~ped*** pękł balon **3.** (*visit*) wpadać ⟨-paść⟩; ***why don't you ~ in for a drink?*** może wpadniesz na drinka? **4.** (*appear*) wyskakiwać ⟨-skoczyć⟩; ***the menu ~s out when you click the mouse*** po kliknięciu myszką pojawia się menu **5.** ***an idea ~ped into his head*** nagle wpadł mu do głowy pewien pomysł **6.** ***his eyes nearly ~ped out*** oczy mu o mało nie wyszły z orbit **III** *v/t* wtykać ⟨wetknąć⟩; ***he ~ped his head into the room and said hello*** zajrzał do pokoju i powiedział „Cześć"; **pop off** *v/i infml* wykorkować; **pop up** *v/i* pojawiać ⟨-wić⟩ się
'pop group *s* zespół *m* popowy; **'pop sing•er** *s* piosenkarz *m* popowy; **'pop song** *s* piosenka *f* pop; **'pop star** *s* gwiaza *f* muzyki pop
pop•corn ['pɒpkɔːn] *s* popcorn *m*
Pope [pəʊp] *s* papież *m*; **Pope•mo•bile** ['pəʊpməbiːl] *s* papamobil *m*
pop-'eyed *adj*: ***be ~*** *infml* wytrzeszczać oczy
'pop•gun *s* (*toy*) pistolet *m* (na kulki lub korki)
pop•py ['pɒpɪ] *s* mak *m*
'pop•py•cock ['pɒpɪkɒk] *s dated* dyrdymały *pl*, androny *pl*
Pop•sicle® ['pɒpsɪkl] *Am* lody *pl* na patyku
pop•u•lar ['pɒpjələ] *adj* **1.** popularny; ***a ~ singer*** popularny piosenkarz; ***make oneself ~ with*** zdobyć popularność u *G* **2.** lubiany **3.** powszechny; ***contrary to ~ belief*** wbrew obiegowym opiniom **4.** rozpowszechniony **5.** ludowy; ***~ support*** poparcie społeczne; **pop•u•lar 'front** *s* front *m* ludowy; **pop•u•lar•i•ty** [pɒpjʊ'lærətɪ] *s* popularność *f*; **pop•u•lar•ize** ['pɒpjələraɪz] *v/t* **1.** popularyzować ⟨s-⟩ **2.** przybliżać ⟨-żyć⟩; **pop•u•lar•iz•er** ['pɒpjələraɪzə] *s* popularyzator *m*; **pop•u•lar•ly** ['pɒpjələlɪ] *adv* powszechnie; ***~ known as*** powszechnie znany jako *N*
pop•u•late ['pɒpjʊleɪt] *v/t* zaludniać ⟨-nić⟩; ***densely ~d*** gęsto zaludniony

P

pop•u•la•tion [pɒpjʊ'leɪʃn] *s* **1.** populacja *f* **2.** ludność *f*; ***one third of the world's ~*** jedna trzecia ludności świata **3.** mieszkańcy *pl*; ***Poland has a ~ of nearly 38 million*** Polska ma prawie 38 milionów mieszkańców
pop•u•lism ['pɒpjəlɪzəm] *s* populizm *m*; **pop•u•list** ['pɒpjəlɪst] **I** *s* populista *f* **II** *adj* populistyczny
pop•u•lous ['pɒpjələs] *adj* **1.** gęsto zaludniony **2.** ludny
porce•lain ['pɔːsəlɪn] *s* porcelana *f*
porch [pɔːtʃ] *s* **1.** ganek *m* **2.** (*church*) przedsionek *m* **3.** *Am* weranda *f*
por•cu•pine ['pɔːkjʊpaɪn] *s* jeżozwierz *m*
pore [pɔː] *s* (*skin*) por *m*; ***blocked ~s*** zatkane pory skóry; **pore over** *v/i* ślęczeć nad *I*
pork [pɔːk] *s* wieprzowina *f*; **pork 'chop** *s* kotlet *m* wieprzowy; **pork 'pie** *s* pasztecik *m* z nadzieniem z wieprzowiny; **pork 'rinds** *pl Am* skórki *pl* wieprzowe; **pork•y** ['pɔːkɪ] **I** *s* ***tell porkies*** *Br infml* wciskać kit **II** *adj infml* spasiony, tłusty
porn [pɔːn] *infml* **I** *s* porno *n* **II** *adj* porno; **porno** ['pɔːnəʊ] *adj infml* porno; **por•nog•raph•ic** [pɔːnə'græfɪk] *adj* pornograficzny; **por•nog•ra•phy** [pɔː'nɒgrəfɪ] *s* pornografia *f*
po•rous ['pɔːrəs] *adj* porowaty
por•poise ['pɔːpəs] *s* morświn *m*
por•ridge ['pɒrɪdʒ] *s Br* owsianka *f*, płatki *pl* owsiane
port[1] [pɔːt] **I** *s* **1.** port *m*; ***come into ~*** wejść do portu; ***leave ~*** wyjść z portu; ***any ~ in the storm*** lepsze to niż nic, na bezrybiu i rak ryba **2.** miasto *n* portowe **II** *adj* portowy
port[2] [~] *s* (*wine*) porto *n*
port[3] [~] *s* lewa burta *f*, bakburta *f*
por•ta•ble ['pɔːtəbl] **I** *adj* przenośny; ***a ~ computer*** przenośny komputer **II** *s* **1.** przenośny telewizor *m* **2.** przenośny komputer *m*
por•tal ['pɔːtl] *s* portal *m*
por•tent ['pɔːtent] *s lit* zapowiedź *f*; **por•ten•tous** [pɔː'tentəs] *adj lit* proroczy
por•ter ['pɔːtə] *s* **1.** bagażowy *m* **2.** portier *m* **3.** odźwierny *m* **4.** sanitarusz *m*; **por•ter•house 'steak** *s* stek *m* z polędwicy
port•fo•li•o [pɔːt'fəʊlɪəʊ] *pl -lios s* **1.** portfolio *n* **2.** POLIT resort *m*, teka *f*; ***a minister without ~*** minister bez teki **3.** teczka *f*, aktówka *f* **4.** ECON portfel *m*; ***an investment ~*** portfel inwestycyjny; ***~ management*** zarządzanie portfelem
port•hole ['pɔːthəʊl] *s* **1.** bulaj *m* **2.** okienko *n* w samolocie
por•ti•co ['pɔːtɪkəʊ] *pl -cos, -coes s* portyk *m*
por•tion ['pɔːʃn] *s* **1.** część *f* **2.** porcja *f* **3.** kawałek *m*; ***cut the cake into six ~s*** pokrój ciasto na sześć kawałków **4.** *credit*: transza *f*; **portion out** *v/t* rozdzielać ⟨-lić⟩ (***among/between*** między *G*)
port•ly ['pɔːtlɪ] *adj man*: korpulentny
por•trait ['pɔːtreɪt] *s* portret *m*; ***a ~ painter*** portrecista; **por•trait•ist** ['pɔːtreɪtɪst] *s* portrecista *m*; **por•trai•ture** ['pɔːtrətʃə] *s* **1.** sztuka *f* portretu, portret *m* **2.** portrety *pl*
por•tray [pɔː'treɪ] *v/t* **1.** przedstawiać ⟨-wić⟩; ***the painting ~s a young woman*** portret przedstawia młodą kobietę **2.** (*actor*) grać ⟨za-⟩ **3.** portretować ⟨s-⟩; **por•tray•al** [pɔː'treɪəl] *s* **1.** obraz *m* **2.** przedstawienie *n* **3.** (*by actor*) interpretacja *f*
Por•tu•gal ['pɔːtʃʊgl] *s* Portugalia *f*; **Por•tu•guese** [pɔːtʃʊ'giːz] **I** *adj* portugalski **II** *s* **1.** Portugalczyk *m*, Portugalka *f*; ***the ~*** Portugalczycy **2.** język *m* portugalski
pose [pəʊz] **I** *s* **1.** poza *f* **2.** pozycja *f* **II** *v/t* **1.** stanowić; ***~ no problem*** nie stanowić problemu **2.** *question*: zadawać ⟨-dać⟩ **III** *v/i* pozować (**as** na *A*); ***~ for a photo*** pozować do zdjęcia; **pos•er** ['pəʊzə] *s* **1.** pozer *m* **2.** *infml* trudny orzech *m* do zgryzienia
posh [pɒʃ] *adj infml* **1.** drogi **2.** elegancki **3.** snobistyczny
po•si•tion [pə'zɪʃn] **I** *s* **1.** pozycja *f*; ***in a sitting ~*** w pozycji siedzącej; ***in an upright ~*** w pozycji pionowej; ***be in a ~ to do s.th.*** być w stanie coś zrobić; ***what ~ does he play?*** na jakiej gra pozycji? **2.** miejsce *n*; ***is everybody in ~?*** czy wszyscy są na swoich miejscach?; ***what would you do in my ~?*** co byś zrobił na moim miejscu? **3.** położenie *n* **4.** sytuacja *f*; ***the company's fi-***

P

nancial ~ sytuacja finansowa spółki **5.** stanowisko *n*; ***take the ~ that*** reprezentować stanowisko, że; ***apply for the ~ of Sales Director*** ubiegać się o stanowisko dyrektora sprzedaży **6.** zdanie *n*; ***she has made her ~ clear*** jasno wyraziła swoje zdanie **II** *v/t* **1.** umieszczać ⟨umieścić⟩ **2.** rozmieszczać ⟨-mieścić⟩ **3.** ***~ oneself*** zająć miejsce, ulokować się

pos•i•tive ['pɒzətɪv] **I** *adj* **1.** pozytywny; ***a ~ response*** pozytywny odzew; ***the test is ~*** wynik testu jest pozytywny; ***she was tested ~ for bird flu*** wykryto u niej wirusa ptasiej grypy; ***try to be more ~*** spróbuj myśleć bardziej pozytywnie **2.** *MATH PHYS* dodatni; ***a ~ charge*** ładunek dodatni; ***a ~ number*** liczba dodatnia **3.** pewny; ***she was ~ that*** była pewna, że **4.** *action*: konkretny **5.** *evidence*: niezbity **II** *s* **1.** ***the ~*** pozytyw **2.** pozytywny wynik *m*; **pos•i•tive•ly** ['pɒzətɪvlɪ] *adv* **1.** pozytywnie **2.** naprawdę; ***some diets may be ~ dangerous*** niektóre diety mogą być naprawdę niebezpieczne **3.** dodatnio; ***~ charged electrons*** elektrony o ładunku dodatnim

pos•sess [pə'zes] *v/t* **1.** posiadać **2.** mieć; **3.** być właścicielem **4.** opętać; ***what ~ed him to do such a thing?*** co go opętało, żeby zrobić coś takiego? **5.** ogarniać ⟨-nąć⟩; ***terrible fear ~ed her*** ogarnęło ją wielkie przerażenie

pos•ses•sion [pə'zeʃn] *s* **1.** posiadanie *n*; ***be in ~ of*** posiadać *A*, być w posiadaniu *G*; ***come into ~ of*** wejść w posiadanie *G*; ***take ~ of*** przejąć *A* **2.** własność *f*; ***personal ~s*** mienie osobiste **3.** opętanie *n*; **pos•ses•sive** [pə'zesɪv] *adj* **1.** zaborczy **2.** zazdrosny (***about*** o *A*); ***she's ~ about her clothes*** nie lubi, gdy ktoś nosi jej ubrania **3.** *pronoun*: dzierżawczy; **posses•sor** [pə'zesə] *s* posiadacz *m*; ***the proud ~ of a driving licence*** dumny posiadacz prawa jazdy

pos•si•bil•i•ty [pɒsə'bɪlətɪ] *s* możliwość *f*; ***there's a ~ that*** możliwe, że; ***there's no ~ that*** niemożliwe, żeby

pos•si•ble ['pɒsəbl] *adj* **1.** możliwy; ***it's ~ to get there by bus*** można tam dojechać autobusem; ***make s.th. ~ for s.o.*** umożliwić coś komuś; ***if ~*** jeżeli to możliwe, w miarę możliwości; ***whenever ~*** kiedy to tylko możliwe; ***as soon as ~*** jak najszybciej, tak szybko, jak to możliwe; ***the best ~*** najlepszy **2.** ewentualny; ***with the ~ exception of*** może z wyjątkiem *G*; **possibly** ['pɒsəblɪ] *adv* **1.** być może; ***this was ~ his worst concert*** bardzo możliwe, że to był jego najgorszy koncert **2.** ***you can't ~ mean that!*** chyba nie mówisz poważnie! **3.** ***could you ~ open the window?*** czy mógłbyś otworzyć okno? **4.** ***I did everything I ~ could*** zrobiłem, co mogłem; zrobiłem wszystko, co w mojej mocy

pos•sum ['pɒsəm] → ***opossum***; ***he's playing ~*** udaje, że śpi

post[1] [pəʊst] *Br* **I** *s* poczta *f*; ***by ~*** listownie **II** *v/t* wysyłać ⟨-słać⟩ (pocztą); ***~ a letter*** wysłać list; ***keep s.o. ~ed about s.th.*** informować kogoś o czymś na bieżąco

post[2] [~] **I** *s* **1.** stanowisko *n*; ***he has held the ~ for three years*** zajmował to stanowisko przez trzy lata; ***resign from a ~*** ustąpić ze stanowiska; ***an observation ~*** punkt obserwacyjny **2.** posterunek *m* **II** *v/t* **1.** wysyłać ⟨-słać⟩ **2.** rozmieszczać ⟨-mieścić⟩ **3.** wywieszać ⟨-wiesić⟩ **4.** ogłaszać ⟨-łosić⟩ **5.** publikować ⟨o-⟩; ***the results will be ~ed on the Internet*** wyniki zostaną opublikowane w Internecie

post[3] [~] *s* **1.** słup *m* **2.** słupek *m*; ***the ball hit the ~*** piłka uderzyła w słupek

post•age ['pəʊstɪdʒ] *s* opłata *f* pocztowa; ***the price includes ~ and packing*** cena obejmuje koszty wysyłki; **'postage stamp** *s* znaczek *m* pocztowy

post•al ['pəʊstl] *adj* pocztowy; ***~ address*** adres pocztowy

'post•box *s* skrzynka *f* pocztowa; **'post•card** *s* kartka *f* pocztowa; **'post•code** *s* kod *m* pocztowy

post•'date *v/t* **1.** postdatować **2.** pochodzić z późniejszego okresu niż *N*; ***some parts of the town ~ the earthquake*** niektóre części miasta pochodzą z okresu po trzęsieniu ziemi

post•er ['pəʊstə] *s* plakat *m*

poste res•tante [pəʊst'restɒnt] *s* *Br* poste restante *n*

P

pos•te•ri•or [pɒ'stɪərɪə] **I** *adj* tylny **II** *s infml* siedzenie *n*
pos•ter•i•ty [pɒ'sterətɪ] *s* przyszłe pokolenia *pl*
post-'free *adv* bez opłaty pocztowej
post•grad•u•ate ['pəʊstgrædʒʊət] *Br* **I** *adj* **1.** magisterski **2.** doktorski **II** *s* **1.** magistrant *m* **2.** doktorant *m*
post•hu•mous ['pɒstjʊməs] *adj* pośmiertny; **post•hu•mous•ly** ['pɒstjʊməslɪ] *adv* pośmiertnie
post•ing ['pəʊstɪŋ] *s employee*: oddelegowanie *n*
'post•man *pl -men s Br* listonosz *m*; **'post•mark I** *s* stempel *m* pocztowy **II** *v/t stamp*: stemplować ⟨o-⟩; **'post•mas•ter** *s* naczelnik *m* poczty
post me•ri•di•em [pəʊstmə'rɪdɪəm] *adv* po południu
post•mod•ern•ism [pəʊst'mɒdənɪzəm] *s* postmodernizm *m*; **post•mod•ern•ist** [pəʊst'mɒdənɪst] *s* postmodernista *m*
post-mor•tem [pəʊst'mɔːtəm] *s* sekcja *f* zwłok, autopsja *f*
post•na•tal [pəʊst'neɪtl] *adj* poporodowy
'post of•fice *s* urząd *m* pocztowy
post•pone [pəʊst'pəʊn] *v/t* przekładać ⟨przełożyć⟩ (na późniejszy termin); ***we have to ~ our meeting to Thursday*** musimy przełożyć nasze spotkanie na czwartek; **post•pone•ment** [pəʊst'pəʊnmənt] *s* przełożenie *n* (na późniejszy termin)
post•script ['pəʊstskrɪpt] *s* post scriptum *n*
pos•tu•late I ['pɒstjʊleɪt] *v/t* **1.** twierdzić ⟨s-⟩ **2.** zakładać ⟨założyć⟩ **II** ['pɒstjʊlət] *s* **1.** twierdzenie *n* **2.** założenie *n* **3.** postulat *m*
pos•ture ['pɒstʃə] **I** *s* **1.** postawa *f* **2.** pozycja *f*; ***sit in an upright ~*** siedzieć prosto **3.** stanowisko *n* **II** *v/i* pozować (**as** na *A*)
post-'war *adj* powojenny
pot[1] [pɒt] **I** *s* **1.** garnek *m*; ***the ~ calling the kettle black*** przyganiał kocioł garnkowi; ***have ~s of money*** *Br infml* mieć kupę forsy; ***go to ~*** *fig* schodzić na psy **2.** *Br* pojemnik *m* **3.** słoik *m* **4.** słój *m* **5.** dzbanek *m*; ***a coffee ~*** dzbanek do kawy **6.** donica *f* **7.** doniczka *f* **8.** (*cards*) **the ~** bank **9.** *infml* trawka *f* **II** *v/t* sadzić ⟨po-⟩ w doniczce; ***a ~ted plant*** roślina doniczkowa
pot[2] [~] **I** *s* **1.** (*billiards*) wbicie *n* **2.** ***take a ~ at*** strzelić na chybił trafił do *G* **II** *v/t* **1.** *the red*: wbijać ⟨-bić⟩ do łuzy **2.** zastrzelić
po•ta•ble ['pəʊtəbl] *adj* nadający się do picia, pitny
po•tas•si•um [pə'tæsɪəm] *s CHEM* potas *m*; **po•tas•si•um cy•a•nide** *s CHEM* cyjanek *m* potasu, *infml* cyjanek *m*
po•ta•to [pə'teɪtəʊ] *pl -toes s* ziemniak *m*; kartofel *m*; **po•'ta•to bee•tle** *Am*, ***po•'ta•to bug*** *Br s* stonka *f* ziemniaczana; **po•'ta•to chips** *Am*, **po•ta•to 'crisps** *Br pl* chipsy *pl* ziemniaczane; **po•'ta•to peel•er** *s* skrobaczka *f* do ziemniaków; **po•ta•to 'sal•ad** *s* sałatka *f* ziemniaczana
pot•bel•ly ['pɒtbelɪ] *s* duży brzuch *m*, *infml* kałdun *m*
po•ten•cy ['pəʊtənsɪ] *s* **1.** siła *f* **2.** potencja *f*
po•tent ['pəʊtənt] *adj* **1.** *medicine*: silny, mający silne działanie **2.** *alcohol*: mocny **3.** *power*: potężny **4.** *argument*: przekonujący; **po•ten•tate** ['pəʊtənteɪt] *s lit* potentat *m*; **po•ten•tial** [pə'tenʃl] **I** *adj* potencjalny **II** *s* **1.** potencjał *m* **2.** możliwości *pl*; **po•ten•tial•ly** [pə'tenʃəlɪ] *adv* potencjalnie
pot•hole ['pɒthəʊl] *s* (*road*) dziura *f*; **pot•holed** ['pɒthəʊld] *adj road*: dziurawy; **pot•hol•er** ['pɒthəʊlə] *s Br* grotołaz *m*; **pot•hol•ing** ['pɒthəʊlɪŋ] *s* eksploracja *f* jaskiń
po•tion ['pəʊʃn] *s* mikstura *f*; ***love ~*** napój *m* miłosny
pot 'luck *s* ***take ~*** zadowolić się tym, co jest
'pot plant *s Br* roślina *f* doniczkowa
'pot roast *s* duszona wołowina *f*
'pot shot *s*: ***take a ~ at*** strzelić na chybił trafił do *G*
pot•ter[1] ['pɒtə] *v/i* (*a.* ***~ around***) leniwie spędzać czas
pot•ter[2] [~] *s* garncarz *m*; ***a ~'s wheel*** koło garncarskie; **pot•ter•y** ['pɒtərɪ] *s* **1.** wyroby *pl* garncarskie **2.** ceramika *f* **3.** garncarstwo *n* **4.** glina *f* garncarska
pot•ty[1] ['pɒtɪ] *adj Br infml* stuknięty; ***be ~ about*** mieć fioła na punkcie *G*;

P

drive s.o. ~ doprowadzać kogoś do szału

pot•ty² [~] *s infml* nocnik *m*; **'pot•ty-trained** *adj*: ***be ~*** **a)** załatwiać się do nocnika **b)** załatwiać się w toalecie

pouch [paʊtʃ] *s* **1.** woreczek *m* **2.** sakiewka *f* **3.** torba *f* na listy **4.** (*kangaroo*) torba *f* **5.** (*hamster*) torba *f* policzkowa

pouf [pʊf], ***pouffe*** [puːf] *s* **1.** puf *m* **2.** podnóżek *m*

poul•tice ['pəʊltɪs] *s MED* okład *m*, kompres *m*

poul•try ['pəʊltrɪ] *s* drób *m*

pounce [paʊns] *v/i* **1.** atakować ⟨za-⟩ (***on*** *A*); ***ready to ~*** gotowy do ataku **2.** rzucać ⟨-cić⟩ się (***on*** na *A*)

pound¹ [paʊnd] *s* **1.** (*currency*) funt *m* **2.** (*0,454 kg*) funt *m*

pound² [~] *s* **1.** schronisko *n* dla psów **2.** parking *m* dla odholowanych przez policję samochodów

pound³ [~] **I** *v/i* **1.** walić ⟨-lnąć⟩; ***heavy rain ~ed on the roof*** deszcz walił o dach **2.** ***my head is ~ing*** głowa mi pęka **3.** ***they ~ed along the pavement*** szli po chodniku, głośno tupiąc **II** *v/t* **1.** walić ⟨-lnąć⟩, okładać; ***she ~ed him with her fists*** waliła go pięściami, okładała go pięściami **2.** ucierać ⟨utrzeć⟩ **3.** bombardować ⟨z-⟩; **pound•ing** ['paʊndɪŋ] *s* **1.** walenie *n*; ***~ on the door*** walenie do drzwi **2.** łomotanie *n*; ***~ of the heart*** łomotanie serca; ***take a ~*** **a)** (*war time*) ucierpieć **b)** (*team*) *infml* dostać łomot; **pound 'ster•ling** *s* (*currency*) funt *m* szterling

P

pour [pɔː] **I** *v/t* **1.** nalewać ⟨-lać⟩ (***into*** do *G*); ***~ the sauce over the pasta*** polej makaron sosem; ***will you ~ the coffee?*** możesz nalać kawę?; ***I've ~ed you a cup of tea*** zrobiłam ci herbatę **2.** sypać ⟨na-⟩ (***into*** do *G*) **II** *v/i* **1.** cieknąć **2.** (*tears*) spływać **3.** ***it's ~ing with rain, it's ~ing*** leje **4.** (*a.* ***~ in***) napływać ⟨-łynąć⟩; **pour out I** *v/i* **1.** wypływać ⟨-łynąć⟩ **2.** wydobywać ⟨-być⟩ się **II** *v/t* **1.** rozlewać ⟨-lać⟩ **2.** nalewać ⟨-lać⟩ **3.** *fig* wyrzucać ⟨-cić⟩ z siebie; ***~ one's troubles to s.o.*** zwierzyć się komuś ze swoich problemów

pout [paʊt] **I** *v/i* wydymać ⟨-dąć⟩ usta **II** *s* wydęcie *n* ust

pov•er•ty ['pɒvətɪ] *s* **1.** bieda *f* **2.** ubóstwo *n* **3.** niedostatek *m*; **'pov•er•ty line** *s* granica *f* ubóstwa *f*; ***live below the ~*** żyć w nędzy; **'pov•er•ty-stricken** *adj* ubogi, cierpiący nędzę

POW [piːəʊ'dʌbljuː] *abbr* (=***prisoner of war***) jeniec *m* wojenny

pow•der ['paʊdə] **I** *s* **1.** proszek *m*; ***washing ~*** proszek do prania; ***baking ~*** proszek do pieczenia **2.** puder *m*; ***face ~*** puder do twarzy **II** *v/t* **1.** pudrować ⟨przy-⟩ **2.** sproszkować: ***~ed milk*** mleko w proszku; **'pow•der keg** *s fig* beczka *f* prochu; **'pow•der puff** *s* puszek *f* do pudru; **'pow•der room** *s* toaleta *f*; **pow•der•y** ['paʊdərɪ] *adj snow*: drobny, sypki

pow•er ['paʊə] **I** *s* **1.** władza *f* (***over*** nad *I*); ***be in ~*** być przy władzy; ***come to ~*** dojść do władzy; ***~ struggle*** walka o władzę; ***be the ~ behind the throne*** być szarą eminencją, pociągać za sznurki **2.** kontrola *f* (***over*** nad *I*) **3.** moc *f*; ***engine ~*** moc silnika; ***I'll do everything in my ~*** zrobię, co w mojej mocy **4.** siła *f* **5.** zdolność *f*; ***mental ~s*** zdolności umysłowe; ***~ of speech*** mowa, dar mowy **6.** możliwość *f*; ***at the height of one's ~s*** u szczytu swoich możliwości **7.** prawo *n*; ***have the ~ to do s.th.*** mieć prawo coś zrobić **8.** uprawnienie *n*; ***~s*** uprawnienia, kompetencje; ***~ of attorney*** pełnomocnictwo **9.** (*country*) mocarstwo *n*, potęga *f* **10.** wpływ *m* **11.** energia *f*, ***solar ~*** energia słoneczna **12.** (*a.* ***~ supply***) zasilanie *n* **13.** *MATH* potęga *f*; ***4 to the ~ of 3*** cztery do trzeciej potęgi; ***raise a number to the third ~*** podnieść liczbę do trzeciej potęgi **II** *v/t* **1.** napędzać ⟨-dzić⟩ **2.** zasilać ⟨-lić⟩; **'pow•er-as•sist•ed steering** → ***power steering***; **'pow•er•boat** *s* łódź *f* motorowa, motorówka *f*; **'pow•er cut** *s Br* przerwa *f* w dostawie prądu; **'pow•er fail•ure** *s* awaria *f* instalacji elektrycznej

pow•er•ful ['paʊəfl] *adj* **1.** potężny **2.** wpływowy **3.** silny **4.** *engine*: o dużej mocy; **pow•er•less** ['paʊəlɪs] *adj* **1.** bezsilny **2.** bezradny; ***I was ~ to help*** nie byłem w stanie pomóc

'pow•er line *s* **1.** linia *f* energetyczna **2.** linia *f* wysokiego napięcia; **'power**

out•age *Am* → ***power cut***; ˈ**pow•er pack** *s* zasilacz *m* sieciowy; ˈ**pow•er plant** *s* elektrownia *f*; ˈ**pow•er point** *s Br* kontakt *m*, gniazdko *n*; ˈ**pow•er sta•tion** → ***power plant***; ˈ**pow•er steer•ing** *s AUTO* układ *m* kierowniczy ze wspomaganiem; ˈ**pow•er tool** *s* narzędzie *n* z napędem elektrycznym; ˈ**pow•er u•nit** *s* **1.** jednostka *f* napędowa, zespół *m* napędowy **2.** zasilacz *m*; ˈ**pow•er walk•ing** *s* szybki marsz *m*

pow•wow [ˈpaʊwaʊ] *s* **1.** rada *f* plemienna **2.** *infml* narada *f*

pox [pɒks] *s* **1.** *dated* franca *f* **2.** ospa *f*; **pox•y** [pɒksi] *adj* bezwartościowy

PR [piːˈɑː] *abbr* (=**public relations**) PR *m*

prac•ti•ca•ble [ˈpræktɪkəbl] *adj* **1.** możliwy do zrealizowania **2.** wykonalny

prac•ti•cal [ˈpræktɪkl] **I** *adj* **1.** praktyczny; ***~ experience*** doświadczenie praktyczne; ***~ application*** praktyczne zastosowanie; ***for all ~ purposes*** praktycznie rzecz biorąc **2.** wykonalny **3.** realny **4.** ***she married a ~ stranger*** wyszła za mąż za człowieka, którego niemal nie znała **II** *s Br infml* **1.** ćwiczenia *pl* **2.** egzamin *m* praktyczny; **prac•ti•cal** ˈ**joke** *s* kawał *m*, figiel *m*; **prac•ti•cally** [ˈpræktɪklɪ] *adv* praktycznie; ***it's ~ impossible*** to praktycznie niemożliwe

prac•tice [ˈpræktɪs] **I** *s* **1.** praktyka *f*; ***theory and ~*** teoria i praktyka; ***put one's ideas into ~*** wprowadzić swoje pomysły w życie; ***in ~*** w praktyce, w rzeczywistości; ***religious ~s*** praktyki religijne; ***get out of ~*** wyjść z wprawy **2.** trening *m*; ***~ makes perfect*** trening czyni mistrza **3.** ćwiczenie *n*; ***it takes a lot of ~ to play the violin well*** trzeba dużo ćwiczyć, żeby dobrze grać na skrzypcach **4.** sposób *m* postępowania; ***common ~*** powszechna praktyka **5.** próba *f* **6.** zwyczaj *m* **II** *v/i Am* → ***practise***; **prac•ticed** *Am* → ***practised***

prac•tise [ˈpræktɪs] **I** *v/t* **1.** ćwiczyć; ***~ the piano*** ćwiczyć na pianinie, grać (wprawki) na pianinie **2.** stosować ⟨za-⟩ **3.** *safe sex*: uprawiać **4.** praktykować; ***a practising Catholic*** praktykujący katolik **5.** wyznawać **6.** ***~ medicine*** być lekarzem **II** *v/i Br* ćwiczyć;

prac•tised [ˈpræktɪsd] *adj Br* wprawny, doświadczony; ***be ~ in*** mieć wprawę w *L*, mieć doświadczenie w *L*

prac•ti•tion•er [prækˈtɪʃənə] *s* **1.** ***a medical ~*** lekarz; ***a general ~*** lekarz rodzinny; ***a legal ~*** prawnik **2.** wyznawca *m* **3.** ***a ~ of tattooing*** artysta tatuażu; ***a ~ of aikido*** ćwiczący aikido, aikidoka

prag•mat•ic [prægˈmætɪk] *adj* pragmatyczny; **prag•ma•tism** [ˈprægmətɪzm] *s* pragmatyzm *m*; **prag•ma•tist** [ˈprægmətɪst] *s* pragmatyk *m*

Prague [prɑːg] *s* Praga *f*

prai•rie [ˈpreərɪ] *s* preria *f*; ˈ**prai•rie dog** *s* piesek *m* preriowy; ˈ**prai•rie schoo•ner** *s* (*Wild West*) wóz *m* pionierów

praise [preɪz] **I** *v/t* chwalić ⟨po-⟩ (***s.o. for*** kogoś za *A*); ***~ s.th. to the skies*** wychwalać coś pod niebiosa **II** *s* **1.** pochwała *f*; ***be full of ~ for s.o.*** bardzo kogoś chwalić, nie szczędzić komuś pochwał; ***poems in ~ of the beauty of nature*** wiersze opiewające piękno przyrody **2.** uznanie *n*; ***win ~*** zyskać uznanie **3.** chwała *f*; **praise•wor•thy** [ˈpreɪzwɜːðɪ] *adj* **1.** godny pochwały **2.** godny uznania

pram [præm] *s Br* wózek *m* dziecięcy

prance [prɑːns] *v/i* **1.** paradować **2.** chodzić tanecznym krokiem **3.** (*horse*) brykać

prank [præŋk] *s* figiel *m*, psikus *m*; ***play a ~ on s.o.*** spłatać komuś figla

prat [præt] *s Br infml* dureń *m*

prat•tle [ˈprætl] *v/i dated* paplać (***on/ about*** o *L*)

prawn [prɔːn] *s* krewetka *f*

pray [preɪ] **I** *v/i* **1.** modlić ⟨po-⟩ się (***for*** o *A*, ***to*** do *G*); ***I ~ed that nobody would notice my mistake*** modliłem się, żeby nikt nie zauważył mojego błędu **2.** błagać; ***he ~ed to be forgiven*** błagał o przebaczenie **II** *adv dated* **1.** proszę; ***~ come closer*** proszę, podejdź bliżej **2.** ***what, ~, is the meaning of all this?*** bądź łaskaw wyjaśnić, co to wszystko ma znaczyć?

prayer [preə] *s* **1.** modlitwa *f*; ***our ~s were answered*** nasze modlitwy zostały wysłuchane; ***Lord's ~*** Modlitwa Pańska **2.** błaganie *n* **3.** nadzieja *f*; ***my ~ is that*** mam nadzieję, że; ˈ**prayer book** *s* książeczka *f* do nabożeństwa; **pray•ing man•tis** *s* [preɪɪŋ'mæntɪs] *s* (*insect*) modliszka *f*

preach [priːtʃ] **I** *v/i* **1.** głosić ⟨wy-⟩ kazanie (***about/on*** o *L*); ***~ to the converted*** *fig* wyważać otwarte drzwi **2.** *fig* prawić kazania, prawić morały; ***~ at s.o.*** prawić komuś kazania **II** *v/t* **1.** głosić ⟨wy-⟩ **2.** wychwalać; **preacher** ['priːtʃə] *s* kaznodzieja *f*

pre•am•ble [priː'æmbl] *s* **1.** wstęp *m* **2.** preambuła *f*

pre•ar•range [priːə'reɪndʒ] *v/t* **1.** uzgadniać ⟨-godnić⟩ **2.** planować ⟨za-⟩

pre•car•i•ous [prɪ'keərɪəs] *adj* **1.** niepewny; ***they are in a financially ~ position*** ich sytuacja finansowa jest niepewna **2.** niebezpieczny; ***the roof was ~*** dach mógł w każdej chwili się zawalić; **pre•car•i•ous•ly** [prɪ'keərɪəslɪ] *adv* niebezpiecznie; ***be ~ close to*** być niebezpiecznie blisko *G*

pre•cau•tion [prɪ'kɔːʃn] *s* środek *m* ostrożności; ***safety ~s*** środki bezpieczeństwa; ***take ~s against fire*** przedsięwziąć środki ostrożności na wypadek pożaru; ***as a ~*** na wszelki wypadek; ***as a ~ against*** dla ochrony przed *I*; **pre•cau•tion•a•ry** [prɪ'kɔːʃənrɪ] *adj* zapobiegawczy; ***~ measures*** środki zapobiegawcze, środki ostrożności

pre•cede [prɪ'siːd] *v/t* **1.** poprzedzać ⟨-dzić⟩; ***the celebration was ~d by lengthy preparations*** uroczystość poprzedziły długie przygotowania; ***~ one's speech with thanks*** rozpocząć przemówienie od podziękowań **2.** być poprzednikiem **3.** być przed *I* **4.** iść przed *I*; ***she ~d him out of the room*** wyszła z pokoju przed nim

pre•ce•dence ['presɪdəns] *s* pierwszeństwo *n*, ważność *f*; ***take ~ over*** mieć pierwszeństwo przed *I*, być ważniejszym od *G*; **pre•ce•dent** ['presɪdənt] *s* JUR precedens *m*; ***set the ~*** ustanowić precedens; ***without ~*** bez precedensu

pre•ce•ding [prɪ'siːdɪŋ] *adj* **1.** poprzedni; ***in the ~ chapter*** w poprzednim rozdziale **2.** poprzedzający

pre•cept ['priːsept] *s* **1.** zasada *f*; ***moral ~*** zasada moralna **2.** nakaz *m*

pre•cinct ['priːsɪŋkt] *s* **1.** *Br* strefa *f* zamknięta dla ruchu kołowego; ***a shopping ~*** pasaż handlowy **2.** *Am* rewir *m* (policyjny) **3.** teren *m*; ***within the ~ of the castle*** na terenie przylegającym do zamku

pre•cious ['preʃəs] **I** *adj* **1.** *a. fig* cenny; ***you're wasting ~ time*** tracisz cenny czas **2.** kosztowny; ***a ~ vase*** kosztowny wazon **3.** szlachetny; ***a ~ stone*** kamień szlachetny; ***~ metal*** metal szlachetny **II** *adv infml* bardzo; ***~ few, ~ little*** bardzo mało, bardzo niewiele

pre•ci•pice ['presɪpɪs] *s* przepaść *f*

pre•cip•i•tate **I** [prɪ'sɪpɪteɪt] *v/t* **1.** doprowadzać ⟨-dzić⟩ do *G* **2.** wywoływać ⟨-łać⟩ **3.** przyśpieszać ⟨-szyć⟩ **4.** *substance*: wytrącać ⟨-cić⟩ **II** [prɪ'sɪpɪteɪt] *v/i* (*of substance*) wytrącać ⟨-cić⟩ się **III** [prɪ'sɪpɪtət] *s* CHEM osad *m* **IV** [prɪ'sɪpɪtət] *adj* **1.** pochopny **2.** nieprzemyślany; **pre•cip•i•ta•tion** [prəsɪpɪ'teɪʃn] *s* **1.** opady *pl* **2.** CHEM wytrącanie *n* (się)

pre•cip•i•tous [prə'sɪpɪtəs] *adj* **1.** urwisty **2.** *action*: gwałtowny **3.** pochopny **4.** nieprzemyślany

pré•cis ['preɪsiː] *pl précis* ['preɪsiːz] *s* streszczenie *n*, abstrakt *m*

pre•cise [prɪ'saɪs] *adj* **1.** dokładny; ***at the ~ moment*** dokładnie w tym momencie; ***to be ~*** ściśle mówiąc **2.** precyzyjny; **pre•cise•ly** [prɪ'saɪslɪ] *adv* **1.** dokładnie; ***they look ~ the same to me*** dla mnie wyglądają dokładnie tak samo **2.** precyzyjnie; **pre•ci•sion** [prɪ'sɪʒn] **I** *s* **1.** dokładność *f*; ***choose one's words with ~*** starannie dobierać słowa **2.** precyzja *f* **II** *adj* precyzyjny

pre•clude [prɪ'kluːd] *v/t* **1.** uniemożliwiać ⟨-wić⟩; ***~ s.o. from doing s.th.*** uniemożliwić komuś zrobienie czegoś **2.** wykluczać ⟨-czyć⟩

pre•co•cious [prɪ'kəʊʃəs] *adj* **1.** nad wiek rozwinięty **2.** przedwcześnie dojrzały

pre•con•ceived [priːkən'siːvd] *adj opinion*: wcześniej wyrobiony; ***~ notions*** **a)** wyrobione zdanie **b)** uprzedzenia; **pre•con•cep•tion** [priːkən'sepʃn] *s* **1.** wyrobione zdanie *n* **2.** uprzedzenie *n*

pre•con•di•tion [priːkən'dɪʃn] *s* warunek *m* wstępny

pre•cook [priː'kʊk] *v/t* wcześniej gotować ⟨u-⟩

P

pre•cur•sor [priːˈkɜːsə] *s* **1.** ***be a precursor to*** poprzedzać *A* **2.** pierwowzór *m* **3.** zwiastun *m* **4.** prekursor *m*
pre•date [priːˈdeɪt] *v/t* **1.** być starszym od *G* **2.** poprzedzać ⟨-dzić⟩ *A* **3.** antydatować
pred•a•tor [ˈpredətə] *s* drapieżnik *m*; **pred•a•to•ry** [ˈpredətrɪ] *adj* drapieżny
pre•de•ces•sor [ˈpriːdɪsesə] *s* poprzednik *m*
pre•des•ti•na•tion [priːdestɪˈneɪʃn] *s* przeznaczenie *n*, predestynacja *f*; **pre•des•tined** [priːˈdestɪnd] *adj* przeznaczony; ***be ~ to failure*** być skazanym na porażkę; ***she was ~ to succeed*** był jej pisany sukces
predetermine [prɪdɪˈtɜːmɪn] *s* określać ⟨-lić⟩ (z góry)
pre•dic•a•ment [priːˈdɪkəmənt] *s* trudna sytuacja *f*; ***a financial ~*** trudna sytuacja finansowa
pred•i•cate [ˈpredɪkət] *s* GRAM orzeczenie *n*; **pred•i•ca•tive** [prɪˈdɪkətɪv] *adj* GRAM predykatywny; ***a ~ adjective*** orzecznik *m* przymiotnikowy
pre•dict [prɪˈdɪkt] *v/t* **1.** przewidywać ⟨-dzieć⟩ **2.** przepowiadać ⟨-wiedzieć⟩; **pre•dict•a•ble** [prɪˈdɪktəbl] *adj* przewidywalny; **pre•dic•tion** [prɪˈdɪkʃn] *s* przewidywanie *n*; ***against all ~s*** wbrew wszystkim przewidywaniom
pre•di•gest•ed [priːdaɪˈdʒestɪd] *adj information*: podany w przystępnej formie
pred•i•lec•tion [priːdɪˈlekʃn] *s* upodobanie *n*, *lit* predylekcja *f*
pre•dis•pose [priːdɪsˈpəʊz] *v/t* **1.** predysponować (***s.o. for*** kogoś do *G*); ***be ~d to*** mieć predyspozycje do *G* **2.** czynić ⟨u-⟩ podatnym (***to*** na *A*); ***be ~d to*** MED być podatnym na *A*; **pre•dis•po•si•tion** [priːdɪspəˈzɪʃn] *s* **1.** skłonność *f* (***to*** do *G*); ***a genetic ~ to obesity*** genetyczna skłonność do otyłości **2.** predyspozycja *f* (***to*** do *G*)
pre•dom•i•nance [prɪˈdɒmɪnəns] *s* **1.** przewaga *f*; ***a ~ of female teachers in elementary schools*** przewaga nauczycielek nad nauczycielami w szkołach podstawowych **2.** dominacja *f*; ***struggle for global ~*** walka o dominację nad światem; **pre•dom•i•nant** [prɪˈdɒmɪnənt] *adj* przeważający, dominujący; ***be ~*** przeważać, dominować; **pre•dom•i•nant•ly** [prɪˈdɒmɪnəntlɪ] *adv* **1.** głównie **2.** przeważająco; **pre•dom•i•nate** [prɪˈdɔmɪneɪt] *v/i* **1.** przeważać ⟨-żyć⟩; ***women ~ in the audience*** na widowni przeważają kobiety **2.** dominować (***over*** nad *I*)
pre-em•i•nent [priːˈemɪnənt] *adj* **1.** najwybitniejszy **2.** najznakomitszy **3.** najważniejszy
pre-empt [priːˈempt] *v/t* **1.** zapobiegać ⟨-biec⟩ **2.** ubiegać ⟨ubiec⟩ **3.** uniemożliwiać ⟨-wić⟩; **pre-emp•tive** [priːˈemptɪv] *adj* **1.** *attack*, *strike*: wyprzedzający **2.** zapobiegawczy **3.** prewencyjny **4.** ***~ right*** prawo pierwokupu
preen [priːn] *v/t* **1.** ***~ oneself*** stroić się **2.** ***~ oneself on*** upajać się *I* **3.** ***~ itself*** (*bird*) czyścić sobie piórka
pre•fab [ˈpriːfæb] *s infml* dom *m* z prefabrykatów; **preˈfab•ri•cate** [priːˈfæbrɪkeɪt] *v/t* **1.** prefabrykować **2.** *building*: budować ⟨z-⟩ z prefabrykatów; **pre•fab•ri•cat•ed** [priːˈfæbrɪkeɪtɪd] *adj* **1.** prefabrykowany **2.** *house*: z prefabrykatów
pref•ace [ˈprefəs] **I** *s* wstęp *m*, przedmowa *f* **II** *v/t* opatrywać ⟨-rzyć⟩ wstępem, opatrywać ⟨-rzyć⟩ przedmową
pre•fer [prɪˈfɜː] *v/t* **1.** woleć; ***do you ~ coffee or tea?*** wolisz kawę czy herbatę?; ***I ~ jazz to rock music*** wolę jazz od muzyki rockowej; ***I'd ~ to stay at home*** wolałbym zostać w domu; ***I'd ~ you not to smoke*** *form* wolałbym, żeby pan nie palił **2.** preferować; ***a local firm is to be ~red*** preferowane będą lokalne firmy; **pre•ferred ˈcred•i•tor** *s* ECON wierzyciel *m* uprzywilejowany; **pref•e•ra•ble** [ˈprefrəbl] *adj* lepszy; ***it would be ~ to employ two people*** lepiej byłoby zatrudnić dwie osoby; ***he finds country life ~ to living in the city*** woli mieszkać na wsi niż w mieście; **pref•e•ra•bly** [ˈprefrəblɪ] *adv* najlepiej; ***we're looking for a new house, ~ one near the beach*** szukamy nowego domu, najlepiej niedaleko plaży; **pref•e•rence** [ˈprefrəns] *s* **1.** preferencja *f*; ***consumer ~s*** preferencje konsumentów; ***it's a matter of personal ~*** to kwestia osobistych pre-

ferencji **2.** pierwszeństwo *n*; ***give s.o. ~ over*** dać komuś pierwszeństwo przed *I*; **pref•er•en•tial** [prefəˈrenʃl] *adj* preferencyjny

pre•fix [ˈpriːfɪks] **I** *s* **1.** przedrostek *m* **2.** prefiks *m*; ***dial the ~ 044*** wybierz prefiks 044 **II** *v/t* **1.** dodawać ⟨-dać⟩ prefiks **2.** poprzedzać ⟨-dzić⟩; ***the number is ~ed with CA*** liczbę poprzedzają litery CA

preg•nan•cy [ˈpregnənsɪ] *s* ciąża *f*; ***a ~ test*** test ciążowy; **preg•nant** [ˈpregnənt] *adj* **1.** w ciąży; ***get ~*** zajść w ciążę; ***she's four months ~*** jest w czwartym miesiącu ciąży **2.** *fig* wymowny

pre•heat [priːˈhiːt] *v/t oven*: nagrzewać ⟨-rzać⟩

pre•his•tor•ic [priːhɪsˈtɒrɪk] *adj* prehistoryczny

pre•in•stalled [priːɪnˈstɔːld] *adj* **1.** preinstalowany **2.** wcześniej zainstalowany

pre•judge [priːˈdʒʌdʒ] *v/t* przedwcześnie osądzać ⟨-dzić⟩

prej•u•dice [ˈpredʒʊdɪs] **I** *s* **1.** uprzedzenie *n* (***against*** do *G*); ***racial ~s*** uprzedzenia rasowe **2.** uprzedzenia *pl* **3.** niechęć *f* (***against*** do *G*) **4.** ***without ~ to*** JUR bez uszczerbku dla *G* **II** *v/t* **1.** uprzedzać ⟨-dzić⟩ (***against*** do *G*) **2.** przynosić ⟨-nieść⟩ szkodę **3.** wpływać ⟨-łynąć⟩ negatywnie na *A*; **prej•u•diced** [ˈpredʒʊdɪst] *adj* uprzedzony (***against*** do *G*); **prej•u•di•cial** [predʒʊˈdɪʃl] *adj*: ***be ~ to*** **a)** być szkodliwym dla *G* **b)** mieć negatywny wpływ na *A*

pre•lim•i•na•ry [prɪˈlɪmɪnerɪ] **I** *adj* **1.** wstępny; ***~ remarks*** uwagi wstępne **2.** początkowy **3.** ***be ~ to*** poprzedzać *A*, być wstępem do *G* **II** *s* **1.** wstęp *m* **2.** przygotowanie *n* **3.** *tournament*: eliminacje *pl*

prel•ude [ˈpreljuːd] *s a. fig* preludium *n*

pre•mar•i•tal [priːˈmærɪtl] *adj* przedmałżeński; ***a ~ agreement*** intercyza

pre•ma•ture [ˈpremətʃʊə] *adj* **1.** przedwczesny; ***the baby was four weeks ~*** dziecko urodziło się cztery tygodnie przed terminem **2.** pochopny; ***it's ~ to talk about success*** jest jeszcze zbyt wcześnie, żeby mówić o sukcesie; **pre•ma•ture ˈba•by** *s* wcześniak *m*; **pre•ma•ture•ly** [ˈpremətʃʊəlɪ] *adv* przedwcześnie; ***her hair became ~ white*** przedwcześnie posiwiała

pre•med•i•tat•ed [priːˈmedɪteɪtɪd] *adj* **1.** (popełniony) z premedytacją **2.** umyślny; **pre•med•i•ˈta•tion** [priːmedɪˈteɪʃn] *s* premedytacja *f*

pre•men•stru•al [priːmenstrʊəl] *adj* przedmiesiączkowy; **pre•ˈmen•stru•al ˈsyn•drome** *s* zespół *m* napięcia przedmiesiączkowego; **pre•men•stru•al ˈten•sion** *s* napięcie *n* przedmiesiączkowe

prem•i•er [ˈpremɪə] **I** *adj* najlepszy **II** *s* premier *m*

prem•i•ère [ˈpremɪeə] **I** *s* premiera *f*; ***the world ~*** światowa premiera **II** *v/t* **1.** *concert*, *play*: wykonywać ⟨-nać⟩ po raz pierwszy; ***the play was ~d in Paris*** premiera sztuki odbyła się w Paryżu **2.** *film*: pokazywać ⟨-zać⟩ po raz pierwszy

pre•mise [ˈpremɪs] *s* przesłanka *f*

prem•is•es [ˈpremɪsɪz] *s pl* **1.** lokal *m* **2.** siedziba *f* **3.** teren *m*; ***on the ~*** **a)** na terenie firmy **b)** w sklepie **c)** w lokalu **d)** na uczelni

pre•mi•um [ˈpriːmɪəm] **I** *s* **1.** składka *f*; ***an insurance ~*** składka ubezpieczeniowa **2.** dopłata *f* **3.** ***at a ~*** **a)** w cenie **b)** *sell*: po wyższej cenie **4.** ***put a high ~ on*** przywiązywać dużą wagę do *G* **II** *adj* **1.** *products*: wysokiej jakości **2.** *quality*: wysoki

pre•mo•ni•tion [preməˈnɪʃn] *s* przeczucie *n*; ***he had a ~ he would never see her again*** miał przeczucie, że już nigdy jej nie zobaczy

pre•na•tal [priːˈneɪtl] *adj* prenatalny

pre•oc•cu•pa•tion [priːɒkjʊˈpeɪʃn] *s* **1.** zajęcie *n*; ***her current ~ is music*** obecnie zajmuje się muzyką **2.** zaabsorbowanie *n* (***with*** *I*) **3.** troska *f* (***with*** o *A*) **4.** zainteresowanie *n* (***with*** *I*); **pre•oc•cu•pied** [prɪˈɒkjʊpaɪd] *adj* **1.** zajęty **2.** zaabsorbowany **3.** pochłonięty; ***~ with one's own thoughts*** pochłonięty własnymi myślami; **pre•oc•cu•py** [priːˈɒkjʊpaɪ] *v/t* **1.** absorbować ⟨za-⟩ **2.** ***~ s.o.*** zaprzątać czyjeś myśli

P

pre•or•dain [priːɔːˈdeɪn] *v/t* przeznaczać ⟨-czyć⟩; ***his success was ~ed*** sukces był mu pisany

prep [prep] *s Br* praca *f* domowa

pre•paid [priːˈpeɪd] *adj* **1.** opłacony z góry **2.** *envelope*: zwrotny **3.** *telephone*: w systemie pre-paid, na kartę **4.** *card*: pre-paid

prep•a•ra•tion [prepəˈreɪʃn] *s* **1.** przygotowanie *n*; ***~ for the exam*** przygotowanie do egzaminu; ***make ~s for*** przygotowywać się do *G* **2.** przygotowania *pl* **3.** preparat *m*; ***~s for the hair and skin*** preparaty do pielęgnacji włosów i skóry

pre•par•a•to•ry [prɪˈpærətrɪ] *adj* **1.** przygotowawczy; ***a ~ course*** kurs przygotowawczy **2.** ***~ to*** przed *I*; **preˈpar•a•to•ry school** *s* **1.** *Br* (prywatna) *f* szkoła podstawowa **2.** *Am* (prywatna) szkoła *f* średnia

pre•pare [prɪˈpeə] **I** *v/t* **1.** przygotowywać ⟨-tować⟩; ***~ oneself for one's journey*** przygotować się do podróży; ***~ oneself for death*** przygotować się na śmierć; ***~ the ground for*** przygotować grunt pod *A* **2.** sporządzać ⟨-dzić⟩; ***~ a report*** sporządzić sprawozdanie **3.** *meal*: przyrządzać ⟨-dzić⟩ **II** *v/i* **1.** przygotowywać ⟨-tować⟩ się **2.** szykować się; ***I was preparing to leave*** szykowałem się do wyjścia; **pre•pared** [prɪˈpeəd] *adj* **1.** przygotowany (***for*** do *G*/na *A*) **2.** gotowy (***to do s.th.*** zrobić coś); **pre•pared•ness** [prɪˈpeədnis] *s* gotowość *f*; ***in a state of ~*** w stanie gotowości, w pogotowiu

pre•pon•der•ance [prɪˈpɒndərəns] *no pl s* **1.** przewaga *f* **2.** dominacja *f*; **pre•pon•der•ant** [prɪˈpɒndərənt] *adj* **1.** przeważający **2.** dominujący

prep•o•si•tion [prepəˈzɪʃn] *s GRAM* przyimek *m*

pre•pos•sess•ing [priːpəˈzesɪŋ] *adj* **1.** atrakcyjny; ***it wasn't a ~ sight*** nie był to zbyt piękny widok **2.** ujmujący

pre•pos•ter•ous [prɪˈpɒstərəs] *adj* niedorzeczny, absurdalny

prep•py [ˈprepɪ] *Am infml* **I** *s* uczeń *m* szkoły prywatnej **II** *adj* wyelegantowany

ˈprep school → ***preparatory school***

pre•re•cord•ed [priːrɪˈkɔːdɪd] *adj* nagrany wcześniej

pre•req•ui•site [priːˈrekwɪzɪt] *s* warunek *m* wstępny

pre•rog•a•tive [prɪˈrɒgətɪv] *s* **1.** przywilej *m* **2.** prawo *n* **3.** prerogatywa *f*

Pres•by•te•ri•an [prezbɪˈtɪərɪən] *REL* **I** *adj* prezbiteriański **II** *s* prezbiterianin *m*

pre•school [ˈpriːskuːl] *s Am* przedszkole *n*; **pre-ˈschool** *adj* przedszkolny

pre•scribe [prɪˈskraɪb] *v/t* **1.** *medicine*: przepisywać ⟨-sać⟩ **2.** wymagać **3.** określać ⟨-lić⟩ **4.** nakazywać ⟨-zać⟩

pre•scrip•tion [prɪˈskrɪpʃn] *s* **1.** recepta *f*; ***antibiotics are only available on ~*** antybiotyki dostępne są wyłącznie na receptę **2.** lek *m* na receptę **3.** *medicine*: przepisywanie *n* **4.** przepis *m* **5.** proponowane rozwiązanie *m*

pres•ence [ˈprezns] *s* obecność *f*; ***in the ~ of*** w obecności *G*; ***he didn't notice my ~*** nie zauważył mojej obecności; ***make one's ~ felt*** dać odczuć swoją obecność; ***the US maintains a military ~ in that country*** w tym kraju stacjonują oddziały sił zbrojnych USA; **pres•ence of ˈmind** *s* przytomność *f* umysłu

pres•ent[1] [ˈpreznt] **I** *adj* **1.** obecny; ***in the ~ situation*** w obecnej sytuacji; ***at the ~ time*** obecnie; ***there were 15 people ~ at the meeting*** w spotkaniu uczestniczyło 15 osób; ***analysis showed that traces of arsenic were ~ in the body*** analiza wykazała obecność śladowych ilości arszeniku w organizmie **2.** aktualny **3.** *GRAM* teraźniejszy; ***the ~ tense*** czas teraźniejszy; ***the ~ participle*** imiesłów czasu teraźniejszego **II** *s* **1.** teraźniejszość *f*; ***at ~*** **a)** obecnie **b)** w tej chwili, teraz **2.** ***the ~*** czas teraźniejszy

pres•ent[2] [prɪˈzent] *v/t* **1.** wręczać ⟨-czyć⟩ (***s.o. with*** komuś *A*, ***s.th. to*** coś *D*) **2.** przekazywać ⟨-zać⟩ (***s.o. with*** komuś *A*, ***s.th. to*** coś *D*) **3.** przedstawiać ⟨-wić⟩; ***may I ~ my husband to you?*** pozwól, że przedstawię ci mojego męża; ***he likes to ~ himself as a radical politician*** lubi

P

kreować się na radykała **4.** prezentować ⟨za-⟩ **5.** stanowić; ***this doesn't ~ us with any problems*** to nie stanowi dla nas problemu **6.** *bill, play*: wystawiać ⟨-wić⟩ **7.** *lecture*: wygłaszać ⟨-łosić⟩ **8.** ***~ oneself for an interview*** przyjść na rozmowę kwalifikacyjną; ***the solution ~ed itself*** pojawiło się rozwiązanie **9.** *TV programme*: prowadzić ⟨po-⟩ **10.** *apology*: składać ⟨złożyć⟩

pre•sent³ ['preznt] *s* prezent *m*; ***a Christmas ~*** prezent gwiazdkowy; ***make s.o. a ~ of*** sprezentować komuś *A*

pre•sent•a•ble [prɪ'zentəbl] *adj* **1.** przyzwoity; ***make oneself ~*** doprowadzić się do porządku **2.** do przyjęcia

pre•sen•ta•tion [prezn'teɪʃn] *s* **1.** wręczenie *n* **2.** przekazanie *n* **3.** przedstawienie *n* **4.** prezentacja *f*; ***give a ~ on*** zaprezentować *A*, przeprowadzić prezentację *G* **5.** okazanie *n*; ***on ~ of a membership card*** po okazaniu karty członkowskiej **6.** *TV programme*: prowadzenie *n*

pres•ent-day [preznt'deɪ] *adj* **1.** dzisiejszy **2.** obecny **3.** współczesny

pre•sent•er [prɪ'zentə] *s* prezenter *m*

pre•sen•ti•ment [prɪ'zentɪmənt] *s* złe przeczucie *n*

pres•ent•ly ['prezntlɪ] *adv* **1.** obecnie **2.** po chwili; ***~, the door opened again*** po chwili drzwi znów się otworzyły **3.** wkrótce; ***she'll be here ~*** wkrótce tu będzie

pres•er•va•tion [prezə'veɪʃn] *s* **1.** ochrona *f*; ***environmental ~*** ochrona środowiska **2.** konserwacja *f* **3.** konserwowanie *n*; ***food ~*** konserwowanie żywności **4.** *status quo*: utrzymanie *n* **5.** zachowanie *n*; ***in a good state of ~*** w dobrym stanie; ***the ~ of jobs*** zachowanie stanowisk pracy

pre•ser•va•tive [prɪ'zɜːvətɪv] *s* **1.** środek *m* konserwujący **2.** konserwant *m*; ***contain no artificial ~s*** nie zawierać konserwantów

pre•serve [prɪ'zɜːv] **I** *v/t* **1.** utrzymywać ⟨-mać⟩; ***~ peace*** utrzymać pokój **2.** zachowywać ⟨-chować⟩; ***a well-~d 14th-century house*** dobrze zachowany dom z XIV wieku **3.** chronić ⟨o-⟩; ***~ endangered species from extinction*** chronić zagrożone gatunki przed wyginięciem **4.** *food, leather*: konserwować ⟨za-⟩ **II** *s* **1.** domena *f*; ***football is no longer the ~ of men*** piłka nożna nie jest już wyłącznie domeną mężczyzn **2.** rezerwat *m* **3.** teren *m* łowiecki **4.** dżem *m* **5.** marynata *f*

pre•side [prɪ'zaɪd] *v/i* przewodniczyć (***at/over*** *D*); ***~ at a meeting*** prowadzić zebranie

pres•i•den•cy ['prezɪdənsɪ] *s* **1.** prezydentura *f*; ***during the Clinton ~*** za prezydentury Clintona **2.** prezesura *f* **3.** *European Union*: prezydencja *f*, przewodnictwo *n*

pres•i•dent ['prezɪdnt] *s* **1.** prezydent *m* **2.** przewodniczący *m* **3.** prezes *m*; **pres•i•den•tial** [prezɪ'denʃl] *adj* **1.** prezydencki **2.** *candidate*: na prezydenta

press [pres] **I** *s* **1.** prasa *f*; ***the story was reported in the ~*** doniesiono o tym w prasie; ***get a good ~*** mieć dobrą prasę; ***it had wide ~ coverage*** dużo o tym pisano w prasie **2.** maszyna *f* drukarska; ***go to ~*** pójść do druku **3.** wydawnictwo *n* **4.** drukarnia *f* **5.** TECH prasa *f* **6.** TECH tłocznia *f* **7.** naciśnięcie *n*; ***give s.th. a ~*** nacisnąć coś **8.** ścisk *m* **II** *v/t* **1.** naciskać ⟨-snąć⟩; ***~ a button*** nacisnąć przycisk; ***they are ~ing us to make a quick decision*** naciskają, żebyśmy szybko podjęli decyzję; ***we're ~ed for time*** czas nas goni **2.** przyciskać ⟨-snąć⟩; ***~ one's nose against a window*** przycisnąć nos do szyby **3.** przykładać ⟨przyłożyć⟩ **4.** ***~ one's lips together*** zacisnąć usta **5.** forsować; ***~ one's demands*** forsować swoje żądania **6.** upierać ⟨uprzeć⟩ się przy *L* **7.** *subject*: drążyć **8.** prasować ⟨s-, u-⟩ **9.** tłoczyć ⟨wy-⟩ **10.** *juice*: wyciskać ⟨-snąć⟩; **press ahead** *v/i* **1.** kontynuować realizację (***with*** *G*) **2.** nie ustawać **3.** jechać ⟨po-⟩ dalej, kontynuować podróż; **press for** *v/i* nalegać na *A*

'press a•gen•cy *s* agencja *f* prasowa; **'press box** *s* loża *f* prasowa; **'press card** *s* legitymacja *f* prasowa; **'press clip•ping** → ***press cutting***; **'press con•fe•rence** *s* konferencja *f* prasowa;

P

'press cut•ting *s* wycinek *m* prasowy; **'press gal•ler•y** *s* galeria *f* prasowa
press•ing ['presɪŋ] *adj* **1.** pilny **2.** *request*: usilny
'press of•fice *s* biuro *n* prasowe; **2.** pracownik *m* biura prasowego; **'press re•lease** *s* komunikat *m* prasowy; **press stud** *s Br* zatrzask *m*; **'press-up** *s* (*exercise*) pompka *f*; ***do* ~*s*** robić pompki
pres•sure ['preʃə] **I** *s* **1.** *a. fig* nacisk *m*; ***put* ~ *on s.o.*** wywierać na kogoś nacisk **2.** PHYS TECH ciśnienie *n*; ***air* ~** ciśnienie powietrza **3.** presja *f* **4.** stres *m* **II** *v/t* **1.** wywierać ⟨-wrzeć⟩ nacisk na *A* **2.** zmuszać ⟨-sić⟩ (***s.o. into*** kogoś do *G*); **'pres•sure cook•er** *s* szybkowar *m*; **'pres•sure gauge** *s* manometr *m*, ciśnieniomierz *m*; **'pres•sure group** *s* grupa *f* nacisku; **'pres•sure suit** *s* skafander *m* ciśnieniowy
pres•sur•ize ['preʃəraɪz] *v/t* **1.** *Br* wywierać ⟨-wrzeć⟩ nacisk na *A*; ***she was* ~*d into doing this*** zrobiła to pod naciskiem **2.** zmuszać ⟨-sić⟩; **pres•sur•ized** ['preʃəraɪzd] *adj cabin*: ciśnieniowy
pres•tige [pre'stiːʒ] **I** *s* **1.** prestiż *m* **2.** status *m* **II** *adj* **1.** prestiżowy **2.** luksusowy; **pres•ti•gious** [pre'stɪdʒəs] *adj* prestiżowy; ***a* ~ *award*** prestiżowa nagroda
pres•to ['prestəʊ] *interj* czary mary!
pre•sum•a•bly [prɪ'zjuːməblɪ] *adv* **1.** przypuszczalnie **2.** prawdopodobnie
pre•sume [prɪ'zjuːm] *v/i* **1.** sądzić, przypuszczać; ***you knew that, I* ~** wiedziałeś o tym, jak sądzę; ***I* ~ *so*** sądzę, że tak; ***it is* ~*d that*** prawdopodobnie **2.** ***he's* ~*d dead*** uznano go za zmarłego **3.** zakładać ⟨założyć⟩; ***a person is* ~*d innocent until proven guilty*** każdego uważa się za niewinnego, dopóki jego wina nie zostanie udowodniona; ***the course* ~*s previous knowledge of the subject*** od uczestników kursu wymaga się podstawowej znajomości tematu **4.** śmieć; ***I wouldn't* ~ *to tell you what to do*** nie śmiałbym mówić ci, co masz zrobić; **presume on** *v/i* **1.** nadużywać ⟨-żyć⟩ **2.** wykorzystywać ⟨-tać⟩
pre•sump•tion [prɪ'zʌmpʃn] *s* **1.** przypuszczenie *n*; ***there's a general* ~ *that*** powszechnie sądzi się, że **2.** założenie *n* **3.** *innocence*: domniemanie *n* **4.** tupet *m*, arogancja *f*; **pre•sump•tu•ous** [prɪ'zʌmptʃʊəs] *adj* **1.** arogancki **2.** bezczelny
pre•sup•pose [priːsə'pəʊz] *v/t* zakładać ⟨założyć⟩; ***teachers often* ~ *a high level of knowledge by their students*** nauczyciele często zakładają, że poziom wiedzy ich uczniów jest wysoki; **pre•sup•po•si•tion** [priːsʌpə'zɪʃn] *s* założenie *n*; ***the theory is based on the* ~ *that*** teoria opiera się na założeniu, że
pre-tax [priː'tæks] *adj income*: przed opodatkowaniem, brutto
pre•tence [prɪ'tens] *Br*, **pre•tense** *Am* *s* **1.** pozory *pl*; ***make a* ~ *of*** udawać *A* **2.** pozór *m* **3.** pretensje *pl*; ***I make no* ~ *of being an expert*** nie twierdzę, że jestem ekspertem
pre•tend [prɪ'tend] **I** *v/t* udawać ⟨udać⟩ **II** *v/i* **1.** udawać ⟨udać⟩; ***she's* ~*ing to be asleep*** udaje, że śpi; ***~ that everything is OK*** udawać, że wszystko jest w porządku **2.** rościć sobie pretensje (**to** do *G*); ***I don't* ~ *to have any musical talent*** nie twierdzę, że mam jakiekolwiek uzdolnienia muzyczne **3.** pretendować (***to be*** do *G*) **III** *adj infml* na niby
pre•tense *Am* → ***pretence***
pre•ten•sion [prɪ'tenʃn] *s* **1.** pretensja *f* **2.** pretensjonalność *f*
pre•ten•tious [prɪ'tenʃəs] *adj* pretensjonalny; **pre•ten•tious•ness** [prɪ'tenʃəsnɪs] *s* pretensjonalność *f*
pre•text ['priːtekst] *s* pretekst *m* (**for** do *G*); ***on the* ~ *of*** pod pretekstem *G*
pret•ty ['prɪtɪ] **I** *adj* **1.** ładny; ***a* ~ *name*** ładne imię; (***as***) ***~ as a picture*** jak z obrazka **2.** śliczny; ***you look* ~ *in that dress*** ślicznie wyglądasz w tej sukience **II** *adv* **1.** dość; ***~ difficult*** dość trudny; ***they look* ~ *much the same*** wyglądają prawie tak samo **2.** całkiem **3.** bardzo; ***the play is* ~ *impressive*** przedstawienie naprawdę robi wrażenie
pre•vail [prɪ'veɪl] *v/i* **1.** panować ⟨za-⟩; ***conditions* ~*ing in prisons*** warunki panujące w więzieniach **2.** być rozpowszechnionym **3.** zwyciężać ⟨-żyć⟩ (***over*** *A*); ***fortunately, common sense***

P

~ed na szczęście zwyciężył zdrowy rozsądek; **prevail on** *v/i* przekonywać ⟨-nać⟩ (***s.o. to do s.th.*** kogoś do zrobienia czegoś); **pre•vail•ing** [prɪ'veɪlɪŋ] *adj* **1.** panujący **2.** istniejący **3.** dominujący

prev•a•lence ['prevələns] *s* częstość *f* występowania; **prev•a•lent** ['prevələnt] *adj* **1.** powszechny **2.** (szeroko) rozpowszechniony **3.** panujący

pre•var•i•cate [prɪ'værɪkeɪt] *v/i* uchylać ⟨-lić⟩ się od odpowiedzi; **pre•var•i•ca•tion** [prɪværɪ'keɪʃn] *s* uchylanie *n* się od odpowiedzi

pre•vent [prɪ'vent] *v/t* **1.** zapobiegać ⟨-biec⟩; ***the accident could have been ~ed*** wypadkowi można było zapobiec **2.** powstrzymywać ⟨-mać⟩; ***nothing will ~ him from telling the truth*** nic nie powstrzyma go od powiedzenia prawdy; **pre•ven•tion** [prɪ'venʃn] *s* **1.** zapobieganie *n*; ***crime ~*** zapobieganie przestępczości; ***~ is better than cure*** lepiej zapobiegać niż leczyć **2.** *JUR* prewencja *f* **3.** *MED* profilaktyka *f*; **pre•ven•tive** [prɪ'ventɪv], **pre•vent•a•tive** [prɪ'ventətɪv] *adj* **1.** zapobiegawczy **2.** prewencyjny

pre•view ['priːvjuː] **I** *s* **1.** pokaz *m* przedpremierowy **2.** zapowiedź *f* **II** *v/t* **1.** opisywać ⟨-sać⟩ **2.** recenzować ⟨z-⟩

pre•vi•ous ['priːvɪəs] *adj* **1.** poprzedni; ***she is his daughter from a ~ marriage*** jest jego córką z poprzedniego małżeństwa **2.** wcześniejszy; ***no ~ experience necessary*** wcześniejsze doświadczenie nie jest wymagane; ***~ to*** przed *I*; **pre•vi•ous•ly** ['priːvɪəslɪ] *adv* **1.** poprzednio **2.** wcześniej

pre-war [priː'wɔː] *adj* przedwojenny

prey [preɪ] **I** *s* **1.** ofiara *f*; ***birds of ~*** ptaki drapieżne; ***fall ~ to s.th.*** paść ofiarą czegoś **2.** łup *m*; ***easy ~ for*** łatwy łup dla *G* **II** *v/i* ***~ on s.o.'s mind*** **a)** nie dawać komuś spokoju **b)** dręczyć kogoś; **prey on** *v/i* **1.** polować na *A* **2.** żerować na *L*

price [praɪs] **I** *s* **1.** cena *f*; ***what is the ~ of the shoes?*** ile kosztują te buty?; ***at a reasonable ~*** w rozsądnej cenie; ***at any ~*** za wszelką cenę; ***come at a ~*** mieć wysoką cenę; ***put a ~ on s.o.'s head*** wyznaczyć nagrodę za czyjąś głowę **2.** *stock*: kurs *m* **3.** (*betting*) stawka *f* **II** *v/t* **1.** ustalać ⟨-lić⟩ cenę; ***be ~d at $200*** kosztować 200 dolarów; ***be ~ed too high*** być zbyt drogim **2.** (*a.* ***~ up***) naklejać ⟨-leić⟩ metki z ceną na *A*; ***all items were ~d*** wszystkie towary miały metki z ceną **3.** porównywać ⟨-nać⟩ ceny; **'price-conscious** *adj*: ***be ~*** zwracać uwagę na cenę, kierować się ceną; **'price cut** *s* obniżka *f* (ceny); **'price fix•ing** *s* **1.** zmowa *f* cenowa **2.** ustalenie *n* cen; **'price freeze** *s* zamrożenie *n* cen; **'price in•fla•tion** *s* inflacja *f* cenowa; **price•less** ['praɪslɪs] *adj* bezcenny; **'price list** *s* cennik *m*; **'price range** *s* zakres *m* cenowy; **'price ratio** *s* wskaźnik *m* cen; **'price tag, 'price ticket** *s* **1.** metka *f* z ceną **2.** cena *f*; **'price war** *s* wojna *f* cenowa; **pricey** ['praɪsɪ] *adj infml* drogi

prick [prɪk] **I** *v/t* **1.** kłuć ⟨u-⟩; ***~ one's finger on a needle*** ukłuć się igłą **2.** nakłuwać ⟨-łuć⟩; ***his conscience ~ed him*** sumienie go gryzło, miał wyrzuty sumienia **3.** *hole*: robić ⟨z-⟩ **4.** ***~ (up) one's ears*** **a)** (*animal*) postawić uszy **b)** (*people*) nadstawić uszu **II** *v/i* kłuć; ***feel a ~ing sensation in one's throat*** mieć uczucie kłucia w gardle **III** *s* **1.** ukłucie *n*; ***~s of conscience*** wyrzuty sumienia **2.** nakłucie *n*; ***give s.th. a ~*** nakłuć coś **3.** *vulg* kutas *m* **4.** *vulg* dupek *m*

prick•le ['prɪkl] **I** *s* **1.** kolec *m*; ***roses have ~s*** róże mają kolce **2.** ciarki *pl*; ***a ~ of excitement*** lekki dreszcz podniecenia **II** *v/t* **1.** (*skin*) cierpnąć ⟨ś-⟩ **2.** jeżyć ⟨z-⟩ się **III** *v/t* **1.** kłuć ⟨u-⟩ **2.** drapać ⟨po-⟩; **prick•ly** ['prɪklɪ] *adj* **1.** kolczasty **2.** kłujący; ***~ sensation*** mrowienie **3.** drapiący **4.** *person*: drażliwy

pride [praɪd] **I** *s* duma *f*; ***fill s.o. with ~*** napawać kogoś dumą; ***take ~ in*** być dumnym z *G*; ***be a blow to s.o.'s ~*** zranić czyjąś dumę; ***swallow one's ~*** schować dumę do kieszeni **II** *v/t* ***~ oneself on*** być dumnym z *G*, szczycić się *I*

priest [priːst] *s* **1.** ksiądz *m* **2.** kapłan *m* **priest•ess** ['priːstes] *s* kapłanka *f*; **priest•hood** ['priːsthʊd] *s* **1.** stan *m*

P

duchowny **2.** duchowieństwo *n*; **priest•ly** [priːstlɪ] *adj* kapłański

prig [prɪg] *s* świętoszek *m*; **prig•gish** ['prɪgɪʃ] *adj* świętoszkowaty

prim [prɪm] *adj* **1.** (*a.* **~ and proper**) *person*: sztywny **2.** *outfit*: stosowny, schludny

pri•ma•cy ['praɪməsɪ] *s* **1.** prymat *m* **2.** wyższość *f* **3.** pierwszeństwo *n*; ***give ~ to facts*** przyznawać pierwszeństwo faktom **4.** godność *f* prymasa, prymasostwo *n*

pri•ma don•na [priːmə'dɒnə] *s* primadonna *f*

pri•mae•val [praɪ'miːvl] → ***primeval***

pri•mal ['praɪml] *adj* **1.** prymitywny **2.** pierwotny **3.** podstawowy

pri•ma•ri•ly [praɪ'merɪlɪ] *adv* **1.** głównie; ***course designed ~ for specialists*** kurs przeznaczony głównie dla specjalistów **2.** przede wszystkim

pri•ma•ry ['praɪmərɪ] **I** *adj* **1.** główny **2.** podstawowy; ***~ causes*** podstawowe przyczyny **3.** najważniejszy; ***of ~ importance*** najważniejszy **4.** *phase*: początkowy **II** *s* prawybory *pl*; **pri•ma•ry 'mar•ket** *s* rynek *m* pierwotny; **'pri•ma•ry school** *s* szkoła *f* podstawowa

prime [praɪm] **I** *adj* **1.** główny; ***a ~ candidate*** główny kandydat **2.** podstawowy **3.** najważniejszy **4.** *example*: typowy **5.** najlepszy, najwyższej jakości **6.** ***in ~ condition*** w doskonałym stanie **II** *s* ***in the ~ of one's life*** w kwiecie wieku; ***be past one's ~*** **a)** najlepsze lata mieć już za sobą **b)** być nie pierwszej świeżości **III** *v/t* **1.** instruować ⟨po-⟩ **2.** gruntować ⟨za-⟩ **3.** *bomb*: uzbrajać ⟨-roić⟩; **prime 'min•is•ter** *s* premier *m*; **prime 'mov•er** *s* inicjator *m*; **prime 'num•ber** *s* MATH liczba *f* pierwsza

prim•er ['praɪmə] *s* **1.** grunt *m* **2.** podręcznik *m* (dla początkujących) **3.** *dated* elementarz *m*

'prime rate *s Am* najlepsza *f* stopa procentowa; **prime 'sus•pect** *s* główny podejrzany *m*; **prime 'tar•get** *s*: ***be a ~ for*** **a)** być najbardziej narażonym na ataki *G* **b)** być najczęstszym celem ataków *G*; **'prime time** *s* czas *m* największej oglądalności

pri•me•val [praɪ'miːvl] *adj* **1.** prastary **2.** pierwotny; **3.** prymitywny; ***~ instincts*** prymitywne instynkty

prim•i•tive ['prɪmɪtɪv] *adj* prymitywny

pri•mor•di•al [praɪ'mɔːdɪəl] → ***primeval***

prim•rose ['prɪmrəʊz] *s* pierwiosnek *m* (pospolity); ***evening ~*** wiesiołek

prim•u•la ['prɪmjʊlə] *s* pierwiosnek *m*

prince [prɪns] *s* książę *m*; ***~ Charming*** książę z bajki; **prince•ly** ['prɪnslɪ] *adj* książęcy; **prin•cess** [prɪn'ses] *s* księżniczka *f*

prin•ci•pal ['prɪnsəpl] **I** *adj* **1.** główny; ***the ~ reason*** główny powód **2.** podstawowy **II** *s* **1.** *Am* dyrektor *m* szkoły **2.** *Br* rektor *m* **3.** odtwórca *m* głównej roli **4.** solista *m* **5.** kapitał *m*

prin•ci•pal•i•ty [prɪnsɪ'pælətɪ] *s* księstwo *n*

prin•ci•pally ['prɪnsəplɪ] *adv* **1.** głównie **2.** przede wszystkim

prin•ci•ple ['prɪnsəpl] *s* **1.** zasada *f*; ***it's against my ~s*** to wbrew moim zasadom; ***on ~*** z zasady; ***stick to one's ~s*** trzymać się swoich zasad **2.** reguła *f* **3.** prawo *n*

print [prɪnt] **I** *v/t* **1.** drukować ⟨wy-⟩; ***we ~ed 1000 copies of the book*** wydrukowaliśmy 1000 egzemplarzy książki; ***the model number is ~ed on the box*** na opakowaniu podany jest numer modelu; ***stickers with our logo ~ed on them*** nalepki z naszym logo **2.** publikować ⟨o-⟩ **3.** pisać ⟨na-⟩ nie łącząc liter; ***~ s.th. in block letters*** napisać coś drukowanymi literami **4.** robić ⟨z-⟩ odbitki z *G*; ***have the pictures developed and ~ed*** wywołać film i zrobić odbitki **5.** odciskać ⟨-snąć⟩ ślady (***in*** na *L*) **6.** nadrukowywać ⟨-kować⟩ **7.** zadrukowywać ⟨-kować⟩ **II** *s* **1.** druk *m*; ***in bold ~*** tłustym drukiem; ***in small ~*** małą czcionką **2.** odcisk *m* **3.** ślad *m* **4.** PHOT odbitka *f* **5.** grafika *f* **6.** nadruk *m*; **print out** *v/t* drukować ⟨wy-⟩

print•a•ble ['prɪntəbl] *adj* nadający się do druku; ***his comment was not ~*** jego komentarz nie nadawał się do druku

printed 'circuit *s* obwód *m* drukowany; ***~ board*** płytka drukowana; **'print•ed mat•ter** *s* druki *pl*; **print•er** ['prɪntə] *s* **1.** drukarka *f* **2.** drukarz *m*; **'print•ing**

ink *s* farba *f* drukarska; '**print•ing press** *s* prasa *f* drukarska; '**print•ing works** *pl* drukarnia *f*; '**print•out** *s* wydruk *m*; '**print run** *s* nakład *m*; **print-shop** *s* drukarnia *f*

pri•or [praɪə] **I** *adj* **1.** wcześniejszy; ***without ~ written consent*** bez wcześniejszej pisemnej zgody; ***appointments by ~ arrangement only*** (*doctor*) tylko umówione wizyty, wizyty tylko po wcześniejszym ustaleniu terminu; ***give s.o. ~ notice*** uprzedzić kogoś **2.** uprzedni **3.** ***~ to*** przed *I* **II** *s* *REL* przeor *m*

pri•o•ri•tize [praɪ'ɒrətaɪz] *v/t* **1.** traktować ⟨po-⟩ priorytetowo **2.** szeregować ⟨u-⟩ według ważności; **pri•or•i•ty** [praɪ'ɒrətɪ] *s* **1.** priorytet *m*; ***give ~ to s.th.*** przyznawać czemuś priorytet, traktować coś priorytetowo; ***you need to get your priorities right*** musisz ustalić swoje priorytety **2.** pierwszeństwo *n*; ***have ~ over*** mieć pierwszeństwo przed *I*; ***have ~ at a junction*** mieć pierwszeństwo na skrzyżowaniu

prise [praɪz] *Br*, **prize** *Am v/t lid*: podważać ⟨-żyć⟩; ***~ s.th. open*** **a)** otworzyć coś **b)** wyważyć coś

prism ['prɪzəm] *s* **1.** *PHYS* pryzmat *m* **2.** *MATH* graniastosłup *m*; **pris•mat•ic** [priz'mætɪk] *adj* pryzmatyczny

pris•on ['prɪzn] *s* więzienie *n*; ***be in ~*** być w więzieniu; '**pris•on camp** *s* obóz *m* jeniecki; '**pris•on cell** *s* więzienna cela *f*; **pris•on•er** ['prɪznə] *s* **1.** więzień *m* **2.** jeniec *m*; ***take s.o. ~*** wziąć kogoś do niewoli; ***hold s.o. ~*** trzymać kogoś w niewoli; **pris•on•er of 'war** *s* jeniec *m* wojenny; **pris•on 'guard** *s* strażnik *m* więzienny; '**prison sen•tence** *s* kara *f* więzienia, kara *f* pozbawienia wolności

pris•sy ['prɪsɪ] *adj* **1.** sztywny **2.** grzeczny i ułożony

pris•tine ['prɪstiːn] *adj* **1.** nieskazitelny **2.** *forest*, *beach*: dziewiczy

priv•a•cy ['prɪvəsɪ] *s* **1.** prywatność *f* **2.** zacisze *n*; ***in the ~ of one's own room*** w zaciszu własnego pokoju

pri•vate ['praɪvət] **I** *adj* **1.** prywatny; ***a ~ detective***, ***a ~ eye*** *infml* prywatny detektyw; ***~ property*** własność prywatna; ***~ lessons*** prywatne lekcje, korepetycje **2.** osobisty **3.** poufny; ***keep it ~*** zachowaj to dla siebie **4.** ***be a ~ person*** być zamkniętym w sobie **II** *s* **1.** (*soldier*) szeregowy *m* **2.** ***can we talk in ~?*** czy możemy porozmawiać na osobności?; **pri•vate 'en•ter•prise** *s* **1.** prywatna przedsiębiorczość *f* **2.** prywatni przedsiębiorcy *pl*; '**pri•vate life** *s* życie *n* prywatne; **pri•vate•ly** ['praɪvətlɪ] *adv* prywatnie; '**pri•vate sec•tor** *s ECON* sektor *m* prywatny

pri•va•tion [praɪ'veɪʃn] *s* **1.** ubóstwo *n* **2.** niedostatek *m*

pri•va•ti•za•tion [praɪvətaɪ'zeɪʃn] *s* prywatyzacja *f*; **pri•va•tize** ['praɪvətaɪz] *v/t* prywatyzować ⟨s-⟩

priv•i•lege ['prɪvɪlɪdʒ] **I** *s* **1.** przywilej *m* **2.** zaszczyt *m*; ***I hope to have the ~ of working with you again*** mam nadzieję, że będę miał zaszczyt ponownie z panem pracować **II** *v/t* faworyzować; **priv•i•leged** ['prɪvɪlɪdʒd] *adj* uprzywilejowany

priv•y ['prɪvɪ] *adj* wtajemniczony (**to** w *A*)

prize [praɪz] **I** *s* **1.** nagroda *f*; ***be awarded the Nobel ~*** otrzymać nagrodę Nobla **2.** wygrana *f* **3.** *fig* nagroda *f* **II** *adj* **1.** nagrodzony **2.** cenny **3.** ***a ~ fool*** kompletny głupiec **III** *v/t* **1.** cenić **2.** *Am* → ***prise***; '**prize•fight•er** *s* zawodowy bokser *m*; '**prize•fight•ing** *s* zawodowy boks *m*; '**prize•giv•ing** *s* wręczenie *n* nagród; '**prize mon•ey** *s* **1.** nagroda *f* pieniężna **2.** pula *f* nagród pieniężnych; '**prize•win•ner** *s* zdobywca *m* nagrody, laureat; '**prize-win•ning** *adj* nagrodzony

pro[1] [prəʊ] **I** *s infml* zawodowiec *m*; ***turn ~*** przejść na zawodowstwo **II** *adj* zawodowy

pro[2] [~] *pl pros s*: ***the ~s and cons*** za i przeciw; ***the ~s and cons of*** zalety i wady *G*, plusy i minusy *G*

pro-am [prəʊ'æm] *adj* dla amatorów i zawodowców

prob•a•bil•i•ty [prɒbə'bɪlətɪ] *s* prawdopodobieństwo *n*; ***a high ~ of success*** wysokie prawdopodobieństwo sukcesu; ***in all ~*** najprawdopodobniej

prob•a•ble ['prɒbəbl] *adj* prawdopodobny; **prob•a•bly** ['prɒbəblɪ] *adv* prawdopodobnie

P

pro•ba•tion [prə'beɪʃn] *s* **1.** ***be put on ~*** zostać oddanym pod dozór kuratora; ***she was given two years' ~*** dostała karę w zawieszeniu na dwa lata i oddana pod dozór kuratora **2.** (*work*) okres *m* próbny; **pro•ba•tion•ar•y** [prə'beɪʃnrɪ] *adj period*: próbny; **pro•ba•tion•er** [prə'beɪʃnə] *s* **1.** stażysta *m* **2.** *osoba pod dozorem kuratorskim*; **pro•'ba•tion of•fi•cer** *s JUR* kurator *m*; **pro•'ba•tion pe•ri•od** *s JUR* okres *m* próby

probe [prəʊb] **I** *s* **1.** *MED TECH* sonda *f* **2.** śledztwo *n* **II** *v/t* **1.** badać ⟨z-⟩ **2.** sondować **III** *v/i* **1.** badać ⟨z-⟩ (***into*** *A*) **2.** *fig* prześwietlać ⟨-lić⟩ (***into*** *A*)

prob•ing ['prəʊbɪŋ] *adj* **1.** *look*: badawczy **2.** *question*: dociekliwy

pro•bi•ty ['prəʊbɪtɪ] *s* uczciwość *f*

prob•lem ['prɒbləm] *s* **1.** problem *m*; ***the only ~ is that*** jedynym problemem jest to, że; ***no ~*** **a)** oczywiście, jasne **b)** nie ma problemu **c)** nie ma za co **2.** *MATH* zadanie *n*; ***solve a ~*** rozwiązać zadanie; ***the teacher set us four ~s to do*** nauczyciel zadał nam cztery zadania; **prob•lem•at•ic** [prɒblə'mætɪk] *adj* **1.** trudny; ***a ~ child*** trudne dziecko; **2.** problematyczny

pro•ce•dur•al [prə'siːdʒərəl] *adj* proceduralny; **pro•ce•dure** [prə'siːdʒə] *s* **1.** procedura *f* **2.** postępowanie *n*

pro•ceed [prə'siːd] *v/i* **1.** kontynuować (***with*** *A*) **2.** postępować ⟨-tąpić⟩; ***work is ~ing slowly*** praca idzie wolno **3.** przystępować ⟨-tąpić⟩ (***to do s.th.*** do *G*); ***she ~ed to discuss the report*** przystąpiła do omawiania sprawozdania **4.** udawać ⟨udać⟩ się; ***passengers for Rome should ~ to gate 22*** pasażerowie odlatujący do Rzymu proszeni są do wyjścia numer 22 **5.** iść ⟨pójść⟩; **proceed against** *v/i JUR* wszczynać ⟨-cząć⟩ postępowanie przeciw *D*; **proceed from** *v/i* wynikać ⟨-knąć⟩ z *G*; → ***proceeds***

pro•ceed•ings [prə'siːdɪŋz] *pl* **1.** postępowanie *n* **2.** wydarzenia *pl*, przebieg wydarzeń **3.** protokół *m* **4.** sprawozdanie *n* **5.** materiały *pl* z konferencji

pro•ceeds ['prəʊsiːdz] *pl* dochód *m*, wpływy *pl*; ***the ~ of the concert will go to charity*** dochód z koncertu zostanie przekazany na cele charytatywne

pro•cess ['prəʊses] **I** *s* proces *m*; ***in the ~ of*** w trakcie *G*; ***we're in the ~ of moving house*** przeprowadzamy się, jesteśmy w trakcie przeprowadzki; ***a manufacturing ~*** proces produkcyjny; ***the aging ~*** proces starzenia **II** *v/t* **1.** przetwarzać ⟨-worzyć⟩; ***~ed food*** przetworzona żywność **2.** *film*: wywoływać ⟨-łać⟩ **3.** *complaint*, *application*: rozpatrywać ⟨-trzyć⟩; **pro•cess•ing** ['prəʊsesɪŋ] *s* **1.** przetwarzanie *n* **2.** *film*: wywołanie *n*

pro•ces•sion [prə'seʃn] *s* **1.** procesja *f* **2.** pochód *m* **3.** *funeral*: kondukt *m* **4.** *wedding*: orszak *m*

pro•ces•sor ['prəʊsesə] *s INF* procesor *m*

pro-'choice *adj* **1.** opowiadający się za prawem do aborcji **2.** na rzecz prawa do aborcji

pro•claim [prə'kleɪm] *v/t* **1.** ogłaszać ⟨-łosić⟩; ***the day was ~ed a public holiday*** dzień ten został ogłoszony dniem wolnym od pracy; ***~ s.o. king*** ogłosić kogoś królem **2.** proklamować; **proc•la•ma•tion** [prɒklə'meɪʃn] *s* **1.** ogłoszenie *n* **2.** proklamacja *f*

pro•cliv•i•ty [prə'klɪvətɪ] *s* **1.** skłonność (***for*** do *G*) *f* **2.** tendencja *f* (***for*** do *G*)

pro•cras•ti•nate [prəʊ'kræstɪneɪt] *v/i* zwlekać; **pro•cras•ti•na•tion** [prəʊkræstɪ'neɪʃn] *s* **1.** zwlekanie *n* **2.** zwłoka *f*

pro•cre•ate ['prəʊkrɪeɪt] *v/i* rozmnażać ⟨-nożyć⟩ się; **pro•cre•a•tion** [prəʊkrɪ'eɪʃn] *s* rozmnażanie się *n*, prokreacja *f*

pro•cure [prə'kjʊə] *v/t* **1.** uzyskiwać ⟨-kać⟩ **2.** wystarać się o *A* **3.** zdobywać ⟨-być⟩; ***I managed to ~ two tickets*** udało mi się zdobyć dwa bilety **4.** stręczyć; **pro•cure•ment** [prə'kjʊrmənt] *s* **1.** zaopatrzenie *n* **2.** zakup *m* **3.** stręczycielstwo *n*

prod [prɒd] **I** *v/t* **1.** dźgać ⟨-gnąć⟩ **2.** dźgać ⟨-gnąć⟩ palcem; ***~ s.o. in the ribs*** dźgnąć kogoś palcem w żebra **3.** trącać ⟨-cić⟩ **4.** skłaniać ⟨-łonić⟩ (***s.o. into*** kogoś do *G*) **5.** mobilizować ⟨z-⟩ (***s.o. into*** kogoś do *G*) **II** *v/i* dłubać (***at*** w *L*); ***~ at one's food with a fork*** dłubać widelcem w jedzeniu

prod•i•gal ['prɒdɪgl] *adj* rozrzutny; **prod•i•gal 'son** *s* syn *m* marnotrawny

pro•di•gious [prə'dɪdʒəs] *adj* **1.** ogromny **2.** niesamowity; **prod•i•gy** ['prɒdɪdʒɪ] *s* cudowne dziecko *n*, mały geniusz *m*

pro•duce I [prə'dju:s] *v/t* **1.** produkować ⟨wy-⟩ **2.** wytwarzać ⟨-worzyć⟩ **3.** *children*: rodzić ⟨u-⟩; ***he is the greatest man this nation has ~d*** jest największym człowiekiem, jakiego wydał ten naród **4.** *result, profit*: przynosić ⟨-nieść⟩ **5.** wyjmować ⟨-jąć⟩; ***he ~d a letter from his pocket*** wyjął list z kieszeni **6.** okazywać ⟨-zać⟩ **7.** przedkładać ⟨-dłożyć⟩ **II** ['prɒdju:s] *s* produkty *pl* rolne

pro•duc•er [prə'dju:sə] *s* **1.** producent *m* **2.** wytwórca *m*

prod•uct ['prɒdʌkt] *s* **1.** produkt *m*; ***gross national ~*** produkt narodowy brutto **2.** wyrób *m* **3.** *MATH* iloraz *m*

pro•duc•tion [prə'dʌkʃn] *s* **1.** produkcja *f* **2.** wytwarzanie *n*; ***be in ~*** być produkowanym; ***go out of ~*** zostać wycofanym z produkcji **3.** okazanie *n*; ***on ~ of*** po okazaniu *G*; **pro•'duc•tion capac•i•ty** *s* **1.** zdolność *f* produkcyjna **2.** wydajność *f*; **pro•'duc•tion costs** *pl* koszty *pl* produkcji; **pro•'duc•tion di•rect•or** *s* dyrektor *m* (ds.) produkcji; **pro•'duc•tion line** *s* linia *f* produkcyjna; **pro•'duc•tion man•ag•er** *s* kierownik *m* produkcji

pro•duc•tive [prə'dʌktɪv] *adj* **1.** produktywny **2.** owocny **3.** ***be ~ of*** **a)** prowadzić do *G* **b)** przyczyniać się do *G* **c)** *profit*: przynosić **d)** *emotion*: wzbudzać; **pro•duc•tiv•i•ty** [prɔdʌk'tɪvətɪ] *s* **1.** wydajność *f* **2.** produktywność *f*

'prod•uct li•a•bil•i•ty *s JUR* odpowiedzialność *f* za produkt; **'prod•uct line** *s* linia *f* produktów; **'prod•uct manag•er** *s* menadżer *m* produktu; **'product mix** *s* mieszanka *f* produktów; **'prod•uct place•ment** *s ECON* plasowanie *n* produktu; **'prod•uct range** *s* **1.** asortyment *m* **2.** oferta *f*

prof [prɒf] *s infml* → ***professor***

pro•fane [prə'feɪn] **I** *adj* **1.** bluźnierczy **2.** świecki **II** *v/t* profanować ⟨s-⟩; **profan•i•ty** [prə'fænətɪ] *s* **1.** profanacja *f* **2.** bluźnierstwo *n* **3.** przekleństwo *n*

pro•fess [prə'fes] *v/i* **1.** twierdzić (***that*** że); ***I don't ~ to be an expert in this subject*** nie twierdzę, że jestem w tej dziedzinie ekspertem **2.** oświadczać ⟨-czyć⟩ (***that*** że) **3.** ***she ~ed innocence*** utrzymywała, że jest niewinna **4.** wyrażać ⟨-razić⟩; ***~ one's admiration for*** wyrazić podziw dla *G*; ***to ~ oneself to be satisfied*** wyrazić swoje zadowolenie **5.** wyznawać ⟨-nać⟩, być wyznawcą; **pro•fessed** [prə'fest] *adj* **1.** zdeklarowany **2.** *reason*: oficjalny

pro•fes•sion [prə'feʃn] *s* **1.** zawód *m*; ***the teaching ~*** zawód nauczyciela; ***by ~*** z zawodu **2.** grupa *f* zawodowa; ***the medical ~*** pracownicy służby zdrowia; ***the legal ~*** prawnicy; ***enter the teaching ~*** zostać nauczycielem **3.** *faith*: wyznanie *n*; **pro•fes•sion•al** [prə'feʃnl] **I** *adj* **1.** zawodowy; ***~ qualifications*** kwalifikacje zawodowe; ***~ development*** rozwój zawodowy; ***a ~ basketball player*** zawodowy koszykarz **2.** profesjonalny **3.** fachowy **II** *s* **1.** zawodowiec *m*; ***turn ~*** przejść na zawodowstwo **2.** profesjonalista *m* **3.** fachowiec *m*; **pro•fes•sion•alism** [prə'feʃənəlɪzəm] *s* **1.** profesjonalizm *m* **2.** *SPORT* zawodowstwo *n*; **profes•sion•al•ly** [prə'feʃnlɪ] *adv* **1.** zawodowo; ***he wants to play ~*** *SPORT* chce przejść na zawodowstwo **2.** profesjonalnie **3.** fachowo

pro•fes•sor [prə'fesə] *s* profesor *m*; **pro•fes•sor•ship** [prə'fesəʃɪp] *s* profesura *f*

prof•fer ['prɒfə] *v/t form* **1.** wręczać ⟨-czyć⟩ **2.** podawać ⟨-dać⟩ **3.** *advice*: dawać ⟨dać⟩

pro•fi•cien•cy [prə'fɪʃnsɪ] *s* biegłość *f*; **pro•fi•cient** [prə'fɪʃnt] *adj* biegły (***in/ at*** w *L*)

pro•file ['prəʊfaɪl] **I** *s* **1.** profil *m*; ***in ~*** z profilu **2.** charakterystyka *f* **3.** opis *m*; ***a job ~*** opis stanowiska **4.** zarys *m*; ***the ~ of a tower against the sky*** zarys wieży na tle nieba **5.** *fig* portret *m*; ***a psychological ~*** portret psychologiczny; ***the magazine published a short ~ of the new mayor*** gazeta opublikowała krótką notkę informacyjną o nowym burmistrzu **6.** ***have a high ~*** **a)** być znanym **b)** odgrywać

P

istotną rolę; ***s.th. has a high ~ in the media*** o czymś jest często mowa w mediach; ***raise the ~ of*** **a)** spopularyzować *A* **b)** podnieść status *G*; ***keep a low ~*** **a)** nie zwracać na siebie uwagi **b)** unikać rozgłosu **II** *v/t* **1.** przedstawiać ⟨-wić⟩ **2.** przedstawiać ⟨-wić⟩ sylwetkę

prof•it ['prɒfɪt] **I** *s* **1.** zysk *m*; ***make a ~*** osiągnąć zysk; ***at a ~*** z zyskiem; ***net ~*** zysk netto **2.** dochód *m* **3.** korzyść *f* **4.** pożytek *m*; ***there is no ~ in doing s.th.*** nie warto czegoś robić **II** *v/i* **1.** ***s.o. is ~ing from s.th.*** coś jest korzystne dla kogoś **2.** czerpać korzyści (***from*** z *G*); ***~ by one's mistakes*** uczyć się na własnych błędach **III** *v/i* być korzystnym dla *G*, przynosić korzyść; **prof•it•a•bil•i•ty** [prɒfɪtə'bɪlətɪ] *s* **1.** zyskowność *f* **2.** rentowność *f*; **prof•it•a•ble** ['prɒfɪtəbl] *adj* **1.** zyskowny **2.** rentowny **3.** pożyteczny; **profit and 'loss statement** *s ECON* rachunek *m* zysków i strat

prof•it•eer [prɒfɪ'tɪə] *s infml* zdzierca *m*; **prof•it•eer•ing** [prɒfɪt'ɪərɪŋ] *s infml* zdzierstwo *n*

'prof•it mar•gin *s ECON* marża *f* zysku; **'profit sharing** *s ECON* udział *m* w zyskach

prof•li•gate ['prɒflɪgət] *adj* **1.** rozrzutny **2.** marnotrawny

pro forma invoice [prəʊ'fɔːməɪnvɔɪs] *s* faktura *f* pro forma

pro•found [prə'faʊnd] *adj* **1.** *fig* głęboki; ***a ~ thought*** głęboka myśl **2.** *influence*: ogromny, przemożny **3.** *knowledge, changes*: gruntowny **4.** *disability*: ciężki; **pro•found•ly** [prə'faʊndlɪ] *adv* **1.** *fig* głęboko **2.** ogromnie, wielce **3.** gruntownie

pro•fuse [prə'fjuːs] *adj* **1.** obfity; ***~ bleeding*** obfite krwawienie **2.** ***s.th. is ~*** czegoś jest mnóstwo, czegoś jest w bród **3.** ***he was ~ in his apologies to them*** wylewnie ich przepraszał **4.** ***be ~ in one's praise for s.o.*** nie żałować komuś pochwał; **pro•'fuse•ly** [prə'fjuːslɪ] *adv* **1.** obficie **2.** *thank*: wylewnie; **pro•fu•sion** [prə'fjuːʒn] *s* **1.** mnóstwo *n*; ***irises grow in ~ in the fields*** na polach rośnie mnóstwo irysów **2.** obfitość *f*

prog•no•sis [prɒg'nəʊsɪs] *pl -ses s* **1.** prognoza *f* **2.** *MED* rokowanie *n*

prog•nos•ti•cate [prɒg'nɒstɪkeɪt] *v/t* **1.** prognozować **2.** rokować

pro•gram ['prəʊgræm] **I** *s* **1.** *INF* program *m* **2.** → ***programme I*** **II** *v/t* **1.** programować ⟨za-⟩; ***in this class students will learn how to ~*** na tych zajęciach uczniowie nauczą się programowania **2.** → ***programme II***; **pro•gram•er** *Am* → ***programmer***; **pro•gram•ing** *Am* → ***programming***

pro•gramme ['prəʊgræm] *Br*, **pro•gram** *Am* **I** *s* program *m*; ***a research ~*** program badań; ***what's the ~ for tomorrow?*** *infml* jakie mamy plany na jutro? **II** *v/t* **1.** programować ⟨za-⟩ **2.** nastawiać ⟨-wić⟩ **3.** planować ⟨za-⟩; ***completion is ~d for 2010*** zakończenie prac planuje się na rok 2010

pro•gram•mer ['prəʊgræmə] *s* programista *m*; **pro•gram•ming** ['prəʊgræmɪŋ] *adj* programowanie *n*; **'pro•gram•ming lang•uage** język *m* programowania

pro•gress I ['prəʊgres] *s* **1.** postęp *m* **2.** postępy *pl*; ***make good ~*** **a)** iść szybko **b)** robić szybkie postępy **3.** posuwanie *n* się; ***they watched her slow ~ down the stairs*** obserwowali, jak wolno schodzi po schodzach **4.** ***be in ~*** trwać **II** [prəʊ'gres] *v/i* **1.** robić ⟨z-⟩ postępy **2.** posuwać ⟨-sunąć⟩ się do przodu **3.** postępować **4.** iść; ***the work is ~ing slowly*** praca idzie wolno **5.** ***as the day ~ed*** w miarę upływu dnia

pro•gres•sion [prəʊ'greʃn] *s* **1.** rozwój *m*; ***a rapid ~ of the disease*** szybki rozwój choroby **2.** ciąg *m* **3.** szereg *m* **4.** seria *f*; **pro•gres•sive** [prəʊ'gresɪv] **I** *adj* **1.** postępowy **2.** nowoczesny **3.** stopniowy **4.** postępujący **5.** *verb form*: ciągły **6.** *rock*: progresywny **II** *s* zwolennik *m* postępu, postępowiec *m*; **pro•gres•sive•ly** [prəʊ'gresɪvlɪ] *adv* **1.** stopniowo **2.** coraz

pro•hib•it [prə'hɪbɪt] *v/t* **1.** zabraniać ⟨-ronić⟩; ***~ s.o. from drinking alcohol*** zabronić komuś pić alkohol; ***they were ~ed from going there*** nie wolno im było tam chodzić **2.** uniemożliwiać ⟨-wić⟩; ***~ s.o. from practising sport*** uniemożliwić komuś uprawianie sportu; **pro•hi•bi•tion** [prəʊhɪ'bɪʃn] *s*

P

1. zakaz *m* 2. ∴ Prohibicja; **pro•hib•i•tive** [prə'hɪbɪtɪv] *adj* 1. *costs*: bardzo wysoki 2. *price*: zaporowy 3. *duty*: prohibicyjny

proj•ect I ['prɒdʒekt] *s* 1. projekt *m*; ***a research ~*** projekt naukowo-badawczy 2. plan *m* 3. inwestycja *f* 4. (*school*) praca *f* 5. POLIT program *m* 6. *Am* osiedle *n* II [prə'dʒekt] *v/t* 1. planować ⟨za-⟩; ***the book is ~ed for publication in May*** książka ma zostać wydana w maju 2. przewidywać ⟨-dzieć⟩; ***an increase of 5% is ~ed*** przewiduje się 5-procentowy wzrost 3. *image*, *shadow*: rzucać ⟨-cić⟩ 4. wyświetlać ⟨-lić⟩ 5. MATH rzutować 6. *image*: tworzyć ⟨s-⟩, kreować ⟨wy-⟩ 7. ***~ oneself as a victim*** kreować się na ofiarę; ***~ oneself as a reformer*** starać się uchodzić za reformatora 8. emanować; ***~ an air of self-confidence*** emanować pewnością siebie 9. *voice*: wydawać ⟨-dać⟩ 10. *missile*: wystrzeliwać ⟨-lić⟩ 11. *personality*: dokonywać ⟨-nać⟩ projekcji III [prə'dʒekt] *v/i* wystawać; **'pro•ject lead•er, pro•ject man•ag•er** *s* kierownik *m* projektu

pro•jec•tile [prə'dʒektaɪl] *s* pocisk *m*

pro•jec•tion [prə'dʒekʃn] *s* 1. prognoza *f* 2. przewidywanie *n* 3. projekcja *f*; ***a ~ room*** sala projekcyjna 4. wyświetlenie *n* 5. MATH rzut *m* 6. wystający element *m* 7. wypustka *f* 8. *of rock*: występ *m* 9. *voice*: emisja *f*; **pro•jec•tion•ist** [prə'dʒekʃnɪst] *s* kinooperator *m*; **pro•jec•tor** [prə'dʒektə] *s* projektor *m*; ***a slide ~*** rzutnik

pro•le•tar•i•an [prəʊlə'teərɪən] I *adj* proletariacki II *s* proletariusz *m*; **pro•le•tar•i•at** [prəʊlə'teərɪət] *s* proletariat *m*

pro-'life *adj movement*: w obronie życia poczętego

pro•lif•er•ate [prə'lɪfəreɪt] *v/i* mnożyć ⟨na-⟩ się; ***Internet companies have ~d*** namnożyło się firm internetowych; ***books on the subject are proliferating*** wydaje się wiele książek na ten temat; **pro•lif•er•a•tion** [prəlɪfə'reɪʃn] *s* 1. gwałtowny wzrost *m* liczby 2. duża liczba *f* 3. ***nuclear ~*** rozprzestrzenianie broni jądrowej *n*

pro•lif•ic [prə'lɪfɪk] *adj* 1. płodny 2. ***a ~ scorer*** bramkostrzelny zawodnik 3. *crops*: obfity 4. *growth*: bujny

pro•logue ['prəʊlɒg] *Br*, **pro•log** *Am s* prolog *m*

pro•long [prə'lɒŋ] *v/t* przedłużać ⟨-żyć⟩; **pro•lon•ga•tion** [prəʊlɒŋ'geɪʃn] *s* przedłużenie *n*; **pro•longed** [prə'lɒŋd] *adj* 1. długi 2. przedłużający się

prom [prɒm] *s* 1. *Am* bal *m* 2. *Br dated infml* promenada *f* 3. *Br infml* koncert *m* promenadowy

prom•e•nade [prɒmə'nɑːd] *dated* I *s* 1. promenada *f* 2. spacer *m* II *v/i* spacerować; **prom•e•'nade con•cert** *s Br* koncert *m* promenadowy; **prom•e•'nade deck** *s* pokład *m* spacerowy

prom•i•nence ['prɒmɪnəns] *s* 1. znaczenie *n*; ***give ~ to*** a) kłaść nacisk na *A* b) poświęcać szczególną uwagę *D* 2. popularność *f*; ***rise to ~*** zyskać popularność 3. wysoka pozycja *f*; **prom•i•nent** ['prɒmɪnənt] *adj* 1. znany 2. znaczący 3. widoczny 4. rzucający się w oczy 5. wystający; **prom•i•nent•ly** ['prɒmɪnəntlɪ] *adv* 1. w widocznym miejscu 2. ***feature ~*** pełnić ważną rolę

prom•is•cu•i•ty [prɒmɪ'skjuːətɪ] *s* swoboda *f* seksualna; **pro•mis•cu•ous** [prə'mɪskjʊəs] *adj* prowadzący bogate życie seksualne

prom•ise ['prɒmɪs] I *s* 1. obietnica *f*; ***make a ~*** obiecać, złożyć obietnicę; ***keep a ~*** dotrzymać obietnicy 2. ***show great ~*** a) być obiecującym b) dobrze się zapowiadać; ***they failed to fulfil their ~*** nie spełnili pokładanych w nich nadziei II *v/t* 1. obiecywać ⟨-cać⟩; ***~ not to tell anyone*** obiecaj, że nikomu nie powiesz; ***I'll see what I can do but I can't ~ anything*** zobaczę, co da się zrobić, ale niczego nie obiecuję 2. zapowiadać, zwiastować; ***dark clouds promising rain*** ciemne chmury zapowiadające deszcz III *v/i* zapowiadać się; ***it ~s to be an interesting few days*** zapowiada się kilka interesujących dni; **prom•ising** ['prɒmɪsɪŋ] *adj* obiecujący; ***the weather doesn't look very ~*** pogoda nie zapowiada się najlepiej

prom•is•so•ry note ['prɒmɪsərɪnəʊt] *s* ECON weksel *m* własny

prom•on•to•ry ['prɒmәntrɪ] *s* cypel *m*
pro•mote [prә'mәʊt] *v/t* **1.** promować ⟨wy-⟩; ***the band ~s their new album*** zespół promuje nową płytę **2.** wspierać ⟨wesprzeć⟩; ***~ economic growth*** wspierać wzrost gospodarczy **3.** reklamować ⟨za-⟩ **4.** awansować (***s.o. to s.o.*** kogoś na stanowisko *G*); ***be ~d*** awansować; **pro•mot•er** [prә'mәʊtә] *s* **1.** propagator *m*; ***be a ~ of*** propagować *A* **2.** organizator *m*; **pro•mo•tion** [prә'mәʊʃn] *s* **1.** awans *m* (***to*** na *A*) **2.** promocja *f* **3.** reklama *f* **4.** wspieranie *n* **5.** propagowanie *n*; ***a society for the ~ of science*** stowarzyszenie na rzecz nauki, stowarzyszenie krzewienia nauki; **pro•mo•tion•al** [prә'mәʊʃәnl] *adj* **1.** promocyjny **2.** reklamowy
prompt [prɒmpt] **I** *adj* **1.** natychmiastowy; ***~ action was required*** niezbędne było podjęcie natychmiastowych działań **2.** niezwłoczny; ***be ~ in doing s.th.*** zrobić coś bez zwłoki **3.** punktualny **II** *adv* **1.** dokładnie **2.** punktualnie; ***at 1 o'clock ~*** punktualnie o pierwszej **III** *s* **1.** podpowiedź *f* **2.** *INF* znak *m* zachęty, znak *m* zgłoszenia **IV** *v/t* **1.** skłaniać ⟨-łonić⟩ (***s.o. to do s.th.*** kogoś do zrobienia czegoś) **2.** wywoływać ⟨-łać⟩ **3.** powodować ⟨s-⟩ **4.** podpowiadać ⟨-wiedzieć⟩; **prompt•er** ['prɒmptә] *s* **1.** *THEAT* sufler *m*; ***a ~'s box*** budka suflera **2.** *TV* teleprompter *m*; **prompt•ly** ['prɒmptlɪ] *adv* **1.** natychmiast **2.** niezwłocznie **3.** punktualnie; **prompt•ness** ['prɒmptnɪs] *s* **1.** szybkość *f* **2.** natychmiastowość *f*
prom•ul•gate ['prɒmlgeɪt] *v/t* **1.** rozpowszechniać ⟨-nić⟩ **2.** ogłaszać ⟨-łosić⟩; **prom•ul•ga•tion** ['prɒml'geɪʃn] *s* **1.** rozpowszechnianie *n* **2.** ogłoszenie *n*
prone [prәʊn] *adj* **1.** podatny (***to*** na *A*); ***~ to infection*** podatny na infekcje **2.** ***be ~ to*** mieć skłonność do *G* **3.** narażony (***to*** na *A*); ***injury-~*** narażony na kontuzje **4.** *lie*: na brzuchu
prong [prɒŋ] *s* (*fork*) ząb *m*
pro•noun ['prәʊnaʊn] *s GRAM* zaimek *m*; ***personal ~*** zaimek osobowy
pro•nounce [prә'naʊns] **I** *v/t* **1.** wymawiać ⟨-mówić⟩ **2.** ogłaszać ⟨-łosić⟩; ***~ sentence*** ogłosić wyrok; ***~ s.o. the winner*** ogłosić kogoś zwycięzcą; ***~ s.o. dead*** stwierdzić czyjś zgon **3.** *opinion*: wygłaszać ⟨-łosić⟩ **II** *v/i* **1.** oświadczać ⟨-czyć⟩ **2.** wydawać ⟨-dać⟩ wyrok; **pronounce on** *v/i* wypowiadać ⟨-wiedzieć⟩ się na temat *G*; **pro•nounced** [prә'naʊnst] *adj* **1.** wyraźny **2.** *view*: zdecydowany; **pro•nounce•ment** [prә'naʊnsmәnt] *s* **1.** oświadczenie *n* **2.** *verdict*: orzeczenie *n*
pron•to ['prɒntәʊ] *adv* natychmiast
pro•nun•ci•a•tion [prәnʌnsɪ'eɪʃn] *s* wymowa *f*
proof [pru:f] **I** *s* **1.** dowód *m*; ***there is no ~ that*** nie ma dowodów na to, że; ***~ of purchase*** dowód zakupu; ***~ of identity*** dowód tożsamości **2.** ***~s*** korekta, odbitki korektorskie **3.** stopień *m* zawartości alkoholu; ***the whisky is 80% ~*** *Br* ta whisky ma 40%, *Am* ta whisky ma 44,6% **4.** próba *f* **II** *adj* odporny (***against*** na *A*) **III** *v/t fabric, wood*: impregnować ⟨za-⟩; '**proof•read•er** *s* korektor *m*
prop [prɒp] **I** *v/t* (*a.* ***~ up***) podpierać ⟨-deprzeć⟩; ***she ~ped the ladder against the wall*** oparła drabinę o ścianę; ***he ~ped himself up on the elbow*** podparł się na łokciu **II** *s* **1.** *a. fig* podpora *f* **2.** (*mine*) stempel *m* **3.** *THEAT* rekwizyt *m*; **prop up** *v/t* **1.** podpierać ⟨-deprzeć⟩ **2.** *fig* wspierać ⟨wesprzeć⟩
prop•a•gan•da [prɒpә'gændә] *s* propaganda *f*; **prop•a•gan•dist** [prɒpә'gændist] *s* propagandysta *m*
prop•a•gate ['prɒpәgeɪt] **I** *v/t* **1.** szerzyć **2.** rozpowszechniać ⟨-nić⟩ **3.** *plant*: rozmnażać ⟨-nożyć⟩ **II** *v/i* (*plant*) rozmnażać ⟨-nożyć⟩ się; **prop•a•ga•tion** [prɒpә'geɪʃn] *s* **1.** szerzenie *n* **2.** rozpowszechnianie *n* **3.** *plant*: rozmnażanie *n* (się)
pro•pane ['prәʊpeɪn] *s* propan *m*
pro•pel [prә'pel] *v/t* **1.** napędzać ⟨-dzić⟩; ***electrically ~led*** o napędzie elektrycznym **2.** ***~ s.o. into action*** pchnąć kogoś do działania, pobudzić kogoś do działania; **pro•pel•lant** [prә'pelәnt] *s* **1.** (*aerosol*) propelent *m*, gaz *m* nośny **2.** paliwo *n* napędowe; **pro•pel•ler** [prә'pelә] *s* **1.** śmi-

P

gło *n* **2.** śruba *f* napędowa; **pro•pel•ling** [prə'pelɪŋ] *adj* **1.** *pencil*: automatyczny **2.** ***~ force*** *fig* motor

pro•pen•si•ty [prə'pensətɪ] *s* skłonność *f*; ***she has a ~ to exaggerate*** ma skłonność do przesady

prop•er ['prɒpə] *adj* **1.** odpowiedni; ***in the ~ way*** w odpowiedni sposób **2.** właściwy; ***put s.th. back in its ~ place*** odłożyć coś na swoje miejsce **3.** należyty **4.** stosowny **5.** *Br infml* porządny; ***get a ~ job*** znaleźć sobie porządną pracę **6.** przyzwoity **7.** ***a ~ noun*** nazwa własna; **prop•er•ly** ['prɒpəlɪ] *adv* **1.** właściwie **2.** odpowiednio **3.** jak należy **4.** stosownie **5.** porządnie **6.** przyzwoicie **7.** ***~ speaking*** ściśle mówiąc, dokładnie rzecz biorąc

prop•er•ty ['prɒpətɪ] *s* **1.** własność *f*; ***be s.o.'s ~*** być czyjąś własnością, należeć do kogoś **2.** nieruchomość *f* **3.** właściwość *f*; **prop•er•ty de•'vel•op•er** *s* **1.** deweloper *m* **2.** firma *f* deweloperska; **'prop•er•ty mar•ket** *s* rynek *m* nieruchomości; **'prop•er•ty tax** *s* podatek *m* od nieruchomości

proph•e•cy ['prɒfəsɪ] *s* **1.** proroctwo *n* **2.** przepowiednia *f* **proph•e•sy** ['prɒfəsaɪ] *v/t* przepowiadać ⟨-wiedzieć⟩

proph•et ['prɒfɪt] *s* **1.** prorok *m*; ***a ~ of doom*** czarnowidz **2.** *fig* apostoł *m*; **proph•et•ess** [prɒfɪ'tes] *s* **1.** prorokini *f* **2.** wieszczka *f*; **pro•phet•ic** [prə'fetɪk] *adj* proroczy

pro•phy•lac•tic [prɒfɪ'læktɪk] **I** *adj* **1.** profilaktyczny **2.** zapobiegawczy **II** *s* **1.** MED środek *m* zapobiegawczy **2.** *Am* prezerwatywa *f*; **pro•phy•lax•is** [prɒfɪ'læksɪs] *s* profilaktyka *f*

pro•po•nent [prə'pəʊnənt] *s* **1.** orędownik *m* **2.** propagator *m*

pro•por•tion [prə'pɔːʃn] *s* **1.** proporcja *f*; ***in ~*** proporcjonalny; ***out of ~*** nieproporcjonalny; ***keep things in ~*** nie popadać w przesadę **2.** stosunek *m*; ***in the ~ 2:1*** w stosunku 2:1 **3.** rozmiar *m*; ***grow to huge ~s*** osiągnąć ogromne rozmiary **4.** wielkość *f*; ***of great ~s*** wielkich rozmiarów; **pro•por•tion•al** [prə'pɔːʃnl] *adj* proporcjonalny (***to*** do *G*); **pro•por•tion•al rep•re•sen•'ta•tion** *s* POLIT system *m* proporcjonalny; **pro•por•tion•ate** [prə'pɔːʃnət] *adj* **1.** proporcjonalny (***to*** do *G*)

pro•pos•al [prə'pəʊzl] *s* **1.** propozycja *f* **2.** projekt *m* **3.** oferta *f* **4.** oświadczyny *pl*; **pro•'pos•al form** *s* wniosek *m*

pro•pose [prə'pəʊz] **I** *v/t* **1.** proponować ⟨za-⟩; ***he ~d changing the name of the company*** zaproponował zmianę nazwy firmy; ***it was ~d that*** zaproponowano, aby **2.** zamierzać, mieć zamiar; ***what do you ~ to do now?*** co teraz zamierzasz zrobić? **3.** występować ⟨-tąpić⟩ z *I* **4.** *toast*: wznosić ⟨wznieść⟩; ***~ to s.o.'s health*** wznieść toast za czyjeś zdrowie **II** *v/i* oświadczać ⟨-czyć⟩ się (***to*** *D*)

prop•o•si•tion [prɒpə'zɪʃn] *s* **1.** propozycja *f*; ***make s.o. a ~*** złożyć komuś propozycję **2.** oferta *f* **3.** sprawa *f*; ***be an easy ~*** być łatwym; ***be an attractive ~*** być atrakcyjnym, być kuszącym **4.** *form* twierdzenie *n* **5.** *Am* POLIT poprawka *f*

pro•pound [prə'paʊnd] *v/t* **1.** wysuwać ⟨-sunąć⟩ **2.** przedstawiać ⟨-wić⟩

pro•pri•e•tar•y [prə'praɪətərɪ] *adj* **1.** *information*, *brand*: zastrzeżony **2.** *rights*: własności; **pro•pri•e•tor** [prə'praɪətə] *s* właściciel *m*; **pro•pri•e•tress** [prə'praɪətrɪs] *s dated* właścicielka *f*

pro•pri•e•ty [prə'praɪətɪ] *s* **1.** dobre wychowanie *n* **2.** przyzwoitość *f* **3.** ***proprieties*** zasady dobrego wychowania, konwenanse

pro•pul•sion [prə'pʌlʃn] *s* napęd *m*

pro ra•ta [prəʊ'rɑːtə] **I** *adj* proporcjonalny **II** *adv* proporcjonalnie

pro•sa•ic [prəʊ'zeɪɪk] *adj* **1.** prozaiczny **2.** przyziemny **3.** nieefektowny

pro•scribe [prə'skraɪb] *v/t form* **1.** zabraniać ⟨-ronić⟩ **2.** delegalizować ⟨z-⟩; **pro•scrip•tion** [prə'skrɪpʃn] *s form* zakaz *m*

prose [prəʊz] *s* proza *f*

pros•e•cute ['prɒsɪkjuːt] *v/t* **1.** wnosić ⟨wnieść⟩ oskarżenie przeciwko *D*; ***a prosecuting attorney*** oskarżyciel; ***trespassers will be ~d*** wstęp wzbroniony **2.** ścigać (sądownie); **pros•e•cu•tion** [prɒsɪ'kjuːʃn] *s* **1.** postępowanie *n* sądowe **2.** sprawa *f* sądowa **3.** oskarżenie *n*; ***bring a ~ against***

wnieść oskarżenie przeciwko *D*; ***a witness for the ~*** świadek oskarżenia; ***be liable for ~*** podlegać odpowiedzialności karnej **4.** ***the ~*** oskarżyciel; **pros•e•cu•tor** ['prɒsɪkjuːtə] *s* **1.** oskarżyciel *m* **2.** prokurator *m*

pros•e•lyt•ize ['prɒsəlɪtaɪz] *v/t* nawracać ⟨-rócić⟩

pros•pect **I** ['prɒspekt] *s* **1.** szansa *f*; ***there is a good ~ that*** istnieje duża szansa, że; ***there is no ~ of peace*** nie ma żadnych szans na pokój **2.** perspektywy *pl*; ***good career ~s*** perspektywy zawodowe **3.** perspektywa *f*; ***a pleasant perspective*** przyjemna perspektywa **4.** kandydat *m* **5.** widok *m* (***of*** na *A*); ***with no ~s*** *fig* bez widoków na przyszłość **II** [prə'spekt] *v/i* szukać (***for*** *G*); **pro•spec•tive** [prə'spektɪv] *adj* **1.** *client*: potencjalny **2.** przyszły **3.** *change*: nadchodzący; **pros•pec•tor** [prə'spektə] *s* poszukiwacz *m*

pros•per ['prɒspə] *v/i* prosperować; **pros•per•i•ty** [prɒ'sperətɪ] *s* **1.** dobrobyt *m* **2.** powodzenie *n* **3.** *of economy*: okres *m* prosperity, rozkwit *m*; **pros•per•ous** ['prɒspərəs] *adj* **1.** dobrze prosperujący **2.** bogaty

pros•tate ['prɒsteɪt] *s* ANAT prostata *f*

pros•the•sis [prɒs'θiːsɪs] *pl -ses s* proteza *f*

pros•ti•tute ['prɒstɪtjuːt] *s* prostytutka *f*; **pros•ti•tu•tion** [prɒstɪ'tjuːʃn] *s* prostytucja *f*

pros•trate **I** ['prɒstreɪt] **I** *adj* **1.** twarzą do ziemi; ***fall ~ before*** paść na twarz przed *I* **2.** *fig* zdruzgotany (***with*** *I*) **3.** w rozpaczliwym stanie **II** [prə'streɪt] *v/t* ***be ~d*** być zdruzgotanym

pro•tag•o•nist [prə'tægənɪst] *s* **1.** *book, play*: główny bohater *m* **2.** protagonista *m* **3.** orędownik *m*

pro•tect [prə'tekt] *v/t* **1.** chronić ⟨o-⟩ (***s.th. against/from*** coś przed *I*) **2.** zabezpieczać ⟨-czyć⟩ (***s.th. against/from*** coś przed *I*) **3.** *interests*: bronić **4.** osłaniać ⟨-łonić⟩; ***~ s.th. from the wind*** osłaniać coś od wiatru

pro•tec•tion [prə'tekʃn] *s* ochrona *f*, osłona *f*, zapezpieczenie *n*; ***~ against the wind and rain*** ochrona przed wiatrem i deszczem; ***under police ~*** pod ochroną policji; **pro•tec•tion•ism** [prə'tekʃnɪzəm] *s* ECON protekcjonizm *m*; **pro•'tec•tion mon•ey** *s infml* haracz *m*; **pro•'tec•tion rack•et** *s infml* wymuszanie *n* haraczu; **pro•tec•tive** [prə'tektɪv] *adj* **1.** ochronny; ***a ~ layer of varnish*** ochronna warstwa lakieru **2.** zabezpieczający **3.** opiekuńczy (***towards*** w stosunku do *G*); ***over-~*** nadopiekuńczy; **pro•tec•tive 'cloth•ing** *s* odzież *f* ochronna; **pro•tec•tive 'cus•to•dy** *s* areszt *m* prewencyjny; **pro•tec•tor** [prə'tektə] *s* **1.** opiekun *m* **2.** obrońca *m* **3.** ochraniacz *m*; ***knee ~s*** nakolanniki; **pro•tec•tor•ate** [prə'tektərət] *s* POLIT protektorat *m*

pro•té•gé ['prɒtəʒeɪ] *s* protegowany *m*; **pro•té•gée** ['prɒtəʒeɪ] *s* protegowana *f*

pro•tein ['prəʊtiːn] *s* białko *n*

pro•test **I** ['prəʊtest] *s* **1.** protest *m*; ***in ~ at*** w proteście przeciwko *D*, na znak protestu przeciwko *D*; ***without ~*** bez protestów, bez sprzeciwu; ***a ~ march*** marsz protestacyjny **2.** sprzeciw *m* **3.** ***under ~*** niechętnie **II** [prə'test] *v/i* **1.** protestować ⟨za-⟩ (***about/against/at*** przeciw *D*) **2.** wyrażać ⟨-zić⟩ niezadowolenie (***about/against/at*** z powodu *G*) **3.** zapewniać ⟨-nić⟩ (***that*** że) **III** [prə'test] *v/t* **1.** protestować ⟨za-⟩ przeciwko *D* **2.** oprotestowywać ⟨-tować⟩ **3.** zapewniać ⟨-nić⟩ o *L*; ***he ~ed his innocence*** zapewniał, że jest niewinny

Prot•es•tant ['prɒtɪstənt] **I** *s* protestant *m*, protestantka *f* **II** *adj* protestancki; **Prot•es•tant•ism** ['prɒtɪstəntɪzəm] *s* protestantyzm *m*

prot•es•ta•tion [prɒtes'teɪʃn] *s* **1.** zapewnienie *n*; ***his ~s of innocence*** jego zapewnienia, że jest niewinny **2.** protest *m*

pro•test•er [prə'testə] *s* protestujący *m*

pro•to•col ['prəʊtəkɒl] *s* protokół *m*; ***diplomatic ~*** protokół dyplomatyczny

pro•ton ['prəʊtɒn] *s* PHYS proton *m*

pro•to•type ['prəʊtətaɪp] *s* prototyp *m*

pro•tract•ed [prə'træktɪd] *adj* **1.** przedłużający się **2.** przeciągający się

pro•trac•tor [prə'træktə] *s* MATH kątomierz *m*

pro•trude [prə'truːd] *v/i* **1.** wystawać **2.** odstawać; **pro•trud•ing** [prə'truː-

P

dıŋ] *adj* **1.** wystający **2.** *ears*: odstający **3.** *eyes*: wypukły, *infml* wyłupiasty; **pro•tru•sion** [prə'tru:ʒn] *s* **1.** *rock*: występ *m* **2.** wypukłość *f*

pro•tu•ber•ance [prə'tju:bərəns] *s* **1.** wypukłość *f* **2.** zgrubienie *n*; **pro•tu•ber•ant** [prə'tju:bərənt] *adj* **1.** wypukły **2.** wystający **3.** *eyes*: wypukły, *infml* wyłupiasty

proud [praʊd] **I** *adj* dumny (**of** z *G*); ***be ~ of oneself*** być z siebie dumnym; ***I feel ~ to be Australian*** jestem dumny, że jestem Australijczykiem **II** *adv* ***do s.o. ~*** *Br dated* potraktować kogoś po królewsku; **proud•ly** ['praʊdlı] *adv* dumnie

prov•a•ble ['pru:vəbl] *adj* (możliwy) do udowodnienia

prove [pru:v] **I** *v/t* (*proved*; *proved/proven*) udowadniać ⟨-wodnić⟩; ***~ oneself*** sprawdzić się; ***he ~d himself to be a good musician*** udowodnił, że jest dobrym muzykiem **II** *v/i* (*proved*; *proved/proven*) okazywać ⟨-zać⟩ się; ***it ~d (to be) difficult to establish the truth*** prawda okazała się trudna do ustalenia; **prov•en** ['pru:vn] **I** *Past Perfect* → **prove II** *adj* **1.** sprawdzony **2.** wypróbowany **3.** udowodniony

prov•e•nance ['prɒvənəns] *s* pochodzenie *n*

prov•erb ['prɒvɜ:b] *s* przysłowie *n*; **pro•ver•bi•al** [prə'vɜ:bıəl] *adj* przysłowiowy

pro•vide [prə'vaıd] **I** *v/t* **1.** dostarczać ⟨-czyć⟩ **2.** zapewniać ⟨-nić⟩ **3.** *service*: świadczyć **4.** *answer*: dawać ⟨dać⟩, dostarczać ⟨-czyć⟩ **5.** stanowić **6.** ***each student is ~d with an identity card*** każdy student otrzymuje legitymację; ***the kitchen is ~d with an electric stove*** kuchnia jest wyposażona w kuchenkę elektryczną; ***the product is ~d with software*** do produktu dołączone jest oprogramowanie **II** *v/i* (*contract*) stanowić, przewidywać (***that*** że); **provide against** *v/i* zabezpieczać ⟨-czyć⟩ się na wypadek *G*; **provide for** *v/i* **1.** przewidywać ⟨-dzieć⟩ **2.** utrzymywać ⟨-mać⟩; ***she has three children to ~*** ma troje dzieci na utrzymaniu **3.** zabezpieczać ⟨-czyć⟩ się na wypadek *G*

provided [prə'vaıdıd] *conj* ***~ (that)***: **a)** o ile **b)** pod warunkiem, że

prov•i•dence ['prɒvıdəns] *s* opatrzność *f*; **prov•i•dent** ['prɒvıdənt] *adj* **1.** przezorny **2.** przewidujący; **prov•i•den•tial** [prɒvı'denʃl] *adj* szczęśliwy; **prov•i•den•tial•ly** [prɒvı'denʃəlı] *adv* **1.** szczęśliwie **2.** szczęśliwym zbiegiem okoliczności

pro•vid•er [prə'vaıdə] *s* **1.** dostawca *m*; ***an Internet ~*** dostawca usług internetowych **2.** żywiciel *m*; ***the family's sole ~*** jedyny żywiciel rodziny; **pro•vid•ing** [prə'vaıdıŋ] → ***provided***

prov•ince ['prɒvıns] *s* **1.** prowincja *f* **2.** ***~s*** prowincja; ***in the ~s*** na prowincji **3.** ***be the ~ of s.o.*** leżeć w czyjejś gestii, podlegać czyjejś kompetencji; ***be outside s.o.'s ~*** nie leżeć w czyjejś gestii, nie należeć do czyichś kompetencji

pro•vin•cial [prə'vınʃl] **I** *adj* **1.** prowincjonalny **2.** zaściankowy **3.** regionalny **II** *s* prowincjusz *m*

pro•vi•sion [prə'vıʒn] **I** *s* **1.** zapewnienie *n*; ***health care ~*** opieka zdrowotna **2.** zaopatrzenie *n* (**of** w *A*) **3.** dostarczanie *n* **4.** *service*: świadczenie *n* **5.** zabezpieczenie *n*; ***make ~s for s.o.*** zabezpieczyć kogoś **6.** ***~s*** *dated* prowiant **7.** (*contract*) warunek *m*; ***under the ~ that*** pod warunkiem, że **II** *v/t* zaopatrywać ⟨-trzyć⟩ (***s.o. with*** kogoś w *A*)

pro•vi•sion•al [prə'vıʒnl] *adj* **1.** tymczasowy; ***a ~ government*** rząd tymczasowy **2.** wstępny; ***let's make a ~ appointment for Thursday*** umówmy się wstępnie na czwartek; **pro•vi•sion•al•ly** [prə'vıʒənlı] *adv* **1.** tymczasowo **2.** wstępnie

pro•vi•so [prə'vaızəʊ] *pl -sos s* warunek *m*; ***with the ~ that*** pod warunkiem, że

prov•o•ca•tion [prɒvə'keıʃn] *s* prowokacja *f*; ***at the slightest ~*** z byle powodu; ***without ~*** bez powodu; **pro•voc•a•tive** [prə'vɒkətıv] *adj* **1.** prowokacyjny **2.** prowokujący

pro•voke [prə'vəʊk] *v/t* **1.** prowokować ⟨s-⟩; ***~ s.o. into doing s.th.*** sprowokować kogoś do zrobienia czegoś; ***she's easily ~d*** łatwo ją sprowokować **2.** *anger*, *reaction*: wywoływać ⟨-łać⟩ **3.** powodować ⟨s-⟩

P

prow [praʊ] *s lit ship*: dziób *m*
prow•ess ['praʊəs] *s* **1.** umiejętności *pl* **2.** ***sexual ~*** jurność *f* **3.** męstwo *n*
prowl [praʊl] **I** *v/i* **1.** skradać się **2.** *fig* grasować **3.** ***~ around*** *infml* kręcić się (w pobliżu) **II** *v/t* ***a muderer ~ing the streets of New Orleans*** morderca siejący postrach na ulicach Nowego Orleanu **III** *s* ***be on the ~*** skradać się; ***be on the ~ for*** poszukiwać *G*; '**prowl car** *s Am* radiowóz *m* patrolowy; **prowl•er** ['praʊlə] *s*: ***there was a ~ outside*** ktoś podejrzany kręcił się koło domu
prox•im•i•ty [prɒk'sɪmətɪ] *s* bliskość *f*; ***in the ~ of*** w pobliżu *G*; ***in close ~ to each other*** niedaleko od siebie
prox•y ['prɒksɪ] *s* **1.** pełnomocnictwo *n* **2.** upoważnienie *n* **3.** pełnomocnik *m*; ***vote by ~*** głosować przez pełnomocnika **4.** osoba *f* upoważniona **5.** prokura *f*
prude [pru:d] *s* osoba *f* pruderyjna; ***be a ~*** być pruderyjnym
pru•dence ['pru:dns] *s* **1.** rozwaga *f* **2.** rozsądek *m*; **pru•dent** ['pru:dnt] *adj* **1.** rozważny **2.** rozsądny; **pru•dent•ly** ['pru:dntlɪ] *adv* **1.** z rozwagą **2.** rozsądnie
prud•er•y ['pru:dərɪ] *s* pruderia *f*; **prud•ish** ['pru:dɪʃ] *adj* pruderyjny
prune[1] [pru:n] *s* suszona śliwka *f*
prune[2] [~] *v/t* **1.** *branches*: przycinać ⟨-ciąć⟩ **2.** *hedge*: przystrzygać ⟨-rzyc⟩ **3.** *text*: skracać ⟨-rócić⟩ **4.** *details*: usuwać ⟨usunąć⟩ **5.** *workforce*: zmniejszać ⟨-szyć⟩
pru•ri•ence ['prʊərɪəns] *s* lubieżność *f*; **pru•ri•ent** ['prʊərɪənt] *adj* **1.** lubieżny **2.** *interest*: chorobliwy
prus•sic ac•id [prʌsɪk'æsɪd] *s CHEM* kwas *m* pruski
pry[1] [praɪ] *Am* → ***prise***
pry[2] [~] *v/i* **1.** ***~ into*** **a)** wtykać nos w *A* **b)** wtrącać się w *A* **2.** ***sorry, I didn't mean to ~*** przepraszam, nie chciałem być wścibski; **pry•ing** ['praɪɪŋ] *adj* wścibski; ***away from the ~ eyes*** z dala od wścibskich spojrzeń
PS [pi:'es] *s* **1.** PS *n* **2.** postscriptum *n*
psalm [sɑ:m] *s REL* psalm *m*
pseud [sju:d] *s Br infml* pozer *m*
pseu•do•nym ['sju:dənɪm] *s* pseudonim *m*; ***under a ~*** pod pseudonimem

pso•ri•a•sis [sə'raɪəsɪs] *s MED* łuszczyca *f*
psy•che ['saɪkɪ] *s* **1.** psychika *f* **2.** *lit* psyche *f*
psy•che•del•ic [saɪkə'delɪk] *adj* **1.** *drug*: halucynogenny **2.** *music*: psychodeliczny
psy•chi•at•ric [saɪkɪ'ætrɪk] *adj* **1.** psychiatryczny **2.** *patient*: chory psychicznie; **psy•chi•a•trist** [saɪ'kaɪətrɪst] *s* psychiatra *m*; **psy•chi•a•try** [saɪ'kaɪətrɪ] *s* psychiatria *f*
psy•chic ['saɪkɪk] **I** *adj* **1.** paranormalny **2.** parapsychologiczny **3.** ponadzmysłowy **4.** ***be ~*** **a)** mieć zdolności paranormalne **b)** być medium; ***I'm not ~!*** *infml* nie jestem jasnowidzem! **5.** *form* psychiczny **II** *s* **1.** osoba *f* mająca zdolności paranormalne **2.** medium *n*
psy•cho•a•nal•y•sis [saɪkəʊə'næləsɪs] *s* psychoanaliza *f*; **psy•cho•an•a•lyst** [saɪkəʊ'ænəlɪst] *s* psychoanalityk *m*
psy•cho•an•a•lyze [saɪkəʊ'ænəlaɪz] *v/t* poddawać ⟨-dać⟩ psychoanalizie
psy•cho•bab•ble ['saɪkəʊbæbl] *s* żargon *m* psychologiczny
psy•cho•log•i•cal [saɪkə'lɒdʒɪkl] *adj* psychologiczny; ***~ warfare*** wojna psychologiczna; **psy•cho•log•i•cal•ly** [saɪkə'lɒdʒɪklɪ] *adv* psychologicznie; **psy•chol•o•gist** [saɪ'kɒlədʒɪst] *s* psycholog *m*; **psy•chol•o•gy** [saɪ'kɒlədʒɪ] *s* psychologia *f*
psy•cho•met•ric [saɪkə'metrɪk] *adj* psychometryczny
psy•cho•path ['saɪkəʊpæθ] *s* psychopata *m*
psy•cho•sis [saɪ'kəʊsɪs] *pl -ses* [~si:z] *s MED* psychoza *f*
psy•cho•so•mat•ic [saɪkəʊsə'mætɪk] *adj* psychosomatyczny
psy•cho•ther•a•pist [saɪkəʊ'θerəpɪst] *s* psychoterapeuta *m*; **psy•cho•ther•a•py** [saɪkəʊ'θerəpɪ] *s* psychoterapia *f*
psy•chot•ic [saɪ'kɒtɪk] *adj* psychotyczny
psych out [saɪk'aʊt] *v/t infml* zastraszać ⟨-szyć⟩, straszyć ⟨prze-⟩; **psych up** [saɪk'ʌp] *v/t*: ***get psyched up for***, ***psych oneself up for*** *infml* przygotowywać ⟨-tować⟩ się psychicznie do *G*

P

PTA [piːtiːˈeɪ] *abbr* (=***parent-teacher association***) komitet *m* rodzicielski

PTO [piːtiːˈəʊ] *abbr* (=***please turn over***) *Br* verte

pub [pʌb] *s* pub *m*; ***go on a ~ crawl*** zrobić rundkę po pubach

pu•ber•ty [ˈpjuːbətɪ] *s* okres *m* dojrzewania (płciowego), pokwitanie *n*; ***reach ~*** wejść w okres dojrzewania

pu•bic [ˈpjuːbɪk] *adj* łonowy

pub•lic [ˈpʌblɪk] **I** *adj* **1.** publiczny; ***a ~ figure*** osoba publiczna; ***make s.th. ~*** ujawnić coś; ***in the ~ interest*** w interesie publicznym **2.** społeczny; ***~ awareness*** świadomość społeczna **II** *s* **1.** ***the ~*** **a)** społeczeństwo **b)** ludzie **c)** zwiedzający; ***the viewing ~*** widzowie **2.** ***in ~*** publicznie; **pub•lic ad•ˈdress sys•tem** *s* system *m* nagłaśniający

pub•li•can [ˈpʌblɪkən] *s Br* **1.** właściciel *m* pubu **2.** kierownik *m* pubu

pub•li•ca•tion [pʌblɪˈkeɪʃn] *s* **1.** wydanie *n*; ***~ date*** data wydania **2.** publikacja *f* **3.** ukazanie *n* się

pub•lic ex•ˈpen•di•ture *s* wydatki *pl* na cele publiczne; **pub•lic ˈhol•i•day** *s* (*dzień wolny od pracy*) święto *n*

pub•li•cist [ˈpʌblɪsɪst] *s* agent *m* reklamowy

pub•lic•i•ty [pʌbˈlɪsətɪ] *s* **1.** reklama *f*; ***she works in ~*** pracuje w reklamie **2.** ***there has been a lot of ~ surrounding the event*** wydarzeniu towarzyszyło duże zainteresowanie mediów; **pub•ˈlic•i•ty cam•paign** *s* kampania *f* promocyjna; **pub•ˈlic•i•ty ma•te•ri•al** *s* materiał *m* reklamowy; **pub•ˈlic•i•ty stunt** *s* chwyt *m* reklamowy

P

pub•li•cize [ˈpʌblɪsaɪz] *v/t* **1.** nagłaśniać ⟨-łośnić⟩ **2.** reklamować ⟨za-⟩

pub•lic li•a•ˈbil•i•ty in•sur•ance *s* ubezpieczenie *n* od odpowiedzialności cywilnej; **pub•lic ˈli•bra•ry** *s* biblioteka *f* publiczna; **pub•lic lim•it•ed ˈcom•pa•ny** *s* spółka *f* akcyjna; **pub•lic•ly** [ˈpʌblɪklɪ] *adv* publicznie; **pub•lic o•ˈpin•ion** *s* opinia *f* publiczna; **pub•lic ˈpros•e•cu•tor** *s Br* prokurator *m*, oskarżyciel *m* publiczny; **pub•lic re•ˈla•tions** *pl* public relations *pl*; **pub•lic ˈschool** *s* **1.** *Br* prywatna szkoła *f* średnia **2.** *Am* szkoła *f* państwowa; **pub•lic ˈsec•tor** *s* sektor *m* prywatny; **pub•lic-ˈspir•it•ed** *adj* **1.** społecznikowski **2.** obywatelski; **pub•lic ˈtrans•port** *s* transport *m* publiczny; **pub•lic u•ˈtil•i•ty** *s* przedsiębiorstwo *n* użyteczności publicznej

pub•lish [ˈpʌblɪʃ] *v/t* **1.** wydawać ⟨-dać⟩ **2.** publikować ⟨o-⟩ **3.** (*internet*) publikować ⟨o-⟩, umieszczać ⟨umieścić⟩; **pub•lish•er** [ˈpʌblɪʃə] *s* wydawca *m*; **pub•lish•ing** [ˈpʌblɪʃɪŋ] *s* **1.** działalność *f* wydawnicza **2.** wydawanie *n* **3.** publikowanie *n*; **ˈpub•lish•ing com•pa•ny**, **ˈpub•lish•ing house** *s* wydawnictwo *n*

puce [pjuːs] *adj* **1.** fioletowobrązowy **2.** ciemnoczerwony **3.** ***~ with embarrassment*** purpurowy ze wstydu

puck [pʌk] *s* SPORT krążek *m* (hokejowy)

puck•er [ˈpʌkə] **I** *v/t* **1.** marszczyć ⟨z-⟩ **2.** krzywić ⟨s-⟩ **3.** ***~ one's lips*** **a)** złożyć usta (w ryjek) **b)** ściągnąć usta **II** *v/i* **1.** marszczyć ⟨z-⟩ się **2.** krzywić ⟨s-⟩ się

pud [pʊd] *Br infml* → ***pudding***

pud•ding [ˈpʊdɪŋ] *s* **1.** *Br* deser *m* **2.** *Br* pudding *m* **3.** *Am* budyń *m*; ***chocolate ~*** budyń czekoladowy, deser czekoladowy

pud•dle [ˈpʌdl] *s* kałuża *f*

pu•er•ile [ˈpjuəraɪl] *adj* **1.** dziecinny **2.** infantylny

puff [pʌf] **I** *v/i* **1.** *pipe*: pykać (**at**/**on** *A*) **2.** *cigarette*: palić, *infml* kurzyć (**at**/**on** *A*) **3.** zaciągać się (**at**/**on** dymem z *G*) **4.** (*smoke*) wydobywać się **5.** dyszeć **II** *v/t* **1.** wypuszczać ⟨-puścić⟩; ***chimneys were ~ing out clouds of smoke*** z kominów unosiły się kłęby dymu **2.** dmuchać ⟨-chnąć⟩ **3.** ***be ~ed up with pride*** pękać z dumy **III** *s* **1.** zaciągnięcie *n* się; ***take a ~ on a cigarette*** zaciągnąć *n* się papierosem **2.** pyknięcie *n*; ***take a ~ on a pipe*** pyknąć z fajki **3.** wdech *m* **4.** *wind*: podmuch *m* **5.** obłok *m*, obłoczek *m* **6.** COOK ptyś *m*; **puff out** *v/t* **1.** *cheeks*: wydymać ⟨-dąć⟩ **2.** nadmuchiwać ⟨-chać⟩; **puff up** *v/i* **1.** puchnąć ⟨s-⟩ **2.** nadymać ⟨-dąć⟩ się **3.** (*dough*) rosnąć ⟨u-⟩; **puffed** [pʌft] *adj Br infml* zdyszany

puf•fin [ˈpʌfɪn] *s* (*bird*) maskonur *m*

puff ˈpas•try *s* ciasto *n* francuskie

puff•y ['pʌfɪ] *adj* **1.** opuchnięty **2.** *eyes*: podpuchnięty, spuchnięty **3.** *clouds*: puszysty

pug [pʌg] *s* (*dog*) mops *m*

pug•na•cious [pʌg'neɪʃəs] *adj* **1.** zadziorny **2.** wojowniczy; **pug•nac•i•ty** [pʌg'næsətɪ] *s* **1.** zadziorność *f* **2.** wojowniczość *f*

puke [pjuːk] *infml* **I** *v/i* (*a.* **~ up**) rzygać **II** *v/t* (*a.* **~ up**) rzygać ⟨wy-⟩ **III** *s* rzygowiny *pl*

pull [pʊl] **I** *v/t* **1.** ciągnąć ⟨po-⟩; **~ *s.o.'s hair*** ciągnąć kogoś za włosy **2.** pociągać ⟨-gnąć⟩ za *A*; ***~ the trigger*** pociągnąć za spust; ***~ a door open*** (***shut***) otworzyć (zamknąć) drzwi; ***~ s.o.'s leg*** *fig* nabierać kogoś; ***~ the strings*** *fig* pociągać za sznurki **3.** wyciągać ⟨-gnąć⟩; ***~ a plug out*** wyciągnąć wtyczkę; ***he ~ed his sweater on*** włożył sweter; ***she ~ed her hand back*** cofnęła rękę **4.** ***~ the curtains*** **a)** rozsunąć zasłony **b)** zasunąć zasłony **5.** *muscle*: naciągać ⟨-gnąć⟩ **6.** *crowd*: przyciągać ⟨-gnąć⟩ **7.** ***~ the car to the left*** skręcić w lewo **8.** ***~ a trick on s.o.*** robić komuś kawał **9.** ***not ~ one's punches*** nie przebierać w słowach **10.** *Br infml* pociągać, *infml* rajcować **11.** *infml* odwoływać ⟨-łać⟩ **II** *v/i* **1.** ciągać ⟨-gnąć⟩; ***don't ~ so hard or the handle will come off*** nie ciągnij tak mocno, bo oderwiesz uchwyt **2.** (*car*, *whells*) skręcać ⟨-cić⟩ **3.** wiosłować **III** *s* **1.** pociągnięcie *n*; ***give s.th. a ~*** pociągnąć za coś **2.** PHYS przyciąganie *n*; ***gravitational ~*** siła ciążenia **3.** *fig* siła *f* przyciągania; ***magnetic ~*** magnetyzm **4.** *infml* wpływy *pl* **5.** zaciągnięcie *n* się; ***take a ~ on*** zaciągnąć się *I* **6.** łyk *m* **7.** *muscles*: naciągnięcie *n* **8.** (*for pulling*) uchwyt *m* **9.** sznurek *m*; **pull ahead** *v/i* **1.** wysuwać ⟨-sunąć⟩ się do przodu **2.** uzyskiwać ⟨-kać⟩ przewagę (***of*** nad *L*); **pull apart** *v/t* rozdzielać ⟨-lić⟩; **pull away** *v/i* ruszać ⟨-szyć⟩ (z miejsca); **pull down** *v/t* **1.** burzyć ⟨z-⟩ **2.** opuszczać ⟨opuścić⟩; **pull in I** *v/i* **1.** zatrzymywać ⟨-mać⟩ się **2.** zjeżdżać ⟨zjechać⟩ na pobocze **3.** (*train*) wjeżdżać ⟨wjechać⟩ na stację **II** *v/t* **1.** *suspect*: zatrzymywać ⟨-mać⟩ **2.** *sum*: *infml* wyciągać ⟨-gnąć⟩, zgarniać ⟨-nąć⟩ **3.** przyciągać ⟨-gnąć⟩; **pull off I** *v/i* ***~ the road*** zjechać na pobocze **II** *v/t* **1.** ***pull the car off the road*** zjechać na pobocze **2.** ***he pulled it off*** *infml* udało mu się; **pull out I** *v/i* **1.** wycofywać ⟨-fać⟩ się (***of*** z *G*) **2.** zmieniać ⟨-nić⟩ pas ruchu **3.** wyjeżdżać ⟨-chać⟩ (***into*** na *A*) **4.** (*train*) odjeżdżać ⟨-jechać⟩ **II** *v/t* *troops*: wycofywać ⟨-fać⟩; **pull over** *v/i* zjeżdżać ⟨zjechać⟩ na pobocze; **pull through** *v/t* **1.** *patient*: stawiać ⟨postawić⟩ na nogi **2.** pomagać ⟨-móc⟩ **3.** ***he'll ~*** *infml* wyjdzie z tego, wyliże się z tego **4.** radzić ⟨po-⟩ sobie; **pull together I** *v/t* ***~ oneself together*** wziąć się w garść, pozbierać się **II** *v/i* współdziałać; **pull up I** *v/i* zatrzymywać ⟨-mać⟩ się **II** *v/t* **1.** *chair*: przysuwać ⟨-sunąć⟩ **2.** (*criticise*) *Br infml* zjechać

pul•ley ['pʊlɪ] *s* TECH krążek *m* (linowy), blok *m*, bloczek *m*

'pull-out *s* **1.** wkładka *f* **2.** wycofanie *n*

pull•o•ver ['pʊləʊvə] *s* pulower *m*

'pull-up *s* podciągnięcie *n* (na drążku); ***do ~s*** podciągać się (na drążku)

pul•mo•nar•y ['pʌlmənərɪ] *adj* płucny

pulp [pʌlp] **I** *s* **1.** papka *f*; ***beat s.o. to a ~*** *fig* zbić kogoś na kwaśne jabłko **2.** miazga *f* **3.** miąższ *m* **II** *v/t* **1.** rozcierać ⟨-zetrzeć⟩ na papkę **2.** rozgniatać ⟨-nieść⟩ na purée; **pulp 'fiction** *s* literatura *f* brukowa, *infml* czytadła *pl*

pul•pit ['pʊlpɪt] *s* (*church*) ambona *f*

'pulp nov•el *s* powieść *f* brukowa

pul•sate [pʌl'seɪt] *v/i* **1.** pulsować; ***a pulsating headache*** pulsujący ból głowy **2.** tętnić; ***streets pulsating with life*** ulice tętniące życiem

pulse [pʌls] **I** *s* **1.** MED tętno *n*, puls *m*; ***take one's ~*** zmierzyć komuś puls **2.** MUS rytm *n* **3.** PHYS impuls *m* **II** *v/i* pulsować

pul•ver•ize ['pʌlvəraɪz] *v/t* **1.** proszkować ⟨s-⟩ **2.** *fig* rozbijać ⟨-bić⟩ w pył

pu•ma ['pjuːmə] *s* puma *f*

pum•ice ['pʌmɪs] *s* GEOL pumeks *m*

pum•mel ['pʌml] *v/t* **1.** okładać pięściami, uderzać ⟨-rzyć⟩ pięściami **2.** ***be ~led*** (*team*, *player*) *fig* dostać cięgi

pump [pʌmp] **I** *s* **1.** pompa *f* **2.** *Am* czółenko *n*, pantofel *m* (damski)

3. *Br* tenisówka *f* **4.** *Br* balerinka *f*, balerina *f* **II** *v/t* **1.** pompować; **~ *out water*** wypompować wodę **2.** **~ *s.o.'s stomach*** zrobić komuś płukanie żołądka **3.** *infml* wyciskać ⟨-snąć⟩; ***see if you can ~ him for more information*** spróbuj wycisnąć z niego więcej informacji **III** *v/i* **1.** tryskać ⟨-snąć⟩; ***blood was ~ing out of the wound*** krew tryskała z rany **2.** (*heart*) walić; **pump into** *v/t* wpompowywać ⟨-pować⟩; **~ *money into*** pakować pieniądze w *A*; **pump up** *v/t* pompować ⟨na-⟩

pump•kin ['pʌmpkɪn] *s* dynia *f*

pun [pʌn] **I** *s* kalambur *m*, gra *f* słów **II** *v/i* tworzyć kalambury

Punch [pʌntʃ] *s*: ***be as pleased as ~*** *Br* cieszyć się jak dziecko

punch[1] [pʌntʃ] **I** *s* **1.** cios *m* pięścią; ***give s.o. a ~*** uderzyć kogoś pięścią **2.** siła *f* wyrazu **II** *v/t* uderzać ⟨-rzyć⟩ pięścią

punch[2] [~] *s* poncz *m*

punch[3] [~] **I** *s* dziurkacz *m* **II** *v/t* **1.** dziurkować ⟨prze-⟩ **2.** kasować ⟨s-⟩ **3.** perforować; **punch in I** *v/t* wpisywać ⟨-sać⟩, *infml* wstukiwać ⟨-kać⟩ **II** *v/i Am* odbijać ⟨-bić⟩ kartę zegarową (przy wejściu do pracy); **punch out I** *v/t* **1.** *number*: wybierać ⟨-brać⟩ **2.** *hole*: robić ⟨z-⟩ **II** *v/i Am* odbijać ⟨-bić⟩ kartę zegarową (przy wyjściu z pracy)

Punch-and-'Ju•dy show *s* (*puppet show*) *Br* przedstawienie *n* Punch and Judy show

'punch•bag *s* worek *m* treningowy; **'punch card** *s* karta *f* perforowana; **'punch•line** *s* puenta *f* (dowcipu); **'punch-up** *s Br infml* bijatyka *f*

punc•til•i•ous [pʌŋk'tɪlɪəs] *adj* o nienagannych manierach: ***be ~ in one's manners*** mieć nienaganne maniery

punc•tu•al ['pʌŋktʃʊəl] *adj* punktualny; ***be ~*** przyjdź punktualnie; **punc•tu•al•i•ty** [pʌŋktʃʊ'ælətɪ] *s* punktualność *f*; **punc•tu•al•ly** ['pʌŋktʃʊəlɪ] *adv* punktualnie

punc•tu•ate ['pʌŋktʃʊeɪt] **I** *v/t* przerywać ⟨-rwać⟩ **II** *v/i* stosować znaki interpunkcyjne; **punc•tu•a•tion** ['pʌŋktʃʊ'eɪʃn] *s* interpunkcja *f*; **punc•tu•'a•tion mark** *s* znak *m* interpunkcyjny

punc•ture ['pʌŋktʃə] **I** *s* **1.** *Br* przebicie *n*; ***have a ~*** *infml* złapać gumę; ***a tyre with a slow ~*** opona, z której powoli uchodzi powietrze **2.** nakłucie *n* **3.** dziurka *f* **II** *v/t* **1.** przebijać ⟨-bić⟩ **2.** przekłuwać ⟨-łuć⟩ **3.** **~ *s.o.'s confidence*** odebrać komuś pewność siebie **III** *v/i* przebijać ⟨-bić⟩ się

pun•dit ['pʌndɪt] *s* ekspert *m*

pun•gen•cy ['pʌndʒənsɪ] *s a. fig* ostrość *f*; **pun•gent** ['pʌndʒənt] *adj* **1.** *smell, taste*: ostry **2.** *remark*: cięty **3.** *analysis*: wnikliwy

pun•ish ['pʌnɪʃ] *v/t* **1.** karać ⟨u-⟩; ***she was severly ~ed*** została surowo ukarana; ***in those days murder was ~ed with death*** w tych czasach morderstwo karano śmiercią **2.** **~ *oneself for*** obwinać się za *A*; **pun•ish•a•ble** ['pʌnɪʃəbl] *adj* karalny; ***a ~ offence*** czyn karalny; **pun•ish•ing** ['pʌnɪʃɪŋ] *adj* **1.** wyczerpujący **2.** bardzo męczący; **pun•ish•ment** ['pʌnɪʃmənt] *s* kara *f* (***for*** za *A*); ***as a ~*** za karę

pu•ni•tive ['pju:nətɪv] *adj* **1.** karny **3.** odwetowy **3.** *tax*: bardzo wysoki

punk [pʌŋk] **I** *s* **1.** punk *m* **2.** *Am* chuligan *m* **II** *adj* punkowy; **'punk rock** ['pʌŋkrɔk] *s* punk rock *m*; **punk 'rock•er** *s* punk *m*

punt[1] [pʌnt] **I** *s* łódź *f* płaskodenna **II** *v/i* pływać łodzią (płaskodenną)

punt[2] [~] *s Br infml* zakład *m*; **punt•er** ['pʌntə] *s Br infml* **1.** klient *m* **2.** gracz *m*

pu•ny ['pju:nɪ] *adj* **1.** drobny **2.** słabiutki **3.** mizerny

pup [pʌp] *s* **1.** szczeniak *m* **2.** (*animal*) młode *n*

pu•pa ['pju:pə] *pl -pae* ['~pi:] *s BIOL* poczwarka *f*

pu•pil[1] ['pju:pl] *s* uczeń *m*

pu•pil[2] [~] *s* źrenica *f*

pup•pet ['pʌpɪt] *s* **1.** *a. fig* marionetka *f* **2.** pacynka *f* **3.** kukiełka *f*, lalka *f*; **pup•pet•eer** [pʌpɪ'tɪə] *s* lalkarz *m*; **'pup•pet gov•ern•ment** *s* rząd *m* marionetkowy; **'pup•pet show** *s* przedstawienie *n* lalkowe

pup•py ['pʌpɪ] *s* **1.** *a. fig* szczeniak *m* **2.** szczenię *n*; **'pup•py fat** *s Br* dziecięcy tłuszczyk *m*; '**pup•py love** *s infml* szczenięca miłość *f*

pur•chase ['pɜːtʃəs] **I** *v/t* **1.** kupować ⟨-pić⟩ **2.** nabywać ⟨-być⟩ **II** *s* **1.** zakup *m*; ***make a ~*** dokonać zakupu; ***proof of ~*** dowód zakupu **2.** nabytek *m*

'**pur•chase in•voice** *s* faktura *f* zakupu; '**pur•chase ledg•er** *s ECON* księga *f* zakupów; '**pur•chase or•der** *s* **1.** zamówienie *n* **2.** zlecenie *n* zakupu; '**pur•chase price** *s* **1.** cena *f* kupna **2.** kurs *m* kupna; **pur•chas•er** ['pɜːtʃəsə] *s* nabywca *m*; '**pur•chas•ing de•part•ment** *s* dział *m* zakupów; '**pur•chas•ing power** *s ECON* siła *f* nabywcza

pure [pjʊə] *adj* **1.** czysty; ***~ wool*** czysta wełna; ***by ~ chance*** przez czysty przypadek, zupełnie przypadkowo; ***lead a ~ life*** żyć w czystości **2.** *happiness*: niczym niezmącony **3.** *truth*: szczery **4.** ***it's blackmail, ~ and simple*** to jest zwykły szantaż; **pure•bred** ['pjʊəbred] *adj* **1.** *horse*: czystej krwi **2.** *dog*: rasowy

pu•rée ['pjʊəreɪ] **I** *s* purée *n* **II** *v/t* robić ⟨z-⟩ purée z *G*

pure•ly ['pjʊəlɪ] *adv* **1.** wyłącznie; ***~ and simply for money*** tylko i wyłącznie dla pieniędzy **2.** czysto **3.** zupełnie; ***~ by chance*** zupełnie przypadkowo, przez czysty przypadek

pur•ga•tive ['pɜːgətɪv] *s* środek *m* przeczyszczający

pur•ga•to•ry ['pɜːgətrɪ] *s* **1.** *REL* czyściec *m* **2.** *fig* piekło *n*

purge [pɜːdʒ] **I** *v/t* **1.** przeprowadzać ⟨-dzić⟩ czystkę w *L* **2.** usuwać ⟨usunąć⟩; ***~ conservatists from a party, ~ a party of conservatists*** usunąć z partii konserwatystów **3.** oczyszczać ⟨oczyścić⟩ **II** *s* czystka *f*

pu•ri•fi•ca•tion [pjʊərɪfɪ'keɪʃn] *s* oczyszczanie *n*; **pu•ri•fi•er** [pjʊərɪ'faɪə] *s* **1.** oczyszczacz *m* **2.** filtr *m*; **pu•ri•fy** ['pjʊərɪfaɪ] *v/t* oczyszczać ⟨oczyścić⟩

pur•ism ['pjʊərɪzəm] *s* puryzm *m*; **pur•ist** ['pjʊərɪst] *s* purysta *m*

Pu•ri•tan ['pjʊərɪtən] *REL* **I** *adj* purytański **II** *s* purytanin *m*

pu•ri•tan ['pjʊərɪtən] *s* purytanin *m*; **pu•ri•tan•i•cal** [pjʊərɪ'tænɪkl] *adj* purytański; **Pu•ri•tan•ism** ['pjʊərɪtənɪzəm] *s REL* purytanizm *m*

pu•ri•ty ['pjʊərɪtɪ] *s* czystość *f*

pur•loin [pɜː'lɔɪn] *v/t* kraść ⟨u-⟩, *infml* podwędzić

pur•ple ['pɜːpl] **I** *adj* **1.** fioletowy **2.** purpurowy; ***his face turned ~*** zrobił się purpurowy na twarzy **II** *s* **1.** fiolet *m*, fioletowy *m* **2.** purpura *f*

pur•port I [pə'pɔːt] *v/i* **1.** ***~ to contain*** rzekomo zawierać; ***~ to be*** rzekomo być **2.** twierdzić; ***they ~ to represent our interests*** twierdzą, że reprezentują nasze interesy **3.** pretendować; ***the book doesn't ~ to be a manual*** książka nie pretenduje do miana podręcznika **II** ['pɜːpɔːt] *s* sens *m*; **pur•port•ed•ly** [pə'pɔːtɪdlɪ] *adv* rzekomo

pur•pose ['pɜːpəs] *s* **1.** cel *m*; ***for the ~ of doing s.th.*** w celu zrobienia czegoś; ***on ~*** celowo, specjalnie; ***to no ~*** bezskutecznie, na próżno; ***to all practical ~s*** praktycznie rzecz biorąc, na dobrą sprawę **2.** zastosowanie *n*; ***have no useful ~*** **a)** niczemu nie służyć **b)** nie mieć żadnego praktycznego zastosowania; ***what's the ~ of this tool?*** do czego służy to narzędzie? **3.** sens *m*; ***give one's life*** (***a sense of***) ***~*** nadawać czyjemuś życiu sens **4.** ***strength of ~*** determinacja, zdecydowanie; **pur•pose•ful** ['pɜːpəsfəl] *adj* **1.** celowy **2.** zdecydowany; '**pur•pose•less** ['pɜːpəslɪs] *adj* **1.** bezcelowy **2.** bezsensowny; **pur•pose•ly** ['pɜːpəslɪ] *adv* celowo

purr [pɜː] *a. fig* **I** *v/i* mruczeć **II** *s* mruczenie *n*

purse [pɜːs] **I** *s* **1.** portmonetka *f*; ***to suit every ~*** *fig* na każdą kieszeń **2.** *Am* (damska) torebka *f* **3.** pieniądze *pl*, fundusze *pl*; ***the public ~*** pieniądze publiczne, fundusze publiczne **4.** *SPORT* nagroda *f* pieniężna **II** *v/t lips*: ściągać ⟨-gnąć⟩

purs•er ['pɜːsə] *s* ochmistrz *m* (pokładowy)

pur•su•ance [pə'sjuːəns] *s*: ***in ~ of his aims*** aby osiągnąć postawione sobie cele; ***in ~ of paragraph 2*** zgodnie z paragrafem 2; ***in ~ of one's duties*** podczas wykonywania swoich obowiązków; **pur•su•ant** [pə'sjuːənt] *adj* zgodnie (***to*** z *I*)

pur•sue [pə'sjuː] *v/t* **1.** *aim*: dążyć do *G* **2.** *strategy*, *policy*: realizować **3.** *studies*: kontynuować **4.** ***~ a teaching***

P

career pracować jako nauczyciel **5.** *interests*: rozwijać **6.** *form* ścigać; ***he was ~d by the police*** ścigała go policja; **pur•su•er** [pə'sjuːə] *s* **1.** prześladowca *m* **2.** ścigający *m*; **pur•suit** [pə'sjuːt] *s* **1.** pościg *m* **2.** *a. fig* pogoń *f*; ***in ~ of profit*** w pogoni za zyskiem **3.** dążenie *n* (**of** do *G*); ***~ of happiness*** dążenie do szczęścia **4.** zajęcie *n* **5.** hobby *n*

pu•ru•lent ['pjʊərələnt] *adj* ropny

pus [pʌs] *s* MED ropa *f*

push [pʊʃ] **I** *v/t* **1.** pchać ⟨pchnąć⟩; ***she ~ed him away*** odepchnęła go ***~ the door open*** otworzyć drzwi; ***be ~ing up the daisies*** *infml* wąchać kwiatki od spodu **2.** popychać ⟨-pchnąć⟩; ***she ~ed the cup towards me*** popchnęła filiżankę w moją stronę **3.** *button*: naciskać ⟨-snąć⟩ **4.** (*urge*) naciskać ⟨-snąć⟩ na *A*; ***no one ~ed her to take the job*** nikt jej nie zmuszał do podjęcia tej pracy **5.** ***~ one's way*** torować sobie drogę, przepychać się **6.** ***~ oneself a little harder*** bardziej się wysilić **7.** ***be ~ing 40*** dobiegać czterdziestki **8.** ***~ one's luck*** igrać z losem **9.** reklamować ⟨za-⟩ **10.** lansować **11.** forsować ⟨prze-⟩ **12.** *infml drugs*: sprzedawać ⟨-dać⟩ **II** *v/i* **1.** pchać; ***you ~ and I'll pull*** ty pchaj, a ja będę ciągnąć **2.** przepychać ⟨-pchnąć⟩ się **3.** (*army*) przeć (do przodu) **III** *s* **1.** pchnięcie *n*; ***give s.th. a ~*** popchnąć coś **2.** naciśnięcie *n* **3.** (*army*) uderzenie *n* **4.** dążenie *n* (**for** do *G*) **5.** zachęta *f* **6.** *sales*: kampania *f*; **push about** → ***push around***; **push ahead** *v/i* **1.** kontynuować (***with*** *A*) **2.** *reforms*: kontynuować realizację (***with*** *G*); **push around** *v/t fig* dyrygować; **push away** *v/t* odpychać ⟨odepchnąć⟩; **push for** *v/i* **1.** domagać się; ***~ a ban on alcohol advertising*** domagać się zakazu reklamowania alkoholu **2.** walczyć o *A*; **push in** *Br v/i* wpychać ⟨wepchnąć⟩ się (do kolejki); **push off** *v/i* **1.** ***~!*** *Br infml* spadaj! **2.** odpychać ⟨odepchnąć⟩ się (**form** od *G*); **push on** *v/i* **1.** iść ⟨pójść⟩ dalej **2.** ruszać ⟨-szyć⟩ w dalszą drogę **3.** nie przestawać; **push out** *v/t* **1.** (*work*) wyrzucać ⟨-cić⟩ **2.** *from market*: wypierać ⟨-przeć⟩ **3.** ***~ cheap products*** zalewać rynek tanimi produktami

'push•bike *s Br dated* rower *m*; **'push but•ton** *s* przycisk *m*; **'push-but•ton** *adj telephone*: z klawiaturą (numeryczną); **'push•cart** *s* wózek *m*; **'push•chair** *s Br* wózek *m* spacerowy, spacerówka *f*

push•er ['pʊʃə] *s infml* diler *m* narkotyków

'push•o•ver *s* **1.** *infml* łatwizna *f*, pestka *f* **2.** ***he's no ~*** niełatwo go przekonać; ***he's a ~*** łatwo go przekonać; **'push-start** *v/t infml car*: zapalać ⟨-lić⟩ na pych; **'push-up** *s* (*exercise*) pompka *f*

push•y ['pʊʃɪ] *adj infml* nachalny

pu•sil•lan•i•mous [pjuːsɪ'lænɪməs] *adj form* bojaźliwy

puss [pʊs] *s Br* kiciuś *m*; ***here, ~!*** kici! kici!

pus•sy [pʊsɪ] *s* **1.** (*a.* ***~ cat***) kotek *m*, kiciuś *m* **2.** *vulg* cipa *f*

pussyfoot ['pʊsɪfʊt] *v/i* (*a.* ***~ about***, ***~ around***) *infml* robić uniki

pustule ['pʌstjuːl] *s* krosta *f*

put [pʊt] (*put*; *put*) *v/t* **1.** kłaść ⟨położyć⟩ (**on** na *L*); ***did you ~ sugar in my coffee?*** osłodziłeś mi kawę?; ***he earned more than all the other players ~ together*** zarobił więcej niż wszyscy pozostali gracze razem wzięci; ***~ s.th. at risk*** narażać coś; ***~ emphasis on*** kłaść nacisk na *A*; ***~ pressure on*** naciskać na *A*; ***~ an end*** (*a.* ***a stop***) ***to*** położyć kres *D* **2.** stawiać ⟨postawić⟩; ***~ yourself in my position*** postaw się na moim miejscu **3.** ***~ s.o. in a good*** (***bad***) ***mood*** wprawić kogoś w dobry (zły) nastrój **4.** pisać ⟨na-⟩; ***I'll ~ it in my diary*** zapiszę to sobie w kalendarzu **5.** nakładać ⟨nałożyć⟩; ***~ a limit on*** ograniczać *A* **6.** ujmować ⟨ująć⟩; ***to ~ it mildly*** łagodnie mówiąc; ***to ~ it another way*** innymi słowy; ***how shall I ~ it*** jak by to powiedzieć; **put about** *v/t gossip*: roznosić; **put across** *v/t* **1.** przekazywać ⟨-zać⟩ **2.** przedstawiać ⟨-wić⟩; **put aside** *v/t* **1.** odkładać ⟨odłożyć⟩ **2.** odkładać ⟨odłożyć⟩ na bok; ***let's ~ our differences*** zapomnijmy (na chwilę) o tym, co nas dzieli; **put away** *v/t* **1.** odstawiać

P

⟨-wić⟩ **2.** odkładać ⟨odłożyć⟩ na miejsce **3.** *money*: odkładać ⟨odłożyć⟩ **4.** (*drink*) *infml* wytrąbić **5.** (*in jail*) *infml* zamykać ⟨-mknąć⟩ **6.** *infml* odsyłać ⟨odesłać⟩ do czubków; **put back** *v/t* **1.** odkładać ⟨odłożyć⟩ na miejsce **2.** opóźniać ⟨-nić⟩ **3.** *meeting*: przekładać ⟨przełożyć⟩ **4.** ***put one's clocks back*** cofnąć wskazówki zegara; **put by** odkładać ⟨odłożyć⟩; **put down I** *v/t* **1.** kłaść ⟨położyć⟩ (***s.th. on*** coś na *L*); ***put it down here*** połóż to tutaj **2.** odkładać ⟨odłożyć⟩; ***put that knife down!*** odłóż ten nóż! **3.** *infml* ośmieszać ⟨-szyć⟩ **4.** zapisywać ⟨-sać⟩ **5.** *deposit*: wpłacać ⟨-cić⟩ **6.** *uprising*: tłumić ⟨s-⟩ **7.** *animal*: usypiać ⟨uśpić⟩ **8.** *child*: kłaść ⟨położyć⟩ spać **9.** ***put s.o. down as*** uważać kogoś za *A* **10.** ***put s.th. down to*** przypisywać coś *D* **II** *v/i* lądować ⟨wy-⟩; **put forward** *v/t* **1.** proponować ⟨za-⟩; ***put s.o.'s name forward for*** zaproponować czyjąś kandydaturę na *A* **2.** *opinion*: przedstawiać ⟨-wić⟩ **3.** *suggestion*: występować ⟨-tąpić⟩ z *I* **4.** *meeting*: przesuwać ⟨-sunąć⟩ na wcześniejszy termin **5.** ***put one's clocks forward*** przesunąć wskazówki zegara do przodu; **put in I** *v/t* **1.** wybierać ⟨-brać⟩ **2.** zakładać ⟨założyć⟩, montować ⟨za-⟩ **3.** wtrącać ⟨-cić⟩ **4.** *claim*: wysuwać ⟨-sunąć⟩ **5.** *a lot of work*: wkładać ⟨włożyć⟩ **6.** *time*: poświęcać ⟨-cić⟩ **II** *v/i* **1.** (*ship*) zawijać ⟨-winąć⟩ do portu (***at*** w *L*) **2.** ubiegać się (***for*** o *A*); **put off** *v/t* **1.** przekładać ⟨przełożyć⟩ **2.** odwoływać ⟨-łać⟩ spotkanie z *I* **3.** zrażać ⟨zrazić⟩; ***don't be ~ by how it looks*** niech cię nie zraża wygląd **4.** odrzucać ⟨-cić⟩ **5.** (*distract*) rozpraszać ⟨-roszyć⟩ **6.** *passenger*: wysadzać ⟨-dzić⟩; **put on** *v/t* **1.** *clothes*: wkładać ⟨włożyć⟩ **2.** *make-up*: robić ⟨z-⟩ **3.** *music*, *radio*: włączać ⟨-czyć⟩ **4.** ***put a kettle on for tea*** nastawić wodę na herbatę **5.** ***~ weight*** przytyć **6.** *play*: wystawiać ⟨-wić⟩ **7.** (*in betting*) stawiać ⟨postawić⟩ (***s.th. for*** coś na *A*) **8.** dodawać ⟨-dać⟩ **9.** udawać; ***he was putting it on*** on udawał; **put out I** *v/t* **1.** gasić ⟨z-⟩ **2.** *rubbish*: wystawiać ⟨-wić⟩ **3.** publikować ⟨o-⟩ **4.** sprawiać ⟨-wić⟩ kłopot **5.** ***be ~*** być obrażonym **6.** *player*: eliminować ⟨wy-⟩ **7.** wybijać ⟨-bić⟩ sobie (ze stawu), wywichnąć **II** *v/i* wypływać ⟨-łynąć⟩ z portu; **put over** → ***put across***; **put through** *v/t* **1.** (*on phone*) łączyć ⟨po-⟩ (***to*** z *I*) **2.** doprowadzać ⟨-dzić⟩ do końca; **put together** *v/t* **1.** składać ⟨złożyć⟩ **2.** tworzyć ⟨s-, u-⟩ **3.** *meal*: przygotowywać ⟨-tować⟩; **put up I** *v/i* wytrzymywać ⟨-mać⟩ (***with*** *A*); ***I don't know how she puts up with him*** nie wiem, jak ona z nim wytrzymuje **II** *v/t* **1.** *building*: wznosić ⟨-nieść⟩ **2.** *fence*: stawiać ⟨postawić⟩ **3.** *tent*: rozbić ⟨-bijać⟩ **4.** wywieszać ⟨-wiesić⟩ **5.** *fee*: podnosić ⟨-nieść⟩ **6.** *money*: wykładać ⟨wyłożyć⟩ **7.** przenocować; ***we can put you up for one night*** możemy cię przenocować przez jedną noc **8.** *candidate*: wystawiać ⟨-wić⟩ **9.** *proposal*: przedstawiać ⟨-wić⟩ **10.** namawiać ⟨-mówić⟩ (***to*** do *G*)

pu•ta•tive ['pjuːtətɪv] *adj form* domniemany

'put-down *s infml* przytyk *m*, złośliwa uwaga *f*; **'put-on** *s Am* blef *m*

pu•tre•fy ['pjuːtrɪfaɪ] *v/i* **1.** gnić ⟨z-⟩ **2.** psuć ⟨ze-⟩ się

pu•trid ['pjuːtrɪd] *adj* **1.** zgniły; ***a ~ smell*** zapach zgnilizny **2.** *infml* ohydny

putsch [pʊtʃ] *s* pucz *m*

putt [pʌt] *v/t ball*: uderzać ⟨-rzyć⟩ po ziemi

putt•er ['pʌtə] **I** *v/i* (*a.* ***~ around***) *Am* → ***potter***[1] **II** *s* (*golf club*) putter *m*

put•ty ['pʌtɪ] *s* kit *m*

'put-up job *s*: ***it was a ~*** *Br infml* to zostało ukartowane

'put-up•on *adj* wykorzystywany

puz•zle ['pʌzl] **I** *s* **1.** zagadka *f* **2.** łamigłówka *f*; ***a crossword ~*** krzyżówka **3.** puzzle *pl*, układanka *f* (obrazkowa) **II** *v/t* zastanawiać; ***what ~s me is why she tricked him*** zastanawia mnie, dlaczego go oszukała; **puzzle out** *v/t mystery*: rozwikłać

puz•zled ['pʌzld] *adj* **1.** zbity z tropu **2.** ***scientists are ~ by this*** naukowcy nie potrafią tego wyjaśnić; ***he was***

~ ***as to why*** nie rozumiał, dlaczego **3.** ***she had a ~ look on her face*** miała zdziwioną minę

puz•zler ['pʌzlə] *s*: ***it's a ~*** *infml* trudno to wyjaśnić; **puz•zling** ['pʌzlɪŋ] *adj* zagadkowy

PVC [piːviː'siː] *s* PCW *m*, polichlorek *m* winylu

Pyg•my ['pɪgmɪ] *s* Pigmej *m*

pyg•my ['pɪgmɪ] **I** *s fig* karzeł *m* **II** *adj* karłowaty

py•ja•ma jack•et [pə'dʒɑːmədʒækɪt] *s* góra *f* od piżamy; **py•ja•ma 'pants** *pl* spodnie *pl* od piżamy; **py•ja•mas** [pə'dʒɑːməz] *pl Br* piżama *f*

py•lon ['paɪlən] *s* (*a.* **electric ~**) słup *m* wysokiego napięcia

pyr•a•mid ['pɪrəmɪd] *s* **1.** piramida *f* **2.** *MATH* ostrosłup *m*; **pyr•a•mid 'scheme** *s* piramida *f* (finansowa)

pyre ['paɪə] *s* stos *m* (pogrzebowy)

py•ro•ma•ni•ac [paɪrəʊ'meɪnɪæk] *s* piroman *m*; **py•ro•tech•nics** [paɪrəʊ'teknɪks] *pl* **1.** sztuczne ognie *pl* **2.** pokaz *m* sztucznych ogni **3.** pirotechnika *f* **4.** popis *m*

Pyr•rhic vic•to•ry [pɪrɪk'vɪktərɪ] *s* pyrrusowe zwycięstwo *n*

py•thon ['paɪθən] *s* pyton *m*

Q

quack[1] [kwæk] **I** *s* kwakanie *n* **II** *v/i* kwakać ⟨-knąć⟩

quack[2] [~] *s* (*a.* ***~ doctor***) **1.** konował *m* **2.** znachor *m*; **quack•er•y** ['~ərɪ] *s* znachorstwo *n*

quad [kwɒd] *s* **1.** wewnętrzny dziedziniec *m* **2. ~s** czworaczki

quad•ran•gle ['kwɒdræŋgl] *s* **1.** czworokąt *m* **2.** wewnętrzny dziedziniec *m*; **quad•ran•gu•lar** [kwɒd'ræŋgjʊlə] *adj* czworokątny

quad•ra•phon•ic [kwɒdrə'fɒnɪk] *adj* kwadrofoniczny

quad•rat•ic e•qua•tion [kwɒdrætɪk ɪ'kweɪʃn] *s* równanie *n* kwadratowe

quad•ri•lat•er•al [kwɒdrɪ'lætərəl] **I** *adj* czworokątny **II** *s* czworobok *m*

quad•ru•ped ['kwɒdruped] *s* czworonóg *m*

quad•ru•ple ['kwɒdrupl] **I** *v/i* zwiększać ⟨-szyć⟩ się czterokrotnie **II** *v/t* zwiększać ⟨-szyć⟩ czterokrotnie **III** *adj* **1.** czterokrotny **2.** poczwórny

quad•ru•plets ['kwɒdruplɪts] *pl* czworaczki *pl*

quag•mire ['kwɒgmaɪə] *s* **1.** bagno *n* **2.** *fig* grząski grunt *m*

quail [kweɪl] **I** *pl quail*, *quails* *s* przepiórka *f* **II** *v/i* drżeć ⟨za-⟩, truchleć ⟨s-⟩

quaint [kweɪnt] *adj* **1.** uroczy **2.** osobliwy

quake [kweɪk] **I** *v/i* **1.** drżeć ⟨za-⟩; ***~ with cold*** drżeć z zimna **2.** trząść ⟨za-⟩ się; ***~ with fear*** trząść się ze strachu; ***the ground ~d*** ziemia zatrzęsła się **II** *s infml* trzęsienie *n* ziemi

Quak•er ['kweɪkə] *s REL* kwakier *m*

qual•i•fi•ca•tion [kwɒlfɪ'keɪʃn] *s* **1.** kwalifikacja *f*; ***professional ~s*** kwalifikacje zawodowe **2.** wymaganie *n*, wymóg *m*; ***experience is a necessary ~ for this job*** od kandydatów na to stanowisko wymaga się doświadczenia **3.** zastrzeżenie *n*; ***without ~s*** bez zastrzeżeń **4.** zakwalifikowanie *n* się; **qual•i•fied** ['kwɒlɪfaɪd] *adj* **1.** wykwalifikowany; ***be well ~*** mieć odpowiednie kwalifikacje **2.** dyplomowany **3.** uprawniony (***to do s.th.*** do *G*), kompetentny (***to do s.th.*** żeby coś zrobić) **4.** obwarowany zastrzeżeniami **5.** *support*: ograniczony; **qual•i•fi•er** ['kwɒlɪfaɪə] *s* **1.** zawodnik *m*, który się zakwalifikował **2.** mecz *m* kwalifikacyjny **3.** *GRAM* określenie *n*; **qual•i•fy** ['kwɒlɪfaɪ] **I** *v/i* **1.** kwalifikować ⟨za-⟩ się (***for*** do *G*) **2.** zdobywać ⟨-być⟩ kwalifikacje (***as*** jako *N*) **3.** uzyskiwać ⟨-kać⟩ dyplom (***as*** *G*) **4.** nadawać ⟨-dać⟩ się (***as*** na *A*) **II** *v/t* **1.** uprawniać (***s.o. for*** kogoś do *G*) **2.** *GRAM* określać ⟨-lić⟩

qual•i•ta•tive ['kwɒlɪtətɪv] *adj* jakościowy

qual•i•ty ['kwɒlətɪ] **I** *s* **1.** jakość *f*; ***of good ~*** dobrej jakości **2.** wysoka jakość *f*; ***writers of ~*** dobrzy pisarze **3.** cecha *f*; ***personal qualities*** cechy charakteru **II** *adj* wysokiej jakości; **'qual•i•ty as•sur•ance** *s* zapewnienie *n* jakości; **'qual•i•ty con•trol** *s* kontrola *f* jakości; **qual•i•ty 'news•pa•per** *s Br* poważna gazeta *f*; **'qual•i•ty time** *s* czas *m* poświęcony rodzinie

qualm [kwɑːm] *s*: ***have no ~s about doing s.th.*** zrobić coś bez skrupułów

quan•da•ry ['kwɒndərɪ] *s* dylemat *m*; ***be in a ~ about what to do*** mieć dylemat, co zrobić

quan•ta ['kwɒntə] *pl* → ***quantum***

quan•ti•fy ['kwɒntɪfaɪ] *v/t* wyrażać ⟨-razić⟩ ilościowo

quan•ti•ta•tive ['kwɒntɪtətɪv] *adj* ilościowy

quan•ti•ty ['kwɒntətɪ] *s* **1.** ilość *f*; ***in large quantities*** w dużych ilościach **2.** duża ilość *f*; ***buy goods in ~*** kupować towary hurtowo **3.** *MATH* wielkość *f*

quan•tum ['kwɒntəm] *pl -ta* ['~tə] *s PHYS* kwant *m*; **quan•tum 'leap** *s fig* milowy krok *m*; **quan•tum 'phys•ics** *s* fizyka *f* kwantowa; **quan•tum me•'chanics** *s* mechanika *f* kwantowa

quar•an•tine ['kwɒrəntiːn] **I** *s* kwarantanna *f* **II** *v/t* poddawać ⟨-dać⟩ kwarantannie

quark [kwɑːk] *s PHYS* kwark *m*

quar•rel ['kwɒrəl] **I** *s* **1.** kłótnia *f* (***about/over*** o *A*); ***they had a ~ about money*** pokłócili się o pieniądze **2.** ***have no ~ with*** zgadzać się z *I* **II** *v/i* kłócić ⟨po-⟩ się (***about/over*** o *A*); **quar•rel with** *v/i* nie zgadzać ⟨zgodzić⟩ się z *I*

quar•rel•some ['kwɒrəlsʌm] *adj* kłótliwy

quar•ry[1] ['kwɒrɪ] **I** *s* kamieniołom *m* **II** *v/t* wydobywać ⟨-być⟩

quar•ry[2] [~] *s* **1.** ścigane zwierzę *n* **2.** ścigany *m*

quart [kwɔːt] *s* (*Br = 1,14 litre*, *Am around 0,92 litre*) kwarta *f*

quar•ter ['kwɔːtə] **I** *s* **1.** ćwiartka *f*, ćwierć *f*; ***cut the apple into ~s*** pokrój jabłko na ćwiartki **2.** kwadrans *m*; ***it's (a) ~ to four*** jest za kwadrans czwarta **3.** kwartał *m* **4.** dzielnica *f*; ***the Latin ~*** Dzielnica Łacińska **5.** ***~s*** *fig* kręgi; ***in some ~s*** w niektórych kręgach **6.** *Am* dwudziestopięciocentówka *f* **7.** *moon*: kwadra *f* **II** *v/t* **1.** dzielić ⟨po-⟩ na ćwiartki **2.** zakwaterowywać ⟨-rować⟩; **'quar•ter•back** *Am* **I** *s* rozgrywający *m* **II** *v/i* grać ⟨za-⟩ na pozycji rozgrywającego; **'quar•ter•deck** *s* pokład *m* rufowy; **quar•ter-'fi•nal** *s* ćwierćfinał *m*; **quar•ter-'fi•nal•ist** *s* ćwierćfinalista *m*

quar•ter•ly ['kwɔːtəlɪ] **I** *adj* kwartalny **II** *adv* raz na kwartał **III** *s* kwartalnik *m*

'quar•ter note *s Am* ćwierćnuta *f*

quar•ters ['kwɔːtəz] *pl* **1.** kwatery *f* **2.** zakwaterowanie *n*

quar•tet [kwɔː'tet] *s MUS* kwartet *m*

quartz [kwɔːts] *s* kwarc *m*; **quartz 'clock** *s* zegarek *m* kwarcowy

quash [kwɒʃ] *v/t* **1.** *verdict*: unieważniać ⟨-nić⟩ **2.** *decision*: odwoływać ⟨-łać⟩

qua•ver ['kweɪvə] **I** *v/i* (*voice*) drżeć ⟨za-⟩ **II** *s* **1.** (*voice*) drżenie *n* **2.** *MUS Br* ósemka *f*

quay [kiː] *s* nabrzeże *n*

quea•sy ['kwiːzɪ] *adj*: ***I feel ~*** niedobrze mi

queen [kwiːn] *s* **1.** królowa *f* **2.** (*chess*) hetman *m* **3.** *vulg* ciota *f*; ***a drag ~*** drag queen; **queen 'bee** *s BIOL* królowa *f*; **queen 'mo•ther** *s* królowa *f* matka; **queen•ly** ['kwiːnlɪ] *adj* królewski

queer [kwɪə] **I** *adj* **1.** osobliwy, dziwny **2.** ***be ~*** *vulg* być ciotą **II** *s vulg* pedał *m* **III** *v/t* ***~ the pitch for s.o.*** *Br infml* pokrzyżować komuś szyki; **queer•ly** ['kwɪrlɪ] *adv* dziwnie, osobliwie

quell [kwel] *v/t uprising*, *revolt*, *doubts*: tłumić ⟨s-⟩

quench [kwentʃ] *v/t* **1.** *thirst*: gasić ⟨u-⟩ **2.** *fire*: tłumić ⟨s-⟩

quer•u•lous ['kweruləs] *adj* **1.** rozdrażniony **2.** poirytowany

que•ry ['kwɪərɪ] **I** *s* **1.** pytanie *n* **2.** znak *m* zapytania **II** *v/t* podawać ⟨-dać⟩ w wątpliwość **III** *v/i* pytać ⟨za-⟩

quest [kwest] **I** *s* poszukiwanie *n*; ***the ~ for happiness*** poszukiwanie szczęścia; ***set off in ~ of adventure*** wyruszyć na poszukiwanie przygód **II** *v/i* szukać (***for*** *G*)

Q

ques•tion ['kwestʃən] **I** *s* **1.** pytanie *n*; ***ask a ~*** zadać pytanie **2.** kwestia *f*; ***it is only a ~ of time*** to tylko kwestia czasu; ***an open ~*** otwarta kwestia **3.** sprawa *f*; ***the point in ~*** sprawa, o którą chodzi, sprawa, o której mowa **4.** wątpliwość *f*; ***out of the ~!*** wykluczone!; ***be beyond ~*** nie ulegać wątpliwości; ***bring s.th. into ~*** podać coś w wątpliwość **II** *v/t* **1.** przesłuchiwać ⟨-chać⟩ **2.** ankietować **3.** kwestionować ⟨za-⟩, podawać ⟨-dać⟩ w wątpliwość; **ques•tion•a•ble** ['kwestʃənəbl] *adj* wątpliwy; **ques•tion•er** ['kwestʃənə] *s* pytający *m*; **ques•tion•ing** ['kwestʃənɪŋ] **I** *s* **1.** pytanie *n* **2.** przesłuchanie *n* **II** *adj look*: pytający; '**ques•tion mark** *s* znak *m* zapytania; **ques•tion•naire** [kwestʃə'neə] *s* ankieta *f*

queue [kjuː] *Br* **I** *s* kolejka *f*; ***join a ~*** stanąć w kolejce **II** *v/i* (*a.* ***~ up***) stać w kolejce (***for*** po *A*)

quib•ble ['kwɪbl] **I** *v/i* sprzeczać ⟨po-⟩ się (***about***/***over*** o *A*) **II** *s* drobne zastrzeżenie *n*

quick [kwɪk] **I** *adj* **1.** szybki; ***be ~!*** pośpiesz się!; ***be ~ to do s.th.*** szybko coś robić; ***be ~ to learn*** szybko się uczyć; ***it's ~er by train*** pociągiem jest szybciej **2.** *journey*, *way*: krótki; ***this is the ~est way*** to najkrótsza droga **3.** *wit*: bystry **4.** ***have a ~ temper*** być porywczym **II** *adv* szybko; ***come as ~ as you can*** przyjdź jak najszybciej **III** *s* ***cut s.o. to the ~*** dotknąć kogoś do żywego; '**quick-act•ing** *adj medicine*: o szybkim działaniu

quick•en ['kwɪkən] **I** *v/t* **1.** przyśpieszać ⟨-szyć⟩; ***he ~ed his pace*** przyśpieszył kroku **2.** zwiększać ⟨-szyć⟩ **II** *v/i* **1.** przyśpieszać ⟨-szyć⟩; ***his heartbeat ~ed*** serce zaczęło mu szybciej bić **2.** zwiększać ⟨-szyć⟩ się **3.** wzrastać ⟨-rosnąć⟩; ***his interest ~ed*** jego zainteresowanie wzrosło

'**quick-fire** *adj*: ***they asked me a series of ~ questions*** zasypali mnie gradem pytań

quick•ie ['kwɪkɪ] *s infml* **1.** (*sex*) szybki numerek *m* **2.** ***have a ~*** strzelić sobie jednego **3.** ***it'll be a ~*** to potrwa tylko chwilkę

quick•ly ['kwɪklɪ] *adv* szybko

'**quick•sand** *s* ruchome piaski *pl*; '**quick•sil•ver I** *s* (*mercury*) *dated* żywe srebro *n* **II** *adj* **1.** porywczy **2.** błyskawiczny; **quick-'tem•pered** *adj* **1.** porywczy **2.** choleryczny; **quick-'wit•ted** *adj* **1.** bystry **2.** szybko myślący

quid [kwɪd] *pl quid s* (*currency*) *Br infml* funt *m*

qui•et ['kwaɪət] **I** *adj* **1.** cichy; ***be ~!*** bądź cicho! **2.** spokojny; ***a ~ street*** spokojna ulica; ***they had a ~ wedding*** wzięli cichy ślub **II** *s* **1.** cisza *f* **2.** spokój *m*; ***peace and ~*** cisza i spokój **3.** ***on the ~*** *fig* w tajemnicy **III** *v/i* → ***quieten*** **IV** *v/t* → ***quieten***

qui•et•en ['kwaɪətn] *Br* **I** *v/i* **1.** uciszać ⟨-szyć⟩ się **2.** uspokajać ⟨-koić⟩ się **II** *v/t* **1.** uciszać ⟨-szyć⟩ **2.** uspokajać ⟨-koić⟩

quiet•ly ['kwaɪətlɪ] *adv* **1.** cicho **2.** spokojnie; **quiet•ness** ['kwaɪətnɪs] *s* **1.** cisza *f* **2.** spokój *m*

quill [kwɪl] *s* **1.** (*a.* ***~ feather***) pióro *n* **2.** (*a.* ***~ pen***) gęsie pióro *n* **3.** *hedgehog*: kolec *m*

quilt [kwɪlt] *s* kołdra *f*; **quilt•ed** ['kwɪltɪd] *adj* pikowany

quins [kwɪns] *pl Br infml* pięcioraczki *pl*

quince [kwɪns] *s* pigwa *f*

quin•ine ['kwɪniːn] *no pl s* chinina *f*

quint•es•sence [kwɪn'tesns] *s* kwintesencja *f*; ***the ~ of Parisian elegance*** kwintesencja paryskiej elegancji; **quint•es•sen•tial** [kwɪntɪ'senʃəl] *adj* typowy

quints [kwɪnts] *pl Am infml* pięcioraczki *pl*

quin•tet [kwɪn'tet] *s* MUS kwintet *m*

quin•tu•plets ['kwɪntjʊpləts] *pl* pięcioraczki *pl*

quip [kwɪp] *s* celna uwaga *f*

quirk [kwɜːk] *s* **1.** osobliwość *f* **2.** ***by a strange ~ of fate*** dziwnym zrządzeniem losu; **quirk•y** ['kwɜːrkɪ] *adj* osobliwy, dziwaczny

quit [kwɪt] *infml* **I** (*quit*/*quitted*; *quit*/*quitted*) *v/t* **1.** rzucać ⟨-cić⟩; ***I ~ smoking*** rzuciłem palenie **2.** opuszczać ⟨opuścić⟩ **3.** wyjeżdżać ⟨-jechać⟩ z *G*; ***they ~ the city*** wyjechali z miasta **4.** (*programme*) wychodzić z *G* **5.** ***~ it!*** przestań!, daj spokój! **II** (*quit*/*quitted*;

Q

quit/quitted) *v/i* odchodzić ⟨odejść⟩; ***he ~ as a coach*** zrezygnował z funkcji trenera
quite [kwaɪt] *adv* **1.** dość; ***~ interesting*** dość interesujący **2.** całkiem, zupełnie; ***~ good*** całkiem niezły, ***he plays ~ well*** gra zupełnie nieźle; ***~ frankly*** zupełnie szczerze; ***I don't ~ understand*** niezupełnie rozumiem **3.** całkowicie; ***you're ~ right*** masz całkowitą rację; ***she's ~ a beauty*** prawdziwa z niej piękność **4.** **~** (**so**) *Br* właśnie
quits [kwɪts] *adj*: **be ~** być kwita
quit•ter ['kwɪtə] *s infml*: **be a ~** łatwo się poddawać
quiv•er[1] ['kwɪvə] **I** *v/i* **1.** drżeć ⟨za-⟩ **2.** trząść ⟨za-⟩ się; ***~ with anger*** trząść się ze złości **II** *s* **1.** drżenie *n*; ***~ in one's voice*** drżenie głosu **2.** dreszcz *m*; ***a ~ of excitement*** dreszczyk podniecenia
quiv•er[2] [~] *s* kołczan *m*
quix•ot•ic [kwɪk'sɒtɪk] *adj* nieżyciowy, idealistyczny
quiz [kwɪz] **I** *pl quizzes s* **1.** quiz *m*; ***a television ~ show*** teleturniej **2.** test *m* **II** *v/t* **1.** wypytywać ⟨-tać⟩, pytać (***s.o. about*** kogoś o *A*) **2.** robić ⟨z-⟩ test; '**quiz mas•ter** *s Br* prowadzący *m* (teleturnej)
quiz•zi•cal ['kwɪzɪkl] *adj look*: pytający
quoit [kwɔɪt] *s* **1.** kółko *n* **2.** **~s** (*game*) rzucanie *n* kółek
quo•rum ['kwɔːrəm] *s* kworum *n*
quo•ta ['kwəʊtə] *s* **1.** ECON kontyngent *m*, kwota *f*; ***a ~ system*** system kwotowy **2.** udział *m* **3.** limit *m* **4.** część *f* **5.** wymagana liczba *f* głosów
quo•ta•ble ['kwəʊtəbl] *adj* wart przytoczenia
quo•ta•tion [kwəʊ'teɪʃn] *s* **1.** cytat *m*; ***a dictionary of ~s*** słownik cytatów **2.** cytowanie *n* **3.** wycena *f* **4.** oferta *f* **5.** (*stock exchange*) notowanie *n*; **quo'ta•tion marks** *pl* cudzysłów *m*; ***put s.th. in ~*** ująć coś w cudzysłów
quote [kwəʊt] **I** *v/t* **1.** cytować ⟨za-⟩; ***he was ~d in the press as saying that*** w prasie przytoczono jego wypowiedź, że; ***~... unquote*** cytuję... koniec cytatu **2.** podawać ⟨-dać⟩ przykład **3.** wyceniać ⟨-nić⟩ (na *A*) **4.** ***be ~d on the Stock Exchange*** być notowanym na giełdzie; ***yesterday the dollar was ~d at PLN 3.82*** wczoraj dolar wart był 3,82 złotego **II** *s* **1.** cytat *m* **2.** **~s** cudzysłów
quo•tient ['kwəʊʃnt] *s* iloraz *m*

R

rab•bi ['ræbaɪ] *s* REL rabin *m*
rab•bit ['ræbɪt] **I** *s* królik *m* **II** *v/i Br infml* ględzić (**on** o *L*); '**rab•bit punch** *s* cios *m* kantem dłoni w kark
rab•ble ['ræbl] *s* motłoch *m*, hołota *f*; **rab•ble-rous•er** ['ræblraʊzə] *s* podżegacz *m*; **rab•ble-rous•ing** ['ræblraʊzɪŋ] *s* podżeganie *n*
rab•id ['ræbɪd] *adj* **1.** fanatyczny **2.** radykalny **3.** zaciekły **4.** MED wściekły, chory na wściekliznę
ra•bies ['reɪbiːz] *s* MED wścieklizna *f*
rac•coon [rə'kuːn] *s* BIOL szop *m* pracz
race[1] [reɪs] *s* rasa *f*; ***a ~ of cattle*** rasa bydła; ***the human ~*** rodzaj ludzki
race[2] [~] **I** *s* **1.** wyścig *m*; ***a ~ against time*** wyścig z czasem **2.** bieg *m* **3.** gonitwa *f* **II** *v/i* **1.** ścigać się (***against*** z *I*) **2.** gnać ⟨po-⟩, pędzić ⟨po-⟩; ***he ~d up the stairs*** pognał po schodach na górę **3.** (*engine*) pracować na zwiększonych obrotach **III** *v/t* **1.** ścigać się z *I* **2.** ***~ s.o. to hospital*** zawieźć kogoś błyskawicznie do szpitala **3.** wystawiać ⟨-wić⟩ do wyścigu
'**race•course** *s Br* tor *m* wyścigów konnych; '**race•horse** *s* koń *m* wyścigowy; '**race meet•ing** *s Br* wyścigi *pl* konne
rac•er ['reɪsə] *s* **1.** koń *m* wyścigowy **2.** biegacz *m* **3.** samochód *m* wyścigowy, *infml* wyścigówka *f* **4.** rower *m* wyścigowy, *infml* wyścigówka *f* **5.** motocykl *m* wyścigowy, *infml* ścigacz *m*
'**race•track** *Am* → ***racecourse***
ra•cial ['reɪʃl] *adj* rasowy; **ra•cial dis•crim•i'na•tion** *s* dyskryminacja *f* ra-

sowa **ra•cial seg•re•'ga•tion** *s* segregacja *f* rasowa

rac•ing ['reɪsɪŋ] **I** *s* **1.** wyścigi *pl*; ***horse ~*** wyścigi konne **2.** regaty *pl* **II** *adj* **1.** wyścigowy **2.** regatowy; **'rac•ing bi•cy•cle** *s* rower *m* wyścigowy; **'rac•ing car** *s Br* samochód *m* wyścigowy; **'rac•ing driv•er** *s* kierowca *m* wyścigowy

rac•ism ['reɪsɪzm] *s* rasism *m*; **ra•cist** ['reɪsɪst] **I** *s* rasista *m* **II** *adj* rasistowski

rack[1] [ræk] **I** *s* **1.** stojak *m*; ***a drying ~*** suszarka *f* **2.** półka *f* (bagażowa) **3.** wieszak *m* **4.** (*car's roof*) bagażnik *m* **5.** stelaż *m* **6.** (*torture*) ława *f* do wyciągania, łoże *n* sprawiedliwości; ***put s.o. on the ~*** łamać kogoś kołem **II** *v/t* dręczyć; ***~ one's brains*** wytężać umysł, łamać sobie głowę

rack[2] [~] *s*: ***go to ~ and ruin*** popaść w ruinę, podupaść

rack•et[1] ['rækɪt] *s SPORT* rakieta *f*

rack•et[2] [~] *s infml* **1.** hałas *m*, harmider *m*; ***make a ~*** hałasować **2.** proceder *m*; ***a drugs ~*** handel narkotykami; ***an extortion ~*** ściąganie haraczu; **rack•et•eer** [rækə'tɪə] *s* reketier *m*

ra•coon [rə'ku:n] → ***raccoon***

rac•y ['reɪsɪ] *adj story*: pikantny

ra•dar ['reɪdɑ:] *s* radar *m*; **'ra•dar screen** *s* ekran *m* radaru; **ra•dar 'speed check** *s* kontrola *f* radarowa

ra•di•al ['reɪdɪəl] **I** *adj* **1.** promienisty **2.** rozchodzący się promieniście **3.** radialny **II** *s* opona *f* radialna; **ra•di•al 'tyre** *Br*, ***ra•di•al* 'tire** *Am*→ **radial II**

R

ra•di•ance ['reɪdɪəns] *s* blask *m*; **ra•di•ant** ['reɪdɪənt] *adj a. fig* promieniujący; ***be ~ with happiness*** promieniować szczęściem

ra•di•ate ['reɪdɪeɪt] **I** *v/t* **1.** *happiness*: promieniować **2.** *confidence*: emanować **3.** *heat*: wydzielać ⟨-lić⟩ **II** *v/i* rozchodzić ⟨-zejść⟩ się promieniście; **ra•di•a•tion** [reɪdɪ'eɪʃn] *s* **1.** promieniowanie *n*; ***~ level*** poziom promieniowania **2.** *MED **~ therapy*** radioterapia *f*; **ra•di•a•tor** ['reɪdɪeɪtə] *s* **1.** grzejnik *m*, kaloryfer *m* **2.** *AUTO* chłodnica *f*; **'ra•di•a•tor grille** *s AUTO* osłona *m* chłodnicy

rad•i•cal ['rædɪkl] **I** *adj* radykalny **II** *s* radykał *m*; **rad•i•cal•ism** ['rædɪkəlɪzm] *s* radykalizm *m*; **rad•i•cal•ize** ['rædɪklaɪz] *v/t* radykalizować ⟨z-⟩; **rad•i•cal•ly** ['rædɪklɪ] *adv* radykalnie

ra•di•i ['reɪdɪaɪ] *pl*→ ***radius***

ra•di•o ['reɪdɪəʊ] **I** *s* radio *n*; ***on the ~*** w radiu; ***turn on the ~*** włączyć radio; ***by ~*** przez radio **II** *adj* radiowy **III** *v/t* przesyłać ⟨-słać⟩ przez radio **IV** *v/i* **1.** łączyć ⟨po-⟩ się przez radio **2.** nadawać ⟨-dać⟩ przez radio; ***~ for help*** wezwać pomoc drogą radiową; **ra•di•o•ac•tive** [reɪdɪəʊ'æktɪv] *adj* radioaktywny, promieniotwórczy; **ra•di•o•ac•tive 'waste** *s* odpady *pl* promieniotwórcze; **ra•di•o•ac•tiv•i•ty** [reɪdɪəʊæk'tɪvətɪ] *s* radioaktywność *f*, promieniotwórczość *f*; **ra•di•o a'larm** *s* radio *n* z budzikiem; **'ra•di•o cab** *s Am* radio-taxi *n*; **ra•di•o 'cas•sette play•er** *s* radioodtwarzacz *m*; **'ra•di•o con•tact** *s* kontakt *m* radiowy; **ra•di•o-con•trolled** [reɪdɪəʊkən'trəʊld] *adj* zdalnie sterowany; **'ra•di•o dra•ma** *s* słuchowisko *n* radiowe

ra•di•og•ra•pher [reɪdɪ'ɔgrəfə] *s MED* technik *m* rentgenowski; **ra•di•og•ra•phy** [reɪdɪ'ɔgrəfɪ] *s MED* radiografia *f*

'ra•di•o ham *s infml* radioamator *m*

ra•di•ol•o•gist [reɪdɪ'ɔlədʒɪst] *s MED* radiolog *m*; **ra•di•ol•o•gy** [reɪdɪ'ɔlədʒɪ] *s MED* radiologia *f*

'ra•di•o link *s* linia *f* radiowa, radiolinia *f*; **'ra•di•o op•er•a•tor** *s* radiooperator *m*; **'ra•di•o pro•gramme** *Br*, ***'ra•di•o pro•gram*** *Am s* program *m* radiowy; **ra•di•o set** *s* odbiornik *m* radiowy; **'ra•di•o sta•tion** *s* stacja *f* radiowa; **'ra•di•o tax•i** *s* radio-taxi *n*; **ra•di•o 'tel•e•phone** *s* radiotelefon *m*; **ra•di•o 'tel•e•scope** *s* radioteleskop *m*; **ra•di•o•'ther•a•py** *s MED* radioterapia *f*; **'ra•di•o traf•fic** *s* radiokomunikacja *f*; **'ra•di•o wave** *s* fala *f* radiowa

rad•ish ['rædɪʃ] *s* rzodkiewka *f*

ra•di•us ['reɪdɪəs] *pl -dii s MATH* promień *m*; ***within a ~ of 50 miles*** w promieniu 50 mil

raf•fle ['ræfl] **I** *s* loteria *f* fantowa **II** *v/t* ***a special prize will be ~d*** można będzie wygrać specjalną nagrodę

raft [rɑ:ft] *s* **1.** tratwa *f* **2.** ponton *m*

raf•ter ['rɑ:ftə] *s* krokiew *m*

rafting ['rɑːftɪŋ] *s SPORT* rafting *m*

rag [ræg] *s* **1.** szmata *f* **2.** ścierka *f* **3.** ***~s*** łachmany; ***dressed in ~s*** ubrany w łachmany; ***from ~s to riches*** od pucybuta do milionera **4.** *infml (newspaper)* szmatławiec *m* **5.** ***be like a red ~ to a bull to*** działać jak czerwona płachta na byka na *A*; **rag•bag** ['rægbæg] *s* miszmasz *m*

rage [reɪdʒ] **I** *s* wściekłość *f*; ***fly into a ~*** wściec się; ***be all the ~*** *infml* być na topie, być trendy **II** *v/i* **1.** wściekać ⟨-ciec⟩ się (***at/against/about*** na *A*) **2.** (*storm, fire*) szaleć **4.** ***a debate ~s on*** wciąż trwa zażarta dyskusja

rag•ged ['rægɪd] *adj* **1.** w strzępach, podarty **2.** w łachmanach, obdarty **3.** nierówny **4.** *infml* wykończony

raid [reɪd] **I** *s* **1.** nalot *m* **2.** atak *m* **3.** napad *m*; ***a bank ~*** napad na bank **II** *v/t* **1.** atakować ⟨za-⟩ **2.** włamywać ⟨-mać⟩ się do *G* **3.** rabować ⟨ob-⟩ **4.** robić ⟨z-⟩ nalot na *A*; **raid•er** ['reɪdə] *s* **1.** rabuś *m* **2.** napastnik *m*

rail[1] [reɪl] *s* **1.** poręcz *f* **2.** barierka *f* **3.** balustrada *f* **4.** (*ship*) reling *m* **5.** wieszak *m*; ***a towel ~*** wieszak na ręczniki **6.** szyna *f*; ***by ~*** koleją; ***go off the ~s*** *fig* zejść na złą drogę, wykoleić się

rail[2] [~] *v/i* złorzeczyć (***at/against*** na *A*)

rail•ings ['reɪlɪŋz] *pl* **1.** ogrodzenie *n* (z metalowych prętów) **2.** barierka *f* **3.** balustrada *f*

'rail•freight *s* transport *m* kolejowy; **'rail pass** *s* wieloprzejazdowy bilet *m* kolejowy; **rail•road** ['reɪlrəʊd] **I** *s Am* → ***railway*** **II** *v/t* **1.** *bill*: przepychać ⟨-pchnąć⟩ **2.** zmuszać ⟨zmusić⟩ (***into*** do *G*); **'rail•road sta•tion** *Am* → ***railway station***

rail•way ['reɪlweɪ] *s Br* **1.** tory *pl* kolejowe **2.** kolej *f* **3.** linia *f* kolejowa; **rail•way sta•tion** *s Br* stacja *f* kolejowa

rain [reɪn] **I** *s* **1.** deszcz *m*; ***in the ~*** w deszczu; ***it looks like ~*** zanosi się na deszcz; ***a ~ of arrows*** grad strzał **2.** ***the ~s*** pora deszczowa **II** *v/i* **1.** ***it's ~ing*** pada (deszcz); ***it never ~s but it pours*** nieszczęścia chodzą parami **2.** (*a.* ***~ down***) spadać ⟨spaść⟩ (***on*** na *A*) **III** *v/t* zasypywać ⟨-pać⟩; ***~ blows on s.o.*** zasypać kogoś ciosami; ***it's ~ing cats and dogs*** leje jak z cebra; **'rain•bow** *s* tęcza *f*; **'rain-check** *s*: ***can I take a ~ on that?*** *Am infml* możemy to odłożyć na inną okazję?, może innym razem?; **'rain-coat** *s* płaszcz *m* przeciwdeszczowy; **'rain•drop** *s* kropla *f* deszczu; **'rain•fall** *s* opady *pl* deszczu; **'rain for•est** *s* tropikalny las *m* deszczowy; **'rain•proof** *adj* nieprzemakalny; **'rain•storm** *s* ulewa *f*; **'rain•wa•ter** *s* deszczówka *f*

rain•y ['reɪnɪ] *adj* deszczowy; ***save s.th. for a ~ day*** trzymać coś na czarną godzinę; **'rain•y sea•son** *s* pora *f* deszczowa

raise [reɪz] **I** *v/t* **1.** podnosić ⟨-nieść⟩; ***~ one's eyebrow*** unieść brew; ***~ eyebrows*** *fig* wywołać zdziwienie; ***~ a hand against*** podnieść rękę na *A*; ***~ one's glass*** wznieść toast; ***~ s.o.'s spirits*** podnieść kogoś na duchu **2.** podwyższać ⟨-szyć⟩ **3.** zwiększać ⟨-szyć⟩ **4.** *money*: zbierać ⟨zebrać⟩ **5.** *issue*: poruszać ⟨-szyć⟩ **6.** *doubts, suspicion*: wzbudzać ⟨-dzić⟩ **7.** *laughter*: wywoływać ⟨-łać⟩ **8.** *dust*: wzniecać ⟨-cić⟩ **9.** wychowywać ⟨-chować⟩; ***I was born and ~d in New York*** urodziłem się i wychowałem w Nowym Jorku **10.** hodować ⟨wy-⟩ **11.** uprawiać **12.** *ban*: znosić ⟨znieść⟩ **13.** kontaktować ⟨s-⟩ się (telefonicznie) z *I* **II** *s Am* podwyżka *f*

rai•sin ['reɪzn] *s COOK* rodzynek *m*, rodzynka *f*

rake [reɪk] **I** *s* **1.** grabie *pl* **2.** *dated* hulaka *f* **II** *v/t* **1.** grabić ⟨za-⟩ **2.** ostrzeliwać ⟨-lać⟩ **3.** omiatać ⟨omieść⟩ (światłami) **4.** drapać ⟨po-⟩; **rake around** *v/i* szperać, grzebać; **rake in** *v/t*: ***~ it in*** *infml* zgarniać kupę kasy; **rake up** *v/t infml past*: odgrzebywać ⟨-bać⟩

'rake-off *s infml* działka *f*, dola *f*

rak•ish ['reɪkɪʃ] *adj* **1.** hulaszczy **2.** ***at a ~ angle*** zawadiacko na bakier

ral•ly ['rælɪ] **I** *s* **1.** wiec *m* **2.** *Br* rajd *m*; ***a car ~*** rajd samochodowy **3.** (*tennis*) wymiana *f* **4.** *ECON* poprawa *f* **II** *v/i* **1.** ***~ to s.o.'s support*** udzielić komuś poparcia **2.** dochodzić ⟨dojść⟩ do siebie **3.** *ECON* zwyżkować **II** *v/t support*: uzyskiwać ⟨-kać⟩; **rally round** *v/i* łączyć ⟨po-⟩ siły

R

RAM [ræm] *abbr* (=***random access memory***) INF pamięć *f* RAM

ram [ræm] **I** *v/t* **1.** taranować ⟨s-⟩ **2.** ***~ s.th. home to*** uzmysłowić coś *D* **II** *v/t* wpychać ⟨wepchnąć⟩ (***into*** do *G*) **III** *s* **1.** baran *m* **2.** taran *m*

ram•ble ['ræmbl] **I** *v/i* **1.** wędrować ⟨po-⟩ **2.** chodzić ⟨pójść⟩, spacerować **3.** mówić bez ładu i składu **4.** rozwodzić się (***about*** na temat *G*) **5.** (*plants*) piąć się **II** *s* **1.** wędrówka *f* **2.** piesza wycieczka *f*; **ram•bler** ['ræmblə] *s* **1.** turysta *f* (pieszy) **2.** pnącze *n*; **ram•bling** ['ræmblıŋ] *adj* **1.** *speech*: bezładny, chaotyczny **2.** *building*: o nieregularnej bryle **3.** *plant*: pnący

ram•i•fi•ca•tions [ræmıfı'keıʃnz] *pl* **1.** reperkusje *pl* **2.** konsekwencje *pl*

ramp [ræmp] *s* **1.** podjazd *m* **2.** rampa *f* **3.** ***an entrance ~*** *Am* wjazd na autostradę; ***an exit ~*** *Am* zjazd z autostrady

ram•page ['ræmpeıdʒ] **I** *s* ***go on the ~*** zacząć szaleć **II** *v/i* szaleć

ram•pant ['ræmpənt] *adj* **1.** *inflation*: szalejący **2.** *corruption*, *unemployment*: szerzący się **3.** *plant*: bujny

ram•part ['ræmpɑːt] *s* wał *m* obronny

ram•shack•le ['ræmʃækl] *adj* **1.** *building*: walący się **2.** *car*: rozklekotany

ran [ræn] *Past Simple* → ***run***

ranch [raːntʃ] *s* ranczo *n*; **ranch•er** ['raːntʃə] *s* ranczer *m*

ran•cid ['rænsıd] *adj butter*: zjełczały

ran•cour ['ræŋkə] *Br*, ***rancor*** *Am s* uraza *f*; **ran•cor•ous** ['ræŋkərəs] *adj* urażony

ran•dom ['rændəm] **I** *adj* **1.** losowy; ***a ~ sample*** próbka losowa; ***in a ~ order*** w kolejności losowej **2.** przypadkowy **II** *s* ***at ~*** na chybił trafił; **ran•dom access mem•o•ry** → ***RAM***

ran•dy ['rændı] *adj Br infml* napalony, nakręcony

rang [ræŋ] *Past Simple* → ***ring***

range [reındʒ] **I** *s* **1.** zakres *m*; ***a full ~ of services*** pełen zakres usług; ***a wide ~ of factors*** wiele różnych czynników; ***in the ~ of 20 to 50 per cent*** w granicach 20-50 procent **2.** asortyment *m*, wybór *m* **3.** zasięg *m*; ***a ~ of 300 miles*** zasięg 300 mil; ***in the ~ of vision*** w polu widzenia **4.** odległość *f* **5.** GEOGR łańcuch *m*; ***a mountain ~*** łańcuch górski **6.** strzelnica *f* **7.** poligon *m* **8.** *Am* kuchenka *f* **9.** *Am* pastwisko *n* **II** *v/i* **1.** mieścić się w zakresie (***between A and B*** pomiędzy A a B); ***their height ~s from 3 inches to 2 feet*** mają wysokość od trzech cali do dwóch stóp; ***she's had a number of different jobs, ranging from babysitter to restaurateur*** imała się różnych zajęć, od niańczenia dzieci po prowadzenie restauracji **2.** wahać się; ***they ~ in price from $30 to $200*** ich cena waha się od trzydziestu do dwustu dolarów **3.** rozciągać się, sięgać **III** *v/t* ustawiać ⟨-wić⟩; **range find•er** ['reındʒfaındə] *s* PHOT dalmierz *m*

rang•er ['reındʒə] *s* strażnik *m* leśny

rank[1] [ræŋk] **I** *s* **1.** pozycja *f*; ***a social ~*** pozycja społeczna **2.** stopień *m*, ranga *f*; ***in the ~ of captain*** w stopniu kapitana, w randze kapitana; ***serve in the ~s*** służyć jako prosty żołnierz **3.** klasa *f*; ***of the first ~*** najwyższej klasy **4.** szereg *m*; ***break ~s*** *fig* wyłamać się z szeregu; ***close ~s*** *fig* zewrzeć szeregi **5.** grono *n*; ***in our ~*** w naszym gronie **II** *v/t* **1.** szeregować ⟨u-⟩ **2.** klasyfikować ⟨s-⟩; ***~ 6th on the list*** zajmować szóste miejsce na liście; ***our university is ~ed number one in the country*** nasz uniwersytet zajmuje pierwsze miejsce w rankingu; **rank among** *v/t* zaliczać się do *G*; ***the hotel ~s among the finest in town*** hotel zalicza się do najlepszych w mieście

rank[2] [~] *adj* **1.** *smell*: obrzydliwy **2.** *outsider*: kompletny **3.** *stupidity*: czysty **4.** *grass*: bujny

rank•ing ['ræŋkıŋ] **I** *s* pozycja *f* w rankingu **II** *adj* **1.** wysoki rangą **2.** najwyższy rangą **3.** ***high-~*** wysoki rangą; ***low-~*** niski rangą; **rank•ings** ['ræŋkıŋz] *pl* ranking *m*

ran•kle ['ræŋkl] *v/i* napełniać ⟨-nić⟩ goryczą (***with*** *A*)

ran•sack ['rænsæk] *v/t* plądrować ⟨s-⟩

ran•som ['rænsəm] **I** *s* okup *m*; ***a ~ demand*** żądanie okupu; ***hold s.o. to ~*** **a)** przetrzymywać kogoś dla okupu **b)** szantażować kogoś **II** *v/t* płacić ⟨za-⟩ okup za *A*

rant [rænt] *v/i* (*a.* ***~ on***, ***~ and rave***) pomstować, ciskać gromy (***about*** na *A*)

R

rap [ræp] **I** *s* **1.** pukanie *n*, stukanie *n*; ***give s.o. a ~ on the knuckles*** *fig* dać komuś po łapach; ***take the ~ for*** *fig* zebrać cięgi za *A* **2.** *MUS* rap *m* **3.** *Am infml* skazanie *n*; ***a ~ sheet*** rejestr skazanych **4.** krytyka *f* **5.** *Am infml* zła sława *f* **II** *v/i* **1.** pukać ⟨za-⟩, stukać ⟨za-⟩; ***~ at the door*** pukać do drzwi **2.** *MUS* rapować **III** *v/t* **1.** krytykować ⟨s-⟩ (**for** za *A*); ***~ s.o. on the knuckles*** *fig* dać komuś po łapach **2.** (*a.* ***~ out***) wykrzykiwać ⟨-rzyczeć⟩

ra•pa•cious [rə'peɪʃəs] *adj* pazerny; **ra•pac•i•ty** [rə'pæsətɪ] *s* pazerność *f*

rape[1] [reɪp] **I** *v/t* gwałcić ⟨z-⟩ **II** *s* gwałt *m*; ***a ~ victim*** ofiara gwałtu

rape[2] [~] *s BIOL* rzepak *m*; ***~*** (***seed***) ***oil*** olej rzepakowy

rap•id ['ræpɪd] *adj* **1.** nagły **2.** gwałtowny **3.** bardzo szybki **4.** błyskawiczny; **'rap•id-fire** *adj* szybkostrzelny

ra•pid•i•ty [rə'pɪdətɪ] *s* **1.** błyskawiczne tempo *n* **2.** szybkość *f*

rap•id•ly ['ræpɪdlɪ] *adv* **1.** bardzo szybko **2.** gwałtownie **3.** błyskawicznie

rap•port [ræ'pɔː] *s*: ***a*** (***good***) ***~*** **a)** dobre stosunki **b)** wzajemne zrozumienie; ***we have a good ~*** dobrze się rozumiemy

rap•proche•ment [ræ'prɒʃmɒŋ] *s POLIT* zbliżenie *n*, ocieplenie *n* stosunków

rapt [ræpt] *adj* **1.** *attention*: wytężony **2.** *person*: skupiony

rap•ture ['ræptʃə] *s* zachwyt *m*; ***go into ~s about*** wpaść w zachwyt nad *I*; **rap•tur•ous** ['ræptʃərəs] *adj* entuzjastyczny

rare [reə] *adj* **1.** rzadki; ***a ~ sight*** rzadki widok **2.** *steak*: krwisty

rar•e•fied ['reərɪfaɪd] *adj* **1.** *air*: rozrzedzony **2.** ekskluzywny, elitarny

rare•ly ['reəlɪ] *adv* rzadko; ***I ~ dance*** rzadko tańczę

rar•ing ['reərɪŋ] *adj*: ***be ~ to do s.th.*** *infml* palić się do *G*

rar•i•ty ['reərətɪ] *s* rzadkość *f*

ras•cal ['ræskl] *s infml* drań *m*, łobuz *m*

rash[1] [ræʃ] *adj* pochopny

rash[2] [~] *s* **1.** *MED* wysypka *f*; ***come out in a ~*** dostać wysypki **2.** *fig* wysyp *m*

rash•er ['ræʃə] *s Br bacon*: plaster *m*

rash•ly ['ræʃlɪ] *adv* pochopnie

rasp [rɑːsp] **I** *s* **1.** zgrzyt *m* **2.** tarka *f* **3.** *TECH* tarnik *m*, raszpla *f* **II** *v/i* zgrzytać ⟨za-⟩ **III** *v/t* **1.** (*a.* ***~ out***) chrypieć ⟨wy-⟩ **2.** obrabiać ⟨-robić⟩ tarnikiem

rasp•ber•ry ['rɑːzbrɪ] *s* malina *f*

rasp•ing ['rɑːspɪŋ] *adj* zgrzytliwy

rat [ræt] *s* szczur *m*; ***smell a ~*** poczuć pismo nosem; **rat on** *v/i infml* **1.** sypać ⟨-pnąć⟩ **2.** *promise*: nie dotrzymywać ⟨-mać⟩

rate [reɪt] **I** *s* **1.** tempo *n*; ***at this ~*** w tym tempie **2.** szybkość *f* **3.** współczynnik *m* **4.** wskaźnik *m*; ***the birth ~*** wskaźnik urodzeń **5.** *ECON* stopa *f*; ***a ~ of interest*** stopa procentowa **6.** kurs *m*; ***a ~ of exchange*** kurs wymiany walut **7.** stawka *f*; ***a ~ of tax*** stawka podatkowa **8.** ***at any ~*** w każdym razie **9.** ***~s*** *Br* podatek od gruntów i nieruchomości **II** *v/t* **1.** oceniać ⟨-nić⟩ **2.** cenić; ***~ high*** wysoko cenić **3.** zasługiwać ⟨-łużyć⟩ na *A*; ***~ a mention in the press*** zasługiwać na wzmiankę w prasie

rather ['ræðə] **I** *adv* **1.** raczej; ***~ a cold night*** raczej zimna noc; ***it was ~ a success*** można to uznać za sukces; ***I'd ~ stay at home*** wolałbym zostać w domu; ***or ~*** czy też raczej **2.** całkiem; ***she's ~ pretty*** jest całkiem ładna **II** *interj Br dated* **1.** oczywiście! **2.** pewnie!

rat•i•fi•ca•tion [rætɪfɪ'keɪʃn] *s* ratyfikacja *f*; **rat•i•fy** ['rætɪfaɪ] *v/t* ratyfikować

rat•ing[1] ['reɪtɪŋ] *s Br* marynarz *m*

rat•ing[2] [~] *s* **1.** ocena *f* **2.** wskaźnik *m*; **rat•ings** ['reɪtɪŋz] *pl* **1.** notowania *pl* **2.** (*TV*) wskaźnik *m* oglądalności; (*radio*) wskaźnik *m* słuchalności

ra•ti•o ['reɪʃɪəʊ] *pl -tios s* **1.** stosunek *m*; ***the ~ of applicants to available places stands at 10:1*** na jedno miejsce przypada dziesięciu chętnych **2.** wskaźnik *m* **3.** proporcja *f*

ra•tion ['ræʃn] **I** *s* **1.** przydział *m* **2.** racja *f*; ***~s*** (*army*) racje żywnościowe **II** *v/t* **1.** racjonować **2.** wydzielać ⟨-lić⟩

ra•tion•al ['ræʃənl] *adj* **1.** racjonalny **2.** rozsądny

ra•tion•ale [ræʃə'nɑːl] *s* **1.** racjonalne podstawy *pl* (**for**/**behind** *G*) **2.** powody *pl* (**for**/**behind** *G*)

ra•tion•al•ism ['ræʃnəlɪzəm] *s* racjonalizm *m*; **ra•tion•al•ist** ['ræʃnəlɪst] *s* racjonalista *m*; **ra•tion•al•'is•tic** *adj* ra-

R

cjonalistyczny; **ra•tion•al•i•ty** [ræʃə'nælɪtɪ] *s* racjonalność *f* **ra•tion•al•i•za•tion** [ræʃənəlaɪ'zeɪʃn] *s* racjonalizacja *f* **ra•tion•al•ize** ['ræʃənəlaɪz] *v/t* **1.** racjonalizować ⟨z-⟩ **2.** uzasadniać ⟨-nić⟩; **ra•tion•al•ly** ['ræʃənlɪ] *adv* racjonalnie

'rat poi•son *s* trutka *f* na szczury; **'rat race** *s*: ***the ~*** *fig* wyścig szczurów

rat•tle ['rætl] **I** *v/i* **1.** grzechotać ⟨za-⟩ **2.** brzęczeć ⟨brzęknąć⟩ **3.** szczękać ⟨-knąć⟩ **4.** stukać ⟨-knąć⟩ **5.** trząść ⟨za-⟩ się **6.** turkotać ⟨za-⟩ **II** *v/t* **1.** trząść ⟨za-⟩ **2.** wytrącać ⟨-cić⟩ z równowagi **III** *s* **1.** grzechotanie *n* **2.** brzęczenie *n*, brzęk *m* **3.** szczękanie *n*, szczęk *m* **4.** stukotanie *n*, stukot *m* **5.** trzęsienie się *n* **6.** turkotanie *n*, turkot *m* **7.** grzechotka *f*; **rattle off** *v/t* recytować ⟨wy-⟩ z pamięci, *infml* wyklepywać ⟨-pać⟩; **rattle on** *v/i* *infml* ględzić (***about*** o *L*)

'rat•tle•snake *s* BIOL grzechotnik *m*

'rat•trap *s* pułapka *f* na szczury

rat•ty ['rætɪ] *adj* **1.** *Br infml* drażliwy **2.** *Am infml* skołtuniony **3.** *Am infml* poszarpany **4.** *eyes*: szczurzy

rau•cous ['rɔːkəs] *adj* **1.** głośny **2.** hałaśliwy **3.** rechotliwy

raun•chy ['rɔːntʃɪ] *adj* **1.** *infml* pikantny; ***a ~ magazine*** świerszczyk **2.** *Am* niechlujny

rav•age ['rævɪdʒ] **I** *v/t* **1.** wyniszczać ⟨-czyć⟩ **2.** pustoszyć ⟨s-⟩ **II** *s* ***~s*** **a)** zniszczenia *pl* **b)** spustoszenia *pl*

rave [reɪv] **I** *v/i* **1.** zachwycać ⟨-cić⟩ się (***about*** *I*) **2.** wrzeszczeć ⟨wrzasnąć⟩ (***at*** na *A*) **3.** bełkotać **II** *s* *infml* **1.** *Br* odjazdowa impreza *f* **2.** *Am* → ***rave review***

R

ra•ven ['reɪvn] **I** *s* kruk *m* **II** *adj hair*: kruczoczarny

rav•e•nous ['rævənəs] *adj* **1.** wygłodzony, wygłodniały; ***I'm ~*** umieram z głodu **2.** *appetite*: wilczy; **rav•e•nous•ly** ['rævənəslɪ] *adv* **1.** *eat*: łapczywie **2.** *hungry*: wściekle, jak wilk

rave re•'view *s* entuzjastyczna recenzja *f*

ra•vine [rə'viːn] *s* GEOGR wąwóz *m*

rav•ing ['reɪvɪŋ] **I** *adj* **1.** *lunatic*: kompletny **2.** *idiot*: skończony **3.** *beauty*: olśniewający **II** *adv* ***she's ~ mad*** to zupełna wariatka **III** *s* ***~s*** bełkot *m*

rav•ish ['rævɪʃ] *v/t* **1.** (*rape*) *lit* niewolić ⟨z-⟩ **2.** olśniewać ⟨-nić⟩; **rav•ish•ing** ['rævɪʃɪŋ] *adj beauty*: olśniewający

raw [rɔː] **I** *adj* **1.** surowy; ***eat s.th. ~*** jeść coś na surowo **2.** w stanie surowym, nieprzetworzony **3.** *emotion*: silny **4.** *skin*: zdarty **5.** *person*: niedoświadczony, *infml* zielony **6.** *wind*: przenikliwie zimny **7.** *description*: naturalistyczny **8.** ***get a ~ deal*** zostać skrzywdzonym **II** *s* ***touch s.o. on the ~*** dotknąć kogoś do żywego; ***life in the ~*** prawdziwe życie; **raw ma•'te•ri•als** *pl* surowce *pl*

ray[1] [reɪ] *s* **1.** promień *m*; ***the sun's ~s*** promienie słoneczne **2.** *a. fig* promyk *m*; ***a ~ of hope*** promyk nadziei

ray[2] [~] *s* BIOL płaszczka *f*

ray•on ['reɪɒn] *s* sztuczny jedwab *m*, rayon *m*

raze [reɪz] *v/t*: ***~ s.th. to the ground*** zrównać coś z ziemią

ra•zor ['reɪzə] *s* **1.** maszynka *f* do golenia **2.** brzytwa *f*; **'ra•zor blade** *s* żyletka *f*; **'ra•zor edge** *s*: ***be on a ~*** być na krawędzi; **'ra•zor-sharp** *adj* **1.** ostry jak brzytwa **2.** błyskotliwy

raz•zle ['ræzl] *s*: ***go on the ~*** *Br infml* iść poszaleć

razz•ma•tazz [ræzmə'tæz] *s infml* (wielka) pompa *f*

re [riː] *prep* (*in letter*) dot.

reach [riːtʃ] **I** *v/t* **1.** docierać ⟨dotrzeć⟩ do *G*; ***the letter didn't ~ him*** list do niego nie dotarł; ***we finally ~ed the border*** w końcu dotarliśmy do granicy **2.** dojeżdżać ⟨-jechać⟩ do *G* **3.** osiągać ⟨-gnąć⟩; ***~ a compromise*** osiągnąć kompromis; ***the temperatures can ~ 45°C*** temperatury mogą dochodzić do 45°C **4.** *conclusion*: dochodzić ⟨dojść⟩ do *G* **5.** *hand*: wyciągać ⟨-gnąć⟩ **6.** sięgać ⟨-gnąć⟩, dosięgać ⟨-gnąć⟩; ***the cable isn't long enough to ~ the socket*** kabel jest zbyt krótki i nie sięga gniazdka **II** *v/i* sięgać ⟨-gnąć⟩; ***~ for a pen*** sięgnąć po długopis; ***~ for the stars*** *fig* wysoko mierzyć **III** *s* **1.** zasięg *m*; ***within ~*** w zasięgu, osiągalny; ***out of the ~*** poza zasięgiem, nieosiągalny; ***within easy ~ of*** blisko *G*; ***keep out of the ~ of children*** chronić przed dziećmi **2.** rozpiętość *f* ramion; ***s.th. is beyond s.o.'s ~***

ktoś nie może czegoś dosięgnąć **3.** ***the upper*** **(*lower*)** ***~es of the river*** GEOGR górny (dolny) bieg rzeki **4.** kraniec *m*; ***the eastern ~es of the continent*** wschodnie krańce kontynentu; **reach out** *v/i* wyciągać ⟨-gnąć⟩ pomocną dłoń (***to*** do *G*)

re•act [rɪ'ækt] *v/i* **1.** reagować ⟨za-⟩ (***to*** na *A*) **2.** buntować ⟨z-⟩ się (***against*** przeciw *D*)

re•ac•tion [rɪ'ækʃn] *s* reakcja *f* (***to*** na *A*); **re•ac•tion•ar•y** [rɪ'ækʃnrɪ] **I** *adj* reakcyjny **II** *s* reakcjonista *m*

re•ac•ti•vate [rɪ'æktɪveɪt] *v/t* reaktywować

re•ac•tive [rɪ'æktɪv] *adj* reaktywny

re•ac•tor [rɪ'æktə] *s nuclear*: reaktor *m*

read[1] [riːd] **I** (*read*; *read*) *v/t* **1.** czytać ⟨prze-⟩; ***learn to ~*** uczyć się czytać; ***~ a book*** czytać książkę; ***I read about it in the papers*** czytałem o tym w gazetach; ***~ s.o.'s mind*** (*a.* ***thoughts***) czytać w czyichś myślach; ***~ s.o.'s lips*** czytać z ruchu czyichś warg; ***~ between the lines*** czytać między wierszami; ***~ s.o. like a book*** *fig* potrafić odgadnąć czyjeś myśli **2.** odczytywać ⟨-tać⟩ **3.** interpretować ⟨z-⟩ **4.** (*meter*) wskazywać ⟨-zać⟩ **5.** (*on radio*) słyszeć; ***do you ~ me?*** czy mnie słyszysz? **6.** *Br* studiować **7.** INF wczytywać ⟨-tać⟩; ***~ a file into a computer*** wczytać plik do komputera **II** (*read*; *read*) *v/i* **1.** brzmieć **2.** czytać się **III** *s* ***be a good ~*** dobrze się czytać; ***have a quiet ~*** spokojnie sobie czytać; **read back** *v/t* odczytywać ⟨-tać⟩; **read into** *v/t*: ***~ too much into*** nadinterpretować *A*; **read out** *v/t* czytać ⟨prze-⟩ na głos, odczytywać ⟨-tać⟩; **read through** *v/t* **1.** czytać ⟨prze-⟩ uważnie **2.** sczytywać ⟨-tać⟩; **read up on** *v/i* **1.** czytać ⟨po-⟩ na temat *G* **2.** uzupełniać ⟨-nić⟩ swoją wiedzę na temat *G*

read[2] [red] **I** *Past Simple and Past Participle* → ***read***[1] **II** *adj* **(*well-*)*~*** oczytany

rea•da•ble ['riːdəbl] *adj* **1.** przyjemny w czytaniu **2.** czytelny

read•er ['riːdə] *s* **1.** czytelnik *m* **2.** czytający *m* **3.** zbór *m* tekstów **4.** *Br* adiunkt *m* **5.** TECH czytnik *m*

read•er•ship ['riːdəʃɪp] *s* **1.** czytelnicy *pl* **2.** *Br* adiunktura *f*

read•i•ly ['redɪlɪ] *adv* **1.** łatwo **2.** chętnie, ochoczo; **read•i•ness** ['redɪnɪs] *s* **1.** gotowość *f* **2.** chęć *f*; ***~ to help*** chęć pomocy

read•ing ['riːdɪŋ] *s* **1.** czytanie *n* **2.** przeczytanie *n* **3.** odczytanie *n* **4.** interpretacja *f* **5.** odczyt *m* **6.** ***be good ~*** dobrze się czytać; **'read•ing glass•es** *pl* okulary *pl* do czytania; **'read•ing lamp** *s* lampka *f* do czytania; **'read•ing mat•ter** *s* lektura *f*; **'read•ing room** *s* czytelnia *f*

re•ad•just [riːə'dʒʌst] **I** *v/i* **1.** przystosowywać ⟨-sować⟩ się (***to*** do *G*) **2.** aklimatyzować ⟨za-⟩ się **II** *v/t* **1.** ustawiać ⟨-wić⟩ **2.** regulować ⟨wy-⟩ **3.** poprawiać ⟨-wić⟩; **re•ad•just•ment** [riːə'dʒʌstmənt] *s* **1.** przystosowanie *n* się **2.** aklimatyzacja *f* **3.** regulacja *f* **4.** zmiana *f*

'read-me doc•u•ment *s* INF plik *m* Readme; **read-'on•ly file** *s* INF plik *m* tylko do odczytu; **read-'on•ly mem•o•ry** *s* INF → ***ROM***; **'read•out** *s* INF **1.** odczyt *m* **2.** (wyświetlona) wartość *f*; **'read-through** *s* THEAT próba *f* czytana; **read-'write head** *s* TECH głowica *f* odczytu-zapisu

read•y ['redɪ] **I** *adj* **1.** gotowy (***for*** na *A*); ***~ to go*** gotowy do wyjścia; ***dinner is ~!*** obiad gotowy!; ***get ~*** przygotować się; ***~, steady, go!*** do biegu, gotowi, start! **2.** chętny; ***he's always ~ to help*** zawsze jest chętny do pomocy **3.** bliski; ***~ to collapse*** bliski załamania **II** *v/t* przygotowywać ⟨-tować⟩; ***~ oneself*** przygotowywać się; **read•y 'cash** *s* gotówka *f*; **read•y-cooked** [redɪ'kʊkt] *adj meal*: gotowy; **ready-made** [redɪ'meɪd] *adj meal, solution*: gotowy; **read•y-to-'wear** *adj clothes*: gotowy; ***~ clothes*** odzież gotowa

re•af•firm [riːə'fɜːm] *v/t* (ponownie) potwierdzać ⟨-dzić⟩; **re•af•fir•ma•tion** [riːæfə'meɪʃn] *s* (ponowne) potwierdzenie *n*

re•af•for•est [riːə'fɒrɪst] *v/t Br* zalesiać ⟨-sić⟩; **re•af•for•est•a•tion** [riːəfɒrɪs'teɪʃn] *s Br* zalesianie *n*

re•a•gent [riː'eɪdʒənt] *s* CHEM odczynnik *m*

R

real [riəl] **I** *adj* **1.** prawdziwy; ***tell me the ~ reason*** podaj mi prawdziwy powód; ***a ~ friend*** prawdziwy przyjaciel; ***he was making a ~ effort*** naprawdę się starał; ***it's for ~*** to się dzieje naprawdę; ***get ~!*** **a)** zejdź na ziemię! **b)** akurat! **2.** realny **3.** rzeczywisty; ***in ~ life*** w rzeczywistości; ***the ~ world*** świat rzeczywisty **4.** poważny **II** *adv Am infml* naprawdę; ***that tastes ~ good*** to jest naprawdę dobre; **'real es•tate** *s* **1.** nieruchomość *f* **2.** nieruchomości *pl* **3.** pośrednictwo *n* w handlu nieruchomościami; **'real es•tate a•gent** *s* agent *m* nieruchomości, pośrednik *m* w handlu nieruchomościami

re•al•ism ['rɪəlɪzəm] *s* realizm *m*; **re•a•list** ['rɪəlɪst] *s* realista *m*; **re•a•lis•tic** [rɪə'lɪstɪk] *adj* realistyczny; **re•a•lis•tic•al•ly** [rɪə'lɪstɪklɪ] *adv* realistycznie

re•al•i•ty [rɪ'ælətɪ] *s* rzeczywistość *f*; ***in ~*** w rzeczywistości; ***face ~*** stawić czoła rzeczywistości; ***become ~*** stać się rzeczywistością; **'re•al•i•ty show** *s* reality show *m*

re•a•li•za•tion [rɪəlaɪ'zeɪʃn] *s* **1.** uświadomienie *n* sobie; ***come to the ~ that*** uświadomić sobie, że **2.** realizacja *f* **3.** spełnienie *n* **4.** *assets*: upłynnienie *n*; **re•a•lize** ['rɪəlaɪz] **I** *v/i* uświadamiać ⟨-domić⟩ sobie, zdawać ⟨zdać⟩ sobie sprawę (***that*** że) **II** *v/t* **1.** uświadamiać ⟨-domić⟩ sobie, zdawać ⟨zdać⟩ sobie sprawę z *G* **2.** realizować ⟨z-⟩ **3.** spełniać ⟨-nić⟩ **4.** *assets*: upłynniać ⟨-nić⟩

real-'life *adj* **1.** prawdziwy **2.** z życia wzięty

real•ly ['rɪəlɪ] *adv* **1.** naprawdę; ***what do you ~ think about her?*** co naprawdę o niej myślisz?; ***now I ~ must go*** teraz naprawdę muszę iść; ***I don't ~ agree*** niezupełnie się zgadzam; ***– 'Did you like the book?' – 'Not ~.'*** – „Podobała ci się książka?" – „Niezbyt."; ***– 'We are going to Japan.' – 'Oh, ~?'*** – „Jedziemy do Japonii." – „Naprawdę?"; ***~, you could have told us before*** no naprawdę, mogłeś nam wcześniej o tym powiedzieć **2.** rzeczywiście

realm [relm] *s* **1.** *lit* królestwo *n* **2.** dziedzina *f* **3.** sfera *f*; ***beyond the ~s of possibility*** niemożliwy

real 'time *s* INF czas *m* rzeczywisty; **real-time** *adj* INF w czasie rzeczywistym; ***~ processing*** przetwarzanie danych w czasie rzeczywistym

reanimate [riː'ænɪmeɪt] *v/t* ożywiać ⟨-wić⟩

reap [riːp] *v/t* **1.** *profit*: czerpać **2.** zbierać ⟨zebrać⟩; ***~ the rewards of one's hard work*** zbierać owoce ciężkiej pracy **3.** kosić ⟨s-⟩; ***you ~ what you sow*** *fig* zbierać, co się zasiało

re•ap•pear [riːə'pɪə] *v/i* **1.** powracać ⟨-rócić⟩ **2.** wracać ⟨wrócić⟩ **3.** pojawiać ⟨-wić⟩ się ponownie; **reappearance** [riːə'pɪərəns] *s* **1.** powrót *m* **2.** ponowne pojawienie *n* się

re•ap•prais•al [riːə'preɪzl] *s* ponowna ocena *f*; **re•ap•praise** [riːə'preɪz] *v/t* ponownie oceniać ⟨-nić⟩

rear[1] [rɪə] *v/t* **1.** wychowywać ⟨-chować⟩ **2.** hodować ⟨wy-⟩

rear[2] [~] **I** *s* **1.** tył *m*; ***the front and the ~*** przód i tył; ***an entrance to the ~*** wejście od tyłu; ***bring up the ~*** *fig* ubezpieczać tyły **2.** *infml* siedzenie *n*, tyłek *m* **II** *adj* tylny **III** *v/i* (*a.* **~ up**) (*horse*) stawać ⟨stanąć⟩ dęba; **rear 'ax•le** *s* TECH tylna oś *f*; **'rear-end** *v/t*: **~ s.o.** *infml* wjechać komuś w tył; **rear 'ex•it** *s* tylne wyjście *n*; **'rear•guard** *s* tylna straż *f*; **rear 'light** *s* AUTO tylne światło *n*

re•arm [riː'ɑːm] *v/t* **1.** ponownie uzbrajać ⟨-roić⟩ **2.** remilitaryzować ⟨z-⟩; **re•ar•ma•ment** [rɪ'ɑːməmənt] *s* **1.** ponowne uzbrajanie *n* **2.** remilitaryzacja *f*

'rear•most *adj* **1.** najbardziej wysunięty do tyłu **2.** ostatni

re•ar•range [riːə'reɪnʒ] *v/t* **1.** *furniture*: przestawiać ⟨-wić⟩ **2.** *meeting*: przekładać ⟨przełożyć⟩ na inny termin

rear-view 'mir•ror *s* AUTO lusterko *n* wsteczne

rear•ward ['rɪəwəd] **I** *adj* **1.** tylni **2.** do tyłu **II** *adv* do tyłu

'rear•wards → ***rearward II***

rear-wheel 'drive *s* AUTO napęd *m* na tylne koła

rear win•dow *s* AUTO tylna szyba *f*; **rear wip•er** *s* AUTO tylna wycieraczka *f*

rea•son ['riːzn] **I** *s* **1.** powód *m*; ***give me a ~ why*** powiedz, dlaczego; ***for some ~*** z jakiegoś powodu; ***for personal ~s*** z powodów osobistych; ***have one's***

R

~s mieć swoje powody; ***we have every ~ to*** mamy wszelkie powody, aby; ***with ~*** nie bez powodu; ***by ~ of*** z powodu *G* **2.** przyczyna *f* **3.** rozum *m*; ***lose one's ~*** postradać rozum **4.** rozsądek *m*; ***listen to ~*** posłuchać głosu rozsądku **II** *v/i* **1.** stwierdzać ⟨-dzić⟩, dochodzić ⟨dojść⟩ do wniosku **2.** ***~ with s.o.*** przekonywać kogoś

rea•so•na•ble ['riːznəbl] *adj* **1.** *person*: rozsądny **2.** *argument*: sensowny **3.** *price*: rozsądny, umiarkowany **4.** *offer*: przyzwoity **5.** *doubt*: uzasadniony **6.** znośny; ***the hotel was ~*** hotel był znośny; **rea•son•a•bly** ['riːznəblɪ] *adv* **1.** dość, dosyć **2.** rozsądnie; ***be ~ priced*** być w rozsądnej cenie **3.** sensownie; **rea•son•ing** ['riːznɪŋ] *s* **1.** rozumowanie *n* **2.** logika *f*

re•as•sem•ble [riːə'sembl] **I** *v/t* (ponownie) składać ⟨złożyć⟩, (ponownie) montować ⟨z-⟩ **II** *v/i* spotykać ⟨-tkać⟩ się (ponownie); ***after lunch, the class ~d*** po lunchu uczniowie wrócili do klasy

re•as•sur•ance [riːə'ʃʊrəns] *s* **1.** zapewnienie *n* **2.** otucha *f* **3.** wsparcie *n*; **re•as•sure** [riːə'ʃʊə] *v/t* **1.** zapewniać ⟨-nić⟩ **2.** dodawać ⟨-dać⟩ otuchy **3.** uspokajać ⟨-koić⟩; **re•as•sur•ing** [riːə'ʃʊərɪŋ] *adj* **1.** pocieszający; ***it's ~ to know that*** pocieszająca jest myśl, że **2.** uspokajający

re•bate ['riːbeɪt] *s* **1.** *taxes*: zwrot *m* **2.** rabat *m*

reb•el[1] ['rebl] *s* **1.** buntownik *m* **2.** rebeliant *m*

re•bel[2] [rɪ'bel] *v/i* buntować ⟨z-⟩ się (***against*** przeciw *D*); **reb•el•lion** [rɪ'belɪən] *s* **1.** bunt *m* **2.** rebelia *f*; **rebel•lious** [rɪ'beljəs] *adj* buntowniczy; **reb•el•lious•ly** [rɪ'belɪəslɪ] *adv* buntowniczo; **reb•el•lious•ness** [rɪ'beljəsnɪs] *s* buntowniczość *f*

re•birth [riː'bɜːθ] *s* odrodzenie *n*

re•boot [riː'buːt] INF **I** *v/i* restartować ⟨z-⟩ **II** *v/i* restartować ⟨z-⟩ się

re•bound [rɪ'baʊnd] **I** *v/i* **1.** (*ball*) odbijać ⟨-bić⟩ się (***from/off*** od *G*) **2.** *fig* odbijać ⟨-bić⟩ się (**on** na *L*) **3.** (*prices*) (ponownie) rosnąć ⟨wz-⟩ **II** ['riːbaʊnd] *s* **1.** ECON ożywienie *n* **2.** odbicie *n* **3.** rykoszet *m* **4.** odbita piłka *f* **5.** ***be on the ~*** przeżywać zawód miłosny

re•buff [rɪ'bʌf] **I** *v/t* **1.** odrzucać ⟨-cić⟩ **2.** odmawiać ⟨-mówić⟩ **II** *s* **1.** odmowa *f*; ***meet with a ~*** spotkać się z odmową **2.** odrzucenie *n*

re•build [riː'bɪld] (*rebuilt*; *rebuilt*) *v/t* **1.** odbudowywać ⟨-dować⟩ **2.** przebudowywać ⟨-dować⟩

re•buke [rɪ'bjuːk] **I** *v/t* **1.** ganić ⟨z-⟩ **2.** udzielać ⟨-lić⟩ nagany **3.** karcić ⟨s-⟩ **II** *s* nagana *f*

re•but [rɪ'bʌt] *v/t* **1.** *accusations*: odpierać ⟨odeprzeć⟩ **2.** dementować ⟨z-⟩; **re•but•tal** [rɪ'bʌtl] *s* **1.** *accusations*: odparcie *n* **2.** zdementowanie *n*

re•cal•ci•trant [rɪ'kælsɪtrənt] *adj child*: krnąbrny

re•call [rɪ'kɔːl] **I** *v/t* **1.** przypominać ⟨-mnieć⟩ sobie **2.** pamiętać; ***I can't ~ his name*** nie pamiętam jego imienia **3.** przypominać **4.** *product*: wycofywać ⟨-fać⟩ ze sprzedaży **5.** (*to team*) (ponownie) powoływać ⟨-łać⟩ **II** *v/i* **1.** przypominać ⟨-mnieć⟩ sobie **2.** pamiętać **III** *s* **1.** pamięć *f* **2.** (*to team*) (ponowne) powołanie *n* **3.** ***lost beyond ~*** bezpowrotnie stracony

re•cap ['riːkæp] **I** *v/t* → ***recapitulate*** **II** *s* → ***recapitulation***

re•ca•pit•u•late [riːkə'pɪtjʊleɪt] *v/t* **1.** reasumować ⟨z-⟩ **2.** podsumowywać ⟨-mować⟩; **re•ca•pit•u•la•tion** [riːkəpɪtjʊ'leɪʃn] *s* podsumowanie *n*

re•cap•ture [riː'kæptʃə] **I** *v/t* **1.** *town*: odzyskiwać ⟨-kać⟩, odbijać ⟨-bić⟩ **2.** *prisoner*: ujmować ⟨-ująć⟩ **3.** *memories*: przywoływać ⟨-łać⟩ **4.** *atmosphere*: odtwarzać ⟨-worzyć⟩ **II** *s* **1.** *town*: odzyskanie *n*, odbicie *n* **2.** *prisoner*: ujęcie *n*

re•cast [riː'kɑːst] (*recast*; *recast*) *v/t* **1.** zmieniać ⟨-nić⟩ obsadę; ***be ~ as*** zostać obsadzonym w roli *G* **2.** przerabiać ⟨-robić⟩ (**as** na *A*) **3.** przeorganizowywać ⟨-zować⟩ **4.** przetapiać ⟨-topić⟩

re•cede [rɪ'siːd] *v/i* **1.** oddalać ⟨-lić⟩ się; ***the prospect of bankruptcy has now ~d*** widmo bankructwa się oddaliło **2.** cofać ⟨-fnąć⟩ się **3.** (*voice*) niknąć **4.** (*hair*) ***his hair is beginning to ~*** zaczyna łysieć **5.** (*pain*) łagodnieć

R

⟨z-⟩; **re•ced•ing** [rɪˈsiːdɪŋ] *adj* **1.** ***with ~ hair*** łysiejący **2.** *jaw*: cofnięty

re•ceipt [rɪˈsiːt] *s* **1.** paragon *m*; ***can I have the ~, please?*** czy mogę prosić o paragon? **2.** pokwitowanie *n* **3.** odbiór *m* **4.** otrzymanie *n*; ***on ~ of*** po otrzymaniu *G* **5.** ***~s*** *ECON* wpływy

re•ceive [rɪˈsiːv] *v/t* **1.** otrzymywać ⟨-mać⟩ **2.** *guests*: przyjmować ⟨-jąć⟩ **3.** *RADIO* odbierać ⟨odebrać⟩; ***are you receiving me?*** czy mnie słyszysz? **4.** spotykać ⟨-tkać⟩ się z *I*; ***~ a warm welcome*** spotkać się z ciepłym przyjęciem **5.** *injuries*: odnosić ⟨-nieść⟩ **6.** (*tennis*) odbierać ⟨odebrać⟩

re•ceiv•er [rɪˈsiːvə] *s* **1.** słuchawka *f*; ***pick up the ~*** podnieść słuchawkę **2.** *RADIO* odbiornik *m* **3.** odbiorca *m* **4.** *ECON* syndyk *m* (masy upadłościowej)

re•ceiv•er•ship [rɪˈsiːvəʃɪp] *s ECON* zarząd *m* przymusowy

re•ceiv•ing [rɪˈsiːvɪŋ] *adj*: ***he was on the ~ end of harsh criticism*** został ostro skrytykowany

re•cent [ˈriːsnt] *adj* **1.** niedawny **2.** ostatni; ***in ~ years*** w ostatnich latach **2.** najnowszy; **re•cent•ly** [ˈriːsntlɪ] *adv* **1.** niedawno; ***as ~ as yesterday*** zaledwie wczoraj; ***until ~*** do niedawna **2.** ostatnio; ***I haven't seen him ~*** ostatnio go nie widziałem

re•cep•ta•cle [rɪˈseptəkl] *s* **1.** pojemnik *m* **2.** zbiornik

re•cep•tion [rɪˈsepʃn] *s* **1.** recepcja *f*; ***at ~*** w recepcji **2.** (*outpatients*) rejestracja *f* **3.** przyjęcie *n*; ***a wedding ~*** przyjęcie weselne; ***give s.o. a warm ~*** zgotować komuś ciepłe przyjęcie; ***meet with an enthusiastic ~*** spotkać się z entuzjastycznym przyjęciem **4.** *TECH* odbiór *m*; **re'cep•tion desk** *s* recepcja *f*

re•cep•tion•ist [rɪˈsepʃnɪst] *s* **1.** recepcjonista *m*, recepcjonistka *f* **2.** (*outpatients*) rejestrator *m*, rejestratorka *f*

re•cep•tive [rɪˈseptɪv] *adj* **1.** *mind*: chłonny **2.** *person*: otwarty; ***~ to new ideas*** otwarty na nowe pomysły

re•cess **I** [rɪˈses] *s* **1.** przerwa *f* **2.** wakacje *pl* parlamentarne **3.** wnęka *f* **4.** zakamarek *m* **5.** zakątek *m* **II** *v/t* **1.** przerywać ⟨-rwać⟩ **2.** umieszczać ⟨umieścić⟩ we wnęce **3.** wbudowywać ⟨-dować⟩ w *A*

re•ces•sion [rɪˈseʃn] *s* **1.** *ECON* recesja *f*; ***be in deep ~*** znajdować się w głębokiej recesji **2.** cofanie się *n* **3.** ustępowanie *n*

re•charge [riːˈtʃɑːdʒ] *v/t battery, gun*: ponownie ładować ⟨na-⟩; **re•charge•a•ble** [riːˈtʃɑːdʒəbl] *adj*: ***a ~ battery*** **a)** akumulator **b)** akumulatorek; ***the battery is ~*** baterię można ładować

re•cid•i•vist [rɪˈsɪdɪvɪst] *s* recydywista *m*

re•ci•pe [ˈresəpɪ] *s* przepis *m*; ***a ~ for s.th*** przepis na coś **ˈre•ci•pe book** *s* książka *f* kucharska

re•cip•i•ent [rɪˈsɪpɪənt] *s* **1.** odbiorca *m* **2.** beneficjent *m* **3.** laureat *m* **4.** biorca *m*

re•cip•ro•cal [rɪˈsɪprəkl] *adj* **1.** wzajemny **2.** obustrony **3.** obopólny; **re•cip•ro•cate** [rɪˈsɪprəkeɪt] **I** *v/t* odwzajemniać ⟨-nić⟩ **II** *v/i* **1.** odwzajemniać ⟨-nić⟩ się (**with** *I*) **2.** *TECH* poruszać się ruchem postępowo-zwrotnym; **re•cip•ro•ca•tion** [rɪsɪprəˈkeɪʃn] *s* **1.** odwzajemnienie *n* **2.** wzajemność *f*

re•cit•al [rɪˈsaɪtl] *s* **1.** *MUS* recital *m* **2.** *fig* litania *f*; **rec•i•ta•tion** [resɪˈteɪʃn] *s* recytacja *f*; **rec•i•ta•tive** [resɪtəˈtiːv] *s MUS* recytatyw *m*; **re•cite** [rɪˈsaɪt] *v/t* **1.** recytować ⟨wy-⟩ **2.** wyliczać ⟨-czyć⟩

reck•less [ˈreklɪs] *adj* **1.** lekkomyślny **2.** *driving*: niebezpieczny; **reck•less•ly** [ˈreklɪslɪ] *adv* **1.** lekkomyślnie **2.** *drive*: niebezpiecznie; **reck•less•ness** [ˈreklɪsnɪs] *s* **1.** lekkomyślność *f* **2.** brawura *f*

reck•on [ˈrekən] **I** *v/i* sądzić, przypuszczać; ***I ~ I'm going to get the job*** sądzę, że dostanę tę pracę; ***what do you ~?*** jak sądzisz?; ***you ~?*** tak sądzisz? **II** *v/t* **1.** ***they are ~ed to be better*** uchodzą za lepszych **2.** ***the age of the earth is ~ed at about 4600 million years*** wiek ziemi szacuje się na około 4,6 mld lat; **reckon on** *v/i* liczyć na; ***~ good weather*** spodziewać się ładnej pogody; **reckon with** *v/t* **1.** liczyć się z *I*; ***political force to be ~ed with*** siła polityczna, z którą trzeba się liczyć

R

reck•on•ing ['rekənɪŋ] *s* **1.** szacunki *pl*, obliczenia *pl*; ***by my ~*** **a)** według moich obliczeń **b)** w mojej ocenie **2.** ***the Day of ~*** Dzień Sądu Ostatecznego

re•claim [rɪ'kleɪm] **I** *v/t* **1.** odbierać ⟨odebrać⟩ **2.** odzyskiwać ⟨-kać⟩ **3.** żądać ⟨za-⟩ zwrotu **4.** *land*: rekultywować ⟨z-⟩ **5.** *rubbish*: utylizować ⟨z-⟩ **II** *v/t* odbiór *m*; ***baggage ~*** odbiór bagażu; **re•cla•ma•tion** [reklə'meɪʃn] *s* **1.** odbiór *m* **2.** rekultywacja *f* **3.** utylizacja *f*

re•cline [rɪ'klaɪn] **I** *v/i* **1.** siedzieć ⟨usiąść⟩ **2.** leżeć, kłaść ⟨położyć⟩ się **3.** mieć regulowane oparcie **4.** (*armchair*) rozkładać ⟨-złożyć⟩ się **II** *v/t* odchylać ⟨-lić⟩ oparcie; **re•clin•er** [rɪ'klaɪnə] *s Am* fotel *m* z regulowanym oparciem

re•cluse [rɪ'klu:s] *s* **1.** samotnik *m* **2.** odludek *m*; **re•clu•sive** [rɪ'klu:sɪv] *adj* **1.** samotniczy **2.** stroniący od ludzi; ***be ~*** być samotnikiem

rec•og•ni•tion [rekəg'nɪʃn] *s* **1.** rozpoznanie *n*; ***the town has changed beyond ~*** miasto zmieniło się nie do poznania **2.** rozpoznawanie *n* **3.** świadomość *f*; ***a growing ~ of the need for reform*** rosnąca świadomość potrzeby reform **4.** uznanie *n*; ***gain ~*** zyskać uznanie; ***in ~ of*** w uznaniu *G*, w dowód uznania za *A*; **rec•og•niz•a•ble** ['rekəgnaɪzəbl] *adj* rozpoznawalny; ***he was hardly ~*** trudno go było poznać

rec•og•nize ['rekəgnaɪz] **I** *v/t* **1.** poznawać ⟨-nać⟩ (***by*** po *L*) **2.** rozpoznawać ⟨-nać⟩ (***by*** po *L*) **3.** uznawać ⟨-nać⟩; ***~ s.o.'s qualifications*** uznać czyjeś kwalifikacje; ***be a ~d authority*** być uznanym autorytetem **4.** uświadamiać ⟨-domić⟩ sobie **II** *v/i* uznawać ⟨-nać⟩

re•coil **I** [rɪ'kɔɪl] *v/i* **1.** cofać ⟨-fnąć⟩ się (***from*** przed *I*) **2.** wzdrygać ⟨-gnąć⟩ się; ***~ at the sight of*** wzdrygnąć się na widok *G*; ***~ at the idea of*** wzdrygnąć się na myśl o *L* **II** ['ri:kɔil] *s gun*: odrzut *m*

rec•ol•lect [rekə'lekt] *v/t* **1.** przypominać ⟨-mnieć⟩ sobie **2.** pamiętać; ***as far as I can ~*** o ile pamiętam; **rec•ol•lec•tion** [rekə'lekʃn] *s* **1.** ***I have no ~ of her*** nie pamiętam jej; ***to the best of my ~*** z tego, co pamiętam **2.** wspomnienie *n*

rec•om•mend [rekə'mend] *v/t* **1.** polecać ⟨-cić⟩; ***can you ~ a good hotel?*** czy może mi pan polecić dobry hotel? **2.** zalecać ⟨-cić⟩; ***a ~ed dose*** zalecana dawka **3.** ***he has little to ~ him*** niewiele dobrego można o nim powiedzieć; **rec•om•mend•a•ble** [rekə'mendəbl] *adj* godny polecenia; **rec•om•men•da•tion** [rekəmen'deɪʃn] *s* **1.** zalecenie *n*; ***a doctor's ~*** zalecenie lekarza **2.** ***I chose the hotel on her ~*** wybrałem ten hotel, bo ona mi go poleciła **3.** rekomendacja *f*; **rec•om•mend•ed re•tail price** [rekəmendɪd'ri:teɪlpraɪs] *s ECON* sugerowana cena *f* detaliczna

rec•om•pense ['rekəmpens] **I** *s* **1.** odszkodowanie *n* (***for*** za *A*) **2.** rekompensata *f* **II** *v/t* **1.** wypłacać ⟨-cić⟩ odszkodowanie (***for*** za *A*) **2.** wynagradzać ⟨-rodzić⟩ (***for*** *A*)

rec•on•cile ['rekənsaɪl] *v/t* godzić ⟨po-⟩; ***~ one's career with one's family life*** pogodzić karierę zawodową z życiem rodzinnym; ***they are ~d*** pogodzili się; ***~ oneself to*** pogodzić się z *I*, zaakceptować *A*; **rec•on•cil•i•a•tion** [rekənsɪlɪ'eɪʃn] *s* **1.** pojednanie *n* **2.** pogodzenie *n* się **3.** godzenie *n*; ***the ~ of one's career with one's family life*** godzenie kariery zawodowej z życiem rodzinnym **4.** pogodzenie *n*

rec•on•dite ['rekəndaɪt] *adj* **1.** hermetyczny **2.** elitarny

re•con•di•tion [ri:kən'dɪʃn] *v/t* **1.** remontować ⟨wy-⟩ **2.** regenerować ⟨z-⟩

re•con•nais•sance [rɪ'kɒnɪsns] *s* **1.** rozpoznanie *n* **2.** zwiad *m* **3.** rekonesans *m*; **re•'con•nais•sance flight** *s* lot *m* zwiadowczy; **re•'con•nais•sance plane** *s* samolot *m* zwiadowczy

rec•on•noi•tre [rekə'nɔɪtə] *Br*, ***rec•on•noi•ter*** *Am* *v/t* przeprowadzać ⟨-dzić⟩ rozpoznanie

re•con•quer [ri:'kɒŋkə] *v/t* **1.** odbijać ⟨-bić⟩ **2.** odzyskiwać ⟨-kać⟩

re•con•sid•er [ri:kən'sɪdə] **I** *v/t* **1.** ponownie przemyśleć **2.** *opinion*: rewidować ⟨z-⟩ **II** *v/i* zmieniać ⟨-nić⟩ zdanie; **re•con•sid•er•a•tion** [ri:kənsɪd-

R

əˈeɪʃn] *s* **1.** ponowne przemyślenie *n* **2.** *opinion*: rewizja *f*

re•con•struct [riːkənˈstrʌkt] *v/t* **1.** odbudowywać ⟨-dować⟩ **2.** rekonstruować ⟨z-⟩; **re•con•struc•tion** [riːkənˈstrʌkʃn] *s* **1.** odbudowa *f* **2.** rekonstrukcja *f*

rec•ord [ˈrekɔːd] **I** *s* **1.** zapis *m*; ***keep a ~ of*** zapisywać *A*; ***keep a ~ of one's expenses*** notować swoje wydatki; ***off the ~*** *fig* nieoficjalnie, prywatnie; ***for the ~*** warto przy okazji wspomnieć, że; ***set the ~ straight*** sprostować nieścisłości **2.** rejestr *m* **3.** protokół *m* **4.** akta *pl* **5.** ***~s*** dokumentacja *f*; ***medical ~s*** dokumentacja medyczna **6.** MUS płyta *f*; ***a ~ company*** firma fonograficzna **7.** rekord *m*; ***set a new ~*** ustanowić nowy rekord; ***break the ~*** pobić rekord **8.** ***she has a strong ~ of achievement*** ma na swoim koncie wiele osiągnięć **9.** ***he has a criminal ~*** był notowany **II** [rɪˈkɔːd] *v/t* **1.** notować ⟨za-⟩ **2.** zapisywać ⟨-sać⟩ **3.** rejestrować ⟨za-⟩ **4.** dokumentować ⟨u-⟩ **5.** protokołować ⟨za-⟩ **6.** *song*, *film*: nagrywać ⟨-rać⟩ **7.** *temperature*: wskazywać ⟨-zać⟩

ˈrec•ord-break•ing *adj* rekordowy

re•cor•der [rɪˈkɔːdə] *s* **1.** nagrywarka *f*; ***a tape ~*** magnetofon; ***a DVD ~*** nagrywarka DVD **2.** MUS flet *m* prosty

ˈrec•ord hold•er *s* rekordzista *m*

re•cord•ing [rɪˈkɔːdɪŋ] *s* **1.** nagranie *n* **2.** nagrywanie *n*; **re•ˈcord•ing en•gi•neer** *s* inżynier *m* dźwięku; **re•ˈcord•ing head** *s* TECH głowica *f* zapisująca; **re•ˈcord•ing stu•di•o** *s* studio *n* nagraniowe

R

ˈrec•ord play•er *s* gramofon *m*

re•count[1] [rɪˈkaʊnt] *v/t* **1.** opowiadać ⟨-wiedzieć⟩ **2.** opisywać ⟨-sać⟩

re•count[2] **I** [ˈriːkaʊnt] *s* ponowne przeliczenie *n* **II** [riːˈkaʊnt] *v/t* ponownie przeliczać ⟨-czyć⟩

re•coup [rɪˈkuːp] *v/t* **1.** ***we hope to ~ our investment in one year*** mamy nadzieję, że nasza inwestycja zwróci się w ciągu roku **2.** *losses*: rekompensować ⟨z-⟩

re•course [rɪˈkɔːs] *s*: ***without ~ to*** nie uciekając się do *G*; ***have ~ to*** uciec się do *G*

re•cov•er [rɪˈkʌvə] **I** *v/i* **1.** zdrowieć ⟨wy-⟩ **2.** dochodzić ⟨dojść⟩ do siebie; ***~ from an operation*** dochodzić do siebie po operacji **3.** wychodzić ⟨wyjść⟩ z kryzysu **II** *v/t* odzyskiwać ⟨-kać⟩; ***the police ~ed the stolen paintings*** policja odzyskała ukradzione obrazy; ***~ consciousness*** odzyskać świadomość; **re•cov•er•y** [rɪˈkʌvərɪ] *s* **1.** powrót *m* do zdrowia, wyzdrowienie *n*; ***make a ~*** wyzdrowieć; ***wish s.o. a quick ~*** życzyć komuś szybkiego powrotu do zdrowia **2.** ożywienie *n*, poprawa *f*; ***an economic ~*** ożywienie gospodarcze **3.** odzyskanie *n* **4.** MED sala *f* pooperacyjna

rec•re•a•tion [rekrɪˈeɪʃn] *s* **1.** rekreacja *f* **2.** ***his ~s include tennis and cycling*** w wolnym czasie gra w tenisa i jeździ na rowerze; **rec•re•a•tion•al** [rekrɪˈeɪʃnl] *adj* rekreacyjny; ***a ~ vehicle*** *Am* samochód turystyczny

re•crim•in•a•tions [rɪkrɪmɪnˈeɪʃnz] *pl* wzajemne oskarżenia *pl*

re•cruit [rɪˈkruːt] **I** *v/t* **1.** rekrutować **2.** werbować ⟨z-⟩ **3.** przyjmować ⟨-jąć⟩ do pracy **II** *s* **1.** rekrut *m* **2.** nowy pracownik *m*; **re•cruit•ment** [rɪˈkruːtmənt] *s* **1.** rekrutacja *f* **2.** nabór *m* **3.** werbowanie *n*, werbunek *m*

rec•ta [ˈrektə] *pl* → ***rectum***

rec•tan•gle [ˈrektæŋgl] *s* prostokąt *m*; **rec•tan•gu•lar** [rekˈtæŋgjʊlə] *adj* prostokątny

rec•ti•fi•ca•tion [rektɪfɪˈkeɪʃn] *s* **1.** poprawienie *n* **2.** naprawa *f*; **rec•ti•fy** [ˈrektɪfaɪ] *v/t* **1.** poprawiać ⟨-wić⟩ **2.** naprawiać ⟨-wić⟩

rec•ti•lin•e•ar [rektɪˈlɪnɪə] *adj movement*: prostoliniowy

rec•ti•tude [ˈrektɪtjuːd] *s* prawość *f*

rec•tor [ˈrektə] *s* **1.** (*Anglican church*) proboszcz *m* **2.** rektor *m* **3.** dyrektor *m*; **rec•to•ry** [ˈrektərɪ] *s* (*Anglican church*) probostwo *n*

rec•tum [ˈrektəm] *pl -tums, -ta s* ANAT odbytnica *f*

re•cu•pe•rate [rɪˈkuːpəreɪt] **I** *v/i* wracać ⟨wrócić⟩ do zdrowia **II** *v/t* odzyskiwać ⟨-kać⟩

re•cur [rɪˈkɜː] *v/t* **1.** powtarzać ⟨-tórzyć⟩ się **2.** powracać ⟨-rócić⟩ **3.** nawracać ⟨-rócić⟩; **re•cur•rence** [rɪˈkʌrəns] *s* **1.** powtórzenie *n* się **2.** *ill-*

ness: nawrót *m*; **re•cur•rent** [rɪ'kʌrənt] *adj* **1.** powtarzający się **2.** powracający

re•cy•cle [riː'saɪkl] *v/t* **1.** utylizować ⟨z-⟩ **2.** przetwarzać ⟨-worzyć⟩; **re•cy•cla•ble** [riː'saɪkləbl] *adj* nadający się do przetworzenia; **re•cy•cling** [riː'saɪklɪŋ] *s* **1.** recycling *m* **2.** utylizacja *f*; **re'cy•cling plant** *s* zakład *m* utylizacji

red [red] **I** *adj* **1.** czerwony; ***the sky went ~*** niebo poczerwieniało; ***she'd go ~*** zaczerwieniłaby się **2.** *hair*: rudy **II** *s* **1.** czerwony *m*, czerwień *f*; ***see ~*** *fig* wściec się; ***be in the ~*** *infml* być na minusie **2.** *infml* czerwony *m*; **red 'car•pet** *s*: ***give s.o. the ~ treatment*** *fig* potraktować kogoś z wszelkimi honorami; **red 'card** *s* SPORT czerwona kartka *f*; **Red 'Cross** *s* Czerwony Krzyż *m*; **red•'cur•rant** *s* czerwona porzeczka *f*

red•den ['redn] **I** *v/i* **1.** czerwienić ⟨za-⟩ się **2.** poczerwienieć **II** *v/t* zabarwiać ⟨-wić⟩ na czerwowo; **red•dish** ['redɪʃ] *adj* **1.** czerwonawy **2.** rudawy

re•dec•o•rate [riː'dekəreɪt] *v/t* **1.** odnawiać ⟨-nowić⟩ **2.** odmalowywać ⟨-lować⟩ **3.** remontować ⟨od-⟩

re•deem [rɪ'diːm] *v/t* **1.** rekompensować ⟨z-⟩; ***she is irritating but her sense of humour is her ~*** jest irytująca, ale ratuje ją poczucie humoru **2.** *situation*: ratować ⟨u-⟩ **3.** ***~ oneself*** zrehabiliować się **4.** REL odkupić **5.** *loan*: spłacać ⟨-cić⟩ **6.** *pawned goods*: wykupywać ⟨-pić⟩ **7.** *coupon*: realizować ⟨z-⟩ **8.** *promise*: spełniać ⟨-nić⟩; **Re•deem•er** [rɪ'diːmə] *s* REL Odkupiciel *m*

re•demp•tion [rɪ'dempʃn] *s* **1.** REL odkupienie *n* **2.** ***s.th. is beyond ~, s.th. is past ~*** czegoś nie da się już uratować **3.** *from pawn*: wykupienie *n*, umorzenie *n*

re•de•vel•op [riːdɪ'veləp] *v/t* **1.** przebudowywać ⟨-dować⟩ **2.** zmieniać ⟨-nić⟩ sposób zagospodarowania; **re•de•vel•op•ment** [riːdɪ'veləpmənt] *s* **1.** przebudowa *f* **2.** zmiana *f* sposobu zagospodarowania

'red eye *s* PHOT efekt *m* czerwonych oczu; **'red-eye (flight)** *s Am infml* nocny lot *m*; **red-hand•ed** [red'hændɪd] *adj*: ***catch s.o. ~*** złapać kogoś na gorącym uczynku; **'red•head** *s* rudzielec *m*; **red-head•ed** [red'hedɪd] *adj* rudy; **red 'her•ring** *s fig* temat *m* zastępczy; **red-'hot** *adj* **1.** rozgrzany do czerwoności **2.** *news*: gorący **3.** ***the ~ favourite*** absolutny faworyt, *infml* pewniak

re•di•al [riː'daɪəl] **I** *v/i* powtórnie wybierać ⟨-brać⟩ numer **II** *v/t number*: powtórnie wybierać ⟨-brać⟩

re•di•rect [riːdɪ'rekt] *v/t* **1.** *resources*: przekierowywać ⟨-rować⟩ **2.** *traffic*: kierować ⟨s-⟩ w inną stronę **3.** *mail*: kierować ⟨s-⟩ na inny adres

re•dis•cov•er [riːdɪ'skʌvə] *v/t* **1.** powtórnie odkrywać ⟨-ryć⟩ **2.** odnajdować ⟨-naleźć⟩; **re•dis•cov•er•y** [riːdɪ'skʌvərɪ] *s* **1.** powtórne odkrycie *n* **2.** odnalezienie *n*

re•dis•trib•ute [riːdɪ'strɪbjuːt] *v/t* **1.** dokonywać ⟨-nać⟩ redystrybucji **2.** ponownie rozdzielać ⟨-lić⟩; **re•dis•trib•u•tion** [riːdɪstrɪ'bjuːʃn] *s* **1.** redystrybucja *f* **2.** ponowne rozdzielenie *n*

red-'let•ter day *s* pamiętny dzień *m*; **red 'light** *s* czerwone światło *n*; ***go through a ~*** przejechać na czerwonym świetle; **red 'light dis•trict** *s* dzielnica *f* domów publicznych; **red 'meat** *s* czerwone mięso *n*; **'red•neck** *s Am infml* wsiok *m* (z Południa); **red•ness** ['rednɪs] *s* **1.** czerwień *f* **2.** zaczerwienienie *n*

re•do [riː'duː] (*redid*; *redone*) *v/t* **1.** robić ⟨z-⟩ jeszcze raz **2.** przerabiać ⟨-robić⟩ **3.** odnawiać ⟨-nowić⟩

re•dou•ble [riː'dʌbl] *v/t* podwajać ⟨-woić⟩

re•doubt•a•ble [rɪ'daʊtəbəl] *adj opponent*: budzący respekt

red 'pep•per *s* czerwona papryka *f*

re•dress [rɪ'dres] **I** *v/t* **1.** *error*: naprawiać ⟨-wić⟩ **2.** *balance*: przywracać ⟨-rócić⟩ **II** *s* zadośćuczynienie *n*

red 'tape *s fig* (nadmierna) biurokracja *f*

re•duce [rɪ'djuːs] *v/t* **1.** zmniejszać ⟨-szyć⟩; ***~ speed*** zmniejszyć prędkość, zwolnić **2.** obniżać ⟨-żyć⟩; ***~ taxes*** obniżyć podatki **3.** redukować ⟨z-⟩ **4.** doprowadzać ⟨-dzić⟩ (***to*** do *G*); ***~ s.o. to tears*** doprowadzić kogoś do płaczu **5.** ***live in ~d circumstances***

R

mieć trudne warunki materialne; **re•duced-e•mis•sion** [rɪdjuːsdɪ'mɪʃn] *adj* o zmniejszonej emisji zanieczyszczeń; **re•duc•tion** [rɪ'dʌkʃn] *s* **1.** zmniejszenie *n* **2.** obniżenie *n* **3.** spadek *m* **4.** redukcja *f* **5.** obniżka *f* **6.** przecena *f* **7.** *PHOT* pomniejszenie *n*

re•dun•dan•cy [rɪ'dʌndənsɪ] *s* **1.** *Br* zwolnienie *n* (z pracy); ***10 ~ies*** redukcja dziesięciu miejsc pracy; ***a ~ payment*** odprawa **2.** *INF* redundancja *f*; **re•dun•dant** [rɪ'dʌndənt] *adj* **1.** *Br worker*: zredukowany ***make s.o. ~*** zwolnić kogoś **2.** *device*: zbędny, zbyteczny

red 'wine *s* czerwone wino *n*

reed [riːd] *s* **1.** *BIOL* trzcina *f* **2.** *MUS* stroik *m*

re-ed•u•cate [riː'edʒʊkeɪt] *v/t* reedukować

reed•y ['riːdɪ] *s voice*: piskliwy

reef [riːf] **I** *s* **1.** rafa *f*; ***a coral ~*** rafa koralowa **2.** (*sail*) ref *m* **II** *v/t sail*: refować ⟨z-⟩; **'reef knot** *s Br* węzeł *m* refowy

reek [riːk] **I** *v/i* cuchnąć, śmierdzieć; ***~ of hypocrisy*** *fig* zalatywać hipokryzją **II** *s* odór *m*

reel[1] [riːl] **I** *v/i* **1.** zataczać się; ***be ~ing from the shock*** *fig* być w głębokim szoku **2.** chwiać się **3.** *fig* wirować; ***the room was ~ing before my eyes*** pokój wirował mi przed oczami; ***my head is ~ing*** kręci mi się w głowie **II** *s* (*Scottish dance*) reel *m*

reel[2] [~] **I** *s* **1.** szpula *f* **2.** szpulka *f* **3.** *wire*: zwój *m* **4.** *PHOT* rolka *f* **5.** *wool*: kłębek *m* **6.** (*fishing rod*) kołowrotek *m* **II** *v/t* ***~ s.th. in*** wyciągać (za pomocą kołowrotka); **reel off** *v/t* recytować ⟨wy-⟩

re-elect [riː'ɪlekt] *v/t* ponownie wybierać ⟨-brać⟩; **re-elec•tion** [riː'ɪlekʃn] *s* ponowny wybór *m*, reelekcja *f*

reel-to-reel *adj tape recorder*: szpulowy

re-en•ter [riː'entə] *v/t* **1.** wracać ⟨wrócić⟩ do *G* **2.** ponownie wchodzić ⟨wejść⟩ do *G*; **re-entry** [riː'entrɪ] *s* **1.** powrót *m* **2.** ponowne wejście *n* **3.** wejście *n* w atmosferę; **re-entry visa** *s* wiza *f* wielokrotna

ref [ref] *infml* → ***referee I.1***

ref. [ref] *abbr* (=***reference***) nr ref.

re•fec•to•ry [rɪ'fektərɪ] *s* refektarz *m*

re•fer [rɪ'fɜː] **I** *v/i* **1.** wspominać ⟨-mnieć⟩ (***to*** *A*); ***the attackers weren't ~red to by name*** nie podano nazwisk napastników **2.** mówić (***to*** o *L*); ***you know who I'm ~ring to*** wiecie, o kim mówię; ***she always ~red to him as 'that nice man'*** zawsze mówiła o nim „ten miły człowiek" **3.** odnosić ⟨-nieść⟩ się (***to*** do *G*) **4.** oznaczać (***to*** *A*); ***what does this term ~s to?*** co oznacza ten termin? **5.** konsultować ⟨s-⟩; ***~ to the dictionary*** sięgnąć do słownika **II** *v/t* **1.** odsyłać ⟨odesłać⟩ (***s.o. to*** kogoś do *G*) **2.** kierować ⟨s-⟩; ***my doctor ~red me to a specialist*** mój lekarz skierował mnie do specjalisty **3.** przekazywać ⟨-zać⟩ (***to*** *D*)

ref•er•ee [refə'riː] **I** *s* **1.** *SPORT* sędzia *m*, arbiter *m* **2.** *Br* osoba *f* wystawiająca referencje **II** *v/t* sędziować

ref•er•ence ['refərəns] *s* **1.** wzmianka *f*; ***she made no ~ to her problems*** nie wspomniała nic o swoich problemach **2.** odniesienie *n*; ***in ~ to*** w odniesieniu do *G*; ***I wrote her number down for future ~*** zapisałem jej numer na wypadek, gdybym kiedyś go potrzebował **3.** konsultacja *f*; ***without ~ to a doctor*** bez konsultacji z lekarzem **4.** numer *m* referencyjny **5.** ***~s*** referencje *pl* **6.** ***~s*** bibliografia *f* **7.** osoba *f* wystawiająca referencje; **'ref•er•ence book** *s* **1.** publikacja *f* encyklopedyczna **2.** słownik *m* **3.** podręcznik *m*; **'ref•er•ence li•bra•ry** *s* księgozbiór *m* podręczny

ref•e•ren•dum [refə'rendəm] *pl -dums, -da s* referendum *n*; ***hold a ~*** zorganizować referendum

re•fill **I** [riː'fɪl] *v/t* ponownie napełniać ⟨-nić⟩; ***she ~ed his wine glass*** dolała mu wina **II** ['riːfɪl] *s* **1.** ***would you like a ~?*** napijesz się jeszcze?, dolać ci jeszcze? **2.** wkład *m* **3.** nabój *m* **4.** uzupełnienie *n*; **'re•fill pack** *s* opakowanie *n* uzupełniające

re•fine [rɪ'faɪn] *v/t* **1.** rafinować **2.** udoskonalać ⟨-lić⟩ **3.** dopracowywać ⟨-cować⟩; **re•fined** [rɪ'faɪnd] *adj* **1.** rafinowany **2.** wyrafinowany **3.** wytworny **4.** dopracowany; **re•fine•ment** [rɪ-

R

'faınmənt] *s* **1.** udoskonalenie *n* **2.** udoskonalanie *n* **3.** udoskonalona wersja *f* **4.** wyrafinowanie *n* **5.** wytworność *f*; **re•fin•e•ry** [rı'faınərı] *s* rafineria *f*

reflect [rı'flekt] **I** *v/t* **1.** odbijać ⟨-bić⟩ **2.** odzwierciedlać ⟨-lić⟩ **II** *v/i* **1.** zastanawiać ⟨-nowić⟩ się (***on*** nad *I*); ***I didn't have time to ~*** nie miałem czasu się zastanowić **2.** świadczyć; ***~ well*** (***badly***) ***on*** dobrze (źle) świadczyć o *L*; **re•flec•tion** [rı'flekʃn] *s* **1.** odbicie *n* **2.** odbijanie *n* **3.** odzwierciedlenie *n*; ***be a ~ of*** odwierciedlać *A* **4.** namysł *m*; ***on ~*** po namyśle; **re•flec•tive** [rı'flektıv] *adj* **1.** refleksyjny **2.** skłonny do zadumy **3.** odbijający światło **4.** odblaskowy **5.** ***be ~ of*** być odzwierciedleniem *G*; **re•flec•tor** [rı'flektə] *s* **1.** reflektor *m* **2.** światełko *n* odblaskowe

re•flex ['ri:fleks] **I** *s* odruch *m*; ***have quick ~s*** mieć (dobry) refleks **II** *adj* odruchowy; **'re•flex ac•tion** *s*: ***as a ~, in a ~*** odruchowo; **'re•flex cam•er•a** *s PHOT* lustrzanka *f*

re•flex•ive [rı'fleksıv] *adj verb*: zwrotny

re•flex•ol•o•gy [ri:flek'sɒlədʒı] *s MED* refleksologia *f*

re•for•est [ri:'fɒrıst] → ***reafforest***; **re•for•est•a•tion** [ri:fɒrıs'teıʃn] → ***reafforestation***

re•form [rı'fɔ:m] **I** *v/t* **1.** reformować ⟨z-⟩ **2.** zmieniać ⟨-nić⟩ (na lepsze) **II** *s* reforma *f*; ***economic ~s*** reformy gospodarcze

ref•or•ma•tion [refə'meıʃn] *s* **1.** reforma *f* **2.** poprawa *f* **3.** zmiana *f* na lepsze **4.** ***the ~*** *REL* Reformacja

re•form•a•to•ry [rı'fɔ:mətərı] *s Am* dom *m* poprawczy

re•form•er [rı'fɔ:mə] *s* reformator *m*

re•fract [rı'frækt] *v/t light*: załamywać ⟨-mać⟩; **re•frac•tion** [rı'frækʃn] *s light*: załamanie *n*

re•frac•to•ry [rı'fræktərı] *adj* **1.** nieposłuszny **2.** uparty **3.** oporny na leczenie

re•frain[1] [rı'freın] *v/i* powstrzymywać ⟨-mać⟩ się (***from*** od *G*); ***please ~ from smoking*** prosimy nie palić

re•frain[2] [~] *s MUS* refren *m*

re•fresh [rı'freʃ] *v/t* **1.** odświeżać ⟨-żyć⟩; ***allow me to ~ your memory*** pozwól, że ci przypomnę **2.** orzeźwiać ⟨-zić⟩ **3.** *Am infml* ponownie napełniać ⟨-nić⟩; ***can I ~ your glass?*** dolać ci jeszcze?; **re•'fresher** *Am* → ***refresher course***; **re•fresh•er course** [rı'freʃəkɔ:s] *s* kurs *m* doszkalający; **re•fresh•ing** [rı'freʃıŋ] *adj* **1.** odświeżający **2.** orzeźwiający **3.** *fig* świeży **4.** ***make a ~ change*** stanowić miłą odmianę; **re•fresh•ing•ly** [rı'freʃıŋlı] *adv* **1.** orzeźwiająco **2.** ***be ~ different*** stanowić miłą odmianę; **re•fresh•ments** [rı'freʃmənts] *pl* napoje i przekąski *pl*; **re•'fresh rate** *s INF* częstotliwość *f* odświeżania

re•frig•er•ate [rı'frıdʒəreıt] *v/t* wkładać ⟨włożyć⟩ do lodówki; ***keep s.th. ~d*** przechowywać coś w lodówce; **re•frig•er•a•tion** [rıfrıdʒər'eıʃn] *s*: ***keep s.th. under ~*** przechowywać coś w lodówce; **re•frig•er•a•tor** [rı'frıdʒəreıtə] *s* **1.** lodówka *f* **2.** chłodziarka *f*

re•fu•el [ri:f'jʊəl] *v/t* **1.** tankować ⟨za-⟩ **2.** uzupełniać ⟨-nić⟩ zapas paliwa w zbiorniku *G*

ref•uge ['refju:dʒ] *s* **1.** schronienie *n*; ***take ~*** schronić się; ***seek ~*** szukać schronienia **2.** *fig* ucieczka *f*; ***take ~ in the work*** szukać ucieczki w pracy

ref•u•gee [refjʊ'dʒi:] *s* uchodźca *m*; **ref•u•'gee camp** *s* obóz *m* dla uchodźców

re•fund I ['ri:fʌnd] *s* zwrot *m* pieniędzy ***a tax ~*** zwrot podatku **II** [rı'fʌnd] *v/t money*: zwracać ⟨-rócić⟩

re•fur•bish [ri:'fɜ:bıʃ] *v/t* **1.** remontować ⟨wy-⟩ **2.** odnawiać ⟨-nowić⟩; **re•fur•bish•ment** [ri:'fɜ:bıʃmənt] *s* **1.** remont *m* **2.** odnowienie *n*

re•fus•al [rı'fju:zl] *s* **1.** odmowa *f* **2.** odrzucenie *n*

re•fuse[1] [rı'fju:z] *v/t* **1.** odmawiać ⟨-mówić⟩; ***she ~d to comment*** odmówiła komentarza; ***he ~d to eat anything*** nie chciał nic jeść **2.** *invitation*: odrzucać ⟨-cić⟩

ref•use[2] ['refju:s] *s* **1.** śmieci *pl* **2.** odpadki *pl*; **3.** odpady *pl* **ref•use dump** ['refju:sdʌmp] *s* wysypisko *n* śmieci; **ref•use skip** ['refju:sskıp] *s* kontener *m* na gruz i odpady

re•fut•a•ble [rı'fju:təbl] *adj* łatwy do obalenia; **ref•u•ta•tion** [refjʊ'teıʃn] *s theory*: obalenie *n*; **re•fute** [rı'fju:t]

R

v/t theory: obalać ⟨-lić⟩; **~ s.o.** udowodnić komuś, że się myli
re•gain [rɪ'geɪn] *v/t* odzyskiwać ⟨-kać⟩; **~ consciousness** odzyskać przytomność; **~ one's strength** odzyskać siły
re•gal ['riːgl] *adj* królewski
re•gale [rɪ'geɪl] *v/t* podejmować ⟨-djąć⟩, raczyć ⟨u-⟩ (**s.o. with** kogoś *I*)
re•ga•li•a [rɪ'geɪlɪə] *s* **1.** insygnia *pl* królewskie **2.** paradny strój *m*
re•gard [rɪ'gɑːd] **I** *v/t* **1.** uznawać ⟨-nać⟩ (**s.o./s.th. as** kogoś/coś za *A*) **2.** uważać; **he ~s himself as an artist** uważa się za artystę **3.** traktować ⟨po-⟩ (**as** jako *A*) **4. as ~s** jeśli chodzi o *A*, co się tyczy *G* **5.** patrzeć ⟨po-⟩; **~ s.o. suspiciously** popatrzeć na kogoś podejrzliwie **II** *s* **1.** szacunek *m*, poważanie *n* **2.** wzgląd *m*; **in that ~** w tym względzie; **with ~ to a)** jeżeli chodzi o *A*, co się tyczy *G* **b)** związany z *I*; **without ~ to** nie zważając na *A* **3.** uwaga *f*; **pay ~ to** zwracać uwagę na *A* **4. best ~s, with kind ~s** (*ending letter*) **a)** serdecznie pozdrawiam **b)** z poważaniem; **give him my best ~s** pozdrów go ode mnie; **re•gard•ing** [rɪ'gɑːdɪŋ] *prep* **1.** w związku z *I*; **issues ~ security** kwestie związane z bezpieczeństwem, kwestie bezpieczeństwa **2.** odnośnie *G*; **re•gard•less** [rɪ'gɑːdlɪs] **I** *adv* mimo to, mimo wszystko **II** *adj* **~ of** niezależnie od *G*, bez względu na *A*
re•gat•ta [rɪ'gætə] *s* SPORT regaty *pl*
re•gen•cy ['riːdʒənsɪ] *s* regencja *f*
re•gen•er•ate [rɪ'dʒenəreɪt] **I** *v/i* **1.** regenerować ⟨z-⟩ się **2.** odrastać ⟨-rosnąć⟩ **II** *v/t* **1.** ożywiać ⟨-wić⟩ **2.** regenerować ⟨z-⟩; **re•gen•er•a•tion** [rɪdʒenər'eɪʃn] *s* **1.** regeneracja *f* **2.** odrośnięcie *n* **3.** ożywienie *n*
re•gent ['riːdʒənt] *s* regent *m*
reg•gae ['regeɪ] *s* MUS reggae *n*
re•gime [reɪ'ʒiːm] *s* **1.** reżim *m* **2.** *tax*: system *m* **3.** → **regimen 2, 3**
reg•i•men ['redʒɪmen] *s* **1.** reżim *m* **2.** *exercise*: program *m* **3. a dietary ~** ścisła dieta
re•gi•ment ['redʒɪmənt] *s* **1.** pułk *m* **2.** *fig* chmara *f* **3.** *fig* zastępy *pl*; **reg•i•men•tal** [redʒɪ'mentl] *adj*: **a ~ flag (colours)** flaga (kolory) pułku; **reg•i•men•ta•tion** [redʒɪmen'teɪʃn] *s* **1.** surowa dyscyplina *f* **2.** reżim *m*
re•gion ['riːdʒən] *s* **1.** region *m* **2.** okolica *f*; **in the ~ of 2000** około 2000 roku **3.** rejon *m*; **re•gion•al** ['riːdʒənl] *adj* **1.** regionalny **2.** okoliczny **3.** rejonowy
re•gis•ter ['redʒɪstə] **I** *v/t* **1.** rejestrować ⟨za-⟩; **~ a company** zarejestrować spółkę **2.** notować ⟨za-⟩; **the stock exchange ~ed losses** giełda zanotowała spadki **3.** zgłaszać ⟨-łosić⟩ **4.** (*instrument*) wskazywać ⟨-zać⟩ **5.** wyrażać ⟨-razić⟩; **her face ~ed disapproval** jej twarz wyrażała dezaprobatę **6.** zauważać ⟨-żyć⟩ **7.** *letter*: nadawać ⟨-dać⟩ jako polecony **II** *v/i* **1.** (*hotel*) meldować ⟨za-⟩ się **2.** (*doctor*) rejestrować ⟨za-⟩ się **3.** (*feelings*) malować ⟨od-⟩ się **III** *s* **1.** rejestr *m* **2.** spis *m* **3.** ewidencja *f* **4.** dziennik *m*; **the teacher called the ~** nauczyciel sprawdził obecność **5.** *Am* kasa *f*; **re•gis•tered let•ter** [redʒɪstəd'letə] *s* list *m* polecony; **reg•is•tered of•fice** [redʒɪstəd'ɔfɪs] *s* siedziba *f* (firmy); **reg•is•tered trade•mark** [redʒɪstəd'treɪdmæk] *s* zastrzeżony znak *m* towarowy
reg•is•trar [redʒɪ'strɑː] *s* **1.** urzędnik *m* stanu cywilnego **2.** *Br* kierownik *m* dziekanatu **3.** *Br* lekarz *m* w trakcie specjalizacji
re•gis•tra•tion [redʒɪ'streɪʃn] *s* **1.** rejestracja *f* **2.** zgłoszenie *n* **3.** zapisy *pl*; **re•gis•'tra•tion num•ber** *s Br* numer *m* rejestracyjny
reg•is•try ['redʒɪstrɪ] *s* archiwum *n*; **'reg•is•try of•fice** *s Br* urząd *m* stanu cywilnego
re•gress [rɪ'gres] *v/i* cofać ⟨-fnąć⟩ się w rozwoju; **re•gres•sion** [rɪ'greʃn] *s* regres *m*; **re•gres•sive** [rɪ'gresɪv] *adj* regresywny
re•gret [rɪ'gret] **I** *v/t* żałować; **I don't ~ a thing** niczego nie żałuję; **I ~ that I am unable to accept your invitation** przykro mi, że nie mogę przyjąć Pańskiego zaproszenia; **we ~ to inform you** z przykrością informujemy **II** *s* żal *m*; **express one's ~** wyrazić żal; **with great ~** z wielkim żalem; **have no ~s** niczego nie żałować; **re•gret•ful**

R

[rɪ'gretfəl] *adj look*: pełen żalu; **re·gret·ful·ly** [rɪ'gretfəlɪ] *adj* **1.** z żalem **2.** niestety; **re·gret·ta·ble** [rɪ'gretəbl] *adj* **1.** *accident*: niefortunny **2.** ***it is ~ that*** szkoda, że; **re·gret·ta·bly** [rɪ'gretəblɪ] *adv* niestety

re·group [riː'gruːp] *v/t* przegrupowywać ⟨-pować⟩

reg·u·lar ['regjʊlə] **I** *adj* **1.** regularny; ***at ~ intervals*** w regularnych odstępach czasu; ***on a ~ basis*** regularnie **2.** często; ***a ~ guest*** częsty gość; ***be a ~ occurrence*** często mieć miejsce **3.** *income, duties, employment*: stały; ***be in ~ employment*** być zatrudnionym na stałe **4.** zwykły **5.** normalny **6.** standardowy **7.** *soldier*: zawodowy **II** *s* **1.** stały klient *m* **2.** stały bywalec *m* **3.** stały uczestnik *m* **4.** żołnierz *m* zawodowy; **reg·u·lar 'cus·tom·er** *s* stały klient *m*; **reg·u·lar 'gas·o·line** *s Am* benzyna *f* zwykła; **reg·u·lar in·come** *s* stały dochód *m*

reg·u·lar·i·ty [regjʊ'lærətɪ] *s* **1.** regularność *f*; **reg·u·lar·ize** ['regjələraɪz] *v/t* legalizować ⟨za-⟩; **reg·u·lar·ly** ['regjələlɪ] *adj* **1.** regularnie **2.** często; **reg·u·lar play·er** *s* gracz *m* zawodowy

reg·u·late ['regjʊleɪt] *v/t* **1.** regulować ⟨u-⟩ **2.** kontrolować ⟨s-⟩ **3.** nastawiać ⟨-wić⟩; **reg·u·la·tion** [regjʊ'leɪʃn] **I** *adj* **1.** przepis *m* **2.** ***~s*** regulamin *m* **3.** kontrola *f* **4.** regulacja *f* **II** *adj outfit*: przepisowy; **reg·u·la·tor** ['regjʊleɪtə] *s* **1.** kontroler *m* **2.** regulator *m*; **reg·u·la·to·ry** [regjʊ'leɪtərɪ] *adj procedure*: kontrolny

re·ha·bil·i·tate [riːə'bɪlɪteɪt] *v/t* **1.** *patient*: rehabilitować ⟨z-⟩, poddawać ⟨-dać⟩ rehabilitacji **2.** *fig* rehabilitować ⟨z-⟩ **3.** resocjalizować ⟨z-⟩; **re·ha·bil·i·ta·tion** [riːəbɪlɪ'teɪʃn] *s* **1.** rehabilitacja *f* **2.** resocjalizacja *f*

re·hash **I** [riː'hæʃ] *v/t* **1.** *old ideas*: odgrzewać ⟨-rzać⟩ **2.** *song*: przerabiać ⟨-robić⟩ **II** ['riːhæʃ] *s* **1.** *old ideas*: odgrzewanie *n* **2.** *songs*: przerabianie *n*

re·hears·al [rɪ'hɜːsl] *s MUS THEAT* próba *f*; ***a dress ~*** próba generalna; **re·hearse** [rɪ'hɜːs] *v/t* **1.** próbować **2.** robić ⟨z-⟩ próbę **3.** ćwiczyć ⟨prze-⟩

reign [reɪn] **I** *s* **1.** rządy *pl*, panowanie *n* **II** *v/i* **1.** rządzić, panować; ***~ over England*** rządzić Anglią **2.** *fig* panować ⟨za-⟩; ***silence ~ed*** zapanowała cisza

re·im·burse [riːɪm'bɜːs] *v/t costs*: zwracać ⟨-rócić⟩, refundować ⟨z-⟩; **re·im·burse·ment** [riːɪm'bɜːsmənt] *s* zwrot *m* (kosztów)

rein [reɪn] *s*: ***~s*** lejce *pl*, wodze *pl*, cugle *pl*; ***give free ~ to one's imagination*** popuścić wodze fantazji; ***give s.o. free ~*** dać komuś wolną rękę; ***keep a tight ~ on spending*** ściśle kontrolować wydatki; ***keep s.o. on a tight ~*** trzymać kogoś w karbach, trzymać kogoś krótko; **rein in** *v/t* **1.** *spending, inflation*: ograniczać ⟨-czyć⟩ **2.** *emotions*: trzymać na wodzy **3.** *horse*: ściągać ⟨-gnąć⟩ cugle

re·in·car·nate [riːɪn'kɑːneɪt] *v/t*: ***be ~d*** odradzać się; **re·in·car·na·tion** [riːɪnkɑː'neɪʃn] *s* reinkarnacja *f*

rein·deer ['reɪndɪə] *pl -deer s* renifer *m*

re·in·force [riːɪn'fɔːs] *v/t* **1.** wzmacniać ⟨-mocnić⟩ **2.** umacniać ⟨umocnić⟩; **re·in·forced con·crete** [riːɪn'fɔːst~] *s TECH* żelbet *m*, żelbeton *m*; **re·in·force·ment** [riːɪn'fɔːsmənt] *s* **1.** ***~s*** (*army*) posiłki *pl* **2.** wzmocnienie *n* **3.** umocnienie *n*

re·in·state [riːɪn'steɪt] *v/t* przywracać ⟨-rócić⟩; ***he was ~d in his post*** został przywrócony na stanowisko

re·in·sur·ance [riːɪn'ʃʊrəns] *s* (*insurance*) reasekuracja *f*; **re·in·sure** [riːɪn'ʃʊə] *v/t* reasekurować

re·in·vent [riːɪn'vent] *v/t* przekształcać ⟨-cić⟩; ***~ the wheel*** *fig* odkrywać Amerykę

re·is·sue [riː'ɪʃuː] **I** *v/t book*: wznawiać ⟨-nowić⟩ **II** *s book*: wznowienie *n*

re·it·e·rate [riː'ɪtəreɪt] *v/t* powtarzać ⟨-tórzyć⟩

re·ject [rɪ'dʒekt] **I** *v/t* odrzucać ⟨-cić⟩ **II** *s* **1.** wyrób *m* wybrakowany, odrzut *m* **2.** wyrzutek *m*; **re·jec·tion** [rɪ'dʒekʃn] *s* odrzucenie *n*

re·joice [rɪ'dʒɔɪs] *v/i* **1.** radować się, cieszyć się (***at/in/over*** *I*) **2.** świętować (***at/in/over*** *A*); **re·joic·ing** [rɪ'dʒɔɪsɪŋ] *s* **1.** radość *f* **2.** świętowanie *n*

re·join[1] [riː'dʒɔɪn] *v/t* **1.** wracać ⟨wrócić⟩ do *G* **2.** ponownie wstępować ⟨-tąpić⟩ do *G*

re•join[2] [rɪ'dʒɔɪn] *v/i* ripostować ⟨z-⟩; **re•join•der** [riː'dʒɔɪndə] *s* riposta *f*, replika *f*

re•ju•ve•nate [rɪ'dʒuːvəneɪt] *v/t* odmładzać ⟨-łodzić⟩; **re•ju•ve•na•tion** [rɪdʒuːvə'neɪʃn] *s* odmłodzenie *n*

re•kin•dle [riː'kɪndl] *v/t feelings, memories*: budzić ⟨o-⟩

re•lapse ['riːlæps] **I** *s* nawrót *m* (choroby) **II** *v/i* **1. she ~d** pogorszyło jej się **2. they ~d into their old habits** wrócili do starych przyzwyczajeń **3. he ~d into silence** ponownie zamilkł **4. ~ into a coma** ponownie zapaść w śpiączkę

re•late [rɪ'leɪt] *v/t* **1.** łączyć ⟨po-⟩ **2.** wiązać ⟨po-⟩ **3.** relacjonować ⟨z-⟩, zdawać ⟨zdać⟩ relację z *G*; **re•late to** *v/i* **1.** być związanym z *I* **2.** wiązać się z *I* **3.** odnosić się do *G* **4.** identyfikować się z *I* **5.** znajdować ⟨znaleźć⟩ wspólny język z *I*

re•lat•ed [rɪ'leɪtɪd] *adj* **1.** związany **2.** powiązany; ***these problems are closely ~*** te problemy są ze sobą ściśle powiązane **3.** spokrewniony (***to*** z *I*) **4.** *species, languages*: pokrewny

re•la•tion [rɪ'leɪʃn] *s* **1.** stosunek *m*; ***diplomatic ~*** stosunki dyplomatyczne **2.** relacja *f* **3.** związek *m*; ***bear no ~ to*** nie mieć związku z *I*; ***in ~ to*** **a)** w związku z *I* **b)** w porównaniu do *G* **4.** powiązanie *n* **5.** krewny *pl*; ***a distant ~*** daleki krewny; ***we're no ~*** nie jesteśmy ze sobą spokrewnieni; **re•la•tion•al da•ta•base** [rɪleɪʃnl 'deɪtəbeɪs] *s INF* relacyjna baza *f* danych

R

re•la•tion•ship [rɪ'leɪʃnʃɪp] *s* **1.** relacja *f*; ***have a close ~ to s.o.*** być z kimś blisko związanym **2.** stosunki *pl* **3.** związek *m* **4.** powiązanie *n* **5.** pokrewieństwo *n*

rel•a•tive ['relətɪv] **I** *adj* **1.** względny; ***~ to*** względem *G*; ***a ~ clause*** zdanie względne **2.** stosunkowy **3. *~ to*** związany z *I* **II** *s* krewny *m*; **rel•a•tive•ly** ['relətɪvlɪ] *adv* **1.** względnie; ***~ easy*** względnie łatwy **2.** stosunkowo; **rel•a•tiv•i•ty** [relə'tɪvɪtɪ] *s* względność *f*; ***the theory of ~*** teoria względności

re•lax [rɪ'læks] **I** *v/i* **1.** relaksować ⟨z-⟩ się **2.** odprężać ⟨-żyć⟩ się **3.** uspokajać ⟨-koić⟩ się; ***~!*** spokojnie! **4.** rozluźniać ⟨-nić⟩ się **II** *v/t* **1.** *grip, muscles*: rozluźniać ⟨-nić⟩ **2.** *law*: łagodzić ⟨z-⟩; **re•lax•a•tion** [riːlæk'seɪʃn] *s* **1.** relaks *m* **2.** odprężenie *n* **3.** *law*: złagodzenie *n*; **re•laxed** [rɪ'lækst] *adj* **1.** zrelaksowany **2.** odprężony **3.** spokojny **4.** rozluźniony **5.** swobodny; **re•lax•ing** [rɪ'læksɪŋ] *adj* **1.** relaksujący **2.** odprężający **3.** rozluźniający

re•lay ['riːleɪ] **I** *v/t* **1.** przekazywać ⟨-zać⟩ **2.** transmitować **II** *s* **1.** *SPORT* sztafeta *f*, bieg *m* sztafetowy **2.** zmiana *f*; ***work in ~s*** pracować na zmianę **3.** *TECH* przekaźnik *m*

re•lease [rɪ'liːs] **I** *v/t* **1.** zwalniać ⟨zwolnić⟩; ***~ s.o. from prison*** zwolnić kogoś z więzienia **2.** wypuszczać ⟨-puścić⟩ **3.** uwalniać ⟨uwolnić⟩ **4.** *emotion*: dawać ⟨dać⟩ upust **5.** *tension*: zmniejszać ⟨-szyć⟩; ***~ the tension in your muscles*** rozluźnij mięśnie **6.** *book*: wydawać ⟨-dać⟩ **7.** publikować ⟨o-⟩ **8. *be ~d*** (*movie*) wejść na ekrany; ***be ~d on DVD*** ukazać się na DVD **II** *s* **1.** zwolnienie *n* **2.** wypuszczenie *n* **3.** uwolnienie *n* **4.** płyta *f* **5.** film *m*; ***a new ~*** nowy film **6.** książka *f* **7.** komunikat *m*; ***a news ~*** komunikat prasowy **8.** *movie*: wejście *n* na ekrany

rel•e•gate ['relɪgeɪt] *v/t* **1.** degradować ⟨z-⟩ **2. *be ~d to the second division*** *SPORT* spaść do drugiej ligi; **rel•e•ga•tion** [relɪ'geɪʃn] *s* **1.** degradacja *f* **2.** *SPORT* spadek *m*

re•lent [rɪ'lent] *v/i* **1.** ustępować ⟨-tąpić⟩ **2.** dawać ⟨dać⟩ za wygraną **3.** (*rain*) zelżeć; **re•lent•less** [rɪ'lentlɪs] *adj* **1.** nieustępliwy **2.** nieustający **3.** niesłabnący; **re•lent•less•ly** [rɪ'lentlɪslɪ] *adv* **1.** nieustępliwie **2.** bez przerwy

rel•e•vance ['reləvəns] *s* **1.** związek *m* (z tematem) **2.** znaczenie *n*; ***be of contemporary ~*** być aktualnym; **rel•e•vant** ['reləvənt] *adj* **1.** istotny; ***be ~ to*** mieć związek z *I* **2.** na temat **3.** odpowiedni **4.** aktualny

re•li•a•bil•i•ty [rɪlaɪə'bɪlətɪ] *s* **1.** niezawodność *f* **2.** solidność *f* **3.** rzetelność *f* **4.** wiarygodność *f*; **re•li•a•ble** [rɪ'laɪəbl] *adj* **1.** niezawodny **2.** solidny

3. rzetelny 4. wiarygodny; **re•li•a•bly** [rɪ'laɪəblɪ] *adv* 1. niezawodnie 2. solidnie 3. rzetelnie

re•li•ance [rɪ'laɪəns] *s* 1. zaufanie *n* (**on** do *G*); ***place ~ on*** polegać na *L* 2. zależność *f* (**on** od *G*) 3. uzależnienie *n* (**on** od *G*); **re•li•ant** [rɪ'laɪənt] *adj* uzależniony (**on** od *G*)

rel•ic ['relɪk] *s* 1. relikt *m* 2. REL relikwia *f*

re•lief [rɪ'li:f] *s* 1. ulga *f*; ***breathe a sigh of ~*** odetchnąć z ulgą; ***what a ~!*** co za ulga! 2. pomoc *f*; ***a ~ organization*** organizacja humanitarna 3. (*group of workers*) zmiana *f* 4. ART relief *m*, płaskorzeźba *f* 5. GEOGR rzeźba *f* terenu, relief *m* 6. kontrast *m*; ***stay out in sharp ~*** mocno kontrastować; **re'lief fund** *s* fundusz *m* pomocowy; **re'lief map** *s* mapa *f* plastyczna; **re'lief road** *s Br* objazd *m*; **re'lief train** *s* pociąg *m* zastępczy

re•lieve [rɪ'li:v] *v/t* 1. łagodzić ⟨z-⟩ 2. przynosić ⟨-nieść⟩ ulgę w *L*; ***she was ~d when*** ulżyło jej, gdy 3. *driver*: zmieniać ⟨-nić⟩ 4. ***~ oneself*** załatwić się 5. uwalniać ⟨uwolnić⟩ (**s.o. of** kogoś od *G*) 6. zwalniać ⟨zwolnić⟩ (**s.o. of** kogoś od *G*)

re•li•gion [rɪ'lɪdʒən] *s* religia *f*

re•li•gious [rɪ'lɪdʒəs] *adj* religijny; ***a ~ faith*** wiara; **re•li•gious•ly** [rɪ'lɪdʒəslɪ] *adv* religijnie; ***follow the instructions ~*** ściśle przestrzegać instrukcji

re•lin•quish [rɪ'lɪŋkwɪʃ] *v/t* 1. rezygnować ⟨z-⟩ z *G* 2. zrzekać ⟨zrzec⟩ się 3. *hope*: porzucać ⟨-cić⟩

rel•ish ['relɪʃ] I *v/t* 1. cieszyć się; ***I don't ~ the prospect of*** nie jestem zachwycony perspektywą *G* 2. przepadać za *I* 3. upajać się II *s* 1. wielka przyjemność *f*, rozkosz *f* 2. COOK *sos ze świeżych lub marynowanych warzyw*

re•live [ri:'lɪv] *v/t* przeżywać ⟨-żyć⟩ na nowo

re•load [ri:'ləʊd] *v/t gun*: ponownie ładować ⟨za-⟩

re•lo•cate [ri:ləʊ'keɪt] I *v/t* przenosić ⟨-nieść⟩ II *v/i* przenosić ⟨-nieść⟩ się; **re•lo•ca•tion** [ri:ləʊ'keɪʃn] *s* 1. przeniesienie *n* 2. przeprowadzka *f* 3. INF relokacja *f*; **re•lo•'ca•tion al•low•ance** *s* dodatek *f* na zagospodarowanie się

re•luc•tance [rɪ'lʌktəns] *s* 1. niechęć *f* 2. wahanie *n*; **re•luc•tant** [rɪ'lʌktənt] *adj* niechętny; ***she was ~ to admit she'd made a mistake*** nie chciała przyznać się do błędu; **re•luc•tant•ly** [rɪ'lʌktəntlɪ] *adv* 1. niechętnie 2. z ociąganiem

re•ly on [rɪ'laɪ] *v/t* 1. zależeć od *G*, być zależnym od *G* 2. polegać na *L*

re•main [rɪ'meɪn] *v/i* 1. zostać ⟨po-⟩, zostawać ⟨-tać⟩; ***~ at home*** zostać w domu; ***there are ten minutes ~ing*** zostało 10 minut; ***a lot ~s to be done*** zostało jeszcze dużo do zrobienia; ***it ~s to be seen*** to się dopiero okaże; ***~ silent*** zachować milczenie; ***~ seated*** nie wstawać; ***~ standing*** nie siadać; ***~ unchanged*** nie zmieniać się; **re•main•der** [rɪ'meɪndə] I *s* reszta *f* II *v/t books*: sprzedawać ⟨-dać⟩ po niższych cenach, wyprzedawać ⟨-dać⟩; **re•main•ing** [rɪ'meɪnɪŋ] *adj* pozostały; **re•mains** [rɪ'meɪnz] *pl* 1. resztki *pl* 2. pozostałości *pl* 3. (*corpse*) szczątki *pl*

re•make I ['ri:meɪk] *s filmu*: remake *m* II [ri:'meɪk] (*remade*; *remade*) *v/t* 1. przerabiać ⟨-robić⟩ 2. *film*: nakręcić nową wersję

re•mand [rɪ'mɑ:nd] I *v/t* ***be ~ed in custody*** przebywać w areszcie śledczym; ***be ~ed on bail*** zostać wypuszczonym na wolność za kaucją II *s* ***on ~*** w areszcie śledczym

re•mark [rɪ'mɑ:k] I *s* uwaga *f* (**on** na temat *G*) II *v/i* 1. zwracać ⟨-rócić⟩ uwagę (**on** na *A*) 2. zauważać ⟨-żyć⟩ 3. mówić ⟨powiedzieć⟩; **re•mar•ka•ble** [rɪ'mɑ:kəbl] *adj* niezwykły; **re•mark•a•bly** [rɪ'mɑ:kəblɪ] *adv* 1. niezwykle 2. niesamowicie

re•mar•riage [ri:'mærɪdʒ] *s* powtórne małżeństwo *n*; **re•mar•ry** [ri:'mærɪ] *v/i* 1. powtórnie wychodzić ⟨wyjść⟩ za mąż 2. powtórnie żenić ⟨o-⟩ się

re•me•di•al [rɪ'mi:djəl] *adj* 1. *measures*: zaradczy 2. leczniczy 3. *class*: wyrównawczy

rem•e•dy ['remədɪ] I *s* 1. *a. fig* lekarstwo *n* (**to/for** na *A*); ***it's beyond ~*** to beznadziejny przypadek 2. rozwiązanie *n* 3 środek *m* zaradczy II *v/t* 1. naprawiać ⟨-wić⟩ 2. zaradzać ⟨-dzić⟩ 3. *problem*: rozwiązywać ⟨-zać⟩

R

re•mem•ber [rɪ'membə] *v/t* **1.** pamiętać ⟨za-⟩; ***I don't ~ saying that*** nie przypominam sobie, żebym to powiedział; ***~ to lock the door*** nie zapomnij zamknąć drzwi; ***~ s.o.'s birthday*** pamiętać o czyichś urodzinach; ***~ me to your wife*** *Br* pozdrów ode mnie żonę **2.** przypominać ⟨-mnieć⟩ sobie; ***if I ~ correctly*** jeśli mnie pamięć nie myli **3.** czcić ⟨u-⟩ pamięć; **re•mem•brance** [rɪ'membrəns] *s* **1.** ***in ~ of*** dla uczczenia pamięci *G*, dla upamiętnienia *G* **2.** wspomnienie *n* **3.** pamiątka *f*

re•mind [rɪ'maɪnd] *v/t* przypominać ⟨-mnieć⟩ (***s.o. about/of*** komuś o *L*); ***you ~ me of my father*** przypominasz mi mojego ojca; ***that ~s me*** à propos; **re•mind•er** [rɪ'maɪndə] *s* **1.** przypomnienie *n* **2.** upomnienie *n*

rem•i•nisce [remɪ'nɪs] *v/i* wspominać ⟨-mnieć⟩ (***about*** *A*); **rem•i•nis•cence** [remɪ'nɪsns] *s* **1.** wspomnienie *n* **2.** wspominanie *n* **3.** ***~s*** reminescencje *pl*; **rem•i•nis•cent** [remɪ'nɪsənt] *adj*: ***be ~ of*** przypominać *A*

re•miss [rɪ'mɪs] *adj*: ***he was ~ in his duties*** zaniedbał swoje obowiązki

re•mis•sion [rɪ'mɪʃn] *s* **1.** *MED* remisja *f* **2.** *Br* zmniejszenie *n* wymiaru kary **3.** *debts*: umorzenie *n* **4.** *fee*: obniżenie *n* (wysokości) **5.** *sins*: odpuszczenie *n*

re•mit [rɪ'mɪt] **I** *v/t* **1.** *money*: przesyłać ⟨-słać⟩ **2.** *debts*: umarzać ⟨umorzyć⟩ **3.** *fee*: obniżać ⟨-żyć⟩ **4.** *sentence*: zmniejszać ⟨-szyć⟩ wymiar **5.** *sins*: odpuszczać ⟨-puścić⟩ **6.** *case*: przekazywać ⟨-zać⟩ **II** *s* **1.** *Br* kompetencje *pl*; ***be outside s.o.'s ~*** wykraczać poza czyjeś kompetencje **2.** *Br* obowiązki *pl*; ***fall within s.o.'s ~*** należeć do czyichś obowiązków; **re•mit•tance** [rɪ'mɪtəns] *s* płatność *f*

rem•nant ['remnənt] *s* **1.** pozostałość *f* **2.** resztka *f*

re•mod•el [riː'mɒdl] *v/t* **1.** zmieniać ⟨-nić⟩ **2.** przebudowywać ⟨-dować⟩ **3.** reorganizować ⟨z-⟩ **4.** przemodelowywać ⟨-lować⟩

re•mold *Am* → ***remould***

re•mon•strance [rɪ'mɒnstrəns] *s* **1.** protest *m* **2.** skarga *f* **3.** zażalenie *n*; **re•mon•strate** ['remənstreɪt] *v/i* **1.** protestować ⟨za-⟩ **2.** składać ⟨złożyć⟩ zażalenie (***about*** na *A*)

re•morse [rɪ'mɔːs] *s* wyrzuty *pl* sumienia; ***feel ~*** mieć wyrzuty sumienia; **re•morse•ful** [rɪ'mɔːsfʊl] *adj* **1.** skruszony **2.** pełen skruchy; **re•morse•less** [rɪ'mɔːslɪs] *adj* **1.** pozbawiony skrupułów **2.** niepowstrzymany **3.** niepohamowany; **re•morse•less•ly** [rɪ'mɔːslɪslɪ] *adv* **1.** niepowstrzymanie **2.** bezlitośnie

re•mote [rɪ'məʊt] **I** *adj* **1.** odległy, daleki; ***in the ~ past*** w zamierzchłej przeszłości; ***a ~ cousin*** daleki kuzyn **2.** oddalony; ***~ from other buildings*** oddalony od innych budynków **3.** odosobniony **4.** *TECH* zdalny **5.** *chance*: niewielki, mały; ***I don't have the ~st idea*** nie mam najmniejszego pojęcia **II** *s infml* → ***remote control 1***; **re•mote 'ac•cess** *s* dostęp *m* zdalny; **re•mote con•'trol** *s* **1.** pilot *m* (do telewizora) **2.** zdalne sterowanie *n*; **re•mote-con•trolled** [rɪməʊtkən'trəʊld] *adj* zdalnie sterowany; **re•mote da•ta en•try** *s* zdalne wprowadzanie *n* danych; **re•mote•ly** [rɪ'məʊtlɪ] *adv* **1.** trochę; ***it wasn't even ~ funny*** nie było w tym nic śmiesznego **2.** na odludziu **3.** zdalnie; **re•mote•ness** [rɪ'məʊtnəs] *s* **1.** oddalenie *n* **2.** odosobnienie *n*

re•mould [riː'məʊld] *Br*, **re•mold** *Am* *v/t* **1.** zmieniać ⟨-nić⟩ **2.** przekształcać ⟨-cić⟩

re•mount [riː'maʊnt] *v/t horse*, *bike*: ponownie wsiadać ⟨wsiąść⟩ na *A*

re•mov•a•ble [rɪ'muːvəbl] *adj* **1.** usuwalny **2.** ruchomy; **re•mov•al** [rɪ'muːvl] *s* **1.** usunięcie *n* **2.** usuwanie *n* **3.** *barrier*: zniesienie *n* **4.** *Br* przeprowadzka *f*

re•move [rɪ'muːv] *v/t* **1.** usuwać ⟨usunąć⟩ **2.** zdejmować ⟨zdjąć⟩ **3.** *barriers*: znosić ⟨znieść⟩; **re•'mov•er** *s*: ***a stain ~*** odplamiacz; ***a nail varnish ~*** zmywacz do paznokci; ***a make-up ~*** płyn do demakijażu

re•mu•ner•ate [rɪ'mjuːnəreɪt] *v/t* płacić ⟨za-⟩ (***s.o. for*** komuś za *A*); **re•mu•ner•a•tion** [rɪmjuːnə'reɪʃn] *s* **1.** wynagrodzenie *n* **2.** pensja *f*; **re•mu•ner•a•tive** [rɪ'mjuːnərətɪv] *adj job*: popłatny, opłacalny

R

Ren•ais•sance [rəˈneɪsəns] *s ART* renesans *m*, odrodzenie *n*; **Ren•ais•sance ˈman** *s* człowiek *m* renesansu

re•nal [ˈriːnl] *adj MED* nerkowy; **~ colic** kolka nerkowa; **~ failure** niewydolność nerek

re•name [riːˈneɪm] *v/t* **1.** zmieniać ⟨-nić⟩ nazwę **2.** przemianowywać ⟨-nować⟩

ren•der [ˈrendə] *v/t* **1.** czynić ⟨u-⟩; **~ s.o. harmless** unieszkodliwić kogoś; **~ s.th. invisible** uczynić coś niewidzialnym; **hundreds of people were ~ed homeless by the earthquake** w wyniku trzęsienia ziemi setki osób straciło dach nad głową **2.** *service*: wykonywać ⟨-nać⟩ **3.** *favour*: świadczyć ⟨wy-⟩ **4.** *aid*: udzielać ⟨-lić⟩ **5.** *report*: przedstawiać ⟨-wić⟩, przedkładać ⟨-dłożyć⟩ **6.** *song*: wykonywać ⟨-nać⟩ **7.** *meaning*: oddawać ⟨-dać⟩ **8.** tłumaczyć ⟨prze-⟩ (**into** na *A*) **9.** *wall*: tynkować ⟨o-⟩ **10.** *verdict*: ogłaszać ⟨-łosić⟩; **ren•der•ing** [ˈrendərɪŋ] *s* **1.** *piece*: interpretacja *f* **2.** *THEAT* interpretacja *f* roli **3.** tłumaczenie *n* **4.** tynk *m*

ren•dez•vous [ˈrɒndɪvuː] **I** *pl -vous s* **1.** spotkanie *n* **2.** *dated* rendez-vous *n* **3.** randka *f*, schadzka *f* **4.** miejsce *n* spotkania **II** *v/i* spotykać ⟨-tkać⟩ się

ren•di•tion [renˈdɪʃn] *s* **1.** interpretacja *f* **2.** wykonanie *n*; **give a live ~ of a song** wykonać utwór na żywo

ren•e•gade [ˈrenɪgeɪd] *s* **1.** zdrajca *m*, renegat *m* **2.** buntownik *m*

re•nege [rɪˈneɪg] *v/i* **1.** *promise*: nie dotrzymywać ⟨-mać⟩ (**on** *G*) **2.** nie wywiązywać ⟨-zać⟩ się z warunków (**on** *G*)

re•new [rɪˈnjuː] *v/t* **1.** ponawiać ⟨-nowić⟩; **with ~ed strength** z nowymi siłami **2.** *negotiations*: wznawiać ⟨-nowić⟩ **3.** *acquaintance*: odnawiać ⟨-nowić⟩ **4.** *visa*: przedłużać ⟨-żyć⟩ **5.** *contract*: przedłużać ⟨-żyć⟩ termin obowiązywania; **re•new•a•ble** [rɪˈnjuːəbl] *adj* **1.** odnawialny; **~ energy sources** odnawialne źródła energii **2.** możliwy do przedłużenia; **the visa is not ~** wizy nie można przedłużyć; **re•new•al** [rɪˈnjuːəl] *s* **1.** wznowienie *n*; **a ~ of interest in** ponowny wzrost zainteresowania *I* **2.** *visa*, *contract*: przedłużenie *n* **3.** odnowienie *n*

re•nounce [rɪˈnaʊns] *v/t* **1.** *title*, *right*: zrzekać ⟨zrzec⟩ się **2.** wyrzekać ⟨-rzec⟩ się **3.** odżegnywać ⟨-nać⟩ się od *G*

ren•o•vate [ˈrenəveɪt] *v/t* **1.** odnawiać ⟨-nowić⟩ **2.** poddawać ⟨-dać⟩ renowacji; **ren•o•va•tion** [renəˈveɪʃn] *s* **1.** renowacja *f* **2.** remont *m*

re•nown [rɪˈnaʊn] *s* **1.** renoma *f* **2.** sława *f*; **re•nowned** [rɪˈnaʊnd] *adj* **1.** znany (**for** z *G*) **2.** renomowany **3.** sławny

rent[1] [rent] **I** *s* czynsz *m*; **for ~** do wynajęcia **II** *v/t* wynajmować ⟨-jąć⟩; **~ s.th. from** wynajmować coś od *G*; **~ s.th. (out) to** wynajmować coś *D*

rent[2] [~] *s* **1.** rozdarcie *n* **2.** pęknięcie *n*

ˈrent-a-car (serv•ice) *s* wynajem *m* samochodów

rent•al [ˈrentl] *s* **1.** wynajem *m* **2.** opłata *f* **3.** czynsz *m* **4.** wynajęty dom *m* **5.** wynajęty samochód *m*; **ˈrent•al a•gree•ment** *s JUR* umowa *f* najmu; **ˈrent•al car** *s* wynajęty samochód *m*

rent•er [ˈrentə] *s* **1.** najemca *m* **2.** *Am* wypożyczalnia *f*

rent-ˈfree *adj house*: wolny od czynszu

re•nun•ci•a•tion [rɪnʌnsɪˈeɪʃn] *s* **1.** wyrzeczenie się *n* **2.** zrzeczenie się *n*

re•o•pen [riːˈəʊpn] **I** *v/t* **1.** *shop*, *school*: ponownie otwierać ⟨-worzyć⟩; **~ old wounds** *fig* rozdrapywać stare rany **2.** wznawiać ⟨-nowić⟩ **II** *v/i* zostać ponownie otwartym

re•or•gan•i•za•tion [riːɔːgənaɪzˈeɪʃn] *s* reorganizacja *f*; **re•or•gan•ize** [riːˈɔːgənaɪz] *v/t* reorganizować ⟨z-⟩

rep [rep] *s infml* przedstawiciel *m*

re•pair [rɪˈpeə] **I** *v/t* naprawiać ⟨-wić⟩ **II** *s* **1.** naprawa *f*; **beyond ~** nie do naprawienia **2.** **in good (state of) ~** w dobrym stanie; **in bad (state of) ~** w złym stanie; **reˈpair•man** *pl -men s*: **a bicycle ~** mechanik *m* rowerowy; **be a TV ~** zajmować się naprawą telewizorów

rep•a•ra•ble [ˈrepərəbl] *adj* możliwy do naprawienia; **rep•a•ra•tion** [repərˈeɪʃn] *s* **1.** **~s** reparacje *pl* **2.** zadośćuczynienie *n* **3.** wynagrodzenie *n*

rep•ar•tee [repɑːˈtiː] *s* riposta *f*

R

re•pa•tri•ate [riːˈpætrɪeɪt] *v/t* repatriować; **re•pa•tri•a•tion** [riːˈpætrɪˈeɪʃn] *s* repatriacja *f*;

re•pay [riːˈpeɪ] *v/t* **1.** spłacać ⟨-cić⟩ **2.** oddawać ⟨-dać⟩ **3.** odwdzięczać ⟨-czyć⟩ się **4.** odwdzięczać ⟨-czyć⟩ się za *A* **5.** ***this movie ~s repeated watching*** warto wielokrotnie obejrzeć ten film; **re•pay•a•ble** [riːˈpeɪəbl] *adj* podlegający zwrotowi; ***the loan is ~ in monthly instalments*** kredyt jest spłacany w miesięcznych ratach; **re•pay•ment** [riːˈpeɪmənt] *s debt*: spłata *f*, zwrot *m*

re•peal [rɪˈpiːl] **I** *v/t law*: uchylać ⟨-lić⟩, znosić ⟨znieść⟩ **II** *s law*: uchylenie *n*, zniesienie *n*

re•peat [rɪˈpiːt] **I** *v/t* powtarzać ⟨-tórzyć⟩; ***history ~s itself*** historia się powtarza; ***~ after me*** powtarzaj za mną; ***the programme will be ~ed*** program zostanie powtórzony **II** *s* powtórka *f*; **re•peat•ed** [rɪˈpiːtɪd] *adj* **1.** wielokrotny **2.** powtarzający się; **re•peat•ed•ly** [rɪˈpiːtɪdlɪ] *adv* wielokrotnie; **re•peat ˈor•der** *s* powtórne zamówienie *n*; **re•peat ˈpur•chase** *s* powtórny zakup *m*

re•pel [rɪˈpel] *v/t* **1.** *attack*: odpierać ⟨odeprzeć⟩ **2.** odpychać ⟨odepchnąć⟩ **3.** odrzucać ⟨-cić⟩ **4.** ***~ water*** nie przepuszczać wody **5.** *insects*: odstraszać ⟨-szyć⟩; **re•pel•lent** [rɪˈpelənt] **I** *adj* **1.** odpychający **2.** wstrętny **3.** ***water-~*** nieprzepuszczający wody **II** *s* ***an insect ~*** środek odstraszający owady

re•pent [rɪˈpent] **I** *v/i* **1.** żałować ⟨po-⟩ **2.** odczuwać ⟨-czuć⟩ skruchę **II** *v/t* żałować ⟨po-⟩

R

re•per•cus•sions [riːpəˈkʌʃnz] *pl* reperkusje *pl*, konsekwencje *pl*

rep•er•toire [ˈrepətwɑː] *s* repertuar *m*

rep•e•ti•tion [repɪˈtɪʃn] *s* **1.** potwórzenie *n* **2.** powtarzanie *n* **3.** powtórka *f*; **re•pet•i•tive** [rɪˈpetɪtɪv] *adj* **1.** powtarzający się **2.** monotonny **3.** powtarzalny

re•phrase [rɪˈfreɪs] *v/t question*: sformułować inaczej

re•place [rɪˈpleɪs] *v/t* **1.** zastępować ⟨-tąpić⟩ (***with*** *I*) **2.** wymieniać ⟨-nić⟩ **3.** odkładać ⟨odłożyć⟩ (na miejsce); ***~ the receiver*** odłożyć słuchawkę; **re•place•ment** [rɪˈpleɪsmənt] *s* **1.** wymiana *f* **2.** zastępca *m*; ***be a ~ for*** zastąpić *A*; **re•place•ment ˈpart** *s* część *f* (zamienna)

re•plant [riːˈplænt] *v/t plant*: przesadzać ⟨-dzić⟩

re•play I [ˈriːpleɪ] *s* **1.** SPORT *Br* powtórzony mecz *m* **2.** powtórka *f* **II** [riːˈpleɪ] *v/t* **1.** *match*: powtarzać ⟨-tórzyć⟩ **2.** *film, music*: puszczać ⟨puścić⟩ jeszcze raz

re•plen•ish [rɪˈplenɪʃ] *v/t* **1.** uzupełniać ⟨-nić⟩ **2.** ponownie napełnić ***~ s.o.'s glass*** dolać komuś

re•plete [rɪˈpliːt] *adj* **1.** pełny **2.** syty

rep•li•ca [ˈreplɪkə] *s* **1.** replika *f* **2.** (dokładna) kopia *f*

re•ply [rɪˈplaɪ] **I** *v/i* **1.** odpowiadać ⟨-wiedzieć⟩ (***to*** na *A*) **2.** reagować ⟨za-⟩ **II** *s* odpowiedź *f*; ***make no ~*** nie odpowiedzieć; ***in ~ to your letter*** w odpowiedzi na Pański list; **re•ply-paid en•ve•lope** *s Br* koperta *f* zwrotna

re•port [rɪˈpɔːt] **I** *v/t* **1.** informować ⟨po-⟩ o *L* **2.** donosić ⟨-nieść⟩ o *L* **3.** relacjonować ⟨z-⟩ **4.** zgłaszać ⟨-łosić⟩; ***she has ~ed her daughter missing*** zgłosiła zaginięcie córki **5.** *profits, losses*: notować ⟨za-⟩ **6.** ***he is ~ed to earn $2 million a year*** podobno zarabia 2 miliony dolarów rocznie; ***the president is ~ed to have said that*** prezydent miał powiedzieć, że **II** *v/i* **1.** składać ⟨złożyć⟩ sprawozdanie (***on*** z *G*) **2.** zgłaszać ⟨-łosić⟩ się (***to*** do *G*); ***~ sick*** zawiadomić przełożonego o chorobie **III** *s* **1.** (*media*) doniesienie *n*, relacja *f*; ***a weather ~*** prognoza pogody **2.** raport *m* **3.** sprawozdanie *n* **4.** zgłoszenie *n* **5.** *Br* świadectwo *n* (szkolne) **6.** *explosion*: huk *m*; **re•ported speech** *s* GRAM mowa *f* zależna

re'port card *s Am* świadectwo *n* (szkolne)

re•port•er [rɪˈpɔːtə] *s* **1.** reporter *m* **2.** sprawozdawca *m*

re•pose [rɪˈpəuz] **I** *s* **1.** *lit* spoczynek *m* **2.** odpoczynek *m* **II** *v/i* **1.** spoczywać ⟨-cząć⟩ **2.** odpoczywać ⟨-cząć⟩

rep•re•hen•si•ble [reprɪˈhensəbl] *adj behaviour*: naganny

rep•re•sent [reprɪˈzent] *v/t* **1.** reprezentować; ***~ the interests of women*** reprezentować interesy kobiet **2.** stanowić; **~ *20% of the annual revenue*** stanowić 20% rocznych dochodów **3.** przedstawiać ⟨-wić⟩ **4.** symbolizować; **rep•re•sen•ta•tion** [reprızen'teıʃn] *s* **1.** przedstawienie *n* **2.** obraz *m* **3.** reprezentacja *f* **4.** przedstawicielstwo *n* **5.** symbol *m*, **rep•re•sen•ta•tion•al** [reprızen'teıʃənl] *adj* **1.** ART figuratywny **2.** przedstawicielski; **rep•re•sen•ta•tive** [reprı'zentətıv] **I** *s* **1.** przedstawiciel *m*; ***a sales*** **~** przedstawiciel handlowy **2.** ***a* ~** *Am* członek Izby Reprezentantów; ***the House of* ~*s*** Izba Reprezentantów **II** *adj* **1.** reprezentatywny **2.** przedstawicielski

re•press [rı'pres] *v/t* **1.** *revolt, anger*: tłumić ⟨s-⟩ **2.** uciskać **3.** represjonować; **re•pres•sion** [rı'preʃn] *s* **1.** tłumienie *n* **2.** *fig* ucisk *m* **3.** represje *pl*; **re•pres•sive** [rı'presıv] *adj regime*: represyjny

re•prieve [rı'pri:v] **I** *v/t prisoner*: ułaskawiać ⟨-wić⟩ **II** *s* ułaskawienie *n*

rep•ri•mand ['reprıma:nd] **I** *v/t* udzielać ⟨-lić⟩ nagany **II** *s* **1.** nagana *f* **2.** reprymenda *f*

re•print **I** ['ri:prınt] *s* **1.** reprint *m* **2.** przedruk *m* **3.** wznowienie *n* **II** [ri:'prınt] *v/t* **1.** przedrukowywać ⟨-kować⟩ **2.** wznawiać ⟨-nowić⟩

re•pri•sal [rı'praızl] *s* odwet *m*

re•proach [rı'prəʊtʃ] **I** *s* wyrzut *m*; ***a look of* ~** spojrzenie pełne wyrzutu; ***beyond* ~, *above* ~** bez zarzutu **II** *v/t* **1.** robić wyrzuty **2.** wyrzucać ⟨-cić⟩ (***s.o. for*** komuś *A*); **re•proach•ful** [rı'prəʊtʃfəl] *adj look*: pełen wyrzutu; **re•proach•ful•ly** [rı'prəʊtʃfəlı] *adv* z wyrzutem

rep•ro•bate ['reprəʊbeıt] *s* **1.** REL potępiony *m* **2.** *infml* drań *m*

re•proc•ess [ri:'prəʊses] *v/t waste*: utylizować ⟨z-⟩; **re•proc•ess•ing plant** [ri:'prəʊsesıŋ pla:nt] *s* zakład *m* utylizacji odpadów radioaktywnych

re•pro•duce [ri:prə'dju:s] **I** *v/t painting*: reprodukować **2.** *atmosphere*: oddawać ⟨-dać⟩ **3.** *accent*: naśladować **4.** *sound*: odtwarzać ⟨-worzyć⟩ **II** *v/i* rozmnażać ⟨-nożyć⟩ się; **re•pro•duc•tion** [ri:prə'dʌkʃn] *s* **1.** BIOL rozmnażanie *n* **2.** *sound*: odtwarzanie *n* **3.** *painting*: reprodukcja *f*; **re•pro•duc•tion 'fur•ni•ture** *s* meble *pl* stylowe; **re•pro•duc•tive** [rıprə'dʌktıv] *adj* reprodukcyjny

re•proof [rı'pru:f] *s* nagana *f*

re•prove [rı'pru:v] *v/t* ganić ⟨z-⟩ (***s.o. for*** kogoś za *A*)

rep•tile ['reptaıl] *s* gad *m*

re•pub•lic [rı'pʌblık] *s* republika *f*; **re•pub•li•can** [rı'pʌblıkn] **I** *s* republikanin *m* **II** *adj* republikański

re•pu•di•ate [rı'pju:dıeıt] *v/t* **1.** odrzucać ⟨-cić⟩ **2.** zaprzeczać ⟨-czyć⟩ **3.** odstępować ⟨-tąpić⟩ od *G*; **~ *an agreement*** odstąpić od umowy **4.** wyrzekać ⟨-rzec⟩ się; **re•pudi•'a•tion** *s* **1.** odrzucenie *n* **2.** zaprzeczenie *n* **3.** (*of contract*) odstąpienie *n* (**of** od *G*) **4.** wyrzeczenie się *n*

re•pug•nance [rı'pʌgnəns] *s* odraza *f* (**for** do *G*) [rı'pʌgnənt] *adj* odrażający

re•pulse [rı'pʌls] *v/t* **1.** napawać wstrętem; ***be* ~*d by*** brzydzić się *I* **2.** *attack*: odpierać ⟨odeprzeć⟩; **re•pul•sion** [rı'pʌlʃn] *s* **1.** wstręt *m* **2.** PHYS odpychanie *n*; **re•pul•sive** [rı'pʌlsıv] *adj* **1.** odpychający **2.** wstrętny

re•pur•chase [ri:'pɜ:tʃəs] *s* **1.** odkup *m* **2.** wykup *m*

rep•u•ta•ble ['repjʊtəbl] *adj* **1.** renomowany **2.** szanowany; **rep•u•ta•tion** [repjʊ'teıʃn] *s* **1.** reputacja *f*; ***have a good*** (***bad***) **~** mieć dobrą (złą) reputację; ***have a* ~ *as a good writer*** uchodzić za dobrego pisarza **2.** renoma *f*; **re•pute** [rı'pju:t] *s* **1.** renoma *f*; ***of* ~** renomowany, cieszący się dobrą renomą **2.** reputacja *f*; **re•put•ed** [rı'pju:tıd] *adj*: ***he is* ~ *to be the best surgeon in the country*** ma opinię najlepszego chirurga w kraju; **re•put•ed•ly** [rı'pju:tıdlı] *adv* rzekomo, podobno

re•quest [rı'kwest] **I** *s* prośba *f*; ***at his* ~** na jego prośbę; ***on* ~** na życzenie; ***make a* ~ *for*** poprosić o *A* **II** *v/t* prosić ⟨po-⟩ o *A*; **~ *permission*** poprosić o pozwolenie; ***you are* ~*ed not to smoke*** uprasza się o niepalenie

re•quiem ['rekwıəm] *s* **1.** REL msza *f* żałobna **2.** MUS requiem *n*

re•quire [rɪ'kwaɪə] *v/t* **1.** wymagać (***s.th. of*** czegoś od *G*); ***be ~d*** być wymaganym **2.** potrzebować; ***if ~d*** w razie potrzeby; **re•quired** [rɪ'kwaɪəd] *adj* **1.** wymagany **2.** potrzebny; **re•quired 'read•ing** *s* lektura *f* obowiązkowa; **re•quire•ment** [rɪ'kwaɪəmənt] *s* **1.** wymaganie *n*; ***meet the ~s*** sprostać wymaganiom **2.** potrzeba *f*; ***satisfy the ~s*** zaspokoić potrzeby

req•ui•site ['rekwɪzɪt] **I** *adj* wymagany **II** *s* **1.** warunek *m* **2.** wymaganie *n* **3.** ***toilet ~s*** przybory toaletowe; **req•ui•si•tion** [rekwɪ'zɪʃn] **I** *v/t* rekwirować ⟨za-⟩ **II** *s* **1.** zapotrzebowanie *n* (***for*** na *A*) **2.** zamówienie *n* **3.** rekwizycja *f*

re•quite [rɪ'kwaɪt] *v/t love*: odwzajemniać ⟨-nić⟩

re-route [riː'ruːt] *v/t* **1.** *flight*, *race*: przekierowywać ⟨-rować⟩ **2.** *traffic*: kierować ⟨s-⟩ inną trasą

re•run **I** ['riːrʌn] *s* powtórka *f* **II** [riː'rʌn] (*reran*; *rerun*) *v/t* powtarzać ⟨-tórzyć⟩

re•sale ['riːseɪl] *s* odsprzedaż *f*; ***not for ~*** bez prawa sprzedaży

re•sched•ule [riː'ʃedjuːl] *v/t* **1.** *date*: zmieniać ⟨-nić⟩ **2.** *repayment*: odraczać ⟨-roczyć⟩ **3.** *credit*: zmieniać ⟨-nić⟩ harmonogram spłaty

re•scind [rɪ'sɪnd] *v/t* **1.** *law*, *decision*: uchylać ⟨-lić⟩ **2.** *contract*: unieważniać ⟨-nić⟩ **3.** odwoływać ⟨-łać⟩; **re•scis•sion** [rɪ'sɪʒn] *s* **1.** uchylenie *n* **2.** unieważnienie *n* **3.** odwołanie *n*

res•cue ['reskjuː] **I** *v/t* ratować ⟨u-⟩ (***from*** przed *I*) **II** *s* **1.** ratunek *m*; ***come to s.o.'s ~*** przyjść komuś na ratunek; ***a ~ squad*** ekipa ratunkowa **2.** akcja *f* ratunkowa; **res•cu•er** ['reskjʊə] *s* **1.** ratownik *m* **2.** wybawca *m*; **'res•cue op•er•a•tion** *s* akcja *f* ratunkowa; **'res•cue par•ty** *s* ekipa *f* ratownicza

re•search [rɪ'sɜːtʃ] **I** *s* **1.** badania *pl* (***into***/***on*** nad *I*); ***carry out ~*** prowadzić badania; ***a ~ worker*** pracownik naukowo-badawczy **2.** badanie *n* **II** *v/t* badać ⟨z-⟩; ***~ the market*** badać rynek **III** *v/i* prowadzić ⟨prze-⟩ badania (***into***/***in***/***on*** nad *I*); **re•search and de•'vel•op•ment** *s* badania i rozwój *pl*; **re•search•er** [rɪ'sɜːtʃə] *s* badacz *m*; **re•'search proj•ect** *s* projekt *m* badawczy

re•sem•blance [rɪ'zembləns] *s* podobieństwo *n* (***between*** między *I*); ***a striking ~ to*** uderzające podobieństwo do *G*; ***bear no ~ to*** nie być podobnym do *G*; **re•sem•ble** [rɪ'zembl] *v/t* **1.** być podobnym do *G* **2.** przypominać *A*

re•sent [rɪ'zent] *v/t* **1.** czuć ⟨po-⟩ się urażonym **2.** ***she ~s being treated like a child*** nie podoba jej się, że jest traktowana jak dziecko **3.** żywić urazę *G*; **re•sent•ful** [rɪ'zentfəl] *adj* **1.** pełen urazy **2.** ***s.o. is ~ of*** komuś się coś nie podoba; **re•sent•ful•ly** [rɪ'zentfəlɪ] *adv* z urazą; **re•sent•ment** [rɪ'zentmənt] *s* **1.** uraza *f* **2.** niezadowolenie *n*

res•er•va•tion [rezə'veɪʃn] *s* **1.** rezerwacja *f*; ***make a ~*** dokonać rezerwacji; ***~ in the name of*** rezerwacja na nazwisko *G* **2.** zastrzeżenie *n*; ***without ~*** bez zastrzeżeń **3.** *American Indians*: rezerwat *m*

re•serve [rɪ'zɜːv] **I** *v/t* **1.** *table*, *room*: rezerwować ⟨za-⟩ **2.** *law*: zastrzegać ⟨-rzec⟩ sobie; ***all rights ~d*** wszystkie prawa zastrzeżone **II** *s* **1.** rezerwa *f*; ***with ~*** z rezerwą **2.** zapas *m* **3.** rezerwat *m*; ***a wildlife ~*** rezerwat przyrody **4.** SPORT zawodnik *m* rezerwowy **5.** ***the ~*** (*army*) rezerwa *f*; **re•served** [rɪ'zɜːvd] *adj person*: powściągliwy

re•serv•ist [rɪ'zɜːvɪst] *s* rezerwista *m*

res•er•voir ['rezəvwɑː] *s* **1.** rezerwuar *m* **2.** zbiornik *m* **3.** *fig* kopalnia *f* **4.** skarbnica *f*

re•set [riː'set] *v/t* **1.** *watch*: przestawiać ⟨-wić⟩ **2.** uruchamiać ⟨-chomić⟩ ponownie, resetować ⟨z-⟩ **3.** *bone*: nastawiać ⟨-wić⟩

re•set•tle [riː'setl] *v/t* **1.** przesiedlać ⟨-lić⟩ **2.** zasiedlać ⟨-lić⟩ na nowo; **re•set•tle•ment** [riː'setlmənt] *s* przesiedlenie *n*

re•shuf•fle ['riːʃʌfl] POLIT **I** *v/t* przeprowadzać ⟨-dzić⟩ przetasowania w *L* **II** *s* przetasowania *pl*

re•side [rɪ'zaɪd] *v/i* **1.** mieszkać **2.** zamieszkiwać ⟨-kać⟩ **3.** (*power*) spoczywać (***with*** w rękach *G*); **res•i•dence** ['rezɪdəns] *s* **1.** zamieszkanie *n*; ***a place of ~*** miejsce zamieszkania; ***take up ~*** zamieszkać **2.** dom *m* **3.** mieszkanie *n* **4.** rezydencja *f* **5.** pobyt *m*; ***permanent ~*** pobyt stały; **'res•i•dence per•mit** *s* pozwolenie *n* na pobyt; **res•i•dent** ['rezɪdənt] **I** *s* mieszkaniec *m* **II** *adj* zamieszkały; ***be ~ abroad*** mieszkać za granicą **3.** *nurse*, *tutor*: mieszkający na miejscu; **res•i•den•tial** [rezɪ'denʃl] *adj* **1.** mieszkalny **2.** *course, post*: z zakwaterowaniem na miejscu

re•sid•u•al [rɪ'zɪdjʊəl] *adj* **1.** szczątkowy **2.** osadowy; **res•i•due** ['rezɪdjuː] *s* **1.** pozostałość *f* **2.** osad *m*

re•sign [rɪ'zaɪn] **I** *v/i* **1.** rezygnować ⟨z-⟩ (***from*** z *G*) **2.** ustępować ⟨-tąpić⟩ (***from*** z *G*) **II** *v/t* **1.** rezygnować ⟨z-⟩ z *G* **2.** ***~ oneself to*** pogodzić się z *I*; **res•ig•na•tion** [rezɪg'neɪʃn] *s* **1.** rezygnacja *f*; ***hand in one's ~*** złożyć rezygnację **2.** ustąpienie *n*; **re•signed** [re'zaɪnd] *adj* zrezygnowany

re•sil•i•ence [rɪ'zɪlɪəns] *s* **1.** wytrzymałość *f* **2.** odporność *f* **3.** TECH sprężystość *f*; **re•sil•i•ent** [rɪ'zɪlɪənt] *adj* **1.** wytrzymały **2.** odporny **3.** TECH sprężysty

res•in ['rezɪn] *s* żywica *f*; **res•in•ous** ['rezɪnəs] *adj* żywiczny

re•sist [rɪ'zɪst] *v/t* **1.** sprzeciwiać ⟨-wić⟩ się; ***they ~ change*** są przeciwni zmianom **2.** opierać ⟨oprzeć⟩ się; ***I couldn't ~ it*** nie mogłem się oprzeć **3.** być odpornym na *A*; **re•sist•ance** [rɪ'zɪstəns] *s* **1.** opór *m*; ***the* ⁓** ruch oporu **2.** sprzeciw *m* **3.** odporność *f* (***to*** na *A*); **re•sis•tant** [rɪ'zɪstənt] *adj* **1.** odporny (***to*** na *A*); ***water-~*** wodoodporny; ***fire-~*** ognioodporny **2.** niechętny; **re•sis•tor** [rɪ'zɪstə] *s* TECH opornik *m*, rezystor *m*

re•sit **I** [riː'sɪt] (*resat*; *resat*) *v/t exam*: powtarzać ⟨-tórzyć⟩ **II** ['riːsɪt] *s* **1.** egzamin *m* **2.** *infml* poprawka *f*

res•o•lute ['rezəluːt] *adj* zdecydowany, stanowczy; **res•o•lu•tion** [rezə'luːʃn] *s* **1.** uchwała *f* **2.** rezolucja *f* **3.** postanowienie *n*; ***make a ~ to do s.th.*** postanowić coś zrobić; ***New Year's ~s*** noworoczne postanowienia **4.** *problem, crisis*: rozwiązanie **5.** zdecydowanie *n*, stanowczość *f* **6.** INF rozdzielczość *f*; **'res•o•lute•ness** → ***resolution***

re•solve [rɪ'zɒlv] **I** *v/t* **1.** *problem*: rozwiązywać ⟨-zać⟩ **2.** rozkładać ⟨-złożyć⟩ (***into*** na *A*) **II** *v/i* **1.** decydować ⟨z-⟩ **2.** postanawiać ⟨-nowić⟩ (***on*** *A*) **3.** rozkładać ⟨-złożyć⟩ się (***into*** na *A*) **III** *s* **1.** postanowienie *n*, determinacja *f*

res•o•nance ['rezənəns] *s* **1.** rezonans *m* **2.** *voice*: moc *f* **3.** *fig* echo *n*; ***the poem has many ~s*** wiersz wywołuje wiele skojarzeń; **res•o•nant** ['rezənənt] *adj* **1.** *voice*: donośny **2.** rezonansowy **3.** ***the poem is ~ with disappointment*** w wierszu pobrzmiewa wyraźna nuta rozczarowania

re•sort [rɪ'zɔːt] **I** *s* **1.** kurort *m* **2.** miejscowość *f* wypoczynkowa **3.** ***without ~ to*** nie uciekając się do *G*; ***the last ~*** ostatnia deska ratunku; ***in the last ~*** ostatecznie **II** *v/i* uciekać ⟨uciec⟩ się (***to*** do *G*)

re•sound [rɪ'zaʊnd] *v/i* rozbrzmiewać ⟨-mieć⟩ (***with*** *I*); ***laughter ~ed through the house*** śmiech rozbrzmiewał w całym domu; **re•sound•ing** [rɪ'zaʊndɪŋ] *adj* **1.** *success*: spektakularny **2.** *defeat*: druzgocący **3.** *voice*: donośny

re•source [rɪ'sɔːs] *s* **1.** ***~s*** zasoby *pl*; ***natural ~s*** bogactwa naturalne **2.** ***financial ~s*** środki pieniężne **3.** pomoc *f* naukowa **4.** ***~s*** zaradność *f*; **re•source•d** *adj*: ***the school is well-~ with modern IT equipment*** szkoła posiada nowoczesny sprzęt komputerowy; **re•source•ful** [rɪ'sɔːsfəl] *adj* **1.** zaradny **2.** przedsiębiorczy

re•spect [rɪ'spekt] **I** *s* **1.** szacunek *m*; ***with all due ~*** z całym szacunkiem; ***out of ~ for*** z szacunku dla *G*; ***pay one's ~s to*** oddać hołd *D*; ***pay one's last ~s to s.o.*** pożegnać zmarłego *A* **2.** wzgląd *m*; ***in this ~*** pod tym względem; ***in some ~s*** pod pewnymi względami; ***in no ~*** pod żadnym względem; ***in ~ of*** **a)** w związku z *I* **b)** pod względem *G* **c)** z tytułu *G*; ***with ~ to*** **a)** pod względem *G* **b)** odnośnie *G* **II** *v/t* **1.** szanować ⟨u-⟩ **2.** *law*: przestrzegać; **re•spect•a•bil•i•ty** [rɪspektə'bɪlətɪ] *s* **1.** przyzwoitość *f* **2.** poważanie *n*; **re•spec•ta•ble** [rɪ'spektəbl] *adj*

R

1. przyzwoity 2. szanowany; **re•spec•ta•bly** [rɪ'spektəblɪ] *adv* 1. przyzwoicie 2. odpowiednio; **re•spect•ful** [rɪ'spektfəl] *adj* 1. ***be ~ of*** szanować *A* 2. pełen szacunku; **re•spect•ful•ly** [rɪ'spektfəlɪ] *adv* z szacunkiem; **re•spec•tive** [rɪ'spektɪv] *adj* odnośny; ***they are each recognized as specialists in their ~ fields*** każdy z nich jest uznawany za specjalistę w swojej dziedzinie; **re•spec•tive•ly** [rɪ'spektɪvlɪ] *adv* odpowiednio; ***Julie and Mark, aged 17 and 19 ~*** Julie i Mark w wieku odpowiednio 17 i 19 lat

res•pi•ra•tion [respɪ'reɪʃn] *s* oddychanie *n*; **res•pi•ra•tor** [respɪ'reɪtə] *s* 1. *MED* respirator *m* 2. maska *f* przeciwgazowa 3. maska *f* ochronna; **res•pi•ra•to•ry** [rɪ'spɪrətrɪ] *adj* oddechowy; ***~ failure*** niewydolność oddechowa; ***the ~ tract*** drogi oddechowe; **res•'pi•ra•to•ry sys•tem** *s ANAT* układ *m* oddechowy

re•spite ['respaɪt] *s* 1. wytchnienie *n*; ***without ~*** bez wytchnienia 2. *debt*: odroczenie *n* spłaty

re•splend•ent [rɪ'splendənt] *adj* olśniewający

re•spond [rɪ'spɒnd] *v/t* 1. odpowiadać ⟨-wiedzieć⟩ (***to*** na *A*) 2. reagować ⟨za-⟩ (***to*** na *A*); ***how did they ~ to the news?*** jak zareagowali na tę wiadomość?; **re•spond•ent** [rɪ'spɒndənt] *s* 1. respondent *m* 2. *JUR* pozwany *m*

re•sponse [rɪ'spɒns] *s* 1. odpowiedź *f*; ***in ~ to your inquiry*** w odpowiedzi na Pańskie zapytanie 2. reakcja *f*

re•spon•si•bil•i•ty [rɪspɒnsɪ'bɪlətɪ] *s* odpowiedzialność *f* (***for*** za *A*); ***on one's own ~*** na własną odpowiedzialność; ***claim ~ for*** przyznawać się do *G*; ***a sense of ~*** poczucie odpowiedzialności; **re•spon•si•ble** [rɪ'spɒnsəbl] *adj* odpowiedzialny (***for*** za *A*, ***to*** przed *I*); ***be held ~ for*** zostać pociągniętym do odpowiedzialności za *A*; **re•spon•sive** [rɪ'spɒnsɪv] *adj* 1. wrażliwy; ***~ to cold*** wrażliwy na zimno 2. czuły 3. ***be ~ to*** reagować na *A*

rest¹ [rest] **I** *s* odpoczynek *m*; ***take a ~*** odpocząć; ***have a good night's ~*** dobrze spać w nocy; ***lay s.th. to ~, put s.th. to rest*** położyć czemuś kres; ***give s.th. a ~*** *infml* dać sobie spokój z *I*; ***lie at ~*** spoczywać w pokoju **II** *v/i* 1. odpoczywać ⟨-cząć⟩; ***~ assured*** być spokojnym; ***you may ~ assured*** niech cię o to głowa nie boli 2. spoczywać ⟨-cząć⟩; ***he won't ~ until he finds the killer*** nie spocznie, dopóki nie znajdzie zabójcy; ***may he ~ in peace*** niech spoczywa w pokoju 3. opierać ⟨oprzeć⟩ się **III** *v/t* opierać ⟨oprzeć⟩ (***against/on*** o *A*); **rest on** *v/i* 1. zależeć od *G* 2. opierać ⟨oprzeć⟩ się o *A*; **rest with** *v/i*: ***it ~s with him to take appropriate action*** jego obowiązkiem jest podjąć odpowiednie działania; ***the decision ~s with the doctors*** decyzja należy do lekarzy

rest² [~] *s* reszta *f*; ***the ~ of the world*** reszta świata

re•start [riː'stɑːt] **I** *v/t* 1. *computer*: restartować ⟨z-⟩ 2. *talks*: wznawiać ⟨-nowić⟩ **II** *v/i* (*talks*) zostawać ⟨-tać⟩ wznowionym

res•tau•rant ['restrɒnt] *s* restauracja *f*; **'res•tau•rant car** *s Br* wagon *m* restauracyjny

rest•ful ['restfəl] *adj* 1. spokojny 2. relaksujący 3. kojący

'rest home *s* dom *m* spokojnej starości

rest•ing place ['restɪŋ~] *s* 1. miejsce *n* wiecznego spoczynku 2. miejsce *n* odpoczynku

res•ti•tu•tion [restɪ'tjuːʃn] *s* restytucja *f*

res•tive ['restɪv] *adj* 1. zniecierpliwiony; ***grow ~*** zaczynać się niecierpliwić 2. niespokojny 3. *horse*: narowisty; **res•tive•ness** ['restɪvnɪs] *s* zniecierpliwienie *n*

rest•less ['restlɪs] *adj* 1. niespokojny 2. zniecierpliwiony; ***get ~*** zaczynać się niecierpliwić; **rest•less•ly** ['restlɪslɪ] *adv* niespokojnie

re•stock [riː'stɒk] *v/t* uzupełniać ⟨-nić⟩ zapasy w *L*

res•to•ra•tion [restə'reɪʃn] *s* 1. renowacja *f* 2. *ART* restauracja *f* 3. przywrócenie *n* 4. *diplomatic relations*: wznowienie *n* 5. zwrot *m* 6. ***the ~*** restauracja *f* Stuartów

re•store [rɪ'stɔː] *v/t* 1. przywracać ⟨-rócić⟩; ***she is ~d to health*** powróciła do zdrowia 2. restaurować ⟨od-⟩ 3. odnawiać ⟨-nowić⟩ 4. zwracać

R

⟨-rócić⟩; **re•stor•er** [rɪ'stɔːrə] *s* konserwator *m*

re•strain [rɪ'streɪn] *v/t* powtrzymywać ⟨-mać⟩ (***s.o. from*** kogoś od *G*); **re•strained** [rɪ'streɪnd] *adj* **1.** opanowany **2.** *laughter*: tłumiony **3.** *light*, *music*: spokojny **4.** *colour*: stonowany; **re•straint** [rɪ'streɪnt] *s* **1.** ograniczenie *n*; ***impose ~s*** nakładać ograniczenia **2.** powściągliwość *f* **3.** spokój *m* **4.** opanowanie *n*

re•strict [rɪ'strɪkt] *v/t* ograniczać ⟨-czyć⟩; ***~ oneself to*** ograniczać się do *G*; **re•strict•ed** [rɪ'strɪktɪd] *adj* **1.** ograniczony (***to*** do *G*) **2.** *information*: poufny; **re•strict•ed 'ar•e•a** *s* **1.** teren *m* zamknięty **2.** strefa *f* ograniczonego dostępu; **re•stric•tion** [rɪ'strɪkʃn] *s* ograniczenie *n*; ***without ~s*** bez ograniczeń; **re•stric•tive** [rɪ'strɪktɪv] *adj* **1.** *law*: restrykcyjny **2.** *clothes*: krępujący

'rest room *s Am* toaleta *f*

re•struc•ture [riː'strʌktʃə] *v/t* restrukturyzować ⟨z-⟩; **re•struc•tur•ing** [riː'strʌktʃərɪŋ] *s* restrukturyzacja *f*

re•sult [rɪ'zʌlt] **I** *s* **1.** wynik *m*; ***as a ~ of*** w wyniku *G* **2.** rezultat *m*; ***without ~*** bez rezultatu **II** *v/i* wynikać ⟨-knąć⟩ (***from*** z *G*); **result in** *v/t* **1.** powodować ⟨s-⟩ **2.** prowadzić ⟨do-⟩ do *G*

ré•su•mé ['rezʊmeɪ] *s* **1.** streszczenie *n* **2.** *Am* życiorys *m*

re•sume [rɪ'zjuːm] **I** *v/t* **1.** wznawiać ⟨-nowić⟩; ***~ driving*** ruszyć w dalszą drogę; ***~ one's seat*** wrócić na miejsce **2.** podejmować ⟨-djąć⟩ na nowo **II** *v/i* **1.** zostawać ⟨-tać⟩ wznowionym **2.** kontynuować; **re•sump•tion** [rɪ'zʌmpʃn] *s* **1.** wznowienie *n* **2.** kontynuacja *f*

re•sur•face [riː'sɜːfɪs] **I** *v/i* **1.** wynurzać ⟨-rzyć⟩ się **2.** *fig* powracać ⟨-rócić⟩ **II** *v/t* kłaść ⟨położyć⟩ nową nawierzchnię

re•sur•gence [rɪ'sɜːdʒəns] *s* **1.** *interests*: odrodzenie się **2.** *popularity*: ponowny wzrost *m* **3.** *energy*: ponowny przypływ *m* **4.** *violence*: ponowny wybuch *m*; **re•sur•gent** [rɪ'sɜːdʒənt] *adj* odradzający się; ***a ~ economy*** ponowny wzrost gospodarczy

res•ur•rect [rezə'rekt] *v/t a. fig* wskrzeszać ⟨-sić⟩ **res•ur•rec•tion** [rezə'rekʃn] *s* **1.** ***the ~*** *REL* Zmartwychwstanie *n* **2.** wskrzeszenie *n* **3.** odrodzenie się *n*

re•sus•ci•tate [rɪ'sʌsɪteɪt] *v/t a. fig* reanimować; **re•sus•ci•ta•tion** [rɪsʌsɪ'teɪʃn] *s a. fig* reanimacja *f*; ***a mouth-to-mouth ~*** sztuczne oddychanie metodą usta-usta

re•tail ['riːteɪl] **I** *s* sprzedaż *f* detaliczna **II** *v/t* sprzedawać ⟨-dać⟩ detalicznie **III** *v/i* ***the book ~s at $20*** cena detaliczna książki wynosi 20 dolarów; **re•tail•er** ['riːteɪlə] *s* detalista *m*; **'re•tail out•let** *s* **1.** punkt *m* sprzedaży detalicznej **2.** sklep *m*; **'re•tail price** *s* cena *f* detaliczna; **re•tail 'price in•dex** *s Br* *ECON* wskaźnik *m* cen detalicznych

re•tain [rɪ'teɪn] *v/t* **1.** zachowywać ⟨-chować⟩ **2.** *water*, *heat*: zatrzymywać ⟨-mać⟩ **3.** zapamiętywać ⟨-tać⟩ **4.** *lawyer*: angażować ⟨za-⟩; **re•tain•er** [rɪ'teɪnə] *s* wynagrodzenie *n* za pozostawanie do dyspozycji klienta

re•take I [riː'teɪk] (*retook*; *retaken*) *v/t* **1.** odzyskiwać ⟨-kać⟩ **2.** *exam*: powtarzać ⟨-tórzyć⟩ **II** ['riːteɪk] *s* **1.** *FILM* powtórka *f* **2.** egzamin *m* poprawkowy, *infml* poprawka *f*

re•tal•i•ate [rɪ'tælɪeɪt] *v/i* brać ⟨wziąć⟩ odwet (***against*** na *L*); **re•tal•i•a•tion** [rɪtælɪ'eɪʃn] *s* odwet *m*; **re•tal•i•a•to•ry** [rɪ'tælɪətɔːrɪ] *adj action*: odwetowy

re•tard I [rɪ'tɑːd] *v/t* **1.** opóźniać ⟨-nić⟩ **2.** spowalniać ⟨-wolnić⟩ **II** ['riːtɑːd] *s infml* kretyn *m*; **re•tard•ed** [rɪ'tɑːdɪd] *adj* upośledzony umysłowo

retch [retʃ] *v/i* mieć odruch wymiotny

re•ten•tion [rɪ'tenʃn] *s* **1.** zatrzymywanie *n*; ***water ~*** *MED* zatrzymywanie wody w organizmie **2.** zatrzymanie *n* **3.** utrzymanie *n* **4.** zapamiętywanie *n*; **re•ten•tive** [rɪ'tentɪv] *adj memory*: dobry

re•think [riː'θɪŋk] (*rethought*; *rethought*) *v/t* przemyśliwać ⟨-leć⟩

re•ti•cence ['retɪsns] *s* małomówność *f*; **re•ti•cent** ['retɪsnt] *adj* małomówny

ret•i•na ['retɪnə] *pl -nas*, *-nae* ['~niː] *s* *ANAT* siatkówka *f*

ret•i•nue ['retɪnjuː] *s* świta *f*

re•tire [rɪ'taɪə] **I** *v/i* **1.** przechodzić ⟨przejść⟩ na emeryturę **2.** *SPORT* kończyć ⟨za-⟩ karierę **3.** (*player*, *army*)

R

wycofywać ⟨-fać⟩ się **4.** oddalać ⟨-lić⟩ się **5.** udawać ⟨udać⟩ się na spoczynek **II** *v/t* wysyłać ⟨-słać⟩ na emeryturę; **re•tired** [rɪ'taɪəd] *adj* **1.** emerytowany **2.** na emeryturze; **re•tire•ment** [rɪ'taɪəmənt] *s* **1.** przejście *n* na emeryturę; ***take early ~*** przejść na wcześniejszą emeryturę **2.** emerytura *f* **3.** SPORT zakończenie *n* kariery; **re•'tire•ment age** *s* wiek *m* emerytalny; **re•tir•ing** [rɪ'taɪərɪŋ] *adj* **1.** nieśmiały **2.** *minister*: ustępujący

re•tort[1] [rɪ'tɔːt] **I** *v/i* ripostować ⟨z-⟩ **II** *s* riposta *f*

re•tort[2] [~] *s* retorta *f*

re•touch [riː'tʌtʃ] *v/t* retuszować ⟨wy-⟩

re•trace [rɪ'treɪs] *v/t* **1.** ***~ one's steps*** wrócić tą samą drogą **2.** *events*: odtwarzać ⟨-worzyć⟩

re•tract [rɪ'trækt] **I** *v/t* **1.** cofać ⟨-fnąć⟩ **2.** odwoływać ⟨-łać⟩ **3.** wycofywać ⟨-fać⟩ **4.** *claws*: chować ⟨s-⟩ **II** *v/i* **1.** wycofywać ⟨-fać⟩ się **2.** chować ⟨s-⟩ się; **re•tract•a•ble** [rɪ'træktəbl] *adj* **1.** *landing gear, aerial*: wysuwany **2.** *roof*: rozsuwany **3.** *measure*: zwijany; **re•trac•tion** [rɪ'trækʃn] *s* **1.** cofnięcie *n* **2.** odwołanie *n* **3.** wycofanie *n* **4.** wsuwanie *n* **5.** schowanie *n*

retrain [riː'treɪn] **I** *v/t* przekwalifikowywać ⟨-kować⟩ **II** *v/i* przekwalifikowywać ⟨-kować⟩ się (***as*** na *A*); **re•training** [riː'treɪnɪŋ] *s* przekwalifikowanie *n*; ***a ~ course*** kurs przekwalifikowania zawodowego

re•tread ['riːtred] *s* opona *f* bieżnikowana

re•treat [rɪ'triːt] **I** *v/i* **1.** wycofywać ⟨-fać⟩ się **2.** cofać ⟨-fnąć⟩ się **3.** oddalać ⟨-lić⟩ się **4.** udawać ⟨udać⟩ się **5.** *fig* uciekać ⟨uciec⟩; ***~ into a world of fantasy*** uciekać w świat fantazji **II** *v/t* (*prices*) spadać ⟨spaść⟩ o *A* **III** *s* **1.** odwrót *m* **2.** wycofanie się *n* **3.** cofanie się *n* **4.** *fig* ucieczka *f* **5.** ustronie *n* **6.** kryjówka *f* **7.** odosobnienie *n* medytacyjne

re•trench [rɪ'trentʃ] *v/i* ograniczać ⟨-czyć⟩ wydatki

re•tri•al ['riːtraɪəl] *s* JUR ponowny proces *m*

ret•ri•bu•tion [retrɪ'bjuːʃn] *s* kara *f*

re•triev•al [rɪ'triːvl] *s* **1.** INF *data*: wyszukiwanie *n*; **2.** odzyskanie *n*; **re•trieve** [rɪ'triːv] **I** *v/t* **1.** odzyskiwać ⟨-kać⟩ **2.** *situation*: ratować ⟨u-⟩ **3.** *data*: wyszukiwać ⟨-kać⟩ **II** *v/i* aportować; **re•triev•er** [rɪ'triːvə] *s* **1.** retriever *m* **2.** pies *m* myśliwski (aportujący)

ret•ro•ac•tive [retrəʊ'æktɪv] *adj law*: działający wstecz; **ret•ro•ac•tive•ly** [retrəʊ'æktɪvlɪ] *adv* wstecz

ret•ro•grade ['retrəgreɪd] *adj*: ***a~ step*** *fig* krok wstecz

ret•ro•gres•sive [retrə'gresɪv] *adj* wsteczny

ret•ro•spect ['retrəspekt] *s*: ***in ~*** patrząc wstecz, z perspektywy czasu; **ret•ro•spec•tive** [retrə'spektɪv] **I** *adj* **1.** retrospektywny **2.** *law*: działający wstecz **II** *s* ART retrospektywa *f*

ret•ro•vi•rus ['retrəʊvaɪrəs] *s* BIOL retrowirus *m*

re•try [riː'traɪ] **I** *v/t* **1.** *person*: ponownie sądzić ⟨o-⟩ **2.** *case*: ponownie rozpatrywać ⟨-rzyć⟩ **II** *v/i* próbować ⟨s-⟩ ponownie

re•turn [rɪ'tɜːn] **I** *v/i* **1.** wracać ⟨wrócić⟩ (***from*** z *G*, ***to*** do *G*); ***~ to normal*** wrócić do normalności **2.** powracać ⟨-rócić⟩ **II** *v/t* **1.** zwracać ⟨-rócić⟩ **2.** oddawać ⟨-dać⟩ **3.** odwzajemniać ⟨-nić⟩; ***~ a phone call*** oddzwonić; ***~ a favour*** odwdzięczyć się **4.** *verdict*: wydawać ⟨-dać⟩; **5.** *loss, profit*: notować ⟨za-⟩ **III** *s* **1.** powrót *m*; ***on one's ~*** po powrocie; ***many happy ~s*** wszystkiego najlepszego (z okazji urodzin) **2.** zwrot *m*; ***a ~ address*** adres zwrotny; ***by ~ of post*** *Br* odwrotną pocztą **3.** ***in ~ for*** w zamian za *A* **4.** *symptoms*: nawrót *m* **5.** zysk *m* **6.** dochód *m* **7.** ***a tax ~*** zeznanie podatkowe **8.** *Br* bilet *m* powrotny; **re•turn•a•ble** [rɪ'tɜːnəbl] *adj* **1.** *bottle*: zwrotny **2.** ***the application is ~ not later than 5 May*** zgłoszenia należy składać do 5 maja; **re•turn 'flight** *s* lot *m* powrotny; **re•turn 'jour•ney** *s* podróż *f* powrotna; **re•'turn key** *s* INF klawisz *m* Enter

re•u•ni•fi•ca•tion [riːjuːnɪfɪ'keɪʃn] *s* ponowne zjednoczenie *n*; **re•u•ni•fy** [riː'juːnɪfaɪ] *v/t* ponownie jednoczyć ⟨z-⟩

re•u•nion [riː'juːnjən] *s* **1.** zjazd *m* **2.** zlot *m* **3.** spotkanie *n*; **re•u•nite**

[riːjuː'naɪt] **I** *v/t* **1.** ***be ~d*** spotykać ⟨-tkać⟩ się **2.** jednoczyć ⟨z-⟩ **II** *v/i* **1.** spotykać ⟨-tkać⟩ się **2.** (*band*) reaktywować się **3.** jednoczyć ⟨z-⟩ się

re•us•a•ble [riː'juːzəbl] *adj*: ***~ packaging*** opakowanie wielokrotnego użytku

rev [rev] **I** (*a.* ***~ up***) *v/t engine*: zwiększać ⟨-szyć⟩ obroty **II** (*a.* ***~ up***) *v/i engine*: zwiększać ⟨-szyć⟩ obroty **III** *s engine*: *infml* obrót *m*

re•val•u•a•tion [riːvæljʊ'eɪʃn] *s* **1.** *currency*: rewaluacja *f* **2.** aktualizacja *f* wyceny

re•vamp [riː'væmp] *v/t* **1.** przerabiać ⟨-robić⟩ **2.** zmieniać ⟨-nić⟩ **3.** ⟨z-⟩ reorganizować

re•veal [rɪ'viːl] *v/t* **1.** ujawniać ⟨-nić⟩ **2.** wyjawiać ⟨-wić⟩ **3.** odsłaniać ⟨-łonić⟩ **4.** ukazywać ⟨-zać⟩; **re•veal•ing** [rɪ'viːlɪŋ] *adj* **1.** odkrywczy **2.** pouczający **3.** *dress*: wydekoltowany

rev•el ['revl] **I** *v/i* hulać **II** *s* hulanka *f*; **revel in** *v/t* **1.** upajać się **2.** rozkoszować się

rev•e•la•tion [revə'leɪʃn] *s* **1.** rewelacja *f* **2.** ujawnienie *n* **3.** odkrycie *n* **4.** *REL* objawienie *n*

rev•el•ler ['revələ] *Br*, **reveler** *Am s*: ***thousand of ~s filled the Trafalgar Square*** tysiące ludzi bawiło się na Trafalgar Square

rev•el•ry ['revlrɪ] *s* hulanka *f*

re•venge [rɪ'vendʒ] **I** *s* **1.** zemsta *f*; ***take ~ on*** zemścić się na *L*; ***be in ~ for*** być zemstą za *A*, być odwetem za *A* **2.** *SPORT* rewanż *m* **II** *v/t* ***~ oneself on*** zemścić się na *L*; **re•venge•ful** [rɪ'vendʒfʊl] *adj* **1.** szukający zemsty **2.** mściwy

rev•e•nue ['revənjuː] *s ECON* **1.** wpływy *pl* **2.** przychód *m* **3.** dochód *m*

re•ver•be•rate [rɪ'vɜːbəreɪt] *v/i* **1.** rozbrzmiewać ⟨-mieć⟩ **2.** rozlegać ⟨-lec⟩ się **3.** drżeć ⟨za-⟩ (***with*** od *G*) **4.** *fig* odbijać ⟨-bić⟩ się szerokim echem; **re•ver•be•ra•tion** [rɪvɜːbə'reɪʃn] *s* **1.** pogłos *m* **2.** echo *n* **3.** ***~s*** *fig* reperkusje *pl*

re•vere [rɪ'vɪə] *v/t* **1.** czcić **2.** wielbić **3.** podziwiać; **rev•e•rence** ['revərəns] *s* **1.** cześć *f* **2.** uwielbienie *n* **3.** podziw *m*; **Rev•e•rend** ['revərənd] *s REL* wielebny *m*

rev•e•rent ['revərənt] *adj* **1.** pełen czci **2.** nabożny; **rev•er•en•tial** [revə'renʃl] → ***reverent***

rev•er•ie ['revərɪ] *s* zaduma *f*; ***jolt s.o. out of ~*** wyrwać kogoś z zadumy

re•ver•sal [rɪ'vɜːsl] *s* **1.** *trend, roles*: odwrócenie *n* **2.** *post*: (radykalna) zmiana *f* **3.** *policy*: (radykalny) zwrot *m* **4.** niepowodzenie *n*; **reverse** [rɪ'vɜːs] **I** *v/t* **1.** odwracać ⟨-rócić⟩ **2.** *policy*: radykalnie zmieniać ⟨-nić⟩ **3.** *decision*: zmieniać ⟨-nić⟩ **4.** *verdict*: unieważniać ⟨-nić⟩ **5.** *car*: cofać ⟨-fnąć⟩ **II** *v/i* cofać ⟨-fnąć⟩ się **III** *s* **1.** odwrotność *f*; ***quite the ~*** zupełnie na odwrót **2.** *coin*: rewers *m* **3.** *page*: odwrotna strona *f* **4.** *garment*: lewa strona *f* **5.** *AUTO* bieg *m* wsteczny; ***put the car in ~*** wrzucić bieg wsteczny **6.** niepowodzenie *n* **IV** *adj* odwrotny; ***in ~ order*** w odwrotnej kolejności; ***the ~ side of a garment*** lewa strona ubrania; **re•vers•i•ble** [rɪ'vɜːsəbl] *adj* **1.** *process*: odwracalny **2.** *jacket*: dwustronny

revert [rɪ'vɜːt] *v/t* powracać ⟨-rócić⟩ (***to*** do *G*); ***~ to the earlier question*** powrócić do wcześniejszego pytania; ***~ to one's maiden name*** powrócić do panieńskiego nazwiska

re•view [rɪ'vjuː] **I** *s* **1.** przegląd *m* **2.** ocena *f*; ***be under ~*** zostać poddanym ocenie **3.** *policy*: rewizja *f* **4.** recenzja *f* **II** *v/t* **1.** *troops*: dokonywać ⟨-nać⟩ przeglądu **2.** oceniać ⟨-nić⟩, poddawać ⟨-dać⟩ ocenie **3.** *policy*: rewidować ⟨z-⟩ **4.** recenzować ⟨z-⟩ **5.** *Am lesson*: powtarzać ⟨-tórzyć⟩; **re•view•er** [rɪ'vjuːə] *s* recenzent *m*

re•vise [rɪ'vaɪz] **I** *v/t* **1.** zmieniać ⟨-nić⟩ **2.** poprawiać ⟨-wić⟩ **3.** *opinion*: rewidować ⟨z-⟩ **4.** *Br lesson*: powtarzać ⟨-tórzyć⟩ **II** *v/i* powtarzać ⟨-tórzyć⟩ wiadomości; **re•vi•sion** [rɪ'vɪʒn] *s* **1.** zmiana *f* **2.** zmiany *pl* **3.** poprawienie *n* **4.** *opinion*: rewizja *f* **5.** *Br subject*: powtórka *f*

re•vi•tal•ize [riː'vaɪtəlaɪz] *v/t* ożywiać ⟨-wić⟩

re•viv•al [rɪ'vaɪvl] *s* **1.** ponowny rozkwit *m* **2.** *fig* renesans *m* **3.** powrót *m* **4.** ożywienie *n* **5.** *THEAT* wznowienie *n*; **re•vive** [rɪ'vaɪv] **I** *v/i* **1.** odżywać ⟨-żyć⟩ **2.** ożywać ⟨ożyć⟩ **II** *v/t* **1.** roz-

R

budzać ⟨-dzić⟩ na nowo **2.** wskrzeszać ⟨-sić⟩ **3.** cucić ⟨o-⟩ **4.** *economy*: ożywiać ⟨-wić⟩ **5.** *hope*: przywracać ⟨-rócić⟩ **6.** *THEAT* wznawiać ⟨-nowić⟩

rev•o•ca•tion [revə'keɪʃn] *s* **1.** *permission*: cofnięcie *n* **2.** uchylenie *n* **3.** unieważnienie *n*

re•voke [rɪ'vəʊk] *v/t* **1.** *permission*: cofać ⟨-fnąć⟩ **2.** uchylać ⟨-lić⟩ **3.** unieważniać ⟨-nić⟩

re•volt [rɪ'vəʊlt] **I** *s* **1.** bunt *m* (***against*** przeciw *D*) **2.** powstanie *n* **II** *v/i* buntować ⟨z-⟩ się **III** *v/t* budzić ⟨o-⟩ odrazę w *L*; **re•volt•ing** [rɪ'vəʊltɪŋ] *adj* **1.** odrażający **2.** wstrętny

rev•o•lu•tion [revə'lu:ʃn] *s* **1.** rewolucja *f*; ***a scientific ~*** rewolucja naukowa **2.** *circle*: obrót *m*; **rev•o•lu•tion•ar•y** [revə'lu:ʃnərɪ] **I** *adj* rewolucyjny **II** *s* rewolucjonista *m*; **rev•o•lu•tion•ize** [revə'lu:ʃnaɪz] *v/t* rewolucjonizować ⟨z-⟩

re•volve [rɪ'vɒlv] *v/i* obracać ⟨-rócić⟩ się (***around*** wokół *G*); ***the earth ~s on its axis*** Ziemia obraca się wokół własnej osi; ***she thinks that the world ~s around her*** myśli, że świat kręci się wokół niej; **re•volv•er** [rɪ'vɒlvə] *s* rewolwer *m*; **re•volv•ing 'door** [rɪ'vɒlvɪŋ] *s* drzwi *pl* obrotowe

re•vue [rɪ'vju:] *s* rewia *f*

re•vul•sion [rɪ'vʌlʃn] *s* **1.** odraza *f* **2.** wstręt *m*

re•ward [rɪ'wɔ:d] **I** *s* nagroda *f*; ***as a ~ for*** w nagrodę za *A*; ***reap the ~s of*** *fig* zbierać owoce *G* **II** *v/t* nagradzać ⟨-rodzić⟩; **re•ward•ing** [rɪ'wɔ:dɪŋ] *adj* **1.** *job*: dający satysfakcję **2.** *experience*: cenny **3.** ***financially ~*** dochodowy

re•word [ri:'wɜ:d] *v/t* przeredagowywać ⟨-gować⟩; ***I'll ~ my question*** zapytam inaczej

re•write [ri:'raɪt] (*rewrote*; *rewritten*) *v/t* **1.** przepisywać ⟨-pisać⟩ **2.** *article, novel*: pisać ⟨na-⟩ na nowo **3.** *play*: przerabiać ⟨-robić⟩ **4.** *text*: redagować ⟨prze-⟩; **re•write•a•ble** *adj*: ***a ~ CD*** płyta CD wielokrotnego zapisu

rhap•so•dize ['ræpsədaɪz] *v/i* **1.** piać z zachwytu (***about***/***over*** nad *I*) **2.** rozpływać się (***about***/***over*** nad *I*)

rhap•so•dy ['ræpsədɪ] *s MUS* rapsodia *f*

rhe•sus fac•tor ['ri:səsfæktə] *s MED* czynnik *m* Rh

rhe•to•ric ['retərɪk] *s* retoryka *f*; **rhe•to•ric•al 'ques•tion** [rɪ'tɒrɪkl'kwestʃən] *s* pytanie *n* retoryczne

rheu•mat•ic [ru:'mætɪk] *adj* reumatyczny; **rheu•ma•tism** ['ru:mətɪzm] *s* reumatyzm *m*

rhi•no ['raɪnəʊ] *pl -nos s infml*, ***rhi•no•ce•ros*** [raɪ'nɒsərəs] *s* nosorożec *m*

rho•do•den•dron [rəʊdə'dendrən] *s BIOL* rododendron *m*

rhom•bus ['rɒmbəs] *pl -buses*, *-bi* ['~baɪ] *s* romb *m*

rhu•barb ['ru:bɑ:b] *s* rabarbar *m*

rhyme [raɪm] **I** *s* **1.** rym *m*; ***a ~ for*** rym do *G*; ***without ~ or reason*** **a)** bez powodu **b)** bez ładu i składu; ***he behaved without ~ or reason*** zachowywał się zupełnie irracjonalnie **2.** wiersz *m* **3.** wierszyk *m* **II** *v/i* rymować ⟨z-⟩ się (***with*** z *I*); ***I prefer poems that ~*** wolę wiersze rymowane **III** *v/t* rymować ⟨z-⟩

rhythm ['rɪðm] *s* rytm *m*; ***play in ~*** grać do rytmu; ***disrupt s.o.'s ~*** wybić kogoś z rytmu; **rhyth•mic**, ***rhyth•mi•cal*** ['rɪðmɪk(l)] *adj* rytmiczny

rib [rɪb] **I** *s* **1.** żebro *n* **2.** *COOK* żeberka *pl* **II** *v/t dated* kpić ⟨za-⟩ (**s.o. *about*/*over*** z kogoś z powodu *G*)

rib•bon ['rɪbən] *s* **1.** wstążka *f* **2.** wstęga *f* **3.** tasiemka *f* **4.** ***tear s.th. to ~s*** podrzeć coś na strzępy

'rib cage *s* klatka *f* piersiowa

rice [raɪs] *s* ryż *m*; **'rice pa•per** *s* papier *m* ryżowy; **'rice pad•dy** *s* pole *n* ryżowe; **rice 'pud•ding** *s COOK* pudding *m* ryżowy

rich [rɪtʃ] **I** *adj* **1.** bogaty; ***~ in vitamin C*** bogaty w witaminę C **2.** pełen; ***~ in contrasts*** pełen kontrastów **3.** *food*: sycący **4.** *colour*: intensywny **5.** *voice*: głęboki **6.** *soil*: żyzny **7.** *life, history*: bogaty **8.** *decoration*: kosztowny **9.** ***that's ~!*** a to ci dopiero! **II** *s* ***the ~*** bogaci *pl*; **rich•es** ['rɪtʃɪz] *pl* **1.** bogactwo *n* **2.** majątek *m*; **rich•ly** ['rɪtʃlɪ] *adv* **1.** bogato **2.** *flavoured*: intensywnie **3.** *reward*: sowicie; **rich•ness** ['rɪtʃnɪs] *s a. fig* bogactwo *n*

rick•ets ['rɪkɪts] *s MED* krzywica *f*; **rick•et•y** ['rɪkətɪ] *adj* **1.** chybotliwy **2.** chwiejny **3.** rozklekotany

rick•shaw ['rɪkʃɔː] *s* riksza *f*

ric•o•chet ['rɪkəʃeɪ] **I** *s* rykoszet *m* **II** *v/i* odbijać 〈-bić〉 się rykoszetem (***off*** od *G*)

rid [rɪd] (*rid*; *rid*) *v/t* uwalniać 〈uwolnić〉 (***of*** od *G*); ***get ~ of*** **a)** pozbyć się *G* **b)** uwolnić się od *G*; ***get ~ of excess weight*** zrzucić nadmiar kilogramów; ***be ~ of*** pozbyć się *G*; ***I'm glad we're ~ of her*** cieszę się, że się jej pozbyliśmy; **rid•dance** ['rɪdns] *s*: ***good ~*** krzyżyk na drogę

rid•den ['rɪdn] **I** *Past Participle* → **ride** **II** *adj* ***s.o. is guilt-~*** kogoś przepełnia poczucie winy; ***debt-~*** tonący w długach

rid•dle ['rɪdl] **I** *s* zagadka *f*; ***speak in ~s*** mówić zagadkami **II** *v/t* dziurawić 〈po-〉; ***be ~d with bullets*** być podziurawionym kulami; ***be ~d with mistakes*** roić się od błędów

ride [raɪd] **I** (*rode*; *ridden*) *v/t* **1.** jeździć; ***I often ~ my bike to work*** często jeżdżę rowerem do pracy **2.** jechać; ***he was riding a white horse*** jechał na białym koniu **3.** *distance*: przejeżdżać 〈-jechać〉 **II** (*rode*; *ridden*) *v/i* **1.** jeździć **2.** jechać **3.** jeździć konno; ***can you ~?*** czy umiesz jeździć konno? **III** *s* **1.** przejażdżka *f*; ***give s.o. a ~*** zabrać kogoś na przejażdżkę; ***go for a ~*** wybrać się na przejażdżkę; ***a horse ~*** przejażdżka konna; ***take s.o. for a ~*** *fig* zrobić kogoś w balona **2.** jazda *f* **3.** karuzela *f*; **ride up** *v/i* (*dress*) podciągać 〈-gnąć〉 się; **rid•er** ['raɪdə] *s* **1.** jeździec *m* **2.** rowerzysta *m* **3.** motocyklista *m*

ridge [rɪdʒ] *s* **1.** *mountain*: grzbiet *m* **2.** kalenica *f* **3.** *earth*: skiba *f* **4.** klin *m* wysokiego ciśnienia

rid•i•cule ['rɪdɪkjuːl] **I** *v/t* wyśmiewać 〈-miać〉 **II** *s* pośmiewisko *n*; ***hold s.o. up to ~*** wyśmiać kogoś; ***an object of ~*** przedmiot kpin; **ri•dic•u•lous** [rɪ'dɪkjʊləs] *adj* **1.** śmieszny **2.** absurdalny; **ri•dic•u•lous•ly** [rɪ'dɪkjʊləslɪ] *adv* **1.** śmiesznie; ***~ cheap*** śmiesznie tani **2.** absurdalnie

rid•ing ['raɪdɪŋ] *s* **1.** jazda *f* konna; ***go ~*** pojeździć konno **2.** jeździectwo *n*; **'rid•ing boots** *pl* buty *pl* do jazdy konnej; **'rid•ing breech•es** *pl* bryczesy *pl*; **'rid•ing school** *s* szkoła *f* jazdy konnej

rife [raɪf] *adj* **1.** ***be ~*** szerzyć się; ***rumours are ~ that*** krążą plotki, że **2.** ***the office was ~ with rumours*** w biurze huczało od plotek

rif•fle ['rɪfl] **I** *v/i* kartkować 〈prze-〉 (***through*** *A*) **II** *v/t pages*: przewracać

riff•raff ['rɪfræf] *s* motłoch *m*, hołota *f*

ri•fle ['raɪfl] **I** *s* **1.** karabin *m* **2.** strzelba *f* **II** *v/i* przetrząsać 〈-snąć〉 (***through*** *A*); **ri•fle range** *s* strzelnica *f*

rift [rɪft] *s* **1.** *fig* rozłam *m* **2.** *fig* rozdźwięk *m* **3.** szczelina *f* **4.** rozpadlina *f*

rig [rɪg] **I** *v/t* **1.** *elections*: fałszować 〈s-〉 **2.** (*sailing*) taklować 〈o-〉 **II** *s* **1.** ożaglowanie *n* **2.** platforma *f* wiertnicza; **rig up** *v/t* klecić 〈s-〉; **rig•ging** ['rɪgɪŋ] *s* **1.** olinowanie *n* **2.** takielunek *m*

right [raɪt] **I** *adj* **1.** prawidłowy, dobry; ***the ~ answer*** prawidłowa odpowiedź; ***the ~ time*** dokładny czas **2.** ***be ~*** mieć rację; ***am I ~?*** czy mam rację? **3.** właściwy; ***do the ~ thing*** postąpić właściwie; ***be in the ~ place at the ~ time*** być we właściwym miejscu, we właściwym czasie **4.** prawdziwy; ***is it ~*** czy to prawda?; ***yes, that's ~*** tak, to prawda, tak, zgadza się **5.** prawy; ***take a ~ turn*** skręć w prawo **6.** *Br infml* zupełny; ***I felt a ~ idiot*** czułem się jak zupełny idiota **II** *adv* **1.** dokładnie; ***~ on time*** punktualnie, dokładnie na czas; ***~ now*** w tym momencie, natychmiast **2.** zaraz; ***I'll be ~ back*** zaraz wracam **3.** dobrze, prawidłowo **4.** w prawo; ***turn ~*** skręć w prawo **5.** zupełnie **III** *s* **1.** dobro *n*; ***~ and wrong*** dobro i zło **2.** prawo *n*; ***you have no ~ to stop me*** nie masz prawa mnie zatrzymać; ***she had every ~ to be angry*** miała prawo być zła; ***human ~s*** prawa człowieka **3.** prawa strona *f*; ***on the ~*** po prawej (stronie) **4.** ***the ~*** POLIT prawica *f* **5.** (*boxing*) prawy *m* **IV** *v/t* **1.** prostować 〈wy-〉 **2.** naprawiać 〈-wić〉; ***~ a wrong*** naprawić wyrządzone zło; **right-'an•gle** *s* kąt *m* prosty; **right-an•gled** ['raɪtæŋgld] *adj* prostokątny

right•eous ['raɪtʃəs] *adj* **1.** prawy **2.** sprawiedliwy **3.** słuszny

right•ful ['raɪtfəl] *adj owner*: prawowity; **'right-hand** *adj side*, *glove*: prawy; **right-hand 'drive** *adj vehicle*: z kie-

R

rownicą po prawej stronie; **right-hand•ed** [raɪt'hændɪd] *adj* praworęczny; **right-hand•er** [raɪt'hændə] *s* **1.** osoba *f* praworęczna **2.** prawy *m*; **right-hand 'man** *s fig* prawa ręka *f*
rightist['raɪtɪst] *s POLIT* prawicowiec *m*
right•ly ['raɪtlɪ] *adv* **1.** słusznie; ***quite ~*** całkiem słusznie; ***~ or wrongly*** słusznie czy nie **2.** dobrze; ***if I remember ~*** jeśli dobrze pamiętam
right of 'way *pl rights of way s* pierwszeństwo *n* (przejazdu)
right 'wing *s* **1.** *POLIT* prawe skrzydło *n* **2.** *SPORT* prawoskrzydłowy *m*; **right-'wing** *adj views*: prawicowy; **right-'wing•er** *s* **1.** *POLIT* prawicowiec *m* **2.** *SPORT* prawoskrzydłowy *m*; **right-wing ex•'trem•ism** *s* skrajna prawica *f*
rig•id ['rɪdʒɪd] *adj* **1.** sztywny **2.** *rules*: rygorystyczny **3.** *control*, *discipline*: ścisły; **ri•gid•i•ty** [rɪ'dʒɪdɪtɪ] *s* **1.** sztywność *f* **2.** rygorystyczność *f* **3.** ścisłość *f*
rig•ma•role ['rɪgmərəʊl] *s fig* **1.** zamieszanie *n* (**of**/**about** związane z *I*) **2.** *infml* zawracanie *n* głowy
rig•or *Am* → ***rigour***
rig•or mor•tis [rɪgə'mɔːtɪs] *s MED* stężenie *n* pośmiertne
rig•or•ous ['rɪgərəs] *adj* **1.** rygorystyczny **2.** surowy **3.** ścisły **4.** wnikliwy; **rig-or•ous•ly** ['rɪgərəslɪ] *adv* **1.** rygorystycznie **2.** ściśle **3.** wnikliwie
rig•our ['rɪgə] *Br*, ***rigor*** *Am s* **1.** rygor *m* **2.** dyscyplina *f* **3.** surowość *f*; ***with the full ~ of the law*** z całą surowością prawa
rile [raɪl] *v/t* denerwować ⟨z-⟩
rim [rɪm] **I** *s* **1.** brzeg *m* **2.** obręcz *f* **3.** obwódka *f* **4.** oprawka *f*; **II** *v/t* ***gold-~med spectacles*** okulary w złotych oprawkach
rind [raɪnd] *s lemon*, *orange*: skórka *f*
ring[1] [rɪŋ] **I** *s* **1.** pierścionek *m*; ***a wedding ~*** obrączka (ślubna) **2.** koło *n* **3.** kółko *n*; ***a key ~*** kółko do kluczy **4.** krąg *m* **5.** (*boxing*) ring *m* **6.** (*circus*) arena *f* **7.** palnik *m* **8.** gang *m* **9.** ***a spy ~*** siatka szpiegowska **II** *v/t* **1.** otaczać ⟨otoczyć⟩ **2.** *birds*: obrączkować ⟨za-⟩ **3.** zakreślać ⟨-lić⟩ kółkiem
ring[2] [~] **I** *s* **1.** (*sound*) dzwonek *m*; ***a ~ at the door*** dzwonek do drzwi; ***give s.o. a ~*** *Br infml* zadzwonić do kogoś **2.** dzwonienie *n* **3.** ***have a familiar ~*** brzmieć znajomo; ***have a hollow ~*** brzmieć niewiarygodnie **II** (*rang*; *rung*) *v/t* dzwonić ⟨za-⟩; ***~ the doorbell*** zadzwonić do drzwi; ***I'll ~ you later*** zadzwonię do ciebie później; ***~ a bell*** *fig* brzmieć znajomo **III** (*rang*; *rung*) *v/i* **1.** rozbrzmiewać ⟨-mieć⟩ (**with** *G*) **2.** ***his voice rang with pride*** w jego głosie brzmiała duma **3.** ***my ears are ~ing*** dzwoni mi w uszach; **ring back** *v/t Br* oddzwaniać ⟨-wonić⟩; **ring in** *v/i Br* dzwonić ⟨za-⟩ (do pracy); **ring off** *v/i Br* **1.** odkładać ⟨odłożyć⟩ słuchawkę **2.** rozłączać ⟨-czyć⟩ się; **ring out** *v/i* rozlegać ⟨-lec⟩ się; **ring up** *v/t* **1.** dzwonić ⟨za-⟩ do *G* **2.** (*shop*) nabijać ⟨-bić⟩ (na kasę)
'ring bind•er *s* segregator *m*; **'ring-fence** *v/t Br money*: rezerwować ⟨za-⟩; **'ring fin•ger** *s* palec *m* serdeczny; **'ring•lead•er** *s* **1.** przywódca *m* **2.** prowodyr *m*; **'ring-pull** *s Br* metalowe kółko do otwierania puszki; **'ring road** *s Br* obwodnica *f*; **'ring-side** *s*: ***at the ~*** w pobliżu ringu
rink [rɪŋk] *s* **1.** lodowisko *n* **2.** tor *m* do jazdy na wrotkach
rinse [rɪns] **I** *v/t* **1.** przepłukiwać ⟨-kać⟩ **2.** wypłukiwać ⟨-kać⟩ **3.** spłukiwać ⟨-kać⟩ (**from** z *G*) **II** *s* **1.** płukanie *n*; ***give a glass a ~*** wypłukać szklankę **2.** płyn *m* do płukania (jamy ustnej) **3.** płukanka *f* do włosów
ri•ot ['raɪət] **I** *s* **1.** rozruchy *pl* **2.** zamieszki *pl*; ***race ~s*** zamieszki na tle rasowym **3.** ***run ~*** szaleć; ***let one's imagination run ~*** puścić wodze fantazji **4.** ***be a ~ of colours*** mienić się wszystkimi kolorami **5.** ***the party was a ~*** *infml* impreza była fantastyczna **II** *v/i* (*prisoners*) buntować ⟨z-⟩ się; **ri•ot•er** ['raɪətə] *s* uczestnik *m* rozruchów; **ri•ot•ous** ['raɪətəs] *adj* **1.** *life*: hulaszczy; ***waste s.th. in ~ living*** przehulać coś **2.** *demonstration*: burzliwy **3.** *crowd*: szalejący **4.** *party*: hałaśliwy; **ri•ot•ous•ly** ['raɪətəslɪ] *adv* bardzo; **'riot police** *s* (*police*) oddziały *pl* prewencji
rip [rɪp] **I** *v/t* **1.** drzeć ⟨po-⟩ **2.** rozdzierać ⟨-zedrzeć⟩ **3.** zdzierać ⟨zedrzeć⟩ (**off** *A*) **II** *v/i* **1.** drzeć ⟨po-⟩ się **2.** roz-

dzierać ⟨-zedrzeć⟩ się; **rip apart** *v/t* **1.** rozdzierać ⟨-zedrzeć⟩ **2.** *fig* niszczyć ⟨z-⟩; **rip off** *v/t infml* **1.** zdzierać ⟨zedrzeć⟩ (z *G*) **2.** (*steal*) podprowadzać ⟨-dzić⟩; **rip up** *v/t* drzeć ⟨po-⟩ na strzępy

'rip cord *s parachute*: linka *f* wyzwalająca

ripe [raɪp] *adj fruit, cheese*: dojrzały; ***live to a ~ old age*** dożyć sędziwego wieku; **rip•en** ['raɪpn] *v/i* dojrzewać ⟨-rzeć⟩; **ripe•ness** ['raɪpnɪs] *s* dojrzałość *f*

'rip-off *s infml* **1.** zdzierstwo *n* **2.** podróbka *f* **3.** przeróbka *f*

ri•poste [rɪ'pɒst] **I** *s* riposta *f* **II** *v/i* ripostować ⟨z-⟩

rip•ple ['rɪpl] **I** *s* **1.** (*on water*) zmarszczka *f* **2.** niewielka fala *f*; ***cause ~ in*** *fig* mieć wpływ na *A* **II** *v/i* **1.** (*water*) marszczyć ⟨z-⟩ się **2.** (*shivers*) przebiegać ⟨-biec⟩ **III** *v/t water*: marszczyć ⟨z-⟩

rise [raɪz] **I** *s* **1.** wzrost *m*; ***a price ~*** wzrost cen **2.** wzrost *m* popularności **3.** *Br* podwyżka *f* **4.** wzniesienie *n* **5.** wnoszenie się *n* **6.** *empire*: narodziny *pl*; ***the ~ and fall of the empire*** narodziny i upadek imperium **7. *a ~ to power*** dojście do władzy **8. *give ~ to*** spowodować *A*; ***give ~ to much speculation*** wywołać falę domysłów **II** (*rose*; *risen*) *v/i* **1.** wstawać ⟨-tać⟩; ***~ from a table*** wstać od stołu; ***~ to the occasion*** stanąć na wysokości zadania **2.** (*prices*) rosnąć ⟨wz-⟩ **3.** wznosić ⟨-nieść⟩ się **4.** (*sun*) wschodzić ⟨wzejść⟩ **5. *~ to power*** dojść do władzy; ***~ in rank*** awansować **6.** (*wind*) wzmagać ⟨-móc⟩ się **7.** powstawać ⟨-tać⟩, buntować ⟨z-⟩ się **8.** (*dough*) rosnąć ⟨u-⟩ **9. *~ from the dead*** zmartwychwstać, *lit* powstać z martwych; **ris•en** ['rɪzn] *Past Participle* → **rise**; **ris•er** ['raɪzə] *s*: ***an early ~*** ranny ptaszek; ***a late ~*** śpioch; **ris•ing** ['raɪzɪŋ] *s* powstanie *n*

risk [rɪsk] **I** *s* **1.** ryzyko *n*; ***at one's own ~*** na własne ryzyko; ***run a ~*** ryzykować; ***take a ~*** podjąć ryzyko; ***a ~ group*** grupa ryzyka **2.** zagrożenie *n* **3.** niebezpieczeństwo *n*; ***be at ~*** być w niebezpieczeństwie; ***put s.o. at ~*** narażać kogoś na niebezpieczeństwo **II** *v/t* ryzykować ⟨za-⟩; ***~ one's life***, ***~ one's neck*** ryzykować życiem; **'risk a•nal•y•sis** *s* ECON analiza *f* ryzyka; **'risk man•age•ment** *s* ECON zarządzanie *n* ryzykiem; **'risk-tak•er** *s* ryzykant *m*; **risk•y** ['rɪskɪ] *adj* **1.** ryzykowny **2.** niebezpieczny

ris•qué [rɪ'skeɪ] *adj* pikantny

ris•sole ['rɪsəʊl] *s Br* kotlet *m* siekany

rite [raɪt] *s* **1.** rytuał *m* **2.** obrzęd *m* **3.** obrządek *m*

rit•u•al ['rɪtʃʊəl] **I** *s* rytuał *m* **II** *adj* rytualny

ritz•y ['rɪtsɪ] *adj infml* szykowny

ri•val ['raɪvl] **I** *s* **1.** konkurent *m*; ***have no ~*** być bezkonkurencyjnym **2.** rywal *m* **II** *adj* **1.** konkurujący **2.** *team*: przeciwny **III** *v/t* **1.** równać się z *I* **2.** dorównywać ⟨-nać⟩; **ri•val•ry** ['raɪvlrɪ] *s* **1.** rywalizacja *f* **2.** współzawodnictwo *n*

riv•er ['rɪvə] *s* rzeka *f*; ***float down the ~*** płynąć w dół rzeki; **'riv•er bank** *s* brzeg *m* rzeki; **'riv•er•bed** *s* koryto *n* rzeki; **'riv•er•side** *s* brzeg *m* rzeki

riv•et ['rɪvɪt] **I** *s* TECH nit *m* **II** *v/t* **1.** *attention*: przykuwać ⟨-kuć⟩ **2. *the book ~ed her*** książka ją wciągnęła **3. *her eyes were ~ed on the ceiling*** jej wzrok był utkwiony w sufit; ***he was ~ed to the ground*** nogi mu wrosły w ziemię **4.** TECH nitować ⟨przy-⟩; **riv•et•ing** ['rɪvɪtɪŋ] *adj* **1.** przykuwający uwagę **2.** bardzo wciągający

RNA [ɑːren'eɪ] *abbr* (=**ribonucleic acid**) RNA *n*, kwas *m* rybonukleinowy

roach [rəʊtʃ] *s* **1.** *Am infml* karaluch *m* **2.** *pl roach* (*fish*) płoć *f*, płotka *f*

road [rəʊd] *s* droga *f*; ***the ~ to success*** droga do sukcesu; ***2 hours by ~*** dwie godziny jazdy; ***hit the ~*** wyruszyć w drogę; ***be on the ~*** (*music band*) być w trasie; ***come on, one for the ~!*** no to strzemiennego!; **'road ac•ci•dent** *s* wypadek *m* drogowy; **'road•block** *s* **1.** blokada *f* drogowa **2.** *Am fig* bariera *f*; **'road hog** *s infml* pirat *m* drogowy; **'road-hold•ing** *s* AUTO przyczepność *f*; **'road•house** *s Am* zajazd *m* przydrożny; **'road map** *s* mapa *f* samochodowa; **road noise** *s* hałas *m* uliczny; **'road rage** *s* agresja *f* na drodze; **road re-**

pairs *pl* roboty *pl* drogowe; ˈ**road·show** *s* objazdowa impreza *f* promocyjna; ˈ**road•side I** *s* pobocze *n* **II** *adj* przydrożny; ˈ**road•sign** *s* znak *m* drogowy; ˈ**road tax** *s* podatek *m* drogowy; ˈ**road test** *s* test *m* (w warunkach drogowych); ˈ**road-test** *v/t* testować ⟨prze-⟩ (w warunkach drogowych); ˈ**road toll** *s* opłata *f* za przejazd autostradą; **road** ˈ**traf•fic** *s* ruch *m* drogowy; ˈ**road•way** *s* jezdnia *f*; ˈ**road•worthy** *adj car*: sprawny

roam [rəʊm] **I** *v/i* włóczyć się **II** *v/t* **1.** włóczyć się po *L* **2.** przemierzać ⟨-rzyć⟩

roar [rɔː] **I** *v/i* **1.** ryczeć ⟨za-, ryknąć⟩ **2.** grzmieć ⟨za-⟩ **3.** (*fire*) buzować **II** *s* **1.** ryk *m* **2.** huk *m*; **roar•ing** [ˈrɔːrɪŋ] *adj* **1.** ryczący; ***do a ~ trade in*** *infml* zrobić świetny interes na *L* **2.** huczący **3.** *fire*: buzujący **4.** *success*: oszałamiający

roast [rəʊst] **I** *v/t* **1.** piec ⟨u-⟩ **2.** *nuts*: prażyć ⟨u-⟩ **3.** *coffee*: palić **II** *v/i* piec ⟨u-⟩ się **III** *s* pieczeń *f*; **roast** ˈ**beef** *s* pieczeń *f* wołowa; **roast•ing** [ˈrəʊstɪŋ] *adj* **1.** do pieczenia **2.** ***~ hot*** skwarny **3.** ***I'm ~*** umieram z gorąca; ˈ**roast•ing dish** *s* brytfanna *f*; **roast** ˈ**pork** *s* pieczeń *f* wieprzowa

rob [rɒb] *v/t* **1.** rabować ⟨ob-⟩ **2.** okradać ⟨-raść⟩ **3.** pozbawiać ⟨-wić⟩ (***s.o. of*** kogoś *G*); **rob•ber** [ˈrɒbə] *s* **1.** bandyta *m* **2.** rabuś *m* **3.** złodziej *m*; **rob•ber•y** [ˈrɒbərɪ] *s* **1.** rabunek *m* **2.** napad *m*

robe [rəʊb] **I** *s* **1.** szata *f* **2.** płaszcz *m* kąpielowy **II** *v/t* ***be ~d in*** być odzianym w *A*

R

rob•in [ˈrɒbɪn] *s* BIOL **1.** rudzik *m* **2.** drozd *m* wędrowny

ro•bot [ˈrəʊbɒt] *s* robot *m*

ro•bust [rəʊˈbʌst] *adj* **1.** silny **2.** krzepki **3.** *furniture*: solidny **4.** *opinions, defence*: zdecydowany

rock [rɒk] **I** *s* **1.** skała *f*; ***caught between a ~ and a hard place*** *fig* między młotem a kowadłem **2.** kamień *m* **3.** głaz *m* **4.** *Am* kamyk *m* **5.** MUS rock *m* **II** *v/i* **1.** kołysać się **2.** (*building*) trząść się **III** *v/t* **1.** kołysać; ***~ a child to sleep*** ukołysać dziecko do snu **2.** (*news, explosion*) wstrząsać ⟨-snąć⟩

rock-and-ˈ**roll** *s* MUS rock and roll *m*

ˈ**rock band** *s* zespół *m* rockowy; **rock** ˈ**bot•tom** *s infml* najniższy poziom *m*; ***hit ~*** *fig* **a)** stoczyć się na dno **b)** przechodzić największy kryzys; ˈ**rock-bot•tom** *adj prices*: najniższy; ˈ**rock climb•er** *s* wspinacz *m*; ˈ**rock climb•ing** *s* wspinaczka *f*

rock•er [ˈrɒkə] *s* **1.** *Am* fotel *m* bujany **2.** *rocking chair*: biegun *m*; ***he's off his ~*** *infml* brakuje mu piątej klepki; ˈ**rock•er arm** → ***rocker 2***

rock•er•y [ˈrɒkərɪ] *s* skalniak *m*, ogródek *m* skalny

rock•et [ˈrɒkɪt] **I** *s* **1.** rakieta *f* **2.** pocisk *m* rakietowy **3.** raca *f* **II** *v/i* **1.** gwałtownie rosnąć ⟨wz-⟩ **2.** (*prices*) *infml* skakać ⟨skoczyć⟩ (w górę) **III** *v/t* przeprowadzać ⟨-dzić⟩ atak rakietowy na *A*

ˈ**rock face** *no pl s* ściana *f* skalna; ˈ**rock-fall** *s* obryw *m* skalny; ˈ**rock gar•den** *s* skalniak *m*, ogródek *m* skalny; ˈ**rock-hard** *adj* twardy jak skała

rock•ing chair [ˈrɒkɪŋtʃeə] *s* fotel *m* bujany; ˈ**rock•ing horse** *s* koń *m* na biegunach

ˈ**rock mu•sic** *s* muzyka *f* rockowa; **rock'n'roll** [rɒknˈrəʊl] *s* MUS rockand-roll *m*; ˈ**rock salt** *s* sól *f* kamienna; **rock-**ˈ**sol•id** *adj* **1.** solidny **2.** *support*: pewny; ˈ**rock star** *s* gwiazda *f* rocka

rock•y[1] [ˈrɒkɪ] *adj* skalisty

rock•y[2] [~] *adj* **1.** chwiejny **2.** niepewny **3.** trudny; ***~ times*** trudne chwile; ***their relationship got off to a ~ start*** początki ich związku były trudne

ro•co•co [rəˈkəʊkəʊ] ART **I** *s* rokoko *n* **II** *adj* rokokowy

rod [rɒd] *s* **1.** pręt *m*; ***a lightning ~*** piorunochron **2.** drążek *m* **3.** kij *m* **4.** wędka *f* **5.** (*gun*) *Am infml* gnat *m*

rode [rəʊd] *Past Simple* → ***ride***

ro•dent [ˈrəʊdnt] *s* gryzoń *m*

ro•de•o [ˈrəʊdɪəʊ] *pl -deos s* rodeo *n*

roe[1] [rəʊ] *s* BIOL COOK ikra *f*

roe[2] [~] → ***roe deer***

ˈ**roe•buck** *pl -buck, -bucks s* kozioł *m* sarny

ˈ**roe deer** *pl -deer s* sarna *f*

rog•er [ˈrɒdʒə] *interj* TEL zrozumiałem!

rogue [rəʊg] **I** *s* **1.** drań *m* **2.** łobuz *m* **3.** *dated* łotr *m* **II** *adj* **1.** kłopotliwy **2.** *programme*: złośliwy **3.** *animal*: samotny

role [rəʊl] *s* rola *f*; ˈ**role mod•el** *s* **1.** wzór *m* **2.** autorytet *m*; ˈ**role play** *s* **1.** (*lesson*) scenka *f* **2.** psychodrama *f*; **role re•ˈver•sal** *s* odwrócenie *n* ról

roll [rəʊl] **I** *v/i* **1.** toczyć ⟨po-⟩ się **2.** tarzać się **3.** zwijać ⟨zwinąć⟩ się **4.** kołysać się **II** *v/t* **1.** toczyć ⟨po-⟩ **2.** obracać ⟨-rócić⟩ **3.** zwijać ⟨zwinąć⟩ **4.** *sleeves*: podwijać ⟨-winąć⟩ **5.** *pastry*: rozwałkowywać ⟨-kować⟩ **6.** walcować **III** *s* **1.** rolka *f* **2.** zwój *m* **3.** zwitek *m* **4.** bela *f* **5.** *fat*: fałda *f* **6.** bułka *f* **7.** przewrót *m* **8.** ***have a ~ in the sunshine*** tarzać się w słońcu **9.** lista *f*, ***call the ~*** odczytać listę obecności **10.** *dice*: rzut *m* **11.** (*sound*) werbel *m*; **roll around**, ***roll about*** *v/i* tarzać się ze śmiechu; **roll back** *v/t* **1.** *prices*: obniżać ⟨-żyć⟩ **2.** cofać ⟨-fnąć⟩ **3.** *enemy*: odpierać ⟨odeprzeć⟩; **roll down** *v/t* **1.** *sleeves*: odwijać ⟨-winąć⟩ **2.** *window*: opuszczać ⟨opuścić⟩; **roll in** *v/i* **1.** napływać ⟨-łynąć⟩ **2.** przychodzić ⟨przyjść⟩ spóźnionym; **roll out** *v/t* **1.** rozwałkowywać ⟨-kować⟩ **2.** *campaign*: rozpoczynać ⟨-cząć⟩ **3.** wprowadzać ⟨-dzić⟩ na rynek; **roll over I** *v/i* **1.** obracać ⟨-rócić⟩ się **2.** przewracać ⟨-rócić⟩ się **II** *v/t* **1.** obracać ⟨-rócić⟩ **2.** przewracać ⟨-rócić⟩; **roll up** *v/t* **1.** *sleeves*: podwijać ⟨-winąć⟩ **2.** *window*: podnosić ⟨-nieść⟩

ˈ**roll call** *s* sprawdzanie *n* listy obecności

roll•er [ˈrəʊlə] *s* **1.** wałek *m* **2.** walec **3.** rolka *f* **4.** krążnik *m* **5.** (wielka) fala *f*; ˈ**Roll•er•blade**® **I** *s* rolka *f* **II** *v/i* jeździć na rolkach; ˈ**roll•er blind** *s* roleta *f*; **roll•er coast•er** [ˈrəʊlekəʊstə] *s* **1.** (*amusement park*) kolejka *f* górska **2.** *fig* huśtawka *f*; ˈ**roll•er skate I** *s* wrotka *f* **II** *v/i* jeździć na wrotkach; ˈ**roll•er skat•er** *s* wrotkarz *m*; ˈ**roll•er skat•ing** *s* jazda *f* na wrotkach; ˈ**roll•er tow•el** *s* ręcznik *m* papierowy (na rolce)

roll•ing mill [ˈrəʊlɪŋmɪl] *s* walcownia *f*; ˈ**roll•ing pin** *s* wałek *m* (do ciasta); ˈ**roll•ing stock** *s* tabor *m* kolejowy

ROM [rɒm] *abbr* (=***read only memory***) INF pamięć *f* ROM

Ro•man [ˈrəʊmən] **I** *adj* rzymski **II** *s* Rzymianin *m*, Rzymianka *f*; **Ro•man ˈCath•o•lic I** *adj* (rzymsko)katolicki **II** *s* katolik *m*

ro•mance [rəʊˈmæns] **I** *s* **1.** romans *m* **2.** romantyzm *m* **II** *v/t* romansować

Ro•mance [rəʊˈmæns] *adj language*: romański

Ro•man•esque [rəʊməˈnesk] *adj* ARCHIT romański

Ro•ma•ni•a [ruːˈmeɪnɪə] *s* Rumunia *f*; **Ro•ma•ni•an** [ruːˈmeɪnjən] **I** *adj* rumuński **II** *s* Rumun *m*, Rumunka *f*

ro•man•tic [rəʊˈmæntɪk] **I** *adj* **1.** romantyczny **2.** miłosny; ***a ~ relationship*** związek (miłosny) **3.** idealistyczny **4.** ≈ ART romantyczny **II** *s* **1.** romantyk *m* **2.** ≈ ART romantyk *m*; **ro•man•tic•al•ly** [rəʊˈmæntɪklɪ] *adv* romantycznie; **ro•man•ti•cism** [rəʊˈmæntɪsɪzəm] *s* **1.** romantyzm *m* **2.** ≈ ART Romantyzm *m*; **ro•man•ti•cize** [rəʊˈmæntɪsaɪz] *v/t past*: idealizować

Rom•a•ny [ˈrɒmənɪ] **I** *s* **1.** Rom *m* **2.** język *m* romski **II** *adj* romski

Rome [rəʊm] *s* Rzym *m*

romp [rɒmp] **I** *v/i* **1.** dokazywać **2.** baraszkować; ***~ through the questions*** *Br infml* odpowiedzieć z łatwością na pytania **II** *s* igraszki *pl*

roof [ruːf] **I** *s* dach *m*; ***the prices went through the ~*** ceny poszły w górę; ***hit the ~*** *fig* wściec się **II** *v/t* ***be ~ed over*** być zadaszonym; ***the house is ~ed with blue tiles*** dom ma dach kryty niebieską dachówką; ˈ**roof gar•den** *s* ogród *m* na dachu; ˈ**roof-rack** *s* bagażnik *m* na dachu; ˈ**roof•top** *s* dach *m*; ***shout s.th. from the ~*** *fig* rozgłaszać coś wszem i wobec

rook[1] [rʊk] *s* gawron *m*

rook[2] [~] *s* (*chess*) wieża *f*

rook•ie [ˈrʊkɪ] *s Am infml* **1.** nowicjusz *m* **2.** (*soldier*) kot *m*

room [ruːm] **I** *s* **1.** pokój *m*; ***in the next ~*** w pokoju obok **2.** pomieszczenie *n* **3.** miejsce *n*; ***is there enough ~ in the car?*** czy w samochodzie jest dość miejsca?; ***make ~ for s.o.*** zrobić komuś miejsce; ***there is still ~ for improvement*** wiele można jeszcze poprawić **II** *v/i* mieszkać w jednym pokoju; **room•ing house** [ˈruːmɪŋhaʊs] *s dom z umeblowanymi pokojami lub mieszkaniami do wynajęcia*

'room•mate *s* współlokator *m*; **'room ser•vice** *s* (*hotel*) obsługa *f* pokoi; **room 'tem•per•a•ture** *s* temperatura *f* pokojowa

room•y ['ru:mɪ] *adj* przestronny

roost [ru:st] **I** *s* grzęda *f* **II** *v/i* **1.** siedzieć na grzędzie **2.** nocować

roost•er ['ru:stə] *s Am* kogut *m*

root [ru:t] **I** *s* **1.** korzeń *m*; ***flamenco has its ~s in Gypsy music*** flamenco wywodzi się z muzyki cygańskiej; ***destroy s.th. ~ and branch*** **a)** doszczętnie coś zniszczyć **b)** wykorzenić coś; ***put down ~s*** **a)** zakorzenić się **b)** *fig* zapuścić korzenie **2.** (*hair*) cebulka *f* **3.** źródło *n*; ***get to the ~ of the problem*** dotrzeć do źródła problemu **4.** podstawa *f* **5.** *word*: rdzeń *m* **6.** MATH pierwiastek *m* **II** *v/i* zakorzeniać ⟨-nić⟩ się; **root around** *v/t* **1.** ryć ⟨z-⟩ **2.** szperać ⟨wy-⟩ (**through** w *L*); **root for** *v/t* **1.** kibicować **2.** trzymać kciuki za *G*; **root out** *v/t* **1.** wykorzeniać ⟨-nić⟩ **2.** wypleniać ⟨-nić⟩ **3.** *culprit*: zdemaskować i ukarać

'root beer *s* (*soft drink*) piwo *n* korzenne; **'root crop** *s* roślina *f* okopowa; **'root di•rec•to•ry** *s* INF katalog *m* główny; **root•ed** *adj* zakorzeniony; ***her problems are ~ in her childhood*** jej problemy mają swoje źródło w dzieciństwie; ***he was ~ to the ground*** *fig* nogi mu wrosły w ziemię

rope [rəʊp] **I** *s* **1.** lina *f*; ***learn the ~s*** *infml* załapać, w czym rzecz; ***know the ~s*** *infml* znać się na rzeczy **2.** sznur *m* **3.** sznurek *m* **II** *v/t* **1.** przywiązywać ⟨-zać⟩ (***s.th. to*** coś do *G*); ***~ s.th. together*** związać coś **2.** obwiązywać ⟨-zać⟩; **rope off** *v/t* odgradzać ⟨-rodzić⟩ (sznurem)

'rope lad•der *s* drabinka *f* sznurowa

rop•(e)y ['rəʊpɪ] *adj Br infml* kiepski; ***I feel ~*** kiepsko się czuję

ro•sa•ry ['rəʊzərɪ] *s* różaniec *m*

rose[1] [rəʊz] **I** *s* **1.** róża *f*; ***everything's coming up ~s*** *infml* wszystko idzie jak po maśle; ***be a bed of ~s*** *fig* być usłanym różami; ***their life together wasn't a bed of ~s*** ich wspólne życie nie było sielanką **2.** róż *m* **3.** (*watering can*) sitko *n* **4.** (*ceiling*) rozeta *f* **II** *adj* ***~ pink*** różowy

rose[2] [~] *Past Simple* → ***rise***

ro•sé ['rəʊzeɪ] *s* różowe wino *n*

'rose•bud *s* pączek *m* róży; **rose•bush** *s* krzew *m* różany

rose-col•oured ['rəʊzkʌləd] *Br*, **rose-col•ored** *Am adj* różowy; ***through ~ spectacles*** przez różowe okulary

'rose•hip *s* owoc *m* dzikiej róży; **rose-hip 'syr•up** *s* syrop *m* z dzikiej róży

rose•ma•ry ['rəʊzmerɪ] *s* BIOL rozmaryn *m*

ro•sette [rəʊ'zet] *s* **1.** (*ribbon*) rozetka *f* **2.** ARCHIT rozeta *f*

ros•in ['rɒzɪn] *s* kalafonia *f*

ros•ter ['rɒstə] *s* **1.** harmonogram *m* pracy **2.** grafik *m* dyżurów

ros•trum ['rɒstrəm] *pl -trums, -tra s* **1.** podium *n* **2.** mównica *f* **3.** katedra *f* **4.** trybuna *f*

ros•y ['rəʊzɪ] *adj* różowy

rot [rɒt] **I** *v/i* **1.** gnić ⟨z-⟩ **2.** butwieć ⟨z-⟩ **3.** psuć ⟨ze-⟩ się **II** *v/t* **1.** psuć ⟨ze-⟩ **2.** niszczyć ⟨z-⟩ **III** *s* **1.** gnicie *n* **2.** butwienie *n* **3.** zepsucie *n*

ro•ta ['rəʊtə] *pl -tas s Br* **1.** harmonogram *m* pracy **2.** grafik *m* dyżurów

ro•ta•ry ['rəʊtərɪ] **I** *adj* obrotowy **II** *s Am* rondo *n*

ro•tate [rəʊ'teɪt] **I** *v/i* **1.** obracać ⟨-rócić⟩ się **2.** kręcić się **3.** ***the position ~s among them*** zmieniają się na tym stanowisku **II** *v/t* **1.** obracać ⟨-rócić⟩ **2.** przekręcać ⟨-cić⟩ **3.** (*posts*) zmieniać ⟨-nić⟩ się na *L*; **ro•ta•tion** [rəʊ'teɪʃn] *s* **1.** obrót *m* **2.** rotacja *f*; ***in ~*** na zmianę; ***crop ~*** płodozmian

rote [rəʊt] *s*: ***learn by ~*** uczyć się czegoś na pamięć; ***~ learning*** uczenie się na pamięć

ro•tor ['rəʊtə] *s* **1.** śmigło *n* **2.** wirnik *m*; **ro•tor blade** *s* **1.** łopatka *f* śmigła **2.** łopatka *f* wirnika

rot•ten ['rɒtn] **I** *adj* **1.** zgniły; ***go ~*** gnić **2.** zbutwiały **3.** zepsuty **4.** *infml* okropny **5.** *infml* cholerny **II** *adv infml* strasznie

ro•tund [rəʊ'tʌnd] *adj* **1.** pulchny **2.** okrągły

rouge [ru:ʒ] *s* róż *m*

rough [rʌf] **I** *adj* **1.** szorstki **2.** chropowaty **3.** nierówny **4.** wyboisty **5.** *figure*: przybliżony **6.** *estimate*: szacunkowy **7.** *plan*: ogólny **8.** ***a ~ draft*** **a)** szkic **b)** robocza wersja **9.** brutalny **10.** *play*: ostry **11.** *treatment*: zły

R

12. prostacki **13.** ciężki; ***we had a ~ time*** przeżyliśmy ciężkie chwile; ***I had a ~ night*** źle spałem **14.** *sea*: wzburzony **15.** *weather*: burzowy **16.** *furniture*: prymitywny **17.** *voice*: zachrypnięty **II** *s* **1.** (*golf*) rough *m* **2.** szkic *m* **3.** robocza wersja *f* **III** *v/t* **1.** ***~ it*** obywać się bez wygód, żyć w prymitywnych warunkach **2.** ***~ s.o. up*** poturbować kogoś **IV** *adv* **1.** brutalnie **2.** *play*: ostro; **rough•age** ['rʌfɪdʒ] *s* błonnik *m*

rough-and-'read•y *adj* **1.** prowizoryczny **2.** *person*: prosty; **rough-and-'tum•ble** *s* **1.** *fig* przepychanki *pl* **2.** szamotanina *f*

rough•en ['rʌfn] **I** *v/i* (*skin*) stawać ⟨stać⟩ się szorstkim **II** *v/t* ***~ the skin*** sprawiać, że skóra staje się szorstka

rough 'es•ti•mate *s* ocena *f* szacunkowa

rough•ly ['rʌflɪ] *adv* **1.** około **2.** mniej więcej **3.** szacunkowo **4.** orientacyjnie **5.** brutalnie **6.** siłą **7.** nierówno

'rough•neck *s infml* prostak *m*

rough•ness ['rʌfnɪs] *s* **1.** szorstkość *f* **2.** chropowatość *f* **3.** nierówność *f* **4.** wyboistość *f* **5.** brutalność *f* **6.** prostactwo *n*

rough•shod ['rʌfʃɒd] *adv*: ***ride ~ over*** sponiewierać *A*

rou•lette [ruː'let] *s* ruletka *f*

round [raʊnd] **I** *adj* **1.** okrągły; ***let's make it a ~ figure, say, forty dollars*** zaokrąglijmy to, powiedzmy, do czterdziestu dolarów; ***in ~ figures*** w zaokrągleniu **2.** zaokrąglony **3.** krągły **II** *adv* **1.** ***turn ~*** odwrócić się **2.** dookoła; ***all the year ~*** przez cały rok; ***~ about*** **a)** w okolicy **b)** około **3.** w kółko **III** *prep* **1.** dookoła *G*; ***~ here*** tutaj **2.** wokół *G*; ***~ the earth*** wokół Ziemi **3.** (*place*) za *I*; ***our house is just ~ the corner*** nasz dom jest tuż za rogiem **4.** (*direction*) zza *G* **IV** *s* **1.** runda *f* **2.** tura *f* **3.** obchód *m* **4.** *golf*: partia *f* **5.** strzał *m* **6.** nabój *m* **7.** (*alcohol*) kolejka *f* **8.** *Br bread*: kromka *f* **V** *v/t* **1.** okrążać ⟨-żyć⟩ **2.** zaokrąglać ⟨-lić⟩ **VI** *v/i* robić ⟨z-⟩ się okrągłym; ***her eyes ~ed with surprise*** oczy jej zrobiły się okrągłe ze zdumienia; **round down** *v/t sum*: zaokrąglać ⟨-lić⟩ w dół; **round off** *v/t* **1.** zakańczać ⟨-kończyć⟩ **2.** *edge*: wygładzać ⟨-dzić⟩; **round up** *v/t* **1.** *sum*: zaokrąglać ⟨-lić⟩ w górę **2.** zbierać ⟨zebrać⟩ **3.** *cattle*: spędzać ⟨-dzić⟩ z pastwiska

round•a•bout ['raʊndəbaʊt] **I** *s* **1.** *Br* rondo *n* **2.** karuzela *f* **II** *adj* okrężny; ***take a ~ route*** pójść okrężną drogą; ***in a ~ way*** nie wprost, w zaowalowany sposób

round•ly ['raʊndlɪ] *adv* **1.** powszechnie **2.** stanowczo **3.** ***be ~ defeated*** ponieść sromotną porażkę

round rob•in *s* **1.** list *m* otwarty **2.** SPORT rozgrywki *pl* w systemie „każdy z każdym"

'round-ta•ble *adj talks*: przy okrągłym stole; **'round-the-clock I** *adj* całodobowy **II** *adv* 24 godziny na dobę; **'round-the-world** *adj journey*: dookoła świata; **round 'trip I** *s* podróż *f* w obie strony **II** *adj* **1.** w obie strony **2.** tam i z powrotem; **round trip 'tick•et** *s* bilet *m* powrotny; **'round-up** *s* **1.** *news*: skrót *m* **2.** zgromadzenie *n* **3.** *cattle*: spęd *m*

rouse [raʊz] *v/t* **1.** wzbudzać ⟨-dzić⟩ **2.** budzić ⟨o-⟩ **3.** *to action*: pobudzać ⟨-dzić⟩; **rous•ing** ['raʊzɪŋ] *adj* **1.** entuzjastyczny **2.** *speech*: porywający

rout [raʊt] **I** *s* pogrom *m* **II** *v/t* rozgramiać ⟨-romić⟩

route [ruːt] **I** *s* **1.** *a. fig* droga *f*; ***a ~ to fame*** droga do sławy **2.** trasa *f*; ***a cycle ~*** trasa rowerowa **3.** szlak *m* **II** *v/t* przesyłać ⟨-słać⟩

rou•tine [ruː'tiːn] **I** *s* **1.** rozkład *m* zajęć; ***daily ~*** rozkład dnia **2.** rutyna *f* **3.** *dance*: układ *m* **II** *adj* **1.** rutynowy; ***a ~ procedure*** rutynowe postępowanie **2.** *fig* nieciekawy; **rou•tine•ly** [ruː'tiːnlɪ] *adv* rutynowo

row[1] [rəʊ] *s* rząd *m*; ***a ~ of trees*** rząd drzew; ***sit in a ~*** siedzieć w rzędzie; ***three times in a ~*** trzy razy pod rząd

row[2] [~] **I** *v/i* wiosłować **II** *v/t* ***~ a boat*** wiosłować; ***they ~ed the boat to the other side*** popłynęli łodzią na drugą stronę **III** *s* ***go for a ~*** iść popływać łodzią

row[3] [~] *Br infml* **I** *s* **1.** awantura *f* (***over*** o *A*) **2.** ostry konflikt *m* **3.** hałas *m* **II** *v/i Br infml* awanturować się

row•boat ['rəʊbəʊt] *s Am* łódź *f* wiosłowa

R

row•dy ['raʊdɪ] *adj* **1.** hałaśliwy **2.** awanturniczy

row house ['rəoʊhaʊs] *s Am* dom *m* szeregowy

roy•al [rɔɪəl] **I** *adj* królewski; ***the ~ family*** rodzina królewska; ***a ~ welcome*** królewskie przyjęcie **II** *s infml* członek *m* rodziny królewskiej; **roy•al•ist** ['rɔɪəlɪst] **I** *s* rojalista *m* **II** *adj* rojalistyczny; **roy•al•ly** *adv receive*: po królewsku; **roy•al•t|y** ['rɔɪəltɪ] *s* **1.** członkowie *pl* rodziny królewskiej **2.** członek *m* rodziny królewskiej **3.** ***~ies*** tantiemy *pl*

RSVP [ɑːresviː'piː] *abbr* (=***répondez s'il vous plaît***) (*please answer*) RSVP

rub [rʌb] **I** *v/t* **1.** trzeć ⟨po-⟩; ***~ s.o. the wrong way*** *Am infml* rozzłościć kogoś **2.** pocierać ⟨potrzeć⟩ **3.** masować ⟨po-⟩ **4.** wcierać ⟨wetrzeć⟩ (***into*** w *A*) **5.** wycierać ⟨wytrzeć⟩ (***off*** z *G*) **6.** *hands*: zacierać ⟨zatrzeć⟩ **II** *v/i* **1.** trzeć ⟨po-⟩ (***at*** *A*) **2.** ocierać ⟨otrzeć⟩ się (***at*** o *A*) **III** *s* **1.** ***give s.th. a ~*** potrzeć coś **2.** ***there lies the ~*** *fig* w tym sęk; **rub down** *v/t* **1.** wycierać ⟨wytrzeć⟩ **2.** polerować ⟨wy-⟩ **3.** *sandpaper*: przecierać ⟨przetrzeć⟩; **rub in** *v/t* **1.** wcierać ⟨wetrzeć⟩ **2.** *fig* ciągle przypominać o *L*; **rub off** **I** *v/i* **1.** ścierać ⟨zetrzeć⟩ się **2.** udzielać ⟨-lić⟩ się (***on*** *D*) **II** *v/t* ścierać ⟨zetrzeć⟩; **rub up** *v/t*: ***rub s.o. up the wrong way*** *Br infml* rozzłościć kogoś

rub•ber ['rʌbə] **I** *s* **1.** guma *f* **2.** kauczuk *m* **3.** *Br* gumka *f* (do mazania) **4.** gąbka *f* do tablicy **II** *adj* gumowy; **rub•ber 'band** *s* gumka *f* (recepturka); **rub•ber 'bul•let** *s* gumowa kula *f*; **rub•ber 'din•ghy** *s* ponton *m*; **rubber gloves** [rʌbə'glʌvz] *pl* gumowe rękawiczki *pl*; **'rub•ber•neck** *v/i Am infml* gapić się; **'rub•ber plant** *s* (*tree*) kauczukowiec *m*; **rub•ber 'stamp** *s* pieczątka *f*; **rub•ber-'stamp** *v/t* zatwierdzać ⟨-dzić⟩; **rub•ber•y** ['rʌbərɪ] *adj* **1.** gumiasty **2.** *legs*: jak z waty

rub•bish ['rʌbɪʃ] **I** *s* **1.** śmieci *pl* **2.** *Br infml* bzdury *pl*; ***~!*** bzdura! **3.** *Br infml* szmira *f* **4.** *Br infml* chłam *m* **II** *v/t Br infml* mieszać ⟨z-⟩ z błotem; **rub•bish•y** ['rʌbɪʃɪ] *adj Br infml* **1.** tandetny

rub•ble ['rʌbl] *s* gruz *m*

ru•bel•la [rʊ'belə] *s MED* różyczka *f*

ru•by ['ruːbɪ] **I** *s* rubin *m* **II** *adj* rubinowy; ***a ~ wedding*** rubinowe gody

ruck [rʌk] *s* **1.** *Br* burda *f*; ***a political ~*** polityczne przepychanki **2.** (*rugby*) otwarty młyn *m* **3.** ***the ~*** szare życie; **ruck up** **I** *v/t* marszczyć ⟨z-⟩ **II** *v/i* marszczyć ⟨z-⟩ się

ruck•sack ['rʌksæk] *s* plecak *m*

ruc•tions ['rʌkʃnz] *infml s* awantura *f*

ruck•us ['rʌkəs] *s Am* zamieszanie *n*

rud•der ['rʌdə] *s* ster *m*

rud•dy ['rʌdɪ] *adj* **1.** rumiany **2.** *Br* dziadowski; ***I can't get the ~ car to start!*** ten dziadowski samochód nie chce zapalić!

rude [ruːd] *adj* **1.** niegrzeczny **2.** nieuprzejmy **3.** *gesture*, *joke*: nieprzyzwoity **4.** *shock*: brutalny, ciężki **5.** *dwelling*: prymitywny; **rude•ly** ['ruːdlɪ] *adv* **1.** niegrzecznie **2.** nieuprzejmie **3.** *wake up*: brutalnie; **rude•ness** ['ruːdnɪs] *s* **1.** niegrzeczność *f* **2.** nieuprzejmość *f*

ru•di•men•ta•ry [ruːdɪ'mentərɪ] *adj* **1.** podstawowy **2.** elementarny **3.** prymitywny; **ru•di•ments** ['ruːdɪmənts] *pl* podstawy *pl*; ***the ~ of mathematics*** podstawy matematyki

rue [ruː] *v/t dated* żałować ⟨po-⟩; **rue•ful** ['ruːfəl] *adj* **1.** smutny **2.** żałosny; **rue•ful•ly** ['ruːfəlɪ] *adv* **1.** z żalem **2.** smutno

ruff [rʌf] *s* kreza *f*

ruf•fle ['rʌfl] **I** *v/t* **1.** mierzwić ⟨z-⟩ **2.** stroszyć ⟨na-⟩ **3.** wyprowadzać ⟨-dzić⟩ z równowagi **II** *s* **1.** falbana *f* **2.** falbanka *f*

rug [rʌg] *s* **1.** dywanik *m* **2.** *Br* pled *m*

rug•by ['rʌgbɪ] *s SPORT* rugby *n*

rug•ged ['rʌgɪd] *adj* **1.** poszarpany **2.** nierówny **3.** *landscape*: surowy **4.** *character*, *personality*: twardy **5.** *vehicle*, *equipment*: wytrzymały

ru•in ['ruːɪn] **I** *v/t* **1.** rujnować ⟨z-⟩ **2.** psuć ⟨ze-⟩ **3.** niszczyć ⟨z-⟩ **4.** *plans*: niweczyć ⟨z-⟩ **II** *s* **1.** ruina *f*; ***~s*** ruiny; ***in ~s*** w ruinie **2.** upadek *m*; **ru•in•a•tion** [ruːɪn'eɪʃn] *s* **1.** zniszczenie *n* **2.** ruina *f*; **ru•in•ous** ['ruːɪnəs] *adj* **1.** *cost*: rujnujący **2.** fatalny w skutkach **3.** zrujnowany; **ru•in•ous•ly**

R

['ruːnəslɪ] *adv expensive*: astronomicznie

rule [ruːl] **I** *s* **1.** reguła *f*; ***as a ~*** z reguły; ***as a ~ of thumb*** można przyjąć, że **2.** zasada *f*; ***break a ~*** złamać zasadę **3.** przepis *m*; ***against the ~s*** wbrew przepisom; ***bend the ~s*** naginać przepisy **4.** rządy *pl*; ***the ~ of the law*** rządy prawa **5.** linijka *f* **II** *v/t* **1.** rządzić; ***~ the roost*** *infml* rządzić **2.** panować; ***when dinosaurs ~d the earth*** gdy na Ziemi panowały dinozaury **3.** ***~ s.th. illegal*** uznać coś za nielegalne **4.** ⟨po-⟩ liniować **III** *v/i* **1.** rządzić (***over*** *I*); ***~ with a rod of iron*** *fig* rządzić żelazną ręką **2.** panować **3.** orzekać ⟨orzec⟩ (***that*** że, ***in favour of*** na korzyść *G*, ***against*** na niekorzyść *G*) **4.** decydować ⟨z-⟩ (***on*** o *L*); **rule out** *v/t* wykluczać ⟨-czyć⟩

rul•er ['ruːlə] *s* **1.** władca *m* **2.** rządzący *m* **3.** linijka *f*; **rul•ing** ['ruːlɪŋ] **I** *s JUR* orzeczenie *n* **II** *adj party*: rządzący

rum [rʌm] *s* rum *m*

Ru•ma•ni•a → ***Romania***

rum•ble ['rʌmbl] **I** *s* **1.** dudnienie *n* **2.** *thunder*: huk *m* **3.** gwar *m* **II** *v/i* **1.** dudnić ⟨za-⟩ **2.** ***my stomach is ~ing*** burczy mi w brzuchu **3.** toczyć ⟨prze-⟩ się z łoskotem **III** *v/t Br infml* demaskować ⟨z-⟩; **'rum•ble strip** *s* (*on road*) *infml pas ostrzegawczy na nawierzchni drogi z punktowych elementów wypukłych*

rum•bus•tious [rʌm'bʌstʃəs] *adj Br infml* hałaśliwy

ru•mi•nant ['ruːmɪnənt] *s BIOL* przeżuwacz *m*; **ru•mi•nate** ['ruːmɪneɪt] *v/i form* rozmyślać (***on***/***over***/***about*** nad *I*); **ru•mi•na•tive** ['ruːmɪnətɪv] *adj* **1.** zamyślony **2.** refleksyjny

rum•mage ['rʌmɪdʒ] **I** *v/i* **1.** grzebać (***in***/***through*** w *L*) **2.** szperać (***in***/***through*** w *L*) **II** *s* ***have a ~ around in*** grzebać w *L*

rum•my ['rʌmɪ] *s* remik *m*

ru•mour ['ruːmə] *Br*, ***rumor*** *Am* **I** *s* **1.** plotka *f*; ***spread ~s*** rozsiewać plotki; ***~ has it that*** plotka głosi, że **2.** pogłoska *f* **II** *v/t* ***it is ~ed that*** chodzą słuchy, że; **ru•mour•mon•ger** ['ruːməmʌŋgə] *Br*, ***ru•mor•mon•ger*** *Am s* plotkarz *m*

rump [rʌmp] *s* **1.** zad *m* **2.** *infml* tyłek *m* **3.** *fig* niedobitki *pl* **4.** (*beef*) krzyżowa *f* **5.** stek *m* z krzyżowej

rum•ple ['rʌmpl] *v/t* **1.** *hair*: targać ⟨po-⟩ **2.** *clothes*: gnieść ⟨po-⟩

rump 'steak *s* **1.** (*beef*) krzyżowa *f* **2.** stek *m* z krzyżowej

run [rʌn] **I** (*ran*; *run*) *v/i* **1.** biec ⟨po-⟩; ***come ~ning*** przybiec; ***a scar ~ning down the cheek*** blizna biegnąca przez policzek **2.** biegać **3.** (*engine*) pracować, być włączonym **4.** (*buses*, *trains*) kursować; ***the trains are ~ning late*** pociągi mają opóźnienie **5.** jechać; ***~ off the road*** zjechać z drogi **6.** (*debate*) ciągnąć się **7.** (*performance*) być granym **8.** (*warranty*) być ważnym **9.** (*tears*) płynąć ⟨po-⟩ **10.** (*fabric*) farbować **11.** rozpuszczać ⟨-puścić⟩ się **12.** *POLIT Am* kandydować; ***~ for president***, ***~ for the presidency*** kandydować na prezydenta **13.** ***we've run short of milk*** skończyło nam się mleko **14.** ***s.o.'s nose is ~ning*** komuś cieknie z nosa **II** (*ran*; *run*) *v/t* **1.** przebiegać ⟨-biec⟩ **2.** *shop*, *hotel*: prowadzić **3.** zarządzać; ***a badly-~ company*** źle zarządzana firma **4.** kierować **5.** *course*, *competition*: organizować ⟨z-⟩ **6.** *course*, *cable*: prowadzić ⟨po-⟩ **7.** ***~ a bath*** napuścić wodę do wanny **8.** *infml* podrzucać ⟨-ucić⟩ **9.** *programme*: uruchamiać ⟨-chomić⟩ **10.** przesuwać ⟨-sunąć⟩; ***she ran her fingers through her hair*** przeczesała palcami włosy **11.** *advert*: zamieszczać ⟨-mieścić⟩ **12.** *gun*: przemycać ⟨-cić⟩ **13.** *test*: przeprowadzać ⟨-dzić⟩ **III** *s* **1.** bieg *m*; ***go for a ~*** iść pobiegać; ***the normal ~ of things*** normalny bieg wydarzeń; ***be on the ~*** *fig* **a)** ukrywać się **b)** być w biegu **2.** ***in the long ~*** na dłuższą metę; ***in the short ~*** na krótszą metę **3.** wyjazd *m* **4.** dojazd *m* **5.** *infml* wypad *m* **6.** seria *f*; ***a ~ of good luck*** dobra passa **7.** ***have a six-month ~*** *THEAT* nie schodzić z afisza przez sześć miesięcy **8.** (*tights*) *Am* oczko *n* **9.** ***make a ~ for president*** *POLIT* ubiegać się o fotel prezydenta; **'run•a•bout** → ***run around***; **run across** *v/i* **1.** natykać ⟨-tknąć⟩ się na *A* **2.** *infml* wpadać

R

⟨wpaść⟩ na *A*; **run after** *v/i* uganiać się za *I*; **run a•long** *v/i*: ~ zmykaj!; **run around with** *v/t* zadawać ⟨-dać⟩ się z *I*; **run away** *v/i* uciekać ⟨uciec⟩; ***her imagination tends to ~ with her*** często ponosi ją wyobraźnia; **run down I** *v/t* **1.** krytykować ⟨s-⟩ **2.** zmniejszać ⟨-szyć⟩ **3.** ograniczać ⟨-czyć⟩ **4.** (*car*) potrącać ⟨-cić⟩ **5.** znajdować ⟨znaleźć⟩ **II** *v/i* (*battery*) wyczerpywać ⟨-pać⟩ się; **run into** *v/i* **1.** natykać ⟨-tknąć⟩ się na *A* **2.** *infml* wpadać ⟨wpaść⟩ na *A* **3.** ***~ debt*** zadłużyć się **4.** (*trouble*) wpadać ⟨wpaść⟩ w *A* **5.** (*income*) sięgać ⟨-gnąć⟩ **6.** wjeżdżać ⟨wjechać⟩ na *A*; **run off I** *v/i* **1.** uciekać ⟨uciec⟩ (***with*** z *I*) **2.** zbiec (***with*** z *I*) **II** *v/t* **1.** *photograph*: robić ⟨z-⟩ **2.** *race*: rozgrywać ⟨-zegrać⟩; **run on I** *v/i* przedłużać ⟨-żyć⟩ się **II** *v/t* rozwodzić się nad *I*; **run out** *v/i* **1.** (*time*) uciekać ⟨uciec⟩ **2.** (*supplies*) kończyć ⟨s-⟩ się; ***we ~ of fuel*** skończyło się nam paliwo **3.** (*contract*) wygasać ⟨-snąć⟩ **4.** tracić ⟨s-⟩ ważność **5.** zostawiać ⟨-wić⟩ (w potrzebie) (***on*** *A*); **run over I** *v/t* **1.** (*car*) przejeżdżać ⟨-jechać⟩ **2.** *notes*: przeglądać ⟨przejrzeć⟩ **II** *v/i* (*water*) przelewać ⟨-lać⟩ się; **run through** *v/i* **1.** powtarzać ⟨-tórzyć⟩ **2.** omawiać ⟨omówić⟩ **3.** ćwiczyć ⟨prze-⟩ **4.** *fig* przebiegać ⟨-biec⟩ (***through*** przez *A*) **5.** przenikać ⟨-knąć⟩ **run up I** *v/t* **1.** ***~ debts*** zadłużyć się **2.** *flag*: wciągać ⟨-gnąć⟩ na maszt **II** *v/i* natknąć się (***against*** na *A*)

run•a•way ['rʌnəweɪ] **I** *s* **1.** *child*: uciekinier *m* **2.** zbieg *m* **II** *adj* **1.** zbiegły; ***a ~ child*** dziecko, które uciekło z domu; ***a ~ horse*** koń, który poniósł **2.** *inflation*: niekontrolowany **3.** *success*: oszałamiający

run-'down *adj* **1.** zaniedbany **2.** podupadły **3.** wyczerpany

rung¹ [rʌŋ] *s a. fig* szczebel *m*

rung² [~] *Past Simple and Past Participle* → **ring**

'run-in *s infml* zatarg *m*; **have a ~ with s.o.** zadrzeć z kimś

run•ner ['rʌnə] *s* **1.** biegacz *m* **2.** koń *m* (wyścigowy) **3.** płoza *f* **4.** goniec *m* **5.** (*plant*) rozłóg *m* **6.** przemytnik *m* **7.** prowadnica *f*; **run•ner 'bean** *s* fasola *f* wielokwiatowa, fasola *f* pnąca; **run•ner-'up** *s* zdobywca *m* drugiego miejsca; ***she was ~*** zdobyła drugie miejsce

run•ning ['rʌnɪŋ] **I** *s* **1.** *SPORT* bieganie *n*; ***make the ~*** *Br fig* dyktować tempo **2.** zarządzanie *n* **3.** kierowanie *n* **4.** prowadzenie *n* **5.** ***drug-~*** przemyt narkotyków **II** *adj* **1.** *year*, *month*: z rzędu **2.** *water*: bieżący **3.** nieustanny **4.** *commentary*: na żywo; ***give a ~ commentary on*** komentować na żywo *A*; **run•ning 'bat•tle** *s*: ***have a ~ with*** prowadzić nieustanną walkę z *I*; **run•ning costs** ['rʌnɪŋkɔsts] *pl* koszty *pl* eksploatacji; **run•ning head** *s* żywa pagina *f*; **'run•ning mate** *s Am POLIT* kandydat *m* na wiceprezydenta; **run•ning shoes** ['rʌnɪŋʃu:z] *pl* buty *pl* do biegania; **run•ning 'wa•ter** *s* bieżąca woda *f*

run•ny ['rʌnɪ] *adj* **1.** ***a ~ nose*** katar **2.** płynny **3.** rzadki

run-of-the-'mill *adj* **1.** przeciętny **2.** zwykły

'run-up *s Br* **1.** rozbieg *m* **2.** okres *m* poprzedzający; **'run•way** *s* **1.** pas *m* startowy **2.** (*fashion*) *Am* wybieg *m*

rup•ture ['rʌptʃə] **I** *s* **1.** pęknięcie *n* **2.** *infml* przepuklina *f* **3.** *in relations*: zerwanie *n* (***in*** *G*) **II** *v/i* pękać ⟨-knąć⟩ **III** *v/t relations*: zrywać ⟨zerwać⟩

ru•ral ['rʊrəl] *adj* **1.** wiejski **2.** *economy*: rolny

ruse [ru:z] *s* podstęp *m*

rush¹ [rʌʃ] *s* sitowie *n*

rush² [~] **I** *v/i* **1.** spieszyć ⟨po-⟩ się **2.** pędzić ⟨po-⟩ **3.** ***~ into a decision*** podjąć pochopną decyzję **II** *v/t* **1.** popędzać ⟨-dzić⟩ **2.** ***~ s.o. to hospital*** szybko zawieźć kogoś do szpitala **3.** spieszyć ⟨po-⟩ się z *I* **4.** szybko jeść ⟨z-⟩ **5.** niezwłocznie wysyłać ⟨-słać⟩ **6.** atakować ⟨za-⟩ **III** *s* **1.** pośpiech *m*; ***be in a ~*** spieszyć się; ***the Christmas ~*** przedświąteczna gorączka **2.** *adrenalin*: przypływ *m* **3.** napływ *m* **4.** gwałtowny wzrost *m* popytu; **rush through** *v/t issue*: szybko załatwiać ⟨-wić⟩

'rush hour *s* godziny *pl* szczytu

rush•es ['rʌʃɪz] *pl FILM* pierwsza kopia *f* robocza

rusk [rʌsk] *s* sucharek *m*

R

Rus•sia ['rʌʃə] *s* Rosja *f*; **Rus•sian** ['rʌʃən] **I** *adj* rosyjski **II** *s* **1.** Rosjanin *m*, Rosjanka *f* **2.** język *m* rosyjski; **Rus•sian rou•'lette** *s* rosyjska ruletka *f*
rust [rʌst] **I** *s* rdza *f* **II** *v/i* rdzewieć ⟨za-⟩
rus•tic ['rʌstɪk] **I** *adj* **1.** wiejski **2.** sielski **3.** rustykalny **II** *s* wieśniak *m*
rus•tle ['rʌsl] **I** *v/i* szeleścić ⟨za-⟩ **II** *v/t* szeleścić ⟨za-⟩ **III** *s* szelest *m*; **rustle up** *v/t* robić ⟨z-⟩ naprędce
'rust-proof *adj* nierdzewny; **rust re•mov•er** ['rʌstrɪmuːvə] *s* odrdzewiacz *m*
rust•y ['rʌstɪ] *adj* zardzewiały; ***my German is very ~*** *infml* prawie zapomniałem, jak się mówi po niemiecku; ***she's a little ~*** trochę wyszła z wprawy
rut[1] [rʌt] *s* BIOL ruja *f*
rut[2] [~] *s* **1.** koleina *f* **2.** *fig* rutyna *f*; ***he's stuck in a ~*** popadł w rutynę
ruth•less ['ruːθlɪs] *adj* bezwzględny; **ruth•less•ly** ['ruːθlɪslɪ] *adv* bezwzględnie; **ruth•less•ness** ['ruːθlɪsnɪs] *s* bezwzględność *f*
RV [ɑː'viː] *abbr* (=***recreational vehicle***) *Am* samochód *m* turystyczny
rye [raɪ] *s* żyto *n*; **'rye bread** *s* chleb *m* żytni; **'rye grass** *s* (*grass*) życica *f*; **rye 'whis•ky** *s* żytnia whisky *f*

S

sab•bath ['sæbəθ] *s* **1.** (*judaism*) szabas *m* **2.** (*christianity*) Dzień *m* Pański
sab•bat•i•cal [sə'bætɪkl] *s* urlop *n* naukowy; ***~ year*** dziekanka; ***he's on ~*** jest na urlopie naukowym
sa•ber ['seɪbə] *s Am* szabla *f*
sa•ble ['seɪbl] *s* **1.** (*animal*) soból *m* **2.** (*fur*) sobole *pl*
sab•o•tage ['sæbətɑːʒ] **I** *s* sabotaż *m* **II** *v/t* **1.** sabotować **2.** uniemożliwiać ⟨-wić⟩ przeprowadzenie **3.** uszkadzać ⟨-kodzić⟩ (w akcie sabotażu); **sab•o•teur** [sæbə'tɜː] *s* sabotażysta *m*
sa•bre ['seɪbə] *s Br* szabla *f*; **sa•bre rat•tling** *s fig* wymachiwanie *n* szabelką
sac•cha•rin ['sækərɪn] *s* CHEM sacharyna *f*
sa•chet [sæ'ʃeɪ] *s* **1.** torebka *f* **2.** saszetka *f*
sack[1] [sæk] **I** *s* worek *m*; ***get the ~*** *infml* zostać wylanym z pracy; ***give s.o. the ~*** *infml* wylać kogoś z pracy; ***hit the ~*** *infml* uderzyć w kimono **II** *v/t* *infml* wylewać ⟨-lać⟩ (z pracy)
sack[2] [~] **I** *s* **1.** złupienie *n*; ***the ~ of Rome*** złupienie Rzymu **2.** splądrowanie *n* **II** *v/t* **1.** łupić ⟨z-⟩ **2.** plądrować ⟨s-⟩
'sack•cloth *s* **1.** tkanina *f* workowa; ***put on ~ and ashes*** pokajać się publicznie **2.** juta *f*
sack•ing ['sækɪŋ] *s infml* wylanie *n* z pracy
sack race *s* (*game*) wyścig *m* w workach
sac•ra•ment ['sækrəmənt] *s* REL sakrament *m*
sa•cred ['seɪkrɪd] *adj* **1.** *sacrament*: święty; ***a ~ cow*** *a. fig* święta krowa **2.** *music*: sakralny
sac•ri•fice ['sækrɪfaɪs] **I** *s* **1.** poświęcenie *n* **2.** wyrzeczenie *n* **3.** REL ofiara *f* **4.** REL składanie *n* ofiar (**of** z *G*) **II** *v/t* **1.** poświęcać ⟨-cić⟩; ***she ~d everything for her children*** poświęciła wszystko dla swoich dzieci **2.** REL ofiarowywać ⟨-rować⟩, składać ⟨złożyć⟩ w ofierze; **sac•ri•fi•cial** [sækrɪ'fɪʃl] *adj* REL ofiarny
sac•ri•lege ['sækrɪlɪdʒ] *s* świętokradztwo *n*; **sac•ri•le•gious** [sækrɪ'lɪdʒəs] *adj* świętokradczy
sac•ris•ty ['sækrɪstɪ] *s* zakrystia *f*
sad [sæd] *adj* **1.** smutny; ***it is ~ that*** to smutne, że; ***~ to say*** niestety **2.** *infml* żałosny; **sad•den** ['sædn] *v/t* zasmucać ⟨-cić⟩
sad•dle ['sædl] **I** *s* **1.** siodło *n*; ***be back in the ~ again*** *fig* powrócić **2.** siodełko *n* **II** *v/t* **1.** siodłać ⟨o-⟩ **2.** obarczać ⟨-czyć⟩ (***s.o. with*** kogoś *I*); **saddle up** *v/t* siodłać ⟨o-⟩; **'sad•dle bag** *s* **1.** sakwa *f* **2.** torba *f* pod siodełko
sa•dism ['seɪdɪzm] *s* sadyzm *m*; **sa•dist** ['seɪdɪst] *s* sadysta *m*; **sa•dis•tic** [sə'dɪstɪk] *adj* sadystyczny
sad•ly ['sædlɪ] *adv* **1.** niestety **2.** smutno; ***be ~ mistaken*** bardzo się mylić; **sad•ness** ['sædnɪs] *s* smutek *m*

S

sae [eseɪ'iː] *abbr* (=***self-addressed envelope***) koperta *f* zwrotna

sa•fa•ri [sə'fɑːrɪ] *s* safari *n*; **sa'fa•ri park** *s* park *m* safari

safe [seɪf] **I** *adj* bezpieczny; ***be in ~ hands*** być w bezpiecznych rękach; ***the child was found ~ and sound*** dziecko odnalazło się całe i zdrowe; ***it's ~ to say*** można śmiało powiedzieć; ***better ~ than sorry*** lepiej dmuchać na zimne; ***just to be on the ~ side*** na wszelki wypadek; ***play ~*** nie ryzykować **II** *s* sejf *m*; **safe•break•er** ['seɪfbreɪkə], ***safe•crack•er*** ['seɪfkrækə] *s infml* kasiarz *m*; **safe de'pos•it box** → ***safety deposit box***; **'safe•guard I** *v/t* **1.** chronić ⟨o-⟩ (***against/from*** przed *I*) **2.** zabezpieczać ⟨-czyć⟩ (***against//from*** przed *I*) **II** *v/i* **1.** zabezpieczać ⟨-czyć⟩ się **2.** chronić ⟨o-⟩ się **III** *s* zabezpieczenie *n*; **safe 'ha•ven** *s* **1.** schronienie *n* **2.** azyl *m*; **'safe•keep•ing** *s*: ***give s.o. s.th. for ~*** dać komuś coś na przechowanie; ***in s.o.'s ~*** pod czyjąś opieką; ***be in the ~*** być w bezpiecznych rękach; **safe•ly** ['seɪflɪ] *adv* bezpiecznie; ***we can ~ say that*** możemy śmiało powiedzieć, że

safe•ty ['seɪftɪ] *s* bezpieczeństwo *n*; ***~ first!*** bezpieczeństwo przede wszystkim!; **'safe•ty belt** *s AUTO* pas *m* bezpieczeństwa; **'safe•ty catch** *s* (*gun*) bezpiecznik *m*; **'safe•ty-con•scious** *adj* dbający o bezpieczeństwo; **'safe•ty cur•tain** *s THEAT* kurtyna *f* przeciwpożarowa; **safe•ty de'pos•it box** *s* skrytka *f* depozytowa; **'safe•ty glass** *s* szkło *n* bezpieczne, szkło *n* bezodpryskowe; **'safe•ty is•land** *s AUTO Am* wysepka *f*; **'safe•ty lock** *s AUTO* automatyczne zamknięcia *n* centralnego zamka; **'safe•ty meas•ure** *s* środek *m* bezpieczeństwa; **'safe•ty net** *s* **1.** siatka *f* asekuracyjna **2.** *fig* zabezpieczenie *n*; **'safe•ty pin** *s* agrafka *f*; **'safe•ty pre•cau•tion** *s* środek *m* ostrożności; **'safe•ty ra•zor** *s* maszynka *f* do golenia; **'safe•ty valve** *s* zawór *m* bezpieczeństwa

saf•fron ['sæfrən] *s* szafran *m*

sag [sæg] *v/i* **1.** obwisać ⟨-snąć⟩ **2.** uginać ⟨-giąć⟩ się **3.** zapadać ⟨-paść⟩ się **4.** (*value*) spadać ⟨-paść⟩

sa•ga ['sɑːgə] *s* **1.** saga *f*; ***a family ~*** saga rodzinna **2.** historia *f*

sa•ga•cious [sə'geɪʃəs] *adj* mądry; **sa•ga•ci•ty** [sə'gæsətɪ] *s* mądrość *f*

sage[1] [seɪdʒ] *s* mędrzec *m*

sage[2] [~] *s* szałwia *f*

Sa•git•tar•i•us [sædʒɪ'teərɪəs] *s ASTR* Strzelec *m*

Sa•ha•ra [sə'hɑːrə] *s* Sahara *f*

said [sed] *Past Simple and Past Perfect* → ***say***

sail [seɪl] **I** *v/i* **1.** żeglować **2.** (*clouds*) płynąć ⟨po-⟩ **3.** (*ball*) szybować ⟨po-⟩ **II** *v/t* **1.** *boat*: pływać ⟨po-⟩ **2.** *sea*: przepływać ⟨-łynąć⟩ **III** *s* żagiel *m*; ***set ~*** wypłynąć w morze; ***in full ~*** na pełnych żaglach; ***go for a ~*** iść popływać; **'sail•board** *s* deska *f* surfingowa; **'sail•board•er** *s* windsurfer *m*; **'sail•board•ing** *s* windsurfing *m*; **'sail•boat** *s Am* żaglówka *f*

sail•ing ['seɪlɪŋ] *s* **1.** żeglarstwo *n*; ***everything was plain ~*** wszystko poszło jak po maśle **2.** rejs *m*; ***when is the next ~?*** kiedy jest następny rejs?; **'sail•ing boat** *s Br* żaglówka *f*; **'sail•ing ship** *s* żaglowiec *m*

sail•or ['seɪlə] *s* **1.** żeglarz *m* **2.** marynarz *m*

'sail•plane *s* szybowiec *m*

saint [seɪnt] *s* święty *m*; **saint•ly** ['seɪntlɪ] *adj* święty; **'saint's day** *s* **1.** dzień *m* świętego patrona **2.** imieniny *pl*

sake [seɪk] *s*: ***for God's ~!***, ***for heaven's ~*** na miłość boską!, na litość boską!; ***for his ~*** dla jego dobra; ***for the children's ~*** ze względu na dzieci; ***art for art's ~*** sztuka dla sztuki

sal•ad ['sæləd] *s* **1.** *COOK* surówka *f* **2.** *COOK* sałatka *f*; **'sal•ad cream** *s Br* sos *m* majonezowy do sałatek; **'sal•ad dress•ing** *s* dressing *m*, sos *m* do sałatek

sal•a•man•der ['sæləmændə] *s* salamandra *f*

sa•la•mi [sə'lɑːmɪ] *s* salami *n*

sal•a•ried ['sælərɪd] *adj employee*: otrzymujący stałą pensję; **sal•a•ry** ['sælərɪ] *s* pensja *f*; **'sal•a•ry scale** *s* taryfikator *m* płac

sale [seɪl] *s* **1.** sprzedaż *f*; ***for ~*** na sprzedaż; ***be on ~*** być w sprzedaży; ***tickets are on ~ from the club*** bilety można kupić w klubie; ***go on ~*** trafić do sprzedaży **2.** wyprzedaż *f*; ***in the ~s*** na wyprzedaży **3.** aukcja *f*; **'sale•a•ble** ['seɪləbl] *Br*, ***sal•able*** *Am adj* **1.** chodliwy **2.** nadający się do sprzedaży

sales [seɪlz] *pl* **1.** sprzedaż *f*; ***~ increased by 8 per cent*** sprzedaż wzrosła o 8%; ***a ~ and marketing director*** dyrektor ds. sprzedaży i marketingu **2.** dział *m* sprzedaży; **'sales clerk** *s Am* sprzedawca *m*, ekspedient *m*; **'sales fig•ures** *pl* wielkość *f* sprzedaży; **'sales force** *s* **1.** agenci *pl* handlowi **2.** personel *m* działu sprzedaży; **'sales•girl** *s* sprzedawczyni *f*, ekspedientka *f*; **'sales•man** *s -men pl* sprzedawca *m*, ekspedient *m*; **sales 'man•ag•er** *s* **1.** kierownik *m* sprzedaży **2.** dyrektor *m* ds. sprzedaży; **sales•man•ship** ['seɪlzmənʃɪp] *s* sztuka *f* sprzedaży; **'sales rep•re•sent•a•tive** *s* przedstawiciel *m* handlowy; **'sales slip** *s Am* paragon *m*; **'sales tax** *s* podatek *m* obrotowy; **'sales•wo•man** *s* sprzedawczyni *f*, ekspedientka *f*

sa•lient ['seɪljənt] *adj* najistotniejszy

sa•line ['seɪlaɪn] **I** *adj* słony; ***a ~ solution*** roztwór soli **II** *s* roztwór *m* soli

sa•li•va [sə'laɪvə] *s* ślina *f*; **sal•i•var•y** ['sælərvərɪ] *adj* ślinowy; ***a ~ gland*** gruczoł ślinowy, ślinianka; **sal•i•vate** ['sælɪveɪt] *v/i* ślinić się

sal•low ['sæləʊ] **I** *adj complexion*: niezdrowy **II** *s* wierzba *f* iwa

salm•on ['sæmən] *pl salmon s* łosoś *m*

sal•mo•nel•la [sælmə'nelə] *s* salmonella *f*; ***~ poisoning*** zatrucie salmonellą

sal•on ['sælɒn] *s* salon *m*; ***a beauty ~*** salon piękności

sa•loon [sə'luːn] *s* **1.** *Br* sedan *m* **2.** (*ship*) salon *m* **3.** *Br* bar *m* wyższej kategorii **4.** *dated* saloon *m*

sal•sa ['sælsə] *s* **1.** *MUS* salsa *f* **2.** *COOK* sos *m* salsa

salt [sɔːlt] **I** *s* sól *f*; ***a pinch of ~*** szczypta soli; ***take s.th. with a pinch of ~*** *fig* traktować coś z przymrużeniem oka; ***bath ~s*** sól kąpielowa; ***smelling ~s*** sole trzeźwiące **II** *v/t* **1.** solić ⟨po-⟩ **2.** *street*: posypywać ⟨-pać⟩ solą **III** *adj water*: słony; **salt away** *v/t* (*on account*) lokować ⟨u-⟩; **salt down** *v/t* solić ⟨za-⟩

'salt•cel•lar *s Br* solniczka *f*; **'salt-free** *adj* bezsolny; **salt•pe•tre** [sɔːlt'piːtə] *Br*, ***salt•pe•ter*** *Am s* saletra *f* potasowa; **salt•shak•er** ['sɔːltʃeɪkə] *s Am* solniczka *f*; **salt 'wa•ter** *s* słona woda *f*; **'salt-wa•ter fish** *s* ryba *f* słonowodna; **salt•y** ['sɔːltɪ] *adj* słony

sa•lu•bri•ous [sə'luːbrɪəs] *adj* **1.** *climate*: zdrowy **2.** *neighbourhood*: dobry

sal•u•tar•y ['sæljʊtərɪ] *adj experience*: pouczający

sal•u•ta•tion [sælju:'teɪʃn] *s* pozdrowienie *n*

sa•lute [sə'luːt] **I** *v/i* salutować ⟨za-⟩ **II** *v/t* **1.** pozdrawiać ⟨-rowić⟩ **2.** salutować ⟨za-⟩ **3.** wyrażać ⟨-razić⟩ uznanie dla *G* **4.** *flag*: oddawać ⟨-dać⟩ honory **5.** oddawać ⟨-dać⟩ hołd **III** *s* **1.** salut *m* **2.** salwa *f* honorowa **3.** pozdrowienie *n* **4.** hołd *m*

sal•vage ['sælvɪdʒ] **I** *v/t* **1.** ratować ⟨u-⟩ **2.** ocalać ⟨-lić⟩ **II** *s* **1.** ocalenie *n*; ***a ~ operation*** operacja ratunkowa **2.** ocalone mienie *n*; **'sal•vage ves•sel** *s* okręt *m* ratowniczy

Sal•va•dor(e)•an [sælvə'dɔːrən] **I** *adj* salwadorski **II** *s* Salwadorczyk *m*

sal•va•tion [sæl'veɪʃn] *s* **1.** *REL* zbawienie *n* **2.** *fig* wybawienie *n*, ratunek *m*; ***be s.o.'s ~*** uratować kogoś; **Sal•va•tion 'Ar•my** *s* Armia *f* Zbawienia; **Sal'va•tion•ist** *s* członek *m* Armii Zbawienia

sal•ver ['sælvə] *s* taca *f*

sal•vo ['sælvəʊ] *pl -vos, -voes s* salwa *f*

Sa•mar•i•tan [sə'mærɪtən] *s* Samarytanin *m*; ***a good ~*** dobry samarytanin

sam•ba ['sæmbə] *s* samba *f*

same [seɪm] **I** *adj* ***the ~*** **a)** ten sam **b)** taki sam; ***live in the ~ house*** mieszkać w tym samym domu; ***I bought exactly the ~ car*** kupiłem dokładnie taki sam samochód **II** *pron* ***the ~*** to samo; ***it's all the ~ to me*** wszystko mi jedno; – ***'I'll have coffee.'*** – ***'~ for me'*** – „Poproszę kawę." – „Dla mnie to samo."; (***the***) ***~ to you*** nawzajem; ***all the ~*** mimo to, mimo wszystko **III** *adv* ***the ~*** tak samo; ***they look the ~*** wyglądają tak samo; **'same•y** ['seɪmɪ] *adj Br infml* monotonny

sam•ple ['sɑːmpl] **I** *s* **1.** próbka *f*; ***a free ~ of shampoo*** darmowa próbka szamponu; ***take ~s of s.o.'s blood*** pobrać komuś krew **2.** próba *f*; ***a repre-***

S

sentative ~ of students reprezentatywna grupa studentów **3.** **~s** *MUS* sample *m* **II** *v/t* **1.** próbować ⟨s-⟩ **2.** skosztować **3.** pobierać ⟨-brać⟩ próbki

san•a•to•ri•um [sænə'tɔːrɪəm] *pl -riums, -ria s* sanatorium *n*

sanc•ti•mo•ni•ous [sæŋktɪ'məʊnɪəs] *adj* świętoszkoway

sanc•tion ['sæŋkʃn] **I** *s* **1.** sankcja *f*; ***economic ~s*** sankcje gospodarcze; ***impose ~s on*** nałożyć sankcje na *A*; ***lift ~s*** znieść sankcje **2.** zgoda *f* **3.** zatwierdzenie *n* **II** *v/t* **1.** wyrażać ⟨-razić⟩ zgodę na *A* **2.** zatwierdzać ⟨-dzić⟩ **3.** sankcjonować ⟨u-⟩ **4.** nakładać ⟨nałożyć⟩ sankcje na *A*

sanc•ti•ty ['sæŋktətɪ] *s* świętość *f*

sanc•tu•a•ry ['sæŋktʃʊerɪ] *s* **1.** sanktuarium *n*, świątynia *f* **2.** schronienie *n* **3.** azyl *m* **4.** rezerwat *m*

sand [sænd] **I** *s* **1.** piasek *m* **2.** plaża *f* **II** *v/t* **~ *s.th.* (*down*)** szlifować coś papierem ściernym

san•dal ['sændl] *s* sandał *m*; **san•dal•wood** ['sændlwʊd] *s* drzewo *n* sandałowe

'sand•bag *s* **I** *s* worek *m* z piaskiem **II** *v/t* obkładać ⟨obłożyć⟩ workami z piaskiem; **'sand•bank** *s* **1.** mielizna *f* **2.** ławica *f* piasku; **'sand•blast** *v/t* piaskować ⟨wy-⟩; **'sand box** *s Am* piaskownica *f*; **'sand•cas•tle** *s* zamek *m* z piasku; **'sand dune** *s* wydma *f*

sand•er ['sændə] *s* szlifierka *f*

'sand•man *s* (*fairy tales*) piaskowy dziadek *m*; **'sand•pa•per** **I** *s* papier *m* ścierny **II** *v/t* szlifować ⟨o-⟩ papierem ściernym; **'sand pit** *s Br* piaskownica *f*; **'sand•stone** *s* piaskowiec *m*; **'sand storm** *s* burza *f* piaskowa

S

sand•wich ['sænwɪtʃ] **I** *s* kanapka *f*; ***a ham ~*** kanapka z szynką **II** *v/t* wciskać ⟨-snąć⟩ (***between*** pomiędzy *I*); **sand•wich course** *s Br* kurs *m* teoretyczno-praktyczny

sand•y ['sændɪ] *adj* **1.** piaszczysty **2.** *hair*: rudoblond

sane [seɪn] *adj* **1.** zdrowy na umyśle **2.** zdrowy psychicznie **3.** rozsądny

sang [sæŋ] *Past Simple* → ***sing***

san•guine ['sæŋgwɪn] *adj* optymistyczny

san•i•tar•i•um [sænɪ'teərɪəm] *Am* → ***sanatorium***; **san•i•ta•ry** ['sænɪterɪ] *adj* **1.** sanitarny **2.** higieniczny; **'san•i•ta•ry towel** *Br*, ***'san•i•ta•ry nap•kin*** *Am s* podpaska *f* (higieniczna); **san•i•ta•tion** [sænɪ'teɪʃn] *s* **1.** warunki *pl* sanitarne **2.** urządzenia *pl* sanitarne; **san•i•'ta•tion de•part•ment** *s* zakład *m* oczyszczania miasta; **san•i•tize** ['sænɪtaɪz] *v/t* **1.** ugrzeczniać ⟨-nić⟩ **2.** cenzurować ⟨o-⟩ **3.** czyścić ⟨wy-⟩; **san•i•ty** ['sænətɪ] *s* **1.** zdrowie *n* psychiczne **2.** zdrowy rozsądek *m*

sank [sæŋk] *Past Simple* → ***sink***

San•ta Claus ['sæntəklɔːz] *s* Święty Mikołaj *m*

sap[1] [sæp] *s* **1.** *BIOL* sok *m* **2.** frajer *m*

sap[2] [~] *v/t* **1.** *health*: nadwątlać ⟨-lić⟩ **2.** *confidence*: nadszarpywać ⟨-pnąć⟩

sap•ling ['sæplɪŋ] *s* młode drzewko *n*

sap•phire ['sæfaɪə] **I** *s* szafir **II** *adj* szafirowy

sar•cas•m ['sɑːkæzm] *s* sarkazm *m*; **sar•cas•tic** [sɑː'kæstɪk] *adj* sarkastyczny; **sar•cas•tic•al•ly** [sɑː'kæstɪklɪ] *adv* sarkastycznie

sar•co•ma [sɑː'kəʊmə] *pl -mas, -mata s MED* mięsak *m*

sar•coph•a•gus [sɑː'kɒfəgəs] *pl -gi* [gaɪ], *-guses* [gəsəz] *s* sarkofag *m*

sar•dine [sɑː'diːn] *s* sardynka *f*

Sar•din•i•a [sɑː'dɪnɪə] *s* Sardynia *f*

sar•don•ic [sɑː'dɒnɪk] *adj laugh*: sardoniczny; **sar•don•ic•al•ly** [sɑː'dɒnɪklɪ] *adv* sardonicznie

sark•y ['sɑːkɪ] *Br infml* → ***sarcastic***

sash[1] [sæʃ] *s* szarfa *f*

sash[2] [~] *s* skrzydło *n* okna przesuwanego (w pionie); **sash 'win•dow** *s* okno *n* przesuwane (w pionie)

sass•y ['sæsɪ] *adj Am infml* **1.** bezczelny **2.** trendy

SAT [eseɪ'tiː] *abbr* **1.** *Am* (=**scholastic aptitude test**) *egzamin, którego wyniki decydują o przyjęciu na studia* **2.** (=***Standard Assessment Task***) **~s** *Br* ujednolicony sprawdzian *m* wiadomości

sat [sæt] *Past Simple and Past Perfect* → ***sit***

Sa•tan ['seɪtn] *s* szatan *m*; **sa•tan•ic** [sə'tænɪk] *s* **1.** satanistyczny **2.** diabelski

satch•el ['sætʃəl] *s* torba *f* (na ramię)

sat•el•lite ['sætəlaɪt] *s* satelita *m*; **'sat•el•lite dish** *s* antena *f* satelitarna; **'sat•el•lite state** *s POLIT* państwo *n* satelitarne; **sat•el•lite T'V** *s* telewizja *f* satelitarna

sa•ti•ate ['seɪʃɪeɪt] *v/t* zaspokajać ⟨-koić⟩

sat•in ['sætɪn] **I** *s* **1.** atłas *m* **2.** satyna *f* **II** *adj* **1.** atłasowy **2.** satynowy

sat•ire ['sætaɪə] *s* satyra *f*; **sa•tir•i•cal** [sə'tɪrɪkl] *adj* satyryczny; **sat•i•rist** ['sætərɪst] *s* satyryk *m*; **sat•ir•ize** ['sætəraɪz] *v/t* ośmieszać ⟨-szyć⟩

sat•is•fac•tion [sætɪs'fækʃn] *s* **1.** zadowolenie *n*; ***to s.o.'s ~*** ku czyjemuś zadowoleniu **2.** satysfakcja *f* **3.** zaspokojenie *n* **4.** *aim*: realizacja *f* **5.** zadośćuczynienie *n*; **sat•is•fac•to•ry** [sætɪs'fæktərɪ] *adj* **1.** zadowalający **2.** satysfakcjonujący

sat•is•fy ['sætɪsfaɪ] *v/t* **1.** satysfakcjonować ⟨u-⟩ **2.** zadowalać ⟨-wolić⟩ **3.** zaspokajać ⟨-koić⟩ **4.** przekonywać ⟨-konać⟩; ***be ~ied that*** być przekonanym, że

sat•u•rate ['sætʃəreɪt] *v/t* **1.** nasycać ⟨-cić⟩ (***with*** *I*); ***~ the market*** nasycić rynek; ***~d acid*** kwas nasycony **2.** ***be ~d with blood*** być przesiąkniętym krwią; **sat•u•ra•tion** [sætʃə'reɪʃn] *s* **1.** nasycenie *n*; ***a ~ point*** punkt nasycenia; ***a ~ bombing*** zmasowane bombardowanie **2.** przesiąknięcie *n*

Sat•ur•day ['sætədeɪ] *s* sobota *f*

Sat•urn ['sætən] *s ASTR* Saturn *m*

sauce [sɔːs] *s* **1.** sos *m* **2.** *Br dated* czelność *f*; **'sauce•pan** *s* rondel *m*

sau•cer ['sɔːsə] *s* **1.** spodek *m*; ***a flying ~*** latający spodek **2.** spodeczek *m*

sauc•y ['sɔːsɪ] *adj* bezczelny

Sa•u•di A•ra•bi•a [saʊdɪə'reɪbɪə] *s* Arabia *f* Saudyjska

sau•er•kraut ['saʊəkraʊt] *s* kiszona *f* kapusta

sau•na ['sɔːnə] *s* sauna *f*

saun•ter ['sɔːntə] *v/i* przechadzać się

saus•age ['sɒsɪdʒ] *s* **1.** kiełbasa *f* **2.** kiełbaska *f*

sau•té [səʊ'teɪ] *COOK* **I** *adj* sauté **II** *v/t* smażyć ⟨u-⟩ na niewielkiej ilości tłuszczu

sav•age ['sævɪdʒ] **I** *adj* **1.** *attack*: brutalny **2.** *criticism*: ostry **3.** dziki **II** *s* dzikus *m* **III** *v/t* **1.** pokiereszować **2.** rozszarpywać ⟨-pać⟩ **3.** ostro krytykować ⟨s-⟩, nie zostawić suchej nitki na *L*; **sav•age•ry** ['sævɪdʒrɪ] *s* **1.** brutalność *f* **2.** okrucieństwo *n* **3.** dzikość *f*

save [seɪv] **I** *v/t* **1.** oszczędzać ⟨-dzić⟩ (***for*** na *A*, ***on*** na *L*); ***~ one's strength*** oszczędzać siły **2.** ratować ⟨u-⟩; ***you ~d my life*** uratowałeś mi życie; ***~ s.o. from drowning*** uratować kogoś przed utonięciem; ***~ one's face*** zachować twarz **3.** zbierać ⟨zebrać⟩ **4.** *SPORT* bronić ⟨o-⟩ **5.** *INF* zapisywać ⟨-sać⟩ **II** *v/t* **1.** oszczędzać ⟨-dzić⟩ (***for*** na *A*, ***on*** na *L*) **2.** *SPORT* bronić ⟨o-⟩ **III** *s* **1.** *SPORT* obrona *f* **2.** *SPORT* interwencja *f* **IV** *prep* ***~*** (***for***) *dated* z wyjątkiem *G* **V** *conj* ***~ that*** *dated* poza tym, że; **save up** *v/i* oszczędzać ⟨-dzić⟩

sav•er ['seɪvə] *s* **1.** oszczędzający *m* **2.** ***be a time*** (***money***) ***~*** oszczędzać czas (pieniądze); **savi•ng** ['seɪvɪŋ] *s* **1.** oszczędność *f*; ***a ~ of $50*** oszczędność 50 dolarów **2.** oszczędzanie *n*; **sav•ing 'grace** *no pl s* jedyny plus *m*; ***his sense of humour is his ~*** ratuje go jedynie poczucie humoru; **sav•ings** ['seɪvɪŋz] *pl* oszczędności *pl*; **'sav•ings ac•count** *s* rachunek *m* oszczędnościowy; **sav•ings and 'loan association** *s Am* kasa *f* budowlana; **'sav•ings bank** *s* bank *m* oszczędnościowy

sa•viour ['seɪvjə] *Br*, **sa•vior** *Am s* **1.** wybawca *m* **2.** zbawca *m* **3.** ***the ~*** *REL* Zbawiciel *m*

sa•vour ['seɪvə] *Br*, **sa•vor** *Am* **I** *v/t* **1.** delektować się **2.** cieszyć się; ***~ every moment*** cieszyć się każdą chwilą **II** *v/i* mieć posmak (***of*** *G*) **III** *s fig* smak *m*; **sa•voury** ['seɪvərɪ] *Br*, **sa•vory** *Am* **I** *adj* **1.** pikantny **2.** słony **3.** smaczny, smakowity **II** *s* (słona) przekąska *f*

Sa•voy [sə'vɔɪ] *s* kapusta *f* włoska

sav•vy ['sævɪ] *infml* **I** *s* **1.** otrzaskanie *n* **2.** *political*: zmysł *m* **II** *adj* **1.** otrzaskany **2.** łebski

saw[1] [sɔː] *Past Simple* → **see**

saw[2] [~] **I** *s* piła *f* **II** (*sawed*; *sawn*/*sawed*) *v/t* piłować ⟨prze-⟩; **saw off** *v/t* odpiłowywać ⟨-łować⟩

'saw•dust *s* trociny *pl*; **'saw•mill** *s* tartak *m*

S

sawn [sɔːn] *Past Participle* → ***saw***[2]
sax [sæks] *s infml* saks *m*
sax•o•phone ['sæksəfəʊn] *s* saksofon *m*; **sax•o•phon•ist** [sæks'ɒfənɪst] *s* saksofonista *m*
say [seɪ] **I** (*said*; *said*) *v/t* mówić, powiedzieć; ***they ~ he's rich*** mówią, że jest bogaty; ***I have something to ~ about it*** mam coś do powiedzenia na ten temat; ***~ what you like*** mów, co chcesz; ***it's hard to ~*** trudno powiedzieć; ***let's ~ that*** powiedzmy, że; ***it goes without ~ing*** to się rozumie samo przez się; ***that is to ~*** to jest, to znaczy; ***to ~ the least*** delikatnie mówiąc; ***who can ~*** któż to wie; ***you can ~ that again*** zgadza się; ***~ yes*** zgodzić się; ***~ no*** odmówić **II** *s* ***have no ~*** nie mieć nic do powiedzenia; ***she has the final ~*** do niej należy ostateczna decyzja; **say•ing** ['seɪɪŋ] *s* powiedzenie *n*; ***as the ~ goes*** zgodnie z powiedzeniem
'say-so *no pl s infml* zgoda *f*; ***he has the final ~*** do niego należy ostateczna decyzja
scab [skæb] *s* **1.** strup *m* **2.** łamistrajk *m*
sca•bies ['skeɪbiːz] *s* świerzb *m*
scaf•fold ['skæfəʊld] *s* **1.** szafot *m* **2.** rusztowanie *n*; **scaf•fold•ing** ['skæfəldɪŋ] *s* rusztowanie *n*
scal•a•wag ['skæləwæg] *Am infml* → ***scallywag***
scald [skɔːld] **I** *v/t* parzyć ⟨po-⟩ **II** *s* poparzenie *n*; **scald•ing** ['skɔːldɪŋ] **I** *adj* parzący **II** *adv* ***~ hot*** bardzo gorący
scale[1] [skeɪl] **I** *s* **1.** łuska *f* **2.** MED kamień *m* nazębny **II** *v/t* **1.** *fish*: skrobać ⟨o-⟩ **2.** usuwać ⟨usunąć⟩ kamień nazębny z *G*
scale[2] [~] *s* **1.** szala *f* wagi **2.** *Am* waga *f*
scale[3] [~] **I** *s* **1.** skala *f*; ***on a large ~*** na dużą skalę; ***the full ~ of the disaster*** pełny rozmiar katastrofy; ***a ~ of 1:250000*** skala 1:250000; ***to ~*** w skali **2.** MUS gama *f* **II** *v/t* **1.** wspinać ⟨-piąć⟩ się na *A* **2.** powiększać ⟨-szyć⟩ i pomniejszać ⟨-szyć⟩ (w skali); ***the image can be ~d to any size*** rozmiar obrazka można dowolnie zmieniać **3.** powiększać ⟨-szyć⟩ **4.** pomniejszać ⟨-szyć⟩; **scale down** *v/t* **1.** zmniejszać ⟨-szyć⟩ **2.** pomniejszać ⟨-szyć⟩ **3.** ograniczać ⟨-czyć⟩; **scale up** *v/t* **1.** zwiększać ⟨-szyć⟩ **2.** powiększać ⟨-szyć⟩
scales [skeɪlz] *pl* waga *f*; ***bathroom ~*** waga łazienkowa
scal•lop ['skɒləp] *s* **1.** (*shellfish*) przegrzebek *m* **2.** ***~s*** obszycie w ząbki
scal•ly•wag ['skælɪwæg] *s Br infml* łobuziak *m*
scalp [skælp] **I** *s* **1.** skóra *f* głowy **2.** skalp *m* **II** *v/t* **1.** skalpować ⟨o-⟩ **2.** *tickets*: sprzedawać ⟨-dać⟩ (po wyższej cenie)
scal•pel ['skælpl] *s* skalpel *m*
scam [skæm] *s infml* przekręt *m*
scamp [skæmp] *s* urwis *m*, łobuziak *m*
scam•per ['skæmpə] *v/i* dreptać ⟨po-⟩
scam•pi ['skæmpɪ] *s Br* **1.** homarce *pl*, langustynki *pl* **2.** krewetki *pl*
scan [skæn] **I** *v/t* **1.** przeglądać ⟨przejrzeć⟩ **2.** przebiegać ⟨-biec⟩ wzrokiem **3.** przyglądać ⟨przyjrzeć⟩ się uważnie **4.** prześwietlać ⟨-lić⟩ **5.** robić ⟨z-⟩ USG **6.** robić ⟨z-⟩ tomografię **7.** skanować ⟨ze-⟩ **II** *v/i* ***this line doesn't ~*** ten wers gubi rytm **II** *s* **1.** prześwietlenie *n* **2.** USG *n* **3.** tomografia *f* **4.** ***have a ~ through s.th.*** przejrzeć coś; **scan in** *v/t* wskanowywać ⟨-nować⟩
scan•dal ['skændl] *s* **1.** skandal *m* **2.** plotki *pl*; **scan•dal•ize** ['skændəlaɪz] *v/t* gorszyć ⟨z-⟩
scan•dal•mon•ger ['skændlmʌŋgə] *s*: ***be a ~*** rozsiewać plotki
scan•dal•ous ['skændələs] *adj* skandaliczny
Scan•di•na•vi•a [skændɪ'neɪvɪə] *s* Skandynawia *f*; **Scan•di•na•vi•an** [skændɪ'neɪvɪən] **I** *adj* skandynawski **II** *s* Skandynaw *m*
scan•ner ['skænə] *s* **1.** skaner *m* **2.** ultrasonograf *m* **3.** tomograf *m* **4.** aparat *m* rentgenowski **5.** antena *f* radarowa
scant [skænt] *adj* niewielki; ***I paid ~ attention*** prawie nie uważałem; ***a ~ few hours*** zaledwie kilka godzin
scant•i•ly ['skæntɪlɪ] *adv* skąpo; ***~ dressed*** skąpo odziany; **scant•y** ['skæntɪ] *adj* skąpy; ***a ~ bikini*** skąpe bikini
scape•goat ['skeɪpgəʊt] *s* kozioł *m* ofiarny; ***make oneself a ~*** zrobić z siebie kozła ofiarnego

scar [skɑː] **I** *s* blizna *f*; ***his years in the concentration camp have left deep ~s*** *fig* pobyt w obozie koncentracyjnym odcisnął głębokie piętno na jego psychice **II** *v/t* okaleczać ⟨-czyć⟩; ***his face was ~red*** jego twarz była pokryta bliznami; ***leave s.o. ~red for life*** *fig* odcisnąć piętno na czyjejś psychice

scarce [skeəs] **I** *adj* **1.** niewystarczający; ***food was ~*** brakowało jedzenia **2.** rzadki; ***good lawyers are ~*** trudno o dobrego prawnika **3.** *infml* ***make oneself ~*** ulotnić się **II** *adv* ledwo; ***I can ~ remember her*** ledwo ją pamiętam; **scarce•ly** ['skeəslɪ] *adv* **1.** ledwo; ***I can ~ believe it*** ledwo mogę w to uwierzyć; ***he had ~ put the phone down when*** ledwo odłożył słuchawkę, gdy **2.** prawie nie; ***I ~ know them*** prawie ich nie znam **3.** zaledwie; ***she was ~ 12*** miała zaledwie 12 lat; **scarce•ness** ['skeəsnɪs] *s* **1.** brak *m* **2.** niewystarczająca ilość *f* **3.** rzadkość *f*

scar•ci•ty ['skeəsətɪ] → ***scarceness***

scare [skeə] **I** *v/t* straszyć ⟨prze-, wy-⟩; ***~ the life out of s.o.*** śmiertelnie kogoś wystraszyć **II** *v/i* ***I don't ~ easily*** niełatwo mnie przestraszyć **III** *s* **1.** panika *f* **2.** ***give s.o. a ~*** napędzić komuś stracha; **scare away** *v/t* **1.** odstraszać ⟨-szyć⟩ **2.** płoszyć ⟨s-⟩

'scare•crow ['skeəkrəʊ] *s* strach *m* na wróble; **scare•mon•ger** ['skeəmʌŋgə] *s*: ***be a ~*** siać panikę

scarf [skɑːf] *pl scarves s* **1.** szalik *m* **2.** chusta *f* **3.** apaszka *f*

scar•let ['skɑːlət] *adj* szkarłatny; **scarlet 'fe•ver** *s* szkarlatyna *f*

scar•per ['skɑːpə] *v/i Br infml* zwiewać ⟨-wiać⟩

scarred [skɑːd] *adj* pokryty bliznami

scarves [skɑːvz] *pl* → ***scarf***

scar•y ['skeərɪ] *adj* straszny; ***a ~ movie*** horror

scath•ing ['skeɪðɪŋ] *adj* **1.** *attack, criticism*: zjadliwy **2.** ***be ~ about*** ostro krytykować *A*

scat•ter ['skætə] **I** *v/t* **1.** (*a.* ***~ about, ~ around***) rozrzucać ⟨-cić⟩, rozsypywać ⟨-pać⟩ **2.** *crowd*: rozpędzać ⟨-dzić⟩ **II** *v/i* rozpraszać ⟨-roszyć⟩ się **III** *s* → ***scattering***; **'scat•ter•brain** *s infml* roztrzepaniec *m*; ***be a ~*** być roztrzepanym, być roztargnionym; **scat•ter•brained** ['skætəbreɪnd] *adj infml* roztrzepany, roztargniony; **scat•tered** ['skætəd] *adj* **1.** rozrzucony **2.** porozrzucany **3.** rozproszony; **scat•ter•ing** ['skætərɪŋ] *s*: ***a ~ of houses*** kilka rozrzuconych domów

scav•enge ['skævɪndʒ] **I** *v/t* **1.** grzebać ⟨wy-⟩ w śmieciach (***for*** w poszukiwaniu *G*) **2.** wygrzebywać ⟨-bać⟩ **3.** *animal*: żywić się padliną *I* **II** *v/i* **1.** grzebać (***through*** w *L*) **2.** żywić się (***on*** *I*); **scav•eng•er** ['skævɪndʒə] *s* **1.** padlinożerca *m* **2.** *infml* śmieciarz *m*

sce•na•ri•o [sɪ'nɑːrɪəʊ] *s* **1.** scenariusz *m*; ***in this nightmare ~*** gdyby taki czarny scenariusz się spełnił **2.** możliwość *f*

scene [siːn] *s* **1.** miejsce *n*; ***the ~ of the accident*** miejsce wypadku **2.** scena *f*; ***a love ~*** scena miłosna; ***the political ~*** scena polityczna; ***make a ~*** zrobić scenę; ***behind the ~s*** za kulisami **3.** widok *m*

sce•ne•ry ['siːnərɪ] *s* **1.** krajobraz *m* **2.** THEAT dekoracje *pl*

sce•nic ['siːnɪk] *adj view, route*: malowniczy

scent [sent] **I** *s* **1.** zapach *m*; ***a ~ of flowers was in the air*** w powietrzu unosił się zapach kwiatów **2.** woń *f* **3.** trop *m*; ***on the ~*** na tropie; ***put s.o. off the ~*** skierować kogoś na fałszywy trop **4.** *Br* perfumy *pl* **II** *v/t* **1.** zwęszyć **2.** wyczuwać ⟨-czuć⟩ **3.** spryskiwać ⟨-kać⟩

scep•tic ['skeptɪk] *Br*, ***skep•tic*** *Am adj* sceptyczny; **scep•tical** ['skeptɪkl] *Br*, ***skep•tical*** *Am adj* sceptyczny; **scep•ti•cism** ['skeptɪsɪzəm] *Br*, ***skep•ti•cism*** *Am s* sceptycyzm *m*

scep•tre ['septə] *s Br*, ***scep•ter*** *Am* berło *n*

sched•ule ['ʃedjuːl] **I** *s* **1.** plan *m*; ***begin on ~*** rozpocząć się zgodnie z planem; ***we are behind ~*** mamy opóźnienie; ***the construction is behind ~*** prace budowlane przebiegają z opóźnieniem; ***the project was finished ahead of ~*** inwestycję zakończono przed terminem **2.** harmonogram *m* **3.** terminarz *m* **4.** plan *m* zajęć **5.** rozkład *m* jazdy **6.** program *m* (telewizyjny) **7.** wykaz *m*; ***a price ~*** cennik **II** *v/t* **1.** planować ⟨za-⟩; ***the meeting is***

S

~d for Friday spotkanie zaplanowano na piątek; **a ~d departure** planowany odjazd **2.** klasyfikować ⟨za-⟩ (**as** jako *A*); **sched•uled 'flight** *s* lot *m* rejsowy

sche•mat•ic [skɪ'mætɪk] *adj* schematyczny

scheme [skiːm] **I** *s* **1.** program *m* **2.** system *m* **3.** plan *m*; **in the overall ~ of things** ogólnie rzecz biorąc, w ogólnej perspektywie **4. a colour ~ a)** kolorystyka **b)** tonacja (kolorystyczna) **II** *v/t* knuć ⟨u-⟩; **schem•er** ['skiːmə] *s* intrygant *m*; **schem•ing** ['skiːmɪŋ] *adj* knujący

schiz•o•phre•ni•a [skɪtsəʊ'friːnɪə] *s* schizofrenia *f*; **schiz•o•phren•ic** [skɪtsəʊ'frenɪk] *s* schizofrenik *m*

schlep [ʃlep] *Am infml* **I** *v/i* wlec się **II** *v/t* wlec

schmaltz [ʃmɒlts] *s infml* ckliwość *f*; **schmaltz•y** ['ʃmɔːltsɪ] *adj infml* ckliwy

schmooze [ʃmuːz] *v/i Am infml* gadać ⟨po-⟩

schnapps [ʃnæps] *s* sznaps *m*

schnit•zel ['ʃnɪtsl] *s* sznycel *m*

schnoz•zle ['ʃnɔːzl] *s infml* kinol *m*

schol•ar ['skɒlə] *s* **1.** uczony *m*; **a classical ~** filolog klasyczny **2.** badacz *m* **3.** stypendysta *m* **4.** *dated* uczeń *m*; **I was never much of a ~** *infml* w szkole nigdy nie byłem orłem; **schol•ar•ly** ['skɒləlɪ] *adj* **1.** naukowy **2.** uczony; **schol•ar•ship** ['skɒləʃɪp] *s* **1.** stypendium *n* **2.** nauka *f* **3.** wiedza *f*

school[1] [skuːl] *s of fish*: ławica *f*

school[2] [~] **I** *s* **1.** szkoła *f*; **at** (*Am a.* **in**) **~** w szkole; **go to ~** chodzić do szkoły; **a language ~** szkoła językowa **2.** *Am infml* college *m*, uniwerek *m*; **go to law ~** studiować prawo **3.** wydział *m* **II** *v/t* **1.** uczyć ⟨na-⟩; **~ed oneself in pa•tience** ćwiczyć cierpliwość **2. be ~ed** *form* uczęszczać do szkoły **3.** *animal*: tresować ⟨wy-⟩; **'school age** *s* wiek *m* szkolny; **'school-age** *adj* w wieku szkolnym; **'school bag** *s* **1.** teczka *f* szkolna **2.** tornister *m* **3.** plecak *m*; **'school•boy** *s* uczeń *m*; **'school bus** *s* szkolny autobus *m*; **'school•child** *pl -children s* uczeń *m*; **'school days** *pl* szkolne lata *pl*; **in my ~** gdy chodziłem do szkoły; **'school friend** *s Br* kolega *m* szkolny; **'school•girl** *s* uczennica *f*

school•ing ['skuːlɪŋ] *s* **1.** nauka *f* **2.** edukacja *f* **3.** wykształcenie *n*

'school kid *s infml* uczeń *m*; **school leav•er** *s Br* absolwent *m*; **'school•mate** *s* kolega *m* ze szkoły; **'school•teach•er** *s* nauczyciel *m*; **'school•work** *s* nauka *f*; **she helps me in my ~** pomaga mi w lekcjach; **'school yard** *s* **1.** szkolny dziedziniec *m* **2.** boisko *n* szkolne

schoon•er ['skuːnə] *s* **1.** szkuner *m* **2.** kieliszek *m* do sherry

sci•at•ic [saɪ'ætɪk] *adj nerve*: kulszowy; **sci•at•i•ca** [saɪ'ætɪkə] *s MED* rwa *f* kulszowa

sci•ence ['saɪəns] *s* **1.** nauka *f*; **social ~** nauki społeczne; **natural ~** nauki przyrodnicze **2.** nauki *pl* ścisłe; **sci•ence 'fic•tion** *s* fantastyka *f* naukowa, science fiction *f*; **'sci•ence park** *s* park *m* naukowy; **sci•en•tif•ic** [saɪən'tɪfɪk] *adj* **1.** naukowy **2.** metodyczny; **sci•en•tist** ['saɪəntɪst] *s* naukowiec *m*, uczony *m*

sci-fi ['saɪfaɪ] *infml* → **science fiction**

scin•til•lat•ing ['sɪntɪleɪtɪŋ] *adj fig* błyskotliwy

scis•sors ['sɪzəz] *pl* nożyczki *pl*

scle•ro•sis [sklɪə'rəʊsɪs] *s MED* **1.** stwardnienie *n*; **multiple ~** stwardnienie rozsiane **2.** miażdżyca *f*

scoff[1] [skɒf] *v/i* szydzić, wyszydzać ⟨-dzić⟩, naśmiewać się (**at** z *G*)

scoff[2] [~] *v/t Br infml* wtranżalać ⟨-żolić⟩, wtrząchać ⟨-chnąć⟩

scold [skəʊld] *v/t* besztać ⟨z-⟩ (**for** za *A*); **scold•ing** ['skəʊldɪŋ] *s* bura *f*; **get a ~** dostać burę

scone [skɒn] *s Br COOK* babeczka *f* (*podawana z masłem*)

scoop [skuːp] **I** *s* **1.** łyżka *f* do lodów **2.** łopatka *f* **3.** *ice-cream*: gałka *f* **4.** sensacyjna wiadomość *f* **II** *v/t* **1.** nakładać ⟨nałożyć⟩ **2.** (*a.* **~ up**) nabierać ⟨-brać⟩ **3.** *hole*: wykopywać ⟨-pać⟩ **4.** wydrążyć

scoot [skuːt] *v/i infml* lecieć ⟨po-⟩, biec ⟨po-⟩; **scoot•er** ['skuːtə] *s* **1.** *Br* skuter *m* **2.** hulajnoga *f*

scope [skəʊp] *s* **1.** zakres *m* **2.** ramy *pl*; **within the ~ of** w ramach *G* **3.** miejsce *n*; **there is not much ~ for originality**

S

nie ma wiele miejsca na oryginalność **4.** zakres *m* kompetencji **5.** możliwości *pl*; ***within one's ~*** w zasięgu czyichś możliwości
scorch [skɔːtʃ] **I** *v/t* **1.** przypalać ⟨-lić⟩ **2.** *grass*: wypalać ⟨-lić⟩ **II** *v/i* **1.** (*leaves*) brązowieć ⟨z-⟩ **2.** przypalać ⟨-lić⟩ się **3.** (*dash*) *Br infml* pruć; **scorch•er** ['skɔːtʃə] *s infml* skwarny dzień *m*; **scorch•ing** ['skɔːtʃɪŋ] *adj infml* skwarny; ***~ heat*** skwar; **scorch mark** *s* wypalony ślad *m*
score [skɔː] **I** *s* **1.** wynik *m*, rezultat *m*; ***what's the ~?*** jaki wynik?; ***the final ~ was 2-1*** mecz zakończył się wynikiem 2:1; ***keep the ~*** zapisywać wyniki; ***settle a ~ with*** *fig* wyrównać porachunki z *I* **2.** *MUS* partytura *f* **3.** muzyka *f* (filmowa) **4.** ***a ~ of cars*** dwadzieścia samochodów; ***two ~ years*** czterdzieści lat; ***~s*** *infml* mnóstwo **5.** nacięcie *n* **6.** ***you don't have to worry on that ~*** nie musisz się z tego powodu martwić **7.** ***I know the ~*** *infml* wiem, jak się rzeczy mają **II** *v/t* **1.** *point*: zdobywać ⟨-być⟩ **2.** *goal*: strzelać ⟨-lić⟩ **3.** *success*: osiągać ⟨-gnąć⟩ **4.** *points*: przyznawać ⟨-nać⟩ **5.** oceniać ⟨-nić⟩ **6.** *passage*: rozpisywać ⟨-sać⟩ (**for** na *A*) **7.** *passage*: aranżować ⟨za-⟩ **8.** *FILM* pisać ⟨na-⟩ muzykę do *G* **9.** nacinać ⟨-ciąć⟩ **III** *v/i* **1.** zdobywać ⟨-być⟩ punkt **2.** strzelać ⟨-lić⟩ gola **3.** liczyć ⟨po-⟩ punkty **4.** notować ⟨za-⟩ wyniki **5.** *infml* zaliczać (**with** *A*); **score out** *v/t* skreślać ⟨-lić⟩; ***score s.o.'s name out on a list*** skreślić kogoś z listy
'**score•board** *s SPORT* tablica *f* wyników; '**score•line** *s Br* wynik *m* (końcowy)
scor•er ['skɔːrə] *s* **1.** (*football*) strzelec *m*; ***a top ~*** najlepszy strzelec, król strzelców **2.** zdobywca *m* punktu **3.** sędzia *m* punktowy
scorn [skɔːn] **I** *s* pogarda *f*; ***pour ~ on*** szydzić z *G* **II** *v/t* **1.** gardzić ⟨wz-⟩ **2.** pogardzać ⟨-dzić⟩; **scorn•ful** ['skɔːrnfl] *adj* pogardliwy; **scorn•ful•ly** ['skɔːnflɪ] *adv* pogardliwie
Scor•pi•o ['skɔːpɪəʊ] *s ASTR* Skorpion *m*
scor•pi•on ['skɔːpɪən] *s* skorpion *m*
Scot [skɒt] *s* Szkot *m*
Scotch [skɒtʃ] *s* (*whisky*) szkocka *f*
Scotch 'tape® *s Am* taśma *f* klejąca
scot-'free *adj*: ***she got off ~*** *infml* upiekło się jej
Scot•land ['skɒtlənd] *s* Szkocja *f*; **Scottish** ['skɒtɪʃ] *adj* szkocki
Scots•man ['skɒtsmən] *pl -men s* Szkot *m*; **Scots•wom•an** ['skɒtswʊmən] *pl -men s* Szkotka *f*
scoun•drel ['skaʊndrəl] *s infml* drań *m*, łajdak *m*
scour[1] ['skaʊə] *v/t* **1.** dokładnie przeszukiwać ⟨-kać⟩ **2.** przeczesywać ⟨-sać⟩
scour[2] [~] *v/t* szorować ⟨wy-⟩
scourge [skɜːdʒ] **I** *s* **1.** plaga *f* **2.** zmora *f* **3.** bicz *m* **II** *v/t* **1.** nękać **2.** trapić
scout [skaʊt] **I** *s* **1.** skaut *m* **2.** harcerz *m*; ***the ~s*** harcerstwo **3.** zwiadowca *m* **4.** łowca *m* talentów **II** *v/t* przeszukiwać ⟨-kać⟩ **III** *v/i* (*a.* ***~ around***) szukać (**for** *G*); **scout out** *v/t* **1.** znajdować ⟨znaleźć⟩ **2.** ***~ around*** rozpoznawać ⟨-nać⟩ teren
scowl [skaʊl] **I** *v/i* **1.** krzywić ⟨s-⟩ się **2.** patrzeć ⟨po-⟩ krzywo (**at** na *A*) **II** *s* **1.** grymas *m* **2.** skrzywiona mina *f*
scrab•ble ['skræbl] *v/i*: ***~ around for*** szukać po omacku *G*
scrag•gy ['skrægɪ] *adj* wychudzony
scram [skræm] *v/i*: ***~!*** *dated infml* spadaj!
scram•ble ['skræmbl] **I** *v/i* **1.** wdrapywać ⟨-pać⟩ się **2.** ***~ to one's feet*** podnieść się pośpiesznie **3.** przedzierać ⟨-drzeć⟩ się **4.** walczyć (**for** o *A*) **II** *v/t* **1.** ***~ a win*** wygrać z trudem **2.** ***~ eggs*** robić jajecznicę **3.** *signal*: szyfrować ⟨za-⟩ **4.** ***~ s.o.'s brain*** mieszać komuś w głowie **III** *s* **1.** wdrapanie się *n* **2.** przepychanka *f* **3.** motocross *m*; **scram•bled 'eggs** ['skræmbld~] *s* jajecznica *f*; **scram•bler** ['skræmblə] *s* szyfrator *m*
scrap[1] [skræp] **I** *s* **1.** skrawek *m*; ***a ~ of paper*** skrawek papieru **2.** ***~s*** resztki *pl* (jedzenia) **3.** strzęp *m* **4.** ***it won't make a ~ of difference*** to nie robi najmniejszej różnicy; ***there's not a ~ of evidence*** nie ma żadnych dowodów **5.** złom *m*; ***for ~*** na złom **II** *v/t* **1.** złomować ⟨ze-⟩ **2.** oddawać ⟨-dać⟩ na złom **3.** odstępować ⟨-tąpić⟩ od *G* **4.** likwidować ⟨z-⟩

S

scrap² [~] *infml* **I** *s* **1.** sprzeczka *f* **2.** bójka *f* **II** *v/i* **1.** sprzeczać ⟨po-⟩ się **2.** bić ⟨po-⟩ się

'scrap•book *s* album *m* z wycinkami

scrape [skreɪp] **I** *v/t* **1.** zdrapywać ⟨-pać⟩, zeskrobywać ⟨-bać⟩ (***s.th. off*** coś z *G*) **2.** *potatoes*: oskrobywać ⟨-bać⟩ **3.** zadrapywać ⟨-pać⟩ **4.** ***~ a win*** wygrać z trudem; ***~ a living*** z trudem wiązać koniec z końcem **5.** *hole*: wykopywać ⟨-pać⟩ **II** *s* **1.** zgrzyt *m* **2.** szuranie *n* **3.** drapanie *n* **4.** zadrapanie *n* **5.** *dated* tarapaty *pl*; ***get into a ~*** wpakować w tarapaty; **scrape along**, ***scrape by*** *v/i* z trudem wiązać koniec z końcem; **scrape off** *v/t* zeskrobywać ⟨-bać⟩; **scrape through** *v/t* *exam*: z trudem zdawać ⟨-dać⟩

scrap•er ['skreɪpə] *s* skrobaczka *f*

'scrap heap *s* złomowisko *n*; **scrap 'met•al** *s* złom *m*; **scrap 'pa•per** *s* **1.** papier *m* do notatek **2.** makulatura *f*

scrap•py ['skræpɪ] *adj* **1.** chaotyczny **2.** *Br* byle jaki

'scrap•yard *s* **1.** skład *m* złomu **2.** złomowisko *n*

scratch [skrætʃ] **I** *v/t* **1.** drapać ⟨po-⟩; ***the dog ~ed itself behind the ear*** pies drapał się za uchem; ***~ one's nose*** podrapać się po nosie; ***~ the car*** porysować samochód; ***~ one's head over*** *fig* łamać sobie głowę nad *I*; ***you ~ my back and I'll ~ yours*** *fig* ręka rękę myje **2.** zadrapywać ⟨-pać⟩ **3.** drasnąć ⟨za-⟩ **4.** wydrapywać ⟨-pać⟩ **5.** rysować ⟨na-⟩ **6.** odwoływać ⟨-łać⟩ **7.** ***~ a living*** z trudem wiązać koniec z końcem **II** *v/i* drapać ⟨po-⟩ się **III** *s* **1.** zadrapanie *n*; ***she escaped without a ~*** wyszła z tego bez szwanku **2.** zadraśnięcie *n* **3.** rysa *f* **4.** zgrzyt *m* **5.** drapanie *n* **6.** ***have a ~*** podrapać się **7.** ***from ~*** od zera, od początku; **scratch off** *v/t* zdrapywać ⟨-pać⟩

'scratch pad *s Am* notatnik *m*; **'scratch pa•per** *s Am* papier *m* do notatek; **scratch•y** ['skrætʃɪ] *adj* **1.** szorstki; ***this scarf is ~*** ten szalik gryzie **2.** niedbały **3.** *record*: trzeszczący

scrawl [skrɔːl] **I** *v/t* bazgrać ⟨na-⟩ **II** *s* bazgroły *pl*

scraw•ny ['skrɔːnɪ] *adj* **1.** chudy **2.** mizerny

scream [skriːm] **I** *v/i* **1.** krzyczeć ⟨krzyknąć⟩ (***at*** na *A*); ***~ with excitement*** krzyknąć z podniecenia; ***~ in terror*** krzyknąć z przerażenia; ***~ for help*** wołać o pomoc **2.** wrzeszczeć ⟨wrzasnąć⟩ **3.** (*siren*) wyć **II** *v/t* wykrzykiwać ⟨-rzyczeć⟩; ***~ blue murder*** *Br* **a)** drzeć się w niebogłosy **b)** głośno protestować **III** *s* **1.** krzyk *m* **2.** wrzask *m* **3.** ***be a ~*** *dated* być przezabawnym

scree [skriː] *s* piarg *m*

screech [skriːtʃ] **I** *v/i* **1.** (*brakes*, *tyres*) piszczeć ⟨za-⟩; ***~ to a halt*** zatrzymać się z piskiem opon **2.** krzyczeć ⟨krzyknąć⟩ piskliwie **II** *v/t* **1.** krzyczeć ⟨krzyknąć⟩ piskliwie **III** *s* **2.** pisk *m*

screed [skriːd] *s* elaborat *m*

screen [skriːn] **I** *s* **1.** ekran *m*; ***adapt a novel for the ~*** przenieść powieść na ekran **2.** parawan *m* **3.** *fig* przykrywka *f*; ***behind a ~ of secrecy*** w tajemnicy **II** *v/t* **1.** osłaniać ⟨-łonić⟩ **2.** zasłaniać ⟨-łonić⟩ **3.** chronić **4.** MED badać ⟨z-⟩ **5.** ***~ s.o.*** prześwietlić czyjś życiorys, sprawdzić kogoś **6.** *film*: wyświetlać ⟨-lić⟩ **7.** *programme*, *film*: emitować ⟨wy-⟩; **screen off** *v/t* **1.** odzielać ⟨-lić⟩ **2.** odzielać ⟨-lić⟩ parawanem

'screen i•dol *s* idol *m* filmowy; **'screen•play** *s* scenariusz *m*; **'screen sav•er** *s* INF wygaszacz *m* ekranu; **'screen test** *s* zdjęcia *pl* próbne

screw [skruː] **I** *s* **1.** śruba *f*; ***he has a ~ loose*** *fig* brak mu piątej klepki; ***put the ~s on*** *fig* przycisnąć *A* **2.** wkręt *m* **3.** ***have a ~*** *vulg* pieprzyć się **II** *v/t* **1.** przykręcać ⟨-cić⟩ **2.** (*fool*) *infml* naciągać ⟨-gnąć⟩ **3.** *vulg* pieprzyć się z *I* **III** *v/i* wkręcać ⟨-cić⟩ się; **screw up** *v/t* **1.** *paper*: miąć ⟨z-⟩ **2.** zakręcać ⟨-cić⟩ **3.** *infml* pieprzyć ⟨s-⟩ **4.** *face*: wykrzywiać ⟨-wić⟩

'screw•ball *s Am infml* świr *m*

'screw•driv•er *s* śrubokręt *m*

screwed-up [skruːd'ʌp] *adj* **1.** *paper*: zmięty **2.** *face*: wykrzywiony **3.** *infml* okaleczony psychicznie

screw-top *adj* zakręcany

screw•y ['skruːɪ] *adj infml* pokręcony

S

scrib•ble ['skrɪbl] **I** *v/t* bazgrać ⟨na-⟩ **II** *s* bazgroły *pl*; **scrib•bler** ['skrɪblə] *s* **1.** gryzipiórek *m* **2.** pismak *m*
scrim•mage ['skrɪmɪdʒ] *s* szamotanina *f*
scrimp [skrɪmp] *v/i fig* zaciskać ⟨-snąć⟩ pasa
script [skrɪpt] **I** *s* **1.** scenariusz *m* **2.** pismo *n* (odręczne) **3.** alfabet *m*; ***Cyryllic ~*** cyrylica **4.** *INF* skrypt *m* **II** *v/t* pisać ⟨na-⟩ scenariusz do *G*
scrip•ture ['skrɪptʃə] *s* **1.** ≈, ***the ≈s*** Biblia *f*, Pismo *n* Święte **2.** ***~s*** święte księgi *pl*
'script•writ•er *s* scenarzysta *m*
scroll [skrəʊl] **I** *s* zwój *m* **II** *v/t INF* ***~ down*** przewijać w dół; ***~ up*** przewijać w górę
Scrooge [skruːdʒ] *s infml* sknera *m/f*
scro•tum ['skrəʊtəm] *pl -tums*, *-ta* [~tə] *s ANAT* moszna *f*
scrounge [skraʊndʒ] *infml* **I** *v/t* wyciągać ⟨-gnąć⟩ (***s.th. from*** coś od *G*) **II** *v/i* sępić (***for*** o *A*) **III** *s* ***be on the ~*** sępić; **scroung•er** ['skraʊndʒə] *s fig* pasożyt *m*
scrub[1] [skrʌb] *s* busz *m*
scrub[2] [~] **I** *v/t* **1.** szorować ⟨wy-⟩ **2.** *infml* odwoływać ⟨-łać⟩ **II** *s* ***give s.th. a ~*** wyszorować coś; **scrub•bing brush** ['skrʌbɪŋbrʌʃ], ***scrub brush*** *Am s* szczotka *f* ryżowa
scrub•by ['skrʌbɪ] *adj* **1.** *tree*: karłowaty **2.** *hill*: porośnięty karłowatymi drzewami i krzewami
scruff [skrʌf] *s* **1.** *Br infml* niechluj *m* **2.** *Br infml* obdartus *m* **3.** ***by the ~ of the neck*** za kark; **scruff•y** ['skrʌfɪ] *adj infml* **1.** niechlujny **2.** obdarty
scrum [skrʌm] *s* **1.** (*rugby*) młyn *m* **2.** tłum *m*; **scrump•tious** ['skrʌmpʃəs] *adj infml* pyszny
scrunch [skrʌntʃ] **I** *v/i* **1.** trzeszczeć ⟨za-⟩ **2.** chrzęścić ⟨za-⟩ **3.** chrupać ⟨-pnąć⟩ **II** (*a.* ***~ up***) *v/t* **1.** gnieść ⟨z-⟩ **2.** zwijać ⟨zwinąć⟩
scru•ple ['skruːpl] **I** *s* ***~s*** skrupuły; ***without ~*** bez skrupułów; ***have no ~s about doing s.th.*** nie mieć oporów przed zrobieniem czegoś **II** *v/i* ***not ~ to do s.th.*** nie mieć oporów przed zrobieniem czegoś; **scru•pu•lous** ['skruːpjələs] *adj* **1.** skrupulatny; ***be ~ in doing s.th.*** robić coś skrupulatnie **2.** sumienny; **scru•pu•lous•ly** ['skruːpjələslɪ] *adv* **1.** skrupulatnie **2.** sumiennie
scru•ti•nize ['skruːtɪnaɪz] *v/t* **1.** przypatrywać ⟨-trzeć⟩ się **2.** analizować ⟨prze-⟩; **scru•ti•ny** ['skruːtɪnɪ] *s* **1.** analiza *f*; ***the documents should be available for public ~*** dokumenty powinny być dostępne do wglądu dla wszystkich zainteresowanych **2.** badanie *n* **3.** obserwacja *f*; ***be under close ~*** być bacznie obserwowanym
scu•ba div•er ['skuːbədaɪvə] *s* płetwonurek *m*; **scu•ba div•ing** *s* nurkowanie *n* z akwalungiem
scuff [skʌf] **I** *v/t* **1.** rysować ⟨po-, za-⟩ **2.** ***~ one's feet*** powłóczyć nogami **II** *v/i* rysować ⟨po-, za-⟩ się
scuf•fle ['skʌfl] **I** *s* starcie *n* **II** *v/i* ścierać ⟨zetrzeć⟩ się (***with*** z *I*)
scull [skʌl] **I** *s* **1.** wiosło *n* krótkie **2.** łódź *f* wiosłowa; ***single ~s*** jedynki; ***double ~s*** dwójki **3.** ***~s*** zawody *pl* wioślarskie **II** *v/i* wiosłować; **'scull•er** *s* wioślarz *m*
sculpt [skʌlpt] **I** *v/t* rzeźbić ⟨wy-⟩ **II** *v/i* rzeźbić; ***~ in marble*** rzeźbić w marmurze
sculp•tor ['skʌlptə] *s* rzeźbiarz *m*; **sculp•ture** ['skʌlptʃə] *s* **1.** rzeźbiarstwo *n* **2.** rzeźba *f*
scum [skʌm] *s* **1.** brudny osad *m* **2.** piana *f* **3.** kożuch *m* **4.** (*offensive*) szumowiny *pl*
scup•per ['skʌpə] *v/t plan*: *Br infml* niweczyć ⟨z-⟩
scur•ri•lous ['skʌrələs] *adj* oszczerczy
scur•ry ['skʌrɪ] *v/i* gnać ⟨po-⟩
scut•tle ['skʌtl] → ***scurry***
scythe [saɪð] **I** *s* kosa *f* **II** *v/t* kosić ⟨s-⟩
sea [siː] *s* morze *n*; ***the open ~*** otwarte morze; ***at ~*** na morzu; ***be all at ~*** *fig* mieć mętlik w głowie, zupełnie nie wiedzieć, o co chodzi; ***by the ~*** nad morzem; ***travel by ~*** podróżować drogą morską; ***go to ~*** zostać marynarzem; ***put*** (***out***) ***to ~*** wyjść w morze; **'sea an•i•mal** *s* zwierzę *n* morskie; **'sea•bed** *s* dno *n* morskie; **'sea•bird** *s* ptak *m* nadmorski; **'sea•board** *s* wybrzeże *n*; **'sea breeze** *s* morska *f* bryza; **'sea change** *no pl s* wyraźna zmiana *f*; **sea•far•ing** ['siːfeərɪŋ] *adj tradition*: żeglarski; ***a ~ nation*** naród żeg-

S

larzy; **a ~ man** żeglarz; **'sea•food** *s* owoce *pl* morza; **'sea•front** *s* nadmorski bulwar *m*; **'sea•go•ing** *adj vessel*: dalekomorski; **'sea•gull** *s* mewa *f*; **'sea horse** *s* konik *m* morski

seal[1] [siːl] *s* foka *f*

seal[2] [~] **I** *s* **1.** pieczęć *f*; ***under ~*** zapieczętowany; ***give s.th. one's ~ of approval*** zatwierdzić coś, wyrazić na coś zgodę; ***set the ~ on*** *fig* przypieczętować *A* **2.** uszczelka *f* **3.** uszczelnienie *n* **4.** plomba *f* **II** *v/t* **1.** *envelope*: zaklejać ⟨-leić⟩ **2.** szczelnie zamykać ⟨-mknąć⟩ **3.** pieczętować ⟨za-, o-⟩ **4.** *friendship, fate*: pieczętować ⟨przy-⟩ **5.** ***~ a deal*** sfinalizować umowę **6.** uszczelniać ⟨-nić⟩ **7.** *surface*: pokrywać ⟨-ryć⟩; **seal off** *v/t* **1.** zamykać ⟨-mknąć⟩ dostęp do *G* **2.** zamykać ⟨-mknąć⟩

seal•ant ['siːlənt] *s* **1.** uszczelniacz *m* **2.** szczeliwo *n* **3.** szpachlówka *f*

'sea lev•el *s* poziom *m* morza

seal•ing wax ['siːlɪŋwæks] *s* lak *m*

'sea li•on *s* lew *m* morski

seam [siːm] *s* **1.** szew *m*; ***be bursting at the ~s*** *fig* pękać w szwach **2.** *gold*: żyła *f* **3.** *coal*: pokład *m* **4.** łączenie *n*

sea•man ['siːmən] *pl -men s* marynarz *m*

seam•stress ['siːmstrɪs] *s* szwaczka *f*

seam•y ['siːmɪ] *adj* **1.** przykry; ***the ~ side of life*** ciemna strona życia **2.** *area*: cieszący się złą sławą

'sea•plane *s* hydroplan *m*; **'sea•port** *s* port *m* morski; **'sea pow•er** *s* potęga *f* morska

sear [sɪə] *v/t* **1.** (*sun, shame*) palić ⟨s-⟩; ***feelings of guilt ~ed him*** dręczyło go poczucie winy **2.** wypalać ⟨-lić⟩ **3.** *meat*: obsmażać ⟨-żyć⟩

search [sɜːtʃ] **I** *s* **1.** poszukiwanie *n* (***for*** *G*); ***in ~ of*** w poszukiwaniu *G* **2.** przeszukiwanie *n* **3.** rewizja *f* **II** *v/i* szukać ⟨po-⟩ (***for*** *G*); ***~ high and low*** szukać wszędzie; ***~ me*** *infml* nie mam pojęcia **III** *v/t* **1.** przeszukiwać ⟨-kać⟩ **2.** przeprowadzać ⟨-dzić⟩ rewizję w *L* **3.** rewidować ⟨z-⟩; **search out** *v/t* odszukiwać ⟨-kać⟩; **search through** *v/i* przeszukiwać ⟨-kać⟩

'search and 'res•cue op•er'a•tion *s* akcja *f* poszukiwawczo-ratunkowa; **'search 'func•tion** *s* INF funkcja *f* wyszukiwania; **search•ing** ['sɜːtʃɪŋ] *adj* **1.** dociekliwy **2.** wnikliwy; **'search•light** *s* reflektor *m*; **'search par•ty** *s* ekipa *f* poszukiwawcza; **'search warrant** *s* nakaz *m* rewizji

'sea•shore *s* brzeg *m* morza; **'sea•sick** *adj*: ***be ~*** cierpieć na chorobę morską; ***get ~*** zapaść na chorobę morską; **'sea•sick•ness** *s* choroba *f* morska; **'sea•side** *s*: ***at the ~*** nad morzem; ***to the ~*** nad morze

sea•son ['siːzn] **I** *s* **1.** pora *f* roku **2.** pora *f*; ***the rainy ~*** pora deszczowa; ***~'s Greetings!*** Wesołych Świąt! **3.** sezon *m*; ***the hunting ~*** sezon polowań; ***during the peak ~*** w sezonie; ***off ~*** poza sezonem **II** *v/t* **1.** przyprawiać ⟨-wić⟩ **2.** doprawiać ⟨-wić⟩; ***~ to taste*** doprawić do smaku; **sea•son•al** ['siːzənl] *adj* **1.** sezonowy **2.** okresowy **3.** świąteczny; **sea•soned** ['siːznd] *adj* **1.** doświadczony **2.** wytrawny **3.** przyprawiony **4.** *wood*: sezonowany; **sea•son•ing** ['siːzənɪŋ] *s* przyprawa *f*; **'sea•son tick•et** *s* bilet *m* okresowy; ***a monthly ~*** bilet miesięczny

seat [siːt] **I** *s* **1.** miejsce *n*; ***take a ~*** zająć miejsce; ***reserve a ~*** zarezerwować miejsce; ***a ~ in Parliament*** miejsce w parlamencie **2.** siedzenie *n* **3.** siodełko *n* **4.** siedziba *f*; ***the ~ of government*** siedziba rządu **II** *v/t* usadzać ⟨-dzić⟩; ***please be ~ed*** proszę usiąść; ***please remain ~ed*** proszę pozostać na miejscach; ***~ oneself*** usiąść **III** *v/i* ***the bus ~s 42*** w autobusie są 42 miejsca siedzące; **'seat belt** *s* pas *m* (bezpieczeństwa); ***fasten one's ~*** zapiąć pas; ***wear a ~*** być przypiętym pasem; ***a ~ tensioner*** napinacz pasa; **seat•er** ['siːtə] *adj*: ***a four-~ (car)*** samochód czteroosobowy; ***ten-~ minibus*** 10-osobowy minibus; **seat•ing** ['siːtɪŋ] *s* miejsca *pl* siedzące; ***a ~ capacity*** liczba miejsc siedzących

'sea ur•chin *s* jeżowiec *m*; **'sea•weed** *s* wodorosty *pl* (morskie); **'sea•wor•thy** *adj ship*: zdatny do żeglugi

sec [sek] *s infml* sekundka; ***just a ~!*** sekundkę!, momencik!

sec•a•teurs [sekə'tɜːz] *pl* sekator *m*

se•cede [sɪ'siːd] *v/i* odłączać ⟨-czyć⟩ się (***from*** od *G*); **se•ces•sion** [sɪ'seʃn] *s* POLIT secesja *f*

S

se•clud•ed [sɪ'klu:dɪd] *adj* **1.** odludny **2.** odosobniony **3.** zaciszny **4.** *life*: samotniczy; **se•clu•sion** [sɪ'klu:ʒn] *s* **1.** odosobnienie *n* **2.** osamotnienie *n*

sec•ond¹ [sɪ'kɒnd] *v/t Br employee*: oddelegowywać ⟨-gować⟩

sec•ond² ['sekənd] *s* sekunda *f*; ***just a ~ !*** jedną chwilę!, moment!; ***have you got a ~?*** masz chwilę?; ***in a ~*** za chwilę

se•cond³ ['səkənd] **I** *adj* **1.** drugi; ***the ~ time*** drugi raz; ***the ~ of June*** drugi czerwca; ***it has become ~ nature for him*** to stało się dla niego drugą naturą; ***be ~ to none*** być nie do pobicia **II** *adv* **2.** jako drugi; ***I agreed to speak ~*** zgodziłem się przemawiać jako drugi; ***come ~ in the marathon*** ukończyć maraton na drugim miejscu **3.** po drugie **III** *s* **1.** ***~s*** dokładka *f*; ***~s, anybody?*** czy ktoś chce dokładkę? **2.** towar *m* drugiego gatunku **3.** AUTO dwójka *f* **4.** sekundant *m* **IV** *v/t* popierać ⟨-przeć⟩

sec•ond•a•ry ['sekəndrɪ] *adj* **1.** drugorzędny **2.** wtórny **3.** *accent*: poboczny **4.** ponadpodstawowy; ***a ~ school*** szkoła średnia; ***a ~ teacher*** nauczyciel w szkole średniej; **sec•ond•a•ry ed•u'ca•tion** *s* szkolnictwo *n* ponadpodstawowe

se•cond 'best I *adj* **1.** drugi po najlepszym **2.** ***come off ~*** odnieść porażkę **II** *adv* **1.** jako drugi **2.** na drugim miejscu **III** *s* ***he doesn't settle for ~*** interesuje go tylko to, co najlepsze, nie zadowoli się namiastką; **sec•ond 'big•gest** *adj* drugi pod względem wielkości; **sec•ond 'class** *s* **1.** druga *f* klasa **2.** przesyłka *f* zwykła; **second-'class** *adj* **1.** drugiej klasy **2.** *citizen*: drugiej kategorii **3.** *letter*: zwykły **4.** podrzędny; **sec•ond 'cous•in** *s* dalszy krewny *m*; **sec•ond-de•'gree** *adj burn*: drugiego stopnia; **sec•ond 'floor** *s* **1.** *Br* drugie piętro *n* **2.** *Am* pierwsze piętro; **sec•ond-'guess** *v/t* **1.** przewidywać ⟨-dzieć⟩ **2.** *Am* krytykować ⟨s-⟩ po fakcie; **sec•ond hand** *s* wskazówka *f* sekundowa, sekundnik *m*; **sec•ond-'hand** *adj* **1.** używany; ***a ~ bookshop*** antykwariat; ***a ~ shop*** second-hand **2.** *information*: z drugiej ręki

sec•ond•ly ['sekəndlɪ] *adv* po drugie

sec•ond-'rate *adj* podrzędny; **second 'thoughts** *pl*: ***on ~*** po namyśle; ***have ~ about*** zmienić zdanie co do *G*

se•cre•cy ['si:krəsɪ] *s* **1.** tajemnica *f*; ***in ~*** w tajemnicy; ***s.th. is shrouded in ~*** coś otacza tajemnica, coś jest utrzymywane w tajemnicy **2.** dyskrecja *f* **3.** tajemniczość *f*

se•cret ['si:krət] **I** *adj* **1.** tajny; ***keep s.th. ~*** utrzymywać coś w tajemnicy **2.** *admirer*, *hope*: cichy; ***have ~ hopes*** mieć cichą nadzieję **3.** *person*: tajemniczy **4.** *passage*: tajemny **II** *s* **1.** sekret *m* **2.** tajemnica *f*; ***in ~*** w tajemnicy; ***the ~ of success*** tajemnica sukcesu; ***keep a ~*** dotrzymać tajemnicy; ***let s.o. in on the ~*** dopuścić kogoś do tajemnicy; ***make no ~s of*** nie ukrywać *G*; **se•cret 'a•gent** *s* tajny agent *m*; **se•cret po•'lice** *s* tajna policja *f*; **secret 'ser•vice** *s* wywiad *m*; **se•cret•ly** ['si:krətlɪ] *adv* potajemnie, w tajemnicy

sec•re•tar•i•al [sekrə'teərɪəl] *adj* sekretarski

sec•re•tar•y ['sekrətrɪ] *s* sekretarz *m*, sekretarka *f*; **sec•re•tar•y-'gen•er•al** *s* sekretarz *m* generalny; **Sec•re•tary of 'State** *s* **1.** (*minister of foreign affairs*) *Am* sekretarz *m* stanu **2.** *Br* minister *m*

se•crete [sɪ'kri:t] *v/t* **1.** wydzielać ⟨-lić⟩ **2.** *form* ukrywać ⟨-ryć⟩; **se•cre•tion** [sɪ'kri:ʃn] *s* **1.** wydzielanie *n* **2.** wydzielina *f*

se•cre•tive ['si:krətɪv] *adj* skryty; ***be ~ about s.th.*** robić z czegoś tajemnicę

sect [sekt] *s* sekta *f*; **sec•tar•i•an** [sek'teərɪən] *adj* **1.** o podłożu religijnym **2.** wyznaniowy **3.** sekciarski

sec•tion ['sekʃn] **I** *s* **1.** część *f* **2.** sekcja *f* **3.** dział *m* **4.** odcinek *m* **5.** fragment *m* **6.** paragraf *m* **7.** *orange*: cząstka *f* **8.** przekrój *m* **9.** wycinek *m* **II** *v/t* **1.** dzielić ⟨po-⟩ **2.** ciąć ⟨po-⟩ **3.** pobierać ⟨-brać⟩ wycinek; **sec•tion•al** ['sekʃənl] *adj* **1.** *interests*: partykularny **2.** *drawing*: przekrojowy

sec•tor ['sektə] *s* sektor *m*; ***the public ~*** sektor państwowy; ***the private ~*** sektor prywatny

sec•u•lar ['sekjʊlə] *adj* świecki; **'sec•u•lar•ize** ['sekjʊləraɪz] *v/t* **1.** sekularyzować ⟨z-⟩ **2.** zeświecczać ⟨-czyć⟩

se•cure [sɪ'kjʊə] **I** *adj* **1.** bezpieczny; ***feel ~*** czuć się bezpiecznie **2.** zabezpieczony (***against*** przed *I*); ***make s.th. ~*** zabezpieczyć coś **3.** *job*, *income*: pewny **4.** solidny **5.** dobrze zamocowany **II** *v/t* **1.** zabezpieczać ⟨-czyć⟩ (***against*** przed *I*) **2.** przymocowywać ⟨-cować⟩ **3.** zapewniać ⟨-nić⟩

se•cu•ri•t|y [sɪ'kjʊrətɪ] *s* **1.** ochrona *f* **2.** bezpieczeństwo *n* **3.** środki *pl* bezpieczeństwa **4.** zabezpieczenie *n* **5.** ***~ies*** papiery *pl* wartościowe; ***the ~ies market*** rynek papierów wartościowych; **se•'cu•ri•ty check** *s* kontrola *f* bezpieczeństwa; **se•'cu•ri•ty-con•scious** *adj* dbający o bezpieczeństwo; **se•'cu•ri•ty forces** *pl* siły *pl* bezpieczeństwa; **se•'cu•ri•ty guard** *s* **1.** ochroniarz *m* **2.** strażnik *m*; **se•'cu•ri•ty risk** *s* zagrożenie *n* bezpieczeństwa

se•dan [sɪ'dæn] *s Am* sedan *m*

se•date [sɪ'deɪt] **I** *adj* **1.** spokojny **2.** niespieszny **II** *v/t* podawać ⟨-dać⟩ środki uspokajające; ***be ~d*** być pod wpływem środków uspokajających; **se•da•tion** [sɪ'deɪʃn] *s*: ***be under ~*** być pod wpływem środków uspokajających; **sed•a•tive** ['sedətɪv] *s* środek *m* uspokajający

sed•en•ta•ry ['sedntrɪ] *adj* **1.** *job*: siedzący **2.** osiadły

sed•i•ment ['sedɪmənt] *s* osad *m*

se•duce [sɪ'dju:s] *v/t* **1.** uwodzić ⟨uwieść⟩ **2.** kusić ⟨s-⟩ (***s.o. into*** kogoś do *G*); **se•duc•tion** [sɪ'dʌkʃn] *s* **1.** uwiedzenie *n* **2.** pokusa *f*; **se•duc•tive** [sɪ'dʌktɪv] *adj* **1.** uwodzicielski **2.** nęcący **3.** kuszący

S

see[1] [si:] **I** (*saw*; *seen*) *v/t* **1.** widzieć; ***did you ~ what happened?*** widziałeś, co się stało?; ***I saw him arrive*** widziałem, jak przyjechał; ***I ~ things differently now*** teraz inaczej na to patrzę; ***as I ~ it*** tak, jak ja to widzę **2.** zobaczyć; ***go and ~ what the kids are doing*** idź zobaczyć, co robią dzieci; ***~ you later!*** na razie!; ***I'll ~ what I can do*** zobaczę, co da się zrobić; ***I hope I never live to ~ the day when*** mam nadzieję, że nie dożyję dnia, kiedy **3.** rozumieć ⟨z-⟩; ***can't you ~ what I mean?*** nie rozumiesz, co mam na myśli?; ***he didn't ~ the joke*** nie zrozumiał dowcipu **4.** oglądać ⟨obejrzeć⟩; ***~ a movie*** obejrzeć film; ***go to ~ a film*** pójść na film **5.** ***~ page 20*** patrz strona 20 **6.** odwiedzać ⟨-dzić⟩; ***come and ~ us*** odwiedź nas **7.** zobaczyć się z *I* **8.** spotykać się z *I*; ***are you ~ing anyone?*** spotykasz się z kimś? **9.** iść ⟨pójść⟩ do *G*; ***you should ~ a doctor*** powinieneś pójść do lekarza **10.** odprowadzać ⟨-dzić⟩; ***~ s.o. home*** odprowadzić kogoś do domu **11.** być świadkiem *G*; ***this stadium has seen many international games*** na tym stadionie rozegrano wiele międzynarodowych meczy **II** (*saw*; *seen*) *v/i* **1.** widzieć; ***~ for yourself*** przekonaj się sam **2.** zobaczyć; ***we'll ~*** zobaczymy; ***let me ~*** popatrzmy **3.** rozumieć ⟨z-⟩; ***I ~*** rozumiem; ***you ~*** no wiesz **4.** ***~ to it that s.th. is done*** dopilnować, żeby coś zostało zrobione; **see about** *v/i* zajmować ⟨-jąć⟩ się *G*; ***we'll ~ that*** zajmiemy się tym; **see in** *v/t* widzieć w *L*; ***I don't know what she sees in him*** nie wiem, co ona w nim widzi; **see off** *v/t* **1.** żegnać ⟨po-⟩ **2.** *Br* pokonywać ⟨-nać⟩; **see out** *v/t winter*: przetrwać; **see over**, **see around** *v/t Br* oglądać ⟨obejrzeć⟩; **see through** *v/t* **1.** przejrzeć **2.** rozszyfrowywać ⟨-rować⟩ **3.** doprowadzać ⟨-dzić⟩ do końca; **see to** *v/t*: ***~ it that s.th. is done*** dopilnować, żeby coś zostało zrobione

see[2] [~] *s* biskupstwo; ***the Holy ~*** Stolica Apostolska

seed [si:d] **I** *s* **1.** nasiono *n*, nasienie *n* **2.** ziarno *n* **3.** *Am* pestka *f* **4.** (*tennis*) ***the number one ~*** gracz rozstawiony z numerem pierwszym **II** *v/t* **1.** obsiewać ⟨-siać⟩ **2.** ***~ oneself*** rozsiewać się **3.** (*tennis*) rozstawiać ⟨-wić⟩; ***be ~ed 7th*** być rozstawionym z numerem siódmym **III** *v/i* wydawać ⟨-dać⟩ nasiona; **'seed•bed** *s* **1.** rozsadnik *m* **2.** *fig* pożywka *f* **3.** *fig* wylęgarnia *f*; **seed•ed** ['si:dɪd] *adj* **1.** *player*: rozstawiony; ***a top-~ player*** najwyżej rozstawiony gracz **2.** *tomatoes*, *grapes*: wypestkowany; **seed•less** ['si:dlɪs] *adj* **1.** bezpestkowy **2.** bez nasion; **seed•ling** ['si:dlɪŋ] *s* sadzonka *f*; **seed•y** ['si:dɪ] *adj* **1.** obskurny **2.** zapuszczony **3.** brudny

see•ing ['si:ɪŋ] *conj* **~ that** ponieważ, zważywszy, że

seek [si:k] **I** (*sought*; *sought*) *v/t* **1.** szukać; **~ help from** poprosić o pomoc *G*, szukać pomocy u *G* **2.** poszukiwać **3.** ubiegać się o *A* **4. ~ s.o.'s advice** zasięgnąć czyjejś rady **II** (*sought*; *sought*) *v/i* **1.** szukać (**for** *G*) **2.** poszukiwać (**for** *G*)

seem [si:m] *v/i* wydawać ⟨-dać⟩ się; ***it ~s impossible to me*** wydaje mi się to niemożliwe; ***he ~s nice*** wydaje się miły; ***it ~s that*** wydaje się, że; ***so it ~s*** tak się wydaje; **seem•ing** ['si:mɪŋ] *adj* **1. *he won with ~ ease*** wydawało się, że wygrana przyszła mu łatwo **2.** pozorny; **seem•ing•ly** ['si:mɪŋlɪ] *adv* **1. *she was ~ indifferent to their suffering*** wydawało się, że jest obojętna na ich cierpienia **2.** pozornie, na pozór **3.** podobno

seen [si:n] *Past Participle* → **see**[1]

seep [si:p] *v/i* **1.** sączyć ⟨prze-⟩ się **2.** ciec ⟨prze-⟩; **seep out** *v/i* (*information*) przeciekać ⟨-ciec⟩, wydostawać ⟨-tać⟩ się na zewnątrz

see•saw ['si:sɔ] **I** *s a. fig* huśtawka *f* **II** *v/i* ***her emotions ~ed*** przeżywała huśtawkę nastrojów

seethe [si:ð] *v/i* **1.** kipieć **2. ~** (***with anger***) kipieć złością **3. *be seething with tourists*** roić się od turystów

see-through ['si:θru:] *adj* **1.** prześwitujący **2.** przezroczysty

seg•ment ['segmənt] **I** *s* **1.** część *f* **2.** segment *m* **3.** człon *m* **4.** *orange*: cząstka *f* **5.** *MATH* odcinek *m* (koła) **II** *v/t* **1.** dzielić ⟨po-⟩ na części **2.** dzielić ⟨po-⟩ na cząstki; **seg•mented** [seg'məntɪd] *adj* **1.** wieloczłonowy; ***the tapeworm has a ~ body*** ciało tasiemca składa się z szeregu segmentów **2.** podzielony na części

seg•re•gate ['segrɪgeɪt] *v/t* **1.** oddzielać ⟨-lić⟩ **2.** rozdzielać ⟨-lić⟩ **3.** segregować ⟨po-⟩; **seg•re•ga•tion** [segrɪ'geɪʃn] *s* **1.** segregacja *f*; ***racial ~*** segregacja rasowa **2.** rozdzielenie *n*

seis•mic ['saɪzmɪk] *adj* sejsmiczny

seis•mo•graph ['saɪzməgrɑ:f] *s* sejsmograf *m*; **seis•mol•o•gist** [saɪz'mɒlədʒɪst] *s* sejsmolog *m*; **seis•mol•o•gy** [saɪz'mɒlədʒɪ] *s* sejsmologia *f*

seize [si:z] *v/t* **1.** chwytać ⟨chwycić⟩; ***he ~d her by her arm*** chwycił ją za ramię; ***panic ~d her*** ogarnęła ją panika; ***~ the day*** korzystaj z dnia **2.** przejmować ⟨-jąć⟩ **3.** *territory*, *property*: zajmować ⟨-jąć⟩ **4.** *criminal*: zatrzymywać ⟨-mać⟩ **5.** przechwytywać ⟨-chwycić⟩ **6.** *chance*, *opportunity*: wykorzystywać ⟨-tać⟩; **seize up** *v/i* **1.** (*engine*) zacierać ⟨zatrzeć⟩ się **2.** (*hand*) odmawiać ⟨-mówić⟩ posłuszeństwa; **sei•zure** ['si:ʒə] *s* **1.** *MED* atak *m* **2.** przejęcie *n* **3.** *territory*, *property*: zajęcie *n* **4.** przechwycenie *n*

sel•dom ['seldəm] *adv* rzadko

se•lect [sɪ'lekt] **I** *v/t* **1.** wybierać ⟨-brać⟩ **2.** selekcjonować ⟨wy-⟩ **II** *adj* **1.** wybrany; ***a ~ few*** garstka wybrańców **2.** wyselekcjonowany **3.** najlepszy **4.** ekskluzywny; **se•lec•tion** [sɪ'lekʃn] *s* **1.** wybór *m*; ***make a ~*** dokonać wyboru; ***a wide ~ of*** szeroki wybór *G* **2.** selekcja *f*; **se'lec•tion pro•cess** *s* proces *m* selekcji; **se•lec•tive** [sɪ'lektɪv] *adj* **1.** selektywny **2.** wybiórczy **3.** wybredny **4. *be ~ about*** wybierać *A*, dokonać wyboru *G*; **se'lec•tive•ly** *adv* selektywnie, wybiórczo

self [self] *pl selves* [selvz] *s* **1.** własne ja *n*; ***my true ~*** moje prawdziwe ja; ***he is back to his old ~*** znowu jest sobą **2.** jaźń *f*; **self-ab'sorbed** *adj* pochłonięty sobą; **self-ad•dressed 'en•ve•lope** [selfə'drest 'envələʊp] *s* koperta *f* zwrotna; **self-ad'he•sive** *adj* samoprzylepny; **self-ap-'point•ed** *adj* samozwańczy; **self-as'sur•ance** *s* pewność *f* siebie; **self-assured** [selfə'ʃʊəd] *adj* pewny siebie; **self-ca•ter•ing** [self'keɪtərɪŋ] *adj Br accomodation*: z wyżywieniem we własnym zakresie; **self-'cen•tred** [self'sentəd] *Br*, ***self-'cen•tered*** *Am adj* egocentryczny; **self-'clean•ing** *adj* samoczyszczący; **self-con•'fessed** [selfkən'fest] *adj* **1.** *criminal*: przyznający się do winy **2.** *alcoholic*: przyznający się do nałogu; **self-'con•fi•dence** *s* pewność *f* siebie; **self-'con-**

fi•dent *adj* pewny siebie; **self-'con•scious** *adj* **1.** skrępowany; ***be ~ about*** wstydzić się *G* **2.** nieśmiały; **self-'con•scious•ness** *s* **1.** skrępowanie *n* **2.** nieśmiałość *n*; **self-contained** [selfkən'teɪnd] *adj* **1.** samowystarczalny **2.** *Br flat*: samodzielny **3.** niezależny; **self-con'trol** *s* **1.** opanowanie *n* **2.** samokontrola *f*; **self-'crit•i•cal** *adj* samokrytyczny; **self-'crit•i•cism** *s* samokrytyka *f*; **self-de•'fence** *Br*, ***self-de'fense*** *Am s* samoobrona *f*; **self-de•struct** [selfdɪ'strʌkt] *v/i* ulegać ⟨-lec⟩ samozniszczeniu; **self-de•ter•mi'na•tion** *s* **1.** samostanowienie *n* **2.** niezależność *f*; **self-'dis•ci•pline** *s* samodyscyplina *f*; **self-'doubt** *s* brak *m* wiary w siebie; **self-'ed•u•cat•ed** *adj*: ***be ~*** być samoukiem; **self-ef•fac•ing** [selfɪ'feɪsɪŋ] *adj* skromny; **self-em•ployed** [selfɪm'plɔɪd] *adj* pracujący na własny rachunek; **self-e•'steem** *s* poczucie *n* własnej wartości; **self-'ev•i•dent** *adj* oczywisty; **self-ex•'pres•sion** *s* wyrażanie *n* siebie; **self-'gov•ern•ment** *s* **1.** autonomia *f* **2.** samorządność *f*; **self-'help** *s* **1.** zaradność *f* **2.** wzajemna pomoc *f*; ***a ~ group*** grupa wzajemnej pomocy; **self-im•'portance** *s* zarozumiałość *f*; **self-im•'portant** *adj* zarozumiały; **self-in•'dulgent** *s*: **1.** ***be ~*** dogadzać sobie, *dated* folgować sobie **2.** *life*: pełen przyjemności; **self-'in•terest** *s* korzyść *f* własna

self•ish ['selfɪʃ] *adj* samolubny

self•less ['selflɪs] *adj* bezinteresowny

self-made 'man [self'meɪd'mæn] *pl -men s* człowiek *m*, który wszystko zawdzięcza sobie, self-made man *m*; **self-'pit•y** *s* użalanie *n* się nad sobą; **self-'por•trait** *s* autoportret *m*; **self-pos•sessed** [selfpə'zest] *adj* opanowany; **self-pos•'ses•sion** *s* opanowanie *n*; **self-pres•er•'va•tion** *s*: ***a ~ instinct***, ***a sense of ~*** instynkt *m* samozachowawczy; **self-pro•claimed** [selfprə'kleɪmd] *adj* samozwańczy; **'self-rais•ing flour** *s Br* mąka *f* z proszkiem do pieczenia; **self-re•'li•ant** *adj* **1.** samodzielny **2.** niezależny; **self-re'spect** *s* szacunek *m* dla samego siebie; **self-re•spect•ing** [selfrɪ'spektɪŋ] *adj* szanujący się; **self-right•eous** [self'raɪtʃəs] *adj* zadufany w sobie; **self-ris•ing flour** *Am* → ***self-raising flour***; **self-'rule** *s* samorządność *f*; **self-'sac•ri•fice** *s* poświęcenie *n*; **self-sat•is•fied** [self'sætɪsfaɪd] *adj* pełen samozadowolenia; **self-seal•ing** [self'siːlɪŋ] *adj envelope*: samoklejący; **self-'ser•vice I** *s* samoobsługa *f* **II** *adj* samoobsługowy; **self-ser•vice 'res•tau•rant** *s* restauracja *f* samoobsługowa; **self-suf•'fi•cient** *adj* samowystarczalny; **self-sup•port•ing** [selfsə'pɔːtɪŋ] *adj* niezależny finansowo; **self-taught** [self'tɔːt] *adj*: ***be ~*** być samoukiem

sell [sel] **I** (*sold*; *sold*) *v/t* sprzedawać ⟨-dać⟩ (**for** za *A*); ***~ the idea to the management*** *fig* sprzedać pomysł dyrekcji; ***~ one's soul to the devil*** sprzedać duszę diabłu **II** (*sold*; *sold*) *v/i* sprzedawać ⟨-dać⟩ się; ***the book ~s well*** książka dobrze się sprzedaje; **sell off** *v/t* wyprzedawać ⟨-dać⟩; **sell out** *v/t* wyprzedawać ⟨-dać⟩; ***we are sold out of bread*** chleba już nie ma; **sell up** *v/i* sprzedawać ⟨-dać⟩ wszystko

'sell-by date *s Br* data *f* ważności; ***this product is past its ~*** termin ważności tego produktu już minął

sell•er ['selə] *s* **1.** sprzedawca *m* **2.** ***be a good ~*** dobrze się sprzedawać; **selling** ['selɪŋ] *adj*: ***a ~ price*** cena sprzedaży; **'sell•ing point** *s* cecha *f* stanowiąca o atrakcyjności towaru

Sel•lo•tape® ['seləteɪp] *s Br* taśma *f* klejąca

'sell•out *s* **1.** ***the concert is a ~*** wszystkie bilety na koncert zostały wyprzedane **2.** *fig* zdrada *f*

selves [selvz] *pl* → **self**

se•man•tic [sɪ'mæntɪk] *adj* semantyczny; **se•man•tics** [sɪ'mæntɪks] *s* semantyka *f*

sem•blance ['sembləns] *s* pozory *pl*; ***a ~ of normality has been restored*** sytuacja pozornie wróciła do normy

se•men ['siːmən] *s* sperma *f*, nasienie *n*

se•mes•ter [sɪ'mestə] *s* semestr *m*; ***the winter ~*** semestr zimowy

sem•i- ['semɪ] (*in combinations*) pół-

sem•i ['semɪ] *pl -mis s* (*house*) *Br infml* połowa *f* bliźniaka

sem•i•breve ['semɪbriːv] *s Br MUS* cała nuta *f*; **'sem•i•cir•cle** *s* **1.** półkole *n* **2.** półokrąg *m*; ***sit in a ~*** siedzieć w półokręgu; **sem•i•'cir•cu•lar** *adj* **1.** półkolisty **2.** półokrągły; **semi-'co•lon** *s* średnik *m*; **sem•i•con'duc•tor** *s* półprzewodnik *m*; **sem•i•de•tached 'house** *s Br* połowa *f* bliźniaka; **semi•'fi•nal** *s* półfinał *m*; **semi•'fi•nal•ist** *s* półfinalista *m*

sem•i•nar ['semɪnɑː] *s* (*university*) seminarium *n*

sem•i•nar•y ['semɪnərɪ] *s* seminarium *n* duchowne

sem•i•of'fi•cial *adj* półoficjalny; **sem•i•pre•cious 'stone** *s* kamień *m* półszlachetny; **sem•i•'skilled** *adj* **1.** *person*: nieposiadający pełnych kwalifikacji **2.** *work*: niewymagający pełnych kwalifikacji; **sem•i•'skimmed 'milk** *s* mleko *n* półtłuste

Sem•ite ['siːmaɪt] *s* Semita *m*; **Sem•it•ic** [sə'mɪtɪk] *adj* semicki

'sem•i•tone *s MUS Br* półton *m*; **'sem•i•trail•er** *s* naczepa *f*

sem•o•li•na [semə'liːnə] *s* **1.** semolina *f* **2.** kasza *f* manna

sen•ate ['senɪt] *s* senat *m*; **sen•a•tor** ['senətə] *s* senator *m*; **sen•a•to•ri•al** [senə'tɔːrɪəl] *adj* senacki

send [send] (*sent*; *sent*) *v/t* **1.** wysyłać ⟨-słać⟩; ***~ s.th. by post*** wysyłać coś pocztą; ***~ word that*** zawiadomić kogoś, że; ***~ s.o. to boarding school*** wysłać kogoś do szkoły z internatem; ***~ s.o. crazy*** doprowadzać kogoś do szału **2.** *greetings*: przesyłać ⟨-słać⟩; **send away** *v/t* **1.** odsyłać ⟨odesłać⟩ **2.** zamawiać ⟨-mówić⟩ (pocztą); **send back** *v/t* odsyłać ⟨odesłać⟩; **send down** *v/t* **1.** *Br infml* posyłać ⟨-słać⟩ za kratki **2.** *dated* relegować z uczelni; **send for** *v/i* **1.** posyłać ⟨-słać⟩ po *A* **2.** *doctor*: wzywać ⟨wezwać⟩; **send in** *v/t* **1.** wysyłać ⟨-słać⟩ **2.** przysyłać ⟨-słać⟩; **send off** *v/t* **1.** wysyłać ⟨-słać⟩ **2.** posyłać ⟨-słać⟩ (***for*** po *A*) **3.** usuwać ⟨usunąć⟩ z boiska; **send on** *v/t* **1.** przesyłać ⟨-słać⟩ (na nowy adres) **2.** *luggage*: wysyłać ⟨-słać⟩ wcześniej; **send out I** *v/t* **1.** rozsyłać ⟨-zesłać⟩ **2.** emitować ⟨wy-⟩ **II** *v/i* zamawiać ⟨-mówić⟩ (***for*** *A*); **send up** *v/t Br infml* parodiować ⟨s-⟩

send•er ['sendə] *s* nadawca *m*

'send-off *s infml* pożegnanie *n*; **'send-up** *s infml* parodia *f*

se•nile ['siːnaɪl] *adj* **1.** *behaviour*, *decay*: starczy **2.** ***get ~*** dziecinnieć na starość; **se•nil•i•ty** [sɪ'nɪlətɪ] *s* otępienie *n* starcze

se•ni•or ['siːnjə] **I** *adj* **1.** starszy **2.** wyższy rangą **3.** zajmujący wyższe stanowisko; ***a ~ manager*** członek ścisłego kierownictwa **4.** *civil servant*: wysokiego szczebla **5.** *position*: wysoki **II** *s* **1.** ***my brother is 2 years my ~*** mój brat jest ode mnie o dwa lata starszy **2.** senior *m*; ***George Bush ~*** George Bush senior; ***a ~ competition*** *SPORT* zawody seniorów; **se•ni•or 'cit•i•zen** *s* emeryt *m*; **se•ni•or•i•ty** [siːnj'ɒrətɪ] *s* **1.** staż *m* pracy **2.** zajmowane stanowisko *n* **3.** starszeństwo *n*

sen•sa•tion [sen'seɪʃn] *s* **1.** uczucie *n*; ***a tingling ~*** łaskotanie **2.** doznanie *n* **3.** wrażenie *n*; ***I had a ~ of falling*** miałem wrażenie, że spadam **4.** czucie *n*; ***lose ~ in one's fingers*** stracić czucie w palcach **5.** sensacja *f*; ***cause a ~*** wzbudzać sensację; **sen•sa•tion•al** [sen'seɪʃnl] *adj* **1.** sensacyjny **2.** *infml* fantastyczny; **sen•sa•tion•al•ism** [sen'seɪʃnəlɪzəm] *s* (celowe) wzbudzanie *n* sensacji; **sen'sa•tion•al•ize** [sen'seɪʃnəlaɪz] *v/t* robić ⟨z-⟩ sensację z *G*

sense [sens] **I** *s* **1.** zmysł *m*; ***the ~ of sight*** zmysł wzroku; ***the ~ of direction*** zmysł orientacji; ***the sixth ~*** szósty zmysł **2.** poczucie *n*; ***a ~ of humour*** poczucie humoru **3.** wyczucie *n* **4.** sens *m*; ***make ~*** mieć sens; ***it doesn't make ~*** to nie ma sensu; ***in a ~*** w pewnym sensie; ***there is no ~ in worrying about it*** nie ma sensu się tym przejmować **5.** znaczenie *n*; ***in every ~ of the word*** w pełnym tego słowa znaczeniu **6.** rozsądek *m*; ***come to one's ~s*** opamiętać się; ***talk some ~ into s.o.*** przemówić komuś do rozsądku **II** *v/t* wyczuwać ⟨-czuć⟩; **sense•less** ['senslɪs] *adj* **1.** bezsensowny **2.** bezmyślny **3.** ***he drank himself ~*** upił się do nieprzytomności

'sense or•gan *s* narząd *m* zmysłu

sen•si•bil•i•t|y [sensɪ'bɪlətɪ] *s* **1.** wrażliwość *f* **2.** ***~ies*** uczucia *pl*; ***offend s.o.'s***

S

religious ~ies obrażać czyjeś uczucia religijne; **sen•si•ble** ['sensəbl] *adj* **1.** rozsądny **2.** sensowny **3.** praktyczny **4.** *form* świadomy; ***I'm ~ of the fact that*** jestem świadomy faktu, że; **sen•si•bly** ['sensəblɪ] *adv* **1.** rozsądnie **2.** sensownie **3.** praktycznie

sen•si•tive ['sensətɪv] *adj* **1.** wrażliwy (***to*** na *A*); ***~ to cold*** wrażliwy na zimno **2.** przeczulony, drażliwy (***about***/***to*** na punkcie *G*) **3.** uwrażliwiony (***to*** na *A*) **4.** *matter*: delikatny, drażliwy **5.** *instrument*: czuły; **sen•si•tiv•i•ty** [sensə'tɪvətɪ] *s* **1.** wrażliwość *f* (***to*** na *A*) **2.** przeczulenie *n*, drażliwość *f* (***about***/***to*** na punkcie *G*) **3.** *of matter*: delikatność *f*, drażliwość *f* **4.** *of instrument*: czułość *f*

sen•si•tize ['sensɪtaɪz] *v/t* uwrażliwiać ⟨-wić⟩

sen•sor ['sensə] *s* czujnik *m*

sen•so•ry ['sensərɪ] *adj* **1.** zmysłowy; ***~ organs*** organy zmysłów **2.** *deprivation*: sensoryczny

sen•su•al ['senʃʊəl] *adj* zmysłowy; **sen•su•al•i•ty** [senʃʊ'ælətɪ] *s* zmysłowość *f*; **sen•su•al•ly** ['senʃʊəlɪ] *adv* zmysłowo

sen•su•ous ['senʃʊəs] → ***sensual***

sent [sent] *Past Simple and Past Participle* → ***send***

sen•tence ['sentəns] **I** *s* **1.** zdanie *n* **2.** wyrok *m*; ***a prison ~*** kara więzienia; ***a death ~*** kara śmierci; ***pass ~*** wydać wyrok; ***serve one's ~*** odbywać wyrok **II** *v/t* skazywać ⟨-zać⟩; ***be ~d to three years in prison*** zostać skazanym na trzy lata więzienia

sen•ten•tious [sen'tenʃəs] *adj* **1.** moralizatorski **2.** sentencjonalny

S

sen•ti•ment ['sentɪmənt] *s* **1.** odczucie *n* **2.** nastrój *n*; ***nationalist ~s*** nastroje nacjonalistyczne **3.** sentymenty *pl* **4.** uczucia *pl*; **sen•ti•ment•al** [sentɪ'mentl] *adj* sentymentalny; ***~ value*** wartość sentymentalna; ***be ~ about*** **a)** mieć sentyment do *G* **b)** roztkliwiać się nad *I*; ***get ~ about*** roztkliwiać się nad *I*; **sen•ti•men•tali•ty** [sentɪmen'tælətɪ] *s* **1.** sentymentalizm *m* **2.** czułostkowość *f*

sen•try ['sentrɪ] *s* wartownik *m*; **'sen•try box** *s* budka *f* wartownika; **'sen•try du•ty** *s* warta *f*; ***be on ~*** stać na warcie

sep•a•ra•ble ['sepərəbl] *adj* **1.** ***be ~ from*** dać się oddzielić od *G* **2.** rozdzielny

sep•a•rate[1] ['sepərət] *adj* **1.** oddzielny **2.** osobny **3.** różny

sep•a•rate[2] ['sepəreɪt] **I** *v/t* **1.** oddzielać ⟨-lić⟩ (***from*** od *G*); ***~ the eggs*** oddzielić żółtka od białek **2.** rozdzielać ⟨-lić⟩ **II** *v/i* **1.** rozdzielać ⟨-lić⟩ się **2.** oddzielać ⟨-lić⟩ się (***from*** od *G*) **3.** rozstawać ⟨-tać⟩ się; ***they ~d after 20 years of marriage*** rozstali się po 20 latach małżeństwa; **sep•a•rat•ed** ['sepəreɪtɪd] *adj* (*couple*) w separacji; **sep•a•rate•ly** ['sepərətlɪ] *adv* **1.** oddzielnie **2.** osobno; **sep•a•ra•tion** [sepə'reɪʃn] *s* **1.** oddzielenie *n* **2.** rozstanie *n* **3.** separacja *f* **4.** rozdział *m*

sep•a•ra•tism ['seprətɪzəm] *s* separatyzm *m*; **sep•a•ra•tist** ['seprətɪst] *adj* separatystyczny

Sep•tem•ber [sep'tembə] *s* wrzesień *m*

sep•tic ['septɪk] *adj* **1.** zakażony; ***go ~*** ulec zakażeniu **2.** septyczny; **'sep•tic tank** *s* szambo *n*

se•quel ['siːkwəl] *s* **1.** kontynuacja *f* **2.** sequel *m* **3.** następstwo *n*; **se•quence** ['siːkwəns] *s* **1.** kolejność *f*; ***the ~ of events*** kolejność wydarzeń; ***in ~*** po kolei; ***out of ~*** nie po kolei **2.** ciąg *m* **3.** seria *f* **4.** pasmo *n* **5.** sekwencja *f* **6.** następstwo *n*; ***the ~ of tenses*** następstwo czasów; **se•quen•tial** [sɪ'kwenʃl] *adj* sekwencyjny; **se•quen•tial•ly** [sɪ'kwenʃəlɪ] *adv* sekwencyjnie

se•ques•ter [sɪ'kwestə] *v/t* **1.** zajmować ⟨-jąć⟩ **2.** obłożyć sekwestrem

se•quin ['siːkwɪn] *s* cekin *m*

se•quoi•a [sɪ'kwɔɪə] *s* sekwoja *f*

Serb [sɜːb] *s* Serb *m*, Serbka *f*; **Ser•bi•a** ['sɜːbɪə] *s* Serbia *f*; **Ser•bi•an** ['sɜːbɪən] **I** *adj* serbski **II** *s* **1.** Serb *m*, Serbka *f* **2.** język *m* serbski

ser•e•nade [serə'neɪd] **I** *s* serenada *f* **II** *v/t* śpiewać ⟨za-⟩ serenadę

se•rene [sɪ'riːn] *adj* **1.** spokojny **2.** *sky*: pogodny; **se•ren•i•ty** [sə'renətɪ] *s* **1.** spokój *m* **2.** pogoda *f*; ***the ~ of her face*** pogoda malująca się na jej twarzy

serf [sɜːf] *s* chłop *m* pańszczyźniany
ser•geant ['sɑːdʒənt] *s* sierżant *m*
se•ri•al ['sɪərɪəl] **I** *s* **1.** serial *m* **2.** powieść *f* w odcinkach **II** *adj* **1.** *killer*, *number*: seryjny **2.** *programme*: w odcinkach **3.** *port*: szeregowy; **se•ri•al•ize** ['sɪərɪəlaɪz] *v/t* **1.** nadawać 〈-dać〉 w odcinkach **2.** publikować 〈o-〉 w odcinkach; **'se•ri•al kill•er** *s* seryjny morderca *m*; **'se•ri•al num•ber** *s* numer *m* seryjny; **'se•ri•al port** *s INF* port *m* szeregowy
se•ries ['sɪəriːz] *pl series s* **1.** szereg *f*, seria *f*; ***a ~ of events*** szereg zdarzeń, seria zdarzeń **2.** pasmo *n* **3.** *television*: serial *m* **4.** cykl *m*
se•ri•ous ['sɪərɪəs] *adj* poważny; ***are you ~?*** mówisz poważnie?; **se•ri•ous•ly** ['sɪərɪəslɪ] *adv* **1.** poważnie; ***take s.th. ~*** potraktować coś poważnie **2.** naprawdę **3.** ale mówiąc poważnie; **se•ri•ous•ness** ['sɪərɪəsnɪs] *s* powaga *f*; ***in all ~*** z całą powagą, zupełnie poważnie
ser•mon ['sɜːmən] *s* kazanie *n*; **'ser•mon•ize** *v/i* prawić kazania
serpent ['sɜːpənt] *s* wąż *m*
ser•rat•ed [sɪ'reɪtɪd] *adj* ząbkowany
se•rum ['siːrəm] *s* surowica *f*
ser•vant ['sɜːvənt] *s* **1.** służący *m* **2.** urzędnik *m*; ***a civil ~*** urzędnik służby cywilnej
serve [sɜːv] **I** *v/t* **1.** służyć 〈po-〉; ***~ no useful purpose*** nie mieć żadnego praktycznego zastosowania; ***~ the interests of*** służyć interesom *G*; ***it ~s you right*** dobrze ci tak **2.** pracować dla *G* **3.** obsługiwać 〈-łużyć〉 **4.** podawać 〈-dać〉, serwować 〈za-〉 **5.** ***~ a prison sentence***, ***~ time*** odbywać karę więzienia, *infml* odsiadywać wyrok; ***he ~d two years in prison*** był dwa lata w więzieniu **6.** *form* doręczać 〈-czyć〉 **II** *v/i* **1.** służyć 〈po-〉 (**as** jako *N*) **2.** odbywać 〈-być〉 służbę **3.** *SPORT* serwować 〈za-〉 **III** *s SPORT* serw *m*; **serve up** *v/t* **1.** podawać 〈-dać〉 **2.** serwować 〈za-〉
serv•er ['sɜːvə] *s* **1.** *INF* serwer *m* **2.** *SPORT* serwujący *m* **3.** *Am* kelner *m* **4.** ministrant *m* **5.** łyżka *f* do nakładania
ser•vice ['sɜːvɪs] **I** *s* **1.** usługa *f*; ***goods and ~s*** towary i usługi; ***at your ~*** do usług **2.** obsługa *f*; ***customer ~*** obsługa klienta **3.** przysługa *f*; ***do s.o. a ~*** wyświadczyć komuś przysługę **4.** służba *f* **5.** praca *f* **6.** ***the ~s*** siły *pl* zbrojne **7.** eksploatacja *f*, użycie *n*; ***the computer gave us a very good ~*** ten komputer dobrze nam służył; ***be in ~*** być używanym; ***be taken out of ~*** zostać wycofanym z użycia; ***'out of ~'*** „nieczynny" **8.** *TECH* przegląd *m* **9.** *TECH* serwis *m* **10.** *REL* nabożeństwo *n* **11.** *bus*, *railway*: połączenie *n* **12.** *SPORT* serwis *m*, podanie *n* **13.** serwis *m*; ***a tea ~*** serwis do herbaty **14.** *form* doręczenie *n* **II** *v/t* **1.** *car*: dokonywać 〈-nać〉 przeglądu **2.** obsługiwać 〈-łużyć〉; **ser•vice•a•ble** ['sɜːvɪsəbl] *adj* **1.** nadający się do użytku **2.** sprawny
'ser•vice ar•e•a *s Br* stacja *f* benzynowa (przy autostradzie); **'ser•vice charge** *s* opłata *f* za obsługę; **'ser•vice in•dus•try** *s* sektor *m* usług, usługi *pl*; **'ser•vice•man** *pl -men s* żołnierz *m*; **'ser•vice pro•vid•er** *s* usługodawca *m*; **'ser•vice sec•tor** *s* sektor *m* usług; **'ser•vice sta•tion** *s* stacja *f* benzynowa
ser•vi•ette [sɜːvɪ'et] *s Br* serwetka *f*
ser•vile ['sɜːvaɪl] *adj* służalczy
serv•ing ['sɜːvɪŋ] *s food*: porcja *f*
ser•vi•tude ['sɜːvɪtjuːd] *s* niewola *f*
ses•a•me ['sesəmɪ] *s* sezam *m*; ***~ oil*** olej sezamowy
ses•sion ['seʃn] **I** *s* **1.** sesja *f* **2.** spotkanie *n* **3.** obrady *pl* **4.** *jury*: posiedzenie *n*; ***the court is in ~*** trwa rozprawa **II** *adj musician*: sesyjny
set [set] **I** (*set*; *set*) *v/t* **1.** ustawiać 〈-wić〉 **2.** umieszczać 〈umieścić〉 **3.** stawiać 〈postawić〉; ***the house is ~ on a hill*** dom stoi na wzgórzu **4.** *date*, *deadline*, *rules*: ustalać 〈-lić〉 **5.** ***~ s.o. free*** uwolnić kogoś; ***~ s.o. at ease*** uspokoić kogoś **6.** ***~ fire to s.th.***, ***~ s.th. on fire*** podpalić coś **7.** nastawiać 〈-wić〉; ***~ the alarm for 6 a.m.*** nastawić budzik na szóstą rano **8.** ***~ s.th. to music*** skomponować muzykę do czegoś **9.** ***~ the table*** nakryć do stołu **10.** *record*: ustanawiać 〈-nowić〉 **11.** *good example*: dawać 〈dać〉 **12.** *task*: zadawać 〈-dać〉 **13.** *hair*: układać 〈ułożyć〉 **14.** *bone*: nasta-

wiać ⟨-wić⟩ **15.** *text*: składać ⟨złożyć⟩ **16.** **~ *an exam*** ułożyć pytania na egzamin **17.** wysadzać ⟨-dzić⟩; ***a bracelet ~ with emeralds*** bransoletka wysadzana szmaragdami **II** (*set*; *set*) *v/i* **1.** (*concrete*) twardnieć ⟨s-⟩, tężeć ⟨s-⟩ **2.** (*glue*) wysychać ⟨-schnąć⟩ **3.** (*sun*, *moon*) zachodzić ⟨zajść⟩ **4.** (*bone*) zrastać ⟨zrosnąć⟩ się **III** *s* **1.** zestaw *m*; ***a chess ~*** szachy **2.** komplet *m*; ***a ~ of six chairs*** komplet sześciu krzeseł; ***a ~ of false teeth*** sztuczna szczęka **3.** zbiór *m* **4.** zespół *m* **5.** grupa *f* **6.** *FILM THEAT* dekoracje *pl* **7.** *FILM* plan *m* **8.** *SPORT* set *m* **9.** *hair*: modelowanie *n* **10.** odbiornik *m*; ***a TV ~*** telewizor, odbiornik telewizyjny **IV** *adj* **1.** określony **2.** ustalony **3.** stały **4.** ***interest rates are ~ to rise*** wszystko wskazuje na to, że stopy procentowe wzrosną **5.** *phrase*: utarty **6.** *ideas*: zdecydowany **7.** ***be ~ against*** być przeciwnym *D*; ***be ~ on doing s.th.*** bardzo chcieć coś zrobić; **set about** *v/i* **1.** zabierać ⟨-brać⟩ się do *G* **2.** przystępować ⟨-tąpić⟩ do *G* **3.** *Br dated* atakować ⟨za-⟩; **set against** *v/t* **1.** nastawiać ⟨-wić⟩ przeciwko *D* **2.** zestawiać ⟨-wić⟩; **~ *s.th.*** w porównaniu z czymś; **set apart** *v/t* **1.** wyróżniać ⟨-nić⟩ (***from*** wśród *G*) **2.** odróżniać ⟨-nić⟩ (***from*** od *G*); **set aside** *v/t* **1.** odkładać ⟨odłożyć⟩ **2.** przeznaczać ⟨-czyć⟩ **3.** *differences*: odkładać ⟨odłożyć⟩ na bok **4.** *decision*: uchylać ⟨-lić⟩; **set back** *v/t* **1.** opóźniać ⟨-nić⟩ **2.** ***the laptop will set you back over 1000 pounds*** *infml* jeśli kupisz tego laptopa, będziesz ponad 1000 funtów do tyłu **3.** ***a house set back from the road*** dom położony z dala od drogi; **set down** *v/t* **1.** *passengers*: *Br* wysadzać ⟨-dzić⟩ **2.** notować ⟨za-⟩ **3.** *rules*: ustalać ⟨-lić⟩; **set in** **I** *v/i* **1.** (*winter*) nastawać ⟨-tać⟩ **2.** ***the rain ~ for good*** rozpadało się na dobre **3.** (*infection*) wdawać ⟨wdać⟩ się **II** *v/t* (*in wall*) wpuszczać ⟨wpuścić⟩, wmurowywać ⟨-rować⟩; **set off** **I** *v/i* wyruszać ⟨-szyć⟩ **II** *v/t* **1.** *bomb*: odpalać ⟨-lić⟩, detonować ⟨z-⟩ **2.** *alarm*: uruchamiać ⟨-chomić⟩ **3.** *panic*: wywoływać ⟨-łać⟩ **4.** *colour*: uwydatniać ⟨-nić⟩, podkreślać ⟨-lić⟩ **5.** ***set s.o. off crying*** doprowadzić kogoś do płaczu; **set out** **I** *v/i* **1.** wyruszać ⟨-szyć⟩ **2.** **~ *to do s.th.*** wyznaczać ⟨-czyć⟩ sobie za cel zrobienie czegoś, postanowić coś zrobić **II** *v/t* **1.** wystawiać ⟨-wić⟩ **2.** przedstawiać ⟨-wić⟩; **set to** *v/t*: **~ *work*** *infml dated* zabrać się do pracy; **set up** **I** *v/t* **1.** *company*: zakładać ⟨założyć⟩ **2.** *commission*: tworzyć ⟨u-⟩ **3.** *stand, blockade*: ustawiać ⟨-wić⟩ **4.** *statue*: wznosić ⟨-nieść⟩ **5.** *meeting*: organizować ⟨z-⟩ **6.** *reaction*: wywoływać ⟨-łać⟩ **7.** stawiać ⟨postawić⟩ na nogi **8.** *infml* wrabiać ⟨wrobić⟩ **II** *v/i* rozpoczynać ⟨-cząć⟩ działalność gospodarczą

'set•back *s* **1.** komplikacja *f* **2.** przeszkoda *f* **3.** pogorszenie *n*; ***a ~ in s.o.'s health*** pogorszenie się czyjegoś stanu zdrowia; **'set de•sign•er** *s* scenograf *m*; **set 'point** *s SPORT* piłka *f* setowa; **'set square** *s Br* ekierka *f*

set•tee [se'tiː] *s Br* sofa *f*

'set the•o•ry *s MATH* teoria *f* zbiorów

set•ting ['setɪŋ] *s* **1.** sceneria *f* **2.** miejsce *n* **3.** otoczenie *n* **4.** *film*, *book*: miejsce *n* akcji **5.** *FILM Am* plan *m* **6.** *diamond*: oprawa *f* **7.** *table*: zastawa *f* **8.** *TECH* ustawienie *n*

set•tle ['setl] **I** *v/t* **1.** *conflict*: rozstrzygać ⟨-gnąć⟩ **2.** *matter*: załatwiać ⟨-wić⟩, porządkować ⟨z-⟩ **3.** ustalać ⟨-lić⟩; ***that ~s it! I'm not coming!*** w takim razie ja nie jadę! **4.** zasiedlać ⟨-lić⟩ **5.** układać ⟨ułożyć⟩ wygodnie **6.** *nerves*: uspokajać ⟨-koić⟩ **7.** *bills*: regulować ⟨u-⟩ **II** *v/i* **1.** dochodzić ⟨dojść⟩ do porozumienia; **~ *out of court*** zawrzeć ugodę pozasądową **2.** osiedlać ⟨-lić⟩ się **3.** układać ⟨ułożyć⟩ się wygodnie, usadawiać ⟨-dowić⟩ się wygodnie **4.** uspokajać ⟨-koić⟩ się **5.** (*dust*) osiadać ⟨osiąść⟩; **settle back** *v/i* usadawiać ⟨-dowić⟩ się wygodnie; **settle down** **I** *v/i* **1.** usadawiać ⟨-dowić⟩ się **2.** ustatkować się **II** *v/t* uspokajać ⟨-koić⟩; **settle for** *v/t* zadowalać ⟨-wolić⟩ się; **settle in** *v/i* **1.** zadomawiać ⟨-mowić⟩ się **2.** adoptować ⟨za-⟩ się (do nowych warunków); **settle on** **I** *v/i* decydować ⟨z-⟩ się na *A* **II** *v/t* zapisywać ⟨-sać⟩ w testamencie (***s.th. on*** coś *D*); **settle up**

S

I *v/t bills*: regulować ⟨u-⟩ II *v/i* rozliczać ⟨-czyć⟩ się
set•tled ['setld] *adj* **1.** *way of life*: uregulowany **2.** ustalony **3.** stabilny **4.** stały
set•tle•ment ['setlmənt] *s* **1.** porozumienie *n*; ***reach a ~*** osiągnąć porozumienie **2.** ugoda *f* **3.** *dispute*: rozstrzygnięcie *n* **4.** *debt*: spłata *f* **5.** *bill*: uregulowanie *n* **6.** osada *f* **7.** zasiedlanie *n* **8.** umowa *f*
set•tler ['setlə] *s* osadnik *m*
'set-to *no pl s Br infml* zgrzyt *m*, sprzeczka *f*; **'set-up** *s* **1.** *infml* sytuacja *f* **2.** ***She didn't do it. It was a ~*** *infml* Nie zrobiła tego – została wrobiona.
sev•en ['sevn] I *num* siedem, siedmiu, siedmioro II *s* siódemka *f*; **sev•en•fold** ['sevnfəʊld] I *adj* siedmiokrotny II *adv* siedmiokrotnie
sev•en•teen [sevn'ti:n] I *num* siedemnaście II *s* siedemnastka *f*; **sev•en•teenth** [sevn'ti:nθ] *adj* siedemnasty
sev•enth ['sevnθ] *adj* siódmy; ***the ~ of May*** siódmy maja
sev•en•ti•eth ['sevntɪəθ] *adj* siedemdziesiąty
'sev•en-time *adj* siedmiokrotny
sev•en•ty ['sevntɪ] I *num* siedemdziesiąt II *s* **1.** siedemdziesiątka *f* **2.** ***the seventies*** lata *pl* siedemdziesiąte; ***be in one's seventies*** być po siedemdziesiątce
sev•er ['sevə] *v/t* **1.** *relations*: zrywać ⟨zerwać⟩ **2.** przecinać ⟨-ciąć⟩ **3.** urywać ⟨-rwać⟩; ***her hand was ~ed from her arm*** urwało jej rękę **4.** przerywać ⟨-rwać⟩
sev•e•ral ['sevrəl] *adj* **1.** kilka; ***he's written ~ books*** napisał kilka książek; ***~ of us*** kilkoro z nas; ***~ times*** kilka razy **2.** parę **3.** szereg *m*
sev•er•ance ['sevərəns] *s of relations*: zerwanie *n*; **sev•er•ance pay** *s* odprawa *f*
se•vere [sɪ'vɪə] *adj* **1.** *damage*: poważny **2.** *punishment*, *person*, *style*: surowy **3.** *period*: trudny, ciężki **4.** *pain*: ostry; **se•vere•ly** [sɪ'vɪəlɪ] *adv* **1.** poważnie **2.** mocno **3.** surowo; ***anyone breaking the law will be ~ punished*** każdy, kto złamie prawo, zostanie surowo ukarany; **se•ver•i•ty** [sɪ'verətɪ] *s* **1.** powaga *f* **2.** waga *f* **3.** surowość *f*
sew [səʊ] (*sewed*; *sewn*/*sewed*) *v/t* **1.** szyć ⟨u-⟩ **2.** przyszywać ⟨-szyć⟩ (**on** do *G*) **3.** ***~ s.th. together*** zszywać ⟨-szyć⟩; **sew on** *v/t* przyszywać ⟨-szyć⟩; **sew up** *v/t* **1.** zszywać ⟨-szyć⟩ **2.** *deal*: *infml* ubijać ⟨-bić⟩; ***have the win sewn up*** *fig* mieć wygraną w kieszeni
sew•age ['su:ɪdʒ] *s* ścieki *pl*; **'sew•age plant** *s Am* oczyszczalnia *f* ścieków
sew•er ['su:ə] *s* **1.** kanał *m* (ściekowy) **2.** ściek *m*; **sew•er•age** ['su:ərɪdʒ] *s* kanalizacja *f*, system *m* kanalizacyjny
sew•ing ['səʊɪŋ] *s* szycie *n*; **'sew•ing ma•chine** *s* maszyna *f* do szycia
sewn [səʊn] *Past Participle* → ***sew***
sex [seks] *s* **1.** płeć *f*; ***the fair ~*** płeć piękna; ***the weaker ~*** słaba płeć; ***~ discrimination*** dyskryminacja ze względu na płeć **2.** seks *m*; ***have ~ with*** **a)** współżyć z *I* **b)** odbyć stosunek z *I* **c)** *infml* pójść do łóżka z *I*; **'sex ap•peal** *s* seksapil *m*; **'sex change** *s* zmiana *f* płci; **'sex crime** *s* przestępstwo *n* na tle seksualnym; **sex edu•'ca•tion** *s* edukacja *f* seksualna
sex•ism ['seksɪzəm] *s* seksizm *m*; **sex•ist** ['seksɪst] I *s* seksista *m* II *adj* seksistowski
'sex life *s* życie *n* seksualne; **'sex ma•ni•ac** *s* maniak *m* seksualny; **'sex ob•ject** *s* obiekt *m* seksualny; **'sex or•gan** *s* narząd *m* płciowy; **'sex shop** *s* sex shop *m*; **'sex sym•bol** *s* symbol *m* seksu
sex•tant ['sekstənt] *s* sekstans *m*
'sex tour•ism *s* turystyka *f* seksualna
sex•tu•plets [seks'tu:pləts] *pl* sześcioraczki *pl*
sex•u•al ['sekʃʊəl] *adj* **1.** seksualny **2.** płciowy; **sex•u•al ha•'rass•ment** *s* molestowanie *n* seksualne; **sex•u•al 'in•ter•course** *s* stosunek *m* płciowy
sex•u•al•ity [sekʃʊ'ælətɪ] *s* seksualność *f*
sex•u•al•ly ['sekʃəlɪ] *adv* **1.** seksualnie **2.** płciowo
sex•y ['seksɪ] *adj* seksowny
SF [es'ef] *abbr* (=**science fiction**) SF
shab•bi•ly ['ʃæbɪlɪ] *adv dressed*: nędznie; **shab•by** ['ʃæbɪ] *adj* **1.** wytarty

2. sfatygowany 3. obdarty 4. zaniedbany 5. *look*: nędzny 6. *behaviour*: podły

shack [ʃæk] **I** *s* 1. buda *f* 2. chałupa *f* **II** *v/i* **~ up with s.o.** *infml* żyć z kimś na kocią łapę

shack•les ['ʃæklz] *pl* 1. kajdany *pl* 2. *fig* pęta *f*

shade [ʃeɪd] **I** *s* 1. cień *m*; **in the ~** w cieniu; **put s.th. in the ~** *fig* usunąć coś w cień 2. abażur *m* 3. *Am* roleta *f* 4. odcień *m* 5. niuans *m*; **~s of meaning** niuanse znaczeniowe 6. **a ~ too short** odrobinę za krótki 7. **~s** *infml* okulary *pl* słoneczne **II** *v/t* 1. ocieniać ⟨-nić⟩ 2. osłaniać ⟨-łonić⟩ od słońca

shad•ow ['ʃædəʊ] **I** *s* cień *m*; **cast a ~ on** rzucać cień na *A*; **beyond a ~ of doubt** bez cienia wątpliwości; **be a ~ of one's former self** być cieniem samego siebie; **be scared of one's own ~** bać się własnego cienia; **have ~s under one's eyes** mieć cienie pod oczami **II** *v/t* 1. śledzić 2. rzucać ⟨-cić⟩ cień na *A*; **shad•ow 'cab•i•net** *s* POLIT gabinet *m* cieni; **shad•ow•y** ['ʃædəʊɪ] *adj* 1. *corridor*: ciemny 2. *figure*: niewyraźny 3. tajemniczy

shad•y ['ʃeɪdɪ] *adj* 1. cienisty 2. zacieniony 3. dający cień 4. *infml* podejrzany

shaft [ʃɑːft] *s* 1. *lift*, *mine*: szyb *m* 2. *hammer*: trzonek *m* 3. *arrow*: drzewce *m* 4. TECH wał *m* 5. *light*: snop *m* 6. dyszel *m*

shag•gy ['ʃægɪ] *adj* 1. kudłaty 2. zmierzwiony 3. potargany

shake [ʃeɪk] **I** (*shook*; *shaken*) *v/t* 1. trząść ⟨za-⟩ 2. potrząsać ⟨-snąć⟩; **~ one's head** potrząsnąć głową, pokręcić głową; **~ hands with s.o.** podać komuś rękę, uścisnąć czyjąś dłoń 3. wstrząsać ⟨-snąć⟩; **~ before use** przed użyciem wstrząsnąć; **~ one's fist at s.o.** grozić komuś pięścią 4. chwiać ⟨za-⟩; **~ s.o.'s faith** zachwiać czyjąś wiarą 5. pozbywać ⟨-być⟩ się 6. *cocktails*: mieszać ⟨z-⟩ **II** (*shook*; *shaken*) *v/i* 1. trząść ⟨za-⟩ się; **~ with fear** trząść się ze strachu 2. drżeć ⟨za-⟩; **~ like a leaf** drżeć jak osika **III** *s* 1. **give s.o. a ~** potrząsnąć kimś; **give a bottle a ~** wstrząsnąć butelką; **with a ~ of one's head** kręcąc głową; **in two ~s** *infml* migiem 2. koktajl *m* (mleczny), shake *m*; **shake down I** *v/t Am infml* 1. przeszukiwać ⟨-kać⟩ 2. *money*: wymuszać ⟨-musić⟩ **II** *v/i infml* wdrażać ⟨-rożyć⟩ się; **shake off** *v/t* 1. *pursuer*: gubić ⟨z-⟩ 2. strząsać ⟨-snąć⟩ 3. pozbywać ⟨-być⟩ się; **shake out** *v/t* trzepać ⟨wy-⟩; **shake up** *v/t* 1. wstrząsać ⟨-snąć⟩ 2. zaskakiwać ⟨-skoczyć⟩ 3. reorganizować ⟨z-⟩

'shake•down *s Am infml* 1. wymuszenie *n* pieniędzy 2. przeszukanie *n*; **give s.o. a ~** przeszukać kogoś 3. rewizja *f*

shak•en ['ʃeɪkən] *Past Participle* → **shake**

'shake•out *s* 1. kryzys *m* 2. → **shake-up**

shak•er ['ʃeɪkə] *s* 1. (*for cocktails*) shaker *m* 2. **a salt ~** solniczka

'shake-up *s* 1. reorganizacja *f* 2. restrukturyzacja *f*

'shak•y ['ʃeɪkɪ] *adj* 1. trzęsący się 2. drżący 3. chwiejny; **be ~ on one's feet** chwiać się na nogach 4. niepewny; **on ~ ground** *fig* na niepewnym gruncie 5. *memories*: mglisty

shale [ʃeɪl] *s* łupek *m*

shall [ʃæl] *v aux* 1. (*future*) **I ~ come** *Br* przyjdę; **she shan't be gone long** *Br* niedługo wróci 2. (*suggestion*) **shall I send you this book?** czy mam ci wysłać tę książkę? 3. (*asking for advice*) **~ I take the job?** czy mam wziąć tę pracę 4. (*command*) **passengers ~ remain in their seats** pasażerowie proszeni są o pozostanie na miejscach

shal•lot [ʃə'lɒt] *s* szalotka *f*

shal•low ['ʃæləʊ] **I** *adj* 1. płytki 2. powierzchowny **II** *s* **the ~s** płycizna

sham [ʃæm] **I** *s* 1. **the figures are a ~** te dane są fałszywe 2. **the election was a ~** wybory były sfałszowane 3. hipokryzja *f* 4. oszust *m* **II** *adj* 1. pozorowany 2. udawany 3. fikcyjny **III** *v/t* 1. udawać ⟨-dać⟩; **he's ~ming** on udaje 2. pozorować

sha•man ['ʃeɪmən] *s* szaman *m*

sham•bles ['ʃæmblz] *s infml* 1. bałagan *m* 2. *infml* bajzel *m*, burdel *m* 3. zamieszanie *n*

sham•bol•ic [ʃæm'bɒlik] *adj Br infml* źle zorganizowany

shame [ʃeım] **I** *s* **1.** wstyd *m*; **~ *on you!*** wstydziłbyś się!; ***she felt no ~*** nie było jej wstyd; ***bring ~ on one's family*** przynosić wstyd rodzinie; ***what a ~!*** ale wstyd! **2. *what a ~!*** jaka szkoda!; ***it's a ~ you couldn't come*** szkoda, że nie mogłeś przyjść **II** *v/t* **1.** zawstydzać ⟨-dzić⟩ **2.** przynosić ⟨-nieść⟩ wstyd

shame•faced ['ʃeımfeıst] *adj* zawstydzony

shame•ful ['ʃeımfəl] *adj* **1.** karygodny **2.** *episode*: wstydliwy **3.** żenujący; **shame•ful•ly** ['ʃeımfəlı] *adv* **1.** karygodnie **2.** żenująco

shame•less ['ʃeımlıs] *adj* bezwstydny; **shame•less•ly** ['ʃeımlıslı] *adv* bezwstydnie

sham•poo [ʃæm'puː] **I** *s* **1.** szampon *m* **2.** mycie *n* (szamponem) **II** *v/t* myć ⟨u-⟩ (szamponem)

sham•rock ['ʃæmrɒk] *s* (*emblem*) trójlistna koniczynka *f*

shan•dy ['ʃændı] *s* piwo *n* z lemoniadą

shank [ʃæŋk] *s* **1.** *knife*: trzonek *m* **2.** *screw*: trzpień *m* **3.** *golf club*: rączka *f* **4.** ANAT podudzie *n*, goleń *f* **5.** COOK pręga *f* tylna

shan't [ʃɑːnt] *contracted form* → ***shall not***

shan•ty[1] ['ʃæntı] *s* MUS szanta *f*

shan•ty[2] [~] *s* slums *m*; **shan•ty town** *s* dzielnica *f* slumsów, slumsy *pl*

shape [ʃeıp] **I** *s* **1.** kształt *m*; ***in the ~ of*** w kształcie *G*; ***triangular in ~*** w kształcie trójkąta; ***s.th. comes in all ~s and sizes*** *infml* czegoś jest do wyboru, do koloru; ***take ~*** *fig* nabierać kształtów **2.** stan *m* **3.** forma *f*, kondycja *f*; ***keep in ~*** trzymać formę; ***she is in good ~ for her age*** dobrze się trzyma, jak na swój wiek **II** *v/t* **1.** kształtować ⟨u-⟩; ***~ the party policy*** kształtować politykę partii **2.** formować ⟨u-⟩; ***~ the dough into a ball*** uformować ciasto w kulę; **shape up** *v/i* **1.** poprawiać ⟨-wić⟩ się **2.** *fig* nabierać ⟨-brać⟩ rumieńców

shaped *adj*: ***~ like*** w kształcie *G*; ***almond-~ eyes*** oczy w kształcie migdałów

shape•less ['ʃeıplıs] *adj* **1.** bezkształtny **2.** nieforemny

shape•ly ['ʃeıplı] *adj* **1.** kształtny **2.** zgrabny

shard [ʃɑːd] *s* skorupa *f*

share [ʃeə] **I** *s* **1.** udział *m*; ***a ~ of the market*** udział w rynku **2.** część *f*; ***we did our ~*** zrobiliśmy naszą część **3.** ECON akcja *f* **4.** ECON udział *m* **II** *v/t* **1.** dzielić; ***~ a room with*** dzielić pokój z *I*; ***~ a house with*** mieszkać w jednym domu z *I*, mieszkać pod jednym dachem z *I* **2.** dzielić ⟨po-⟩ się; ***~ chocolate with other kids*** podzielić się czekoladą z innymi dziećmi **3.** podzielać ⟨-lić⟩; ***we ~ a common interest in music*** oboje interesujemy się muzyką **III** *v/i* dzielić ⟨po-⟩ się; **share in** *v/t* **1.** ***~ the housework*** wykonywać część prac domowych **2.** mieć swój udział w *L*; **share out** *v/t* rozdzielać ⟨-lić⟩ (***between*** między *A*)

'share•crop•per *s Am* dzierżawca *m* gruntu

shared [ʃeəd] *adj* **1.** wspólny **2.** *values*: ten sam

'share•hold•er *s* **1.** akcjonariusz *m* **2.** udziałowiec *m*; **'share index** *s* ECON indeks *m* giełdowy

'share-out *s Br* rozdział *m*

'share•ware *s* INF shareware *m*, oprogramowanie *n* typu shareware

shark [ʃɑːk] *s* rekin *m*

sharp [ʃɑːp] **I** *adj* **1.** ostry **2.** *fall*: nagły, gwałtowny **3.** *tongue*: cięty **4.** *person*: bystry **5.** *taste*: wyrazisty, gorzki **6.** *clothes*: modny **7.** *note*: podwyższony o pół tonu, z krzyżykiem; ***in C ~ minor*** w tonacji cis moll **II** *s* MUS krzyżyk *m* **III** *adv* ***at seven o'clock ~*** punktualnie o siódmej, *infml* punkt o siódmej; **sharp•en** ['ʃɑːpn] **I** *v/t* **1.** ostrzyć ⟨na-⟩ **2.** temperować ⟨za-⟩ **3.** *appetite*: zaostrzać ⟨-rzyć⟩ **4.** *senses*: wyostrzać ⟨-rzyć⟩ **5.** *skills*: podnosić ⟨-nieść⟩, udoskonalać ⟨-lić⟩ **II** *v/i* **1.** (*skills*) wzrastać ⟨-rosnąć⟩ **2.** (*difference*) powiększać ⟨-szyć⟩ się **3.** (*senses*) wyostrzać ⟨-rzyć⟩ się; **'sharp•en•er** ['ʃɑːpnə] *s* **1.** temperówka *f* **2.** ostrzarka *f*; **sharp•ly** ['ʃɑːplı] *adv* **1.** ostro **2.** gwałtownie, nagle; **sharp•ness** ['ʃɑːpnıs] *s* **1.** ostrość *f* **2.** bystrość *f*

sharp 'prac•tice *s* cwaniactwo *n*; **sharp•shoot•er** ['ʃɑːpʃuːtə] *s* strzelec *m* wyborowy

shat [ʃæt] *Past Simple and Past Participle* → **shit**

shat•ter ['ʃætə] **I** *v/i* roztrzaskiwać ⟨-kać⟩ się; ***my whole world ~ed into a million pieces*** cały mój świat legł w gruzach **II** *v/t* **1.** rozbijać ⟨-bić⟩ **2.** roztrzaskiwać ⟨-kać⟩ **3.** *life*: rujnować ⟨z-⟩ **4.** *dreams*: rozwiewać ⟨-zwiać⟩ **5.** *illusion*: pozbawiać ⟨-wić⟩ **6.** *person*: wstrząsać ⟨-snąć⟩; **shat•tered** ['ʃætəd] *adj* **1.** *person*: zdruzgotany, wstrząśnięty **2.** *dreams*: rozwiany **3.** *illusion*: stracony **4.** *Br infml* wykończony; **shat•ter•ing** ['ʃætərɪŋ] *adj* **1.** *news*: wstrząsający **2.** *blow*: straszny **3.** *noise*: ogłuszający; **'shat•ter•proof** *adj glass*: bezodpryskowy, bezpieczny

shave [ʃeɪv] **I** *v/i* golić ⟨o-⟩ się **II** *v/t* golić ⟨o-⟩; **shave off** *v/t beard*: golić ⟨z-⟩

shav•en ['ʃeɪvn] *adj* **1.** ogolony **2.** wygolony; **shav•er** ['ʃeɪvə] *s* maszynka *f* do golenia, golarka *f*; **shav•ing brush** ['ʃeɪvɪŋbrʌʃ] *s* pędzel *m* do golenia; **shav•ing foam** *s* pianka *f* do golenia; **shav•ing soap** *s* mydło *n* do golenia

shawl [ʃɔːl] *s* **1.** szal *m* **2.** chusta *f*

she [ʃiː] **I** *pron* ona **II** *s* ***a ~-bear*** niedźwiedzica; ***a ~-wolf*** wilczyca

sheaf [ʃiːf] *pl sheaves* [ʃiːvz] *s* **1.** *corn*: snopek *m*, snop *m* **2.** *paper*: plik *m*

shear [ʃɪə] (*scheared*; *shorn*) *v/t sheep*: strzyc ⟨o-⟩; **shear off** *v/i* urywać ⟨-rwać⟩ się

shears [ʃɪəz] *pl* nożyce *pl* (ogrodnicze)

sheath [ʃiːθ] *s* **1.** (*of knife*, *sword*) pochwa *f* **2.** osłona *f* **3.** *Br* prezerwatywa *f*

sheathe [ʃiːð] *v/t* **1.** *knife*, *sword*: chować ⟨s-⟩ do pochwy **2.** ***~d in*** pokryty *I*

S

'sheath knife *s* nóż *m* fiński, *infml* finka *f*

sheaves [ʃiːvz] *pl* → **sheaf**

she•bang [ʃɪ'bæŋ] *s*: ***the whole ~*** **a)** to wszystko **b)** cała ta sprawa

she'd [ʃiːd] *contracted form* → ***she would***, ***she had***

shed[1] [ʃed] (*shed*; *shed*) *v/t* **1.** *light*: rzucać ⟨-cić⟩ **2.** *leaves*, *skin*: zrzucać ⟨-cić⟩ **3.** pozbywać ⟨-być⟩ się **4.** likwidować ⟨z-⟩; ***the company will ~ 200 jobs*** firma zlikwiduje 200 miejsc pracy **5.** *tears*: ronić ⟨u-⟩ **6.** *blood*: przelewać ⟨-lać⟩

shed[2] [~] *s* **1.** szopa *f* **2.** altana *f* **3.** hangar *m*

sheen [ʃiːn] *s* połysk *m*

sheep [ʃiːp] *pl sheep* owca *f*; **'sheep-dog** *s* pies *m* pasterski; **sheep-herd-er** ['ʃiːphɜːdə] *s Am* pasterz *m*

sheep•ish ['ʃiːpɪʃ] *adj* **1.** zawstydzony **2.** zażenowany

'sheep•skin *s* **1.** owcza skóra *f* **2.** kożuch *m*

sheer [ʃɪə] **I** *adj* **1.** czysty; ***a ~ delight*** czysta przyjemność; ***we were impressed by the ~ size of the cathedral*** sam rozmiar katedry zrobił na nas wrażenie **2.** urwisty **3.** przezroczysty **II** *adv* bardzo stromo

sheet [ʃiːt] *s* **1.** prześcieradło *n* **2.** ***~s*** pościel *m*; ***have you changed the ~s?*** czy zmieniłeś pościel? **3.** *paper*: kartka *f* **4.** *steel*, *paper*: arkusz *m* **5.** blacha *f*; ***~ metal*** blacha karoseryjna **6.** *glass*, *ice*: tafla *f*; **'sheet lightning** *s* błyskawica *f* rozświetlająca całe niebo; **'sheet mu•sic** *s* MUS nuty *pl*

sheikh [ʃeɪk] *s* szejk *m*; **'sheikh•dom** ['ʃeɪkdəm] *s* szejkanat *m*

shelf [ʃelf] *pl shelves* [ʃelvz] *s* półka *f*; **'shelf life** *s* **1.** okres *m* przechowywania **2.** okres *m* trwałości

shell [ʃel] **I** *s* **1.** muszla *f* **2.** muszelka *f* **3.** *eggs*: skorupka *f* **4.** *nut*: łupina *f* **5.** pocisk *m* **6.** *building*: szkielet *m* **7.** *fig* skorupa *f*; ***come out of one's ~*** **a)** otworzyć się **b)** wyjść ze swojej skorupy **II** *v/t* **1.** ostrzeliwać ⟨-lać⟩ **2.** *nuts*, *peas*: łuskać **3.** obierać ⟨-brać⟩; **shell out** *v/t infml* bulić ⟨wy-⟩ (**for** za *A*)

she'll [ʃiːl] *contracted form* → ***she will***

'shell•fire *s* ostrzał *m*; **'shell•fish** *pl* **1.** skorupiaki *pl* **2.** COOK owoce *pl* morza; **'shell shock** *s* nerwica *f* frontowa; **'shell shocked** *adj* cierpiący na nerwicę frontową; **'shell suit** *s Br* dres *m* ortalionowy

shel•ter ['ʃeltə] **I** *s* **1.** dach *m* nad głową **2.** schronienie *n*; ***take ~ from the rain*** schronić się przed deszczem **3.** schronisko *n* **4.** schron *m* **5.** osłona *f* **II** *v/t* **1.** osłaniać ⟨-łonić⟩ **2.** *refugee*: ukrywać ⟨-ryć⟩ **3.** dawać ⟨dać⟩ schronienie **III** *v/i* chronić ⟨s-⟩ się; **shel•tered** [ˈʃeltəd] *adj* **1.** osłonięty **2.** *fig* pod kloszem

shelve [ʃelv] **I** *v/t fig* odkładać ⟨odłożyć⟩ do szuflady **II** *v/i* (*beach*) opadać ⟨opaść⟩

shelves [ʃelvz] *pl* → ***shelf***

shelv•ing [ˈʃelvɪŋ] *s* **1.** półki *pl* **2.** regały *pl*

shep•herd [ˈʃepəd] **I** *s* pasterz *m* **II** *v/t* prowadzić ⟨za-⟩; **shep•herd's pie** *s Br* zapiekanka *f* z mielonego mięsa i ziemniaków

sher•iff [ˈʃerɪf] *s* szeryf *m*

sher•ry [ˈʃerɪ] *s* sherry *n*

she's [ʃiːz] *contracted form* → **she is; she has**

shield [ʃiːld] **I** *s* **1.** tarcza *f*; ***a human ~*** żywa tarcza **2.** tarcza *f* herbowa **3.** *of indifference*: maska *f* **4.** *SPORT* trofeum *m* **5.** *Am* odznaka *f* policyjna **6.** *TECH* osłona *f* **7.** *TECH* ekran *m* ochronny **III** *v/t* osłaniać ⟨-łonić⟩ (***from*** przed *I*)

shift [ʃɪft] **I** *v/t* **1.** przenosić ⟨-nieść⟩ **2.** przesuwać ⟨-sunąć⟩ **3.** *blame*: zrzucać ⟨-cić⟩ (***onto*** na *A*) **4.** *opinion*: zmieniać ⟨-nić⟩ **5.** *stains*: usuwać ⟨usunąć⟩ **II** *v/i* **1.** przesuwać ⟨-sunąć⟩ się **2.** (*opinion*) zmieniać ⟨-nić⟩ się **3.** ***~ into second gear*** *Am* wrzucić dwójkę **III** *s* **1.** zmiana *f*; ***a ~ in policy*** zmiana polityki; ***day ~*** dzienna zmiana **2.** przesunięcie *n* **3.** przejście *n* **4.** *INF* klawisz *m* Shift; ˈ**shift work** *s* praca *f* zmianowa; ˈ**shift work•er** *s* pracownik *m* zmianowy; **shift•y** [ˈʃɪftɪ] *adj infml* niebudzący zaufania; ***he has ~ eyes*** źle mu z oczu patrzy

shil•ly-shal•ly [ˈʃɪlɪʃælɪ] *v/i infml* wahać się; ***stop ~ing!*** zdecyduj się!

shim•mer [ˈʃɪmə] **I** *v/i* **1.** mienić się **2.** lśnić **3.** (*air*) drżeć **II** *s* **1.** blask *m* **2.** połyskiwanie *n*

shin [ʃɪn] **I** *s ANAT* goleń *f* **II** *v/i* ***~ up s.th.*** *Br infml* wspinać się po czymś; ***~ down s.th.*** *Br infml* schodzić w dół po czymś; ˈ**shin•bone** *s ANAT* piszczel *f*

shine[1] [ʃaɪn] **I** (*shone*; *shone*) *v/i* **1.** świecić; ***the sun is shining*** świeci słońce **2.** *surface*: błyszczeć; ***her eyes shone with excitement*** jej oczy błyszczały z podniecenia **II** (*shone*; *shone*) *v/t* świecić ⟨za-⟩ **III** *s* **1.** blask *m*; ***take a ~ to s.o.*** *infml* od razu kogoś polubić **2.** połysk *m*

shine[2] [~] *v/t* **1.** polerować ⟨wy-⟩ **2.** *infml shoes*: glansować ⟨wy-⟩

shin•gle [ˈʃɪŋgl] *s* **1.** kamyki *pl* **2.** gont *m* **3.** *Am* tabliczka *f*

shin•gles [ˈʃɪŋglz] *s MED* półpasiec *m*

shin•gly [ˈʃɪŋglɪ] *adj beach*: kamienisty

shin•y [ˈʃaɪnɪ] *adj* **1.** błyszczący **2.** lśniący **3.** pełen blasku

ship [ʃɪp] **I** *s* statek *m*; ***by ~*** statkiem, drogą morską; ***on board ~*** na pokładzie **II** *v/t* **1.** wysyłać ⟨-słać⟩ **2.** przewozić ⟨-wieźć⟩ **3.** przewozić ⟨-wieźć⟩ drogą morską; ˈ**ship•build•er** *s* **1.** stocznia *f* **2.** budowniczy *m* okrętów **3.** stoczniowiec *m*; ˈ**ship•build•ing** *s* budownictwo *n* okrętowe

ship•ment [ˈʃɪpmənt] *s* **1.** wysyłka *f* **2.** transport *m* **3.** przesyłka *f*

ˈ**ship•own•er** *s* armator *m*

ship•per [ˈʃɪpə] *s* spedytor *m*; **shipping** [ˈʃɪpɪŋ] *s* **1.** spedycja *f* **2.** transport *m* **3.** koszty *pl* transportu; ˈ**shipping com•pa•ny** *s* **1.** przedsiębiorstwo *n* żeglugowe **2.** firma *f* spedycyjna; **ship•ping costs** *pl* koszty *pl* transportu; ˈ**ship•ping fore•cast** *s*: ***a ~ for the Baltic Sea*** prognoza pogody dla Bałtyku; ˈ**ship•ping lane** *s* szlak *m* żeglugowy

ship•ˈshape *adj*: ***keep one's room ~*** utrzymywać swój pokój w idealnym porządku

ˈ**ship•wreck** **I** *s* **1.** wrak *m* (statku) **2.** katastrofa *f* (morska) **II** *v/t* ***be ~ed*** rozbić się; ˈ**ship•yard** *s* stocznia *f*

shirk [ʃɜːk] *v/i* **1.** uchylać ⟨-lić⟩ się (***from*** od *G*) **2.** *infml* migać ⟨wy-⟩ się (***from*** od *G*) **3.** *infml* obijać się; **shirk•er** [ˈʃɜːkə] *s* **1.** *infml* obibok *m* **2.** ***be a ~*** uchylać się od obowiązków

shirt [ʃɜːt] *s* koszula *f*; ***keep your ~ on*** *infml* nie denerwuj się

shirt•y [ˈʃɜːtɪ] *adj Br infml* wkurzony (***with*** na *A*)

shit [ʃɪt] *vulg* **I** *s* **1.** gówno *n*; ***have a ~*** wysrać się; ***talk ~*** pieprzyć; ***have the ~s*** mieć sraczkę; ***be in deep ~*** siedzieć po uszy w gównie; ***I don't give a ~ about it*** mam to w dupie, gówno mnie to obchodzi **2.** dupek *m* **II** *interj*

S

cholera! **III** (*shat*; *shat*) *v/i* srać **IV** (*shat*; *shat*) *v/t* **~ oneself a)** wysrać się, obsrywać ⟨-rać⟩ się **b)** *fig* zrobić w gacie ze strachu

shit•ty [ˈʃɪtɪ] *adj vulg* gówniany

shiv•er [ˈʃɪvə] **I** *v/i* **1.** drżeć ⟨za-⟩; **~ *with cold*** drżeć z zimna **2.** trząść ⟨za-⟩ się **II** *s* **1.** drżenie *n* **2. ~s** dreszcze

shoal [ʃəʊl] *s* ławica *f*

shock[1] [ʃɒk] **I** *s* **1.** szok *m*; ***in (a state of) ~*** w szoku; ***the news came as a ~ to us*** ta wiadomość była dla nas szokiem **2.** wstrząs *m* **3.** wstrząsy *pl* **4.** porażenie *n* prądem; ***she got a ~*** poraził ją prąd **II** *v/t* szokować ⟨za-⟩

shock[2] [~] *s*: ***a ~ of hair*** gęsta czupryna

shock ab•sorb•er [ˈʃɒkəbsɔːbə] *s* amortyzator *m*

shock•ing [ˈʃɒkɪŋ] *adj* **1.** szokujący **2.** *infml* fatalny; **shock•ing•ly** [ˈʃɒkɪŋlɪ] *adv* **1.** szokująco **2.** *infml* fatalnie; **shock•ing pink I** *adj* jaskraworóżowy **II** *s* jaskrawy róż *m*; ˈ**shock•proof** *s* odporny na wstrząsy, wstrząsoodporny; ˈ**shock wave** *s* fala *f* uderzeniowa

shod [ʃɒd] **I** *v Past Simple and Past Participle* → ***shoe II*** **II** *adj* **1.** obuty; ***she was ~ in black boots*** na nogach miała czarne kozaczki **2.** podkuty

shod•dy [ˈʃɒdɪ] *adj* **1.** *product*: tandetny **2.** *service*, *behaviour*: zły **3.** *work*: niedbały

shoe [ʃuː] **I** *s* **1.** but *m*; ***if I were in your ~s*** gdybym był na twoim miejscu; ***put oneself in s.o.'s ~s*** postawić się na czyimś miejscu **2.** podkowa *f* **II** (*shod*; *shod*) *v/t* podkuwać ⟨-kuć⟩; ˈ**shoebox** *s* pudełko *n* do butów; ˈ**shoehorn I** *s* łyżka *f* do butów **II** *v/t* **1.** upakowywać ⟨-kować⟩ **2.** *infml* wciskać ⟨-snąć⟩; ˈ**shoelace** *s* sznurówka *f*, sznurowadło *n*; ˈ**shoe•mak•er** *s* szewc *m*; ˈ**shoe•shine boy** *s* pucybut *m*; ˈ**shoe•store** *s* sklep *m* z butami, sklep *m* obuwniczy; ˈ**shoe•string** *s*: ***on a ~*** *infml* małym kosztem, za małe pieniądze; ***live on a ~*** *infml* ledwo wiązać koniec z końcem

shone [ʃɒn] *Past Simple and Past Participle* → ***shine***

shoo [ʃuː] **I** *v/t* **1.** wyganiać ⟨-gonić⟩ **2.** przeganiać ⟨-gonić⟩ **II** *interj* sio!

shook [ʃʊk] *Past Simple* → ***shake***

shoot [ʃuːt] **I** (*shot*; *shot*) *v/i* strzelać ⟨-lić⟩ (**at** do *G*); **~!** *Am infml* wal śmiało! **II** (*shot*; *shot*) *v/t* **1.** postrzelić **2.** zastrzelić; ***he was shot dead*** został zastrzelony **3.** *bullet*: wystrzelić **4.** rozstrzeliwać ⟨-lać⟩ **5.** polować ⟨za-⟩ na *A* **6.** *film*: kręcić ⟨na-⟩ **7.** *look*: rzucać ⟨-cić⟩ **III** *s* **1.** kiełek *m* **2.** pęd *m* **3.** FILM zdjęcia *pl* **4.** *of photographs*: sesja *f* **5.** *Br* polowanie *n*; **shoot down** *v/t* **1.** zestrzeliwać ⟨-lić⟩ **2.** zastrzelić **3.** *fig* torpedować ⟨s-⟩ **4.** *theory*: obalać ⟨-lić⟩; **shoot off** *v/i infml* zmywać ⟨zmyć⟩ się; **shoot up I** *v/i* **1.** gwałtownie wzrastać ⟨-rosnąć⟩ **2.** (*prices*) podskoczyć **3.** *infml* dawać ⟨dać⟩ sobie w żyłę **II** *v/t* **1.** ostrzeliwać ⟨-lać⟩ **2.** wstrzykiwać ⟨-knąć⟩ (sobie)

shoot•er [ˈʃuːtə] *s* **1.** strzelec *m* **2.** *infml* pukawka *f*

shoot•ing [ˈʃuːtɪŋ] *s* **1.** strzelanina *f* **2.** zabójstwo *n* **3.** polowanie *n* **4.** FILM zdjęcia *pl*; ˈ**shoot•ing gal•ler•y** *s* strzelnica *f*; ˈ**shoot•ing range** *s* strzelnica *f*; **shoot•ing** ˈ**star** *s* spadająca gwiazda *f*

ˈ**shoot-out** *s* **1.** strzelanina *f* **2.** SPORT rzuty *pl* karne

shop [ʃɒp] **I** *s* **1.** sklep *m* **2.** warsztat *m* **3.** *Br infml* zakupy *pl* **4. *talk ~*** rozmawiać o sprawach zawodowych **II** *v/i* **1.** robić ⟨z-⟩ zakupy; ***go ~ping*** iść na zakupy **2.** kupować ⟨-pić⟩ (***for*** *A*); **~ *for food*** kupować jedzenie **III** *v/i Br infml* donosić ⟨-nieść⟩ na *G*; **shop around** *v/i* rozglądać ⟨-zejrzeć⟩ się (***for*** za *I*)

ˈ**shop as•sist•ant** *s Br* sprzedawca *m*, ekspedient *m*; **shop** ˈ**floor** *s Br* **1.** załoga *f*, pracownicy *pl* produkcji **2.** zakład *m*; **~ *workers*** załoga

shop•ping [ˈʃɒpɪŋ] *s* zakupy *pl*; ***do the ~*** robić zakupy; ˈ**shop•ping bag** *s* torba *f* na zakupy; ˈ**shop•ping bas•ket** *s* koszyk *m* na zakupy; ˈ**shop•ping cart** *s* wózek *m* na zakupy; ˈ**shop•ping centre** *Br*, ˈ***shop•ping cen•ter*** *Am s* centrum *n* handlowe; ˈ**shop•ping list** *s* lista *f* zakupów; ˈ**shop•ping mall** *s* centrum *n* handlowe

shop•keep•er [ˈʃɒkiːpə] *s* sklepikarz *m*; **shop•lift•er** [ˈʃɒplɪftə] *s* złodziej *m* (sklepowy); **shop•lift•ing** [ˈʃɒplɪftɪŋ] *s* kradzież *f* sklepowa; **shop•per** ['ʃɒpə] *s* **1.** klient *m* **2.** kupujący *m*; **shop 'stew•ard** *s Br* przedstawiciel *m* załogi; **shop 'win•dow** *s* wystawa *f* (sklepowa), witryna *f* (sklepowa); **shop-'soiled** *Br*, **'*shop•worn*** *Am adj* zleżały

shore[1] [ʃɔː] *s* **1.** brzeg *m* **2.** ląd *m*; ***on ~*** na lądzie; ***a ~ leave*** przepustka

shore[2] [~] **I** *s* **1.** podpora *f* **2.** stempel *m* **II** *v/t* **~ *s.th. up*** **a)** podeprzeć coś **b)** *fig* wzmocnić coś

shorn [ʃɔːn] *Past Participle* → ***shear***

short [ʃɔːt] **I** *adj* **1.** krótki; ***a ~ time ago*** niedawno; ***in the ~ run*** na krótką metę **2.** *person*: niski **3.** ***s.o. is ~ of s.th.*** komuś brakuje czegoś; ***I'm ~ of money*** nie mam pieniędzy; ***she's never ~ of excuses*** zawsze znajdzie jakąś wymówkę **4.** ***it's ~ for*** to skrót od *G* **5.** opryskliwy, szorstki **II** *adv* **1.** krótko; ***in ~*** krótko mówiąc; ***cut s.th. ~*** przerwać coś **2.** ***they've run ~ of petrol*** skończyła im się benzyna; ***we're running ~ of time*** mamy coraz mniej czasu; ***fall ~ of s.o.'s expectations*** zawieść czyjeś oczekiwania **III** *s* **1.** film *m* krótkometrażowy **2.** *Br* mocny alkohol *m* **3.** zwarcie *n*; **short•age** ['ʃɔːtɪdʒ] *s* **1.** brak *m* **2.** niedobór *m*

'short•bread *s* kruche ciastko *n*; **short•cake** *s* **1.** *Br* → ***shortbread*** **2.** ciastko *n* z bitą śmietaną i owocami; **short-'change** *v/t* wydawać ⟨-dać⟩ za mało (reszty); **short 'cir•cuit** *s* spięcie *n*, zwarcie *n*; **short•com•ing** ['ʃɔːtkʌmɪŋ] *s* **1.** wada *f* **2.** defekt *m*; **'short cut** *s* **1.** skrót *m*; ***take a ~*** pójść na skróty **2.** *fig* droga *f* na skróty

short•en ['ʃɔːtn] **I** *v/t* skracać ⟨-rócić⟩ **II** *v/i* **1.** skracać ⟨-rócić⟩ się **2.** stawać ⟨-tać⟩ się krótszym; **short•en•ing** ['ʃɔːtnɪŋ] *s* **1.** tłuszcz *m* (do pieczenia) **1.** skrócenie *n*

'short•fall *s* **1.** niedobór *m* **2.** deficyt *m*; **short-haired** ['ʃɔːtheəd] *adj* **1.** z krótkimi włosami **2.** krótkowłosy; **'short•hand** *s* **1.** stenografia *f*; ***a ~ typist*** stenotypistka **2** skrót *m* myślowy; **short-hand•ed** [ʃɔːt'hændɪd] → ***short-staffed***

'short list I *s* ostateczna lista *f* kandydatów **II** *v/t* umieszczać ⟨umieścić⟩ na ostatecznej liście kandydatów; **short-lived** ['ʃɔːtlɪvd] *adj* krótkotrwały; ***the hopes were ~*** nadzieje szybko się rozwiały

short•ly ['ʃɔːtlɪ] *adv* **1.** krótko; ***~ after us*** krótko po nas **2.** wkrótce **3.** zaraz **4.** opryskliwie, szorstko; **short•ness** ['ʃɔːtnɪs] *s* **1.** krótkość *f*; ***remind s.o. of the ~ of life*** przypominać komuś o tym, że życie jest krótkie **2.** niski wzrost *m* **3.** ***~ of breath*** zadyszka

'short-range *adj* **1.** *missile*: bliskiego zasięgu **2.** *forecast*, *plan*: krótkoterminowy

shorts [ʃɔːts] *pl* **1.** szorty *pl*, (krótkie) spodenki *pl* **2.** bokserki *pl*

short•sight•ed [ʃɔːt'saɪtɪd] *adj a. fig* krótkowzroczny; **short-sleeved** ['ʃɔːtsliːvd] *adj shirt*: z krótkim rękawem; **short-staffed** [ʃɔːt'stæft] *adj*: ***hospitals are ~*** w szpitalach brakuje personelu; **short 'sto•ry** *s* opowiadanie *n*; **short-tem•pered** [ʃɔːt'tempəd] *adj* wybuchowy; **'short-term** *adj* **1.** *credit*: krótkoterminowy **2.** *memory*: krótkotrwały; **'short time** *s* skrócony czas *m* pracy; **'short wave** *s RADIO* fale *pl* krótkie; **'short-wave** *adj* **1.** na falach krótkich **2.** odbierający fale krótkie

shot[1] [ʃɒt] *s* **1.** strzał *m*; ***fire a ~*** strzelić; ***have a ~ at goal*** oddać strzał na bramkę; ***~ in the dark*** *fig* strzał w ciemno; ***like a ~*** migiem **2.** wystrzał *m* **3.** strzelec *m*; ***a good ~*** dobry strzelec; ***a big ~*** *fig* gruba ryba **4.** śrut *m* **5.** ***I'll have a ~ at it*** *infml* spróbuję; ***at the first ~*** za pierwszym razem **6.** (*basketball*) rzut *m* **7.** (*tennis*) uderzenie *n* **8.** *FILM* ujęcie *n* **9.** zdjęcie *n* **10.** *Am infml drug*: działka *f* **11.** *infml vodka*: kieliszek *m* **12.** *SPORT* kula *f* **13.** zastrzyk *m*

shot[2] [~] **I** *v Past Simple and Past Participle* → ***shoot*** **II** *adj* ***be ~ of*** *Br infml* pozbyć się czegoś

'shot•gun *s* śrutówka *f*; **'shot-put** *s*: ***the ~*** *SPORT* pchnięcie *n* kulą; **shot•put•ter** ['ʃɒtpʊtə] *s SPORT* miotacz *m* (kulą), kulomiot *m*

should [ʃəd] *strong form* [ʃʊd] *v aux* **1.** (*obligation*) ***you ~ be more careful*** powinieneś bardziej uważać; ***you shouldn't drink*** nie powinieneś pić **2.** (*advice*) ***~ I call him?*** powinnam do niego zadzwonić?; ***I ~ wait a little longer if I were you*** na twoim

S

miejscu poczekałbym jeszcze trochę **3.** (*expectation*) ***we ~ arrive before dark*** powinniśmy dotrzeć przed zmrokiem; ***the bus ~ have arrived 10 minutes ago*** autobus powinien przyjechać już 10 minut temu

shoul•der ['ʃəʊldə] **I** *s* **1.** ANAT bark *m* **2.** ramię *n*; ***look back over one's ~*** obejrzeć się przez ramię; ***shrug one's ~s*** wzruszyć ramionami; ***~ to ~*** ramię w ramię; ***give s.o. the cold ~*** **a)** potraktować kogoś ozięble **b)** *fig* odwrócić się do kogoś plecami **II** *v/t* **1.** *responsibility*: brać ⟨wziąć⟩ na swoje barki **2.** *blame*: brać ⟨wziąć⟩ na siebie **3.** *bag*: zarzucać ⟨-cić⟩ na ramię **4.** ***~ one's way*** przepychać się, przeciskać się; '**shoul•der bag** *s* torba *f* na ramię; '**shoul•der blade** *s* ANAT łopatka *f*; '**shoul•der-length** *adj hair*: do ramion; '**shoul•der pad** *s* **1.** (*of blouse*) poduszka *f* **2.** SPORT ochraniacz *m* barku; '**shoul•der strap** *s* **1.** *of dress*: ramiączko *n* **2.** *of bag*: pasek *m*

should•n't ['ʃʊdnt] *contracted form* → ***should not***

shout [ʃaʊt] **I** *v/i* krzyczeć ⟨krzyknąć⟩ (***at*** na *A*); ***~ for help*** wołać o pomoc **II** *v/t* wykrzykiwać ⟨-rzyczeć⟩; ***~ orders*** wykrzykiwać rozkazy **III** *s* **1.** krzyk *m*; ***give me a ~*** zawołaj mnie **2.** okrzyk *m*; **shout down** *v/t* zakrzykiwać ⟨-rzyczeć⟩

shout•ing ['ʃaʊtɪŋ] *s* **1.** krzyki *pl* **2.** okrzyki *pl*

shove [ʃʌv] **I** *v/i* **1.** pchać ⟨pchnąć⟩ **2.** rozpychać się **II** *v/t* **1.** popychać ⟨-pchnąć⟩ **2.** wpychać ⟨wepchnąć⟩ **3.** wciskać ⟨-snąć⟩ **III** *s* ***give s.o. a ~*** popchnąć kogoś; **shove off** *v/i infml* spływać; ***~!*** spływaj!

S

shov•el ['ʃʌvl] **I** *s* **1.** łopata *f* **2.** szufla *f* **3.** łopatka *f* **4.** łyżka *f* (koparki) **II** *v/t* **1.** odgarniać ⟨-nąć⟩ (łopatą) **2.** ładować ⟨za-⟩ (łopatą)

show [ʃəʊ] **I** (*showed*; *shown*) *v/t* **1.** pokazywać ⟨-zać⟩; ***I'll ~ you!*** ja ci pokażę!; ***~ s.o. the door*** *fig* pokazać komuś drzwi; ***~ them who's the boss*** pokaż im, kto tu rządzi **2.** (*painting*, *novel*) przedstawiać ⟨-wić⟩ **3.** *place*: wskazywać ⟨-zać⟩ **4.** prowadzić ⟨za-⟩ **5.** *courage*: wykazywać ⟨-zać⟩ **6.** *respect*: okazywać ⟨-zać⟩ **7.** *collection*: wystawiać ⟨-wić⟩ **II** (*showed*; *shown*) *v/i* **1.** pokazywać ⟨-zać⟩ się **2.** być widocznym; ***it ~s*** to widać **3.** (*film*) być pokazywanym, być wyświetlanym **4.** ***it just goes to ~ that*** to tylko świadczy o tym, że **III** *s* **1.** program *m* **2.** show *m* **3.** przedstawienie *n* **4.** spektakl *m* **5.** seans *m* **6.** wystawa *f*; ***on ~*** wystawiony, na wystawie **7.** pokaz *m*; ***for ~*** na pokaz **8.** okazanie *n* **9.** demonstracja *f*; **show around** *v/t* oprowadzać ⟨-dzić⟩; **show in** *v/t* **1.** wprowadzać ⟨-dzić⟩ **2.** wpuszczać ⟨wpuścić⟩; **show off I** *v/i infml* popisywać ⟨-sać⟩ się **II** *v/t* **1.** *infml* popisywać ⟨-sać⟩ się **2.** chwalić ⟨po-⟩ się **3.** uwydatniać ⟨-nić⟩; **show out** *v/t* **1.** wyprowadzać ⟨-dzić⟩ **2.** wypuszczać ⟨-puścić⟩; **show round** → ***show around***; **show up I** *v/i* **1.** pojawiać ⟨-wić⟩ się **2.** *infml* zjawiać ⟨-wić⟩ się **3.** być widocznym **II** *v/t* **1.** pokazywać ⟨-zać⟩ **2.** ***show s.o. up*** *Br infml* narobić komuś wstydu

show biz ['ʃəʊbɪz], '***show busi•ness*** *s* show-business *m*, przemysł *m* rozrywkowy; '**show•case** *s* **1.** gablota *f* **2.** okazja *f* do zaprezentowania (się); '**show•down** *s* ostateczna rozgrywka *f*

show•er ['ʃaʊə] **I** *s* **1.** prysznic *m*; ***take a ~, have a ~*** wziąć prysznic **2.** przelotny deszcz *m* **3.** *of praise*: deszcz *m* **4.** *of bullets*: grad *m* **II** *v/i* brać ⟨wziąć⟩ prysznic **III** *v/t* obsypywać ⟨-pać⟩ (***s.o. with*** kogoś *I*); **show•er cab•i•net** *s* kabina *f* prysznicowa; '**show•er cap** *s* czepek *m* kąpielowy; '**show•er cur•tain** *s* zasłona *f* prysznicowa; **show•er gel** *s* żel *m* pod prysznic; '**show•er•proof** *adj* przeciwdeszczowy

'**show•girl** *s* tancerka *f* rewiowa, *infml* girlsa *f*; '**show•jump•ing** *s* (*horse riding*) skoki *pl* przez przeszkody; **show•man** ['ʃəʊmən] *pl -men s* showman *m*; **show•man•ship** ['ʃəʊmənʃɪp] *s* umiejętność *f* zabawiania publiczności

shown [ʃəʊn] *Past Partciple* → ***show***

'**show-off** *s*: ***he's a ~*** lubi się popisywać; '**show•piece** *s* **1.** doskonały przykład *m* **2.** majstersztyk *m* **3.** *fig* wizytówka *f*; **a ~** pokazowa szkoła; ˈ**show•room** *s* salon *m*

show•y [ˈʃəʊɪ] *adj* **1.** krzykliwy **2.** *infml* efekciarski

shrank [ʃræŋk] *Past Simple* → **shrink**

shred [ʃred] **I** *v/t* **1.** drzeć ⟨po-⟩ **2.** *vegetables*: szatkować ⟨po-⟩, siekać ⟨po-⟩ **3.** niszczyć ⟨z-⟩ (w niszczarce) **II** *s* **1.** strzęp *m*; ***tear s.th. to ~s*** podrzeć coś na strzępy **2.** *of truth*: krzta *f*, odrobina *f* **3.** *evidence*: cień *m*; **shredder** [ˈʃredə] *s* **1.** niszczarka *f* dokumentów **2.** COOK szatkownica *f*

shrewd [ʃruːd] *adj* **1.** bystry **2.** przenikliwy **3.** *move, investment*: dobry; **shrewd•ness** [ˈʃruːdnɪs] *s* **1.** bystrość *f* **2.** przenikliwość *f*

shriek [ʃriːk] **I** *v/i* **1.** wrzeszczeć ⟨wrzasnąć⟩ **2.** piszczeć ⟨-snąć⟩ **II** *s* **1.** wrzask *m* **2.** pisk *m*

shrift [ʃrɪft] *s*: ***give s.o. a short ~*** zbyć kogoś

shrill [ʃrɪl] **I** *adj* **1.** *sound*: przenikliwy **2.** *protest*: ostry **II** *v/i* piszczeć ⟨za-⟩

shrimp [ʃrɪmp] *pl shrimp, shrimps s* krewetka *f*

shrine [ʃraɪn] *s* **1.** sanktuarium *n* **2.** kaplica *f* **3.** *fig* mekka *f*

shrink[1] [ʃrɪŋk] **I** (*shrank/shrunk; shrunk*) *v/i* **1.** kurczyć ⟨s-⟩ się **2.** zbiegać ⟨zbiec⟩ się **3.** zmniejszać ⟨-szyć⟩ się **4.** wzbraniać się (***from*** przed *I*) **II** (*shrank/shrunk; shrunk*) *v/t* **1.** zmniejszać ⟨-szyć⟩ **2.** powodować ⟨s-⟩ kurczenie się

shrink[2] [~] *s infml* psychiatra *m*

ˈ**shrink•age** *s* **1.** kurczenie się *n* **2.** zbieganie się *n* **3.** zmniejszanie się *n*; **shrink•ing** [ˈʃrɪŋkɪŋ] *adj* **1.** kurczący się; ***be a ~ violet*** być bardzo nieśmiałym; ***she's no ~*** nie należy do osób nieśmiałych **2.** zmniejszający się; ˈ**shrink-wrap** *v/t* pakować ⟨za-⟩ w folię (termokurczliwą); ˈ**shrink-wrap•ping** *s* **1.** pakowanie *n* w folię termokurczliwą **2.** folia *f* (termokurczliwa)

shriv•el [ˈʃrɪvl] **I** *v/t* wysuszać ⟨-szyć⟩ **II** *v/i* schnąć ⟨wy-⟩, suszyć ⟨wy-⟩ się

shroud [ʃraʊd] **I** *s* całun *m*; ***under a ~ of secrecy*** w tajemnicy **II** *v/t* pokrywać ⟨-ryć⟩; ***~ed in mist*** spowity mgłą; ***~ed in mystery*** owiany tajemnicą

Shrove Tues•day [ʃrəʊvtjuzdːː] *s* ostatki *pl*

shrub [ʃrʌb] *s* krzew *m*; **shrub•be•ry** [ˈʃrʌbərɪ] *s* krzewy *pl*

shrug [ʃrʌg] **I** *v/i* wzruszać ⟨-szyć⟩ ramionami **II** *v/t* ***~ one's shoulders*** wzruszyć ramionami **III** *s* wzruszenie *n* ramion; ***give a ~*** wzruszyć ramionami; **shrug off** *v/t* **1.** **1.** ignorować ⟨z-⟩ **2.** bagatelizować ⟨z-⟩

shrunk [ʃrʌŋk] *Past Simple and Past Participle* → **shrink**

shuck [ʃʌk] *Am* **I** *s* **1.** *oysters*: muszla *f* **2.** *nut*: łupina *f* **II** *v/t* **1.** wyjmować ⟨-jąć⟩ z muszli **2.** łuskać

shucks [ʃʌks] *interj Am infml* **1.** a niech to! **2.** e tam!

shud•der [ˈʃʌdə] **I** *v/i* **1.** trząść ⟨za-⟩ się **2.** dygotać ⟨za-⟩ **3.** wzdrygać ⟨-gnąć⟩ się **II** *s* **1.** dreszcz *m* **2.** ***give a ~*** zadygotać

shuf•fle [ˈʃʌfl] **I** *v/i* **1.** powłóczyć nogami **2.** wlec się **II** *v/t* **1.** ***~ one's feet*** powłóczyć nogami **2.** *cards*: tasować ⟨po-⟩ **3.** przekładać ⟨po-⟩ **III** *s* **1.** ***walk with a ~*** iść powłócząc nogami **2.** ***give the cards a ~*** potasować karty; ˈ**shuffle•board** *s gra polegająca na trafianiu krążkami w oznaczone cyframi pola*

shun [ʃʌn] *v/t* **1.** unikać ⟨-knąć⟩ **2.** stronić od *G*

shunt [ʃʌnt] *v/t* **1.** *train*: przestawiać ⟨-wić⟩ na inny tor **2.** *employee*: przenosić ⟨-nieść⟩

shut [ʃʌt] **I** (*shut; shut*) *v/t* zamykać ⟨-mknąć⟩; ***~ your mouth!***, ***~ your face!*** *vulg* zamknij gębę!; ***~ one's finger in the door*** przytrzasnąć sobie palec drzwiami **II** (*shut; shut*) *v/i* zamykać ⟨-mknąć⟩ się; ***the window won't ~*** okno nie chce się zamknąć **III** *adj* zamknięty; **shut away** *v/t* zamykać ⟨-mknąć⟩; **shut down** **I** *v/i* **1.** zostawać ⟨-tać⟩ zlikwidowanym **2.** kończyć ⟨za-⟩ działalność **3.** (*computer*) wyłączać ⟨-czyć⟩ się **II** *v/t* **1.** zamykać ⟨-mknąć⟩ **2.** *computer*: wyłączać ⟨-czyć⟩; **shut off** *v/t* **1.** wyłączać ⟨-czyć⟩ **2.** *water, gas*: odłączać ⟨-czyć⟩; ***the valve that shuts off the gas*** zawór, który odcina dopływ gazu **3.** ***~ oneself from the world*** odgrodzić się od świata, odizolować

S

się od świata; **shut out** *v/t* **1.** nie wpuszczać ⟨wpuścić⟩ do *G* **2.** nie przepuszczać ⟨-puścić⟩ **3.** zasłaniać ⟨-łonić⟩ **4.** *thought*: nie dopuszczać ⟨-puścić⟩ **5.** *emotion*: tłumić ⟨s-⟩; **shut up I** *v/i* zamykać ⟨-mknąć⟩ się **II** *v/t* zamykać ⟨-mknąć⟩

'shut•down *s* **1.** zamknięcie *n* **2.** likwidacja *f* **3.** *machine*: wyłączenie *n*

'shut-eye *s*: ***get some ~*** *infml* przespać się

shut•ter ['ʃʌtə] *s* **1.** okiennica *f* **2.** żaluzja *f* **3.** PHOT migawka *f*; **'shut•ter speed** *s* PHOT czas *m* naświetlania

shut•tle ['ʃʌtl] **I** *s* **1.** autobus *m* wahadłowy **2.** pociąg *m* wahadłowy **3.** wahadłowiec *m*, prom *m* kosmiczny **4.** TECH czółenko *n* **II** *v/i* kursować; (***between*** pomiędzy *I*) **III** *v/t* przewozić ⟨-wieźć⟩; **'shut•tle•bus** *s* autobus *m* wahadłowy; **'shut•tle•cock** *s* SPORT lotka *f*; **'shut•tle ser•vice** *s* połączenie *n* wahadłowe; ***a ~ bus between London and Leeds*** autobusowe połączenie wahadłowe pomiędzy Londynem i Leeds

shy [ʃaɪ] **I** *adj* **1.** nieśmiały; ***be ~ of women*** być nieśmiałym wobec kobiet; ***not be ~ of doing s.th.*** nie wahać się czegoś zrobić **2.** *animal*: płochliwy **II** *v/i* płoszyć ⟨s-⟩ się; **shy away** *v/i* **1.** uchylać ⟨-lić⟩ się (***from*** od *G*) **2.** wzbraniać się (***from*** przed *I*)

shy•ness ['ʃaɪnɪs] *s* **1.** nieśmiałość *f* **2.** płochliwość *f*

shy•ster ['ʃaɪstə] *s Am infml* krętacz *m*

Si•a•mese twins [saɪəmiːz'twɪnz] *pl* bliźnięta *pl* syjamskie

Si•ber•i•a [saɪ'bɪərɪə] *s* Syberia *f*

sib•ling ['sɪblɪŋ] *s* **1.** ***~s*** rodzeństwo **2.** brat *m* **3.** siostra *f*

Si•ci•ly [sɪsɪlɪ] *s* Sycylia *f*

sick [sɪk] **I** *adj* **1.** chory; ***she's off ~*** nie ma jej w pracy z powodu choroby; ***she called in ~*** zadzwoniła i powiedziała, że nie przyjdzie do pracy, bo jest chora **2.** ***be ~*** *Br* zwymiotować; ***I'll be ~*** robi mi się niedobrze, zaraz zwymiotuję **3.** ***I'm ~ of waiting*** mam dość czekania **4.** ***you make me ~*** *infml* jesteś obrzydliwy **II** *s* **1.** *Br infml* wymiociny *pl*, paw *m* **2.** ***the ~*** chorzy *pl* **III** *v/t* ***~ s.th. up*** *infml* zwymiotować coś; **'sick bag** *s* torba *f* chorobowa; **'sick bay** *s* izba *f* chorych; **'sick•bed** *s* łóżko *n* chorego

sick•en ['sɪkn] *Br v/t* napawać obrzydzeniem; **sick•en•ing** ['sɪknɪŋ] *adj* **1.** obrzydliwy **2.** szokujący **3.** okropny

sick•le ['sɪkl] *s* sierp *m*

'sick leave *s* zwolnienie *n* lekarskie; ***be on ~*** być na zwolnieniu; **sick•ly** ['sɪklɪ] *adv* **1.** chorowity **2.** *smell*: mdły **3.** *colour*: obrzydliwy; **sick•ness** ['sɪknɪs] *s* **1.** choroba *f* **2.** *Br* wymioty *pl*; **'sick-note** *s* zwolnienie *n* lekarskie; **'sick pay** *s* wynagrodzenie *n* za okres choroby, *infml* chorobowe *n*

side [saɪd] **I** *s* **1.** strona *f*; ***the right ~ of the road*** prawa strona drogi; ***cross to the other ~ of the road*** przejść na drugą stronę ulicy; ***by my ~*** u mojego boku, obok mnie; ***~ by ~*** obok siebie; ***be on s.o.'s ~*** *fig* być po czyjejś stronie, popierać kogoś; ***take ~s*** opowiedzieć się po czyjejś stronie; ***my grandparents on my father's ~*** dziadkowie ze strony mojego ojca **2.** ANAT MATH bok *m* **3.** *mountain*: zbocze *n* **II** *v/i* ***~ with s.o. against*** brać czyjąś stronę przeciw *D*; **'side•board** *s* kredens *m*; **'sideburns** *pl* baczki *pl*, baki *pl*; **'side-car** *s* przyczepa *f* motocyklowa; **'side dish** *s* przystawka *f*; **'side door** *s* boczne drzwi *pl*; **'side ef•fect** *s* skutek *m* uboczny; **'side im•pact pro•tec•tion** *s* AUTO system *m* chroniący przed skutkami uderzeń z boku; **'side issue** *s* **1.** kwestia *f* poboczna **2.** sprawa *f* drugorzędna; **'side•light** *s* **1.** *Br* światło *n* postojowe przednie **2.** *infml* dygresja *f*; **'side•line I** *s* **1.** dodatkowe zajęcie *n* **2.** SPORT linia *f* boczna; ***watch from the ~s*** *fig* patrzeć z boku **II** *v/t* **1.** ***be ~d by injury*** SPORT pauzować z powodu kontuzji **2.** *fig* odsuwać ⟨-sunąć⟩ na boczny tor; **'side-long** *adj look*: ukradkowy; **'side road** *s* boczna droga *f*; **'side•sad•dle I** *s* siodło *n* damskie **II** *adv ride a horse*: po damsku; **'side show** *s* impreza *f* towarzysząca; **side•split•ting** ['saɪdsplɪtɪŋ] *adj* śmieszny, że boki zrywać; **'side•step** *v/t* **1.** omijać ⟨ominąć⟩ **2.** *infml* wymigiwać ⟨-gać⟩ się od odpowiedzi na *A*; **'side street** *s* boczna uliczka *f*; **'side•swipe** *s* **1.** *Am* uderzenie *n* w bok **2.** krytyczny komen-

S

tarz *m*; ***take a ~ at*** przy okazji kogoś skrytykować; **'side•track** *v/t* **1.** odwracać ⟨-rócić⟩ uwagę **2.** odchodzić ⟨odejść⟩ od tematu; **'side•walk** *s Am* chodnik *m*; **side•walk 'caf•é** *s* ogródek *m* kawiarniany

side•ward ['saɪdwəd] **I** *adj* **1.** w bok **2.** z ukosa; ***give s.o. a ~ glance*** spojrzeć na kogoś z ukosa **II** *adv* w bok; **side•wards** ['saɪdwədz] → ***sideward I.2***; **side•ways** ['saɪdweɪz] **I** *adv* **1.** w bok **2.** na bok **3.** z ukosa **4.** na równorzędne stanowisko **II** *adj* **1.** w bok **2.** z ukosa; ***give s.o. a ~ glance*** spojrzeć na kogoś z ukosa

sid•ing ['saɪdɪŋ] *s* **1.** bocznica *f* kolejowa **2.** siding *m*, deskowanie *n* zewnętrzne

si•dle ['saɪdl] *v/i*: ***~ up to*** podejść chyłkiem do *G*

siege [siːdʒ] *s* oblężenie *n*; ***under ~*** oblegany; ***lay ~ to*** oblegać

sieve [sɪv] **I** *s* **1.** sito *n*; ***have a memory like a ~*** mieć dziurawą pamięć **2.** sitko *n* **II** *v/t* przesiewać ⟨-siać⟩

sift [sɪft] *v/t* **1.** przesiewać ⟨-siać⟩ **2.** przeszukiwać ⟨-kać⟩; **sift out** *v/t* oddzielać ⟨-lić⟩ (***from*** od *G*); **sift through** *v/t* **1.** przeszukiwać ⟨-kać⟩ **2.** przeglądać ⟨przejrzeć⟩

sigh [saɪ] **I** *v/i* wzdychać ⟨westchnąć⟩ **II** *s* westchnienie *n*; ***a ~ of relief*** westchnienie ulgi; ***breathe a ~ of relief*** odetchnąć z ulgą

sight [saɪt] **I** *s* **1.** wzrok *m*; ***lose one's ~*** stracić wzrok **2.** widok *m*; ***a sorry ~*** przykry widok; ***at the ~ of*** na widok *G*; ***at first ~*** na pierwszy rzut oka; ***love at first ~*** miłość od pierwszego wejrzenia; ***lose ~ of s.o.*** stracić kogoś z oczu; ***out of ~, out of mind*** co z oczu, to z serca; ***it's a ~ for sore eyes*** *infml* przyjemnie na to popatrzeć; ***know s.o. by ~*** znać kogoś z widzenia **3.** (*field of vision*) ***in ~*** w zasięgu wzroku; ***there was no one in ~*** nikogo nie było widać; ***get out of my ~!*** zejdź mi z oczu! **4.** ***~s*** celownik *m*; ***have s.o. in one's ~s*** mieć kogoś na muszce **5.** ***~s*** atrakcje *pl* turystyczne **II** *v/t lit* ujrzeć; **sight•ed** ['saɪtɪd] *adj* widzący; ***partially ~*** niedowidzący; ***short-~*** krótkowzroczny

sight•ing ['saɪtɪŋ] *s*: ***there were several ~s of a lonely leopard in the area*** w okolicy kilkakrotnie widziano samotną panterę

'sight-read (*sightread*; *sightread*) *v/t* **1.** grać ⟨za-⟩ a vista **2.** śpiewać ⟨za-⟩ a vista

sight•see•ing ['saɪtsiːɪŋ] *s* zwiedzanie *n*; ***go ~*** zwiedzać; **'sight•see•ing bus** *s* autobus *m* turystyczny; **'sight•see•ing tour** *s* zwiedzanie *n*; ***guided ~*** zwiedzanie z przewodnikiem; **sight-seer** ['saɪtsiːə] *s* zwiedzający *m*

sign [saɪn] **I** *s* **1.** znak *m*; ***a traffic ~*** znak drogowy; ***a ~ of the times*** znak czasu **2.** oznaka *f*; ***no ~s of life*** brak oznak życia; ***headaches may be a ~ of depression*** bóle głowy mogą być objawem depresji; ***all the ~s are that*** wszystko wskazuje na to, że **3.** symbol *m* **4.** napis *m* **5.** gest *m* **II** *v/t* **1.** podpisywać ⟨-sać⟩ **2.** *autographs*: rozdawać ⟨-dać⟩ **III** *v/i* **1.** podpisywać ⟨-sać⟩ się **2.** dawać ⟨dać⟩ znak (***to*** *D*) **3.** używać ⟨użyć⟩ języka migowego, migać; **sign away** *v/t* zrzekać ⟨zrzec⟩ się (na piśmie); **sign for** *v/i* kwitować ⟨po-⟩; **sign in I** *v/i* **1.** meldować ⟨za-⟩ się **2.** wpisywać ⟨-sać⟩ się na listę **II** *v/t* **1.** meldować ⟨za-⟩ **2.** wpisywać ⟨-sać⟩ na listę; **sign off I** *v/i* zatwierdzać ⟨-dzić⟩ **II** *v/i* **1.** *Br* kończyć ⟨za-⟩ list (***with*** *I*) **2.** kończyć ⟨za-⟩ emisję; **sign out I** *v/i* **1.** wymeldowywać ⟨-dować⟩ się **2.** podpisywać ⟨-sać⟩ listę (przed wyjściem) **II** *v/t* wymeldowywać ⟨-dować⟩; **sign over** *v/t property*: przepisywać ⟨-sać⟩ (***to*** na *A*); **sign up I** *v/t* werbować ⟨z-⟩ **II** *v/i* zapisywać ⟨-sać⟩ się (***for*** na *A*)

sig•nal ['sɪgnl] **I** *s* **1.** sygnał *m*; ***traffic ~s*** sygnalizacja świetlna **2.** znak *m* **3.** semafor *m* **II** *v/t* **1.** sygnalizować ⟨za-⟩ **2.** wskazywać ⟨-zać⟩ na *A* **3.** zapowiadać ⟨-wiedzieć⟩ **III** *v/i* **1.** dawać ⟨dać⟩ sygnał **2.** włączać ⟨-czyć⟩ kierunkowskaz **IV** *adj* **1.** *success*: istotny **2.** *failure*: wyraźny

sig•na•to•ry ['sɪgnətrɪ] *s* sygnatariusz *m*

sig•na•ture ['sɪgnətʃə] *s* podpis *m*; **sig•na•ture 'tune** *s* RADIO sygnał *m* dźwiękowy

sig•net ring ['sɪgnɪtrɪŋ] *s* sygnet *m*

S

sig•nif•i•cance [sɪg'nɪfɪkəns] *s* **1.** znaczenie *n*; ***be of great ~ to*** mieć duże znaczenie dla *G* **2.** ważność *f*; **sig•nif•i•cant** [sɪg'nɪfɪkənt] *adj* **1.** znaczący **2.** ważny; **sig•nif•i•cant•ly** [sɪg'nɪfɪkəntlɪ] *adv* **1.** znacznie **2.** co istotne **3.** znacząco

sig•ni•fy ['sɪgnɪfaɪ] **I** *v/t* **1.** znaczyć **2.** oznaczać **II** *v/i* **1.** dawać ⟨dać⟩ do zrozumienia (***that*** że) **2.** mieć znaczenie

'sign lan•guage *s* język *m* migowy; **'sign•post** *s* **1.** drogowskaz *m* **2.** *fig* wskazówka *f*

si•lage ['saɪlɪdʒ] *s* kiszonka *f*

si•lence ['saɪləns] **I** *s* **1.** cisza *f*; ***~!*** cisza!; ***in ~*** w ciszy **2.** milczenie *n*; ***a one-minute ~*** minuta milczenia; ***~ is golden*** milczenie jest złotem **II** *v/t* uciszać ⟨-szyć⟩; **si•lenc•er** ['saɪlənsə] *s* tłumik *m*

si•lent ['saɪlənt] *adj* **1.** cichy **2.** milczący; ***be ~*** milczeć, nie odzywać się **3.** małomówny **4.** *film*, *letter*: niemy

sil•hou•ette [sɪlu:'et] **I** *s* **1.** sylwetka *f* **2.** zarys *m* **II** *v/t* ***~d against*** odcinający się na tle *G*, rysujący się na tle *G*

sil•i•con ['sɪlɪkən] *s* krzem *m*; **sil•i•con 'chip** *s* (krzemowy) układ *m* scalony; **Sil•i•con 'Val•ley** *s* Dolina *f* Krzemowa

sil•i•cone ['sɪlɪkəʊn] *s* silikon *m*

sil•i•co•sis [sɪlɪ'kəʊsɪs] *s* MED krzemica *f*, pylica *f* krzemowa płuc

silk [sɪlk] **I** *s* jedwab *m* **II** *adj* jedwabny; **'silk•worm** *s* BIOL jedwabnik *m*; **silk•y** ['sɪlkɪ] *adj* **1.** *hair*: jedwabisty **2.** *voice*: aksamitny

sill [sɪl] *s* **1.** parapet *m* (okienny) **2.** próg *m*

S

sil•li•ness ['sɪlɪnɪs] *s* głupota *f*

sil•ly ['sɪlɪ] **I** *adj* **1.** niemądry; ***don't be ~*** nie bądź niemądry **2.** głupi **II** *s infml* głuptas *m*

si•lo ['saɪləʊ] *s* **1.** silos *m* **2.** podziemna wyrzutnia *f* rakietowa

silt [sɪlt] **I** *s* **1.** muł *m* **2.** szlam *m* **II** *v/t* ***~ s.th. up*** zamulić coś

sil•ver ['sɪlvə] **I** *s* **1.** srebro *n*; ***hand s.o. s.th. on a ~ platter*** *fig* podać coś komuś na tacy **2.** srebra *pl*; ***the family ~*** srebra rodzinne **3.** bilon *m* **II** *adj* srebrny **III** *v/t* posrebrzać ⟨-rzyć⟩; **'sil•ver•fish** *pl silverfish s* (*insect*) rybik *m* cukrowy; **sil•ver 'foil** *s Br* folia *f* aluminiowa; **sil•ver-haired** ['sɪlvəheəd] *adj* siwowłosy; **sil•ver ju•bi•lee** [sɪlvər'dʒu:bɪli:] *s* srebrny jubileusz *m*; **sil•ver 'med•al** *s* srebrny medal *m*; **sil•ver 'med•al•list** *Br*, ***sil•ver 'med•a•list*** *Am s* srebrny medalista *m*; **sil•ver 'pa•per** *s Br* folia *f* aluminiowa; **sil•ver-plat•ed** [sɪlvə'pleɪtɪd] *adj* posrebrzany; **sil•ver 'screen** *s* **1.** (wielki) ekran *m* **2.** kino *n*; **sil•ver smith** ['sɪlvəsmɪθ] *s* złotnik *m*; **sil•ver•ware** ['sɪlvərweə] *s* **1.** srebro *n* stołowe **2.** *Am* sztućce *pl* **3.** *Br infml* trofeum *n*; **sil•ver 'wed•ding** *s* srebrne wesele *n*

sim•i•lar ['sɪmɪlə] *adj* podobny (***to*** do *G*); **sim•i•lar•i•ty** [sɪmɪ'lærətɪ] *s* podobieństwo *n*; ***a striking ~*** uderzające podobieństwo; **sim•i•lar•ly** ['sɪmələlɪ] *adv* **1.** podobnie **2.** w podobny sposób

sim•i•le ['sɪmɪlɪ] *s* porównanie *n*

sim•mer ['sɪmə] **I** *v/t* **1.** dusić na wolnym ogniu **2.** gotować na wolnym ogniu **II** *v/i* **1.** dusić się na wolnym ogniu **2.** gotować się na wolnym ogniu **3.** ~ (***with anger***) kipieć ze złości **III** *s* ***bring s.th. to a ~*** doprowadzić coś do lekkiego wrzenia; **simmer down** *v/i infml* uspokajać ⟨-koić⟩ się

sim•per ['sɪmpə] *v/i* głupio się uśmiechać ⟨-chnąć⟩

sim•ple ['sɪmpl] *adj* **1.** prosty; ***for the ~ reason*** z tego prostego powodu **2.** łatwy **3.** zwykły, zwyczajny; **sim•ple-mind•ed** [sɪmpl'maɪndɪd] *adj* **1.** niemądry **2.** *opinions*: naiwny

sim•pli•ci•ty [sɪm'plɪsətɪ] *s* **1.** prostota *f* **2.** łatwość *f*

sim•pli•fi•ca•tion [sɪmplɪfɪ'keɪʃn] *s* uproszczenie *n*; **sim•pli•fy** ['sɪmplɪfaɪ] *v/t* upraszczać ⟨-rościć⟩

sim•plis•tic [sɪm'plɪstɪk] *adj* zbyt uproszczony

sim•ply ['sɪmplɪ] *adv* **1.** po prostu; ***to put it ~*** mówiąc po prostu **2.** prosto; ***live ~*** żyć zwyczajnie

sim•u•late ['sɪmjʊleɪt] *v/t* **1.** udawać ⟨-dać⟩ **2.** symulować; **sim•u•la•tion** [sɪmjʊ'leɪʃn] *s* **1.** udawanie *n* **2.** symulowanie *n* **3.** TECH symulacja *f*; ***a computer ~*** symulacja komputerowa; **sim•u•la•tor** ['sɪmjʊleɪtə] *s* symulator *m*

sim•ul•ta•ne•ous [saɪml'teɪnɪəs] *adj* **1.** jednoczesny **2.** równoczesny; ***a ~ interpreter*** tłumacz symultaniczny; **sim•ul•ta•ne•ous•ly** [saɪml'teɪnɪəslɪ] *adv* **1.** jednocześnie **2.** równocześnie

sin [sɪn] **I** *s* grzech *m*; ***as ugly as ~*** brzydki jak noc **II** *v/t* grzeszyć ⟨z-⟩

since [sɪns] **I** *prep* (*moment*) od *G*; ***~ breakfast*** od śniadania; ***~ when?*** od kiedy? **II** *conj* **1.** odkąd, od kiedy, od czasu, gdy; ***Cathy hasn't phoned ~ she went to London*** Cathy nie dzwoniła od czasu, gdy wyjechała do Londynu **2.** ponieważ, jako że **III** *adv* (*a.* ***~ then***, **ever ~**) od tej pory, od tego czasu

sin•cere [sɪn'sɪə] *adj* szczery; **sin•cere•ly** [sɪn'sɪəlɪ] *adv* **1.** szczerze; ***Yours ~***, ⁂ Z poważaniem; **sin•cer•i•ty** [sɪn'serətɪ] *s* **1.** szczerość *f* **2.** uczciwość *f*

sine [saɪn] *s MATH* sinus *m*

si•ne qua non [sɪneɪkwɑː'nəʊn] *s* warunek *m* konieczny, warunek *m* sine qua non

sin•ew ['sɪnjuː] *s ANAT* ścięgno *n*; **'sin•ew•y** *adj* **1.** muskularny **2.** *meat*: żylasty

sin•ful ['sɪnfəl] *adj* grzeszny

sing [sɪŋ] (*sang*; *sung*) *v/t* śpiewać ⟨za-⟩; **sing along with** *v/t* śpiewać ⟨za-⟩ razem z *I*

singe [sɪndʒ] *v/t* przypalać ⟨-lić⟩

sing•er ['sɪŋə] *s* **1.** śpiewak *m* **2.** piosenkarz *m* **3.** wokalista *f* **4.** ***be a good ~*** umieć śpiewać; **sing•er-'song•writ•er** *s* autor i wykonawca piosenek; **sing•ing** ['sɪŋɪŋ] *s* **1.** śpiewanie *n*; ***have a beautiful ~ voice*** mieć piękny głos **2.** śpiew *m*; ***a ~ lesson*** lekcja śpiewu

sin•gle ['sɪŋgl] **I** *adj* **1.** jeden; ***not a ~ one*** ani jeden **2.** pojedynczy **3.** wolny, *form* stanu wolnego; ***he's ~*** jest nieżonaty; ***she's ~*** jest niezamężna **4.** *ticket*: w jedną stronę **II** *s* **1.** bilet *m* w jedną stronę **2.** *MUS* singiel *m* **3.** pokój *m* jednoosobowy, *infml* jedynka *f* **4.** ***~s*** ludzie samotni, *infml* single **III** *v/t* ***~ s.th. out*** wybierać ⟨-brać⟩ coś; **sin•gle-breast•ed** [sɪŋgl'brestɪd] *adj jacket*: jednorzędowy; **sin•gle cream** *s* śmietana *f* o niskiej zawartości tłuszczu; **sin•gle cur•ren•cy** *s* wspólna waluta *f*; **sin•gle 'file** *s*: ***in ~*** gęsiego; **sin•gle-'hand•ed** [sɪŋgl'hændɪd] *adj* **1.** samodzielnie **2.** bez niczyjej pomocy **3.** samotnie; ***sail around the world ~*** samotnie opłynąć świat; **sin•gle-mind•ed** [sɪŋgl'maɪndɪd] *adj*: **be ~** mieć tylko jeden cel; **sin•gle 'mar•ket** *s* jednolity rynek *m*; **sin•gle 'moth•er** *s* samotna matka *f*; **sin•gle 'pa•rent** *s* samotny rodzic *m*; **sin•gle pa•rent 'fam•i•ly** *s* niepełna *f* rodzina; **sin•gle 'room** *s* pokój *m* jednoosobowy

sin•gles bar ['sɪŋglzbɑː] *s* bar *m* dla samotnych

'sing•song I *s Br* wspólne śpiewanie *n* **II** *adj* śpiewny

sin•gu•lar ['sɪŋgjʊlə] **I** *s GRAM* liczba *f* pojedyncza **II** *adj* **1.** *form*: pojedynczy **2.** niezwykły **3.** *lit* osobliwy; **sin•gu•lar•ly** ['sɪŋgjələlɪ] *adv* **1.** bardzo **2.** niezwykle

sin•is•ter ['sɪnɪstə] *adj* **1.** złowrogi **2.** złowieszczy **3.** ponury

sink [sɪŋk] **I** (*sank*; *sunk*) *v/i* **1.** tonąć ⟨za-, u-⟩ **2.** opadać ⟨opaść⟩; ***~ into an armchair*** opaść na fotel **3.** osuwać ⟨osunąć⟩ się; ***~ to one's knees*** osunąć się na kolana **4.** (*profits*) spadać ⟨spaść⟩ **5.** (*sun*) zachodzić ⟨zajść⟩ **6.** (*building*) osiadać ⟨osiąść⟩ **7.** (*land*) zapadać ⟨-paść⟩ się **8.** ***his voice sank to a whisper*** *lit* zniżył głos do szeptu **9.** *fig* upadać ⟨upaść⟩; ***how could you ~ so low?*** jak mogłeś upaść tak nisko? **II** (*sank*; *sunk*) *v/t* **1.** topić ⟨za-⟩; ***be sunk in thoughts*** być zatopionym w myślach **2.** kopać ⟨wy-⟩ **3.** zakopywać ⟨-pać⟩ **4.** wkopywać ⟨-pać⟩ **5.** ***~ one's teeth into*** zatopić zęby w *L* **6.** *infml chances*: pogrzebać **7.** *infml beer*: obalać ⟨-lić⟩ **8.** *infml glass*: wychylać ⟨-lić⟩ **III** *s* **1.** zlewozmywak *m*, zlew *m* **2.** *Am* umywalka *f*; **sink in** *v/i* **1.** wsiąkać ⟨-knąć⟩ **2.** ***it took a while to ~*** dopiero po jakimś czasie dotarło to do mnie

'sink•er *s* (*on fishing rod*) ciężarek *m*; **sink•ing** ['sɪŋkɪŋ] *adj*: ***I got that ~ feeling*** poczułam ucisk w żołądku

sin•ner ['sɪnə] *s* grzesznik *m*

S

si•nus ['saɪnəs] *s ANAT* zatoka *f*; **si•nus•i•tis** [saɪnə'saɪtɪs] *s MED* zapalenie *n* zatok

Sioux [suː] *pl Sioux* [suːz] *s* Siuks *m*

sip [sɪp] **I** *v/t* **1.** sączyć **2.** popijać **II** *v/i* **1.** sączyć (**at** *A*) **2.** popijać (**at** *A*) **III** *s* **1.** łyk *m* **2.** łyczek *m*

siphon ['saɪfn] **I** *s* syfon *m* **II** (*a.* **~ off**) *v/t* **1.** *liquid*: spuszczać ⟨spuścić⟩ **2.** *money*: wyprowadzać ⟨-dzić⟩

sir [sɜː] *s* **1.** (*addressing man*) pan *m*; ***good morning, ~*** dzień dobry panu; ***Dear ~*** (*letters*) Szanowny Panie **2.** (*noble title*) ***~ Winston Churchill*** Sir Winston Churchill

si•ren ['saɪrən] *s* syrena *f*

sir•loin ['sɜːlɔɪn] *s* polędwica *f* (wołowa); **sir•loin steak** *s* befsztyk *m* z polędwicy

sis [sɪs] *s infml* siostra *f*

sis•sy ['sɪsɪ] *s infml* mięczak *m*

sis•ter ['sɪstə] *s* siostra *f*, ***my little ~*** moja siostrzyczka; **sis•ter•hood** ['sɪstəhʊd] *s* zakon *m* żeński; **'sis•ter-in-law** *s* **1.** szwagierka *f* **2.** bratowa *f*; **sis•ter•ly** ['sɪstəlɪ] *adj* siostrzany

sit [sɪt] (*sat*; *sat*) *v/i* **1.** siedzieć; ***just ~ still!*** siedź spokojnie **2.** siadać ⟨usiąść⟩; ***may I ~ here?*** czy mogę tu usiąść?; (*dog*) ***~!*** siad! **3.** *magazine, letter*: leżeć **4.** *books, furniture*: stać **5.** zasiadać; ***~ on a committee*** zasiadać w komisji **6.** → ***babysit*** **II** (*sat*; *sat*) *v/t* **7.** *Br exam*: zdawać; **sit around** *v/i*: ***~ doing nothing*** *Br infml* siedzieć i nic nie robić; **sit back** *v/i* rozsiadać ⟨-siąść⟩ się; **sit by** *v/i fig* siedzieć z założonymi rękami; **sit down** *v/i* siadać ⟨usiąść⟩; **sit for** *v/i* **1.** pozować do *G* **2.** pozować *D*; **sit in for** *v/i* zastępować ⟨-tąpić⟩; **sit in on** *v/i* być obecnym na *L*; **sit on** *v/i* przetrzymywać ⟨-mać⟩; **sit out** *v/t* przeczekiwać ⟨-kać⟩; **sit up** *v/i* **1.** (*raise oneself up*) siadać ⟨usiąść⟩, podnosić ⟨-nieść⟩ się **2.** siedzieć do późna **3.** prostować ⟨wy-⟩ się

sit•com ['sɪtkɒm] *s* sitcom *m*

'sit-down *s* **1.** ***I need a ~*** *Br infml* muszę usiąść i odpocząć **2.** strajk *m* okupacyjny

site [saɪt] **I** *s* **1.** miejsce *n* **2.** teren *m* **3.** plac *m*; ***a building ~*** plac budowy, budowa **4.** *battle*: pole *n* **5.** *INF* witryna *f* **II** *v/t* **1.** lokalizować ⟨z-⟩ **2.** rozmieszczać ⟨-mieścić⟩

'sit-in *s* strajk *m* okupacyjny

sit•ter ['sɪtə] *s* **1.** model *m*, modelka *f* **2.** → ***babysitter***; **sit•ting** ['sɪtɪŋ] *adj* **1.** posiedzenie *n*; ***in one ~*** za jednym posiedzeniem **2.** *PHOT ART* sesja *f* **3.** (*meal*) tura *f*; **sit•ting 'duck** *s fig* łatwy cel *m*; **'sit•ting room** *s* (*room*) *Br* salon *m*

sit•u•at•ed ['sɪtʃʊeɪtɪd] *adj* **1.** zlokalizowany; ***be ~*** znajdować się **2.** położony; ***the house is beautifully ~*** dom jest pięknie położony **3.** ***be well ~*** *form* być dobrze sytuowanym; **sit•u•a•tion** [sɪtʃʊ'eɪʃn] *s* **1.** sytuacja *f* **2.** *lit* położenie *n*; ***be in a beautiful ~*** być pięknie położonym **3.** *dated* posada *f*; ***'~s vacant'*** „oferty pracy"; **sit•u•a•tion 'com•e•dy** *s* komedia *f* sytuacyjna

sit-ups ['sɪtʌps] *pl infml* (*exercise*) brzuszki *pl*

six [sɪks] **I** *num* sześć, sześciu, sześcioro **II** *s* szóstka *f*; ***we've been at ~es and sevens in the office*** *infml* w pracy mieliśmy straszny kołowrót; **six•fold** ['siksfəʊld] *adj* sześciokrotny **II** *adv* sześciokrotnie

sixth [sɪksθ] *adj* szósty; ***the ~ sense*** szósty zmysł

'six-pack *s* sześciopak *m*

six•teen [sɪks'tiːn] **I** *num* szesnaście **II** *s* szesnastka *f*

six•teenth [sɪks'tiːnθ] *adj* szesnasty

six•ti•eth ['sɪkstɪɪθ] *adj* sześćdziesiąty

'six-time *adj* sześciokrotny

six•ty ['sɪkstɪ] **I** *num* sześćdziesiąt **II** *s* sześćdziesiątka *f*; ***be in one's sixties*** być po sześćdziesiątce; ***in the sixties*** w latach sześćdziesiątych

size [saɪz] **I** *s* **1.** wielkość *f* **2.** rozmiar *m*; ***what ~ do you take?*** jaki ma pani rozmiar? **3.** numer *m*; ***a shoe ~*** numer butów **4.** wymiary *pl* **II** *v/t* **1.** podawać ⟨-dać⟩ rozmiar **2.** zmieniać ⟨-nić⟩ rozmiar; **size up** *v/t infml* **1.** oceniać ⟨-nić⟩ **2.** mierzyć ⟨z-⟩ wzrokiem

size•a•ble ['saɪzəbl] *adj* **1.** znaczny **2.** spory **3.** pokaźny

siz•zle ['sɪzl] *v/i* skwierczeć ⟨za-⟩; **'siz•zler** *s* skwarny dzień *m*

S

skate[1] [skeɪt] *pl skate, skates s* BIOL płaszczka *f*

skate[2] [~] **I** *v/i* **1.** jeździć na łyżwach **2.** jeździć na rolkach **3.** jeździć na wrotkach **4.** jeździć na deskorolce **II** *s* **1.** łyżwa *f* **2.** rolka *f* **3.** wrotka *f*; **skate around, *skate over*** *v/i fig* omijać ⟨ominąć⟩

skate•board ['skeɪtbɔːd] **I** *s* deskorolka *f* **II** *v/i* jeździć na deskorolce; **skate•board•er** ['skeɪtbɔːdə] *s* deskorolkarz *m*; **skate•board•ing** ['skeɪtbɔːdɪŋ] *s* jazda *f* na deskorolce; **skat•er** ['skeɪtə] *s* **1.** łyżwiarz *m* **2.** rolkarz *m* **3.** wrotkarz *m*; **skat•ing** ['skeɪtɪŋ] *s* **1.** łyżwiarstwo *n* **2.** jazda *f* na rolkach **3.** wrotkarstwo *n*; **'skat•ing rink** *s* **1.** lodowisko *n* **2.** tor *m* wrotkarski

skel•e•ton ['skelɪtn] *s* **1.** szkielet *m*; ***a ~ in the cupboard*** *Br fig* trup w szafie **2.** zarys *m*; **'skel•e•ton key** *s* klucz *m* uniwersalny

skep•tic *Am* → ***sceptic***; **skep•ti•cal** *Am* → ***sceptical***; **skep•ti•cism** *Am* → ***scepticism***

sketch [sketʃ] **I** *s* **1.** szkicować ⟨na-⟩ **2.** *plan*: kreślić ⟨na-⟩ **II** *s* **1.** szkic *m* **2.** skecz *m*; **sketch out** *v/t fig* przedstawiać ⟨-wić⟩ w zarysie

'sketch pad, *'sketch•book* *s* szkicownik *m*; **sketch•y** ['sketʃɪ] *adj* **1.** szkicowy **2.** pobieżny

skew [skjuː] *v/t* **1.** zniekszałcać ⟨-cić⟩ **2.** przekrzywiać ⟨-wić⟩; **skewed** ['skjuːd] *adj* **1.** zniekształcony **2.** przekrzywiony; **skew•er** ['skjʊə] *s* COOK **1.** rożen *m* **2.** szpikulec *m*

ski [skiː] **I** *v/i* jeździć na nartach **II** *s* narta *f* **III** *adj* narciarski; **'ski boots** *pl* buty *pl* narciarskie

skid [skɪd] **I** *v/i* wpadać ⟨wpaść⟩ w poślizg **II** *s* poślizg *m*; ***go into a ~*** wpaść w poślizg

ski•er ['skiːə] *s* narciarz *m*

skiff [skɪf] *s* **1.** lekka łódź *f* **2.** SPORT skif *m*, jedynka *f*

ski gog•gles ['skiːgɒglz] *pl* gogle *pl* narciarskie

ski•ing ['skiːɪŋ] *s* jazda *f* na nartach; ***let's go ~*** chodźmy na narty; **'ski in•struc•tor** *s* instruktor *m* jazdy na nartach; **'ski jump** *s* **1.** skocznia *f* narciarska **2.** skok *m* narciarski; **'ski jump•er** *s* skoczek *m* narciarski; **'ski jump•ing** *s* skoki *pl* narciarskie

skil•ful ['skɪlfəl] *Br*, ***'skill•ful*** *Am adj* **1.** *player, driver*: sprawny **2.** zręczny; **skil•ful•ly** *Br* ['skɪlfəlɪ], ***skill•ful•ly*** *Am adv* **1.** umiejętnie **2.** zręcznie **3.** wprawnie

'ski lift *s* wyciąg *m* narciarski

skill [skɪl] *s* **1.** umiejętność *f* **2.** zręczność *f* **3.** wprawa *f*; **skilled** [skɪld] *adj* **1.** *player, driver*: sprawny **2.** ***be ~ at doing s.th.*** umiejętnie coś robić **3.** zręczny **4.** *employee*: wykwalifikowany **5.** *work*: wymagający kwalifikacji

skil•let ['skɪlɪt] *s Am* patelnia *f*

skim [skɪm] **I** *v/t* **1.** (*a.* ***~ off***) *fat*: zbierać ⟨zebrać⟩ **2.** zbierać ⟨zebrać⟩ śmietankę z *G* **II** *v/t* prześlizgiwać ⟨-gnąć⟩ się po *L* **III** *v/i* (*a.* ***~ through***) *text*: przeglądać ⟨przejrzeć⟩; **skimmed milk** [skɪmd'mɪlk] *Br*, ***skim 'milk*** *Am s* chude mleko *n*, mleko *n* odtłuszczone

skimp [skɪmp] *v/i* **1.** oszczędzać ⟨-dzić⟩ (***on*** na *L*) **2.** skąpić ⟨po-⟩ (***on*** na *A*); **skimp•y** ['skɪmpɪ] *adj* **1.** *swimsuit*: skąpy **2.** *skirt*: kusy **3.** *money*: marny

skin [skɪn] **I** *s* **1.** skóra *f*; ***by the ~ of one's teeth*** *infml* z trudem, z ledwością; ***get under one's ~*** *fig* zajść komuś za skórę; ***I've got her under my ~*** szaleję za nią; ***be drenched to the ~*** być przemoczonym do suchej nitki; ***save one's ~*** ratować własną skórę **2.** *fruit*: skórka *f* **3.** (*on milk*) kożuch *m* **4.** *paint*: powłoka *f* **II** *v/t* **1.** obierać ⟨-brać⟩ ze skórki **2.** ściągać ⟨-gnąć⟩ skórę z *G* **3.** ***~ one's knees*** obetrzeć sobie kolana; ***~ one's hands*** zedrzeć sobie skórę z dłoni; **'skin care** *s* pielęgnacja *f* skóry; **skin-'deep** *adj* powierzchowny; ***beauty is only ~*** uroda to nie wszystko; **'skin div•er** *s* nurek *m*; **'skin div•ing** *s* nurkowanie *n* (bez skafandra); **'skin flick** *s infml* pornos *m*; **skin•flint** ['skɪnflɪnt] *s infml* sknera *m/f*

'skin•head *s* skinhead *m*, *infml* skin *m*

skin•ny ['skɪnɪ] *adj infml* **1.** kościsty **2.** strasznie chudy **3.** *trousers*: obcisły; **skin•ny-dip•ping** ['skɪnɪdɪpɪŋ] *s infml* kąpiel *f* na golasa

skint [skɪnt] *adj Br infml* spłukany

'skin-tight *adj trousers*: obcisły

skip [skɪp] **I** *v/i* **1.** podskakiwać ⟨-skoczyć⟩ **2.** skakać przez skakankę **3.** *~ from one topic to another fig* przeskakiwać z tematu na temat **II** *v/t* **1.** pomijać ⟨-minąć⟩; *~ breakfast* nie jeść śniadania **2.** opuszczać ⟨opuścić⟩; *~ lessons* opuszczać lekcje; *~ school* nie pójść do szkoły **3.** *~ stones* puszczać kaczki **III** *s* **1.** podskok *m* **2.** *Br* kontener *m* na gruz; **skip off** *v/i infml* zwiewać ⟨zwiać⟩; **skip over** *v/t* **1.** pomijać ⟨-minąć⟩ **2.** opuszczać ⟨opuścić⟩

skip•per ['skɪpə] *s* **1.** szyper *m* **2.** SPORT *infml* kapitan *m*; **skip•ping rope** ['skɪpɪŋrəʊp] *s Br* skakanka *f*

skir•mish ['skɜːmɪʃ] *s* **1.** potyczka *f* **2.** utarczka *f* słowna

skirt [skɜːt] **I** *s* spódnica *f* **II** *v/t* **1.** okrążać ⟨-żyć⟩ **2.** (*a.* *~ around*) *subject*: unikać ⟨-knąć⟩; **'skirt•ing board** *s Br* listwa *f* przypodłogowa

skit [skɪt] *s* parodia *f* (**on** *G*)

skive [skaɪv] *Br infml* **I** *v/i* (*a.* *~ off*) **1.** wagarować **2.** obijać się **3.** zrywać ⟨zerwać⟩ się wcześniej z pracy **II** *v/t* **1.** *~ school* wagarować **2.** zrywać ⟨zerwać⟩ się z *G*

skul•dug•ger•y [skʌl'dʌgərɪ] *s infml* machlojki *pl*

skulk [skʌlk] *v/i* **1.** skradać się **2.** przyczaić się

skull [skʌl] *s* czaszka *f*; **'skull cap** *s* **1.** jarmułka *f*, mycka *f* **2.** piuska *f*

skunk [skʌŋk] *s* BIOL skunks *m*

sky [skaɪ] *s* niebo *n*; *in the ~* na niebie; *praise s.o. to the skies* wychwalać kogoś pod niebiosa; **sky-'blue** *adj* błękitny; **'sky•div•er** *s* spadochroniarz *m*; **'sky-div•ing** *s* spadochroniarstwo *n*; **sky-'high I** *adj prices*: astronomiczny, niebotyczny **II** *adv* ***go ~*** (*prices*) poszybować w górę; **'sky•light** *s* (*roof*) świetlik *m*; **'sky•line** *s* **1.** linia *f* horyzontu **2.** kontury *pl* budynków (na tle nieba); **'sky•rock•et** *v/i* (*prices*) szybować ⟨po-⟩ w górę; **sky•scrap•er** ['skaɪskreɪpə] *s* drapacz *m* chmur

slab [slæb] *s* **1.** *stone, concrete*: płyta *f* **2.** *meat*: kawał *m* **3.** *chocolate*: tabliczka *f*

slack [slæk] **I** *adj* **1.** luźny **2.** *discipline*: słaby **3.** *period*: spokojny **4.** *skin*: zwiotczały **5.** *person*: niedbały **II** *s* luz *m*; *there's too much ~ in these ropes* te liny są za słabo naciągnięte **III** *v/i* obijać się; **slack off** *v/i* zwalniać ⟨zwolnić⟩ tempo

slack•en ['slækn] **I** *v/i* **1.** (*rope*) rozluźniać ⟨-nić⟩ się **2.** *his grip ~ed* zwolnił uścisk **3.** (*a.* *~ off*) *fig* zwalniać ⟨zwolnić⟩ **4.** (*a.* *~ off*) (*rain*) słabnąć ⟨o-⟩ **II** *v/t* **1.** *rope, grip*: zwalniać ⟨zwolnić⟩ **2.** zwalniać ⟨zwolnić⟩; *~ one's pace* zwolnić kroku

slag [slæg] **I** *s* **1.** żużel *m* **2.** (*woman*) *infml* zdzira *f* **II** *v/t* ***~ s.o. off*** *Br infml* obsmarowac kogoś

slain [sleɪn] *Past Participle →* **slay**

slake [sleɪk] *v/t* **1.** *thirst*: gasić ⟨u-⟩ **2.** *needs, desire*: zaspokajać ⟨-koić⟩

sla•lom ['slɑːləm] *s* slalom *m*

slam [slæm] **I** *v/t* **1.** trzaskać ⟨-snąć⟩; *to ~ s.th. shut* zatrzymać coś **2.** *~ on the brakes infml* ostro zahamować **3.** rzucać ⟨-cić⟩; *~ down the phone* rzucić słuchawkę **4.** ostro krytykować ⟨s-⟩, *infml* zjechać (**for** za *A*) **II** *v/i* **1.** zatrzaskiwać ⟨-snąć⟩ się **2.** z impetem uderzać ⟨-rzyć⟩ (**into** w *A*)

slan•der ['slɑːndə] **I** *s* **1.** pomówienie *n* **2.** zniesławienie *n* **3.** oszczerstwo *n* **II** *v/t* **1.** pomawiać ⟨-mówić⟩ **2.** zniesławiać ⟨-wić⟩; **slan•der•ous** ['slɑːndərəs] *adj* **1.** zniesławiający **2.** oszczerczy

slang [slɑːŋ] *s* slang *m*; **'slang•ing match** *s Br infml* pyskówka *f*

slant [slɑːnt] **I** *v/i* nachylać ⟨-lić⟩ się **II** *v/t* **1.** nachylać ⟨-lić⟩ **2.** *fig* naginać ⟨-giąć⟩ **III** *s* **1.** nachylenie *n*, pochylenie *n*; *the floor is on a ~* podłoga jest pochyła **2.** spojrzenie *n*; *put a new ~ on* zaprezentować nowy punkt widzenia na *A* **3.** *fig* skrzywienie *n*; **slant•ing** ['slɑːntɪŋ] *adj* **1.** pochyły **2.** *eyes*: skośny **3.** *rain*: zacinający

slap [slæp] **I** *v/t* **1.** *~ s.o. across the face*, *~ s.o.'s face* uderzyć kogoś w twarz, spoliczkować kogoś **2.** *~ s.o. on the back* poklepać kogoś po plecach **3.** dawać ⟨dać⟩ klapsa **4.** rzucać ⟨-cić⟩; *~ some paint on the wall* chlapnąć trochę farby na ścianę **II** *v/i* *the water ~ped against the rocks* fale z pluskiem uderzały o skały

III *s* **1.** ***a ~*** (***in the face***) policzek **2.** klaps *m* **3.** klepnięcie *n* **IV** (*a.* **~ 'bang**) *adv infml* **1.** prosto **2.** ***~ in the middle*** w samym środku; **'slap•dash** *adj* **1.** niedbały **2.** byle jaki; **'slap•stick** *s* slapstick *m*; ***a ~ comedy*** komedia slapstickowa; **'slap-up** *adj*: ***a ~ meal*** *Br infml* wyżerka

slash [slæʃ] **I** *v/t* **1.** ciąć ⟨po-⟩; ***~ one's wrists*** podciąć sobie żyły **2.** przecinać ⟨-ciąć⟩ **3.** *throat*: podrzynać ⟨-derżnąć⟩ **4.** *costs*: ciąć ⟨ob-⟩, drastycznie obniżać ⟨-żyć⟩ **II** *s* **1.** cięcie *n* **2.** rana *f* cięta **3.** (*punctuation*) ukośnik *m*

slate[1] [sleɪt] **I** *s* **1.** łupek *m* **2.** (łupkowa) płytka *f* dachowa **3.** *Am* POLIT lista *f* kandydatów **4.** (*for writing*) tabliczka *f* **II** *v/t* planować ⟨za-⟩; ***the next meeting is ~d for March*** następne spotkanie odbędzie się w marcu; ***be ~d for demolition*** być przeznaczonym do rozbiórki

slate[2] [~] *v/t infml* zmieszać z błotem

slaugh•ter ['slɔːtə] **I** *s* **1.** ubój *m* **2.** rzeź *f* **II** *v/t* **1.** *animals*: ubijać ⟨-bić⟩ **2.** *people*: mordować ⟨wy-⟩; **'slaugh•ter-house** *s* rzeźnia *f*

Slav [slɑːv] *s* Słowianin *m*

slave [sleɪv] **I** *s* niewolnik *m* **II** *v/i* harować (**at** nad *I*); **'slave-driv•er** *s* **1.** *fig* gnębiciel *m* **2.** poganiacz *m* niewolników; **slave 'la•bour** *Br*, ***slave labor*** *Am* praca *f* niewolnicza

slav•er ['slævə] *v/i* ślinić się

slav•er•y ['sleɪvərɪ] *s* **1.** niewolnictwo *n* **2.** niewola *f*

'slave trade, ***'slave traf•fic*** *s* handel *m* niewolnikami

Slavic ['slaːvɪk] → ***Slavonic***

slav•ish ['sleɪvɪʃ] *adj* **1.** *copy*: (niemal) identyczny **2.** *devotion*: niewolniczy **3.** *follower*, *fan*: bezkrytyczny **4.** ***be a ~ follower of fashion*** niewolniczo podążać za modą

Sla•von•ic [slə'vɒnɪk] *adj* słowiański

slay [sleɪ] (*slew*; *slain*) *v/t* **1.** *lit* zabijać ⟨-bić⟩ **2.** uśmiercać ⟨-cić⟩ **3.** *Am* mordować ⟨za-⟩ **4.** *Am fig* rzucać ⟨-cić⟩ na kolana; **slay•er** ['sleɪə] *s* zabójca *m*

sleaze [sliːz] *s* **1.** zepsucie *n* **2.** brud *m* moralny

slea•zy ['sliːzɪ] *adj infml* **1.** obskurny **2.** zepsuty

sled [sled] *Am* → ***sledge***

sledge [sledʒ] **I** *s* **1.** sanki *pl* **2.** sanie *pl* **II** *v/i* **1.** jeździć na sankach **2.** jeździć saniami; **'sledge-ham•mer** *s* młot *m* oburęczny

sleek [sliːk] *adj* **1.** *hair*: lśniący **2.** *car*: elegancki

sleep [sliːp] **I** (*slept*; *slept*) *v/i* spać; ***~ late*** spać do późna; ***~ like a log*** spać jak suseł; ***let ~ing dogs lie*** nie wywołuj wilka z lasu **II** (*slept*; *slept*) *v/t* ***we can ~ six*** możemy przenocować sześć osób; ***the apartment ~s six*** w mieszkaniu jest sześć miejsc do spania **III** *s* sen *m*; ***in one's ~*** we śnie; ***I couldn't get to ~*** nie mogłem zasnąć; ***get to ~*** zasnąć; ***did you have a good ~?*** dobrze spałeś?; ***put s.o. to ~*** uśpić kogoś; **sleep around** *v/i infml* puszczać się na prawo i lewo; **sleep in** *v/i* spać ⟨po-⟩ dłużej; **sleep off** *v/t* odsypiać ⟨odespać⟩; **sleep on** *v/i* (*think over*) przespać się z *I*; **sleep over** *v/i* nocować ⟨prze-⟩; **sleep through** *v/i* przesypiać ⟨-spać⟩; **sleep together** *v/i* spać ze sobą; **sleep with** *v/i* spać z *I*

sleep•er ['sliːpə] *s* **1.** śpiący *m* **2.** ***be a light ~*** mieć lekki sen **3.** wagon *m* sypialny **4.** pociąg *m* z wagonami sypialnymi **5.** *Br* podkład *m* kolejowy

sleep•i•ly ['sliːpɪlɪ] *adv* sennie

'sleep•ing bag ['sliːpɪŋbæg] *s* śpiwór *m*; **'sleep•ing car** *s* wagon *m* sypialny; **'sleep•ing part•ner** *s* ECON cichy wspólnik *m*; **'sleep•ing pill** *s* tabletka *f* nasenna; **sleep•ing po•lice•man** *s Br infml* próg *m* zwalniający; **'sleep•ing sick•ness** *s* MED śpiączka *f*; **'sleep-ing tab•let** *s* tabletka *f* nasenna

sleep•less ['sliːpləs] *adj* bezsenny

'sleep•walk *v/i* chodzić we śnie; **'sleep-walk•er** *s* lunatyk *m*; **'sleep walk•ing** *s* lunatyzm *m*

sleep•y ['sliːpɪ] *adj* **1.** śpiący **2.** senny; **'sleep•y•head** *s* śpioch *m*

sleet [sliːt] **I** *s* deszcz *m* ze śniegiem **II** *v/i* ***it's ~ing*** pada deszcz ze śniegiem

sleeve [sliːv] *s* **1.** rękaw *m*; ***have s.th. up one's ~ fig*** mieć coś w zanadrzu; ***laugh up one's ~*** śmiać się w kułak **2.** TECH tuleja *f*; **sleeve•less** ['sliːvləs] *adj* bez rękawów

sleigh [sleɪ] *s* sanie *pl*

S

sleight of hand [slaɪtəv'hænd] *s* **1.** zręczne ręce *pl* **2.** sztuczka *f*
slen•der ['slendə] *adj* **1.** szczupły **2.** smukły **3.** *amount*, *height*: niewielki **4.** *majority*: nieznaczny
slept [slept] *Past Simple and Past Participle* → **sleep**
sleuth [slu:θ] *s* detektyw *m*
slew [slu:] *Past Simple* → **slay**
slice [slaɪs] **I** *s* **1.** kromka *f* **2.** plaster *m* **3.** plasterek *m* **4.** część *f* **5.** (*cake*) łopatka *f* **6.** (*tennis*) slajs *m* **II** *v/t* **1.** kroić ⟨po-⟩ **2.** kroić ⟨po-⟩ na plastry; **slice off** *v/t* odcinać ⟨-ciąć⟩; **slice up** *v/t* kroić ⟨po-⟩
slick [slɪk] **I** *adj* **1.** zgrabny **2.** zręczny **3.** *person*: wygadany **4.** *movement*: płynny **5.** *surface*: śliski **II** *s* plama *f* ropy **III** *v/t hair*: przygładzać ⟨-dzić⟩; **slick•er** [slɪkə] *s Am* płaszcz *m* przeciwdeszczowy
slid [slɪd] *Past Simple and Past Participle* → **slide**
slide [slaɪd] **I** (*slid*; *slid*) *v/i* **1.** ślizgać się **2.** sunąć **3.** wślizgiwać ⟨-znąć⟩ się (***into*** do *G*) **4.** ***~ out*** wyśliznąć się **5.** ***~ in and out*** wsuwać się i wysuwać **6.** (*prices*) spadać ⟨-paść⟩ **7** (*dollar*, *euro*) słabnąć ⟨o-⟩, tanieć ⟨po-⟩ **8.** ***let s.th ~*** zaniedbać coś **II** (*slid*; *slid*) *v/t* **1.** przesuwać ⟨-sunąć⟩ **2.** wsuwać ⟨wsunąć⟩ (***into*** do *G*) **3.** ***~ s.th. out*** wysunąć coś **III** *s* **1.** spadek *m* **2.** ***the economy is on the ~*** gospodarka podupada **3.** ślizgawka *f* **4.** zjeżdżalnia *f* **5.** PHOT slajd *m*, przeźrocze *n* **6.** szkiełko *n* (mikroskopu) **7.** wsuwka *f* **8.** lawina *f* kamieni; **'slide pro•jec•tor** *s* rzutnik *m*; **slide rule** *s* suwak *m* logarytmiczny
slid•ing door ['slaɪdɪŋdɔ:] *s* rozsuwane drzwi *pl*; **slid•ing 'scale** *s* skala *f* ruchoma
slight [slaɪt] **I** *adj* **1.** niewielki; ***I haven't got the ~est idea*** nie mam najmniejszego pojęcia **2.** nieznaczny **3.** *person*: drobny **3.** *form* niewarty uwagi **II** *s* **1.** obraza *f* (***on*** *G*) **2.** afront *m* **III** *v/t* obrażać ⟨-razić⟩; **slight•ly** ['slaɪtlɪ] *adv* **1.** trochę **2.** nieco **3.** nieznacznie
slim [slɪm] **I** *adj* **1.** szczupły **2.** cienki **3.** *chance*: niewielki, nikły **4.** *hope*: znikomy, nikły **II** *v/i* odchudzać ⟨-dzić⟩ się; **slim down I** *v/i* chudnąć ⟨s-⟩; ***~ to 60 kilos*** schudnąć do 60 kilo **II** *v/t* **1.** *fig* odchudzać ⟨-dzić⟩ **2.** ograniczać ⟨-czyć⟩ działalność
slime [slaɪm] *s* **1.** muł *m* **2.** szlam *m* **2.** śluz *m*
slim•ming ['slɪmɪŋ] *s Br* odchudzanie *n*
slim•y ['slaɪmɪ] *adj* **1.** *a. fig* oślizły **2.** mulisty **3.** mazisty
sling [slɪŋ] **I** (*slung*; *slung*) *v/t* **1.** rzucać ⟨-cić⟩ **2.** wieszać ⟨powiesić⟩ **3.** przewieszać ⟨-wiesić⟩ **II** *s* **1.** temblak *m*; ***in a ~*** na temblaku **2.** (*child*) nosidełko *n* **3.** proca *f*
slink [slɪŋk] (*slunk*; *slunk*) *v/i* wślizgiwać ⟨-znąć⟩ się (***into*** do *G*); ***~ away*** oddalić się chyłkiem
slip[1] [slɪp] *adj* **1.** karteczka *f*; ***a ~ of paper*** kawałek papieru **2.** świstek *m* **3.** odcinek *m* **4.** paragon *m*
slip[2] [~] **I** *v/i* **1.** potykać ⟨-tknąć⟩ się (***over*** o *A*) **2.** ześlizgiwać ⟨-znąć⟩ się **3.** wyślizgiwać ⟨-znąć⟩ się (***out of*** z *G*) **4.** wślizgiwać ⟨-znąć⟩ się (***into*** do *G*) **5.** ***~ free*** uwolnić się **6.** ***~ out*** wymknąć się **7.** ***time is ~ping away*** czas ucieka **8.** (*popularity*, *profits*) spadać ⟨spaść⟩ **9.** ***~ into a coma*** zapaść w śpiączkę; ***~ into debt*** popaść w długi **II** *v/t* **1.** wsuwać ⟨wsunąć⟩; ***~ the letter into the envelope*** wsunąć list do koperty **2.** *coat*: narzucać ⟨-cić⟩ (***over*** na *A*) **3.** ***let a chance ~ through one's fingers*** przepuścić okazję **4.** ***it ~ped my mind*** wypadło mi to z głowy **III** *s* **1.** pomyłka *f*; ***a ~ of the tongue*** przejęzyczenie **2.** błąd *m* **3.** potknięcie *n* **4.** gafa *f* **5.** poślizgnięcie *n* **6.** halka *f*; **slip away** *v/i* **1.** wymykać ⟨-mknąć⟩ się **2.** zanikać ⟨-knąć⟩; **slip by** *v/i* (*time*) upływać ⟨-łynąć⟩; **slip off** *v/t clothes*: zrzucać ⟨-cić⟩; **slip on** *v/t clothes*: narzucać ⟨-cić⟩; **slip out** *v/i* **1.** wymykać ⟨-mknąć⟩ się **2.** ***it just slipped out*** wyrwało mi się; **slip up** *v/i infml* mylić ⟨po-⟩ się
'slip•cov•er *s Am* pokrowiec *m*; **slip•page** ['slɪpɪdʒ] *s* **1.** *prices*: spadek *m* **2.** (*time*) *infml* poślizg *m*; **slip-ons** ['slɪpɒnz] *pl* wsuwane buty *pl*
slip•per ['slɪpə] *s* pantofel *m* domowy, *infml* kapeć *m*
slip•per•y ['slɪpərɪ] *adj* śliski

slip road *s Br* **1.** zjazd *m* z autostrady **2.** wjazd *m* na autostradę; **slip•shod** ['slɪpʃɒd] *adj* **1.** niedbały **2.** byle jaki; **'slip•stream** *s* cień *m* aerodynamiczny; **'slip-up** *s infml* potknięcie *n*

slit [slɪt] **I** *s* **1.** (*skirt*) rozcięcie *n* **2.** szpara *f* **II** *v/t* **1.** rozcinać ⟨-ciąć⟩ **2.** *~ s.o.'s throat* poderżnąć komuś gardło

sliv•er ['slɪvə] *s* **1.** drzazga *f* **2.** *glass*: odłamek *m*

slob [slɒb] **I** *s infml* flejtuch *m* **II** *v/i ~ around, ~ out Br infml* obijać się; **slob•ber** ['slɔbə] *v/i* ślinić się

slog [slɒg] *infml* **I** *v/i* **1.** (*a. ~ away*) harować (***at*** nad *I*) **2.** brnąć ⟨prze-⟩ (***through*** przez *A*) **II** *s* harówa *f*

slo•gan ['sləʊgən] *s* slogan *m*

slop [slɒp] **I** *v/i* **1.** przelewać ⟨-lać⟩ się **2.** wylewać ⟨-lać⟩ się **II** *v/t* wylewać ⟨-lać⟩ **III** *s* pomyje *pl*; **slop about, *slop around*** *v/i Br infml* snuć się

slope [sləʊp] **I** *s* **1.** zbocze *n* **2.** stok *m* **3.** nachylenie *n* **II** *v/i* (*path*) opadać ⟨-paść⟩; ***the path ~s gently down*** ścieżka łagodnie opada; **slope off** *v/i infml* zmywać ⟨-myć⟩ się

slop•py ['slɒpɪ] *adj* **1.** niedbały **2.** niechlujny **3.** *film*: ckliwy **4.** *infml kiss*: soczysty

slosh [slɒʃ] **I** *v/i* **1.** chlupać **2.** *~ out* wylewać ⟨-lać⟩ się **3.** taplać się **II** *v/t* **1.** rozlewać ⟨-lać⟩ **2.** chlapać

sloshed [slɒʃt] *adj infml* zalany

slot [slɔt] **I** *s* **1.** otwór *m*; ***put a coin into the ~*** wrzucić monetę do automatu **2.** miejsce *n* **3.** (*TV programme*) okienko *n*; ***be broadcast at a peak viewing ~*** być nadawanym w porze największej oglądalności **4.** INF gniazdo *n*, slot *m* **II** *v/t* wkładać ⟨włożyć⟩ (***into*** do *G*) **III** *v/i* pasować do *G*; **slot in** *v/t* rezerwować ⟨za-⟩ czas dla *G*

'slot ma•chine *s* (*with drinks, cigarettes*) automat *m*

slouch [slaʊtʃ] **I** *v/i* garbić ⟨z-⟩ się **II** *s* **1.** niedbała postawa *f* **2.** ***he's no ~ at the guitar*** *infml* jest naprawdę niezłym gitarzystą

slough [slʌf] *v/t* **1.** *skin*: zmieniać ⟨-nić⟩ **2.** *~ s.th. off* pozbyć się czegoś

Slo•vak ['sləʊvæk] **I** *adj* słowacki **II** *s* **1.** Słowak *m*, Słowaczka *f* **2.** język *m* słowacki; **Slo•va•ki•a** [slə'vækɪə] *s* Słowacja *f*

Slo•ve•ni•a [slə'viːnjə] *s* Słowenia *f*; **Slo•ve•ni•an** [slə'viːnjən] **I** *adj* słoweński **II** *s* **1.** Słoweniec *m*, Słowenka *f* **2.** język *m* słoweński; **Slo•vene** ['sləʊviːn] → ***Slovenian***

slov•en•ly ['slʌvnlɪ] *adj* niechlujny

slow [sləʊ] **I** *adj* **1.** wolny, powolny; ***be ~ to do s.th.*** nie spieszyć się ze zrobieniem czegoś; ***he wasn't ~ to realise what was going on*** szybko zdał sobie sprawę, co się dzieje **2.** ***my watch is 5 minutes ~*** mój zegarek późni się o 5 minut **3.** niezbyt bystry **4.** *sale*: niski **5.** ***the market is ~*** na rynku panuje zastój **II** *adv* **1.** wolno **2.** powoli; ***drive ~!*** jedź powoli! **III** *v/i* (*a. ~ down*) zwalniać ⟨zwolnić⟩; ***~ down to a halt*** zatrzymać się **IV** *v/t* spowalniać ⟨-wolnić⟩; **'slow•coach** *s Br infml* ślamazara *f*; **'slow•down** *s* **1.** zwolnienie *n* **2.** spowolnienie *n*; **slow•ly** ['sləʊlɪ] *adv* **1.** wolno **2.** powoli; **slow 'mo•tion** *s*: ***in ~*** w zwolnionym tempie; **slow-mov•ing** ['sləʊmuːvɪŋ] *adj* powolny; **slow•ness** ['sləʊnɪs] *s* **1.** powolność *f* **2.** wolne tempo *n*; **'slow•poke** *s Am infml s* ślamazara *m/f*; **'slow•worm** *s* padalec *m*

sludge [slʌdʒ] *s* **1.** osad *m* **2.** szlam *m* **3.** muł *m* **4.** ścieki *pl*

slug[1] [slʌg] *s* ślimak *m* nagi

slug[2] [~] *s infml alcohol*: łyk *m*

slug[3] [~] *s Am infml* kulka *f*

slug[4] [~] *v/t infml* **1.** walić ⟨-lnąć⟩ **2.** zdzielać ⟨-lić⟩

slug•gish ['slʌgɪʃ] *adj* **1.** leniwy **2.** powolny **3.** ociężały **4.** ***be ~*** ECON znajdować się w zastoju

sluice [sluːs] **I** *s* śluza *f* **II** *v/t* **1.** spłukiwać ⟨-kać⟩ **2.** przemywać ⟨-myć⟩ **3.** ***~ s.th. out*** wypłukać coś; **'sluice gate** *s* wrota *pl* śluzy

slum [slʌm] *s* (*a. ~s*) slumsy *pl*

slump [slʌmp] **I** *v/i* **1.** (*prices, value*) gwałtownie spadać ⟨-paść⟩ **2.** siadać ⟨usiąść⟩ ciężko **II** *s* **1.** gwałtowny spadek *m* **2.** kryzys *m*; ***be in a ~*** przeżywać kryzys **3.** załamanie *n*

slung [slʌŋ] *Past Simple and Past Participle* → ***sling***

slunk [slʌŋk] *Past Simple and Past Participle* → **slink**

slur [slɜː] **I** *v/t* **1.** bełkotać ⟨wy-⟩; ***~ one's words*** mówić niewyraźnie **2.** *MUS* grać ⟨za-⟩ legato **II** *s* **1.** oszczerstwo *n* **2.** *MUS* legato *n*

slurp [slɜːp] *v/t* siorbać

slurred [slɜːd] *adj* bełkotliwy

slush [slʌʃ] *s* **1.** błoto *n* (pośniegowe) **2.** *infml* ckliwe bzdury *pl*; **'slush fund** *s* fundusz *n* łapówkowy; **slush•y** ['slʌʃɪ] *adj* **1.** błotnisty **2.** rozmokły **3.** ckliwy

slut [slʌt] *s* **1.** dziwka *f* **2.** (*woman*) flądra *f*

sly [slaɪ] *adj* przebiegły; ***on the ~*** po kryjomu

smack [smæk] **I** *v/t* **1.** *Br* dawać ⟨dać⟩ klapsa; ***it's wrong to ~ children*** nie powinno się bić dzieci **2.** walić ⟨-lnąć⟩; ***~ one's hand down on to the table*** walnąć ręką w stół **II** *v/i* walić ⟨-lnąć⟩ (***into*** w *A*); ***~ into each other*** zderzyć się **III** *s* **1.** klaps *m* **2.** policzek *m* **3.** trzask *m* **4.** *infml* (głośny) całus *m*, cmoknięcie *n*; ***give s.o. a ~ on*** cmoknąć kogoś w *A* **5.** *infml* hera *f*, heroina *f* **IV** *adv* **1.** prosto **2.** ***~ in the middle*** w samym środku; **smack of** *v/t* trącić; ***~ hypocrisy*** trącić hipokryzją

smack•er ['smækə] *s infml* **1.** (głośny) całus *m*, cmoknięcie *n* **2.** *Br* funciak *m* **3.** *Am* dolec *m*; **smack•ing** ['smækɪŋ] *s Br* lanie *n*; ***give s.o. a good ~*** sprawić komuś porządne lanie

small [smɔːl] **I** *adj* **1.** mały; ***it's a ~ world*** jaki ten świat mały **2.** niewielki **3.** drobny; ***~ business*** drobna przedsiębiorczość; ***~ ads*** ogłoszenia drobne **II** *adv* **1.** *chop*: drobno **2.** drobnym pismem **III** *s* ***~ of the back*** *ANAT* krzyż; **small caps** [smɔːl'kæps] *pl* (*font*) kapitaliki *pl*; **small 'change** *s* (*coins*) drobne *pl*; **small 'hours** *pl* późne godziny *pl* nocne; **'small•hold•ing** *s* małe gospodarstwo *n* rolne; **small-mind•ed** [smɔːl'maɪndɪd] *adj* małostkowy; **small•pox** ['smɔːlpɒks] *s MED* ospa *f* wietrzna; **'small print** *s Br* **1.** ***the ~*** adnotacje drobnym drukiem **2.** drobny druk *m*; **'small talk** *s* rozmowa *f* towarzyska; **'small-time** *adj criminal*: drobny; **'small-town** *adj* małomiasteczkowy

smarm•y ['smɑːmɪ] *adj Br infml* lizusowki, wazeliniarski

smart [smɑːt] **I** *adj* **1.** elegancki **2.** bystry **3.** *restaurant*: modny **4.** *pace*: żwawy **II** *v/i* **1.** piec ⟨za-⟩; ***his eyes were ~ing from the smoke*** oczy piekły go od dymu **2.** ***be ~ing from one's defeat*** odczuwać gorycz porażki; **smart al•ec** [smɑːt'ælɪk] *Br*, ***smart aleck*** *Am s infml* mądrala *m*; **'smart ass** *Am* → ***smart alec***; **'smart bomb** *s* inteligentna bomba *f*; **'smart card** *s* karta *f* chipowa

smart•en ['smɑːtn] *v/t*: *infml* ***~ s.th. up*** **a)** ogarnąć coś **b)** odświeżyć coś; ***~ oneself up*** ogarnąć się

smart•ly ['smɑːtlɪ] *adv* **1.** energicznie **2.** elegancko; **'smart•ness** *s* **1.** elegancja *f* **2.** bystrość *f*

smash [smæʃ] **I** *v/t* **1.** roztrzaskiwać ⟨-skać⟩ **2.** rozbijać ⟨-bić⟩; ***~ s.th. into pieces*** rozbić coś na kawałki **3.** *record*: pobijać ⟨-bić⟩ **4.** *fist*: walić ⟨-lnąć⟩; ***~ one's fist down on a table*** walnąć pięścią w stół **5.** *ball*: ścinać ⟨ściąć⟩ **II** *v/i* **1.** roztrzaskiwać ⟨-skać⟩ się **2.** rozbijać ⟨-bić⟩ się **3.** uderzać ⟨-rzyć⟩ w *A* **III** *s* **1.** huk *m* **2.** trzask *m* **3.** *Br* kraksa *f* **4.** (*tennis*) smecz *m* **5.** wielki hit *m*; **smash down** *v/t door*: wyważać ⟨-żyć⟩; **smash up** *v/t* demolować ⟨z-⟩

smashed [smæʃt] *adj infml* zalany: **smash•er** ['smæʃə] *s*: ***be a ~*** *Br infml* być naprawdę super, być fantastycznym; ***she's a ~*** *Br infml* ślicznotka z niej; **smash 'hit** *s* prawdziwy hit *m*; **smash•ing** ['smæʃɪŋ] *adj Br infml* **1.** kapitalny **2.** fantastyczny

smat•ter•ing ['smætərɪŋ] *s* odrobina *f*; ***have a ~ of French*** mówić trochę po francusku

smear [smɪə] **I** *v/t* **1.** smarować ⟨wy-⟩; ***~ mud on the walls*** wysmarować ściany błotem **2.** rozsmarowywać ⟨-rować⟩ (***s.th. on/over*** coś na *L*) **3.** mazać ⟨po-⟩ (***s.th. with*** coś *I*) **4.** *fig* oczerniać ⟨-nić⟩ **5.** *reputation*: szargać ⟨z-⟩ **II** *s* **1.** plama *f* **2.** oszczerstwo *n* **3.** *MED* wymaz *m*; **'smear campaign** *s* kampania *f* oszczerstw; **'smear test** *s* wymaz *m*, *infml* cytologia *f*

S

smell [smel] **I** (*smelt*; *smelt*) *v/i* **1.** pachnieć; **~ *good*** ładnie pachnieć **2.** śmierdzieć **3.** czuć; ***she said she could ~ the gas*** powiedziała, że czuć było gaz **4.** mieć węch **II** (*smelt*; *smelt*) *v/t* **1.** czuć ⟨po-⟩; ***can you ~ something burning?*** czy czujesz spaleniznę?; ***I can ~ trouble*** czuję, że będą kłopoty; **~ *a rat* a)** *infml* czuć, że coś jest nie tak **b)** węszyć podstęp **2.** wąchać ⟨po-⟩ **III** *s* **1.** węch *m*; ***the sense of ~*** zmysł węchu **2.** powonienie *n* **3.** zapach *m* **4.** smród *m*; **smell out** *v/t* **1.** wyczuwać ⟨-czuć⟩ **2.** węszyć ⟨wy-⟩

'smell•ing *adj*: **~ *salts*** sole trzeźwiące

smell•y ['smelɪ] *adj* śmierdzący

smelt [smelt] **I** *Past Simple and Past Participle* → ***smell*** **II** *v/t metal*: wytapiać ⟨-topić⟩

smile [smaɪl] **I** *v/i* uśmiechać ⟨-chnąć⟩ się (***at*** do *G*) **II** *s* uśmiech *m*; ***he's all ~s again*** wrócił mu dobry humor

smirk [smɜːk] **I** *v/i* uśmiechać ⟨-chnąć⟩ się z wyższością **II** *s* uśmieszek *m* (wyższości)

smite [smaɪt] (*smote*; *smitten*) *v/t lit* **1.** grzmotnąć **2.** uderzać ⟨-rzyć⟩ **3.** karać ⟨u-⟩

smith [smɪθ] *s* kowal *m*

smith•er•eens [smɪðə'riːnz] *s*: ***smash s.th. to ~*** rozbić coś w drobny mak

smith•y ['smɪðɪ] *s* kuźnia *f*

smit•ten ['smɪtn] *adj* **1.** zadurzony (***with***/***by*** w *L*) **2.** ***he was ~ with remorse*** ogarnęły go wyrzuty sumienia

smock [smɒk] *s* **1.** fartuch *m*, kitel *m* **2.** bluzka *f*

smog [smɒg] *s* smog *m*; **smog a•lert** *s* alarm *m* smogowy

smoke [sməʊk] **I** *s* dym *m*; ***there is no ~ without fire*** nie ma dymu bez ognia; ***go up in ~* a)** pójść z dymem **b)** spalić na panewce **II** *v/t* **1.** *cigarettes*: palić **2.** *fish*, *meat*: wędzić ⟨u-⟩ **III** *v/i* **1.** palić (papierosy) **2.** dymić ⟨za-⟩; **smoke out** *v/t* **1.** wykurzać ⟨-rzyć⟩ **2.** *fig* demaskować ⟨z-⟩ **3.** *fig* wykrywać ⟨-ryć⟩

'smoke a•larm *s* czujnik *m* dymu; **smoke bomb** *s* bomba *f* dymna

smoked [sməʊkt] *adj* **1.** wędzony **2.** *glass*: dymny

'smoke de•tec•tor *s* czujnik *m* dymu

smok•er ['sməʊkə] *s* palacz *m*

'smoke•screen *s a. fig* zasłona *f* dymna; **'smoke•stack** *s* komin *m* (fabryczny)

smok•ing ['sməʊkɪŋ] *s* palenie *n* tytoniu; ***'No ~'*** „Palenie wzbronione"; **'smok•ing com•part•ment** *s* przedział *m* dla palących

smok•y ['sməʊkɪ] *adj* **1.** *room*: zadymiony **2.** *chimney*: dymiący **3.** *glass*: dymny

smooch [smuːtʃ] *v/i infml* obściskiwać się

smooth [smuːð] **I** *adj* **1.** gładki **2.** *flight*: spokojny **3.** *movement*: płynny **4.** *taste*: łagodny **5.** *music*: przyjemny **6.** *breath*: regularny **7.** *journey*: komfortowy **8.** *person*: ugrzeczniony **II** *v/t* **1.** (*t* **~ *out***, **~ *down***) wygładzać ⟨-dzić⟩, wyrównywać ⟨-nać⟩ **2.** (*a.* **~ *back***, **~ *down***) *hair*: przygładzać ⟨-dzić⟩ **3.** rozsmarowywać ⟨-rować⟩; **smooth away**, ***smooth out*** *v/t problems*: usuwać ⟨usunąć⟩; **smooth over** *v/t situation*: łagodzić ⟨za-⟩

smooth•ly ['smuːðlɪ] *adj* **1.** gładko **2.** płynnie

smote [sməʊt] *Past Simple* → ***smite***

smoth•er ['smʌðə] *v/t* **1.** dusić ⟨u-⟩; **~ *s.o. with kisses*** *fig* obsypać kogoś pocałunkami **2.** tłumić ⟨s-⟩ **3.** *cream*: pokrywać ⟨-ryć⟩

smoul•der ['sməʊldə] *Br*, **smol•der** *Am* *v/i* tlić się

smudge [smʌdʒ] **I** *s* **1.** plama *f* **2.** brudny ślad *m* **II** *v/t* **1.** rozmazywać ⟨-zać⟩ **2.** brudzić ⟨po-⟩ **3.** mazać ⟨po-⟩ **III** *v/i* rozmazywać ⟨-zać⟩ się

smug [smʌg] *adj* zadowolony z siebie; **~ *smile*** uśmiech (samo)zadowolenia

smug•gle ['smʌgl] *v/t* przemycać ⟨-cić⟩, *infml* szmuglować ⟨prze-⟩; **smug•gler** ['smʌglə] *s* przemytnik *m*, *infml* szmugler *m*; **smug•gling** ['smʌglɪŋ] *adj* przemyt *m*

smug•ly ['smʌglɪ] *adv* z samozadowoleniem

smut [smʌt] *s* **1.** *infml* świństwa *f* **2.** sadza *f* **3.** zabrudzenie *n*; **smut•ty** ['smʌtɪ] *adj infml* sprośny

snack [snæk] **I** *s* przekąska *f* **II** *v/i* przekąszać ⟨-kąsić⟩ (***on*** *A*); **'snack bar** *s* bar *m* z przekąskami, snack bar *m*

S

snaf•fle ['snæfl] *v/t Br infml* **1.** zagarniać ⟨-nąć⟩ **2.** *award*: zgarniać ⟨-nąć⟩

sna•fu ['snæfuː] *s Am infml* **1.** bałagan *m* **2.** kołomyja *f*

snag [snæg] **I** *s* drobny problem *m* **II** *v/t* **1.** zaczepiać ⟨-pić⟩ (**on** o *A*) **2.** rozdzierać ⟨-zedrzeć⟩ **III** *v/i* zaczepiać ⟨-pić⟩ się (**on** o *A*)

snail [sneɪl] *s* ślimak *m*; ***at a ~'s pace*** w żółwim tempie

snake [sneɪk] **I** *s* BIOL wąż *m* **II** *v/i* (*road*) wić się; **'snake•bite** *s* ukąszenie *n* węża; **snake charm•er** ['sneɪktʃɑːmə] *s* zaklinacz *m* węży; **'snake-skin** *s* wężowa skóra *f*

snak•y ['sneɪkɪ] *adj road*: wijący się

snap [snæp] **I** *v/t* **1.** łamać ⟨z-⟩ **2.** *rope*: zrywać ⟨zerwać⟩ **3.** ***~ one's fingers*** pstrykać palcami **4.** ***~ s.th. open*** otworzyć coś (z trzaskiem) **5.** ***~ s.th. shut*** zatrzasnąć coś **6.** (*person*) fuknąć, warknąć **7.** *infml photograph*: pstrykać ⟨-knąć⟩ **II** *v/i* **1.** łamać ⟨z-⟩ się **2.** zrywać ⟨zerwać⟩ się **3.** ***~ open*** otworzyć się (z trzaskiem) **4.** ***~ shut*** zatrzasnąć się **5.** kłapać ⟨-pnąć⟩ paszczą **6.** chwytać ⟨-cić⟩ zębami (**at** *A*) **7.** (*patience*) kończyć ⟨s-⟩ się **III** *s* **1.** trzask *m* **2.** *infml* fotka *f* **3.** *Am* zatrzask *m* **IV** *adj decision*: pospieszny, szybki; **snap off I** *v/t* **1.** odłamywać ⟨-mać⟩ **2.** odrywać ⟨oderwać⟩ **II** *v/i* **1.** odłamywać ⟨-mać⟩ się **2.** odrywać ⟨oderwać⟩ się; **snap up** *v/t* rozchwytywać, wykupywać ⟨-pić⟩

'snap drag•on *s* (*plant*) lwia paszcza *f*; **snap fast•en•er** ['snæpfæsnə] *s* zatrzask *m*

'snap-on *adj* **1.** zaciskany **2.** mocowany na wcisk

snap•py ['snæpɪ] *adj* **1.** *slogan*: chwytliwy **2.** *infml* modny **3.** żwawy **4.** opryskliwy

'snap•shot *s* zdjęcie *n*

snare [sneə] **I** *s* **1.** sidła *pl*, wnyki *pl* **2.** *fig* pułapka *f* **II** *v/t* **1.** łapać ⟨z-⟩ w sidła **2.** *rich husband*: złapać, upolować

snarl [snɑːl] **I** *v/i* warczeć ⟨-rknąć⟩ (**at** na *A*) **II** *s* **1.** warknięcie *n* **2.** warczenie *n*; ***with a ~*** warcząc; **snarl up** *v/t* **1.** wstrzymywać ⟨-mać⟩ **2.** blokować ⟨za-⟩

'snarl-up *s* zator *m*

snatch [snætʃ] **I** *v/t* **1.** chwytać ⟨-wycić⟩ **2.** wyrywać ⟨-rwać⟩; ***~ s.th. from s.o.'s hand*** wyrwać coś komuś z ręki **3.** *opportunity*: korzystać ⟨s-⟩ z *G* **II** *s* **1.** *conversation*: strzęp *m* **2.** urywek *m*; **snatch at** *v/t* **1.** rzucać ⟨-cić⟩ się na *A* **2.** próbować chwycić **3.** *opportunity*: korzystać ⟨s-⟩ z *G*

snaz•zy ['snæzɪ] *adj infml* odlotowy

sneak [sniːk] **I** *v/i* **1.** (*a.* ***~ around***) skradać się; ***~ up*** podkraść się **2.** ***~ in*** wkraść się **3.** ***~ out*** wymknąć się **4.** *Br dated* skarżyć ⟨po-⟩ się (**on** na *A*) **II** *v/t* **1.** przemycać ⟨-cić⟩ **2.** ***~ a look at*** rzucić ukradkowe spojrzenie na *A* **III** *s Br dated* skarżypyta *m/f* **IV** *adj attack*: znienacka

sneak•er ['sniːkə] *s Am* tenisówka *f*

sneak•ing ['sniːkɪŋ] *adj*: ***I have a ~ feeling that*** podejrzewam, że

sneak 'pre•view *s* pokaz *m* przedpremierowy

sneak•y ['sniːkɪ] *adj* ukradkowy

sneer [sniːə] **I** *v/i* **1.** uśmiechać ⟨-chnąć⟩ się szyderczo **2.** szydzić (**at** z *G*) **II** *s* **1.** szyderczy uśmiech *m* **2.** drwina *f* **3.** szyderstwo *n*

sneeze [sniːz] **I** *v/i* kichać ⟨-chnąć⟩; ***not to be ~d at*** nie do pogardzenia **II** *s* kichnięcie *n*

snick•er ['snɪkə] **I** *s* chichot *m* **II** *v/i* → ***snigger***

snide [snaɪd] *adj* złośliwy

sniff [snɪf] **I** *v/i* **1.** pociągać ⟨-gnąć⟩ nosem **2.** węszyć **3.** obwąchiwać (**at** *A*) **4.** *fig* prychać ⟨-chnąć⟩; ***not to be ~ed at*** nie do pogardzenia **II** *v/t* **1.** czuć ⟨po-⟩ zapach **2.** *air*: wciągać ⟨-gnąć⟩ **3.** *glue*: wąchać **III** *s* **1.** ***take a ~ at*** powąchać *A* **2.** pociągnięcie *n* nosem; **sniff out** *v/i* **1.** wywęszyć **2.** węszyć ⟨z-⟩ **3.** tropić ⟨wy-⟩

snif•fer dog ['snɪfədɒg] *s Br infml* pies *m* policyjny (*wyszkolony do wykrywania narkotyków lub materiałów wybuchowych*)

snif•fle ['snɪfl] **I** *v/i* pociągać ⟨-gnąć⟩ nosem **II** *s* pociąganie *n* nosem; ***have the ~s*** być przeziębionym

snif•fy ['snɪfɪ] *adj* wybredny

snif•ter ['snɪftə] *s Br* kieliszek *m* do koniaku

snig•ger ['snɪgər] **I** *v/i* **1.** chichotać **2.** podśmiewać się (**at** z *G*) **II** *s* chichot *m*

snip [snɪp] **I** *v/t* **1.** wycinać ⟨-ciąć⟩ **2.** przecinać ⟨-ciąć⟩ **3.** odcinać ⟨-ciąć⟩ **II** *s* **1.** cięcie *n* **2.** *infml* ciachnięcie *n* **3.** **~, ~** ciach, ciach **4.** **~s** nożyce do blachy **5.** *Br infml* okazja *f*; **snip off** *v/t* odcinać ⟨-ciąć⟩

snipe [snaɪp] **I** *v/i* **1.** strzelać ⟨-lić⟩ (z ukrycia) (**at** do *G*) **2.** krytykować ⟨s-⟩ **3.** *infml* dogryzać **II** *pl snipe s* (*bird*) bekas *m*

snip•er ['snaɪpə] *s* snajper *m*

snip•pet ['snɪpɪt] *s* **1.** urywek *m* **2.** strzęp *m*

snitch [snɪtʃ] *infml* **I** *v/i* skarżyć ⟨na-⟩, kablować ⟨za-⟩ (**on** na *A*) **II** *s* skarżypyta *m/f*

sniv•el ['snɪvl] *v/i* pochlipywać

snob [snɒb] *s* snob *m*; **snob•ber•y** ['snɒbərɪ] *s* snobizm *m*; **snob•bish** ['snɒbɪʃ] *adj* snobistyczny

snog [snɒg] *infml v/i* obcałowywać się

snook [snuːk] *s*: ***cock a ~ at s.o.*** zagrać komuś na nosie

snook•er ['snuːkə] **I** *s* snooker *m* **II** *v/t plans*: krzyżować ⟨po-⟩

snoop [snuːp] **I** *v/i* **1.** (*a.* ***~ around***, ***~ about***) myszkować **2.** szpiegować (**on** *A*) **II** *s infml* szpicel *m*; '**snoop•er** → ***snoop II***

snoot•y ['snuːtɪ] *adj* **1.** przemądrzały **2.** ***be ~*** zadzierać nosa

snooze [snuːz] **I** *v/i* drzemać **II** *s* drzemka *f*; ***have a ~*** zdrzemnąć się

snore [snɔː] **I** *v/i* chrapać **II** *s* chrapanie *n*

'**snor•er** *s*: ***be a ~*** chrapać; **snor•ing** ['snɔːrɪŋ] *s* chrapanie *n*

snor•kel ['snɔːkl] *s* (*diving*) rurka *f*, fajka *f*; **snor•kel•ling** ['snɔːklɪŋ] *Br*, ***snor•kel•ing*** *Am s* nurkowanie *n* z rurką

snort [snɔːt] **I** *v/i* **1.** parskać ⟨-knąć⟩ **2.** prychać ⟨-chnąć⟩ **II** *v/t infml cocaine*: wciągać ⟨-gnąć⟩ **III** *s* **1.** parsknięcie *n* **2.** prychnięcie *n* **3.** *infml* niuch *m*; ***take a ~ of cocaine*** wciągnąć kokainę

snot [snɒt] *s* smarki *pl*; **snot•ty** ['snɒtɪ] *adj* **1.** zasmarkany **2.** → ***snooty***

snot•ty-nosed ['snɒtɪnəʊzd] → ***snooty***

snout [snaʊt] *s* **1.** ryj *m* **2.** pysk *m* **3.** *infml* kapuś *m*

snow [snəʊ] **I** *s* śnieg *m* **II** *v/i* ***it's ~ing*** pada śnieg **III** *v/t* **1.** ***we are ~ed in*** zasypało nas; ***the road is ~ed up*** droga jest zasypana **2.** ***be ~ed under with work*** być zawalonym pracą; '**snow•ball I** *s* **1.** śnieżka *f*; ***a ~ fight*** bitwa na śnieżki **2.** ***a ~ effect*** efekt śnieżnej kuli **II** *v/i* **1.** toczyć ⟨po-⟩ się lawinowo **2.** bardzo się rozrastać ⟨-rosnąć⟩; '**snow•board** *s* deska *f* snowboardowa, snowboard *m*; **snow•board•er** ['snəʊbɔːdə] *s* snowboardzista *m*; **snow•board•ing** *s* snowboarding *m*; '**snow•bound** *adj road, building*: zasypany (śniegiem); **snow•capped** ['snəʊkæpt] *adj summit*: ośnieżony; **snow chains** *pl* łańcuchy *pl* na koła; '**snow•drift** *s* zaspa *f* śnieżna; '**snow-drop** *s* przebiśnieg *m*; '**snow•fall** *s* opad *m* śniegu; '**snow•flake** *s* płatek *m* śniegu; '**snow•man** *pl -men s* bałwan *m*; '**snow•plough** *s Br*, ***snow plow*** *Am* pług *m* śnieżny; '**snow-shoe** *s* rakieta *f* śnieżna; '**snow•storm** *s* zamieć *f*; '**snow•suit** *s* kombinezon *m* narciarski

snow•y ['snəʊɪ] *adj* **1.** ośnieżony **2.** śnieżny **3.** zaśnieżony **4.** śnieżnobiały

snub[1] [snʌb] **I** *v/t* **1.** ignorować ⟨z-⟩ **2.** bojkotować ⟨z-⟩ **II** *s* **1.** afront *m* **2.** obraza *f*

snub[2] [~] *adj nose*: zadarty; **snub-nosed** ['snʌbnəʊzd] *adj* z zadartym nosem

snuck [snʌk] *Past Simple and Past Participle* → ***sneak***

snuff[1] [snʌf] *v/t* (*a.* ***~ out***) *candle*: gasić ⟨z-⟩

snuff[2] [~] **I** *v/t* węszyć ⟨z-⟩ **II** *s* tabaka *f*

snuf•fle ['snʌfl] **I** *v/i* **1.** ciężko oddychać **2.** sapać **II** *s* sapanie *n*; ***have the ~s*** *infml* być przeziębionym

snug [snʌg] *adj* **1.** przytulny **2.** ciepły **3.** dopasowany; ***be a ~ fit*** leżeć jak ulał **4.** ciasny

snug•gle ['snʌgl] *v/i* **1.** przytulać ⟨-lić⟩ się (**up to** do *G*) **2.** wtulać ⟨-lić⟩ się (**into** w *A*) **3.** ***~ down under the bedclothes*** ułożyć się wygodnie pod kołdrą

so [səʊ] **I** *adv* **1.** tak; ***she spoke ~ quietly that*** mówiła tak cicho, że; ***I hope ~*** mam nadzieję, że tak; ***I think ~*** tak sądzę; ***I don't think ~*** nie sądzę; ***if ~*** jeśli tak; ***is that ~?*** czy to prawda?; ***or ~ he says*** tak przynajmniej mówi; ***and ~ on*** i tak dalej; ***~ be it*** niech tak będzie; ***~ much money*** tyle pieniędzy **2.** taki; ***I'm not ~ stupid*** nie jestem taki głupi **3.** tak (bardzo); ***I'm ~ glad*** tak (bardzo) się cieszę **4.** też; ***he likes cats and ~ do I*** on lubi koty i ja też **5.** ***twenty or ~*** około dwudziestu **II** *conj* **1.** więc; ***my knee hurt, ~ I went to a doctor*** bolało mnie kolano, więc poszedłem do lekarza **2.** ***~ that*** aby, żeby; ***~ that you don't get lost*** żebyś się nie zgubił; ***~ as to do s.th.*** żeby coś zrobić **3.** tak więc; ***~ what?*** i co z tego?

soak [səʊk] **I** *v/t* **1.** namaczać ⟨-moczyć⟩ **2.** przemaczać ⟨-moczyć⟩ **II** *v/i* **1.** moczyć ⟨na-⟩ się; ***leave s.th. to ~*** zostawić coś, żeby się namoczyło **2.** nasiąkać ⟨-knąć⟩ **3.** ***~ through*** przesiąknąć przez *A* **III** *s* **1.** ***give s.th. a good ~*** dobrze coś namoczyć **2.** *infml* kąpiel *f*; **soak up** *v/t* **1.** wchłaniać ⟨-łonąć⟩ **2.** *fig* chłonąć

soaked [səʊkt] *adj* **1.** przemoczony; ***get ~*** przemoknąć; ***~ to the skin*** przemoczony do suchej nitki **2.** nasiąknięty **3.** przesiąknięty **4.** namoczony; **soak•ing (wet)** ['səʊkɪŋ] *adj* przemoczony

so-and-so ['səʊənsəʊ] *pl -sos s* **1.** taki a taki *m* **2.** ***you ~!*** ty taki owaki!

soap [səʊp] **I** *s* mydło *n* **II** *v/t* namydlać ⟨-lić⟩; **'soap bub•ble** *s* bańka *f* mydlana; **'soap dish** *s* mydelniczka *f*; **'soap op•e•ra** *s* telenowela *f*, opera *f* mydlana; **'soap pow•der** *s* proszek *m* do prania; **'soap•suds** *pl*, piana *f* (mydlana)

soap•y ['səʊpɪ] *adj* **1.** mydlany **2.** namydlony

soar [sɔː] *v/i* **1.** (*value*, *prices*) gwałtownie wzrastać ⟨-rosnąć⟩ **2.** (*prices*) iść ⟨pójść⟩ w górę **3.** wzbijać ⟨-bić⟩ się w powietrze **4.** szybować, unosić się w powietrzu **5.** (*buildings*) wznosić się

sob [sɒb] **I** *v/i* szlochać **II** *v/t* **1.** szlochać ⟨wy-⟩ **2.** ***~ one's heart out*** wypłakiwać sobie oczy **III** *s* szloch *m*; ***give a ~*** zaszlochać

so•ber ['səʊbə] **I** *adj* **1.** trzeźwy **2.** *behaviour*: poważny **3.** *colour*: stonowany, spokojny **II** *v/i* poważnieć ⟨s-⟩; **sober up** *v/i* trzeźwieć ⟨wy-⟩

so•ber•ing ['səʊbərɪŋ] *adj* otrzeźwiający

'sob sto•ry *s* wzruszająca historia *f*

so-'called *adj* tak zwany

soc•cer ['sɒkə] *s* SPORT *Br* piłka *f* nożna

so•cia•ble ['səʊʃəbl] *adj* towarzyski

so•cial ['səʊʃl] **I** *adj* **1.** społeczny; ***~ security*** **a)** system ubezpieczeń społecznych **b)** ubezpieczenie społeczne **c)** zasiłek **2.** *benefit*, *reform*: socjalny **3.** *life*, *event*: towarzyski **4.** *animal*: stadny **II** *s dated* spotkanie *n* towarzyskie; **so•cial 'climb•er** *s* karierowicz *m*; **so•cial 'dem•o•crat** *s* socjaldemokrata *m*

so•cial•ism ['səʊʃəlɪzm] *s* socjalizm *m*; **so•cial•ist** ['səʊʃəlɪst] **I** *s* socjalista *m* **II** *adj* socjalistyczny

so•cial•i•za•tion [səʊʃəlaɪ'zeɪʃn] *s* socjalizacja *f*; **so•cial•ize** ['səʊʃəlaɪz] **I** *v/i* **1.** udzielać się towarzysko **2.** spotykać ⟨-tkać⟩ się (***with*** z *I*) **II** *v/t child*: uspołeczniać ⟨-nić⟩

'so•cial life *s* życie *n* towarzyskie

so•cial•ly ['səʊʃəlɪ] *adv* **1.** społecznie **2.** towarzysko

so•cial 'sci•ence *s* nauki *pl* społeczne; **'so•cial work** *s* praca *f* w opiece społecznej; **'so•cial work•er** *s* pracownik *m* opieki społecznej

so•ci•e•ty [sə'saɪətɪ] *s* **1.** społeczeństwo *n* **2.** towarzystwo *n* **3.** stowarzyszenie *n*

so•ci•o•log•i•cal [səʊsɪə'lɒdʒɪkl] *adj* socjologiczny; **so•ci•ol•o•gist** [səʊsɪ'ɒlədʒɪst] *s* socjolog *m*; **so•ci•ol•o•gy** [səʊsɪ'ɒlədʒɪ] *s* socjologia *f*

sock[1] [sɒk] *s* **1.** skarpeta *f* **2.** skarpetka *f*

sock[2] [~] *v/t* walić ⟨-lnąć⟩

sock•et ['sɒkɪt] *s* **1.** *Br* gniazdko *n*, kontakt *m* **2.** (*bulb*) oprawka *f* **3.** ANAT panewka *f* **4.** ***an eye ~*** oczodół; ***a tooth ~*** zębodół

sod [sɒd] **I** *s* **1.** *Br vulg* sukinsyn *m* **2.** darń *f* **II** *v/t* ***~ it!*** *infml* niech to diabli!; ***~ off!*** *vulg* odpieprz się!

S

so•da ['səʊdə] *s* **1.** woda *f* sodowa; ***whisky and ~, please*** poproszę whisky z wodą sodową **2.** *Am* napój *m* gazowany **3.** *CHEM* soda *f*; '**so•da wa•ter** *s* woda *f* sodowa

sod•den ['sɒdn] *adj* **1.** rozmokły **2.** przemoczony

so•di•um ['səʊdɪəm] *s CHEM* sód *m*

so•do•my ['sɒdəmɪ] *s* seks *m* analny

so•fa ['səʊfə] *s* **1.** kanapa *f* **2.** sofa *f*; '**so•fa-bed** *s* rozkładana *f* kanapa

soft [sɒft] *adj* **1.** miękki; ***become ~, get ~*** zmięknąć; ***have a ~ spot for*** mieć słabość do *G* **2.** gładki **3.** *voice, wind*: łagodny **4.** *colour*: stonowany **5.** pobłażliwy **6.** *infml* przygłupi; **soft-boiled** ['sɒftbɔɪld] *adj egg*: na miękko; '**soft drink** *s* napój *m* bezalkoholowy; '**soft drug** *s* miękki narkotyk *m*

soft•en ['sɒfn] **I** *v/i* **1.** mięknąć ⟨z-⟩ **2.** łagodnieć ⟨z-⟩; ***his face ~ed*** twarz mu złagodniała **II** *v/t* **1.** zmiękczać ⟨-czyć⟩ **2.** łagodzić ⟨z-⟩ **3.** *blow*: amortyzować ⟨z-⟩; **soften up I** *v/i* mięknąć ⟨z-⟩ **II** *v/t* **1.** *fig* zmiękczać ⟨-czyć⟩ **2.** *enemy*: osłabiać ⟨-bić⟩

soft•en•er ['sɒfnə] *s* **1.** (*a.* **water ~**) środek *m* do zmiękczania wody **2.** środek *m* do zmiękczania tkanin

soft•heart•ed ['sɒfthɑːtɪd] *adj* **1.** o miękkim sercu **2.** *teacher*: pobłażliwy

soft•ie ['sɒftɪ] *s*: ***be a ~*** mieć miękkie serce

soft•ly ['sɒftlɪ] *adv* **1.** miękko **2.** łagodnie **3.** delikatnie **4.** lekko **5.** *say*: miękkim głosem

'**soft-ped•al** *v/t infml* łagodzić ⟨z-⟩; '**soft sell** *s* nieagresywna reklama *f*; '**soft-soap** *infml* **I** *v/t* kadzić **II** *s infml* kadzenie *n*; **soft-spo•ken** ['sɒftspəʊkn] *adj*: **be ~** mieć miękki głos; **soft** '**toy** *s Br* pluszowa zabawka *f*

soft•ware ['sɒftweə] *s* oprogramowanie *n* komputerowe, software *m*

soft•y → ***softie***

sog•gy ['sɒgɪ] *adj* **1.** rozmokły **2.** rozmiękły

soil [sɔɪl] **I** *s* **1.** gleba *f* **2.** ziemia *f* **II** *v/t* brudzić ⟨za-⟩; ***~ one's hands*** *fig* ubrudzić sobie ręce

so•journ ['sɒdʒən] *s lit* pobyt *m*

sol•ace ['sɒləs] *s* **1.** ukojenie *n* **2.** pocieszenie *n*

so•lar [səʊlə] *adj* słoneczny; **so•lar cell** *s TECH* ogniwo *n* słoneczne; **so•lar e-'clipse** *s* zaćmienie *n* słońca; **so•lar** '**en•er•gy** *s* energia *f* słoneczna; '**so-lar pan•el** *s TECH* płytka *f* ogniwa słonecznego; **so•lar plex•us** [səʊlə 'pleksəs] *s* splot *m* słoneczny; '**so•lar sys•tem** *s* układ *m* słoneczny

so•lar•i•um [sə'leərɪəm] *pl -ria* [~ɪə], *-riums s* solarium *m*

sold [səʊld] *Past Simple and Past Participle* → **sell**

sol•der ['səʊldə] *TECH* **I** *s* lut *m* **II** *v/t* lutować ⟨z-, przy-⟩; '**sol•der•ing i•ron** *s TECH* lutownica *f*

sol•dier ['səʊldʒə] **I** *s* żołnierz *m* **II** *v/i* ***~ on*** nie poddawać się; ***~ on doing s.th.*** wytrwale coś robić

sole[1] [səʊl] *adj* **1.** jedyny; ***the ~ reason*** jedyny powód **2.** wyłączny; ***the ~ owner*** wyłączny właściciel

sole[2] [~] **I** *s* (*shoe, foot*) podeszwa *f* **II** *v/t* wymieniać ⟨-nić⟩ podeszwę

sole[3] [~] *s* (*fish*) sola *f*

sole•ly ['səʊllɪ] *adv* **1.** tylko **2.** jedynie **3.** wyłącznie

sol•emn ['sɒləm] *adj* **1.** poważny **2.** uroczysty **3.** *promise*: solenny; **so•lem•ni•ty** [sə'lemnətɪ] *s* **1.** powaga *f* **2.** ***solemnities*** uroczystości *pl*; **sol•emn•ly** ['sɒləmlɪ] *adv* **1.** poważnie **2.** uroczyście **3.** *promise*: solennie

so•lic•it [sə'lɪsɪt] **I** *v/t* **1.** zabiegać o *A*; ***~ s.o.'s help*** szukać pomocy u kogoś **2.** prosić ⟨po-⟩ o *A* **II** *v/i* (*prostitutes*) nagabywać klientów

so•lic•i•tor [sə'lɪsɪtə] *s Br* **1.** notariusz *m* **2.** radca *f* prawny **3.** adwokat *m*

so•lic•i•tous [sə'lɪsɪtəs] *adj* troskliwy; ***be ~ of*** troszczyć się o *G*

sol•id ['sɒlɪd] **I** *adj* **1.** *body, food, substance*: stały **2.** *rock*: lity **3.** *gold*: czysty **4.** *table, roof*: solidny, mocny **5.** rzetelny **6.** ***he's a ~ player*** nie schodzi poniżej pewnego poziomu **7.** *tyre*: pełny **8.** jednomyślny **9.** ***for two hours ~*** przez bite dwie godziny **10.** ***a ~ figure*** *MATH* bryła **II** *s* **1.** *PHYS* ciało *n* stałe **2.** ***~s*** pokarmy *pl* stałe **3.** *MATH* bryła *f*

sol•i•dar•i•ty [sɒlɪ'dærətɪ] *s* solidarność *f*

so•lid•i•fy [sə'lɪdɪfaɪ] **I** *v/t* **1.** zestalać ⟨-lić⟩ się **2.** tężeć ⟨s-⟩ **3.** krzepnąć

S

⟨s-⟩ **4.** umacniać ⟨umocnić⟩ się **II** *v/t* umacniać ⟨umocnić⟩

sol•id•ly ['sɒlɪdlɪ] *adv* **1.** solidnie **2.** porządnie **3.** mocno **4.** *rain*: bez przerwy **5.** zdecydowanie; ***her colleges were ~ behind her*** jej koledzy stanęli za nią murem

so•lil•o•quy [sə'lɪləkwɪ] *s* monolog *m*

sol•i•taire [sɒlɪ'teə] *s* **1.** pasjans *m* **2.** (*gem*) soliter *m*

sol•i•ta•ry ['sɒlɪtrɪ] **I** *adj* **1.** *walk*: samotny **2.** *life*: samotniczy **3.** *person*: lubiący samotność **4.** *case*: odosobniony **5.** ***not a ~*** ani jeden; ***there was not a ~ shred of evidence*** nie było ani cienia dowodu **II** *s* samotnik *m*; **sol•i•ta•ry con•'fine•ment** *s* więzienna izolatka *f*

sol•i•tude ['sɒlɪtjuːd] *s* samotność *f*

so•lo ['səʊləʊ] **I** *adj* **1.** samodzielny **2.** solowy **3.** solo; ***a piece for ~ guitar*** utwór na gitarę solo **4.** *artist*: występujący solo **II** *adv* **1.** samodzielnie **2.** w pojedynkę **3.** solo **III** *s* **1.** solo *n* **2.** partia *f* solowa **3.** solówka *f*; **so•lo•ist** ['səʊləʊɪst] *s* MUS solista *m*

sol•stice ['sɒlstɪs] *s* ASTR przesilenie *n*

sol•u•ble ['sɒljəbl] *adj* **1.** rozpuszczalny; ***~ in water*** rozpuszczalny w wodzie **2.** *problem*: możliwy do rozwiązania

so•lu•tion [sə'luːʃn] *s* **1.** *problem, puzzle*: rozwiązanie *n* **2.** CHEM roztwór *m* **3.** CHEM rozpuszczanie *n*

solv•a•ble ['sɒlvəbl] *adj* MATH rozwiązywalny

solve [sɒlv] *v/t problem, puzzle*: rozwiązywać ⟨-zać⟩

sol•ven•cy ['sɒlvənsɪ] *s* ECON wypłacalność *f*; **sol•vent** ['sɒlvənt] **I** *s* rozpuszczalnik *m* **II** *adj* **1.** ECON wypłacalny **2.** rozpuszczalny

som•bre ['sɒmbə] *Br*, **som•ber** *Am adj* **1.** ponury **2.** posępny

som•bre•ro [sɒm'brerəʊ] *pl -ros s* sombrero *n*

some [sʌm] **I** *adj* **1.** trochę; ***there is ~ wine in the bottle*** jest jeszcze trochę wina w butelce; ***have ~ more coffee*** napij się jeszcze trochę kawy **2.** kilka; ***~ biscuits*** kilka herbatników **3.** parę; ***for ~ years*** od paru lat **4.** niektóry; ***~ people think that*** niektórzy ludzie myślą, że **5.** jakiś; ***for ~ time*** przez jakiś czas **6.** pewien **II** *pron* niektórzy; ***here are ~ of our suggestions*** oto niektóre z naszych propozycji **III** *adv* jakiś; ***~ 30 people*** jakieś 30 osób

some•bod•y ['sʌmbədɪ] *pron* ktoś; ***~ else*** ktoś inny; **'some•day** *adv* **1.** pewnego dnia **2.** kiedyś; **'some•how** *adv* jakoś; ***~ or other*** w ten czy inny sposób; **'some•one** → ***somebody***; **'some•place** *Am* → ***somewhere***

som•er•sault ['sʌməsɔːlt] **I** *s* **1.** salto *n*; ***turn a ~*** wykonać salto **2.** przewrót *m* **3.** *infml* fikołek *m* **II** *v/i* (*car*) koziołkować ⟨prze-⟩

'some•thing *pron* coś; ***~ to eat*** coś do jedzenia; ***or ~ like that*** *infml* lub coś w tym stylu; ***~ around 15 dollars*** *infml* coś koło piętnastu dolarów; ***thirty-~s*** *infml* trzydziestolatkowie, osoby po trzydziestce; **'some•time I** *adv* **1.** kiedyś **2.** któregoś dnia **II** *adj* były

'some•times ['sʌmtaɪmz] *adv* **1.** czasami **2.** od czasu do czasu

'some•way *Am* → ***somehow***; **'some•what** *adv* **1.** nieco **2.** raczej **3.** trochę; ***how it occurs is ~ of a mystery*** mechanizm tego zjawiska nie jest do końca wyjaśniony; **'some•where** *adv* gdzieś; ***I've seen him ~ before*** gdzieś już go wcześniej widziałem; ***~ around two thousand dollars*** gdzieś około dwóch tysięcy dolarów

som•no•lent ['sɒmnələnt] *adj lit* senny

son [sʌn] *s* syn *m*

so•na•ta [sə'nɑːtə] *s* MUS sonata *f*

song [sɒŋ] *s* **1.** piosenka *f* **2.** pieśń *f* **3.** ***for a ~*** *infml* za pół darmo **4.** *bird*: śpiew *m*; **'song•bird** *s* ptak *m* śpiewający; **'song•book** *s* śpiewnik *m*; **'song•writ•er** *s* autor *m* piosenek

son•ic ['sɒnɪk] *adj wave*: dźwiękowy

'son-in-law *pl sons-in-law s* zięć *m*

'son•net ['sɒnɪt] *s* sonet *m*

son of a 'bitch *pl sons of a bitch s vulg* skurwysyn *m*

so•no•rous ['sɒnərəs] *adj voice*: dźwięczny

soon [suːn] *adv* **1.** wkrótce; ***see you ~*** do zobaczenia wkrótce; ***see you ~!*** na razie! **2.** niedługo **3.** wcześnie; ***it's too ~ to talk about it*** za wcześnie o tym mówić **4.** szybko; ***as ~ as possib-***

le jak najszybciej; ***the ~er the better*** im szybciej, tym lepiej; ***~ or later*** prędzej czy później; ***no ~er had she moved in than*** ledwo się wprowadziła, kiedy **5.** ***I'd ~er*** wolałbym

soot [sʊt] *s* sadza *f*

soothe [suːð] *v/t* **1.** koić ⟨u-⟩ **2.** łagodzić ⟨z-⟩ **3.** uspokajać ⟨-koić⟩

soot•y ['sʊtɪ] *adj* **1.** pokryty sadzą **2.** usmolony **3.** czarny (jak smoła)

sop [sɒp] *s fig* ochłap *m*

soph•ism ['sɒfɪzəm] *s* sofizm *m*

so•phis•ti•cat•ed [sə'fɪstɪkeɪtɪd] *adj* **1.** *audience*: wyrobiony **2.** *person*: o wysokiej kulturze osobistej, wyrobiony towarzysko **3.** *technology*: zaawansowany, nowoczesny **4.** *mechanism*: skomplikowany **5.** *style*: wyrafinowany, wyszukany **6.** wytworny; **so•phis•ti•ca•tion** [sə'fɪstɪkeɪʃn] *s* **1.** wyrobienie *n* **2.** wysoka kultura *f* osobista **3.** wyrafinowanie *n* **4.** *technology*: zaawansowanie *n* **5.** wytworność *f*

soph•o•more ['sɒfəmɔː] *s Am* **1.** student *m* drugiego roku **2.** uczeń *m* drugiej klasy

sop•o•rif•ic [sɒpə'rɪfɪk] **I** *adj effect*: usypiający, ***~ drugs*** środki nasenne **II** *s* środek *m* nasenny

sop•ping ['sɒpɪŋ] *adj infml* całkiem mokry

sop•py ['sɒpɪ] *adj Br infml* ckliwy

so•pra•no [sə'prænəʊ] MUS **I** *s* sopran *m* **II** *adj* sopranowy

sor•bet ['sɒːbeɪ] *s* sorbet *m*

sor•cer•er ['sɔːsərə] *s* czarnoksiężnik *m*; **sor•cer•y** ['sɔːsərɪ] *s* **1.** czarnoksięstwo *n* **2.** czary *pl*

sor•did ['sɒːdɪd] *adj* **1.** wstrętny **2.** ohydny **3.** zapuszczony

sore [sɒː] **I** *adj* **1.** ***be ~*** boleć; ***he is ~ all over*** wszystko go boli; ***I have a ~ throat*** boli mnie gardło; ***my stomach is ~*** boli mnie brzuch **2.** urażony **3.** ***a ~ point*** czuły punkt **II** *s* **1.** rana *f* **2.** *fig* utrapienie *n*; **sore•ly** ['sɔːlɪ] *adv* **1.** ***he'll be ~ missed*** będzie nam go bardzo brakowało **2.** *needed*: pilnie

so•ror•i•ty [sə'rɒrətɪ] *s Am* korporacja *f* studentek

sor•row ['sɒrəʊ] **I** *s* **1.** smutek *m*; ***joys and ~s*** radości i smutki **2.** żal *m* **II** *v/i* ***the ~ing relatives*** pogrążeni w żalu krewni; **sor•row•ful** ['sɒrəʊfl] *adj lit* **1.** przepełniony smutkiem **2.** smutny

sor•ry ['sɒrɪ] **I** *adj* **1.** ***I'm ~*** **a)** przepraszam **b)** przykro mi; ***we're ~ to hear it*** przykro nam to słyszeć; ***I'm ~ about what's happened*** przykro mi, że to się stało; ***feel ~ for s.o.*** współczuć komuś; ***you'll be ~ if I catch you*** pożałujesz, jak cię złapię **2.** żałosny **3.** ***in a ~ state*** w pożałowania godnym stanie **4.** *view*: przykry **II** *interj* przepraszam

sort [sɔːt] **I** *s* **1.** rodzaj *m*; ***what ~ of music do you like?*** jaki rodzaj muzyki lubisz?; ***all ~s of things*** najprzeróżniejsze rzeczy; ***nothing of the ~!*** nic podobnego!; ***~ of*** w pewnym sensie, tak jakoś; ***I ~ of expected it*** właściwie to się tego spodziewałem; ***be out of ~s*** *infml* być nie w sosie **2.** typ *m* **3.** ***people of that ~*** ludzie tego pokroju, tacy ludzie **II** *v/t* **1.** sortować ⟨po-⟩ **2.** segregować ⟨po-⟩ **3.** ***we'll soon have this ~ed*** *Br infml* wkrótce sobie z tym poradzimy; **sort out** *v/t* **1.** porządkować ⟨u-⟩; ***it will all ~ itself out*** wszystko się jakoś ułoży **2.** robić ⟨z-⟩ porządek z *I* **3.** załatwiać ⟨-wić⟩ **4.** zajmować ⟨-jąć⟩ się; **sort through** *v/i* przeglądać ⟨-dnąć⟩

sor•tie ['sɔːtiː] *s* wypad *m*

SOS [esəʊ'es] *s* SOS *m*, sygnał *m* SOS

so-'so *infml* **I** *adj* taki sobie **II** *adv* tak sobie

souf•flé ['suːfleɪ] *s* COOK suflet *m*

sought [sɒt] *Past Simple and Past Participle* → **seek**

'sought-af•ter *adj* **1.** poszukiwany **2.** rozchwytywany **3.** wzięty

soul [səʊl] *s* **1.** dusza *f*; ***there wasn't a ~ on the street*** na ulicy nie było żywej duszy **2.** MUS soul *m*; **soul-de•stroy•ing** ['səʊldɪstrɔɪɪŋ] *adj* **1.** przygnębiający **2.** śmiertelnie nudny; **soul•ful** ['səʊlfl] *adj* smutny; **soul•less** ['səʊlləs] *adj* **1.** bezduszny **2.** pozbawiony wyrazu; **'soul mate** *s* bratnia dusza *f*; **'soul mu•sic** *s* MUS soul *m*; **soul-search•ing** ['səʊlsɜːtʃɪŋ] *s*: ***I've done a lot of ~ lately*** wiele ostatnio myślałem nad sobą

sound[1] [saʊnd] **I** *adj* **1.** *structure*: mocny **2.** *basis*: solidny **3.** sensowny

S

4. rozsądny 5. *knowledge*: dogłębny 6. zdrowy; ***arrive home save and ~*** dotrzeć do domu cało i zdrowo 7. ***of ~ mind*** zdrowy na umyśle 8. *sleep*: głęboki 9. *investment*: pewny, bezpieczny **II** *adv* ***be ~ asleep*** spać głęboko

sound² [~] *s* przesmyk *m*

sound³ [~] **I** *s* 1. dźwięk *m*; ***I don't like the ~ of it*** *fig* to mi się nie podoba 2. odgłos *m* 3. brzmienie *n* 4. sonda *f* **II** *v/i* 1. brzmieć ⟨za-⟩; ***it ~s reasonable*** to brzmi rozsądnie; ***she didn't ~ surprised*** nie wydawała się zdziwiona; ***you ~ just like your father*** mówisz zupełnie jak twój ojciec 2. (*alarm*) rozlegać ⟨-lec⟩ się **III** *v/t* 1. *alarm*: włączać ⟨-czyć⟩ 2. ***~ one's horn*** zatrąbić 3. sondować ⟨wy-⟩; **sound off** *v/t*: ***~ about*** wypowiadać się o *L*; **sound out** *v/t* 1. badać ⟨wy-⟩ 2. sondować ⟨wy-⟩

'sound bar•ri•er *s* PHYS bariera *f* dźwięku; **'sound card** *s* INF karta *f* dźwiękowa

sound•ly ['saʊndlɪ] *adv* 1. ***he was ~ beaten*** a) dostał porządne lanie b) odniósł dotkliwą porażkę 2. *sleep*: głęboko 3. ***~ built*** solidnie 4. ***~ based argument***: oparty na solidnych przesłankach

sound•ness ['saʊndnɪs] *s* 1. solidność *f* 2. zdrowie *f* 3. racjonalność *f* 4. *knowledge*: dogłębność *f*

'sound•proof I *adj* dźwiękoszczelny **II** *v/t* 1. wyciszać ⟨-szyć⟩ 2. izolować ⟨wy-⟩ akustycznie; **sound•proof•ing** ['saʊndpru:fɪŋ] *s* 1. izolacja *f* akustyczna 2. wyciszenie *n*; **'sound sys•tem** *s* zestaw *m* nagłaśniający; **'sound•track** *s* ścieżka *f* dźwiękowa

S

soup [su:p] **I** *s* zupa *f* **II** *v/t* ***~ s.th. up*** *infml* podrasowywać ⟨-sować⟩; **souped-up** ['su:ptʌp] *adj infml* podrasowany; **'soup kitch•en** *s* jadłodajnia *f* dla ubogich; **'soup plate** *s* głęboki talerz *m*; **'soup spoon** *s* łyżka *f* do zupy

sour [saʊə] **I** *adj* 1. kwaśny; ***turn ~*** skwaśnieć 2. *person*: zgorzkniały **II** *v/i* 1. kwaśnieć ⟨s-⟩ 2. (*atmosphere, relations*) psuć ⟨po-⟩ się; **sour 'cream, soured 'cream** *s* kwaśna śmietana *f*; **sour 'grapes** *pl fig* kwaśne winogrona *pl*

source [sɔ:s] *s* 1. źródło *n*; ***a ~ of information*** źródło informacji; ***an energy ~*** źródło energii; ***at ~*** u źródła; ***I have it from a reliable ~ that*** wiem z wiarygodnego źródła, że; **'source file** *s* INF plik *m* źródłowy; **'source lan•guage** *s* język *m* oryginału

sour•puss ['saʊəpʊs] *s infml* ponurak *m*

south [saʊθ] **I** *s* południe *n*; ***in the ~*** na południu; ***to the ~ of*** na południe od *G* **II** *adj* południowy; ***a ~ wind*** wiatr południowy **III** *adv* na południe; **South 'Af•ric•a** *s* Afryka *f* Południowa; **South 'Af•ri•can** *adj* południowoafrykański; **South A•'mer•i•ca** *s* Ameryka *f* Południowa; **South A•'mer•i•can** *adj* południowoamerykański

'south•bound *adj* 1. prowadzący na południe 2. jadący na południe

south•'east I *s* południowy wschód *m* **II** *adj* południowo-wschodni **III** *adv* na południowy wschód; **South•east 'A•sia** *s* Azja *f* południowo-wschodnia; **south•'east•ern** *adj* południowo-wschodni

south•er•ly ['sʌðəlɪ] **I** *adj* południowy **II** *s* wiatr *m* południowy

south•ern ['sʌðən] *adj* południowy; **south•ern•er** ['sʌðənə] *s* południowiec *m*

south•ern•most ['sʌðənməʊst] *adj* najbardziej wysunięty na południe

south•ward ['saʊθwəd] **I** *adj* południowy; ***in ~ direction*** w kierunku południowym **II** *adv* na południe

south•'west I *s* południowy zachód *m* **II** *adj* południowo-zachodni **III** *adv* na południowy zachód; **south•'west•ern** *adj* południowo-zachodni

sou•ve•nir [su:və'nɪə] *s* pamiątka *f*

sove•reign ['sɒvrɪn] **I** *s* 1. władca *m* 2. monarcha *f* 3. (*coin*) suweren *m* **II** *adj* 1. suwerenny 2. *power*: najwyższy; **sove•reign•ty** ['sɒvrɪntɪ] *s* 1. władza *f* 2. panowanie *n* 3. suwerenność *f*

So•vi•et ['səʊvɪət] *adj* sowiecki; **So•vi•et 'U•nion** *s*: ***the ~s*** Związek Radziecki

sow[1] [səʊ] (*sowed*; *sowed/sown*) *v/t* **1.** *a. fig* siać ⟨za-⟩; **~ wheat** siać pszenicę; **~ doubt in s.o.'s mind** zasiać w kimś wątpliwości **2.** obsiewać ⟨-siać⟩
sow[2] [saʊ] *s* BIOL maciora *f*, locha *f*
sown [səʊn] *Past Participle* → **sow**[1]
soya [sɔɪə] *Br*, **soy** *Am s* soja *f*; **soy·bean** *s Am* soja *f*; **'soy sauce** *s Am* sos *m* sojowy
spa [spɑː] *s* **1.** uzdrowisko *n* **2.** *Am* centrum *n* odnowy biologicznej
space [speɪs] **I** *s* **1.** przestrzeń *f*; ***time and ~*** czas i przestrzeń; ***in the ~ of five days*** na przestrzeni pięciu dni, w przeciągu pięciu dni **2.** miejsce *n*; ***make ~*** zrobić miejsce **3.** przestrzeń *f* kosmiczna, kosmos *m* **4.** INF spacja *f* **II** *v/t* **1.** (*a.* **~ out**) rozmieszczać ⟨-mieścić⟩; ***evenly ~d plants*** równomiernie rozmieszczone rośliny **2.** rozkładać ⟨-złożyć⟩ **3.** rozstawiać ⟨-wić⟩; **'space-age** *adj* supernowoczesny; **'space bar** *s* INF klawisz *m* spacji; **'space ca•det** *s*: ***she's a bit of a ~*** *infml* jest trochę dziwna; **'space•craft** *pl -craft s* pojazd *m* kosmiczny
'space•flight *s* **1.** lot *m* kosmiczny **2.** loty *pl* kosmiczne; **'space heat•er** *s* grzejnik *m*; **'space•lab** *s* laboratorium *n* kosmiczne; **space•man** ['speɪsmæn] *pl -men s infml* astronauta *m*; **'space probe** *s* sonda *f* kosmiczna; **'space•ship** *s* statek *m* kosmiczny; **'space shut•tle** *s* prom *m* kosmiczny, wahadłowiec *m*; **'space sta•tion** *s* stacja *f* kosmiczna; **'space•suit** *s* skafander *m* kosmiczny; **'space trav•el** *s* podróże *pl* kosmiczne; **'space•walk** *s* spacer *m* w kosmosie; **'space•wom•an** *pl -men s* astronautka *f*
spac•ing ['speɪsɪŋ] *s* **1.** odstępy *pl*; ***in double ~*** z podwójnym odstępem **2.** rozmieszczenie *n*
spa•cious ['speɪʃəs] *adj* przestronny
spade [speɪd] *s* **1.** szpadel *m*; ***call a ~ a ~*** nazywać rzeczy po imieniu **2.** łopata *f* **3.** łopatka *f* **4. ~s** (*cards*) pik *m*, *infml* wino *n*; ***the queen of ~s*** królowa pik
spa•ghet•ti [spə'getɪ] *s* COOK spaghetti *n*
Spain [speɪn] *s* Hiszpania *f*
spam [spæm] *s* **1. ~**® mielonka *f* (konserwowa) **2.** INF spam *m*
span [spæn] **I** *s* **1.** okres *m*; ***over a ~ of six months*** przez sześć miesięcy; ***an attention ~*** czas koncentracji uwagi **2.** *wings*: rozpiętość *f* **3.** TECH przęsło *n* **II** *v/t* **1.** obejmować ⟨objąć⟩; ***her career ~ned almost half a century*** jej kariera trwała prawie pół wieku **2.** przerzucać ⟨-rzucić⟩ most przez *A*
span•gle ['spæŋgl] **I** *v/t* dekorować ⟨u-⟩ **II** *s* **1.** cekin *m* **2.** pajetka *f*
Span•iard ['spænjəd] *s* Hiszpan *m*
span•iel ['spænjəl] *s* spaniel *m*
Span•ish ['spænɪʃ] **I** *adj* hiszpański **II** *s* język *m* hiszpański; ***the ~*** Hiszpanie
spank [spæŋk] *v/t* dawać ⟨dać⟩ klapsa; **spank•ing** ['spæŋkɪŋ] **I** *s* lanie *n*; ***give s.o. a ~*** sprawić komuś lanie **II** *adv* ***~ new*** *infml* nowiusieńki **III** *adj* ***at a ~ pace*** *infml* pędem
span•ner ['spænə] *s* TECH *Br* klucz *m*; ***an adjustable ~*** klucz nastawny
spar [spɑː] **I** *v/i* **1.** (*boxing*) odbywać ⟨-być⟩ sparing (**with** z *I*) **2.** sprzeczać ⟨po-⟩ się (**with** z *I*) **II** *s* **1.** *mast*: drzewce *n* **2.** *wing*: dźwigar *m*
spare [speə] **I** *adj* **1.** wolny; ***a ~ room*** pokój gościnny **2.** zapasowy **II** *v/t* **1.** poświęcać ⟨-cić⟩; ***~ s.o. a few minutes*** poświęcić komuś kilka minut; ***I can't ~ the time just now*** w tej chwili nie mam czasu **2.** oszczędzać ⟨-dzić⟩; ***~ me the details*** oszczędź mi szczegółów; ***not ~ oneself*** nie oszczędzać się **3.** ***to ~*** w zapasie; ***she had 10 minutes to ~*** miała jeszcze 10 minut **4.** poradzić sobie bez *G* **5.** szczędzić; ***~ no effort*** nie szczędzić wysiłków **III** *s* **1.** koło *n* zapasowe **2.** część *f* zamienna; **spare 'part** *s* część *f* zapasowa, część *f* zamienna; **spare 'ribs** *pl* COOK żeberka *pl*; **spare 'time** *s* czas *m* wolny; **spare 'tyre** *Br*, ***spare*** **'tire** *Am s* koło *n* zapasowe
spar•ing ['speərɪŋ] *adj use*: oszczędny; ***be ~ with praise*** być oszczędnym w pochwałach; **spa•ring•ly** ['speərɪŋlɪ] *adv* oszczędnie
spark [spɑːk] **I** *s* **1.** iskra *f* **2.** *hopes*: iskierka *f* **3.** *fig* odrobina *f* **II** *v/t* (*a.* **~ off**) *fire*, *protest*: wywoływać ⟨-łać⟩ **III** *v/i* iskrzyć ⟨za-⟩

S

spar•kle ['spɑːkl] **I** *v/i* **1.** skrzyć się **2.** lśnić **3.** błyszczeć się **4.** mienić się **5.** tryskać energią i humorem **II** *s* **1.** blask *m* **2.** błysk *m* **3.** *fig* iskra *f*; **spar•kler** ['spɑːklə] *s* **~s** zimne ognie *pl*; **spar•kling** ['spɑːklɪŋ] *adj* **1.** skrzący się **2.** błyszczący **3.** mieniący się **4.** *drink*: gazowany **5.** *conversation*: błyskotliwy **6.** *condition*: wyśmienity; **spar•kling 'wine** *s* wino *n* musujące

'spark plug *s AUTO* świeca *f* zapłonowa

spar•ring ['spɑːrɪŋ] *adj*: ***a ~ partner*** (*boxing*) sparing partner

spar•row ['spærəʊ] *s* wróbel *m*

sparse [spɑːs] *adj* **1.** nieliczny; ***the population of the island is ~*** wyspa jest słabo zaludniona **2.** skąpy; ***the information on the subject is ~*** niewiele jest na ten temat informacji **3.** rzadki; **sparse•ly** ['spɑːslɪ] *adv* **1.** *wooded, furnished*: słabo **2.** skąpo; ***the service was ~ attended*** na nabożeństwo przyszło niewiele osób

spar•tan ['spɑːtn] *adj conditions*: spartański

spasm ['spæzəm] *s* **1.** skurcz *m* **2.** kurcz *m*, spazm *m* **3.** *pain*: paroksyzm *m*; **spas•mod•ic** [spæz'mɒdɪk] *adj* **1.** sporadyczny **2.** spazmatyczny

spas•tic ['spæstɪk] *MED* **I** *adj* spastyczny **II** *s* osoba z porażeniem spastycznym

spat[1] [spæt] *Past Simple and Past Participle* → **spit**

spat[2] [~] *s infml* sprzeczka *f*

spat[3] [~] *s*: **~s** getry *pl*

spate [speɪt] *s* **1.** seria *f* **2.** ***in*** (***full***) **~** *river*: wezbrany

spa•tial ['speɪʃl] *adj* przestrzenny

spat•ter ['spætə] **I** *v/t* ochlapywać ⟨-pać⟩ (***s.o. with*** kogoś *I*) **II** *v/i* **1.** rozpryskiwać ⟨-snąć⟩ się **2.** (*rain*) bębnić (***on*** o *A*)

S

spat•u•la ['spætjʊlə] *s* **1.** *COOK* łopatka *f* **2.** *MED* szpatułka *f*

spawn [spɔːn] **I** *v/i* **1.** składać ⟨złożyć⟩ ikrę **2.** składać ⟨złożyć⟩ skrzek **3.** dawać ⟨dać⟩ początek **II** *s* **1.** ikra *f* **2.** skrzek *m*

spay [speɪ] *v/t she-cat*: sterylizować ⟨wy-⟩

speak [spiːk] **I** (*spoke*; *spoken*) *v/i* **1.** mówić (***to*** do *G*, ***about*** o *L*); ***~ with a foreign accent*** mówić z obcym akcentem; ***Ella ~ing*** tu Ella, mówi Ella; ***– 'Is that Mr Jones?' – '~ing.'*** – „Czy Pan Jones?" – „Przy telefonie."; ***~ing of travelling*** skoro mowa o podróżach; ***so to ~*** że tak powiem; ***it ~s for itself*** to mówi samo za siebie; ***~ for yourself*** mów za siebie; ***~ well*** (***ill***) ***of*** mówić dobrze (źle) o *L* **2.** rozmawiać (***to/with*** z *I*, ***about*** o *L*); ***we don't ~ to each other*** nie rozmawiamy ze sobą **3.** przemawiać ⟨-mówić⟩ **4.** zabierać ⟨-brać⟩ głos **II** (*spoke*; *spoken*) *v/t* mówić; ***do you ~ English?*** czy mówisz po angielsku?; ***~ the truth*** mówić prawdę; **speak for** *v/i* mówić w imieniu *G*; **speak out** *v/i* **1.** zabierać ⟨-brać⟩ głos **2.** wypowiadać ⟨-wiedzieć⟩ się (publicznie); **speak up** *v/i* mówić głośniej; **speak up for** *v/i* ujmować ⟨ująć⟩ się za *I*

speak•er ['spiːkə] *s* **1.** mówiący *m*; ***an English ~*** osoba znająca angielski; ***native ~s of French*** rodzimi użytkownicy języka francuskiego **2.** mówca *m* **3.** głośnik *m*; **speak•ing** ['spiːkɪŋ] *adj* mówiący; ***a ~ clock*** zegarynka; ***We are not on ~ terms*** nie rozmawiamy ze sobą

spear [spɪə] **I** *s* włócznia *f* **II** *v/t* dźgać ⟨dźgnąć⟩ włócznią; **spear•head** ['spɪəhed] **I** *v/t* **1.** prowadzić ⟨po-⟩ **2.** inicjować ⟨za-⟩ **II** *s* ***be at the ~ of a campaign*** stać na czele kampanii; **spear•mint** ['spɪəmɪnt] *s* mięta *f* kędzierzawa

spec [spek] *s* ***on ~*** *Br infml* w ciemno

spe•cial ['speʃl] **I** *adj* **1.** specjalny **2.** szczególny **II** *s* **1.** danie *n* dnia **2.** wydanie *n* specjalne **3.** *Am infml* promocja *f*; **spe•cial ef•fects** *pl* efekty *pl* specjalne

spe•cial•ist ['speʃlɪst] **I** *s* specjalista *m* **II** *adj* specjalistyczny; **spe•ci•al•i•ty** [speʃɪ'ælətɪ] *Br*, **spe•cial•ty** ['speʃəltɪ] *Am s* specjalność *f*; ***a local ~*** miejscowa specjalność; ***my ~ is international tax law*** specjalizuję się w międzynarodowym prawie podatkowym; **spe•cial•i•za•tion** [speʃəlaɪ'zeɪʃn] *s* specjalizacja *f*; **spe•cial•ize** ['speʃəlaɪz] *v/i* specjalizować ⟨wy-⟩ się (***in*** w *L*); **spe•cial•ly** ['speʃəlɪ] *adj* **1.** specjalnie; ***we came ~ to see you*** przyjechaliśmy specjalnie, żeby cię zobaczyć **2.** *infml* szczególnie

spe•cies ['spi:ʃi:z] *pl species s* BIOL gatunek *m*; ***endangered ~*** zagrożone gatunki

spe•cif•ic [spə'sɪfɪk] *adj* **1.** określony **2.** konkretny; ***can you be more ~?*** czy możesz wyrażać się jaśniej? **3.** dokładny **4.** szczegółowy **5.** ścisły **6.** specyficzny (***to*** dla *G*) **7.** charakterystyczny (***to*** dla *G*); **spe•cif•i•cal•ly** [spə'sɪfɪklɪ] *adv* **1.** wyraźnie; ***I ~ told you*** powiedziałem ci wyraźnie **2.** dokładnie; ***the newspaper, or more ~ the editor*** gazeta, a dokładniej wydawca **3.** specjalnie

spe•ci•fi•ca•tion [spesɪfɪ'keɪʃn] *s* **1.** specyfikacja *f* **2.** dokumentacja *f*; **spe•ci•fy** ['spesɪfaɪ] *v/t* **1.** określać ⟨-lić⟩ **2.** wyszczególniać ⟨-nić⟩

spe•ci•men ['spesɪmən] *s* **1.** próbka *f* **2.** okaz *m*; ***interesting ~s of tropical fish*** interesujące okazy ryb tropikalnych **3.** *document*: wzór *m*

spe•cious ['spi:ʃəs] *adj* **1.** *appearance*: zwodniczy **2.** *argument*: pozornie słuszny

speck [spek] *s* **1.** plamka *f* **2.** punkcik *m* **3.** drobinka *f*; **speck•led** ['spekld] *adj* **1.** nakrapiany **2.** w plamki

specs [speks] *pl Br infml* okulary *pl*

spec•ta•cle ['spektəkl] **I** *s* **1.** **~s** okulary *pl* **2.** widowisko *n*; ***make a ~ of oneself*** robić z siebie widowisko **3.** widok *m* **II** *adj* ***~ frames*** oprawki okularów

spec•tac•u•lar [spek'tækjʊlə] **I** *adj* **1.** widowiskowy **2.** spektakularny **3.** efektowny **II** *s* widowisko *n*

spec•ta•tor [spek'teɪtə] *s* widz *m*

spec•tra *pl* → ***spectrum***

spec•tral ['spektrəl] *adj* **1.** widmowy **2.** spektralny

spec•tre ['spektə] *Br*, **spec•ter** *Am s* widmo *n*; ***the ~ of civil war*** widmo wojny domowej

spec•trum ['spektrəm] *pl -tra s* **1.** PHYS widmo *n* **2.** zakres *m* **3.** spektrum *n* **4.** wachlarz *m*; ***a broad ~ of possibilities*** szeroki wachlarz możliwości

spec•u•late ['spekjʊleɪt] *v/i* **1.** spekulować (***about***/***on*** na temat *G*) **2.** snuć ⟨wy-⟩ domysły (***about***/***on*** na temat *G*) **3.** przypuszczać ⟨-puścić⟩ **4.** (*stock exchange*) spekulować; **spec•u•la•tion** [spekjʊ'leɪʃn] *s* **1.** domysły *pl* **2** spekulacje *pl* **3.** przypuszczenia *pl* **4.** ECON spekulacja *f*; **spec•u•la•tive** ['spekjələtɪv] *adj* **1.** oparty na domysłach **2.** oparty na przypuszczeniach **3.** ECON spekulacyjny; **spec•u•la•tor** ['spekjəleɪtə] *s* ECON spekulant *m*

sped [sped] *Past Simple and Past Participle* → ***speed***

speech [spi:tʃ] *s* **1.** mowa *f* **2.** przemówienie *n*; ***give a ~*** wygłosić przemówienie **3.** język *m* mówiony; **'speech de•fect** *s* zaburzenie *n* mowy; **'speech im•ped•i•ment** → ***speech defect***; **'speech ther•a•pist** *s* logopeda *m*; **speech ther•a•py** *s* logopedia *f*; **speech•less** ['spi:tʃlɪs] *adj*: ***leave s.o. ~*** odjąć komuś mowę; ***be ~ with wonder*** oniemieć z zachwytu

speed [spi:d] **I** *s* **1.** szybkość *f* **2.** prędkość *f*; ***at a ~ of*** z prędkością *G*; ***at full ~*** z maksymalną prędkością; ***full ~ ahead!*** cała naprzód! **3.** tempo *n* **4.** AUTO bieg *m*; ***a four-~ gearbox*** czterobiegowa skrzynia biegów **5.** (*bike*) przerzutka *f* **6.** PHOT czułość *f* **7.** (*drug*) *infml* speed *m* **II** *v/i* **1.** (*sped*; *sped*) pędzić ⟨po-⟩ **2.** (*sped*; *sped*) mknąć ⟨po-⟩ **3.** (*speeded*; *speeded*) przekraczać ⟨-roczyć⟩ dozwoloną prędkość **III** (*sped/speeded*; *sped/speeded*) *v/t* (*a.* ***~ up***) przyspieszać ⟨-szyć⟩; **'speed•boat** *s* ślizgacz *m*; **'speed hump** *Br*, ***speed bump*** *Am s* próg *m* zwalniający

speed•i•ly ['spi:dɪlɪ] *adv* pospiesznie

speed•ing ['spi:dɪŋ] *s* AUTO przekroczenie *n* (dozwolonej) prędkości

'speed lim•it *s* ograniczenie *n* prędkości; **speed•om•e•ter** [spi:'dɒmɪtə] *s* prędkościomierz *m*; **'speed trap** *s* miejsce *n* kontroli radarowej

speed•y ['spi:dɪ] *adj* szybki; ***a ~ recovery*** szybki powrót do zdrowia

spell[1] [spel] **I** (*spelled/spelt*; *spelled/spelt*) *v/t* **1.** literować ⟨prze-⟩; ***could you ~ your name, please?*** czy mógłby pan przeliterować swoje nazwisko? **2.** pisać ⟨na-⟩ **3.** zapowiadać ⟨-wiedzieć⟩ **4.** zwiastować **II** (*spelled/spelt*; *spelled/spelt*) *v/i* pisać (poprawnie); **spell out** *v/t* **1.** literować ⟨prze-⟩ **2.** wyjaśniać ⟨-nić⟩

spell[2] [~] *s* **1.** okres *m*; ***hot ~s*** upały; ***she had a ~ as an actress*** przez pe-

S

wien czas parała się aktorstwem **2.** pobyt *m*

spell[3] [~] *s* **1.** urok *m*; ***be under s.o.'s ~*** być pod czyimś urokiem **2.** czar *m*; ***cast a ~*** rzucić czar **3.** zaklęcie *n*

spell•bind•ing ['spelbaɪndɪŋ] *adj* przykuwający uwagę; '**spell•bound** *adj* oczarowany; '**spell•check** *INF* **I** *v/t* sprawdzać ⟨-dzić⟩ pisownię **II** *s* funkcja *f* sprawdzania pisowni *m*; '**spell-check•er** *s INF* funkcja *f* sprawdzania pisowni

spell•er ['spelə] *s*: ***be a good***/(***bad***) ~ być dobrym (słabym) z ortografii

spell•ing ['spelɪŋ] *s* **1.** pisownia *f* **2.** ortografia *f*; ***a ~ mistake*** błąd ortograficzny

spelt [spelt] *Past Simple and Past Participle* → ***spell***[1]

spend [spend] (*spent*; *spent*) *v/t* **1.** *money*: wydawać ⟨-dać⟩ **2.** *time*: spędzać ⟨-dzić⟩; ***~ too much time watching TV*** poświęcać za dużo czasu na oglądanie telewizji **3.** *energy*: poświęcać ⟨-cić⟩; **spend•er** ['spendə] *s*: ***be a big ~*** szastać pieniędzmi; **spend•ing** ['spendɪŋ] *s* wydatki *pl*; '**spend•ing mon•ey** *s* pieniądze *pl* na drobne wydatki

'**spend•thrift** **I** *s* rozrzutnik *m* **II** *adj* rozrzutny

spent [spent] **I** *Past Simple and Past Participle* → ***spend*** **II** *adj* zużyty

sperm [spɜːm] *s pl sperm*, *sperms* **1.** plemnik *m* **2.** sperma *f* **3.** nasienie *n*; '**sperm bank** *s* bank *m* spermy

spew [spjuː] **I** *v/t* **1.** *smoke*, *lava*: wypluwać ⟨-luć⟩; wyrzucać ⟨-cić⟩ **2.** (*a.* ***~ up***) *Br infml* wymiotować ⟨z-⟩ **II** *v/i* **1.** wydobywać ⟨-być⟩ się **2.** wypływać ⟨-łynąć⟩

sphere [sfɪə] *s* **1.** *MATH* kula *f* **2.** sfera *f* **3.** dziedzina *f* **4.** obszar *m*; **spher•i-cal** ['sferɪkl] *adj* **1.** kulisty **2.** sferyczny

sphinc•ter ['sfɪŋktə] *s ANAT* zwieracz *m*

spice [spaɪs] **I** *s* **1.** przyprawa *f* **2.** *fig* pikanteria *f* **II** (*a.* ***~ up***) *v/t* **1.** przyprawiać ⟨-wić⟩ **2.** *fig* dodawać ⟨-dać⟩ pikanterii **3.** *fig* urozmaicać ⟨-cić⟩; **spice rack** ['spaɪsræk] *s* **1.** stojak *m* na przyprawy **2.** półka *f* na przyprawy

spick-and-span [spɪkən'spæn] *adj* lśniący czystością

spic•y ['spaɪsɪ] *adj* **1.** ostry **2.** *a. fig* pikantny

spi•der ['spaɪdə] *s* pająk *m*; '**spi•der's-web** ['spaɪdəzweb] *s* pajęczyna *f*, pajęcza sieć *f*

spiel [ʃpiːl] *s infml* gadka *f*

spike [spaɪk] **I** *s* **1.** szpikulec *m* **2.** szpic *m* **3.** kolec *m*; ***~s*** *SPORT* kolce **4.** kłos *m* **II** *v/t* **1.** nabijać ⟨-bić⟩ **2.** nadziewać ⟨-dziać⟩ **3.** zaprawiać ⟨-wić⟩; '**spike heel** *s Am* (*of shoe*) szpilka *f*

spik•y ['spaɪkɪ] *adj* **1.** spiczasty **2.** ostry **3.** kłujący **4.** kolczasty **5.** *Br person*: drażliwy

spill [spɪl] **I** (*spilled*/*spilt*; *spilled*/*spilt*) *v/t* rozlewać ⟨-lać⟩; ***~ one's coffee over one's trousers*** wylać sobie kawę na spodnie; ***~ blood*** przelewać krew; ***~ the beans*** *fig* puścić farbę **II** (*spilled*/*spilt*; *spilled*/*spilt*) *v/i* **1.** rozlewać ⟨-lać⟩ się **2.** wylewać ⟨-lać⟩ się **3.** wysypywać ⟨-pać⟩ się; ***people ~ed into the street*** *fig* ludzie wylegli na ulicę **III** *s* **1.** wyciek *m* **2.** plama *f* **3.** upadek *m*; ***take a ~*** upaść; **spill out** *v/t* wyrzucać ⟨-cić⟩ z siebie; **spill over** *v/i* **1.** przelewać ⟨-lać⟩ się **2.** przenosić ⟨-nieść⟩ się (***into*** na *A*)

spilt [spɪlt] *Past Simple and Past Participle* → ***spill***

spin [spɪn] **I** (*spun*; *spun*) *v/t* **1.** kręcić się **2.** wirować **3.** (*a.* ***~ round***, ***~ around***) obracać ⟨-rócić⟩ się szybko **4.** pędzić ⟨po-⟩ **II** (*spun*; *spun*) *v/t* **1.** obracać ⟨-rócić⟩ **2.** kręcić ⟨za-⟩ **3.** *wool*: prząść; ***~ a yarn*** *fig* opowiadać niestworzone historie **4.** *web*: tkać ⟨u-⟩ **5.** *washing*: odwirowywać ⟨-rować⟩ **III** *s* **1.** obrót *m* **2.** obracanie się *n* **3.** wirowanie *n*; ***give s.th. a ~*** odwirować coś **4.** (*aircraft*) korkociąg *m* **5.** (*tennis*) rotacja *f* **6.** *dated* przejażdżka *f* **7.** ***put one's own ~ on s.th.*** **a)** przedstawiać coś w korzystnym dla siebie świetle **b)** interpretować coś na swój sposób; **spin around** *v/i* **1.** kręcić się **2.** wirować; **spin out** *v/t* **1.** przeciągać ⟨-gnąć⟩ **2.** przedłużać ⟨-żyć⟩

spin•ach ['spɪnɪtʃ] *s* szpinak *m*

spin•al ['spaɪnl] *adj* kręgowy; **spin•al 'col•umn** *s* kręgosłup *m*; **spin•al 'cord** *s* rdzeń *m* kręgowy

S

spin•dle ['spɪndl] *s* **1.** wrzeciono *n* **2.** trzpień *m* obrotowy **3.** wałek *m*
spin•dly ['spɪndlɪ] *adj infml* patykowaty
'**spin doc•tor** *s infml* rzecznik *m* prasowy; '**spin-dry** *v/t Br* odwirowywać ⟨-rować⟩; **spin-'dri•er** *s* wirówka *f*
spine [spaɪn] *s* **1.** ANAT kręgosłup *m* **2.** *book*: grzbiet *m* **3.** kolec *m*; **spine-chill•ing** ['spaɪntʃɪlɪŋ] *adj* mrożący krew w żyłach; **spine•less** ['spaɪnlɪs] *adj* **1.** bezkręgowy **2.** *infml* tchórzliwy
spin•na•ker ['spɪnəkə] *s* (*sailing*) spinaker *m*
spin•ney ['spɪnɪ] *s Br* zagajnik *m*
spin•ning mill ['spɪnɪŋmɪl] *s* przędzalnia *f*; **spin•ning wheel** ['spɪnɪŋwiːl] *s* kołowrotek *m*
'**spin-off** *s* **1.** (pozytywny) produkt *m* uboczny **2.** (pozytywny) efekt *m* uboczny **3.** wersja *f* **4.** kontynuacja *f*
spin•ster ['spɪnstə] *s* stara panna *f*; **spin•ster•ish** ['spɪnstərɪʃ] *adj* staropanieński
spin•y ['spaɪnɪ] *adj* kolczasty
spi•ral ['spaɪrəl] **I** *s* spirala *f* **II** *adj* **1.** spiralny **2.** kręty; **spi•ral 'stair•case** *s* schody *pl* kręcone
spire [spaɪə] *s* ARCHIT iglica *f*
spir•it ['spɪrɪt] **I** *s* **1.** duch *m*; ***a community ~*** duch wspólnoty; ***the Holy ~*** Duch Święty; ***be in ~ with*** być myślami z *I* **2.** nastrój *m* **3.** humor *m*; ***be in low ~s*** być nie w humorze; ***be in high ~s*** być w dobrym nastroju **4.** nastawienie *n* **5.** odwaga *f* **6.** charakter *m* **7.** *Br* alkohol *m* wysokoprocentowy; ***~s*** wysokoprocentowe napoje alkoholowe **8.** spirytus *m* **II** *v/i* (*a.* ***~ away***) zabierać ⟨-brać⟩ niepostrzeżenie; **spir•it•ed** ['spɪrɪtɪd] *adj* **1.** odważny **2.** zdeterminowany **3.** *discussion*: ożywiony
'**spir•it lev•el** *s* TECH poziomica *f*
spir•it•u•al ['spɪrɪtʃʊəl] **I** *adj* duchowy **II** *s* MUS spirituals *pl*; **spir•it•u•al•ism** ['spɪrɪtʃʊəlɪzm] *s* spirytyzm *m*; **spir•it•u•al•ist** ['spɪrɪtʃʊəlɪst] *s* spirytysta *m*; **spir•it•u•al•is•tic** [spɪrɪtʃʊəl'ɪstɪk] *adj* spirytystyczny
spit[1] [spɪt] **I** (*spat*; *spat*) *v/t* **1.** pluć ⟨wy-⟩; ***~ blood*** pluć krwią; ***~ it out!*** *fig* wyrzuć to z siebie!; ***~ venom*** *fig* pluć jadem **2.** *curses*: obrzucać ⟨-cić⟩ **II** (*spat*; *spat*) *v/i* **1.** opluwać ⟨-luć⟩ (***at*** *A*) **2.** pluć ⟨plunąć⟩ **3.** spluwać ⟨splunąć⟩ **4.** skwierczeć **5.** (*fire*) trzaskać **6.** ***it's ~ting*** siąpi **III** *s* **1.** ślina *f* **2.** plwocina
spit[2] [spɪt] *s* **1.** rożen *m* **2.** szpikulec *m* rożna **3.** mierzeja *f*, kosa *f* **4.** cypel *m*
spite [spaɪt] **I** *s* **1.** złośliwość *f* **2.** przekora *f* **3.** ***in ~ of*** pomimo *G*; ***in ~ of the fact that*** pomimo tego, że; ***in ~ of oneself*** wbrew sobie **II** *v/t* robić ⟨z-⟩ komuś na złość; **spite•ful** ['spaɪtfəl] *adj* złośliwy; **spite•ful•ly** ['spaɪtfəlɪ] *adv* złośliwie
spit•ting ['spɪtɪŋ] *adj*: ***within ~ distance*** o rzut kamieniem; **spit•ting 'im•age** *s*: ***he's the ~ of his father*** wykapany ojciec
spit•tle ['spɪtl] *s dated* ślina *f*
splash [splæʃ] **I** *v/t* **1.** ochlapywać ⟨-pać⟩ **2.** rozchlapywać ⟨-pać⟩ **II** *v/i* **1.** chlapać **2.** rozpryskiwać ⟨-kać⟩ się **3.** pluskać się **III** *s* **1.** plusk *m* **2.** plama *f*; **splash down** *v/i* (*spaceship*) wodować; **splash out** *infml* **I** *v/t money*: wydawać ⟨-dać⟩ (***on*** na *A*) **II** *v/i* szaleć ⟨za-⟩
'**splash•down** *s spaceship*: wodowanie *n*
splat [splæt] *s* plaśnięcie *n*
splat•ter ['splætə] → ***spatter***
splay [spleɪ] *v/t* (*a.* ***~ out***) **1.** *feet*, *legs*: rozstawiać ⟨-wić⟩ **2.** *legs*, *hands*: rozkładać ⟨-złożyć⟩ **3.** *fingers*: rozcapierzać ⟨-rzyć⟩
spleen [spliːn] *s* śledziona *f*
splen•did ['splendɪd] *adj* **1.** wspaniały **2.** znakomity
splen•dour ['splendə] *Br*, **splen•dor** *Am s* **1.** świetność *f* **2.** wspaniałość *f* **3.** okazałość *f*
splice [splaɪs] **I** *v/t* **1.** kleić ⟨s-⟩ **2.** splatać ⟨-leść⟩ **3.** łączyć ⟨po-⟩ **II** *s* **1.** sklejenie *n* **2.** splot *m* **3.** połączenie *n*
splint [splɪnt] *s* MED szyna *f*
splin•ter ['splɪntə] **I** *s* **1.** odłamek *m* **2.** drzazga *f* **II** *v/t* **1.** rozbijać ⟨-bić⟩ **2.** rozłupywać ⟨-pać⟩ **III** *v/i* **1.** rozbijać ⟨-bić⟩ się **2.** rozpadać ⟨-paść⟩ się; '**splin•ter group** *s* POLIT odłam *m*
split [splɪt] **I** (*split*; *split*) *v/i* **1.** pękać ⟨-knąć⟩ **2.** łamać ⟨z-⟩ się **3.** rozdzie-

S

rać ⟨-zedrzeć⟩ się **4.** dzielić ⟨po-⟩ się **5.** zrywać ⟨zerwać⟩ (**with** z *I*) **6.** *infml* zmywać ⟨-myć⟩ się **II** (*split*; *split*) *v/t* **1.** rozłupywać ⟨-pać⟩ **2.** rozdzierać ⟨-zedrzeć⟩ **3.** rozcinać ⟨-ciąć⟩ **4.** dzielić ⟨po-⟩; **~ *the bills*** płacić rachunki po połowie **5.** dzielić ⟨po-⟩ się (**with** z *I*); **~ *a win*** podzielić się wygraną **III** *s* **1.** rozłam *m* **2.** podział *m* **3.** część *f* **4.** zerwanie *n* **5.** pęknięcie *n* **6.** rozdarcie *n* **7.** rozcięcie *n* **8.** (*gymnastics*) ***the ~s*** szpagat *m*; **split up I** *v/i* **1.** zrywać ⟨zerwać⟩ (**with** z *I*) **2.** dzielić ⟨po-⟩ się **II** *v/t* **1.** poróżniać ⟨-nić⟩ **2.** dzielić ⟨po-⟩

split ends [splɪt'endz] *pl* (*hair*) rozdwajające się końce *pl*; **split-'level** *adj flat*: dwupoziomowy; **split per•son•'al•i•ty** *s* rozdwojenie *n* jaźni; **split 'screen** *s INF* **1.** dzielony ekran *m* **2.** podział *m* ekranu; **split 'sec•ond** *s* ułamek *m* sekundy; ***in a ~*** w ułamku sekundy; **split•ting** ['splɪtɪŋ] *adj pain*: przeszywający; ***I have a ~ headache*** głowa mi pęka

splodge [splɒdʒ], ***splotch*** [splɒtʃ] *s* plama *f*

splurge [splɜːdʒ] *infml* **I** *v/t money*: wydawać ⟨-dać⟩ mnóstwo (**on** na *A*) **II** *v/i* wydawać ⟨-dać⟩ mnóstwo pieniędzy (**on** na *A*)

splut•ter ['splʌtə] → ***sputter***

spoil [spɔɪl] **I** (*spoiled/spoilt*; *spoiled/spoilt*) *v/t* **1.** psuć ⟨ze-, po-⟩ **2.** niszczyć ⟨z-⟩ **3.** *child*: rozpieszczać ⟨-pieścić⟩, psuć **II** (*spoiled/spoilt*; *spoiled/spoilt*) *v/i* **1.** psuć ⟨ze-, po-⟩ się **2. *be ~ing for a fight*** szukać zaczepki

spoil•er ['spɔɪlə] *s AUTO* spoiler *m*

'spoil•sport *s*: ***don't be such a ~*** *infml* nie psuj ludziom zabawy

S

spoilt [spɔɪlt] *Past Simple and Past Participle* → ***spoil***

spoke[1] [spəʊk] *s* szprycha *f*

spoke[2] [~] *Past Simple* → ***speak***

spo•ken ['spəʊkən] **I** *Past Participle* → ***speak*** **II** *adj* **1.** *language*: mówiony **2.** *command*: ustny

spokes•man ['spəʊksmən] *pl -men s* rzecznik *m*; **spokes•per•son** ['spəʊkspɜːsən] *s* rzecznik *m*; **spokes•wom•an** ['spəʊkswʊmən] *pl -men s* rzeczniczka *f*

sponge [spʌndʒ] **I** *s* **1.** gąbka *f* **2.** *COOK* biszkopt *m* **II** *v/t* (*a.* **~ *down***) przecierać ⟨przetrzeć⟩ gąbką; **sponge off**, ***sponge on*** *v/i infml* żerować na *L*

'sponge bag *s Br* kosmetyczka *f*; **'sponge cake** *s COOK* biszkopt *m*

spong•er ['spʌndʒə] *s infml fig* pasożyt *m*

spong•y ['spʌndʒɪ] *adj* gąbczasty

spon•sor ['spɒnsə] *s* **1.** sponsor *m* **2.** rodzic *m* chrzestny **3.** wnioskodawca *m*; **spon•sor•ship** ['spɒnsəʃɪp] *s* **1.** sponsorowanie *n* **2.** sponsoring *m* **3.** patronat *m*

spon•ta•ne•i•ty [spɒntə'neɪətɪ] *s* spontaniczność *f*; **spon•ta•ne•ous** [spɒn'teɪnɪəs] *adj* **1.** spontaniczny **2.** samorzutny; **spon•ta•ne•ous•ly** [spɒn'teɪnɪəslɪ] *adj* **1.** spontanicznie **2.** samorzutnie

spoof [spuːf] *s* parodia *f* (**of/on** *G*)

spook [spuːk] *infml* **I** *s* **1.** duch *m* **2.** *Am* szpieg *m* **II** *v/t* wystraszyć **III** *v/i* wystraszyć się; **spook•y** ['spuːkɪ] *adj* **1.** straszny **2.** *house*: nawiedzony

spool [spuːl] *s* **1.** szpula *f* **2.** szpulka *f* **3.** kołowrotek *m*

spoon [spuːn] *s* łyżka *f*; **'spoon•feed** *v/t* **1.** karmić ⟨na-⟩ łyżeczką **2.** *fig* podawać ⟨-dać⟩ na tacy; **spoon•ful** ['spuːnfʊl] *s* łyżka *f*; ***two ~s of sugar*** dwie łyżki cukru

spo•rad•ic [spə'rædɪk] *adj* sporadyczny; **spo•rad•i•cal•ly** [spə'rædɪklɪ] *adv* sporadycznie

spore [spɔː] *s BIOL* zarodnik *m*, spora *f*

sport [spɔːt] **I** *s* **1.** sport *m* **2.** dyscyplina *f* (sportowa) **3.** wychowanie *n* fizyczne **4.** zabawa *f*; ***make ~ of s.o.*** bawić się czyimś kosztem **5. *what's up, ~?*** *infml* co słychać, stary? **II** *v/t* **1.** obnosić się z *I* **2.** paradować z *I*; **sport•ing** ['spɔːtɪŋ] *adj* **1.** sportowy **2.** *chance*: spory

'sports car [spɔːtskɑː] *s* samochód *m* sportowy; **'sports•cast** *s Am* transmisja *f* sportowa; **'sports cen•tre** *Br*, ***'sports cen•ter*** *Am s* kompleks *m* sportowy; **'sports jack•et** *s* sportowa marynarka *f*; **sports 'jour•nal•ist** *s* dziennikarz *m* sportowy; **'sports•man** *pl -men s* sportowiec *m*; **sports•man•like** ['spɔːtsmənlaɪk] *adj* sportowy; **sports•man•ship** ['spɔːtsmənʃɪp] *s* sportowa postawa *f*; ˈ**sports page** *s* (*newspaper*) dział *m* sportowy; ˈ**sports•wear** *s* odzież *f* sportowa; ˈ**sports•wom•an** *pl -men s* sportsmenka *f*

sport•y [ˈspɔːtɪ] *adj infml* **1.** wysportowany **2.** *clothes*, *car*: sportowy

spot [spɒt] **I** *s* **1.** miejsce *n*; ***on the ~*** **a)** na miejscu **b)** z miejsca, natychmiast **c)** w miejscu; ***he was rooted to the ~*** *fig* nogi wrosły mu w ziemię; ***have a weak ~ for*** mieć słabość do *G* **2.** kropka *f* **3.** cętka *f* **4.** plamka *f* **5.** plama *f* **6.** pryszcz *m* **7.** odrobina *f*; ***a ~ of*** trochę *G* **8.** reklama *f* **9.** *infml* reflektor *m* punktowy **II** *v/t* **1.** dostrzegać ⟨-rzec⟩ **2.** zauważać ⟨-żyć⟩; **spot** ˈ**check** *s* wyrywkowa kontrola *f*

spot•less [ˈspɒtlɪs] *adj* **1.** nieskazitelnie czysty **2.** ***be ~*** lśnić czystością **3.** bez skazy

ˈ**spot•light** [ˈspɒtlaɪt] **I** *s* **1.** reflektor *m* punktowy **2.** światło *n* punktowe **3.** ***be in the ~*** *fig* być w centrum uwagi; ***turn the ~ on*** *fig* zwrócić uwagę na *A* **II** *v/t* (*spotlighted/spotlit*; *spotlighted/spotlit*) **1.** oświetlać ⟨-lić⟩ reflektorem punktowym **2.** *fig* zwracać ⟨-rócić⟩ uwagę na *A*; **spot-**ˈ**on** *adj Br infml* **1.** bezbłędny **2.** trafiony w dziesiątkę **3.** ***~!*** doskonale!

spot•ted [ˈspɒtɪd] *adj* **1.** w kropki **2.** cętkowany **3.** nakrapiany; **spot•ty** [ˈspɒtɪ] *adj* **1.** *Br* pryszczaty **2.** *Am* wyrywkowy, niepełny **3.** *Am* nierówny

spouse [spaʊz] *s* **1.** małżonek *m* **2.** małżonka *f*

spout [spaʊt] **I** *s* **1.** struga *f* **2.** dziobek *m*; ***go up the ~*** *Br infml* wziąć w łeb **3.** wylot *m* **4.** końcówka *f* **II** *v/i* tryskać ⟨-snąć⟩ **III** *v/t* tryskać ⟨-snąć⟩

sprain [spreɪn] **I** *v/t* skręcać ⟨-cić⟩; ***~ one's ankle*** skręcić nogę w kostce **II** *s MED* skręcenie *n*

sprang [spræŋ] *Past Simple* → ***spring***

sprat [spræt] *s* szprot *m*

sprawl [sprɔːl] **I** *v/i* **1.** rozkładać ⟨-złożyć⟩ się, *infml* rozwalać ⟨-lić⟩ się; ***he was ~ing on the sofa*** *infml* leżał rozwalony na kanapie **2.** rozciągać się **II** *s* **1.** rozrastanie się *n* **2.** aglomeracja *f*; **sprawl•ing** [ˈsprɔːlɪŋ] *adj* **1.** rozległy **2.** ogromny

spray[1] [spreɪ] *s* **1.** gałązka *f* **2.** wiązanka *f*

spray[2] [~] **I** *s* **1.** spray *m* **2.** rozpylacz *m* **3.** aerozol *m* **4.** mgła *f* wodna **5.** pył *m* wodny **6.** *bullets*: grad *m* **7.** pryskanie *n*; ***give s.th. a ~*** spryskać coś **II** *v/t* **1.** spryskiwać ⟨-kać⟩ **2.** pryskać ⟨-snąć⟩ **III** *v/i* **1.** rozpryskiwać ⟨-snąć⟩ się **2.** tryskać ⟨-snąć⟩; ˈ**spray can** *s* **1.** spray *m* **2.** aerozol *m*; ˈ**spray•gun** *s* pistolet *m* natryskowy; **spray paint** *s* farba *f* w sprayu

spread [spred] **I** (*spread*; *spread*) *v/t* **1.** (*a.* ***~ out***) rozkładać ⟨-złożyć⟩ (***on*** na *L*) **2.** *butter*: rozsmarowywać ⟨-rować⟩ **3.** *knowledge*: rozpowszechniać ⟨-nić⟩ **4.** *gossip*: rozsiewać ⟨-siać⟩ **5.** *lies*: rozpowiadać ⟨-wiedzieć⟩ **6.** ***~ the word, that*** rozgłosić, że **II** (*spread*; *spread*) *v/i* **1.** (*area*) rozciągać się **2.** rozpościerać się **3.** (*illness*, *fire*) rozprzestrzeniać ⟨-nić⟩ się **4.** (*gossip*) rozchodzić ⟨-zejść⟩ się; ***~ like wildfire*** rozchodzić się lotem błyskawicy **5.** rozsmarowywać ⟨-rować⟩ się **III** *s* **1.** rozprzestrzenianie się *n* **2.** rozpowszechnianie *n* **3.** rozchodzenie się *n* **4.** wachlarz *m* **5.** spektrum *m* **6.** *wings*: rozpiętość *f* **7.** rozkładówka *f* **8.** *infml* uczta *f* **9.** *COOK* pasta *f*; ***low-fat ~*** margaryna z niską zawartością tłuszczu **10.** *Am* narzuta *f*; **spread out** *v/i* **1.** rozciągać ⟨-gnąć⟩ się **2.** rozkładać ⟨-złożyć⟩ się **3.** rozdzielać ⟨-lić⟩ się

spread-ea•gled [spredˈiːgld] *adj Br lie*: z rozrzuconymi nogami i ramionami; ˈ**spread•sheet** *s INF* arkusz *m* kalkulacyjny

spree [spriː] *s*: ***go on a ~*** iść zaszaleć

sprig [sprɪg] *s* gałązka *f*

spright•ly [ˈspraɪtlɪ] *adj* **1.** żwawy **2.** dziarski

spring[1] [sprɪŋ] *s* wiosna *f*; ***in (the) ~*** wiosną

spring[2] [~] **I** *s* **1.** sprężyna *f* **2.** źródło *n* **3.** skok *m* **4.** (*a.* **coil ~**) resor *m* (sprężynowy) **5.** sprężystość *f*; ***walk with a ~ in one's step*** iść sprężystym krokiem **II** (*sprang*; *sprung*) *v/i* **1.** skakać ⟨skoczyć⟩; ***~ to one's feet*** zerwać się na równe nogi; ***~ into life*** budzić się do życia; ***~ open*** (*lid*) odskoczyć **2.** pojawiać ⟨-wić⟩ się **III** (*sprang*;

S

sprung) *v/t* zaskakiwać ⟨-skoczyć⟩ (***s.th. on*** czymś *A*); **spring back** *v/i* **1.** odskakiwać ⟨-skoczyć⟩ (do tyłu) **2.** (*twig*) prostować ⟨wy-⟩ się; **spring from I** *v/t* wynikać ⟨-knąć⟩ z *G* **II** *v/i* pojawiać ⟨-wić⟩ się; ***where on earth did you ~?*** *infml* skądże u diabła się tu wziąłeś?; **spring up** *v/i* **1.** wyrastać ⟨-rosnąć⟩ jak grzyby po deszczu **2.** pojawiać ⟨-wić⟩ się nagle; **'spring•board** *s* **1.** SPORT trampolina *f* **2.** *fig* odskocznia *f* (***to*** do *G*)

spring 'chick•en *s*: ***be no ~*** być nie pierwszej młodości; **spring-'clean** *v/t* gruntownie sprzątać ⟨po-⟩; **spring-'clean•ing** *s* gruntowne sprzątanie *n*; **spring 'on•ion** *s Br* dymka *f*; **spring 'roll** *s* COOK sajgonka *f*; **'spring•time** *s* wiosna *f*

spring•y ['sprɪŋɪ] *adj* **1.** sprężysty **2.** sprężynujący

sprin•kle ['sprɪŋkl] **I** *v/t* **1.** posypywać ⟨-pać⟩; ***~ strawberries with sugar*** posypać truskawki cukrem **2.** skrapiać ⟨-ropić⟩ **3.** *fig* okraszać ⟨-rasić⟩ **II** *v/i* ***it's sprinkling*** *Am* kropi, mży **III** *s* **1.** szczypta *f* **2.** ***a ~ of*** kilka kropel *G* **3.** *Am* mżawka *f*; **sprin•kler** ['sprɪŋklə] *s* **1.** zraszacz *m* **2.** tryskacz *m*; **sprin•kler sys•tem** *s* instalacja *f* tryskaczowa; **sprin•kling** ['sprɪŋklɪŋ] *adj* **1.** szczypta *f* **2.** odrobina *f* **3.** ***a ~ of*** trochę *G*

sprint [sprɪnt] **I** *v/i* biec ⟨po-⟩ sprintem **II** *s* sprint *m*; **sprint•er** ['sprɪntə] *s* sprinter *m*

sprite [spraɪt] *s* **1.** duszek *m* **2.** chochlik *m*

spritz [sprɪts] *v/t Am* skrapiać ⟨-ropić⟩

spritz•er ['sprɪtsə] *s* szprycer *m*

sprout [spraʊt] **I** *v/i* **1.** kiełkować ⟨wy-⟩ **2.** (*leaves*) wyrastać ⟨-rosnąć⟩ **II** *v/t* **1.** *shoots*: puszczać ⟨wy-⟩ **2.** *beard*: zapuszczać ⟨-puścić⟩ **III** *s* **1.** kiełek *m* **2.** brukselka *f*

spruce[1] [spruːs] *s* świerk *m*

spruce[2] [~] **I** *adj* elegancki **II** *v/t* ***~ oneself up*** *infml* wyszykować się

sprung [sprʌŋ] *Past Participle* → ***spring***

spry [spraɪ] → ***sprightly***

spud [spʌd] *s Br infml* ziemniak *m*

spun [spʌn] *Past Participle* → ***spin***

spunk [spʌŋk] *s infml* **1.** odwaga *f* **2.** przebojowość *f*; **spunk•y** ['spʌŋkɪ] *adj* **1.** odważny **2.** przebojowy

spur [spɜː] **I** *s* **1.** ostroga *f* **2.** bodziec *m*; ***on the ~ of the moment*** pod wpływem chwili **3.** zachęta *f* **II** *v/t* **1.** (*a.* ***~ on***) zachęcać ⟨-cić⟩ **2.** pobudzać ⟨-dzić⟩ **3.** *horse*: spinać ⟨spiąć⟩

spu•ri•ous ['spjʊərɪəs] *adj* **1.** złudny **2.** błędny **3.** fałszywy

spurn [spɜːn] *v/t* **1.** wzgardzać ⟨-dzić⟩ **2.** odrzucać ⟨-cić⟩

spurt [spɜːt] **I** *v/i* **1.** (*blood*) tryskać ⟨-snąć⟩ **2.** (*flames*) buchać ⟨-chnąć⟩ **3.** przyśpieszać ⟨-szyć⟩ **II** *v/t* **1.** *blood*: tryskać ⟨-snąć⟩ **2.** *lava*: wyrzucać ⟨-cić⟩ **III** *s* **1.** *water*: struga *f* **2.** *anger*: przypływ *m*, wybuch *m*

sput•ter ['spʌtə] *v/i* **1.** trzaskać ⟨-snąć⟩ **2.** (*engine*) charczeć ⟨za-⟩ **3.** bełkotać ⟨wy-⟩

spy [spaɪ] **I** *s* szpieg *m* **II** *v/i* szpiegować (***for*** na rzecz *G*) **III** *v/t lit* dostrzegać ⟨-rzec⟩; **spy on** *v/i* **1.** (po kryjomu) obserwować **2.** szpiegować

squab•ble ['skwɒbl] **I** *v/i* sprzeczać ⟨po-⟩ się (***with*** z *I*, ***about***/***over*** o *A*) **II** *s* sprzeczka *f*

squad [skwɒd] *s* **1.** oddział *m*; ***an anti-terrorist ~*** brygada antyterrorystyczna; ***a firing ~*** pluton egzekucyjny **2.** wydział *m*; ***a drugs ~*** wydział ds. narkotyków **3.** SPORT kadra *f*, reprezentacja *f*; ***a national ~*** kadra narodowa; **'squad car** *s* samochód *m* policyjny

squad•ron ['skwɒdrən] *s* **1.** dywizjon *m* **2.** (*navy*) eskadra *f* **3.** szwadron *m*

squal•id ['skwɒlɪd] *s* **1.** zapuszczony **2.** nędzny **3.** *fig* podejrzany

squall[1] [skwɔːl] *s* szkwał *m*

squall[2] [~] *v/i* (*cry*) ryczeć

squal•or ['skwɒlə] *s*: ***live in ~*** żyć w brudzie i nędzy

squan•der ['skwɒndə] *v/t* **1.** trwonić ⟨roz-⟩ **2.** zaprzepaszczać ⟨-paścić⟩

square [skweə] **I** *s* **1.** kwadrat *m*; ***the ~ of 7 is 49*** 7 podniesione do kwadratu równa się 49; ***we're back to ~ one*** *fig* wróciliśmy do punktu wyjścia **2.** plac *m* **3.** *infml* nudziarz *m*, sztywniak *m* **II** *adj* **1.** kwadratowy; ***a ~ bracket*** nawias kwadratowy; ***36 ~ metres*** 36 metrów kwadratowych; ***be a ~ peg in a round hole*** pasować jak kwiatek do kożucha **2.** ***a man of ~ build*** krępy mężczyzna **3.** równoległy (***with*** do *G*) **4.** prostopadły (***with*** do *G*) **5.** ***be ~*** *infml* być kwita **6.** ***be ~*** *SPORT* remisować, mieć tyle samo punktów **7.** uczciwy (***with*** wobec *G*) **8.** zgodny (***with*** z *I*) **9.** staroświecki **III** *v/t* **1.** (*a.* ***~ off***) ***be ~d off at the end*** mieć kwadratowy tył **2.** podnosić ⟨-nieść⟩ do kwadratu; ***two ~d*** dwa (podniesione) do kwadratu **3.** wyrównywać ⟨-nać⟩; ***~ the game 1-1*** wyrównać na 1:1 **4.** *infml* dawać ⟨dać⟩ łapówkę; **square up** *v/i* rozliczać ⟨-czyć⟩ się (***with*** z *I*); **square up to** *v/i* mierzyć ⟨z-⟩ się z *I*

'square dance *s* taniec *m* w cztery pary

squared pa•per [skweəd'peɪpə] *s* papier *m* w kratkę

square•ly ['skweəlɪ] *adv* **1.** prosto; ***look ~ into s.o.'s eyes*** popatrzeć komuś prosto w oczy **2.** ***face a problem ~*** stanąć twarzą w twarz z problemem

square 'root *s* *MATH* pierwiastek *m* kwadratowy

squash[1] [skwɒʃ] **I** *v/t* **1.** zgniatać ⟨-nieść⟩ **2.** rozgniatać ⟨-nieść⟩ **3.** wciskać ⟨-snąć⟩ **4.** *revolt*: dusić ⟨z-⟩, tłumić ⟨s-⟩ **II** *v/i* **1.** gnieść ⟨z-⟩ się **2.** wciskać ⟨-snąć⟩ się **III** *s* **1.** ścisk *m* **2.** *Br* zagęszczony sok *m* owocowy

squash[2] [~] *s* *SPORT* squash *m*

squash[3] [~] *s* *pl squash*, *squashes* **1.** dynia *f* **2.** kabaczek *m* **3.** cukinia *f* **4.** patison *m*

'squash court *s* sala *f* do squasha; **'squash rack•et** *s* rakieta *f* do squasha

squash•y ['skwɒʃɪ] *adj fruit*: miękki

squat [skwɒt] **I** *v/i* **1.** (*a.* ***~ down***) kucać ⟨-cnąć⟩ **2.** mieszkać na dziko **II** *s* **1.** kucki *pl* **2.** nielegalnie zajmowany budynek *m*, *infml* squat *m* **III** *adj* przysadzisty; **squat•ter** ['skwɔtə] *s* dziki lokator *m*

squaw [skwɔː] *s Am* Indianka *f*, squaw *f*

squawk [skwɔːk] *v/i* skrzeczeć ⟨za-⟩

squeak [skwiːk] **I** *v/i* **1.** skrzypieć ⟨za-⟩ **2.** piszczeć ⟨-snąć⟩ **II** *s* **1.** skrzypnięcie *n* **2.** pisk *m*; **squeak•y** ['skwiːkɪ] *adj* skrzypiący; **'squeak•y clean** *adj infml* **1.** lśniąco czysty **2.** nieskazitelny

squeal [skwiːl] **I** *v/i* **1.** kwiczeć ⟨za-⟩ **2.** piszczeć ⟨za-⟩ **3.** *infml* donosić ⟨-nieść⟩, *infml* kablować ⟨na-⟩ (***on*** na *A*) **II** *s* **1.** kwik *m* **2.** pisk *m*

squeam•ish ['skwiːmɪʃ] *adj* **1.** wrażliwy **2.** delikatny

squeeze [skwiːz] **I** *v/t* **1.** ściskać ⟨-snąć, uścisnąć⟩; ***~ s.o.'s hand*** uścisnąć komuś dłoń **2.** wyciskać ⟨-snąć⟩ **3.** wciskać ⟨-snąć⟩ (***into/in*** do *G*) **4.** wyduszać ⟨-sić⟩ (***out of*** z *G*) **II** *v/i* wciskać ⟨-snąć⟩ się **III** *s* **1.** uścisk *m*; ***he gave my hand a ~*** uścisnął mi dłoń **2.** odrobina *f* **3.** ścisk *m*; **squeeze in** *v/t* **1.** wciskać ⟨-snąć⟩ **2.** *fig* znaleźć czas dla *G*; **squeeze out** *v/t* **1.** wyciskać ⟨-snąć⟩ **2.** *confession*: wydobywać ⟨-być⟩ **3.** wypierać ⟨-przeć⟩ z rynku; **squeeze up** *v/i* ściskać ⟨-snąć⟩ się

'squeez•er *s* wyciskacz *m*; ***a lemon ~*** wyciskacz do cytryn

squelch [skweltʃ] *v/i* **1.** chlupać ⟨za-⟩ **2.** chlupotać ⟨za-⟩

squib [skwɪb] *s* petarda *f*

squid [skwɪd] *s pl squid*, *squids* kałamarnica *f*

squig•gle ['skwɪgl] *s* **1.** zawijas *m* **2.** gryzmoły *pl*

squint [skwɪnt] **I** *v/i* **1.** patrzeć ⟨po-⟩ spod przymrużonych powiek **2.** ***his right eye ~s*** ma zeza w prawym oku **3.** mieć zeza **II** *v/t eyes*: mrużyć ⟨z-⟩ **III** *s* zez *m*

squirm [skwɜːm] *v/i* **1.** wiercić się **2.** ***~ free*** wywijać ⟨-winąć⟩ się **3.** ***~ with embarrassment*** nie wiedzieć, gdzie się podziać ze wstydu

squir•rel ['skwɪrəl] **I** *s* wiewiórka *f* **II** *v/t* ***~ away*** *infml* chomikować

squirt [skwɜːt] **I** *v/i* tryskać ⟨-snąć⟩ **II** *v/t* **1.** strzykać ⟨-knąć⟩ **2.** pryskać ⟨-snąć⟩ **III** *s* **1.** strumień *m* **2.** odrobina *f* **3.** *infml* gnojek *m*

Sri Lan•ka [sriː'læŋkə] *s* Sri Lanka *f*

stab [stæb] **I** *v/t* dźgać ⟨-gnąć⟩; ***~ s.o. with a knife*** pchnąć kogoś nożem; ***~ s.o. to death*** zakłuć kogoś, *infml* zadźgać kogoś; ***~ one's finger at s.o.'s arm*** dźgnąć kogoś palcem w ramię; ***~ s.o. in the back*** *fig* wbić komuś nóż w plecy **II** *s* **1.** dźgnięcie *n* **2.** pchnięcie *n* nożem; ***a ~ in the back*** *fig* nóż w plecy **3.** ukłucie *n*; ***a ~ of pain*** ukłucie bólu **4.** *infml* próba *f*;

stab•bing ['stæbɪŋ] **I** *s* atak *m* z użyciem noża **II** *adj pain*: kłujący
sta•bil•i•ty [stə'bɪlətɪ] *s* stabilność *f*
sta•bi•li•za•tion [steɪbəlaɪ'zeɪʃn] *s* stabilizacja *f*; **sta•bil•ize** ['steɪbəlaɪz] **I** *v/i* stabilizować ⟨u-⟩ się **II** *v/t* stabilizować ⟨u-⟩; **sta•bi•liz•er** ['steɪbəlaɪzə] *s* **1.** stabilizator *m* **2.** statecznik *m*
sta•ble[1] ['steɪbl] *adj* **1.** stabilny **2.** *person*: zrównoważony **3.** *job*: stały
sta•ble[2] [~] *s* stajnia *f*
stack [stæk] **I** *s* **1.** sterta *f*; ***~s of money*** *infml* kupa pieniędzy **2.** stos *m* **3.** stóg *m* **4.** komin *m* **II** *v/t* **1.** (*a.* ***~ up***) układać ⟨ułożyć⟩ w stos **2.** *shelves*: zapełniać ⟨-nić⟩ (***with*** *I*); **stack up** *v/i* gromadzić ⟨na-⟩ się; **stack up against** *v/t* *infml* porównywać ⟨-nać⟩ do *G*
sta•di•um ['steɪdɪəm] *pl -diums*, *-dia s* stadion *n*
staff[1] [stæf] *s* MUS *pl* ***staves*** [steɪvz] pięciolinia *f*
staff[2] [~] *s pl* ***staves*** [steɪvz] laska *f*
staff[3] [~] **I** *s* **1.** personel *m* **2.** pracownicy *pl*; ***teaching ~*** *Br* grono pedagogiczne **3.** sztab *m* **II** *v/t position*: obsadzać ⟨-dzić⟩; '**staff of•fi•cer** *s* oficer *m* sztabowy; '**staff•room** *s* pokój *m* nauczycielski
stag [stæg] *s* jeleń *m*
stage[1] [steɪdʒ] **I** *s* **1.** scena *f*; ***the political ~*** scena polityczna; ***go on the ~*** *fig* zostać aktorem; ***set the ~ for*** przygotować grunt dla *G* **2.** estrada *f* **3.** podium *n* **II** *v/t* **1.** wystawiać ⟨-wić⟩ (na scenie) **2.** *exhibition*, *strike*: organizować ⟨z-⟩
stage[2] [~] *s* **1.** etap *m*; ***at this ~*** na tym etapie; ***in ~s*** etapami **2.** faza *f* **3.** stadium *n*; '**stage di•rec•tions** *pl* didaskalia *pl*; **stage** '**door** *s* THEAT wejście *n* dla aktorów; '**stage fright** *s* trema *f*; '**stage hand** *s* THEAT maszynista *m* sceny; '**stage man•ag•er** *s* THEAT inspicjent *m*; '**stage name** *s* pseudonim *m* artystyczny; **stage•y** ['steɪdʒɪ] *adj* **1.** udawany **2.** teatralny
stag•ger ['stægə] **I** *v/i* **1.** słaniać się **2.** chwiać się **II** *v/t* **1.** zdumiewać ⟨-mieć⟩ **2.** szokować ⟨za-⟩ **3.** rozkładać ⟨-złożyć⟩ w czasie; **stag•ger•ing** ['stægərɪŋ] *adj* **1.** zdumiewający **2.** oszałamiający
stag•nant ['stægnənt] *adj* **1.** *water*: stojący **2.** w zastoju; **stag•nate** [stæg'neɪt] *v/i* **1.** popadać ⟨-paść⟩ w zastój **2.** przestawać ⟨-tać⟩ się rozwijać **3.** (*water*) zatrzymywać ⟨-mać⟩ się, przestawać ⟨-tać⟩ płynąć; **stag•na•tion** [stæg'neɪʃn] *s* **1.** stagnacja *f* **2.** zastój *m*
'**stag par•ty** *s* wieczór *m* kawalerski
staid [steɪd] *adj* **1.** tradycyjny **2.** stateczny
stain [steɪn] **I** *v/t* **1.** plamić ⟨po-⟩ **2.** brudzić ⟨po-⟩ **3.** barwić ⟨za-⟩ **4.** *wood*: bejcować ⟨za-⟩ **5.** *reputation*: szkodzić ⟨za-⟩ **II** *v/i* brudzić ⟨po-⟩ się **III** *s* **1.** plama *f* **2.** barwnik *m* **3.** bejca *f* **4.** *fig* skaza *f*; **stained-glass window** [steɪndglɑːs'wɪndəʊ] *s* witraż *m*; **stain•less steel** ['steɪnlɪs'stiːl] *s* stal *m* nierdzewna; **stain re•mov•er** ['steɪnrɪ'muːvə] *s* odplamiacz *m*, środek *m* do wywabiania plam
stair [steə] *s* **1.** ~**s** schody; ***a flight of ~s*** kondygnacja schodów **2.** schodek *m*; '**stair car•pet** *s* chodnik *m* (na schody); '**stair•case**, '**stair•way** *s* klatka *f* schodowa, schody *pl*
stake[1] [steɪk] **I** *s* **1.** stawka *f*; ***people's life is at ~*** stawką jest ludzkie życie; ***play for high ~s*** grać o duże pieniądze **2.** ECON udział *m* **II** *v/t* stawiać ⟨postawić⟩ (***on*** na *A*); ***I'd ~ my life on it*** *fig* dałbym sobie za to rękę uciąć
stake[2] [~] **I** *s* **1.** palik *m* **2.** kołek *m* **3.** słupek *m* **4.** słup *m* **5.** HIST stos *m*; ***be burnt at the ~*** zostać spalonym na stosie **II** *v/t* podpierać ⟨-deprzeć⟩ palikiem; **stake out** *v/t* (*police*) obserwować
'**stake•out** *s* (*police*) obserwacja *f*
sta•lac•tite ['stæləktaɪt] *s* stalaktyt *m*; **sta•lag•mite** ['stæləgmaɪt] *s* stalagmit *m*
stale [steɪl] *adj* **1.** *bread*: czerstwy **2.** *air*: zatęchły, stęchły **3.** *phrase*: wytarty **4.** *joke*: z brodą **5.** *news*: nieaktualny **6.** *person*: wypalony; '**stale•mate** *s* pat *m*
stalk[1] [stɔːk] *s* **1.** łodyga *f* **2.** *apple*: ogonek *m* **3.** *mushroom*: nóżka *f* **4.** *cabbage*: głąb *m*
stalk[2] [~] **I** *v/t* **1.** tropić ⟨wy-⟩ **2.** śledzić ⟨wy-⟩ **3.** prześladować **4.** krążyć po *L*; ***~ a building*** krążyć po budyn-

S

ku **II** *v/i* kroczyć dumnie; **stalk•er** ['stɔːkə] *s* **1.** tropiciel *m* **2.** prześladowca *m*

stall[1] [stɔːl] **I** *s* **1.** stoisko *n* **2.** stragan *m* **3.** boks *m* **4.** (*animals*) przegroda *f* **II** *v/i* (*engine*) gasnąć ⟨z-⟩ **III** *v/t* ***he ~ed the car*** zgasł mu silnik

stall[2] [~] **I** *v/i* **1.** wykręcać ⟨-cić⟩ się **2.** ***~ for time*** grać na zwłokę **II** *v/t* **1.** zatrzymywać ⟨-mać⟩ **2.** opóźniać ⟨-nić⟩ **3.** zajmować ⟨-jąć⟩

stalls [stɔːlz] *pl* **1.** THEAT *Br* parter *m*, miejsca *pl* na parterze **2.** ARCHIT stalle *pl*

stal•li•on ['stæljən] *s* ogier *m*

stal•wart ['stɔːlwərt] **I** *adj* **1.** wierny **2.** oddany **II** *s* **1.** aktywista *m* **2.** wierny zwolennik *m*

stam•i•na ['stæmɪnə] *s* wytrzymałość *f*

stam•mer ['stæmə] **I** *v/i* jąkać się **III** *s* jąkanie *n*; **stammer out** *v/t* wyjąkać

stam•mer•er ['stæmərə] *s infml* jąkała *m*

stamp [stæmp] **I** *s* **1.** znaczek *m*; ***a postage ~*** znaczek pocztowy **2.** pieczątka *f* **3.** stempel *m* **4.** *fig* znamię *n*; ***bear the ~ of*** nosić znamię *G* **5.** *fig* piętno *n* **6.** tupnięcie *n* **II** *v/t* **1.** ***~ one's foot*** tupnąć nogą **2.** wykazywać ⟨-zać⟩; ***their faces were ~ed with sadness*** na ich twarzach malował się smutek **3.** przybijać ⟨-bić⟩ pieczątkę na *L* **4.** stemplować ⟨o-⟩ **5.** *letter*: frankować ⟨o-⟩; **stamp out** *v/t* **1.** wytłaczać ⟨-łoczyć⟩ **2.** wyciskać ⟨-snąć⟩ **3.** *coins*: bić ⟨wy-⟩ **4.** *revolt*: tłumić ⟨s-⟩ **5.** wypleniać ⟨-nić⟩

'stamp al•bum *s* klaser *m*; **'stamp collec•ting** *s* filatelistyka *f*; **'stamp col•lec•tion** *s* kolekcja *f* znaczków; **'stamp col•lec•tor** *s* filatelista *m*; **'stamp du•ty** *s Br* opłata *f* skarbowa

stam•pede [stæm'piːd] **I** *s* popłoch *m*, panika *f* **II** *v/i* uciekać ⟨uciec⟩ w popłochu **III** *v/t* ***~ s.o. into doing s.th.*** ponaglać kogoś do zrobienia czegoś

stamp•ing ground ['stæmpɪŋgraʊnd] *s infml* ulubione miejsce *n*

stance [stæns] *s* **1.** postawa *f* **2.** stanowisko *n*

stand [stænd] **I** (*stood*; *stood*) *v/i* **1.** stać; ***~ still*** stać nieruchomo; ***a castle stood here*** tutaj stał kiedyś zamek; ***my offer still ~s*** moja oferta jest nadal aktualna; ***~ at 3%*** wynosić 3% **2.** *Br* kandydować (**as** na *A*, ***for*** do *G*); ***~ for parliament*** kandydować do parlamentu **II** (*stood*; *stood*) *v/t* **1.** ustawiać ⟨-wić⟩ **2.** znosić ⟨znieść⟩; ***I can't ~ him*** nie znoszę go **3.** *cold*, *stress*: wytrzymywać ⟨-mać⟩ **4.** *low temperature*: być odpornym na *A* **5.** stawiać ⟨postawić⟩; ***~ s.o. a dinner*** postawić komuś kolację **III** *s* **1.** stanowisko *n* **2.** *Br* stoisko *n* **3.** budka *f* **4.** kiosk *m*; ***a newspaper ~*** kiosk (z gazetami) **5.** stojak *m*; ***a bicycle ~*** stojak na rowery **6.** SPORT trybuna *f* **7.** (*in court*) miejsce *n* dla świadka **8.** (*orchestra*) podium *m* **9.** *taxi*: postój *m*; **stand back** *v/i* **1.** odsuwać ⟨-sunąć⟩ się (***from*** od *G*) **2.** być oddalonym **3.** *fig* dystansować ⟨z-⟩ się, spoglądać ⟨spojrzeć⟩ z dystansem; **stand by** *v/i* **1.** być w pogotowiu **2.** być gotowym do akcji **3.** stać z założonymi rękami **4.** trwać przy *L* **5.** *principles*: być wiernym *D* **6.** *offer*: podtrzymywać ⟨-mać⟩; **stand down** *v/i* (*position*) ustępować ⟨-tąpić⟩; **stand for** *v/i* **1.** (*initials*) oznaczać; ***what does the 'T.C.' ~?*** co oznacza skrót „T.C."? **2.** reprezentować, uosabiać **3.** pozwalać ⟨-wolić⟩ na *A*; **stand in for** *v/i* zastępować ⟨-tąpić⟩; **stand out** *v/i* **1.** odcinać ⟨-ciąć⟩ się; ***~ against a dark background*** odcinać się od ciemnego tła **2.** wyróżniać się; ***~ in a crowd*** wyróżniać się z tłumu; **stand over** *v/i* **1.** stać nad *I* **2.** obserwować; **stand together** *v/i* trzymać się razem; **stand up I** *v/i* **1.** wstawać ⟨-tać⟩ **2.** stanąć **II** *v/t infml* wystawiać ⟨-wić⟩ do wiatru; **stand up for** *v/i* **1.** stawać ⟨stanąć⟩ w obronie **2.** walczyć o *A* **3.** bronić; **stand up to** *v/i* **1.** *criticism*: wytrzymywać ⟨-mać⟩ **2.** stawiać ⟨-wić⟩ czoła

'stand-a•lone *adj* INF autonomiczny

stan•dard ['stændəd] **I** *s* **1.** standard *m*; ***maintain high ~s*** utrzymywać wysokie standardy **2.** norma *f*; ***set the ~s*** ustanawiać normy; ***meet the ~s*** spełniać normy **3.** poziom *m*; ***~ of living*** poziom życia **4.** wzorzec *m* **5.** sztandar *m* **II** *adj* **1.** standardowy **2.** typowy **3.** znormalizowany **4.** wzorcowy; **stan•dard•i•za•tion** [stændədaɪ-

S

'zeɪʃn] *s* **1.** standaryzacja *f* **2.** normalizacja *f*; **stan•dard•ize** ['stændədaɪz] *v/t* **1.** standaryzować **2.** normalizować ⟨z-⟩

'**stan•dard lamp** *s Br* lampa *f* stojąca

'**stand•by** **I** *pl -bys s* **1.** rezerwa *f*; ***keep s.th. as a ~*** trzymać coś na wszelki wypadek **2.** stan *m* gotowości; ***on ~*** w stanie gotowości, w pogotowiu; ***be put on ~*** zostać postawionym w stan gotowości **II** *adj* **1.** awaryjny **2.** rezerwowy **3.** ***a ~ ticket*** bilet bez rezerwacji miejsca

'**stand-in** *s* **1.** zastępca *m* **2.** FILM dubler *m*

stand•ing ['stændɪŋ] **I** *adj* **1.** stały; ***a ~ order*** zlecenie stałe **2.** stojący **3.** *ovation*: na stojąco **II** *s* **1.** pozycja *f* **2.** status *m*; ***legal ~*** status prawny **3.** sytuacja *f*; ***financial ~*** sytuacja finansowa **4.** renoma *f* **5.** popularność *f* **6.** ***of ten years' ~*** dziesięcioletni; '**stand•ing room** *s* miejsca *pl* stojące

'**stand•off** *s* impas *m*; **stand•off•ish** [stænd'ɒfɪʃ] *adj infml* wyniosły; '**stand•point** *s* punkt *m* widzenia; ***from my ~*** z mojego punktu widzenia; '**stand•still** *s* **1.** bezruch *m*; ***come to a ~*** zatrzymać się **2.** zastój *m*; ***at a ~*** w zastoju

stand-up ('com•edy) *s* monolog *m* przed publicznością; **stand-up 'fight** *s* ostra kłótnia *f*

stank [stæŋk] *Past Simple* → ***stink***

stan•za ['stænzə] *s* zwrotka *f*

sta•ple¹ ['steɪpl] **I** *s* **1.** zszywka *f* **2.** klamra *f* **II** *v/t documents*: zszywać ⟨zszyć⟩

sta•ple² [~] **I** *adj* podstawowy **II** *s* **1.** podstawowy produkt *m* żywnościowy **2.** (*a.* ***~ diet***) ***rice is their ~*** (***food***) podstawę ich wyżywienia stanowi ryż

'**sta•ple gun** *s* tacker *m*

sta•pler ['steɪplə] *s* zszywacz *m*

staple remover *s* rozszywacz *m*

star [stɑː] **I** *s* gwiazda *f*; ***camp under the ~s*** obozować pod gołym niebem; ***a five-~ hotel*** hotel pięciogwiazdkowy; ***be born under a lucky ~*** urodzić się pod szczęśliwą gwiazdą; ***see ~s*** *fig* zobaczyć wszystkie gwiazdy **II** *v/i* **1.** grać ⟨za-⟩ główną rolę **2.** występować ⟨-tąpić⟩ (***as*** jako *N*) **III** *v/t* **1.** ***a film ~ring Tom Cruise*** film z Tomem Cruise'em w roli głównej **2.** oznaczać ⟨-czyć⟩ gwiazdką; '**star•board** *s* sterburta *f*, prawa burta *f*

starch [stɑːtʃ] **I** *s* **1.** skrobia *f* **2.** krochmal *m* **II** *v/t* krochmalić ⟨wy-⟩; **starch•y** ['stɑːtʃɪ] *adj* bogaty w skrobię

star•dom ['stɑːdəm] *s* **1.** status *m* gwiazdy; ***rise to ~*** stać się gwiazdą **2.** sława *f*

stare [steə] **I** *v/i* **1.** wpatrywać się **2.** *infml* gapić się; ***what are you staring at?*** na co się gapisz?; ***the answer was staring us in the face*** *infml* odpowiedź była na wyciągnięcie ręki **II** *s* spojrzenie *n*

'**star•fish** *pl -fish s* rozgwiazda *f*

stark [stɑːk] **I** *adj* **1.** surowy **2.** *reality*: brutalny **3.** *contrast*: jaskrawy **4.** ***be in ~ contrast*** jaskrawo kontrastować **5.** *warning*: poważny **II** *adv naked*: całkiem; **stark•ers** ['stɑːkəz] *adj Br infml* golusieńki

star•let ['stɑːlət] *s* (*woman*) gwiazdka *f*

'**star•light** *s* światło *n* gwiazd

star•ling ['stɑːlɪŋ] *s* drozd *m*

'**star•lit** *adj lit sky*: rozgwieżdżony

star•ry ['stɑːrɪ] *adj* **1.** *sky*: gwiaździsty **2.** *eyes*: roziskrzony; **star•ry-eyed** [stɑːrɪ'aɪd]] *adj*: ***be ~*** *infml* chodzić z głową w chmurach

Stars and 'Stripes *s* flaga *f* Stanów Zjednoczonych

Star-Span•gled Ban•ner [stɑːspæŋgld'bænə] *s* (*US flag and anthem*) Gwiaździsty Sztandar *m*

start [stɑːt] **I** *v/t* **1.** zaczynać ⟨-cząć⟩, rozpoczynać ⟨-cząć⟩; ***it ~ed to rain*** zaczęło padać; ***she ~ed laughing*** zaczęła się śmiać; ***don't ~!*** nie zaczynaj!; ***he ~ed it!*** to on zaczął!; ***to ~ with*** **a)** po pierwsze **b)** przede wszystkim **2.** powodować ⟨s-⟩; ***~ a fire*** **a)** zaprószyć ogień **b)** podłożyć ogień **3.** uruchamiać ⟨-chomić⟩ **II** *v/i* **1.** zaczynać ⟨-cząć⟩ się, rozpoczynać ⟨-cząć⟩ się **2.** (*engine*) zapalać ⟨-lić⟩ **3.** ruszać ⟨-szyć⟩; ***~ for the door*** ruszyć w kierunku drzwi **4.** wyruszać ⟨-szyć⟩ **5.** odjeżdżać ⟨-jechać⟩ **III** *s* **1.** początek *m*; ***from ~ to finish*** od początku do końca; ***make a fresh ~*** zacząć wszystko od początku; ***for a ~*** *infml* po pierwsze **2.** start *m* **3.** ***you gave me quite a ~!*** ale mnie przestraszyłeś!; **start off I** *v/i* **1.** ruszać ⟨-szyć⟩ **2.** rozpoczynać ⟨-cząć⟩ się **3.** zaczynać ⟨-cząć⟩ **II** *v/t* **1.** wywoływać ⟨-łać⟩ **2.** powodować ⟨s-⟩ **3.** ***start s.o. off laughing*** rozśmieszyć kogoś; **start out** *v/i* **1.** rozpoczynać ⟨-cząć⟩ (**on** *A*); ***~ in business*** rozpocząć działalność gospodarczą **2.** ***~ out to do s.th.*** zacząć z zamiarem zrobienia czegoś; **start up** *v/t* **1.** uruchamiać ⟨-chomić⟩ **2.** *computer*: włączać ⟨-czyć⟩ **3.** *engine*: zapalać ⟨-lić⟩ **4.** *business*: zakładać ⟨założyć⟩ **5.** *gossip*: puszczać ⟨puścić⟩

start•er ['stɑːtə] *s* **1.** COOK *Br* przystawka *f* **2.** SPORT startujący *m* **3.** SPORT starter *m* **4.** AUTO rozrusznik *m* **5.** ***she was a late ~ in acting*** późno rozpoczęła karierę aktorską

start•ing blocks ['stɑːtɪŋblɒks] *pl* SPORT blok *m* startowy; **'start•ing gate** *s* (*horse racing*) maszyna *f* startowa; **'start•ing point** *s* **1.** punkt *m* startowy **2.** punkt *m* wyjścia

start•le ['stɑːtl] *v/t* straszyć ⟨wy-⟩; **start•ling** ['stɑːtlɪŋ] *adj* **1.** zaskakujący **2.** jaskrawy; ***~-blue*** jaskrawoniebieski

starv•a•tion [stɑː'veɪʃn] *s* śmierć *f* głodowa; ***die of ~*** umrzeć z głodu; ***~ wages*** głodowa płaca

starve [stɑːv] **I** *v/i* głodować; ***~ to death*** umrzeć z głodu; ***I'm starving*** umieram z głodu **II** *v/t* ***~ oneself*** głodzić się

star wars ['stɑːwɔːz] *pl* gwiezdne wojny *pl*

stash [stæʃ] **I** *v/t* (*a.* ***~ away***) ukrywać ⟨-ryć⟩ **II** *s* ***a ~ of money*** ukryte pieniądze

state[1] [steɪt] **I** *s* **1.** stan *m*; ***a ~ of mind*** stan umysłu; ***a ~ of affairs*** stan rzeczy, sytuacja; ***be in a ~ of war with*** być w stanie wojny z *I*; ***she was in a real ~*** *Br infml* była cała w nerwach; ***the 2s*** Stany, USA **2.** państwo *n* **II** *adj* **1.** państwowy **2.** stanowy **3.** oficjalny

state[2] [~] **I** *v/t* **1.** stwierdzać ⟨-dzić⟩; ***it was ~d that*** stwierdzono, że **2.** podawać ⟨-dać⟩ **3.** określać ⟨-lić⟩; ***at the time ~d*** w określonym terminie **II** *v/t* stwierdzać ⟨-dzić⟩ (***that*** że); **'State De•part•ment** *s Am* (*ministry of foreign affairs*) Departament *m* Stanu; **state•less** ['steɪtlɪs] *adj* bezpaństwowy; ***a ~ person*** bezpaństwowiec; **state•ly** ['steɪtlɪ] *adj* **1.** okazały **2.** majestatyczny **3.** dostojny

state•ment ['steɪtmənt] *s* **1.** oświadczenie *n*; ***a press ~*** oświadczenie prasowe; ***make a ~*** wygłosić oświadczenie **2.** stwierdzenie *n* **3.** wypowiedź *f* **4.** JUR zeznanie *n* **5.** wyciąg *m*; ***a bank ~*** wyciąg bankowy **6.** FIN sprawozdanie *n*

state of e'mer•gen•cy *s* stan *m* wyjątkowy; **state-of-the-'art** *adj* **1.** najnowocześniejszy **2.** supernowoczesny

states•man ['steɪtsmən] *pl -men s* mąż *m* stanu; **states•man•like** ['steɪtsmənlaɪk] *adj* godny męża stanu

stat•ic ['stætɪk] **I** *adj* **1.** nieruchomy **2.** statyczny **II** *s* **1.** RADIO zakłócenia *pl* **2.** ***~s*** PHYS statyka *f* **3.** elektryczność *f* statyczna; ***my hair gets full of ~ when I brush it*** włosy mi się elektryzują, kiedy się czeszę

sta•tion ['steɪʃn] **I** *s* **1.** stacja *f*, ***a research ~*** stacja badawcza; ***an electric power ~*** elektrownia **2.** dworzec *m*; ***a railway*** (***bus***) ***~*** dworzec kolejowy (autobusowy) **3.** posterunek *m*; ***a police ~*** komisariat policji, posterunek policji **4.** stanowisko *n* **5.** pozycja *f* **6.** *military*: baza *f* **II** *v/t* **1.** ***be ~ed*** (*troops*) stacjonować **2.** ***be ~ed*** (*soldier*) służyć **3.** rozmieszczać ⟨-mieścić⟩ **4.** ***he ~ed himself at the window*** *form* zajął miejsce przy oknie

sta•tion•a•ry ['steɪʃənrɪ] *adj* **1.** nieruchomy; ***remain ~*** nie ruszać się **2.** stojący w miejscu **3.** stały **4.** niezmienny **5.** stacjonarny

sta•tion•er ['steɪʃənə] *s* **1.** właściciel *m* sklepu papierniczego **2.** kierownik *m* sklepu papierniczego **3.** ***a ~'s*** sklep papierniczy

sta•tion•er•y ['steɪʃənrɪ] *s* **1.** materiały *pl* piśmienne **2.** materiały *pl* biurowe **3.** papeteria *f*

'sta•tion house *s Am* komisariat *m* policji; **sta•tion 'man•ag•er**, ***'sta•tion mas•ter*** *Br s* zawiadowca *m* stacji, naczelnik *m* stacji; **'sta•tion wag•on** *s Am* samochód *m* kombi

S

sta•tis•tic [stə'tɪstɪk] *s*: ***particular ~s*** poszczególne dane statystyczne; **sta•tis•ti•cal** [stə'tɪstɪkl] *adj* statystyczny; **sta•tis•ti•cal•ly** [stə'tɪstɪklɪ] *adv* statystycznie; **sta•tis•ti•cian** [stætɪs'tɪʃn] *s* statystyk *m*; **sta•tis•tics** [stə'tɪstɪks] *pl* **1.** statystyka **2.** statystyki *pl*; ***~ show that*** statystyki mówią, że

stat•ue ['stætʃuː] *s* **1.** posąg *m* **2.** statua *f*

stat•ure ['stætʃə] *s* **1.** postura *f*; ***of short ~*** niskiej postury **2.** *fig* format *m* **3.** pozycja *f*

sta•tus ['steɪtəs] *s* **1.** status *m*; ***legal ~*** status prawny **2.** pozycja *f* **3.** prestiż *m*; **'sta•tus bar** *s* INF pasek *m* stanu; **sta•tus quo** [steɪtəs'kwəʊ] *s* status quo *n*; **'sta•tus sym•bol** *s* wyznacznik *m* statusu społecznego

stat•ute ['stætjuːt] *s* **1.** ustawa *f*; ***by ~*** ustawowo **2. *~s*** statut *m*; **'stat•ute book** *s* JUR kodeks *m*; **stat•ute law** *s* JUR prawo *n* pisane, prawo *n* stanowione

stat•u•to•ry ['stætjʊtrɪ] *adj* ustawowy; ***~ duties*** obowiązki ustawowe

staunch[1] [stɔːntʃ] *v/t Am blood*: tamować ⟨za-⟩

staunch[2] [~] *adj* **1.** wierny **2.** zagorzały

stave [steɪv] *s* **1.** kij *m* **2.** klepka *f* **3.** sztacheta *f* **4.** MUS *Br* pięciolinia *f*; **stave off** *v/i* **1.** powstrzymywać ⟨-mać⟩ **2.** pokonywać ⟨-nać⟩ **3.** odsuwać ⟨-sunąć⟩

stay [steɪ] **I** *v/i* **1.** zostawać ⟨-tać⟩; ***~ for lunch*** zostać na lunch; ***~ angry*** nadal się złościć; ***the stores ~ open all day*** sklepy są otwarte cały dzień; ***~ friends*** pozostać przyjaciółmi **2.** mieszkać ⟨za-⟩; ***~ at a hotel*** mieszkać w hotelu; ***~ with friends*** mieszkać u przyjaciół **II** *v/t* ***~ the night*** przenocować **III** *s* **1.** pobyt *m*; ***a ~ in hospital*** pobyt w szpitalu **2. *a ~ of execution*** JUR zawieszenie *n* egzekucji; **stay away** *v/i* trzymać się z dala (***from*** od *G*); **stay behind** *v/i* zostawać ⟨-tać⟩; **stay in** *v/i* zostawać ⟨-tać⟩ w domu; ***I feel like staying in*** nie mam ochoty wychodzić z domu; **stay on** *v/i* **1.** zostawać ⟨-tać⟩ dłużej **2.** zostawać ⟨-tać⟩; **stay out** *v/i* **1.** nie wracać ⟨wrócić⟩ do domu; ***he stayed out until 1 o'clock*** wrócił do domu o pierwszej **2.** kontynuować strajk **3.** nie mieszać ⟨w-⟩ się (***of*** w *A*); ***~ of my business!*** nie mieszaj się w nieswoje sprawy!; ***~ of trouble*** unikać kłopotów; **stay over** *v/i* nocować ⟨prze-⟩; **stay up** *v/i* nie kłaść ⟨położyć⟩ się spać; ***~ late*** późno położyć się spać

'stay-at-home *s infml* domator *m*

stay•ing pow•er ['steɪɪŋpaʊə] *s* wytrzymałość *f*

STD [estiː'diː] *abbr* (=***sexually transmitted disease***) choroba *f* przenoszona drogą płciową

stead [sted] *s*: ***in s.o.'s ~*** *form* zamiast kogoś

stead•fast ['stedfæst] *adj* **1.** wierny **2.** niewzruszony **3.** niezłomny

stead•i•ly ['stedɪlɪ] *adv* **1.** stale **2.** ciągle **3.** równo **4.** *breathe*: regularnie; **stead•y** ['stedɪ] **I** *adj* **1.** stały **2.** ciągły **3.** równy **4.** *breath, income*: regularny **5.** *move*: pewny, spokojny **6.** *table*: stabilny **7.** *grip*: mocny **8. *he's ~*** można na nim polegać **II** *v/t* ***~ one's nerves*** uspokajać ⟨-koić⟩ się **III** *v/i* **1.** uspokajać ⟨-koić⟩ się **2.** zatrzymywać ⟨-mać⟩ się **3.** stabilizować ⟨u-⟩ się **IV** *adv* FIN ***hold ~*** (*interest rates*) utrzymywać się na stałym poziomie **V** *interj* **1. *~ on!*** hola! **2. *~*** uwaga!

steak [steɪk] *s* **1.** befsztyk *m* **2.** stek *m* **3.** kotlet *m* **4.** *fish*: filet *m*

steal [stiːl] **I** (*stole*; *stolen*) *v/t* kraść ⟨u-⟩; ***~ a glance at*** rzucić ukradkowe spojrzenie na *A*; ***~ the show*** wzbudzać największe zainteresowanie **II** (*stole*; *stolen*) *v/i* wymykać ⟨-mknąć⟩ się (***out of*** z *G*)

stealth [stelθ] *s*: ***by ~*** ukradkiem; **'stealth bomb•er** *s* bombowiec *m* niewidzialny dla radaru; **stealth•y** ['stelθɪ] *adj* ukradkowy

steam [stiːm] **I** *s* para *f* wodna; ***go full ~ ahead*** *fig* ruszyć pełną parą; ***run out of ~*** *fig* **a)** opaść z sił **b)** stracić zapał; ***let off ~*** *infml* wyładować się, wyżyć się **II** *v/i* **1.** parować **2.** dymić **3. *~ up*** zaparowywać ⟨-wać⟩ **III** *v/t* **1.** gotować ⟨u-⟩ na parze **2. *~ a letter open*** otworzyć list nad parą **3. *get ~ed up about*** *infml* wkurzać się o *A*; **steam•er** ['stiːmə] *s* **1.** parowiec *m* **2.** garnek *n* do gotowania na parze

S

3. wkładka *f* do gotowania na parze; **'steam i•ron** *s* żelazko *n* z nawilżaczem; **'steam roll•er** *s* walec *m* drogowy; **'steam ship** *s* statek *m* parowy; **steam•y** ['stiːmɪ] *adj* **1.** zaparowany **2.** parny **3.** parujący **4.** *infml affair*: namiętny

steel [stiːl] **I** *s* stal *f* **II** *v/t* **~ *oneself for*** przygotowywać się do *G*; **steel 'wool** *s* **1.** druciak *m* **2.** wełna *f* stalowa; **'steel•work•er** *s* hutnik *m*; **'steel-works** *pl -works s* huta *f* stali; **steel•y** ['stiːlɪ] *adj* stalowy

steep[1] [stiːp] *adj* **1.** stromy **2.** *fall, rise*: gwałtowny **3.** *price*: wygórowany

steep[2] [~] *v/t* **1.** namaczać ⟨-moczyć⟩ **2. ~ *oneself in fig*** zagłębiać się w *A* **3. *be ~ed in history*** mieć bogatą historię

steep•en ['stiːpən] *v/i* stawać ⟨stać⟩ się bardziej stromym

stee•ple ['stiːpl] *s* (strzelista) wieża *f*; **'stee•ple•chase** *s* **1.** gonitwa *f* z przeszkodami **2.** bieg *m* z przeszkodami; **steep•ly** ['stiːplɪ] *adv* **1.** stromo **2.** *increase*: gwałtownie

steer[1] [stɪə] *s* wół *m* opasowy

steer[2] [~] **I** *v/t* **1.** kierować ⟨s-⟩; **~ *the conversation away*** skierować rozmowę na inne tory **2.** sterować **3.** prowadzić ⟨po-⟩; **~ *a team to victory*** poprowadzić drużynę do zwycięstwa **II** *v/i* **1.** kierować ⟨po-⟩ się **2.** płynąć ⟨s-⟩; **steer•ing** ['stɪərɪŋ] *s* **1.** układ *m* kierowniczy **2.** sterowanie *n*; **'steer-ing wheel** *s* kierownica *f*

stel•lar ['stelə] *adj* **1.** gwiezdny **2.** *fig* znakomity

stem[1] [stem] **I** *s* **1.** łodyga *f* **2.** *glass*: nożka *f* **3.** *pipe*: cybuch *m* **4.** (*part of word*) temat *m* **II** *v/i* **~ *from* a)** wynikać z *G* **b)** wywodzić się z *G*

stem[2] [~] *v/***1.** tamować ⟨za-⟩ **2.** powstrzymywać ⟨-mać⟩

stench [stentʃ] *s* **1.** smród *m* **2.** odór *m*

sten•cil ['stensɪl] *s* **1.** szablon *m* **2.** wzór *m*

ste•nog•ra•pher [stə'nɒgrəfə] *s Am* stenograf *m*

step [step] **I** *s* **1.** krok *m*; ***take a ~*** zrobić krok; ***take ~s*** podjąć kroki; **~ *by ~*** krok po kroku; ***it's just a few ~s to the shop*** do sklepu jest tylko kilka kroków; ***a ~ in the right direction*** krok we właściwym kierunku; ***watch your ~* a)** uważaj, jak idziesz, patrz pod nogi **b)** *fig* uważaj **2.** stopień *m*, schodek *m*; ***up the ~s*** po schodach na górę **3. *~s*** *Br* drabina *f* **II** *v/i* **1.** stąpać, iść **2.** nadeptywać ⟨-pnąć⟩ (***on*** na *A*) **3. ~ *into a room*** wejść do pokoju; **~ *off a bus*** wysiąść z autobusu; **~ *out of a shower*** wyjść spod prysznica; **~ *into s.o.'s shoes*** *fig* przejąć czyjeś obowiązki; **step aside** *v/i* **1.** odsuwać ⟨-sunąć⟩ się na bok **2.** → ***step down***; **step down** *v/i* ustępować ⟨-tąpić⟩ (***in favour of*** na rzecz *G*); **step forward** *v/i* **1.** występować ⟨-tąpić⟩ naprzód **2.** zgłaszać ⟨-łosić⟩ się; **step in** *v/i* wkraczać ⟨-roczyć⟩; **step out** *v/i* wychodzić ⟨wyjść⟩; **step up I** *v/i* **1.** występować ⟨-tąpić⟩ (naprzód) **2.** zbliżać ⟨-żyć⟩ się **II** *v/t* **1.** zwiększać ⟨-szyć⟩ **2.** wzmacniać ⟨-mocnić⟩; **~ *security*** wzmocnić środki bezpieczeństwa **3.** *effort*: wzmagać ⟨wzmóc⟩

'step•broth•er *s* przyrodni brat *m*; **'step•child** *s* **1.** pasierb *m* **2.** pasierbica *f*; **'step•daugh•ter** *s* pasierbica *f*; **'step•fa•ther** *s* ojczym *m*; **'step•lad-der** *s* drabina *f*; **'step•moth•er** *s* macocha *f*

steppe [step] *s* step *m*

step•ping stone ['stepɪŋstəʊn] *s fig* trampolina *f*, odskocznia *f*

'step•sis•ter *s* przyrodnia siostra *f*; **'step•son** *s* pasierb *m*

ster•e•o ['sterɪəʊ] **I** *pl -reos s* **1.** stereo *n* **2.** odtwarzacz *m* stereo **3.** zestaw *m* stereo **II** *adj* stereo, stereofoniczny

ster•e•o•type ['sterɪəʊtaɪp] **I** *s* stereotyp *m* **II** *v/t* postrzegać sterotypowo; **ster•e•o•typed** ['sterɪəʊtaɪpt] *adj* stereotypowy; **ster•e•o•typ•i•cal** [sterɪəʊ'tɪpɪkl] *adj* stereotypowy

ster•ile ['steraɪl] *adj* **1.** bezpłodny **2.** *a. fig* jałowy **3.** sterylny; **ste•ril•i-ty** [stə'rɪlətɪ] *s* **1.** bezpłodność *f* **2.** jałowość *f*; **ster•i•li•za•tion** [sterəlaɪ'zeɪʃn] *s* **1.** sterylizacja *f* **2.** wyjaławianie *n*; **ster•il•ize** ['sterəlaɪz] *v/t* **1.** sterylizować ⟨wy-⟩ **2.** wyjaławiać ⟨-łowić⟩

ster•ling ['stɜːlɪŋ] *s Br* funt *m* szterling

stern[1] [stɜːn] *s* rufa *f*

S

stern² [~] *adj* **1.** *face*, *voice*: surowy, srogi **2.** *warning*: poważny; **sternly** ['stɜːnlɪ] *adv* **1.** surowo **2.** srogo **3.** poważnie

ster•num ['stɜːnəm] *pl -nums*, *-na s* ANAT mostek *m*

ster•oids ['sterɔɪdz] *pl* MED CHEM sterydy *pl*, steroidy *pl*

steth•o•scope ['steθəskəʊp] *s* stetoskop *m*

stet•son® ['stetsn] *s Am* kapelusz *m* kowbojski, stetson *m*

ste•ve•dore ['stiːvədɔː] *s* doker *m*

stew [stjuː] COOK **I** *s* **1.** mięso *n* duszone z jarzynami **2.** potrawka *f* **II** *v/t* dusić ⟨u-⟩ **III** *v/i* dusić ⟨u-⟩ się

stew•ard ['stjuːəd] *s* **1.** steward *m* **2.** zarządca *m* **3.** *Br* intendent *m* **4.** *Br* organizator *m*; **stew•ard•ess** [stjuːər'des] *s* stewardesa *f*; **stew•ard•ship** ['stjuːədʃɪp] *s* **1.** zarząd *m* **2.** nadzór *m*

stick¹ [stɪk] *s* **1.** patyk *m* **2.** patyczek *m* **3.** kij *m*; ***a hockey ~*** kij hokejowy **4.** laska *f*; ***walk on a ~*** chodzić o lasce **5.** *carrot*: korzeń *m* **6.** *Am infml* drążek *m* sterowniczy **7.** *Am infml* dźwignia *f* zmiany biegów **8.** sztyft *m*; ***a glue ~*** klej w sztyfcie **9.** MUS pałeczka *f*, batuta *f*

stick² [~] **I** (*stuck*; *stuck*) *v/t* **1.** wkładać ⟨włożyć⟩ **2.** wsadzać ⟨-dzić⟩ **3.** wtykać ⟨wetknąć⟩ **4.** wbijać ⟨wbić⟩ (***into*** w *A*) **5.** *stamps*: przyklejać ⟨-leić⟩ **6.** *Br infml* znosić ⟨znieść⟩; ***I can't ~ it any longer*** dłużej już tego nie zniosę **II** (*stuck*; *stuck*) *v/i* **1.** kleić się **2.** przyklejać ⟨-leić⟩ się **3.** utknąć **4.** klinować ⟨za-⟩ się **5.** utkwić; ***~ in s.o.'s mind*** zapaść komuś w pamięć; **stick around** *v/i* kręcić się w pobliżu; **stick by** *v/i* **1.** nie opuszczać ⟨opuścić⟩ **2.** trwać wiernie przy *L* **3.** *decision*: trzymać się; **stick out I** *v/i* **1.** wystawać **2.** (*ears*) odstawać **II** *v/t tongue*, *hand*: wystawiać ⟨-wić⟩; **stick out for** *v/i* domagać się; **stick to** *v/t* **1.** trzymać się; ***let's ~ Saturday*** pozostańmy przy sobocie; ***~ one's word*** dotrzymać słowa **2.** *diet*: przestrzegać **2.** obstawać przy *L*; **stick together I** *v/t* kleić ⟨s-⟩ **II** *v/i infml* trzymać się razem; **stick up** *v/i* wystawać; **stick up for** *v/i* bronić; **stick with** *v/i* trzymać się

stick•er ['stɪkə] *s* naklejka *f*, nalepka *f*; **'stick•er price** *s car*: cena *f* sugerowana (przez producenta); **stick•ing plas•ter** ['stɪkɪŋplɑːstə] *s Br* plaster *m*; **'stick•ing point** *s* kwestia *f* sporna

'stick-in-the-mud *s infml* **1.** tradycjonalista *m* **2.** nudziarz *m*

stick•ler ['stɪklə] *s*: ***be a ~ for*** *infml* mieć fioła na punkcie *G*

'stick-on *adj plaster*, *sticker*: samoprzylepny; **'stick•pin** *s Am* spinka *f* do krawata; **'stick shift** *s Am* **1.** dźwignia *f* zmiany biegów **2.** samochód *m* z ręczną skrzynią biegów

stick•y ['stɪkɪ] *adj* **1.** lepki; ***have ~ fingers*** *fig* mieć lepkie ręce **2.** klejący się **3.** *tape*: klejący, samoprzylepny **4.** *infml* parny **5.** *infml problem*: delikatny, trudny

stiff [stɪf] **I** *adj* **1.** sztywny; ***whisk the egg whites until ~*** ubić białka na sztywną pianę **2.** zesztywniały **3.** zdrętwiały **4.** *punishment*: surowy **5.** *objections*: ostry **6.** *wind*: silny **7.** *atmosphere*: sztywny, wymuszony **8.** *infml price*: wygórowany **9.** *alcohol*: mocny **II** *adv* ***be bored ~*** śmiertelnie się nudzić; ***be scared ~*** być śmiertelnie przerażonym; ***be frozen ~*** **a)** zamarznąć na kamień **b)** zmarznąć na kość **III** *s infml* trup *m*; **stiffen** ['stɪfn] **I** (*a.* ***~ up***) *v/i* **1.** sztywnieć ⟨ze-⟩ **2.** drętwieć ⟨z-⟩ **II** *v/t* **1.** usztywniać ⟨-nić⟩ **2.** *regulations*: zaostrzać ⟨-rzyć⟩; **stiff•ly** ['stɪflɪ] *adv* sztywno; **stiff•ness** ['stɪfnəs] *s* sztywność *f*

sti•fle ['staɪfl] **I** *v/t* **1.** tłumić ⟨s-⟩ **2.** dusić ⟨z-⟩ **3.** powstrzymywać ⟨-mać⟩ **II** *v/i* dusić ⟨u-⟩ się; **sti•fling** ['staɪflɪŋ] *adj* **1.** duszny **2.** duszący

stig•ma ['stɪgmə] *s* piętno *n*; **stig•ma•ta** [stɪg'mɑːtə] *pl* REL stygmaty *pl*; **stig•ma•tize** ['stɪgmətaɪz] *v/t* piętnować ⟨na-⟩

sti•let•to [stɪ'letəʊ] *pl -tos*, *-toes s* **1.** sztylet *m* **2.** (*shoe*) szpilka *f*; ***~s*** szpilki; **sti•let•to heel** [stɪletəʊ'hiːl] *s* (*of shoe*) szpilka *f*

still¹ [stɪl] *adv* **1.** wciąż; ***I'm ~ hungry*** wciąż jestem głodny **2.** nadal; ***do you ~ live in London?*** nadal mieszkasz w Londynie? **3.** ciągle **4.** jeszcze;

S

the next day was warmer ~ następny dzień był jeszcze cieplejszy; ***~ more*** jeszcze więcej **5.** mimo to; ***the weather was cold, ~, we had a great time*** było zimno, ale mimo to dobrze się bawiliśmy

still[2] [~] **I** *adj* **1.** nieruchomy; ***keep ~*** nie ruszać się; ***stand ~*** stać bez ruchu, nie ruszać się; ***sit ~!*** siedź spokojnie!; ***~ water*** woda stojąca; ***~ waters run deep*** *fig* cicha woda brzegi rwie **2.** bezwietrzny **3.** *water*: niegazowany **II** *s* **1.** fotos *m* **2.** zdjęcie *n* **III** *v/i* uspokajać ⟨-koić⟩ się **IV** *v/t* **1.** uspokajać ⟨-koić⟩ **2.** *doubts*: rozwiewać ⟨-zwiać⟩

still[3] [~] *s* destylator *m*

'still•birth *s* urodzenie *n* martwego dziecka; **'still•born** *adj* **1.** *child*: martwy **2.** nieudany; **still 'life** *s* ART martwa natura *f*

stilt•ed ['stɪltɪd] *adj style*: koturnowy

stilts [stɪlts] *pl* szczudła *pl*; ***walk on ~*** chodzić na szczudłach

stim•u•lant ['stɪmjʊlənt] *s* **1.** środek *m* pobudzający **2.** używka *f* **3.** zachęta *f*, doping *m*; **stim•u•late** ['stɪmjʊleɪt] *v/t* **1.** pobudzać ⟨-dzić⟩ **2.** stymulować **3.** *interest*: wzbudzać ⟨-dzić⟩ **4.** dopingować ⟨z-⟩ **5.** zachęcać ⟨-cić⟩; **stim•u•lat•ing** ['stɪmjʊleɪtɪŋ] *adj* **1.** stymulujący **2.** pobudzający **3.** inspirujący; **stim•u•la•tion** [stɪmjʊ'leɪʃn] *s* **1.** stymulacja *f* **2.** pobudzenie *n* **3.** podnieta *f*; **stim•u•lus** ['stɪmjʊləs] *pl -li* [~laɪ] *s a. fig* bodziec *m*

sting [stɪŋ] **I** (*stung*; *stung*) *v/t* **1.** żądlić ⟨u-⟩ **2.** (*nettle*) parzyć ⟨po-⟩ **3.** *eyes*: szczypać w *A* **4.** *fig* dotykać ⟨-tknąć⟩ **5.** *infml* naciągać ⟨-gnąć⟩; ***I got stung for $100*** zostałem naciągnięty na 100 dolarów **II** (*stung*; *stung*) *v/i* (*eyes*) szczypać, piec **III** *s* **1.** żądło *n*; ***take the ~ out of*** *fig* złagodzić *A* **2.** użądlenie *n* **3.** ukłucie *n* **4.** pieczenie *n*, piekący ból *m*; **sting•ing** ['stɪŋɪŋ] *adj* **1.** piekący **2.** szczypiący **3.** jadowity **4.** *attack*: agresywny; **'sting•ing net•tle** *s* pokrzywa *f*

sting•y ['stɪndʒɪ] *adj infml* skąpy

stink [stɪŋk] **I** (*stank*; *stunk*) *v/i a. fig* śmierdzieć (**of** *I*) **II** *s* smród *m*; ***kick up a ~*** *infml* zrobić aferę; **stink bomb** *s* pojemnik *m* z cuchnącą substancją; **stink•er** ['stɪŋkə] *s infml* **1.** śmierdziel *m* **2.** ***a ~ of a movie*** beznadziejny film; **stink•ing** ['stɪŋkɪŋ] **I** *adj* **1.** śmierdzący **2.** *Br infml* okropny, fatalny **II** *adv infml rich*: obrzydliwie

stint[1] [stɪnt] *s* **1.** pobyt *m*; ***she did a two-year ~ as an editor*** dwa lata pracowała jako redaktor; ***I've done my ~ for today*** zrobiłem już swoje na dzisiaj

stint[2] [~] *v/i*: **~ on a)** oszczędzać na *L* **b)** żałować *G*

stip•u•la•tion [stɪpjʊ'leɪʃn] *s* **1.** warunek *m* **2.** zastrzeżenie *n* **3.** postanowienie *n*; **stip•u•late** ['stɪpjʊleɪt] *v/t* **1.** określać ⟨-lić⟩ **2.** przewidywać ⟨-dzieć⟩ **3.** stwierdzać ⟨-dzić⟩

stir [stɜː] **I** *v/t* **1.** mieszać ⟨za-⟩ **2.** poruszać ⟨-szyć⟩; ***~ s.o. from sleep*** wyrwać kogoś ze snu; ***~ s.o. into action*** zmobilizować kogoś do działania **3.** poruszać ⟨-szyć⟩ **4.** wzbudzać ⟨-dzić⟩ **II** *v/i* poruszać ⟨-szyć⟩ się **III** *s* **1.** ***give s.th. a ~*** zamieszać coś **2.** *fig* poruszenie *n*; **stir up** *v/t* **1.** wzbijać ⟨-bić⟩ **2.** wzbudzać ⟨-dzić⟩ **3.** *trouble*: powodować ⟨s-⟩ **4.** podburzać ⟨-rzyć⟩ **5.** mobilizować ⟨z-⟩

stir-fry I *v/t* smażyć ⟨u-⟩ na sposób chiński **II** *adj* smażony na sposób chiński

stir•ring ['stɜːrɪŋ] **I** *s* ***she felt a ~ of interest*** obudziła się w niej ciekawość; ***the first ~s of spring*** pierwsze oznaki wiosny **II** *adj fig* poruszający

stir•rup ['stɪrəp] *s* strzemię *n*

stitch [stɪtʃ] **I** *s* **1.** MED szew *m*; ***he had his ~es out yesterday*** wczoraj miał zdjęte szwy **2.** ścieg *m* **3.** oczko *n*; ***drop a ~*** spuścić oczko **4.** MED kolka *f*; ***be in ~es*** *fig* śmiać się do rozpuku **II** *v/t* (*a.* **~ up**) zszywać ⟨-szyć⟩; ***~ s.th. hastily together*** *fig* sklecić coś naprędce; **stitch up** *v/t Br infml* wrabiać ⟨wrobić⟩

stitch•ing ['stɪtʃɪŋ] *s* szew *m*

stock [stɒk] **I** *s* **1.** zapas *m*; ***food ~s*** zapasy żywności **2.** COMM towar *m*; ***be in ~*** być na składzie; ***be out of ~*** być wyprzedanym **3.** ECON akcja *f* **4.** ECON udział *m* **5.** ECON kapitał *m* akcyjny **6.** (*animals*) inwentarz *m* **7.** bulion *m* **8.** ***the ~s*** dyby *pl* **II** *v/t* **1.** prowadzić sprzedaż **2.** zaopatrywać ⟨-trzyć⟩ (**with** w *A*) **III** *adj* **1.** standardowy

S

2. typowy; **stock up** *v/i* robić ⟨z-⟩ zapasy (***on*** *G*)

'stock•breed•er *s* hodowca *m* bydła; **'stock•breed•ing** *s* hodowla *f* bydła; **'stock•brok•er** *s* makler *m* giełdowy; **'stock com•pa•ny** *s* spółka *f* akcyjna; **'stock cube** *s* kostka *f* rosołowa; **'stock ex•change** *s* giełda *f* (papierów wartościowych); **'stock•hold•er** *s* **1.** akcjonariusz *m* **2.** udziałowiec *m*

stock•ing ['stɒkɪŋ] *s* pończocha *f*; **stock•ing 'mask** *s* (*on criminal's head*) pończocha *f*

stock-in-'trade *s fig* chleb *m* powszedni; **stock•ist** ['stɒkɪst] *s* sklep *m* (specjalistyczny); **'stock mar•ket** *s* **1.** giełda *f* (papierów wartościowych) **2.** rynek *m* papierów wartościowych; **stock•mar•ket crash** *s* krach *m* na giełdzie; **'stock•pile I** *s* **1.** zapas *m* **2.** wielka ilość *f* **II** *v/t* **1.** gromadzić ⟨z-⟩ **2.** składować; **'stock•room** *s* magazyn *m*; **stock-'still** *adv* nieruchomo, bez ruchu; **'stock•tak•ing** *s* **1.** inwentaryzacja *f*, remanent *m* **2.** przemyślenia *pl*

'stock•y ['stɒkɪ] *adj* **1.** przysadzisty **2.** krępy

sto•i•cal ['stəʊɪkl] *adj* stoicki; **sto•i•cism** ['stəʊɪsɪzm] *s* stoicyzm *m*

stoke [stəʊk] *v/t* (*a.* ***~ up***) **1.** *fire*: dokładać ⟨dołożyć⟩ do *G* **2.** *interest*: podsycać ⟨-cić⟩; **stoke up** *v/i* najadać ⟨-jeść⟩ się na zapas (***on/with*** *I*); **'stok•er** *s* (*ship*) palacz *m*

stole[1] [stəʊl] *s* **1.** REL stuła *f* **2.** etola *f* **3.** szal *m*

stole[2] [~] *Past Simple* → ***steal***

stol•en ['stəʊlən] *Past Participle* → ***steal***

stol•id ['stɒlɪd] *adj face expression*: beznamiętny

stom•ach ['stʌmək] **I** *s* **1.** żołądek *m*; ***on an empty ~*** na pusty żołądek; ***have no ~ to do s.th.*** nie mieć odwagi czegoś zrobić **2.** *infml* brzuch *m* **II** *v/t* znosić ⟨znieść⟩; **'stom•ach ache** *s* ból *m* brzucha; ***I've got a ~*** boli mnie brzuch; **stom•ach up•set** *s* rozstrój *m* żołądka

stomp [stɒmp] *v/i*: ***he ~ed up the stairs*** wszedł po schodach, głośno tupiąc

stone [stəʊn] **I** *s* **1.** kamień *m*; ***a precious ~*** kamień szlachetny; ***kidney ~s*** kamienie nerkowe; ***have a heart of ~*** *fig* mieć serce z kamienia; ***leave no ~ unturned*** *fig* poruszyć niebo i ziemię **2.** *Br* pestka *f* **3.** *pl stone* (*unit of weight*) *Br* 6,35 kg **II** *v/t* **1.** obrzucać ⟨-cić⟩ kamieniami **2.** kamienować ⟨u-⟩; ***~ s.o. to death*** ukamienować kogoś; ***~ me!*** *dated* a niech mnie kule biją! **3.** *Br* drylować ⟨wy-⟩; **'Stone Age** *s* epoka *f* kamienna; **stone-'broke** *Am* → ***stony broke***; **stone-'cold** *adj* **1.** zimny jak lód **2.** *sober*: zupełnie

stoned [stəʊnd] *adj infml* **1.** naćpany **2.** na bani

stone-'dead *adj martwy*; **stone-deaf** *adj* głuchy jak pień; **'stone•ma•son** *s* kamieniarz *m*; **'stone•wall** *v/t* **1.** blokować ⟨za-⟩ **2.** *questions*: unikać odpowiedzi na *A*; **'stone•ware** *s* wyroby *pl* kamionkowe; **'stone•work** *s* kamieniarka *f*

ston•y ['stəʊnɪ] *adj* **1.** kamienisty **2.** kamienny; ***~ silence*** kamienna cisza; **ston•y 'broke** *adj infml* całkiem spłukany

stood [stuːd] *Past Simple and Past Participle* → ***stand***

stool [stuːl] *s* **1** stołek *m* **2.** MED stolec *m*

stoop[1] [stuːp] *v/i* **1.** pochylać ⟨-lić⟩ się **2.** nachylać ⟨-lić⟩ się **3.** garbić ⟨z-⟩ się **4.** *fig* upaść; ***~ so low*** upaść tak nisko (***to do s.th.*** by coś zrobić); **stoop to** *v/t* zniżać ⟨-żyć⟩ się do *G*

stoop[2] [~] *s* ***have a ~*** garbić się

stop [stɒp] **I** *v/i* **1.** zatrzymywać ⟨-mać⟩ się; ***~ to do s.th.*** zatrzymać się, aby coś zrobić; ***~ at nothing*** nie cofnąć się przed niczym **2.** stawać ⟨stanąć⟩ **3.** kończyć ⟨s-⟩ się **II** *v/t* **1.** zatrzymywać ⟨-mać⟩ **2.** przestawać ⟨-tać⟩; ***~ crying*** przestać płakać; ***~ it!*** przestań! **3.** przerywać ⟨-rwać⟩ **4.** powstrzymywać ⟨-mać⟩ (***s.o. from*** kogoś od *G*) **5.** zatykać ⟨-tkać⟩; ***~ one's ears*** zatkać uszy **III** *s* **1.** postój *m*; ***come to a ~*** zatrzymać się **2.** przystanek *m* **3.** przerwa *f*; ***put a ~ to*** położyć kres *D* **4.** (*punctuation*) *Br* kropka *f*; **stop around**, **stop by** *v/i infml* wpadać ⟨wpaść⟩ (do *G*); **stop in** *v/i Br* zostawać ⟨-tać⟩ w domu; **stop off**,

S

stop over *v/i* zatrzymywać ⟨-mać⟩ się; **stop up** *v/t* zatykać ⟨-tkać⟩

'stop•cock *s* zawór *m* odcinający; **'stop•gap** *s* tymczasowe rozwiązanie *n*; **'stop•light** *s* **1.** *Br* czerwone światło *n* **2.** *AUTO Am* światło *n* stopu; **'stop•o•ver** *s* przerwa *f* w podróży

stop•page ['stɒpɪdʒ] *s* **1.** strajk *m* **2.** *SPORT* przerwa *f*; ***~ time*** doliczony czas gry **3.** *MED* zator *m*; **stop•per** ['stɒpə] *s* **1.** korek *m* **2.** zatyczka *f*

stop press *s* wiadomość *f* z ostatniej chwili; **'stop•watch** *s* stoper *m*

stor•age ['stɔːrɪdʒ] *s* **1.** przechowywanie *n*; ***data ~*** przechowywanie danych **2.** magazynowanie *n*; ***~ facilities*** magazyny **3.** składowanie *n*; **'stor•age heat•er** *s TECH Br* grzejnik *m* akumulacyjny

store [stɔː] **I** *s* **1.** sklep *m*; ***a department ~*** dom *m* towarowy **2.** zapas *m* **3.** magazyn *m*; ***a surprise lay in ~ for her*** *fig* czekała ją niespodzianka **4.** skład *m* **5.** ***put great ~ to*** przykładać wielką wagę do *G* **II** (*a.* ***~ up***) *v/t* **1.** przechowywać ⟨-chować⟩ **2.** gromadzić ⟨z-⟩ **3.** robić ⟨z-⟩ zapas; **'store•card** *s* karta *f* kredytowa (*wydawana przez sklep*); **'store de•tec•tive** *s* detektyw *m* sklepowy; **'store•house** *s* **1.** magazyn *m* **2.** skład *m* **3.** *fig* skarbnica *f*; **'store•keep•er** *s Am* **1.** sklepikarz *m* **2.** właściciel *m* sklepu; **'store•room** *s* **1.** magazyn *m* **2.** składzik *m*; **store 'win•dow** *s Am* witryna *f* sklepowa

sto•rey ['stɔːrɪ] *Br*, ***story*** *Am s* piętro *n*; ***a three-~ building*** dwupiętrowy budynek

stork [stɔːk] *s* bocian *m*

storm [stɔːm] **I** *s* **1.** burza *f*; ***a ~ in a teacup*** burza w szklance wody **2.** sztorm *m* **3.** ***take s.th. by ~*** wziąć coś szturmem **II** *v/t* **1.** szturmować **2.** brać ⟨wziąć⟩ szturmem **III** *v/i* wpadać ⟨-paść⟩ jak burza (***into*** do *G*); **'storm cloud** *s* chmura *f* burzowa; **'storm drain** *s* kanał *m* burzowy; **'storm warn•ing** *s* ostrzeżenie *n* sztormowe

storm•y ['stɔːmɪ] *adj* **1.** *weather*: burzowy **2.** *debate*: burzliwy

sto•ry ['stɔːrɪ] *s* **1.** historia *f*; ***that's another ~*** to już inna historia; ***to cut a long ~ short*** mówiąc krótko; ***it's the same old ~*** to stara śpiewka **2.** opowieść *f*; ***a bedtime ~*** bajka na dobranoc **3.** opowiadanie *n* **4.** historyjka *f* **5.** artykuł *m*; **'sto•ry book** *s* historyjki *pl* dla dzieci; **'sto•ry line** *s* fabuła *f*

stoup [stuːp] *s REL* kropielnica *f*

stout [staʊt] **I** *adj* **1.** *person*: tęgi **2.** *shoes*: mocny **3.** *resistance*: zacięty **II** *s* mocne, ciemne piwo *n* typu stout

stove [stəʊv] *s* **1.** piec *m* **2.** piecyk *m* **3.** *Am* kuchenka *f*

stow [stəʊ] *v/t* **1.** wkładać ⟨włożyć⟩ (***in*** do *G*) **2.** chować ⟨s-⟩; **stow away** *v/i* **1.** podróżować na gapę **2.** ukrywać ⟨-ryć⟩ się

'stow•a•way *s* pasażer *m* na gapę

strad•dle ['strædl] *v/t* **1.** *border*: leżeć po obu stronach **2.** siedzieć okrakiem na *L* **3.** stać w rozkroku nad *I*

strag•gle ['strægl] *v/i* **1.** (*hair*) opadać w nieładzie (***over*** na *A*) **2.** być rozrzuconym **3.** wlec ⟨po-⟩ się; **strag•gler** ['stræglə] *s*: ***be a ~*** wlec się w ogonie; **strag•gly** ['stræglɪ] *adj win*: rozwichrzony

straight [streɪt] **I** *adj* **1.** prosty; ***in a ~ line*** w prostej linii; ***get s.th. ~*** *fig* wyjaśnić coś; ***keep a ~ face*** zachować powagę **2.** szczery **3.** uczciwy **4.** *win*: z rzędu **5.** *whisky*: czysty **6.** *infml* zwykły **7.** *infml* hetero **II** *adv* **1.** prosto; ***~ ahead*** prosto przed siebie; ***come ~ home*** wrócić prosto do domu; ***~ away*** natychmiast, od razu; ***play it ~*** grać fair; ***he's going ~*** (*former criminal*) prowadzić uczciwe życie; ***say s.th. ~ from the shoulder*** *Am infml* powiedzieć coś prosto z mostu **2.** wprost **3.** bez przerwy **III** *s* **1.** *infml* hetero *m* **2.** prosta *f*

straight•en ['streɪtn] **I** *v/t* **1.** prostować ⟨wy-⟩ **2.** *tie*: poprawiać ⟨-wić⟩ **II** *v/i* **1.** (*a.* ***~ out***) prostować ⟨wy-⟩ się **2.** (*a.* ***~ up***) wyciągać ⟨-gnąć⟩ się, rozciągać ⟨-gnąć⟩ się; **straighten out** *v/t* **1.** prostować ⟨wy-⟩ **2.** wyjaśniać ⟨-nić⟩ **3.** porządkować ⟨u-⟩; **straighten up** *v/t* **1.** poprawiać ⟨-wić⟩ **2.** doprowadzać ⟨-dzić⟩ do porządku

straight'for•ward *adj* **1.** prosty **2.** zrozumiały **3.** *person*: prostolinijny

strain[1] [streɪn] **I** *s* **1.** obciążenie *n* **2.** napięcie *n*; ***the couple is under great***

S

~ przechodzą ciężki okres **3.** stres *m* **4.** wysiłek *m* **5.** uszkodzenie *n* powysiłkowe **6.** nadwyrężenie *n* **7.** naderwanie *n* **8.** rys *m*; ***she had a ~ of snobbery in her*** była snobką, miała skłonność do snobizmu **9.** **~s** *form* dźwięki **II** *v/t* **1.** uszkadzać ⟨-kodzić⟩ nadwyrężać ⟨-żyć⟩; ***~ s.o.'s patience*** wystawiać na próbę czyjąś cierpliwość **3.** nadrywać ⟨-derwać⟩ **4.** naprężać ⟨-żyć⟩; ***~ one's ears*** natężać słuch; ***~ one's neck*** wyciągać szyję **5.** odcedzać ⟨-dzić⟩ **III** *v/i* ***~ at the leash*** szarpać się na smyczy

strain[2] [~] *s bacteria*: szczep *m*

strained [streɪnd] *adj* **1.** spięty, zestresowany **2.** *situation*: napięty **3.** *laughter*: wymuszony

strain•er ['streɪnə] *s* sitko *n*

strait [streɪt] *s* **1.** cieśnina *f* **2.** **~s** kłopoty *pl*; ***be in dire ~s*** mieć poważne kłopoty, być w tarapatach; **'strait•jack•et** *s* kaftan *m* bezpieczeństwa; **strait-laced** [streɪt'leɪst] *adj* pruderyjny

strand[1] [strænd] *s* **1.** *hair*: pasmo *n* **2.** nić *f* **3.** *pearls*: sznur *m* **4.** *cable*: żyła *f* **5.** wątek *m*

strand[2] [~] *v/t* **1.** wyrzucać ⟨-cić⟩ (na brzeg) **2.** ***many drivers were ~ed by heavy snow*** wielu kierowców utknęło w zaspach; ***be ~ed by flood waters*** być odciętym od świata w wyniku powodzi

strange [streɪndʒ] *adj* **1.** dziwny; ***~ to say*** może to zabrzmi dziwnie, ale **2.** osobliwy **3.** obcy, nieznany (***to*** dla *G*); **strange•ly** ['streɪndʒlɪ] *adv* **1.** dziwnie **2.** osobliwie **3.** obco; **strang•er** ['streɪndʒə] *s* obcy *m*; ***a complete ~*** zupełnie obcy człowiek; ***I'm a ~ here*** nie jestem stąd

S

stran•gle ['stræŋgl] *v/t* **1.** dusić ⟨u-⟩ **2.** *laughter*: tłumić ⟨s-⟩ **3.** hamować ⟨za-⟩ rozwój **4.** *inflation*: zdusić; **stran•gled** *adj* **1.** stłumiony **2.** *voices*: przytłumiony; **'stran•gle•hold** *s* dławiący uścisk *m*; ***have a ~ on*** *fig* mieć całkowitą kontrolę nad *I*

stran•gu•la•tion [stræŋgjʊ'leɪʃn] *s* **1.** uduszenie *n* **2.** zduszenie *n* **3.** stłumienie *n* **4.** zdławienie *n*

strap [stræp] **I** *s* **1.** pas *m* **2.** pasek *m* **3.** rzemień *m* **4.** (*dress*) ramiączko *n* **II** *v/t* **1.** przypinać ⟨-piąć⟩ **2.** przywiązywać ⟨-zać⟩ **3.** (*a.* ***~ up***) opatrywać ⟨-trzeć⟩; **strap in** *v/t* przypinać ⟨-piąć⟩ (pasami); ***~ oneself in*** zapiąć pasy

'strap•less ['stræplɪs] *s dress*: bez ramiączek

strapped [stræpt] *adj*: ***I'm ~ for cash*** *infml* kiepsko u mnie z gotówką; ***be financially ~*** *infml* mieć kłopoty finansowe

stra•ta ['strɑːtə] *pl* → ***stratum***

strat•a•gem ['strætədʒəm] *s* **1.** fortel *m* **2.** sztuczka *f* **3.** metoda *f*

stra•te•gic [strə'tiːdʒɪk] *adj* strategiczny; **strat•e•gist** ['strætədʒɪst] *s* strateg *m*; **strat•e•gy** ['strætədʒɪ] *s* strategia *f*

strat•i•fied ['strætɪfaɪd] *adj* **1.** warstwowy **2.** rozwarstwiony

strat•o•sphere ['strætəsfɪə] *s* stratosfera *f*

stra•tum ['strɑːtəm] *pl strata* ['strɑːtə] *s* warstwa *f*

straw [strɔː] *s* **1.** słoma *f* **2.** źdźbło *n* słomy; ***clutch at ~s***, ***grasp at ~s*** *fig* chwytać się brzytwy; ***the ~ that breaks the camel's back*** kropla, która przelała czarę **3.** słomka *f*

straw•ber•ry ['strɔːbərɪ] *s* truskawka *f*; ***wild ~*** poziomka; **'straw•ber•ry mark** *s* (czerwone) znamię *n*

straw 'hat *s* słomkowy kapelusz *m*; **'straw man** *pl -men s fig* figurant *m*; **straw 'poll** *s* badanie *n* opinii publicznej

stray [streɪ] **I** *v/i* **1.** błądzić ⟨za-⟩ **2.** błąkać ⟨za-⟩ się **3.** ***~ from the theme of the debate*** odchodzić od tematu dyskusji; ***my mind kept ~ing back to our last talk*** myślami wracałem wciąż do naszej ostatniej rozmowy **4.** popełniać ⟨-nić⟩ zdradę **II** *adj* **1.** bezpański **2.** zabłąkany **3.** pojedynczy **4.** *bullet*: przypadkowy **III** *s* **1.** bezpańskie zwierzę *n* **2.** zabłąkane zwierzę *n*

streak [striːk] **I** *s* **1.** smuga *f*; ***a ~ of lighting*** zygzak błyskawicy **2.** pasmo *n*; ***a winning*** (***losing***) ***~*** dobra (zła) passa **3.** pasemko *n* **4.** ***he had a paranoid ~*** miał cechy paranoika; ***she has a mean ~*** jest wredna **II** *v/t* **1.** robić ⟨z-⟩ smugi; ***his face was ~ed with mud*** na twarzy miał smugi błota **2.** ***she's had her hair ~ed*** zrobiła sobie pasemka; **streak•y** ['stri:kɪ] *adj*: ***be ~ with grease*** mieć tłuste smugi

stream [stri:m] **I** *s* **1.** strumień *m* **2.** (*at school*) grupa *f* **II** *v/i* **1.** płynąć **2.** spływać ⟨-łynąć⟩; ***tears were ~ing down her face*** łzy spływały jej po twarzy **3.** wypływać ⟨-łynąć⟩ (***out of*** z *G*) **4.** wydostawać ⟨-stać⟩ się (***out of*** z *G*) **5.** powiewać; ***~ in the wind*** powiewać na wietrze **III** *v/t* (*at school*) dzielić ⟨po-⟩ na grupy; **stream•er** ['stri:mə] *s* **1.** serpentyna *f* **2.** wstęga *f* **3.** wstążka *f*; **stream•ing** ['stri:mɪŋ] *s Br* dzielenie *n* uczniów na grupy w zależności od poziomu

'stream•line *v/t* **1.** nadawać ⟨-dać⟩ opływowy kształt **2.** *production*: racjonalizować ⟨z-⟩ **3.** usprawniać ⟨-nić⟩; **'stream•lined** *adj* **1.** opływowy **2.** aerodynamiczny

street [stri:t] *s* ulica *f*; ***in the ~, on the ~*** na ulicy; ***the job is right up her ~*** *infml* to praca w sam raz dla niej; **'street•car** *s Am* tramwaj *m*; **street cred** ['stri:tkred] *s infml* **1.** wiarygodność *f* **2.** akceptacja *f* rówieśników; **'street kid** *s* dziecko *n* ulicy; **'street lamp**, **'street light** *s* latarnia *f* uliczna; **'street light•ing** *s* oświetlenie *n* ulic; **'street map** *s* plan *m* miasta; **'street mu•si•cian** *s* muzyk *m* uliczny; **'street peo•ple** *pl Am* ludzie *pl* ulicy, bezdomni *pl*; **'street val•ue** *s* wartość *f* rynkowa; **'street vend•or** *s* handlarz *m* uliczny; **'street•walk•er** *s dated* prostytutka *f*, ulicznica *f*; **'street-wise** *adj infml* cwany

strength [streŋθ] *s* **1.** siła *f*; ***~ of wind*** siła wiatru; ***~ of will*** siła woli; ***a show of ~*** manifestacja siły; ***on the ~ of*** **a)** dzięki *D* **b)** na mocy *G*; ***go from ~ to ~*** odnosić coraz większe sukcesy **2.** siły *pl* **3.** wytrzymałość *f* **4.** moc *f* **5.** mocna strona *f* **6.** zaleta **7.** *currency*: wartość *f* **8.** CHEM stężenie *n* **9.** liczba *f*; ***at full ~*** SPORT w pełnym składzie; **strength•en** ['streŋθn] **I** *v/t* **1.** wzmacniać ⟨-mocnić⟩ **2.** umacniać ⟨umocnić⟩ **II** *v/i* **1.** wzmacniać ⟨-mocnić⟩ się **2.** umacniać ⟨umocnić⟩ się **3.** wzmagać ⟨-móc⟩ się

stren•u•ous ['strenjʊəs] *adj* **1.** wyczerpujący **2.** forsowny **3.** *effort*: wytężony; **stren•u•ous•ly** ['strenjʊəslɪ] *adv* **1.** z wysiłkiem **2.** ciężko **3.** *deny*: stanowczo

stress [stres] **I** *s* **1.** stres *m*; ***under ~*** w stresie, zestresowany **2.** napięcie *n* **3.** obciążenie *n* **4.** nacisk *m*; ***lay ~ on*** kłaść nacisk na *A* **5.** akcent *m* **II** *v/t* **1.** kłaść ⟨położyć⟩ nacisk na *A* **2.** podkreślać ⟨-lić⟩ **3.** akcentować ⟨za-⟩; **stressed** [strest] *adj* **1.** zestresowany **2.** akcentowany; **stressed out** [stresd'aʊt] *adj* zestresowany; **stress•ful** ['stresfəl] *adj* stresujący; **'stress-free** *adj* bezstresowy

stretch [stretʃ] **I** *v/t* **1.** rozciągać ⟨-gnąć⟩; ***~ one's legs*** rozprostować nogi **2.** *line*: naciągać ⟨-gnąć⟩ **4.** (*a.* ***~ out***) *hand*: wyciągać ⟨-gnąć⟩ **5.** *facts*: naginać ⟨-giąć⟩ **II** *v/i* **1.** rozciągać ⟨-gnąć⟩ się; ***fields ~ed out as far as we could see*** jak okiem sięgnąć rozpościerały się pola **2.** ciągnąć się **3.** wyciągać ⟨-gnąć⟩ się; ***he ~ed and yawned*** przeciągnął się i ziewnął **4.** ***the history of the town ~es back to 1564*** historia miasta sięga roku 1564 **5.** (*talks*) przeciągać ⟨-gnąć⟩ się **6.** (*money*) wystarczać ⟨-czyć⟩ (***to*** na *A*) **III** *s* **1.** *road, river*: odcinek *m* **2.** okres *m*; ***at a ~*** bez przerwy **3.** *infml* odsiadka *f* **4.** ***do ~es*** rozciągać się **5.** rozciągliwość *f* **6.** ***by any ~ of the imagination*** w żadnym razie; **stretch•er** ['stretʃə] **I** *s* nosze *pl* **II** *v/t* nieść ⟨nosić⟩ na noszach; ***~ s.o. off the pitch*** znieść kogoś z boiska na noszach; **'stretch marks** *pl* rozstępy *pl*; **stretch•y** ['stretʃɪ] *adj* rozciągliwy

strick•en ['strɪkən] *adj* **1.** dotknięty (***with*** *I*); ***~ with disease*** dotknięty chorobą **2.** *area*: dotknięty klęską żywiołową

strict [strɪkt] *adj* **1.** surowy; ***be ~ with*** być surowym dla *G* **2.** rygorystyczny **3.** *diet, instructions*: ścisły **4.** ortodoksyjny **5.** bezwzględny; ***in the ~est confidence*** w największym zaufaniu; **strict•ly** ['strɪktlɪ] *adv* **1.** surowo; ***~ forbidden*** surowo wzbronione; ***be ~ brought up*** otrzymać surowe wychowanie **2.** rygorystycznie **3.** ściśle; ***~ speaking*** ściśle mówiąc **4.** wyłącznie

stride [straɪd] **I** (*strode*; *stridden*) *v/i* iść wielkimi krokami **II** *s* **1.** krok *m*; ***take s.th. in (one's) ~*** *fig* nie przejąć się czymś; ***get into one's ~***, ***hit one's ~*** *fig* znaleźć swój rytm **2.** chód *m* **3.** postęp *m*; ***make great ~s*** robić wielkie postępy

stri•dent ['straɪdnt] *adj sound*: ostry, przenikliwy

strid•den ['strɪdn] *Past Participle* → ***stride I***

strife [straɪf] *s lit* **1.** konflikty *pl* **2.** kłótnie *pl*

strike [straɪk] **I** (*struck*; *struck*) *v/t* **1.** uderzać ⟨-rzyć⟩; ***the tree was struck by lightning*** w drzewo uderzył piorun; ***it suddenly struck me that*** nagle uświadomiłem sobie, że; ***~ while the iron is hot*** kuj żelazo póki gorące **2.** *blow*: zadawać ⟨-dać⟩ **3.** ***~ a deal*** dobić targu **4.** ***~ a balance between*** znaleźć złoty środek pomiędzy *I* **5.** atakować ⟨za-⟩ **6.** ***the town was struck by an epidemic*** w mieście wybuchła epidemia **7.** *matches*: zapalać ⟨-lić⟩ **8.** *six o'clock*: wybijać ⟨-bić⟩ **9.** *tune*: grać ⟨za-⟩ **10.** *gold, oil*: odkrywać ⟨-ryć⟩, natrafiać ⟨-fić⟩ na *A* **11.** ***be struck dumb*** oniemieć; ***be struck blind*** oślepnąć; ***be struck deaf*** ogłuchnąć **II** (*struck*; *struck*) *v/i* **1.** uderzać ⟨-rzyć⟩ **2.** atakować ⟨za-⟩ **3.** (*disaster*) wydarzyć się **4.** strajkować ⟨za-⟩ **III** *s* **1.** strajk *m*; ***go on ~*** zastrajkować **2.** uderzenie *n* **3.** atak *m*; **strike back** *v/i* **1.** odpowiadać ⟨-wiedzieć⟩ atakiem na atak **2.** zrewanżować się; **strike down** *v/t* **1.** powalać ⟨-lić⟩ **2.** ***be struck down by a heart attack*** dostać ataku serca **3.** *law*: uchylać ⟨-lić⟩; **strike off** *v/t* (*on list*) usuwać ⟨usunąć⟩, skreślać ⟨-lić⟩; **strike out I** *v/i* **1.** ***~ on one's own*** usamodzielniać ⟨-nić⟩ się **2.** atakować ⟨za-⟩ (***at*** *A*) **3.** wyruszać ⟨-szyć⟩ **II** *v/t* wykreślać ⟨-lić⟩; **strike up** *v/t* **1.** *conversation*: rozpoczynać ⟨-cząć⟩ **2.** ***~ a friendship with*** zaprzyjaźnić się z *I*)

'strike•bound *adj* sparaliżowany przez strajk; **'strike•break•er** *s* łamistrajk *m*; **strike call** *s* wezwanie *n* do strajku; **'strike pay** *s* zasiłek *m* strajkowy (wypłacany przez związek zawodowy)

strik•er ['straɪkə] *s* **1.** strajkujący *m* **2.** (*football*) napastnik *m*; **strik•ing** ['straɪkɪŋ] *adj* **1.** uderzający **2.** rzucający się w oczy **3.** *beauty*: niezwykły

string [strɪŋ] **I** *s* **1.** sznurek *m* **2.** żyłka *f* **3.** *pearls*: sznur *m* **4.** seria *f* **5.** pasmo *n* **6.** INF ciąg *m*, łańcuch *m* **7.** MUS struna *f*; ***the ~s*** instrumenty strunowe, *infml* smyczki **8.** (*racket*) struna *f*, naciąg *m* **II** *adj* **1.** *instrument*: strunowy **2.** sznurkowy; ***a ~ bag*** siatka **3.** siatkowy **III** *v/t* **1.** wieszać ⟨powiesić⟩ **2.** nizać ⟨na-⟩ (***on*** na *A*) **3.** zakładać ⟨założyć⟩ naciąg w *L*; **string along I** *v/t infml* zwodzić ⟨zwieść⟩ **II** *v/i Br* włóczyć się (***with*** z *I*); **string out** *v/t talks*: przeciągać ⟨-gnąć⟩; **string together** *v/t sentences*: klecić ⟨s-⟩; **string up** *v/t infml* wieszać ⟨powiesić⟩

string 'bean *s* fasolka *f* szparagowa

stringed in•stru•ment [strɪŋd 'instrʊmənt] *s* instrument *m* strunowy

strin•gent ['strɪndʒnt] *adj* **1.** surowy **2.** rygorystyczny

'string play•er *s* muzyk *m* grający na instrumentach strunowych

string•y ['strɪŋɪ] *adj* **1.** *hair*: zlepiony w strąki **2.** *hair*: rzadki **3.** *meat*: włóknisty **4.** *neck*: chudy

strip [strɪp] **I** *v/i* (*a.* ***~ off***) rozbierać ⟨-zebrać⟩ się **II** *v/t* **1.** (*a.* ***~ off***) rozbierać ⟨-zebrać⟩; ***~ to the waist*** rozebrać się do pasa **2.** *paint*: zdrapywać ⟨-pać⟩ **3.** *wallpaper*: zrywać ⟨zerwać⟩, zdzierać ⟨zedrzeć⟩ **4.** ***~ the beds*** ściągnąć pościel **5.** *mechanism*: rozbierać ⟨-zebrać⟩ (na kawałki) **6.** pozbawiać ⟨-wić⟩ (***of*** *G*) **III** *s* **1.** pasek *m* **2.** *land, water*: pas *m* **3.** SPORT stroje *pl* **4.** striptiz *m*; **strip car'•toon** *s Br* historyjka *f* obrazkowa, komiks *m*; **'strip club** *s* klub *m* ze striptizem

stripe [straɪp] *s* **1.** pas *m*; ***white tablecloth with red ~s*** biały obrus w czerwone pasy **2.** pasek *m* **3.** prążek *m* **4.** naszywka *f* **5.** (*band-like*) belka *f*; **striped** [straɪpt] *adj* **1.** w paski **2.** w pasy **3.** prążkowany **4.** pręgowany

'strip joint *Am* → ***strip club***; **'strip light** *s* świetlówka *f*; **strip•per** ['strɪpə] *s* striptizer *m*, striptizerka *f*; **strip'tease** *s* striptiz *m*

S

strive [straɪv] *v/i* (*strived/strove*; *striven*) dążyć (***for*** do *G*)
striv•en ['strɪvn] *Past Participle* → **strive**
strobe (light) [strəʊb] *s* stroboskop *m*
strode [strəʊd] *Past Simple* → **stride**
stroke [strəʊk] **I** *s* **1.** uderzenie *n*; ***a ~ of genius*** przebłysk geniuszu; ***it was a ~ of luck that I met you*** miałem szczęście, że cię spotkałem; ***on the ~ of three*** z wybiciem trzeciej; ***at a ~*** za jednym zamachem **2.** (*swimming*) styl *m* **3.** ruch *m* **4.** ***give s.o. a ~*** pogłaskać kogoś **5.** pociągnięcie *n*; ***a brush ~*** pociągnięcie pędzlem **6.** MED udar *m* **7.** TECH suw *m*; ***a four-~ engine*** silnik czterosuwowy **II** *v/t* **1.** głaskać ⟨po-⟩ **2.** *infml* przymilać ⟨-lić⟩ się do *G*
stroll [strəʊl] **I** *v/i* przechadzać ⟨przejść⟩ się, spacerować **II** *s* przechadzka *f*, spacer *m*; **stroll•er** ['strəʊlə] *s* **1.** spacerowicz *m* **2.** (*pushchair*) *Am* wózek *m* spacerowy, *infml* spacerówka *f*
strong [strɒŋ] *adj* **1.** silny **2.** mocny **3.** *clothes, house*: solidny **4.** *taste*: intensywny **5.** *colour*: żywy **6.** *opponent*: zdecydowany **7.** *fan*: zagorzały **8.** *language*: dosadny **9.** *verb*: nieregularny **10.** ***a 2000-~ crowd*** dwutysięczny tłum; '**strong•box** *s* kasa *f* pancerna, sejf *m*; '**strong•hold** *s* **1.** twierdza *f* **2.** *fig* bastion *m*; **strong•ly** ['strɒŋlɪ] *adv* **1.** silnie **2.** mocno **3.** ***~-built*** *man*: dobrze zbudowany **4.** intensywnie **5.** dosadnie **6.** ***be ~ opposed to*** być zdecydowanym przeciwnikiem *G*; **strong-mind•ed** [strɒŋ'maɪndɪd] *adj* zdecydowany; '**strong•room** *s* skarbiec *m*; **strong-willed** [strɒŋ'wɪld] *adj* uparty
stron•ti•um ['strɒntɪəm] *s* CHEM stront *m*
strove [strəʊv] *Past Simple* → **strive**
struck [strʌk] *Past Simple and Past Participle* → **strike**
struc•tur•al ['strʌktʃərl] *adj* **1.** strukturalny **2.** konstrukcyjny; **struc•tur•al•ly** ['strʌktʃərəlɪ] *adv* **1.** strukturalnie **2.** konstrukcyjnie; **struc•ture** ['strʌktʃə] **I** *s* **1.** struktura *f* **2.** budowa *f* **3.** konstrukcja *f* **4.** budowla *f* **II** *v/t* **1.** organizować ⟨z-⟩ **2.** układać ⟨ułożyć⟩
strug•gle ['strʌgl] **I** *v/i* **1.** walczyć (***for*** o *A*); ***~ for freedom*** walczyć o wolność; ***~ for breath*** próbować złapać oddech **2.** dążyć (***for*** do *G*) **3.** zmagać się (***with/against*** z *I*) **4.** mocować się (***with*** z *I*); ***~ free*** wyrwać się **5.** ***~ up the hill*** z trudem wchodzić pod górę **II** *s* walka *f*; ***a ~ for survival*** walka o przetrwanie; **struggle on** *v/i* **1.** nie poddawać się **2.** radzić sobie (w trudnej sytuacji)
strum [strʌm] **I** *v/i* grać (***on*** na *L*); ***~ a guitar*** grać na gitarze **II** *v/t* grać (na *L*)
strung [strʌŋ] *Past Simple and Past Participle* → **string**
strut[1] [strʌt] *v/i* **1.** paradować **2.** kroczyć dumnie
strut[2] [~] *s* podpora *f*
strych•nine ['strɪkni:n] *s* strychnina *f*
stub [stʌb] **I** *s* **1.** niedopałek *m* **2.** *ticket*: odcinek *m* **II** *v/t* ***~ one's toe*** uderzyć się w palec (u nogi) (***against*** o *A*); **stub out** *v/t cigarette*: gasić ⟨z-⟩
stub•ble ['stʌbl] *s* **1.** ściernisko *n*, rżysko *n* **2.** kilkudniowy zarost *m*, *fig* szczecina *f*; **stub•bly** ['stʌblɪ] *adj* nieogolony
stub•born ['stʌbən] *adj* **1.** uparty **2.** *stain*: uporczywy
stub•by ['stʌbɪ] *adj*: ***~ fingers*** krótkie, grube palce
stuc•co ['stʌkəʊ] *s* **1.** tynk *m* (szlachetny) **2.** stiuk *m*
stuck [stʌk] **I** *Past Simple and Past Participle* → **stick** **II** *adj* **1.** zablokowany; ***get ~*** utknąć; ***their car got ~ in the snow*** ich samochód ugrzązł w śniegu; ***be ~ in traffic*** tkwić w korku **2.** zaklinowany **3.** ***I'm ~ for words*** nie wiem, co powiedzieć **4.** ***be ~ with s.o.*** *infml* być skazanym na kogoś **5.** ***get ~ into*** zabrać się ochoczo do *G*; **stuck-'up** *adj infml* nadęty
stud[1] [stʌd] *s* **1.** ćwiek *m* **2.** gwóźdź *m* (ozdobny) **3.** kolczyk *m* **4.** (*part of football shoe*) korek *m* **5.** śruba *f* dwustronna
stud[2] [~] *s* **1.** *a. fig* ogier *m* **2.** stadnina *f*
stu•dent ['stju:dnt] *s* **1.** student *m*; ***~(s') union*** *Br* samorząd studencki

2. uczeń *m*; **stu•dent 'driv•er** *s Am* początkujący kierowca *m*
'stud farm *s* stadnina *f*
stud•ied ['stʌdɪd] *adj* wystudiowany
stu•di•o ['stu:dɪəʊ] *pl -dios s* **1.** studio *n* **2.** pracownia *f* **3.** kawalerka *f*; **stu•di-o 'au•di•ence** *s* publiczność *f* w studio; **'stu•di•o couch** *s* rozkładana kanapa *f*; **'stu•di•o flat** *Br*, ***'stu•di•o apart•ment*** *Am* → ***studio 3***
stu•di•ous ['stu:dɪəs] *adj student*: pilny
stud•y ['stʌdɪ] **I** *v/t* **1.** uczyć ⟨na-⟩ się; ***~ English*** uczyć się angielskiego **2.** studiować ⟨prze-⟩; ***~ at a university*** studiować na uniwersytecie **3.** badać ⟨z-⟩ **II** *s* **1.** nauka *f* **2.** ***studies*** studia *pl* **3.** badanie *n* **4.** badania *pl*; ***make a ~ of***, ***carry out a ~ of*** zbadać *A*, przeprowadzić badania *G* **5.** praca *f* **6.** studium *n* **7.** gabinet *m* **8.** MUS *Br* etiuda *f*
stuff [stʌf] **I** *s* **1.** *infml* rzecz *f*; ***they're made of some weird plastic ~*** są zrobione z jakiegoś dziwnego plastiku; ***this wine is good ~*** niezłe to wino; ***it's expensive ~*** to droga rzecz; ***they know their ~*** są dobrzy w tym, co robią **2.** *infml* rzeczy *pl*; ***where's my ~?*** gdzie są moje rzeczy?; ***I've got lots of ~ to do today*** mam dziś mnóstwo roboty **3.** *infml* towar *m* **4.** ***s.th. has become the ~ of legend*** coś stało się legendarne **II** *v/t* **1.** wypychać ⟨-pchać⟩ (***with*** *I*); ***the fridge is ~ed to bursting*** lodówka pęka w szwach **2.** upychać ⟨upchać⟩ **3.** nadziewać ⟨-dziać⟩ **4.** ***~ oneself*** *infml* opychać się, objadać się; **stuffed** [stʌft] *adj* **1.** *infml* napchany **2.** nadziewany; **stuffed shirt** *s infml* nadęty nudziarz *m*; **stuff•ing** ['stʌfɪŋ] *s* **1.** farsz *m* **2.** nadzienie *n* **3.** wypełnienie *n*
stuff•y ['stʌfɪ] *adj* **1.** duszny; ***it's ~ in here*** tu jest duszno **2.** *infml* sztywny **3.** *infml* niemodny
stum•ble ['stʌmbl] *v/i* **1.** potykać ⟨-tknąć⟩ się (***on/over*** o *A*) **2.** iść ⟨pójść⟩ niepewnym krokiem **3.** ***~ over a word*** zaciąć się; **stumble across** *v/i* natykać ⟨-tknąć⟩ się na *A*
stum•bling-block ['stʌmblɪŋblɒk] *s* przeszkoda *f*
stump [stʌmp] **I** *s* **1.** pień *m* **2.** kikut *m* **3.** *infml pencil*: ogryzek *m* **4.** kawałek *m* **II** *v/t* ***~ s.o.*** zabić komuś ćwieka; ***I'm ~ed*** **a)** nie wiem, o co chodzi **b)** jestem w kropce **III** *v/i* ***~ out of the room*** wyjść ciężkim krokiem z pokoju; **stump up** *v/i Br infml* bulić ⟨za-⟩ (***for*** za *A*)
stump•y ['stʌmpɪ] *adj*: ***~ fingers*** krótkie, grube palce
stun [stʌn] *v/t* **1.** ogłuszać ⟨-szyć⟩ **2.** oszałamiać ⟨oszołomić⟩
stung [stʌŋ] *Past Simple and Past Participle* → ***sting***
stunk [stʌŋk] *Past Simple and Past Participle* → ***stink***
stun•ner ['stʌnə] *s*: ***be a ~*** *infml* być fantastycznym; ***she's a ~*** *infml* powala na kolana; **stun•ning** ['stʌnɪŋ] *adj* oszałamiający
stunt¹ [stʌnt] *s* **1.** wyczyn *m* kaskaderski **2.** chwyt *m*; ***a publicity ~*** chwyt reklamowy **3.** *infml* wygłup *m*
stunt² [~] *v/t* hamować ⟨za-⟩
stunt fly•ing *s* akrobacja *f* lotnicza; **stunt•man** ['stʌntmæn] *pl -men s* kaskader *m*; **'stunt wom•an** *pl -men s* kaskaderka *f*
stu•pe•fy ['stju:pɪfaɪ] *v/t* **1.** oszałamiać ⟨oszołomić⟩ **2.** szokować ⟨za-⟩
stu•pen•dous [stju:'pendəs] *adj* **1.** ogromny **2.** olbrzymi **3.** imponujący **4.** kolosalny
stu•pid ['stju:pɪd] **I** *adj* głupi; ***it was ~ of you*** to było głupie z twojej strony **II** *s infml* głuptas *m*; ***yes, ~, I'm talking to you*** tak, głuptasie, mówię do ciebie; **stu•pid•i•ty** [stju:'pɪdətɪ] *s* głupota *f*
stu•por ['stju:pə] *s* **1.** otępienie *n* **2.** osłupienie *n*, stupor *m* **3.** zamroczenie *n*; ***in a drunken ~*** w zamroczeniu alkoholowym
stur•dy ['stɜ:dɪ] *adj* **1.** mocny; ***of ~ build*** mocno zbudowany **2.** solidny **3.** *person*: silny
stur•geon ['stɜ:dʒən] *pl -geon, geons s* BIOL jesiotr *m*
stut•ter ['stʌtə] **I** *v/i* **1.** jąkać się **2.** ***~ along*** wlec się **II** *v/t* wyjąkać **III** *s* jąkanie się *n*; ***have a ~*** jąkać się; **stut•ter•er** ['stʌtərə] *s* jąkała *m/f*
sty¹ [staɪ] *s* chlew *m*
sty² [~] *s* MED jęczmyk *m*, jęczmień *m*
style [staɪl] **I** *s* **1.** styl *m*; ***the Gothic ~*** styl gotycki; ***it's not my ~*** to nie w moim stylu **2.** model *m* **3.** fason

S

m **II** *v/t* **1.** stylizować ⟨wy-⟩ **2.** *hair*: modelować ⟨wy-⟩; ***styling mousse*** pianka do włosów
styl•ish ['staılıʃ] *adj* **1.** stylowy **2.** elegancki; **styl•ist** ['staılıst] *s* stylista *m*; **sty•lis•tic** [staı'lıstık] *adj* stylistyczny
styl•ized *adj* stylizowany
sty•lus ['staıləs] *pl -luses s* igła *f* (gramofonowa)
sty•mie ['staımı] *v/t plan*: udaremniać ⟨-nić⟩
styp•tic ['stıptık] *s MED* środek *m* ściągający
Sty•ro•foam® ['staırəfəʊm] *s Am* styropian *m*
suave [swɑːv] *adj person*: gładki w obyciu
sub [sʌb] *s infml* **1.** łódź *f* podwodna **2.** *SPORT* rezerwowy *m* **3.** *Br* składka *f*
sub•com•mit•tee ['sʌbkəmıtı] *s* podkomisja *f*
sub•con•scious [sʌb'kɒnʃəs] **I** *adj* podświadomy **II** *s* ***the ~*** podświadomość *f*; **sub•con•scious•ly** [sʌb'kɒnʃəslı] *adv* podświadomie
sub•con•ti•nent [sʌb'kɒntınənt] *s* subkontynent *m*
sub•con•tract I [sʌbkən'trækt] *v/t* **1.** zlecać ⟨-cić⟩ podwykonanie **2.** ***~ a company to do the work*** zlecić roboty podwykonawcy **II** [sʌb'kɒntrækt] *s* umowa *f* o podwykonawstwo; **sub•con•trac•tor** [sʌbkɒn'træktə] *s* podwykonawca *m*
sub•cul•ture ['sʌbkʌltʃə] *s* subkultura *f*
sub•cu•ta•ne•ous [sʌbkjuː'teınıəs] *adj injection*: podskórny
sub•di•vide [sʌbdı'vaıd] *v/t* dzielić ⟨po-⟩ (na mniejsze części); **sub•di•vi•sion** [sʌbdı'vıʒn] *s* (dalszy) podział *m*
sub•due [səb'djuː] *v/t* **1.** tłumić ⟨s-⟩ **2.** poskramiać ⟨-romić⟩ **3.** *fear*: przełamywać ⟨-mać⟩ **4.** *inflation*: zdławić; **sub•dued** [səb'djuːd] *adj* **1.** *person*: przygaszony **2.** *light, sound*: przytłumiony **3.** *colour*: stonowany
sub•ed•i•tor ['sʌbedıtə] *s* **1.** zastępca *m* redaktora **2.** asystent *m* redaktora
sub•head•ing ['sʌbhedıŋ] *s* śródtytuł *m*
sub•hu•man [sʌb'hjuːmən] *adj* nieludzki
sub•ject ['sʌbdʒıkt] **I** *s* **1.** temat *m*; ***change the ~*** zmienić temat; ***get off the ~*** zboczyć z tematu **2.** (*school*) przedmiot *m* **3.** obiekt *m* **4.** poddany *m* **5.** *GRAM* podmiot *m* **II** *adj* **1.** ***be ~ to*** podlegać *D*; ***be ~ to copyright law*** podlegać przepisom prawa autorskiego **2.** narażony (**to** na *A*) **3.** zależny (**to** od *G*); ***all advertising copy is ~ to editorial approval*** treść materiałów reklamowych musi zostać zaakceptowana przez redaktora **4.** poddany (**to** *D*) **III** *v/t* **1.** poddawać ⟨-dać⟩ (**to** *D*) **2.** narażać ⟨-zić⟩ (**to** na *A*) **3.** *country*: podporządkowywać ⟨-kować⟩; **sub•jec•tion** [səb'dʒekʃn] *s* podporządkowanie *n*; **sub•jec•tive** [səb'dʒektıv] *adj* subiektywny; **'sub•ject mat•ter** *s* **1.** temat *m* **2.** tematyka *f* **3.** przedmiot *m*
sub•ju•gate ['sʌbdʒʊgeıt] *v/t* podporządkowywać ⟨-kować⟩ (**s.th. to** coś *D*)
sub•junc•tive (mood) [səb'dʒʌŋktıv] *s* tryb *m* łączący
sub•lease [sʌb'liːs] *v/t* **1.** podnajmować ⟨-nająć⟩ **2.** poddzierżawiać ⟨-wić⟩
sub•let [sʌb'let] (*sublet*; *sublet*) *v/t* **1.** podnajmować ⟨-nająć⟩ **2.** poddzierżawiać ⟨-wić⟩
sub•lime [sə'blaım] **I** *adj* **1.** *beauty*: niezwykły **2.** cudowny **3.** *confidence*: wyjątkowy **II** *s* ***from the ~ to the ridiculous*** od wzniosłości do śmieszności; **sub•lim•i•nal** [sʌb'lımınl] *adj* podświadomy
sub•ma'chine gun [sʌbmə'ʃiːngʌn] *s* (ręczny) pistolet *m* maszynowy
sub•ma•rine ['sʌbməriːn] **I** *s* łódź *f* podwodna **II** *adj life, plant*: podwodny; **sub•ma•rin•er** [sʌb'mærınə] *s* marynarz *m* z załogi łodzi podwodnej, *infml* podwodniak *m*
sub•merge [səb'mɜːdʒ] **I** *v/i* zanurzać ⟨-rzyć⟩ się **II** *v/t* **1.** zanurzać ⟨-rzyć⟩ **2.** *field*: zalewać ⟨-lać⟩ **3.** *feelings*: ukrywać ⟨-ryć⟩
sub•mis•sion [səb'mıʃn] *s* **1.** uległość *f* **2.** poddanie się *n* **3.** złożenie *n* **4.** przedłożenie *n*; **sub•mis•sive** [səb'mısıv] *adj* **1.** uległy **2.** posłuszny
sub•mit [səb'mıt] *v/t* **1.** składać ⟨złożyć⟩ **2.** przedkładać ⟨-dłożyć⟩ **3.** poddawać ⟨-dać⟩ się (**to** *D*)
sub•nor•mal [sʌb'nɔːml] *adj person*: opóźniony w rozwoju

sub•or•di•nate [sə'bɔːdɪnət] **I** *adj* **1.** podporządkowany **2.** podrzędny **3.** niższej rangi **4.** ***be ~ to*** podlegać *D* **II** *s* podwładny *m* **III** *v/t* podporządkowywać ⟨-kować⟩ (***to*** *D*)

sub•plot ['sʌbplɒt] *s* wątek *m* poboczny

sub•poe•na [səb'piːnə] **I** *s* wezwanie *n* do sądu **II** *v/t* wzywać ⟨wezwać⟩; ***~ s.o. to appear as a witness*** wezwać kogoś na świadka

sub•scribe [səb'skraɪb] *v/i* **1.** zgadzać ⟨zgodzić⟩ się (***to*** z *I*) **2.** *theory*: uznawać ⟨-nać⟩ (***to*** *A*) **3.** prenumerować (***to*** *A*) **4.** abonować (***to*** *A*) **5.** subskrybować (***to*** *A*) **6.** opłacać ⟨-cić⟩ składki (***to*** na rzecz *G*) **7.** wspierać ⟨wesprzeć⟩ finansowo (***to*** *A*) **8.** (*shares*) zapisywać ⟨-sać⟩ się (***for*** na *A*); **sub•scrib•er** [səb'skraɪbə] *s* **1.** prenumerator *m* **2.** abonent *m* **3.** subskrybent *m*; **sub•scrip•tion** [səb'skrɪpʃn] *s* **1.** prenumerata *f* **2.** abonament *m* **3.** składka *f* (członkowska) **4.** subskrypcja *f* **5.** datek *m*

sub•sec•tion ['sʌbsekʃn] *s* podpunkt *m*

sub•se•quent ['sʌbsɪkwənt] *adj* **1.** następny **2.** późniejszy; ***~ to*** po *L*; ***~ to the meeting*** po spotkaniu; **sub•se•quent•ly** ['sʌbsɪkwəntlɪ] *adv* **1.** następnie **2.** później

sub•ser•vi•ence [səb'sɜːvɪəns] **1.** służalczość *f* **2.** uległość *f*; **sub•ser•vi•ent** [səb'sɜːvɪənt] *adj* **1.** służalczy **2.** podrzędny (***to*** w stosunku do *G*)

sub•side [səb'saɪd] *v/i* **1.** zelżeć **2.** (*water*) opadać ⟨opaść⟩ **3.** (*house*) osiadać ⟨osiąść⟩ **4.** zapadać ⟨-paść⟩ się

sub•sid•ence ['səbsaɪdəns] *s* **1.** *house*: osiadanie *n* **2.** zapadanie się *n*

sub•sid•i•ar•i•ty [səbsɪdɪ'ærɪtɪ] *s* subsydiarność *f*, pomocniczość *f*; ***the principle of ~*** zasada subsydiarności

S

sub•sid•i•a•ry [səb'sɪdɪərɪ] **I** *adj* **1.** drugorzędny **2.** pomocniczy **3.** *subject*: uzupełniający **4.** ***a ~ company*** spółka zależna **II** *s* spółka *f* zależna

sub•si•dize ['sʌbsɪdaɪz] *v/t* **1.** dotować **2.** wspierać ⟨wesprzeć⟩ finansowo

sub•si•dy ['sʌbsɪdɪ] *s* **1.** dotacja *f* **2.** subwencja *f*

sub•sist [sʌb'sɪst] *v/i* **1.** utrzymywać ⟨-mać⟩ się (***on*** z *G*) **2.** przeżywać ⟨-żyć⟩ **3.** pozostawać w mocy; **sub•sist•ence** [səb'sɪstəns] *s* utrzymanie się *n* (przy życiu); **sub'sist•ence level** *s* minimum *n* egzystencji

sub•stance ['sʌbstəns] *s* **1.** substancja *f* **2.** środek *m* **3.** ***allegations without ~*** bezpodstawne zarzuty; ***there is some ~ in what he says*** w tym, co mówi, jest trochę prawdy **4.** treść *f* **5.** istota *f* **6.** waga *f* **7.** ***a man of ~*** człowiek zamożny

sub•stan•dard [sʌb'stændəd] *adj* **1.** niespełniający wymagań jakościowych **2.** złej jakości

sub•stan•tial [səb'stænʃl] *adj* **1.** znaczny **2.** istotny **3.** *breakfast*: obfity **4.** *damage*: poważny **5.** *damages*: wysoki **6.** pokaźnych rozmiarów; **sub•stan•tial•ly** [səb'stænʃlɪ] *adv* **1.** znacznie **2.** istotnie **3.** *damage*: poważnie **4.** bardzo **5.** w zasadzie

sub•stan•ti•ate [səb'stænʃɪeɪt] *v/t form* **1.** potwierdzać ⟨-dzić⟩ **2.** popierać ⟨poprzeć⟩ dowodami

sub•stan•tive [sʌb'stæntɪv] **I** *adj* **1.** istotny **2.** poważny **3.** konkretny **II** *s dated* rzeczownik *m*

sub•sti•tute ['sʌbstɪtjuːt] **I** *s* **1.** substytut *m*, zamiennik *m*; ***there is no ~ for practical experience*** nic nie zastąpi praktyki **2.** zastępca *m* **3.** SPORT rezerwowy *m*; ***the ~s' bench*** ławka rezerwowych **II** *adj* **1.** zastępczy **2.** rezerwowy **III** *v/t* zastępować ⟨-tąpić⟩; ***~ margarine for butter*** zastąpić masło margaryną; **sub•sti•tu•tion** [sʌbstɪ'tjuːʃn] *s* **1.** zastąpienie *n* **2.** zmiana *f*

'sub•struc•ture ['sʌbstrʌktʃə] *s* **1.** podbudowa *f* **2.** *fig* fundament *m*

sub•ten•ant [sʌb'tenənt] *s* **1.** podnajemca *m* **2.** poddzierżawca *m*

sub•ter•fuge ['sʌbtəfjuːdʒ] *s* **1.** wybieg *m* **2.** podstęp *m*

sub•ter•ra•ne•an [sʌbtə'reɪnɪən] *adj* podziemny

sub•ti•tle ['sʌbtaɪtl] **I** *s* **1.** podtytuł *m* **2.** ***~s*** FILM napisy *pl* **II** *v/t* **1.** ***be ~d*** (*book*) nosić podtytuł **2.** ***an Icelandic film ~d in English*** islandzki film z angielskimi napisami

sub•tle ['sʌtl] *adj* subtelny; **sub•tle•ty** ['sʌtltɪ] *s* subtelność *f*

sub•to•tal ['sʌbtəʊtl] *s* suma *f* częściowa

sub•tract [səb'trækt] *v/t* odejmować ⟨odjąć⟩; **sub•trac•tion** [səb'trækʃn] *s* odejmowanie *n*

sub•trop•i•cal [sʌb'trɒpɪkl] *adj* podzwrotnikowy

sub•urb ['sʌbɜːb] *s* przedmieście *n*; **~s** przedmieścia; ***she lives in the ~s*** mieszka na przedmieściu

sub•ur•ban [sə'bɜːbən] *adj* **1.** *street*: podmiejski **2.** *houses*: na przedmieściach **3.** drobnomieszczański

sub•ur•bi•a [sə'bɜːbɪə] *s* przedmieścia *pl*

sub•ver•sion [səb'vɜːʃn] *s* działalność *f* wywrotowa; **sub•ver•sive** [səb'vɜːsɪv] *adj* wywrotowy

sub•vert [sʌb'vɜːt] *v/t* **1.** obalać ⟨-lić⟩ **2.** *belief*: podważać ⟨-żyć⟩

sub•way ['sʌbweɪ] *s* **1.** *Br* przejście *n* podziemne **2.** *Am* metro *n*

suc•ceed [sək'siːd] **I** *v/i* **1.** udawać ⟨udać⟩ się **2.** powieść się; ***our plan ~ed*** nasz plan się powiódł **3.** ***I ~ed in doing it*** udało mi się to zrobić **4.** osiągać ⟨-gnąć⟩ sukces (***in*** w *L*, ***as*** jako *N*) **5.** *throne*: obejmować ⟨objąć⟩ (***to*** *A*) **6.** *title*: dziedziczyć ⟨o-⟩ (***to*** *A*) **II** *v/t* następować ⟨-tąpić⟩ po *L*; ***~ s.o. as president*** objąć po kimś urząd prezydenta; **suc•ceed•ing** [sək'siːdɪŋ] *adj* następny

suc•cess [sək'ses] *s* **1.** sukces *m*; ***the key to ~*** klucz do sukcesu; ***have ~*** osiągnąć sukces; ***meet with ~*** zakończyć się sukcesem **2.** powodzenie *n*; ***without ~*** bez powodzenia; **suc•cess•ful** [sək'sesfl] *adj* **1.** udany **2.** pomyślny **3.** ***the play was very ~*** sztuka odniosła wielki sukces; ***he was ~ in convincing her*** udało mu się ją przekonać **4.** *company*: prosperujący **5.** ***a ~ writer*** pisarz, który odniósł sukces; **suc•cess•ful•ly** [sək'sesfəlɪ] *adv* **1.** pomyślnie **2.** ***the spacecraft has been ~ launched*** start pojazdu kosmicznego powiódł się

suc•ces•sion [sək'seʃn] *s* **1.** seria *f*; ***a ~ of events*** seria następujących po sobie wydarzeń; ***in rapid ~*** jeden po drugim; ***three years in ~*** trzy lata z rzędu **2.** następowanie *n* po sobie **3.** sukcesja *f*; **suc•ces•sive** [sək'sesɪv] *adj* **1.** z rzędu **2.** kolejny; **suc•ces•sor** [sək'sesə] *s* **1.** następca *m* **2.** sukcesor *m*

suc•cinct [sək'sɪŋkt] *adj* zwięzły

suc•cu•lent ['sʌkjʊlənt] **I** *adj* soczysty **II** *s* BIOL sukulent *m*, roślina *f* gruboszowata

suc•cumb [sə'kʌm] *v/i* **1.** poddawać ⟨-dać⟩ się **2.** ulegać ⟨-lec⟩

such [sʌtʃ] **I** *adj* taki; ***~ a person*** taka osoba; ***there is no ~ thing*** nie ma czegoś takiego; ***in ~ a way*** w taki sposób; ***it's ~ a beautiful day!*** jaki piękny dzień! **II** *pron* taki; ***~ as*** **a)** taki jak **b)** na przykład; ***~ as this*** taki jak; ***as ~*** jako taki; ***and ~*** i tym podobne; '**such•like I** *pron* ***and ~*** i tym podobne **II** *adj* i tym podobny

suck [sʌk] **I** *v/t* **1.** ssać **2.** wysysać ⟨wyssać⟩ (***out of*** z *G*) **3.** zasysać ⟨zassać⟩ **II** *v/t* **1.** (*baby*): ssać **2.** *Am infml* ***it ~s!*** to jest do dupy; **suck up to** *v/i infml* podlizywać się *D*

suck•er ['sʌkə] *s* **1.** *infml* frajer *m* **2.** przyssawka *f* **3.** (*plant*) odrost *m*

suck•le ['sʌkl] **I** *v/t* **1.** (*woman*) karmić ⟨na-⟩ piersią **2.** (*animal*) karmić ⟨na-⟩ mlekiem **II** *v/i* ssać (pierś); **suckling pig** [sʌklɪŋ'pɪg] *s* prosię *n* (ssące)

suc•tion ['sʌkʃn] *s* ssanie *n*; '**suc•tion pump** *s* pompa *f* ssąca

Su•dan [suː'dɑːn] *s* Sudan *m*

sud•den ['sʌdn] *adj* nagły; **sud•den•ly** ['sʌdnlɪ] *adv* **1.** nagle **2.** nieoczekiwanie **3.** znienacka

suds [sʌdz] *pl* mydliny *pl*

sue [suː] **I** *v/t* **1.** pozywać ⟨-zwać⟩ (do sądu); ***~ s.o. for damages*** wnieść przeciw komuś powództwo o odszkodowanie **2.** zaskarżać ⟨-żyć⟩ **II** *v/i* wnosić ⟨wnieść⟩ sprawę do sądu; ***~ for divorce*** wnieść pozew o rozwód

suede [sweɪd] **I** *s* zamsz *m* **II** *adj* zamszowy

su•et ['sʊɪt] *s* łój *m*

suf•fer ['sʌfə] **I** *v/i* cierpieć ⟨u-⟩; ***~ from asthma*** cierpieć na astmę, mieć astmę; ***be ~ing from a cold*** być przeziębionym; ***he's ~ing from shock*** doznał szoku **II** *v/t* **1.** *defeat*: doznawać ⟨-nać⟩ **2.** *heart attack*: mieć **3.** *loss*: ponosić ⟨-nieść⟩; **suf•fer•er** ['sʌfərə] *s* chory *m*; ***asthma ~s*** chorzy na astmę; **suf•fer•ing** ['sʌfərɪŋ] *s* cierpienie *n*

suf•fice [sə'faɪs] *v/i* wystarczać ⟨-czyć⟩; ***a phone call will ~*** wystarczy telefon

S

suf•fi•cient [sə'fɪʃnt] *adj* **1.** wystarczający; ***is 200 dollars ~ for our expenses?*** czy 200 dolarów wystarczy na nasze wydatki? **2.** dostateczny; ***there wasn't ~ evidence to convict her*** nie było dostatecznych dowodów, aby ją skazać; **suf•fi•cient•ly** [sə'fɪʃntlɪ] *adv* **1.** wystarczająco **2.** dostatecznie

suf•fix ['sʌfɪks] *s* sufiks *m*, przyrostek *m*

suf•fo•cate ['sʌfəkeɪt] **I** *v/i* dusić ⟨u-⟩ się; ***it's suffocating in here*** strasznie tu duszno **II** *v/t* dusić ⟨u-⟩; **suf•fo•ca•tion** [sʌfə'keɪʃn] *s* uduszenie *n*

suf•frage ['sʌfrɪdʒ] prawa *pl* wyborcze

suf•fuse [sə'fjuːz] *v/t lit* **1.** nasycać ⟨-cić⟩ **2.** przesycać ⟨-cić⟩ **3.** ***be ~d with inner glow*** jaśnieć wewnętrznym blaskiem

sug•ar ['ʃʊgə] **I** *s* **1.** cukier *m*; ***do you take ~ in your tea?*** słodzisz herbatę? **2.** ***see you later, ~*** do zobaczenia, skarbie **II** *v/t* słodzić ⟨po-, o-⟩; **'sug•ar beet** *s* burak *m* cukrowy; **'sug•ar bowl** *s* cukierniczka *f*; **'sug•ar cane** *s* trzcina *f* cukrowa; **'sug•ar cu•be** *s* kostka *f* cukru; **sug•ar•y** ['ʃʊgərɪ] *adj* **1.** słodki **2.** *fig* cukierkowy

sug•gest [sə'dʒest] *v/t* **1.** proponować ⟨za-⟩ (***s.th. to*** coś *D*); ***I ~ that we (should) go to the cinema*** proponuję pójść do kina; ***I ~ going home*** proponuję wrócić do domu **2.** polecać ⟨-cić⟩; ***can you ~ a good dictionary?*** czy możesz polecić jakiś dobry słownik? **3.** sugerować ⟨za-⟩; ***are you ~ing that I'm boring*** czy chciałeś przez to powiedzieć, że jestem nudny? **4.** wskazywać ⟨-zać⟩ na *A*; ***~ that*** wskazywać na to, że; **sug•gest•i•ble** [sə'dʒestəbl] *adj* łatwo ulegający wpływom

sug•ges•tion [sə'dʒestʃən] *s* **1.** propozycja *f*; ***we are open to ~s*** jesteśmy otawarci na propozycje **2.** sugestia *f*; ***at s.o.'s ~*** zgodnie z czyjąś sugestią **3.** ***there is no ~ that*** nic nie wskazuje na to, że **4.** ***with a ~ of a smile*** lekko się uśmiechając; **sug•ges•tive** [sə'dʒestɪv] *adj* **1.** sugestywny; ***be ~ of s.th.*** przywodzić coś na myśl **2.** dwuznaczny

S

su•i•ci•dal [suɪ'saɪdl] *adj* samobójczy; **su•i•cide** ['suːɪsaɪd] *s* **1.** samobójstwo *n* **2.** samobójca *m*

suit [suːt] **I** *s* **1.** (*man's*) garnitur *m* **2.** (*woman's*) kostium *m* **3.** strój *m*; ***a bathing ~*** strój kąpielowy **4.** kombinezon *m* **5.** (*cards*) kolor *m* **6.** JUR proces *m*; ***file a ~ against*** wnieść powództwo przeciw *D* **II** *v/t* **1.** pasować **2.** odpowiadać; ***that ~s me fine*** to mi odpowiada **3.** ***this coat ~s you*** w tym płaszczu jest ci do twarzy **4.** ***~ yourself*** rób, jak chcesz

sui•ta•ble ['suːtəbl] *adj* odpowiedni, ***is Friday ~ for you?*** czy piątek ci pasuje?; **sui•ta•bly** ['suːtəblɪ] *adv* odpowiednio

'suit•case *s* ['suːtkeɪs] walizka *f*

suite [swiːt] *s* **1.** (*hotel*) apartament *m* **2.** komplet *m* (mebli) **3.** komplet *m* wypoczynkowy **4.** MUS suita *f* **5.** INF pakiet *m*

suit•or ['suːtə] *s* **1.** *fig* zalotnik *m*, konkurent *m* **2.** ECON *firma zainteresowana przejęciem innej firmy*

sul•fate *Am* → **sulphate**; **sul•fide** *Am* → **sulphide**; **sul•fur** *Am* → **sulphur**

sulk [sʌlk] **I** *v/i* dąsać się **II** *s* dąsy *pl*; **sulk•y** ['sʌlkɪ] *adj* nadąsany

sul•len ['sʌlən] *adj* ponury

sul•phate ['sʌlfeɪt] *Br*, ***sul•fate*** *Am s* CHEM siarczan *m*; **sul•phide** ['sʌlfaɪd] *Br*, ***sul•fide*** *Am s* CHEM siarczek *m*; **sul•phur** ['sʌlfə] *Br*, ***sul•fur*** *Am s* siarka *f*; **sul•phur di•ox•ide** [sʌlfədaɪ'ɒksaɪd] *Br*, ***sul•fur di•oxi•de*** *Am s* CHEM dwutlenek *m* siarki; **sul•phur•ic ac•id** [sʌlfjuːrɪk'æsɪd] *Br*, ***sul•furic ac•id*** *Am s* kwas *m* siarkowy; **sul•phu•rous ac•id** [sʌlfərəs'æsɪd] *Br*, ***sul•furous ac•id*** *Am s* kwas *m* siarkowy

sul•try ['sʌltrɪ] *adj* **1.** parny **2.** ponętny

sum [sʌm] *s* **1.** suma *f*; ***in ~*** **a)** krótko mówiąc **b)** podsumowując **2.** kwota *f* **3.** ***if my ~s are right*** jeżeli dobrze policzyłem; **sum up** *v/t* **1.** podsumowywać ⟨-mować⟩; ***to ~ up*** podsumowując **2.** oceniać ⟨-nić⟩

sum•mar•ize ['sʌməraɪz] *v/t* **1.** streszczać ⟨-reścić⟩ **2.** podsumowywać ⟨-mować⟩; **sum•ma•ry** ['sʌmərɪ] **I** *s* **1.** streszczenie *n* **2.** podsumowanie *n* **II** *adj* **1.** skrótowy **2.** doraźny **3.** w trybie doraźnym

sum•mer ['sʌmə] *s* lato *n*; ***in (the) ~*** latem; ***Indian ~*** babie lato; '**sum•mer camp** *s* obóz *m* letni, kolonie *pl*; **sum•mer 'hol•i•days** *pl* wakacje *pl* (letnie); '**sum•mer house** *s* altana *f*; '**sum•mer school** *s* szkoła *f* letnia; **sum•mer time** *s Br* czas *m* letni; '**sum•mer•time** *s lit* lato *n*; **sum•mer va•'ca•tion** *pl Am* wakacje *pl* (letnie)
sum•mer•y ['sʌmərɪ] *adj* letni
sum•ming-up [sʌmɪŋ'ʌp] *pl summings-up s* **1.** podsumowanie *n* **2.** *JUR* podsumowanie *n* wyników postępowania
sum•mit ['sʌmɪt] *s* szczyt *m*; '**sum•mit meet•ing** *s* spotkanie *n* na szczycie
sum•mon ['sʌmən] *v/t* **1.** wzywać ⟨wezwać⟩; ***be ~ed to appear in court*** otrzymać wezwanie do stawienia się w sądzie **2.** przywoływać ⟨-łać⟩ **3.** *conference*: zwoływać ⟨-łać⟩; **summon up** *v/t* **1.** *courage*: zbierać ⟨zebrać⟩ **2.** *memories*: przywoływać ⟨-łać⟩, budzić ⟨o-⟩
sum•mons ['sʌmənz] **I** *pl -monses s* **1.** *JUR* wezwanie *n* do sądu **2.** wezwanie *n* **II** *v/t* wzywać ⟨wezwać⟩ do sądu
sump [sʌmp] *s TECH* miska *f* olejowa
sump•tu•ous ['sʌmptʃʊəs] *adj* **1.** okazały **2.** wspaniały **3.** urządzony z przepychem **4.** wystawny
sun [sʌn] **I** *s* ***the ~*** słońce *n*; ***get up with the ~*** *fig* wstawać z kurami **II** *v/t* ***~ oneself*** wygrzewać się na słońcu; '**sunbathe** *v/i* opalać ⟨-lić⟩ się; '**sunbed** *s* (*with sunlamp*) łóżko *n* do opalania; '**sun•block** *s* krem *m* z filtrem przeciwsłonecznym; '**sun•burn** *s* oparzenie *n* słoneczne; '**sun•burnt** *adj* **1.** poparzony (przez słońce) **2.** *Br* opalony; '**sun•cream** *s* krem *m* do opalania
sun•dae ['sʌndeɪ] *s* deser *m* lodowy
Sun•day ['sʌndɪ] *s* niedziela *f*; ***on ~*** w niedzielę; **Sun•day 'best** *s*: ***in one's ~*** *infml* odświętnie ubrany; '**Sun•day school** *s* szkółka *f* niedzielna
'**sun•dial** *s* zegar *m* słoneczny; '**sundown** → ***sunset***; **sun-dried** ['sʌndraɪd] *adj tomatoes*: suszony na słońcu; **sun•dries** ['sʌndrɪz] *pl* **1.** różności *pl* **2.** artykuły *pl* różne; **sun•dry** ['sʌndrɪ] *adj* **1.** różny **2.** rozmaity **3.** ***all and ~*** *infml* wszyscy (bez wyjątku); '**sun•flow•er** *s* słonecznik *m*; ***~ oil*** olej słonecznikowy; '**sun•glass•es** *pl* okulary *pl* przeciwsłoneczne
sung [sʌŋ] *Past Participle* → ***sing***
'**sun god** *s* bóg *m* słońca; '**sun hat** *s* kapelusz *m* od słońca
sunk [sʌŋk] *Past Participle* → ***sink***
sunk•en ['sʌŋkn] *adj* **1.** *ship*, *treasure*: zatopiony **2.** *eyes*: zapadnięty **3.** *bath*: wpuszczony w podłogę **4.** położony na niższym poziomie
'**sun•lamp** *s* lampa *f* kwarcowa; '**sunlight** *s* światło *n* słoneczne; '**sun•lit** *adj* **1.** *room*: słoneczny **2.** nasłoneczniony
sun•ny ['sʌnɪ] *adj* **1.** *day*: słoneczny **2.** *person*: pogodny
'**sun•rise** *s* wschód *m* słońca; ***at ~*** o wschodzie słońca; '**sun•roof** *s AUTO* szyberdach *m*; '**sun•screen** *s* (*cream*) filtr *m* przeciwsłoneczny; '**sun•set** *s* zachód *m* słońca; '**sun•shade** *s* **1.** *Br* parasol *m* (od słońca) **2.** parasolka *f* (od słońca) **3.** *Am* markiza *f* **4.** ***~s*** okulary przeciwsłoneczne; '**sun•shine** *s* **1.** światło *n* słoneczne **2.** *infml* radość *f* **3.** (*addressing s.o.*) *infml* słonko *n*, słoneczko *n*; '**sun•spot** *s ASTR* plama *f* słoneczna, plama *f* na słońcu; '**sun•stroke** *s MED* udar *m* słoneczny; '**sun•tan** *s* opalenizna *f*; '**suntanned** *adj* opalony; '**sun•up** → ***sunrise***; '**sun vi•sor** *s* **1.** daszek *m* **2.** *AUTO* osłona *f* przeciwsłoneczna
su•per ['suːpə] *adj* **1.** super **2.** świetny
su•per- ['suːpə] (*in combinations*) super-, nad-
su•per•a'bun•dance *s* nadmiar *m*
su•per•an•nu•at•ed [suːpə'rænjʊeɪtɪd] *adj* **1.** przestarzały **2.** podstarzały
su•perb [suː'pɜːb] *adj* **1.** znakomity **2.** doskonały **3.** wyśmienity
su•per•bug *s* bakteria *f* odporna na antybiotyki
su•per•cil•i•ous [suːpə'sɪlɪəs] *adj* wyniosły
su•per•fi•cial [suːpə'fɪʃl] *adj* **1.** powierzchowny **2.** płytki; **su•per•fi•ci•al•i•ty** [suːpəfɪʃɪ'æləti] *s* **1.** powierzchowność *f* **2.** płytkość *f*
su•per•flu•ous [suː'pɜːflʊəs] *adj* zbyteczny
su•per'hu•man *adj* nadludzki

su•per•im'pose [suːpərɪm'pəʊz] *v/t* nakładać ⟨nałożyć⟩ (***s.th. on*** coś na *A*)

su•per•in•tend•ent [suːpərɪn'tendənt] *s* **1.** (*police*) *Br* komisarz *m* **2.** (*police*) *Am* szef *m*, naczelnik *m* **3.** dyrektor *m* **4.** kierownik *m* **5.** *Am* dozorca *m* **6.** *Am* kurator *m*

su•pe•ri•or [suː'pɪərɪə] **I** *adj* **1.** lepszy **2.** *status*: wyższy **3.** *knowledge*: większy **4.** wybitny **5.** najwyższej jakości **6.** wyższy rangą, starszy **7.** wyniosły **II** *s* przełożony *m*; **su•pe•ri•or•i•ty** [suːpɪərɪ'ɒrətɪ] *s* **1.** wyższość *f* **2.** przewaga *f*

su•per•la•tive [suː'pɜːlətɪv] **I** *adj* **1.** znakomity **2.** *of adjective*: najwyższy **II** *s* GRAM stopień *m* najwyższy

'su•per•man *pl -men s* **1.** nadczłowiek *m* **2.** superman *m*

'su•per•mar•ket *s* supermarket *m*

su•per•'nat•u•ral **I** *adj* **1.** nadprzyrodzony **2.** nadnaturalny **II** *s* ***the*** ~ siły *pl* nadprzyrodzone

su•per•nu•mer•ar•y [suːpə'njuːmərərɪ] *adj* dodatkowy

'su•per•pow•er *s* supermocarstwo *n*

su•per•sede [suːpə'siːd] *v/t* **1.** wypierać ⟨-przeć⟩ **2.** zastępować ⟨-tąpić⟩ **3.** zajmować ⟨-jąć⟩ miejsce

su•per•son•ic [suːpə'sɒnɪk] *adj* (po)naddźwiękowy

'su•per•star *s fig* megagwiazda *f*

su•per•sti•tion [suːpə'stɪʃn] *s* przesąd *m*; **su•per•sti•tious** [suːpə'stɪʃəs] *adj* przesądny

'su•per•struc•ture *s a. fig* nadbudowa *f*

su•per•vise ['suːpəvaɪz] *v/t* **1.** nadzorować **2.** pilnować ⟨po-⟩; **su•per•vi•sion** [suːpə'vɪʒn] *s* **1.** nadzór *m* **2.** pilnowanie *n*

su•per•vi•sor ['suːpəvaɪzə] *s* **1.** kierownik *m* **2.** nadzorca *m* **3.** (*university*) promotor *m*, opiekun *m*; **su•per•vi•so•ry** [suːpə'vaɪzərɪ] *adj* **1.** nadzorczy **2.** kierowniczy

sup•per ['sʌpə] *s* kolacja *f*; ***have*** ~ jeść kolację

sup•plant [sə'plɑːnt] *v/t form* **1.** zastępować ⟨-tąpić⟩ **2.** zajmować ⟨-jąć⟩ miejsce

sup•ple ['sʌpl] *adj* **1.** wygimnastykowany **2.** giętki **3.** gibki **4.** elastyczny **5.** *skin*: jędrny

sup•ple•ment ['sʌplɪmənt] **I** *s* **1.** uzupełnienie *n* **2.** dodatek *m* **3.** suplement *m* **4.** dopłata *f* **II** *v/t* uzupełniać ⟨-nić⟩; **sup•ple•men•ta•ry** [sʌplɪ'mentərɪ] *Br*, ***sup•ple•men•tal*** *Am adj Br* **1.** dodatkowy **2.** uzupełniający

sup•pli•er [sə'plaɪə] *s* dostawca *m*

sup•ply [sə'plaɪ] **I** *s* **1.** dostawa *f*; ***the power ~ system*** instalacja elektryczna; ***the quality of water ~*** jakość wody (dostarczanej do mieszkań) **2.** zaopatrzenie *n* **3.** zapas *m*; ***food supplies*** zapasy żywności **4.** *blood*: dopływ *m* **5.** źródło *n*; ***a power ~*** źródło *n* zasilania **6.** ECON podaż *f*; ***~ and demand*** podaż i popyt **II** *v/t* **1.** dostarczać ⟨-czyć⟩ (***to*** *D*) **2.** zaopatrywać ⟨-trzyć⟩ (***with*** w *A*) **3.** podawać ⟨-dać⟩; **sup•'ply teach•er** *s Br* nauczyciel *m* na zastępstwie

sup•port [sə'pɔːt] **I** *v/t* **1.** popierać ⟨-przeć⟩ **2.** wspierać ⟨wesprzeć⟩ **3.** finansować ⟨s-⟩ **4.** *family*: utrzymywać ⟨-mać⟩ **5.** podtrzymywać ⟨-mać⟩, utrzymywać ⟨-mać⟩ ciężar **6.** *Br* kibicować **7.** *statement*: potwierdzać ⟨-dzić⟩ **8.** INF *format*, *standard*: obsługiwać **II** *s* **1.** poparcie *n* **2.** wsparcie *n*; ***moral ~*** wsparcie moralne; ***a ~ group*** grupa wsparcia **3.** pomoc *f* **4.** *a. fig* podpora *f* **5.** (*for knee*, *ankle*) opaska *f* elastyczna, stabilizator *m* **6.** podparcie *n* **7.** INF obsługa *f*; **sup•port•er** [sə'pɔːtə] *s* **1.** zwolennik *m* **2.** stronnik *m* **3.** *Br* kibic *m*; **sup•port•ing** [sə'pɔːtɪŋ] *adj* **1.** *role*: drugoplanowy **2.** TECH podpierający; ***a ~ wall*** ściana nośna **3.** ***~ evidence*** **a)** dowody **b)** materiał dowodowy; **sup•port•ive** [sə'pɔːtɪv] *adj* pomocny; ***he was very ~ to us*** **a)** bardzo nam pomógł **b)** okazał nam wiele serca; ***they were ~ of each other*** nawzajem się wspierali

sup•pose [sə'pəʊz] **I** *v/i* **1.** sądzić; ***I ~ so*** sądzę, że tak; ***there is no reason to ~ she's lying*** nie ma powodu sądzić, że kłamie **2.** przypuszczać; ***it's not that simple, I ~*** przypuszczam, że to nie takie proste **II** *v/t* **1.** zakładać ⟨założyć⟩; ***~ the hotels are fully booked, what will you do?*** a jeśli nie będzie już wolnych miejsc w żadnym hotelu, co wtedy zrobisz?; ***the theory ~s the***

S

existence of life on Mars teoria ta zakłada istnienie życia na Marsie **2.** ***be ~d to do s.th.*** mieć coś zrobić; ***you were ~d to be here an hour ago*** miałeś tu być godzinę temu; ***you're not ~d to smoke here*** tu nie wolno palić; ***what is that ~d to mean?*** co to ma znaczyć? **3.** ***it's ~d to be a good film*** to podobno dobry film; ***he's ~d to be rich*** podobno jest bogaty; **sup•posed** [sə'pəʊzd] *adj* **1.** domniemany **2.** rzekomy; **sup•pos•ed•ly** [sə'pəʊzɪdlɪ] *adv* **1.** podobno **2.** ponoć

sup•pos•ing [sə'pəʊzɪŋ] *conj* **1.** a jeżeli; ***~ you are wrong*** a jeżeli się mylisz? **2.** przypuśćmy, że

sup•po•si•tion [sʌpə'zɪʃn] *s* **1.** domniemanie *n* **2.** przypuszczenie *n* **3.** założenie *n*; ***based on the ~ that*** oparty na założeniu, że

sup•pos•i•to•ry [sə'pɒzətrɪ] *s MED* czopek *m*

sup•press [sə'pres] *v/t* **1.** *revolt, yawning*: tłumić ⟨s-⟩ **2.** *smile*: powstrzymywać ⟨-mać⟩ **3.** *anger*: opanowywać ⟨-nować⟩ **4.** *information*: zatajać ⟨-taić⟩ **5.** *scandal*: tuszować ⟨za-⟩; **sup•pres•sion** [sə'preʃn] *s* **1.** stłumienie *n* **2.** tłumienie *n* **3.** zatajanie *n* **4.** tuszowanie *n*

su•prem•a•cy [suː'preməsɪ] *s* **1.** panowanie *n* (***over/on*** nad *I*) **2.** dominacja *f* (***over/on*** nad *I*) **3.** przewaga *f* (***over/on*** nad *I*)

su•preme [suː'priːm] *adj* **1.** najwyższy **2.** największy **3.** ogromny **4.** ***it's an event in which she reigns ~*** w tej konkurencji nie ma sobie równych; **su•preme•ly** [suː'priːmlɪ] *adv* **1.** niezwykle **2.** bardzo

sur•charge ['sɜːtʃɑːdʒ] **I** *s* dopłata *f* **II** *v/t* obciążać ⟨-żyć⟩ dodatkową opłatą

sure [ʃɔː] **I** *adj* pewny; ***~ of oneself*** pewny siebie; ***~ of victory*** pewny zwycięstwa; ***for ~*** *infml* na pewno; ***I'm ~*** jestem pewien; ***you're ~ to like this film*** ten film na pewno ci się spodoba; ***be ~ to lock the door*** nie zapomnij zamknąć drzwi; ***make ~ that*** **a)** upewnić się, że **b)** sprawdzić, czy **c)** dopilnować, żeby **II** *adv* **1.** – ***'Will you open the wine?' – '~.'*** – „Otworzysz wino?" – „Pewnie." **2.** faktycznie **3.** rzeczywiście **4.** ***I said she'd forget and ~ enough she did*** mówiłem, że zapomni i, oczywiście, zapomniała; **'sure-fire** *adj method, success*: pewny; **sure-foot•ed** [ʃɔː'fʊtɪd] *adj* **1.** ***be ~*** trzymać się pewnie na nogach **2.** pewny siebie

sure•ly ['ʃɔːlɪ] *adv* **1.** z pewnością; ***it's ~ only a matter of time*** to z pewnością tylko kwestia czasu **2.** (*surprise*) chyba; ***~ you don't think*** (***that***) chyba nie myślisz, że

sur•e•ty ['ʃɔːrətɪ] *s* **1.** poręczenie *n* **2.** zabezpieczenie *n* **3.** gwarancja *f* **4.** kaucja *f* **5.** poręczyciel *m*

surf [sɜːf] **I** *s* **1.** fale *pl* (przyboju) **2.** morska piana *f* **II** *v/i* surfować **III** *v/t* ***~ the Internet*** surfować po Internecie

sur•face ['sɜːfɪs] **I** *s* **1.** powierzchnia *f*; ***on the ~*** *fig* pozornie **2.** nawierzchnia *f* **II** *v/i* **1.** wynurzać ⟨-rzyć⟩ się **2.** wypływać ⟨-łynąć⟩ na powierzchnię **3.** *fig* pojawiać ⟨-wić⟩ się; **'sur•face mail** *s* poczta *f* lądowo-morska, poczta *f* zwykła; **sur•face-to-'air** *adj rocket*: ziemia-powietrze; **sur•face-to-'sur•face** *adj rocket*: ziemia-ziemia

'surf•board *s SPORT* deska *f* surfingowa

sur•feit ['sɜːfɪt] *s form* nadmiar *m* (***of*** *G*)

surf•er ['sɜːfə] *s* **1.** *SPORT* surfer *m* **2.** internauta *m*; **surf•ing** ['sɜːfɪŋ] *s* **1.** *SPORT* surfing *m* **2.** (*in Internet*) surfowanie *n*

surge [sɜːdʒ] **I** *v/i* **1.** (*prices*) gwałtownie wzrastać ⟨-rosnąć⟩ **2.** (*water, crowd*) wdzierać ⟨wedrzeć⟩ się (***into*** do *G*) **3.** (*anger*) wzbierać ⟨wezbrać⟩ (***through*** w *L*) **4.** ***panic ~d through her*** ogarnęła ją panika **II** *s* **1.** *prices*: gwałtowny wzrost *m* **2.** *anger*: nagły przypływ *m* **3.** *tide*: fala *f*

sur•geon ['sɜːdʒən] *s* chirurg *m*; **Sur•geon 'Gen•e•ral** *s*: ***the ~*** *Am* minister zdrowia; **sur•ge•ry** ['sɜːdʒərɪ] *s* **1.** zabieg *m* **2.** operacja *f* **3.** chirurgia *f* **4.** *Br* godziny *pl* przyjęć **5.** *Br* dyżur *m* **6.** *Br* gabinet *m*; **sur•gi•cal** ['sɜːdʒɪkl] *adj* **1.** operacyjny **2.** chirurgiczny; **sur•gi•cal•ly** ['sɜːdʒɪklɪ] *adv* **1.** operacyjnie **2.** chirurgicznie

sur•ly ['sɜːlɪ] *adj* **1.** gburowaty **2.** opryskliwy

S

sur•mise **I** [sɜː'maɪz] *v/i* **1.** domyślać ⟨-lić⟩ się **2.** przypuszczać **II** ['sɜːmaɪz] *s* **1.** domysł *m* **2.** przypuszczenie *n*

sur•mount [sɜ'maʊnt] *v/t* **1.** *difficulties*: pokonywać ⟨-nać⟩, przezwyciężać ⟨-żyć⟩ **2.** zwieńczać ⟨-czyć⟩; ***the building is ~ed by a dome*** budowlę wieńczy kopuła

sur•name ['sɜːneɪm] *s* nazwisko *n*

sur•pass [sə'pæs] *v/t* przekraczać ⟨-roczyć⟩; ***she ~ed herself*** przeszła samą siebie **2.** *record*: pobijać ⟨-bić⟩

sur•plus ['sɜːpləs] **I** *s* **1.** nadwyżka *f*; ***trade ~*** nadwyżka w handlu **2.** nadmiar *m* **II** *adj* **1.** ***~ food*** nadwyżka żywności **2.** *value*: dodatkowy **3.** ***be ~ to s.o.'s needs*** być komuś zbędnym

sur•prise [sə'praɪz] **I** *s* **1.** niespodzianka *f* **2.** zaskoczenie *n*; ***to my ~*** ku mojemu zaskoczeniu; ***take s.o. by ~*** zaskoczyć kogoś; ***it came as a complete ~ to them that she won*** jej zwycięstwo zupełnie ich zaskoczyło **II** *v/t* zaskakiwać ⟨-skoczyć⟩; **sur•pris•ing** [sə'praɪzɪŋ] *adj* **1.** zaskakujący **2.** niespodziewany; **sur•pris•ing•ly** [sə'praɪzɪŋlɪ] *adv* **1.** zaskakująco **2.** niespodziewanie

sur•re•al [sə'riːəl] *adj* surrealistyczny; **sur•re•al•ism** [sə'riːəlɪzəm] *s ART* surrealizm; **sur•re•al•ist** [sə'riːəlɪst] *ART* **I** *s* surrealista *m* **II** *adj* surrealistyczny; **sur•re•al•is•tic** [səriːəl'ɪstɪk] *adj ART* surrealistyczny

sur•ren•der [sə'rendə] **I** *v/i* **1.** poddawać ⟨-dać⟩ się; ***~ to the police*** oddać się w ręce policji **2.** kapitulować ⟨s-⟩ **II** *v/t* **1.** zrzekać ⟨zrzec⟩ się *G* **2.** oddawać ⟨-dać⟩ **3.** poddawać ⟨-dać⟩ **III** *s* **1.** kapitulacja *f* **2.** poddanie się *n* **3.** oddanie *n*

sur•rep•ti•tious [sʌrəp'tɪʃəs] *adj* ukradkowy; **sur•rep•ti•tious•ly** [sʌrəp'tɪʃəslɪ] *adv* ukradkiem

sur•ro•gate moth•er ['sʌrəgət'mʌðə] *s* matka *f* zastępcza

sur•round [sə'raʊnd] **I** *v/t* **1.** otaczać ⟨otoczyć⟩ (***by/with*** *I*); ***be ~ed by*** być otoczonym *I*; ***~ oneself with*** otaczać się *I* **2.** okrążać ⟨-żyć⟩ **II** *s fireplace*: obramowanie *n*; **sur•round•ing** [sə'raʊndɪŋ] *adj* okoliczny; ***the ~ area*** okolica; **sur•round•ings** [sə'raʊndɪŋz] *pl* **1.** okolica *f* **2.** otoczenie *n*

sur•veil•lance [sɜː'veɪləns] *s* obserwacja *f*; ***~ cameras*** kamery monitorujące **2.** inwigilacja *f*; ***be under ~*** być inwigilowanym

sur•vey **I** ['sɜːveɪ] *s* **1.** badanie *n* **2.** sondaż *m* **3.** przegląd *m* **4.** pomiary *pl* **5.** oględziny *pl* **II** [sə'veɪ] *v/t* **1.** badać ⟨z-⟩ **2.** przeprowadzać ⟨-dzić⟩ sondaż wśród *G*; ***all persons ~ed*** wszyscy uczestnicy sondażu **3.** przyglądać ⟨przyjrzeć⟩ się **4.** dokonywać ⟨-nać⟩ oględzin **5.** dokonywać ⟨-nać⟩ pomiarów; **sur•vey•or** [sɜː'veɪə] *s* **1.** geodeta *m* **2.** *Br* rzeczoznawca *m* (budowlany)

sur•viv•al [sə'vaɪvl] *s* **1.** przetrwanie *n*; ***fight for ~*** walka o przetrwanie **2.** przeżycie *n* **3.** relikt *m* **4.** pozostałość *f*

sur•vive [sə'vaɪv] *v/t* **1.** przetrwać **2.** przeżyć; **sur•vi•vor** [sə'vaɪvə] *s* ocalały *m*; ***there were no ~s*** nikt nie ocalał

sus•cep•ti•ble [sə'septəbl] *adj* **1.** podatny (***to*** na *A*) **2.** wrażliwy (***to*** na *A*) **3.** ***~ to flattery*** łasy na pochlebstwa

sus•pect **I** [sə'spekt] *v/t* podejrzewać; ***be ~ed of*** być podejrzanym o *A*; ***~ing nothing*** niczego nie podejrzewając **II** ['sʌspekt] *s* podejrzany *m*; ***the prime ~*** główny podejrzany **III** ['sʌspekt] *adj* podejrzany; **sus•pect•ed** [sə'spektɪd] *adj*: ***~ terrorists*** podejrzani o terroryzm; ***a patient with ~ asthma*** pacjent, u którego podejrzewa się astmę

sus•pend [sə'spend] *v/t* **1.** zawieszać ⟨-wiesić⟩; ***the police officer was ~ed from duty*** policjant został zawieszony w czynnościach służbowych; ***he was given a two-year ~ed sentence*** został skazany na dwa lata w zawieszeniu **2.** wstrzymywać ⟨-mać⟩; ***~ one's judgement*** wstrzymać się z oceną; **sus•pend•er belt** [sə'spendə belt] *s Br* pas *m* do pończoch; **sus•pend•er** [sə'spendə] *s Br* podwiązka *f*

sus•pense [sə'spens] *s* **1.** napięcie *n* **2.** niepewność *f*; ***keep s.o. in ~*** trzymać kogoś w niepewności **3.** suspens *m*; **sus•pen•sion** [sə'spenʃn] *s* **1.** zawieszenie *n* **2.** wstrzymanie *n* **3.** ***~ bridge*** most wiszący

sus•pi•cion [sə'spɪʃn] *s* **1.** podejrzenie *n*; ***be above ~, be beyond ~*** być poza

S

podejrzeniami; ***be under ~ of murder*** być podejrzanym o morderstwo; ***I have a ~ that*** podejrzewam, że **2.** nieufność *f*; ***with ~*** nieufnie; **sus•pi•cious** [sə'spɪʃəs] *adj* **1.** podejrzliwy; ***become ~*** powziąć podejrzenia; ***be ~ of*** odnosić się podejrzliwie do *G* **2.** nieufny; **sus•pi•cious•ly** [sə'spɪʃəslɪ] *adv* **1.** podejrzliwie **2.** nieufnie **3.** podejrzanie **4.** *behave*: w podejrzany sposób

sus•tain [sə'steɪn] *v/t* **1.** podtrzymywać ⟨-mać⟩; ***a ~ed economic growth*** stały wzrost gospodarczy; ***'objection ~ed'*** JUR „sprzeciw podtrzymany" **2.** krzepić ⟨po-⟩ **3.** *injury*: odnosić ⟨-nieść⟩ **4.** *loss*: ponosić ⟨-nieść⟩ **5.** ***~ damage*** zostać uszkodzonym **6.** *weight*: utrzymywać ⟨-mać⟩; **sus•tain•a•ble** [sə'steɪnəbl] *adj* **1.** *development*: zrównoważony **2.** *growth*: stały **3.** *resources*: odnawialny **4.** trwały; **sus•tained** [sə'steɪnd] *adj* **1.** ciągły **2.** stały **3.** nieprzerwany **4.** *effort*: ustawiczny

sus•te•nance ['sʌstənəns] *s* wartości *f* odżywcze

su•ture ['suːtʃə] MED **I** *s* szew *m* **II** *v/t wound*: zszywać ⟨-szyć⟩

svelte [svelt] *adj* smukły

swab [swɒb] **I** *s* **1.** wacik *m* **2.** gazik *m* **3.** patyczek *m* higieniczny **4.** wymaz *m* **II** *v/t* **1.** *wound*: oczyszczać ⟨oczyścić⟩ **2.** *floor*: myć ⟨wy-⟩

swag•ger ['swægə] **I** *v/i* kroczyć ⟨w-⟩ (lekko) rozkołysanym krokiem **II** *s* **1.** ***with a ~*** (lekko) rozkołysanym krokiem **2.** pewność *f* siebie

swal•low[1] ['swɒləʊ] *s* jaskółka *f*

swal•low[2] [~] **I** *v/t* **1.** *a. fig* przełykać ⟨-łknąć⟩; ***~ one's pride*** schować dumę do kieszeni **2.** *savings*: pochłaniać ⟨-łonąć⟩ **II** *v/i* przełykać ⟨-łknąć⟩ ślinę; ***~ hard*** głośno przełknąć ślinę **III** *s* **1.** łyk *m*; ***take a ~ of coffee*** wypić łyk kawy **2.** kęs *m*

swam [swæm] *Past Simple* → **swim**

swamp [swɒmp] **I** *s* bagno *n* **II** *v/t* **1.** *a. fig* zalewać ⟨-lać⟩ **2.** ***be ~ed with work*** *infml* być zawalonym pracą **3.** ***be ~ed with letters*** zostać zasypanym listami; **swamp•y** ['swɒmpɪ] *adj* bagnisty

swan [swɒn] *s* łabędź *m*; **'swan song** *s fig* łabędzi śpiew *m*

swank [swæŋk] *v/i Br dated* **1.** szpanować ⟨za-⟩ (**about** *I*) **1.** popisywać ⟨-pisać⟩ się (**about** *I*); **swank•y** ['swæŋkɪ] *adj Br infml* **1.** modny **2.** drogi **3.** szpanerski

swap [swɒp] **I** *v/t* **1.** zamieniać ⟨-nić⟩; ***~ places*** zamienić się miejscami **2.** wymieniać ⟨-nić⟩ (***s.th.*** **for** coś na *A*) **II** *v/i* **1.** zamieniać ⟨-nić⟩ się; ***can I ~ with you?*** mogę się z tobą zamienić?; ***I'll drive first and then we'll ~ over*** najpierw ja poprowadzę, a potem się zamienimy **2.** wymieniać ⟨-nić⟩ się **III** *s* **1.** zamiana *f*; ***do a ~*** zamienić się **2.** wymiana *f*

swarm [swɔːm] **I** *s* **1.** rój *m* **2.** mrowie *n* **II** *v/i* **1.** roić się **2.** tłoczyć się **3.** wylegać ⟨-lec⟩ (**into**/**onto** na *A*); ***thousands of people ~ed into the streets*** tysiące ludzi wyległo na ulice

swar•thy ['swɔːðɪ] *adj* **1.** śniady **2.** smagły

swash•buck•ling ['swɒʃbʌklɪŋ] *adj* **1.** *tale*: awanturniczy **2.** *hero*: zawadiacki

swat [swɔt] *v/t fly*: pacnąć

swatch [swɒtʃ] *s* próbka *f* (materiału)

swathe [sweɪð] **I** *s* **1.** pas *m* **2.** pasmo *n* **II** *v/t* **1.** owijać ⟨owinąć⟩ (**in** *I*) **2.** opatulać ⟨-lić⟩ (**in** *I*)

sway [sweɪ] **I** *v/i* **1.** kołysać ⟨za-⟩ się **2.** chwiać ⟨za-⟩ się **II** *v/t* **1.** kołysać ⟨za-⟩ **2.** wpływać ⟨-łynąć⟩ na *A*; ***she wasn't ~ed by his promises*** nie dała się zwieść jego obietnicom **III** *s* **1.** kołysanie *n* **2.** kontrola *f*; ***s.o. holds ~ over s.th.*** coś znajduje się w czyichś rękach, ktoś ma kontrolę nad czymś

swear [sweə] **I** (*swore*; *sworn*) *v/i* **1.** przeklinać ⟨-ląć⟩ **2.** kląć (**at** na *A*) **II** (*swore*; *sworn*) *v/t* **1.** przysięgać ⟨-siąc⟩; ***~ revenge*** przysiąc zemstę; ***I could have sworn*** mógłbym przysiąc; ***~ to God*** przysięgać na Boga; ***~ to tell the truth*** przysiąc mówić prawdę **2.** zobowiązywać ⟨-zać⟩; ***~ s.o. to secrecy*** zobowiązać kogoś do zachowania tajemnicy **3.** *oath*: składać ⟨złożyć⟩; **swear by** *v/i* **1.** przysięgać ⟨-siąc⟩ na *A* **2.** *infml* wierzyć w *A*; **swear in** *v/t president*: zaprzysięgać ⟨-siąc⟩

'swear•word *s* przekleństwo *n*

S

sweat [swet] **I** *s* **1.** pot *m*; ***break a ~*** spocić się; ***break out in a ~*** *fig* oblewać się zimnym potem; ***earn one's bread by the ~ of one's brow*** *lit* ciężko pracować na chleb; ***no ~!*** *infml* nie ma sprawy! **2. *~s*** *Am infml* dres *m* **II** *v/i* **1.** pocić ⟨s-⟩ się **2.** męczyć się (***over*** nad *I*); **sweat out** *v/t*: ***~ it out*** zacisnąć zęby i przeczekać

'sweat•band *s SPORT* **1.** opaska *f* (na czoło) **2.** frotka *f*

sweat•er ['swetə] *s* sweter *m*

'sweat gland *s ANAT* gruczoł *m* potowy; **'sweat•shirt** *s* bluza *f* dresowa

sweat•y ['swetɪ] *adj* **1.** spocony **2.** przepocony **3.** duszny **4.** męczący

Swede [swiːd] *s* Szwed *m*, Szwedka *f*

Swe•den ['swiːdn] *s* Szwecja *f*; **Swedish** ['swiːdɪʃ] **I** *adj* szwedzki **II** *s* język *m* szwedzki

sweep [swiːp] **I** (*swept*; *swept*) *v/t* **1.** *floor*: zamiatać ⟨-mieść⟩ **2.** *dust*: zmiatać ⟨zmieść⟩ **3.** *area*: przeczesywać ⟨-sać⟩ **4.** *sky*: omiatać ⟨omieść⟩ **5.** wchodzić ⟨wejść⟩ pewnym krokiem (***into*** do *G*) **6.** wychodzić ⟨wyjść⟩ pewnym krokiem (***out of*** z *G*) **7. *~ one's hair back*** zaczesać włosy do tyłu **8.** przetaczać ⟨-toczyć⟩ się **9. *~ s.o. off s.o.'s feet*** *fig* zawrócić komuś w głowie **10. *~ the board*** **a)** odnieść spektakularne zwycięstwo **b)** *infml* zgarnąć wszystko **II** (*swept*; *swept*) *v/i* **1.** zamiatać ⟨-mieść⟩ **2.** *fig* płynąć ⟨prze-⟩ **3.** mknąć ⟨prze-⟩ **4.** (*panic*) ogarniać ⟨-nąć⟩ (***through*** *A*) **5.** (*rumour*) rozchodzić ⟨-zejść⟩ się **6. *his gaze swept around the room*** omiótł wzrokiem pokój **7.** (*area*) rozciągać się **III** *s* **1. *give a room a ~*** zamieść pokój **2.** (zamaszysty) ruch *m* **3.** machnięcie *n* **4.** łuk *m* **5.** połać *f* **6.** odcinek *m* **7. *make a ~ of*** przeczesać *A* **8.** *history*: panorama *f* **9.** kominiarz *m*; **sweep along** *v/t*: ***be swept along by the force of one's emotions*** dać się ponieść emocjom; **sweep aside** *v/t* całkowicie ignorować ⟨z-⟩; **sweep away** *v/t* **1.** porywać ⟨-rwać⟩ **2. *be swept away*** (*doubts*) rozwiać się **3. *he was swept away by her beauty*** jej uroda zrobiła na nim ogromne wrażenie; **sweep up I** *v/i* zamiatać ⟨-mieść⟩ **II** *v/i* **1.** zmiatać ⟨zmieść⟩ **2. *sweep s.o. up in one's arms*** wziąć kogoś na ręce

sweep•er ['swiːpə] *s* **1.** zamiatacz *m* **2.** *TECH* zamiatarka *f* **3. *a carpet ~*** szczotka do dywanów; **sweep•ing** ['swiːpɪŋ] *adj* **1.** *changes*: gruntowny, szeroko zakrojony **2.** *gesture*: zamaszysty **3.** *victory*: miażdżący **4.** *generalisation*: pochopny

sweet [swiːt] **I** *adj* słodki; ***~ dreams!*** słodkich snów!; ***have a ~ tooth*** być łasym na słodycze; ***~ nothings*** czułe słówka **II** *s* **1.** *Br* cukierek *m* **2.** *Br* deser *m* **3. *~s*** słodycze *pl* **4. *my ~*** *dated* skarbie; **sweet and 'sour** *adj sauce*: słodko-kwaśny; **'sweet•corn** *s* kukurydza *f* cukrowa

sweet•en ['swiːtn] *v/t* **1.** słodzić ⟨po-⟩ **2.** *fig* osładzać ⟨-łodzić⟩ **3.** uatrakcyjniać ⟨-nić⟩ **4.** (*a.* ***~ up***) *infml* urabiać ⟨urobić⟩; **sweet•en•er** ['swiːtnə] *s* **1.** słodzik *m* **2.** *infml* łapówka *f*

'sweet•heart *s* **1. *thank you, ~*** dziękuję, kochanie **2.** *dated* ukochany *m*

sweet•ie ['swiːtɪ] *s*: ***hi, ~!*** cześć, skarbie!

sweet•ly ['swiːtlɪ] *adv* **1.** słodko **2.** ślicznie **3.** *go*: gładko **4.** bez wysiłku

'sweet•meat *s dated* **1.** słodki przysmak *m* **2.** słodycze *pl*; **sweet 'pea** *s* groszek *m* pachnący; **sweet po•'ta•to** *s* batat *m*; słodki ziemniak *m*; **'sweet-talk** *v/t* nakłaniać ⟨-łonić⟩; ***~ s.o. into doing s.th.*** nakłonić kogoś do zrobienia czegoś

swell [swel] **I** (*swelled*; *swollen*/*swelled*) *v/i* **1.** (*a.* ***~ up***) puchnąć ⟨s-⟩ **2.** (*a.* ***~ up***) pęcznieć ⟨na-⟩ **3.** (*a.* ***~ out***) (*sail*) wydymać ⟨-dąć⟩ się **4.** (*profit*) wzrastać ⟨-rosnąć⟩ **5.** (*noise*) wzmagać ⟨-móc⟩ się **6. *they ~ed with pride*** przepełniała ich duma **II** (*swelled*; *swollen*/*swelled*) *v/t* **1.** powiększać ⟨-szyć⟩; ***~ the ranks of*** zasilić szeregi *G* **2.** (*a.* ***~ out***) *sail*: wydymać ⟨-dąć⟩ **III** *adj Am* świetny; ***I had a ~ time*** świetnie się bawiłem; **swell•ing** ['swelɪŋ] *s* **1.** opuchlizna *f* **2.** guz *m*

swel•ter ['sweltə] *v/i infml* gotować się; **swel•ter•ing** ['sweltərɪŋ] *adj* skwarny; ***~ heat*** skwar

swept [swept] *Past Simple and Past Participle* → **sweep**

S

swerve [swɜːv] **I** *v/i* (*car*) gwałtownie skręcać ⟨-cić⟩ **II** *s* gwałtowny skręt *m*

swift[1] [swɪft] *s* (*bird*) jerzyk *m*

swift[2] [~] *adj* **1.** szybki; ***be ~ to act*** szybko podjąć działania **2.** prędki **3.** *current*: wartki **4.** *move*: zwinny; **swift•ly** ['swɪftlɪ] *adv* **1.** szybko **2.** prędko **3.** zwinnie; **swift•ness** ['swɪftnɪs] *s* **1.** szybkość *f* **2.** zwinność *f*

swig [swɪg] **I** *v/t* pić ⟨wy-⟩ dużymi łykami **II** *s* duży łyk *m*; ***take a ~ from a bottle*** pociągnąć z butelki

swill [swɪl] **I** *v/t* **1.** (*a.* ***~ out***) płukać ⟨wy-⟩ **2.** (*a.* ***~ down***) spłukiwać ⟨-kać⟩ **3.** *infml* chlać ⟨wy-⟩ **II** *s* pomyje *pl*

swim [swɪm] **I** (*swam*; *swum*) *v/i* **1.** pływać; ***I can't ~*** nie umiem pływać **2.** płynąć ⟨po-⟩ **3.** przepływać ⟨-łynąć⟩ **4.** rozmazywać się przed oczami **5.** ***my head is ~ming*** kręci mi się w głowie **II** (*swam*; *swum*) *v/t* **1.** przepływać ⟨-łynąć⟩ **2.** *crawl*, *breaststroke*: pływać **III** *s* ***let's go for a ~*** chodźmy popływać; **swim•mer** ['swɪmə] *s* pływak *m*; ***be a good ~*** dobrze pływać; **swim•ming** ['swɪmɪŋ] **I** *s* pływanie *n* **II** *adj* pływacki; ***~ lessons*** lekcje pływania; **'swim•ming pool** *s* basen *m* (pływacki); **'swim•ming trunks** *pl* kąpielówki *pl*; **'swim•suit** *s* kostium *m* kąpielowy; **'swim•wear** *s* stroje *pl* kąpielowe

swin•dle ['swɪndl] **I** *v/t* **1.** oszukiwać ⟨-kać⟩ (***s.o. out of*** kogoś na *A*) **2.** wyłudzać ⟨-dzić⟩ **II** *s* oszustwo *n*; **swindler** ['swɪndlə] *s* oszust *m*

swine [swaɪn] *pl swine*, *swines s infml fig* świnia *f*

swing [swɪŋ] **I** (*swung*; *swung*) *v/i* **1.** kołysać ⟨za-⟩ się **2.** huśtać ⟨roz-⟩ się **3.** wahać się (***between*** między *I*) **4.** skręcać ⟨-cić⟩ **5.** swingować **II** (*swung*; *swung*) *v/t* **1.** machać **2.** wymachiwać; ***~ one's legs*** wymachiwać nogami **3.** *infml* załatwiać ⟨-wić⟩ **III** *s* **1.** kołysanie *n* **2.** ruch *m* **3.** *mood*: zmiana *f* **4.** huśtawka *f* **5.** *MUS* swing *m* **6.** ***the party was in full ~*** zabawa trwała w najlepsze; **swing-'door** *s Br* drzwi *pl* wahadłowe

swinge•ing ['swɪndʒɪŋ] *adj* **1.** *attack*: gwałtowny **2.** *criticism*: druzgocący **3.** *cuts*: ostry, drastyczny

swing•ing ['swɪŋɪŋ] *adj music*: swingujący; **swing•ing 'motion** *s* **1.** kołysanie *n* **2.** ruch *m* wahadłowy; **swinging 'door** *s Am* drzwi *pl* wahadłowe

swipe [swaɪp] **I** *v/i* **1.** zamachnąć się (***at*** na *A*) **2.** uderzać ⟨-rzyć⟩ (***at*** *A*) **II** *v/t* **1.** *infml* podwędzić **2.** *credit card*: przeciągać ⟨-gnąć⟩ przez czytnik **III** *s* **1.** zamach *m*; ***take a ~ at*** zamachnąć się na *A* **2.** atak *m*; ***he took a ~ at her*** zamierzył się na nią

swirl [swɜːl] **I** *v/i* wirować ⟨za-⟩ **II** *s* **1.** wir *m* **2.** wirowanie *n* **3.** *smoke*: kłąb *m*

swish [swɪʃ] **I** *v/i* **1.** świstać ⟨-snąć⟩ **2.** świszczeć **3.** szeleścić ⟨za-⟩ **II** *s* **1.** świst *m* **2.** szelest *m*

Swiss [swɪs] **I** *s* ***the ~*** Szwajcarzy *pl* **II** *adj* szwajcarski; ***a ~ roll*** rolada

switch [swɪtʃ] **I** *s* **1.** włącznik *m* **2.** wyłącznik *m* **3.** przełącznik *m* **4.** kontakt *m* **5.** zmiana *f* **6.** przejście *n* (***to*** na *A*) **7.** *Am* zwrotnica *f* **8.** szpicruta *f* **II** *v/i* **1.** przechodzić ⟨przejść⟩ (***to*** na *A*) **2.** zamieniać ⟨-nić⟩ się (***with*** z *I*) **III** *v/t* **1.** zamieniać ⟨-nić⟩ (miejscami) **2.** ***~ jobs*** zmienić pracę; **switch off** **I** *v/t* wyłączać ⟨-czyć⟩ **II** *v/i* wyłączać ⟨-czyć⟩ się; **switch on** **I** *v/t* włączać ⟨-czyć⟩ **II** *v/i* włączać ⟨-czyć⟩ się; **switch over** *v/i* **1.** przełączać ⟨-czyć⟩ (***to*** na *A*) **2.** przechodzić ⟨przejść⟩ (***to*** na *A*)

'switch•back *s* (*road*) serpentyna *f*; **'switch•blade** *s Am* nóż *m* sprężynowy; **'switch•board** *s* **1.** centrala *f* telefoniczna; ***a ~ operator*** telefonistka **2.** tablica *f* rozdzielcza; **'switch•o•ver** *s* przejście *n* (***to*** na *A*)

Swit•zer•land ['swɪtsələnd] *s* Szwajcaria *f*

swiv•el ['swɪvl] **I** *v/t* obracać ⟨-rócić⟩; ***she ~led her chair around to look at him*** obróciła się na krześle, żeby na niego spojrzeć **II** *v/i* obracać ⟨-rócić⟩ się; **'swiv•el chair** *s* krzesło *n* obrotowe

swol•len ['swəʊlən] **I** *Past Participle* → **swell** **II** *adj* **1.** spuchnięty **2.** *gland*: powiększony **3.** *river*: wezbrany

swoon [swuːn] *v/i* mdleć (z zachwytu) (***over*** na widok *G*)

swoop [swuːp] **I** *v/i* **1.** (*a.* ***~ down***) (*plane*, *bird*) nurkować ⟨za-⟩ **2.** (*police*)

robić ⟨z-⟩ nalot (***on*** na *A*) **II** *s* **1.** lot *m* nurkowy **2.** nalot *m* (policyjny)
swop → ***swap***
sword [sɔːd] *s* miecz *m*; '**sword•fish** *pl -fish*, *-fishes s* (*fish*) miecznik *m*
swore [swɔː] *Past Simple* → ***swear***
sworn [swɔːn] *Past Participle* → ***swear***
swot [swɒt] *Br infml* **I** *s* kujon *m* **II** *v/i* (*learn*) kuć; **swot up** *v/t Br infml* kuć
swum [swʌm] *Past Participle* → ***swim***
swung [swʌŋ] *Past Simple and Past Participle* → ***swing***
syc•o•phant ['sɪkəfænt] *s* pochlebca *m*
syl•la•bi ['sɪləbaɪ] *pl* → ***syllabus***
syl•lab•ic [sɪ'læbɪk] *adj* sylabiczny; **syl•la•ble** ['sɪləbl] *s* sylaba *f*
syl•la•bus ['sɪləbəs] *pl -bi*, *-buses s* program *m* (nauczania)
sym•bi•o•sis [sɪmbaɪ'əʊsɪs] *s* symbioza *f*
sym•bol ['sɪmbl] *s* symbol *m*; **sym•bol•ic** [sɪm'bɒlɪk] *adj* symboliczny; **sym•bol•i•cal•ly** [sɪm'bɒɪklɪ] *adv* symbolicznie; **sym•bol•ism** ['sɪmbəlɪzm] *s* symbolizm *m*; **sym•bol•ist** ['sɪmbəlɪst] *s* symbolista *m*; **sym•bol•ize** ['sɪmbəlaɪz] *v/t* symbolizować
sym•met•ric [sɪ'metrɪk], ***sym•met•ri•cal*** [sɪ'metrɪkl] *adj* symetryczny; **sym•me•try** ['sɪmətrɪ] *s* symetria *f*
sym•pa•thet•ic [sɪmpə'θetɪk] *adj* **1.** pełen zrozumienia **2.** ***be ~ to***, ***be ~ towards*** współczuć *D* **3.** pełen współczucia **4.** życzliwy (***to***/***towards*** *D*) **5.** przychylny (***to***/***towards*** *D*); ***be ~ to*** **a)** popierać *A* **b)** sympatyzować z *I* **6.** sympatyczny; **sym•pa•thize** ['sɪmpəθaɪz] *v/i* **1.** współczuć (***with*** *D*) **2.** *opinions*: podzielać (***with*** *A*) **3.** sympatyzować (***with*** z *I*); **sym•pa•thiz•er** ['sɪmpəθaɪzə] *s* **1.** sympatyk *m* **2.** zwolennik *m*
sym•pa•thy ['sɪmpəθɪ] *s* **1.** współczucie *n* (***for*** dla *G*); ***have ~ for*** współczuć *D*; ***offer one's deepest sympathies to s.o.*** złożyć komuś wyrazy najgłębszego współczucia; ***a letter of ~*** list z kondolencjami **2.** sympatia *f*; ***political symphaties*** sympatie polityczne **3.** ***strike in ~ with*** zastrajkować na znak solidarności z *I* **4.** poparcie *n* **5.** życzliwość *f*
sym•phon•ic [sɪm'fɒnɪk] *adj* symfoniczny; **sym•pho•ny** ['sɪmfənɪ] *s* symfonia *f*; '**sym•pho•ny or•ches•tra** *s* orkiestra *f* symfoniczna
sym•po•si•um [sɪm'pəʊzɪəm] *pl -siums* [~zɪəmz], *-sia* [~zɪə] *s* sympozjum *n*
symp•tom ['sɪmptəm] *s* **1.** objaw *m* **2.** symptom *m* **3.** oznaka *f* **4.** przejaw *m*; **symp•to•mat•ic** [sɪmptə'mætɪk] *adj* **1.** znamienny **2.** symptomatyczny
syn•a•gogue ['sɪnəgɔg] *s* synagoga *f*
syn•chro•nize ['sɪŋkrənaɪz] **I** *v/t* synchronizować ⟨z-⟩ **II** *v/i* być zsynchronizowanym (***with*** z *I*)
syn•di•cate ['sɪndɪkət] *s ECON* **1.** konsorcjum *n* **2.** syndykat *m*
syn•drome ['sɪndrəʊm] *s MED* **1.** zespół *m* **2.** *a. fig* syndrom *m*
syn•er•gy ['sɪnədʒɪ] *s* synergia *f*
syn•od ['sɪnəd] *s REL* synod *m*
syn•o•nym ['sɪnənɪm] *s* synonim *m*; **sy•non•y•mous** [sɪ'nɒnɪməs] *adj* synonimiczny; ***be ~ with*** być równoznacznym z *I*
syn•op•sis [sɪ'nɒpsɪs] *pl -ses* [~siːz] *s* streszczenie *n*
syn•tac•tic [sɪn'tæktɪk] *adj* **1.** składniowy **2.** syntaktyczny; **syn•tax** ['sɪntæks] *s* składnia *f*
syn•the•sis ['sɪnθəsɪs] *pl -ses* [~siːz] *s* synteza *f*; **syn•the•size** ['sɪnθəsaɪz] *v/t* syntetyzować ⟨z-⟩; **syn•the•siz•er** ['sɪnθəsaɪzə] *s* syntezator *m*
syn•thet•ic [sɪn'θetɪk] **I** *adj* syntetyczny **II** *s* syntetyk *m*
syph•i•lis ['sɪfɪlɪs] *s MED* syfilis *m*
sy•phon → ***siphon***
Syr•ia ['sɪrɪə] *s* Syria *f*
sy•ringe [sɪ'rɪndʒ] *s* strzykawka *f*
syr•up ['sɪrəp] *s* syrop *m*; **syr•up•y** ['sɪrəpɪ] *adj* **1.** o konsystencji syropu **2.** gęsty **3.** *fig* ckliwy
sys•tem ['sɪstəm] *s* **1.** system *m*; ***a computer ~*** system komputerowy; ***a ~ error*** *INF* błąd systemowy **2.** organizm *m*; ***get s.th. out of one's ~*** *fig* wyrzucić coś z siebie **3.** *MED* układ *m*; ***the respiratory ~*** układ oddechowy; **sys•te•mat•ic** [sɪstə'mætɪk] *adj* systematyczny; **sys•tem•at•i•cal•ly** [sɪstə'mætɪklɪ] *adv* systematycznie; **sys•tem•a•tize** ['sɪstəmətaɪz] *v/t* systematyzować ⟨u-⟩; **sys•tems 'an•a•lyst** ['sɪstəmz,ænəlɪst] *s* analityk *m* systemów komputerowych

S

T

T [tiː]: ***fit to a ~*** leżeć jak ulał; ***this job suits him to a ~*** ta praca jest dla niego stworzona

tab [tæb] *s* **1.** etykietka *f* **2.** naszywka *f* **3.** wieszak *m*, pętelka *f* **4.** *infml* rachunek *m*; ***pick up the ~*** zapłacić rachunek **5.** *INF* tabulator *m* **6.** ***keep ~s on s.o.*** mieć kogoś na oku; **tab stop** *s INF* tabulator *m*

ta•ble ['teɪbl] **I** *s* **1.** stół *m*; ***at the ~*** przy stole; ***set*** (*a.* ***lay***) ***the ~*** nakryć do stołu; ***clear the ~*** sprzątnąć ze stołu; ***turn the ~s*** *fig* odwrócić sytuację; ***a ~ of contents*** spis rzeczy **2.** tabela *f* **3.** *MATH* tabliczka *f* mnożenia **II** *v/t* **1.** *Br proposal*: przedstawiać ⟨-wić⟩ **2.** *Am motion*, *bill*: odkładać ⟨odłożyć⟩ rozpatrzenie; **'ta•ble•cloth** *s* obrus *m*; **'table lamp** *s* lampa *f* stołowa; **'ta•ble man•ners** *pl* dobre maniery *pl* przy stole; **'ta•ble•mat** *s Br* podstawka *f* pod garnek; **'ta•ble•spoon** *s* łyżka *f* stołowa; **'ta•ble ten•nis** *s SPORT* tenis *m* stołowy; **'ta•ble wine** *s* wino *n* stołowe; **ta•ble•ware** ['teɪblweə] *s* zastawa *f* stołowa

ta•blet ['tæblɪt] *s* **1.** tabletka *f* **2.** tablica *f*; ***a memorial ~*** tablica *f* pamiątkowa

tab•loid ['tæblɔɪd] *s* gazeta *f* brukowa; **tab•loid 'press** *s* prasa *f* brukowa

ta•boo [tə'buː] **I** *s* tabu *n* **II** *adj topic*: zakazany, tabu

tab•u•lar ['tæbjʊlə] *adj* tabelaryczny; ***in ~ form*** w formie tabeli; **tab•u•late** ['tæbjʊleɪt] *v/t* przedstawiać ⟨-wić⟩ w postaci tabeli

tach•o•graph ['tækəgræf] *s AUTO* tachograf *m*

ta•chom•e•ter [tæk'ɔmɪtə] *s TECH* obrotomierz *m*

ta•cit ['tæsɪt] *adj* milczący; **ta•ci•turn** ['tæsɪtɜːn] *adj* **1.** małomówny **2.** milczący

tack [tæk] **I** *s* **1.** taktyka *f* **2.** *fig* kurs *m* **3.** pinezka *f* **4.** (*sailing*) hals *m* **5.** fastryga *f* **II** *v/t* **1.** przypinać ⟨-piąć⟩ **2.** fastrygować ⟨s-⟩ **III** *v/i* halsować; **tack on** *v/t* **1.** dołączać ⟨-czyć⟩ **2.** dorzucać ⟨-cić⟩

tack•le ['tækl] **I** *v/t* **1.** stawiać ⟨-wić⟩ czoła *D* **2.** zabierać ⟨-brać⟩ się za *A* **3.** (*football*) blokować ⟨za-⟩, próbować ⟨s-⟩ odebrać piłkę **II** *s* **1.** sprzęt *m* wędkarski **2.** (*football*) zablokowanie *n*, wejście *n*

tack•y ['tækɪ] *adj* **1.** *infml* tandetny **2.** *paint*: lepki

tact [tækt] *s* takt *m*; **tact•ful** ['tæktfəl] *adj* taktowny; **tact•ful•ly** ['tæktfəlɪ] *adv* taktownie

tac•tic ['tæktɪk] → ***tactics***; **tac•tic•al** ['tæktɪkl] *adj* taktyczny; **tac•ti•cian** [tæk'tɪʃn] *s* strateg *m*; **tac•tics** ['tæktɪks] *pl* taktyka *f*, strategia *f*

tact•less ['tæktlɪs] *adj* nietaktowny

tad•pole ['tædpəʊl] *s* kijanka *f*

taf•fe•ta ['tæfɪtə] *s* tafta *f*

taf•fy ['tæfɪ] *s Am* tofi *n*

tag [tæg] **I** *s* **1.** metka *f* **2.** *a. fig* etykietka *f* **3.** etykieta *f* **4.** (*with name*) identyfikator *m* **5.** *INF* znacznik *m* **6.** sentencja *f*, powiedzenie *n* **7.** (*game*) berek *m* **II** *v/t a. fig* przyczepiać ⟨-pić⟩ etykietkę; **tag along** *v/i* zabierać ⟨-brać⟩ się z *I*; **tag on** *v/t* **1.** dołączać ⟨-czyć⟩ **2.** dodawać ⟨-dać⟩ **3.** dorzucać ⟨-cić⟩

tail [teɪl] **I** *s* **1.** ogon *m*; ***with one's ~ between one's legs*** *fig* jak niepyszny, *infml* z podkulonym ogonem **2.** ***~s*** frak *m* **3.** (*of coin*) ***~s*** orzeł *m*; ***heads or ~s?*** orzeł czy reszka? **II** *v/t* śledzić; **tail back** *v/i infml AUTO* korkować ⟨za-⟩ się; **tail off** *v/i Br* spadać ⟨spaść⟩, zmniejszać ⟨-szyć⟩ się

'tail•back *s Br* (*on road*) korek *m*; **'tail coat** *s* frak *m*; **'tail end** *s* koniec *m*; **'tail•gate I** *s* **1.** klapa *f* bagażnika **2.** klapa *f* tylna **II** *v/t Am infml* siedzieć na ogonie; **'tail•light** *s* tylne światło *n*

tai•lor ['teɪlə] **I** *s* krawiec *m* męski **II** *v/t* przystosowywać ⟨-sować⟩; ***~ the programme to s.o.'s needs*** przystosować program do czyichś potrzeb; **tai•lor-made** [teɪlə'meɪd] *adj* **1.** dopasowany do indywidualnych wymagań **2.** stworzony

'tail•pipe *s Am* rura *f* wydechowa; **'tail•spin** *s* (*aircraft*) korkociąg *m*; **'tail•wind** *s* wiatr *m* w plecy

taint•ed ['teɪntɪd] *adj water*: skażony

take [teɪk] **I** (*took*; *taken*) *v/t* **1.** brać ⟨wziąć⟩, zabierać ⟨-brać⟩; ***someone***

has taken my scarf ktoś wziął mój szalik; ***I'll ~ the black jacket*** wezmę tę czarną kurtkę; ***I'll ~ you by car*** podwiozę cię; ***do you ~ sugar in your coffee?*** pijesz kawę z cukrem?; ***~ a bath*** wziąć kąpiel; ***~ a seat*** usiąść; ***~ an interest in*** interesować się; ***~ offence*** obrazić się; ***~ the bus*** pojechać autobusem; ***~ the second road on the right*** skręcić w drugą ulicę po prawej; ***~ the blame*** wziąć winę na siebie **2.** zajmować ⟨-jąć⟩; ***it ~s half an hour to get to the airport*** dotarcie do lotniska zajmuje pół godziny; ***it won't ~ long*** to nie potrwa długo **3.** *picture*: robić ⟨z-⟩ **4.** *decision*, *action*: podejmować ⟨-djąć⟩ **5.** *break*: robić ⟨z-⟩ sobie **6.** akceptować ⟨za-⟩, przyjmować ⟨-jąć⟩; ***do you ~ credit cards?*** czy mogę zapłacić kartą?; ***~ s.o.'s advice*** posłuchać czyjejś rady **7.** traktować ⟨po-⟩; ***~ s.o. seriously*** traktować kogoś poważnie; ***what do you ~ me for?*** za kogo mnie masz? **8.** rozumieć ⟨z-⟩ **9.** odejmować ⟨odjąć⟩; ***~ 5 from 12*** odejmij 5 od 12 **10.** zapisywać ⟨-sać⟩, notować ⟨za-⟩ **11.** *pulse*: badać ⟨z-⟩ **12.** *temperature*: mierzyć ⟨z-⟩ **13.** *form*: przyjmować ⟨-jąć⟩ **14.** potrzebować; ***it doesn't ~ much*** nie trzeba wiele **15.** (*exam*) podchodzić ⟨-dejść⟩ do *G* **II** *s* **1.** *FILM* ujęcie *n* **2.** *fig* spojrzenie *n* (**on** na *A*); **take after** *v/t* **1.** przypominać **2.** być podobnym do *G*; **take apart** *v/t* **1.** rozkładać ⟨-złożyć⟩ na części **2.** rozgramiać ⟨-romić⟩ **3.** nie pozostawić na kimś suchej nitki; **take away I** *v/t* **1.** *pain*: łagodzić ⟨z-⟩ **2.** *Br* kupować ⟨-pić⟩ na wynos: ***a hamburger to ~ please*** poproszę hamburgera na wynos **II** *v/i* umniejszać ⟨-szyć⟩ (***from*** *A*); ***~ from s.o.'s achievements*** umniejszać czyjeś osiągnięcia; **take back** *v/t* **1.** przyjmować ⟨-jąć⟩ z powrotem **2.** (*cause to remember*) przenosić ⟨-nieść⟩; ***take s.o. back to s.o.'s childhood*** przenieść kogoś w lata dzieciństwa **3.** *goods*: zwracać ⟨-rócić⟩ **4.** *words*: odwoływać ⟨-łać⟩, cofać ⟨-fnąć⟩; **take down** *v/t* **1.** *tent*: składać ⟨złożyć⟩ **2.** *scaffolding*: demontować ⟨z-⟩, rozbierać ⟨-zebrać⟩ **3.** *trousers*: zsuwać ⟨zsunąć⟩ **4.** notować ⟨za-⟩; **take in** *v/t* **1.** przygarniać ⟨-nąć⟩ **2.** *lodger*: brać ⟨wziąć⟩ **3.** (*deceive*) nabierać ⟨-brać⟩ **4.** *oxygen*: pobierać ⟨-brać⟩, wchłaniać ⟨-łonąć⟩ **5.** *clothes*: zwężać ⟨zwęzić⟩ **6.** (*encompass*) obejmować ⟨objąć⟩ **7.** pojmować ⟨-jąć⟩, rozumieć ⟨z-⟩; **take off I** *v/i* **1.** (*plane*) startować ⟨wy-⟩ **2.** *infml* wyruszać ⟨-szyć⟩, wybierać ⟨-brać⟩ się **3.** (*idea*) chwytać ⟨-wycić⟩, przyjmować ⟨-jąć⟩ się **4.** (*career*) nabierać ⟨-brać⟩ tempa **II** *v/t* **1.** naśladować **2.** przedrzeźniać **3.** zabierać ⟨-brać⟩; ***take the book off the table!*** zabierz tę książkę ze stołu! **4.** *clothes*: zdejmować ⟨zdjąć⟩ **5.** *make-up*: usuwać ⟨usunąć⟩ **6.** *performance*: zdejmować ⟨zdjąć⟩ z afisza **7.** *programme*: odwoływać ⟨-łać⟩ **8.** (*post*) usuwać ⟨usunąć⟩ **9.** (*case*) odsuwać ⟨-sunąć⟩ **10.** *goods*: wycofywać ⟨-fać⟩ **11.** odejmować ⟨odjąć⟩; ***take $10 off the bill*** odliczyć 10 dolarów od rachunku; **take on** *v/t* **1.** zatrudniać ⟨-nić⟩ **2.** *tone*: przyjmować ⟨-jąć⟩ **3.** *work*: przyjmować ⟨-jąć⟩, podejmować ⟨-djąć⟩ się **4.** *passengers*: brać ⟨wziąć⟩; **take out** *v/t* **1.** zabierać ⟨-brać⟩; ***he took me out to a restaurant*** zabrał mnie do restauracji **2.** wyjmować ⟨-jąć⟩ **3.** usuwać ⟨usunąć⟩ **4.** *credit*: uzyskiwać ⟨-kać⟩, brać ⟨wziąć⟩ **5.** *insurance*: wykupywać ⟨-pić⟩ **6.** *money*: wyjmować ⟨-jąć⟩ z konta, podejmować ⟨-djąć⟩ **7.** (*salary*) odciągać ⟨-gnąć⟩ **8.** ***take it out on*** wyżywać się na *L*, wyładowywać się na *L* **9.** *Am* → ***take away 2*** **10.** ***take s.o. out of himself*** rozweselić kogoś; **take over I** *v/i* **1.** zastępować ⟨-tąpić⟩ (***from*** *A*) **2.** przejmować ⟨-jąć⟩ obowiązki (***from*** od *G*) **II** *v/t* **1.** przejmować ⟨-jąć⟩ władzę **2.** *company*: przejmować ⟨-jąć⟩; **take to** *v/i* **1.** przyzwyczajać ⟨-czaić⟩ się do *G* **2.** nabierać ⟨-brać⟩ zwyczaju; ***he took to drinking*** zaczął pić **3.** polubić; **take up** *v/t* **1.** *time*, *space*: zabierać ⟨-brać⟩ **2.** zainteresować się, zająć się **3.** *job*, *story*: podejmować ⟨-djąć⟩ **4.** zaczynać ⟨-cząć⟩ **5.** *post*: obejmować ⟨objąć⟩ **6.** *position*: zajmować ⟨-jąć⟩ **7.** *proposal*, *challenge*: przyjmować ⟨-jąć⟩ **8.** *issue*: omawiać ⟨omówić⟩

9. *trousers*: skracać ⟨-rócić⟩ **10.** ***be taken up with s.th.*** poświęcać czemuś całą energię, być czymś pochłoniętym
'take•a•way *s Br* **1.** danie *n* na wynos **2.** restauracja *f* przygotowująca dania na wynos
'take-home pay *s* pensja *f* netto
tak•en ['teɪkən] *Past Participle* → ***take***
'take•off *s* **1.** *plane*: start *m* **2.** podskok *m*
'take•out *Am* → ***takeaway***
'take•o•ver *s* **1.** ECON przejęcie *n* **2.** *country*: zajęcie *n*; **'take•o•ver bid** *s* ECON oferta *f* przejęcia
tak•er ['teɪkə] *s* **1.** chętny *m* **2.** ***a drug ~*** narkoman **3.** ***she's a risk ~*** ona lubi ryzyko
tak•ings ['teɪkɪŋz] *pl* wpływy *pl*
talc [tælk] *s* talk *m*
tal•cum pow•der ['tælkəmpaʊdə] *s* talk *m*
tale [teɪl] *s* **1.** opowieść *f* **2.** historia *f* **3.** opowiadanie *n* **4.** baśń *f* **5.** bajeczka *f*, bujda *f*
tal•ent ['tælənt] *s* talent *m*; ***artistic ~*** talent artystyczny; ***a ~ contest*** konkurs talentów; **tal•ent•ed** ['tæləntɪd] *adj* utalentowany; **'tal•ent scout** *s* łowca *f* talentów
tal•is•man ['tælɪzmən] *s* talizman *m*
talk [tɔːk] **I** *v/i* **1.** rozmawiać (***to/with*** z *I*, ***about*** o *L*); ***what are you ~ing about?*** o czym ty mówisz?; ***we need to ~*** musimy porozmawiać; ***~ in Chinese*** rozmawiać po chińsku; ***~ one's way of doing s.th.*** wykręcić się od czegoś; ***get oneself ~ed about*** dostać się na języki; ***~ing of*** skoro już mowa o *L*; ***~ s.o. into doing s.th.*** namówić kogoś do zrobienia *G*; ***she ~ed me out of going there*** przekonała mnie, żebym tam nie szedł; ***look who's ~ing, you can ~, you're a fine one to ~*** przyganiał kocioł garnkowi **2.** plotkować, gadać **II** *v/t* ***~ business*** rozmawiać o interesach; ***~ nonsense*** *infml* pleść bzdury **III** *s* **1.** rozmowa *f* (***with s.o. about*** z kimś o *L*); ***have a long ~ with*** długo rozmawiać z *I*; ***hold ~s*** prowadzić rozmowy **2.** przemówienie *n* **3.** referat *m*; ***give a ~*** wygłosić referat **4.** gadanie *n*; ***she's all ~*** ona tylko tak mówi **5.** plotki *pl*; ***there's been ~ that*** chodzą plotki, że; **talk around** *v/i* krążyć wokół *G*; **talk back** *v/i infml* odszczekiwać ⟨-kać⟩ (***to*** *D*); **talk down** *v/t* umniejszać ⟨-szyć⟩; **talk down to** *v/i* traktować ⟨po-⟩ z góry; **talk over** *v/t* omawiać ⟨omówić⟩; **talk through** *v/t* dyskutować ⟨prze-⟩
talk•a•tive ['tɔːkətɪv] *adj* **1.** rozmowny **2.** gadatliwy; **talk•er** ['tɔkə] *s* **1.** mówca *m* **2.** gaduła *m*; ***he's a great ~*** jest gadułą, dużo mówi; **talk•ing** ['tɔːkɪŋ] **I** *s* mówienie *n*; ***she did (all) the ~*** (tylko) ona mówiła **II** *adj* mówiący; ***a ~ doll*** mówiąca lalka; **'talk•ing point** *s* **1.** *Br* (powszechny) temat *m* rozmów **2.** *Am* temat *m*; **talk•ing-to** *s infml* bura *f*, reprymenda *f*; ***give s.o. a ~*** dać komuś burę
talk show *s* talk-show *m*
tall [tɔːl] *adj* wysoki; ***how ~ are you?*** ile masz wzrostu?; **tall 'or•der** *s infml* trudna sprawa *f*; **tall 'sto•ry** *s Br* historia *f* wyssana z palca
tal•low ['tæləʊ] *s* łój *m*
tal•ly ['tælɪ] **I** *s* **1.** liczba *f* **2.** wynik *m* **3.** ***keep a ~ of how much you spend*** kontroluj, ile wydajesz **II** *v/i* zgadzać się (***with*** z *I*); **tal•ly up** *v/t* liczyć ⟨po-⟩
tal•on ['tælən] *s* **1.** szpon *m* **2.** pazur *m*
tam•bou•rine [tæmbə'riːn] *s* tamburyn *m*
tame [teɪm] **I** *adj* **1.** oswojony **2.** *infml* nudny **3.** *person*: zgodny, uległy **II** *v/t* **1.** *animal*: oswajać ⟨-woić⟩ **2.** *anger*: hamować ⟨po-⟩
tam•per with ['tæmpə] *v/t* majstrować przy *L*; **'tam•per-proof** *adj* zabezpieczony
tam•pon ['tæmpɒn] *s* tampon *m*
tan [tæn] **I** *s* **1.** opalenizna *f*; ***get a ~*** opalić się **2.** (*colour*) brązowożółty *m* **II** *v/i* opalać ⟨-lić⟩ się **III** *v/t skin*: garbować **IV** *adj* brązowożółty
tan•dem ['tændəm] *s* tandem *m*; ***in ~ with*** wraz z *I*
tang [tæŋ] *s* **1.** cierpki smak *m* **2.** ostry zapach *m*
tan•gent ['tændʒənt] *s* MATH **1.** styczna *f*; ***go off on a ~*** *fig* **a)** zboczyć z tematu **b)** przeskoczyć na inny temat **2.** tangens *m*
tan•ge•rine [tændʒə'riːn] **I** *s* mandarynka *f* **II** *adj colour*: pomarańczowy

T

tan•gi•ble ['tændʒɪbl] *adj* **1.** wyraźny **2.** widoczny **3.** namacalny **4.** uchwytny

tan•gle ['tæŋgl] **I** *s* **1.** plątanina *f*, gąszcz *m* **2.** *fig infml* mętlik *m* **II** (*a.* **~ up**) *v/t* zaplątywać ⟨-tać⟩ **III** (*a.* **~ up**) *v/i* zaplątywać ⟨-tać⟩ się; **tangle with** *v/t* **1.** kłócić ⟨po-⟩ się z *I* **2.** popadać ⟨-paść⟩ w konflikt z *I*

tan•go ['tæŋgəʊ] **I** *pl -gos s* tango *n* **II** *v/i* tańczyć ⟨za-⟩ tango; ***it takes two to ~*** do tanga trzeba dwojga

tank [tæŋk] *s* **1.** zbiornik *m*; ***a fuel ~*** zbiornik na paliwo **2.** czołg *m*

tank•ard ['tæŋkəd] *s* kufel *m*

tank•er ['tæŋkə] *s* **1.** tankowiec *m* **2.** cysterna *f*

'tank top *s* bezrękawnik *m*

tan•ned [tænd] *adj* opalony

tan•ta•lize ['tæntəlaɪz] *v/t* **1.** zwodzić ⟨zwieść⟩, mamić ⟨o-⟩ **2.** kusić ⟨s-⟩; **tan•ta•liz•ing** ['tæntəlaɪzɪŋ] *adj* **1.** kuszący **2.** zwodniczy

tan•ta•mount ['tæntəmaʊnt] *adj* równoznaczy; ***be ~ to*** być równoznacznym z *I*

tan•trum ['tæntrəm] *s* napad *m* złości; ***throw a ~*** dostać napadu złości

Tan•za•nia [tænzə'nɪə] *s* Tanzania *f*

tap [tæp] **I** *v/t* **1.** klepać ⟨po-⟩; ***~ s.o. on the shoulder*** poklepać kogoś po ramieniu **2.** stukać ⟨-knąć⟩; ***~ at the door*** pukać do drzwi; ***~ at the computer*** stukać w klawiaturę; ***~ one's fingers on the table*** bębnić palcami w stół **3.** *resources*: wykorzystywać ⟨-tać⟩ **4.** ***s.o's phone is ~ped*** czyjś telefon jest na podsłuchu **II** *s* **1.** *Br* kran *m*, kurek *m*; ***turn the ~ on*** odkręcić kran; ***on ~*** **a)** pod ręką **b)** *beer*: z beczki **2.** klepnięcie *n* **3.** stukanie *n*, pukanie *n* **4.** podsłuch *m* (telefoniczny); **tap into** *v/t* wykorzystywać ⟨-tać⟩, korzystać ⟨s-⟩ z *G*

'tap dance, **'*tap-danc•ing*** *s* stepowanie *n*

tape [teɪp] **I** *s* **1.** taśma **2.** kaseta *f*; ***on ~*** na kasecie **3.** tasiemka *f* **II** *v/t* **1.** nagrywać ⟨-rać⟩ (na kasetę) **2.** oklejać ⟨-leić⟩ taśmą (klejącą) **3.** przyklejać ⟨-leić⟩ taśmą (klejącą); **tape up** *v/t Am* bandażować ⟨za-⟩

'tape deck *s* magnetofon *m*, kasetowy; **'tape drive** *s* napęd *m* taśmy; **'tape meas•ure** *s* centymetr *m* krawiecki

tap•er ['teɪpə] **I** *v/i* zwężać ⟨zwęzić⟩ się **II** *v/t* zwężać ⟨zwęzić⟩ **III** *s* cienka świeca *f*; **taper off I** *v/i* zmniejszać ⟨-szyć⟩ się, maleć ⟨z-⟩ **II** *v/t* zmniejszać ⟨-szyć⟩ stopniowo

'tape-re•cord *v/t* nagrywać ⟨-rać⟩; **'tape re•cor•der** *s* magnetofon *m*; **'tape re•cor•ding** *s* nagranie *n* magnetofonowe

ta•pes•try ['tæpɪstrɪ] *s* gobelin *m*

'tape•worm *s* BIOL tasiemiec *m*

'tap wa•ter *s* woda *f* z kranu

tar [tɑː] **I** *s* smoła *f*; ***low-~ cigarettes*** papierosy o niskiej zawartości substancji smolistych **II** *v/t* smołować; ***be ~red with the same brush*** być ulepionym z tej samej gliny

ta•ran•tu•la [tə'ræntjʊlə] *s* BIOL tarantula *f*

tar•dy ['tɑːdɪ] *adj* **1.** późny **2.** spóźniony; ***be ~ in doing s.th.*** spóźniać się z czymś

tare [teə] *s* tara *f*

tar•get ['tɑːgɪt] **I** *s* **1.** cel *m*; ***aim at a ~*** mierzyć do celu; ***set oneself a ~*** wyznaczyć sobie cel; ***meet one's ~*** osiągnąć (swój) cel **2.** łup *m*; ***an easy ~ for burglars*** łatwy łup dla włamywaczy **3.** obiekt *m*; ***a ~ of criticism*** obiekt krytyki **II** *v/t* **1.** kierować ⟨s-⟩ (***at/on*** do *G*) **2.** wymierzać ⟨-rzyć⟩; ***the missiles were ~ed at*** rakiety były wymierzone w *A* **3.** być przeznaczonym dla *G*, być zaadresowanym do *G*; **tar•get 'au•di•ence**, **'tar•get group** *s* grupa *f* docelowa; **'tar•get lan•guage** *s* język *m* docelowy; **'tar•get mar•ket** *s* rynek *m* docelowy

tar•iff ['tærɪf] *s* **1.** cło *n* **2.** cennik *m*

tar•mac ['tɑːmæk] *s* **1.** asfalt **2.** płyta *f* lotniska

tar•mac ['tɑːmæk] *v/t* asfaltować ⟨wy-⟩

tar•nish ['tɑːnɪʃ] **I** *v/i* matowieć ⟨z-⟩ **II** *v/t reputation*: nadszarpywać ⟨-pnąć⟩ **III** *s* **1.** nalot *m* **2.** śniedź *f*

ta•rot ['tɑːrəʊ] *s* tarot *m*

tar•pau•lin [tɑː'pɔːlɪn] *s* brezent *m*

tar•ra•gon ['tærəgən] *s* estragon *m*

tar•ry ['tɑːrɪ] *v/i* zwlekać

tart[1] [tɑːt] *adj* cierpki

tart[2] [~] **I** *s* **1.** COOK tarta *f* **2.** *vulg* dziwka *f* **II** *v/i* **~ *oneself*** stroić się, *infml*

T

odpicować się; **tart up** *v/t Br infml* upiększać ⟨-szyć⟩, odpicowywać ⟨-cować⟩
tar•tan ['tɑːtn] *s* tartan *m*
tar•tar ['tɑːtə] *s* kamień *m* nazębny
tar•tare sauce [tɑːtə'sɔːs] *s COOK* sos *m* tatarski
task [tɑːsk] *s* zadanie *n*; ***a thankless ~*** niewdzięczne zadanie; ***take s.o. to ~ for*** zganić kogoś *A*, skrytykować kogoś za *A*; '**task force** *s* **1.** grupa *f* zadaniowa **2.** oddział *m* specjalny; **task mas•ter** *s*: ***be a hard ~*** być bardzo wymagającym
tas•sel ['tɑːsl] *s* frędzel *m*
taste [teɪst] **I** *s* **1.** smak *m*; ***sweet ~*** słodki smak; ***have a ~ of*** spróbować; ***have no ~*** być bez smaku; ***add salt to ~*** dodać soli do smaku; ***a ~ of things to come*** zapowiedź przyszłych wydarzeń **2.** zmysł *m* smaku **3.** smak *m*, gust *m*; ***furnished with ~*** umeblowany ze smakiem; ***be in bad ~*** być w złym guście **4.** zamiłowanie *n* **II** *v/i* smakować, mieć smak; ***it ~s sweet*** smakuje słodko; ***what does it ~ like?*** jak to smakuje? **III** *v/t* **1.** wyczuwać ⟨-czuć⟩ smak **2.** próbować ⟨s-⟩, kosztować ⟨s-⟩; ***~ it*** spróbuj tego; **taste•ful** ['teɪstfʊl] *adj* gustowny; **taste•ful•ly** ['teɪstfʊlɪ] *adv* **1.** gustownie **2.** w dobrym guście; **taste•less** ['teɪstlɪs] *adj* **1.** bez smaku **2.** *joke*: niesmaczny **3.** niegustowny
tast•y ['teɪstɪ] *adj* **1.** smaczny, pyszny **2.** *Br infml woman*: apetyczny
tat [tæt] → ***tit***[1]
tat•tered ['tætəd] *adj* **1.** zniszczony **2.** podarty **3.** postrzępiony **4.** *opinion*: zszargany
tat•ters ['tætərz] *pl* łachmany; ***in ~*** w strzępach
tat•too[1] [tə'tuː] **I** *pl -toos s* tatuaż *m* **II** *v/t* tatuować ⟨wy-⟩
tat•too[2] [~] *s* capstrzyk *m*
tat•ty ['tætɪ] *adj Br infml* niechlujny
taught [tɔt] *Past Simple and Past Participle* → **teach**
taunt [tɔːnt] **I** *v/t* szydzić ⟨wyszydzać⟩, drwić ⟨wy-⟩ **II** *s* szyderstwo *n*, drwina *f*
Taur•us ['tɔːrəs] *s ASTR* Byk *m*
taut [tɔːt] *adj* **1.** napięty **2.** naprężony **3.** *film*: trzymający w napięciu; **taut•en** ['tɔːtn] **I** *v/i* napinać ⟨-piąć⟩ się, naprężać ⟨-żyć⟩ się **II** *v/t* napinać ⟨-piąć⟩, naprężać ⟨-żyć⟩
taw•dry ['tɔːdrɪ] *adj* **1.** tandetny **2.** lichy **3.** tani
taw•ny ['tɔːnɪ] *adj* płowy
tax [tæks] **I** *s* podatek *m*; ***before ~*** przed opodatkowaniem; ***after ~*** po opodatkowaniu **II** *v/t* **1.** opodatkowywać ⟨-kować⟩ **2.** nadwyrężać ⟨-żyć⟩; ***the problem is currently ~ing the brains of the experts*** eksperci właśnie łamią sobie głowę nad tym problemem; **tax•a•ble 'in•come** *s* dochód *m* podlegający opodatkowaniu
ta•x•ation [tæk'seɪʃn] *s* opodatkowanie *n*
'**tax avoid•ance** *s* obchodzenie *n* przepisów podatkowych; '**tax brack•et** *s* próg *m* podatkowy; '**tax break** *s Am* ulga *f* podatkowa; '**tax bur•den** *s* obciążenie *n* podatkowe; '**tax de•duct•i•ble** *adj costs*: możliwy do odliczenia (od podatku); '**tax disc** *s Br* winieta *f*; '**tax eva•sion** *s* uchylanie się *n* od płacenia podatków; '**tax-free** *adj* wolny od podatku; '**tax haven** *s* raj *m* podatkowy
tax•i ['tæksɪ] **I** *s* taksówka *f*; ***by ~*** taksówką **II** *v/i* (*plane*) kołować; '**tax•i dri•ver** *s* taksówkarz *m*
tax•ing ['tæksɪŋ] *adj* wymagający;
'**tax•i rank**, ***tax•i stand*** *s* postój *m* taksówek
'**tax in•spect•or** *s Br* inspektor *m* podatkowy
tax•man ['tæksmæn] *pl -men s infml* fiskus *m*; '**tax•pay•er** *s* podatnik *m*; '**tax rate** *s* stawka *f* podatkowa; '**tax re•lief** *s* ulga *f* podatkowa; '**tax re•turn** *s* deklaracja *f* podatkowa; '**tax year** *s* rok *m* podatkowy
TB [tiː'biː] *abbr* (=**tuberculosis**) *MED* gruźlica *f*
T-bone steak [tiːbəʊn'steɪk] *s COOK* stek *m* z kością
tea [tiː] *s* **1.** herbata *f*; ***would you like a cup of ~?*** zrobić ci herbaty?; ***not for all the ~ in China*** za żadne skarby świata **2.** *Br* podwieczorek *m*; **tea•bag** ['tiːbæg] *s* torebka *f* herbaty ekspresowej; '**tea break** *s Br* przerwa *f* na herbatę; '**tea cad•dy** *s Br* pojemnik *m* na herbatę

teach [tiːtʃ] (*tought*; *tought*) *v/t* **1.** uczyć ⟨na-⟩, nauczać; **~ *English in primary school*** uczyć angielskiego w szkole podstawowej; **~ *s.o. to swim*** uczyć kogoś pływać **2.** oduczać ⟨-czyć⟩; ***that'll ~ you to lie*** to cię oduczy kłamać; ***you can't ~ an old dog new tricks*** *fig* czego Jaś się nie nauczy, tego Jan nie będzie umiał

tea•cher ['tiːtʃə] *s* nauczyciel *m*; **teacher 'train•ing** *s* kształcenie *n* nauczycieli; **tea•ching** ['tiːtʃɪŋ] *s* **1.** nauczanie *n*; ***he wants to go into ~*** on chce zostać nauczycielem **2.** nauka *f*; **'tea•ching aids** *pl* pomoce *pl* naukowe

'tea cloth *Br* → ***tea towel***; **'tea co•sy** *Br s* ocieplacz *m* (na dzbanek do herbaty); **'tea•cup** *s* filiżanka *f* do herbaty; **'tea drink•er** *s* amator *m* herbaty; **'tea•house** *s* herbaciarnia *f*

teak [tiːk] *s* drewno *m* tekowe

'tea•ket•tle *s* czajnik *m* do herbaty; **'tea leaf** *pl* *leaves* *s* liść *m* herbaty

team [tiːm] *s* **1.** drużyna *f*; ***a football ~*** drużyna piłkarska **2.** zespół *m*; ***a ~ member*** członek zespołu **3.** zaprzęg *m*; **team up with** *v/i* **1.** łączyć ⟨po-⟩ siły z *I* **2.** dołączać ⟨-czyć⟩ do *G* **3.** tworzyć ⟨u-⟩ zespół z *I*

team 'ef•fort *s* wspólny wysiłek *m*; ***by ~*** wspólnymi siłami; **'team game** *s* SPORT gra *f* zespołowa; **'team•mate** *s* kolega z drużyny; **team 'spirit** *s* duch *m* współpracy

team•ster ['tiːmstə] *s Am* kierowca *m* ciężarówki

'team•work *s* praca *f* zespołowa

'tea par•ty *s* spotkanie *n* przy herbacie; **'tea•pot** *s* dzbanek *m* do herbaty

tear[1] [tɪə] *s* łza *f*; ***burst into ~s*** wybuchnąć płaczem; ***move s.o. to ~s*** wzruszyć kogoś do łez; ***fight back the ~s*** powstrzymywać płacz; ***~s of joy*** łzy radości

tear[2] [~] **I** (*tore*; *torn*) *v/t* **1.** drzeć ⟨po-⟩; ***he tore the letter in two*** przedarł list na pół; ***~ one's hair out*** wyrywać włosy z głowy; ***be torn between*** być rozdartym pomiędzy *I* **2.** wyrywać ⟨-rwać⟩ (***from*** z *D*); **3.** *muscle*: naciągać ⟨-gnąć⟩ **II** (*tore*; *torn*) *v/i* **1.** drzeć ⟨po-⟩ się **2.** mknąć ⟨prze-⟩, pędzić ⟨po-⟩ **III** *s* **1.** rozdarcie *n* **2.** dziura *f*; **tear a•way** *v/t* odrywać ⟨oderwać⟩; ***tear oneself away from the TV*** oderwać się od telewizora; **tear down** *v/t* burzyć ⟨z-⟩; **tear off** *v/t* **1.** odrywać ⟨oderwać⟩ **2.** zrywać ⟨zerwać⟩; ***the storm nearly tore the roof off*** burza niemal zerwała dach **3.** ***~ one's clothes*** zrzucić z siebie ubranie; **tear up** *v/t* **1.** drzeć ⟨po-⟩ **2.** niszczyć ⟨z-⟩

tear•a•way ['teərəweɪ] *s infml* narwaniec *m*

tear•drop ['tɪədrɒp] *s* łza *f*

tear•ful ['tɪəfʊl] *adj* **1.** zapłakany **2.** rzewny

'tear gas *s* gaz *m* łzawiący

tear•ing ['teərɪŋ] *adj*: ***be in a ~ hurry*** strasznie się spieszyć

tear-jerk•er ['tɪədʒɜːkə] *s* (*film*, *book*) *infml* wyciskacz *m* łez

tear•off ['teərɒf] *adj*: ***a ~ calendar*** kalendarz z wyrywanymi kartkami, *infml* zdzierak

'tea room *s Br* herbaciarnia *f*

tease [tiːz] **I** *v/i* droczyć się z *I*, przekomarzać się z *I* **II** *v/t* **1.** dokuczać ⟨-czyć⟩ **2.** wyśmiewać się z *G* **3.** drażnić **III** *s* **1.** kpiarz *m* **2.** droczenie się *n*, przekomarzanie się *n* **3.** dokuczanie *n*

'teas•er [tiːzə] *s* **1.** łamigłówka *f* **2.** trudny orzech *m* do zgryzienia

'tea ser•vice, **'*tea set*** *s* serwis *m* do herbaty; **'tea•spoon** *s* łyżeczka *f* (do herbaty)

teat [tiːt] *s* **1.** *Br* smoczek *m* **2.** ANAT sutek *m*, brodawka *f* sutkowa

'tea tow•el *s* ściereczka *f* do naczyń; **'tea trol•ley** *Br*, **'*tea wag•on*** *Am s* stolik *m* na kółkach

tech•ni•cal ['teknɪkl] *adj* **1.** techniczny; ***~ support*** pomoc techniczna **2.** fachowy, specjalistyczny; ***~ terms*** terminy fachowe; **tech•ni•cal•i•ty** [teknɪ'kælətɪ] *s* szczegół *m* techniczny; **tech•ni•cal•ly** ['teknɪklɪ] *adv* **1.** technicznie; ***it's ~ possible*** technicznie jest to możliwe **2.** pod względem technicznym **3.** formalnie; ***~ speaking*** formalnie rzecz biorąc; **tech•ni•cian** [tek'nɪʃn] *s* technik *m*

tech•nique [tek'niːk] *s* technika *f*; ***management ~s*** techniki zarządzania

tech•no ['teknəʊ] *s* MUS techno *n*

T

tech•no•crat ['teknəʊkræt] *s* technokrata *m*
tech•no•log•i•cal [teknə'lɒdʒɪkl] *adj* **1.** technologiczny **2.** techniczny; **tech•nol•ogist** [tek'nɒlədʒɪst] *s* technolog *m*
tech•no•lo•gy [tek'nɒlədʒɪ] *s* technologia *f*; **tech'no•lo•gy park** *s* park *m* technologiczny
tech•no•phobe ['teknəfəʊb] *s* technofob *m*; **tech•no•phob•i•a** [teknə'fəʊbɪə] *s* technofobia *f*
ted•dy bear ['tedɪbeə] *s* pluszowy miś *m*
te•di•ous ['tiːdjəs] *adj* **1.** nudny **2.** nużący; **te•di•um** ['tiːdjəm] *s* **1.** nuda *f* **2.** znużenie *n*
teem [tiːm] *v/i* **1.** (*rain*) lać; ***it was ~ing with rain*** lał deszcz; ***the rain was ~ing down*** lało **2.** ***the streets were ~ing with tourists*** na ulicach roiło się od turystów
teen•age ['tiːneɪdʒ] *adj* nastoletni; **teen•ag•er** ['tiːneɪdʒə] *s* nastolatek *m*, nastolatka *f*
teens [tiːnz] *pl*: ***be in one's ~*** mieć naście lat
tee•ny ['tiːnɪ] *adj* drobny, malutki
tee•ny-wee•ny [tɪːnɪ'wiːnɪ] → ***teeny***
tee-shirt ['tiːʃɜːt] *s* koszulka *f* (z krótkim rękawem), T-shirt *m*, tiszert *m*
tee•ter ['tiːtə] *v/i* chwiać ⟨za-⟩ się; ***~ on the brink of*** stać na krawędzi *G*
teeth [tiːθ] *pl* → ***tooth***
teethe [tiːð] *v/i* ząbkować; **teething problems** ['tiːðɪŋprɒbləmz] *pl* początkowe trudności *pl*
tee•to•tal•ler [tiː'təʊtlə] *Br*, ***tee•to•tal•er*** *Am s* abstynent *m*
tel•e•cast ['telɪkɑːst] *Am* **I** *s* transmisja *f* **II** *v/t* transmitować
tel•e•com•mu•ni•ca•tions [telɪkəmjuːnɪ'keɪʃnz] *pl* telekomunikacja *f*; **tel•e•com•mu•ni•ca•tions sat•el•lite** *s* satelita *m* telekomunikacyjny
tel•e•com•mute ['telɪkəmjuːt] *v/i* pracować zawodowo przy domowym terminalu; **tel•e•com•mut•er** ['telɪkəmjuːtə] *s* telepracownik *m*; **tel•e•com•mut•ing** ['telɪkəmjuːtɪŋ] *s* telepraca *f*
tel•e•gram ['telɪgræm] *s* telegram *m*
tel•e•graph ['telɪgrɑːf] **I** *s* telegraf *m* **II** *v/t* telegrafować ⟨za-⟩; **tel•e•graph•ic** [telɪ'græfɪk] *adj* telegraficzny; **tel•e•graph pole** ['telɪgræf~] *s* słup *m* telegraficzny
tel•e•path•ic [telɪ'pæθɪk] *adj* telepatyczny; **te•lep•a•thy** [tɪ'lepəθɪ] *s* telepatia *f*
tel•e•phone ['telɪfəʊn] **I** *s* telefon *m*; ***make a ~ call*** zadzwonić; ***by ~*** przez telefon, telefonicznie; ***be on the ~*** **a)** rozmawiać przez telefon **b)** *Br* mieć telefon **II** *v/t Br* telefonować ⟨za-⟩, dzwonić ⟨za-⟩; **'tel•e•phone bank•ing** *s* bankowość *f* telefoniczna; **'tel•e•phone bill** *s* rachunek *m* za telefon; **'tel•e•phone book** *s* książka *f* telefoniczna; **'tel•e•phone booth** *s* budka *f* telefoniczna; **'tel•e•phone call** *s* rozmowa *f* telefoniczna; **'tel•e•phone di•rec•to•ry** *s* → ***telephone book***; **'tel•e•phone ex•change** *s* centrala *f* telefoniczna; **'tel•e•phone num•ber** *s* numer *m* telefoniczny
te•leph•o•nist [tə'lefənɪst] *s Br* telefonista *m*
te•le•pho•ny [tə'lefənɪ] *s* telefonia *f*
tel•e•pho•to lens [telɪ'fəʊtəʊlenz] *s* PHOT teleobiektyw *m*
tel•e•pro•cess•ing [telɪ'prəʊsesɪŋ] *s* INF zdalne przetwarzanie *n* danych
tel•e•sales ['telɪseɪlz] *Br* telesprzedaż *f*
tel•e•scope ['telɪskəʊp] **I** *s* teleskop *m*, luneta *f* **II** *v/t* **1.** składać ⟨złożyć⟩ **2.** skracać ⟨-rócić⟩ **III** *v/i* składać ⟨złożyć⟩ się; **tel•e•scop•ic** [telɪ'skɒpɪk] *adj* **1.** teleskopowy **2.** składany; **tel•e•scop•ic an•'ten•na** *s* antena *f* teleskopowa; **tel•e•scop•ic um•'brel•la** *s* parasolka *f* składana
tel•e•shop•ping ['telɪshɒpɪŋ] *s* teleshopping *m*
tel•e•text ['telɪtekst] *s* **1.** telegazeta *f* **2.** teletekst *m*
tel•e•vise ['telɪvaɪz] *v/t* **1.** emitować ⟨wy-⟩ **2.** transmitować
tel•e•vi•sion ['telɪvɪʒn] *s* **1.** telewizor *m* **2.** telewizja *f*; ***on ~*** w telewizji; ***watch ~*** oglądać telewizję; ***work in ~*** pracować w telewizji;
tel•e•work•er ['telɪwɜːkə] *s* telepracownik *m*; **tel•e•work•ing** ['telɪwɜːkɪŋ] *s* telepraca *f*
tel•ex ['teleks] **I** *s* teleks *m* **II** *v/t* teleksować ⟨prze-⟩

tell [tel] **I** (*told*; *told*) *v/t* **1.** powiedzieć (**to** *D*); ***did she ~ you her name?*** czy powiedziała ci, jak ma na imię?; ***~ the truth*** powiedzieć prawdę; ***can you ~ me the time?*** czy możesz mi powiedzieć, która godzina? **2.** *story*: opowiadać ⟨-wiedzieć⟩ **3.** kazać; ***do as you were told*** rób, co ci kazano **4.** odróżniać ⟨-nić⟩; ***can you ~ Tom from his brother?*** potrafisz odróżnić Toma od jego brata?; ***~ the difference between A and B*** odróżnić A od B **II** (*told*; *told*) *v/i* ***it's hard to ~*** trudno powiedzieć; ***you never can ~*** nigdy nic nie wiadomo; ***I could ~ he was angry*** widać było, że jest zły; **tell off** *v/t* skrzyczeć, *infml* ochrzanić (**for** za *A*)

tell•er ['telə] *s Am* **1.** kasjer *m* **2.** ***an automatic ~ machine*** bankomat

tell•ing ['telɪŋ] *s* **1.** *comment*: wymowny **2.** pouczający; **tell•ing-'off** *pl tellings-of s Br infml* awantura *f*

tell•tale ['telteɪl] **I** *adj* wymowny **II** *s Br* skarżypyta *m*

tel•ly ['telɪ] *s Br infml* **1.** telewizja *f* **2.** telewizor *m*

te•mer•i•ty [tɪ'merətɪ] *s* czelność *f*; ***have the ~ to*** mieć czelność, żeby

temp [temp] **I** *s* pracownik *m* tymczasowy **II** *v/i* pracować tymczasowo **III** *abbr* (=**temperature**) temp.

tem•per ['tempə] **I** *s* **1.** humor *m*; ***be in a bad ~*** być w złym humorze **2.** usposobienie *n*; ***have a quick ~*** łatwo wpadać w gniew; ***keep one's ~*** zachować zimną krew; ***loose one's ~*** stracić panowanie nad sobą **3.** gniew *m*, wściekłość *f*, złość *f* **II** *v/t* **1.** łagodzić ⟨z-⟩ **2.** *steel*: hartować ⟨za-⟩ **3.** *steel*: odpuszczać ⟨-puścić⟩, odhartowywać ⟨-tować⟩

tem•per•a•ment ['temprəmənt] *s* **1.** temperament *m* **2.** usposobienie *n* **3.** złość *f*; **tem•per•a•men•tal** [temprə'mentl] *adj* **1.** humorzasty **2.** ***~ differences*** różnice w usposobieniu; **tem•per•a•men•tal•ly** [temprə'mentəlɪ] *adv* **1.** z natury **2.** z usposobienia

tem•pe•rate ['tempərət] *adj climate*, *optimism*: umiarkowany

tem•pe•ra•ture ['temprətʃə] *s* **1.** temperatura *f*; ***at a room ~*** w temperaturze pokojowej; ***take s.o.'s ~*** zmierzyć komuś temperaturę **2.** temperatura *f*, gorączka *f*; ***have a ~*** mieć temperaturę

tem•pest ['tempɪst] *s* burza *f*; ***a ~ in a teapot*** burza w szklance wody; **tem•pes•tu•ous** [tem'pestjʊəs] *adj a. fig* burzliwy

tem•pi ['tempɪː] *pl* → ***tempo***

tem•plate ['templeɪt] *s* szablon *m*

tem•ple[1] ['templ] *s* świątynia *f*

tem•ple[2] [~] *s ANAT* skroń *f*

tem•po ['tempəʊ] *pl -pos*, *-pi s* tempo *n*; ***a ~ of life*** tempo życia

tem•po•ral[1] ['tempərəl] *adj* **1.** czasowy **2.** ziemski **3.** doczesny **4.** świecki

tem•po•ral[2] [~] *adj ANAT* skroniowy

tem•po•ra•ry ['tempərərɪ] *adj* **1.** tymczasowy **2.** czasowy **3.** przejściowy; **tem•po•rar•i•ly** [tempə'rərɪlɪ] *adv* **1.** tymczasowo **2.** czasowo **3.** przejściowo

tempt [tempt] *v/t* **1.** kusić ⟨s-⟩; ***don't ~ fate*** nie kuś losu **2.** zachęcać ⟨-cić⟩ **3.** *REL* kusić ⟨s-⟩, wodzić na pokuszenie; **temp•ta•tion** [temp'teɪʃn] *s* **1.** pokusa *f*; ***resist the ~*** oprzeć się pokusie **2.** zachęta *f*; **tempt•er** ['temptə] *s* kusiciel *m*; **tempt•ing** ['temptɪŋ] *adj* kuszący; **tempt•ress** ['temptres] *s* kusicielka *f*

ten [ten] *num* dziesięć; ***~ to one*** dziesięć do jednego

ten•a•ble ['tenəbl] *adj argument*: dający się obronić

te•na•cious [tɪ'neɪʃəs] *adj* **1.** zdecydowany **2.** nieustępliwy **3.** *grip*: mocny **4.** trwały **5.** głęboko zakorzeniony **6.** utrzymujący się; **te•nac•i•ty** [tɪ'næsətɪ] *s* **1.** zdecydowanie *n* **2.** upór *m* **3.** nieustępliwość *f*

ten•an•cy ['tenənsɪ] *s* **1.** najem *m* **2.** dzierżawa *f*

ten•ant ['tenənt] *s* **1.** najemca *m*, lokator *m* **2.** dzierżawca *m*

tend[1] [tend] *v/i* mieć tendencję, skłaniać się (**to** do *G*); ***women ~ to live longer than men*** kobiety na ogół żyją dłużej od mężczyzn

tend[2] [~] *v/t* **1.** opiekować się; ***~ the injured*** opiekować się rannymi **2.** doglądać; ***~ the sheep*** doglądać owiec **3.** *Am* ***~ the bar*** być barmanem

ten•den•cy ['tendənsɪ] *s* **1.** tendencja *f* **2.** skłonność *f* (**to** do *G*); ***artistic ten-***

T

dencies ciągoty artystyczne; **ten•den•tious** [ten'denʃəs] *adj* tendencyjny
ten•der¹ ['tendə] **I** *s* **1.** *ECON* oferta *f* (przetargowa); ***s.th. has been put out to ~*** rozpisać przetarg na *A* **2.** ***legal ~*** środek płatniczy **II** *v/i* składać ⟨złożyć⟩ ofertę (przetargową) (***for*** na *A*) **III** *v/t resignation*: składać ⟨złożyć⟩
ten•der² [~] *adj* **1.** czuły **2.** delikatny **3.** *meat*: miękki, kruchy **4.** *age*: młody **5.** *plant*: delikatny, wrażliwy
ten•der³ [~] *s* **1.** tender *m* **2.** tender *m*, łódź *f* towarzysząca
'ten•der•foot *pl -feet, -foots s* żółtodziób *m*; **ten•der•heart•ed** [tendə'hærtɪd] *adj* **1.** wrażliwy **2.** ***be ~*** mieć miękkie serce
ten•der•ize ['tendəraɪz] *v/t meat*: zmiękczać ⟨-czyć⟩
'ten•der•loin *s COOK* polędwica *f*
ten•der•ness ['tendərnɪs] *s* **1.** czułość *f* **2.** wrażliwość *f* **3.** *meat*: miękkość *f*, kruchość *f*
ten•don ['tendən] *s ANAT* ścięgno *n*
ten•dril ['tendrəl] *s* **1.** *plant*: wąs *m* **2.** kosmyk *m*
ten•e•ment ['tenəmənt] *s* kamienica *f* czynszowa
ten•fold ['tenfəʊld] **I** *adj* dziesięciokrotny **II** *adv* dziesięciokrotnie
ten•ner ['tenə] *s* (*10 pounds*) *Br infml* dziesiątka *f*, dziesiątak *m*
ten•nis ['tenɪs] *s SPORT* tenis *m*; **'ten•nis ball** *s* piłka *f* tenisowa; **'ten•nis court** *s* kort *m* tenisowy; **ten•nis 'el•bow** *s MED* łokieć *m* tenisisty; **'ten•nis play•er** *s* tenisista *m*; **'ten•nis rack•et** *s* rakieta *f* tenisowa; **'ten•nis shoe** *s* tenisówka *f*
ten•or ['tenə] **I** *s* **1.** *MUS* tenor *m* **2.** *fig* wydźwięk *m* **3.** *fig* charakter *m* **II** *adj* tenorowy
'ten•pin *s* kręgiel *m*; **ten•pin 'bowl•ing** *s* (*game*) kręgle *pl*
tense¹ [tens] *s GRAM* czas *m*
tense² [~] **I** *adj* **1.** napięty **2.** *person*: nerwowy, spięty **3.** *situation*: nerwowy, napięty **4.** *rope*: napięty, naciągnięty **II** (*a.* ***~ up***) *v/t* **1.** *muscles*: napinać ⟨-piąć⟩, naprężać ⟨-żyć⟩ **2.** ***be ~d up*** być spiętym
ten•sile ['tensaɪl] *adj* **1.** rozciągliwy **2.** rozciągalny **3.** ciągliwy
ten•sion ['tenʃn] **I** *s* **1.** napięcie *n*; ***muscular ~*** napięcie mięśni; ***political ~s*** napięcia polityczne **2.** naprężenie *n* **3.** nerwowość *f* **II** *v/t* napinać ⟨-piąć⟩
tent [tent] *s* namiot *m*; ***put up a ~*** rozbić namiot
ten•ta•cle ['tentəkl] *s* macka *f*
ten•ta•tive ['tentətɪv] *adj* **1.** prowizoryczny **2.** *smile*: niepewny; **ten•ta•tive•ly** ['tentətɪvlɪ] *adv* **1.** prowizorycznie **2.** niepewnie
ten•ter•hooks ['tentəhʊks] *pl*: ***be on ~*** siedzieć jak na szpilkach
tenth [tenθ] **I** *adj* dziesiąty; ***the ~ of May*** dziesiąty maja **II** *s* jedna dziesiąta *f*; ***in a ~ of a second*** w ułamku sekundy
'tent•peg *s* (*tent*) śledź *m*; **'tent•pole** *s* maszt *m* namiotu
ten•u•ous ['tenjʊəs] *adj* **1.** bardzo słaby **2.** wiotki
ten•ure ['tenjʊə] *s* **1.** kadencja *f* **2.** urzędowanie *n* **3.** dożywotnia posada *f* **4.** prawo *n* użytkowania
tep•id ['tepɪd] *adj* **1.** *tea*: letni **2.** *enthusiasm*: umiarkowany
term [tɜːm] **I** *s* **1.** termin *m*, określenie *n*; ***legal ~s*** terminy prawnicze **2.** semestr *m* **3.** okres *m*; ***a ~ of office*** okres urzędowania; ***during the president's first ~ in office*** za pierwszej kadencji prezydenta; ***in the long*** (***short***) ***~*** na dłuższą (krótszą) metę **4.** ***~s*** warunki *pl*; ***in economic ~*** w kategoriach ekonomicznych; ***in ~s of*** pod względem *G*; ***be on good ~ with*** być w dobrych stosunkach z *I* **II** *v/t* **1.** nazywać ⟨-zwać⟩ **2.** określać ⟨-lić⟩
ter•mi•nal ['tɜːmɪnl] **I** *s* **1.** terminal *m* **2.** ostatnia stacja *f*, pętla *f* **3.** końcówka *f* **4.** zacisk *m* **5.** przyłącze *n* **II** *adj* **1.** *disease*: nieuleczalny **2.** *patient*: nieuleczalnie chory **3.** końcowy; **ter•mi•nal•ly** ['tɜːmɪnəlɪ] *adv ill*: nieuleczalnie
ter•mi•nate ['tɜːmɪneɪt] **I** *v/i* **1.** kończyć ⟨s-⟩ się **2.** (*bus, train*) kończyć ⟨s-⟩ bieg **II** *v/t* **1.** kończyć ⟨s-⟩ **2.** *contract*: rozwiązywać ⟨-zać⟩; **ter•mi•na•tion** [tɜːmɪ'neɪʃn] *s* **1.** zakończenie *n*, koniec *m* **2.** *contract*: rozwiązanie *n* **3.** *MED* aborcja *f*
ter•mi•ni ['tɜːmɪnaɪ] *pl* → ***terminus***
ter•mi•nol•o•gy [tɜːmɪ'nɒlədʒɪ] *s* terminologia *f*

T

ter•mi•nus ['tɜːmɪnəs] *pl termini s* pętla *f*, stacja *f* końcowa
ter•mite ['tɜːmaɪt] *s BIOL* termit *m*
ter•race ['terəs] *s* **1.** taras *m* **2.** *SPORT* trybuna *f* (stojąca); **ter•raced house** ['terəsdhaʊs] *s Br* dom *m* w zabudowie szeregowej
ter•ra cot•ta [terə'kɒtə] *s* **1.** (*earthenware*) terakota *f* **2.** (*colour*) ceglasty *m*
ter•rain [te'reɪn] *s* teren *m*
ter•res•tri•al [te'restrɪəl] *adj* **1.** ziemski **2.** *animals*: lądowy
ter•ri•ble ['terəbl] *adj* straszny, okropny; **ter•ri•bly** ['terəblɪ] *adv* strasznie, okropnie
ter•ri•er ['terɪə] *s* terier *m*
ter•rif•ic [tə'rɪfɪk] *adj* **1.** wspaniały **2.** niesamowity **3.** ogromny; **ter•rif•i•cal•ly** [tə'rɪfɪklɪ] *adv infml* strasznie, niesamowicie; **~ *exciting*** strasznie ekscytujący
ter•ri•fy ['terɪfaɪ] *v/t* przerażać ⟨-razić⟩; ***I am ~ied of spiders*** panicznie boję się pająków; **ter•ri•fy•ing** ['terɪfaɪɪŋ] *adj* przerażajcy
ter•ri•to•ri•al [terɪ'tɔːrɪəl] *adj* terytorialny; **ter•ri•to•ri•al 'wa•ters** *pl* wody *pl* terytorialne
ter•ri•to•ry ['terɪtərɪ] *s* **1.** terytorium *n* **2.** *fig* teren *m*; ***stress goes with the ~ in this job*** stres jest nieodłączną częścią tej pracy
ter•ror ['terə] *s* **1.** przerażenie *n*; ***in ~*** w strachu; ***have a ~ of*** panicznie bać się **2.** terror *m* **3.** *infml* (*child*) diabelec *m*; **ter•ror•ism** ['terərɪzm] *s* terroryzm *m*; **ter•ror•ist** ['terərɪst] *s* terrorysta *m*; **'ter•ror•ist at•tack** *s* atak *m* terrorystyczny; **'ter•ror•ist or•gan•i•za•tion** *s* organizacja *f* terrorystyczna; **ter•ror•ize** ['terəraɪz] *v/t* terroryzować ⟨s-⟩
ter•ry (cloth) ['terɪklɒθ] *s* frotté *n*
terse [tɜːs] *adj* **1.** zwięzły **2.** lakoniczny
test [test] **I** *s* **1.** test *m*; **2.** egzamin *m* **3.** sprawdzian *m* **4.** badanie *n* **5.** próba *f*; ***put s.th. to the ~*** wystawić coś na próbę; ***stand the ~ of time*** przetrwać próbę czasu **6.** *blood*, *urine*: analiza *f* **II** *v/t* **1.** testować ⟨prze-⟩; ***~ s.o.'s endurance*** sprawdzać czyjąś wytrzymałość **2.** badać ⟨z-⟩; ***the water is regularly ~ed for purity*** czystość wody jest regularnie badana; ***~ s.o. for*** przebadać kogoś na obecność *G* **3.** egzaminować ⟨prze-⟩
tes•ta•ment ['testəmənt] *s* **1.** testament *m* **2.** dowód *m*, świadectwo *n* **3.** ***the Old ~*** *REL* Stary Testament; ***the New ~*** *REL* Nowy Testament; **tes•ta•men•ta•ry** [testə'mentərɪ] *adj* testamentowy
test card *s TEL* plansza *f* kontrolna; **'test case** *s JUR* precedens *m* (sądowy); **test drive** *s* jazda *f* próbna; **'test-drive** (*testdrove*; *testdriven*) *v/t* odbywać ⟨-być⟩ jazdę próbną
tes•ter ['testə] *s* **1.** tester *m* **2.** kontroler *m* **3.** próbka *f*
tes•ti•cle ['testɪkl] *s ANAT* jądro *n*
tes•ti•fy ['testɪfaɪ] *v/i* **1.** zeznawać ⟨-nać⟩ (***against*** przeciw *D*) **2.** poświadczać ⟨-czyć⟩ **3.** być dowodem (***to*** *G*)
tes•ti•mo•ni•al [testɪ'məʊnɪəl] *s* **1.** referencje *pl* **2.** dowód *m* uznania; **tes•ti•mo•ny** ['testɪmənɪ] *s* **1.** dowód *m* **2.** świadectwo *n* **3.** *JUR* zeznanie *n*
test•ing ['testɪŋ] **I** *s* **1.** testowanie *n* **2.** sprawdzanie *n* **II** *adj time*: trudny
test pat•tern *Am* → ***test card***; **'test pi•lot** *s* oblatywacz *m*; **'test tube** *s* probówka *f*; **'test-tube ba•by** *s* dziecko *n* z probówki
tes•ty ['testɪ] *adj* drażliwy
te•ta•nus ['tetənəs] *s MED* tężec *m*
tetch•y ['tetʃɪ] *adj* drażliwy
teth•er ['teðə] **I** *v/t dog*: przywiązywać ⟨-zać⟩ **II** *s* **1.** łańcuch *m* **2.** postronek *m*; ***to be at the end of one's ~*** *fig* być u kresu wytrzymałości
Teu•ton•ic [tjuː'tɒnɪk] *adj* **1.** niemiecki **2.** germański **3.** ***~ Knights*** Krzyżacy *pl*
text [tekst] **I** *s* **1.** tekst *m* **2.** ***a set ~*** lektura **II** *v/t* wysyłać ⟨-słać⟩ SMS; ***~ a message*** napisać SMS; **'text•book I** *s* podręcznik *m* **II** *adj example*: podręcznikowy
tex•tile ['tekstəl] *s*: ***~s*** wyroby *pl* włókiennicze; ***the ~ industry***, ***~s*** przemysł włókienniczy
tex•tu•al ['tekstjʊəl] *adj* **1.** tekstowy **2.** w tekście; **tex•tu•al an'al•y•sis** *pl -ses s* analiza *f* tekstu
tex•ture ['tekstʃə] *s* **1.** faktura *f* **2.** konsystencja *f* **3.** *rock*: tekstura *f* **4.** *soil*: struktura
Thai [taɪ] **I** *adj* tajski **II** *s* Taj *m*, Tajka *f*; **Thai•land** ['taɪlænd] *s* Tajlandia *f*

T

Thames [temz] *s* Tamiza *f*

than [ðən] *strong form* [ðæn] **I** *conj* niż; ***it was much better ~ I expected*** było o wiele lepiej, niż się spodziewałem **II** *prep* od *G*, niż *N*; ***I'm older ~ her*** jestem od niej starszy; ***there were fewer ~ twenty people*** było mniej niż 20 osób

thank [θæŋk] *v/t* dziękować ⟨po-⟩ (***s.o. for*** komuś za *A*); ***~ you very much*** bardzo dziękuję, serdecznie dziękuję; ***no, ~ you*** nie, dziękuję; ***I have my parents to ~ for my success*** swój sukces zawdzięczam rodzicom; ***~ goodness***, ***~ God*** dzięki Bogu; **thank•ful** ['θæŋkfəl] *adj* wdzięczny (***for*** za *A*); **thank•ful•ly** ['θæŋkfəlɪ] *adv* **1.** na szczęście; ***~ no one was hurt*** na szczęście nikomu nic się nie stało **2.** z wdzięcznością **3.** z radością; **thank•less** ['θæŋklɪs] *adj task*: niewdzięczny

thanks [θæŋks] **I** *interj* dziękuję, *infml* dzięki; ***~ a lot for*** bardzo dziękuję za *A* **II** *s* **1.** podziękowania *pl* **2.** wdzięczność *f*; ***express one's ~*** wyrazić swoją wdzięczność **3.** ***~ to*** dzięki *D*

Thanks•giv•ing (Day) [θæŋks'gɪvɪŋdeɪ] *s Am* Święto *n* Dziękczynienia

'**thank-you** *s* podziękowanie *n*; '**thank-you let•ter** *s* list *m* z podziękowaniami

that [ðæt] **I** *pron* **1.** ten, ta, to **2.** tamten, tamta, tamto; ***look at ~ man over there*** spójrz na tamtego mężczyznę **3.** to; ***who's ~?*** kto to jest?; ***~'s Peter*** to Peter; ***~ is to say*** to znaczy, to jest; ***~'s ~*** to jest to; ***he's always been like ~*** zawsze taki był **4.** który; ***where's the letter ~ came yesterday?*** gdzie jest list, który wczoraj przyszedł? **II** *conj* że; ***it's possible ~*** możliwe, że; ***she said ~ the story was true*** powiedziała, że ta historia jest prawdziwa **III** *adv* **1.** (aż) tak; ***it's not ~ far*** to nie jest aż tak daleko; ***I was ~ scared that*** byłem tak przerażony, że **2.** (aż) taki; ***it's about ~ long*** to jest mniej więcej takiej długości

thatch [θætʃ] **I** *s* strzecha *f* **II** *v/t* kryć ⟨po-⟩ strzechą; **thatched** [θætʃd] *adj house*: kryty strzechą

thaw [θɔː] **I** *v/i* **1.** topnieć, topić ⟨s-⟩ się; ***it ~s*** jest odwilż **2.** rozmrażać ⟨-rozić⟩ się **3.** (*relations*) *fig* poprawiać ⟨-wić⟩ się **II** *v/t* rozmrażać ⟨-rozić⟩ **III** *s a. fig* odwilż *f*

the [ðə] *befor vowels* [ði] *strong form* [ðiː] *art* **1.** ***He has a cat and two dogs. ~ cat's name is Max.*** On ma kota i dwa psy. Kot ma na imię Max; ***~ second*** drugi; ***~ rich and ~ poor*** bogaci i biedni; **2.** ***~ more ~ better*** im więcej, tym lepiej

the•a•tre ['θɪətə] *Br*, **the•a•ter** *Am s* **1.** teatr *m*; ***go to the ~*** iść do teatru **2.** *Br* sala *f* operacyjna; **the•a•tre•go•er** ['θɪətəgəʊə] *Br*, **the•a•ter•go•er** *Am s* teatroman *m*; '**the•a•tre crit•ic** *s* krytyk *m* teatralny

the•at•ri•cal [θɪ'ætrɪkl] *adj a. fig* teatralny

theft [θeft] *s* kradzież *f*

their [ðeə] *poss* ich; ***~ daughter studies medicine*** ich córka studiuje medycynę; ***everyone took ~ seats*** każdy zajął swoje miejsce

theirs [ðeəz] *poss* ich; ***a friend of ~*** ich przyjaciel; ***our children and ~*** nasze dzieci i ich

them [ðəm] *pron* **1.** ich; ***I saw ~ yesterday*** widziałem ich wczoraj; ***I'll call ~*** zadzwonię do nich; → ***they*** **2.** im; ***tell ~*** powiedz im; → ***they*** **3.** (*emphasis*) oni; ***it's ~*** to oni

theme [θiːm] *s* **1.** temat *m* **2.** motyw *m*; ***the central ~ of Greek art*** główny motyw sztuki greckiej **3.** MUS temat *m*; '**theme park** *s* park *m* tematyczny, tematyczny park *m* rozrywki; '**theme song** *s* motyw *m* przewodni; **theme tune** → ***theme song***

them•selves [ðəm'selvz] *pron* **1.** (*emphasis*) oni sami; ***Don and Julie paid for it ~*** Don i Julie sami za to zapłacili **2.** się, sobie; ***they enjoyed ~*** dobrze się bawili; ***they bought ~ a new car*** kupili sobie nowy samochód

then [ðen] **I** *adv* **1.** wtedy, wówczas; ***since ~*** od tego czasu; ***by ~*** do tego czasu; ***just ~*** właśnie wtedy; ***from ~ on*** od tamtego czasu; ***there and ~***, ***~ and there*** natychmiast **2.** potem, następnie; ***first..., then*** najpierw..., potem **3.** (to) wtedy, to; ***if you miss the bus ~ you'll have to get a taxi*** jeżeli spóźnisz się na autobus to będziesz musiał wziąć taksówkę **4.** więc **5.** ***but ~ again*** ale z drugiej strony **II** *adj* ówczesny; ***the ~ president*** ówczesny prezydent

the•o•lo•gian [θɪə'ləʊdʒən] *s* teolog *m*; **the•o•log•i•cal** [θɪə'lɒdʒɪkl] *adj* teologiczny; ***a ~ college*** seminarium duchowne; **the•ol•o•gy** [θɪ'ɒlədʒɪ] *s* teologia *f*

the•o•rem ['θɪərəm] *s* MATH twierdzenie *n*

the•o•ret•i•cal [θɪə'retɪkl] *adj* teoretyczny; ***it's a ~ possibility*** teoretycznie jest to możliwe; **the•o•ret•i•cal•ly** [θɪə'retɪklɪ] *adv* teoretycznie; **the•o•rist** ['θɪərɪst] *s* teoretyk *m*; **the•o•rize** ['θɪəraɪz] *v/i* teoretyzować (***about/on*** na temat *G*); **the•o•ry** ['θɪərɪ] *s* teoria *f*

ther•a•peu•tic [θerə'pju:tɪk] *s* **1.** leczniczy **2.** terapeutyczny **3.** relaksujący; **ther•a•pist** ['θerəpɪst] *s* **1.** terapeuta *m* **2.** psychoterapeuta *m*; **ther•a•py** ['θerəpɪ] *s* **1.** leczenie *n* **2.** terapia *f* **3.** psychoterapia *f*

there [ðeə] **I** *adv* **1.** tam; ***I was ~*** byłem tam; ***~ and back*** tam i z powrotem; ***over ~*** tam; ***~ and then*** natychmiast; ***~ you are, ~ you go*** bardzo proszę; ***~ it is*** tak właśnie jest; ***~ you go again!*** nie zaczynaj znowu! **2.** ***~ is, ~ are*** jest; ***~ is a book on the table*** na stole leży książka; ***~ are two people waiting for you*** czekają na ciebie dwie osoby; ***~ are only four days left*** zostały tylko cztery dni; ***is ~ a restaurant over here?*** czy jest tu jakaś restauracja? **II** *interj* (*satisfaction*) no proszę, no i co; ***~! What did I tell you?*** No i co, nie miałem racji?; ***~! You've woken the baby!*** Widzisz? Obudziłeś dziecko!; ***~, ~*** (*to child*) (no) już dobrze; **there•a•bouts** [ðerə'baʊts] *adv* **1.** ***he comes from London or ~*** pochodzi z Londynu lub okolic **2.** ***$1 million or ~*** około miliona dolarów; **there•aft•er** [ðeər'æftə] *adv* **1.** potem; ***shortly ~*** wkrótce potem **2.** po tym; **there•by** [ðeər'baɪ] *adv* w ten sposób

there•fore ['ðeəfɔ:] *adv* dlatego; ***he is only 17 and ~ not eligible to vote*** ma dopiero 17 lat i dlatego nie może głosować

there•up•on [ðeərə'pɒn] *adv* **1.** po tym **2.** (zaraz) potem

ther•mal ['θɜ:ml] **I** *adj* **1.** cieplny **2.** termiczny **3.** *clothes*: ocieplany **4.** *spring*: gorący, termalny **II** *s* **1.** prąd *m* termiczny **2.** ***~s*** bielizna *f* termoaktywna

ther•mo•mat ['θɜ:məmæt] *s* termookładka *f*

ther•mom•e•ter [θə'mɒmɪtə] *s* termometr *m*

ther•mo•nu•cle•ar [θɜ:məʊ'nju:klɪə] *adj* termojądrowy

ther•mos bot•tle, ['θɜ:məsbɒtl] ***thermos flask***® *s* termos *m*

ther•mo•stat ['θɜ:məʊstæt] *s* termostat *m*

these [ði:z] *pl* → ***this***

the•sis ['θi:sɪs] *pl -ses* ['θi:si:z] *s* **1.** praca *f* naukowa; *f*; ***an MA ~*** praca magisterska **2.** rozprawa *f*; ***a PhD ~*** rozprawa doktorska **3.** teza *f*

they [ðeɪ] *pron* **1.** oni; ***~ went for a walk*** poszli na spacer **2.** (*impersonal*) ***~ say the red wine is good for you*** podobno czerwone wino jest zdrowe

they'd [ðeɪd] *contracted form* → ***they would***, **they had**

they'll [ðeɪl] *contracted form* → ***they will***

they're [ðeə] *contracted form* → ***they are***

they've [ðeɪv] *contracted form* → ***they have***

thick [θɪk] **I** *adj* **1.** gruby; ***be 2 inches ~*** mieć dwa cale grubości; ***give s.o. a ~ ear*** *infml* dać komuś w ucho **2.** gęsty; ***~ with smoke*** zadymiony; ***the furniture was ~ with dust*** meble były pokryte grubą warstwą kurzu; ***the streets were ~ with tourists*** na ulicach było pełno turystów **3.** *Br infml* głupi **4.** *accent*: wyraźny, mocny **5.** ***be very ~ (with each other)*** *infml* być zżytym (ze sobą) **II** *adv* grubo **III** *s* ***in the ~ of the fight*** w wirze walki; ***through ~ and thin*** w dobrych i złych czasach; **thicken** ['θɪkən] **I** *v/i* gęstnieć ⟨z-⟩ **II** *v/t sauce*: zagęszczać ⟨-gęścić⟩; **thick•et** ['θɪkɪt] *s a. fig* gąszcz *m*

thick•head•ed [θɪk'hedɪd] *adj infml* tępy

thick•ness ['θɪknɪs] *s* **1.** grubość *f*; ***be two inches in ~*** mieć dwa cale grubości **2.** gęstość **3.** warstwa *f*
thick•set ['θikset] *adj* przysadzisty;
thick•skinned [θɪk'skɪnd] *adj fig* niewrażliwy na krytykę
thief [θi:f] *pl thieves* [θi:vz] *s* złodziej *m*
thigh [θaɪ] *s* **1.** *ANAT* udo *n* **2.** *COOK* udko *n*
thim•ble ['θɪmbl] *s* naparstek *m*
thin [θɪn] **I** *adj* **1.** cienki; ***disappear into ~ air*** rozpłynąć sie w powietrzu; ***out of ~ air*** **a)** znikąd **b)** nie wiadomo skąd **2.** *person*: chudy **3.** *hair*: rzadki **4.** *sauce*: wodnisty **5.** *voice*, *smile*: słaby **6.** *argument*: nieprzekonujący **II** *adv* cienko; ***slice bread ~*** cienko kroić chleb **III** *v/t* **1.** rozcieńczać ⟨-czyć⟩ **2.** przerzedzać ⟨-dzić⟩ **IV** *v/i* przerzedzić ⟨-dzić⟩ się
thing [θɪŋ] *s* **1.** rzecz *f*; ***what's this ~?*** co to jest?; ***first ~ tomorrow morning*** jutro z samego rana; ***for one ~..., and for another*** z jednej strony..., z drugiej; ***know a ~ or two*** wiedzieć to i owo **2.** przedmiot *m* **3.** ***I couldn't see a ~*** niczego nie widziałam; ***it doesn't mean a ~*** to nic nie znaczy **4.** sprawa *f*; ***a funny ~*** śmieszna sprawa; ***I like swimming and that sort of ~*** lubię pływanie i tego typu sprawy; ***how are ~s?*** jak leci?, co słychać? **5.** stworzenie *n*; ***poor ~*** biedactwo
think [θɪŋk] **I** (*thought*; *thought*) *v/i* **1.** myśleć; ***do you ~ she'll come?*** myślisz, że przyjdzie?; ***come to ~ of it, he did call me*** teraz sobie przypominam, że do mnie zadzwonił; ***~ highly of*** mieć wysokie mniemanie o *L*; ***what are you ~ing about?*** o czym myślisz?; ***who could have thought it's possible*** kto by pomyślał, że to możliwe; ***I have to ~ about it*** muszę to przemyśleć; ***let me ~*** niech pomyślę **2.** sądzić, uważać; ***what do you ~ about it?*** co o tym sądzisz?; ***I ~ this is his house*** sądzę, że to jego dom; ***I ~ so*** tak sądzę; ***I ~ not*** nie sądzę **3.** przypominać ⟨-mnieć⟩ sobie; ***I can't ~ of his name*** nie mogę sobie przypomnieć jego nazwiska **4.** zamierzać; ***I'm ~ing of taking a bath*** chyba wezmę kąpiel **II** (*thought*; *thought*) *v/t* **1.** uważać za *A*; ***you ~ yourself clever?*** uważasz się na sprytnego? **2.** myśleć ⟨po-⟩ **3.** wyobrażać ⟨-razić⟩ sobie; ***my mother always ~s the worst*** moja matka zawsze wyobraża sobie najgorsze **III** *s* ***have a ~ about*** przemyśleć; ***you've got another ~ coming*** *infml* musisz to jeszcze przemyśleć; **think back** *v/i* powracać ⟨-rócić⟩ myślami (***to*** do *G*); **think out** *v/t* przemyśleć; **think over** *v/t* **1.** przemyśleć **2.** rozważać ⟨-żyć⟩; **think through** *v/t* przemyśleć; **think up** *v/t infml* wymyślać ⟨-lić⟩
think•er ['θɪŋkə] *s* myśliciel *m*; **think•ing** ['θɪŋkɪŋ] **I** *s* myślenie *n*; ***do some ~*** pomyśleć; ***to my way of ~*** moim zdaniem **II** *adj* **1.** myślący **2.** inteligentny **3.** rozumny
think tank *s* grupa *f* ekspertów, zespół *m* doradców
thin•ner ['θɪnə] *s* rozcieńczalnik *m*
thin-skinned [θɪn'skɪnd] *adj* **1.** wrażliwy na krytykę **2.** *fruit*: o cienkiej skórce
third [θɜ:d] *adj* trzeci; ***the ~ of May*** trzeci maja; ***~ time lucky*** do trzech razy sztuka '**third-class** *adj* **1.** trzeciej klasy **2.** trzeciej kategorii; **third de•'gree** *s*: ***give s.o. the ~*** *infml* przemaglować kogoś; '**third-de•gree** *adj burn*: trzeciego stopnia
third•ly ['θɜ:dlɪ] *adv* po trzecie
third 'par•ty *s JUR* osoby *pl* trzecie; **third-par•ty in•'sur•ance** *s* ubezpieczenie *n* od odpowiedzialności cywilnej; **third-par•ty li•a•'bil•ity** *s* odpowiedzialność *f* cywilna; **third 'per•son** *s* (*grammar*) trzecia osoba *f*; '**third-rate** *adj* **1.** trzeciorzędny **2.** kiepski
thirst [θɜ:st] **I** *s* pragnienie *n*; ***die of ~*** umrzeć z pragnienia; ***a ~ for knowledge*** żądza wiedzy **II** *v/i* ***~ for*** pragnąć *G*, pożądać *G*; **thirst-quench•ing** ['θɜ:stkwenʃɪŋ] *adj* gaszący pragnienie; **thirst•y** ['θɜ:stɪ] *adj* **1.** spragniony **2.** *fig* żądny; ***~ for power*** żądny władzy
thir•teen [θɜ:'ti:n] *num* trzynaście
thir•teenth [θɜ:'ti:nθ] *adj* trzynasty
thir•ti•eth ['θɜ:tɪɪθ] *num* trzydziesty
thir•ty ['θɜ:tɪ] **I** *num* trzydzieści **II** *s* (*years*) trzydziestka *f*; ***in the 30s*** w latach trzydziestych; ***be in one's thirties*** być po trzydziestce
this [ðɪs] **I** *pron* **1.** ten, ta, to; ***~ one or that one?*** ten czy tamten?; ***is ~ your***

bag? czy to twoja torba?; ***~ is Kate*** to jest Kate; ***~ is what I expected*** właśnie tego się spodziewałem **2.** (*with time expressions*) ten; ***~ week*** w tym tygodniu; ***~ year*** w tym roku; ***~ morning*** dzisiaj rano; ***do it ~ minute*** zrób to w tej chwili **II** *adv* tak; ***it's about ~ high*** jest mniej więcej tak wysoki; ***I didn't think we would get ~ far*** nie sądziłem, że zajdziemy tak daleko

this•tle ['θɪsl] *s* oset *m*

thong [θɒŋ] *s* **1.** rzemień *m* **2.** stringi *pl* **3.** ***~s*** *Am* japonki

tho•rax ['θɔːræks] *pl -raxes, -races s* **1.** klatka *f* piersiowa **2.** *insect*: tułów *m*

thorn [θɔːn] *s* kolec *m*, cierń *m*; ***be a ~ in s.o.'s flesh*** (*a.* ***side***) być komuś solą w oku

thorn•y ['θɔːnɪ] *adj* **1.** kolczasty, ciernisty **2.** *question*: drażliwy

thor•ough ['θʌrəʊ] *adj* **1.** gruntowny **2.** dokładny **3.** drobiazgowy **4.** *mess*: straszny

thor•ough•bred ['θʌrəʊbred] *s* koń *m* czystej krwi

thor•ough•fare ['θʌrəʊfeə] *s*: ***a main ~*** główna ulica *f*

thor•ough•ly ['θʌrəlɪ] *adv* **1.** dokładnie **2.** gruntownie **3.** bardzo **4.** całkowicie

those [ðəʊz] *pl* → ***that I***

though [ðəʊ] **I** *conj* **1.** chociaż, choć; ***Anne was fond of Tim, ~ he often annoyed her*** Anne lubiła Tima, chociaż często ją denerwował **2.** mimo to, ale; ***he'll probably say no, ~ it's worth asking*** prawdopodobnie odmówi, ale warto zapytać **II** *adv* jednak; ***Our team lost. It was a very good game, ~.*** Nasza drużyna przegrała, ale sam mecz był bardzo dobry.

thought[1] [θɔːt] *Past Simple and Past Participle* → ***think***

T

thought[2] [~] *s* **1.** myśl *f*; ***the very ~ of it makes me want to cry*** na samą myśl o tym chce mi się płakać; ***that's a ~!*** to jest myśl!; ***lost in one's ~s*** zatopiony w myślach; ***on second ~*** po namyśle, po zastanowieniu; ***without a second ~*** natychmiast, bez namysłu **2.** zamiar *m*; **thought•ful** ['θɔːtfəl] *adj* **1.** zamyślony **2.** troskliwy, miły; ***it was ~ of you to help her*** to miło z twojej strony, że jej pomogłaś **3.** przemyślany; **thought•less** ['θɔːtlɪs] *adj* bezmyślny

thou•sand ['θaʊznd] **I** *num* tysiąc **II** *s* tysiąc *m*; ***~s of times*** tysiące razy

thou•sandth ['θaʊzndθ] **I** *adj* tysięczny **II** *s* jedna tysięczna *f*; ***in a ~ of a second*** w ułamku sekundy

thrash [θræʃ] **I** *v/t* **1.** lać ⟨z-⟩, tłuc ⟨s-⟩ **2.** rozgramiać ⟨-romić⟩, pobić na głowę **II** *v/i* (*a.* ***~ about***, ***~ around***) rzucać się, miotać się **III** *s MUS* thrash *m*, thrash metal *m*; **thrash out** *v/t problem*: przedyskutować, omawiać ⟨omówić⟩; **thrash•ing** ['θræʃɪŋ] *s* lanie *n*, *infml* baty *pl*; ***give s.o. a ~*** sprawić komuś lanie

thread [θred] **I** *s* **1.** nić *f*, nitka *f* **2.** wątek *m*; ***loose the ~*** stracić wątek **3.** *of light*: smużka *f* **4.** *TECH* gwint *m* **II** *v/t* **1.** nawlekać ⟨-lec⟩ **2.** ***~ one's way*** przemykać (***through*** pomiędzy *I*); **thread•bare** ['θredbeə] *adj* **1.** wytarty **2.** *argument*: wyświechtany

threat [θret] *s* **1.** groźba *f*; ***carry out one's ~*** spełnić groźbę; ***under ~*** zagrożony **2.** zagrożenie *n*; ***pose a ~ to*** stanowić zagrożenie dla *G*

threat•en ['θretn] **I** *v/t* **1.** grozić; ***~ s.o. with a gun*** grozić komuś pistoletem **2.** zagrażać ⟨-rozić⟩; ***be ~ed with extinction*** być zagrożonym wyginięciem **II** *v/i* (*danger*) grozić; ***the dispute ~ed to split the party*** istniało niebezpieczeństwo, że ten spór doprowadzi do rozłamu w partii; **threat•ening** ['θretnɪŋ] *adj* groźny

three [θriː] **I** *num* trzy, trzej, troje **II** *s* trójka *f*; ***the ~ of hearts*** trójka kier; **'three-act** *adj* trzyaktowy; ***a ~ play*** sztuka w trzech aktach; **three-'cornered** *adj* trójkątny; **three-di•men•sion•al** [θriːdaɪ'menʃnəl] *adj* trójwymiarowy

three•fold ['θriːfəʊld] **I** *adj* trzykrotny **II** *adv* trzykrotnie

'three-piece *adj* trzyczęściowy; **three-piece 'suit** *s* garnitur *m* trzyczęściowy; **three-piece 'suite** *s Br* zestaw *m* wypoczynkowy

three-ply *adj* **1.** trójwarstwowy **2.** *thread*: potrójny

thresh [θreʃ] *v/t grain*: młócić ⟨wy-⟩; **thresh•ing ma•chine** ['θreʃɪŋməʃiːn] *s* młockarnia *f*, młocarnia *f*

thresh•old ['θreʃhəʊld] *s a. fig* próg *m*; ***on the ~ of a new life*** na progu nowego życia; ***a pain ~*** próg bólu
threw [θruː] *Past Simple* → ***throw***
thrift [θrɪft] *s* oszczędność *f*; **thrift•y** ['θrɪftɪ] *adj* oszczędny
thrill [θrɪl] **I** *s* **1.** dreszczyk *m* emocji **2.** ogromna przyjemność *f* **3.** dreszcz *m* **II** *v/t* ekscytować; ***be ~ed*** być podekscytowanym; ***I was ~ed to hear that*** niezmiernie ucieszyłem się na wieść, że **III** *v/i* ***~ to*** ekscytować się *I*; **thrill•er** ['θrɪlə] *s FILM* dreszczowiec *m*, thriller *m*; **thrill•ing** ['θrɪlɪŋ] *adj* ekscytujący
thrive [θraɪv] *v/i a. fig* kwitnąć; **thrive on** *v/t*: ***he ~s on hard work*** ciężka praca (dobrze) mu służy; **thriving** *adj business*: kwitnący
throat [θrəʊt] *s* gardło *n*; ***I have a sore ~*** boli mnie gardło; ***force s.th. down s.o.'s ~*** *infml* wpychać coś komuś na siłę; '**throat loz•enge** *s MED* pastylka *f* do ssania (na gardło); **throat•y** ['θrəʊtɪ] *adj sound*: gardłowy
throb [θrɒb] **I** *v/i* **1.** (*pain*, *blood*) pulsować **2.** (*heart*) walić **3.** (*muscles*) rwać **4.** (*machine*) warczeć **II** *s* **1.** pulsowanie *n* **2.** walenie *n* **3.** rwanie *n* **4.** warkot *m*
throes [θrəʊz] *pl* **1.** ***death ~*** **a)** drgawki *pl* przedśmiertne **b)** *fig* agonia *f* **2.** ***in the ~ of*** *fig* w wirze *G*, w ferworze *G*; ***in the ~ of passion*** w namiętnym uniesieniu, w wirze namiętności
throm•bo•sis [θrɒm'bəʊsɪs] *pl -ses s MED* zakrzepica *f*
throne [θrəʊn] *s* tron *m*; ***on the ~*** na tronie; ***come to the ~*** zasiąść na tronie
throng [θrɒŋ] **I** *s* tłum *m* **II** *v/i* **1.** tłoczyć się **2.** pchać się **III** *v/t streets*: wypełniać ⟨-nić⟩
throt•tle ['θrɒtl] **I** *v/t* dusić ⟨u-⟩ **II** *s* **1.** *TECH* przepustnica *f*, zawór *m* dławiący **2.** ***at full ~*** z maksymalną prędkością, *infml* na pełnym gazie; **throttle back** *v/i* zwalniać ⟨zwolnić⟩, zmniejszać ⟨-szyć⟩ prędkość
through [θruː] **I** *prep* **1.** przez *A*; ***~ the window*** przez okno; ***get ~ the exams*** zdać egzaminy; ***he will not live ~ the night*** nie przeżyje nocy **2.** do *G*; ***Monday ~ Friday*** od poniedziałku do piątku **3.** przez *A*, za pomocą *G*; ***achieve success ~ hard work*** osiągnąć sukces ciężką pracą **II** *adv* **1.** ***drive ~*** przejechać; ***read ~*** przeczytać; ***go ~*** przechodzić **2.** ***the train goes ~ to New York*** pociąg zatrzymuje się dopiero w Nowym Jorku **3.** zupełnie, całkowicie; ***get wet ~ and ~*** przemoknąć do suchej nitki; ***he's British ~ and ~*** jest stuprocentowym Brytyjczykiem **III** *adj* **1.** *train*: bezpośredni **2.** *road*, *street*: przejazdowy; ***No ~ road*** Ślepa ulica **3.** ***are you ~ with the newspaper?*** *infml* skończyłeś czytać gazetę?; ***be ~ with*** zerwać z *I*; '**through flight** *s* lot *m* bezpośredni
through•out [θruː'aʊt] **I** *prep* **1.** (*time*) przez *A*; ***~ the night*** przez całą noc **2.** (*place*) w całym *L*, na całym *L*; ***~ the country*** w całym kraju; ***~ the world*** na całym świecie **II** *adv* **1.** (*time*) od początku do końca **2.** (*place*) wszędzie; '**through•route** *s* trasa *f* przejazdowa; '**through traf•fic** *s* tranzyt *m*, ruch *m* tranzytowy; '**through train** *s* pociąg *m* bezpośredni; '**through•way** *s* **1.** przejście *n* **2.** przejazd *m*
throw [θrəʊ] **I** (*threw*; *thrown*) *v/t* **1.** rzucać ⟨-cić⟩; ***~ stones at the window*** rzucać kamieniami w okno; ***~ the door open*** (gwałtownie) otworzyć drzwi; ***~ the dice*** rzucić kostką; ***~ oneself at s.o.*** rzucić się komuś na szyję **2.** *blame*: zrzucać ⟨-cić⟩ **3.** *arms*: zarzucać ⟨-cić⟩ **4.** powalić **5.** *pottery*: toczyć, formować ⟨u-⟩ **6.** *fit of anger*: dostawać ⟨-tać⟩ **7.** *infml party*: urządzać ⟨-dzić⟩ **II** *s* rzut *m*; **throw about, throw around** *v/t money*: szastać; **throw away** *v/t* **1.** wyrzucać ⟨-cić⟩ **2.** marnować ⟨z-⟩ **3.** zaprzepaszczać ⟨-paścić⟩; **throw back** *v/t* **1.** wyrzucać ⟨-cić⟩ (***at*** *D*) **2.** polegać (***on*** na *L*); **throw in** *v/t* **1.** dorzucać ⟨-cić⟩ **2.** dodawać ⟨-dać⟩; **throw off** *v/t* **1.** zrzucać ⟨-cić⟩ **2.** otrząsać ⟨-snąć⟩ się z *G* **3.** *chase*: gubić ⟨z-⟩ **4.** wydzielać ⟨-lić⟩; **throw on** *v/t* **1.** narzucać ⟨-cić⟩ **2.** ubierać ⟨ubrać⟩; **throw out** *v/t* **1.** wyrzucać ⟨-cić⟩ **2.** *idea*: rzucać ⟨-cić⟩ **3.** *proposal*: odrzucać ⟨-cić⟩ **4.** wydzielać ⟨-lić⟩; **throw to•geth•er**

T

v/t **1.** *people*: stykać ⟨zetknąć⟩ ze sobą **2.** przygotowywać ⟨-tować⟩ w pośpiechu **3.** *infml* klecić ⟨s-⟩ **4.** *infml meal*: pichcić ⟨u-⟩; **throw up** *v/t* **1.** wymiotować ⟨z-⟩ **2.** *work*: rzucać ⟨-cić⟩

'throw-a•way *adj* **1.** jednorazowy **2.** *remark*: rzucony mimochodem

throw•er ['θrəʊə] *s SPORT* miotacz *m*

'throw-in *s* (*football*) rzut *m* z autu

thrown [θrəʊn] *Past Participle* → ***throw***

thru [θruː] *Am infml* → ***through***

thrush[1] [θrʌʃ] *s* drozd *m*

thrush[2] [~] *s MED* **1.** pleśniawka *f* **2.** *Br* grzybica *f* pochwy

thrust [θrʌst] **I** (*thrust*; *thrust*) *v/t* **1.** pchać ⟨pchnąć⟩ **2.** rzucać ⟨-cić⟩ **3.** wpychać ⟨wepchnąć⟩ **II** (*thrust*; *thrust*) *v/i* rzucać ⟨-cić⟩ się (***at*** na *A*) **III** *s* **1.** pchnięcie *n* **2.** ruch *m* do przodu **3.** *fig* zasadnicza myśl *f* **4.** *TECH* ciąg *m*, siła *f* ciągu

'thru•way *Am* → ***throughway***

thud [θʌd] **I** *s* głuche uderzenie *n* **II** *v/i* uderzać ⟨-rzyć⟩ głucho

thug [θʌg] *s* bandyta *m*, *infml* zbir *m*

thumb [θʌm] **I** *s* kciuk *m*; ***be all ~s*** mieć dwie lewe ręce; ***give s.th. the ~s up*** (***down***) zaakceptować (odrzucić) coś; ***stick out like a sore ~*** rzucać się w oczy **II** *v/t* jechać ⟨jeździć⟩ autostopem; ***~ a lift*** *Br* łapać okazję; **thumb through** *v/t book*: przeglądać ⟨przejrzeć⟩, wertować ⟨prze-⟩

'thumb in•dex *pl* ***~ indices*** *s* (*dictionary*) *indeks w postaci wcięć w bloku książki*; **'thumb•nail** *s* paznokieć *m* kciuka; **thumb•nail 'sketch** *s* zarys *m*; **'thumb•screw** *s TECH* **1.** śruba *f* radełkowana **2.** śruba *f* skrzydełkowa; **'thumb•tack** *s Am* pinezka *f*

thump [θʌmp] **I** *v/t* **1.** uderzać ⟨-rzyć⟩ pięścią **2.** walić ⟨-lnąć⟩ **II** *v/i* **1.** upadać ⟨upaść⟩ **2.** (*heart*) walić, łomotać **III** *s* **1.** łupnięcie *n* **2.** głuche uderzenie *n* **3.** walnięcie *n*, grzmotnięcie *n*; **thump out** *v/t* **1.** grać ⟨za-⟩ głośno **2.** bębnić; **thump•ing** ['θʌmpɪŋ] *adj infml* **1.** *majority*: miażdżący **2.** *defeat*: druzgocący **3.** ogromny

thun•der ['θʌndə] **I** *s* grzmot *m* **II** *v/i* **1.** grzmieć ⟨za-⟩; ***it ~s*** grzmi **2.** (*sound*) dudnić **3.** jechać ⟨jeździć⟩ z hukiem **4.** krzyczeć ⟨krzyknąć⟩, grzmieć ⟨za-⟩; **thun•der out** *v/t* wykrzykiwać ⟨-rzyczeć⟩

'thun•der•bolt *s* piorun *m*; **'thun•der•clap** *s* grzmot *m* (pioruna); **'thunder•cloud** *s* chmura *f* burzowa

thun•der•ous ['θʌndərəs] *adj* **1.** *applause*: gromki **2.** *look*: piorunujący **3.** *face expression*: gniewny

thun•der•storm ['θʌndəstɔːm] *s* burza *f* z piorunami; **'thun•der•struck** *adj* jak rażony gromem

thun•der•y ['θʌndərɪ] *adj weather*: burzowy

Thurs•day ['θɜːzdeɪ] *s* czwartek *m*

thus [ðʌs] *adv* **1.** w ten sposób **2.** tak więc, a zatem

thwart [θwɔːt] *v/t plans*: udaremniać ⟨-nić⟩

thyme [taɪm] *s* tymianek *m*

thy•roid gland ['θaɪrɔɪdglænd] *s ANAT* tarczyca *f*

ti•ar•a [tɪ'ɑːrə] *s* tiara *f*

Ti•bet [tɪ'bet] *s* Tybet

tic [tɪk] *s* tik *m*

tick[1] [tɪk] *s* kleszcz *m*

tick[2] [~] **I** *s* **1.** (*mark*) ptaszek *m* **2.** tykanie *n* **3.** *Br infml* moment *m*, chwila *f* **4.** (*credit*) ***on ~*** *Br dated* na krechę **II** *v/t* odhaczać ⟨-czyć⟩ **III** *v/i* tykać; **tick away** *v/i* (*time*) mijać ⟨minąć⟩; **tick off** *v/t* **1.** *Br infml* ochrzanić **2.** *Br* odhaczać ⟨-czyć⟩; **tick over** *v/i Br* **1.** (*engine*) chodzić na jałowym biegu **2.** *infml* (*company*) pracować na pół gwizdka

tick•er ['tɪkə] *s infml* serce *n*

tick•et ['tɪkɪt] **I** *s* **1.** bilet *m*; ***a bus ~*** bilet autobusowy; ***a plane ~*** bilet na samolot **2.** mandat *m* **3.** etykieta *f* **4.** *Am* lista *f* wyborcza **II** *v/t* ***be ~ed for*** dostać mandat za *A*; **'ti•cket col•lec•tor** *s* **1.** konduktor *m* **2.** bileter *m*

'ti•cket in•spec•tor *s* kontroler *m* biletów; **'ti•cket ma•chine** *s* automat *m* biletowy; **'ti•cket of•fice** *s* kasa *f* biletowa; **'tick•et tout** *s Br infml* konik *m*

tick•ing ['tɪkɪŋ] *s* **1.** tykanie *n* **2.** (*fabric*) inlet *m*; **tick•ing 'off** *s infml* bura *f*, ochrzan *m*

tick•le ['tɪkl] **I** *v/t* **1.** łaskotać ⟨po-⟩ **2.** łechtać ⟨po-⟩; ***~ s.o.'s fancy*** połechtać czyjąś próżność; ***be ~d pink*** zostać mile połechtanym **II** *s* łaskotanie *n*; **tickl•ish** ['tɪklɪʃ] *adj* **1.** ***be ~*** mieć łaskotki **2.** łaskoczący **3.** *problem*: drażliwy

tid•al ['taɪdl] *adj* pływowy; **ti•dal wave** ['taɪdlweɪv] *s* **1.** fala *f* pływowa **2.** *criminality*: fala *f*

tid•bit ['tɪdbɪt] *s Am a. fig* okruch *m*, okruszek *m*

tid•dly•winks ['tɪdlɪwɪŋks] *s* (*game*) pchełki *pl*

tide [taɪd] **I** *s* **1.** pływ *m*; ***high ~*** przypływ; ***low ~*** odpływ; ***at high ~*** w czasie przypływu **2.** *fig* fala *f*; ***a ~ of crime*** fala przestępczości **3.** *fig* prąd *m*; ***go with the ~*** płynąć z prądem **II** *v/t* ***~ s.o. over*** pomóc komuś przetrwać trudne czasy

ti•di•ness ['taɪdɪnɪs] *s* **1.** czystość *f* **2.** porządek *m*

ti•dy ['taɪdɪ] **I** *adj* **1.** posprzątany, uporządkowany; ***keep one's room ~*** utrzymywać porządek w pokoju **2.** schludny; ***neat and ~*** czysty i schludny **3.** staranny **4.** *infml sum*: ładny, spory **II** *v/t* **1.** sprzątać ⟨po-⟩ **2.** porządkować ⟨u-⟩; **tidy away** *v/t Br* **1.** uprzątać ⟨-tnąć⟩ **2.** odkładać ⟨odłożyć⟩ na miejsce; **tidy up** *v/t* **1.** sprzątać ⟨po-⟩ **2.** porządkować ⟨u-⟩ **3.** dopracowywać ⟨-cować⟩

tie [taɪ] **I** *s* **1.** krawat *m* **2.** więź *f*; ***family ~s*** więzi rodzinne; ***diplomatic ~s*** stosunki dyplomatyczne **3.** *SPORT* remis *m*; ***end in a ~*** zakończyć się remisem **4.** *SPORT* mecz *m* **6.** *MUS* łącznik *m* **7.** *Am* podkład *m* (kolejowy) **II** *v/t* **1.** wiązać ⟨z-⟩; ***~ back one's hair*** związać włosy; ***my hands are ~d*** *fig* mam związane ręce **2.** zawiązywać ⟨-zać⟩; ***~ a ribbon*** zawiązać kokardę **3.** łączyć ⟨po-⟩ **4.** uzależniać ⟨-nić⟩; ***pay increases are ~d to inflation*** podwyżki płac są uzależnione od inflacji **5.** *fig* uwiązywać ⟨-zać⟩; ***be ~d to the house with the baby*** być uwiązanym z dzieckiem w domu **III** *v/i* **1.** wiązać się, być wiązanym **2.** remisować ⟨z-⟩; **tie down** *v/t fig* **1.** uwiązywać ⟨-zać⟩ **2.** ograniczać ⟨-czyć⟩; **tie in with** *v/i* **1.** zgadzać się z *I* **2.** mieć związek z *I*; **tie up** *v/t* **1.** wiązać ⟨z-⟩ **2.** *hands, legs*: związywać ⟨-zać⟩, krępować ⟨s-⟩ **3.** *dog*: uwiązywać ⟨-zać⟩ **4.** *boat*: cumować ⟨przy-⟩ **5.** ***be tied up*** **a)** być zajętym **b)** być związanym (***with*** z *I*) **c)** (*money*) być ulokowanym **6.** finalizować ⟨s-⟩

'tie•break *Br*, **'tie•break•er** *Am s* (*tennis*) tie-break *m*; **'tie•pin** *s* spinka *f* do krawata

tier [tɪə] *s* **1.** warstwa *f* **2.** poziom *m* **3.** szczebel *m* **4.** kondygnacja *f*

'tie-up *s* **1.** *ECON* połączenie *n*, fuzja *f* **2.** *Br* związek *m*; ***the ~ between politics and economy*** związki polityki z gospodarką **3.** *Am* zastój *m* **4.** ***a traffic ~*** *Am* korek *m*

tiff [tɪf] *s* sprzeczka *f*

ti•ger ['taɪgə] *s* tygrys *m*

tight [taɪt] **I** *adj* **1.** ciasny; ***twist one's hair into a ~ knot*** ciasno związać włosy **2.** obcisły; ***a ~ pair of jeans*** obcisłe dżinsy **3.** naciągnięty **4.** napięty **5.** *grip*: mocny **6.** *screw*: mocno dokręcony **7.** *throat*: ściśnięty **8.** *control*: dokładny **9.** *turning*: ostry **10.** *infml* skąpy **11.** (*drunk*) *infml* wstawiony **II** *adv* **1.** mocno; ***hold s.o. ~*** mocno kogoś objąć **2.** ciasno; ***packed ~*** ciasno zapakowany **3.** dobrze; ***sleep ~!*** śpij dobrze!; **tight•en** ['taɪtn] **I** *v/t* **1.** napinać ⟨-piąć⟩, naprężać ⟨-żyć⟩ **2.** dokręcać ⟨-cić⟩ **3.** *grip*: zacieśniać ⟨-nić⟩ **4.** *restrictions*: zaostrzać ⟨-rzyć⟩ **5.** ***~ one's belt*** *fig* zaciskać pasa **II** *v/i* **1.** zaciskać ⟨-snąć⟩ się **2.** napinać ⟨-piąć⟩ się; **tighten up** *v/i* (*restrictions, legislation*) zostać zaostrzonym

tightfist•ed [taɪt'fɪstɪd] *adj* skąpy; **tight•fit•ting** [taɪt'fɪtɪŋ] *adj clothes*: obcisły; **tight'knit** *adj community*: zżyty; **tight-lipped** [taɪt'lɪpt] *adj* **1.** ***be ~ about*** nie chcieć mówić o *L* **2.** z zaciśniętymi ustami

tight•ly ['taɪtlɪ] → ***tight II***

tight•rope ['taɪtrəʊp] *s* lina *f* (do akrobacji); ***walk a ~*** *fig* balansować na linie; **'tight•rope walk•er** *s* linoskoczek *m*

tights [taɪts] *pl Br* rajstopy *pl*

'tight•wad *s Am infml* kutwa *m/f*

ti•gress ['taɪgrɪs] *s* tygrysica *f*

tile [taɪl] **I** *s* **1.** dachówka *f* **2.** płytka *f* ceramiczna, kafelek *m* **II** *v/t* **1.** kryć ⟨po-⟩ dachówką **2.** kafelkować ⟨wy-⟩, wykładać ⟨wyłożyć⟩ kafelkami; **'til•er** *s* **1.** dekarz *m* **2.** glazurnik *m*

till[1] [tɪl] → ***until***

till[2] [~] *s Br* kasa *f* sklepowa; ***pay at the ~*** płacić przy kasie

till[3] [~] *v/t land*: uprawiać

tilt [tɪlt] **I** *v/i* **1.** przechylać ⟨-lić⟩ się **2.** ***~ at windmills*** walczyć z wiatrakami **II** *v/t* przechylać ⟨-lić⟩ **III** *s* **1.** przechylenie *n* **2.** ***at full ~*** **a)** z maksymalną prędkością **b)** co sił w nogach **c)** pełną parą

tim•ber ['tɪmbə] *s* **1.** drewno *n* **2.** drewniany bal *m* **3.** drewniana belka *f*

time [taɪm] **I** *s* **1.** czas *m*; ***some ~ ago*** jakiś czas temu; ***all the ~*** (przez) cały czas; ***at the ~*** wówczas, wtedy; ***at ~s*** czasami; ***at the same ~*** w tym samym czasie, jednocześnie; ***for the ~ being*** na razie, tymczasowo; ***from ~ to ~*** od czasu do czasu; ***on ~*** punktualnie; ***in ~ for dinner*** w sam raz na obiad; ***be ahead of one's ~*** wyprzedzać swoje czasy; ***keep up with the ~s*** iść z duchem czasu; ***take one's ~*** nie spieszyć się; ***have a good ~*** dobrze się bawić; ***there is no ~ to lose*** nie ma czasu do stracenia; ***in record ~*** w rekordowym czasie **2.** godzina *f*; ***what's the ~?*** która godzina?; ***can you tell me the ~?*** czy możesz mi powiedzieć, która godzina?; ***what ~?*** o której godzinie?; ***this ~ tomorrow*** jutro o tej porze **3.** raz *m*; ***next ~*** następnym razem; ***how many ~s?*** ile razy?; ***every ~ I hear that song*** zawsze, kiedy słyszę tę piosenkę; ***~ and ~ again***, ***~ after ~*** ciągle, stale; ***this ~*** tym razem; ***three ~s*** trzy razy **4.** *MUS* takt *m*, ***in ~*** do taktu **5.** rytm *m*; ***in ~ with the music*** w rytm muzyki; ***beat ~*** wybijać rytm; ***clap one's hands to keep ~*** klaskać do rytmu **6.** tempo *n*; ***keep ~*** trzymać tempo **II** *v/t* **1.** planować ⟨za-⟩ godzinę **2.** planować ⟨za-⟩ termin **3.** *moment*: wybierać ⟨-brać⟩; ***~ s.th. well*** (***badly***) wybrać dobry (zły) moment na coś; ***his attack was badly ~d*** zaatakował w złym momencie **10.** mierzyć ⟨z-⟩ czas; **'time bomb** *s* **1.** bomba *f* zegarowa **2.** *fig* bomba *f* z opóźnionym zapłonem; **'time cap•sule** *s* kapsuła *f* czasu (*pojemnik z dokumentami z epoki*); **'time•card** *s Am* karta *f* kontrolna pracownika; **'time clock** *s* zegar *m* kontrolny (czasu pracy); **'time-con•sum•ing** *adj* czasochłonny; **'time dif•fer•ence** *s* różnica *f* czasu; **'time-hon•oured** *Br*, **'*time-honored*** *Am adj* uświęcony tradycją; **'time-keep•er** *s* **1.** *SPORT* sędzia *m* czasowy **2.** ***be a good*** (***bad***) **~** przychodzić do pracy punktualnie (niepunktualnie); **'time-lag** *s* zwłoka *f*, opóźnienie *n*; **time-lapse photography** *s* ekspozycja *f* poklatkowa

time•less ['taɪmlɪs] *adj* **1.** ponadczasowy **2.** wieczny

'time lim•it *s* termin *m*

time•ly ['taɪmlɪ] *adj* w samą porę

'time ma•chine *s* wehikuł *m* czasu

'time•out *s SPORT* **1.** czas *m* **2.** przerwa *f*

tim•er ['taɪmə] *s* **1.** minutnik *m* **2.** regulator *m* czasowy

'time•sav•ing *adj* pozwalający zaoszczędzić czas; **'time•scale** *s* okres *m*; ***within a six-month ~*** w przeciągu sześciu miesięcy; **time shar•ing**, **'*time share*** *s* współwłasność *f* nieruchomości (z prawem użytkowania przez część roku); **'time sig•nal** *s RADIO* sygnał *m* czasu; **'time switch** *s* wyłącznik *m* zegarowy

'time•ta•ble ['taɪmteɪbl] **I** *s* **1.** rozkład *m* jazdy **2.** plan *m* zajęć **3.** program *m* **II** *v/t* planować ⟨za-⟩ termin; **'time warp** *s* dziura *f* czasowa; **'time zone** *s* strefa *f* czasowa

tim•id ['tɪmɪd] *adj* nieśmiały

tim•ing ['taɪmɪŋ] *s* **1.** wyczucie *n* czasu **2.** wybór *m* czasu; ***the ~ of his resignation was completely wrong*** wybrał fatalny moment na złożenie rezygnacji

tin [tɪn] *s* **1.** *CHEM* cyna *f* **2.** *Br* puszka *f*; ***a ~ of beans*** puszka fasoli; **3.** *Br* blacha *f* do pieczenia

tinc•ture ['tɪŋktʃə] *s MED* nalewka *f*

tin•der ['tɪndə] *s* podpałka *f*; **'tin•der-box** *s fig* beczka *f* prochu; **tin•der-'dry** *adj* suchy jak pieprz

tine [taɪn] *s* **1.** *fork*: ząb *m* **2.** ostre zakończenie *n*

tin•foil ['tɪnfɔɪl] *s* folia *f* aluminiowa

tinge [tɪndʒ] **I** *v/t* zabarwiać ⟨-wić⟩; ***surprise ~d with disapproval*** zaskoczenie połączone z dezaprobatą **II** *s* **1.** zabarwienie *n*, odcień *m* **2.** domieszka *f* **3.** *fig* nuta *f*

tin•gle ['tɪŋgl] **I** *v/i* **1.** ***his feet ~d*** czuł

T

mrowienie w stopach **2.** ***the cold made her nose ~*** mróz szczypał ją w nos **3.** ***~ with*** drżeć z *G* **II** *s* **1.** mrowienie *n* **2.** szczypanie *n* **3.** dreszczyk *m* (emocji)

tin 'hat *s* hełm *m*

tin•ker ['tɪŋkə] *v/i*: ***~ with*** majstrować przy *L*

tin•kle ['tɪŋkl] **I** *s* **1.** brzęk *m* **2.** dzwonek *m* **II** *v/i* **1.** brzęczeć ⟨za-⟩ **2.** dzwonić ⟨za-⟩; ***give s.o. a ~*** *Br infml* przekręcić do kogoś

tinned [tɪnd] *adj Br* w puszce, konserwowy; ***~ food*** konserwy

tin•ni•tus [tɪ'naɪtəs] *s* MED dzwonienie *n* w uszach

tin•ny ['tɪnɪ] *adj Br sound*: metaliczny

'tin o•pen•er *s* otwieracz *m* do puszek

tin•sel ['tɪnsl] *s* lameta *f*

tint [tɪnt] **I** *s* **1.** odcień *m*, zabarwienie *n* **2.** farba *f* do włosów **II** *v/t* **1.** *hair*: farbować ⟨u-⟩ **2.** *glass*: barwić ⟨zabarwić⟩; **tint•ed** ['tɪntɪd] *adj* **1.** *hair*: farbowany **2.** *glass*: barwiony

ti•ny ['taɪnɪ] *adj* **1.** malutki **2.** drobny

tip[1] [tɪp] *s* **1.** końcówka *f* **2.** koniuszek *m*; ***it's on the ~ of my tongue*** mam to na końcu języka **3.** czubek *m*; ***the ~ of the iceberg*** *fig* wierzchołek góry lodowej

tip[2] [~] **I** *s* **1.** rada *f*, porada *f* **2.** wskazówka *f* **3.** napiwek *m* **II** *v/t* dawać ⟨dać⟩ napiwek

tip[3] [~] **I** *v/t* **1.** przechylać ⟨-lić⟩ **2.** przewracać ⟨-rócić⟩ **3.** *rubbish*: wyrzucać ⟨-cić⟩ **4.** wylewać ⟨-lać⟩ **5.** wysypywać ⟨-pać⟩ **6.** typować ⟨wy-⟩ **II** *v/i* **1.** przechylać ⟨-lić⟩ się **2.** przewracać ⟨-rócić⟩ się **III** *s* **1.** *Br* wysypisko *n* (śmieci) **2.** *Br fig* chlew *m*; **tip off** *v/t* **1.** informować ⟨po-⟩ **2.** *infml* dawać ⟨dać⟩ cynk; **tip over I** *v/i* przewracać ⟨-rócić⟩ się **II** *v/t* przewracać ⟨-rócić⟩

'tip-off *s* **1.** poufna informacja *f* **2.** *infml* cynk *m*

tipped [tɪpt] *adj cigarette*: z filtrem

tip•ple ['tɪpl] *s infml* (*alcoholic*) drink *m*

tip•sy ['tɪpsɪ] *adj infml* (lekko) wstawiony, podchmielony

'tip•toe I *s* ***on ~(s)*** na palcach **II** *v/i* iść ⟨chodzić⟩ na palcach; **'tip•top** *adj* pierwszorzędny, doskonały; ***in ~ condition*** w doskonałym stanie

ti•rade [taɪ'reɪd] *s* tyrada *f*

tire[1] [taɪə] *Am* → ***tyre***

tire[2] [~] **I** *v/t* męczyć ⟨z-⟩ **II** *v/i* męczyć ⟨z-⟩ się; **tire out** *v/t* **1.** wyczerpywać ⟨-pać⟩ **2.** bardzo męczyć ⟨z-⟩; **tired** [taɪəd] *adj* **1.** zmęczony; ***be ~ of*** mieć dość **2.** *phrase*: wyświechtany; **tiredness** ['taɪədnɪs] *s* zmęczenie *n*

tire•less ['taɪəlɪs] *adj* **1.** niestrudzony **2.** niezmordowany

tire•some ['taɪəsəm] *adj* **1.** męczący **2.** denerwujący

tir•ing ['taɪərɪŋ] *adj* męczący

ti•ro → ***tyro***

tis•sue ['tɪʃuː] *s* **1.** ANAT tkanka *f* **2.** chusteczka *f* higieniczna **3.** → ***tissue paper*** **4.** ***a ~ of lies*** stek kłamstw; **'tis•sue pa•per** *s* bibułka *f*

tit[1] [tɪt] *s vulg* cycek *m*

tit[2] [~] *s* BIOL sikora *f*

tit[3] [~] *s*: ***~ for tat*** wet za wet

ti•tan•ic [taɪ'tænɪk] *adj* **1.** tytaniczny **2.** ogromny

ti•tan•i•um [taɪ'teɪnɪəm] *s* CHEM tytan *m*

tit•bit ['tɪtbɪt] *s Br* smakołyk *m*

tit•il•late ['tɪtɪleɪt] *v/t* podniecać ⟨-cić⟩

ti•tle ['taɪtl] **I** *s* **1.** tytuł *m* **2.** SPORT tytuł *m* (mistrzowski); ***a world ~*** tytuł mistrza świata **3.** JUR tytuł *m* własności **4.** prawo *n* **II** *v/t* tytułować ⟨za-⟩, nadawać ⟨-dać⟩ tytuł; **ti•tle deed** *s* JUR tytuł *m* własności; **'ti•tle fight** *s* (*boxing*) walka *f* o tytuł mistrzowski; **'ti•tle•hold•er** *s* **1.** SPORT mistrz *m* **2.** posiadacz *m* tytułu własności; **'ti•tle page** *s* strona *f* tytułowa; **'ti•tle role** *s* rola *f* tytułowa

'tit•mouse *pl -mice s* BIOL sikora *f*

tit•ter ['tɪtə] **I** *v/i* chichotać ⟨za-⟩ **II** *s* chichot *m*

tit•tle-tat•tle ['tɪtltætl] *s infml* ploteczki *pl*

tit•u•lar ['tɪtjʊlə] *adj* **1.** nominalny **2.** tytularny

tiz•zy ['tɪzɪ] *s infml* zdenerwowanie *n*; ***be in a ~*** denerwować się

to [tə] *strong form* [tʊ; tuː] **I** *prep* **1.** (*direction, aim*) do *G*, na *A*; ***~ school*** do szkoły; ***~ Paris*** do Paryża; ***fall ~ the ground*** upaść na ziemię; ***travel from place ~ place*** podróżować z miejsca na miejsce **2.** (*aim, result*) do *G*; ***~ perfection*** do perfekcji; ***~ tears*** do łez; ***come to s.o.'s aid***

T

przyjść komuś z pomocą; **~ *my surprise*** ku mojemu zdziwieniu; ***sentence s.o. ~ death*** skazać kogoś na śmierć **3.** (*scope*) do *G*; ***he is 25 ~ 30 years old*** ma około 25-30 lat; ***from opera ~ rock*** od opery do rocka **4.** (*hour*) za *A*; ***it's five ~ ten*** jest za pięć dziesiąta **5.** (*dative*) *D*; ***he gave the book ~ his sister*** dał tę książkę swojej siostrze; ***I am grateful ~ my parents*** jestem wdzięczny swoim rodzicom **6.** (*in comparisons*) niż *N*, od *G*; ***I prefer walking ~ jogging*** wolę spacerować niż biegać **7.** (*toast*) za *A*; ***drink ~ s.o.*** wypić za czyjeś zdrowie **II** *particle* **1.** (*infinitive*) **~ *go*** iść; ***easy ~ understand*** łatwy do zrozumienia **2.** aby, żeby; ***he only does it ~ earn money*** robi to tylko dla pieniędzy; ***I went out ~ buy some food*** wyszedłem kupić coś do jedzenia; ***I did it ~ help you*** zrobiłem to, żeby ci pomóc **III** *adv* ***push the door ~*** zamknąć drzwi; **~ *and fro*** tam i z powrotem

toad [təʊd] *s* ropucha *f*; **toad•stool** ['təʊdstu:l] *s* muchomor *m*

toad•y ['təʊdɪ] **I** *s* lizus *m* **II** *v/i* podlizywać ⟨-zać⟩ się (**to** *D*)

toast [təʊst] **I 1.** *s* tost *m*, grzanka *f* **2.** toast *m*; ***propose a ~ to*** wznieść toast za *A* **II** *v/t* **1.** opiekać ⟨opiec⟩ **2.** rumienić ⟨przy-⟩ **3.** wznosić ⟨wznieść⟩ toast za *A*; **toast•er** ['təʊstə] *s* toster *m*, opiekacz *m*

to•bac•co [tə'bækəʊ] *pl -cos s* tytoń *m*; **to•bac•co•nist** [tə'bækənɪst] *s* właściciel *m* sklepu tytoniowego; ***a ~'s***, **~*s*** sklep tytoniowy

to•bog•gan [tə'bɒgən] *s* **1.** sanki *pl* **2.** tobogan *m*

tod [tɒd] *s*: ***on your ~*** *infml* sam jak palec

to•day [tə'deɪ] **I** *adv* **1.** dzisiaj, dziś **2.** w dzisiejszych czasach, obecnie **II** *s* dzisiaj *n*, dziś *n*; **~ *week***, ***a week ~*** od dziś za tydzień; **~*'s paper*** dzisiejsza gazeta

T

tod•dle ['tɒdl] *v/i* (*child*) **1.** dreptać **2.** chodzić; **tod•dler** ['tɒdlə] *s* dziecko *n* uczące się chodzić

tod•dy ['tɒdɪ] *s* grog *m*

to-do [tə'du:] *s infml* zamieszanie *n*

toe [təʊ] **I** *s* palec *m* u nogi; ***keep s.o. on his ~s*** trzymać kogoś w pogotowiu **II** *v/t* **~ *the line*** podporządkować się; **toe•nail** ['təʊneɪl] *s* paznokieć *m* u nogi

tof•fee ['tɒfɪ] *s* toffi *n*; **'tof•fee ap•ple** *s Br* jabłko *n* na patyku w polewie z toffi; **tof•fee-nosed** ['tɒfɪnəʊzd] *adj*: ***be ~*** *Br infml* zadzierać nosa

tof•fy → ***toffee***

to•geth•er [tə'geðə] **I** *adv* **1.** razem; ***we grew up ~*** razem dorastaliśmy; ***he has more money than the rest of us put ~*** ma więcej pieniędzy niż my wszyscy razem wzięci **2.** ze sobą; ***mix the sand and cement ~*** wymieszać piasek z cementem **II** *adj person*: (dobrze) zorganizowany; **to•geth•er•ness** [tə'geðənɪs] *s* poczucie *n* wspólnoty

tog•gle ['tɒgl] **I** *s* **1.** (*fastening*) kołek *m* **2.** TECH przełącznik *m* **II** *v/i* INF przełączać ⟨-czyć⟩ się (**between** pomiędzy *I*); **'tog•gle key** *s* INF klawisz *m* przełączający; **'tog•gle switch** *s* TECH przełącznik *m* (dwustabilny)

toil [tɔɪl] **I** *v/i* **1.** trudzić się, pracować z mozołem **2.** poruszać ⟨-szyć⟩ się z trudem **II** *s* mozolna praca *f*, trud *m*

toi•let ['tɔɪlɪt] *s* toaleta *f*, ubikacja *f*; ***go to the ~*** iść do toalety; **'toi•let bag** *s* (*bag*) kosmetyczka *f*; **toil•et•ries** ['tɔɪlɪtrɪz] *pl* przybory *pl* toaletowe; **'toil•et pa•per** *s* papier toaletowy; **'toi•let roll** *s Br* rolka *f* papieru toaletowego

to•ken ['təʊkən] **I** *s* **1.** żeton *m* **2.** *Br* kupon *m* **3.** symbol *m*, znak *m*; ***as a ~ of our gratitude*** na znak naszej wdzięczności; ***by the same ~*** z tych samych powodów **II** *adj gesture*, *sum*: symboliczny; **'to•ken strike** *s* strajk *m* ostrzegawczy

told [təʊld] *Past Simple and Past Participle* → ***tell***

tol•e•ra•ble ['tɒlərəbl] *adj* **1.** *heat*: do zniesienia, znośny **2.** *meal*: całkiem spory, przyzwoity; **tol•er•a•bly** ['tɒlərəblɪ] *adv* **1.** całkiem, znośnie **2.** przyzwoicie; **tol•e•rance** ['tɒlərəns] **1.** tolerancja *f* **2.** odporność *f* (**to** na *A*); **tol•e•rant** ['tɒlərənt] *adj* **1.** tolerancyjny **2.** odporny; **tol•e•rate** ['tɒləreɪt] *v/t* **1.** tolerować, znosić ⟨znieść⟩ **2.** wytrzymywać ⟨-mać⟩

toll[1] [təʊl] *s* **1.** opłata *f* za przejazd **2.** liczba *f* ofiar; ***the death ~*** liczba ofiar śmiertelnych **3.** ***take a heavy ~*** *fig* zebrać obfite żniwo; ***take its ~ on s.o.*** dać się komuś we znaki **4.** *Am* opłata *f* za połączenie międzymiastowe

toll² [~] **I** *v/i* (*bell*) bić; ***for whom the bell ~s*** komu bije dzwon **II** *v/t hours*: wybijać ⟨-bić⟩

'toll booth *s* punkt *m* pobierania opłaty za przejazd autostradą; **'toll bridge** *s* płatny most *m*; **toll-'free** *adj Am telephone number*: bezpłatny; **'toll road** *s* płatna droga *f*

tom [tɒm] → ***tomcat***

to•ma•to [tə'mɑːtəʊ] *pl -toes s* pomidor *m*; **to•'ma•to juice** *s* sok *m* pomidorowy; **to•ma•to 'ketch•up** *s* keczup *m*; **to•ma•to 'sauce** *s* sos *m* pomidorowy

tomb [tuːm] *s* **1.** grobowiec *m* **2.** grób *m*

tom•boy ['tɒmbɔɪ] *s* chłopczyca *f*

tomb•stone ['tuːmstəʊn] *s* nagrobek *m*

tom•cat ['tɒmkæt] *s* kocur *m*

tome [təʊm] *s* **1.** tom *m* **2.** tomisko *n*

tom•fool•er•y [tɒm'fuːlərɪ] *s* wygłupy *pl*

to•mog•ra•phy [tə'mɒgrəfɪ] *s MED* tomografia *f*; ***computer ~*** tomografia komputerowa

to•mor•row [tə'mɒrəʊ] **I** *adv* jutro; ***~ night*** jutro wieczorem **II** *s* jutro *n*; ***~ week, a week ~*** od jutra za tydzień; ***the day after ~*** pojutrze; ***~'s paper*** jutrzejsza gazeta; ***as if there's no ~*** jakby świat miał się zaraz skończyć

ton [tʌn] *s pl ton, tons* tona *f*; ***~s of money*** *infml* kupa forsy; ***hit s.o. like a ~ of bricks*** *fig* uderzyć kogoś jak obuchem

tone [təʊn] **I** *s* **1.** ton *m*; ***a ~ of voice*** ton głosu; ***the ~ of her words was ironic*** ton jej wypowiedzi był ironiczny **2.** barwa *f* dźwięku **3.** odcień *m* **4.** *TEL* sygnał *m* **5.** tonus *m* **II** *v/t* (*a.* ***~ up***) *muscles*: wyrabiać ⟨-robić⟩ **III** *v/i* (*a.* ***~ in***) **1.** pasować (***with*** z *I*) **2.** współgrać (***with*** z *I*); **tone down** *v/t* **1.** tonować ⟨s-⟩ **2.** łagodzić ⟨z-⟩ **3.** *colour*: rozjaśniać ⟨-nić⟩

tone•less ['təʊnləs] *adj voice*: bezbarwny

ton•er ['təʊnə] *s* **1.** (*printer, photocopier*) toner *m* **2.** (*cosmetic*) tonik *m*; **'ton•er cart•ridge** *s* wkład *m* drukujący

tongs [tɒŋz] *pl* **1.** szczypce *pl* **2.** lokówka *f*

tongue [tʌŋ] *s* **1.** język *m*; ***stick one's ~ out*** wystawiać język; ***bite one's ~*** ugryźć się w język; ***hold one's ~*** trzymać język za zębami; ***with one's ~ in one's cheek*** żartem, żartobliwie **2.** *lit* język *m*; ***mother ~*** język ojczysty; **'tongue twist•er** *s* łamaniec *m* językowy

ton•ic ['tɒnɪk] *s* **1.** (*drink*) tonik *m* **2.** (*cosmetic*) tonik *m* **3.** *MUS* tonika *f*; **'ton•ic wa•ter** → ***tonic 1***

to•night [tə'naɪt] **I** *adv* dziś wieczorem **II** *s* dzisiejszy wieczór *m*

ton•sil ['tɒnsl] *s ANAT* migdałek *m*; **ton•sil•li•tis** [tɒnsə'laɪtɪs] *s MED* zapalenie *n* migdałków

too [tuː] *adv* **1.** też, także; ***can I come ~?*** mogę też przyjść? **2.** za, zbyt; ***he's ~ young*** jest za młody **3.** a do tego, a co więcej; ***she broke her leg, and on her birthday ~!*** złamała nogę, i to w swoje urodziny!

took [tuːk] *Past Simple* → ***take***

tool [tuːl] *s* **1.** narzędzie *n*; ***the ~s of one's trade*** czyjeś narzędzia pracy **2.** *fig* marionetka *f* **3.** *vulg* (*penis*) interes *m*; **'tool•bag** *s* torba *f* na narzędzia; **'tool•bar** *s INF* pasek *m* narzędzi; **'tool•box** *s* skrzynka *f* na narzędzia; **'tool•kit** *s* zestaw *m* narzędzi; **'tool•shed** *s* szopa *f* na narzędzia

toot [tuːt] **I** *s* (*car-horn sound*) trąbienie *n*; ***give a ~*** zatrąbić **II** *v/i* trąbić ⟨za-⟩ **III** *v/t* ***~ one's horn*** trąbić ⟨za-⟩

tooth [tuːθ] *pl teeth* [tiːθ] *s* ząb *m*; ***brush one's teeth*** myć zęby; ***through clenched teeth*** przez zaciśnięte zęby; ***in the teeth of*** *fig* pomimo *G*; ***get one's teeth into*** *fig* wgryzać się w *A*; ***fight ~ and nail*** *fig* walczyć zaciecie

'tooth•ache *s* ból *m* zęba; **'tooth•brush** *s* szczoteczka *f* do zębów; **tooth•less** ['tuːθlɪs] *adj* bezzębny; **'tooth•paste** *s* pasta *f* do zębów; **'tooth•pick** *s* wykałaczka *f*

top [tɒp] **I** *s* **1.** (*highest part*) góra *f*; ***at the ~ of the page*** u góry strony; ***fill the glass to the ~*** napełnić szklankę po brzegi; ***on ~ of*** na *L*; ***from ~ to toe*** od stóp do głów; ***from ~ to bottom*** od góry do dołu, z góry na dół; ***on ~ of***

T

each other jeden na drugim **2.** *mountain*: szczyt *m* **3.** *tree*: wierzchołek *m*, czubek *m* **4.** *table*: blat *m* **5.** top *m*, bluzka *f* **6.** *fig* góra *f*; ***the decision came from the ~*** decyzja przyszła z góry **7.** zakrętka *f* **8.** pokrywka *f* **9.** wieczko *n* **10.** (*toy*) bąk *m* **II** *adj* **1.** najwyższy; ***live on the ~ floor*** mieszkać na najwyższym piętrze **2.** najlepszy; ***~ marks*** najlepsze stopnie **III** *v/t* **1.** przekraczać ⟨-roczyć⟩; ***the sales ~ped $1 million*** sprzedaż przekroczyła milion dolarów **2.** przewyższać ⟨-szyć⟩ **3.** znajdować ⟨znaleźć⟩ się na szczycie **4.** *offer*: przebijać ⟨-bić⟩ **5.** pokrywać ⟨-ryć⟩; **top off** *v/t* **1.** kończyć ⟨za-⟩ **2.** zwieńczać ⟨-czyć⟩; **top up** *v/t Br* **1.** uzupełniać ⟨-nić⟩ **2.** zwiększać ⟨-szyć⟩ **3.** dolewać ⟨-lać⟩; ***can I top you up?*** dolać ci?

'top•flight *adj* najlepszy; **top 'hat** *s* cylinder *m*; **top 'heav•y** *adj* **1.** zbyt ciężki u góry, źle wyważony **2.** *fig* z przerostem stanowisk kierowniczych

top•ic ['tɒpɪk] *s* temat *m*; ***a ~ of conversation*** temat rozmowy; **top•ic•al** ['tɒpɪkl] *adj* aktualny, na czasie

top•less ['tɒplɪs] *adj* toples, topless

top-'lev•el *adj* **1.** *meeting*: na szczycie **2.** *performance*: na najwyższym poziomie; **'top•most** *adj* najwyższy; **top-'notch** *adj infml* pierwszorzędny, pierwsza klasa

to•pog•ra•phy [tə'pɒgrəfɪ] *s* topografia *f*

top•per ['tɒpə] *s infml* cylinder *m*

top•ping ['tɒpɪŋ] *s* COOK **1.** ***with a ~ of whipped cream*** z bitą śmietaną (na wierzchu) **2.** posypka *f* **3.** polewa *f* **4.** przybranie *n*

top•ple ['tɒpl] **I** *v/i* przewracać ⟨-rócić⟩ się **II** *v/t* **1.** przewracać ⟨-rócić⟩ **2.** *dictatorship*: obalać ⟨-lić⟩

top-'qual•i•ty *adj* najwyższej jakości; **top 'se•cret** *adj* ściśle tajny; **'top•soil** *s* górna warstwa *f* gleby; **'top•spin** *s* (*tennis*) topspin *m*

top•sy-tur•vy [tɒpsɪ'tɜːvɪ] *adj* **1.** do góry nogami **2.** *fig* na głowie; ***turn ~*** stanąć na głowie

torch [tɔːtʃ] *s* **1.** *Br* latarka *f* **2.** pochodnia *f* **3.** znicz *m*; ***the Olympic ~*** znicz olimpijski **4.** TECH *Am* opalarka *f*; **'torch•light** *s* **1.** światło *n* latarki; ***by ~*** przy świetle latarki **2.** światło *n* pochodni

tore [tɔː] *Past Simple* → ***tear***

tor•ment ['tɔːment] **I** *s* męczarnie *pl* **II** *v/t* dręczyć ⟨za-⟩, męczyć ⟨za-⟩; ***he was ~ed by uncertainty*** dręczyła go niepewność

torn [tɔːn] *Past Participle* → ***tear***

tor•na•do [tɔː'neɪdəʊ] *pl -does, -dos s* tornado *n*

tor•pe•do [tɔː'piːdəʊ] **I** *pl -does s* torpeda *f* **II** *v/t a. fig* torpedować ⟨s-⟩; **tor'pe•do boat** *s* kuter *m* torpedowy

tor•pid ['tɔːpɪd] *adj* apatyczny, odrętwiały; **tor•por** ['tɔːpə] *s* apatia *f*, odrętwienie *n*

torque [tɔːk] *s* PHYS moment *m* obrotowy

tor•rent ['tɒrənt] *s* **1.** strumień *m*, potok *m*; ***the rain was coming down in ~s*** lało jak z cebra **2.** *questions*: grad *m* **3.** *criticism*: fala *f*; **tor•ren•tial** [tə'renʃl] *adj rain*: ulewny

tor•rid ['tɒrɪd] *s* **1.** *affair*: namiętny **2.** *climate*: gorący

tor•sion ['tɔːʃn] *s* **1.** skręcanie *n* **2.** skręcenie *n*

tor•so ['tɔːsəʊ] *pl -sos s* **1.** tułów *m* **2.** tors *m*

tor•toise ['tɔːtəs] *s* żółw *m*; **'tor•toise•shell** *s* szylkret *m*

tor•tu•ous ['tɔːtʃʊəs] *adj* **1.** zawiły, skomplikowany **2.** pokrętny **3.** *road*: kręty

tor•ture ['tɔːtʃə] **I** *s* **1.** tortury *pl* **2.** tortura *f* **3.** *fig* tortura *f*, męczarnia *f* **II** *v/t* **1.** torturować **2.** zamęczać ⟨-czyć⟩, zadręczać ⟨-czyć⟩; ***he was ~d by memories*** dręczyły go wspomnienia; **'tor•ture cham•ber** *s* izba *f* tortur

To•ry ['tɔːrɪ] *Br* **I** *s* torys *m*, konserwatysta *m* **II** *adj* torysowski, konserwatywny

toss [tɒs] **I** *v/t* **1.** rzucać ⟨-cić⟩; ***~ the coin*** rzucić monetą **2.** odrzucać ⟨-cić⟩ do tyłu; ***~ one's head*** odrzucić głowę do tyłu **3.** kołysać **4.** mieszać ⟨wy-⟩ **5.** *pancake*: podrzucać ⟨-cić⟩ **II** *v/i* **1.** kołysać się **2.** przewracać się; ***~ and turn*** przewracać się z boku na bok **3.** (*a.* ***~ up***) rzucać ⟨-cić⟩ monetą **III** *s* **1.** *coin*: rzut *m*; ***I don't give a***

T

~ about it** infml* mam to gdzieś **2. *with a ~ of one's head odrzucając głowę do tyłu

'toss-up *s* **1.** rzut *m* monetą **2. *it's a ~ whether the prices will go up or down*** i wzrost, i spadek cen są równie prawdopodobne

tot [tɒt] **I** *s* **1.** (*child*) maluch *m*, brzdąc *m* **2.** *Br whisky*: kropla *f*, kapka *f* **II** *v/t* **~ *up*** *Br infml* dodawać, sumować

to•tal ['təʊtl] **I** *adj* **1.** *of figures*: łączny **2.** całkowity, zupełny **II** *s* suma *f*; ***in ~*** w sumie **III** *v/t* **1.** wynosić ⟨-nieść⟩; ***~ $1.5 million*** wynieść 1,5 miliona dolarów **2.** dodawać ⟨-dać⟩, sumować ⟨z-⟩

to•tal•i•tar•i•an [təʊtælı'terıən] *adj system*: totalitarny

to•tal•ly ['təʊtəlı] *adv* zupełnie, całkowicie

tote[1] [təʊt] *s* **1.** zakłady *pl* konne

tote[2] [~] *v/t* **2.** *Am infml* nosić ⟨nieść⟩; **tote bag** ['təʊtbæg] *s Am* torba *f* na ramię

to•tem pole ['təʊtəmpəʊl] *s* totem *m* słup *m* totemiczny

tot•ter ['tɔtə] *v/i* **1.** zataczać ⟨-toczyć⟩ się **2.** chwiać ⟨za-⟩ się (na nogach) **3.** (*government*, *regime*) chwiać ⟨za-⟩ się w posadach; **tot•ter•y** ['tɔtərı] *adj* chwiejny

touch [tʌtʃ] **I** *v/t* **1.** dotykać ⟨-tknąć⟩; ***~ wood*** *fig* odpukać w niemalowane drewno **2.** tykać ⟨tknąć⟩; ***you have hardly ~ed your food*** prawie nie tknąłeś jedzenia **3.** ruszać ⟨-szyć⟩; ***don't ~ my things!*** nie ruszaj moich rzeczy! **4.** wzruszać ⟨-szyć⟩, poruszać ⟨-szyć⟩ **5.** dotykać ⟨-tknąć⟩ się *G*, zabierać ⟨-brać⟩ się do *G*; ***everything she ~es turns to disaster*** wszystko, czego się dotknie, kończy się katastrofą **6.** dosięgać ⟨-gnąć⟩ **7.** osiągać ⟨-gnąć⟩ **II** *v/i* dotykać ⟨-tknąć⟩ się **III** *s* **1.** dotyk *m*; ***cold to the ~*** zimny w dotyku **2.** kontakt *m*; ***keep in ~ with*** być w kontakcie z *I*; ***be out of ~ with*** stracić kontakt z *I* **3.** dotknięcie *n*; ***put the finishing ~ to*** wykańczać **4.** charakter *m*; ***a more personal ~*** bardziej osobisty charakter **5.** podejście *n* **6.** odrobina *f*; ***a ~ too loud*** odrobinę za głośny **7.** ślad *m*; **touch down** *v/i* (*plane*) lądować ⟨wy-⟩; **touch off** *v/t fire*, *crisis*: wywoływać ⟨-łać⟩; **touch on** *v/i* **1.** dotykać ⟨-tknąć⟩ **2.** wspominać ⟨-mnieć⟩; **touch up** *v/t* **1.** *make-up*: poprawiać ⟨-wić⟩ **2.** retuszować ⟨pod-⟩ **3.** *Br infml* obmacywać

touch-and-'go *adj* **1.** niepewny **2.** krytyczny; **touch•down** ['tʌtʃdaʊn] *s* lądowanie *n*

tou•ché ['tu:ʃeı] *interj* **1.** (*fencing*) trafienie! **2.** *fig* punkt dla ciebie!

touched [tʌtʃt] *adj* wzruszony, poruszony; **touch•ing** ['tʌtʃıŋ] *adj* wzruszający, poruszający

touch•line ['tʌtʃlaın] SPORT linia *f* boczna, linia *f* autowa; **'touch screen** *s* ekran *m* dotykowy; **'touch•stone** *s* **1.** wzór *m* **2.** punkt *m* odniesienia; **'touch-type** *v/i* pisać ⟨na-⟩ metodą bezwzrokową (na klawiaturze)

touch•y ['tʌtʃı] *adj* **1.** *person*: drażliwy, przewrażliwiony (***about*** na punkcie *G*) **2.** *topic*: drażliwy, delikatny

tough [tʌf] *adj* **1.** trudny, ciężki **2.** twardy; ***~ luck*** *Br* trudno **3.** *shoes*, *rope*: mocny **4.** *person*: twardy, silny; **tough•en (up)** ['tʌfn] *v/t* **1.** *glass*, *character*: hartować ⟨za-⟩ **2.** *policy*: zaostrzać ⟨-rzyć⟩; **'tough guy** *s infml* twardziel *m*

tour [tʊə] **I** *s* **1.** podróż *f* **2.** wycieczka *f* **3.** zwiedzanie *n*; ***take s.o. on a ~*** oprowadzić kogoś **a ~ of inspection** inspekcja **4.** tournée *n*; ***the band is on ~ in France*** zespół jest na tournée we Francji **II** (*a.* ***~ around***) *v/t* **1.** odbywać ⟨-być⟩ tournée po *L* **2.** jeździć po *L*, podróżować po *L* **III** (*a.* ***~ around***) *v/i* odbywać ⟨-być⟩ tournée

'tour guide *s* przewodnik *m* (wycieczek)

tour•i•sm ['tʊrızm] *s* turystyka *f*; **tour•i•st** ['tʊrıst] *s* turysta *m*; **'tour•ist at•trac•tion** *s* atrakcja *f* turystyczna; **'tour•ist class** *s* klasa *f* turystyczna; **'tour•ist in•dus•try** *s* branża *f* turystyczna; **tour•i•st in•for•'ma•tion of•fice** *s* biuro *n* informacji turystycznej; **'tour•ist sea•son** *s* sezon *m* turystyczny; **'tour•ist trade** → ***tourist industry***; **tour•ist•y** ['tʊrıstı] *adj infml* **1.** nastawiony na turystów **2.** dla turystów

tour•na•ment ['tɔ:nəmənt] *s* turniej *m*

T

'tour op•er•a•tor *s* **1.** biuro *n* turystyczne **2.** organizator *m* wycieczek
tous•led ['taʊzld] *adj hair*: potargany
tout [taʊt] **I** *v/t* **1.** zachwalać, wychwalać **2.** reklamować **3.** ***~ business*** szukać klientów **4.** *tickets*: sprzedawać ⟨-dać⟩ po zawyżonej cenie **II** *s Br infml* konik *m*
tow [təʊ] **I** *v/t* holować; ***~ a car away*** odholować samochód **II** *s* hol *m*; ***take a ship in ~*** wziąć statek na hol; ***with his girlfriend in ~*** *fig* ze swoją dziewczyną, w towarzystwie swojej dziewczyny
to•wards [tə'wɔːdz] *Br*, ***to•ward*** *Am prep* **1.** w kierunku *G*, w stronę *G*, do *G*; ***~ the German border*** w stronę niemieckiej granicy **2.** około *G*; ***~ the end of April*** pod koniec kwietnia **3.** do *G*, w stosunku do *G*; ***be warm ~ s.o.*** być uprzejmym dla kogoś
tow•el ['taʊəl] **I** *s* ręcznik *m* **II** (*a.* ***~ down***) *v/t* wycierać ⟨-trzeć⟩ ręcznikiem; **'tow•el rail** *s Br* wieszak *m* na ręczniki
tow•er ['taʊə] **I** *s* wieża *f*; ***a ~ of strength*** *fig* opoka, ostoja **II** *v/t a. fig* górować (***over***/***above*** nad *I*); **tow•er block** *s Br* wieżowiec *m*; **tow•er•ing** ['taʊərɪŋ] *adj* **1.** ogromny **2.** górujący (nad okolicą) **3.** doskonały
town [taʊn] *s* **1.** miasto *n*; ***home ~*** miasto rodzinne; ***go to ~*** pojechać do miasta; ***go out on the ~*** wyjść na miasto **2.** miasteczko *n*; **town 'cen•tre** *Br* centrum *m* miasta; **town 'coun•cil** *s* rada *f* miejska; **town 'hall** *s* ratusz *m*; **'town house** *s* **1.** *Br* miejska rezydencja *f* **2.** dom *m* jednorodzinny w zabudowie szeregowej; **town planning** [taʊn'plænɪŋ] *s* urbanistyka *f*; **town•ship** ['taʊnʃɪp] *s* (*USA and Canada*) gmina *f* miejska
towns•folk ['taʊnzfəʊk] → ***townspeople***; **towns•peo•ple** ['taʊnzpiːpl] *pl* mieszkańcy *pl* miasta
'tow•rope *s* lina *f* holownicza; **'tow truck** *s Am* samochód *m* pomocy drogowej
tox•ic ['tɒksɪk] *adj* **1.** toksyczny **2.** trujący; **tox•ic 'waste** *s* odpady *pl* toksyczne
toxi•co•logi•cal [tɒksɪkə'lɒdʒɪkl] *adj* toksykologiczny
tox•in ['tɒksɪn] *s* **1.** toksyna *f* **2.** trucizna *f*
toy [tɔɪ] **I** *s* zabawka *f* **II** *v/i* **1.** bawić się (***with*** *I*); ***~ nervously with one's pen*** nerwowo bawić się długopisem **2.** rozważać ⟨-żyć⟩ (***with*** *A*) **III** *adj* miniaturowy; ***a ~ poodle*** pudel miniaturka; **'toy store** *s* sklep *m* z zabawkami
trace [treɪs] **I** *s* **1.** ślad *m*, trop *m*; ***without a ~*** bez śladu **2.** ślad *m*; ***~s of poison*** śladowe ilości trucizny **II** *v/t* **1.** tropić ⟨wy-⟩, szukać ⟨od-⟩; ***he was ~d to*** jego ślady prowadziły do *G* **2.** (*a.* ***~ back***) śledzić ⟨prze-⟩; ***~ back the family tree to the 16th century*** prześledzić drzewo genealogiczne do XVI wieku **3.** znajdować ⟨znaleźć⟩ **4.** *phone call*: namierzać ⟨-rzyć⟩ **5.** odrysowywać ⟨-sować⟩, kalkować ⟨prze-⟩; **'trace el•e•ment** *s* pierwiastek *m* śladowy
tra•che•a [trə'kiːə] *pl -cheae* [~iː] *s ANAT* tchawica *f*
trac•ing ['treɪsɪŋ] *s* kopia *f* (na kalce technicznej), kalka *f*; **trac•ing pa•per** ['treɪsɪŋpeɪpə] *s* kalka *f* kreślarska
track [træk] **I** *s* **1.** trop *m*; ***be on the right ~*** być na właściwym tropie; ***keep ~ of*** być na bieżąco z *I*; ***get one's life back on ~*** na nowo ułożyć sobie życie; ***get a relationship back on ~*** naprawić stosunki **2.** droga *f* gruntowa **3.** ślad *m*; ***~s in the snow*** ślady na śniegu **4.** *train*: tor *m* **5.** utwór *m* **6.** *TECH* ścieżka *f* **7.** *SPORT* bieżnia *f* **8.** *TECH* gąsienica *f* **II** *v/t* **1.** tropić ⟨wy-⟩ **2.** śledzić (tor lotu) **3.** obserwować ⟨za-⟩ **4.** *Am* zostawiać ⟨-wić⟩ ślady; **track down** *v/t criminal*: tropić ⟨wy-⟩
track-and-'field *s SPORT Am* lekkoatletyka *f*; **track-and-'field e•vents** *pl SPORT* konkurencje *pl* lekkoatletyczne
'track•ball *s* (*notebook*) trackball *m*, manipulator *m* kulkowy
tracked [trækt] *adj vehicle*: gąsienicowy
'track•er dog *s* pies *m* tropiciel
track e•vents *pl SPORT* biegi *pl*
'track•ing sta•tion *s* stacja *f* śledzenia (lotu)
track 'rec•ord *s*: ***have a good ~*** mieć na swoim koncie wiele osiągnięć

T

'track•suit *s* dres *m*

tract[1] [trækt] *s* **1.** *ANAT* drogi *pl*, układ *m*; ***the respiratory*** **~** drogi oddechowe **2.** teren *m*

tract[2] [~] *s* traktat *m*

trac•ta•ble ['træktəbl] *adj* **1.** możliwy do rozwiązania **2.** łatwy do wykonania **3.** łatwy **4.** posłuszny

trac•tion ['trækʃn] *s* **1.** *TECH* trakcja *f* **2.** *MED* wyciąg *m*; ***with his leg in*** **~** z nogą na wyciągu **3.** *wheels*: przyczepność *f*; **trac•tion en•gine** *s* silnik *m* trakcyjny

trac•tor ['træktə] *s* traktor *m*, ciągnik *m*

trade [treɪd] **I** *s* **1.** handel *m*; ***foreign*** **~** handel zagraniczny **2.** branża *f*; ***the food*** **~** branża spożywcza; ***a*** **~** ***magazine*** magazyn branżowy **3.** interesy *pl*; ***the*** **~** ***was good last month*** w zeszłym miesiącu interesy szły dobrze **4.** zawód *m*, fach *m* **II** *v/i* **1.** handlować (**in** *I*) **2.** prowadzić działalność (gospodarczą) **3.** (*shares*) być wycenianym na *A* **III** *v/t* **1.** sprzedawać ⟨-dać⟩; ***our products are*** **~*d*** ***worldwide*** nasze produkty są sprzedawane na całym świecie **2.** *shares*: obracać **3.** wymieniać ⟨-nić⟩ (**for** na *A*); **trade in** *v/t*: **~** ***an old car for a new one*** kupić nowy samochód, w rozliczeniu oddając stary; **trade on** *v/i image*, *name*: wykorzystywać ⟨-tać⟩

'trade a•gree•ment *s* umowa *f* handlowa; **'trade bar•ri•er** *s* bariera *f* handlowa; **'trade def•i•cit** *s* deficyt *m* handlowy; **'trade fair** *s* targi *pl* (handlowe); **'trade•mark** *s* znak *m* towarowy; **'trade name** *s* **1.** nazwa *f* handlowa **2.** znak *m* rozpoznawczy; **'trade-off** *s* kompromis *m*; **'trade price** *s* cena *f* hurtowa

trad•er ['treɪdə] *s* handlowiec *m*

trade 'se•cret *s* tajemnica *f* handlowa

trades•man ['treɪdzmən] *pl* ***-men*** *s* **1.** akwizytor *m* **2.** właściciel *m* sklepu **3.** rzemieślnik *m*

trade sur•plus *s* *ECON* nadwyżka *f* w handlu; **trade 'un•ion** *s* związek *m* zawodowy; **trade 'un•ion•ist** *s* związkowiec *m*; **'trade wind** *s* (*wind*) pasat *m*

trad•ing part•ner ['treɪdɪŋpaːtnə] *s* partner *m* handlowy

tra•di•tion [trə'dɪʃn] *s* tradycja *f*; ***break with*** **~** zerwać z tradycją; ***by*** **~** zgodnie z tradycją; **tra•di•tion•al** [trə'dɪʃnl] *adj* tradycyjny; **tra•di•tion•al•ly** [trə'dɪʃnlɪ] *adv* tradycyjnie

traf•fic ['træfɪk] **I** *s* **1.** ruch *m* uliczny; ***get stuck in*** **~** utknąć w korku **2.** (nielegalny) handel *m*; **~** ***in drugs*** handel narkotykami **II** *v/i* **~** ***in*** (nielegalnie) handlować; **'traf•fic cha•os** *s* chaos *m* komunikacyjny; **'traf•fic cir•cle** *s Am* rondo *n*; **'traf•fic cone** *s* (*in street*) pachołek *m*; **'traf•fic is•land** *s* (*in street*) wysepka *f*; **'traf•fic jam** *s* (*in street*) korek *m*

traf•fick•er ['træfɪkə] *s* handlarz *m*, diler *m*; ***a drugs*** **~** handlarz narkotykami, diler narkotykowy

'traf•fic lights *pl* (*in street*) sygnalizacja *f* świetlna, *infml* światła *pl*; **traf•fic offence** *Br*, **traf•fic of•fense** *Am* *s* wykroczenie *n* drogowe; **'traf•fic police** *s* policja *f* drogowa, *infml* drogówka *f*; **'traf•fic vi•o•la•tion** *s* złamanie *n* przepisów drogowych; **'traffic war•den** *s Br* strażnik *m* miejski

trag•e•dy ['trædʒədɪ] *s* tragedia *f*

trag•ic ['trædʒɪk] *adj* tragiczny; **trag•i•cal•ly** ['trædʒɪklɪ] *adv* tragicznie

trag•i•com•e•dy [trædʒɪ'kɒmədɪ] *s* *THEAT* tragikomedia *f*; **trag•i•'com•ic** *adj* *THEAT* tragikomiczny

trail [treɪl] **I** *s* **1.** ślad *m*, trop *m*; ***be on s.o.'s*** **~** być na czyimś tropie **2.** (*path*) szlak *m* **3.** *smoke*: smuga *f* **II** *v/t* **1.** ciągnąć za sobą **2.** przegrywać ⟨-rać⟩ z *I* **3.** śledzić ⟨wy-⟩ **III** *v/i* **1.** ciągnąć się **2.** wlec się **3.** przegrywać ⟨-rać⟩ **4.** (*plants*) zwieszać się; **trail•er** ['treɪlə] *s* **1.** przyczepa *f* **2.** *Am* przyczepa *f* kempingowa **3.** zwiastun *m* (filmowy)

train [treɪn] **I** *s* **1.** pociąg *m*; ***by*** **~** pociągiem; ***on the*** **~** w pociągu; ***a*** **~** ***set*** (*toy*) kolejka **2.** sznur *m* **3.** *vehicles*: kolumna *f* **4.** *events*: ciąg *m*, łańcuch *m* **5.** tok *m*; ***a*** **~** ***of thought*** tok myśli **6.** (*dress*) tren *m* **II** *v/t* **1.** szkolić ⟨wy-⟩ **2.** kształcić ⟨wy-⟩ **3.** trenować ⟨wy-⟩ **4.** *gun*: celować ⟨wy-⟩ (**on** na *A*) **5.** *camera*: kierować ⟨s-⟩ (**on** na *A*) **III** *v/i* **1.** szkolić ⟨wy-⟩ się (**as** na *A*) **2.** trenować

train•ee [treɪ'niː] *s* **1.** praktykant *m* **2.** stażysta *m*; **train•er** ['treɪnə] *s* **1.** trener *m* **2.** treser *m* **3.** *Br* adidas *m*

T

train•ing [treɪnɪŋ] *s* **1.** szkolenie *n* **2.** trening *m*; **'train•ing course** *s* kurs *m* szkoleniowy; **'train•ing scheme** *s* plan *m* szkoleń
'train sta•tion *s* stacja *f* kolejowa
'trainspot•ting *s* (*hobby*) zapisywanie *n* numerów przejeżdżających lokomotyw
traipse [treɪps] *v/i* włóczyć ⟨po-⟩ się
trait [treɪt] *s* cecha *f*; ***a personality ~*** cecha charakteru
trai•tor ['treɪtə] *s* zdrajca *f*
tra•jec•to•ry [trə'dʒektərɪ] *s PHYS* trajektoria *f*
tramp [træmp] **I** *s* **1.** włóczęga *f*, tramp *m* **2.** odgłos *m* ciężkich kroków **3.** wędrówka *f* **4.** *Am dated* dziwka *f* **II** *v/i* **1.** wędrować **2.** iść ⟨pójść⟩ **III** *v/t streets*: przemierzać ⟨-rzyć⟩
tram•ple ['træmpl] **I** *v/t* **1.** deptać ⟨po-⟩ **2.** tratować ⟨s-⟩; ***they were ~d to death*** zostali stratowani na śmierć **II** *v/i* **1.** deptać ⟨po-⟩ (***on*** po *L*) **2.** *fig* nic sobie nie robić (***on*** z *G*)
tram•po•line ['træmpəli:n] *s* trampolina *f*
trance [træns] *s* trans *m*; ***fall into a ~*** wpaść w trans
tran•quil ['træŋkwɪl] *adj* spokojny; **tran•quil•li•ty** [træŋ'kwɪlətɪ] *Br*, ***tran•quil•ity*** *Am s* spokój *m*; **'tran•quil•lize** *Br*, ***'tran•quil•ize*** *Am v/t* uspokajać ⟨-koić⟩; **tran•quil•liz•er** ['træŋkwɪlaɪzə] *Br*, ***tran•qul•iz•er*** *Am s* środek *m* uspokajający
trans•act [træn'zækt] *v/t*: ***~ business*** prowadzić interesy; **trans•ac•tion** [træn'zækʃn] *s* **1.** transakcja *f* **2.** operacja *f* **3.** interes *m*
trans•at•lan•tic [trænzət'læntɪk] *adj* transatlantycki
tran•scen•den•tal [trænsen'dentl] *adj* transcendentalny
trans•ceiv•er [træn'si:və] *s* urządzenie *n* nadawczo-odbiorcze, nadajnik-odbiornik *m*
trans•con•ti•nen•tal [trænzkɒntɪ'nentl] *adj* transkontynentalny
tran•scribe [træn'skraɪb] *v/t* transkrybować ⟨s, prze-⟩
tran•script ['trænskrɪpt] *s* transkrypcja *f*; **tran•scrip•tion** [træn'skrɪpʃn] *s* transkrypcja *f*
tran•sept ['trænsept] *s ARCHIT* transept *m*, nawa *f* poprzeczna
trans•fer [træns'fɜ:] **I** *v/t* **1.** przenosić ⟨-nieść⟩ **2.** przewozić ⟨-wieźć⟩ **3.** *money*: przelewać ⟨-lać⟩ **II** *v/i* **1.** przenosić ⟨-nieść⟩ się **2.** przeprowadzać ⟨-dzić⟩ się **3.** (*travel*) przesiadać ⟨-siąść⟩ się **III** ['trænsfɜ:] *s* **1.** *INF* transfer *m*, przesył *m* **2.** *FIN* przelew *m* **3.** przewóz *m* **4.** *SPORT* transfer *m*; **trans•fer•a•ble** [træns'fɜ:rəbl] *adj JUR* zbywalny; ***the tickets are not ~*** biletów nie można odsprzedawać; **'trans•fer fee** *s* prowizja *f* za przelew
trans•fig•ure [træns'fɪgə] *v/t* przeobrażać ⟨-razić⟩
trans•fix [træns'fɪks] *v/t* **1.** paraliżować ⟨s-⟩; ***be ~ed with fear*** być sparaliżowanym strachem **2.** nieruchomieć ⟨z-⟩
trans•form [træns'fɔ:m] *v/t* przekształcać ⟨-cić⟩ (***into*** w *A*); **trans•form•a•tion** [trænsfə'meɪʃn] *s* **1.** przekształcenie *n* **2.** transformacja *f*; **trans•form•er** [træns'fɔ:mə] *s* transformator *m*
trans•fu•sion [træns'fju:ʒn] *s MED* transfuzja *f*
trans•gress [træns'gres] *v/t* przekraczać ⟨-roczyć⟩, naruszać ⟨-szyć⟩; ***~ the norms of social behaviour*** naruszyć normy społecznego zachowania
tran•si•ent ['trænzɪənt] *adj* **1.** przemijający **2.** przelotny
tran•sis•tor [træn'zɪstə] *s TECH* tranzystor *m*
tran•sit ['trænzɪt] *s* **1.** tranzyt *m*; ***a ~ visa*** wiza tranzytowa **2.** transport *m*; ***in ~*** w czasie transportu; **'tran•sit lounge** *s* (*airport*) hala *f* tranzytowa
tran•si•tion [træn'sɪʃn] *s* przejście *n*; ***a period of ~*** okres przejściowy; **tran•si•tion•al** [træn'sɪʃnl] *adj* przejściowy
tran•si•tive ['trænsətɪv] *adj verb*: przechodni
tran•si•to•ry ['trænsɪtərɪ] → ***transient***
trans•lat•a•ble [træns'leɪtəbl] *adj* przetłumaczalny
trans•late [træns'leɪt] **I** *v/t* **1.** tłumaczyć ⟨prze-⟩, przekładać ⟨przełożyć⟩; ***~ from English into Polish*** tłumaczyć z angielskiego na polski **2.** *fig* przekładać ⟨przełożyć⟩; ***~ words into ac-***

T

tion przekładać słowa na czyny **II** *v/i* **1.** tłumaczyć się **2.** dawać ⟨dać⟩ się przetłumaczyć

trans•la•tion [træns'leɪʃn] *s* tłumaczenie *n*, przekład *m*; **trans•'la•tion com•pa•ny** *s* biuro *n* tłumaczeń; **trans•'la•tion soft•ware** *s* oprogramowanie *n* tłumaczeniowe; **trans•la•tor** [træns'leɪtə] *s* tłumacz *m*

trans•lu•cent [trænz'lu:snt] *adj* półprzezroczysty

trans•mi•gra•tion [trænzmaɪ'greɪʃn] *s* wędrówka *f* dusz, transmigracja *f*

trans•mis•sion [trænz'mɪʃn] *s* **1.** transmisja *f* **2.** nadawanie *n* **3.** przekazywanie *n* **4.** przesyłanie *n* **5.** TECH przekładnia *f*; ***automatic ~*** automatyczna skrzynia biegów

trans•mit [trænz'mɪt] *v/t* **1.** przesyłać ⟨-słać⟩ **2.** nadawać ⟨-dać⟩ **3.** *programme*: transmitować ⟨prze-⟩ **4.** wysyłać ⟨-słać⟩ **5.** *disease*: przenosić ⟨-nieść⟩ **6.** *electricity*: przewodzić **7.** *light*: przepuszczać ⟨-puścić⟩; **trans•mit•ter** [trænz'mɪtə] *s* **1.** nadajnik *m* **2.** przekaźnik *m* **3.** *fig* nadawca *f*

trans•par•en•cy [træns'pærənsɪ] *s* **1.** PHOT przezrocze *n*, slajd *m* **2.** (*projector*) foliogram *m* **3.** przezroczystość *f* **4.** przejrzystość *f* **5.** zrozumiałość *f*; **trans•par•ent** [træns'pærənt] *adj* **1.** przezroczysty **2.** przejrzysty **3.** zrozumiały

tran•spi•ra•tion [trænspɪ'reɪʃn] *s* pocenie się *n*; **tran•spire** [træns'paɪə] *v/i* **1.** okazywać ⟨-zać⟩ się; ***it ~d that*** okazało się, że **2.** zdarzać ⟨-rzyć⟩ się, wydarzać ⟨-rzyć⟩ się **3.** pocić ⟨s-⟩ się

trans•plant **I** [træns'plɑ:nt] *v/t* **1.** przeszczepiać ⟨-pić⟩ **2.** *plant*: przesadzać ⟨-dzić⟩ **3.** przenosić ⟨-nieść⟩ **II** ['trænsplɑ:nt] *s* **1.** przeszczep *m* **2.** transplantacja *f*; **trans•plan•'ta•tion** → ***transplant II***

trans•port **I** [træns'pɔ:t] *v/t* **1.** transportować ⟨prze-⟩ **2.** przewozić ⟨-wieźć⟩ **3.** przenosić ⟨-nieść⟩; ***blood ~s oxygen*** krew przenosi tlen **II** ['trænspɔ:t] *s* **1.** transport *m*; ***public ~*** transport publiczny **2.** przejazd *m* **3.** transporter *m* **4.** transportowiec *m*; **trans•por•ta•tion** [trænspɔ:'teɪʃn] *Am s* transport *m*; **trans•port•er** [træns'pɔ:tə] *s* **1.** transporter *m* **2.** transportowiec *m*

trans•sex•u•al [træns'sekʃʊəl] **I** *s* transseksualista *m* **II** *adj* transseksualny

trans•verse ['trænsvɜ:s] *adj* poprzeczny; **trans•'verse•ly** ['trænsvɜ:slɪ] *adv* w poprzek

trans•ves•tite [træns'vestaɪt] *s* transwestyta *m*

trap [træp] **I** *s* **1.** *a. fig* pułapka *f*; ***set a ~ for*** zastawić pułapkę na *A* **2.** *a. fig* sidła *pl*; ***fall into s.o.'s ~*** wpaść w czyjeś sidła **3.** dwukółka *f* **4.** *infml* gęba *f*, morda *f*; ***shut your ~!*** zamknij się! **II** *v/t* **1.** *fig* chwytać ⟨s-⟩ (w pułapkę), łapać ⟨z-⟩ (w pułapkę); ***be ~ped*** być w pułapce **2.** więzić ⟨u-⟩; ***he was ~ped in the burning building*** był uwięziony w płonącym budynku **3.** przytrzaskiwać ⟨-snąć⟩; ***he ~ped his finger in the door*** przytrzasnął sobie palec w drzwiach; **trap•door** ['træpdɔ:] *s* **1.** (*stage*) zapadnia *f* **2.** klapa *f* **3.** drzwi *pl* zapadowe

tra•peze [trə'pi:z] *s* (*circus*) trapez *m*; **tra•'peze ar•tist** *s* akrobata *m* na trapezie; **tra•'pe•zi•um** [trə'pi:zjəm] *pl -ziums, -zia* [~zjə] *s* MATH **1.** *Br* trapez *m* **2.** *Am* trapezoid *m*; **trap•e•zoid** ['træpɪzɔɪd] *s* MATH **1.** *Br* trapezoid *m* **2.** *Am* trapez *m*

trap•per ['træpə] *s* traper *m*

trap•pings ['træpɪŋz] *s* przywileje *pl*

trash [træʃ] **I** *s* **1.** *Am* śmieci *pl* **2.** *Br* bzdury *pl*, nonsens *m* **3.** *Br infml* szmira *f* **II** *v/t* **1.** *Am* wyrzucać ⟨-cić⟩ (do śmieci) **2.** *infml* niszczyć ⟨z-⟩, demolować ⟨z-⟩; **trash•can** *s Am* kosz *m* na śmieci; **trash•y** [træʃɪ] *adj* **1.** *infml* szmirowaty **2.** tandetny

trau•ma ['trɔ:mə] *s* **1.** uraz *m* **2.** trauma *f*; **trau•mat•ic** [trɔ:'mætɪk] *adj* **1.** urazowy **2.** traumatyczny; **trau•ma•tize** ['traʊmətaɪz] *v/t* powodować ⟨s-⟩ uraz u *G*

trav•el ['trævl] **I** *v/i* **1.** podróżować; ***~ around the world*** podróżować dookoła świata; ***~ light*** podróżować z niewielkim bagażem **2.** jechać ⟨po-⟩; ***~ by train*** jechać pociągiem **3.** (*vehicles*) poruszać ⟨-szyć⟩ się **4.** (*information*) rozchodzić ⟨-zejść⟩ się **II** *v/t* **1.** przebywać ⟨-być⟩ **2.** prze-

T

jeździć ⟨-jechać⟩ **III** *s* podróż *f*; **'trav•el a•gen•cy** *s* biuro *n* podróży; **'trav•el a•gent** *s* pracownik *m* biura podróży; **~ agent's** biuro *n* podróży

trav•el•ler ['trævələ] *Br*, ***trav•el•er*** *Am s* podróżny *m*; **'trav•el•ler's cheque** *Br*, ***'trav•el•er's check*** *Am s* czek *m* podróżny

'trav•el•ling *Br*, ***trav•el•ing*** *Am* **I** *adj* **1.** podróżujący **2.** podróżny **II** *s* podróżowanie *n*; **trav•el•ling sales•man** [trævlɪŋ'seɪlzmən] *Br*, ***trav•el•ing sales•man*** *Am pl -men s dated* komiwojażer *m*

trav•e•logue ['trævəlɒg] *Br*, ***trav•e•log*** *Am s* **1.** książka *f* podróżnicza **2.** film *m* podróżniczy

'trav•el pro•gramme *Br*, ***'trav•el program*** *Am s* program *m* podróżniczy

'trav•el•sick *adj*: **be ~** cierpieć na chorobę lokomocyjną; **'trav•el•sick•ness** *s* choroba *f* lokomocyjna

trav•erse [trə'vɜːs] *v/t country*: przemierzać ⟨-rzyć⟩

trav•es•ty ['trævəstɪ] **1.** trawestacja *f* **2.** *fig* parodia *f*; ***the trial was a ~ of justice*** to była parodia procesu

trav•o•la•tor ['trævəleɪtə] *s* ruchomy chodnik *m*

trawl ['trɔːl] **I** *v/t* **1.** przetrząsać ⟨-snąć⟩ (***for*** w poszukiwaniu *G*) **2.** przeszukiwać ⟨-kać⟩ **II** *v/i* trałować **III** *s* **1.** poszukiwanie *n* **2.** (*net*) trał *m*; **trawl•er** ['trɔːlə] *s* trawler *m*

tray [treɪ] *s* **1.** taca *f* **2.** tacka *f* **3.** pojemnik *m* **4.** (*baking*) blacha *f* **5.** kuweta *f*

treach•er•ous ['tretʃərəs] *adj* **1.** zdradziecki **2.** zdradliwy; **treach•er•y** ['tretʃərɪ] *s* zdrada *f*

trea•cle ['triːkl] *s* melasa *f*; **'trea•cly** *adj* **1.** ckliwy **2.** przesłodzony

tread [tred] **I** (*trod*; *trodden*) *v/i* nadeptywać ⟨-pnąć⟩ (**on** na *A*) **II** (*trod*; *trodden*) *v/t* **1.** deptać ⟨po-⟩; **~ *s.th. in*** wdeptać coś w *A* **2.** *path*: iść, kroczyć, stąpać **III** *s* **1.** krok *m*, kroki *pl* **2.** *tyres*: bieżnik *m*; **'tread•mill** *s* **1.** żarna *pl* **2.** *fig* kierat *m* **3.** (ruchoma) bieżnia *f*

trea•son ['triːzn] *s* zdrada *f*

trea•sure ['treʒə] **I** *s* skarb *m* **II** *v/t* **1.** cenić, doceniać ⟨-nić⟩ **2.** *friendship*: pielęgnować; **trea•sur•er** ['treʒərə] *s* skarbnik *m*; **treas•ure trove** [treʒə'trəʊv] *s* skarb *m*; **Trea•sur•y De•part•ment** ['treʒərɪdɪ'pɑːtmənt] *s* Ministerstwo *n* Finansów

treat [triːt] **I** *v/t* **1.** traktować ⟨po-⟩; ***my parents still ~ me like a child*** moi rodzice nadal traktują mnie jak dziecko; **~ *s.th. as a joke*** potraktować coś jako żart **2.** MED leczyć ⟨wy-⟩ **3.** poddawać ⟨-dać⟩ działaniu **4.** obrabiać ⟨-robić⟩ **5.** *sewage*: oczyszczać ⟨oczyścić⟩ **6.** fundować ⟨za-⟩, stawiać ⟨postawić⟩; **~ *s.o. to lunch*** postawić komuś lunch **II** *s* **1.** prawdziwa przyjemność *f* **2.** *fig* uczta *f* **3.** smakołyk *m* **4.** ***let's go out for lunch, my ~*** chodźmy na lunch, ja stawiam

trea•tise ['triːtɪz] *s* traktat *m*

treat•ment ['triːtmənt] *s* **1.** traktowanie *n* **2.** potraktowanie *n* **3.** MED leczenie *n* **4.** kuracja *f* **5.** TECH obróbka *f* **6.** *sewage*: oczyszczanie *n*

treat•y ['triːtɪ] *s* POL traktat *m*; ***the ~ of Maastricht*** traktat z Maastricht

tre•ble[1] ['trebl] **I** *s* **1.** sopran *m* **2.** dyszkant *m* **3.** wysokie tony *pl* **II** *adj* **1.** sopranowy; ***the ~ clef*** klucz wiolinowy **2.** dyszkantowy

tre•ble[2] [~] **I** *adj* potrójny **II** *v/t* potrajać ⟨-roić⟩ **III** *v/i* potrajać ⟨-roić⟩ się

tree [triː] *s* drzewo *n*; **'tree•less** *adj* pozbawiony drzew; **'tree line** *s* linia *f* drzew; **tree-lined** [triː'laɪnd] *adj* wysadzany drzewami; **'tree sur•geon** *s* chirurg *m* drzew; **'tree trunk** *s* pień *m* drzewa

trek [trek] **I** *s* **1.** wędrówka *f* **2.** wyprawa *f* **II** *v/i* wędrować

trel•lis ['trelɪs] *s* treliaż *m*, krata *f*, kratownica *f*

trem•ble ['trembl] **I** *v/i* drżeć ⟨za-⟩, trząść ⟨za-⟩ się; **~ *at the thought of*** drżeć na myśl o *L* **II** *s* drżenie *n*

tre•men•dous [trɪ'mendəs] *adj* **1.** ogromny, olbrzymi **2.** niesamowity **3.** wspaniały; **tre•men•dous•ly** [trɪ'mendəslɪ] *adv* **1.** ogromnie **2.** bardzo

trem•or ['tremə] *s* **1.** drżenie *n* **2.** dreszcz *m* **3.** (*earthquake*) wstrząs *m*

trench [trentʃ] *s* **1.** rów *m* **2.** okop *m*; **'trench coat** *s* (*coat*) trencz *m*

trend [trend] *s* trend *m*, tendencja *f*; **trend•set•ter** ['trendsetə] *s*: ***be a ~*** wyznaczać trendy

T

trend•y ['trendɪ] *adj* **1.** modny **2.** na czasie

tres•pass ['trespəs] **I** *v/i* **1.** wkraczać ⟨-roczyć⟩ (**on** na *A*); ***no ~ing*** wstęp wzbroniony **2.** ***~ on s.o.'s time*** nadużywać czyjegoś czasu **II** *s* **1.** wkroczenie *n* na cudzy teren **2.** *JUR* naruszenie *n* własności; **tres•pass•er** ['trespəsə] *s*: ***~s will be prosecuted*** wstęp wzbroniony

tri•al ['traɪəl] **I** *s* **1.** *JUR* proces *m*; ***a murder ~*** proces o morderstwo; ***stand ~ for***, ***go on ~ for*** stanąć przed sądem za *A*; ***bring s.o. to ~*** postawić kogoś przed sądem **2.** próba *f*; ***by ~ and error*** metodą prób i błędów **3.** test *m*; ***be on ~*** być testowanym **4.** badanie *n*; ***clinical ~s*** badania kliniczne **4.** (*selection*) *Br* eliminacje *pl*, kwalifikacje *pl* **5.** utrapienie *n* **II** *v/t* *Br* testować ⟨prze-⟩; **tri•al 'pe•ri•od** *s* (*work*) okres *m* próbny; **tri•al 'run** *s* **1.** próba *f* **2.** *AUTO* jazda *f* próbna; **tri•al sep•a•'ra•tion** *s* *JUR* separacja *f*

tri•an•gle ['traɪæŋgl] *s* **1.** trójkąt *m* **2.** *Am* ekierka *f*; **tri•an•gu•lar** [traɪ'æŋgjʊlə] *adj* trójkątny

tri•ath•lon [traɪ'æθlən] *s* *SPORT* trójbój *m*, triatlon *m*

trib•al ['traɪbl] *adj* plemienny; **tribe** [traɪb] *s* plemię *n*; **'tribes•man** *pl -men* *s* członek *m* plemienia; **'tribes•wom•an** *pl -men* *s* członkini *f* plemienia

tri•bu•nal [traɪ'bjuːnl] *s* trybunał *m*

tri•bu•ta•ry ['trɪbjʊtərɪ] *s* (*river*) dopływ *m*

trib•ute ['trɪbjuːt] *s* **1.** hołd *m* **2.** wyrazy *pl* uznania; ***pay ~ to*** wyrazić uznanie dla *G*

trice [traɪs] *s*: ***in a ~*** w okamgnieniu

tri•ceps ['traɪseps] *pl* *triceps* *s* *ANAT* triceps *m*

trick [trɪk] **I** *s* **1.** podstęp *m* **2.** kawał *m*, figiel *m*; ***play a ~ on s.o.*** zrobić komuś kawał, spłatać komuś figla **3.** trik *m*, sztuczka *f*; ***the ~ is to*** cała sztuka polega na tym, aby; ***that will do the ~ for you*** to rozwiąże twój problem; ***if this doesn't do the ~, call me*** jeśli to nie pomoże, zadzwoń do mnie; ***the ~s of the trade*** tajniki zawodu **4.** (*cards*) lewa *f* **II** *v/t* oszukiwać ⟨-kać⟩; ***~ s.o. into doing s.th.*** podstępem skłonić kogoś do zrobienia czegoś; ***~ s.o. out of s.th.*** podstępem pozbawić kogoś czegoś; **trick 'ques•tion** *s* podchwytliwe pytanie *n*

trick•e•ry ['trɪkərɪ] *s* **1.** oszustwo *n* **2.** sztuczki *pl*

trick•le ['trɪkl] **I** *v/i* **1.** ciec ⟨wy-⟩ **2.** spływać ⟨-łynąć⟩ **3.** ***~ out*** wyciekać **4.** ***~ into the assembly hall*** wchodzić powoli do sali zebrań **II** *v/t* lać powoli

trick•ster ['trɪkstə] *s* **1.** oszust *m* **2.** naciągacz *m*

trick•y ['trɪkɪ] *adj* **1.** podchwytliwy **2.** skomplikowany **3.** podstępny, sprytny

tri•cy•cle ['traɪsɪkl] *s* rower *m* trójkołowy

tri•fle ['traɪfl] **I** *s* **1.** drobnostka *f* **2.** ***a ~ boring*** troszeczkę nudne **3.** *Br* biszkopt *m* nasączony sherry z dodatkiem owoców, galaretki i kremu **II** *v/i* **1.** bawić się (***with*** *I*) **2.** stroić sobie żarty; **tri•fling** ['traɪflɪŋ] *adj* banalny, trywialny

trig•ger ['trɪgə] **I** *s* **1.** (*gun*) spust *m*, *infml* cyngiel *m*; ***pull the ~*** pociągnąć za spust **2.** (*bomb*) zapalnik *m* **3.** *fig* powód *m*, przyczyna *f* **II** *v/t* **1.** (*a.* ***~ off***) *reaction*: wywoływać ⟨-łać⟩ **2.** *alarm*: uruchamiać ⟨-chomić⟩; **'trig•ger-hap•py** *adj* ***be ~*** *infml* szybko chwytać za broń

trig•o•nom•e•try [trɪgə'nɒmətrɪ] *s* *MATH* trygonometria *f*

trike [traɪk] (*bike*) trójkołowiec *m*

tril•by ['trɪlbɪ] *s* kapelusz *m* filcowy

tril•lion ['trɪlɪən] *s* **1.** *Am* bilion *m* **2.** *Br* trylion *m*

tril•o•gy ['trɪlədʒɪ] *s* trylogia *f*

trim [trɪm] **I** *v/t* **1.** przycinać ⟨-ciąć⟩ **2.** podcinać ⟨-ciąć⟩ **3.** wykańczać ⟨-kończyć⟩; ***gloves ~med with fur*** rękawiczki wykończone futerkiem **II** *s* **1.** ***the hedge needs a ~*** trzeba przyciąć żywopłot **2.** strzyżenie *n*, podcięcie *n*; ***have a ~*** podciąć włosy **3.** wykończenie *n*; ***blue jacket with a white ~*** niebieska kurtka z białą lamówką **III** *adj* **1.** zadbany **2.** starannie utrzymany; **trim off** *v/t* odcinać ⟨-ciąć⟩

trim•ming ['trɪmɪŋ] *s* **1.** *COOK* przybranie *n*; ***with all the ~s*** z dodatkami

T

2. ~s resztki, ścinki *pl*, skrawki *pl* **3.** lamówka *f*

Trin•i•ty ['trɪnɪtɪ] *s REL* ***the ~*** Trójca *f* Święta

trin•ket ['trɪŋkɪt] *s* błyskotka *f*, świecidełko *n*

tri•o ['triːəʊ] *s MUS* trio *n*

trip [trɪp] **I** *s* **1.** podróż *f*; ***a business ~*** delegacja *f*, podróż *f* służbowa **2.** wycieczka *f*; ***go on a ~*** pojechać na wycieczkę **3.** (*after drugs*) *infml* odlot *m*; ***be on a ~*** odlatywać **4.** potknięcie *n* **II** *v/i* **1.** potykać ⟨-tknąć⟩ się (***over/ on*** o *A*); ***someone will ~ over that cable*** ktoś potknie się o ten kabel **2.** *infml* mieć odlot **III** *v/t* **1.** podstawiać ⟨-wić⟩ nogę **2.** *switch*: zwalniać ⟨zwolnić⟩ **3.** *alarm*: uruchamiać ⟨-chomić⟩; **trip up I** *v/i* potykać ⟨-tknąć⟩ się **II** *v/t Br* podstawiać ⟨-wić⟩ komuś nogę

tripe [traɪp] *s* **1.** *COOK* flaki *pl*, flaczki *pl* **2.** bzdury *pl*

trip•le ['trɪpl] **I** *adj* **1.** potrójny **2.** trzykrotny **3.** trzy razy większy niż *N* **4.** trójstronny **II** *v/t* potrajać ⟨-roić⟩ **III** *v/i* potrajać ⟨-roić⟩ się; **'trip•le jump** *s SPORT* trójskok *m*; **'trip•le jump•er** *s SPORT* trójskoczek *m*

trip•lets ['trɪplɪts] *pl* trojaczki *pl*

trip•li•cate ['trɪplɪkət] *s*: ***in ~*** **a)** trzy razy **b)** w trzech egzemplarzach

tri•pod ['traɪpɔd] *s* (*stand*) trójnóg *m*

'trip•wire *s* (*trap*) drut *m* przeciągnięty nisko nad ziemią

trite [traɪt] *adj* **1.** wyświechtany **2.** oklepany **3.** banalny

tri•umph ['traɪəmf] **I** *s* tryumf *m* **II** *v/i* tryumfować ⟨za-⟩ (***over*** nad *I*); **tri•um•phal** [traɪ'ʌmfl] *adj* tryumfalny; ***a ~ arch*** łuk tryumfalny; **tri•um•phant** [traɪ'ʌmfənt] *adj* tryumfujący

triv•i•al ['trɪvɪəl] *adj* **1.** trywialny **2.** banalny **3** błahy; **triv•i•al•i•ty** [trɪvɪ'ælətɪ] *s* **1.** błahostka *f* **2.** banał *m*

T

trod [trɒd] *Past Simple* → ***tread***

trod•den ['trɒdn] *Past Participle* → ***tread***

trol•ley ['trɒlɪ] *s* **1.** (*shop, airport*) *Br* wózek *m* (na zakupy) **2.** *Br* stolik *m* na kółkach **3.** *Am* tramwaj *m*

trom•bone [trɒm'bəʊn] *s MUS* puzon *m*; **trom•bon•ist** [trɒm'bəʊnɪst] *s MUS* puzonista *m*

troop [truːp] **I** *s* **1.** oddział *m* **2. ~s** żołnierze *pl* **3.** grupa *f* **4.** gromada *f* **II** *v/i* iść ⟨pójść⟩ gromadnie; **'troop carr•i•er** *s* (*plane, vessel*) transportowiec *m*

troop•er ['truːpə] *s* **1.** szeregowiec *m*; ***swear like a ~*** kląć jak szewc **2.** kawalerzysta *m* **3.** *Am* policjant *m*

tro•phy ['trəʊfɪ] *s* trofeum *m*

tro•pic ['trɒpɪk] *s* **1.** *GEOGR* zwrotnik *m*; ***the ≈ of Cancer*** Zwrotnik Raka **2.** ***the ~s*** tropiki *pl*; **trop•i•cal** ['trɒpɪkl] *adj* tropikalny; **trop•i•cal 'for•est** *s* las *m* tropikalny; **trop•i•cal 'rain•for•est** *s* tropikalny las *m* deszczowy

trot [trɒt] **I** *v/i* **1.** (*horse, rider*) kłusować **2.** dreptać, truchtać **II** *v/t* ***~ one's horse*** jechać kłusem **III** *s* **1.** kłus *m* **2.** dreptanie *n*, trucht *m* **3.** ***on the ~*** z rzędu, pod rząd; **trot out** *v/t infml* powtarzać ⟨-tórzyć⟩

trou•ble ['trʌbl] **I** *s* **1.** kłopot *m* **2.** kłopoty *pl*; ***he is in ~ with the police*** ma kłopoty z policją; ***run into ~*** wpaść w kłopoty; ***be in ~*** mieć kłopoty; ***look for ~*** szukać guza; ***it's no ~!*** to żaden kłopot! **3.** problem *m*; ***the ~ is that*** problem w tym, że; ***an eye ~*** problemy z oczami **4.** zmartwienie *n* **5.** zamieszki *pl* **6.** trud *m*; ***take a lot of ~ to do s.th.*** zadać sobie dużo trudu, aby; ***save s.o. the ~*** zaoszczędzić komuś trudu **II** *v/t* **1.** kłopotać, sprawiać ⟨-wić⟩ kłopot; ***sorry to ~ you*** przepraszam za kłopot **2.** martwić ⟨z-⟩; ***be ~d by*** martwić się *I* **3.** boleć, dokuczać; ***my back's been troubling me again*** znowu bolą mnie plecy **III** *v/i* zadawać ⟨-dać⟩ sobie trud; ***he rushed into the room without troubling to knock*** wpadł do pokoju bez pukania; **'trou•ble-free** *adj* bezproblemowy; **'trou•ble-mak•er** *s* wichrzyciel *m*; **'trou•ble-shoot•er** *s* rozjemca *m*, mediator *m*; **'trou•ble•shoot•ing** *s* **1.** mediacje *pl* **2.** *TECH* usuwanie *n* usterek **3.** rozwiązywanie *n* problemów

trou•ble•some ['trʌblsəm] *adj* **1.** dokuczliwy **2.** nieznośny

'trou•ble spot *s* punkt *m* zapalny

trough [trɒf] *s* **1.** koryto *n*, żłób *m*; ***in the ~*** *fig* przy korycie **2.** kryzys *m*

3. spadek *m*; ***peaks and ~s*** wzrosty i spadki (wartości)

trounce [traʊns] *v/t SPORT* rozgramiać ⟨-gromić⟩

troupe [truːp] *s THEAT* trupa *f*

trou•sers ['traʊzəz] *pl Br* spodnie *pl*; **trou•ser suit** ['traʊzəsuːt] *s Br* spodnium *m*

trous•seau ['truːsəʊ] *pl -seaux* [~ 'səʊ], *-seaus* [~' səʊz] *s* wiano *n*, posag *m*

trout [traʊt] *s pl trout* pstrąg *m*

trow•el ['traʊəl] *s* **1.** łopatka *f* ogrodnicza **2.** kielnia *f*; ***lay it on with a ~*** przesadzać

tru•ant ['truːənt] *s* wagarowicz *m*; ***play ~*** wagarować

truce [truːs] *s* rozejm *m*

truck[1] [trʌk] **I** *s* **1.** ciężarówka *f*, samochód *m* ciężarowy **2.** *Br* wagon *m* towarowy **II** *v/t Am* przewozić ⟨-wieźć⟩ ciężarówką

truck[2] [~] *s*: ***want no ~ with*** *Br* nie chcieć mieć nic wspólnego z *I*

'truck driv•er *s* kierowca *m* ciężarówki

truck•er ['trʌkə] *infml* → ***truck driver***

'truck farm *s Am* gospodarstwo *n* warzywnicze; **'truck stop** *s Am* zajazd *m* przydrożny (dla kierowców ciężarówek)

truc•u•lent ['trʌkjʊlənt] *adj* zaczepny, zadziorny

trudge [trʌdʒ] *v/i* wlec się, iść z trudem

true [truː] *adj* **1.** prawdziwy; ***is it ~ that*** czy to prawda, że; ***a ~ story*** prawdziwa historia; ***come ~*** spełnić się; ***it's too good to be ~*** to zbyt piękne, aby było prawdziwe; ***s.o.'s ~ character*** czyjś prawdziwy charakter; ***~ love*** prawdziwa miłość **2.** faktyczny, rzeczywisty **3.** wierny; ***be ~ to oneself*** być wiernym sobie; ***be ~ to one's word*** dotrzymać słowa; ***~ to life*** z życia wzięty, wiernie oddający rzeczywistość

truf•fle ['trʌfl] *s* trufla *f*

tru•ism ['truːɪzəm] *s* truizm *m*

trul•y ['truːlɪ] *adv* naprawdę; ***I'm ~ sorry*** jest mi naprawdę przykro; ***really and ~*** tak naprawdę, prawdę mówiąc; ***Yours ~*** *Am* Z poważaniem

trump [trʌmp] **I** *s* **1.** *a. fig* atut *m*, karta *f* atutowa **2. ~s** kolor *m* atutowy **II** *v/t* **1.** przebijać ⟨-bić⟩ atutem **2.** *fig* przebijać ⟨-bić⟩; **trump up** *v/t* fabrykować ⟨s-⟩, fingować ⟨s-⟩

trum•pet ['trʌmpɪt] **I** *s MUS* trąbka *f*; ***blow one's own ~*** *fig* chwalić się **II** *v/t* **1.** rozgłaszać ⟨-łosić⟩ **2.** wychwalać **III** *v/i* (*elephant*) trąbić; **trum•pet•er** ['trʌmpɪtə] *s MUS* trębacz *m*

trun•cate [trʌŋ'keɪt] *v/t* skracać ⟨-rócić⟩

trun•cheon ['trʌntʃən] *s Br* pałka *f* (policyjna)

trun•dle ['trʌndl] *v/i* toczyć się

trunk [trʌŋk] *s* **1.** pień *m* **2.** *AUTO Am* bagażnik *m* **3.** *elephant*: trąba *f* **4.** kufer *m*, skrzynia *f* **5. ~s** kąpielówki *pl* **6.** *ANAT* tułów *m*; **'trunk road** *Br* droga *f* główna

truss[1] [trʌs] *s MED* pas *m* przepuklinowy

truss[2] [~] **I** *s TECH* kratownica *f*, konstrukcja *f* kratowa **II** (*a.* ***~ up***) *v/t hands and legs*: związywać ⟨-zać⟩

trust [trʌst] **I** *s* **1.** zaufanie *n* (***in*** do *A*); ***place one's ~ in s.o.*** zaufać komuś **2.** opieka *f*; ***in s.o.'s ~*** pod czyjąś opieką **3.** odpowiedzialność *f*; ***a position of ~*** odpowiedzialne stanowisko **4.** *JUR* zarząd *m* powierniczy **5.** *ECON* trust *m* **II** *v/t* **1.** ufać ⟨za-⟩, mieć zaufanie do *G*, polegać na *L*; ***you can ~ me not to tell anyone*** możesz mi zaufać, że nikomu nie powiem; ***not ~ s.o. an inch*** nie mieć za grosz zaufania do *G* **2.** wierzyć ⟨u-⟩; ***don't ~ what the newspapers say*** nie wierz w to, co piszą w gazetach **III** *v/i* ~ (***that***) mieć nadzieję, że; ***I ~ you have no objections*** mam nadzieję, że nie masz nic przeciwko; **trust in** *v/i* **1.** ufać ⟨za-⟩ **2.** wierzyć ⟨u-⟩ w *A*; ***~ one's own abilities*** wierzyć w swoje możliwości; **trust to** *v/i* liczyć na *A*; ***~ luck*** liczyć na łut szczęścia; **trusted** ['trʌstɪd] *adj* zaufany **trust•ee** [trʌs'tiː] *s* **1.** *JUR* powiernik *m* **2.** (*board member*) członek *m* zarządu; **trust•ful** ['trʌstfʊl] *adj* ufny **'trust fund** *s ECON* fundusz *m* powierniczy; **trust•ing** ['trʌstɪŋ] *adj* łatwowierny, ufny; **trust•wor•thy** ['trʌstwɜːðɪ] *adj* godny zaufania

truth [truːθ] *s* **1.** prawda *f*; ***tell the ~*** mówić prawdę; ***the ~ is that*** prawda jest taka, że; ***there is not a grain of ~ in what he says*** w tym, co mówi, nie

T

ma ziarna prawdy **2.** prawda *f*, fakt *m*; **truth•ful** ['truːθfəl] *adj* **1.** prawdomówny **2.** szczery, prawdziwy, zgodny z prawdą

try [traɪ] **I** *v/t* **1.** próbować ⟨s-⟩; ***~ to do s.th.*** próbować coś zrobić; ***have you tried the cake?*** próbowałeś ciasta?; ***she tried the door but it was closed*** pociągnęła za drzwi, ale były zamknięte **2.** starać ⟨po-⟩ się; ***she tried her best*** starała się, jak mogła **3.** wypróbowywać ⟨-bować⟩ **4.** *suspect*: sądzić ⟨o-⟩; ***he was tried for murder*** był sądzony za morderstwo **5.** *case*: rozstrzygać ⟨-gnąć⟩ **II** *s* **1.** próba *f*; ***have a ~*** spróbować; ***it's worth a ~*** warto spróbować **2.** (*rugby*) przyłożenie *n*; **try for** *v/i* próbować ⟨s-⟩; **try on** *v/t clothes*: przymierzać ⟨-rzyć⟩; **try out** *v/t* wypróbowywć ⟨-bować⟩; **try out for** *v/i Am* ubiegać się o *A*

try•ing ['traɪɪŋ] *adj* **1.** trudny **2.** męczący

'try•out *s* **1.** próba *f* **2.** test *m*

tsar [zɑː] *s* car *m*

tsarina [zɑː'riːnə] *s* caryca *f*

T-shirt ['tiːʃɜːt] *s* koszulka *f* z krótkimi rękawami, T-shirt *m*, tiszert *m*

tub [tʌb] *s* **1.** balia *f* **2.** kadź *f* **3.** donica *f* **4.** *Am* wanna *f* **5.** *for margarine*: pudełko *n*

tub•by ['tʌbɪ] *adj infml* pulchny

tube [tjuːb] *s* **1.** rura *f* **2.** rurka *f* **3.** tubka *f* **4.** ANAT przewód *m* **5.** ***the ~*** *Br* metro *n*; ***by ~*** metrem; ***a ~ station*** stacja metra **6.** ***the ~*** *Am infml* telewizja **7.** dętka *f*; **tube•less** ['tjuːblɪs] *adj tyre*: bezdętkowy

tu•ber ['tjuːbə] *s* bulwa *f*

tu•ber•cu•lo•sis [tuːbɜːkjʊ'ləʊsɪs] *s* MED gruźlica *f*

tu•bu•lar ['tjuːbjələ] *adj* **1.** rurowy **2.** cylindryczny **3.** z rurek

tuck [tʌk] **I** *v/t* **1.** (*a.* ***~ up***) zakasywać ⟨-sać⟩, podwijać ⟨-winąć⟩ **2.** (*a.* ***~ in***) wsuwać ⟨wsunąć⟩, wkładać ⟨włożyć⟩ **3.** zakładać ⟨założyć⟩ **4.** owijać ⟨owinąć⟩ (***around*** wokół *G*) **II** *s* zakładka *f*, fałda *f*; **tuck away** *v/t* **1.** *a. fig* ukrywać ⟨-ryć⟩, chować ⟨s-⟩; ***a shop ~ed away down a backstreet*** sklepik ukryty przy jednej z bocznych uliczek **2.** *Br infml* wcinać ⟨wciąć⟩; **tuck in** *v/t Br infml food*: wcinać ⟨wciąć⟩, wsuwać ⟨wsunąć⟩; **tuck into** → ***tuck in***; **tuck up** *v/t* przykrywać ⟨-ryć⟩ przed snem

Tues•day ['tjuːzdɪ] *s* wtorek *m*

tuft [tʌft] *s grass*, *hair*: kępka *f*

tug [tʌg] **I** *v/i* **1.** ciągnąć ⟨po-⟩ (***at*** za *A*) **2.** szarpać ⟨-pnąć⟩ (***at*** za *A*) **II** *v/t* **1.** ciągnąć ⟨po-⟩ za *A* **2.** szarpać ⟨-pnąć⟩ za *A*; ***~ s.o.'s hair*** szarpać kogoś za włosy **II** *s* **1.** holownik *m* **2.** pociągnięcie *n* **3.** szarpnięcie *n* **4.** *jealousy*: ukłucie *n*; **tug of 'war** *s a. fig* przeciąganie *n* liny

tu•i•tion [tjuː'ɪʃn] *s* **1.** lekcje *pl*, korepetycje *pl* **2.** *Am* czesne *pl*

tu•lip ['tjuːlɪp] *s* BIOL tulipan *m*

tulle [tjuːl] *s* tiul *m*

tum•ble ['tʌmbl] **I** *v/i* **1.** przewracać ⟨-rócić⟩ się, upadać ⟨upaść⟩ **2.** (*prices*) gwałtownie spadać ⟨spaść⟩ **3.** (*a.* ***~ down***) walić ⟨za-⟩ się **II** *s* **1.** upadek *m* **2.** *prices*: gwałtowny spadek *m*; **tumble to** *v/t Br infml* kapować ⟨s-⟩

'tum•ble•down *adj building*: walący się, w ruinie; **'tum•ble-dry•er** *s Br* suszarka *f* do bielizny

tum•bler ['tʌmblə] *s* szklanka *f*

tum•my ['tʌmɪ] *s infml* brzuszek *m*, brzuch *m*; **'tum•my ache** *s infml* ból *m* brzucha

tu•mour ['tjuːmə] *Br*, ***tu•mor*** *Am s* MED guz *m*, nowotwór *m*; ***a benign*** (***malignant***) ***~*** nowotwór łagodny (złośliwy)

tu•mult ['tjuːmʌlt] *s* tumult *m*, zgiełk *m*, zamęt *m*; **tu•mul•tu•ous** [tjuː'mʌltʃʊəs] *adj applause*, *period*: burzliwy

tu•na ['tjuːnə] *pl tuna*, *tunas s* tuńczyk *m*

tune [tjuːn] **I** *s* melodia *f*; ***the piano is out of ~*** fortepian jest rozstrojony; ***sing in ~*** śpiewać czysto; ***sing out of ~*** fałszować; ***sing to the ~ of*** śpiewać na melodię *G*; ***be in ~ with*** *fig* być w zgodzie z *I*; ***be out of ~ with*** *fig* stać w sprzeczności z *I*; ***an investment to the ~ of a million dollars*** *infml* inwestycja w wysokości miliona dolarów **II** *v/t* **1.** *instrument*: stroić ⟨na-⟩ **2.** dostrajać ⟨-roić⟩, dostosowywać ⟨-sować⟩ (***to*** do *G*) **3.** *radio*: nastawiać ⟨-wić⟩ (***to*** na *A*) **4.** *engine*: regulować ⟨wy-⟩; **tune in** *v/t radio*: nastawiać

⟨-wić⟩; **tune in to** *v/t* **1.** *radio*: nastawiać ⟨-wić⟩ na *A* **2.** *programme*: włączać ⟨-czyć⟩ **3.** wczuwać ⟨wczuć⟩ się w *A*; **tune up** *v/i*: ***the orchestra was tuning up*** muzycy stroili instrumenty

tune•ful [ˈtjuːnfʊl] *adj* melodyjny; **tune•less** [ˈtjuːnlɪs] *adj* niemelodyjny

tun•er [ˈtjuːnə] *s* **1.** TECH tuner *m* **2.** stroiciel *m*

tun•ing fork [ˈtjuːnɪŋfɔːk] *s* MUS kamerton *m* (widełkowy), widełki *pl* strojowe

Tu•ni•si•a [tjuːˈnɪzɪə] *s* Tunezja *f*

tun•nel [ˈtʌnl] **I** *s* tunel *m* **II** *v/i* kopać ⟨prze-⟩ tunel

tun•ny [ˈtʌnɪ] *pl tunny s Br* tuńczyk

tur•bid [ˈtɜːbɪd] *adj water*: mętny

tur•bine [ˈtɜːbaɪn] *s* TECH turbina *f*

tur•bo [ˈtɜːbəʊ] *pl -bos* [~bəʊz] *s infml* → ***turbocharger***; **tur•bo•charg•er** [ˈtɜːbəʊtʃɑːdʒə] *s* TECH turbosprężarka *f*; ˈ**tur•bo•jet** *s* TECH **1.** silnik *m* turboodrzutowy **2.** samolot *m* z silnikiem turboodrzutowym; ˈ**tur•bo•prop** *s* TECH **1.** silnik *m* turbośmigłowy **2.** samolot *m* z silnikiem turbośmigłowym

tur•bot [ˈtɜːbət] *pl turbot, turbots s* (*fish*) turbot *m*

tur•bu•lence [ˈtɜːbjʊləns] *s* **1.** turbulencja *f* **2.** turbulencje *pl*; **tur•bu•lent** [ˈtɜːbjʊlənt] *adj a. fig* burzliwy

turd [tɜːd] *s vulg* gówno *n*

tu•reen [təˈriːn] *s* waza *f*

turf [tɜːf] *pl turfs, turves s* **1.** darń *f* **2.** SPORT murawa *f*; ***on home ~*** *infml* na własnym boisku, u siebie **3.** ***the ~*** SPORT wyścigi *pl* konne **4.** torf *m*; **turf out** *v/t Br infml* wyrzucać ⟨-cić⟩, wywalać ⟨-lić⟩

tur•gid [ˈtɜːdʒɪd] *adj* **1.** zawiły, mętny, pokrętny **2.** *water*: wezbrany

Turk [tɜːk] *s* Turek *m*, Turczynka *f*

Tur•key [ˈtɜːkɪ] *s* Turcja *f*

tur•key [ˈtɜːkɪ] *pl -keys s* **1.** indyk *m* **2.** *Am infml* klapa *f*, fiasko *n*

Turk•ish [ˈtɜːkɪʃ] **I** *adj* turecki **II** *s* język *m* turecki; **Turk•ish ˈbath** *s* łaźnia *f* turecka; **Turk•ish de•ˈlight** *s* COOK rachatłukum *n*

tur•mer•ic [ˈtɜːmərɪk] *s* COOK kurkuma *f*

tur•moil [ˈtɜːmɔɪl] *s* **1.** zamęt *m* **2.** chaos *m*

turn [tɜːn] **I** *v/i* **1.** skręcać ⟨-cić⟩; ***~ into a narrow street*** skręcić w wąską uliczkę; ***the road ~s to the left*** droga skręca w lewo **2.** obracać ⟨-rócić⟩ się, odwracać ⟨-rócić⟩ się **3.** robić ⟨z-⟩ się, stawać ⟨stać⟩ się; ***~ brown*** brązowieć; ***the weather has ~ed cold*** zrobiło się zimno **4.** kończyć ⟨s-⟩; ***she ~s 21 in June*** w czerwcu kończy 21 lat **5.** ***my stomach ~s*** robi mi się niedobrze **II** *v/t* **1.** *key*: przekręcać ⟨-cić⟩ **2.** obracać ⟨-rócić⟩ **3.** *page*: przewracać ⟨-rócić⟩ **4.** kierować ⟨s-⟩; ***~ one's attention to*** zwrócić uwagę na *A* **5.** ***the heat ~ed the milk sour*** było gorąco i mleko skwaśniało; ***he's a lawyer ~ed politician*** to prawnik, który zajął się polityką **6.** *somersault*: robić ⟨z-⟩ **7.** (*lathe*) toczyć **III** *s* **1.** zakręt *m*; ***make a ~ right*** skręcić w prawo **2.** obrót *m*; ***take a ~ for the better*** polepszyć się; ***a ~ of events*** obrót wypadków **3.** kolej *m*; ***please wait your ~*** proszę poczekać na swoją kolej; ***it's my ~*** moja kolej; ***miss a ~*** stracić kolejkę; ***take ~s at doing s.th.*** robić coś na zmianę; ***in ~s*** na zmianę **4.** przełom *m*; ***at the ~ of the century*** na przełomie wieków **5.** (*on stage*) numer *m* **6.** *illness*: atak *m*; **turn a•gainst I** *v/i* zwracać ⟨-rócić⟩ się przeciw *D* **II** *v/t* buntować ⟨z-⟩ przeciw *D*; **turn around I** *v/i* **1.** odwracać ⟨-rócić⟩ się **2.** ***the economy turned around*** kryzys się skończył **II** *v/t* odwracać ⟨-rócić⟩; **turn away** *v/t* zawracać ⟨-rócić⟩, odsyłać ⟨odesłać⟩; **turn back I** *v/i* zawracać ⟨-rócić⟩, wracać ⟨wrócić⟩ **II** *v/t* zawracać ⟨-rócić⟩; **turn down** *v/t* **1.** *offer, invitation*: odrzucać ⟨-cić⟩ **2.** *radio, television*: ściszać ⟨-szyć⟩ **3.** ***turn the lights down*** przygasić światło, przyciemnić światło; **turn in I** *v/t* **1.** *infml* donosić ⟨-nieść⟩ na *A* **2.** *infml* ***turn oneself in*** oddać się w ręce policji **3.** zwracać ⟨-rócić⟩, oddawać ⟨-dać⟩ **4.** składać ⟨złożyć⟩ **5.** *profit*: osiągać ⟨-gnąć⟩ **II** *v/i dated* iść ⟨pójść⟩ spać; **turn off I** *v/t* **1.** *light, television*: wyłączać ⟨-czyć⟩ **2.** *gas, water*: zakręcać ⟨-cić⟩ **3.** zniechęcać ⟨-cić⟩ do *G* **4.** obrzydzać ⟨-dzić⟩

T

II *v/i* **1.** skręcać ⟨-cić⟩; ***~ the main road*** zjechać z głównej drogi **2.** *fig* (*stop listening*) wyłączać ⟨-czyć⟩; **turn on I** *v/t* **1.** *light, heating*: włączać ⟨-czyć⟩ **2.** *infml* podniecać ⟨-cić⟩, kręcić **3.** interesować ⟨za-⟩ (**to** *I*) **II** *v/i* **1.** atakować ⟨za-⟩ **2.** *Br* zależeć od *G*; **turn out I** *v/i* **1.** okazywać ⟨-zać⟩ się; ***everything turned out well*** wszystko dobrze się skończyło **2.** przybywać ⟨-być⟩, przychodzić ⟨przyjść⟩ **II** *v/t* **1.** produkować ⟨wy-⟩ **2.** wyrzucać ⟨-cić⟩ **3.** *light*: gasić ⟨z-⟩, wyłączać ⟨-czyć⟩ **4.** *pockets*: opróżniać ⟨-nić⟩; **turn over I** *v/i* **1.** przewracać ⟨-rócić⟩ się na drugi bok **2.** wywracać ⟨-rócić⟩ się **3.** dachować **4.** (*television*) zmieniać ⟨-nić⟩ kanał **5.** zwracać ⟨-rócić⟩ się (**to** do *G*) **II** *v/t* **1.** odwracać ⟨-rócić⟩, obracać ⟨-rócić⟩ na drugą stronę **2.** ***the company turns over $50 million a year*** roczne obroty firmy wynoszą 50 milionów dolarów **3.** rozważać ⟨-żyć⟩ **4.** przekazywać ⟨-zać⟩ (**to** *D*) **5.** przekazywać ⟨-zać⟩ w ręce (**to** *D*) **6.** *production*: przestawiać ⟨-wić⟩ (**to** na *A*); **turn up I** *v/i* **1.** (*person*) pojawiać ⟨-wić⟩ się, zjawiać ⟨-wić⟩ się **2.** (*opportunity*) nadarzać ⟨-rzyć⟩ się, pojawiać ⟨-wić⟩ się **3.** znajdować ⟨znaleźć⟩ się **II** *v/t* **1.** podgłaśniać ⟨-łośnić⟩ **2.** *Br trousers*: skracać ⟨-rócić⟩

'turn•a•bout, 'turn•a•round *s* **1.** zwrot *m* **2.** zmiana *f*

'turn•coat *s* **1.** zdrajca *m* **2.** renegat *m* **3.** odstępca *m*

turn•ing ['tɜːnɪŋ] *s* zakręt *m*; ***take a wrong ~*** źle skręcić; **'turn•ing cir•cle** *s* średnica *f* skrętu; **'turn•ing point** *s fig* punkt *m* zwrotny

tur•nip ['tɜːnɪp] *s* rzepa *f*

'turn•off *s* **1.** skręt *m* **2.** ***be a ~*** *infml* być odpychającym; ***be a ~ to potential buyers*** zniechęcać potencjalnych klientów; **'turn-on** *s*: ***be a ~*** *infml* być podniecającym; **'turn•out** *s* **1.** liczba *f* uczestników **2.** (*elections*) frekwencja *f*; **'turn•o•ver** *s* **1.** *ECON* obrót *m*, obroty *pl* **2.** *staff*: fluktuacja *f*; **'turn-pike** *s Am* płatna autostrada *f*; **'turn sig•nal** *s Am* kierunkowskaz *m*; **'turn•stile** *s* bramka *f* obrotowa, kołowrót *m*; **'turn•ta•ble** *s* **1.** (*record player*) talerz *m* obrotowy **2.** gramofon *m*

tur•pen•tine ['tɜːpəntaɪn] *s CHEM* terpentyna *f*

turps [tɜːps] *infml* → ***turpentine***

tur•quoise ['tɜːkwɔɪz] **I** *s* turkus *m* **II** *adj* turkusowy

tur•ret ['tʌrɪt] *s* **1.** *ARCHIT* wieża *f* **2.** *tank, ship*: wieża *f*, wieżyczka *f*

tur•tle ['tɜːtl] *s* żółw *m*; ***turn ~*** *fig* przewrócić się do góry dnem; **tur•tle-neck** (**'sweater**) *s* golf *m*, sweter *m* z golfem

turves [tɜːvz] *pl* → ***turf***

tusk [tʌsk] *s* kieł *m* (słoniowy)

tus•sle ['tʌsl] **I** *s* **1.** bójka *f* (**for** o *A*) **2.** walka *f*, spór *m* (**for** o *A*) **II** *v/i* **1.** bić się **2.** spierać się **3.** zmagać się

tus•sock ['tʌsək] *s* kępa *f* (trawy)

tu•te•lage ['tjuːtɪlɪdʒ] *s* **1.** uczenie *n*, nauczanie *n* **2.** *JUR* opieka *f*

tu•tor ['tjuːtə] **I** *s* **1.** korepetytor *m* **2.** *Br* wykładowca *m* **3.** *Br* nauczyciel *m* **4.** *Br* opiekun *m* studenta **5.** *Br* opiekun *m* grupy **6.** (*university*) *Am* asystent *m* **7.** samouczek *m* **II** *v/t* **1.** uczyć **2.** wykładać

tux [tʌks] *infml* → ***tuxedo***

tu•xe•do [tʌk'siːdəʊ] *pl -dos s Am* smoking *m*

TV [tiː'viː] *abbr* (=***television***) telewizja *f*; ***what's on ~ tonight?*** co jest dzisiaj w telewizji?; ***watch ~*** oglądać telewizję; ***a ~ set*** telewizor; **T'V din•ner** *s* gotowy posiłek *m*; **T'V guide** *s* program *m* telewizyjny

twad•dle ['twɒdl] *s dated* bzdura *f*, banialuki *pl*

twang [twæŋ] *s*: ***speak with a ~*** mówić przez nos

tweak [twiːk] *v/t* **1.** wykręcać ⟨-cić⟩ **2.** ***~ s.o.'s ear*** pociągnąć kogoś za ucho **3.** *infml* podrasowywać ⟨-sować⟩

tweed [twiːd] *s* tweed *m*

tweet [twiːt] *s* **1.** świergot *m* **2.** ćwierkanie *n*; **tweet•er** ['twiːtə] *s* głośnik *m* wysokotonowy

tweez•ers ['twiːzəz] *pl* pęseta *f*

twelfth [twelfθ] *adj* dwunasty

twelve [twelv] **I** *num* dwanaście **II** *s* dwunastka *f*

twen•ti•eth ['twentɪəθ] *adj* dwudziesty

twen•ty ['twentɪ] **I** *num* dwadzieścia

II *s* dwudziestka *f*; ***be in one's ~ies*** mieć dwadzieścia kilka lat; ***in the ~ies*** w latach dwudziestych

twerp [twɜːp] *s infml* przygłup *m*

twice [twaɪs] *adv* dwa razy, dwukrotnie; ***~ as much*** dwa razy tyle; ***I only met him ~*** spotkałem go tylko dwa razy; ***he's ~ her age*** jest od niej dwa razy starszy

twid•dle [ˈtwɪdl] *v/t* **1.** kręcić; ***~ one's ring on one's finger*** obracać pierścionek na palcu; ***~ one's thumbs*** **a)** kręcić młynka palcami **b)** *fig* zbijać bąki **2.** bawić się

twig[1] [twɪg] *s* gałązka *f*

twig[2] [~] *v/i* (*understand*) *Br infml* kapować ⟨s-⟩

twi•light [ˈtwaɪlaɪt] **I** *s a. fig* zmierzch *m*; ***at ~*** o zmierzchu; ***in the ~ of his career*** u schyłku swojej kariery **II** *adj* **1.** tajemniczy **2.** niejasny; ***a ~ zone*** *fig* granica, pogranicze

twin [twɪn] **I** *s* bliźniak *m* **II** *adj* bliźniaczy; ***a ~ brother*** brat bliźniak; ***a ~ sister*** siostra bliźniaczka; **twin-ˈbed•ded** *adj room*: z dwoma łóżkami (jednoosobowymi); **ˈtwin beds** *pl* dwa łóżka *pl* jednoosobowe; **twin ˈroom** *s* pokój *m* z dwoma łóżkami (jednoosobowymi); **ˈtwin town** *s* miasto *m* bliźniacze

twine [twaɪn] **I** *s* szpagat *m*, sznurek *m* **II** *v/t* **1.** owijać ⟨owinąć⟩ **2.** ***~ one's arms around s.o.'s neck*** opleść kogoś ramionami **III** *v/i* wić się (***around*** wokół *G*)

twin-en•gined [ˈtwɪnendʒɪnd] *adj* TECH dwusilnikowy

twinge [twɪndʒ] *s a. fig* ukłucie *n*; ***a ~ of envy*** ukłucie zazdrości; ***a ~ of conscience*** wyrzut sumienia

twin•kle [ˈtwɪŋkl] **I** *v/i* **1.** migotać **2.** migać **3.** (*eyes*) błyszczeć, skrzyć się (***with*** *I*) **II** *s* **1.** błysk *m*, iskra *f*; ***with a ~ in one's eye*** z błyskiem w oku **2.** migotanie *n* **3.** miganie *n*; **twin•kling** [ˈtwɪŋklɪŋ] *s* **1.** okamgnienie *n*; ***in the ~ of an eye*** w mgnieniu oka **2.** migotanie *n* **3.** miganie *n*

twirl [twɜːl] **I** *v/i* **1.** wirować ⟨za-⟩ **2.** kręcić ⟨za-⟩ się **3.** obracać ⟨-rócić⟩ się; ***she ~ed around in front of the mirror*** robiła obroty przed lustrem **II** *v/t* **1.** obracać ⟨-rócić⟩ **2.** *moustache*: podkręcać ⟨-cić⟩ **3.** *hair*: kręcić ⟨s-⟩ **III** *s* obrót *m*

twist [twɪst] **I** *v/i* **1.** skręcać ⟨-cić⟩ się **2.** wykrzywiać ⟨-wić⟩ się; ***his face ~ed in pain*** jego twarz wykrzywiła się w grymasie bólu **3.** (*road*, *river*) wić się **II** *v/t* **1.** *metal*: wyginać ⟨-giąć⟩ **2.** *ankle*: skręcać ⟨-cić⟩ **3.** *arm*: wykręcać ⟨-cić⟩ **4.** *hair*: wiązać ⟨z-⟩ **5.** okręcać ⟨-cić⟩; ***~ s.o. round one's little finger*** *fig* okręcić sobie kogoś wokół małego palca **6.** ***~ one's head around*** odwrócić głowę **7.** *switch*: przekręcać ⟨-cić⟩ **8.** kręcić, obracać **9.** *facts*: przeinaczać ⟨-czyć⟩ **10.** *s.o.'s words*: przekręcać ⟨-cić⟩ **11.** owijać ⟨owinąć⟩ **III** *s* **1.** skręt *m* **2.** przekręcenie *n* **3.** zwrot *m*; ***by a curious ~ of fate*** dziwnym zrządzeniem losu **4.** (ostry) zakręt *m* **5.** *paper*: zwitek *m* **6.** *wire*: zwój *m* **7.** (*dance*) twist *m*; **twist off** *v/t lid*: odkręcać ⟨-cić⟩

twist•er [ˈtwɪstə] *s Am infml* tornado *n*

twist•y [ˈtwɪstɪ] *adj road*: kręty, wijący się

twit [twɪt] *s Br infml* pacan *m*, głąb *m*

twitch [twɪtʃ] **I** *v/i* drgać ⟨-gnąć⟩ **II** *v/t* szarpać ⟨-pnąć⟩ **III** *s* **1.** tik *m* **2.** drgnięcie *n* **3.** drganie *n* **4.** szarpnięcie *n*

twit•ter [ˈtwɪtə] **I** *v/i* **1.** ćwierkać **2.** paplać, szwargotać (***about*** o *L*) **II** *s* **1.** ćwierkanie *n* **2.** *infml* paplanina *f*

two [tuː] **I** *num* dwa, dwaj, dwoje; ***in a day or ~*** za dzień lub dwa, za kilka dni; ***it's ~ (o'clock)*** jest druga; ***break s.th. in ~*** przełamać coś na pół; ***the ~ cars*** oba samochody **II** *s* dwójka *f*; ***the ~ of us*** my oboje; ***in ~s*** dwójkami, parami; ***put ~ and ~ together*** *fig* skojarzyć fakty; ***it takes ~ to tango*** do tanga trzeba dwojga; **ˈtwo-act** *adj play*: w dwóch aktach; **ˈtwo-bit** *adj Am infml* **1.** marny **2.** byle jaki; **two-faced** [ˈtuːfeɪst] *adj* dwulicowy

two•fold [ˈtuːfəʊld] **I** *adj* **1.** dwojaki **2.** dwukrotny **II** *adv* dwa razy, dwukrotnie; ***increase ~*** podwoić się

two-hand•ed [tuːˈhændɪd] *adj* **1.** *backhand*, *person*: oburęczny **2.** *sword*: dwuręczny; **two•pence** [ˈtʌpəns] *s Br* dwupensówka *f*; **two•pen•ny** [ˈtʌpənɪ] *adj Br* dwupensowy, za dwa pensy;

'**two-piece** *adj swimsuit*: dwuczęściowy; **two-seat•er** ['tuːsiːtə] *s* **1.** samochód *m* dwuosobowy **2.** samolot *m* dwumiejscowy **3.** kanapa *f* dwuosobowa **4.** fotel *m* dwuosobowy; '**two-stroke** *adj engine*: dwusuwowy; '**two-time** *v/t* zdradzać ⟨-dzić⟩; '**two-way** *adj* **1.** *road*: dwukierunkowy **2.** *device*: nadawczo-odbiorczy **3.** *relation*: dwustronny; **two-way** '**traf•fic** *s* ruch *m* dwukierunkowy

ty•coon [taɪ'kuːn] *s* magnat *m*, baron *m*

tym•pa•num ['tɪmpənəm] *-na* ['~nə], *-nums* ['~nəms] *s ARCHIT* tympanon *m*

type [taɪp] **I** *s* **1.** typ *m*; ***she's not my ~*** ona nie jest w moim typie **2.** rodzaj *m*; ***of this ~*** tego rodzaju **3.** czcionka *f* **4.** ***blood ~*** grupa krwi **II** *v/t* **1.** pisać ⟨na-⟩ na maszynie **2.** ***~ s.o.'s blood*** oznaczać ⟨-czyć⟩ czyjąś grupę krwi; '**type•cast** (*typecast*; *typecast*) *v/t actor*: szufladkować ⟨za-⟩; '**type•face** *s* krój *m* pisma; '**type•script** *s* maszynopis *m*; '**type•set** (*typeset*; *typeset*) *v/t* składać ⟨złożyć⟩ (do druku); **type•set•ter** ['taɪpsetə] *s* składacz *m*; **type•writ•er** ['taɪpraɪtə] *s* maszyna *f* do pisania; **type•writ•ten** ['taɪprɪtn] *adj* napisany na maszynie

ty•phoid ['taɪfɔɪd] *s MED* dur *m* brzuszny, tyfus *m* brzuszny

ty•phoon [taɪ'fuːn] *s* tajfun *m*

ty•phus ['taɪfəs] *s MED* dur *m* plamisty, tyfus *m* plamisty

typ•i•cal ['tɪpɪkl] *adj* typowy (**of** dla *G*) **typ•i•cal•ly** ['tɪpɪklɪ] *adv* **1.** zwykle, zazwyczaj **2.** typowo; ***~ Polish hospitality*** typowo polska gościnność **3.** jak zwykle; ***~, she couldn't find her keys*** jak zwykle nie mogła znaleźć kluczy

typ•i•fy ['tɪpɪfaɪ] *v/t* **1.** być typowym dla *G* **2.** być cechą charakterystyczną *G* **3.** być uosobieniem *G*

typ•ing ['taɪpɪŋ] *s* pisanie *n* na maszynie; '**typ•ing er•ror** *s* literówka *f*

typ•ist ['taɪpɪst] *s* maszynistka *f*

ty•po•graph•ic [taɪpə'græfɪk] *adj* **1.** typograficzny **2.** drukarski; **ty•pog•ra•phy** [taɪ'pɒgrəfɪ] *s* typografia *f*

ty•ran•ni•cal [tɪ'rænɪkl] *adj* tyrański; **ty•ran•nize** ['tɪrənaɪz] *v/t* tyranizować; **ty•ran•ny** ['tɪrənɪ] *s* tyrania *f*; **ty•rant** ['taɪrənt] *s* tyran *m*

tyre [taɪə] *s Br* opona *f*

ty•ro ['taɪrəʊ] *-ros* ['~rəʊz] *s* początkujący *m*, nowicjusz *m*

tzar [zɑː] → ***tsar***

U

u•biq•ui•tous [juː'bɪkwɪtəs] *s* wszechobecny

ud•der ['ʌdə] *s* wymię *n*

UEFA [juː'eɪfə] *abbr* (=***Union of European Football Associations***) UEFA *f*

UFO [juːef'əʊ] *pl UFO's*, *UFOs abbr* (=***Unidentified Flying Object***) UFO *n*

ugh [ʌg] *interj* fuj!

ug•li•ness ['ʌglɪnɪs] *s* brzydota *f*

ug•ly ['ʌglɪ] *adj* **1.** brzydki; ***the ~ duckling*** brzydkie kaczątko **2.** *accident*: paskudny

UHT [juːeɪtʃ'tiː] *abbr* (=***ultra-heat-treated***) *milk*: UHT

UK [juː'keɪ] *abbr* (=***United Kingdom***) Zjednoczone Królestwo *n*

U•kraine [juː'kreɪn] *s* (*a.* ***the ~***) Ukraina *f*

ul•cer ['ʌlsə] *s MED* wrzód *m*

ul•te•ri•or [ʌl'tɪərɪə] *adj motive*: ukryty

ul•ti•mate ['ʌltɪmət] **I** *adj* **1.** największy, najwyższy, najlepszy **2.** ostateczny **3.** fundamentalny **II** *s* ***the ~ in luxury*** szczyt luksusu; **ul•ti•mate•ly** ['ʌltɪmətlɪ] *adv* w końcu, ostatecznie

ul•ti•ma•tum [ʌltɪ'meɪtəm] *pl -tums*, *-ta s* ultimatum *n*; ***give s.o. an ~*** postawić komuś ultimatum

ul•tra•high [ʌltrə'haɪ] *adj* **1.** niezwykle wysoki **2.** *frequency*: UHF, ultrawysoki; **ul•tra•son•ic** [ʌltrə'sɒnɪk] *adj* ultradźwiękowy; **ul•tra•sound** ['ʌltrəsaʊnd] *s PHYS* ultradźwięk *m*; ***~ scan*** *MED* ultrasonografia, USG; ***~ scanner*** *MED* ultrasonograf *m*; **ul-**

tra•vi•o•let [ʌltrəˈvaɪələt] *adj* ultrafioletowy, nadfioletowy
um•bil•i•cal cord [ʌmˈbɪlɪklkɔːd] *s* ANAT pępowina *f*
um•brage [ˈʌmbrɪdʒ] *s*: ***take ~ at*** poczuć się urażonym z powodu *G*
um•brel•la [ʌmˈbrelə] *s* **1.** parasol *m* **2.** parasolka *f* **3.** *fig* parasol *m* ochronny; ***under the ~ of*** pod egidą *G*; **um•ˈbrel•la or•gan•iza•tion** *s* organizacja *f* patronacka; **um•ˈbrel•la stand** *s* stojak *m* na parasole
um•pire [ˈʌmpaɪə] SPORT **I** *s* sędzia *m*, arbiter *m* **II** *v/i* sędziować
ump•teen [ʌmpˈtiːn] *adj* wiele razy; ***I've told you ~ times*** *infml* mówiłem ci setki razy; **ump•teenth** [ʌmpˈtiːnθ] *adj* po raz któryś z rzędu
UN [juːˈen] *abbr* (=***United Nations***) ONZ *f*
un•a•bashed [ʌnəˈbæʃt] *adj* niespeszony
un•a•bat•ed [ʌnəˈbeɪtəd] *adj* niesłabnący; ***the rain continued ~*** deszcz nie słabł
un•a•ble [ʌnˈeɪbl] *adj*: ***to be ~ to do s.th.*** nie móc czegoś zrobić, nie być w stanie czegoś zrobić, nie potrafić czegoś zrobić
un•a•bridged [ʌnəˈbrɪdʒd] *adj novel, article*: pełny, nieskrócony
un•ac•cept•a•ble [ʌnəkˈseptəbl] *adj* nie do przyjęcia, niedopuszczalny
un•ac•com•pa•nied [ʌnəˈkʌmpənɪd] *adj* **1.** bez opieki; ***no ~ children allowed*** dzieciom bez opieki wstęp wzbroniony **2.** bez akompaniamentu
un•ac•count•a•ble [ʌnəˈkaʊntəbl] *adj* niewyjaśniony
un•ac•count•ed [ʌnəˈkaʊntɪd] *adj*: ***~ for*** brakujący, zaginiony
un•ac•cus•tomed [ʌnəˈkʌstəmd] *adj* **1.** nieprzyzwyczajony; ***be ~ to*** nie być przyzwyczajonym do *G* **2.** niezwykły, nietypowy
un•ac•knowl•edged [ʌnəkˈnɒlɪdʒd] *adj* **1.** niepotwierdzony **2.** oficjalnie nieuznawany **3.** nieuznany
un•ac•quaint•ed [ʌnəˈkweɪntɪd] *adj* ***be ~ with*** nie znać *G*, nie być zaznajomionym z *I*
un•a•dul•ter•at•ed [ʌnəˈdʌltəreɪtɪd] *adj* **1.** czysty; ***~ pleasure*** czysta przyjemność **2.** nieskażony
un•af•fect•ed [ʌnəˈfektɪd] *adj* **1.** naturalny **2.** szczery **3.** niewymuszony **4.** bezpretensjonalny **5.** niezmieniony
un•a•fraid [ʌnəˈfreɪd] *adj*: ***be ~ of*** nie bać się *G*
un•aid•ed [ʌnˈeɪdɪd] *adj* bez pomocy
un•al•tered [ʌnˈɔːltəd] *adj* niezmieniony
un•am•big•u•ous [ʌnæmˈbɪgjʊəs] *adj* niedwuznaczny, jednoznaczny
un-A•mer•i•can [ʌnəˈmerɪkən] *adj* **1.** nieamerykański **2.** antyamerykański
u•na•nim•i•ty [juːnəˈnɪmɪtɪ] *s* **1.** jednomyślność *f* **2.** zgodność *f*
u•nan•i•mous [juːˈnænɪməs] *adj* **1.** jednogłośny **2.** jednomyślny; ***be ~ in condemning s.th.*** jednomyślnie potępić coś **3.** zgodny; **u•nan•i•mous•ly** [juːˈnænɪməslɪ] *adv* **1.** jednogłośnie; ***by a ~ decision*** jednogłośnie **2.** jednomyślnie **3.** zgodnie
un•an•nounced [ʌnəˈnaʊnst] *adj* bez zapowiedzi
un•an•swer•a•ble [ʌnˈænsərəbl] *adj* **1.** niekwestionowany **2.** *question*: bez odpowiedzi
un•ap•peal•ing [ʌnəˈpiːlɪŋ] *adj* nieatrakcyjny, nieciekawy
un•ap•proach•a•ble [ʌnəˈprəʊtʃəbl] *adj* nieprzystępny
un•armed [ʌnˈɑːmd] *adj* nieuzbrojony
un•asked [ʌnˈɑːskt] *adj* **1.** niepytany **2.** *question*: niezadany
un•as•sist•ed [ʌnəˈsɪstɪd] *adj* samodzielny
un•as•sum•ing [ʌnəˈsjuːmɪŋ] *adj* skromny
un•at•tached [ʌnəˈtætʃt] *adj* wolny; stanu wolnego
un•attain•able [ʌnəˈteɪnəbl] *adj* nieosiągalny
un•at•tend•ed [ʌnəˈtendɪd] *adj* niepilnowany, bez opieki
un•at•trac•tive [ʌnəˈtræktɪv] *adj* nieatrakcyjny
un•au•thor•ized [ʌnˈɔːθəraɪzd] *adj* **1.** nieuprawniony **2.** nielegalny **3.** nieupoważniony; ***no ~ entry*** nieupoważnionym wstęp wzbroniony
un•a•vail•a•ble [ʌnəˈveɪləbl] *adj* **1.** niedostępny **2.** nieosiągalny

un•a•void•a•ble [ʌnəˈvɔɪdəbl] *adj* nieunikniony; **un•a•void•a•bly** [ʌnəˈvɔɪdəblɪ] *adv* w nieunikniony sposób
un•a•ware [ʌnəˈweə] *adj* nieświadomy; ***be ~ of*** być nieświadomym *G*, nie być świadomym *G*; ***be ~ that*** nie zdawać sobie sprawy, że; **un•a•wares** [ʌnəˈweəz] *adv* znienacka, z zaskoczenia
un•bal•ance [ʌnˈbæləns] *v/t* wytrącać ⟨-cić⟩ z równowagi; **un•bal•anced** [ʌnˈbælənst] *adj person*, *meal*: niezrównoważony
un•bear•a•ble [ʌnˈbeərəbl] *adj* nieznośny, nie do zniesienia, nie do wytrzymania
un•beat•a•ble [ʌnˈbiːtəbl] *adj* **1.** *team*: nie do pokonania, niepokonany **2.** *offer*: bezkonkurencyjny
un•beat•en [ʌnˈbiːtn] *adj* **1.** *team*, *army*: niepokonany, niezwyciężony **2.** *record*: niepobity
un•be•com•ing [ʌnbɪˈkʌmɪŋ] *adj* **1.** *behaviour*: niestosowny; ***behaviour ~ to an officer*** zachowanie niegodne oficera **2.** *colour*: nietwarzowy
un•be•known [ʌnbɪˈnəʊn], ***un•be-knownst*** [ʌnbɪˈnəʊnst] *adj*: ***~ to*** bez wiedzy *G*
un•be•lie•va•ble [ʌnbɪˈliːvəbl] *adj* niewiarygodny, nie do wiary; **unbelievably** [ʌnbɪˈliːvəblɪ] *adv* niewiarygodnie
un•bend [ʌnˈbend] **I** (*unbent*; *unbent*) *v/i* **1.** rozluźniać ⟨-nić⟩ się **2.** prostować ⟨wy-⟩ się **II** (*unbent*; *unbent*) *v/t* prostować ⟨wy-⟩; **unbend•ing** [ʌnˈbendɪŋ] *adj* nieugięty
un•bi•as(s)ed [ʌnˈbaɪəst] *adj* **1.** nieuprzedzony **2.** bezstronny
un•blem•ished [ʌnˈblemɪʃt] *adj* **1.** nieskalany **2.** *reputation*: nieposzlakowany
un•block [ʌnˈblɒk] *v/t sink*, *pipe*: przetykać ⟨-tkać⟩
un•born [ʌnˈbɔːn] *adj* nienarodzony
un•break•a•ble [ʌnˈbreɪkəbl] *adj* **1.** *glass*: niełtłukący **2.** *toy*: niezniszczalny **3.** *spirit*: niezłomny
un•bri•dled [ʌnˈbraɪdld] *adj* **1.** niepohamowany **2.** nieokiełznany
un•bro•ken [ʌnˈbrəʊkən] *adj* **1.** *record*: niepobity **2.** nieprzerwany **3.** *pottery*: nieuszkodzony

U

un•buck•le [ʌnˈbʌkl] *v/t* rozpinać ⟨-piąć⟩
un•bur•den [ʌnˈbɜːdn] *v/t*: ***~ oneself to*** wyżalić się *D*, wygadać się przed *I*
un•but•ton [ʌnˈbʌtn] *v/t shirt*: rozpinać ⟨-piąć⟩
un•called for [ʌnˈkɔːldfɔː] *adj remark*: nie na miejscu
un•can•ny [ʌnˈkænɪ] *adj* **1.** dziwny, osobliwy **2.** niesamowity
un•ceas•ing [ʌnˈsiːsɪŋ] *adj* nieustający
un•cer•e•mo•ni•ous•ly [ʌnserɪˈməʊnɪəslɪ] *adv* bezceremonialnie
un•cer•tain [ʌnˈsɜːtn] *adj* **1.** niepewny; ***be ~ about*** (*a.* ***of***) być niepewnym *G*, nie być pewnym *G*; ***be ~ how to do s.th.*** nie być pewnym, jak coś zrobić **2.** niezdecydowany; **un•cer•tain•ty** [ʌnˈsɜːtntɪ] *s* **1.** niepewność *f* **2.** niewiadoma *f*
un•chain [ʌnˈtʃeɪn] *v/t* **1.** odczepiać ⟨-pić⟩ **2.** spuszczać ⟨spuścić⟩ z łańcucha
un•changed [ʌnˈtʃeɪndʒd] *adj* niezmieniony; **un•chang•ing** [ʌnˈtʃeɪndʒɪŋ] *adj* niezmienny
un•char•ac•ter•is•tic [ʌnkærɪktəˈrɪstɪk] *adj* nietypowy
un•char•i•ta•ble [ʌnˈtʃærɪtəbl] *adj* nieżyczliwy
un•checked [ʌnˈtʃekt] *adj* **1.** niekontrolowany **2.** niesprawdzony
un•civ•il [ʌnˈsɪvl] *adj lit* niegrzeczny, nieuprzejmy
un•civ•i•lized [ʌnˈsɪvɪlaɪzd] *adj* **1.** niecywilizowany **2.** *fig* barbarzyński
unclaimed [ʌnˈkleɪmd] *adj luggage*: nieodebrany, po który nikt się nie zgłosił
un•cle [ˈʌŋkl] *s* wuj *m*, wujek *m*; **Uncle Sam** [ʌŋklˈsæm] *s* (*USA*) Wuj *m* Sam
un•clear [ʌnˈklɪə] *s* **1.** niejasny; ***it's ~ whether*** nie (do końca) wiadomo, czy; nie jest jasne, czy **2.** *plan*: niesprecyzowany **3.** niepewny; ***I'm ~ about what you want me to do*** nie jestem (do końca) pewna, czego ode mnie chcesz
un•com•for•ta•ble [ʌnˈkʌmftəbl] *adj* **1.** *shoes*: niewygodny **2.** *silence*: niezręczny **3.** *person*: spięty, nieswój
un•com•mit•ted [ʌnkəˈmɪtɪd] *adj* **1.** neutralny **2.** *voter*: niezdecydowany **3.** niezaangażowany

un•com•mon [ʌn'kɒmən] *adj* **1.** rzadki **2.** niezwykły; ***not to be ~*** nie być niczym niezwykłym
un•com•mu•ni•ca•tive [ʌnkə'mjuːnɪkətɪv] *adj* **1.** niekomunikatywny **2.** małomówny
un•com•plain•ing [ʌnkəm'pleɪnɪŋ] *adj* nieskarżący się; **un•com•plain•ing•ly** [ʌnkəm'pleɪnɪŋlɪ] *adv* bez skargi
un•com•pli•cat•ed [ʌn'kɔmplɪkeɪtɪd] *adj* nieskomplikowany
un•com•pro•mis•ing [ʌn'kɒmprəmaɪzɪŋ] *adj* bezkompromisowy
un•con•cerned [ʌnkən'sɜːnd] *adj*: ***be ~ about*** nie przejmować się *I*; ***be ~ with*** nie interesować się *I*
un•con•di•tion•al [ʌnkən'dɪʃnl] *adj* bezwarunkowy
un•con•firmed [ʌnkən'fɜːmd] *adj* niepotwierdzony
un•con•scious [ʌn'kɒnʃəs] *adj* **1.** *MED* nieprzytomny **2.** nieświadomy; ***be ~ of*** być nieświadomym *G*, nie być świadomym *G*; **un•con•scious•ness** *s* **1.** nieprzytomność *f* **2.** nieświadomość *f*
un•con•sti•tu•tion•al ['ʌnkɒnstə'tuːʃənl] *adj* niezgodny z konstytucją, niekonstytucyjny
un•con•trol•la•ble [ʌnkən'trəʊləbl] *adj* **1.** nieokiełznany **2.** nieposkromiony **3.** nie do opanowania **4.** nieposłuszny; **un•con•trolled** [ʌnkən'trəʊld] *adj* **1.** niekontrolowany **2.** nieopanowany **3.** niepohamowany
un•con•ven•tion•al [ʌnkən'venʃnl] *adj* niekonwencjonalny
un•con•vinced [ʌnkən'vɪnst] *adj* nieprzekonany; ***be ~ about*** nie być przekonanym do *G*; **un•convinc•ing** [ʌnkən'vɪnsɪŋ] *adj argument*: nieprzekonujący
un•cooked [ʌn'kʊkt] *adj* niegotowany, surowy
un•count•a•ble [ʌn'kaʊntəbl] *adj noun*: niepoliczalny; **un•'count•ed** *adj* **1.** niepoliczony **2.** niezliczony
un•cou•ple [ʌn'kʌpl] *v/t* **1.** odczepiać ⟨-pić⟩ **2.** odłączać ⟨-czyć⟩ **3.** rozłączać ⟨-czyć⟩
un•couth [ʌn'kuːθ] *adj person, behaviour*: nieokrzesany
un•cov•er [ʌn'kʌvə] *v/t* odkrywać ⟨-ryć⟩
un•crit•i•cal [ʌn'krɪtɪkl] *adj* bezkrytyczny
un•crowned [ʌn'kraʊnd] *adj a. fig* niekoronowany
unc•tion ['ʌŋkʃn] *s REL* namaszczenie *n*
unc•tu•ous ['ʌŋktjʊəs] *adj* obłudny
un•cut [ʌn'kʌt] *adj* **1.** *grass*: nieprzycięty **2.** *bread*: niepokrojony **3.** *version*: pełny **4.** *film*: w pełnej wersji **5.** *diamond*: nieoszlifowany
un•dam•aged [ʌn'dæmɪdʒd] *adj* nieuszkodzony
un•dat•ed [ʌn'deɪtɪd] *adj* **1.** *letter*: niedatowany **2.** z nieznanego okresu
un•de•cid•ed [ʌndɪ'saɪdɪd] *adj* **1.** niezdecydowany **2.** nierozstrzygnięty
un•de•mand•ing [ʌndɪ'mændɪŋ] *adj* **1.** niewymagający **2.** *work*: niewymagający wysiłku **3.** *pupil*: mało absorbujący
un•de•ni•a•ble [ʌndɪ'naɪəbl] *adj* niezaprzeczalny; **un•de•ni•a•bly** [ʌndɪ'naɪəblɪ] *adv* niezaprzeczalnie
un•der ['ʌndə] **I** *prep* **1.** pod *I*; ***~ the table*** pod stołem; ***~ the government of*** pod rządami *G*; ***~ the pseudonym*** pod pseudonimem; ***check ~ 'sport'*** sprawdź pod „sport" **2.** poniżej *G*; ***it costs ~ $10*** to kosztuje poniżej 10 dolarów **3.** zgodnie z *I*; ***~ the agreement*** zgodnie z umową, zgodnie z postanowieniami umowy **4.** w trakcie *G*; ***~ construction*** w budowie **5.** pod wpływem *G*; ***~ stress*** pod wpływem stresu **II** *adv* **1.** pod spodem, pod spód **2.** pod wodą **3.** poniżej; ***children aged two and ~*** dzieci w wieku do dwóch lat **III** *adj layer*: spodni, dolny; **un•der•'age** *adj* nieletni, niepełnoletni; **'un•der•arm I** *adj* **1.** *throw*: od dołu **2.** *deodorant*: do stosowania pod pachami **II** *adv* od dołu; **'un•derbrush** *Am* → ***undergrowth***; **un•der•car•riage** *s* (*plane*) podwozie *n*; **un•der•'charge** *v/t* liczyć ⟨po-⟩ za mało; **'un•der•clothes** → ***underwear***; **'un•der•coat** *s* (*paint layer*) podkład *m*; **'un•der•cov•er I** *adj* tajny; ***an ~ agent*** tajny agent **II** *adv* ***work ~*** działać w ukryciu; **'un•der•cur•rent** *s*: ***an ~ of racism*** ukryty rasizm, utajony rasizm; **un•der•'cut** (*undercut*; *undercut*) *v/t* **1.** oferować ⟨za-⟩ niższe ceny od *G* **2.** *prices*: oferować

U

⟨za-⟩ niższy; **un•der•'devel•oped** *adj* słabo rozwinięty, zacofany; **'un•der•dog** *s* słabszy *m*, gorszy *m*; **un•der•'done** *adj dish*: niedogotowany; **un•der•'es•ti•mate I** *v/t* **1.** zbyt nisko oszacowywać ⟨-cować⟩ **2.** nie doceniać ⟨-nić⟩ **II** *s* zbyt niskie oszacowanie *n*; **un•der•ex•'pose** *v/t* PHOT nie doświetlać ⟨-lić⟩; **un•der•ex•'posed** *adj* PHOT niedoświetlony; **un•der•'fed** *adj* niedożywiony; **'un•der•floor** *adj* (umieszczony) pod podłogą, podpodłogowy; *~ heating* ogrzewanie podłogowe; **un•der•'foot** *adv* pod nogami; **un•der•'go** (*underwent*; *undergone*) *v/t* przechodzić ⟨przejść⟩; *~ an operation* przejść operację; **un•der•grad** ['ʌndərgræd] *infml* → ***undergraduate***; **un•der•'grad•u•ate** *s* student *m* (na studiach licencjackich)

'un•der•ground I *adj a. fig* podziemny; ***an ~ car park*** podziemny parking; ***an ~ resistance movement*** podziemny ruch oporu **II** *adv* pod ziemią, pod ziemię; ***go ~*** *fig* zaszyć się, ukryć się **III** *s* **1.** *Br* metro *n*; ***travel by ~*** jeździć metrem **2.** *fig* podziemie *n*; **'un•der•growth** *s* **1.** (*forest*) podszycie *n* leśne **2.** zarośla *pl*; **un•der•'hand** *adj* podstępny; **un•der•'lie** (*underlay*; *underlain*) *v/i* **1.** leżeć u źródła **2.** stanowić podstawę; **un•der•'line** *v/t a. fig* podkreślać ⟨-lić⟩

un•der•ling ['ʌndəlɪŋ] *s* podwładny *m*

un•der•ly•ing [ʌndə'laɪɪŋ] *adj* **1.** leżący u podstaw **2.** zasadniczy **3.** podstawowy; **un•der•manned** [ʌndə'mænd] *adj factory*, *hospital*: mający niedobór personelu; **un•der•men•tioned** [ʌndə'menʃnd] *adj* wymieniony poniżej; **un•der•'mine** *v/t a. fig* podkopywać ⟨-pać⟩; ***~ s.o.'s authority*** podkopywać czyjś autorytet

un•der•neath [ʌndə'ni:θ] **I** *prep* pod *I* **II** *s* spód *m*

un•der•nour•ished [ʌndə'nʌrɪʃd] *adj* niedożywiony; **un•der•'paid** *adj* źle opłacany; **'un•der•pants** *pl* **1.** majtki *pl* **2.** slipy *pl*; **'un•der•pass** *s* **1.** przejście *n* podziemne **2.** przejazd *m* podziemny (w skrzyżowaniu dwupoziomowym); **un•der•'pay** (*underpaid*; *underpaid*) *v/t* źle opłacać ⟨-cić⟩; **un•der•'play** *v/t* umniejszać ⟨-szyć⟩ znaczenie; **un•der•priv•i•leged** [ʌndə'prɪvɪlɪdʒd] *adj* społecznie i ekonomicznie upośledzony; **un•der•'rate** *v/t* nie doceniać ⟨-nić⟩; **un•der•'score** *Am* → ***underline***; **'un•der•sea** *adj* podwodny; **un•der•'sec•re•tar•y** *s* POLIT podsekretarz *m*; **un•der•'sell** (*undersold*; *undersold*) *v/t* sprzedawać ⟨-dać⟩ po niższych cenach niż *N*; **'un•der•shirt** *s Am* podkoszulek *m*; **'un•der•side** *s* **1.** dół *m* **2.** spód *m*; **un•der•signed** [ʌndə'saɪnd] *s*: ***the ~*** **a)** niżej podpisany **b)** niżej podpisani; **un•der•sized** [ʌndə'saɪzd] *adj* zbyt mały; **'un•der•skirt** *s* halka *f*; **un•der•staffed** [ʌndə'stɑ:ft] → ***undermanned***

un•der•stand [ʌndə'stænd] (*understood*; *understood*) *v/t* **1.** rozumieć ⟨z-⟩; ***can you ~ French?*** rozumiesz po francusku?; ***nobody ~s me*** nikt mnie nie rozumie; ***make oneself understood*** porozumieć się, dogadać się; ***am I to ~ that*** czy mam rozumieć, że; ***give s.o. to ~*** dać komuś do zrozumienia **2.** uważać; ***it is understood that*** uważa się, że; **un•der•stand•able** [ʌndə'stændəbl] *adj* zrozumiały; **un•der•stand•ably** [ʌndə'stændəblɪ] *adv* co zrozumiałe; **un•der•stand•ing** [ʌndə'stændɪŋ] **I** *s* **1.** rozumienie *n*, zrozumienie *n* **2.** porozumienie *n*; ***come to an ~*** dojść do porozumienia; ***on the ~ that*** pod warunkiem, że **3.** znajomość *f* **4.** wyrozumiałość *f* **II** *adj* wyrozumiały; **un•der•'state** *v/t* **1.** *significance*: umniejszać ⟨-szyć⟩ **2.** *cost*: zaniżać ⟨-żyć⟩; **un•der•stat•ed** [ʌndə'steɪtɪd] *adj style*, *colour*: subtelny, dyskretny; **'un•der•state•ment** *s* niedomówienie *n*, niedopowiedzenie; ***it's an ~!*** to mało powiedziane!; **'un•der•stud•y** THEAT **I** *s* dubler *m* **II** *v/t* dublować; **un•der•'take I** (*undertook*; *undertaken*) *v/t* podejmować ⟨-djąć⟩ **II** (*undertook*; *undertaken*) *v/i* **1.** podejmować ⟨-djąć⟩ się **2.** zobowiązywać ⟨-zać⟩ się; **un•der•tak•er** ['ʌndəteɪkə] *s* przedsiębiorca *m* pogrzebowy; **'un•der•tak•ing** *s* **1.** przedsięwzięcie *n* **2.** *form* zobowiązanie *n* **3.** usługi *pl* pogrzebowe; **un•der-the-'count•er** *adj infml* **1.** nielegalny **2.** pokątny

3. spod lady; '**un•der•tone** *s* **1.** ***in an ~*** półgłosem **2.** *fig* zabarwienie *n*, podtekst *m*; **un•der•'val•ue** *v/t* **1.** nie doceniać ⟨-nić⟩ **2.** zbyt nisko wyceniać ⟨-nić⟩; **un•der•'wa•ter I** *adj* podwodny **II** *adv* pod wodą; **un•der•'way** *adj*: ***be ~*** być w trakcie, trwać; '**un•der•wear** *s* bielizna *f*; **un•der•'weight** *adj*; ***be ~*** mieć niedowagę; '**un•der•world** *s* **1.** półświatek *m*, świat *m* przestępczy **2.** ***the ~*** kraina *f* cieni; **un•der•'write** (*underwrote*; *underwritten*) *v/t* **1.** ubezpieczać ⟨-czyć⟩ **2.** asekurować **3.** gwarantować ⟨za-⟩ **4.** *shares*: subskrybować

un•de•served [ʌndɪ'zɜːvd] *adj* niezasłużony; **un•de•serv•ed•ly** [ʌndɪ'zɜːvɪdlɪ] *adv* niezasłużenie

un•de•sir•a•ble [ʌndɪ'zaɪərəbl] *adj* niepożądany

un•dies ['ʌndɪz] *pl infml* bielizna *f*

un•dig•ni•fied [ʌn'dɪgnɪfaɪd] *adj* **1.** *behaviour*: niegodny **2.** *word*: nieprzyzwoity

un•dis•ci•plined [ʌn'dɪsɪplɪnd] *adj* niezdyscyplinowany

un•dis•cov•ered [ʌndɪ'skʌvəd] *adj* nieodkryty

un•dis•guised [ʌndɪs'gaɪzd] *adj* nieskrywany, nieukrywany

un•dis•put•ed [ʌndɪ'spjuːtɪd] *adj* niepodlegający dyskusji, bezdyskusyjny, bezsporny

un•dis•turbed [ʌndɪs'tɜːbd] *adj* **1.** nieprzerwany **2.** niezakłócony **3.** nienaruszony **4.** ***be ~*** nie przejmować się, nie martwić się

un•di•vid•ed [ʌndɪ'vaɪdɪd] *adj* **1.** niepodzielony **2.** cały

un•do [ʌn'duː] (*undid*; *undone*) *v/t* **1.** *button*, *zip*: rozpinać ⟨-piąć⟩ **2.** *shoe lace*: rozwiązywać ⟨-zać⟩ **3.** *harm*: naprawiać ⟨-wić⟩ **4.** *effort*: niweczyć ⟨z-⟩ **5.** *order*: cofać ⟨-fnąć⟩ **6.** *team*: pokonywać ⟨-nać⟩

un•done [ʌn'dʌn] *adj* **1.** rozpięty **2.** rozwiązany **3.** *work*: niedokończony

un•doubt•ed [ʌn'daʊtɪd] *adj* niewątpliwy; **un•doubt•ed•ly** [ʌn'daʊtɪdlɪ] *adv* niewątpliwie

un•dreamed-of [ʌn'driːmdəv] *adj* o którym się nawet nie śniło

un•dress [ʌn'dres] **I** *v/i* rozbierać ⟨-zebrać⟩ się **II** *v/t* rozbierać ⟨-zebrać⟩

un•due [ʌn'djuː] *adj* zbytni, nadmierny

un•du•lat•ing ['ʌndjʊleɪtɪŋ] *adj hills*: łagodny

un•du•ly [ʌn'djuːlɪ] *adv* zbytnio, nadmiernie

un•dy•ing [ʌn'daɪɪŋ] *adj* dozgonny, wieczny, nieśmiertelny

un•earth [ʌn'ɜːθ] *v/t* **1.** wykopywać ⟨-pać⟩, odkopywać ⟨-pać⟩ **2.** *fig* odgrzebywać ⟨-bać⟩, wydobywać ⟨-być⟩ na światło dzienne; **un•earth•ly** [ʌn'ɜːθlɪ] *adj* nieziemski, nie z tej ziemi, niesamowity; ***at an ~ hour*** o nieludzkiej godzinie

un•eas•i•ness [ʌn'iːzɪnəs] *s* niepokój *m*; **un•eas•y** [ʌn'iːzɪ] *adj* **1.** niespokojny; ***be ~ about*** niepokoić się o *A* **2.** niepewny

un•eat•a•ble [ʌn'iːtəbl] *adj* niejadalny

un•e•co•nom•ic [ʌniːkə'nɒmɪk] *adj* nierentowny, nieopłacalny

un•ed•u•cat•ed [ʌn'edʒəkeɪtɪd] *adj* niewykształcony

un•e•mo•tion•al [ʌnɪ'məʊʃənl] *adj* **1.** powściągliwy **2.** spokojny **3.** pozbawiony emocji **4.** nieporuszony; ***be ~ about*** nie przejmować się *I*

un•em•ployed [ʌnɪm'plɔɪd] **I** *adj* bezrobotny **II** *s* ***the ~*** bezrobotni; **un•em•ploy•ment** [ʌnɪm'plɔɪmənt] *s* bezrobocie *n*; ***~ benefit***, ***~ compensation*** zasiłek dla bezrobotnych

un•end•ing [ʌn'endɪŋ] *adj* niekończący się

un•en•dur•a•ble [ʌnɪn'djʊərəbl] *adj* nieznośny, nie do zniesienia

un-Eng•lish [ʌn'ɪŋglɪʃ] *adj* nieangielski

un•en•vi•a•ble [ʌn'envɪəbl] *adj* **1.** *task*: niewdzięczny **2.** nie do pozazdroszczenia

un•e•qual [ʌn'iːkwəl] *adj* **1.** nierówny **2.** różny; ***~ in length*** różnej długości **3.** ***he's ~ to the task*** *form* to zadanie go przerasta; **un•e•qualled** [ʌn'iːkwəld] *Br*, ***un•e•qualed*** *Am adj* niezrównany, niedościgniony

un•e•quiv•o•cal [ʌnɪ'kwɪvəkl] *adj* jednoznaczny, niedwuznaczny

un•er•ring [ʌn'erɪŋ] *adj instinct*: nieomylny

un•e•ven [ʌn'iːvn] *adj* **1.** nierówny **2.** *breath*: nieregularny; **un•e•ven•ly** [ʌn'iːvnlɪ] *adv* nierówno

U

un•e•vent•ful [ʌnɪ'ventfəl] *adj* **1.** spokojny **2.** nieciekawy
un•ex•pec•ted [ʌnɪk'spektɪd] *adj* nieoczekiwany; **un•ex•pec•ted•ly** [ʌnɪk'spektɪdlɪ] *adv* nieoczekiwanie
un•ex•plained [ʌnɪk'spleɪnd] *adj* niewyjaśniony
un•ex•plored [ʌnɪk'splɔːd] *adj* niezbadany
un•fail•ing [ʌn'feɪlɪŋ] *adj* niezawodny
un•fair [ʌn'feə] *adj* niesprawiedliwy; **un•fair•ness** [ʌn'feənɪs] *s* niesprawiedliwość *f*
un•faith•ful [ʌn'feɪθfəl] *adj* niewierny
un•fal•ter•ing [ʌn'fɔːltərɪŋ] *adj calmness*: niewzruszony
un•fa•mil•i•ar [ʌnfə'mɪljə] *adj* nieznany; ***be ~ with*** nie znać *G*
un•fash•ion•a•ble [ʌn'fɑːʃnəbl] *adj* niemodny
un•fas•ten [ʌn'fɑːsn] *v/t* odpinać ⟨-piąć⟩
un•fa•vou•ra•ble [ʌn'feɪvərəbl] *Br*, ***unfa•vo•ra•ble*** *Am* niesprzyjający; ***~ conditions*** niesprzyjające warunki; ***show s.o. in an ~ light*** przedstawiać kogoś w niekorzystnym świetle
un•feel•ing [ʌn'fiːlɪŋ] *adj* nieczuły, bezduszny
un•fet•tered [ʌn'fetəd] *adj form* **1.** nieograniczony **2.** wolny
un•fin•ished [ʌn'fɪnɪʃt] *adj* niedokończony, nieskończony
un•fit [ʌn'fɪt] *adj* **1.** nienadający się, nieodpowiedni **2.** niezdolny; ***~ for work*** niezdolny do pracy **3.** *person*: nie w formie, w słabej kondycji
un•flag•ging [ʌn'flægɪŋ] *adj interest*: niesłabnący
un•flat•ter•ing [ʌn'flætərɪŋ] *adj* **1.** *haircut*: nietwarzowy **2.** *remark*: niepochlebny
un•fold [ʌn'fəʊld] **I** *v/t* **1.** *map, tablecloth, arms*: rozkładać ⟨-złożyć⟩ **2.** rozwijać ⟨-winąć⟩ **II** *v/i* rozwijać ⟨-winąć⟩ się
un•fore•seen [ʌnfɔː'siːn] *adj* nieoczekiwany
un•for•get•ta•ble [ʌnfə'getəbl] *adj* niezapomniany
un•for•giv•a•ble [ʌnfə'gɪvəbl] *adj* niewybaczalny
un•for•tu•nate [ʌn'fɔːtʃənət] *adj* **1.** *accident*: nieszczęśliwy **2.** *decision*: niefortunny; **un•for•tu•nate•ly** [ʌn'fɔːtʃənətlɪ] *adv* niestety
un•found•ed [ʌn'faʊndɪd] *adj* nieuzasadniony
un•fre•quent•ed [ʌnfrɪ'kwentɪd] *adj* mało uczęszczany
un•friend•ly [ʌn'frendlɪ] *adj* **1.** niemiły **2.** nieprzyjemny **3.** nieprzyjazny **4.** ***environmentally ~*** szkodliwy dla środowiska
un•ful•filled [ʌnfʊl'fɪld] *adj wish, condition*: niespełniony; ***to feel ~*** czuć się niespełnionym
un•furl [ʌn'fɜːl] **I** *v/t* rozwijać ⟨-winąć⟩, rozpościerać ⟨-postrzec⟩ **II** *v/i* (*buds*) otwierać ⟨-worzyć⟩ się
un•fur•nished [ʌn'fɜːnɪʃt] *adj* nieumeblowany
un•gain•ly [ʌn'geɪnlɪ] *adj* niezgrabny, niezręczny
un•gen•tle•man•like [ʌn'dʒentlmənlaɪk], ***un•'gen•tle•man•ly*** *adj* niedżentelmeński
un•god•ly [ʌn'gɒdlɪ] *adj dated* nieboski; ***at an ~ hour*** o nieludzkiej godzinie
un•grate•ful [ʌn'greɪtfəl] *adj* niewdzięczny
un•guard•ed [ʌn'gɑːdɪd] *adj* **1.** niestrzeżony **2.** *remark*: nieprzemyślany **3.** nieuważny; ***in an ~ moment*** w chwili nieuwagi
un•hap•pi•ness [ʌn'hæpɪnɪs] *s* **1.** bycie *n* nieszczęśliwym; ***we all experience moments of ~*** każdy czasem czuje się nieszczęśliwy **2.** niezadowolenie *n* **3.** smutek *m*
un•hap•py [ʌn'hæpɪ] *adj* **1.** smutny **2.** nieszczęśliwy **3.** niezadowolony (***with*** z *G*) **4.** pechowy
un•harmed [ʌn'hɑːmd] *adj* bez szwanku
un•health•y [ʌn'helθɪ] *adj* **1.** *person*: chory **2.** *area*: niezdrowy **3.** *interest*: chorobliwy
un•heard [ʌn'hɜːd] *adj* **1.** ***go ~*** przejść bez echa, przejść niezauważonym **2.** *cassette*: nieprzesłuchany; **unheard-of** [ʌn'hɜːdəv] *adj* niespotykany
un•help•ful [ʌn'helpfl] *adj* nieprzydatny
un•hes•i•tat•ing [ʌn'hezɪteɪtɪŋ] *adj* stanowczy
un•hinge [ʌn'hɪndʒ] *v/t* **1.** zdjąć z zawiasów **2.** *fig* wytrącać ⟨-cić⟩ z równowagi

un•ho•ly [ʌn'həʊlɪ] *adj* **1.** niebezpieczny **2.** *infml* straszny
un•hurt [ʌn'hɜːt] *adj* bez szwanku
u•ni ['juːnɪ] *s infml* uniwerek *m*
un•i•den•ti•fied [ʌnaɪ'dentɪfaɪd] *adj* nieokreślony, niezidentyfikowany; **un•i•den•ti•fied fly•ing 'ob•ject** *s* niezidentyfikowany obiekt *m* latający, UFO *n*
u•ni•fi•ca•tion [juːnɪfɪ'keɪʃn] *s* **2.** zjednoczenie *n* **2.** połączenie *n* **3.** ujednolicenie *n* **4.** unifikacja *f*
u•ni•form ['juːnɪfɔːm] **I** *adj* jednolity **II** *s* mundur *m*; **u•ni•formed** ['juːnɪfɔːmd] *adj* w mundurze; **u•ni•form•i•ty** [juːnɪ'fɔːmətɪ] *s* jednolitość *f*
u•ni•fy ['juːnɪfaɪ] *v/t* **1.** łączyć ⟨po-⟩ **2.** jednoczyć ⟨z-⟩ **3.** ujednolicać ⟨-cić⟩
u•ni•lat•e•ral [juːnɪ'lætərəl] *adj* jednostronny
un•i•ma•gi•na•ble [ʌnɪ'mædʒɪnəbl] *adj* niewyobrażalny; **un•i•ma•gi•na•tive** [ʌnɪ'mædʒɪnətɪv] *adj* **1.** bez wyobraźni **2.** mało oryginalny **3.** bez polotu
un•im•por•tant [ʌnɪm'pɔːtənt] *adj* nieważny
un•im•pressed [ʌnɪm'prest] *adj*: ***she was ~ by his story*** jego opowieść nie zrobiła na niej wrażenia
un•in•hab•i•ta•ble [ʌnɪn'hæbɪtəbl] *adj* nienadający się do zamieszkania; **un•in•hab•it•ed** [ʌnɪn'hæbɪtɪd] *adj* **1.** niezamieszkany, niezamieszkały **2.** bezludny
un•in•hib•it•ed [ʌnɪn'hɪbɪtɪd] *adj* nieskrępowany, swobodny, bez zahamowań
un•in•jured [ʌn'ɪndʒəd] *adj* bez szwanku, bez szkody
un•in•spir•ing [ʌnɪn'spaɪərɪŋ] *adj* **1.** nieciekawy **2.** bezbarwny
un•in•sured [ʌnɪn'ʃʊəd] *adj* nieubezpieczony
un•in•tel•li•gi•ble [ʌnɪn'telɪdʒəbl] *adj* niezrozumiały
un•in•tend•ed [ʌnɪn'tendɪd] *adj* niezamierzony
un•in•ten•tion•al [ʌnɪn'tenʃnl] *adj* niezamierzony; **un•in•ten•tion•al•ly** [ʌnɪn'tenʃnlɪ] *adv* niechcący
un•in•ter•est•ed [ʌn'ɪntrəstɪd] *adj*: ***be ~ in*** nie interesować się *I*; **un•in•te•rest•ing** [ʌn'ɪntrəstɪŋ] *adj* nieciekawy
un•in•ter•rupt•ed [ʌnɪntə'rʌptɪd] *adj* nieprzerwany
un•in•vit•ed [ʌnɪn'vaɪtɪd] **I** *adj* nieproszony **II** *adv* bez zaproszenia
u•nion ['juːnjən] *s* **1.** związek *m* **2.** unia *f*; ***the European ~*** Unia Europejska; ***a monetary ~*** unia monetarna **3.** samorząd *m*; ***a students' ~*** samorząd studencki **4.** (*a.* **trade ~**) związek *m* zawodowy; **un•ion•ist** ['juːniənɪst] *s* związkowiec *m*
u•nique [ju'niːk] *adj* jedyny w swoim rodzaju, niepowtarzalny, wyjątkowy, unikalny
u•ni•sex ['juːnɪseks] *adj* uniseks
u•ni•son ['juːnɪzn] *s*: ***in ~*** zgodnie, wspólnie
u•nit ['juːnɪt] *s* **1.** jednostka *f* **2.** komórka *f*; ***the basic ~ of society*** podstawowa komórka społeczna **3.** (*hospital*) oddział *m* **4.** szafka *f* **5.** segment *m* **6.** blok *m*
u•nite [juː'naɪt] **I** *v/t* **1.** łączyć ⟨po-⟩ **2.** jednoczyć ⟨z-⟩ **II** *v/i* **1.** łączyć ⟨po-⟩ się **2.** jednoczyć ⟨z-⟩ się
u•nit•ed [juː'naɪtɪd] *adj* zjednoczony; **U•nit•ed 'King•dom** *s* Zjednoczone Królestwo *n*; **U•nit•ed 'Na•tions** *pl* Organizacja *f* Narodów Zjednoczonych; **U•nit•ed 'States (of A'mer•i•ca)** *pl* Stany *pl* Zjednoczone (Ameryki)
u•ni•ty ['juːnətɪ] *s* jedność *f*
u•ni•ver•sal [juːnɪ'vɜːsl] *adj* **1.** uniwersalny **2.** powszechny; **u•ni•ver•sal•ly** [juːnɪ'vɜːsəlɪ] *adv* powszechnie
u•ni•verse ['juːnɪvɜːs] *s* wszechświat *m*
u•ni•ver•si•ty [juːnɪ'vɜːsətɪ] *s* uniwersytet *m*; ***go to ~*** iść na uniwersytet
un•just [ʌn'dʒʌst] *adj* niesprawiedliwy
un•jus•ti•fi•a•ble [ʌndʒʌstɪ'faɪəbl] *adj* **1.** nieusprawiedliwiony **2.** nieuzasadniony
un•kempt [ʌn'kempt] *adj* **1.** *hair*: rozczochrany **2.** *appearance*: niechlujny **3.** zaniedbany
un•kind [ʌn'kaɪnd] *adj* niemiły, nieżyczliwy
un•known [ʌn'nəʊn] **I** *adj* **1.** nieznany, niewiadomy; ***for some ~ reasons*** z niewiadomych powodów **2.** nieznajomy **II** *s* niewiadoma *f*
un•la•dy•like [ʌn'leɪdɪlaɪk] *adj*: ***behave ~*** zachowywać się w sposób niegodny damy

un•law•ful [ʌn'lɔːfl] *adj* **1.** bezprawny **2.** nielegalny
un•lead•ed [ʌn'ledɪd] *adj petrol*: bezołowiowy
un•learn [ʌn'lɜːn] (*unlearned; unlearnt*) *v/t* oduczać ⟨-czyć⟩ się *G*
un•leash [ʌn'liːʃ] *v/t emotion*: uwalniać ⟨uwolnić⟩; ***all his anger was ~ed on her*** wyładował na niej całą swoją złość
un•leav•ened [ʌn'levnd] *adj bread*: przaśny
un•less [ən'les] *conj* **1.** jeżeli nie, chyba że; ***I'll see you tomorrow ~ something unexpected happens*** zobaczymy się jutro, chyba że zdarzy się coś nieoczekiwanego **2.** o ile nie; ***~ I'm mistaken*** o ile się nie mylę
un•like [ʌn'laɪk] **I** *prep* **1.** w przeciwieństwie do *G* **2.** niepodobny do *G*; ***he is very ~ his father*** jest zupełnie niepodobny do swojego ojca; ***that's very ~him*** to do niego zupełnie niepodobne **II** *adj* różny, inny; **un•like•ly** [ʌn'laɪklɪ] *adj* **1.** mało prawdopodobny; ***it's ~ that she'll arrive*** najprawdopodobniej nie przyjedzie; jest mało prawdopodobne, żeby przyjechała **2.** nieprawdopodobny
un•lim•it•ed [ʌn'lɪmɪtɪd] *adj* **1.** nieograniczony **2.** bezgraniczny
un•list•ed [ʌn'lɪstɪd] *adj* **1.** nienotowany na giełdzie **2.** *number*: zastrzeżony
un•lit [ʌn'lɪt] *adj* **1.** nieoświetlony **2.** niezapalony
un•load [ʌn'ləʊd] *v/t* **1.** *luggage*: wyładowywać ⟨-dować⟩ **2.** *car*: rozładowywać ⟨-dować⟩ **3.** *infml responsibility, task*: zwalać ⟨-lić⟩; ***~ one's problems on(to) s.o.*** zwierzyć się komuś ze swoich problemów
un•lock [ʌn'lɒk] *v/t* otwierać ⟨-worzyć⟩; **un•locked** *adj* otwarty; ***never leave the door ~*** zawsze zamykaj drzwi na klucz
un•loved [ʌn'lʌvd] *adj* niekochany
un•luck•i•ly [ʌn'lʌkɪlɪ] *adv* niestety, na nieszczęście; **un•luck•y** [ʌn'lʌkɪ] *adj* pechowy; ***it's ~ to walk under a ladder*** przechodzenie pod drabiną przynosi pecha
un•made [ʌn'meɪd] *adj bed*: niepościelony
un•man•age•a•ble [ʌn'mænɪdʒəbl] *adj* **1.** ***s.th. is ~*** z czymś nie można sobie poradzić **2.** nie do opanowania **3.** nieposłuszny
un•man•ly [ʌn'mænlɪ] *adj* niemęski
un•manned [ʌn'mænd] *adj* bezzałogowy
un•marked [ʌn'mɑːkt] *adj* **1.** nieoznakowany **2.** nieoznaczony
un•mar•ried [ʌn'mærɪd] *adj* **1.** nieżonaty **2.** niezamężny **3.** *status*: wolny
un•mask [ʌn'mɑːsk] *v/t* demaskować ⟨z-⟩
un•matched [ʌn'mætʃt] *adj* niezrównany
un•men•tion•a•ble [ʌn'menʃnəbl] *adj topic*: tabu
un•mer•ci•ful•ly [ʌn'mɜːsɪflɪ] *adv* bezlitośnie
un•mis•ta•ka•ble [ʌnmɪ'steɪkəbl] *adj voice*: charakterystyczny
un•mit•i•gat•ed [ʌn'mɪtɪgeɪtɪd] *adj* zupełny, kompletny, totalny; ***an ~ disaster*** kompletna katastrofa
un•moved [ʌn'muːvd] *adj* niewzruszony, obojętny
un•mu•si•cal [ʌn'mjuːzɪkl] *adj* niemuzykalny
un•named [ʌn'neɪmd] *adj* nienazwany
un•nat•u•ral [ʌn'nætʃrəl] *adj* nienaturalny
un•ne•ces•sa•ry [ʌn'nesəserɪ] *adj* niepotrzebny
un•nerve [ʌn'nɜːv] *v/t* denerwować ⟨z-⟩; **un•nerv•ing** [ʌn'nɜːvɪŋ] *adj* denerwujący
un•no•ticed [ʌn'nəʊtɪst] *adj* niezauważony; ***go ~*** przejść niezauważonym
un•num•bered [ʌn'nʌmbəd] *adj* **1.** nienumerowany **2.** bez numeru
un•ob•tain•a•ble [ʌnəb'teɪnəbl] *adj* nieosiągalny
un•ob•tru•sive [ʌnəb'truːsɪv] *adj* dyskretny
un•oc•cu•pied [ʌn'ɒkjʊpaɪd] *adj* **1.** *place*: wolny **2.** *house*: niezamieszkany
un•of•fi•cial [ʌnə'fɪʃl] *adj* nieoficjalny; **un•of•fi•cial•ly** [ʌnə'fɪʃlɪ] *adv* nieoficjalnie
un•or•tho•dox [ʌn'ɔːθədɒks] *adj* **1.** nieortodoksyjny **2.** niekonwencjonalny
un•pack [ʌn'pæk] **I** *v/t* rozpakowywać ⟨-kować⟩ **II** *v/i* rozpakowywać ⟨-kować⟩ się

un•paid [ʌn'peɪd] *adj* **1.** niezapłacony **2.** *credit*: niespłacony **3.** *job*: nieodpłatny **4.** *leave*: bezpłatny
un•pal•at•a•ble [ʌn'pælətəbl] *adj* **1.** *food*: niesmaczny **2.** *truth*: przykry, trudny do przełknięcia
un•par•al•leled [ʌn'pærəleld] *adj* niezrównany, nieporównywalny
un•par•don•a•ble [ʌn'pɑːdnəbl] *adj* niewybaczalny
un•pick [ʌn'pɪk] *v/t* pruć ⟨s-⟩
un•pleas•ant [ʌn'pleznt] *adj* nieprzyjemny, niemiły; **un•pleas•ant•ness** [ʌn'plezntnɪs] *s* nieprzyjemności *pl*
un•plug [ʌn'plʌg] *v/t* **1.** wyłączać ⟨-czyć⟩ z sieci **2.** odłączać ⟨-czyć⟩
un•po•lished [ʌn'pɒlɪʃt] *adj* **1.** *shoes, floor*: niewypastowany **2.** *fig person*: bez ogłady, nieokrzesany
un•pol•lut•ed [ʌnpə'luːtɪd] *adj* **1.** *air, water*: niezanieczyszczony **2.** *mind*: nieskażony
un•pop•u•lar [ʌn'pɒpjələ] *adj* niepopularny; ***make oneself ~ with*** narazić się *D*
un•prac•ti•cal [ʌn'præktɪkl] *adj* niepraktyczny
un•pre•ce•den•ted [ʌn'presɪdentɪd] *adj situation*: bez precedensu
un•pre•dict•a•ble [ʌnprɪ'dɪktəbl] *adj* nieprzewidywalny
un•prej•u•diced [ʌn'predʒʊdɪst] *adj* bez uprzedzeń
un•pre•pared [ʌnprɪ'peəd] *adj* **1.** nieprzygotowany **2.** niegotowy; ***he was ~ to accept the truth*** nie był gotowy na przyjęcie prawdy
un•pre•ten•tious [ʌnprɪ'tenʃəs] *adj* bezpretensjonalny
un•prin•ci•pled [ʌn'prɪnsɪpld] *adj* pozbawiony zasad moralnych
un•print•a•ble [ʌn'prɪntəbl] *adj fig* nienadający się do druku
un•pro•duc•tive [ʌnprə'dʌktɪv] *adj* bezproduktywny, jałowy
un•pro•fes•sion•al [ʌnprə'feʃnl] *adj* **1.** nieprofesjonalny **2.** sprzeczny z etyką zawodową
un•prof•i•ta•ble [ʌn'prɒfɪtəbl] *adj* **1.** nierentowny **2.** nieopłacalny
un•prompt•ed [ʌn'prɒmptɪd] *adj* spontaniczny
un•pro•nounce•a•ble [ʌnprə'naʊnsəbl] *adj* nie do wymówienia
un•pro•tect•ed [ʌnprə'tektɪd] *adj* **1.** niechroniony **2.** niezabezpieczony **3.** *sex*: bez zabezpieczenia
un•proved [ʌn'pruːvd], ***un•prov•en*** [ʌn'pruːvn] *adj* nieudowodniony
un•pro•voked [ʌnprə'vəʊkt] *adj* **1.** niesprowokowany **2.** nieuzasadniony
un•pub•lished [ʌn'pʌblɪʃt] *adj* niepublikowany
un•pun•ished [ʌn'pʌnɪʃt] *adj* niekarany; ***not go ~*** nie ujść bezkarnie
un•qual•i•fied [ʌn'kwɒlɪfaɪd] *adj* **1.** niewykwalifikowany; ***I feel ~ to comment*** nie czuję się kompetentna, żeby się wypowiadać **2.** *success*: pełny **3.** bezwarunkowy
un•ques•tio•na•bly [ʌn'kwestʃnəblɪ] *adv* niewątpliwie, bezsprzecznie; **un•ques•tion•ing** [ʌn'kwestʃnɪŋ] *adj* **1.** bezwarunkowy **2.** *fig* ślepy
un•rav•el [ʌn'rævl] **I** *v/t* **1.** *puzzle*: rozwikłać **2.** rozplątywać ⟨-tać⟩ **3.** pruć ⟨s-⟩ **II** *v/i* **1.** rozplątywać ⟨-tać⟩ się **2.** pruć ⟨s-⟩ się
un•rea•da•ble [ʌn'riːdəbl] *adj* **1.** ***s.th. is ~*** *fig* czegoś się nie da czytać, coś się nie nadaje do czytania **2.** nieczytelny
un•re•al [ʌn'rɪəl] *adj* **1.** nierealny, nierzeczywisty **2.** nierealistyczny; **un•rea•lis•tic** [ʌnrɪə'lɪstɪk] *adj* nierealistyczny
un•rea•so•na•ble [ʌn'riːznəbl] *adj* **1.** nierozsądny **2.** niedorzeczny **3.** wygórowany
un•rec•og•niz•a•ble [ʌnrekəg'naɪzəbl] *adj* nie do poznania
un•re•fined [ʌnrɪ'faɪnd] *adj* **1.** *sugar, oil*: nierafinowany **2.** *person*: nieobyty, nieokrzesany
un•re•lat•ed [ʌnrɪ'leɪtɪd] *adj* **1.** niespokrewniony **2.** bez związku; ***be ~ to*** nie mieć związku z *I*
un•re•lent•ing [ʌnrɪ'lentɪŋ] *adj* **1.** nieustający, niesłabnący **2.** uporczywy **3.** nieubłagany, bezlitosny
un•rel•i•a•ble [ʌnrɪ'laɪəbl] *adj* **1.** niegodny zaufania **2.** niesolidny **3.** zawodny
un•re•lieved [ʌnrɪ'liːvd] *adj* beznadziejny
un•re•mit•ting [ʌnrɪ'mɪtɪŋ] *adj* nieustający, nieustanny
un•rep•re•sen•ta•tive [ʌnreprɪ'zentətɪv] *adj* niereprezentatywny

un•re•quit•ed [ʌnrɪˈkwaɪtɪd] *adj love*: nieodwzajemniony
un•re•served [ʌnrɪˈzɜːvd] *adj* **1.** niezarezerwowany **2.** całkowity **3.** szczery; **unre•serv•ed•ly** [ʌnrɪˈzɜːvdɪdlɪ] *adv* całkowicie, szczerze
un•rest [ʌnˈrest] *s* zamieszki *pl*, rozruchy *pl*
un•re•strained [ʌnrɪˈstreɪnd] *adj* niepohamowany
un•re•strict•ed [ʌnrɪˈstrɪktɪd] *adj* nieograniczony
un•re•ward•ing [ʌnrɪˈwɔːdɪŋ] *adj* niesatysfakcjonujący
un•ripe [ʌnˈraɪp] *adj fruit*: niedojrzały
un•ri•valled [ʌnˈraɪvld] *Br*, ***un•ri•valed*** *Am adj* niezrównany
un•roll [ʌnˈrəʊl] **I** *v/t* rozwijać ⟨-winąć⟩ **II** *v/i* rozwijać ⟨-winąć⟩ się
un•ru•ly [ʌnˈruːlɪ] *adj child*, *hair*: niesforny
un•sad•dle [ʌnˈsædl] *v/t* **1.** *horse*: rozsiodłać **2.** *rider*: zrzucać ⟨-cić⟩ z siodła
un•safe [ʌnˈseɪf] *adj* **1.** niebezpieczny **2.** niepewny **3.** zagrożony
un•said [ʌnˈsed] *adj* niewypowiedziany; ***leave s.th. ~*** przemilczeć coś
un•sal(e)•a•ble [ʌnˈseɪləbl] *adj* nie do sprzedania, niechodliwy
un•salt•ed [ʌnˈsɔːltɪd] *adj* niesolony
un•sat•is•fac•to•ry [ʌnsætɪsˈfæktərɪ] *adj* niezadowalający, niesatysfakcjonujący; **un•sat•is•fied** [ʌnˈsætɪsfaɪd] *adj* **1.** *need*: niezaspokojony **2.** niezadowolony, nieusatysfakcjonowany (***with*** *I*); **un•sat•is•fy•ing** [ʌnˈsætɪsfaɪɪŋ] → ***unsatisfactory***
un•sa•vou•ry [ʌnˈseɪvərɪ] *Br*, ***un•sa•vo•ry*** *Am adj* **1.** *individual*: nieciekawy **2.** *reputation*: nienajlepszy, marny
un•scathed [ʌnˈskeɪðd] *adj* bez szwanku, nietknięty
un•sci•en•tif•ic [ʌnsaɪənˈtɪfɪk] *adj* nienaukowy
un•screw [ʌnˈskruː] *v/t screw*, *lid*: odkręcać ⟨-cić⟩
un•script•ed [ʌnˈskrɪptɪd] *adj speech*: improwizowany
un•scru•pu•lous [ʌnˈskruːpjʊləs] *adj* pozbawiony skrupułów, bez skrupułów
un•seat [ʌnˈsiːt] *v/t* **1.** odsuwać ⟨-sunąć⟩ od władzy **2.** *rider*: zrzucać ⟨-cić⟩
un•seed•ed [ʌnˈsiːdɪd] *adj player*: nierozstawiony
un•seem•ly [ʌnˈsiːmlɪ] *adj dated* nieodpowiedni, niestosowny
un•seen [ʌnˈsiːn] *adj* **1.** niewidoczny **2.** ukryty **3.** niezauważony
un•self•ish [ʌnˈselfɪʃ] *adj* niesamolubny, bezinteresowny
un•sen•ti•men•tal [ʌnsentɪˈmentl] *adj* **1.** pozbawiony sentymentów **2.** beznamiętny
un•set•tle [ʌnˈsetl] *v/t* **1.** niepokoić ⟨za-⟩ **2.** zakłócać ⟨-cić⟩ spokój; **unset•tled** [ʌnˈsetld] *adj* **1.** *times*: niespokojny **2.** *weather*: zmienny **3.** *person*: podenerwowany; ***have an ~ stomach*** mieć rozstrój żołądka **4.** *issue*: nierozstrzygnięty **5.** *bill*: nieuregulowany
un•shak(e)•a•ble [ʌnˈʃeɪkəbl] *adj certainty*: niezachwiany, niewzruszony
un•shav•en [ʌnˈʃeɪvn] *adj* nieogolony
un•sight•ly [ʌnˈsaɪtlɪ] *adj* brzydki, szpetny
un•signed [ʌnˈsaɪnd] *adj* niepodpisany
un•skilled [ʌnˈskɪld] *adj* niewykwalifikowany
un•so•cia•ble [ʌnˈsəʊʃəbl] *adj* nietowarzyski
un•so•cial [ʌnˈsəʊʃl] *adj*: ***work ~ hours*** pracować w nietypowych godzinach
un•sold [ʌnˈsəʊld] *adj* niesprzedany
un•so•lic•it•ed [ʌnsəˈlɪsɪtɪd] *adj* **1.** nieproszony **2.** niezamawiany **3.** niechciany, niepożądany
un•solved [ʌnˈsɒlvd] *adj* nierozwiązany, nierozwikłany
un•so•phis•ti•cat•ed [ʌnsəˈfɪstɪkeɪtɪd] *adj* prosty, niewyrafinowany, nieskomplikowany
un•sound [ʌnˈsaʊnd] *adj* **1.** nierzetelny, niesolidny **2.** błędny **3.** oparty na błędnych przesłankach **4.** ***environmentally ~*** szkodliwy dla środowiska
un•spar•ing [ʌnˈspeərɪŋ] *adj* **1.** surowy, bezwzględny (***in*** w *L*) **2.** szczodry; ***be ~ of*** nie szczędzić *G*
un•speak•a•ble [ʌnˈspiːkəbl] *adj* niewypowiedziany, niewymowny, nie do opisania
un•spec•i•fied [ʌnˈspesɪfaɪd] *adj* nieokreślony
un•spoiled [ʌnˈspɒɪld], ***un•spoilt*** [ʌnˈspɔɪlt] *Br adj* **1.** niezepsuty **2.** nieroz-

U

pieszczony **3.** zachowany w naturalnym stanie **4.** *wildlife*: nieskażony

un•spo•ken [ʌn'spəʊkən] *adj agreement*: milczący

un•sport•ing [ʌn'spɔːtɪŋ], ***un•sportsman•like*** [ʌn'spɔːtsmənlaɪk] *adj behaviour*: niesportowy, nie fair

un•sta•ble [ʌn'steɪbl] *adj* **1.** niestabilny **2.** chwiejny **3.** *person*: niezrównoważony **4.** *weather*: zmienny

un•stead•y [ʌn'stedɪ] *adj* niepewny

un•stint•ing [ʌn'stɪntɪŋ] *adj* szczodry; ***be ~ in*** nie szczędzić *G*

un•stop•pa•ble [ʌn'stɒpəbl] *adj* nie do zatrzymania

un•stressed [ʌn'strest] *adj syllable*: nieakcentowany

un•stuck [ʌn'stʌk] *adj*: **come ~ a)** oderwać się, odkleić się **b)** (*person*) *Br infml* zawieść

un•suc•cess•ful [ʌnsək'sesfl] *adj* nieudany; ***be ~*** zakończyć się niepowodzeniem; ***he was ~*** nie udało mu się; **un•suc•cess•ful•ly** [ʌnsək'sesflɪ] *adv* bez powodzenia

un•suit•a•ble [ʌn'suːtəbl] *adj* nieodpowiedni; **un•suit•a•bly** [ʌn'suːtəblɪ] *adv* nieodpowiednio

un•sure [ʌn'ʃʊə] *adj* niepewny; ***he was ~ of what to do next*** nie był pewien, co ma dalej robić

un•sur•passed [ʌnsə'pɑːst] *adj* niezrównany

un•sus•pect•ed [ʌnsə'spektɪd] *adj* **1.** nieoczekiwany **2.** *illness*: niezdiagnozowany; **un•sus•pect•ing** [ʌnsə'spektɪŋ] *adj* niczego niepodejrzewający

un•sweet•ened [ʌn'swiːtnd] *adj* niesłodzony

un•swerv•ing [ʌn'swɜːvɪŋ] *adj lit* niezachwiany

un•sym•pa•thet•ic [ʌnsɪmpə'θetɪk] *adj* **1.** nieczuły; ***be ~ to s.o.*** nie okazać komuś współczucia **2.** obojętny; ***~ to public opinion*** obojętny na głos opinii publicznej **3.** niesympatyczny

un•tan•gle [ʌn'tæŋgl] *v/t* **1.** rozplątywać ⟨-tać⟩ **2.** *fig* rozwikłać

un•tapped [ʌn'tæpt] *adj resources*: niewykorzystany

un•ten•a•ble [ʌn'tenəbl] *adj standpoint*: nie do obrony

un•think•a•ble [ʌn'θɪŋkəbl] *adj* nie do pomyślenia; **un•think•ing•ly** [ʌn'θɪŋkɪŋlɪ] *adv* bezmyślnie

un•ti•dy [ʌn'taɪdɪ] *adj* **1.** nieporządny, bałaganiarski **2.** nieposprzątany; ***his room was ~*** w jego pokoju był bałagan

un•tie [ʌn'taɪ] *v/t* rozwiązywać ⟨-zać⟩

un•til [ən'tɪl] **I** *prep* do *G*; ***from morning ~ night*** od rana do nocy; ***not ~ Monday*** dopiero w poniedziałek, najwcześniej w poniedziałek **II** *conj* dopóki; ***~ the rain stops*** dopóki nie przestanie padać

un•time•ly [ʌn'taɪmlɪ] *adj* **1.** przedwczesny **2.** w niewłaściwym czasie, nie w porę

un•tir•ing [ʌn'taɪərɪŋ] *adj* niezmordowany

un•told [ʌn'təʊld] *adj* **1.** nieopisany **2.** ogromny **3.** nieopowiedziany

un•touched [ʌn'tʌtʃt] *adj* **1.** nietknięty; ***she left her food ~*** nie tknęła jedzenia **2.** niezmieniony **3.** nienaruszony

un•trans•lat•a•ble [ʌntræns'leɪtəbl] *adj* nieprzetłumaczalny

un•treat•ed [ʌn'triːtɪd] *adj* **1.** *illness*: nieleczony **2.** *water*: nieoczyszczony

un•trou•bled [ʌn'trʌbld] *adj* spokojny; ***be ~ by*** nie przejmować się *I*

un•true [ʌn'truː] *adj* **1.** nieprawdziwy **2.** niewierny

un•trust•wor•thy [ʌn'trʌstwɜːðɪ] *adj* niegodny zaufania

un•truth [ʌn'truːθ] *s* nieprawda *f*, kłamstwo *n*

un•used[1] [ʌn'juːzd] *adj* nieużywany

un•used[2] [ʌn'juːst] *adj* nieprzyzwyczajony; ***I'm ~ to drinking alcohol*** nie jestem przyzwyczajony do picia alkoholu

un•u•su•al [ʌn'juːʒl] *adj* **1.** niezwykły **2.** niecodzienny **3.** osobliwy; **un•u•su•al•ly** [ʌn'juːʒəlɪ] *adv* **1.** niezwykle **2.** wyjątkowo; ***it's ~ for him*** to do niego niepodobne

un•ut•ter•a•ble [ʌn'ʌtərəbl] *adj* niewypowiedziany, niewymowny

un•var•nished [ʌn'vɑːnɪʃt] *adj* **1.** *wood*: nielakierowany **2.** *fig truth*: nagi

un•var•y•ing [ʌn'veərɪɪŋ] *adj* **1.** niezmienny **2.** jednostajny

un•veil [ʌn'veɪl] *v/t* **1.** odsłaniać ⟨-łonić⟩ **2.** prezentować ⟨za-⟩

un•voiced [ʌn'vɔɪst] *adj* **1.** niewypowiedziany **2.** *consonant*: bezdźwięczny
un•want•ed [ʌn'wɒntɪd] *adj* niechciany
un•war•rant•ed [ʌn'wɒrəntɪd] *adj* **1.** nieuzasadniony **2.** nieusprawiedliwiony
un•wa•ver•ing [ʌn'weɪvərɪŋ] *adj* niesłabnący, niezachwiany, niezłomny
un•wel•come [ʌn'welkəm] *adj* **1.** niechciany **2.** niemile widziany
un•well [ʌn'wel] *adj* chory; ***feel ~*** źle się czuć, czuć się niedobrze
un•whole•some [ʌn'həʊlsəm] *adj* niezdrowy
un•wield•y [ʌn'wiːldɪ] *adj* nieporęczny
un•will•ing [ʌn'wɪlɪŋ] *adj* niechętny, oporny; ***be ~ to do s.th.*** nie mieć ochoty czegoś zrobić; **un•will•ing•ly** [ʌn'wɪlɪŋlɪ] *adv* niechętnie
un•wind [ʌn'waɪnd] (*unwound*; *unwound*) **I** *v/t* **1.** odwijać ⟨-winąć⟩ **2.** rozwijać ⟨-winąć⟩ **II** *v/i* **1.** odwijać ⟨-winąć⟩ się **2.** rozwijać ⟨-winąć⟩ się **3.** odprężać ⟨-żyć⟩ się, relaksować ⟨z-⟩ się
un•wise [ʌn'waɪz] *adj* niemądry
un•wit•ting [ʌn'wɪtɪŋ] *adj* **1.** nieświadomy **2.** bezwiedny; **un•wit•ting•ly** [ʌn'wɪtɪŋlɪ] *adv* **1.** nieświadomie **2.** bezwiednie
un•wont•ed [ʌn'wəʊntɪd] *adj* **1.** niezwykły **2.** niespodziewany
un•wor•thy [ʌn'wɜːðɪ] *adj* niegodny; ***be ~ of*** nie zasługiwać na *A*; ***such opinions are ~ of a lady*** takie poglądy nie przystoją damie
un•work•a•ble [ʌn'wɜːkəbl] *adj* niewykonalny
un•wrap [ʌn'ræp] *v/t* rozpakowywać ⟨-kować⟩
un•writ•ten [ʌn'rɪtn] *adj* **1.** niepisany **2.** nienapisany
un•yield•ing [ʌn'jiːldɪŋ] *adj* niezłomny
un•zip [ʌn'zɪp] *v/t* **1.** rozpinać ⟨-piąć⟩ **2.** INF *file*: rozpakowywać ⟨-kować⟩
up [ʌp] **I** *adv* **1.** do góry, w górę, w górze, na górze; ***~ and down*** w górę i w dół; ***prices are going ~*** ceny idą w górę; ***they live ~ in the mountains*** mieszkają wysoko w górach **2.** (*direction towards*) ***the car drove ~*** podjechał samochód; ***she went ~ to the door*** podeszła do drzwi **3.** (*finished*) ***we ate all the food ~*** zjedliśmy wszystko **4.** ***time's ~*** czas minął **5.** (*awake*) ***I stayed ~ late last night*** wczoraj późno położyłem się spać, wczoraj byłem na nogach do późna **6.** (*in phrases*) ***what's ~?*** co słychać?; ***it's ~ to you*** ty zdecyduj, to zależy od ciebie; ***he's ~ to no good*** on coś knuje; ***~ to now*** do tej pory **II** *prep* **1.** w górę *G*; ***a cruise ~ the Thames*** rejs w górę Tamizy; ***we live ~ the road*** mieszkamy dalej na tej ulicy **2.** na *A*; ***go ~ the hill*** wejść na wzgórze **3.** po *L*; ***go ~ the stairs*** wchodzić po schodach **III** *adj* **1.** w górę **2.** *mood*: dobry **IV** *s* ***~s and downs*** wzloty *pl* i upadki *pl* **V** *v/t prices*: podnosić ⟨-nieść⟩; **up-and-com•ing** [ʌpən'kʌmɪŋ] *adj infml* dobrze zapowiadający się; **'up•beat** *adj infml* optymistyczny, pozytywny; **up•bring•ing** ['ʌpbrɪŋɪŋ] *s* wychowanie *n*; **up•com•ing** ['ʌpkʌmɪŋ] *adj elections*: nadchodzący, zbliżający się; **up•'date** *v/t* uaktualniać ⟨-nić⟩; ***~ s.o. on*** udzielić komuś najświeższych informacji o *L*; **'up•date** *s* uaktualnienie *n*; **up•'end** *v/t* przewracać ⟨-rócić⟩ do góry nogami; **up•'front** *adj* **1.** szczery, otwarty **2.** *payment*: z góry; **up•'grade** *v/t* **1.** modernizować ⟨z-⟩ **2.** ulepszać ⟨-szyć⟩ **3.** awansować; **up•heav•al** [ʌp'hiːvl] *s* **1.** przewrót *m* **2.** rewolucja *f*; **up•hill** [ʌp'hɪl] **I** *adj* **1.** *road*: (prowadzący) pod górę **2.** ***be an ~ struggle*** wymagać wiele wysiłku, nie być łatwym **II** *adv* pod górę; **up'hold** (*upheld*; *upheld*) *v/t* **1.** *law*: przestrzegać **2.** *objection*: podtrzymywać ⟨-mać⟩; **up•hol•ster** [ʌp'həʊlstə] *v/t furniture*: obijać ⟨obić⟩ (tapicerką); **up•hol•stered** [ʌp'həʊlstəd] *adj* tapicerowany; **up•hol•ster•y** [ʌp'həʊlstərɪ] *s* obicie *n*, tapicerka *f*; **'up•keep** *s* utrzymanie *n*, koszty *pl* utrzymania; **up•lift•ing** [ʌp'lɪftɪŋ] *adj* podnoszący na duchu; **up•'mar•ket** *adj clothes, hotel*: luksusowy, ekskluzywny
up•on [ə'pɒn] → ***on***
up•per ['ʌpə] **I** *adj* górny; ***the ~ jaw*** szczęka górna; ***the ~ deck*** górny pokład; ***gain the ~ hand*** zyskać przewagę **II** *s* **1.** cholewka *f* **2.** *infml* środek *m* pobudzający; **'up•per•case I** *s* ***in ~*** wielkimi literami, wersalikami

II *adj letters*: wielki, drukowany; **upper 'class** *s* klasa *f* wyższa; **'up•per•cut** *s* (*boxing*) hak *m*

up•per•most ['ʌpəməʊst] **I** *adj* najwyższy **II** *adv* najwyżej, na samej górze

up•pish ['ʌpɪʃ], ***up•pi•ty*** ['ʌpətɪ] *adj dated* zadzierający nosa

'up•right ['ʌpraɪt] *adj* **1.** wyprostowany **2.** pionowy **3.** prawy, uczciwy; **'upright (pi'an•o)** *s MUS* pianino *n*

up•ris•ing ['ʌpraɪzɪŋ] *s* powstanie *n*; ***crush an ~*** stłumić powstanie

'up•roar ['ʌprɔː] *s* **1.** poruszenie *n* **2.** wrzawa *f*, hałas *m*

up•root [ʌp'ruːt] *v/t* **1.** *plant*: wyrywać ⟨-rwać⟩ **2.** wysiedlać ⟨-lić⟩

'up•shot ['ʌpʃɒt] *no pl s* rezultat *m*; ***the ~ was that*** skończyło się na tym, że

up•set **I** [ʌp'set] (*upset*; *upset*) *v/t* **1.** martwić ⟨z-⟩ **2.** smucić ⟨za-⟩ **3.** denerwować ⟨z-⟩ **4.** *plan*: psuć ⟨ze-⟩ **5.** *glass*: przewracać ⟨-rócić⟩ **II** [ʌp'set] *adj* **1.** zmartwiony, zdenerwowany; ***get ~, be ~*** zmartwić się, zdenerwować się **2.** smutny **3.** *stomach*: rozstrojony **III** ['ʌpset] *s* **1.** problem *m* **2.** trudna sytuacja *f* **3.** (niespodziewana) porażka *f* **4.** ***a stomach ~*** rozstrój *m* żołądka; **up'set•ting** *adj* **1.** przykry **2.** denerwujący

up•side 'down *adv* do góry nogami

up•'stairs [ʌp'steəz] **I** *adv* na górze, na piętrze, na górę, na piętro **II** *adj room*: na piętrze, na górze **III** *s* piętro *n*, góra *f*

'up•start *s* ['ʌpstɑːt] nowicjusz *m*, nowy *m*

up•'stream [ʌp'striːm] *adv* w górę rzeki

'up•surge ['ʌpsɜːdʒ] *s* **1.** nagły wzrost *m* **2.** *enthusiasm*: przypływ *m*

'up•swing [ʌp'swɪŋ] *s* **1.** poprawa *f* **2.** wzrost *m*

'up•take ['ʌpteɪk] *s* absorpcja *f*; ***be quick (slow) on the ~*** *infml* szybko (wolno) chwytać

up•'tight [ʌp'taɪt] *adj infml* **1.** zdenerwowany (***about*** *I*) **2.** spięty

up-to-'date [ʌptə'deɪt] *adj* **1.** aktualny **2.** najnowszy **3.** nowoczesny

up-to-the-'min•ute [ʌptəðə'mɪnɪt] *adj* **1.** najświeższy **2.** najmodniejszy

'up•town [ʌp'taʊn] *adv* **1.** poza centrum **2.** na przedmieściach

'up•turn ['ʌptɜːn] *s* poprawa *f*, zmiana *f* na lepsze; **up•turned** [ʌp'tɜːnd] *adj* **1.** przewrócony **2.** odwrócony **3.** *nose*: zadarty

up•ward ['ʌpwəd] *adj* do góry, w górę; ***face ~*** twarzą do góry

u•ra•ni•um [jʊ'reɪnɪəm] *s CHEM* uran *m*

ur•ban ['ɜːbən] *adj* miejski; **ur•ban•i•za•tion** [ɜːbənaɪ'zeɪʃn] *s* urbanizacja *f*

ur•bane [ɜː'beɪn] *adj* **1.** dobrze wychowany **2.** swobodny

ur•chin ['ɜːtʃɪn] *s* **1.** *dated* urwis *m* **2.** *BIOL* jeżowiec *m*

u•re•thra [jʊ'riːθrə] *pl -thrae* [~θriː], *-thras s ANAT* cewka *f* moczowa

urge [ɜːdʒ] **I** *v/t* **1.** nakłaniać ⟨-łonić⟩ **2.** namawiać ⟨-mówić⟩; ***she ~d him to stay*** namawiała go, żeby został **3.** zachęcać ⟨-cić⟩; ***~ s.o. to do s.th.*** zachęcać kogoś do zrobienia czegoś **4.** zalecać ⟨-cić⟩; ***~ caution*** zalecać ostrożność **II** *s* chęć *f*, pragnienie *n*; **ur•gen•cy** ['ɜːdʒənsɪ] *s* pilna potrzeba *f*

ur•gent ['ɜːdʒənt] *adj* pilny, nie cierpiący zwłoki; ***be in ~ need of*** pilnie potrzebować *G*

u•ri•nal ['jʊrənl] *s* pisuar *m*; **u•ri•nar•y** ['jʊrənərɪ] *adj* moczowy; **u•ri•nate** ['jʊrəneɪt] *v/i* oddawać ⟨-dać⟩ mocz; **u•rine** ['jʊərɪn] *s* mocz *m*

urn [ɜːn] *s* (*for ashes*) urna *f*

u•rol•o•gist [jʊə'rɔlədʒɪst] *s MED* urolog *m*

U•ru•guay ['jʊrəgwaɪ] *s* Urugwaj *m*

us [əs] *stressed* [ʌs] *pron* **1.** nam; ***give ~*** daj nam **2.** nas **3.** nami; ***with ~*** z nami **4.** ***both of ~*** my oboje; ***it's ~*** to my **5.** siebie; ***we looked around ~*** rozglądaliśmy się wokół siebie

US [juː'es] *abbr* (=***United States***) → ***USA***

USA [juːes'eɪ] *abbr* (=***United States of America***) USA *pl*

us•a•ble ['juːzəbl] *adj* nadający się do użytku

us•age ['juːzɪdʒ] *s* **1.** użycie *n* **2.** używanie *n*

use **I** [juːz] *v/t* **1.** używać ⟨użyć⟩; ***I could ~ a drink*** chętnie bym się czegoś napił; ***~ your head*** rusz głową **2.** stosować ⟨za-⟩ **3.** korzystać ⟨s-⟩ z *G*; ***can I ~ the phone?*** mogę skorzystać z telefonu? **4.** wykorzystywać ⟨-tać⟩; ***I felt ~d*** czułem się wykorzystany **5.** zużywać ⟨-żyć⟩ **6.** *drugs*: brać ⟨wziąć⟩ **II** [juːs] *s* **1.** użycie *n*; ***go out of ~*** wyjść z użycia; ***make ~ of*** korzystać z *G*, używać *A* **2.** zastosowanie *n*; ***have many ~s*** mieć wiele zastosowań; ***be of ~*** być przydatnym; ***it's no ~ complaining*** narzekanie nic nie da; **use up** *v/t* zużywać ⟨-żyć⟩

used[1] [juːzd] *adj* (*objects*): używany

used[2] [juːst] *adj* przyzwyczajony (***to*** do *G*); ***I got ~ to it*** przyzwyczaiłem się do tego

used[3] [juːst] *v/i*: ***I ~ to live in London*** wcześniej mieszkałem w Londynie; ***we ~ to go sailing in the summer*** w lecie zwykle wyjeżdżaliśmy na żagle

use•ful ['juːsfl] *adj* przydatny, użyteczny; ***make oneself ~*** starać się być użytecznym; **use•ful•ness** ['juːsfəlnɪs] *s* przydatność *f*, użyteczność *f*

use•less ['juːslɪs] *adj* **1.** nieprzydatny, nieużyteczny **2.** *infml* beznadziejny (***at*** w *L*); **use•less•ness** ['juːslɪsnɪs] *s* bezużyteczność *f*

us•er ['juːzə] *s* użytkownik *m*; **us•er-'friend•ly** *adj* przyjazny dla użytkownika

ush•er ['ʌʃə] **I** *s osoba wprowadzająca i sadzająca gości w teatrze, na weselu itp.* **II** *v/t* wprowadzać ⟨-dzić⟩; **usher in** *v/t* **1.** inicjować ⟨za-⟩ **2.** wprowadzać ⟨-dzić⟩; **ush•er•ette** [ʌʃə'ret] bileterka *f*

USSR *abbr* (=***Union of Soviet Socialist Republics***) ZSRR *m*

u•su•al ['juːʒuəl] **I** *adj* zwykły, zwyczajny; ***as ~*** jak zwykle; ***it's not ~ for him to be so late*** zwykle nie przychodzi tak późno **II** *s infml* (*bar*, *restaurant*) ***the ~*** to, co zwykle

u•su•al•ly ['juːʒuəlɪ] *adv* zwykle, zazwyczaj

u•su•rer ['juːʒərə] *s* lichwiarz *m*

u•surp [juː'zɜːp] *v/t* uzurpować sobie

u•su•ry ['juːʒərɪ] *s* lichwa *f*

u•ten•sil [juː'tensl] *s*: przyrząd *m*; ***kitchen ~s*** utensylia kuchenne

u•te•rus ['juːtərəs] *s ANAT* macica *f*

u•til•i•tar•i•an [juːtɪlɪ'terɪən] *adj* **1.** praktyczny **2.** funkcjonalny **3.** utylitarystyczny

u•til•i•ty [juː'tɪlətɪ] *s* **1.** ***public utilities*** *Am* usługi *pl* komunalne **2.** użyteczność *f* **3.** *INF* program *m* narzędziowy

u•til•ize ['juːtɪlaɪz] *v/t* **1.** używać ⟨-żyć⟩ **2.** stosować ⟨za-⟩ **3.** wykorzystywać ⟨-tać⟩

ut•most ['ʌtməʊst] **I** *adj* **1.** najwyższy; ***a matter of ~ importance*** sprawa najwyższej wagi **2.** największy **II** *s* ***to the ~*** do granic możliwości; ***he did his ~*** zrobił, co w jego mocy

ut•ter ['ʌtə] **I** *adj* **1.** zupełny; ***it's ~ nonsense*** to zupełna bzdura **2.** całkowity **3.** totalny **II** *v/t* **1.** *words*: wypowiadać ⟨-wiedzieć⟩ **2.** *cry*: wydawać ⟨-dać⟩; **ut•ter•ly** ['ʌtəlɪ] *adv* **1.** zupełnie **2.** całkowicie; **ut•ter•ance** ['ʌtərəns] *s* **1.** wypowiedź *f* **2.** wypowiedzenie *n*

U-turn ['juːtɜːn] *s* **1.** zawracanie *n*; ***do a ~*** zawrócić **2.** *fig* zwrot *m* o 180 stopni

u•vu•la ['juːvjʊlə] *pl -lae s ANAT* języczek *m*

V

V

va•can•cy ['veɪkənsɪ] *s* **1.** wakat *m*, wolny etat *m*; ***he filled the ~y for Project Manager*** został zatrudniony jako kierownik projektu **2.** wolny pokój *m*; ***sorry, we have no ~ies*** niestety, nie mamy wolnych pokoi **3.** wolne miejsce *n* **4.** bezmyślność *f*; **va•cant** ['veɪkənt] *adj* **1.** wolny; ***the seat next to him was ~*** miejsce obok niego było wolne **2.** *face expression*: obojętny; **va•cant•ly** ['veɪkəntlɪ] *adv* obojętnie

va•cate [veɪ'keɪt] *v/t* **1.** *room*: opuszczać ⟨opuścić⟩ **2.** *post*: zwalniać ⟨zwolnić⟩

va•ca•tion [və'keɪʃn] **I** *s* **1.** wakacje *pl*; ***be on ~*** być na wakacjach **2.** *Am* urlop *m* **II** *v/i* spędzać ⟨-dzić⟩ urlop; **va-**

ca•tion•er [və'keɪʃənə] *s Am* urlopowicz *m*

vac•cin•ate ['væksɪneɪt] *v/t* szczepić ⟨za-⟩ (***against*** przeciw *D*); **vac•cin•a•tion** [væksɪ'neɪʃn] *s* szczepienie *n*; **vac•cine** ['væksiːn] *s* szczepionka *f*

vac•il•late ['væsɪleɪt] *v/i* wahać się (***between*** między *I*); **vac•il•la•tion** [væsɪ'leɪʃn] *s* niezdecydowanie *n*, wahanie *n*

vac•u•ous ['vækjuəs] *adj expression, smile*: bezmyślny, tępy

vac•u•um ['vækjuəm] **I** *s* **1.** próżnia *f* **2.** odkurzanie *n*; ***give the room a ~*** odkurzyć pokój **II** *v/t* odkurzać ⟨-rzyć⟩; '**vac•u•um bot•tle** *Am* → ***vacuum flask***; '**vac•u•um clean•er** *s* odkurzacz *m*; '**vac•u•um flask** *Br* termos *m*; **vac•u•um-'packed** *adj* pakowany próżniowo

vag•a•bond ['vægəbɒnd] *s* włóczęga *m*, tramp *m*

va•gar•ies ['veɪgəriz] *pl weather, fashion*: kaprysy *pl*

va•gi•na [və'dʒaɪnə] *s* ANAT pochwa *f*, wagina *f*; **va•gi•nal** [və'dʒaɪnl] *adj* pochwowy, waginalny

va•gran•cy ['veɪgrənsi] *s* włóczęgostwo *n*

va•grant ['veɪgrənt] *s* włóczęga *m*

vague [veɪg] *adj* **1.** niewyraźny **2.** mglisty; ***have ~ memories of s.th.*** mgliście coś pamiętać, pamiętać coś jak przez mgłę **3.** niejasny; ***be ~ about*** mówić wymijająco o *L*, mówić mało konkretnie o *L* **4.** *description*: mało precyzyjny, ogólnikowy **5.** rozmyty **6.** *look*: błędny, bezmyślny; **vague•ly** ['veɪglɪ] *adv* **1.** niewyraźnie **2.** niejasno **3.** mgliście; ***~ remember s.th.*** mgliście coś pamiętać, pamiętać coś jak przez mgłę; ***s.th. seems ~ familiar*** coś wydaje się (jakby) znajome **4.** nieco **5.** *look*: błędnym wzrokiem

vain [veɪn] *adj* **1.** daremny, bezskuteczny; ***in a ~ attempt to hold back the tears*** bezskutecznie próbując powstrzymać łzy; ***in ~*** nadaremnie, bezskutecznie **2.** próżny

va•len•cy ['veɪlənsɪ] *s* walencja *f*

val•en•tine ['væləntaɪn] *Br*, **va•lence** *Am s* walentynka *f*; '**val•en•tine card** *s* kartka *f* walentynkowa

va•le•ri•an [və'lɪərɪən] *s* waleriana *f*

val•et ['væleɪ] **I** *s* **1.** służący *m*, osobisty kamerdyner *m* **2.** (*hotel*) *Br* czyszczący *m* ubrania **3.** (*hotel, restaurant*) *Am* odprowadzający *m* samochody na parking **II** *v/t car, clothes*: czyścić ⟨wy-⟩; '**val•et park•ing** *s* (*hotel, restaurant*) odprowadzanie *n* samochodów na parking '**val•et service** *s* (*hotel*) czyszczenie *n* ubrań

val•iant ['væljənt] *adj* **1.** dzielny **2.** waleczny; **val•iant•ly** ['væljəntlɪ] *adv* **1.** dzielnie **2.** walecznie

val•id ['vælɪd] *adj* **1.** ważny **2.** *rule*: obowiązujący **3.** *consent*: prawomocny **4.** *document*: ważny **5.** *reason*: uzasadniony

val•i•date ['vælɪdeɪt] *v/t* **1.** potwierdzać ⟨-dzić⟩ **2.** uprawomocniać ⟨-nić⟩ **3.** aprobować ⟨za-⟩; **va•lid•i•ty** [və'lɪdətɪ] *s* **1.** ważność *f* **2.** obowiązywanie *n*; ***the period of ~ the agreement*** okres obowiązywania umowy **3.** zasadność *f*

val•ley ['vælɪ] *s* dolina *f*; ***the Loire ≈*** Dolina Loary

val•our ['vælə] *Br*, **val•or** *Am s* odwaga *f*, męstwo *n*

val•u•a•ble ['væljuəbl] **I** *adj* **1.** wartościowy; ***~ information*** wartościowe informacje **2.** cenny **3.** kosztowny **II** *s* ***~s*** kosztowności *pl*, przedmioty *pl* wartościowe

val•u•a•tion [vælju'eɪʃn] *s* **1.** wycena *f*; ***carry out a ~*** dokonać wyceny **2.** oszacowanie *n* wartości **3.** wartość *f*; ***put a high ~ on*** przykładać wielką wagę do *G*

val•ue ['væljuː] **I** *s* **1.** wartość *f*; ***s.th. rose in ~*** wzrosła wartość czegoś; ***s.th. fell in ~*** spadła wartość czegoś; ***sentimental ~*** wartość sentymentalna; ***cultural ~s*** wartości kulturowe; ***a set of ~s*** system wartości **2.** cena *f*; ***be ~ for money*** być wartym swojej ceny **3.** waga *f* **II** *v/t* **1.** cenić; ***I ~ him as a friend*** cenię go jako przyjaciela **2.** wyceniać ⟨-nić⟩ (***at*** na *A*) **3.** oszacowywać ⟨-cować⟩ wartość (***at*** na *A*); **val•ue-ad•ded tax** [væljuː'ædɪdtæks] *s* podatek *m* od wartości dodanej, podatek *m* VAT; **val•ued** ['væljuːd] *adj* ceniony; '**val•ue judg(e)•ment** *s* ocena *f* wartościująca; **val•ue•less** ['væljuːləs] *adj* bezwartościowy; **val-**

V

u•er ['væljuːə] *s* **1.** rzeczoznawca *m* majątkowy **2.** taksator *m*
valve [vælv] *s* **1.** *TECH* zawór *m* **2.** *ANAT* zastawka *f* **3.** wentyl *m*
vamp [væmp] *s* wamp *m*, kobieta *f* wamp
vam•pire ['væmpaɪə] *s* wampir *m*; **'vam•pire bat** *s BIOL* nietoperz *m* wampir
van [væn] *s* **1.** van *m*; ***a delivery ~*** samochód dostawczy **2.** furgonetka *f* **3.** *Br* wagon *m* bagażowy
van•dal ['vændl] *s* wandal *m*; **van•dal•ism** ['vændəlɪzm] *s* wandalizm *m*; **van•dal•ize** ['vændəlaɪz] *v/t* demolować ⟨z-⟩
vane [veɪn] *s* skrzydło *n* (wiatraka)
van•guard ['vængɑːd] *s* **1.** awangarda *f*; ***be in the ~ of progress*** być w awangardzie postępu **2.** (*troops*) straż *f* przednia, awangarda *f*
va•nil•la [və'nɪlə] **I** *s* wanilia *f* **II** *adj* waniliowy
van•ish ['vænɪʃ] *v/i* znikać ⟨-knąć⟩; ***~ without a trace*** zniknąć bez śladu; ***all hopes had now ~ed*** przepadły wszelkie nadzieje
van•i•ty ['vænətɪ] *s* **1.** próżność *f* **2.** marność *f* **3.** daremność *f*, bezskuteczność *f*; **'van•i•ty case** *s* kosmetyczka *f*; **'van•i•ty ta•ble** *s Am* toaletka *f* (z lustrem)
van•quish ['væŋkwɪʃ] *v/t lit* **1.** pokonywać ⟨-nać⟩ **2.** rozgramiać ⟨-romić⟩
van•tage point ['væntɪdʒpɔɪnt] *s* **1.** punkt *m* obserwacyjny **2.** *fig* punkt *m* widzenia
va•por•ize ['veɪpəraɪz] **I** *v/i* parować ⟨wy-⟩ **II** *v/i* odparowywać ⟨-rować⟩
va•pour ['veɪpə] *Br*, **va•por** *Am s* **1.** para *f* (wodna) **2.** opary *pl*; **'va•pour trail** *Br*, **va•por trail** *Am s* (*plane*) smuga kondensacyjna
var•i•a•ble ['veərɪəbl] **I** *s* zmienna *f* **II** *adj* **1.** zmienny **2.** niestały **3.** regulowany; **var•i•ance** ['veərɪəns] *s* różnica *f*; ***a ~ in temperature*** różnica temperatur; ***be at ~ with*** nie zgadzać się z *I*; kłócić się z *I*; **var•i•ant** ['veərɪənt] **I** *s* **1.** wariant *m* **2.** odmiana *f* **II** *adj* **1.** alternatywny **2.** ***a ~ form*** odmiana, wariant; **var•i•a•tion** [veərɪ'eɪʃn] *s* **1.** zmiana *f* **2.** zmiany *pl* **3.** wahania *pl* **4.** odmiana *f*; ***a regional ~*** odmiana regionalna **5.** *MUS* wariacja *f*
var•i•cose vein ['værɪkəʊs 'veɪn] *s MED* żylak *m*
var•ied ['veərɪd] *adj* **1.** różnorodny **2.** zróżnicowany **3.** urozmaicony
var•i•e•gat•ed ['veərɪgeɪtɪd] *adj* **1.** kolorowy **2.** nakrapiany **3.** różnorodny **4.** zróżnicowany **5.** urozmaicony
va•ri•e•ty [və'raɪətɪ] *s* **1.** ***for a ~ of reasons*** z różnych powodów **2.** wybór *m*; ***a wide ~ of dishes*** duży wybór dań **3.** urozmaicenie *n*; ***add ~ to*** urozmaicać *A* **4.** odmiana *f*; ***a rare ~ of orchid*** rzadka odmiana orchidei **5.** rewia *f*
var•i•ous ['veərɪəs] *adj* **1.** różny; ***for ~ reasons*** z różnych powodów **2.** różnorodny, rozmaity
var•nish ['vɑːnɪʃ] **I** *s* lakier *m* **II** *v/t* lakierować ⟨po-⟩
var•y ['veərɪ] *v/i* **1.** różnić się; ***~ in quality*** różnić się jakością; ***with ~ing degrees of success*** z różnym powodzeniem; ***prices ~ according to*** ceny różnią się w zależności od **2.** zmieniać ⟨-nić⟩ się; ***the menu varies with the season*** jadłospis zmienia się zależnie od pory roku **3.** wahać się; ***~ between 25 and 30*** wahać się między 25 a 30
vas•cu•lar ['væskjʊlə] *adj MED* naczyniowy
vase [vɑːz] *s* wazon *m*
vast [vɑːst] *adj* **1.** ogromny; ***a ~ amount of information*** ogromna ilość informacji; ***arrive in ~ numbers*** przybyć bardzo licznie **2.** rozległy; ***a ~ area*** rozległy obszar; **vast•ly** ['vɑːstlɪ] *adv* **1.** bardzo **2.** ogromnie
VAT [viːeɪ'tiː, væt] *abbr* (=***value added tax***) VAT *m*, podatek *m* VAT
vat [væt] *s* **1.** kadź *f* **2.** zbiornik *m*
Vat•i•can ['vætɪkən] *s **the ~*** Watykan *m*
vau•de•ville ['vɔːdəvɪl] *s* **1.** wodewil *m* **2.** *Am* rewia *f*
vault[1] [vɔːlt] *s* **1.** (*bank*) skarbiec *m* **2.** krypta *f* **3.** sklepienie *n*
vault[2] [~] **I** *v/i* przeskakiwać ⟨-koczyć⟩ (***over*** nad *I*) **II** *v/t* przeskakiwać ⟨-koczyć⟩ przez *A* **III** *s* skok *m*
vault•ed ['vɔːltɪd] *adj ARCHIT* sklepiony
vault•ing horse ['vɔːltɪŋhɔːs] *s SPORT* koń *m*

V

VCR [viːsiːˈɑː] *abbr* (=***video cassette recorder***) magnetowid *m*, *infml* wideo *n*
VD [viːˈdiː] *abbr* (=***veneral disease***) choroba *f* weneryczna
VDU [viːdiːˈjuː] *abbr* (=***visual display unit***) *Br* monitor *m*
veal [viːl] *s* COOK cielęcina *f*
vec•tor [ˈvektə] *s* **1.** MATH PHYS wektor *m* **2.** BIOL nosiciel *m*, wektor *m*
veer [vɪə] *v/i* **1.** gwałtownie skręcać ⟨-cić⟩; ~ ***off course*** zboczyć z kursu; ***the debate*** ~***ed away from the topic*** dyskusja odeszła od tematu **2.** (*wind*) zmieniać ⟨-nić⟩ kierunek
ve•gan [ˈviːgən] *s* weganin *m*
veg•e•burg•er® [ˈvedʒɪbɜːgə] → ***veggie burger***
veg•e•ta•ble [ˈvedʒtəbl] **I** *s* **1.** warzywo *n*; ***a salad of raw*** ~***s*** surówka warzywna **2.** *infml* (*person*) roślina *f*, warzywo *n* **II** *adj* **1.** warzywny; ***a*** ~ ***garden*** ogród warzywny **2.** roślinny; ~ ***oil*** olej roślinny
veg•e•tar•i•an [vedʒəˈteərɪən] *s* wegetarianin *m*; **veg•e•tar•i•an•ism** [vedʒəˈteərɪənɪzm] *s* wegetarianizm *m*
veg•e•tate [ˈvedʒɪteɪt] *v/i* wegetować; **veg•e•ta•tion** [vedʒɪˈteɪʃn] *s* wegetacja *f*
veg•gie bur•ger [ˈvedʒɪbɜːgə] *s* hamburger *m* wegetariański
ve•he•mence [ˈviːəməns] *s* gwałtowność *f*; **ve•he•ment** [ˈviːəmənt] *adj* **1.** gwałtowny **2.** zaciekły; **ve•he•ment•ly** [ˈviːəməntlɪ] *adv* **1.** gwałtownie **2.** zaciekle
ve•hi•cle [ˈviːɪkl] *s* **1.** pojazd *m* **2.** *fig* środek *m*, medium *n*
veil [veɪl] **I** *s* **1.** welon *m* **2.** *fig* zasłona *f*; ***behind a*** ~ ***of secrecy*** w tajemnicy; ***draw a*** ~ ***over*** spuścić zasłonę milczenia na *A* **II** *v/t* **1.** zasłaniać ⟨-łonić⟩ **2.** przesłaniać ⟨-łonić⟩
vein [veɪn] *s* **1.** żyła *f*; ***a*** ~ ***of gold*** żyła złota **2.** żyłka *f*
Vel•cro® [ˈvelkrəʊ] *s* rzep *m*, zapięcie *n* na rzep
ve•loc•i•ty [vɪˈlɒsətɪ] *s* prędkość *f*; ***the*** ~ ***of light*** prędkość światła
vel•vet [ˈvelvɪt] *s* aksamit *m*; ***as smooth as*** ~ miękki jak aksamit; **vel•vet•y** [ˈvelvɪtɪ] *adj* aksamitny; ~ ***skin*** aksamitna skóra
vend•er → ***vendor***
ven•det•ta [venˈdetə] *s* **1.** wojna *f* **2.** wendeta *f*
vend•ing ma•chine [ˈvendɪŋ məʃiːn] *s* (*coffee, cigarettes*) automat *m*
ve•neer [vəˈnɪə] **I** *s* **1.** okleina *f* **2.** fornir *m* **3.** *fig* fasada *f* **II** *v/t* oklejać ⟨-leić⟩ fornirem, fornirować
vend•or [ˈvendə] *s* **1.** sprzedawca *m*; ***a street*** ~ uliczny sprzedawca **2.** JUR sprzedający *m*
ven•e•ra•ble [ˈvenərəbl] *adj* **1.** szacowny **2.** czcigodny **3.** (*Catholic Church*) ***the*** ~ Sługa Boży; **ven•e•rate** [ˈvenəreɪt] *v/t* szanować, poważać; **ven•e•ra•tion** [venəˈreɪʃn] *s* szacunek *m*, poważanie *n*
ven•e•re•al dis•ease [vɪˈnɪərɪəl dɪˈziːz] *s* MED choroba *f* weneryczna
ve•ne•tian ˈblind *s* żaluzja *f*
Ven•e•zue•la [venɪˈzweɪlə] *s* Wenezuela *f*
ven•geance [ˈvendʒəns] *s* zemsta *f*; ***take a*** ~ ***on*** zemścić się na *L*; ***with a*** ~ *infml* z większą siłą, ze zdwojoną siłą; **venge•ful** [ˈvendʒfʊl] *adj* dyszący zemstą
Venice [venɪs] *s* Wenecja *f*
ven•i•son [ˈvenɪsn] *s* COOK **1.** dziczyzna *f* **2.** sarnina *f*
ven•om [ˈvenəm] *s* jad *m*; ***in a voice full of*** ~ *fig* głosem pełnym jadu; **ven•om•ous** [ˈvenəməs] *adj* **1.** jadowity **2.** nienawistny
vent [vent] **I** *s* **1.** otwór *m* wentylacyjny **2.** wylot *m* **3.** ujście *n*; ***give*** ~ ***to*** dać upust *D* **4.** ANAT otwór *m* odbytu **5.** (*jacket*) rozcięcie **II** *v/t* **1.** dawać ⟨dać⟩ upust **2.** wyładowywać ⟨-dować⟩ (***on*** na *L*)
ven•ti•late [ˈventɪleɪt] *v/t* **1.** wietrzyć ⟨wy-⟩ **2.** przewietrzać ⟨-trzyć⟩; **ven•ti•la•tion** [ventɪˈleɪʃn] *s* **1.** wentylacja *f* **2.** wietrzenie *n*; **ven•ti•ˈla•tion shaft** *s* TECH szyb *m* wentylacyjny; **ven•ti•la•tor** [ˈventɪleɪtə] *s* **1.** MED respirator *m* **2.** wentylator *m* **3.** wywietrznik *m*
ven•tral [ˈventrəl] *adj* ANAT brzuszny
ven•tri•cle [ˈventrɪkl] *s* ANAT komora *f*; ***a heart*** ~ komora serca; ***cerebral*** ~***s*** komory mózgu
ven•tril•o•quism [venˈtrɪləkwɪzəm] *s* brzuchomówstwo *n*; **ven•tril•o•quist** [venˈtrɪləkwɪst] *s* brzuchomówca *m*

ven•ture ['ventʃə] **I** *s* przedsięwzięcie *n* **II** *v/i* **1.** odważyć się; ***they ~d into the water*** odważyli się wejść do wody **2.** ośmielić się; ***I ~d to suggest*** ośmieliłem się zauważyć **III** *v/t* ryzykować ⟨za-⟩; ***~ one's opinion*** ośmielić się wypowiedzieć swoje zdanie; ***nothing ~d, nothing gained*** bez ryzyka nie ma sukcesu; **ven•ture cap•i•tal** *s ECON* kapitał *m* wysokiego ryzyka

ven•ue ['venju:] *s* miejsce *n* (spotkania, koncertu)

Ve•nus ['vi:nəs] *s ASTR* Wenus *f*

ve•ran•da [və'rændə] *s Br* weranda *f*

verb [vɜ:b] *s GRAM* czasownik *m*; **verb•al** ['vɜ:bl] *adj* **1.** werbalny, słowny; ***non-~ communication*** komunikacja niewerbalna **2.** *agreement*: ustny **3.** *noun*: odczasownikowy; **ver•bal•ize** ['vɜ:bəlaɪz] *v/t* werbalizować ⟨z-⟩, wyrażać ⟨-razić⟩ słowami; **ver•bal•ly** ['vɜ:bəlɪ] *adv* ustnie; **ver•ba•tim** [və'beɪtɪm] **I** *adj* dosłowny **II** *adv* dosłownie, słowo w słowo; **ver•bi•age** ['vɜ:bɪɪdʒ] *s* wielosłowie *n*; **ver•bose** [vɜ:'bəʊs] *adj* **1.** wielosłowny **2.** gadatliwy **3.** rozwlekły

ver•dict ['vɜ:dɪkt] *s* werdykt *m*; ***reach a ~*** uzgodnić werdykt; ***return a ~ of guilty*** ogłosić werdykt skazujący

ver•di•gris ['vɜ:dɪgrɪs] *s CHEM* patyna *f*, śniedź *f*

verge [vɜ:dʒ] **I** *s* **1.** brzeg *m*; ***on the ~ of tears*** na granicy łez; ***they are on the ~ of signing the contract*** są o krok od podpisania umowy **2.** skraj *m*; ***on the ~ of*** na skraju *G* **II** *v/i* graniczyć (**on** z *I*); ***a dislike verging on contempt*** niechęć granicząca z pogardą

verg•er ['vɜ:dʒə] *s* (*Anglican Church*) kościelny *m*

ver•i•fi•a•ble ['verɪfaɪəbl] *adj* sprawdzalny; **ver•i•fi•ca•tion** [verɪfɪ'keɪʃn] *s* **1.** weryfikacja *f* **2.** sprawdzenie *n* **3.** potwierdzenie *n*; **ver•i•fy** ['verɪfaɪ] *v/t* **1.** weryfikować ⟨z-⟩ **2.** sprawdzać ⟨-dzić⟩ **3.** potwierdzać ⟨-dzić⟩

V

ver•i•ta•ble ['verɪtəbl] *adj* prawdziwy; ***the meal is a ~ banquet*** ten posiłek to prawdziwa uczta

ver•mil•ion [və'mɪlɪən] *adj* karminowy

ver•min ['vɜ:mɪn] *s* **1.** szkodnik *m* **2.** *a. fig* pasożyt *m*; **ver•min•ous** ['vɜ:mɪnəs] *adj* **1.** pełen robactwa **2.** zapchlony **3.** zawszony

ver•mouth ['vɜ:məθ] *s* wermut *m*

ver•nac•u•lar [və'nækjʊlə] **I** *s* **1.** język *m* narodowy **2.** dialekt *m* lokalny **II** *adj* ***a ~ language*** → ***vernacular I***

ver•nis•sage [vɜ:nɪ'sɑ:ʒ] *s* wernisaż *m*

ver•sa•tile ['vɜ:sətaɪl] *adj* **1.** wszechstronny **2.** uniwersalny **3.** ***be ~*** mieć wiele zastosowań; **ver•sa•til•i•ty** [vɜ:sə'tɪlətɪ] *s* **1.** wszechstronność *f* **2.** uniwersalność *f*

verse [vɜ:s] *s* **1.** poezja *f*; ***in ~*** wierszem **2.** strofa *f* **3.** (*Bible*) werset *m*; **versed** [vɜ:st] *adj*: ***be ~ in*** znać się na *L*, być obeznanym w *L*

ver•sion ['vɜ:ʃn] *s* wersja *f*; ***the new ~ of the Volkswagen Golf*** nowa wersja volkswagena golfa; ***the film ~ of 'War and Peace'*** filmowa adaptacja „Wojny i Pokoju"; ***the English ~ of the novel*** angielski przekład powieści; ***their ~s conflict*** ich wersje wydarzeń są ze sobą sprzeczne

ver•sus ['vɜ:səs] *prep* **1.** przeciw *D*, przeciwko *D* **2.** versus *N*

ver•te•bra ['vɜ:tɪbrə] *pl -brae s ANAT* kręg *m*; **ver•te•bral** *adj* kręgowy; **ver•te•brate** ['vɜ:tɪbreɪt] *s BIOL* kręgowiec *m*

ver•tex ['vɜ:teks] *pl -tices* ['~tɪsi:z], *-texes s MATH* wierzchołek *m*

ver•ti•cal ['vɜ:tɪkl] **I** *adj* pionowy **II** *s* pion *m*, linia *f* pionowa

ver•ti•go ['vɜ:tɪgəʊ] *s* zawroty *pl* głowy

verve [vɜ:v] *s* werwa *f*

ver•y ['verɪ] **I** *adv* **1.** bardzo; ***~ small*** bardzo mały; ***I like it ~ much*** bardzo mi się to podoba; ***I'm not ~ impressed*** nie wywiera to na mnie większego wrażenia; ***I ~ much hope*** mam wielką nadzieję **2.** (*emphatic*) naprawdę; ***the ~ best quality*** najlepsza jakość; ***for the ~ last time*** naprawdę ostatni raz; ***at the ~ least*** przynajmniej **II** *adj* **1.** (*emphatic*) dokładny; ***at this ~ moment*** dokładnie w tej chwili; ***the ~ thing I need*** dokładnie to, czego potrzebuję **2.** sam; ***at the ~ beginning*** na samym początku; ***the ~ thought of s.th.*** sama myśl o czymś

ves•i•cle ['vesɪkl] *s* **1.** *BIOL* pęcherzyk *m* **2.** *MED* pęcherz *m*, bąbel *m*

ves•sel ['vesl] *s* **1.** statek *m* **2.** łódź *f* **3.** naczynie *n*; ***blood ~s*** naczynia krwionośne

vest [vest] **I** *s* **1.** *Br* podkoszulek *m* **2.** *Am* kamizelka *f* **3.** ***a bullet-proof ~*** kamizelka kuloodporna **II** *v/t* ***overall authority is ~ed in the Supreme Council*** cała władza spoczywa w rękach Rady Najwyższej **III** *v/i* (*power*) spoczywać (***in*** w rękach *G*); **vest•ed in•ter•est** [vestɪd'ɪntrəst] *s* własny interes *m*

ves•ti•bule ['vestɪbjuːl] *s* **1.** przedsionek *m* **2.** westybul *m*

ves•tige ['vestɪdʒ] *s* **1.** pozostałość *m* **2.** ***there is not a ~ of truth in this story*** w tej historii nie ma za grosz prawdy

ves•try ['vestrɪ] *s* REL zakrystia *f*

vet[1] [vet] *s* weterynarz *m*

vet[2] [~] *s Am infml* weteran *m*, kombatant *m*

vet[3] [~] *v/t Br* sprawdzać ⟨-dzić⟩

vet•e•ran ['vetərən] **I** *s* weteran *m*, kombatant *m* **II** *adj* **1.** doświadczony; ***a ~ jazz musician*** weteran sceny jazzowej **2.** stary **3.** zaprawiony

vet•e•ri•nar•i•an [vetərɪ'neərɪən] *s* weterynarz *m*; **vet•er•i•nar•y** ['vetərənərɪ] *adj* weterynaryjny; '**vet•er•i•nar•y med•i•cine** *s* weterynaria *f*; '**vet•er•i•nar•y sur•geon** *s Br form* weterynarz *m*

ve•to ['viːtəʊ] **I** *pl -toes s* weto *n*; ***the right of ~*** prawo weta **II** *v/t* wetować ⟨za-⟩

vex [veks] *v/t form* **1.** denerwować ⟨z-⟩ **2.** drażnić ⟨roz-⟩ **3.** dręczyć; **vexed** [vekst] *adj form* **1.** zdenerwowany **2.** rozdrażniony **3.** *problem*: trudny

vi•a ['vaɪə] *prep* przez *A*

vi•a•ble ['vaɪəbl] *adj* **1.** wykonalny, możliwy; ***financially ~*** realny z finansowego punktu widzenia **2.** rentowny **3.** opłacalny **4.** BIOL zdolny do przeżycia

vi•a•duct ['vaɪədʌkt] *s* wiadukt *m*

vi•al ['vaɪəl] *s* fiolka *f*

vibes [vaɪbz] *pl infml* **1.** wibracje *pl*, atmosfera *f*; ***good ~*** pozytywne wibracje **2.** MUS wibrafon *m*

vi•brant ['vaɪbrənt] *adj* **1.** tętniący życiem **2.** tryskający energią **3.** *colour*: żywy

vi•bra•phone ['vaɪbrəfəʊn] *s* MUS wibrafon *m*

vi•brate [vaɪ'breɪt] *v/i* **1.** drżeć **2.** drgać **3.** wibrować **4.** ***the city ~s with life*** miasto tętni życiem; **vi•bra•tion** [vaɪ'breɪʃn] *s* **1.** drżenie *n* **2.** drganie *n* **3.** wibracja *f* **4.** → ***vibes***; **vi•bra•tor** [vaɪ'breɪtə] *s* wibrator *m*

vic•ar ['vɪkə] *s* (*Anglican Church*) pastor *m*; **vic•ar•age** ['vɪkərɪdʒ] *s* plebania *f*

vi•car•i•ous [vɪ'keərɪəs] *adj* zastępczy

vice[1] [vaɪs] *Br*, **vise** *Am s* TECH imadło *n*

vice[2] [~] *s* wada *f*, przywara *f*

vice[3] [~] (*in combinations*) wice-; **vice 'pres•i•dent** *s* **1.** POL wiceprezydent *m* **2.** ECON wiceprezes *m*; '**vice squad** *s* policja *f* obyczajowa, *infml* obyczajówka *f*

vi•ce ver•sa [vaɪsɪ'vɜːrsə] *adj* **1.** vice versa, odwrotnie

vi•cin•i•ty [vɪ'sɪnətɪ] *s* okolica *f*; ***in the ~ of*** w pobliżu *G*, w sąsiedztwie *G*; ***in the ~ of 40*** około 40

vi•cious ['vɪʃəs] *adj* **1.** brutalny **2.** *dog*: niebezpieczny, zły **3.** złośliwy, zjadliwy **4.** *words*: jadowity, kąśliwy **5.** gwałtowny **6.** *headache*: *infml* potworny; **vi•cious 'cir•cle** *s* błędne koło *n*; **vi•cious•ly** ['vɪʃəslɪ] *adv* **1.** brutalnie **2.** złośliwie, zjadliwie **3.** gwałtownie

vi•cis•si•tudes [vɪ'sɪsɪtjuːdz] *pl form* zmienne koleje *pl*

vic•tim ['vɪktɪm] *s* ofiara *f*; ***earthquake ~s*** ofiary trzęsienia ziemi; ***fall ~ to*** paść ofiarą *G*; **vic•tim•ize** ['vɪktɪmaɪz] *v/t* **1.** krzywdzić ⟨s-⟩ **2.** szykanować

vic•tor ['vɪktə] *s* zwycięzca *m*

Vic•to•ri•an [vɪk'tɔːrɪən] *adj* wiktoriański; **vic•to•ri•ous** [vɪk'tɔːrɪəs] *adj* zwycięski

vic•to•ry ['vɪktərɪ] *s* zwycięstwo *n* (***over/against*** nad *I*); ***a ~ ceremony*** SPORT ceremonia dekoracji zwycięzców

vid•e•o ['vɪdɪəʊ] **I** *s* **1.** wideo *n* **2.** kaseta *f* wideo; ***on ~*** na kasetach wideo **3.** film *m* wideo **4.** *Br* magnetowid *m* **II** *v/t* **1.** nagrywać ⟨-rać⟩ (na wideo) **2.** filmować ⟨s-⟩ (na wideo); '**vid•e•o cam•e•ra** *s* kamera *f* wideo; **vid•e•o-**

cas•'sette *s* kaseta *f* wideo; **vid•e•o-cas•'sette re•cord•er** *s* odtwarzacz *m* kaset wideo, magnetowid *m*; **'vid•e•o clip** *s* wideoklip *m*, teledysk *m*; **'vid•e•o con•fer•ence** *s* wideokonferencja *f*; **'vid•e•o•disk** *s* **1.** dysk *m* wideo **2.** płyta *f* DVD; **'vid•e•o 'nas•ty** *s Br infml* **1.** horror *m* **2.** film *m* zawierający sceny drastyczne; **'vid•e•o•phone** *s* wideofon *m*; **'vid•e•o re•cord•er** *s* magnetowid *m*, odtwarzacz *m* kaset wideo; **'vid•e•o•tape** *s* taśma *f* wideo

vie [vaɪ] *v/i* **1.** rywalizować (**for** o *A*) **2.** walczyć (**for** o *A*)

Vi•en•na [vɪ'enə] *s* Wiedeń *m*

Vi•et•nam [vjet'næm] *s* Wietnam *m*; **Vi•et•nam•ese** [vjetnə'miːz] **I** *adj* wietnamski **II** *s* Wietnamczyk *m*, Wietnamka *f*

view [vjuː] **I** *s* **1.** pogląd *m*; ***have strong political ~s*** mieć zdecydowane poglądy polityczne **2.** zdanie *n*, opinia *f*; ***in my ~*** moim zdaniem **3.** spojrzenie *n*; ***an optimistic ~ of life*** optymistyczne spojrzenie na życie **4.** widok *m*; ***come into ~*** pojawić się; ***disappear from ~*** zniknąć z pola widzenia; ***there was nobody in ~*** nikogo nie było widać; ***block one's ~*** zasłaniać komuś widok; ***in full ~ of*** na oczach *G* **5.** ***in ~ of*** mając na względzie *A*, ze względu na *A*; ***with a ~ to*** z myślą o *L* **6.** fotografia *f*, zdjęcie *n* **7.** pokaz *m*; ***a private ~*** prywatny pokaz; ***over 150 works are on ~*** ekspozycja obejmuje ponad 150 dzieł; ***the sculpture is on ~ in the Tate Modern*** rzeźbę można obejrzeć w Tate Modern **II** *v/t* **1.** uznawać (**as** za *A*) **2.** traktować ⟨po-⟩ (**as** jako *A*) **3.** oceniać ⟨-nić⟩ **4.** oglądać, obejrzeć, patrzeć ⟨po-⟩; ***~ing platform*** platforma widokowa **5.** oglądać ⟨obejrzeć⟩; **view•er** ['vjuːə] *s* **1.** widz *m* **2.** oglądający *m* **3.** obserwator *m* **4.** przeglądarka *f* (do przezroczy); **'view•find•er** *s PHOT* wizjer *m*; **'view•point** *s* punkt *m* widzenia (**on** na *A*); ***from the practical ~*** z praktycznego punktu widzenia

vig•il ['vɪdʒɪl] *s* czuwanie *n*; ***keep a ~ at s.o.'s bedside*** czuwać przy czyimś łóżku; **vig•i•lance** ['vɪdʒɪləns] *s* czujność *f*; **vig•i•lant** ['vɪdʒɪlənt] *adj* czujny; **vig•i•lan•te** [vɪdʒɪl'æntɪ] *s* członek *m* straży obywatelskiej

vig•our ['vɪgə] *Br*, **vig•or** *Am s* **1.** wigor *m* **2.** energia *f*; **vig•or•ous** ['vɪgərəs] *adj* **1.** energiczny **2.** pełen wigoru **3.** *fan*: gorący; **vig•or•ous•ly** ['vɪgərəslɪ] *adv* **1.** energicznie **2.** z wigorem **3.** żarliwie

vile [vaɪl] *adj* **1.** *infml* paskudny, obrzydliwy **2.** *form* podły, zły, nikczemny

vil•i•fy ['vɪlɪfaɪ] *v/t* szkalować ⟨o-⟩

vil•la ['vɪlə] *s* **1.** dom *m* (letniskowy) **2.** willa *f*

vil•lage ['vɪlɪdʒ] *s* wieś, wioska *f*; **vil•lag•er** ['vɪlɪdʒə] *s* mieszkaniec *m* wsi

vil•lain ['vɪlən] *s* **1.** (*novel*, *film*) czarny charakter *m* **2.** łotr *m* **3.** *Br infml* przestępca *m*

vin•di•cate ['vɪndɪkeɪt] *v/t* **1.** potwierdzać ⟨-dzić⟩ słuszność; ***our fears were ~d*** nasze obawy okazały się słuszne **2.** oczyszczać ⟨oczyścić⟩ z zarzutów; **vindication** [vɪndɪ'keɪʃn] *s* **1.** potwierdzenie *n* słuszności **2.** oczyszczenie *n* z zarzutów

vin•dic•tive [vɪn'dɪktɪv] *adj* mściwy; **vin•dic•tive•ly** [vɪn'dɪktɪvlɪ] *adv* mściwie

vine [vaɪn] *s* **1.** winorośl *f* **2.** roślina *f* pnąca **3.** pnącze *n*

vin•e•gar ['vɪnɪgə] *s* ocet *m*; ***wine ~*** ocet winny

'vine•grow•er *s* właściciel *m* winnicy; **vine•yard** ['vɪnjɑːd] *s* winnica *f*

vi•no ['viːnəʊ] *pl -nos* ['~nəʊz] *s infml* wino *n*

vin•tage ['vɪntɪdʒ] **I** *s* **1.** rocznik *m* **2.** zbiór *m*, winobranie *n* **II** *adj* **1.** *wine*: z dobrego rocznika **2.** *Br* (*car*) wyprodukowany w latach 1917–1930; ***a ~ car*** oldtimer, samochód zabytkowy **3.** klasyczny **4.** ***a ~ year*** dobry rok

vint•ner ['vɪntnə] *s form* sprzedawca *m* win

vi•o•la [vɪ'əʊlə] *s MUS* altówka *f*

vi•o•late ['vaɪəleɪt] *v/t* **1.** *law*: naruszać ⟨-szyć⟩; pogwałcić **2.** *grave*: beszcześcić ⟨z-⟩; **vi•o•la•tion** [vaɪə'leɪʃn] *s* **1.** *law*: naruszenie *n*, pogwałcenie *n* **2.** zbeszczeszczenie *n*

vi•o•lence ['vaɪələns] *s* **1.** przemoc *f*; ***domestic ~*** przemoc w rodzinie **2.** siła

V

f; ***the use of ~*** użycie siły; **vi•o•lent** ['vaɪələnt] *adj* **1.** gwałtowny; ***die a ~ death*** zginąć gwałtowną śmiercią **2.** agresywny **3.** brutalny, z użyciem przemocy; ***a ~ crime*** przestępstwo z użyciem przemocy **4.** ***a ~ pink*** jaskraworóżowy; **vi•o•lent•ly** ['vaɪələntlɪ] *adv* **1.** gwałtownie **2.** mocno **3.** bardzo **4.** agresywnie

vi•o•let ['vaɪələt] **I** *s* **1.** *BIOL* fiołek *m* **2.** (*colour*) fiolet *m* **II** *adj* fioletowy

vi•o•lin [vaɪə'lɪn] *s MUS* skrzypce *pl*; ***vi•o•lin•ist*** [vaɪə'lɪnɪst] *s* skrzypek *m*

vi•o•lon•cel•lo [vaɪələn'tʃeləʊ] *pl -los s* wiolonczela *f*

VIP [viːaɪ'piː] *abbr* (=***very important person***) VIP *m*, ważna osobistość *m*

vi•per ['vaɪpə] *s* żmija *f*

vi•ral ['vaɪərəl] *adj* wirusowy; ***a ~ infection*** infekcja wirusowa

vir•gin ['vɜːdʒɪn] **I** *s* dziewica *f*; ***the ~*** *REL* Maryja *f* Dziewica **II** *adj* **1.** dziewiczy **2.** nietknięty, nienaruszony

vir•gin•i•ty [vɜː'dʒɪnətɪ] *s* dziewictwo *n*

Vir•go ['vɜːgəʊ] *s ASTR* Panna *f*

vir•ile ['vɪraɪl] *adj* **1.** męski **2.** jurny; **vi•ril•i•ty** [və'rɪlətɪ] *s* **1.** męskość *f* **2.** jurność *f*

vir•tu•al ['vɜːtʃʊəl] *adj* **1.** ***he's a ~ alcoholic*** praktycznie jest alkoholikiem; ***it's a ~ certainty that*** jest niemal pewne, że **2.** *INF* wirtualny; **vir•tu•al•ly** ['vɜːtʃʊəlɪ] *adv* **1.** niemal, prawie; ***~ all students*** niemal wszyscy studenci **2.** praktycznie **3.** *INF* wirtualnie; **vir•tu•al re'al•i•ty** *s* wirtualna rzeczywistość *f*

vir•tue ['vɜːʃtuː] *s* **1.** cnota *f* **2.** zaleta *f* **3.** korzyść *f*; ***make a ~ of necessity*** obrócić sytuację na swoją korzyść **4.** ***by ~ of*** z racji *G*, ze względu na *A*

vir•tu•o•so [vɜːtjʊː'əʊzəʊ] **I** *pl -sos, -si s MUS* wirtuoz *m* **II** *adj* wirtuozerski

vir•tu•ous ['vɜːtʃʊəs] *adj* **1.** cnotliwy **2.** dobry

vir•u•lent ['vɪrʊlənt] *adj* **1.** *virus*: zjadliwy **2.** *illness*: złośliwy **3.** *poison*: silny **4.** *criticism*, *attack*: jadowity, zjadliwy

vi•rus ['vaɪrəs] *s* wirus *m*; **'vi•rus pro•tec•tion** *s INF* ochrona *f* antywirusowa; **'vi•rus scan•ner** *s INF* skaner *m* antywirusowy

vi•sa ['viːzə] *s* wiza *f*

vis-à-vis [viːzɑː'viː] *prep* **1.** w odniesieniu do *G* **2.** wobec *G* **3.** w porównaniu do *G*

vis•cer•a ['vɪsərə] *pl MED* wnętrzności *pl*, trzewia *pl*; **vis•cer•al** ['vɪsərəl] *adj* **1.** emocjonalny **2.** instynktowny **3.** *hatred, dislike*: organiczny **4.** trzewiowy, trzewny

vis•count ['vaɪkaʊnt] *s Br* wicehrabia *m*; **'vis•count•ess** *s Br* wicehrabina *f*

vis•cous ['vɪskəs] *adj* lepki

vise [vaɪs] *Am* → **vice**

vis•i•bil•i•ty [vɪzə'bɪlətɪ] *s* widoczność *f*; **vis•i•ble** ['vɪzəbl] *adj* **1.** widoczny; ***~ to the naked eye*** widoczny gołym okiem **2.** wyraźny; **vis•i•bly** ['vɪzəblɪ] *adv* **1.** widocznie **2.** wyraźnie

vi•sion ['vɪʒn] *s* **1.** wzrok *m*; ***have a good ~*** mieć dobry wzrok **2.** wizja *f*; ***a ~ of the future*** wizja przyszłości **3.** wyobraźnia *f* **4.** *TEL* wizja *f*, obraz *m*; **vi•sion•ar•y** ['vɪʒnərɪ] **I** *s* wizjoner *m* **II** *adj* wizjonerski

vis•it ['vɪzɪt] **I** *v/t* **1.** odwiedzać ⟨-dzić⟩ **2.** składać ⟨złożyć⟩ wizytę w *L* **3.** iść ⟨pójść⟩ do *G*; ***~ the doctor*** pójść do lekarza **4.** zwiedzać ⟨-dzić⟩ **5.** dokonywać ⟨-nać⟩ wizytacji w *L* **6.** przeprowadzać ⟨-dzić⟩ inspekcję w *L* **II** *s* **1.** wizyta *f*; ***pay s.o. a ~*** złożyć komuś wizytę **2.** odwiedziny *pl* **3.** pobyt *m* **4.** ***pay a ~ to a museum*** zwiedzić muzeum; **visit with s.o.** *v/t Am* odwiedzać ⟨-dzić⟩ kogoś

vis•it•a•tion [vɪzɪ'teɪʃn] *s* **1.** wizytacja *f* **2.** inspekcja *f* **3.** nawiedzenie *n* **4.** *JUR Am* odwiedziny *pl*; **vis•it•ing card** ['vɪzɪtɪŋkɑːd] *s* wizytówka *f*; **'vis•it•ing hours** *pl* godziny *pl* odwiedzin

vis•i•tor ['vɪzɪtə] *s* **1.** odwiedzający *m*; ***~s to England*** osoby przyjeżdżające do Anglii **2.** gość *m* **3.** zwiedzający *m*; **vis•i•tors' book** ['vɪzɪtəzbʊk] *s* księga *f* gości

vi•sor ['vaɪzə] *s* **1.** osłona *f* **2.** *Am* daszek *m* **3.** *AUTO* osłona *f* przeciwsłoneczna **4.** przyłbica *f*

vis•ta ['vɪstə] *s* **1.** widok *m* **2.** *fig* widoki *pl*, perspektywy *pl*; ***open up new ~s for*** otworzyć nowe perspektywy przed *I*

vis•u•al ['vɪʒʊəl] **I** *adj* **1.** wzrokowy; ***~ memory*** pamięć wzrokowa **2.** wizualny **II** *s* **1.** → ***visual aid*** **2.** ***~s*** *FILM* zdjęcia *pl*; **vis•u•al 'aid** *s* pomoc *m* wizualna; **vis•u•al 'arts** *pl* ART sztuki *pl* wizualne; **vis•u•al dis•'play u•nit** *s* INF monitor *m*; **vis•u•al•ize** ['vɪʒʊəlaɪz] *v/t* wyobrażać ⟨-razić⟩ sobie (**as** jako *A*); **vis•u•al•ly** ['vɪʒʊlɪ] *adv* **1.** wzrokowo **2.** wizualnie; **vis•u•al•ly im'paired** *adj* niedowidzący

vi•tal ['vaɪtl] *adj* **1.** niezbędny **2.** zasadniczy; ***play a ~ role*** odgrywać zasadniczą rolę **3.** podstawowy **4.** decydujący **5.** *organ*: niezbędny do życia, podstawowy **6.** *person*: pełen wigoru; **vi•tal•i•ty** [vaɪ'tælətɪ] *s* witalność *f*; **vi•tal•ly** ['vaɪtəlɪ] *adv* **1.** niezmiernie **2.** bardzo; **vi•tal sta•'tis•tics** *pl* **1.** statystyka *f* urodzin, zgonów, małżeństw i rozwodów, dane *pl* demograficzne **2.** *Br infml* wymiary *pl*

vit•a•min ['vaɪtəmɪn] *s* witamina *f*; **'vit•a•min pill** *s* (*pill*) witamina *f*

vit•re•ous ['vɪtrɪəs] *adj* szklisty

vit•ri•ol•ic [vɪtrɪ'ɒlɪk] *adj lit* jadowity, zjadliwy

vi•va•cious [vɪ'veɪʃəs] *adj* **1.** żywy **2.** pełen życia; **vi•vac•i•ty** [vɪ'væsətɪ] *s* żywość *f*, żywy temperament *m*

vi•va vo•ce [vaivə'vəʊsɪ] *s Br* egzamin *m* ustny

viv•id ['vɪvɪd] *adj* **1.** *memory*: żywy, wyraźny **2.** *description*: barwny **3.** *imagination*: bujny **4.** *colour*, *light*: jaskrawy; **viv•id•ly** ['vɪvɪdlɪ] *adv* **1.** wyraźnie **2.** barwnie **3.** jaskrawo

viv•i•sec•tion [vɪvɪ'sekʃn] *s* wiwisekcja *f*

V-neck ['viːnek] *s* dekolt *m* w serek

vix•en ['vɪksən] *s* **1.** lisica *f* **2.** jędza *f*

vo•cab ['vəʊkæb] *infml* → ***vocabulary***; **vo•cab•u•la•ry** [vəʊ'kæbjʊlərɪ] *s* **1.** słownictwo *n* **2.** słowniczek *m*

vo•cal ['vəʊkl] **I** *adj* **1.** głosowy **2.** wokalny **3.** głośny; ***be ~ in one's opposition*** głośno wyrażać sprzeciw **II** *s* **1.** wokal *m*; ***the backing ~s*** podkład wokalny **2.** śpiew *m*; **'vo•cal cords** *pl* ANAT struny *pl* głosowe; **'vo•cal group** *s* MUS grupa *f* wokalna; **vo•cal•ist** ['vəʊkəlɪst] *s* wokalista *m*

vo•ca•tion [vəʊ'keɪʃn] *s* powołanie *n*; ***miss one's ~*** minąć się z powołaniem; **vo•ca•tion•al** [vəʊ'keɪʃnl] *adj* zawodowy; ***~ training*** szkolenie zawodowe

vo•cif•er•ous [vəʊ'sɪfərəs] *adj* **1.** głośny **2.** głośno wyrażany

vod•ka ['vɒdkə] *s* wódka *f*

vogue [vəʊg] *s* moda *f*; ***be in ~*** być w modzie

voice [vɔɪs] **I** *s* **1.** głos *m*; ***raise one's ~*** podnieść głos; ***lower one's ~*** zniżyć głos; ***the ~ of reason*** głos rozsądku; ***with one ~*** jednogłośnie, zgodnym chórem; ***give one's ~ to*** wyrazić *A* **2.** prawo *n* głosu **3.** GRAM strona *f*; ***the active ~*** strona czynna; ***the passive ~*** strona bierna **II** *v/t opinion, feeling*: wyrażać ⟨-razić⟩; **'voice box** *s* ANAT krtań *f*; **voiced** [vɔɪst] *adj sound*: dźwięczny; **voice•less** ['vɔɪslɪs] *adj sound*: bezdźwięczny; **'voice mail** *s* poczta *f* głosowa; **voice-o•ver** *s* głos *m* lektora; ***do ~s*** pracować jako lektor; ***she did ~s in several cartoons*** użyczała głosu postaciom w kilku filmach animowanych

void [vɔɪd] **I** *s* **1.** *lit* pustka *f* **2.** *lit* otchłań *f* **II** *adj* **1.** *form* pozbawiony (***of*** *G*) **2.** JUR nieważny **3.** *form* pusty **III** *v/t* JUR unieważniać ⟨-nić⟩

vol•a•tile ['vɒlətəl] *adj* **1.** zmienny **2.** niestabilny **3.** chimeryczny **4.** *substance*: lotny

vol•can•ic [vɒl'kænɪk] *adj* wulkaniczny; **vol•ca•no** [vɒl'keɪnəʊ] *pl -nos, -noes s* wulkan *m*

vole [vəʊl] *s* BIOL nornik *m*

vo•li•tion [vəʊ'lɪʃn] *s* wola *f*; ***on one's own ~*** z własnej woli, dobrowolnie

vol•ley ['vɒlɪ] **I** *s* **1.** SPORT wolej *m* **2.** salwa *f*; ***a ~ of questions*** grad pytań; **'vol•ley•ball** *s* siatkówka *f*

volt [vəʊlt] *s* PHYS wolt *m*; **volt•age** ['vəltɪdʒ] *s* PHYS napięcie *n*

vol•u•ble ['vɒljʊbl] *adj* **1.** rozmowny, gadatliwy **2.** wymowny, elokwentny

vol•ume ['vɒljəm] *s* **1.** objętość *f* **2.** pojemność *f* **3.** głośność *f*; ***turn the ~ up*** pogłośnić; ***turn the ~ down*** przyciszyć; ***at full ~*** na cały regulator **4.** tom *m*; ***in 20 ~s*** w 20 tomach **5.** ilość *f* **6.** rozmiar *m*, wielkość *f* **7.** masa *f* **8.** zakres *m* **9.** natężenie *n*; **vol•ume con•'trol** *s* regulator *m* głośności; **vo•lu•mi•nous** [və'luːmɪnəs] *adj* **1.** (bardzo) obszerny **2.** pojemny **3.** *armchair*: wielki

vol•un•tar•i•ly [vɒlən'terılı] *adv* **1.** dobrowolnie **2.** ochotniczo **3.** nieodpłatnie; **vol•un•ta•ry** ['vɒlənterı] **1.** dobrowolny **2.** ochotniczy; ***work on a ~ basis*** pracować jako wolontariusz **3.** nieobowiązkowy **4.** niepłatny **5.** *move*: świadomy; **vol•un•ta•ry redun•dancy** *s*: ***take ~*** *Br* odejść z pracy na własną prośbę
vol•un•teer [vɒlən'tıə] **I** *s* **1.** ochotnik *m* **2.** wolontariusz *m* **II** *v/t help*: oferować ⟨za-⟩, proponować ⟨za-⟩ **III** *v/i* zgłaszać ⟨-łosić⟩ się na ochotnika; ***she ~ed to stay*** zaoferowała się, że zostanie
vo•lup•tu•ous [və'lʌpʃʊəs] *adj* **1.** ***be ~*** mieć bujne kształty **2.** *body*: krągły **3.** *lips*: pełny **4.** *smell*: zmysłowy
vom•it ['vɒmət] **I** *v/t* (*a.* ***~ up***) wymiotować ⟨z-⟩ **II** *s* wymiociny *pl*
voo•doo ['vu:du:] *s* wudo *n*, voodoo *n*
vo•ra•cious [və'reıʃəs] *adj* **1.** żarłoczny **2.** *appetite*: ogromny, wilczy; **vo•ra•cious•ly** [və'reıʃəslı] *adv* żarłocznie
vor•tex ['vɔ:teks] *pl -texes*, *-tices* ['~tısi:z] *s a. fig* wir *m*
vote [vəʊt] **I** *s* **1.** głos *m* (***for*** za *I*, ***against*** przeciw *D*); ***cast a ~*** oddać głos, zagłosować **2.** głosowanie *n* (***on*** nad *I*); ***put s.th. to the ~*** poddać coś pod głosowanie **3.** ***the ~*** głosy *pl*, całkowita liczba *f* głosów **4.** ***the ~*** prawo *n* do głosowania **II** *v/i* głosować ⟨za-⟩ (***for*** za *I*, ***against*** przeciw *D*) **III** *v/t* **1.** głosować ⟨za-⟩ na *A*; ***~ Democrat*** zagłosować na demokratów **2.** wybierać ⟨-brać⟩ **3.** przegłosować; ***~ a pay increase*** przegłosować podwyżkę płac; **vote in** *v/t* wybierać ⟨-brać⟩ (w głosowaniu); **vote out** *v/t* odwoływać ⟨-łać⟩ (w głosowaniu)
vot•er ['vəʊtə] *s* **1.** wyborca *m* **2.** głosujący *m*; **vot•ing** ['vəʊtıŋ] *s* głosowanie *n*; **'vot•ing booth** *s* kabina *n* do głosowania
vouch•er ['vaʊtʃə] *s* **1.** kupon *m* **2.** bon *m* **3.** talon *m* **4.** kwit *m* **5.** potwierdzenie *n*; **vouch for** [vaʊtʃfɔ:] *v/t* ręczyć ⟨po-⟩ za *A*
vow [vaʊ] **I** *s* **1.** ślubowanie *n* **2.** przysięga *f*; ***marriage ~s*** przysięga małżeńska **II** *v/t* **1.** ślubować **2.** przysięgać ⟨-siąc⟩
vow•el [vaʊəl] *s* samogłoska *f*
voy•age ['vɔııdz] *s* **1.** podróż *f* (morska) **2.** rejs *m*
voy•eur [vwaı'ɜ:] *s* podglądacz *m*
VP [vi:'pi:] *abbr* (=***vice president***) **1.** wiceprezydent *m* **2.** *Am* dyrektor *m*
vul•can•ize ['vʌlkənaız] *v/t* TECH wulkanizować ⟨z-⟩; **vul•can•ized rub•ber** [vʌlkənaızd'rʌbə] *s* guma *f* wulkanizowana
vul•gar ['vʌlgə] *adj* **1.** prostacki **2.** ordynarny, wulgarny **3.** bez gustu **4.** niewybredny; **vul•gar•i•ty** [vʌl'gærətı] *s* **1.** prostactwo *n* **2.** ordynarność *f*, wulgarność *f* **3.** bezguście *n*
vul•ne•ra•ble ['vʌlnərəbl] *adj* **1.** podatny (***to*** na *A*) **2.** wrażliwy (***to*** na *A*) **3.** narażony (***to*** na *A*) **4.** bezbronny; **vul•ner•a•bil•i•ty** [vʌlnərə'bılətı] *s* **1.** podatność *f* **2.** wrażliwość *f* **3.** słabość *f*
vul•ture ['vʌltʃə] *s a. fig* sęp *m*

W

wack•y ['wækı] *adj infml* stuknięty
wad [wɒd] *s* **1.** *banknotes*, *documents*: plik *m* **2.** *banknotes*: zwitek *m* **3.** wacik *m*
wad•ding ['wɒdıŋ] *s* **1.** watowanie *n* **2.** wyściółka *f* **3.** watolina *f*
wad•dle ['wɒdl] *v/i* chodzić, kołysząc się
wade [weıd] **I** *v/i* **1.** brodzić (***through*** przez *A*); ***~ into the water*** wejść do wody **2.** brnąć ⟨prze-⟩ (***through*** przez *A*) **3.** przedzierać ⟨-drzeć⟩ się (***through*** przez *A*) **II** *v/t* przechodzić ⟨przejść⟩ w bród przez *A*; **wade in** *v/t infml* **1.** mieszać ⟨w-⟩ się w *A* **2.** rzucać ⟨-cić⟩ się na *A*; **wade through** *v/t fig* przedzierać ⟨-drzeć⟩ się przez *A*
wad•er [weıdə] *s* ptak *m* brodzący
wad•ers [weıdəz] *pl* wodery *pl*, buty *pl* wędkarskie
wad•ing pool ['weıdıŋpu:l] *s Am* brodzik *m*

wa•fer ['weɪfə] *s* **1.** wafel *m* **2.** REL opłatek *m*; '**wa•fer-thin** *adj* **1.** *wall*: bardzo cienki **2.** *slice*: cienki jak opłatek

waf•fle[1] ['wɒfl] *s* gofr *m*

waf•fle[2] [~] *Br infml* **I** *v/i* **1.** ględzić (**on** o *L*) **2.** rozwodzić się (**on** o *L*) **II** *s infml* mowa-trawa *f*

waft [wɒft] **I** *v/i* **1.** unosić się **2.** rozchodzić się **II** *v/t smell*: nieść **III** *s* **1.** zapach *m* **2.** powiew *m* **3.** *smoke*: smużka *f*

wag[1] [wæg] **I** *v/t* **1.** merdać; ***the dog ~ged its tail*** pies merdał ogonem **2.** ***~ one's finger at s.o.*** grozić komuś palcem; ***tongues will ~*** ludzie rozpuszczą języki **II** *s* merdanie *n* (ogonem)

wag[2] [~] *s infml* kawalarz *m*

wage[1] [weɪdʒ] *v/t war*: prowadzić, toczyć (***against*** przeciw *D*)

wage[2] [~] *s* (*a.* ***~s***) **1.** pensja *f* **2.** płaca *f* **3.** zarobki *pl* **4.** wynagrodzenie *n*; '**wage claim** *s* żądanie *n* płacowe; '**wage de•mand** → ***wage claim***; '**wage earn•er** *s* **1.** osoba *f* pracująca **2.** żywiciel *m* rodziny; '**wage freeze** *s* zamrożenie *n* płac; '**wage ne•go•ti•a•tions** *pl* negocjacje *pl* płacowe; '**wage pack•et** *s Br fig* wypłata *f*; '**wage rise** *s Br* podwyżka *f* płac

wa•ger ['weɪdʒə] **I** *s form* zakład *m* **II** *v/t* **1.** *form* stawiać ⟨postawić⟩ (**on** na *A*) **2.** zakładać ⟨założyć⟩ się o *A* **III** *v/i infml* założyć się; ***I'll ~ that*** założę się, że

wag•gle ['wægl] *v/t infml* ruszać ⟨po-⟩; ***can you ~ your ears?*** umiesz ruszać uszami?

wag•gon *Br* → ***wagon 2***

wag•on ['wægən] *s* **1.** *Br* wagon *n* (towarowy) **2.** wóz *m* **3.** furmanka *f* **4.** *Am* kombi *n*

wail [weɪl] **I** *v/i* **1.** zawodzić **2.** płakać **3.** (*complain*) jęczeć **4.** (*siren*) wyć **II** *s* **1.** zawodzenie *n* **2.** płacz *m* **3.** *siren*: wycie *n*

wain•scot•ting ['weɪnskətɪŋ] *s* boazeria *f*

waist [weɪst] *s* **1.** pas *m*; ***from ~ down*** od pasa w dół **2.** talia *f*; '**waist•band** *s* (*trousers*, *skirt*) pasek *m* (wszywany); '**waist•coat** *s Br* kamizelka *f*; **waist-'deep I** *adj* głęboki do pasa; ***the water was ~*** woda sięgała do pasa **II** *adv* do pasa; ***they waded ~ in water*** szli po pas zanurzeni w wodzie; **waist-'high** *adj grass*, *rye*: wysoki do pasa; '**waist•line** *s* talia *f*; ***I'm watching my ~*** dbam o linię

wait [weɪt] **I** *v/i* **1.** czekać (**for** na *A*); ***I ~ed*** (**for**) ***10 minutes*** czekałem 10 minut; ***~ for s.o. to do s.th.*** czekać, aż ktoś coś zrobi; ***this can ~*** to może poczekać; ***keep s.o. ~ing*** kazać komuś czekać; ***~ a moment*** chwileczkę; ***I can't ~ to see him*** nie mogę się doczekać, kiedy się z nim zobaczę; ***~ and see!*** zaczekaj, to zobaczysz! **2.** ***~ at table*** podawać do stołu **II** *v/t* czekać ⟨po-⟩ na *A*; ***~ one's turn*** poczekać na swoją kolej **III** *s* **1.** czekanie *n*; ***have a long ~*** długo czekać **2.** oczekiwanie *n*; **wait on** *v/i* **1.** służyć **2.** pracować jako służący; **wait up** *v/i* czekać ⟨za-⟩; ***don't ~ for me*** nie czekaj na mnie, idź spać

wait•er ['weɪtə] *s* kelner *m*; **wait•ing** ['weɪtɪŋ] **I** *s* czekanie *n*, oczekiwanie *n*; ***no ~*** AUTO zakaz postoju **II** *adj* czekający, oczekujący; '**wait•ing list** *s* lista *f* oczekujących; '**wait•ing room** *s* poczekalnia *f*

wait•ress ['weɪtrɪs] *s* kelnerka *f*

waive [weɪv] *v/t* **1.** uchylać ⟨-lić⟩ **2.** zrzekać ⟨zrzec⟩ się *G* **3.** odstępować ⟨-tąpić⟩ od *G* **4.** *tax*: zaniechać poboru; **waiv•er** ['weɪvə] *s* **1.** zrzeczenie się *n* **2.** odstąpienie *n*

wake[1] [weɪk] (*woke*; *woken*) **I** *v/t* (*a.* ***~ up***) budzić ⟨o-⟩; ***~ the baby up*** obudzić dziecko; ***~ up to*** *fig* zdać sobie sprawę z *G* **II** *v/i* (*a.* ***~ up***) budzić ⟨o-⟩ się; ***~ up! It's 8 o'clock!*** Wstawaj! Jest ósma!

wake[2] [~] *s* czuwanie *n* przy zwłokach; ***in the ~ of s.th*** w ślad za czymś; **wake•ful** ['weɪkfʊl] *adj* bezsenny

wak•en ['weɪkən] *lit* **I** *v/i* (*a.* ***~ up***) budzić ⟨o-⟩ się **II** *v/t* (*a.* ***~ up***) budzić ⟨o-⟩ się; **wak•ing** ['weɪkɪŋ] *adj*: ***he spends all his ~ hours studying*** uczy się całymi dniami

'**wake-up call** *s* (*hotel*) budzenie *n*

Wales [weɪlz] *s* Walia *f*

walk [wɔːk] **I** *v/i* **1.** chodzić; ***the baby is learning to ~*** dziecko uczy się chodzić; ***she had to ~ home*** musiała pójść do domu piechotą **2.** spacerować **II** *v/t* **1.** odprowadzać ⟨-dzić⟩; **~ *s.o. home*** odprowadzić kogoś do domu **2.** *dog*: wyprowadzać ⟨-dzić⟩ na spacer **III** *s* **1.** spacer *m*; ***go for a ~*** pójść na spacer; ***take a dog for a ~*** wyprowadzić psa na spacer; ***the church is just a five-minute ~ from here*** kościół jest zaledwie pięć minut drogi stąd **2.** trasa *f* (spacerowa) **3.** droga *f* **4.** chód *m*; **walk off with** *v/i infml* **1.** *infml award*: zgarniać ⟨-nąć⟩ **2. ~ *off with a win*** odnieść łatwe zwycięstwo **3.** *infml* (*steal*) zwędzić; **walk out** *v/i* **1.** strajkować ⟨za-⟩ **2.** wychodzić ⟨wyjść⟩; **~ *of a meeting*** wyjść z zebrania **3.** opuszczać ⟨opuścić⟩; **walk out on** *v/i* zostawiać ⟨-wić⟩

walk•a•bout ['wɔːkəbaʊt] *s*: ***go on a ~*** *Br* wmieszać się w tłum; **walk•a•way** ['wɔːkəweɪ] *s* łatwe zwycięstwo *n*; **walk•er** ['wɔːkə] *s* **1.** piechur *m*; ***be a fast ~*** szybko chodzić **2.** spacerowicz *m* **3.** SPORT chodziarz *m*; **walk•ie-'talk•ie** [wɔːkɪ'tɔːkɪ] *s* radiotelefon *m*, *infml* walkie-talkie *n*; **walk-in 'clos•et** *s* garderoba *f*; **walk•ing** ['wɔːkɪŋ] **I** *s* **1.** chodzenie *n* **2.** spacerowanie *n* **3.** SPORT chodziarstwo *n* **II** *adj* chodzący; ***a ~ encyclopaedia*** chodząca encyklopedia; **'walk•ing stick** *s* laska *f*; **'walk•ing tour** *s* wycieczka *f* piesza; **'Walk•man®** *s* walkman *m*; **'walk-on part** *s* THEAT (*role*) epizod *f*; **'walk•out** *s* **1.** strajk *m* **2.** wyjście *n* z sali na znak protestu; **'walk•o•ver** *s* łatwe zwycięstwo *n*; **'walk-up** *s Am* **1.** budynek *m* bez windy **2.** mieszkanie *n* w budynku bez windy

wall [wɔːl] **I** *s* **1.** ściana *f*; ***~s have ears*** ściany mają uszy; ***drive s.o. up the ~*** *fig* doprowadzać kogoś do szału; ***off the ~*** *fig* zwariowany; ***a ~ of fire*** ściana ognia; ***a ~ of silence*** mur milczenia **2.** ścianka *f* **II** *v/t* **1.** ogradzać ⟨-rodzić⟩ murem; **~ *s.th. off*** odgrodzić coś murem **2.** otaczać ⟨otoczyć⟩ murem; **~ *s.th. up*** zamurować coś

'wall•chart *s* plansza *f*

wal•let ['wɒlɪt] *s* **1.** portfel *m* **2.** aktówka *f*

'wall•flow•er ['wɔːlflaʊə] *s* (*flower*) lak *m* pospolity; ***be a ~*** podpierać ściany (podczas zabawy tanecznej);

wal•lop ['wɔːləp] *infml* **I** *v/t* **1.** przywalić **2.** (*win*) rozgromić **II** *s* fanga *f*; ***give s.o. a ~*** przywalić komuś

wal•low ['wɔːləʊ] *v/i* **1.** nurzać się; **~ *in luxury*** pławić się w luksusie; **~ *in self-pity*** użalać się nad sobą **2.** wylegiwać się

'wall paint•ing *s* fresk *m*; **'wall•pa•per I** *s* tapeta *f* **II** *v/t* tapetować ⟨wy-⟩; **wall-to-wall 'car•pet** *s* wykładzina *f* dywanowa

wal•nut ['wɔːlnʌt] *s* orzech *m* włoski

wal•rus ['wɔːlrəs] *pl -ruses* ['~rəsɪz] *s* (*animal*) mors *m*; **wal•rus 'mous•tache** *s* sumiaste wąsy *pl*

waltz [wɔːlts] *s* MUS walc *m*

wand [wɒnd] *s* różdżka *f*

wand•er ['wɒndə] **I** *v/i* **1.** wędrować ⟨po-⟩ **2.** szwendać się **3.** nieśpiesznie iść ⟨pójść⟩ **4. ~ *off the subject*** *fig* zboczyć z tematu; ***don't let your mind ~*** nie rozpraszaj się; ***her thoughts ~ed back to her youth*** powróciła myślami do czasów swojej młodości; ***she let her gaze ~*** błądziła wzrokiem **II** *s* spacer *m*; ***have a ~*** przejść się; **wan•der•ings** ['wɒndərɪŋz] *pl* **1.** wędrówki *pl* **2.** podróże *pl*

wane [weɪn] **I** *v/i* **1.** maleć ⟨z-⟩; ***the moon ~s*** księżyca ubywa **2.** słabnąć ⟨o-⟩ **II** *s* ***be on the ~*** **a)** maleć **b)** słabnąć

wan•gle ['wæŋgl] *v/t infml* **1.** załatwiać ⟨-wić⟩; **~ *one's way out of*** wykręcić się z *G* **2.** wydębiać ⟨-bić⟩; ***I'll try to ~ some money out of my parents*** spróbuję wydębić trochę pieniędzy od rodziców

wank [wæŋk] *v/t Br infml* onanizować się; **wanker** ['wæŋkə] *s Br infml* palant *m*

wan•na ['wɒnə] *infml* → **want**; **~ *drink?*** masz ochotę się napić?; ***I ~ stay*** chcę zostać

wan•na•be ['wɒnəbɪ] *infml* **I** *s* kiepski naśladowca *m* **II** *adj* niedoszły

want [wɒnt] **I** *v/t* **1.** chcieć; ***he knows what he ~s*** on wie, czego chce; **~ *to do s.th.*** chcieć coś zrobić; **~ *s.o. to do s.th.*** chcieć, aby ktoś coś zrobił; **~ *s.th. done*** chcieć, aby coś zostało zrobione; **~ *in*** (***out***) chcieć wejść (wyjść) **2.** pragnąć; ***I ~ you*** pragnę cię **3.** potrzebować; ***you're ~ed on the phone*** jest pan proszony do tele-

W

fonu; ***this house ~s a good clean*** *infml* ten dom trzeba porządnie posprzątać; ***he doesn't ~ anything*** niczego mu nie brakuje **4.** (*advice*) ***you ~ to avoid alcohol*** *infml* powinnaś unikać alkoholu **II** *s* **1.** potrzeba *f*; ***be in ~ of*** potrzebować *G* **2.** pragnienie *n* **3.** brak *m* (***of*** *G*); ***for ~ of*** z braku *G* **4.** ubóstwo *n*; ***live in ~*** żyć w ubóstwie; **'want ad** *s Br* ogłoszenie *n* drobne

want•ed ['wɒntɪd] *adj* poszukiwany (przez policję); **want•ing** ['wɒntɪŋ] *adj* **1.** brakujący; ***they are not ~ in enthusiasm*** nie brakuje im entuzjazmu **2.** niezadowalający

wan•ton ['wɒntən] *adj* **1.** *violence, destruction*: bezsensowny **2.** *dated* wyuzdany

war [wɔː] *s* wojna *f* (***against*** przeciw *D*); ***the Second World ~*** druga wojna światowa; ***be at ~ with*** być w stanie wojny z *I*; ***declare ~ on*** wypowiedzieć wojnę *D*; **'war crime** *s* przestępstwo *n* wojenne; **'war crim•i•nal** *s* przestępca *m* wojenny; **'war cry** *s* okrzyk *m* wojenny; **'war me•mo•ri•al** *s* pomnik *m* ku czci poległych; **'war•paint** *s* **1.** barwy *pl* wojenne **2.** (*make-up*) *infml* tapeta *f*; **'war•path** *s*: ***on the ~*** na wojennej ścieżce; **'war•plane** *s* samolot *m* wojskowy; **'war•ship** *s* okręt *m* wojenny; **'war•time I** *s* **1.** czas *m* wojny; ***in ~*** w czasie wojny **2.** wojna *f* **II** *adj* podczas wojny

war•ble ['wɔːbl] *v/i* **1.** świergotać ⟨za-⟩ **2.** śpiewać ⟨za-⟩

ward [wɔːd] *s* **1.** (*hospital*) oddział *m* **2.** (*hospital*) sala *f* **3.** POLIT *Br* okręg *m* **4.** JUR podopieczny *m*; **ward off** *v/t* **1.** odpierać ⟨odeprzeć⟩ **2.** bronić ⟨o-⟩ się przed *I*; **war•den** ['wɔːdn] *s* **1.** strażnik *m*; ***a traffic ~*** strażnik miejski **2.** dozorca *m* **3.** strażnik *m* więzienny **4.** *Am* naczelnik *m* więzienia

'ward•robe ['wɔːdrəʊb] *s* **1.** szafa *f* **2.** garderoba *f*

ware [weə] *s* (*in combinations*) **1.** wyroby *pl* **2.** naczynia *pl*; ***silverware*** srebra; ***kitchenware*** naczynia kuchenne; **ware•house** ['weəhaʊs] *s* **1.** magazyn *m* **2.** hurtownia *f*; **wares** [weəz] *pl dated* towary *pl*

'war•fare *s* **1.** wojna *f* **2.** działania *pl* wojenne

'war•head *s* głowica *f* (bojowa)

war•i•ly ['weəɪlɪ] *adv* **1.** podejrzliwie **2.** nieufnie

'war•like *adj* **1.** wojowniczy **2.** wojenny; **'war•lord** *s* watażka *m*

warm [wɔːm] **I** *adj* **1.** ciepły; ***I'm ~*** jest mi ciepło **2.** serdeczny; ***a ~ welcome*** serdeczne przyjęcie **II** *adv* ciepło **III** *v/t* (*a.* ***~ up***) **1.** podgrzewać ⟨-rzać⟩; ***I'll ~ up some milk*** podgrzeję mleko **2.** rozgrzewać ⟨-rzać⟩ **3.** ogrzewać ⟨-rzać⟩ **IV** *v/i* (*a.* ***~ up***) **1.** podgrzewać ⟨-rzać⟩ się; ***the climate ~s up*** klimat się ociepla **2.** rozgrzewać ⟨-rzać⟩ się **3.** ogrzewać ⟨-rzać⟩ się **V** *s* ***the ~*** ciepło *n*; **warm up I** *v/i* **1.** → ***warm IV*** **2.** SPORT rozgrzewać ⟨-rzać⟩ się **3.** (*party*) rozkręcać ⟨-cić⟩ się **II** *v/t party*: rozkręcać ⟨-cić⟩

warm•blood•ed [wɔːm'blʌdɪd] *adj* BIOL stałocieplny

warm•heart•ed ['wɔːmhɑːtɪd] *adj* serdeczny

warm•ly ['wɔːmlɪ] *adv* **1.** ciepło; ***~ dressed*** ciepło ubrany **2.** serdecznie

war•mon•ger ['wɔːmʌŋgə] *s* podżegacz *m* wojenny

warmth [wɔːmθ] *s* **1.** ciepło *n* **2.** serdeczność *f*

'warm-up *s* SPORT rozgrzewka *f*

warn [wɔːn] *v/t* **1.** ostrzegać ⟨-rzec⟩ (***of/ against*** przed *I*); ***~ s.o. to keep away from*** ostrzec kogoś, aby trzymał się z daleka od *G*; ***~ s.o. against pickpockets*** ostrzec kogoś przed kieszonkowcami; ***~ s.o. off s.th.*** odradzić komuś coś **2.** uprzedzać ⟨-dzić⟩; ***she was ~ed that if she did it again she'd lose her job*** została uprzedzona, że jeżeli zrobi to raz jeszcze, straci pracę; **warn•ing** ['wɔːnɪŋ] **I** *s* ostrzeżenie *n*; ***without ~*** bez ostrzeżenia; ***the final ~*** ostatnie ostrzeżenie **II** *adj* ostrzegawczy; ***a ~ triangle*** trójkąt ostrzegawczy; ***fire a ~ shot*** oddać strzał ostrzegawczy

warp [wɔːp] **I** *v/i* **1.** wypaczać ⟨-czyć⟩ się **2.** odkształcać ⟨-cić⟩ się **3.** wyginać ⟨-giąć⟩ się **II** *v/t* **1.** wypaczać ⟨-czyć⟩ **2.** odkształcać ⟨-cić⟩ **3.** wyginać ⟨-giąć⟩; **warped** [wɔːpt] *adj*

W

1. wypaczony **2.** spaczony **3.** odkształcony **4.** wygięty
war•rant ['wɔːrənt] **I** *s* **1.** *JUR* nakaz *m* sądowy; ***issue a ~ for arrest*** wydać nakaz aresztowania **2.** upoważnienie *n* **3.** usprawiedliwienie *n*; ***there is no ~ for such criticism*** nie ma usprawiedliwienia dla takiej krytyki **II** *v/t* wymagać; ***further investigation is ~ed*** niezbędne jest dalsze dochodzenie; **war•ran•ty** ['wɔːrəntɪ] *s* gwarancja *f*; ***under ~*** na gwarancji
war•ri•or ['wɔːrɪə] *s* wojownik *m*
wart [wɔːt] *s ANAT* brodawka *f*; ***~s and all*** ze wszystkimi wadami
war•y ['weərɪ] *adj* **1.** ostrożny **2.** nieufny; ***be ~ of s.o.*** nie ufać komuś **3.** podejrzliwy
was [wɒz] *Past Simple* → ***be***
wash [wɒʃ] **I** *v/t* **1.** myć ⟨u-⟩; ***~ your hands*** umyj ręce; ***~ the car*** umyć samochód; ***~ one's hands of*** *fig* umywać od czegoś ręce; ***s.th. doesn't ~*** *infml* coś nie trzyma się kupy **2.** prać ⟨wy-⟩; ***~ the jeans*** wyprać dżinsy **3.** zmywać ⟨zmyć⟩; ***~ the dishes*** zmyć naczynia **II** *v/i* **1.** myć ⟨u-⟩ się; ***I ~ed and changed*** umyłem się i przebrałem **2.** (*clothes*) prać się **III** *s* **1.** mycie *n*; ***have a ~*** umyć się **2.** pranie *n*; ***your shirt is in the ~*** twoja koszula jest w praniu; ***it will come out in the ~*** *infml* to się okaże w praniu **3.** zmywanie *n* **4.** *paint*: warstwa *f* **5.** płyn *m* do mycia **6.** żel *m* myjący; **wash up I** *v/i* **1.** *Br* zmywać ⟨zmyć⟩ naczynia **2.** *Am* myć ⟨u-⟩ się **II** *v/t* **1.** *Br dishes*: zmywać ⟨zmyć⟩ **2.** wyrzucać ⟨-cić⟩ na brzeg
wash•a•ble ['wɒʃəbl] *adj* **1.** zmywalny **2.** nadający się do prania; ***'machine ~'*** „można prać w pralce"
'**wash•bag** *s Br* kosmetyczka *f*; '**wash-ba•sin**, '***wash•bowl*** *Am s* umywalka *f*; '**wash•cloth** *s Am* **1.** ścierka *f* **2.** ściereczka *f*; '**wash•day** *s* dzień *m* prania
washed-out [wɒʃt'aʊt] *adj* **1.** sprany **2.** *person*: wykończony; **washed-up** [wɒʃt'ʌp] *adj infml career*: skończony
wash•er ['wɒʃə] *s* **1.** *TECH* podkładka *f* **2.** *infml* pralka *f*
wash•ing ['wɒʃɪŋ] *s* **1.** pranie *n*; ***do the ~*** zrobić pranie; ***hang the ~ out*** rozwiesić pranie **2.** mycie *n*; ***a shampoo for frequent ~*** szampon do częstego stosowania; '**wash•ing line** *s* sznur *m* na bieliznę; '**wash•ing ma•chine** *s* pralka *f*
'**wash•out** *s infml* klapa *f*; '**wash•room** *s Am dated* toaleta *f*
was•n't ['wɒznt] *contracted form* → ***was not***
wasp [wɒsp] *s* osa *f*; **wasp•ish** ['wɒspɪʃ] *adj* **1.** *remark*: kąśliwy **2.** *look*: ostry, kłujący
waste [weɪst] **I** *v/t* **1.** marnować ⟨z-⟩; ***you're ~d as a teacher*** marnujesz się jako nauczyciel; ***don't ~ your sympathy on him*** nie żałuj go **2.** tracić ⟨s-⟩ **II** *s* **1.** strata *f*; ***a ~ of time*** strata czasu **2.** marnowanie *n* **3.** marnotrawstwo *n* **4.** odpady *pl* **5.** pustkowie *n*; **waste away** *v/i* marnieć ⟨z-⟩
'**waste•bas•ket** *s Am* kosz *m* na śmieci; '**waste dis•pos•al (unit)** *s Br* młynek *m* zlewozmywakowy; **wast•ed** ['weɪstɪd] *adj* **1.** zmarnowany **2.** daremny; ***she had a ~ trip – they weren't in*** pojechała tam na darmo – nie było ich w domu **3.** wychudzony **4.** *infml* narąbany, nawalony; **waste•ful** ['weɪstfʊl] *adj* **1.** rozrzutny **2.** nieekonomiczny; '**waste•land** *s* **1.** nieużytki *pl* **2.** teren *m* niezagospodarowany; **waste'pa•per** *s* makulatura *f*; **waste•pa•per 'bas•ket** *Br* kosz *m* na śmieci; '**waste pipe** *s* rura *f* kanalizacyjna; **waste prod•uct** *s* odpad *m* produkcyjny
wast•er ['weɪstə] *s* marnotrawca *m*; ***he's a time ~*** marnuje czas
watch [wɒtʃ] **I** *s* **1.** (*hand*) zegarek *m* **2.** obserwacja *f*; ***keep a ~ on*** obserwować *A*; ***keep ~*** pilnować **3.** wachta *f* **II** *v/t* **1.** oglądać ⟨obejrzeć⟩; ***~ television*** oglądać telewizję **2.** przyglądać się; ***~ s.o. doing s.th.*** przyglądać się, jak ktoś coś robi **3.** obserwować **4.** pilnować ⟨po-⟩ **5.** uważać na *A*; ***~ yourself*** uważaj na siebie; ***~ one's step*** uważać; ***~ your bag*** uważaj na swoją torbę; ***~ every penny*** *fig* liczyć każdy grosz; **watch for** *v/i* czekać na *A*; **watch out** *v/i* uważać; **watch out for** *v/i* uważać na *A*
'**watch•band** *s Am* → ***watch strap***; '**watch•dog** *s* niezależna organizacja *f* pozarządowa; ***a consumer ~*** organi-

zacja ochrony praw konsumentów; **watch•ful** ['wɒθful] *adj* **1.** czujny **2.** uważny; **'watch•mak•er** *s* zegarmistrz *m*; **watch•man** ['wɒtʃmən] *pl -men s dated* stróż *m*; **'watch strap** *s Br* pasek *m* do zegarka; **'watch•tow•er** *s* wieża *f* strażnicza, strażnica *f*; **'watch•word** *s* **1.** dewiza *f* **2.** hasło *n*

wa•ter ['wɔːtə] **I** *s* woda *f*; ***a glass of ~*** szklanka wody; ***drinking ~*** woda pitna; ***running ~*** woda bieżąca; ***dive under the ~*** zanurkować; ***it's all ~ under the bridge*** było, minęło; ***territorial ~s*** wody terytorialne **II** *v/t* **1.** podlewać ⟨-lać⟩ **2.** poić ⟨na-⟩ **3.** nawadniać ⟨-wodnić⟩; ***~ s.th. down*** rozcieńczyć coś wodą **III** *v/i* **1.** (*eyes*) łzawić **2.** ***the smell makes my mouth ~*** gdy czuję ten zapach, to aż cieknie mi ślinka; **'wa•ter bed** *s* łóżko *n* wodne; **'wa•ter bird** *s* ptak *m* wodny; **'wa•ter bot•tle** *s* **1.** bidon *m* **2.** manierka *f* **3.** butelka *f* na wodę; **'wa•ter buf•fa•lo** *s* bawół *m* domowy; **'wa•ter butt** *s* zbiornik *m* na deszczówkę; **'wa•ter can•non** *s* działko *n* wodne; **'wa•ter•col•our** *Br*, ***'wa•ter•col•or*** *Am s* akwarela *f*; **'wa•ter cool•er** *s* **1.** urządzenie *n* do chłodzenia wody **2.** *INF* zestaw *m* do chłodzenia wodą; **'wa•ter•course** *s* **1.** ciek *m* **2.** droga *f* wodna **3.** koryto *n* (rzeki); **'wa•ter•cress** *s* **1.** *BIOL* rukiew *f* wodna **2.** *COOK* rzeżucha *f*

wa•tered-down [wɔːtəd'daʊn] *adj* rozcieńczony

'wa•ter•fall *s* wodospad *m*; **'wa•ter•front I** *s* **1.** nadbrzeże *n* **2.** nabrzeże *n* **II** *adj* nadbrzeżny; **'wa•ter hole** *s* wodopój *m*; **'wa•ter ice** *s Br* sorbet *m*

wa•ter•ing can ['wɔːtərɪŋkʌn] *s* konewka *f*; **'wa•ter•ing hole** → ***water hole***; **'wa•ter•ing pot** *s Am* → ***watering can***

'wa•ter jump *s SPORT* rów *m* z wodą; **'wa•ter lev•el** *s* poziom *m* wody; **'wa•ter lil•y** *s* lilia *f* wodna; **'wa•ter•line** *s* lina *f* wodna, wodnica *f*; **wa•ter•logged** ['wɒtəlɒgd] *adj* **1.** rozmokły **2.** *boat*: pełen wody; **'wa•ter main** *s* magistrala *f* wodociągowa; **'wa•ter•mark** *s* znak *m* wodny; **'wa•ter•mel•on** *s* arbuz *m*; **'wa•ter me•ter** *s* wodomierz *m*; **'wa•ter pipe** *s* **1.** rura *f* wodociągowa **2.** fajka *f* wodna; **'wa•ter pis•tol** *s* pistolet *m* na wodę; **'wa•ter pol•lu•tion** *s* zanieczyszczenie *n* wody; **'wa•ter po•lo** *s SPORT* waterpolo *n*, piłka *f* wodna; **'wa•ter•proof I** *adj* **1.** nieprzemakalny **2.** wodoodporny **II** *s* **1.** płaszcz *m* nieprzemakalny **2.** **~s** odzież *f* nieprzemakalna **III** *v/t* impregnować ⟨za-⟩; **'wa•ter•shed** *s* **1.** *fig* punkt *m* zwrotny **2.** *GEOGR* dział *m* wodny; **'wa•ter•side I** *s* **1.** brzeg *m* **2.** nadbrzeże *n* **II** *adj* nadbrzeżny; **'wa•ter-ski** *v/i* jeździć na nartach wodnych; **'wa•ter-ski•ing** *s* **1.** jazda *f* na nartach wodnych **2.** narciarstwo *n* wodne; **'wa•ter sup•ply** *s* **1.** woda *f* **2.** zaopatrzenie *n* w wodę **3.** zapasy *pl* wody; **'wa•ter ta•ble** *s* poziom *m* wód gruntowych; **'wa•ter•tight** *adj* **1.** wodoszczelny **2.** niepodważalny **3.** *alibi*: żelazny; **'wa•ter va•pour** *Br*, ***'wa•ter va•por*** *Am s* para *f* wodna; **'wa•ter•way** *s* droga *f* wodna; **'wa•ter wheel** *s* koło *n* wodne; **'wa•ter•wings** *pl* rękawki *pl* do pływania; **wa•ter•works** ['wɔːtərwɜrks] *pl* **1.** zakłady *pl* wodociągowe **2.** wodociągi *pl*

wa•ter•y ['wɔːtərɪ] *adj* wodnisty

watt [wɒt] *s PHYS* wat

wave [weɪv] **I** *v/t* **1.** machać ⟨po-⟩; ***~ one's hand*** pomachać ręką; ***I ~d her goodbye*** pomachałem jej na pożegnanie; ***~ s.th. away*** odrzucić coś **2.** wymachiwać **II** *v/i* **1.** machać ⟨po-⟩ (***at/to*** *D*) **2.** (*flag*) powiewać **3.** (*hair*) układać ⟨ułożyć⟩ się w fale **III** *s* **1.** *a. fig* fala *f*; ***radio ~s*** fale radiowe; ***sound ~*** fale dźwiękowe; ***a ~ of protest*** fala protestów; ***a crime ~*** fala przestępczości **2.** machnięcie *n*; ***give s.o. a ~*** pomachać komuś ręką; **'wave band** *s RADIO* pasmo *n* (częstotliwości); **'wave•length** *s* **1.** długość *f* fali **2.** częstotliwość *f*; ***be on the same ~*** *fig* nadawać na tych samych falach

wa•ver ['weɪvə] **I** *v/i* **1.** wahać ⟨za-⟩ się (***between*** między *I*) **2.** (*voice*) drżeć ⟨za-⟩ **3.** (*light*) migotać ⟨za-⟩ **4.** (*determination*) słabnąć ⟨o-⟩ **II** *s* niezdecydowany *m*

wav•y ['weɪvɪ] *adj hair*: falujący

wax[1] [wæks] **I** *s* wosk *m* **II** *v/t* **1.** woskować ⟨na-⟩ **2.** depilować ⟨wy-⟩ woskiem

W

wax[2] [~] *v/i* **1.** ***the moon ~es*** księżyca przybywa **2.** stawać się; ***~ sentimental*** stawać się sentymentalnym

wax•en ['wæksən] *adj* **1.** woskowy **2.** z wosku

'wax mu•se•um *s* muzeum *m* figur woskowych; **'wax•work** *s* figura *f* woskowa; ***~s*** *Br* muzeum figur woskowych

wax•y ['wæksɪ] *adj* **1.** woskowy **2.** woskowaty

way [weɪ] **I** *s* **1.** droga *f*; ***can you tell me the ~ to the station?*** czy może mi pan powiedzieć, jak dojść na dworzec?; ***the ~ back*** droga powrotna; ***the ~ home*** droga do domu; ***the ~ in*** wejście; ***the ~ out*** wyjście; ***get out of my ~!*** z drogi!; ***be on the ~*** być w drodze; ***give ~*** AUTO ustąpić pierwszeństwa przejazdu; ***lose one's ~*** zgubić się; ***make ~*** zrobić miejsce; ***by way of*** **a)** przez *A* **a)** tytułem *G* **c)** jako *N*; ***by ~ of introduction*** tytułem wstępu; ***by the ~*** przy okazji, à propos **2.** sposób *m*; ***infectious diseases can be acquired in several ~s*** chorobami zakaźnymi można się zarazić na kilka sposobów; ***I'll do it my ~*** zrobię to po swojemu; ***one ~ or another*** tak czy inaczej; ***in a ~*** w pewnym sensie; ***no ~!*** nic z tego! **3.** kierunek *m*; ***this ~*** tędy, w tym kierunku **4.** strona *f*; ***which ~?*** w którą stronę? **5.** zwyczaj *m* **6.** sposób *m* bycia **7.** odległość *f*; ***be a long ~ from*** być daleko od *G*; ***Easter is still a long ~ off*** do Wielkanocy jeszcze daleko **II** *adv* ***~ behind*** daleko w tyle; ***it's ~ past his bedtime*** już dawno powinien być w łóżku; ***~ too long*** o wiele za długi; ***~ back*** dawno temu; **'way•bill** *s* list *m* przewozowy; **way•'lay** (*waylaid*; *waylaid*) *v/t* zatrzymywać ⟨-mać⟩ (w drodze); **'way•side I** *s* pobocze *n*; ***by the ~*** przy drodze; ***fall by the ~*** (*plan*) spalić na panewce, *infml* nie wypalić **II** *adv hotel*: przydrożny; **way•ward** ['weɪwəd] *adj* **1.** niesforny **2.** przekorny

we [wiː] *pron* my

weak [wiːk] *adj* słaby; ***~ in maths*** słaby z matematyki; ***in a ~ moment*** w chwili słabości; **weak•en** ['wiːkn] **I** *v/t* osłabiać ⟨-bić⟩ **II** *v/i* **1.** słabnąć ⟨o-⟩ **2.** (*person*) *infml* mięknąć ⟨z-⟩

weak-kneed [wiːk'niːd] *adj infml* bojaźliwy

weak•ling ['wiːklɪŋ] *s* słabeusz *m*; **weak•ly** ['wiːklɪ] *adv* słabo; **weak•ness** ['wiːknɪs] *s* słabość *f*; ***a sign of ~*** oznaka słabości; ***have a ~ for*** mieć słabość do

weal [wiːl] *s Br* **1.** pręga *f* **2.** ślad *m* po uderzeniu

wealth [welθ] *s* **1.** bogactwo *n* **2.** zamożność *f* **3.** majątek *m* **4.** obfitość *f*; ***a ~ of information*** mnóstwo informacji; **wealth•y** ['welθɪ] *adj* **1.** bogaty; ***the ~*** bogaci **2.** zamożny

wean [wiːn] *v/t* **1.** odstawiać ⟨-wić⟩ od piersi **2.** odzwyczajać ⟨-czaić⟩ (***s.o. off/from*** kogoś od *G*) **3.** ***be ~ed on*** być wychowanym na *L*

weap•on ['wepən] *s a. fig* broń *f*; ***a murder ~*** narzędzie zbrodni; **weap•on•ry** ['wepənrɪ] *s* broń *f*

wear [weə] **I** (*wore*; *worn*) *v/t* **1.** nosić; ***she always ~s black*** zawsze ubiera się na czarno **2.** *face expression*: mieć; ***~ a smile*** uśmiechać się; ***~ an angry expression*** wyglądać na rozgniewanego **3.** *hole*: robić ⟨z-⟩ **II** (*wore*; *worn*) *v/i* **1.** niszczyć ⟨z-⟩ się **2.** wycierać ⟨wytrzeć⟩ się **3.** zużywać ⟨-żyć⟩ się **III** *s* **1.** odzież *f*; ***ladies' ~*** odzież damska **2.** ubiór *m* **3.** noszenie *n* **4.** zużycie *n*; ***~ and tear*** normalne zużycie; **wear away I** *v/i* **1.** wycierać ⟨wytrzeć⟩ się **2.** ścierać ⟨zetrzeć⟩ się **II** *v/t* **1.** wycierać ⟨wytrzeć⟩ **2.** ścierać ⟨zetrzeć⟩; **wear down I** *v/t* **1.** ścierać ⟨zetrzeć⟩ **2.** osłabiać ⟨-bić⟩ **3.** męczyć ⟨z-⟩ **II** *v/i* **1.** ścierać ⟨zetrzeć⟩ się **2.** zużywać ⟨-żyć⟩ się; **wear off** *v/i* **1.** ***the effects of the drug ~ after 12 hours*** działanie leku utrzymuje się przez 12 godzin **2.** przestawać ⟨-tać⟩ działać **3.** ścierać ⟨zetrzeć⟩ się; **wear on** *v/i* (*time*) wlec się; **wear out I** *v/i* **1.** niszczyć ⟨z-⟩ się **2.** zużywać ⟨-żyć⟩ się **3.** (*patience*) wyczerpywać ⟨-pać⟩ się **II** *v/t* **1.** niszczyć ⟨z-⟩ **2.** zużywać ⟨-żyć⟩ **3.** *infml* wykańczać ⟨-kończyć⟩ **4.** męczyć ⟨wy-⟩

wea•ri•ly ['wɪərɪlɪ] *adj* ze znużeniem; ***tread ~*** wlec się

wear•ing ['weərɪŋ] *adj* **1.** wyczerpujący **2.** bardzo męczący

wea•ri•some ['wɪərɪsəm] *adj* nużący

wear•y ['wɪərɪ] **I** *adj* **1.** wyczerpany **2.** bardzo zmęczony **3.** znużony (***of*** *I*) **4.** znudzony (***of*** *I*) **II** *v/t* **1.** męczyć ⟨z-⟩ **2.** nużyć ⟨z-⟩ **3.** nudzić ⟨z-⟩
wea•sel ['wi:zl] **I** *s* łasica *f* **II** *v/i infml* wykręcać ⟨-cić⟩ się (***out of*** od *G*)
weath•er ['weðə] **I** *s* pogoda *f*; ***did you have good ~?*** mieliście ładną pogodę?; ***in this ~*** w taką pogodę; ***if the ~ holds*** jeżeli pogoda się utrzyma; ***~ permitting*** jeżeli pogoda pozwoli; ***in all ~s*** bez względu na pogodę; ***feel under the ~*** *infml* nie czuć się najlepiej **II** *v/t* **1.** *recession*: przetrwać **2.** ***his face was ~ed by the sun*** jego twarz była ogorzała od słońca **III** *v/i* wietrzeć ⟨z-⟩; '**weath•er-beat•en** *adj face*: ogorzały; '**weath•er chart** *s* mapa *f* pogody; '**weath•er cock** *s* wiatrowskaz *m* (w kształcie koguta); '**weath•er eye** *s*: ***keep a ~ on*** mieć oko na *A*; '**weath•er fore•cast** *s* prognoza *f* pogody; '**weath•er•man** *pl* **-men** *s infml* prezenter *m* prognozy pogody; '**weath•er map** *s* mapa *f* pogody; '**weath•er•proof** *adj* **1.** nieprzemakalny **2.** wodoszczelny **3.** odporny na wpływy atmosferyczne; '**weath•er sat•el•lite** *s* satelita *m* meteorologiczny; '**weath•er sta•tion** *s* stacja *f* meteorologiczna; '**weath•er vane** *s* wiatrowskaz *m*
weave [wi:v] **I** (*wove*; *woven*) *v/t* **1.** tkać ⟨u-⟩ **2.** pleść ⟨u-⟩, wyplatać **3.** *story*: snuć **4.** ***~ one's way between the tables*** przejść zygzakiem między stołami **II** (*wove*; *woven*) *v/i* (*river*) wić się **III** *s* splot *m*; **weav•er** ['wi:və] *s* tkacz *m*
web [web] *s* **1.** pajęczyna *f* **2.** sieć *f* **3.** *streets*: labirynt **4.** błona *f* pławna **4.** ***the ~*** *INF* Internet, *infml* sieć; '**web page** *s INF* strona *f* internetowa; '**web site** → ***web page***
wed [wed] (*wedded*/*wed*; *wedded*/*wed*) **I** *v/t* poślubiać ⟨-bić⟩ **II** *v/i* pobierać ⟨-brać⟩ się
we'd [wi:d] *contracted form* → ***we had, we would***

W

wed•ding ['wedɪŋ] **I** *s* **1.** ślub *m* **2.** wesele *n* **II** *adj* **1.** ślubny **2.** weselny; '**wed•ding an•ni•ver•sa•ry** *s* rocznica *f* ślubu; '**wed•ding cake** *s* tort *m* weselny; '**wed•ding day** *s* dzień *m* ślubu; '**wed•ding dress** *s* suknia *f* ślubna; '**wed•ding ring** *s* obrączka *f*
wedge [wedʒ] **I** *s* **1.** klin *m*; ***drive a ~ between*** *fig* wbić klin pomiędzy x i y **2.** *cake*, *orange*: (trójkątny) kawałek *m* **II** *v/t* ***he was ~d in a narrow corridor*** zaklinował się w wąskim korytarzu; ***~ a door*** zaklinować drzwi, żeby się nie zamknęły; '**wedge-shaped** *adj* w kształcie klina
wed•lock ['wedlɔk] *s dated* związek *m* małżeński; ***she was born out of ~*** jest nieślubnym dzieckiem
Wed•nes•day ['wenzdeɪ] *s* środa *f*
wee[1] [wi:] *adj* malutki; ***a ~ bit*** odrobinka
wee[2] [~] *infml* **I** *s* siku *n* **II** *v/i* robić ⟨z-⟩ siku
weed [wi:d] **I** *s* **1.** chwast *m* **2.** ***the ~*** *infml* tytoń *m*; ***give up the ~*** rzucić palenie **3.** (*marijuana*) *infml* trawka *f* **4.** *Br infml* mięczak *m* **5.** *Br infml* cherlak *m* **II** *v/t* pielić ⟨wy-⟩; **weed out** *v/t* wyplenić; '**weed-kill•er** *s* środek *m* chwastobójczy; **weed•y** ['wi:dɪ] *adj* **1.** *Br infml* cherlawy **2.** zachwaszczony
week [wi:k] *s* tydzień *m*; ***~ after ~*** *infml* przez wiele tygodni; ***~ by ~*** tydzień po tygodniu; ***a ~ from tomorrow*** od jutra za tydzień; ***we'll see Monday week*** *Br* zobaczymy się za tydzień, licząc od poniedziałku; '**week•day** *s* dzień *m* roboczy; **week•'end** **I** *s* weekend *m*; ***at the ~*** w weekend **II** *v/i* spędzać ⟨-dzić⟩ weekend; '**week•long** *adj* tygodniowy; **week•ly** ['wi:klɪ] **I** *adj* **1.** tygodniowy **2.** cotygodniowy; ***a ~ magazine*** tygodnik **II** *adj* **1.** co tydzień; ***twice ~*** dwa razy w tygodniu **2.** raz na tydzień **III** *s* tygodnik *m*
wee•ny ['wi:nɪ] *adj infml* malutki
weep [wi:p] **I** (*wept*; *wept*) *v/i* **1.** szlochać, (***over*** nad *I*, z powodu *G*) **2.** płakać (***over*** nad *I*, z powodu *G*) **3.** opłakiwać (***for*** *A*) **4.** ropieć **5.** krwawić **II** *s* ***have a ~*** płakać, wypłakać się; '**weep•ing wil•low** *s* wierzba *f* płacząca; **weep•y** ['wi:pɪ] **I** *adj* płaczliwy **II** *s* (*film*, *book*) *infml* wyciskacz *m* łez
'**wee-wee** → **wee**[2]
weft [weft] *s* nić *f* wątkowa, wątek *m*
weigh [weɪ] **I** *v/i* **1.** ważyć; ***how much do you ~?*** ile ważysz? **2.** ***~ against***

przemawiać przeciwko *D* **II** *v/t* **1.** ważyć ⟨z-⟩ **2.** odważać ⟨-żyć⟩ **3.** (*a.* **~up**) rozważać ⟨-żyć⟩; ***~ up the pros and cons*** rozważyć wszelkie za i przeciw **4.** ***~ one's words*** starannie dobierać słowa **5.** ***~ anchor*** podnieść kotwicę; **weigh down** *v/t* **1.** przygniatać ⟨-nieść⟩; ***I was weighed down with baggage*** miałem bardzo ciężki bagaż **2.** ***one's responsibilities weigh s.o. down*** ktoś ugina się pod ciężarem obowiązków; ***he was weighed down with guilt*** dręczyło go głębokie poczucie winy; **weigh on** *v/t*: ***the responsibilities weigh heavily on her*** ugina się pod ciężarem obowiązków; **weigh up** *v/t* **1.** taksować **2.** oceniać ⟨-nić⟩

weight [weɪt] **I** *s* **1.** waga *f*; ***lose ~*** schudnąć, stracić na wadze; ***put on ~*** przytyć, przybrać na wadze; ***watch one's ~*** dbać o linię **2.** ciężar *m*; ***his decision took a ~ off my mind*** *fig* ulżyło mi, kiedy podjął decyzję **3.** ciężarek *m* **4.** waga *f*, znaczenie *n* **II** *v/t* **1.** obciążać ⟨-żyć⟩ (***s.th. with*** coś *I*) **2.** wyważać ⟨-żyć⟩; **'weight cat•e•go•ry, 'weight di•vi•sion** *s* SPORT kategoria *f* wagowa; **'weight•less** ['weɪtləs] *adj* PHYS znajdujący się w stanie nieważkości; **'weight•less•ness** ['weɪtləsnəs] *s* PHYS nieważkość *f*; **'weight-lift•er** *s* SPORT ciężarowiec *m*; **'weight-lift•ing** *s* SPORT podnoszenie *n* ciężarów; **'weight train•ing** *s* ćwiczenia *pl* siłowe; **weight•y** ['weɪtɪ] *adj* **1.** ważki **2.** ważny **3.** ciężki

weir [wɪə] *s* jaz *m*

weird [wɪəd] *adj* **1.** dziwny **2.** dziwaczny **3.** niesamowity; **weird•ly** ['wɪədlɪ] *adv* **1.** dziwnie **2.** dziwacznie **3.** niesamowicie; **weird•o** ['wɪədəʊ] *pl -dos s* **1.** dziwak *m* **2.** oryginał *m*

wel•come ['welkəm] **I** *interj* witamy!, witam!; ***~ home*** witaj w domu; ***~ to London*** witamy w Londynie **II** *s* **1.** powitanie *n* **2.** przyjęcie *n*; ***give s.o. a warm ~*** przyjąć kogoś serdecznie; ***outstay one's ~*** nadużywać czyjejś gościnności **III** *adj* **1.** mile widziany; ***I had the feeling we were not ~*** miałem wrażenie, że nie byliśmy mile widziani; ***they are ~ to stay*** będzie mi miło, jak zostaną **2.** (*response*) ***you're ~!*** proszę bardzo!, nie ma za co! **IV** *v/t* **1.** witać ⟨przy-, po-⟩ **2.** przyjmować ⟨-jąć⟩; ***~ s.o. with open arms*** przyjąć kogoś z otwartymi ramionami; ***I'd ~ any suggestions*** będę wdzięczny za wszelkie sugestie

weld [weld] **I** *v/t* **1.** spawać ⟨ze-, przy-⟩ **2.** zgrzewać ⟨-rzać⟩ **3.** *fig* łączyć ⟨po-⟩ **4.** *fig* jednoczyć ⟨z-⟩ **II** *s* **1.** spaw *m* **2.** spoina *f*; **weld•er** ['weldə] *s* spawacz *m*

wel•fare ['welfeə] *s* **1.** dobro *n* **2.** dobrobyt *m* **3.** opieka *f* społeczna **4.** zasiłek *m*; ***live on ~*** żyć z zasiłku; **wel•fare 'state** *s* państwo *n* opiekuńcze; **'wel•fare work•er** *s* pracownik *m* opieki społecznej

well[1] [wel] **I** (*better*; *best*) *adv* **1.** dobrze; ***~ done!*** bardzo dobrze!, dobra robota!; ***be doing ~*** **a)** mieć się dobrze **b)** dobrze sobie radzić; ***be ~ aware of*** dobrze sobie zdawać sprawę z *G*; ***I could very ~ leave now*** równie dobrze mógłbym teraz wyjść; ***as ~*** także, również; ***as ~ as*** oraz **2.** dużo; ***~ in advance*** dużo wcześniej **3.** bardzo, mocno; ***he was driving ~ over the speed limit*** jechał z prędkością znacznie wyższą od dozwolonej; ***I like him ~ enough*** nawet go lubię **II** *interj* **1.** cóż; ***oh, ~*** no cóż; ***~, ~!*** no proszę! **2.** a więc **III** (*better*; *best*) *adj* zdrowy; ***I don't feel very ~*** nie najlepiej się czuję; ***all's ~ that ends ~*** wszystko dobre, co się dobrze kończy; ***it's all very ~ for you to criticize*** łatwo ci krytykować; ***that's all ~ and good but*** to wszystko ładnie, ale

well[2] [~] **I** *s* **1.** studnia *f* **2.** szyb *m* **3.** odwiert *m* **II** *v/i* (*a.* **~ up**) napływać ⟨-łynąć⟩; ***tears were ~ing up in her eyes*** łzy napływały jej do oczu

we'll [wiːl] *contracted form* → ***we will***

well-ad'vised *adj* rozsądny; **well-ap'point•ed** *adj* komfortowo wyposażony; **well-'bal•anced** *adj* **1.** *person*: zrównoważony **2.** *meal*: dobrze zbilansowany; **well-be•'haved** *adj child*: dobrze wychowany; **well-'be•ing** *s* dobre samopoczucie *n*; ***the economic ~ of a nation*** dobrobyt kraju; **3.** dobrostan *n*; **well-'born** *adj* dobrze urodzony; **well-'built** *adj* **1.** *person*: dobrze zbudowany **2.** *building*: solidny; **well-dis•'posed** *adj* przychylnie nastawiony (***towards*** do *G*); **well-'done** *adj steak*: dobrze wysmażony; **well-'dressed** *adj* elegancko ubrany; **well-'earned** *adj rest*: zasłużony; **well-'found•ed** *adj suspicion*: uzasadniony; **well-'groomed** *adj* zadbany; **well-'heeled** *adj* (*rich*) *infml* nadziany; **well-in'formed** *adj* dobrze poinformowany; **well-in'ten•tioned** *adj* **1.** ***be*** **~** mieć dobre intencje **2.** *project, action*: wynikający z dobrych intencji; **well-'kept** *adj* **1.** *garden*: dobrze utrzymany **2.** *secret*: pilnie strzeżony; **well-'known** *adj* znany, sławny; **well-'made** *adj* **1.** *person, animal*: dobrze zbudowany **2.** *object*: solidnie wykonany; **well-'man•nered** *adj form* **1.** uprzejmy **2.** dobrze wychowany; **well-'mean•ing** *adj* **1.** ***be*** **~** mieć dobre intencje **2.** *try*: wynikający z dobrych intencji; **well-'meant** *adj* **1.** *offer*: złożony w dobrej wierze **2.** wynikający z dobrych intencji; **well-nigh** ['welnaɪ] *adv form* niemal; **well-'off** *adj* dobrze sytuowany; **well-'paid** *adj* **1.** *job*: dobrze płatny **2.** *person*: dobrze opłacany; **well-pro'por•tioned** *adj* proporcjonalny; **well-'read** *adj* oczytany; **well-'thought-of** *adj* **1.** ceniony **2.** poważany; **well-'timed** *adj action*: podjęty w porę; **well-to-'do** *adj* zamożny; **'well-wish•er** *s* życzliwy *m*; **well-'worn** *adj* **1.** znoszony **2.** *fig* oklepany

welsh [welʃ] *v/i*: ***~ on one's promise*** *infml* nie dotrzymać słowa

Welsh [welʃ] **I** *adj* walijski **II** *s* **1.** język *m* walijski **2.** ***the ~*** Walijczycy *pl*; ***Welsh•man*** ['welʃmən] *pl -men s* Walijczyk *m*; **'Welsh•wom•an** *pl -men s* Walijka *f*

welt [welt] *s* **1.** ślad *m* po uderzeniu **2.** pręga *f* **3.** obrzęk *m*

wel•ter•weight ['weltəweɪt] *s* SPORT **1.** waga *f* półśrednia **2.** bokser *m* wagi półśredniej

W

went [went] *Past Simple* → **go**

wept [wept] *Past Simple and Past Participle* → **weep**

we're [wɪə] *contracted form* → **we are**

were [wə] *Past Simple* → **be**

weren't [wɜnt] *contracted form* → ***were not***

were•wolf ['weəwʊlf] *pl -wolves s* wilkołak *m*

west [west] **I** *s* ***the ~*** zachód *m*; ***in the ~*** na zachodzie; ***to the ~ of*** na zachód od *G*; ***the ~*** Zachód **II** *adj* zachodni **III** *adv* na zachód; ***the window faces ~*** okno wychodzi na zachód; **'west-bound** *adj* **1.** prowadzący na zachód **2.** jadący na zachód

west•er•ly ['westəlɪ] **I** *adj* zachodni **II** *s* wiatr *m* zachodni

west•ern ['westən] **I** *adj* zachodni; ***~ Spain*** zachodnia Hiszpania **II** FILM *s* western *m*; **west•ern•er** ['westənə] *s* mieszkaniec *m* Zachodu; **west•ern-most** ['westənməʊst] *adj* najbardziej wysunięty na zachód

west•ward ['westwəd] **I** *adj* zachodni **II** *adv* na zachód

wet [wet] **I** *adj* **1.** mokry; ***you'll get ~*** zmokniesz; ***it's ~ outside*** na dworze jest mokro; ***~ through*** przemoczony do suchej nitki; ***'~ paint'*** „świeżo malowane"; ***~ behind the ears*** *fig* zielony, niedoświadczony **2.** wilgotny **3.** *weather*: deszczowy **4.** *Br infml person*: miękki; ***don't be so ~!*** nie bądź mięczakiem! **II** *v/t* **1.** moczyć 〈z-〉; ***~ one's bed*** zmoczyć się w nocy; ***~ oneself*** zmoczyć się **2.** zwilżać 〈-żyć〉 **III** *s* **1.** ***the ~*** deszcz *m* **2.** ***the ~*** woda *f* **3.** *Br infml* mięczak *m*; **wet 'blan•ket** *s infml* smutas *m*; ***don't be such a ~!*** nie psuj zabawy!; **'wet suit** *s* kombinezon *m* piankowy, *infml* pianka *f*

we've [wiːv] *contracted form* → ***we have***

whack [wæk] **I** *v/t infml* **1.** walić 〈-lnąć〉 **2.** przywalić **II** *s infml* **1.** walnięcie *n*; ***give s.o. a ~*** przywalić komuś **2.** *Br infml* działka *f*, część *f*; ***do one's ~*** zrobić swoje **3.** ***be out of ~*** *Am infml* fiksować; **whacked** [wækt] *adj Br infml* skonany; **whack•ing** ['wækɪŋ] *adj Br infml* **1.** ogromny **2.** wielgachny; **whack•y** ['wækɪ] *adj* stuknięty

whale [weɪl] *s* wieloryb *m*; ***have a ~ of time*** świetnie się bawić

whal•er ['weɪlə] *s* wielorybnik *m*; **whal-ing** ['weɪlɪŋ] *s* wielorybnictwo *n*

wharf [wɔːf] *pl wharves s* nabrzeże *n*
what [wɒt] *pron* co; **~'s for lunch?** co jest na lunch?; **~ for?** po co?; **~ about a game of tennis?** może zagramy w tenisa?; **~ if...** a co wtedy, jeśli...; **he told me ~ to do** powiedział mi, co mam robić; **know ~'s ~** wiedzieć, o co chodzi; **~ luck!** co za szczęście!; **~ a beautiful house!** jaki ładny dom!; **~ a pity!** jaka szkoda!
what•ev•er [wɒt'evə] **I** *pron* **1.** cokolwiek; **do ~ you like** rób, co chcesz; **don't tell her, ~ you do!** pod żadnym pozorem jej o tym nie mów! **2.** *infml* wszystko jedno **II** *adv* **1. none ~** absolutnie żaden; **they received no help ~** nie otrzymali absolutnie żadnej pomocy **2.** *infml* cokolwiek się stanie
whats•it ['wɒtsɪt] *s Br infml* dynks *m*; **where's the ~ you change channels with?** gdzie jest to – jak to się nazywa – czym zmienia się programy?
what•so•ev•er [wɒtsəʊ'evə] → **whatever II.1**
wheat [wiːt] *s* pszenica *f*; **separate the ~ from the chaff** *fig* oddzielić ziarno od plew
whee•dle ['wiːdl] *v/t* **1.** *money*: *infml* wyciągać ⟨-gnąć⟩ (**out of** od *G*) **2. ~ s.o. into doing s.th.** nakłonić kogoś do zrobienia czegoś
wheel [wiːl] *s* **I** *s* **1.** koło *n*; **my own ~s** *infml* moje własne cztery kółka **2.** kierownica *f*, *infml* kółko *n*; **behind the ~** za kierownicą **II** *v/t* **1.** pchać ⟨pchnąć⟩ **2.** *bike*: prowadzić **3.** wieźć ⟨przy-⟩ (na wózku) **III** *v/i* (*birds*) krążyć; **wheel around** *v/i* odwracać ⟨-rócić⟩ się
'wheel•bar•row *s* taczka *f*; **'wheel•base** *s AUTO* rozstaw *m* osi; **'wheel•chair** *s* wózek *m* inwalidzki; **confined to a ~** przykuty do wózka inwalidzkiego; **'wheel clamp** *s* blokada *f* na koła
wheeled [wiːld] *adj*: **a sixteen-~ lorry** szesnastokołowa ciężarówka
wheel•er-deal•er [wiːlə'diːle] *s infml* kombinator *m*
wheel•ie bin ['wiːlɪ bɪn] *s* pojemnik *m* na śmieci na kółkach
wheel•ing and deal•ing [wiːlɪŋən'diːlɪŋ] *s* **1.** kombinacje *pl* **2.** machinacje *pl*
wheeze [wiːz] **I** *v/i* **1.** mieć świszczący oddech **2.** rzęzić **II** *s* **1.** świszczący oddech *m* **2.** rzężenie *n*
when [wen] **I** *adv* kiedy; **~ can I see you?** kiedy możemy się zobaczyć?; **the day ~** dzień, w którym **II** *pron* kiedy; **until ~ can you stay?** do kiedy możesz zostać?; **since ~?** od kiedy? **III** *conj* kiedy; **call me ~ you have finished** zadzwoń do mnie, kiedy skończysz
whence [wens] *adv dated* skąd; **they returned ~ they had come** wrócili tam, skąd przyszli
when•ev•er [wen'evə] **I** *conj* **1.** kiedykolwiek; **~ you want** kiedy tylko chcesz **2.** zawsze kiedy **3.** obojętnie kiedy **II** *adv* (*surprise*) kiedy(ż)
where [weə] **I** *adv* gdzie; **~ do you live?** gdzie mieszkasz?; **~ from?** skąd?; **~ to?** dokąd? **II** *conj* **1.** gdzie; **this is ~ I live** to tu mieszkam; **sit ~ I can see you** usiądź tam, gdzie będę mógł cię widzieć **2.** dokąd
where•a•bouts [werə'baʊts] **I** *s* miejsce *n* pobytu **II** *adv* **1.** gdzie **2.** w którym miejscu
where•as *conj* podczas gdy
where'by *adv* **1.** dzięki któremu **2.** w ramach którego **3.** wskutek czego **4.** *JUR* zgodnie z którym, na mocy którego
where•up'on *conj lit* na co, po czym
wher•ev•er [wer'evə] **I** *conj* **1.** gdziekolwiek; **sit ~ you like** usiądź, gdzie chcesz **2.** obojętnie gdzie **3.** gdzie **II** *adv* (*surprise*) gdzie(ż)
whet [wet] *v/t* **1.** zwiększać ⟨-szyć⟩ **2.** *appetite*: zaostrzać ⟨-rzyć⟩
wheth•er ['weðə] *conj* czy; **I don't know ~ she loves me or not** nie wiem, czy mnie kocha, czy nie
whey [weɪ] *s* serwatka *f*
which [wɪtʃ] *pron* który; **~ of them is better?** który z nich jest lepszy?; **the house ~ we bought** dom, który kupiliśmy; **which•ev•er** [wɪtʃ'evə] *adj* **1.** którykolwiek **2.** obojętnie który
whiff [wɪf] *s* **1.** woń *f*, zapach *m*; **he caught a ~ of her perfume** dobiegła go woń jej perfum **2.** *success*: posmak *m*
while [waɪl] **I** *conj* **1.** kiedy, gdy **2.** podczas gdy **3.** chociaż **II** *s* **1.** jakiś czas *m*; **I haven't seen her for a ~** nie

W

widziałem jej już jakiś czas **2.** chwila *f*; ***I'll be back in a little ~*** zaraz wrócę; **while away** *v/t time*: spędzać ⟨-dzić⟩
whilst [waɪlst] → ***while***
whim [wɪm] *s* **1.** kaprys *m* **2.** zachcianka *f*
whim•per ['wɪmpə] **I** *s* **1.** kwilenie *n* **2.** skomlenie *n* **II** *v/i* **1.** kwilić ⟨za-⟩ **2.** skomleć ⟨za-⟩ **3.** (*complain*) *infml* jęczeć ⟨jęknąć⟩
whim•si•cal ['wɪmzɪkl] *adj* **1.** kapryśny **2.** fantazyjny **3.** wymyślny **4.** żartobliwy
whim•sy ['wɪmzɪ] *s* fantazja *f*
whine [waɪn] **I** *v/i* **1.** (*person*) jęczeć **2.** (*dog*) skomleć ⟨za-⟩ **II** *s* **1.** jęk *m* **2.** skomlenie *n*
whin•er ['waɪnə] *s* maruda *m*, jęczydusza *m*
whin•ny ['wɪnɪ] **I** *v/i* cicho rżeć ⟨za-⟩ **II** *s* ciche rżenie *n*
whip [wɪp] **I** *s* **1.** bicz *m* **2.** bat *m* **3.** *COOK* mus *m* **4.** deputowany *m* pilnujący przestrzegania dyscypliny partyjnej **II** *v/t* **1.** chłostać ⟨wy-⟩ **2.** uderzać ⟨-rzyć⟩ biczem **3.** smagać ⟨-gnąć⟩ batem **4.** smagać ⟨-gnąć⟩ **5.** *cream*: ubijać ⟨ubić⟩; **whip off** *v/t clothes*: zerwać ⟨zrywać⟩ z siebie; **whip up** *v/t infml* **1.** *emotion*: rozbudzać ⟨-dzić⟩ **2.** *interest*: wzbudzać ⟨-dzić⟩ **3.** pitrasić ⟨u-⟩
'whip•cord *s* sznur *m* od bicza; **'whip•lash** *s* **1.** smagnięcie *n* biczem **2.** *MED* odgięciowy uraz *m* kręgosłupa szyjnego
'whipped cream [wɪptkriːm] *s* bita śmietana *f*
whip•ping ['wɪpɪŋ] *s* chłosta *f*; **'whipping boy** *s infml* chłopiec *m* do bicia; **'whip•ping cream** *s* śmietana *f* kremowa, *infml* kremówka *f*
'whip•round *s Br infml* zrzutka *f*
whir *Am* → ***whirr***
whirl [wɜːrl] **I** *v/i* **1.** wirować ⟨za-⟩ **2.** obracać ⟨-rócić⟩ się gwałtownie **II** *v/t* kręcić ⟨za-⟩ **III** *s* **1.** wir *m*; ***a ~ of leaves*** wirujące liście **2.** ***give s.th. a ~*** *infml* wypróbować coś
whirl•i•gig ['wɜːlɪgɪg] *s* **1.** *fig* karuzela *f* **2.** *dated* wir *m*
whirl•pool *s* wir *m*; **'whirl•wind** *s* **1.** trąba *f* powietrzna **2.** *fig* wir *m*; ***I threw myself into a ~ of activities*** rzuciłem się w wir zajęć
whirr [wɜː] **I** *v/i* **1.** (*engine*) warczeć **2.** (*wings*) furkotać **II** *s* **1.** warkot *m* **2.** furkotanie *n*
whisk [wɪsk] **I** *v/t eggs*: ubijać ⟨ubić⟩ **II** *s* trzepaczka *f*; **whisk away** *v/t* zabierać ⟨-brać⟩
whis•kers ['wɪskəz] *pl* **1.** (*cat*) wąsy *pl* **2.** (*man*) baki *pl*, baczki *pl*
whis•ky ['wɪskɪ] *Br*, ***whis•key*** *Am s* whisky *f*
whis•per ['wɪspə] **I** *v/i* szeptać ⟨wy-⟩ **II** *s* **1.** szept *m*; ***speak in ~s*** mówić szeptem **2.** pogłoska *f* **3.** plotka *f*; **whis•per•ing cam•paign** ['wɪspərɪŋkæmpeɪn] *s* rozpowszechnianie *n* fałszywych pogłosek
whist [wɪst] *s* (*cards game*) wist *m*
whis•tle ['wɪsl] **I** *v/i* gwizdać ⟨-dnąć⟩; ***~ to a dog*** gwizdnąć na psa **II** *v/t* gwizdać ⟨za-⟩ **III** *s* **1.** gwizdek *m*; ***blow a ~*** zagwizdać **2.** gwizd *m*; **whis•tle-blow•er** ['wɪslbloʊə] *s* informator *m* (*pracownik ujawniający nieprawidłowości w firmie*); **whis•tle-stop 'tour** *s* **1.** wycieczka *f* objazdowa **2.** ***go on a ~ of a country*** *POLIT* jeździć po kraju na spotkania z wyborcami
white [waɪt] **I** *adj* **1.** biały; ***~ coffee*** biała kawa, kawa z mlekiem **II** *s* **1.** biel *f* **2.** *egg, eye*: białko *n* **3.** ***~s*** białe ubrania; **'white•board** *s* (biała) tablica *f*; **white-col•lar 'crime** *s* przestępstwo *n* gospodarcze; **white-col•lar 'work•er** *s* pracownik *m* umysłowy; **white 'el•e•phant** *s fig* chybiona inwestycja *f*; **white-'hot** *adj* rozgrzany do białości; **white 'lie** *s* niewinne kłamstwo *n*, kłamstewko *n*; **white 'trash** *s* biała biedota *f*; **'white•wash I** *s* **1.** wapno *n* (do bielenia) **2.** próba *f* ukrycia faktów **3.** *SPORT* rozgromienie *n*, porażka *f* do zera **II** *v/t* **1.** *walls*: bielić ⟨po-⟩ **2.** *fig* tuszować ⟨za-⟩ **3.** rozgramiać ⟨-romić⟩; **white-wa•ter ca•noe•ing** [waɪtwɒtərkə'nuːɪŋ] *s* kajakarstwo *n* górskie; **white-wa•ter raft•ing** [waɪtwɒtə'ræftɪŋ] *s SPORT* rafting *m*; **white 'wed•ding** *s* ślub *m* kościelny; **white 'wine** *s* białe wino *n*
whit•en ['waɪtn] **I** *v/i* bieleć ⟨z-⟩ **II** *v/t* **1.** bielić ⟨wy-, po-⟩ **2.** blednąć ⟨z-⟩

whit•ish ['waɪtɪʃ] *adj* białawy

Whit•sun ['wɪtsn] *s REL* Zielone Świątki *pl*

whit•tle ['wɪtl] *v/t* strugać ⟨wy-⟩; ***whittle away*** *v/t* **1.** uszczuplać ⟨-lić⟩ **2.** zmniejszać ⟨-szyć⟩; **whit•tle down** *v/t* **1.** ograniczać ⟨-czyć⟩ liczbę **2.** ograniczać ⟨-czyć⟩

whizz [wɪz] *Br*, ***whiz*** *Am* **I** *v/i* **1.** świstać ⟨-snąć⟩ **2.** śmigać ⟨-gnąć⟩ **II** *s infml* **1.** spec *m* **2.** mistrz *m*; ***he's a ~ at cooking*** genialnie gotuje; **'whizz•kid** *Br*, ***whiz•kid*** *Am infml s* genialne dziecko *n*

who [hu:] *pron* **1.** kto; ***~ are you?*** kim jesteś?; ***~ do you think you are?*** za kogo się uważasz? **2.** który; ***Mary, ~ is a teacher*** Mary, która jest nauczycielką

who'd [hu:d] *contracted form* → ***who had***, **who would**

who•dunn•it [hu:'dʌnɪt] *Br*, ***who•dun•it*** *Am s infml* (*book*, *film*) kryminał *m*

who•ev•er [hu:'evə] *pron* **1.** ktokolwiek **2.** każdy, kto **3.** wszyscy, którzy **4.** (*surprise*) kto, któż

whole [həʊl] **I** *adj* cały; ***the ~ of the town*** całe miasto **II** *s* całość *f*; ***as a ~*** **a)** w całości **b)** jako całość; ***for the region as a ~*** dla całego regionu; ***on the ~*** ogólnie rzecz biorąc; **'whole•food** *s* zdrowa żywność *f*; **whole-heart•ed** [həʊl'hɑ:tɪd] *adj* **1.** entuzjastyczny **2.** całkowity; **whole-heart•ed•ly** [həʊl'hɑ:tɪdlɪ] *adv* **1.** entuzjastycznie **2.** całkowicie; **whole•meal 'bread** *s* chleb *m* razowy; **'whole note** *s MUS Am* cała nuta *f*; **'whole•sale I** *adj* **1.** hurtowy **2.** *destruction*: masowy **II** *adv* hurtowo, hurtem; **whole•sal•er** ['həʊlseɪlə] *s* hurtownik *m*; **whole•some** ['həʊlsəm] *adj a. fig* zdrowy; **'whole-wheat** *adj bread*: razowy

who'll [hu:l] *contracted form* → ***who will***

whol•ly ['həʊlɪ] *adv* całkowicie, zupełnie; **whol•ly owned 'sub•sid•i•ar•y** *s* spółka *f* w pełni zależna

whom [hu:m] *pron* **1.** (*object*) kogo; ***~ did they invite?*** kogo zaprosili? **2.** (*with preposition*) który; ***the author ~ you criticize*** autor, którego krytykujesz; ***the children, most of ~ were tired*** dzieci, z których większość była zmęczona

whoop [wu:p] **I** *s* okrzyk *m* (radości) **II** *v/i* krzyczeć ⟨krzyknąć⟩ (z radości); **whoop•ing cough** ['hu:pɪŋkɒf] *s MED* koklusz *m*

whoops [wʊps] *interj* oj!

whoosh [wʊʃ] **I** *s* **1.** świst *m* **2.** szum *m* **II** *v/i* śmigać ⟨-gnąć⟩ **III** *interj* oj!

whop•per ['wɒpə] *s infml* **1.** gigant *m* **2.** bujda *f*; **whop•ping** ['wɒpɪŋ] *adj infml* **1.** *money*: kolosalny **2.** *majority*: przytłaczający

whore [hɔ:] *s vulg* kurwa *f*; **'whorehouse** *s dated* burdel *m*

whorl [wɜ:l] *s* **1.** spirala *f* **2.** wzór *m* wirowy **3.** *leaves*: okółek *m*

who's [hu:z] *contracted form* → ***who has***

whose [hu:z] *pron* **1.** czyj; ***~ house is that?*** czyj to dom? **2.** którego; ***he's a man ~ opinion I respect*** to człowiek, którego zdanie szanuję

why [waɪ] **I** *adv* dlaczego; ***~ were you late?*** dlaczego się spóźniłeś?; ***~ on earth?*** na litość boską, dlaczego? **II** *interj* (*surprise*) ***why Jane, it's you!*** o mój Boże, Jane, to ty!

wick [wɪk] *s* knot *m*; ***get on s.o.'s ~*** *Br infml* działać komuś na nerwy

wick•ed ['wɪkɪd] *adj* **1.** zły **2.** podły **3.** *smile*: szelmowski **4.** *blow*: groźny **5.** *infml* super

wick•er ['wɪkə] *s* wilkina *f*; **wick•er 'bas•ket** *s* wiklinowy kosz *m*; **wick•er 'chair** *s* wiklinowe krzesło *n*; **'wick•er•work** *s* wyroby *pl* z wikliny

wick•et ['wɪkɪt] *s* **1.** (*cricket*) bramka *f* **2.** (*cricket*) obszar *m* pomiędzy bramkami

wide [waɪd] **I** *adj* **1.** szeroki; ***a ~ road*** szeroka droga; ***a ~ choice of goods*** szeroki wybór towarów; ***it received ~ media coverage*** było o tym głośno w mediach **2.** *eyes*: szeroko otwarty **3.** ***the ball was ~*** piłka wyszła na aut **II** *adv* **1.** szeroko; ***the door was ~ open*** drzwi były szeroko otwarte **2.** zupełnie; ***~ awake*** zupełnie rozbudzony; **wide-an•gle 'lens** *s PHOT* obiektyw *m* szerokokątny; **wide-eyed** [waɪd'aɪd] *adj* **1.** ***be ~*** wytrzeszczać oczy; ***stare at s.th. in ~ amazement*** gapić się na coś z wytrzeszczo-

W

nymi ze zdumienia oczami **2.** *fig* naiwny

wide•ly ['waɪdlɪ] *adv* **1.** powszechnie; ***~ available*** powszechnie dostępny **2.** szeroko **3.** znacznie; ***they have travelled ~*** wiele podróżowali **4.** bardzo; ***he's ~-read*** jest bardzo oczytany

wid•en ['waɪdn] **I** *v/t* **1.** poszerzać ⟨-rzyć⟩ **2.** rozszerzać ⟨-rzyć⟩ **II** *v/i* **1.** poszerzać ⟨-rzyć⟩ się **2.** rozszerzać ⟨-rzyć⟩ się

wide-'rang•ing *adj* **1.** szeroki; ***the commission has ~ powers*** komisja posiada szerokie kompetencje **2.** różnorodny **3.** daleko idący; **'wide•spread** *adj* **1.** powszechny **2.** *support*: szeroki **3.** rozległy

widg•et ['wɪdʒɪt] *s infml* dynks *m*

wid•ow ['wɪdəʊ] *s* wdowa *f*; **'wid•owed** *adj* owdowiały; **wid•ow•er** ['wɪdəʊə] *s* wdowiec *m*

width [wɪdθ] *s* szerokość *f*; ***be about 10 metres in ~*** mieć około 10 metrów szerokości

wield [wi:ld] *v/t* **1.** *power*: posiadać, dzierżyć **2.** *knife*: dzierżyć **3.** *influence*: mieć

wife [waɪf] *pl wives* [waɪvz] *s* żona *f*, małżonka *f*

wig [wɪg] *s* peruka *f*

wig•gle ['wɪgl] **I** *v/i* **1.** wić się **2.** ***her hips ~d as she walked*** szła, kołysząc biodrami **II** *v/t* **1.** kręcić **2.** *fingers*: szybko poruszać ⟨-szyć⟩, przebierać

wig•wam ['wɪgwæm] *s* wigwam *m*

wild [waɪld] **I** *adj* **1.** dziki; ***~ rabbit*** dziki królik; ***a ~ laughter*** dziki śmiech; ***not in my ~est dreams did I think that*** nawet w najśmielszych marzeniach nie wyobrażałem sobie, że; ***run ~*** **a)** (*garden*) zarosnąć **b)** rozrabiać **2.** ***it was a ~ guess*** strzelałem **3.** *sea*, *affair*: burzliwy **4.** *infml* wściekły **5.** *infml* super **6.** ***she's ~ about him*** *infml* ma bzika na jego punkcie, szaleje za nim **II** *s* ***animals living in the ~*** zwierzęta żyjące na swobodzie; ***survive in the ~*** przeżyć w naturalnym środowisku; ***the call of the ~*** zew natury; ***in the ~s*** *infml* w dziczy; **wild 'boar** *s* dzik *m*; **'wild card** *s* **1.** *fig* niewiadoma *f* **2.** (*tennis*) dzika karta *f* **3.** (*cards*) dżoker *m* **4.** INF znak *m* specjalny, gwiazdka *f*; **'wild•cat** *s* żbik *m*

wil•der•ness ['wɪldərnɪs] *s* **1.** odludzie *n* **2.** pustkowie *n* **3.** puszcza *f*

'wild•fire *s*: ***spread like ~*** (*news*) rozchodzić się lotem błyskawicy: **wild-'goose chase** *s* szukanie *n* wiatru w polu; **'wild•life** *s* **1.** (dzika) fauna *f* i flora *f* **2.** dzika przyroda *f*

wild•ly ['waɪldlɪ] *adv* **1.** dziko **2.** gwałtownie **3.** wściekle **4.** burzliwie **5.** bardzo

wil•ful ['wɪlfʊl] *Br*, ***will•ful*** *Am adj* **1.** umyślny **2.** *child*: uparty

will[1] [wɪl] *s* **1.** wola *f*; ***impose one's ~ on other people*** narzucać innym swoją wolę; ***against my ~*** wbrew mojej woli; ***at ~*** do woli; ***you can arrange the furniture at ~*** możesz ustawić meble, jak chcesz; ***where there's a ~ there's a way*** dla chcącego nie ma nic trudnego **3.** testament *m*

will[2] [~] *v aux* **1.** (*future tense*) ***I'll come*** przyjdę; ***you ~ be in time if you hurry*** nie spóźnisz się, jeżeli się pospieszysz; ***how long ~ you be staying in Paris?*** jak długo będziesz w Paryżu? **2.** (*willingness, consent*) ***they won't lend us any more money*** nie pożyczą nam więcej pieniędzy **3.** (*request*) ***~ you send this letter for me?*** mógłbyś wysłać dla mnie ten list? **4.** (*commands*) ***~ you be quiet!*** bądźże cicho! **5.** (*assumption*) ***this ~ be my husband*** to pewnie mój mąż **6.** (*general fact*) ***accidents ~ happen*** wypadków nie da się uniknąć

will[3] [~] *v/t* **1.** *dated* chcieć **2.** zmuszać ⟨-sić⟩ się; ***she ~ed herself to smile*** zmusiła się do uśmiechu; ***he ~ed himself not to panic*** zapanował nad ogarniającym go uczuciem paniki **3.** zapisywać ⟨-sać⟩ w testamencie

will•ful → ***wilful***

wil•lies ['wɪlɪz] *pl*: ***it give me the ~*** boję się tego

will•ing ['wɪlɪŋ] *adj* **1.** chętny **2.** gotowy; ***I'm ~ to discuss the problem*** jestem gotowy przedyskutować tę kwestię **3.** ochoczy; **will•ing•ly** ['wɪlɪŋlɪ] *adv* **1.** chętnie **2.** dobrowolnie; **will•ing•ness** ['wɪlɪŋnɪs] *s* **1.** chęć *f* **2.** gotowość *f*

wil•low ['wɪləʊ] *s* **1.** wierzba *f* **2.** wierzbina *f*; **wil•low•y** ['wɪləʊɪ] *adj* smukły i gibki

'**will•pow•er** *s* siła *f* woli

wil•ly-nil•ly [wɪlɪ'nɪlɪ] *adv infml* **1.** chcąc nie chcąc **2.** bezmyślnie

wilt [wɪlt] *v/i a. fig* więdnąć ⟨z-⟩

wi•ly ['waɪlɪ] *adj* przebiegły, podstępny

wimp [wɪmp] *s infml* mięczak *m*

win [wɪn] **I** (*won*; *won*) *v/i* wygrywać ⟨-rać⟩; ***~ at chess*** wygrać w szachy **II** (*won*; *won*) *v/t* **1.** wygrywać ⟨-rać⟩ **2.** *medal*, *goal*: zdobywać ⟨-być⟩ **3.** *support*: zdobywać ⟨-być⟩ **II** *s* wygrana *f*, zwycięstwo *n*; **win back** *v/t* odzyskiwać ⟨-kać⟩

wince [wɪns] *v/i* krzywić ⟨s-⟩ się

winch [wɪntʃ] **I** *s* wciągarka *f* **II** *v/t* wciągać ⟨-gnąć⟩

wind[1] [wɪnd] **I** *s* **1.** wiatr *m*; ***the ~ is blowing from the south*** wieje wiatr z południa; ***there is something in the ~*** *fig* coś wisi w powietrzu; ***s.o. got ~ of s.th.*** *infml* coś doszło do czyichś uszu; ***put the ~ up s.o.*** *Br infml* napędzić komuś stracha; ***take the ~ out of s.o.'s sails*** *fig* podciąć komuś skrzydła **2.** oddech *m* **3.** *MUS* instrumenty *pl* dęte **4.** ***break ~*** puszczać wiatry **II** *v/t* ***he was momentarily ~ed*** na chwilę zaparło mu dech w piersi

wind[2] [waɪnd] (*wound*; *wound*) **I** *v/i* (*road*) wić się **II** *v/t* **1.** nawijać ⟨-winąć⟩ (***on*** na *A*) **2.** owijać ⟨owinąć⟩ (***around*** wokół *A*) **3.** zawijać ⟨-winąć⟩ (***into*** w *A*) **4.** (*a.* ***~ up***) *watch*, *clock*: nakręcać ⟨-cić⟩ **5.** przewijać ⟨-winąć⟩; ***~ s.th. forward*** przewijać coś do przodu; ***~ s.th. back*** przewijać coś do tyłu **III** *s* ***give a clock a ~*** nakręcić zegar; **wind down I** *v/i* **1.** odprężać ⟨-żyć⟩ się **2.** być w trakcie likwidacji **II** *v/t* **1.** (stopniowo) likwidować ⟨z-⟩ **2.** *window*: otwierać ⟨-worzyć⟩; **wind up I** *v/i* (*person*) kończyć ⟨s-⟩, lądować ⟨wy-⟩; ***he will ~ in prison*** skończy w więzieniu **II** *v/t* **1.** kończyć ⟨za-⟩ **2.** *Br infml* prowokować ⟨s-⟩ **3.** *window*: zamykać ⟨-mknąć⟩

'**wind•bag** *s infml* gaduła *f/m*; '**wind•break** *s* **1.** wiatrochron *m* **2.** pas *m* wiatrochronny; '**wind•fall** *s* **1.** nieoczekiwany przypływ *m* gotówki **2.** (*fruit*) spad *m*

wind•ing ['waɪndɪŋ] *adj road*: wijący się, kręty

'**wind in•stru•ment** *s MUS* instrument *m* dęty

wind•lass ['wɪndləs] *s TECH* kołowrót *m*

wind•less ['wɪndlɪs] *adj* bezwietrzny

'**wind•mill** *s* wiatrak *m*

win•dow ['wɪndəʊ] *s* **1.** okno *n*; ***a stained-glass ~*** witraż **2.** witryna *f*, wystawa *f* **3.** (*post office*, *bank*) okienko *n*; '**win•dow box** *s* skrzynka *f* na kwiaty; '**win•dow clean•er** *s* **1.** osoba *f* myjąca okna **2.** płyn *m* do mycia szyb; '**win•dow dress•ing** *s* **1.** aranżacja *f* wystaw sklepowych **2.** *fig* pozory *pl*; '**win•dow en•ve•lope** *s* koperta *f* z okienkiem; '**win•dow•pane** *s* szyba *f* (okienna); '**win•dow seat** *s* miejsce *n* przy oknie; '**win•dow shade** *s Am* roleta *f*; '**win•dow-shop** *v/i*: ***go ~ping*** oglądać wystawy sklepowe; **win•dow•sill** ['wɪndəʊsɪl] *s* parapet *m* (okienny)

'**wind•pipe** *s ANAT* tchawica *f*; '**wind pow•er** *s* energia *f* wiatru; '**wind•screen** *s AUTO Br* przednia szyba *f*; '**wind•shield** *Am* → ***windscreen***; '**wind•shield wip•er** *s AUTO Br* wycieraczka *f*; '**wind•sock** *s* rękaw *m* (lotniskowy); '**wind•surf•er** *s* **1.** deska *f* surfingowa **2.** windsurfer *m*; '**wind•surf•ing** *s SPORT* windsurfing *m*; **wind-swept** ['wɪndswept] *adj* **1.** wietrzny **2.** *lit* smagany wiatrem **3.** *hair*: potargany; '**wind tun•nel** *s* tunel *m* aerodynamiczny

wind•up ['waɪndʌp] **I** *adj* **1.** nakręcany **2.** na korbkę **II** *s Br* kawał *m*

wind•ward ['wɪndwəd] **I** *adj* nawietrzny **II** *adv* pod wiatr

wind•y ['wɪndɪ] *adj* wietrzny

wine [waɪn] *s* wino; '**wine bar** *s* winiarnia *f*; '**wine bot•tle** *s* **1.** butelka *f* po winie **2.** butelka *f* wina; '**wine cel•lar** *s* piwnica *f* do przechowywania wina; '**wine glass** *s* kieliszek *m* do wina; '**wine list** *s* karta *f* win

win•ery ['waɪnərɪ] *s Am* winnica *f*

wing [wɪŋ] *s* **1.** skrzydło *n*; ***take s.o. under one's ~*** wziąć kogoś pod swoje skrzydła **2.** *AUTO Br* błotnik *m* **3.** *SPORT* skrzydłowy *m* **4.** ***the ~s*** *THEAT* kulisy *pl*; **wing•er** ['wɪŋə] *s* SPORT skrzydłowy *m*

'wing mir•ror *s* lusterko *n* boczne; **'wing•span** *s* rozpiętość *f* skrzydeł

wink [wɪŋk] **I** *v/i* mrugać ⟨-gnąć⟩ (***at*** na *A*) **II** *s* mrugnięcie *n*; ***not have a ~ of sleep, not sleep a ~*** całą noc nie zmrużyć oka; ***give s.o. a ~*** *infml* puścić do kogoś oko

win•kle ['wɪŋkl] *s* (*animal*) pobrzeżek *m*; **winkle out** *v/t* wyciągać ⟨-gnąć⟩

win•ner ['wɪnə] *s* **1.** zwycięzca *m*, wygrany *m* **2.** *medal*: zdobywca *m* **3.** (*tennis*) piłka *f* kończąca; **winning** ['wɪnɪŋ] *adj* **1.** zwycięski **2.** wygrywający **3.** *smile*: ujmujący; **'winning post** *s Br* meta *f*; **win•nings** ['wɪnɪŋz] *pl* wygrana *f*

win•now ['wɪnəʊ] *v/t rye*: przewiewać ⟨-wiać⟩

win•o ['waɪnəʊ] *pl -nos* ['~əʊz] *s infml* pijaczek *m*, pijaczyna *m*

win•ter ['wɪntə] **I** *s* zima *f* **II** *v/i* zimować ⟨prze-⟩; **win•ter•ize** ['wɪntəraɪz] *v/t Am car*: przygotowywać ⟨-tować⟩ na zimę; **win•ter sports** [wɪntə'spɔːts] *pl* sporty *pl* zimowe; **'win•ter•time** *s* **1.** zima *f* **2.** okres *m* zimowy

win•try ['wɪntrɪ] *adj* **1.** zimowy **2.** *smile*: lodowaty

wipe [waɪp] **I** *v/t* **1.** wycierać ⟨wytrzeć⟩; ***~ your feet on the mat*** wytrzyj buty na wycieraczce **2.** ocierać ⟨otrzeć⟩; ***~ the sweat from one's forhead*** otrzeć pot z czoła **3.** (*a.* ***~ off***) *film*: kasować ⟨s-⟩ **4.** ***~ s.th. from one's mind*** wymazać coś z pamięci **II** *s* **1.** ***give s.th. a ~*** wytrzeć coś **2.** chusteczka *f*; ***baby ~s*** chusteczki dla niemowląt; **wipe out** *v/t* **1.** zrównywać ⟨-nać⟩ z ziemią **2.** tępić ⟨wy-⟩ **3.** wymazywać ⟨-zać⟩; ***wipe up*** *v/t* wycierać ⟨wytrzeć⟩

wip•er ['waɪpə] *s* wycieraczka *f*

wire [waɪə] **I** *s* **1.** drut *m* **2.** przewód *m* **3.** kabel *m* **4.** *Am infml* telegram *m* **II** *v/t* **1.** (*a.* ***~ up***) podłączać ⟨-czyć⟩ **2.** (*a.* ***~ up***) zakładać ⟨założyć⟩ instalację elektryczną w *L* **3.** *Am* przesyłać ⟨-słać⟩ telegraficznie **4.** ***~ money to s.o.*** przelać pieniądze na czyjeś konto; **wire cut•ters** ['waɪəkʌtəz] *pl* szczypce *pl* do cięcia drutu; **wire•less** ['waɪrlɪs] *adj* bezprzewodowy; **wire 'net•ting** *s* siatka *f* druciana; **'wire•tap I** *v/t* podsłuchiwać ⟨-chać⟩ rozmowy telefoniczne **II** *s* podsłuch *m* telefoniczny; **wire 'wool** *s Br* wełna *f* stalowa, wata *f* stalowa

wir•ing ['waɪrɪŋ] *s* **1.** instalacja *f* elektryczna **2.** okablowanie *n*

wir•y ['waɪrɪ] *adj* **1.** *person*: silny **2.** *hair*: sztywny **3.** *coat of animal*: szorstki

wis•dom ['wɪzdəm] *s* mądrość *f*; **'wisdom tooth** *s* ząb *m* mądrości

wise [waɪz] **I** *adj* mądry; ***it was a ~ thing to do*** to było mądre posunięcie; ***be ~ after the event*** być mądrym po szkodzie; ***be none the ~r*** nie być mądrzejszym niż przedtem; ***get ~ to s.o.*** *infml* przejrzeć kogoś **II** *v/i* ***~ up to the fact that*** *infml* zorientować się, że; **'wise•crack** *s infml* żart *f*; **'wise guy** *s Am infml* mądrala *m*

wise•ly ['waɪzlɪ] *adv* mądrze

wish [wɪʃ] **I** *s* **1.** życzenie *n*; ***make a ~*** wyrazić życzenie; ***against one's parents' ~es*** wbrew życzeniom rodziców; (***with***) ***best ~es*** (*letter ending*) z serdecznymi pozdrowieniami; ***your ~ is my command*** twoje życzenie jest dla mnie rozkazem **2.** pragnienie *n* **II** *v/i* **1.** chcieć; ***you may stay if you ~*** możesz zostać, jeśli chcesz; ***I ~ I was taller*** chciałbym być wyższy, żałuję, że nie jestem wyższy; ***just as you ~*** jak chcesz; ***I ~ to speak to the manager*** chciałbym porozmawiać z kierownikiem; ***he has everything he could ~ for*** ma wszystko, czego tylko mógłby chcieć **2.** pragnąć **III** *v/t* **1.** chcieć; ***~ s.o. away*** chcieć, aby ktoś sobie poszedł **2.** pragnąć **3.** życzyć; ***~ s.o. well*** dobrze komuś życzyć; ***~ s.o. a happy birthday*** złożyć komuś życzenia urodzinowe; ***I wouldn't ~ that on my worst enemy*** nie życzyłbym tego najgorszemu wrogowi; **'wish•bone** *s* widełki (*zrośnięte obojczyki u ptaków*) *pl*

wish•ful think•ing [wɪʃfəl'θɪŋkɪŋ] *s* pobożne życzenia *pl*

wish•y-wash•y ['wɪʃɪwɒʃɪ] *adj* **1.** *colour*: rozmyty **2.** *person*: nijaki, mało konkretny

wisp [wɪsp] *s* **1.** *hair*: kosmyk *m* **2.** *smoke*: smuga *f* **3.** *hay*: wiązka *f*

W

wist•ful ['wɪstfʊl] *adj* **1.** tęskny **2.** smutny; **wist•ful•ly** ['wɪstfəlɪ] *adv* **1.** tęsknie **2.** ze smutkiem

wit [wɪt] *s* **1.** dowcip *m*; ***a woman of ~ and intelligence*** dowcipna i inteligentna kobieta **2.** humorysta *m* **3. *~s*** inteligencja *f* **4.** rozum *m*; ***at least you had the ~ to ask for help*** przynajmniej miałeś dość rozumu, żeby poprosić o pomoc; ***be at one's ~s' end*** nie wiedzieć, co począć; ***be frightened out of one's ~s*** odchodzić od zmysłów ze strachu; ***keep one's ~s about one*** mieć się na baczności

witch [wɪtʃ] *s* **1.** czarownica *f* **2.** wiedźma *f*; '**witch•craft** *s* czary *pl*; '**witch doc•tor** *s* szaman *m*; '**witch•hunt** *s fig* polowanie *n* na czarownice, nagonka *f*

with [wɪð] *prep* **1.** z *I*; ***she lives ~ her parents*** mieszka z rodzicami; ***a war ~ a neighbouring country*** wojna z sąsiadującym państwem; ***I'll be ~ you in a moment*** zaraz się panem zajmę **2.** (*using*); ***cut it ~ a knife*** przetnij to nożem **3.** (*reason*) z *G*; ***she blushed ~ embarrassment*** zarumieniła się ze wstydu

with•draw [wɪð'drɔː] (*withdrew*; *withdrawn*) **I** *v/t* **1.** wycofywać ⟨-fać⟩ (***from*** z *G*); ***~ from the market*** wycofać z rynku **2.** *money*: podejmować ⟨-djąć⟩ **3.** *motion*: cofać ⟨wy-⟩ **II** *v/i* wycofywać ⟨-fać⟩ się; **with•draw•al** [wɪð'drɔːəl] *s* **1.** wycofanie *n* **2.** wycofanie się *n* **3.** *money*: podjęcie *n* **4.** wypłata *f*; **with•'draw•al symp•toms** *pl* MED **1.** objawy *pl* abstynencyjne **2.** objawy *pl* głodu narkotycznego; **withdrawn** [wɪð'dɒɒn] **I** *Past Participle* → ***withdraw*** **II** *adj* zamknięty w sobie

with•er ['wɪðə] *v/i* usychać ⟨uschnąć⟩; **with•er•ing** ['wɪðərɪŋ] *adj look*: piorunujący

with•'hold (*withheld*; *whithheld*) *v/t* **1.** *information*: zatajać ⟨-taić⟩ **2.** *payment*: wstrzymywać ⟨-mać⟩

with•'in **I** *prep* **1.** w (prze)ciągu *G*; ***you'll receive a reply ~ seven days*** otrzymasz odpowiedź w ciągu siedmiu dni **2.** nie dalej niż *A*; ***~ a mile from home*** nie dalej niż milę od domu **3.** w obrębie *G* **4.** w zasięgu *G*; ***~ sight*** w zasięgu wzroku **5.** w *L*; ***from ~ a building*** z budynku; ***remain within the limit of*** nie przekraczać *G* **II** *adv* wewnątrz, w środku

with•'out **I** *prep* bez *G*; ***~ enthusiasm*** bez entuzjazmu; ***can you see ~ your glasses?*** widzisz bez okularów?; ***he left ~ saying goodbye*** wyszedł bez pożegnania **II** *adv* bez; ***do you want a room with bath or ~?*** chce pan pokój z łazienką czy bez?

with•'stand (*withstood*; *withstood*) *v/t* wytrzymywać ⟨-mać⟩

wit•less ['wɪtlɪs] *adj* niemądry

wit•ness ['wɪtnɪs] **I** *s* **1.** świadek *m*; ***a ~ for the defence*** świadek obrony; ***a ~ for the prosecution*** świadek oskarżenia **2.** *lit* świadectwo *n*; ***bear ~ to*** **a)** stanowić świadectwo *G* **b)** świadczyć o *L* **II** *v/t* **1.** być świadkiem *G* **2.** *signature*: poświadczać ⟨-czyć⟩; '**wit•ness box** *Br*, '***wit•ness stand*** *Am s* (*court*) miejsce *n* dla świadka

wit•ti•cism ['wɪtɪsɪzm] *s* dowcipna uwaga *f*

wit•ty ['wɪtɪ] *adj* dowcipny

wives [waɪvz] *pl* → ***wife***

wiz•ard ['wɪzəd] *s* **1.** czarodziej *m* **2.** ***a computer ~*** spec od komputerów

wiz•ened ['wɪznd] *adj skin*: pomarszczony

wob•ble ['wɒbl] **I** *v/i* **1.** chwiać ⟨za-⟩ się **2.** trząść ⟨za-⟩ się **3.** iść ⟨pójść⟩ chwiejnym krokiem **4.** (*voice*) drżeć ⟨za-⟩ **II** *v/t* potrząsać ⟨-snąć⟩; **wobbly** ['wɒblɪ] *adj* **1.** chwiejny **2.** chwiejący się **3.** drżący **4.** trzęsący się

woe [wəʊ] *s dated* **1.** niedola *f* **2.** nieszczęście *n* **3. *~s*** kłopoty *pl*; ***woe•ful*** ['wəʊfʊl] *adj* **1.** żałosny **2.** zgnębiony **3.** nieszczęśliwy

wok [wɒk] *s* COOK wok *m*

woke [wəʊk] *Past Simple* → ***wake***

wok•en ['wəʊkn] *Past Participle* → ***wake***

wolf [wʊlf] **I** *pl wolves* [wʊlvz] *s* wilk *m*; ***a ~ in sheep's clothing*** *fig* wilk w owczej skórze **II** (*a.* ***~ down***) *v/t food*: pożerać ⟨-żreć⟩; '**wolf whis•tle** *s* gwizd *m* podziwu; '**wolf-whis•tle** *v/i* gwizdać ⟨za-⟩ z podziwem

wom•an ['wʊmən] *pl -men* ['wɪmɪn] *s* kobieta *f*; **wom•an 'doc•tor** *s* lekarka *f*; **wom•an 'driv•er** *s* (*woman*) kierowca *m*; **wom•an hat•er** ['wʊmənheɪtə] *s*

W

mizogin *m*; **wom•an•hood** ['wʊmənhʊd] *s* kobiecość *f*
wom•an•ize ['wʊmənaɪz] *v/i* uganiać się za kobietami; **wom•an•iz•er** ['wʊmənaɪzə] *s* kobieciarz *m*
wom•an•kind [wʊmən'kaɪnd] *s dated* kobiety *pl*; **wom•an•ly** ['wʊmənlɪ] *adj* kobiecy
womb [wuːm] *s* **1.** *ANAT* macica *f* **2.** *fig* łono *n*
wom•en [wɪmɪn] *pl* → ***woman***; **women's lib** [wɪmɪnz'lɪb] *s infml* ruch *m* wyzwolenia kobiet; **wom•en's libber** [wɪmɪnz'lɪbə] *s* działaczka *f* ruchu wyzwolenia kobiet, feministka *f*
won [wʌn] *Past Simple and Past Participle* → ***win***
won•der ['wʌndə] **I** *v/i* **1.** zastanawiać ⟨-nowić⟩ się; ***I ~ if you could help me*** może mógłbyś mi pomóc? **2.** dziwić się (***at*** *D*) **II** *s* **1.** zdziwienie *n*; ***it's no ~ that*** nic dziwnego, że **2.** zdumienie *n*; ***in ~*** w zdumieniu **3.** cud *m*; ***work ~s*** zdziałać cuda; **won•der•ful** ['wʌndəfəl] *adj* **1.** cudowny **2.** wspaniały **3.** zdumiewający; **won•der•ful•ly** ['wʌndəfəlɪ] *adv* **1.** cudownie **2.** wspaniale **3.** zdumiewająco; '**won•der•land** *s* **1.** kraina *f* czarów **2.** *fig* raj *m*
won•ky ['wɒŋkɪ] *adj Br infml* **1.** chwiejny **2.** przekrzywiony
wont [wəʊnt] *dated* **I** *adj* ***be ~ to do s.th.*** mieć zwyczaj coś robić **II** *s* zwyczaj *m*
won't [wəʊnt] *contracted form* → ***will not***
woo [wuː] *v/t* **1.** nęcić ⟨z-⟩ (***s.o. with*** kogoś *I*) **2.** zalecać się do *G* **3.** zabiegać o *A*
wood [wʊd] *s* **1.** drewno *n*; ***made of ~*** drewniany **2.** las *m*; ***be not out of the ~*** *fig* uporać się z problemami; ***he can't see the ~ for the trees*** *fig* szczegóły przesłaniają mu istotę rzeczy; '**wood•cut** *s* drzeworyt *m*; '**wood•cutter** *s* drwal *m*
wood•ed ['wʊdɪd] *adj* **1.** leśny **2.** zalesiony
wood•en ['wʊdn] *adj* **1.** *a. fig* drewniany **2.** z drewna
wood•land ['wʊdlənd] *s* **1.** las *m* **2.** teren *m* leśny; '**wood•louse** *pl -lice s* stonoga *f*; **wood•peck•er** ['wʊdpekə] *s* dzięcioł *m*; '**wood•pile** *s* stos *m* drewna; '**wood•shed** *s* **1.** szopa *f* na drewno **2.** drewutnia *f*; '**wood•wind** *s MUS* instrumenty *pl* dęte drewniane; '**wood•work** *s* stolarka *f*; ***hit the ~*** *SPORT* **a)** strzelić w słupek **b)** strzelić w poprzeczkę; '**wood•worm** *s* (*animal*) czerw *m* drzewny
wood•y ['wʊdɪ] *adj* **1.** zdrewniały **2.** zalesiony **3.** porośnięty drzewami **4.** ***with a ~ note*** (*wine*) z nutą drewna
woof [wʊf] **I** *interj* hau! **II** *v/i* szczekać ⟨za-⟩ **III** *s* **1.** szczeknięcie *n* **2.** szczekanie *n*; **woof•er** ['wʊfə] *s* głośnik *m* niskotonowy, woofer *m*
wool [wʊl] *s* wełna *f*; **wool•len** ['wʊlən] *Br*, ***wool•en*** *Am adj* wełniany; ***a ~ coat*** wełniany płaszcz; **wool•ly** ['wʊlɪ] *Br*, ***woo•ly*** *Am adj* **1.** wełniany **2.** wełnisty **3.** *thinking*: mętny
word [wɜːd] **I** *s* **1.** słowo *n*; ***by ~ of mouth*** ustnie; ***~ for ~*** słowo w słowo; ***in a ~*** jednym słowem; ***in other ~s*** innymi słowy; ***in one's own ~s*** własnymi słowami; ***~s fail me*** brak mi słów; ***have a ~ with*** zamienić słowo z *I*; ***he always has to have the last ~*** zawsze musi mieć ostatnie słowo; ***put s.th. into ~s*** ująć coś w słowa; ***I give you my ~ that*** daję słowo, że, obiecuję, że; ***keep one's ~*** dotrzymać słowa; ***break one's ~*** złamać słowo; ***take s.o.'s ~ for it*** uwierzyć komuś na słowo **2.** wieść *f*, wiadomość *f*; ***there has been no ~ from her for 2 months*** nie odzywa się od dwóch miesięcy **II** *v/t* **1.** ujmować ⟨ująć⟩ w słowa **2.** formułować ⟨s-⟩ **3.** wyrażać ⟨-razić⟩; **word•ing** ['wɜːdɪŋ] *s* **1.** sformułowanie *n* **2.** dobór *m* słów
word or•der *s* szyk *m* wyrazów; '**word•play** *s* gra *f* słów
word 'pro•cess•ing *s INF* przetwarzanie *n* tekstu; **word 'pro•ces•sor** *s INF* procesor *m* tekstu
word•y ['wɜːdɪ] *adj* **1.** rozwlekły **2.** przegadany **3.** wielomówny
wore [wɔː] *Past Simple* → ***wear***
work [wɜːk] **I** *v/i* **1.** pracować (***on*** nad *I*) **2.** (*device, medicine*) działać ⟨za-⟩ **3.** (*plan*) udać się **II** *v/t* **1.** obrabiać ⟨-robić⟩ **2.** *device*: obsługiwać **3.** *land*: uprawiać **4.** *miracles*: działać ⟨z-⟩ **III** *s* **1.** praca *f*; ***at ~*** w pracy; ***be***

W

out of ~ być bez pracy, być bezrobotnym; ***set to ~*** zabrać się do pracy **2.** dzieło *n* **3.** utwór *m* **4.** ***~s*** fabryka *f* **5.** ***~s*** zakład *m* produkcyjny **6.** ***the ~s*** mechanizm *m*; **work off** *v/t* **1.** *anger*: wyładowywać ⟨-dować⟩ **2.** odpracowywać ⟨-cować⟩; **work out I** *v/i* **1.** ćwiczyć **2.** udawać ⟨-dać⟩ się **3.** układać ⟨ułożyć⟩ się; ***things ~ed out well for her*** wszystko jej się dobrze ułożyło **4.** przybierać ⟨-brać⟩ pomyślny obrót **II** *v/t* **1.** *answer*: znajdować ⟨znaleźć⟩ **2.** *problem*: rozwiązywać ⟨-zać⟩ **3.** *person*: rozgryzać ⟨-ryźć⟩ **4.** *plan*: opracowywać ⟨-cować⟩ **5.** *compromise*: osiągać ⟨-gnąć⟩; **work up** *v/t* **1.** ***~ oneself up*** denerwować się; ***be ~ed up*** być zdenerwowanym **2.** podniecać ⟨-cić⟩ **2.** wykrzesać z siebie **3.** *courage*: zdobyć się na *A* **4.** opracowywać ⟨-cować⟩ **5.** sporządzać ⟨-dzić⟩

work•a•ble ['wɜːkəbl] *adj* **1.** wykonalny **2.** nadający się do zastosowania **3.** *substance*: plastyczny

work•a•day ['wɜːkədeɪ] *adj* **1.** zwyczajny **2.** codzienny

work•a•hol•ic [wɜːkə'hɔlɪk] *s* pracoholik *m*

'work•bench *s* stół *m* warsztatowy; **'work•book** *s* zeszyt *m* ćwiczeń, ćwiczenia *pl*; **'work camp** *s* obóz *m* pracy; **'work•day** *s Am* dzień *m* roboczy

work•er ['wɜːkə] *s* pracownik *m*; ***be a hard ~*** ciężko pracować

'work•force *s* **1.** pracownicy *pl* **2.** siła *f* robocza; **'work hours** *pl* godziny *pl* pracy

work•ing ['wɜːkɪŋ] **I** *adj* **1.** pracujący **2.** czynny zawodowo **3.** ***a ~ man*** robotnik **4.** zawodowy **5.** roboczy **6.** *knowledge*: podstawowy **7.** działający **8.** sprawny; ***in full ~ order*** w pełni sprawny **II** *s* **1.** ***~s*** działanie *n* **2.** ***~s*** funkcjonowanie *n*; **'work•ing class** *s*: ***the ~*** klasa robotnicza; **'work•ing-class** *adj* robotniczy; **'work•ing con•di•tions** *pl* warunki *pl* pracy; **work•ing 'day** *Br* → ***workday***; **'work•ing hours** → ***workhours***; **work•ing 'knowl•edge** *s* podstawowa znajomość *f*; **work•ing 'moth•er** *s* pracująca matka *f*

'work•load *s* obciążenie *n* pracą; ***have a heavy ~*** mieć dużo pracy; **'work•man** *pl -men s* robotnik *m*; **'work•man•like** *adj* **1.** solidny **2.** porządny; **'work•man•ship** *s* wykonanie *n*; **'work•mate** *s* kolega *f* z pracy

work of 'art *pl works of art s* dzieło *n* sztuki

'work•out *s* trening *m*; **'work per•mit** *s* pozwolenie *n* na pracę; **'work•place** *s* miejsce *n* pracy; **'work•room** *s* **1.** warsztat *m* **2.** pracownia *f*; **'work sheet** *s* (*school*) kartka *f* z ćwiczeniami; **'work•shop** *s* **1.** (*place*) warsztat *m* **2.** warsztaty *pl*; ***a poetry ~*** warsztaty poetyckie; **'work•shy** *adj Br* leniwy; **'work•sta•tion** *s* stacja *f* robocza; **work sur•face** → ***worktop***; **'work•top** *s* blat *m* kuchenny

work-to-'rule *s* strajk *m* włoski

world [wɜːld] **I** *s* świat *m*; ***all over the ~, throughout the ~*** na całym świecie; ***the best in the ~*** najlepszy na świecie; ***the next ~*** tamten świat; ***be all the ~ to s.o.*** być dla kogoś całym światem; ***a man of the ~*** światowiec; ***be ~s apart*** być zupełnie różnym; ***the rest did him a ~ of good*** odpoczynek bardzo dobrze mu zrobił; ***not for all the ~*** za żadne skarby świata; ***what in the ~ is that?*** co to na litość boską ma być? **II** *adj* światowy; ***a ~ champion*** mistrz świata; ***~ championship*** mistrzostwo świata; **world-'class** *adj* światowej klasy; **World 'Cup** *s* Mistrzostwa *pl* Świata (w Piłce Nożnej); **world-'fa•mous** *adj* światowej sławy; **world 'pow•er** *s* POLIT światowe mocarstwo *n*, światowa potęga *f*; **world 're•cord** *s* rekord *m* świata; **world 'war** *s* wojna *f* światowa; **'world•wide I** *adv* na całym świecie **II** *adj* **1.** światowy **2.** ogólnoświatowy

world•ly ['wɜːldlɪ] *adj* **1.** ziemski **2.** doczesny **3.** światowy

worm [wɜːm] **I** *s* robak *m* **II** *v/t* **1.** odrobaczać ⟨-czyć⟩ **2.** ***~ one's way*** torować sobie drogę; ***~ one's way*** (*a.* ***oneself***) ***into s.o.'s heart*** wkraść się w czyjeś łaski; ***~ s.th. out of*** wyciągnąć coś od *G*; **worm-eat•en** ['wɜːmiːtn] *adj* **1.** robaczywy **2.** stoczony przez robaki

worn [wɔːn] *Past Participle* → ***wear***; **worn-'out** *adj* **1.** zużyty **2.** zniszczony **3.** znoszony **4.** *fig* wyświechtany

5. *person*: wyczerpany, *infml* wykończony

wor•ried ['wʌrɪd] *adj* **1.** zmartwiony; ***be ~ about*** martwić się *I* **2.** zaniepokojony; **wor•ried•ly** ['wʌrɪdlɪ] *adv* z niepokojem; **wor•ri•some** ['wʌrɪsəm] *adj Am* niepokojący

wor•ry ['wʌrɪ] **I** *v/i* **1.** martwić ⟨z-⟩ się; ***don't ~ about me*** nie martw się o mnie; ***not to ~*** *infml* nie przejmuj się, nie ma problemu **2.** niepokoić ⟨za-⟩ się **3.** ***~ at*** **a)** *lip*: przygryzać **b)** *fig* gryźć się *I* **II** *v/t* **1.** martwić ⟨z-⟩ **2.** niepokoić ⟨za-⟩ **III** *s* **1.** troska *f* **2.** niepokój *m* **3.** zmartwienie *n*; **wor•ry•ing** ['wʌrɪɪŋ] *adj* niepokojący

worse [wɜːs] **I** *adj comp* → ***bad*** gorszy; ***to make matters ~*** co gorsza; ***he's getting steadily ~*** jego stan stale się pogarsza **II** *adv comp* → ***bad*** gorzej; ***you could do ~ than that*** mogło być gorzej **III** *s* gorsze *n*; ***a change for the ~*** zmiana na gorsze; ***there is ~ to come*** będzie (jeszcze) gorzej; **wors•en** ['wɜːsn] **I** *v/i* pogarszać ⟨-gorszyć⟩ się **II** *v/t* **1.** pogarszać ⟨-gorszyć⟩ **2.** szkodzić ⟨za-⟩

wor•ship ['wɜːʃɪp] **I** *s* **1.** kult *m*; ***a place of ~*** miejsce kultu **2.** uwielbienie *n* **3.** nabożeństwo *n* **II** *v/t* **1.** oddawać ⟨-dać⟩ cześć **2.** wielbić **3.** uwielbiać **III** *v/i* chodzić do kościoła; **wor•ship•per** ['wɜːʃɪpə] *Br*, ***wor•ship•er*** *Am s* **1.** wierny *m* **2.** wyznawca *m*

worst [wɜːst] **I** *adj superl* → ***bad*** najgorszy; ***of the ~ kind*** najgorszego rodzaju; ***come off ~ in a survey*** wypaść najgorzej w sondażu **II** *adv superl* → ***bad*** najgorzej; ***~ of all*** a co najgorsze **III** *s* najgorsze *n*; ***the ~ is over*** najgorsze za nami; ***if the ~ comes to the ~*** w najgorszym razie

worth [wɜːθ] **I** *adj* warty; ***it's ~ $10*** to jest warte 10 dolarów; ***it's ~ a try*** warto spróbować; ***it isn't ~ it*** nie warto, nie opłaca się; ***~ mentioning*** warty wzmianki; ***it's not ~ mentioning*** nie warto o tym mówić; ***it isn't ~ waiting any longer*** nie warto już dłużej czekać; ***the game is not ~ the candle*** gra nie jest warta świeczki **II** *s* wartość *f*; **worth•less** ['wɜθlɪs] *adj* **1.** bezwartościowy **2.** nic nie wart; **worth•'while** *adj* **1.** wart zachodu; ***it's ~ to do s.th.*** warto coś zrobić **2.** interesujący **3.** *discussion*: owocny; **worth•y** ['wɜːðɪ] *adj* **1.** godny; ***~ of mention*** godny wzmianki; ***be ~ of*** zasługiwać na *A* **2.** *aim*: szlachetny

would [wʊd] *v aux* **1.** (*reported speech*) ***he said he ~ come*** powiedział, że przyjdzie; ***she asked if I ~ help*** zapytała, czy pomogę **2.** (*conditional sentences*) ***she'd look better with short hair*** lepiej by jej było w krótkich włosach; ***if you went to see him, he ~ be delighted*** gdybyś go odwiedził, bardzo by się ucieszył; ***what ~ you do if*** co byś zrobił, gdyby **3.** (*request, suggestion*) ***~ you open the door, please?*** czy mógłbyś otworzyć drzwi?; ***~ you like a sandwich?*** masz ochotę na kanapkę? **4.** (*wish*) ***I wish you'd stay*** chciałbym, żebyś został **5.** (*refusing*) ***the door wouldn't shut*** drzwi nie chciały się zamknąć **5.** (*routine*) ***he ~ take a walk after the supper*** po kolacji udawał się na spacer

'would-be *adj*: ***~ actors*** ci, którzy chcą zostać aktorami

would•n't ['wʊdnt] *contracted form* → ***would not***

wound[1] [wuːnd] **I** *s* **1.** rana *f*; ***open old ~s*** *fig* rozdrapywać stare rany **2.** skaleczenie *n* **II** *v/t* ranić ⟨z-⟩; ***he was ~ed in the arm*** został ranny w ramię; ***her feelings were ~ed*** *fig* zraniono jej uczucia

wound[2] [waʊnd] *Past Simple and Past Participle* → ***wind***[2]

woun•ded ['wuːndɪd] *adj* **1.** ranny; ***a ~ soldier*** ranny żołnierz; ***the ~*** ranni **2.** *a. fig* zraniony; ***~ pride*** zraniona duma

wove [wəʊv] *Past Simple* → ***weave***

wo•ven ['wəʊvn] *Past Participle* → ***weave***

wow [waʊ] *interj* u!, ojoj!

wran•gle ['ræŋgl] **I** *s* **1.** spór *m* **2.** kłótnia *f* **II** *v/i* spierać się (***with s.o. over/about*** z kimś o *A*)

wrap [ræp] **I** *v/t* **1.** (*a.* ***~ up***) pakować ⟨za-, o-⟩; ***~ up the presents*** pakować prezenty **2.** (*a.* ***~ up***) owijać ⟨owinąć⟩; ***~ the baby up in a blanket*** owinąć dziecko kocem **II** *s* **1.** papier *m* do pakowania **2.** opakowanie *n* **3.** narzutka *f* **4.** szal *m*; **wrap up I** *v/i* (*a.* ~

W

warm) ubierać ⟨ubrać⟩ się ciepło **II** *v/t infml* **1.** kończyć ⟨za-⟩ **2.** finalizować ⟨s-⟩ **3.** *business*: ubijać ⟨ubić⟩

wrap•per ['ræpə] *s* **1.** papierek *m* **2.** opakowanie *n*; **wrap•ping** ['ræpɪŋ] *s* opakowanie *n*; **'wrap•ping pa•per** *s* papier *m* do pakowania

wrath [ræθ] *s* gniew *m*

wreak [ri:k] *v/t*: ***~ havoc*** wyrządzić wielkie szkody; ***~ vengeance on*** zemścić się na *L*

wreath [ri:θ] *s* **1.** wieniec *m* **2.** wianek *m*

wreathe [ri:ð] *v/t*: ***the mountain tops were ~d in mist*** *lit* szczyty gór spowijała mgła

wreck [rek] **I** *s a. fig* wrak *m*; ***be a nervous ~*** mieć zszargane nerwy **II** *v/t* **1.** niszczyć ⟨z-⟩ **2.** *car*: rozbijać ⟨-bić⟩ **3.** *plans*: niweczyć ⟨z-⟩; **wreck•age** ['rekɪdʒ] *s* szczątki *pl*; **wreck•er** ['rekə] *s Am* (*salvage truck*) samochód *m* pomocy drogowej

wren [ren] *s* (*bird*) strzyżyk *m*

wrench [rentʃ] **I** *v/t* **1.** wyrywać ⟨-rwać⟩ (***s.th. from*** coś *D*); ***~ s.th. off*** **a)** oderwać coś **b)** zerwać coś; ***~ the door open*** szarpnięciem otworzyć drzwi; ***she managed to ~ free*** udało jej się wyrwać **2.** *ankle*: skręcać ⟨-cić⟩ **II** *s* **1.** MED skręcenie *n* **2.** szarpnięcie *n* **3.** TECH klucz *m* francuski

wrest [rest] *v/t* **1.** przejmować ⟨-jąć⟩; ***~ control of a town*** przejąć kontrolę nad miastem **2.** wydzierać ⟨-drzeć⟩ (***s.th. from*** komuś coś) **3.** wyrywać ⟨-rwać⟩ (***s.th. from*** komuś coś)

wres•tle ['resl] *v/i* **1.** SPORT trenować zapasy **2.** walczyć (***with*** z *I*) **3.** zmagać się (***with*** z *I*); **wres•tler** ['reslə] *s* SPORT zapaśnik *m*; **wrest•ling** ['reslɪŋ] *s* SPORT zapasy *pl*; **'wres•tling match** *s* SPORT walka *f* zapaśnicza

wretch [retʃ] *s* nędznik *m*, nieszczęśnik *m*; ***poor ~!*** biedaczek!; **wretch•ed** ['retʃɪd] *adj* **1.** okropny, fatalny, straszny; ***I feel ~*** okropnie się czuję **2.** nędzny, nieszczęsny, biedny

wrig•gle ['rɪgl] **I** *v/i* **1.** wiercić się **2.** wić się **3.** rzucać się **II** *v/t fingers*: szybko poruszać, przebierać; **wriggle out of** *v/i* wykręcić się z *G*

wring (out) [rɪŋ] (*wrung; wrung*) *v/t* wykręcać ⟨-cić⟩, wyciskać ⟨-snąć⟩; ***~ s.o.'s hand*** mocno ścisnąć komuś dłoń; ***~ one's hands*** załamywać ręce; ***~ s.th. out of*** *money, information*: wyciągnąć coś od *G*; **wring•ing** ['rɪŋɪŋ] *adv*: ***~ wet*** ociekający wodą

wrin•kle ['rɪŋkl] **I** *s* zmarszczka *f* **II** *v/t* marszczyć ⟨z-⟩; ***he ~d his forehead*** zmarszczył czoło **III** *v/i* marszczyć ⟨z-⟩ się

wrist [rɪst] *s* ANAT nadgarstek *m*; **'wrist•band** *s* **1.** pasek *m* (do zegarka) **2.** frotka *f*; **'wrist•watch** *s* zegarek *m* na rękę

writ [rɪt] *s* nakaz *m* sądowy

write [raɪt] (*wrote; written*) **I** *v/t* **1.** pisać ⟨na-⟩; ***~ a letter to*** napisać list do *G*; ***guilt was written all over his face*** miał winę wypisaną na twarzy **2.** (*a.* ***~ out***) *cheque*: wypisywać ⟨-sać⟩ **3.** *data*: zapisywać ⟨-sać⟩ **II** *v/i* pisać; **write down** *v/t* zapisywać ⟨-sać⟩; **write off** *v/t* **1.** *debt*: umarzać ⟨umorzyć⟩ **2.** *car*: *Br* kasować ⟨s-⟩ **3.** spisywać ⟨-sać⟩ na straty; **write up** *v/t* pisać ⟨na-⟩ na czysto

'write-off *s* **1.** *debt*: umorzenie *n* **2.** ***the car was a ~*** samochód nadawał się tylko na złom **3.** *infml* strata *f* czasu

writ•er ['raɪtə] *s* pisarz *m*

writhe [raɪð] *v/i* (*in pain*) wić się, skręcać się

writ•ing ['raɪtɪŋ] *s* **1.** pisanie *n* **2.** pismo *n*; ***in ~*** na piśmie, pisemnie **3.** ***~s*** dzieła *pl*, utwory *pl*; **'writ•ing desk** *s* biurko *n*; **'writ•ing pa•per** *s* papeteria *f*

writ•ten ['rɪtn] **I** *Past Participle* → ***write*** **II** *adj exam*: pisemny

wrong [rɒŋ] **I** *adj* **1.** zły; ***the ~ answer*** zła odpowiedź; ***you've dialled the ~ number*** to pomyłka **2.** błędny; ***I got the answer wrong*** podałem błędną odpowiedź **3.** ***be ~*** nie mieć racji, mylić się; ***correct me if I'm ~*** popraw mnie, jeśli się mylę **4.** niewłaściwy; ***fall into the ~ hands*** wpaść w niewłaściwe ręce **5.** nie w porządku; ***there is something ~ with the printer*** coś jest nie tak z tą drukarką; ***what's ~ with you?*** co się z tobą dzieje? **II** *adv* źle; ***get s.o. ~*** źle kogoś zrozumieć; ***go ~*** **a)** popełnić błąd **b)** psuć się **c)** (*watch*) źle chodzić **III** *s* **1.** zło *n* **2.** krzywda *f* **IV** *v/t* krzywdzić ⟨s-⟩; **wrong•do•er** ['rɒŋdu:ə] *s*

1. przestępca *m* 2. winny *m*; **wrong·do·ing** ['rɒŋdu:ɪŋ] *s* 1. przestępstwo *n* 2. czyn *m* karygodny
wrong'foot *v/t* zaskakiwać ⟨-skoczyć⟩
wrong·ful ['rɒŋfəl] *adj* bezprawny
wrong·ly ['rɒŋlɪ] *adv* 1. źle 2. błędnie
wrote [rəʊt] *Past Simple* → ***write***
wrought 'i·ron [rɔ:taɪən] *s* kute żelazo *n* zgrzewne; **wrought-'i·ron** *adj* z kutego żelaza
wrung [rʌŋ] *Past Simple and Past Participle* → ***wring***
wry [raɪ] *adj* 1. *smile*: gorzki 2. *humour*: ironiczny, gorzki
WWW ['dʌblju:dʌblju:dʌblju:] *abbr* (=***world wide web***) www

X

xen·o·pho·bi·a [zenə'fəʊbɪə] *s* ksenofobia *f*; **xen·o·pho·bic** [zenə'fəʊbɪk] *adj* ksenofobiczny
X·mas ['krɪsməs, 'eksməs] → ***Christmas***
X-rat·ed ['eksreɪtɪd] *adj film*: dozwolony od lat 18
X-ray ['eksreɪ] **I** *s* 1. **~s** promieniowanie *n* rentgenowskie 2. zdjęcie *n* rentgenowskie, *infml* rentgen *m* 3. prześwietlenie *n*; ***have an ~*** zrobić sobie prześwietlenie **II** *v/t* prześwietlać ⟨-lić⟩
xy·lo·phone ['zaɪləfəʊn] *s* MUS ksylofon *m*

Y

yacht [jɒt] *s* jacht *m*; **yacht·ing** ['jɒtɪŋ] *s* żeglarstwo *n*, jachting *m*
yachts·man ['jɔtsmən] *pl -men s* żeglarz *m*; **yachts·wom·an** ['jɒtswʊmən] *pl -men s* żeglarka *f*
yak [jæk] **I** *s* (*animal*) jak *m* **II** *v/i infml* paplać
yank [jæŋk] *v/t infml* 1. przyciągać ⟨-gnąć⟩ 2. pociągać ⟨-gnąć⟩
Yank [jæŋk] *s Br infml* Jankes *m*
Yan·kee ['jæŋkɪ] *s* Jankes *m*
yap [jæp] **I** *v/i* 1. szczekać, ujadać 2. *infml* trajkotać, paplać **II** *s* 1. szczekanie *n*, ujadanie *n* 2. trajkotanie *n*, paplanina *f*
yard[1] [jɑ:d] *s* 1. *Br* podwórko *n*, podwórze *n* 2. *Br* dziedziniec *m* 3. *Am* ogródek *m* 4. (*sailing*) reja *f*
yard[2] [~] *s* (*0,9144 metre*) jard *m*
'yard·sale *s Am podwórkowa wyprzedaż wyposażenia domu*; **'yard·stick** *s fig* miara *f*; ***the ~ for success*** miara sukcesu
yarn [jɑ:n] *s* 1. przędza *f* 2. *fig* opowieść *f*, bajka *f*; ***spin a ~*** a) snuć opowieści b) opowiadać bajki, zmyślać
yawn [jɔ:n] **I** *v/i* 1. ziewać ⟨-wnąć⟩ 2. (*abyss*) ziać; zionąć; ***a precipice ~ed at their feet*** u ich stóp ziała przepaść; ***the ~ing gap between the rich and poor*** *fig* przepaść między bogatymi i biednymi **II** *s* 1. ziewnięcie *n* 2. ***be a big ~*** *infml* być okropnie nudnym; **yawn·ing** ['jɔ:nɪŋ] **I** *s* ziewanie *n* **II** *adj precipice*: ziejący
yeah [jeə] *interj infml* tak!
year [jɪə] *s* rok *m*; ***the school ~*** rok szkolny; ***all the ~ round*** przez cały rok; ***he is 14 ~s old*** ma czternaście lat; ***they haven't seen her for ~s*** nie widzieli jej od lat; ***the man of the ~*** człowiek roku; ***not in a hundred ~s!*** nigdy w życiu!; ***~ in, ~ out*** rok w rok; **'year·long** *adj* roczny, trwający rok; **year·ly** ['jɪəlɪ] **I** *adj* roczny; ***a ~ income*** roczny dochód; ***on a ~ basis*** co rok **II** *adv* rocznie, corocznie; ***the magazine is issued twice ~*** magazyn ukazuje się dwa razy do roku
yearn [jɜ:n] *v/i* 1. tęsknić (**for** za *I*) 2. pragnąć (**for** *G*); ***people ~ed for peace*** ludzie pragnęli pokoju; **yearn·ing** ['jɜ:nɪŋ] **I** *s* 1. tęsknota *f* (**for** za *I*) 2. pragnienie *n* (**for** *G*, **to do s.th.** zrobienia czegoś) **II** *s look*: tęskny
yeast [ji:st] *s* drożdże *pl*
yell [jel] **I** *v/i* krzyczeć ⟨krzyknąć⟩,

wrzeszczeć ⟨wrzasnąć⟩ (**at** na *A*) **II** *v/t* wykrzykiwać ⟨-rzyczeć⟩; **~ *encouragement*** wydawać okrzyki zachęty **III** *s* **1.** okrzyk *m*; ***a ~ of surprise*** okrzyk zdziwienia **2.** krzyk *m*, wrzask *m*

yel•low ['jeləʊ] **I** *adj* **1.** żółty **2.** *infml* tchórzliwy **II** *s* (*colour*) żółty *m*, żółć *f* **III** *v/i* zabarwiać ⟨-wić⟩ się na żółto; **yel•low 'card** *s SPORT* żółta kartka *f*; **yel•low 'fe•ver** *s MED* żółta febra *f*; **yel•low 'pag•es** *pl* **1.** branżowa książka *f* telefoniczna **2.** *infml* żółte strony *pl*

yelp [jelp] *v/i* skampleć ⟨za-⟩, skowyczeć ⟨za-⟩

yep [jep] *interj* (*affirmation*) *infml* no

yes [jes] **I** *interj* tak; ***~ or no?*** tak czy nie?; ***~, please*** tak, poproszę; ***say ~*** zgodzić się; ***~, ~, I'm coming*** dobrze już, dobrze, idę **II** *s* **1.** zgoda *f* **2.** głos *m* na tak **3.** odpowiedź *f* na tak; **'yes-man** *pl -men s* potakiwacz *m*

yes•ter•day ['jestədeɪ] **I** *adv* wczoraj, ***the day before ~*** przedwczoraj; ***~ morning*** wczoraj rano; ***I wasn't born ~*** **a)** akurat **b)** nie jestem taki naiwny **II** *s* wczoraj *n*; ***~ was Monday*** wczoraj był poniedziałek; ***~'s newspaper*** wczorajsza gazeta

yet [jet] **I** *adv* **1.** jeszcze; ***I haven't read the book ~*** jeszcze nie przeczytałem tej książki; – ***'Are you ready?' – 'No, not ~.'*** – „Jesteś gotowy?" – „Nie, jeszcze nie."; ***don't go ~*** nie idź jeszcze; ***we may win ~*** jeszcze możemy wygrać; ***~ worse*** jeszcze gorzej; ***~ more*** jeszcze więcej **2.** do tej pory; ***the highest building ~ constructed*** najwyższy budynek, jaki do tej pory zbudowano; ***as ~*** do tej pory, dotychczas **II** *conj* jednak, mimo to; ***she has a good job, and ~ she does not seem happy*** ma dobrą pracę, a jednak nie wydaje się szczęśliwa

ye•ti ['jetɪ] *s* yeti *m*

yew [juː] *s* (*bush, tree*) cis *m*

Y-fronts ['waɪfrʌnts] *pl Br* slipy *pl*

Yid•dish ['jɪdɪʃ] *s* jidysz *m*

yield [jiːld] **I** *v/t* **1.** *profits, results*: dawać ⟨dać⟩ **2.** *fruit*: wydawać ⟨-dać⟩; ***a tree that no longer ~s fruit*** drzewo, które już nie owocuje **3.** poddawać ⟨-dać⟩ (**s.th. to** coś *D*) **II** *v/i* **1.** poddawać ⟨-dać⟩ się (**to** *D*); ***the town was forced to ~*** miasto musiało się poddać **2.** ulegać ⟨ulec⟩ (**to** *D*); ***~ to temptation*** ulec pokusie **3.** ustępować ⟨-tąpić⟩; ***the lock would not ~*** zamek nie chciał się otworzyć **4.** zostawać ⟨-tać⟩ zastąpionym (**to** przez *A*) **5.** *Am* ustępować ⟨-tąpić⟩ pierwszeństwa

YMCA [waɪemsiː'eɪ] *abbr* (=***Young Men's Christian Association***) Chrześcijańskie Stowarzyszenie *n* Młodzieży Męskiej

yo•ga ['jəʊgə] *s* joga *f*

yog•hurt ['jɒʊgət] *s* jogurt *m*

yolk [jəʊk] *s* żółtko *n* (jajka)

you [ju] *stressed* [juː] *pron* **1.** ty; ***~ said ~ knew the way*** mówiłeś, że znasz drogę; ***can I sit next to ~*** mogę usiąść koło ciebie?; ***I thought she told ~*** myślałem, że ci powiedziała **2.** wy; ***~ girls, stop talking*** dziewczyny, przestańcie gadać **3.** (*polite form*) pan; ***excuse me, can ~ tell me what time it is?*** przepraszam, czy mógłby mi pan powiedzieć, która godzina? **4.** ***you can learn a language faster if you read a lot*** języka można się nauczyć szybciej, jeśli się dużo czyta; ***~ must*** trzeba; ***~ should*** należy; ***~ never know*** nigdy nie wiadomo; ***drinking red wine is good for ~*** picie czerwonego wina jest zdrowe

you'd [juːd] *contracted form* → **you would, you had**

you'll [juːl] *contracted form* → **you will**

young [jʌŋ] **I** *adj* **1.** młody; ***~ people*** młodzież, młodzi ludzie; ***she married ~*** młodo wyszła za mąż; ***I think you owe me an apology, ~ man*** myślę, że jesteś mi winien przeprosiny, młody człowieku **2.** mały; ***~ children*** małe dzieci **II** *s* **1.** (*people*) młodzi *pl*, ***a book for ~ and old*** książka dla młodych i starych **2.** (*animal*) młode *pl*; **young•ish** ['jʌŋɪʃ] *adj* dość młody, niestary; **young•ster** ['jʌŋstə] *s infml* **1.** dziecko *n* **2.** nastolatek *m*; ***for ~s*** dla młodzieży

your [jɔː] *poss* **1.** twój; ***I like ~ shoes*** podobają mi się twoje buty **2.** wasz; ***is this ~ house?*** to wasz dom?; ***2 Majesty*** Wasza Wysokość **3.** swój

you're [jʊə] *contracted form* → ***you are***
yours [jɔːz] *poss* **1.** ***a friend of ~*** twój przyjaciel **2.** ***a house of ~*** wasz dom **3.** ***excuse me, is that book ~?*** przepraszam, czy to pana książka? **4.** ***~ sincerely, ~ faithfully*** (*letter ending*) z poważaniem
your•self [jɔː'self] *pron* **1.** (*stressed*) (ty) sam; ***do it ~*** zrób to sam; ***you ~ told me*** sam mi to powiedziałeś; ***by ~*** sam **2.** się; ***have you hurt ~?*** skaleczyłeś się?; ***you don't seem quite ~ today*** wydajesz się dziś jakiś nieswój; ***be ~*** bądź sobą
your•selves [jɔː'selvz] *pron* **1.** (*stressed*) (wy) sami; ***you can try it out for ~*** wypróbujcie sami **2.** się; ***enjoy ~!*** bawcie się dobrze!
youth [juːθ] *s* **1.** młodość *f*; ***in my ~*** w mojej młodości **2.** młody chłopak *m*, nastolatek *m* **3.** młodzież *f*; **'youth club** *s* klub *m* dla młodzieży; **youth•ful** ['juːθfəl] *adj* młodzieńczy; ***~ enthusiasm*** młodzieńczy zapał; **'youth hos•tel** *s* schronisko *n* młodzieżowe
you've [juːv] *contracted form* → ***you have***
yo-yo ['jəʊjəʊ] *pl yo-yos s* (*toy*) jojo *n*
yuck [jʌk] *interj infml* (*disgust*) fu!, fuj!; **yuck•y** ['jʌkɪ] *adj infml* obrzydliwy, wstrętny
Yu•go•slav•i•a [juːgəʊ'slɑːvɪə] *s* Jugosławia *f*
Yule•tide ['juːltaɪd] *s lit* okres *m* bożonarodzeniowy
yum•my ['jʌmɪ] *adj infml* pyszny, palce lizać
yup•pie ['jʌpɪ] *s* yuppi *m*
YWCA [waɪdʌbljuːsiː'eɪ] *abbr* (=***Young Women's Christian Association***) Chrześcijańskie Stowarzyszenie Młodzieży Żeńskiej

Z

Zam•bi•a ['zæmbɪə] *s* Zambia *f*
za•ny ['zeɪnɪ] *adj infml* zwariowany, *infml* zakręcony
zap [zæp] **I** *v/t infml* **1.** (*kill*) rozwalać ⟨-lić⟩ **2.** walić ⟨-lnąć⟩ **II** *v/i* **1.** ***~ TV channels*** skakać po kanałach **2.** pędzić ⟨po-⟩, mknąć ⟨prze-⟩; ***the racing cars ~ped past us*** samochody rajdowe przemknęły obok nas
zap•per ['zæpə] *s* (*TV*) *infml* pilot *m*
zap•py ['zæpɪ] *adj melody*: skoczny
zeal [ziːl] *s* zapał *m*, entuzjazm *m*; **zeal•ous** ['zeləs] *adj* zapalony, pełen entuzjazmu
ze•bra ['zebrə] *pl zebra, zebras s* zebra *f*; **ze•bra 'cross•ing** *s Br* przejście *n* dla pieszych
ze•ro ['zɪrəʊ] **I** *s* zero *n*; ***ten degrees below ~*** dziesięć stopni poniżej zera **II** *s* zerowy **III** *v/t* zerować ⟨wy-⟩; **zero in on** *v/i* **1.** skupiać ⟨-pić⟩ się na *L* **2.** celować ⟨wy-⟩ w *A*; **ze•ro-e•'mis•sion** *adj* ekologiczny, o zerowej emisji zanieczyszczeń; **ze•ro-'tol•er•ance** *s* (*attitude*) zero *n* tolerancji
zest [zest] *s* **1.** pasja *f*, zamiłowanie *n*; ***a great ~ for life*** wielka radość życia **2.** *fig* pikanteria *f*, smaczek *m* **3.** COOK skórka *f*; ***orange ~*** starta skórka pomarańczowa
zig•zag ['zɪgzæg] **I** *s* zygzak *m* **II** *adj* zygzakowaty **III** *v/i* **1.** wić się **2.** poruszać się zygzakiem
zilch [zɪltʃ] *s infml* nic *n*; ***with ~*** z niczym
zil•lion ['zɪlɪən] *s*: ***I've told you a ~ times that*** *Am infml* mówiłem ci już miliony razy, że; ***there were ~s of reporters there*** *Am infml* był tam tłum reporterów
Zim•ba•bwe [zɪm'bɑːbweɪ] *s* Zimbabwe *n*
zinc [zɪŋk] *s* CHEM cynk *m*
zip [zɪp] **I** *s* **1.** zamek *m* (błyskawiczny), suwak *m*; ***do up a ~*** zasunąć zamek (błyskawiczny) **2.** *infml* energia *f* **3.** *Am infml* zero *n*; ***we won four ~*** wygraliśmy cztery do zera **II** *v/t* **1.** zapinać ⟨-piąć⟩ (na zamek błyskawiczny) **2.** INF *file*: pakować ⟨s-⟩ **III** *v/i* *infml* pędzić ⟨po-⟩; ***I ~ped to town to buy some food*** popędziłem do miasta kupić coś do jedzenia; **zip up I** *v/t* zapinać ⟨-piąć⟩ (na zamek błys-

kawiczny); ~ ***s.o. up*** zapiąć komuś zamek (błyskawiczny), **II** *v/i* zapinać ⟨-piąć⟩ się (na zamek błyskawiczny)

'zip code *s Am* kod *m* pocztowy; **'zip fas•ten•er** *Br* → ***zip I.1***; **zip•per** ['zɪpə] *Am* → ***zip I.1***

zit [zɪt] *s infml* pryszcz *m*

zo•di•ac ['zəʊdɪæk] *s* zodiak *m*; ***signs of the ~*** znaki zodiaku

zom•bie ['zɒmbɪ] *s* zombi *m*

zone [zəʊn] **I** *s* strefa *f* **II** *v/t* **1.** wydzielać ⟨-lić⟩ **2.** dzielić ⟨po-⟩ na strefy

zonked [zɒŋkt] *adj infml* **1.** wykończony **2.** skacowany

zoo [zuː] *pl zoos s* zoo *n*

zo•o•log•i•cal [zəʊə'lɒdʒɪkl] *adj* zoologiczny; **zo•ol•o•gist** [zəʊ'ɔlədʒɪst] *s* zoolog *m*; **zo•ol•o•gy** [zəʊ'ɔlədʒɪ] *s* zoologia *f*

zoom [zuːm] **I** *s* PHOT zoom *m*, obiektyw *m* zmiennoogniskowy **II** *v/i* **1.** mknąć ⟨prze-⟩, śmigać ⟨-gnąć⟩ **2.** (*a.* ~ **up**) (*prices*) podskakiwać ⟨-skoczyć⟩; **zoom in** *v/i* PHOT robić ⟨z-⟩ zbliżenie (***on*** na *A*); **zoom out** *v/i* PHOT oddalać ⟨-lić⟩ się, pomniejszać ⟨-szyć⟩ obraz

zoom 'lens *pl* PHOT obiektyw *m* zmiennoogniskowy

zuc•chi•ni [zu'kiːnɪ] *pl zucchini, zucchinis s* cukinia

Summary of Polish Grammar

A. Declension

Declension is the inflection of nouns, adjectives, numerals, pronouns and adjectival participles by using endings that indicate case, number and gender. Note: nouns and substantival pronouns are not inflected according to gender. They appear in a specified gender: masculine, feminine or neuter.

The Declension of Nouns

The following declensions are distinguished according to the kind of noun: masculine, feminine or neuter.

The Masculine Declension

I. The table below shows the declension of masculine nouns whose stem ends in a hard consonant: *-b, -d, -f, -ł, -t, -m, -n, -p, -r, -s, -t, -w, -z.*

		N	G	D	A	I	L	V
sg.	*anim.*	syn-ϕ	syn-a	syn-owi	= Gsyn	-em	syn-u	= L
	inanim.	sen-ϕ	sn-u	sn-owi	= N	sn-em	śn(i)-e	= L
	inanim.	dom-ϕ	dom-u	dom-owi	= N	dom-em	dom-u	= L
pl.	*anim.*	syn-owie	syn-ów	syn-om	= Gsyn	-ami	syn-ach	= N
	inanim.	sn-y	sn-ów	sn-om	= N	sn-ami	sn-ach	= N
	inanim.	dom-y	dom-ów	dom-om	= N	dom-ami	dom-ach	= N

II. The table below shows the declension of masculine nouns whose stem ends in a soft consonant: *-ć, -dź, -j, -l, -ń, -ś,* or a functionally soft consonant: *-c, -cz, -dz, -dż, -rz, -sz, -ż* and *-g, -ch, -k.*

		N	G	D	A	I	L	V
sg.	*anim.*	harcerz-ϕ	harcerz-a	harcerz-owi	= Gha	rcerz-em	harcerz-u	= L
	anim.	dziadek-ϕ	dziadk-a	dziadk-owi	= Gdz	iadk-iem	dziadk-u	= L
	inanim.	ból-ϕ	ból-u	ból-owi	= N	ból-em	ból-u	= L
pl.	*anim.*	harcerz-e	harcerz-y	harcerz-om	= Gh	arcerz-ami	harcerz-ach	= N
	anim.	dziadk-owie	dziadk-ów	dziadk-om	= Gdz	iadk-ami	dziadk-ach	= N
	inanim.	ból-e	ból-ów	ból-om	= N	ból-ami	ból-ach	= N

III. List of endings of the masculine declension

	sg.	*pl.*
N	-ϕ, -o	-owie, -i, -y, -e
G-a	, -u	-ów, -i, -y
D	-a, -owi	-om
A	-a, -ϕ	-ów, -i, -y, -e
I	-em	-ami, -mi
L	-e, -u	-ach
V	-e, -u	-owie, -i, -y, -e

IV. Summary of noun inflectional endings: masculine declension

1. Nominative sg.: **-ϕ**, *syn-ϕ*, *ból-ϕ* (diminutive forms are exceptions, e.g. *Józi-o, dzia-dzi-o,* which end in **-o**).
2. Genitive sg.: **-a** for animate nouns, e.g. *harcerz-a*, *ps-a* and for nouns denoting the names of tools and parts of the body, e.g. *talerz-a*, *kolan-a*; **-u** for inanimate nouns, e.g. *ból-u, dom-u, sn-u.*
3. Locative sg.: **-e** for hard-stemmed nouns, e.g. *śni-e*, (exceptions: *dom-u*, *syn-u*); **-u** for soft-stemmed nouns and for those whose stem ends in *-k*, *-g*, *-ch*, np. *chłopc-u, ból-u.*
4. Vocative sg. has the same endings as locative sg. Exception: nouns that end in *-ec*, e.g. *chłopiec – chłopcz-e*!
5. Nominative pl.: **-e** for soft-stemmed and for functionally soft-stemmed nouns, e.g.: *harcerz-e*, *ból-e*; **-y, -i** for hard-stemmed nouns, but **-y** is characteristic of inanimate nouns: *dom-y*, *sn-y*, **-i** for animate nouns: *chłop-i*, (exception: nouns which end in *-k*, *-g*, *-ch*, and *-ec*, e.g.: *Polak – Polac-y*, *Norweg – Norwedz-y*, *chłopiec – chłopc-y*); **-owie** for words which denote the names of degrees of relationships; e.g.: *sędzi-owie, syn-owie.*
6. Genitive pl.: **-ów** for nouns ending in a hard stem, e.g.: *syn-ów, dom-ów*; **-i, -y** for soft-stemmed and for functionally soft nouns, e.g.: *harcerz-y*; **-ϕ** is rare, e.g. *mieszczan-ϕ.*
7. Accusative pl. for animate nouns A = Gpl ., e.g. *harcerz-y*, *chłopc-ów*; for inanimate nouns A = N pl., e.g.: *sn-y*, *ból-e.*

The Feminine Declension

I. The table below shows the declension of feminine nouns whose stem ends in a hard consonant: *-ba, -cha, -da, -fa, -ła, -ta, -ma, -na, -pa, -ra, -sa, -ta, -wa, -za.*

	N	G	D	A	I	L	V
sg.	wdow-a	wdow-y	wdow(i)-e	wdow-ę	wdow-ą	wdow(i)-e	wdow-o!
	wizyt-a	wizyt-y	wizyc(i)-e	wizyt-ę	wizyt-ą	wizyc(i)-e	wizyt-o!
pl.	wdow-y	wdów-ϕ	wdow-om	= N	wdow-ami	wdow-ach	= N
	wizyt-y	wizyt-ϕ	wizyt-om	= N	wizyt-ami	wizyt-ach	= N

II. The table below shows the declension of feminine nouns whose stem ends in a soft consonant or a functionally soft consonant or *-k*, *-g*, *-ch*. They end as follows: *-ca, -cza, -dza, -dża, -rza, -sza, -ża, -la, -bia, -cia, -dzia, -fia, -gia, -ja, -kia, -lia, -mia, -nia, -pia, -ria, -sia, -tia, -wia, -zia.*

	N	G	D	A	I	L	V
sg.	niani- a	nian-i	nian-i	niani-ę	niani-ą	nian-i	niani-u!
	wież-a	wież-y	wież-y	wież-ę	wież-ą	wież-y	wież-o!
pl.	niani-e	nian-ϕ	niani-om	= N	niani-ami	niani-ach	= N
	wież-e	wież-ϕ	wież-om	= N	wież-ami	wież-ach	= N

III. The table below shows the declension of feminine nouns that end in a consonant in the nominative sg.

	N	G	D	A	I	L	V
sg.	brew-ϕ	brw-i	brw-i	= N	brwi-ą	brw-i	= G
	noc-ϕ	noc-y	noc-y	= N	noc-ą	noc-y	= G
pl.	brw-i	brw-i	brwi-om	= N	brwi-ami	brwi-ach	= N
	noc-e	noc-y	noc-om	= N	noc-ami	noc-ach	= N

IV. List of endings of the feminine declension

	sg.	*pl.*
N	-a, -i, -ϕ	-y, -i, -e
G-y	, -i	-ϕ, -i, -y
D	-e, -i, -y	-om
A	-ę, -ϕ	= N
I	-ą	-ami,-mi
L	= G-a	ch
V	-o, -i, -y	= N

V. Summary of noun inflectional endings: feminine declension

1. Nominative sg.: **-a** for nouns with a hard stem, e.g.: *wdow-a*; **-i** for nouns with a soft stem, e.g.: *pan-i*; **-ϕ** for nouns ending in a consonant, e.g.: *noc-ϕ*.
2. Genitive sg.: -**y** for nouns with a hard stem, e.g.: *wizyt-y*; **-i** for nouns ending in -*k*, -*g*, e.g. *matk-i, nog-i*; and such nouns whose stem ends in a soft consonant: nominative sg. *dłoń*-ϕ, genitive sg. *dłon-i*.
3. Accusative sg.: **-ę**, e.g. *matk-ę,* apart from nouns ending in a consonant in the nominative sg., e.g.: *noc-ϕ* (A sg. = N sg.). Exception: **-ą,** *pani-ą.*
4. In the genitive pl. most nouns take the form of the stem, e.g.: *wdów-*ϕ, *niań-*ϕ. Nouns which end in: *-alnia*, *-arnia*, *-ernia*, *-ja* have the ending **-i**, e.g. *księgarnia – księgarn-i, cukiernia – cukiern-i, transmisja – transmisj-i.* Nouns that end in a consonant in the nominative sg. take the following endings: **-y, -i,** e.g. *noc – noc-y, dłoń – dłon-i.*
5. Instrumental pl.: **-ami,** e.g.: *wdow-ami, noc-ami*, with the exception of nouns with the suffix *-ość* which take the ending **-mi**, e.g.: *kość – kość-mi.*

The Neuter Declension

I. The table below shows the declension of neuter nouns with the ending *-o* in the nominative sg.

	N	G	D	A	I	L	V
sg.	okn-o	okn-a	okn-u	= N	okn-em	okni-e	= N
	lat-o	lat-a	lat-u	= N	lat-em	leci-e	= N
pl.	okn-a	okien-ϕ	okn-om	= N	okn-ami	okn-ach	= N
	lat-a	lat-ϕ	lat-om	= N	lat-ami	lat-ach	= N

II. The table below shows the declension of neuter nouns with the ending *-e* in the nominative sg.

	N	G	D	A	I	L	V
sg.	pol-e	pol-a	pol-u	= N	pol-em	pol-u	= N
	zboże	zboż-a	zboż-u	= N	zboż-em	zboż-u	= N
pl.	pol-a	pól-ϕ	pol-om	= N	pol-ami	pol-ach	= N
	zboż-a	zbóż-ϕ	zboż-om	= N	zboż-ami	zboż-ach	= N

III. The table below shows the declension of neuter nouns with the ending *-ę* in the nominative sg.

	N	G	D	A	I	L	V
sg.	ciel-ę	ciel-ęci-a	ciel-ęci-u	= N	ciel-ęci-em	ciel-ęci-u	= N
	źrebi-ę	źrebi-ęci-a	źrebi-ęci-u	= N	źrebi-ęci-em	źrebi-ęci-u	= N
pl.	ciel-ę-ta	ciel-ąt-ϕ	ciel-ęt-om	= N	ciel-ęt-ami	ciel-ęt-ach	= N
	źrebi-ęt-a	źrebi-ąt-ϕ	źrebi-ęt-om	= N	źrebi-ęt-ami	źrebi-ęt-ach	= N

IV. List of endings of neuter declension

	sg.	*pl.*
N	-o, -e, -ę	-a
G-a		-ϕ, -i, -y
D	-u	-om
A	= N	= N
I	-em	-ami
L	-e, -u	-ach
V	= N	= N

V. Summary of noun inflectional endings: neuter declension

1. Genitive pl.: **-ϕ**, e.g.: *okien-ϕ, pól-ϕ, cieląt-ϕ,* but nouns ending in *-e* in the nominative sg. have the genitive pl. **-i, -y**, e.g. *narzędzie – narzędz-i, wybrzeże – wybrzeż-y.*
2. The nouns which end in *-um* in the nominative sg. are indeclinable in the singular and declined as follows in the plural:

	N	G	D	A	I	L	V
pl.	lice-a	lice-ów	lice-om	= N	lice-ami	lice-ach	= N

Declension of nouns – some peculiarities

1. Masculine nouns ending in *-a* (*poeta, znawca*) decline in the singular like feminine nouns, and in the plural like masculine nouns.
2. The following nouns are indeclinable: *kakao, boa, menu, salami, jury, alibi*
3. Plural nouns, e.g. *rodzice, państwo, usta, drzwi, nożyce, okulary, fusy, imieniny, perfumy* are declined as follows:

	N	G	D	A	I	L	V
pl.	skrzypc-e	skrzypc-ów	skrzypc-om	skrzypc-e	skrzypc-ami	skrzypc-ach	skrzypc-e!
pl.	obcęg-i	obcęg-ów	obcęg-om	obcęg-i	obcęg-ami	obcęg-ach	obcęg-i!

The Declension of Adjectives

Adjectives are declined by using endings that indicate case, number and gender. In the singular, they occur in three forms e.g. *zdrow-y, zdrow-a, zdrow-e*. In the plural adjectives have two forms: masculine, which describes masculine nouns, e.g.: *zdrow-i mężczyźni, zdrow-i uczniowie*; and non-masculine, which describes feminine, neuter and inanimate masculine nouns, e.g.: *zdrow-e kobiety, zdrow-e cielęta, zdrow-e owoce.*

I. The table below shows the declension of adjectives.

	sg.	*sg.*	*sg.*	*pl.*	*pl.*
	masculine	*feminine*	*neuter*	*masculine*	*non-masculine*
N	tan-i mił-y	tani-a mił-a	tani-e mił-e	tan-i mil-i	tani-e mił-e
Gta	ni-ego mił-ego	tani-ej mił-ej	tani-ego mił-ego	tan-ich mił-ych	tan-ich mił-ych
D	tani-emu mił-emu	tani-ej mił-ej	tani-emu mił-emu	tan-im mił-ym	tan-im mił-ym
A	tan-i mił-ego	tani-ą mił-ą	tani-e mił-e	tan-ich mił-ych	tani-e mił-e
I	tan-im mił-ym	tani-ą mił-ą	tan-im mił-ym	tan-imi mił-ymi	tan-imi mił-ymi
L	tan-im mił-ym	tani-ej mił-ej	tan-im mił-ym	tan-ich mił-ych	tan-ich mił-ych
V	tan-i! mił-y!	tani-a! mił-a!	tani-e! mił-e!	tan-i! mil-i!	tani-e! mił-e!

II. List of endings of the adjective declension

	sg.	*sg.*	*sg.*	*pl.*	*pl.*
	masculine	*feminine*	*neuter*	*masculine*	*non-masculine*
N	-y, -i	-a	-e	-i, -y	-e
G-e	go	-ej	-ego	-ich, -ych	-ich, -ych
D	-emu	-ej	-emu	-im, -ym	-im, -ym
A	-y, -i, -ego	-ą	-e	-ich, -ych	-e
I	-im, -ym	-ą	-im, -ym	-imi, -ymi	-imi, -ymi
L	-im, -ym	-ej	-im, -ym	-ich, -ych	-ich, -ych
V	= N	= N	= N	= N	= N

III. Summary of inflectional endings of adjectives

1. The differentiation between endings of the same case (e.g. locative sg. masc. has parallel endings ***-im, -ym***), depends on the stem of the adjective. An adjective whose stem ends in a soft consonant has ***-i*** in its ending and ***-y*** if it ends in a hard consonant.

2. The nominative sg. masc. has the following endings: ***-i*** for adjectives whose stem ends in a soft consonant *-k*, *-g*, *-ch*, e.g.: *tan-i, dług-i;* ***-y*** for adjectives whose stem ends in a hard consonant e.g.: *chciw-y.*

3. The accusative sg. of adjectives denoting animate nouns is the same as the genitive e.g. *dobr-ego człowieka,* The accusative sg. of adjectives denoting inanimate nouns is the same as the nominative, e.g. *now-y samochód.*

4. In the nominative pl. masculine, hard consonants change into soft ones: ***-py*** – ***-pi***, ***-by*** – ***-bi***, ***-wy*** – ***-wi***, ***-ny*** – ***-ni***, ***-dy*** – ***-dzi***, ***-ty*** – ***-ci***, e.g.: *równy – równi, garbaty – garbaci.* Additionally, the following consonants change: ***-k*** – ***-c***, ***-g*** – ***-dz***, ***-ch*** – ***-s***, e.g.: *wysoki – wysocy, ubogi – ubodzy, cichy – cisi.*

5. Simple adjectives: *zdrów-ϕ, wesół-ϕ, ciekaw-ϕ, pewien-ϕ, gotów-ϕ,* take only the masculine form of the nominative sg., e.g. *Chłopiec jest zdrów.*

IV. Degrees of comparison in adjectives

The comparative is formed by adding the endings ***-szy, -si*** to the stem of the basic form of the adjective, e.g. sg. *młod-y – młod-szy,* pl. *młodz-i – młod-si.* The superlative is formed by adding the prefix *naj-* to the comparative form of the adjective, e.g.: *młodszy – naj-młodszy.*

V. Irregular adjectives:

duży – większy – największy

mały – mniejszy – najmniejszy

dobry – lepszy – najlepszy

zły – gorszy – najgorszy

The Declension of Pronouns

I. The declension of personal pronouns

In the declension of personal pronouns, oblique cases are not formed by using the nominative stem. Within the same case there are variant forms (stressed – longer, and unstressed – shorter), e.g. in the nominative sg. *mnie – mi*, *tobie* – ci.

N	ja	ty
Gmn	ie	ciebie
D	mnie, mi	tobie, ci
A	mnie, mię	ciebie, cię
I	mną	tobą
L	mnie	tobie

II. The declension of possessive pronouns

Possessive pronouns e.g. *mój, twój, nasz, wasz* are declined in the same way as adjectives. Oblique cases are not formed by using the nominative stem. Variant forms also occur.

	sg.	*sg.*	*sg.*	*pl.*	*pl.*
	masculine	*feminine*	*neuter*	*masculine*	*non-masculine*
N	on	ona	ono	oni	one
Gje	go, go, niego	jej, niej	jego, go, niego	ich, nich	ich, nich
D	jemu, mu, niemu	jej, niej	jemu, mu, niemu	im, nim	im, nim
A	jego, go, niego	ją, nią	je, nie	ich, nich	je, nie
I	nim	nią	nim	nimi	nimi
L	nim	niej	nim	nich	nich

The declension of numerals

I. The numeral *jeden* has the same forms as the personal pronoun *on*. It is declined in the same way as adjectives e.g.: *jeden uczeń, jedna uczennica, jedno dziecko, jedni uczniowie, jedne uczennice*.

II. The numeral *dwa* occurs in three forms: masculine (*dwaj uczniowie*), feminine (*dwie uczennice*) and non-masculine and neuter (*dwa zeszyty*).

III. The numerals from *trzech* to *tysiąc* have only two forms: masculine (*trzej uczniowie*) and non-masculine (*trzy uczennice, trzy zeszyty*).

IV. Collective numerals, e.g. *dwoje, troje, czworo*, etc. are declined in the same way as neuter nouns in the singular, e.g.: *troj-e ludzi, trojg-a ludzi, trojg-u ludziom, trojgi-em ludzi*.

V. Ordinal numbers, e.g. *pierwszy, drugi, trzeci*, etc. are declined in the same way as adjectives, e.g. *pierwszy uczeń, pierwszego ucznia, pierwszemu uczniowi*, etc.

B. Conjugation

Polish verbs fall into 11 conjugations according to thematic suffixes.

Group I verbs with the thematic suffix ***-a-***
e.g. *kochać, biegać, czytać*, the ending of the infinitive is ***-ać*,**

infinitive	*1st pers., sg., present tense*	*3rd pers., sg., present tense*	*3rd pers., pl., present tense*	*imperative*	*3rd pers., sg., m, f, n, past tense*	*adverbial simultaneous participle*
czyt-a-ć	czyt-a-m	czyt-a	czyt-aj-ą	czyt-a-j!	czyt-a-ł(a, -o)	czyt-aj-ąc

In the third person plural present tense, the imperative and the simultaneous participle, the suffix ***-a-*** undergoes extension to ***-aj-***, e.g. *czyt-aj-ą.*

Group II verbs with the thematic suffix ***-e-***
e.g. *umieć, rozumieć*, the ending of the infinitive is ***-eć***

infinitive	*1st pers., sg., present tense*	*3rd pers., sg., present tense*	*3rd pers., pl., present tense*	*imperative*	*3rd pers., sg., m, f, n, past tense*	*adverbial simultaneous participle*
umi-e-ć	umi-e-m	umie	umi-ej-ą	umi-ej!	umi-a-ł(a, -o)	umi-ej-ąc

In the third person plural present tense, the imperative and the simultaneous participle, the suffix ***-e-*** undergoes extension to ***-ej-***, e.g. *umi-ej-ą.*

Group III verbs with the thematic suffix ***-eje-***
e.g. *szaleć, maleć, posmutnieć*, the ending of the infinitive is ***-eć***

infinitive	*1st pers., sg., present tense*	*3rd pers., sg., present tense*	*3rd pers., pl., present tense*	*imperative*	*3rd pers., sg., m, f, n, past tense*	*adverbial simultaneous participle*
mal-e-ć	mal-ej-ę	mal-ej-e	mal-ej-ą	mal-ej!	mal-a-ł(a, -o)	mal-ej-ąc

The thematic suffix ***-eje-*** shortens to ***-ej-*** before vowels, e.g. (*on*) *mal-ej-e*; before consonants it takes the following form: ***-eje-*** e.g. (*ty*) *mal-eje-sz*, (*my*) *mal--eje-my*.

Group IV verbs with the thematic suffix ***-uje-***
e.g. *pracować, malować*, the ending of the infinitive is ***-ować***

infinitive	*1st pers., sg., present tense*	*3rd pers., sg., present tense*	*3rd pers., pl., present tense*	*impera-tive*	*3rd pers., sg., m, f, n, past tense*	*adverbial simulta-neous participle*
prac-owa-ć	prac-uj-ę	prac-uj-e	prac-uj-ą	prac-uj!	prac-owa-ł(a, -o)	prac-uj-ąc

The thematic suffix ***-uje-*** gets shortened to ***-uj-*** before vowels, e.g. (*on*) *prac--uj-e.*

Group V verbs with the thematic suffix: ***-nie-***, ***-nę-*** or ***-ną-***
e.g. *puchnąć, chudnąć, sunąć*, the ending of the infinitive is ***-nąć***

infinitive	*1st pers., sg., present tense*	*3rd pers., sg., present tense*	*3rd pers., pl., present tense*	*impera-tive*	*3rd pers., sg., m, f, n, past tense*	*adverbial simulta-neous participle*
ciąg-ną-ć	ciąg-n-ę	ciąg-nie	ciąg-n-ą	ciąg-nij!	ciąg-ną-ł (-ęła, -ęło)	ciąg-n-ąc
su-ną-ć	su-n-ę	su-nie	su-n-ą	su-ń!	su-ną-ł (-ęła, -ęło)	su-n-ąc
gi-ną-ć	gi-n-ę	gi-nie	gi-n-ą	gi-ń!	gi-ną-ł (-ęła, -ęło)	gi-nąc

Group VI verbs with the thematic suffix: ***-i-*** or ***-y-***
e.g. *topić, mierzyć*, the ending of the infinitive is ***-ić, -yć***

infinitive	*1st pers., sg., present tense*	*3rd pers., sg., present tense*	*3rd pers., pl., present tense*	*impera-tive*	*3rd pers., sg., m, f, n, past tense*	*adverbial simulta-neous participle*
top-i-ć	top-i-ę	top-i	top-i-ą	top!	top-i-ł(a, -o)	top-i-ąc
mierz-y-ć	mierz-ę	mierz-y	mierz-ą	mierz!	mierz-y-ł(a, -o)	mierz-ąc

Group VII verbs with the thematic suffix: ***-e*** in the infinitive, ***-i-*** or ***-y-*** in the present tense
e.g. *myśleć, usłyszeć*, the ending of the infinitive is ***-ić, -yć***

infinitive	*1st pers., sg., present tense*	*3rd pers., sg., present tense*	*3rd pers., pl., present tense*	*impera-tive*	*3rd pers., sg., m, f, n, past tense*	*adverbial simulta-neous participle*
myśl-e-ć	myśl-ę	myśl-i	myśl-ą	myśl!	myśl-a-ł(a, -o)	myśl-ąc
usłysz-e-ć	usłysz-ę*	usłysz-y*	usłysz-ą*	usłysz!	usłysz-a-ł(a, -o)	–

* forms of the future simple tense

Group VIII verbs with the thematic suffix: ***-ywa-, -iwa-***
e.g. *widywać, wymachiwać,* the ending of the infinitive is ***-ywać*** or ***-iwać***,

infinitive	*1st pers., sg., present tense*	*3rd pers., sg., present tense*	*3rd pers., pl., present tense*	*impera-tive*	*3rd pers., sg., m, f, n, past tense*	*adverbial simulta-neous participle*
wid-ywa-ć	wid-uj-ę	wid-uj-e	wid-uj-ą	widuj!	wid-ywa-ł(a, -o)	wid-uj-ąc
wymach-iwa-ć	wymach-uj-ę	wymach-uj-e	wymach-uj-ą	wymach-uj!	wymach-iwa-ł(a,-o)	wymach-uj-ąc

In the present tense verbs have the following suffix ***-uje-***, e.g. (*ja*) *wymach-uj-ę,* (*ty*) *wymach-uje-sz.*

Group IX verbs with the thematic suffix: ***-a-*** in the infinitive, ***-e-*** in the present tense
e.g. *łapać, pisać, chrapać*, the ending of the infinitive is ***-ać***

infinitive	*1st pers., sg., present tense*	*3rd pers., sg., present tense*	*3rd pers., pl., present tense*	*impera-tive*	*3rd pers., sg., m, f, n, past tense*	*adverbial simulta-neous participle*
łap-a-ć	łapi-ę	łapi-e	łapi-ą	łap!	łap-a-ł(a, -o)	łapi-ąc

Group X comprises various verbs: with the thematic suffix: ***-a-*** in the infinitive, ***-e-*** in the present tense:

Xa – the stem of the verbs ends in ***-i, -y, -u***;

Xb – they have the thematic suffix ***-eje-*** in the present tense, ***-a-*** in the past tense and in the infinitive;

Xc – there is a change in the stem from ***-n-***, ***-m-*** into ***-ą-*** e.g. *dąć – dmie*, *tchnąć – tchnie.*

infinitive	*1st pers., sg., present tense*	*3rd pers., sg., present tense*	*3rd pers., pl., present tense*	*impera-tive*	*3rd pers., sg., m, f, n, past tense*	*adverbial simulta-neous participle*
ży-ć	żyj-ę	żyj-e	żyj-ą	żyj!	żył(a, -o)	żyj-ąc
grz-a-ć	grz-ej-ę	grz-ej-e	grz-ej-ą	grzej!	grzał(a, -o)	grz-ej-ąc
dą-ć	dm-ę	dmi-e	dm-ą	dmij!	dął (-ęła, -ęło)	dmi-ąc

Group XI verbs with the thematic suffix: ***-e-*** in the present tense (*wiezi-e-sz, tłucz-e-my).*
There is no suffix in the infinitive.

infinitive	*1st pers., sg., present tense*	*3rd pers., sg., present tense*	*3rd pers., pl., present tense*	*impera-tive*	*3rd pers., sg., m, f, n, past tense*	*adverbial simulta-neous participle*
wieś-ć	wioz-ę	wiezi-e	wioz-ą	wieź!	wiózł(a, -o)	wioz-ąc
tłuc	tłuk-ę	tłucz-e	tłuk-ą	tłucz!	tłukł(a, -o)	tłuk-ąc

Rules for forming conjugations

The Past Simple Tense (the forms are based on the stem of the verb in the past tense)

sg. m, f, n	*pl. m, non-m*
1. czytał-em, -am	1. czytali-śmy, czytały-śmy
2. czytał-eś, -aś	2. czytali-ście, czytały-ście
3. czytał-ϕ, -a, -o	3. czytali-ϕ, czytały-ϕ

The Present Simple Tense (only imperfect verbs; the forms are based on the stem of the verb in the present tense)

sg.	*pl.*
1. czyta-m	1. czyta-my
2. czyta-sz	2. czyta-cie
3. czyta-ϕ	3. czyta-ją

The Future Simple Tense (only perfect verbs; the forms are based on the stem of the verb in the present tense)

sg.	*pl.*
1. przeczyta-m	1. przeczyta-my
2. przeczyta-sz	2. przeczyta-cie
3. przeczyta-ϕ	3. przeczyta-ją

The Future Tense type I (only imperfect verbs; the forms are based on the stem of the verb in the past tense)

sg.	*pl.*
1. będ-ę czytać	1. będzie-my czytać
2. będzie-sz czytać	2. będzie-cie czytać
3. będzie-ϕ czytać	3. będ-ą czytać

The Future Tense type II

sg. m, f, n	*pl. m, non-m*
1. będę pisał, -a,	1. będziemy pisali, będziemy pisały
2. będziesz pisał, -a	2. będziecie pisali, będziecie pisały
3. będzie pisał, -a, -o	3. będą pisali, będą pisały

Declensional forms of the verb

1. Active and passive participles are declined according to the adjectival declension.
   a) The active participle is formed by adding the following to the stem of the verb in the third person plural of the present tense: the suffix ***-ąc-*** and the appropriate case ending, e.g. N sg. *czytaj-ąc-a kobieta, czytaj-ąc-y chłopiec*, G sg. *czytaj-ąc-ej kobiety, czytaj-ąc-ego chłopca*, etc.
   b) The passive participle is formed by adding the following to the stem of the verb in the past tense: the suffix ***-n-***, ***-on-***, ***-t-*** and the appropriate case ending, e.g. N sg. *czyta-n-a książka*, Gsg . *czyta-n-ej książki*, etc.
2. Gerunds are declined according to the noun declension. They are formed by adding the following to the stem: the suffixes ***-nie***, **-(*i*)*enie***, ***-cie***, **-(*i*)*ęcie***, **-(*ie*)*nie*** and the appropriate case ending, e.g. *czyta-nie, macha-nie, widywa-nie, d-ęcie.*

Indeclinable forms of the verb

1. Infinitives
2. Adverbial participles
   a) Simultaneous participle – is formed by adding the suffix ***-ąc*** to the stem of the verb in the 3rd person plural in the present tense, e.g. *czytaj-ąc, widz-ąc*
   b) Anticipatory participle – is formed by adding the following suffixes to the stem of the verb in the past tense: ***-łszy*** (if the stem ends in a consonant), e.g. *zjadłszy, podniósłszy*; or ***-wszy*** (if the stem ends in a vowel), e.g. *dojecha-wszy, przeczyta-wszy.*
3. Modal verbs, e.g.: *trzeba, warto, można, wolno.*

Numerals – Liczebniki

Cardinal Numerals – Liczebniki główne

0 *nought*, zero
telefon: *O*, zero
1 *one* jeden, jedna, jedno
2 *two* dwa, dwie
3 *three* trzy
4 *four* cztery
5 *five* pięć
6 *six* sześć
7 *seven* siedem
8 *eight* osiem
9 *nine* dziewięć
10 *ten* dziesięć
11 *eleven* jedenaście
12 *twelve* dwanaście
13 *thirteen* trzynaście
14 *fourteen* czternaście
15 *fifteen* piętnaście
16 *sixteen* szesnaście
17 *seventeen* siedemnaście
18 *eighteen* osiemnaście
19 *nineteen* dziewiętnaście
20 *twenty* dwadzieścia
21 *twenty-one* dwadzieścia jeden
22 *twenty-two* dwadzieścia dwa
30 *thirty* trzydzieści
31 *thirty-one* trzydzieści jeden
40 *forty* czterdzieści
41 *forty-one* czterdzieści jeden
50 *fifty* pięćdziesiąt
51 *fifty-one* pięćdziesiąt jeden
60 *sixty* sześćdziesiąt
61 *sixty-one* sześćdziesiąt jeden
70 *seventy* siedemdziesiąt
71 *seventy-one* siedemdziesiąt jeden
80 *eighty* osiemdziesiąt
81 *eighty-one* osiemdziesiąt jeden
90 *ninety* dziewięćdziesiąt
91 *ninety-one* dziewięćdziesiąt jeden
100 *a hundred*, *one hundred* sto
101 *a/one hundred and one* sto jeden
200 *two hundred* dwieście
300 *three hundred* trzysta
572 *five hundred and seventy-two* pięćset siedemdziesiąt dwa
1000 *a thousand*, *one thousand* tysiąc
2000 *two thousand* dwa tysiące
5000 *five thousand* pięć tysięcy
1,000,000 *a million*, *one million* milion
2,000,000 *two million* dwa miliony
1,000,000,000 *a billion*, *one billion* miliard

Ordinal Numerals – Liczebniki porządkowe

1st *first* pierwszy
2nd *second* drugi
3rd *third* trzeci
4th *fourth* czwarty
5th *fifth* piąty
6th *sixth* szósty
7th *seventh* siódmy
8th *eighth* ósmy
9th *ninth* dziewiąty
10th *tenth* dziesiąty
11th *eleventh* jedenasty
12th *twelfth* dwunasty
13th *thirteenth* trzynasty
14th *fourteenth* czternasty
15th *fifteenth* piętnasty
16th *sixteenth* szesnasty
17th *seventeenth* siedemnasty
18th *eighteenth* osiemnasty
19th *nineteenth* dziewiętnasty
20th *twentieth* dwudziesty
21st *twenty-first* dwudziesty pierwszy
22nd *twenty-second* dwudziesty drugi
23rd *twenty-third* dwudziesty trzeci
30th *thirtieth* trzydziesty
31st *thirty-first* trzydziesty pierwszy
40th *fortieth* czterdziesty
41st *forty-first* czterdziesty pierwszy
50th *fiftieth* pięćdziesiąty
51st *fifty-first* pięćdziesiąty pierwszy
60th *sixtieth* sześćdziesiąty
61st *sixty-first* sześćdziesiąty pierwszy
70th *seventieth* siedemdziesiąty
71st *seventy-first* siedemdziesiąty pierwszy
80th *eightieth* osiemdziesiąty
81st *eighty-first* osiemdziesiąty pierwszy
90th *ninetieth* dziewięćdziesiąty
100th (*one*) *hundredth* setny
101st *hundred and first* sto pierwszy
200th *two hundredth* dwusetny *lub* dwóchsetny
300th *three hundredth* trzechsetny
572nd *five hundred and seventy-second* pięćset siedemdziesiąty drugi
1000th (*one*) *thousandth* tysięczny
1950th *nineteen hundred and fiftieth* tysiąc dziewięćset pięćdziesiąty
2000th *two thousandth* dwutysięczny
1,000,000th *millionth* milionowy
2,000,000th *two millionth* dwumilionowy

Fractions – Ułamki

$^{1}/_{2}$ *one half* lub *a half* pół *lub* jedna druga

$1^{1}/_{2}$ *one and a half* półtora *lub* jeden i jedna druga

$2^{1}/_{2}$ *two and a half* dwa i pół *lub* dwa i jedna druga

$^{1}/_{3}$ *one third, a third* jedna trzecia

$^{2}/_{3}$ *two thirds* dwie trzecie

$^{1}/_{4}$ *one a quarter, one fourth* ćwierć *lub* jedna czwarta

$^{3}/_{4}$ *three quarters, three fourths* trzy czwarte

$^{1}/_{5}$ *one fifth lub **a fifth*** jedna piąta

$3^{4}/_{5}$ *three and four fifths* trzy (całe) i cztery piąte

$^{5}/_{8}$ *five eighths* pięć ósmych

0.45 (*nought*) *point four five* zero przecinek czterdzieści pięć *lub* czterdzieści pięć setnych

2.5 *two point five* dwa przecinek pięć *lub* dwa i pięć dziesiątych *lub* dwa i pół

once raz

twice dwa razy

*three **times*** trzy razy

*four **times*** cztery razy

*twice **as much*** dwa razy tyle (*przy rzeczownikach niepoliczalnych*)

*twice **as many*** dwa razy tyle (*przy rzeczownikach policzalnych*)

firstly, ***in the first place*** po pierwsze

secondly, ***in the second place*** po drugie

thirdly, ***in the third place*** po trzecie

Krótka gramatyka języka angielskiego

Użycie przedimka – a/an

Przedimek nieokreślony **a** występuje przed rzeczownikami policzalnymi w liczbie pojedynczej, zaczynającymi się od spółgłoski. Rzeczowniki policzalne zaczynające się od samogłoski poprzedza się przedimkiem **an**. Przedimka tego używamy głównie do określenia rzeczy/przedmiotu należącego do jakiejś klasy rzeczy.

This is a university. = To jest uniwersytet. (pewien budynek należący do klasy „uniwersytet".)
He has a car. = On ma samochód. (jakiś przedmiot należący do kategorii „samochód")
She's an architect. = Ona jest architektem. (jest kimś kogo się zwie „architekt".)
I need an umbrella. = Potrzebna mi parasolka. (potrzeba mi czegokolwiek co się zwie „parasol".)

Użycie przedimka – the

Przedimek określony **the** stosowany jest przed rzeczownikiem, który jest w jakiś sposób określony:

– jest jeden taki obiekt:
the sun, the moon = słońce, księżyc
– został on wcześniej wspomniany:
I've bought a cat. The cat is black. = Kupiłam kota. Ten kot jest czarny.
– kiedy wiadomo, o którą rzecz chodzi:
Please close the door. = Proszę, zamknij drzwi.

Liczba mnoga rzeczowników

Liczbę mnogą rzeczowników tworzy się najczęściej za pomocą końcówki ***-s***:

a boy – boys **a car – cars**
a day – days **a horse – horses**

Niektóre rzeczowniki tworzą liczbę mnogą w sposób nieregularny:

a woman – women **a deer – deer**
a child – children **a sheep – sheep**

Dopełniacz

Przynależność do kogoś lub czegoś można wyrazić za pomocą tzw. **Saxon genitive** (forma ta jest preferowana w przypadku rzeczowników żywotnych):

my mother's hat = kapelusz mojej matki
your father's car = samochód twego ojca

lub za pomocą **of**:(f orma ta jest preferowana w przypadku rzeczowników nieżywotnych)
the capital of Poland = stolica Polski
the top of the hill = szczyt góry

Zaimki

Zaimki osobowe w języku angielskim mogą być używane jako podmiot lub dopełnienie

Podmiot	Dopełnienie
I (ja)	**me** (mi)
you (ty)	**you** (ciebie, tobie)
he (on)	**him** (jego, jemu)
she (ona)	**her** (jej, ją)
it (ono)	**it** (jego, jemu)
we (my)	**us** (nas, nam)
you (wy)	**you** (was, wam)
they (oni, one)	**them** (ich, im)

Zaimki dzierżawcze przymiotnikowe

my (mój)
your (twój)
his (jego)
her (jej)
its (jego)
our (nasz)
your (wasz)
their (ich)

Zaimki dzierżawcze rzeczownikowe

mine (moja, moje)
yours (twoja, twoje)
his (jego)
its (jej)
ours (nasz, nasze)
yours (wasz, wasze)
theirs (ich)

Zaimki zwrotne

Zaimek zwrotny w języku angielskim odpowiada polskiemu „się".
myself
yourself
himself
herself
itself
ourselves
yourselves
themselves

Zaimki wskazujące

Zaimki wskazyjące **this** i **these** odnoszą się do przedmiotów i osób, które znajdują się bliżej osoby mówiącej. Zaimki **that** i **those** odnoszą się do osób i przedmiotów znajdujących się dalej.

Do you like this music? = Czy lubisz tę muzykę?
What was that? = Co to (tamto) było?
These apples are very sweet. = Te jabłka są bardzo słodkie.
Who are those people over there? = Kim są tamci ludzie?

Zaimki pytające

Who knows? = Kto wie?
What are you reading? = Co czytasz?
Which boxer won? = Który bokser wygrał?
Whose is this? = Czyje to jest?
Whom did you see? = Kogo widziałeś?
Where is my pen? = Gdzie jest mój długopis?

Zaimki nieokreślone

Zaimka **some** przeważnie używa się w zdaniachtwi erdzących. Natomiast zaimek **any** jest używany w pytaniach i przeczeniach.

I need some money. = Potrzebuję trochę pieniędzy.

Have you got any money? = Masz jakieś pieniądze?

I haven't got any time. = Nie mam czasu.

Przymiotniki – stopniowanie

Stopniowanie regularne przymiotników jednosylabowych:

tall – taller – the tallest = wysoki – wyższy – najwyższy

safe – safer – the safest = bezpieczny – bezpieczniejszy – najbezpieczniejszy

big – bigger – biggest = duży – większy – największy

Stopniowanie regularne przymiotników wielosylabowych:

beautiful – more beautiful – the most beautiful =
piękny – piękniejszy – najpięknieszy

comfortable – more comfortable – the most comfortable =
wygodny – wygodniejszy – najwygodniejszy

expensive – more expensive – the most expensive =
drogi – droższy – najdroższy

Stopniowanie nieregularne:

good – better – the best = dobry – lepszy – najlepszy

bad – worse – the worst = zły – gorszy – najgorszy

Tworzenie przysłówków

Regularne tworzenie przysłówków:

nice – nicely = miły – miło

noisy – noisily = głośny – głośno

perfect – perfectly = doskonały – doskonale

Nieregularne tworzenie przysłówków:

far – far = daleki – daleko

fast – fast = szybki – szybko

good – well = dobry – dobrze

Czasy

Czas teraźniejszy prosty – Present simple

I work.	I do not work.	Do I work?
You work.	You do not work.	Do you work?
He/she/it works.	He/she/it does not work.	Does he/she/it work?
We work.	We do not work.	Do we work?
You work.	You do not work.	Do you work?
They work.	They do not work.	Do they work?

Czasu tego używamy najczęściej do wyrażania nawyków lub prawd ogólnych.

He works as a teacher. = On pracuje jako nauczyciel.
Cats do not bark. = Koty nie szczekają.
What do pigs eat? = Co jedzą świnie?

Czas teraźniejszy ciągły – Present continous

I am working.	I am not working.	Am I working?
You are working.	You are not working.	Are you working?
He/she/it is working.	He/she/it is not working.	Is he/she/it working?
We are working.	We are not working.	Are we working?
You are working.	You are not working.	Are you working?
They are working.	They are not working.	Are they working?

Czasu tego używamy do opisania czynności, które odbywają się w chwili, kiedy o nichm ówimy.

I'm watching TV now. = Teraz oglądam telewizję.
He's not crying now. = On teraz nie płacze.
Where are you going? = Dokąd idziesz?

Czas przeszły prosty – Past simple

I worked.	I did not work.	Did I work?
You worked.	You did not work.	Did you work?
He/she/it worked.	He/she/it did not work.	Did he/she/it work?
We worked.	We did not work.	Did we work?
You worked.	You did not work.	Did you work?
They worked.	They did not work.	Did they work?

Czasu tego używamy mówiąc o czynnościach, które miały miejsce w przeszłości.

Shakespeare wrote many plays. = Szekspir napisał wiele sztuk.
When did you arrive? = Kiedy przyjechałeś?
He didn't do it. = On tego nie zrobił.

W przypadku czasowników nieregularnychst osujemy drugą formę czasownika z listy czasowników nieregularnych.

I watched TV last night. = Wczoraj wieczorem oglądałem telewizję.
I saw a horror film last night. = Wczoraj wieczorem oglądałem horror.

Czas przeszły ciągły – Past continuous

I was working.	I was not working.	Was I working?
You were working.	You were not working.	Was you working?
He/she/it was working.	He/she/it was not working.	Was he/she/it working?
We were working.	We were not working.	Were we working?

You were working.	You were not working.	Were you working?
They were working.	They were not working.	Were they working?

Czasu tego używamy, gdy mówimy o czynności, która odbywała się w pewnym momencie w przeszłości.

What were you doing at 10 o'clock yesterday? = Co robiłeś wczoraj o dziesiątej?

The phone rang while I was having a bath. = Telefon zadzwonił kiedy się kąpałem.

What did you say? I wasn't listening. = Co powiedziałeś? Nie słuchałem.

Czas teraźniejszy dokonany – Present perfect

I have worked.	I have not worked.	Have I worked?
You have worked.	You have not worked.	Have you worked?
He/she/it has worked.	He/she/it has not worked.	Has he/she/it worked?
We have worked.	We have not worked.	Have we worked?
You have worked.	You have not worked.	Have you worked?
They have worked.	They have not worked.	Have they worked?

Czasu tego używamy mówiąc o czynnościach, które odbyły się w przeszłości i których skutki ważne są w teraźniejszości.

I haven't read the book yet. = Nie przeczytałem jeszcze tej książki. (Nie wiem, o czym ona jest.)

I can't walk. – I've broken my leg. = Nie mogę chodzić. Złamałem nogę.

Have you passed your exam? = Zdałeś egzamin?

Czas zaprzeszły – Past perfect

I had worked.	I had not worked.	Had I worked?
You had worked.	You had not worked.	Had you worked?
He/she/it had worked.	He/she/it had not worked.	Had he/she/it worked?
We had worked.	We had not worked.	Had we worked?
You had worked.	You had not worked.	Had you worked?
They had worked.	They had not worked.	Had they worked?

Czasu tego używamy mówiąc o wydarzeniach, które miały miejsce przed innym wydarzeniem w przeszłości.

I couldn't remember where I had hidden the money. = Nie mogłem sobie przypomnieć, gdzie schowałem pieniądze.

When he had done his homework, he decided to have a rest. = Kiedy odrobił pracę domową, postanowił odpocząć.

He was upset because Mary hadn't called. = Był zmartwiony, ponieważ Mary nie zadzwoniła.

Czas przyszły prosty – Future simple

I will work.	I will not work.	Will I work?
You will work.	You will not work.	Will you work?
He/she/it will works.	He/she/it will not work.	Will he/she/it work?
We will work.	We will not work.	Will we work?
You will work.	You will not work.	Will you work?
They will work.	They will not work.	Will they work?

Czasu tego używamy do wyrażania decyzji w momencie ichpod ejmowania lub do informowania, że coś wydarzy się w przyszłości.

I'll help you. = Pomogę ci.
I think I'll have a piece of cake. = Myślę, że zjem kawałek ciasta.

Czasowniki modalne

Czasowniki modalne **can, could, may, might, should, must, need** występują z czasownikiem głównym w formie podstawowej.

Can you help me? = Czy możesz mi pomóc?
I can't do it. = Nie mogę tego zrobić.

I could swim when I was a child. = Potrafiłem pływać jako dziecko.
Could you help me? = Czy mógłbyś mi pomóc?

May I use the telephone? = Czy mogę skorzystać z telefonu?
That may be true. = To może być prawda.
Might I use the phone? = Czy mógłbym skorzystać z telefonu?
It might rain. = Być może będzie padać.

You should give up smoking. = Powinieneś rzucić palenie.
You shouldn't steal. = Nie powinieneś kraść.
She must give up smoking. = Ona musi rzucić palenie.
Must I do it? = Czy muszę to robić?

Uwaga:w połączeniu z **not,** czasownik **must** nie znaczy *nie musieć* ale *nie wolno.*
You mustn't park here. = Nie wolno tu parkować.

Jeśli chcemy wyrazić brak konieczności lub przymusu używamy **need not.**
You needn't pay now. = Nie musisz teraz płacić.

Czasowniki modalne w czasie przeszłym
modal + have + past participle

He had to go home. = Musiał pójść do domu. (Taka była konieczność.)
He must have gone home. = Musiał pójść do domu. (Ponieważ go tutaj nie ma.)

You shouldn't bring wine. = Nie powinnaś przynosić wina. (Nie przynoś.)
You shouldn't have brought wine. = Nie powinnaś (była) przynosić wina. (Ale przyniosłaś. Trudno.)

Strona czynna i bierna

Present Simple – **I do my homework.** = Homework is done.
Present Continuous - **I am doing my homework**. = Homework is being done.
Past Simple – **I did my homework.** = Homework was done.
Past Continuous – **I was doing my homework.** = Homework was being done.
Present Perfect – **I've done my homework.** = Homework has been done.
Past Perfect – **I'd done my homework.** = Homework had been done.
Future Simple – **I will do my homework.** = Homework will be done.

Mowa zależna

I like her. = Lubię ją.
He said he liked her. = On powiedział, że ją lubi.

I liked her. = Lubiłem ją.
He said he had liked her. = On powiedział, że ją lubił.

I'm learning English. = Uczę się angielskiego.
She told me she was learning English. = Powiedziała mi, że uczy się angielskiego.
Do they like me? = Czy oni mnie lubią?
I wondered if they liked me. = Zastanawiałem się, czy mnie lubią.

Okresy warunkowe

If I become President, I'll raise taxes. = Kiedy zostanę prezydentem, podniosę podatki.

If I became President, I'd raise taxes. = Gdybym został prezydentem, podniósłbym podatki.

If I had become President, I'd have raised taxes. = Gdybym wtedy został prezydentem, podniósłbym podatki.

Wyrażenie to be going to

Wyrażenia **to be going to** używamy mówiąc o zamiarze dokonania czegoś w przyszłości lub do przewidywania przyszłości.
She is going to have a baby. = Ona będzie miała dziecko. (przewidywanie)
He is going to be a pilot. = On będzie pilotem. (zamiar)
When are you going to have your hair cut? = Kiedy obetniesz włosy? (pytanie o zamiar)

Konstrukcja kauzatywna have + object + verb

He is having his house built. = On buduje dom.
When did you last have your hair cut? = Kiedy ostatnio obcinałeś włosy?
Do we need to have the car serviced? = Czy musimy oddać samochód do naprawy?

Wyrażenie had better

You'd better not say that. = Lepiej tego nie mów.
He'd better come on time. = Lepiej, żeby przyszedł na czas.

Wyrażenie used to

I used to drink wine. = Kiedyś piłem wino.
They used to live in Warsaw. = Kiedyś mieszkali w Warszawie.

Wyrażenie to be supposed to

This looks strange. What is it supposed to be? = To wygląda dziwnie. Co to ma być?
They were supposed to be here two hours ago. = Mieli tu być dwie godziny temu.

Wyrażenie verb + object + infinitive

I want you to do it. = Chcę, abyś to zrobił.
He wants me to help her. = Ona chce, abym jej pomógł.

Wyrażenie there is/are

There's a table in the middle of the room. = Na środku pokoju znajduje się stół.
There are a lot of people there. = Tam jest dużo ludzi.
Are there any potatoes? = Czy są ziemniaki?
There will be rain tonight. = Dziś wieczorem będzie padać.

Wyrażenie wish

I wish he didn't smoke. = Szkoda, że on pali.
I wish he hadn't smoked. = Szkoda, że on palił.

I wish I spoke Japanese. = Szkoda, że nie mówię po japońsku.
I wish I had spoken Japanese. = Szkoda, że nie mówiłem po japońsku.

Wyrażenie it's time

It's time we got started. = Czas zacząć.
It's time to start our lesson. = Czas zacząć lekcję.

Wyrażenie I'd rather

I'd rather stay at home. = Wolałbym zostać w domu.
I'd rather you stayed at home. = Wolałbym, abyś został w domu.
I'd rather not help you. = Wolałbym ci nie pomagać.
I'd rather she didn't phone me. = Wolałbym, żeby ona do mnie nie dzwoniła.

Wykaz angielskich czasowników nieregularnych

Poniższe zestawienie zawiera listę najważniejszych czasowników nieregularnych. W pierwszej kolumnie podano bezokolicznik (infinitive),w drugiej znaczenie (meaning),w trzeciej formę czasu przeszłego (past tense) a w czwartej imiesłów bierny (past participle).

Infinitive	Meaning	Past tense	Past participle
arise	*powstawać*	arose	arisen
awake	*budzić (się)*	awoke	awoken
be	*być*	was *albo* were	been
bear	*nosić/rodzić*	bore	borne/born
beat	*bić*	beat beaten	
become	*stawać się*	became	become
beget	*począć*	begot	begotten
begin	*zaczynać*	began	begun
bend	*zginać (się)*	bent	bent
bet	*zakładać się*	bet *lub* betted	bet *lub* betted
bid[1]	*oferować*	bid	bid
bid[2]	*mówić*	bade *lub* bid	bidden
bind	*wiązać*	bound	bound
bite	*gryźć*	bit	bitten
bleed	*krwawić*	bled	bled
blow	*wiać/dmuchać*	blew	blown
break	*łamać*	broke	broken
breed	*hodować*	bred	bred
bring	*przynosić*	brought	brought
broadcast	*radio i TV: nadawać*	broadcast	broadcast
build	*budować*	built	built
burn	*palić (się)/oparzyć (się)*	burnt *lub* burned	burnt *lub* burned
burst	*pękać*	burst	burst
buy	*kupować*	bought	bought
can	*móc, umieć*	could	–
cast	*rzucać*	cast	cast
catch	*łapać*	caught	caught

choose	*wybierać*	chose	chosen
cling	*przywierać*	clung	clung
come	*przychodzić*	came	come
cost	*kosztować*	cost	cost
creep	*skradać się/pełzać*	crept	crept
cut	*ciąć*	cut	cut
deal	*handlować/zajmować się*	dealt	dealt
dig	*kopać*	dug	dug
dive	*skakać/nurkować*	dived, *AE* dove	dived
do	*robić*	did	done
draw	*ciągnąć/rysować*	drew	drawn
dream	*śnić/marzyć*	dreamt *lub* dreamed	dreamt *lub* dreamed
drink	*pić*	drank	drunk
drive	*prowadzić (pojazd)*	drove	driven
dwell	*mieszkać*	dwelt *lub* dwelled	dwelt *lub* dwelled
eat	*jeść*	ate	eaten
fall	*padać*	fell	fallen
feed	*karmić*	fed	fed
feel	*czuć*	felt	felt
fight	*walczyć*	fought	fought
find	*znajdować*	found	found
fit	*pasować*	fitted, *AE też* fit	fitted, *AE też* fit
flee	*uciekać*	fled	fled
fling	*rzucać*	flung	flung
fly	*latać*	flew	flown
forbid	*zakazywać*	forbade *lub* forbad	forbidden
forecast	*prognozować*	forecast	forecast
foresee	*przewidywać*	foresaw	foreseen
forget	*zapominać*	forgot	forgotten
forgive	*wybaczać*	forgave	forgiven
freeze	*zamarzać/zamrażać*	froze	frozen
get	*dostawać*	got	got, *AE też* gotten
give	*dać/dawać*	gave	given

go	*iść/jechać*	went	gone
grind	*mielić/ostrzyć*	ground	ground
grow	*rosnąć/uprawiać*	grew	grown
hang[1]	*wisieć/wieszać*	hung	hung
hang[1]	*powiesić (człowieka)*	hanged	hanged
have	*mieć*	had	had
hear	*słyszeć*	heard	heard
hide	*ukrywać (się)*	hid	hidden
hit	*uderzać/trafić*	hit	hit
hold	*trzymać*	held	held
hurt	*boleć/ranić*	hurt	hurt
keep	*trzymać*	kept	kept
kneel	*klęczeć*	knelt, *AM* kneeled	knelt, *AM* kneeled
knit	*robić na drutach*	knitted, knit	knitted, knit
know	*wiedzieć/znać*	knew	known
lay	*kłaść/znosić (jajka)*	laid	laid
lead	*prowadzić*	led	led
lean	*opierać (się)*	leaned, leant	leaned, leant
leap	*skakać*	leapt, *AM* leaped	leapt, *AM* leaped
learn	*uczyć się*	learned, learnt	learned, learnt
leave	*wyjeżdżać/zostawiać*	left	left
lend	*pożyczać (komuś)*	lent	lent
let	*pozwalać*	let	let
lie	*leżeć*	lay	lain
light	*oświetlić/zapalić (się)*	lit, lighted	lit, lighted
lose	*zgubić/przegrać*	lost	lost
make	*robić*	made	made
mean	*znaczyć*	meant	meant
meet	*spotykać (się)*	met	met
mislead	*wprowadzać w błąd*	misled	misled
mistake	*pomylić*	mistook	mistaken
misunderstand	*źle zrozumieć*	misunderstood	misunderstood

mow	*kosić*	mowed	mown, mowed
outdo	*przewyższać*	outdid	outdone
outgrow	*wyrastać*	outgrew	outgrown
overcome	*pokonać*	overcame	overcome
overdo	*przesadzać (z czymś)*	overdid	overdone
overhear	*przypadkowo usłyszeć*	overheard	overheard
oversleep	*zaspać*	overslept	overslept
overtake	*wyprzedzać*	overtook	overtaken
pay	*płacić*	paid	paid
plead	*błagać*	pleaded, *AM* pled	pleaded, *AM* pled
prove	*udowodnić*	proved	proved, *AM* proven
put	*kłaść/stawiać*	put	put
read	*czytać*	read	read
resit	*ponownie zdawać*	resat	resat
rewind	*przewijać*	rewound	rewound
ride	*jeździć/jechać*	rode	ridden
ring	*dzwonić/telefonować*	rang	rung
rise	*wzrastać/wschodzić*	rose	risen
run	*biec*	ran	run
saw	*piłować*	sawed	sawn, sawed
say	*powiedzieć/mówić*	said	said
see	*widzieć/zobaczyć*	saw	seen
seek	*szukać*	sought	sought
sell	*sprzedawać (się)*	sold	sold
send	*wysyłać*	sent	sent
set	*umieścić/nastawić*	set	set
sew	*szyć/przyszyć*	sewed	sewn, sewed
shake	*trząść (się)*	shook	shaken
shine	*świecić/polerować*	shone, shined	shone, shined
shoot	*strzelać*	shot	shot
show	*pokazywać*	showed	shown
shrink	*kurczyć się*	shrank, shrunk	shrunk
shut	*zamykać (się)*	shut	shut

sing	*śpiewać*	sang	sung
sink	*tonąć/zatopić*	sank	sunk
sit	*siedzieć*	sat	sat
sleep	*spać*	slept	slept
slide	*ślizgać się/przesuwać*	slid	slid
smell	*pachnieć/wąchać*	smelt, *AM* smelled	smelt, *AM* smelled
sow	*siać*	sowed	sown, sowed
speak	*mówić/rozmawiać*	spoke	spoken
spell	*pisać/literować*	spelt, spelled	spelt, spelled
spill	*rozlać (się)*	spilt, *AM* spilled	spilt, *AM* spilled
spin	*wirować/obracać*	spun, span	spun
spit	*pluć*	spat, *AM* spit	spat, *AM* spit
split	*rozczepiać (się)*	split	split
spoil	*psuć/niszczyć/ rozpieszczać*	spoilt, *AM* spoiled	spoilt, *AM* spoiled
spread	*rozkładać/rozpościerać*	spread	spread
spring	*skoczyć*	sprang, *AM* sprung	sprung
stand	*stać/stawiać*	stood	stood
steal	*kraść*	stole	stolen
stick	*wbijać/przyklejać (się)*	stuck	stuck
sting	*żądlić*	stung	stung
stink	*śmierdzieć*	stank, stunk	stunk
strike	*atakować/uderzać*	struck	struck
strive	*dokładać starań*	strove, strived	striven, strived
swear	*kląć/przysięgać*	swore	sworn
sweep	*zamiatać/zgarniać*	swept	swept
swell	*powiększać (się)/puchnąć*	swelled	swollen, swelled
swim	*płynąć*	swam	swum
swing	*hustać się/kołysać się*	swung	swung
take	*brać/przyjmować*	took	taken
teach	*uczyć/nauczać*	taught	taught
tear	*rwać/odrywać*	tore	torn
tell	*powiedzieć/opowiadać*	told	told
think	*myśleć*	thought	thought

throw	*rzucać*	threw	thrown
tread	*kroczyć*	trod	trodden, trod
understand	*rozumieć*	understood	understood
undertake	*podejmować się*	undertook	undertaken
undo	*rozpinać*	undid	undone
upset	*sprawić przykrość*	upset	upset
wake	*budzić (się)*	woke, waked	woken, waked
wear	*nosić (ubranie)*	wore	worn
weave	*tkać/wyplatać*	wove	woven
wed	*poślubić*	wedded, wed	wedded, wed
weep	*płakać/łkać*	wept	wept
win	*wygrać/zwyciężyć*	won	won
wind	*nawijać/wić się*	wound	wound
withdraw	*wycofać się*	withdrew	withdrawn
wring	*wykręcać*	wrung	wrung
write	*pisać*	wrote	written

Najważniejsze miary i wagi

Miary długości

1 inch (in) *cal* = 2,54 cm
1 foot (ft) *stopa* = 12 cali = 30,48 cm
1 yard (yd) *jard* = 3 stopy = 91,44 cm
1 (statute) mile *mila* = 1760 jardów = 1,609 km

Lotnictwo i marynarka:

1 nautical mile *mila morska* = 1,852 km

Miary powierzchni

1 square inch (sq in) *cal kwadratowy* = 6,452 cm^2
1 square foot (sq ft) *stopa kwadratowa* = 144 cale kw. = 929,029 cm^2
1 square yard (sq yd) *jard kwadratowy* = 9 stóp kw. = 8361,26 cm^2
1 square mile *mila kwadratowa* = 259 ha = 2,59 km^2

Miary objetości

1 cubic inch (cu in) *cal sześcienny* = 16,387 cm^3
1 cubic foot (cu ft) *stopa sześcienna* = 1728 cali sześciennych = 0,02832 m^3
1 cubic yard *jard sześcienny* = 27 stóp sześciennych = 0,7646 m^3

Brytyjskie miary objętości płynów

1 pint (pt) *pół kwarty* = 0,568 l
1 quart (qt) *kwarta* = 1,136 l
1 gallon (gall) *galon* = 4 kwarty = 4,546 l

Amerykańskie miary objętości płynów

1 pint (pt) *pół kwarty* = 0,4732 l
1 quart (qt) *kwarta* = 0,9464 l
1 gallon (gall) *galon* = 4 kwarty = 3,7853 l
1 barrel petroleum *baryłka* = 42 galony = 158,97 l

Jednostki wagi stosowane w handlu

1 ounce (oz) *uncja* = 28,35 g
1 pound (lb) *funt* = 16 uncji = 453,59 g
1 stone (st) *kamień* = 14 funtów = 6,356 kg
1 hundredweight (cwt) *cetnar:*
BE = 112 funtów = 50,802 kg,
AE = 100 funtów = 45,359 kg
1 longton *tona angielska* = 20 cetnarów (*BE*) = 1016,05 kg
1 short ton *tona amerykańska* = 20 cetnarów (*AE*) = 907,185 kg
1 metric ton *tona metryczna* = 1000 kg

1 października 1995 r. Wielka Brytania przeszła na system metryczny.
W użyciu pozostaną jednak, przynajmniej przez jakiś czas, pół kwarty (**pint**) w odniesieniu do piwa i mleka oraz mile przy podawaniu odległości na tablicach drogowych.